The Steinsaltz Humash

Humash Translation and Commentary

Commentary by

Rabbi Adin Even-Israel Steinsaltz

Steinsaltz Center

KOREN

Koren Publishers Jerusalem

Steinsaltz Center

Executive Director, Steinsaltz Center
Rabbi Meni Even-Israel

Executive Editors
Rabbi Joshua Schreier
Rabbi Dr. Joshua Amaru

Editors
Rabbi Ayal Geffon, *Senior Content Editor*
Rabbi Yedidya Naveh, *Senior Editor*
Rabbi Michael Siev, *Senior Editor*
Rabbi Avi Grossman, *Senior Editor*
Rabbi Aryeh Sklar, *Content Curator*
Rabbi Alan Haber
Yisrael Kalker
Elisha Loewenstern
Rabbi Eli Ozarowski
Avi Steinhart
Rabbi David Strauss

Hebrew Edition Editors
Sara Friedland Ben Arza
Rabbi Yossi Ben Arza
Rabbi Meir Klein
Rabbi Daniel Eliav

Technical Staff
Tani Bednarsh
Adena Frazer
Shaltiel Shmidman

Editor in Chief
Rabbi Jason Rappoport

Copy Editors
Caryn Meltz, *Manager*
Aliza Israel, *Consultant*
Ita Olesker, *Senior Copy Editor*
Debbie Ismailoff, *Senior Proofreader*
   and Language Consultant
Chava Boylan
Suri Brand
Ilana Brown
Carolyn Budow Ben-David
Rachelle Emanuel
Shira Finson
Charmaine Gruber
Deborah Meghnagi Bailey
Deena Nataf
Dvora Rhein
Elisheva Ruffer
Ilana Sobel

Language Experts
Dr. Stéphanie E. Binder, *Greek & Latin*
Rabbi Yaakov Hoffman, *Arabic*
Shira Shmidman, *Aramaic*

KOREN

Design & Typesetting
Avishai Magence, *Production Manager*
Eliyahu Misgav, *Art Director*
Bentzi Binder, *Design & Typesetting*
Estie Dishon, *Typesetting*

This book is dedicated in loving memory to

Louis Weisfeld *z"l*

**who observed God's work,
who strove to emulate His ways and to walk along His path.**

והיאך היא הדרך לאהבתו ויראתו?
בשעה שיתבונן האדם במעשיו וברואיו הנפלאים הגדולים....

רמב"ם ספר המדע, הלכות יסודי התורה ב:ב

What is the way that leads to the love of Him and to
reverence for Him? ... a person who contemplates
His great and wondrous acts and creations ....

Mishne Torah, Sefer HaMadda, Hilkhot Yesodei HaTorah 2:2

Gabi Weisfeld

This book is dedicated in loving memory to

Louis Weisfeld z"l

who observed God's work,
who strove to emulate His ways and to walk along His path.

ועתה ישראל מה ה' אלקיך שואל מעמך
כי אם ליראה את ה' אלקיך ללכת בכל דרכיו ולאהבה אותו...

דברים י:יב

What is the way that leads to the love of Him and to
reverence for Him? ... a person who contemplates
His great and wondrous acts and creations...

Mishne Torah, Sefer HaMadda, Hilkhot Yesodei HaTorah 2:2

Gabi Weisfeld

Table of Contents

Introduction to the Steinsaltz Humash

Scholars and lay readers alike are aware that writing a new commentary on the Bible requires assistance and blessings from Above, as well as substantial effort from below. Two fundamental challenges stand before one who seeks to write a commentary on the Torah: First, the aspiration to relate to the loftiest and holiest text and to explain it faithfully risks hubris. Second, a huge number of commentaries on the Bible have been composed over the course of the past three thousand years by the greatest people in our history. Who has the audacity to attempt to join this holy assembly or even grasp its coattails?

Sanction for undertaking this daunting task can be found in Rashi's statement to his grandson Rashbam, himself the author of an important commentary on the Torah. Rashbam reports Rashi to have said that if he had had the strength, he would have written another commentary in accordance with the "plain meanings that are renewed every day" (Rashbam, Genesis 38:2).

In every generation and on each passing day, fresh light can be shed on the verses of the Bible and new perspectives can be found. Not only are new answers offered to old questions, but in every era additional questions are raised by students of the Bible, due to both the diversity of the personalities, and the differing interests and perspectives, of each era. Throughout the ages, the great commentaries have discussed a wide range of different issues. To this day, thank God, there are many scholars and students of the Bible raising unique questions and challenges that require attention, analysis, and investigation. All these illuminate the eternal words of the Torah through a range of viewpoints and give rise to "plain meanings that are renewed every day."

This commentary seeks to offer the reader the plain meaning of the text, the *peshat*. Ostensibly, this is the simplest level of interpretation, but the elucidation of the plain meaning is actually the most difficult type of interpretation. Other kinds of interpretation, based on allusion [*remez*], midrashic hermeneutics [*derash*], or esoteric, mystical traditions [*sod*] are free to forge links between the text and the sources from which they draw and are not constrained by the language and concepts of the Bible. In contrast, discovering the plain meaning of the text requires the interpreter to adhere closely to the literal meaning of the words while paying attention to syntax and context. The best way to go about this has always been a matter of debate, and the elucidation of the plain meaning of the Torah as a holistic entity will never be fully achieved (see, e.g., Ibn Ezra's introduction to his commentary on the Torah).

Finally, there is a fundamental problem that is unique to interpretation of the Torah: The aim of finding the plain meaning is related to the author's intent, yet the infinite consciousness of the Giver of the Torah is unfathomable and boundless (see Ramban's introduction to the Torah).

Although this commentary includes references to many other commentaries, it is not an anthology. It was not intended to provide a comprehensive array of interpretations from across the generations. The aim of the references is to show that a suggested interpretation is based on earlier sources or discusses a similar question. Moreover, this work does not aspire to be revolutionary or novel. Rather, it aims to present what might be called a "transparent" commentary, one whose explanations should go almost unnoticed and serve only to give the reader and student the sense that there is no barrier between him or her and the text. The aim is to let the Torah speak for itself, to allow the prophets to prophesy and the wise men to impart their wisdom. In order to enable the "voice" of the verses to be heard, the annotations are brief, serving as a thin, barely perceptible screen rather than a heavy, concealing coat of armor.

At Mount Sinai, the entire Jewish people heard "a great voice" (Deuteronomy 5:18), which the Sages interpret to mean a voice that has never ceased (*Targum Onkelos*; *Sanhedrin* 17a). It is my hope that this project will help people hear the voice of the Torah even in our busy, noisy world.

Rabbi Adin Even-Israel Steinsaltz

Introduction by the Hebrew Editors

The purpose of this commentary is to assist the contemporary reader by bridging the gaps in language, outlook, and culture between us and the world of the Bible. As far as possible, it seeks to clarify ambiguities, elucidate problematic passages, and remove obstacles to understanding while dealing with both explicit and implicit difficulties.

The commentary consists of several parts, which complement but are independent of one another. The literal translation of the verses appears in boldface. Woven into the biblical text in non-bold typeface are brief explanatory comments and elaborations. Below the text are notes that offer more elaborate discussion of topics that appear in the verses as well as insights into the general context and scientific and historical realia that surround the biblical text.

The biblical text is divided into units based on subject matter, which do not always accord with the standard division into chapters. Each unit is prefaced by a heading and a short introduction. This structure should not be viewed as a definitive partition of the biblical text but as a suggestion, part of the commentary, for the reader's convenience and orientation.

The commentary seeks to concisely clarify the language and context at the most basic level so as not to encumber the reader. Consequently, it is not committed to a particular exegetical method and does not systematically defer to any particular commentator. In cases where there are differing explanations of a passage, alternative explanations may be cited. In cases where the halakhic tradition expounds a verse in a manner not consistent with the plain meaning, this will be noted and explained briefly in the annotations themselves or by means of a reference, allowing the plain meaning of the text to be preserved while not disregarding the interpretation of the Oral Law.

It must be stated that even when written without qualification, the interpretations offered are not meant to be seen as authoritative. They are no more than suggestions, occasionally novel ones, which are compatible with the simple meaning of the text and which speak to the average reader. There are no systematic exegetical considerations behind the decision to adopt any particular interpretation.

Much thought and labor has been invested to ensure that the design of this work is as aesthetically pleasing and convenient for the user as possible. This design is the fruit of an ongoing collaboration between the team at the Institute for Talmudic Publications and Koren Publishers. Our thanks to Rabbi Meir Hanegbi, whose wisdom, conviviality, and efficiency contributed greatly to the success of the project. Rabbi Hanokh Ben Arza, may his memory be for a blessing, was the father of the two editors in chief of the Hebrew edition; his spirit and respect for the written word inspired them in their work.

The Editors

Introduction by the Translators

ON THE TRANSLATION OF THE TORAH

The English translation of the *Steinsaltz Commentary on the Humash* includes a completely new translation of the Humash based on Rabbi Adin Even-Israel Steinsaltz's Hebrew commentary. Translation is necessarily an act of interpretation. In general, we have done our best, at Rabbi Steinsaltz's behest, to stay as close as possible to the original Hebrew verses so that the English reader will encounter the complexities of the text directly. In the course of translating, we have consulted other English translations, as well as relying heavily upon Onkelos' Aramaic translation and the classic medieval Jewish commentaries of the Torah: Rav Se'adya Gaon, Rashi, Ibn Ezra, Ramban, and Rashbam. Our goal throughout has been to produce a translation that is true to the original Hebrew text and commentary, yet at the same time is readable and accessible to a broad range of readers, from those who are familiar with Hebrew and seek to deepen their understanding of the Torah to those who will gain access to the text only by reading it in English. The commentary and notes are written in modern American English. In the spirit of the Hebrew edition, we have tried to preserve the lofty register of the biblical text while providing a commentary that is relevant and inspiring to our own generation. We hope that the Author of the Torah has aided us in achieving this goal.

THE LAYOUT OF THIS EDITION

On the left-hand side of each set of facing pages is the Hebrew text of the Bible with the traditional cantillation marks, meticulously edited over decades by the team at Koren Publishers, Jerusalem. Below it is Rashi's classic commentary in Hebrew, also fully vocalized and punctuated. The text of Rashi's commentary reproduced here is also taken from the Koren edition of the Bible, drawing from the most reliable manuscripts. On the facing page, the Steinsaltz translation of the Bible appears in boldface with the commentary interspersed between the words of the text in non-bold typeface. This enables the reader to easily follow either the direct translation alone or the translation augmented by the elucidated text.

Three traditional divisions of the Torah are marked: the weekly portion, the *aliyot* of the Torah reading on both the Hebrew and English sides, where the reading is paused on Shabbat morning, and the "open" and "closed" sections [*parashot*] as they appear in a Torah scroll. The weekly readings from the Prophets, the *haftarot*, are printed at the end of the Humash, accompanied by a direct translation of the verses and an introduction before each *haftara* that offers a connection between the *haftara* and the weekly Torah reading. To preserve space, the Steinsaltz commentary to the *haftarot* is not included.

The notes at the foot of the page are divided into two categories. Discussion notes provide background material, internal biblical parallels, alternative explanations, and a wealth of midrashic and philosophical ideas from Jewish commentaries over the generations. Background notes provide linguistic, historical, archaeological, and scientific information that is relevant to places, nations, flora and fauna, and other realia mentioned in the verses. Integrated into both the commentary and the notes are pictures, maps, and other graphics to aid the reader in grasping the biblical text.

References and sources for the commentary appear as endnotes, while the references and sources for the notes are interspersed throughout the notes themselves in parentheses. These references and sources, compiled by the Hebrew editors, include citations of other verses in the Bible, commentary elsewhere in the Bible, insights of the rabbinic Sages in the Talmud and *midrashim*, interpretations of the classical biblical commentaries, and citations of philosophical works and responsa by the early authorities [*rishonim*].

The translation of the verses of the Torah and most of the *haftarot* was undertaken by Rabbi Joshua Schreier and reviewed meticulously by Rabbi Dr. Joshua Amaru. The verses of the *haftarot* from Jeremiah and Ezekiel were reviewed by Rabbi Ayal

Geffon. Many talented editors and translators participated in the translation of the commentary and notes as listed in the credits. We thank Matthew Miller, Avishai Magence, and the devoted and gifted team at Koren Publishers. We are grateful to Rabbi Meni Even-Israel, Executive Director of the Steinsaltz Center, whose wisdom and guidance have made the publication of this Humash possible. We also thank Rabbi Dr. Natan Slifkin of the Biblical Museum of Natural History in Beit Shemesh for his help in identifying some animals and providing suitable images.

TRANSLITERATION

In general, we have tried to keep transliteration to a minimum and have relied upon it only for proper nouns and in places where a point of commentary relates to a Hebrew term. In the case of proper nouns, we have sought a middle ground between a rigorous adherence to Hebrew phonology and the use of anglicized versions of names taken from earlier translations of the Bible. For familiar names of both places and people, where encountering a transliteration would be jarring to many readers, we have used the well-known anglicized versions, such as Canaan, Egypt, Abraham, and Moses. Otherwise, proper nouns are transliterated according to the rules listed below. These transliterations offer the English reader an experience that is closer to that of the Hebrew reader.

Of course, determining which names count as familiar and which are not is not an exact science; the policy has been to use the anglicized names of familiar figures from the early chapters in Genesis, the names of prophets and books of the Bible, and some other well-known characters and place-names. The transliteration scheme generally follows modern Israeli Hebrew pronunciation, but note the following points:

- For proper nouns and names of the *parashot*, no special characters are used to designate sounds that do not exist in English. For example, the name אֲחִיעֶזֶר will not be rendered Aḥiezer (with a diacritic for the letter *ḥet* that is used for the transliteration of Hebrew terms that are not proper nouns) but rather Ahiezer. Consequently, the letter ח is rendered as *h* (like the letter ה).

- The letter *h*, representing the Hebrew letter ה, has been omitted at the end of a word unless its omission could lead to mispronunciation. For example, שלה is written Shela, while נינוה is written Nineveh.

- The soft letter כ is rendered as *kh*.

- No distinction has been made between a letter containing a *dagesh ḥazak* (elsewhere represented by a double consonant) and one without. For example, it is Hukat as opposed to Hukkat.

- Apostrophes indicating glottal stops are employed only where a name could be mispronounced without them. For example, it is Se'ir as opposed to Seir.

- We have maintained a more technical transliteration scheme for citations, including the diacritic *ḥ* and consonant doubling for cases of a *dagesh*. For example, in the citation *Tanḥuma, Korah 5, Tanḥuma* retains the diacritic *ḥ*, whereas *Korah* does not.

On behalf of the team of inspired and dedicated translators, editors, and copy editors with whom it has been a great privilege to work, I express my hope that the decisions we have made have produced a translation that is faithful to the Hebrew, readable, accessible, and useful to the reader.

Jason Rappoport
Editor in Chief

Blessings for Reading the Torah (Ashkenazic Custom)

The reader shows the oleh the section to be read. The oleh touches the scroll at that place with the tzitzit of his tallit, which he then kisses. Grasping the handles of the scroll, he recites:

Oleh: Bless the LORD, the blessed One.

Cong: Bless the LORD, the blessed One, for ever and all time.

Oleh: Bless the LORD, the blessed One, for ever and all time.

Blessed are You, LORD our God, King of the Universe,
who has chosen us from all peoples and has given us His Torah.
Blessed are You, LORD, Giver of the Torah.

After the reading, the oleh recites:

Oleh: Blessed are You, LORD our God, King of the Universe,
who has given us the Torah of truth, and everlasting life He has planted in our midst.
Blessed are You, LORD, Giver of the Torah.

Blessings for Reading the Haftara

Before reading the Haftara, the person called up for Maftir recites:

בָּרוּךְ Blessed are You, LORD our God, King of the Universe, who chose good prophets and was pleased with their words, spoken in truth. Blessed are You, LORD, who chooses the Torah, His servant Moses, His people Israel, and the prophets of truth and righteousness.

After the Haftara, the person called up for Maftir recites the following blessings:

בָּרוּךְ Blessed are You, LORD our God King of the Universe, Rock of all worlds, righteous for all generations, the faithful God who says and does, speaks and fulfills, all of whose words are truth and righteousness. You are faithful, LORD our God, and faithful are Your words, not one of which returns unfulfilled, for You, God, are a faithful (and compassionate) King. Blessed are You, LORD, faithful in all His words.

רַחֵם Have compassion on Zion for it is the source of our life, and save the one grieved in spirit swiftly in our days. Blessed are You, LORD, who makes Zion rejoice in her children.

שַׂמְּחֵנוּ Grant us joy, LORD our God, through Elijah the prophet Your servant, and through the kingdom of the house of David Your anointed – may he soon come and gladden our hearts. May no stranger sit on his throne, and may others no longer inherit his glory, for You took an oath to him by Your holy name that his light would never be extinguished. Blessed are You, LORD, Shield of David.

עַל הַתּוֹרָה For the Torah, for divine worship, for the prophets, and for this Sabbath day which You, LORD our God, have given us for holiness and rest, honor and glory – for all these we thank and bless You, LORD our God, and may Your name be blessed by the mouth of all that lives, continually, for ever and all time. Blessed are You, LORD, who sanctifies the Sabbath.

ברכות התורה לאשכנזים

קודם הברכה על העולה לראות היכן קוראים ולנשק את ספר התורה.
בשעת הברכה העולה אוחז בעמודי הספר.

עולה: בָּרְכוּ אֶת יהוה הַמְבֹרָךְ.

קהל: בָּרוּךְ יהוה הַמְבֹרָךְ לְעוֹלָם וָעֶד.

עולה: בָּרוּךְ יהוה הַמְבֹרָךְ לְעוֹלָם וָעֶד.

בָּרוּךְ אַתָּה יהוה, אֱלֹהֵינוּ מֶלֶךְ הָעוֹלָם,
אֲשֶׁר בָּחַר בָּנוּ מִכָּל הָעַמִּים וְנָתַן לָנוּ אֶת תּוֹרָתוֹ.
בָּרוּךְ אַתָּה יהוה, נוֹתֵן הַתּוֹרָה.

לאחר הקריאה העולה מנשק את ספר התורה ומברך:

בָּרוּךְ אַתָּה יהוה, אֱלֹהֵינוּ מֶלֶךְ הָעוֹלָם,
אֲשֶׁר נָתַן לָנוּ תּוֹרַת אֱמֶת וְחַיֵּי עוֹלָם נָטַע בְּתוֹכֵנוּ.
בָּרוּךְ אַתָּה יהוה, נוֹתֵן הַתּוֹרָה.

ברכות ההפטרה

לפני קריאת ההפטרה המפטיר מברך:

בָּרוּךְ אַתָּה יהוה אֱלֹהֵינוּ מֶלֶךְ הָעוֹלָם אֲשֶׁר בָּחַר בִּנְבִיאִים טוֹבִים, וְרָצָה בְדִבְרֵיהֶם הַנֶּאֱמָרִים בֶּאֱמֶת.
בָּרוּךְ אַתָּה יהוה, הַבּוֹחֵר בַּתּוֹרָה וּבְמֹשֶׁה עַבְדּוֹ וּבְיִשְׂרָאֵל עַמּוֹ וּבִנְבִיאֵי הָאֱמֶת וָצֶדֶק.

אחר קריאת ההפטרה המפטיר מברך:

בָּרוּךְ אַתָּה יהוה, אֱלֹהֵינוּ מֶלֶךְ הָעוֹלָם, צוּר כָּל הָעוֹלָמִים, צַדִּיק בְּכָל הַדּוֹרוֹת, הָאֵל הַנֶּאֱמָן, הָאוֹמֵר וְעוֹשֶׂה, הַמְדַבֵּר וּמְקַיֵּם, שֶׁכָּל דְּבָרָיו אֱמֶת וָצֶדֶק. נֶאֱמָן אַתָּה הוּא יהוה אֱלֹהֵינוּ וְנֶאֱמָנִים דְּבָרֶיךָ, וְדָבָר אֶחָד מִדְּבָרֶיךָ אָחוֹר לֹא יָשׁוּב רֵיקָם, כִּי אֵל מֶלֶךְ נֶאֱמָן (וְרַחֲמָן) אָתָּה. בָּרוּךְ אַתָּה יהוה, הָאֵל הַנֶּאֱמָן בְּכָל דְּבָרָיו.

רַחֵם עַל צִיּוֹן כִּי הִיא בֵּית חַיֵּינוּ, וְלַעֲלוּבַת נֶפֶשׁ תּוֹשִׁיעַ בִּמְהֵרָה בְיָמֵינוּ. בָּרוּךְ אַתָּה יהוה, מְשַׂמֵּחַ צִיּוֹן בְּבָנֶיהָ.

שַׂמְּחֵנוּ יהוה אֱלֹהֵינוּ בְּאֵלִיָּהוּ הַנָּבִיא עַבְדֶּךָ, וּבְמַלְכוּת בֵּית דָּוִד מְשִׁיחֶךָ, בִּמְהֵרָה יָבוֹא וְיָגֵל לִבֵּנוּ. עַל כִּסְאוֹ לֹא יֵשֶׁב זָר, וְלֹא יִנְחֲלוּ עוֹד אֲחֵרִים אֶת כְּבוֹדוֹ, כִּי בְשֵׁם קָדְשְׁךָ נִשְׁבַּעְתָּ לּוֹ שֶׁלֹּא יִכְבֶּה נֵרוֹ לְעוֹלָם וָעֶד. בָּרוּךְ אַתָּה יהוה, מָגֵן דָּוִד.

עַל הַתּוֹרָה וְעַל הָעֲבוֹדָה וְעַל הַנְּבִיאִים וְעַל יוֹם הַשַּׁבָּת הַזֶּה, שֶׁנָּתַתָּ לָּנוּ יהוה אֱלֹהֵינוּ לִקְדֻשָּׁה וְלִמְנוּחָה, לְכָבוֹד וּלְתִפְאָרֶת. עַל הַכֹּל יהוה אֱלֹהֵינוּ אֲנַחְנוּ מוֹדִים לָךְ וּמְבָרְכִים אוֹתָךְ, יִתְבָּרַךְ שִׁמְךָ בְּפִי כָּל חַי תָּמִיד לְעוֹלָם וָעֶד. בָּרוּךְ אַתָּה יהוה, מְקַדֵּשׁ הַשַּׁבָּת.

Blessings for Reading the Torah (Sephardic Custom)

The reader shows the oleh the section to be read. The oleh touches the scroll at that place with the tzitzit of his tallit, which he then kisses. Grasping the Torah with a cloth, he recites:

Oleh: The LORD is with you   *Cong:* May the LORD bless you

Oleh: Bless the LORD, the blessed One.

Cong: Bless the LORD, the blessed One, for ever and all time.

Oleh: Bless the LORD, the blessed One, for ever and all time.

Blessed are You, LORD our God, King of the Universe,
who has chosen us from all peoples and has given us His Torah.
Blessed are You, LORD, Giver of the Torah.

After the reading, the oleh recites:

Oleh: Blessed are You, LORD our God, King of the Universe,
who has given us His Torah, the Torah of truth, and everlasting life He has planted in our midst.
Blessed are You, LORD, Giver of the Torah.

Blessings for Reading the Haftara

Before reading the Haftara, the person called up for Maftir recites:

בָּרוּךְ Blessed are You, LORD our God, King of the Universe, who chose good prophets and was pleased with their words, spoken in truth. Blessed are You, LORD, who chose the Torah, His servant Moses, His people Israel, and the prophets of truth and righteousness.

After reading the Haftara, he recites:

גֹּאֲלֵנוּ Our Redeemer, the LORD of hosts is His name, Holy One of Israel   *Isaiah 47*

בָּרוּךְ Blessed are You, LORD our God, King of the Universe, Rock of all worlds, righteous for all generations, the faithful God who says and does, speaks and fulfills, all of whose words are truth and righteousness. You are faithful, LORD our God, and faithful are Your words, not one of which returns unfulfilled, for You, God, are a faithful (and compassionate) King. Blessed are You, LORD, faithful in all His words.

רַחֵם Have compassion on Zion for it is the source of our life, and save the one grieved in spirit swiftly in our days. Blessed are You, LORD, who makes Zion rejoice in her children.

שַׂמְּחֵנוּ Grant us joy, LORD our God, through Elijah the prophet Your servant, and through the kingdom of the house of David Your anointed – may he soon come and gladden our hearts. May no stranger sit on his throne, and may others no longer inherit his glory, for You took an oath to him by Your holy name that his light would never be extinguished. Blessed are You, LORD, Shield of David.

עַל הַתּוֹרָה For the Torah, for divine worship, for the prophets, and for this Sabbath day which You, LORD our God, have given us for holiness and rest, honor and glory – for all these we thank and bless You, LORD our God, and may Your name be blessed by the mouth of all that lives, continually, for ever and all time. Blessed are You, LORD, who sanctifies the Sabbath.

ברכות התורה לספרדים

קודם הברכה על העולה לראות היכן קוראים ולנשק את ספר התורה.
בשעת הברכה העולה אוחז בספר באמצעות מטפחת.

עולה: **יהוה עִמָּכֶם** קהל: **יְבָרֶכְךָ יהוה**

עולה: (רַבָּנַן) בָּרְכוּ אֶת יהוה הַמְבֹרָךְ.

קהל: בָּרוּךְ יהוה הַמְבֹרָךְ לְעוֹלָם וָעֶד.

עולה: בָּרוּךְ יהוה הַמְבֹרָךְ לְעוֹלָם וָעֶד.

בָּרוּךְ אַתָּה יהוה, אֱלֹהֵינוּ מֶלֶךְ הָעוֹלָם,
אֲשֶׁר בָּחַר בָּנוּ מִכָּל הָעַמִּים, וְנָתַן לָנוּ אֶת תּוֹרָתוֹ.
בָּרוּךְ אַתָּה יהוה, נוֹתֵן הַתּוֹרָה.

לאחר הקריאה העולה מנשק את ספר התורה ומברך:

בָּרוּךְ אַתָּה יהוה, אֱלֹהֵינוּ מֶלֶךְ הָעוֹלָם,
אֲשֶׁר נָתַן לָנוּ (אֶת) תּוֹרָתוֹ תּוֹרַת אֱמֶת, וְחַיֵּי עוֹלָם נָטַע בְּתוֹכֵנוּ.
בָּרוּךְ אַתָּה יהוה, נוֹתֵן הַתּוֹרָה.

ברכות ההפטרה

לפני קריאת ההפטרה המפטיר מברך:

בָּרוּךְ אַתָּה יהוה אֱלֹהֵינוּ מֶלֶךְ הָעוֹלָם אֲשֶׁר בָּחַר בִּנְבִיאִים טוֹבִים, וְרָצָה בְדִבְרֵיהֶם הַנֶּאֱמָרִים בֶּאֱמֶת.
בָּרוּךְ אַתָּה יהוה, הַבּוֹחֵר בַּתּוֹרָה וּבְמֹשֶׁה עַבְדּוֹ וּבְיִשְׂרָאֵל עַמּוֹ וּבִנְבִיאֵי הָאֱמֶת וָצֶדֶק.

אחרי קריאת ההפטרה המפטיר מוסיף פסוק זה קודם הברכה:

גֹּאֲלֵנוּ יהוה צְבָאוֹת שְׁמוֹ, קְדוֹשׁ יִשְׂרָאֵל: ישעיה מז

בָּרוּךְ אַתָּה יהוה, אֱלֹהֵינוּ מֶלֶךְ הָעוֹלָם, צוּר כָּל הָעוֹלָמִים, צַדִּיק בְּכָל הַדּוֹרוֹת, הָאֵל הַנֶּאֱמָן, הָאוֹמֵר וְעוֹשֶׂה, מְדַבֵּר וּמְקַיֵּם, כִּי כָל דְּבָרָיו אֱמֶת וָצֶדֶק. נֶאֱמָן אַתָּה הוּא יהוה אֱלֹהֵינוּ וְנֶאֱמָנִים דְּבָרֶיךָ, וְדָבָר אֶחָד מִדְּבָרֶיךָ אָחוֹר לֹא יָשׁוּב רֵיקָם, כִּי אֵל מֶלֶךְ נֶאֱמָן (וְרַחֲמָן) אָתָּה. בָּרוּךְ אַתָּה יהוה, הָאֵל הַנֶּאֱמָן בְּכָל דְּבָרָיו.

רַחֵם עַל צִיּוֹן כִּי הִיא בֵּית חַיֵּינוּ, וְלַעֲלוּבַת נֶפֶשׁ תּוֹשִׁיעַ בִּמְהֵרָה בְיָמֵינוּ. בָּרוּךְ אַתָּה יהוה, מְשַׂמֵּחַ צִיּוֹן בְּבָנֶיהָ.

שַׂמְּחֵנוּ יהוה אֱלֹהֵינוּ בְּאֵלִיָּהוּ הַנָּבִיא עַבְדֶּךָ, וּבְמַלְכוּת בֵּית דָּוִד מְשִׁיחָךְ, בִּמְהֵרָה יָבוֹא וְיָגֵל לִבֵּנוּ. עַל כִּסְאוֹ לֹא יֵשֵׁב זָר, וְלֹא יִנְחֲלוּ עוֹד אֲחֵרִים אֶת כְּבוֹדוֹ, כִּי בְשֵׁם קָדְשְׁךָ נִשְׁבַּעְתָּ לּוֹ שֶׁלֹּא יִכְבֶּה נֵרוֹ לְעוֹלָם וָעֶד. בָּרוּךְ אַתָּה יהוה, מָגֵן דָּוִד.

עַל הַתּוֹרָה וְעַל הָעֲבוֹדָה וְעַל הַנְּבִיאִים וְעַל יוֹם הַשַּׁבָּת הַזֶּה, שֶׁנָּתַתָּ לָּנוּ יהוה אֱלֹהֵינוּ לִקְדֻשָּׁה וְלִמְנוּחָה, לְכָבוֹד וּלְתִפְאָרֶת. עַל הַכֹּל יהוה אֱלֹהֵינוּ אֲנַחְנוּ מוֹדִים לָךְ וּמְבָרְכִים אוֹתָךְ, יִתְבָּרַךְ שִׁמְךָ בְּפִי כָּל חַי תָּמִיד לְעוֹלָם וָעֶד. בָּרוּךְ אַתָּה יהוה, מְקַדֵּשׁ הַשַּׁבָּת. אָמֵן.

Cantillation Marks (*Trop*)

שמות הטעמים וסימניהם

אשכנזים:

מֵרְכָ֥א טִפְּחָ֖א מֻנַּ֣ח אֶתְנַחְתָּ֑א מֵרְכָ֥א טִפְּחָ֖א סוֹף־פָּסֽוּק

מַהְפַּ֤ךְ פַּשְׁטָא֙ מֻנַּ֣ח זָקֵף־קָטֹ֔ן זָקֵף־גָּד֕וֹל מֻנַּ֣ח | מֻנַּ֣ח רְבִ֗יעַ

קַדְמָ֨א דַּרְגָּ֧א תְּבִ֛יר מֻנַּ֣ח זַרְקָא֮ מֻנַּ֣ח סֶגּוֹל֒ תְּ֠לִישָׁא־גְדוֹלָה

תְּלִישָׁא־קְטַנָּה֩ קַדְמָ֨א וְאַזְלָ֨א אַזְלָא־גֵּ֜רֵשׁ גֵּרְשַׁ֞יִם פָּזֵ֡ר

יְ֚תִיב שַׁלְשֶׁ֓לֶת גַּלְגַּ֪ל קַרְנֵי־פָרָ֟ה מֵרְכָא־כְפוּלָ֦ה

לְגַרְמֵ֣ה ׀ סוֹף־פָּסֽוּק

ספרדים:

זַרְקָא֮ מַקַּף־שׁוֹפָר־הוֹלֵ֣ךְ סְגוֹלְתָּא֒ פָּזֵר־גָּד֡וֹל

תְּ֠לְשָׁא תִּילְשָׁא֩ אַזְלָא־גֵּ֜רִישׁ פָּסֵק׀ רָבִ֗יעַ שְׁנֵי־גֵרְשִׁ֞ין

דַּרְגָּ֧א תְּבִ֛יר מַאֲרִ֥יךְ טַרְחָ֖א אַתְנָ֑ח שׁוֹפָר־מְהֻפָּ֤ךְ

קַדְמָ֨א תְּרֵי־קַדְמִ֨ין זָקֵף־קָטֹ֔ן זָקֵף־גָּד֕וֹל שַׁלְשֶׁ֓לֶת

גַּלְגַּ֪ל קַרְנֵי־פָרָ֟ה תְּרֵי־טַעֲמֵ֦י יְ֚תִיב סוֹף־פָּסֽוּק

אות קורן ואות רש״י

א	א
ב	ב
ג	ג
ד	ד
ה	ה
ו	ו
ז	ז
ח	ח
ט	ט
י	י
כ	כ
ל	ל
מ	מ
נ	נ
ס	ס
ע	ע
פ	פ
צ	צ
ק	ק
ר	ר
ש	ש
ת	ת
ם	ם
ן	ן
ץ	ץ
ף	ף
ך	ך

Book of
Genesis

GENESIS

This book is dedicated to

my parents and grandparents, and to their parents and grandparents, and those who came before.

It is they on whose shoulders I stand.
If it were not for them, their sacrifices and wisdom,
I would be but dust in the wind.

William A. Ackman

Bereshit

INTRODUCTION TO GENESIS

The book of Genesis is the book of beginnings and roots. It covers a far greater time period than all the other books of the Torah combined, surveying thousands of years, whereas the other books of the Torah deal with events that occurred over the course of 120 years. The early sections of Genesis skim over some two thousand years without much comment, although the narrative interrupts its general survey to focus on specific details and stories. These particulars do not merely add interest and color to the general picture, but together constitute the essential part of the overall tapestry of the book.

Genesis differs from the other books of the Torah in that it is virtually all narrative accounts of events, with very few commandments. In the manner of the Bible, it does not explicitly discuss philosophical or theoretical topics; rather, its contents are presented to the reader in the form of stories. Through its stories, the book deals with numerous fundamental human problems. Thus, the book of Genesis stands on its own, because it is relevant to all people. Rarely can one find in the book definitive positive or negative judgments. The stories mainly relate what happened.

That said, even when the Torah does not offer an explicit judgment, its opinion frequently can be inferred from the verses themselves. Direct messages, insights and revelations, discussions and analyses, questions and answers, are rarely found explicitly in the book. Instead, they are planted in the mind of the learner and left to take root and develop intellectually and emotionally within his or her soul, in accordance with his or her abilities.

At first glance it might seem that Genesis is an orderly book, as it stays faithful to the time line of the events it describes. However, a more careful examination of the sequence of the verses shows that there are invariably aspects of the text that are not fully elucidated. Some of the missing details are vital for a proper understanding, while others merely arouse the reader's curiosity. Even the opening verse, which apparently deals with the very beginning of all beginnings, "In the beginning, God created the heavens and the earth," actually occurs in the middle of the story. After all, the undoubted first and central "protagonist" of the book, as indicated by the number of mentions of His name, is God Himself, and yet He appears in the first verse of the book without any introduction or explanation. Indeed, God is the beginning of existence not only in the chronological sense, but also in the manner described in philosophical literature as the Primary Cause. Similarly, on more than one occasion, other important characters in the book, human or otherwise, appear on the scene with no background information provided, and their actions are generally described without any accompanying explanatory comments. Granted, over the generations, the Sages have elucidated these stories with various interpretations, but the stories of the Torah flow without such glosses, as though saying to the reader: The rest is commentary; go learn.

The three main topics of the book are the creation of the world in general, humanity as a whole, and the seeds of the development of God's elected people, Israel. However, the attention paid to the three subjects is unequal. The stories with the widest scope are short and obscure; the more an incident is focused and limited in scope, the more detail the text provides.

The first topic, the creation of the world in general, is found mainly in the first chapter, which depicts the formation of various cosmic entities and creatures from a primeval state of being. The book describes a world built on internal contrasts yet whose discrete beings somehow unite into a single essence. These accounts also evoke thoughts on the relationship between creation as a whole, with its many creatures, and the rational being that is man; the reproductive urges and will to dominate that define the biological world; and the complex and problematic nature of man, who is tasked with further developing God's creation.

The sections of the book that deal with humanity in general touch upon the basic issues of philosophy: human consciousness; the struggle between primitive nature and artifice; the temptations and dangers of the developing mind, as well as the problems of

desire and sin, lust and law breaking, jealousy and murder; responsibility and punishment; human creativity and those problems resulting from the very existence and stratification of human society. However, as stated above, these issues are not analyzed through a series of philosophical observations, but arise from the narrative accounts. The stories in the first chapters, *Parashat Bereshit* and *Parashat Noaḥ*, can be read as parables, as introductions or keys to an entire world of human thought.

The sections of the book that concentrate on its third topic, the origins of the chosen people, contain the stories of the patriarchs and the nation's first generations. The individuals depicted are presented in their full humanity. Their lives are full of exertions, confrontations, and trials. The forefathers of the Jewish people must deal with the same problems that occupy humanity as a whole: love and hate, jealousy and competition, errors and their consequences. They are not spared pain, enslavement, or internal and external strife, but they also experience forgiveness and absolution. Nevertheless, alongside the human, personal, and familial aspects of the lives of the patriarchs, the book of Genesis depicts their relationship with God, together with their commitment and extreme devotion to the covenant with Him. Their personalities are molded through all of these factors. God's elect are capable not only of asking questions, but also of receiving answers and instructions, and these figures create the foundations for the rest of the books of the Torah.

Parashat
Bereshit

The Seven Days of Creation
GENESIS 1:1–2:3

It is commonly thought that the beginning of the book of Genesis presents a cosmogony, a theory of how the universe came to exist. While this is mostly correct, the account of Creation appearing in Genesis diverges from other recorded accounts in that it disregards the question of what was the starting point of existence itself. For this reason, the Torah begins the account of Creation with the word *bereshit*, which literally means "in the beginning of." The account begins at the beginning of some preexisting process. Had the verse stated *bareshit*, it would have been understood as meaning simply "in the beginning." By contrast, the term *bereshit* indicates the beginning of some specific, unnamed process. It appears that a fundamental message lies hidden in this first word: At some early stage in the mysterious process of creating existence, God created the heavens and the earth.

1 **1** **In the beginning, God created the heavens and the earth.** The opening verse takes the existence of God as a given. It does not address questions about God's origin or nature; rather, God is understood to be the absolute existence from which everything begins. Already at the beginning of the account of Creation, heaven and earth appear as distinct entities and as a framework for all of creation, as detailed in the rest of the chapter.

2 **The earth was unformed and empty**[D] **[*tohu vavohu*].** The earth was completely lacking any structure or order. The heavens too were unformed and empty, but the verse initially focuses on the earth, its structure and content. Although these two terms appear together in other places in the Bible, the precise meaning of the word *vohu* is difficult to ascertain; it is even uncertain whether *vohu* refers to a distinct concept. **And darkness was upon the face of the deep.** The deep may refer to deep waters, or to the unstructured universe, that existed at the time. At this early stage of Creation, nothing had yet to receive definite shape; nothing had been revealed. Therefore, the darkness upon the face of the deep was merely the absence of the light that was about to be created. Some commentaries maintain that the darkness was not the absence of light, but an entity in itself, based on the verse "I form the light, and create darkness." **And the spirit of God hovered over the surface of the water.** Water is the first actual substance mentioned in the Torah, as the heaven and the earth are not substances but general entities or zones. The verse does not discuss the creation of the primeval substance that served as the foundation for all of existence. In any case, the Torah indicates that God's power, or will, exists in some form in this reality. God is not located within these entities, and He certainly is not to be identified with them; rather, He hovers close by while remaining separate from them.

3 The process of Creation begins: **God said: Let there be light, and there was light.**[D] It is difficult to understand the meaning or significance of the phrase "God said." The most that can be understood from this cryptic description is that God transmitted a kind of message that there should be light, and His instruction came to pass. Light was the first creation to emerge from *tohu vavohu*. It was unlike any form of light known to mankind; it did not emanate from a prior source. Perhaps it was not even a physical light, but a unique phenomenon.

4 **God saw the light that it was good.**[D] As soon as the light emerged from the unformed universe, God evaluated it and distinguished between good and bad. **And God divided between the light and the darkness.** Once light was created and discerned as good, the next phase of its creation began, namely, the stage of separation, which established the light as a clearly defined entity. The act of discerning and separating between good and bad would continue till the end of time and manifest itself also in human history and civilization.

5 **God called the light day.** From the inception of the concepts of light and day, there was some measure of synonymy between them. Nevertheless, they are clearly and independently defined. Aside from day's association with daylight, the day denotes a specific period of time. At this early stage of the Creation, with the formation of light comes the establishment of time. Until this point, the universe was in a raw state, completely unstructured and undefined; even space and time were not yet defined. These concepts came into being when God willed it. **And to the darkness He called night.** Darkness as well is removed from its previous status as a description of space alone and placed in a framework of time. The concepts of day and night as they appear in this verse express what the Sages called the order of time, in other words, the notions of before and after, relative concepts that did not apply when the earth was

פרשת

בראשית

א ב בְּרֵאשִׁית בָּרָא אֱלֹהִים אֵת הַשָּׁמַיִם וְאֵת הָאָרֶץ: וְהָאָרֶץ הָיְתָה תֹהוּ וָבֹהוּ וְחֹשֶׁךְ א
ג עַל־פְּנֵי תְהוֹם וְרוּחַ אֱלֹהִים מְרַחֶפֶת עַל־פְּנֵי הַמָּיִם: וַיֹּאמֶר אֱלֹהִים יְהִי־אוֹר
ד וַיְהִי־אוֹר: וַיַּרְא אֱלֹהִים אֶת־הָאוֹר כִּי־טוֹב וַיַּבְדֵּל אֱלֹהִים בֵּין הָאוֹר וּבֵין הַחֹשֶׁךְ:
ה וַיִּקְרָא אֱלֹהִים ׀ לָאוֹר יוֹם וְלַחֹשֶׁךְ קָרָא לָיְלָה וַיְהִי־עֶרֶב וַיְהִי־בֹקֶר יוֹם אֶחָד:

רש"י

פרק א

א| **בראשית.** אמר רבי יצחק: לא היה צריך להתחיל את התורה אלא מ"החדש הזה לכם" (שמות יב, ב) שהיא מצוה ראשונה שנצטוו ישראל. ומה טעם פתח ב"בראשית" – משום "כח מעשיו הגיד לעמו לתת להם נחלת גוים" (תהלים קיא, ו), שאם יאמרו אמות העולם לישראל: לסטים אתם שכבשתם ארצות שבעה גוים, הם אומרים להם: כל הארץ של הקדוש ברוך הוא היא, הוא בראה ונתנה לאשר ישר בעיניו, ברצונו נתנה להם, וברצונו נטלה מהם ונתנה לנו: **בראשית ברא.** אין המקרא הזה אומר אלא דרשני, כמו שדרשוהו רבותינו ז"ל: בשביל התורה שנקראת "ראשית דרכו" (משלי ח, כב), ובשביל ישראל שנקראו "ראשית תבואתה" (ירמיה ב, ג). ואם באת לפרשו כפשוטו, כך פרשהו: בראשית בריאת שמים וארץ, והארץ היתה תהו ובהו וחשך, ויאמר אלהים יהי אור. ולא בא המקרא להורות סדר הבריאה לומר שאלו קדמו, שאם בא להורות כך, היה לו לכתב: בראשונה ברא את השמים וגו', שאין לך 'ראשית' במקרא שאינו דבוק לתבה של אחריו, כמו: "בראשית ממלכת יהויקם" (שם כז, א), "ראשית ממלכתו" (בראשית י, י), "ראשית דגנך" (דברים יח, ד). אף כאן אתה אומר: "בראשית ברא אלהים" וגו' כמו: 'בראשית ברא', ודומה לו: "תחלת דבר ה' בהושע", כלומר תחלת דבורו של הקדוש ברוך הוא בהושע, "ויאמר ה' אל הושע" וגו' (הושע א, ב). ואם תאמר, להורות בא שאלו תחלה נבראו, ופרושו: 'בראשית הכל ברא אלו', ויש לך מקראות שמקצרים לשונם וממעטים תבה אחת, כמו: "כי לא סגר דלתי בטני" (איוב ג, י) ולא פרש מי הסוגר, וכמו: "ישא את חיל דמשק" (ישעיה ח, ד) ולא פרש מי ישאנו, וכמו: "אם יחרוש בבקרים" (עמוס ו, יב) ולא פרש 'אם יחרוש אדם בבקרים', וכמו: "מגיד מראשית אחרית" (ישעיה מו, י) ולא פרש 'מגיד מראשית דבר אחרית דבר' – אם כן תמה על עצמך שהרי המים קדמו, שהרי כתיב: "ורוח אלהים מרחפת על פני המים" (להלן פסוק ב), ועדין לא גלה המקרא בריאת המים מתי היתה, למדת שקדמו לארץ, ועוד שהשמים מאש וממים נבראו, על כרחך לא למד המקרא בסדר המקדמים והמאחרים כלום: **ברא אלהים.** ולא אמר 'ברא ה'', שבתחלה עלה במחשבה לבראתו במדת הדין, וראה שאין מתקים, והקדים מדת רחמים ושתפה למדת הדין, והינו דכתיב: "ביום עשות ה' אלהים ארץ ושמים" (להלן ב, ד):

ב| **תהו ובהו.** תהו לשון תמה ושממון, שאדם תוהה ומשתומם על בהו שבה: **תהו.** אישטורדישו"ן בלעז: **בהו.** לשון ריקות וצדו: **על פני תהום.** על פני המים שעל הארץ: **ורוח אלהים מרחפת.** כסא הכבוד עומד באויר ומרחף על פני המים ברוח פיו של הקדוש ברוך הוא ובמאמרו, כיונה המרחפת על הקן, אקוביטי"ר בלעז:

ד| **וירא אלהים את האור כי טוב ויבדל.** אף בזה אנו צריכים לדברי אגדה, ראהו שאינו כדאי להשתמש בו רשעים והבדילו לצדיקים לעתיד לבא. ולפי פשוטו, כך פרשהו: ראהו כי טוב ואין נאה לו ולחשך שיהיו משתמשים בערבוביא, וקבע לזה תחומו ביום ולזה תחומו בלילה:

ה| **יום אחד.** לפי סדר לשון הפרשה היה לו לכתב: יום ראשון, כמו שכתוב בשאר הימים: שני, שלישי, רביעי. למה כתב "אחד"? על שם שהיה הקדוש ברוך הוא יחיד

DISCUSSION

1:2| **The earth was unformed and empty:** Some of the commentaries maintain that heaven and earth contained all the components of Creation from the outset in a chaotic jumble (see Ramban, verse 1; *Bereshit Rabba* 1:14). According to this opinion, the process of Creation essentially involved the arrangement of these various components, specifically the establishment of the location, status, and function of each and every entity.

1:3| **And there was light:** If one assumes that the light was indeed physical, it can be described as radiating from all of existence. There were no boundaries to it; it spread over the entire universe. Not for naught did the Sages teach that with this light one could see from one end of the world to the other (*Ḥagiga* 12a).

1:4| **That it was good:** The process of appraisal and judgment will appear in the subsequent stages of Creation as well. It is a fundamental part not only of the book of Genesis but of the other books of the Bible too, and can even be considered a foundational principle of Judaism itself (see introduction to commentary on Leviticus). Consequently, the evaluative term "good" is among the first words of the Torah and is the first abstract idea mentioned in the Torah.

The concept of good can refer to a positive evaluation on a number of levels. Earlier generations differentiated between the moral good, the opposite of which is evil; the practical good, or the effective; and the pleasant (see *Rambam's Introduction to Avot 5*; *Sefer HaIkkarim* 3:35). The Bible also refers to the aesthetically beautiful as good. It seems that throughout the recounting of the process of Creation, the descriptive term "good" is used in all its various meanings.

still unformed and empty. The verse introduces additional new concepts: **It was evening and it was morning,**[D] **one day.** The essence of time is comprised of evening, which is related to darkness and night, and morning, which is related to light and day. After the passage of evening and morning, one day comes to an end. Therefore, the term "day," which previously referred specifically to the hours of light and was even identified with light, now receives an additional meaning: A unit of time that includes both the hours of light and darkness. The verse refers to this first day of Creation as "one day" instead of the first day, as the day itself is a distinct entity. In other words, the existence of one day did not indicate the existence of a second. The acts of creation that followed occurred spontaneously. Consequently, the next day may be considered the second day only in the sense that there was already one day preceding it; its existence did not derive from the existence of the first day. The creation of light, therefore, was unique, as its appearance allowed for the basic arrangement of space and time.

6 **God said: Let there be a firmament in the midst of the water.** This was not a geographical division, but a metaphysical one. **And let it divide between water and water.** The breaking up of the all-encompassing primordial waters was vital to the continuation of Creation. These waters would be confined and transformed into two separate entities, with the firmament separating them from one another.

7 **God made the firmament and divided**[D] **between the water that was under the firmament and the water that was above the firmament; and it was so.** This division served to separate between the material and spiritual planes. From this point forward, physical matter and spirit became distinguishable from one another. They would now exist separately, in some ways interconnected but essentially independent from one another.

8 **God called the firmament heavens**[D] **[*shamayim*].** Some expound the word *shamayim* as *sham mayim,* meaning "water is there." However, it is more likely that *shamayim* is the double form of *sham,* there there, meaning that it is located beyond. The second day of Creation also brought with it an element of measurement not with regard to space but with regard to time: **It was evening and it was morning, a second day.** On this day, the universe achieved a new structure. Although it did not yet resemble the universe as we know it, it now contained a hierarchical structure in addition to light.

9 **God said: Let the water under the heavens be gathered.** This refers to the physical water under the firmament, similar to the water of today. The lower waters were called upon to be gathered **to one place, and let the dry land appear.** When the water was collected in one place, the dry land underneath would be exposed. **And it was so.**

10 **God called the dry land earth.** It should not be inferred from these verses that the dry land already existed as a distinct entity, albeit under water. Rather, it seems more likely that just as the light burst forth from within the darkness, so too the dry land was initially incorporated within the water, as it were. Only on the third day did the land dry, consolidate, and become a separate entity that would now be called earth. **And the gathering of the waters He called seas.**[D] The place in which the waters gathered would become a distinct entity. This includes not only actual seas, but also discrete bodies of water, such as lakes of any size. Even the basin in the Temple, which King Solomon fashioned so the priests could wash their hands and feet, is known as a sea. From this point forward, the earth and the sea would be the two largest entities in the world. **And God saw that it was good.** Unlike the mystifying creation of the first day, or the traumatic separation of the second, the creations of the third day were already the beginnings of the fully formed universe. The earth and the seas were given their own space and unique characteristics that would enable the flourishing of those creatures that would inhabit each of them respectively. The existence of the earth and the seas was possible only because they had been separated from each other. This combination of dry land and water, and their subsequent division, was seen by God as good.

11 From an outsider's perspective, the exposure of dry land, with its tall mountains, plains, and ravines, would have seemed a most dramatic event. However, on the very same day there was another creation, even more significant for humanity: **God said: Let the earth sprout grasses.** The earth was commanded to bring forth various types of vegetation. If until now the Torah dealt with metaphysics and physics, the third day introduced the concept of biology. The novelty of this creation was not in the actual growth or spread of the grass; such processes occur even in a puddle of water or a mound of earth. Rather, the sprouting of the grass was unique in that it contained within it

---

DISCUSSION

1:5 | It was evening and it was morning: When does the day begin? Intuitively it begins with morning's first light. According to contemporary convention, a new day begins at midnight. The biblical account of Creation, however, indicates that the unit of time known as day begins in the evening, so that darkness precedes light (see also Leviticus 22:7, 23:32; *Berakhot* 2a). This definition represents a worldview in which absence precedes existence (see *Tzidkat HaTzaddik* 11). That is, darkness is perceived as a more primordial reality from which its antithesis, light, emerges. The day begins with the evening and continues through the morning light, just as the beginning of all existence was hidden in its absence. This idea also conveys a message of hope: From a dark and concealed beginning light shall emerge.

ז ויאמר אלהים יהי רקיע בתוך המים ויהי מבדיל בין מים למים: ויעש אלהים
את־הרקיע ויבדל בין המים אשר מתחת לרקיע ובין המים אשר מעל לרקיע
ח ויהי־כן: ויקרא אלהים לרקיע שמים ויהי־ערב ויהי־בקר יום שני:
ט ויאמר אלהים יקוו המים מתחת השמים אל־מקום אחד ותראה היבשה
י ויהי־כן: ויקרא אלהים ׀ ליבשה ארץ ולמקוה המים קרא ימים וירא
יא אלהים כי־טוב: ויאמר אלהים תדשא הארץ דשא עשב מזריע זרע עץ פרי

רש"י

בעולמו, שלא נבראו המלאכים עד יום שני. כך מפרש בבראשית רבה (ג, ח):

ו| **יהי רקיע.** יחזק הרקיע, שאף על פי שנבראו שמים ביום ראשון, עדין לחים היו, וקרשו בשני מגערת הקדוש ברוך הוא באמרו: "יהי רקיע", וזהו שכתוב: "עמודי שמים ירופפו" (איוב כו, יא) כל יום ראשון, ובשני – "ויתמהו מגערתו" (שם), כאדם שמשתומם ועומד מגערת המאיים עליו: **בתוך המים.** באמצע המים, שיש הפרש בין מים העליונים לרקיע כמו בין הרקיע למים שעל הארץ. הא למדת שהם תלויים במאמרו של מלך:

ז| **ויעש אלהים את הרקיע.** תקנו על עמדו והיא עשייתו, כמו: "ועשתה את צפרניה" (דברים כא, יב): **מעל לרקיע.** 'על הרקיע' לא נאמר אלא "מעל", לפי שהן תלויין באויר. ומפני מה לא נאמר 'כי טוב' בשני? לפי שלא נגמרה מלאכת המים עד יום שלישי והרי התחיל בה בשני, ודבר שלא נגמר אינו במלואו וטובו, ובשלישי שנגמרה מלאכת המים והתחיל וגמר מלאכה אחרת, כפל בו 'כי טוב' שני פעמים (להלן פסוקים י; יב): אחת לגמר מלאכת השני ואחת לגמר מלאכת היום:

ח| **ויקרא אלהים לרקיע שמים.** שא מים, שם מים, אש ומים שערבן זה בזה ועשה מהם שמים:

ט| **יקוו המים.** שהיו שטוחים על פני כל הארץ, והקום באוקינוס, הוא הים הגדול שבכל הימים:

י| **קרא ימים.** והלא ים אחד הוא? אלא אינו דומה טעם דג העולה מן הים בעכו לטעם דג העולה מן הים באספמיא:

יא| **תדשא הארץ דשא עשב.** לא דשא לשון עשב ולא עשב לשון דשא, ולא היה לשון המקרא לומר: 'תעשיב הארץ', שמיני דשאין מחלקין, כל אחד לעצמו נקרא עשב פלוני, ואין לשון למדבר לומר דשא פלוני, שלשון דשא הוא לבישת הארץ כשהיא מתמלאת בדשאים: **תדשא.** תתמלא ותתכסה לבוש עשבים. בלשון לעז נקרא דשא אירבידי"ן, כלן בערבוביא, וכל שרש לעצמו נקרא עשב: **מזריע זרע.** שיגדל בו זרעו לזרוע ממנו במקום אחר: **עץ פרי.** שיהא טעם העץ כטעם הפרי. והיא לא

DISCUSSION

1:7| **And divided:** The Sages teach that the lower waters cried out: We too wish to be before the King (*Tikkunei Zohar* 19:2; see Rabbeinu Baḥya, Leviticus 2:13). In other words, the physical world bemoaned the fact that due to the separation it was no longer a spiritual entity, and it yearned for the primordial existence, where matter and spirit were one.

The Sages note that all the stages of Creation were considered by God as good except for the work of the second day; only on the second day is the phrase "it was good" absent (*Pesaḥim* 54a). Distinction and separation are essential for the existence of the universe. The world is not a fixed, unchanging reality; rather, it constantly moves on a continuum between opposing poles. The second day, on which all of existence was divided, enabled movement in different directions, progress, and ultimately life. Although the concept of division already appeared on the first day, the second day added a more profound form of separation: The division between the upper and the lower elements of a single entity. The hierarchical structure of existence established by this division, between what is above and what is below, emphasizes the concepts of sanctity and superiority but also allows for the existence of inferiority and impurity. Weaving this dichotomy into the fabric of the universe allowed for the existence of non-neutral entities. Consequently, the division on the second day may be considered good only from a utilitarian perspective: It is a necessary separation on account of the benefit it provides, but it comes at a cost. The separation between the upper and the lower elements of existence did not make the universe better in moral or aesthetic terms, nor did it create a more pleasant existence. Therefore, the goodness of the second day goes unmentioned.

1:8| **Heavens:** Heaven is not the atmosphere or the sky, but a different entity altogether. This accounts for the expression "the heavens and the heavens of heavens" (Deuteronomy 10:14). The tension between mankind, situated on earth, and the great beyond of heaven, is not only a piece of the account of Creation, but a fundamental part of human history as well. The creation of heaven stretches a dividing line between the material, which is perceivable and existent among mankind, and the spiritual, which is elusive and beyond man's reach. The existence of the firmament is not as simple as that of light, as the firmament includes within itself a distinction between above and below.

1:10| **God called the dry land earth, and the gathering of the waters He called seas:** Henceforth there will be a complex relationship of opposition and combination between land and water. On the one hand, the dry land is defined as a place without water; understood in this sense, the dry land and the water are two distinct entities that complement and oppose one another. Several verses in the Bible refer to the constant struggle between the sea and the land. The sea seeks to flood the land and erode the earth, but it is blocked by the shores (see,

a novelty known in classical philosophy as the vegetative soul. The grass was the basis for all higher life forms that would be created later, not only because the latter depend upon vegetation in order to survive, but because they are themselves more advanced forms of things that grow. The creation of biology includes not only growth but also proliferation: **Vegetation yielding seed, and fruit tree bearing fruit in its kind, in which there is its seed, upon the earth.** The definition of the biological system according to a process in which a cell or group of cells start to grow, and indeed to propagate, is not new. Although this phenomenon of growth and reproduction runs counter to all considerations of physics, as it violates the laws of entropy, it is nevertheless the very definition of life. **And it was so.**

12 **The earth produced grasses, vegetation yielding seed in its kind, and a tree bearing fruit in which there was its seed in its kind.** The Torah does not classify the various species of vegetation; it does not even provide the criteria for categorizing them. The verse instead emphasizes that each of these creations was a species to itself; the creation of plant life was a deliberate, ordered process. **And God saw that it was good.** In addition to being the day on which the dry land was exposed, the third day was the day on which life was first brought forth. The significance of the emergence of life on the third day is expressed in the double appearance of the phrase "it was good" (see verse 10). Before the third day, the universe consisted only of inanimate entities; on the third day life began, even if it was not yet intelligent. Although vegetation does not share all the characteristics of more complex life forms, it possesses the foundation and source of life, namely, the ability to tend to its own survival, to grow, and to multiply.

13 **It was evening and it was morning, a third day.**

14 **God said: Let there be lights**[D] **in the firmament of the heavens.** From this point objects would exist that would generate and emit light. These were distinct from light itself, which was created on the first day. The addition on the fourth day of entities responsible for the light was part of the continued structuring and ordering of the universe. These lights would exist **to distinguish between the day and the night.** The division between day and night was significant not only from a celestial perspective, but also in establishing the rhythm of time. The function of the lights is first and foremost to measure time and divide it into segments. Specifically, **let them be for signs,** phenomena which occur in heaven and on earth, **and for seasons, and for days and years.**

15 **Let them be for lights in the firmament of the heavens to give light upon the earth;**[D] **and it was so.**

16 **God made the two great lights,** as they appear today: **the greater light,** the sun, **to rule the day, and the lesser light,** the moon, **to rule the night, and the stars.**

17 **God set them in the firmament of the heavens to give light upon the earth**

18 **and to rule during the day and during the night.** The sun and moon appear to human beings as rulers over day and night, as it is impossible for one to fail to notice the presence of the sun or its absence, and it is likewise impossible to miss the appearance or disappearance of the moon. **And** these lights also serve **to divide between the light and the darkness.** Although earlier verses already referred to day and night, and to morning and evening, and connected them to light and darkness, these entities were not completely defined until now. **And God saw that it was good.**

19 **It was evening and it was morning, a fourth day.**

20 From vegetation and the heavenly bodies, the verse addresses the creation of animals: **God said: Let the water swarm with swarms [*sheretz*] of living creatures [*nefesh ḥaya*].** These creatures would not grow and develop blindly, like vegetation, but would have the ability to move and some measure of will. The word *sheretz* may allude to wanting, *retziya*, or running, *ritza*. Note that the first appearance of the phrase *nefesh ḥaya* is in connection with aquatic creatures; it appears again only later with regard to land animals. Perhaps this is because water is the first source for creation and for the continued existence of life. **And let birds fly above the earth on the face of the firmament of the heavens.**

21 **God created the great serpents [*taninim*].** In several places in the Bible, the *tanin* is identified with the *livyatan* or some creature resembling it. In modern Hebrew, *livyatan* refers to a whale while *tanin* refers to an alligator, but these are not their biblical meanings. Rather, the *tanin* and *livyatan* are mysterious aquatic creatures that were created in the water and whose relationship to our world is unclear. In several places in the Bible they are depicted as enormously powerful monsters, which at times do not accept the authority even of God. **And every**

DISCUSSION

e.g., Job 7:12, 26:10; Jeremiah 5:22). On the other hand, there is a profound, symbiotic relationship between them: The dry land cannot exist without the waters of the sea, and the sea requires the dry land in order to contain and establish

boundaries for its waters, and to provide water through the various springs and rivers streaming through the dry land. This mutual dependency can be inferred from several descriptions of rain and rivers, both of which are manifestations of

the connection between the land and the sea (see, e.g., Deuteronomy 11:10–12; Ecclesiastes 1:7; *Ta'anit* 9b; *Sanhedrin* 108a).

1:14 | **Lights:** The heavenly bodies are the foundation of all human measurements of time, and ◂▸

עֹשֶׂה פְּרִי לְמִינוֹ אֲשֶׁר זַרְעוֹ־בוֹ עַל־הָאָרֶץ וַיְהִי־כֵן: וַתּוֹצֵא הָאָרֶץ דֶּשֶׁא עֵשֶׂב
מַזְרִיעַ זֶרַע לְמִינֵהוּ וְעֵץ עֹשֶׂה־פְּרִי אֲשֶׁר זַרְעוֹ־בוֹ לְמִינֵהוּ וַיַּרְא אֱלֹהִים כִּי־טוֹב:
יג וַיְהִי־עֶרֶב וַיְהִי־בֹקֶר יוֹם שְׁלִישִׁי:
יד וַיֹּאמֶר אֱלֹהִים יְהִי מְאֹרֹת בִּרְקִיעַ הַשָּׁמַיִם לְהַבְדִּיל בֵּין הַיּוֹם וּבֵין הַלָּיְלָה וְהָיוּ
לְאֹתֹת וּלְמוֹעֲדִים וּלְיָמִים וְשָׁנִים: טו וְהָיוּ לִמְאוֹרֹת בִּרְקִיעַ הַשָּׁמַיִם לְהָאִיר עַל־
הָאָרֶץ וַיְהִי־כֵן: טז וַיַּעַשׂ אֱלֹהִים אֶת־שְׁנֵי הַמְּאֹרֹת הַגְּדֹלִים אֶת־הַמָּאוֹר הַגָּדֹל
לְמֶמְשֶׁלֶת הַיּוֹם וְאֶת־הַמָּאוֹר הַקָּטֹן לְמֶמְשֶׁלֶת הַלַּיְלָה וְאֵת הַכּוֹכָבִים: יז וַיִּתֵּן
אֹתָם אֱלֹהִים בִּרְקִיעַ הַשָּׁמַיִם לְהָאִיר עַל־הָאָרֶץ: יח וְלִמְשֹׁל בַּיּוֹם וּבַלַּיְלָה וּלְהַבְדִּיל
בֵּין הָאוֹר וּבֵין הַחֹשֶׁךְ וַיַּרְא אֱלֹהִים כִּי־טוֹב: יט וַיְהִי־עֶרֶב וַיְהִי־בֹקֶר יוֹם רְבִיעִי:
כ וַיֹּאמֶר אֱלֹהִים יִשְׁרְצוּ הַמַּיִם שֶׁרֶץ נֶפֶשׁ חַיָּה וְעוֹף יְעוֹפֵף עַל־הָאָרֶץ עַל־פְּנֵי רְקִיעַ
הַשָּׁמָיִם: כא וַיִּבְרָא אֱלֹהִים אֶת־הַתַּנִּינִם הַגְּדֹלִים וְאֵת כָּל־נֶפֶשׁ הַחַיָּה ׀ הָרֹמֶשֶׂת

רש״י

עֲשָׂתָה כֵּן, חֶלֶף וַתּוֹצֵא הָאָרֶץ עֵץ עֹשֶׂה פְּרִי, וְלֹא הָעֵץ פְּרִי, לְפִיכָךְ כְּשֶׁנִּתְקַלֵּל אָדָם עַל עֲוֹנוֹ נִפְקְדָה גַם הִיא עַל עֲוֹנָהּ וְנִתְקַלְּלָה: אֲשֶׁר זַרְעוֹ בוֹ. הֵן גַּרְעִינֵי כָּל פְּרִי שֶׁמֵּהֶן הָאִילָן צוֹמֵחַ כְּשֶׁנּוֹטְעִין אוֹתָן:

יב | וַתּוֹצֵא הָאָרֶץ וְגוֹ'. אַף עַל פִּי שֶׁלֹּא נֶאֱמַר 'לְמִינֵהוּ' בַּדֶּשָׁאִין בְּצִוּוּיֵיהֶן, שָׁמְעוּ שֶׁנִּצְטַוּוּ הָאִילָנוֹת עַל כָּךְ, וְנָשְׂאוּ קַל וָחֹמֶר בְּעַצְמָן, כַּמְפֹרָשׁ בְּאַגָּדָה בִּשְׁחִיטַת חֻלִּין (חולין ס ע״א):

יד | יְהִי מְאֹרֹת וְגוֹ'. מִיּוֹם רִאשׁוֹן נִבְרְאוּ, וּבָרְבִיעִי צִוָּה עֲלֵיהֶם לְהִתָּלוֹת בָּרָקִיעַ, וְכֵן כָּל תּוֹלְדוֹת שָׁמַיִם וָאָרֶץ נִבְרְאוּ מִיּוֹם רִאשׁוֹן וְכָל אֶחָד וְאֶחָד נִקְבַּע בַּיּוֹם שֶׁנִּגְזַר עָלָיו, הוּא שֶׁכָּתוּב (לעיל פסוק א) "אֵת הַשָּׁמַיִם" – לְרַבּוֹת תּוֹלְדוֹתֵיהֶם, "וְאֵת הָאָרֶץ" – לְרַבּוֹת תּוֹלְדוֹתֶיהָ: יְהִי

מְאֹרֹת. חָסֵר וי״ו כְּתִיב, עַל שֶׁהוּא יוֹם מְאֵרָה לִפֹּל אַסְכָּרָה בַּתִּינוֹקוֹת, הוּא שֶׁשָּׁנִינוּ: בָּרְבִיעִי הָיוּ מִתְעַנִּים עַל אַסְכָּרָה שֶׁלֹּא תִפֹּל בַּתִּינוֹקוֹת (תענית כז ע״ב): לְהַבְדִּיל בֵּין הַיּוֹם וּבֵין הַלָּיְלָה. מִשֶּׁנִּגְנַז הָאוֹר הָרִאשׁוֹן, אֲבָל בְּשֵׁבַעַת יְמֵי בְרֵאשִׁית שִׁמְּשׁוּ הָאוֹר וְהַחֹשֶׁךְ זֶה בַּיּוֹם וְזֶה בַּלָּיְלָה: וְהָיוּ לְאֹתֹת. כְּשֶׁהַמְּאוֹרוֹת לוֹקִין סִימָן רַע הוּא לָעוֹלָם, שֶׁנֶּאֱמַר: "וּמֵאֹתוֹת הַשָּׁמַיִם אַל תֵּחָתּוּ" (ירמיה י, ב), בַּעֲשׂוֹתְכֶם רְצוֹן הַקָּדוֹשׁ בָּרוּךְ הוּא אֵין אַתֶּם צְרִיכִים לִדְאֹג מִן הַפֻּרְעָנוּת: וּלְמוֹעֲדִים. עַל שֵׁם הֶעָתִיד, שֶׁעֲתִידִים יִשְׂרָאֵל לְהִצְטַוּוֹת עַל הַמּוֹעֲדוֹת, וְהֵם נִמְנִים לְמוֹלַד הַלְּבָנָה: וּלְיָמִים. שִׁמּוּשׁ הַחַמָּה חֲצִי יוֹם וְשִׁמּוּשׁ הַלְּבָנָה חֶצְיוֹ, הֲרֵי יוֹם שָׁלֵם: וְשָׁנִים. לְסוֹף שְׁלֹשׁ מֵאוֹת וְשִׁשִּׁים וַחֲמִשָּׁה יָמִים יִגָּמְרוּ מַהֲלָכָתָן בִּשְׁנֵים עָשָׂר מַזָּלוֹת הַמְּשָׁרְתִים אוֹתָם, וְהִיא שָׁנָה:

טו | וְהָיוּ לִמְאוֹרֹת. עוֹד זֹאת יְשַׁמְּשׁוּ, שֶׁיָּאִירוּ לָעוֹלָם:

טז | הַמְּאֹרֹת הַגְּדֹלִים. שָׁוִים נִבְרְאוּ, וְנִתְמַעֲטָה הַלְּבָנָה עַל שֶׁקִּטְרְגָה וְאָמְרָה: אִי אֶפְשָׁר לִשְׁנֵי מְלָכִים שֶׁיִּשְׁתַּמְּשׁוּ בְּכֶתֶר אֶחָד: וְאֵת הַכּוֹכָבִים. עַל יְדֵי שֶׁמִּעֵט אֶת הַלְּבָנָה הִרְבָּה צְבָאֶיהָ לְהָפִיס דַּעְתָּהּ:

כ | נֶפֶשׁ חַיָּה. שֶׁיֵּשׁ בָּהּ חַיּוּת: שֶׁרֶץ. כָּל דָּבָר חַי שֶׁאֵינוֹ גָּבוֹהַּ מִן הָאָרֶץ קָרוּי שֶׁרֶץ, בָּעוֹף – כְּגוֹן זְבוּבִים, בַּשְּׁקָצִים – כְּגוֹן נְמָלִים וְחִפּוּשִׁית וְתוֹלָעִים, וּבַבְּרִיּוֹת – כְּגוֹן חֹלֶד וְעַכְבָּר וְחֹמֶט וְכַיּוֹצֵא בָהֶם, וְכָל הַדָּגִים:

כא | הַתַּנִּינִם. דָּגִים גְּדוֹלִים שֶׁבַּיָּם, וּבְדִבְרֵי אַגָּדָה הוּא לִוְיָתָן וּבֶן זוּגוֹ, שֶׁבְּרָאָם זָכָר וּנְקֵבָה וְהָרַג אֶת הַנְּקֵבָה וּמְלָחָהּ לַצַּדִּיקִים לֶעָתִיד לָבֹא, שֶׁאִם יִפְרוּ וְיִרְבּוּ לֹא יִתְקַיֵּם הָעוֹלָם בִּפְנֵיהֶם: נֶפֶשׁ חַיָּה. נֶפֶשׁ שֶׁיֵּשׁ בָּהּ חַיּוּת:

DISCUSSION

this is their primary function. While it is also true that the sun is the source of the earth's energy, in principle the world could exist if there were another source to provide energy or light for the earth, independent of the sun. Theoretically, there could be a source of light and energy that is not concentrated in one place but scattered throughout the firmament.

1:15 | For lights in the firmament of the heavens to give light upon the earth: The book of Genesis is not the story of the entire universe; rather, it is "the book of the legacy of Adam" (5:1). Since it deals with man, his problems, his manner of living, and his purpose, the world is described from mankind's perspective, and only with regard to those aspects relevant to him. Accordingly, although the difference in size between these massive lights and the planet Earth was known even in ancient times, it is no surprise that the heavenly bodies are portrayed in the verse without any reference to their true size or to their function, beyond the fact that man uses them to measure time and that they provide light. Since other stars, which are located light-years away from us, have no practical connection to human existence on earth, the Torah does not mention them.

living creature that crawls, with which the water swarmed in their kinds. The variety of living creatures ranges from tiny fish that fill rivers, lakes, and streams to powerful sharks, and even to the great sea monsters, whose existence borders on the abstract and which may possess some form of intelligence. **And every winged bird in its kind,** a myriad of species. **And God saw that it was good.**

22 **God blessed them, saying: Be fruitful, and multiply, and fill the water in the seas, and let birds multiply on the earth.** Vegetation propagates automatically; it does not require action on its own part to multiply. By contrast, the reproductive processes of animals, whether flying, aquatic, or amphibious, involve the search for a mate. Consequently, they required a special blessing that would instill within them the active drive to be fruitful and multiply.

23 **It was evening and it was morning, a fifth day.**

24 Up to this point, God had created aquatic creatures and birds, the latter being either more advanced forms of sea life or creatures formed from swamps, a combination of land and sea. On the sixth day, God created land creatures: **God said: Let the earth produce living creatures in its kind, animals** of many types, not just domesticated ones, **and crawling creatures.** This is not meant as a zoological definition, but as a description of animal life from a human perspective. That is to say, the term "crawling creatures" refers to the small animals that swarm on the ground, such as mice and snakes. **And let the earth produce beasts of the earth in its kind.** The Torah distinguishes between animals [*behema*] and beasts [*ḥaya*]. Some suggest that *ḥaya* refers to predatory animals, whereas *behema* refers to herbivores. **And it was so.**

25 **God made the beasts of the earth in its kind, and the animals in its kind, and every creature that crawls upon the ground in its kind; and God saw that it was good.**

26 This verse is the climax of the entire account of Creation: **God said: Let Us make Man**[D] **in Our image, in Our likeness.** Although in a physiological sense man is very similar to other living creatures, he is nevertheless a category of being to

himself. Unlike other creations, man was fashioned in the image of God, not in terms of his appearance, but in terms of his essence. Aside from man's superior intelligence, this likeness is expressed principally in man's freedom to choose. This quality is unique to man and God. The rest of creation moves within its respective circles, always subject to a long chain of cause and effect. Humans are not bound by these chains. **And let them dominate**[D] **over the fish of the sea, and over the birds of the heavens, and over the animals, and over all the earth,**[D] meaning over the inanimate substances, **and over every crawling creature that crawls upon the earth.**

27 **God created man in His own image,** granting him freedom and the capacity to expand and alter his surroundings; **in the image of God He created him.** The verse notes: **Male and female He created them.** The Torah will later elaborate on this statement. In theory, man could have been created as one, just as God is one. The fact that man was created male and female indicates that mankind is part of the world's system of living creatures. The Torah's emphasis on this fact indicates that it does not refer to man as an individual, but as a species, whose beginnings are described in this verse. On the other hand, although the other creatures were also created male and female, the Torah mentions the creation of male and female counterparts only with regard to mankind. This serves to emphasize that the difference between man and woman is not merely biological, but fundamental as well.

28 **God blessed them; and God** also **said to them: Be fruitful, and multiply.** Since the propagation of mankind, unlike that of plants, requires a conscious reproductive act, this was the first command addressed to man as a subject with free will. The second commandment is: **And fill the earth.** It is not enough for man to be fruitful and multiply. He must also spread out across the entire planet, settle it, **and subdue it.** Of course this does not negate the presence of other creatures on the earth. Nevertheless, man has a special obligation to populate the world, to cultivate and tame it. **And** finally, you must **rule over**

DISCUSSION

1:26 | **Let Us make man:** Many explanations have been offered for the verse's use of the plural form "Us." One explanation is that in addition to man's living soul, which gives him his will, the creation of man introduced a new concept into the universe, namely, the ability to choose freely and affect the world. Creation, which until this point was a delicately balanced ecosystem, was suddenly exposed to a free, independent being, man. In considering the introduction of this foreign element, whose unique character will be

revealed later, the Midrash suggests that God sought the advice of His angels, as it were, and asked their opinion with regard to the creation of man (see *Bereshit Rabba* 17:19).

A more poetic explanation appears in an early midrash: God turned to the entire world and said: Let us all make man. Since man incorporates all of Creation, all creatures have some connection to him. For the creation of man, the lion donated some of its might, the fox gave part of its cunning, the snake its poison, the lamb its

innocence, and the butterfly its flight. According to this midrash, man was created in the image and likeness of all the creatures of the world (see *Zohar* 3:238b; *Yalkut Shimoni, Bereshit* 13).

And let them dominate: It was not by chance that mankind gained dominion over the other creatures. Even if for many generations man would struggle against them, ultimately he would achieve total mastery over the natural world. This is one of the tasks imposed upon mankind due to its extreme, uninhibited nature,

אֲשֶׁר שָׁרְצוּ הַמַּיִם לְמִינֵהֶם וְאֵת כָּל־עוֹף כָּנָף לְמִינֵהוּ וַיַּרְא אֱלֹהִים כִּי־טוֹב׃
כב וַיְבָרֶךְ אֹתָם אֱלֹהִים לֵאמֹר פְּרוּ וּרְבוּ וּמִלְאוּ אֶת־הַמַּיִם בַּיַּמִּים וְהָעוֹף יִרֶב בָּאָרֶץ׃
כג וַיְהִי־עֶרֶב וַיְהִי־בֹקֶר יוֹם חֲמִישִׁי׃
כד וַיֹּאמֶר אֱלֹהִים תּוֹצֵא הָאָרֶץ נֶפֶשׁ חַיָּה לְמִינָהּ בְּהֵמָה וָרֶמֶשׂ וְחַיְתוֹ־אֶרֶץ לְמִינָהּ
כה וַיְהִי־כֵן׃ וַיַּעַשׂ אֱלֹהִים אֶת־חַיַּת הָאָרֶץ לְמִינָהּ וְאֶת־הַבְּהֵמָה לְמִינָהּ וְאֵת כָּל־
כו רֶמֶשׂ הָאֲדָמָה לְמִינֵהוּ וַיַּרְא אֱלֹהִים כִּי־טוֹב׃ וַיֹּאמֶר אֱלֹהִים נַעֲשֶׂה אָדָם בְּצַלְמֵנוּ
כִּדְמוּתֵנוּ וְיִרְדּוּ בִדְגַת הַיָּם וּבְעוֹף הַשָּׁמַיִם וּבַבְּהֵמָה וּבְכָל־הָאָרֶץ וּבְכָל־הָרֶמֶשׂ
כז הָרֹמֵשׂ עַל־הָאָרֶץ׃ וַיִּבְרָא אֱלֹהִים ׀ אֶת־הָאָדָם בְּצַלְמוֹ בְּצֶלֶם אֱלֹהִים בָּרָא
כח אֹתוֹ זָכָר וּנְקֵבָה בָּרָא אֹתָם׃ וַיְבָרֶךְ אֹתָם אֱלֹהִים וַיֹּאמֶר לָהֶם אֱלֹהִים פְּרוּ וּרְבוּ

רש"י

כב| **וַיְבָרֶךְ אֹתָם.** לְפִי שֶׁמְּחַסְּרִים אוֹתָם וְצָדִין מֵהֶן וְאוֹכְלִין אוֹתָם, הֻצְרְכוּ לִבְרָכָה. וְאַף הַחַיּוֹת הֻצְרְכוּ לִבְרָכָה, אֶלָּא מִפְּנֵי הַנָּחָשׁ הֶעָתִיד לִקְלָלָה, לְכָךְ לֹא בֵּרְכָן, שֶׁלֹּא יְהֵא הוּא בַּכְּלָל: **פְּרוּ.** לְשׁוֹן פְּרִי, כְּלוֹמַר עֲשׂוּ פֵּרוֹת:

כד| **תּוֹצֵא הָאָרֶץ.** הוּא שֶׁפֵּרַשְׁתִּי (לעיל פסוק יד) שֶׁהַכֹּל נִבְרָא מִיּוֹם רִאשׁוֹן וְלֹא הֻצְרְכוּ אֶלָּא לְהוֹצִיאָם: **נֶפֶשׁ חַיָּה.** שֶׁיֵּשׁ בָּהּ חִיּוּת: **וָרֶמֶשׂ.** הֵם שְׁרָצִים שֶׁהֵם נְמוּכִים וְרוֹמְשִׂים עַל הָאָרֶץ, וְנִרְאִים כְּאִלּוּ נִגְרָרִין שֶׁאֵין הִלּוּכָן נִכָּר, כָּל לְשׁוֹן רֶמֶשׂ וְשֶׁרֶץ בְּלַשׁוֹנֵנוּ קונמוברי"ש:

כה| **וַיַּעַשׂ.** תִּקֵּן לִצְבְיוֹנָן בְּקוֹמָתָן:

כו| **נַעֲשֶׂה אָדָם.** עַנְוְתָנוּתוֹ שֶׁל הַקָּדוֹשׁ בָּרוּךְ הוּא לָמַדְנוּ מִכָּאן, לְפִי שֶׁהָאָדָם בִּדְמוּת הַמַּלְאָכִים וְיִתְקַנְּאוּ בּוֹ, לְפִיכָךְ נִמְלַךְ בָּהֶם. וּכְשֶׁהוּא דָּן אֶת הַמְּלָכִים הוּא נִמְלָךְ בְּפָמַלְיָא שֶׁלּוֹ, שֶׁכֵּן מָצִינוּ בְּאַחְאָב שֶׁאָמַר לוֹ מִיכָה: "רָאִיתִי אֶת ה' יֹשֵׁב עַל כִּסְאוֹ וְכָל צְבָא הַשָּׁמַיִם עֹמֵד עָלָיו מִימִינוֹ וּמִשְּׂמֹאלוֹ" (מלכים א' כב, יט), וְכִי יֵשׁ יָמִין וּשְׂמֹאל לְפָנָיו? אֶלָּא אֵלּוּ מַיְמִינִים לִזְכוּת וְאֵלּוּ מַשְׂמְאִילִים לְחוֹבָה, וְכֵן: "בִּגְזֵרַת עִירִין פִּתְגָמָא וּמֵאמַר קַדִּישִׁין שְׁאֵלְתָא" (דניאל ד, יד), אַף כָּאן בְּפָמַלְיָא שֶׁלּוֹ נָטַל רְשׁוּת. אָמַר לָהֶם: יֵשׁ בָּעֶלְיוֹנִים כִּדְמוּתִי, אִם אֵין בַּתַּחְתּוֹנִים כִּדְמוּתִי הֲרֵי יֵשׁ קִנְאָה בְּמַעֲשֵׂה בְרֵאשִׁית: **נַעֲשֶׂה אָדָם.** אַף עַל פִּי שֶׁלֹּא סִיְּעוּהוּ בִּיצִירָתוֹ, וְיֵשׁ מָקוֹם לַמִּינִים לִרְדּוֹת, לֹא נִמְנַע הַכָּתוּב מִלְּלַמֵּד דֶּרֶךְ אֶרֶץ וּמִדַּת עֲנָוָה, שֶׁיְּהֵא הַגָּדוֹל נִמְלָךְ וְנוֹטֵל רְשׁוּת מִן הַקָּטָן. וְאִם כָּתַב 'אֶעֱשֶׂה אָדָם' לֹא לָמַדְנוּ שֶׁהָיָה מְדַבֵּר עִם בֵּית דִּינוֹ, אֶלָּא עִם עַצְמוֹ. וּתְשׁוּבַת הַמִּינִים כָּתַב בְּצִדּוֹ: "וַיִּבְרָא אֱלֹהִים אֶת הָאָדָם", וְלֹא כָּתַב 'וַיִּבְרְאוּ': **בְּצַלְמֵנוּ.** בִּדְפוּס שֶׁלָּנוּ: **כִּדְמוּתֵנוּ.** לְהָבִין וּלְהַשְׂכִּיל:

וְיִרְדּוּ בִדְגַת הַיָּם. יֵשׁ בַּלָּשׁוֹן הַזֶּה לְשׁוֹן רִדּוּי וּלְשׁוֹן יְרִידָה, זָכָה – רוֹדֶה בַּחַיּוֹת וּבַבְּהֵמוֹת, לֹא זָכָה – נַעֲשֶׂה יָרוּד לִפְנֵיהֶם וְהַחַיָּה מוֹשֶׁלֶת בּוֹ:

כז| **וַיִּבְרָא אֱלֹהִים אֶת הָאָדָם בְּצַלְמוֹ.** בִּדְפוּס הֶעָשׂוּי לוֹ, שֶׁהַכֹּל נִבְרָא בְּמַאֲמָר וְהוּא בְּיָדַיִם, שֶׁנֶּאֱמַר: "וַתָּשֶׁת עָלַי כַּפֶּכָה" (תהלים קלט, ה). נַעֲשָׂה בְּחוֹתָם כְּמַטְבֵּעַ הָעֲשׂוּיָה עַל יְדֵי רֹשֶׁם, שֶׁקּוֹרִין קוי"ן בְּלַעַז, וְכֵן הוּא אוֹמֵר: "תִּתְהַפֵּךְ כְּחֹמֶר חוֹתָם" (איוב לח, יד): **בְּצֶלֶם אֱלֹהִים בָּרָא אוֹתוֹ.** פֵּרֵשׁ לְךָ שֶׁאוֹתוֹ צֶלֶם הַמְּתֻקָּן לוֹ צֶלֶם דְּיוֹקַן יוֹצְרוֹ הוּא: **זָכָר וּנְקֵבָה בָּרָא אֹתָם.** וּלְהַלָּן הוּא אוֹמֵר: "וַיִּקַּח אַחַת מִצַּלְעֹתָיו" וְגוֹ' (להלן ב, כא)! מִדְרַשׁ אַגָּדָה, שֶׁבְּרָאוֹ שְׁנֵי פַּרְצוּפִים בִּבְרִיאָה רִאשׁוֹנָה, וְאַחַר כָּךְ חִלְּקוֹ. וּפְשׁוּטוֹ שֶׁל מִקְרָא: כָּאן הוֹדִיעֲךָ שֶׁנִּבְרְאוּ שְׁנֵיהֶם בַּשִּׁשִּׁי, וְלֹא פֵּרֵשׁ לְךָ כֵּיצַד בְּרִיָּתָן, וּפֵרֵשׁ לְךָ בְּמָקוֹם אַחֵר:

DISCUSSION

which combines strength, force of will, desire, freedom of choice, and even a certain madness. Earthquakes, volcanoes, and floods are all minor phenomena in comparison to the actions of humanity, the entity that makes the greatest impact on living beings and the world itself. From this stems the question raised by the psalmist: "What is a mortal, that You remember him, a man, that You take him into account? For You have made him a little less than divine, crowning him with honor and glory. You have made him ruler over the works of Your hands; You placed all things at his feet" (Psalms 8:5–7). That is, why did God choose man and place the entire world under his control? In the forthcoming chapters, the Torah will address this question: Is this creation, man, sufficiently stable to rule? Do his powers of destruction pose too great a danger to himself and to the world? Indeed, this question will be raised throughout human history.

And let them dominate over the fish of the sea, and over the birds of the heavens, and over the animals, and over all the earth: Man was tasked with a general obligation to rule over the world and subjugate it. He is to construct bridges over rivers, boats to cross seas, airplanes to fly in the sky, and spaceships to venture far beyond Earth. All these accomplishments are considered not products of man's unhealthy inclinations or desire for power but positive fulfillments of a divine command. Man is commanded to become master of the world, and his ability to fulfill this task constantly grows.

the fish of the sea, and over the birds of the heavens, and over every living creature that crawls upon the earth.

29 **God said: Behold, I have given you,** for now at least, **all vegetation yielding seed**[D] **that is upon the face of all the earth, and every tree, in which there is the fruit of a tree yielding seed; to you it shall be for food.** You may take your sustenance from all types of plants, herbs, vegetables, and fruit, as you see fit.

30 **And to every beast of the earth, and to every bird of the heavens, and to everything that crawls upon the earth, in which there is a living soul,** I have given **all green vegetation for food. And it was so.** It is possible that when all life forms were first created, they were herbivorous. However, perhaps there was no prohibition against receiving sustenance from living creatures or their carcasses, only against killing living creatures. It is permitted for man and beast to derive their sustenance from vegetation, because they each possess an animate soul, making them superior to plants.

31 **God saw everything that He had made,** in its entirety, from light to man, **and, behold, it was very good.**[D] **It was evening and it was morning, the sixth day.**

2 1 **The heavens and the earth and their entire host,** the abundance of creatures contained within them, with all their abilities and roles, **were completed.**

2 **God completed on the seventh day His works that He had made** on the previous six days; **He rested on the seventh day from all His works that He had made.** Concluded is the process in which new, unique creations were formed on each day. From this point forward, the world will continue its existence according to the order that has been determined for it.

3 Due to the unique nature of the Sabbath, **God blessed the seventh day and sanctified it**[D] with additional holiness; **because on it He rested from all His works that God created to make.**

The Second Account of Creation

GENESIS 2:4–3:24

This section is one of the most dramatic, mystifying, and challenging sections in the entire Torah. Some of its details can be understood only vaguely. Following the sweeping description of the Creation above, which dealt with the universe on a broad scale, the Torah now provides a detailed description of the process of creating all that emerged from nothing. This account is more tangible than the abstract, conceptual depiction of the first chapter. Even the divine name of God differs in this account from the previous one. In the first version, God is called *Elohim*, a term which on the one hand expresses God's authority and power, and on the other His all-encompassing, impersonal essence. By contrast, in the next two chapters, God is called *Adonai Elohim*, the Lord God, the first word of which is spelled *yud-heh-vav-heh*, the Tetragrammaton, the personal name of God, as it were. In this account, God is not merely an abstract philosophical or theological entity, as He functioned in the first chapter, which focused on the large-scale plan of Creation. Rather, God attends to the specific details of the Creation process.

4 **This is the legacy of the heavens and of the earth when they**
Second aliya **were created, on the day that the Lord God made earth and heaven.**

5 At this stage the world was still incomplete, as **no shrub of the field was yet in the earth, and no vegetation of the field had yet sprouted; because the Lord God had not caused it to rain upon the earth.** Although rain is a part of the natural order of the world, it was not mentioned in the previous chapter alongside the formation of the seas, dry land, or vegetation. Since it had not yet rained, the plants were unable to fully grow. The Sages teach that the plants initially only barely emerged from the ground. When the first man was created, he prayed for them, and the first rains came, causing the plants to sprout and grow. **And there was no man to till the ground.** People can work the land even when there is no rainfall, by drawing water

DISCUSSION

1:29 | Behold, I have given you all vegetation yielding seed: The necessity for this command stems from man's ability to choose, and from the endless possibilities open before him. As a result, man requires guidance even with regard to the simplest aspects of his life. A cow or a fish does not struggle with the question of what it should eat. It seems that man needs clear and specific instructions.

1:31 | Everything that He had made, and behold, it was very good: Is the world truly very good, lacking anything bad? This question is particularly salient in light of the existence of man, whose freedom of choice makes him a loose cannon in a delicate universe. If humanity has the capacity to act in a negative manner, can it too be called "very good"? From the many interpretations, expositions, and midrashim that have been composed regarding this verse, it seems that there is a distinction to be made between good, which is simply the opposite of evil, and very good, which relates to the complex entirety of the world, including darkness and light, the growth and withering of vegetation, the rising and setting of the sun, creation and death (see *Bereshit Rabba* 9:5, 12; *Shemot Rabba* 10:11; *Zohar* 1:144b).

2:3 | God blessed the seventh day and sanctified it: There are places in the world where people refrain from work on the seventh day because they consider it a day of bad fortune. The Torah, however, stresses the opposite: The seventh day is a day of blessing, of holiness, of

וּמִלְאוּ אֶת־הָאָרֶץ וְכִבְשֻׁהָ וּרְדוּ בִּדְגַת הַיָּם וּבְעוֹף הַשָּׁמַיִם וּבְכָל־חַיָּה הָרֹמֶשֶׂת
כט עַל־הָאָרֶץ: וַיֹּאמֶר אֱלֹהִים הִנֵּה נָתַתִּי לָכֶם אֶת־כָּל־עֵשֶׂב ׀ זֹרֵעַ זֶרַע אֲשֶׁר עַל־
פְּנֵי כָל־הָאָרֶץ וְאֶת־כָּל־הָעֵץ אֲשֶׁר־בּוֹ פְרִי־עֵץ זֹרֵעַ זָרַע לָכֶם יִהְיֶה לְאָכְלָה:
ל וּֽלְכָל־חַיַּת הָאָרֶץ וּלְכָל־עוֹף הַשָּׁמַיִם וּלְכֹל ׀ רוֹמֵשׂ עַל־הָאָרֶץ אֲשֶׁר־בּוֹ נֶפֶשׁ
לא חַיָּה אֶת־כָּל־יֶרֶק עֵשֶׂב לְאָכְלָה וַֽיְהִי־כֵן: וַיַּרְא אֱלֹהִים אֶת־כָּל־אֲשֶׁר עָשָׂה
וְהִנֵּה־טוֹב מְאֹד וַֽיְהִי־עֶרֶב וַֽיְהִי־בֹקֶר יוֹם הַשִּׁשִּׁי:
ב א וַיְכֻלּוּ הַשָּׁמַיִם וְהָאָרֶץ וְכָל־צְבָאָם: ב וַיְכַל אֱלֹהִים בַּיּוֹם הַשְּׁבִיעִי מְלַאכְתּוֹ אֲשֶׁר
ג עָשָׂה וַיִּשְׁבֹּת בַּיּוֹם הַשְּׁבִיעִי מִכָּל־מְלַאכְתּוֹ אֲשֶׁר עָשָׂה: וַיְבָרֶךְ אֱלֹהִים אֶת־יוֹם
הַשְּׁבִיעִי וַיְקַדֵּשׁ אֹתוֹ כִּי בוֹ שָׁבַת מִכָּל־מְלַאכְתּוֹ אֲשֶׁר־בָּרָא אֱלֹהִים לַעֲשׂוֹת:
ד אֵלֶּה תוֹלְדוֹת הַשָּׁמַיִם וְהָאָרֶץ בְּהִבָּרְאָם בְּיוֹם עֲשׂוֹת יהוה אֱלֹהִים אֶרֶץ ב שני
ה וְשָׁמָיִם: וְכֹל ׀ שִׂיחַ הַשָּׂדֶה טֶרֶם יִהְיֶה בָאָרֶץ וְכָל־עֵשֶׂב הַשָּׂדֶה טֶרֶם יִצְמָח
כִּי לֹא הִמְטִיר יהוה אֱלֹהִים עַל־הָאָרֶץ וְאָדָם אַיִן לַעֲבֹד אֶת־הָאֲדָמָה:

רש״י

כח | **וְכִבְשֻׁהָ.** חָסֵר וָי״ו, לְלַמֶּדְךָ שֶׁהַזָּכָר כּוֹבֵשׁ אֶת הַנְּקֵבָה שֶׁלֹּא תְּהֵא יַצְאָנִית. וְעוֹד לְלַמֶּדְךָ, שֶׁהָאִישׁ שֶׁדַּרְכּוֹ לִכְבֹּשׁ מְצֻוֶּה עַל פְּרִיָּה וּרְבִיָּה וְלֹא הָאִשָּׁה:

כט-ל | **לָכֶם יִהְיֶה לְאָכְלָה וּלְכָל חַיַּת הָאָרֶץ.** הִשְׁוָה לָהֶם הַכָּתוּב בְּהֵמוֹת וְחַיּוֹת לְמַאֲכָל, וְלֹא הִרְשָׁה לְאָדָם וּלְאִשְׁתּוֹ לְהָמִית בְּרִיָּה וְלֶאֱכֹל בָּשָׂר, אַךְ כָּל יֶרֶק עֵשֶׂב יֹאכְלוּ יַחַד כֻּלָּם. וּכְשֶׁבָּאוּ בְּנֵי נֹחַ, הִתִּיר לָהֶם בָּשָׂר, שֶׁנֶּאֱמַר: ״כָּל רֶמֶשׂ אֲשֶׁר הוּא חַי וְגוֹ׳ כְּיֶרֶק עֵשֶׂב״ שֶׁהִתַּרְתִּי לְאָדָם הָרִאשׁוֹן ״נָתַתִּי לָכֶם אֶת כֹּל״ (להלן ט, ג):

לא | **יוֹם הַשִּׁשִּׁי.** הוֹסִיף ה״א בַּשִּׁשִּׁי בִּגְמַר מַעֲשֵׂה בְרֵאשִׁית, לוֹמַר שֶׁהִתְנָה עִמָּהֶם עַל מְנָת שֶׁיְּקַבְּלוּ עֲלֵיהֶם יִשְׂרָאֵל חֲמִשָּׁה חֻמְשֵׁי תוֹרָה. דָּבָר אַחֵר, ״יוֹם הַשִּׁשִּׁי״, כֻּלָּם תְּלוּיִים וְעוֹמְדִים עַד יוֹם הַשִּׁשִּׁי, הוּא שִׁשִּׁי בְּסִיוָן הַמּוּכָן לְמַתַּן תּוֹרָה:

פרק ב

ב | **וַיְכַל אֱלֹהִים בַּיּוֹם הַשְּׁבִיעִי.** רַבִּי שִׁמְעוֹן אוֹמֵר: בָּשָׂר וָדָם שֶׁאֵינוֹ יוֹדֵעַ עִתָּיו וּרְגָעָיו צָרִיךְ לְהוֹסִיף מֵחוֹל עַל הַקֹּדֶשׁ, הַקָּדוֹשׁ בָּרוּךְ הוּא שֶׁיּוֹדֵעַ עִתָּיו וּרְגָעָיו, נִכְנַס בּוֹ כְּחוּט הַשַּׂעֲרָה, וְנִרְאָה כְּאִלּוּ כִּלָּה בּוֹ בַּיּוֹם. דָּבָר אַחֵר: מֶה הָיָה הָעוֹלָם חָסֵר? מְנוּחָה, בָּאת שַׁבָּת בָּאת מְנוּחָה, כָּלְתָה וְנִגְמְרָה הַמְּלָאכָה:

ג | **וַיְבָרֶךְ וַיְקַדֵּשׁ.** בֵּרְכוֹ בַּמָּן, שֶׁכָּל יְמוֹת הַשָּׁבוּעַ יוֹרֵד לָהֶם עֹמֶר לַגֻּלְגֹּלֶת, וּבַשִּׁשִּׁי לֶחֶם מִשְׁנֶה. וְקִדְּשׁוֹ בַּמָּן שֶׁלֹּא יָרַד בּוֹ מָן כְּלָל, וְהַמִּקְרָא כָּתוּב עַל הֶעָתִיד: **אֲשֶׁר בָּרָא אֱלֹהִים לַעֲשׂוֹת.** הַמְּלָאכָה שֶׁהָיְתָה רְאוּיָה לַעֲשׂוֹת בַּשַּׁבָּת כָּפַל וַעֲשָׂאָהּ בַּשִּׁשִּׁי, כְּמוֹ שֶׁמְּפֹרָשׁ בִּבְרֵאשִׁית רַבָּה (יא, ט):

ד | **אֵלֶּה.** הָאֲמוּרִים לְמַעְלָה ״תּוֹלְדוֹת הַשָּׁמַיִם וְהָאָרֶץ״: **בְּהִבָּרְאָם בְּיוֹם עֲשׂוֹת ה׳.** לְלַמֶּדְךָ שֶׁכֻּלָּם נִבְרְאוּ בָּרִאשׁוֹן. דָּבָר אַחֵר, ״בְּהִבָּרְאָם״, בְּהֵ״א בְּרָאָם, שֶׁנֶּאֱמַר: ״כִּי בְּיָהּ ה׳ צוּר עוֹלָמִים״ (ישעיה כו, ד), בִּשְׁתֵּי אוֹתִיּוֹת הַלָּלוּ שֶׁל הַשֵּׁם יָצַר שְׁנֵי עוֹלָמִים, וְלִמֶּדְךָ כָּאן שֶׁהָעוֹלָם הַזֶּה נִבְרָא בְּהֵ״א, רֶמֶז שֶׁיֵּרְדוּ הָרְשָׁעִים לְמַטָּה לִרְאוֹת שַׁחַת, כְּהֵ״א זֹאת שֶׁסְּתוּמָה מִכָּל הַצְּדָדִים וּפְתוּחָה לְמַטָּה לָרֶדֶת דֶּרֶךְ שָׁם:

ה | **טֶרֶם יִהְיֶה בָאָרֶץ.** כָּל ׳טֶרֶם׳ שֶׁבַּמִּקְרָא לְשׁוֹן ׳עַד לֹא׳ הוּא, וְאֵינוֹ לְשׁוֹן קֹדֶם, וְאֵינוֹ נִפְעָל לוֹמַר: הִטְרִים, כַּאֲשֶׁר יֵאָמֵר: הִקְדִּים, וְזֶה מוֹכִיחַ, וְעוֹד אַחֵר: ״כִּי טֶרֶם תִּירְאוּן״ (שמות ט, ל), עֲדַיִן לֹא תִּירָאוּן. וְאַף זֶה תְּפָרֵשׁ: עֲדַיִן לֹא הָיָה בָאָרֶץ כְּשֶׁנִּגְמְרָה בְּרִיאַת הָעוֹלָם בַּשִּׁשִּׁי קֹדֶם שֶׁנִּבְרָא אָדָם, וְכָל עֵשֶׂב הַשָּׂדֶה עֲדַיִן לֹא צָמַח. וּבַשְּׁלִישִׁי שֶׁכָּתוּב: ״וַתּוֹצֵא הָאָרֶץ״ (לעיל א, יב), עַל פֶּתַח קַרְקַע עָמְדוּ עַד יוֹם שִׁשִּׁי: **כִּי לֹא הִמְטִיר.** וּמַה טַּעַם לֹא הִמְטִיר? לְפִי שֶׁאָדָם אַיִן לַעֲבֹד אֶת הָאֲדָמָה וְאֵין מַכִּיר בְּטוֹבָתָם שֶׁל גְּשָׁמִים. וּכְשֶׁבָּא אָדָם וְיָדַע שֶׁהֵם צֹרֶךְ לָעוֹלָם הִתְפַּלֵּל עֲלֵיהֶם וְיָרְדוּ, וְצָמְחוּ הָאִילָנוֹת וְהַדְּשָׁאִים: **ה׳ אֱלֹהִים.** ה׳ הוּא שְׁמוֹ, אֱלֹהִים – שֶׁהוּא שַׁלִּיט וְשׁוֹפֵט עַל כֹּל, וְכֵן פֵּרוּשׁ זֶה בְּכָל מָקוֹם לְפִי פְּשׁוּטוֹ: ה׳ שֶׁהוּא אֱלֹהִים:

DISCUSSION

→ completion. Only on the seventh day did the world attain its proper form, as it includes not only production but also abstention from labor; it contains not only days of speech, but also a day of silence. This silence and abstention are derived from the sense that on the Sabbath day, the world is complete; nothing is lacking.

from elsewhere. Without man, however, the land remained unworked.

6 **A mist would rise from the earth, and water the entire surface of the ground.** The essence of rain already existed, but the complete hydrological cycle was not yet in place. The Torah here describes a primordial water cycle: Mist would rise from the earth, condense, and fall to water the ground.

7 The creation of vegetation, which occurred on the third day of Creation, will soon be described in detail. But first the Torah elaborates on the creation and actions of a far more important entity, man, whose formation was previously depicted only in general terms: **The Lord God formed man of dust from the ground.** Unlike the other created beings, which were fashioned in one step, God created man in stages: First he was a lump of earth, a purely physical entity known by the Sages as a *golem*. **And** He then **breathed into his nostrils the breath of life,**^D giving life to this inanimate object. **Man became a living creature.** The soul of man is living not only in the sense that it is not dead, but also in that it contains a special vitality: It is a speaking soul. The breath of life within man is not just an abstract entity or form of sanctity concealed inside him; rather, it radiates outward from within him.

8 As part of the Creation process, **the Lord God planted a garden, in** the place known as **Eden to the east**. Although Eden refers to a place, the word itself means pleasure. The ambiguity and mystery regarding this location is further accentuated by the fact that the verse describes it as located eastward without offering any point of reference. This place is a lost world outside

the realm of our current experience. **He placed there the man whom He** had **formed.**

9 **The Lord God grew from the ground** in the Garden of Eden **every tree that is pleasant to the sight and good for food, and the tree of life,** which will be discussed later, **in the midst of the garden,** in the center, **and the tree of the knowledge**^D **of good and evil.**^D

10 **A river emerged from Eden to water the garden; and from there it,** the river, **would part and would become four headwaters.**

11 **The name of the one is Pishon; it is that which encircles the entire land of Havila, where the gold is** found. Pishon is generally identified with the Nile.

12 **The gold** in the deposits **of that land is** of particularly **good** quality; **there is** also **bdellium and the onyx stone.**

13 **The name of the second river is Gihon;**^D **it is that which encircles the entire land of Kush.** It is possible that Kush is modern-day Ethiopia. Some identify Kush as the mountain range known today as the Hindu Kush, which stretches between modern-day Afghanistan and Pakistan.

Possible locations of Pishon and Gihon

DISCUSSION

2:7 | And breathed into his nostrils the breath of life: Perhaps this phrase can be understood as an allusion to the notion that the soul of man is a part of God Himself, as it were. In the words of *Sefer HaKaneh*: One who breathes into another imbues him with his own breath. This is the source of man's unique status as the only being created in the image and likeness of God.

2:9 | And the tree of life in the midst of the garden and the tree of the knowledge: The verse does not mention the location of the tree of the knowledge of good and evil. Only later does the woman note that it is in the midst of the garden (Genesis 3:3). It is possible that the tree of life and the tree of the knowledge of good and evil were not separate trees, but different sides of the same tree, two branches or trunks that grew from a single root (see Ramban).

And the tree of the knowledge of good and evil: Several fundamental questions lie at the root of this story: Does the tree actually provide knowledge of good and evil? If so, why did God prohibit man from partaking of its fruit? Did God wish to prevent him from attaining knowledge, to stunt his development?

Many commentaries explain that the knowledge to be gained from partaking of the tree's fruit was not intelligence or wisdom, but knowledge of evil. Indeed, the tree is never called simply the tree of knowledge but the tree of the knowledge of good and evil precisely because the tree had no influence on objective knowledge such as mathematics. Indeed, this story addresses the essence of the definition of evil. Evil is possible, but it is not necessary. The performance of evil is rooted, among other things, in man's ability to choose his own way. Evil involves distortion, and yet this distortion is not too far

removed from the essence of human creativity, a capacity that stems from the ability to perceive reality beyond its obvious form. Man's freedom to reflect anew upon matters opens doors to myriad possibilities of creation and recombination. In this sense, knowledge of good and evil is not necessarily a recognition of the abyss of evil, but an awareness that one need not always act appropriately. Why would one choose to act improperly? Perhaps out of desire, or out of curiosity, or simply out of spite. Such motivations are expressions of evil.

God prohibited man from partaking of the fruit of the tree of the knowledge of good and evil because man cannot acquire knowledge of good and evil without being attracted to some extent to evil. Human knowledge, unlike that of the angels, cannot be completely objective. By its very nature, human knowledge contains biases and emotional attachments. Indeed, the

ו ז וְאֵד יַעֲלֶה מִן־הָאָרֶץ וְהִשְׁקָה אֶת־כָּל־פְּנֵי הָאֲדָמָה: וַיִּיצֶר יְהוָה אֱלֹהִים
אֶת־הָאָדָם עָפָר מִן־הָאֲדָמָה וַיִּפַּח בְּאַפָּיו נִשְׁמַת חַיִּים וַיְהִי הָאָדָם לְנֶפֶשׁ
ח חַיָּה: וַיִּטַּע יְהוָה אֱלֹהִים גַּן בְּעֵדֶן מִקֶּדֶם וַיָּשֶׂם שָׁם אֶת־הָאָדָם אֲשֶׁר יָצָר:
ט וַיַּצְמַח יְהוָה אֱלֹהִים מִן־הָאֲדָמָה כָּל־עֵץ נֶחְמָד לְמַרְאֶה וְטוֹב לְמַאֲכָל וְעֵץ
י הַחַיִּים בְּתוֹךְ הַגָּן וְעֵץ הַדַּעַת טוֹב וָרָע: וְנָהָר יֹצֵא מֵעֵדֶן לְהַשְׁקוֹת אֶת־
יא הַגָּן וּמִשָּׁם יִפָּרֵד וְהָיָה לְאַרְבָּעָה רָאשִׁים: שֵׁם הָאֶחָד פִּישׁוֹן הוּא הַסֹּבֵב אֵת
יב כָּל־אֶרֶץ הַחֲוִילָה אֲשֶׁר־שָׁם הַזָּהָב: וּזֲהַב הָאָרֶץ הַהִוא טוֹב שָׁם הַבְּדֹלַח
יג וְאֶבֶן הַשֹּׁהַם: וְשֵׁם־הַנָּהָר הַשֵּׁנִי גִּיחוֹן הוּא הַסּוֹבֵב אֵת כָּל־אֶרֶץ כּוּשׁ:

רש״י

ו| **וְאֵד יַעֲלֶה.** לְעִנְיַן בְּרִיָּתוֹ שֶׁל אָדָם, הֶעֱלָה הַתְּהוֹם וְהִשְׁקָה עֲנָנִים לִשְׁרוֹת הֶעָפָר וְנִבְרָא אָדָם, כְּגַבָּל זֶה שֶׁנּוֹתֵן מַיִם וְאַחַר כָּךְ לָשׁ אֶת הָעִסָּה, אַף כָּאן "וְהִשְׁקָה" וְאַחַר כָּךְ "וַיִּיצֶר":

ז| **וַיִּיצֶר.** שְׁתֵּי יְצִירוֹת, יְצִירָה לָעוֹלָם הַזֶּה וִיצִירָה לִתְחִיַּת הַמֵּתִים, אֲבָל בַּבְּהֵמָה שֶׁאֵינָהּ עוֹמֶדֶת לַדִּין, לֹא נִכְתַּב בִּיצִירָתָהּ שְׁנֵי יוּדִי"ן: **עָפָר מִן הָאֲדָמָה.** צָבַר עֲפָרוֹ מִכָּל הָאֲדָמָה מֵאַרְבַּע רוּחוֹת, שֶׁכָּל מָקוֹם שֶׁיָּמוּת שָׁם תְּהֵא קוֹלַטְתּוֹ לִקְבוּרָה. דָּבָר אַחֵר, נָטַל עֲפָרוֹ מִמָּקוֹם שֶׁנֶּאֱמַר בּוֹ: "מִזְבַּח אֲדָמָה תַּעֲשֶׂה לִּי" (שמות כ, כא), הַלְוַאי תְּהֵא לוֹ כַּפָּרָה וְיוּכַל לַעֲמֹד: **וַיִּפַּח בְּאַפָּיו.** עֲשָׂאוֹ מִן הַתַּחְתּוֹנִים וּמִן הָעֶלְיוֹנִים, גּוּף מִן הַתַּחְתּוֹנִים וּנְשָׁמָה מִן הָעֶלְיוֹנִים. לְפִי שֶׁבְּיוֹם רִאשׁוֹן נִבְרְאוּ שָׁמַיִם וָאָרֶץ, בַּשֵּׁנִי בָּרָא רָקִיעַ לָעֶלְיוֹנִים, בַּשְּׁלִישִׁי "תֵּרָאֶה הַיַּבָּשָׁה" לַתַּחְתּוֹנִים, בָּרְבִיעִי בָּרָא מְאוֹרוֹת לָעֶלְיוֹנִים, בַּחֲמִישִׁי "יִשְׁרְצוּ הַמַּיִם" לַתַּחְתּוֹנִים, הֻזְקַק הַשִּׁשִּׁי לִבְרֹאות בּוֹ בָּעֶלְיוֹנִים וּבַתַּחְתּוֹנִים, וְאִם לָאו יֵשׁ קִנְאָה בְּמַעֲשֵׂה בְרֵאשִׁית, שֶׁיִּהְיוּ אֵלּוּ רַבִּים עַל אֵלּוּ בִּבְרִיאַת יוֹם אֶחָד: **לְנֶפֶשׁ חַיָּה.** אַף בְּהֵמָה וְחַיָּה נִקְרְאוּ 'נֶפֶשׁ חַיָּה', אַךְ זוֹ שֶׁל אָדָם חַיָּה שֶׁבְּכֻלָּן, שֶׁנִּתּוֹסֵף בּוֹ דֵּעָה וְדִבּוּר:

ח| **מִקֶּדֶם.** בְּמִזְרָחוֹ שֶׁל עֵדֶן נָטַע אֶת הַגָּן. וְאִם תֹּאמַר, הֲרֵי כְּבָר כָּתַב: "וַיִּבְרָא... אֶת הָאָדָם" וְגוֹ' (לעיל א, כז)? רָאִיתִי בִּבְרַיְתָא שֶׁל רַבִּי אֱלִיעֶזֶר בְּנוֹ שֶׁל רַבִּי יוֹסֵי הַגְּלִילִי מִשְּׁלֹשִׁים וּשְׁתַּיִם מִדּוֹת הָאַגָּדָה נִדְרֶשֶׁת, וְזוֹ אַחַת מֵהֶן: כְּלָל שֶׁלְּאַחֲרָיו מַעֲשֶׂה, הוּא פְּרָטוֹ שֶׁל רִאשׁוֹן. "וַיִּבְרָא... אֶת הָאָדָם" – זֶהוּ כְּלָל, סָתַם בְּרִיָּתוֹ מֵהֵיכָן וְסָתַם מַעֲשָׂיו. חָזַר וּפֵרַשׁ: "וַיִּיצֶר ה' אֱלֹהִים" וְגוֹ', וַיַּצְמַח לוֹ גַּן עֵדֶן וַיַּנִּיחֵהוּ בְּגַן עֵדֶן וַיַּפֵּל עָלָיו תַּרְדֵּמָה, הַשּׁוֹמֵעַ סָבוּר שֶׁהוּא מַעֲשֶׂה אַחֵר וְאֵינוֹ אֶלָּא פְּרָטוֹ שֶׁל רִאשׁוֹן. וְכֵן אֵצֶל הַבְּהֵמָה חָזַר וְכָתַב: "וַיִּצֶר ה' וְגוֹ' מִן הָאֲדָמָה כָּל חַיַּת הַשָּׂדֶה" (להלן פסוק יט), כְּדֵי לְפָרֵשׁ: "וַיָּבֵא אֶל הָאָדָם" לִקְרוֹת שֵׁם, וּלְלַמֵּד עַל הָעוֹפוֹת שֶׁנִּבְרְאוּ מִן הָרְקָק:

ט| **וַיַּצְמַח.** לְעִנְיַן הַגָּן הַכָּתוּב מְדַבֵּר: **בְּתוֹךְ הַגָּן.** בְּאֶמְצַע הַגָּן:

יא| **פִּישׁוֹן.** הוּא נִילוּס נְהַר מִצְרַיִם, וְעַל שֵׁם שֶׁמֵּימָיו מִתְבָּרְכִין וְעוֹלִין וּמַשְׁקִין אֶת הָאָרֶץ נִקְרָא "פִּישׁוֹן", כְּמוֹ: "וּפָשׁוּ פָּרָשָׁיו" (חבקוק א, ח). דָּבָר אַחֵר, "פִּישׁוֹן", שֶׁהוּא מְגַדֵּל פִּשְׁתָּן, הוּא שֶׁנֶּאֱמַר בִּישַׁעְיָה אֵצֶל מִצְרַיִם: "וּבֹשׁוּ עֹבְדֵי פִשְׁתִּים" (ישעיה יט, ט):

יג–יד| **גִּיחוֹן.** שֶׁהָיָה הוֹלֵךְ וְהוֹמֶה וְהֶמְיָתוֹ גְּדוֹלָה מְאֹד,

DISCUSSION

term *daat*, knowledge, is used in reference to emotional or intimate awareness (see 4:1; see also Rabbeinu Bahya; Abravanel; Exodus 2:25). Perhaps a man who knows good and evil becomes like God. Nevertheless, that man would be completely different from God, as his knowledge is intertwined with his involvement with the objects of his knowledge. Therefore, unlike God, man cannot remain truly impartial.

The Sages teach that the serpent, who enticed Eve to eat the fruit of the tree (chap. 3), was one of three characters mentioned in the Torah who spoke only the truth (*Pirka deRabbeinu HaKadosh, Bava deShlosha* 16). Although the serpent clearly spoke words of incitement, it did not lie. It enticed Eve with exposure to the complete expanse of knowledge, which is not itself wholly bad. God, however, did not want to subject man to the tests presented by possessing this knowledge, at least not at this stage. This concept is intuitive. Educators attempt to shield their young students from exposure to certain truths that they cannot yet digest. This is not an act of deception; the educator merely wishes to wait until the child is capable of grasping evil without being drawn to or influenced by it. He will expose the child to evil only when the child is mature enough to handle it. A similar idea is expressed by the Sages, who suggest that at the end of the sixth day, God might have permitted Adam and Eve to partake of the fruit of the tree of the knowledge of good and evil (*Bereshit Rabba* 21:7). However, since they failed to obey His command for even one hour and ate from the tree prematurely, their consumption of its fruit had a deleterious effect on them.

2:11, 13| **Pishon...Gihon:** Based on the fact that the Pishon and Gihon Rivers surround the lands of Havila and Kush, respectively, these rivers apparently flow in the lands that will be bequeathed to the descendants of Ham (see 10:6–7). Accordingly, many scholars identify them with different tributaries of the Nile. However, in light of the fact that the Torah states that all four rivers have a single source, some claim that they

14 **The name of the third river is Tigris;**[B] **it is that which goes east of Ashur.** The Tigris is an immense river in Mesopotamia, known even today by this name. **And the fourth river is Euphrates.**[D] There is no need for the verse to elaborate on the location of the Euphrates, as throughout virtually the entire Bible, whenever a verse mentions a river without further specification, it refers to the Euphrates. This river serves as the border between the lands of the Middle East and the surrounding lands. This is also the meaning of the expression "beyond the river," which appears throughout the Bible and rabbinic literature, as well as in archaeological findings.

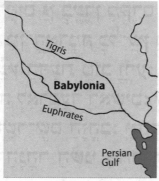

Locations of the Tigris and Euphrates

15 **The Lord God took the man, and placed him in the Garden of Eden to cultivate it and to keep it.** In contrast to the other creations scattered throughout the garden, the man was placed there for a particular purpose, namely, to cultivate the ground and to keep it. Just as in the previous chapter man was commanded to rule over the entire world, here man is given responsibility over a part of this otherworldly place. The world was not yet functioning in its fixed manner; perhaps rain never fell in the Garden of Eden, which instead drew all its sustenance from the river flowing through it and required the care of man. Consequently, it was of great importance for the man to cultivate the garden and to protect it from harm.

16 **The Lord God commanded the man, saying: From every tree of the garden you may eat,** and from them you shall draw your sustenance.

17 **But of the tree of the knowledge of good and evil, you shall not eat; for on the day that you eat of it you shall die.** If you eat from this tree, you will die.

18 **The Lord God said: It is not good that the man shall be alone.** All living creatures were created male and female, and they were meant to multiply. Only man was created without a

mate. Is one to conclude, then, that man was never meant to procreate? Perhaps God created man in His image, with intelligence and free will, as His parallel in this world. If so, just as God is alone above, man was likewise alone below, and this is how he was meant to fulfill his duties. To rule out this understanding, the Torah states that it is not good, neither for man himself nor for the world, for him to be alone. God continued: Therefore, **I will make for him a helper alongside him,** someone who completes him. Man requires a partnership with another being; this partnership would signify the beginning of humanity.

19 To that end, **the Lord God formed from the ground every beast of the field and every bird of the heavens and brought them to the man,** master of creation below, **to see what he would call it. Whatever the man would call every living creature, that was its name.**

20 **The man called names**[D] **for every animal, and for the birds of the heavens and for the beasts of the field; but** after all the animals passed before him to receive their names, it became apparent that **for Adam, he did not find a helper to be alongside him;** there was no other human being. In a world without nomenclature, each entity was completely unique and uncategorized. The ability to categorize similar creatures into groups and species and apply names to them is contingent on the cognitive abilities of association. Before he began to use these faculties, it is possible that Adam was unaware that he was alone. He lived in a world without classification and considered himself to be just another one of a myriad of creatures. Once Adam began to categorize the types of vegetation and male and female animals, he became acutely aware of his aloneness, as he realized that none of the individual creatures he encountered was suitable for him.

Third aliya

21 **The Lord God cast a deep sleep upon the man, and he slept; He took one of his sides [***tzalotav***].** Although many commentaries interpret the word *tzela* as rib, it seems more likely *tzela* refers to a whole side of the body. If so, one must conclude that the man was originally created with a double body, one half of which was separated from him now. **And** God **closed with flesh in its place,** where He had removed this side.

22 **The Lord God built the side that He took from the man into a woman,**[D] whose form differed from that of a man, **and brought her to the man** after he awakened.

─────────────────── BACKGROUND ───────────────────

2:14 | **Tigris:** From the Akkadian *Idiglat*. In the book of Daniel (10:4), the Tigris is referred to as the great river; indeed, it is almost 2,000 km long and is one of the two important rivers constituting the borders of Mesopotamia, together with the Euphrates. Characterized by its strong current, the Tigris rises in the Taurus Mountains of Turkey and flows parallel to the Zagros Mountains before emptying into the Persian Gulf.

יד וְשֵׁם הַנָּהָר הַשְּׁלִישִׁי חִדֶּקֶל הוּא הַהֹלֵךְ קִדְמַת אַשּׁוּר וְהַנָּהָר הָרְבִיעִי הוּא פְרָת:
טו טז וַיִּקַּח יהוה אֱלֹהִים אֶת־הָאָדָם וַיַּנִּחֵהוּ בְגַן־עֵדֶן לְעָבְדָהּ וּלְשָׁמְרָהּ: וַיְצַו יהוה
יז אֱלֹהִים עַל־הָאָדָם לֵאמֹר מִכֹּל עֵץ־הַגָּן אָכֹל תֹּאכֵל: וּמֵעֵץ הַדַּעַת טוֹב וָרָע
יח לֹא תֹאכַל מִמֶּנּוּ כִּי בְּיוֹם אֲכָלְךָ מִמֶּנּוּ מוֹת תָּמוּת: וַיֹּאמֶר יהוה אֱלֹהִים לֹא־
יט טוֹב הֱיוֹת הָאָדָם לְבַדּוֹ אֶעֱשֶׂה־לּוֹ עֵזֶר כְּנֶגְדּוֹ: וַיִּצֶר יהוה אֱלֹהִים מִן־הָאֲדָמָה
כָּל־חַיַּת הַשָּׂדֶה וְאֵת כָּל־עוֹף הַשָּׁמַיִם וַיָּבֵא אֶל־הָאָדָם לִרְאוֹת מַה־יִּקְרָא־לוֹ
כ וְכֹל אֲשֶׁר יִקְרָא־לוֹ הָאָדָם נֶפֶשׁ חַיָּה הוּא שְׁמוֹ: וַיִּקְרָא הָאָדָם שֵׁמוֹת לְכָל־ שלישי
כא הַבְּהֵמָה וּלְעוֹף הַשָּׁמַיִם וּלְכֹל חַיַּת הַשָּׂדֶה וּלְאָדָם לֹא־מָצָא עֵזֶר כְּנֶגְדּוֹ: וַיַּפֵּל
יהוה אֱלֹהִים ׀ תַּרְדֵּמָה עַל־הָאָדָם וַיִּישָׁן וַיִּקַּח אַחַת מִצַּלְעֹתָיו וַיִּסְגֹּר בָּשָׂר
כב תַּחְתֶּנָּה: וַיִּבֶן יהוה אֱלֹהִים ׀ אֶת־הַצֵּלָע אֲשֶׁר־לָקַח מִן־הָאָדָם לְאִשָּׁה וַיְבִאֶהָ

רש"י

כמו: "וכי יגח" (שמות כא, כח), שמנגח והולך והומה: **חדקל.** שמימיו חדין וקלין: **פרת.** שמימיו פרין ורבין ומברין את האדם: **כוש ואשור** - עדין לא היו, ונכתב מקרא על העתיד: **קדמת אשור.** למזרחה של אשור: **הוא פרת.** החשוב על כלם, הנזכר על שם ארץ ישראל:

טו| **ויקח.** לקחו בדברים נאים ופתהו לכנס:

יח| **לא טוב היות וגו'.** שלא יאמרו שתי רשויות הן, הקדוש ברוך הוא בעליונים יחיד ואין לו זוג וזה בתחתונים אין לו זוג: **עזר כנגדו.** זכה - 'עזר', לא זכה - 'כנגדו' להלחם:

יט| **ויצר... מן האדמה.** היא יצירה היא עשיה האמורה למעלה: "ויעש אלהים את חית הארץ" וגו' (לעיל א, כה), אלא בא ופרש שהעופות נבראו מן הרקק, לפי שאמר למעלה (לעיל א, כ) מן המים נבראו, וכאן אמר מן הארץ נבראו. ועוד למדך כאן, שבשעת יצירתן מיד בו ביום הביאם אל האדם לקרות להם שם. ובדברי אגדה יצירה זו לשון רדוי וכבוש, כמו: "כי תצור אל עיר" (דברים כ, יט), שכבשן תחת ידו של אדם: **וכל אשר יקרא לו האדם נפש חיה וגו'.** סרסהו ופרשהו: כל נפש חיה אשר יקרא לו האדם שם, הוא שמו לעולם:

כ-כא| **ולאדם לא מצא עזר. ויפל ה' אלהים תרדמה.** כשהביאן, הביאן לפניו כל מין ומין זכר ונקבה, אמר: לכלם יש בן זוג ולי אין בן זוג, מיד "ויפל": **מצלעתיו.** מסטריו, כמו: "ולצלע המשכן" (שמות כו, כ), זהו שאמרנו (ברכות סא ע"א): שני פרצופין נבראו: **ויסגר.** מקום החתך: **ויישן ויקח.** שלא יראה חתיכת הבשר שממנו נבראת ותתבזה עליו:

כב| **ויבן.** כבנין, רחבה מלמטה וקצרה מלמעלה לקבל הולד, כאוצר של חטים שהוא רחב מלמטה וקצר מלמעלה שלא יכביד משאו על קירותיו:

DISCUSSION

must all be on a single continent. Therefore, the Pishon and Gihon must be large rivers in Asia, near the other two rivers mentioned here, the Euphrates and the Tigris.

2:14| **And the fourth river is Euphrates:** If Pishon is indeed the Nile, which flows from south to north through the African continent, then it has absolutely no connection with either the Euphrates or the Tigris, which are located in Asia and flow from north to south. Indeed, it is precisely the identification of these four rivers that hints to the notion that the Garden of Eden is not a physical place with a geographic, albeit hidden, location. Only in a supernatural garden can a river flow that branches into locations so distant from one another.

2:20| **The man called names:** The midrashim describe this as an expression of man's wisdom as opposed to that of angels. Humanity is defined by its ability to speak. However, man's intelligence and speech are characterized not by the technical ability to produce sounds, but by the capacity to represent reality through symbols. When man scrutinized all the creatures of the world and gave each of them its name, he created hundreds of thousands of symbols. The angels could not do this because, among other reasons, they lack the power of imagination. Man's unique status lies in his capacity to formulate novel concepts (see *Bereshit Rabba* 17:19; *Avot deRabbi Natan* 8).

2:22| **The Lord God built the side that He took from the man into a woman:** Man was initially created as a single being with two sides, not yet divided into male and female, as described by the verse below: "Male and female He created them…and He called their name Man, on the day they were created" (5:2). In that state, man did not have clear male or female features; rather, he had both a male and a female side. These sides were closer to one another than conjoined twins, as the sides of man were connected in mind and body alike. This perfect creature thought with a single mind (see *Berakhot* 61a). Perhaps this primordial androgynous person embodied the idea that every male has a feminine side and vice versa.

23 Before the man fell into a deep sleep the woman was part of him. Only at this point, **the man said: This time,** this particular entity, is **a bone from my bones, and flesh from my flesh.** On the one hand, the man realized that the woman was a part of his original composition; on the other hand, he knew that she was a stranger to him. What was once a single being was now divided into two separate entities that were capable of relating to one another. **This shall be called woman [*isha*], because this was taken from man [*ish*].** The linguistic similarity between the terms representing man and woman, *ish* and *isha*, attests to the resemblance between them.

24 Since man and woman were not created as separate beings, their relationship is unique among creations. Unlike the males and females of the animal world, which have always been separate entities that develop independently, man and woman were once a single person. This unique status is what creates the special bond of love between a man and a woman and gives meaning to the institution of marriage. **Therefore, a man shall leave his father and his mother, and he shall cleave to his wife, and they shall become one flesh.**[D] Initially, the strongest bond between members of a family is the bond between a child and his parents. Nevertheless, the bond between husband and wife surpasses even the bond between a person and the family of his childhood. One's bond with one's parents certainly remains even after marrying, but it grows weaker.

25 The verse provides some background for events that will be described below: **They were both naked, the man and his wife, and they were not ashamed.** Like the other living creatures, the man and his wife did not need clothing in the Garden of Eden. As part of the natural world, humanity was originally bare and exposed.

3 1 **The serpent was more cunning**[D] **than any beast of the field that the Lord God had made.** The serpent was clever; it possessed intelligence. Although the word "cunning" [*arum*] usually has negative connotations in modern Hebrew, in the Bible it is a neutral term. Furthermore, this primeval serpent was not the same as the diminished snake we know today, but a wholly intelligent creature. **He said to the woman: Did God actually say: You shall not eat of any tree of the garden?** Perhaps the serpent chose to address the woman because God did not speak directly to her but to the man, reasoning that since she had heard of the prohibition only through an intermediary, it would be easier to incite and deceive her. Although when God forbade man

from partaking of the tree of the knowledge of good and evil the woman was still a part of him, one must conclude that only the male side heard the command directly from God.

A more profound reason that the serpent chose the woman is that it sought to arouse her curiosity. Perhaps curiosity was more characteristic of the woman and rendered her more susceptible to seduction, either because she desired to understand the ways of the world, or precisely because the seduction was not purely intellectual but included emotional and experiential aspects as well, as indicated by the verses below, and these aspects were more developed in the woman than in the man. With its cunning, the serpent concocted a complex plan: Although its question indicated that it was uncertain about the precise content of God's command, in fact the serpent knew that God did not actually prohibit all the trees of the garden for consumption. Nevertheless, the question it posed to the woman demanded a response, thus enabling its conversation with the woman to continue.

2 **The woman said to the serpent: From the fruit of the trees of the garden we may eat.** God did not prohibit us from eating the fruit of the garden.

3 **But from the fruit of the tree that is in the midst,** the middle, **of the garden, God said: You shall not eat of it, nor shall you touch it, lest you die.** This is a dangerous tree. It is prohibited for us to eat from this tree, or even to touch it, as death resides within it.

4 In response to this claim, **the serpent said to the woman: You will not die.** There is no need for you to fear that you might die, as the tree of the knowledge of good and evil does not cause death. The serpent could speak to the woman about this matter with the confidence of being a reliable source, because man was created last, and consequently all the other creatures had more life experience than he had.

5 The serpent now revealed the ostensible motivation for the divine prohibition: **For God knows that on the day you eat from it, then your eyes shall be opened, and you shall be as God, knowers of good and evil.** God does not want you to eat from this tree, not because it is dangerous, but because by consuming it you will be raised to a higher level. God seeks to prevent you from acquiring the knowledge of good and evil that He possesses.

6 **The woman saw that the tree was good for eating.**[D] The woman began to submit to temptation, thus marking the

---

DISCUSSION

2:24 | **And he shall cleave to his wife, and they shall become one flesh:** With this verse, the essence of marriage is articulated for the first time. The marital bond is not based on

passion alone, nor on the instinct to procreate. Rather, the essence of marriage is a unique and personal connection between a particular man and a particular woman. This is the basis for all

the rights, obligations, and foundations of the institution of marriage, including the relationship between a couple's childhood families and their own blossoming family. At this stage, the ◀▶

כג אֶל־הָאָדָם: וַיֹּאמֶר הָאָדָם זֹאת הַפַּעַם עֶצֶם מֵעֲצָמַי וּבָשָׂר מִבְּשָׂרִי לְזֹאת יִקָּרֵא
כד אִשָּׁה כִּי מֵאִישׁ לֻקֳחָה־זֹּאת: עַל־כֵּן יַעֲזָב־אִישׁ אֶת־אָבִיו וְאֶת־אִמּוֹ וְדָבַק בְּאִשְׁתּוֹ
כה ג א וְהָיוּ לְבָשָׂר אֶחָד: וַיִּהְיוּ שְׁנֵיהֶם עֲרוּמִּים הָאָדָם וְאִשְׁתּוֹ וְלֹא יִתְבֹּשָׁשׁוּ: וְהַנָּחָשׁ
הָיָה עָרוּם מִכֹּל חַיַּת הַשָּׂדֶה אֲשֶׁר עָשָׂה יְהוָה אֱלֹהִים וַיֹּאמֶר אֶל־הָאִשָּׁה אַף
ב כִּי־אָמַר אֱלֹהִים לֹא תֹאכְלוּ מִכֹּל עֵץ הַגָּן: וַתֹּאמֶר הָאִשָּׁה אֶל־הַנָּחָשׁ מִפְּרִי
ג עֵץ־הַגָּן נֹאכֵל: וּמִפְּרִי הָעֵץ אֲשֶׁר בְּתוֹךְ־הַגָּן אָמַר אֱלֹהִים לֹא תֹאכְלוּ מִמֶּנּוּ
ד ה וְלֹא תִגְּעוּ בּוֹ פֶּן תְּמֻתוּן: וַיֹּאמֶר הַנָּחָשׁ אֶל־הָאִשָּׁה לֹא־מוֹת תְּמֻתוּן: כִּי יֹדֵעַ
אֱלֹהִים כִּי בְּיוֹם אֲכָלְכֶם מִמֶּנּוּ וְנִפְקְחוּ עֵינֵיכֶם וִהְיִיתֶם כֵּאלֹהִים יֹדְעֵי טוֹב
ו וָרָע: וַתֵּרֶא הָאִשָּׁה כִּי טוֹב הָעֵץ לְמַאֲכָל וְכִי תַאֲוָה־הוּא לָעֵינַיִם וְנֶחְמָד הָעֵץ

רש"י

ויבן... את הצלע... לאשה. להיות אשה, כמו: "ויעש אותו גדעון לאפוד" (שופטים ח, כז), להיות אפוד:

כג | **זאת הפעם.** מלמד שבא אדם על כל בהמה וחיה ולא נתקררה דעתו בהם: **לזאת יקרא אשה כי מאיש וגו'.** לשון נופל על לשון, מכאן שנברא העולם בלשון הקדש:

כד | **על כן יעזב איש.** רוח הקדש אומרת כן, לאסור על בני נח עריות: **לבשר אחד.** הולד נוצר על ידי שניהם, ושם נעשה בשרם אחד:

כה | **ולא יתבששו.** שלא היו יודעים דרך צניעות להבחין בין טוב לרע, ואף על פי שנתנה בו דעה לקרוא שמות, לא נתן בו יצר הרע עד אכלו מן העץ, ונכנס בו יצר הרע וידע מה בין טוב לרע:

פרק ג

א | **והנחש היה ערום.** מה ענין זה לכאן? היה לו לסמוך: "ויעש... לאדם ולאשתו כתנות עור וילבשם" (להלן פסוק כא)! אלא למדך מאיזו עצה קפץ הנחש עליהם, ראה אותם ערמים ועוסקים בתשמיש לעין כל ונתאוה לה: **ערום מכל.** לפי ערמתו וגדלתו היתה מפלתו, ערום מכל, ארור מכל (להלן פסוק יד): **אף כי אמר וגו'.** שמא אמר לכם: "לא תאכלו מכל" וגו', ואף על פי שראה אותם אוכלים משאר פרות, הרבה עליה דברים כדי שתשיבנו ויבא לדבר באותו העץ:

ג | **ולא תגעו בו.** הוסיפה על הצווי לפיכך באה לידי גרעון, הוא שנאמר: "אל תוסף על דבריו" (משלי ל, ו):

ד | **לא מות תמתון.** דחפה עד שנגעה בו. אמר לה: כשם שאין מיתה בנגיעה, כך אין מיתה באכילה:

ה | **כי ידע.** כל אומן שונא את בני אומנותו, מן העץ אכל וברא את העולם: **והייתם כאלהים.** יוצרי עולמות:

ו | **ותרא האשה.** ראתה דבריו של נחש והנאו לה והאמינתו: **כי טוב העץ.** להיות כאלהים: **וכי תאוה הוא לעינים.** "ונפקחו עיניכם" (לעיל פסוק ה): **ונחמד...**

DISCUSSION

Torah states only the general principle underlying the special relationship between man and woman; the statutes, laws, and ordinances that result from this relationship will be delineated at a later stage.

3:1 | **The serpent was more cunning:** The Torah does not disclose the serpent's motives for seducing the woman. Perhaps it sought to usurp man's position atop the hierarchy in the Garden of Eden (see *Bereshit Rabba* 20:5). It is also possible that the serpent had absolutely no personal motive; it was simply the embodiment of evil. The Midrash depicts Satan as riding on the back of the serpent; the serpent was an instrument in the hands of absolute evil (*Pirkei deRabbi Eliezer* 12). However, even if the serpent's actions are ascribed to Satan, it is still difficult to fathom the existence of such evil in the world. Indeed, the mystery surrounding the serpent's motivation remains unsolved (see *Zohar* 1:35b).

Whatever the motivation, the serpent wanted evil, negation of the laws of reality. And yet, it seems that the serpent itself was unable to eat from the fruit of the tree of the knowledge of good and evil. Like the other creatures, it was unable to contravene these laws. Since only the man and the woman had the freedom to violate the laws, the serpent turned to them. Alternatively, perhaps the serpent was cunning precisely because it happened to eat from the fruit of the tree of the knowledge of good and evil, as it was not prohibited from doing so (see *Ḥizkuni*).

3:6 | **The tree was good for eating:** One who is attracted to evil assumes that there are forms of good in this world that do not necessarily fall within the rigid category of the morally good. Such forms of good include that which is beautiful, that which is pleasant, or that which is effective. Before the woman gazed upon the tree,

beginning of the sin. Of course the root of this sin preceded its execution; it was based on the willingness to even consider the possibility of violating a divine command. This did not occur to the woman on her own; it was the serpent who presented her with the option of defiance. Perhaps before the serpent spoke to her she was afraid of the tree and refrained from gazing at it or from reflecting on its nature and the effect of its fruit. But after it spoke to her she saw that the tree was as good as all the others, **and that it was an enticement to the eyes, and that the tree was attractive to apprehend.** There was something intriguing about this tree that made one desire to approach and understand it. **She took from its fruit and ate; she also gave to her husband with her, and he ate.** In the manner of a good wife who loves her husband, she immediately shared her great discovery with him.

7 **The eyes of both of them were opened, and they knew that they were naked.** Obviously, the man and woman were always aware of their nakedness. Indeed, their nakedness is already mentioned, as a matter of fact, at the end of the previous chapter. However, at first they were not ashamed of their naked state, just as people are not embarrassed to expose their noses or their eyes. Like the animals, all parts of their bodies were considered equal in their eyes. Partaking of the fruit of the tree of the knowledge of good and evil injected something new into their consciousness: A separation of the various forms of good, namely, aesthetics, pleasure, utility, and morality. This new awareness does not mean that until this point they were unaware of their sexuality. However, before eating of the fruit of the tree, they engaged in the sexual act as animals do, with complete innocence and unselfconsciousness. Now they became aware of the unique nature of human sexuality, and into their world was introduced a new sort of inclination. Unlike the sexual drive of animals, which is part of their biological compulsion and limited by objective factors of need and satiation, the human sexual urge is based on a potentially boundless erotic desire. The man and woman were suddenly faced with their ability to choose to what extent to indulge these newly discovered inclinations, and thus found themselves before a gaping chasm. Consequently, **they sewed fig leaves, and made themselves loincloths.** Since their nakedness was no longer a neutral state but a source of provocation and temptation, it was not to be publicly displayed; they therefore hurried to cover themselves.

8 It is difficult to appreciate the severity of the sin of the first man, who violated the sole command God had imposed upon him. From this point forward, humanity's penchant for sinning would fall to the greatest depths. Perhaps the first man foresaw this and recoiled. It is possible that the man and woman were perplexed, even dazed and intoxicated, by the fruit of the tree of the knowledge of good and evil. **They heard the voice of the Lord God** as though it were **moving in the garden with the day breeze.** The Divine Presence was particularly manifest in the Garden of Eden. **The man and his wife hid from the presence of the Lord God among the trees of the garden.** Before sinning, the man and his wife were like young children, who do only what they are supposed to do and are therefore not ashamed of their actions. For the first time, they sensed that they had acted improperly and felt ashamed and sought to hide.

9 **The Lord God called to the man, and said to him: Where are you?** This question is, of course, not designed to elicit information. It is a summons: Where are you? Stand before Me!

10 **He,** the man, apologized and **said: I heard Your voice in the garden, and I was afraid because I was naked, and I hid.** I am not standing in the open, because I am confused and ashamed. I hid because I did not want to be seen in my nakedness.

11 **He,** God, **said: Who told you that you were naked,** that there is something wrong with your nakedness? You were naked beforehand as well, and yet you were not ashamed. Clearly, God was not referring to man's physical nakedness, as even an animal could have discerned this. **Did you eat from the tree from which I commanded you not to eat?** This was also a rhetorical question, meant to test the man's response.

12 Despite all he had learned about good and evil, the man had not yet learned how to lie. His response was therefore not a distortion of reality. However, it was also not a direct response. Having internalized the serpent's cunning, the man did not respond: Yes, or: I sinned. Rather, **the man said: The woman whom You gave to be with me, she gave me from the tree, and I ate.** You created a woman for me, and she gave me the fruit. By referring to his wife as the woman whom God gave to be with him, the man shirked responsibility for his actions and sought to shift the blame onto her and onto God.

13 **The Lord God said to the woman: What is this you have done?** Why did you consume the fruit, and why did you give it to your husband? **The woman said: The serpent enticed me, and I ate.** She also absolved herself of responsibility, although her response was indeed very close to the truth. The woman claimed that she herself would never have conceived of such a deed. Rather, another entity, the serpent, persuaded her with its crafty ways to eat from the fruit. Nevertheless, the woman did not seek to blame God.

14 **The Lord God said to the serpent.** God did not ask the serpent why it behaved as it did, because unlike the man and his wife, the serpent had no justification for its actions. It acted out of a profound wickedness whose purpose was to break open the depths of evil, or simply for its amusement. Even if the serpent did not intend to bring about the tremendous upheaval in the world that resulted from its actions or the expulsion from the Garden of Eden, the serpent's words stemmed from the malicious thought: Perhaps we should do the very opposite of

לְהַשְׂכִּיל וַתִּקַּח מִפִּרְיוֹ וַתֹּאכַל וַתִּתֵּן גַּם־לְאִישָׁהּ עִמָּהּ וַיֹּאכַל: וַתִּפָּקַחְנָה עֵינֵי ז
שְׁנֵיהֶם וַיֵּדְעוּ כִּי עֵירֻמִּם הֵם וַיִּתְפְּרוּ עֲלֵה תְאֵנָה וַיַּעֲשׂוּ לָהֶם חֲגֹרֹת: וַיִּשְׁמְעוּ ח
אֶת־קוֹל יְהוָה אֱלֹהִים מִתְהַלֵּךְ בַּגָּן לְרוּחַ הַיּוֹם וַיִּתְחַבֵּא הָאָדָם וְאִשְׁתּוֹ מִפְּנֵי
יְהוָה אֱלֹהִים בְּתוֹךְ עֵץ הַגָּן: וַיִּקְרָא יְהוָה אֱלֹהִים אֶל־הָאָדָם וַיֹּאמֶר לוֹ אַיֶּכָּה: ט
וַיֹּאמֶר אֶת־קֹלְךָ שָׁמַעְתִּי בַּגָּן וָאִירָא כִּי־עֵירֹם אָנֹכִי וָאֵחָבֵא: וַיֹּאמֶר מִי הִגִּיד לְךָ י יא
כִּי עֵירֹם אָתָּה הֲמִן־הָעֵץ אֲשֶׁר צִוִּיתִיךָ לְבִלְתִּי אֲכָל־מִמֶּנּוּ אָכָלְתָּ: וַיֹּאמֶר הָאָדָם יב
הָאִשָּׁה אֲשֶׁר נָתַתָּה עִמָּדִי הִוא נָתְנָה־לִּי מִן־הָעֵץ וָאֹכֵל: וַיֹּאמֶר יְהוָה אֱלֹהִים יג
לָאִשָּׁה מַה־זֹּאת עָשִׂית וַתֹּאמֶר הָאִשָּׁה הַנָּחָשׁ הִשִּׁיאַנִי וָאֹכֵל: וַיֹּאמֶר יְהוָה יד
אֱלֹהִים ׀ אֶל־הַנָּחָשׁ כִּי עָשִׂיתָ זֹּאת אָרוּר אַתָּה מִכָּל־הַבְּהֵמָה וּמִכֹּל חַיַּת הַשָּׂדֶה
עַל־גְּחֹנְךָ תֵלֵךְ וְעָפָר תֹּאכַל כָּל־יְמֵי חַיֶּיךָ: וְאֵיבָה ׀ אָשִׁית בֵּינְךָ וּבֵין הָאִשָּׁה וּבֵין טו

רש״י

לְהַשְׂכִּיל. "יֹדְעֵי טוֹב וָרָע" (שם): וַתִּתֵּן גַּם לְאִישָׁהּ. שֶׁלֹּא תָּמוּת הִיא וְיִחְיֶה הוּא וְיִשָּׂא אַחֶרֶת: גַּם. לְרַבּוֹת בְּהֵמָה וְחַיָּה:

ז | וַתִּפָּקַחְנָה וְגוֹ׳. לְעִנְיַן הַחָכְמָה דִּבֵּר הַכָּתוּב וְלֹא לְעִנְיַן רְאִיָּה מַמָּשׁ, וְסוֹף הַמִּקְרָא מוֹכִיחַ: "וַיֵּדְעוּ כִּי עֵירֻמִּם הֵם" – אַף הַסּוּמָא יוֹדֵעַ כְּשֶׁהוּא עָרֹם!: וַיֵּדְעוּ כִּי עֵירֻמִּם הֵם. מִצְוָה אַחַת הָיְתָה בְּיָדָם וְנִתְעַרְטְלוּ הֵימֶנָּה: עֲלֵה תְאֵנָה. הוּא הָעֵץ שֶׁאָכְלוּ מִמֶּנּוּ, בַּדָּבָר שֶׁנִּתְקַלְקְלוּ בּוֹ נִתְקְנוּ, אֲבָל שְׁאָר הָעֵצִים מְנָעוּם מִלִּטֹּל עֲלֵיהֶם. וּמִפְּנֵי מָה לֹא נִתְפַּרְסֵם הָעֵץ? שֶׁאֵין הַקָּדוֹשׁ בָּרוּךְ הוּא חָפֵץ לְהוֹנוֹת בְּרִיָּה, שֶׁלֹּא יַכְלִימוּהוּ וְיֹאמְרוּ: זֶהוּ שֶׁלָּקָה הָעוֹלָם עַל יָדוֹ. מִדְרַשׁ רַבִּי תַּנְחוּמָא (וירא יד):

ח | וַיִּשְׁמְעוּ. יֵשׁ מִדְרְשֵׁי אַגָּדָה רַבִּים, וּכְבָר סִדְּרוּם רַבּוֹתֵינוּ עַל מְכוֹנָם בִּבְרֵאשִׁית רַבָּה וּבִשְׁאָר מִדְרָשׁוֹת, וַאֲנִי לֹא בָּאתִי אֶלָּא לִפְשׁוּטוֹ שֶׁל מִקְרָא וּלְאַגָּדָה הַמְיַשֶּׁבֶת דִּבְרֵי הַמִּקְרָא דָּבָר דָּבוּר עַל אָפְנָיו. וּמַשְׁמָעוֹ, שָׁמְעוּ אֶת קוֹל הַקָּדוֹשׁ בָּרוּךְ הוּא שֶׁהָיָה מִתְהַלֵּךְ בַּגָּן: לְרוּחַ הַיּוֹם. לְאוֹתוֹ רוּחַ שֶׁהַשֶּׁמֶשׁ בָּאָה מִשָּׁם, וְזוֹ הִיא מַעֲרָבִית, שֶׁלִּפְנוֹת עֶרֶב חַמָּה בַּמַּעֲרָב, וְהֵם סָרְחוּ בָּעֲשִׂירִית:

ט | אַיֶּכָּה. יוֹדֵעַ הָיָה הֵיכָן הוּא, אֶלָּא לִכָּנֵס עִמּוֹ בִּדְבָרִים, שֶׁלֹּא יְהֵא נִבְהָל לְהָשִׁיב אִם יַעֲנִישֵׁהוּ פִּתְאוֹם. וְכֵן בְּקַיִן אָמַר לוֹ: "אֵי הֶבֶל אָחִיךָ" (להלן ד, ט), וְכֵן בְּבִלְעָם: "מִי הָאֲנָשִׁים הָאֵלֶּה עִמָּךְ" (במדבר כב, ט), לִכָּנֵס עִמָּהֶם בִּדְבָרִים, וְכֵן בְּחִזְקִיָּהוּ בִּשְׁלוּחֵי אֱוִיל מְרוֹדַךְ:

יא | מִי הִגִּיד לְךָ. מֵאַיִן לְךָ לָדַעַת מַה בֹּשֶׁת יֵשׁ בָּעוֹמֵד עָרֹם?: הֲמִן הָעֵץ. בִּתְמִיהָ:

יב | אֲשֶׁר נָתַתָּה עִמָּדִי. כָּאן כָּפַר בַּטּוֹבָה:

יג | הִשִּׁיאַנִי. הִטְעַנִי, כְּמוֹ: "אַל יַשִּׁיא אֶתְכֶם חִזְקִיָּהוּ" (דברי הימים ב׳ לב, טו):

יד | כִּי עָשִׂיתָ זֹּאת. מִכָּאן שֶׁאֵין מְהַפְּכִים בִּזְכוּתוֹ שֶׁל מֵסִית, שֶׁאִלּוּ שְׁאָלוֹ: לָמָּה עָשִׂיתָ זֹאת? הָיָה לוֹ לְהָשִׁיב: דִּבְרֵי הָרַב וְדִבְרֵי הַתַּלְמִיד, דִּבְרֵי מִי שׁוֹמְעִין?: מִכָּל הַבְּהֵמָה וּמִכֹּל חַיַּת הַשָּׂדֶה. אִם מִבְּהֵמָה נִתְקַלֵּל, מֵחַיָּה לֹא כָּל שֶׁכֵּן?! הֶעֱמִידוּ רַבּוֹתֵינוּ מִדְרָשׁ זֶה בְּמַסֶּכֶת בְּכוֹרוֹת (דף ח ע״א) לְלַמֵּד שֶׁיְּמֵי עִבּוּרוֹ שֶׁל נָחָשׁ שֶׁבַע שָׁנִים: עַל גְּחֹנְךָ תֵלֵךְ. רַגְלַיִם הָיוּ לוֹ וְנִקְצְצוּ:

טו | וְאֵיבָה אָשִׁית. אַתָּה לֹא נִתְכַּוַּנְתָּ אֶלָּא שֶׁיָּמוּת אָדָם, שֶׁיֹּאכַל הוּא תְּחִלָּה וְתִשָּׂא אֶת חַוָּה, וְלֹא בָאתָ לְדַבֵּר אֶל

God's wishes. God therefore cursed the serpent: **Because you did this, cursed are you from among all the animals, and from all the beasts of the field; upon your belly shall you go, and dust shall you eat all the days of your life.** It can be inferred from the verse that the serpent previously walked on legs.

15 God declared an additional punishment: **I will place enmity between you and the woman, and between your descendants and her descendants.** If, for whatever reason, you sought to establish a connection with the woman, your efforts will be unsuccessful. Henceforth, an irrational hatred will prevail

DISCUSSION

the various forms of good, such as aesthetics, pleasure, utility, and morality, were all united. The discovery that the forbidden tree was good for eating shattered this unity between the different forms of good. Suddenly, there was a choice that, while not morally good, as it entailed a rebellion against the command of God, nonetheless incorporated an abundance of all the other aspects of the good (see Sforno, Genesis 2:9; *Minḥa Belula*).

between you and the woman, and between your descendants and hers. This hatred will be expressed by the fact that **he shall strike your head, and you shall strike his heel.**

16 **To the woman He said.** The curses placed upon the woman distinguish the female human from the females of the animal kingdom: **I will increase your suffering;** your life will involve much pain. Some explain this as a reference to the menstrual cycle, which has no counterpart in most animals and which is unpleasant and sometimes even painful. **And** I will increase the difficulty of **your pregnancy.** Human pregnancy is not as simple or straightforward as that of other creatures. This is partly due to human psychology and partly due to physiology. The same applies to childbirth: **In pain you shall give birth to children. And** furthermore, **your desire shall be for your husband.** Since you initiated this action, that is, you were proactive in tempting your husband and attempting to create a new reality, you will henceforth yearn for your husband. Although this is not an adverse state of affairs, it involves a measure of passivity on the woman's part. **And he shall rule over you,** not necessarily in terms of a social order, but in the context of sexual relations. The woman was cursed that man and woman would no longer be equal partners. Since the woman wanted to know evil, she would experience suffering; since she sought to lead her husband, she would now be led by him.

17 **And to Adam He said: Because you heeded the voice of your wife, and ate from the tree that I commanded you, saying: You shall not eat from it,** your sin is more severe, as you heeded the voice of your wife despite hearing the prohibition directly from Me. Therefore, **cursed is the ground on your account.** No longer will the ground be like the fertile soil of the Garden of Eden, which gave forth produce without any toil on your part, and which you only had to protect from damage. From now on, mankind's relationship with the ground will be different: **In suffering,** through toil, **shall you eat of it all the days of your life.**

18 **And** unlike in the Garden of Eden, if you wait for the ground to produce its fruit spontaneously, then **thorns and thistles shall it grow for you; and you shall eat the vegetation of the field,** which will not always be edible in its natural state.

19 In order for the vegetation of the field to be fit for consumption, you will have to toil over its growth. You will no longer be able to consume all produce in its natural state. Rather, **by the sweat of your brow shall you eat bread.** Until now you have lived in a world in which everything was prepared for you. Henceforth, you will have to exert great effort to produce your food, **until you return to the ground; for from it were you taken.** Ultimately, you will die. **For you are dust, and to dust shall you return.**[D]

20 **The man called the name of his wife Eve [Ḥavva].** Before the man imagined that other people would inhabit the earth, there was no reason for him to give his wife a name. He was man and she was woman, and that was sufficient. After learning of their mortality and that the woman would give birth to other people who would replace them, he gave her a name. He chose this name **because she was the mother of all living [*ḥai*].** There is much affection and love in the selection of this particular name. Adam could have chosen many other names; he could even have given her a name that reflected some resentment toward her. Despite everything, he called her Ḥavva, as if to say to her: From you life will come to the world.

21 **The Lord God made for Adam and for his wife hide tunics**[D] **and clothed them.** God took into account the shame and vulnerability that Adam and Eve felt in the wake of their sin. He wished to assist them on their new path, so He clothed them.

22 **The Lord God said: Behold, the man has become as one of**
Fourth aliya **us,** like one of the heavenly beings, as he has the capacity **to know good and evil.** Man no longer acts solely based on instinct or what he is told, but in accordance with his own free will. **And now, lest he put forth his hand, and take also from the tree of life, and eat, and live forever.** Although the tree of life was in the garden the entire time, it seems that it did not attract the attention of Adam or Eve. Unlike the enticing tree of the knowledge of good and evil, whose fruits were particularly desirable, perhaps the tree of life was a simple tree whose fruit was unimpressive. However, following man's recent dramatic awareness of his mortality, he might have sought ways to avoid death. It is possible that no prohibition or threat would prevent him from making use of that which could grant him eternal life.

23 **Therefore, the Lord God sent him out from the Garden of Eden, to cultivate the ground from which he was taken.** Man returned to the unremarkable land outside the Garden of Eden.

24 The man was not sent from the garden in a leisurely manner; rather, **He,** God, **banished the man; He stationed the**

DISCUSSION

3:19 | **For you are dust, and to dust shall you return:** Was it ever possible that man would live forever? From his very creation, man was an anomaly; the combination of dust and the breath of life from God does not exist among any other creature. It is therefore possible that this extraordinary being was initially not supposed to die, and that man became part of the standard life cycle only after he sinned. Since all life in this world participates in the cycle of formation and decay, mankind would henceforth be mortal. The knowledge that one's life will eventually come to an end is a formative and highly significant part of the human condition; man's mortality is an inescapable truth that

טו זַרְעֲךָ וּבֵין זַרְעָהּ הוּא יְשׁוּפְךָ רֹאשׁ וְאַתָּה תְּשׁוּפֶנּוּ עָקֵב: אֶל־הָאִשָּׁה
אָמַר הַרְבָּה אַרְבֶּה עִצְּבוֹנֵךְ וְהֵרֹנֵךְ בְּעֶצֶב תֵּלְדִי בָנִים וְאֶל־אִישֵׁךְ תְּשׁוּקָתֵךְ וְהוּא
יז יִמְשָׁל־בָּךְ: וּלְאָדָם אָמַר כִּי שָׁמַעְתָּ לְקוֹל אִשְׁתֶּךָ וַתֹּאכַל מִן־הָעֵץ
אֲשֶׁר צִוִּיתִיךָ לֵאמֹר לֹא תֹאכַל מִמֶּנּוּ אֲרוּרָה הָאֲדָמָה בַּעֲבוּרֶךָ בְּעִצָּבוֹן תֹּאכֲלֶנָּה
יח יט כֹּל יְמֵי חַיֶּיךָ: וְקוֹץ וְדַרְדַּר תַּצְמִיחַ לָךְ וְאָכַלְתָּ אֶת־עֵשֶׂב הַשָּׂדֶה: בְּזֵעַת אַפֶּיךָ
תֹּאכַל לֶחֶם עַד שׁוּבְךָ אֶל־הָאֲדָמָה כִּי מִמֶּנָּה לֻקָּחְתָּ כִּי־עָפָר אַתָּה וְאֶל־עָפָר
כ כא תָּשׁוּב: וַיִּקְרָא הָאָדָם שֵׁם אִשְׁתּוֹ חַוָּה כִּי הִוא הָיְתָה אֵם כָּל־חָי: וַיַּעַשׂ יְהוָה
אֱלֹהִים לְאָדָם וּלְאִשְׁתּוֹ כָּתְנוֹת עוֹר וַיַּלְבִּשֵׁם:
כב וַיֹּאמֶר ׀ יְהוָה אֱלֹהִים הֵן הָאָדָם הָיָה כְּאַחַד מִמֶּנּוּ לָדַעַת טוֹב וָרָע וְעַתָּה ׀ ג רביעי
כג פֶּן־יִשְׁלַח יָדוֹ וְלָקַח גַּם מֵעֵץ הַחַיִּים וְאָכַל וָחַי לְעֹלָם: וַיְשַׁלְּחֵהוּ יְהוָה אֱלֹהִים

רש״י

חַוָּה תְּחִלָּה אֶלָּא לְפִי שֶׁהַנָּשִׁים קַלּוֹת לְהִתְפַּתּוֹת וְיוֹדְעוֹת לְפַתּוֹת בַּעְלֵיהֶן, לְפִיכָךְ "וְאֵיבָה אָשִׁית": **יְשׁוּפְךָ.** יְכַתֶּתְךָ, כְּמוֹ: "וָאֶכֹּת אֹתוֹ" (דברים ט, כא), וְתַרְגּוּמוֹ: "וְשָׁפִית יָתֵיהּ": **וְאַתָּה תְּשׁוּפֶנּוּ עָקֵב.** לֹא יְהֵא לְךָ קוֹמָה, וְתִשְּׁכֶנּוּ בַּעֲקֵבוֹ וְאַף מִשָּׁם תְּמִיתֶנּוּ. וּלְשׁוֹן 'תְּשׁוּפֶנּוּ' כְּמוֹ: "נָשַׁף בָּהֶם" (ישעיה מ, כד), כְּשֶׁהַנָּחָשׁ בָּא לְנְשֹׁךְ הוּא נוֹשֵׁף כְּמִין שְׁרִיקָה, וּלְפִי שֶׁהַלָּשׁוֹן נוֹפֵל עַל הַלָּשׁוֹן כָּתַב לְשׁוֹן נְשִׁיפָה בִּשְׁנֵיהֶם:

טז **עִצְּבוֹנֵךְ.** זֶה צַעַר גִּדּוּל בָּנִים: **וְהֵרֹנֵךְ.** זֶה צַעַר הָעִבּוּר: **בְּעֶצֶב תֵּלְדִי בָנִים.** זֶה צַעַר הַלֵּדָה: **וְאֶל אִישֵׁךְ תְּשׁוּקָתֵךְ.** לְתַשְׁמִישׁ, וְאַף עַל פִּי כֵן אֵין לָךְ מֵצַח לְתָבְעוֹ בַּפֶּה אֶלָּא "הוּא יִמְשָׁל בָּךְ", הַכֹּל מִמֶּנּוּ וְלֹא מִמֵּךְ: **תְּשׁוּקָתֵךְ.** תַּאֲוָתֵךְ, כְּמוֹ: "וְנַפְשׁוֹ שׁוֹקֵקָה" (ישעיה כט, ח):

יז **אֲרוּרָה הָאֲדָמָה בַּעֲבוּרֶךָ.** מַעֲלָה לְךָ דְּבָרִים אֲרוּרִים, כְּגוֹן זְבוּבִים וּפַרְעוֹשִׁים וּנְמָלִים. מָשָׁל לְיוֹצֵא לְתַרְבּוּת רָעָה וְהַבְּרִיּוֹת מְקַלְּלוֹת שָׁדַיִם שֶׁיָּנַק מֵהֶם:

יח **וְקוֹץ וְדַרְדַּר תַּצְמִיחַ לָךְ.** הָאָרֶץ, כְּשֶׁתִּזְרָעֶנָּה מִינֵי זְרָעִים תַּצְמִיחַ קוֹץ וְדַרְדַּר, קוּנְדָס וְעַכָּבִיּוֹת, וְהֵן נֶאֱכָלִין עַל יְדֵי תִּקּוּן: **וְאָכַלְתָּ אֶת עֵשֶׂב הַשָּׂדֶה.** וּמַה קְּלָלָה הִיא זוֹ? וַהֲלֹא בִּבְרָכָה נֶאֱמַר לוֹ: "הִנֵּה נָתַתִּי לָכֶם אֶת כָּל עֵשֶׂב זֹרֵעַ זֶרַע" וְגוֹ' (לעיל א, כט)? אֶלָּא מָה אָמוּר כָּאן בָּרֹאשׁ הָעִנְיָן: "אֲרוּרָה הָאֲדָמָה בַּעֲבוּרֶךָ בְּעִצָּבוֹן תֹּאכֲלֶנָּה", וְאַחַר הָעִצָּבוֹן: "וְקוֹץ וְדַרְדַּר תַּצְמִיחַ לָךְ", כְּשֶׁתִּזְרָעֶנָּה קִטְנִית אוֹ יַרְקוֹת גִּנָּה, הִיא תַּצְמִיחַ לְךָ קוֹצִים וְדַרְדָּרִים וּשְׁאָר עִשְׂבֵי שָׂדֶה, וְעַל כָּרְחֲךָ תֹּאכְלֵם:

יט **בְּזֵעַת אַפֶּיךָ.** לְאַחַר שֶׁתִּטְרַח בּוֹ הַרְבֵּה:

כ **וַיִּקְרָא הָאָדָם.** חָזַר הַכָּתוּב לְעִנְיָנוֹ הָרִאשׁוֹן: "וַיִּקְרָא הָאָדָם שֵׁמוֹת" (לעיל ב, כ), וְלֹא הִפְסִיק אֶלָּא לְלַמֶּדְךָ שֶׁעַל יְדֵי קְרִיאַת שֵׁמוֹת נִזְדַּוְּגָה לוֹ חַוָּה, כְּמוֹ שֶׁכָּתוּב: "וּלְאָדָם לֹא מָצָא עֵזֶר כְּנֶגְדּוֹ" (שם), לְפִיכָךְ "וַיַּפֵּל... תַּרְדֵּמָה" (שם, כא), וְעַל יְדֵי שֶׁכָּתַב: "וַיִּהְיוּ שְׁנֵיהֶם עֲרוּמִּים" (שם, כה) סָמַךְ לוֹ פָּרָשַׁת הַנָּחָשׁ, לְהוֹדִיעֲךָ שֶׁמִּתּוֹךְ שֶׁרָאָה עֶרְוָתָהּ וְרָאָה אוֹתָם עֲסוּקִים בְּתַשְׁמִישׁ נִתְאַוָּה לָהּ, וּבָא עֲלֵיהֶם בְּמַחֲשָׁבָה וּבְמִרְמָה: **חַוָּה.** נוֹפֵל עַל לְשׁוֹן 'חַיָּה' שֶׁמְּחַיָּה אֶת וַלְדוֹתֶיהָ, כַּאֲשֶׁר תֹּאמַר: "מֶה הֹוֶה לָאָדָם" (קהלת ב, כב) בִּלְשׁוֹן 'הָיָה':

כא **כָּתְנוֹת עוֹר.** יֵשׁ דִּבְרֵי אַגָּדָה אוֹמְרִים: חֲלָקִים כְּצִפֹּרֶן מְדֻבָּקִין עַל עוֹרָן. וְיֵשׁ אוֹמְרִים: דָּבָר הַבָּא מִן הָעוֹר, כְּגוֹן צֶמֶר אַרְנָבִים שֶׁהוּא רַךְ וְחַם, וְעָשָׂה לָהֶם כֻּתֳּנוֹת מִמֶּנּוּ:

כב **הָיָה כְּאַחַד מִמֶּנּוּ.** הֲרֵי הוּא יָחִיד בַּתַּחְתּוֹנִים כְּמוֹ שֶׁאֲנִי יָחִיד בָּעֶלְיוֹנִים, וּמַה הִיא יְחִידוּתוֹ? "לָדַעַת טוֹב וָרָע", מַה שֶּׁאֵין כֵּן בַּבְּהֵמָה וּבַחַיָּה: **וְעַתָּה פֶּן יִשְׁלַח יָדוֹ** וְגוֹ'. וּמִשֶּׁיִּחְיֶה לְעוֹלָם הֲרֵי הוּא קָרוֹב לְהַטְעוֹת הַבְּרִיּוֹת אַחֲרָיו וְלוֹמַר אַף הוּא אֱלוֹהַּ. וְיֵשׁ מִדְרְשֵׁי אַגָּדָה, אֲבָל אֵין מְיֻשָּׁבִין עַל פְּשׁוּטוֹ:

DISCUSSION

remains embedded in his consciousness. Were man to have lived forever, there would not have been much significance to the consequences of the sin in general and to the toil with which man was cursed in particular (see *Responsa of the Radbaz* 257).

3:21 | **Hide tunics:** According to one midrash, these garments were made of the serpent's hide (*Pirkei deRabbi Eliezer* 20; *Midrash Tehillim* 92:6). Indeed, the Midrash teaches that one of the serpent's punishments was the shedding of its skin (*Pirkei deRabbi Eliezer* 14). From the hide shed by the creature who caused the sin, God prepared garments to conceal the shame felt by Adam and Eve over their sin.

cherubs, a type of angel, **east [***kedem***] of the Garden of Eden.** Perhaps the entrance to the garden was on its eastern side, as was the case in the Temple. Alternatively, *kedem* simply refers to the front of the garden, in whatever direction it may have been. **And** He placed **the blade of the ever-turning sword,** which blocked the way, **to guard the path to the tree of life,** at

least for the time being, until God decides to return the man to the Garden of Eden. Angels and heavenly forces of deterrence removed the possibility of immortality from man's grasp. The man understood that he could no longer return to the garden, and that he had to seek his destiny elsewhere.

The Family of Adam and Eve
GENESIS 4:1–26

This chapter marks the beginning of the story of Adam and his family outside the Garden of Eden. After their banishment from the garden, Adam and Eve begin a new life with all its complexities. Their family must deal with some of the fundamental issues facing humanity, one of which is relations between siblings. The story opens with two brothers, each living in his own manner and in his own realm. From the outset, they are different from one another, and perhaps there is some friction between them, but each remains in his own world. Eventually, however, their worlds collide.

4 **1** **The man had been intimate**[D] **with Eve his wife** while they were still in the Garden of Eden. Since Eve gave birth after their banishment, the verse relates the entire story here. **And she conceived and gave birth to Cain and said: I have acquired [***kaniti***] a man with the Lord.** Eve was amazed by the first human birth, at the fact that she, together with God, created a man that until now did not exist. Eve felt that she could not create man by herself; she was instead a partner with God in giving birth to this new being. To this day, women in labor, and indeed people in general, express similar astonishment at the wonder of childbirth.

2 **She continued to give birth to his brother,** who was called **Abel.** In contrast to Cain, no reason is given for the choice of Abel's name. Many explain that the name alludes to Abel's sad demise; like *hevel*, vapor, nothing was left of him. His name can also be interpreted in a positive manner, as a reference to a breath of wind, as if the birth of Abel revealed something of a spiritual nature. If so, this passage touches on the foundations of human existence: The first child, Cain, sparked amazement at the birth process itself, whereas the second child, Abel, revealed the wonder of diversity, which is inherent in the human spirit. Although mankind would eventually become accustomed to these marvels, for Adam and Eve the fact that such diverse children could emerge from the same parents was truly remarkable. It is unknown how these two children differed from one another at birth, although the differences between them eventually manifested themselves in behavior: **Abel was a shepherd;** he would milk the sheep and shear their wool, but he did not eat their meat; **and Cain was a cultivator of the ground.**[D]

3 **It happened, after some time,** perhaps years later. According to one opinion, this occurred forty years after the birth of Cain and Abel. **Cain brought from the fruit of the ground an offering to the Lord.** In contrast to various theories claiming otherwise, this episode indicates the fundamental nature of bringing an offering and that this concept was not introduced by foreign cultures. From the very beginnings of humanity,

people felt the need to bring gifts to God. Later, these gift offerings would be called burnt offerings, as they were burnt in their entirety in God's honor. These offerings were not considered a tax; they were not even obligatory. Although the Recipient of the gift has no need for it, the gift offering allows the giver to express his feelings toward Him.

4 **And Abel, he too brought** an offering to God **from the firstborn of his flock and from the choicest of them; and the Lord turned toward Abel and to his offering.** The verse does not explain how this acceptance expressed itself. Perhaps a fire descended from heaven upon Abel's offering, as occurred in other instances, or perhaps it was evident that Abel's offering was accepted because he was in high spirits or experienced some euphoric state.

5 **But toward Cain and to his offering He did not turn.** The two brothers were presumably close in age and had similar characteristics. God's preference for one brother over the other was therefore highly upsetting for the one who was rejected. **Cain was very incensed, and his face became downcast.** Understood literally, this expression is an accurate and straightforward description of the behavior of a shamed, disappointed, and angry individual, who lowers his face toward the ground.

6 **The Lord said to Cain: Why are you incensed, and why did your face become downcast?** While it is true that I chose Abel, why are you angry? Although you were not chosen, I did not harm you. Why, then, do you feel despised and ashamed? God reproved Cain for his jealousy, an emotion that easily leads to unjustified rage.

7 **Truly, if you do good, you will be elevated.** If you improve your deeds and behave properly, you will be elevated. This phrase might be an indication that Cain did not bring his offering wholeheartedly, or that he did not select his choicest produce, as expounded by the Sages. **And if you do not do good,** remember that **sin crouches at the entrance.** Beyond the very existence of evil is the concept of sin, which is the introduction of evil into the world through the deeds of man. In this figurative representation, sin is depicted as a living creature

כד מגן־עדן לעבד את־האדמה אשר לקח משם: ויגרש את־האדם וישכן
מקדם לגן־עדן את־הכרבים ואת להט החרב המתהפכת לשמר את־דרך
ד א עץ החיים: והאדם ידע את־חוה אשתו ותהר ותלד את־קין
ב ותאמר קניתי איש את־יהוה: ותסף ללדת את־אחיו את־הבל ויהי־הבל
ג רעה צאן וקין היה עבד אדמה: ויהי מקץ ימים ויבא קין מפרי האדמה
ד מנחה ליהוה: והבל הביא גם־הוא מבכרות צאנו ומחלבהן וישע יהוה אל־
ה הבל ואל־מנחתו: ואל־קין ואל־מנחתו לא שעה ויחר לקין מאד ויפלו
ו ז פניו: ויאמר יהוה אל־קין למה חרה לך ולמה נפלו פניך: הלוא אם־תיטיב
שאת ואם לא תיטיב לפתח חטאת רבץ ואליך תשוקתו ואתה תמשל־בו:

רש"י

כד | מקדם לגן עדן. במזרחו של גן עדן חוץ לגן: את הכרבים. מלאכי חבלה, וחרב מתהפכת ולה להט, לאיים עליו מלהכנס עוד לגן. תרגום 'להט' – "שנן", והוא כמו "שלף שננא" בסנהדרין (דף פב ע"א) ובלשון לעז למ"א. ומדרשי אגדה יש, ואני איני בא אלא לפשוטו:

פרק ד

א–ב | והאדם ידע. כבר קודם ענין של מעלה, קודם שחטא ונטרד מגן עדן, וכן ההריון והלידה, שאם כתב 'וידע אדם' נשמע שלאחר שנטרד היו לו בנים: קין. על שם "קניתי": את ה'. עם ה', כשברא אותי ואת אישי לבדו בראנו, אבל בזה שותפים אנו עמו: את קין, את אחיו את הבל. שלשה 'אתים' רבויים הם, מלמד שתאומה נולדה עם קין, ועם הבל נולדו שתים, לכך נאמר: "ותסף": רעה צאן. לפי שנתקללה האדמה, פירש לו מעבודתה:

ג | מפרי האדמה. מן הגרוע, ויש אגדה שאומרת זרע פשתן היה:

ד | וישע. ויפן, וכן: "שעה מעליו" (איוב יד, ו) פנה מעליו: וישע. ירדה אש ולחכה מנחתו:

ה | לא שעה. לא פנה, וכן: "אל ישעו" (שמות ה, ט) אל יפנו:

ז | הלא אם תיטיב. כתרגומו פרושו: לפתח חטאת רבץ. לפתח קברך חטאך שמור: ואליך תשוקתו. של חטאת, הוא יצר הרע, תמיד שוקק ומתאוה להכשילך: ואתה תמשל בו. אם תרצה תתגבר עליו:

that prowls at an entrance and seeks to enter. Behind this verse lies the perception that when a person acts properly, he thereby prevents sin from controlling him, while if he does not, even if he does not actually perform evil, sin crouches at the entrance. **And its desire is for you.** In contrast to the common perception of man as the one who desires to sin, the verse describes the personified sin as seeking to control man. **But you may rule over it.**[D] It is within man's potential to rule over sin. He must keep in mind that sin is ever present, and that it seeks to build itself and grow powerful by attaching itself to him. As long as man is the one in control, and he does not let it conquer him, his existence is assured.

8 Although Cain heard the words of God, he did not internalize them at all and held firm to his jealousy: **Cain said to Abel his**

DISCUSSION

4:1 | The man had been intimate [*yada*]: This form of the verb indicates that Adam was already intimate with Eve while they were still in the garden, and this is stated explicitly by the Sages (see *Pirkei deRabbi Eliezer* 11; see also Rashi; *Responsa of the Rashbatz* 222).

4:2 | Abel was a shepherd, and Cain was a cultivator of the ground: For much of history, the divide between shepherds and farmers has been significant. Quarrels would sometimes break out between followers of these two lifestyles when shepherds, who were generally desert dwellers, encroached with their flock on the cultivated fields of farmers. The rivalry sometimes developed into war between tribes and nations over settled lands and pasture.

4:7 | But you may rule over it: The declaration that man is always capable of controlling sin has serious implications with regard to the principle of free choice and the perception of good and evil. God declares that nothing forces one to sin; transgression occurs only when a person decides to submit to sin.

It can be inferred from God's statement to Cain that sin, far more than the primeval serpent, is a kind of parasitic entity that exists only by clinging to man, which is why its desire is directed toward man. Sin is a kind of empty space, a framework devoid of substance; it requires man to give it content.

brother. The verse does not specify what Cain said to Abel. Perhaps he suggested that they travel somewhere together. Maybe he leveled harsh accusations against him or informed him of God's statement. In any case, there was some conversation between Cain and Abel that amplified the friction between them: **It happened when they were in the field,** when they happened to be alone, that **Cain arose against Abel his brother and killed him.**[D] In his overpowering rage, Cain fell upon Abel and killed him.

9 At the dawn of humanity, man was still capable of hearing the word of God directly: **The Lord said to Cain: Where is Abel your brother?** Similar to the question posed to Adam on the heels of his transgression: Where are you? God turned to Cain with a question following his sin. There were many possible responses to God's question. Cain could have broken down in tears and admitted that he had committed a terrible crime. Instead, he feigned ignorance: **He said: I do not know.** It is unknown what Cain did with Abel's body after killing him. Perhaps he threw it aside, or buried it, or maybe he simply left it untouched. It is entirely possible that Cain's response was sincere, as this was the first human death. If so, his response bears relevance to one of mankind's burning questions: What happens to a person after he dies? Nevertheless, the conclusion of his response indicates a denial of responsibility: **Am I my brother's keeper?**[D]

10 He, God, **said** to Cain: **What have you done?** Think about your actions. Do not behave like those individuals, and this includes criminals, who attempt to justify or rationalize their behavior by claiming: It happened spontaneously, or: I lost my temper. **The voice of your brother's blood cries out to Me from the ground.**[D] The murder itself calls out with the cry of unfulfilled life. The spilled blood screams out not only over the pain and the injustice but also for the loss of life itself.

11 **Now, cursed are you from the ground that opened its mouth to take your brother's blood from your hand.** In contrast to the various midrashim that discuss how the blood of certain murder victims was not swallowed up by and continued to bubble up on the ground, Abel's blood was accepted by the ground, as it were, and absorbed by it. The ground is therefore involved in Cain's curse.

12 **When you cultivate the ground, it shall not continue giving its strength to you.** The ground is cursed on your account; it shall cease to be a source of life for you. Instead, **restless and itinerant shall you be on the earth.**[D] You shall wander the earth and suffice with what you find during your travels. You are not banished from the ground itself, but from its produce. You no longer have any share in the life stored in the ground.

13 **Cain said to the Lord: My punishment [*avoni*] is greater than I can bear.** Although the word *avon* is usually interpreted as iniquity, it seems more likely that Cain was referring to his punishment rather than the deed itself. Indeed, there are many instances in which the words *avon*, iniquity, *ḥet*, transgression, and *pesha*, sin, are used in reference to a punishment instead of a deed. This interpretation suits the continuation of Cain's statement:

14 **Behold, You have banished me this day from the face of the land.** The ground no longer accepts me, and I feel as though the land is burning beneath my feet. Consequently, I cannot settle anywhere. **And from Your face shall I be hidden.** How will I be able to present myself before You? Cain was warned that sin crouches at the entrance (4:7). Now, after allowing sin to control him to such an extent that he killed his brother, he was too ashamed to bare his face before God. **I shall be restless and itinerant on the earth, and anyone who finds me will kill me.** I am now exposed to all the dangers of the world. I will find no security anywhere on earth; I cannot even take shelter in Your presence, and I am unprotected from other living creatures. Cain's statement expresses the loneliness of a murderer, who feels that the entire world despises him.

15 **The Lord said to him: Therefore, anyone who kills Cain, vengeance shall be taken on him sevenfold.** Although you sinned, you will not be punished with immediate death. Rather, you shall be provided with some form of protection, so that you will be able to continue living. **The Lord placed a sign for Cain, so that anyone who finds him shall not smite him.** This sign, whatever it was, somehow enabled Cain to bear his punishment.

16 **Cain departed from the presence of the Lord and lived in the land of Nod, east of Eden.** Some commentaries hold that this was an actual land called Nod. Others interpret the verse as meaning that Cain attempted to settle in various lands, but he was cast out of each one. Consequently, he was left to wander [*noded*] from land to land. According to this explanation, the emphasis on the fact that Cain dwelled east of Eden serves to further highlight Cain's broken state: Cain was from the second generation following the banishment from the Garden of Eden, and now he himself had been exiled.

--- DISCUSSION ---

4:8 | **And killed him:** The first crime in history was fratricide. Despite the fact that the entire human race then consisted of one small family, Cain still committed murder. This act was motivated by simple jealousy. Jealousy, however, can lead to hatred, which in turn can lead one to commit a crime, even the severest crime of all: murder.

ח ויאמר קין אל-הבל אחיו ויהי בהיותם בשדה ויקם קין אל-הבל אחיו ויהרגהו:
ט ויאמר יהוה אל-קין אי הבל אחיך ויאמר לא ידעתי השמר אחי אנכי:
י יא ויאמר מה עשית קול דמי אחיך צעקים אלי מן-האדמה: ועתה ארור אתה
יב מן-האדמה אשר פצתה את-פיה לקחת את-דמי אחיך מידך: כי תעבד את-
יג האדמה לא-תסף תת-כחה לך נע ונד תהיה בארץ: ויאמר קין אל-יהוה גדול
יד עוני מנשוא: הן גרשת אתי היום מעל פני האדמה ומפניך אסתר והייתי נע
טו ונד בארץ והיה כל-מצאי יהרגני: ויאמר לו יהוה לכן כל-הרג קין שבעתים
טז יקם וישם יהוה לקין אות לבלתי הכות-אתו כל-מצאו: ויצא קין מלפני יהוה

רש"י

ח| **ויאמר קין אל הבל.** נכנס עמו בדברי ריב ומצה להתגולל עליו ולהרגו. ויש בזה מדרשי אגדה, אך זה ישובו של מקרא:

ט| **אי הבל אחיך.** להכנס עמו בדברי נחת, אולי ישיב: אני הרגתיו וחטאתי לך: **לא ידעתי.** נעשה כגונב דעת העליונה: **השמר אחי.** לשון תמה הוא, וכן כל ה"א הנקודה בחטף פתח:

י| **דמי אחיך.** דמו ודם זרעיותיו. דבר אחר, שעשה בו פצעים הרבה, שלא היה יודע מהיכן נפשו יוצאה:

יא-יב| **מן האדמה.** יותר ממה שנתקללה היא כבר בעונה, וגם בזו הוסיפה לחטוא "אשר פצתה את פיה לקחת את דמי אחיך" וגו', והנני מוסיף לה קללה אצלך: "לא תסף תת כחה": **נע ונד.** אין לך רשות לדור במקום אחד:

יג| **גדול עוני מנשוא.** בתמיה, אתה טוען עליונים ותחתונים ועוני אי אפשר לטעון?!:

טו| **לכן כל הרג קין.** זה אחד מן המקראות שקצרו דבריהם ורמזו ולא פרשו: "לכן כל הרג קין" לשון גערה, כה יעשה לו, כך וכך ענשו, ולא פרש ענשו: **שבעתים יקם.** איני רוצה להנקם מקין עכשיו, לסוף שבעה דורות אני נוקם נקמתי ממנו, שיעמוד למך מבני בניו ויהרגהו. וסוף המקרא שאמר: "שבעתים יקם", והיא נקמת הבל מקין, הוא למדנו שתחלת מקרא לשון גערה היא שלא תהא בריה מזיקתו. וכיוצא בו: "ויאמר דוד... כל מכה יבסי ויגע בצנור" (שמואל ב' ה, ח) ולא פרש מה יעשה לו, אבל דבר הכתוב ברמז: כל מכה יבוסי ויגע בצנור ויקרב אל השער ויכבשנו, "ואת העורים" וגו', וגם אותם יכה על אשר אמרו העור והפסח: לא יבא דוד אל תוך הבית; המכה את אלו אני אעשנו ראש ושר. כאן קצר דבריו, ובדברי הימים (א' יא, ו) פרש: "יהיה לראש ולשר": **וישם ה' לקין אות.** חקק לו אות משמו במצחו:

טז| **ויצא קין.** יצא בהכנעה כגונב דעת העליונה:

DISCUSSION

4:9| **Am I my brother's keeper:** This statement is more than just an avoidance of blame; it also reveals the root of his sin. Cain's crime arose from his feelings of alienation toward his brother, which allowed him to say with feigned indifference: Am I my brother's keeper? Indeed, throughout the Torah narrative as well as in its commandments, one encounters the underlying principle that man is in fact his brother's keeper. The perception of one's brother as a stranger is the root of jealousy, hatred, and ultimately murder.

4:10| **The voice of your brother's blood cries out to Me from the ground:** This cry is repeated many times in the Torah, such as in the case of the law of the heifer whose neck is broken (see Deuteronomy 21:1–9), which echoes this episode. In that case, if a murder victim is discovered and the perpetrator is unknown, the community located nearest to the corpse must perform a specific ritual involving a heifer, through which that community assumes collective responsibility for the death. There is a need for acknowledgment, or performance of a rite, to atone for the cries of the victim's blood.

4:12| **Restless and itinerant shall you be on the earth:** Cain was initially described as a cultivator of the ground (4:2). Indeed, his desire to develop a connection with the ground is also evident from the verses below. Cain sought to find a place for himself, and his punishment was that he would find no such place on the face of the earth. The very person who wanted to establish a permanent dwelling Is sentenced to a nomadic life, unable to settle down.

Later, the Torah states that one who murders unwittingly is exiled from his land (Numbers 35:9–34). The Sages teach that the similarity between this law and Cain's punishment is due to the fact that although Cain acted intentionally, his actions may be likened to those of one who murders unwittingly. Cain was humanity's first murderer, and it seems that he was not completely aware of what he was doing. At that time, it was prohibited to harm any creature in the world, and it is quite possible that Cain did not know how to kill. Perhaps he continued to strike Abel even after his brother was long dead. Due to the unwitting aspect of this murder, Cain was granted the protection of exile (see *Devarim Rabba*, Lieberman, ed., *Va'ethanan*, s.v. *az yavdil*).

17 At this stage, the propagation of the human race was effected through marriage between siblings. Adam and Eve begot girls, who became their brothers' wives: **Cain was intimate with his wife and she conceived, and gave birth to** a son called **Hanokh; he,** Cain, **was the builder of a city.**[D] Cain was not just the cursed son; he was also the creative son. As the preceding verses will describe, this creativity was apparent in his descendants as well. **And he,** Cain, **called the name of the city after the name of his son Hanokh.** This name alludes to *ḥanikha*, beginning. Cain chose this name for the city because it marked the beginning of the craft of building. It may also serve as an indication that Cain became educated [*hitḥanekh*]. However, Cain's central motive in building a city was his desire to connect to a place and establish roots within it. However, due to the curse imposed upon him, he was unable to actually live in this city. Indeed, the Torah refers to Cain's construction of the city in the progressive tense, indicating that it was never definitely completed. Rather, throughout his wanderings to and from the land of Nod, he would return to this place to add a stone or two. In this manner, the city was slowly built.

18 The verse lists Cain's descendants. A son called **Irad was born to Hanokh; and Irad begot Mehuyael; and Mehuyael begot Metushael; and Metushael begot Lemekh.** A comparison with the genealogy in the following chapter reveals that the descendants of Seth had names that were similar to those of the descendants of Cain. Apparently, in those times, many children born in the same generation were called by similar names.

19 The verse momentarily dwells on Lemekh on account of his unique behavior: **Lemekh took for himself two wives.** This is possibly the first instance of polygamy. At first each man married just one woman. This was never explicitly commanded by God, but arose from a basic intuition. Still, by taking two wives Lemekh breached the existing boundaries. This is a further expression of the ambition of Cain's family to grow and create, although it is possible that Lemekh simply lusted after more than one woman or that he married his second wife because the first had yet to produce children. **The name of one was Ada, and the name of the other Tzila.**

Fifth aliya

20 **Ada gave birth to Yaval; he was the forerunner of those who dwell in tents and raise livestock.** Yaval, like his father Lemekh, introduced a new practice. Perhaps he was trying to continue Abel's legacy; indeed, even their names are similar. Although shepherding was already introduced by Abel, he left no descendants, vanishing from the world like *hevel*, vapor. As a result, a culture of shepherding had yet to develop. By contrast, Cain sought to establish a stable agricultural society, and it can be assumed that his sons followed him and cultivated the ground as well. In addition, Cain sought to build a city, a permanent settlement. Here, one of Cain's descendants returned to the practice of shepherding and developed it into a distinct culture, thus becoming the forerunner of those who dwell in tents and among livestock.

21 **And the name of his brother was Yuval.** Yuval, like many of Cain's progeny, was a creative individual; **he was the forerunner of all those who grasp the harp and pipe.** He was the first musician, the inventor of the first musical instruments.

22 **And Tzila, she too gave birth to Tuval Cain.** Just as the names Yaval and Yuval are reminiscent of Abel, the name Tuval Cain combines Abel with Cain, patriarch of this family. Tuval Cain was the **forger of every sharp instrument of bronze and iron;** he was the first metalworker. Until Tuval Cain, people relied on the simplest materials that were readily available in nature. Tuval Cain's revolutionary discovery was the extraction of copper and iron from the earth. Although some have criticized Tuval Cain for being responsible for introducing armaments into the world, the verse refers explicitly only to the creative act of metalworking, with no mention of weapons. **And the sister of Tuval Cain was Naama.**[D]

23 **Lemekh said to his wives.** This is the first poem in the Torah. It is structured in the form of parallels between pairs of phrases, as is common in the poetry of the Bible: **Ada and Tzila, hear my voice; wives of Lemekh, listen to my speech; for I have slain a man for my wound and a child for my injury.** The Torah does not provide the background for Lemekh's poem. According to one midrash, Lemekh killed Cain unwittingly, and the phrase "I have slain a man" is Lemekh's confession. Some commentaries maintain that Lemekh's statement is not an expression of regret but a boast, as if to say: One who wounds me or bruises me I will kill. It is possible that Lemekh was confessing to his wives that he too participated in some act of killing, not necessarily the murder of Cain, but that he acted unwittingly.

24 Therefore, **as Cain shall be avenged sevenfold, and Lemekh seventy-seven-fold.** If God had pity upon Cain and assured

DISCUSSION

4:17| **He was the builder of a city:** The fact that it was Cain who built the first city might be an indication that the construction of a city is not a laudable act. This can also be seen in God's response to the city and tower built in Babylon by the generation of the dispersion (see chap. 11). Furthermore, the Bible contains numerous expressions of nostalgia for the period when the nation of Israel wandered in the wilderness, when they were a nation of shepherds rather than urban dwellers. With all the advantages provided by a city, it also leads to many problems, many of which stem from human nature (see commentary on Isaiah 23:17).

יז וַיֵּשֶׁב בְּאֶרֶץ־נוֹד קִדְמַת־עֵדֶן: וַיֵּדַע קַיִן אֶת־אִשְׁתּוֹ וַתַּהַר וַתֵּלֶד אֶת־חֲנוֹךְ וַיְהִי
יח בֹּנֶה עִיר וַיִּקְרָא שֵׁם הָעִיר כְּשֵׁם בְּנוֹ חֲנוֹךְ: וַיִּוָּלֵד לַחֲנוֹךְ אֶת־עִירָד וְעִירָד יָלַד
יט אֶת־מְחוּיָאֵל וּמְחִיָּיאֵל יָלַד אֶת־מְתוּשָׁאֵל וּמְתוּשָׁאֵל יָלַד אֶת־לָמֶךְ: וַיִּקַּח־לוֹ חמישי
כ לֶמֶךְ שְׁתֵּי נָשִׁים שֵׁם הָאַחַת עָדָה וְשֵׁם הַשֵּׁנִית צִלָּה: וַתֵּלֶד עָדָה אֶת־יָבָל הוּא
כא הָיָה אֲבִי יֹשֵׁב אֹהֶל וּמִקְנֶה: וְשֵׁם אָחִיו יוּבָל הוּא הָיָה אֲבִי כָּל־תֹּפֵשׂ כִּנּוֹר וְעוּגָב:
כב וְצִלָּה גַם־הִוא יָלְדָה אֶת־תּוּבַל קַיִן לֹטֵשׁ כָּל־חֹרֵשׁ נְחֹשֶׁת וּבַרְזֶל וַאֲחוֹת תּוּבַל־
כג קַיִן נַעֲמָה: וַיֹּאמֶר לֶמֶךְ לְנָשָׁיו עָדָה וְצִלָּה שְׁמַעַן קוֹלִי נְשֵׁי לֶמֶךְ הַאְזֵנָּה אִמְרָתִי כִּי

רש״י

בארץ נוד. בארץ שכל הגולים נדים שם: קדמת עדן. שם גלה אביו כשגרש מגן עדן, שנאמר: "וישכן מקדם לגן עדן" (לעיל ג, כד) את שמירת דרך מבוא הגן – יש לך ללמד שהיה אדם שם. ומצינו רוח מזרחית קולטת בכל מקום את הרוצחים: "אז יבדיל משה וגו' מזרחה שמש" (דברים ד, מא). דבר אחר, "בארץ נוד", כל מקום שהולך היתה הארץ מזדעזעת מתחתיו, והבריות אומרות: סורו מעליו, זהו שהרג את אחיו:

יז | ויהי. קין בונה עיר, ויקרא שם העיר לזכר בנו חנוך:

יח | ועירד ילד. יש מקום שהוא אומר בזכר 'הוליד' ויש מקום שהוא אומר 'ילד', שהלידה משמשת שתי לשונות, לדת האשה נייסטר"א בלעז, וזריעת תולדות האיש אינינדרי"ר בלעז; כשהוא אומר 'הוליד' בלשון הפעיל, מדבר בלדת האשה, פלוני הוליד את אשתו בן או בת, כשהוא אומר 'ילד' מדבר בזריעת האיש:

יט | ויקח לו למך. לא היה לו לפרש כל זה, אלא ללמדנו מסוף הענין שקיים הקדוש ברוך הוא הבטחתו שאמר: "שבעתים יקם קין", עמד למך לאחר שהוליד בנים ועשה דור שביעי והרג את קין. זהו שאמר: "כי איש הרגתי לפצעי" וגו': שתי נשים. כך היה דרכן של דור המבול, אחת לפריה ורביה ואחת לתשמיש. זו שהיא לתשמיש משקה כוס של עקרין כדי שתעקר, ומקשטה ככלה ומאכילה מעדנים, וחברתה נזופה ואבלה כאלמנה, וזהו שפירש איוב (כד, כא): "רעה עקרה לא תלד ואלמנה לא ייטיב", כמו שמפורש באגדת 'חלק'. עדה. היא של פריה ורביה, על שם שמגונה עליו ומוסרת מאצלו, "עדה" תרגום של סורה: צלה. היא של תשמיש, על שם שיושבת תמיד בצלו. דברי אגדה הם בבראשית רבה (כג, ב):

כ | אבי ישב אהל ומקנה. הוא היה הראשון לרועי בהמות במדברות, ויושב אהלים חדש כאן וחדש כאן; כשכלה המרעה לצאנו במקום זה הולך ותוקע אהלו במקום אחר. ומדרש אגדה: בונה בתים לעבודה זרה, כמה דאת אמר: "סמל הקנאה המקנה" (יחזקאל ח, ג), וכן אחיו "תפש כנור ועוגב" לזמר לעבודה זרה:

כב | תובל קין. לשון תבלין, תבל והתקין אומנותו של קין לעשות כלי זין לרוצחים: לטש כל חרש נחשת וברזל. מחדד אומנות נחשת וברזל, כמו: "ילטוש עיניו לי" (איוב טז, ט). 'חרש' אינו לשון פעל, אלא לשון פועל, שהרי נקוד קמץ (צירי) וטעמו למטה, כלומר מחדד ומצחצח כל כלי אומנות נחשת וברזל: נעמה. היא אשתו של נח. בבראשית רבה (כג, ג):

כג-כד | שמען קולי. שהיו נשיו פורשות ממנו מתשמיש לפי שהרג את קין ואת תובל קין בנו, שהיה למך סומא ותובל קין מושכו, וראה את קין ונדמה לו כחיה, ואמר לאביו למשוך בקשת, והרגו. וכיון שידע שהוא קין זקנו הכה כף אל כף וספק את בנו ביניהן והרגו. והיו נשיו פורשות ממנו והוא מפייסן: "שמען קולי" להשמע לי; וכי "איש" אשר "הרגתי, לפצעי" הוא נהרג? וכי אני פצעתיו מזיד שיהא הפצע קרוי על שמי? "וילד" אשר הרגתי, "לחבורתי" נהרג? כלומר על ידי חבורתי? בתמיה; והלא שוגג אני, לא זהו פצעי ולא זהו חבורתי. פצע – מכת חרב או חץ, נברידור"א בלעז: כי שבעתים יקם קין. קין שהרג מזיד נתלה לו עד שבעה דורות, אני שהרגתי שוגג כל שכן שיתלה לי שביעיות הרבה:

DISCUSSION

4:22 | **And the sister of Tuval Cain was Naama:** While the Torah provides no additional information about Naama, the Sages offer varying accounts relating to her identity and deeds. According to one opinion, Naama too was an innovator, as she introduced the concept of prostitution to the world. The Torah, however, did not want to mention this (*Yalkut Shimoni*, *Bereshit* 161). Another opinion states that Naama was in fact Noah's wife (*Bereshit Rabba* 23:3). If so, this means that Cain's seed was not completely eliminated during the flood, as it survived through Naama. To this day, mankind contains within it the spirit of Cain. Although the episode of Cain and Abel seems to paint an unambiguous picture, this does not indicate that the essence embodied by Cain was objectively negative. Unlike the duo of the serpent and Adam, Cain and Abel do not represent diametrically opposed concepts of good and evil. Rather, Abel's character is more abstract, softer, and perhaps purer, whereas Cain's is more instinctive and creative. In kabbalistic literature, certain personalities are considered to come from the so-called root of Cain (*Sha'ar HaGilgulim*, introduction, 35–36). That is to say, such individuals possess great power, which lies in their ability to create items that are generally good, but these inventions may also become tools of destruction.

him that he would be avenged sevenfold, then I, who killed unwittingly, deserve even greater protection than that provided to Cain (verse 15).

25 At first, Adam and Eve had two sons, until one killed the other. It is possible that because of this terrible tragedy of the first murder in the first family, the couple did not immediately want to reproduce. Perhaps they wondered whether they even wanted to bring another child into the world. It took some time until they recovered, after which **Adam was intimate with his wife again and she gave birth to a son, and she called his name Seth [Shet]: As God has provided [*shat*] me with another offspring in place of Abel, as Cain killed him.** From the continuation of the record of human history, it emerges that Seth was the foundation of mankind. All of humanity descended from him, effectively making him the father of the human race. This is why the Bible uses the expression "sons of Seth" as a synonym for sons of Adam, or people.

26 **And to Seth too a son was born; and he called his name Enosh.** The name Enosh is also used as a synonym for mankind. **Then commenced [*huhal*] proclaiming the name of the Lord.** There are two opposing interpretations of this statement. According to one opinion, this means that during the period of Enosh, people began to institute prayer and organized worship. Previously, Cain and Abel brought offerings out of a spontaneous religious awakening, without any temple or established structure for worship. Only in the generation of Enosh, when human society grew, did there develop an orderly forum for calling in the name of God. According to the second opinion, the term *huhal* relates to the words *ḥullin*, non-sacred, and *ḥillul*, desecration. That is, in the days of Enosh people began to desecrate the name of God by introducing idol worship. Initially, idolaters believed in the oneness of God, but they thought that entities through which His power is expressed, either through impressive force, beauty, or some unique quality, were also worthy of reverence. It is only a short leap from such a belief to deifying the entities themselves. The calling of various objects and powers in the name of God, whether this occurred at once or as a gradual process of deterioration that merely began in the generation of Enosh, is at the root of idol worship.

The Book of the Descendants of Adam

GENESIS 5:1–32

This passage consists of a brief chronology of the first ten generations of man, descendants of Seth. It encompasses a period of roughly one thousand seven hundred years.

5 1 **This is the book of the legacy of Adam.** Although the Torah already discussed the events of Adam's life, that was not a historical record with any chronological context. Until here, the Torah has presented fundamental paradigms: the Garden of Eden, the sin and its punishment, choosing evil, the first children, sibling rivalry, the first murder, and regret. This chapter provides a short survey of many generations, beginning with the dawn of human history. This process began **on the day that God created man, in the likeness of God He made him.** The uniqueness of man is that he was created in the likeness of God, and his history therefore merits special attention.

Sixth aliya

2 **Male and female He created them.** Earlier, the Torah detailed the complex process of creating man. Here it simply states that the male and the female were initially created together. Though this might seem to contradict the previous account, wherein the woman was built from the man while he was in a deep sleep (2:21–22), that was merely a procedure in which the theretofore unified male and female forms were separated from one another. **He blessed them, and He called their name Man [Adam], on the day they were created.** Of the various terms for human beings, including Adam, *ish*, Enosh, and *gever*, Adam is the primary name for the human race and most representative of its essence, both because man was created from the *adama*, ground (2:7), and because he was formed in the *demut*, likeness, of God (see verse 1; 1:26). Indeed, this is how the Sages explain the verse: "I will be like [*edammeh*] the Most High."

3 **Adam lived one hundred and thirty years, and begot a son in his likeness, after his image.** Some commentaries maintain that before this time, he begot defective offspring who were not in his likeness or after his image. However, the plain meaning of the text is that the child born after 130 years resembled Adam, and this has no bearing on any kind of defect in other offspring. **And he called his name Seth [Shet].** This name resembles the word *tashtit*, foundation, as humanity was founded upon him.

4 The Torah now provides an extremely brief list of the generations until the time of the flood: **The days of Adam after he begot Seth were eight hundred years; and** during this time **he begot sons and daughters.** The Torah does not provide the names of these children or any details of their lives, as they have no importance for the reader.

5 **All the days that Adam lived were nine hundred and thirty years;**[D] **and he died.**

6 **Seth lived one hundred and five years, and he begot Enosh.**

7 **Seth lived after he begot Enosh eight hundred and seven years; and he begot sons and daughters.**

8 **All the days that Seth lived were nine hundred and twelve years; and he died.** It is unknown if all the sons listed by name in this genealogical record were specifically firstborn offspring. It is possible that the Torah mentions only the first son by

כד אִישׁ הָרַגְתִּי לְפִצְעִי וְיֶלֶד לְחַבֻּרָתִי: כִּי שִׁבְעָתַיִם יֻקַּם־קָיִן וְלֶמֶךְ שִׁבְעִים וְשִׁבְעָה:
כה וַיֵּדַע אָדָם עוֹד אֶת־אִשְׁתּוֹ וַתֵּלֶד בֵּן וַתִּקְרָא אֶת־שְׁמוֹ שֵׁת כִּי שָׁת־לִי אֱלֹהִים זֶרַע
כו אַחֵר תַּחַת הֶבֶל כִּי הֲרָגוֹ קָיִן: וּלְשֵׁת גַּם־הוּא יֻלַּד־בֵּן וַיִּקְרָא אֶת־שְׁמוֹ אֱנוֹשׁ אָז
ה א הוּחַל לִקְרֹא בְּשֵׁם יְהוָה: זֶה סֵפֶר תּוֹלְדֹת אָדָם בְּיוֹם בְּרֹא אֱלֹהִים ד ששי
ב אָדָם בִּדְמוּת אֱלֹהִים עָשָׂה אֹתוֹ: זָכָר וּנְקֵבָה בְּרָאָם וַיְבָרֶךְ אֹתָם וַיִּקְרָא אֶת־
ג שְׁמָם אָדָם בְּיוֹם הִבָּרְאָם: וַיְחִי אָדָם שְׁלֹשִׁים וּמְאַת שָׁנָה וַיּוֹלֶד בִּדְמוּתוֹ כְּצַלְמוֹ
ד וַיִּקְרָא אֶת־שְׁמוֹ שֵׁת: וַיִּהְיוּ יְמֵי־אָדָם אַחֲרֵי הוֹלִידוֹ אֶת־שֵׁת שְׁמֹנֶה מֵאֹת שָׁנָה
ה וַיּוֹלֶד בָּנִים וּבָנוֹת: וַיִּהְיוּ כָּל־יְמֵי אָדָם אֲשֶׁר־חַי תְּשַׁע מֵאוֹת שָׁנָה וּשְׁלֹשִׁים שָׁנָה
ו ז וַיָּמֹת: וַיְחִי־שֵׁת חָמֵשׁ שָׁנִים וּמְאַת שָׁנָה וַיּוֹלֶד אֶת־אֱנוֹשׁ: וַיְחִי־
שֵׁת אַחֲרֵי הוֹלִידוֹ אֶת־אֱנוֹשׁ שֶׁבַע שָׁנִים וּשְׁמֹנֶה מֵאוֹת שָׁנָה וַיּוֹלֶד בָּנִים וּבָנוֹת:
ח וַיִּהְיוּ כָּל־יְמֵי־שֵׁת שְׁתֵּים עֶשְׂרֵה שָׁנָה וּתְשַׁע מֵאוֹת שָׁנָה וַיָּמֹת:

רש״י

שִׁבְעִים וְשִׁבְעָה. לְשׁוֹן רִבּוּי שְׁבִיעִיּוֹת אָחַז לוֹ, כָּךְ דָּרַשׁ רַבִּי תַּנְחוּמָא (יא). וּמִדְרַשׁ בְּרֵאשִׁית רַבָּה: לֹא הָרַג לֶמֶךְ כְּלוּם, וְנָשָׁיו פּוֹרְשׁוֹת מִמֶּנּוּ מִשֶּׁקִּיְּמוּ פְּרִיָּה וּרְבִיָּה, לְפִי שֶׁנִּגְזְרָה גְּזֵרָה לְכַלּוֹת זַרְעוֹ שֶׁל קַיִן לְשִׁבְעָה דוֹרוֹת, אָמְרוּ: מָה אָנוּ יוֹלְדוֹת לַבֶּהָלָה? לְמָחָר הַמַּבּוּל בָּא וְשׁוֹטֵף אֶת הַכֹּל. וְהוּא אוֹמֵר לָהֶן: ״וְכִי אִישׁ הָרַגְתִּי לְפִצְעִי״? וְכִי אֲנִי הָרַגְתִּי אֶת הֶבֶל שֶׁהוּא אִישׁ בְּקוֹמָה וְיֶלֶד בְּשָׁנִים שֶׁיְּהֵא זַרְעִי כָּלֶה בְּאוֹתוֹ עָוֹן? וּמַה קַּיִן שֶׁהָרַג, נִתְלוּ לוֹ שִׁבְעָה דוֹרוֹת, אֲנִי שֶׁלֹּא הָרַגְתִּי לֹא כָּל שֶׁכֵּן שֶׁיִּתָּלוּ לִי שְׁבִיעִיּוֹת הַרְבֵּה? וְזֶהוּ קַל וָחֹמֶר שֶׁל שְׁטוּת, אִם כֵּן אֵין הַקָּדוֹשׁ בָּרוּךְ הוּא גּוֹבֶה אֶת חוֹבוֹ וּמְקַיֵּם אֶת דְּבָרוֹ:

כה| וַיֵּדַע אָדָם וְגוֹ׳. בָּא לוֹ לֶמֶךְ אֵצֶל אָדָם הָרִאשׁוֹן וְקָבַל עַל נָשָׁיו. אָמַר לָהֶם: וְכִי עֲלֵיכֶם לְדַקְדֵּק עַל גְּזֵרָתוֹ שֶׁל מָקוֹם? אַתֶּם עֲשׂוּ מִצְוַתְכֶם וְהוּא יַעֲשֶׂה אֶת שֶׁלּוֹ! אָמְרוּ לוֹ: קְשׁוֹט עַצְמְךָ תְּחִלָּה, וַהֲלֹא פָּרַשְׁתָּ מֵאִשְׁתְּךָ זֶה מֵאָה וּשְׁלֹשִׁים שָׁנָה מִשֶּׁנִּקְנְסָה מִיתָה עַל יָדְךָ! מִיָּד – ״וַיֵּדַע אָדָם״ וְגוֹ׳, וּמַהוּ ״עוֹד״? מְלַמֵּד שֶׁנִּתּוֹסְפָה לוֹ תַּאֲוָה עַל תַּאֲוָתוֹ. בִּבְרֵאשִׁית רַבָּה (כג, ד–ה):

כו| אָז הוּחַל לִקְרֹא. אֶת שְׁמוֹת הָאָדָם וְאֶת שְׁמוֹת הָעֲצַבִּים בִּשְׁמוֹ שֶׁל הַקָּדוֹשׁ בָּרוּךְ הוּא, לַעֲשׂוֹתָן עֲבוֹדָה זָרָה וְלִקְרוֹתָן אֱלֹהוֹת:

פרק ה

א| זֶה סֵפֶר תּוֹלְדֹת אָדָם. זוֹ הִיא סְפִירַת תּוֹלְדוֹת אָדָם. וּמִדְרְשֵׁי אַגָּדָה יֵשׁ רַבִּים: בְּיוֹם בְּרֹא וְגוֹ׳. מַגִּיד שֶׁבַּיּוֹם שֶׁנִּבְרָא הוֹלִיד:

ג| שְׁלֹשִׁים וּמְאַת שָׁנָה. עַד כָּאן פֵּרַשׁ מִן הָאִשָּׁה:

DISCUSSION

5:5| **All the days that Adam lived were nine hundred and thirty years:** The extraordinarily long lives of these early generations are quite astonishing. Rambam suggests that the early humans were exceptionally great people. It is likewise possible to attribute their unusually long life spans to differences between the ancient world and the one experienced by modern man. Some maintain that it was a more complete world, and therefore all its creatures, including man, were healthier (see Sforno, Genesis 6:13). Alternatively, man still has the natural capacity to live to exceptionally advanced ages, and the fact that people die far younger is due to their lifestyle, which are affected by factors such as the climate in which they live, their diet, or the activities in which they engage.

One can also explain their exceedingly long lives from another perspective: The modern world is built upon knowledge that has developed over the millennia. The fact that modern man is educated with the accumulated knowledge of past generations allows him to more easily overcome the challenges posed by this world. By contrast, the early generations, lacking any preexisting foundation, required long lives in order to develop culture, science, and models for sustained living.

name, as his birth divides the father's life into two periods, before becoming a father and after. There may be other reasons why each son is mentioned by name. In any case, the family line continues through each of these sons until the birth of Noah.

9 **Enosh lived ninety years, and he begot Kenan.** This name, like Cain's, relates to ownership and acquisition [*kinyan*].

10 **Enosh lived after he begot Kenan eight hundred and fifteen years; and he begot sons and daughters.**

11 **All the days of Enosh were nine hundred and five years; and he died.**

12 **Kenan lived seventy years, and he begot Mahalalel.**

13 **Kenan lived after he begot Mahalalel eight hundred and forty years; and he begot sons and daughters.**

14 **All the days of Kenan were nine hundred and ten years; and he died.**

15 **Mahalalel lived sixty-five years, and he begot Yered.**

16 **Mahalalel lived after he begot Yered eight hundred and thirty years; and he begot sons and daughters.**

17 **All the days of Mahalalel were eight hundred and ninety-five years; and he died.**

18 **Yered lived one hundred and sixty-two years, and he begot Hanokh.**

19 **Yered lived after he begot Hanokh eight hundred years; and he begot sons and daughters.**

20 **All the days of Yered were nine hundred and sixty-two years; and he died.**

21 **Hanokh lived sixty-five years, and he begot Methuselah.**

22 **Hanokh walked with God after he begot Methuselah three hundred years; and he begot sons and daughters.** The concept of walking with God appears throughout the Bible, and denotes a close relationship with God. Hanokh was close to God and was occupied with His worship. Hanokh was possibly a prophet or an exceedingly righteous man.

23 **All the days of Hanokh were three hundred and sixty-five years,** far fewer than those of his father or his son.

24 **Hanokh walked with God and he was not, for God took him.** Hanokh was an exceptional and mysterious figure. It is possible that God took him up to Heaven alive just as He took the prophet Elijah. Indeed, various sources state that to this day, Hanokh remains in Heaven, as a kind of angel, similar to Elijah. Perhaps God brought him into His court because he did not belong in this world.

25 *Seventh aliya* **Methuselah lived one hundred and eighty-seven years, and he begot Lemekh.**

26 **Methuselah lived after he begot Lemekh seven hundred and eighty-two years; and he begot sons and daughters.**

27 **All the days of Methuselah were nine hundred and sixty-nine years; and he died.** Methuselah is the oldest person recorded in the Bible.

28 **Lemekh lived one hundred and eighty-two years, and he begot a son.**

29 **He called his name Noah,**[D] **saying: This shall relieve us from** the suffering of **our work and from the misery of our hands, from the ground, which the Lord has cursed.** Noah received this name because already from birth he was recognized as special. The commentaries and midrashim discuss what might have made Noah so unique. Noah was named after a prophecy, or after the hope, or as a prayer, that there would be relief from the toil and suffering. Indeed, the events of his life proved that Noah was the hope of humanity. Nevertheless, he did not provide relief for all of humanity, as only Noah and his family were spared during the flood. He did not bring salvation to the rest of mankind.

30 **Lemekh lived after he begot Noah five hundred and ninety-five years; and he begot sons and daughters.**

31 **All the days of Lemekh were seven hundred and seventy-seven years; and he died.**

DISCUSSION

5:29| **Noah:** Although all human beings today are descended from Adam, that lineage is through Noah. This led to the term "Sons of Noah," or "Noahides," which appears frequently in rabbinic literature (see, e.g., Mishna *Nedarim* 3:11; *Bava Kamma* 38a; *Sanhedrin* 59a). This expression emphasizes the fact that man descends from an individual who lived in a particularly wicked generation yet chose to follow a path that found favor in the eyes of God.

ט ויחי אנוש תשעים שנה ויולד את־קינן: ויחי אנוש אחרי הולידו את־קינן
יא חמש עשרה שנה ושמנה מאות שנה ויולד בנים ובנות: ויהיו כל־ימי אנוש
יב חמש שנים ותשע מאות שנה וימת: ויחי קינן שבעים שנה ויולד
יג את־מהללאל: ויחי קינן אחרי הולידו את־מהללאל ארבעים שנה ושמנה
יד מאות שנה ויולד בנים ובנות: ויהיו כל־ימי קינן עשר שנים ותשע מאות
טו שנה וימת: ויחי מהללאל חמש שנים וששים שנה ויולד את־ירד:
טז ויחי מהללאל אחרי הולידו את־ירד שלשים שנה ושמנה מאות שנה ויולד
יז בנים ובנות: ויהיו כל־ימי מהללאל חמש ותשעים שנה ושמנה מאות שנה
יח וימת: ויחי־ירד שתים וששים שנה ומאת שנה ויולד את־חנוך:
יט כ ויחי־ירד אחרי הולידו את־חנוך שמנה מאות שנה ויולד בנים ובנות: ויהיו
כא כל־ימי־ירד שתים וששים שנה ותשע מאות שנה וימת: ויחי חנוך
כב חמש וששים שנה ויולד את־מתושלח: ויתהלך חנוך את־האלהים אחרי
כג הולידו את־מתושלח שלש מאות שנה ויולד בנים ובנות: ויהי כל־ימי חנוך
כד חמש וששים שנה ושלש מאות שנה: ויתהלך חנוך את־האלהים ואיננו כי־
כה לקח אתו אלהים: ויחי מתושלח שבע ושמנים שנה ומאת שנה שביעי
כו ויולד את־למך: ויחי מתושלח אחרי הולידו את־למך שתים ושמונים שנה
כז ושבע מאות שנה ויולד בנים ובנות: ויהיו כל־ימי מתושלח תשע וששים
כח שנה ותשע מאות שנה וימת: ויחי־למך שתים ושמנים שנה
כט ומאת שנה ויולד בן: ויקרא את־שמו נח לאמר זה ינחמנו ממעשנו ומעצבון
ל ידינו מן־האדמה אשר אררה יהוה: ויחי־למך אחרי הולידו את־נח חמש
לא ותשעים שנה וחמש מאת שנה ויולד בנים ובנות: ויהי כל־ימי־למך שבע

רש״י

כד) ויתהלך חנוך. צדיק היה וקל בדעתו לשוב להרשיע, לפיכך מהר הקדוש ברוך הוא וסלקו והמיתו קדם זמנו, וזהו ששנה הכתוב במיתתו, לכתב: "ואיננו" בעולם למלאות שנותיו: כי לקח אתו. לפני זמנו, כמו: "הנני לקח ממך את מחמד עיניך" (יחזקאל כד, טז).

כח) ויולד בן. שממנו נבנה העולם.

כט) זה ינחמנו. ינח ממנו את עצבון ידינו, עד שלא בא נח לא היה להם כלי מחרשה והוא הכין להם, והיתה הארץ מוציאה קוצים ודרדרים כשזורעים חטים, מקללתו של אדם הראשון, ובימי נח נחה, וזהו 'ינחמנו' – ינח ממנו.

32 Noah was five hundred years old; and Noah begot Shem, Ham, and Yefet. The Sages debate whether this listing reflects the order of their births. The verse marks the conclusion of the book of the descendants of Adam, which contains the names of representatives of the ten generations from Adam to Noah, but it provides almost no information about them. This "book of the legacy of Adam" concludes in a generation that underwent a great transformation. For this reason, the Torah goes into detail with regard to Noah and notes that already at his birth he was made a locus for humanity's hope, by a prophecy that through him the world would be rectified. A new world would indeed begin with him, albeit in an unexpected manner.

Humanity Disappoints

GENESIS 6:1–8

Adam and Eve gained knowledge of good and evil by eating from the fruit of the tree of the knowledge of good and evil. When their descendants choose the path of evil, they undermine the justification for their existence and the existence of all living creatures.

6 1 It was, when men began to multiply on the face of the earth, and daughters were born to them;

2 the sons of the great ones [*benei ha'elohim*] saw that the daughters of man were fair. Some explain that with the proliferation of the human race came the development of a social hierarchy. The term *benei ha'elohim* refers to members of an upper class that grew apart from the rest of humanity. According to this understanding, the daughters of man were women of the lower classes. According to another interpretation, the sons of God were angels who arrived in this world and were granted human bodies and qualities as a kind of test, which they failed. Although they ceased to be angels, they still retained their supernatural powers alongside their human urges. According to this opinion, the daughters of man refers to mortal women. **And they took for themselves wives, from whomever they chose,** whether young or old, single or married, without consideration for laws of any kind.

3 Society turned a blind eye to lawlessness. No one interfered with or objected to the breaching of boundaries. Therefore, **the Lord said: My spirit shall not abide in man forever.** According to many commentaries, the verse means: My spirit shall not fight and complain about man forever, **for he too is flesh.** Man has repeatedly failed to actualize his superiority over other creatures; therefore, he too is only flesh. **And his days shall be one hundred and twenty years.** I will grant mankind an extension of 120 years before sealing its fate. If man does not change, humanity will cease to exist in its current form.

4 The verse notes: **The giants [*nefilim*] were on the earth in those days, and also thereafter.** It is possible that they were called *nefilim* because they fell [*nafelu*] from their position of greatness, or because they were more wondrous [*nifla*] than the rest of humanity. The *nefilim* are mentioned much later as well, some as mythical creatures, others as actual people, perhaps remnants of the primeval giants mentioned in this verse. The *nefilim* were born **when the sons of the great ones consorted with the daughters of man, and they bore them children.** Although the *nefilim* were not themselves "sons of the great ones" in either sense mentioned above, as their children they were nonetheless great and powerful. Although few in number, the *nefilim* ruled over many places in the world. For example, Og, king of Bashan, was described as one of the last surviving descendants of these giants. He was killed by the children of Israel in his kingdom, the Bashan, in the present-day Golan Heights. **They were the mighty who were from ancient times, the men of renown,** those who made a name for themselves and were remembered by later generations. When people spoke of the mighty men of yore, they were referring to these *nefilim*.

5 **The Lord saw that the wickedness of man was great on the**
Maftir **earth, and that every inclination of the thoughts of his heart was only evil all the time.** One's inclinations are not necessarily evil; they are the proactive and creative force within man, which can lead him in various directions. Indeed, the Sages speak of a good inclination. The verse, however, refers to an inclination that is completely evil. That is, man chose to utilize his inclination exclusively for evil.

6 **The Lord regretted,** as it were, **that He had made man on the earth.** The hopes placed upon man, who was granted free will, were dashed. **And He was saddened in His heart.** The verse employs anthropomorphic expressions toward God, meant to convey that the creation of man was a failure. Some explain the verse as follows: The Lord considered and decided with regard to the man that He had made on the earth, and He brought sadness to the heart of man.

7 **The Lord said: I will obliterate man whom I have created from the face of the earth; from man to animal, to crawling creatures, to birds of the heavens; for I regret that I made them.** Man is not simply the pinnacle of creation, but the very purpose of it. Only man can direct the many objects and creatures of the world to their collective purpose. Consequently, in his absence, all of creation loses its reason for being. The Sages teach a parable to illustrate this idea: A man fashioned a wedding canopy for his son and prepared many types of food for the wedding feast. Sometime later, before the wedding, his son died. The father then dismantled the canopy, saying: I fashioned all this only for my son. Now that he is dead, why do I need a wedding canopy? Similarly, the Holy One, blessed be He, said: I created all the animals only for man. Now that man sins, why do I need these creatures?

8 **But** from the entire human race, only **Noah found favor in the eyes of the Lord.** After being disappointed by the rest of Adam's descendants, God chose Noah as the father of the new humanity, due to his special qualities.

לב וְשִׁבְעִים שָׁנָה וּשְׁבַע מֵאוֹת שָׁנָה וַיָּמֹת׃ וַיְהִי־נֹחַ בֶּן־חֲמֵשׁ מֵאוֹת
ו א שָׁנָה וַיּוֹלֶד נֹחַ אֶת־שֵׁם אֶת־חָם וְאֶת־יָפֶת׃ וַיְהִי כִּי־הֵחֵל הָאָדָם לָרֹב עַל־פְּנֵי
ב הָאֲדָמָה וּבָנוֹת יֻלְּדוּ לָהֶם׃ וַיִּרְאוּ בְנֵי־הָאֱלֹהִים אֶת־בְּנוֹת הָאָדָם כִּי טֹבֹת הֵנָּה
ג וַיִּקְחוּ לָהֶם נָשִׁים מִכֹּל אֲשֶׁר בָּחָרוּ׃ וַיֹּאמֶר יהוה לֹא־יָדוֹן רוּחִי בָאָדָם לְעֹלָם
ד בְּשַׁגַּם הוּא בָשָׂר וְהָיוּ יָמָיו מֵאָה וְעֶשְׂרִים שָׁנָה׃ הַנְּפִלִים הָיוּ בָאָרֶץ בַּיָּמִים
הָהֵם וְגַם אַחֲרֵי־כֵן אֲשֶׁר יָבֹאוּ בְּנֵי הָאֱלֹהִים אֶל־בְּנוֹת הָאָדָם וְיָלְדוּ לָהֶם הֵמָּה
הַגִּבֹּרִים אֲשֶׁר מֵעוֹלָם אַנְשֵׁי הַשֵּׁם׃
ה וַיַּרְא יהוה כִּי רַבָּה רָעַת הָאָדָם בָּאָרֶץ וְכָל־יֵצֶר מַחְשְׁבֹת לִבּוֹ רַק רַע כָּל־הַיּוֹם׃ מפטיר
ו ז וַיִּנָּחֶם יהוה כִּי־עָשָׂה אֶת־הָאָדָם בָּאָרֶץ וַיִּתְעַצֵּב אֶל־לִבּוֹ׃ וַיֹּאמֶר יהוה אֶמְחֶה
אֶת־הָאָדָם אֲשֶׁר־בָּרָאתִי מֵעַל פְּנֵי הָאֲדָמָה מֵאָדָם עַד־בְּהֵמָה עַד־רֶמֶשׂ וְעַד־
ח עוֹף הַשָּׁמָיִם כִּי נִחַמְתִּי כִּי עֲשִׂיתִם׃ וְנֹחַ מָצָא חֵן בְּעֵינֵי יהוה׃

רש״י

וְאִם לֹא תְּפָרְשֵׁהוּ כָּךְ, אֵין טַעַם הַלָּשׁוֹן נוֹפֵל עַל הַשֵּׁם, וְהָיְתָה צָרִיךְ לִקְרוֹת שְׁמוֹ מְנַחֵם:

לב | **בֶּן חֲמֵשׁ מֵאוֹת שָׁנָה.** אָמַר רַבִּי יוּדָן: מַה טַּעַם כָּל הַדּוֹרוֹת הוֹלִידוּ לְמֵאָה שָׁנָה וְזֶה לַחֲמֵשׁ מֵאוֹת? אָמַר הַקָּדוֹשׁ בָּרוּךְ הוּא: אִם רְשָׁעִים הֵם יֹאבְדוּ בַּמַּיִם וְרַע לְצַדִּיק זֶה, וְאִם צַדִּיקִים הֵם אַטְרִיחַ עָלָיו לַעֲשׂוֹת תֵּבוֹת הַרְבֵּה, כָּבַשׁ אֶת מַעְיָנוֹ וְלֹא הוֹלִיד עַד חֲמֵשׁ מֵאוֹת שָׁנָה, כְּדֵי שֶׁלֹּא יְהֵא יֶפֶת הַגָּדוֹל שֶׁבְּבָנָיו רָאוּי לָעֳנָשִׁין לִפְנֵי הַמַּבּוּל, דִּכְתִיב: "כִּי הַנַּעַר בֶּן מֵאָה שָׁנָה יָמוּת" (ישעיה סה, כ) – רָאוּי לְעֹנֶשׁ לֶעָתִיד, וְכֵן לִפְנֵי מַתַּן תּוֹרָה: **אֶת שֵׁם אֶת חָם וְאֶת יָפֶת.** וַהֲלֹא יֶפֶת הַגָּדוֹל הוּא! אֶלָּא בַּתְּחִלָּה אַתָּה דוֹרֵשׁ אֶת שֶׁהוּא צַדִּיק, וְנוֹלַד כְּשֶׁהוּא מָהוּל, וְשֶׁאַבְרָהָם יָצָא מִמֶּנּוּ וְכוּ׳. בְּבְרֵאשִׁית רַבָּה (כו, ג):

פרק ו

ב | **בְּנֵי הָאֱלֹהִים.** בְּנֵי הַשָּׂרִים וְהַשּׁוֹפְטִים. דָּבָר אַחֵר, "בְּנֵי הָאֱלֹהִים", הֵם הַשָּׂרִים הַהוֹלְכִים בִּשְׁלִיחוּתוֹ שֶׁל מָקוֹם, אַף הֵם הָיוּ מִתְעָרְבִים בָּהֶם. כָּל 'אֱלֹהִים' שֶׁבַּמִּקְרָא לְשׁוֹן מָרוּת, וְזֶה יוֹכִיחַ: "וְאַתָּה תִּהְיֶה לּוֹ לֵאלֹהִים" (שמות ד, טז), "רְאֵה נְתַתִּיךָ אֱלֹהִים" (שם ז, א): **כִּי טֹבֹת הֵנָּה.** אָמַר רַבִּי יוּדָן: "טבת" כְּתִיב, מִשֶּׁהָיוּ מְטִיבִין אוֹתָהּ מְקֻשֶּׁטֶת לִכָּנֵס לַחֻפָּה, הָיָה גָּדוֹל נִכְנָס וּבוֹעֲלָהּ תְּחִלָּה: **מִכֹּל אֲשֶׁר בָּחָרוּ.** אַף בְּעוּלַת בַּעַל, אַף הַזָּכָר וְהַבְּהֵמָה:

ג | **לֹא יָדוֹן רוּחִי בָאָדָם.** לֹא יִתְרַעֵם וְיָרִיב רוּחִי עָלַי בִּשְׁבִיל הָאָדָם: **לְעֹלָם.** לְאֹרֶךְ יָמִים; הִנֵּה רוּחִי נָדוֹן בְּקִרְבִּי אִם לְהַשְׁחִית וְאִם לְרַחֵם, לֹא יִהְיֶה מָדוֹן זֶה בְּרוּחִי לְעוֹלָם, כְּלוֹמַר לְאֹרֶךְ יָמִים: **בְּשַׁגַּם הוּא בָשָׂר.** כְּמוֹ 'בְּשֶׁגַּם', כְּלוֹמַר בִּשְׁבִיל שֶׁגַּם זֹאת בּוֹ שֶׁהוּא בָּשָׂר וְאַף עַל פִּי כֵן אֵינוֹ נִכְנָע לְפָנַי, וּמָה אִם יִהְיֶה אֵשׁ אוֹ דָּבָר קָשֶׁה. כַּיּוֹצֵא בוֹ: "עַד שַׁקַּמְתִּי דְּבוֹרָה" (שופטים ה, ז) כְּמוֹ 'שֶׁקַּמְתִּי', וְכֵן: "שָׁאַתָּה מְדַבֵּר עִמִּי" (שם ו, יז) כְּמוֹ 'שֶׁאַתָּה', אַף 'בְּשַׁגַּם' כְּמוֹ 'בְּשֶׁגַּם': **וְהָיוּ יָמָיו וְגוֹ׳.** עַד מֵאָה וְעֶשְׂרִים שָׁנָה אַאֲרִיךְ לָהֶם אַפִּי, וְאִם לֹא יָשׁוּבוּ – אָבִיא עֲלֵיהֶם מַבּוּל. וְאִם תֹּאמַר, מִשֶּׁנּוֹלַד יֶפֶת עַד הַמַּבּוּל אֵינוֹ אֶלָּא מֵאָה שָׁנָה? אֵין מֻקְדָּם וּמְאֻחָר בַּתּוֹרָה, כְּבָר הָיְתָה הַגְּזֵרָה גְּזוּרָה עֶשְׂרִים שָׁנָה קֹדֶם שֶׁהוֹלִיד נֹחַ תּוֹלָדוֹת, וְכֵן מָצִינוּ בְּסֵדֶר עוֹלָם (סוף פכ״ח). יֵשׁ מִדְרְשֵׁי אַגָּדָה רַבִּים בְּ"לֹא יָדוֹן", אֲבָל זֶה צַחוּת פְּשׁוּטוֹ:

ד | **הַנְּפִלִים.** עַל שֵׁם שֶׁנָּפְלוּ וְהִפִּילוּ אֶת הָעוֹלָם, וּבִלְשׁוֹן עִבְרִית לְשׁוֹן עֲנָקִים הוּא: **בַּיָּמִים הָהֵם.** בִּימֵי דוֹר אֱנוֹשׁ וּבְנֵי קַיִן: **וְגַם אַחֲרֵי כֵן.** אַף עַל פִּי שֶׁרָאוּ בְּאָבְדָן שֶׁל דּוֹר אֱנוֹשׁ, שֶׁעָלָה אוֹקְיָנוֹס וְהֵצִיף שְׁלִישׁ הָעוֹלָם, לֹא נִכְנַע דּוֹר הַמַּבּוּל לִלְמֹד מֵהֶם: **אֲשֶׁר יָבֹאוּ.** הָיוּ יוֹלְדוֹת עֲנָקִים כְּמוֹתָם: **הַגִּבֹּרִים.** לִמְרֹד בַּמָּקוֹם: **אַנְשֵׁי הַשֵּׁם.** אוֹתָם שֶׁנִּקְּבוּ בְּשֵׁמוֹת: עִירָד מְחוּיָאֵל מְתוּשָׁאֵל, שֶׁנִּקְרְאוּ עַל שֵׁם אָבְדָן, שֶׁנִּמּוֹחוּ וְהֻתְּשׁוּ. דָּבָר אַחֵר, אַנְשֵׁי שְׁמָמוֹן, שֶׁשִּׁמְּמוּ אֶת הָעוֹלָם:

ו | **וַיִּנָּחֶם ה׳ כִּי עָשָׂה.** נֶחָמָה הָיְתָה לְפָנָיו שֶׁבְּרָאוֹ בַּתַּחְתּוֹנִים, שֶׁאִלּוּ הָיָה מִן הָעֶלְיוֹנִים הָיָה מַמְרִידָן, בִּבְרֵאשִׁית רַבָּה (כז, ד): **וַיִּתְעַצֵּב.** הָאָדָם "אֶל לִבּוֹ" שֶׁל מָקוֹם, עָלָה בְּמַחֲשַׁבְתּוֹ שֶׁל מָקוֹם לְהַעֲצִיבוֹ, זֶהוּ תַּרְגּוּם אוּנְקְלוֹס. דָּבָר אַחֵר, "וַיִּנָּחֶם", נֶהֶפְכָה מַחֲשַׁבְתּוֹ שֶׁל מָקוֹם מִמִּדַּת רַחֲמִים לְמִדַּת הַדִּין, עָלָה בְּמַחֲשָׁבָה לְפָנָיו מַה לַּעֲשׂוֹת בָּאָדָם שֶׁעָשָׂה בָּאָרֶץ, וְכֵן כָּל לְשׁוֹן נִחוּם שֶׁבַּמִּקְרָא לְשׁוֹן נִמְלָךְ מַה לַּעֲשׂוֹת: "וּבֶן אָדָם וְיִתְנֶחָם" (במדבר כג, יט), "וְעַל עֲבָדָיו יִתְנֶחָם" (דברים לב, לו), "וַיִּנָּחֶם ה׳ עַל הָרָעָה" (שמות לב, יד), "נִחַמְתִּי כִּי הִמְלַכְתִּי" (שמואל א׳ טו, יא), כֻּלָּם לְשׁוֹן מַחֲשָׁבָה אַחֶרֶת הֵם. "וַיִּתְעַצֵּב אֶל לִבּוֹ" – נִתְאַבֵּל עַל אָבְדַן מַעֲשֵׂה יָדָיו, כְּמוֹ: "נֶעֱצַב הַמֶּלֶךְ עַל בְּנוֹ" (שמואל ב׳ יט, ג). וְזוֹ כָּתַבְתִּי לִתְשׁוּבַת הַמִּינִים: גּוֹי אֶחָד שָׁאַל אֶת רַבִּי יְהוֹשֻׁעַ בֶּן קָרְחָה, אָמַר לוֹ: אֵין אַתֶּם מוֹדִים שֶׁהַקָּדוֹשׁ בָּרוּךְ הוּא רוֹאֶה אֶת הַנּוֹלָד? אָמַר לוֹ: הֵן. אָמַר לוֹ: וְהָא כְּתִיב: "וַיִּתְעַצֵּב אֶל לִבּוֹ"? אָמַר לוֹ: נוֹלַד לְךָ בֵּן זָכָר מִיָּמֶיךָ? אָמַר לוֹ: הֵן. אָמַר לוֹ: וּמֶה עָשִׂיתָ? אָמַר לוֹ: שָׂמַחְתִּי וְשִׂמַּחְתִּי אֶת הַכֹּל. אָמַר לוֹ: וְלֹא הָיִיתָ יוֹדֵעַ שֶׁסּוֹפוֹ לָמוּת? אָמַר לוֹ: בִּשְׁעַת חֶדְוָתָא חֶדְוָתָא, בִּשְׁעַת אֶבְלָא אֶבְלָא. אָמַר לוֹ: כָּךְ מַעֲשֵׂה לִפְנֵי הַקָּדוֹשׁ בָּרוּךְ הוּא, אַף עַל פִּי שֶׁגָּלוּי לְפָנָיו שֶׁסּוֹפָן לַחֲטֹא וּלְאַבְּדָן לֹא נִמְנַע מִלְּבָרְאָן, בִּשְׁבִיל הַצַּדִּיקִים הָעֲתִידִים לַעֲמֹד מֵהֶם:

ז | **וַיֹּאמֶר ה׳ אֶמְחֶה אֶת הָאָדָם.** הוּא עָפָר וְאָבִיא עָלָיו מַיִם וְאֶמְחֶה אוֹתוֹ, לְכָךְ נֶאֱמַר לְשׁוֹן מְחוּי: **מֵאָדָם עַד בְּהֵמָה.** אַף הֵם הִשְׁחִיתוּ דַרְכָּם. דָּבָר אַחֵר, הַכֹּל נִבְרָא בִּשְׁבִיל הָאָדָם, וְכֵיוָן שֶׁהוּא כָּלֶה מַה צֹּרֶךְ בְּאֵלּוּ: **כִּי נִחַמְתִּי כִּי עֲשִׂיתִם.** חָשַׁבְתִּי מַה לַּעֲשׂוֹת עַל אֲשֶׁר עֲשִׂיתִים:

Parashat
Noah

The Impending Flood

GENESIS 6:9–7:6

In addition to the sin of sexual promiscuity mentioned at the end of the previous section, theft was rampant among mankind as well. For this reason, humans, and along with them all animals living on dry land, were doomed to perish in a flood. Only a few representatives of each species would be saved from the calamity and form the nucleus of a new world.

9 **This is the legacy of Noah,** the story of his life in brief. **Noah was a righteous, wholehearted man in his generations;** in contrast to those surrounding him, **Noah walked with God.** Noah was connected to God, as he contemplated Him and lived with an awareness of the Divine. During this period, when mankind had not yet received God's commandments, one's relationship with God was not expressed in mandated actions. It is stated about Noah, as well as Hanokh before him and Abraham after him, that they walked with or before God (5:22, 17:1). This means that God was the subject of their lives, and they had a special relationship with Him.

10 **Noah begot three sons: Shem, Ham, and Yefet.**

11 After a brief description of Noah as a private individual, the focus returns to the history of the world and Noah's important role in the unfolding events. **The earth was corrupted before God, and the earth was filled with villainy.** The absence of law and order, described above in relation to men taking women as they chose (verse 2), was not limited to the sexual sphere. This corruption also found expression in the manner in which the powerful exerted control over the weak, as people began to steal and snatch property from one another without compunction. As a result, the very possibility of possession and ownership was eliminated.

12 **God saw the earth, and behold, it was corrupted, as all flesh corrupted its path upon the earth.** People's lives in the environment of the time were apparently quiet and comfortable, with abundant food and water.[1] However, instead of being happy with their lot, the people exploited the abundance that was in easy reach by stealing from one another and refusing to recognize property laws and social conventions. Limits and boundaries did not exist for them.

13 **God said to Noah: The end of all flesh has come before Me.** According to My reckoning, the end of all living creatures has arrived, **as the earth is filled with villainy because of them; and behold, I will destroy them with the earth.** I will destroy them together with the earth itself. However, you have been chosen to continue humanity.

14 Therefore, **make for you an ark of** the relatively light **gopher wood;**[B] separate **compartments shall you make the ark, and you shall coat it within and without with pitch,** a kind of tar from which asphalt is produced. The tar will serve as a waterproofing substance.

Cedar tree

Cypress tree

15 **And this is how you shall make it: Three hundred cubits shall be the length of the ark, fifty cubits its breadth, and thirty cubits its height.** This is a huge structure, of exceptional proportions even in comparison to structures built on land.

16 **You shall make a window for the ark,** to allow the entrance of light. **And to a cubit shall you complete it at the top;** the sides of the ark shall form a kind of trapezoid, with the roof of the ark one cubit long. **And the entrance of the ark you shall place in its side,** for entering and exiting. **Lower, second, and third stories you shall make it;** the ark shall have three floors.

17 **And behold, I am bringing the flood [*mabbul*].** The term *mabbul* is commonly translated as flood, based on the context.[2] However, it is likely that the word actually means "judgment" or "sentence."[3] In other words, God is bringing a sentence of judgment in the form of **water upon the earth to destroy all flesh in which there is the breath of life, from under the heavens.** In those waters, **everything that is on the earth,** everything that is generally found on dry land, **shall perish.**

18 **But** at this juncture **I will keep My covenant with you,** which will be confirmed and fulfilled at a later point (see 9:9–11). **You shall come to the ark: you, and your sons, and your wife, and your sons' wives with you.**

BACKGROUND

6:14 | **Gopher wood:** Some identify the gopher tree with the cypress, *Cupressus*, whose wood is water-resistant and suitable for shipbuilding. Others suggest that it is the cedar tree (Onkelos). The Septuagint translation renders gopher as squared and planed.

פרשת

נֹחַ

ט אֵ֣לֶּה תּוֹלְדֹ֣ת נֹ֗חַ נֹ֚חַ אִ֥ישׁ צַדִּ֛יק תָּמִ֥ים הָיָ֖ה בְּדֹֽרֹתָ֑יו אֶת־הָֽאֱלֹהִ֖ים הִֽתְהַלֶּךְ־נֹֽחַ: ה

י וַיּ֥וֹלֶד נֹ֖חַ שְׁלֹשָׁ֣ה בָנִ֑ים אֶת־שֵׁ֖ם אֶת־חָ֥ם וְאֶת־יָֽפֶת: יא וַתִּשָּׁחֵ֥ת הָאָ֖רֶץ לִפְנֵ֣י הָֽאֱלֹהִ֑ים

יב וַתִּמָּלֵ֥א הָאָ֖רֶץ חָמָֽס: וַיַּ֧רְא אֱלֹהִ֛ים אֶת־הָאָ֖רֶץ וְהִנֵּ֣ה נִשְׁחָ֑תָה כִּֽי־הִשְׁחִ֧ית כָּל־

בָּשָׂ֛ר אֶת־דַּרְכּ֖וֹ עַל־הָאָֽרֶץ: יג וַיֹּ֨אמֶר אֱלֹהִ֜ים לְנֹ֗חַ קֵ֤ץ כָּל־בָּשָׂר֙ בָּ֣א

לְפָנַ֔י כִּֽי־מָלְאָ֥ה הָאָ֛רֶץ חָמָ֖ס מִפְּנֵיהֶ֑ם וְהִנְנִ֥י מַשְׁחִיתָ֖ם אֶת־הָאָֽרֶץ: עֲשֵׂ֤ה לְךָ֙

יד תֵּבַ֣ת עֲצֵי־גֹ֔פֶר קִנִּ֖ים תַּֽעֲשֶׂ֣ה אֶת־הַתֵּבָ֑ה וְכָֽפַרְתָּ֤ אֹתָהּ֙ מִבַּ֣יִת וּמִח֔וּץ בַּכֹּֽפֶר: וְזֶ֕ה

טו אֲשֶׁ֥ר תַּֽעֲשֶׂ֖ה אֹתָ֑הּ שְׁלֹ֧שׁ מֵא֣וֹת אַמָּ֗ה אֹ֚רֶךְ הַתֵּבָ֔ה חֲמִשִּׁ֤ים אַמָּה֙ רָחְבָּ֔הּ וּשְׁלֹשִׁ֥ים

אַמָּ֖ה קֽוֹמָתָֽהּ: צֹ֣הַר ׀ תַּֽעֲשֶׂ֣ה לַתֵּבָ֗ה וְאֶל־אַמָּה֙ תְּכַלֶּ֣נָּה מִלְמַ֔עְלָה וּפֶ֥תַח הַתֵּבָ֖ה

טז בְּצִדָּ֣הּ תָּשִׂ֑ים תַּחְתִּיִּ֛ם שְׁנִיִּ֥ם וּשְׁלִשִׁ֖ים תַּֽעֲשֶֽׂהָ: וַֽאֲנִ֗י הִֽנְנִי֩ מֵבִ֨יא אֶת־הַמַּבּ֥וּל מַ֨יִם֙

יז עַל־הָאָ֔רֶץ לְשַׁחֵ֣ת כָּל־בָּשָׂ֗ר אֲשֶׁר־בּוֹ֙ ר֣וּחַ חַיִּ֔ים מִתַּ֖חַת הַשָּׁמָ֑יִם כֹּ֥ל אֲשֶׁר־בָּאָ֖רֶץ

יח יִגְוָֽע: וַֽהֲקִֽמֹתִ֥י אֶת־בְּרִיתִ֖י אִתָּ֑ךְ וּבָאתָ֙ אֶל־הַתֵּבָ֔ה אַתָּ֕ה וּבָנֶ֛יךָ וְאִשְׁתְּךָ֥ וּנְשֵֽׁי־

רש״י

ט אֵלֶּה תּוֹלְדֹת נֹחַ נֹחַ אִישׁ צַדִּיק. הוֹאִיל וְהִזְכִּירוֹ סִפֵּר
בְּשִׁבְחוֹ, שֶׁנֶּאֱמַר: "זֵכֶר צַדִּיק לִבְרָכָה" (משלי י, ז). דָּבָר אַחֵר,
לְלַמֶּדְךָ שֶׁעִקַּר תּוֹלְדוֹתֵיהֶם שֶׁל צַדִּיקִים מַעֲשִׂים טוֹבִים:
בְּדֹרֹתָיו. יֵשׁ מֵרַבּוֹתֵינוּ דּוֹרְשִׁים אוֹתוֹ לְשֶׁבַח: כָּל שֶׁכֵּן
אִלּוּ הָיָה בְדוֹר צַדִּיקִים הָיָה צַדִּיק יוֹתֵר. וְיֵשׁ שֶׁדּוֹרְשִׁים
אוֹתוֹ לִגְנַאי: לְפִי דוֹרוֹ הָיָה צַדִּיק, וְאִלּוּ הָיָה בְדוֹרוֹ שֶׁל
אַבְרָהָם לֹא הָיָה נֶחְשָׁב לִכְלוּם: אֶת הָאֱלֹהִים הִתְהַלֶּךְ
נֹחַ. וּבְאַבְרָהָם הוּא אוֹמֵר: "אֲשֶׁר הִתְהַלַּכְתִּי לְפָנָיו" (להלן
כד, מ). נֹחַ הָיָה צָרִיךְ סַעַד לְתָמְכוֹ, אֲבָל אַבְרָהָם הָיָה
מִתְחַזֵּק וּמְהַלֵּךְ בְּצִדְקוֹ מֵאֵלָיו: הִתְהַלֶּךְ. לְשׁוֹן עָבָר. וְזֶהוּ
שִׁמּוּשׁוֹ שֶׁל לָמֶ״ד בִּלְשׁוֹן כָּבֵד, מְשַׁמֶּשֶׁת לְהַבָּא וּלְשֶׁעָבַר
בְּלָשׁוֹן אֶחָד: "קוּם הִתְהַלֵּךְ" (להלן יג, יז) לְהַבָּא, "הִתְהַלֶּךְ־
נֹחַ" לְשֶׁעָבַר, "הִתְפַּלֵּל בְּעַד עֲבָדֶיךָ" (שמואל־א יב, יט),
לְהַבָּא, "וּבָא וְהִתְפַּלֵּל אֶל הַבַּיִת הַזֶּה" (מלכים־א ח, מב)
לְשׁוֹן עָבָר, אֶלָּא שֶׁהַוָּי״ו שֶׁבְּרֹאשׁוֹ הוֹכְכוֹ לְהַבָּא:

יא וַתִּשָּׁחֵת. לְשׁוֹן עֶרְוָה וַעֲבוֹדָה זָרָה, כְּמוֹ: "פֶּן
תַּשְׁחִתוּן" (דברים ד, טז), "כִּי הִשְׁחִית כָּל בָּשָׂר" (להלן פסוק
יב): וַתִּמָּלֵא הָאָרֶץ חָמָס. גָּזֵל:

יב כִּי הִשְׁחִית כָּל בָּשָׂר. אֲפִלּוּ בְּהֵמָה חַיָּה וָעוֹף נִזְקָקִין
לְשֶׁאֵינָן מִינָן:

יג קֵץ כָּל בָּשָׂר. כָּל מָקוֹם שֶׁאַתָּה מוֹצֵא זְנוּת,
אַנְדְּרָלַמּוּסְיָא בָּאָה לָעוֹלָם וְהוֹרֶגֶת טוֹבִים וְרָעִים: כִּי
מָלְאָה הָאָרֶץ חָמָס. לֹא נֶחְתַּם גְּזַר דִּינָם אֶלָּא עַל
הַגָּזֵל: אֶת הָאָרֶץ. כְּמוֹ מִן הָאָרֶץ, וְדוֹמֶה לוֹ: "כְּצֵאתִי
אֶת הָעִיר" (שמות ט, כט) מִן הָעִיר, "חַלָּה אֶת רַגְלָיו"
(מלכים־א טו, כג) מִן רַגְלָיו. דָּבָר אַחֵר, "אֶת הָאָרֶץ", עִם
הָאָרֶץ, שֶׁאַף שְׁלֹשָׁה טְפָחִים שֶׁל עֹמֶק הַמַּחֲרֵשָׁה נִמּוֹחוּ
וְנִטְשְׁטְשׁוּ:

יד עֲשֵׂה לְךָ תֵּבַת. הַרְבֵּה רֶוַח וְהַצָּלָה לְפָנָיו, וְלָמָּה
הִטְרִיחוֹ בְּבִנְיָן זֶה? כְּדֵי שֶׁיִּרְאוּהוּ אַנְשֵׁי דוֹר הַמַּבּוּל
עוֹסֵק בָּהּ מֵאָה וְעֶשְׂרִים שָׁנָה וְשׁוֹאֲלִין אוֹתוֹ: מַה זֹּאת לְךָ?
וְהוּא אוֹמֵר לָהֶם: עָתִיד הַקָּדוֹשׁ בָּרוּךְ הוּא לְהָבִיא מַבּוּל
לָעוֹלָם, אוּלַי יָשׁוּבוּ: עֲצֵי גֹפֶר. כָּךְ שְׁמוֹ. וְלָמָּה מִמִּין זֶה?
עַל שֵׁם גָּפְרִית שֶׁנִּגְזַר עֲלֵיהֶם לִמְחוֹת בּוֹ: קִנִּים. מְדוֹרִים
מְדוֹרִים לְכָל בְּהֵמָה וְחַיָּה: בַּכֹּפֶר. זֶפֶת בִּלְשׁוֹן אֲרַמִּי.
וּמָצִינוּ בַּתַּלְמוּד "כּוּפְרָא". בִּתֵּבָתוֹ שֶׁל מֹשֶׁה, עַל יְדֵי שֶׁהָיוּ
הַמַּיִם תַּשִּׁים, דַּיָּה בְּחֹמֶר מִבִּפְנִים וְזֶפֶת מִבַּחוּץ, וְעוֹד כְּדֵי

טו צֹהַר. יֵשׁ אוֹמְרִים חַלּוֹן, וְיֵשׁ אוֹמְרִים אֶבֶן טוֹבָה
הַמְּאִירָה לָהֶם: וְאֶל אַמָּה תְּכַלֶּנָּה מִלְמַעְלָה. כִּסּוּיָהּ
מְשֻׁפָּע וְעוֹלֶה עַד שֶׁהוּא קָצָר מִלְמַעְלָה וְעוֹמֵד עַל אַמָּה,
כְּדֵי שֶׁיָּזוּבוּ הַמַּיִם לְמַטָּה מִכָּאן וּמִכָּאן: בְּצִדָּהּ תָּשִׂים.
שֶׁלֹּא יִפְּלוּ גְּשָׁמִים בָּהּ: תַּחְתִּיִּם שְׁנִיִּם וּשְׁלִשִׁים. שָׁלֹשׁ
עֲלִיּוֹת זוֹ עַל גַּב זוֹ, עֶלְיוֹנִים לָאָדָם אֶמְצָעִיִּים לְמָדוֹר
הַבְּהֵמוֹת תַּחְתִּיִּים לְזֶבֶל:

יז וַאֲנִי הִנְנִי מֵבִיא. הִנְנִי מוּכָן לְהַסְכִּים עִם אוֹתָם
שֶׁזֵּרְזוּנִי כְּבָר: "מָה אֱנוֹשׁ כִּי תִזְכְּרֶנּוּ" (תהלים ח, ה): מַבּוּל.
שֶׁבִּלָּה אֶת הַכֹּל, שֶׁבִּלְבֵּל אֶת הַכֹּל, שֶׁהוֹבִיל אֶת הַכֹּל מִן
הַגָּבוֹהַּ לַנָּמוּךְ. וְזֶהוּ שֶׁתִּרְגֵּם אוּנְקְלוֹס: "טוּפָנָא", שֶׁהֵצִיף
אֶת הַכֹּל וְהֶבִיאָם לְבָבֶל שֶׁהִיא עֲמֻקָּה, לְכָךְ נִקְרֵאת
'שִׁנְעָר', שֶׁכָּל מֵתֵי מַבּוּל נִנְעֲרוּ לְשָׁם:

יח וַהֲקִמֹתִי אֶת בְּרִיתִי. בְּרִית הָיָה צָרִיךְ עַל הַפֵּרוֹת
שֶׁלֹּא יֵרָקְבוּ וְיַעֲפְשׁוּ, וְשֶׁלֹּא יַהַרְגֻהוּ רְשָׁעִים שֶׁבַּדּוֹר: אַתָּה
וּבָנֶיךָ וְאִשְׁתְּךָ. הָאֲנָשִׁים לְבַד וְהַנָּשִׁים לְבַד, מִכָּאן שֶׁנֶּאֶסְרוּ
בְּתַשְׁמִישׁ הַמִּטָּה:

19 **From every living being of all flesh, two of each you shall bring to the ark to keep alive with you; they shall be male and female.** You must bring into the ark the living beings that will form the basis of the future existence of both mankind and the animal kingdom.

20 **From the birds according to their kind, and from the animals according to their kind, from every crawling creature of the ground according to its kind, two of each shall come to you.** You are not commanded to hunt them; rather, I will make them come to you in pairs.[4] The aim is **to keep** all of the species of the world **alive** from them. Although you are not required to gather the animals into the ark, there is another duty which you are obligated to perform:

21 **You, take for you from all food that is eaten.** You must collect enough appropriate food for you and all the animals that will be living in the ark. **And gather it to you; and it shall be for you and for them for food.**

22 **Noah did according to all that God had commanded him; so he did.** It should not be inferred from the brevity of the account that this was a simple process. Various *midrashim* describe at length Noah's difficulties during the years of the construction of the ark.[5] For over one hundred years Noah was occupied with building an enormous structure.[6] The ark that he built did not have a steering wheel, mast, sail, or oar. It resembled neither a ship nor a building. It was not meant to sail in any particular direction, but merely to float. It is easy to imagine the practical and social difficulties of this effort, and the halting efforts that Noah might have made to explain the purpose of his work to others.

7 1 **The Lord said to Noah: Come you and your entire household into the ark, for I have seen you to be righteous before Me in this generation.** Unlike the animals, who were selected at random to enter the ark, you were chosen from all humans because of your righteousness.

Second aliya

2 **From every pure animal you shall take to you seven pairs,** each pair composed of **a male and his mate.** It is commonly explained that this is referring to animals that would later be considered pure, kosher according to *halakha*. It is possible, however, that the distinction between pure and impure animals is an ancient one, which predates the giving of the Torah. **And of the animals that are not pure, two, a male and his mate;** literally, a man and his wife. Since the Torah is speaking of specific pairs of animals, who are to be the sole survivors of that species, it refers to the male and female animal with the unusual expression of a man and his wife.

3 **Also from the birds of the heavens,** take with you **seven each, male and female,** in order **to keep offspring alive on the face of all the earth.**

4 **For in seven more days, I will make it rain upon the earth forty days and forty nights, and I will obliterate all existence that I made,** everything that lives, **from the face of the earth.**

5 **Noah did according to all that the Lord had commanded him.** Although Noah had not yet seen any actual flooding, he still entered the ark in obedience with God's command, as he believed His word.

6 **Noah was six hundred years old** at that time, **and the flood,** or sentence of judgment, **was water upon the earth.**

The Flood

GENESIS 7:7–24

In contrast to life inside the free-floating ark, disconnected from all information and sense of time and place, the Torah anchors the story of the flood with precise dates and lengths of time.

7 **Noah, and his sons, and his wife, and his sons' wives with him, came into the ark, because of the water of the flood.**

8 **From the pure animal, and from the animal that is not pure, and from the birds, and from every creature that crawls upon the ground,**

9 **two at a time they came** by themselves **to Noah into the ark, male and female, as God had commanded Noah.** In the case of most species they came in pairs, while from certain species there were sets of seven pairs. It is these animals that survived in the ark.

10 **It was after the passage of seven days that the water of the flood was upon the earth.** The water began to cover the earth.

11 **In the six hundredth year of the life of Noah, during the second month:** It is possible that this is referring to the second month after Noah's birthday. However, the Sages maintain that it means the second month of the calendar year, which follows the Creation of the world. They disagree whether this is the month of Iyar, which is second after Nisan, or Marḥeshvan, which follows Tishrei.[7] **On the seventeenth day of the month, on that day all the wellsprings of the great depth,** which ordinarily flow slowly and in moderation, **were breached, and the windows of the heavens were opened.** This was not a sprinkle, as water gushed out and inundated the land.

יט בָּנֶיךָ אִתָּךְ: וּמִכָּל־הָחַי מִכָּל־בָּשָׂר שְׁנַיִם מִכֹּל תָּבִיא אֶל־הַתֵּבָה לְהַחֲיֹת אִתָּךְ
כ זָכָר וּנְקֵבָה יִהְיוּ: מֵהָעוֹף לְמִינֵהוּ וּמִן־הַבְּהֵמָה לְמִינָהּ מִכֹּל רֶמֶשׂ הָאֲדָמָה לְמִינֵהוּ
כא שְׁנַיִם מִכֹּל יָבֹאוּ אֵלֶיךָ לְהַחֲיוֹת: וְאַתָּה קַח־לְךָ מִכָּל־מַאֲכָל אֲשֶׁר יֵאָכֵל וְאָסַפְתָּ
כב אֵלֶיךָ וְהָיָה לְךָ וְלָהֶם לְאָכְלָה: וַיַּעַשׂ נֹחַ כְּכֹל אֲשֶׁר צִוָּה אֹתוֹ אֱלֹהִים כֵּן עָשָׂה:
ז א וַיֹּאמֶר יְהוָה לְנֹחַ בֹּא־אַתָּה וְכָל־בֵּיתְךָ אֶל־הַתֵּבָה כִּי־אֹתְךָ רָאִיתִי צַדִּיק לְפָנַי שני
ב בַּדּוֹר הַזֶּה: מִכֹּל ׀ הַבְּהֵמָה הַטְּהוֹרָה תִּקַּח־לְךָ שִׁבְעָה שִׁבְעָה אִישׁ וְאִשְׁתּוֹ וּמִן־
ג הַבְּהֵמָה אֲשֶׁר לֹא טְהֹרָה הִוא שְׁנַיִם אִישׁ וְאִשְׁתּוֹ: גַּם מֵעוֹף הַשָּׁמַיִם שִׁבְעָה
ד שִׁבְעָה זָכָר וּנְקֵבָה לְחַיּוֹת זֶרַע עַל־פְּנֵי כָל־הָאָרֶץ: כִּי לְיָמִים עוֹד שִׁבְעָה אָנֹכִי
מַמְטִיר עַל־הָאָרֶץ אַרְבָּעִים יוֹם וְאַרְבָּעִים לָיְלָה וּמָחִיתִי אֶת־כָּל־הַיְקוּם אֲשֶׁר
ה עָשִׂיתִי מֵעַל פְּנֵי הָאֲדָמָה: וַיַּעַשׂ נֹחַ כְּכֹל אֲשֶׁר־צִוָּהוּ יְהוָה: וְנֹחַ בֶּן־שֵׁשׁ מֵאוֹת
ו
ז שָׁנָה וְהַמַּבּוּל הָיָה מַיִם עַל־הָאָרֶץ: וַיָּבֹא נֹחַ וּבָנָיו וְאִשְׁתּוֹ וּנְשֵׁי־בָנָיו אִתּוֹ אֶל־
ח הַתֵּבָה מִפְּנֵי מֵי הַמַּבּוּל: מִן־הַבְּהֵמָה הַטְּהוֹרָה וּמִן־הַבְּהֵמָה אֲשֶׁר אֵינֶנָּה טְהֹרָה
ט וּמִן־הָעוֹף וְכֹל אֲשֶׁר־רֹמֵשׂ עַל־הָאֲדָמָה: שְׁנַיִם שְׁנַיִם בָּאוּ אֶל־נֹחַ אֶל־הַתֵּבָה
י זָכָר וּנְקֵבָה כַּאֲשֶׁר צִוָּה אֱלֹהִים אֶת־נֹחַ: וַיְהִי לְשִׁבְעַת הַיָּמִים וּמֵי הַמַּבּוּל הָיוּ
יא עַל־הָאָרֶץ: בִּשְׁנַת שֵׁשׁ־מֵאוֹת שָׁנָה לְחַיֵּי־נֹחַ בַּחֹדֶשׁ הַשֵּׁנִי בְּשִׁבְעָה־עָשָׂר יוֹם
לַחֹדֶשׁ בַּיּוֹם הַזֶּה נִבְקְעוּ כָּל־מַעְיְנֹת תְּהוֹם רַבָּה וַאֲרֻבֹּת הַשָּׁמַיִם נִפְתָּחוּ:

רש"י

יט | **וּמִכָּל הָחַי.** אֲפִלּוּ שֵׁדִים: **שְׁנַיִם מִכֹּל.** מִן הַפָּחוּת שֶׁבָּהֶם לֹא פָּחֲתוּ מִשְּׁנַיִם, אֶחָד זָכָר וְאֶחָד נְקֵבָה:

כ | **מֵהָעוֹף לְמִינֵהוּ.** אוֹתָן שֶׁדָּבְקוּ בְּמִינֵיהֶם וְלֹא הִשְׁחִיתוּ דַּרְכָּם; וּמֵאֲלֵיהֶן בָּאוּ, וְכָל שֶׁהַתֵּבָה קוֹלַטְתּוֹ הִכְנִיס בָּהּ:

כב | **וַיַּעַשׂ נֹחַ.** זֶה בִּנְיַן הַתֵּבָה:

פרק ז

א | **רָאִיתִי צַדִּיק.** וְלֹא נֶאֱמַר 'צַדִּיק תָּמִים', מִכָּאן שֶׁאוֹמְרִים מִקְצַת שִׁבְחוֹ שֶׁל אָדָם בְּפָנָיו וְכֻלּוֹ שֶׁלֹּא בְּפָנָיו:

ב | **הַטְּהוֹרָה.** הָעֲתִידָה לִהְיוֹת טְהוֹרָה לְיִשְׂרָאֵל, לָמַדְנוּ שֶׁלָּמַד נֹחַ תּוֹרָה: **שִׁבְעָה שִׁבְעָה.** כְּדֵי שֶׁיַּקְרִיב מֵהֶם קָרְבָּן בְּצֵאתוֹ:

ג | **גַּם מֵעוֹף הַשָּׁמַיִם וְגוֹ'.** בַּטְּהוֹרִים דִּבֵּר הַכָּתוּב, וְיִלָּמֵד סָתוּם מִן הַמְפֹרָשׁ:

ד | **כִּי לְיָמִים עוֹד שִׁבְעָה.** אֵלּוּ שִׁבְעַת יְמֵי אֶבְלוֹ שֶׁל מְתוּשֶׁלַח הַצַּדִּיק, שֶׁחָס הַקָּדוֹשׁ בָּרוּךְ הוּא עַל כְּבוֹדוֹ וְעִכֵּב אֶת הַפֻּרְעָנוּת. צֵא וַחֲשֹׁב שְׁנוֹתָיו שֶׁל מְתוּשֶׁלַח וְתִמְצָא שֶׁהֵם כָּלִים בִּשְׁנַת שֵׁשׁ מֵאוֹת שָׁנָה לְחַיֵּי נֹחַ: **כִּי לְיָמִים עוֹד.** מַהוּ "עוֹד"? זְמַן אַחַר זְמַן זֶה, נוֹסָף עַל מֵאָה וְעֶשְׂרִים שָׁנָה: **אַרְבָּעִים יוֹם.** כְּנֶגֶד יְצִירַת הַוָּלָד, שֶׁקִּלְקְלוּ לְהַטְרִיחַ לְיוֹצְרָם לָצוּר צוּרַת מַמְזֵרִים:

ה | **וַיַּעַשׂ נֹחַ.** זֶה בִּיאָתוֹ לַתֵּבָה:

ז | **נֹחַ וּבָנָיו.** הָאֲנָשִׁים לְבַד וְהַנָּשִׁים לְבַד, לְפִי שֶׁנֶּאֶסְרוּ בְּתַשְׁמִישׁ הַמִּטָּה מִפְּנֵי שֶׁהָעוֹלָם שָׁרוּי בְּצַעַר: **מִפְּנֵי מֵי הַמַּבּוּל.** אַף נֹחַ מִקְּטַנֵּי אֲמָנָה הָיָה, מַאֲמִין וְאֵינוֹ מַאֲמִין שֶׁיָּבֹא הַמַּבּוּל, וְלֹא נִכְנַס לַתֵּבָה עַד שֶׁדְּחָקוּהוּ הַמַּיִם:

ט | **בָּאוּ אֶל נֹחַ.** מֵאֲלֵיהֶן: **שְׁנַיִם שְׁנַיִם.** כֻּלָּם הֻשְׁווּ בְּמִנְיָן זֶה, מִן הַפָּחוּת הָיוּ שְׁנַיִם:

יא | **בַּחֹדֶשׁ הַשֵּׁנִי.** רַבִּי אֱלִיעֶזֶר אוֹמֵר: זֶה מַרְחֶשְׁוָן, רַבִּי יְהוֹשֻׁעַ אוֹמֵר: זֶה אִיָּר: **נִבְקְעוּ.** לְהוֹצִיא מֵימֵיהֶן: **תְּהוֹם רַבָּה.** מִדָּה כְּנֶגֶד מִדָּה, הֵם חָטְאוּ בְּ"רַבָּה רָעַת הָאָדָם" (לעיל ו, ה) וְלָקוּ בִּ"תְהוֹם רַבָּה":

12 **The rain was upon the earth** for **forty** consecutive **days and forty nights.**
13 **On that very day, Noah, and Shem, and Ham, and Yefet, the sons of Noah, and Noah's wife, and the three wives of his sons with them, entered into the ark;**
14 **they, and every beast according to its kind, and every animal according to its kind, and every crawling creature that crawls upon the earth according to its kind, and every flying thing according to its kind, every bird, every winged creature,** even winged insects.[8]
15 **They came to Noah to the ark, two each from all flesh in which there is the breath of life.**
16 **And they that came, male and female from all flesh came, as God had commanded him; and the Lord shut it for him.** Due to the unparalleled intensity of the waters of the flood, which came from above and below, God's own special closing of the ark, as it were, was required to prevent water from penetrating inside.
17 *Third aliya* **The flood was forty days upon the earth; and the water increased, and lifted the ark, and it was raised above the earth.** After forty days of incessant flooding, the ark, which was undoubtedly very heavy, began to rise above the earth.
18 **The water accumulated and increased greatly upon the earth, and the ark went upon the face of the water.** The ark began to float. Since it was not a ship and there was no way to direct it, the ark simply drifted along, drawn by the flow and movement of the water.
19 **The water accumulated exceedingly upon the earth, and all the high mountains under the entire heavens were covered.**
20 **Fifteen cubits upward the water accumulated, and the mountains were covered.**
21 **All flesh that crawls upon the earth, of the birds, and of the animals, and of the beasts, and of all the swarming creatures that swarm upon the earth, and all mankind, perished.**
22 **All in whose nostrils was the breath of the spirit of life, from all that was on the dry land, died.** All creatures living in dry places passed away.[9] The force of the water, its quantity, and according to the Sages, even its heat,[10] destroyed all the living creatures. Presumably the animals that could swim tried to do so, but they could not withstand the overpowering water. The people certainly tried to find a hiding place or grab onto planks to stay afloat, but all such material was washed away.
23 **He obliterated all existence that was upon the face of the earth, from man, to animal, to crawling creature, to birds of the heavens; they were obliterated from the earth. Only Noah remained and they that were with him in the ark.**
24 **The water accumulated upon the earth one hundred and fifty days.** Over the course of these one hundred and fifty days, perhaps the rain continued to fall, and the wellsprings did not stop up, but the force of the water weakened. During this period, everything flowed and intermingled: The oceans surged past the coastline and the seas broke their boundaries. For almost half a year, there was nothing in the world except for water and the ark floating somewhere upon it. Its occupants did not know where they were, and possibly they could not even know how much time had elapsed since they had shut themselves in the ark, as time calculations in those days depended on the celestial bodies. It is doubtful whether they could even distinguish between day and night.[11]

The End of the Flood and Exit from the Ark

GENESIS 8:1–19

This section describes the gradual conclusion of the flood and the cautious exit of the ark's inhabitants into the world, after more than a year had passed since they entered it.

8 1 **God remembered Noah and all the beasts and all the animals that were with him in the ark; God caused a wind to pass over the earth, and the water subsided.** The water rested from its rage and did not descend anymore in the form of rain nor surge from the depths.

יב יג וַיְהִי הַגֶּשֶׁם עַל־הָאָרֶץ אַרְבָּעִים יוֹם וְאַרְבָּעִים לָיְלָה: בְּעֶצֶם הַיּוֹם הַזֶּה בָּא נֹחַ
יד וְשֵׁם־וְחָם וָיֶפֶת בְּנֵי־נֹחַ וְאֵשֶׁת נֹחַ וּשְׁלֹשֶׁת נְשֵׁי־בָנָיו אִתָּם אֶל־הַתֵּבָה: הֵמָּה
וְכָל־הַחַיָּה לְמִינָהּ וְכָל־הַבְּהֵמָה לְמִינָהּ וְכָל־הָרֶמֶשׂ הָרֹמֵשׂ עַל־הָאָרֶץ לְמִינֵהוּ
טו וְכָל־הָעוֹף לְמִינֵהוּ כֹּל צִפּוֹר כָּל־כָּנָף: וַיָּבֹאוּ אֶל־נֹחַ אֶל־הַתֵּבָה שְׁנַיִם שְׁנַיִם
טז מִכָּל־הַבָּשָׂר אֲשֶׁר־בּוֹ רוּחַ חַיִּים: וְהַבָּאִים זָכָר וּנְקֵבָה מִכָּל־בָּשָׂר בָּאוּ כַּאֲשֶׁר
יז צִוָּה אֹתוֹ אֱלֹהִים וַיִּסְגֹּר יְהוָה בַּעֲדוֹ: וַיְהִי הַמַּבּוּל אַרְבָּעִים יוֹם עַל־הָאָרֶץ וַיִּרְבּוּ שלישי
יח הַמַּיִם וַיִּשְׂאוּ אֶת־הַתֵּבָה וַתָּרָם מֵעַל הָאָרֶץ: וַיִּגְבְּרוּ הַמַּיִם וַיִּרְבּוּ מְאֹד עַל־הָאָרֶץ
יט וַתֵּלֶךְ הַתֵּבָה עַל־פְּנֵי הַמָּיִם: וְהַמַּיִם גָּבְרוּ מְאֹד מְאֹד עַל־הָאָרֶץ וַיְכֻסּוּ כָּל־הֶהָרִים
כ הַגְּבֹהִים אֲשֶׁר־תַּחַת כָּל־הַשָּׁמָיִם: חֲמֵשׁ עֶשְׂרֵה אַמָּה מִלְמַעְלָה גָּבְרוּ הַמָּיִם
כא וַיְכֻסּוּ הֶהָרִים: וַיִּגְוַע כָּל־בָּשָׂר ׀ הָרֹמֵשׂ עַל־הָאָרֶץ בָּעוֹף וּבַבְּהֵמָה וּבַחַיָּה וּבְכָל־
כב הַשֶּׁרֶץ הַשֹּׁרֵץ עַל־הָאָרֶץ וְכֹל הָאָדָם: כֹּל אֲשֶׁר נִשְׁמַת־רוּחַ חַיִּים בְּאַפָּיו מִכֹּל
כג אֲשֶׁר בֶּחָרָבָה מֵתוּ: וַיִּמַח אֶת־כָּל־הַיְקוּם ׀ אֲשֶׁר ׀ עַל־פְּנֵי הָאֲדָמָה מֵאָדָם עַד־
בְּהֵמָה עַד־רֶמֶשׂ וְעַד־עוֹף הַשָּׁמַיִם וַיִּמָּחוּ מִן־הָאָרֶץ וַיִּשָּׁאֶר אַךְ־נֹחַ וַאֲשֶׁר אִתּוֹ
כד ח א בַּתֵּבָה: וַיִּגְבְּרוּ הַמַּיִם עַל־הָאָרֶץ חֲמִשִּׁים וּמְאַת יוֹם: וַיִּזְכֹּר אֱלֹהִים אֶת־נֹחַ וְאֵת ׀
כָּל־הַחַיָּה וְאֶת־כָּל־הַבְּהֵמָה אֲשֶׁר אִתּוֹ בַּתֵּבָה וַיַּעֲבֵר אֱלֹהִים רוּחַ עַל־הָאָרֶץ

רש"י

יב | **וַיְהִי הַגֶּשֶׁם עַל הָאָרֶץ.** וּלְהַלָּן (פסוק יז) הוּא אוֹמֵר: "וַיְהִי הַמַּבּוּל"? אֶלָּא כְּשֶׁהוֹרִידָן הוֹרִידָן בְּרַחֲמִים שֶׁאִם יַחְזְרוּ יִהְיוּ גִּשְׁמֵי בְרָכָה, כְּשֶׁלֹּא חָזְרוּ הָיוּ לְמַבּוּל: **אַרְבָּעִים יוֹם וְגוֹ'.** אֵין יוֹם רִאשׁוֹן מִן הַמִּנְיָן, לְפִי שֶׁאֵין לֵילוֹ עִמּוֹ, שֶׁהֲרֵי כָּתוּב: "בַּיּוֹם הַזֶּה נִבְקְעוּ כָּל מַעְיְנוֹת" (לעיל פסוק יא), נִמְצְאוּ אַרְבָּעִים יוֹם כָּלִים בְּכ"ח בְּכִסְלֵו לְרַבִּי אֱלִיעֶזֶר, שֶׁהֶחֳדָשִׁים נִמְנִין כְּסִדְרָן אֶחָד מָלֵא וְאֶחָד חָסֵר, הֲרֵי שְׁנֵים עָשָׂר מִמַּרְחֶשְׁוָן וְעֶשְׂרִים וּשְׁמוֹנָה מִכִּסְלֵו:

יג | **בְּעֶצֶם הַיּוֹם הַזֶּה.** לִמֶּדְךָ הַכָּתוּב שֶׁהָיוּ בְּנֵי דוֹרוֹ אוֹמְרִים: אִלּוּ אָנוּ רוֹאִים אוֹתוֹ נִכְנָס לַתֵּבָה אָנוּ שׁוֹבְרִין אוֹתָהּ וְהוֹרְגִין אוֹתוֹ. אָמַר הַקָּדוֹשׁ בָּרוּךְ הוּא: אֲנִי מַכְנִיסוֹ לְעֵינֵי כֻּלָּם, וְנִרְאֶה דְּבַר מִי יָקוּם:

יד | **צִפּוֹר כָּל כָּנָף.** דָּבוּק הוּא, צִפּוֹר שֶׁל כָּל מִין כָּנָף, לְרַבּוֹת חֲגָבִים:

טז | **וַיִּסְגֹּר ה' בַּעֲדוֹ.** הֵגֵן עָלָיו שֶׁלֹּא שְׁבָרוּהָ, הִקִּיף הַתֵּבָה דֻּבִּים וַאֲרָיוֹת וְהָיוּ הוֹרְגִים בָּהֶם. וּפְשׁוּטוֹ שֶׁל מִקְרָא, סָגַר כְּנֶגְדּוֹ מִן הַמַּיִם, וְכֵן כָּל 'בְּעַד' שֶׁבַּמִּקְרָא לְשׁוֹן 'כְּנֶגֶד' הוּא: "בְּעַד כָּל רֶחֶם" (להלן כ, יח), "בַּעֲדֵךְ וּבְעַד בָּנַיִךְ" (מלכים ב' ד, ד), "עוֹר בְּעַד עוֹר" (איוב ב, ד), "מָגֵן בַּעֲדִי" (תהלים ג, ד), "הִתְפַּלֵּל בְּעַד עֲבָדֶיךָ" (שמואל א' יב, יט), כְּנֶגֶד עֲבָדֶיךָ:

יז | **וַתָּרָם מֵעַל הָאָרֶץ.** מְשֻׁקַּעַת הָיְתָה בַּמַּיִם אַחַת עֶשְׂרֵה אַמָּה, כִּסְפִינָה טְעוּנָה שֶׁמְּשֻׁקַּעַת מִקְצָתָהּ בַּמַּיִם, וּמִקְרָאוֹת שֶׁלְּפָנֵינוּ יוֹכִיחוּ:

יח | **וַיִּגְבְּרוּ.** מֵאֲלֵיהֶן:

כ | **חֲמֵשׁ עֶשְׂרֵה אַמָּה מִלְמַעְלָה.** לְמַעְלָה שֶׁל גֹּבַהּ כָּל הֶהָרִים לְאַחַר שֶׁהֻשְׁווּ הַמַּיִם לְרָאשֵׁי הֶהָרִים:

כב | **נִשְׁמַת רוּחַ חַיִּים.** נְשָׁמָה שֶׁל רוּחַ חַיִּים: **אֲשֶׁר בֶּחָרָבָה.** וְלֹא דָּגִים שֶׁבַּיָּם:

כג | **וַיִּמַח.** לְשׁוֹן וַיִּפְעַל הוּא וְאֵינוֹ לְשׁוֹן וַיִּפָּעֵל, וְהוּא מִגִּזְרַת 'וַיִּפֶן' 'וַיִּבֶן'. כָּל תֵּבָה שֶׁסּוֹפָהּ הֵ"א, כְּגוֹן בָּנָה, מָחָה, קָנָה, כְּשֶׁהוּא נוֹתֵן וָי"ו יוּ"ד בְּרֹאשָׁהּ נָקוּד בְּחִירִק תַּחַת הַיּוּ"ד: **אַךְ נֹחַ.** לְבַד נֹחַ, זֶהוּ פְּשׁוּטוֹ. וּמִדְרַשׁ אַגָּדָה, גּוֹנֵחַ וְכוֹהֶה דָּם מִטֹּרַח הַבְּהֵמוֹת וְהַחַיּוֹת. וְיֵשׁ אוֹמְרִים שֶׁאִחַר מְזוֹנוֹת לָאֲרִי וְהִכִּישׁוֹ, וְעָלָיו נֶאֱמַר: "הֵן צַדִּיק בָּאָרֶץ יְשֻׁלָּם" (משלי יא, לא):

פרק ח

א | **וַיִּזְכֹּר אֱלֹהִים.** זֶה הַשֵּׁם מִדַּת הַדִּין הוּא, וְנֶהֶפְכָה לְמִדַּת רַחֲמִים עַל יְדֵי תְּפִלַּת הַצַּדִּיקִים. וְרִשְׁעָתָן שֶׁל רְשָׁעִים הוֹפֶכֶת מִדַּת רַחֲמִים לְמִדַּת הַדִּין, שֶׁנֶּאֱמַר: "וַיַּרְא ה' כִּי רַבָּה רָעַת הָאָדָם וְגוֹ' וַיֹּאמֶר ה' אֶמְחֶה" (לעיל ו, ה-ז), וְהוּא שֵׁם מִדַּת רַחֲמִים: **וַיִּזְכֹּר אֱלֹהִים אֶת נֹחַ וְגוֹ'.** מָה זָכַר לָהֶם לַבְּהֵמוֹת? זְכוּת שֶׁלֹּא הִשְׁחִיתוּ דַּרְכָּם קֹדֶם לָכֵן, וְשֶׁלֹּא שִׁמְּשׁוּ בַּתֵּבָה: **וַיַּעֲבֵר אֱלֹהִים רוּחַ.** רוּחַ תַּנְחוּמִין וַהֲנָחָה עָבְרָה לְפָנָיו: **עַל הָאָרֶץ.** עַל עִסְקֵי הָאָרֶץ:

2 **The wellsprings of the depth and the windows of the heavens were dammed,** closed, **and the rain from the heavens was terminated.**

3 **The water receded from upon the earth gradually.** The water that had swelled and risen above the mountains descended into the valleys, from where it flowed into the sea. These processes took time, as the entire world was inundated with water. **And the water was diminished at the end of one hundred and fifty days.** After one hundred and fifty days of flooding, the water began to diminish.

4 **The ark rested during the seventh month, on the seventeenth day of the month,** at the conclusion of one hundred and fifty days starting from the second month, **upon the mountains of Ararat.**[B] The water level receded until the ark rested once again on the earth, although not in the place where Noah had built it. The ark was presumably constructed

in a then-inhabited area, in or around modern-day Iraq, and it drifted a considerable distance to the high mountains of Ararat, which are likely close to the mountains called by that name today.[12]

5 **And the water gradually receded until the tenth month; during the tenth month, on the first of the month, the peaks of the mountains were** revealed and **seen.** Since the ark was exceedingly heavy and deeply immersed in the water, it took additional time from when it rested on the peak until the mountains themselves were exposed.

6 **It was at the end of forty days** from the time that the tops of the mountains could first be seen. Only after the mountaintops became visible could it be known with certainty that the water was gradually receding. **Noah opened the window of the ark that he made.**

7 **He sent the raven.** Noah chose to send a raven, on the assumption that a bird which feeds on carrion would be the first to find itself something to eat. Were it to find food, Noah would know that the water level had diminished.[13] **And it went to and fro,** without bringing back any sign, **until the drying of the water from upon the earth.**

8 **He sent the dove from him,** as this bird is also capable of flying long distances, **to see if the waters** had **abated from upon the surface of the ground.**

9 **But the dove did not find rest for its foot, and it returned to him to the ark, as water was on the face of the entire earth; and he extended his hand and took it, and brought it to him to the ark.**

10 **He waited yet another seven days and again sent the dove from the ark.**

11 **The dove came in to him at evening time,** after it had been sent off in the morning, **and behold, it had plucked**[14] **an olive leaf in its mouth.** Since olive leaves are relatively tough, they did not rot in the water. **And Noah knew that the waters had abated [*kallu*],** that they had become light [*kal*] and diminished **from upon the earth.**

12 **He waited yet another seven days and sent the dove, and it did not return again to him anymore,** as it found rest in one of the spots that had dried up in the meantime.

Mountains of Ararat

BACKGROUND

8:4 | Mountains of Ararat: A high mountain range, whose peaks reach above 5,000 m, northeast of Lake Van in eastern Turkey. The mountains of Ararat and the kingdom of Ararat west of Lake Van, are mentioned in the Bible as a region lying north of Babylon and Assyria. Onkelos renders it as *Turei Kardo*, the mountains of the Kurds, and Josephus explains likewise (*Antiquities of the Jews* I:3:6).

ב וַיָּשֹׁכּוּ הַמָּיִם׃ וַיִּסָּכְרוּ מַעְיְנֹת תְּהוֹם וַאֲרֻבֹּת הַשָּׁמָיִם וַיִּכָּלֵא הַגֶּשֶׁם מִן־הַשָּׁמָיִם׃
ג וַיָּשֻׁבוּ הַמַּיִם מֵעַל הָאָרֶץ הָלוֹךְ וָשׁוֹב וַיַּחְסְרוּ הַמַּיִם מִקְצֵה חֲמִשִּׁים וּמְאַת יוֹם׃
ד ה וַתָּנַח הַתֵּבָה בַּחֹדֶשׁ הַשְּׁבִיעִי בְּשִׁבְעָה־עָשָׂר יוֹם לַחֹדֶשׁ עַל הָרֵי אֲרָרָט׃ וְהַמַּיִם
הָיוּ הָלוֹךְ וְחָסוֹר עַד הַחֹדֶשׁ הָעֲשִׂירִי בָּעֲשִׂירִי בְּאֶחָד לַחֹדֶשׁ נִרְאוּ רָאשֵׁי הֶהָרִים׃
ו ז וַיְהִי מִקֵּץ אַרְבָּעִים יוֹם וַיִּפְתַּח נֹחַ אֶת־חַלּוֹן הַתֵּבָה אֲשֶׁר עָשָׂה׃ וַיְשַׁלַּח אֶת־
ח הָעֹרֵב וַיֵּצֵא יָצוֹא וָשׁוֹב עַד־יְבֹשֶׁת הַמַּיִם מֵעַל הָאָרֶץ׃ וַיְשַׁלַּח אֶת־הַיּוֹנָה מֵאִתּוֹ
ט לִרְאוֹת הֲקַלּוּ הַמַּיִם מֵעַל פְּנֵי הָאֲדָמָה׃ וְלֹא־מָצְאָה הַיּוֹנָה מָנוֹחַ לְכַף־רַגְלָהּ
וַתָּשָׁב אֵלָיו אֶל־הַתֵּבָה כִּי־מַיִם עַל־פְּנֵי כָל־הָאָרֶץ וַיִּשְׁלַח יָדוֹ וַיִּקָּחֶהָ וַיָּבֵא אֹתָהּ
י אֵלָיו אֶל־הַתֵּבָה׃ וַיָּחֶל עוֹד שִׁבְעַת יָמִים אֲחֵרִים וַיֹּסֶף שַׁלַּח אֶת־הַיּוֹנָה מִן־
יא הַתֵּבָה׃ וַתָּבֹא אֵלָיו הַיּוֹנָה לְעֵת עֶרֶב וְהִנֵּה עֲלֵה־זַיִת טָרָף בְּפִיהָ וַיֵּדַע נֹחַ כִּי־קַלּוּ
יב הַמַּיִם מֵעַל הָאָרֶץ׃ וַיִּיָּחֶל עוֹד שִׁבְעַת יָמִים אֲחֵרִים וַיְשַׁלַּח אֶת־הַיּוֹנָה וְלֹא־

רש״י

וישכו. כמו: "כשך חמת המלך" (אסתר ב, א), לשון הנחת חמה:

ב| ויסכרו מעינת. כשנפתחו כתיב: "כל מעינות" (לעיל ז, יא) וכאן אין כתיב 'כל', לפי שנשתיירו מהם אותן שיש בהם צרך לעולם, כגון חמי טבריה וכיוצא בהן: ויכלא. וימנע, כמו: "לא תכלא רחמיך" (תהלים מ, יב), "לא יכלה ממך" (להלן כג, ו):

ג| מקצה חמשים ומאת יום. התחילו לחסר, והוא אחד בסיון, כיצד? בעשרים ושבעה בכסלו פסקו הגשמים, הרי שלשה מכסלו ועשרים ותשעה מטבת הרי שלשים ושנים, ושבט ואדר וניסן ואייר מאה ושמונה עשר, הרי מאה וחמשים:

ד| בחדש השביעי. סיון, והוא שביעי לכסלו שבו פסקו הגשמים: בשבעה עשר יום. מכאן אתה למד שהיתה התבה משקעת במים אחת עשרה אמה, שהרי כתיב: "בעשירי באחד לחדש נראו ראשי ההרים", זה אב שהוא עשירי למרחשון לירידת גשמים, והם היו גבוהים על ההרים חמש עשרה אמה, וחסרו מיום אחד בסיון עד אחד באב חמש עשרה אמה לששים יום, הרי אמה לארבעה ימים, נמצא שבששה עשר של סיון לא חסרו אלא ארבע אמות, ונחה התבה ליום המחרת, למדת שהיתה משקעת אחת עשרה אמה במים שעל ראשי ההרים:

ה| בעשירי... נראו ראשי ההרים. זה אב שהוא עשירי למרחשון שהתחיל הגשם. ואם תאמר, הוא אלול ועשירי לכסלו שפסק הגשם, כשם שאתה אומר "בחדש השביעי" סיון והוא שביעי להפסקה – אי אפשר לומר כן, על כרחך שביעי אי אתה מונה אלא להפסקה, שהרי לא כלו ארבעים יום של ירידת גשמים ומאה וחמשים של תגברת המים עד אחד בסיון. ואם אתה אומר שביעי לירידה אין זה סיון. והעשירי אי אפשר למנות אלא לירידה, שאם אתה אומר להפסקה והוא אלול, אי אתה מוצא "בראשון באחד לחדש חרבו המים מעל הארץ" (להלן פסוק יג), שהרי מקץ ארבעים יום משנראו ראשי ההרים שלח את העורב, ועשרים ואחת יום הוחיל בשליחות היונה, הרי ששים יום משנראו ראשי ההרים עד שחרבו פני האדמה. ואם תאמר באלול נראו, נמצא שחרבו במרחשון, והוא קורא אותו ראשון?! ואין זה אלא תשרי שהוא ראשון לבריאת עולם, ולרבי יהושע הוא ניסן:

ו| מקץ ארבעים יום. משנראו ראשי ההרים: את חלון התבה אשר עשה. לצהר, ולא זה פתח התבה העשוי לביאה ויציאה:

ז| יצוא ושוב. הולך ומקיף סביבות התבה, ולא הלך בשליחותו, שהיה חושדו על בת זוגו, כמו שמצינו באגדת 'חלק' (סנהדרין קח ע"ב): עד יבשת המים. פשוטו כמשמעו. אבל מדרש אגדה: מוכן היה העורב לשליחות אחרת בעצירת גשמים בימי אליהו, שנאמר: "והערבים מביאים לו לחם ובשר" (מלכים א' יז, ו):

ח| וישלח את היונה. לסוף שבעה ימים, שהרי כתיב (להלן פסוק י): "ויחל עוד שבעת ימים אחרים", מכלל זה אתה למד שאף בראשונה הוחיל שבעה ימים: וישלח. אין זה לשון שליחות אלא לשון שלוח, שלחה ללכת לדרכה, ובזו יראה אם קלו המים, שאם תמצא מנוח לא תשוב אליו:

י| ויחל. לשון המתנה, וכן: "לי שמעו ויחלו" (איוב כט, כא), והרבה יש במקרא:

יא| טרף בפיה. אומר אני שזכר היה, לכך הוא קוראהו פעמים לשון זכר ופעמים לשון נקבה, לפי שכל יונה שבמקרא לשון נקבה, כמו: "כיוני הגאיות כלם המות" (יחזקאל ז, טז), וכן: "כיונה פותה" (הושע ז, יא): טרף. חטף. ומדרש אגדה לשון מזון, ודרשו "בפיה" לשון מאמר, אמרה: יהיו מזונותי מרורין כזית זו בידו של הקדוש ברוך הוא ולא יהו מתוקים כדבש ביד בשר ודם:

יב| וייחל. הוא לשון 'ויחל' (לעיל פסוק י), אלא שזה לשון ויפעל וזה לשון ויתפעל, 'ויחל' וימתן, 'וייחל' ויתמתן:

13 **It was in the six hundred and first year, during the first month on the first of the month; the water dried from upon the earth,** those areas that had been dry land prior to the flood. **Noah removed the cover of the ark,** as apparently the window was very small and he was able to see out only after removing the cover; **and he saw, and behold, the surface of the ground dried.** The water had disappeared, but the ground was still sodden.

14 **During the second month, on the twenty-seventh day of the month, the earth dried.** It took a long time until the ground fully dried up, to the extent that it was possible to tread upon it.

15 Nevertheless, Noah remained in the ark. Just as he did not enter
Fourth aliya the ark of his own initiative, so too, now he waited for a divine command to exit it.[15] And indeed, **God spoke to Noah, saying:**

16 **Go out of the ark: You, and your wife, and your sons, and your sons' wives with you.**

17 **Every living being that is with you from all flesh, of the birds, and of the animals, and of every crawling creature that crawls on the earth, bring out with you.** Remove them forcibly, as the animals had become accustomed to life in the ark. Although they were confined there, they had easy access to food. Moreover, some of them may have been in a state of hibernation due to the conditions. It was therefore necessary to compel them to leave. **And they will teem [*veshartzu*] on the earth,** by increasing greatly in number so that they will be found everywhere, like creeping animals [*sheratzim*],[16] **and be fruitful and multiply upon the earth.** In this manner the world will be populated afresh.

18 **Noah emerged, and his sons, and his wife, and his sons' wives with him.**

19 **Every beast, every crawling creature and every bird, every creature that crawls on the earth, after their families, emerged from the ark.**

In the Wake of the Flood: A Renewal of the Connection between God and the Creatures on Earth

GENESIS 8:20–9:17

Here, for the first time, God enacts a covenant between Himself and man, along with all living beings. This covenant includes a promise, as well as a sign of its implementation. After the flood, man's power over animals is increased, but at the same time certain restrictions and obligations are placed upon him.

20 **Noah built an altar to the Lord, and he took from every pure animal and from every pure bird, and sacrificed burnt offerings on the altar.**

21 **The Lord smelled the pleasing aroma.** This is a symbolic expression, which appears elsewhere in connection with offerings. Its plain meaning is satisfaction. **And the Lord said in His heart,** an anthropomorphic expression denoting divine contemplation: **I will not continue to curse the ground anymore on account of man,** as I did with the flood, **as the inclination of man's heart is evil from his youth [*mine'urav*].**[D] The Sages expound: From when he stirs himself [*ninar*] and emerges into the world, from birth.[17] Man is not by nature evil. But he is given freedom to choose and is subject to constant temptation. **And** therefore **I will not continue to smite every living being anymore, as I did.** In order to repair the corruption of the evil inclination, mankind requires a fixed and stable world. Therefore, human history will know no more all-encompassing, catastrophic events like the flood, but rather there will be relatively moderate rises and falls.

22 **As long as the earth endures, planting and harvest, and cold and heat, and summer and winter,**[D] **and day and night shall not cease.** During the flood, the seasons of the year and the alternation between day and night came to a stop. Afterward, God reestablished regular time and its units, and determined that they shall not cease again. The world will follow its natural path, the human race will survive, and never again will there be a total flood.

9 1 To establish the above promise, God turns to Noah and his family with blessings and commandments. In rabbinic and later literature these are called the seven Noahide mitzvot. **God blessed Noah and his sons, and He said to them: Be fruitful and multiply, and fill the earth.** This blessing had already

DISCUSSION

8:21 | **As the inclination of man's heart is evil from his youth:** It is interesting that this same fact, that the inclination of man's heart is evil, was earlier cited as the cause for the flood: "The Lord saw that the wickedness of man was great on the earth, and that every inclination of the thoughts of his heart was only evil all the time. The Lord regretted that He had made man on the earth" (see 6:5–6). Here, however, this rationale is used as an excuse for mankind. Indeed, the existence of the evil inclination in man can be a cause for despair and lead him to the brink of destruction. Nevertheless, as this inclination is planted within him from his youth, from his very birth, he should not be entirely blamed.

8:22 | **Planting and harvest, and cold and heat, and summer and winter:** Some Sages derive from this verse that a year comprises six

יג יָסְפָה שׁוּב־אֵלָיו עוֹד׃ וַיְהִי בְּאַחַת וְשֵׁשׁ־מֵאוֹת שָׁנָה בָּרִאשׁוֹן בְּאֶחָד לַחֹדֶשׁ
חָרְבוּ הַמַּיִם מֵעַל הָאָרֶץ וַיָּסַר נֹחַ אֶת־מִכְסֵה הַתֵּבָה וַיַּרְא וְהִנֵּה חָרְבוּ פְּנֵי
יד הָאֲדָמָה׃ וּבַחֹדֶשׁ הַשֵּׁנִי בְּשִׁבְעָה וְעֶשְׂרִים יוֹם לַחֹדֶשׁ יָבְשָׁה הָאָרֶץ׃
טו טז וַיְדַבֵּר אֱלֹהִים אֶל־נֹחַ לֵאמֹר׃ צֵא מִן־הַתֵּבָה אַתָּה וְאִשְׁתְּךָ וּבָנֶיךָ וּנְשֵׁי־בָנֶיךָ ז רביעי
יז אִתָּךְ׃ כָּל־הַחַיָּה אֲשֶׁר־אִתְּךָ מִכָּל־בָּשָׂר בָּעוֹף וּבַבְּהֵמָה וּבְכָל־הָרֶמֶשׂ הָרֹמֵשׂ
יח עַל־הָאָרֶץ הוצא אִתָּךְ וְשָׁרְצוּ בָאָרֶץ וּפָרוּ וְרָבוּ עַל־הָאָרֶץ׃ וַיֵּצֵא־נֹחַ וּבָנָיו הַיְצֵא
יט וְאִשְׁתּוֹ וּנְשֵׁי־בָנָיו אִתּוֹ׃ כָּל־הַחַיָּה כָּל־הָרֶמֶשׂ וְכָל־הָעוֹף כֹּל רוֹמֵשׂ עַל־הָאָרֶץ
כ לְמִשְׁפְּחֹתֵיהֶם יָצְאוּ מִן־הַתֵּבָה׃ וַיִּבֶן נֹחַ מִזְבֵּחַ לַיהוָה וַיִּקַּח מִכֹּל ׀ הַבְּהֵמָה
כא הַטְּהֹרָה וּמִכֹּל הָעוֹף הַטָּהֹר וַיַּעַל עֹלֹת בַּמִּזְבֵּחַ׃ וַיָּרַח יְהוָה אֶת־רֵיחַ הַנִּיחֹחַ
וַיֹּאמֶר יְהוָה אֶל־לִבּוֹ לֹא אֹסִף לְקַלֵּל עוֹד אֶת־הָאֲדָמָה בַּעֲבוּר הָאָדָם כִּי יֵצֶר
כב לֵב הָאָדָם רַע מִנְּעֻרָיו וְלֹא־אֹסִף עוֹד לְהַכּוֹת אֶת־כָּל־חַי כַּאֲשֶׁר עָשִׂיתִי׃ עֹד
ט א כָּל־יְמֵי הָאָרֶץ זֶרַע וְקָצִיר וְקֹר וָחֹם וְקַיִץ וָחֹרֶף וְיוֹם וָלַיְלָה לֹא יִשְׁבֹּתוּ׃ וַיְבָרֶךְ

רש"י

יג| **בראשון.** לרבי אליעזר הוא תשרי ולרבי יהושע הוא ניסן: **חרבו.** נעשה כמין טיט, שקרמו פניה של מעלה:

יד| **יבשה.** נעשית גריד כהלכתה. **בשבעה ועשרים,** וירידתו בחדש השני בשבעה עשר, אלו אחד עשר ימים שהחמה יתרה על הלבנה, שמשפט דור המבול שנה תמימה היה:

טז| **אתה ואשתך וגו'.** איש ואשתו, כאן התיר להם תשמיש המטה:

יז| **הוצא.** כתיב, 'היצא' קרי. "היצא" – אמור להם שיצאו, "הוצא" – אם אין רוצים לצאת הוציאם אתה: **ושרצו בארץ.** ולא בתבה, מגיד שאף הבהמה והעוף נאסרו בתשמיש:

יט| **למשפחתיהם.** קבלו עליהם על מנת לדבק במינן:

כ| **מכל הבהמה הטהרה.** אמר: לא צוה לי הקדוש ברוך הוא להכניס מאלו שבעה שבעה אלא כדי להקריב קרבן מהם:

כא| **מנעריו.** 'מנעריו' כתיב, משננער לצאת ממעי אמו נתן בו יצר הרע: **לא אסף, ולא אסף.** כפל הדבר לשבועה, הוא שכתוב (ישעיה נד, ט): "אשר נשבעתי מעבר מי נח", ולא מצינו בה שבועה אלא זו שכפל דבריו והיא שבועה, וכן דרשו חכמים במסכת שבועות (דף לו ע"א):

כב| **עד כל ימי הארץ וגו' לא ישבתו.** ששה עתים הללו, שני חדשים לכל אחד ואחד, כמו ששנינו: חצי תשרי ומרחשון וחצי כסלו – זרע, חצי כסלו וטבת וחצי שבט – קר וכו', בבבא מציעא (דף קו ע"ב): **קר.** קשה מחרף: **וחרף.** עת זרע שעורים וקטניות החריפין להתבשל מהר, והוא חצי שבט ואדר וחצי ניסן. **קיץ.** הוא זמן לקיטת תאנים וזמן שמייבשין אותן בשדות, ושמו קיץ, כמו: "והלחם והקיץ לאכול הנערים" (שמואל ב' טז, ב): **חם.** הוא סוף ימות החמה, חצי אב ואלול וחצי תשרי, שהעולם חם ביותר, כמו ששנינו במסכת יומא (דף כט ע"א) שלהי קיטא קשי מקיטא: **ויום ולילה לא ישבתו.** מכלל ששבתו כל ימות המבול, שלא שמשו המזלות ולא נכר בין יום ולילה: **לא ישבתו.** לא יפסקו כל אלה מלהתנהג כסדרן:

DISCUSSION

short seasons, with different weather conditions, each of which is associated with different agricultural tasks (*Bava Metzia* 106b). This verse accords with the climate of the Land of Israel, which has only two seasons: a hot, dry summer and a moderate, rainy winter. In biblical Hebrew, the word *setav* refers to winter, even though it has come to mean autumn in modern times (see Song of Songs 2:11, and Rashi ad loc.).

been given to Adam, but it seems that God canceled it with the flood. Therefore, this blessing is granted here once again.

2 **Fear of you and dread of you shall be upon every beast of the earth, upon every bird of the heavens, upon all that crawls on the ground, and upon all fish of the sea. Into your hand they are** all **given.** Before the flood, relations between man and the animals were mostly peaceful. Although man had been given dominion over the animal world (1:28), and some engaged in animal husbandry, people were prohibited to exploit animals for food, and apparently they refrained from causing them any harm. Here God casts dread of man upon all other living creatures.

3 And in addition, **every crawling creature that lives shall be yours for food;** from now on you are permitted to eat animals. **Like green vegetation I have given you everything;** until now both you and animals were vegetarians,[18] whereas now you are given permission to eat everything in the world.

4 After God has granted permission to eat animal flesh, He now places limits on this allowance. **But flesh with its life, its blood, you shall not eat.** One may not eat the flesh of an animal when it is still connected to its soul. This is the prohibition against eating a limb cut from a living animal.[19] Although man is permitted to eat animals, this does not give him the right to act in a cruel manner.

5 This verse states another limitation: **But I will demand your blood of your lives,**[D] as your right to kill other creatures does not extend to people. Human beings cannot be compared to other living things. If someone's blood is spilled, the responsibility is upon the person who spilled it. And similarly, **from every beast I will demand it.** Animals are held responsible for shedding human blood just as people are. When the Torah will be given, it will include a *halakha* that the court must sentence and put to death an ox or any other animal that kills a human being.[20] **And,** as stated, **from man, from every man for**

shedding the blood of **his brother,**[21] **will I demand the life of man.**

6 **One who sheds the blood of man, by man shall his blood be shed.** This is the first appearance of the death penalty, which is imposed on a murderer. The verse provides the reason for all these commands: **As He made man in the image of God.** Man is not merely one of the creatures of the zoological system. Since he was created in the image of God, he must be treated with greater respect.

7 **And you, be fruitful and multiply; teem on the earth, and multiply on it.** Some of the instructions that were given to Adam are still valid. Nevertheless, new commands are stated here that are appropriate for a changed world.

Fifth aliya

8 **God spoke to Noah, and to his sons with him, saying:** You must observe these obligations that I have imposed upon you.

9 **And I hereby establish,** set up and enact, **My covenant with you, and with your descendants after you;**

10 **and with every living soul that is with you, with the birds, and with the animals, and with every beast of the earth** that is **with you; from all that emerged from the ark.** The covenant applies **to every beast of the earth;** it is valid with respect to all living creatures in the world.[22]

11 **And I will establish My covenant with you,** which in essence is that **all flesh shall not be excised again by water of the flood; there shall not be a flood anymore to destroy the earth.**

12 **God said: This is the sign of the covenant that I place between Me and you and every living soul that is with you, for eternal generations:**

13 **My rainbow I have set in the cloud, and it shall be as a sign of a covenant between Me and the earth.**[D] The rainbow shall signify the covenant between Me and the earth's inhabitants.

14 **It shall be when I bring a cloud over the earth, and the rainbow will be seen in the cloud,**

DISCUSSION

9:5 | But I will demand your blood of your lives: The first and last clauses of the verse both appear to warn against murder. The Sages resolve this apparent redundancy by interpreting the first clause as a warning against suicide (*Bava Kama* 91b).

9:13 | My rainbow I have set in the cloud, and it shall be as a sign of a covenant: Already in antiquity it was known that a rainbow is caused by the refractive dispersion of sunlight in drops of rain or mist, and that its colors can also be seen in the refraction of light in water, glass, or the like. But if a rainbow is a simple natural

phenomenon, how can it be produced as a sign of a covenant? It has been suggested that after the flood, a change was introduced not only in the moral laws, as mentioned above, but also in nature, and that prior to the flood, rainbows did not appear. However, it is likely that the rainbow was not in fact created at this juncture. Rather, it was chosen from all natural phenomena to serve as a token of the covenant. When people enter into covenants, they sometimes select some object found in their environment and use it as a sign of that covenant. A rainbow, which appears naturally after rain or the formation of

dense clouds, was chosen here as an appropriate sign of the covenant and of God's commitment that there would no similar flood (see Ramban, verse 12).

In addition to the above considerations, the choice of a rainbow as a sign of the covenant symbolizes the calming of God's anger, as the bow, which is an instrument of war whose arch is usually angled away from the bowman, reverses itself and becomes a sign of moderation and peaceful relations with the earth (see Ramban; *Ḥizkuni*; see also *Bereshit Rabba* 35:3).

ב אֱלֹהִים אֶת־נֹחַ וְאֶת־בָּנָיו וַיֹּאמֶר לָהֶם פְּרוּ וּרְבוּ וּמִלְאוּ אֶת־הָאָרֶץ: וּמוֹרַאֲכֶם
וְחִתְּכֶם יִהְיֶה עַל כָּל־חַיַּת הָאָרֶץ וְעַל כָּל־עוֹף הַשָּׁמָיִם בְּכֹל אֲשֶׁר תִּרְמֹשׂ הָאֲדָמָה
ג וּבְכָל־דְּגֵי הַיָּם בְּיֶדְכֶם נִתָּנוּ: כָּל־רֶמֶשׂ אֲשֶׁר הוּא־חַי לָכֶם יִהְיֶה לְאָכְלָה כְּיֶרֶק
ד ה עֵשֶׂב נָתַתִּי לָכֶם אֶת־כֹּל: אַךְ־בָּשָׂר בְּנַפְשׁוֹ דָמוֹ לֹא תֹאכֵלוּ: וְאַךְ אֶת־דִּמְכֶם
לְנַפְשֹׁתֵיכֶם אֶדְרֹשׁ מִיַּד כָּל־חַיָּה אֶדְרְשֶׁנּוּ וּמִיַּד הָאָדָם מִיַּד אִישׁ אָחִיו אֶדְרֹשׁ
ו אֶת־נֶפֶשׁ הָאָדָם: שֹׁפֵךְ דַּם הָאָדָם בָּאָדָם דָּמוֹ יִשָּׁפֵךְ כִּי בְּצֶלֶם אֱלֹהִים עָשָׂה
ז ח אֶת־הָאָדָם: וְאַתֶּם פְּרוּ וּרְבוּ שִׁרְצוּ בָאָרֶץ וּרְבוּ־בָהּ: וַיֹּאמֶר אֱלֹהִים חמישי
ט אֶל־נֹחַ וְאֶל־בָּנָיו אִתּוֹ לֵאמֹר: וַאֲנִי הִנְנִי מֵקִים אֶת־בְּרִיתִי אִתְּכֶם וְאֶת־זַרְעֲכֶם
י אַחֲרֵיכֶם: וְאֵת כָּל־נֶפֶשׁ הַחַיָּה אֲשֶׁר אִתְּכֶם בָּעוֹף בַּבְּהֵמָה וּבְכָל־חַיַּת הָאָרֶץ
יא אִתְּכֶם מִכֹּל יֹצְאֵי הַתֵּבָה לְכֹל חַיַּת הָאָרֶץ: וַהֲקִמֹתִי אֶת־בְּרִיתִי אִתְּכֶם וְלֹא־
יב יִכָּרֵת כָּל־בָּשָׂר עוֹד מִמֵּי הַמַּבּוּל וְלֹא־יִהְיֶה עוֹד מַבּוּל לְשַׁחֵת הָאָרֶץ: וַיֹּאמֶר
אֱלֹהִים זֹאת אוֹת־הַבְּרִית אֲשֶׁר־אֲנִי נֹתֵן בֵּינִי וּבֵינֵיכֶם וּבֵין כָּל־נֶפֶשׁ חַיָּה אֲשֶׁר
יג אִתְּכֶם לְדֹרֹת עוֹלָם: אֶת־קַשְׁתִּי נָתַתִּי בֶּעָנָן וְהָיְתָה לְאוֹת בְּרִית בֵּינִי וּבֵין הָאָרֶץ:
יד טו וְהָיָה בְּעַנְנִי עָנָן עַל־הָאָרֶץ וְנִרְאֲתָה הַקֶּשֶׁת בֶּעָנָן: וְזָכַרְתִּי אֶת־בְּרִיתִי אֲשֶׁר

רש״י

פרק ט

ב| וְחִתְּכֶם. וְאֵימַתְכֶם, כְּמוֹ: "תִּרְאוּ חֲתַת" (איוב ו, כא). וְאַגָּדָה: לְשׁוֹן חִיּוּת, שֶׁכָּל זְמַן שֶׁתִּינוֹק בֶּן יוֹמוֹ חַי אֵין צָרִיךְ לְשָׁמְרוֹ מִן הָעַכְבָּרִים, עוֹג מֶלֶךְ הַבָּשָׁן מֵת צָרִיךְ לְשָׁמְרוֹ מִן הָעַכְבָּרִים, שֶׁנֶּאֱמַר: "וּמוֹרַאֲכֶם וְחִתְּכֶם יִהְיֶה", אֵימָתַי יִהְיֶה מוֹרַאֲכֶם עַל הַחַיּוֹת? כָּל זְמַן שֶׁאַתֶּם חַיִּים:

ג| לָכֶם יִהְיֶה לְאָכְלָה. שֶׁלֹּא הִרְשֵׁיתִי לְאָדָם הָרִאשׁוֹן לֶאֱכֹל בָּשָׂר אֶלָּא יֶרֶק עֵשֶׂב, וְלָכֶם – "כְּיֶרֶק עֵשֶׂב" שֶׁהִפְקַרְתִּי לְאָדָם הָרִאשׁוֹן "נָתַתִּי לָכֶם אֶת כֹּל":

ד| בְּנַפְשׁוֹ דָמוֹ. אָסַר לָהֶם אֵבֶר מִן הַחַי, כְּלוֹמַר כָּל זְמַן שֶׁנַּפְשׁוֹ בְּדָמוֹ לֹא תֹאכְלוּ הַבָּשָׂר: בְּנַפְשׁוֹ דָמוֹ. בְּעוֹד נַפְשׁוֹ בּוֹ: בָּשָׂר בְּנַפְשׁוֹ לֹא תֹאכֵלוּ. הֲרֵי אֵבֶר מִן הַחַי, וְאַף "דָּמוֹ לֹא תֹאכֵלוּ" הֲרֵי דָּם מִן הַחַי:

ה| וְאַךְ אֶת דִּמְכֶם. אַף עַל פִּי שֶׁהִתַּרְתִּי לָכֶם נְטִילַת נְשָׁמָה בִּבְהֵמָה, "אֶת דִּמְכֶם... אֶדְרֹשׁ" – הַשּׁוֹפֵךְ דַּם עַצְמוֹ, "לְנַפְשֹׁתֵיכֶם" – אַף הַחוֹנֵק עַצְמוֹ, אַף עַל פִּי שֶׁלֹּא יָצָא מִמֶּנּוּ דָּם: מִיַּד כָּל חַיָּה. לְפִי שֶׁחָטְאוּ דּוֹר הַמַּבּוּל וְהֻפְקְרוּ לְמַאֲכַל חַיּוֹת רָעוֹת לִשְׁלֹט בָּהֶן, שֶׁנֶּאֱמַר: "נִמְשַׁל כַּבְּהֵמוֹת נִדְמוּ" (תהלים מט, כא), לְפִיכָךְ הֻצְרַךְ לְהַזְהִיר עֲלֵיהֶן אֶת הַחַיּוֹת: וּמִיַּד הָאָדָם. מִיַּד הַהוֹרֵג בְּמֵזִיד וְאֵין עֵדִים, אֲנִי אֶדְרֹשׁ: מִיַּד אִישׁ אָחִיו. שֶׁהוּא אוֹהֵב לוֹ כְּאָח וַהֲרָגוֹ שׁוֹגֵג, אֲנִי אֶדְרֹשׁ אִם לֹא יִגְלֶה וִיבַקֵּשׁ עַל עֲוֹנוֹ לִמָּחֵל, שֶׁאַף הַשּׁוֹגֵג צָרִיךְ כַּפָּרָה, וְאִם אֵין עֵדִים לְחַיְּבוֹ גָּלוּת וְהוּא אֵינוֹ נִכְנָע הַקָּדוֹשׁ בָּרוּךְ הוּא דּוֹרֵשׁ מִמֶּנּוּ, כְּמוֹ שֶׁדָּרְשׁוּ רַבּוֹתֵינוּ "וְהָאֱלֹהִים אִנָּה לְיָדוֹ" (שמות כא, יג) בְּמַסֶּכֶת מַכּוֹת (דף י ע״ב): הַקָּדוֹשׁ בָּרוּךְ הוּא מְזַמְּנָן לְפֻנְדָּק אֶחָד וְכוּ':

ו| בָּאָדָם דָּמוֹ יִשָּׁפֵךְ. אִם יֵשׁ עֵדִים הֲמִיתוּהוּ אַתֶּם, לָמָּה? "כִּי בְּצֶלֶם אֱלֹהִים עָשָׂה אֶת הָאָדָם", וְזֶה מִקְרָא חָסֵר: עָשָׂה הָעוֹשֶׂה אֶת הָאָדָם, וְכֵן הַרְבֵּה בַּמִּקְרָא:

ז| וְאַתֶּם פְּרוּ וּרְבוּ. לְפִי פְּשׁוּטוֹ, הָרִאשׁוֹנָה לִבְרָכָה וְכָאן לְצִוּוּי. וּלְפִי מִדְרָשׁוֹ, לְהַקִּישׁ מִי שֶׁאֵינוֹ עוֹסֵק בִּפְרִיָּה וּרְבִיָּה לְשׁוֹפֵךְ דָּמִים:

ט| וַאֲנִי הִנְנִי. מַסְכִּים אֲנִי עִמְּךָ; שֶׁהָיָה נֹחַ דּוֹאֵג לַעֲסֹק בִּפְרִיָּה וּרְבִיָּה עַד שֶׁהִבְטִיחוֹ הַקָּדוֹשׁ בָּרוּךְ הוּא שֶׁלֹּא לְשַׁחֵת הָעוֹלָם עוֹד, וְכֵן עָשָׂה. בָּאַחֲרוֹנָה אָמַר לוֹ: הִנְנִי מַסְכִּים לַעֲשׂוֹת קִיּוּם וְחִזּוּק בְּרִית לְהַבְטָחָתִי וְאֶתֵּן לְךָ אוֹת:

י| חַיַּת הָאָרֶץ אִתְּכֶם. הֵם הַמִּתְהַלְּכִים עִם הַבְּרִיּוֹת: מִכֹּל יֹצְאֵי הַתֵּבָה. לְהָבִיא שְׁקָצִים וּרְמָשִׂים: לְכֹל חַיַּת הָאָרֶץ. לְהָבִיא הַמַּזִּיקִין שֶׁאֵינָן בִּכְלַל "הַחַיָּה אֲשֶׁר אִתְּכֶם", שֶׁאֵין הִלּוּכָן עִם הַבְּרִיּוֹת:

יא| וַהֲקִמֹתִי. אֶעֱשֶׂה קִיּוּם לִבְרִיתִי, וּמַהוּ קִיּוּמוֹ? אוֹת הַקֶּשֶׁת, כְּמוֹ שֶׁמְּסַיֵּם וְהוֹלֵךְ:

יב| לְדֹרֹת עוֹלָם. נִכְתַּב חָסֵר, שֶׁיֵּשׁ דּוֹרוֹת שֶׁלֹּא הֻצְרְכוּ לְאוֹת לְפִי שֶׁצַּדִּיקִים גְּמוּרִים הָיוּ, כְּמוֹ דּוֹרוֹ שֶׁל חִזְקִיָּהוּ מֶלֶךְ יְהוּדָה וְדוֹרוֹ שֶׁל רַבִּי שִׁמְעוֹן בֶּן יוֹחַאי:

יד| בְּעַנְנִי עָנָן. כְּשֶׁתַּעֲלֶה בְמַחֲשָׁבָה לְפָנַי לְהָבִיא חֹשֶׁךְ וַאֲבַדּוֹן לָעוֹלָם:

15 **I will remember My covenant that is between Me and you and every living soul of all flesh, and the water shall not become a flood anymore to destroy all flesh.**

16 **The rainbow shall be in the cloud, and I will see it, to remember the eternal covenant between God and every living creature of all flesh that is upon the earth.**

17 **God said to Noah: This is the sign of the covenant that I have established between Me and all flesh that is upon the earth.** The rainbow represents the covenant between God and mankind. Since it can also be viewed as a sign of God's revelation in the world, the Sages instructed that one must treat a rainbow with proper respect, and one must take care not to gaze upon it.[23]

Noah's Family after the Flood

GENESIS 9:18–29

The first actions which the survivors of the flood, Noah's family, perform in the new world involve the loss of consciousness caused by drinking wine, and as a result, the exposing and eventual covering of the body. This can be seen as an inverse parallel to the beginning of the old world, where Adam and Eve acquired knowledge of good and evil through eating fruit that was forbidden to them, and as result they became ashamed of their nakedness and covered themselves up.

18 *Sixth aliya* **The sons of Noah, who emerged from the ark, were Shem, and Ham, and Yefet; and Ham was the father of Canaan.** This additional mention of one of their children is important for the continuation of the story.

19 **These three were the sons of Noah, and from these the whole earth was dispersed.** The sons of Noah multiplied until they filled the entire world.

20 **Noah, man of the soil, began, and he planted a vineyard.** As related earlier (see 5:29), Noah was a farmer. One of his first actions after the flood was to plant a vineyard. Apparently, Noah chose a vineyard over essential grains or fruit trees necessary for his survival. This is meant as a criticism of Noah, as he decided to produce a luxury item.[24] It is possible that he planted a vineyard because he actively wanted to get drunk; after the entire world that he was familiar with had been destroyed, he sought to blur his mind in order to overcome the trauma.

21 **He drank of the wine and became drunk.** Since he was drunk and lying on the ground, his clothes, which were presumably flowing robes, fell off him, **and he was exposed**[D] and left naked **inside his tent.**

22 **Ham, father of Canaan, saw the nakedness of his father.** Canaan is mentioned here due to his involvement in the affair, as maintained by the Sages. Either Ham was the one who glanced inside the tent and went off and told his brothers, or he performed even worse actions.[25] The phrase "to see nakedness" is similar to the expression "to reveal nakedness," which appears in the Torah in halakhic contexts not in its literal sense, but as referring to forbidden sexual contact.[26] Accordingly, this might be an indication that Ham or his son Canaan performed some sexual act upon Noah.[27] It is possible that Ham merely saw Noah's nakedness; however, rather than concealing his father's shame, he did the opposite and humiliated him,[28] **and told his two brothers outside.**

23 **Shem and Yefet took the garment,** a broad cloth that would cover Noah's entire body, and **they placed it upon both their shoulders. They walked backward,** so as not to disgrace their father. Furthermore, they treated him with great modesty: **And they covered the nakedness of their father. They faced backward, and they did not see the nakedness of their father.**

24 **Noah awoke from his wine, and knew.** Noah was not so drunk that when he woke up he had no memory of what had happened in his drunken stupor. While intoxicated, he behaved abnormally and was unaware of his actions, but once he sobered up, he was able to recall **what his youngest son,** Ham, or his grandson, Canaan, **had done to him.**[29]

25 **He,** Noah, **said: Cursed be Canaan** and his descendants; **a slave of slaves,** a slave among slaves, an absolute slave in every sense,[30] **shall he be to his brothers.**

26 **He said: Blessed be the Lord, God of Shem; and Canaan shall be their servant,** a servant to the descendants of Shem.

27 **May God expand [*yaft*]** and enlarge the borders of the inheritance of **Yefet;** *yaft* is an alliterative play on words. **And He,** God, **shall dwell in the tents of Shem;**[D] indeed, the Divine Presence rested upon the seed of Abraham, a descendant of Shem. **And Canaan shall be their servant,** as Canaan shall remain the servant of both Shem and Yefet.

DISCUSSION

9:21 | **And he was exposed:** Unlike ancient Greece and other cultures, Judaism across the generations has had a negative attitude toward nudity. In the Jewish world, nakedness has been perceived as shameful, from the day that Adam and Eve ate of the tree of knowledge of good and evil. Thus the words *ervah*, nakedness, and *arom*, naked, are terms of disgrace and weakness (see, e.g., Deuteronomy 23:15; Hosea 2:5; see also commentary on Leviticus 18:1).

9:27 | **May God expand Yefet, and He shall dwell in the tents of Shem:** Some expound *yaft* as related to *yofi*, beauty. According to this interpretation, Noah bestows the blessing of sanctity and ethics upon Shem, and the blessing of wealth and aesthetics upon Yefet (see *Megilla* 9b), but he curses Canaan. Although Canaan's progeny were destined to become a

בֵּינִי וּבֵינֵיכֶם וּבֵין כָּל־נֶפֶשׁ חַיָּה בְּכָל־בָּשָׂר וְלֹא־יִהְיֶה עוֹד הַמַּיִם לְמַבּוּל לְשַׁחֵת
טז כָּל־בָּשָׂר: וְהָיְתָה הַקֶּשֶׁת בֶּעָנָן וּרְאִיתִיהָ לִזְכֹּר בְּרִית עוֹלָם בֵּין אֱלֹהִים וּבֵין
יז כָּל־נֶפֶשׁ חַיָּה בְּכָל־בָּשָׂר אֲשֶׁר עַל־הָאָרֶץ: וַיֹּאמֶר אֱלֹהִים אֶל־נֹחַ זֹאת אוֹת־
הַבְּרִית אֲשֶׁר הֲקִמֹתִי בֵּינִי וּבֵין כָּל־בָּשָׂר אֲשֶׁר עַל־הָאָרֶץ:
יח יט וַיִּהְיוּ בְנֵי־נֹחַ הַיֹּצְאִים מִן־הַתֵּבָה שֵׁם וְחָם וָיָפֶת וְחָם הוּא אֲבִי כְנָעַן: שְׁלֹשָׁה ח ששי
כ כא אֵלֶּה בְּנֵי־נֹחַ וּמֵאֵלֶּה נָפְצָה כָל־הָאָרֶץ: וַיָּחֶל נֹחַ אִישׁ הָאֲדָמָה וַיִּטַּע כָּרֶם: וַיֵּשְׁתְּ
כב מִן־הַיַּיִן וַיִּשְׁכָּר וַיִּתְגַּל בְּתוֹךְ אָהֳלֹה: וַיַּרְא חָם אֲבִי כְנַעַן אֵת עֶרְוַת אָבִיו וַיַּגֵּד
כג לִשְׁנֵי־אֶחָיו בַּחוּץ: וַיִּקַּח שֵׁם וָיֶפֶת אֶת־הַשִּׂמְלָה וַיָּשִׂימוּ עַל־שְׁכֶם שְׁנֵיהֶם וַיֵּלְכוּ
כד אֲחֹרַנִּית וַיְכַסּוּ אֵת עֶרְוַת אֲבִיהֶם וּפְנֵיהֶם אֲחֹרַנִּית וְעֶרְוַת אֲבִיהֶם לֹא רָאוּ: וַיִּיקֶץ
כה נֹחַ מִיֵּינוֹ וַיֵּדַע אֵת אֲשֶׁר־עָשָׂה־לוֹ בְּנוֹ הַקָּטָן: וַיֹּאמֶר אָרוּר כְּנָעַן עֶבֶד עֲבָדִים
כו כז יִהְיֶה לְאֶחָיו: וַיֹּאמֶר בָּרוּךְ יהוה אֱלֹהֵי שֵׁם וִיהִי כְנַעַן עֶבֶד לָמוֹ: יַפְתְּ אֱלֹהִים

רש״י

טז| **בין אלהים ובין כל נפש חיה.** בֵּין מִדַּת הַדִּין שֶׁל מַעְלָה וּבֵינֵיכֶם; שֶׁהָיָה לוֹ לִכְתֹּב: ׳בֵּינִי וּבֵין כָּל נֶפֶשׁ חַיָּה׳, אֶלָּא זֶהוּ מִדְרָשׁוֹ: כְּשֶׁתָּבֹא מִדַּת הַדִּין לְקַטְרֵג עֲלֵיכֶם לְחַיֵּב אֶתְכֶם, אֲנִי רוֹאֶה אֶת הָאוֹת וְנִזְכָּר:

יז| **זאת אות הברית.** הֶרְאָהוּ הַקֶּשֶׁת וְאָמַר לוֹ: הֲרֵי הָאוֹת שֶׁאָמַרְתִּי:

יח| **וחם הוא אבי כנען.** לָמָּה הֻצְרַךְ לוֹמַר כָּאן? לְפִי שֶׁהַפָּרָשָׁה עֲסוּקָה וּבָאָה בְּשִׁכְרוּתוֹ שֶׁל נֹחַ שֶׁקִּלְקֵל בָּהּ חָם וְעַל יָדוֹ נִתְקַלֵּל כְּנַעַן, וַעֲדַיִן לֹא כָּתַב תּוֹלְדוֹת חָם וְלֹא יָדַעְנוּ שֶׁכְּנַעַן בְּנוֹ, לְפִיכָךְ הֻצְרַךְ לוֹמַר כָּאן: ״וְחָם הוּא אֲבִי כְנָעַן״:

כ| **ויחל.** עָשָׂה עַצְמוֹ חֻלִּין, שֶׁהָיָה לוֹ לַעֲסֹק תְּחִלָּה בִּנְטִיעָה אַחֶרֶת: **איש האדמה.** אֲדוֹנֵי הָאֲדָמָה, כְּמוֹ: ״אִישׁ נָעֳמִי״ (רות א, ג): **ויטע כרם.** כְּשֶׁנִּכְנַס לַתֵּבָה הִכְנִיס עִמּוֹ זְמוֹרוֹת וְיִחוּרֵי תְּאֵנִים:

כא| **אהלה.** ״אָהֳלָה״ כְּתִיב, רֶמֶז לַעֲשָׂרָה שְׁבָטִים שֶׁנִּקְרְאוּ עַל שֵׁם שׁוֹמְרוֹן שֶׁנִּקְרֵאת אָהֳלָה, שֶׁגָּלוּ עַל עִסְקֵי יַיִן, שֶׁנֶּאֱמַר: ״הַשֹּׁתִים בְּמִזְרְקֵי יַיִן״ (עמוס ו, ו): **ויתגל.** לְשׁוֹן וַיִּתְפַּעֵל:

כב| **וירא חם אבי כנען.** יֵשׁ מֵרַבּוֹתֵינוּ אוֹמְרִים, כְּנַעַן רָאָה וְהִגִּיד לְאָבִיו, לְכָךְ הֻזְכַּר עַל הַדָּבָר וְנִתְקַלֵּל: **וירא... את ערות אביו.** יֵשׁ אוֹמְרִים סֵרְסוֹ, וְיֵשׁ אוֹמְרִים רְבָעוֹ:

כג| **ויקח שם ויפת.** אֵין כְּתִיב ׳וַיִּקְחוּ׳ אֶלָּא ״וַיִּקַּח״, לִמֵּד עַל שֵׁם שֶׁנִּתְאַמֵּץ בַּמִּצְוָה יוֹתֵר מִיֶּפֶת, לְכָךְ זָכוּ בָנָיו לְטַלִּית שֶׁל צִיצִית, וְיֶפֶת זָכָה לִקְבוּרָה לְבָנָיו, שֶׁנֶּאֱמַר: ״אֶתֵּן לְגוֹג מְקוֹם שָׁם קֶבֶר״ (יחזקאל לט, יא). וְחָם שֶׁבִּזָּה אֶת אָבִיו, נֶאֱמַר בְּזַרְעוֹ: ״כֵּן יִנְהַג מֶלֶךְ אַשּׁוּר אֶת שְׁבִי מִצְרַיִם וְאֶת גָּלוּת כּוּשׁ נְעָרִים וּזְקֵנִים עָרוֹם וְיָחֵף וַחֲשׂוּפַי שֵׁת״ וְגוֹ׳ (ישעיה כ, ד): **ופניהם אחרנית.** לָמָּה נֶאֱמַר פַּעַם שְׁנִיָּה? לְלַמֵּד שֶׁכְּשֶׁקָּרְבוּ אֶצְלוֹ וְהֻצְרְכוּ לַהֲפֹךְ עַצְמָם לְכַסּוֹתוֹ, הָפְכוּ פְּנֵיהֶם אֲחוֹרַנִּית:

כד| **בנו הקטן.** הַפָּסוּל וְהַבָּזוּי, כְּמוֹ: ״הִנֵּה קָטֹן נְתַתִּיךָ בַּגּוֹיִם בָּזוּי״ (ירמיה מט, טו; עובדיה א, ב):

כה| **ארור כנען.** אַתָּה גָּרַמְתָּ לִי שֶׁלֹּא אוֹלִיד בֵּן רְבִיעִי אַחֵר לְשַׁמְּשֵׁנִי, אָרוּר בִּנְךָ רְבִיעִי לִהְיוֹת מְשַׁמֵּשׁ אֶת זַרְעָם שֶׁל אֵלּוּ הַגְּדוֹלִים שֶׁהֻטַּל עֲלֵיהֶם טֹרַח עֲבוֹדָתִי מֵעַתָּה. וּמָה רָאָה חָם שֶׁסֵּרְסוֹ? אָמַר לָהֶם לְאֶחָיו: אָדָם הָרִאשׁוֹן שְׁנֵי בָנִים הָיוּ לוֹ, וְהָרַג זֶה אֶת זֶה בִּשְׁבִיל יְרֻשַּׁת הָעוֹלָם, וְאָבִינוּ יֵשׁ לוֹ שְׁלֹשָׁה בָנִים וְעוֹדֶנּוּ מְבַקֵּשׁ בֵּן רְבִיעִי:

כו| **ברוך ה׳ אלהי שם.** שֶׁעָתִיד לִשְׁמֹר הַבְטָחָתוֹ לְזַרְעוֹ לָתֵת לָהֶם אֶת אֶרֶץ כְּנַעַן: **ויהי.** לָהֶם כְּנַעַן לְמַס עוֹבֵד:

כז| **יפת אלהים ליפת.** מְתֻרְגָּם: ״יַפְתֵּי״, יַרְחִיב:

DISCUSSION

nation of slaves, they did not immediately acquire that status. This passage also serves as the background for subsequent events, as Abraham would be given the Land of Canaan (Ramban). For this reason, Canaan is the only one of Ham's sons whose borders are delineated below (see 10:19, and *Ḥizkuni* ad loc.).

28 **Noah lived after the flood three hundred and fifty years.**

29 **All the days of Noah were nine hundred and fifty years; and he died.** Noah passed away without fathering any more

children, perhaps as a result of what Canaan had done to him. The entire future course of history will unfold from Noah's three sons, who were together with him in the ark.

Noah's Descendants and the Development of the Nations
GENESIS 10:1–32

The Torah presents a list of Noah's descendants, including families that developed into nations. These families are divided "after their families, in/after their tongues, in their lands" (verses 20, 31), in accordance with familial, linguistic, and national criteria. This chapter is the source of the accepted number of seventy nations. The list consists only of tribes that came directly from the land of Shinar; it does not include other nations, as those were very remote and had no direct contact with the children of Israel.

10 1 **This is the legacy of the sons of Noah: Shem, Ham, and Yefet; sons were born to them after the flood.** It stands to reason that they had children beforehand as well, but the majority of their sons were born after the flood.

2 **The sons of Yefet were Gomer,**[B] **Magog,**[B] **Madai, Yavan, Tuval,**[B] **Meshekh,**[B] **and Tiras.**[B] One can do no more than speculate about these names and the ones listed below. For example, the identification of Magog is unclear, despite the fact that he is also mentioned elsewhere: "Direct your attention to Gog, of the land of Magog."[31] In some cases, the name of the father of a nation is preserved in the name of its country. For example, the locations of Madai, or Medea, and Yavan, Greece, are known. In contrast, Tuval, Meshekh, and Tiras have not been identified. It has been suggested that Tiras is Persia.[32]

3 **The sons of Gomer were Ashkenaz,**[B] **Rifat,**[B] **and Togarma.**[B] In later generations, Ashkenaz was identified, linguistically, with Germany, and Togarma with Turkey, but here too there is no certainty.

4 **And the sons of Yavan were Elisha,**[B] which is reminiscent of the ancient name of Greece, Hellas; **Tarshish,**[B] which should perhaps be identified with Tartessos, a city and state on the southern coast of the Iberian Peninsula;[33] **Kitim,**[B] who were possibly succeeded by the Romans;[34] **and Dodanim.**[B]

5 **From these the island nations were divided into their lands, each after its language, after its families, in their nations.** These are all nations that developed from the descendants of Yefet. These peoples apparently spoke different languages, as

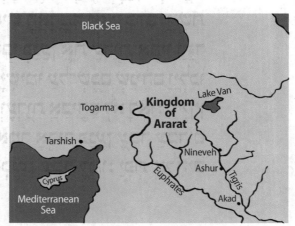
Togarma and Tarshish in Asia Minor

there was no territorial continuity between them. They spread over various islands and multiplied there, with each nation going to a different place, as the entire earth was open before them.

6 **The sons of Ham were Kush, Mitzrayim, Put,**[B] **and Canaan.**

7 **The sons of Kush were Seva,**[B] **Havila,**[B] **Savta, Raama, and Savtekha;**[B] **and the sons of Raama**[B] **were Sheva**[B] **and Dedan.** These are apparently all places in eastern Africa.

─── BACKGROUND ───

10:2 | **Gomer:** Gomer is also mentioned in Ezekiel (38:6) as a northern people. The Sages (*Yoma* 10a) identify Gomer as Germamiya of Rome, the Germanic tribes. Assyrian documents from the eighth century BCE mention the land of Gamir, near the kingdom of Urartu in the vicinity of Lake Van in the Ararat Mountains in Armenia. According to Herodotus, fifth century BCE, this

is the Kimri people who settled in the Crimean Peninsula. According to Josephus, they are the Galatians, from central Asia Minor.

Magog: Magog is also mentioned in Ezekiel (39:6) together with the inhabitants of the Greek islands: "I will send fire against Magog and against those who live in security in the lands of the sea." This place is identified in *Yoma* (10a)

as Candia, Crete; and in the Jerusalem Talmud (*Megilla* 1:9) as Gothia, the land of the Germanic tribe of the Goths. Josephus identifies Magog as the Scythians, a nomadic people that dwelled north of the Black Sea.

Tuval: In Isaiah (66:19) Tuval is listed together with Yavan, Greece: "Tuval and Yavan, the distant lands of the sea," and likewise in Ezekiel ◄●

כח לְיֶפֶת וְיִשְׁכֹּן בְּאׇהֳלֵי־שֵׁם וִיהִי כְנַעַן עֶבֶד לָמוֹ: וַיְחִי־נֹחַ אַחַר הַמַּבּוּל שְׁלֹשׁ מֵאוֹת
כט שָׁנָה וַחֲמִשִּׁים שָׁנָה: וַיְהִי כׇּל־יְמֵי־נֹחַ תְּשַׁע מֵאוֹת שָׁנָה וַחֲמִשִּׁים שָׁנָה וַיָּמֹת:
י א ב וְאֵלֶּה תּוֹלְדֹת בְּנֵי־נֹחַ שֵׁם חָם וָיָפֶת וַיִּוָּלְדוּ לָהֶם בָּנִים אַחַר הַמַּבּוּל: בְּנֵי יֶפֶת
ג גֹּמֶר וּמָגוֹג וּמָדַי וְיָוָן וְתֻבָל וּמֶשֶׁךְ וְתִירָס: וּבְנֵי גֹּמֶר אַשְׁכְּנַז וְרִיפַת וְתֹגַרְמָה:
ד ה וּבְנֵי יָוָן אֱלִישָׁה וְתַרְשִׁישׁ כִּתִּים וְדֹדָנִים: מֵאֵלֶּה נִפְרְדוּ אִיֵּי הַגּוֹיִם בְּאַרְצֹתָם אִישׁ
ו ז לִלְשֹׁנוֹ לְמִשְׁפְּחֹתָם בְּגוֹיֵהֶם: וּבְנֵי חָם כּוּשׁ וּמִצְרַיִם וּפוּט וּכְנָעַן: וּבְנֵי כוּשׁ סְבָא

רש״י

וְיִשְׁכֹּן בְּאׇהֳלֵי שֵׁם. יַשְׁרֶה שְׁכִינָתוֹ בְּיִשְׂרָאֵל. וּמִדְרַשׁ חֲכָמִים, אַף עַל פִּי שֶׁ״יַּפְתְּ אֱלֹהִים לְיֶפֶת״, שֶׁבָּנָה כּוֹרֶשׁ שֶׁהָיָה מִבְּנֵי יֶפֶת בַּיִת שֵׁנִי, לֹא שָׁרְתָה בּוֹ שְׁכִינָה; וְהֵיכָן שָׁרְתָה? בְּמִקְדָּשׁ רִאשׁוֹן שֶׁבָּנָה שְׁלֹמֹה שֶׁהָיָה מִבְּנֵי שֵׁם: וִיהִי כְנַעַן עֶבֶד. אַף מִשֶּׁיִּגְלוּ בְּנֵי שֵׁם יִמָּכְרוּ לָהֶם עֲבָדִים מִבְּנֵי כְנַעַן:

פרק י

ב | וְתִירָס. זוֹ פָּרַס:

BACKGROUND

(27:13): "Yavan, Tuval, and Meshekh, they were your traders." The name is mentioned in Assyrian documents dating from the ninth and eighth centuries BCE as a people living in central and southern Asia Minor. Tuval is identified by Herodotus as the Tibareni tribe, which dwelled along the coast of the Black Sea, and by the Sages as Beit Unaiki, the land of Bithynia, in northwest Asia Minor along the coast of the Black Sea (*Yoma* 10a).

Meshekh: Meshekh appears in Ezekiel (see 27:13; 32:26; 38:2) alongside Tuval, under the common rule of Magog. Assyrian documents refer to a people with a similar name who lived in Asia Minor and in the Caucasus Mountains east of the Black Sea in modern day Abkhazia.

Tiras: Some Sages identify Tiras as Persia, others as Beit Teraiki, which is Thrace, the eastern portion of the Balkan Peninsula, northeast of Greece (*Yoma* 10a). Ancient Egyptian documents dating back to the end of the thirteenth century BCE list Teresh among the sea peoples, the Philistines.

10:3| **Ashkenaz:** Ashkenaz is mentioned in Jeremiah (51:27) as one of the kingdoms of Ararat. The Sages (Jerusalem Talmud, *Megilla* 1:9) identify it with Asya, central Asia Minor. Some modern scholars say that Ashkenaz refers to the Scythians, a group of nomadic tribes that lived in the plains north of the Black and Caspian Seas.

Rifat: The name appears in I Chronicles (1:6) as Difat. The Sages identify Rifat with the kingdom of Adiabene on the east bank of the Tigris River, or with the Ural Mountains, which were formerly called the Riphean Mountains (*Bereshit Rabba* 37:1; Jerusalem Talmud, *Megilla* 1:9). According to the *Jerusalem Targum*, Rifat is Parkhon, or Parkhoi, southeast of the Caspian Sea. Josephus maintains that it is Paphlagonia in the north-central part of Asia Minor along the Black Sea Coast, east of Bithynia.

Togarma: Togarma is listed in Ezekiel (27:14) as a country in the far north that traded in horses. It is also mentioned in Assyrian documents as a major commercial city in central Asia Minor. Some identify it with the city of Gürün in Turkey; others say it is Barbaria in northern Africa (*Targum Yonatan*).

10:4| **Elisha:** In Ezekiel (27:7), Elisha is the name of a group of islands that traded with Tyre. The Midrash (*Bereshit Rabba* 37:4) identifies Elisha with Ellas. Many scholars suggest that this is Cyprus, while Josephus claims that this is referring to the Aeolian Islands, the Lipari Islands between Italy and Sicily. *Targum Yonatan* likewise translates it as Italia.

Tarshish: Tarshish has been identified with Tarsus in southeastern Asia Minor, or with Tartessos in the southwestern part of the Iberian Peninsula.

Kitim: The Kitim are mentioned in several places in the Bible (Isaiah 23:12; Ezekiel 27:6), as island dwellers linked to the Sidonians and Tyrians, or as Phoenicians, who engaged in maritime trade. According to the Jerusalem Talmud (*Megilla* 1:9) they are the Achaeans, residents of the northern part of the Peloponnesian Peninsula in Ancient Greece. The commentaries identify the Kitim with the residents of Rome. It has been suggested that they lived in the ancient port city of Kiton in Larnaca on the eastern coast of Cyprus, which according to the archaeological evidence was a city populated by Phoenicians (*Antiquities*: I:6:1)

Dodanim: The name appears in I Chronicles (1:7) as Rodanim. Phoenician documents from the eighth century BCE refer to Orakh king of Dananim and his city Adana in southern Cilicia in Asia Minor. The Septuagint identifies Dodanim with Rhodes.

10:6| **Put:** Put is described as a people of military men, experts in defense, who were allies of Egypt (Ezekiel 38:5; see Jeremiah 46:9; Nahum 3:9). Put has been identified with a tribe located in Libya or with the so-called land of Punt, south of Egypt, which is mentioned in ancient Egyptian documents.

10:7| **Seva:** The inhabitants of Seva are mentioned in Isaiah (45:14) as men of stature who engaged in commerce, and in Psalms (72:10) as merchants. Accordingly, they have been identified with the Nubians of Kush, a nation of strong individuals who lived in Meroe, north of Khartum, in modern-day Sudan.

8 Among his other children, **Kush begot Nimrod.** Since he was such an extraordinary figure, Nimrod is mentioned by himself, not in connection with any particular nation. **He began to be a mighty one on the earth.** Nimrod was a king who left his mark on the memory of future generations. Several rabbinic legends identify him with Amrafel and other characters.[35] However, the biblical text itself provides comparatively little detail about his life.

9 **He was a mighty hunter before the Lord;** Nimrod was considered a hero not only in his immediate surroundings, but also on a global scale.[36] **Therefore it is said** over the course of the generations, as a kind of popular folk saying: **Like Nimrod, a mighty hunter before the Lord.** When people speak of an outstanding hunter, a great hero, or a mighty king, they compare him to Nimrod.

10 **The beginning of his kingdom was Babel, Erekh,**[B] **Akad,**[B] **and Kalne,**[B] **in the land of Shinar.**[B] These are cities and regions in Mesopotamia.

11 **From that land** around Mesopotamia **Ashur emerged.** Ashur is mentioned below as one of the sons of Shem. This verse might mean that Ashur withdrew from the tyrannous domain of Nimrod, the mighty hunter who descended from Ham, and went to build and develop cities.[37] According to another explanation, it was Nimrod who went out to Ashur,[38] **and he built Nineveh,**[B] the largest city in the history of Ashur, **the city of Rehovot, Kalah,**[B]

12 **and Resen between Nineveh and Kalah; that is the great city.** Although one could infer otherwise from the verse, the great city is not Kalah but Nineveh, as indicated in other places.[39] These cities were built by the Assyrians. Apparently Ashur went out toward the east, in the direction of the Tigris River, to the region of the future Assyrian empire.

13 **Mitzrayim begot Ludim,**[B] **Anamim,**[B] **Lehavim,**[B] **Naftuhim,**[B]

14 **Patrusim,**[B] whose connection to Egypt can also be inferred from the Prophets,[40] **and Kasluhim,**[B] **from which the Philistines emerged, and Kaftorim.** Although the Philistines settled in Canaan, they were actually a foreign nation that arrived from overseas. They were part of the group of nations that scholars refer to as the Sea Peoples. Apparently, they came from the area of the Aegean Sea to the coast of the Mediterranean Sea, as far as Egypt. Kaftor is probably the island of Crete, which the ancient Egyptians called Keftiu.

15 **Canaan begot Sidon his firstborn, and Het,**[B] who fathered one of the tribes living in the Land of Canaan when the people of Israel arrived there;

16 **and the Yevusite,**[B] **the Emorite,**[B] **the Girgashite,**[B] also Canaanite tribes,

BACKGROUND

Havila: Havila appears as the name of a region rich in gold, surrounded by the Pishon River (2:11); as one of the descendants of Shem (verse 29); and as the home of the children of Yishmael (25:18). The Havila located in today's Sudan, home of the descendants of Ham, is not the same Havila that lies in the desert east of Egypt, where the children of Yishmael lived. Some scholars argue that Havila is not a place name at all; rather, it comes from the root *ḥet-vav-lamed*, meaning sand, and is a general term for deserts.

Savta, Savtekha: Some say that these are peoples and tribes that lived south of the Sudan. Savta refers to the Semburai, while Savtekha is the Lezingai, who might be members of the Zande tribe (*Targum Yonatan*). Josephus identifies them with the Estabri, who lived along the Black Nile in Sudan. Alternatively, these are Scythian tribes, nomadic Asiatic peoples located north of the Caspian and Black Seas (*Yoma* 10a).

Raama: Raama is also mentioned in Ezekiel 27:22 together with Sheva as a city of merchants. It has been identified with Regmah, a major city located on the trade route between Sheva and Dodan, which appears in ancient South Arabian inscriptions as well. Alternative suggestions include Libya and Moritinos, which is a place of unknown identification (*Targum Yonatan*).

Sheva: This name appears several times in the Bible, as one of the descendants of Shem (verse 28); a descendant of Abraham and Ketura (25:3); and the name of a kingdom in the southwestern part of the Arabian Peninsula, which was the source of trade in gold, precious stones, and spices (I Kings 10:1; Jeremiah 6:20; Ezekiel 27:22; Psalms 72:15). Elsewhere the Shevans are described as a nomadic people that raided permanent settlements, traded in slaves, and dwelled in the Syrian Arabian desert (Joel 4:8; Job 6:19). It is likely that Sheva, from the descendants of Kush, dwelled in eastern Africa near the Red Sea, Ethiopia, since two locations in that region bear names similar to "Sheba."

10:10| **Erekh:** This is identified with the archaeological site Tel Uruk in southern Babylonia. It is considered one of the largest and oldest cities ever discovered. In Babylonian documents, Uruk is listed as the first city built after the flood.

Akad: This is the name of a region in northern Mesopotamia, as well as a royal city which is presumed to have been located some 50 km southwest of Baghdad. In the Talmud (*Yoma* 10a), Rav Yosef identifies this as the settlement Baskar, located close to what is now the city of Kut, on the Tigris River, about 110 km east of the site of ancient Babylon.

Kalne: This is a city in northern Syria, apparently Nippur, whose remains are located about 90 km south of the city of Babylon (see *Yoma* 10a). The name also appears in Amos (6:2) and with a slight variation in Isaiah 10:9.

The land of Shinar: This is an ancient name for the region of the Babylonian Empire, found also in Egyptian and Hitite documents. Some have identified it with the Sinjar Valley in northern Babylonia, about 100 km west of Nineveh. It is also mentioned as the valley which mankind settled after the flood (11:2), as well as the seat of King Amrafel (14:1), whom the Sages identify with Nimrod (*Eiruvin* 53a).

10:11| **Nineveh:** This is the Assyrian capital, located on the Tigris River, and called "the

ח וַחֲוִילָה וְסַבְתָּה וְרַעְמָה וְסַבְתְּכָא וּבְנֵי רַעְמָה שְׁבָא וּדְדָן: וְכוּשׁ יָלַד אֶת־
ט נִמְרֹד הוּא הֵחֵל לִהְיוֹת גִּבֹּר בָּאָרֶץ: הוּא־הָיָה גִבֹּר־צַיִד לִפְנֵי יְהוָה עַל־כֵּן
י יֵאָמַר כְּנִמְרֹד גִּבּוֹר צַיִד לִפְנֵי יְהוָה: וַתְּהִי רֵאשִׁית מַמְלַכְתּוֹ בָּבֶל וְאֶרֶךְ וְאַכַּד
יא וְכַלְנֵה בְּאֶרֶץ שִׁנְעָר: מִן־הָאָרֶץ הַהִוא יָצָא אַשּׁוּר וַיִּבֶן אֶת־נִינְוֵה וְאֶת־רְחֹבֹת
יב יג עִיר וְאֶת־כָּלַח: וְאֶת־רֶסֶן בֵּין נִינְוֵה וּבֵין כָּלַח הִוא הָעִיר הַגְּדֹלָה: וּמִצְרַיִם
יד יָלַד אֶת־לוּדִים וְאֶת־עֲנָמִים וְאֶת־לְהָבִים וְאֶת־נַפְתֻּחִים: וְאֶת־פַּתְרֻסִים
טו וְאֶת־כַּסְלֻחִים אֲשֶׁר יָצְאוּ מִשָּׁם פְּלִשְׁתִּים וְאֶת־כַּפְתֹּרִים: וּכְנַעַן
טז יָלַד אֶת־צִידֹן בְּכֹרוֹ וְאֶת־חֵת: וְאֶת־הַיְבוּסִי וְאֶת־הָאֱמֹרִי וְאֵת הַגִּרְגָּשִׁי:

רש״י

ח| **לִהְיוֹת גִּבֹּר.** לְהַמְרִיד כָּל הָעוֹלָם עַל הַקָּדוֹשׁ בָּרוּךְ הוּא בַּעֲצַת דּוֹר הַפַּלָּגָה:

ט| **גִּבֹּר צַיִד.** צָד דַּעְתָּן שֶׁל בְּרִיּוֹת בְּפִיו וּמַטְעָן לִמְרֹד בַּמָּקוֹם: **לִפְנֵי ה׳.** מִתְכַּוֵּן לְהַקְנִיטוֹ עַל פָּנָיו: **עַל כֵּן יֵאָמַר.** עַל כָּל אָדָם מַרְשִׁיעַ בְּעַזּוּת פָּנִים, יוֹדֵעַ רִבּוֹנוֹ וּמִתְכַּוֵּן לִמְרֹד בּוֹ, יֵאָמֵר: זֶה כְּנִמְרֹד גִּבּוֹר צַיִד:

יא| **מִן הָאָרֶץ.** כֵּיוָן שֶׁרָאָה אַשּׁוּר אֶת בָּנָיו שׁוֹמְעִין לְנִמְרוֹד וּמוֹרְדִין בַּמָּקוֹם לִבְנוֹת הַמִּגְדָּל, יָצָא מִתּוֹכָם:

יב| **הָעִיר הַגְּדֹלָה.** הִיא נִינְוֵה, שֶׁנֶּאֱמַר: "וְנִינְוֵה הָיְתָה עִיר גְּדוֹלָה לֵאלֹהִים" (יונה ג, ג):

יג| **לְהָבִים.** שֶׁפְּנֵיהֶם דּוֹמִים לְלַהַב:

יד| **וְאֶת פַּתְרֻסִים וְאֶת כַּסְלֻחִים אֲשֶׁר יָצְאוּ מִשָּׁם פְּלִשְׁתִּים.** מִשְּׁנֵיהֶם יָצְאוּ, שֶׁהָיוּ פַּתְרוּסִים וְכַסְלוּחִים מַחֲלִיפִין מִשְׁכַּב נְשׁוֹתֵיהֶם אֵלּוּ לָאֵלּוּ, וְיָצְאוּ מֵהֶם פְּלִשְׁתִּים:

BACKGROUND

great city (see verse 12 and Jonah 1:2). Its walls stretched for 12 km, and it comprised an area of 7.5 sq km.

Kalah: Kalah is identified with Tel Nimrod, located about 30 km south of the site of ancient Nineveh. According to Assyrian documents, Kalah was an important administrative and military center, and even served as the Assyrian capital during the ninth to seventh centuries BCE.

10:13| **Ludim:** Ludim is elsewhere mentioned together with the nations of Kush and Put, who lived close to Egypt (Isaiah 66:19; Ezekiel 27:10, 30:5). The Ludim are also depicted as mercenary soldiers in the service of the Tyrians, the Sidonians, and the Egyptians.

Anamim: This is a nation that lived in the region of Alexandria, Lower Egypt (see *Targum Yonatan* and Rav Se'adya Gaon).

Lehavim: This name has no parallels in the Bible or in external documents. Some have identified Lehavim with the Libyans, who lived to the west of Egypt (Septuagint; Josephus).

Naftuhim: This name has no parallels in the Bible either, or in external documents. The Septuagint and *Targum Yonatan* identify the Naftuhim with the residents of the northeastern part of the Nile delta.

10:14| **Patrusim:** Patros in Egyptian means the southern country, Upper Egypt. The verse "I will restore the returnees of Egypt, and I will return them to the land of Patros, to the land of their origins" (Ezekiel 29:14) indicates that Patros is the original land of the Egyptians. According to the *Jerusalem Targum*, they are the Plosai, who lived in the northeastern part of the Nile delta.

Kasluhim: No parallel to this name is found in the Bible or in external documents. *Targum Yonatan* calls them Penatsakhnaei, residents of the region of Cyrenaica in Libya.

10:15| **Het:** In the Torah, the children of Het lived in Hebron (see chap. 23) and in the mountains (Numbers 13:29). The book of Samuel (I Samuel 26:6; II Samuel 11:3) refers to Ahimelekh and Uriya the Hitites, who served in King David's army. According to the book of Kings (I Kings 10:29; II Kings 7:6) and external documents, the Hitite Empire was located in Asia Minor and northern Syria, and it was destroyed toward the end of the second millennium BCE. The Hitites in the Bible were descendants of emigrants from the Hitite Empire, or they were a local people of the same name.

10:16| **Yevusite:** The Yevusites are mentioned in Numbers (13:29) as a nation that dwelled in the mountains. In the Prophets (Joshua 15:63; Judges 1:21; II Samuel 24:16) they lived in Jerusalem, and the city is called Yevus after them (Judges 19:10). Some argue that the Yevusites descended from the Hitites (see Ezekiel 16:3).

Emorite: Emorite is the name of a nation, as well as a group of nations in Canaan (Joshua 10:5; Judges 1:34), and the name of a region on the east bank of the Jordan (Numbers 21:26; Joshua 24:8). According to Egyptian documents, the Emorites also lived on Mount Lebanon, and their name appears in Sumerian inscriptions in reference to the area west of the Euphrates.

17 and **the Hivite,**[B] **the Arkite, the Sinite,**
18 **the Arvadite,**[B] **the Tzemarite,**[B] **and the Hamatite,**[B] six Phoenician-Syrian city-states. **And then the families of the Canaanite dispersed.**

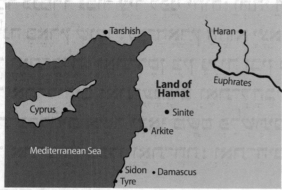

Land of Hamat

19 **The border of the Canaanite was from Sidon** in the north, **as you come** on the way leading **toward Gerar**[B] in the south, **until Gaza; as you come toward Sodom and Gomorrah and Adma and Tzevoyim,**[B] **until Lasha.**[B] The descendants of Ham populated a considerable part of the world in several different regions.
20 **These are the sons of Ham, after their families, after their tongues, in their lands, in their nations.**
21 **And to Shem, father of all the children of Ever, brother of Yefet, the eldest, children were also born.** The verse is

ambiguous, as it is unclear whether Shem is the older brother of Yefet, or vice versa.[41] Contrary to the usual order in which the sons of Noah are presented: Shem, Ham, and Yefet, here the order is Yefet, Ham, and Shem. The reason is possibly because the book of Genesis and the rest of the Torah will focus on the descendants of Shem. Therefore, although Shem might not have been the youngest of Noah's children, his family is presented last in order to connect it to the continuation of the story.[42]

22 **The sons of Shem** were **Elam;**[B] **Ashur;**[B] **Arpakhshad,**[B] whom some consider the father of the Chaldeans, the Babylonians; and **Lud.** This name is related to Lydia, a region in Asia Minor, not the Ludim, mentioned above among the children of Mitzrayim. **And** the last son of Shem is **Aram.**[B]
23 **The sons of Aram** were **Utz,**[B] who appears in the book of Job and elsewhere,[43] **Hul, Geter, and Mash.**
24 **And Arpakhshad begot Shela; and Shela begot Ever.** This is the family line most significant for the continuation of the story from the children of Shem.
25 **And to Ever were born two sons; the name of the one was Peleg, as in his days the earth was divided** [*niflega*], as will be explained at length in the next section; **and the name of his brother was Yoktan.**
26 **Yoktan begot Almodad, Shelef, Hatzarmavet,**[B] **Yerah,**
27 **Hadoram, Uzal, Dikla,**
28 **Oval, Avimael, Sheva,** also mentioned in other places in the Bible,[44]
29 **Ofir, Havila, and Yovav; all these were sons of Yoktan.**
30 **Their dwelling was from Mesha, as you come toward Sefar, the mountain of the east.** These tribes settled in the southern part of the Arabian Peninsula.

BACKGROUND

Girgashite: According to the Sages (Jerusalem Talmud, *Shevi'it* 6:1; *Vayikra Rabba* 17:6), upon the Israelites' entry into Canaan, the Girgashite people left the country for Africa. The Septuagint (Deuteronomy 3:14; Joshua 13:11) identifies the Girgashites with the Geshurites, whom Joshua did not conquer, and who lived east of the Sea of Galilee, apparently in Gargerashah. Some argue that they originated in the city of Karkashta, in western Asia Minor (see *Midrash Shir HaShirim* 1:4).

10:17| **Hivite:** This name includes several groups of people that lived in different places: in Shekhem (34:2); in the north of Jerusalem, as the Givonites (Joshua 9:7); and in the region of the Hermon and the Lebanon (Joshua 11:3; Judges 3:3). This name is not found in external sources.

10:18| **Arvadite:** Arvad is mentioned in Ezekiel (27:8, 11) as a city of sailors and soldiers. It has been identified with Arwad, a port island 3 km from the city of Tartus in Syria. This important port city is mentioned in Egyptian and Assyrian documents as a center of trade with Egypt.

Tzemarite: Tzemar, which was south of Arvad, is also mentioned in Egyptian and Assyrian documents.

Hamatite: Hamat, or Hama, was one of the most important kingdoms in central Syria, located along the Orontes River.

10:19| **Gerar:** This was the name of a city and a region in the eastern Negev. The city of Gerar was located on the northern bank of Wadi Gerar, and has been identified with Tel Gamma near

Kibbutz Re'im, or with Tel Harur, south of Melilot in the northern Negev.

Sodom, Gomorrah, Adma, Tzevoyim: These cities were located in the plain of the Jordan (13:10; 19:28), in the region of the Dead Sea. They could be seen from the mountains of Benjamin and Hebron (13:10; 19:28). The archaeological surveys suggest that they were located in the southern basin of the Dead Sea.

Lasha: The Sages identify Lasha with Callirrhoe, approximately 2.5 km south of the spot where Wadi Zarqa meets the eastern shore of the Dead Sea (see Onkelos; *Targum Yonatan*; Jerusalem Talmud, *Megilla* 1:9). Modern research identifies it with Tzo'ar, south of the Dead Sea.

יז יח ואת־החוי ואת־הערקי ואת־הסיני: ואת־הארודי ואת־הצמרי ואת־החמתי
יט ואחר נפצו משפחות הכנעני: ויהי גבול הכנעני מצידן באכה גררה עד־עזה
כ באכה סדמה ועמרה ואדמה וצבים עד־לשע: אלה בני־חם למשפחתם
כא ללשנתם בארצתם בגויהם: ולשם ילד גם־הוא אבי כל־בני־
כב כג עבר אחי יפת הגדול: בני שם עילם ואשור וארפכשד ולוד וארם: ובני ארם
כד כה עוץ וחול וגתר ומש: וארפכשד ילד את־שלח ושלח ילד את־עבר: ולעבר
כו ילד שני בנים שם האחד פלג כי בימיו נפלגה הארץ ושם אחיו יקטן: ויקטן
כז ילד את־אלמודד ואת־שלף ואת־חצרמות ואת־ירח: ואת־הדורם ואת־אוזל
כח כט ואת־דקלה: ואת־עובל ואת־אבימאל ואת־שבא: ואת־אופר ואת־חוילה
ל ואת־יובב כל־אלה בני יקטן: ויהי מושבם ממשא באכה ספרה הר הקדם:

רש"י

יח| **ואחר נפצו.** מאלה נפוצו משפחות הרבה:

יט| **גבול הכנעני.** גבול סוף ארצו. כל 'גבול' לשון סוף וקצה: **באכה.** שם דבר. ולי נראה, כאדם האומר לחברו: גבול זה מגיע עד אשר תבא למקום פלוני:

כ| **ללשנתם בארצתם.** אף על פי שנחלקו ללשונות וארצות, כלם בני חם הם:

כא| **אבי כל בני עבר.** הנהר, היה שם: **אחי יפת הגדול.** איני יודע אם יפת הגדול אם שם. כשהוא אומר: "שם בן מאת שנה וגו' שנתים אחר המבול" (להלן יא, י), הוי אומר יפת הגדול, שהרי בן חמש מאות שנה היה נח כשהתחיל להוליד, והמבול היה בשנת שש מאות שנה, נמצא שהגדול בבניו היה בן מאה שנה, ושם לא הגיע למאה עד שנתים אחר המבול: **אחי יפת.** ולא אחי חם, שאלו שניהם כבדו את אביהם וזה בזהו:

כה| **נפלגה.** נתבלבלו הלשונות ונפוצו מן הבקעה ונתפלגו בכל העולם. למדנו שהיה עבר נביא, שקרא שם בנו על שם העתיד. ושנינו בסדר עולם שבסוף ימיו נתפלגו, שאם תאמר בתחלת ימיו, הרי יקטן אחיו צעיר ממנו והוליד כמה משפחות קודם לכן, שנאמר: "ויקטן ילד" וגו' (להלן פסוק כו) ואחר כך: "ויהי כל הארץ שפה אחת" (להלן יא, א). ואם תאמר באמצע ימיו, לא בא הכתוב לסתום אלא לפרש; הא למדת שבשנת מות פלג נתפלגו: **יקטן.** שהיה ענו ומקטין עצמו, לכך זכה להעמיד כל המשפחות הללו:

כו| **חצרמות.** על שם מקומו, דברי אגדה:

BACKGROUND

10:22| **Elam:** This nation was located northeast of the Persian Gulf, in southwestern Iran. Its capital was Shushan (Daniel 8:2). Elam was a significant player in Mesopotamia, and it fought repeatedly with Babylonia and Assyria. From the end of the eighth century BCE, it weakened, disintegrated, and eventually became part of the Persian Empire.

Ashur: This was the name of a city and a kingdom. The city was located between the Great Zab River and the Little Zab River, on the west bank of the Tigris. The Assyrian kingdom stretched across the northwestern part of Mesopotamia between the kingdoms of Ararat in the north, Babylonia in the south, Aram Naharayim in the west, and Madai in the east.

Arpakhshad: Arpakhshad founded Ur Kasdim (*Antiquities* 1:6:4; Naftali Tur Sinai), which was a city and kingdom in southern Mesopotamia. The name is an amalgamation of Ur, p, and Kasd. The letter p in Egyptian serves as a definite article.

Aram: This was a nation that dwelled between Canaan and the Euphrates. It was split into several kingdoms: Aram Damesek, Aram Tzova, Aram Beit Rehov, and Aram Naharayim. Its origins are Kir in eastern Babylonia (Amos 1:5).

10:23| **Utz:** This was one of the lands of the east (Job 1:1, 3). The mention of this name among the children of Se'ir (36:28) and in a verse in Lamentations (4:21): "Be glad and rejoice, daughter of Edom, who resides in the land of Utz," indicates that it was located near Edom. The ancient historians placed it in the Bashan region near Aram (see Josephus).

10:26| **Hatzarmavet:** Hatzarmavet is the only place on this list that is known by that same name today, Hadhramaut in English. It is located in southern Yemen on the coast of the Indian Ocean. Even among the Arabs, the ancient tribes that live there are considered to be of noble lineage with a well-developed language and culture.

31 **These are the sons of Shem,** as they gradually spread: **After their families,** clans and tribes; **after their tongues,** as each family developed a language of its own; **in their lands,** since afterward they spread out over a geographical expanse; and **after their nations,** for each became a nation in its own right.

32 **These are the families of the sons of Noah, in their legacy, in their nations; and from these the nations were dispersed on the earth after the flood,** over the course of the generations.

The Generation of the Dispersion

GENESIS 11:1–9

By this time most of the world was filled with plants and animals, but remained empty of humans. Since people could settle wherever they pleased, there was no need for wars. There was still no conceptual distance or sense of alienation between cultures, and unfettered collaboration led to swift technological progress. God responded to this effort by dispersing mankind all over the earth.

11 1 **The entire earth was of one language and of common words,** similar discourse. People could talk to each other about any topic, as they knew each other and came from comparable backgrounds. They were all descendants of Noah. There were still no major linguistic or cultural differences that could create divisions among the peoples. All of the world's inhabitants constituted a single unit.

Seventh aliya

2 **It was as they traveled from** some place in **the east.** This is not referring to all humanity, but to a certain large group of people. **And they found a plain.** Unlike in modern Hebrew, the word *bik'a* does not mean a valley, but a plain, a low, level expanse of land.[45] The plain was **in the land of Shinar,** which lies between the rivers of Babylonia, and is indeed a flat expanse suitable for the events described below; **and they settled there.**

3 **Each man said to his counterpart: Come, let us make bricks and burn them thoroughly.** In the land of Shinar there were not many stones, but there was an abundant supply of clay. Consequently, already in ancient times clay was used for building houses. **The brick was for them as stone.** The bricks fashioned from blocks of clay were molded into a fixed shape and burned in fire, and thereby turned into a building material that served the same function as stone. **And the clay was for them as mortar** for sticking the bricks together, and for covering the inner face of the walls. Since they had large amounts of the material, they could build many buildings solely out of such bricks, as was common in most areas of Europe for many years. However, they were not satisfied with the abundance of clay.

4 **They said: Come, let us build a city for ourselves, and a tower with** the tower's **top in the heavens, and let us make a name for ourselves, lest we be dispersed abroad upon the face of the entire earth.** The tower will be visible from vast distances, and it will serve as our center, so that we will not become scattered throughout the world. We can travel far from the city provided that we can still see the tower and know how to return to it. This will ensure that we will not lose contact with each other.

5 **The Lord came down to see the city,** in whose construction all the people were partners, **and the tower that the children of man built,** not for a practical or technical purpose.

6 **The Lord said: Behold, they are one people, and there is one language for them all.** They are united like a nation, a single unit with a shared idea; **and this is what they have begun to do.** The unity of the people and language has urged on their ambitions. **Now nothing of all that they plotted to do will be prevented from them.** It is now in their power to do everything. Since the inclination of the heart of man is evil, in such a state of unity, evil is liable to develop in this society without constraints.

7 Therefore, **come, let us descend and muddle their language there, so that one will not understand the language of his counterpart,** and we will thereby disrupt their unity.

8 **The Lord dispersed them from there upon the face of the entire earth, and they ceased to build the city.** Their languages became confused, and new forms of expression were created. As a result, people could no longer live together, and therefore they became dispersed throughout the world.

9 **Therefore, its name,** the city's name, **was called Babel, because the Lord confounded [*balal*] the language of all the earth there;**[D] **and from there the Lord dispersed them on the face of the entire earth.** Mankind developed and settled the entire world.

DISCUSSION

11:9| **Because the Lord confounded [*balal*] the language of all the earth there:** The commentaries ask: What was the sin of the people who built the city and the tower? Some maintain that the phrase "with its top in the heavens" alludes to their intention to reach the heavens, but the text does not explain what they wanted to do there. On the contrary, it offers a rather different explanation: "And let us make a name for ourselves, lest we be dispersed abroad upon the face of the entire earth," which means that they wished to create a center that would prevent their dispersion. The people wanted to remain a single society living in a defined locale. To this end they built a huge city, a kind of a megalopolis, with a tower in it that symbolized their unity and their aspirations to stay together as a single group.

לא לב אֵלֶּה בְנֵי־שֵׁם לְמִשְׁפְּחֹתָם לִלְשֹׁנֹתָם בְּאַרְצֹתָם לְגוֹיֵהֶם: אֵלֶּה מִשְׁפְּחֹת בְּנֵי־נֹחַ
לְתוֹלְדֹתָם בְּגוֹיֵהֶם וּמֵאֵלֶּה נִפְרְדוּ הַגּוֹיִם בָּאָרֶץ אַחַר הַמַּבּוּל:

יא א ב וַיְהִי כָל־הָאָרֶץ שָׂפָה אֶחָת וּדְבָרִים אֲחָדִים: וַיְהִי בְּנָסְעָם מִקֶּדֶם וַיִּמְצְאוּ בִקְעָה ט שביעי
ג בְּאֶרֶץ שִׁנְעָר וַיֵּשְׁבוּ שָׁם: וַיֹּאמְרוּ אִישׁ אֶל־רֵעֵהוּ הָבָה נִלְבְּנָה לְבֵנִים וְנִשְׂרְפָה
ד לִשְׂרֵפָה וַתְּהִי לָהֶם הַלְּבֵנָה לְאָבֶן וְהַחֵמָר הָיָה לָהֶם לַחֹמֶר: וַיֹּאמְרוּ הָבָה נִבְנֶה־
לָּנוּ עִיר וּמִגְדָּל וְרֹאשׁוֹ בַשָּׁמַיִם וְנַעֲשֶׂה־לָּנוּ שֵׁם פֶּן־נָפוּץ עַל־פְּנֵי כָל־הָאָרֶץ:
ה ו וַיֵּרֶד יְהוָה לִרְאֹת אֶת־הָעִיר וְאֶת־הַמִּגְדָּל אֲשֶׁר בָּנוּ בְּנֵי הָאָדָם: וַיֹּאמֶר יְהוָה
הֵן עַם אֶחָד וְשָׂפָה אַחַת לְכֻלָּם וְזֶה הַחִלָּם לַעֲשׂוֹת וְעַתָּה לֹא־יִבָּצֵר מֵהֶם כֹּל
ז אֲשֶׁר יָזְמוּ לַעֲשׂוֹת: הָבָה נֵרְדָה וְנָבְלָה שָׁם שְׂפָתָם אֲשֶׁר לֹא יִשְׁמְעוּ אִישׁ שְׂפַת
ח ט רֵעֵהוּ: וַיָּפֶץ יְהוָה אֹתָם מִשָּׁם עַל־פְּנֵי כָל־הָאָרֶץ וַיַּחְדְּלוּ לִבְנֹת הָעִיר: עַל־כֵּן
קָרָא שְׁמָהּ בָּבֶל כִּי־שָׁם בָּלַל יְהוָה שְׂפַת כָּל־הָאָרֶץ וּמִשָּׁם הֱפִיצָם יְהוָה עַל־
פְּנֵי כָּל־הָאָרֶץ:

רש"י

פרק יא

א| שפה אחת. לשון הקדש: ודברים אחדים. באו בעצה אחת ואמרו: לא כל הימנו שיבור לו את העליונים, נעלה לרקיע ונעשה עמו מלחמה. דבר אחר, על יחידו של עולם. דבר אחר, "ודברים אחדים", אמרו: אחת לאלף ותרנ"ו שנים הרקיע מתמוטט כשם שעשה בימי המבול, באו ונעשה לו סמוכות. בראשית רבה (לח, ו):

ב| בנסעם מקדם. שהיו יושבים שם, כדכתיב למעלה: "ויהי מושבם וגו' הר הקדם" (לעיל י, ל), ונסעו משם לתור להם מקום להחזיק את כלם, ולא מצאו אלא שנער:

ג| איש אל רעהו. אמה לאמה, מצרים לכוש וכוש לפוט ופוט לכנען: הבה. הזמינו עצמכם. כל 'הבה' לשון הזמנה הוא, שמכינים עצמן ומתחברים למלאכה או לעצה או למשא. הבה – הזמינו, אפריילי"ר בלעז: לבנים. שאין אבנים בבבל, שהיא בקעה: ונשרפה לשרפה. כך עושין הלבנים שקורים טיוול"ש, שורפים אותן בכבשן: לחמר. לטוח הקיר:

ד| פן נפוץ. שלא יביא עלינו שום מכה להפיצנו מכאן:

ה| וירד ה' לראות. לא הוצרך לכך, אלא ללמד לדיינים שלא ירשיעו הנדון עד שיראו ויבינו. מדרש רבי תנחומא (יח): בני האדם. אלא בני מי? שמא בני חמורים וגמלים?! אלא בני אדם הראשון שכפה את הטובה ואמר: "האשה אשר נתתה עמדי" (לעיל ג, יב), אף אלו כפו בטובה למרוד במי שהשפיעם טובה ומלטם מן המבול:

ו| הן עם אחד. כל טובה זו יש עמהם, שעם אחד הם ושפה אחת לכלם, ודבר זה החלו לעשות: החלם. כמו 'אמרם' 'עשותם', להתחיל הם לעשות: לא יבצר. בתמיה. "יבצר" לשון מניעה כתרגומו, ודומה לו: "יבצר רוח נגידים" (תהלים עו, יג):

ז| הבה נרדה. בבית דינו נמלך מענותנותו יתרה: הבה. מדה כנגד מדה, הם אמרו: "הבה נבנה", והוא כנגדם מדד ואמר: "הבה נרדה": ונבלה. ונבלבל, נו"ן משמש בלשון רבים, והה"א אחרונה יתרה כה"א של 'נרדה': לא ישמעו. זה שואל לבנה וזה מביא טיט, וזה עומד עליו ופוצע את מוחו:

ח| ויפץ ה' אותם משם. בעולם הזה. מה שאמרו "פן נפוץ" (לעיל פסוק ד) נתקיים עליהם, הוא שאמר שלמה: "מגורת רשע היא תבואנו" (משלי י, כד):

ט| ומשם הפיצם. למד שאין להם חלק לעולם הבא. וכי אי זו קשה, של דור המבול או של דור הפלגה? אלו לא פשטו יד בעקר ואלו פשטו יד בעקר להלחם בו, ואלו

DISCUSSION

This generation expressed the very human desire to gather in large urban centers that hold all their power, control, and technology. Their unity enabled them to build these huge centers. Such centers, however, are designed for preservation rather than progress The world they tried to build is a frightening one. Indeed, it brings to mind the world we live in today, a world that is becoming increasingly uniform, in which many languages are succumbing to one dominant language, where one type of dialogue and one set of aspirations rule. Such a powerful society

The Family Line of Shem

GENESIS 11:10–32

This section provides a brief historical account covering many generations, which leads to the heroes of the biblical story.

10 **This is the legacy of Shem. Shem was one hundred years old, and he begot Arpakhshad, two years after the flood.**[D]

11 **Shem lived after he begot Arpakhshad five hundred years; and he begot sons and daughters.**

12 **Arpakhshad lived thirty-five years, and he begot Shela.**

13 **Arpakhshad lived after he begot Shela four hundred and three years; and he begot sons and daughters.**

14 **Shela lived thirty years, and he begot Ever.**

15 **Shela lived after he begot Ever four hundred and three years; and he begot sons and daughters.**

16 **Ever lived thirty-four years, and he begot Peleg.**

17 **Ever lived after he begot Peleg four hundred and thirty years; and he begot sons and daughters.**

18 **Peleg lived thirty years, and he begot Re'u.**

19 **Peleg lived after he begot Re'u two hundred and nine years; and he begot sons and daughters.**

20 **Re'u lived thirty-two years, and he begot Serug.**

21 **Re'u lived after he begot Peleg two hundred and seven years; and he begot sons and daughters.**

22 **Serug lived thirty years, and he begot Nahor.**

23 **Serug lived after he begot Nahor two hundred years; and he begot sons and daughters.**

24 **Nahor lived twenty-nine years, and he begot Terah.**

25 **Nahor lived after he begot Terah one hundred and nineteen years; and he begot sons and daughters.**

26 **Terah lived seventy years, and** during those years **he begot Abram, Nahor, and Haran.**

27 **This is the legacy of Terah: Terah begot Abram, Nahor, and Haran; and Haran,** who was likely the youngest son, **begot Lot.** These characters will be important for the continuation of the story.

28 **Haran died during the lifetime of Terah his father.** It was apparently uncommon for a son to pass away during his father's lifetime.[46] He passed away **in the land of his birth, in Ur of the Chaldeans.**

29 *Maftir* **Abram and Nahor took wives for themselves; the name of Abram's wife was Sarai; and the name of Nahor's wife was Milka, daughter of** his brother **Haran,** who was the **father of Milka and the father of Yiska.**[D]

30 **Sarai was barren.** In contrast to Nahor, who together with Milka gave rise to an entire dynasty, as will be described below (22:20–24), **she,** Sarai, **had no child.**

DISCUSSION

does not allow anything different to develop within it, and therefore individuals cannot free themselves from its chains. In a homogeneous technological society, nothing new will grow. Only when its frameworks are broken will a few individuals be able to venture out, act, and influence others. By forming a uniform pattern of life and society, these people were acting against God's intention that there should be a rich, multifaceted world in which the differences between people lead to progress and blessing. God wanted the entire world to be settled and for people to construct productive societies. Therefore, He dispersed mankind across the entire earth. For this reason, this generation is called the Generation of the Dispersion (see *Geon HaGe'onim* 20:34, Rav Se'adya Gaon; Rashi, verse 1; Rashbam and Ibn Ezra, verse 4).

11:10| **Shem was one hundred years old, and he begot Arpakhshad, two years after the flood:** The genealogical tables indicate that after the flood people began to die at a younger age. Life expectancy prior to the flood approached one thousand years, whereas now, although people are still living many years, their lives are less than half that length. Apparently the entire world has changed; in the antediluvian world there was a certain perfection of form, whereas the post-flood world sees the appearance of diseases and other factors that shorten people's lives.

11:29| **Yiska:** Milka is identified here, but it is unclear who Yiska was, as this name does not appear anywhere else in the Bible. According to the Sages, Yiska is another name for Sarai, who is mentioned here (*Megilla* 14a; *Sanhedrin* 69a). In those days people would adopt names associated with a rise to power or the selection of a certain path in life. If so, it is possible that Yiska was her original name, but Abram later called her Sarai, meaning "mistress" or "ruler" (see also commentary on 17:15).

י אֵלֶּה תּוֹלְדֹת שֵׁם שֵׁם בֶּן־מְאַת שָׁנָה וַיּוֹלֶד אֶת־אַרְפַּכְשָׁד שְׁנָתַיִם אַחַר

יא הַמַּבּוּל׃ וַיְחִי־שֵׁם אַחֲרֵי הוֹלִידוֹ אֶת־אַרְפַּכְשָׁד חֲמֵשׁ מֵאוֹת שָׁנָה וַיּוֹלֶד בָּנִים

יב יג וּבָנוֹת׃ וְאַרְפַּכְשַׁד חַי חָמֵשׁ וּשְׁלֹשִׁים שָׁנָה וַיּוֹלֶד אֶת־שָׁלַח׃ וַיְחִי

אַרְפַּכְשַׁד אַחֲרֵי הוֹלִידוֹ אֶת־שֶׁלַח שָׁלֹשׁ שָׁנִים וְאַרְבַּע מֵאוֹת שָׁנָה וַיּוֹלֶד

יד טו בָּנִים וּבָנוֹת׃ וְשֶׁלַח חַי שְׁלֹשִׁים שָׁנָה וַיּוֹלֶד אֶת־עֵבֶר׃ וַיְחִי־שֶׁלַח

אַחֲרֵי הוֹלִידוֹ אֶת־עֵבֶר שָׁלֹשׁ שָׁנִים וְאַרְבַּע מֵאוֹת שָׁנָה וַיּוֹלֶד בָּנִים וּבָנוֹת׃

טז יז וַיְחִי־עֵבֶר אַרְבַּע וּשְׁלֹשִׁים שָׁנָה וַיּוֹלֶד אֶת־פָּלֶג׃ וַיְחִי־עֵבֶר אַחֲרֵי הוֹלִידוֹ אֶת־

יח פֶּלֶג שְׁלֹשִׁים שָׁנָה וְאַרְבַּע מֵאוֹת שָׁנָה וַיּוֹלֶד בָּנִים וּבָנוֹת׃ וַיְחִי־פֶלֶג

יט שְׁלֹשִׁים שָׁנָה וַיּוֹלֶד אֶת־רְעוּ׃ וַיְחִי־פֶלֶג אַחֲרֵי הוֹלִידוֹ אֶת־רְעוּ תֵּשַׁע שָׁנִים

כ וּמָאתַיִם שָׁנָה וַיּוֹלֶד בָּנִים וּבָנוֹת׃ וַיְחִי רְעוּ שְׁתַּיִם וּשְׁלֹשִׁים שָׁנָה וַיּוֹלֶד

כא אֶת־שְׂרוּג׃ וַיְחִי רְעוּ אַחֲרֵי הוֹלִידוֹ אֶת־שְׂרוּג שֶׁבַע שָׁנִים וּמָאתַיִם שָׁנָה וַיּוֹלֶד בָּנִים

כב כג וּבָנוֹת׃ וַיְחִי שְׂרוּג שְׁלֹשִׁים שָׁנָה וַיּוֹלֶד אֶת־נָחוֹר׃ וַיְחִי שְׂרוּג אַחֲרֵי

כד הוֹלִידוֹ אֶת־נָחוֹר מָאתַיִם שָׁנָה וַיּוֹלֶד בָּנִים וּבָנוֹת׃ וַיְחִי נָחוֹר תֵּשַׁע

כה וְעֶשְׂרִים שָׁנָה וַיּוֹלֶד אֶת־תָּרַח׃ וַיְחִי נָחוֹר אַחֲרֵי הוֹלִידוֹ אֶת־תֶּרַח תְּשַׁע־עֶשְׂרֵה

כו שָׁנָה וּמְאַת שָׁנָה וַיּוֹלֶד בָּנִים וּבָנוֹת׃ וַיְחִי־תֶרַח שִׁבְעִים שָׁנָה וַיּוֹלֶד

כז אֶת־אַבְרָם אֶת־נָחוֹר וְאֶת־הָרָן׃ וְאֵלֶּה תּוֹלְדֹת תֶּרַח תֶּרַח הוֹלִיד אֶת־אַבְרָם

כח אֶת־נָחוֹר וְאֶת־הָרָן וְהָרָן הוֹלִיד אֶת־לוֹט׃ וַיָּמָת הָרָן עַל־פְּנֵי תֶּרַח אָבִיו בְּאֶרֶץ

כט מוֹלַדְתּוֹ בְּאוּר כַּשְׂדִּים׃ וַיִּקַּח אַבְרָם וְנָחוֹר לָהֶם נָשִׁים שֵׁם אֵשֶׁת־אַבְרָם שָׂרָי מפטיר

ל וְשֵׁם אֵשֶׁת־נָחוֹר מִלְכָּה בַּת־הָרָן אֲבִי־מִלְכָּה וַאֲבִי יִסְכָּה׃ וַתְּהִי שָׂרַי עֲקָרָה אֵין

רש"י

נִשְׁטְפוּ, וְאֵלּוּ לֹא נֶאֶבְדוּ מִן הָעוֹלָם! אֶלָּא שֶׁדּוֹר הַמַּבּוּל הָיוּ גַּזְלָנִים וְהָיְתָה מְרִיבָה בֵּינֵיהֶם, וְאֵלּוּ הָיוּ נוֹהֲגִים אַהֲבָה וְרֵעוּת בֵּינֵיהֶם, שֶׁנֶּאֱמַר: "שָׂפָה אֶחָת וּדְבָרִים אֲחָדִים" (לעיל פסוק א). לָמַדְתָּ שֶׁשְּׂנוּאוּי הַמַּחֲלֹקֶת וְגָדוֹל הַשָּׁלוֹם:

י | שֵׁם בֶּן מְאַת שָׁנָה. כְּשֶׁהוֹלִיד אֶת אַרְפַּכְשַׁד שְׁנָתַיִם אַחַר הַמַּבּוּל:

כח | עַל פְּנֵי תֶּרַח אָבִיו. בְּחַיֵּי אָבִיו. וּמִדְרַשׁ אַגָּדָה אוֹמֵר, שֶׁעַל יְדֵי אָבִיו מֵת, שֶׁקָּבַל תֶּרַח עַל אַבְרָם בְּנוֹ לִפְנֵי נִמְרוֹד עַל שֶׁכִּתֵּת אֶת צְלָמָיו, וְהִשְׁלִיכוֹ לְכִבְשַׁן הָאֵשׁ, וְהָרָן יוֹשֵׁב וְאוֹמֵר בְּלִבּוֹ: אִם אַבְרָם נוֹצֵחַ אֲנִי מִשֶּׁלּוֹ, וְאִם נִמְרוֹד נוֹצֵחַ אֲנִי מִשֶּׁלּוֹ. וּכְשֶׁנִּצַּל אַבְרָם אָמְרוּ לוֹ לְהָרָן: מִשֶּׁל מִי אַתָּה? אָמַר לָהֶם הָרָן: מִשֶּׁל אַבְרָם אֲנִי. הִשְׁלִיכוּהוּ לְכִבְשַׁן הָאֵשׁ וְנִשְׂרַף, וְזֶהוּ: "אוּר כַּשְׂדִּים". וּמְנַחֵם פֵּרֵשׁ "אוּר" בִּקְעָה, וְכֵן: "בָּאֻרִים כַּבְּדוּ ה'" (ישעיה כד, טו), וְכֵן: "מְאוּרַת צִפְעוֹנִי" (שם יא, ח), כָּל חוֹר וּבֶקַע עָמֹק קָרוּי 'אוּר':

כט | יִסְכָּה. זוֹ שָׂרָה, עַל שֵׁם שֶׁסּוֹכָה בְּרוּחַ הַקֹּדֶשׁ, וְשֶׁהַכֹּל סוֹכִין בְּיָפְיָהּ. וּלְשׁוֹן נְסִיכוּת, כְּמוֹ 'שָׂרָה' לְשׁוֹן שְׂרָרָה:

31 **Terah took Abram his son, and Lot, son of Haran, the son of his son, and Sarai, his daughter-in-law, the wife of his son Abram, and they departed with them from Ur of the Chaldeans**[B] **to go to the land of Canaan.**[D] It is not at all clear why they left Ur of the Chaldeans, which is probably located in southern Mesopotamia, modern Iraq, to go to the land of Canaan, which was very far away. Even as the crow flies, this is a huge distance, about 1,000 km. Furthermore, between the two locations lies the Syrian Desert, which can be crossed only in large convoys and after special preparation. In order to reach Canaan, one would have to turn north and come close to the Euphrates River in northern Syria. **And they came until Haran,**[B] **and settled there** for the time being, despite the fact that it was not in Canaan.

32 **The days of Terah were two hundred and five years; and Terah died in Haran.** It is clear from a comparison of the dates given here and below that Terah's death at the age of 205 occurred much later than the events described in the next section. However, the Torah supplies this detail here in order to conclude the story of the descendants of Shem. From now on, the focus will be on Abram, the tenth generation from Noah. Abram, together with his descendants, is at the center of the book of Genesis.

DISCUSSION

11:31 | **And they departed with them from Ur of the Chaldeans to go to the land of Canaan:** Why did the family seek to go to Canaan? The account here might be anticipating later events, as it is clear from the continuation that Abram was instructed to go to the land of Canaan. Perhaps only Abram wanted to travel, and it was his journey that caused the rest of the family to undertake the move. Abram was the oldest son, and possibly the most active and successful member of the family. Consequently, when he announced his intention to leave for Canaan, the rest of the family, which was not that large, decided to accompany him.

Parashat
Lekh Lekha

Abram's Journey to Canaan at God's Command and with His Blessing
GENESIS 12:1–9

The Torah reveals almost nothing about Abram's youth and early life, other than a few basic details such as the names of his father and family members, his place of birth, and the fact that his family set out in the direction of Canaan before halting along the way in Haran.

Furthermore, the account of Abram's selection by God appears with absolutely no description of his character. This stands in sharp contrast to Noah, who is defined as "righteous" and "wholehearted" (6:9), explaining why he was chosen to continue the human race.

The Sages fill in some of the missing details through various traditions recorded in *midrashim*. The most common idea is that Abram discovers God and develops faith in Him independently, rejecting the idolatrous worship of the surrounding society. As the narrative progresses, it becomes clear that he considers it his personal mission to manifest his faith everywhere through prayer and sacrifice, and to put his faith into practice through good deeds. Due to these qualities, he receives prophetic revelations and hears the divine voice.

12 1 **The Lord said to Abram: Go you from your land,** the geographic location where you were born; **and from your birthplace,** the place for which you harbor a sense of closeness and belonging; **and from your father's house,** and travel **to the land,** currently unknown to you, **that I will show you.** You will be told only the general direction you must travel, and you will be informed when you reach your destination.

2 You embark on this journey as an individual who is merely the head of a family or tribe. Nevertheless, I assure you that in the place where you are going **I will make you** into a **great nation and I will bless you and I will make your name great** as you will be renowned, **and you shall be a blessing,** meaning that people will use you as a paradigm for blessings. When they bless one another, they will say: May you merit to be like Abram.

3 **I will bless those who bless you, and he who curses you I will curse; and all the families of the earth,** not only the families of your descendants or your neighbors, **shall be blessed**

לֹא לָהּ וָלָד: וַיִּקַּח תֶּרַח אֶת־אַבְרָם בְּנוֹ וְאֶת־לוֹט בֶּן־הָרָן בֶּן־בְּנוֹ וְאֵת שָׂרַי כַּלָּתוֹ אֵשֶׁת אַבְרָם בְּנוֹ וַיֵּצְאוּ אִתָּם מֵאוּר כַּשְׂדִּים לָלֶכֶת אַרְצָה כְּנַעַן וַיָּבֹאוּ עַד־חָרָן

לֹב וַיֵּשְׁבוּ שָׁם: וַיִּהְיוּ יְמֵי־תֶרַח חָמֵשׁ שָׁנִים וּמָאתַיִם שָׁנָה וַיָּמָת תֶּרַח בְּחָרָן:

רש"י

לֹא] וַיֵּצְאוּ אִתָּם. וַיֵּצְאוּ תֶּרַח וְאַבְרָם עִם לוֹט וְשָׂרָי:

לֹב] וַיָּמָת תֶּרַח בְּחָרָן. לְאַחַר שֶׁיָּצָא אַבְרָם מֵחָרָן וּבָא לְאֶרֶץ כְּנַעַן, הָיָה שָׁם יוֹתֵר מִשִּׁשִּׁים שָׁנָה, שֶׁהֲרֵי כָּתוּב:

"וְאַבְרָם בֶּן חָמֵשׁ וְשִׁבְעִים שָׁנָה הָיָה בְּצֵאתוֹ מֵחָרָן" (להלן יב, ד), וְתֶרַח בֶּן שִׁבְעִים שָׁנָה הָיָה כְּשֶׁנּוֹלַד אַבְרָם, הֲרֵי קמ"ה לְתֶרַח כְּשֶׁיָּצָא אַבְרָם מִמֶּנּוּ, נִשְׁאֲרוּ מִשְּׁנוֹתָיו הַרְבֵּה. וְלָמָּה הִקְדִּים הַכָּתוּב מִיתָתוֹ שֶׁל תֶּרַח לִיצִיאָתוֹ

שֶׁל אַבְרָהָם? שֶׁלֹּא יְהֵא הַדָּבָר מְפֻרְסָם לַכֹּל, וְיֹאמְרוּ: לֹא קִיֵּם אַבְרָהָם כִּבּוּד אָבִיו שֶׁהִנִּיחוֹ זָקֵן וְהָלַךְ לוֹ. לְפִיכָךְ קְרָאוֹ הַכָּתוּב מֵת, שֶׁהָרְשָׁעִים אַף בְּחַיֵּיהֶם קְרוּיִים מֵתִים, וְהַצַּדִּיקִים בְּמִיתָתָן קְרוּיִים חַיִּים:

11:31 | Ur of the Chaldeans: Affiliated with Tel al-Shukeiri, one of the oldest cultural centers in the south of Babylon. Ur and Haran were two major centers in the worship of Sin, the Babylonian god of the moon.

Haran: Haran was a city of major economic importance, as well as one of the chief seats of the worship of the Babylonian god of the moon. It was located along the upper part of the Balikh River, one of the main tributaries of the Euphrates.

פרשת
לך לך

ב א וַיֹּאמֶר יְהוָה אֶל־אַבְרָם לֶךְ־לְךָ מֵאַרְצְךָ וּמִמּוֹלַדְתְּךָ וּמִבֵּית אָבִיךָ אֶל־ י

ב הָאָרֶץ אֲשֶׁר אַרְאֶךָּ: וְאֶעֶשְׂךָ לְגוֹי גָּדוֹל וַאֲבָרֶכְךָ וַאֲגַדְּלָה שְׁמֶךָ וֶהְיֵה

ג בְּרָכָה: וַאֲבָרֲכָה מְבָרֲכֶיךָ וּמְקַלֶּלְךָ אָאֹר וְנִבְרְכוּ בְךָ כֹּל מִשְׁפְּחֹת הָאֲדָמָה:

רש"י

א-ב] לֶךְ לְךָ. לַהֲנָאָתְךָ וּלְטוֹבָתְךָ, וְשָׁם אֶעֶשְׂךָ לְגוֹי גָּדוֹל, וְכָאן אִי אַתָּה זוֹכֶה לְבָנִים. וְעוֹד, שֶׁאוֹדִיעַ טִבְעֲךָ בָּעוֹלָם: וְאֶעֶשְׂךָ לְגוֹי גָּדוֹל. לְפִי שֶׁהַדֶּרֶךְ גּוֹרֶמֶת לִשְׁלֹשָׁה דְבָרִים: מְמַעֶטֶת פְּרִיָּה וּרְבִיָּה, וּמְמַעֶטֶת אֶת הַמָּמוֹן, וּמְמַעֶטֶת אֶת הַשֵּׁם; לְכָךְ הֻזְקַק לִשְׁלֹשׁ בִּרְכוֹת הַלָּלוּ, שֶׁהִבְטִיחוֹ עַל הַבָּנִים וְעַל הַמָּמוֹן וְעַל הַשֵּׁם: וַאֲבָרֶכְךָ. בַּמָּמוֹן, בְּרֵאשִׁית רַבָּה (לט, יא): וְהְיֵה בְּרָכָה. הַבְּרָכוֹת נְתוּנוֹת בְּיָדֶךָ. עַד עַכְשָׁו הָיוּ בְיָדִי, בֵּרַכְתִּי לְאָדָם וְנֹחַ, וּמֵעַכְשָׁו אַתָּה תְּבָרֵךְ אֶת אֲשֶׁר תַּחְפֹּץ. בְּרֵאשִׁית רַבָּה

(סס). דָּבָר אַחֵר, "וְאֶעֶשְׂךָ לְגוֹי גָּדוֹל", זֶה שֶׁאוֹמְרִים אֱלֹהֵי אַבְרָהָם, "וַאֲבָרֶכְךָ", זֶה שֶׁאוֹמְרִים אֱלֹהֵי יִצְחָק, "וַאֲגַדְּלָה שְׁמֶךָ", זֶה שֶׁאוֹמְרִים אֱלֹהֵי יַעֲקֹב. יָכוֹל יְהוּ חוֹתְמִין בְּכֻלָּן? תַּלְמוּד לוֹמַר: "וֶהְיֵה בְּרָכָה", בְּךָ חוֹתְמִין וְלֹא בָהֶם: מֵאַרְצְךָ. וַהֲלֹא כְּבָר יָצָא מִשָּׁם עִם אָבִיו וּבָא עַד חָרָן? אֶלָּא כָּךְ אָמַר לוֹ: הִתְרַחֵק עוֹד מִשָּׁם וְצֵא מִבֵּית אָבִיךָ. אֲשֶׁר אַרְאֶךָּ. לֹא גִלָּה לוֹ הָאָרֶץ מִיָּד, כְּדֵי לְחַבְּבָהּ בְּעֵינָיו וְלָתֵת לוֹ שָׂכָר עַל כָּל דִּבּוּר וְדִבּוּר. כַּיּוֹצֵא בוֹ: "אֶת בִּנְךָ אֶת יְחִידְךָ אֲשֶׁר אָהַבְתָּ" (להלן כב, ב), כַּיּוֹצֵא

בּוֹ: "עַל אַחַד הֶהָרִים אֲשֶׁר אֹמַר אֵלֶיךָ" (שם), כַּיּוֹצֵא בּוֹ: "וּקְרָא אֵלֶיהָ אֶת הַקְּרִיאָה אֲשֶׁר אָנֹכִי דֹּבֵר אֵלֶיךָ" (יונה ג, ב):

ג] וְנִבְרְכוּ בְךָ. יֵשׁ אַגָּדוֹת רַבּוֹת, וְזֶהוּ פְשׁוּטוֹ: אָדָם אוֹמֵר לִבְנוֹ תְּהֵא כְּאַבְרָהָם. וְכֵן כָּל "וְנִבְרְכוּ בְךָ" שֶׁבַּמִּקְרָא, וְזֶה מוֹכִיחַ: "בְּךָ יְבָרֵךְ יִשְׂרָאֵל לֵאמֹר יְשִׂמְךָ אֱלֹהִים כְּאֶפְרַיִם וְכִמְנַשֶּׁה" (להלן מח, כ):

---

in, or through, **you.** From this point forward, Abram would not live his life for himself alone as a private individual; he would become a symbol and a model for all.

4 **Abram went, as the Lord had spoken to him.** He set out on his way and left most of his family, who had also initially planned to go to Canaan, behind in Haran. **And Lot,** the son of his brother Haran, **went with him.**[D] **Abram was five years and seventy years old upon his departure from Haran.**

5 **Abram took Sarai his wife, and Lot, son of his brother, and all their property that they had acquired, and the people that they had acquired in Haran;**[D] **they departed to go to the land of Canaan; and they came to the land of Canaan.** The Torah does not specify the route they took, but it can be assumed that they either traveled through Syria and then along the coast of the Mediterranean, or along the international road that traversed present-day Iraq and Syria to Damascus, and then turned south across the Golan Heights until they crossed over the Jordan River into the land of Canaan via one of several possible crossing points.

6 **Abram passed through the land to the place of Shekhem,** the site where the city of Shekhem would later be built,[1] **until the plain [*elon*] of Moreh.**[D] **And the Canaanites were then in the land.** This observation, which is important for the continuation of the story, explains that the land to which Abram came was not desolate and empty of inhabitants, as were many

regions at the time. Rather, it had been inhabited for many years by the Canaanite people.

7 **The Lord appeared to Abram** upon his arrival in Canaan, **and said: To your descendants I will give this land.** Earlier, when Abram was commanded to travel, he had been given a general blessing. At this point, God promised him a specific gift, that his descendants would inherit the land of Canaan. **He built there an altar to the Lord, who had appeared to him.** Abram built the first altar to God after His revelation to him.[2] The altar was to serve as a reminder that God had revealed Himself to Abram in this place.

8 **He,** Abram, then **moved from there to the mountains, east of** the city of **Beit El, and he pitched his tent** there. **Beit El** was **to the west** of his place of encampment, **and Ai to the east.** For many years, Abram and his family were primarily nomadic shepherds who lived in tents. It can be assumed that much of the land was uninhabited at the time, leaving large empty areas suitable for grazing. Abram found pasture for his flock between Beit El and Ai. **He** also **built there an altar to the Lord, and proclaimed the name of the Lord.**[D]

9 **Abram journeyed, steadily journeying to the Negev.** Since he had not been told where to stop, and as he had not yet found a place where he felt sufficiently comfortable, he left Beit El and continued southward.

Abram in Egypt
GENESIS 12:10–20

Although he had received a blessing upon his departure from Haran, Abram encounters many difficulties and challenges when he arrives. He was promised the land of Canaan, but cannot continue living there due to famine. Likewise, God had assured him that all the nations would be blessed through him, but then he has to cope with his wife being taken against her will to the house of the king of Egypt.

10 **There was famine in the land,** due to lack of rainfall, which had a negative impact upon both the produce required for human sustenance and the vegetation used for animal pasture. **And** therefore, **Abram descended to Egypt to reside there** temporarily, but not to remain there as a permanent resident;[3] **as the famine was severe in the land.** Egypt, which is dependent upon the Nile rather than on rainfall, was generally immune from the effects of a famine of this kind.[4]

11 **It was when he,** his camp,[5] **drew near to come to Egypt,** that **he said to Sarai his wife: Behold, I know** and have become fully aware **now that you are a beautiful woman,** and that in addition to your external beauty you also have a strong personality and presence.

12 **It will be, when** you come with me to Egypt and **the Egyptians see you, they will say: This is his wife. And** then **they will kill me** out of desire for you, **and keep you alive.** Abram was

---

DISCUSSION

12:4| **And Lot went with him:** Haran probably died young. According to a *midrash*, Lot was Abram's brother-in-law as well as his nephew, since Haran was also Sarai's father (*Megilla* 14a). Due to their double connection, Lot, who was too young to stand at the head of his own family, went along with Abram.

12:5| **And the people that they had acquired in Haran:** According to the simple reading of the text, this expression refers to slaves. However, several *midrashim* understand it as a reference to individuals who had converted under their guidance.

It is possible that both interpretations are correct and that these were people subject to

Abram's authority whom he influenced spiritually as well. Abram was not merely the head of a small family; he was also the leader of a nomadic tribe that owned property and herds. It is likely that his holdings included people who were enslaved, subjugated, or subordinate to him in various degrees. In addition to the economic ◄●

ד וַיֵּלֶךְ אַבְרָם כַּאֲשֶׁר דִּבֶּר אֵלָיו יְהוָה וַיֵּלֶךְ אִתּוֹ לוֹט וְאַבְרָם בֶּן־חָמֵשׁ שָׁנִים
ה וְשִׁבְעִים שָׁנָה בְּצֵאתוֹ מֵחָרָן: וַיִּקַּח אַבְרָם אֶת־שָׂרַי אִשְׁתּוֹ וְאֶת־לוֹט בֶּן־אָחִיו
וְאֶת־כָּל־רְכוּשָׁם אֲשֶׁר רָכָשׁוּ וְאֶת־הַנֶּפֶשׁ אֲשֶׁר־עָשׂוּ בְחָרָן וַיֵּצְאוּ לָלֶכֶת אַרְצָה
ו כְּנַעַן וַיָּבֹאוּ אַרְצָה כְּנָעַן: וַיַּעֲבֹר אַבְרָם בָּאָרֶץ עַד מְקוֹם שְׁכֶם עַד אֵלוֹן מוֹרֶה
ז וְהַכְּנַעֲנִי אָז בָּאָרֶץ: וַיֵּרָא יְהוָה אֶל־אַבְרָם וַיֹּאמֶר לְזַרְעֲךָ אֶתֵּן אֶת־הָאָרֶץ הַזֹּאת
ח וַיִּבֶן שָׁם מִזְבֵּחַ לַיהוָה הַנִּרְאֶה אֵלָיו: וַיַּעְתֵּק מִשָּׁם הָהָרָה מִקֶּדֶם לְבֵית־אֵל וַיֵּט
אָהֳלֹה בֵּית־אֵל מִיָּם וְהָעַי מִקֶּדֶם וַיִּבֶן־שָׁם מִזְבֵּחַ לַיהוָה וַיִּקְרָא בְּשֵׁם יְהוָה:
ט וַיִּסַּע אַבְרָם הָלוֹךְ וְנָסוֹעַ הַנֶּגְבָּה:
י יא וַיְהִי רָעָב בָּאָרֶץ וַיֵּרֶד אַבְרָם מִצְרַיְמָה לָגוּר שָׁם כִּי־כָבֵד הָרָעָב בָּאָרֶץ: וַיְהִי
כַּאֲשֶׁר הִקְרִיב לָבוֹא מִצְרָיְמָה וַיֹּאמֶר אֶל־שָׂרַי אִשְׁתּוֹ הִנֵּה־נָא יָדַעְתִּי כִּי אִשָּׁה
יב יְפַת־מַרְאֶה אָתְּ: וְהָיָה כִּי־יִרְאוּ אֹתָךְ הַמִּצְרִים וְאָמְרוּ אִשְׁתּוֹ זֹאת וְהָרְגוּ אֹתִי

רש״י

ה | **אֲשֶׁר עָשׂוּ בְחָרָן.** שֶׁהִכְנִיסָם תַּחַת כַּנְפֵי הַשְּׁכִינָה, אַבְרָהָם מְגַיֵּר אֶת הָאֲנָשִׁים וְשָׂרָה מְגַיֶּרֶת הַנָּשִׁים, וּמַעֲלֶה עֲלֵיהֶם הַכָּתוּב כְּאִלּוּ עֲשָׂאוּם. וּפְשׁוּטוֹ שֶׁל מִקְרָא: עֲבָדִים וּשְׁפָחוֹת שֶׁקָּנוּ לָהֶם, כְּמוֹ: ״עָשָׂה אֵת כָּל הַכָּבֹד הַזֶּה״ (להלן לא, א), ״וְיִשְׂרָאֵל עֹשֶׂה חָיִל״ (במדבר כד, יח) לְשׁוֹן קוֹנֶה וְכוֹנֵס:

ו | **וַיַּעֲבֹר אַבְרָם בָּאָרֶץ.** נִכְנַס לְתוֹכָהּ: **עַד מְקוֹם שְׁכֶם.** לְהִתְפַּלֵּל עַל בְּנֵי יַעֲקֹב כְּשֶׁיָּבֹאוּ לְהִלָּחֵם בִּשְׁכֶם: **אֵלוֹן מוֹרֶה.** הוּא שְׁכֶם. הֶרְאָהוּ הַר גְּרִזִים וְהַר עֵיבָל שֶׁשָּׁם קִבְּלוּ יִשְׂרָאֵל שְׁבוּעַת הַתּוֹרָה: **וְהַכְּנַעֲנִי אָז בָּאָרֶץ.** הָיָה הוֹלֵךְ וְכוֹבֵשׁ אֶת אֶרֶץ יִשְׂרָאֵל מִזַּרְעוֹ שֶׁל שֵׁם, שֶׁבְּחֶלְקוֹ שֶׁל שֵׁם נָפְלָה כְּשֶׁחִלֵּק נֹחַ אֶת הָאָרֶץ לְבָנָיו, שֶׁנֶּאֱמַר: ״וּמַלְכִּי צֶדֶק מֶלֶךְ שָׁלֵם״ (להלן יד, יח); לְפִיכָךְ ״וַיֹּאמֶר – אֶל אַבְרָם – לְזַרְעֲךָ אֶתֵּן אֶת הָאָרֶץ הַזֹּאת״ (להלן פסוק ז), עָתִיד אֲנִי לְהַחֲזִירָהּ לְבָנֶיךָ שֶׁהֵם מִזַּרְעוֹ שֶׁל שֵׁם:

ז | **וַיִּבֶן שָׁם מִזְבֵּחַ.** עַל בְּשׂוֹרַת הַזֶּרַע וְעַל בְּשׂוֹרַת אֶרֶץ יִשְׂרָאֵל:

ח | **וַיַּעְתֵּק מִשָּׁם.** אָהֳלוֹ: **מִקֶּדֶם לְבֵית אֵל.** בְּמִזְרָחָהּ שֶׁל בֵּית אֵל, נִמְצֵאת בֵּית אֵל בְּמַעֲרָבוֹ, הוּא שֶׁנֶּאֱמַר: ״בֵּית אֵל מִיָּם״: **אָהֳלֹה.** אָהֳלָהּ כְּתִיב, בַּתְּחִלָּה נָטָה אֶת אֹהֶל אִשְׁתּוֹ וְאַחַר כָּךְ אֶת שֶׁלּוֹ. בְּרֵאשִׁית רַבָּה (לט, טו): **וַיִּבֶן שָׁם מִזְבֵּחַ.** נִתְנַבֵּא שֶׁעֲתִידִין בָּנָיו לְהִכָּשֵׁל שָׁם עַל עֲוֹן עָכָן וְהִתְפַּלֵּל עֲלֵיהֶם:

ט | **הָלוֹךְ וְנָסוֹעַ.** לִפְרָקִים, יוֹשֵׁב כָּאן חֹדֶשׁ אוֹ יוֹתֵר וְנוֹסֵעַ מִשָּׁם וְנוֹטֶה אָהֳלוֹ בְּמָקוֹם אַחֵר, וְכָל מַסָּעָיו ״הַנֶּגְבָּה״, לָלֶכֶת לְדָרוֹמָהּ שֶׁל אֶרֶץ יִשְׂרָאֵל, וְהוּא בְּחֶלְקוֹ שֶׁל יְהוּדָה שֶׁנָּטְלוּ בִּדְרוֹמָהּ שֶׁל אֶרֶץ יִשְׂרָאֵל, וְהוּא לְצַד יְרוּשָׁלַיִם, הַר הַמּוֹרִיָּה. בְּרֵאשִׁית רַבָּה (לט, טז):

י | **רָעָב בָּאָרֶץ.** בְּאוֹתָהּ הָאָרֶץ לְבַדָּהּ, לְנַסּוֹתוֹ אִם יְהַרְהֵר אַחַר דְּבָרָיו שֶׁל הַקָּדוֹשׁ בָּרוּךְ הוּא, שֶׁאָמַר לוֹ לָלֶכֶת אֶל אֶרֶץ כְּנַעַן וְעַכְשָׁו מַשִּׂיאוֹ לָצֵאת מִמֶּנָּה:

יא | **הִנֵּה נָא יָדַעְתִּי.** מִדְרַשׁ אַגָּדָה: עַד עַכְשָׁיו לֹא הִכִּיר בָּהּ מִתּוֹךְ צְנִיעוּת שֶׁבִּשְׁנֵיהֶם, וְעַכְשָׁיו הִכִּיר בָּהּ עַל יְדֵי מַעֲשֶׂה. דָּבָר אַחֵר, מִנְהַג הָעוֹלָם שֶׁעַל יְדֵי טֹרַח הַדֶּרֶךְ אָדָם מִתְבַּזֶּה, וְזֹאת עָמְדָה בְּיָפְיָהּ. וּפְשׁוּטוֹ שֶׁל מִקְרָא: הִנֵּה נָא הִגִּיעָה שָׁעָה שֶׁיֵּשׁ לִדְאֹג עַל יָפְיֵךְ; יָדַעְתִּי זֶה יָמִים כִּי יְפַת מַרְאֶה אַתְּ, וְעַכְשָׁיו אָנוּ בָּאִים בֵּין אֲנָשִׁים שְׁחוֹרִים וּמְכֹעָרִים, אֲחֵיהֶם שֶׁל כּוּשִׁים, וְלֹא הֻרְגְּלוּ בְּאִשָּׁה יָפָה. וְדוֹמֶה לוֹ: ״הִנֵּה נָּא אֲדֹנַי סוּרוּ נָא״ (להלן יט, ב):

DISCUSSION

services they provided for Abram, they also adopted the beliefs and values of his household.

12:6| **The plain [*elon*] of Moreh:** It is almost certain that this expression does not refer to an oak tree [*alon*]. Rather, in all probability it is either the name of the city adjacent to Shekhem, or it means "the plain of Moreh" (see Targum Yonatan, Ibn Ezra, and Ramban).

12:8| **And proclaimed the name of the Lord:** This expression, which appears on several occasions (e.g., 13:4, 21:33), refers to a public announcement or declaration. While Abram moved from place to place according to the needs of his flock, he understood that the real purpose of his wanderings was to teach about God and publicize His name.

concerned that he would be attacked, both due to Sarai's beauty and charming personality, and because of his great wealth.[6]

13 **Please say** to the residents of Egypt that **you are my sister; so that it may be well with me for your sake;** as your brother, no one will have cause to harm me. **And my soul shall live because of you.**

Second aliya
14 Indeed, Abram's concern was justified, as **it was upon Abram's arrival in Egypt, the Egyptians saw the woman that she was very fair.**

15 **Pharaoh's officers saw her,** and **they praised her to Pharaoh**[D] king of Egypt, informing him that there was an exceptionally beautiful woman among the visitors who had arrived from distant lands. **And the woman was taken to Pharaoh's house**[D] to be one of his wives. It seems that Sarai was not able to object, as she and Abram claimed to be siblings.

16 **And he,** Pharaoh, **benefited Abram for her sake,** as the brother of the woman he sought for himself. **He,** Abram, **acquired,** of his own property as well as from all the gifts he received, **sheep, oxen, donkeys, slaves, maidservants, female donkeys, and camels.**

17 But in the meantime, **the Lord afflicted Pharaoh and his household,** his family and those surrounding him, **with great afflictions over the matter of Sarai, Abram's wife.**[D]

18 Pharaoh called Abram, and he said: **What is this that you have done to me? Why did you not tell me that she was your wife?**

19 **Why did you say: She is my sister? I took her for myself as my wife.** Since you claimed to be her brother, I intended to take her as my wife. I acted properly; I did not rape her or take her by force. On the contrary, I treated her with full respect and wished to marry her. It is only now that I have become aware that I took your wife from you. **And** therefore **now, here is your wife.** She is too great a temptation for the men who live here. We want neither her nor the troubles and plagues she has brought upon us, so **take her and go.**

20 **Pharaoh commanded men regarding him** to accompany Abram. The escort was provided not merely as a mark of honor; their mission was to compel Abram to leave their place. **And so they sent forth him, and his wife, and everything that was his.**

Abram and Lot in Canaan

GENESIS 13:1–18

In the previous section, Abram had to contend with the forced separation from his wife Sarai. Now, on his own initiative, Abram separates from her brother Lot, who has accompanied him until this point.

13 1 **Abram ascended**[D] northward **from Egypt, he, and his wife, and everything that was his, and Lot with him, to the Negev.**

2 **And Abram was very wealthy in livestock, in silver, and in gold.** Abram was successful in his business dealings and became very wealthy over time. The significance of this detail will become apparent as the narrative progresses.

3 **He went on his journeys from the Negev to Beit El, to the place where his tent had been initially, between Beit El and Ai.** He retraced his steps along the same route he had previously taken, in order to reacquaint himself with the inhabitants of those places, or to pay his debts, as explained by the Sages.[7]

4 He came **to the place of the altar that he prepared there at first;** and again **Abram proclaimed there the name of the Lord.** Perhaps this means that he called a public assembly, prayed, and gave speeches, with the aim of making the name of God known in the world.

Third aliya
5 **Lot, who went with Abram, also had flocks, and cattle, and tents.** Lot left Ur of the Chaldeans as the heir of his father, Haran. Consequently, he had property of his own. Although he traveled alongside his uncle Abram, he was not subservient to him.

DISCUSSION

12:15 | **Pharaoh:** This is not the actual name of the king of Egypt, but rather his official title (see Rashbam 41:10). The literal meaning of the word seems to be "the large house," which apparently referred to the royal palace. In a similar fashion, the Ottoman Sultan was called the Sublime Porte, or High Gate. Even today, metonyms of this kind are used for governmental positions, e.g., referring to the president of the United States as the White House.

And the woman was taken to Pharaoh's house: Sarai was a striking individual, noted for

her physical beauty as well as her other unusual qualities. It seems that she remained beautiful even many years after she was taken to Pharaoh's house, as this was not the only time she underwent an experience of this nature (see verse 20; *Bereshit Rabba* 45:4; *Shir HaShirim Rabba* 2:14).

It is possible that Abram's status as the leader of a large tribe was another reason she was taken. As related below (verse 20), at one point he even organized a small but significant

military force of his own. For these reasons too, the Pharaoh of Egypt might have wanted Sarai.

The Sages list this story as one of the trials Abram endured. Abram suffered both physically and mentally from his wife's abduction. He had recently been blessed and given many promises, and yet he now encountered famine and the taking of his wife. Nevertheless, Abram maintained his faith in God, and did not question His promises or complain (see *Avot deRabbi Natan*, chap. 33).

יג וְאֹתָךְ יְחַיּוּ: אִמְרִי־נָא אֲחֹתִי אָתְּ לְמַעַן יִיטַב־לִי בַעֲבוּרֵךְ וְחָיְתָה נַפְשִׁי בִּגְלָלֵךְ:
יד טו וַיְהִי כְּבוֹא אַבְרָם מִצְרָיְמָה וַיִּרְאוּ הַמִּצְרִים אֶת־הָאִשָּׁה כִּי־יָפָה הִוא מְאֹד: וַיִּרְאוּ שני
טז אֹתָהּ שָׂרֵי פַרְעֹה וַיְהַלְלוּ אֹתָהּ אֶל־פַּרְעֹה וַתֻּקַּח הָאִשָּׁה בֵּית פַּרְעֹה: וּלְאַבְרָם
הֵיטִיב בַּעֲבוּרָהּ וַיְהִי־לוֹ צֹאן־וּבָקָר וַחֲמֹרִים וַעֲבָדִים וּשְׁפָחֹת וַאֲתֹנֹת וּגְמַלִּים:
יז וַיְנַגַּע יְהוָה ׀ אֶת־פַּרְעֹה נְגָעִים גְּדֹלִים וְאֶת־בֵּיתוֹ עַל־דְּבַר שָׂרַי אֵשֶׁת אַבְרָם:
יח וַיִּקְרָא פַרְעֹה לְאַבְרָם וַיֹּאמֶר מַה־זֹּאת עָשִׂיתָ לִּי לָמָּה לֹא־הִגַּדְתָּ לִּי כִּי אִשְׁתְּךָ
יט הִוא: לָמָה אָמַרְתָּ אֲחֹתִי הִוא וָאֶקַּח אֹתָהּ לִי לְאִשָּׁה וְעַתָּה הִנֵּה אִשְׁתְּךָ קַח
כ א ג וָלֵךְ: וַיְצַו עָלָיו פַּרְעֹה אֲנָשִׁים וַיְשַׁלְּחוּ אֹתוֹ וְאֶת־אִשְׁתּוֹ וְאֶת־כָּל־אֲשֶׁר־לוֹ: וַיַּעַל
ב אַבְרָם מִמִּצְרַיִם הוּא וְאִשְׁתּוֹ וְכָל־אֲשֶׁר־לוֹ וְלוֹט עִמּוֹ הַנֶּגְבָּה: וְאַבְרָם כָּבֵד מְאֹד
ג בַּמִּקְנֶה בַּכֶּסֶף וּבַזָּהָב: וַיֵּלֶךְ לְמַסָּעָיו מִנֶּגֶב וְעַד־בֵּית־אֵל עַד־הַמָּקוֹם אֲשֶׁר־הָיָה
ד שָׁם אָהֳלֹה בַּתְּחִלָּה בֵּין בֵּית־אֵל וּבֵין הָעָי: אֶל־מְקוֹם הַמִּזְבֵּחַ אֲשֶׁר־עָשָׂה שָׁם
ה בָּרִאשֹׁנָה וַיִּקְרָא שָׁם אַבְרָם בְּשֵׁם יְהוָה: וְגַם־לְלוֹט הַהֹלֵךְ אֶת־אַבְרָם הָיָה צֹאן־ שלישי

רש״י

יג| לְמַעַן יִיטַב לִי בַעֲבוּרֵךְ. יִתְּנוּ לִי מַתָּנוֹת:

יד| וַיְהִי כְּבוֹא אַבְרָם מִצְרָיְמָה. הָיָה לוֹ לוֹמַר ״כְּבוֹאָם מִצְרָיְמָה״, אֶלָּא לָמֵד שֶׁהִטְמִין אוֹתָהּ בְּתֵבָה, וְעַל יְדֵי שֶׁתָּבְעוּ אֶת הַמֶּכֶס פָּתְחוּ וְרָאוּ אוֹתָהּ:

טו| וַיְהַלְלוּ אֹתָהּ אֶל פַּרְעֹה. הִלְּלוּהָ בֵּינֵיהֶם לוֹמַר, הֲגוּנָה זוֹ לַמֶּלֶךְ:

טז| וּלְאַבְרָם הֵיטִיב. פַּרְעֹה בַּעֲבוּרָהּ:

יז| וַיְנַגַּע. בְּמַכַּת רָאתָן לָקָה שֶׁהַתַּשְׁמִישׁ קָשֶׁה לוֹ. בִּבְרֵאשִׁית רַבָּה (מא, ב): עַל דְּבַר שָׂרַי. עַל פִּי דִּבּוּרָהּ, אוֹמֶרֶת לַמַּלְאָךְ הַךְ, וְהוּא מַכֶּה:

יט| קַח וָלֵךְ. לֹא כַּאֲבִימֶלֶךְ שֶׁאָמַר לוֹ: ״הִנֵּה אַרְצִי לְפָנֶיךָ״ (להלן כ, טו), אֶלָּא אָמַר לוֹ: לֵךְ וְאַל תַּעֲמֹד, שֶׁהַמִּצְרִים שְׁטוּפֵי זִמָּה הֵם, שֶׁנֶּאֱמַר: ״וְזִרְמַת סוּסִים זִרְמָתָם״ (יחזקאל כג, כ):

כ| וַיְצַו עָלָיו. עַל אוֹדוֹתָיו, לְשַׁלְּחוֹ וּלְשָׁמְרוֹ: וַיְשַׁלְּחוּ. כְּתַרְגּוּמוֹ: ״וְאַלְוִיאוּ״:

פרק יג

א-ב| כָּבֵד מְאֹד. טָעוּן מַשָּׂאוֹת: וַיַּעַל אַבְרָם... הַנֶּגְבָּה. לָבֹא לִדְרוֹמָהּ שֶׁל אֶרֶץ יִשְׂרָאֵל, כְּמוֹ שֶׁאָמַר לְמַעְלָה: ״הָלוֹךְ וְנָסוֹעַ הַנֶּגְבָּה״ (לעיל יב, ט) לְהַר הַמּוֹרִיָּה, וּמִכָּל מָקוֹם כְּשֶׁהוּא הוֹלֵךְ מִמִּצְרַיִם לְאֶרֶץ כְּנַעַן מִדָּרוֹם לַצָּפוֹן הוּא מְהַלֵּךְ, שֶׁאֶרֶץ מִצְרַיִם בִּדְרוֹמָהּ שֶׁל אֶרֶץ יִשְׂרָאֵל, כְּמוֹ שֶׁמּוֹכִיחַ בְּמַסָּעוֹת וּבִגְבוּלֵי הָאָרֶץ:

ג| וַיֵּלֶךְ לְמַסָּעָיו. כְּשֶׁחָזַר הָיָה לָן בָּאַכְסַנְיוֹת שֶׁלָּן בָּהֶן כְּשֶׁהָלַךְ לְשָׁם. לָמֵד דֶּרֶךְ אֶרֶץ שֶׁלֹּא יְשַׁנֶּה אָדָם מֵאַכְסַנְיָה שֶׁלּוֹ. דָּבָר אַחֵר, בַּחֲזָרָתוֹ פָּרַע הַקָּפוֹתָיו: מִנֶּגֶב. אֶרֶץ מִצְרַיִם בִּדְרוֹמָהּ שֶׁל אֶרֶץ כְּנַעַן:

ד| אֲשֶׁר עָשָׂה שָׁם בָּרִאשֹׁנָה. וַאֲשֶׁר קָרָא ״שָׁם אַבְרָם בְּשֵׁם ה׳״. וְגַם יֵשׁ לוֹמַר ״וַיִּקְרָא שָׁם״ עַכְשָׁיו ״בְּשֵׁם ה׳״:

ה| הַהֹלֵךְ אֶת אַבְרָם. מִי גָּרַם לוֹ שֶׁהָיָה לוֹ זֹאת? הִלּוּכוֹ עִם אַבְרָם:

DISCUSSION

12:17| **Over the matter of Sarai, Abram's wife:** It is not readily apparent how Pharaoh knew that his taking of Sarai was the cause of his suffering. It is possible that the plagues appeared immediately upon her arrival, or that Sarai explained to him that they were a punishment, or that after she refused his advances he realized that the troubles he and his household were experiencing coincided with his kidnapping of the stranger. In any case, Pharaoh ultimately discovered the truth, and Sarai told him that she was Abram's wife, not his sister (*Zohar* I,113:1; Rashi; Ramban, verse 18).

13:1| **Ascended:** Here, and in many other places in the Bible, this verb refers to a movement from south to north (see, e.g., Exodus 13:18; Numbers 13:17, 21:33; Joshua 15:3). Elsewhere it denotes a journey into the Land of Israel from outside (e.g., II Samuel 5:17, II Kings 18:9, Isaiah 36:10, Zechariah 14:16–17, Ezra 2:1; see *Kiddushin* 69b), or an ascent to a higher elevation (see commentary on Joshua 15:3).

6 **And the land could not support them to live together, as their property was substantial, and they were unable to live together.** Although at the time the land was relatively uninhabited with large areas available for pasture, the size of flocks that grazed near a settlement was generally in proportion with the size of the settlement. In this situation, when the tribe of nomads arrived with Abram's large flocks and Lot's large flocks in addition to those of the locals, there was not enough land available for all of them. However, in addition to these objective limitations, there was another significant factor preventing them from living together.

7 **There was** also **a quarrel between the herdsmen of Abram's livestock and the herdsmen of Lot's livestock.**[D] **And** in this context, the verse notes that **the Canaanites and the Perizites then lived in the land.** Since Abram did not yet own the land, and other tribes lived there, the quarrel between his herdsmen and Lot's was potentially dangerous, as the local inhabitants could take advantage of their dispute and attack them.

8 **Abram said to Lot: Please, let there be no quarrel between me and you and between my herdsmen and your herdsmen; for we are brethren.** When herdsmen disagree with one another, each group complains to their master, which could eventually lead to a fight between the heads of the two groups, Abram and Lot. Abram did not wish to become embroiled in a conflict with his relative.

9 **Isn't the whole land before you?** Since Abram and Lot were not looking to settle down, but were merely seeking pasture, the entire land was available to them, without restrictions. **Please, part from me,** and we will head in different directions; we do not need to dwell in the same place. So choose which territory you would like: **If you go to the left, I will go** to the **right; and if** you go **to the right, I will go left.**

10 At the time, Abram and Lot were situated in the southern Judean hills. **Lot raised his eyes, and** from that vantage point he **saw** the expansive view of the valley below, **the entire** area south of the Jordan River, known as the **plain of the Jordan,** and saw **that it was all watered.** This plain was a large, very low area, extremely rich in water. Even nowadays there are fertile areas south of the Dead Sea, where the climate is almost tropical, but **before the Lord destroyed Sodom and Gomorrah,** the climate in the region was different. At that time, the entire area of what is today called the Dead Sea was one large, well-watered vale. Because of the heat and water, it was **like the garden of the Lord, like the land of Egypt,** an area rich in vegetation that does not receive its water from rain but from rivers and irrigation canals. This description applied to the entire plain **as,** until, **you come to** the small town of **Tzoar.**

11 **Lot** accepted Abram's suggestion and **chose for himself all the plain of the Jordan,** a lush, fertile area large enough for his flocks and herds. **Lot journeyed from the east** of the place where he and Abram were situated, the side that faced the Dead Sea.[8] **And they parted one from another,** each following a different path.

12 **Abram lived in the land of Canaan, and Lot lived in,** among, and between, **the cities of the plain** of Jordan, **and** Lot **pitched his tent as far as Sodom.** At this stage Lot was not yet a resident of Sodom, but a tent-dwelling shepherd who lived near the city and under its patronage.

13 At this point, the text notes the moral qualities of the inhabitants of Sodom, among whom Lot had chosen to live: **And** even at that time **the men of Sodom**[D] **were** known to be **extremely wicked and sinful to the Lord.**

14 **The Lord said to Abram, after Lot parted from him:**[D] **Raise now your eyes, and look from the place where you are, northward, southward, eastward, and westward;**

15 **for all the land that you see, I will give to you, and to your descendants forever.**

16 **I will render your descendants** numerous **like the dust of the earth;** so that only **if a man could count the dust of the earth, so your descendants shall be counted.**

DISCUSSION

13:7 | There was a quarrel between the herdsmen of Abram's livestock and the herdsmen of Lot's livestock: There is a fundamental and perpetual conflict, dating back to ancient times (see 4:2–8), between nomadic shepherds and the farmers who till the land, as flocks of sheep would frequently damage produce growing in fields. The problematic relationship between shepherds and farmers was also discussed and debated many generations later in the period of the Mishna and Talmud (see, e.g., *Bava Kamma,* chap. 6).

Some commentators quote midrashic traditions that suggest that this conflict was not merely a squabble over land, but had a moral dimension as well. According to these traditions, Abram had ordered his shepherds to take strict measures to prevent any damage to neighboring fields, whereas Lot's shepherds were far less careful about this. Abram's herdsmen then rebuked Lot's, telling them that shepherds must act in an honest manner by preventing their sheep from grazing on property belonging to others (*Bereshit Rabba* 41:5).

13:13 | The men of Sodom: Later, the prophet Ezekiel would describe the evil of Sodom in the following way: Behold, this was the iniquity of your sister Sodom: She and her daughters had pride, surfeit of bread and tranquil calm, but she did not support the hand of the poor and indigent. They were haughty and performed an abomination before Me (Ezekiel 16:49–50).

The extremely wealthy cities of the plain developed an ideology of rapacious, merciless avarice. Strangers were unwanted, and Sodom apparently established a harsh legal system

ו וּבָקָר וְאֹהָלִים׃ וְלֹא־נָשָׂא אֹתָם הָאָרֶץ לָשֶׁבֶת יַחְדָּו כִּי־הָיָה רְכוּשָׁם רָב וְלֹא
ז יָכְלוּ לָשֶׁבֶת יַחְדָּו׃ וַיְהִי־רִיב בֵּין רֹעֵי מִקְנֵה־אַבְרָם וּבֵין רֹעֵי מִקְנֵה־לוֹט וְהַכְּנַעֲנִי
ח וְהַפְּרִזִּי אָז יֹשֵׁב בָּאָרֶץ׃ וַיֹּאמֶר אַבְרָם אֶל־לוֹט אַל־נָא תְהִי מְרִיבָה בֵּינִי וּבֵינֶךָ
ט וּבֵין רֹעַי וּבֵין רֹעֶיךָ כִּי־אֲנָשִׁים אַחִים אֲנָחְנוּ׃ הֲלֹא כָל־הָאָרֶץ לְפָנֶיךָ הִפָּרֶד נָא
י מֵעָלָי אִם־הַשְּׂמֹאל וְאֵימִנָה וְאִם־הַיָּמִין וְאַשְׂמְאִילָה׃ וַיִּשָּׂא־לוֹט אֶת־עֵינָיו וַיַּרְא
אֶת־כָּל־כִּכַּר הַיַּרְדֵּן כִּי כֻלָּהּ מַשְׁקֶה לִפְנֵי ׀ שַׁחֵת יְהוָה אֶת־סְדֹם וְאֶת־עֲמֹרָה
יא כְּגַן־יְהוָה כְּאֶרֶץ מִצְרַיִם בֹּאֲכָה צֹעַר׃ וַיִּבְחַר־לוֹ לוֹט אֵת כָּל־כִּכַּר הַיַּרְדֵּן וַיִּסַּע
יב לוֹט מִקֶּדֶם וַיִּפָּרְדוּ אִישׁ מֵעַל אָחִיו׃ אַבְרָם יָשַׁב בְּאֶרֶץ־כְּנָעַן וְלוֹט יָשַׁב בְּעָרֵי
יג יד הַכִּכָּר וַיֶּאֱהַל עַד־סְדֹם׃ וְאַנְשֵׁי סְדֹם רָעִים וְחַטָּאִים לַיהוָה מְאֹד׃ וַיהוָה אָמַר
אֶל־אַבְרָם אַחֲרֵי הִפָּרֶד־לוֹט מֵעִמּוֹ שָׂא־נָא עֵינֶיךָ וּרְאֵה מִן־הַמָּקוֹם אֲשֶׁר־
טו אַתָּה שָׁם צָפֹנָה וָנֶגְבָּה וָקֵדְמָה וָיָמָּה׃ כִּי אֶת־כָּל־הָאָרֶץ אֲשֶׁר־אַתָּה רֹאֶה לְךָ
טז אֶתְּנֶנָּה וּלְזַרְעֲךָ עַד־עוֹלָם׃ וְשַׂמְתִּי אֶת־זַרְעֲךָ כַּעֲפַר הָאָרֶץ אֲשֶׁר ׀ אִם־יוּכַל

רש"י

ו| **וְלֹא נָשָׂא.** לֹא הָיְתָה יְכוֹלָה לְהַסְפִּיק מִרְעֶה לְמִקְנֵיהֶם: **וְלֹא נָשָׂא אֹתָם.** לְשׁוֹן קָצָר הוּא וְצָרִיךְ לְהוֹסִיף עָלָיו, כְּמוֹ: 'וְלֹא נָשָׂא אוֹתָם מִרְעֵה הָאָרֶץ', לְפִיכָךְ כָּתַב: "וְלֹא נָשָׂא" בִּלְשׁוֹן זָכָר:

ז| **וַיְהִי רִיב.** לְפִי שֶׁהָיוּ רוֹעָיו שֶׁל לוֹט רְשָׁעִים וּמַרְעִים בֶּהֱמְתָּם בִּשְׂדוֹת אֲחֵרִים, וְרוֹעֵי אַבְרָם מוֹכִיחִים אוֹתָם עַל הַגָּזֵל, וְהֵם אוֹמְרִים: נִתְּנָה הָאָרֶץ לְאַבְרָם, וְלוֹ אֵין יוֹרֵשׁ וְלוֹט יוֹרְשׁוֹ, וְאֵין זֶה גָּזֵל; וְהַכָּתוּב אוֹמֵר: "וְהַכְּנַעֲנִי וְהַפְּרִזִּי אָז יֹשֵׁב בָּאָרֶץ", וְלֹא זָכָה בָּהּ אַבְרָם עֲדַיִן:

ח| **אֲנָשִׁים אַחִים.** קְרוֹבִים. וּמִדְרַשׁ אַגָּדָה, דּוֹמִין בְּקַלַסְתֵּר פָּנִים:

ט| **אִם הַשְּׂמֹאל וְאֵימִנָה.** בְּכָל אֲשֶׁר תֵּשֵׁב לֹא אֶתְרַחֵק מִמְּךָ וְאֶעֱמֹד לְךָ לְמָגֵן וּלְעֵזֶר. וְסוֹף דָּבָר הֻצְרַךְ לוֹ, שֶׁנֶּאֱמַר: "וַיִּשְׁמַע אַבְרָם כִּי נִשְׁבָּה אָחִיו" וְגוֹ' (להלן יד, יד): **וְאֵימִנָה.** אַיְמִין אֶת עַצְמִי, כְּמוֹ "וְאַשְׂמְאִילָה" – אַשְׂמְאִיל אֶת עַצְמִי. וְאִם תֹּאמַר, הָיָה לוֹ לִנָּקֵד וְאֵימִינָה, כָּךְ מָצִינוּ בְּמָקוֹם אַחֵר: "אִם אִשׁ לְהֵמִין" (שמואל ב' יד, יט) וְאֵין נָקוּד 'לְהַיְמִין':

י| **כִּי כֻלָּהּ מַשְׁקֶה.** אֶרֶץ נַחֲלֵי מַיִם: **לִפְנֵי שַׁחֵת ה' אֶת סְדֹם וְאֶת עֲמֹרָה.** הָיָה אוֹתוֹ מִישׁוֹר "כְּגַן ה'" – לָאִילָנוֹת; "כְּאֶרֶץ מִצְרַיִם" – לַזְּרָעִים: **בֹּאֲכָה צֹעַר.** עַד צֹעַר. וּמִדְרַשׁ אַגָּדָה דּוֹרְשׁוֹ לִגְנַאי, עַל שֶׁהָיוּ שְׁטוּפֵי זִמָּה בָּחַר לוֹ לוֹט בִּשְׁכוּנָתָם. בְּמַסֶּכֶת הוֹרָיוֹת (דף י ע"ב):

יא| **כִּכַּר.** מִישׁוֹר, כְּתַרְגּוּמוֹ: **מִקֶּדֶם.** נָסַע מֵאֵצֶל אַבְרָם וְהָלַךְ לוֹ לְמַעֲרָבוֹ שֶׁל אַבְרָם, נִמְצָא נוֹסֵעַ מִמִּזְרָח לְמַעֲרָב. וּמִדְרַשׁ אַגָּדָה, הִסִּיעַ עַצְמוֹ מִקַּדְמוֹנוֹ שֶׁל עוֹלָם, אָמַר: אִי אֶפְשִׁי לֹא בְּאַבְרָם וְלֹא בֵּאלֹהָיו:

יב| **וַיֶּאֱהַל.** נָטָה אֹהָלִים לְרוֹעָיו וּלְמִקְנֵהוּ "עַד סְדֹם":

יג| **וְאַנְשֵׁי סְדֹם רָעִים.** וְאַף עַל פִּי כֵן לֹא נִמְנַע לוֹט מִלִּשְׁכֹּן עִמָּהֶם. וְרַבּוֹתֵינוּ לָמְדוּ מִכָּאן: "שֵׁם רְשָׁעִים יִרְקָב" (משלי י, ז): **רָעִים.** בְּגוּפָם: **וְחַטָּאִים.** בְּמָמוֹנָם: **לַה' מְאֹד.** יוֹדְעִים רִבּוֹנָם וּמִתְכַּוְּנִים לִמְרֹד בּוֹ:

יד| **אַחֲרֵי הִפָּרֶד לוֹט.** כָּל זְמַן שֶׁהָרָשָׁע עִמּוֹ הָיָה הַדִּבּוּר פּוֹרֵשׁ מִמֶּנּוּ:

DISCUSSION

→ designed to protect its citizens' property at all costs. Lot was not particularly troubled by his neighbors' character. It is possible that he was accepted in Sodom because he arrived there as an individual of means, rather than as a needy traveler. As such, he was able to establish a peaceful and mutually beneficial relationship with the residents of the city.

13:14| **After Lot parted from him:** The family ties between Abram and Lot are recalled in the Bible many generations later, in the time of Moses and even later. However, relations between their descendants were not always friendly. The verse emphasizes the promise of the land that was given to Abram after Lot's departure, as Lot did not merit sharing the inheritance of Canaan. The entire Land of Israel, including the plain of the Jordan chosen by Lot, is an everlasting inheritance for Abram and his descendants.

17 So therefore, **arise, walk in the land to its length and to its breadth, as to you I will give it.**[D] Even though the land is currently inhabited by others and is not yet in your possession, you can feel as comfortable in it as a landowner strolling through his estate.

18 **Abram** did not remain between Beit El and Ai, but he also did not continue wandering. Rather, he turned southward and decided to encamp. He **pitched his tent, and came and settled in the plains [*elonei*] of Mamre,**[B] **which are in Hebron. And he built there an altar to the Lord.** While on the move seeking pasture for his flock, Abram spread his faith by constructing altars and publicizing the name of God.

Abram and the War of the Kings
GENESIS 14:1–24

The story of the great war in the area known today as the Dead Sea reveals additional aspects of Abram's character. Whereas until now he has been portrayed as a simple shepherd who preached and taught during his wanderings, this chapter shows him as a military leader and successful warrior. His daring attack against the powerful kings is not motivated by political interest or hope of personal gain; rather, it is an expression of his familial duty and sense of responsibility for his nephew Lot.

14 1 *Fourth aliya* **It was in the days of Amrafel king of Shinar,**[BD] a large kingdom in the area of Babylonia;[9] **Ariokh king of Elasar,**[B] probably a region northeast of Babylonia; **Kedorlaomer king of Elam,**[B] also northeast of Babylonia; **and Tidal king of Goyim.** It is possible that this title means that Tidal reigned over a conglomeration of different tribes or nations [*goyim*], a phenomenon known even in ancient times.

2 **They,** those kings, **waged war with Bera king of Sodom, and with Birsha king of Gomorrah, Shinab king of Adma, and Shemever king of Tzevoyim, and the king of Bela, which is** the same city that was later called **Tzoar.**[D]

3 **All these,** the kings of Sodom, Gomorrah, Adma, Tzevoyim and Bela, **joined forces at the valley of Sidim,** one of the plural forms of *sadeh*, meaning field, **which is** in the place[10] now known as **the Dead Sea.**[D]

4 For **twelve years they served Kedorlaomer,** who is singled out probably because he was the strongest member of the coalition of northern kings. It can be assumed that these areas had been conquered by the kings of the north prior to Abram's arrival in Canaan. **And in the thirteenth year, they rebelled.**[11] It appears that in addition to the kings of the five cities previously mentioned, the entire region revolted against these foreign rulers with their strange language and culture, who had come from afar with imperialist aspirations. Similarly, many years later, when Nebuchadnezzar took control of the Land of Israel, its various leaders came together and established alliances in order to strengthen one another against the foreign ruler and restore their independence.

5 **And in the fourteenth year, Kedorlaomer and the kings that were with him came** to suppress these rebellions, **and smote** the **Refaim,** remnants of the Anakim, **in Ashterot Karnayim,**[B] northern modern-day Jordan, **and the Zuzim,** another name for

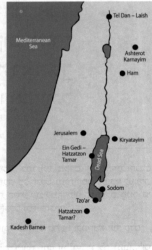

Locations relevant to the War of the Kings

DISCUSSION

13:17| **Arise, walk in the land to its length and to its breadth, as to you I will give it:** Abram's walk through the land is an example of the midrashic-historic idea, emphasized by the Ramban in his commentary to Genesis: The deeds of the fathers are a sign for the children. According to this concept, certain deeds performed or undergone by the forefathers foreshadow similar events that their descendants would experience hundreds of years later (*Bereshit Rabba* 48:7, 68:10; Ramban, 12:6).

Although he did not perform any act of conquest during this excursion, Abram journeyed along the same paths where his offspring would march generations later. Throughout the generations, his traversal of the land has been interpreted as a symbolic expression of his offspring's future control over it. Some even ascribed to it legal significance as an act of acquisition (see *Bava Batra* 100a).

14:1| **It was in the days of Amrafel king of Shinar:** Over the centuries, both before Abram's time and long afterwards, the Land of Israel attracted the attention of empires to its north, such as Aram, Assyria, Babylon, Greece, and Rome. Thousands of years later in the nineteenth and early twentieth centuries, European powers, most notably France and Britain, vied for control of the area after the collapse of the Ottoman Empire. Many of these powers from the north saw the land as a southern province ◄●

אִישׁ לִמְנוֹת אֶת־עֲפַר הָאָרֶץ גַּם־זַרְעֲךָ יִמָּנֶה: קוּם הִתְהַלֵּךְ בָּאָרֶץ לְאָרְכָּהּ יז
יח וּלְרָחְבָּהּ כִּי לְךָ אֶתְּנֶנָּה: וַיֶּאֱהַל אַבְרָם וַיָּבֹא וַיֵּשֶׁב בְּאֵלֹנֵי מַמְרֵא אֲשֶׁר בְּחֶבְרוֹן
וַיִּבֶן־שָׁם מִזְבֵּחַ לַיהוָה:

ד א וַיְהִי בִּימֵי אַמְרָפֶל מֶלֶךְ־שִׁנְעָר אַרְיוֹךְ מֶלֶךְ אֶלָּסָר כְּדָרְלָעֹמֶר מֶלֶךְ עֵילָם וְתִדְעָל יא רביעי
ב מֶלֶךְ גּוֹיִם: עָשׂוּ מִלְחָמָה אֶת־בֶּרַע מֶלֶךְ סְדֹם וְאֶת־בִּרְשַׁע מֶלֶךְ עֲמֹרָה שִׁנְאָב ׀
ג מֶלֶךְ אַדְמָה וְשֶׁמְאֵבֶר מֶלֶךְ צְבֹיִים וּמֶלֶךְ בֶּלַע הִיא־צֹעַר: כָּל־אֵלֶּה חָבְרוּ אֶל־ צְבוֹיִם
ד עֵמֶק הַשִּׂדִּים הוּא יָם הַמֶּלַח: שְׁתֵּים עֶשְׂרֵה שָׁנָה עָבְדוּ אֶת־כְּדָרְלָעֹמֶר וּשְׁלֹשׁ־
ה עֶשְׂרֵה שָׁנָה מָרָדוּ: וּבְאַרְבַּע עֶשְׂרֵה שָׁנָה בָּא כְדָרְלָעֹמֶר וְהַמְּלָכִים אֲשֶׁר אִתּוֹ

רש״י

טז| אֲשֶׁר אִם יוּכַל אִישׁ. כְּשֵׁם שֶׁאִי אֶפְשָׁר לֶעָפָר לִמָּנוֹת, כָּךְ זַרְעֲךָ לֹא יִמָּנֶה:

יח| מַמְרֵא. שֵׁם אָדָם:

פרק יד

א| אַמְרָפֶל. הוּא נִמְרוֹד, שֶׁאָמַר לְאַבְרָהָם: פֹּל לְתוֹךְ כִּבְשַׁן הָאֵשׁ: מֶלֶךְ גּוֹיִם. מָקוֹם יֵשׁ שֶׁשְּׁמוֹ 'גּוֹיִם' עַל שֵׁם שֶׁנִּקְבְּצוּ שָׁמָּה מִכַּמָּה אֻמּוֹת וּמְקוֹמוֹת, וְהִמְלִיכוּ אִישׁ עֲלֵיהֶם וּשְׁמוֹ תִּדְעָל. בְּרֵאשִׁית רַבָּה (מב, ד):

ב| בֶּרַע. רַע לַשָּׁמַיִם וְרַע לַבְּרִיּוֹת: בִּרְשַׁע. שֶׁנִּתְעַלָּה בְּרֶשַׁע: שִׁנְאָב. שׁוֹנֵא אָבִיו שֶׁבַּשָּׁמַיִם: שֶׁמְאֵבֶר. שָׂם אֵבֶר לָעוּף וְלִקְפֹּץ וְלִמְרֹד בְּהַקָּדוֹשׁ בָּרוּךְ הוּא: בֶּלַע. שֵׁם הָעִיר:

ג| עֵמֶק הַשִּׂדִּים. כָּךְ שְׁמוֹ, עַל שֵׁם שֶׁהָיוּ בּוֹ שָׂדוֹת הַרְבֵּה. הוּא יָם הַמֶּלַח. לְאַחַר זְמַן נִמְשַׁךְ הַיָּם לְתוֹכוֹ וְנַעֲשָׂה יָם הַמֶּלַח. וּמִדְרַשׁ אַגָּדָה: אוֹמֵר, שֶׁנִּתְבַּקְּעוּ הַצּוּרִים סְבִיבוֹתָיו וְנִמְשְׁכוּ יְאוֹרִים לְתוֹכוֹ:

ד| שְׁתֵּים עֶשְׂרֵה שָׁנָה עָבְדוּ. חֲמִשָּׁה מְלָכִים הַלָּלוּ "אֶת כְּדָרְלָעֹמֶר":

ה| וּבְאַרְבַּע עֶשְׂרֵה שָׁנָה. לְמָרְדָן: בָּא כְדָרְלָעֹמֶר. לְפִי שֶׁהוּא הָיָה בַּעַל הַמַּעֲשֶׂה נִכְנַס בְּעֳבִי הַקּוֹרָה: וְהַמְּלָכִים

DISCUSSION

of Syria. At other points in time, various rulers of Egypt aspired to control it as a northern extension of their own kingdom.

The aggressive kings of the north described in this verse formed an alliance in order to conquer and rule over distant lands, far from their own borders. Their dominion extended over a great distance, as they presumably conquered large sections of Syria before reaching the southeastern part of Canaan. Nevertheless, this military campaign is not discussed by the Torah. The Torah's narrative is concerned only with the story of Abram and those close to him, and from his perspective those conquests were of little significance until the incident involving Lot.

14:2| **Which is Tzoar:** As indicated below (19:20–22), Sodom, Gomorrah, Adma, and Tzevoyim were important cities, whereas Tzoar was a small town adjacent to those central locations. All of them were situated in the plain of the Jordan River, along the banks of today's Dead Sea. Although there was no comparison between the kings of the north, who reigned over such powerful kingdoms as Elam and Shinar, and the rulers of these small cities, nevertheless those kings traveled from the north to fight these local chieftains. The motive for the war will be explained in the coming verses.

14:3| **The Dead Sea:** The Dead Sea that is familiar to us did not exist at the time; at most there was a small saltwater lake there. The Torah will later explain the catastrophic events that transformed the watered, fertile valley of Sidim into a largely desolate area.

BACKGROUND

13:18| **The plains of Mamre:** As indicated below (14:24), Mamre was the name of a person. Consequently, the name, the plains of Mamre, refers to flat lands in his possession (Onkelos), identified with Haram Ramet el-Khalil, roughly 3.5 km north of Hebron.

14:1| **Shinar:** This was the ancient name of the region later known as the kingdom of Babylon. The term also appears in Egyptian and Hitite documents. The valley of Shinar was settled after the flood (11:2). Some identify it with the plain of Sanjar in northern Babylonia, approximately 100 km west of Nineveh. According to *Targum Yonatan*, it is Pontus, in the north of Asia Minor, on the southern coast of the Black Sea.

Elasar: Some identify Elasar with the important city of Larsa, also known as Tel as-Senkereh or Sankarah, in southern Babylonia. Others say it is the same as the site mentioned later, called: Telasar (see II Kings 19:12; Isaiah 37:12).

Eilam: Although Elam was an independent empire with its own language, over the course of time it was incorporated into the Persian Empire (see commentary on 10:22).

14:5| **Ashterot Karnayim:** Identified near today's Al Shaykh

Refaim[12] **in a place called Ham,**[B] **and the Eimim,** yet another name for Refaim[13] **in Shaveh Kiryatayim.**[B] Moving from place to place, the kings of the north waged battles against local rulers and defeated them one after the other.

6 **And the Horites,** an important nation among the early settlers of Canaan, one of whose tribes lived **in their mountain Se'ir,** in the land of Edom.[14] Later Esau and his family conquered the area from this tribe and intermingled with them. It seems that the army of the coalition of kings advanced from north to south along the eastern side of the Jordan River. They routed all the kings and tribes they encountered there, **until Eil Paran, which is adjacent to,** at the edge of, **the wilderness** of Sinai.

7 **They** then **turned back, and came to En Mishpat, which is** also called **Kadesh.**[B] After defeating all the rulers on the eastern side of the Jordan River, the kings turned northward again **and smote the entire field of the Amalekites,** a region in Edom. Although Amalek was not yet born, his descendants would later live there, and the place is described according to its future name. **And** they **also** smote **the Emorites, who lived in Hatzatzon Tamar,**[B] another name for Ein Gedi.[15] The kings of the north traveled from place to place, striking any nation or tribe that stood in their way. Their vast experience and military might undoubtedly gave them a substantial advantage over the local kings of small fiefdoms.

8 **The king of Sodom, the king of Gomorrah, the king of Adma, the king of Tzevoyim, and the king of Bela, which is Tzoar, went out; and they waged a war with them,** the kings of the north, **in the valley of Sidim,** which was a flat area suitable for combat.

9 They fought **with Kedorlaomer king of Elam, and Tidal king of Goyim, and Amrafel king of Shinar, and Ariokh king of Elasar; four kings against the five.** Although the local kings outnumbered the foreign ones, the actual balance of power dramatically favored the kings of the north, who represented four powerful kingdoms against the rulers of five small cities. It should be noted, however, that as was customary among mighty kings at the time, the king himself did not participate in the battle. He simply sent a spearhead force to quash the rebellion.

10 **The valley of Sidim,** albeit fertile, **was full of clay pits,**[B] **and the kings of Sodom and Gomorrah fled, and they fell there,**[D] into the pits; **and those who remained,** who had not fallen into the pits, **fled to the highlands.**

11 **They,** the four kings from the north, **took all the property of Sodom and Gomorrah,** Adma, Tzevoyim, and Tzoar. They passed through these cities without meeting any resistance and looted their property, **and all their food,** which they fed to their armies. **And they** then turned away and **went** northward back toward their place of origin.

12 **They took Lot,** who was the **son of Abram's brother, and his property and they went; and he lived in Sodom.** Since he had not long been associated with residents of these cities, Lot apparently did not want to get involved in the war. He did not even take an interest when the kings of Elam and Shinar fought the nearby king of Sodom. Nevertheless, the soldiers of Kedorlaomer and Amrafel did not care that Lot was a nomad who had also come from the north. As he was living in the place of the rebellion and he owned property, they captured him as well and plundered his possessions.

13 **The survivor,** an unidentified individual, had fled from the battlefield and escaped the war, as always happens during military conflicts. According to the Talmud, this refugee was Og king of Bashan.[16] He **came and told Abram the Hebrew;**[D] **and he was dwelling on the plains of Mamre the Emorite,** who was the **brother of Eshkol, and** the **brother of Aner, and they were allies of Abram.** Abram had developed close relationships with

BACKGROUND

Saad, this was the capital city of the land of Bashan, which was allotted to half the tribe of Manasseh (Joshua 13:12). Og King of Bashan lived there (Deuteronomy 1:4).

Ham: The village of Tel Ham, 5.5 km southwest of Irbid, in modern-day Jordan.

Shaveh Kiryatayim: This name means "the plain of the city of Kiryatayim," as *shaveh* means level. Kiryatayim, mentioned in Numbers 32:37 and Joshua 13:19, was located in Moav and included in the inheritance of Reuben. It also appears in the Mesha Stele (ninth century BCE). Modern researchers have offered several hypotheses as to the location of this place.

DISCUSSION

14:10| **And they fell there:** Their fall into the pits was the very thing that saved them. The kings of the north did not spend time chasing them, as they came to punish and to quell the rebellion, not to conquer. Therefore, once their enemies' strength was broken, they continued on their way.

14:13| **Abram the Hebrew [*Ivri*]:** The commentaries suggest two main explanations for this name. The name may simply reflect the fact that Abram was from the family of Ever, the descendants of Shem. Alternatively, it may mean that he came from beyond, or the other side [*ever*] of the river. The rulers of the great northern powers made a sharp distinction between their lands on the eastern side of the Euphrates (Mesopotamia, Assyria, and Persia) and the areas on its western bank. The western area, known as the Fertile Crescent, was also called *Ever HaNahar*, meaning "beyond the river." This region bore the same name even one thousand years later (see Joshua 24:2, I Kings 5:4, Ezra 4:16, 8:36). Although Abram had originally come from Ur of the Chaldeans, on the eastern side of the Euphrates, his family had lived for a considerable time in Haran, which is on the western side. Perhaps for this reason, he was called a Hebrew (see *Bereshit Rabba* 42:8).

It is likely that the term "Hebrew" appears in this particular context because the refugee

וַיַּכּוּ אֶת־רְפָאִים בְּעַשְׁתְּרֹת קַרְנַיִם וְאֶת־הַזּוּזִים בְּהָם וְאֵת הָאֵימִים בְּשָׁוֵה קִרְיָתָיִם׃
ו ז וְאֶת־הַחֹרִי בְּהַרְרָם שֵׂעִיר עַד אֵיל פָּארָן אֲשֶׁר עַל־הַמִּדְבָּר׃ וַיָּשֻׁבוּ וַיָּבֹאוּ אֶל־
עֵין מִשְׁפָּט הִוא קָדֵשׁ וַיַּכּוּ אֶת־כָּל־שְׂדֵה הָעֲמָלֵקִי וְגַם אֶת־הָאֱמֹרִי הַיֹּשֵׁב בְּחַצְצֹן
ח תָּמָר׃ וַיֵּצֵא מֶלֶךְ־סְדֹם וּמֶלֶךְ עֲמֹרָה וּמֶלֶךְ אַדְמָה וּמֶלֶךְ צְבֹיִים וּמֶלֶךְ בֶּלַע צבוים
ט הִוא־צֹעַר וַיַּעַרְכוּ אִתָּם מִלְחָמָה בְּעֵמֶק הַשִּׂדִּים׃ אֵת כְּדָרְלָעֹמֶר מֶלֶךְ עֵילָם
וְתִדְעָל מֶלֶךְ גּוֹיִם וְאַמְרָפֶל מֶלֶךְ שִׁנְעָר וְאַרְיוֹךְ מֶלֶךְ אֶלָּסָר אַרְבָּעָה מְלָכִים
י אֶת־הַחֲמִשָּׁה׃ וְעֵמֶק הַשִּׂדִּים בֶּאֱרֹת בֶּאֱרֹת חֵמָר וַיָּנֻסוּ מֶלֶךְ־סְדֹם וַעֲמֹרָה
יא וַיִּפְּלוּ־שָׁמָּה וְהַנִּשְׁאָרִים הֶרָה נָּסוּ׃ וַיִּקְחוּ אֶת־כָּל־רְכֻשׁ סְדֹם וַעֲמֹרָה וְאֶת־כָּל־
יב אָכְלָם וַיֵּלֵכוּ׃ וַיִּקְחוּ אֶת־לוֹט וְאֶת־רְכֻשׁוֹ בֶּן־אֲחִי אַבְרָם וַיֵּלֵכוּ וְהוּא יֹשֵׁב בִּסְדֹם׃
יג וַיָּבֹא הַפָּלִיט וַיַּגֵּד לְאַבְרָם הָעִבְרִי וְהוּא שֹׁכֵן בְּאֵלֹנֵי מַמְרֵא הָאֱמֹרִי אֲחִי אֶשְׁכֹּל

רש"י

אֲשֶׁר אִתּוֹ. אֵלֶּה שְׁלֹשָׁה מְלָכִים: **זוּזִים.** הֵם זַמְזֻמִּים (דברים ב, כ):

ו| **בְּהַרְרָם.** בְּהַר שֶׁלָּהֶם: **אֵיל פָּארָן.** כְּתַרְגּוּמוֹ: "מֵישַׁר". וְאוֹמֵר אֲנִי שֶׁאֵין 'אֵיל' לְשׁוֹן מִישׁוֹר, אֶלָּא מִישׁוֹר שֶׁל פָּארָן 'אֵיל' שְׁמוֹ, וְשֶׁל מַמְרֵא 'אֵלוֹנֵי' שְׁמוֹ, וְשֶׁל יַרְדֵּן 'כִּכָּר' שְׁמוֹ, וְשֶׁל שִׁטִּים 'אָבֵל' שְׁמוֹ, "אָבֵל הַשִּׁטִּים" (במדבר לג, מט), וְכֵן "בַּעַל גָּד" (יהושע יא, יז) 'בַּעַל' שְׁמוֹ, וְכֻלָּם מְתַרְגְּמִין "מֵישַׁר" וְכָל אֶחָד שְׁמוֹ עָלָיו: **עַל הַמִּדְבָּר.** אֵצֶל הַמִּדְבָּר, כְּמוֹ: "וְעָלָיו מַטֵּה מְנַשֶּׁה" (במדבר ב, כ):

ז| **עֵין מִשְׁפָּט הִוא קָדֵשׁ.** עַל שֵׁם הֶעָתִיד, שֶׁעֲתִידִים מֹשֶׁה וְאַהֲרֹן לְהִשָּׁפֵט שָׁם עַל עִסְקֵי אוֹתוֹ הָעַיִן, וְהֵם מֵי מְרִיבָה. וְאוּנְקְלוֹס תִּרְגְּמוֹ כִּפְשׁוּטוֹ, מָקוֹם שֶׁהָיוּ בְּנֵי הַמְּדִינָה מִתְקַבְּצִים שָׁם לְכָל מִשְׁפָּט: **שְׂדֵה הָעֲמָלֵקִי.** עֲדַיִן לֹא נוֹלַד עֲמָלֵק, וְנִקְרָא עַל שֵׁם הֶעָתִיד: **בְּחַצְצֹן תָּמָר.** הוּא עֵין גֶּדִי, מִקְרָא מָלֵא בְּדִבְרֵי הַיָּמִים (ב׳ כ, ב) בִּיהוֹשָׁפָט:

ט| **אַרְבָּעָה מְלָכִים אֶת הַחֲמִשָּׁה.** וְאַף עַל פִּי כֵן נִצְּחוּ הַמּוּעָטִים, לְהוֹדִיעֲךָ שֶׁגִּבּוֹרִים הָיוּ, וְאַף עַל פִּי כֵן לֹא נִמְנַע אַבְרָהָם מִלִּרְדֹּף אַחֲרֵיהֶם:

י| **בֶּאֱרֹת בֶּאֱרֹת חֵמָר.** בֶּאֱרוֹת הַרְבֵּה הָיוּ שָׁם שֶׁנּוֹטְלִין מִשָּׁם אֲדָמָה לְטִיט שֶׁל בִּנְיָן. וּמִדְרַשׁ אַגָּדָה, שֶׁהָיָה הַטִּיט בָּהֶם, וְנַעֲשָׂה נֵס לְמֶלֶךְ סְדוֹם שֶׁיָּצָא מִשָּׁם, לְפִי שֶׁהָיוּ בְּאֻמּוֹת מִקְצָתָן שֶׁלֹּא הָיוּ מַאֲמִינִין שֶׁנִּצַּל אַבְרָהָם מֵאוּר כַּשְׂדִּים מִכִּבְשַׁן הָאֵשׁ, וְכֵיוָן שֶׁיָּצָא זֶה מִן הַחֵמָר הֶאֱמִינוּ בְאַבְרָהָם לְמַפְרֵעַ: **הֶרָה נָּסוּ.** לָהַר נָסוּ. 'הֶרָה' כְּמוֹ 'לָהַר', כָּל תֵּבָה שֶׁצְּרִיכָה לָמֶ"ד בִּתְחִלָּתָהּ הִטִּיל לָהּ הֵ"א בְּסוֹפָהּ. וְיֵשׁ חִלּוּק בֵּין 'הָרָה' לְ'הָהָרָה', שֶׁהֵ"א שֶׁבְּסוֹף הַתֵּבָה עוֹמֶדֶת בִּמְקוֹם לָמֶ"ד שֶׁבְּרֹאשָׁהּ, אֲבָל אֵינָהּ עוֹמֶדֶת בִּמְקוֹם לָמֶ"ד וּנְקוּדָה פַּתָּח תַּחְתֶּיהָ, וַהֲרֵי 'הֶרָה' כְּמוֹ 'לְהַר' אוֹ כְּמוֹ 'אֶל הַר' וְאֵינוֹ מְפֹרָשׁ לְאֵיזֶה הַר, אֶלָּא בְּחֶסֶר מָנָה תְּחִלָּה, וּכְשֶׁהוּא נוֹתֵן הֵ"א בְּרֹאשָׁהּ לִכְתֹּב 'הָהָרָה', 'הַמִּדְבָּרָה', פִּתְרוֹנוֹ כְּמוֹ 'אֶל הָהָר' אוֹ כְּמוֹ 'לָהָר', וּמַשְׁמַע לְאוֹתוֹ הַר הַיָּדוּעַ וּמְפֹרָשׁ בַּפָּרָשָׁה:

יב| **וְהוּא יֹשֵׁב בִּסְדֹם.** מִי גָּרַם לוֹ זֹאת? יְשִׁיבָתוֹ בִּסְדוֹם:

יג| **וַיָּבֹא הַפָּלִיט.** זֶה עוֹג שֶׁפָּלַט מִן הַמִּלְחָמָה, וְזֶהוּ: "נִשְׁאַר מִיֶּתֶר הָרְפָאִים" (דברים ג, יא) – 'נִשְׁאַר' שֶׁלֹּא הֲרָגוּהוּ אַמְרָפֶל וַחֲבֵרָיו כְּשֶׁהִכּוּ הָרְפָאִים בְּעַשְׁתְּרֹת קַרְנַיִם. תַּנְחוּמָא (חקת כה). וּבִבְרֵאשִׁית רַבָּה: זֶה עוֹג שֶׁפָּלַט מִדּוֹר הַמַּבּוּל, וְזֶהוּ "מִיֶּתֶר הָרְפָאִים", שֶׁנֶּאֱמַר: "הַנְּפִלִים

BACKGROUND

14:7| **En Mishpat, which is Kadesh:** These are two names for the same place, a city near the southern border of the Land of Israel (16:14; 20:1; Numbers 33:36). This city might be identical to the place called Kadesh Barnea, identified with Ein Al Qudeirat, an important crossroads roughly 25 km south of Nitzana in the Negev. There is a group of springs in the surrounding area, one of which is called Ein Al Qadis, perhaps preserving the name Kadesh.

There were also other places called Kadesh, or Kedesh, in the north of the country. Cities with these names are later mentioned in the portions of the tribes of Judah, in the south, and Naftali and Issachar, in the north (see Joshua 15:23, 19:37; I Chronicles 6:57).

Hatzatzon Tamar: According to II Chronicles 20:2, this is Ein Gedi, identified with Tel Goren, north of Nahal Arugot. Some claim that Tamar is the name of the entire province (B. Mazar). It is also the name of a southern border town, one of those built by King Solomon (I Kings 9:18; see Ezekiel 47:19), which has been identified with Ein Hatzeva, in the Arava valley, about 30 km south of the Dead Sea.

14:10| **Clay pits:** There are deposits of bitumen under the soil in the area of the Dead Sea, especially at its southern end. These release pieces of bitumen that float in the sea, and were collected and used for producing pitch. This process is described by historians from the early centuries of the Common Era (*Targum Yonatan*; Ibn Ezra; see also Onkelos).

his neighbors, Mamre and his men, who ruled over Hebron or the nearby plains of Mamre. These relations included a mutual pact for protection. The support of his allies apparently strengthened Abram's resolve.

14 **Abram heard that his brother had been taken captive.** The war itself did not interest Abram; it was the capture of Lot that spurred him into action. **And he marshaled his retainers,** called upon them to leave their homes and join him. At least some of these men had been **born in his house** and grown up in his camp.[17] The group of soldiers who answered his call amounted to a total of **three hundred and eighteen.**[D] **And** Abram **pursued** the kings' camp, which had headed north after finishing their business in Sodom, **until Dan,** a region in northern Canaan also called by a later name reflecting the area's inhabitants centuries later.[18]

15 On returning from their string of victories, during which they had vanquished the rebels, the kings encamped near Dan. This well-watered region was perfectly suited for a short stay. The kings were likely pleased by their successes and rested complacently. **He,** Abram, **arrayed** his men **against them at night,**[D] **he and his servants, and smote them,**[D] **and pursued them until Hova.** The location of Hova is unknown. The only detail the verse provides is that it is a place **which is to the left,** north, **of Damascus.**[D]

16 **He returned all the goods.** The looted property was there for the taking, as the soldiers who fled for their lives left it behind. **And also his brother Lot and his property he returned, and also the women and the people.** Plundered goods and captives were part of the victors' spoils in military campaigns of this type. The kings of the north took men for slaves, and women for all their needs. Abram released all these captives and returned to the Hebron region.

17 **The king of Sodom,** who was presumably disheveled and suffering from war wounds, **went out to meet him,** Abram, perhaps from one of the bitumen pits. The king of Sodom hoped to restore some of his losses through negotiations with Abram, who was now the rising power in the region, **after his return from smiting Kedorlaomer and the kings who were with him, to the valley of Shaveh, which is the valley of the king.**

18 **And Malkitzedek king of Shalem,**[D] another name for Jerusalem,[19] **brought out bread and wine,** a customary ritual performed as a festive greeting. In this manner Malkitzedek, who was from a different region than the king of Sodom, also sought to honor Abram as a great hero after his victory over the kings of the north. **And he,** Malkitzedek, **was** not only a king, but also **a priest of God, the Most High.** Although he lived among the local pagans, he was one of the few who worshipped the one God, referred to as El, the Most High. El is translated here as simply God. Thus Malkitzedek, who is identified by rabbinic tradition as Shem son of Noah[20] was one of a small group of individuals who did not worship idols, and whose faith was close to that of Abram.

19 As a priest, **he,** Malkitzedek **blessed him.** It is possible that Abram did not wish to be blessed by the king of Sodom, but as Malkitzedek was a priest of God, Abram accepted his blessing. **And he said: Blessed is Abram to God, the Most High, master of heaven and earth,**

20 **and blessed is God, the Most High, who delivered**[D] **your enemies into your hand.** Malkitzedek formally blessed both Abram for his character, which was blessed by God, and God for providing the victory. **He gave him a tenth of everything.** Abram treated the priest with respect and bestowed upon him a substantial gift, a tenth of all the property he had restored.[21]

21 *Fifth aliya* After seeing Abram's considerable generosity in his gift to Malkitzedek, **the king of Sodom said to Abram: Give me the**

DISCUSSION

addressed Abram as such. Abram had not participated in the war and had presumably remained largely unaffected by it. The mention of his identity as a Hebrew alludes to the fact that he was from the other side of the region, opposite the area controlled by the aggressive kings. Thus, the refugee appealed to Abram as one who had a stake in this conflict, and should oppose the kings of the north.

14:14| **Three hundred and eighteen:** Abram was able, immediately and without great effort, to gather together several hundred soldiers. It can therefore be assumed that his camp did not consist of a single family together with a few others. Rather, he was the leader of a large tribe from which he could marshal a small but significant army.

14:15| **He arrayed [*vayehalek*] against them at night, he and his servants:** He divided [*hilek*] his small army into several different forces which attacked from different directions simultaneously (Ramban; Sforno). Others interpret the phrase to mean that he divided the nighttime against them by attacking in the middle of the night.

Although the kings' camp was a large one, it was not fortified or organized for protection. It seems that it never occurred to them that they would be attacked at this juncture. The element of surprise led the kings to flee, as they had no idea who was behind the attack, or the size of the attacking force. Several incidents using a similar tactic by a small number of soldiers to defeat numerous enemies in a surprise attack at night occurred generations later: The judge Gideon, together with a small, focused band of warriors, surprised a large army of unprepared Midyanites and wiped them out (Judges 7); Yonatan son of Saul and his armor-bearer were able to confuse a huge camp of Philistines on their own, causing them to flee (I Samuel 14).

At night, he and his servants, and smote them: Abram's nighttime attack was entirely unforeseen. Had Lot not been captured, Abram would not have involved himself in the matter

יד וְאַחִי עָנֵר וְהֵם בַּעֲלֵי בְרִית־אַבְרָם: וַיִּשְׁמַע אַבְרָם כִּי נִשְׁבָּה אָחִיו וַיָּרֶק

טו אֶת־חֲנִיכָיו יְלִידֵי בֵיתוֹ שְׁמֹנָה עָשָׂר וּשְׁלֹשׁ מֵאוֹת וַיִּרְדֹּף עַד־דָּן: וַיֵּחָלֵק

טז עֲלֵיהֶם | לַיְלָה הוּא וַעֲבָדָיו וַיַּכֵּם וַיִּרְדְּפֵם עַד־חוֹבָה אֲשֶׁר מִשְּׂמֹאל לְדַמָּשֶׂק:

יז וַיָּשֶׁב אֵת כָּל־הָרְכֻשׁ וְגַם אֶת־לוֹט אָחִיו וּרְכֻשׁוֹ הֵשִׁיב וְגַם אֶת־הַנָּשִׁים

וְאֶת־הָעָם: וַיֵּצֵא מֶלֶךְ־סְדֹם לִקְרָאתוֹ אַחֲרֵי שׁוּבוֹ מֵהַכּוֹת אֶת־כְּדָרְלָעֹמֶר

יח וְאֶת־הַמְּלָכִים אֲשֶׁר אִתּוֹ אֶל־עֵמֶק שָׁוֵה הוּא עֵמֶק הַמֶּלֶךְ: וּמַלְכִּי־צֶדֶק

יט מֶלֶךְ שָׁלֵם הוֹצִיא לֶחֶם וָיָיִן וְהוּא כֹהֵן לְאֵל עֶלְיוֹן: וַיְבָרְכֵהוּ וַיֹּאמַר בָּרוּךְ אַבְרָם

כ לְאֵל עֶלְיוֹן קֹנֵה שָׁמַיִם וָאָרֶץ: וּבָרוּךְ אֵל עֶלְיוֹן אֲשֶׁר־מִגֵּן צָרֶיךָ בְּיָדֶךָ וַיִּתֶּן־

כא לוֹ מַעֲשֵׂר מִכֹּל: וַיֹּאמֶר מֶלֶךְ־סְדֹם אֶל־אַבְרָם תֶּן־לִי הַנֶּפֶשׁ וְהָרְכֻשׁ קַח־לָךְ: חמישי

רש"י

הָיוּ בְחֶלְקוֹ" וְגוֹ' (לעיל ו, ד). וּמְתֻכָּן שֶׁיִּהְיוּ אַבְרָם וְיֵשַׁע אֶת שָׂרָה: הָעִבְרִי. שֶׁבָּא מֵעֵבֶר הַנָּהָר: בַּעֲלֵי בְרִית אַבְרָם. שֶׁכָּרְתוּ עִמּוֹ בְּרִית:

יד וַיָּרֶק. כְּתַרְגּוּמוֹ "וְזָרֵיז", וְכֵן: "וַהֲרִיקֹתִי אַחֲרֵיכֶם חָרֶב" (ויקרא כו, לג), אֶזְדַּיֵּן בְּחַרְבִּי עֲלֵיכֶם, וְכֵן: "אָרִיק חַרְבִּי" (שמות טו, ט), וְכֵן: "וְהָרֵק חֲנִית וּסְגֹר" (תהלים לה, ג): חֲנִיכָיו. שֶׁחִנְּכוֹ לְמִצְוֹת, וְהוּא לְשׁוֹן הַתְחָלַת כְּנִיסַת הָאָדָם אוֹ כְּלִי לְאֻמָּנוּת שֶׁהוּא עָתִיד לַעֲמֹד בָּהּ. וְכֵן: "חֲנֹךְ לַנַּעַר" (משלי כב, ו), "חֲנֻכַּת הַמִּזְבֵּחַ" (במדבר ז, י), "חֲנֻכַּת הַבַּיִת" (תהלים ל, א), וּבְלַעַז קוֹרִין לוֹ אנציניי"ר: שְׁמֹנָה עָשָׂר וְגוֹ'. רַבּוֹתֵינוּ אָמְרוּ: אֱלִיעֶזֶר לְבַדּוֹ הָיָה, וְהוּא מִנְיַן גִּימַטְרִיָּא שֶׁל שְׁמוֹ: עַד דָּן. שָׁם תָּשַׁשׁ כֹּחוֹ, שֶׁרָאָה שֶׁעֲתִידִים בָּנָיו לְהַעֲמִיד שָׁם עֵגֶל:

טו וַיֵּחָלֵק עֲלֵיהֶם. לְפִי פְשׁוּטוֹ סָרֵס הַמִּקְרָא: "וַיֵּחָלֵק הוּא וַעֲבָדָיו עֲלֵיהֶם לַיְלָה" כְּדֶרֶךְ הָרוֹדְפִים שֶׁמִּתְפַּלְּגִים אַחַר הַנִּרְדָּפִים כְּשֶׁבּוֹרְחִים זֶה לְכָאן וְזֶה לְכָאן: לָיְלָה. כְּלוֹמַר, אַחַר שֶׁחָשְׁכָה לֹא נִמְנַע מִלְּרָדְפָם. וּמִדְרַשׁ אַגָּדָה שֶׁנֶּחֱלַק הַלַּיְלָה, וּבַחֲצִי הָרִאשׁוֹן שֶׁלּוֹ נַעֲשָׂה לוֹ נֵס, וְחֶצְיוֹ הַשֵּׁנִי נִשְׁמַר וּבָא לַחֲצוֹת לַיְלָה שֶׁל מִצְרַיִם: עַד חוֹבָה. אֵין מָקוֹם שֶׁשְּׁמוֹ "חוֹבָה", וְדָן קוֹרֵא "חוֹבָה" עַל שֵׁם עֲבוֹדָה זָרָה שֶׁעֲתִידָה לִהְיוֹת שָׁם:

יז עֵמֶק שָׁוֵה. כָּךְ שְׁמוֹ, כְּתַרְגּוּמוֹ: "לְמֵישַׁר מִפְנָא" פְּנוּי מֵאִילָנוֹת וּמִכָּל מִכְשׁוֹל: עֵמֶק הַמֶּלֶךְ. בֵּית רֵיסָא דְמַלְכָּא" (אונקלוס), בֵּית רִיס אֶחָד, שֶׁהוּא שְׁלֹשִׁים קָנִים שֶׁהָיָה מְיֻחָד לַמֶּלֶךְ לְשַׂחֵק שָׁם. וּמִדְרַשׁ אַגָּדָה, עֵמֶק

שֶׁהֻשְׁווּ שָׁם כָּל הָאֻמּוֹת וְהִמְלִיכוּ אֶת אַבְרָהָם עֲלֵיהֶם לִנְשִׂיא אֱלֹהִים וּלְקָצִין:

יח וּמַלְכִּי צֶדֶק. מִדְרַשׁ אַגָּדָה, הוּא שֵׁם בֶּן נֹחַ: לֶחֶם וָיָיִן. כָּךְ עוֹשִׂים לִיגֵעֵי מִלְחָמָה, וְהֶרְאָה לוֹ שֶׁאֵין בְּלִבּוֹ עָלָיו עַל שֶׁהָרַג אֶת בָּנָיו. וּמִדְרַשׁ אַגָּדָה, רָמַז לוֹ עַל הַמְּנָחוֹת וְעַל הַנְּסָכִים שֶׁיַּקְרִיבוּ שָׁם בָּנָיו:

יט קֹנֵה שָׁמַיִם וָאָרֶץ. כְּמוֹ: עֹשֵׂה שָׁמַיִם וָאָרֶץ, עַל יְדֵי עֲשִׂיָּתָן קְנָאָן לִהְיוֹת שֶׁלּוֹ:

כ אֲשֶׁר מִגֵּן. אֲשֶׁר הִסְגִּיר, וְכֵן: "הֲמַגֶּנְךָ יִשְׂרָאֵל" (הושע יא, ח): וַיִּתֶּן לוֹ. אַבְרָם: מַעֲשֵׂר מִכֹּל. אֲשֶׁר לוֹ, לְפִי שֶׁהָיָה כֹהֵן:

כא תֶּן לִי הַנֶּפֶשׁ. מִן הַשְּׁבִי שֶׁלִּי שֶׁהִצַּלְתָּ, הַחֲזֵר לִי הַגּוּפִים לְבַדָּם:

DISCUSSION

➤ at all. Nevertheless, the Sages suggest another motive for Abram's involvement in the war: His unresolved account with Amrafel dating back to the days when Abram was living in Ur of the Chaldeans, in Shinar (see *Eiruvin* 53a).

To the left of Damascus: The names of the directions in the Bible are oriented based on the perspective of an individual facing east. Thus, east is called *kedem*, meaning the front. Interestingly, the English word orientation also comes from Orient, meaning east, as the east was apparently used as the reference point for

measurements. Similarly, many ancient maps are drawn with east at the top.

The west, sometimes called *yam*, meaning sea, is also known as *ahor*, meaning back, and the Mediterranean Sea is called *HaYam HaAharon*, the sea to the rear. For the same reason, south is called *Teiman*, as it is to the right [*yamin*], and consequently north can be termed left [*smol*], as in this verse. Even today, in Arabic north is called *shimāl*.

14:18 | Malkitzedek King of Shalem: Other kings who later reigned in Jerusalem, such as

Adoni Tzedek (Joshua 10:1), also had the suffix *zedek*, meaning righteous, as part of their names. In a similar fashion, some explain the use of the name Malkitzedek in Psalms 110:4 as a reference to David (Radak). Perhaps these names were given specifically to the kings of this city, which would later (Isaiah 1:26) be called "the city of righteousness" (*Bereshit Rabba* 43:6; Ramban; Rashbam 41:10; Radak, Joshua 10:1).

14:20 | Delivered [*migen*]: Some explain that *migen* means that God broke or overthrew the enemies (see Hosea 11:8; Lamentations 3:65).

people, and take the property for yourself. Let me have the residents of my city, Sodom, as I am responsible for them, and we will waive any claim to the plunder. You can keep any property the kings looted from us, which you rescued from them.

22 **Abram said to the king of Sodom: I have raised my hand to the Lord, God Most High, master of heaven and earth.** The raising of one's hand or hands to the heavens is a gesture indicating an oath.[22]

23 **Surely, be it** even **a thread** of a garment **or a shoelace, I will not take of anything that is yours,** so **that you will not say: I made Abram rich.** I do not want my wealth to be attributed to you and to the property of Sodom. Consequently, I shall return all the property to you

24 **without regard to me,** leave me out of the calculations, do not take me into account (see also 41:16). **Only that which the young men have** already **eaten** from the property we have restored, as they needed it for their sustenance on their way back from the north to Jerusalem; this property shall not be restored. **And** also **the portion of the men who went with me, Aner, Eshkol, and Mamre,** Abram's friends and allies, who were probably not among his three hundred and eighteen soldiers. Since they joined with Abram and supported his cause, they deserved a portion of the spoils and Abram did not wish to deprive them of it. Therefore, he said: I insist that **they shall take their portion.** But as for me, although as the victorious commander I am rightfully entitled to the majority of the spoils, I relinquish my entire portion.

The Vision and the Covenant between the Parts

GENESIS 15:1–21

Both parts of this section deal with Abram's future. First, he is promised that he will have descendants to continue after him. In the second part, which depicts the symbolic enactment of a covenant, God provides him with some details regarding the future of those descendants, and promises him that they will ultimately inherit the land of Canaan.

15 1 **After these matters,** after Abram's war with the great kings of the north, he may have been concerned that the powerful rulers might return to Canaan for another military campaign in order to take revenge. And so **the word of the Lord came to Abram in a** prophetic **vision, saying: Fear not, Abram, I am a shield for you,** and I will protect you from all harm. Additionally, **your** future **reward** for your deeds **is very great.**

2 **Abram said: My Lord God, what will You give me? I go childless.** You have promised me an exceedingly great reward, but what can I do with it when I have no children? **And the steward of my house,** the one in charge of all my dealings since I have no son, **is Eliezer of,** who comes from,[23] **Damascus.**

3 **Abram said: Behold, to me You have not given descendants, and a member of my household is my heir.** Since I do not have a son, and my steward will inherit me, this reward has no meaning for me. Although Eliezer is indeed a faithful and decent man, he is not my child.

4 **Behold, the word of the Lord came to him, saying:**[D] **This man** who is the steward of your house **shall not be your heir; rather, one who shall emerge from your loins, he shall be your heir.**

5 **He took him,** or instructed him to go, **outside, and said: Look now toward the heavens, and count the stars,** and see **if you can count them. And** after Abram had looked toward the heavens, **He said to him: So shall be your descendants;** they will be as numerous as the stars.

6 Although this seemed impossible to Abram, as he and his wife were elderly, **he believed in the Lord; and He,** God, **considered it,** Abram's faith,[244] **for him as righteousness,**[D] as a correct, upright, and proper act.

7 **He said to him: I am the Lord who took you out of Ur of the Chaldeans,** among other reasons, in order **to give you this land to inherit it.**

Sixth aliya

8 **He said: My Lord God, how shall I know that I shall inherit it?** This statement does not indicate a lack of faith in the fulfillment of God's promise. However, the promise would come to pass only for Abram's descendants, none of whom had yet been born, while in the present there was no practical expression of his possession of the land. Hence, Abram requested some sort of assurance or deed that would serve as a confirmation and reinforcement of the covenant.

9 **He said to him: Take Me a triple heifer, and a triple female goat, and a triple ram,**[D] **and a dove, and a young pigeon.**[D]

DISCUSSION

15:4| **Saying:** Generally, this common term means "thus" or "in these words and in this manner." Nowadays, we would typically replace it with punctuation that introduces a quotation.

15:6| **Righteousness [*tzedaka*]:** Here the term *tzedaka* does not mean charity, a gift to the poor, as it usually does in contemporary usage. On many occasions in the Bible, its meaning is closer to the word *tzedek*, justice, indicating the right and appropriate deed. For example, in Deuteronomy 33:21 it is used in parallel to *mishpat*, meaning justice: He executed the righteousness [*tzidkat*] of the Lord and His ordinances [*mishpatav*] in Israel (see also Isaiah 5:16, and commentary ad loc.).

15:9| **A triple heifer, and a triple female goat, and a triple ram:** Some commentaries explain this term to mean a choice animal of

כב וַיֹּאמֶר אַבְרָם אֶל־מֶלֶךְ סְדֹם הֲרִמֹתִי יָדִי אֶל־יְהוָה אֵל עֶלְיוֹן קֹנֵה שָׁמַיִם וָאָרֶץ׃
כג אִם־מִחוּט וְעַד שְׂרוֹךְ־נַעַל וְאִם־אֶקַּח מִכָּל־אֲשֶׁר־לָךְ וְלֹא תֹאמַר אֲנִי הֶעֱשַׁרְתִּי
כד אֶת־אַבְרָם׃ בִּלְעָדַי רַק אֲשֶׁר אָכְלוּ הַנְּעָרִים וְחֵלֶק הָאֲנָשִׁים אֲשֶׁר הָלְכוּ אִתִּי
טו א עָנֵר אֶשְׁכֹּל וּמַמְרֵא הֵם יִקְחוּ חֶלְקָם׃ אַחַר | הַדְּבָרִים הָאֵלֶּה הָיָה יב
דְבַר־יְהוָה אֶל־אַבְרָם בַּמַּחֲזֶה לֵאמֹר אַל־תִּירָא אַבְרָם אָנֹכִי מָגֵן לָךְ שְׂכָרְךָ
ב הַרְבֵּה מְאֹד׃ וַיֹּאמֶר אַבְרָם אֲדֹנָי יֱהוִה מַה־תִּתֶּן־לִי וְאָנֹכִי הוֹלֵךְ עֲרִירִי וּבֶן־
ג מֶשֶׁק בֵּיתִי הוּא דַּמֶּשֶׂק אֱלִיעֶזֶר׃ וַיֹּאמֶר אַבְרָם הֵן לִי לֹא נָתַתָּה זָרַע וְהִנֵּה
ד בֶן־בֵּיתִי יוֹרֵשׁ אֹתִי׃ וְהִנֵּה דְבַר־יְהוָה אֵלָיו לֵאמֹר לֹא יִירָשְׁךָ זֶה כִּי־אִם אֲשֶׁר
ה יֵצֵא מִמֵּעֶיךָ הוּא יִירָשֶׁךָ׃ וַיּוֹצֵא אֹתוֹ הַחוּצָה וַיֹּאמֶר הַבֶּט־נָא הַשָּׁמַיְמָה וּסְפֹר
ו הַכּוֹכָבִים אִם־תּוּכַל לִסְפֹּר אֹתָם וַיֹּאמֶר לוֹ כֹּה יִהְיֶה זַרְעֶךָ׃ וְהֶאֱמִן בַּיהוָה
ז וַיַּחְשְׁבֶהָ לּוֹ צְדָקָה׃ וַיֹּאמֶר אֵלָיו אֲנִי יְהוָה אֲשֶׁר הוֹצֵאתִיךָ מֵאוּר כַּשְׂדִּים לָתֶת ששי
ח לְךָ אֶת־הָאָרֶץ הַזֹּאת לְרִשְׁתָּהּ׃ וַיֹּאמַר אֲדֹנָי יֱהוִה בַּמָּה אֵדַע כִּי אִירָשֶׁנָּה׃
ט וַיֹּאמֶר אֵלָיו קְחָה לִי עֶגְלָה מְשֻׁלֶּשֶׁת וְעֵז מְשֻׁלֶּשֶׁת וְאַיִל מְשֻׁלָּשׁ וְתֹר וְגוֹזָל׃

רש"י

כב| הֲרִמֹתִי יָדִי. לְשׁוֹן שְׁבוּעָה, מֵרִים אֲנִי אֶת יָדִי לָאֵל עֶלְיוֹן, וְכֵן: "בִּי נִשְׁבַּעְתִּי" (להלן כב, טז) – נִשְׁבָּע אֲנִי. וְכֵן: "נָתַתִּי כֶּסֶף הַשָּׂדֶה קַח מִמֶּנִּי" (להלן כג, יג) – נוֹתֵן אֲנִי לְךָ כֶּסֶף הַשָּׂדֶה וְקָחֵהוּ מִמֶּנִּי:

כג| אִם מִחוּט וְעַד שְׂרוֹךְ נַעַל. אֲעַכֵּב לְעַצְמִי מִן הַשֶּׁבִי: וְאִם אֶקַּח מִכָּל אֲשֶׁר לָךְ. אִם תֹּאמַר לָתֵת לִי שָׂכָר מִבֵּית גְּנָזֶיךָ: וְלֹא תֹאמַר וְגוֹ'. שֶׁהַקָּדוֹשׁ בָּרוּךְ הוּא הִבְטִיחַנִי לְעַשְּׁרֵנִי, שֶׁנֶּאֱמַר: "וַאֲבָרֶכְךָ וַאֲגַדְּלָה שְׁמֶךָ" (לעיל יב, ב):

כד| הַנְּעָרִים. עֲבָדַי אֲשֶׁר הָלְכוּ אִתִּי, וְעוֹד "עָנֵר אֶשְׁכֹּל וּמַמְרֵא" וְגוֹ'; אַף עַל פִּי שֶׁעֲבָדַי נִכְנְסוּ לַמִּלְחָמָה, שֶׁנֶּאֱמַר: "וַיִּרְדֹּף עַד דָּן" (לעיל פסוק יד), וְעָנֵר וַחֲבֵרָיו יָשְׁבוּ עַל הַכֵּלִים לִשְׁמֹר. וּמִמֶּנּוּ לָמַד דָּוִד שֶׁאָמַר: "כְּחֵלֶק הַיֹּרֵד בַּמִּלְחָמָה וּכְחֵלֶק הַיֹּשֵׁב עַל הַכֵּלִים יַחְדָּו יַחֲלֹקוּ" (שמואל א' ל, כד), וּלְכָךְ נֶאֱמַר: "וַיְהִי מֵהַיּוֹם הַהוּא וָמַעְלָה וַיְשִׂמֶהָ לְחֹק וּלְמִשְׁפָּט" (שם פסוק כה), וְלֹא נֶאֱמַר 'וָהָלְאָה', לְפִי שֶׁכְּבָר נִתַּן הַחֹק בִּימֵי אַבְרָהָם:

פרק טו

א| אַחַר הַדְּבָרִים הָאֵלֶּה. כָּל מָקוֹם שֶׁנֶּאֱמַר 'אַחַר' – סָמוּךְ, 'אַחֲרֵי' – מֻפְלָג. בְּרֵאשִׁית רַבָּה (מד, ה). אַחַר שֶׁנַּעֲשָׂה לוֹ נֵס זֶה שֶׁהָרַג אֶת הַמְּלָכִים, וְהָיָה דוֹאֵג וְאוֹמֵר: שֶׁמָּא קִבַּלְתִּי שָׂכָר עַל כָּל צִדְקוֹתַי? לְכָךְ אָמַר לוֹ הַמָּקוֹם: "אַל תִּירָא": אָנֹכִי מָגֵן לָךְ. מִן הָעֹנֶשׁ, שֶׁלֹּא תֵּעָנֵשׁ עַל כָּל אוֹתָן נְפָשׁוֹת שֶׁהָרַגְתָּ. וּמַה שֶּׁאַתָּה דוֹאֵג עַל קִבּוּל שְׂכָרְךָ – "שְׂכָרְךָ הַרְבֵּה מְאֹד":

ב| הוֹלֵךְ עֲרִירִי. מְנַחֵם בֶּן סָרוּק פֵּרְשׁוֹ לְשׁוֹן יוֹרֵשׁ, וְחִבֵּר לוֹ: "עֵר וְעֹנֶה" (מלאכי ב, יב). 'עֲרִירִי' – בְּלֹא יוֹרֵשׁ, כַּאֲשֶׁר תֹּאמַר: "וּבְכָל תְּבוּאָתִי תְשָׁרֵשׁ" (איוב לא, יב) – תַּעֲקֹר שָׁרָשֶׁיהָ, כָּךְ לְשׁוֹן עֲרִירִי – אֲשֶׁר בָּנִים, וּבְלַעַז דישאנפנטי"ץ. וְלִי נִרְאֶה, "עֵר וְעֹנֶה" מִגִּזְרַת "וְלִבִּי עֵר" (שיר השירים ה, ב), וַעֲרִירִי לְשׁוֹן חֻרְבָּן, וְכֵן: "עָרוּ עָרוּ" (תהלים קלז, ז), וְכֵן: "עָרוֹת יְסוֹד" (חבקוק ג, יג), וְכֵן: "עַרְעֵר תִּתְעַרְעַר" (ירמיה נא, נח), וְכֵן: "כִּי אַרְזָה עֵרָה" (צפניה ב, יד): וּבֶן מֶשֶׁק בֵּיתִי. כְּתַרְגּוּמוֹ, כָּל בֵּיתִי נִזּוֹן עַל פִּיו, כְּמוֹ: "וְעַל פִּיךָ יִשַּׁק" (להלן מא, מ), אַפּוֹטְרוֹפּוֹס שֶׁלִּי; וְאִלּוּ הָיָה לִי בֵּן, הָיָה בְּנִי מְמֻנֶּה עַל שֶׁלִּי: דַּמֶּשֶׂק. לְפִי הַתַּרְגּוּם מִדַּמֶּשֶׂק הָיָה; וּלְפִי מִדְרַשׁ אַגָּדָה, שֶׁרָדַף הַמְּלָכִים עַד דַּמֶּשֶׂק. וּבַתַּלְמוּד שֶׁלָּנוּ (יומא כח ע"ב) דּוֹרְשׁוֹ נוֹטָרִיקוֹן: דּוֹלֶה וּמַשְׁקֶה מִתּוֹרַת רַבּוֹ לַאֲחֵרִים:

ג| הֵן לִי לֹא נָתַתָּה זָרַע. וּמַה תּוֹעֶלֶת בְּכָל אֲשֶׁר תִּתֵּן לִי?:

ה| וַיּוֹצֵא אֹתוֹ הַחוּצָה. לְפִי פְשׁוּטוֹ, הוֹצִיאוֹ מֵאָהֳלוֹ לַחוּץ לִרְאוֹת הַכּוֹכָבִים. וּלְפִי מִדְרָשׁוֹ, אָמַר לוֹ: צֵא מֵאִצְטַגְנִינוּת שֶׁלְּךָ, שֶׁרָאִיתָ בַּמַּזָּלוֹת שֶׁאֵינְךָ עָתִיד לְהַעֲמִיד בֵּן – אַבְרָם אֵין לוֹ בֵּן, אֲבָל אַבְרָהָם יֵשׁ לוֹ בֵּן; שָׂרַי לֹא תֵלֵד, אֲבָל שָׂרָה תֵּלֵד – אֲנִי קוֹרֵא לָכֶם שֵׁם אַחֵר וְיִשְׁתַּנֶּה הַמַּזָּל. דָּבָר אַחֵר, הוֹצִיאוֹ מֵחֲלָלוֹ שֶׁל עוֹלָם וְהִגְבִּיהוֹ לְמַעְלָה מִן הַכּוֹכָבִים; וְזֶהוּ לְשׁוֹן הַבָּטָה, מִלְמַעְלָה לְמַטָּה:

ו| וְהֶאֱמִן בַּה'. לֹא שָׁאַל לוֹ אוֹת עַל זֹאת, אֲבָל עַל יְרֻשַּׁת הָאָרֶץ שָׁאַל לוֹ אוֹת וְאָמַר לוֹ: "בַּמָּה אֵדַע" (להלן פסוק ח): וַיַּחְשְׁבֶהָ לּוֹ צְדָקָה. הַקָּדוֹשׁ בָּרוּךְ הוּא חֲשָׁבָהּ לְאַבְרָהָם לִזְכוּת וְלִצְדָקָה עַל הָאֱמוּנָה שֶׁהֶאֱמִין בּוֹ. דָּבָר אַחֵר, "בַּמָּה אֵדַע" – לֹא שָׁאַל לוֹ אוֹת, אֶלָּא אָמַר לְפָנָיו: הוֹדִיעֵנִי בְּאֵיזֶה זְכוּת יִתְקַיְּמוּ בָהּ; וְאָמַר לוֹ הַקָּדוֹשׁ בָּרוּךְ הוּא: בִּזְכוּת הַקָּרְבָּנוֹת:

ט| עֶגְלָה מְשֻׁלֶּשֶׁת. שְׁלֹשָׁה עֲגָלִים, רֶמֶז לִשְׁלֹשָׁה פָּרִים: פַּר יוֹם הַכִּפּוּרִים, וּפַר הֶעְלֵם דָּבָר שֶׁל צִבּוּר וְעֶגְלָה עֲרוּפָה: וְעֵז מְשֻׁלֶּשֶׁת. רֶמֶז לְשָׂעִיר הַנַּעֲשֶׂה בִּפְנִים, וּשְׂעִירֵי מוּסָפִין שֶׁל מוֹעֵד, וּשְׂעִירַת חַטָּאת יָחִיד: וְאַיִל מְשֻׁלָּשׁ. אָשָׁם וַדַּאי וְאָשָׁם תָּלוּי וְכִבְשָׂה שֶׁל חַטָּאת יָחִיד: וְתֹר וְגוֹזָל. תּוֹרִים וּבְנֵי יוֹנָה:

10 **He took all these for him** after they had each been slaughtered, **divided them in the middle** into approximately equal halves, **and placed each half opposite the other,** with a gap separating them. **But the birds,** the dove and young pigeon,[25] **he did not divide.**[D]

11 **The birds of prey,** no specific bird, but birds of prey in general, **descended onto the carcasses.** These birds represent enemies who attempt to undermine the covenant. **And Abram drove them away.** He sought to fight these symbolic enemies and expel them. This indicates that the covenant and its fulfillment would encounter many future difficulties and threats, which must be opposed. Some explain that Abram put the pieces back to their initial state and miraculously restored them to life, as a sign of future renewal and resurrection.[26]

12 This episode involved three stages: First came the initial prophetic vision, which Abram apparently experienced at night; this was followed by the preparations for the covenantal ritual and the descent of the birds of prey upon the carcasses, which occurred during the day. Then came the third and final stage, which is described in this verse: **It was when the sun was setting; a deep sleep fell upon Abram.** This was not an ordinary sleep due to tiredness, but an absolute inability to stay awake, as though an external factor put him in a trance. **And behold,** together with the deep sleep, **a dread, a great darkness,**[D] a terrible fear devoid of specific content or meaning, **fell upon him.**

13 Here the covenant is formulated as a detailed, defined prophecy.

He, God, **said to Abram: Know that your descendants shall be strangers in a land that is not theirs.** Indeed you will father children and will ultimately inherit the land, but your descendants shall not receive it immediately. The covenant will not be fulfilled in a smooth, straightforward manner. Beforehand, they will be foreigners and nomads like you are. However, in contrast to you, their wanderings will not be in this land that they are destined to inherit, but rather in a foreign place that is not their own. **And** furthermore, **they shall be enslaved to them,** the inhabitants of that foreign land; **and they shall oppress them** for **four hundred years.**[D] The content of this prophecy fits the dread that Abram felt, but straightaway, God encouraged him with a promise:

14 **And also that nation that they shall serve, I will judge.**[D] Your descendants will suffer there for reasons of My own, but the nation that enslaves them will be punished for doing so. **And afterwards,** when the designated hour arrives, **they,** your children, **will emerge with great property.**

15 But these travails will not affect you personally, **and you** will not be exiled or suffer, but rather, you **shall go to your fathers,** you will die and be united with your ancestors **in peace,** and **you shall** even **be buried at a good old age;** you will live a long and peaceful life.

16 **And the fourth generation** of your descendants **shall return here** to inherit the promised land, **for the iniquity of the Emorite is not complete until then.**[D]

— DISCUSSION —

the best quality, with a price three times that of an ordinary one (*Tosafot* on *Gittin* 56a). Others maintain that God commanded Abram to take three heifers, three female goats, and three rams (Onkelos; Rashi).

Heifer, goat, ram, dove, young pigeon: Abram could understand only some of the various details of the symbolism contained in this covenant. The significance of other aspects of the vision would become clear only to later generations.

The commentaries note that all the types of animals mentioned here – cattle, goats, rams, doves, and young pigeons – are among those that the Torah would later mandate for offerings in the Temple. This allusion was probably lost on Abram at the time, although there was apparently a tradition from the days of Noah with regard to the difference between ritually pure and impure animals (see 7:2). Possible allusions and references to various offerings would become meaningful at another time and under other

circumstances (see *Bereshit Rabba* 44:14; *Shemot Rabba* 51:7).

15:10 | But the birds, he did not divide: The division of animals was a customary feature of a covenantal agreement, a kind of formal, binding contract. Many years later, in the generation of the destruction of the First Temple, a ritual would also be performed involving parts of animals (Jeremiah 34:18).

The division of animals into two parts symbolizes the presentation of the two parties as parts of a single, binding entity, an aspect rendered more prominent when the animalistic aspects of human existence, which separate people from one another, are torn asunder (see *Beit Ya'akov, Lekh Lekha* 1). In the ritual described by Jeremiah, the parties to the covenant pass between the pieces of the animals, and through this symbolic act they implement a covenant.

Since this was an accepted manner of enacting a covenant, God's command to take the

animals can be seen as a response to Abram's request for confirmation of His promise.

15:12 | A dread, a great darkness: The Bible does not record many accounts of the emotions experienced by prophets while receiving their prophetic revelations. Nevertheless, the dread depicted here is fundamentally similar to several other descriptions of prophets falling upon their faces or losing their strength.

It seems that the great terror that is also described elsewhere as accompanying the prophetic experience is not a part of the prophecy itself (see I Samuel 19:24, Ezekiel 1:28, Daniel 10:7–9). Rather, it occurs in advance of, and as part of, the prophet's preparation for the revelation. The lofty experience of prophecy is not a comfortable and relaxing one. On the contrary, it is an awesome experience emptying the person of all awareness of himself as a separate individual. It overwhelms and silences the prophet, similar to an anesthetic administered before surgery.

וַיִּקַּח־לוֹ אֶת־כָּל־אֵלֶּה וַיְבַתֵּר אֹתָם בַּתָּוֶךְ וַיִּתֵּן אִישׁ־בִּתְרוֹ לִקְרַאת רֵעֵהוּ
וְאֶת־הַצִּפֹּר לֹא בָתָר: וַיֵּרֶד הָעַיִט עַל־הַפְּגָרִים וַיַּשֵּׁב אֹתָם אַבְרָם: וַיְהִי הַשֶּׁמֶשׁ
לָבוֹא וְתַרְדֵּמָה נָפְלָה עַל־אַבְרָם וְהִנֵּה אֵימָה חֲשֵׁכָה גְדֹלָה נֹפֶלֶת עָלָיו: וַיֹּאמֶר
לְאַבְרָם יָדֹעַ תֵּדַע כִּי־גֵר ׀ יִהְיֶה זַרְעֲךָ בְּאֶרֶץ לֹא לָהֶם וַעֲבָדוּם וְעִנּוּ אֹתָם אַרְבַּע
מֵאוֹת שָׁנָה: וְגַם אֶת־הַגּוֹי אֲשֶׁר יַעֲבֹדוּ דָּן אָנֹכִי וְאַחֲרֵי־כֵן יֵצְאוּ בִּרְכֻשׁ גָּדוֹל:
וְאַתָּה תָּבוֹא אֶל־אֲבֹתֶיךָ בְּשָׁלוֹם תִּקָּבֵר בְּשֵׂיבָה טוֹבָה: וְדוֹר רְבִיעִי יָשׁוּבוּ הֵנָּה

רש"י

יו **וַיְבַתֵּר אֹתָם.** חִלֵּק כָּל אֶחָד לִשְׁנֵי חֲלָקִים; וְאֵין הַמִּקְרָא יוֹצֵא מִידֵי פְשׁוּטוֹ, לְפִי שֶׁהָיָה כּוֹרֵת בְּרִית עִמּוֹ לִשְׁמֹר הַבְטָחָתוֹ לְהוֹרִישׁ לְבָנָיו אֶת הָאָרֶץ, כְּדִכְתִיב: "בַּיּוֹם הַהוּא כָּרַת ה' אֶת אַבְרָם בְּרִית לֵאמֹר" וְגוֹ' (להלן פסוק יח), וְדֶרֶךְ כּוֹרְתֵי בְּרִית לַחַלֵּק בְּהֵמָה וְלַעֲבֹר בֵּין בְּתָרֶיהָ, כְּמָה שֶׁנֶּאֱמַר לְהַלָּן: "הָעֹבְרִים בֵּין בִּתְרֵי הָעֵגֶל" (ירמיה לד, יט), אַף כָּאן: "תַּנּוּר עָשָׁן וְלַפִּיד אֵשׁ אֲשֶׁר עָבַר בֵּין הַגְּזָרִים" (להלן פסוק יז) הוּא שְׁלוּחוֹ שֶׁל שְׁכִינָה שֶׁהִיא אֵשׁ: **וְאֶת הַצִּפֹּר לֹא בָתָר.** לְפִי שֶׁהָאֻמּוֹת נִמְשְׁלוּ לְפָרִים וְאֵילִים וּשְׂעִירִים, שֶׁנֶּאֱמַר: "סְבָבוּנִי פָּרִים רַבִּים" וְגוֹ' (תהלים כב, יג), וְאוֹמֵר: "הָאַיִל אֲשֶׁר רָאִיתָ בַּעַל הַקְּרָנַיִם מַלְכֵי מָדַי וּפָרָס" (דניאל ח, כ), וְאוֹמֵר: "וְהַצָּפִיר הַשָּׂעִיר מֶלֶךְ יָוָן" (שם כא), וְיִשְׂרָאֵל נִמְשְׁלוּ לִבְנֵי יוֹנָה, שֶׁנֶּאֱמַר: "יוֹנָתִי בְּחַגְוֵי הַסֶּלַע" (שיר השירים ב, יד), לְפִיכָךְ בִּתֵּר הַבְּהֵמוֹת, רֶמֶז שֶׁיִּהְיוּ הָאֻמּוֹת כָּלִין וְהוֹלְכִין, "וְאֶת הַצִּפֹּר לֹא בָתָר" – רֶמֶז שֶׁיִּהְיוּ יִשְׂרָאֵל קַיָּמִין לְעוֹלָם:

יא **הָעַיִט.** הוּא עוֹף, וְעַל שֵׁם שֶׁהוּא עָט וְשׁוֹאֵף אֶל הַנְּבֵלוֹת לָטוּשׂ עֲלֵי אֹכֶל, כְּמוֹ: "וַתַּעַט אֶל הַשָּׁלָל" (שמואל

חי טו, יט): עַל הַפְּגָרִים. עַל הַבְּתָרִים: **וַיַּשֵּׁב.** לְשׁוֹן נְשִׁיבָה וְהַפְרָחָה, כְּמוֹ: "יַשֵּׁב רוּחוֹ" (תהלים קמז, יח), רֶמֶז שֶׁיָּבֹא דָוִד בֶּן יִשַׁי לְכַלּוֹתָם, וְאֵין מַנִּיחִין אוֹתוֹ מִן הַשָּׁמַיִם עַד שֶׁיָּבֹא מֶלֶךְ הַמָּשִׁיחַ:

יב **וְהִנֵּה אֵימָה וְגוֹ'.** רֶמֶז לְצָרוֹת וְחֹשֶׁךְ שֶׁל גָּלֻיּוֹת:

יג **כִּי גֵר יִהְיֶה זַרְעֲךָ.** מִשֶּׁנּוֹלַד יִצְחָק עַד שֶׁיָּצְאוּ יִשְׂרָאֵל מִמִּצְרַיִם אַרְבַּע מֵאוֹת שָׁנָה. כֵּיצַד? יִצְחָק בֶּן שִׁשִּׁים שָׁנָה כְּשֶׁנּוֹלַד יַעֲקֹב, וְיַעֲקֹב כְּשֶׁיָּרַד לְמִצְרַיִם אָמַר: "יְמֵי שְׁנֵי מְגוּרַי שְׁלֹשִׁים וּמְאַת שָׁנָה" (להלן מז, ט), הֲרֵי מֵאָה וְתִשְׁעִים, וּבְמִצְרַיִם הָיוּ מָאתַיִם וְעֶשֶׂר כְּמִנְיַן "רְדוּ", הֲרֵי אַרְבַּע מֵאוֹת שָׁנָה. וְאִם תֹּאמַר, בְּמִצְרַיִם הָיוּ אַרְבַּע מֵאוֹת – הֲרֵי קְהָת מִיּוֹרְדֵי מִצְרַיִם הָיָה, צֵא וַחֲשֹׁב שְׁנוֹתָיו שֶׁל קְהָת וְשֶׁל עַמְרָם וּשְׁמוֹנִים שֶׁל מֹשֶׁה שֶׁהָיָה כְּשֶׁיָּצְאוּ יִשְׂרָאֵל מִמִּצְרַיִם, אֵין אַתָּה מוֹצֵא חֲלָק שֶׁל שְׁלֹשׁ מֵאוֹת וַחֲמִשִּׁים, וְאַתָּה צָרִיךְ לְהוֹצִיא מֵהֶן כָּל הַשָּׁנִים שֶׁחַי קְהָת אַחַר לֵדַת עַמְרָם, וְשֶׁחַי עַמְרָם אַחַר לֵדַת מֹשֶׁה. בְּאֶרֶץ לֹא לָהֶם. וְלֹא נֶאֱמַר "בְּאֶרֶץ מִצְרַיִם" אֶלָּא "לֹא

לָהֶם", וּמִשֶּׁנּוֹלַד יִצְחָק: "וַיָּגָר אַבְרָהָם" וְגוֹ' (להלן כא, לד), וּבְיִצְחָק – "וַיָּגָר בִּגְרָר" (להלן כו, א), "וַיַּעֲקֹב גָּר בְּאֶרֶץ חָם" (תהלים קה, כג), "לָגוּר בָּאָרֶץ בָּאנוּ" (להלן מז, ד):

יד **וְגַם אֶת הַגּוֹי.** "וְגַם" לְרַבּוֹת אַרְבַּע מַלְכֻיּוֹת, שֶׁאַף הֵן כָּלִים עַל שֶׁשִּׁעְבְּדוּ אֶת יִשְׂרָאֵל: **דָּן אָנֹכִי.** בְּעֶשֶׂר מַכּוֹת: **בִּרְכֻשׁ גָּדוֹל.** בְּמָמוֹן גָּדוֹל, כְּמוֹ שֶׁנֶּאֱמַר: "וַיְנַצְּלוּ אֶת מִצְרָיִם" (שמות יב, לו):

טו **וְאַתָּה תָּבוֹא אֶל אֲבֹתֶיךָ.** אָבִיו עוֹבֵד עֲבוֹדָה זָרָה וְהוּא מְבַשְּׂרוֹ שֶׁיָּבֹא אֵלָיו?! לִמֶּדְךָ שֶׁעָשָׂה תֶּרַח תְּשׁוּבָה: **תִּקָּבֵר בְּשֵׂיבָה טוֹבָה.** בִּשְּׂרוֹ שֶׁיַּעֲשֶׂה יִשְׁמָעֵאל תְּשׁוּבָה בְּיָמָיו, וְלֹא יֵצֵא עֵשָׂו לְתַרְבּוּת רָעָה בְּיָמָיו, וּלְפִיכָךְ מֵת חָמֵשׁ שָׁנִים קֹדֶם זְמַנּוֹ, וּבוֹ בַּיּוֹם מָרַד עֵשָׂו:

טז **וְדוֹר רְבִיעִי.** לְאַחַר שֶׁיִּגְלוּ לְמִצְרַיִם יִהְיוּ שָׁם שְׁלֹשָׁה דוֹרוֹת, וְהָרְבִיעִי יָשׁוּבוּ לָאָרֶץ הַזֹּאת, לְפִי שֶׁבְּאֶרֶץ כְּנַעַן הָיָה מְדַבֵּר עִמּוֹ וְכוֹרֵת בְּרִית זוֹ, כְּדִכְתִיב: "לָתֶת לְךָ אֶת הָאָרֶץ הַזֹּאת לְרִשְׁתָּהּ" (לעיל פסוק ז). וְכֵן הָיָה – יַעֲקֹב יָרַד

DISCUSSION

15:13 | Four hundred years: As the Sages demonstrated, this count includes the entire process, starting from the birth of Abram's seed in Canaan, a land that at that time was not their own. The period of actual servitude in Egypt lasted two hundred and ten years (Rashi; Ramban).

15:14 | And also that nation that they shall serve, I will judge: If Abram's descendants were to be exiled by divine decree, why should the nations who fulfilled this decree be punished? Many answers to this philosophical dilemma have been suggested. According to the Rambam, man essentially has free choice, but sometimes it appears that the scope of his choice is narrowed, such as in a situation where an individual is swept up with a rioting mob. However, even when there are factors strongly pressing an individual to act in a particular way, this does not negate that individual's responsibility for his actions.

In this case, while it was decreed that Abram's descendants would be exiled and enslaved, and this decree may well have tempted kings and politicians, none of the protagonists were personally obligated to fulfill the decree. Consequently, they were punished for their deeds. In a certain sense, this is comparable to traffic accidents: There is a statistical probability that a certain number of people will die each year on the roads, but this does not mean that one who negligently runs over a child on the street should not be held accountable (see Rambam, *Sefer HaMadda*, *Hilkhot Teshuva* 6:3).

15:16 | For the iniquity of the Emorite is not complete until then: The fulfillment of the

17 As stated above, the vision started when the sun began to set. **It was when the sun had set, and there was extreme darkness, and behold,** there was an appearance of **a smoking furnace,** a thick cloud of smoke, like the smoke that emerges from a furnace,[27] **and a flaming torch that passed between those pieces.** The smoking furnace and smoking torch represent the Divine Presence passing between the pieces, thereby completing the covenantal ritual.

18 As befitting a formal covenant, its content is summarized in clear terms. **On that day, the Lord established a covenant with Abram, saying: To your descendants I have given this land** according to its greatest and fullest scope, **from the river of Egypt,** a name referring to the eastern branch of the Nile, often called the ravine of Egypt,[28] which serves as the southwestern border of Canaan, **until the great river,**[D] **the Euphrates River,** at its northeastern edge.

19 The promise of the inheritance of the land includes the removal of the nations currently living there: **the Kenites, the Kenizzites,** and **the Kadmonites.** The identity of these peoples is unknown, but it can be assumed that they dwelled outside the standard area known as Canaan.

20 **And the Hitites, the Perizites,** Canaanite nations; and **the Refaim,** the Anakim, mentioned above (14:5), and on several occasions in Deuteronomy (2:11, 20–21);

21 **the Emorites, the Canaanites, the Girgashites, and the Yevusites.**

Hagar's Pregnancy and the Birth of Ishmael

GENESIS 16:1–16

This story can be seen as a continuation of part of the previous dialogue between Abram and God, which focused mainly on the problem of Abram's succession and his progeny.

16 **1** **And Sarai, Abram's wife, bore him no children,** despite the fact that they had been married for many years. According to some traditions, Abram was twenty-five years old, or even younger, when he married Sarai.[29] **And she had an Egyptian maidservant,**[D] **and her name was Hagar.** Hagar was apparently Sarai's personal maidservant.

2 **Sarai said to Abram: Please, behold, the Lord has kept me from bearing** children; I cannot give birth. **Please, consort with my maidservant; perhaps I shall be built** and have children **through her.**[D] Sarai may have felt that she was nearing the end of her years of fertility, and she hoped that this act would cause her to give birth as well. **Abram heeded the voice of Sarai.** He did not initiate the matter or act for his own reasons, but cooperated with his wife, and complied for her sake alone.

3 **Sarai, Abram's wife, took Hagar the Egyptian, her maidservant, at the conclusion of ten years**[D] **of Abram's residence in the land of Canaan.** Sarai's suggestion came after she and Abram had experienced many long journeys together. Ten years had passed since they had arrived in Canaan and they were still childless. **And she gave her to Abram her husband as a wife.**[D] Hagar was apparently a full-fledged wife, not merely a maidservant or concubine. However, this change of status caused problems afterwards.

DISCUSSION

promise must be delayed, among other reasons, due to calculations in God's management of history. The Emorites and the other nations dwelling in Canaan were not acting appropriately. Their despicable deeds, involving idol worship and promiscuous sexual behavior, were gradually accumulating. When the time would come for their punishment, Abram's descendants would conquer the land and serve as God's instrument of retribution.

The theological issues raised by the Covenant between the Parts involve not only the punishment of those who would enslave the children of Israel, but also the punishment of the Emorites. Various accounts with regard to different nations' merit and guilt are interwoven with one another. Consequently, the actualization of the covenant involved considerations of personal responsibility and the effects of general events, including the relationship between the broad decree imposed from the outset by God and the details of its fulfillment in practice.

15:18 | From the river of Egypt until the great river: The inheritance described here is far larger than any political definition of Canaan at any period in history. It includes the majority of the Fertile Crescent, all the land west of the Euphrates, which was known in biblical times as *Ever HaNahar*, meaning "beyond the river."

At no point in time was this area entirely under the dominion of Israel, not even in the days of King David and his son Solomon, whose kingdom's borders approached the Euphrates.

16:1 | And she had an Egyptian maidservant: Although we do not know the precise legal arrangements followed by the forefathers' families, it can be assumed that they were similar to those of the local nations in whose environs Abram and Sarai lived, such as the Code of Hammurabi, the Laws of Eshnunna, and the Laws of Mari. According to these laws, women were not under the absolute authority of their husbands. Rather, they had their own personal and legal status. Here too it is evident that Sarai ◄●

יז כי לא־שלם עון האמרי עד־הנה: ויהי השמש באה ועלטה היה והנה תנור
יח עשן ולפיד אש אשר עבר בין הגזרים האלה: ביום ההוא כרת יהוה את־אברם
ברית לאמר לזרעך נתתי את־הארץ הזאת מנהר מצרים עד־הנהר הגדל
יט כ נהר־פרת: את־הקיני ואת־הקנזי ואת הקדמני: ואת־החתי ואת־הפרזי ואת־
כא הרפאים: ואת־האמרי ואת־הכנעני ואת־הגרגשי ואת־היבוסי:
טז א ב ושרי אשת אברם לא ילדה לו ולה שפחה מצרית ושמה הגר: ותאמר שרי יג
אל־אברם הנה־נא עצרני יהוה מלדת בא־נא אל־שפחתי אולי אבנה ממנה
ג וישמע אברם לקול שרי: ותקח שרי | אשת אברם את־הגר המצרית שפחתה
מקץ עשר שנים לשבת אברם בארץ כנען ותתן אתה לאברם אישה לו

רש"י

למצרים, נח וחשב דורותיו – יהודה פרץ וחצרון, וכלב בן חצרון מבאי הארץ היה: כי לא שלם עון האמרי. להיות משתלח מארצו עד אותו זמן, שאין הקדוש ברוך הוא נפרע מאומה עד שתתמלא סאתה, שנאמר: "בסאסאה בשלחה תריבנה" (ישעיה כז, ח):

יז | ויהי השמש באה. כמו: "ויהי הם מריקים שקיהם" (להלן מב, לה), "ויהי הם קברים איש" (מלכים ב' יג, כא), כלומר, ויהי דבר זה: השמש באה. שקעה: ועלטה היה. חשך היום: והנה תנור עשן וגו'. רמז לו שיפלו המלכיות בגיהנם: באה. טעמו למעלה, לכך הוא מבאר שבאה כבר. ואם היה טעמו למטה באל"ף, היה מבאר כשהיא שוקעת; ואי אפשר כן, שהרי כבר כתב: "ויהי השמש לבוא" (לעיל פסוק יב), והעברת תנור עשן לאחר מכאן היתה, נמצא שכבר שקעה. וזה חלוק בכל תבה לשון נקבה שיסודה שתי אותיות, כשהטעם למעלה לשון שעבר הוא, כגון זה, וכגון: "ורחל באה" (להלן כט, ט), "קמה אלמתי" (להלן לז, ז), "הנה שבה יבמתך" (רות א, טו), וכשהטעם למטה הוא לשון הווה, דבר שנעשה עכשיו והולך, כמו: "באה עם הצאן" (להלן כט, ו), "קמה בחמה" (מיכה ז, ו), "ובבקר היא שבה" (אסתר ב, יד):

יח | לזרעך נתתי. אמירתו של הקדוש ברוך הוא כאלו היא עשויה: הנהר הגדל. לפי שהוא דבוק לארץ ישראל קראהו גדול, אף על פי שהוא מאחר בארבעה נהרות היוצאים מעדן, שנאמר: "והנהר הרביעי הוא פרת" (לעיל ב, יד); משל הדיוט: עבד מלך – מלך, הדבק לשחור וישתחוו לך:

יט | את הקיני. עשר אמות יש כאן, ולא נתן להם אלא שבעה גוים, והשלשה אדום ומואב ועמון, והם קיני קנזי קדמני, ועתידים להיות ירשה לעתיד, שנאמר: "אדום ומואב משלוח ידם ובני עמון משמעתם" (ישעיה יא, יד):

כ | ואת הרפאים. ארץ עוג, שנאמר בה: "ההוא יקרא ארץ רפאים" (דברים ג, יג):

פרק טז

א | שפחה מצרית. בת פרעה היתה, כשראה נסים שנעשו לשרה, אמר: מוטב שתהא בתי שפחה בבית זה ולא גבירה בבית אחר:

ב | אולי אבנה ממנה. למד על מי שאין לו בנים שאינו בנוי אלא הרוס: אבנה ממנה. בזכות שאכניס צרתי לביתי: לקול שרי. לרוח הקדש שבה:

ג | ותקח שרי. לקחתה בדברים: אשריך שזכית לדבק בגוף קדוש כזה: מקץ עשר שנים. מועד הקבוע לאשה

DISCUSSION

had rights to her own property, including an Egyptian maidservant.

16:2 | **Perhaps I shall be built through her:** On several occasions, the Bible relates that a barren woman brought a child into the family, usually born to a maidservant or another woman subservient to the barren wife, and that she was subsequently blessed with offspring. While this custom was a folk remedy for barrenness, there are many documented cases of childless couples in modern times who brought a child into their home and were subsequently blessed with a pregnancy of their own.

The verses hint that the newborn baby would actually be placed on the knees of the adopting mother (see 30:3; 50:23). This symbolic act is also documented in other accounts from the ancient East. It is also possible that the phrase "built [*ibaneh*] through her" means that the childless woman sat on the birth stool [*ovnayim*] alongside the woman in labor.

16:3 | **At the conclusion of ten years:** This is also the period of time later fixed by Jewish law for determining whether a woman can become pregnant (see *Yevamot* 64a; Rambam, *Sefer Nashim*, *Hilkhot Ishut* 15:7).

And she gave her to Abram her husband as a wife: The relationship between Abram and Sarai was not merely a legal or formal one; they had a close emotional relationship. It is clear from the stories involving Sarai that she was a woman of initiative who made independent decisions, and

4 **He**, Abram, **consorted with Hagar, and** in a short time **she conceived; she saw that she conceived, and her mistress was diminished in her eyes.** Hagar saw her pregnancy as a sign of a new status. According to some Sages, she considered her conception an indication of moral superiority over her mistress.[30] However, the change in her attitude toward Sarai can also be explained in a different manner. According to the laws and customs of several nations in ancient times, if a woman married to a man who has more than one wife bears him a child, especially a son, she becomes the primary wife. According to this, Hagar's pregnancy strengthened her position, and even if she did not openly disparage her mistress, her self-esteem would increase.[31]

5 The situation was very delicate for Sarai, and her emotional response to Hagar's pregnancy was ambivalent. **Sarai said to Abram: The villainy done to me [***ḥamasi***] is on you;** you have done me wrong. In this context *ḥamas* does not bear its usual meaning of theft or robbery, but merely indicates an illegal or improper act. Sarai said: Of my own volition, **I gave my maidservant into your bosom. And** then **she saw that she conceived and I was diminished in her eyes.** Therefore, **the Lord shall judge between me and you.** This was not an outright accusation that Abram had harmed her, but a demand that he stand by her side in a more conspicuous manner.

6 **Abram said to Sarai: Behold, your maid is in your hand.** Although she is pregnant with my child, I will not defend her; you can take her back as a maidservant. Apparently, Abram had not developed close ties with Hagar, or even if he had, he was willing to give her up for Sarai. **Do to her that which is favorable in your eyes.** So **Sarai treated her harshly.**[D] The verse does not specify whether this harassment was mental or physical, if it involved reprimands, curses, the imposition of hard labor, or some other form of persecution. **And she,** Hagar, **fled from her.**

7 **The angel of the Lord found her in the wilderness at,** or next to, **the spring of water on the way to Shur,**[B] in the Negev.

8 **He said: Hagar, Sarai's maidservant.** The angel addressed her by name; he knew who she was. **From where did you come, and where will you go? She said: From my mistress Sarai I flee.**

9 **The angel of the Lord said to her: Return to your mistress, and suffer under her hands.** So it has been decreed upon you, and this is the best thing for you.

10 **The angel of the Lord said to her: I will multiply your descendants;** the child in your womb will grow into a great nation. **And they shall not be counted due to their great number.** Hagar's child would also receive the blessing of fertility and strength granted to Abram.

11 **The angel of the Lord said to her:**[D] **Behold,** as you already know, **you are with child, and** I am hereby informing you that you **shall bear a son,** not a daughter. **You shall call his name Ishmael, as the Lord has heard [***shama***] your suffering.**

12 **He shall be a wild man.** He will have a reputation as a wild, uncontrolled, and unsettled figure. **His hand shall be against everyone and everyone's hand against him;** he will be continually involved in fights, quarrels, and wars. Perhaps the angel was alluding to the tendency of Ishmael and his descendants to choose the life of the nomad. As is typical of the nomadic existence, they would be drawn to banditry and suffer from endless conflicts. **And yet, he shall dwell among all his brethren.** He will achieve greatness in the eyes of his brothers and the members of his family.

13 Realizing that that the angel was no more than a messenger, **she called,** described, **the name of the Lord who spoke to her** as: **You are the God of my vision,** the God who is seen, the God who reveals Himself. It is hard to ascertain much about the character of the quiet Hagar, but as one who came from the house of Abram, she must have absorbed something of his worldview. She was therefore aware that the angel was not a god, but a mouthpiece of God. **For she said: Have I seen** a revelation **here too, after my vision,** in addition to those I saw in Abram's house? Hagar had some prior familiarity with angels, as she had lived in a spiritual environment. She exclaimed in

---

DISCUSSION

that Abram had great respect for her sensitivities and opinion. It is never simple for a woman to suggest to her husband to take another wife, and this is especially true for a woman with her own independent status. Furthermore, the fact that the other woman was her own maidservant, with whom she perhaps felt a degree of intimacy, must have made it even more difficult.

16:6 | **Sarai treated her harshly:** The Ramban criticizes Sarai for treating Hagar improperly, and Abram for allowing it. It should be noted, though, that according to the laws of the ancient world, such as the Code of Hammurabi, a maidservant who conceived from her master and began to deride the honor of her mistress was liable to be punished. If so, Sarai acted in accordance with the accepted law. Nevertheless,

such behavior would not be expected from a merciful matriarch. Even if Sarai's misery is understandable, this does not justify her deeds from a moral perspective.

16:11 | **The angel of the Lord said to her:** The Sages derived from the three repetitions of this phrase that a different angel appeared to her each time (*Bereshit Rabba* 45:7). It is also possible ◂●

ד ה לְאִשָּׁה: וַיָּבֹא אֶל־הָגָר וַתַּהַר וַתֵּרֶא כִּי הָרָתָה וַתֵּקַל גְּבִרְתָּהּ בְּעֵינֶיהָ: וַתֹּאמֶר
שָׂרַי אֶל־אַבְרָם חֲמָסִי עָלֶיךָ אָנֹכִי נָתַתִּי שִׁפְחָתִי בְּחֵיקֶךָ וַתֵּרֶא כִּי הָרָתָה וָאֵקַל
ו בְּעֵינֶיהָ יִשְׁפֹּט יהוה בֵּינִי וּבֵינֶיךָ: וַיֹּאמֶר אַבְרָם אֶל־שָׂרַי הִנֵּה שִׁפְחָתֵךְ בְּיָדֵךְ
ז עֲשִׂי־לָהּ הַטּוֹב בְּעֵינָיִךְ וַתְּעַנֶּהָ שָׂרַי וַתִּבְרַח מִפָּנֶיהָ: וַיִּמְצָאָהּ מַלְאַךְ יהוה עַל־
ח עֵין הַמַּיִם בַּמִּדְבָּר עַל־הָעַיִן בְּדֶרֶךְ שׁוּר: וַיֹּאמַר הָגָר שִׁפְחַת שָׂרַי אֵי־מִזֶּה בָאת
ט וְאָנָה תֵלֵכִי וַתֹּאמֶר מִפְּנֵי שָׂרַי גְּבִרְתִּי אָנֹכִי בֹּרַחַת: וַיֹּאמֶר לָהּ מַלְאַךְ יהוה שׁוּבִי
י אֶל־גְּבִרְתֵּךְ וְהִתְעַנִּי תַּחַת יָדֶיהָ: וַיֹּאמֶר לָהּ מַלְאַךְ יהוה הַרְבָּה אַרְבֶּה אֶת־זַרְעֵךְ
יא וְלֹא יִסָּפֵר מֵרֹב: וַיֹּאמֶר לָהּ מַלְאַךְ יהוה הִנָּךְ הָרָה וְיֹלַדְתְּ בֵּן וְקָרָאת שְׁמוֹ
יב יִשְׁמָעֵאל כִּי־שָׁמַע יהוה אֶל־עָנְיֵךְ: וְהוּא יִהְיֶה פֶּרֶא אָדָם יָדוֹ בַכֹּל וְיַד כֹּל בּוֹ
יג וְעַל־פְּנֵי כָל־אֶחָיו יִשְׁכֹּן: וַתִּקְרָא שֵׁם־יהוה הַדֹּבֵר אֵלֶיהָ אַתָּה אֵל רֳאִי כִּי אָמְרָה

רש״י

שֶׁשָּׁהֲתָה עֶשֶׂר שָׁנִים וְלֹא יָלְדָה לְבַעְלָהּ, חַיָּב לִשָּׂא אַחֶרֶת: לְשֶׁבֶת אַבְרָם וְגוֹ׳. מַגִּיד שֶׁאֵין יְשִׁיבַת חוּצָה לָאָרֶץ עוֹלָה לוֹ מִן הַמִּנְיָן, לְפִי שֶׁלֹּא נֶאֱמַר לוֹ: ״וְאֶעֶשְׂךָ לְגוֹי גָּדוֹל״ (לעיל יב, ב) עַד שֶׁיָּבֹא לְאֶרֶץ יִשְׂרָאֵל:

ד| **וַיָּבֹא אֶל הָגָר וַתַּהַר.** מִבִּיאָה רִאשׁוֹנָה: **וַתֵּקַל גְּבִרְתָּהּ בְּעֵינֶיהָ.** אָמְרָה: שָׂרָה זוֹ אֵין סִתְרָהּ כְּגִלּוּיָהּ, מַרְאָה עַצְמָהּ כְּאִלּוּ הִיא צַדֶּקֶת וְאֵינָהּ צַדֶּקֶת, שֶׁלֹּא זָכְתָה לְהֵרָיוֹן כָּל הַשָּׁנִים הַלָּלוּ, וַאֲנִי נִתְעַבַּרְתִּי מִבִּיאָה רִאשׁוֹנָה:

ה| **חֲמָסִי עָלֶיךָ.** חָמָס הֶעָשׂוּי לִי, עָלֶיךָ אֲנִי מַטִּילָה הָעֹנֶשׁ; כְּשֶׁהִתְפַּלַּלְתָּ לְהַקָּדוֹשׁ בָּרוּךְ הוּא: ״מַה תִּתֶּן לִי וְאָנֹכִי הוֹלֵךְ עֲרִירִי״ (לעיל טו, ב) לֹא הִתְפַּלַּלְתָּ אֶלָּא עָלֶיךָ, וְהָיָה לְךָ לְהִתְפַּלֵּל עַל שְׁנֵינוּ וְהָיִיתִי אֲנִי נִפְקֶדֶת עִמָּךְ. וְעוֹד, דְּבָרֶיךָ אַתָּה חוֹמֵס מִמֶּנִּי, שֶׁאַתָּה שׁוֹמֵעַ בִּזְיוֹנִי וְשׁוֹתֵק: **אָנֹכִי נָתַתִּי שִׁפְחָתִי וְגוֹ׳ בֵּינִי וּבֵינֶיךָ.** כָּל ׳בֵּינְךָ׳ שֶׁבַּמִּקְרָא חָסֵר וְזֶה מָלֵא, קְרִי בֵּיהּ: ׳וּבֵינֵיךְ׳, שֶׁהִכְנִיסָה עַיִן הָרָע בְּעִבּוּרָהּ שֶׁל הָגָר וְהִפִּילָה עֻבָּרָהּ. הוּא שֶׁהַמַּלְאָךְ אוֹמֵר לְהָגָר: ״הִנָּךְ הָרָה״ (להלן פסוק יא), וַהֲלֹא כְּבָר הָרְתָה, וְהוּא מְבַשֵּׂר לָהּ שֶׁתַּהַר?! אֶלָּא מְלַמֵּד שֶׁהִפִּילָה הֵרָיוֹן הָרִאשׁוֹן:

ו| **וַתְּעַנֶּהָ שָׂרַי.** הָיְתָה מְשַׁעְבֶּדֶת בָּהּ בְּקֹשִׁי:

ח| **אֵי מִזֶּה בָאת.** מֵהֵיכָן בָּאת. יוֹדֵעַ הָיָה, אֶלָּא לִתֵּן לָהּ פֶּתַח לִכָּנֵס עִמָּהּ בִּדְבָרִים. וּלְשׁוֹן ״אֵי מִזֶּה״, אַיֵּה הַמָּקוֹם שֶׁתֹּאמַר עָלָיו ״מִזֶּה״ אַתְּ בָּאָה:

ט| **וַיֹּאמֶר לָהּ מַלְאַךְ וְגוֹ׳.** עַל כָּל אֲמִירָה הָיָה שָׁלוּחַ לָהּ מַלְאָךְ אַחֵר מַלְאָךְ, לְכָךְ נֶאֱמַר ׳מַלְאָךְ׳ בְּכָל אֲמִירָה וַאֲמִירָה:

יא| **הִנָּךְ הָרָה.** כְּשֶׁתָּשׁוּבִי תַּהֲרִי, כְּמוֹ: ״הִנָּךְ הָרָה״ (שופטים יג, ה) דְּאֵשֶׁת מָנוֹחַ: **וְיֹלַדְתְּ בֵּן.** כְּמוֹ ׳וְיוֹלֶדֶת׳. וְדוֹמֶה לוֹ: ״יֹשַׁבְתְּ בַּלְּבָנוֹן מְקֻנַּנְתְּ בָּאֲרָזִים״ (ירמיה כב, כג): **וְקָרָאת שְׁמוֹ.** צִוּוּי הוּא, כְּמוֹ שֶׁאוֹמֵר לַזָּכָר: ״וְקָרָאתָ אֶת שְׁמוֹ יִצְחָק״ (להלן יז, יט):

יב| **פֶּרֶא אָדָם.** אוֹהֵב מִדְבָּרוֹת לָצוּד חַיּוֹת, כְּמוֹ שֶׁכָּתוּב: ״וַיֵּשֶׁב בַּמִּדְבָּר וַיְהִי רֹבֶה קַשָּׁת״ (להלן כא, כ): **יָדוֹ בַכֹּל.** לִסְטִים: **וְיַד כֹּל בּוֹ.** הַכֹּל שׂוֹנְאִין אוֹתוֹ וּמִתְגָּרִין בּוֹ: **וְעַל פְּנֵי כָל אֶחָיו יִשְׁכֹּן.** שֶׁיְּהֵא זַרְעוֹ גָּדוֹל:

יג| **אַתָּה אֵל רֳאִי.** נָקוּד חֲטַף קָמַץ מִפְּנֵי שֶׁהוּא שֵׁם דָּבָר, אֱלוֹהַּ הָרְאִיָּה, שֶׁרוֹאֶה בְּעֶלְבּוֹן שֶׁל עֲלוּבִין: **הֲגַם הֲלֹם.** לְשׁוֹן תֵּמַהּ, וְכִי סְבוּרָה הָיִיתִי שֶׁאַף הֲלוֹם בַּמִּדְבָּרוֹת רָאִיתִי שְׁלוּחוֹ שֶׁל מָקוֹם, ״אַחֲרֵי רֹאִי״ אוֹתָם בְּבֵיתוֹ שֶׁל אַבְרָהָם שֶׁשָּׁם הָיִיתִי רְגִילָה לִרְאוֹת מַלְאָכִים? וְתֵדַע שֶׁהָיְתָה רְגִילָה לִרְאוֹתָם, שֶׁהֲרֵי מָנוֹחַ רָאָה אֶת הַמַּלְאָךְ פַּעַם אַחַת וְאָמַר: ״מוֹת נָמוּת״ (שופטים יג, כב), וְזוֹ רָאֲתָה אַרְבָּעָה זֶה אַחַר זֶה וְלֹא חָרְדָה:

DISCUSSION

that it was the same angel, but the statements are presented separately because he spoke from a different perspective and served a different function in each address. First, he posed a question to Hagar, then he commanded her to act, and finally he blessed her offspring and prophesied about his future.

BACKGROUND

16:7| **On the way to Shur:** Shur is located between Kadesh Barnea and Bered, and is identified with Bir el-Hasana in central Sinai. It is also the name of a desert east of Egypt (25:18; Exodus 15:22). Consequently, the road mentioned here is assumed to be the route through central Sinai, which extends from Beersheba through Kadesh Barnea, Bered, and Refidim, all the way to present-day Ismailia in Egypt. In Aramaic, *shur* means wall or fortification. The route was called by this name due to the fortresses on the eastern border of Egypt, along the line of today's Suez Canal.

surprise that even here, in a distant wilderness, the God she had seen and known in her home had revealed Himself to her.

14 **Therefore, one**[32] **called the cistern Be'er Laḥai Roi,** meaning the well [*be'er*] of the living [*ḥai*] God of my vision [*ro'i*]. **Behold,** this well is still known, and is mentioned several times later (24:62; 25:11); **it is** located **between Kadesh and Bered,**[B] to the south of Canaan.

15 After returning home as instructed by the angel, **Hagar** ultimately **bore to Abram a son; Abram called the name of his**

son, whom Hagar bore, Ishmael. It is possible that he had not heard from Hagar that this was the name recommended by the angel, and yet he selected it of his own accord, as the Lord had heard [*shama*] him and his misery as well, and had given him his firstborn son.

16 **And Abram was eighty-six years old,**[D] **when Hagar bore Ishmael to Abram.**

The Covenant of Circumcision
GENESIS 17:1–27

This passage, which discusses another significant incident in Abram's history, can been seen as a major turning point in his life. God changes his name and establishes a covenant with him whose signs would be etched onto the flesh of his offspring, in the form of the removal of the foreskin.

Here Abraham is presented as the third major founding figure in the history of humanity: Adam, the first man; Noah, from whom everyone descended after the flood; and now Abraham, who forges a new path and is considered the father of many kings and nations.

17 1 **Abram was ninety-nine years old, and the Lord appeared to Abram; He said to him: I am God Almighty.** According to the majority of commentaries, this name denotes God's might and involvement in reality, as the One who destroys and rebuilds new systems in the world.[33] **Walk before Me,** serve Me, **and be wholehearted,** perfect. God had already established the Covenant between the Parts with Abram, a covenant that consisted of the eternal acquisition of the land of Canaan, and the continuation of his lineage. The covenant established here was a more personal one.

2 **I shall establish My covenant between Me and you.** This covenant was established with Abram as a private individual, and also with each of his descendants personally. **And I will multiply you exceedingly.**

3 **Abram fell upon his face,** in awe, due to the prophecy, and as an expression of his complete submission to whatever God was about to tell him, as the promise would no doubt include an obligation as well. **And God spoke with him, saying:**

4 **I, My covenant is hereby** being established **with you, and you shall be the father of a multitude of nations.**

5 This is a new status, and therefore **your name shall no longer be called Abram,** with its simple meaning of lofty [*ram*] father [*av*]. **But** rather, **your name shall be Abraham; for I have made you the father of a multitude of nations.**[D] As part of the covenant, the name given to him by his parents was exchanged for a name chosen by God. The meaning of this name is far more complex, and the verse itself explains it: The father of a multitude [*av hamon*], or the lofty father of a multitude.

6 God promised Abraham: As the father of a multitude of nations, **I will make you exceedingly fruitful, I will make you into** the progenitor of various **nations, and kings shall emerge from you** and rule, each in his own realm.

7 **I will establish My covenant,** a private, personal connection **between Me and you and your descendants after you throughout their generations for an eternal covenant, to be your God and for your descendants after you.** The God and King of the universe, who created the entire universe with all of the planets and stars, now established a personal, family covenant with Abraham and his descendants. This covenant expresses a unique relationship with them, different from His relationship with the rest of humanity, other creatures, and worlds.

Seventh aliya

8 As part of this covenant, **I will give to you and to your descendants after you the land of your residence, the entire land of Canaan, for an eternal portion.** Here God repeats His earlier promise, thereby declaring that this covenant does not replace the Covenant between the Parts as a new spiritual arrangement. Rather, it exists in addition to the previous covenant. **And** He added an additional promise: **I will be their God.** From this point onward one finds the phrase, God of Abraham.[34] From now on God is not only the Creator of heaven and earth (14:19, 22), but also our God, the God of Abraham's descendants.

9 **God said to Abraham: And you, you shall observe My covenant; you, and your descendants after you throughout their generations,** as it includes an obligation on your part as well:

── BACKGROUND ──
16:14| **Bered:** According to *Targum Yonatan,* this is Ḥaluza, north of Kadesh Barnea. However, contemporary researchers identify it with Bir el-Ḥasana, in the center of the Sinai Peninsula.

── DISCUSSION ──
16:16| **Abram was eighty-six years old:** The mention of Abram's age at Ishmael's birth is important for determining the order of events and the time that elapsed between them, since

the Bible is not necessarily written in chronological order. For example, it is unclear when the Covenant between the Parts took place relative to Abram's arrival in Canaan. The first time

יד הַגַּם הֲלֹם רָאִיתִי אַחֲרֵי רֹאִי: עַל־כֵּן קָרָא לַבְּאֵר בְּאֵר לַחַי רֹאִי הִנֵּה בֵין־קָדֵשׁ
טו וּבֵין בָּרֶד: וַתֵּלֶד הָגָר לְאַבְרָם בֵּן וַיִּקְרָא אַבְרָם שֶׁם־בְּנוֹ אֲשֶׁר־יָלְדָה הָגָר
טז יִשְׁמָעֵאל: וְאַבְרָם בֶּן־שְׁמֹנִים שָׁנָה וְשֵׁשׁ שָׁנִים בְּלֶדֶת־הָגָר אֶת־יִשְׁמָעֵאל
יז א לְאַבְרָם: וַיְהִי אַבְרָם בֶּן־תִּשְׁעִים שָׁנָה וְתֵשַׁע שָׁנִים וַיֵּרָא יְהוָה אֶל־ יד
ב אַבְרָם וַיֹּאמֶר אֵלָיו אֲנִי־אֵל שַׁדַּי הִתְהַלֵּךְ לְפָנַי וֶהְיֵה תָמִים: וְאֶתְּנָה בְרִיתִי בֵּינִי
ג וּבֵינֶךָ וְאַרְבֶּה אוֹתְךָ בִּמְאֹד מְאֹד: וַיִּפֹּל אַבְרָם עַל־פָּנָיו וַיְדַבֵּר אִתּוֹ אֱלֹהִים
ד ה לֵאמֹר: אֲנִי הִנֵּה בְרִיתִי אִתָּךְ וְהָיִיתָ לְאַב הֲמוֹן גּוֹיִם: וְלֹא־יִקָּרֵא עוֹד אֶת־שִׁמְךָ
ו אַבְרָם וְהָיָה שִׁמְךָ אַבְרָהָם כִּי אַב־הֲמוֹן גּוֹיִם נְתַתִּיךָ: וְהִפְרֵתִי אֹתְךָ בִּמְאֹד מְאֹד
ז וּנְתַתִּיךָ לְגוֹיִם וּמְלָכִים מִמְּךָ יֵצֵאוּ: וַהֲקִמֹתִי אֶת־בְּרִיתִי בֵּינִי וּבֵינֶךָ וּבֵין זַרְעֲךָ שביעי
ח אַחֲרֶיךָ לְדֹרֹתָם לִבְרִית עוֹלָם לִהְיוֹת לְךָ לֵאלֹהִים וּלְזַרְעֲךָ אַחֲרֶיךָ: וְנָתַתִּי לְךָ
וּלְזַרְעֲךָ אַחֲרֶיךָ אֵת ׀ אֶרֶץ מְגֻרֶיךָ אֵת כָּל־אֶרֶץ כְּנַעַן לַאֲחֻזַּת עוֹלָם וְהָיִיתִי לָהֶם
ט לֵאלֹהִים: וַיֹּאמֶר אֱלֹהִים אֶל־אַבְרָהָם וְאַתָּה אֶת־בְּרִיתִי תִשְׁמֹר אַתָּה וְזַרְעֲךָ

רש"י

יד| **באר לחי ראי.** כתרגומו: "דמלאך קימא אתחזי עלה":

טו| **ויקרא אברם שם וגו'.** אף על פי שלא שמע אברהם דברי המלאך שאמר: "וקראת שמו ישמעאל" (לעיל פסוק יא), שרתה רוח הקדש עליו וקראו ישמעאל:

טז| **ואברם בן שמנים וגו'.** לשבחו של ישמעאל נכתב, להודיע שהיה בן שלש עשרה שנה כשנמול ולא עכב:

פרק יז

א| **אני אל שדי.** אני הוא שיש די באלהותי לכל בריה, לפיכך "התהלך לפני" ואהיה לך לאלוה ולפטרון. וכן כל מקום שהוא במקרא, פרושו: די שלו, לפי הענין: **התהלך לפני.** כתרגומו: "פלח קדמי", הדבק בעבודתי:

והיה תמים. אף זה צווי אחר צווי, היה שלם בכל נסיונותי. ולפי מדרשו, "התהלך לפני" במצות מילה, ובדבר הזה תהיה תמים, שכל זמן שהערלה בך אתה בעל מום לפני. דבר אחר, "והיה תמים", מוסיף אני אות על שמך ויהיו מנין אותיותיך רמ"ח כמנין איבריך:

ב| **ואתנה בריתי.** ברית של אהבה וברית הארץ להורישה לך על ידי מצוה זו:

ג| **ויפל אברם על פניו.** ממורא השכינה, שעד שלא מל לא היה בו כח לעמד ורוח הקדש נצבת עליו. וזהו שנאמר בבלעם: "נפל וגלוי עינים" (במדבר כד, ד). בברייתא דרבי אליעזר:

ה| **כי אב המון גוים.** לשון נוטריקון של שמו, וריי"ש שהיתה בו בתחלה, שלא היה אב אלא לארם שהוא מקומו, ועכשיו אב לכל העולם. ואף יו"ד של שרי נתרעמה על השכינה עד שהוסיפה ליהושע, שנאמר: "ויקרא משה להושע בן נון יהושע" (במדבר יג, טז):

ו| **ונתתיך לגוים.** ישראל ואדום, שהרי ישמעאל כבר היה לו ולא היה מבשרו עליו:

ז| **והקמתי את בריתי.** ומה היא הברית? "להיות לך לאלהים":

ח| **לאחזת עולם.** ושם אהיה לכם לאלהים, אבל הדר בחוצה לארץ כמי שאין לו אלוה:

ט-י| **ואתה.** וי"ו זו מוסף על ענין ראשון, "אני הנה בריתי אתך" (לעיל פסוק ד), ואתה הוי זהיר לשמרו, ומה

DISCUSSION

Abram's age is mentioned is upon his departure from Haran. Here, when his first son was born, his age is stated again, roughly eleven years after his arrival in Canaan.

17:5| **For I have made you the father of a multitude of nations:** In contrast to Noah, who is described upon first appearance as "a righteous, wholehearted man" (6:9), no clear assessment of Abram's character has yet been provided by the Torah. Instead, it has described a series of events in his life . The change from being known by his birth name, Abram, to a name he earned through his deeds and way of life, Abraham, expresses the transformation of his personality.

10 **This is My covenant that you shall observe, between Me and you and between your descendants after you: Circumcise every male among you.**[D]

11 **You shall circumcise the flesh of your foreskin; and it,** this cutting of the flesh, **shall be a mark of a covenant between Me and you.**[D] The covenant is the relationship itself, while the circumcision serves as a concrete symbol, an indication of, and reminder about the covenant.

12 This verse constitutes a normative commandment that forms a binding obligation in Jewish law, similar in style to the many commandments found in the later books of the Torah: **And one who is eight days old shall be circumcised among you, every male throughout your generations,** whether **born in the house,** an actual member of the family or anyone else born into the household, even if not a biological descendant of Abraham, **or purchased with silver,** a slave purchased **from any foreigner, who is not of your descendants.** Not only must Abraham's descendants be circumcised, but all males who are his property. The covenant applies to these people from the moment of their birth, although the mark of the covenant is placed on their flesh only on the eighth day.

13 **Circumcise those born in your house, or those purchased with your silver, and** the mark of **My covenant shall be in your flesh for an eternal covenant** throughout the generations.

14 **And the uncircumcised male** among your descendants **who shall not circumcise the flesh of his foreskin, that soul shall be excised from his people.** This is the most severe of punishments; the soul is cut off and destroyed, a penalty that begins with death and continues in the world of the souls after death.[35] An individual who chooses to remain uncircumcised is deserving of such a severe punishment, since **he has breached My covenant,** by essentially declaring that he wants no part in it.

15 **God said to Abraham,** referring to him by his new name, by which he was to be forever known from that moment forward: **Sarai your wife,**[D] **you shall not call her name Sarai, as Sarah is her name.**[D]

16 **I will bless her** with various blessings, **and I will also give you a son from her; I will bless her, and she** too **shall become nations** [*goyim*]. The word *goyim* can also mean tribes or leaders (see 20:4, 25:23). **Kings of peoples shall be** descended **from her.**[D]

17 In the wake of these declarations, **Abraham fell upon his face** in submission, **and he laughed.**[D] He said in his heart: **Shall a child be born to one who is one hundred years old?** Abraham was ninety-nine at the time. If Sarah were to become pregnant immediately, he would be one hundred years old at the time of the child's birth. **And if it is Sarah, shall a ninety-year-old woman give birth?** This certainly goes against the laws of nature.

18 **Abraham said to God: If only Ishmael shall live before You.** You have promised me miracles, which go against the laws of nature. However, I already have a son, Ishmael. If only he could be considered my son and receive this blessing.

DISCUSSION

17:10 | Circumcise every male among you: As is the case nowadays, in Abraham's time as well there were also other groups who practiced circumcision, as well as many others who were uncircumcised. Accordingly, circumcision does not distinguish the descendants of Abraham from the rest of humanity. Rather, it is a sign embedded in our flesh, to remind us of the covenant and to bring it forward in our consciousness.

17:11 | Shall be a mark of a covenant between Me and you: The circumcision ceremony is known in Hebrew as *berit mila*, which literally means "covenant of circumcision." However, the circumcision itself does not constitute the substance of the covenant or its formal enactment; it is nothing other than a mark or sign of the covenant's existence. This physical symbol engraved in the flesh of Abraham's descendants constitutes a very different example of a somewhat similar phenomenon, the practice of branding the hides of animals with a sign indicating that they belong to their owners. The sign of the covenant placed on the people's bodies is not there for God's sake. Rather, it serves as an indicator for the people themselves, reminding them of God, who has established His covenant with them. In this regard it is similar to the rainbow that serves to remind the world that God is faithful to His covenant with mankind (9:13).

17:15 | Sarai your wife: Sarai was not merely Abraham's wife, but his partner, with a status equal or similar to that of her husband. Therefore, although circumcision as a physical symbol of the covenant was given only to Abraham and his sons after him, the covenant itself and the close relationship between God and the people applied equally to Sarai and their female descendants. Since Sarai was to establish the people and the continuation of the covenant together with Abraham, her name was also changed at the same time.

Sarah is her name: The name Sarai can be interpreted as "my princess" or "my queen ruler." The possessive form indicates a certain limitation. Just as her husband's name was changed from that of a private individual to one that described him as the father of a multitude of nations, so too the name Sarai, meaning my princess or my queen, became Sarah, the princess or queen of all.

17:16 | Kings of peoples shall be from her: The granting of a new name is indicative of one's advancement to a new status. In those days it was customary to give a new name to kings who had ascended to the throne, to express their lofty position. This practice is still observed today in some places where such forms of leadership exist.

In Sarah's case, the name also signified that she would bear a child to Abraham. Alongside

◄●

י אחריך לדרתם: זאת בריתי אשר תשמרו ביני וביניכם ובין זרעך אחריך המול
יא לכם כל־זכר: ונמלתם את בשר ערלתכם והיה לאות ברית ביני וביניכם:
יב ובן־שמנת ימים ימול לכם כל־זכר לדרתיכם יליד בית ומקנת־כסף מכל בן־
יג נכר אשר לא מזרעך הוא: המול | ימול יליד ביתך ומקנת כספך והיתה בריתי
יד בבשרכם לברית עולם: וערל | זכר אשר לא־ימול את־בשר ערלתו ונכרתה
טו הנפש ההוא מעמיה את־בריתי הפר: ויאמר אלהים אל־אברהם
טז שרי אשתך לא־תקרא את־שמה שרי כי שרה שמה: וברכתי אתה וגם
יז נתתי ממנה לך בן וברכתיה והיתה לגוים מלכי עמים ממנה יהיו: ויפל
אברהם על־פניו ויצחק ויאמר בלבו הלבן מאה־שנה יולד ואם־שרה הבת־
יח תשעים שנה תלד: ויאמר אברהם אל־האלהים לו ישמעאל יחיה לפניך:

רש"י

היא שמירתו? "זאת בריתי אשר תשמרו... המול לכם" וגו': ביני וביניכם. אותם של עכשיו: ובין זרעך אחריך. העתידין להולד אחריך: המול. כמו 'להמול', כמו שאתה אומר 'עשות' כמו 'לעשות':

יא| ונמלתם. כמו 'ומלתם', והנו"ן בו יתרה ליסוד הנופל בו לפרקים, כמו נו"ן של 'נושך' ונו"ן של 'נושא'. 'ונמלתם' כמו 'ונשאתם' (להלן מה, יט), אבל 'ימול' לשון יפעל, כמו: יעשה, יאכל:

יב| יליד בית. שילדתו השפחה בבית: ומקנת כסף. שקנאו משנולד:

יג| המול ימול יליד ביתך. כאן כפל עליו ולא אמר לשמנה ימים, ללמדך שיש יליד בית נמול לאחד, וכמו שמפורש במסכת שבת (דף קלה ע"ב):

יד| וערל זכר. כאן למד שהמילה באותו מקום שהוא מבדיל בין זכר לנקבה: אשר לא ימול. משיגיע לכלל עונשין – "ונכרתה". אבל אביו אין ענוש עליו כרת, אבל עובר בעשה: ונכרתה הנפש. הולך ערירי ומת קודם זמנו:

טו| לא תקרא את שמה שרי. דמשמע שרי לי ולא לאחרים, "כי שרה" סתם "שמה", שתהא שרה על כל:

טז| וברכתי אתה. ומה היא הברכה? שחזרה לנערותה, שנאמר: "היתה לי עדנה" (להלן יח, יב): וברכתיה. בהנקת שדים כשנצרכה לכך, ביום משתה יצחק, שהיו מרננים עליהם שהביאו אסופי מן השוק ואומרים בננו הוא, והביאה כל אחת בנה עמה ומניקתה לא הביאה, והיא הניקה את כלם. הוא שנאמר: "היניקה בנים שרה" (להלן כא, ז). בראשית רבה רמזו במקצת (מז, ט):

יז| ויפל אברהם על פניו ויצחק. זה תרגם אונקלוס לשון שמחה: 'וחדי', ושל שרה לשון מחוך (להלן יח, יב), למדת שאברהם האמין ושמח, ושרה לא האמינה ולגלגה, וזהו שהקפיד הקדוש ברוך הוא על שרה ולא הקפיד על אברהם: הלבן. יש תמיהות שהן קיימות, כמו: "הנגלה נגליתי" (שמואל א' ב, כז), "הראה אתה" (שמואל ב' טו, כז), אף זו קיימת, וכך אמר בלבו: הנעשה חסד זה לאחר, מה שהקדוש ברוך הוא עושה לי?: ואם שרה הבת תשעים שנה. היתה כדאי לילד? ואף על פי שדורות הראשונים היו מולידין בני חמש מאות שנה, בימי אברהם נתמעטו השנים כבר ובא תשות כח לעולם; וצא ולמד מעשרה דורות שמנח ועד אברהם שמהרו תולדותיהן בני שלשים ובני שבעים:

יח| לו ישמעאל יחיה. הלואי שיחיה ישמעאל, איני כדאי לקבל מתן שכר כזה: יחיה לפניך. יחיה ביראתך, כמו: "התהלך לפני" (לעיל פסוק א) – "פלח קדמי":

DISCUSSION

the personal significance of Sarah's blessing of a son, she also received the news that she would become the mother of an entire nation.

17:17| **And he laughed:** Abraham's laughter was not an expression of amusement, but of astonishment and wonder at the incredible news he had heard. His laughter stemmed from the good news he had heard, as if to say: See what a wonder can happen in the world! Therefore, the Aramaic translations render this phrase as: He rejoiced (Onkelos), or: He was astonished (*Targum Yonatan*). The precise nature of Abraham's laugh will be analyzed in greater detail in the next chapter, in comparison to Sarah's laughter (18:12).

19 **God said: But**[D] indeed, in truth, **Sarah your wife shall bear you a son, and you shall call his name Isaac.** This name, which means "he will laugh," is undoubtedly connected to Abraham's laughter, as well as to that of Sarah, as seen below. **And I will keep My covenant with him for an eternal covenant for his descendants after him.** He, and not Ishmael, is the son through whom the special covenant will be preserved.

20 **And** as **for** your request with regard to **Ishmael, I have heard you,** and your wish shall not be entirely unfulfilled. **Behold, I** have **blessed him, I will make him fruitful, and I will multiply him exceedingly; twelve princes shall he beget, and I will make him** too into **a great nation.**

21 **But My covenant I will keep with Isaac.** God stressed the difference between Abraham's two sons. Ishmael, his first son, who was raised in his home and was undoubtedly beloved by his father, was blessed with great fertility and power. However, the unique personal connection embodied by the covenant was reserved for Isaac alone, **whom Sarah shall bear** to **you at the designated time,** on the same date, **in another year.**

22 **He,** God, **concluded speaking with him, and God ascended from upon Abraham.** By speaking to the prophet, God, as it were, descends to him, and when the prophecy concludes, He ascends back to the heights.

23 **Abraham took Ishmael his son, and all those born in his house, and all those purchased with his silver, every male among the people of Abraham's household, and he circumcised the flesh of their foreskin on that very day,**[D] the same day on which he had received God's command, **as God had spoken with him,** in spite of his advanced age.

24 *Maftir* **Abraham was ninety-nine years old when he was circumcised in the flesh of his foreskin.**

25 **And Ishmael his son was thirteen years old when he was circumcised in the flesh of his foreskin.** Although significantly younger than his father, circumcision is difficult at that age as well, for a variety of reasons.

26 **On that very day, Abraham was circumcised, and Ishmael his son.**

DISCUSSION

17:19 | **But [*aval*]:** In some of the later books of the Bible (see, e.g., Ezra 10:12–13) and in modern Hebrew, this word is a simple term of negation. But in the Torah, such a meaning is indicated by the word *akh* or *ulam,* whereas the term *aval* means "indeed" or "in truth." At times, the Sages used the word in this manner as well.

17:23 | **On that very day:** In various contexts, the Torah describes how Abraham was zealous and did not even briefly delay taking action to fulfill God's command. Generally, he obeyed immediately after hearing a command from God, without hesitation and without questioning it or engaging in philosophical reflections. When God changed his name, he immediately adopted the new one, and as soon as he was commanded to circumcise himself, his family, and his servants, he fulfilled that very difficult command on the same day.

יט וַיֹּאמֶר אֱלֹהִים אֲבָל שָׂרָה אִשְׁתְּךָ יֹלֶדֶת לְךָ בֵּן וְקָרָאתָ אֶת־שְׁמוֹ יִצְחָק וַהֲקִמֹתִי
כ אֶת־בְּרִיתִי אִתּוֹ לִבְרִית עוֹלָם לְזַרְעוֹ אַחֲרָיו: וּלְיִשְׁמָעֵאל שְׁמַעְתִּיךָ הִנֵּה | בֵּרַכְתִּי
אֹתוֹ וְהִפְרֵיתִי אֹתוֹ וְהִרְבֵּיתִי אֹתוֹ בִּמְאֹד מְאֹד שְׁנֵים־עָשָׂר נְשִׂיאִם יוֹלִיד וּנְתַתִּיו
כא לְגוֹי גָּדוֹל: וְאֶת־בְּרִיתִי אָקִים אֶת־יִצְחָק אֲשֶׁר תֵּלֵד לְךָ שָׂרָה לַמּוֹעֵד הַזֶּה בַּשָּׁנָה
כב כג הָאַחֶרֶת: וַיְכַל לְדַבֵּר אִתּוֹ וַיַּעַל אֱלֹהִים מֵעַל אַבְרָהָם: וַיִּקַּח אַבְרָהָם אֶת־
יִשְׁמָעֵאל בְּנוֹ וְאֵת כָּל־יְלִידֵי בֵיתוֹ וְאֵת כָּל־מִקְנַת כַּסְפּוֹ כָּל־זָכָר בְּאַנְשֵׁי בֵּית
אַבְרָהָם וַיָּמָל אֶת־בְּשַׂר עָרְלָתָם בְּעֶצֶם הַיּוֹם הַזֶּה כַּאֲשֶׁר דִּבֶּר אִתּוֹ אֱלֹהִים:
כד כה וְאַבְרָהָם בֶּן־תִּשְׁעִים וָתֵשַׁע שָׁנָה בְּהִמֹּלוֹ בְּשַׂר עָרְלָתוֹ: וְיִשְׁמָעֵאל בְּנוֹ בֶּן־שְׁלֹשׁ מפטיר
כו עֶשְׂרֵה שָׁנָה בְּהִמֹּלוֹ אֵת בְּשַׂר עָרְלָתוֹ: בְּעֶצֶם הַיּוֹם הַזֶּה נִמּוֹל אַבְרָהָם וְיִשְׁמָעֵאל
כז בְּנוֹ: וְכָל־אַנְשֵׁי בֵיתוֹ יְלִיד בָּיִת וּמִקְנַת־כֶּסֶף מֵאֵת בֶּן־נֵכָר נִמֹּלוּ אִתּוֹ:

רש"י

יט | **אֲבָל.** לְשׁוֹן אֲמִתַּת דְּבָרִים, וְכֵן: "אֲבָל אֲשֵׁמִים אֲנַחְנוּ" (להלן מב, כא), "אֲבָל בֵּן אֵין לָהּ" (מלכים ב׳ ד, יד): **וְקָרָאתָ אֶת שְׁמוֹ יִצְחָק.** עַל שֵׁם הַצְּחוֹק; וְאַל שֵׁם עֲשָׂרָה נִסְיוֹנוֹת, וְתִשְׁעִים שָׁנָה שֶׁל שָׂרָה, וּשְׁמוֹנָה יָמִים שֶׁנִּמּוֹל, וּמֵאָה שָׁנָה שֶׁל אַבְרָהָם: **אֶת בְּרִיתִי.** בְּרִית הַמִּילָה תְּהֵא מְסוּרָה לְזַרְעוֹ:

כ | **שְׁנֵים עָשָׂר נְשִׂיאִם.** כַּעֲנָנִים יִכְלוּ, כְּמוֹ: "נְשִׂיאִים וְרוּחַ" (משלי כה, יד):

כב | **מֵעַל אַבְרָהָם.** לָשׁוֹן נְקִיָּה הוּא כְּלַפֵּי שְׁכִינָה, וְלָמַדְנוּ שֶׁהַצַּדִּיקִים מֶרְכַּבְתּוֹ שֶׁל מָקוֹם:

כג | **בְּעֶצֶם הַיּוֹם.** בּוֹ בַּיּוֹם שֶׁנִּצְטַוָּה, בַּיּוֹם וְלֹא בַּלַּיְלָה, לֹא נִתְיָרֵא לֹא מִן הַגּוֹיִם וְלֹא מִן הַלֵּיצָנִים, וְשֶׁלֹּא יִהְיוּ אוֹיְבָיו וּבְנֵי דוֹרוֹ אוֹמְרִים: אִלּוּ רְאִינוּהוּ לֹא הִנַּחְנוּהוּ לָמוּל וּלְקַיֵּם מִצְוָתוֹ שֶׁל מָקוֹם: **וַיָּמָל.** לְשׁוֹן וַיִּפְעַל:

כד | **בְּהִמֹּלוֹ.** בְּהִפָּעֲלוֹ, כְּמוֹ: "בְּהִבָּרְאָם" (לעיל ב, ד): **בְּהִמֹּלוֹ בְּשַׂר עָרְלָתוֹ.** בְּאַבְרָהָם לֹא נֶאֱמַר 'אֵת' לְפִי שֶׁלֹּא הָיָה חָסֵר אֶלָּא חִתּוּךְ בָּשָׂר, שֶׁכְּבָר נִתְמַעֵךְ עַל יְדֵי תַּשְׁמִישׁ, אֲבָל יִשְׁמָעֵאל שֶׁהָיָה יֶלֶד הֻזְקַק לַחְתֹּךְ עָרְלָה וְלִפְרֹעַ הַמִּילָה, לְכָךְ נֶאֱמַר בּוֹ 'אֵת' (להלן פסוק כה):

כו | **בְּעֶצֶם הַיּוֹם הַזֶּה.** שֶׁמָּלְאוּ לְאַבְרָהָם תִּשְׁעִים וָתֵשַׁע שָׁנָה וּלְיִשְׁמָעֵאל שְׁלֹשׁ עֶשְׂרֵה שָׁנִים, "נִמּוֹל אַבְרָהָם וְיִשְׁמָעֵאל בְּנוֹ":

Parashat
Vayera

God's Revelation and the Angels' Visit to Abraham
GENESIS 18:1–33

In this section, two parallel events occur: God reveals Himself to Abraham and visitors arrive at Abraham's tent. The passage begins with a detailed description of Abraham's generous conduct with his guests, despite the fact that he is apparently leaving the Divine Presence in favor of earthly pursuits. But when the guests foretell the birth of Abraham and Sarah's son, it becomes apparent that God Himself is participating in the conversation. When the visitors move on toward Sodom, God reveals to Abraham His intention of destroying the city. By now it is clear that the guests are in fact angels, messengers of God sent to Abraham to bring him news of a child and to bring an end to Sodom.

Abraham's traits of kindness and alacrity are highlighted in this story, both in his treatment of the guests and in his subsequent effort to convince God to spare the inhabitants of the city of Sodom.

The text does not specify the time of year when the circumcision of Abraham and his household occurred, but there is a tradition that it took place at the time of the festival of Passover.

18 1 Not long after Abraham's circumcision, **the Lord appeared to him in the plains of Mamre, and** this occurred when **he,** Abraham, **sat at the entrance of the tent as the day grew hot.**

2 **He,** Abraham, **lifted his eyes and saw, and behold, three men were standing before him.** He had not noticed the men approaching, and he was surprised to see them suddenly so near him. **He saw** them **and ran toward them**[D] **from the entrance of the tent and prostrated himself to the earth.** He did not wait for them to reach the tent before greeting them; rather, he approached them warmly and ran to welcome them, thereby showing them great respect.

3 **He said: My Lord, please, if I have found favor in Your eyes,** if You wish, **please do not depart from upon your servant.** Most commentaries maintain that this statement was addressed to God, who had just revealed Himself to Abraham.[1] As Abraham rushed toward the guests, he begged God to wait until he had properly welcomed them.

4 Abraham turned to the men and said: **Please, let a little water be taken, and wash your feet,** since you have come from afar, and you certainly need to rest. Washing one's feet, whether he wore shoes or not, was one of the first steps a traveler took to relax. **And recline beneath the tree,** in the shade.

5 **I will take a portion of bread, and you shall sustain your heart,** meaning to satisfy your hunger, **thereafter depart.** I have no wish to delay you greatly; after you have rested and

eaten a bit, feel free to go on your way.[2] **As for this you have happened upon your servant.** Since you happened to arrive here, take the opportunity to stay with me. **They said** courteously: **Do so,** but only **as you have said.** Give us some bread and water and let us sit under the tree, as that will be enough for us.[3]

6 Despite his guests' comment, Abraham acted otherwise, in his dedication and zeal. **Abraham hurried to the tent to Sarah and said: Hurry** and take **three se'a,** a significant amount, **of high-quality flour,** which is flour produced by the coarse grinding of wheat kernels, **knead** dough, **and make cakes,** a type of round bread.

7 **Abraham ran to the cattle and took a bullock, tender,** young, **and good, and gave it to the lad** standing there; he commanded the young man to slaughter the calf, skin it, and ready it for the meal. **And he,** the lad, **hurried to prepare it.**

8 **He took butter, milk, and the bullock that he prepared and placed it before them,** the visitors. In his delight at the opportunity to welcome guests, Abraham himself ran to provide for all their needs. Although his household presumably had bread stored away, he wanted fresh bread for his visitors. The baking of bread and the slaughter of cattle in honor of guests were also ceremonial acts that displayed the host's enthusiasm and goodwill. **He stood over them,** by serving them,[4] **beneath the tree, and they ate.**

DISCUSSION

18:2 | **He saw and ran toward them:** The Sages learn from Abraham's behavior here that gracious hospitality is greater than receiving the Divine Presence (*Shabbat* 127a). God does not get hungry, nor is He susceptible to sickness or the elements. The welcoming of guests, by contrast, is an opportunity to provide for very real and immediate needs.

פרשת
וירא

ח א ב וַיֵּרָא אֵלָיו יהוה בְּאֵלֹנֵי מַמְרֵא וְהוּא יֹשֵׁב פֶּתַח־הָאֹהֶל כְּחֹם הַיּוֹם: וַיִּשָּׂא עֵינָיו טו
וַיַּרְא וְהִנֵּה שְׁלֹשָׁה אֲנָשִׁים נִצָּבִים עָלָיו וַיַּרְא וַיָּרָץ לִקְרָאתָם מִפֶּתַח הָאֹהֶל
ג וַיִּשְׁתַּחוּ אָרְצָה: וַיֹּאמַר אֲדֹנָי אִם־נָא מָצָאתִי חֵן בְּעֵינֶיךָ אַל־נָא תַעֲבֹר מֵעַל
ד ה עַבְדֶּךָ: יֻקַּח־נָא מְעַט־מַיִם וְרַחֲצוּ רַגְלֵיכֶם וְהִשָּׁעֲנוּ תַּחַת הָעֵץ: וְאֶקְחָה
פַת־לֶחֶם וְסַעֲדוּ לִבְּכֶם אַחַר תַּעֲבֹרוּ כִּי־עַל־כֵּן עֲבַרְתֶּם עַל־עַבְדְּכֶם וַיֹּאמְרוּ
ו כֵּן תַּעֲשֶׂה כַּאֲשֶׁר דִּבַּרְתָּ: וַיְמַהֵר אַבְרָהָם הָאֹהֱלָה אֶל־שָׂרָה וַיֹּאמֶר מַהֲרִי
ז שְׁלֹשׁ סְאִים קֶמַח סֹלֶת לוּשִׁי וַעֲשִׂי עֻגוֹת: וְאֶל־הַבָּקָר רָץ אַבְרָהָם וַיִּקַּח
ח בֶּן־בָּקָר רַךְ וָטוֹב וַיִּתֵּן אֶל־הַנַּעַר וַיְמַהֵר לַעֲשׂוֹת אֹתוֹ: וַיִּקַּח חֶמְאָה וְחָלָב
וּבֶן־הַבָּקָר אֲשֶׁר עָשָׂה וַיִּתֵּן לִפְנֵיהֶם וְהוּא עֹמֵד עֲלֵיהֶם תַּחַת הָעֵץ וַיֹּאכֵלוּ:

רש"י

א| **וַיֵּרָא אֵלָיו.** לְבַקֵּר אֶת הַחוֹלֶה. אָמַר רַבִּי חָמָא בַּר חֲנִינָא: יוֹם שְׁלִישִׁי לְמִילָתוֹ הָיָה, וּבָא הַקָּדוֹשׁ בָּרוּךְ הוּא וְשָׁאַל בּוֹ: **בְּאֵלֹנֵי מַמְרֵא.** הוּא שֶׁנָּתַן לוֹ עֵצָה עַל הַמִּילָה, לְפִיכָךְ נִגְלָה עָלָיו בְּחֶלְקוֹ: **יֹשֵׁב.** 'יָשַׁב' כְּתִיב, בִּקֵּשׁ לַעֲמֹד, אָמַר לוֹ הַקָּדוֹשׁ בָּרוּךְ הוּא: שֵׁב, וַאֲנִי אֶעֱמֹד, וְאַתָּה סִימָן לְבָנֶיךָ שֶׁעָתִיד אֲנִי לְהִתְיַצֵּב בַּעֲדַת הַדַּיָּנִים וְהֵן יוֹשְׁבִים: **פֶּתַח הָאֹהֶל.** לִרְאוֹת אִם יֵשׁ עוֹבֵר וָשָׁב, וְיַכְנִיסֵם בְּבֵיתוֹ: **כְּחֹם הַיּוֹם.** הוֹצִיא הַקָּדוֹשׁ בָּרוּךְ הוּא חַמָּה מִנַּרְתִּיקָהּ שֶׁלֹּא לְהַטְרִיחוֹ בְּאוֹרְחִים, וּלְפִי שֶׁרָאָהוּ מִצְטַעֵר שֶׁלֹּא הָיוּ אוֹרְחִים בָּאִים, הֵבִיא הַמַּלְאָכִים עָלָיו בִּדְמוּת אֲנָשִׁים:

ב| **וְהִנֵּה שְׁלֹשָׁה אֲנָשִׁים.** אֶחָד לְבַשֵּׂר אֶת שָׂרָה וְאֶחָד לַהֲפֹךְ אֶת סְדוֹם וְאֶחָד לְרַפְּאוֹת אֶת אַבְרָהָם, שֶׁאֵין מַלְאָךְ אֶחָד עוֹשֶׂה שְׁתֵּי שְׁלִיחוּיוֹת, תֵּדַע לְךָ שֶׁכֵּן כָּל הַפָּרָשָׁה הוּא מַזְכִּירָן בִּלְשׁוֹן רַבִּים, "וַיֹּאכֵלוּ" (להלן פסוק ח), "וַיֹּאמְרוּ אֵלָיו" (שם פסוק ט), וּבַבְּשׂוֹרָה נֶאֱמַר: "וַיֹּאמֶר שׁוֹב אָשׁוּב" (שם פסוק י), וּבַהֲפִיכַת סְדוֹם הוּא אוֹמֵר: "כִּי לֹא אוּכַל לַעֲשׂוֹת דָּבָר" (להלן יט, כב), "לְבִלְתִּי הָפְכִּי" (שם פסוק כא). וּרְפָאֵל שֶׁרִפֵּא אֶת אַבְרָהָם הָלַךְ מִשָּׁם לְהַצִּיל אֶת לוֹט, הוּא שֶׁנֶּאֱמַר: "וַיְהִי כְהוֹצִיאָם אֹתָם הַחוּצָה וַיֹּאמֶר הִמָּלֵט עַל נַפְשֶׁךָ" (שם פסוק יז), לָמַדְתָּ שֶׁהָאֶחָד הָיָה מַצִּיל: **נִצָּבִים עָלָיו.** לְפָנָיו, אֲבָל לָשׁוֹן נְקִיָּה הוּא כְּלַפֵּי הַמַּלְאָכִים: **וַיַּרְא.** מַהוּ "וַיַּרְא... וַיַּרְא" שְׁנֵי פְּעָמִים? הָרִאשׁוֹן כְּמַשְׁמָעוֹ, וְהַשֵּׁנִי לְשׁוֹן הֲבָנָה – נִסְתַּכֵּל שֶׁהָיוּ נִצָּבִים בְּמָקוֹם אֶחָד וְהֵבִין שֶׁלֹּא הָיוּ רוֹצִים לְהַטְרִיחוֹ, וְקָדַם הוּא וְרָץ לִקְרָאתָם. בְּבָבָא מְצִיעָא (דף פו ע"ב): כְּתִיב "נִצָּבִים עָלָיו" וּכְתִיב "וַיָּרָץ לִקְרָאתָם", כַּד חַזְיוּהּ דַּהֲוָה שָׁרֵי וְאָסַר, פֵּרְשׁוּ הֵימֶנּוּ. מִיָּד – "וַיָּרָץ לִקְרָאתָם":

ג| **וַיֹּאמַר אֲדֹנָי אִם נָא וְגוֹ'.** לַגָּדוֹל שֶׁבָּהֶם אָמַר, וּקְרָאָם כֻּלָּם אֲדוֹנִים, וְלַגָּדוֹל אָמַר: "אַל נָא תַעֲבֹר", וְכֵיוָן שֶׁלֹּא יַעֲבֹר הוּא יַעַמְדוּ חֲבֵרָיו עִמּוֹ, וּבְלָשׁוֹן זֶה הוּא חוֹל. דָּבָר אַחֵר, קֹדֶשׁ הוּא, וְהָיָה אוֹמֵר לְהַקָּדוֹשׁ בָּרוּךְ הוּא לְהַמְתִּין לוֹ עַד שֶׁיָּרוּץ וְיַכְנִיס אֶת הָאוֹרְחִים, וְאַף עַל פִּי שֶׁכָּתוּב אַחַר "וַיָּרָץ לִקְרָאתָם", הָאֲמִירָה קֹדֶם לָכֵן הָיְתָה, וְדֶרֶךְ הַמִּקְרָאוֹת לְדַבֵּר כֵּן, כְּמוֹ שֶׁפֵּרַשְׁתִּי אֵצֶל "לֹא יָדוֹן רוּחִי בָאָדָם" (לעיל ו, ג) שֶׁנִּכְתַּב אַחַר "וַיּוֹלֶד נֹחַ" (לעיל ה, לב), וְאִי אֶפְשָׁר לוֹמַר אֶלָּא אִם כֵּן קֹדֶם הַגְּזֵרָה עֶשְׂרִים שָׁנָה. וּשְׁתֵּי הַלְּשׁוֹנוֹת בִּבְרֵאשִׁית רַבָּה (מח, י; מט, ז):

ד| **יֻקַּח נָא.** עַל יְדֵי שָׁלִיחַ, וְהַקָּדוֹשׁ בָּרוּךְ הוּא שִׁלֵּם לְבָנָיו עַל יְדֵי שָׁלִיחַ, שֶׁנֶּאֱמַר: "וַיָּרֶם מֹשֶׁה אֶת יָדוֹ וַיַּךְ אֶת הַסֶּלַע" (במדבר כ, יא): **וְרַחֲצוּ רַגְלֵיכֶם.** כִּסְבוּר שֶׁהֵם עַרְבִיִּים שֶׁמִּשְׁתַּחֲוִים לַאֲבַק רַגְלֵיהֶם וְהִקְפִּיד שֶׁלֹּא לְהַכְנִיס עֲבוֹדָה זָרָה לְבֵיתוֹ. אֲבָל לוֹט שֶׁלֹּא הִקְפִּיד הִקְדִּים לִינָה לִרְחִיצָה, שֶׁנֶּאֱמַר: "וְלִינוּ וְרַחֲצוּ רַגְלֵיכֶם" (להלן יט, ב): **תַּחַת הָעֵץ.** תַּחַת הָאִילָן:

ה| **וְסַעֲדוּ לִבְּכֶם.** בַּתּוֹרָה בַּנְּבִיאִים וּבַכְּתוּבִים מָצִינוּ דְּפִתָּא סַעְדְּתָא דְּלִבָּא. בַּתּוֹרָה: "וְסַעֲדוּ לִבְּכֶם", בַּנְּבִיאִים: "סְעָד לִבְּךָ פַּת לֶחֶם" (שופטים יט, ה), בַּכְּתוּבִים: "וְלֶחֶם לְבַב אֱנוֹשׁ יִסְעָד" (תהלים קד, טו). אָמַר רַבִּי חָמָא: 'לְבַבְכֶם' אֵין כְּתִיב כָּאן אֶלָּא 'לִבְּכֶם', מַגִּיד שֶׁאֵין יֵצֶר הָרָע שׁוֹלֵט בַּמַּלְאָכִים: **אַחַר תַּעֲבֹרוּ.** אַחַר כֵּן תֵּלֵכוּ: **כִּי עַל כֵּן עֲבַרְתֶּם.** כִּי הַדָּבָר הַזֶּה אֲנִי מְבַקֵּשׁ מִכֶּם מֵאַחַר שֶׁעֲבַרְתֶּם עָלַי לְכְבוֹדִי. "כִּי עַל כֵּן" – כְּמוֹ: 'עַל אֲשֶׁר', וְכֵן כָּל 'כִּי עַל כֵּן' שֶׁבַּמִּקְרָא: "כִּי עַל כֵּן בָּאוּ בְּצֵל קֹרָתִי" (להלן יט, ח), "כִּי עַל כֵּן רָאִיתִי פָנֶיךָ" (להלן לג, י), "כִּי עַל כֵּן לֹא נְתַתִּיהָ" (להלן לח, כו), "כִּי עַל כֵּן יָדַעְתָּ חֲנֹתֵנוּ" (במדבר י, לא):

ו| **קֶמַח סֹלֶת.** סֹלֶת לְעוּגוֹת, קֶמַח לַעֲמִילָן שֶׁל טַבָּחִים לְכַסּוֹת אֶת הַקְּדֵרָה לִשְׁאֹב אֶת הַזֻּהֲמָא:

ז| **בֶּן בָּקָר רַךְ וָטוֹב.** שְׁלֹשָׁה פָּרִים הָיוּ, כְּדֵי לְהַאֲכִילָן שָׁלֹשׁ לְשׁוֹנוֹת בְּחַרְדָּל: **אֶל הַנַּעַר.** זֶה יִשְׁמָעֵאל, לְחַנְּכוֹ בְּמִצְוֹת:

ח| **וַיִּקַּח חֶמְאָה וְגוֹ'.** וְלֶחֶם לֹא הֵבִיא, לְפִי שֶׁפֵּרְסָה שָׂרָה נִדָּה שֶׁחָזַר לָהּ אֹרַח כַּנָּשִׁים אוֹתוֹ הַיּוֹם, וְנִטְמֵאת הָעִסָּה: **חֶמְאָה.** שׁוּמָן הֶחָלָב שֶׁקּוֹלְטִין מֵעַל פָּנָיו: **וּבֶן הַבָּקָר אֲשֶׁר עָשָׂה.** אֲשֶׁר תִּקֵּן. קַמָּא קַמָּא שֶׁתִּקֵּן אַמְטֵי וְאַיְתִי קַמַּיְהוּ: **וַיֹּאכֵלוּ.** נִרְאוּ כְּמוֹ שֶׁאָכְלוּ, מִכָּאן שֶׁלֹּא יְשַׁנֶּה אָדָם מִן הַמִּנְהָג:

9 **They said to him: Where is Sarah, your wife?** Although these were ostensibly passersby, they could have known about Abraham. They may have asked about Sarah because it was customary for the mistress of the household to welcome important guests. **He said: Behold,** she is **in the tent.** She does not want to interfere with this ceremony.

10 **He,** the leader of the guests, **said: I will return to you at this time next year, and behold, a son for Sarah, your wife. And Sarah was listening at the entrance of the tent,** not far from the tree. **And he was behind it.** Apparently the man was standing behind the entrance of the tent,[5] facing away, and consequently did not notice that Sarah was seeing and hearing everything.

11 **Abraham and Sarah were old, advanced in years.** Abraham was ninety-nine years old, while Sarah was ninety. **It had ceased to be with Sarah the manner of women,** meaning that she no longer experienced a menstrual cycle.

12 Therefore, when **Sarah,** who was alone, heard this, she **laughed inside herself** silently, **saying: After my languishing, shall I have youth?** Now that I am old and my menstrual cycle has ceased, shall my body become young again? This process is irreversible, **and** furthermore, **my lord** Abraham **is old.**

13 **The Lord said to Abraham.** The speaker was one of the visitors. At this point it became apparent that they were actually angels, messengers of God, who appeared in human form. Angels are sometimes referred to as: The Lord.[6] Alternatively, this was the voice of God Himself, as Abraham was still before the Divine Presence when he tended to his guests.[7] According to this interpretation, when God interrupted the conversation between Abraham and the visitors, He revealed that they were His messengers. **Why is it that Sarah laughed, saying: Shall I indeed bear a child, and I grew old?** Her laughter indicates a lack of faith in the prophecy.

14 **Is any matter beyond the** power of the **Lord? At the designated time I will return to you, at this time next year, and Sarah shall have a son.** This will indeed occur, and then I will reveal Myself to you again.

15 *Second aliya* **Sarah denied it, saying: I did not laugh.** Apparently Abraham, who had been standing close to the tent, came inside to speak with her. He reacted differently to the prophecy. Therefore, since God had told him that Sarah had laughed, he asked her why she had done so. Having laughed silently, Sarah denied that she had laughed, **for she was afraid** to admit to doubting the promise. Her denial demonstrates that she had indeed laughed out of ridicule, rather than joy. **He,** Abraham or God,[8] **said: No, but you did laugh.**

16 The exchange between Abraham and Sarah occurred while the guests were eating. Afterward, **the men arose from there and looked** out from the hills **toward Sodom,** in the Jordan Valley far below. **And Abraham was walking with them to see them off,** as befitting a host.

17 **The Lord said** to Himself:[9] **Shall I conceal from Abraham that which I am doing?**

18 He is dear to Me, **and Abraham shall become a great and mighty nation.** He will be a central figure in history, **and all the nations of the earth shall be blessed in him.** They will all consider themselves his successors.

19 **For I love him,**[D] **so that he shall command his children and his household after him, and they will observe the way of the Lord, to perform righteousness and justice; so that the Lord will bring upon Abraham that which He spoke of him.** God's purpose would be realized through Abraham, as he was chosen to be the father of the nation that would receive numerous blessings and inherit the land of Canaan. Since Canaan was promised to Abraham's descendants, it was fitting that Abraham be informed of God's plans for the land.

20 **The Lord said: Because** I hear **the outcry of Sodom and Gomorrah,** and it **is great** and increasing, **and because their sin,** evident from the cries of the oppressed individuals there, **is very heavy,**[D]

21 **I will descend now and see if they have acted in accordance with the outcry that has reached Me.** The bare fact that certain people are suffering under the law does not necessarily mean that it is part of an evil regime. At times the suffering is

DISCUSSION

18:19 | **For I love him [*yedativ*]:** In addition to its common meaning of conceptual knowledge, *yeda* can also refer to emotional knowledge of another, love and intimacy (see 4:1).

18:20 | **And because their sin is very heavy:** The Sages' detailed description of the sins of Sodom accords well with the account in the Torah (see, e.g., *Sanhedrin* 109a). The Sages teach that the Sodomites held a distorted view of justice that was exceedingly harsh and unyielding toward individuals. Formally, Sodom functioned under the rule of law. The evil there was not spontaneous or driven by passions, but ingrained in the fabric of society. Nazi Germany was similar: In contrast to anti-Semitism in other times and places, German Jew-hatred in the Nazi era was deeply institutionalized and organized. The precise time of a pogrom would often be published in the newspaper and the riot would be executed exactly as planned. One survivor of Kristallnacht reported that two hours afterward he met a German who had participated in the attacks who politely tipped his hat to him, as though once a pogrom ended, life could return to normal.

ט וַיֹּאמְרוּ אֵלָיו אַיֵּה שָׂרָה אִשְׁתֶּךָ וַיֹּאמֶר הִנֵּה בָאֹהֶל: וַיֹּאמֶר שׁוֹב אָשׁוּב אֵלֶיךָ

י כָּעֵת חַיָּה וְהִנֵּה־בֵן לְשָׂרָה אִשְׁתֶּךָ וְשָׂרָה שֹׁמַעַת פֶּתַח הָאֹהֶל וְהוּא אַחֲרָיו:

יא יב וְאַבְרָהָם וְשָׂרָה זְקֵנִים בָּאִים בַּיָּמִים חָדַל לִהְיוֹת לְשָׂרָה אֹרַח כַּנָּשִׁים: וַתִּצְחַק

יג שָׂרָה בְּקִרְבָּהּ לֵאמֹר אַחֲרֵי בְלֹתִי הָיְתָה־לִּי עֶדְנָה וַאדֹנִי זָקֵן: וַיֹּאמֶר יְהוָה אֶל־

יד אַבְרָהָם לָמָּה זֶּה צָחֲקָה שָׂרָה לֵאמֹר הַאַף אֻמְנָם אֵלֵד וַאֲנִי זָקַנְתִּי: הֲיִפָּלֵא

טו מֵיְהוָה דָּבָר לַמּוֹעֵד אָשׁוּב אֵלֶיךָ כָּעֵת חַיָּה וּלְשָׂרָה בֵן: וַתְּכַחֵשׁ שָׂרָה לֵאמֹר שני

טז לֹא צָחַקְתִּי כִּי ׀ יָרֵאָה וַיֹּאמֶר ׀ לֹא כִּי צָחָקְתְּ: וַיָּקֻמוּ מִשָּׁם הָאֲנָשִׁים וַיַּשְׁקִפוּ

יז עַל־פְּנֵי סְדֹם וְאַבְרָהָם הֹלֵךְ עִמָּם לְשַׁלְּחָם: וַיהוָה אָמָר הַמְכַסֶּה אֲנִי מֵאַבְרָהָם

יח אֲשֶׁר אֲנִי עֹשֶׂה: וְאַבְרָהָם הָיוֹ יִהְיֶה לְגוֹי גָּדוֹל וְעָצוּם וְנִבְרְכוּ־בוֹ כֹּל גּוֹיֵי הָאָרֶץ:

יט כִּי יְדַעְתִּיו לְמַעַן אֲשֶׁר יְצַוֶּה אֶת־בָּנָיו וְאֶת־בֵּיתוֹ אַחֲרָיו וְשָׁמְרוּ דֶּרֶךְ יְהוָה לַעֲשׂוֹת

כ צְדָקָה וּמִשְׁפָּט לְמַעַן הָבִיא יְהוָה עַל־אַבְרָהָם אֵת אֲשֶׁר־דִּבֶּר עָלָיו: וַיֹּאמֶר

כא יְהוָה זַעֲקַת סְדֹם וַעֲמֹרָה כִּי־רָבָּה וְחַטָּאתָם כִּי כָבְדָה מְאֹד: אֵרְדָה־נָּא וְאֶרְאֶה

רש"י

ט | **וַיֹּאמְרוּ אֵלָיו.** נָקוּד עַל אי"ו, וְתַנְיָא, רַבִּי שִׁמְעוֹן בֶּן אֶלְעָזָר אוֹמֵר: כָּל מָקוֹם שֶׁהַכְּתָב רַבָּה עַל הַנְּקֻדָּה אַתָּה דּוֹרֵשׁ הַכְּתָב, וְכָאן נְקֻדָּה רַבָּה עַל הַכְּתָב וְאַתָּה דּוֹרֵשׁ הַנְּקֻדָּה, שֶׁאַף לְשָׂרָה שָׁאֲלוּ: אַיּוֹ אַבְרָהָם? לָמַדְנוּ שֶׁיִּשְׁאַל אָדָם בְּאַכְסַנְיָא שֶׁלּוֹ לָאִישׁ עַל הָאִשָּׁה וְלָאִשָּׁה עַל הָאִישׁ. בְּבָבָא מְצִיעָא (דף פז ע"א) אוֹמְרִים: יוֹדְעִים הָיוּ מַלְאֲכֵי הַשָּׁרֵת שָׂרָה אִמֵּנוּ הֵיכָן הָיְתָה, אֶלָּא לְהוֹדִיעַ שֶׁצְּנוּעָה הָיְתָה כְּדֵי לְחַבְּבָהּ עַל בַּעְלָהּ. אָמַר רַבִּי יוֹסֵי בְּרַבִּי חֲנִינָא: כְּדֵי לְשַׁגֵּר לָהּ כּוֹס שֶׁל בְּרָכָה: **הִנֵּה בָאֹהֶל.** צְנוּעָה הִיא:

י | **כָּעֵת חַיָּה.** כָּעֵת הַזֹּאת לַשָּׁנָה הַבָּאָה, וּפֶסַח הָיָה, וְלַפֶּסַח הַבָּא נוֹלַד יִצְחָק, מִדְּלָא קָרֵינָן כְּעֵת חַיָּה: **כָּעֵת חַיָּה.** כָּעֵת הַזֹּאת שֶׁתְּהֵא חַיָּה לָכֶם, שֶׁתִּהְיוּ כֻּלְּכֶם שְׁלֵמִים וְקַיָּמִים: **שׁוֹב אָשׁוּב.** לֹא בִּשְּׂרוֹ הַמַּלְאָךְ שֶׁיָּשׁוּב אֵלָיו, אֶלָּא בִּשְׁלִיחוּתוֹ שֶׁל מָקוֹם אָמַר לוֹ, כְּמוֹ: "וַיֹּאמֶר לָהּ מַלְאַךְ ה' הַרְבָּה אַרְבֶּה" (לעיל טז, י) וְהוּא אֵין בְּיָדוֹ לְהַרְבּוֹת, אֶלָּא בִּשְׁלִיחוּתוֹ שֶׁל מָקוֹם אָמַר לָהּ, אַף כָּאן בִּשְׁלִיחוּתוֹ שֶׁל מָקוֹם אָמַר לוֹ: **וְהוּא אַחֲרָיו.** הַפֶּתַח הָיָה אַחַר הַמַּלְאָךְ:

יא | **חָדַל לִהְיוֹת.** פָּסַק מִמֶּנָּה דֶּרֶךְ נָשִׁים – נִדּוּת:

יב | **בְּקִרְבָּהּ לֵאמֹר.** מִסְתַּכֶּלֶת בְּמֵעֶיהָ: אֶפְשָׁר הַקְּרָבַיִם הַלָּלוּ טוֹעֲנִין וָלָד? הַשָּׁדַיִם הַלָּלוּ שֶׁצָּמְקוּ מוֹשְׁכִין חָלָב? תַּנְחוּמָא (שופטים יח): **עֶדְנָה.** צַחְצוּחַ בָּשָׂר, וּלְשׁוֹן מִשְׁנָה: "מַשִּׁיר אֶת הַשֵּׂעָר וּמְעַדֵּן אֶת הַבָּשָׂר". דָּבָר אַחֵר, לְשׁוֹן עִדָּן, זְמַן וֶסֶת נִדּוּת:

יג | **הַאַף אֻמְנָם.** הֲגַם אֱמֶת "אֵלֵד": **וַאֲנִי זָקַנְתִּי.** שִׁנָּה הַכָּתוּב מִפְּנֵי הַשָּׁלוֹם, שֶׁהֲרֵי הִיא אָמְרָה: "וַאדֹנִי זָקֵן":

יד | **הֲיִפָּלֵא.** כְּתַרְגּוּמוֹ, "הֲיִתְכַּסֵּי", וְכִי שׁוּם דָּבָר מֻפְלָא וּמֻפְרָד וּמְכֻסֶּה מִמֶּנִּי מִלַּעֲשׂוֹת כִּרְצוֹנִי?: **לַמּוֹעֵד.** לְאוֹתוֹ מוֹעֵד הַמְיֻחָד שֶׁקָּבַעְתִּי לְךָ אֶתְמוֹל, "לַמּוֹעֵד הַזֶּה בַּשָּׁנָה הָאַחֶרֶת" (לעיל יז, כא):

טו | **כִּי יָרֵאָה. כִּי צָחָקְתְּ.** הָרִאשׁוֹן מְשַׁמֵּשׁ לְשׁוֹן 'דְּהָא', שֶׁהוּא נוֹתֵן טַעַם לַדָּבָר: וַתְּכַחֵשׁ שָׂרָה לְפִי שֶׁיָּרְאָה. וְהַשֵּׁנִי מְשַׁמֵּשׁ בִּלְשׁוֹן 'אֶלָּא': וַיֹּאמֶר, לֹא כִּדְבָרַיִךְ הוּא, אֶלָּא צָחַקְתְּ; שֶׁאָמְרוּ רַבּוֹתֵינוּ: 'כִּי' מְשַׁמֵּשׁ בְּאַרְבַּע לְשׁוֹנוֹת, אִי, דִּלְמָא, אֶלָּא, דְּהָא:

טז | **וַיַּשְׁקִפוּ.** כָּל הַשְׁקָפָה שֶׁבַּמִּקְרָא לְרָעָה, חוּץ מֵ"הַשְׁקִיפָה מִמְּעוֹן קָדְשְׁךָ" (דברים כו, טו), שֶׁגָּדוֹל כֹּחַ מַתְּנוֹת עֲנִיִּים שֶׁהוֹפֵךְ מִדַּת הָרֹגֶז לְרַחֲמִים: **לְשַׁלְּחָם.** לְלַוּוֹתָם, כִּסְבוּר אוֹרְחִים הֵם:

יז | **הַמְכַסֶּה אֲנִי.** בִּתְמִיָּה, מַה שֶּׁאֲנִי עוֹשֶׂה בִּסְדוֹם?! לֹא יָפֶה לִי לַעֲשׂוֹת דָּבָר זֶה שֶׁלֹּא מִדַּעְתּוֹ! אֲנִי נָתַתִּי לוֹ אֶת הָאָרֶץ הַזֹּאת וַחֲמִשָּׁה כְּרַכִּין הַלָּלוּ שֶׁלּוֹ הֵן, שֶׁנֶּאֱמַר: "גְּבוּל הַכְּנַעֲנִי מִצִּידֹן... בֹּאֲכָה סְדֹמָה וַעֲמֹרָה" וְגוֹ' (לעיל י, יט), קָרָאתִי אוֹתוֹ אַבְרָהָם, "אַב הֲמוֹן גּוֹיִם" (לעיל יז, ה), וְאַשְׁמִיד אֶת הַבָּנִים וְלֹא אוֹדִיעַ לָאָב שֶׁהוּא אוֹהֲבִי?!:

יח | **וְאַבְרָהָם הָיוֹ יִהְיֶה.** מִדְרַשׁ אַגָּדָה, "זֵכֶר צַדִּיק לִבְרָכָה" (משלי י, ז), הוֹאִיל וְהִזְכִּירוֹ בֵּרְכוֹ. וּפְשׁוּטוֹ, וְכִי מִמֶּנּוּ אֲנִי מַעְלִים? וַהֲרֵי הוּא חָבִיב לְפָנַי לִהְיוֹת לְגוֹי גָּדוֹל וּלְהִתְבָּרֵךְ בּוֹ כָּל גּוֹיֵי הָאָרֶץ:

יט | **כִּי יְדַעְתִּיו.** לְשׁוֹן חִבָּה, כְּמוֹ: "מוֹדַע לְאִישָׁהּ" (רות ב, א), "הֲלֹא בֹעַז מֹדַעְתָּנוּ" (שם ג, ב), "וָאֵדָעֲךָ בְּשֵׁם" (שמות לג, יז). וְאָמְנָם עִקַּר לְשׁוֹן כֻּלָּם אֵינוֹ אֶלָּא לְשׁוֹן יְדִיעָה, שֶׁהַמְחַבֵּב אֶת הָאָדָם מְקָרְבוֹ אֶצְלוֹ וְיוֹדְעוֹ וּמַכִּירוֹ. וְלָמָּה יְדַעְתִּיו? "לְמַעַן אֲשֶׁר יְצַוֶּה", לְפִי שֶׁהוּא מְצַוֶּה אֶת בָּנָיו עָלַי לִשְׁמֹר דְּרָכַי. וְאִם תְּפָרְשֵׁהוּ כְּתַרְגּוּמוֹ: יוֹדֵעַ אֲנִי בּוֹ שֶׁיְּצַוֶּה אֶת בָּנָיו וְגוֹ', אֵין 'לְמַעַן' נוֹפֵל עַל הַלָּשׁוֹן: **יְצַוֶּה.** לְשׁוֹן הֹוֶה, כְּמוֹ: "כָּכָה יַעֲשֶׂה אִיּוֹב" (איוב א, ה): **לְמַעַן הָבִיא.** כָּךְ הוּא מְצַוֶּה לְבָנָיו: שִׁמְרוּ דֶּרֶךְ ה' כְּדֵי שֶׁיָּבִיא ה' עַל אַבְרָהָם וְגוֹ'; 'עַל בֵּית אַבְרָהָם' לֹא נֶאֱמַר אֶלָּא "עַל אַבְרָהָם", לָמַדְנוּ כָּל הַמַּעֲמִיד בֵּן צַדִּיק כְּאִלּוּ אֵינוֹ מֵת:

כ | **וַיֹּאמֶר ה'.** אֶל אַבְרָהָם: זַעֲקַת סְדֹם וְגוֹ'. **כִּי רָבָּה.** כָּל 'רַבָּה' שֶׁבַּמִּקְרָא הַטַּעַם בַּבֵּי"ת, לְפִי שֶׁהֵן מִתְרַגְּמִין 'גְּדוֹלָה' אוֹ 'גְּדֵלָה וְהוֹלֶכֶת', אֲבָל זֶה טַעְמוֹ לְמַעְלָה בָּרֵי"שׁ לְפִי שֶׁמִּתַּרְגֵּם 'גְּדֵלָה' כְּבָר, כְּמוֹ שֶׁפֵּרַשְׁתִּי: "וַיְהִי הַשֶּׁמֶשׁ בָּאָה" (לעיל טו, יז), "הִנֵּה שָׁבָה יְבִמְתֵּךְ" (רות א, טו):

כא | **אֵרְדָה נָּא.** לִמֵּד לַדַּיָּנִים שֶׁלֹּא יִפְסְקוּ דִּינֵי נְפָשׁוֹת אֶלָּא בִּרְאִיָּה, הַכֹּל כְּמוֹ שֶׁפֵּרַשְׁתִּי בְּפָרָשַׁת הַפַּלָּגָה (לעיל

due to problems of inefficiency, or insensitivity, rather than actual malfeasance. If the actions of Sodom are so evil that they justify the outcry, I will bring **destruction** upon them; **and if not, I will know** exactly what is happening there.

22 **The men turned from there,** after being escorted by Abraham, **and went to Sodom; and Abraham was still standing before the Lord.** The revelation or conversation between God and Abraham was still in progress.[10] Alternatively, this phrase has the same meaning as: The Lord was still standing before Abraham.[11]

23 After God made His plans for Sodom known to Abraham, **Abraham approached, and he said: Will You destroy even the righteous with the wicked?**

23 **Perhaps there are fifty righteous people within the city; will You even destroy, and not tolerate the place for the sake of the fifty righteous people who are within it?** All populations contain different types of people. There must be some righteous individuals in Sodom.

25 If so, **it is inconceivable for You to do a thing like this, to kill the righteous with the wicked, and** that **the righteous shall be** given the same fate **as the wicked. It is inconceivable for You; shall the Judge of all the earth not practice justice?**

26 **The Lord said: If I find in Sodom fifty righteous people within the city, I will tolerate the entire place for their sake.**

27 **Abraham** attempted to bargain. He **responded and said: Behold, I have presumed to speak to my Lord, and** yet **I am** mere **dust and ashes,** a lowly being.

28 **Perhaps the fifty righteous people will lack five,** as there might be only forty-five righteous people in Sodom. **Will You destroy the entire city for the** lack of only **five? He,** God, **said: I will not destroy** it, **if I find there forty-five.**

29 **He continued to speak to Him and said: Perhaps forty** righteous people **shall be found there. He said: I will not do it,** even **for the sake of the forty.**

30 **He said: Let my Lord please not be incensed, and I will speak. Perhaps thirty shall be found there. He said: I will not do it, if I find thirty there.**

31 **He said: Behold, I have presumed to speak to my Lord, perhaps twenty shall be found there. He said: I will not destroy, for the twenty.**

32 **He said: Please, let my Lord not be incensed, and I will speak only this time. Perhaps ten shall be found there. He said: I will not destroy, for the ten.**[D] Ten righteous people is apparently the smallest community that can save the city.

33 **The Lord went,** He ascended, as it were, **when He concluded speaking to Abraham, and Abraham returned to his place,** presumably worried and preoccupied by the coming events.

DISCUSSION

18:32 | I will not destroy for the ten: If there are fewer than ten righteous people, it might be possible to save them individually, but the city as a whole will not escape punishment. Later it was established as *halakha* that the minimum number of individuals required for a congregation, a community, or a quorum, to pray communally or to perform certain other religious rituals, is ten.

Shall the Judge of All the Earth Not Practice Justice?: In the philosophy of religion in general, and in Jewish philosophy in particular, the question arises: Is there morality independent of God?[12] While many sources may be cited relating to this issue, it appears that the clearest proof that there is an independent ethic is from the verse: "It is inconceivable for You to do a thing like this, to kill the righteous with the wicked, and the righteous shall be as the wicked; it is inconceivable for You; shall the Judge of all the earth not practice justice?" (18:25). If God is the

exclusive source of morality, the rhetorical question "Shall the Judge of all the earth not practice justice?" is logically impossible. By definition, that which God practices is just.

According to the Rambam,[13] Abraham did not address that question to God. In his opinion, any episode in the biblical narrative that involves angels is a dream or a prophetic vision. *Parashat Vayera* begins with God appearing to Abraham. It continues with the description of the visit of three men, the angels. Two of the angels subsequently continue to Sodom and destroy the city and rescue Lot. The Sodom story concludes with the verse: "His wife looked behind him, and she became a pillar of salt" (19:26). The following verse begins: "Abraham arose early in the morning," connoting, according to the Rambam, the end of the prophetic dream.

Perhaps the Rambam can refute the proof that there is morality independent of God based on the Gemara in *Berakhot* (55a): Rabbi Yoḥanan said in the name of Rabbi Shimon bar Yoḥai:

Just as it is impossible for grain to grow without straw, so too it is impossible to dream without idle matters.

In his prophetic dream, Abraham received the tidings that he would father a son from Sarah rewarding his kindness, exemplified by his hospitality toward the three nomads. Similarly, he was shown that Sodom would be destroyed, but his nephew Lot would be rescued due to the merit of his uncle Abraham. That is the grain.

According to this understanding of the Rambam, the rhetorical question, "Shall the Judge of all the earth not practice justice?" and the protracted negotiation between Abraham and God recorded in the Torah originated with Abraham, not with God. That is the straw, the idle matters of the prophetic dream, as the Gemara in *Berakhot* (55b) explains: Rabbi Shmuel bar Naḥmani said that Rabbi Yonatan said: A person is shown in his dream only the thoughts of his heart when he was awake.

כב הַכְּצַעֲקָתָהּ הַבָּאָה אֵלַי עָשׂוּ | כָּלָה וְאִם־לֹא אֵדָעָה: וַיִּפְנוּ מִשָּׁם הָאֲנָשִׁים וַיֵּלְכוּ
כג סְדֹמָה וְאַבְרָהָם עוֹדֶנּוּ עֹמֵד לִפְנֵי יהוה: וַיִּגַּשׁ אַבְרָהָם וַיֹּאמַר הַאַף תִּסְפֶּה צַדִּיק
כד עִם־רָשָׁע: אוּלַי יֵשׁ חֲמִשִּׁים צַדִּיקִם בְּתוֹךְ הָעִיר הַאַף תִּסְפֶּה וְלֹא־תִשָּׂא לַמָּקוֹם
כה לְמַעַן חֲמִשִּׁים הַצַּדִּיקִם אֲשֶׁר בְּקִרְבָּהּ: חָלִלָה לְּךָ מֵעֲשֹׂת | כַּדָּבָר הַזֶּה לְהָמִית
צַדִּיק עִם־רָשָׁע וְהָיָה כַצַּדִּיק כָּרָשָׁע חָלִלָה לָּךְ הֲשֹׁפֵט כָּל־הָאָרֶץ לֹא יַעֲשֶׂה
כו מִשְׁפָּט: וַיֹּאמֶר יהוה אִם־אֶמְצָא בִסְדֹם חֲמִשִּׁים צַדִּיקִם בְּתוֹךְ הָעִיר וְנָשָׂאתִי
כז לְכָל־הַמָּקוֹם בַּעֲבוּרָם: וַיַּעַן אַבְרָהָם וַיֹּאמַר הִנֵּה־נָא הוֹאַלְתִּי לְדַבֵּר אֶל־אֲדֹנָי
כח וְאָנֹכִי עָפָר וָאֵפֶר: אוּלַי יַחְסְרוּן חֲמִשִּׁים הַצַּדִּיקִם חֲמִשָּׁה הֲתַשְׁחִית בַּחֲמִשָּׁה
כט אֶת־כָּל־הָעִיר וַיֹּאמֶר לֹא אַשְׁחִית אִם־אֶמְצָא שָׁם אַרְבָּעִים וַחֲמִשָּׁה: וַיֹּסֶף עוֹד
לְדַבֵּר אֵלָיו וַיֹּאמַר אוּלַי יִמָּצְאוּן שָׁם אַרְבָּעִים וַיֹּאמֶר לֹא אֶעֱשֶׂה בַּעֲבוּר
ל הָאַרְבָּעִים: וַיֹּאמֶר אַל־נָא יִחַר לַאדֹנָי וַאֲדַבֵּרָה אוּלַי יִמָּצְאוּן שָׁם שְׁלֹשִׁים וַיֹּאמֶר
לא לֹא אֶעֱשֶׂה אִם־אֶמְצָא שָׁם שְׁלֹשִׁים: וַיֹּאמֶר הִנֵּה־נָא הוֹאַלְתִּי לְדַבֵּר אֶל־אֲדֹנָי
לב אוּלַי יִמָּצְאוּן שָׁם עֶשְׂרִים וַיֹּאמֶר לֹא אַשְׁחִית בַּעֲבוּר הָעֶשְׂרִים: וַיֹּאמֶר אַל־נָא
יִחַר לַאדֹנָי וַאֲדַבְּרָה אַךְ־הַפַּעַם אוּלַי יִמָּצְאוּן שָׁם עֲשָׂרָה וַיֹּאמֶר לֹא אַשְׁחִית
לג בַּעֲבוּר הָעֲשָׂרָה: וַיֵּלֶךְ יהוה כַּאֲשֶׁר כִּלָּה לְדַבֵּר אֶל־אַבְרָהָם וְאַבְרָהָם שָׁב

רש"י

יח, ה). דָּבָר אַחֵר, "חָלִלָה נָא" לְסוֹף מַעֲשֵׂיהֶם: **הַכְּצַעֲקָתָהּ.** שֶׁל מְדִינָה: **הַבָּאָה אֵלַי עָשׂוּ.** וְכֵן עוֹמְדִים בְּמִרְדָּם – "כָּלָה" אֲנִי עוֹשֶׂה בָּהֶם, "וְאִם לֹא" יַעַמְדוּ בְּמִרְדָּם – "אֵדָעָה" מָה אֶעֱשֶׂה, לְהִפָּרַע מֵהֶם בְּיִסּוּרִין, וְלֹא אֲכַלֶּה אוֹתָם. וְכַיּוֹצֵא בוֹ מָצִינוּ בְּמָקוֹם אַחֵר: "וְעַתָּה הוֹרֵד עֶדְיְךָ מֵעָלֶיךָ וְאֵדְעָה מָה אֶעֱשֶׂה לָּךְ" (שמות לג, ה). וּלְפִיכָךְ יֵשׁ הֶפְסֵק נְקֻדַּת פָּסֵק בֵּין 'עָשׂוּ' לְ'כָלָה', כְּדֵי לְהַפְרִידָם זֶה מֵחֶבְרָתָהּ. וְרַבּוֹתֵינוּ דָּרְשׁוּ: "הַכְּצַעֲקָתָהּ", צַעֲקַת רִיבָה אַחַת שֶׁהָרְגוּהָ מִיתָה מְשֻׁנָּה עַל שֶׁנָּתְנָה מָזוֹן לְעָנִי, כִּמְבֹאָר בְּ'חֵלֶק' (סנהדרין קט ע"ב):

כב| **וַיִּפְנוּ מִשָּׁם.** מִמָּקוֹם שֶׁאַבְרָהָם לִוָּם שָׁם: **עוֹדֶנּוּ עֹמֵד וְגוֹ'.** וַהֲלֹא לֹא הָלַךְ לַעֲמֹד לְפָנָיו, אֶלָּא הַקָּדוֹשׁ בָּרוּךְ הוּא בָּא אֶצְלוֹ וְאָמַר לוֹ: "זַעֲקַת סְדֹם וַעֲמֹרָה" וְגוֹ' (לעיל פסוק כ), וְהָיָה לוֹ לִכְתֹּב: 'וַה' עוֹדֶנּוּ עוֹמֵד עַל אַבְרָהָם'? אֶלָּא תִּקּוּן סוֹפְרִים הוּא זֶה:

כג| **וַיִּגַּשׁ אַבְרָהָם.** מָצִינוּ הַגָּשָׁה לְמִלְחָמָה: "וַיִּגַּשׁ יוֹאָב" וְגוֹ' (דברי הימים א' יט, יד); הַגָּשָׁה לְפִיּוּס: "וַיִּגַּשׁ אֵלָיו יְהוּדָה" (להלן מד, יח); וְהַגָּשָׁה לִתְפִלָּה: "וַיִּגַּשׁ אֵלִיָּהוּ הַנָּבִיא" (מלכים א' יח, לו); וּלְכָל אֵלֶּה נִכְנַס אַבְרָהָם: לְדַבֵּר קָשׁוֹת וּלְפִיּוּס וְלִתְפִלָּה: **הַאַף תִּסְפֶּה.** הֲגַם תִּסְפֶּה. וּלְתַרְגּוּם שֶׁל אוּנְקְלוֹס שֶׁתִּרְגְּמוֹ לְשׁוֹן רֹגֶז, כָּךְ פֵּרוּשׁוֹ: הַאַף יַשִּׂיאֲךָ שֶׁתִּסְפֶּה צַדִּיק עִם רָשָׁע?

כד| **חֲמִשִּׁים צַדִּיקִם.** עֲשָׂרָה צַדִּיקִים לְכָל כְּרַךְ וּכְרַךְ, חֲמִשָּׁה מְקוֹמוֹת יֵשׁ.

כה| **חָלִלָה לְּךָ.** וְאִם תֹּאמַר, לֹא יַצִּילוּ הַצַּדִּיקִים אֶת הָרְשָׁעִים, לָמָּה תָּמִית הַצַּדִּיקִים? חֻלִּין הוּא לָךְ! יֹאמְרוּ: כָּךְ הִיא אֻמָּנוּתוֹ, שׁוֹטֵף הַכֹּל, צַדִּיקִים וּרְשָׁעִים; כָּךְ עָשִׂיתָ לְדוֹר הַמַּבּוּל וּלְדוֹר הַפַּלָּגָה: **כַּדָּבָר הַזֶּה.** לֹא הוּא וְלֹא כַּיּוֹצֵא בוֹ: **חָלִלָה לָּךְ.** לָעוֹלָם הַבָּא: **הֲשֹׁפֵט כָּל הָאָרֶץ.** נָקוּד בַּחֲטַף פַּתָּח הֵ"א שֶׁל 'הֲשֹׁפֵט', לְשׁוֹן תְּמִיהָה, וְכִי מִי שֶׁהוּא שׁוֹפֵט לֹא יַעֲשֶׂה מִשְׁפַּט אֱמֶת?!

כו| **אִם אֶמְצָא בִסְדֹם וְגוֹ'.** לְפִי שֶׁסְּדוֹם הָיְתָה מֶטְרוֹפּוֹלִין וַחֲשׁוּבָה מִכֻּלָּם, תָּלָה בָהּ הַכָּתוּב:

כח| **הֲתַשְׁחִית בַּחֲמִשָּׁה.** וַהֲלֹא הֵן תִּשְׁעָה לְכָל כְּרַךְ, וְאַתָּה צַדִּיקוֹ שֶׁל עוֹלָם תִּצְטָרֵף עִמָּהֶם:

כט| **אוּלַי יִמָּצְאוּן שָׁם אַרְבָּעִים.** וְיִמָּלְטוּ אַרְבָּעָה הַכְּרַכִּים. וְכֵן שְׁלֹשִׁים יַצִּילוּ שְׁלֹשָׁה מֵהֶם, אוֹ עֶשְׂרִים יַצִּילוּ שְׁנַיִם מֵהֶם, אוֹ עֲשָׂרָה יַצִּילוּ אֶחָד מֵהֶם:

לא| **הוֹאַלְתִּי.** רָצִיתִי, כְּמוֹ: "וַיּוֹאֶל מֹשֶׁה" (שמות ב, כא):

לב| **אוּלַי יִמָּצְאוּן שָׁם עֲשָׂרָה.** עַל הַפָּחוֹת לֹא בִקֵּשׁ, אָמַר: דּוֹר הַמַּבּוּל הָיוּ שְׁמוֹנָה, נֹחַ וּבָנָיו וּנְשֵׁיהֶם, וְלֹא הִצִּילוּ עַל דּוֹרָם. וְעַל תִּשְׁעָה עַל יְדֵי צֵרוּף כְּבָר בִּקֵּשׁ וְלֹא מָצָא:

לג| **וַיֵּלֶךְ ה' וְגוֹ'.** כֵּיוָן שֶׁנִּשְׁתַּתֵּק הַסָּנֵגוֹר הָלַךְ לוֹ הַדַּיָּן: **וְאַבְרָהָם שָׁב לִמְקוֹמוֹ.** נִסְתַּלֵּק הַדַּיָּן נִסְתַּלֵּק הַסָּנֵגוֹר,

Destruction of Sodom and the Rescue of Lot and His Family

GENESIS 19:1–38

Two of the angels who visited Abraham come to Lot in Sodom. Since the two stories of their visits are presented consecutively, the characters of Abraham and his nephew, Lot, may be compared and contrasted in stark detail. Once the complex natures of Lot and his family have been revealed, it can be concluded that their relationship to Abraham was the primary reason they merited rescue from Sodom.

19 **1** *Third aliya* **The two angels came to Sodom in the evening.** The Sages teach that the third angel did not travel to Sodom, because his mission had been fulfilled in informing Abraham and Sarah of their forthcoming son. The two other angels had tasks to perform in Sodom. **And Lot was sitting at the gate of Sodom.** Sitting at the gate of a city was typically a sign of high status, as that was where the judges and town elders convened. **Lot saw them and rose to meet them, and he prostrated himself with his face to the earth.** Lot had either learned the attribute of hospitality from Abraham, or they had both learned it as a family tradition.

2 **He said: Behold now my lords; please turn aside to your servant's house, stay the night, and wash your feet, and you shall awaken early and go on your way.** Lot's proposal was less generous than that of Abraham, who had included food and drink as well. Nevertheless, Lot did offer them a place to rest. **They said: No, for we will stay the night in the street.**

3 **He implored them greatly, and** eventually **they turned aside to him and entered his house; he prepared a feast for them, he baked unleavened bread, and they ate.** He gave them food and drink as well, despite the fact that he did not initially refer to provisions.

4 **Before they,** the angels, **lay down** to sleep, **the men of the city, the men of Sodom, surrounded the house, from young to old, all the people from every quarter.** The mention of the men of Sodom evokes the earlier verse: "The men of Sodom were extremely wicked and sinful to the Lord" (13:13).

5 **They called to Lot, and said to him: Where are the men who came to you tonight? Bring them out to us, and we will be intimate with them.** The residents of the city demanded that Lot bring out his guests so that they could exploit them sexually. It was not clear at this point whether their demand was based on sexual desire or to demonstrate their absolute intolerance of

guests.[14] The only person in Sodom who accepted guests was Lot, who was not a native of the city.

6 **Lot went out to them,** the residents of the city, **to the entrance** of his home, **and he closed the door behind him,** to prevent them from entering the house.

7 **He said: Please, my brethren, do not do evil.** He requested that they forgo their wicked demand.

8 **Here now are my two** virgin **daughters**[D] **who have not been intimate with a man; I will now bring them out to you, and you may do to them as is fit in your eyes. Only to these men do nothing, as for this they came under the shelter of my roof.**

9 **They said: Move aside. And they said: This one came to reside, and he sits in judgment?** You are not a native of the city, but merely a sojourner who came to live here temporarily. How do you presume to pass judgment on our behavior? **Now we will treat you worse than them.** If you insist on protecting them, we will inflict an even worse punishment on you. It can be inferred from this statement that those surrounding the house were not motivated by sexual desire, but by a wish to inflict pain and humiliation on the guests. **They implored the man, Lot, and** when that attempt proved unsuccessful, they **approached to break the door,** which had been locked from the inside.

10 **The men,** the angels, who had the appearance of men, **extended their hand and brought Lot to them, to the house, and closed the door.** With their ability to perform miracles, the angels were able to spirit Lot into the house without letting the mob force its way inside.

11 **They smote the men who were at the entrance of the house with blindness** or blurred vision, **from small to great, so that they,** the residents, **were unable to find the entrance.** Consequently, the crowd ceased to pose a threat to Lot and his guests.

DISCUSSION

19:8 | Here now are my two daughters: Lot believed that he was obligated to do everything in his power to protect the welfare of the guests sheltered in his house. He was even prepared to give up his daughters for their sake. Similar stories are known, primarily from Arab culture, of the readiness of a host to sacrifice everything for his guests. Although Lot's offer here illustrates his dedication as a host, it also indicates moral perversion as well as imbalanced priorities and values.

ט א למקמו: ויבאו שני המלאכים סדמה בערב ולוט ישב בשער־סדם וירא־לוט טז שלישי
ב ויקם לקראתם וישתחו אפים ארצה: ויאמר הנה נא־אדני סורו נא אל־בית
עבדכם ולינו ורחצו רגליכם והשכמתם והלכתם לדרככם ויאמרו לא כי ברחוב
ג נלין: ויפצר־בם מאד ויסרו אליו ויבאו אל־ביתו ויעש להם משתה ומצות
ד אפה ויאכלו: טרם ישכבו ואנשי העיר אנשי סדם נסבו על־הבית מנער ועד־
ה זקן כל־העם מקצה: ויקראו אל־לוט ויאמרו לו איה האנשים אשר־באו אליך
ו הלילה הוציאם אלינו ונדעה אתם: ויצא אלהם לוט הפתחה והדלת סגר
ז ח אחריו: ויאמר אל־נא אחי תרעו: הנה־נא לי שתי בנות אשר לא־ידעו איש
אוציאה־נא אתהן אליכם ועשו להן כטוב בעיניכם רק לאנשים האל אל־
ט תעשו דבר כי־על־כן באו בצל קרתי: ויאמרו גש־הלאה ויאמרו האחד
בא־לגור וישפט שפוט עתה נרע לך מהם ויפצרו באיש בלוט מאד ויגשו
י לשבר הדלת: וישלחו האנשים את־ידם ויביאו את־לוט אליהם הביתה ואת־
יא הדלת סגרו: ואת־האנשים אשר־פתח הבית הכו בסנורים מקטן ועד־גדול

רש"י

והקטגור מקטרג, לפיכך "ויבאו שני המלאכים סדמה" (להלן יט, א), להשחית.

פרק יט

א| ויבאו שני. והשלישי שבא לבשר את שרה, כיון שעשה שליחותו נסתלק לו: המלאכים. ולהלן (לעיל יח, ב) קראם 'אנשים'; כשהיתה שכינה עמהם קראם 'אנשים'. דבר אחר, אצל אברהם שכחו גדול והיו המלאכים תדירין אצלו כאנשים, קראם 'אנשים', ואצל לוט קראם 'מלאכים': בערב. וכי כל כך שהו המלאכים מחברון לסדום? אלא מלאכי רחמים היו וממתינים שמא יוכל אברהם ללמד עליהם סנגוריא: ולוט ישב בשער סדם. 'ישב' כתיב, אותו היום מנוהו שופט על השופטים: וירא לוט וגו'. מבית אברהם למד לחזר על האורחים:

ב| הנה נא אדני. הנה נא אתם אדונים לי אחר שעברתם עלי. דבר אחר, "הנה נא", צריכים אתם לתת לב על הרשעים הללו שלא יכירו בכם; וזו היא עצה נכונה: "סורו נא" וגו' – עקמו את הדרך לביתי דרך עקלתון, שלא יכירו שאתם נכנסים שם, לכך נאמר "סורו". בראשית רבה (נ, ד): ויאמרו לא. לאברהם אמרו: "כן תעשה" (לעיל יח, ה), מכאן שמסרבין לקטן ואין מסרבין לגדול: כי ברחוב נלין. הרי 'כי' משמש בלשון 'אלא', שאמרו: לא נסור אל ביתך אלא ברחובה של עיר נלין:

ג| ויסרו אליו. עקמו את הדרך לצד ביתו: ומצות אפה. פסח היה:

ד| טרם ישכבו ואנשי העיר אנשי סדם. כך נדרש בבראשית רבה (נ, ה): "טרם ישכבו ואנשי העיר" היו בפיהם של מלאכים, שהיו שואלים ללוט: מה טיבם ומעשיהם? והוא אומר להם: רבם רשעים. עודם מדברים בהם, ו"אנשי סדם נסבו" וגו'. ופשוטו של מקרא: ואנשי העיר, אנשי רשע, נסבו על הבית; על שהיו רשעים נקראים "אנשי סדם", כמו שאמר הכתוב: "ואנשי סדם רעים וחטאים" (לעיל יג, יג): כל העם מקצה. מקצה העיר עד הקצה, שאין אחד מוחה בידם, שאפלו צדיק אחד אין בהם:

ה| ונדעה אתם. במשכב זכור, כמו: "אשר לא ידעו איש" (להלן פסוק ח):

ח| האל. כמו 'האלה': כי על כן באו. כי הטובה הזאת תעשו לכבודי על אשר "באו בצל קרתי", "בטלל שריתי", תרגום של 'קורה' – שריתא:

ט| גש הלאה. כשאמר להם על הבנות, אמרו לו: "גש הלאה", לשון נחת. ועל שאתה מלין על האורחין, אמרו לו: איך מלאך לבך? "האחד בא לגור" – אדם נכרי יחידי אתה בינינו שבאת לגור, "וישפט שפוט" – נעשית מוכיח אותנו [ור' יוסף בר' שמעון (קרא) אומר הלא "גש הלאה" אינו אלא לשון דחיה ודחיפה, כמו "קרב אליך אל תגש בי" (ישעיה סה, ה) וכמו "ואת האש זרה הלאה" (במדבר יז, ב) וכמו "והגליתי אתכם מהלאה לדמשק" (עמוס ה, כז) שאף כאן לוט היה מתחבט לפניהם על האכסנאים, והם אומרים לו: קרב אליך אל תפגע בנו; שאם אתה אומר קרב אלינו ושמע דברינו הוא, מה צורך לדבר זה? והלא לוט קרוב אליהם עומד, כמו שמצינו "ויצא אלהם לוט הפתחה" (לעיל פסוק ו)! אלא על כרחך לשון הרחקה הוא, כלומר, לך מעמנו. והודה המורה לדבריו]: הדלת. הסובבת לנעל ולפתח:

יא| פתח. הוא החלל שבו נכנסין ויוצאין: בסנורים. מכת עורון: מקטן ועד גדול. הקטנים התחילו בעבירה תחלה,

12 The angels had yet to perform the tasks for which they were sent: the destruction of Sodom and the rescue of Lot. Although Lot was not altogether righteous, he was saved due to Abraham, his uncle. **The men said to Lot: Who else have you here?** Do you have any family in the city? **A son-in-law, and your sons, and your daughters, and everyone whom you have in the city, remove from the place.**

13 **For we are destroying this place, as their outcry,** that of the oppressed and ill-treated in the city, **has amassed before the Lord, and the Lord sent us to destroy it.**

14 **Lot came out, and spoke to his sons-in-law, who had betrothed his daughters.** Lot told his sons-in-law, who were certainly natives of the city, what was about to happen. **And** he **said: Arise, depart from this place, for the Lord is destroying the city. But he seemed as one who jests in the eyes of his sons-in-law.** They did not believe him and ignored his warning.

15 **About when the dawn broke, the angels urged Lot, saying: Arise; take your wife and your two daughters who are present, lest you** too **be destroyed in the iniquity of the city.** There is nothing we can do to save the rest of your family, whom you were unable to convince to flee. The time has arrived to leave the city.

16 Perhaps Lot himself did not completely believe the angels' warning. Their power to strike the residents of the city with blindness would certainly have impressed him, but he may still not not have entirely placed his confidence in them, and he may also have harbored concern about his uncertain future outside the city. Therefore, **he hesitated. And the men** forcefully **grasped his hand, the hand of his wife, and the hand of his two daughters** who were in the house. All this was performed **out of the compassion of the Lord for him;** although he was unworthy of being saved, it was the angels' task to save him, even against his will. **They took him out and placed him outside the city.** They led him by foot to the entrance to the city or supernaturally transported him to the city's outskirts.

17 **It was when they took them out** that **he,** one of the angels, **said: Flee for your life; do not look**[D] **behind you and do not stay in the entire plain** of the Jordan, which encircled Sodom. **Flee to the highlands** surrounding the plain, **lest you be destroyed.**

18 **Lot said to them: Please, no, my lords.**

19 **Please, behold, your servant has found favor in your eyes, and you have increased your kindness that you have done with me to save my life. But I will not be able to flee to the highlands;** it is too far, the climb is exhausting and dangerous, and I am too old for such a challenging expedition. But I cannot remain on the plain either, **lest the evil overtake me and I die.**

20 **Here now, this city is near to flee there, and it is small; please, I will flee there.** Although it is a city with its own king (see 14:2), **is it not small** enough to escape destruction, **and** perhaps there **my life will be saved?**

21 *Fourth aliya* **He,** the angel, **said to him: Behold,** not only have I taken you out of the city, but **I have granted your request for this matter as well, not to overturn the city of which you spoke.** I will destroy only the large cities on the plain, Sodom, Gomorrah, Adma, and Tzevoyim, but I will leave standing the city to which you referred.

DISCUSSION

19:17| **Do not look:** The destruction of Sodom was no mere natural disaster, but a punishment inflicted directly by God. Despite its cataclysmic character, it was an act of divine revelation, and as with other revelations in the Bible, human beings were not able to gaze upon it directly (see, e.g., Exodus 3:6, 33:20; I Kings 19:13; Isaiah 6:5).

יב וַיִּלְאוּ לִמְצֹא הַפָּתַח: וַיֹּאמְרוּ הָאֲנָשִׁים אֶל־לוֹט עֹד מִי־לְךָ פֹה חָתָן וּבָנֶיךָ וּבְנֹתֶיךָ
יג וְכֹל אֲשֶׁר־לְךָ בָּעִיר הוֹצֵא מִן־הַמָּקוֹם: כִּי־מַשְׁחִתִים אֲנַחְנוּ אֶת־הַמָּקוֹם הַזֶּה
יד כִּי־גָדְלָה צַעֲקָתָם אֶת־פְּנֵי יְהוָה וַיְשַׁלְּחֵנוּ יְהוָה לְשַׁחֲתָהּ: וַיֵּצֵא לוֹט וַיְדַבֵּר ׀
אֶל־חֲתָנָיו ׀ לֹקְחֵי בְנֹתָיו וַיֹּאמֶר קוּמוּ צְּאוּ מִן־הַמָּקוֹם הַזֶּה כִּי־מַשְׁחִית יְהוָה
טו אֶת־הָעִיר וַיְהִי כִמְצַחֵק בְּעֵינֵי חֲתָנָיו: וּכְמוֹ הַשַּׁחַר עָלָה וַיָּאִיצוּ הַמַּלְאָכִים בְּלוֹט
לֵאמֹר קוּם קַח אֶת־אִשְׁתְּךָ וְאֶת־שְׁתֵּי בְנֹתֶיךָ הַנִּמְצָאֹת פֶּן־תִּסָּפֶה בַּעֲוֺן הָעִיר:
טז וַיִּתְמַהְמָהּ ׀ וַיַּחֲזִיקוּ הָאֲנָשִׁים בְּיָדוֹ וּבְיַד־אִשְׁתּוֹ וּבְיַד שְׁתֵּי בְנֹתָיו בְּחֶמְלַת יְהוָה
יז עָלָיו וַיֹּצִאֻהוּ וַיַּנִּחֻהוּ מִחוּץ לָעִיר: וַיְהִי כְהוֹצִיאָם אֹתָם הַחוּצָה וַיֹּאמֶר הִמָּלֵט
עַל־נַפְשֶׁךָ אַל־תַּבִּיט אַחֲרֶיךָ וְאַל־תַּעֲמֹד בְּכָל־הַכִּכָּר הָהָרָה הִמָּלֵט פֶּן־תִּסָּפֶה:
יח יט וַיֹּאמֶר לוֹט אֲלֵהֶם אַל־נָא אֲדֹנָי: הִנֵּה־נָא מָצָא עַבְדְּךָ חֵן בְּעֵינֶיךָ וַתַּגְדֵּל חַסְדְּךָ
אֲשֶׁר עָשִׂיתָ עִמָּדִי לְהַחֲיוֹת אֶת־נַפְשִׁי וְאָנֹכִי לֹא אוּכַל לְהִמָּלֵט הָהָרָה פֶּן־
כ תִּדְבָּקַנִי הָרָעָה וָמַתִּי: הִנֵּה־נָא הָעִיר הַזֹּאת קְרֹבָה לָנוּס שָׁמָּה וְהִוא מִצְעָר
כא אִמָּלְטָה נָּא שָׁמָּה הֲלֹא מִצְעָר הִוא וּתְחִי נַפְשִׁי: וַיֹּאמֶר אֵלָיו הִנֵּה נָשָׂאתִי פָנֶיךָ רביעי

רש"י

שנאמר: "מנער ועד זקן" (לעיל פסוק ד), לפיכך התחילה הפרענות מהם:

יב| **עד מי לך פה.** פשוטו של מקרא, מי יש לך עוד בעיר הזאת חוץ מאשתך ובנותיך שבבית: **חתן ובניך ובנתיך.** אם יש לך חתן או בנים ובנות, "הוצא מן המקום": **ובניך.** בני בנותיך הנשואות. ומדרש אגדה, "עד" – מאחר שעושין נבלה כזאת, "מי לך" פתחון פה ללמד סניגוריא עליהם, שכל הלילה היה מלין עליהם טובות. קרי ביה: 'מי לך פה':

יד| **חתניו.** שתי בנות נשואות היו לו בעיר: **לקחי בנתיו.** שאותן שבבית ארוסות להם:

טו| **ויאיצו.** כתרגומו 'ודחיקו', מהרוהו: **הנמצאת.** המזמנות לך בבית להצילם. ומדרש אגדה יש, וזה ישובו של מקרא: **תספה.** תהיה כלה; "עד תם כל הדור" (דברים ב, יד) מתרגם: "עד דסף":

טז| **ויתמהמה.** כדי להציל את ממונו: **ויחזיקו.** אחד מהם היה שליח להצילו, וחברו להפך את סדום, לכך נאמר: "ויאמר המלט" (להלן פסוק יז) ולא נאמר 'ויאמרו':

יז| **המלט על נפשך.** דייך להציל נפשות, אל תחוס על הממון: **אל תביט אחריך.** אתה הרשעת עמהם ובזכות אברהם אתה נצול, אינך כדאי לראות בפרענותם ואתה נצול: **בכל הככר.** ככר הירדן: **ההרה המלט.** אצל אברהם ברח שהיה יושב בהר, שנאמר: "ויעתק משם ההרה" (לעיל יב, ח), ואף עכשיו היה יושב שם, שנאמר: "עד המקום אשר היה שם אהלה בתחלה" (לעיל יג, ג); ואף על פי שכתוב: "ויאהל אברם" וגו' (שם יח), אהלים הרבה היו לו ונמשכו עד חברון: **המלט.** לשון השמטה, וכן כל המלטה שבמקרא אשמוטי"ר בלעז, וכן: "והמליטה זכר" (ישעיה סו, ז), שנשמט העובר מן הרחם, "כצפור נמלטה" (תהלים קכד, ז), "לא יכלו מלט משא" (ישעיה מו, ב), להשמיט משא הרעי שבנקביהם:

יח| **אל נא אדני.** רבותינו אמרו שזה קדש, שנאמר בו: "להחיות את נפשי" (להלן פסוק יט) – מי שיש בידו להמית ולהחיות, ותרגומו "בבעו כען ה'": **אל נא.** אל תאמרו אלי להמלט ההרה: **נא.** לשון בקשה:

יט| **פן תדבקני הרעה.** כשהייתי אצל אנשי סדום היה הקדוש ברוך הוא רואה מעשי ומעשה בני עירי והייתי נראה צדיק וכדאי להנצל, וכשאבוא אצל צדיק אני כרשע. וכן אמרה הצרפית לאליהו: "באת אלי להזכיר את עוני" (מלכים א' יז, יח) – עד שלא באת אצלי היה הקדוש ברוך הוא רואה מעשי ומעשה עמי ואני צדקת ביניהם, ומשבאת אצלי, לפי מעשיך אני רשעה:

כ| **העיר הזאת קרבה.** ישיבתה קרובה, ולא נתמלאת סאתה עדין. ומה היא קריבתה? מדור הפלגה, שנתפלגו האנשים והתחילו להתישב איש איש במקומו, והיא היתה בשנת מות פלג, ומשם עד כאן חמשים ושתים שנה, שפלג מת בשנת ארבעים ושמנה לאברהם. כיצד? פלג חי אחרי הולידו את רעו מאתים ותשע שנה, מהם כלו שלשים ושתים כשנולד שרוג ומשרוג עד שנולד נחור שלשים, הרי ששים ושתים, ומנחור עד שנולד תרח עשרים ותשע, הרי תשעים ואחת, ומשם עד שנולד אברהם שבעים, הרי מאה ששים ואחת, תן להם ארבעים ושמנה, הרי מאתים ותשע, ואותה שנה היתה שנת הפלגה. וכשנחרבה סדום היה אברהם בן תשעים ותשע שנה, הרי מדור הפלגה עד כאן חמשים ושתים שנה. ונוער אחרה ישיבתה אחרי ישיבת סדום וחברותיה שנה אחת, הוא שנאמר: "אמלטה נא", 'נא' בגימטריא חמשים ואחת: **הלא מצער הוא.** עוונותיה מועטין ויכול אתה להניחה "ותחי נפשי" בה, זהו מדרשו. ופשוטו של מקרא, הלא עיר קטנה היא ואנשים בה מעט, אין לך להקפיד אם תניחנה "ותחי נפשי" בה:

22 **Hurry** and **flee there, as I will not be able to do anything until your arrival there.** Since an angel is only a messenger of God, he has no choice but to obey the instructions given to him. These angels had been directed to destroy the sinful cities and to save Lot. They could not strike the cities if that would put Lot in danger. The Torah notes: **Therefore,** because the city was small [*mitz'ar*], **he called the name of the city Tzoar.** This became an additional name of the city.

23 Lot and his family left at daybreak. A short while later, **the sun rose upon the earth, and Lot came to Tzoar.**

24 **The Lord rained brimstone and fire upon Sodom and upon Gomorrah,** as well as on Adma and Tzevoyim, **from the Lord from the heavens.**

25 Furthermore, **He overturned those cities, the entire plain, all the inhabitants of the cities, and the vegetation of the earth.** Apart from the fire and brimstone, there was a massive earthquake that overturned the entire area, until nothing remained as it had been.

26 **His,** Lot's, **wife looked behind him,** despite the angel's warning. She had been rescued due to her relationship with Lot, but she may have been a native of Sodom, and apparently still felt connected to the city. Whether out of curiosity or emotional distress, she turned to look at her city, **and she became a pillar of salt.** This could be meant literally or metaphorically that she froze in place and died.

27 **Abraham arose early in the morning to the place where he stood before the Lord.**

28 **He looked over Sodom and Gomorrah, and over all the land of the plain** of the Jordan, the region that is currently the Dead Sea. **And he saw** that **behold, the smoke of the earth rose** thickly and in abundance, **like the smoke of a kiln.** In addition to the destruction wreaked by the earthquake, the entire plain was burnt, leaving no trace of anything that had stood there.

29 The Torah summarizes the previous events: **It was when God destroyed the cities of the plain,** and **God remembered Abraham. And** due to Abraham's merit, **He sent Lot from the midst of the upheaval, as He overturned the cities in which Lot lived.**

30 **Lot ascended from Tzoar and lived in the hills, and his two daughters with him, because he feared to live in Tzoar.** Lot had stayed in Tzoar on the first night, but he was afraid to remain there, as it was one of the cities of the plain that had originally been intended for punishment. As Lot suspected that its destruction had been merely delayed due to his presence and request, he felt anxious. Therefore, he eventually ascended into the mountains, as the angel had originally instructed him. **And he lived in a cave, he and his two daughters.**

31 Lot and his two daughters stayed alone in the cave, surrounded by total desolation. The destruction of Sodom and Gomorrah presumably prevented any traveler from approaching the area. Lot's daughters did not know that the destruction was limited to Sodom and its environs. They assumed that a global catastrophe like the flood had occurred and that they were the only survivors. As stated earlier (verse 8), both were young and unmarried. Therefore, **the elder said to the younger: Our father is old;** we cannot expect that he will have use of his faculties for long. **And there is no man on the earth** aside from him **to consort with us in the way of the world.** The continuation of the human race depends on us. Although we are his daughters, we must act like the family of Adam, the first man, and procreate from family members, in order to prevent the extinction of humanity.

32 **Let us give our father wine to drink** so that he will be drunk, **and we will lie with him, and we will give life to offspring from our father.** Lot's daughters chose to intoxicate their father rather than plan with him, whether out of concern that he would react negatively or because they were embarrassed to discuss the idea with him.

33 **They gave their father wine to drink that night.** The wine was likely brought from Tzoar, along with the other provisions they had taken for their survival. **The elder came and lay with her father, and** in his drunken state, **he did not know when she lay or when she arose.**

כב גַּם לַדָּבָר הַזֶּה לְבִלְתִּי הָפְכִּי אֶת־הָעִיר אֲשֶׁר דִּבַּרְתָּ׃ מַהֵר הִמָּלֵט שָׁמָּה כִּי לֹא
כג אוּכַל לַעֲשׂוֹת דָּבָר עַד־בֹּאֲךָ שָׁמָּה עַל־כֵּן קָרָא שֵׁם־הָעִיר צוֹעַר׃ הַשֶּׁמֶשׁ יָצָא
כד עַל־הָאָרֶץ וְלוֹט בָּא צֹעֲרָה׃ וַיהוה הִמְטִיר עַל־סְדֹם וְעַל־עֲמֹרָה גָּפְרִית וָאֵשׁ
כה מֵאֵת יהוה מִן־הַשָּׁמָיִם׃ וַיַּהֲפֹךְ אֶת־הֶעָרִים הָאֵל וְאֵת כָּל־הַכִּכָּר וְאֵת כָּל־יֹשְׁבֵי
כו כז הֶעָרִים וְצֶמַח הָאֲדָמָה׃ וַתַּבֵּט אִשְׁתּוֹ מֵאַחֲרָיו וַתְּהִי נְצִיב מֶלַח׃ וַיַּשְׁכֵּם אַבְרָהָם
כח בַּבֹּקֶר אֶל־הַמָּקוֹם אֲשֶׁר־עָמַד שָׁם אֶת־פְּנֵי יהוה׃ וַיַּשְׁקֵף עַל־פְּנֵי סְדֹם וַעֲמֹרָה
כט וְעַל כָּל־פְּנֵי אֶרֶץ הַכִּכָּר וַיַּרְא וְהִנֵּה עָלָה קִיטֹר הָאָרֶץ כְּקִיטֹר הַכִּבְשָׁן׃ וַיְהִי
בְּשַׁחֵת אֱלֹהִים אֶת־עָרֵי הַכִּכָּר וַיִּזְכֹּר אֱלֹהִים אֶת־אַבְרָהָם וַיְשַׁלַּח אֶת־לוֹט
ל מִתּוֹךְ הַהֲפֵכָה בַּהֲפֹךְ אֶת־הֶעָרִים אֲשֶׁר־יָשַׁב בָּהֵן לוֹט׃ וַיַּעַל לוֹט מִצּוֹעַר וַיֵּשֶׁב
בָּהָר וּשְׁתֵּי בְנֹתָיו עִמּוֹ כִּי יָרֵא לָשֶׁבֶת בְּצוֹעַר וַיֵּשֶׁב בַּמְּעָרָה הוּא וּשְׁתֵּי בְנֹתָיו׃
לא וַתֹּאמֶר הַבְּכִירָה אֶל־הַצְּעִירָה אָבִינוּ זָקֵן וְאִישׁ אֵין בָּאָרֶץ לָבוֹא עָלֵינוּ כְּדֶרֶךְ
לב לג כָּל־הָאָרֶץ׃ לְכָה נַשְׁקֶה אֶת־אָבִינוּ יַיִן וְנִשְׁכְּבָה עִמּוֹ וּנְחַיֶּה מֵאָבִינוּ זָרַע׃ וַתַּשְׁקֶיןָ
אֶת־אֲבִיהֶן יַיִן בַּלַּיְלָה הוּא וַתָּבֹא הַבְּכִירָה וַתִּשְׁכַּב אֶת־אָבִיהָ וְלֹא־יָדַע בְּשִׁכְבָהּ

רש"י

כא| **גַּם לַדָּבָר הַזֶּה.** לֹא דַּיֶּךָ שֶׁאַתָּה נִצּוֹל אֶלָּא אַף כָּל הָעִיר אַצִּיל בִּגְלָלְךָ: **הָפְכִּי.** הוֹפֵךְ אֲנִי, כְּמוֹ "עַד בֹּאִי" (להלן מח, ה), "אַחֲרֵי רֹאִי" (לעיל טז, יג), "מִדֵּי דַבְּרִי בּוֹ" (ירמיה לא, יט):

כב| **כִּי לֹא אוּכַל לַעֲשׂוֹת.** זֶה עָנְשָׁן שֶׁל מַלְאָכִים עַל שֶׁאָמְרוּ: "כִּי מַשְׁחִתִים אֲנַחְנוּ" (לעיל פסוק יג) וְתָלוּ הַדָּבָר בְּעַצְמָן, לְפִיכָךְ לֹא זָזוּ מִשָּׁם עַד שֶׁהֻזְקְקוּ לוֹמַר שֶׁאֵין הַדָּבָר בִּרְשׁוּתָן: **כִּי לֹא אוּכַל.** לְשׁוֹן יָחִיד, מִכָּאן אַתָּה לָמֵד שֶׁהָאֶחָד הוֹפֵךְ וְהָאֶחָד מַצִּיל, שֶׁאֵין שְׁנֵי מַלְאָכִים נִשְׁלָחִים לְדָבָר אֶחָד: **עַל כֵּן קָרָא שֵׁם הָעִיר צוֹעַר.** עַל שֵׁם "וְהִיא מִצְעָר" (לעיל פסוק כ):

כד| **וַה' הִמְטִיר.** כָּל מָקוֹם שֶׁנֶּאֱמַר "וַה'" – הוּא וּבֵית דִּינוֹ: **הִמְטִיר עַל סְדֹם.** בַּעֲלוֹת הַשַּׁחַר, כְּמוֹ שֶׁנֶּאֱמַר: "וּכְמוֹ הַשַּׁחַר עָלָה" (לעיל פסוק טו). שָׁעָה שֶׁהַלְּבָנָה עוֹמֶדֶת בָּרָקִיעַ עִם הַחַמָּה, לְפִי שֶׁהָיוּ מֵהֶם עוֹבְדִים לַחַמָּה וּמֵהֶם לַלְּבָנָה, אָמַר הַקָּדוֹשׁ בָּרוּךְ הוּא: אִם אֶפָּרַע מֵהֶם בַּיּוֹם יִהְיוּ עוֹבְדֵי לְבָנָה אוֹמְרִים, אִלּוּ לְבָנָה מוֹשֶׁלֶת לֹא הָיִינוּ חֲרֵבִין; וְאִם אֶפָּרַע מֵהֶם בַּלַּיְלָה יִהְיוּ עוֹבְדֵי הַחַמָּה אוֹמְרִים, אִלּוּ הָיָה בַּיּוֹם כְּשֶׁהַחַמָּה מוֹשֶׁלֶת לֹא הָיִינוּ חֲרֵבִין; לְכָךְ כְּתִיב: "וּכְמוֹ הַשַּׁחַר עָלָה", וְנִפְרַע מֵהֶם בְּשָׁעָה שֶׁהַחַמָּה וְהַלְּבָנָה מוֹשְׁלִים: **הִמְטִיר... גָּפְרִית וָאֵשׁ.** בַּתְּחִלָּה מָטָר וְנַעֲשָׂה גָּפְרִית וָאֵשׁ: **מֵאֵת ה'.** דֶּרֶךְ מִקְרָאוֹת לְדַבֵּר כֵּן, כְּמוֹ: "נְשֵׁי לֶמֶךְ" (לעיל ד, כג) וְלֹא אָמַר 'נָשַׁי'; וְכֵן אָמַר דָּוִד: "קְחוּ עִמָּכֶם אֶת עַבְדֵי אֲדֹנֵיכֶם" (מלכים א' א, לג) וְלֹא אָמַר 'אֶת עֲבָדַי'; וְכֵן בַּאֲחַשְׁוֵרוֹשׁ: "בְּשֵׁם הַמֶּלֶךְ" (אסתר ח, ח) וְלֹא אָמַר 'בִּשְׁמִי'; אַף כָּאן אָמַר: "מֵאֵת ה'" וְלֹא אָמַר 'מֵאִתּוֹ': **מִן הַשָּׁמָיִם.** הוּא שֶׁאָמַר הַכָּתוּב: "כִּי בָם יָדִין עַמִּים" וְגוֹ' (איוב לו, לא). כְּשֶׁבָּא לְיַסֵּר הַבְּרִיּוֹת מֵבִיא עֲלֵיהֶם אֵשׁ מִן הַשָּׁמַיִם כְּמוֹ שֶׁעָשָׂה לִסְדוֹם, וּכְשֶׁבָּא לְהוֹרִיד הַמָּן – מִן הַשָּׁמַיִם, "הִנְנִי מַמְטִיר לָכֶם לֶחֶם מִן הַשָּׁמָיִם" (שמות טז, ד):

כה| **וַיַּהֲפֹךְ אֶת הֶעָרִים וְגוֹ'.** אַרְבַּעְתָּן יוֹשְׁבוֹת בְּסֶלַע אֶחָד וַהֲפָכָן מִלְמַעְלָה לְמַטָּה, שֶׁנֶּאֱמַר: "בַּחַלָּמִישׁ שָׁלַח יָדוֹ" וְגוֹ' (איוב כח, ט):

כו| **וַתַּבֵּט אִשְׁתּוֹ מֵאַחֲרָיו.** מֵאַחֲרָיו שֶׁל לוֹט: **וַתְּהִי נְצִיב מֶלַח.** בְּמֶלַח חָטְאָה וּבְמֶלַח לָקְתָה; אָמַר לָהּ: תְּנִי מְעַט מֶלַח לָאוֹרְחִים הַלָּלוּ, אָמְרָה לוֹ: אַף הַמִּנְהָג הָרַע הַזֶּה אַתָּה בָּא לְהַנְהִיג בַּמָּקוֹם הַזֶּה?!:

כח| **קִיטֹר.** תִּמּוּר שֶׁל עָשָׁן, טורק"א בְּלַעַז: **כִּבְשָׁן.** חֲפִירָה שֶׁשּׂוֹרְפִין בָּהּ אֶת הָאֲבָנִים לְסִיד, וְכֵן כָּל 'כִּבְשָׁן' שֶׁבַּתּוֹרָה:

כט| **וַיִּזְכֹּר אֱלֹהִים אֶת אַבְרָהָם.** מָה הִיא זְכִירָתוֹ שֶׁל אַבְרָהָם עַל לוֹט? נִזְכַּר, שֶׁהָיָה יוֹדֵעַ שֶׁשָּׂרָה אִשְׁתּוֹ שֶׁל אַבְרָהָם, וְשָׁמַע שֶׁאָמַר אַבְרָהָם בְּמִצְרַיִם עַל שָׂרָה: "אֲחוֹתִי הוּא" (לעיל יב, יט) וְלֹא גִלָּה הַדָּבָר, שֶׁהָיָה חָס עָלָיו, לְפִיכָךְ חָס הַקָּדוֹשׁ בָּרוּךְ הוּא עָלָיו:

ל| **כִּי יָרֵא לָשֶׁבֶת בְּצוֹעַר.** לְפִי שֶׁהָיְתָה קְרוֹבָה לִסְדוֹם:

לא| **אָבִינוּ זָקֵן.** וְאִם לֹא עַכְשָׁיו אֵימָתַי? שֶׁמָּא יָמוּת אוֹ יִפְסֹק מִלֵּדָה: **וְאִישׁ אֵין בָּאָרֶץ.** סְבוּרוֹת הָיוּ שֶׁכָּל הָעוֹלָם נֶחֱרַב כְּמוֹ בְּדוֹר הַמַּבּוּל. בְּרֵאשִׁית רַבָּה (נא, ח):

לג| **וַתַּשְׁקֶיןָ וְגוֹ'.** יַיִן נִזְדַּמֵּן לָהֶן בַּמְּעָרָה לְהוֹצִיא מֵהֶן שְׁתֵּי אֻמּוֹת: **וַתִּשְׁכַּב אֶת אָבִיהָ.** וּבַצְּעִירָה כְּתִיב: "וַתִּשְׁכַּב עִמּוֹ" (להלן פסוק לה). צְעִירָה לְפִי שֶׁלֹּא פָּתְחָה בִּזְנוּת אֶלָּא אֲחוֹתָהּ לִמְּדַתָּה, חִסֵּךְ עָלֶיהָ הַכָּתוּב וְלֹא פֵּרֵשׁ גְּנוּתָהּ, אֲבָל בְּכִירָה שֶׁפָּתְחָה בִּזְנוּת פִּרְסְמָהּ הַכָּתוּב בִּמְפֹרָשׁ. "וּבְקוּמָהּ" שֶׁל בְּכִירָה נָקוּד, הֲרֵי הוּא כְּאִלּוּ לֹא נִכְתַּב, לוֹמַר שֶׁבְּקוּמָהּ יָדַע, וְאַף עַל פִּי כֵן לֹא נִשְׁמַר לֵיל שֵׁנִי מִלִּשְׁתּוֹת:

34 **It was the next day, and the elder said to the younger: Behold, I lay last night with my father.** Since I have already broken the taboo, **let us give him wine to drink tonight as well, and** you **come and lie with him; and we will give life to offspring from our father.** We cannot know yet if I have become pregnant. Since we must guarantee the survival of the human race, we will improve our chances of success if you lie with him as well.

35 **They gave their father wine to drink that night as well. The younger arose and lay with him, and he did not know when she lay or when she arose.**

36 **Lot's two daughters conceived from their father.**

37 **The elder gave birth to a son and called his name Moav; he is the ancestor of the Moavites to this day.** The name Moav can be understood to mean: From father [*me'av*].

38 **The younger too gave birth to a son, and called his name Ben Ami,** which has a similar meaning, as the word *ami* can denote a close familial relationship (see, e.g., 49:29). Nevertheless, this was a more subtle reference to his sordid origins than Moav. **He is the ancestor of the descendants of Amon**[D] **to this day.**

Abraham and Sarah in Gerar
GENESIS 20:1–18

The Torah returns to the story of Abraham and Sarah, whose journey to Gerar brings them into a situation similar to the one they experienced earlier in Egypt. The Sages note the juxtaposition of this episode to the destruction of Sodom, and suggest that Abraham may have left Hebron due to the effects of the calamity on the surrounding area. If the actions of Lot and his daughters had become widely known, the rumors alone could have prompted Abraham to migrate.

20 1 **Abraham journeyed from there to the land of the south; he lived between Kadesh and Shur,** in the Negev; **and he resided in Gerar,** one of the cities of the Philistines.

2 **Abraham said of Sarah his wife: She is my sister.** Although they arrived in a location that was smaller and less powerful than Egypt, nevertheless, Abraham adopted the same precautions he had used there. **Avimelekh king of Gerar sent** messengers **and took Sarah,** either for personal reasons or due to political and economic considerations.

3 Unlike in Egypt, **God came to Avimelekh in a dream at night, and He said to him: Behold, you shall die, because of the woman that you have taken, and she is married to a husband.**

4 **Avimelekh had not approached her;** even before God spoke to him, he had not engaged in sexual relations with Sarah. **He said,** either in the dream or while awake: **Lord, will You kill** me when I am **a nation,** a king, **who is also righteous?** Avimelekh pleaded for his life: Why must I die? I have done no wrong.

5 **Did he,** Abraham, **not say to me: She is my sister? And she,** Sarah, **she too** as much as **said: He is my brother. In the innocence of my heart and in the cleanliness of my hands I did this.**

6 **God said to him in the dream: I also knew that in the innocence of your heart you did this, and I also prevented you from sinning to Me.** Although you were able to take her, I kept you from sinning further. **Therefore,** after you took her **I did not allow you to touch her.**

7 **Now, restore the man's wife, as he is a prophet, and he shall pray for you, and you will live.** The fact that Abraham is a prophet is not the reason Avimelekh must return his wife. Rather, God is saying that as Abraham is a prophet and a holy individual, his prayer has the power to ensure that Avimelekh will be spared. Therefore, the king would be advised not merely to return Sarah, but to ask Abraham to pray for him. **And if you do not restore her, know that you shall die, you and all that is yours.**

8 **Avimelekh rose early in the morning, and he called all his servants and spoke all these matters in their ears; and the men were very frightened,** due to the threat to their king's life.

9 **Avimelekh called Abraham, and said to him: What have you done to us, and what have I sinned to you, that you have brought upon me and upon my kingdom a great sin? Deeds that may not be done you have done to me.** Abraham did not answer Avimelekh's accusation, as he himself was not to blame.

DISCUSSION

19:38 | **Amon:** These sons were the forefathers of Moav and Amon, two nations that lived east of the Dead Sea for many generations. The descendants of Abraham, the Jewish people, interacted closely and frequently with them throughout their history. However, due to their deficiencies in interpersonal relations, which may have resulted from their dubious ancestry, relations between them and the Jewish people were never entirely friendly.

לד ובקומה: ויהי ממחרת ותאמר הבכירה אל־הצעירה הן־שכבתי אמש את־
לה אבי נשקנו יין גם־הלילה ובאי שכבי עמו ונחיה מאבינו זרע: ותשקין גם
בלילה ההוא את־אביהן יין ותקם הצעירה ותשכב עמו ולא־ידע בשכבה
לו לז ובקמה: ותהרין שתי בנות־לוט מאביהן: ותלד הבכירה בן ותקרא שמו מואב
לח הוא אבי־מואב עד־היום: והצעירה גם־הוא ילדה בן ותקרא שמו בן־עמי
כ א הוא אבי בני־עמון עד־היום: ויסע משם אברהם ארצה הנגב וישב בין־קדש יז
ב ובין שור ויגר בגרר: ויאמר אברהם אל־שרה אשתו אחתי הוא וישלח
ג אבימלך מלך גרר ויקח את־שרה: ויבא אלהים אל־אבימלך בחלום הלילה
ד ויאמר לו הנך מת על־האשה אשר־לקחת והוא בעלת בעל: ואבימלך לא
ה קרב אליה ויאמר אדני הגוי גם־צדיק תהרג: הלא הוא אמר־לי אחתי הוא
ו והיא־גם־הוא אמרה אחי הוא בתם־לבבי ובנקין כפי עשיתי זאת: ויאמר
אליו האלהים בחלם גם אנכי ידעתי כי בתם־לבבך עשית זאת ואחשך גם־
ז אנכי אותך מחטו־לי על־כן לא־נתתיך לנגע אליה: ועתה השב אשת־האיש
כי־נביא הוא ויתפלל בעדך וחיה ואם־אינך משיב דע כי־מות תמות אתה
ח וכל־אשר־לך: וישכם אבימלך בבקר ויקרא לכל־עבדיו וידבר את־כל־
ט הדברים האלה באזניהם וייראו האנשים מאד: ויקרא אבימלך לאברהם
ויאמר לו מה־עשית לנו ומה־חטאתי לך כי־הבאת עלי ועל־ממלכתי חטאה

רש"י

לו| **ותהרין.** אף על פי שאין האשה מתעברת מביאה ראשונה, אלו שלטו בעצמן והוציאו ערותן לחוץ ועברו מביאה ראשונה:

לז| **מואב.** זו שלא היתה צנועה פרשה שמאביה הוא, אבל צעירה קראתו בלשון נקיה, וקבלו שכר בימי משה, שנאמר בבני עמון: "ואל תתגר בם" (דברים ב, יט) כלל, ובמואב לא הזהיר אלא שלא ילחם בם, אבל לצערן התיר לו:

פרק כ

א| **ויסע משם אברהם.** כשראה שחרבו הכרכים ופסקו העוברים והשבים נסע לו משם. דבר אחר, להתרחק מלוט שיצא עליו שם רע שבא על בנותיו:

ב| **ויאמר אברהם.** כאן לא נטל רשות, אלא על כרחה שלא בטובתה, לפי שכבר לקחה לבית פרעה על ידי כן: **אל שרה אשתו.** על שרה אשתו. כיוצא בו: "אל הלקח ארון וגו' ואל חמיה" (שמואל א׳ ד, כא), שניהם בלשון 'על':

ד| **לא קרב אליה.** המלאך מנעו, כמה שנאמר: "לא נתתיך לנגע אליה" (להלן פסוק ו): **הגוי גם צדיק תהרג.** אף אם הוא צדיק תהרגנו? שמא כך דרכך לאבד אומות חנם? כך עשית לדור המבול ולדור הפלגה, אף אני אומר שהרגתם על לא דבר כשם שאתה אומר להרגני:

ה| **גם הוא.** לרבות עבדים וגמלים וחמרים שלה, את כלם שאלתי ואמרו לי: אחיה הוא: **בתם לבבי.** שלא דמיתי לחטוא: **ובנקין כפי.** נקי אני מן החטא, שלא נגעתי בה:

ו| **ידעתי כי בתם לבבך וגו'.** אמת שלא דמית מתחלה לחטוא, אבל נקיון כפים אין כאן שלא ממך היה שלא נגעת בה, אלא אני חשכתי אותך מחטוא: **לא נתתיך.** לא נתתי לך כח, וכן: "ולא נתנו אלהים להרע" (להלן לא, ז), וכן: "ולא נתנו אביה לבוא" (שופטים טו, א) – לא נתן לו מקום:

ז| **השב אשת האיש.** ואל תהא סבור שתתגנה בעיניו ולא יקבלנה, או ששנאך ולא יתפלל עליך: **כי נביא הוא.** ויודע שלא נגעת בה, לפיכך "ויתפלל בעדך":

While Abraham had omitted some pertinent details, Avimelekh had taken Sarah without Abraham's express permission.

10 When Abraham did not respond to his accusation, Avimelekh sought to determine his motive. **Avimelekh said to Abraham: What did you see that you did this thing?**

11 **Abraham said: Because I said: Surely there is no fear of God in this place.** Although I am unfamiliar with this area, the impression I received is that there is no fear of God. In such an environment no one heeds moral norms in the fundamental areas of murder and forbidden sexual relationships. **And** I thought: If I tell the truth about Sarah, **they will kill me over the matter of my wife.**

12 **Also,** I did not actually lie. **Indeed, she is my sister, the daughter of my father,**[D] **but** she is **not the daughter of my mother.** Apparently, even then it was considered taboo to marry a maternal sister.[15] **And she became my wife.**

13 **It was, when God caused me to wander from my father's house** and live as a nomad, that **I said to her: This is your kindness that you shall perform for me; at every place that we shall come, say of me: He is my brother.**

14 **Avimelekh took flocks and cattle, and slaves and maidservants, and he gave them to Abraham** as a gift, **and he restored his wife Sarah to him.**

15 **Avimelekh said: Behold, my land is before you: Live where it is fit in your eyes.** I will not hold this episode against you, and I grant you permission to stay here if you wish.

16 **And to Sarah he said:** The appearance of having left your husband's house and stayed with another man could cause a scandal. Therefore, **behold, I have given your brother** Abraham sheep, cattle, slaves, and maidservants worth a large sum, **a thousand pieces of silver;**[16] **behold, it,** the gift, **is for you a covering of the eyes for all who are with you,** and it will cover the eyes of all who would look at you in a disparaging manner and malign you, **and for all** people **it is proven** by the compensation that you have behaved honorably and need not be ashamed.

17 **Abraham prayed to God,** as God had predicted to Avimelekh; **and God healed Avimelekh, his wife, and his maidservants, and they bore children.**

18 The Torah explains why Avimelekh submitted so quickly to God's command: **For the Lord had obstructed all wombs of the house of Avimelekh,**[D] **over the matter of Sarah, Abraham's wife.** During the time that Sarah was in Avimelekh's house, no children were born to the household, neither to Avimelekh's wives nor to his maidservants. Avimelekh feared that this condition would become even more serious. Once Abraham prayed for him, this affliction in Avimelekh's household abated.

Isaac from Birth to Weaning

GENESIS 21:1–8

Surrounded by prose sections, which describe a sequence of events, the celebratory first verse of the next passage, and likewise Sarah's joyous comments in verses 6–7, stand out for their poetry, employing parallelism. They emphasize the dramatic importance of the birth of Sarah's promised son, heir to the house of Abraham.

21 1 **The Lord remembered [*pakad*] Sarah.** The term *pakad* refers to remembering to fulfill a need or a lack.[17] The Lord blessed her with a pregnancy **as He had said, and the Lord did to Sarah as He had spoken.**

2 **Sarah conceived, and bore Abraham a son in his old age, at the designated time that God had told him,** one year after the angels had visited his tent.

DISCUSSION

20:12 | **Indeed she is my sister, the daughter of my father:** Although Sarah's precise lineage is unclear from the Torah, the Sages teach that she was the daughter of Abraham's brother Haran (*Megilla* 14a). Accordingly, Abraham could say that she was his sister, as she was a descendant of his father, Terah. Just as Abraham had said about his nephew Lot: We are brethren [*aḥim*] (13:8), and as Jacob remarked to his cousin Rachel on their initial meeting that he was her father's brother (29:12), so too, Sarah could be considered Abraham's sister. Similarly, Hanamel was called Jeremiah's brother, despite the fact that they were actually cousins (see Jeremiah 32:7–8).

20:18 | **Avimelekh:** Earlier, when Sarai was taken into the house of Pharaoh in Egypt, the incident between Pharaoh and Abram was never resolved. Pharaoh, stricken with illness and frightened, simply banished Abram and Sarai from the country immediately. Avimelekh, by contrast, considered himself a good and just king, and demanded an explanation from Abraham, who was compelled to defend his behavior. Furthermore, unlike Pharaoh, Avimelekh was interested in maintaining an ongoing relationship with Abraham. Later, the Torah further depicts Avimelekh's desire to remain close to Abraham and even to enter into a covenant with him.

י גדלה מעשים אשר לא־יעשו עשית עמדי: ויאמר אבימלך אל־אברהם מה
יא ראית כי עשית את־הדבר הזה: ויאמר אברהם כי אמרתי רק אין־יראת
יב אלהים במקום הזה והרגוני על־דבר אשתי: וגם־אמנה אחתי בת־אבי הוא
יג אך לא בת־אמי ותהי־לי לאשה: ויהי כאשר התעו אתי אלהים מבית אבי
ואמר לה זה חסדך אשר תעשי עמדי אל כל־המקום אשר נבוא שמה אמרי־
יד לי אחי הוא: ויקח אבימלך צאן ובקר ועבדים ושפחת ויתן לאברהם וישב
טו לו את שרה אשתו: ויאמר אבימלך הנה ארצי לפניך בטוב בעיניך שב:
טז ולשרה אמר הנה נתתי אלף כסף לאחיך הנה הוא־לך כסות עינים לכל אשר
יז אתך ואת־כל ונכחת: ויתפלל אברהם אל־האלהים וירפא אלהים את־
יח אבימלך ואת־אשתו ואמהתיו וילדו: כי־עצר עצר יהוה בעד כל־רחם לבית
א אבימלך על־דבר שרה אשת אברהם: ויהוה פקד את־שרה כאשר אמר
ב ויעש יהוה לשרה כאשר דבר: ותהר ותלד שרה לאברהם בן לזקניו למועד

רש"י

ט | **מעשים אשר לא יעשו.** מכה אשר לא הרגלה לבא על בריה באה לנו על ידך – עצירת כל נקבים של זרע ושל קטנים ורעי ואזנים וחטם:

יא | **רק אין יראת אלהים.** אכסנאי שבא לעיר, על עסקי אכילה ושתיה שואלין אותו או על עסקי אשתו שואלין אותו, אשתך היא או אחותך היא?

יב | **אחותי בת אבי היא.** ובת אב מותרת לבן נח, שאין אב לגוי; וכדי לאמת דבריו השיבם כן. ואם תאמר, והלא בת אחיו היתה! בני בנים הרי הם כבנים והרי היא בתו של תרח, וכך הוא אומר ללוט: "כי אנשים אחים אנחנו" (לעיל יג, ח): **אך לא בת אמי.** הרן מאם אחרת היה:

יג | **ויהי כאשר התעו אותי וגו'.** אונקלוס תרגם מה שתרגם; ויש ליישבו עוד דבר דבור על אפניו: כשהוציאני הקדוש ברוך הוא מבית אבי להיות משוטט ונד ממקום למקום וידעתי שאעבור במקום רשעים, "ואמר לה זה חסדך": **כאשר התעו.** לשון רבים. ואל תתמה, כי הרבה מקומות לשון אלהות ולשון מרות קרוי בלשון רבים: "אשר הלכו אלהים" (שמואל ב' ז, כג), "אלהים חיים" (דברים ה, כג), "אלהים קדשים" (יהושע כד, יט), וכל לשון 'אלהים' לשון רבים. וכן: "ויקח אדני יוסף" (להלן לט, כ), "ואדני האדנים" (דברים י, יז), "אדני הארץ" (להלן מב, לג); וכן: "בעליו עמו" (שמות כב, יד), "והועד בבעליו" (שם כא, כט). ואם תאמר, מהו לשון 'התעו'? כל הגולה ממקומו ואינו מיושב קרוי 'תועה', כמו: "ותלך ותתע" (להלן כא, יד), "תעיתי כשה אבד" (תהלים קיט, קעו), "יתעו לבלי אכל" (איוב לח, מא), יצאו ויתעו לבקש אכלם: **אמרי לי.** עלי, וכן: "וישאלו אנשי המקום לאשתו" (להלן כו, ז) על אשתו, וכן: "ואמר פרעה לבני ישראל" (שמות יד, ג), "פן יאמרו לי אשה הרגתהו" (שופטים ט, נד):

יד | **ויתן לאברהם.** כדי שיתפיס ויתפלל עליו:

טו | **הנה ארצי לפניך.** אבל פרעה אמר לו: "הנה אשתך קח ולך" (לעיל יב, יט), לפי שנתירא, שהמצרים שטופי זמה:

טז | **ולשרה אמר.** אבימלך לכבודה, כדי לפייסה: הנה עשיתי לך כבוד זה, נתתי ממון לאחיך שאמרת עליו "אחי הוא", הנה הכבוד הזה לך "כסות עינים לכל אשר אתך" – יכסה עיניהם שלא יקלוך, שאלו השיבותיך ריקנית יש להם לומר, לאחר שנתעלל בה החזירה, עכשיו שהצרכתי לבזבז ממון ולפייסך, יודעים יהיו שעל כרחי השיבותיך ועל ידי נס: **ואת כל.** ועם כל באי עולם: **ונכחת.** יהא לך פתחון פה להתוכח ולהראות דברים נכרים הללו. ולשון 'הוכחה' בכל מקום ברור דברים, ובלעז אספרובי"ר. ואונקלוס תרגם בפנים אחרים, ולשון המקרא כך הוא נופל על תרגומו של אונקלוס: הנה הוא לך כסות של כבוד על העינים שלי ששלטו בך ובכל אשר אתך, ועל כן תרגם: "וחזית יתיך וית כל דעמיך". ויש מדרשי אגדה, אבל ישוב לשון המקרא פרשתי:

יז | **וילדו.** כתרגומו "ואתרוחו", נפתחו נקביהם והוציאו, והיא לדה שלהם:

יח | **בעד כל רחם.** כנגד כל פתח: **על דבר שרה.** על פי דבורה של שרה:

פרק כא

א | **וה' פקד את שרה.** סמך פרשה זו לכאן, ללמדך שכל המבקש רחמים על חברו והוא צריך לאותו דבר הוא נענה תחלה, שנאמר: "ויתפלל" וגו' (לעיל כ, יז) "וה' פקד את שרה", שפקד כבר קודם שרפא את אבימלך: **פקד.** בהריון: **כאשר דבר.** בלדה. ומה היא אמירה והיכן הוא דבור? אמירה: "ויאמר אלהים אבל שרה אשתך" וגו' (לעיל יז, יט), דבור: "היה דבר ה' אל אברם" (לעיל טו, א) בברית בין הבתרים, שם נאמר: "לא יירשך זה" וגו' (שם ד), והביא היורש משרה: **ויעש ה' לשרה כאשר דבר.** לאברהם:

3 **Abraham called the name of his son that was born to him, whom Sarah bore to him, Isaac,** as God had commanded. Isaac, whose name means: He will laugh, was born in the wake of the laughter of both Abraham (17:17) and Sarah (18:12). Moreover, his name alludes both to his character and to later events in his life.[18]

4 **Abraham circumcised his son Isaac when he was eight days old, as God had commanded him** above (17:12). Isaac was the first child of Abraham to be born after God's commandment with regard to circumcision, and was therefore the first to be circumcised on the eighth day.

5 **Abraham was one hundred years old when his son Isaac was**
Fifth aliya **born to him.**

6 **Sarah said: God has made laughter for me.** This is a strange and happy occurrence, prompting laughter. **Everyone who hears will laugh for me.** The unlikely event of this birth and the gladness it brings me will cause everyone who hears of it to share in my joy.

7 **She said: Who would have said of Abraham that Sarah would nurse children,** as has happened? I have been married to Abraham for many years without children, and now the impossible has occurred, **as I bore** him **a son for his old age.**

8 **The child grew and was weaned.** It is unclear when this occurred, as nursing sometimes continued until age three. **Abraham made a great feast on the day Isaac was weaned,** in accordance with the prevalent custom to celebrate a child's weaning.[19]

The Banishment of Hagar and Ishmael

GENESIS 21:9–21

The proper development of Isaac, Abraham's heir and successor, necessitates the banishment of Abraham's firstborn son, Ishmael. Sarah is the driving force behind the exile of Ishmael and his mother Hagar in response to the boy's problematic conduct, which she fears will adversely affect Isaac. It is notable that the term for Ishmael's immoral behavior, *tzeḥok*, shares the same root as Isaac's name, *Yitzḥak*.

9 **Sarah saw** Ishmael, **the son of Hagar the Egyptian, whom she,** Hagar, **bore to Abraham, playing.**[D]

10 **She said to Abraham: Banish this maidservant and her son.** By rights you should banish only the son, but as he is young and needs his mother, you must send her away as well. **For the son of this maidservant shall not inherit**[D] **with my son, with Isaac.**

11 **The matter was very grave in the eyes of Abraham, on account of his son.** Abraham was more pained about banishing Ishmael than about banishing Hagar. He may also have better understood Sarah's discomfort with Hagar's presence than he did her objection to Ishmael.

12 But **God said to Abraham: Let it not be grave in your eyes about the lad and about your maidservant.** Significantly, God included Hagar in this statement. **Everything that Sarah says to you, heed her voice.**[D] Whether or not you understand and identify with Sarah's demand, it is My will that you should listen to her, **for it is through Isaac that descendants will be accounted to you.** You have a son from Sarah, and even if you have other biological children, only Isaac will be your heir and successor, and only his descendants will be attributed to you.

13 **Also the son of the maidservant I will make a nation.**[D] He is not simply being discarded, **because he is your descendant,** and your merit stands in his favor. He too will be the father of a great people, although they will not be known as Abraham's unique descendants.

14 **Abraham rose early in the morning;**[D] he **took bread and a skin of water and gave it to Hagar, placed it on her shoulder,**

DISCUSSION

21:9| **Playing [*metzaḥek*]:** In this context, the term indicates behavior of either an explicitly or implicitly sexual nature. Later (26:8), this verb is used in an explicitly sexual sense (see *Bereshit Rabba* 53:11).

21:10| **Inherit:** Sarah's demand did not refer merely to inheritance, as Abraham, not Sarah, had the power to decide who his heir would be (see 25:5–6). Rather, the core of the issue was the relationship between the two children. Sarah did not want Isaac and Ishmael to live together, befriend each other, and see themselves as brothers.

21:12| **Heed her voice:** In light of this story, the Sages state that Sarah was a greater prophet than Abraham (*Tanḥuma*, *Shemot* 1). They also identify Sarah with Yiska (11:29), as she saw [*sakhta*] by means of divine inspiration (*Megilla* 14a; see Jerusalem Talmud, *Sota* 7:5; *Lekaḥ Tov*, Genesis 23:1). God here affirmed that Isaac was to be raised as an only child, with Ishmael sent elsewhere, thereby fulfilling the prophecy of the angel to Hagar earlier that Ishmael would live in the wilderness (16:12). It can similarly be argued that Rebecca was a greater prophet than Isaac (see *Shoḥer Tov* 9:7; *Yalkut Shimoni*, *Ḥayei Sarah* 109). Both of these women apparently had a clearer view of the future than their husbands.

21:13| **Also the son of the maidservant I will make a nation:** The story of Ishmael teaches that God's providence is neither straightforward nor one-sided. From God's order to banish Hagar and her son one might easily receive the impression that they were of no importance. Nevertheless, later God would notice Ishmael's suffering, answer his cries, and miraculously save him from death. There is no contradiction between these events: God supported Sarah's judgment, but He also cared for the welfare of

ג אשר־דבר אתו אלהים: ויקרא אברהם את־שם־בנו הנולד־לו אשר־ילדה־
ד לו שרה יצחק: וימל אברהם את־יצחק בנו בן־שמנת ימים כאשר צוה אתו
ה אלהים: ואברהם בן־מאת שנה בהולד לו את יצחק בנו: חמישי
ו ז ותאמר שרה צחק עשה לי אלהים כל־השמע יצחק־לי: ותאמר מי מלל
ח לאברהם היניקה בנים שרה כי־ילדתי בן לזקניו: ויגדל הילד ויגמל ויעש
ט אברהם משתה גדול ביום הגמל את־יצחק: ותרא שרה את־בן־הגר המצרית
י אשר־ילדה לאברהם מצחק: ותאמר לאברהם גרש האמה הזאת ואת־בנה
יא כי לא יירש בן־האמה הזאת עם־בני עם־יצחק: וירע הדבר מאד בעיני אברהם
יב על אודת בנו: ויאמר אלהים אל־אברהם אל־ירע בעיניך על־הנער ועל־
יג אמתך כל אשר תאמר אליך שרה שמע בקלה כי ביצחק יקרא לך זרע: וגם
יד את־בן־האמה לגוי אשימנו כי זרעך הוא: וישכם אברהם | בבקר ויקח־לחם
וחמת מים ויתן אל־הגר שם על־שכמה ואת־הילד וישלחה ותלך ותתע

רש"י

ב | **למועד אשר דבר אתו.** "דמליל יתיה", את המועד דבר וקבע כשאמר לו: "למועד אשוב אליך" (לעיל יח, יד), שרט לו שריטה בכותל, אמר לו: כשתגיע חמה לשריטה זו בשנה האחרת – תלד:

ו | **יצחק לי.** ישמח עלי. ומדרש אגדה, הרבה עקרות נפקדו עמה, הרבה חולים נתרפאו בו ביום, הרבה תפלות נענו עמה, ורב שחוק היה בעולם:

ז | **מי מלל לאברהם.** לשון שבח וחשיבות, ראו מי הוא וכמה הוא גדול, שומר הבטחתו, ומבטיח ועושה: **מלל.** שנה הכתוב ולא אמר 'דבר', גימטריא שלו מאה, כלומר לסוף מאה לאברהם "היניקה בנים שרה". ומהו 'בנים' לשון רבים? ביום המשתה הביאו השרות בניהן עמהן, שהיו אומרות: לא ילדה שרה, אלא אסופי הביאה מן השוק – והיניקה אותם:

ח | **ויגמל.** לסוף עשרים וארבעה חדש: **משתה גדול.** שהיו שם גדולי הדור, שם ועבר ואבימלך:

ט | **מצחק.** לשון עבודה זרה, שנאמר: "ויקמו לצחק" (שמות לב, ו); לשון רציחה, "יקומו נא הנערים וישחקו לפנינו" (שמואל ב' ב, יד); לשון גלוי עריות, כמו: "לצחק בי" (להלן לט, יז). היה מריב עם יצחק על הירשה ואומר: אני בכור ונוטל פי שנים, ויוצאים לשדה ונוטל קשתו ויורה בו חצים, כמה דאת אמר: "כמתלהלה הירה זקים וגו' ואמר הלא משחק אני" (משלי כו, יח-יט):

י | **עם בני עם יצחק.** מכיון שהוא בני אפילו אם איננו הגון כיצחק, או הגון כיצחק אפילו איננו בני, אין זה כדאי לירש עמו, קל וחומר "עם בני עם יצחק", ששתיהם בו:

יא | **על אודות בנו.** ששמע שיצא לתרבות רעה. ופשוטו, על שאומרת לו לשלחו:

יב | **שמע בקלה.** למדנו שהיה אברהם טפל לשרה בנביאות:

יד | **לחם וחמת מים.** ולא כסף וזהב, לפי שהיה שונאו על שיצא לתרבות רעה: **ואת הילד.** אף הילד "שם על שכמה", שהכניסה בו שרה עין רעה, ואחזתו חמה ולא יכל לילך ברגליו: **ותלך ותתע.** חזרה לגלולי בית אביה:

DISCUSSION

➞ Hagar and Ishmael. In this story, there is no clear demarcation between absolute good and absolute evil, but rather a nuanced approach to dealing with characters who were on different paths.

21:14 | **Abraham rose early in the morning:** When Abraham received an order from God, he did not wait for a convenient time to carry it out, but set about the task immediately. This was not the first nor the last time that Abraham's diligence was highlighted (see 17:22–23, and Rashi ad loc.; 22:3; *Ḥullin* 16a).

Placed it on her shoulder, and the child: Bearing in mind Ishmael's age at the time, it is surprising that Hagar would have to hold him. He was at least fifteen years old, as more than two years had passed since he was circumcised, at age thirteen. The Sages explain that Ishmael was ill at the time, and his mother had to care for him constantly and even carry him when he became weary. Ishmael's expulsion from his home in this condition was a more severe ordeal (see *Bereshit Rabba* 53:13; Rashi; Radak).

and gave her[20] **the child,**[D] **and sent her away. She went and wandered in the wilderness of Beersheba.** Although she may have planned on traveling to her native Egypt, in any event, she wandered in the wilderness instead of reaching any place of human habitation.

15 Eventually, **the water in the skin** Abraham had given her **was finished, and she cast the child** into the shade **beneath one of the bushes** in the desert. This description supports the opinion that Ishmael was sick, as perhaps he had fainted and was unable to walk.

16 **She went and sat herself down at a far distance, approximately a bowshot removed.** In biblical times, an arrow could be shot approximately 170 m.[21] She was at a distance from her son but presumably could still see him and hear his cries. **For she said: I** do not want to sit close to him, so that I **will not see the death of the child. She sat at a distance, raised her voice, and wept.**

17 **God heard the voice of the lad; the angel of God called to Hagar from the heavens and said to her: What is it with you,** **Hagar?**[D] **Fear not, as God has heard the voice of the lad as he is there.** His cries and needs are heard above. In all places and whatever the circumstances, God protects Ishmael.

18 **Rise, lift up the lad,** since he is too weak to walk on his own, **and hold him with your hand** to support him, **for I will make of him a great nation.** He will not die yet, as a mighty nation will descend from him.

19 **God opened her eyes, and she saw a well of water; she went and filled the skin with water, and gave the lad to drink.** This drink revived the dehydrated Ishmael.

20 **God was with the lad, and he grew; he lived in the wilderness and became an archer,** skilled at hunting with bow and arrows.

21 **He lived in the wilderness of Paran, and his mother took him a wife from the land of Egypt,** her native land. Here, in the wilderness of Paran, the career of Ishmael began, and he ultimately became the patriarch of a great nation.

Abraham and Avimelekh Seal a Covenant

GENESIS 21:22–34

Before Abraham fathered children, he was considered an individual who would eventually die and leave the world much as he found it. Now that he has an heir, those around him realize that he cannot be disregarded. Even after he dies, the tribe that he establishes will remain.

22 **It was at that time,** after Abraham had fathered a son, that

Sixth aliya **Avimelekh and Pikhol,**[D] **the captain of his guard, said to Abraham, saying:** Although you are not the ruler of a great kingdom, we see that **God is with you in all that you do.** They began this political discussion by invoking God.

23 **Now take an oath to me here by God that you shall not deceive** or betray **me, or my son,**[D] **or my son's son; like the kindness that I have done with you** in allowing you to live within my territory and in taking a certain responsibility for your welfare, **do with me** personally, **and also with the land in which you resided.**

24 **Abraham said: I will** agree to **take an oath** and pledge to be trustworthy in my relations with your people and country.

25 On this same occasion, **Abraham reprimanded Avimelekh with regard to the well of water that Avimelekh's** **servants had stolen.** Abraham had previously dug a well, which Avimelekh's servants then took by force. Abraham had not complained at that point, but once he was negotiating a covenant with Avimelekh, he decided to raise the matter. Since Avimelekh had publicly declared that he had a positive relationship with Abraham and had treated him with kindness, Abraham found it appropriate to note the unresolved issues in their relationship and try to reconcile them.

26 **Avimelekh said: I do not know who did this thing; and you also did not tell me** it had happened, **nor did I hear of it, other than today.** I can take no responsibility for the incident. I did not send those people, and I never heard anything about this incident until now. By this statement, Avimelekh conceded that the well belonged to Abraham.

27 **Abraham took flocks and cattle and gave them to Avimelekh**

DISCUSSION

21:17 | Hagar: This was not the first time Hagar conversed with angels (see 16:7–13). The revelations she experienced led the Sages to extol her virtues. Various circumstances may have caused her to come into conflict with Sarah, and the fact that she was expelled was not necessarily an indication of a personal failing on her part.

It could even have been precisely Hagar's exceptional personality that aroused Sarah's resentment (*Bereshit Rabba* 45:1, 7, 10; *Yalkut Shimoni,* Joshua 9).

21:22 | Pikhol: This could be his name or a Philistine term for a military leader.

21:23 | Or my son [*nini*]: In modern Hebrew, *nin* means a great-grandson. In biblical usage, as indicated by the word order in this verse, it can refer to a son (Onkelos) or any descendant (see Isaiah 14:22; Job 18:19; Rashi, Proverbs 29:21).

טו בְּמִדְבַּר בְּאֵר שָׁבַע: וַיִּכְלוּ הַמַּיִם מִן־הַחֵמֶת וַתַּשְׁלֵךְ אֶת־הַיֶּלֶד תַּחַת אַחַד
טז הַשִּׂיחִם: וַתֵּלֶךְ וַתֵּשֶׁב לָהּ מִנֶּגֶד הַרְחֵק כִּמְטַחֲוֵי קֶשֶׁת כִּי אָמְרָה אַל־אֶרְאֶה
יז בְּמוֹת הַיָּלֶד וַתֵּשֶׁב מִנֶּגֶד וַתִּשָּׂא אֶת־קֹלָהּ וַתֵּבְךְּ: וַיִּשְׁמַע אֱלֹהִים אֶת־קוֹל הַנַּעַר
וַיִּקְרָא מַלְאַךְ אֱלֹהִים ׀ אֶל־הָגָר מִן־הַשָּׁמַיִם וַיֹּאמֶר לָהּ מַה־לָּךְ הָגָר אַל־תִּירְאִי
יח כִּי־שָׁמַע אֱלֹהִים אֶל־קוֹל הַנַּעַר בַּאֲשֶׁר הוּא־שָׁם: קוּמִי שְׂאִי אֶת־הַנַּעַר וְהַחֲזִיקִי
יט אֶת־יָדֵךְ בּוֹ כִּי־לְגוֹי גָּדוֹל אֲשִׂימֶנּוּ: וַיִּפְקַח אֱלֹהִים אֶת־עֵינֶיהָ וַתֵּרֶא בְּאֵר מָיִם
כ וַתֵּלֶךְ וַתְּמַלֵּא אֶת־הַחֵמֶת מַיִם וַתַּשְׁקְ אֶת־הַנָּעַר: וַיְהִי אֱלֹהִים אֶת־הַנַּעַר וַיִּגְדָּל
כא וַיֵּשֶׁב בַּמִּדְבָּר וַיְהִי רֹבֶה קַשָּׁת: וַיֵּשֶׁב בְּמִדְבַּר פָּארָן וַתִּקַּח־לוֹ אִמּוֹ אִשָּׁה מֵאֶרֶץ
מִצְרָיִם:

כב וַיְהִי בָּעֵת הַהִוא וַיֹּאמֶר אֲבִימֶלֶךְ וּפִיכֹל שַׂר־צְבָאוֹ אֶל־אַבְרָהָם לֵאמֹר אֱלֹהִים ששי
כג עִמְּךָ בְּכֹל אֲשֶׁר־אַתָּה עֹשֶׂה: וְעַתָּה הִשָּׁבְעָה לִּי בֵאלֹהִים הֵנָּה אִם־תִּשְׁקֹר לִי
וּלְנִינִי וּלְנֶכְדִּי כַּחֶסֶד אֲשֶׁר־עָשִׂיתִי עִמְּךָ תַּעֲשֶׂה עִמָּדִי וְעִם־הָאָרֶץ אֲשֶׁר־גַּרְתָּה
כד כה בָהּ: וַיֹּאמֶר אַבְרָהָם אָנֹכִי אִשָּׁבֵעַ: וְהוֹכִחַ אַבְרָהָם אֶת־אֲבִימֶלֶךְ עַל־אֹדוֹת בְּאֵר
כו הַמַּיִם אֲשֶׁר גָּזְלוּ עַבְדֵי אֲבִימֶלֶךְ: וַיֹּאמֶר אֲבִימֶלֶךְ לֹא יָדַעְתִּי מִי עָשָׂה אֶת־הַדָּבָר
כז הַזֶּה וְגַם־אַתָּה לֹא־הִגַּדְתָּ לִּי וְגַם אָנֹכִי לֹא שָׁמַעְתִּי בִּלְתִּי הַיּוֹם: וַיִּקַּח אַבְרָהָם

רש"י

טו| וַיִּכְלוּ הַמַּיִם. לְפִי שֶׁדֶּרֶךְ חוֹלִים לִשְׁתּוֹת הַרְבֵּה:

טז| מִנֶּגֶד. מֵרָחוֹק: כִּמְטַחֲוֵי קֶשֶׁת. כִּשְׁתֵּי טִיחוֹת, וְהוּא לְשׁוֹן יְרִיַּת חֵץ. בִּלְשׁוֹן מִשְׁנָה: "שֶׁהִטִּיחַ בְּאִשְׁתּוֹ", עַל שֵׁם שֶׁהַזֶּרַע יוֹרֶה כַּחֵץ. וְאִם תֹּאמַר, הָיָה לוֹ לִכְתֹּב 'כִּמְטַחֵי קֶשֶׁת'! מִשְׁפַּט הַוָּי"ו לִכָּנֵס לְכָאן, כְּמוֹ: "בְּחַגְוֵי הַסֶּלַע" (שיר השירים ב, יד) מִגִּזְרַת: "וְהָיְתָה אַדְמַת יְהוּדָה לְמִצְרַיִם לְחָגָּא" (ישעיה יט, יז) וּמִגִּזְרַת: "יָחוֹגּוּ וְיָנוּעוּ כַּשִּׁכּוֹר" (תהלים קז, כז), וְכֵן: "קַצְוֵי אֶרֶץ" (שם סה, ו) מִגִּזְרַת 'קָצֶה': וַתֵּשֶׁב מִנֶּגֶד. כֵּיוָן שֶׁקָּרַב לָמוּת הוֹסִיפָה לְהִתְרַחֵק:

יז| אֶת קוֹל הַנַּעַר. מִכָּאן שֶׁיָּפָה תְּפִלַּת הַחוֹלֶה מִתְּפִלַּת אֲחֵרִים עָלָיו, וְהִיא קוֹדֶמֶת לְהִתְקַבֵּל: בַּאֲשֶׁר הוּא שָׁם. לְפִי מַעֲשִׂים שֶׁהוּא עוֹשֶׂה עַכְשָׁיו הוּא נִדּוֹן, וְלֹא לְפִי מַה שֶּׁהוּא עָתִיד לַעֲשׂוֹת; לְפִי שֶׁהָיוּ מַלְאֲכֵי הַשָּׁרֵת מְקַטְרְגִים וְאוֹמְרִים: רִבּוֹנוֹ שֶׁל עוֹלָם, מִי שֶׁעָתִיד לְהָמִית בָּנֶיךָ בַּצָּמָא אַתָּה מַעֲלֶה לוֹ בְּאֵר? וְהוּא מְשִׁיבָם: עַכְשָׁיו מַה הוּא, צַדִּיק אוֹ רָשָׁע? אָמְרוּ לוֹ: צַדִּיק. אָמַר לָהֶם: לְפִי מַעֲשָׂיו שֶׁל עַכְשָׁיו אֲנִי דָּנוֹ, וְזֶהוּ "בַּאֲשֶׁר הוּא שָׁם". וְהֵיכָן הֵמִית אֶת יִשְׂרָאֵל בַּצָּמָא? כְּשֶׁהִגְלָם נְבוּכַדְנֶצַּר, שֶׁנֶּאֱמַר: "מַשָּׂא בַּעְרָב וְגוֹ' לִקְרַאת צָמֵא הֵתָיוּ מָיִם" וְגוֹ' (ישעיה כא, יג-יד), כְּשֶׁהָיוּ מוֹלִיכִין אוֹתָן אֵצֶל עַרְבִיִּים הָיוּ יִשְׂרָאֵל אוֹמְרִים לַשַּׁבָּאִים, בְּבַקָּשָׁה מִכֶּם הוֹלִיכוּנוּ אֵצֶל בְּנֵי דּוֹדֵנוּ יִשְׁמָעֵאל וִירַחֲמוּ עָלֵינוּ, שֶׁנֶּאֱמַר: "אֹרְחוֹת דְּדָנִים" (שם), אַל תִּקְרֵי דְּדָנִים אֶלָּא דּוֹדִים; וְאֵלּוּ יוֹצְאִים לִקְרָאתָם וּמְבִיאִין לָהֶם בָּשָׂר מָלִיחַ וְנוֹדוֹת נְפוּחִים, כִּסְבוּרִים יִשְׂרָאֵל שֶׁהֵם מְלֵאִים מַיִם, וּכְשֶׁמַּכְנִיסוֹ לְתוֹךְ פִּיו וּפוֹתְחוֹ, הָרוּחַ נִכְנֶסֶת בְּגוּפוֹ וּמֵת:

כ| רֹבֶה קַשָּׁת. יוֹרֶה חִצִּים בַּקֶּשֶׁת: קַשָּׁת. עַל שֵׁם הָאֻמָּנוּת, כְּמוֹ: חַמָּר, גַּמָּל, צַיָּד, לְפִיכָךְ הַשִּׁי"ן מְדֻגֶּשֶׁת. הָיָה יוֹשֵׁב בַּמִּדְבָּר וּמְלַסְטֵם אֶת הָעוֹבְרִים, הוּא שֶׁנֶּאֱמַר: "יָדוֹ בַכֹּל" וְגוֹ' (לעיל טז, יב):

כא| מֵאֶרֶץ מִצְרָיִם. מִמְּקוֹם גִּדּוּלֶיהָ, שֶׁנֶּאֱמַר: "וְלָהּ שִׁפְחָה מִצְרִית" וְגוֹ' (לעיל טז, א), הַיְנוּ דְּאָמְרֵי אֱנָשֵׁי: זְרֹק חוּטְרָא לַאֲוִירָא, אַעִקָּרֵיהּ קָאֵי:

כב| אֱלֹהִים עִמְּךָ. לְפִי שֶׁרָאוּ שֶׁיָּצָא מִשְּׁכוּנַת סְדוֹם לְשָׁלוֹם, וְעִם הַמְּלָכִים נִלְחַם וְנָפְלוּ בְּיָדוֹ, וְנִפְקְדָה אִשְׁתּוֹ לִזְקוּנָיו:

כג| וּלְנִינִי וּלְנֶכְדִּי. עַד כָּאן רַחֲמֵי הָאָב עַל הַבֵּן: כַּחֶסֶד אֲשֶׁר עָשִׂיתִי עִמְּךָ תַּעֲשֶׂה עִמָּדִי. שֶׁאָמַרְתִּי לְךָ: "הִנֵּה אַרְצִי לְפָנֶיךָ" (לעיל כ, טו):

כה| וְהוֹכִחַ. נִתְוַכַּח עִמּוֹ עַל כָּךְ:

as a gift and as his contribution to the feast prepared there. **And the two of them established a covenant.** The covenant may have been formalized by a ceremony in which the animals were cut in half.[22]

28 **Abraham placed,** set aside, **seven ewes of the flock** he had given as a gift **by themselves.**

29 **Avimelekh said to Abraham: What are these seven ewes that you have placed by themselves?** If you intend to give them to me or to contribute them to the feast, why did you separate them from the rest of the flock?

30 **He,** Abraham, **said: Because you shall take seven ewes from me, so that it will be for me as a testament, that I dug this well.** These seven sheep will symbolize your consent that the well belongs to me, like an addendum to our covenant. By accepting them you give your assurance that your servants will not steal the well from me again.

31 **Therefore he called that place Beersheba, because both of them took an oath there.** The name evokes both the oath [*shevua*] about the well [*be'er*] and the number seven [*sheva*].

32 **They established a covenant in Beersheba.** Then **Avimelekh and Pikhol, the captain of his guard, arose, and they returned to the land of the Philistines,**[D] from where they had traveled to the place of Abraham's encampment.

33 **He,** Abraham, **planted a tamarisk in Beersheba, and he proclaimed there the name of the Lord, God of the Universe.** This was Abraham's practice throughout his travels. Wherever he encamped, he would build an altar, teach the residents of that place about God, and make His name known to them.

34 **Abraham** did not return immediately to Hebron, but **resided in the land of the Philistines** for **many days.**

The Binding of Isaac

GENESIS 22:1–19

The binding of Isaac is one of the most dramatic episodes in the Bible. It occurs shortly after the events recounted above, suggesting a connection between the stories. Abraham has achieved a measure of stability. After sending Ishmael away, there is quiet in his household, his heir is growing to maturity, and he has made peace with the neighboring kingdom. It is now, when his life has finally stabilized, that the test of the binding of Isaac will shake the very foundations of his existence.

22 1 **It was** not long **after these** previous **matters;**[23] **God tested** *Seventh aliya* **Abraham.** This is the first event explicitly described as a test planned by God. **And** God **said to him: Abraham; and he said: Here I am.** Abraham's response indicates not only that he has heard God's call but that he is ready to receive His command.

2 **He,** God, **said: Take now your son, your only one,**[D] as Abraham's other son had been banished and was not considered an heir, **whom you love: Isaac.** This long string of descriptions serves to underscore the monumental demand God is about to make. **And go you to the land of Moriah,** traditionally associated with the area of Jerusalem, **and offer him up there as a burnt offering upon one of the mountains that I will tell you.**

3 Once again, **Abraham** wasted no time. Since he had received the command only at night or just before, he **awoke early in the morning and saddled his donkey,** to carry the items he required for the journey. **He took two of his young men with him, and Isaac his son;** and **he cleaved the wood for the burnt offering,** as he could not know if he would find more wood on the way.[24] He **arose, and** he **went,** striding purposefully **to the place that God told him,** as he knew where it was.

DISCUSSION

21:32| **They returned to the land of the Philistines:** Beersheba, where Abraham was living at the time, was in Philistine territory, as indicated in verse 34. This phrase means that Avimelekh returned to the country's capital, from where he had come (Ramban; see Sforno).

22:2| **Take now your son, your only one:** God asked Abraham to make the ultimate sacrifice. Although child sacrifice was practiced in many cultures in antiquity, it was unusual for one to relinquish his son if he had no other children. Here this aspect is itself emphasized: "Your son, your only one," as though to say: You have no other children, and most likely you never will.

כח צֹאן וּבָקָר וַיִּתֵּן לַאֲבִימֶלֶךְ וַיִּכְרְתוּ שְׁנֵיהֶם בְּרִית: וַיַּצֵּב אַבְרָהָם אֶת־שֶׁבַע כִּבְשֹׂת
כט הַצֹּאן לְבַדְּהֶן: וַיֹּאמֶר אֲבִימֶלֶךְ אֶל־אַבְרָהָם מָה הֵנָּה שֶׁבַע כְּבָשֹׂת הָאֵלֶּה אֲשֶׁר
ל הִצַּבְתָּ לְבַדָּנָה: וַיֹּאמֶר כִּי אֶת־שֶׁבַע כְּבָשֹׂת תִּקַּח מִיָּדִי בַּעֲבוּר תִּהְיֶה־לִּי לְעֵדָה
לא כִּי חָפַרְתִּי אֶת־הַבְּאֵר הַזֹּאת: עַל־כֵּן קָרָא לַמָּקוֹם הַהוּא בְּאֵר שָׁבַע כִּי שָׁם
לב נִשְׁבְּעוּ שְׁנֵיהֶם: וַיִּכְרְתוּ בְרִית בִּבְאֵר שָׁבַע וַיָּקָם אֲבִימֶלֶךְ וּפִיכֹל שַׂר־צְבָאוֹ
לג וַיָּשֻׁבוּ אֶל־אֶרֶץ פְּלִשְׁתִּים: וַיִּטַּע אֶשֶׁל בִּבְאֵר שָׁבַע וַיִּקְרָא־שָׁם בְּשֵׁם יְהוָה אֵל
לד עוֹלָם: וַיָּגָר אַבְרָהָם בְּאֶרֶץ פְּלִשְׁתִּים יָמִים רַבִּים:

כב א וַיְהִי אַחַר הַדְּבָרִים הָאֵלֶּה וְהָאֱלֹהִים נִסָּה אֶת־אַבְרָהָם וַיֹּאמֶר אֵלָיו אַבְרָהָם יט שביעי
ב וַיֹּאמֶר הִנֵּנִי: וַיֹּאמֶר קַח־נָא אֶת־בִּנְךָ אֶת־יְחִידְךָ אֲשֶׁר־אָהַבְתָּ אֶת־יִצְחָק
וְלֶךְ־לְךָ אֶל־אֶרֶץ הַמֹּרִיָּה וְהַעֲלֵהוּ שָׁם לְעֹלָה עַל אַחַד הֶהָרִים אֲשֶׁר אֹמַר
ג אֵלֶיךָ: וַיַּשְׁכֵּם אַבְרָהָם בַּבֹּקֶר וַיַּחֲבֹשׁ אֶת־חֲמֹרוֹ וַיִּקַּח אֶת־שְׁנֵי נְעָרָיו אִתּוֹ וְאֵת
יִצְחָק בְּנוֹ וַיְבַקַּע עֲצֵי עֹלָה וַיָּקָם וַיֵּלֶךְ אֶל־הַמָּקוֹם אֲשֶׁר־אָמַר־לוֹ הָאֱלֹהִים:

רש"י

ל | **בעבור תהיה לי.** זאת, "לעדה" – לשון עדות של נקבה, כמו: "ועדה המצבה" (להלן לא, נב): **כי חפרתי את הבאר.** מריבים היו עליה רועי אבימלך ואומרים: אנחנו חפרנוה; אמרו ביניהם, כל מי שיתראה על הבאר ויעלו המים לקראתו שלו היא, ועלו לקראת אברהם:

לג | **אשל.** רב ושמואל, חד אמר: פרדס להביא ממנו פרות לאורחים בסעודה; וחד אמר: פונדק לאכסניא ובו כל מיני פרות. ומצינו לשון נטיעה באהלים, שנאמר: "ויטע אהלי אפדנו" (דניאל יא, מה): **ויקרא שם וגו'.** על ידי אותו אשל הקרא שמו של הקדוש ברוך הוא אלוה לכל העולם; לאחר שאוכלים ושותים אומר להם: ברכו למי שאכלתם משלו; סבורים אתם שמשלי אכלתם? משל מי שאמר והיה העולם אכלתם:

לד | **ימים רבים.** מרבים על של חברון; בחברון עשה עשרים וחמש שנה וכאן עשרים ושש, שהרי בן שבעים וחמש שנה היה בצאתו מחרן, אותה שנה "ויאהל וישב באלני ממרא" (לעיל יג, יח), שלא מצינו קדם לכן שנתישב אלא שם, שבכל מקומותיו היה כאורח חונה ונוסע והולך, שנאמר: "ויעבר אברם" (לעיל יב, ו), "ויעתק משם" (שם פסוק ח), "ויהי רעב בארץ וירד אברם מצרימה" (שם פסוק י), ובמצרים לא עשה אלא שלשה חדשים, שהרי שלחו פרעה, מיד "וילך למסעיו" (לעיל יג, ג) עד "ויאהל וישב באלני ממרא אשר בחברון" (שם פסוק יח), שם ישב עד שנהפכה סדום, מיד "ויסע משם אברהם" (לעיל כ, א) מפני בושה של לוט, ובא לארץ פלשתים, ובן תשעים ותשע שנה היה, שהרי בשלישי למילתו באו אצלו המלאכים, הרי עשרים וחמש שנה, וכאן כתיב: "ימים רבים" – מרבים על הראשונים, ולא בא הכתוב לסתום אלא לפרש, ואם היו מרבים עליהם שתי שנים או יותר היה מפרשם, על כרחך אינם יתרים יותר משנה, הרי עשרים ושש שנה. מיד יצא משם וחזר לחברון, ואותה שנה קדמה לפני עקדתו של יצחק שתים עשרה שנים. כך שנויה בסדר עולם:

פרק כב

א | **אחר הדברים האלה.** יש מרבותינו אומרים: אחר דבריו של שטן שהיה מקטרג ואומר: מכל סעודה שעשה אברהם לא הקריב לפניך פר אחד או איל אחד. אמר לו: כלום עשה אלא בשביל בנו, אלו הייתי אומר לו: זבח אותו לפני, לא היה מעכב. ויש אומרים: אחר דבריו של ישמעאל שהיה מתפאר על יצחק, שמל בן שלש עשרה שנה ולא מחה. אמר לו יצחק: באבר אחד אתה מיראני, אלו אמר לי הקדוש ברוך הוא: זבח עצמך לפני, לא הייתי מעכב: **הנני.** כך היא ענותם של חסידים, לשון ענוה הוא ולשון זמון:

ב | **קח נא.** אין 'נא' אלא לשון בקשה, אמר לו: בבקשה ממך עמד לי בזו, שלא יאמרו: הראשונות לא היה בהן ממש: **את בנך.** אמר לו: שני בנים יש לי. אמר לו: "את יחידך". אמר לו: זה יחיד לאמו וזה יחיד לאמו. אמר לו: "אשר אהבת". אמר לו: שניהם אני אוהב. אמר לו: "את יצחק". ולמה לא גלה לו מתחלה? שלא לערבבו פתאום ותזוח דעתו עליו ותטרף, וכדי לחבב עליו את המצוה וליתן לו שכר על כל דבור ודבור: **ארץ המריה.** ירושלים. וכן בדברי הימים (ב' ג, א): "לבנות את בית ה' בירושלם בהר המוריה". ורבותינו פרשו, על שם שמשם הוראה יוצאה לישראל. ואונקלוס תרגמו על שם עבודת הקטרת שיש בו מור נרד ושאר בשמים: **והעלהו.** לא אמר לו 'שחטהו', לפי שלא היה חפץ הקדוש ברוך הוא לשחטו אלא יעלהו להר לעשותו עולה, ומשהעלהו אמר לו הורידהו: **אחד ההרים.** הקדוש ברוך הוא מתהא הצדיקים ואחר כך מגלה להם, וכל זה כדי להרבות שכרן, וכן: "אל הארץ אשר אראך" (לעיל יב, א), וכן ביונה: "וקרא אליה את הקריאה" (יונה ג, ב):

ג | **וישכם.** נזדרז למצוה: **ויחבש.** הוא בעצמו, ולא צוה לאחד מעבדיו, שהאהבה מקלקלת השורה: **את שני נעריו.** ישמעאל ואליעזר, שאין אדם חשוב רשאי לצאת לדרך בלא שני אנשים, שאם יצטרך האחד לנקביו ויתרחק יהיה השני עמו: **ויבקע.** "ויבקע", כמו: "וצלחו הירדן" (שמואל ב' יט, יח), לשון בקוע, פינדר"א בלעז:

4 Abraham started his journey in Beersheba,[25] many hours from Jerusalem, on foot. Since he and Isaac had only one donkey and were traveling together, the journey took three days. **On the third day Abraham lifted up his eyes and saw the place**[D] **from afar.**

5 **Abraham said to his young men: Stay here with the donkey** and wait for me, **and I and the lad will go there; we will prostrate ourselves,** pray or sacrifice an offering, **and will return to you.** Abraham does not reveal his intention to sacrifice his son. Instead, he gives his attendants the impression that he and Isaac will sacrifice an offering together and then return.

6 **Abraham took the wood of the burnt offering and placed it upon Isaac his son.**[D] By carrying the wood, Isaac was already participating in the sacrifice. **He, Abraham, took in his hand the fire,** the kindling, **and the knife, and the two of them went together.**[D]

7 Now that they were alone **Isaac said to Abraham his father; he said: My father. He,** Abraham, **said** to him, as he had responded earlier to God: **Here I am, my son,** ready and attentive. Abraham has not become any less fatherly toward Isaac, and he listens with a loving ear, despite the knowledge that he must sacrifice him. **He,** Isaac, **said: Here are the fire and the wood, but** if our intention is to sacrifice an animal, **where is the lamb for a burnt offering?**

8 **Abraham said,**[D] in a poignant response: **God will Himself see to the lamb for a burnt offering, my son.** At this point,

Isaac surely began to ponder: What if we do not find a lamb? The juxtaposition of "burnt offering" and "my son" would have rung in his ears, as Isaac was no doubt aware of the practice of human sacrifice among the surrounding peoples. Nevertheless, the verse repeats the phrase indicating their solidarity: **And the two of them went together.** Earlier, Abraham was deeply troubled and Isaac was entirely innocent, and they went together. Now Isaac has heard Abraham's frightening words, but he continues to walk with his father, without any attempt to escape.

9 **They came to the place that God had told him; Abraham built the altar there, arranged the wood, and bound** the hands and feet of **Isaac his son**[D] to prevent him from moving, **and he placed him on the altar upon the wood.** He completed his preparation of Isaac as an offering.

10 **Abraham raised his hand**[D] **and took the knife to slaughter his son.**

11 **The angel of the Lord called to him from the heavens.** Since the angel is a messenger of God, its statement is the word of God. **And he said: Abraham, Abraham.** Again, **he,** Abraham, **said: Here I am,** always ready to be commanded, even in the midst of such a superhuman effort as this.

12 **He said: Do not raise your hand to the lad, and do not do anything to him;**[D] **for now I know that you are God-fearing,**[D] **and you did not withhold your son, your only one, from Me.**

DISCUSSION

22:4 | And saw the place: It is unclear what exactly Abraham saw. While he may have been able to identify the land of Moriah, he would still have been unable to pinpoint the precise spot of his destination. The Temple Mount rises above the city of Jerusalem, but it does not rise above the surrounding hills and is unremarkable to the casual onlooker. The Sages explain that the hill was marked by a heavenly sign, such as a cloud (see *Pirkei deRabbi Eliezer* 31; *Tanḥuma, Vayera* 46; Ramban).

22:6 | And placed it upon Isaac his son: The Sages, in light of the juxtaposition of this story to the death of Sarah mentioned soon afterward (23:2), maintain that the two events occurred at the same period. If so, Isaac would have been thirty-seven years old at the time (*Seder Olam Rabba* 1; *Vayikra Rabba* 20:2; *Tanḥuma, Vayera* 23). However, from the details of the events and the conversation between Abraham and Isaac it appears that Isaac was quite young, perhaps ten to twelve years old. He could not have been much younger, as he was old enough to carry

wood a considerable distance (see Ibn Ezra, verse 4).

The two of them went together: The word "together" recurs three times in this story. In this verse, it underscores the heartrending nature of their journey together. Father and son walked together, one agonizingly aware of the purpose of their journey, and the other entirely innocent, under the assumption he was about to participate in a religious ritual, but utterly unaware that he was to be the offering.

22:8 | Abraham said: One powerful aspect of the story of the binding of Isaac is the silence of the Torah with regard to Abraham's thoughts and emotions throughout the ordeal, as well as those of Isaac. Abraham could not perform his task immediately, but was obligated to complete a journey of several days, all the while nursing the thought that he would be required to kill his own son when he would reach his destination (see Ramban, verse 2). For him, those days would have been emotionally and psychologically devastating (see *Bereshit Rabba* 55:5).

One issue that must have struck Abraham was the apparent contradiction between God's earlier promise: "It is through Isaac that descendants will be accounted to you" (21:12), and His command to sacrifice Isaac as a burnt offering. Apart from the personal sacrifice and the contradiction between God's statements, the sheer moral repugnance of what he was being asked to do must also have weighed on Abraham, who was familiar with child sacrifice as one of the abominations of the Canaanites (see Deuteronomy 12:31).

Abraham was thrust into a personal crisis, facing the impending loss of his beloved only son and heir, and simultaneously into a crisis of faith, forcing him to reexamine both his relationship with God and the ideals in which he believed. The test of the binding of Isaac highlighted Abraham's profound compliance with God's instructions. When God commanded him to perform this act, he obeyed, without question or complaint (see *Tanḥuma, Vayera* 46).

ד ה ביום השלישי וישא אברהם את־עיניו וירא את־המקום מרחק: ויאמר אברהם
אל־נעריו שבו־לכם פה עם־החמור ואני והנער נלכה עד־כה ונשתחוה ונשובה
ו אליכם: ויקח אברהם את־עצי העלה וישם על־יצחק בנו ויקח בידו את־האש
ז ואת־המאכלת וילכו שניהם יחדו: ויאמר יצחק אל־אברהם אביו ויאמר אבי
ח ויאמר הנני בני ויאמר הנה האש והעצים ואיה השה לעלה: ויאמר אברהם
ט אלהים יראה־לו השה לעלה בני וילכו שניהם יחדו: ויבאו אל־המקום אשר
אמר־לו האלהים ויבן שם אברהם את־המזבח ויערך את־העצים ויעקד את־
י יצחק בנו וישם אתו על־המזבח ממעל לעצים: וישלח אברהם את־ידו ויקח
יא את־המאכלת לשחט את־בנו: ויקרא אליו מלאך יהוה מן־השמים ויאמר
יב אברהם | אברהם ויאמר הנני: ויאמר אל־תשלח ידך אל־הנער ואל־תעש לו
מאומה כי | עתה ידעתי כי־ירא אלהים אתה ולא חשכת את־בנך את־יחידך

רש"י

ד| **ביום השלישי.** למה איחר מלהראותו מיד? כדי שלא יאמרו: הממו ועירבבו פתאום וטרף דעתו, ואילו היה לו שהות להמלך אל לבו לא היה עושה: **וירא את המקום.** ראה ענן קשור על ההר:

ה| **עד כה.** כלומר, דרך מועט למקום אשר לפנינו. ומדרש אגדה, אראה היכן הוא מה שאמר לי המקום: "כה יהיה זרעך" (לעיל טו, ה): **ונשובה.** נתנבא שישובו שניהם:

ו| **המאכלת.** סכין, על שם שאוכלת את הבשר, כמה דתימא: "ואכלי תאכל בשר" (דברים לב, מב), ושמכשרת בשר לאכילה. דבר אחר, זאת נקראת מאכלת, על שם שישראל אוכלים מתן שכרה: **וילכו שניהם יחדו.** אברהם שהיה יודע שהולך לשחט את בנו, היה הולך ברצון ושמחה כיצחק שלא היה מרגיש בדבר:

ח| **יראה לו השה.** כלומר, יראה ויבחר לו השה, ואם אין שה – "לעולה בני". ואף על פי שהבין יצחק שהוא הולך להשחט, "וילכו שניהם יחדו" בלב שוה:

ט| **ויעקד.** ידיו ורגליו מאחוריו. הידים והרגלים ביחד היא עקדה, והוא לשון 'עקדים' (להלן ל, לט) שהיו קרסליהם לבנים, מקום שעוקדים אותן בו היה נכר:

יא| **אברהם אברהם.** לשון חבה הוא, שכופל את שמו:

יב| **אל תשלח.** לשחט. אמר לו: אלא לחנם באתי לכאן? אעשה בו חבלה ואוציא מעט דם! אמר לו: "אל תעש לו מאומה": **כי עתה ידעתי.** מעתה יש לי מה אשיב לשטן ולאומות, התמהים מה היא חבתי אצלך, ידעתי לי פתחון פה עכשיו, שרואים "כי ירא אלהים אתה":

DISCUSSION

22:9| **And bound Isaac his son:** The Torah does not describe Isaac's reaction. Did he scream or cry? Did he resign himself to his fate? Many commentaries take this silence, and his lack of any opposition or attempt to flee reported in the Torah, as an indication that Isaac willingly consented to serve as the burnt offering. From this moment, the relationship between God and Abraham's family took on a new dimension. The descendants of Abraham became not just descendants of a particular individual, but a group of people with a unique heritage and destiny, whose roots can be found in Isaac's selfless devotion.

22:10| **Abraham raised his hand:** The action is drawn out in this verse, not due to any hesitation on Abraham's part, but in order to emphasize the difficulty of the trial. Every movement had independent significance, and the fact that the reader's attention is drawn to every part of the act accentuates the difficulty of the test.

22:12| **Do not do anything to him:** Do not slaughter him or wound him in any way, even symbolically. Child sacrifice in the ancient world was sometimes performed by a token gesture, such as passing one's son through fire without actually burning him.

Now I know that you are God-fearing: Until the binding of Isaac, Abraham had always performed God's will out of love; see Isaiah 41:8, where God refers to "Abraham who loved Me." This episode emphasizes Abraham's fear of God, and his willingness to obey any command God would give him. The term "fear" in this context does not mean that Abraham was frightened. Rather, it denotes obedience even in the

13 **Abraham lifted his eyes and saw that behold, there was a ram after it had been caught in the thicket by its horns.** Rams, even those with long horns, are typically able to avoid being caught in thickets. Furthermore, this ram was in unusually close proximity to humans. Abraham immediately understood that this was no coincidence, but a sign.[26] Therefore, **Abraham went, took the ram, and offered it up as a burnt offering in place of his son.**[D]

14 **Abraham called the name of that place** where this occurred: **The Lord will see, as it is said to this day** with regard to that mountain: **On the mount where the Lord will be seen.**[D]

15 **The angel of the Lord called to Abraham a second time from the heavens.**

16 **He said: By Myself I have taken an oath – the utterance of the Lord – for because you have done this thing, and did not withhold your son, your only one,**

17 **for that I will bless you**[D] **and multiply your descendants as the stars of the heavens and as the sand that is upon the seashore, and your descendants shall inherit the gate of their enemies;**

18 **and all the nations of the earth shall bless themselves by your descendants,** meaning that they will bless each other with the prayer that they be like your descendants, **since you heeded My voice.**

19 **Abraham returned to his young men, and they arose and went together**[D] **to Beersheba; and Abraham lived** for some years more **in Beersheba.**

The Descendants of Nahor and the Birth of Rebecca

GENESIS 22:20–24

Immediately following the binding of Isaac, the Torah presents the family tree of Nahor, Abraham's brother. At first glance this appears unrelated to the preceding story, but the information is important for Isaac's future. The episode at Mount Moriah was not an ending, but the beginning of a new stage of life, which also had roots in a faraway land. Abraham's descendants survived and would multiply through Isaac, whom he had bound on the altar, and Rebecca, Isaac's future wife, born meanwhile in Haran.

20 *Maftir* **It was after these matters that it was told to Abraham, saying: Behold, Milka,** wife of Nahor, **she too has borne children to your brother Nahor.** This particular form of the word "after" indicates that considerable time had passed between the two events.[27] The news reached Abraham from Haran, on the border of modern-day Turkey and Syria, where Nahor and his family lived.

21 Nahor fathered several sons: **Utz,**[D] with a traditional Aramaic name, who was **his firstborn, Buz his brother, and Kemuel, father of Aram,** who was apparently an important Aramean leader. Apart from Abraham, Terah's descendants became Arameans.

22 **Kesed, Hazo, Pildash, Yidlaf, and Betuel,** Nahor's youngest son.

23 **Betuel begot Rebecca.** He had other children as well, and the Torah later introduces his son Laban, who was older than Rebecca. Nevertheless, in this context the birth of Rebecca is of more significance, as she will marry Isaac.[28] At this point

DISCUSSION

absence of understanding, benefit, or pleasure at what he was commanded do. It involves an acceptance that God's word is the ultimate law, above all other statutes, thoughts, and plans that one may have.

22:13 | **And offered it up as a burnt offering in place of his son:** Abraham sacrificed this ram with all of the devotion and loyalty he had mustered to sacrifice his son. Consequently, the ram served merely as a physical replacement for Isaac, and is not considered a separate offering (see *Bemidbar Rabba* 17:2, 55:5). This idea helps explain the surprising statement of the Sages that the ashes of Isaac are piled on the altar (see, e.g., Jerusalem Talmud, *Ta'anit* 2:1). Although Isaac himself was not actually slaughtered, it is as though he was sacrificed, because the ram merely took his place on the altar.

Many commentaries suggest that the concept underlying all animal sacrifice is that the animal substitutes for the person bringing the offering (see, e.g., Ramban, Leviticus 1:9; *Sefer HaḤinnukh*, 95). The animal's owner sacrifices himself symbolically, in effect saying: I am willing to offer myself completely to God. Since I may not sacrifice myself, I perform the act instead through this animal.

22:14 | **On the mount where the Lord will be seen:** Although this is referring to Mount Moriah, it can also be seen as an allusion to Mount Sinai, as God revealed Himself there as well (see Exodus 24:10). There is a midrash that the two mountains were one and the same, and that the Temple Mount was temporarily transported from Canaan to the Sinai desert for the giving of the Torah (*Shoḥer Tov* 68:9). The midrash vividly illustrates the idea that Abraham's willingness to deliver Isaac's soul to heaven on Mount Moriah led conceptually and spiritually to God's descent upon Mount Sinai to give the Torah to their descendants.

22:17 | **I will bless you:** The reward for the binding of Isaac was to extend to many generations of Abraham's descendants, as this episode was a turning point in which the character of

יג מִמֶּנִּי: וַיִּשָּׂא אַבְרָהָם אֶת־עֵינָיו וַיַּרְא וְהִנֵּה־אַיִל אַחַר נֶאֱחַז בַּסְּבַךְ בְּקַרְנָיו וַיֵּלֶךְ
יד אַבְרָהָם וַיִּקַּח אֶת־הָאַיִל וַיַּעֲלֵהוּ לְעֹלָה תַּחַת בְּנוֹ: וַיִּקְרָא אַבְרָהָם שֵׁם־הַמָּקוֹם
טו הַהוּא יְהוָה ׀ יִרְאֶה אֲשֶׁר יֵאָמֵר הַיּוֹם בְּהַר יְהוָה יֵרָאֶה: וַיִּקְרָא מַלְאַךְ יְהוָה אֶל־
טז אַבְרָהָם שֵׁנִית מִן־הַשָּׁמָיִם: וַיֹּאמֶר בִּי נִשְׁבַּעְתִּי נְאֻם־יְהוָה כִּי יַעַן אֲשֶׁר עָשִׂיתָ
יז אֶת־הַדָּבָר הַזֶּה וְלֹא חָשַׂכְתָּ אֶת־בִּנְךָ אֶת־יְחִידֶךָ: כִּי־בָרֵךְ אֲבָרֶכְךָ וְהַרְבָּה אַרְבֶּה
אֶת־זַרְעֲךָ כְּכוֹכְבֵי הַשָּׁמַיִם וְכַחוֹל אֲשֶׁר עַל־שְׂפַת הַיָּם וְיִרַשׁ זַרְעֲךָ אֵת שַׁעַר
יח יט אֹיְבָיו: וְהִתְבָּרְכוּ בְזַרְעֲךָ כֹּל גּוֹיֵי הָאָרֶץ עֵקֶב אֲשֶׁר שָׁמַעְתָּ בְּקֹלִי: וַיָּשָׁב אַבְרָהָם
אֶל־נְעָרָיו וַיָּקֻמוּ וַיֵּלְכוּ יַחְדָּו אֶל־בְּאֵר שָׁבַע וַיֵּשֶׁב אַבְרָהָם בִּבְאֵר שָׁבַע:
כ וַיְהִי אַחֲרֵי הַדְּבָרִים הָאֵלֶּה וַיֻּגַּד לְאַבְרָהָם לֵאמֹר הִנֵּה יָלְדָה מִלְכָּה גַם־הִוא בָּנִים מפטיר
כא כב לְנָחוֹר אָחִיךָ: אֶת־עוּץ בְּכֹרוֹ וְאֶת־בּוּז אָחִיו וְאֶת־קְמוּאֵל אֲבִי אֲרָם: וְאֶת־כֶּשֶׂד

רש"י

יג| וְהִנֵּה אַיִל. מוּכָן הָיָה לְכָךְ מִשֵּׁשֶׁת יְמֵי בְרֵאשִׁית: אַחַר. אַחֲרֵי שֶׁאָמַר לוֹ הַמַּלְאָךְ: "אַל תִּשְׁלַח יָדְךָ" רָאָהוּ כְּשֶׁהוּא נֶאֱחָז, וְהוּא שֶׁמְּתַרְגְּמִינַן: "וּזְקַף אַבְרָהָם יָת עֵינוֹהִי בָּתַר אִלֵּין": בַּסְּבַךְ. אִילָן: בְּקַרְנָיו. שֶׁהָיָה רָץ אֵצֶל אַבְרָהָם, וְהַשָּׂטָן סוֹכְכוֹ וּמְעַרְבְּבוֹ בָּאִילָנוֹת: תַּחַת בְּנוֹ. מֵאַחַר שֶׁכָּתוּב: "וַיַּעֲלֵהוּ לְעֹלָה" לֹא חָסֵר הַמִּקְרָא כְּלוּם, מַהוּ "תַּחַת בְּנוֹ"? עַל כָּל עֲבוֹדָה שֶׁעָשָׂה מִמֶּנּוּ הָיָה מִתְפַּלֵּל וְאוֹמֵר: יְהִי רָצוֹן שֶׁתְּהֵא זוֹ כְּאִלּוּ הִיא עֲשׂוּיָה בִּבְנִי, כְּאִלּוּ בְּנִי שָׁחוּט, כְּאִלּוּ דָּמוֹ זָרוּק, כְּאִלּוּ בְּנִי מֻפְשָׁט, כְּאִלּוּ הוּא נִקְטָר וְעָשׂוּי דֶּשֶׁן:

יד| ה' יִרְאֶה. פְּשׁוּטוֹ כְּתַרְגּוּמוֹ: ה' יִבְחַר וְיִרְאֶה לוֹ אֶת הַמָּקוֹם הַזֶּה לְהַשְׁרוֹת בּוֹ שְׁכִינָתוֹ וּלְהַקְרִיב כָּאן קָרְבָּנוֹת:

אֲשֶׁר יֵאָמֵר הַיּוֹם. שֶׁיֹּאמְרוּ לִימֵי הַדּוֹרוֹת עָלָיו: בְּהַר זֶה יֵרָאֶה הַקָּדוֹשׁ בָּרוּךְ הוּא לְעַמּוֹ: הַיּוֹם. הַיָּמִים הָעֲתִידִים, כְּמוֹ 'עַד הַיּוֹם הַזֶּה' שֶׁבְּכָל הַמִּקְרָא, שֶׁדּוֹרוֹת הַבָּאִים הַקּוֹרְאִים אֶת הַמִּקְרָא אוֹמְרִים עַל יוֹם שֶׁעוֹמְדִים בּוֹ: 'הַיּוֹם הַזֶּה'. וּמִדְרַשׁ אַגָּדָה, "ה' יִרְאֶה" עֲקֵדָה זוֹ לִסְלֹחַ לְיִשְׂרָאֵל בְּכָל שָׁנָה וּלְהַצִּילָם מִן הַפֻּרְעָנוּת, כְּדֵי שֶׁיֵּאָמֵר הַיּוֹם הַזֶּה בְּכָל דּוֹרוֹת הַבָּאִים: בְּהַר ה' יֵרָאֶה אֶפְרוֹ שֶׁל יִצְחָק צָבוּר וְעוֹמֵד לְכַפָּרָה:

יז| בָּרֵךְ אֲבָרֶכְךָ. אַחַת לְאָב וְאַחַת לַבֵּן: וְהַרְבָּה אַרְבֶּה. אַחַת לְאָב וְאַחַת לַבֵּן:

יט| וַיֵּשֶׁב אַבְרָהָם בִּבְאֵר שָׁבַע. לֹא יְשִׁיבָה מַמָּשׁ, שֶׁהֲרֵי בְּחֶבְרוֹן הָיָה יוֹשֵׁב. שְׁתֵּים עֶשְׂרֵה שָׁנִים לִפְנֵי עֲקֵדָתוֹ שֶׁל יִצְחָק יָצָא מִבְּאֵר שֶׁבַע וּבָא לוֹ לְחֶבְרוֹן, כְּמוֹ שֶׁנֶּאֱמַר: "וַיָּגָר אַבְרָהָם בְּאֶרֶץ פְּלִשְׁתִּים יָמִים רַבִּים" (לעיל כא, לד), מְרֻבִּים מִשֶּׁל חֶבְרוֹן הָרִאשׁוֹנִים, וְהֵם עֶשְׂרִים וָשֵׁשׁ שָׁנָה כְּמוֹ שֶׁפֵּרַשְׁנוּ לְמַעְלָה:

כ| אַחֲרֵי הַדְּבָרִים הָאֵלֶּה וַיֻּגַּד וְגוֹ'. בְּשׁוּבוֹ מֵהַר הַמּוֹרִיָּה הָיָה אַבְרָהָם מְהַרְהֵר וְאוֹמֵר: אִלּוּ הָיָה בְּנִי שָׁחוּט כְּבָר הָיָה הוֹלֵךְ בְּלֹא בָנִים, הָיָה לִי לְהַשִּׂיאוֹ אִשָּׁה מִבְּנוֹת עָנֵר אֶשְׁכּוֹל וּמַמְרֵא; בִּשְּׂרוֹ הַקָּדוֹשׁ בָּרוּךְ הוּא שֶׁנּוֹלְדָה רִבְקָה בַּת זוּגוֹ. וְזֶהוּ "הַדְּבָרִים הָאֵלֶּה", הִרְהוּרֵי דְּבָרִים שֶׁהָיוּ עַל יְדֵי הָעֲקֵדָה: גַּם הִוא. אַף הִיא הִשְׁוַת מִשְׁפְּחוֹתֶיהָ לְמִשְׁפְּחוֹת אַבְרָהָם שְׁתֵּים עֶשְׂרֵה, מָה אַבְרָהָם, שְׁבָטִים

DISCUSSION

Abraham and his descendants was fundamentally transformed.

22:19| **And went together:** Yet again, Abraham and Isaac are described as walking silently together. Each now carries his own memories and experiences from that day, while they walk together with the attendants, who know nothing of the event. The binding of Isaac was exclusive to the participants: father, son, and God.

22:21| **Utz:** Earlier, Utz was listed as the first-born son of Aram, son of Shem (10:23). The same name was also given to the firstborn of Dishan, son of Se'ir the Horite, and a younger son was called Aran (36:28). Evidently, the name Utz was commonly given in families who also favored the name Aram or Aran. It may be surmised that the land of Utz, mentioned in the beginning of the book of Job, could have been located in the region of Aram (see Rashi, Job 1:1). Although there is a different verse which refers to a land of Utz located within Edom (Lamentations 4:21), it is possible that Utz was a tribe that originated in Aramean territory, and some of its members later migrated southward to Edom.

Abraham knew that there was at least one woman in the family eligible for Isaac, and he may have had Rebecca in mind when he later sent a messenger to Haran to seek a wife for his son

(chap. 24). **These eight** sons **Milka bore to Nahor, Abraham's brother.**

24 **And his,** Nahor's, **concubine, and her name was Re'uma, she too**[D] **bore** sons: **Tevah, Gaham, Tahash, and Maakha.**

DISCUSSION

22:24 | **She too:** The naming of all of Nahor's sons is significant, as their number amounts to twelve, the same as the number of Jacob's sons.

Twelve is considered a complete number. Just like Abraham's family, Nahor's family, which included both leaders and ordinary individuals,

was a complete unit (*Bereshit Rabba* 57:3; see Rashi, verse 20).

Parashat
Hayei Sarah

The Death of Sarah and Her Burial
GENESIS 23:1–20

It might be inferred from the juxtaposition of the death of Sarah to the story of the binding of Isaac that Sarah's death immediately followed the binding of her son. The Sages maintain that this was indeed the case. However, a straightforward reading of the verses indicates that Isaac was a young boy at the time of the binding. If so, a long time passed from then until his mother's death.

Although nothing is stated about the events of Sarah's life after the birth of Isaac, one can assume that she was busy raising him. During this period, Sarah likely lived in Hebron, where she died, while Abraham wandered between several locations.

This section relates Abraham's initial purchase of property in the land of Canaan, the very first example of ownership of the land by the Jewish people. The Torah provides precise details of the transaction, including the location of the property purchased for the burial of Sarah, where future generations of the family would also be buried, the person from whom it was purchased, as well the public and ceremonious nature of the event.

23 1 **The lifetime of Sarah was one hundred and twenty-seven years, the years of the life of Sarah.** A literal rendition of the verse would read: The lifetime of Sarah was one hundred years and twenty years, and seven years, the years of the life of Sarah. Some commentaries explain that the repetition of "years" in the verse teaches that at each stage of her life, whether she was seven, twenty-seven, or one hundred, Sarah exhibited the same good qualities.[1] The concluding phrase, "the years of the life of Sarah," indicates that in each of those stages she lived a full and complete life.

2 **Sarah died in Kiryat Arba, which is Hebron, in the land of Canaan; Abraham came** from Beersheba, where he lived before and after the binding of Isaac, **to lament Sarah,** as is customary when mourning someone, **and to weep** and move others to weep **for her.**

3 After mourning for Sarah, her husband must find a place to bury her. **Abraham arose from before his dead, and he spoke to the children of Het,**[D] their leaders and elders, who sat at the entrance to the city of Hebron, **saying:**

4 Although **I am a foreigner** here, my family and I have lived here for many years. **And** in addition, I am **a resident alien**

כג וְאֶת־חֲזוֹ וְאֶת־פִּלְדָּשׁ וְאֶת־יִדְלָף וְאֵת בְּתוּאֵל: וּבְתוּאֵל יָלַד אֶת־רִבְקָה שְׁמֹנָה

כד אֵלֶּה יָלְדָה מִלְכָּה לְנָחוֹר אֲחִי אַבְרָהָם: וּפִילַגְשׁוֹ וּשְׁמָהּ רְאוּמָה וַתֵּלֶד גַּם־הִוא אֶת־טֶבַח וְאֶת־גַּחַם וְאֶת־תַּחַשׁ וְאֶת־מַעֲכָה:

רש"י

כג | וּבְתוּאֵל יָלַד אֶת־רִבְקָה. כָּל הַיִּחוּסִין הַלָּלוּ לֹא נִכְתְּבוּ אֶלָּא בִּשְׁבִיל פָּסוּק זֶה:

שֶׁיָּצְאוּ מִיַּעֲקֹב שְׁמֹנָה בְּנֵי הַגְּבִירוֹת וְאַרְבָּעָה בְּנֵי שְׁפָחוֹת, אַף חֵלּוּ שְׁמֹנָה בְּנֵי גְּבִירוֹת וְאַרְבָּעָה בְּנֵי פִילַגֶשׁ:

פרשת

חיי שרה

א וַיִּהְיוּ חַיֵּי שָׂרָה מֵאָה שָׁנָה וְעֶשְׂרִים שָׁנָה וְשֶׁבַע שָׁנִים שְׁנֵי חַיֵּי שָׂרָה: וַתָּמָת שָׂרָה

ב בְּקִרְיַת אַרְבַּע הִוא חֶבְרוֹן בְּאֶרֶץ כְּנָעַן וַיָּבֹא אַבְרָהָם לִסְפֹּד לְשָׂרָה וְלִבְכֹּתָהּ:

ג וַיָּקָם אַבְרָהָם מֵעַל פְּנֵי מֵתוֹ וַיְדַבֵּר אֶל־בְּנֵי־חֵת לֵאמֹר: גֵּר־וְתוֹשָׁב אָנֹכִי עִמָּכֶם

רש"י

א | וַיִּהְיוּ חַיֵּי שָׂרָה מֵאָה שָׁנָה וְעֶשְׂרִים שָׁנָה וְשֶׁבַע שָׁנִים. לְכָךְ נִכְתַּב שָׁנָה בְּכָל כְּלָל וּכְלָל, לוֹמַר לְךָ שֶׁכָּל אֶחָד נִדְרָשׁ לְעַצְמוֹ: בַּת מֵאָה כְּבַת עֶשְׂרִים לְחֵטְא, מַה בַּת עֶשְׂרִים לֹא חָטְאָה שֶׁהֲרֵי אֵינָהּ בַּת עָנְשִׁין, אַף בַּת מֵאָה בְּלֹא חֵטְא, וּבַת עֶשְׂרִים כְּבַת שֶׁבַע לְיֹפִי: שְׁנֵי חַיֵּי שָׂרָה. כֻּלָּן שָׁוִין לְטוֹבָה:

ב | בְּקִרְיַת אַרְבַּע. עַל שֵׁם אַרְבָּעָה עֲנָקִים שֶׁהָיוּ שָׁם אֲחִימָן שֵׁשַׁי וְתַלְמַי וַאֲחִיהֶם, דָּבָר אַחֵר, עַל שֵׁם אַרְבָּעָה זוּגוֹת שֶׁנִּקְבְּרוּ שָׁם, אִישׁ וְאִשְׁתּוֹ: אָדָם וְחַוָּה, אַבְרָהָם וְשָׂרָה, יִצְחָק וְרִבְקָה, יַעֲקֹב וְלֵאָה: מִפְּנֵי שֶׁבַע "לִסְפֹּד לְשָׂרָה וְלִבְכֹּתָהּ". וְנִסְמְכָה מִיתַת שָׂרָה

ד | גֵּר־וְתוֹשָׁב אָנֹכִי עִמָּכֶם. גֵּר מֵאֶרֶץ אַחֶרֶת וְנִתְיַשַּׁבְתִּי עִמָּכֶם. וּמִדְרַשׁ אַגָּדָה: אִם תִּרְצוּ, הֲרֵינִי גֵּר, וְאִם לָאו, אֶהְיֶה תוֹשָׁב וְאֶטְּלֶנָּה מִן הַדִּין, שֶׁאָמַר לִי הַקָּדוֹשׁ בָּרוּךְ

לַעֲקֵדַת יִצְחָק, לְפִי שֶׁעַל יְדֵי בְּשׂוֹרַת הָעֲקֵדָה שֶׁנִּזְדַּמֵּן בְּנָהּ לִשְׁחִיטָה וְכִמְעַט שֶׁלֹּא נִשְׁחַט, פָּרְחָה נִשְׁמָתָהּ וּמֵתָה:

DISCUSSION

23:3 | And he spoke to the children of Het: Although the children of Het lived in Canaan at the time and were considered one of the Canaanite nations, they were originally part of the Hitite nation that resided north of Canaan. They were called "the children of Het" or "the smaller Hitites," because they were a branch of

the larger Hitite nation. The children of Het presumably spoke in the Canaanite language rather than Hitite. However, they apparently preserved some of their ancestral customs as well as their legal system, which was similar to that of the residents of Haran, the land of Abraham's origin. Haran was not far from the area in Asia Minor

where the Hitites dwelled, which is known today as Anatolia. Consequently, it is possible that Abraham was on friendly terms with the children of Het, aside from the personal relationships he had developed with certain individuals from Kiryat Arba (see 14:13, 24).

with you: I do not have rights in this place, but I am an old acquaintance of yours. Therefore, **give me** a portion of your land that can serve as **a burial portion**[D] **with you, and I will bury my dead from before me.**

5 **The children of Het answered Abraham, saying to him.** It is possible that they discussed the matter among themselves first, before providing him with an official response.

6 **Hear us, my lord:** Although you say that you are a foreigner and a resident alien, you are not merely an ordinary person. Rather, **you are a prince of God**[D] **in our midst,** as your status is greater than that of the head of a small tribe. Therefore, **in the choicest of our graves bury your dead; none of us shall withhold his grave from you, from burying your dead,** as you may choose a burial plot in any place that you desire. The local residents thereby declared that they have given Abraham informal rights to their land.

7 **Abraham arose, and prostrated himself,** or bowed his head,[2] in a formal gesture of respect and gratitude, **before the people of the land, before the children of Het.**

8 Despite his expression of gratitude, Abraham did not wish to bury his wife in the land of the children of Het. Rather, he wanted to purchase a separate piece of property. **He spoke with them, saying: If you are** truly **willing to** fulfill my request and **bury my dead from before me, heed me, and intercede for me with** a specific individual, **Efron son of Tzohar,**

9 that he will give me the Cave of Makhpela,[D] which was so called because it is a double [*kefula*] cave, **that is his, which is at the edge of his field; he shall give it to me for a full price in your midst for a burial portion.** Despite their offer to allow him to use any property he chose, Abraham insisted on purchasing a plot at full price, as he wanted it to be property held by the family in perpetuity. With regard to the retention of an

ancestral inheritance, see, e.g., I Kings 21:1–3 and Nehemiah 2:2–5.

10 **And Efron,** who was not necessarily an important member of the city, **was living** at that time **among the children of Het; and Efron the Hitite answered Abraham in hearing of the children of Het, of all those coming to his city gate.** He too conducted himself ceremoniously, as he approached the city council and issued a public declaration, **saying:**

11 **No, my lord,** you offered to purchase a portion of my field, but I cannot accept that proposal. Rather, **heed me: The** entire **field I have given to you,**[3] **and the cave that is in it, I have given it to you; in the eyes of my people,** who are all listening to my declaration, **I have given it to you** and will not deter you from taking it. I will clear the land for such a distinguished man as yourself, and the entire plot will belong to you; go **bury your dead.**

12 **Abraham prostrated himself** a second time **before the people of the land,**[D] thereby formally expressing his gratitude for Efron's generous offer.

13 Despite the offer, **he,** Abraham, **spoke to Efron in the hearing of the people of the land, saying: Rather, if only you will heed me,** when you originally said: No, my lord, heed me, I indeed listened to you. Now it is my turn to request that you listen to me: **I have given you,** that is, I am giving you, **the silver for the field** in order to purchase it; please **take it from me, and I will bury my dead there.**

14 Until this point, Efron had spoken generally about the matter; now he must set a price. Therefore, **Efron responded to Abraham, saying to him:**

15 **My lord, heed me.** This **land** is **worth four hundred shekels of silver,**[D] **between me and you what is it?** We are close friends, and consequently such a small plot of land should not

---

DISCUSSION

23:4 | Give me a burial portion: Abraham did not request a plot inside their cemetery, but an independent portion of land that could be used for burial. The phrase "burial portion" means an important familial plot of land that passes down as an inheritance. In other words, Abraham sought to purchase not only a burial place for Sarah, but also a plot where his descendants could be buried in the future, as indeed occurred.

23:6 | You are a prince of God: Avimelekh was also informed in a dream that Abraham was a prophet (20:7). It is likely that Abraham had gained a reputation as a holy man. The special honor the Hitites accord him is reminiscent of

the description of Malkitzedek king of Shalem: Not merely a king, but a king who is also a priest to the Most High (14:18).

23:9 | The Cave of Makhpela: Since no one has entered the actual Cave of Makhpela for a long time, its inner structure is not definitively known. Even in the past it was uncertain whether it was called a double cave because there is an additional cave inside, whether it consists of two caves adjacent to one another, or if one cave is on top of the other (see Rashi; Ibn Ezra; *Eiruvin* 53a).

Some Sages claim that this was the ancient burial cave where Adam and Eve were buried. Abraham was aware of its existence, and as

he lived in Hebron, he even knew the identity of its owner. Perhaps this is why he wanted to bury Sarah specifically there, and was willing to pay its full price (*Yalkut Shimoni*, Joshua 28). It is further possible that Abraham had already contemplated purchasing this cave, as he did not know whether he or Sarah would die first, but had not yet actually done so. Indeed, the fact that he arrived from afar and was not in Hebron at the time might indicate that her death came as a surprise to him.

23:12 | Abraham prostrated himself before the people of the land: This ceremony is very similar to the standard manner of purchase in the Middle East, which follows the traditional ↤

ה תְּנוּ לִי אֲחֻזַּת־קֶבֶר עִמָּכֶם וְאֶקְבְּרָה מֵתִי מִלְּפָנָי: וַיַּעֲנוּ בְנֵי־חֵת אֶת־אַבְרָהָם
ו לֵאמֹר לוֹ: שְׁמָעֵנוּ ׀ אֲדֹנִי נְשִׂיא אֱלֹהִים אַתָּה בְּתוֹכֵנוּ בְּמִבְחַר קְבָרֵינוּ קְבֹר
ז אֶת־מֵתֶךָ אִישׁ מִמֶּנּוּ אֶת־קִבְרוֹ לֹא־יִכְלֶה מִמְּךָ מִקְּבֹר מֵתֶךָ: וַיָּקָם אַבְרָהָם
ח וַיִּשְׁתַּחוּ לְעַם־הָאָרֶץ לִבְנֵי־חֵת: וַיְדַבֵּר אִתָּם לֵאמֹר אִם־יֵשׁ אֶת־נַפְשְׁכֶם לִקְבֹּר
ט אֶת־מֵתִי מִלְּפָנַי שְׁמָעוּנִי וּפִגְעוּ־לִי בְּעֶפְרוֹן בֶּן־צֹחַר: וְיִתֶּן־לִי אֶת־מְעָרַת
הַמַּכְפֵּלָה אֲשֶׁר־לוֹ אֲשֶׁר בִּקְצֵה שָׂדֵהוּ בְּכֶסֶף מָלֵא יִתְּנֶנָּה לִּי בְּתוֹכְכֶם לַאֲחֻזַּת־
י קָבֶר: וְעֶפְרוֹן יֹשֵׁב בְּתוֹךְ בְּנֵי־חֵת וַיַּעַן עֶפְרוֹן הַחִתִּי אֶת־אַבְרָהָם בְּאָזְנֵי בְנֵי־חֵת
יא לְכֹל בָּאֵי שַׁעַר־עִירוֹ לֵאמֹר: לֹא־אֲדֹנִי שְׁמָעֵנִי הַשָּׂדֶה נָתַתִּי לָךְ וְהַמְּעָרָה אֲשֶׁר־
יב בּוֹ לְךָ נְתַתִּיהָ לְעֵינֵי בְנֵי־עַמִּי נְתַתִּיהָ לָּךְ קְבֹר מֵתֶךָ: וַיִּשְׁתַּחוּ אַבְרָהָם לִפְנֵי
יג עַם־הָאָרֶץ: וַיְדַבֵּר אֶל־עֶפְרוֹן בְּאָזְנֵי עַם־הָאָרֶץ לֵאמֹר אַךְ אִם־אַתָּה לוּ שְׁמָעֵנִי
יד נָתַתִּי כֶּסֶף הַשָּׂדֶה קַח מִמֶּנִּי וְאֶקְבְּרָה אֶת־מֵתִי שָׁמָּה: וַיַּעַן עֶפְרוֹן אֶת־אַבְרָהָם
טו לֵאמֹר לוֹ: אֲדֹנִי שְׁמָעֵנִי אֶרֶץ אַרְבַּע מֵאֹת שֶׁקֶל־כֶּסֶף בֵּינִי וּבֵינְךָ מַה־הִוא וְאֶת־

רש״י

הוּא: "לְזַרְעֲךָ אֶתֵּן אֶת הָאָרֶץ הַזֹּאת" (לעיל יב, ז): אֲחֻזַּת קֶבֶר. אֲחֻזַּת קַרְקַע לְבֵית הַקְּבָרוֹת:

ו] לֹא יִכְלֶה. לֹא יִמְנַע, כְּמוֹ: "לֹא תִכְלָא רַחֲמֶיךָ" (תהלים מ, יב), וּכְמוֹ: "וַיִּכָּלֵא הַגֶּשֶׁם" (לעיל ח, ב):

ח] נַפְשְׁכֶם. רְצוֹנְכֶם: וּפִגְעוּ לִי. לְשׁוֹן בַּקָּשָׁה, כְּמוֹ: "אַל תִּפְגְּעִי בִי" (רות א, טז):

ט] הַמַּכְפֵּלָה. בַּיִת וַעֲלִיָּה עַל גַּבָּיו. דָּבָר אַחֵר, שֶׁכְּפוּלָה בְּזוּגוֹת: בְּכֶסֶף מָלֵא. שָׁלֵם, כָּל שָׁוְיָהּ:

י] וְעֶפְרוֹן יֹשֵׁב. כְּתִיב חָסֵר, אוֹתוֹ הַיּוֹם מִנּוּהוּ שׁוֹטֵר עֲלֵיהֶם; מִפְּנֵי חֲשִׁיבוּתוֹ שֶׁל אַבְרָהָם שֶׁהָיָה צָרִיךְ לוֹ, עָלָה לִגְדֻלָּה: לְכֹל בָּאֵי שַׁעַר עִירוֹ. שֶׁכֻּלָּן בִּטְּלוּ מִמְּלַאכְתָּן וּבָאוּ לִגְמֹל חֶסֶד לְשָׂרָה:

יא] לֹא אֲדֹנִי. לֹא תִקְנֶה אוֹתָהּ בְּדָמִים: נָתַתִּי לָךְ. הֲרֵי הִיא כְּמוֹ שֶׁנְּתַתִּיהָ לָךְ:

יג] אַךְ אִם אַתָּה לוּ שְׁמָעֵנִי. אַתָּה אוֹמֵר לִי לִשְׁמֹעַ לָךְ וְלִקַּח חִנָּם, אֲנִי אֵי אֶפְשִׁי בְּכָךְ. אַךְ אִם אַתָּה לוּ שְׁמָעֵנִי. הַלְוַאי וְתִשְׁמָעֵנִי: נָתַתִּי. דּוֹנִי״ בְּלַעַז, מוּכָן הוּא אֶצְלִי וְהַלְוַאי נְתַתִּיו לְךָ כְּבָר:

טו] בֵּינִי וּבֵינְךָ. בֵּין שְׁנֵי אוֹהֲבִים כְּמוֹתֵנוּ "מַה הִיא" – חֲשׁוּבָה לִכְלוּם, אֶלָּא הַנַּח אֶת הַמֶּכֶר "וְאֶת מֵתְךָ קְבֹר":

DISCUSSION

system of the marketplaces of the region. An individual approaches a seller and requests to purchase an item. The seller responds by saying that the prospective buyer is such a good friend that he will not sell it to him, but he will give it to him as a gift. This response, however, is not necessarily indicative of good will on his part. The purchaser, who understands that this response is not to be taken literally but is merely ceremonious, continues to insist that he would like to purchase the item, and begs the seller to set a price for it. The seller would then typically stipulate a high price, which was occasionally ten times the actual value of the item, after which the negotiations for the purchase would begin. The sale was concluded when they established a price with which both sides were satisfied. If these formal rules were not followed during a purchase, both buyer and seller might feel that the transaction had not been conducted properly. This conversation between Abraham and Efron is possibly the first official documentation of this method of purchase; however, it did not proceed precisely along the lines described above, as will be seen.

23:15| **Four hundred shekels of silver:** Although the precise property values in those times are unknown, it can be inferred from elsewhere that the value of a very large plot of

concern us; **and** therefore **bury your dead,** and let us not suffer delays over the price.

16 **Abraham heeded Efron; and Abraham weighed for Efron the silver that he spoke in the hearing of the children of Het.** It is almost certain that this silver was not in the form of minted coins; it was more likely a collection of metal pieces whose value was determined by weight. Abraham surprised Efron, who expected him to suggest a much lower price, after which the negotiations would continue until the two sides agreed upon a compromise sum. However, Abraham chose to refrain from the formal method of purchase, and instead immediately paid the entire sum, which was **four hundred shekels of** pure, choice **silver, ready currency** that would be accepted by anyone in the world.

17 *Second aliya* **The field of Efron that was in Makhpela,** the field that surrounded the Cave of Makhpela, **that was before Mamre, the field and the cave that was in it, and every tree that was in the field, that was within its border all around, were established** as Abraham's property. Abraham was not satisfied in purchasing the cave alone; he also acquired the surrounding area and an access path to the cave.

18 All of this was transferred **as a possession for Abraham in the eyes of the children of Het, of all coming to his city gate.**[D]

19 **And thereafter,** after the property was transferred to his ownership, **Abraham buried Sarah his wife in**[4] **the cave of the field of Makhpela opposite Mamre, which is Hebron, in the land of Canaan.**

20 **The field and the cave that was in it were established as a burial portion for Abraham,** for his family, which he had purchased from **the children of Het.**

A Wife for Isaac

GENESIS 24:1–67

The story of how a wife is found for Isaac is related in this chapter in greater detail than any comparable account in the Bible. In this regard, the Sages said that the ordinary conversation of the servants of the patriarchs is more beloved before God than the Torah of their sons, as the section dealing with Eliezer is repeated in the Torah, whereas many fundamentals of the Torah are taught only through allusion.[5] In this section, the chain of events is described down to the smallest detail: The precise conversations between the parties are recorded, as well as the journey and the lodging, the care given to the camels, the hospitality granted to Abraham's servant, and other such matters. All of these events are accompanied by divine assistance, as their occurrence is miraculously arranged in the most advantageous manner. This story includes a large element of human initiative and kindness, but it also highlights the crucial role of divine providence in achieving the goal of finding a wife for Isaac.

24 1 **And Abraham was old, advanced in years.** Isaac at that time was thirty-seven or thirty-eight years old; Abraham was therefore one hundred and thirty-seven or slightly older. It is possible that this introductory phrase reflects Abraham's perception of himself. **And the Lord blessed Abraham with everything,** including rest and tranquility from troubles and from his nomadic travels.

2 **Abraham said to his servant,**[D] **the elder of his household.** This individual was not necessarily elderly, but was the senior and most distinguished attendant, **who oversaw everything that he had,** the general administrator of finances in Abraham's household. Abraham said to him: **Please, place your hand under my thigh,** which was an ancient manner of taking an oath. In contrast to grasping or shaking hands, which expresses a commitment between two individuals of similar social status, an oath accepted by placing one's hand under the thigh of a seated person was typically used in the case of an agreement between an individual with a senior status and someone under his jurisdiction. By this action, the taker of the vow expresses his commitment to perform the bidding of the one administering the oath.[6]

3 **And I will administer an oath to you by the Lord, God of the heavens and the God of the earth,** who is all-powerful, **that you shall not take a wife for my son from the daughters of the Canaanites, in whose midst I live.** Abraham did not know how many years he had left, and whether he would succeed in marrying off Isaac himself. He therefore requested that his servant promise not to marry off his son to one of the daughters of the Canaanites after his death.

4 **Rather, you shall go to my land,** Aram Naharayim, **and to my birthplace,** Haran, where my extended family is located, the tribe into which I was born, **and take** from there **a wife for my son, for Isaac.**

5 **The servant said to him: Perhaps the woman will not wish to follow me to this land,** as it is a long journey to Canaan from Haran, which is located on the southern border of modern-day

DISCUSSION

agricultural land was much smaller than this (see 33:19). Moreover, this property was rocky terrain, as a cave and its surrounding area are not suitable for planting or harvesting. Consequently, the price that Efron suggested was far higher than the actual value of the property. However,

טז מֵתְךָ קְבֹר: וַיִּשְׁמַע אַבְרָהָם אֶל־עֶפְרוֹן וַיִּשְׁקֹל אַבְרָהָם לְעֶפְרֹן אֶת־הַכֶּסֶף אֲשֶׁר
יז דִּבֶּר בְּאָזְנֵי בְנֵי־חֵת אַרְבַּע מֵאוֹת שֶׁקֶל כֶּסֶף עֹבֵר לַסֹּחֵר: וַיָּקָם ׀ שְׂדֵה עֶפְרוֹן שני
אֲשֶׁר בַּמַּכְפֵּלָה אֲשֶׁר לִפְנֵי מַמְרֵא הַשָּׂדֶה וְהַמְּעָרָה אֲשֶׁר־בּוֹ וְכָל־הָעֵץ אֲשֶׁר
יח בַּשָּׂדֶה אֲשֶׁר בְּכָל־גְּבֻלוֹ סָבִיב: לְאַבְרָהָם לְמִקְנָה לְעֵינֵי בְנֵי־חֵת בְּכֹל בָּאֵי שַׁעַר־
יט עִירוֹ: וְאַחֲרֵי־כֵן קָבַר אַבְרָהָם אֶת־שָׂרָה אִשְׁתּוֹ אֶל־מְעָרַת שְׂדֵה הַמַּכְפֵּלָה
כ עַל־פְּנֵי מַמְרֵא הִוא חֶבְרוֹן בְּאֶרֶץ כְּנָעַן: וַיָּקָם הַשָּׂדֶה וְהַמְּעָרָה אֲשֶׁר־בּוֹ לְאַבְרָהָם
כד א לַאֲחֻזַּת־קָבֶר מֵאֵת בְּנֵי־חֵת: וְאַבְרָהָם זָקֵן בָּא בַּיָּמִים וַיהוה בֵּרַךְ אֶת־אַבְרָהָם כ
ב בַּכֹּל: וַיֹּאמֶר אַבְרָהָם אֶל־עַבְדּוֹ זְקַן בֵּיתוֹ הַמֹּשֵׁל בְּכָל־אֲשֶׁר־לוֹ שִׂים־נָא יָדְךָ
ג תַּחַת יְרֵכִי: וְאַשְׁבִּיעֲךָ בַּיהוה אֱלֹהֵי הַשָּׁמַיִם וֵאלֹהֵי הָאָרֶץ אֲשֶׁר לֹא־תִקַּח אִשָּׁה
ד לִבְנִי מִבְּנוֹת הַכְּנַעֲנִי אֲשֶׁר אָנֹכִי יוֹשֵׁב בְּקִרְבּוֹ: כִּי אֶל־אַרְצִי וְאֶל־מוֹלַדְתִּי תֵּלֵךְ
ה וְלָקַחְתָּ אִשָּׁה לִבְנִי לְיִצְחָק: וַיֹּאמֶר אֵלָיו הָעֶבֶד אוּלַי לֹא־תֹאבֶה הָאִשָּׁה לָלֶכֶת
אַחֲרַי אֶל־הָאָרֶץ הַזֹּאת הֶהָשֵׁב אָשִׁיב אֶת־בִּנְךָ אֶל־הָאָרֶץ אֲשֶׁר־יָצָאתָ מִשָּׁם:

רש״י

טז| וַיִּשְׁקֹל אַבְרָהָם לְעֶפְרֹן. חָסֵר וָי״ו, לְפִי שֶׁאָמַר הַרְבֵּה וַאֲפִלּוּ מְעַט לֹא עָשָׂה, שֶׁנָּטַל מִמֶּנּוּ שְׁקָלִים גְּדוֹלִים שֶׁהֵן קַנְטָרִין, שֶׁנֶּאֱמַר: "עֹבֵר לַסֹּחֵר", שֶׁמִּתְקַבְּלִים בְּשֶׁקֶל בְּכָל מָקוֹם, וְיֵשׁ מָקוֹם שֶׁשִּׁקְלֵיהֶן גְּדוֹלִים שֶׁהֵן קַנְטָרִין, גנטינא״ר בְּלַעַז:

יז-יח| וַיָּקָם שְׂדֵה עֶפְרוֹן. תְּקוּמָה הָיְתָה לוֹ שֶׁיָּצָא מִיַּד הֶדְיוֹט לְיַד מֶלֶךְ. וּפְשׁוּטוֹ שֶׁל מִקְרָא: וַיָּקָם הַשָּׂדֶה וְהַמְּעָרָה אֲשֶׁר בּוֹ וְכָל הָעֵץ לְאַבְרָהָם לְמִקְנָה וְגוֹ׳: בְּכֹל בָּאֵי שַׁעַר עִירוֹ. בְּקֶרֶב כֻּלָּם וּבְמַעֲמַד כֻּלָּם הִקְנָהוּ לוֹ:

פרק כד

א| בֵּרַךְ אֶת אַבְרָהָם בַּכֹּל. 'בַּכֹּל' עוֹלֶה בְּגִימַטְרִיָּא 'בֵּן', וּמֵאַחַר שֶׁהָיָה לוֹ בֵּן הָיָה צָרִיךְ לְהַשִּׂיאוֹ אִשָּׁה:

ב| זְקַן בֵּיתוֹ. לְפִי שֶׁהוּא דָּבוּק נָקוּד 'זְקַן': תַּחַת יְרֵכִי. לְפִי שֶׁהַנִּשְׁבָּע צָרִיךְ לִטֹּל בְּיָדוֹ חֵפֶץ שֶׁל מִצְוָה כְּגוֹן סֵפֶר תּוֹרָה אוֹ תְּפִלִּין, וְהַמִּילָה הָיְתָה מִצְוָה רִאשׁוֹנָה לוֹ, וּבָאָה לוֹ עַל יְדֵי צַעַר וְהָיְתָה חֲבִיבָה עָלָיו, וּנְטָלָהּ:

DISCUSSION

as explained above, Efron did not expect to receive this entire sum, and merely stated an exaggerated price in accordance with the accepted procedure for the sale of property at the time.

23:18| **In the eyes of the children of Het, of all coming to his city gate:** The verse again emphasizes that the first act of acquisition of Abraham in Canaan was not performed by force or against anyone's will. Rather, it was conducted with the complete desire and consent of all the relevant parties. Not only was the seller satisfied with the purchase, but all the city residents also agreed. Since they were present, any of them could have expressed opposition to the sale of land in their territory to a foreigner. Instead, they accepted the official public transfer of the property (see Sforno, verse 20).

24:2| **Abraham said to his servant:** The name of Abraham's servant is not mentioned in this entire passage. According to the tradition of the Sages, this servant is Eliezer (*Yoma* 28b; see also *Targum Yonatan*, verse 2). This is based upon a comparison between these verses and Abraham's earlier description of his servant: "And the steward of my house is Eliezer of Damascus.... Behold, to me You have not given me descendants, and a member of my household is my heir" (15:2–3).

Turkey. What should I do if she refuses to leave her home to come here? **Shall I return your son to the land from which you departed?**

6 **Abraham said to him: Beware lest you return my son there.** It was not my choice to distance myself from the land of my birth. Therefore,

7 **the Lord, God of the heavens, who took me from my father's house, and from my birthplace, and who spoke to me** in a prophecy, **and who took an oath to me, saying: To your descendants I will give this land; He will send His angel before you** to assist you, **and you will** successfully find and **take a wife for my son from there.**

8 **And if the woman will not wish to follow you, you shall be absolved from this oath of mine,** and you need not continue searching for a wife for Isaac; **only you shall not return my son there,**[D] as he must remain in this land. God gave me this land, and He commanded me to dwell here; therefore, my son may not leave it either.[7]

9 **The servant placed his hand under the thigh of Abraham his master, and took an oath to him with regard to this matter.**

10 *Third aliya* **The servant took ten of his master's camels** for the extended journey from the south of Canaan to Haran, **and he went with all of his master's goods in his hand.**[D] He took gifts and other unique articles that would convey Abraham's status and power, as well as various items he would need during the journey. **He arose and went to Aram Naharayim, to the city of Nahor.**

11 At the end of his journey, **he had the camels kneel,** in contrast to horses and donkeys that generally drink while standing, **outside the city by the well of water at evening time, at the time the women who draw water come out.** Since the servant could not knock on every door searching for an appropriate wife for his master, he thought that visiting the well at this time of day would give him a good opportunity to see the local girls.

12 **He said** in prayer: **Lord, God of my master Abraham, please arrange it for me today, and perform kindness with my master Abraham,** on his behalf and in his honor.

13 **Behold, I stand by the spring of water; and the daughters of the men of the city come out to draw water.**

14 **It shall be that the girl to whom I shall say: Tilt your jug please,** while it is still on your shoulder, which was the accepted method of giving another to drink, **that I may drink, and she,** that girl, **shall say: Drink, and I will also give your camels to drink;** I will know that **it is she You have** thereby **confirmed** to be a wife **for Your servant, for Isaac; and through her,** if I find such a girl, **I shall know that You have shown kindness to my master.**[D]

15 **It was before he concluded to speak,** while he was still praying; **behold, Rebecca,** who was mentioned earlier (22:23), **was coming out.** Either she arrived first, before the other girls, or she stood out in some manner. The verse proceeds to restate her lineage: It was Rebecca **who was born to Betuel, son of Milka,** the primary **wife,** rather than a concubine, **of Nahor, brother of Abraham.** This is Abraham's closest family (see 22:24). **And her jug was on her shoulder** as she came.

16 **And the girl was good-looking, a virgin, and a man had not been intimate with her,** which indicates that she was modest. Naturally, the servant became aware of these facts only later. **She descended to the spring, she filled her jug, and ascended** from the spring, which was slightly lower than the area surrounding it.

17 The girl, whose dress likely indicated that she was unmarried, and who appeared to him to be the appropriate age for Isaac, impressed Abraham's servant. Therefore, **the servant ran toward her, and he said: Please allow me to sip a little water from your jug.**

18 **She said: Drink, my lord, and she hurried and lowered her jug on her hand, and gave him to drink.** Instead of tilting the

DISCUSSION

24:8| **Only you shall not return my son there:** Isaac remained within the borders of Canaan for his entire life, and was the only one of the three forefathers who never left the land of Canaan. Perhaps this is because he was bound upon the altar as an offering, and was therefore considered sacred to God (see Rashi, 26:2).

24:10| **All of his master's goods in his hand:** According to one midrash, the servant also took Abraham's deed of inheritance, in which he bequeathed all of his assets to Isaac (see Rashi; *Midrash Tanḥuma, Vayetze* 3).

24:14| **And through her I shall know that You have shown kindness to my master:** Abraham's servant was a stranger in this place, and it was natural for him to request a drink. Therefore, he could expect to find a girl who would accede to his request and give him some water. However, providing water for all his camels was a far more difficult task, as the large amount of water necessary for them also would have to be drawn from the well. Any girl who offers to do this also would thereby demonstrate an exceptionally generous nature and a strong desire to help strangers, far beyond the requirements of common courtesy. The servant sought a girl who was unusually kind, and truly willing to offer assistance and hospitality toward guests. This character trait would render her an appropriate counterpart for Isaac and member of the house of Abraham, who himself excelled in his hospitality toward guests (see Rashi).

ו וַיֹּאמֶר אֵלָיו אַבְרָהָם הִשָּׁמֶר לְךָ פֶּן־תָּשִׁיב אֶת־בְּנִי שָׁמָּה:

ז יְהוָה ׀ אֱלֹהֵי הַשָּׁמַיִם אֲשֶׁר לְקָחַנִי מִבֵּית אָבִי וּמֵאֶרֶץ מוֹלַדְתִּי וַאֲשֶׁר דִּבֶּר־לִי וַאֲשֶׁר נִשְׁבַּע־לִי לֵאמֹר לְזַרְעֲךָ אֶתֵּן אֶת־הָאָרֶץ הַזֹּאת הוּא יִשְׁלַח מַלְאָכוֹ לְפָנֶיךָ

ח וְלָקַחְתָּ אִשָּׁה לִבְנִי מִשָּׁם: וְאִם־לֹא תֹאבֶה הָאִשָּׁה לָלֶכֶת אַחֲרֶיךָ וְנִקִּיתָ מִשְּׁבֻעָתִי זֹאת רַק אֶת־בְּנִי לֹא תָשֵׁב שָׁמָּה:

ט וַיָּשֶׂם הָעֶבֶד אֶת־יָדוֹ תַּחַת יֶרֶךְ אַבְרָהָם אֲדֹנָיו וַיִּשָּׁבַע לוֹ עַל־הַדָּבָר הַזֶּה:

י וַיִּקַּח הָעֶבֶד עֲשָׂרָה גְמַלִּים מִגְּמַלֵּי אֲדֹנָיו וַיֵּלֶךְ וְכָל־טוּב אֲדֹנָיו בְּיָדוֹ וַיָּקָם וַיֵּלֶךְ אֶל־אֲרַם נַהֲרַיִם אֶל־עִיר נָחוֹר:

יא וַיַּבְרֵךְ הַגְּמַלִּים מִחוּץ לָעִיר אֶל־בְּאֵר הַמָּיִם לְעֵת עֶרֶב לְעֵת צֵאת הַשֹּׁאֲבֹת:

יב וַיֹּאמַר ׀ יְהוָה אֱלֹהֵי אֲדֹנִי אַבְרָהָם הַקְרֵה־נָא לְפָנַי הַיּוֹם וַעֲשֵׂה־חֶסֶד עִם אֲדֹנִי אַבְרָהָם:

יג הִנֵּה אָנֹכִי נִצָּב עַל־עֵין הַמָּיִם וּבְנוֹת אַנְשֵׁי הָעִיר יֹצְאֹת לִשְׁאֹב מָיִם:

יד וְהָיָה הַנַּעֲרָ אֲשֶׁר אֹמַר אֵלֶיהָ הַטִּי־נָא כַדֵּךְ וְאֶשְׁתֶּה וְאָמְרָה שְׁתֵה וְגַם־גְּמַלֶּיךָ אַשְׁקֶה אֹתָהּ הֹכַחְתָּ לְעַבְדְּךָ לְיִצְחָק וּבָהּ אֵדַע כִּי־עָשִׂיתָ חֶסֶד עִם־אֲדֹנִי:

טו וַיְהִי־הוּא טֶרֶם כִּלָּה לְדַבֵּר וְהִנֵּה רִבְקָה יֹצֵאת אֲשֶׁר יֻלְּדָה לִבְתוּאֵל בֶּן־מִלְכָּה אֵשֶׁת נָחוֹר אֲחִי אַבְרָהָם וְכַדָּהּ עַל־שִׁכְמָהּ:

טז וְהַנַּעֲרָ טֹבַת מַרְאֶה מְאֹד בְּתוּלָה וְאִישׁ לֹא יְדָעָהּ וַתֵּרֶד הָעַיְנָה וַתְּמַלֵּא כַדָּהּ וַתָּעַל:

יז וַיָּרָץ הָעֶבֶד לִקְרָאתָהּ וַיֹּאמֶר הַגְמִיאִינִי נָא מְעַט־מַיִם מִכַּדֵּךְ:

יח וַתֹּאמֶר שְׁתֵה אֲדֹנִי וַתְּמַהֵר וַתֹּרֶד כַּדָּהּ עַל־יָדָהּ וַתַּשְׁקֵהוּ:

ז] אֱלֹהֵי הַשָּׁמַיִם אֲשֶׁר לְקָחַנִי מִבֵּית אָבִי. וְלֹא אָמַר 'וֵאלֹהֵי הָאָרֶץ', וּלְמַעְלָה (לעיל פסוק ג) אָמַר: "וְאַשְׁבִּיעֲךָ" וְגוֹ'. אָמַר לוֹ: עַכְשָׁיו הוּא אֱלֹהֵי הַשָּׁמַיִם וֵאלֹהֵי הָאָרֶץ, שֶׁהִרְגַּלְתִּיו בְּפִי הַבְּרִיּוֹת, אֲבָל כְּשֶׁלְּקָחַנִי מִבֵּית אָבִי הָיָה אֱלֹהֵי הַשָּׁמַיִם וְלֹא אֱלֹהֵי הָאָרֶץ, שֶׁלֹּא הָיוּ בָאֵי עוֹלָם מַכִּירִים בּוֹ: מִבֵּית אָבִי. מֵחָרָן: וּמֵאֶרֶץ מוֹלַדְתִּי. מֵאוּר כַּשְׂדִּים: וַאֲשֶׁר דִּבֶּר־לִי. לְצָרְכִּי, כְּמוֹ: "אֲשֶׁר דִּבֶּר עָלַי". וְכֵן כָּל 'לִי' וְ'לוֹ' וְ'לָהֶם' הַסְּמוּכִים אֵצֶל דִּבּוּר מְפֹרָשִׁים בִּלְשׁוֹן 'עַל', וְתַרְגּוּם שֶׁלָּהֶם: 'עֲלַי' 'עֲלוֹהִי', שֶׁאֵין נוֹפֵל אֵצֶל דִּבּוּר לְשׁוֹן לִי וְלוֹ וְלָהֶם, אֶלָּא 'אֵלַי' 'אֵלָיו' 'אֲלֵיהֶם', וְתַרְגּוּם שֶׁלָּהֶם: 'עִמִּי' 'עִמֵּיהּ' 'עִמְּהוֹן'. אֲבָל אֵצֶל אֲמִירָה נוֹפֵל לְשׁוֹן לִי וְלוֹ וְלָהֶם: וַאֲשֶׁר נִשְׁבַּע־לִי. בֵּין הַבְּתָרִים:

ח] וְנִקִּיתָ מִשְּׁבֻעָתִי. וְקַח לוֹ אִשָּׁה מִבְּנוֹת עָנֵר אֶשְׁכֹּל וּמַמְרֵא: רַק אֶת־בְּנִי וְגוֹ'. 'רַק' מִעוּט הוּא – בְּנִי אֵינוֹ חוֹזֵר, אֲבָל יַעֲקֹב בֶּן בְּנִי סוֹפוֹ לַחֲזֹר.

י] מִגְּמַלֵּי אֲדֹנָיו. נִכָּרִין הָיוּ מִשְּׁאָר גְּמַלִּים, שֶׁהָיוּ יוֹצְאִין זְמוּמִין מִפְּנֵי הַגָּזֵל שֶׁלֹּא יִרְעוּ בִּשְׂדוֹת אֲחֵרִים: וְכָל טוּב אֲדֹנָיו בְּיָדוֹ. שְׁטַר מַתָּנָה כָּתַב לְיִצְחָק עַל כָּל אֲשֶׁר לוֹ, כְּדֵי שֶׁיִּקְפְּצוּ לִשְׁלֹחַ לוֹ בִּתָּם: אֲרַם נַהֲרַיִם. בֵּין שְׁתֵּי נְהָרוֹת יוֹשֶׁבֶת:

יא] וַיַּבְרֵךְ הַגְּמַלִּים. הִרְבִּיצָם:

יד] אֹתָהּ הֹכַחְתָּ. רְאוּיָה הִיא לוֹ, שֶׁתְּהֵא גּוֹמֶלֶת חֲסָדִים וּכְדַאי לִכָּנֵס בְּבֵיתוֹ שֶׁל אַבְרָהָם. וּלְשׁוֹן 'הוֹכַחְתָּ' בֵּרַרְתָּ,

אפרוביס"ט בְּלַעַז: וּבָהּ אֵדַע. לְשׁוֹן תְּחִנָּה, הוֹדַע לִי בָּהּ: כִּי עָשִׂיתָ חֶסֶד. אִם תִּהְיֶה מִמִּשְׁפַּחְתּוֹ וְהוֹגֶנֶת לוֹ אֵדַע כִּי עָשִׂיתָ חֶסֶד:

טז] בְּתוּלָה. מִמְּקוֹם בְּתוּלִים: וְאִישׁ לֹא יְדָעָהּ. כְּדַרְכָּהּ, לְפִי שֶׁבְּנוֹת הַגּוֹיִם מְשַׁמְּרוֹת מְקוֹם בְּתוּלֵיהֶן וּמַפְקִירוֹת עַצְמָן מִמָּקוֹם אַחֵר, הֵעִיד עַל זוֹ שֶׁנְּקִיָּה מִכֹּל:

יז] וַיָּרָץ הָעֶבֶד לִקְרָאתָהּ. לְפִי שֶׁרָאָה שֶׁעָלוּ הַמַּיִם לִקְרָאתָהּ: הַגְמִיאִינִי. לְשׁוֹן גְּמִיעָה, הומי"ר בְּלַעַז:

יח] וַתֹּרֶד כַּדָּהּ. מֵעַל שִׁכְמָהּ:

jug while it was still on her shoulder, Rebecca took the extra effort of removing the heavy container from her shoulder, so that it would be easier for the servant to drink.[8]

19 **She concluded giving him to drink, and** after he had drunk his fill **she said:** It is not enough for you alone to drink; **I will draw for your camels** and give them to drink **as well, until they conclude to drink** and their thirst is satiated.

20 **She hurried, emptied** the water that remained in **her jug into the trough, ran again to the well to draw, and drew for all his camels.** It is no simple matter to give ten camels all the water they require; even a single camel that has traveled a long distance will consume a tremendous amount of water.

21 Therefore, **the man** stared at her as she ran back and forth from the well to the trough and **was astonished at her. He was** still **silent,** waiting **to know whether the Lord had made his journey successful or not.** In light of her actions, he was certainly wondering about her identity and her family background, and thinking how he could learn more about her.

22 **It was when the camels concluded to drink; the man took a gold nose ring,** a kind of medallion placed on one's nose or forehead, **whose weight was one half shekel, and two bracelets** that were to be strapped **on her hands, whose weight was ten gold shekels.** Based on comparisons with other sources, these were large and expensive pieces of jewelry. The servant initially removed the ornaments from his bag, then asked her for her identity, and only upon receiving a satisfactory answer did he give her the ring and bracelets. This is the interpretation of the Rashbam and the Ramban, although Rashi (verse 23) explains the sequence of events differently.

23 The servant then asked Rebecca two questions: First, **he said: Whose daughter are you; please tell me.** It was not considered proper etiquette for a stranger to ask a girl's name; therefore he inquired into the identity of her family. Second, he asked: **Is there room in your father's house for us to stay the night,** as it is evident from your behavior that you come from a family that is hospitable to guests.

24 **She said to him: I am the daughter of Betuel, son of Milka, whom she bore to Nahor.**

25 **She** then **said to him:** With regard to your second question, **both straw and feed is plentiful with us, as well as room to stay the night.** She responded to the questions in the order in which they were asked. As noted by the Sages, it is considered the trait of a wise person to answer questions in the same order that they were posed.[9]

26 The condition that the servant had earlier stipulated (verse 14) was merely divination, and its fulfillment alone did not prove that this girl was destined to marry Isaac.[10] However, once it became clear that the same girl who fulfilled his conditions was also a close relative of Abraham, **the man bowed and prostrated himself to the Lord.**

27 He said: Blessed is the Lord, God of my master Abraham, *Fourth aliya* **who did not withhold His kindness and His truth from my master. I have been guided by the Lord on the** proper and correct **way,** and He ensured that I traveled **to the** very **house of my master's brethren.**

28 **The girl ran and told her mother's household**[D] akin to these **matters.**

29 **Rebecca had a brother and his name was Laban.** It can be inferred from the continuation of the story that Laban was the firstborn, as well as the dominant figure in the family. **And Laban ran out to the man, to the spring.** After Rebecca ran to her home, her brother ran from the house to discover more about the mysterious man who had arrived from afar, given gifts to his sister, questioned her, and requested to lodge in their house.

30 Perhaps in his role as the older brother Laban wanted to ensure that everything would transpire in an appropriate and ethical manner, and it was for this reason that he ran to greet the servant. However, it is also possible that his motivations were less pure. **It was when he saw the nose ring and the bracelets upon his sister's hands,** an indication of wealth, **and when he heard the words of Rebecca his sister, saying: So spoke the man to me,** that he asked me certain questions, prayed, and engaged in other activities, but he did not relate any information about himself, that **he,** Laban, **came to the man and behold, he was standing beside the camels at the spring.**

31 **He, Laban, said: Come, blessed of the Lord; why do you stand outside when I have cleared the house** so that there will be room for you and your entourage to stay? Abraham's servant was accompanied by other subordinates, as is evident from the next verse. Laban continues: **And** in addition, there is even a **place for the** ten **camels,** who take up a large area.

32 **The man came to the house and he,** Laban,[11] **unloaded the camels; he gave straw and feed for the camels, and,** as was customary in honor of a guest after a long journey, Laban gave him **water to wash his feet and the feet of the men who were with him.**

DISCUSSION

24:28 | **The girl ran and told her mother's household:** Although the Torah does not disclose Rebecca's exact age, it can be inferred from her conduct and the fact that she is called a girl [*na'ara*], that she was approximately eleven or twelve. In addition, her reaction to meeting the servant who gave her the jewelry, running home to relate her experiences to her mother, is typical of a girl that age (see also *Yevamot* 61b, Ramban, and Rashba ad loc.; *Midrash HaGadol* 25:20; Abravanel 25:19).

יט כ וַתְּכַל לְהַשְׁקֹתוֹ וַתֹּאמֶר גַּם לִגְמַלֶּיךָ אֶשְׁאָב עַד אִם־כִּלּוּ לִשְׁתֹּת: וַתְּמַהֵר וַתְּעַר
כא כַּדָּהּ אֶל־הַשֹּׁקֶת וַתָּרָץ עוֹד אֶל־הַבְּאֵר לִשְׁאֹב וַתִּשְׁאַב לְכָל־גְּמַלָּיו: וְהָאִישׁ
כב מִשְׁתָּאֵה לָהּ מַחֲרִישׁ לָדַעַת הַהִצְלִיחַ יְהוָה דַּרְכּוֹ אִם־לֹא: וַיְהִי כַּאֲשֶׁר כִּלּוּ
הַגְּמַלִּים לִשְׁתּוֹת וַיִּקַּח הָאִישׁ נֶזֶם זָהָב בֶּקַע מִשְׁקָלוֹ וּשְׁנֵי צְמִידִים עַל־יָדֶיהָ
כג עֲשָׂרָה זָהָב מִשְׁקָלָם: וַיֹּאמֶר בַּת־מִי אַתְּ הַגִּידִי נָא לִי הֲיֵשׁ בֵּית־אָבִיךְ מָקוֹם
כד כה לָנוּ לָלִין: וַתֹּאמֶר אֵלָיו בַּת־בְּתוּאֵל אָנֹכִי בֶּן־מִלְכָּה אֲשֶׁר יָלְדָה לְנָחוֹר: וַתֹּאמֶר
כו אֵלָיו גַּם־תֶּבֶן גַּם־מִסְפּוֹא רַב עִמָּנוּ גַּם־מָקוֹם לָלוּן: וַיִּקֹּד הָאִישׁ וַיִּשְׁתַּחוּ לַיהוָה:
כז וַיֹּאמֶר בָּרוּךְ יְהוָה אֱלֹהֵי אֲדֹנִי אַבְרָהָם אֲשֶׁר לֹא־עָזַב חַסְדּוֹ וַאֲמִתּוֹ מֵעִם אֲדֹנִי רביעי
כח אָנֹכִי בַּדֶּרֶךְ נָחַנִי יְהוָה בֵּית אֲחֵי אֲדֹנִי: וַתָּרָץ הַנַּעַר וַתַּגֵּד לְבֵית אִמָּהּ כַּדְּבָרִים
כט ל הָאֵלֶּה: וּלְרִבְקָה אָח וּשְׁמוֹ לָבָן וַיָּרָץ לָבָן אֶל־הָאִישׁ הַחוּצָה אֶל־הָעָיִן: וַיְהִי ׀
כִּרְאֹת אֶת־הַנֶּזֶם וְאֶת־הַצְּמִדִים עַל־יְדֵי אֲחֹתוֹ וּכְשָׁמְעוֹ אֶת־דִּבְרֵי רִבְקָה אֲחֹתוֹ
לֵאמֹר כֹּה־דִבֶּר אֵלַי הָאִישׁ וַיָּבֹא אֶל־הָאִישׁ וְהִנֵּה עֹמֵד עַל־הַגְּמַלִּים עַל־הָעָיִן:
לא וַיֹּאמֶר בּוֹא בְּרוּךְ יְהוָה לָמָּה תַעֲמֹד בַּחוּץ וְאָנֹכִי פִּנִּיתִי הַבַּיִת וּמָקוֹם לַגְּמַלִּים:
לב וַיָּבֹא הָאִישׁ הַבַּיְתָה וַיְפַתַּח הַגְּמַלִּים וַיִּתֵּן תֶּבֶן וּמִסְפּוֹא לַגְּמַלִּים וּמַיִם לִרְחֹץ

רש"י

יט] עד אם כלו. הרי 'אם' משמש בלשון 'אשר': אם כלו. "דיספיקון", שזו היא גמר שתייתן כששתו די ספוקן.

כ] ותער. לשון נפיצה, והרבה יש בלשון משנה: "המערה מכלי אל כלי" (עבודה זרה עב ע"א), ובמקרא יש לו דומה: "אל תער נפשי" (תהלים קמא, ח), "אשר הערה למות נפשו" (ישעיה נג, יב): השקת. אבן חלולה ששותים בה הגמלים:

כא] משתאה. לשון שאיה, כמו: "שאו ערים", "תשאה שממה" (ישעיה ו, יא): משתאה. משתומם ומתבהל על שראה דברו קרוב להצליח, אבל אינו יודע אם ממשפחת אברהם היא אם לאו. ואל תתמה בתי"ו של "משתאה", שאין לך תבה שתחלת יסודה שי"ן ומדברת בלשון מתפעל שאין תי"ו מפרידה בין שתי אותיות של עקר היסוד, כגון: "משתאה", "משתולל", מגזרת 'שולל', "וישתומם" (שם פסוק טז) מגזרת 'שממה', "וישתמר חקות עמרי" (מיכה ו, טז) מגזרת 'וישמר', אף כאן "משתאה" מגזרת 'תשאה'. וכשם שהתה מוצא לשון משומם בהלם ובהל ונעלם ובעל מחשבות, כמו: "על יומו נשמו אחרנים" (איוב יח, כ), "שמו שמים" (ירמיה ב, יב), "אשתומם כשעה חדה" (דניאל ד, טז), כך תפרש לשון 'שאיה' בהלם בהול ובעל מחשבות. ואונקלוס תרגם לשון 'שהיה', "וגברא שהי", שוהא ועומד במקום אחד לראות "ההצליח ה' דרכו". ואין לתרגם 'שתי', שהרי אינו לשון שתיה, שאין אל"ף נופלת בלשון שתיה: משתאה לה. משתומם עליה, כמו: "אמרי לי אחי הוא" (לעיל כ, יג), "אנשי המקום לאשתו" (להלן כו, ז).

כב] בקע. רמז לשקלי ישראל בקע לגלגלת (שמות לח, כו): ושני צמידים. רמז לשני לוחות מצמדות: עשרה זהב משקלם. רמז לעשרת הדברות שבהן:

כג] ויאמר בת מי את. לאחר שנתן לה שאלה, לפי שהיה בטוח בזכותו של אברהם שהצליח הקדוש ברוך הוא דרכו: ללין. לינה אחת, 'לין' שם דבר, והיא אמרה "ללון" (להלן פסוק כה), כמה לינות אתה יכול ללון אצלנו:

כד] בת בתואל. השיבתו על ראשון ראשון ועל אחרון אחרון:

כה] מספוא. כל מאכל הגמלים קרוי 'מספוא', כגון תבן ושעורים:

כז] בדרך. דרך המזמן, דרך הישר, באותו דרך שהייתי צריך. וכן כל בי"ת ולמ"ד וה"א המשמשים בראש התבה ונקודים בפתח, מדברים בדבר הפשוט שנזכר כבר במקום אחר, או שהוא מבֹרר ונכר באיזו הוא מדבר:

כח] לבית אמה. דרך הנשים היתה להיות להן בית לישב בו למלאכתן, ואין הבת מגדת אלא לאמה:

כט] וירץ. למה וירץ ועל מה רץ? "ויהי כראת את הנזם" (בפסוק הבא), אמר: עשיר הוא זה, ונתן עיניו בממון:

ל] על הגמלים. לשמרן, כמו: "והוא עמד עליהם" (לעיל יח, ח) לשמשם:

לא] פניתי הבית. מעבודה זרה:

לב] ויפתח. התיר זמם שלהם, שהיה סותם את פיהם שלא ירעו בדרך בשדות אחרים:

33 Following the greeting he received, Abraham's servant entered the house. **Food was placed before him to eat, and he said: I will not eat until I have spoken my words.** If the servant were to eat and lodge in the house, he would already feel a certain debt of gratitude to his hosts. Therefore, he insists on first explaining the purpose of his visit and his intentions, and only then will he eat. **He,** Laban, **said: Speak.**

34 **He said: I am Abraham's servant,**[D] and I am responsible for all matters in my master's household.

35 **The Lord has greatly blessed my master; and he became** much more **wealthy** than when he lived in Haran with your family. **He,** God, **gave him flocks and cattle, and silver and gold, and slaves and maidservants, and camels and donkeys.** In addition, Abraham and Sarah were childless when they left Haran and already advanced in age, but since then,

36 **Sarah, my master's wife,** whom you know well, as she too is from your family, **bore a son to my master after her old age. And** as my master is Abraham's foremost son, **he gave to him everything that he has.**

37 The previous comments invite an obvious question: If Abraham is such an illustrious and wealthy individual, and all of his wealth will be inherited by this one son, why has he sent his servant so far away to find a wife for that son? The servant therefore explains: **My master administered an oath to me, saying: You shall not take a wife for my son from the daughters of the Canaanites, in whose land I live.**

38 **Rather, you shall go to my father's house and to my family, and take a wife for my son** from there. Since my master desires to remain within the framework of his family, he insisted that I should not find a wife for his son from any other nation, but only from his family.

39 **I said to my master: Perhaps the woman will not follow me.** The mention of this exchange is significant for the continuation of the story.

40 **He said to me: The Lord, before whom I walked,** whom I served, **will send His angel with you and will make your path successful; and you shall take a wife for my son from my family, and from my father's house.**

41 If you take such a wife, **then you shall be absolved of my oath,**[D] **when you come to my family** and request from them a wife for my son; **and if they do not give her to you, you shall** likewise **be absolved of my oath.**

42 **I came this day to the spring, and I said: Lord, God of my master Abraham, if You would please make the path upon which I am going successful.**

43 **Behold, I am standing beside the spring of water; and there will be the young woman who comes out to draw, that I say to her: Please give me a little water to drink from your jug;**

44 **and she will say to me: You too drink, and I will draw for your camels as well; she is the woman whom the Lord has confirmed for my master's son.**

45 **Before I concluded to speak to my heart, behold, Rebecca came out with her jug on her shoulder; and she descended to the spring, and drew. I said to her: Please give me drink.**

46 **She hurried and lowered her pitcher from her shoulder, and said: Drink, and I will give to your camels to drink as well. I drank and she gave to the camels to drink as well.**

47 I then **asked her and said: Whose daughter are you?**[D] She said: **Daughter of Betuel, son of Nahor, whom Milka bore to him. I** subsequently **placed the ring on her nose, and the bracelets on her arms.**

DISCUSSION

24:34 | I am Abraham's servant: Identifying oneself as the servant of a distinguished individual was not necessarily an expression of inferiority. After all, Moses himself is called the servant of God (Deuteronomy 34:5), in a complimentary sense. Furthermore, elegant seals have been excavated in Israel with the title of "Servant of the King," and the like.

24:41 | Then you shall be absolved of my oath [*alati*]: The term for oath here is *ala*, which means a curse. The reason is that every oath contains the implicit threat of a curse if the one accepting the oath violates it.

24:47 | I asked her and said: Whose daughter are you: Abraham's servant's intent in recounting the story in such detail is to prevent potential skepticism on the part of Rebecca's family, as the episode is somewhat unusual. In order to prevent their anticipated resistance, the servant says to them: See how the angel that God sent was helping me, and how this wondrous story unfolded before all our eyes.

לג רַגְלָיו וְרַגְלֵי הָאֲנָשִׁים אֲשֶׁר אִתּוֹ: וַיִּישֶׂם לְפָנָיו לֶאֱכֹל וַיֹּאמֶר לֹא אֹכַל עַד אִם־ וַיּוּשַׂם
לד לה דִּבַּרְתִּי דְּבָרָי וַיֹּאמֶר דַּבֵּר: וַיֹּאמַר עֶבֶד אַבְרָהָם אָנֹכִי: וַיהוָה בֵּרַךְ אֶת־אֲדֹנִי
מְאֹד וַיִּגְדָּל וַיִּתֶּן־לוֹ צֹאן וּבָקָר וְכֶסֶף וְזָהָב וַעֲבָדִם וּשְׁפָחֹת וּגְמַלִּים וַחֲמֹרִים:
לו וַתֵּלֶד שָׂרָה אֵשֶׁת אֲדֹנִי בֵן לַאדֹנִי אַחֲרֵי זִקְנָתָהּ וַיִּתֶּן־לוֹ אֶת־כָּל־אֲשֶׁר־לוֹ:
לז וַיַּשְׁבִּעֵנִי אֲדֹנִי לֵאמֹר לֹא־תִקַּח אִשָּׁה לִבְנִי מִבְּנוֹת הַכְּנַעֲנִי אֲשֶׁר אָנֹכִי יֹשֵׁב
לח לט בְּאַרְצוֹ: אִם־לֹא אֶל־בֵּית־אָבִי תֵּלֵךְ וְאֶל־מִשְׁפַּחְתִּי וְלָקַחְתָּ אִשָּׁה לִבְנִי: וָאֹמַר
מ אֶל־אֲדֹנִי אֻלַי לֹא־תֵלֵךְ הָאִשָּׁה אַחֲרָי: וַיֹּאמֶר אֵלָי יְהוָה אֲשֶׁר־הִתְהַלַּכְתִּי לְפָנָיו
יִשְׁלַח מַלְאָכוֹ אִתָּךְ וְהִצְלִיחַ דַּרְכֶּךָ וְלָקַחְתָּ אִשָּׁה לִבְנִי מִמִּשְׁפַּחְתִּי וּמִבֵּית אָבִי:
מא אָז תִּנָּקֶה מֵאָלָתִי כִּי תָבוֹא אֶל־מִשְׁפַּחְתִּי וְאִם־לֹא יִתְּנוּ לָךְ וְהָיִיתָ נָקִי מֵאָלָתִי:
מב וָאָבֹא הַיּוֹם אֶל־הָעָיִן וָאֹמַר יְהוָה אֱלֹהֵי אֲדֹנִי אַבְרָהָם אִם־יֶשְׁךָ־נָּא מַצְלִיחַ כא
מג דַּרְכִּי אֲשֶׁר אָנֹכִי הֹלֵךְ עָלֶיהָ: הִנֵּה אָנֹכִי נִצָּב עַל־עֵין הַמָּיִם וְהָיָה הָעַלְמָה
מד הַיֹּצֵאת לִשְׁאֹב וְאָמַרְתִּי אֵלֶיהָ הַשְׁקִינִי־נָא מְעַט־מַיִם מִכַּדֵּךְ: וְאָמְרָה אֵלַי גַּם־
מה אַתָּה שְׁתֵה וְגַם לִגְמַלֶּיךָ אֶשְׁאָב הִוא הָאִשָּׁה אֲשֶׁר־הֹכִיחַ יְהוָה לְבֶן־אֲדֹנִי: אֲנִי
טֶרֶם אֲכַלֶּה לְדַבֵּר אֶל־לִבִּי וְהִנֵּה רִבְקָה יֹצֵאת וְכַדָּהּ עַל־שִׁכְמָהּ וַתֵּרֶד הָעַיְנָה
מו וַתִּשְׁאָב וָאֹמַר אֵלֶיהָ הַשְׁקִינִי נָא: וַתְּמַהֵר וַתּוֹרֶד כַּדָּהּ מֵעָלֶיהָ וַתֹּאמֶר שְׁתֵה
מז וְגַם־גְּמַלֶּיךָ אַשְׁקֶה וָאֵשְׁתְּ וְגַם הַגְּמַלִּים הִשְׁקָתָה: וָאֶשְׁאַל אֹתָהּ וָאֹמַר בַּת־מִי
אַתְּ וַתֹּאמֶר בַּת־בְּתוּאֵל בֶּן־נָחוֹר אֲשֶׁר יָלְדָה־לּוֹ מִלְכָּה וָאָשִׂם הַנֶּזֶם עַל־אַפָּהּ

רש״י

לג] **עד אם דברתי.** הֲרֵי 'אִם' מְשַׁמֵּשׁ בִּלְשׁוֹן 'אֲשֶׁר' וּבִלְשׁוֹן 'כִּי', כְּמוֹ: "עַד כִּי יָבֹא שִׁילֹה" (להלן מט, י), וְזֶהוּ שֶׁאָמְרוּ חֲכָמִים: 'כִּי' מְשַׁמֵּשׁ בְּאַרְבַּע לְשׁוֹנוֹת, וְהָאֶחָד 'אִי' וְהוּא 'אִם'.

לו] **ויתן לו את כל אשר לו.** שְׁטַר מַתָּנָה בְּיָדִי:

לז-לח] **לא תקח אשה לבני מבנות הכנעני.** אִם לֹא תֵּלֵךְ תְּחִלָּה אֶל בֵּית אָבִי וְלֹא תֹאבֶה לָלֶכֶת אַחֲרֶיךָ:

לט] **אלי לא תלך האשה.** 'אֻלַי' כְּתִיב, בַּת הָיְתָה לוֹ לֶאֱלִיעֶזֶר, וְהָיָה מְחַזֵּר לִמְצֹא עִלָּה שֶׁיֹּאמַר לוֹ אַבְרָהָם לִפְנוֹת אֵלָיו לְהַשִּׂיאוֹ בִּתּוֹ. אָמַר לוֹ אַבְרָהָם: בְּנִי בָּרוּךְ וְאַתָּה אָרוּר, וְאֵין אָרוּר מִדַּבֵּק בְּבָרוּךְ.

מב] **ואבא היום.** הַיּוֹם יָצָאתִי וְהַיּוֹם בָּאתִי; מִכָּאן שֶׁקָּפְצָה לוֹ הָאָרֶץ. אָמַר רַבִּי אַחָא: יָפָה שִׂיחָתָן שֶׁל עַבְדֵי אָבוֹת לִפְנֵי הַמָּקוֹם מִתּוֹרָתָן שֶׁל בָּנִים, שֶׁהֲרֵי פָּרָשָׁה שֶׁל אֱלִיעֶזֶר כְּפוּלָה בַּתּוֹרָה, וְהַרְבֵּה גּוּפֵי תוֹרָה לֹא נִתְּנוּ אֶלָּא בִּרְמִיזָה:

מד] **גם אתה.** 'גַּם' לְרַבּוֹת אֲנָשִׁים שֶׁעִמּוֹ: **הוכיח.** בֵּרֵר וְהוֹדִיעַ, וְכֵן כָּל הוֹכָחָה שֶׁבַּמִּקְרָא בֵּרוּר דָּבָר.

מה] **טרם אכלה.** טֶרֶם שֶׁאֲנִי מְכַלֶּה, וְכֵן כָּל לָשׁוֹן הַזֶּה, פְּעָמִים שֶׁהוּא מְדַבֵּר בִּלְשׁוֹן עָבָר, וְיָכוֹל לִכְתֹּב 'טֶרֶם כִּלִּיתִי', וּפְעָמִים שֶׁמְּדַבֵּר בִּלְשׁוֹן עָתִיד; כְּמוֹ: "כִּי אָמַר אִיּוֹב" (איוב א, ה) הֲרֵי לְשׁוֹן עָבָר, "כָּכָה יַעֲשֶׂה אִיּוֹב" (שם) הֲרֵי לְשׁוֹן עָתִיד, וּפֵרוּשׁ שְׁנֵיהֶם לָשׁוֹן הֹוֶה: כִּי אוֹמֵר הָיָה אִיּוֹב: "אוּלַי חָטְאוּ בָנַי" וְגוֹ' (שם) וְהָיָה עוֹשֶׂה כָּךְ:

מז] **ואשאל... ואשם.** שִׁנָּה הַסֵּדֶר, שֶׁהֲרֵי הוּא תְּחִלָּה נָתַן וְאַחַר כָּךְ שָׁאַל, אֶלָּא שֶׁלֹּא יִתְפְּשׂוּהוּ בִּדְבָרָיו וְיֹאמְרוּ: הֵיאַךְ נָתַתָּ לָהּ וַעֲדַיִן אֵינְךָ יוֹדֵעַ מִי הִיא?

48 **I bowed and prostrated myself to the Lord, and blessed the Lord, God of my master Abraham, who guided me in the true path to take the daughter of my master's brother for his son.** This concludes the servant's narration of the events that led him to his hosts.

49 **And now** he submits his request: **If you will do kindness and truth with my master** and agree to give the girl in marriage to the son of my master, **tell me. And if** you do **not** desire this match, likewise **tell me; and I will turn to the right or to the left.** I shall search elsewhere for a wife for the son of my master, as I can ask other family members as well.

50 **Laban and Betuel answered and said: The matter comes from the Lord,** and evidently it is destined in Heaven for Rebecca to marry Isaac; **we can speak to you neither bad nor good.** The mention of Laban's name before his father's is indicative of his central role; perhaps Betuel was weak or ill at the time.

51 **Behold, Rebecca is before you, take her, and go, and she shall be a wife for your master's son, as the Lord has spoken.**

52 **It was when Abraham's servant heard their statement** of consent, **he prostrated himself to the earth to the Lord,** again expressing his thanks for the success of his mission.

53 **The servant produced vessels of silver, vessels of gold, and garments, and he gave them to Rebecca; and he gave her brother and her mother precious objects,** food or gifts, as a tribute for the match.

Fifth aliya

54 **He and the men who were with him ate and drank and stayed the night,** as the previous events and discussions all took place during the evening hours: He met Rebecca toward the end of the day before the sun set (verse 11). They most likely reached her house in the early evening hours, after which he dined with her family. **They arose in the morning, and he,** the servant, **said: Send me to my master.** I wish to return to him and fulfill his request. His implicit intention was that they should send the girl with him, and thereby allow him to complete his mission.

55 **Her brother,** who again spoke first, **and her mother said: Let the girl remain with us** for a full period, **one year, or ten months; afterward she shall go.** It is preferable that she remain here in the meantime; she may leave after all of the necessary preparations for her departure and her wedding have been completed.

56 **He said to them: Do not delay me,**[D] **as the Lord has made my path successful; send me and I will go to my master.**

57 **They said: We will call the girl and ask her response.**

58 **They called Rebecca and said to her: Will you go with this man?** Some commentaries suggest that their use of the term "this man" instead of referring to him as the servant of Abraham, was a veiled warning: Do you really agree to undertake a long journey with this unfamiliar man?[12] **She said: I will go.**[D]

59 After Rebecca's response, her family were left with no choice, and therefore **they sent Rebecca their sister, and her nursemaid,**[D] **and Abraham's servant, and his men.**

60 **They blessed Rebecca, and said to her: Our sister, may you become thousands and ten thousands.** We wish that a great nation should come from you, **and let your descendants** defeat and **inherit the gate of their enemies.**

61 **Rebecca and her young women rose.** Since Nahor's family was noble and wealthy, Rebecca was sent with her nursemaid and other girls to accompany her. **And** they **rode upon the camels, and followed the man.** Rebecca's nursemaid and servants rode on the camels that were led by Abraham's other subordinates, while **the servant took Rebecca** himself, personally overseeing her well-being, **and went.**

62 **Isaac came from going to** visit the area of **Be'er Lahai Roi,** the location where the angel of God had found Hagar. This name was due to Hagar's vision of God there; it means the well [*be'er*] of the living [*ḥai*] God of my vision [*ro'i*] (see 16:14). **And he,** Isaac, **was living in the land of the South.**

63 **Isaac went out to walk [*lasuaḥ*] in the field** among the bushes [*siḥim*][13] **toward evening; and he lifted his eyes, and behold, he saw camels coming.**

DISCUSSION

24:56| **Do not delay me:** If her family had insisted on delaying Rebecca's departure, perhaps the servant would have been compelled to remain there and wait for her. Presumably he reiterated to them that Abraham was the eldest surviving member of the family, as Nahor does not appear in the story. They too would have been aware of this fact, as they could simply calculate the ages of the various family members. The servant can therefore justify his hurry to return, not only to bring the girl to Isaac, but also to report to the elderly Abraham that a wife has been found for his son.

24:58| **I will go:** This is one of the first examples of Rebecca's sense of independence, a quality that will come to the fore in future episodes as well. Up to this point, the servant had seen her as a young girl with a good heart who was hospitable toward guests. He had also witnessed her thoughtfulness, and how she spoke clearly and to the point. He now sees evidence of her independent personality as well.

24:59| **Her nursemaid:** As was typical for a distinguished family, Rebecca had a nursemaid who had cared for her from infancy. After the nursemaid was no longer needed for nursing, she would become the child's caregiver. In this particular case, the nursemaid accompanied Rebecca for nearly her entire life. Although the Torah does not relate much about this nursemaid, it does state that when she died many years later, Jacob, Rebecca's son, cried for her (see 35:8; *Pirkei deRabbi Eliezer* 16). Moreover, the later verse mentions that she was called Deborah. The name of such a minor character in the Bible is a rarity, and is likely an indication of her prominent status within the family.

מח וְהַצְּמִידִים עַל־יָדֶיהָ: וָאֶקֹּד וָאֶשְׁתַּחֲוֶה לַיהוָה וָאֲבָרֵךְ אֶת־יְהוָה אֱלֹהֵי אֲדֹנִי

מט אַבְרָהָם אֲשֶׁר הִנְחַנִי בְּדֶרֶךְ אֱמֶת לָקַחַת אֶת־בַּת־אֲחִי אֲדֹנִי לִבְנוֹ: וְעַתָּה אִם־

יֶשְׁכֶם עֹשִׂים חֶסֶד וֶאֱמֶת אֶת־אֲדֹנִי הַגִּידוּ לִי וְאִם־לֹא הַגִּידוּ לִי וְאֶפְנֶה עַל־יָמִין

נ אוֹ עַל־שְׂמֹאל: וַיַּעַן לָבָן וּבְתוּאֵל וַיֹּאמְרוּ מֵיְהוָה יָצָא הַדָּבָר לֹא נוּכַל דַּבֵּר אֵלֶיךָ

נא רַע אוֹ־טוֹב: הִנֵּה־רִבְקָה לְפָנֶיךָ קַח וָלֵךְ וּתְהִי אִשָּׁה לְבֶן־אֲדֹנֶיךָ כַּאֲשֶׁר דִּבֶּר

נב יְהוָה: וַיְהִי כַּאֲשֶׁר שָׁמַע עֶבֶד אַבְרָהָם אֶת־דִּבְרֵיהֶם וַיִּשְׁתַּחוּ אַרְצָה לַיהוָה:

נג וַיּוֹצֵא הָעֶבֶד כְּלֵי־כֶסֶף וּכְלֵי זָהָב וּבְגָדִים וַיִּתֵּן לְרִבְקָה וּמִגְדָּנֹת נָתַן לְאָחִיהָ חמישי

נד וּלְאִמָּהּ: וַיֹּאכְלוּ וַיִּשְׁתּוּ הוּא וְהָאֲנָשִׁים אֲשֶׁר־עִמּוֹ וַיָּלִינוּ וַיָּקוּמוּ בַבֹּקֶר וַיֹּאמֶר

נה שַׁלְּחֻנִי לַאדֹנִי: וַיֹּאמֶר אָחִיהָ וְאִמָּהּ תֵּשֵׁב הַנַּעֲרָ אִתָּנוּ יָמִים אוֹ עָשׂוֹר אַחַר תֵּלֵךְ:

נו וַיֹּאמֶר אֲלֵהֶם אַל־תְּאַחֲרוּ אֹתִי וַיהוָה הִצְלִיחַ דַּרְכִּי שַׁלְּחוּנִי וְאֵלְכָה לַאדֹנִי:

נז וַיֹּאמְרוּ נִקְרָא לַנַּעֲרָ וְנִשְׁאֲלָה אֶת־פִּיהָ: וַיִּקְרְאוּ לְרִבְקָה וַיֹּאמְרוּ אֵלֶיהָ הֲתֵלְכִי

נח עִם־הָאִישׁ הַזֶּה וַתֹּאמֶר אֵלֵךְ: וַיְשַׁלְּחוּ אֶת־רִבְקָה אֲחֹתָם וְאֶת־מֵנִקְתָּהּ וְאֶת־

נט עֶבֶד אַבְרָהָם וְאֶת־אֲנָשָׁיו: וַיְבָרֲכוּ אֶת־רִבְקָה וַיֹּאמְרוּ לָהּ אֲחֹתֵנוּ אַתְּ הֲיִי לְאַלְפֵי

ס רְבָבָה וְיִירַשׁ זַרְעֵךְ אֵת שַׁעַר שֹׂנְאָיו: וַתָּקָם רִבְקָה וְנַעֲרֹתֶיהָ וַתִּרְכַּבְנָה עַל־

סא הַגְּמַלִּים וַתֵּלַכְנָה אַחֲרֵי הָאִישׁ וַיִּקַּח הָעֶבֶד אֶת־רִבְקָה וַיֵּלַךְ: וְיִצְחָק בָּא מִבּוֹא

סב בְּאֵר לַחַי רֹאִי וְהוּא יוֹשֵׁב בְּאֶרֶץ הַנֶּגֶב: וַיֵּצֵא יִצְחָק לָשׂוּחַ בַּשָּׂדֶה לִפְנוֹת עָרֶב

סג

מט אֶת הַיֵי לְאַלְפֵי רְבָבָה. אַתְּ וְזַרְעֵךְ תְּקַבְּלוּ אוֹתָהּ בְּרָכָה שֶׁנֶּאֱמַר לְאַבְרָהָם בְּהַר הַמּוֹרִיָּה: "הַרְבָּה אַרְבֶּה אֶת־זַרְעֲךָ" וְגו' (לעיל כב, יז), יְהִי רָצוֹן שֶׁיְּהֵא הַזֶּרַע מִמֵּךְ וְלֹא מֵאִשָּׁה אַחֶרֶת:

סב מִבּוֹא בְּאֵר לַחַי רֹאִי. שֶׁהָלַךְ לְהָבִיא הָגָר לְאַבְרָהָם אָבִיו שֶׁיִּשָּׂאֶנָּה: יוֹשֵׁב בְּאֶרֶץ הַנֶּגֶב. קָרוֹב לְאוֹתוֹ בְּאֵר, שֶׁנֶּאֱמַר: "וַיֵּלֶךְ אַבְרָהָם מִשָּׁם אַרְצָה הַנֶּגֶב וַיֵּשֶׁב בֵּין־קָדֵשׁ וּבֵין שׁוּר" (לעיל כ, א) וְשָׁם הָיָה הַבְּאֵר, שֶׁנֶּאֱמַר: "הִנֵּה בֵין־קָדֵשׁ וּבֵין בָּרֶד" (לעיל טז, יד):

סג לָשׂוּחַ. לְשׁוֹן תְּפִלָּה, כְּמוֹ "יִשְׁפֹּךְ שִׂיחוֹ" (תהלים קב, א):

נד וַיָּלִינוּ. כָּל לִינָה שֶׁבַּמִּקְרָא לִינַת לַיְלָה אֶחָד:

נה וַיֹּאמֶר אָחִיהָ וְאִמָּהּ. וּבְתוּאֵל הֵיכָן הָיָה? רוֹצֶה הָיָה לְעַכֵּב וּבָא מַלְאָךְ וֶהֱמִיתוֹ: יָמִים. כְּמוֹ: "יָמִים תִּהְיֶה גְאֻלָּתוֹ" (ויקרא כה, כט), שֶׁכֵּךְ נוֹתְנִים לִבְתוּלָה זְמַן שְׁנֵים עָשָׂר חֹדֶשׁ לְפַרְנֵס עַצְמָהּ בְּתַכְשִׁיטֶיהָ: אוֹ עָשׂוֹר. עֲשָׂרָה חֳדָשִׁים. וְאִם תֹּאמַר יָמִים מַמָּשׁ, אֵין דֶּרֶךְ הַמְבַקְּשִׁים לְבַקֵּשׁ דָּבָר מוּעָט, וְאִם תֹּאמַר תֵּרֵד – תֶּן לָנוּ מִרְפֶּה מַה:

נז וְנִשְׁאֲלָה אֶת פִּיהָ. מִכָּאן שֶׁאֵין מַשִּׂיאִין אֶת הָאִשָּׁה אֶלָּא מִדַּעְתָּהּ:

נח וַתֹּאמֶר אֵלֵךְ. מֵעַצְמִי, וְאַף אִם אֵינְכֶם רוֹצִים:

מט עַל יָמִין. מִבְּנוֹת יִשְׁמָעֵאל: עַל שְׂמֹאל. מִבְּנוֹת לוֹט, שֶׁהָיָה יוֹשֵׁב לִשְׂמֹאלוֹ שֶׁל אַבְרָהָם. בְּרֵאשִׁית רַבָּה (ס, ט):

נ וַיַּעַן לָבָן וּבְתוּאֵל. רָשָׁע הָיָה וְקָפַץ לְהָשִׁיב לִפְנֵי אָבִיו: לֹא נוּכַל דַּבֵּר אֵלֶיךָ. לְמָאֵן בַּדָּבָר הַזֶּה, לֹא עַל יְדֵי תְּשׁוּבַת דָּבָר רַע וְלֹא עַל יְדֵי תְּשׁוּבַת דָּבָר הָגוּן וְנִכָּר, לְפִי שֶׁמָּה יָצָא הַדָּבָר לְפִי דְּבָרֶיךָ שֶׁזִּמְּנָה לְךָ:

נב וַיִּשְׁתַּחוּ אַרְצָה. מִכָּאן שֶׁמּוֹדִים עַל בְּשׂוֹרָה טוֹבָה:

נג וּמִגְדָּנֹת. מְגָדִים, שֶׁהֵבִיא עִמּוֹ מִינֵי פֵרוֹת שֶׁל אֶרֶץ יִשְׂרָאֵל:

129

64 Presumably realizing that their caravan was approaching their destination, **Rebecca lifted her eyes,** and **she saw Isaac.** Perhaps his appearance had been previously described to her, or she possibly identified him by his dress and manner as a noble individual, as he was strolling in the field rather than working. She might have intuitively sensed that he was Isaac. In any event, she was excited, **and she fell from the camel.**[D] This probably means that she leaned toward the servant, who was walking next to her and leading the camel.

65 **She said to the servant,** as she leaned toward him: **Who is that man who walks in the field toward us?** He appears to me to be an exceptional individual. Although Rebecca had apparently already identified Isaac, perhaps she wanted her suspicions confirmed. Alternatively, the dialogue in this verse preceded the events of the previous verse.[14] **The servant said: He is my master,** Isaac. **She took the veil and covered herself.**[D] Since her journey was complete, and she was now about to meet her future husband, she covered herself with a veil in a formal manner.

66 **The servant related to Isaac all the matters that he had done,** his own actions, as well as the miraculous fashion in which his mission was accomplished.

67 **Isaac brought her into the tent of his mother Sarah.** As a distinguished woman, Sarah likely had her own tent, in which she kept her personal possessions. This tent, located in Hebron, remained empty after her death, and it was here that Isaac brought Rebecca. It is possible that this is the tent referred to earlier, in the story of Abraham's hospitality to the angels (18:9–10). **He took Rebecca, she became his wife, and he loved her. Isaac was comforted after his mother.** Evidently, his mother had died not long before. As Sarah's only son, Isaac felt a deep inner void upon her passing. Upon the arrival of Rebecca, he finally felt that he could be comforted after his mother's demise. He brought Rebecca to Sarah's tent because she was expected to take over the matriarchal role in the family, a function that she would indeed fulfill in an important sense later.

The Other Descendants of Abraham; the Deaths of Abraham and Ishmael

GENESIS 25:1–18

Following the marriage of Isaac and Rebecca, before the Torah discusses their descendants at length, it provides a short summary of the last years of Abraham's life. Although he continued to live for more than thirty years after Isaac's marriage, few details are related about those years, as the focus of the narrative switches to Isaac.

The stage of Abraham's life in which he built the foundation for the Jewish people is complete. He now establishes many additional families, and thereby begins to fulfill his destiny as the father of many nations. Abraham then sends his many sons, who will become heads of nations, to the east, together with gifts, while everything else in his possession he gives to Isaac. Finally, the Torah relates the death of Abraham at a fine old age, as well as the death of Ishmael, and then lists his descendants.

25 1 *Sixth aliya* Following the banishment of Ishmael to the desert with Hagar, the death of Sarah, and the marriage of Isaac, **Abraham,** who was left alone, **took another wife, and her name was Ketura.**[D]

2 **She bore him Zimran, and Yokshan, and Medan, and Midyan,**[D] **and Yishbak, and Shuah.**

3 **And Yokshan begot Sheva and Dedan.** These tribes possibly lived in the southern Arabian peninsula.[15] Sheva and Dedan also appear in the list of the sons of Raama, son of Kush, son of Ham (see 10:7). **And the sons of Dedan were Ashurim, and Letushim, and Le'umim.** These are either simply the names of the tribes,[16] or descriptions of their character traits, which mean, respectively: Those who dwell in encampments, those who are swift, and those who form nation-units.[17]

4 **And the sons of Midyan,** who is listed here among the sons of Abraham, were: **Ephah, and Efer, and Hanokh, and Avida, and Eldaa. All these were the children of Ketura.** Since Abraham was very old and had been infertile until the births of Ishmael and Isaac, some commentaries suggest that these were the sons of Ketura alone, and were not Abraham's, although he raised them in his house.[18] However, this explanation is not particularly convincing. It seems more likely that whereas Abraham considered himself elderly and advanced in age, he was still quite capable of procreation and he himself fathered a number of children from Ketura. It can also be inferred from here and from the story of the birth of Ishmael that it was Sarah who was infertile.

5 Although these additional offspring were born to him, **Abraham gave all that was his to Isaac.**

6 **And to the sons of the concubines of Abraham,** Hagar and Ketura, **Abraham gave gifts.** Since he did not deem them his

DISCUSSION

24:64 | **And she fell [*vatipol*] from the camel:** In many instances in the Bible, this verb does not indicate that the individual in question dropped to the ground against his will, which is the common usage and is the case in modern Hebrew. Instead, it can refer to an intentional act of descent, and sometimes it simply means bending over (see Rashi; II Kings 5:21).

24:65 | **She took the veil and covered herself:** This is possibly the origin of a custom that is practiced to this day of a bride covering her face with a veil before meeting her groom at the

סד וַיִּשָּׂא עֵינָיו וַיַּרְא וְהִנֵּה גְמַלִּים בָּאִים׃ וַתִּשָּׂא רִבְקָה אֶת־עֵינֶיהָ וַתֵּרֶא אֶת־יִצְחָק
סה וַתִּפֹּל מֵעַל הַגָּמָל׃ וַתֹּאמֶר אֶל־הָעֶבֶד מִי־הָאִישׁ הַלָּזֶה הַהֹלֵךְ בַּשָּׂדֶה לִקְרָאתֵנוּ
סו וַיֹּאמֶר הָעֶבֶד הוּא אֲדֹנִי וַתִּקַּח הַצָּעִיף וַתִּתְכָּס׃ וַיְסַפֵּר הָעֶבֶד לְיִצְחָק אֵת כָּל־
סז הַדְּבָרִים אֲשֶׁר עָשָׂה׃ וַיְבִאֶהָ יִצְחָק הָאֹהֱלָה שָׂרָה אִמּוֹ וַיִּקַּח אֶת־רִבְקָה וַתְּהִי־
לוֹ לְאִשָּׁה וַיֶּאֱהָבֶהָ וַיִּנָּחֵם יִצְחָק אַחֲרֵי אִמּוֹ׃

ה א ב וַיֹּסֶף אַבְרָהָם וַיִּקַּח אִשָּׁה וּשְׁמָהּ קְטוּרָה׃ וַתֵּלֶד לוֹ אֶת־זִמְרָן וְאֶת־יָקְשָׁן וְאֶת־ כב ששי
ג מְדָן וְאֶת־מִדְיָן וְאֶת־יִשְׁבָּק וְאֶת־שׁוּחַ׃ וְיָקְשָׁן יָלַד אֶת־שְׁבָא וְאֶת־דְּדָן וּבְנֵי דְדָן
ד הָיוּ אַשּׁוּרִם וּלְטוּשִׁם וּלְאֻמִּים׃ וּבְנֵי מִדְיָן עֵיפָה וָעֵפֶר וַחֲנֹךְ וַאֲבִידָע וְאֶלְדָּעָה
ה ו כָּל־אֵלֶּה בְּנֵי קְטוּרָה׃ וַיִּתֵּן אַבְרָהָם אֶת־כָּל־אֲשֶׁר־לוֹ לְיִצְחָק׃ וְלִבְנֵי הַפִּילַגְשִׁים
אֲשֶׁר לְאַבְרָהָם נָתַן אַבְרָהָם מַתָּנֹת וַיְשַׁלְּחֵם מֵעַל יִצְחָק בְּנוֹ בְּעוֹדֶנּוּ חַי קֵדְמָה

רש״י

סד| וַתֵּרֶא אֶת יִצְחָק. רָאֲתָה אוֹתוֹ הָדוּר וְתָוְהָה מִפָּנָיו: וַתִּפֹּל. הִשְׁמִיטָה עַצְמָהּ לָאָרֶץ, כְּתַרְגּוּמוֹ: "וְאִתְרְכִינַת", הִטַּת עַצְמָהּ לָאָרֶץ וְלֹא הִגִּיעָה עַד הַקַּרְקַע, כְּמוֹ: "הַטִּי נָא כַדֵּךְ" (לעיל פסוק יד) "אַרְכִּינִי", "וַיֵּט שָׁמַיִם" (שמואל ב' כב, י; תהלים יח, י) "וְאַרְכֵּין", לְשׁוֹן מֻטֶּה לָאָרֶץ, וְדוֹמֶה לוֹ: "כִּי יִפֹּל לֹא יוּטָל" (תהלים לז, כד), כְּלוֹמַר, אִם יִטֶּה לָאָרֶץ לֹא יַגִּיעַ עַד הַקַּרְקַע:

סה| וַתִּתְכָּס. לְשׁוֹן מִתְפַּעֵל, כְּמוֹ: "וַתִּקָּבֵר" (להלן לה, ח), "וַתִּלָּכֵד" (שמואל א' י, כא), "וַתִּשָּׁבֵר" (שם ד, יח):

סו| וַיְסַפֵּר הָעֶבֶד. גִּלָּה לוֹ נִסִּים שֶׁנַּעֲשׂוּ לוֹ, שֶׁקָּפְצָה לוֹ הָאָרֶץ וְשֶׁנִּזְדַּמְּנָה לוֹ רִבְקָה בִּתְפִלָּתוֹ:

סז| הָאֹהֱלָה שָׂרָה אִמּוֹ. וַיְבִאֶהָ הָאֹהֱלָה וְנַעֲשֵׂית דֻּגְמַת שָׂרָה אִמּוֹ, כְּלוֹמַר, וַהֲרֵי הִיא שָׂרָה אִמּוֹ, שֶׁכָּל זְמַן שֶׁשָּׂרָה קַיֶּמֶת הָיָה נֵר דָּלוּק מֵעֶרֶב שַׁבָּת לְעֶרֶב שַׁבָּת וּבְרָכָה מְצוּיָה בָּעִסָּה וְעָנָן קָשׁוּר עַל הָאֹהֶל, וּמִשֶּׁמֵּתָה פָּסְקוּ, וּכְשֶׁבָּאת רִבְקָה חָזְרוּ. בִּרְאשִׁית רַבָּה (ס, טז): אַחֲרֵי אִמּוֹ. דֶּרֶךְ אֶרֶץ, כָּל זְמַן שֶׁאִמּוֹ שֶׁל אָדָם קַיֶּמֶת כָּרוּךְ הוּא אֶצְלָהּ, וּמִשֶּׁמֵּתָה – הוּא מִתְנַחֵם בְּאִשְׁתּוֹ:

פרק כה

א| קְטוּרָה. זוֹ הָגָר, וְנִקְרֵאת קְטוּרָה עַל שֵׁם שֶׁנָּאִים מַעֲשֶׂיהָ כִּקְטֹרֶת, וְשֶׁקָּשְׁרָה פִּתְחָהּ, שֶׁלֹּא נִזְדַּוְּגָה לְאָדָם מִיּוֹם שֶׁפֵּרְשָׁה מֵאַבְרָהָם:

ג| אַשּׁוּרִם וּלְטוּשִׁם. שֵׁם רָאשֵׁי אֻמּוֹת. וְתַרְגּוּם שֶׁל אוּנְקְלוֹס אֵין לִי לְיַשְּׁבוֹ עַל לְשׁוֹן הַמִּקְרָא:

ה| וַיִּתֵּן אַבְרָהָם וְגוֹ׳. אָמַר רַבִּי נְחֶמְיָה: בְּרָכָה וּדְיַתִּיקִי נָתַן לוֹ. שֶׁאָמַר לוֹ הַקָּדוֹשׁ בָּרוּךְ הוּא לְאַבְרָהָם: "וֶהְיֵה בְּרָכָה" (לעיל יב, ב), הַבְּרָכוֹת מְסוּרוֹת בְּיָדְךָ לְבָרֵךְ אֶת מִי שֶׁתִּרְצֶה, וְאַבְרָהָם מְסָרָן לְיִצְחָק:

ו| הַפִּילַגְשִׁים. חָסֵר כְּתִיב, שֶׁלֹּא הָיְתָה אֶלָּא פִּילֶגֶשׁ אַחַת, הִיא הָגָר הִיא קְטוּרָה. נָשִׁים בִּכְתֻבָּה, פִּילַגְשִׁים בְּלֹא כְתֻבָּה, כִּדְאָמְרִינַן בְּסַנְהֶדְרִין בְּנָשִׁים וּפִילַגְשִׁים דְּדָוִד: נָתַן אַבְרָהָם מַתָּנֹת. פֵּרְשׁוּ רַבּוֹתֵינוּ, שֵׁם טֻמְאָה מָסַר לָהֶם:

DISCUSSION

wedding. This story includes several other allusions to matrimonial customs that would be observed for thousands of years afterward, such as sending presents to the bride, and the granting of twelve months to a virgin to prepare herself before her wedding.

25:1| **Ketura:** A straightforward reading of the verse indicates that this is a new wife (see Rashbam; Ibn Ezra; *Yalkut Shimoni*, Job 904). However, some suggest that Ketura is another name for Hagar, whom Abraham restored to his residence to live with him at this juncture (*Bereshit Rabba* 61:4; *Targum Yonatan*; Rashi).

25:2| **Midyan:** The tribes of Midyan, who wandered in the eastern portion of Canaan, are often mentioned as enemies of the Jewish people (see, e.g., Numbers 25:17–18; Judges 7). They appear in other contexts as well. For instance, the Medanites and Midyanites were instrumental in the sale of Joseph (see 37:28, 36), and the wife of Moses was a Midyanite (see Exodus 2:16–21).

inheritors, he instead gave them presents, in the form of money or valuables, but not property. **And** he **sent them away from Isaac his son, while he was still alive,** so that they should not contest Isaac's inheritance. They traveled **eastward, to the east country.** The nations that have been identified from this list indeed lived on the eastern side of the Jordan River, and reached as far as the southern portion of the Negev, perhaps even to the Arabian Peninsula. These nations were sent eastward, and dwelled together with the descendants of Ishmael, and do not feature in the main narrative of the Torah.

7 **These are the days of the years of Abraham's life that he lived, one hundred and seventy-five years.** Abraham lived for many years after his wife Sarah passed away.

8 **Abraham expired and died at a good old age.** His later years were pleasant, without battles, struggles, or tension in his family. He was **aged** in years **and content** with his life. **And he was gathered to his people,** his soul returned to its source. This expression is used by the Bible only in reference to the passing of righteous individuals.

9 **Isaac and Ishmael, his** eldest **sons, buried him in the Cave of Makhpela, in the field of Efron son of Tzohar the Hitite, that is** located **before Mamre.** They knew that Abraham had purchased this land for a burial plot and that he had buried Sarah there.

10 **The field that Abraham purchased from the children of Het; there Abraham was buried, and Sarah his wife.** Their descendants would later be buried there as well.

11 **It was after the death of Abraham, God blessed Isaac his son; and Isaac lived beside Be'er Lahai Roi** in the Negev, where he was engaged primarily in shepherding sheep. The Torah will later relate that he also worked in agriculture (26:12).

12 *Seventh aliya* Following the completion of the story of Abraham's life, the Torah deals briefly with his secondary offspring, thereby rounding out the picture with regard to his children. **These are the descendants of Ishmael son of Abraham, whom Hagar the Egyptian, Sarah's maidservant, bore to Abraham.**

13 **And these are the names of the sons of Ishmael, by their names, according to their birth: The firstborn of Ishmael was Nevayot.**[D] **And** the other sons of Ishmael, some of whom became heads of families, tribes, or small nations, are: **Kedar, Adbe'el, Mivsam,**

14 **Mishma, Duma, Masa,**

15 **Hadad, Temah, Yetur, Nafish, and Kedem.**

16 *Maftir* **These are the sons of Ishmael and these are their names.** The sons of Ishmael typically did not construct permanent settlements. Rather, they dwelled **in their enclosures,** which were considered semi-permanent living places, **and in their fortifications,** structures that were capable of shielding them when necessary. The sum total of the sons of Ishmael was **twelve princes**[D] **of their nations.** Each one of them was the prince of a small nation.

17 **These are the years of the life of Ishmael:** He lived for **one hundred and thirty-seven years; and he expired and died; and he was gathered to his people.**[D]

18 **They,** the sons of Ishmael, **dwelled from Havila,**[19] **until Shur that is adjacent to Egypt, all the way to Ashur: He resided [*nafal*] adjacent to all his brethren.** Alternatively: His portion was ultimately adjacent to his brethren. The term *nafal* here possibly means conquest, so that the tribes of Ishmael ruled over their brethren, the children of Ketura.

DISCUSSION

25:13| **Nevayot:** The descendants of Nevayot have been identified as the Arab tribe called the Nabaiates, which dwelled on the frontier of Canaan. They are not to be confused with the Arab tribes known today as the Nabateans, who lived in northern Arabia. That name was given to this nomadic group at a later period by the Greeks.

25:16| **Twelve princes:** As was the case with the family of Nahor (see 22:23–24 and the commentary), the number of sons of Ishmael is significant, as it is the same as the number of sons of Jacob (see, e.g., 35:22). In general, twelve is considered a number that represents wholeness.

25:17| **And he expired and died; and he was gathered to his people:** Ishmael's death is described in a similar manner to the passing of the righteous, without any negative overtones. In fact, the Sages maintain that toward the end of his life Ishmael accepted upon himself the authority of Isaac as the leader, despite the fact that he himself was the elder brother (*Bava Batra* 16b). It is likely that although Ishmael did not entirely transmit the tradition of Abraham to his children, in his old age he conducted himself partially in accordance with its values. He certainly transmitted to his sons the importance of hospitality as practiced in the family, and he even instructed them to be circumcised, a custom that his descendants and all that follow in their ways continue to observe to this day.

ז אֶל־אֶרֶץ קֶדֶם: וְאֵלֶּה יְמֵי שְׁנֵי־חַיֵּי אַבְרָהָם אֲשֶׁר־חָי מְאַת שָׁנָה וְשִׁבְעִים שָׁנָה
ח וְחָמֵשׁ שָׁנִים: וַיִּגְוַע וַיָּמָת אַבְרָהָם בְּשֵׂיבָה טוֹבָה זָקֵן וְשָׂבֵעַ וַיֵּאָסֶף אֶל־עַמָּיו:
ט וַיִּקְבְּרוּ אֹתוֹ יִצְחָק וְיִשְׁמָעֵאל בָּנָיו אֶל־מְעָרַת הַמַּכְפֵּלָה אֶל־שְׂדֵה עֶפְרֹן בֶּן־צֹחַר
י הַחִתִּי אֲשֶׁר עַל־פְּנֵי מַמְרֵא: הַשָּׂדֶה אֲשֶׁר־קָנָה אַבְרָהָם מֵאֵת בְּנֵי־חֵת שָׁמָּה
יא קֻבַּר אַבְרָהָם וְשָׂרָה אִשְׁתּוֹ: וַיְהִי אַחֲרֵי מוֹת אַבְרָהָם וַיְבָרֶךְ אֱלֹהִים אֶת־יִצְחָק
בְּנוֹ וַיֵּשֶׁב יִצְחָק עִם־בְּאֵר לַחַי רֹאִי:

שביעי

יב וְאֵלֶּה תֹּלְדֹת יִשְׁמָעֵאל בֶּן־אַבְרָהָם אֲשֶׁר יָלְדָה הָגָר הַמִּצְרִית שִׁפְחַת שָׂרָה
יג לְאַבְרָהָם: וְאֵלֶּה שְׁמוֹת בְּנֵי יִשְׁמָעֵאל בִּשְׁמֹתָם לְתוֹלְדֹתָם בְּכֹר יִשְׁמָעֵאל נְבָיֹת
יד טו וְקֵדָר וְאַדְבְּאֵל וּמִבְשָׂם: וּמִשְׁמָע וְדוּמָה וּמַשָּׂא: חֲדַד וְתֵימָא יְטוּר נָפִישׁ וָקֵדְמָה:

מפטיר

טז אֵלֶּה הֵם בְּנֵי יִשְׁמָעֵאל וְאֵלֶּה שְׁמֹתָם בְּחַצְרֵיהֶם וּבְטִירֹתָם שְׁנֵים־עָשָׂר נְשִׂיאִם
יז לְאֻמֹּתָם: וְאֵלֶּה שְׁנֵי חַיֵּי יִשְׁמָעֵאל מְאַת שָׁנָה וּשְׁלֹשִׁים שָׁנָה וְשֶׁבַע שָׁנִים וַיִּגְוַע
יח וַיָּמָת וַיֵּאָסֶף אֶל־עַמָּיו: וַיִּשְׁכְּנוּ מֵחֲוִילָה עַד־שׁוּר אֲשֶׁר עַל־פְּנֵי מִצְרַיִם בֹּאֲכָה
אַשּׁוּרָה עַל־פְּנֵי כָל־אֶחָיו נָפָל:

רש"י

ז| **מְאַת שָׁנָה וְשִׁבְעִים שָׁנָה וְחָמֵשׁ שָׁנִים.** בֶּן מֵאָה כְּבֶן שִׁבְעִים, וּבֶן שִׁבְעִים כְּבֶן חָמֵשׁ בְּלֹא חֵטְא:

ט| **יִצְחָק וְיִשְׁמָעֵאל.** מִכָּאן שֶׁעָשָׂה יִשְׁמָעֵאל תְּשׁוּבָה וְהוֹלִיךְ אֶת יִצְחָק לְפָנָיו, וְהִיא "שֵׂיבָה טוֹבָה" (לעיל טו, טו) שֶׁנֶּאֶמְרָה בְּאַבְרָהָם:

יא| **וַיְהִי אַחֲרֵי מוֹת אַבְרָהָם וַיְבָרֶךְ וְגוֹ'.** נִחֲמוֹ תַּנְחוּמֵי אֲבֵלִים. דָּבָר אַחֵר, אַף עַל פִּי שֶׁמָּסַר הַקָּדוֹשׁ בָּרוּךְ הוּא אֶת הַבְּרָכוֹת לְאַבְרָהָם, נִתְיָרֵא לְבָרֵךְ אֶת יִצְחָק, מִפְּנֵי שֶׁצָּפָה אֶת עֵשָׂו יוֹצֵא מִמֶּנּוּ. אָמַר: יָבֹא בַּעַל הָעוֹלָם וִיבָרֵךְ אֶת אֲשֶׁר יִיטַב בְּעֵינָיו. וּבָא הַקָּדוֹשׁ בָּרוּךְ הוּא וּבֵרְכוֹ:

יג| **בִּשְׁמֹתָם לְתוֹלְדֹתָם.** סֵדֶר לֵדָתָן זֶה אַחַר זֶה:

טז| **בְּחַצְרֵיהֶם.** כְּרַכִּים שֶׁאֵין לָהֶם חוֹמָה, כְּתַרְגּוּמוֹ: "בְּפַצְחֵיהוֹן", שֶׁהֵם מְפֻצָּחִים, לְשׁוֹן פְּתִיחָה, כְּמוֹ: "פִּצְחוּ וְרַנְּנוּ" (תהלים צח, ד):

יז| **וְאֵלֶּה שְׁנֵי חַיֵּי יִשְׁמָעֵאל וְגוֹ'.** אָמַר רַבִּי חִיָּא בַּר אַבָּא: לָמָּה נִמְנוּ שְׁנוֹתָיו שֶׁל יִשְׁמָעֵאל? כְּדֵי לְיַחֵס בָּהֶם שְׁנוֹתָיו שֶׁל יַעֲקֹב. מִשְּׁנוֹתָיו שֶׁל יִשְׁמָעֵאל לָמַדְנוּ שֶׁשִּׁמֵּשׁ יַעֲקֹב בְּבֵית עֵבֶר אַרְבַּע עֶשְׂרֵה שָׁנָה כְּשֶׁפֵּרַשׁ מֵאָבִיו קֹדֶם שֶׁבָּא אֵצֶל לָבָן, שֶׁהֲרֵי כְּשֶׁפֵּרַשׁ יַעֲקֹב מֵאָבִיו מֵת יִשְׁמָעֵאל, שֶׁנֶּאֱמַר: "וַיֵּלֶךְ עֵשָׂו אֶל יִשְׁמָעֵאל" וְגוֹ' (להלן כח, ט), כְּמוֹ שֶׁמְּפֹרָשׁ בְּסוֹף 'מְגִלָּה נִקְרֵאת' (מגילה יז ע"א): **וַיִּגְוַע.** לֹא נֶאֶמְרָה 'גְּוִיעָה' אֶלָּא בַּצַּדִּיקִים:

יח| **נָפָל.** שָׁכַן, כְּמוֹ: "וּמִדְיָן וַעֲמָלֵק וְכָל בְּנֵי קֶדֶם נֹפְלִים בָּעֵמֶק" (שופטים ז, יב). כָּאן הוּא אוֹמֵר לְשׁוֹן נְפִילָה, וּלְהַלָּן הוּא אוֹמֵר: "עַל פְּנֵי כָל אֶחָיו יִשְׁכֹּן" (לעיל טז, יב), עַד שֶׁלֹּא מֵת אַבְרָהָם – "יִשְׁכֹּן", מִשֶּׁמֵּת אַבְרָהָם – "נָפָל":

Parashat
Toledot

Jacob, Esau, and the Birthright
GENESIS 25:19–34

After enumerating Ishmael's descendants in brief, the Torah focuses at length on the generations of Isaac. Here the description is not merely a list of descendants but the story of Isaac's life, especially the issue of which of his two sons, Jacob or Esau, will be his successor. Although the incident depicted in this chapter involving the sale of the birthright is of little importance to Esau, Jacob considers it a matter of great significance, as it signals his position as the leader of the family after Isaac's death.

19 **And this is the legacy,** the events in the life, **of Isaac, Abraham's son: Abraham begot Isaac.**^D

20 **Isaac was forty years old when he took Rebecca, daughter of Betuel the Aramean, from Padan Aram,** who was the **sister of Laban the Aramean,**^D **to be his wife.** *Padan* means field; there is a similar word in Arabic.¹

21 **Isaac entreated** and prayed fervently to **the Lord on behalf of his wife** while standing opposite her, **because** he understood from the fact that she had not given birth in the many years since they were married (see verse 26) that **she was barren. The Lord acceded to his entreaty, and Rebecca his wife conceived.**

22 During her pregnancy **the children were agitated within her.** It will soon become clear that she was bearing fraternal twins. Sensing that something was abnormal and cause for concern, **she said: If so,** if the pregnancy is so difficult, **why am I like this,** why do I want it? Alternatively, this means: If my suffering is so great, what is the point of living? **And she went to inquire of the Lord.**^D At the time, there were distinguished individuals who accepted the faith of Abraham and his family, such as Malkitzedek king of Shalem (see 14:18–20). Rebecca sought prophetic instruction from such a man.²

23 **The Lord said to her: Two peoples,** or national leaders (see, e.g., 17:16), **are in your womb, and two nations shall be separated from your innards.** From the moment they are born it will be clear that they are very different from one another. **One nation will prevail over the other nation,** as the struggle between them, which you sense within your womb, will continue after they are born. **And the elder shall serve the younger.** Even in the case of twins, one is born before the other and is the elder.

24 **Her days to give birth were complete, and behold, there were twins in her womb.**

25 **The first emerged** with **red** skin, redder than that of an average person.³ And he was covered, **all of him like a cloak of hair,** as he was very hairy. **And they called his name Esau,** perhaps due to his hair [*se'ar*], or because he appeared mature, like an object that is fully fashioned [*asui*].⁴

26 **And thereafter his brother emerged.** Their birth, like her pregnancy, was unusual, as **his hand** was **grasping Esau's heel** [*akev*]; **and he called his name Jacob** [*Ya'akov*].^D **Isaac was sixty years old when she bore them.** Since he married Rebecca at the age of forty, evidently they had lived twenty years as a childless couple.

DISCUSSION

25:19 | The legacy of Isaac, Abraham's son, Abraham begot Isaac: One explanation of this apparent repetition is that the two were similar in appearance. In other words, the fact that Abraham begot Isaac was evident to all, as Isaac's face clearly resembled his father's (*Bava Metzia* 87a; *Targum Yonatan*; Rashi; Abravanel). Furthermore, throughout his life Isaac saw himself as heir to Abraham's path. For Isaac, his status as Abraham's son was of particular importance. The phrase "Isaac, Abraham's son" merely states his name, whereas the emphasis that "Abraham begot Isaac" indicates that Isaac was born and groomed as his heir and successor (Ramban).

25:20 | Daughter of Betuel the Aramean... sister of Laban the Aramean: The mention of Rebecca's father and brother highlights the contrast between her behavior and that of her family. Both Betuel and Laban are highly dubious characters. Betuel the Aramean from Padan Aram is presented as a weak and vacillating individual (see 24:50, 29:5), while Laban the Aramean will be shown in a later chapter to be a scheming and guileful fellow. Notwithstanding her problematic background, Rebecca developed into a very different person (see *Bereshit Rabba*; Rashi).

25:22 | And she went to inquire of the Lord: It is unclear whether Rebecca discussed her pain with her husband. It is possible that Isaac was unaware of both her distress and her inquiry of God. She appears to have been granted a private prophecy, which she kept to herself, although she would later act in accordance with its contents (see *Ḥizkuni*).

25:26 | And he called his name Jacob [*Ya'akov*]: In addition to the idea that Jacob was call Ya'akov because he was grasping Esau's heel [*akev*], the root *ayin-kuf-bet* means cunning or crooked. See Isaiah 40:4: "The crooked [*he'akov*] will become straight." This meaning will come

פרשת

תולדת

יט כ וְאֵלֶּה תּוֹלְדֹת יִצְחָק בֶּן־אַבְרָהָם אַבְרָהָם הוֹלִיד אֶת־יִצְחָק: וַיְהִי יִצְחָק בֶּן־ כג
אַרְבָּעִים שָׁנָה בְּקַחְתּוֹ אֶת־רִבְקָה בַּת־בְּתוּאֵל הָאֲרַמִּי מִפַּדַּן אֲרָם אֲחוֹת לָבָן
כא הָאֲרַמִּי לוֹ לְאִשָּׁה: וַיֶּעְתַּר יִצְחָק לַיהוה לְנֹכַח אִשְׁתּוֹ כִּי עֲקָרָה הִוא וַיֵּעָתֶר לוֹ
כב יהוה וַתַּהַר רִבְקָה אִשְׁתּוֹ: וַיִּתְרֹצְצוּ הַבָּנִים בְּקִרְבָּהּ וַתֹּאמֶר אִם־כֵּן לָמָּה זֶּה
כג אָנֹכִי וַתֵּלֶךְ לִדְרֹשׁ אֶת־יהוה: וַיֹּאמֶר יהוה לָהּ שְׁנֵי גֹיִים בְּבִטְנֵךְ וּשְׁנֵי לְאֻמִּים גוים
כד מִמֵּעַיִךְ יִפָּרֵדוּ וּלְאֹם מִלְאֹם יֶאֱמָץ וְרַב יַעֲבֹד צָעִיר: וַיִּמְלְאוּ יָמֶיהָ לָלֶדֶת וְהִנֵּה
כה תוֹמִם בְּבִטְנָהּ: וַיֵּצֵא הָרִאשׁוֹן אַדְמוֹנִי כֻּלּוֹ כְּאַדֶּרֶת שֵׂעָר וַיִּקְרְאוּ שְׁמוֹ עֵשָׂו:
כו וְאַחֲרֵי־כֵן יָצָא אָחִיו וְיָדוֹ אֹחֶזֶת בַּעֲקֵב עֵשָׂו וַיִּקְרָא שְׁמוֹ יַעֲקֹב וְיִצְחָק בֶּן־שִׁשִּׁים

רש״י

יט| **ואלה תולדת יצחק.** יעקב ועשו האמורים בפרשה; ועל ידי שכתב הכתוב: "יצחק בן אברהם" הזקק לומר: "אברהם הוליד את יצחק", לפי שהיו ליצני הדור אומרים: מאבימלך נתעברה שרה, שהרי כמה שנים שהתה עם אברהם ולא נתעברה הימנו. מה עשה הקדוש ברוך הוא? צר קלסתר פניו של יצחק דומה לאברהם, והעידו הכל: אברהם הוליד את יצחק. וזהו שכתוב כאן: "יצחק בן אברהם", שהרי עדות יש ש"אברהם הוליד את יצחק":

כ| **בן ארבעים שנה.** שהרי כשהיה בא אברהם מהר המוריה נתבשר שנולדה רבקה, ויצחק היה בן שלשים ושבע שנה, שהרי בו בפרק מתה שרה, ומשנולד יצחק עד שמתה שרה שלשים ושבע שנים היו – בת תשעים היתה כשנולד, ובת מאה עשרים ושבע שנה היתה כשמתה, שנאמר: "ויהיו חיי שרה" וגו' (לעיל כג, א), הרי ליצחק שלשים ושבע שנים. ובו בפרק נולדה רבקה. המתין לה עד שתהא ראויה לביאה שלש שנים ונשאה: **בת בתואל מפדן ארם אחות לבן.** וכי עדין לא נכתב שהיא בת בתואל ואחות לבן ומפדן ארם? אלא להגיד שבחה, שהיתה בת רשע ואחות רשע ומקומה אנשי רשע, ולא למדה ממעשיהם: **מפדן ארם.** על שם ששני ארם היו, ארם נהרים וארם צובה, קורא אותו 'פדן', לשון: "צמד בקר" (שמואל א' יא, ז) תרגום: "פדן תורין". ויש פותרים 'פדן ארם' כמו "שדה ארם" (הושע יב, יג), שבלשון ישמעאל קורין לשדה 'פדן':

כא| **ויעתר.** הרבה והפציר בתפלה: **ויעתר לו.** נתפצר לו ונתפתה לו. ואומר אני, כל לשון 'עתר' לשון הפצרה ורבוי הוא, וכן: "ועתר ענן הקטרת" (יחזקאל ח, יא) – מרבית עלית העשן, וכן: "והעתרתם עלי דבריכם" (שם לה, יג), וכן: "ונעתרות נשיקות שונא" (משלי כז, ו) – דומות למרבות והנם למשא, אנקריסמנ"ט בלעז: **לנכח אשתו.** זה עומד בזוית זו ומתפלל, וזו עומדת בזוית זו ומתפללת: **ויעתר לו.** ולא לה, שאין דומה תפלת צדיק בן רשע לתפלת צדיק בן צדיק, לפיכך לו ולא לה:

כב| **ויתרצצו.** על כרחך המקרא הזה אומר דרשני, שסתם מה היא רציצה זו וכתב: "אם כן למה זה אנכי". רבותינו דרשוהו לשון ריצה: כשהיתה עוברת על פתחי תורה של שם ועבר יעקב רץ ומפרכס לצאת, עוברת על פתח עבודה זרה ועשו מפרכס לצאת. דבר אחר, מתרוצצים זה עם זה ומריבים בנחלת שני עולמות: **ותאמר אם כן.** גדול צער העבור, "למה זה אנכי" מתאוה ומתפללת על הריון: **ותלך לדרש.** לבית מדרשו של שם: **לדרש את ה'.** להגיד לה מה תהא בסופה:

כג| **ויאמר ה' לה.** על ידי שליח, לשם אמר ברוח הקדש והוא אמר לה: **שני גוים בבטנך.** 'גיים' כתיב, אלו אנטונינוס ורבי, שלא פסקו מעל שלחנם לא צנון ולא חזרת לא בימות החמה ולא בימות הגשמים: **ושני לאמים.** אין 'לאם' אלא מלכות: **ממעיך יפרדו.** מן המעים הם נפרדים, זה לרשעו וזה לתמו: **מלאם יאמץ.** לא ישוו בגדלה, כשזה קם זה נופל, וכן הוא אומר: "אמלאה החרבה" (יחזקאל כו, ב) – לא נתמלאה צר אלא מחרבנה של ירושלים:

כד| **וימלאו ימיה.** אבל בתמר כתיב: "ויהי בעת לדתה" (להלן לח, כז), שלא מלאו ימיה כי לשבעה חדשים ילדתם: **והנה תומם.** חסר. ובתמר "תאומים" מלא, לפי ששניהם צדיקים, אבל כאן אחד צדיק ואחד רשע:

כה| **אדמוני.** סימן הוא שיהא שופך דמים: **כלו כאדרת שער.** מלא שער כטלית של צמר המלאה שער, פלוקיד"א בלעז: **ויקראו שמו עשו.** הכל קראו לו כן, לפי שהיה נעשה ונגמר בשערו כבן שנים הרבה:

כו| **בעקב עשו.** סימן שאין זה מספיק לגמר מלכותו עד שזה עומד ונוטלה הימנו: **ויקרא שמו יעקב.** הקדוש ברוך הוא. דבר אחר, אביו קרא לו יעקב על שם אחיזת העקב: **בן ששים שנה.** עשר שנים משנשאה עד שנעשית בת שלש עשרה שנה וראויה להריון, ועשר שנים הללו צפה והמתין לה כמו שעשה אביו לשרה (לעיל טז, ג). כיון שלא נתעברה ידע שהיא עקרה והתפלל עליה. ושפחה לא רצה לשא, לפי שנתקדש בהר המוריה להיות עולה תמימה:

27 **The lads grew,**[D] and the prophecy that they would follow different paths indeed came to pass. Alongside their joint family obligations in housekeeping and agriculture, their diverse natures began to show: **Esau was a man who knew hunting,** an adventurer who was dissatisfied with domestic tasks and ventured out to hunt animals, **a man of the large field,** of the open plains. **And Jacob was a guileless man,** uninterested in the ruses of hunting, in ambushes and setting traps.[5] He led a sedentary lifestyle, **living in tents.** Alternatively, the verse could mean that he was a shepherd, expert in tending flocks, as can be seen from later events in his life.[6]

28 **And Isaac loved Esau because of the game in his mouth, and Rebecca loved Jacob.**[D] It is possible that Rebecca's preference for Jacob was due to the fact that he lived at home, in close proximity to her.

29 One day **Jacob,** who was home much of the time, **stewed a stew. Esau came from the field,** probably after an unsuccessful hunting expedition, **and he was weary,** exhausted and thirsty.[7]

30 **Esau said to Jacob: Feed me please from that red, red [*adom ha'adom*] dish.** Esau did not know what red food was in the pot. He said: Please feed me, **as I am** so **weary** that it is too hard for me to bring a spoon to my own mouth. In this connection the verse notes: **Therefore his name is called Edom.** This incident, in which Esau connected himself to a red [*adom*] dish, stuck to him for the rest of his life and to his descendants for many later generations, to the point that Edom became his alternate designation.

31 **Jacob said:** Just as you have a request from me, I too have something to ask of you. **Sell me your birthright this day,** meaning now.

32 **And Esau said: Behold, I am going to die;** I am so tired that I feel that I am about to collapse. **For what do I need a birthright?** Even if some sort of financial benefit will accrue from the birthright, it will be actualized only in the distant future, and Esau the hunter is not a calculating individual who makes long-term plans.

33 **Jacob said:** I am not satisfied with a simple declaration that you don't care about the birthright. Rather, **take an oath to me this day** that you are transferring it to me. **He took an oath to him** that the birthright would belong to him, **and he sold his birthright to Jacob.** It is possible that the stew was given in payment for the birthright. However, it can be argued that as part of the family meal, the stew was not Jacob's to sell to his brother. If so, perhaps Esau sold the birthright for a substantial sum, which Jacob handed over immediately or promised to give at a later time.[8]

34 **And Jacob gave Esau bread and a stew of lentils.** Jacob fed Esau, in accordance with the custom to eat a meal at the conclusion of an acquisition.[9] By serving a meal, Jacob exhibited the seriousness of the purchase of the birthright for him. **He,** Esau, **ate** and **he drank,** and after he recovered and realized that he was not going to die, **he arose, and he went, and Esau scorned the birthright.**[D] He remembered the sale, but he considered the entire incident ridiculous, pointless, and meaningless.

Isaac and the Land
GENESIS 26:1–33

After the previous story, which dealt with the initial tension between the two brothers and the sale of the birthright, the Torah focuses on Isaac. Up to this point, the verses have provided mostly factual information about Isaac, where he lived, whom he married, and the like. However, almost nothing has been stated about his personality. Here God appears to Isaac for the first time, and Isaac's special relationship with the land of Canaan is also presented. In contrast to his father Abraham and his son Jacob, Isaac remained in the Land of Canaan his entire life. This chapter describes how he gained a foothold in the land, his success in finding water, and his cultivation of its produce. Isaac advances in economic and social status, as he establishes his family's settlement in the land promised to his father.

26 1 **There was a famine in the land,**[D] **besides the first famine that was during the days of Abraham. Isaac,** who was a shepherd living in the south of the land of Canaan, **went to Avimelekh king of the Philistines, to Gerar.**[D] Avimelekh was one of the

---

DISCUSSION

to the fore in Jacob's relationship with Esau (see 27:36). At a later stage God will change Jacob's name to Yisrael, or Israel (32:28), which means almost the opposite, straight [*yashar*].

25:27 | **The lads grew:** The Sages maintain that Jacob and Esau were fifteen years old when the following story occurred (see *Bava Batra* 16b; *Targum Yonatan,* verse 29; *Tanḥuma, Toledot* 2). This is the age at which the unique characteristics of children start to become evident, despite

the fact that they have yet to mature fully in behavior and reasoning.

25:28 | **And Isaac loved Esau, because of the game in his mouth, and Rebecca loved Jacob:** Isaac's and Rebecca's respective preferences are of the type that occur naturally in families, when children develop significant personality differences. This verse is not critical of Esau: As the son who went out into the wild, Esau would hunt game, and out of love and respect for his

father, he would serve him meals from the animals he had caught. Perhaps Isaac preferred the taste of game animals over that of domesticated animals. These gifts, which Isaac found especially tasty, strengthened the special bond between father and his older son (see Ramban; Radak).

It may also be that, like Jacob, Isaac too was an introvert of sorts who dwelled in tents, but for this very reason he was impressed by the son who was so different from him. Alternatively, it ◄◄

כז שנה בלדת אתם: ויגדלו הנערים ויהי עשו איש ידע ציד איש שדה ויעקב
כח איש תם ישב אהלים: ויאהב יצחק את־עשו כי־ציד בפיו ורבקה אהבת את־
כט ל יעקב: ויזד יעקב נזיד ויבא עשו מן־השדה והוא עיף: ויאמר עשו אל־יעקב
הלעיטני נא מן־האדם האדם הזה כי עיף אנכי על־כן קרא־שמו אדום:
לא לב ויאמר יעקב מכרה כיום את־בכרתך לי: ויאמר עשו הנה אנכי הולך למות
לג ולמה־זה לי בכרה: ויאמר יעקב השבעה לי כיום וישבע לו וימכר את־בכרתו
לד ליעקב: ויעקב נתן לעשו לחם ונזיד עדשים ויאכל וישת ויקם וילך ויבז עשו
את־הבכרה:

כו א ויהי רעב בארץ מלבד הרעב הראשון אשר היה בימי אברהם וילך יצחק

רש"י

כז| ויגדלו הנערים ויהי עשו. כל זמן שהיו קטנים לא היו נכרים במעשיהם ואין אדם מדקדק בהם מה טיבם. כיון שנעשו בני שלש עשרה שנה, זה פירש לבתי מדרשות וזה פירש לעבודה זרה: ידע ציד. לצוד ולרמות את אביו בפיו, ושואל: אבא, היאך מעשרין את המלח? היאך מעשרין את התבן? כסבור אביו שהוא מדקדק במצות: איש שדה. כמשמעו, אדם בטל, וצודה בקשתו חיות ועופות: תם. אינו בקי בכל אלה, כלבו כן פיו. מי שאינו חריף לרמות קרוי 'תם': ישב אהלים. אהלו של שם ואהלו של עבר:

כח| בפיו. כתרגומו, בפיו של יצחק. ומדרשו, בפיו של עשו, שהיה צד אותו ומרמהו בדבריו:

כט| ויזד. לשון בשול, כתרגומו: והוא עיף. ברציחה, כמה דתימר: "כי עיפה נפשי להרגים" (ירמיה ד, לא):

ל| הלעיטני. אפתח פי ושפך הרבה לתוכה, כמו ששנינו: "אין אובסין את הגמל אבל מלעיטין אותו" (שבת קנה ע"ב): מן האדם האדם. עדשים אדמות, ואותו היום מת אברהם שלא יראה את עשו בן בנו יוצא לתרבות רעה, ואין זו "שיבה טובה" שהבטיחו הקדוש ברוך הוא (לעיל טו, טו), לפיכך קצר הקדוש ברוך הוא חמש שנים משנותיו, שיצחק חי מאה ושמנים שנה וזה מאה ושבעים וחמש שנה, ובשל יעקב עדשים להברות את האבל. ולמה עדשים? שדומות לגלגל, שהאבלות גלגל שחוזר בעולם:

לא| מכרה כיום. כתרגומו: "כיום דלהן", כיום שהוא ברור כך מכר לי מכירה ברורה: בכרתך. לפי שהעבודה בבכורות, אמר יעקב: אין רשע זה כדאי שיקריב להקדוש ברוך הוא:

לב| הנה אנכי הולך למות. אמר עשו: מה טיבה של עבודה זו? אמר לו: כמה אזהרות ועונשין ומיתות תלויין בה, כאותה ששנינו: אלו הן שבמיתה, שתויי יין ופרועי ראש. אמר: אני הולך למות על ידה, אם כן מה חפץ לי בה?

לד| ויבז עשו. העיד הכתוב על רשעו שבזה עבודתו של מקום:

DISCUSSION

may be suggested that Isaac and Esau were actually similar, as they were both men of the field (see 26:12), and it was due to this similarity that they grew close.

25:34| **The birthright:** Despite the many indications scattered throughout the Torah that the status of a firstborn is greater than that of his brothers, it is likely that in the time of the forefathers the firstborn's double portion in his father's inheritance was not yet established (see Deuteronomy 21:17). It is possible that the firstborn would receive only slightly more than his brothers, rather than a full portion. Consequently, Jacob's acquisition of the birthright did not necessarily grant him any clearly defined economic privileges (see Ramban). Nevertheless, the eldest brother would take his father's place as head of the family, and in this regard his superior status is evident. It should be noted that Jacob and Esau's ancestors lived long lives, and therefore it was likely that the inheritance and its accompanying tensions would become relevant only a century later. Esau is also well aware that his lifestyle is full of exploits that place him at risk, and therefore he might not last that long (see Ibn Ezra; Rashbam). In sum, this is not a practical quarrel or a fight over money. Jacob sought to acquire from Esau his preferential position, to be the elder brother rather than the younger.

26:1| **There was a famine in the land:** Owing to its location, there is often insufficient rainfall in the Land of Israel. In times of increased and continued drought, its soil cannot sustain the flocks and the people living there, and there is widespread famine.

local rulers of the Philistines, and perhaps he was king over all the Philistines at the time.[10]

2 **The Lord appeared to him, and said: Do not go down to Egypt; dwell in the land that I will tell you.** Like the other forefathers, Isaac too merited a divine revelation.

3 **Reside in this land, and I will be with you, and I will bless you; for I will give all these lands to you and to your descendants, and I will keep the oath that I took to Abraham your father.** You belong to this land, and it belongs to you and your descendants, and therefore you must stay here and live here.

4 **And I will multiply your descendants like the stars of the heavens, and I will give to your descendants all these lands; and all the nations of the earth shall be blessed through your descendants.**

5 However, your right to the land is not due exclusively to your own merit; rather, it originated **because Abraham heeded My voice, and kept My commission, My commandments, My statutes, and My laws.**[D]

Second aliya
6 **Isaac lived in Gerar.** Since he was prohibited from leaving for Egypt, Isaac remained in Gerar.

7 **The men of the place asked him with regard to his wife. He said: She is my sister.** Isaac thereby followed Abraham's example (12:13, 20:2). In a sense his claim was justified, as Rebecca was related to him. It is possible that Isaac and Rebecca were similar enough in appearance that this contention would be accepted. **As he was afraid to say:** She is **my wife,** for he said to himself: **Lest the men of the place kill me over Rebecca,**[D] **because she is of fair appearance.** An earlier verse already mentioned Rebecca's beauty as a young girl (24:16), but her age at the time of this incident is not stated. Perhaps due to the negative experience of the residents of Gerar during Abraham's

earlier visit (20:1–18), they accepted Isaac's claim at face value, and were careful not to take a woman from his tribe.

8 Yet, **it was when the days he was there were extended,** and Isaac was less careful; **Avimelekh king of the Philistines looked out through the window,** as he presumably lived in a palace that was taller than the surrounding buildings, **and behold, he saw Isaac** in his house **playing,** engaging in sexual activity, **with Rebecca his wife.**

9 **Avimelekh summoned Isaac and said: Behold,** I have seen that **she is your wife; how did you say: She is my sister?** Why did you deceive me? **Isaac said to him: Because I said,** or I thought to myself: **Lest I die over her.** If I reveal that she is my wife, they might kill me and take her.

10 **Avimelekh said: What is this that you have done to us,** by cheating us? **One of** the men of **the people**[D] **almost lay with your wife; you would have brought guilt,** sin, **upon us.** Whether this is the same Avimelekh as in the days of Abraham or a different individual,[11] what unfolded when Sarah was taken (see chap. 20) had not been forgotten in Avimelekh's household. Therefore, Isaac did not rely on the moral probity of the residents of Gerar.

11 **Avimelekh commanded all the people, saying: Anyone who touches this man or his wife,** as it has now been established that Rebecca is Isaac's wife, **shall be put to death.**

12 Up to this point, the incidents in Isaac's life parallel events that occurred in Abraham's life. The focus now turns to deeds performed by Isaac that were apparently not done by his father. It is likely that Abraham the nomad was occupied mainly with shepherding. In contrast, Isaac, who lived in Gerar, engaged also in agriculture. **Isaac sowed in that land and found in that year one hundredfold.** He reaped one hundred times what he

---

DISCUSSION

And Isaac went...to Gerar: Isaac moved to Gerar, which was close to the coast (see 10:19). He thought he would go from there to Egypt by way of the ancient trade route down the coast of the land of Canaan called Via Maris, which connected Syria in the north with Egypt in the south. Those fleeing a famine in Canaan would turn to Egypt, which was irrigated by the Nile, whose sources are far in the south. For this reason Egypt did not suffer from droughts; even when famine prevailed in Canaan, the land in Egypt might be fertile and its crops bounteous.

26:5 | **And kept My commission, My commandments, My statutes, and My laws:** In all the stories of his travels, his journeys, and his wanderings from one land to another, it is

evident that Abraham heeded the voice of God. God Himself confirmed this trait of Abraham: "For I love him, so that he shall command his children and his household after him, and they will observe the way of the Lord, to perform righteousness and justice" (18:19). However, in this verse, the phrase "My observances, My commandments, My statutes, and My laws" is much more specific than that. Abraham was not merely a man of a religious spirit, enthused by the revelations and prophetic visions he received, while letting the divine voice influence his life only in a general manner. Rather, he and his household observed God's law, a complex system of commandments and statutes. This system to which he adhered provided a practical, intelligent way

of living: The laws refer to the study of the Torah, the statutes are the divine decrees, while the observances and commandments involve the practical side of what should and should not be done, such as commands that can be rationally understood. Based on this verse, the Sages state that Abraham observed the entire Torah before it was given (Mishna *Kiddushin* 4:14). The statutes of the Torah may already have been revealed to select individuals and small groups of people well before the Torah was given to all of Israel in a public manner at Sinai.

26:7 | **Lest the men of the place kill me over Rebecca:** Both Abraham and Isaac were aware that their neighbors observed no commandments, statutes, or laws similar to those to which ◄●

ב אֶל־אֲבִימֶלֶךְ מֶלֶךְ־פְּלִשְׁתִּים גְּרָרָה: וַיֵּרָא אֵלָיו יְהוָה וַיֹּאמֶר אַל־תֵּרֵד מִצְרָיְמָה
ג שְׁכֹן בָּאָרֶץ אֲשֶׁר אֹמַר אֵלֶיךָ: גּוּר בָּאָרֶץ הַזֹּאת וְאֶהְיֶה עִמְּךָ וַאֲבָרְכֶךָּ כִּי־לְךָ
וּלְזַרְעֲךָ אֶתֵּן אֶת־כָּל־הָאֲרָצֹת הָאֵל וַהֲקִמֹתִי אֶת־הַשְּׁבֻעָה אֲשֶׁר נִשְׁבַּעְתִּי
ד לְאַבְרָהָם אָבִיךָ: וְהִרְבֵּיתִי אֶת־זַרְעֲךָ כְּכוֹכְבֵי הַשָּׁמַיִם וְנָתַתִּי לְזַרְעֲךָ אֵת כָּל־
ה הָאֲרָצֹת הָאֵל וְהִתְבָּרְכוּ בְזַרְעֲךָ כֹּל גּוֹיֵי הָאָרֶץ: עֵקֶב אֲשֶׁר־שָׁמַע אַבְרָהָם בְּקֹלִי
ו ז וַיִּשְׁמֹר מִשְׁמַרְתִּי מִצְוֹתַי חֻקּוֹתַי וְתוֹרֹתָי: וַיֵּשֶׁב יִצְחָק בִּגְרָר: וַיִּשְׁאֲלוּ אַנְשֵׁי שני
הַמָּקוֹם לְאִשְׁתּוֹ וַיֹּאמֶר אֲחֹתִי הִוא כִּי יָרֵא לֵאמֹר אִשְׁתִּי פֶּן־יַהַרְגֻנִי אַנְשֵׁי הַמָּקוֹם
ח עַל־רִבְקָה כִּי־טוֹבַת מַרְאֶה הִוא: וַיְהִי כִּי־אָרְכוּ־לוֹ שָׁם הַיָּמִים וַיַּשְׁקֵף אֲבִימֶלֶךְ
מֶלֶךְ פְּלִשְׁתִּים בְּעַד הַחַלּוֹן וַיַּרְא וְהִנֵּה יִצְחָק מְצַחֵק אֵת רִבְקָה אִשְׁתּוֹ:
ט וַיִּקְרָא אֲבִימֶלֶךְ לְיִצְחָק וַיֹּאמֶר אַךְ הִנֵּה אִשְׁתְּךָ הִוא וְאֵיךְ אָמַרְתָּ אֲחֹתִי
י הִוא וַיֹּאמֶר אֵלָיו יִצְחָק כִּי אָמַרְתִּי פֶּן־אָמוּת עָלֶיהָ: וַיֹּאמֶר אֲבִימֶלֶךְ מַה־זֹּאת
יא עָשִׂיתָ לָּנוּ כִּמְעַט שָׁכַב אַחַד הָעָם אֶת־אִשְׁתֶּךָ וְהֵבֵאתָ עָלֵינוּ אָשָׁם: וַיְצַו אֲבִימֶלֶךְ
יב אֶת־כָּל־הָעָם לֵאמֹר הַנֹּגֵעַ בָּאִישׁ הַזֶּה וּבְאִשְׁתּוֹ מוֹת יוּמָת: וַיִּזְרַע יִצְחָק

רש״י

פרק כו

ב] **אַל תֵּרֵד מִצְרָיְמָה.** שֶׁהָיָה דַּעְתּוֹ לָרֶדֶת מִצְרַיִם כְּמוֹ שֶׁיָּרַד אָבִיו בִּימֵי הָרָעָב. **אַל תֵּרֵד מִצְרָיְמָה.** שֶׁאַתָּה עוֹלָה תְּמִימָה וְאֵין חוּצָה לָאָרֶץ כְּדַאי לְךָ:

ג] **הָאֵל.** כְּמוֹ ״הָאֵלֶּה״:

ד] **וְהִתְבָּרְכוּ בְזַרְעֲךָ.** אָדָם אוֹמֵר לִבְנוֹ: יְהֵא זַרְעֲךָ כְּזַרְעוֹ שֶׁל יִצְחָק, וְכֵן בְּכָל הַמִּקְרָא, וְזֶה אָב לְכֻלָּן: ״בְּךָ יְבָרֵךְ יִשְׂרָאֵל לֵאמֹר״ וְגוֹ׳ (להלן מח, כ). וְאַף לְעִנְיַן הַקְּלָלָה מָצִינוּ כֵּן: ״וְהָיְתָה הָאִשָּׁה לְאָלָה״ (במדבר ה, כז), שֶׁהַמְקַלֵּל שׂוֹנְאוֹ אוֹמֵר: תְּהֵא כִּפְלוֹנִית; וְכֵן: ״וְהִנַּחְתֶּם שִׁמְכֶם לִשְׁבוּעָה לִבְחִירַי״ (ישעיה סה, טו), שֶׁהַנִּשְׁבָּע אוֹמֵר: אֱהֵא כִּפְלוֹנִי אִם עָשִׂיתִי כָּךְ וְכָךְ:

ה] **שָׁמַע אַבְרָהָם בְּקֹלִי.** כְּשֶׁנִּסִּיתִי אוֹתוֹ: **וַיִּשְׁמֹר מִשְׁמַרְתִּי.** גְּזֵרוֹת לְהַרְחָקָה עַל אַזְהָרוֹת שֶׁבַּתּוֹרָה, כְּגוֹן שְׁנִיּוֹת לָעֲרָיוֹת וּשְׁבוּת לַשַּׁבָּת: **מִצְוֹתַי.** דְּבָרִים שֶׁאִלּוּ לֹא נִכְתְּבוּ רְאוּיִין הֵם לְהִצְטַוּוֹת, כְּגוֹן גָּזֵל וּשְׁפִיכוּת דָּמִים: **חֻקּוֹתַי.** דְּבָרִים שֶׁיֵּצֶר הָרָע וְאֻמּוֹת הָעוֹלָם מְשִׁיבִים עֲלֵיהֶם, כְּגוֹן אֲכִילַת חֲזִיר וּלְבִישַׁת שַׁעַטְנֵז, שֶׁאֵין טַעַם בַּדָּבָר אֶלָּא הַמֶּלֶךְ גָּזַר חֻקָּיו עַל עֲבָדָיו: **וְתוֹרֹתָי.** לְהָבִיא תּוֹרָה שֶׁבְּעַל פֶּה, הֲלָכָה לְמֹשֶׁה מִסִּינַי:

ז] **לְאִשְׁתּוֹ.** עַל אִשְׁתּוֹ, כְּמוֹ: ״אִמְרִי לִי אָחִי הוּא״ (לעיל כ, יג):

ח] **כִּי אָרְכוּ.** אָמַר: מֵעַתָּה אֵין לִי לִדְאֹג מֵאַחַר שֶׁלֹּא אֲנָסוּהָ עַד עַכְשָׁיו, וְלֹא נִזְהַר לִהְיוֹת נִשְׁמָר: **וַיַּשְׁקֵף אֲבִימֶלֶךְ.** רָאָהוּ מְשַׁמֵּשׁ מִטָּתוֹ:

י] **אַחַד הָעָם.** הַמְיֻחָד בָּעָם, זֶה הַמֶּלֶךְ: **וְהֵבֵאתָ עָלֵינוּ אָשָׁם.** אִם שָׁכַב, כְּבָר הֵבֵאתָ אָשָׁם עָלֵינוּ:

DISCUSSION

they faithfully observed. Even if a legal system existed, it is hard to know the extent to which laws were enforced in practice. Furthermore, such laws were often applied only to the simple folk, leaving the leaders and kings to follow their whims unrestricted. In this context, it is notable that the Torah's approach is that not even a king, the supreme ruler, is exempt from the law (Deuteronomy 17:18–20; II Samuel 12:1–13; see commentary on Leviticus 4:22). This concept was not accepted in many places even thousands of years after the period of the patriarchs.

26:10| **One of the people:** Some commentaries maintain that the expression "one of the people" refers to the king himself or to one of his ministers (Rashi; *Targum Yonatan*). If so, the king is delicately alluding to the possibility that he too might have slept with Isaac's wife, as he likewise thought she was unattached.

sowed, a very respectable yield even nowadays. **And** the explanation for this unusually large crop is that **the Lord blessed him.**

13 *Third aliya* **The man grew wealthy, and continued to grow until he became very wealthy.** Since Isaac grew more crops than he required, he sold the surplus and became wealthy as a result.

14 **He had livestock of flocks, and livestock of cattle, and a great household,** a general term covering slaves, maidservants, and all his household staff;[12] **the Philistines envied him,** as his neighbors were not similarly blessed in their fields.

15 Here the chapter inserts a comment that will be important for the continuation of the story: **All the cisterns that his father's servants dug in the days of Abraham, his father, the Philistines sealed them**[D] after Abraham left Gerar, **and filled them with earth.** Isaac was uncomfortable in Gerar not only due to his great wealth, which aroused envy among his neighbors, but also because his father's wells had been filled with earth.

16 The envy and general resentment of the residents of Gerar toward Isaac also finds expression in a statement of the king, which represents the overall feeling of the public. **Avimelekh said to Isaac: Leave us, for you have grown much mightier than we.** You are too strong for us; one who grows wealthy in such an irregular manner is liable to upset the social and political balance in our community.

17 **Isaac left there,** probably southward, **and he encamped in the Valley of Gerar**[B] **and settled there.**

18 As he required water in his new place, **Isaac again dug the cisterns of water that they had dug in the days of Abraham, his father, and that the Philistines had sealed after the death of Abraham.** There were certainly sufficient markers by which he could locate the wells. **He called them names like the names that his father called them.** Due to their importance, the serviceable wells were given names.

19 **Isaac's servants dug in the valley,** as it is easy to find ground water in the channels of streams, **and they found there a well of fresh water.**

20 **The herdsmen of Gerar quarreled with Isaac's herdsmen, saying: The water is ours.** Since you are residing near our city of Gerar, in our territory, the water belongs to us. **He called the name of the well Esek, because they involved themselves [*hitasseku*],** fought, **with him.**

21 **They,** Isaac's servants, **dug another well, and they,** the Philistines, **quarreled over it as well. He called it Sitna,** accusation.[13]

22 Again **he,** Isaac, **moved from there and dug another well, and they did not quarrel over it. He called its name Rehovot, and he said: As now the Lord has expanded space [*hirḥiv*] for us, and we shall be fruitful in the land;** now we can dwell in our place in peace. Isaac assumed that the herdsmen of Gerar would likely leave this particular well alone, as they preferred to tend their flocks nearer to their city, and the well was situated far from their territory.

23 *Fourth aliya* **He,** Isaac, **ascended from there to Beersheba,** which was at a higher altitude than his previous location in the Valley of Gerar, as Beersheba was built on a raised area. It is also possible that Isaac's move to Beersheba is described as an ascension due to the importance of the city.

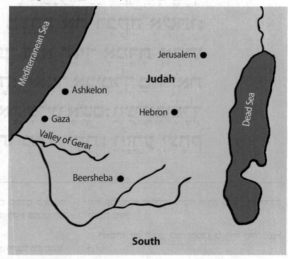

Locations of Beersheba and the Valley of Gerar

24 **The Lord appeared to him that night and said: I am the God of Abraham your father. Fear not,** despite the fact that you have been forced to move due to the provocations of the Philistines, **as I am with you; I will bless you and multiply your descendants for the sake of My servant Abraham.**

25 **He built an altar there and proclaimed the name of the Lord.** Like Abraham, Isaac performed a ceremony or prayer in which he publicly invoked God's name. **And he pitched**

DISCUSSION

26:15 | **The Philistines sealed them:** The context suggests that this was not a personal vendetta directed against Abraham, as he no longer lived in proximity to the Philistines. Rather, it is likely that they considered all wells located outside the city a security risk, since their water could be used by any enemy who came to besiege Gerar (Rashi).

יג בארץ ההוא וימצא בשנה ההוא מאה שערים ויברכהו יהוה: ויגדל האיש שלישי
יד וילך הלוך וגדל עד כי־גדל מאד: ויהי־לו מקנה־צאן ומקנה בקר ועבדה רבה
טו ויקנאו אתו פלשתים: וכל־הבארת אשר חפרו עבדי אביו בימי אברהם אביו
טז סתמום פלשתים וימלאום עפר: ויאמר אבימלך אל־יצחק לך מעמנו כי־
יז יח עצמת ממנו מאד: וילך משם יצחק ויחן בנחל־גרר וישב שם: וישב יצחק
ויחפר | את־בארת המים אשר חפרו בימי אברהם אביו ויסתמום פלשתים
יט אחרי מות אברהם ויקרא להן שמות כשמת אשר־קרא להן אביו: ויחפרו
כ עבדי־יצחק בנחל וימצאו־שם באר מים חיים: ויריבו רעי גרר עם־רעי יצחק
כא לאמר לנו המים ויקרא שם־הבאר עשק כי התעשקו עמו: ויחפרו באר אחרת
כב ויריבו גם־עליה ויקרא שמה שטנה: ויעתק משם ויחפר באר אחרת ולא רבו
עליה ויקרא שמה רחבות ויאמר כי־עתה הרחיב יהוה לנו ופרינו בארץ:
כג כד ויעל משם באר שבע: וירא אליו יהוה בלילה ההוא ויאמר אנכי אלהי אברהם רביעי
אביך אל־תירא כי־אתך אנכי וברכתיך והרביתי את־זרעך בעבור אברהם
כה עבדי: ויבן שם מזבח ויקרא בשם יהוה ויט־שם אהלו ויכרו־שם עבדי־יצחק

רש"י

יב | בארץ ההוא. אף על פי שאינה חשובה כארץ ישראל עצמה, כארץ שבעה גוים: בארץ ההוא בשנה ההוא. הארץ קשה והשנה קשה: בשנה ההוא. אף על פי שאינה כתקנה, שהיתה שנת רעבון: מאה שערים. שאמדוה כמה ראויה לעשות, ועשתה על אחת שאמדוה מאה. ורבותינו אמרו: אמד זה למעשרות היה:

יג | כי גדל מאד. שהיו אומרים: זבל פרדותיו של יצחק ולא כספו וזהבו של אבימלך:

יד | ועבדה רבה. פעלה רבה, בלשון לעז אוברינ"א. 'עבודה' משמע עבודה אחת, 'עבדה' משמע פעלה רבה:

טו | סתמום פלשתים. מפני שאמרו: תקלה הם לנו מפני הגיסות הבאות עלינו. "טמונון פלשתאי", לשון סתימה, ובלשון משנה: "מטמטם את הלב" (פסחים מב ע"א):

יז | בנחל גרר. רחוק מן העיר:

יח | וישב ויחפר. את הבארות אשר חפרו בימי אברהם אביו ופלשתים סתמום קדם שנסע יצחק מגרר, חזר וחפרן:

כ | עשק. ערער: התעשקו. נתעסקו עמו עליה במריבה וערער:

כא | שטנה. נוישמנ"ט:

כב | ופרינו בארץ. כתרגומו: "ונפוש בארעא":

BACKGROUND

26:17 | **The Valley of Gerar:** This refers to one of the main wadis in the Negev, the southern portion of Israel, one that also serves as a geographic and climatic border between inhabited regions and the desert. The wadi begins in the South Hebron Hills before joining the Besor Stream. The ground water in the area is high and accessible. There are roughly fifty springs in its middle section, and the remains of many settlements have been discovered nearby.

his tent there. And Isaac's servants dug a well there, near Beersheba.
26 Later, **Avimelekh** king of the Philistines **went to him,** Isaac, **from Gerar, with a group of his associates**[D] **and Pikhol the captain of his guard.**
27 Upon seeing the arrival of a friendly delegation, **Isaac said to them: Why did you come to me?** After all, **you hated me, and you sent me from among you.**
28 **They said: We saw that the Lord was with you,** since you grew and prospered beyond the status of a private individual, **and** therefore **we said: Let there please be an oath** of a covenant **between us, between us and you; we will establish a covenant with you:**
29 **If you will** or so that you will[14] **do us no harm, when we have not touched you, and when we have done only good with you, and we sent you in peace.** While it is true that we feared you and banished you from our land, nevertheless you lived among us for a certain period and were not sent away in a violent manner or with hatred. Perhaps we were mistaken in dismissing you; in any case we see that **you are now the blessed of the Lord,**[D] and therefore we wish to establish a covenant with you.
30 *Fifth aliya* Isaac agreed, and **he made a feast for them, and they ate and drank,** in accordance with the custom after establishing a covenant.
31 **They awoke in the morning and took oaths to one another** that they would keep the covenant and maintain friendly relations from that time forward. **Isaac sent them** back, **and they went from him in peace.**
32 **It was on that day** that Avimelekh left, and **Isaac's servants came and told him with regard to the well that they had dug.** Isaac's servants had continued digging wells. **They said to him: We have** again **found water.**
33 **He called it Shiva,** in allusion to the oath [*shevua*]; **therefore, the name of the city is Beersheba to this day.**[D]

Jacob, Esau, and the Blessings

GENESIS 26:34–28:9

This portion, which deals with Isaac's blessings, begins by mentioning Esau's marriage to Hitite women and ends with his marriage to Ishmael's daughter. In his choice of wives Esau strays from Abraham's path, as Abraham instructed his servant not to take a wife for his son from the women of Canaan (24:3).

The central issue in this portion is who will merit the blessings of Isaac, and to whom the blessing of Abraham will pass. In contrast to the uniformity of Isaac and Rebecca's negative response to Esau's wives, they disagree over the appropriate recipient of the blessings. Despite Jacob's use of deception to receive the blessings that Isaac intended to give to Esau, Isaac initiates granting the blessing of Abraham to Jacob before he leaves for Haran.

34 **Esau was forty years old.** Esau tried to imitate his father, at least on the superficial level. Just as Isaac married at forty, at an age when one's mind is already settled,[15] Esau did the same. **And he took as a wife Yehudit, daughter of Be'eri the Hitite, and Basmat, daughter of Eilon the Hitite,** who were two Hitite women.
35 The Torah attests: **They were a source of bitterness**[D] **to Isaac and to Rebecca.**
27 1 **It was when Isaac was old, and his eyes dimmed from seeing,** as he became blind, or his sight diminished considerably; **he summoned Esau, his elder son, and said to him: My son. He,** Esau, **said to him: Here I am.** Esau responded in the proper manner, as there was a mutually positive relationship between father and son.
2 **He,** Isaac, **said: Behold, I have now**[16] **grown old; I do not know the day of my death.** In actuality, Isaac lived far longer than he expected, for as it follows from various calculations, he did not die until many years after this episode. Perhaps due to his blindness and inactive life, he felt old and frail before his time.
3 **Now, please take your** hunting **gear, your quiver,** which is

DISCUSSION

26:26 | **With a group [*aḥuzat*] of his associates:** The term *aḥuza*, which primarily denotes an inheritance, is used here in a more abstract sense (see Onkelos; Rashi; Rashbam). Alternatively, Aḥuzat is the name of a close associate of Avimelekh (*Bereshit Rabba* 64; *Da'at Zekenim* of *Tosafot*; *Ḥizkuni*), his advisor and confidant (see I Kings 4:5; I Chronicles 27:33).

26:29 | **You are now the blessed of the Lord:** Although Gerar was only one of many Philistine cities, it is possible that Avimelekh was the king over all the Philistines, while the other cities were under the control of his captains, the local rulers. Isaac's banishment is understandable if one takes into account the fact that he settled in a major city, but one that was neither large nor strong. His increasing wealth and stature threatened the delicate social and political balance there. While Avimelekh's comments are hardly diplomatic, they are honest and fair. He admits that he and his men banned Isaac from their land, but justifies his decision, since a subject who has grown so powerful can undermine the status quo in the city.

26:33 | **Therefore the name of the city is Beersheba to this day:** It was already stated in an earlier chapter (21:28–31) that the city was named for the oath and the seven [*sheva*] sheep of Abraham, who established a similar covenant with Avimelekh (see commentary on 35:15). Here

כו כז באר: ואבימלך הלך אליו מגרר ואחזת מרעהו ופיכל שר־צבאו: ויאמר
כח אלהם יצחק מדוע באתם אלי ואתם שנאתם אתי ותשלחוני מאתכם: ויאמרו
ראו ראינו כי־היה יהוה | עמך ונאמר תהי נא אלה בינותינו בינינו ובינך
כט ונכרתה ברית עמך: אם־תעשה עמנו רעה כאשר לא נגענוך וכאשר עשינו
ל עמך רק־טוב ונשלחך בשלום אתה עתה ברוך יהוה: ויעש להם משתה חמישי
לא ויאכלו וישתו: וישכימו בבקר וישבעו איש לאחיו וישלחם יצחק וילכו מאתו
לב בשלום: ויהי | ביום ההוא ויבאו עבדי יצחק ויגדו לו על־אדות הבאר אשר
לג חפרו ויאמרו לו מצאנו מים: ויקרא אתה שבעה על־כן שם־העיר באר שבע
לד עד היום הזה: ויהי עשו בן־ארבעים שנה ויקח אשה את־יהודית בת־בארי
לה כז א החתי ואת־בשמת בת־אילן החתי: ותהיין מרת רוח ליצחק ולרבקה: ויהי כד
כי־זקן יצחק ותכהין עיניו מראת ויקרא את־עשו בנו הגדל ויאמר אליו בני
ב ג ויאמר אליו הנני: ויאמר הנה־נא זקנתי לא ידעתי יום מותי: ועתה שא־נא

רש״י

כו| ואחזת מרעהו. "סיעת מרחמוהי", סיעה מאוהביו. ויש תתמה על תי"ו שב'אחזת' ואף על פי שאינה תבה דבוקה לחברתה, יש דגמתה במקרא: "הבה לנו עזרת מצר" (תהלים ס, יג), "ושכרת ולא מיין" (ישעיה נא, כא). ויש פותרים 'מרעהו' המ"ם מיסוד התבה, כמו "שלשים מרעים" (שופטים יד, יא) דשמשון, כדי לעשות 'ואחזת' תבה דבוקה, ומתרגמין "סיעת רחמוהי": אחזת. לשון קבוצה ואגדה, שנאחזים יחד:

כח| ראו ראינו. ראו באביך, ראינו בך: תהי נא אלה בינותינו. תהי האלה אשר בינותינו מימי אביך, תהי גם עתה בינינו ובינך:

כט| לא נגענוך. כשאמרנו לך: "לך מעמנו" (לעיל פסוק טז): אתה. גם אתה עשה לנו כן:

לג| שבעה. על שם הברית:

לד| בן ארבעים שנה. עשו נמשל לחזיר, שנאמר: "יכרסמנה חזיר מיער" (תהלים פ, יד); החזיר הזה כשהוא שוכב פושט טלפיו לומר: ראו שאני טהור, כך אלו גוזלים וחומסים ומראים עצמם כשרים. כל ארבעים שנה היה עשו צד נשים תחת בעליהן ומענה אותן; כשהיה בן ארבעים אמר: אבא בן ארבעים שנה נשא אשה, אף אני כן:

לה| מרת רוח. לשון: "ממרים הייתם" (דברים ט, כד), כל מעשיהן היו לעצבון "ליצחק ולרבקה", שהיו עובדות עבודה זרה:

פרק כז

א| ותכהין. בעשן של אלו. דבר אחר, כדי שיטול יעקב את הברכות:

ב| לא ידעתי יום מותי. אמר רבי יהושע בן קרחה: אם מגיע אדם לפרק אבותיו ידאג חמש שנים לפני כן וחמש לאחר כן, ויצחק היה בן מאה ועשרים ושלש, אמר: שמא לפרק אמי אני מגיע והיא מתה בת מאה ועשרים ושבע, והריני בחמש שנים סמוך לפרקה, לפיכך "לא ידעתי יום מותי", שמא לפרק אמי שמא לפרק אבא:

DISCUSSION

the name was reinforced; the city itself had perhaps grown in stature in the meantime as well (see Radak). It is possible that it was due to Isaac calling the well Shiva that the city retained its name "to this day"; although Abraham initially gave the city its name, its affirmation by Isaac perpetuated this name.

26:35| **They were a source of bitterness:** It is probable that Esau's parents disliked his wives not for personal reasons, but due to the fact that they came from a different culture. Local women were unsuited for the customs of the tribe of Abraham, rooted as it was in a distant land. Their distance from the family's way of life was the cause of bitterness for Isaac and Rebecca.

hung on one's back, **and your bow, and go out to the field and hunt game for me.**

4 **Prepare for me tasty food** from the animals you capture, **such as I like.** As stated above (25:28), Esau would regularly feed Isaac from the animals he hunted, and Isaac enjoyed such meals. **And bring it to me, and I will eat, so that my soul will bless you**[D] **before I die.**

5 **Rebecca heard as Isaac spoke to Esau his son. Esau went to the field,** in accordance with his father's command, **to hunt game** in order **to bring** it to him.

6 **Rebecca said to Jacob her son, saying: Behold, I heard your father speak to Esau your brother, saying** as follows:

7 **Bring me game and prepare for me tasty food, and I will eat, and I will bless you before the Lord before my death.**

8 **Now, my son, heed my voice to that which I command you.** Rebecca invokes her authority in her address to her son, as she is telling him to perform a complicated and ostensibly questionable maneuver.

9 **Please go to the flock and take for me from there two fine goat kids.** Rebecca assumed that Esau would return from his hunt with a deer or two. Consequently, she asked Jacob to bring two goat kids, which are similar in taste to deer.[17] **And I will make them tasty food for your father, such as he likes.** Since she knew how to cook for her husband and was familiar with his sensitivities, it was likely that she could prepare him a dish of goat meat whose taste he would be unable to distinguish from that of deer meat.

10 **You shall bring it to your father and he will eat, so that he will bless you before his death.**

11 **And Jacob said to Rebecca his mother:** I cannot approach my father as Esau, as **behold, Esau my brother is a hairy man.** Covered with hair already at birth, Esau had become even more hairy over the years. **And I am a man of smooth skin.** Jacob might not have been entirely hairless, but he was smooth-skinned in comparison to Esau.

12 **Perhaps my father will feel me,** not necessarily to discover my identity, but innocently, due to our physical proximity;[18] **and I shall be in his eyes as a deceiver,** a trickster, as he will realize

that I have disguised myself as Esau. **And** this is dangerous, as **I shall bring upon myself a curse and not a blessing.**

13 **His mother said to him:** If you will be cursed, **your curse is upon me, my son.** This is a rhetorical expression of her acceptance of responsibility for the curse.[19] **Only** in the meantime **heed my voice, and go, take** the goat kids **for me,** as I have commanded you.

14 **He went, and took** the kids, **and brought** them **to his mother,** as she requested; **and his mother made tasty food, such as his father liked.**

15 In response to the problem Jacob had raised, **Rebecca took the fine garments,** the best clothes, reserved for special occasions, **of Esau, her elder son, that were with her in the house, and she dressed Jacob, her younger son,** in them.

16 **The hides of the kids of the goats she placed** as sleeves **on his hands and on the smooth of his neck,** as these are the exposed areas of the body where the difference between the brothers is likely to be most noticeable. When the blind Isaac felt the hides, he would assume that it was Esau standing before him.

17 **She gave the tasty food and the bread that she prepared into the hand of Jacob her son.**

18 **He came to his father and said: My father. He,** Isaac, **said: Here I am; who are you, my son?** It is possible that the voices of the twins, Jacob and Esau, were very similar, and therefore Isaac would always ask this question upon their arrival.

19 **Jacob said to his father: I am Esau your firstborn; I did as you spoke to me. Arise now, sit and eat from my game, so that your soul will bless me.**

20 Since Jacob did not go out hunting but simply took goat kids from the goat shed, he arrived sooner than his father had anticipated. Therefore, **Isaac said to his son: How is it that you hastened so to find it, my son?** According to my calculation, the hunt and the preparation of the dish should have taken longer. **He,** Jacob, **said: Because the Lord your God coordinated it,** the outcome, so that the game appeared **before me** without delay.

21 Sensing that something strange was going on, **Isaac said to Jacob: Please approach, that I may feel you, my son,** so that

---

DISCUSSION

27:4 | That my soul will bless you: Isaac's blessing is not a perfunctory wish, but a prophecy. For the spirit of prophecy to rest on a prophet, he must be free from all anger or worry, and

utter his blessing in a relaxed, content state of mind. As indicated elsewhere in the Bible, certain prophets required the playing of music in order to achieve this state of mind (see II Kings

3:15). Isaac asked Esau to bring him dishes prepared to his taste so that he would feel comfortable and serene, and able to bestow upon him an appropriate blessing.

ד כֵּלֶיךָ תֶּלְיְךָ וְקַשְׁתֶּךָ וְצֵא הַשָּׂדֶה וְצוּדָה לִּי צידה: וַעֲשֵׂה־לִי מַטְעַמִּים כַּאֲשֶׁר
ה אָהַבְתִּי וְהָבִיאָה לִּי וְאֹכֵלָה בַּעֲבוּר תְּבָרֶכְךָ נַפְשִׁי בְּטֶרֶם אָמוּת: וְרִבְקָה שֹׁמַעַת
ו בְּדַבֵּר יִצְחָק אֶל־עֵשָׂו בְּנוֹ וַיֵּלֶךְ עֵשָׂו הַשָּׂדֶה לָצוּד צַיִד לְהָבִיא: וְרִבְקָה אָמְרָה
אֶל־יַעֲקֹב בְּנָהּ לֵאמֹר הִנֵּה שָׁמַעְתִּי אֶת־אָבִיךָ מְדַבֵּר אֶל־עֵשָׂו אָחִיךָ לֵאמֹר:
ז הָבִיאָה לִּי צַיִד וַעֲשֵׂה־לִי מַטְעַמִּים וְאֹכֵלָה וַאֲבָרֶכְכָה לִפְנֵי יְהוָה לִפְנֵי מוֹתִי:
ח ט וְעַתָּה בְנִי שְׁמַע בְּקֹלִי לַאֲשֶׁר אֲנִי מְצַוָּה אֹתָךְ: לֶךְ־נָא אֶל־הַצֹּאן וְקַח־לִי מִשָּׁם
י שְׁנֵי גְּדָיֵי עִזִּים טֹבִים וְאֶעֱשֶׂה אֹתָם מַטְעַמִּים לְאָבִיךָ כַּאֲשֶׁר אָהֵב: וְהֵבֵאתָ
יא לְאָבִיךָ וְאָכָל בַּעֲבֻר אֲשֶׁר יְבָרֶכְךָ לִפְנֵי מוֹתוֹ: וַיֹּאמֶר יַעֲקֹב אֶל־רִבְקָה אִמּוֹ
יב הֵן עֵשָׂו אָחִי אִישׁ שָׂעִר וְאָנֹכִי אִישׁ חָלָק: אוּלַי יְמֻשֵּׁנִי אָבִי וְהָיִיתִי בְעֵינָיו
יג כִּמְתַעְתֵּעַ וְהֵבֵאתִי עָלַי קְלָלָה וְלֹא בְרָכָה: וַתֹּאמֶר לוֹ אִמּוֹ עָלַי קִלְלָתְךָ בְּנִי
יד אַךְ שְׁמַע בְּקֹלִי וְלֵךְ קַח־לִי: וַיֵּלֶךְ וַיִּקַּח וַיָּבֵא לְאִמּוֹ וַתַּעַשׂ אִמּוֹ מַטְעַמִּים כַּאֲשֶׁר
טו אָהֵב אָבִיו: וַתִּקַּח רִבְקָה אֶת־בִּגְדֵי עֵשָׂו בְּנָהּ הַגָּדֹל הַחֲמֻדֹת אֲשֶׁר אִתָּהּ בַּבָּיִת
טז וַתַּלְבֵּשׁ אֶת־יַעֲקֹב בְּנָהּ הַקָּטָן: וְאֵת עֹרֹת גְּדָיֵי הָעִזִּים הִלְבִּישָׁה עַל־יָדָיו וְעַל
יז חֶלְקַת צַוָּארָיו: וַתִּתֵּן אֶת־הַמַּטְעַמִּים וְאֶת־הַלֶּחֶם אֲשֶׁר עָשָׂתָה בְּיַד יַעֲקֹב
יח יט בְּנָהּ: וַיָּבֹא אֶל־אָבִיו וַיֹּאמֶר אָבִי וַיֹּאמֶר הִנֶּנִּי מִי אַתָּה בְּנִי: וַיֹּאמֶר יַעֲקֹב
אֶל־אָבִיו אָנֹכִי עֵשָׂו בְּכֹרֶךָ עָשִׂיתִי כַּאֲשֶׁר דִּבַּרְתָּ אֵלָי קוּם־נָא שְׁבָה וְאָכְלָה
כ מִצֵּידִי בַּעֲבוּר תְּבָרְכַנִּי נַפְשֶׁךָ: וַיֹּאמֶר יִצְחָק אֶל־בְּנוֹ מַה־זֶּה מִהַרְתָּ לִמְצֹא
כא בְּנִי וַיֹּאמֶר כִּי הִקְרָה יְהוָה אֱלֹהֶיךָ לְפָנָי: וַיֹּאמֶר יִצְחָק אֶל־יַעֲקֹב גְּשָׁה־נָּא

רש״י

ג | תֶּלְיְךָ. חַרְבְּךָ שֶׁדֶּרֶךְ לְתָלוֹתָהּ: שָׂא נָא. לְשׁוֹן הַשְׁחָזָה, כְּמוֹ שֶׁשָּׁנִינוּ: "אֵין מַשְׁחִיזִין אֶת הַסַּכִּין אֲבָל מַשִּׂיאָהּ עַל גַּבֵּי חֲבֶרְתָּהּ" (ביצה כח ע"א), חַדֵּד סַכִּינְךָ וּשְׁחֹט יָפֶה, שֶׁלֹּא תַּאֲכִילֵנִי נְבֵלָה: וְצוּדָה לִּי. מִן הַהֶפְקֵר וְלֹא מִן הַגָּזֵל:

ה | לָצוּד צַיִד לְהָבִיא. מַהוּ "לְהָבִיא"? אִם לֹא יִמְצָא צַיִד – יָבִיא מִן הַגָּזֵל:

ז | לִפְנֵי ה׳. בִּרְשׁוּתוֹ, שֶׁיַּסְכִּים עַל יָדִי:

ט | וְקַח לִי. מִשֶּׁלִּי הֵם וְאֵינָם גָּזֵל, שֶׁכָּךְ כָּתַב לָהּ יִצְחָק בִּכְתֻבָּתָהּ לִטֹּל שְׁנֵי גְּדָיֵי עִזִּים בְּכָל יוֹם. בְּרֵאשִׁית רַבָּה (סה):

יא | אִישׁ שָׂעִר. בַּעַל שֵׂעָר:

יב | יְמֻשֵּׁנִי. כְּמוֹ: "מְמַשֵּׁשׁ בַּצָּהֳרַיִם" (דברים כח, כט):

טו | הַחֲמֻדֹת. הַנְּקִיּוֹת, "דַּכְיָתָא". דָּבָר אַחֵר, שֶׁחָמַד אוֹתָן מִן נִמְרוֹד: אֲשֶׁר אִתָּהּ בַּבָּיִת. וַהֲלֹא כַּמָּה נָשִׁים הָיוּ לוֹ וְהוּא מַפְקִיד אֵצֶל אִמּוֹ? אֶלָּא שֶׁהָיְתָה בְּקִיאָה בְּמַעֲשֵׂיהֶן וְחוֹשַׁדְתָּן:

יט | אָנֹכִי. הַמֵּבִיא לְךָ, וְעֵשָׂו הוּא בְּכֹרֶךָ: עָשִׂיתִי. כַּמָּה דְּבָרִים כַּאֲשֶׁר דִּבַּרְתָּ אֵלָי: שְׁבָה. לְשׁוֹן מֵסֵב עַל הַשֻּׁלְחָן, לְכָךְ מְתֻרְגָּם "אַסְתְּחַר":

כא | גְּשָׁה נָּא וַאֲמֻשְׁךָ. אָמַר בְּלִבּוֹ: אֵין דֶּרֶךְ עֵשָׂו לִהְיוֹת שֵׁם שָׁמַיִם שָׁגוּר בְּפִיו, וְזֶה אוֹמֵר: "כִּי הִקְרָה ה׳ אֱלֹהֶיךָ" (לעיל פסוק כ):

I will know: **Are you my son Esau or not?** Due to his faulty eyesight, Isaac was unable to tell the twins apart.

22 **Jacob approached Isaac his father, and he,** Isaac, **felt him. He said: The voice is the voice of Jacob,** as the subtleties of the voice bring to mind the voice of Jacob, **but the hands are the hands of Esau.**

23 **He did not recognize him, because his hands were hairy like the hands of his brother, Esau; and he blessed him.**[D] Although Jacob's voice unnerved Isaac, his hands felt like those of Esau. Some say that Jacob's vocabulary was also identical to that of Esau.[20]

24 **He said: Are you my son Esau?** Isaac sought further confirmation of his identity. **He said: I am.**

25 **He said,** in a somewhat ceremonial fashion: **Serve me, and I will eat from my son's game so that my soul will bless you. He served him, and he ate, and he brought him wine, and he drank.**

26 After eating, Isaac's spirits lifted, and he sensed a closeness to his son. And **Isaac his father said to him: Approach and kiss me, my son.**

27 **He,** Jacob, **approached and kissed him. He,** Isaac, **smelled the scent of his,** Esau's, fine **garments,** which had absorbed the scent of one who frequents the fields, **and he blessed him and said:**[D] **See, the scent of my son is as the scent of a field that the Lord blessed.** The Sages suggest that Isaac smelled the scent of an orchard,[21] as a field of grain does not emit a pleasant fragrance, whereas one can smell the fruit in an area planted with trees.

28 *Sixth aliya* While smelling the scent of the blessed field in the present, Isaac blesses Jacob with successful fields throughout his life. **God will give you**[D] **from the dew of the heavens, from the fat of the earth, and an abundance of grain and wine.**

29 From bread and wine, the blessing turns to the nation that will descend from Jacob. **Peoples will serve you, and nations will prostrate themselves to you. Be a lord** and leader **to your brethren,** conquer them, **and your mother's sons will prostrate themselves to you.**[D] **Cursed be one who curses you, and blessed be one that blesses you.**

30 **It was when Isaac concluded blessing Jacob, and Jacob had just departed from the presence of Isaac his father, that Esau his brother came from his hunt.** Fortunately, Esau arrived only after Jacob had received the blessings and left the room.

31 **He,** Esau, **too made tasty food, and brought it to his father. He said to his father: Let my father arise, and eat from his son's game, so that your soul will bless me.**

32 **Isaac his father said to him: Who are you?** Isaac was confused by this second entrance. **He said: I am your son, your firstborn, Esau.**

33 **Isaac was overcome with great trembling,** as he realized something terrible had occurred. **And he said: Who is it then who hunted game and brought it to me? I ate from** it **all before you came, and I blessed him; indeed, he shall be blessed.**[D] I know that the blessing has taken effect.

34 **When Esau heard the words of his father, he cried a very great and bitter cry,** in disappointment, anger, and frustration. **And he said to his father: Bless me too, my father.**[D]

DISCUSSION

27:23 | **And he blessed him:** Isaac rejected the possibility that Jacob had suddenly become hairy, and so he assumed that he had misidentified his son's voice. Unlike the guileless Isaac, Rebecca was familiar with the ways of deception, perhaps because she grew up in a culture where tricks and ruses were commonplace (see 29:12–25).

27:27 | **He smelled the scent of his garment, and he blessed him and said:** Isaac's blessing was not a prophetic revelation detached from reality. Rather, it drew upon his physical surroundings and emotional state: His proximity to his son, the food he had been served, and the overall connection between father and son, with all the love and affection that this aroused. Isaac's blessing grew out of these feelings, until it turned into a powerful prophecy.

27:28 | **God will give you:** There are similarities between these blessings and God's blessings to Abraham in chapter 12. As in God's blessings there, Isaac mentions the land and alludes to its inheritance, and he refers to those who bless and curse him. Isaac thereby provides his son with the power of Abraham's inheritance. Later in the chapter it will be explicitly stated that after giving Jacob a personal blessing, Isaac also transfers to him the blessing he received from Abraham.

27:29 | **Be a lord to your brethren, and your mother's sons will prostrate themselves before you:** It is unclear what is added by "your mother's sons," after the mention of "your brethren," as both expressions are apparent references to Esau. Perhaps Isaac and Rebecca had other sons who are not mentioned because they are not important to the story, or this might be a metonymy, meaning Esau's sons or the children of Rebecca's brother (see Ibn Ezra; *Targum Yonatan*).

27:33 | **Indeed, he shall be blessed:** As stated above, Rebecca's efforts to ensure that Jacob received the blessing were due to her assumption that Isaac's blessing was not merely an expression of his wishes, but a revelation of sorts, which had the power to influence future events. Apparently, in addition to giving the blessing, Isaac was able to sense whether it had taken effect. He therefore states that he knows that the blessing he gave to Jacob would indeed be realized.

Nowhere does Isaac rebuke Jacob for his deception. Perhaps he sensed that the blessing had taken effect on Jacob, which he took as a sign that his younger son was in truth the more deserving one, even if he did take the blessing

כב נא ואמשך בני האתה זה בני עשו אם־לא: ויגש יעקב אל־יצחק אביו וימשהו
כג ויאמר הקל קול יעקב והידים ידי עשו: ולא הכירו כי־היו ידיו כידי עשו אחיו
כד כה שערת ויברכהו: ויאמר אתה זה בני עשו ויאמר אני: ויאמר הגשה לי ואכלה
כו מציד בני למען תברכך נפשי ויגש־לו ויאכל ויבא לו יין וישת: ויאמר אליו
כז יצחק אביו גשה־נא ושקה־לי בני: ויגש וישק־לו וירח את־ריח בגדיו ויברכהו
כח ויאמר ראה ריח בני כריח שדה אשר ברכו יהוה: ויתן־לך האלהים מטל כה ששי
כט השמים ומשמני הארץ ורב דגן ותירש: יעבדוך עמים וישתחו לך לאמים
ל הוה גביר לאחיך וישתחוו לך בני אמך ארריך ארור ומברכיך ברוך: ויהי
כאשר כלה יצחק לברך את־יעקב ויהי אך יצא יצא יעקב מאת פני יצחק
לא אביו ועשו אחיו בא מצידו: ויעש גם־הוא מטעמים ויבא לאביו ויאמר לאביו
לב יקם אבי ויאכל מציד בנו בעבור תברכני נפשך: ויאמר לו יצחק אביו מי־אתה
לג ויאמר אני בנך בכרך עשו: ויחרד יצחק חרדה גדלה עד־מאד ויאמר מי־
אפוא הוא הצד־ציד ויבא לי ואכל מכל בטרם תבוא ואברכהו גם־ברוך
לד יהיה: כשמע עשו את־דברי אביו ויצעק צעקה גדלה ומרה עד־מאד ויאמר

רש״י

כב | **קול יעקב.** שמדבר בלשון תחנונים, "קום נא" (לעיל פסוק יט), אבל עשו בלשון קנטוריא דבר, "יקם אבי" (להלן פסוק לא):

כד | **ויאמר אני.** לא אמר 'אני עשו', אלא "אני":

כז | **וירח.** והלא אין ריח רע יותר משטף העזים? אלא מלמד שנכנסה עמו גן עדן: **כריח שדה אשר ברכו ה'.** שנתן בו ריח טוב, וזהו שדה תפוחים. כך דרשו רבותינו זכרונם לברכה:

כח | **ויתן לך.** יתן ויחזור ויתן. בראשית רבה (סו, ג). ולפי פשוטו מוסף לענין ראשון: ריח בני אשר נתן לך הקדוש ברוך הוא כריח שדה וגו', ועוד יתן לך מטל השמים וגו' כמשמעו. ומדרשי אגדה יש הרבה לכמה פנים:

כט | **בני אמך.** ויעקב אמר ליהודה: "בני אביך" (להלן מט, ח), לפי שהיו לו בנים מכמה אמהות, וכאן שלא נשא אלא אשה אחת אמר: "בני אמך": **ארריך ארור ומברכיך ברוך.** ובבלעם הוא אומר: "מברכיך ברוך ואורריך ארור" (במדבר כד, ט)? הצדיקים – תחלתם יסורים וסופן שלוה ואורריהם ומצעריהם קודמים למברכיהם, לפיכך יצחק הקדים קללת אוררים לברכת מברכים; והרשעים – תחלתם שלוה וסופן יסורין, לפיכך בלעם הקדים ברכה לקללה:

ל | **יצא יצא.** זה יוצא וזה בא:

לג | **ויחרד.** כמשמעו, לשון תמיה. ומדרשו, ראה גיהנם פתוחה מתחתיו: **מי אפוא.** לשון לעצמו, משמש עם כמה דברים: "אפוא" – איה פה, מי הוא ואיפה הוא הצד ציד?: **ואכל מכל.** מכל טעמים שבקשתי לטעם טעמתי בו: **גם ברוך יהיה.** שלא תאמר, אלולי שרמה יעקב לאביו לא נטל את הברכות, לכך הסכים וברכו מדעתו:

DISCUSSION

→ by deception. Isaac knows that it is God, not him, who decides who is his worthy successor, and therefore he accepts this decision and does not object to the outcome.

27:34| **Bless me too, my father:** Since Esau had not heard the content of the blessing Jacob had received, he did not know that it rendered him subservient to his younger brother. His request for a blessing of his own stemmed from his belief in its prophetic power, and from the fact that a blessing expresses the personal ties between father and son.

35 **He,** Isaac, **said** to him: **Your brother came with deceit, and he took your blessing.** The blessing has already taken effect and I cannot retract it. What's done is done.

36 **He,** Esau, **said** in anger: **Is it for this that his name was called Jacob [*Ya'akov*]?** Although Jacob was originally named for the manner in which he held on to Esau's heel [*akev*] at birth (see 25:26), and thus was born on his brother's heels, here Esau uses the same root in its meaning of deceit and cheating. **As he deceived me [*vayakveni*] these two times:**[D] **He took my birthright,** as he purchased it from me with deception, **and behold, now he** also **took my blessing.** Having been told that Isaac cannot undo what he had done, **he said: Have you not reserved a blessing for me?** There must be some kind of blessing left for me. You could not have granted Jacob all possible blessings.

37 **Isaac answered and he said to Esau: Behold, I have made him a lord to you; I have given to him all his brethren as servants; and I have supported him with grain and wine;** I have blessed him that produce and wine should be easily available to him. **For you then, what shall I do, my son?** Since I am unable to negate his blessing, what blessing can I bestow upon you that will correspond to that which Jacob received?

38 **Esau said to his father: Have you but one blessing, my father?** There must be a blessing that does not conflict with the one you have already bestowed upon Jacob. **Bless me too, my father,** with some sort of blessing. **And** in his despair, **Esau raised his voice and wept.**

39 Ultimately, Isaac finds a way to bless his elder son as well. **And Isaac his father answered and said to him: Behold, from the fat of the earth shall be your dwelling,** you too shall inherit a fertile portion, **and from the dew of the heavens above.**

40 **By your sword you shall live.** Since you are not the firstborn, you do not enjoy full rights to your place of dwelling, and therefore you will constantly have to fight for it. **And you shall serve your brother. But it will be when you revolt** that you will free yourself from him, **and you will remove his yoke from your neck.**[D] However, in the basic state of affairs, he will be the lord and you will be his slave.

41 **Esau hated Jacob because of the blessing that his father blessed him,** and for the results of that blessing. **Esau said in his heart: The days of mourning for my father will approach,** or my father will die, **and I will kill my brother Jacob.** Out of respect for his father, whom he accepted as a figure of authority, Esau would not dare to harm his brother while Isaac was still alive.

42 **The words of Esau her elder son were told to Rebecca;**[D] **she sent and summoned Jacob her younger son and said to him: Behold, your brother Esau consoles himself in your regard to kill you.** He consoles himself with the thought that he will kill you.[22]

43 **Now my son, heed my voice.** Just as you listened to me and took the blessing, which brought you into this problematic situation, you should once again obey me, this time in order to get you out of it. **And arise, flee to Laban my brother, to Haran,** where you can take refuge.

44 **Live with him a few years, until your brother's anger subsides;**

45 **until your brother's anger subsides from you, and he forgets that which you did to him,** and until the matter of the blessings ceases to bother him. Once I see that his anger has calmed, **I will send** a messenger **and take you from there,** Haran. If you do not leave and keep away, you are liable to fight and even kill each other. **Why should I be bereaved of both of you on one day?**[D]

DISCUSSION

27:36 | As he deceived me [*vayakveni*] these two times: In his anger, Esau speaks carelessly. His mention of the sale of the birthright is not in his best interests (*Tanḥuma, Toledot* 23; Rashi). If Jacob acquired the birthright, then the blessing is rightfully his. Although Esau complains about his brother's repeated deceptions, the first act of deception justifies the second.

27:40 | It will be when you revolt, and you will remove his yoke from your neck: This prophecy was fulfilled over the generations: The land in which the descendants of Esau, the people of Edom, lived, sufficed for most of their needs. For a long period they were subservient to the kings of Judea, but from time to time they attempted to rebel against the control of Jacob's descendants, and they were occasionally successful in this endeavor (see 36:39; *Derashot HaRan* 2).

27:42 | The words of Esau her elder son were told to Rebecca: How did Rebecca know about Esau's plan? It is possible that Esau did not keep his feelings to himself. As an extrovert, it is likely that Esau was regularly surrounded with friends, to whom he confided his plans perhaps when he was drunk, and reports of his comments reached Rebecca. Some commentaries claim that although Esau did in fact keep his thoughts to himself, Rebecca discovered them through her prophetic spirit (*Bereshit Rabba* 67; *Targum Yonatan*; Rashi).

27:45 | Why should I be bereaved of both of you on one day: It is often assumed that Esau was a large, powerful man, while his younger brother Jacob was thin and weak. However, from the fact that Isaac had to feel the twins' skin in order to distinguish between them, and was unable to discern by touch any difference in their height or build, it may be inferred that they ◄►

לה לו לְאָבִיו בָּרְכֵנִי גַם־אָנִי אָבִי: וַיֹּאמֶר בָּא אָחִיךָ בְּמִרְמָה וַיִּקַּח בִּרְכָתֶךָ: וַיֹּאמֶר הֲכִי
קָרָא שְׁמוֹ יַעֲקֹב וַיַּעְקְבֵנִי זֶה פַעֲמַיִם אֶת־בְּכֹרָתִי לָקָח וְהִנֵּה עַתָּה לָקַח בִּרְכָתִי
לז וַיֹּאמַר הֲלֹא־אָצַלְתָּ לִּי בְּרָכָה: וַיַּעַן יִצְחָק וַיֹּאמֶר לְעֵשָׂו הֵן גְּבִיר שַׂמְתִּיו לָךְ
וְאֶת־כָּל־אֶחָיו נָתַתִּי לוֹ לַעֲבָדִים וְדָגָן וְתִירֹשׁ סְמַכְתִּיו וּלְכָה אֵפוֹא מָה אֶעֱשֶׂה
לח בְּנִי: וַיֹּאמֶר עֵשָׂו אֶל־אָבִיו הַבְרָכָה אַחַת הִוא־לְךָ אָבִי בָּרְכֵנִי גַם־אָנִי אָבִי וַיִּשָּׂא
לט עֵשָׂו קֹלוֹ וַיֵּבְךְּ: וַיַּעַן יִצְחָק אָבִיו וַיֹּאמֶר אֵלָיו הִנֵּה מִשְׁמַנֵּי הָאָרֶץ יִהְיֶה מוֹשָׁבֶךָ
מ וּמִטַּל הַשָּׁמַיִם מֵעָל: וְעַל־חַרְבְּךָ תִחְיֶה וְאֶת־אָחִיךָ תַּעֲבֹד וְהָיָה כַּאֲשֶׁר תָּרִיד
מא וּפָרַקְתָּ עֻלּוֹ מֵעַל צַוָּארֶךָ: וַיִּשְׂטֹם עֵשָׂו אֶת־יַעֲקֹב עַל־הַבְּרָכָה אֲשֶׁר בֵּרְכוֹ אָבִיו
מב וַיֹּאמֶר עֵשָׂו בְּלִבּוֹ יִקְרְבוּ יְמֵי אֵבֶל אָבִי וְאַהַרְגָה אֶת־יַעֲקֹב אָחִי: וַיֻּגַּד לְרִבְקָה
אֶת־דִּבְרֵי עֵשָׂו בְּנָהּ הַגָּדֹל וַתִּשְׁלַח וַתִּקְרָא לְיַעֲקֹב בְּנָהּ הַקָּטָן וַתֹּאמֶר אֵלָיו
מג הִנֵּה עֵשָׂו אָחִיךָ מִתְנַחֵם לְךָ לְהָרְגֶךָ: וְעַתָּה בְנִי שְׁמַע בְּקֹלִי וְקוּם בְּרַח־לְךָ אֶל־
מד מה לָבָן אָחִי חָרָנָה: וְיָשַׁבְתָּ עִמּוֹ יָמִים אֲחָדִים עַד אֲשֶׁר־תָּשׁוּב חֲמַת אָחִיךָ: עַד־שׁוּב
אַף־אָחִיךָ מִמְּךָ וְשָׁכַח אֵת אֲשֶׁר־עָשִׂיתָ לּוֹ וְשָׁלַחְתִּי וּלְקַחְתִּיךָ מִשָּׁם לָמָה אֶשְׁכַּל

רש״י

לה | **בְּמִרְמָה.** בְּחָכְמָה:

לו | **הֲכִי קָרָא שְׁמוֹ.** לְשׁוֹן תֵּמַהּ הוּא, כְּמוֹ: ״הֲכִי אָחִי אַתָּה״ (להלן כט, טו), שֶׁמָּא לְכָךְ נִקְרָא שְׁמוֹ יַעֲקֹב, עַל שֵׁם סוֹפוֹ, שֶׁהוּא עָתִיד לְעָקְבֵנִי. תַּנְחוּמָא (תנחומא ישן כג): לָמָּה חָרַד יִצְחָק? אָמַר: שֶׁמָּא עָוֹן יֵשׁ בִּי שֶׁבֵּרַכְתִּי קָטָן לִפְנֵי גָּדוֹל וְשִׁנִּיתִי סֵדֶר הַיִּחוּס, הִתְחִיל עֵשָׂו מְצַעֵק: ״וַיַּעְקְבֵנִי זֶה פַעֲמַיִם״, אָמַר לוֹ אָבִיו: מָה עָשָׂה לְךָ? אָמַר לוֹ: ״אֶת בְּכֹרָתִי לָקָח״. אָמַר: בְּכָךְ הָיִיתִי מֵצֵר וְחָרֵד שֶׁמָּא עָבַרְתִּי עַל שׁוּרַת הַדִּין, עַכְשָׁיו לַבְּכוֹר בֵּרַכְתִּי, ״גַּם בָּרוּךְ יִהְיֶה״: **וַיַּעְקְבֵנִי.** כְּתַרְגּוּמוֹ: ״וְכַמְנִי״ חַכְמַנִי. ״וְאָרַב״ (דברים יט, יא) – ״וְכַמַן״. וְיֵשׁ מְתַרְגְּמִין: ״וְחַכְמַנִי״, נִתְחַכֵּם לִי: **אָצַלְתָּ.** לְשׁוֹן הַפְרָשָׁה, כְּמוֹ: ״וַיָּאצֶל״ (במדבר יא, כה):

לז | **הֵן גְּבִיר.** בְּרָכָה זוֹ שְׁבִיעִית הִיא וְהוּא עוֹשֶׂה אוֹתָהּ רִאשׁוֹנָה? אֶלָּא אָמַר לוֹ: מַה תּוֹעֶלֶת לְךָ בִּבְרָכָה? אִם תִּקְנֶה נְכָסִים שֶׁלּוֹ הֵם, שֶׁהֲרֵי גְּבִיר שַׂמְתִּיו לָךְ, וּמַה שֶּׁקָּנָה עֶבֶד קָנָה רַבּוֹ: **וּלְכָה אֵפוֹא מָה אֶעֱשֶׂה.** אַיֵּה אֵיפֹה אֲבַקֵּשׁ מַה לַּעֲשׂוֹת לְךָ?:

לח | **הַבְרָכָה אַחַת.** הֵ״א זוֹ מְשַׁמֶּשֶׁת לְשׁוֹן תְּמִיָּה, כְּמוֹ: ״הַבְּמַחֲנִים״ (במדבר יג, יט), ״הַשְּׁמֵנָה הִוא״ (שם כ), ״הַכְּמוֹת נָבָל״ (שמואל ב׳ ג, לג):

לט | **מִשְׁמַנֵּי הָאָרֶץ וְגוֹ׳.** זוֹ אִיטַלְיָא שֶׁל יָוָן:

מ | **וְעַל חַרְבְּךָ.** כְּמוֹ: ׳בְּחַרְבְּךָ׳, יֵשׁ ׳עַל׳ שֶׁהוּא אֶלָּא בִּמְקוֹם אוֹת אַחַת, כְּגוֹן ״עֲמַדְתֶּם עַל חַרְבְּכֶם״ (יחזקאל לג, כו) ׳בְּחַרְבְּכֶם׳, ״עַל צִבְאֹתָם״ (שמות ו, כו) ׳בְּצִבְאֹתָם׳: **וְהָיָה כַּאֲשֶׁר תָּרִיד.** לְשׁוֹן צַעַר, כְּמוֹ: ״אָרִיד בְּשִׂיחִי״ (תהלים נה, ג), כְּלוֹמַר, כְּשֶׁיַּעַבְרוּ יִשְׂרָאֵל עַל הַתּוֹרָה וְיִהְיֶה לְךָ פִּתְחוֹן פֶּה לְהִצְטַעֵר עַל הַבְּרָכוֹת שֶׁנָּטַל – ״וּפָרַקְתָּ עֻלּוֹ״ וְגוֹ׳:

מא | **יִקְרְבוּ יְמֵי אֵבֶל אָבִי.** כְּמַשְׁמָעוֹ, שֶׁלֹּא אֲצַעֵר אֶת אַבָּא. וּמִדְרַשׁ אַגָּדָה לְכַמָּה פָּנִים יֵשׁ:

מב | **וַיֻּגַּד לְרִבְקָה.** בְּרוּחַ הַקֹּדֶשׁ הֻגַּד לָהּ מַה שֶּׁעֵשָׂו מְהַרְהֵר בְּלִבּוֹ: **מִתְנַחֵם.** נִחָם עַל הָאַחֲוָה לַחְשֹׁב מַחֲשָׁבָה אַחֶרֶת לְהִתְנַכֵּר לְךָ ״לְהָרְגֶךָ״. וּמִדְרַשׁ אַגָּדָה, כְּבָר אַתָּה מֵת בְּעֵינָיו וְשָׁתָה עָלֶיךָ כּוֹס תַּנְחוּמִים. לְשׁוֹן אַחֵר לִפְשׁוּטוֹ, לְשׁוֹן תַּנְחוּמִים, מִתְנַחֵם הוּא עַל הַבְּרָכוֹת בַּהֲרִיגָתְךָ:

מד | **אֲחָדִים.** מוּעָטִים:

מה | **לָמָה אֶשְׁכַּל.** אֶהְיֶה שְׁכוּלָה מִשְּׁנֵיכֶם; הַקּוֹבֵר אֶת בָּנָיו קָרוּי ׳שַׁכּוּל׳, וְכֵן יַעֲקֹב אָמַר: ״כַּאֲשֶׁר שָׁכֹלְתִּי שָׁכָלְתִּי״

DISCUSSION

were similar in physical build. Rebecca's observation here, that if Esau tries to kill Jacob they might both die in the ensuing struggle, also indicates that Jacob was by no means a frail and vulnerable individual (see also 29:10).

46 **Rebecca said to Isaac:**[D] **I loathe my life,** I am tired of life, **due to the daughters of Het,** whom Esau married (see 26:34–35). **If Jacob takes a wife from the daughters of Het, like these, from the daughters of the land, why do I need life?** Rebecca hints to Isaac that he should suggest that Jacob follow his example and take a wife from his family who live far away, rather than from the local daughters of Het.

28 **1** As a result of Rebecca's statement, or perhaps after arriving at this decision independently, **Isaac summoned Jacob. He blessed him, and he commanded him; he said to him: Do not take a wife from the daughters of Canaan,** in the manner of your brother.

2 **Arise, go to Padan Aram, to the house of Betuel, father of your mother, and take yourself a wife from there, from the daughters of Laban, brother of your mother.** Apparently Isaac knew that Laban had daughters, as some sort of contact was maintained between the families.

3 Isaac now bestows another blessing upon Jacob: **May God Almighty,** a name of God that expresses His might and His many deeds, **bless you, and make you fruitful and multiply you; may you be an assembly of peoples,** meaning that your descendants will become a great nation;

4 **may He give you the blessing of Abraham – to you, and to your descendants with you – to inherit the land of your residence, which God gave to Abraham.**[D] With this statement, Isaac reaffirms the initial blessing he gave his younger son: Indeed, Jacob will inherit Abraham's legacy.

5 *Seventh aliya* **Isaac sent Jacob, and he went to Padan Aram,**[D] **to Laban, son of Betuel the Aramean, brother of Rebecca, mother of Jacob and Esau.**

6 **Esau saw that Isaac blessed Jacob and sent him to Padan Aram, to take himself a wife from there. In blessing him he commanded him, saying: Do not take a wife from the daughters of Canaan.**

7 *Maftir* **Jacob heeded his father and his mother, and he went to Padan Aram.**

8 **Esau saw that the daughters of Canaan were objectionable in the eyes of Isaac his father.** Until this point, Esau thought that the main objection to his marrying women from Canaan came from his mother. It was only now that he realized how displeased his father was with his choice.

9 Therefore, **Esau went to** his uncle **Ishmael, and took Mahalat, the daughter of Ishmael son of Abraham, sister of Nevayot,**[D] Ishmael's firstborn, **in addition to his** previous **wives, as his wife.** In this manner, he too married his cousin, as was planned for Jacob.

DISCUSSION

27:46 | **Rebecca said to Isaac:** The events surrounding the blessings were uncomfortable for all members of the family. When addressing her husband here, Rebecca does not mention them. Perhaps she sought to spare Isaac the pain he would undoubtedly feel if he were aware of the great tension between the brothers and Esau's plans for revenge. Instead, she prefers to prepare the ground for Jacob's departure by other means.

28:4 | **To inherit the land of your residence, which God gave to Abraham:** Here Isaac explicitly grants Jacob the inheritance of Abraham, which indicates that he clearly accepted his younger son as his undisputed successor. Indeed, Esau leaves the land of Canaan for another land (36:6), as he realizes that Canaan was not his inheritance.

28:5 | **Isaac sent Jacob, and he went to Padan Aram:** The phrase "mother of Jacob and Esau" seems to be superfluous. Perhaps it serves to emphasize that although Rebecca was the mother of Esau as well, only Jacob went to her family in Haran in order to find a wife. According to the Sages, Laban's daughters were aware of a tacit understanding between the families that they would marry Rebecca's sons (*Bava Batra* 123a; see Rashi, 29:17). However, Esau was disinclined to undertake such a lengthy journey in search of a mate, when he had already married two Hitite women.

Although the family of Abraham had not yet developed into a distinct people, the forefathers were alienated from the inhabitants of Canaan and considered themselves connected to their tribe of origin, the family of Nahor. Admittedly, Isaac did not know what Laban's daughters were like, but he assumed that they would be more suitable for his son than the neighboring women of Canaan, whose character he knew only too well. In this manner, the forefathers preserved the unique nature of their family, which was gradually establishing itself as a distinct nation.

28:9 | **Sister of Nevayot:** In several places in the East it was customary to attribute the lineage of some of one's children to his eldest brother. It is also possible that Ishmael was no longer alive at the time, and as his firstborn Nevayot was now in charge of the home, Mahalat was referred to as his sister (*Megilla* 17b; Rashi; see Rashbam).

מו גַּם־שְׁנֵיכֶם יוֹם אֶחָד: וַתֹּאמֶר רִבְקָה אֶל־יִצְחָק קַצְתִּי בְחַיַּי מִפְּנֵי בְּנוֹת חֵת אִם־
כח א לֹקֵחַ יַעֲקֹב אִשָּׁה מִבְּנוֹת־חֵת כָּאֵלֶּה מִבְּנוֹת הָאָרֶץ לָמָּה לִּי חַיִּים: וַיִּקְרָא יִצְחָק
ב אֶל־יַעֲקֹב וַיְבָרֶךְ אֹתוֹ וַיְצַוֵּהוּ וַיֹּאמֶר לוֹ לֹא־תִקַּח אִשָּׁה מִבְּנוֹת כְּנָעַן: קוּם לֵךְ
פַּדֶּנָה אֲרָם בֵּיתָה בְתוּאֵל אֲבִי אִמֶּךָ וְקַח־לְךָ מִשָּׁם אִשָּׁה מִבְּנוֹת לָבָן אֲחִי אִמֶּךָ:
ג ד וְאֵל שַׁדַּי יְבָרֵךְ אֹתְךָ וְיַפְרְךָ וְיַרְבֶּךָ וְהָיִיתָ לִקְהַל עַמִּים: וְיִתֶּן־לְךָ אֶת־בִּרְכַּת
אַבְרָהָם לְךָ וּלְזַרְעֲךָ אִתָּךְ לְרִשְׁתְּךָ אֶת־אֶרֶץ מְגֻרֶיךָ אֲשֶׁר־נָתַן אֱלֹהִים לְאַבְרָהָם:
ה וַיִּשְׁלַח יִצְחָק אֶת־יַעֲקֹב וַיֵּלֶךְ פַּדֶּנָה אֲרָם אֶל־לָבָן בֶּן־בְּתוּאֵל הָאֲרַמִּי אֲחִי שביעי
ו רִבְקָה אֵם יַעֲקֹב וְעֵשָׂו: וַיַּרְא עֵשָׂו כִּי־בֵרַךְ יִצְחָק אֶת־יַעֲקֹב וְשִׁלַּח אֹתוֹ פַּדֶּנָה
אֲרָם לָקַחַת־לוֹ מִשָּׁם אִשָּׁה בְּבָרְכוֹ אֹתוֹ וַיְצַו עָלָיו לֵאמֹר לֹא־תִקַּח אִשָּׁה מִבְּנוֹת
ז ח כְּנָעַן: וַיִּשְׁמַע יַעֲקֹב אֶל־אָבִיו וְאֶל־אִמּוֹ וַיֵּלֶךְ פַּדֶּנָה אֲרָם: וַיַּרְא עֵשָׂו כִּי רָעוֹת מפטיר
ט בְּנוֹת כְּנָעַן בְּעֵינֵי יִצְחָק אָבִיו: וַיֵּלֶךְ עֵשָׂו אֶל־יִשְׁמָעֵאל וַיִּקַּח אֶת־מָחֲלַת ׀ בַּת־
יִשְׁמָעֵאל בֶּן־אַבְרָהָם אֲחוֹת נְבָיוֹת עַל־נָשָׁיו לוֹ לְאִשָּׁה:

רש"י

(להלן מג, יד): **גם שניכם.** אם יקום עליך ואתה תהרגנו יעמדו בניו ויהרגוך. ורוח הקדש נזרקה בה ונתנבאה שביום אחד ימותו, כמו שמפרש ב'המקנא לאשתו' (סוטה יג ע"א):

מו| **קצתי בחיי.** מאסתי בחיי:

פרק כח

ב| **פדנה.** כמו 'לפדן': **ביתה בתואל.** לבית בתואל, כל תבה שצריכה למ"ד בתחלתה הטיל לה ה"א בסופה:

ג| **ואל שדי.** מי שדי בברכותיו למתברכין מפיו יברך אותך:

ד| **את ברכת אברהם.** שאמר לו: "ואעשך לגוי גדול" (לעיל יב, ב), "והתברכו בזרעך" (לעיל כב, יח) – יהיו אותן ברכות אמורות בשבילך, ממך יצא אותו הגוי ואותו הזרע המברך:

ה| **אם יעקב ועשו.** איני יודע מה מלמדנו:

ז| **וישמע יעקב.** מחבר לענין של מעלה: "וירא עשו כי ברך יצחק" וגו' וכי שלח אותו פדנה ארם וכי שמע יעקב אל אביו והלך פדנה ארם וכי רעות בנות כנען, והלך גם הוא אל ישמעאל:

ט| **אחות נביות.** ממשמע שנאמר: "בת ישמעאל" איני יודע שהיא "אחות נביות"? אלא למדנו שמת ישמעאל משיעדה לעשו קדם נשואין, והשיאה נביות אחיה. ולמדנו שהיה יעקב באותו הפרק בן ששים ושלש שנים, שהרי ישמעאל בן שבעים ושבע שנים היה כשנולד יעקב – ארבע עשרה שנה היה גדול ישמעאל מיצחק, "ויצחק בן ששים שנה בלדת אתם" (לעיל כה, כו), הרי שבעים וארבע – ושנותיו היו מאה ושלשים ושבע, שנאמר: "ואלה שני חיי ישמעאל" וגו' (לעיל כה, יז), נמצא יעקב כשמת ישמעאל בן ששים ושלש שנים היה. ולמדנו מכאן שנטמן בבית עבר ארבע עשרה שנה ואחר כך הלך לחרן, שהרי לא שהה בבית לבן לפני לדתו של יוסף אלא ארבע עשרה שנה, שנאמר: "עבדתיך ארבע עשרה שנה בשתי בנתיך ושש שנים בצאנך" (להלן לא, מא), ושכר הצאן משנולד יוסף היה, שנאמר: "ויהי כאשר ילדה רחל את יוסף" וגו' (להלן ל, כה). וכתוב: "ויוסף בן שלשים שנה" (להלן מא, מו) כשמלך, ומשם עד שירד יעקב למצרים תשע שנים, שבע של שבע ושתים של רעב, ויעקב אמר לפרעה: "ימי שני מגורי שלשים ומאת שנה" (להלן מז, ט). צא וחשב ארבע עשרה שנה שלפני לדת יוסף ושלשים של יוסף ותשע משמלך עד שבא יעקב, הרי חמשים ושלש, וכשפרש מאביו היה בן ששים ושלש, הרי מאה ושש עשרה, והוא אומר: "שלשים ומאת שנה", הרי חסרים ארבע עשרה שנים. הא למדת שאחר שקבל הברכות נטמן בבית עבר ארבע עשרה שנה: **על נשיו.** הוסיף רשעה על רשעתו, שלא גרש את הראשונות:

Parashat
Vayetze

Jacob in Beit El – His Dream and Vow

GENESIS 28:10–22

Jacob flees from his brother, leaves his parents, and ventures alone as an exile from the land he was to inherit. Only now does his independent adult life begin. During his stay overnight in Beit El he is granted a vision that will strengthen him on his path to a new life in a foreign place. Although it is an opaque night vision rather than a clear prophecy, this unique revelation symbolizes the start of his making his own way in the world and his ability to hear the word of God.

10 The Torah had interrupted the story of Jacob's departure from
Beersheba to mention Esau's additional marriages. Now the
story of Jacob continues. **Jacob departed from Beersheba**[D]
and went to Haran.
11 **He came upon the place,** meaning that he reached a certain
location that was later revealed to be an important place, **and**
stayed the night there, because the sun had set, and it would
have been dangerous to travel at night. **And he took one of the**

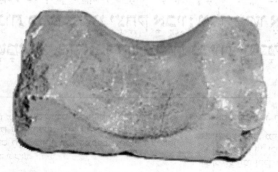

Ancient stone pillow from Mesopotamia

stones from the place, and placed it beneath his head[D] as a
pillow, **and lay in that place.**
12 **He dreamed, and behold,** in his dream, **a ladder was set on**
the earth, and its top reaching to the heavens; and behold,
the angels of God were ascending and descending on it, the
ladder.
13 **And, behold, the Lord,** without the angels, **stood over him,**
Jacob, **and said: I am the Lord, God of Abraham your father,**
and the God of Isaac. The land upon which you lie, the land
of Canaan, **to you I will give it,**[D] **and to your descendants.**
14 **Your descendants will be as** innumerable as **the dust of the**
earth, and you shall spread out **to the west, to the east, to the**
north, and to the south. And all the families, the nations, **of**
the earth shall be blessed in you and your descendants.
15 **And, behold, I am with you; I will keep you wherever you**
go, and I will bring you back from Haran **to this land** of
Canaan. **For I will not leave you until I have done that which**
I spoke to you, returning you from there greater and stronger,
and having begun to form your nation.
16 **Jacob awoke from his sleep, and he said: Indeed, the Lord is**
in this place.[D] It is due to His presence here that I experienced
a dream in which He and His angels were revealed to me. **And**
I did not know. Beforehand, I saw this place as a mere piece of
land upon which I could rest.
17 **He was awestruck, and he said: How awesome,** lofty and
awe-inspiring **is this place; this is nothing other than the**
house of God, as it is worthy to be the house of God, **and this**

DISCUSSION

28:10 | **Jacob departed from Beersheba:** Jacob's journey from his parents' home in Hebron to Beersheba is not mentioned. It is likely that before leaving for Haran he wanted to visit the place of the altar built by his grandfather and father in Beersheba (see Rabbeinu Baḥya). Jacob will conduct himself similarly near the end of his life when he leaves Canaan for Egypt (46:1–5).

28:11 | **And placed it beneath his head:** There is evidence of the practice of resting one's head on a hard pillow, made from wood or similar materials, among the ancient Egyptians, Babylonians, and Chinese, as well as other nations.

28:13 | **The land upon which you lie, to you I will give it:** Jacob received the divine blessing in stages. First, he acquired the birthright, then he took the blessing from his father by deceit. It was only just before his departure that he was given the blessing of Abraham by his father, including the inheritance of the land of Canaan, in a direct, open manner (verses 1–4). Now that promise is confirmed by God.

28:16 | **Indeed, the Lord is in this place:** Dreams are affected by the thoughts of the dreamer. Nevertheless, many biblical stories

פרשת ויצא

י יא ויצא יעקב מבאר שבע וילך חרנה: ויפגע במקום וילן שם כי־בא השמש כו
יב ויקח מאבני המקום וישם מראשתיו וישכב במקום ההוא: ויחלם והנה סלם
יג מצב ארצה וראשו מגיע השמימה והנה מלאכי אלהים עלים וירדים בו: והנה
יהוה נצב עליו ויאמר אני יהוה אלהי אברהם אביך ואלהי יצחק הארץ אשר
יד אתה שכב עליה לך אתננה ולזרעך: והיה זרעך כעפר הארץ ופרצת ימה
טו וקדמה וצפנה ונגבה ונברכו בך כל־משפחת האדמה ובזרעך: והנה אנכי
עמך ושמרתיך בכל אשר־תלך והשבתיך אל־האדמה הזאת כי לא אעזבך
טז עד אשר אם־עשיתי את אשר־דברתי לך: וייקץ יעקב משנתו ויאמר אכן
יז יש יהוה במקום הזה ואנכי לא ידעתי: ויירא ויאמר מה־נורא המקום הזה

רש"י

י| **ויצא יעקב.** על ידי שבשביל שרעות בנות כנען בעיני יצחק אביו הלך עשו אל ישמעאל, הפסיק הענין בפרשתו של יעקב וכתב: "וירא עשו כי ברך" וגו' (לעיל פסוק ו), ומשגמר – חזר לענין הראשון: **ויצא.** לא היה צריך לכתב אלא 'וילך יעקב חרנה', ולמה הזכיר יציאתו? אלא מגיד שיציאת צדיק מן המקום עושה רשם, שבזמן שהצדיק בעיר הוא הודה הוא זיוה הוא הדרה; יצא משם, פנה הודה פנה זיוה פנה הדרה, וכן: "ותצא מן המקום" (רות א, ז) האמור בנעמי ורות: **וילך חרנה.** יצא ללכת לחרן:

יא| **ויפגע במקום.** לא הזכיר הכתוב באיזה מקום, אלא במקום הנזכר במקום אחר, הוא הר המוריה שנאמר בו: "וירא את המקום מרחוק" (לעיל כב, ד): **ויפגע.** כמו: "ופגע ביריחו" (יהושע טז, ז), "ופגע בדבשת" (שם יט, יא). ורבותינו פרשו לשון תפלה, כמו: "ואל תפגע בי" (ירמיה ז, טז), ולמדנו שתקן תפלת ערבית. ושנה הכתוב ולא כתב 'ויתפלל', ללמדך שקפצה לו הארץ, כמו שמפרש בפרק 'גיד הנשה' (חולין צא ע"ב): **כי בא השמש.** היה לו לכתב: 'ויבא השמש וילן שם', "כי בא השמש" משמע ששקעה לו חמה פתאום שלא בעונתה, כדי שילין שם: **וישם מראשתיו.** עשאן כמין מרזב סביב לראשו מפני חיות רעות. התחילו מריבות זו עם זו, זאת אומרת: עלי יניח צדיק את ראשו, וזאת אומרת: עלי יניח. מיד עשאן הקדוש ברוך הוא אבן אחת, וזהו שנאמר: "ויקח את האבן אשר שם מראשתיו" (להלן פסוק יח): **וישכב במקום ההוא.** לשון מעוט – באותו מקום שכב, אבל ארבע עשרה שנים ששמש בבית עבר לא שכב בלילה, שהיה עוסק בתורה:

יב| **עלים וירדים.** עולים תחלה ואחר כך יורדים? מלאכים שלווהו בארץ אין יוצאים חוצה לארץ, ועלו לרקיע, וירדו מלאכי חוצה לארץ ללוותו:

יג| **נצב עליו.** לשמרו: **ואלהי יצחק.** אף על פי שלא מצינו במקרא שיחד הקדוש ברוך הוא שמו על הצדיקים בחייהם לכתב 'אלהי פלוני', משום שנאמר: "הן בקדשו לא יאמין" (איוב טו, טו), כאן יחד שמו על יצחק, לפי שכהו עיניו וכלוא בבית והרי הוא כמת, ויצר הרע פסק ממנו. תנחומא (תולדות ז): **שכב עליה.** קפל הקדוש ברוך הוא כל ארץ ישראל תחתיו, כדי שתהא נוחה לכבש לבניו:

יד| **ופרצת.** וחזקת, כמו: "וכן יפרץ" (שמות א, יב):

טו| **אנכי עמך.** לפי שהיה ירא מעשו ומלבן: **עד אשר אם עשיתי.** 'אם' משמש בלשון 'כי': **דברתי לך.** לצרכך ועליך, מה שהבטחתי לאברהם על זרעו לך הבטחתי ולא לעשו, שלא אמרתי לו: 'כי יצחק יקרא לך זרע' אלא "כי ביצחק" (לעיל כא, יב) ולא כל יצחק. וכן כל 'לי' ו'לך' ו'לו' ו'להם' הסמוכים אצל דבור משמשים לשון 'על', וזה יוכיח, שהרי עם יעקב לא דבר קדם לכן:

טז| **ואנכי לא ידעתי.** שאם ידעתי לא ישנתי במקום קדוש כזה:

DISCUSSION

indicate that they can serve as a medium for divine messages, albeit in a manner more vague than a prophecy received when awake. Jacob is convinced of the truth of what he heard in the dream; however, he does not know its precise interpretation, or even if it has a precise meaning at all.

is the gate of the heavens.[D] It is likely that Jacob woke from his dream in the middle of the night and did not immediately arise from his place of rest, as dawn only arrives in the next verse.

18 **Jacob awoke early in the morning, and** as a mark of gratitude to God for His revelation and His promise to continue accompanying him, and out of a sense of obligation, **he took the stone that he had placed beneath his head and established it as a monument,** a stone of worship, **and poured oil,** which he had presumably brought for dipping his bread, **on the top of it,** the monument, to anoint and sanctify it.

19 **He,** Jacob, **called the name of that place Beit El**[D] from that point onward. **However, Luz was the name of the city initially.**[B] It is possible that Jacob thought he was sleeping in an entirely vacant area, but later realized that he was near the settlement of Luz, which will be mentioned on several occasions in the Bible. Jacob changed its name to Beit El.

20 **Jacob took a vow, saying: If God will** indeed **be with me,**[D] as I heard in my dream, **and He will keep me on this path that I go, and will give me bread to eat and a garment to wear,** if He will grant me the basic requirements for life,

21 **and** if **I return to my father's house in peace,** then **the Lord shall be my God;** I will dedicate myself to His service. Certainly Jacob believed in God beforehand, but here he pledges himself to His worship as a personal obligation;

22 **and this stone that I have established as a monument, shall be the house of God.** Jacob vows to establish a site of worship similar to a temple, which will stand for generations. **And everything that You will give me I will tithe to You.**

Jacob's Marriages in Haran

GENESIS 29:1–30

The Torah does not relate Jacob's precise route to Haran, but it can be assumed that he followed a similar path to the one he would later use upon his return to Canaan, crossing the Jordan River and then heading northward. Like Abraham's servant, who sought a wife for his father Isaac, Jacob will find a wife near a well in Haran. However, this similarity only serves to highlight Jacob's more complicated situation. Unlike his grandfather's servant, he is on the run with nowhere else to go, and he must deal with Laban's deceit equipped with only his wits.

29 1 Although Jacob left Beersheba as a refugee, his mood improved after the vision he received in Beit El. Therefore, **Jacob lifted his feet,** as his travel felt light, and now he sensed he was accompanied, protected, and shielded by God.[1] **And** he **went to the land of the people of the east,** specifically, the Arameans.

Second aliya

2 Nearing Haran, **he saw, and behold, a well in the field, and behold, three flocks of sheep lying alongside it,** the well, **since from that well they watered the flocks, and the great stone was on the mouth of the well.** The opening of the well, which was designed to be used exclusively by the inhabitants of the city and their flocks, was blocked with a large stone to prevent strangers from drawing its water.

3 **All the flocks would gather there and they would roll the stone from the mouth of the well.** Only all the shepherds together had the strength to roll the heavy stone. **And** therefore, when they would all arrive they would **give the sheep to drink, and they would return the stone upon the mouth of the well to its place.**

4 Although Jacob knows the general direction in which he is headed, he is unsure of the precise place where he has arrived. **Jacob said to them: My brethren, from where are you? They said: We are from Haran.**

5 **He said to them: Do you know Laban son of Nahor,** who lives in Haran? The attribution of Laban to Nahor his grandfather rather than to Betuel his father provides support for the theory that Betuel was not an important figure.[2] **They said: We know** him.

6 **He said to them: Is he well? They said: He is well, and here is Rachel his daughter coming with the sheep.** If you wish to

DISCUSSION

28:17| **And this is the gate of the heavens:** Jacob calls it the gate of the heavens because he had seen a ladder there that reached to heaven, and the heavens had opened up before him. The image of a ladder that connects earth to heaven can be considered a basic metaphor for God's Temple.

28:19| **Beit El:** Jacob decided that this place should be sanctified. Luz, which became Beit El, is mentioned at a later stage as a border city in the territory of the tribe of Ephraim (Joshua 16:2, and commentaries ad loc.). For close to eight hundred years Beit El remained consecrated, even though no Temple was built there, and despite the fact that it was not always used for worthy purposes (see Judges 20:18–27; I Samuel 7:16; I Kings 12:29; II Kings 2:1–23). Some Sages identify this Beit El with the location of the Temple in Jerusalem (see *Targum Yonatan*, verse 11; *Pesaḥim* 88a; *Ḥullin* 91a; Rashi, verse 17).

28:20| **If God will be with me:** Jacob was uncertain whether he had dreamed an ordinary dream, influenced by his subjective desires, or whether he had experienced a prophetic revelation. Therefore, he stipulated a condition: If the promises of the dream indeed came to pass, he would turn that place into a fixed site of worship. It can be assumed that until his return Jacob harbored doubts and was uncertain whether his dream was an authentic prophecy. He became convinced of its prophetic nature only after God's statements to him in the dream came true.

יח אֵין זֶה כִּי אִם־בֵּית אֱלֹהִים וְזֶה שַׁעַר הַשָּׁמָיִם: וַיַּשְׁכֵּם יַעֲקֹב בַּבֹּקֶר וַיִּקַּח אֶת־
הָאֶבֶן אֲשֶׁר־שָׂם מְרַאֲשֹׁתָיו וַיָּשֶׂם אֹתָהּ מַצֵּבָה וַיִּצֹק שֶׁמֶן עַל־רֹאשָׁהּ:
יט כ וַיִּקְרָא אֶת־שֵׁם־הַמָּקוֹם הַהוּא בֵּית־אֵל וְאוּלָם לוּז שֵׁם־הָעִיר לָרִאשֹׁנָה: וַיִּדַּר
יַעֲקֹב נֶדֶר לֵאמֹר אִם־יִהְיֶה אֱלֹהִים עִמָּדִי וּשְׁמָרַנִי בַּדֶּרֶךְ הַזֶּה אֲשֶׁר אָנֹכִי הוֹלֵךְ
כא וְנָתַן־לִי לֶחֶם לֶאֱכֹל וּבֶגֶד לִלְבֹּשׁ: וְשַׁבְתִּי בְשָׁלוֹם אֶל־בֵּית אָבִי וְהָיָה יְהוָה לִי
כב לֵאלֹהִים: וְהָאֶבֶן הַזֹּאת אֲשֶׁר־שַׂמְתִּי מַצֵּבָה יִהְיֶה בֵּית אֱלֹהִים וְכֹל אֲשֶׁר תִּתֶּן־
ט א ב לִי עַשֵּׂר אֲעַשְּׂרֶנּוּ לָךְ: וַיִּשָּׂא יַעֲקֹב רַגְלָיו וַיֵּלֶךְ אַרְצָה בְנֵי־קֶדֶם: וַיַּרְא וְהִנֵּה בְאֵר שני
בַּשָּׂדֶה וְהִנֵּה־שָׁם שְׁלֹשָׁה עֶדְרֵי־צֹאן רֹבְצִים עָלֶיהָ כִּי מִן־הַבְּאֵר הַהִוא יַשְׁקוּ
ג הָעֲדָרִים וְהָאֶבֶן גְּדֹלָה עַל־פִּי הַבְּאֵר: וְנֶאֶסְפוּ־שָׁמָּה כָל־הָעֲדָרִים וְגָלְלוּ אֶת־
הָאֶבֶן מֵעַל פִּי הַבְּאֵר וְהִשְׁקוּ אֶת־הַצֹּאן וְהֵשִׁיבוּ אֶת־הָאֶבֶן עַל־פִּי הַבְּאֵר
ד ה לִמְקֹמָהּ: וַיֹּאמֶר לָהֶם יַעֲקֹב אַחַי מֵאַיִן אַתֶּם וַיֹּאמְרוּ מֵחָרָן אֲנָחְנוּ: וַיֹּאמֶר לָהֶם
ו הַיְדַעְתֶּם אֶת־לָבָן בֶּן־נָחוֹר וַיֹּאמְרוּ יָדָעְנוּ: וַיֹּאמֶר לָהֶם הֲשָׁלוֹם לוֹ וַיֹּאמְרוּ

רש״י

יז| **כי אם בית אלהים.** אמר רבי אלעזר בשם רבי יוסי בן זמרא: הסלם הזה עומד בבאר שבע ואמצעו מגיע כנגד בית המקדש, שבאר שבע עומד בדרומו של יהודה, וירושלים בצפונו בגבול שבין יהודה ובנימין, ובית אל היה בצפון של נחלת בנימין בגבול שבין בנימין ובין בני יוסף; נמצא סלם שרגליו בבאר שבע וראשו בבית אל מגיע אמצעו נגד ירושלים. ולפי שאמרו רבותינו שאמר הקדוש ברוך הוא, צדיק זה בא לבית מלוני ויפטר בלא לינה?, ועוד אמרו, יעקב קראו בית אל, וזו לוז היא ולא ירושלים, ומהיכן למדו לומר כן? אני אומר שנעקר הר המוריה ובא לכאן, וזו היא קפיצת הארץ האמורה בשחיטת חולין (חולין צא ע״ב), שבא בית המקדש לקראתו עד בית אל, וזהו ״ויפגע במקום״ (לעיל פסוק יא): **מה נורא.** תרגום: ״מה דחילו אתרא הדין״. ׳דחילו׳ שם דבר הוא, כמו ׳סובלתנו׳ ׳וכסו למלבש׳: **וזה שער השמים.** מקום תפלה לעלות תפלתם השמימה. ומדרשו, שבית המקדש של מעלה מכון כנגד בית המקדש של מטה:

כ-כא| **אם יהיה אלהים עמדי.** אם ישמר לי הבטחות הללו שהבטיחני להיות עמדי, כמו שאמר לי: ״והנה אנכי עמך״ (לעיל פסוק טו): **ושמרני.** כמו שאמר לי: ״ושמרתיך בכל אשר תלך״ (שם): **ונתן לי לחם לאכל.** כמו שאמר: ״כי לא אעזבך״ (שם), והמבקש לחם הוא קרוי נעזב, שנאמר: ״ולא ראיתי צדיק נעזב וזרעו מבקש לחם״ (תהלים לז, כה): **ושבתי.** כמו שאמר לי: ״והשבתיך אל האדמה״ (לעיל פסוק טו): **בשלום.** שלם מן החטא, שלא אלמד מדרכי לבן: **והיה ה׳ לי לאלהים.** שיחול שמו עלי מתחלה ועד סוף, שלא ימצא פסול בזרעי כמו שאמר: ״אשר דברתי לך״ (שם); והבטחה זו הבטיח לאברהם, שנאמר: ״להיות לך לאלהים ולזרעך אחריך״ (לעיל יז, ז):

כב| **והאבן הזאת.** כך תפרש וי״ו זו של ׳והאבן׳: אם תעשה לי את אלה ואף אני אעשה זאת: **והאבן הזאת אשר שמתי מצבה וגו׳.** כתרגומו: ״אהי פלח עלה קדם ה׳״. וכן עשה בשובו מפדן ארם כשאמר לו: ״קום עלה בית אל״ (להלן לה, א), מה נאמר שם? ״ויצב יעקב מצבה וגו׳ ויסך עליה נסך״ (פסוק יד):

פרק כט

א| **וישא יעקב רגליו.** משנתבשר בשורה טובה והבטח בשמירה, נשא לבו את רגליו ונעשה קל ללכת. כך מפרש בבראשית רבה (ע, ח):

ב| **ישקו העדרים.** משקים הרועים את העדרים, והמקרא דבר בלשון קצרה:

ג| **ונאספו.** רגילים היו להאסף, לפי שהיתה האבן גדולה: **וגללו.** וגוללין, ותרגומו: ״ומגנדרין״. כל לשון הוה משתנה לדבר בלשון עתיד ובלשון עבר, לפי שכל דבר ההוה תמיד כבר היה ועתיד להיות: **והשיבו.** ״ומתיבין״:

BACKGROUND

28:19| Beit El, however, Luz was the name of the city initially: This identification of Luz and Beit El appears elsewhere as well (see, e.g., Joshua 18:13; Judges 1:23). Some suggest that the consecrated area of Beit El was near the city of Luz (see Joshua 16:2).

know more, ask her. Apparently, these shepherds were not keen to speak with a stranger.

7 Jacob does not leave the shepherds alone, but addresses them a second time. **He said: Behold, the day is still great, it is not time for the livestock to be gathered.** Since it is not yet dark, you should continue your work. **Give the sheep to drink, and go and herd.** Why are you waiting here?

8 **They said:** We would like to water the sheep, but **we cannot,** as the stone is too heavy. Therefore, we must wait **until all the flocks are gathered, and they,** the shepherds of all the flocks, **will** together **roll the stone from the mouth of the well; then we give the sheep to drink.**

9 Earlier, the shepherds had told Jacob that Rachel was nearing the well. In the meantime, **he was still speaking with them, and Rachel came,** arriving **with her father's flock; for she was a shepherdess.**[D] This was her responsibility in the family.

10 **It was when Jacob saw Rachel, the daughter of Laban his mother's brother,** a close relative, **and the flock of Laban his mother's brother,** a flock that belonged to his relative, **that Jacob approached and** unaided **rolled the stone**[D] **from the mouth of the well, and gave the sheep of Laban his mother's brother to drink.** Jacob was so strong that he was able to lift a stone that three shepherds together could not budge.

11 **Jacob kissed Rachel** chastely, as one would a young family relation.[3] **And** he **raised his voice, and wept** out of emotion. After a journey of hundreds of miles, which certainly took him several months, spending each night in a different place, he had finally met a member of his family.

12 After this greeting, Jacob began to speak. **Jacob told Rachel that he was her father's brother,** kinsman, **and that he was Rebecca's son.** Rachel must have heard about her aunt who had traveled to a distant land, and now she had met her aunt's son. The young girl was excited about the news, **and** therefore **she ran and told her father.**

13 **It was when Laban heard the news of** the arrival of **Jacob, his sister's son,** that **he ran to meet him, embraced him, kissed him, and brought him to his house,** as befitting a family member. In light of Laban's unsavory nature, as evident from the continuation of the story, some commentaries explain that he had ulterior motives for this friendly welcome.[4] **He,** Jacob, **related to Laban all these matters.**[D] He told him that he had arrived with the aim of establishing contact with his family, and perhaps also informed him of the circumstances of his flight from home.[5]

14 **Laban said to him: Indeed, you are my bone and my flesh,** a family relative. **And** so **he lived with him a month's time.** While staying with Laban, Jacob began to help him, as he felt an obligation toward his family member.

15 **Laban said to Jacob,** after the passage of a month: Merely **because you are my brother,** kinsman, **shall you work for me for nothing?** Since you wish to labor, let us set up a formal arrangement. **Tell me, what is your salary?**

16 Here the Torah notes: **Laban had two daughters: The name of the elder was Leah, and the name of the younger was Rachel.**

17 **Leah's eyes were delicate,** there was some problem with her eyes. Perhaps they were sensitive, not allowing her to shepherd outside. It is also possible that she had blue eyes, which were considered more sensitive to the rays of the sun.[6] **And Rachel was of fine form, and beautiful.**[7]

18 *Third aliya* **Jacob loved Rachel.** Either he fell in love with her when he first saw her approach with the sheep, or his love had developed during the month he had lived in Laban's home. **And he said: I will work for you seven years for Rachel your younger daughter,** in addition to my food and lodgings. Since Jacob had brought no money, dowry, or gifts, he had to pay with his service. Apparently, Laban considered seven years of work to be suitable payment for Rachel, and he accepted Jacob's offer.

19 **Laban said: Better that I give her to you, than I give her to another man;**[D] **live with me.** Your suggestion and terms are acceptable to me.

DISCUSSION

29:9| **For she was a shepherdess:** It was unusual to send a young woman to herd the family flock. Perhaps it may be inferred that Laban had no sons at the time, or that they were older or lived too far away to tend the sheep. Rachel was probably no older than ten or eleven. It is likely that Laban preferred to send her among the shepherds rather than her elder sister, Leah, who was of age (see Ramban).

29:10| **And rolled the stone:** Although it is possible that the shepherds, as hired workers, did not make much of an effort to remove the stone themselves, Jacob's act is nonetheless impressive. Perhaps he rolled the stone in his great excitement, or in order to demonstrate his physical and spiritual prowess.

29:13| **He related to Laban all these matters:** It is informative to compare this story to the episode involving Abraham's servant, which Laban doubtless remembered well. Abraham's servant came laden with silver, camels, and gifts, and was therefore in a position to negotiate for their daughter immediately upon his arrival. Jacob, in sharp contrast, appeared alone, with only his status as a family member to his credit.

29:19| **Better that I give her to you, than I give her to another man:** Laban's reply to Jacob is essentially as follows: Since in any case I must marry Rachel off, I prefer to accept your offer and let her marry you rather than a stranger. Although Laban agrees and states that the arrangement is in his interest, his tone is cautious, and he displays no affection toward Jacob. On

ז שלום והנה רחל בתו באה עם־הצאן: ויאמר הן עוד היום גדול לא־עת האסף
ח המקנה השקו הצאן ולכו רעו: ויאמרו לא נוכל עד אשר יאספו כל־העדרים
ט וגללו את־האבן מעל פי הבאר והשקינו הצאן: עודנו מדבר עמם ורחל ׀
י באה עם־הצאן אשר לאביה כי רעה הוא: ויהי כאשר ראה יעקב את־רחל
בת־לבן אחי אמו ואת־צאן לבן אחי אמו ויגש יעקב ויגל את־האבן מעל פי
יא הבאר וישק את־צאן לבן אחי אמו: וישק יעקב לרחל וישא את־קלו ויבך:
יב ויגד יעקב לרחל כי אחי אביה הוא וכי בן־רבקה הוא ותרץ ותגד לאביה:
יג ויהי כשמע לבן את־שמע ׀ יעקב בן־אחתו וירץ לקראתו ויחבק־לו וינשק־
יד לו ויביאהו אל־ביתו ויספר ללבן את כל־הדברים האלה: ויאמר לו לבן אך
טו עצמי ובשרי אתה וישב עמו חדש ימים: ויאמר לבן ליעקב הכי־אחי אתה
טז ועבדתני חנם הגידה לי מה־משכרתך: וללבן שתי בנות שם הגדלה לאה
יז יח ושם הקטנה רחל: ועיני לאה רכות ורחל היתה יפת־תאר ויפת מראה: ויאהב שלישי
יט יעקב את־רחל ויאמר אעבדך שבע שנים ברחל בתך הקטנה: ויאמר לבן
כ טוב תתי אתה לך מתתי אתה לאיש אחר שבה עמדי: ויעבד יעקב ברחל

רש"י

ו| **באה עם הצאן.** הטעם בה"א, ותרגומו: "אתיא"; "ורחל באה" (להלן פסוק ט) הטעם למעלה בבי"ת ותרגומו: "אתת", הראשון לשון 'עושה' והשני לשון 'עשתה':

ז| **הן עוד היום גדול.** לפי שראה אותם רובצים, כסבור שרוצים לאסוף המקנה הביתה ולא ירעו עוד. אמר להם: "הן עוד היום גדול", אם שכירים אתם – לא השלמתם פעלת היום, ואם הבהמות שלכם – אף על פי כן "לא עת האסף המקנה" וגו'. כבראשית רבה (ע, יא):

ח| **לא נוכל.** להשקות, לפי שהאבן גדולה: **וגללו.** זה מתרגם: "ויגנדרון", לפי שהוא לשון עתיד:

י| **ויגש יעקב ויגל.** כאדם שמעביר את הפקק מעל פי צלוחית, להודיעך שכחו גדול:

יא| **ויבך.** לפי שצפה ברוח הקדש שאינה נכנסת עמו לקבורה. דבר אחר, לפי שבא בידים ריקניות, אמר: אליעזר עבד אבי אבא היו בידיו נזמים וצמידים ומגדנות, ואני אין בידי כלום. לפי שרדף אליפז בן עשו במצות אביו אחריו להרגו, והשיגו, ולפי שגדל אליפז בחיקו של יצחק משך ידו. אמר לו: מה אעשה לצווי של אבא? אמר לו יעקב: טול מה שבידי, והעני חשוב כמת:

יב| **כי אחי אביה הוא.** קרוב לאביה, כמו: "אנשים אחים אנחנו" (לעיל יג, ח). ומדרשו: אם לרמאות הוא בא – גם אני אחיו ברמאות, ואם אדם כשר הוא – גם אני "בן רבקה" אחותו הכשרה: **ותגד לאביה.** אמה מתה ולא היה לה להגיד אלא לו:

יג| **וירץ לקראתו.** כסבור ממון הוא טעון, שהרי עבד הבית בא לכאן בעשרה גמלים טעונין: **ויחבק.** כשלא ראה עמו כלום אמר: שמא זהובים הביא והנם בחיקו: **וינשק לו.** אמר: שמא מרגליות הביא והנם בפיו: **ויספר ללבן.** שלא בא אלא מתוך אנס אחיו, ושנטלו ממונו ממנו:

יד| **אך עצמי ובשרי.** מעתה אין לי לאספך הביתה, הואיל ואין בידך כלום, אלא מפני קרבה אטפל בך חדש ימים, וכן עשה, ואף זו לא לחנם, שהיה רועה צאנו:

טו| **הכי אחי אתה.** לשון תמה, וכי בשביל שאחי אתה תעבדני חנם?: **ועבדתני.** כמו 'ותעבדני'. וכן כל תבה שהיא לשון עבר, הוסף וי"ו בראשה והיא הופכת התבה להבא:

יז| **רכות.** שהיתה סבורה לעלות בגורלו של עשו ובוכה, שהיו הכל אומרים: שני בנים לרבקה ושתי בנות ללבן, הגדולה לגדול והקטנה לקטן: **תאר.** הוא צורת הפרצוף, לשון: "יתארהו בשרד" (ישעיה מד, יג), קונפא"ס בלעז: **מראה.** הוא זיו קלסתר:

יח| **אעבדך שבע שנים.** הם "ימים אחדים" שאמרה לו אמו: "וישבת עמו ימים אחדים" (לעיל כז, מד), ותדע שכן הוא, שהרי כתיב: "ויהיו בעיניו כימים אחדים" (להלן פסוק כ): **ברחל בתך הקטנה.** כל הסימנים הללו למה? לפי שיודע בו שהוא רמאי, אמר לו: "אעבדך ברחל", ושמא תאמר רחל אחרת מן השוק, תלמוד לומר: "בתך", ושמא תאמר אחליף ללאה שמה ואקרא שמה רחל, תלמוד לומר: "הקטנה". ואף על פי כן לא הועיל:

20 **Jacob worked seven years for Rachel; they were in his eyes but a few days, in his love of her.** Since Jacob loved Rachel, seven years of work seemed to him a fair price for her hand in marriage.

21 **Jacob said to Laban: Give me my wife,** in accordance with our agreement, **as my time is fulfilled;** I have performed the amount of work we stipulated. **And I will consort with her.** Throughout that entire period Rachel was designated for Jacob, even engaged to him in a certain sense. Now Jacob sought to consummate this through marriage.

22 **Laban gathered all the people of the place, and made a** wedding **feast.**

23 **It was in the evening,**D **and he,** Laban, **took Leah his** older **daughter and brought her to him,** Jacob; **and he consorted with her,** assuming that she was Rachel.

24 **Laban gave Zilpa,**D **his maidservant, to his daughter Leah as a maidservant,** as one of his wedding gifts.

25 **It was in the morning and** Jacob discovered: **Behold, she was Leah. He said to Laban: What is this that you did to me? Didn't I work with you for Rachel, and why did you deceive me?**

26 **Laban said: It is not done thus in our place, to give the younger before the elder.** According to our custom, the elder must be married before her younger sister.

27 I offer a package deal: **Complete the** wedding **week for this one** bride, **and we will give you that one too,** the other sister, in exchange **for the work that you will work with me another seven additional years.** My daughters are equally dear to me, and each of them is separately worth seven years of work. While you thought you were laboring for Rachel, you were actually working for Leah. If Leah is not enough for you, you must work another seven years.

28 **Jacob,** an isolated stranger with no other recourse, **did so,** as he had no choice but to accept Laban's terms. **And he completed that week,**D the week of celebration for the marriage of Leah, **and he,** Laban, **gave him Rachel his daughter for a wife.** Laban did not want Rachel to wait another seven years. Apparently, she had already come of age.

29 **Laban gave to his daughter Rachel, Bilha his maidservant as a maidservant.**

30 **He also consorted with Rachel, he also loved Rachel more than Leah,** even though she was not his first wife. **And** Jacob **worked with him another seven additional years,** as he had agreed.

The Birth of Jacob's Eleven Sons and Daughter

GENESIS 29:31–30:24

The overwhelming majority of Jacob's descendants, during his lifetime, were born outside the land of Canaan. Through his two wives and their maidservants he established the twelve tribes. The names given to his sons, and the explanations for these names, reveal the internal world of the mothers.

31 **The Lord saw**D **that Leah was hated,**D **and** therefore **He** came to her aid and immediately **opened her womb,** and she conceived. **And Rachel,** however, **was barren.** Since they married Jacob within seven days of each other, it was conspicuous that while Leah was pregnant, Rachel was left without children.

32 **Leah conceived and bore a son, and she called his name Reuben; she said: Because the Lord saw** [*ra'a*] **my affliction; for now my husband will love me,**D for I am the mother of his son.

DISCUSSION

the contrary, he seems a seasoned businessman involved in negotiations.

29:23 | It was in the evening, etc.: The women and men celebrated the wedding feast separately. Furthermore, the custom was to cover the bride's face with a veil, which meant that the bridegroom did not see his bride during the wedding itself. It is possible that the two sisters were similar in physical build and tone of voice. According to one opinion, they were twins (*Seder Olam* 2). Their resemblance to one another aided Laban in his plot to give Jacob Leah instead of Rachel.

Laban swapped his daughters because he wanted to take advantage of the opportunity to marry off Leah, while gaining extra years of service. The Sages assume that although Laban initiated the fraud, a certain measure of cooperation on the part of Rachel was necessary to prevent Jacob from noticing the difference between the sisters. Laban's exchange of Leah for Rachel in the darkness is reminiscent of Rebecca's deception of her husband. There the two brothers, Jacob and Esau, were swapped with the help of metaphorical darkness, Isaac's blindness (see *Bava Batra* 123a).

29:24 | Zilpa: The name Zilpa means "pearl shell." The Sages maintain that Zilpa and Bilha were young daughters of Laban' born from a concubine (*Pirkei deRabbi Eliezer* 36; *Bereshit Rabba* 74:13; Rashi, 31:50). The fact that she had loftier status and was not a lowly slave is relevant for the continuation of the story.

29:28 | And he completed that week: Some of the marriage customs that appear here are observed by the Jewish people to this day. In addition to the basic custom of celebrating a wedding with a public feast, the custom to continue celebrations for seven days is based on this

כא שֶׁבַע שָׁנִים וַיִּהְיוּ בְעֵינָיו כְּיָמִים אֲחָדִים בְּאַהֲבָתוֹ אֹתָהּ: וַיֹּאמֶר יַעֲקֹב אֶל־לָבָן
כב הָבָה אֶת־אִשְׁתִּי כִּי מָלְאוּ יָמָי וְאָבוֹאָה אֵלֶיהָ: וַיֶּאֱסֹף לָבָן אֶת־כָּל־אַנְשֵׁי הַמָּקוֹם
כג וַיַּעַשׂ מִשְׁתֶּה: וַיְהִי בָעֶרֶב וַיִּקַּח אֶת־לֵאָה בִתּוֹ וַיָּבֵא אֹתָהּ אֵלָיו וַיָּבֹא אֵלֶיהָ:
כד כה וַיִּתֵּן לָבָן לָהּ אֶת־זִלְפָּה שִׁפְחָתוֹ לְלֵאָה בִתּוֹ שִׁפְחָה: וַיְהִי בַבֹּקֶר וְהִנֵּה־הִוא
לֵאָה וַיֹּאמֶר אֶל־לָבָן מַה־זֹּאת עָשִׂיתָ לִּי הֲלֹא בְרָחֵל עָבַדְתִּי עִמָּךְ וְלָמָּה רִמִּיתָנִי:
כו כז וַיֹּאמֶר לָבָן לֹא־יֵעָשֶׂה כֵן בִּמְקוֹמֵנוּ לָתֵת הַצְּעִירָה לִפְנֵי הַבְּכִירָה: מַלֵּא שְׁבֻעַ
זֹאת וְנִתְּנָה לְךָ גַּם־אֶת־זֹאת בַּעֲבֹדָה אֲשֶׁר תַּעֲבֹד עִמָּדִי עוֹד שֶׁבַע־שָׁנִים
כח אֲחֵרוֹת: וַיַּעַשׂ יַעֲקֹב כֵּן וַיְמַלֵּא שְׁבֻעַ זֹאת וַיִּתֶּן־לוֹ אֶת־רָחֵל בִּתּוֹ לוֹ לְאִשָּׁה:
כט ל וַיִּתֵּן לָבָן לְרָחֵל בִּתּוֹ אֶת־בִּלְהָה שִׁפְחָתוֹ לָהּ לְשִׁפְחָה: וַיָּבֹא גַּם אֶל־רָחֵל וַיֶּאֱהַב
לא גַּם־אֶת־רָחֵל מִלֵּאָה וַיַּעֲבֹד עִמּוֹ עוֹד שֶׁבַע־שָׁנִים אֲחֵרוֹת: וַיַּרְא יהוה כִּי־שְׂנוּאָה
לב לֵאָה וַיִּפְתַּח אֶת־רַחְמָהּ וְרָחֵל עֲקָרָה: וַתַּהַר לֵאָה וַתֵּלֶד בֵּן וַתִּקְרָא שְׁמוֹ רְאוּבֵן
לג כִּי אָמְרָה כִּי־רָאָה יהוה בְּעָנְיִי כִּי עַתָּה יֶאֱהָבַנִי אִישִׁי: וַתַּהַר עוֹד וַתֵּלֶד בֵּן

רש״י

כא| מָלְאוּ יָמָי. שֶׁאָמְרָה לִי אִמִּי. וְעוֹד, ״מָלְאוּ יָמַי״, שֶׁהֲרֵי אֲנִי בֶּן שְׁמֹנִים וְאַרְבַּע שָׁנָה, וְאֵימָתַי אַעֲמִיד שְׁנֵים עָשָׂר שְׁבָטִים? וְזֶהוּ שֶׁאָמַר: ״וְאָבוֹאָה אֵלֶיהָ״, וַהֲלֹא קַל שֶׁבְּקַלִּים אֵינוֹ אוֹמֵר כֵּן! אֶלָּא לְהוֹלִיד תּוֹלָדוֹת אָמַר כֵּן:

כה| וַיְהִי בַבֹּקֶר וְהִנֵּה הִיא לֵאָה. אֲבָל בַּלַּיְלָה לֹא הָיְתָה לֵאָה, לְפִי שֶׁמָּסַר יַעֲקֹב סִימָנִים לְרָחֵל, וּכְשֶׁרָאֲתָה שֶׁמַּכְנִיסִין לוֹ לֵאָה, אָמְרָה: עַכְשָׁיו תִּכָּלֵם אֲחוֹתִי. עָמְדָה וּמָסְרָה לָהּ אוֹתָן סִימָנִים:

כז| מַלֵּא שְׁבֻעַ זֹאת. דָּבוּק הוּא, שֶׁהֲרֵי נָקוּד בַּחֲטָף, שְׁבוּעַ שֶׁל זֹאת, וְהֵן שִׁבְעַת יְמֵי הַמִּשְׁתֶּה. בְּתַלְמוּד יְרוּשַׁלְמִי בְּמוֹעֵד קָטָן (א, ז): וְנִתְּנָה לְךָ. לְשׁוֹן רַבִּים, כְּמוֹ: ״נֵרְדָה וְנָבְלָה״ (לעיל יא, ז), ״וְנִשְׂרְפָה״ (שם פסוק ג), אַף זֶה לְשׁוֹן ׳וְנִתֵּן׳:

גַּם אֶת זֹאת. מִיָּד לְאַחַר שִׁבְעַת יְמֵי הַמִּשְׁתֶּה, וְתַעֲבֹד לְאַחַר נִשּׂוּאֶיהָ:

ל| שֶׁבַע שָׁנִים אֲחֵרוֹת. אֲחֵרוֹת הִקִּישָׁן לָרִאשׁוֹנוֹת, מָה רִאשׁוֹנוֹת בֶּאֱמוּנָה אַף הָאַחֲרוֹנוֹת בֶּאֱמוּנָה, וְאַף עַל פִּי שֶׁבִּרְמָּאוּת בָּא עָלָיו:

DISCUSSION

episode, and does not appear elsewhere in the Torah (see Judges 14:12).

29:31| **The Lord saw that Leah was hated:** It is possible that Leah loved Jacob even before their marriage, as he was her relative and had many evident fine qualities. She was compelled to love him in silence, dreaming for seven years of winning his hand. If so, she might have conspired with her father in his act of deception. Jacob would have complained to her for not revealing her true identity (see Ramban). Although Jacob always treated Leah properly, Rachel was his favorite. This is similar to the story of Hanna and Penina, the two wives of Elkana (I Samuel 1:1–5). Elkana also loved his barren wife more while he treated the mother of his children in a formal manner.

Leah was hated [*senu'a*]: In modern Hebrew the word *senu'a* means hated. Here however, the Torah means that Leah was unloved relative to Rachel, as indicated in the previous verse. Elsewhere, in a passage dealing with the inheritance of the firstborn, the Torah likewise mentions a case involving two wives, one beloved and the other hated (Deuteronomy 21:15–17). There too, the second woman is apparently not really hated, for if she were, the husband could simply divorce her. Rather, she is less loved than the first wife (see Ramban; *Tzeror HaMor*; Rabbi Samson Raphael Hirsch).

29:32| **Now my husband will love me:** When a son was born to a ruler or in a family of noblemen, the status of the woman who had given birth to him often changed, and she became the primary wife (see 16:4; commentary on I Samuel 1:6).

33 Not long afterward, **she conceived again and bore a son, and said: Because the Lord heard** [*shama*] **that I am hated, He gave me this son as well. She called his name Simeon** [**Shimon**]. Leah's statement here is more explicit than at the birth of Reuben, perhaps because by now the family dynamic had become even clearer. The birth of Reuben did not change Jacob's attitude toward Leah in any substantial manner, and therefore the name of her second son does not express her hope to become his beloved, but confirms her status as unloved.

34 She conceived again and bore a son, and said: Now, this time, my husband will certainly **accompany** [*yillaveh*] and become close to **me, as I have borne him three sons.** Jacob will be pleased that I have given him three sons, as these are important steps in the fulfillment of his destiny. The more sons he has, the quicker his family will become a nation. **Therefore, he,** Jacob, **called his name Levi,** as he too was pleased with the addition of a third son to the family.[8]

35 She conceived again and bore a son, and said: This time I will thank [*odeh*] **the Lord** for the joy in bearing so many sons and in the experience of motherhood. **Therefore, she called his name Judah.**[D] **And** after giving birth to one child a year **she ceased bearing.**[9] For a time she remained the mother of four sons, and did not continue bearing children at the same pace.

30 1 In sharp contrast to Leah's fertility, **Rachel saw that she did not bear for Jacob.** Consequently, **Rachel envied her sister;**

and she said to Jacob: Give me children, and if I will not bear children I am as one dead.

2 Jacob was incensed at Rachel;[D] he said: **Am I in place of God who withheld from you fruit of the womb?**[D] You should not turn to me, as I have been given children by God. If you are deprived of fertility, it is between you and Him.[10]

3 She said: **Here is my maid Bilha, consort with her and she shall bear upon my knees, and I shall be built through her.**[D]

4 Jacob did not object. **She gave him Bilha, her maidservant, as a wife, and Jacob consorted with her.**

5 Bilha conceived and bore Jacob a son.

6 Rachel treated the child as her own son, and therefore was the one who named him. She **said: God judged me** [*dananni*] as to whether I am worthy of children, **and also heard my voice, and gave me a son; therefore she called his name Dan.**

7 Bilha, Rachel's maidservant, conceived again, and bore Jacob a second son.

8 Rachel said: I engaged in a great struggle [*naftulei*] **with my sister.** I fought with her in a primal, mighty battle over children. **And I also prevailed,** as another son was born to me. **She called his name Naphtali.** Although these were not her biological children, Rachel treated them as her own.

9 Leah saw that she had ceased bearing after the birth of Judah; **she took Zilpa her maidservant and gave her to Jacob as a wife.**[D]

10 Zilpa, Leah's maidservant, bore[D] **Jacob a son.**

DISCUSSION

29:35 | Judah: It is reasonable to assume that the names of Leah's children were not of her own invention. Rather, they existed beforehand, and she chose them because they suited the situation. For example, one of Esau's wives was called Yehudit, a name similar to Judah (Yehuda in Hebrew) (26:34). Still, Leah called her son by this particular name due to the gratitude she felt after his birth.

30:2 | Jacob was incensed at Rachel: Jacob was not angry with Rachel for her desire to have children, and he certainly did not refrain from keeping company with his favorite wife. Rather, his anger was aroused by her demanding, indulgent tone, and her assumption that he could cure her barrenness through supernatural means if necessary (see Ramban and Radak).

Am I in place of God who withheld from you fruit of the womb: The Sages are critical of Jacob's response to Rachel, stating in the Midrash: Is this how one responds to a person

in distress? After all, Rachel was simply a distraught young woman (see *Bereshit Rabba* 71:7).

30:3 | And she shall bear upon my knees, and I shall be built through her: This method had been employed earlier by Sarah, who had also been barren. Sarah gave her maidservant to Abraham, not so that he should have a child, but so that Sarah's own line would be built through her (see chap. 16). It is possible that the labor of a maidservant upon the knees of her mistress was an actual ritual in which the woman giving birth literally sat on the knees of the barren woman, as though they were both experiencing the birth. This was supposed to bring fertility to the barren woman herself. Even if the precise mechanism of this remedy is unknown, there are many documented cases today of barren couples who adopted a child into their home and were subsequently blessed with pregnancy themselves.

30:4 | She gave him Bilha her maidservant as a wife: As mentioned earlier, according to some

Sages both Zilpa and Bilha were Laban's daughters, born out of wedlock (see *Bereshit Rabba* 74:13; Rashi, 31:50). Bilha who was a maidservant was liberated and became Jacob's full-fledged wife, which had ramifications for the status of her future sons (see Sforno).

30:9 | And gave her to Jacob as a wife: Jacob cooperated with Leah's decision and fathered children with Zilpa. Apparently, Leah wanted her maidservant to bear children for the same reason as Rachel, to stimulate her own fertility. Some say that his wives knew that as the future heir to the land of Canaan, Jacob could not remain the head of a small family, and therefore they sought to encourage the birth of as many sons as possible by giving their maidservants to their husband. If so, Leah's act stems from her dedication to the ideal of a large family, despite the consequent lessening of her share in the household. Alternatively, one can understand that Leah was engaged in a tacit competition with her sister, and the sons of her maidservant

וַתֹּאמֶר כִּי־שָׁמַע יהוה כִּי־שְׂנוּאָה אָנֹכִי וַיִּתֶּן־לִי גַּם־אֶת־זֶה וַתִּקְרָא שְׁמוֹ שִׁמְעוֹן:

לד וַתַּהַר עוֹד וַתֵּלֶד בֵּן וַתֹּאמֶר עַתָּה הַפַּעַם יִלָּוֶה אִישִׁי אֵלַי כִּי־יָלַדְתִּי לוֹ שְׁלֹשָׁה

לה בָנִים עַל־כֵּן קָרָא־שְׁמוֹ לֵוִי: וַתַּהַר עוֹד וַתֵּלֶד בֵּן וַתֹּאמֶר הַפַּעַם אוֹדֶה אֶת־יהוה

א עַל־כֵּן קָרְאָה שְׁמוֹ יְהוּדָה וַתַּעֲמֹד מִלֶּדֶת: וַתֵּרֶא רָחֵל כִּי לֹא יָלְדָה לְיַעֲקֹב

וַתְּקַנֵּא רָחֵל בַּאֲחֹתָהּ וַתֹּאמֶר אֶל־יַעֲקֹב הָבָה־לִּי בָנִים וְאִם־אַיִן מֵתָה אָנֹכִי:

ב וַיִּחַר־אַף יַעֲקֹב בְּרָחֵל וַיֹּאמֶר הֲתַחַת אֱלֹהִים אָנֹכִי אֲשֶׁר־מָנַע מִמֵּךְ פְּרִי־בָטֶן:

ג וַתֹּאמֶר הִנֵּה אֲמָתִי בִלְהָה בֹּא אֵלֶיהָ וְתֵלֵד עַל־בִּרְכַּי וְאִבָּנֶה גַם־אָנֹכִי מִמֶּנָּה:

ד וַתִּתֶּן־לוֹ אֶת־בִּלְהָה שִׁפְחָתָהּ לְאִשָּׁה וַיָּבֹא אֵלֶיהָ יַעֲקֹב: וַתַּהַר בִּלְהָה וַתֵּלֶד לְיַעֲקֹב

ה בֵּן: וַתֹּאמֶר רָחֵל דָּנַנִּי אֱלֹהִים וְגַם שָׁמַע בְּקֹלִי וַיִּתֶּן־לִי בֵּן עַל־כֵּן קָרְאָה שְׁמוֹ

ו דָּן: וַתַּהַר עוֹד וַתֵּלֶד בִּלְהָה שִׁפְחַת רָחֵל בֵּן שֵׁנִי לְיַעֲקֹב: וַתֹּאמֶר רָחֵל נַפְתּוּלֵי

ז אֱלֹהִים ׀ נִפְתַּלְתִּי עִם־אֲחֹתִי גַּם־יָכֹלְתִּי וַתִּקְרָא שְׁמוֹ נַפְתָּלִי: וַתֵּרֶא לֵאָה כִּי עָמְדָה

ח מִלֶּדֶת וַתִּקַּח אֶת־זִלְפָּה שִׁפְחָתָהּ וַתִּתֵּן אֹתָהּ לְיַעֲקֹב לְאִשָּׁה: וַתֵּלֶד זִלְפָּה

רש"י

ו ׀ דָּנַנִּי אֱלֹהִים. דָּנַנִי וְזִכַּנִי:

ח ׀ נַפְתּוּלֵי אֱלֹהִים. מְנַחֵם בֶּן סָרוּק פֵּרְשׁוֹ בְּמַחְבֶּרֶת "צָמִיד פָּתִיל" (במדבר יט, טו), חִבּוּרִים מֵאֵת הַמָּקוֹם נִתְחַבַּרְתִּי עִם אֲחוֹתִי לִזְכּוֹת לְבָנִים. וַאֲנִי מְפָרְשׁוֹ לְשׁוֹן "עִקֵּשׁ וּפְתַלְתֹּל" (דברים לב, ה), נִתְעַקַּשְׁתִּי וְהִפְצַרְתִּי פְּצִירוֹת וְנַפְתּוּלִים לַמָּקוֹם לִהְיוֹת שָׁוָה לַאֲחוֹתִי. **גַּם יָכֹלְתִּי** – הִסְכִּים עַל יָדִי. וְאוּנְקְלוֹס תִּרְגֵּם לְשׁוֹן תְּפִלָּה, כְּמוֹ נִפּוּלֵי אֱלֹהִים נִתְפַּלַּלְתִּי – בַּקָּשׁוֹת הַחֲבִיבוֹת לְפָנָיו נִתְקַבַּלְתִּי וְנֶעֱתַרְתִּי כַּאֲחוֹתִי. **"נִפְתַּלְתִּי"** – נִתְקַבְּלָה תְּפִלָּתִי. וּמִדְרְשֵׁי אַגָּדָה יֵשׁ רַבִּים בִּלְשׁוֹן נוֹטָרִיקוֹן:

י ׀ וַתֵּלֶד זִלְפָּה. בְּכֻלָּן נֶאֱמַר הֵרָיוֹן חוּץ מִזִּלְפָּה, לְפִי שֶׁהָיְתָה בְּחוּרָה בַּת וּתְנוּקֶת בַּשָּׁנִים וְאֵין הֵרָיוֹן נִכָּר בָּהּ. וּכְדֵי לְרַמּוֹת אֶת יַעֲקֹב נְתָנָהּ לָבָן לְלֵאָה, שֶׁלֹּא יָבִין

פרק ל

א ׀ וַתְּקַנֵּא רָחֵל בַּאֲחֹתָהּ. קִנְּאָה בְּמַעֲשֶׂיהָ, אָמְרָה: אִלּוּלֵי שֶׁצָּדְקָה מִמֶּנִּי לֹא זָכְתָה לְבָנִים: **הָבָה־לִּי.** וְכִי כָךְ עָשָׂה אָבִיךָ לְאִמֶּךָ? וַהֲלֹא הִתְפַּלֵּל עָלֶיהָ: **מֵתָה אָנֹכִי.** מִכָּאן לְמִי שֶׁאֵין לוֹ בָנִים שֶׁחָשׁוּב כַּמֵּת:

ב ׀ הֲתַחַת. וְכִי בִּמְקוֹמוֹ אֲנִי? **אֲשֶׁר מָנַע מִמֵּךְ.** אַתְּ אוֹמֶרֶת שֶׁאֶעֱשֶׂה כְּאַבָּא, אֲנִי אֵינִי כְּאַבָּא, אַבָּא לֹא הָיוּ לוֹ בָנִים, אֲנִי יֵשׁ לִי בָנִים, מִמֵּךְ מָנַע וְלֹא מִמֶּנִּי:

ג ׀ עַל בִּרְכַּי. כְּתַרְגּוּמוֹ: "יָחֲדָן חֲרַבִּי": מַהוּ עַל? **אָמְרָה לוֹ:** זָקֵן, אַבְרָהָם הָיוּ לוֹ בָנִים מֵהָגָר וְחָגַר מָתְנָיו כְּנֶגֶד שָׂרָה. אָמַר לָהּ: זְקֵנַתִּי הִכְנִיסָה צָרָתָהּ לְבֵיתָהּ. אָמְרָה לוֹ: אִם הַדָּבָר הַזֶּה מְעַכֵּב "הִנֵּה אֲמָתִי" "וְאִבָּנֶה גַם אָנֹכִי מִמֶּנָּה" כְּשָׂרָה:

לד ׀ הַפַּעַם יִלָּוֶה אִישִׁי. לְפִי שֶׁהָאִמָּהוֹת נְבִיאוֹת הָיוּ וְיוֹדְעוֹת שֶׁשְּׁנֵים עָשָׂר שְׁבָטִים יוֹצְאִים מִיַּעֲקֹב וְאַרְבַּע נָשִׁים יִשָּׂא, אָמְרָה: מֵעַתָּה אֵין לוֹ פִּתְחוֹן פֶּה עָלַי, שֶׁהֲרֵי נָטַלְתִּי כָּל חֶלְקִי בַּבָּנִים: עַל כֵּן. כָּל מִי שֶׁנֶּאֱמַר בּוֹ "עַל כֵּן" מְרֻבֶּה בְּאֻכְלוֹסִין, חוּץ מִלֵּוִי, שֶׁהָאָרוֹן הָיָה מְכַלֶּה בָּהֶם: קָרָא שְׁמוֹ לֵוִי. תָּמַהְתִּי, שֶׁכָּתוּב כְּתִיב: "וַתִּקְרָא" וְזֶה כָּתַב בּוֹ: "קָרָא"! וְיֵשׁ מִדְרַשׁ אַגָּדָה בְּאֵלֶּה הַדְּבָרִים רַבָּה, שֶׁשָּׁלַח הַקָּדוֹשׁ בָּרוּךְ הוּא גַבְרִיאֵל וֶהֱבִיאוֹ לְפָנָיו וְקָרָא לוֹ שֵׁם זֶה, וְנָתַן לוֹ עֶשְׂרִים וְאַרְבַּע מַתְּנוֹת כְּהֻנָּה, וְעַל שֵׁם שֶׁלִּוָּהוּ בְּמַתָּנוֹת קְרָאוֹ לֵוִי:

לה ׀ הַפַּעַם אוֹדֶה. שֶׁנָּטַלְתִּי יוֹתֵר מֵחֶלְקִי, מֵעַתָּה יֵשׁ לִי לְהוֹדוֹת:

→ Zilpa were considered like her own children in this respect (see Ramban). The evident tension here between Rachel and Leah will later develop into an open breach between their respective descendants, the house of Judah, the seed of

DISCUSSION

Leah, and the house of Joseph, the descendants of Rachel (see Joshua 18:5; Zechariah 10:6).

30:10 | Zilpa bore: The verse does not state that Zilpa conceived. For this reason, the Sages maintain that she was the youngest of the four

wives, and her pregnancy was barely noticeable (*Bereshit Rabba* 71:9). Alternatively, her pregnancy was of unusually short duration, and the sudden birth of her son surprised the rest of the family.

11 Leah said: Fortune [*gad*] has come;^D she called his name Gad.

12 Zilpa, Leah's maidservant, bore a second son to Jacob.

13 Leah said: In my happiness [*be'oshri*], as women will be happy for me and encourage and strengthen me. She called his name Asher.

14 Here the Torah relates a short story-within-a-story about Jacob's growing family. **Reuben,** who was probably around four years old at the time,¹¹ **went during the days of wheat harvest, found mandrakes in the field, and brought them** as a gift **to Leah, his mother.** As her firstborn son, Reuben was very close to his mother, as indicated by the name she gave him. **Rachel said to Leah: Please give me from your son's mandrakes.**^{BD} While some commentaries maintain that mandrakes were a folk remedy for barrenness, it is more likely that Rachel wanted them for the same reason as Reuben, for their beauty and fragrance.¹²

Fourth aliya

Mandrake

15 **She,** Leah, **said to her: Is the taking of my husband insignificant?** Is it not enough for you that you have taken my husband? Rachel had seized Jacob's affections and attention. **And you wish to take also my son's mandrakes? Rachel said: Therefore, he shall lie with you tonight in exchange for your son's mandrakes.** Following the order apparently arranged between the women, that night was Rachel's turn. Rachel suggested that she would give up Jacob for that night in exchange for the mandrakes, and Leah agreed.

16 For reasons of custom and modesty, each of the wives had their own tent. **Jacob came** home **from the field in the evening. Leah came out to meet him** before he turned to Rachel's tent, **and said: You will consort with me for I have hired you** from my sister **with my son's mandrakes. He lay with her that night.** Jacob accepted the agreement between his wives.

17 **God heeded Leah, and she conceived, and** after a time without bearing children, she **bore Jacob a fifth son.**

18 **Leah said: God has given my reward [*sekhari*], that I gave my maidservant to my husband. She called his name Issachar.** This name also alludes to Jacob's hiring [*sekhira*] by Leah, but she explicitly emphasizes her reward from Heaven for giving Zilpa to her husband.

19 **Leah conceived again and bore a sixth son to Jacob.**

20 **Leah said: God has granted me a fine gift; now my husband will reside with me [*yizbeleni*],** and his main residence will be with me, **because I bore him six sons.** Whether or not she was informed in a vision that Jacob would have twelve sons, as claimed by one tradition, six is still a substantial number. **She called his name Zebulun.**

21 **And then she bore a daughter, and she called her name Dina.**

22 After so many births by Jacob's other wives, and after Rachel had prayed extensively for children, **God remembered Rachel, and God heeded her, and He opened her womb.**

23 **She conceived and bore a son, and said: God has removed [*asaf*] my disgrace.**^D

24 **She called his name Joseph, saying: May the Lord add [*yosef*] another son for me** after Joseph. She did not choose the name Asaf, which would accord only with her earlier statement. The name Joseph alludes both to the removal of her disgrace and her wish for another son.

—— BACKGROUND ——

30:14 | Mandrakes: The medicinal mandrake, *Mandragora autumnalis*, is a multiannual plant whose leaves branch out in a rosette on the ground. The fruit of the mandrake appear like small golden apples, weighing approximately 25 g each. They emit a pleasant, pungent fragrance when ripening during the season of the wheat harvest. The fruit, and especially their seeds, contain substances that can be used for pain relief. The mandrake is considered a folk remedy for fertility.

—— DISCUSSION ——

30:11 | Fortune has come [*ba gad*]: See *Sanhedrin* 20a. Gad was the name of a Canaanite god, but the name was also used in its broader meaning to denote fortune (see Isaiah 65:11; *Shabbat* 67b). In its written form in a Torah scroll, this appears as a single word, *bagad*. This anomaly alludes to the notion of betrayal, *begida*, alongside the standard meaning of fortune. Leah is possibly alluding to her sense of betrayal at Jacob's too-eager acceptance of her proposal to marry her maidservant (see Rashi).

30:14 | Mandrakes: There are many legends surrounding this mysterious plant, mostly involving its elongated, twisted roots that evoke the image of a person. Throughout the generations, the root of the mandrake has been used as a talisman for fertility.

Still, it is likely that Reuben, who gathered the fruit of the mandrake rather than its roots, did not do so because of any medicinal qualities it might possess, but for a more obvious reason: He was attracted by the beauty of the fruit, which have the appearance of small golden balls and a pleasing odor (see Song of Songs 7:14). Although these fruits are concealed under leaves, a young, curious child with time on his hands can find them (see Ibn Ezra and Ramban).

30:23 | God has removed my disgrace: Rachel's comment is based on the outlook that motherhood is the main role of women, and a childless woman is in a state of disgrace (see also discussion on I Samuel 1:1–10).

יא יב שִׁפְחַת לֵאָה לְיַעֲקֹב בֵּן: וַתֹּאמֶר לֵאָה בגד וַתִּקְרָא אֶת־שְׁמוֹ גָּד: וַתֵּלֶד זִלְפָּה בָּא גָד
יג שִׁפְחַת לֵאָה בֵּן שֵׁנִי לְיַעֲקֹב: וַתֹּאמֶר לֵאָה בְּאָשְׁרִי כִּי אִשְּׁרוּנִי בָּנוֹת וַתִּקְרָא
יד אֶת־שְׁמוֹ אָשֵׁר: וַיֵּלֶךְ רְאוּבֵן בִּימֵי קְצִיר־חִטִּים וַיִּמְצָא דוּדָאִים בַּשָּׂדֶה וַיָּבֵא רביעי
אֹתָם אֶל־לֵאָה אִמּוֹ וַתֹּאמֶר רָחֵל אֶל־לֵאָה תְּנִי־נָא לִי מִדּוּדָאֵי בְּנֵךְ:
טו וַתֹּאמֶר לָהּ הַמְעַט קַחְתֵּךְ אֶת־אִישִׁי וְלָקַחַת גַּם אֶת־דּוּדָאֵי בְּנִי וַתֹּאמֶר רָחֵל
טז לָכֵן יִשְׁכַּב עִמָּךְ הַלַּיְלָה תַּחַת דּוּדָאֵי בְנֵךְ: וַיָּבֹא יַעֲקֹב מִן־הַשָּׂדֶה בָּעֶרֶב
וַתֵּצֵא לֵאָה לִקְרָאתוֹ וַתֹּאמֶר אֵלַי תָּבוֹא כִּי שָׂכֹר שְׂכַרְתִּיךָ בְּדוּדָאֵי בְּנִי וַיִּשְׁכַּב
יז עִמָּהּ בַּלַּיְלָה הוּא: וַיִּשְׁמַע אֱלֹהִים אֶל־לֵאָה וַתַּהַר וַתֵּלֶד לְיַעֲקֹב בֵּן
יח חֲמִישִׁי: וַתֹּאמֶר לֵאָה נָתַן אֱלֹהִים שְׂכָרִי אֲשֶׁר־נָתַתִּי שִׁפְחָתִי לְאִישִׁי וַתִּקְרָא
יט כ שְׁמוֹ יִשָּׂשכָר: וַתַּהַר עוֹד לֵאָה וַתֵּלֶד בֵּן־שִׁשִּׁי לְיַעֲקֹב: וַתֹּאמֶר לֵאָה זְבָדַנִי
אֱלֹהִים ׀ אֹתִי זֵבֶד טוֹב הַפַּעַם יִזְבְּלֵנִי אִישִׁי כִּי־יָלַדְתִּי לוֹ שִׁשָּׁה בָנִים וַתִּקְרָא
כא כב אֶת־שְׁמוֹ זְבֻלוּן: וְאַחַר יָלְדָה בַּת וַתִּקְרָא אֶת־שְׁמָהּ דִּינָה: וַיִּזְכֹּר אֱלֹהִים אֶת־ כח
כג רָחֵל וַיִּשְׁמַע אֵלֶיהָ אֱלֹהִים וַיִּפְתַּח אֶת־רַחְמָהּ: וַתַּהַר וַתֵּלֶד בֵּן וַתֹּאמֶר אָסַף
כד אֱלֹהִים אֶת־חֶרְפָּתִי: וַתִּקְרָא אֶת־שְׁמוֹ יוֹסֵף לֵאמֹר יֹסֵף יְהוָה לִי בֵּן אַחֵר:

רש"י

שמכניסין לו את לאה, שכך מנהג לתן שפחה הגדולה לגדולה והקטנה לקטנה:

יא | **בא גד.** בא מזל טוב לי, כמו: "גד גדי וסנוק לא" (שבת סז ע"ב). ומדרש אגדה שנולד מהול, כמו: "גדו אילנא" (דניאל ד, יא), ולא ידעתי על מה נכתב תבה אחת.

יד | **בימי קציר חטים.** להגיד שבחן של שבטים, שעת הקציר היה, ולא פשט ידו בגזל להביא חטים ושעורים, אלא דבר ההפקר שאין אדם מקפיד בו: **דודאים.** סיגלי, עשב הוא, ובלשון ישמעאל יסמין:

טו | **ולקחת גם את דודאי בני.** בתמיה, ולעשות עוד זאת לקח גם את דודאי בני? ותרגומו: "ולמסב": **לכן ישכב עמך הלילה.** שלי היתה שכיבת לילה זו, ואני נותנה לך תחת דודאי בנך. ולפי שזלזלה במשכב הצדיק לא זכתה לקבר עמו:

טז | **שכר שכרתיך.** נתתי לרחל שכרה: **בלילה הוא.** הקדוש ברוך הוא סיע בו שיצא משם יששכר:

יז | **וישמע אלהים אל לאה.** שהיתה מתאוה ומחזרת להרבות שבטים:

כ | **זבד טוב.** כתרגומו: **יזבלני.** לשון 'בית זבל' (מלכים א' ח, יג), הירבידירייר"א בלעז, בית מדור. מעתה לא תהא עקר דירתו אלא עמי, שיש לי בנים כנגד כל נשיו:

כא | **דינה.** פרשו רבותינו שדנה לאה דין בעצמה: אם זה זכר לא תהא רחל אחותי כאחת השפחות, ונתפללה עליו ונהפך לנקבה:

כב | **ויזכר אלהים את רחל.** זכר לה שמסרה סימניה לאחותה, ושהיתה מצרה שמא תעלה בגורלו של עשו, שמא יגרשנה יעקב לפי שאין לה בנים; ואף עשו הרשע כך עלה בלבו כששמע שאין לה בנים. הוא שיסד הפיט:

"האדמון כבא שלא חלה, צפה לקחתה לו ונתבהלה" (כפיוט "אז חוג" בקרובות ליום א' דר"ה שחרית):

כג | **אסף.** הכניסה במקום שלא תראה. וכן: "אסף חרפתנו" (ישעיה ד, א), "ולא יאסף הביתה" (שמות ט, יט), "אספו נגהם" (יואל ד, טו), "וירחך לא יאסף" (ישעיה ס, כ), לא יטמן: **חרפתי.** שהייתי לחרפה על שאני עקרה, והיו אומרים עלי שאעלה לחלקו של עשו הרשע. ואגדה, כל זמן שאין לאשה בן אין לה במי לתלות סרחונה, משיש לה בן תולה בו: מי שבר כלי זה? בנך! מי אכל תאנים אלו? בנך!:

כד | **יסף ה' לי בן אחר.** יודעת היתה בנבואה שאין יעקב עתיד להעמיד אלא שנים עשר שבטים; אמרה: יהי רצון שאותו שהוא עתיד להעמיד יהא ממני, לכך לא נתפללה אלא על "בן אחר":

Jacob's Departure from Laban

GENESIS 30:25–31:55

It is likely that Jacob has wanted to return home for a long time, but he waits until he has completed the fourteen years of service he owes Laban, and perhaps also until Rachel has had a child of her own. Perhaps he thought that it would be easier for his favorite wife to become pregnant in familiar surroundings. Now, with the birth of Joseph, Jacob seeks to leave Laban.

Extricating himself from his father-in-law and employer is no simple task. Along with settling financial arrangements between them, many complex emotional issues have to be addressed. Even after the property has been divided between them, they cannot come to an agreement in Haran for Jacob's departure, and he ends up taking flight. But even this does not ultimately succeed in separating the two, as Rachel hides Laban's household idols in the cushion on her camel. The final parting, which includes a covenant between Jacob's family and that of Laban, occurs only far from Haran, at Mount Gilad.

25 **It was when Rachel bore Joseph, that Jacob said to Laban:** I have stayed and worked with you for years; now **release me, and I will go to my place and to my land.**

26 **Give me my wives and my children,** those wives **for whom I have worked for you, and I will go; for you know my labor that I performed for you.** I have fulfilled all my obligations.

27 **Laban said to him: If now I have found favor in your eyes,** please, **I have divined,** in an effort to unearth the cause of my financial success, **and** I have discovered that **the Lord has blessed me on your account.**

28 **He,** Laban, **said** to Jacob: You yourself **stipulate your wages**
Fifth
aliya **for me,** to which you feel you are entitled, **and I will give it.** Up to this point you worked in exchange for two wives, but now that I realize that you have brought me good luck, you may state any amount you wish.

29 **He,** Jacob, **said to him: You know how I have served you, and how your livestock was with me.**

30 **For the little that you had before me has increased abundantly; and the Lord has blessed you on my account.** Jacob confirms Laban's statement, but stresses that one need not resort to the occult arts to understand why Laban's affairs have been blessed since his arrival.[13] **And now when shall I provide for my household as well?** Apart from my wives and children I have nothing of my own, as I have worked all this time for you.

31 **He,** Laban, **said** to Jacob: **What shall I give you?** What do you want? **Jacob said: You do not give me anything.** Do not pay me with silver or the equivalent from your current possessions. **If you will do this matter for me: I will return and** work for you. I will **herd your flock and keep it.**

32 **I will pass** with you **through all your flock today; remove from there,** among the flock, **every speckled and spotted**

lamb with brown patches. The color of most of the sheep in the region was white, but there would sometimes occur a sheep with patches on its skin.[14] **And likewise, every brown lamb among the sheep** that you find, **and the spotted and speckled among the goats.** Generally, goats are entirely black, but some have colorful patches. **And it,** all these unusual animals, if they should be born in the flock from now onward, after you have removed the ones currently there, **shall be my wages.**

33 Jacob suggested a way in which his wages could be set unambiguously, so that no arguments could arise. **My honesty shall speak on my behalf on a future day, when you shall go over my wages before you:** Upon paying me my wages you will know for certain that **every one that is not speckled and spotted among the goats, and brown among the sheep is stolen with me.**

34 **Laban said: Indeed, if only it will be in accordance with your statement.** Laban considered this an excellent offer, as there were relatively few animals of the types described by Jacob.

35 So that no more spotted or speckled sheep and goats would be born by interbreeding, **he,** Laban, **removed that day the streaked,** those which had various types of stripes in the area where the ankles are bound, **and spotted** older **goats, and all the speckled and spotted** birthing **female goats, each goat that had white in it, and all the brown among the sheep, and gave them into the possession of his sons,** in a distant location, so that they should not be mixed with Jacob's flock.

36 **He established a path of three days,** a large distance for flock, **between himself and Jacob. And Jacob herded the remaining flock of Laban** elsewhere.

כה ויהי כאשר ילדה רחל את־יוסף ויאמר יעקב אל־לבן שלחני ואלכה אל־
כו מקומי ולארצי: תנה את־נשי ואת־ילדי אשר עבדתי אתך בהן ואלכה כי
כז אתה ידעת את־עבדתי אשר עבדתיך: ויאמר אליו לבן אם־נא מצאתי חן
כח כט בעיניך נחשתי ויברכני יהוה בגללך: ויאמר נקבה שכרך עלי ואתנה: ויאמר חמישי
ל אליו אתה ידעת את אשר עבדתיך ואת אשר־היה מקנך אתי: כי מעט
אשר־היה לך לפני ויפרץ לרב ויברך יהוה אתך לרגלי ועתה מתי אעשה
לא גם־אנכי לביתי: ויאמר מה אתן־לך ויאמר יעקב לא־תתן־לי מאומה אם־
לב תעשה־לי הדבר הזה אשובה ארעה צאנך אשמר: אעבר בכל־צאנך היום
הסר משם כל־שה ׀ נקד וטלוא וכל־שה־חום בכשבים וטלוא ונקד בעזים
לג והיה שכרי: וענתה־בי צדקתי ביום מחר כי־תבוא על־שכרי לפניך כל אשר־
לד איננו נקד וטלוא בעזים וחום בכשבים גנוב הוא אתי: ויאמר לבן הן לו יהי
לה כדברך: ויסר ביום ההוא את־התישים העקדים והטלאים ואת כל־העזים
לו הנקדות והטלאת כל אשר־לבן בו וכל־חום בכשבים ויתן ביד־בניו: וישם
דרך שלשת ימים בינו ובין יעקב ויעקב רעה את־צאן לבן הנותרת:

רש"י

כה| **כאשר ילדה רחל את יוסף.** משנולד שטנו של עשו, שנאמר: "והיה בית יעקב אש ובית יוסף להבה ובית עשו לקש" (עובדיה א, יח), אש בלא להבה אינו שולט למרחוק; משנולד יוסף בטח יעקב בהקדוש ברוך הוא ורצה לשוב:

כו| **תנה את נשי.** איני רוצה לצאת כי אם ברשות:

כז| **נחשתי.** מנחש הייתי; נסיתי בנחוש שלי שעל ידך באה לי ברכה; כשבאתי לכאן לא היו לי בנים, שנאמר: "והנה רחל בתו באה עם הצאן" (לעיל כט, ו), אפשר יש לו בנים והוא שולח בתו אצל הרועים? עכשיו היו לו בנים, שנאמר: "וישמע את דברי בני לבן" (להלן לא, א):

כח| **נקבה שכרך.** כתרגומו: "פרש אגרך":

כט| **ואת אשר היה מקנך אתי.** את חשבון מעוט מקנך שבא לידי מתחלה, כמה היו:

ל| **לרגלי.** עם רגלי, בשביל ביאת רגלי באת אצלך הברכה, כמו: "העם אשר ברגליך" (שמות יא, ח), "לעם אשר ברגלי" (שופטים ח, ה) – הבאים עמי: **גם אנכי לביתי.** לצרך ביתי; עכשיו אין עושין לצרכי אלא בני, וצריך אני להיות עושה גם אני עמהם וסומכן, וזהו 'גם':

לב| **נקד.** מנמר בחברבורות דקות כמו נקדה, פונטור"א בלעז: **וטלוא.** לשון טלאי, חברבורות רחבות: **חום.** "שחום", דומה לאדום, רו"ס בלעז, לשון משנה: "שחמתית ונמצאת לבנה" (בבא בתרא פג ע"ב) לענין התבואה: **והיה שכרי.** אותן שיולדו מכאן ולהבא נקדים וטלואים בעזים ושחומים בכשבים יהיו שלי, ואותן שישנן עכשיו הפרש מהם והפקידם ביד בניך, שלא תאמר לי על הנולדים מעתה: אלו היו שם מתחלה; ועוד, שלא תאמר לי: על ידי הזכרים שהם נקדים וטלואים תלדנה הנקבות דגמתן מכאן ואילך:

לג| **וענתה בי וגו'.** אם תחשדני שאני נוטל משלך כלום, תענה בי צדקתי, "כי תבוא" צדקתי ותעיד "על שכרי לפניך", שלא תמצא בעדרי כי אם נקדים וטלואים, וכל שתמצא בהן שאינו נקד או טלוא או חום, בידוע שגנבתיו לך ובגנבה הוא שרוי אצלי:

לד| **הן.** לשון הין, קבלת דברים: **לו יהי כדברך.** הלואי שתחפץ בכך:

לה| **ויסר.** לבן "ביום ההוא" וגו': **התישים.** עזים זכרים: **כל אשר לבן בו.** כל אשר היתה בו חברבורת לבנה: **ויתן.** לבן "ביד בניו":

לו| **הנותרת.** הרעועות שבהן, החולות והעקרות שאינן אלא שירים, אותן מסר לו:

37 **Jacob took for himself rods** from trees, **of fresh poplar,**[B] **and almond,**[B] **and plane;**[B] **he peeled white streaks in them** by removing some of the bark, thereby **exposing the white** of the tree **that was in the rods.**

38 **He displayed the rods that he peeled in the receptacles of the water troughs from which the flocks would come to drink, facing the flocks,** opposite the other sheep. This was the place where the flock was gathered together. And **they,** the flock, **would come into heat** to mate **when they came to drink.**

Water trough

Plane

White poplar

Styrax shrub

39 **The flocks came into heat due to the rods, and the flocks gave birth to streaked, speckled, and spotted** young.

40 **And Jacob separated the lambs and he placed the faces of the flocks toward the streaked and all the brown in the flocks of Laban,** meaning that he positioned these at the head of the flock, **and he established for himself droves alone, and did not place them with the flocks of Laban.** In accordance with the conditions set between them, these were Jacob's droves.

41 **And it was, whenever the strong flocks,**[D] the best animals, **would come into heat,** in that season, **Jacob would place the rods before the eyes of the flocks at the troughs, to have them come into heat with the rods,** when they saw them.

42 **When the flocks were feeble** and weak, when they were not in heat, **he would not place them,** the rods. Others interpret: When the sheep's tails were not tied up and were in their natural state.[15] Thus **the feeble** sheep and goats, which were not in heat at the proper time, **were for Laban and the strong,** the best animals, which multiplied well, were **for Jacob,**[D] who did not want to expend effort upon the weaker ones.

43 **The man,** Jacob, **became exceedingly prosperous, and he had many flocks, and** as he did not need them all, he bartered with them for other property, including **maidservants and slaves, and camels and donkeys,** and he became the head of a tribe.

31

1 Since Jacob was living near Laban's family, **he heard the words of Laban's sons, saying: Jacob has taken everything that is our father's, and from that which is our father's he has accumulated all this wealth.** Among themselves, Laban's sons cast aspersions upon Jacob, contending that he had grown rich at their father's expense.

2 Apparently, Laban himself also heard these accusations, as **Jacob saw the countenance of Laban, and behold, it was not toward him as in the past.** Even if Laban was not convinced by these claims, he became suspicious of Jacob and his behavior toward him indicated as much.

3 At this point, **the Lord said to Jacob: Return to the land of your fathers, and to the land of your birth, and I will be with**

DISCUSSION

30:41 | **The strong [*mekusharot*] flocks:** This term means the best of the flock, perhaps because they were tied [*keshurot*] for breeding during this period. Alternatively, it could refer to a practice of tying the tails of the best females, so that males could easily mount them (Rabbi Samson Raphael Hirsch, based on *Shabbat* 53).

30:42 | **And the feeble were for Laban and the strong for Jacob:** Since the natural color of a flock of sheep or goats is not uniform, the result of random interbreeding will be sheep and goats with various colors and stripes. Though he presumably could not explain it in terms of dominant genes, Jacob, an experienced shepherd from a young age (see Rashbam, 25:27), would have known that even solid colored animals will frequently give birth to multicolored animals with or without the use of rods. His use of the rods, then, was merely symbolic, a kind of substitute for the animals removed by Laban. Although Laban might have thought that the rods themselves held Jacob's secret, the rods were not essential to Jacob's breeding a flock of multi-colored animals. Jacob did not swindle Laban, and when Laban later accuses Jacob of wrongdoing (31:26–30), he does not mention Jacob's use of the rods.

לז וַיִּקַּח־לוֹ יַעֲקֹב מַקַּל לִבְנֶה לַח וְלוּז וְעַרְמוֹן וַיְפַצֵּל בָּהֵן פְּצָלוֹת לְבָנוֹת מַחְשֹׂף
לח הַלָּבָן אֲשֶׁר עַל־הַמַּקְלוֹת: וַיַּצֵּג אֶת־הַמַּקְלוֹת אֲשֶׁר פִּצֵּל בָּרֳהָטִים בְּשִׁקֲתוֹת
לט הַמָּיִם אֲשֶׁר תָּבֹאןָ הַצֹּאן לִשְׁתּוֹת לְנֹכַח הַצֹּאן וַיֵּחַמְנָה בְּבֹאָן לִשְׁתּוֹת: וַיֶּחֱמוּ
מ הַצֹּאן אֶל־הַמַּקְלוֹת וַתֵּלַדְןָ הַצֹּאן עֲקֻדִּים נְקֻדִּים וּטְלֻאִים: וְהַכְּשָׂבִים הִפְרִיד
יַעֲקֹב וַיִּתֵּן פְּנֵי הַצֹּאן אֶל־עָקֹד וְכָל־חוּם בְּצֹאן לָבָן וַיָּשֶׁת לוֹ עֲדָרִים לְבַדּוֹ וְלֹא
מא שָׁתָם עַל־צֹאן לָבָן: וְהָיָה בְּכָל־יַחֵם הַצֹּאן הַמְקֻשָּׁרוֹת וְשָׂם יַעֲקֹב אֶת־הַמַּקְלוֹת
מב לְעֵינֵי הַצֹּאן בָּרֳהָטִים לְיַחְמֵנָּה בַּמַּקְלוֹת: וּבְהַעֲטִיף הַצֹּאן לֹא יָשִׂים וְהָיָה
מג הָעֲטֻפִים לְלָבָן וְהַקְּשֻׁרִים לְיַעֲקֹב: וַיִּפְרֹץ הָאִישׁ מְאֹד מְאֹד וַיְהִי־לוֹ צֹאן רַבּוֹת
א וּשְׁפָחוֹת וַעֲבָדִים וּגְמַלִּים וַחֲמֹרִים: וַיִּשְׁמַע אֶת־דִּבְרֵי בְנֵי־לָבָן לֵאמֹר לָקַח יַעֲקֹב
ב אֵת כָּל־אֲשֶׁר לְאָבִינוּ וּמֵאֲשֶׁר לְאָבִינוּ עָשָׂה אֵת כָּל־הַכָּבֹד הַזֶּה: וַיַּרְא יַעֲקֹב
ג אֶת־פְּנֵי לָבָן וְהִנֵּה אֵינֶנּוּ עִמּוֹ כִּתְמוֹל שִׁלְשׁוֹם: וַיֹּאמֶר יהוה אֶל־יַעֲקֹב כט

רש"י

לז| **מקל לבנה.** עץ הוא ושמו 'לבנה', כמה דאת אמר: "תחת אלון ולבנה" (הושע ד, יג). ואומר אני, הוא שקורין טרינבל"א שהוא לבן: **לח.** כשהוא רטב: **ולוז.** ועוד לקח מקל לוז, עץ שגדלין בו אגוזים דקים, קולדר"י בלעז: **וערמון.** קשטניי"ר בלעז: **פצלות.** קלופים קלופים, שהיה עושהו מנמר: **מחשף הלבן.** גלוי לבן של מקל, כשהיה קולפו היה נראה ונגלה לבן שלו במקום הקלוף:

לח| **ויצג.** "ודעיץ", לשון תחיבה ונעיצה הוא בלשון ארמי, והרבה יש בתלמוד: "דצה ושלפה" (שבת נ ע"ב), "דץ ביה מידי" (חולין נג ע"ב), 'דצה' כמו 'דעצה', אלא שמקצר את לשונו: **ברהטים.** במרוצות המים, בברכות העשויות בארץ להשקות שם הצאן: **אשר תבאן וגו'.** ברהטים אשר תבאן הצאן לשתות, שם הציג המקלות "לנכח הצאן": **ויחמנה.** הבהמה רואה את המקלות והיא נרתעת לאחוריה, והזכר רובעה ויולדת כיוצא בו. רבי הושעיא אומר: המים נעשין זרע במעיהן ולא היו צריכות לזכר, וזהו "ויחמנה" וגו':

לט| **אל המקלות.** אל מראית המקלות: **עקדים.** משנים במקום עקדתם, הם קרסלי ידיהם ורגליהם:

מ| **והכשבים הפריד יעקב.** הנולדים עקדים ונקדים הבדיל והפריש לעצמן ועשה אותן עדר עדר לבדו, והוליך אותו העדר העקד לפני הצאן, ופני הצאן ההולכות אחריהם צופות אליהם, וזהו שאמר: "ויתן פני הצאן אל עקד", שהיו פני הצאן אל העקדים ואל "כל חום" שמצא "בצאן לבן": **וישת לו עדרים.** כמו שפרשתי:

מא| **המקשרות.** כתרגומו, הבכירות, ואין לי עד במקרא. ומנחם חברו עם "אחיתפל בקשרים" (שמואל ב' טו, לא), "ויהי הקשר אמץ" (שם פסוק יב) – אותן המתקשרות יחד למהר עבורן:

מב| **ובהעטיף.** לשון איחור, כתרגומו "ובלקישות". ומנחם חברו עם "המחלצות והמעטפות" (ישעיה ג, כב), לשון עטיפת כסות, כלומר, מתעטפות בעורן ובצמרן ואינן מתאוות להתיחם על ידי הזכרים:

מג| **צאן רבות.** פרות ורבות משאר צאן: **ושפחות ועבדים.** מוכר צאנו בדמים יקרים ולוקח לו כל אלה:

פרק לא

א| **עשה.** כנס, כמו: "ויעש חיל ויך את עמלק" (שמואל א' יד, מח):

BACKGROUND

30:37| **Poplar [*livneh*]:** The tree *livneh* is mentioned in Hosea (4:13) together with the oak and terebinth. Some identify it with the silver poplar, *Populus alba*, a tree 30 m tall, whose branches can easily be peeled. Others say the word denotes the styrax, *Styrax officinalis*, a shrub that grows up to 6 m in height and has white leaves and flowers.

Almond [*luz*]: The *luz* is the almond tree; it has the same name in Aramaic and Arabic. In modern Hebrew, the word *luz* refers to hazelnut.

Plane [*armon*]: The *armon* is mentioned in Ezekiel (31:8) alongside the cedar and cypress trees. It is identified by translations as the oriental plane, *Platanus orientalis*, a tall, impressive-looking tree with a smooth, bright appearance once its bark has been removed. In modern Hebrew, the word *armon* refers to the chestnut, genus *Castanea*.

you. God instructed him to return, but did not specify when exactly he should do so.

4 **Jacob sent and summoned Rachel and Leah to the field to his flocks,** for a private discussion and consultation. He took them out to the field because he knew it would be an emotionally charged exchange.[16]

5 **He said to them: I see your father's countenance and it is not toward me as in the past.** His behavior toward me has changed. **And the God of my father was with me.**

6 **And you know that with all my strength I have served your father.**

7 **But your father has cheated me,** as he has not stood by our agreements, **and changed** the conditions of **my wages ten times,** amounting to numerous times. **But** even so, **God did not allow him to harm me.**

8 **If he,** Laban, **said this: The speckled shall be your wages,** that I would receive as my wages all the flock with that particular mark, **then all the flocks bore speckled** young, and I gained. **And if he said that: The streaked shall be your wages, all the flocks bore streaked** young. From Jacob's statement, it is evident that Laban sought to change the contract between them time after time, but it eventually became clear that Jacob was blessed.

9 **God has diverted the livestock of your father, and given it to me.** It was God who transferred the animals from your father's flock to my possession.

10 **It was at the time that the flock was in heat, I lifted my eyes, and saw in a dream, and behold, the males that mounted** and impregnated **the flock were streaked, speckled, and mottled.** They were a variety of mixed colors, even if that was not always the case in reality.

11 **The angel of God said to me in the dream: Jacob, and I said: Here I am.**

12 **He said: Please lift your eyes, and see, all the males that mount the flock are streaked, speckled, and mottled for I have seen all that Laban is doing to you,** and therefore I have come to help you. The vision in your dream will come true, and the animals that will be born will have patches and spots on their skin.

13 **I am the God of** your encounter in **Beit El, where you anointed a monument** with oil to sanctify it, and **where you took a vow to Me,** as described above (28:18–22). **Now arise, leave this land,** since it is time for you to fulfill your vow, **and return to the land of your birth.**

14 Jacob's wives were more than willing to cooperate. **Rachel and Leah answered and said to him: Is there still a share or inheritance for us in our father's house?** We feel no attachment to our father's family.

15 **Are we not considered foreigners by him, as he sold us** for your service? It was not an ordinary marriage arrangement, in which lavish gifts are exchanged between the couple, but a business deal for him. **And he also consumed our silver;** he did not even give us part of that money, but appropriated it all for himself without the slightest hesitation.

16 **As all the wealth that God salvaged from our father, it is for us and for our children.** All the riches and property in your possession is ours and our children's. **And now, everything that God said to you, do.** We are ready to leave our homeland and travel with you.

Sixth aliya

17 **Jacob arose and placed his sons and his wives upon the camels.**

18 **He led all his livestock and all his property that he attained, his acquisitions that he acquired, which he attained in Padan Aram, to come to Isaac his father, to the land of Canaan.**

ד שׁוּב אֶל־אֶרֶץ אֲבוֹתֶיךָ וּלְמוֹלַדְתֶּךָ וְאֶהְיֶה עִמָּךְ: וַיִּשְׁלַח יַעֲקֹב וַיִּקְרָא לְרָחֵל

ה וּלְלֵאָה הַשָּׂדֶה אֶל־צֹאנוֹ: וַיֹּאמֶר לָהֶן רֹאֶה אָנֹכִי אֶת־פְּנֵי אֲבִיכֶן כִּי־אֵינֶנּוּ אֵלַי

ו כִּתְמֹל שִׁלְשֹׁם וֵאלֹהֵי אָבִי הָיָה עִמָּדִי: וְאַתֵּנָה יְדַעְתֶּן כִּי בְּכָל־כֹּחִי עָבַדְתִּי אֶת־

ז אֲבִיכֶן: וַאֲבִיכֶן הֵתֶל בִּי וְהֶחֱלִף אֶת־מַשְׂכֻּרְתִּי עֲשֶׂרֶת מֹנִים וְלֹא־נְתָנוֹ אֱלֹהִים

ח לְהָרַע עִמָּדִי: אִם־כֹּה יֹאמַר נְקֻדִּים יִהְיֶה שְׂכָרֶךָ וְיָלְדוּ כָל־הַצֹּאן נְקֻדִּים וְאִם־כֹּה

ט יֹאמַר עֲקֻדִּים יִהְיֶה שְׂכָרֶךָ וְיָלְדוּ כָל־הַצֹּאן עֲקֻדִּים: וַיַּצֵּל אֱלֹהִים אֶת־מִקְנֵה

י אֲבִיכֶם וַיִּתֶּן־לִי: וַיְהִי בְּעֵת יַחֵם הַצֹּאן וָאֶשָּׂא עֵינַי וָאֵרֶא בַּחֲלוֹם וְהִנֵּה הָעַתֻּדִים

יא הָעֹלִים עַל־הַצֹּאן עֲקֻדִּים נְקֻדִּים וּבְרֻדִּים: וַיֹּאמֶר אֵלַי מַלְאַךְ הָאֱלֹהִים בַּחֲלוֹם

יב יַעֲקֹב וָאֹמַר הִנֵּנִי: וַיֹּאמֶר שָׂא־נָא עֵינֶיךָ וּרְאֵה כָּל־הָעַתֻּדִים הָעֹלִים עַל־הַצֹּאן

יג עֲקֻדִּים נְקֻדִּים וּבְרֻדִּים כִּי רָאִיתִי אֵת כָּל־אֲשֶׁר לָבָן עֹשֶׂה לָּךְ: אָנֹכִי הָאֵל בֵּית־

אֵל אֲשֶׁר מָשַׁחְתָּ שָּׁם מַצֵּבָה אֲשֶׁר נָדַרְתָּ לִּי שָׁם נֶדֶר עַתָּה קוּם צֵא מִן־הָאָרֶץ

יד הַזֹּאת וְשׁוּב אֶל־אֶרֶץ מוֹלַדְתֶּךָ: וַתַּעַן רָחֵל וְלֵאָה וַתֹּאמַרְנָה לוֹ הַעוֹד לָנוּ חֵלֶק

טו וְנַחֲלָה בְּבֵית אָבִינוּ: הֲלוֹא נָכְרִיּוֹת נֶחְשַׁבְנוּ לוֹ כִּי מְכָרָנוּ וַיֹּאכַל גַּם־אָכוֹל אֶת־

טז כַּסְפֵּנוּ: כִּי כָל־הָעֹשֶׁר אֲשֶׁר הִצִּיל אֱלֹהִים מֵאָבִינוּ לָנוּ הוּא וּלְבָנֵינוּ וְעַתָּה כֹּל

יז אֲשֶׁר אָמַר אֱלֹהִים אֵלֶיךָ עֲשֵׂה: וַיָּקָם יַעֲקֹב וַיִּשָּׂא אֶת־בָּנָיו וְאֶת־נָשָׁיו עַל־ שׁשׁי

יח הַגְּמַלִּים: וַיִּנְהַג אֶת־כָּל־מִקְנֵהוּ וְאֶת־כָּל־רְכֻשׁוֹ אֲשֶׁר רָכָשׁ מִקְנֵה קִנְיָנוֹ אֲשֶׁר

רש״י

ג שׁוּב אֶל אֶרֶץ אֲבוֹתֶיךָ. וְשָׁם "אֶהְיֶה עִמָּךְ", אֲבָל בְּעוֹדְךָ מְחֻבָּר לַטָּמֵא אִי אֶפְשָׁר לְהַשְׁרוֹת שְׁכִינָתִי עָלֶיךָ:

ד וַיִּקְרָא לְרָחֵל וּלְלֵאָה. לְרָחֵל תְּחִלָּה וְאַחַר כָּךְ לְלֵאָה, שֶׁהִיא הָיְתָה עִקַּר הַבַּיִת, שֶׁבִּשְׁבִילָהּ נִזְדַּוֵּג יַעֲקֹב עִם לָבָן. וְאַף בְּנֵי לֵאָה מוֹדִים בַּדָּבָר, שֶׁהֲרֵי בֹּעַז וּבֵית דִּינוֹ מִשֵּׁבֶט יְהוּדָה אוֹמְרִים: "כְּרָחֵל וּכְלֵאָה אֲשֶׁר בָּנוּ שְׁתֵּיהֶם" וְגוֹ' (רות ד, יא), הִקְדִּימוּ רָחֵל לְלֵאָה:

ז עֲשֶׂרֶת מֹנִים. אֵין 'מוֹנֶה' פָּחוֹת מֵעֲשָׂרָה. מוֹנִים. לְשׁוֹן סְכוּם כְּלַל הַחֶשְׁבּוֹן, וְהֵן עֲשִׂירִיּוֹת, לַמֵּדְךָ שֶׁהֶחֱלִיף תְּנַאי מֵאָה פְּעָמִים:

יא וְהִנֵּה הָעַתֻּדִים. אַף עַל פִּי שֶׁהִבְדִּילָם לָבָן כֻּלָּם שֶׁלֹּא יִתְעַבְּרוּ הַצֹּאן דֻּגְמָתָן, הָיוּ הַמַּלְאָכִים מְבִיאִין אוֹתָן מֵעֵדֶר הַמָּסוּר בְּיַד בְּנֵי לָבָן לָעֵדֶר שֶׁבְּיַד יַעֲקֹב: וּבְרֻדִּים. כְּתַרְגּוּמוֹ "וּמְפַצְּחִין", פייש�"יד בְּלַעַז, חוּט שֶׁל לָבָן מַקִּיף אֶת גּוּפוֹ

סָבִיב, חֲבַרְבֻּרוֹת שֶׁלּוֹ פְּתוּחָה וּמֻפְלֶשֶׁת מִזֶּה אֶל זֶה, וְאֵין לִי לְהָבִיא לוֹ עֵד מִן הַמִּקְרָא:

יג הָאֵל בֵּית אֵל. כְּמוֹ 'אֵל בֵּית אֵל', הַה״א יְתֵרָה, וְדֶרֶךְ מִקְרָאוֹת לְדַבֵּר כֵּן, כְּמוֹ: "כִּי אַתֶּם בָּאִים אֶל הָאָרֶץ כְּנָעַן" (במדבר לד, ב): מָשַׁחְתָּ שָּׁם. לְשׁוֹן רִבּוּי וּגְדֻלָּה כְּמִנְהַג לַמַּלְכוּת, כָּךְ "וַיִּצֹק שֶׁמֶן עַל רֹאשָׁהּ" (לעיל כח, יח) לִהְיוֹת מְשׁוּחָה לַמִּזְבֵּחַ: אֲשֶׁר נָדַרְתָּ לִּי. וְצָרִיךְ אַתָּה לְשַׁלְּמוֹ (סס), שֶׁאָמַרְתָּ: "יִהְיֶה בֵּית אֱלֹהִים" (לעיל כח, כב), שֶׁתַּקְרִיב שָׁם קָרְבָּנוֹת:

יד הַעוֹד לָנוּ. לָמָּה נְעַכֵּב עַל יָדְךָ מִלָּשׁוּב, כְּלוּם אָנוּ מְיַחֲלוֹת לִירַשׁ מִנִּכְסֵי אָבִינוּ כְּלוּם בֵּין הַזְּכָרִים?

טו הֲלוֹא נָכְרִיּוֹת נֶחְשַׁבְנוּ לוֹ. אֲפִלּוּ בְּשָׁעָה שֶׁדֶּרֶךְ בְּנֵי אָדָם לָתֵת לָאָדָם נְדוּנְיָא לִבְנוֹתָיו, בִּשְׁעַת נִשּׂוּאִין, נָהַג עִמָּנוּ

כְּנָכְרִיּוֹת, "כִּי מְכָרָנוּ" לְךָ בִּשְׂכַר הַפְּעֻלָּה: אֶת כַּסְפֵּנוּ. שֶׁעִכֵּב דְּמֵי שְׂכַר פְּעֻלָּתֶךָ:

טז כִּי כָל הָעֹשֶׁר. "כִּי" זֶה מְשַׁמֵּשׁ בִּלְשׁוֹן 'אֶלָּא', כְּלוֹמַר מִשֶּׁל אָבִינוּ אֵין לָנוּ כְּלוּם, אֶלָּא מַה שֶּׁהִצִּיל הַקָּדוֹשׁ בָּרוּךְ הוּא מֵאָבִינוּ שֶׁלָּנוּ הוּא: הִצִּיל. לְשׁוֹן הִפְרִישׁ, וְכֵן כָּל לְשׁוֹן הַצָּלָה שֶׁבַּמִּקְרָא לְשׁוֹן הַפְרָשָׁה, שֶׁמַּפְרִישׁוֹ מִן הָרָעָה וּמִן הָאוֹיֵב:

יז אֶת בָּנָיו וְאֶת נָשָׁיו. הִקְדִּים זְכָרִים לִנְקֵבוֹת, וְעֵשָׂו הִקְדִּים נְקֵבוֹת לִזְכָרִים, שֶׁנֶּאֱמַר: "וַיִּקַּח עֵשָׂו אֶת נָשָׁיו וְגוֹ' " (להלן לו, ו):

יח מִקְנֵה קִנְיָנוֹ. מַה שֶּׁקָּנָה מִצֹּאנוֹ, עֲבָדִים וּשְׁפָחוֹת וּגְמַלִּים וַחֲמוֹרִים:

169

19 The preparations for the journey were aided by the absence of Laban and his sons, as **Laban went to shear his sheep.** As stated earlier (30:36), Laban's flock was purposely placed far from Jacob's. Since the shearing of a whole flock of sheep takes several days, Jacob seized this opportunity. **And Rachel stole the household idols**[D] **that were her father's.** These might have been small idols in human form, used for sorcery.[17]

20 **Jacob deceived Laban the Aramean in that he did not tell him that he was fleeing.** Jacob did not indicate by his statements or actions that he planned to leave.

21 **He fled, he and all that he had,** his descendants and possessions; **and he arose and crossed the river,** the Euphrates, then turned southwest **and headed toward the highlands of Gilad.** Jacob sought to return to Canaan by the easiest path, via the eastern bank of the Jordan River.

22 **It was told to Laban on the third day** after this departure **that Jacob** had **fled.**

23 **He took his brethren,** his close family members, **with him, and pursued him a distance of seven days.**[D] **He,** Laban, **reached him in the highlands of Gilad.** He was able to cover such a distance in a shorter time than Jacob because he and his accomplices were not burdened with their families and livestock in their care. It is also likely that they rode upon animals.

24 **God came to Laban the Aramean in a dream of the night, and He said to him: Beware lest you speak**[D] **to Jacob from good,** tempting, seductive offers, **to bad** statements, threats. Laban was not forbidden from talking to Jacob at all, but he had to refrain from pressuring him.

25 **Laban caught up with Jacob. Jacob had pitched his tent in the highlands,** Gilad, **and Laban** also **pitched** the tents of **his brethren in the highlands of Gilad.** The two encampments were close enough to each other for Laban to enter Jacob's camp.

26 **Laban said to Jacob: What did you do that you deceived me and led my daughters like captives of the sword?** Laban might have realized that his daughters had not been taken against their will, but in his anger he was happy to fling accusations at Jacob. Since Laban viewed Jacob as the reason for his success (see 30:27), his sudden flight upset him.

27 **Why did you flee surreptitiously and deceive me; and you did not tell me.** Had you informed me, **I would have sent you** in a dignified, celebratory manner, **with joy and with songs, with drum and with harp.**

28 **You did not allow me to kiss my sons,** grandsons, **and my daughters.** Due to his dream, Laban initially sought to avoid threatening Jacob, and made do with a rebuke. **Now you have acted foolishly.** If you had made your intentions known, I would have respected your wishes.

29 Ultimately, Laban was unable to control himself and issued a threat. **It is in my power,** and in that of my men, **to do you harm. But** I refrained from doing so. Laban admitted: **The God of your father said to me last night, saying: Beware of speaking with Jacob from good to bad.**

30 **And now,** even if **you have gone because you longed for your father's house** after a twenty-year absence and a lack of contact with your family, **why did you steal my gods?**

31 **Jacob answered and said to Laban:** With regard to your question as to why I fled, it was **because I feared** you, **because I said: Lest you would rob your daughters from me.** I was apprehensive that you would force me to leave alone, just as I arrived.

32 And as for the claim of stolen idols, **with whomever you find your gods, he shall not live,** but will be put to death. **Before our brethren, identify what is with me;** you may search my property, **and** if you find anything I have wrongfully taken, **take** it back **for yourself.** The word "brethren" refers to the members of Jacob's family as well as Laban's family, who he considered to be his own relatives, especially in light of Jacob's lengthy stay in Haran. **And** his reaction was fierce denial, as **Jacob did not know that Rachel stole them.** Had he known, he would not have placed a curse on the thief, but would have promised to return the idols and perhaps compensate Laban. Jacob assumed that Laban came with false accusations, seeking an excuse to play the role of the offended party and clear himself of all suspicion.

33 Having received permission to conduct a search for any objects belonging to him, **Laban came into Jacob's tent, and into Leah's tent, and into the tent of the two maidservants, but**

DISCUSSION

31:19 | And Rachel stole the household idols: Similar to the various talismanic items placed nowadays in many homes for good luck, such household idols were on the border between actual idols and objects of superstition that supposedly protected their owners from afflictions (see also discussion on I Samuel 19:13).

Rachel's motivation was possibly to cause her father ill fortune. Perhaps she was concerned that the idols would reveal secrets to Laban, and therefore she made sure that he could not use them. However, she did not immediately dispose of the idols, but took them with her, indicating that her aim was not merely to remove them from Laban's possession, but that she

wanted them for herself (see Ibn Ezra ad loc., and 35:2).

31:23 | And pursued him a distance of seven days: Like Jacob, Laban required time to prepare before he could undertake the chase. Since he assumed that Jacob had left for Canaan, he and his men chased him in that direction. Not only did they have to cover the three days' distance ◄●

יט דְכֻשׁ בְּפַדַּן אֲרָם לָבוֹא אֶל־יִצְחָק אָבִיו אַרְצָה כְּנָעַן: וְלָבָן הָלַךְ לִגְזֹז אֶת־צֹאנוֹ

כ וַתִּגְנֹב רָחֵל אֶת־הַתְּרָפִים אֲשֶׁר לְאָבִיהָ: וַיִּגְנֹב יַעֲקֹב אֶת־לֵב לָבָן הָאֲרַמִּי עַל־

כא בְּלִי הִגִּיד לוֹ כִּי בֹרֵחַ הוּא: וַיִּבְרַח הוּא וְכָל־אֲשֶׁר־לוֹ וַיָּקָם וַיַּעֲבֹר אֶת־הַנָּהָר

כב וַיָּשֶׂם אֶת־פָּנָיו הַר הַגִּלְעָד: וַיֻּגַּד לְלָבָן בַּיּוֹם הַשְּׁלִישִׁי כִּי בָרַח יַעֲקֹב: וַיִּקַּח אֶת־

כג אֶחָיו עִמּוֹ וַיִּרְדֹּף אַחֲרָיו דֶּרֶךְ שִׁבְעַת יָמִים וַיַּדְבֵּק אֹתוֹ בְּהַר הַגִּלְעָד: וַיָּבֹא אֱלֹהִים

כד אֶל־לָבָן הָאֲרַמִּי בַּחֲלֹם הַלָּיְלָה וַיֹּאמֶר לוֹ הִשָּׁמֶר לְךָ פֶּן־תְּדַבֵּר עִם־יַעֲקֹב מִטּוֹב

כה עַד־רָע: וַיַּשֵּׂג לָבָן אֶת־יַעֲקֹב וְיַעֲקֹב תָּקַע אֶת־אָהֳלוֹ בָּהָר וְלָבָן תָּקַע אֶת־אֶחָיו

כו בְּהַר הַגִּלְעָד: וַיֹּאמֶר לָבָן לְיַעֲקֹב מֶה עָשִׂיתָ וַתִּגְנֹב אֶת־לְבָבִי וַתְּנַהֵג אֶת־בְּנֹתַי

כז כִּשְׁבֻיוֹת חָרֶב: לָמָּה נַחְבֵּאתָ לִבְרֹחַ וַתִּגְנֹב אֹתִי וְלֹא־הִגַּדְתָּ לִּי וָאֲשַׁלֵּחֲךָ בְּשִׂמְחָה

כח וּבְשִׁרִים בְּתֹף וּבְכִנּוֹר: וְלֹא נְטַשְׁתַּנִי לְנַשֵּׁק לְבָנַי וְלִבְנֹתָי עַתָּה הִסְכַּלְתָּ עֲשׂוֹ:

כט יֶשׁ־לְאֵל יָדִי לַעֲשׂוֹת עִמָּכֶם רָע וֵאלֹהֵי אֲבִיכֶם אֶמֶשׁ ׀ אָמַר אֵלַי לֵאמֹר הִשָּׁמֶר

ל לְךָ מִדַּבֵּר עִם־יַעֲקֹב מִטּוֹב עַד־רָע: וְעַתָּה הָלֹךְ הָלַכְתָּ כִּי־נִכְסֹף נִכְסַפְתָּה לְבֵית

לא אָבִיךָ לָמָּה גָנַבְתָּ אֶת־אֱלֹהָי: וַיַּעַן יַעֲקֹב וַיֹּאמֶר לְלָבָן כִּי יָרֵאתִי כִּי אָמַרְתִּי פֶּן־

לב תִּגְזֹל אֶת־בְּנוֹתֶיךָ מֵעִמִּי: עִם אֲשֶׁר תִּמְצָא אֶת־אֱלֹהֶיךָ לֹא יִחְיֶה נֶגֶד אַחֵינוּ

לג הַכֶּר־לְךָ מָה עִמָּדִי וְקַח־לָךְ וְלֹא־יָדַע יַעֲקֹב כִּי רָחֵל גְּנָבָתַם: וַיָּבֹא לָבָן בְּאֹהֶל־

יַעֲקֹב ׀ וּבְאֹהֶל לֵאָה וּבְאֹהֶל שְׁתֵּי הָאֲמָהֹת וְלֹא מָצָא וַיֵּצֵא מֵאֹהֶל לֵאָה וַיָּבֹא

יט לָגֹז אֶת צֹאנוֹ. שֶׁנָּתַן בְּיַד בָּנָיו דֶּרֶךְ שְׁלֹשֶׁת יָמִים בֵּינוֹ וּבֵין יַעֲקֹב: וַתִּגְנֹב רָחֵל אֶת הַתְּרָפִים. לְהַפְרִישׁ אֶת אָבִיהָ מֵעֲבוֹדָה זָרָה נִתְכַּוְּנָה:

כב בַּיּוֹם הַשְּׁלִישִׁי. שֶׁהֲרֵי דֶּרֶךְ שְׁלֹשֶׁת יָמִים הָיָה בֵּינֵיהֶם:

כג אֶת אֶחָיו. קְרוֹבָיו: דֶּרֶךְ שִׁבְעַת יָמִים. כָּל אוֹתָן שְׁלֹשָׁה יָמִים שֶׁהָלַךְ הַמַּגִּיד לְהַגִּיד לְלָבָן הָלַךְ יַעֲקֹב לְדַרְכּוֹ, נִמְצָא יַעֲקֹב רָחוֹק מִלָּבָן שִׁשָּׁה יָמִים, וּבַשְּׁבִיעִי הִשִּׂיגוֹ לָבָן. לָמַדְנוּ שֶׁכָּל מַה שֶּׁהָלַךְ יַעֲקֹב בְּשִׁבְעָה יָמִים הָלַךְ לָבָן בְּיוֹם אֶחָד.

כד מִטּוֹב עַד רָע. כָּל טוֹבָתָן שֶׁל רְשָׁעִים רָעָה הִיא אֵצֶל הַצַּדִּיקִים:

כז כִּשְׁבֻיוֹת חָרֶב. כָּל חַיִל הַבָּא לַמִּלְחָמָה קְרוּי חֶרֶב:

כז וַתִּגְנֹב אֹתִי. גָּנַבְתָּ אֶת דַּעְתִּי:

כט יֶשׁ לְאֵל יָדִי. יֵשׁ כֹּחַ וְחַיִל בְּיָדִי לַעֲשׂוֹת עִמָּכֶם רָע, וְכָל 'אֵל' שֶׁהוּא קֹדֶשׁ, עַל שֵׁם עֹז וְרֹב אוֹנִים הוּא:

ל נִכְסַפְתָּה. חָמַדְתָּ, וְהַרְבֵּה יֵשׁ בַּמִּקְרָא: "נִכְסְפָה וְגַם

כלְתָה נַפְשִׁי" (תהלים פד, ג), "לְמַעֲשֵׂה יָדֶיךָ תִּכְסֹף" (איוב יד, טו):

לא כִּי יָרֵאתִי וְגוֹ'. הֱשִׁיבוֹ עַל רִאשׁוֹן רִאשׁוֹן, שֶׁאָמַר לוֹ: "וַתְּנַהֵג אֶת בְּנֹתַי" וְגוֹ' (לעיל פסוק כו):

לב לֹא יִחְיֶה. וּמֵאוֹתָהּ קְלָלָה מֵתָה רָחֵל בַּדֶּרֶךְ: מָה עִמָּדִי. מִשֶּׁלְּךָ:

לג בְּאֹהֶל יַעֲקֹב. הוּא אֹהֶל רָחֵל שֶׁהָיָה יַעֲקֹב תָּדִיר אֶצְלָהּ, וְכֵן הוּא אוֹמֵר: "בְּנֵי רָחֵל אֵשֶׁת יַעֲקֹב" (להלן מו):

➤ between them from the outset (see 30:36) but also the additional gap that Jacob had created

in the meantime. Consequently, the pursuit took seven days.

DISCUSSION

31:24 | **Lest you speak** [*tedabber*]: *Dibbur* is a harsher form of speech than the more neutral *amira* (Makkot 11a).

he did not find the idols; **he emerged from Leah's tent and came into Rachel's tent.** As stated earlier, Jacob's wives each had their own tent.[18]

34 **Rachel took the household idols** and **placed them in the cushion of the camel.** For a lengthy journey they would not merely place a small saddle on the camels, but a large, heavily padded cushion. Rachel put the idols under this cushion. **And she sat upon them. Laban felt throughout the tent and did not find** them.

Cushion of the camel

Camel saddle

35 Whether Rachel still desired to keep the idols, or if she now regretted taking them, she refused to admit the theft. **She said to her father: Let my lord not be angry, as I cannot arise before you because the manner of women is upon me.** I am menstruating, and it is hard for me to stand. Perhaps it was customary at the time to refrain from speaking with a woman during her menstruation period, or at least to converse with her as briefly as possible.[19] Therefore, Laban did not continue talking to her and did not ask her to rise. **He searched** in the other areas of the tent **but did not find the household gods.**

36 Convinced that there was no basis for the accusation of theft, Jacob felt dishonored by Laban's intrusive search in his and his wives' tents. **Jacob was angry and quarreled with Laban. Jacob responded and said to Laban: What is my transgression, what is my sin that you have pursued after me?**

37 **For you felt all my vessels, what have you found of all the vessels of your household?** If you discovered any object of yours, **place it here before my brethren and your brethren.** There are people here who know us both and who would recognize your property. **And they will determine between the two of us.** Jacob was not necessarily interested in negotiating, but in his anger he laid out his claims against his employer.

38 **These twenty years I have been with you; your ewes and your female goats have not miscarried.** Through all these years of service, your flocks were blessed. Jacob's statement can also be interpreted as a claim that he had accepted all responsibility for such unfortunate occurrences, that he invariably paid for such deaths from his own pocket. **And the rams of your flock I have not eaten.**

39 **I did not bring** the remains of **a mauled animal,** one torn apart by wild beasts, **to you** with the claim that it was not my fault. The standard custom was that a shepherd was not held responsible for attacks of this kind. Even so, when an animal was mauled **I bore its loss** and would pay for it; **from me you could demand it, whether stolen from me by day or stolen from me by night.** Whether an item was stolen from me by day or night, I accepted responsibility for all damages.

40 **Thus I was:** When I shepherded your flock **in the day dehydration consumed me, and the frost by night; and my sleep fled from my eyes,** as I had to guard your property without respite.

41 **These are twenty years for me in your house: I worked for you fourteen years for your two daughters, and six years for** a portion of **your flocks; and you changed my wages ten times,** as Jacob had related to his wives (verse 7).

42 **If the God of my father, the God of Abraham, and the Fear of Isaac,** God, whom Isaac feared[20] **had not been with me then, you would have sent me away now empty-handed. God saw my hardship and the** faithful **toil of my hands and proved it last night.** When He spoke to you last night He confirmed the rightfulness of my claims.

43 Laban did not agree with Jacob's argument, but rather reemphasized his own claim. **Laban responded and said to Jacob: The girls,** your wives, **are my daughters, and the boys,** their children, **are my sons, and the flocks are my flocks, and everything that you see is mine.** All that you have here you took from me, and therefore it is all my property. **And to my daughters, what can I do to them today, or to their children whom they have borne?** I cannot fight against them, as they are my daughters and grandchildren. In truth it is all mine, but I could not harm my family.

Seventh aliya

44 We shall shortly conclude our involvement with each other and will not see one another again. **And now,** for the sake of the future, **come, let us establish a covenant, I and you; and let it be as a witness between me and you.**

45 **Jacob took a stone and established it as a** commemorative **monument.**

46 **Jacob said to his brethren,** his sons, who were perhaps already strong enough to help, as well as his servants and the other members of his camp: **Gather stones. And they took stones,**

לד בְּאֹהֶל רָחֵל: וְרָחֵל לָקְחָה אֶת־הַתְּרָפִים וַתְּשִׂמֵם בְּכַר הַגָּמָל וַתֵּשֶׁב עֲלֵיהֶם
לה וַיְמַשֵּׁשׁ לָבָן אֶת־כָּל־הָאֹהֶל וְלֹא מָצָא: וַתֹּאמֶר אֶל־אָבִיהָ אַל־יִחַר בְּעֵינֵי אֲדֹנִי
כִּי לוֹא אוּכַל לָקוּם מִפָּנֶיךָ כִּי־דֶרֶךְ נָשִׁים לִי וַיְחַפֵּשׂ וְלֹא מָצָא אֶת־הַתְּרָפִים:
לו וַיִּחַר לְיַעֲקֹב וַיָּרֶב בְּלָבָן וַיַּעַן יַעֲקֹב וַיֹּאמֶר לְלָבָן מַה־פִּשְׁעִי מַה חַטָּאתִי כִּי
לז דָלַקְתָּ אַחֲרָי: כִּי־מִשַּׁשְׁתָּ אֶת־כָּל־כֵּלַי מַה־מָּצָאתָ מִכֹּל כְּלֵי־בֵיתֶךָ שִׂים כֹּה נֶגֶד
לח אַחַי וְאַחֶיךָ וְיוֹכִיחוּ בֵּין שְׁנֵינוּ: זֶה עֶשְׂרִים שָׁנָה אָנֹכִי עִמָּךְ רְחֵלֶיךָ וְעִזֶּיךָ לֹא
לט שִׁכֵּלוּ וְאֵילֵי צֹאנְךָ לֹא אָכָלְתִּי: טְרֵפָה לֹא־הֵבֵאתִי אֵלֶיךָ אָנֹכִי אֲחַטֶּנָּה מִיָּדִי
מ תְּבַקְשֶׁנָּה גְּנֻבְתִי יוֹם וּגְנֻבְתִי לָיְלָה: הָיִיתִי בַיּוֹם אֲכָלַנִי חֹרֶב וְקֶרַח בַּלָּיְלָה וַתִּדַּד
מא שְׁנָתִי מֵעֵינָי: זֶה־לִּי עֶשְׂרִים שָׁנָה בְּבֵיתֶךָ עֲבַדְתִּיךָ אַרְבַּע־עֶשְׂרֵה שָׁנָה בִּשְׁתֵּי
מב בְנֹתֶיךָ וְשֵׁשׁ שָׁנִים בְּצֹאנֶךָ וַתַּחֲלֵף אֶת־מַשְׂכֻּרְתִּי עֲשֶׂרֶת מֹנִים: לוּלֵי אֱלֹהֵי אָבִי
אֱלֹהֵי אַבְרָהָם וּפַחַד יִצְחָק הָיָה לִי כִּי עַתָּה רֵיקָם שִׁלַּחְתָּנִי אֶת־עָנְיִי וְאֶת־יְגִיעַ
מג כַּפַּי רָאָה אֱלֹהִים וַיּוֹכַח אָמֶשׁ: וַיַּעַן לָבָן וַיֹּאמֶר אֶל־יַעֲקֹב הַבָּנוֹת בְּנֹתַי וְהַבָּנִים שביעי
בָּנַי וְהַצֹּאן צֹאנִי וְכֹל אֲשֶׁר־אַתָּה רֹאֶה לִי־הוּא וְלִבְנֹתַי מָה־אֶעֱשֶׂה לָאֵלֶּה הַיּוֹם
מד אוֹ לִבְנֵיהֶן אֲשֶׁר יָלָדוּ: וְעַתָּה לְכָה נִכְרְתָה בְרִית אֲנִי וָאָתָּה וְהָיָה לְעֵד בֵּינִי
מה מו וּבֵינֶךָ: וַיִּקַּח יַעֲקֹב אָבֶן וַיְרִימֶהָ מַצֵּבָה: וַיֹּאמֶר יַעֲקֹב לְאֶחָיו לִקְטוּ אֲבָנִים וַיִּקְחוּ

רש״י

יט), וּבִכְלָן לֹא נֶאֱמַר 'אֵשֶׁת יַעֲקֹב': וַיָּבֹא בְּאֹהֶל רָחֵל. כְּשֶׁיָּצָא מֵאֹהֶל לֵאָה חָזַר לוֹ לְאֹהֶל רָחֵל קֹדֶם שֶׁחִפֵּשׂ בְּאֹהֶל הָאֲמָהוֹת. וְכָל כָּךְ לָמָּה? לְפִי שֶׁהָיָה מַכִּיר בָּהּ שֶׁהִיא מַשְׁמְשָׁנִית:

לד| בְּכַר הַגָּמָל. לְשׁוֹן כָּרִים וּכְסָתוֹת, כְּתַרְגּוּמוֹ: "בַּעֲבִיטָא דְּגַמְלָא", וְהִיא מַרְדַּעַת הָעֲשׂוּיָה כְּמִין כַּר. וּבְעֵרוּבִין שָׁנִינוּ: "הִקִּיפוּהָ בַּעֲבִיטִין" (דף טו ע"א), וְהֵן עֲבִיטֵי גְּמַלִּים, בשטי"ל בְּלַעַז:

לו| דָלַקְתָּ. רָדַפְתָּ, כְּמוֹ: "עַל הֶהָרִים דְּלָקוּנוּ" (איכה ד, יט), וּכְמוֹ: "מִדְּלֹק אַחֲרֵי פְלִשְׁתִּים" (שמואל א' יז, נג):

לז| וְיוֹכִיחוּ. וִיבָרְרוּ עִם מִי הַדִּין, אפרובי"ר בְּלַעַז:

לח| לֹא שִׁכֵּלוּ. לֹא הִפִּילוּ עֻבָּרָם, כְּמוֹ: "רֶחֶם מַשְׁכִּיל" (הושע ט, יד), "תְּפַלֵּט פָּרָתוֹ וְלֹא תְשַׁכֵּל" (איוב כא, י): וְאֵילֵי צֹאנְךָ. מִכָּאן אָמְרוּ: אַיִל בֶּן יוֹמוֹ קָרוּי אַיִל, שֶׁאִם לֹא כֵן מַה שִּׁבְחוֹ? אֵילִים לֹא אָכַל אֲבָל כְּבָשִׂים אָכַל – אִם כֵּן גַּזְלָן הוּא!:

לט| טְרֵפָה. עַל יְדֵי אֲרִי וּזְאֵב: אָנֹכִי אֲחַטֶּנָּה. לְשׁוֹן: "אֶל הַשַּׂעֲרָה וְלֹא יַחֲטִא" (שופטים כ, טז), "אֲנִי וּבְנִי שְׁלֹמֹה חַטָּאִים" (מלכים א' א, כא) – חֲסֵרִים. אָנֹכִי אֲחַסְּרֶנָּה, אִם חָסְרָה חָסְרָה לִי, שֶׁ"מִיָּדִי תְּבַקְשֶׁנָּה": גְּנֻבְתִי יוֹם וּגְנֻבְתִי לָיְלָה. גְּנוּבַת יוֹם אוֹ גְּנוּבַת לַיְלָה, הַכֹּל שִׁלַּמְתִּי: גְּנֻבְתִי. כְּמוֹ: "רַבָּתִי בַגּוֹיִם שָׂרָתִי בַּמְּדִינוֹת" (איכה א, א), "מְלֵאֲתִי מִשְׁפָּט" (ישעיה א, כא), "אֹהַבְתִּי לָדוּשׁ" (הושע י, יא):

מ| אֲכָלַנִי חֹרֶב. לְשׁוֹן "אֵשׁ אֹכְלָה" (דברים ד, כד): וְקֶרַח. כְּמוֹ: "מַשְׁלִיךְ קַרְחוֹ" (תהלים קמז, יז), תַּרְגּוּמוֹ: "גְּלִידָא": שְׁנָתִי. לְשׁוֹן שֵׁנָה:

מא| וַתַּחֲלֵף אֶת מַשְׂכֻּרְתִּי. הָיִיתָ מְשַׁנֶּה תְּנַאי שֶׁבֵּינֵינוּ, מִנָּקֹד לְטָלוּא, לַעֲקֻדִּים, לִבְרֻדִּים:

מב| וּפַחַד יִצְחָק. לֹא רָצָה לוֹמַר 'אֱלֹהֵי יִצְחָק', שֶׁאֵין הַקָּדוֹשׁ בָּרוּךְ הוּא מְיַחֵד שְׁמוֹ עַל הַצַּדִּיקִים בְּחַיֵּיהֶם, וְאַף עַל פִּי שֶׁאָמַר לוֹ בְּצֵאתוֹ מִבְּאֵר שֶׁבַע: "אֲנִי ה' אֱלֹהֵי אַבְרָהָם אָבִיךָ וֵאלֹהֵי יִצְחָק" (לעיל כח, יג) בִּשְׁבִיל שֶׁכָּהוּ עֵינָיו וַהֲרֵי הוּא כְּמֵת, יַעֲקֹב נִתְיָרֵא לוֹמַר: וַיּוֹכַח. לְשׁוֹן תּוֹכָחָה הוּא וְלֹא לְשׁוֹן הוֹכָחָה:

מג| מָה אֶעֱשֶׂה לָאֵלֶּה. אֵיךְ תַּעֲלֶה עַל לִבִּי לְהָרַע לָהֶן?:

מד| וְהָיָה לְעֵד. הַקָּדוֹשׁ בָּרוּךְ הוּא:

מו| לְאֶחָיו. הֵם בָּנָיו, שֶׁהָיוּ לוֹ אַחִים נִגָּשִׁים לְצָרָה וּלְמִלְחָמָה עָלָיו:

and made a pile around the pillar, **and they ate there on the pile,**[D] which was part of the ritual of establishing a covenant.

47 **Laban called** this pile **Yegar Sahaduta,** which in Laban's language, ancient Aramaic, means "pile of testimony," *gal edut* in Hebrew;[21] **and Jacob called it Gal'ed.**

48 As the head of the tribe, **Laban** gave an official speech and **said: This pile is witness between me and you today. Therefore he called its name Gal'ed;**

49 **and the Mitzpa,**[B] the name of a nearby place, will also testify to the same,[22] **as he,** Laban, **said: The Lord will observe [*yitzef*] between me and you, because we will be concealed one from another.** Since we will no longer be able to see each other, God will watch over to ensure that all is conducted properly.

50 God will know **if you shall afflict my daughters, or if you shall take** more **wives in addition to my daughters,** thereby depriving them of their share. I cannot enforce your compliance with this commitment, as **no man is with us** to investigate and report back to me. Instead, **see, God is witness between me and you.**

51 **Laban said to Jacob: Here is this pile and here is the monument that I have established between me and you.**[23] Although it was not Laban who established the pillar or pile, he took credit for both.

52 **This pile is witness, and the monument is witness, that I will not pass this pile to you, and that you shall not pass this pile and this monument to me, for harm.** We may meet again in the future, but not as belligerents.

53 **The God of Abraham, and the God of Nahor,** and also **the God of their father, shall judge between us.** For Laban, the God of Abraham, the God of Nahor, and the God of Terah, are all one and the same. **Jacob took an oath** that he would uphold this agreement, **by the Fear,** the God, **of his father Isaac.**

54 **Jacob slaughtered for a feast on the highland, and summoned his brethren to eat bread** in a more celebratory feast than the previous meal, with the participation of all those present. **They ate bread, and stayed the night on the highland.**

55 *Maftir* **Laban awoke early in the morning, and kissed his sons and his daughters and blessed them.** The goodbyes of which he claimed to have been deprived in Haran he now issued at the mountains of Gilad. **Laban went and returned to his place,** with peaceful relations established between him and Jacob.

Mahanayim

GENESIS 32:1–2

This short account completes the portion of *Vayetze*, which deals entirely with Jacob's first exile. Just as he had a vision of angels upon his departure from Canaan, ascending and descending a ladder, so too on his return he encounters angels. One can see that Jacob was strengthened by his travels, as initially he merely dreamed of angels but now, and later on as well, he sees them with his waking eyes. As in his dream, his meeting with the angels reminds him that God is accompanying him on his journey, emboldening him for the upcoming encounter with his brother Esau.

32 1 After his final departure from Laban, **Jacob went on his way** with his camp from Gilad. He had a long way ahead of him to reach the house of his father, who was living in Beersheba or Hebron. **And angels of God encountered him.**

2 **Jacob said when he saw them:** These are not a mere few angels, but an entire camp; **this is the camp [*maḥaneh*] of God.** Therefore, **he called the name of that place Mahanayim,**[B] meaning "two camps," in reference to his camp and God's camp. Mahanayim remained the name of a place located south of Gilad on the eastern side of the Jordan River.[24]

BACKGROUND

31:49 | **The Mitzpa:** The term *mitzpa* was used for settlements built on the tops of mountains and hills. It appears in the names of three locations east of the Jordan River: Ramat Mitzpe in the north of the inheritance of the tribe of Gad (Joshua 13:26), Mitzpe of Gilad (Judges 11:29), and the Mitzpa (Judges 20:1). The Mitzpa mentioned here was probably north of and adjacent to the Yabok River, now called the Zarqa River.

32:2 | **Mahanayim:** This was one of the cities of the tribe of Gad, which was given to the Levites (Joshua 13:26, 30; 21:36). It was a major city in the middle section of the lands ruled by Solomon east of the Jordan River (I Kings 4:14). It is conjectured that it corresponds to modern-day Tel ed-Dahab, situated on the northern bank of the Zarqa River, or Khirbet Mahneh, 20 km north of the Zarqa River and 4 km north of Ajloun.

מז אֲבָנִים וַיַּעֲשׂוּ־גָל וַיֹּאכְלוּ שָׁם עַל־הַגָּל׃ וַיִּקְרָא־לוֹ לָבָן יְגַר שָׂהֲדוּתָא וְיַעֲקֹב קָרָא
מח לוֹ גַּלְעֵד׃ וַיֹּאמֶר לָבָן הַגַּל הַזֶּה עֵד בֵּינִי וּבֵינְךָ הַיּוֹם עַל־כֵּן קָרָא־שְׁמוֹ גַּלְעֵד׃
מט נ וְהַמִּצְפָּה אֲשֶׁר אָמַר יִצֶף יְהוָה בֵּינִי וּבֵינֶךָ כִּי נִסָּתֵר אִישׁ מֵרֵעֵהוּ׃ אִם־תְּעַנֶּה
אֶת־בְּנֹתַי וְאִם־תִּקַּח נָשִׁים עַל־בְּנֹתַי אֵין אִישׁ עִמָּנוּ רְאֵה אֱלֹהִים עֵד בֵּינִי וּבֵינֶךָ׃
נא נב וַיֹּאמֶר לָבָן לְיַעֲקֹב הִנֵּה ׀ הַגַּל הַזֶּה וְהִנֵּה הַמַּצֵּבָה אֲשֶׁר יָרִיתִי בֵּינִי וּבֵינֶךָ׃ עֵד
הַגַּל הַזֶּה וְעֵדָה הַמַּצֵּבָה אִם־אָנִי לֹא־אֶעֱבֹר אֵלֶיךָ אֶת־הַגַּל הַזֶּה וְאִם־אַתָּה
נג לֹא־תַעֲבֹר אֵלַי אֶת־הַגַּל הַזֶּה וְאֶת־הַמַּצֵּבָה הַזֹּאת לְרָעָה׃ אֱלֹהֵי אַבְרָהָם וֵאלֹהֵי
נד נָחוֹר יִשְׁפְּטוּ בֵינֵינוּ אֱלֹהֵי אֲבִיהֶם וַיִּשָּׁבַע יַעֲקֹב בְּפַחַד אָבִיו יִצְחָק׃ וַיִּזְבַּח יַעֲקֹב
נה זֶבַח בָּהָר וַיִּקְרָא לְאֶחָיו לֶאֱכָל־לָחֶם וַיֹּאכְלוּ לֶחֶם וַיָּלִינוּ בָּהָר׃ וַיַּשְׁכֵּם לָבָן בַּבֹּקֶר מפטיר
א וַיְנַשֵּׁק לְבָנָיו וְלִבְנוֹתָיו וַיְבָרֶךְ אֶתְהֶם וַיֵּלֶךְ וַיָּשָׁב לָבָן לִמְקֹמוֹ׃ וְיַעֲקֹב הָלַךְ לְדַרְכּוֹ
ב וַיִּפְגְּעוּ־בוֹ מַלְאֲכֵי אֱלֹהִים׃ וַיֹּאמֶר יַעֲקֹב כַּאֲשֶׁר רָאָם מַחֲנֵה אֱלֹהִים זֶה וַיִּקְרָא
שֵׁם־הַמָּקוֹם הַהוּא מַחֲנָיִם׃

רש״י

מז-מח | יְגַר. תַּרְגּוּם שֶׁל גַּל: גַּלְעֵד. גַּל עֵד:

מט | וְהַמִּצְפָּה אֲשֶׁר אָמַר וְגוֹ׳. וְהַמִּצְפָּה אֲשֶׁר בְּהַר הַגִּלְעָד, כְּמוֹ שֶׁכָּתוּב: "וַיַּעֲבֹר אֶת מִצְפֵּה גִלְעָד" (שופטים יא, כט), וְלָמָּה נִקְרֵאת שְׁמָהּ 'מִצְפָּה'? לְפִי שֶׁאָמַר כָּל אֶחָד מֵהֶם לַחֲבֵרוֹ: "יִצֶף ה׳ בֵּינִי וּבֵינֶךָ" אִם תַּעֲבֹר אֶת הַבְּרִית: כִּי נִסָּתֵר. וְלֹא נִרְאֶה אִישׁ אֶת רֵעֵהוּ:

נ | בְּנֹתַי... בְּנֹתַי. שְׁתֵּי פְּעָמִים, אַף בִּלְהָה וְזִלְפָּה בְּנוֹתָיו הָיוּ מִפִּילֶגֶשׁ: אִם תְּעַנֶּה אֶת בְּנֹתַי. לִמְנוֹעַ מֵהֶן עוֹנַת תַּשְׁמִישׁ:

נא | יָרִיתִי. כְּמוֹ: "יָרָה בַיָּם" (שמות טו, ד), כָּזֶה שֶׁהוּא יוֹרֶה חֲנִית:

נב | אִם אָנִי. הֲרֵי 'אִם' מְשַׁמֵּשׁ בִּלְשׁוֹן 'אֲשֶׁר', כְּמוֹ: "עַד אִם דִּבַּרְתִּי דְּבָרָי" (לעיל כד, לג): לְרָעָה. לְרָעָה אִי אַתָּה עוֹבֵר, אֲבָל אַתָּה עוֹבֵר לִפְרַקְמַטְיָא:

נג | אֱלֹהֵי אַבְרָהָם. קֹדֶשׁ: וֵאלֹהֵי נָחוֹר. חֹל: אֱלֹהֵי אֲבִיהֶם. חֹל:

נד | וַיִּזְבַּח יַעֲקֹב זֶבַח. שָׁחַט בְּהֵמוֹת לְמִשְׁתֶּה: לְאֶחָיו. לְאוֹהֲבָיו שֶׁעִם לָבָן: לֶאֱכָל לָחֶם. כָּל דְּבַר מַאֲכָל קָרוּי לֶחֶם, כְּמוֹ: "עֲבַד לְחֶם רַב" (דניאל ה, א), "נַשְׁחִיתָה עֵץ בְּלַחְמוֹ" (ירמיה יא, יט):

פרק לב

א | וַיִּפְגְּעוּ בוֹ מַלְאֲכֵי אֱלֹהִים. מַלְאָכִים שֶׁל אֶרֶץ יִשְׂרָאֵל בָּאוּ לִקְרָאתוֹ לְלַוּוֹתוֹ לָאָרֶץ:

ב | מַחֲנָיִם. שְׁתֵּי מַחֲנוֹת, שֶׁל חוּצָה לָאָרֶץ שֶׁבָּאוּ עִמּוֹ עַד כָּאן, וְשֶׁל אֶרֶץ יִשְׂרָאֵל שֶׁבָּאוּ לִקְרָאתוֹ:

DISCUSSION

31:46 | **And they ate there on the pile:** The parties to a covenant would cut slaughtered animals into two pieces and then eat the pieces. This was considered to be an offering as well as a meal and would confirm the covenant (see 21:27; 26:28–31; Leviticus 24:8).

Parashat
Vayishlah

Jacob's Preparations for His Encounter with Esau

GENESIS 32:3–21

Jacob, upon returning from exile in Haran, readies himself for a charged encounter with his brother Esau, from whom he had fled years before in fear of his life. In anticipation of this confrontation, Jacob prays to God. He also takes practical measures, as he both attempts to placate his brother and at the same time prepares for a possible armed conflict.

3 To inform him of their impending meeting, **Jacob sent messengers[1] before him to Esau his brother to the land of Se'ir, the field,** region,[2] **of Edom.**[D] The word for messengers, *malakhim,* can also mean angels. Some commentaries maintain that Jacob sent actual angels from the camp that he had just encountered.[3]

4 **He commanded them, saying: So shall you say to my lord, to Esau: So says your servant Jacob: I have resided with Laban, and tarried until now.**[D] Since Jacob wanted the messengers to understand the complexity of his relationship with Esau, he described himself as a servant addressing his master.

5 **I have oxen, donkeys,**[D] **flocks, slaves, and maidservants.** I have become financially secure since we last met, and I do not need your support. I can even offer you assistance, if you wish.[4] **And I have sent to tell my lord,** so **that I may find favor in your eyes,** in the manner of loving brothers anticipating their reunion.

6 **The messengers returned to Jacob, saying: We came to your brother, to Esau; moreover he is coming to meet you, and four hundred men** are **with him.** Since this was a large battalion, Jacob suspected that it was not merely a guard of honor. Esau did not respond directly to the petition brought by the messengers; they simply observed him heading in Jacob's direction.

7 Faced with Esau's clear numerical advantage, **Jacob was very frightened** of the prospect of bloodshed, **and** furthermore he was **distressed,** as he had nothing against Esau personally.[5] Consequently, **he** prepared to defend himself and **divided the people who were with him,** including the slaves and maidservants, his comrades, and other people who had joined him due to his success in Haran, **and the flocks, the cattle, and the camels, into two camps.**

8 **He said** to his traveling companions, or to himself: **If Esau will come** to wage war **upon the one camp, and smite it,** we may not be capable of defending ourselves; however, at least **the remaining camp will escape;** it will be spared.

9 **Jacob** then prayed, and **said: God of my father Abraham, and God of my father Isaac,**[D] **Lord, who says to me: Return to your land, and to the land of your birth, and I will benefit you.** I turn to You now because You commanded me to return home.

10 Despite the dangers he faces, Jacob begins his prayer with thanksgiving: **I am unworthy of all the kindnesses and of all the truth that You have performed for Your servant; for with my staff** alone **I crossed this Jordan** River when I fled from Canaan. I was by myself and I had nothing, **and now I have become two camps.** I am therefore grateful.

DISCUSSION

32:3 | To Esau his brother to the land of Se'ir, the field of Edom: During Jacob's long stay with Laban, Esau emigrated from Canaan, which was promised to Jacob, and settled in the land of Se'ir. This land was called by the name of the tribes that had lived there previously; it was later named Edom, after Esau. Esau may have taken advantage of his marriage to daughters of the local tribes in order to take control over the land (see chap. 36).

32:4 | And tarried until now: Jacob did not wish to rehash the past with his brother, but to present their relationship in a new light. He was

aware that Esau might still be angry with him, not only due to the episode with the blessings but also for taking the birthright with all of its privileges (see chaps. 25 and 27). Therefore he treats Esau with respect, as the firstborn to whom he is subservient (Ramban).

32:5 | I have oxen, donkeys: In the Hebrew, these items are in the singular. This is not problematic because Jacob is referring to the general category of ox and donkey. It is also possible that Jacob chose this form in order to minimize the description of his property as he did not wish to present himself as overly wealthy.

32:9 | God of my father Abraham, and God of my father Isaac: Unlike previous instances, when Jacob called God the Fear of his father Isaac, here he says: "God of my father Isaac." This expression is reminiscent of God's introduction of Himself to Jacob in his dream upon traveling to Haran: I am the Lord, God of Abraham your father, and the God of Isaac…and, behold, I am with you, and will keep you wherever you will go, and will bring you back to this land. The formula at the beginning of the *Amida* prayer is similar to Jacob's introduction to his prayer (28:13–15, and Rashi ad loc.).

פרשת
וישלח

ג ד וַיִּשְׁלַח יַעֲקֹב מַלְאָכִים לְפָנָיו אֶל־עֵשָׂו אָחִיו אַרְצָה שֵׂעִיר שְׂדֵה אֱדוֹם: וַיְצַו
אֹתָם לֵאמֹר כֹּה תֹאמְרוּן לַאדֹנִי לְעֵשָׂו כֹּה אָמַר עַבְדְּךָ יַעֲקֹב עִם־לָבָן גַּרְתִּי
ה וָאֵחַר עַד־עָתָּה: וַיְהִי־לִי שׁוֹר וַחֲמוֹר צֹאן וְעֶבֶד וְשִׁפְחָה וָאֶשְׁלְחָה לְהַגִּיד לַאדֹנִי
ו לִמְצֹא־חֵן בְּעֵינֶיךָ: וַיָּשֻׁבוּ הַמַּלְאָכִים אֶל־יַעֲקֹב לֵאמֹר בָּאנוּ אֶל־אָחִיךָ אֶל־עֵשָׂו
ז וְגַם הֹלֵךְ לִקְרָאתְךָ וְאַרְבַּע־מֵאוֹת אִישׁ עִמּוֹ: וַיִּירָא יַעֲקֹב מְאֹד וַיֵּצֶר לוֹ וַיַּחַץ
ח אֶת־הָעָם אֲשֶׁר־אִתּוֹ וְאֶת־הַצֹּאן וְאֶת־הַבָּקָר וְהַגְּמַלִּים לִשְׁנֵי מַחֲנוֹת: וַיֹּאמֶר
אִם־יָבוֹא עֵשָׂו אֶל־הַמַּחֲנֶה הָאַחַת וְהִכָּהוּ וְהָיָה הַמַּחֲנֶה הַנִּשְׁאָר לִפְלֵיטָה:
ט וַיֹּאמֶר יַעֲקֹב אֱלֹהֵי אָבִי אַבְרָהָם וֵאלֹהֵי אָבִי יִצְחָק יְהוָה הָאֹמֵר אֵלַי שׁוּב לְאַרְצְךָ
י וּלְמוֹלַדְתְּךָ וְאֵיטִיבָה עִמָּךְ: קָטֹנְתִּי מִכֹּל הַחֲסָדִים וּמִכָּל־הָאֱמֶת אֲשֶׁר עָשִׂיתָ
אֶת־עַבְדֶּךָ כִּי בְמַקְלִי עָבַרְתִּי אֶת־הַיַּרְדֵּן הַזֶּה וְעַתָּה הָיִיתִי לִשְׁנֵי מַחֲנוֹת:

רש"י

ג| **וישלח יעקב מלאכים.** מלאכים ממש: **ארצה שעיר.** לארץ שעיר, כל תיבה שצריכה למ"ד בתחלתה הטיל לה ה"א בסופה:

ד| **גרתי.** לא נעשיתי שר וחשוב אלא גר, אינך כדאי לשנוא אותי על ברכות אביך, שאמר לי "הוה גביר לאחיך" (לעיל כז, כט) – לא נתקיימה בי. דבר אחר, "גרתי" בגימטריא תרי"ג, כלומר, עם לבן הרשע גרתי ותרי"ג מצוות שמרתי, ולא למדתי ממעשיו הרעים:

ה| **ויהי לי שור וחמור.** אבא אמר לי: "מטל השמים ומשמני הארץ" (לעיל כז, כח); זו אינה לא מן השמים ולא מן הארץ: **שור וחמור.** דרך ארץ לומר על שורים הרבה 'שור'; אדם אומר לחבירו: בלילה קרא התרנגול, ואינו אומר: קראו התרנגולים: **ואשלחה להגיד לאדני.** להודיע שאני בא אליך: **למצא חן בעיניך.** שאני שלם עמך ומבקש אהבתך:

ו| **באנו אל אחיך אל עשו.** שהיית אומר אחי הוא, אבל הוא נוהג עמך כעשו, עודנו בשנאתו:

ז| **ויירא... ויצר.** "ויירא" שמא יהרג, "ויצר לו" אם יהרוג הוא את אחרים:

ח| **המחנה האחת והכהו.** 'מחנה' משמש לשון זכר ולשון נקבה, "אם תחנה עלי מחנה" (תהלים כז, ג) הרי נקבה, "המחנה הזה" (להלן לג, ח) הרי זכר. וכן יש אחר דברים משמשים לשון זכר ולשון נקבה: "השמש יצא על הארץ" (לעיל יט, כג), "מקצה השמים מוצאו" (תהלים יט, ז) הרי זכר, "והשמש זרחה על המים" (מלכים ב' ג, כב) הרי נקבה; וכן רוח, "והנה רוח גדולה באה" (איוב א, יט) הרי נקבה, "ויגע בארבע פנות הבית" (שם) הרי זכר, "ורוח גדולה וחזק מפרק הרים" (מלכים א' יט, יא) הרי זכר ונקבה: **והיה המחנה הנשאר לפליטה.** על כרחו, כי אלחם עמו. התקין עצמו לשלשה דברים: לדורון לתפלה ולמלחמה. לדורון, "ותעבר המנחה על פניו" (להלן פסוק כב). לתפלה, "אלהי אבי אברהם" (להלן פסוק ט). למלחמה, "והיה המחנה הנשאר לפליטה":

ט| **ואלהי אבי יצחק.** ולהלן הוא אומר: "ופחד יצחק" (לעיל לא, מב)! ועוד, מהו שחזר והזכיר שם המיוחד? היה לו לכתוב: 'האומר אלי שוב לארצך' וגו'! אלא כך אמר יעקב לפני הקדוש ברוך הוא: שתי הבטחות הבטחתני, אחת בצאתי מבית אבא אמרת לי: "אני ה' אלהי אברהם אביך ואלהי יצחק" (לעיל כח, יג), ושם אמרת לי: "ושמרתיך בכל אשר תלך" (שם טו); ובבית לבן אמרת לי: "שוב אל ארץ אבותיך ולמולדתך ואהיה עמך" (לעיל לא, ג), ושם נגלית אלי בשם המיוחד לבדו, שנאמר: "ויאמר ה' אל יעקב שוב אל ארץ אבותיך" וגו' – בשתי הבטחות הללו אני בא לפניך:

י| **קטנתי מכל החסדים.** נתמעטו זכיותי על ידי החסדים והאמת שעשית עמי, לכך אני ירא, שמא משהבטחתני נתלכלכתי בחטא ויגרם לי להמסר ביד עשו: **ומכל האמת.** אמיתת דבריך ששמרת לי כל ההבטחות שהבטחתני: **כי במקלי.** לא היה עמי לא כסף ולא זהב ולא מקנה אלא מקלי לבדו. ומדרש אגדה, נתן מקלו בירדן ונבקע הירדן:

11 However, I am now in trouble: **Deliver me please from the hand of my brother, from the hand of Esau; for I fear him, lest he come and smite me, mother and children alike.** He is liable to kill all of us.

12 **And You said** in the vision of the ladder at Beit El: **I will benefit you, and render your descendants as the sand of the sea, which cannot be enumerated for multitude.** You promised to shield me, and I am now in need of Your protection.

Second aliya

13 **He stayed there that night; he took from that which was in his possession a gift for Esau his brother:**

14 **Two hundred female goats and twenty male goats, two hundred ewes and twenty rams,**

15 **thirty nursing camels and their offspring, forty cows and ten bulls, twenty female donkeys and ten male donkeys.** Of every species that Jacob sent, he included both males and females, so that they would be able to reproduce. This is also the reason for the various proportions between the males and females, as different ratios are more suitable for the reproduction of different animals. One can infer from the impressive size of the present that Jacob must have owned an enormous amount of livestock.

16 **He placed them in the charge of his servants, each drove by itself,** handled by a different cattle herder. And **he,** Jacob, **said to his servants: Go ahead of me,** to reach my brother before me, **and make space between one drove and the other drove.** The gift was spread out so that it would appear even more impressive to Esau.

17 **He commanded the** shepherd of the **first** herd, **saying: When Esau my brother meets you, and asks you, saying: To whom do you belong, and where are you going, and whose are these** animals **before you?**

18 **You shall say: They are from your servant, Jacob;** and as for this collection of animals, **it is a gift sent to my lord, to Esau, and behold, he,** Jacob, **too, is behind us.** He is sending you these gifts in anticipation of your meeting.

19 **He commanded also the second, and also the third, and also all that followed the droves, saying: In this manner shall you speak to Esau when you find him.** You shall tell him that you are Jacob's servants, and that this entire herd is a gift to his lord, Esau.

20 **You shall say: Moreover, here is your servant Jacob** coming **behind us** to meet you. He is not running away, and there is no need to chase him. **For he,** Jacob, **said** to himself: **I will appease him,** Esau, **with the gift**[D] **that goes before me, and thereafter,** when he has received the gift, **I will see his face; perhaps he will favor me** for what I have done for him.

21 **The gift went before him,** Jacob, for his inspection; **and he stayed that night in the camp.**

The Nocturnal Battle

GENESIS 32:22–32

Between his preparations for the meeting with his brother and the encounter itself, Jacob is confronted alone by a mysterious figure who fights him. This struggle, which unfolds in the darkness of the night, is clearly meant to prepare Jacob for his meeting with Esau. The Sages consider it symbolic of the perpetual spiritual clash between Jacob and Esau; they refer to the figure as Esau's Angel.

Just as Jacob met angels in his dream when he left Canaan, he now encounters metaphysical forces at night upon his return to the land. In fact, Jacob had already met angels at an earlier station on his approach to Canaan, in Mahanayim (verse 2). When he sees this lone man at night, Jacob realizes that he possesses metaphysical powers. However, as opposed to the angels in Mahanayim, this angelic being fights and injures Jacob. Ultimately, Jacob subdues his adversary and compels him to grant him a blessing. As in Mahanayim, Jacob names the location after the encounter.

22 **He,** Jacob, **arose during that night,** after sending off the gifts, **and he** personally **took his two wives, his two maidservants, and his eleven children, and crossed the ford of the Yabok.** The exact location of the ford is unknown, but there is still a stream called Yabok in central present-day Jordan, nowadays also called the Zarqa River. The river, which is not deep, can be crossed by foot.

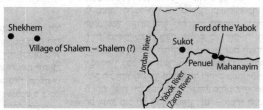

Location of the Yabok

DISCUSSION

32:20 | **I will appease him with the gift:** Jacob's meticulously planned, ceremonial presentation of presents is based on the assumption that the significance of a gift is not determined by its objective worth, or even its subjective value to the beneficiary, but by the positive emotional effect that the giver's act of giving has on the recipient. This is also the psychological effect of accepting a bribe. Jacob sought to arouse in Esau positive feelings of brotherhood and to reduce the impact of the past.

יא הַצִּילֵנִי נָא מִיַּד אָחִי מִיַּד עֵשָׂו כִּי־יָרֵא אָנֹכִי אֹתוֹ פֶּן־יָבוֹא וְהִכַּנִי אֵם עַל־בָּנִים׃
יב וְאַתָּה אָמַרְתָּ הֵיטֵב אֵיטִיב עִמָּךְ וְשַׂמְתִּי אֶת־זַרְעֲךָ כְּחוֹל הַיָּם אֲשֶׁר לֹא־יִסָּפֵר
יג יד מֵרֹב׃ וַיָּלֶן שָׁם בַּלַּיְלָה הַהוּא וַיִּקַּח מִן־הַבָּא בְיָדוֹ מִנְחָה לְעֵשָׂו אָחִיו׃ עִזִּים שני
טו מָאתַיִם וּתְיָשִׁים עֶשְׂרִים רְחֵלִים מָאתַיִם וְאֵילִים עֶשְׂרִים׃ גְּמַלִּים מֵינִיקוֹת וּבְנֵיהֶם
טז שְׁלֹשִׁים פָּרוֹת אַרְבָּעִים וּפָרִים עֲשָׂרָה אֲתֹנֹת עֶשְׂרִים וַעְיָרִם עֲשָׂרָה׃ וַיִּתֵּן בְּיַד־
עֲבָדָיו עֵדֶר עֵדֶר לְבַדּוֹ וַיֹּאמֶר אֶל־עֲבָדָיו עִבְרוּ לְפָנַי וְרֶוַח תָּשִׂימוּ בֵּין עֵדֶר וּבֵין
יז עֵדֶר׃ וַיְצַו אֶת־הָרִאשׁוֹן לֵאמֹר כִּי יִפְגָשְׁךָ עֵשָׂו אָחִי וּשְׁאֵלְךָ לֵאמֹר לְמִי־אַתָּה
יח וְאָנָה תֵלֵךְ וּלְמִי אֵלֶּה לְפָנֶיךָ׃ וְאָמַרְתָּ לְעַבְדְּךָ לְיַעֲקֹב מִנְחָה הִוא שְׁלוּחָה לַאדֹנִי
יט לְעֵשָׂו וְהִנֵּה גַם־הוּא אַחֲרֵינוּ׃ וַיְצַו גַּם אֶת־הַשֵּׁנִי גַּם אֶת־הַשְּׁלִישִׁי גַּם אֶת־כָּל־
הַהֹלְכִים אַחֲרֵי הָעֲדָרִים לֵאמֹר כַּדָּבָר הַזֶּה תְּדַבְּרוּן אֶל־עֵשָׂו בְּמֹצַאֲכֶם אֹתוֹ׃
כ וַאֲמַרְתֶּם גַּם הִנֵּה עַבְדְּךָ יַעֲקֹב אַחֲרֵינוּ כִּי־אָמַר אֲכַפְּרָה פָנָיו בַּמִּנְחָה הַהֹלֶכֶת
כא לְפָנָי וְאַחֲרֵי־כֵן אֶרְאֶה פָנָיו אוּלַי יִשָּׂא פָנָי׃ וַתַּעֲבֹר הַמִּנְחָה עַל־פָּנָיו וְהוּא לָן
כב בַּלַּיְלָה־הַהוּא בַּמַּחֲנֶה׃ וַיָּקָם ׀ בַּלַּיְלָה הוּא וַיִּקַּח אֶת־שְׁתֵּי נָשָׁיו וְאֶת־שְׁתֵּי
כג שִׁפְחֹתָיו וְאֶת־אַחַד עָשָׂר יְלָדָיו וַיַּעֲבֹר אֵת מַעֲבַר יַבֹּק׃ וַיִּקָּחֵם וַיַּעֲבִרֵם אֶת־

רש"י

יא| **מִיַּד אָחִי מִיַּד עֵשָׂו.** מִיַּד אָחִי שֶׁאֵין נוֹהֵג עִמִּי כְּאָח אֶלָּא כְּעֵשָׂו הָרָשָׁע:

יב| **הֵיטֵב אֵיטִיב.** "הֵיטֵב" בִּזְכוּתְךָ, "אֵיטִיב" בִּזְכוּת אֲבוֹתֶיךָ: **וְשַׂמְתִּי אֶת זַרְעֲךָ כְּחוֹל הַיָּם.** וְהֵיכָן אָמַר לוֹ כֵּן? וַהֲלֹא לֹא אָמַר לוֹ אֶלָּא "וְהָיָה זַרְעֲךָ כַּעֲפַר הָאָרֶץ" (לעיל כח, יד)! אֶלָּא שֶׁאָמַר לוֹ: "כִּי לֹא אֶעֱזָבְךָ עַד אֲשֶׁר אִם עָשִׂיתִי אֵת אֲשֶׁר דִּבַּרְתִּי לָךְ" (שם פסוק טו), וּלְאַבְרָהָם אָמַר: "וְהַרְבָּה אַרְבֶּה אֶת זַרְעֲךָ כְּכוֹכְבֵי הַשָּׁמַיִם וְכַחוֹל אֲשֶׁר עַל שְׂפַת הַיָּם" (לעיל כב, יז):

יג| **הַבָּא בְיָדוֹ.** בִּרְשׁוּתוֹ, וְכֵן "וַיִּקַּח אֶת כָּל אַרְצוֹ מִיָּדוֹ" (במדבר כא, כו). וּמִדְרַשׁ אַגָּדָה, "מִן הַבָּא בְיָדוֹ", אֲבָנִים טוֹבוֹת וּמַרְגָּלִיּוֹת שֶׁאָדָם צָר בִּצְרוֹר וְנוֹשְׂאָם בְּיָדוֹ:

יד| **עִזִּים מָאתַיִם וּתְיָשִׁים עֶשְׂרִים.** מָאתַיִם עִזִּים צְרִיכוֹת עֶשְׂרִים תְּיָשִׁים, וְכֵן כֻּלָּם הַזְּכָרִים כְּדֵי צֹרֶךְ הַנְּקֵבוֹת. וּבִבְרֵאשִׁית רַבָּה (עו, ז) דּוֹרֵשׁ מִכָּאן לְעוֹנָה הָאֲמוּרָה בַּתּוֹרָה, הַטַּיָּלִים בְּכָל יוֹם, הַפּוֹעֲלִים שְׁתַּיִם בְּשַׁבָּת, הַחַמָּרִים אַחַת בְּשַׁבָּת, הַגַּמָּלִים אַחַת לִשְׁלֹשִׁים יוֹם, הַסַּפָּנִים אַחַת לְשִׁשָּׁה חֳדָשִׁים. וְאֵינִי יוֹדֵעַ לְכַוֵּן הַמִּדְרָשׁ הַזֶּה בְּכִוּוּן, אַךְ נִרְאֶה בְּעֵינַי שֶׁלָּמַדְנוּ מִכָּאן שֶׁאֵין הָעוֹנָה שָׁוָה בְּכָל אָדָם אֶלָּא לְפִי טֹרַח הַמֻּטָּל עָלָיו, שֶׁמָּצִינוּ כָּאן שֶׁמָּסַר לְכָל תַּיִשׁ עֶשֶׂר עִזִּים, וְכֵן לְכָל אַיִל, לְפִי שֶׁהֵם פְּנוּיִים מִמְּלָאכָה דַּרְכָּן לְהַרְבּוֹת תַּשְׁמִישׁ וּלְעַבֵּר עֶשֶׂר נְקֵבוֹת, וּבְהֵמָה מִשֶּׁנִּתְעַבְּרָה אֵינָהּ מְקַבֶּלֶת זָכָר; וּפָרִים שֶׁעוֹסְקִין בִּמְלָאכָה לֹא מָסַר לְזָכָר אֶלָּא אַרְבַּע נְקֵבוֹת; וְלַחֲמוֹר שֶׁהוֹלֵךְ בְּדֶרֶךְ רְחוֹקָה – שְׁתֵּי נְקֵבוֹת לְזָכָר; וְלַגְּמַלִּים שֶׁהוֹלְכִים דֶּרֶךְ יוֹתֵר רְחוֹקָה – נְקֵבָה אַחַת לְזָכָר:

טו| **גְּמַלִּים מֵינִיקוֹת... שְׁלֹשִׁים.** וּבְנֵיהֶם עִמָּהֶם. וּמִדְרַשׁ אַגָּדָה, "וּבְנֵיהֶם", בַּנָּאֵיהֶם, זָכָר כְּנֶגֶד נְקֵבָה, וּלְפִי שֶׁצָּנוּעַ בְּתַשְׁמִישׁ לֹא פִּרְסְמוֹ הַכָּתוּב: **וַעְיָרִם.** חֲמוֹרִים זְכָרִים:

טז| **עֵדֶר עֵדֶר לְבַדּוֹ.** כָּל מִין וּמִין לְעַצְמוֹ: **עִבְרוּ לְפָנַי.** דֶּרֶךְ יוֹם אוֹ פָּחוֹת, וַאֲנִי אָבוֹא אַחֲרֵיכֶם: **וְרֶוַח תָּשִׂימוּ.** עֵדֶר לִפְנֵי חֲבֵרוֹ מְלֹא עַיִן, כְּדֵי לְהַשְׂבִּיעַ עֵינוֹ שֶׁל רָשָׁע וּלְתַמְּהוֹ עַל רִבּוּי הַדּוֹרוֹן:

יז| **לְמִי אַתָּה.** שֶׁל מִי אַתָּה? מִי שׁוֹלַחֲךָ? וְתַרְגּוּמוֹ: "דְּמַאן אַתְּ": **וּלְמִי אֵלֶּה.** לְמִי הַמִּנְחָה הַזֹּאת שְׁלוּחָה? לָמֶ"ד מְשַׁמֶּשֶׁת בְּרֹאשׁ הַתֵּבָה בִּמְקוֹם 'שֶׁל'; כְּמוֹ: "וְכֹל אֲשֶׁר אַתָּה רֹאֶה לִי הוּא" (לעיל לא, מג), שֶׁלִּי הוּא, "לַה' הָאָרֶץ וּמְלוֹאָהּ" (תהלים כד, א), שֶׁל ה':

יח| **וְאָמַרְתָּ לְעַבְדְּךָ לְיַעֲקֹב.** עַל רִאשׁוֹן רִאשׁוֹן וְעַל אַחֲרוֹן אַחֲרוֹן. שֶׁשָּׁאַלְתָּ "לְמִי אַתָּה" – "לְעַבְדְּךָ לְיַעֲקֹב" אֲנִי, וְתַרְגּוּמוֹ: "דְּעַבְדָּךְ דְּיַעֲקֹב". וְשֶׁשָּׁאַלְתָּ "וּלְמִי אֵלֶּה לְפָנֶיךָ" – "מִנְחָה הִיא שְׁלוּחָה" וְגוֹ': **וְהִנֵּה גַם הוּא.** יַעֲקֹב:

כ| **אֲכַפְּרָה פָנָיו.** אֲבַטֵּל רָגְזוֹ, וְכֵן: "וְכֻפַּר בְּרִיתְכֶם אֶת מָוֶת" (ישעיה כח, יח), "לֹא תוּכְלִי כַּפְּרָהּ" (שם מז, יא). וְנִרְאֶה בְּעֵינַי שֶׁכָּל כַּפָּרָה שֶׁאֵצֶל עָוֹן וְחֵטְא וְאֵצֶל פָּנִים, כֻּלָּן לְשׁוֹן קִנּוּחַ וְהַעֲבָרָה הֵן, וְלָשׁוֹן אֲרַמִּי הוּא, וְהַרְבֵּה בַּתַּלְמוּד: "וְכַפַּר יְדֵיהּ" (בבא מציעא כד ע"א) "בָּעֵי לְכַפּוּרֵי יְדֵיהּ בְּהַהוּא גַּבְרָא" (גיטין נו ע"א). וְגַם בִּלְשׁוֹן הַמִּקְרָא נִקְרָאִים הַמִּזְרָקִים שֶׁל קֹדֶשׁ "כְּפוֹרֵי זָהָב" (עזרא א, י), עַל שֵׁם שֶׁהַכֹּהֵן מְקַנֵּחַ יָדָיו בָּהֶן בִּשְׂפַת הַמִּזְרָק:

כא| **עַל פָּנָיו.** כְּמוֹ לְפָנָיו, וְכֵן: "חָמָס וָשֹׁד יִשָּׁמַע בָּהּ עַל פָּנַי תָּמִיד" (ירמיה ו, ז), וְכֵן: "הַמַּכְעִסִים אוֹתִי עַל פָּנַי" (ישעיה סה, ג). וּמִדְרַשׁ אַגָּדָה, "עַל פָּנָיו", אַף הוּא שָׁרוּי בְּכַעַס שֶׁהָיָה צָרִיךְ לְכָל זֶה:

כב| **וְאֶת אַחַד עָשָׂר יְלָדָיו.** וְדִינָה הֵיכָן הָיְתָה? נְתָנָהּ בְּתֵבָה וְנָעַל בְּפָנֶיהָ, שֶׁלֹּא יִתֵּן בָּהּ עֵשָׂו עֵינָיו, וּלְכָךְ נֶעֱנַשׁ יַעֲקֹב שֶׁמְּנָעָהּ מֵאָחִיו, שֶׁמָּא תַּחֲזִירֶנּוּ לְמוּטָב, וְנָפְלָה בְּיַד שְׁכֶם: **יַבֹּק.** שֵׁם הַנָּהָר:

23 **He took them, and brought them over the stream, and brought over that which he had** in order to meet Esau south of the Yabok River. Obviously, Jacob did not cross the river with all his wives, children of different ages, and his belongings all at once. Instead, he made the crossing several times.
24 Eventually, after the entire camp had crossed, **Jacob remained alone** on the riverbank; **and a** mysterious, unnamed **man wrestled with him**[D] **until dawn.**
25 **He,** the man, **saw that he could not prevail against him, and** therefore **he touched,** struck, Jacob and injured **the joint of his thigh;** and **the joint of Jacob's thigh was dislocated as he wrestled with him.** Despite the great pain, Jacob remained standing and refused to be defeated.
26 While the pair were grappling each other, **he,** the man, **said: Release me, for the dawn has broken.** I cannot remain here for I am a nocturnal being. Here the verse clearly indicates that the strange figure was a spiritual entity. Nevertheless, Jacob felt that he was capable of subduing him, and **he said: I will not release you unless you bless me.** Jacob demanded neither surrender nor apology, but submission, expressed in the form of a blessing. The stranger's agreement to the request, and the bestowal of a blessing, would indicate his acceptance of Jacob.
27 **He,** the angel, **said to him: What is your name? He said: Jacob.** Had this been a normal conversation between people, Jacob presumably would have asked the figure why he attacked him if he was unaware of his identity. However, he understood that the angel knew his name, and his question was a ceremonial introduction to his blessing.
28 **He,** the angel, **said: No more shall Jacob be said to be your name; rather,** you shall be called **Israel;**[D] **for you have striven** [*sarita*] **with God** [*elohim*], an angel, a supernatural force, **and with men, and you have prevailed.**
29 **Jacob asked** the angel **and said: Tell me, please, your name,** your essence or function. This request was not merely due to curiosity; rather, Jacob sought to clarify the meaning of the fight. Jacob did not know whether this angel represented Esau or his own alter-ego, and whether their confrontation was a trial from God or an actual threat from dark heavenly forces. **He said: Why is it that you ask of my name?**[D] It is unnecessary for you to know my name. **And he,** the angel, **blessed him there** again.
30 **Jacob named the place Peniel: For I have seen God**[D] **face-**
Third aliya **to-face and my life was saved.** Other people who saw angels expressed fear that they might perish. In the book of Judges, after Mano'ah and his wife encounter an angel, he says: "We will die, because we have seen God."[6] Jacob, by contrast, knew that his life had been spared despite knowing for certain that he had met an angel face-to-face.
31 The angel left Jacob at daybreak. **The sun** then **rose upon him as he passed Penuel, and he was limping on his thigh.** Jacob was certainly shaken both by the encounter itself and from his injury.
32 At this juncture, the Torah inserts a legal statement: **Therefore, the children of Israel do not eat the sciatic nerve, which is**

DISCUSSION

32:24| **And a man wrestled with him:** While Jacob was preoccupied and weary from the journey, he found himself forced to fight a being that appeared to him out of nowhere, a man who was not a man. The confrontation is depicted as a physical fight without any weapons; part battle, part mystical encounter (*Bereshit Rabba* 77:2–3; see Rashbam; *Ḥizkuni*). The entire episode is shrouded in mystery. At first they apparently fought in complete silence. Does this mean that the man knew Jacob?

It eventually became clear that the figure was an angel or some other heavenly being in human form; perhaps he had the appearance of Esau. Jacob's battle with him therefore takes on symbolic or psychological significance: As his encounter with Esau approached, Jacob had to deal with an internal battle over his independence and identity. He struggled to retain his basic self-identity without surrendering or giving in to his dark, half-spiritual alter-ego, represented by this being.

This figure is both similar to Jacob and diametrically opposed to him; this is a struggle between equals. Whether he represents Jacob's twin brother Esau or his alter-ego, the closeness between the two explains why they fought in silence; clearly they were familiar with each other. This confrontation can also be described by means of the yin and yang symbolism, the black and white polar opposites that encompass one another.

32:28| **No more shall Jacob be said to be your name, rather, Israel:** He was called Jacob [Ya'akov] because at his birth he was holding the heel [*akev*] of his firstborn brother (25:26). This name was later interpreted by Esau as symbolic of the deceit his brother employed against him (27:36). After Jacob won their battle, the angel informed him that from now onward he would no longer be the one who follows behind [*okev*], the secondary brother who had to resort to subterfuge. His new name, Israel [Yisrael], is explained as referring to his successful contention with the angel and with man. The name also means straightness [*yosher*], as the twisted [*akov*] person had become straight. After having overcome the hurdle of his secondary status, Jacob was now the primary son and could therefore behave in a straightforward manner. This meaning of the name Yisrael is more pronounced in its synonym Yeshurun (see, e.g., Deuteronomy 33:5).

32:29| **Why is it that you ask of my name:** The concealment of the angel's name is part of the mysterious nature of this confrontation. Generally, the names of angels are not stated in the Bible, although in later books certain names appear, such as Mikhael and Gavriel (see, e.g., Daniel 9:21, 12:1). Since angels are not

כד הַנָּחַל וַיַּעֲבֵר אֶת־אֲשֶׁר־לוֹ׃ וַיִּוָּתֵר יַעֲקֹב לְבַדּוֹ וַיֵּאָבֵק אִישׁ עִמּוֹ עַד עֲלוֹת

כה הַשָּׁחַר׃ וַיַּרְא כִּי לֹא יָכֹל לוֹ וַיִּגַּע בְּכַף־יְרֵכוֹ וַתֵּקַע כַּף־יֶרֶךְ יַעֲקֹב בְּהֵאָבְקוֹ עִמּוֹ׃

כו כז וַיֹּאמֶר שַׁלְּחֵנִי כִּי עָלָה הַשָּׁחַר וַיֹּאמֶר לֹא אֲשַׁלֵּחֲךָ כִּי אִם־בֵּרַכְתָּנִי׃ וַיֹּאמֶר אֵלָיו

כח מַה־שְּׁמֶךָ וַיֹּאמֶר יַעֲקֹב׃ וַיֹּאמֶר לֹא יַעֲקֹב יֵאָמֵר עוֹד שִׁמְךָ כִּי אִם־יִשְׂרָאֵל כִּי־

כט שָׂרִיתָ עִם־אֱלֹהִים וְעִם־אֲנָשִׁים וַתּוּכָל׃ וַיִּשְׁאַל יַעֲקֹב וַיֹּאמֶר הַגִּידָה־נָּא שְׁמֶךָ

ל וַיֹּאמֶר לָמָּה זֶּה תִּשְׁאַל לִשְׁמִי וַיְבָרֶךְ אֹתוֹ שָׁם׃ וַיִּקְרָא יַעֲקֹב שֵׁם הַמָּקוֹם פְּנִיאֵל שלישי

לא כִּי־רָאִיתִי אֱלֹהִים פָּנִים אֶל־פָּנִים וַתִּנָּצֵל נַפְשִׁי׃ וַיִּזְרַח־לוֹ הַשֶּׁמֶשׁ כַּאֲשֶׁר עָבַר

לב אֶת־פְּנוּאֵל וְהוּא צֹלֵעַ עַל־יְרֵכוֹ׃ עַל־כֵּן לֹא־יֹאכְלוּ בְנֵי־יִשְׂרָאֵל אֶת־גִּיד הַנָּשֶׁה

רש"י

כג| **אֵת אֲשֶׁר לוֹ.** הַבְּהֵמָה וְהַמִּטַּלְטְלִים, עָשָׂה עַצְמוֹ כְּגֶשֶׁר, נוֹטֵל מִכָּאן וּמַנִּיחַ כָּאן:

כד| **וַיִּוָּתֵר יַעֲקֹב.** שָׁכַח פַּכִּים קְטַנִּים וְחָזַר עֲלֵיהֶם: **וַיֵּאָבֵק אִישׁ.** מְנַחֵם פֵּרֵשׁ, וַיִּתְעַפֵּר אִישׁ, לְשׁוֹן אָבָק שֶׁהָיוּ מַעֲלִים עָפָר בְּרַגְלֵיהֶם עַל יְדֵי נִעְנוּעָם. וְלִי נִרְאֶה שֶׁהוּא לְשׁוֹן 'וַיִּתְקַשֵּׁר' (מלכים ב׳ ט, יד), וּלְשׁוֹן אֲרַמִּי הוּא: "בָּתַר דַּאֲבִיקוּ בֵּיהּ" (סנהדרין מג ע״א) "וְאָבֵיק לֵיהּ מֵיבַק" (מנחות מב ע״א) – לְשׁוֹן עֲנִיבָה, שֶׁכֵּן דֶּרֶךְ שְׁנַיִם שֶׁמִּתְעַצְּמִים לְהַפִּיל אִישׁ אֶת רֵעֵהוּ שֶׁחוֹבְקוֹ וְאוֹבְקוֹ בִּזְרוֹעוֹתָיו. וּפֵרְשׁוּ רַבּוֹתֵינוּ שֶׁהוּא שָׂרוֹ שֶׁל עֵשָׂו:

כה| **וַתֵּקַע.** נִתְקַעְקְעָה מִמְּקוֹם מַחְבַּרְתָּהּ. וְדוֹמֶה לוֹ: "פֶּן תֵּקַע נַפְשִׁי מִמֵּךְ" (ירמיה ו, ח), לְשׁוֹן הֲסָרָה. וּבַמִּשְׁנָה: "לְקַעְקֵעַ בֵּיצָתָן", לְשָׁרֵשׁ שָׁרְשֵׁיהֶן:

כו| **כִּי עָלָה הַשָּׁחַר.** וְצָרִיךְ אֲנִי לוֹמַר שִׁירָה: **בֵּרַכְתָּנִי.** הוֹדֶה לִי עַל הַבְּרָכוֹת שֶׁבֵּרְכַנִי אָבִי, שֶׁעֵשָׂו מְעַרְעֵר עֲלֵיהֶן:

כח| **לֹא יַעֲקֹב.** לֹא יֵאָמֵר עוֹד שֶׁהַבְּרָכוֹת בָּאוּ לְךָ בְּעָקְבָה וּרְמִיָּה, כִּי אִם בִּשְׂרָרָה וְגִלּוּי פָּנִים, וְסוֹפְךָ שֶׁהַקָּדוֹשׁ בָּרוּךְ הוּא נִגְלֶה עָלֶיךָ בְּבֵית אֵל וּמַחֲלִיף שִׁמְךָ וְשָׁם הוּא מְבָרֶכְךָ, וַאֲנִי שָׁם אֶהְיֶה וְאוֹדֶה לְךָ עֲלֵיהֶן, וְזֶה שֶׁכָּתוּב: "וַיָּשַׂר אֶל מַלְאָךְ וַיֻּכָל בָּכָה וַיִּתְחַנֶּן לוֹ" (הושע יב, ה) – בָּכָה הַמַּלְאָךְ וַיִּתְחַנֶּן לוֹ, וּמַה נִּתְחַנֵּן לוֹ? "בֵּית אֵל יִמְצָאֶנּוּ וְשָׁם יְדַבֵּר עִמָּנוּ" (שם) – הַמְתֵּן לִי עַד שֶׁיְּדַבֵּר עִמָּנוּ שָׁם. וְלֹא רָצָה יַעֲקֹב, וְעַל כָּרְחוֹ הוֹדָה לוֹ עֲלֵיהֶן, וְזֶהוּ "וַיְבָרֶךְ אֹתוֹ שָׁם", שֶׁהָיָה מִתְחַנֵּן לְהַמְתִּין לוֹ וְלֹא רָצָה: **וְעִם אֲנָשִׁים.** עֵשָׂו וְלָבָן: **וַתּוּכָל.** לָהֶם:

כט| **לָמָּה זֶּה תִּשְׁאַל.** אֵין לָנוּ שֵׁם קָבוּעַ, מִשְׁתַּנִּים הֵם שְׁמוֹתֵינוּ הַכֹּל לְפִי מִצְוַת עֲבוֹדַת הַשְּׁלִיחוּת שֶׁאָנוּ מִשְׁתַּלְּחִים:

לא-לב| **וַיִּזְרַח לוֹ.** לְצָרְכּוֹ, לְרַפְּאוֹת אֶת צַלְעָתוֹ, כְּמָה דְּאַתְּ אָמַר: "שֶׁמֶשׁ צְדָקָה וּמַרְפֵּא בִּכְנָפֶיהָ" (מלאכי ג, כ). וְאוֹתָן שָׁעוֹת שֶׁמִּהֲרָה לִשְׁקֹעַ כְּשֶׁיָּצָא מִבְּאֵר שֶׁבַע מִהֲרָה לִזְרֹחַ בִּשְׁבִילוֹ, **וְהוּא** הָיָה צוֹלֵעַ כְּשֶׁזָּרְחָה הַשֶּׁמֶשׁ:

לב| **גִּיד הַנָּשֶׁה.** לָמָּה נִקְרָא שְׁמוֹ 'גִּיד הַנָּשֶׁה'? שֶׁנָּשָׁה מִמְּקוֹמוֹ וְעָלָה, וְהוּא לְשׁוֹן קְפִיצָה, וְכֵן: "נָשְׁתָה גְבוּרָתָם"

DISCUSSION

independent entities, but divine emissaries and embodiments of heavenly forces, they do not have fixed names. When the name of an angel is mentioned, it serves to express his current mission, and is therefore a temporary designation (Rashi).

Although Jacob's adversary is generally called Esau's angel (*Bereshit Rabba* 77:3), there are other opinions with regard to the identity of this being (see, e.g., *Bereshit Rabba* 78; *Zohar, Bo* 41b).

32:30| **I have seen God:** Jacob's encounter with the mysterious man had both a physical aspect, as Jacob was injured in the fight, and also a metaphysical dimension, as the adversary disappeared at daybreak, never to be seen again.

The reality of angels, which exist between the physical and metaphysical realms and appear in the form of human beings, is also evident in the episode of Abraham's guests, who later went to Lot. At first they seemed to be ordinary human beings, but they were eventually shown to be powerful angels who destroyed an entire city.

The appearances of angels in Abraham's tent and at the ford of Yabok are both related to changes in the names of the patriarchs. Angels appeared to Abraham after God changed his name from Abram, signifying a transformation in his identity to a historical figure with a divine mission. The angels informed him that God's promise of offspring was about to be fulfilled (chaps. 18–19).

Jacob received his new name from an angel. As opposed to his grandfather Abraham, who received his name without any violent upheaval, Jacob earned his new name after a battle. This was typical of Jacob's turbulent life, as nothing came easily to him. By changing his name the angel prophesied Jacob's historical potential: Just as he emerged victorious from this confrontation, so too his descendants would never surrender. Even if they are wounded at certain points in history, they will never capitulate (see Ramban).

upon the joint of the thigh, the large nerve that extends along the entire thigh and leg all the way to the heel, **to this day, because he touched the joint of Jacob's thigh, at the sciatic nerve,**[B] a vulnerable area of the body. Due to Jacob's injury, his

descendants are prohibited from eating the sciatic nerve of animals throughout their generations.

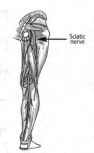

"Because he touched the joint of Jacob's thigh"

The Encounter between Jacob and Esau

GENESIS 33:1–20

After all of Jacob's preparations, on the diplomatic, military, and spiritual planes, by day and by night, the encounter he had feared for so many years finally arrives.

33 1 Jacob had fought with a mysterious man until dawn. After sunrise, when people began to move about the camp, **Jacob lifted his eyes and saw, and behold, Esau came, and with him four hundred men.** Opposed to Jacob's relatively small family camp, which included slaves, maidservants, and possessions, he saw a large military procession. **He divided the children among Leah, Rachel, and the two maidservants.** Jacob arranged his camp so that each mother could watch over her own children.

2 **He placed the maidservants and their children first, Leah and her children next, and Rachel and Joseph last.**[D] Since Jacob was worried about Esau's possibly hostile behavior, he positioned his family in the opposite order of their importance in his eyes. He placed the maidservants and their children in front, behind them Leah and her children, followed lastly by his most beloved wife, Rachel, and her son.

3 **And he,** Jacob, **passed before them,** his family members, **and prostrated himself earthward seven times,** which is a symbolic number, **until his approach to his brother.** This manner of approaching, by stopping for several prostrations, was an expression of honor and submission toward Esau, even before a word had passed between them.

4 **Esau ran to meet him, embraced him,**[D] **fell upon his neck, and kissed him; and they wept** together.

5 **He,** Esau, **lifted his eyes, saw the women and the children,** walking behind Jacob, **and said: Who are these to you?** Although his brother could have guessed, **he,** Jacob, **said: The children with whom God has graced your servant.** These are my children. Jacob repeatedly referred to himself as Esau's

servant. He opted to flatter Esau in order to preserve their cordial relationship.

Fourth aliya 6 **The maidservants approached, they and their children, and they prostrated themselves,** following Jacob's lead.

7 **Leah, too, and her children approached, and prostrated themselves; and afterward Joseph and Rachel also approached, and prostrated themselves.**

8 **He,** Esau, **said: For whom do you intend this entire camp** of flocks of sheep, cattle, camels, and the other animals, **that I met? He,** Jacob, **said: To find favor in the eyes of my lord.** I have brought you a gift of reconciliation, which I hope you will accept.

9 **Esau said: I have plenty, my brother.** I do not need your present. Esau was almost certainly speaking the truth, as he ruled over a small state. **That which is yours shall be yours.** Keep the gift for yourself.

10 **Jacob said: Please, no, if I have found favor in your eyes,** and we indeed have a good relationship, **receive my gift from me,** since the acceptance of a gift is an expression of kinship. **For therefore, I have seen your face, as the sight of the face of angels.** I consider you like a marvelous being, **and you welcomed me.** You are so noble in my eyes that it would be an honor for me for my gift to be accepted by you.

11 **Please, take my gift that was brought to you.** I realize that you do not need the present, but I am offering it to you anyway, **as God has graced me, and because I have everything.** I lose nothing by giving you this gift. Apparently, Esau did not realize the extent of Jacob's wealth. He did not ask about Jacob's whole

---

— BACKGROUND —

32:32 | The sciatic nerve: This is the central nerve of the leg, *nervus ischiadicus*, which runs from the lower back all the way down to the heel. A severe blow to this nerve can be very painful and even lead to partial paralysis.

— DISCUSSION —

33:2 | Rachel and Joseph last: The Sages derive from here the general principle that whatever comes last is more precious.

33:4 | Esau ran to meet him, embraced him: Twin brothers often share an especially intimate relationship. Jacob and Esau were both overcome

by emotion in their reunion. Even if Esau did not entirely relinquish his hatred, it is not at all manifest here. Perhaps he was mollified by the manner in which Jacob presented himself as his brother's submissive servant. Esau may have felt that his honor and power had been restored.

לג א אֲשֶׁר עַל־כַּף הַיָּרֵךְ עַד הַיּוֹם הַזֶּה כִּי נָגַע בְּכַף־יֶרֶךְ יַעֲקֹב בְּגִיד הַנָּשֶׁה: וַיִּשָּׂא
יַעֲקֹב עֵינָיו וַיַּרְא וְהִנֵּה עֵשָׂו בָּא וְעִמּוֹ אַרְבַּע מֵאוֹת אִישׁ וַיַּחַץ אֶת־הַיְלָדִים
ב עַל־לֵאָה וְעַל־רָחֵל וְעַל שְׁתֵּי הַשְּׁפָחוֹת: וַיָּשֶׂם אֶת־הַשְּׁפָחוֹת וְאֶת־יַלְדֵיהֶן
ג רִאשֹׁנָה וְאֶת־לֵאָה וִילָדֶיהָ אַחֲרֹנִים וְאֶת־רָחֵל וְאֶת־יוֹסֵף אַחֲרֹנִים: וְהוּא
ד עָבַר לִפְנֵיהֶם וַיִּשְׁתַּחוּ אַרְצָה שֶׁבַע פְּעָמִים עַד־גִּשְׁתּוֹ עַד־אָחִיו: וַיָּרָץ
ה עֵשָׂו לִקְרָאתוֹ וַיְחַבְּקֵהוּ וַיִּפֹּל עַל־צַוָּארָו וַיִּשָּׁקֵהוּ וַיִּבְכּוּ: וַיִּשָּׂא אֶת־עֵינָיו
וַיַּרְא אֶת־הַנָּשִׁים וְאֶת־הַיְלָדִים וַיֹּאמֶר מִי־אֵלֶּה לָּךְ וַיֹּאמַר הַיְלָדִים אֲשֶׁר־חָנַן
ו ז אֱלֹהִים אֶת־עַבְדֶּךָ: וַתִּגַּשְׁןָ הַשְּׁפָחוֹת הֵנָּה וְיַלְדֵיהֶן וַתִּשְׁתַּחֲוֶיןָ: וַתִּגַּשׁ גַּם־
ח לֵאָה וִילָדֶיהָ וַיִּשְׁתַּחֲווּ וְאַחַר נִגַּשׁ יוֹסֵף וְרָחֵל וַיִּשְׁתַּחֲווּ: וַיֹּאמֶר מִי לְךָ כָּל־הַמַּחֲנֶה
ט הַזֶּה אֲשֶׁר פָּגָשְׁתִּי וַיֹּאמֶר לִמְצֹא־חֵן בְּעֵינֵי אֲדֹנִי: וַיֹּאמֶר עֵשָׂו יֶשׁ־לִי רָב
י אָחִי יְהִי לְךָ אֲשֶׁר־לָךְ: וַיֹּאמֶר יַעֲקֹב אַל־נָא אִם־נָא מָצָאתִי חֵן בְּעֵינֶיךָ וְלָקַחְתָּ
יא מִנְחָתִי מִיָּדִי כִּי עַל־כֵּן רָאִיתִי פָנֶיךָ כִּרְאֹת פְּנֵי אֱלֹהִים וַתִּרְצֵנִי: קַח־נָא
אֶת־בִּרְכָתִי אֲשֶׁר הֻבָאת לָךְ כִּי־חַנַּנִי אֱלֹהִים וְכִי יֶשׁ־לִי־כֹל וַיִּפְצַר־בּוֹ וַיִּקָּח:

רש״י

(ירמיה נא, ל), וכן: "כי נשני אלהים את כל עמלי" (להלן מא, נא).

פרק לג

ב] ואת לאה וילדיה אחרנים. אחרון אחרון חביב.

ג] עבר לפניהם. אמר, אם יבא אותו רשע להלחם, ילחם בי תחלה.

ד] ויחבקהו. נתגלגלו רחמיו כשראהו משתחוה כל השתחואות הללו. וישקהו. נקוד עליו. ויש חולקין בדבר הזה בברייתא דספרי (בהעלתך סט): יש שדרשו נקדה זו לומר שלא נשקו בכל לבו; אמר רבי שמעון בן יוחאי: הלכה היא בידוע שעשו שונא ליעקב, אלא שנכמרו רחמיו באותה שעה ונשקו בכל לבו.

ה] מי אלה לך. מי אלה להיות שלך?

ז] נגש יוסף ורחל. בכלן האמהות נגשות לפני הבנים, אבל ברחל – יוסף נגש לפניה; אמר: אמי יפת תאר, שמא יתלה בה עיניו אותו רשע, אעמד כנגדה ואעכבנו מלהסתכל בה. מכאן זכה יוסף לברכת "עלי עין" (להלן מט, כב).

ח] מי לך כל המחנה. מי כל המחנה אשר פגשתי שהוא שלך? כלומר, למה הוא לך? פשוטו של מקרא על מוליכי המנחה; ומדרשו, כתות של מלאכים פגעו שהיו דוחפין אותו ואת אנשיו ואומרים להם: של מי אתם? והם אומרים להם: של עשו. והם אומרים: הכו הכו. ואלו אומרים: בנו של יצחק הוא, ולא היו משגיחים; בנו של אברהם, ולא היו משגיחים; אחיו של יעקב הוא, ואלו אומרים להם: אם כן משלנו אתם.

ט] יהי לך אשר לך. כאן הודה לו על הברכות.

י] אל נא. אל נא תאמר לי כן: אם נא מצאתי חן בעיניך ולקחת מנחתי מידי כי על כן ראיתי פניך וגו'. כי כדאי והגון לך שתקבל מנחתי, על אשר ראיתי פניך והן חשובין לי כראית פני המלאך, שראיתי שר שלך, ועוד, על שנתרצית לי למחול על סרחני. ולמה הזכיר לו ראית המלאך? כדי שיתירא הימנו ויאמר: ראה מלאכים ונצול, איני יכול לו מעתה. ותרצני. נתפיסת לי, וכן כל רצון שבמקרא לשון פיוס, אפיימנ"ט בלעז; "כי לא לרצון יהיה לכם" (ויקרא כב, כ) – הקרבנות באות לפיס ולרצות, "שפתי צדיק ידעון רצון" (משלי י, לב) – יודעים לפיס ולרצות.

יא] ברכתי. מנחה זו הבאה על ראית פנים ולפרקים, אינה באה אלא לשאלת שלום, וכל ברכה שהיא לראית פנים, כגון: "ויברך יעקב את פרעה" (להלן מז, י), "עשו אתי ברכה" (מלכים ב' יח, לא) דסנחריב, וכן: "לשאל לו לשלום ולברכו" (שמואל ב' ח, י) דתעי מלך חמת, כלם לשון ברכת שלום הן, שקורין בלעז סלודי"ר, אף זו "ברכתי" – מו"ן סלו"ד: אשר הבאת לך. לא טרחת בה ואני יגעתי להגיעה עד שבאה לידך: חנני. נו"ן ראשונה מדגשת לפי שהיא משמשת במקום שתי נוני"ן, שהיה לו לומר 'חננני', שאין 'חנן' בלא שתי נוני"ן, והשלישית לשמוש כמו 'עשני' (ישעיה כג, טז), 'זבדני' (לעיל ל, כ): יש לי כל. כל ספוקי, ועשו דבר בלשון גאוה: "יש לי רב" (לעיל פסוק ט), יותר ויותר מכדי צרכי.

camp and flocks, perhaps because Jacob had cautiously left them behind. **He,** Jacob, **urged him,** Esau, to accept his present, **and he took it.**

12 Ever since Esau's anger and animosity toward Jacob had been aroused many years ago, Jacob had avoided this encounter. Nevertheless, Jacob's gift and gestures of submission were sufficient to subdue Esau's resentment and restore their brotherhood. **He,** Esau, **said: We will travel, and we will go, and I will go along with you.** Let us continue together on the same road, as you are my brother. From Jacob's subsequent response it is apparent that he understood Esau's comment as an invitation to visit him or even to live with him in the place where he ruled.

13 **He,** Jacob, **said to him: My lord knows that the children are tender.** You can see that the children are young. Reuben, Jacob's firstborn son, was about thirteen years old at the time. **And** you know **that** the responsibilities of attending to the needs of **the nursing flocks and cattle are upon me; if they drive them hard one day, all the flocks will die.** With my large family and many sheep, I cannot keep up with your troops.

14 **Please, my lord will pass before his servant.** You go first, **and I will advance slowly, according to the pace of the property that is before me and according to the pace of the children, until I will come to my lord to Se'ir.** There is a long way ahead of us until we reach your land.

15 **And Esau said:** If so, **please, I will place with you some of the people who are with me** to protect you and your family. **He,** Jacob, **said: Why do that? I will find favor in the eyes of my lord.**[D] I am independent; I have no need for such assistance. Furthermore, I do not wish to burden you by accepting this service.

16 **Esau returned on that day** with his entourage and the animals he had received **on his way to Se'ir.**

17 **Jacob traveled to** a location named **Sukot,**[B] **and built him a house, and established booths for his livestock. Therefore, he called the name of the place Sukot.** This was a temporary lodging, where Jacob stayed until he decided upon his next destination.

18 **Jacob came unharmed**[B] and without losses **to the city of Shekhem,**[B] **which is in the land of Canaan, upon his arrival from Padan Aram.** He intended to make Shekhem his permanent residence. **And he encamped before the city;** not inside, but close enough to form a relationship with the local residents.

19 Since this was a populated area, it would have been inappropriate for Jacob to establish his residence on land that he did not own. Therefore, upon his arrival **he purchased a tract of the field where he had pitched his tent, from the possession of the children of Hamor, father of Shekhem,** who was the mayor of the city of Shekhem, **for one hundred kesita,**[B] a certain sum of money.[7] Alternatively, *kesita* means sheep and the like.

20 **He established there an altar, and called it El Elohei Israel,** meaning the Strong God of Israel.[8] Naming an altar in this manner was not unusual, as they were not treated as mere instrumental structures, but were anthropomorphized, given a name and identity. The commentaries note that Moses similarly named an altar "The Lord Is My Standard"[9] and Jerusalem was called "The Lord Is There."[10]

The Incident of Dina

GENESIS 34:1–31

The travails of Jacob's family have not ended. After an extended exile, feuds with the extended family, wanderings, struggles, and fear, Jacob and his family finally return to the land of Canaan. However, they do not merit to dwell there in tranquility, as Jacob's only daughter is raped in Shekhem by the prince of the city. For the first time, two of Jacob's sons, Simeon and Levi, initiate a bold move. Their zealous response to the rape of their sister provokes criticism from their father. There is a renewed sense of danger threatening the household that has been created with great hardships.

34 1 *Fifth aliya* Since Jacob and his family were residing near the city of Shekhem, **Dina,** the young **daughter of Leah, whom she bore to Jacob, went out to see the daughters of the land.** Having lived until that point mostly as a nomad in the desert, Dina

DISCUSSION

33:15| **Why do that? I will find favor in the eyes of my lord:** Jacob wanted to end his encounter with Esau as smoothly and pleasantly as possible, without receiving any benefits from his brother. He did not wish to accept Esau's gestures of kinship, but merely to maintain a distant relationship of respect and conciliation.

BACKGROUND

33:17| **Sukot:** A city in the portion of the tribe of Gad, on the eastern side of the Jordan River. It is identified with Deir Alla, which is located in the valley of Sukot (see Psalms 60:8), near an estuary of the Zarqa River.

33:18| **Jacob came unharmed [*shalem*]:** According to one opinion, Shalem is the name of a town located on the road between the Jordan Valley and Shekhem. Its name is preserved in the Arab village of Shalem, about 6 km east of Shekhem.

Shekhem: Shekhem is identified with Tel Balata, which is located on a major intersection in the center of Samaria, on "the path of the setting sun" (Deuteronomy 11:30). This path extends from the Jordan Valley to the Mediterranean coast through the Samarian hills. Remains of massive walls have been found there. According to archaeological findings, the city was founded at the beginning of the second millennium BCE, and it is mentioned in Egyptian documents dating from that period.

33:19| ***Kesita*:** At that time there were presumably no standard coins; therefore, it is likely that this is not referring to a sum of money but to some other item of

יב ויאמר נסעה ונלכה ואלכה לנגדך: ויאמר אליו אדני ידע כי־הילדים רכים יג
יד והצאן והבקר עלות עלי ודפקום יום אחד ומתו כל־הצאן: יעבר־נא אדני
לפני עבדו ואני אתנהלה לאטי לרגל המלאכה אשר־לפני ולרגל הילדים עד
טו אשר־אבא אל־אדני שעירה: ויאמר עשו אציגה־נא עמך מן־העם אשר אתי
טז ויאמר למה זה אמצא־חן בעיני אדני: וישב ביום ההוא עשו לדרכו שעירה:
יז ויעקב נסע סכתה ויבן לו בית ולמקנהו עשה סכת על־כן קרא שם־המקום
יח סכות: ויבא יעקב שלם עיר שכם אשר בארץ כנען בבאו מפדן לא
יט ארם ויחן את־פני העיר: ויקן את־חלקת השדה אשר נטה־שם אהלו מיד
כ בני־חמור אבי שכם במאה קשיטה: ויצב־שם מזבח ויקרא־לו אל אלהי
ד
א ישראל: ותצא דינה בת־לאה אשר ילדה ליעקב לראות בבנות חמישי

רש"י

יב| נסעה. כמו: "שמעה" (תהלים לט, יג), "סלחה" (להלן מג, ח) שהוא כמו 'שמע', 'סלח', אף 'נסעה' כמו 'נסע', והנו"ן יסוד בתבה. ותרגום של אונקלוס: "טול ונהך", עשו אמר ליעקב, נסע מכאן ונלך: ואלכה לנגדך. בשוה לך, טובה זו אעשה לך שאאריך ימי מהלכתי ללכת לאט כאשר אתה צריך, וזהו "לנגדך" – בשוה לך:

יג| עלות עלי. הצאן והבקר שהן "עלות", מטלות "עלי", לנהלן לאט: עלות. מגדלות עולליהן, לשון "עולל ויונק" (ירמיה מד, ז; איכה ב, יא), "עול ימים" (ישעיה סה, כ), "ושתי פרות עלות" (שמואל א' ו, ז), ובלעז אנפנטיי"ש: ודפקום יום אחד. ליגעם בדרך במרוצה, "ומתו כל הצאן": ודפקום. כמו: "קול דודי דופק" (שיר השירים ה, ב), נוקש בדלת:

יד| יעבר נא אדני. אל נא תאריך ימי הליכתך, עבר כפי דרכך ואף אם תתרחק: אתנהלה. אתנהל, הה"א יתרה, כמו: 'ארדה' (לעיל יח, כא), 'אשמעה' (ירמיה ד, כא; תהלים פה, ט): לאטי. לאט שלי, לשון נחת, "ההולכים לאט" (ישעיה ח, ו), "לאט לי לנער" (שמואל ב' יח, ה): לאטי. הלמ"ד מן היסוד ואינה משמשת, אתנהל נחת שלי: לרגל המלאכה. לפי צרך הליכת רגלי המלאכה המטלת לפני להוליך: ולרגל הילדים. לפי רגליהם שהם יכולים ללכת: עד אשר אבא אל אדני שעירה. הרחיב לו הדרך, שלא היה דעתו ללכת אלא עד סכות, אמר: אם דעתו לעשות לי רעה ימתין עד בואי אצלו. והוא לא הלך, ואימתי ילך? בימי המשיח, שנאמר: "ועלו מושיעים בהר ציון לשפט את הר עשו" (עובדיה א, כא). ומדרשי אגדה יש לפרשה זו רבים:

טו| ויאמר למה זה. תעשה לי טובה זו שאיני צריך לה; "אמצא חן" בעיניך ולא תשלם לי עתה שום גמול:

טז| וישב ביום ההוא עשו לדרכו. עשו לבדו, וארבע מאות איש שהלכו עמו נשמטו מאצלו אחד אחד. והיכן פרע להם הקדוש ברוך הוא? בימי דוד, שנאמר: "כי אם ארבע מאות איש נער אשר רכבו על הגמלים" (שמואל א' ל, יז):

יז| ויבן לו בית. שהה שם שמונה עשר חדש, קיץ וחורף וקיץ; קיץ – 'סכת', חורף – 'בית', וקיץ – 'סכת':

יח| שלם. שלם בגופו, שנתרפא מצלעתו; שלם בממונו, שלא חסר כלום מכל אותו דורון; שלם בתורתו, שלא שכח תלמודו בבית לבן: עיר שכם. כמו 'לעיר', וכמוהו: "עד בואנה בית לחם" (רות א, יט): בבאו מפדן ארם. כאדם האומר לחברו, יצא פלוני מבין שני אריות ובא שלם, אף כאן: ויבא שלם מפדן ארם, מלבן ומעשו שנזדווגו לו בדרך:

יט| קשיטה. מעה. אמר רבי עקיבא: כשהלכתי לכרכי הים היו קורין למעה 'קשיטה':

כ| ויקרא לו אל אלהי ישראל. לא שהמזבח קרוי "אלהי ישראל", אלא על שם שהיה הקדוש ברוך הוא עמו והצילו קרא שם המזבח על שם הנס, להיות שבחו של מקום נזכר בקריאת השם, כלומר, מי שהוא אל, הוא הקדוש ברוך הוא, הוא לאלהים לי ששמי ישראל. וכן מצינו במשה: "ויקרא שמו ה' נסי" (שמות יז, טו), לא שהמזבח קרוי ה', אלא על שם הנס קרא שם המזבח להזכיר שבחו של הקדוש ברוך הוא, ה' הוא נסי. ורבותינו אמרו שהקדוש ברוך הוא קראו ליעקב 'אל'. ודברי תורה "כפטיש יפצץ סלע" (ירמיה כג, כט), מתחלקים לכמה טעמים, ואני ליישב פשוטו של מקרא באתי:

פרק לד

א| בת לאה. ולא בת יעקב? אלא על שם יציאתה

BACKGROUND

value. See the verse: "Each gave him one *kesita*, and each one gold ring" (Job 42:11). The ancient translations of Onkelos, the Dead Sea Scrolls, and the Septuagint render the word as sheep. A similar word in Akkadian, *sikkultu*, means sheep or a valuable item. Interestingly, the term *ḥayyil*, which in biblical Hebrew refers to wealth and property, means a horse in other Semitic languages. An etymological transition of this type, from sheep to money, occurs in Latin as well; the Latin term for money, *pecunia*, is derived from its word for sheep (see also Rav Se'adya Gaon; *Midrash Sekhel Tov*; Ibn Ezra, Job 42:11). However, Rabbi Akiva attests in the Talmud: When I went to Africa, they would call a *ma'a*, which is a type of coin, a *kesita* (*Rosh HaShana* 26a). Some claim that *kesita* was a unit of weight.

became acquainted for the first time with an urban environment, and she socialized with the local girls.

2 **Shekhem, son of Hamor the Hivite, prince of the land, saw her and** was attracted to this young foreign woman. **He took her, and lay with her, and raped her.**

3 Presumably, this was not the first woman whom Shekhem had abused in this manner, by taking advantage of his social status. However, on this occasion he did not abandon her afterward; rather, **his soul was drawn to Dina, daughter of Jacob, and he loved the young woman, and** furthermore he **spoke soothingly to the young woman.** Although Shekhem was certainly more powerful than the young woman, he wanted her to consent to marriage.

4 **Shekhem spoke to his father Hamor, saying: Take for me this girl as a wife.**

5 **Jacob heard that he had defiled Dina his daughter.** The news reached him at home, **and his sons were with his livestock in the field; and Jacob kept silent.** He did nothing about the matter **until their arrival.**

6 Meanwhile, **Hamor, father of Shekhem, went out to Jacob to speak with him** about the possibility of marriage. Were it not for the prior act of rape, there would have been nothing inappropriate about this proposal.

7 **And the sons of Jacob came from the field** immediately **when they heard it; and the men were saddened** over the pain and shame inflicted upon their sister, **and** furthermore **they became very angry, as he,** Shekhem, had **performed an abomination in** the family of **Israel to lie with Jacob's daughter; and so shall not be done** to anyone, certainly not the daughter of an esteemed person.

8 **Hamor,** the prince of the land, **spoke with them, saying: The soul of my son Shekhem longs for your daughter. Please, give her to him as a wife.**

9 In addition to this marriage proposal, Hamor also suggests a political union; perhaps he sought to make amends with the girl's father for his son's misbehavior. **And marry with us; give your daughters to us, and take our daughters for you.** The individual engagement can become a collective one. We will form one family, or at least maintain very close relations.

10 **And you shall live with us** permanently; **and the land shall be before you; live and trade in it.** Use it as though it is your own land, for business or pleasure, **and settle in it.** So far you have managed to buy one small field in exchange for a large sum of money. Now I am offering you free residency, as well as commercial and social unification. Hamor, who was presumably sent by his son, ignored the appalling incident that led to this proposal, and with regard to the marriage he spoke like an ordinary man who wishes to set up his son with his neighbor's daughter.

11 The young **Shekhem** did not wait to hear Jacob's response from his father. Rather, he too came to their house and **said to her father and to her brothers: Let me find favor in your eyes, and that which you shall say to me I will give.** Unlike Hamor, who attempted to act within the bounds of decorum, Shekhem spoke out of passion.

12 **Increase bridal payment and gift, and I will give in accordance with what you shall say to me.** I will agree to pay any amount you see fit; **and** all I ask is that you **give me the young woman as a wife.**

13 Jacob himself did not respond. This might have been due to his grief over the incident, or he had possibly developed a passive personality over the years, perhaps as a result of his encounter with the angel. **The sons of Jacob answered Shekhem and Hamor his father with guile, and spoke** in their father's name. They spoke with cunning, **as he,** Shekhem, had **defiled Dina their sister.** In contrast to Shekhem and Hamor, who ignored the rape and acted as though they were presenting a normal marriage proposal, Jacob's sons emphasized the insult, so that the severity of the harm would be taken into account in the subsequent agreement.

14 The malicious guile in their response lies in the following suggestion. **They said to them: We cannot do this thing, to give our sister to a man who has a foreskin, as** in our eyes the uncircumcised state is not merely a physical matter, but **it is a disgrace for us.**[11] Therefore, it is impossible to speak of marriage at this stage.

15 **Only with this will we accede to you: If you become like us to have every male among you circumcised.**[D] Since it is a disgrace for us to be uncircumcised, we cannot become like you. Consequently, you must agree to become similar to us.

16 **We will give our daughters to you, and we will take your daughters for us, and we will live with you, and we will become one people.**

17 **If you do not heed us, to be circumcised, we will take our daughter** home, **and we will go.** Since the brothers are speaking in their father's name, they call Dina their daughter.[12]

DISCUSSION

34:15 | If you will become like us to have every male among you circumcised: Nowadays, circumcision is generally considered a custom unique to the descendants of Abraham. Indeed, the Philistines and the local inhabitants of Canaan did not circumcise their sons. However, among the Egyptians and some Arab tribes there were many who did. Consequently, this demand would not have been unthinkable to the residents of Shekhem (see commentary on Joshua 5:9).

ב הָאָרֶץ: וַיַּרְא אֹתָהּ שְׁכֶם בֶּן־חֲמוֹר הַחִוִּי נְשִׂיא הָאָרֶץ וַיִּקַּח אֹתָהּ וַיִּשְׁכַּב אֹתָהּ

ג וַיְעַנֶּהָ: וַתִּדְבַּק נַפְשׁוֹ בְּדִינָה בַּת־יַעֲקֹב וַיֶּאֱהַב אֶת־הַנַּעֲרָ וַיְדַבֵּר עַל־לֵב הַנַּעֲרָ:

ד וַיֹּאמֶר שְׁכֶם אֶל־חֲמוֹר אָבִיו לֵאמֹר קַח־לִי אֶת־הַיַּלְדָּה הַזֹּאת לְאִשָּׁה: וְיַעֲקֹב

ה שָׁמַע כִּי טִמֵּא אֶת־דִּינָה בִתּוֹ וּבָנָיו הָיוּ אֶת־מִקְנֵהוּ בַּשָּׂדֶה וְהֶחֱרִשׁ יַעֲקֹב עַד־

ו בֹּאָם: וַיֵּצֵא חֲמוֹר אֲבִי־שְׁכֶם אֶל־יַעֲקֹב לְדַבֵּר אִתּוֹ: וּבְנֵי יַעֲקֹב בָּאוּ מִן־הַשָּׂדֶה

ז כְּשָׁמְעָם וַיִּתְעַצְּבוּ הָאֲנָשִׁים וַיִּחַר לָהֶם מְאֹד כִּי־נְבָלָה עָשָׂה בְיִשְׂרָאֵל לִשְׁכַּב

ח אֶת־בַּת־יַעֲקֹב וְכֵן לֹא יֵעָשֶׂה: וַיְדַבֵּר חֲמוֹר אִתָּם לֵאמֹר שְׁכֶם בְּנִי חָשְׁקָה נַפְשׁוֹ

ט בְּבִתְּכֶם תְּנוּ נָא אֹתָהּ לוֹ לְאִשָּׁה: וְהִתְחַתְּנוּ אֹתָנוּ בְּנֹתֵיכֶם תִּתְּנוּ־לָנוּ וְאֶת־

י בְּנֹתֵינוּ תִּקְחוּ לָכֶם: וְאִתָּנוּ תֵּשֵׁבוּ וְהָאָרֶץ תִּהְיֶה לִפְנֵיכֶם שְׁבוּ וּסְחָרוּהָ וְהֵאָחֲזוּ

יא בָּהּ: וַיֹּאמֶר שְׁכֶם אֶל־אָבִיהָ וְאֶל־אַחֶיהָ אֶמְצָא־חֵן בְּעֵינֵיכֶם וַאֲשֶׁר תֹּאמְרוּ אֵלַי

יב אֶתֵּן: הַרְבּוּ עָלַי מְאֹד מֹהַר וּמַתָּן וְאֶתְּנָה כַּאֲשֶׁר תֹּאמְרוּ אֵלָי וּתְנוּ־לִי אֶת־

יג הַנַּעֲרָ לְאִשָּׁה: וַיַּעֲנוּ בְנֵי־יַעֲקֹב אֶת־שְׁכֶם וְאֶת־חֲמוֹר אָבִיו בְּמִרְמָה וַיְדַבֵּרוּ אֲשֶׁר

יד טִמֵּא אֵת דִּינָה אֲחֹתָם: וַיֹּאמְרוּ אֲלֵיהֶם לֹא נוּכַל לַעֲשׂוֹת הַדָּבָר הַזֶּה לָתֵת

טו אֶת־אֲחֹתֵנוּ לְאִישׁ אֲשֶׁר־לוֹ עָרְלָה כִּי־חֶרְפָּה הִוא לָנוּ: אַךְ־בְּזֹאת נֵאוֹת לָכֶם

טז אִם תִּהְיוּ כָמֹנוּ לְהִמֹּל לָכֶם כָּל־זָכָר: וְנָתַנּוּ אֶת־בְּנֹתֵינוּ לָכֶם וְאֶת־בְּנֹתֵיכֶם נִקַּח־

יז לָנוּ וְיָשַׁבְנוּ אִתְּכֶם וְהָיִינוּ לְעַם אֶחָד: וְאִם־לֹא תִשְׁמְעוּ אֵלֵינוּ לְהִמּוֹל וְלָקַחְנוּ

רש"י

נִקְרֵאת 'בַּת לָאָה', שֶׁאַף הִיא יַצְאָנִית – "וַתֵּצֵא לֵאָה לִקְרָאתוֹ" (לעיל ל, טז):

ב] וַיִּשְׁכַּב אֹתָהּ. כְּדַרְכָּהּ: וַיְעַנֶּהָ. שֶׁלֹּא כְדַרְכָּהּ:

ג] עַל לֵב הַנַּעֲרָ. דְּבָרִים הַמִּתְיַשְּׁבִים עַל הַלֵּב: אָבִיךְ בְּחֶלְקַת שָׂדֶה קְטַנָּה רְאִי כַּמָּה מָמוֹן בִּזְבֵּז, מַחָה קְשִׁיטָה, אֲנִי אֲשַׂדֵּךְ וְתִקְנֶה כָּל הָעִיר וְכָל שְׂדוֹתֶיהָ:

ז] וְכֵן לֹא יֵעָשֶׂה. לְעַנּוֹת אֶת הַבְּתוּלוֹת, שֶׁהָאֻמּוֹת גָּדְרוּ עַצְמָן מִן הָעֲרָיוֹת עַל יְדֵי הַמַּבּוּל:

ח] חָשְׁקָה. חָפְצָה:

יב] מֹהַר. כְּתֻבָּה:

יג] בְּמִרְמָה. בְּחָכְמָה. הַכָּתוּב אוֹמֵר שֶׁלֹּא הָיְתָה רְמִיָּה, שֶׁהֲרֵי "טִמֵּא אֵת דִּינָה אֲחֹתָם":

יד] חֶרְפָּה הִוא. שֶׁמֶן הוּא אֶצְלֵנוּ, הַבָּא לְחָרֵף אֶת חֲבֵרוֹ אוֹמֵר לוֹ: עָרֵל אַתָּה, אוֹ בֶּן עָרֵל, "חֶרְפָּה" בְּכָל מָקוֹם – גִּדּוּף:

טו] נֵאוֹת. נִתְרַצֶּה, לְשׁוֹן "וַיֵּאֹתוּ" (מלכים ב' יב, ט): לְהִמּוֹל. לִהְיוֹת נִמּוֹל. אֵינוֹ לְשׁוֹן לִפְעֹל אֶלָּא לְשׁוֹן לְהִפָּעֵל:

טז] וְנָתַנּוּ. עַ"ן שֶׁנָּנוּ מֻדְגֶּשֶׁת לְפִי שֶׁהִיא מְשַׁמֶּשֶׁת בִּמְקוֹם שְׁתֵּי נוּנִי"ן, "וְנָתַנּוּ", "וְאֶת־בְּנֹתֵיכֶם נִקַּח לָנוּ": אַתָּה מוֹצֵא בַּתִּירוּ שֶׁאָמַר חֲמוֹר לַעֲקֹב וּבִתְשׁוּבַת בְּנֵי יַעֲקֹב לַחֲמוֹר, שֶׁתָּלוּ הַחֲשִׁיבוּת בְּבֵן יַעֲקֹב לָקַח שְׁכֶם בְּנוֹת בְּנֵי יַעֲקֹב, שֶׁנָּבְחֲרוּ לָהֶם וּבְנֹתֵיהֶם יִתְּנוּ לָהֶם לְפִי דַעְתָּם, דִּכְתִיב: "וְנָתַנּוּ אֶת בְּנֹתֵינוּ" – לְפִי דַעְתֵּנוּ, "וְאֶת בְּנֹתֵיכֶם נִקַּח לָנוּ" – בְּכָל אֲשֶׁר נַחְפֹּץ. וּכְשֶׁדִּבְּרוּ חֲמוֹר וּשְׁכֶם בְּנוֹ אֶל יוֹשְׁבֵי עִירָם הָפְכוּ הַדְּבָרִים: "אֵת בְּנֹתָם נִקַּח לָנוּ לְנָשִׁים וְאֶת בְּנֹתֵינוּ נִתֵּן לָהֶם" (להלן פסוק כא), כְּדֵי לְרַצּוֹתָם שֶׁיֵּאוֹתוּ לְהִמּוֹל:

18 **Their statement was favorable in the eyes of Hamor, and in the eyes of Shekhem son of Hamor.** They concluded from the response of Jacob's sons that their proposal had been accepted on the condition that they circumcise themselves.

19 **The lad did not tarry to perform the matter, because he desired Jacob's daughter. And he was more respected than all the house of his father.** It would seem that Shekhem was the firstborn, his father's heir.

20 **Hamor and Shekhem his son came to the gate of their city.** Generally, behind the gate of a city there was a square, where its important residents would convene.[13] **And they spoke with the men of their city,** presenting the deal to them. They omitted Shekhem's love for Dina, which did not concern the city residents, and which would certainly not have helped convince them to undertake such an extreme measure as circumcision. Rather, they laid out before them only the political and commercial elements of the deal, **saying:**

21 **These men are peaceful with us, and** it is beneficial for us that **they will live in the land and trade in it; behold, the land is spacious before them.** Shekhem was a small city at the time, surrounded by large tracts of land, so there was plenty of room for everybody. **Their daughters we will take as wives for us, and our daughters we will give to them.** In a rhetorically persuasive tactic, Hamor and Shekhem adjusted their proposal to Jacob, in which they said: Give your daughters to us, and take our daughters for you (verse 9). It can be inferred from their original statement that Jacob's family would have the discretion with regard to proposals of intermarriage, whereas here they indicate that the residents of Shekhem would have the choice.[14]

22 **Only with this condition will the men accede to us, to live with us, to become one people, with every male being circumcised, as they are circumcised.** There should be no such clear physical distinction between the two populations.

23 **Aren't their livestock and their property and all their animals ours?** We will devour them economically and culturally, and we will thereby enrich ourselves. **We only must accede to them, and they will live with us.** This ethnic and economic merge does not require us to pay a heavy price; all it takes is the fulfillment of one small condition.

24 **All who emerged from the gate of his city heeded Hamor and Shekhem his son; every male, all who emerged from the gate of his city, was circumcised.** In several cultures, males are circumcised in adulthood; however, this is an uncomfortable and even painful operation, far more so than when performed upon infants.

25 **It was on the third day, when they were in** so much pain that they could not leave their homes. Although the pain did not

paralyze them, it limited their ability to move and act. **The two sons of Jacob, Simeon and Levi, Dina's brothers, each** man **took his sword.** These brothers took the initiative because they had a special relationship with Dina, who was their maternal as well as their paternal sister. It is unclear why their elder brother Reuben did not participate. **And** they **came upon the city confidently,** as its residents were not prepared to have to defend themselves against Jacob's family, with whom they were expecting to unite. Furthermore, the recently circumcised men were limited in their physical capabilities. Simeon and Levi went from house to house **and killed all the males.**

26 **And they killed Hamor and Shekhem his son by sword.** Their death was apparently more conspicuous than that of the other men; perhaps they were beheaded in the formal manner of an execution. Throughout this entire episode, Dina had remained imprisoned in Shekhem's house; she was possibly granted the status of a future bride. **And** now, Simeon and Levi **took Dina from the house of Shekhem and departed.**

27 Then **the** other **sons of Jacob,** who did not participate in the killing,[15] **beset the slain** to take their valuables **and looted the city,** with the justification **that** its residents had **defiled their sister.** Even if the other men had not actively assisted in the rape, they were rendered passive accomplices by their failure to stop Shekhem.[16] After all, he did not seduce her gently, but took her by force from the group of girls with whom she was socializing, presumably in public.

28 **They took their flocks, their cattle, and their donkeys, and that which was in the city and that which was in the field.**

29 **And all their wealth, and all their offspring,** their little children, **and their wives, they took captive and looted, and everything that was in the house.** As in war, they took captives and plundered the property.

30 **Jacob said to Simeon and Levi:** Until now I was considered clean and acceptable, but now **you have sullied me,**[D] **to render me loathsome to the inhabitants of the land, the Canaanites and the Perizites. I am few in number.** Since we are foreigners and we have attacked one of the Canaanite nations, the neighboring population might try to avenge the destruction of Shekhem, or seek to deter us from behaving in like manner toward other cities. To this end **they will mobilize against me and smite me, and I and my household shall be destroyed.**

31 **They,** the two sons, **said: Shall he render our sister as a harlot?** Simeon and Levi argue that the marriage proposal presented by Hamor and Shekhem was disingenuous. They refused to come to terms with the treatment of their sister as merchandise in a financial deal.

יט אֶת־בִּתֵּנוּ וְהָלָכְנוּ: וַיִּיטְבוּ דִבְרֵיהֶם בְּעֵינֵי חֲמוֹר וּבְעֵינֵי שְׁכֶם בֶּן־חֲמוֹר: וְלֹא־
אֵחַר הַנַּעַר לַעֲשׂוֹת הַדָּבָר כִּי חָפֵץ בְּבַת־יַעֲקֹב וְהוּא נִכְבָּד מִכֹּל בֵּית אָבִיו:

כ וַיָּבֹא חֲמוֹר וּשְׁכֶם בְּנוֹ אֶל־שַׁעַר עִירָם וַיְדַבְּרוּ אֶל־אַנְשֵׁי עִירָם לֵאמֹר: הָאֲנָשִׁים
הָאֵלֶּה שְׁלֵמִים הֵם אִתָּנוּ וְיֵשְׁבוּ בָאָרֶץ וְיִסְחֲרוּ אֹתָהּ וְהָאָרֶץ הִנֵּה רַחֲבַת־יָדַיִם
לִפְנֵיהֶם אֶת־בְּנֹתָם נִקַּח־לָנוּ לְנָשִׁים וְאֶת־בְּנֹתֵינוּ נִתֵּן לָהֶם: אַךְ־בְּזֹאת יֵאֹתוּ
לָנוּ הָאֲנָשִׁים לָשֶׁבֶת אִתָּנוּ לִהְיוֹת לְעַם אֶחָד בְּהִמּוֹל לָנוּ כָּל־זָכָר כַּאֲשֶׁר הֵם
נִמֹּלִים: מִקְנֵהֶם וְקִנְיָנָם וְכָל־בְּהֶמְתָּם הֲלוֹא לָנוּ הֵם אַךְ נֵאוֹתָה לָהֶם וְיֵשְׁבוּ
כד אִתָּנוּ: וַיִּשְׁמְעוּ אֶל־חֲמוֹר וְאֶל־שְׁכֶם בְּנוֹ כָּל־יֹצְאֵי שַׁעַר עִירוֹ וַיִּמֹּלוּ כָּל־זָכָר
כה כָּל־יֹצְאֵי שַׁעַר עִירוֹ: וַיְהִי בַיּוֹם הַשְּׁלִישִׁי בִּהְיוֹתָם כֹּאֲבִים וַיִּקְחוּ שְׁנֵי־בְנֵי־יַעֲקֹב
שִׁמְעוֹן וְלֵוִי אֲחֵי דִינָה אִישׁ חַרְבּוֹ וַיָּבֹאוּ עַל־הָעִיר בֶּטַח וַיַּהַרְגוּ כָּל־זָכָר: וְאֶת־
כו חֲמוֹר וְאֶת־שְׁכֶם בְּנוֹ הָרְגוּ לְפִי־חָרֶב וַיִּקְחוּ אֶת־דִּינָה מִבֵּית שְׁכֶם וַיֵּצֵאוּ: בְּנֵי
כח יַעֲקֹב בָּאוּ עַל־הַחֲלָלִים וַיָּבֹזּוּ הָעִיר אֲשֶׁר טִמְּאוּ אֲחוֹתָם: אֶת־צֹאנָם וְאֶת־בְּקָרָם
וְאֶת־חֲמֹרֵיהֶם וְאֵת אֲשֶׁר־בָּעִיר וְאֶת־אֲשֶׁר בַּשָּׂדֶה לָקָחוּ: וְאֶת־כָּל־חֵילָם וְאֶת־
ל כָּל־טַפָּם וְאֶת־נְשֵׁיהֶם שָׁבוּ וַיָּבֹזּוּ וְאֵת כָּל־אֲשֶׁר בַּבָּיִת: וַיֹּאמֶר יַעֲקֹב אֶל־שִׁמְעוֹן
וְאֶל־לֵוִי עֲכַרְתֶּם אֹתִי לְהַבְאִישֵׁנִי בְּיֹשֵׁב הָאָרֶץ בַּכְּנַעֲנִי וּבַפְּרִזִּי וַאֲנִי מְתֵי מִסְפָּר
לא וְנֶאֶסְפוּ עָלַי וְהִכּוּנִי וְנִשְׁמַדְתִּי אֲנִי וּבֵיתִי: וַיֹּאמְרוּ הַכְזוֹנָה יַעֲשֶׂה אֶת־אֲחוֹתֵנוּ:

רש"י

כא| **שְׁלֵמִים.** בְּשָׁלוֹם וּבְלֵב שָׁלֵם. **וְהָאָרֶץ הִנֵּה רַחֲבַת
יָדַיִם.** כְּאָדָם שֶׁיָּדוֹ רְחָבָה וּוַתְרָנִית, כְּלוֹמַר, לֹא תַפְסִידוּ
כְּלוּם, פְּרַקְמַטְיָא הַרְבֵּה בָּאָה לְכָאן וְאֵין לָהּ קוֹנִים:

כב| **בְּהִמּוֹל** נְמּוֹל:

כג| **אַךְ נֵאוֹתָה לָהֶם.** לִדְבַר זֶה, וְעַל יְדֵי כֵן יֵשְׁבוּ אִתָּנוּ:

כה| **שְׁנֵי בְנֵי יַעֲקֹב.** בָּנָיו הָיוּ, וְאַף עַל פִּי כֵן נָהֲגוּ עַצְמָן
"שִׁמְעוֹן וְלֵוִי" – כִּשְׁאָר אֲנָשִׁים שֶׁאֵינָם בָּנָיו, שֶׁלֹּא נָטְלוּ

עֵצָה הֵימֶנּוּ: **אֲחֵי דִינָה.** לְפִי שֶׁמָּסְרוּ עַצְמָן עָלֶיהָ נִקְרְאוּ
אַחֶיהָ: **בֶּטַח.** שֶׁהָיוּ כּוֹאֲבִים. וּמִדְרַשׁ אַגָּדָה, בְּטוּחִים עַל
כֹּחוֹ שֶׁל זָקֵן:

כו| **עַל הַחֲלָלִים.** לִפְשֹׁט אֶת הַחֲלָלִים:

כט| **חֵילָם.** מָמוֹנָם, וְכֵן, "עָשָׂה לִי אֶת הַחַיִל הַזֶּה" (דברים
ח, יז), "וְיִשְׂרָאֵל עֹשֶׂה חָיִל" (במדבר כד, יח), "וְעָזְבוּ לַאֲחֵרִים

חֵילָם" (תהלים מט, יא): **שָׁבוּ.** לְשׁוֹן שְׁבִיָּה, לְפִיכָךְ טַעְמוֹ
מִלְרַע:

ל| **עֲכַרְתֶּם.** לְשׁוֹן מַיִם עֲכוּרִים, אֵין דַּעְתִּי צְלוּלָה עַכְשָׁיו.
וְאַגָּדָה, צְלוּלָה הָיְתָה הֶחָבִית וַעֲכַרְתֶּם אוֹתָהּ. מָסֹרֶת
הָיְתָה בְּיַד כְּנַעֲנִים שֶׁיִּפְּלוּ בְּיַד בְּנֵי יַעֲקֹב, אֶלָּא שֶׁהָיוּ
אוֹמְרִים: "עַד אֲשֶׁר תִּפְרֶה וְנָחַלְתָּ אֶת הָאָרֶץ" (שמות כג,
ל), לְפִיכָךְ הָיוּ שׁוֹתְקִין: **מְתֵי מִסְפָּר.** אֲנָשִׁים מוּעָטִים:

לא| **הַכְזוֹנָה.** הֶפְקֵר: **אֶת אֲחוֹתֵנוּ.** "יָת אֲחָתַנָא":

DISCUSSION

34:30 | You have sullied me: Jacob was clearly
very angry, but he did not fully express his rage
at this point. He will hold these two sons to full
account on his deathbed, when he will criticize them and curse their anger for their morally dubious killing (49:5–7). Here he focuses on
the political problems they have created (see
Ramban, verse 13).

Jacob's Fulfillment of His Vow
GENESIS 35:1–15

Beit El was a significant stop in Jacob's journey to Haran, as he experienced the dream of the ladder there when God promised to protect him on his journey. He subsequently vowed that the stone he established there as a monument would become a house of God (28:22). Now that Jacob has returned to Canaan, he fulfills his vow. God appears to him again in Beit El, changes his name to Israel, and bestows upon him the blessing of offspring and the inheritance of the land.

35 1 **God said to Jacob: Arise, ascend to Beit El, and settle there; and make there an altar to the God who appeared to you when you fled from Esau your brother.**

2 **Jacob said to his household and to all who were with him,** including his slaves and maidservants: **Remove the foreign gods that are in your midst** that were looted from Shekhem or belonged to people who accompanied their camp. **And** furthermore, **purify yourselves** by immersion in water **and change your garments.**

3 **And we will arise and ascend to Beit El; and I will make there an altar to the God who answers me on the day of my distress. He was with me on the path upon which I went.**

4 **They indeed gave to Jacob all the foreign gods that were in their possession, and** even **the rings that were in their ears,** which were not actually objects of idol worship but some of which were decorated with such articles. Alternatively, this is referring to the rings that were in the ears of the idols.[17] **And Jacob interred them beneath the terebinth** tree **that is near Shekhem.**

5 **They traveled;** and despite Jacob's fear that the cities surrounding Shekhem might try to avenge the deaths of the people of Shekhem, nevertheless, **the dread of God,** an inexplicable sensation of alarm, **was upon the cities that were surrounding them, and they did not pursue after the sons of Jacob.** There were also sound logical reasons for the hesitation of the neighboring cities: They did not know the size of Jacob's camp, and when they heard that two of his sons had destroyed Shekhem, the residents were afraid of them. Presumably, the residents were not aware of the entire background of the event. Furthermore, it may be assumed that the relationships between different cities were weak, as their residents were not from the same nation. Consequently, many of these local inhabitants were certainly indifferent to the affair, and chose to refrain from getting involved in a matter that was not their concern.

6 **Jacob came to Luz, which is in the land of Canaan, it is Beit El, he and all the people who were with him.**

7 **He erected there an altar, and he called the place** of the altar[18] **El Beit El,** the God of Beit El. El is the name by which God identified Himself to Jacob in Haran.[19] Jacob called the place by this name **because** it was **there** that **God was revealed to him when he fled from his brother.**

8 The Torah relates incidentally that **Deborah, Rebecca's nurse, died.** Deborah was clearly very old at the time, as many years had passed since she had accompanied Rebecca from Haran to the land of Canaan. As Rebecca's lifelong associate, she had a higher status in the family than that of the other maidservants and was therefore accorded respect and treated with great affection. **And she was buried below** the hill upon which **Beit El** was located, **beneath the oak** tree **that stood there; and he called its name Alon Bakhut,**[D] Tree of Weeping, as a sign of mourning for her.

9 **God appeared to Jacob again, already upon his arrival from Padan Aram,**[B] **and He blessed him.** God appeared to him in Beit El, in the same location as when he left for Haran.

10 **God said to him: Your name is** currently **Jacob.** However, **your name shall no longer be called Jacob; rather, Israel shall be your name; and He called his name Israel.** Although Jacob had already been informed of the change of his name (32:29), at that stage he had heard it only from an angel, and in the context of a struggle. Now, the new name is confirmed

---

DISCUSSION

35:8 | Alon Bakhut: It is reasonable to assume that Deborah had cared for Jacob as a baby. It is possible that Rebecca sent her to Jacob in Haran after hearing of his marriage to Laban's daughters, which is how she joined his camp (Rashi). Alternatively, she remained in Haran after Rebecca left as a young girl, and later assisted Jacob in taking care of his children following his marriage to Laban's daughters and their maidservants. If so, this was not Rebecca's nurse who was sent by Rebecca's family to accompany her to the land of Canaan (24:59; see Ramban). Yet

another possibility is that Deborah accompanied Rebecca to Canaan and stayed there, and now had come to greet Jacob after hearing that he was approaching his parents' home.

Some commentaries maintain that this verse alludes to the death of Rebecca herself (*Bereshit Rabba* 81:5; *Targum Yonatan*). It has been suggested that Rebecca's death is not mentioned because her death and burial were kept secret (*Pesikta deRav Kahana* 3:1; *Midrash Tanḥuma, Ki Tetze* 4; see Ramban). Rebecca was buried in the Cave of Makhpela. Due to Isaac's blindness, he

was incapable of organizing a large ceremony; Jacob lived far away and was unable to attend; and her only remaining son, Esau, had a difficult relationship with her and might not have come. Consequently, she was probably buried discreetly by members of Isaac's household. It is therefore possible that the death of Deborah, which occurred around the same time, left a greater impression than the passing of Rebecca, as Jacob and his family were aware of it and mourned her.

ה א וַיֹּאמֶר אֱלֹהִים אֶל־יַעֲקֹב קוּם עֲלֵה בֵית־אֵל וְשֶׁב־שָׁם וַעֲשֵׂה־שָׁם מִזְבֵּחַ לָאֵל

ב הַנִּרְאֶה אֵלֶיךָ בְּבָרְחֲךָ מִפְּנֵי עֵשָׂו אָחִיךָ: וַיֹּאמֶר יַעֲקֹב אֶל־בֵּיתוֹ וְאֶל כָּל־אֲשֶׁר

ג עִמּוֹ הָסִרוּ אֶת־אֱלֹהֵי הַנֵּכָר אֲשֶׁר בְּתֹכְכֶם וְהִטַּהֲרוּ וְהַחֲלִיפוּ שִׂמְלֹתֵיכֶם: וְנָקוּמָה

וְנַעֲלֶה בֵּית־אֵל וְאֶעֱשֶׂה־שָּׁם מִזְבֵּחַ לָאֵל הָעֹנֶה אֹתִי בְּיוֹם צָרָתִי וַיְהִי עִמָּדִי

ד בַּדֶּרֶךְ אֲשֶׁר הָלָכְתִּי: וַיִּתְּנוּ אֶל־יַעֲקֹב אֵת כָּל־אֱלֹהֵי הַנֵּכָר אֲשֶׁר בְּיָדָם וְאֶת־

ה הַנְּזָמִים אֲשֶׁר בְּאָזְנֵיהֶם וַיִּטְמֹן אֹתָם יַעֲקֹב תַּחַת הָאֵלָה אֲשֶׁר עִם־שְׁכֶם: וַיִּסָּעוּ

וַיְהִי ׀ חִתַּת אֱלֹהִים עַל־הֶעָרִים אֲשֶׁר סְבִיבוֹתֵיהֶם וְלֹא רָדְפוּ אַחֲרֵי בְּנֵי יַעֲקֹב:

ו וַיָּבֹא יַעֲקֹב לוּזָה אֲשֶׁר בְּאֶרֶץ כְּנַעַן הִוא בֵּית־אֵל הוּא וְכָל־הָעָם אֲשֶׁר־עִמּוֹ:

ז וַיִּבֶן שָׁם מִזְבֵּחַ וַיִּקְרָא לַמָּקוֹם אֵל בֵּית־אֵל כִּי שָׁם נִגְלוּ אֵלָיו הָאֱלֹהִים בְּבָרְחוֹ

ח מִפְּנֵי אָחִיו: וַתָּמָת דְּבֹרָה מֵינֶקֶת רִבְקָה וַתִּקָּבֵר מִתַּחַת לְבֵית־אֵל תַּחַת הָאַלּוֹן

וַיִּקְרָא שְׁמוֹ אַלּוֹן בָּכוּת:

ט וַיֵּרָא אֱלֹהִים אֶל־יַעֲקֹב עוֹד בְּבֹאוֹ מִפַּדַּן אֲרָם וַיְבָרֶךְ אֹתוֹ: וַיֹּאמֶר־לוֹ אֱלֹהִים לֹא

שִׁמְךָ יַעֲקֹב לֹא־יִקָּרֵא שִׁמְךָ עוֹד יַעֲקֹב כִּי אִם־יִשְׂרָאֵל יִהְיֶה שְׁמֶךָ וַיִּקְרָא אֶת־

רש"י

פרק לה

א קוּם עֲלֵה. לְפִי שֶׁאֵחַרְתָּ בַּדֶּרֶךְ נֶעֱנַשְׁתָּ וּבָא לְךָ זֹאת מִבִּתְּךָ:

ב הַנֵּכָר. שֶׁיֵּשׁ בְּיֶדְכֶם מִשְּׁלַל שֶׁל שְׁכֶם: **וְהִטַּהֲרוּ.** מֵעֲבוֹדָה זָרָה: **וְהַחֲלִיפוּ שִׂמְלֹתֵיכֶם.** שֶׁמָּא יֵשׁ בְּיֶדְכֶם כְּסוּת שֶׁל עֲבוֹדָה זָרָה:

ד הָאֵלָה. מִין אִילָן סְרָק: **עִם שְׁכֶם.** אֵצֶל שְׁכֶם:

ה חִתַּת. פַּחַד:

ז אֵל בֵּית אֵל. הַקָּדוֹשׁ בָּרוּךְ הוּא בְּבֵית אֵל, גִּלּוּי שְׁכִינָתוֹ בְּבֵית אֵל. יֵשׁ תֵּבָה חֲסֵרָה בֵּי"ת הַמְשַׁמֶּשֶׁת בְּרֹאשָׁהּ, כְּמוֹ

"הִנֵּה הוּא בֵּית מָכִיר בֶּן עַמִּיאֵל" (שמואל ב' ט, ד) כְּמוֹ: "בְּבֵית מָכִיר", "בֵּית אָבִיךְ" (להלן לח, יא) כְּמוֹ "בְּבֵית אָבִיךְ": **נִגְלוּ אֵלָיו הָאֱלֹהִים.** בִּמְקוֹמוֹת הַרְבֵּה יֵשׁ שֵׁם אֱלֹהוּת וַאֲדוֹנוּת בִּלְשׁוֹן רַבִּים, כְּמוֹ: "אֲדֹנֵי יוֹסֵף" (להלן לט, כ), "אִם בְּעָלָיו עִמּוֹ" (שמות כב, יד) וְלֹא נֶאֱמַר "בַּעֲלוֹ", וְכֵן אֱלֹהוּת שֶׁהוּא לְשׁוֹן שׁוֹפֵט וּמָרוּת נִזְכָּר בִּלְשׁוֹן רַבִּים, אֲבָל אֶחָד מִכָּל שְׁאָר הַשֵּׁמוֹת לֹא תִּמְצָא בִּלְשׁוֹן רַבִּים:

ח וַתָּמָת דְּבֹרָה. מֶה עִנְיַן דְּבוֹרָה בְּבֵית יַעֲקֹב? אֶלָּא לְפִי שֶׁאָמְרָה רִבְקָה לְיַעֲקֹב "וְשָׁלַחְתִּי וּלְקַחְתִּיךָ מִשָּׁם" (לעיל כז, מה) שָׁלְחָה דְּבוֹרָה אֶצְלוֹ לְפַדַּן אֲרָם לָצֵאת מִשָּׁם, וּמֵתָה בַּדֶּרֶךְ. מִדִּבְרֵי רַבִּי מֹשֶׁה הַדַּרְשָׁן לְמַדְתִּיהָ: **מִתַּחַת לְבֵית אֵל.** הָעִיר יוֹשֶׁבֶת בָּהָר וְנִקְבְּרָה בְּרַגְלֵי הָהָר: **תַּחַת**

הָאַלּוֹן. "בְּשִׁפּוּלֵי מִישְׁרָא", שֶׁהָיָה מִישׁוֹר מִלְמַעְלָה בְּשִׁפּוּעַ הָהָר וְהַקְּבוּרָה מִלְּמַטָּה. וּמִישׁוֹר שֶׁל בֵּית אֵל הָיוּ קוֹרִין לוֹ "אַלּוֹן". וְאַגָּדָה, נִתְבַּשֵּׂר שָׁם בְּאֵבֶל שֵׁנִי, שֶׁהֻגַּד לוֹ עַל אִמּוֹ שֶׁמֵּתָה, וְ"אַלּוֹן" בִּלְשׁוֹן יְוָנִי – "אַחֵר", וּלְפִי שֶׁהֶעֱלִימוּ אֶת יוֹם מוֹתָהּ, שֶׁלֹּא יְקַלְלוּ הַבְּרִיּוֹת כֶּרֶס שֶׁיָּצָא עֵשָׂו מִמֶּנּוּ, אַף הַכָּתוּב לֹא פִּרְסְמָהּ:

ט עוֹד. פַּעַם שֵׁנִי בַּמָּקוֹם הַזֶּה, אֶחָד בְּלֶכְתּוֹ וְאֶחָד בְּשׁוּבוֹ: **וַיְבָרֶךְ אֹתוֹ.** בִּרְכַּת אֲבֵלִים:

י לֹא יִקָּרֵא שִׁמְךָ עוֹד יַעֲקֹב. לְשׁוֹן אָדָם הַבָּא מִמַּאֲרָב וְעָקְבָה, אֶלָּא לְשׁוֹן שַׂר וְנָגִיד:

BACKGROUND

35:9 | Padan Aram: *Padan* means plowed field in Aramaic and Arabic. The meaning of the compound name Padan Aram is the region of Aram, as in the verse: Jacob fled to the field of Aram (Hosea 12:13). This is apparently referring to the general area of Haran; however, some commentaries maintain that the reference is specifically to the city of Haran.

by God Himself. Similarly, Ishmael's name was originally announced before his birth by an angel (16:11) and was later given to him officially (16:15).

11 **God said to him: I am God Almighty.** This name alludes to God's might and His power to grant offspring. **Be fruitful and multiply; a nation and an assembly of nations shall be from you, and kings shall emerge from your loins.** Your offspring will merit greatness.

12 **And the land that I gave to Abraham and Isaac, I will give it to you, and to your descendants after you I will give the land.**

Sixth aliya

13 **God ascended from upon him in the place that He spoke with him.**

14 Apparently, Jacob did not sacrifice an offering as soon as he reached Beit El, but only after he had stayed there a while. **Jacob established a monument in the place that He spoke with him, a monument of stone, and he poured out a libation** of wine **upon it,**[20] **and poured oil upon it** in commemoration of this further revelation.

15 **Jacob** again **called the name of the place where God had spoken with him Beit El,** to reiterate that the place was a house of God where the Divine Presence rested (see 28:17–22). The city of Beersheba is likewise named twice.[21]

The Birth of Benjamin and Rachel's Death

GENESIS 35:16–20

Rachel was the only matriarch who was not buried in the family burial plot in the Cave of Makhpela in Hebron. Tragically, Rachel, who had said to Jacob: "Give me children, and if not, I am dead" (30:1), passed away while giving birth to her second child.

The Sages, with their keen powers of observation, associate Rachel's death with the fulfillment of the unwitting curse that Jacob uttered while Laban was searching for his idols in Jacob's camp. In complete faith that no one from his family could have stolen the idols, Jacob declared: "With whomever you find your gods, he shall not live" (31:32). Alas, it was Rachel who stole them, and due to this mistaken curse she died prematurely.

16 **They traveled** south **from Beit El; and it was still some distance**[22] **to** when they would **arrive at** the city of **Efrat; and Rachel was in childbirth, and she had difficulty in her childbirth.**

17 **It was as she was having difficulty in her childbirth,** that **the midwife said to her: Fear not, for this too is a son for you.**

18 **It was with the departure of her soul, for she was dying** in childbirth, that **she called his name Ben Oni,** son of my pain and anguish. **And** yet **his father** did not wish to call him by that name. Instead, he chose to interpret his wife's statement in a positive manner, that *oni* meant my might, rather than my anguish. He therefore **called him Benjamin,** the right-hand son, or the strong son.[23]

19 **Rachel died, and she was buried on the path to Efrat, it is Bethlehem.** Had Rachel given birth in a populated area, people might have been able to help her. However, she died on the road, and Jacob buried her there rather than in the city.

20 **Jacob established a monument upon her grave; it is the monument of Rachel's grave**[B] **until today.** This monument lasted for many generations. Although its appearance possibly changed over the course of time, it remained standing and is mentioned elsewhere.[24]

21 **Israel traveled, and pitched his tent beyond Migdal Eder,**[B] south of Bethlehem.[25]

Summaries Involving Jacob's Family

GENESIS 35:22–29

A major chapter in the life of Jacob, which incorporated his departure to Haran and his return to Canaan, has ended. This section, which lists the chieftains of Esau's family, separates the accounts of Jacob's two exiles: His first exile, during which he established his family until his return to Canaan, and the events that will ultimately lead to his second exile, together with his family, to Egypt.

The tension between Jacob's two main wives, Rachel and Leah, persists through the next generation and becomes the major cause of the unfortunate incidents that shape the family's future.

22 **It was when Israel dwelled in that land,** Canaan, on his way to his father's home, **that Reuben went and lay with Bilha,**[D] **his father's concubine.** The fact that the verse calls her a concubine might be a reflection of Reuben's opinion, as he perhaps

DISCUSSION

35:22| **And lay with Bilha:** According to one opinion, Reuben did not actually have relations with Bilha; rather, he "disturbed her bedding." The Sages explain that after Rachel's death, her maidservant Bilha took her place as Jacob's chief wife. Reuben, Leah's firstborn son, outraged at the insult to his mother, entered Bilha's tent and disturbed her bed linens. This was either a sort of symbolic protest to his father or perhaps an attempt to give the impression that Bilha had had relations with him, rendering her forbidden to Jacob (Shabbat 55b; Targum Yonatan; Rashi; Ramban).

יא | שְׁמוֹ יִשְׂרָאֵל: וַיֹּאמֶר לוֹ אֱלֹהִים אֲנִי אֵל שַׁדַּי פְּרֵה וּרְבֵה גּוֹי וּקְהַל גּוֹיִם יִהְיֶה

יב | מִמֶּךָּ וּמְלָכִים מֵחֲלָצֶיךָ יֵצֵאוּ: וְאֶת־הָאָרֶץ אֲשֶׁר נָתַתִּי לְאַבְרָהָם וּלְיִצְחָק לְךָ

יג | אֶתְּנֶנָּה וּלְזַרְעֲךָ אַחֲרֶיךָ אֶתֵּן אֶת־הָאָרֶץ: וַיַּעַל מֵעָלָיו אֱלֹהִים בַּמָּקוֹם אֲשֶׁר־

יד | דִּבֶּר אִתּוֹ: וַיַּצֵּב יַעֲקֹב מַצֵּבָה בַּמָּקוֹם אֲשֶׁר־דִּבֶּר אִתּוֹ מַצֶּבֶת אָבֶן וַיַּסֵּךְ עָלֶיהָ

טו | נֶסֶךְ וַיִּצֹק עָלֶיהָ שָׁמֶן: וַיִּקְרָא יַעֲקֹב אֶת־שֵׁם הַמָּקוֹם אֲשֶׁר דִּבֶּר אִתּוֹ שָׁם אֱלֹהִים

טז | בֵּית־אֵל: וַיִּסְעוּ מִבֵּית אֵל וַיְהִי־עוֹד כִּבְרַת־הָאָרֶץ לָבוֹא אֶפְרָתָה וַתֵּלֶד רָחֵל

יז | וַתְּקַשׁ בְּלִדְתָּהּ: וַיְהִי בְהַקְשֹׁתָהּ בְּלִדְתָּהּ וַתֹּאמֶר לָהּ הַמְיַלֶּדֶת אַל־תִּירְאִי כִּי־

יח | גַם־זֶה לָךְ בֵּן: וַיְהִי בְּצֵאת נַפְשָׁהּ כִּי מֵתָה וַתִּקְרָא שְׁמוֹ בֶּן־אוֹנִי וְאָבִיו קָרָא־לוֹ

יט | בִנְיָמִין: וַתָּמָת רָחֵל וַתִּקָּבֵר בְּדֶרֶךְ אֶפְרָתָה הִוא בֵּית לָחֶם: וַיַּצֵּב יַעֲקֹב מַצֵּבָה

כ | עַל־קְבֻרָתָהּ הִוא מַצֶּבֶת קְבֻרַת־רָחֵל עַד־הַיּוֹם: וַיִּסַּע יִשְׂרָאֵל וַיֵּט אָהֳלֹה מֵהָלְאָה

כב | לְמִגְדַּל־עֵדֶר: וַיְהִי בִּשְׁכֹּן יִשְׂרָאֵל בָּאָרֶץ הַהִוא וַיֵּלֶךְ רְאוּבֵן וַיִּשְׁכַּב אֶת־בִּלְהָה

רש"י

יא | אֲנִי אֵל שַׁדַּי. שֶׁאֲנִי כְדַאי לְבָרֵךְ, שֶׁהַבְּרָכוֹת שֶׁלִּי: **פְּרֵה וּרְבֵה.** עַל שֵׁם שֶׁעֲדַיִן לֹא נוֹלַד בִּנְיָמִין, וְאַף עַל פִּי שֶׁכְּבָר נִתְעַבְּרָה מִמֶּנּוּ: **גּוֹי. בִּנְיָמִין: גּוֹיִם.** מְנַשֶּׁה וְאֶפְרַיִם שֶׁעֲתִידִים לָצֵאת מִיּוֹסֵף וְהֵם בְּמִנְיַן הַשְּׁבָטִים: **וּמְלָכִים.** שָׁאוּל וְאִישׁ בֹּשֶׁת שֶׁהָיוּ מִשֵּׁבֶט בִּנְיָמִין שֶׁעֲדַיִן לֹא נוֹלַד:

יד | בַּמָּקוֹם אֲשֶׁר דִּבֶּר אִתּוֹ. אֵינִי יוֹדֵעַ מַה מְלַמְּדֵנוּ:

טו | כִּבְרַת הָאָרֶץ. מְנַחֵם פֵּרַשׁ לְשׁוֹן כַּבִּיר, רִבּוּי, מַהֲלַךְ רַב. וּמִדְרַשׁ אַגָּדָה, בִּזְמַן שֶׁקָּרְקַע חֲלוּלָה כַּכְּבָרָה, שֶׁהַנִּיר מָצוּי, הַסְּתָו עָבַר וְהַשָּׁרָב עֲדַיִן לֹא בָּא. וְאֵין זֶה פְּשׁוּטוֹ שֶׁל מִקְרָא, שֶׁהֲרֵי בְּנַעֲמָן מָצִינוּ: "וַיֵּלֶךְ מֵאִתּוֹ כִּבְרַת אָרֶץ"

(מלכים ב' ה, יט). וְאוֹמֵר אֲנִי שֶׁהוּא שֵׁם מִדַּת קַרְקַע, כְּמוֹ מַהֲלַךְ פַּרְסָה אוֹ יוֹתֵר, כְּמוֹ שֶׁאַתָּה אוֹמֵר: צֶמֶד כֶּרֶם, 'חֶלְקַת שָׂדֶה', כָּךְ בְּמַהֲלַךְ אָדָם נָתַן שֵׁם מִדָּה – כִּבְרַת אָרֶץ:

יז | כִּי גַם זֶה. נוֹסָף לָךְ עַל יוֹסֵף. וְרַבּוֹתֵינוּ דָּרְשׁוּ, עִם כָּל שֵׁבֶט נוֹלְדָה תְּאוֹמָה, וְעִם בִּנְיָמִין נוֹלְדָה תְּאוֹמָה יְתֵרָה:

יח | בֶּן אוֹנִי. בֶּן צַעֲרִי: **בִנְיָמִין.** נִרְאֶה בְעֵינַי לְפִי שֶׁהוּא לְבַדּוֹ נוֹלַד בְּאֶרֶץ כְּנַעַן שֶׁהִיא בַּנֶּגֶב כְּשֶׁאָדָם בָּא מֵאֲרַם נַהֲרַיִם, כְּמוֹ שֶׁנֶּאֱמַר: "בַּנֶּגֶב בְּאֶרֶץ כְּנָעַן" (במדבר לג, מ),

"הָלוֹךְ וְנָסוֹעַ הַנֶּגְבָּה" (לעיל יב, ט). 'בִּנְיָמִין' – בֶּן יָמִין, לְשׁוֹן "צָפוֹן וְיָמִין אַתָּה בְרָאתָם" (תהלים פט, יג), לְפִיכָךְ הוּא מָלֵא:

כב | בִּשְׁכֹּן יִשְׂרָאֵל בָּאָרֶץ הַהִוא. עַד שֶׁלֹּא בָּא לְחֶבְרוֹן אֵצֶל יִצְחָק אֵרְעוּהוּ כָּל אֵלֶּה: **וַיִּשְׁכַּב.** מִתּוֹךְ שֶׁבִּלְבֵּל מִשְׁכָּבוֹ מַעֲלֶה עָלָיו הַכָּתוּב כְּאִלּוּ שְׁכָבָהּ. וְלָמָּה בִּלְבֵּל וְחִלֵּל יְצוּעָיו? שֶׁכְּשֶׁמֵּתָה רָחֵל נָטַל יַעֲקֹב מִטָּתוֹ שֶׁהָיְתָה נְתוּנָה תָּדִיר בְּאֹהֶל רָחֵל וְלֹא בִּשְׁאָר אֹהָלִים, וּנְתָנָהּ בְּאֹהֶל בִּלְהָה. בָּא רְאוּבֵן וְתָבַע עֶלְבּוֹן אִמּוֹ, אָמַר: אִם אֲחוֹת אִמִּי הָיְתָה צָרָה לְאִמִּי, שִׁפְחַת אֲחוֹת אִמִּי תְּהֵא

BACKGROUND

35:20| **The monument of Rachel's grave:** Commentaries and historians disagree with regard to the location of Rachel's grave. The accepted tradition, based on the verses here, is that she was buried near Bethlehem. This location is also mentioned in travel logs dating back to the fourth century CE. However, some claim that Ra-

chel was buried in Al Ram, which is in the portion of Benjamin, north of Jerusalem, as indicated by I Samuel 10:2 and Jeremiah 31:14.

35:21 | **Migdal Eder:** This location is mentioned in the rabbinic literature as a village near Jerusalem (Mishna *Shekalim* 7:4; *Avot deRabbi Natan* version B, chap. 29). Some experts suggest

that it is Khirbat el Bireh, near Solomon's Pools, about 5 km south of Bethlehem. Others suggest that Migdal Eder is south of Beit El, based on the Septuagint and the text of the Bubastite Portal at Karnak (Egypt, tenth century BCE). In this relief, Migdal is listed among the cities north of Jerusalem conquered by Shishak, or Shoshenq I.

did not consider Bilha, who was presumably younger than his mother, his father's legal wife. **And Israel heard.**[D] Although he was clearly distressed and humiliated by this deed, Jacob chose not to react immediately. Only on his deathbed did he respond by cursing Reuben (49:3–4). The verse concludes: **The sons of Jacob were twelve.** Jacob did not banish his sinful son; he continued to be counted among his sons.

23 The chapter lists all of Jacob's sons. **The sons of Leah** were **Reuben,** who is still **Jacob's firstborn,** although on his deathbed Jacob will dismiss him from this status, **and Simeon, Levi, Judah, Issachar, and Zebulun.**

24 **The sons of Rachel** were **Joseph and Benjamin.**

25 **The sons of Bilha, Rachel's maidservant,** were **Dan and Naftali.**

26 **And the sons of Zilpa, Leah's maidservant,** were **Gad and Asher. These are the sons of Jacob, who were born to him in**

Padan Aram, apart from Benjamin, who was born in the land of Canaan.

27 **Jacob** continued southward and **came to Isaac his father at Mamre, Kiryat Ha'arba, which is Hebron, where Abraham and Isaac resided.** The verse records Jacob's return to his father's home, but relates nothing about their reunion or any events that transpired in Isaac's last years.

28 **The days of Isaac were one hundred years and eighty years.**

29 **Isaac expired, and he died, and he was gathered to his people.** When a person passes away, he returns, as it were, to the souls of his parents and family. Isaac died **old and full of days;** he had reached a very advanced age. **Esau and Jacob his sons buried him.** Esau came from the land of Se'ir to bury his father together with Jacob, in the Cave of Makhpela in Hebron.

The Descendants of Esau
GENESIS 36:1–43

After the Torah finished telling the story of Abraham's life, a short passage was devoted to Ishmael's family (25:12–18). Here, following the description of Isaac's death, whose burial was attended by both his sons, this section lists Esau's descendants and relates their history. Before continuing with the primary Torah narrative, which follows Jacob and his family, the Torah digresses and focuses on Esau's descendants. Esau had also received a blessing from his father, and this section describes its fulfillment, as his descendants ruled over a land of their own through an independent government. It is notable that the history of Esau's children was intertwined with that of Jacob's descendants for many generations, alternating between the roles of allies and adversaries.

36 1 **These are the descendants of Esau who is Edom.** As mentioned earlier, Esau was nicknamed Edom after the red [*adom*] stew he requested from Jacob (25:25–30). Presumably, the name was also due to his red hair.

2 **Esau took his wives from the daughters of Canaan,** as stated above (26:34–35): **Ada, daughter of Eilon the Hitite, and Oholivama, daughter of Ana, daughter of Tzivon the Hivite.**

3 After marrying two Canaanite women, Esau subsequently acquiesced to his parents' desire that he take a wife from the family, **and** he married his cousin **Basmat, daughter of Ishmael, sister of Nevayot.**

4 **Ada bore Elifaz to Esau,** his firstborn son; **and Basmat bore Re'uel;**

5 **and Oholivama bore Yeush, Ya'elam, and Korah; these are the sons of Esau, who were born to him** while he still lived **in the land of Canaan.**

6 However, **Esau** subsequently **took his wives, his sons, his daughters, all the members of his household, his livestock, all his animals, and all his possessions that he** had **acquired in the land of Canaan, and went to a land,**[D] a different region, **due to his brother Jacob,**

7 because their property was too great for living together, and the land of their residence could not support them due to their livestock. Although Isaac was a farmer, his two sons

DISCUSSION

And Israel heard: The verse does not state why Jacob did not respond immediately, leaving the matter open to speculation. Whatever the reason, the traditional masoretic text of the Bible leaves an empty space in the middle of this verse. This rare phenomenon indicates that there is much to be said about the serious matter discussed in this verse, but the chapter itself does not go into the details (see Joshua 4:1).

36:6 | And went to a land: Esau left Canaan before Jacob's return and settled in the land of Se'ir (32:4, 33:16). Sometime after Jacob fled to Haran, Esau moved east of the Jordan River with his family and belongings, perhaps because he realized that his father had designated the land of Canaan for Jacob. It is possible that Esau established his kingdom in Se'ir because that land is adjacent to Canaan, even if it is not part of it, as it is located between his father's home in Canaan

and his father-in-law Ishmael's place in Paran. Perhaps Esau returned to live near his father in Isaac's old age, or he maintained a home in both places and would alternate between them. If so, this verse is stating that Esau left Canaan permanently when Jacob returned with his family and cattle to live alongside his father (see Ramban; Radak, here and 32:4).

כג פִּילֶגֶשׁ אָבִיו וַיִּשְׁמַע יִשְׂרָאֵל וַיִּהְיוּ בְנֵי־יַעֲקֹב שְׁנֵים עָשָׂר: בְּנֵי לֵאָה בְּכוֹר יַעֲקֹב
כד כה רְאוּבֵן וְשִׁמְעוֹן וְלֵוִי וִיהוּדָה וְיִשָּׂשכָר וּזְבוּלֻן: בְּנֵי רָחֵל יוֹסֵף וּבִנְיָמִן: וּבְנֵי בִלְהָה
כו שִׁפְחַת רָחֵל דָּן וְנַפְתָּלִי: וּבְנֵי זִלְפָּה שִׁפְחַת לֵאָה גָּד וְאָשֵׁר אֵלֶּה בְּנֵי יַעֲקֹב אֲשֶׁר
כז יֻלַּד־לוֹ בְּפַדַּן אֲרָם: וַיָּבֹא יַעֲקֹב אֶל־יִצְחָק אָבִיו מַמְרֵא קִרְיַת הָאַרְבַּע הִוא חֶבְרוֹן
כח כט אֲשֶׁר־גָּר־שָׁם אַבְרָהָם וְיִצְחָק: וַיִּהְיוּ יְמֵי יִצְחָק מְאַת שָׁנָה וּשְׁמֹנִים שָׁנָה: וַיִּגְוַע
יִצְחָק וַיָּמָת וַיֵּאָסֶף אֶל־עַמָּיו זָקֵן וּשְׂבַע יָמִים וַיִּקְבְּרוּ אֹתוֹ עֵשָׂו וְיַעֲקֹב בָּנָיו:
ו א ב וְאֵלֶּה תֹּלְדוֹת עֵשָׂו הוּא אֱדוֹם: עֵשָׂו לָקַח אֶת־נָשָׁיו מִבְּנוֹת כְּנָעַן אֶת־עָדָה
ג בַּת־אֵילוֹן הַחִתִּי וְאֶת־אָהֳלִיבָמָה בַּת־עֲנָה בַּת־צִבְעוֹן הַחִוִּי: וְאֶת־בָּשְׂמַת
ד בַּת־יִשְׁמָעֵאל אֲחוֹת נְבָיוֹת: וַתֵּלֶד עָדָה לְעֵשָׂו אֶת־אֱלִיפָז וּבָשְׂמַת יָלְדָה
ה אֶת־רְעוּאֵל: וְאָהֳלִיבָמָה יָלְדָה אֶת־יעיש וְאֶת־יַעְלָם וְאֶת־קֹרַח אֵלֶּה יְעוּשׁ
ו בְּנֵי עֵשָׂו אֲשֶׁר יֻלְּדוּ־לוֹ בְּאֶרֶץ כְּנָעַן: וַיִּקַּח עֵשָׂו אֶת־נָשָׁיו וְאֶת־בָּנָיו וְאֶת־
בְּנֹתָיו וְאֶת־כָּל־נַפְשׁוֹת בֵּיתוֹ וְאֶת־מִקְנֵהוּ וְאֶת־כָּל־בְּהֶמְתּוֹ וְאֵת כָּל־קִנְיָנוֹ
ז אֲשֶׁר רָכַשׁ בְּאֶרֶץ כְּנָעַן וַיֵּלֶךְ אֶל־אֶרֶץ מִפְּנֵי יַעֲקֹב אָחִיו: כִּי־הָיָה רְכוּשָׁם
רָב מִשֶּׁבֶת יַחְדָּו וְלֹא יָכְלָה אֶרֶץ מְגוּרֵיהֶם לָשֵׂאת אֹתָם מִפְּנֵי מִקְנֵיהֶם:

רש"י

נִרְאָה לְאָמָּהּ?: **וַיִּהְיוּ בְנֵי יַעֲקֹב שְׁנֵים עָשָׂר.** מַתְחִיל לְעִנְיָן רִאשׁוֹן: מִשֶּׁנּוֹלַד בִּנְיָמִין נִשְׁלְמָה הַמִּטָּה וּמֵעַתָּה רְאוּיִים לְהִמָּנוֹת, וּמְנָאָן. וְרַבּוֹתֵינוּ דָּרְשׁוּ, לְלַמְּדֵנוּ בָּא שֶׁכֻּלָּם שָׁוִים וְכֻלָּם צַדִּיקִים, שֶׁלֹּא חָטָא רְאוּבֵן:

כג| **בְּכוֹר יַעֲקֹב.** אֲפִלּוּ בִּשְׁעַת הַקַּלְקָלָה קְרָאוֹ בְּכוֹר: **בְּכוֹר יַעֲקֹב.** בְּכוֹר לְנַחֲלָה, בְּכוֹר לַעֲבוֹדָה, בְּכוֹר לַמִּנְיָן. וְלֹא נִתְּנָה בְּכוֹרָה לְיוֹסֵף אֶלָּא לְעִנְיַן הַשְּׁבָטִים, שֶׁנַּעֲשָׂה לִשְׁנֵי שְׁבָטִים:

כז| **מַמְרֵא.** שֵׁם הַמִּישׁוֹר: **קִרְיַת הָאַרְבַּע.** שֵׁם הָעִיר: **מַמְרֵא קִרְיַת הָאַרְבַּע.** אֶל מִישׁוֹר שֶׁל קִרְיַת אַרְבַּע. וְאִם תֹּאמַר, הָיָה לוֹ לִכְתֹּב 'מַמְרֵא הַקִּרְיַת אַרְבַּע'? כֵּן דֶּרֶךְ הַמִּקְרָא בְּכָל דָּבָר שֶׁשְּׁמוֹ כָּפוּל, כְּגוֹן זֶה, וּכְגוֹן: בֵּית לֶחֶם, אֲבִי עֶזֶר, בֵּית אֵל, אִם הֻצְרַךְ לְהַטִּיל בּוֹ הֵ"א נוֹתְנָהּ בְּרֹאשׁ תֵּבָה הַשְּׁנִיָּה: "בֵּית הַלַּחְמִי" (שמואל א' טז, א), "בְּעָפְרַת אֲבִי הָעֶזְרִי" (שופטים ו, כד), "בָּנָה חִיאֵל בֵּית הָאֱלִי" (מלכים א' טז, לד):

כט| **וַיִּגְוַע יִצְחָק.** אֵין מֻקְדָּם וּמְאֻחָר בַּתּוֹרָה; מְכִירָתוֹ שֶׁל יוֹסֵף קָדְמָה לְמִיתָתוֹ שֶׁל יִצְחָק שְׁתֵּים עֶשְׂרֵה שָׁנָה, שֶׁהֲרֵי יִצְחָק מֵת בִּשְׁנַת מֵאָה וְעֶשְׂרִים לְיַעֲקֹב, שֶׁנֶּאֱמַר: "וְיִצְחָק בֶּן שִׁשִּׁים שָׁנָה בְּלֶדֶת אֹתָם" (לעיל כה, כו), צֵא שִׁשִּׁים מִמֵּאָה וּשְׁמוֹנִים נִשְׁאֲרוּ מֵאָה וְעֶשְׂרִים; וְיוֹסֵף נִמְכַּר בֶּן שֶׁבַע עֶשְׂרֵה שָׁנָה, וְאוֹתָהּ שָׁנָה שְׁנַת מֵאָה וּשְׁמוֹנֶה לְיַעֲקֹב, כֵּיצַד? בֶּן שִׁשִּׁים וְשָׁלֹשׁ נִתְבָּרֵךְ, אַרְבַּע עֶשְׂרֵה שָׁנָה נִטְמַן בְּבֵית עֵבֶר, הֲרֵי שִׁבְעִים וְשֶׁבַע, וְאַרְבַּע עֶשְׂרֵה עָבַד בְּאִשָּׁה, וּבְסוֹף אַרְבַּע עֶשְׂרֵה נוֹלַד יוֹסֵף, שֶׁנֶּאֱמַר: "וַיְהִי כַּאֲשֶׁר יָלְדָה רָחֵל אֶת יוֹסֵף" וְגוֹ' (לעיל ל, כה), הֲרֵי תִּשְׁעִים וְאַחַת, וּשְׁבַע עֶשְׂרֵה עַד שֶׁלֹּא נִמְכַּר, הֲרֵי מֵאָה וּשְׁמוֹנֶה:

פרק לו

ב| **עָדָה בַּת אֵילוֹן.** הִיא "בָּשְׂמַת בַּת אֵילֹן" (לעיל כו, לד), וְנִקְרֵאת בָּשְׂמַת עַל שֵׁם שֶׁהָיְתָה מְקַטֶּרֶת בְּשָׂמִים לַעֲבוֹדָה זָרָה: **אָהֳלִיבָמָה.** הִיא יְהוּדִית, וְאוֹתוֹ רָשָׁע כִּנָּה שְׁמָהּ יְהוּדִית לוֹמַר שֶׁהִיא כּוֹפֶרֶת בַּעֲבוֹדָה זָרָה כְּדֵי לְהַטְעוֹת אֶת אָבִיו: **בַּת עֲנָה בַּת צִבְעוֹן.** אִם בַּת עֲנָה לֹא בַּת צִבְעוֹן? עֲנָה בְּנוֹ שֶׁל צִבְעוֹן, שֶׁנֶּאֱמַר: "וְאֵלֶּה בְנֵי צִבְעוֹן וְאַיָּה וַעֲנָה" (להלן פסוק כד)! מְלַמֵּד שֶׁבָּא צִבְעוֹן עַל כַּלָּתוֹ אֵשֶׁת עֲנָה וְיָצְאָה אָהֳלִיבָמָה מִבֵּין שְׁנֵיהֶם, וְהוֹדִיעֲךָ הַכָּתוּב שֶׁכֻּלָּן בְּנֵי מַמְזֵרוּת הָיוּ:

ג| **בָּשְׂמַת בַּת יִשְׁמָעֵאל.** וּלְהַלָּן קוֹרֵא לָהּ 'מָחֲלַת' (לעיל כח, ט)? מָצָאתִי בְּאַגָּדַת מִדְרַשׁ סֵפֶר שְׁמוּאֵל (פרק יז), שְׁלֹשָׁה מוֹחֲלִים לָהֶן עֲווֹנוֹתֵיהֶן: גֵּר שֶׁנִּתְגַּיֵּר, וְהָעוֹלֶה לִגְדֻלָּה, וְהַנּוֹשֵׂא אִשָּׁה. וְלָמַד הַטַּעַם מִכָּאן, לְכָךְ נִקְרֵאת 'מָחֲלַת', שֶׁנִּמְחֲלוּ עֲווֹנוֹתָיו: **אֲחוֹת נְבָיוֹת.** עַל שֵׁם שֶׁהוּא הִשִּׂיאָהּ לוֹ מִשֶּׁמֵּת יִשְׁמָעֵאל:

ה| **וְאָהֳלִיבָמָה יָלְדָה וְגוֹ'.** קֹרַח זֶה מַמְזֵר הָיָה, וּבֶן אֱלִיפַז הָיָה שֶׁבָּא עַל אֵשֶׁת אָבִיו, שֶׁהֲרֵי הוּא מָנוּי עִם אַלּוּפֵי אֱלִיפַז בְּסוֹף הָעִנְיָן:

ו| **וַיֵּלֶךְ אֶל אֶרֶץ.** לָגוּר בַּאֲשֶׁר יִמְצָא:

ז| **וְלֹא יָכְלָה אֶרֶץ מְגוּרֵיהֶם.** לְהַסְפִּיק מִרְעֶה לַבְּהֵמוֹת שֶׁלָּהֶם. וּמִדְרַשׁ אַגָּדָה, "מִפְּנֵי יַעֲקֹב אָחִיו", מִפְּנֵי שְׁטָר חוֹב שֶׁל גְּזֵרַת "כִּי גֵר יִהְיֶה זַרְעֲךָ" (לעיל טו, יג) הַמֻּטָּל

were shepherds. Since both were successful and owned large herds, they were compelled to live far from each other.

8 **Esau settled on Mount Se'ir; Esau who is Edom,** and consequently his descendants are called Edomites.

9 **And this is the legacy of Esau, father of Edom on Mount Se'ir.**

10 **These are the names of** all of **Esau's sons,** those who were born in Canaan and those born in Se'ir: **Elifaz, son of Ada, wife of Esau; Re'uel, son of Basmat, wife of Esau.**

11 **The sons of Elifaz were Teman, Omar, Tzefo, and Gatam, and Kenaz.**

12 **And Timna,** who was probably from a local ruling family, **was a concubine of Elifaz son of Esau and she bore Amalek to Elifaz.**[D] **These are the sons of Ada, wife of Esau.**

13 **And these are the sons of Re'uel: Nahat, and Zerah, Shama, and Mitza; these were the sons of Basmat, wife of Esau.**

14 **And these were the sons of Oholivama, daughter of Ana, daughter of Tzivon, Esau's wife.** It is clarified below that Oholivama was a native of Se'ir (verses 20–25), from the nation that lived there before Esau's arrival. It may be suggested that Esau went there due to this marriage, and on account of this wife he claimed ownership of land on Mount Se'ir. **She bore to Esau Yeush, Ya'elam, and Korah.**

15 **These are the chieftains,**[D] the petty rulers **of** the various tribes that descended from **the sons of Esau,** who did not lose their status even after the kingdom of Edom was established: The chieftains of **the sons of Elifaz, firstborn of Esau,** were **the chieftain of Teman, the chieftain of Omar, the chieftain of Tzefo, the chieftain of Kenaz,** his aforementioned sons (verse 11). As the families grew, each of them was headed by a chief. The name of the patriarch of the family, who was their first chieftain, subsequently became the name of the entire family, e.g., the governor of Teman's descendants was referred to as the chieftain of Teman.

16 **The chieftain of Korah, the chieftain of Gatam, the chieftain of Amalek. These are the chieftains of Elifaz in the land of Edom. These are the sons of Ada.**

17 **And these are the sons of Re'uel son of Esau: The chieftain of Nahat, the chieftain of Zerah, the chieftain of Shama, the chieftain of Mitza; these are the chieftains of Re'uel in the land of Edom, these are the sons of Basmat, wife of Esau.**

18 **And these are the sons of Oholivama, wife of Esau: The chieftain of Yeush, the chieftain of Ya'elam, the chieftain of Korah; these are the chieftains of Oholivama, daughter of Ana, wife of Esau.**

19 **These are the sons of Esau, and these are their chieftains; he is Edom.**

20 **These are the sons of Se'ir the Horite,**[B] the original **inhabitants of the land.** Alongside the Edomite rulers, the native rulers retained a measure of authority: **Lotan, Shoval, Tzivon, Ana,**

Seventh aliya

21 **Dishon, Ezer, and Dishan; these are the chieftains of the Horites, sons of Se'ir in the land of Edom.** This is referring either to actual Horite chieftains who retained their chiefdom to some degree after Esau's family came into power, or to Edomite chieftains who adopted this title from the Horites.

22 **The children of Lotan were Hori and Hemam; and Lotan's sister was Timna,** the concubine of Elifaz, son of Esau (verse 12). Timna, Amalek's mother, is one of the few women mentioned in this section.

23 **And these are the children of Shoval: Alvan, and Manahat, and Eval, Shepho, and Onam.**

24 **And these are the children of Tzivon: Aya and Ana; he is Ana, who found the Yemim in the wilderness.** The word *yemim* is either the name of a nation that descended from primeval giants,[26] or it means mules.[27] **As he was herding the donkeys of Tzivon his father.** The significance of this incident depends on the interpretation of the word *yemim*. If Yemim are giants, the likely explanation is that they tried to steal the donkeys, and Ana stood up to them bravely, for which he became renowned. If they are mules, the statement that Ana found the *yemim* means that he invented them by crossbreeding donkeys and horses, either intentionally or by accident. The verse notes that this happened while he was herding donkeys.

BACKGROUND

36:20 | The Horite: According to Hitite, Ugaritic, and Egyptian documents from the third and second millenniums BCE, this was a nation that originated in Mesopotamia. The Horites wandered and spread out, and their influence was felt throughout the Middle East. Some of them settled in Mount Se'ir, and later assimilated into Esau's family, which had taken over there.

DISCUSSION

36:12 | Amalek: Amalek would play a distinctive historical role. On one hand, he was a member of the family closest to Israel; on the other hand, he was an illegitimate child of Esau's family. This led him and his family to separate from Esau's other descendants and live as nomads. Over the course of history, the Amalekites engaged in many clashes with the Jewish people. It is unclear why they were so hostile toward the Israelites. The Talmud writes that Amalek was perpetually offended by

his mother's inferior status, and blamed it on the arrogance of Jacob's children (*Sanhedrin* 99b).

36:15 | Chieftains [*allufim*]: In modern Hebrew, the word *aluf* denotes a high-ranking army officer; here, however, it means a chieftain or governor. It is possible that the rulers called themselves by this name due to the original meaning of *aluf*, bull (see Psalms 144:14; *Targum Yonatan* and Rashi, Deuteronomy 28:4).

ח ט וַיֵּשֶׁב עֵשָׂו בְּהַר שֵׂעִיר עֵשָׂו הוּא אֱדוֹם: וְאֵלֶּה תֹּלְדוֹת עֵשָׂו אֲבִי אֱדוֹם בְּהַר
י שֵׂעִיר: אֵלֶּה שְׁמוֹת בְּנֵי־עֵשָׂו אֱלִיפַז בֶּן־עָדָה אֵשֶׁת עֵשָׂו רְעוּאֵל בֶּן־בָּשְׂמַת
יא יב אֵשֶׁת עֵשָׂו: וַיִּהְיוּ בְּנֵי אֱלִיפָז תֵּימָן אוֹמָר צְפוֹ וְגַעְתָּם וּקְנַז: וְתִמְנַע ׀ הָיְתָה
פִילֶגֶשׁ לֶאֱלִיפַז בֶּן־עֵשָׂו וַתֵּלֶד לֶאֱלִיפַז אֶת־עֲמָלֵק אֵלֶּה בְּנֵי עָדָה אֵשֶׁת עֵשָׂו:
יג וְאֵלֶּה בְּנֵי רְעוּאֵל נַחַת וָזֶרַח שַׁמָּה וּמִזָּה אֵלֶּה הָיוּ בְּנֵי בָשְׂמַת אֵשֶׁת עֵשָׂו:
יד וְאֵלֶּה הָיוּ בְּנֵי אָהֳלִיבָמָה בַת־עֲנָה בַּת־צִבְעוֹן אֵשֶׁת עֵשָׂו וַתֵּלֶד לְעֵשָׂו אֶת־
טו יעיש וְאֶת־יַעְלָם וְאֶת־קֹרַח: אֵלֶּה אַלּוּפֵי בְנֵי־עֵשָׂו בְּנֵי אֱלִיפַז בְּכוֹר עֵשָׂו יְעוּשׁ
טז אַלּוּף תֵּימָן אַלּוּף אוֹמָר אַלּוּף צְפוֹ אַלּוּף קְנַז: אַלּוּף־קֹרַח אַלּוּף גַּעְתָּם אַלּוּף
יז עֲמָלֵק אֵלֶּה אַלּוּפֵי אֱלִיפַז בְּאֶרֶץ אֱדוֹם אֵלֶּה בְּנֵי עָדָה: וְאֵלֶּה בְּנֵי רְעוּאֵל בֶּן־
עֵשָׂו אַלּוּף נַחַת אַלּוּף זֶרַח אַלּוּף שַׁמָּה אַלּוּף מִזָּה אֵלֶּה אַלּוּפֵי רְעוּאֵל בְּאֶרֶץ
יח אֱדוֹם אֵלֶּה בְּנֵי בָשְׂמַת אֵשֶׁת עֵשָׂו: וְאֵלֶּה בְּנֵי אָהֳלִיבָמָה אֵשֶׁת עֵשָׂו אַלּוּף
יְעוּשׁ אַלּוּף יַעְלָם אַלּוּף קֹרַח אֵלֶּה אַלּוּפֵי אָהֳלִיבָמָה בַּת־עֲנָה אֵשֶׁת עֵשָׂו:
יט כ אֵלֶּה בְנֵי־עֵשָׂו וְאֵלֶּה אַלּוּפֵיהֶם הוּא אֱדוֹם: אֵלֶּה בְנֵי־שֵׂעִיר שביעי
כא הַחֹרִי יֹשְׁבֵי הָאָרֶץ לוֹטָן וְשׁוֹבָל וְצִבְעוֹן וַעֲנָה: וְדִשׁוֹן וְאֵצֶר וְדִישָׁן אֵלֶּה אַלּוּפֵי
כב הַחֹרִי בְּנֵי שֵׂעִיר בְּאֶרֶץ אֱדוֹם: וַיִּהְיוּ בְנֵי־לוֹטָן חֹרִי וְהֵימָם וַאֲחוֹת לוֹטָן תִּמְנָע:
כג כד וְאֵלֶּה בְּנֵי שׁוֹבָל עַלְוָן וּמָנַחַת וְעֵיבָל שְׁפוֹ וְאוֹנָם: וְאֵלֶּה בְנֵי־צִבְעוֹן וְאַיָּה וַעֲנָה
הוּא עֲנָה אֲשֶׁר מָצָא אֶת־הַיֵּמִם בַּמִּדְבָּר בִּרְעֹתוֹ אֶת־הַחֲמֹרִים לְצִבְעוֹן אָבִיו:

רש״י

עַל זַרְעוֹ שֶׁל יִצְחָק, אָמַר: אֵלֵךְ לִי מִכָּאן, אֵין לִי חֵלֶק לֹא בַּמַּתָּנָה שֶׁנִּתְּנָה לוֹ הָאָרֶץ הַזֹּאת וְלֹא בְּפִרְעוֹן הַשְּׁטָר, וּמִפְּנֵי הַבּוּשָׁה שֶׁמָּכַר בְּכוֹרָתוֹ:

ט | **וְאֵלֶּה.** הַתּוֹלָדוֹת שֶׁהוֹלִידוּ בָּנָיו מִשֶּׁהָלַךְ לְשֵׂעִיר:

יב | **וְתִמְנַע הָיְתָה פִילֶגֶשׁ.** לְהוֹדִיעַ גְּדֻלָּתוֹ שֶׁל אַבְרָהָם כַּמָּה הָיוּ תְּאֵבִים לִדָּבֵק בְּזַרְעוֹ. תִּמְנַע זוֹ בַּת אַלּוּפִים הָיְתָה, שֶׁנֶּאֱמַר: ״וַאֲחוֹת לוֹטָן תִּמְנָע״ (להלן פסוק כב), וְלוֹטָן מֵאַלּוּפֵי יוֹשְׁבֵי שֵׂעִיר הָיָה, מִן הַחוֹרִים שֶׁיָּשְׁבוּ בָהּ לְפָנִים; אָמְרָה: אֵינִי זוֹכָה לְהִנָּשֵׂא לְךָ, הַלְוַאי וְאֶהְיֶה פִּילֶגֶשׁ. וּבְדִבְרֵי הַיָּמִים (א׳ א, לו) מוֹנֶה אוֹתָהּ בִּבְנָיו שֶׁל אֱלִיפַז! מְלַמֵּד שֶׁבָּא עַל אִשְׁתּוֹ שֶׁל שֵׂעִיר וְיָצְאָה תִּמְנַע מִבֵּינֵיהֶם, וּכְשֶׁגָּדְלָה נַעֲשֵׂית פִּילַגְשׁוֹ; וְזֶהוּ ״וַאֲחוֹת לוֹטָן תִּמְנָע״ וְלֹא מְנָאָהּ עִם בְּנֵי שֵׂעִיר, שֶׁהָיְתָה אֲחוֹתוֹ מִן הָאֵם וְלֹא מִן הָאָב:

טו | **אֵלֶּה אַלּוּפֵי בְנֵי עֵשָׂו.** רָאשֵׁי מִשְׁפָּחוֹת:

כ | **יֹשְׁבֵי הָאָרֶץ.** שֶׁהָיוּ יוֹשְׁבֶיהָ קֹדֶם שֶׁבָּא עֵשָׂו לְשָׁם. וְרַבּוֹתֵינוּ דָּרְשׁוּ, שֶׁהָיוּ בְּקִיאִין בְּיִשּׁוּבָהּ שֶׁל אֶרֶץ – מְלֹא קָנֶה זֶה לְזֵיתִים מְלֹא קָנֶה זֶה לִגְפָנִים, שֶׁהָיוּ טוֹעֲמִין הֶעָפָר וְיוֹדְעִין אֵי זוֹ נְטִיעָה רְאוּיָה לוֹ:

כד | **וְאַיָּה וַעֲנָה.** וָי״ו יְתֵרָה, וְהוּא כְּמוֹ אַיָּה וַעֲנָה. וְהַרְבֵּה יֵשׁ בַּמִּקְרָא: ״תֵּת וְקֹדֶשׁ וְצָבָא מִרְמָס״ (דניאל ח, יג), ״נִרְדָּם וְרֶכֶב וָסוּס״ (תהלים עו, ז): **הוּא עֲנָה.** הָאָמוּר לְמַעְלָה שֶׁהוּא אָחִיו שֶׁל צִבְעוֹן, וְכָאן הוּא קוֹרֵא אוֹתוֹ בְּנוֹ! מְלַמֵּד שֶׁבָּא צִבְעוֹן עַל אִמּוֹ וְהוֹלִיד אֶת עֲנָה: **אֶת הַיֵּמִם.** פְּרָדִים, הִרְבִּיעַ חֲמוֹר עַל סוּס נְקֵבָה וְיָלְדָה פֶּרֶד, וְהוּא הָיָה מַמְזֵר וְהֵבִיא פְּסוּלִין לָעוֹלָם. וְלָמָּה נִקְרָא שְׁמָם ׳יֵמִים׳? שֶׁאֵימָתָן מֻטֶּלֶת עַל הַבְּרִיּוֹת, דְּאָמַר רַבִּי חֲנִינָא: מִיָּמַי לֹא שְׁאָלַנִי אָדָם עַל מַכַּת פִּרְדָּה לְבָנָה וְחָיָה. לֹא נִזְקַק לִכְתֹּב לָנוּ מִשְׁפְּחוֹת הַחוֹרִי אֶלָּא מִפְּנֵי תִּמְנַע, וּלְהוֹדִיעַ גְּדֻלַּת אַבְרָהָם כְּמוֹ שֶׁפֵּרַשְׁתִּי לְמַעְלָה (לעיל פסוק יב):

25 **And these are the children of Ana: Dishon and** a girl, **Oholivama, daughter of Ana.** She is mentioned because she was Esau's wife.[28]

26 **And these are the children of Dishon: Hemdan, Eshban, Yitran, and Keran.**

27 **These are the children of Ezer: Bilhan, Zaavan, and Akan.**

28 **These are the children of Dishan: Utz and Aran.** The name Utz also appears in the list of the sons of Aram (10:23). Consequently, it is uncertain whether the land of Utz belonged to the Arameans or Edomites.[29]

29 **These are the chieftains of the Horites: the chieftain of Lotan, the chieftain of Shoval, the chieftain of Tzivon, the chieftain of Ana,**

30 **the chieftain of Dishon, the chieftain of Ezer, the chieftain of Dishan; these are the chieftains of the Horites, according to their chieftains in the land of Se'ir.**

31 Thus far, the chapter has listed the chieftains of the Edomite and Horite tribes. When kings began to rule in Edom, the system of government became more centralized. **And these are the kings who reigned in the land of Edom, before the reign of a king for the children of Israel.** During the years when Esau's descendants developed as an independent nation with a central government, Jacob's children were in exile in Egypt and could not appoint a king over themselves. It is possible that the Israelite king to which the verse alludes is Moses, who led the entire Jewish nation. It is similarly stated: "He became king in Yeshurun, when the heads of the people were assembled, the tribes of Israel together."[30]

32 **Bela son of Beor reigned in Edom.** Due to the similarity between their names, some commentaries identify this ruler with Bilam son of Beor.[31] However, the context and chronology suggest otherwise.[32] **And the name of his city was Dinhava.** The mention of these kings' cities indicates that they did not inherit the throne from one another, in the manner of a dynasty.[33]

33 **Bela died, and Yovav son of Zerah, of Botzra,**[B] another city in Edom, **reigned in his stead.**

34 **Yovav died, and Husham of the land of the Temanites reigned in his stead.** Teman was one of the Edomite chieftains mentioned above (verse 15).

35 **Husham died, and Hadad son of Bedad, who** had one notable accomplishment in that he **smote Midyan,** a mainly nomadic tribe that had settled temporarily near Edom and Moav, **in the field of Moav,** was the king who **reigned in his stead. And the name of his city was Avit.**

36 **Hadad died, and Samla of Masreka reigned in his stead.**

37 **Samla died, and Shaul of Rehovot on the** Euphrates **river reigned in his stead.**

38 **Shaul died, and Baal Hanan son of Akhbor reigned in his stead.**

39 **And Baal Hanan son of Akhbor died, and Hadar reigned in his stead,**[D] **and the name of the city was Pa'u; and his wife's name was Mehetavel, daughter of Matred, daughter of Mei Zahav.** It is unclear why the name of his wife and her lineage are mentioned here. Mei Zahav is either simply a name without any particular significance, a title meaning goldsmith,[34] or an epithet for a very rich person. Perhaps the wealth of Mehetavel's grandfather enabled Hadad to stabilize his reign.

40 *Maftir* **And these are the names of the chieftains of Esau, according to their families, according to their places, by their names,** as the chieftains of Esau's descendants ruled in different areas. **The chieftain of Timna, the chieftain of Alva, the chieftain of Yetet.** Some of these names were already mentioned above, but there are some differences here. For example, the name Timna did not appear earlier as a man's name.[35]

41 **The chieftain of Oholivama;** although this is the name of one of Esau's wives, perhaps the entire tribe or its chieftain was named after her. **The chieftain of Ela, the chieftain of Pinon,**

42 **the chieftain of Kenaz, the chieftain of Teman, the chieftain of Mivtzar,**

43 **the chieftain of Magdiel, the chieftain of Iram. These are the chieftains of Edom, according to their settlements in their apportioned land. He is Esau, father of Edom.**[D]

DISCUSSION

36:39| **The kings of Edom:** Although the monarchy in Edom lasted for many years, it was not continuous. There were eras when Edom was ruled by governors appointed by the Judean king (see II Samuel 8:14; I Kings 11:15–16; I Chronicles 18:12–13), and other periods when the Edomites rebelled against Judea and reclaimed their independent government (see II Kings 8:20–22; Psalms 137:7). It is possible that Hadar was the last significant Edomite king of that period, as no kings are mentioned in the rest of this section (see Rashi; *Sermons of the Ran*, chap. 2; *Peri Tzaddik*, beginning of *Vayishlaḥ*).

36:43| **He is Esau, father of Edom:** The significance of this list of Edomite kings is unclear. There is no evident reason why this chronology is mentioned in the Torah, as it does not appear to be relevant in any way to the history of the Jewish people. In the mystical works of the Kabbala, this is interpreted as an important list of mysterious, fundamental symbols, which allude to heavenly forces that existed before the world as we know it came into being. Furthermore, the rise of a monarchy in Edom before there was an Israelite king reflects the depth of the relationship between the twin brothers, Esau and Jacob. In many aspects, Esau is the shadow of Jacob (see, e.g., Zohar, part 1, 177:1–2; part 3, 135:1; *Etz Ḥayyim* 18:1; *Peri Tzaddik*, beginning of *Vayishlaḥ*).

וְאֵ֥לֶּה בְנֵֽי־עֲנָ֖ה דִּשֹׁ֑ן וְאָהֳלִֽיבָמָ֖ה בַּת־עֲנָֽה: וְאֵ֖לֶּה בְּנֵ֣י דִישָׁ֑ן חֶמְדָּ֥ן וְאֶשְׁבָּ֖ן וְיִתְרָ֥ן כה כו

וּכְרָ֑ן: אֵ֥לֶּה בְּנֵֽי־אֵ֖צֶר בִּלְהָ֥ן וְזַעֲוָ֖ן וַעֲקָ֑ן: אֵ֥לֶּה בְנֵֽי־דִישָׁ֖ן ע֥וּץ וַאֲרָֽן: אֵ֖לֶּה אַלּוּפֵ֣י כז כח כט

הַחֹרִ֑י אַלּ֤וּף לוֹטָן֙ אַלּ֣וּף שׁוֹבָ֔ל אַלּ֥וּף צִבְע֖וֹן אַלּ֥וּף עֲנָֽה: אַלּ֥וּף דִּשֹׁ֛ן אַלּ֥וּף אֵ֖צֶר ל

אַלּ֣וּף דִּישָׁ֑ן אֵ֣לֶּה אַלּוּפֵ֧י הַחֹרִ֛י לְאַלֻּפֵיהֶ֖ם בְּאֶ֥רֶץ שֵׂעִֽיר:

וְאֵ֙לֶּה֙ הַמְּלָכִ֔ים אֲשֶׁ֥ר מָלְכ֖וּ בְּאֶ֣רֶץ אֱד֑וֹם לִפְנֵ֥י מְלָךְ־מֶ֖לֶךְ לִבְנֵ֥י יִשְׂרָאֵֽל: וַיִּמְלֹ֣ךְ לא לב

בֶּֽאֱד֔וֹם בֶּ֖לַע בֶּן־בְּע֑וֹר וְשֵׁ֥ם עִיר֖וֹ דִּנְהָֽבָה: וַיָּ֖מָת בָּ֑לַע וַיִּמְלֹ֣ךְ תַּחְתָּ֔יו יוֹבָ֥ב בֶּן־ לג

זֶ֖רַח מִבָּצְרָֽה: וַיָּ֖מָת יוֹבָ֑ב וַיִּמְלֹ֣ךְ תַּחְתָּ֔יו חֻשָׁ֖ם מֵאֶ֥רֶץ הַתֵּימָנִֽי: וַיָּ֖מָת חֻשָׁ֑ם לד לה

וַיִּמְלֹ֣ךְ תַּחְתָּ֗יו הֲדַ֤ד בֶּן־בְּדַד֙ הַמַּכֶּ֤ה אֶת־מִדְיָן֙ בִּשְׂדֵ֣ה מוֹאָ֔ב וְשֵׁ֥ם עִיר֖וֹ עֲוִֽית: לו

וַיָּ֖מָת הֲדָ֑ד וַיִּמְלֹ֣ךְ תַּחְתָּ֔יו שַׂמְלָ֖ה מִמַּשְׂרֵקָֽה: וַיָּ֖מָת שַׂמְלָ֑ה וַיִּמְלֹ֣ךְ תַּחְתָּ֔יו שָׁא֖וּל לז

מֵרְחֹב֥וֹת הַנָּהָֽר: וַיָּ֖מָת שָׁא֑וּל וַיִּמְלֹ֣ךְ תַּחְתָּ֔יו בַּ֥עַל חָנָ֖ן בֶּן־עַכְבּֽוֹר: וַיָּ֡מָת בַּ֣עַל לח לט

חָנָן֩ בֶּן־עַכְבּ֨וֹר וַיִּמְלֹ֤ךְ תַּחְתָּיו֙ הֲדַ֔ר וְשֵׁ֥ם עִיר֖וֹ פָּ֑עוּ וְשֵׁ֨ם אִשְׁתּ֤וֹ מְהֵֽיטַבְאֵל֙ בַּת־

מַטְרֵ֔ד בַּ֖ת מֵ֥י זָהָֽב: וְ֠אֵ֠לֶּה שְׁמ֞וֹת אַלּוּפֵ֤י עֵשָׂו֙ לְמִשְׁפְּחֹתָ֔ם לִמְקֹמֹתָ֖ם בִּשְׁמֹתָ֑ם מ מפטיר

אַלּ֥וּף תִּמְנָ֛ע אַלּ֥וּף עַֽלְוָ֖ה אַלּ֥וּף יְתֵֽת: אַלּ֧וּף אָהֳלִֽיבָמָ֛ה אַלּ֥וּף אֵלָ֖ה אַלּ֥וּף פִּינֹֽן: מא

אַלּ֥וּף קְנַ֛ז אַלּ֥וּף תֵּימָ֖ן אַלּ֥וּף מִבְצָֽר: אַלּ֥וּף מַגְדִּיאֵ֖ל אַלּ֣וּף עִירָ֑ם אֵ֣לֶּה ׀ אַלּוּפֵ֣י מב מג

אֱד֗וֹם לְמֹֽשְׁבֹתָם֙ בְּאֶ֣רֶץ אֲחֻזָּתָ֔ם ה֥וּא עֵשָׂ֖ו אֲבִ֥י אֱדֽוֹם:

רש"י

לא) וְאֵלֶּה הַמְּלָכִים וְגו'. שְׁמֹנָה הָיוּ, וּכְנֶגְדָּן הֶעֱמִיד יַעֲקֹב וּבִטֵּל מַלְכוּת עֵשָׂו בִּימֵיהֶם, וְאֵלּוּ הֵן: שָׁאוּל וְאִישׁ בֹּשֶׁת, דָּוִד וּשְׁלֹמֹה, רְחַבְעָם, אֲבִיָּה, אָסָא, יְהוֹשָׁפָט, וּבִימֵי יוֹרָם בְּנוֹ כְּתִיב: "בְּיָמָיו פָּשַׁע אֱדוֹם מִתַּחַת יַד יְהוּדָה וַיַּמְלִיכוּ עֲלֵיהֶם מֶלֶךְ" (מלכים ב' ח, כ), וּבִימֵי שָׁאוּל כְּתִיב: "וּמֶלֶךְ אֵין בֶּאֱדוֹם נִצָּב מֶלֶךְ" (מלכים א' כב, מח).

לו) יוֹבָב בֶּן זֶרַח מִבָּצְרָה. בָּצְרָה מֵעָרֵי מוֹאָב הִיא, שֶׁנֶּאֱמַר: "וְעַל קְרִיּוֹת וְעַל בָּצְרָה וְגו'" (ירמיה מח, כד), וּלְפִי שֶׁהֶעֱמִידָה מֶלֶךְ לֶאֱדוֹם עֲתִידָה לִלְקוֹת עִמָּהֶם, עִמָּהֶם, שֶׁנֶּאֱמַר: "כִּי זֶבַח בְּבָצְרָה" (ישעיה לד, ו).

לה) הַמַּכֶּה אֶת מִדְיָן בִּשְׂדֵה מוֹאָב. שֶׁבָּא מִדְיָן עַל מוֹאָב לַמִּלְחָמָה וְהָלַךְ מֶלֶךְ אֱדוֹם לַעֲזֹר אֶת מוֹאָב. וּמִכָּאן אָנוּ לְמֵדִים שֶׁהָיוּ מִדְיָן וּמוֹאָב מְרִיבִים זֶה עִם זֶה, וּבִימֵי בִלְעָם עָשׂוּ שָׁלוֹם לְהִתְקַשֵּׁר עַל יִשְׂרָאֵל.

מ) וְאֵלֶּה שְׁמוֹת אַלּוּפֵי עֵשָׂו. שֶׁנִּקְרְאוּ עַל שֵׁם מְדִינוֹתֵיהֶם לְאַחַר שֶׁמֵּת הֲדַד וּפָסְקָה מֵהֶם מַלְכוּת, וְהָרִאשׁוֹנִים הַנִּזְכָּרִים לְמַעְלָה הֵם שְׁמוֹת תּוֹלְדוֹתָם, וְכֵן מְפֹרָשׁ בְּדִבְרֵי הַיָּמִים: "וַיָּמָת הֲדָד וַיִּהְיוּ אַלּוּפֵי אֱדוֹם אַלּוּף תִּמְנָע וְגו'" (דברי הימים א' א, נא).

מג) מַגְדִּיאֵל. הִיא רוֹמִי:

לט) בַּת מֵי זָהָב. מַהוּ זָהָב? עָשִׁיר הָיָה זָהָב חָשׁוּב בְּעֵינָיו לִכְלוּם:

BACKGROUND

36:33 | Botzra: The capital of ancient Edom, which was used as a name for the entire country (see Isaiah 34:6; Jeremiah 49:13; Amos 1:12). It is identified as Bouseira, which is 11 km south of Tafilah, the biblical Tofel. Botzra overlooks the main highway of Edom, which extends along the western slope of Mount Se'ir.

Parashat
Vayeshev

The Sale of Joseph
GENESIS 37:1–36

After concluding the narrative of Isaac's life, and after briefly listing the descendants of Esau, the Torah returns its focus to Jacob and the events of his life. The seeds of Jacob's eventual second exile from Canaan lie in his relationship with his wives and his twelve sons. His preference for Joseph son of Rachel sets in motion the events that ultimately lead to the family's exile in Egypt.

37 1 Unlike Esau, who left Canaan to settle on Mount Se'ir, **Jacob settled,** while his father was still alive, **in the land of his father's residence, in the land of Canaan.**

2 **This is the legacy of Jacob.** Although Jacob remained active upon his return to Canaan, his contributions as a leader and builder started to decrease. Therefore the narrative shifts its primary focus to Joseph. **Joseph, seventeen years old, was herding the flock** of his household **with his brothers,** thereby continuing the traditional occupation of their family (see 46:32). **And he was a lad,** or assistant, **with the sons of Bilha, and with the sons of Zilpa, his father's wives.** Jacob himself gave no indication that the sons of the maidservants, Bilha and Zilpa, were of lesser status than the sons of Leah and Rachel. On the contrary, when Jacob blessed his sons, he equated the status of all of them (see 49:16). In practice, however, a disparity existed between them. Joseph became close to the sons of Bilha and Zilpa because he was closer in age to them. Yet **Joseph brought evil report of them to their father,** slandering their inappropriate behavior.[1]

3 **Israel,** Jacob, **loved Joseph more than all his sons, because he was a son of his old age [** *ben zekunim* **].** Although Benjamin was even younger than Joseph, and also a son of Jacob's beloved wife Rachel, his personality was less prominent. Jacob favored Joseph due to his outstanding personality, which becomes apparent in the continuation of the narrative. In fact, Onkelos translates *ben zekunim* as a wise son. Additionally, Joseph resembled Jacob's beloved wife Rachel, who had recently died. The verse describes Joseph as being "of fine form, and of fair appearance," just like his mother (29:17, 39:6). Indeed, Joseph is the only male to be described in such terms by the Torah. Perhaps Joseph's facial features reminded Jacob of Rachel. It is also easy to imagine that Joseph was preferred over Jacob's older children because of their problematic behavior: Reuven defiled the family, and Simeon and Levi's actions in Shekhem were met with Jacob's disapproval. **He,** Jacob, **made him a fine tunic,** a special garment that was distinct from the clothing of the other brothers.

4 **His brothers saw that their father loved him more than all his brothers.** Jacob's preference for Joseph was conspicuous, whether through the way he related to Joseph or from the special tunic that he made for him. **And they hated him, and could not speak peaceably to him.** They were incapable of maintaining any sort of peaceful dialogue with Joseph. They avoided all conversation with him and distanced themselves from him as much as possible.

5 **Joseph dreamed a dream, and he told it to his brothers, and they hated him even more.** Their hatred of Joseph increased because he related to them the details of his dream.

6 **He said to them: Please, hear this dream that I dreamed:**

7 **Behold, we were binding sheaves in the field,** as we normally do. Although the sons of Jacob were primarily shepherds, they also owned fields. **And behold,** instead of resting alongside the other sheaves, **my sheaf arose, and also stood upright; and behold, your sheaves gathered around, and prostrated themselves to my sheaf.**

8 **His brothers,** who understood the dream as a metaphor suggesting Joseph's dominance over them, **said to him: Will you reign over us? Will you have dominion over us?** There is no chance for that. **They hated him even more for his dreams, and for his words.** The brother's hatred of Joseph, which stemmed from his status as favorite son and from the negative reports about them that he would bring to Jacob, was further intensified by the arrogance he expressed through his dreams. Now, in addition to dealing with the fact that Joseph was favored by Jacob, the brothers must contend with a person who entertained megalomaniacal aspirations.

9 **He dreamed yet another dream,**[D] presumably on another night,[2] **and he related it to his brothers. He said: Behold, I dreamed another dream, and behold, the sun, the moon, and eleven stars prostrated themselves to me.**

פרשת
וישב

לז א ב וַיֵּשֶׁב יַעֲקֹב בְּאֶרֶץ מְגוּרֵי אָבִיו בְּאֶרֶץ כְּנָעַן: אֵלֶּה ׀ תֹּלְדוֹת יַעֲקֹב יוֹסֵף בֶּן־שְׁבַע־ לג
עֶשְׂרֵה שָׁנָה הָיָה רֹעֶה אֶת־אֶחָיו בַּצֹּאן וְהוּא נַעַר אֶת־בְּנֵי בִלְהָה וְאֶת־בְּנֵי זִלְפָּה
ג נְשֵׁי אָבִיו וַיָּבֵא יוֹסֵף אֶת־דִּבָּתָם רָעָה אֶל־אֲבִיהֶם: וְיִשְׂרָאֵל אָהַב אֶת־יוֹסֵף מִכָּל־
ד בָּנָיו כִּי־בֶן־זְקֻנִים הוּא לוֹ וְעָשָׂה לוֹ כְּתֹנֶת פַּסִּים: וַיִּרְאוּ אֶחָיו כִּי־אֹתוֹ אָהַב אֲבִיהֶם
ה מִכָּל־אֶחָיו וַיִּשְׂנְאוּ אֹתוֹ וְלֹא יָכְלוּ דַּבְּרוֹ לְשָׁלֹם: וַיַּחֲלֹם יוֹסֵף חֲלוֹם וַיַּגֵּד לְאֶחָיו
ו וַיּוֹסִפוּ עוֹד שְׂנֹא אֹתוֹ: וַיֹּאמֶר אֲלֵיהֶם שִׁמְעוּ־נָא הַחֲלוֹם הַזֶּה אֲשֶׁר חָלָמְתִּי:
ז וְהִנֵּה אֲנַחְנוּ מְאַלְּמִים אֲלֻמִּים בְּתוֹךְ הַשָּׂדֶה וְהִנֵּה קָמָה אֲלֻמָּתִי וְגַם־נִצָּבָה וְהִנֵּה
ח תְסֻבֶּינָה אֲלֻמֹּתֵיכֶם וַתִּשְׁתַּחֲוֶיןָ לַאֲלֻמָּתִי: וַיֹּאמְרוּ לוֹ אֶחָיו הֲמָלֹךְ תִּמְלֹךְ עָלֵינוּ
ט אִם־מָשׁוֹל תִּמְשֹׁל בָּנוּ וַיּוֹסִפוּ עוֹד שְׂנֹא אֹתוֹ עַל־חֲלֹמֹתָיו וְעַל־דְּבָרָיו: וַיַּחֲלֹם
עוֹד חֲלוֹם אַחֵר וַיְסַפֵּר אֹתוֹ לְאֶחָיו וַיֹּאמֶר הִנֵּה חָלַמְתִּי חֲלוֹם עוֹד וְהִנֵּה הַשֶּׁמֶשׁ

רש"י

א| **וַיֵּשֶׁב יַעֲקֹב.** אַחַר שֶׁכָּתַב לְךָ יִשּׁוּבֵי עֵשָׂו וְתוֹלְדוֹתָיו בְּדֶרֶךְ קְצָרָה, שֶׁלֹּא הָיוּ סְפוּנִים וַחֲשׁוּבִים לְפָרֵשׁ הֵיאַךְ נִתְיַשְּׁבוּ וְסֵדֶר מִלְחֲמוֹתֵיהֶם אֵיךְ הוֹרִישׁוּ אֶת הַחוֹרִי, פֵּרֵשׁ לְךָ יִשּׁוּבֵי יַעֲקֹב וְתוֹלְדוֹתָיו בְּדֶרֶךְ אֲרֻכָּה, כָּל גִּלְגּוּלֵי סִבָּתָם, לְפִי שֶׁהֵם חֲשׁוּבִים לִפְנֵי הַמָּקוֹם לְהַאֲרִיךְ בָּהֶם. וְכֵן אַתָּה מוֹצֵא בַּעֲשָׂרָה דוֹרוֹת שֶׁמֵּאָדָם וְעַד נֹחַ, פְּלוֹנִי הוֹלִיד פְּלוֹנִי, וּכְשֶׁבָּא לְנֹחַ הֶאֱרִיךְ בּוֹ. וְכֵן בַּעֲשָׂרָה דוֹרוֹת שֶׁמִּנֹּחַ וְעַד אַבְרָהָם קִצֵּר בָּהֶם, וּמִשֶּׁהִגִּיעַ אֵצֶל אַבְרָהָם הֶאֱרִיךְ בּוֹ. מָשָׁל לְמַרְגָּלִית שֶׁנָּפְלָה בֵּין הַחוֹל, אָדָם מְמַשְׁמֵשׁ בַּחוֹל וְכוֹבְרוֹ בִּכְבָרָה עַד שֶׁמּוֹצֵא אֶת הַמַּרְגָּלִית, וּמִשֶּׁמְּצָאָהּ הוּא מַשְׁלִיךְ אֶת הַצְּרוֹרוֹת מִיָּדוֹ וְנוֹטֵל הַמַּרְגָּלִית:

ב| **אֵלֶּה תֹּלְדוֹת יַעֲקֹב.** וְאֵלֶּה שֶׁל תּוֹלְדוֹת יַעֲקֹב, אֵלֶּה יִשּׁוּבֵיהֶם וְגִלְגּוּלֵיהֶם עַד שֶׁבָּאוּ לִכְלַל יִשּׁוּב; סִבָּה רִאשׁוֹנָה: "יוֹסֵף בֶּן שְׁבַע עֶשְׂרֵה" וְגוֹ', עַל יְדֵי זֶה נִתְגַּלְגְּלוּ וְיָרְדוּ לְמִצְרַיִם. זֶהוּ אַחַר יִשּׁוּב פְּשׁוּטוֹ שֶׁל מִקְרָא לִהְיוֹת דָּבוּר עַל אָפְנָיו. וּמִדְרַשׁ אַגָּדָה דּוֹרֵשׁ, תָּלָה הַכָּתוּב תּוֹלְדוֹת יַעֲקֹב בְּיוֹסֵף מִפְּנֵי כַּמָּה דְּבָרִים: אַחַת, שֶׁכָּל עַצְמוֹ שֶׁל יַעֲקֹב לֹא עָבַד אֵצֶל לָבָן אֶלָּא בְּרָחֵל, וְשֶׁהָיָה זִיו אִיקוֹנִין שֶׁל יוֹסֵף דּוֹמֶה לוֹ, וְכָל מַה שֶּׁאֵרַע לְיַעֲקֹב אֵרַע לְיוֹסֵף: זֶה נִשְׂטַם וְזֶה נִשְׂטַם, זֶה אָחִיו מְבַקֵּשׁ לְהָרְגוֹ וְזֶה אֶחָיו מְבַקְשִׁים לְהָרְגוֹ, וְכֵן הַרְבֵּה בִּבְרֵאשִׁית רַבָּה (פד, ו): **וְהוּא נַעַר.** שֶׁהָיָה עוֹשֶׂה מַעֲשֵׂה נַעֲרוּת, מְתַקֵּן בִּשְׂעָרוֹ, מְמַשְׁמֵשׁ בְּעֵינָיו, כְּדֵי שֶׁיִּהְיֶה נִרְאֶה יָפֶה: **אֶת בְּנֵי בִלְהָה.** כְּלוֹמַר, וְרָגִיל אֵצֶל בְּנֵי בִלְהָה, לְפִי שֶׁהָיוּ אֶחָיו מְבַזִּין אוֹתָן וְהוּא מְקָרְבָן: **אֶת דִּבָּתָם רָעָה.** כָּל רָעָה שֶׁהָיָה רוֹאֶה בְּאֶחָיו בְּנֵי לֵאָה הָיָה מַגִּיד לְאָבִיו, שֶׁהָיוּ אוֹכְלִין אֵבֶר מִן הַחַי, וּמְזַלְזְלִין בִּבְנֵי הַשְּׁפָחוֹת לִקְרוֹתָן עֲבָדִים, וַחֲשׁוּדִים עַל הָעֲרָיוֹת. וּבִשְׁלָשְׁתָּן לָקָה: "וַיִּשְׁחֲטוּ שְׂעִיר עִזִּים" (להלן פסוק לא) בִּמְכִירָתוֹ, וְלֹא אֲכָלוּהוּ חַי; וְעַל דִּבָּה שֶׁסִּפֵּר עֲלֵיהֶם שֶׁקּוֹרִין לַאֲחֵיהֶם עֲבָדִים – "לְעֶבֶד נִמְכַּר יוֹסֵף" (תהלים קה, יז); וְעַל הָעֲרָיוֹת שֶׁסִּפֵּר עֲלֵיהֶם – "וַתִּשָּׂא אֵשֶׁת אֲדֹנָיו" וְגוֹ' (להלן לט, ז): **דִּבָּתָם.** כָּל לְשׁוֹן דִּבָּה פרלדי"ן בְּלַעַז. כָּל מַה שֶּׁהָיָה יָכוֹל לְדַבֵּר בָּהֶם רָעָה הָיָה מְסַפֵּר. 'דִּבָּה' – לְשׁוֹן "דּוֹבֵב שִׂפְתֵי יְשֵׁנִים" (שיר השירים ז, י):

ג| **בֶּן זְקֻנִים.** שֶׁנּוֹלַד לוֹ לְעֵת זִקְנָתוֹ. וְאוּנְקְלוֹס תִּרְגֵּם: "בַּר חַכִּים הוּא לֵיהּ", כָּל מַה שֶּׁלָּמַד מִשֵּׁם וְעֵבֶר מָסַר לוֹ. דָּבָר אַחֵר, שֶׁהָיָה זִיו אִיקוֹנִין שֶׁלּוֹ דּוֹמֶה לוֹ: **פַּסִּים.** לְשׁוֹן כְּלֵי מֵילָת, כְּמוֹ: "כַּרְפַּס וּתְכֵלֶת" (אסתר א, ו), וּכְמוֹ: "כְּתֹנֶת הַפַּסִּים" (שמואל ב' יג, יח) דְּתָמָר וְאַמְנוֹן. וּמִדְרַשׁ אַגָּדָה, עַל שֵׁם צָרוֹתָיו, שֶׁנִּמְכַּר לְפוֹטִיפַר וְלַסּוֹחֲרִים וְלַיִּשְׁמְעֵאלִים וְלַמִּדְיָנִים:

ד| **וְלֹא יָכְלוּ דַּבְּרוֹ לְשָׁלֹם.** מִתּוֹךְ גְּנוּתָם לָמַדְנוּ שִׁבְחָם, שֶׁלֹּא דִּבְּרוּ אַחַת בַּפֶּה וְאַחַת בַּלֵּב. **דַּבְּרוֹ.** לְדַבֵּר עִמּוֹ:

ז| **מְאַלְּמִים אֲלֻמִּים.** כְּתַרְגּוּמוֹ: "מְאַסְּרִין אֱסָרַן", עֳמָרִין, וְכֵן: "נֹשֵׂא אֲלֻמֹּתָיו" (תהלים קכו, ו), וְכָמוֹהוּ בִּלְשׁוֹן מִשְׁנָה: "וְהָאֲלֻמּוֹת נוֹטֵל וּמַכְרִיז" (בבא מציעא כב ע"ב): **קָמָה אֲלֻמָּתִי.** נִזְקְפָה: **וְגַם נִצָּבָה.** לַעֲמֹד עַל עָמְדָהּ בִּזְקִיפָה:

ח| **וְעַל דְּבָרָיו.** עַל דִּבָּתָם רָעָה שֶׁהָיָה מֵבִיא לַאֲבִיהֶם:

DISCUSSION

37:9| **He dreamed yet another dream:** From his relatively innocuous first dream, Joseph progressed to one that was equally transparent, yet far more extreme in scope. The imagery of this dream points to Joseph ruling not only over his brothers, but over the entire world.

10 **He related it to his father and to his brothers.**[D] Unlike in the first dream, Jacob is represented in this dream. For this reason, Joseph also related the dream to his father.[3] **And his father rebuked him, and said to him: What is this dream that you dreamed?** This is certainly not a meaningful dream. Considering that the sun and the moon are metaphors for one's parents, **will I and your mother and your brothers come to prostrate ourselves to you to the earth?** Surely we will not. Your mother is already dead.

11 **His brothers envied him,** whether on account of his abnormal dreams, or because of their father's relatively mild response. Unlike Joseph's brothers, Jacob did not rebuke Joseph for expressing undeserved arrogance; he claimed only that the dream could never come to fruition. **But his father kept the matter in mind.** Despite his stated assertion that Joseph's dreams were mere fantasy, Jacob kept them in mind, as he believed that there was some significance to them.

Second aliya 12 **His brothers went to herd their father's flock in Shekhem.**

13 **Israel said to Joseph: Aren't your brothers herding in Shekhem? Go, and I will send you to them.** It is normal for a flock to spend weeks or even months outside its pen. Jacob wished to maintain contact with his sons, who had wandered with the flock all the way from Hebron to Shekhem. **He,** Joseph, **said to him: Here I am.**

14 **He said to him: Go now, see the status of your brothers and the status of the flock and bring back word. He sent him from the Valley of Hebron.**[B] Although Hebron itself is situated on mountainous terrain, it is possible that Jacob's family dwelled in the valley below. Alternatively, the family lived in Hebron itself, but Jacob accompanied his son until they reached the valley, at which point Jacob sent Joseph on his own.[4] **And he,** Joseph, **came to Shekhem.**

15 **A man found him, and behold, he was wandering in the field.** Despite the fact that Joseph was seeking an entire group of shepherds herding a large flock, he could not locate them. **The man asked him, saying: What do you seek?**

16 **He said: I seek my brothers. Please tell me where they are herding.** Joseph undoubtedly described their appearances to the man.

17 **The man said: They traveled from here; for I heard them saying** to each other: **We shall go to Dotan,**[B] and it is likely that they arrived there. **Joseph went after his brothers, and he found them in Dotan.**

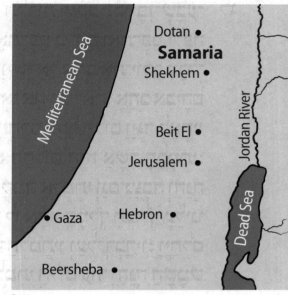

Dotan

18 **They saw him from afar,** and he was alone and likely in an isolated place, **and before he approached them, they conspired against him to kill him.** Their hatred of Joseph was so intense that once they encountered him alone and outside their father's home, they were stirred to rid themselves of him.

19 **They said one to another: Here comes that dreamer.** Joseph's dreams caused the brothers' hatred toward him to intensify. By mockingly referring to Joseph as "that dreamer," the brothers expressed their deep animosity toward him. Furthermore, the word "that" indicates that the brothers viewed Joseph as a hostile stranger, and not as their brother.

DISCUSSION

37:10 | He related it to his father and to his brothers: As the story unfolds, Joseph is revealed as a talented diplomat who demonstrates skill in negotiation and prowess in relating to different types of people, while never being overly submissive or resorting to flattery. The question therefore arises: If Joseph always had these qualities, why did he not have the sense to keep the contents of his dreams to himself? What prompted him to reveal such extreme and transparent dreams to his brothers, especially when considering the fact that they already had an extreme dislike of him?

To answer this question, one must first address another issue pertaining to all dreams recorded in the Bible: Are dreams merely a physiological expression of the dreamer's personal aspirations, as one might conclude from Isaiah 29:8, or are they prophetic portents of future events? Joseph, like his father Jacob (see 28:12–16), was certain that his dreams were prophetic, as they did not portend random events or provide a pleasurable imaginary experience, but contained a clear message. Therefore, he

י והירח ואחד עשר כוכבים משתחוים לי: ויספר אל־אביו ואל־אחיו ויגער־
בו אביו ויאמר לו מה החלום הזה אשר חלמת הבוא נבוא אני ואמך ואחיך
יא יב להשתחות לך ארצה: ויקנאו־בו אחיו ואביו שמר את־הדבר: וילכו אחיו שני
יג לרעות את־צאן אביהם בשכם: ויאמר ישראל אל־יוסף הלוא אחיך רעים
יד בשכם לכה ואשלחך אליהם ויאמר לו הנני: ויאמר לו לך־נא ראה את־שלום
אחיך ואת־שלום הצאן והשבני דבר וישלחהו מעמק חברון ויבא שכמה:
טו טז וימצאהו איש והנה תעה בשדה וישאלהו האיש לאמר מה־תבקש: ויאמר
יז את־אחי אנכי מבקש הגידה־נא לי איפה הם רעים: ויאמר האיש נסעו מזה
יח כי שמעתי אמרים נלכה דתינה וילך יוסף אחר אחיו וימצאם בדתן: ויראו
יט אתו מרחק ובטרם יקרב אליהם ויתנכלו אתו להמיתו: ויאמרו איש אל־אחיו

רש״י

י | **ויספר אל אביו ואל אחיו.** לאחר שספר אותו לאחיו חזר וספרו לאביו בפניהם: **ויגער בו.** לפי שהיה מטיל שנאה עליו: **הבוא נבוא.** והלא אמך כבר מתה! והוא לא היה יודע שהדברים מגיעין לבלהה שגדלתו כאמו. ורבותינו למדו מכאן שאין חלום בלא דברים בטלים, ויעקב נתכוון להוציא הדבר מלב בניו שלא יקנאוהו, לכך אמר לו: "הבוא נבוא" וגו', כשם שאי אפשר באמך כך השאר בטל:

יא | **שמר את הדבר.** היה ממתין ומצפה מתי יבוא, וכן: "שומר אמונים" (ישעיה כו, ב), וכן: "לא תשמור על חטאתי" (איוב יד, טז) – לא תמתין:

יב | **לרעות את צאן.** נקוד על 'את', שלא הלכו אלא לרעות את עצמן:

יג | **הנני.** לשון ענוה וזריזות; נזדרז למצות אביו, ואף על פי שהיה יודע באחיו ששונאין אותו:

יד | **מעמק חברון.** והלא חברון בהר, שנאמר: "ויעלו בנגב ויבא עד חברון" (במדבר יג, כב)? אלא מעצה עמוקה של אותו צדיק הקבור בחברון, לקיים מה שנאמר לאברהם בין הבתרים: "כי גר יהיה זרעך": **ויבא שכמה.** מקום מוכן לפורענות, שם קלקלו השבטים, שם ענו את דינה, שם נחלקה מלכות בית דוד, שנאמר: "וילך רחבעם שכמה" (דברי הימים ב' י, א):

טו | **וימצאהו איש.** זה גבריאל:

יז | **נסעו מזה.** הסיעו עצמן מן האחוה: **נלכה דתינה.** לבקש לך נכלי דתות שימיתוך בהם. ולפי פשוטו שם מקום הוא, ואין מקרא יוצא מידי פשוטו:

יח | **ויתנכלו.** נתמלאו נכלים וערמומיות: **אתו.** כמו 'אתו' 'עמו', כלומר אליו:

DISCUSSION

➞ felt compelled to relate them to his brothers so that they could prepare for their realization, and perhaps in the hope that they would help expedite the prophecy. In his mind, Joseph saw a scenario in which the brothers would accept his leadership and assist him on his way. It was this possibility that motivated him to share his dreams with them.

It would appear that as time progressed, Joseph became increasingly convinced that his dreams would be realized, and actively took steps to bring about their fulfillment (see 42:9).

BACKGROUND

37:14| **The Valley of Hebron:** Biblical Hebron was situated on a mountain known today as Tel Rumeida. From archaeological excavations of the mountain, it appears that Hebron was built during the Middle Bronze Age, between 1750–1650 BCE. Like Shekhem, it was characterized by thick walls constructed from massive stones. The Valley of Hebron is identified with Wadi al Kina to the east of Tel Rumeida, which continues into Wadi al Tuffah.

37:17| **Dotan:** This likely refers to the Dotan Valley, the largest valley in Samaria, measuring approximately 10 km long and 3 km wide. Through this valley once ran an important road connecting the eastern side of the Jordan River with the northern coastal plain. Dotan, which lies in the center of the valley, is generally identified with present-day Tel Dotan, located about 8 km southwest of Jenin. The city is mentioned in II Kings (6:13), and in Egyptian records from the fifteenth century BCE. Based on archaeological excavations, it would appear that during the period of the patriarchs, the city of Dotan was a large settlement surrounded by a wall.

20 **Now let us go and kill him and cast him into one of the** nearby **pits, and we will say: A wild beast devoured him.**[D] Since wild animals are commonly found in uninhabited areas, if someone inquires about the fate of Joseph, we will claim that his death was caused by a predatory animal in the area. **And we shall see what will become of his dreams.**

21 **Reuben,** the oldest son, **heard, and delivered him from their hand,** as he felt responsible for whatever was about to take place; **and** he **said: Let us not smite him mortally;** there is no need for us to kill him.

22 **Reuben said to them: Do not shed blood; cast him into this pit that is in the wilderness, but do not lay a hand on him.** Left alone, he will die of starvation; there is no need for us to kill him with our own hands. The verse points out that Reuben suggested this course of action only **in order to deliver him from their hand, to restore him to his father.** Perhaps Reuben did not join his brothers in their hatred of Joseph, and he therefore urged the brothers not to murder Joseph. He then attempted to convince them to cast Joseph into a pit, with the intention to later return and extract Joseph from the pit and bring him home.[5]

Third aliya **23** **It was when Joseph came to his brothers that they stripped Joseph of his tunic, the fine tunic that was upon him.**

24 **They took him and cast him into the pit; and the pit was empty, there was no water in it.** It is not known during which season this event transpired. However, given that the brothers had gone out to pasture their flocks, it would seem that this incident occurred at the beginning of the summer, at the very latest. During this time of year, it is still possible to find pits filled with rainwater. Nevertheless, the brothers refrained from drowning Joseph in such a pit.[6]

25 **They sat to eat bread.** The brothers saw no fault in their actions, nor did they consider their actions something done in a moment of weakness. Their consciences did not prevent them from sitting down for a meal while their brother cried out from the pit.[7] **And they lifted their eyes and saw, and behold, a caravan of Ishmaelites was coming from Gilad** on the eastern side of the Jordan River. Until recent times, it was common practice for those traveling from the north down to Egypt, to cross the Jordan River and continue through the Dotan Valley, which borders the Yizre'el Valley, and then on toward the

coastal plain. **And their camels were bearing** various **spices [*nekhot*];**[8] alternatively, *nekhot* refers to a specific spice. They were also bearing **balm,**[B] a very valuable spice, **and labdanum,**[B] a plant used for manufacturing perfume. The caravan was **going to take them,** these spices, **down to Egypt** to sell them there.

Arabian balsam tree   Labdanum

26 **Judah said to his brothers: What profit is it,** what would we gain,[9] **if we kill our brother and conceal his blood?**

27 **Go and we will sell him** as a slave **to the** arriving **Ishmaelites.** They will take him far away from here, **and** at the very least, **let our hand not be** directly **upon him, as** after all, **he is our brother, our flesh,** and we should not harm him. **His brothers heeded**[D] Judah's suggestion.

28 **Midyanite men, merchants, passed by, and they pulled and lifted Joseph from the pit.** Some commentaries identify the Midyanite merchants with the group of Ishmaelites mentioned previously. The name "Midyanite" can refer generally to nomadic merchants.[10] Others explain that the Midyanites and Ishmaelites were two distinct groups.[11] **They sold Joseph to the Ishmaelites.** If the Midyanites are not identified with the Ishmaelites, then the brothers sold Joseph to the Ishmaelites who subsequently sold him to the Midyanites.[12] According to another interpretation, the brothers did not actually sell Joseph, and may even have been unaware of the sale; rather, the Midyanites came along while the brothers were eating, extracted him from the pit and sold him to the Ishmaelites. A third possibility is that the brothers had the Midyanites extract Joseph from the pit, and then the brothers themselves sold Joseph.[13] Joseph was sold **for twenty silver pieces,** a considerable amount, that they divided among themselves. According to the prophet Amos, it was enough for each of them to buy a pair of shoes;[14] **and they brought Joseph to Egypt.**

DISCUSSION

37:20 | And we will say: A wild beast devoured him: The Bible records several episodes in which individuals were attacked by lions (see, e.g., Judges 14:5; I Samuel 17:34; I Kings 13:24). It is known that lions were present in the Land of Israel until the Crusader period.

37:27 | His brothers heeded: It is possible that the brothers were not in full agreement with regard to Reuben's suggestion. Perhaps they decided to confine Joseph in the pit while they deliberated about his fate. In this context, Judah suggested the possibility of taking advantage of the passing caravan of Ishmaelites to rid themselves of Joseph.

כ הִנֵּה בַּעַל הַחֲלֹמוֹת הַלָּזֶה בָּא׃ וְעַתָּה ׀ לְכוּ וְנַהַרְגֵהוּ וְנַשְׁלִכֵהוּ בְּאַחַד הַבֹּרוֹת
כא וְאָמַרְנוּ חַיָּה רָעָה אֲכָלָתְהוּ וְנִרְאֶה מַה־יִּהְיוּ חֲלֹמֹתָיו׃ וַיִּשְׁמַע רְאוּבֵן וַיַּצִּלֵהוּ
כב מִיָּדָם וַיֹּאמֶר לֹא נַכֶּנּוּ נָפֶשׁ׃ וַיֹּאמֶר אֲלֵהֶם ׀ רְאוּבֵן אַל־תִּשְׁפְּכוּ־דָם הַשְׁלִיכוּ
אֹתוֹ אֶל־הַבּוֹר הַזֶּה אֲשֶׁר בַּמִּדְבָּר וְיָד אַל־תִּשְׁלְחוּ־בוֹ לְמַעַן הַצִּיל אֹתוֹ מִיָּדָם
כג לַהֲשִׁיבוֹ אֶל־אָבִיו׃ וַיְהִי כַּאֲשֶׁר־בָּא יוֹסֵף אֶל־אֶחָיו וַיַּפְשִׁיטוּ אֶת־יוֹסֵף אֶת־ שלישי
כד כֻּתָּנְתּוֹ אֶת־כְּתֹנֶת הַפַּסִּים אֲשֶׁר עָלָיו׃ וַיִּקָּחֻהוּ וַיַּשְׁלִכוּ אֹתוֹ הַבֹּרָה וְהַבּוֹר רֵק
כה אֵין בּוֹ מָיִם׃ וַיֵּשְׁבוּ לֶאֱכָל־לֶחֶם וַיִּשְׂאוּ עֵינֵיהֶם וַיִּרְאוּ וְהִנֵּה אֹרְחַת יִשְׁמְעֵאלִים
בָּאָה מִגִּלְעָד וּגְמַלֵּיהֶם נֹשְׂאִים נְכֹאת וּצְרִי וָלֹט הוֹלְכִים לְהוֹרִיד מִצְרָיְמָה׃
כו כז וַיֹּאמֶר יְהוּדָה אֶל־אֶחָיו מַה־בֶּצַע כִּי נַהֲרֹג אֶת־אָחִינוּ וְכִסִּינוּ אֶת־דָּמוֹ׃ לְכוּ
וְנִמְכְּרֶנּוּ לַיִּשְׁמְעֵאלִים וְיָדֵנוּ אַל־תְּהִי־בוֹ כִּי־אָחִינוּ בְשָׂרֵנוּ הוּא וַיִּשְׁמְעוּ אֶחָיו׃
כח וַיַּעַבְרוּ אֲנָשִׁים מִדְיָנִים סֹחֲרִים וַיִּמְשְׁכוּ וַיַּעֲלוּ אֶת־יוֹסֵף מִן־הַבּוֹר וַיִּמְכְּרוּ אֶת־

רש״י

כ| **וְנִרְאֶה מַה יִּהְיוּ חֲלֹמֹתָיו.** אָמַר רַבִּי יִצְחָק: מִקְרָא זֶה אוֹמֵר דָּרְשֵׁנִי, רוּחַ הַקֹּדֶשׁ אוֹמֶרֶת כֵּן, הֵם אוֹמְרִים ״נַהַרְגֵהוּ״, וְהַכָּתוּב מְסַיֵּם ״וְנִרְאֶה מַה יִּהְיוּ חֲלֹמֹתָיו״ – נִרְאֶה דְּבַר מִי יָקוּם, אִם שֶׁלָּכֶם אוֹ שֶׁלִּי. וְאִי אֶפְשָׁר שֶׁיֹּאמְרוּ הֵם: ״וְנִרְאֶה מַה יִּהְיוּ חֲלֹמֹתָיו״, שֶׁמִּכֵּיוָן שֶׁיַּהַרְגוּהוּ בָּטְלוּ חֲלוֹמוֹתָיו:

כא| **לֹא נַכֶּנּוּ נָפֶשׁ.** מַכַּת נֶפֶשׁ, זוֹ הִיא מִיתָה:

כב| **לְמַעַן הַצִּיל אֹתוֹ.** רוּחַ הַקֹּדֶשׁ מְעִידָה עַל רְאוּבֵן שֶׁלֹּא אָמַר זֹאת אֶלָּא לְהַצִּיל אוֹתוֹ, שֶׁיָּבֹא הוּא וְיַעֲלֶנּוּ מִשָּׁם. אָמַר: אֲנִי בְּכוֹר וְגָדוֹל שֶׁבְּכֻלָּן, לֹא יִתָּלֶה הַסָּרְחוֹן אֶלָּא בִּי:

כג| **אֶת כֻּתָּנְתּוֹ.** זֶה חָלוּק: **אֶת כְּתֹנֶת הַפַּסִּים.** הוּא שֶׁהוֹסִיף לוֹ אָבִיו יוֹתֵר עַל אֶחָיו:

כד| **וְהַבּוֹר רֵק אֵין בּוֹ מָיִם.** מִמַּשְׁמַע שֶׁנֶּאֱמַר: ״וְהַבּוֹר רֵק״ אֵינִי יוֹדֵעַ שֶׁאֵין בּוֹ מַיִם? מַה תַּלְמוּד לוֹמַר: ״אֵין בּוֹ מָיִם״? מַיִם אֵין בּוֹ, אֲבָל נְחָשִׁים וְעַקְרַבִּים יֵשׁ בּוֹ:

כה| **אֹרְחַת.** כְּתַרְגּוּמוֹ: ״שַׁיָּרַת״, עַל שֵׁם הוֹלְכֵי אֹרַח: **וּגְמַלֵּיהֶם נֹשְׂאִים וְגוֹ׳.** לָמָּה פִּרְסֵם הַכָּתוּב אֶת מַשָּׂאָם? לְהוֹדִיעַ מַתַּן שְׂכָרָן שֶׁל צַדִּיקִים, שֶׁאֵין דַּרְכָּן שֶׁל עַרְבִיִּים לָשֵׂאת אֶלָּא נֵפְט וְעִטְרָן שֶׁרֵיחָן רַע, וְלָזֶה נִזְדַּמְּנוּ בְּשָׂמִים שֶׁלֹּא יֻזַּק מֵרֵיחַ רַע: **נְכֹאת.** כָּל כִּנּוּסֵי בְּשָׂמִים הַרְבֵּה קָרוּי ׳נְכֹאת׳, וְכֵן: ״וַיַּרְאֵם אֶת כָּל בֵּית נְכֹתֹה״ (מלכים ב׳ כ, יג) – מִרְקַחַת בְּשָׂמָיו. וְאוּנְקְלוֹס תִּרְגֵּם לְשׁוֹן שַׁעֲוָה: **וּצְרִי.** שְׂרָף הַנּוֹטֵף מֵעֲצֵי הַקְּטָף, וְהוּא נָטָף (שמות ל, לד) הַנִּמְנֶה עִם סַמָּנֵי הַקְּטֹרֶת: **וָלֹט.** ׳לוֹטֶס׳ שְׁמוֹ בִּלְשׁוֹן מִשְׁנָה (שביעית ז, ו), וְרַבּוֹתַי פֵּרְשׁוּהוּ לִי: שֹׁרֶשׁ עֵשֶׂב וּשְׁמוֹ אשטורוזי״ה בְּמַסֶּכֶת נִדָּה (דף ח ע״א):

כו| **מַה בֶּצַע.** מַה מָּמוֹן, כְּתַרְגּוּמוֹ: **וְכִסִּינוּ אֶת דָּמוֹ.** וְנַעֲלִים אֶת מִיתָתוֹ:

כז| **וַיִּשְׁמְעוּ.** ״וְקַבִּילוּ מִנֵּיהּ״, וְכָל שְׁמִיעָה שֶׁהִיא קַבָּלַת דְּבָרִים, כְּגוֹן זֶה, וּכְגוֹן: ״וַיִּשְׁמַע יַעֲקֹב אֶל אָבִיו״ (לעיל כח, ז), ״נַעֲשֶׂה וְנִשְׁמָע״ (שמות כד, ז), מְתַרְגְּמִין: ׳וְקַבִּילוּ׳. וְכָל שֶׁהִיא שְׁמִיעַת הָאֹזֶן, כְּגוֹן: ״וַיִּשְׁמְעוּ אֶת קוֹל ה׳ אֱלֹהִים מִתְהַלֵּךְ בַּגָּן״ (לעיל ג, ח), ״וְרִבְקָה שֹׁמַעַת״ (לעיל כז, ה), ״וַיִּשְׁמַע יִשְׂרָאֵל״ (לעיל לה, כב), ״שָׁמַעְתִּי אֶת תְּלוּנֹּת״ (שמות טז, יב), כֻּלָּן מְתַרְגְּמִין: וּשְׁמַעוּ, וּשְׁמַעַת, וּשְׁמַע, שְׁמִיעַ קֳדָמַי:

כח| **וַיַּעַבְרוּ אֲנָשִׁים מִדְיָנִים.** זוֹ הִיא שַׁיָּרָה אַחֶרֶת, וְהוֹדִיעֲךָ הַכָּתוּב שֶׁנִּמְכַּר פְּעָמִים הַרְבֵּה: **וַיִּמְשְׁכוּ.** בְּנֵי יַעֲקֹב אֶת יוֹסֵף מִן הַבּוֹר וַיִּמְכְּרוּהוּ לַיִּשְׁמְעֵאלִים, וְהַיִּשְׁמְעֵאלִים לַמִּדְיָנִים, ״וְהַמְּדָנִים מָכְרוּ אֹתוֹ אֶל מִצְרָיִם״ (להלן פסוק לו):

BACKGROUND

37:25 | Balm [*tzeri*]: *Tzeri* is mentioned several times in the Bible (see, e.g., Genesis 43:11; Jeremiah 8:22; Ezekiel 27:17). Some identify this with the oil produced from the Arabian balsam tree, *Commiphora gileadensis*, a valuable fragrant plant that grows in the Jordan Valley region. This oil was an essential ingredient in the manufacture of perfumes in the ancient Near East. During the Second Temple period, the Land of Israel was famous for its production of the oil. The balm from the Gilad region was particularly famous (see Jeremiah 8:22, 46:11). However, some claim that the Gileadean *tzeri* mentioned in the Bible, which grows in cooler, mountainous regions, is different from the *tzeri* mentioned by the Sages, and only the latter is related to the balsam tree.

Labdanum [*lot*]: Researchers identify *lot* as the plant known in Arabic as *lādan*, and in Persian as *lathen*, labdanum, *Cistus ladanifer*. Labdanum is a perennial plant which reaches heights of 40–60 cm. From this plant, one would extract a red aromatic resin which was used in perfumes and cosmetics.

29 **Reuben returned to the pit.** Evidently, Reuben was not present at the time of the sale. **And behold, Joseph was not in the pit; he rent his garments** due to his concern regarding Joseph's fate.

30 **He returned to his brothers, and said: The boy is not there; and I, where do I go?** What will happen to me? As the oldest brother, Reuben felt that the responsibility for Joseph rested on his shoulders.

31 Selling one's own brother is an especially egregious act. By Torah law, kidnapping and selling any member of Israel into slavery, let alone one's relative, is a capital offense. The brothers therefore sought to prepare a cover story for Joseph's disappearance: **They took Joseph's tunic, slaughtered a goat,** whose blood resembles human blood, **and dipped the tunic in the blood** of the goat.

32 **They sent the fine tunic**[D] to Jacob, **and they brought it to their father and they said: We found this. Identify now: Is it your son's tunic or not?** Clearly this is a fine tunic, but is it Joseph's? We never paid attention to the details of his tunic, but since you made it, you must recognize it.

33 **He identified it, and said:** This is **my son's tunic;** clearly **an evil beast devoured him; Joseph was mauled.** The brothers told Jacob that they discovered only the tunic. They found no traces of Joseph's body, as the wild beast would have dragged it to its lair. Since the animal would not consume the tunic, it was left and therefore recovered.

34 **Jacob rent his garments** in mourning, **placed sackcloth on his loins, and mourned his son many days.**

35 **All his sons and all his daughters**[D] **arose to console him; but he refused to be consoled** despite the efforts of those around him. **He said:** Nothing will change the present reality; **for I will descend mourning to the grave, to my son. His father wept for him.** Although Jacob did not have absolute proof that Joseph died as his body was not recovered, there was significant circumstantial evidence that Joseph was mauled.

36 The verse turns its focus back to Joseph: **The Midyanites, [*medanim*],**[15] **sold him,** Joseph, **to Egypt** as a slave **to Potifar,** who was a **courtier [*seris*] of Pharaoh.** Although *seris* literally refers to a eunuch, this is not necessarily its meaning in the verse. Rather, the verse uses it to refer to an officer with a position in the royal palace.[16] Potifar was the **chief executioner.**[17] It is likely that Joseph was considered quality merchandise. He was of fine form, only seventeen years old, and his health had never been strained by hard work. He would have been sold only to a wealthy individual who could afford Joseph's worth.

The Incident of Judah and Tamar

GENESIS 38:1–30

The Torah interrupts its narrative of Joseph's life to focus on an altogether unrelated story involving Judah, one of Joseph's older brothers, who will eventually emerge as the most dominant of the brothers. This chapter, which describes the unique circumstances that lead to the births of Judah's primary successors, also reveals Judah's character. Judah does not initially act with perfect righteousness; however, when faced with a difficult situation, he accepts responsibility for his actions and displays true greatness. As the narrative continues, this behavior will emerge as a common feature of Judah's personality. Although Judah errs, he knows how to rectify and correct his failures. This quality will eventually become the hallmark of the tribe that descends from him.

The details of this seemingly tangential episode underscore an important principle concerning the great characters of the Bible: The Bible does not seek to cover up imperfections; it tells the truth, even though it may be unpleasant. An individual's successes and failures are each related in their entirety, without omission or bias. Consequently, the complete story of Judah is recorded in the Torah: His descent, the details of his unseemly actions, and ultimately, the rectification of those actions.

38 1 **It was at that time; Judah descended from his brothers.**
Fourth aliya Based on chronological considerations, this incident took place shortly before the sale of Joseph.[18] Even after the brothers married and established families of their own, they continued to live in close proximity to one another and worked together. It is unclear whether each brother owned his own property, or if they were partners in a family business. In any case, Judah now left the presence of his brothers to establish his own private business. Judah reached Adulam, a city in the south of Judea, **and he turned to an Adulamite man** and befriended him, **and his name was Hira.**

2 **Judah saw there,** in Adulam, **the daughter of a Canaanite man,**[D] **and his name was Shua. He took her** in marriage, **and engaged in intercourse with her.**

3 **She conceived and she bore a son; he called his name Er.**

DISCUSSION

37:32| **They sent [*vayeshaleḥu*] the fine tunic:** According to one opinion, the word *vayeshaleḥu* is related to *shelaḥ*, a sword or spear. That is, the brothers used a sharp implement to pierce the tunic in order to create the impression that a wild beast mauled whoever was wearing it (see Ramban).

37:35| **And all his daughters:** This refers to all the women of his household, including his daughters-in-law. According to the Torah, Jacob had only one daughter, Dina, and it is uncertain

כט יוֹסֵף לַיִּשְׁמְעֵאלִים בְּעֶשְׂרִים כָּסֶף וַיָּבִיאוּ אֶת־יוֹסֵף מִצְרָיְמָה: וַיָּשָׁב רְאוּבֵן אֶל־
ל הַבּוֹר וְהִנֵּה אֵין־יוֹסֵף בַּבּוֹר וַיִּקְרַע אֶת־בְּגָדָיו: וַיָּשָׁב אֶל־אֶחָיו וַיֹּאמַר הַיֶּלֶד
לא אֵינֶנּוּ וַאֲנִי אָנָה אֲנִי־בָא: וַיִּקְחוּ אֶת־כְּתֹנֶת יוֹסֵף וַיִּשְׁחֲטוּ שְׂעִיר עִזִּים וַיִּטְבְּלוּ
לב אֶת־הַכֻּתֹּנֶת בַּדָּם: וַיְשַׁלְּחוּ אֶת־כְּתֹנֶת הַפַּסִּים וַיָּבִיאוּ אֶל־אֲבִיהֶם וַיֹּאמְרוּ זֹאת
לג מָצָאנוּ הַכֶּר־נָא הַכְּתֹנֶת בִּנְךָ הִוא אִם־לֹא: וַיַּכִּירָהּ וַיֹּאמֶר כְּתֹנֶת בְּנִי חַיָּה רָעָה
לד אֲכָלָתְהוּ טָרֹף טֹרַף יוֹסֵף: וַיִּקְרַע יַעֲקֹב שִׂמְלֹתָיו וַיָּשֶׂם שַׂק בְּמָתְנָיו וַיִּתְאַבֵּל
לה עַל־בְּנוֹ יָמִים רַבִּים: וַיָּקֻמוּ כָל־בָּנָיו וְכָל־בְּנֹתָיו לְנַחֲמוֹ וַיְמָאֵן לְהִתְנַחֵם וַיֹּאמֶר
לו כִּי־אֵרֵד אֶל־בְּנִי אָבֵל שְׁאֹלָה וַיֵּבְךְּ אֹתוֹ אָבִיו: וְהַמְּדָנִים מָכְרוּ אֹתוֹ אֶל־מִצְרָיִם
לְפוֹטִיפַר סְרִיס פַּרְעֹה שַׂר הַטַּבָּחִים:

א וַיְהִי בָּעֵת הַהִוא וַיֵּרֶד יְהוּדָה מֵאֵת אֶחָיו וַיֵּט עַד־אִישׁ עֲדֻלָּמִי וּשְׁמוֹ חִירָה: לח רביעי
ב ג וַיַּרְא־שָׁם יְהוּדָה בַּת־אִישׁ כְּנַעֲנִי וּשְׁמוֹ שׁוּעַ וַיִּקָּחֶהָ וַיָּבֹא אֵלֶיהָ: וַתַּהַר וַתֵּלֶד

רש״י

כט | וַיָּשָׁב רְאוּבֵן. וּבִמְכִירָתוֹ לֹא הָיָה שָׁם, שֶׁהִגִּיעַ יוֹמוֹ לֵילֵךְ וּלְשַׁמֵּשׁ אֶת אָבִיו. דָּבָר אַחֵר, עָסוּק הָיָה בְּשַׂקּוֹ וּבְתַעֲנִיתוֹ עַל שֶׁבִּלְבֵּל יְצוּעֵי אָבִיו:

ל | אָנָה אֲנִי בָא. אָנָה אֶבְרַח מִצַּעֲרוֹ שֶׁל אַבָּא:

לא | שְׂעִיר עִזִּים. דָּמוֹ דּוֹמֶה לְשֶׁל אָדָם: הַכֻּתֹּנֶת. זֶה שְׁמָהּ, וּכְשֶׁהִיא דְּבוּקָה לְתֵבָה אַחֶרֶת, כְּגוֹן ״כְּתֹנֶת יוֹסֵף״, ״כְּתֹנֶת פַּסִּים״ (לעיל פסוק ג), ״כְּתֹנֶת בַּד״ (ויקרא טז, ד), נָקוּד ׳כְּתֹנֶת׳:

לג | וַיֹּאמֶר כְּתֹנֶת בְּנִי. הִיא זוֹ: חַיָּה רָעָה אֲכָלָתְהוּ. נִצְנְצָה בּוֹ רוּחַ הַקֹּדֶשׁ, סוֹפוֹ שֶׁתִּתְגָּרֶה בּוֹ אֵשֶׁת פּוֹטִיפַר. וְלָמָּה לֹא גִּלָּה לוֹ הַקָּדוֹשׁ בָּרוּךְ הוּא? לְפִי שֶׁהֶחֱרִימוּ וְקִלְּלוּ אֶת כָּל מִי שֶׁיְּגַלֶּה, וְשִׁתְּפוּ לְהַקָּדוֹשׁ בָּרוּךְ הוּא עִמָּהֶם. אֲבָל יִצְחָק הָיָה יוֹדֵעַ שֶׁהוּא חַי, אָמַר: הֵיאַךְ אֲגַלֶּה וְהַקָּדוֹשׁ בָּרוּךְ הוּא אֵינוֹ רוֹצֶה לְגַלּוֹת לוֹ?

לד | יָמִים רַבִּים. עֶשְׂרִים וּשְׁתַּיִם שָׁנָה מִשֶּׁפֵּרַשׁ מִמֶּנּוּ עַד שֶׁיָּרַד יַעֲקֹב לְמִצְרַיִם, שֶׁנֶּאֱמַר: ״יוֹסֵף בֶּן שְׁבַע עֶשְׂרֵה שָׁנָה״ וְגוֹ׳ (לעיל פסוק ב), וּבֶן שְׁלֹשִׁים שָׁנָה הָיָה בְּעָמְדוֹ לִפְנֵי פַרְעֹה (להלן מא, מו), וְשֶׁבַע שְׁנֵי הַשָּׂבָע, וְ״כִּי זֶה שְׁנָתַיִם הָרָעָב״ (להלן מה, ו) כְּשֶׁבָּא יַעֲקֹב לְמִצְרַיִם, הֲרֵי עֶשְׂרִים וּשְׁתַּיִם, כְּנֶגֶד עֶשְׂרִים וּשְׁתַּיִם שֶׁלֹּא קִיֵּם יַעֲקֹב כִּבּוּד אָב וָאֵם: עֶשְׂרִים שָׁנָה שֶׁהָיָה בְּבֵית לָבָן, וּשְׁתֵּי שָׁנִים בַּדֶּרֶךְ בְּשׁוּבוֹ מִבֵּית לָבָן, שָׁנָה וָחֵצִי בְּסֻכּוֹת וְשִׁשָּׁה חֳדָשִׁים בְּבֵית אֵל. וְזֶהוּ שֶׁאָמַר לְלָבָן: ״זֶה לִּי עֶשְׂרִים שָׁנָה בְּבֵיתֶךָ״ (לעיל לא, מא) – לִי הֵן, עָלַי הֵן, סוֹפִי לִלְקוֹת כְּנֶגְדָּן:

לה | וְכָל בְּנֹתָיו. רַבִּי יְהוּדָה אוֹמֵר: אֲחָיוֹת תְּאוֹמוֹת נוֹלְדוּ עִם כָּל שֵׁבֶט וְשֵׁבֶט וּנְשָׂאוּם. רַבִּי נְחֶמְיָה אוֹמֵר: כְּנַעֲנִיּוֹת הָיוּ, אֶלָּא מַהוּ ״וְכָל בְּנוֹתָיו״? כַּלּוֹתָיו, שֶׁאֵין אָדָם נִמְנָע מִלִּקְרֹא לַחֲתָנוֹ בְּנוֹ וּלְכַלָּתוֹ בִּתּוֹ: וַיְמָאֵן לְהִתְנַחֵם. אֵין אָדָם יָכוֹל לְקַבֵּל תַּנְחוּמִין עַל הַחַי וְסָבוּר שֶׁמֵּת, שֶׁעַל הַמֵּת נִגְזְרָה גְּזֵרָה שֶׁיִּשְׁתַּכַּח מִן הַלֵּב וְלֹא עַל הַחַי: אֵרֵד אֶל בְּנִי. כְּמוֹ ׳עַל בְּנִי׳, וְהַרְבֵּה ׳אֶל׳ שֶׁמְּשַׁמְּשִׁין בִּלְשׁוֹן ׳עַל׳, ״אֶל שָׁאוּל וְאֶל בֵּית הַדָּמִים״ (שמואל ב׳ כא, א), ״אֶל הִלָּקַח אֲרוֹן הָאֱלֹהִים וְאֶל חָמִיהָ וְאִישָׁהּ״ (שמואל א׳ ד, כא): אָבֵל שְׁאֹלָה. כִּפְשׁוּטוֹ לְשׁוֹן קֶבֶר הוּא, בְּאֶבְלִי אֶקָּבֵר וְלֹא אֶתְנַחֵם כָּל יָמַי. וּבְמִדְרָשׁוֹ: גֵּיהִנָּם; סִימָן זֶה הָיָה מָסוּר בְּיָדִי מִפִּי הַגְּבוּרָה, אִם לֹא יָמוּת אֶחָד מִבָּנַי בְּחַיַּי מֻבְטָח אֲנִי שֶׁאֵינִי רוֹאֶה גֵּיהִנָּם: וַיֵּבְךְּ אֹתוֹ אָבִיו. יִצְחָק בּוֹכֶה הָיָה מִפְּנֵי צָרָתוֹ שֶׁל יַעֲקֹב, אֲבָל לֹא הָיָה מִתְאַבֵּל, שֶׁהָיָה יוֹדֵעַ שֶׁהוּא חַי:

לו | הַטַּבָּחִים. שׁוֹחֲטֵי בַּהֲמוֹת הַמֶּלֶךְ:

פרק לח

א | וַיְהִי בָּעֵת הַהִוא. לָמָּה נִסְמְכָה פָּרָשָׁה זוֹ לְכָאן וְהִפְסִיק בְּפָרָשָׁתוֹ שֶׁל יוֹסֵף? לְלַמֵּד שֶׁהוֹרִידוּהוּ אֶחָיו מִגְּדֻלָּתוֹ כְּשֶׁרָאוּ בְּצָרַת אֲבִיהֶם, אָמְרוּ: אַתָּה אָמַרְתָּ לְמָכְרוֹ, אִלּוּ אָמַרְתָּ לַהֲשִׁיבוֹ הָיִינוּ שׁוֹמְעִים לָךְ: וַיֵּט. מֵאֵת אֶחָיו: עַד אִישׁ עֲדֻלָּמִי. נִשְׁתַּתֵּף עִמּוֹ:

ב | כְּנַעֲנִי. תַּגְּרָא:

DISCUSSION

whether she lived in Jacob's home. The Midrash, however, suggests that each of the twelve tribes was born with a twin sister (*Bereshit Rabba* 84; *Pirkei deRabbi Eliezer* 39; see also Genesis 46:7).

38:2 | **A Canaanite man [*kena'ani*]:** The Bible sometimes uses the word *kena'ani* in reference to a merchant, indicative of the fact that Hebrews were not extensively engaged in trade during the biblical period (see commentary on Isaiah 23:8, 17). That seems to be its meaning in this context as well. It would be incorrect to assume that the Torah is informing us of Shua's ethnicity, as apart from Jacob and his family, everyone in the surrounding area was a member of some Canaanite tribe. Consequently, identifying Shua as a Canaanite man would be trivial. If, however, the verse means to state that Shua was a merchant, it is possible that he was not of Canaanite descent, as merchants often traveled from foreign lands (see Ramban). Nevertheless, it would

4 **She conceived again and bore a son; she called his name Onan.** This name might derive from the similar Hebrew word for might or vitality.

5 **She continued and bore a son again, and** she **called his name Shela. He,** Judah, **was at** the place known as **Keziv,**[B] **when she bore him.** Perhaps this parenthetical comment is meant to explain why Shua's daughter, rather than Judah, named both their second and third sons. Perhaps the standard custom was for parents to alternate naming rights, such that Judah was supposed to name their third son. However, since Judah was in Keziv, his wife named the child.

6 **Judah took a wife for Er his firstborn, and her name was Tamar.** Nothing is known of her origins or ethnicity. It is possible that the absence of any background information alludes to the fact that Tamar was not from the local population. Indeed, the Sages identify her as a descendant of Shem.[19] Some suggest she was from Aram Naharayim.[20]

7 **Er, Judah's firstborn, was wicked in the eyes of the Lord; and** as punishment for his sins **the Lord put him to death** while he was still young.

8 **Judah said to Onan: Engage in intercourse with your brother's wife, and consummate levirate marriage with her.**[D] **Establish offspring for your brother.** The children born from this levirate marriage will be considered the children of the deceased brother. Although the surviving brother is certainly the biological father of these children, he is merely a substitute for his deceased bother.[21]

9 **Onan knew that the offspring would not be his,** and that any children born from this marriage would not be called by his name, but by the name of his deceased brother. Therefore, **it was when he engaged in intercourse with his brother's wife; he would spill it on the ground,** practiced coitus interruptus, **so as not to give offspring for his brother**. Out of envy, Onan preferred to have no children rather than have children who would be regarded as his brother's.

10 **That which he did was evil in the eyes of the Lord.** Unlike his brother, Onan's transgression is explicitly stated by the verse. **And He put him to death too,** and Onan died at a young age.

11 **Judah said to Tamar, his daughter-in-law:** Do not remain in my house; rather, **remain a widow,** alone **in your father's house, until Shela my** third **son matures.** It would appear that Shela had not yet reached marriageable age. Although Shela was supposed to perform levirate marriage when coming of age, Judah was not interested in allowing a marriage between Shela and Tamar, **for he said: Lest he too die, like his brothers.** He was concerned that Tamar was somehow a dangerous woman who caused the deaths of his first two sons. To protect his youngest son, Judah sent Tamar from his house.[22] So **Tamar went and lived in her father's house.**

12 **The days** and years **accumulated and the** unnamed **daughter of Shua, wife of Judah, died.** After mourning over her death, **Judah was comforted** and ceased to mourn, **and** he **went up to** visit **his sheepshearers,** who were apparently located a significant distance from Judah's home. Among other reasons, Judah sought to relieve the grief due to his wife's death by participating in the shearing of his sheep, typically a festive and joyous occasion. **He and Hira, his friend the Adulamite,** came **to Timna.**[B] Perhaps Judah's close friend came to comfort him, and then decided to accompany Judah to the sheep shearing.

13 **It was told to Tamar, saying: Behold, your father-in-law is going up to Timna to shear his sheep.** As Tamar belonged to Judah's family, she was informed of his trip. She decided to take drastic action.

14 **She removed the garments of her widowhood from upon her.** It was customary for widows to wear distinctive garments testifying to their familial status.[23] This custom was especially significant in the case of a widow like Tamar, who was awaiting levirate marriage and was unable to marry whomever she wished. **She covered herself with a** large **veil** concealing her entire body, **wrapped herself,** covering herself completely in the manor of harlots, who wore loose-fitting garments. **And she sat at the entrance of** a place called **Einayim, which is on the road to Timna.** Perhaps Einayim was called by this name because there were *ma'ayanot*, springs, there.[24] Tamar knew that Judah would need to pass through Einayim, so she waited for him there. Her behavior did not stem from some character flaw, but from despair, **for she saw that Shela had matured** and reached marriageable age, **but** yet **she had not been given to him as a wife.** Tamar understood that Judah did not want her to be married to Shela, which meant that she could remain a widow for the rest of her life.

DISCUSSION

seem that most of Jacob's daughters-in-law were of Canaanite descent.

38:8 | Consummate levirate marriage with her: The fact that Judah saw levirate marriage as the obvious course of action indicates that the institution of levirate marriage, which later appears as a divine commandment (Deuteronomy 25:5–6), was already practiced in some form before the giving of the Torah. Various forms of levirate marriage also existed in other societies. Underlying all forms of levirate marriage is the basic premise that if a man dies childless, one of his relatives shall take his widow as a wife. In ancient times, various relatives were viewed as entitled to, or responsible for, performing levirate marriage. In this instance, as is the case by Torah law, only the brothers of the deceased were expected to perform levirate marriage (see also Ramban).

ה בֵּן וַיִּקְרָא אֶת־שְׁמוֹ עֵר: וַתַּהַר עוֹד וַתֵּלֶד בֵּן וַתִּקְרָא אֶת־שְׁמוֹ אוֹנָן: וַתֹּסֶף

ו עוֹד וַתֵּלֶד בֵּן וַתִּקְרָא אֶת־שְׁמוֹ שֵׁלָה וְהָיָה בִכְזִיב בְּלִדְתָּהּ אֹתוֹ: וַיִּקַּח יְהוּדָה

ז אִשָּׁה לְעֵר בְּכוֹרוֹ וּשְׁמָהּ תָּמָר: וַיְהִי עֵר בְּכוֹר יְהוּדָה רַע בְּעֵינֵי יְהוָה וַיְמִתֵהוּ

ח יְהוָה: וַיֹּאמֶר יְהוּדָה לְאוֹנָן בֹּא אֶל־אֵשֶׁת אָחִיךָ וְיַבֵּם אֹתָהּ וְהָקֵם זֶרַע לְאָחִיךָ:

ט וַיֵּדַע אוֹנָן כִּי לֹא לוֹ יִהְיֶה הַזָּרַע וְהָיָה אִם־בָּא אֶל־אֵשֶׁת אָחִיו וְשִׁחֵת אַרְצָה

י לְבִלְתִּי נְתָן־זֶרַע לְאָחִיו: וַיֵּרַע בְּעֵינֵי יְהוָה אֲשֶׁר עָשָׂה וַיָּמֶת גַּם־אֹתוֹ: וַיֹּאמֶר

יא יְהוּדָה לְתָמָר כַּלָּתוֹ שְׁבִי אַלְמָנָה בֵית־אָבִיךְ עַד־יִגְדַּל שֵׁלָה בְנִי כִּי אָמַר

יב פֶּן־יָמוּת גַּם־הוּא כְּאֶחָיו וַתֵּלֶךְ תָּמָר וַתֵּשֶׁב בֵּית אָבִיהָ: וַיִּרְבּוּ הַיָּמִים וַתָּמָת

יג בַּת־שׁוּעַ אֵשֶׁת־יְהוּדָה וַיִּנָּחֶם יְהוּדָה וַיַּעַל עַל־גֹּזֲזֵי צֹאנוֹ הוּא וְחִירָה רֵעֵהוּ

יד הָעֲדֻלָּמִי תִּמְנָתָה: וַיֻּגַּד לְתָמָר לֵאמֹר הִנֵּה חָמִיךְ עֹלֶה תִמְנָתָה לָגֹז צֹאנוֹ:

וַתָּסַר בִּגְדֵי אַלְמְנוּתָהּ מֵעָלֶיהָ וַתְּכַס בַּצָּעִיף וַתִּתְעַלָּף וַתֵּשֶׁב בְּפֶתַח עֵינַיִם

אֲשֶׁר עַל־דֶּרֶךְ תִּמְנָתָה כִּי רָאֲתָה כִּי־גָדַל שֵׁלָה וְהִוא לֹא־נִתְּנָה לוֹ לְאִשָּׁה:

רש"י

ה | וְהָיָה בִכְזִיב. שֵׁם הַמָּקוֹם. וְאוֹמֵר אֲנִי, עַל שֵׁם שֶׁפָּסְקָה מִלֶּדֶת נִקְרָא "כְּזִיב", לְשׁוֹן: "הָיוֹ תִהְיֶה לִי כְּמוֹ אַכְזָב" (ירמיה טו, יח), "אֲשֶׁר לֹא יְכַזְּבוּ מֵימָיו" (ישעיה נח, יא), וְאִם לֹא כֵן מַה בָּא לְהוֹדִיעֵנוּ? וּבְבְרֵאשִׁית רַבָּה (פה, ד) רָאִיתִי: "וַתִּקְרָא שְׁמוֹ שֵׁלָה וְגו' – פְּסָקַת.

ז | רַע בְּעֵינֵי ה'. כְּרָעָתוֹ שֶׁל אוֹנָן, מַשְׁחִית זַרְעוֹ, שֶׁנֶּאֱמַר בְּאוֹנָן: "וַיָּמֶת גַּם אֹתוֹ" (להלן פסוק י), כְּמִיתָתוֹ שֶׁל עֵר מִיתָתוֹ שֶׁל אוֹנָן. וְלָמָּה הָיָה עֵר מַשְׁחִית זַרְעוֹ? כְּדֵי שֶׁלֹּא תִתְעַבֵּר וְיַכְחִישׁ יָפְיָהּ:

ח | וְהָקֵם זֶרַע. הַבֵּן יִקָּרֵא עַל שֵׁם הַמֵּת:

ט | וְשִׁחֵת אַרְצָה. דָּשׁ מִבִּפְנִים וְזוֹרֶה מִבַּחוּץ:

יא | כִּי אָמַר וְגו'. כְּלוֹמַר, דּוֹחֶה הָיָה אוֹתָהּ בְּקַשׁ, שֶׁלֹּא הָיָה בְּדַעְתּוֹ לְהַשִּׂיאָהּ לוֹ: כִּי אָמַר פֶּן יָמוּת. מֻחְזֶקֶת הִיא זוֹ שֶׁיָּמוּתוּ אֲנָשֶׁיהָ:

יב | וַיַּעַל עַל גֹּזֲזֵי צֹאנוֹ. וַיַּעַל תִּמְנָתָה לַעֲמֹד עַל גֹּזֲזֵי צֹאנוֹ:

יג | עֹלֶה תִמְנָתָה. וּבְשִׁמְשׁוֹן הוּא אוֹמֵר: "וַיֵּרֶד שִׁמְשׁוֹן

תִּמְנָתָה" (שופטים יד, א) בִּשְׁפוּעַ הָהָר הָיְתָה יוֹשֶׁבֶת, עוֹלִין לָהּ מִכָּאן וְיוֹרְדִין לָהּ מִכָּאן:

יד | וַתִּתְעַלָּף. כִּסְּתָה פָנֶיהָ, שֶׁלֹּא יַכִּיר בָּהּ: וַתֵּשֶׁב בְּפֶתַח עֵינַיִם. בִּפְתִיחַת עֵינַיִם, בְּפָרָשַׁת דְּרָכִים שֶׁעַל דֶּרֶךְ תִּמְנָתָה. וְרַבּוֹתֵינוּ דָּרְשׁוּ, בְּפִתְחוֹ שֶׁל אַבְרָהָם אָבִינוּ שֶׁכָּל עֵינַיִם מְצַפּוֹת לִרְאוֹתוֹ: כִּי רָאֲתָה כִּי גָדַל שֵׁלָה וְגו'. לְפִיכָךְ הִפְקִירָה עַצְמָהּ אֵצֶל יְהוּדָה, שֶׁהָיְתָה מִתְאַוָּה לְהַעֲמִיד מִמֶּנּוּ בָּנִים:

BACKGROUND

38:5 | Keziv: This refers to a village in the Judean plains, mentioned in Joshua (15:44) and Micah (1:14). Some identify it with the Al-Kazbah spring, located near the present-day Etziona junction. Others identify it with Khirbit Lavnin, which is situated north of Nehusha. This is based on accounts in Joshua and Micah

that place Livna, Adulam, Maresha, and Keziv in close proximity to one another.

38:12 | Timna: This is a city located between ancient Beit Shemesh and Ekron, on the northern border of Judah's portion of the Land of Israel (Joshua 15:10–11). During the era of Samson, it was populated by the Philistines (Judges

14:1). Today, it is identified with Tel Batash, which lies to the south of one of the channels of the Sorek River, and about 7 km west of Beit Shemesh. Archeological excavations there have uncovered Canaanite artifacts from the eighteenth century BCE, and Philistine artifacts from the twelfth century BCE.

15 **Judah saw her** on the road **and thought her to be a harlot because she covered her face.** Evidently, harlots were known to partially cover their faces.

16 Because Judah was a lonely widower, when he saw her **he turned to her by the road, and he said: Please, let me engage in intercourse with you; for he did not know that she was his daughter-in-law.** By Torah law, relations between a father-in-law and daughter-in-law are strictly prohibited, even after the son's death. Although this incident took place before the Torah was given, it is clear that the laws of the time would have prevented a father-in-law from marrying his daughter-in-law.[25] Therefore, there is no doubt that had Judah known the true identity of this woman, he would not have turned to her. **She said: What will you give me that you will engage in intercourse with me?** As she was impersonating a harlot, Tamar demanded payment.

17 **He said: I will send you a kid from the flock** as payment. **She said: If you give me collateral until your sending.** To ensure that you provide payment, give me collateral to hold until I receive the kid.

18 **He said: What is the collateral that I should give you? She said: Your signet,** which was either on his ring or otherwise held close to his body, **and your belt, and your staff that is in your hand.** This appears to be a ruler's staff, as the preceding verses indicate that Judah held some minor governing capacity. **He gave them to her, engaged in intercourse with her, and she conceived by him.** The fact that Judah gave this unknown woman various personal items including his signet, an item not normally given out or lent, as it is used to certify legal documents, demonstrates that Judah was not acting judiciously at that time.

19 After Judah left, **she arose, went, and removed her veil from upon her, and she donned the garments of her widowhood.** Tamar achieved her goal: Through her actions, she effectively guaranteed that Judah would consummate a levirate marriage with her. She succeeded in changing her status from barren widow to married mother, and she fulfilled her desire to be the wife of a member of Judah's family.

20 After some time, out of a sense of obligation and a desire to retrieve his collateral, **Judah sent the kid** to Tamar **in the hand of his friend the Adulamite.** Since Hira was a close friend,

Judah trusted his discretion and was not ashamed to send him on this mission. However, Hira came to the place where Judah initially met the woman, **to take the collateral from the woman, but he did not find her.**

21 **He asked the men of her place, saying: Where is the harlot,**[D] **who was at Einayim on the way? They said: There was no harlot here.**

22 **He returned to Judah, and said: I did not find her. The men of the place also said: There was no harlot here.**

23 **Judah said:** If so, let her **take it,** the collateral, **for her, lest we become a laughingstock; behold, I sent this kid, and you did not find her.** If she does not want or is unable to claim her payment, then let the collateral remain with her. Although the items Judah deposited with the woman were of importance to him, he did not wish to continue searching for her.

24 **It was some three months later,** after Judah's encounter with Tamar, **that it was told to Judah, saying: Tamar, your daughter-in-law, acted licentiously; moreover,** this is evidenced by the fact that **behold, she conceived through harlotry.** Tamar had no qualms about what she had done, as she felt that she had fulfilled the spirit of the law of levirate marriage. She therefore made no attempt to conceal her pregnancy. Nevertheless, since she seduced Judah in a deceitful manner, such that the identity of the father of the fetus was unknown to all except Tamar, she was susceptible to severe consequences, as she was tethered to Judah's family with a marriage-like bond. The Sages refer to such a woman as a widow awaiting her brother-in-law.[26] Since it was assumed that she became pregnant through a man not from Judah's family, her fate was to be that of an adulterous woman. Therefore, **Judah,** her father-in-law, the patriarch of his family, and a distinguished member of his community, **said: Take her out, and she shall be burned.**[D]

25 **She was taken out** to receive her punishment. Since she was imprisoned, she wrapped the items she received from Judah **and she sent** them by messenger **to her father-in-law, saying: By the man whose these are I am with child. She said: Recognize, please, whose signet, belt, and staff are these.**

26 **Judah recognized them,** his possessions, **and said: She is more righteous than I;**[D] **because indeed, I did not give her to Shela my son.** She had some right to be with me, as I did not give her to Shela. Therefore, she cannot be accused

---

DISCUSSION

38:21 | The harlot [*kedeisha*]: The term *kedeisha* originally referred to prostitutes employed by priests to work in pagan temples, and their actions were considered part of the idolatrous rites. Eventually, the term came to be used more broadly as a synonym for all prostitutes.

38:24 | And she shall be burned: Some commentaries have made the anachronistic claim that this refers to branding a symbol of disgrace onto her body using a hot iron. Such a practice was once common in Europe, but not in the

ancient Near East (see Rav Yehuda HaḤasid; Ba'al HaTurim).

38:26 | She is more righteous than I: Like Rebecca, also a mother of twins, Tamar was a resolute individual who set her sights on a goal and pursued it, albeit through unconventional means. ◄●

טו טז ויראה יהודה ויחשבה לזונה כי כסתה פניה: ויט אליה אל־הדרך ויאמר הבה
נא אבואה אליך כי לא ידע כי כלתו הוא ותאמר מה־תתן־לי כי תבוא אלי:
יז ויאמר אנכי אשלח גדי־עזים מן־הצאן ותאמר אם־תתן ערבון עד שלחך:
יח ויאמר מה הערבון אשר אתן־לך ותאמר חתמך ופתילך ומטך אשר בידך
יט ויתן־לה ויבא אליה ותהר לו: ותקם ותלך ותסר צעיפה מעליה ותלבש בגדי
כ אלמנותה: וישלח יהודה את־גדי העזים ביד רעהו העדלמי לקחת הערבון מיד
כא האשה ולא מצאה: וישאל את־אנשי מקמה לאמר איה הקדשה הוא בעינים
כב על־הדרך ויאמרו לא־היתה בזה קדשה: וישב אל־יהודה ויאמר לא מצאתיה
כג וגם אנשי המקום אמרו לא־היתה בזה קדשה: ויאמר יהודה תקח־לה פן נהיה
כד לבוז הנה שלחתי הגדי הזה ואתה לא מצאתה: ויהי | כמשלש חדשים ויגד
ליהודה לאמר זנתה תמר כלתך וגם הנה הרה לזנונים ויאמר יהודה הוציאוה
כה ותשרף: הוא מוצאת והיא שלחה אל־חמיה לאמר לאיש אשר־אלה לו אנכי
כו הרה ותאמר הכר־נא למי החתמת והפתילים והמטה האלה: ויכר יהודה
ויאמר צדקה ממני כי־על־כן לא־נתתיה לשלה בני ולא־יסף עוד לדעתה:

רש"י

טו| **ויחשבה לזונה.** לפי שיושבת בפרשת דרכים: **כי כסתה פניה.** ולא יכול לראותה ולהכירה. ומדרש רבותינו, "כי כסתה פניה", כשהיתה בבית חמיה היתה צנועה, לפיכך לא חשדה:

טז| **ויט אליה אל הדרך.** מדרך שהיה בה נטה אל הדרך אשר היא בה. ובלשון לעז דישטורני"ר: **הבה נא.** הכיני עצמך ודעתך לכך. כל לשון 'הבה' לשון הזמנה הוא, חוץ ממקום שיש לתרגמו בלשון נתינה, ואף אותן של הזמנה קרובים ללשון נתינה הם:

יז| **ערבון.** משכון:

יח| **חתמך ופתילך.** "עזקתך ושושיפך", טבעת שאתה חותם בה ושמלתך שאתה מתכסה בה: **ותהר לו.** גבורים כיוצא בו, צדיקים כיוצא בו:

כא| **הקדשה.** מקדשת ומזמנת לזנות:

כג| **תקח לה.** יהיה שלה מה שבידה: **פן נהיה לבוז.** אם תבקשנה עוד יתפרסם הדבר ויהיה גנאי, כי מה עלי עוד לעשות לאמת דברי? "הנה שלחתי הגדי הזה" וגו'! ולפי שרמה יהודה את אביו בגדי עזים שהטביל כתנת יוסף בדמו, רמוהו גם הוא בגדי עזים:

כד| **כמשלש חדשים.** רבו של ראשון ורבו של אחרון ואמצעי שלם. ולשון "כמשלש חדשים" כהשתלש החדשים, כמו: "ומשלח מנות" (אסתר ט, יט), "משלוח ידם" (ישעיה יא, יד), וכן תרגם אונקלוס: "כתלתות ירחיא": **הרה לזנונים.** שם דבר, מעוברת, כמו: "אשה הרה" (שמות כא, כב), וכמו: "ברה כחמה" (שיר השירים ו, י): **ותשרף.** אמר אפרים מקשאה משום רבי מאיר: בתו של שם היתה שהוא כהן, לפיכך דנוה בשרפה (ב"ר פה, י):

כה| **הוא מוצאת.** לשרף: **והיא שלחה אל חמיה.** לא רצתה להלבין פניו ולומר: ממך אני מעוברת! אלא "לאיש אשר אלה לו". אמרה: אם יודה – יודה מעצמו, ואם לאו – ישרפוני ואל אלבין פניו. מכאן אמרו: נוח לו לאדם שיפילוהו לכבשן האש ואל ילבין פני חברו ברבים: **הכר נא.** אין 'נא' אלא לשון בקשה: הכר נא בוראך ואל תאבד שלש נפשות:

כו| **צדקה.** בדבריה: **ממני.** היא מעוברת. ורבותינו זכרונם לברכה דרשו שיצתה בת קול ואמרה: ממני ומאתי יצאו הדברים, לפי שהיתה צנועה בבית חמיה גזרתי שיצאו ממנה מלכים, ומשבט יהודה גזרתי להעמיד מלכים בישראל: **כי על כן לא נתתיה.** כי בדין עשתה על אשר לא נתתיה לשלה בני: **ולא יסף עוד.** יש אומרים לא הוסיף, ויש אומרים לא פסק:

DISCUSSION

→ She acted boldly, despite the danger and without consideration of the social consequences of her actions. From a historical perspective, Tamar earned the approval of God, as her son Peretz was ultimately the progenitor of the distinguished Davidic dynasty.

of committing adultery. **And he was not intimate with her anymore,** as he already fulfilled his obligation toward Tamar. Although Judah recognized the legality of Tamar's actions and the legitimacy of her fetus, he was uninterested in continuing a relationship with her.

27 **It was at the time of her giving birth, and behold, twins were in her womb.**

28 **It was as she was giving birth,** that **one** of the twins **extended a hand** outside the womb. Faced with this unusual situation, **the midwife took and bound upon his hand a crimson thread, saying,** indicating: **This one emerged first** and was the firstborn.

29 However, **it was, as he retracted his hand** back inside the womb**, and behold, his brother emerged** from the womb first. Thus, the brother without the crimson thread was ultimately the firstborn. **And she said** to the child that emerged first: **What breach [*paretz*] have you breached for yourself?** Your brother was already poised to emerge first. Therefore, **he,** Judah, **called his name Peretz.**

30 **Afterward his brother emerged, on whose hand was the crimson thread; he called his name Zerah,** literally, "glow," alluding to the gleaming red thread tied to his hand.

Joseph: From Potifar's House to Imprisonment

GENESIS 39:1–23

The previous passage followed the path of Judah, the most prominent of Leah's sons, interrupting the main plot focusing on Joseph, Rachel's firstborn. At this point in the narrative, the Torah continues Joseph's story from the time of his arrival in Egypt.

39 1 *Fifth aliya* **Joseph was brought down to Egypt** as a slave devoid of rights. **Potifar, the courtier of Pharaoh, chief executioner, an Egyptian, bought him from the Ishmaelites, who had brought him down there.**

2 **The Lord was with Joseph, and he was a successful man** in the house of Potifar. Joseph arrived in Egypt as an inexperienced youth and with no knowledge of the Egyptian language. He also needed to cross the cultural divide between his upbringing in a small village to life in a developed city. Nevertheless, his success was evident for all to see. **And he was in the house of his master, the Egyptian.**

3 After some time, **his master saw that the Lord was with him, and all that he did, the Lord made his undertaking successful.** Potifar took notice of Joseph's success.

4 **Joseph found favor in his eyes, and he served him** as his personal attendant. Following that, Potifar promoted him and **he appointed him overseer of his household, and everything that was his he placed in his charge,** as Potifar saw Joseph's successes as well as his honesty.

5 **It was once he appointed him overseer of his household and over everything that was his; the Lord blessed the Egyptian's house for Joseph's sake. The blessing of the Lord was in all that he had, in the house and in the field.** In addition to Joseph's personal success, Potifar noticed that he too became prosperous. He sensed that this was due to Joseph's presence, just as Laban had known to attribute his prosperity to Jacob a generation earlier (see also 30:27).

6 Therefore, **he left everything that he had in Joseph's charge; and he did not know anything about his doings except the bread that he would eat.** In other words, Potifar found it unnecessary for himself to be involved in the affairs of his household, as he trusted Joseph completely; he was therefore present only for his personal needs, such as eating.[27] The Torah adds a comment that will be important in the continuation of the narrative: **Joseph,** who was probably around eighteen or twenty years old at the time, **was of fine form, and handsome.** As previously discussed, he bore a resemblance to his mother, who was also described in such terms.[28]

7 *Sixth aliya* **It was after these matters,** after Joseph was promoted above Potifar's other servants and presumably began to dress in more impressive clothing, **that his master's wife cast her eyes upon Joseph;** she desired him. **And she said: Lie with me.** Despite his elevated status, Joseph was still a slave. She therefore spoke directly and in unequivocal terms.

8 **He refused** to lie with her; **and** in order not to offend her, Joseph explained that his refusal was not because of her appearance or some other reason. **He said to his master's wife: Behold, my master** Potifar **does not know anything about what is in the house.** He trusts me to such a degree that he has no idea what I do in this house, **and he has placed everything that he has in my charge.**

9 **There is no one greater in this house than I;** he has provided good living conditions for me **and he has not withheld anything from me but you, as you are his wife.** Furthermore, aside from the fact that lying with you would constitute a betrayal of my master's trust and a complete lack of appreciation for all that he has provided me, there are also religious grounds for my refusal: **How can I do this great wickedness, and sin to God?**[D]

כז כח וַיְהִי בְּעֵת לִדְתָּהּ וְהִנֵּה תְאוֹמִים בְּבִטְנָהּ: וַיְהִי בְלִדְתָּהּ וַיִּתֶּן־יָד וַתִּקַּח הַמְיַלֶּדֶת
כט וַתִּקְשֹׁר עַל־יָדוֹ שָׁנִי לֵאמֹר זֶה יָצָא רִאשֹׁנָה: וַיְהִי ׀ כְּמֵשִׁיב יָדוֹ וְהִנֵּה יָצָא אָחִיו
ל וַתֹּאמֶר מַה־פָּרַצְתָּ עָלֶיךָ פָּרֶץ וַיִּקְרָא שְׁמוֹ פָּרֶץ: וְאַחַר יָצָא אָחִיו אֲשֶׁר עַל־יָדוֹ
לט א הַשָּׁנִי וַיִּקְרָא שְׁמוֹ זָרַח: וְיוֹסֵף הוּרַד מִצְרָיְמָה וַיִּקְנֵהוּ פּוֹטִיפַר סְרִיס לה חמישי
ב פַּרְעֹה שַׂר הַטַּבָּחִים אִישׁ מִצְרִי מִיַּד הַיִּשְׁמְעֵאלִים אֲשֶׁר הוֹרִדֻהוּ שָׁמָּה: וַיְהִי
ג יְהוָה אֶת־יוֹסֵף וַיְהִי אִישׁ מַצְלִיחַ וַיְהִי בְּבֵית אֲדֹנָיו הַמִּצְרִי: וַיַּרְא אֲדֹנָיו כִּי יְהוָה
ד אִתּוֹ וְכֹל אֲשֶׁר־הוּא עֹשֶׂה יְהוָה מַצְלִיחַ בְּיָדוֹ: וַיִּמְצָא יוֹסֵף חֵן בְּעֵינָיו וַיְשָׁרֶת
ה אֹתוֹ וַיַּפְקִדֵהוּ עַל־בֵּיתוֹ וְכָל־יֶשׁ־לוֹ נָתַן בְּיָדוֹ: וַיְהִי מֵאָז הִפְקִיד אֹתוֹ בְּבֵיתוֹ
וְעַל כָּל־אֲשֶׁר יֶשׁ־לוֹ וַיְבָרֶךְ יְהוָה אֶת־בֵּית הַמִּצְרִי בִּגְלַל יוֹסֵף וַיְהִי בִּרְכַּת יְהוָה
ו בְּכָל־אֲשֶׁר יֶשׁ־לוֹ בַּבַּיִת וּבַשָּׂדֶה: וַיַּעֲזֹב כָּל־אֲשֶׁר־לוֹ בְּיַד־יוֹסֵף וְלֹא־יָדַע אִתּוֹ
ז מְאוּמָה כִּי אִם־הַלֶּחֶם אֲשֶׁר־הוּא אוֹכֵל וַיְהִי יוֹסֵף יְפֵה־תֹאַר וִיפֵה מַרְאֶה: וַיְהִי ששי
אַחַר הַדְּבָרִים הָאֵלֶּה וַתִּשָּׂא אֵשֶׁת־אֲדֹנָיו אֶת־עֵינֶיהָ אֶל־יוֹסֵף וַתֹּאמֶר שִׁכְבָה
ח עִמִּי: וַיְמָאֵן ׀ וַיֹּאמֶר אֶל־אֵשֶׁת אֲדֹנָיו הֵן אֲדֹנִי לֹא־יָדַע אִתִּי מַה־בַּבָּיִת וְכֹל
ט אֲשֶׁר־יֶשׁ־לוֹ נָתַן בְּיָדִי: אֵינֶנּוּ גָדוֹל בַּבַּיִת הַזֶּה מִמֶּנִּי וְלֹא־חָשַׂךְ מִמֶּנִּי מְאוּמָה
כִּי אִם־אוֹתָךְ בַּאֲשֶׁר אַתְּ־אִשְׁתּוֹ וְאֵיךְ אֶעֱשֶׂה הָרָעָה הַגְּדֹלָה הַזֹּאת וְחָטָאתִי

רש"י

כז| **בעת לדתה.** ובִרבקה הוא אומר: "וימלאו ימיה ללדת" (לעיל כה, כד), להלן למלאים וכאן לחסרים: **והנה תאומים.** מלא, ולהלן (לעיל כה, כד) "תומם" חסר, לפי שהאחד רשע, אבל אלו שניהם צדיקים:

כח| **ויתן יד.** הוציא האחד ידו לחוץ, ולאחר שקשרה על ידו השני החזירה:

כט| **פרצת.** חזקת, עליך חוזק:

ל| **אשר על ידו השני.** ארבע ידות כתובות כאן, כנגד ארבעה חרמים שמעל עכן שיצא ממנו. ויש אומרים: כנגד ארבעה דברים שלקח: אדרת שנער, ושתי חתיכות כסף של מאתים שקלים, ולשון זהב (יהושע ז, כא). בראשית רבה (פה, יד): **ויקרא שמו זרח.** על שם זריחת מראית השני:

פרק לט

א| **ויוסף הורד.** חוזר לענין ראשון, אלא שהפסיק בו כדי לסמוך ירידתו של יהודה למכירתו של יוסף, לומר שבשבילו הורידוהו מגדלתו. ועוד, כדי לסמוך מעשה אשתו של פוטיפר למעשה תמר, לומר לך, מה זו לשם שמים אף זו לשם שמים, שראתה באצטרולוגין שלה שעתידה להעמיד בנים ממנו, ואינה יודעת אם ממנה אם מבתה:

ג| **כי ה' אתו.** שם שמים שגור בפיו:

ד| **וכל יש לו.** הרי לשון קצרה, חסר 'אשר':

ו-ז| **ולא ידע אתו מאומה.** לא היה נותן לבו לכלום: **כי אם הלחם.** היא אשתו, אלא שדבר בלשון נקיה: **ויהי יוסף יפה תאר.** כיון שראה עצמו מושל, התחיל אוכל ושותה ומסלסל בשערו. אמר הקדוש ברוך הוא: אביך מתאבל, ואתה מסלסל בשערך?! אני מגרה בך את הדב! מיד – "ותשא אשת אדניו" וגו', כל מקום שנאמר 'אחר' – סמוך:

ט| **וחטאתי לאלהים.** בני נח נצטוו על העריות:

DISCUSSION

39:9| **And sin to God:** Even outside the family of Abraham, relations with a married woman was considered a sin (see, e.g., 20:9). This was also true in Egypt (see 12:12).

10 Despite Joseph's refusal, she persisted: **It was as she spoke to Joseph day after day, and he did not heed her to lie with her, to be with her.** At first, she tried to the best of her ability to seduce Joseph. When he refused, she requested that he lie in her bed beside her.[29] Joseph was torn between temptation and the restraint demanded by his religion and his conscience. Nevertheless, the more she pushed to be with Joseph, the more he took effort to avoid her.[30]

11 **It was on a certain day,** a festive occasion,[31] that **he,** Joseph, **went into the house to perform his labor, and none of the people of the household were there in the house.** Perhaps everyone went to partake in whatever celebrations were taking place on that day.[32] Joseph, as a faithful servant, remained in the house. Potifar's wife also remained, as she had plans of her own:

12 **She seized him by his garment, saying: Lie with me. He left his garment in her hand.** At that time, people wore robes that wrapped around their bodies. Accordingly, when she grabbed Joseph's garment, he was able to unravel himself from it, leaving it in her hand. Joseph **fled, and went outside.**

13 **It was when she saw that he had left his garment in her hand, and had fled outside.** When she realized that even now, Joseph refused to lie with her, she could no longer rationalize his refusal by claiming that it was as an attempt to tease her, or that he rejected her until a more opportune time would present itself. She now felt immensely insulted, whether because she failed to achieve her desire, or because the lowly servant Joseph had the audacity to refuse her demands.

14 Potifar's wife sought to protect her dignity and simultaneously take revenge against Joseph. **She called to the people of her household, and spoke to them, saying: See, he,** Potifar, **brought to us a Hebrew man**[D] **to ridicule us** (see 19:14). Alternatively, the verse means: He brought to us a Hebrew man to abuse us.[33] **He came to me to lie with me, and I,** being a decent woman, **cried** out immediately **with a loud voice.**

15 **It was when he heard; I raised my voice and cried. He left his garment with me, fled, and went outside.**

16 Potifar's wife did not suffice with relating this tale to the members of the household; rather, **she placed his garment beside her, until his master's arrival to his home.**

17 **She spoke to him these words, saying: The Hebrew slave whom you brought to us** and whom you promoted, **came to me to mock me.**

18 **It was as I raised my voice and cried that he left his garment with me and fled outside.**

19 **It was when his master heard the words of his wife that she spoke to him, saying: Your slave did to me in this manner,** he attempted to rape me, **he,** Potifar, **was incensed.** It should be noted that the verse does not state with whom he was incensed.

20 **Joseph's master took him,** without any judicial process, **and placed him in the prison**[D] in order to punish him, in **the place where the king's prisoners were incarcerated.** It later becomes apparent that this prison housed distinguished political prisoners, not convicted criminals. **And he was there in the prison** as one of the prisoners.

21 **The Lord was with Joseph, and granted him appeal, and put his favor in the eyes of the commandant of the prison.** Joseph had the ability to ingratiate himself with people outside of his family.

22 Joseph's charm was effective even on the commandant of the prison. He took notice of Joseph, and after some time **the commandant of the prison put in Joseph's charge all the prisoners that were in the prison.** Even though Joseph was still a prisoner, he again earned an administrative position. He was considered a loyal and trustworthy prisoner, and an excellent administrator. He was therefore appointed to oversee all the other prisoners. **And everything that they did there, he, Joseph, would determine.** Joseph was in charge of the daily routine of the prison: meal times, recreational times, and all other daily activities of the prisoners.

23 Eventually, **the commandant of the prison did not oversee anything in his charge.** The commandant trusted Joseph completely and did not scrutinize his actions, **for** all could see that **the Lord was with him. That which he did, the Lord made successful.** Joseph was not simply a man of fine appearance. His charm captured everyone around him: Potifar, Potifar's wife, and the commandant of the prison. Later in the narrative, others are also captivated by his charm. Aside from his extraordinary effectiveness, something about Joseph's personality conveyed to those around him that God was with him, and that he was somehow connected to supreme holiness.

DISCUSSION

39:14 | Hebrew man: Aside from its plain meaning, this phrase was also considered a slur in ancient Egypt. Ancient Egyptian documents indicate that the Egyptians held the Hebrews in contempt (see 43:32). The Hebrews were a distinct race with a different culture, and the Egyptians regarded them as repulsive and primitive.

39:20 | And placed him in the prison: Potifar's moderate response to his wife's story should cast light on how he viewed the incident. In those days, the life of a person, let alone a slave, was not considered to be of much value. Consequently, it would certainly have been acceptable for someone accused of attempting to rape a married woman to receive a severe punishment. Nevertheless, Potifar merely

י לֵאלֹהִים: וַיְהִי כְּדַבְּרָהּ אֶל־יוֹסֵף יוֹם ׀ יוֹם וְלֹא־שָׁמַע אֵלֶיהָ לִשְׁכַּב אֶצְלָהּ לִהְיוֹת
יא עִמָּהּ: וַיְהִי כְּהַיּוֹם הַזֶּה וַיָּבֹא הַבַּיְתָה לַעֲשׂוֹת מְלַאכְתּוֹ וְאֵין אִישׁ מֵאַנְשֵׁי הַבַּיִת
יב שָׁם בַּבָּיִת: וַתִּתְפְּשֵׂהוּ בְּבִגְדוֹ לֵאמֹר שִׁכְבָה עִמִּי וַיַּעֲזֹב בִּגְדוֹ בְּיָדָהּ וַיָּנָס וַיֵּצֵא
יג יד הַחוּצָה: וַיְהִי כִּרְאוֹתָהּ כִּי־עָזַב בִּגְדוֹ בְּיָדָהּ וַיָּנָס הַחוּצָה: וַתִּקְרָא לְאַנְשֵׁי בֵיתָהּ
וַתֹּאמֶר לָהֶם לֵאמֹר רְאוּ הֵבִיא לָנוּ אִישׁ עִבְרִי לְצַחֶק בָּנוּ בָּא אֵלַי לִשְׁכַּב עִמִּי
טו וָאֶקְרָא בְּקוֹל גָּדוֹל: וַיְהִי כְשָׁמְעוֹ כִּי־הֲרִימֹתִי קוֹלִי וָאֶקְרָא וַיַּעֲזֹב בִּגְדוֹ אֶצְלִי
טז יז וַיָּנָס וַיֵּצֵא הַחוּצָה: וַתַּנַּח בִּגְדוֹ אֶצְלָהּ עַד־בּוֹא אֲדֹנָיו אֶל־בֵּיתוֹ: וַתְּדַבֵּר אֵלָיו
כַּדְּבָרִים הָאֵלֶּה לֵאמֹר בָּא אֵלַי הָעֶבֶד הָעִבְרִי אֲשֶׁר־הֵבֵאתָ לָּנוּ לְצַחֶק בִּי:
יח יט וַיְהִי כַּהֲרִימִי קוֹלִי וָאֶקְרָא וַיַּעֲזֹב בִּגְדוֹ אֶצְלִי וַיָּנָס הַחוּצָה: וַיְהִי כִשְׁמֹעַ אֲדֹנָיו
אֶת־דִּבְרֵי אִשְׁתּוֹ אֲשֶׁר דִּבְּרָה אֵלָיו לֵאמֹר כַּדְּבָרִים הָאֵלֶּה עָשָׂה לִי עַבְדֶּךָ וַיִּחַר
כ אַפּוֹ: וַיִּקַּח אֲדֹנֵי יוֹסֵף אֹתוֹ וַיִּתְּנֵהוּ אֶל־בֵּית הַסֹּהַר מְקוֹם אֲשֶׁר־אסורי הַמֶּלֶךְ אֲסִירֵי
כא אֲסוּרִים וַיְהִי־שָׁם בְּבֵית הַסֹּהַר: וַיְהִי יהוה אֶת־יוֹסֵף וַיֵּט אֵלָיו חָסֶד וַיִּתֵּן חִנּוֹ
כב בְּעֵינֵי שַׂר בֵּית־הַסֹּהַר: וַיִּתֵּן שַׂר בֵּית־הַסֹּהַר בְּיַד־יוֹסֵף אֵת כָּל־הָאֲסִירִם אֲשֶׁר
כג בְּבֵית הַסֹּהַר וְאֵת כָּל־אֲשֶׁר עֹשִׂים שָׁם הוּא הָיָה עֹשֶׂה: אֵין ׀ שַׂר בֵּית־הַסֹּהַר
רֹאֶה אֶת־כָּל־מְאוּמָה בְּיָדוֹ בַּאֲשֶׁר יהוה אִתּוֹ וַאֲשֶׁר־הוּא עֹשֶׂה יהוה מַצְלִיחַ:

רש"י

י | **לִשְׁכַּב אֶצְלָהּ.** אֲפִלּוּ בְּלֹא תַּשְׁמִישׁ: **לִהְיוֹת עִמָּהּ.** לָעוֹלָם הַבָּא:

יא | **וַיְהִי כְּהַיּוֹם הַזֶּה.** כְּלוֹמַר, וַיְהִי כַּאֲשֶׁר הִגִּיעַ יוֹם מְיֻחָד, יוֹם צָחוֹק, יוֹם אֵיד שֶׁלָּהֶם, שֶׁהָלְכוּ כֻּלָּם לְבֵית עֲבוֹדָה זָרָה, אָמְרָה: אֵין לִי יוֹם הָגוּן לְהִזָּקֵק לְיוֹסֵף כְּהַיּוֹם הַזֶּה. אָמְרָה לָהֶם: חוֹלָה אֲנִי וְאֵינִי יְכוֹלָה לֵילֵךְ: **לַעֲשׂוֹת מְלַאכְתּוֹ.** רַב וּשְׁמוּאֵל, חַד אָמַר: מְלַאכְתּוֹ מַמָּשׁ, וְחַד אָמַר: לַעֲשׂוֹת צְרָכָיו עִמָּהּ, אֶלָּא שֶׁנִּרְאֵית לוֹ דְּמוּת דְּיוֹקְנוֹ שֶׁל אָבִיו וְכוּ', כִּדְאִיתָא בְּמַסֶּכֶת סוֹטָה (דף לו ע"ב):

יד | **רְאוּ הֵבִיא לָנוּ.** הֲרֵי זֶה לְשׁוֹן קְצָרָה, "הֵבִיא לָנוּ" וְלֹא פֵּרֵשׁ מִי הֱבִיאוֹ, וְעַל בַּעְלָהּ הִיא אוֹמֶרֶת כֵּן: **עִבְרִי.** מֵעֵבֶר הַנָּהָר, מִבְּנֵי עֵבֶר:

טז | **אֲדֹנָיו.** שֶׁל יוֹסֵף:

יז | **בָּא אֵלַי.** לְצַחֶק בִּי, הָעֶבֶד הָעִבְרִי אֲשֶׁר הֵבֵאתָ לָנוּ:

יט | **וַיְהִי כִּשְׁמֹעַ אֲדֹנָיו.** בִּשְׁעַת תַּשְׁמִישׁ אָמְרָה לוֹ, וְזֶהוּ שֶׁאָמְרָה: "כַּדְּבָרִים הָאֵלֶּה עָשָׂה לִי עַבְדֶּךָ" – עִנְיְנֵי תַּשְׁמִישׁ כָּאֵלֶּה:

כא | **וַיֵּט אֵלָיו חָסֶד.** שֶׁהָיָה מְקֻבָּל לְכָל רוֹאָיו, לְשׁוֹן 'כַּלָּה נָאָה וַחֲסוּדָה' שֶׁבַּמִּשְׁנָה (כתובות יז ע"א):

כב | **הוּא הָיָה עֹשֶׂה.** כְּתַרְגּוּמוֹ: "בְּמֵימְרֵיהּ הֲוָה מִתְעֲבִיד":

כג | **בַּאֲשֶׁר ה' אִתּוֹ.** בִּשְׁבִיל ה' אִתּוֹ:

DISCUSSION

→ imprisoned Joseph despite the serious accusations against him. Furthermore, the verse does not even give clear indication regarding the direction of Potifar's anger. Was he angry with Joseph; with himself, for causing this embarrassing situation by elevating Joseph; or was he angry with his wife? It is possible that from the outset, Potifar was suspicious about the veracity of his wife's story, and that he considered Joseph's version of events more accurate than hers (see Ibn Ezra).

Joseph, Interpreter of Dreams
GENESIS 40:1–23

From the beginning of Joseph's story, when his own dreams led his brothers to refer to him as a dreamer (37:19), the dramatic events of his life have led to this defining moment, when he will start interpreting dreams for others. Joseph's initial decision to share his dreams with his brothers was a significant factor in his exile from home and descent to Egypt. At first glance, it would seem that this exile only distanced Joseph from the greatness foretold in his dreams. Ultimately, however, the realization of his dreams will come through the dreams of others. In this passage, Joseph interprets the dreams of his fellow prisoners. His success in accurately interpreting their dreams will eventually pave the way to a meeting with Pharaoh, who will require an interpreter for his own dreams.

40 Seventh aliya

1 **It was after these matters,** after Joseph received an important position in the prison, that **the butler of the king of Egypt,** who was responsible for providing the king with drink, **and the baker**[D] of the king, **sinned against their master, against the king of Egypt.**

2 **Pharaoh became angry at his two courtiers, at the chief butler and at the chief baker.** The Torah does not elaborate as to why he was angry at them. The Midrash relates that Pharaoh became angry because he discovered foreign objects in his bread and wine.[34]

3 **He placed them in custody in the household of the chief executioner,**[35] **in the prison, the place where Joseph was incarcerated.** This prison held distinguished prisoners. Since the courtiers of Pharaoh were men of status who might someday return to their lofty positions, they were provided special privileges.

4 **The chief executioner,** Potifar, **charged Joseph with them, and he served them, and they were in custody one year.**[36]

5 **They,** the butler and the baker, **dreamed a dream both of them – each man his dream during one night, each man in accordance with the interpretation of his dream.** The eventual interpretation of each man's dream, that of **the butler and** that of **the baker of the king of Egypt, who were incarcerated in the prison,** would match its content.[37]

6 **Joseph came to them in the morning** to serve them, **and saw them, and behold, they were distressed.** As their attendant, Joseph was able to sense the change in their demeanor.

7 **He asked Pharaoh's courtiers who were with him in the custody of his master's house, saying: Why are your faces wretched today?**

8 **They said to him: We dreamed a dream, and there is no interpreter for it.** We sense that our dreams contain an important message, but we are unable to decipher them. **Joseph said to them: Aren't interpretations for God?** The interpretation of a dream and its realization lie solely in the hands of God; He can inform us of its meaning.[38] Therefore, **please, relate it to me;** perhaps I will succeed in interpreting it.

9 Joseph succeeding in ingratiating himself with these ministers, and they trusted him: **The chief butler told his dream to Joseph, and said to him: In my dream, behold, a vine was before me.**

10 **On the vine were three tendrils, and it was as though it was budding.** Then **its blossoms emerged, and its clusters produced ripe grapes.**

11 **Pharaoh's cup was in my hand; I took the grapes, pressed them into Pharaoh's cup, and I gave the cup into Pharaoh's hand.**

12 **Joseph said to him: This is its interpretation: The three tendrils are three days;**[D]

13 **In three more days Pharaoh shall raise your head,** your status, **and restore you to your** original **position.** Then your dream will materialize in a literal sense, as **you will give Pharaoh's cup into his hand, like the former circumstance where you would provide him with drink.**

DISCUSSION

40:1 | The butler...and the baker: These were considered prominent positions, not only because they served the needs of the king, but because they were positions that required trust. The food and drink of the king were the easiest mediums through which to poison him. Consequently, only those whose loyalty was unquestioned could be appointed to such positions.

An example of the high esteem in which a butler was regarded can be found in Nehemiah, who was the butler of the king of Persia. He used his position to make requests of the king that no one else could have dared to request (Nehemiah 1:11–2:9).

40:12 | The three tendrils are three days: Joseph correctly recognized that the butler's dream was prophetic, and he therefore informed the butler that he would soon be restored to his previous position. The only truly remarkable part of Joseph's interpretation is his explanation regarding the meaning of the three tendrils. How did Joseph know that the three tendrils symbolized three days and not, say, three months? It would seem that Joseph, like the rest of Egypt, was aware that Pharaoh's birthday celebration was three days away (see verse 20). He knew that on this day, the king offers retrials and pardons for prior offenses. Joseph incorporated this knowledge into his interpretation of the dream (see Ibn Ezra; Ramban, verse 10).

מ

א וַיְהִ֗י אַחַר֙ הַדְּבָרִ֣ים הָאֵ֔לֶּה חָֽטְא֛וּ מַשְׁקֵ֥ה מֶֽלֶךְ־מִצְרַ֖יִם וְהָאֹפֶ֑ה לַאֲדֹנֵיהֶ֖ם לְמֶ֥לֶךְ   שביעי

ב מִצְרָֽיִם: ג וַיִּקְצֹ֣ף פַּרְעֹ֔ה עַ֖ל שְׁנֵ֣י סָֽרִיסָ֑יו עַ֚ל שַׂ֣ר הַמַּשְׁקִ֔ים וְעַ֖ל שַׂ֥ר הָאוֹפִֽים: וַיִּתֵּן֩

אֹתָ֨ם בְּמִשְׁמַ֜ר בֵּ֣ית שַׂ֤ר הַטַּבָּחִים֙ אֶל־בֵּ֣ית הַסֹּ֔הַר מְק֕וֹם אֲשֶׁ֥ר יוֹסֵ֖ף אָס֥וּר שָֽׁם:

ד וַיִּ֠פְקֹ֠ד שַׂ֣ר הַטַּבָּחִ֧ים אֶת־יוֹסֵ֛ף אִתָּ֖ם וַיְשָׁ֣רֶת אֹתָ֑ם וַיִּהְי֥וּ יָמִ֖ים בְּמִשְׁמָֽר: ה וַיַּֽחַלְמוּ֩

חֲל֨וֹם שְׁנֵיהֶ֜ם אִ֣ישׁ חֲלֹמ֗וֹ בְּלַ֤יְלָה אֶחָד֙ אִ֣ישׁ כְּפִתְר֣וֹן חֲלֹמ֔וֹ הַמַּשְׁקֶ֣ה וְהָאֹפֶ֗ה אֲשֶׁר֙

לְמֶ֣לֶךְ מִצְרַ֔יִם אֲשֶׁ֥ר אֲסוּרִ֖ים בְּבֵ֥ית הַסֹּֽהַר: ו וַיָּבֹ֧א אֲלֵיהֶ֛ם יוֹסֵ֖ף בַּבֹּ֑קֶר וַיַּ֣רְא אֹתָ֔ם

וְהִנָּ֖ם זֹֽעֲפִֽים: ז וַיִּשְׁאַ֞ל אֶת־סְרִיסֵ֣י פַרְעֹ֗ה אֲשֶׁ֨ר אִתּ֧וֹ בְמִשְׁמַ֛ר בֵּ֥ית אֲדֹנָ֖יו לֵאמֹ֑ר

מַדּ֛וּעַ פְּנֵיכֶ֥ם רָעִ֖ים הַיּֽוֹם: ח וַיֹּֽאמְר֣וּ אֵלָ֗יו חֲל֤וֹם חָלַ֨מְנוּ֙ וּפֹתֵ֣ר אֵ֣ין אֹת֔וֹ וַיֹּ֤אמֶר אֲלֵהֶם֙

יוֹסֵ֔ף הֲל֤וֹא לֵֽאלֹהִים֙ פִּתְרֹנִ֔ים סַפְּרוּ־נָ֖א לִ֑י: ט וַיְסַפֵּ֧ר שַׂר־הַמַּשְׁקִ֛ים אֶת־חֲלֹמ֖וֹ

לְיוֹסֵ֑ף וַיֹּ֣אמֶר ל֔וֹ בַּֽחֲלוֹמִ֕י וְהִנֵּה־גֶ֖פֶן לְפָנָֽי: י וּבַגֶּ֖פֶן שְׁלֹשָׁ֣ה שָֽׂרִיגִ֑ם וְהִ֤וא כְפֹרַ֨חַת֙

עָֽלְתָ֣ה נִצָּ֔הּ הִבְשִׁ֥ילוּ אַשְׁכְּלֹתֶ֖יהָ עֲנָבִֽים: יא וְכ֥וֹס פַּרְעֹ֖ה בְּיָדִ֑י וָֽאֶקַּ֣ח אֶת־הָֽעֲנָבִ֗ים

וָֽאֶשְׂחַ֤ט אֹתָם֙ אֶל־כּ֣וֹס פַּרְעֹ֔ה וָֽאֶתֵּ֥ן אֶת־הַכּ֖וֹס עַל־כַּ֥ף פַּרְעֹֽה: יב וַיֹּ֤אמֶר לוֹ֙ יוֹסֵ֔ף

זֶ֖ה פִּתְרֹנ֑וֹ שְׁלֹ֨שֶׁת֙ הַשָּׂ֣רִגִ֔ים שְׁלֹ֥שֶׁת יָמִ֖ים הֵֽם: יג בְּע֣וֹד ׀ שְׁלֹ֣שֶׁת יָמִ֗ים יִשָּׂ֤א פַרְעֹה֙

אֶת־רֹאשֶׁ֔ךָ וַֽהֲשִֽׁיבְךָ֖ עַל־כַּנֶּ֑ךָ וְנָֽתַתָּ֤ כוֹס־פַּרְעֹה֙ בְּיָד֔וֹ כַּמִּשְׁפָּט֙ הָֽרִאשׁ֔וֹן אֲשֶׁ֥ר הָיִ֖יתָ

רש״י

פרק מ

א| אַחַר הַדְּבָרִים הָאֵלֶּה. לְפִי שֶׁהִרְגִּילָה אוֹתָהּ אֲרוּרָה
אֶת הַצַּדִּיק בְּפִי כֻלָּם לְדַבֵּר בּוֹ, הֵבִיא לָהֶם הַקָּדוֹשׁ בָּרוּךְ
הוּא סֻרְחָנָם שֶׁל אֵלּוּ, שֶׁיִּפְנוּ אֲלֵיהֶם וְלֹא אֵלָיו; וְעוֹד
שֶׁתָּבוֹא הָרְוָחָה לַצַּדִּיק עַל יְדֵיהֶם. חָטְאוּ. זֶה נִמְצָא
זְבוּב בְּפָיְלֵי פוֹטִירִין שֶׁלּוֹ, וְזֶה נִמְצָא צְרוֹר בַּגְּלוּסְקִין
שֶׁלּוֹ: וְהָאֹפֶה. אֶת פַּת הַמֶּלֶךְ, וְאֵין לְשׁוֹן אֲפִיָּה אֶלָּא
בְּפַת, וּבְלַעַז פיסטו״ר:

ד| וַיִּפְקֹד שַׂר הַטַּבָּחִים אֶת יוֹסֵף. לִהְיוֹת "אִתָּם": וַיִּהְיוּ
יָמִים בְּמִשְׁמָר. שְׁנֵים עָשָׂר חֹדֶשׁ:

ה| וַיַּחַלְמוּ חֲלוֹם שְׁנֵיהֶם. וַיַּחַלְמוּ שְׁנֵיהֶם חֲלוֹם, זֶהוּ
פְּשׁוּטוֹ. וּמִדְרָשׁוֹ, כָּל אֶחָד חָלַם חֲלוֹם שְׁנֵיהֶם – שֶׁחָלַם
אֶת חֲלוֹמוֹ וּפִתְרוֹן חֲבֵרוֹ, וְזֶהוּ שֶׁנֶּאֱמַר: "וַיַּרְא שַׂר הָאֹפִים
כִּי טוֹב פָּתָר": אִישׁ כְּפִתְרוֹן חֲלֹמוֹ. כָּל אֶחָד חָלַם חֲלוֹם
הַדּוֹמֶה לַפִּתְרוֹן הֶעָתִיד לָבֹא עֲלֵיהֶם:

ו| זֹעֲפִים. עֲצֵבִים, כְּמוֹ: "סַר וְזָעֵף" (מלכים א׳ כ, מג), "וְזַעַף
ה׳ אֶשָּׂא" (מיכה ז, ט):

י| שָׂרִיגִם. זְמוֹרוֹת אֲרֻכּוֹת שֶׁקּוֹרִין וידי״ץ: וְהִוא כְפֹרַחַת.
דוֹמָה לְפוֹרַחַת, "וְהִוא כְפֹרַחַת" – נִדְמֵית לִי בַּחֲלוֹמִי
כְּאִלּוּ הִיא פוֹרַחַת, וְאַחַר הַפֶּרַח "עָלְתָה נִצָּהּ" וְנַעֲשׂוּ

סְמָדַר, אשפני״ר בְּלַעַז, וְאַחַר כָּךְ "הִבְשִׁילוּ". "וְהִיא כַד
אֲפִרַחַת אֲפִיקַת לַבְלְבִין", עַד כָּאן תַּרְגּוּם שֶׁל "פֹּרַחַת":
נֵץ גָּדוֹל מִפֶּרַח, כְּדִכְתִיב: "וּבֹסֶר גֹּמֵל יִהְיֶה נִצָּה" (ישעיה
יח, ה), וּכְתִיב: "וַיֵּצֵא פֶרַח" וְחַד "וַיָּצֵץ צִיץ" (במדבר יז, כג):

יא| וָאֶשְׂחַט. כְּתַרְגּוּמוֹ "וַעֲצָרִית", וְהַרְבֵּה יֵשׁ בִּלְשׁוֹן מִשְׁנָה:

יב| שְׁלֹשֶׁת יָמִים הֵם. סִימָן הֵם לְךָ לִשְׁלֹשֶׁת יָמִים, וְיֵשׁ
מִדְרְשֵׁי אַגָּדָה הַרְבֵּה:

יג| יִשָּׂא פַרְעֹה אֶת רֹאשֶׁךָ. לְשׁוֹן חֶשְׁבּוֹן, כְּשֶׁיִּפְקֹד שְׁאָר
עֲבָדָיו לְשָׁרֵת לְפָנָיו בַּסְּעוּדָה, יִמְנֶה אוֹתְךָ עִמָּהֶם: כַּנֶּךָ.
בָּסִיס שֶׁלְּךָ וּמוֹשָׁבֶךָ:

14 Joseph demonstrated just how certain he was of the correctness of his interpretation. He requested of the butler: **If only you remember me when it shall be well for you,** when your dream is realized and you are reinstalled in your position, **and please, perform kindness with me and mention me to Pharaoh, and** you will thereby help **take me out of this house,** this prison.

15 **For I was abducted from the land of the Hebrews.** I was not born a slave; I am a freeman who was kidnapped. **And here too I have done nothing** wrong to justify the fact **that they placed me in the pit.**

16 **The chief baker saw that he interpreted well.** Joseph's interpretation seemed pleasing and accurate to the baker. Some opinions maintain that in addition to their own respective dreams, each minister dreamed the interpretation of the other. Consequently, the baker knew that Joseph correctly interpreted the butler's dream.[39] **And he said to Joseph: I too, in my dream,** dreamed that **behold, there were three wicker baskets** stacked one upon the other **on my head.** Wicker baskets are typically used to hold baked goods, as the gaps in the weaves allow for air to pass to the goods inside them.

17 **In the uppermost basket there was all manner of food for Pharaoh, baked products; and the birds were eating them from the basket above my head.**

18 **Joseph answered and said: This is its interpretation: The three baskets are three days.**

19 **In three more days Pharaoh shall raise,** remove, **your head from upon you, and shall hang you on a tree. The birds shall eat your flesh from upon you.** Part of the dream will indeed be fulfilled, as the birds will eat. However, instead of consuming the contents of the wicker baskets, they will consume your flesh. In this dream, unlike in the butler's dream, the baker's hoped-for restoration does not occur. Rather, the birds partake of the baked goods in place of Pharaoh.

20 *Maftir* **It was on the third day,** the day of **Pharaoh's** public **birthday** celebration, that **he made a feast for all his servants; and** during that feast he **raised the head of the chief butler and the head of the chief baker among his servants.** While Pharaoh sat with his entourage, he was reminded of the absence of the butler and the baker. It seems that when the butler and baker committed their offenses, Pharaoh was angered and had them imprisoned without judgement. Now, Pharaoh issued a ruling: He concluded that the chief butler properly executed his duties and was therefore innocent, while the chief baker acted improperly and was therefore guilty.

21 Accordingly, **he,** Pharaoh, **restored the chief butler to his butlership, and he gave the cup into Pharaoh's hand;**

22 **and he hanged the chief baker, as Joseph interpreted for them.**

23 **But** despite the fact that the chief butler witnessed the complete accuracy of Joseph's interpretation, **the chief butler did not** immediately **remember** the request that **Joseph** made of him. Rather, as time progressed **he forgot him,** as he no longer had any interaction with him.

Maftir on Hanukkah is read from the respective day's portion in Numbers, chap. 7.

יד מַשְׁקֵהוּ: כִּי אִם־זְכַרְתַּנִי אִתְּךָ כַּאֲשֶׁר יִיטַב לָךְ וְעָשִׂיתָ־נָּא עִמָּדִי חָסֶד וְהִזְכַּרְתַּנִי
טו אֶל־פַּרְעֹה וְהוֹצֵאתַנִי מִן־הַבַּיִת הַזֶּה: כִּי־גֻנֹּב גֻּנַּבְתִּי מֵאֶרֶץ הָעִבְרִים וְגַם־פֹּה
טז לֹא־עָשִׂיתִי מְאוּמָה כִּי־שָׂמוּ אֹתִי בַּבּוֹר: וַיַּרְא שַׂר־הָאֹפִים כִּי טוֹב פָּתָר וַיֹּאמֶר
יז אֶל־יוֹסֵף אַף־אֲנִי בַּחֲלוֹמִי וְהִנֵּה שְׁלֹשָׁה סַלֵּי חֹרִי עַל־רֹאשִׁי: וּבַסַּל הָעֶלְיוֹן מִכֹּל
יח מַאֲכַל פַּרְעֹה מַעֲשֵׂה אֹפֶה וְהָעוֹף אֹכֵל אֹתָם מִן־הַסַּל מֵעַל רֹאשִׁי: וַיַּעַן יוֹסֵף
יט וַיֹּאמֶר זֶה פִּתְרֹנוֹ שְׁלֹשֶׁת הַסַּלִּים שְׁלֹשֶׁת יָמִים הֵם: בְּעוֹד | שְׁלֹשֶׁת יָמִים יִשָּׂא
פַרְעֹה אֶת־רֹאשְׁךָ מֵעָלֶיךָ וְתָלָה אוֹתְךָ עַל־עֵץ וְאָכַל הָעוֹף אֶת־בְּשָׂרְךָ מֵעָלֶיךָ:
כ וַיְהִי | בַּיּוֹם הַשְּׁלִישִׁי יוֹם הֻלֶּדֶת אֶת־פַּרְעֹה וַיַּעַשׂ מִשְׁתֶּה לְכָל־עֲבָדָיו וַיִּשָּׂא מפטיר
כא אֶת־רֹאשׁ | שַׂר הַמַּשְׁקִים וְאֶת־רֹאשׁ שַׂר הָאֹפִים בְּתוֹךְ עֲבָדָיו: וַיָּשֶׁב אֶת־שַׂר
כב הַמַּשְׁקִים עַל־מַשְׁקֵהוּ וַיִּתֵּן הַכּוֹס עַל־כַּף פַּרְעֹה: וְאֵת שַׂר הָאֹפִים תָּלָה כַּאֲשֶׁר
כג פָּתַר לָהֶם יוֹסֵף: וְלֹא־זָכַר שַׂר־הַמַּשְׁקִים אֶת־יוֹסֵף וַיִּשְׁכָּחֵהוּ:

רש"י

יד) כִּי אִם זְכַרְתַּנִי אִתְּךָ. אַחַר שֶׁיִּיטַב לְךָ כְּפִתְרוֹנִי: וְעָשִׂיתָ נָּא עִמָּדִי חָסֶד. אֵין 'נָא' אֶלָּא לְשׁוֹן בַּקָּשָׁה [הֲרֵי אַתָּה עוֹשֶׂה עִמִּי חֶסֶד]:

טז) סַלֵּי חֹרִי. סַלִּים שֶׁל נְצָרִים קְלוּפִים חוֹרִין חוֹרִין, וּבִמְקוֹמֵנוּ יֵשׁ הַרְבֵּה, וְדֶרֶךְ מוֹכְרֵי פַּת כִּסָּנִין שֶׁקּוֹרִין אוֹבלי"ש לְתִתָּם בְּאוֹתָם סַלִּים:

כ) יוֹם הֻלֶּדֶת אֶת פַּרְעֹה. יוֹם לֵדָתוֹ, וְקוֹרִין לוֹ יוֹם גֵּנוּסְיָא. וּלְשׁוֹן 'הֻלֶּדֶת', לְפִי שֶׁאֵין הַוָּלָד נוֹלָד אֶלָּא עַל יְדֵי אֲחֵרִים, שֶׁהַחַיָּה מְיַלֶּדֶת אֶת הָאִשָּׁה, וְעַל כֵּן הִיא נִקְרֵאת 'מְיַלֶּדֶת'. וְכֵן: "וּמוֹלְדוֹתַיִךְ בְּיוֹם הוּלֶּדֶת אוֹתָךְ" (יחזקאל טז, ד), וְכֵן: "אַחֲרֵי הֻכַּבֵּס אֶת הַנֶּגַע" (ויקרא יג, נה), שֶׁכִּבּוּסוֹ עַל יְדֵי אֲחֵרִים: וַיִּשָּׂא אֶת רֹאשׁ וְגוֹ'. מְנָאָם עִם שְׁאָר עֲבָדָיו, שֶׁהָיָה מוֹנֶה הַמְשָׁרְתִים שֶׁיְּשָׁרְתוּ לוֹ בִּסְעֻדָּתוֹ וְזָכַר אֶת אֵלּוּ בְּתוֹכָם, כְּמוֹ: "שְׂאוּ אֶת רֹאשׁ" (במדבר א, ב), לְשׁוֹן מִנְיָן:

כג) וְלֹא זָכַר שַׂר הַמַּשְׁקִים. בּוֹ בַּיּוֹם: וַיִּשְׁכָּחֵהוּ. לְאַחַר מִכָּאן, מִפְּנֵי שֶׁתָּלָה בּוֹ יוֹסֵף בִּטָּחוֹן לְזָכְרוֹ הֻזְקַק לִהְיוֹת אָסוּר שְׁתֵּי שָׁנִים, שֶׁנֶּאֱמַר: "אַשְׁרֵי הַגֶּבֶר אֲשֶׁר שָׂם ה' מִבְטַחוֹ וְלֹא פָנָה אֶל רְהָבִים" (תהלים מ, ה), וְלֹא בָּטַח עַל מִצְרִים הַקְּרוּיִים רַהַב:

Parashat
Miketz

Joseph's Rise to Greatness in Egypt
GENESIS 41:1–57

The upheavals in Joseph's life have taken him from the pit into which he was cast by his brothers to the dungeon in Egypt. Joseph has placed his trust in the chief butler, requesting that he put in a good word for him to Pharaoh, after Joseph correctly interpreted the butler's dream. In this manner he hoped to be rescued from his plight. However, as is common with powerful officials, as soon as the chief butler is restored to his post, he forgets about Joseph. Joseph's release from the dark prison will occur in a different manner.

41 1 **It was at the conclusion of two years** since the chief butler had been restored to his post; **Pharaoh was dreaming: Behold,** in his dream **he stood at the Nile** River, upon which all life in Egypt depended.

2 **Behold, coming up from the Nile were seven cows, fair and fat fleshed, and they grazed in the pasture.**

3 **Behold, seven other cows were coming up after them from the river,** and they were **unsightly and lean fleshed, and they stood alongside the other cows on the bank of the Nile.**

4 **The unsightly and lean-fleshed cows ate the seven fair and fat cows, and Pharaoh awoke.** Presumably, Pharaoh woke up from the shock of seeing cows eat other cows.

5 **He slept and dreamed a second time** that same night, **and behold, seven ears of grain were growing on one stalk.** In years of especially fertile harvests, two or three ears might grow from a single stalk. The vision Pharaoh saw in his dream of seven ears on a single stalk is most unusual. These ears were **plump and good.**

6 **Behold,** he saw **seven ears, thin and blighted by the** dry **east wind.** These inferior ears **were growing after them.**

7 **The thin ears swallowed the seven plump and full ears.** This dream is even stranger than the previous one, as in the first dream, cows were eating, and in this dream, ears of grain are eating. **And Pharaoh awoke, and behold,** this too was only **a dream.**[1]

8 **It was in the morning and his spirit was troubled.** Pharaoh was upset by the strong impression the dreams had left upon him. **He sent and called for all the magicians of Egypt,**[B] its priests, who also engaged in science and medicine, **and all its wise men; Pharaoh related his dream to them, but no one could interpret them for Pharaoh.** Some commentaries explain that although his advisors were able to suggest interpretations, all of their ideas appeared unsuitable to Pharaoh.[2]

9 **The chief butler spoke to Pharaoh, saying: I mention my sins today.** Although what I am about to say will include a mention of earlier sins of mine, it is important that I issue my statement nonetheless.

10 **Pharaoh became angry with his servants, and he placed me in the custody of the house of the chief executioner, me and the chief baker.**

11 **We dreamed a dream one night, I and he; each of us dreamed in accordance with the interpretation of his dream;** we both had dreams that came to pass.

12 **There with us was a Hebrew lad, a slave**[D] **of the chief executioner; we told him** the dreams, **and he interpreted our dreams for us; each of us in accordance with his own dream**

—— BACKGROUND ——

41:8 | The magicians [*ḥartumei*] of Egypt: The word *ḥartumim* is derived from an ancient Egyptian term referring to members of the priestly caste, who were considered particularly knowledgeable in witchcraft. Magic was an important element of all realms of life in ancient Egypt.

—— DISCUSSION ——

41:12 | A Hebrew lad, a slave: The Sages note the unflattering portrayal of Joseph in the chief butler's presentation to Pharaoh. He calls him a Hebrew, a title that would elicit disdain and perhaps even disgust from all Egyptians; a lad, an inexperienced youngster; and finally, he identifies him as a slave of the chief executioner (*Tanḥuma, Miketz* 3). A plain reading indicates that the chief butler wanted to diminish Joseph's stature. However, it is also possible that he sought to emphasize that Joseph's ability to interpret dreams did not stem from education or training but was a supernatural gift: Although he is a Hebrew, a lad, and a slave, he possesses exceptional skills in interpreting dreams. Seeing that Pharaoh had despaired of a solution from his wise, educated experts, the chief butler suggests that he might receive a better result from this unlikely source.

פרשת

מקץ

א ב ויהי מקץ שנתים ימים ופרעה חלם והנה עמד על־היאר: והנה מן־היאר עלת
ג שבע פרות יפות מראה ובריאת בשר ותרעינה באחו: והנה שבע פרות
אחרות עלות אחריהן מן־היאר רעות מראה ודקות בשר ותעמדנה אצל
ד הפרות על־שפת היאר: ותאכלנה הפרות רעות המראה ודקת הבשר את
ה שבע הפרות יפת המראה והבריאת וייקץ פרעה: ויישן ויחלם שנית והנה ׀
ו שבע שבלים עלות בקנה אחד בריאות וטבות: והנה שבע שבלים דקות
ז ושדופת קדים צמחות אחריהן: ותבלענה השבלים הדקות את שבע השבלים
ח הבריאות והמלאות וייקץ פרעה והנה חלום: ויהי בבקר ותפעם רוחו וישלח
ויקרא את־כל־חרטמי מצרים ואת־כל־חכמיה ויספר פרעה להם את־חלמו
ט ואין־פותר אותם לפרעה: וידבר שר המשקים את־פרעה לאמר את־חטאי
י אני מזכיר היום: פרעה קצף על־עבדיו ויתן אתי במשמר בית שר הטבחים
יא אתי ואת שר האפים: ונחלמה חלום בלילה אחד אני והוא איש כפתרון חלמו
יב חלמנו: ושם אתנו נער עברי עבד לשר הטבחים ונספר־לו ויפתר־לנו את־

רש"י

א| **ויהי מקץ.** כתרגומו "מסוף", וכל לשון 'קץ' סוף הוא: **על היאר.** כל שאר נהרות אינם קרויין יאורים חוץ מנילוס, מפני שכל הארץ עשויה יאורים יאורים בידי אדם ונילוס עולה בתוכם ומשקה אותם, לפי שאין גשמים יורדין במצרים תדיר כשאר ארצות:

ב| **יפות מראה.** סימן הוא לימי שבע, שהבריות נראות יפות זו לזו, שאין עין בריה צרה בחברתה: **באחו.** באגם, מריש"ק בלעז, כמו: "ישגא אחו" (איוב ח, יא):

ג| **ודקות בשר.** טינבי"ש בלעז, לשון דק:

ד| **ותאכלנה.** סימן שתהא כל שמחת השבע נשכחת בימי הרעב:

ה| **בקנה אחד.** טודי"ל בלעז: **בריאות.** סיינ"ש בלעז:

ו| **ושדופת.** השליד"ש בלעז, "שקיפן קדום", חבוטות, לשון משקוף החבוט תמיד על ידי הדלת המכה עליו: **קדים.** רוח מזרחית שקורין ביס"א:

ז| **הבריאות.** סיינ"ש בלעז: **והנה חלום.** והנה נשלם חלום שלם לפניו והערך לפותרים:

ח| **ותפעם רוחו.** "ומטרפא רוחיה", מקשקשת בתוכו כפעמון. ובנבוכדנצר אומר: "ותתפעם רוחו" (דניאל ב, א), לפי שהיו שם שתי פעימות: שכחת החלום והעלמת פתרונו: **חרטמי.** הנחרים בטימי מתים, ששואלים בעצמות. 'טימי' הן עצמות בלשון ארמי, ובמשנה: בית שהוא מלא טימיא – מלא עצמות: **ואין פותר אותם לפרעה.** פותרים היו אותם, אבל לא לפרעה, שלא היה קולן נכנס באזניו ולא היה לו קורת רוח בפתרונם, שהיו אומרים: שבע בנות אתה מוליד, שבע בנות אתה קובר:

יא| **איש כפתרון חלמו.** חלום הראוי לפתרון שנפתר לנו ודומה לו:

יב| **נער עברי עבד.** ארורים הרשעים שאין טובתם שלמה, מזכירו בלשון בזיון: "נער" – שוטה ואין ראוי לגדולה. "עברי" – אפילו לשוננו אינו מכיר. "עבד" –

he interpreted, so that each dream and its interpretation suited each other.

13 Furthermore, **it was that as he interpreted to us, so it was.** Not only did the interpretation sound convincing, it came true as well: **Me, he,** Pharaoh, **restored to my position, and him,** the chief baker, **he hanged.**

14 Since he was anxious to find the correct interpretation of his dream, **Pharaoh sent and summoned Joseph, and they rushed him from the dungeon. He shaved,** so that he would not appear unkempt when he appeared before the king after his lengthy period of imprisonment, he **changed his garments** to decent clothing, **and came to Pharaoh.**

15 **Pharaoh said to Joseph: I dreamed a dream, and there is no interpreter of it; and I heard about you, saying: You will hear a dream to interpret it.**

Second aliya

16 **Joseph answered Pharaoh, saying: Not by me.** You do not need my skills, as I am not the interpreter. Rather, **God will respond for Pharaoh's peace.** At most, I can serve as an intermediary.

17 **Pharaoh spoke to Joseph: In my dream, behold, I am standing on the bank of the Nile.**

18 **Behold, seven cows, fat fleshed and fair, come up from the Nile, and they grazed in the pasture.**

19 **Behold, seven other cows come up after them, scrawny, very unsightly, and lean fleshed.** Here Pharaoh adds his own impression of the sight: **I have not seen like them in all the land of Egypt for deficiency.**

20 **The lean and unsightly cows ate the first seven fat cows.**

21 Pharaoh adds another observation: **They came into their innards, but it was not apparent that they came into their innards,** as no change was discernible in the scrawny cows; **and their appearance was** just as **unsightly as** it was **at first, and I awoke.**

22 **I saw in my dream, and behold, seven ears of grain growing on one stalk, plump and good.**

23 **Behold, seven ears of grain, parched, thin, and blighted by the east wind, growing after them.**

24 **The thin ears swallowed the seven good ears. I told it to the magicians, but no one could tell me.** Since I have not received a satisfactory interpretation from the magicians, I await your response.

25 **Joseph said to Pharaoh:** Although you saw two different dreams, in fact **the dream of Pharaoh is one; that which God does, He told Pharaoh.**[D] It is a prophetic dream in which you were informed of future events.

26 **The seven good cows are seven years and the seven good ears are seven years: It is one dream.** The fact that the two visions are part of one dream is significant, as it bundles the cows and ears together. The cows symbolize growth, life, and abundance, whereas the ears stand for the cycles of growth because, in contrast to the cows, whose productivity is not dependent on the cycle of the year, the crop of grain is renewed on a yearly basis. Thus the seven ears define the timeframe for the abundance represented by the seven cows.

27 **The seven scrawny and unsightly cows that come up after them are seven years, and the seven empty ears blighted by the east wind shall be seven years of famine.** In contrast to the polite hesitance with which Joseph began his speech to Pharaoh, here he speaks decisively and in a dramatic, almost poetic style.

28 **That is the matter that I spoke to Pharaoh: That which God does, He showed Pharaoh.**

29 **Behold, seven years are coming** in which there will be **great plenty throughout the land of Egypt.** These are represented by the fat cows and the good ears.

30 However, **seven years of famine shall arise after them.** These are represented by the unsightly cows and the blighted ears. **And all the plenty in the land of Egypt shall be forgotten; the famine shall devastate the land.**

DISCUSSION

41:25 | **That which God does, He told Pharaoh:** Joseph had been very close with his father, "a son of his old age" (37:3). It is likely that he learned from Jacob how to distinguish between a dream that simply expresses the desires of the dreamer or one that is mere nonsense, and a dream that contains a message from Heaven. Here Joseph senses that Pharaoh's dream is in fact a prophetic revelation.

יג חֲלֹמֹתֵינוּ אִישׁ כַּחֲלֹמוֹ פָּתָר: וַיְהִי כַּאֲשֶׁר פָּתַר־לָנוּ כֵּן הָיָה אֹתִי הֵשִׁיב עַל־כַּנִּי
יד וְאֹתוֹ תָלָה: וַיִּשְׁלַח פַּרְעֹה וַיִּקְרָא אֶת־יוֹסֵף וַיְרִיצֻהוּ מִן־הַבּוֹר וַיְגַלַּח וַיְחַלֵּף
טו שִׂמְלֹתָיו וַיָּבֹא אֶל־פַּרְעֹה: וַיֹּאמֶר פַּרְעֹה אֶל־יוֹסֵף חֲלוֹם חָלַמְתִּי וּפֹתֵר אֵין אֹתוֹ שני
טז וַאֲנִי שָׁמַעְתִּי עָלֶיךָ לֵאמֹר תִּשְׁמַע חֲלוֹם לִפְתֹּר אֹתוֹ: וַיַּעַן יוֹסֵף אֶת־פַּרְעֹה לֵאמֹר
יז בִּלְעָדָי אֱלֹהִים יַעֲנֶה אֶת־שְׁלוֹם פַּרְעֹה: וַיְדַבֵּר פַּרְעֹה אֶל־יוֹסֵף בַּחֲלֹמִי הִנְנִי
יח עֹמֵד עַל־שְׂפַת הַיְאֹר: וְהִנֵּה מִן־הַיְאֹר עֹלֹת שֶׁבַע פָּרוֹת בְּרִיאוֹת בָּשָׂר וִיפֹת
יט תֹּאַר וַתִּרְעֶינָה בָּאָחוּ: וְהִנֵּה שֶׁבַע פָּרוֹת אֲחֵרוֹת עֹלוֹת אַחֲרֵיהֶן דַּלּוֹת וְרָעוֹת
כ תֹּאַר מְאֹד וְרַקּוֹת בָּשָׂר לֹא־רָאִיתִי כָהֵנָּה בְּכָל־אֶרֶץ מִצְרַיִם לָרֹעַ: וַתֹּאכַלְנָה
כא הַפָּרוֹת הָרַקּוֹת וְהָרָעוֹת אֵת שֶׁבַע הַפָּרוֹת הָרִאשֹׁנוֹת הַבְּרִיאֹת: וַתָּבֹאנָה אֶל־
קִרְבֶּנָה וְלֹא נוֹדַע כִּי־בָאוּ אֶל־קִרְבֶּנָה וּמַרְאֵיהֶן רַע כַּאֲשֶׁר בַּתְּחִלָּה וָאִיקָץ:
כב כג וָאֵרֶא בַּחֲלֹמִי וְהִנֵּה ׀ שֶׁבַע שִׁבֳּלִים עֹלֹת בְּקָנֶה אֶחָד מְלֵאֹת וְטֹבוֹת: וְהִנֵּה
כד שֶׁבַע שִׁבֳּלִים צְנֻמוֹת דַּקּוֹת שְׁדֻפוֹת קָדִים צֹמְחוֹת אַחֲרֵיהֶם: וַתִּבְלַעְןָ הַשִּׁבֳּלִים
כה הַדַּקֹּת אֵת שֶׁבַע הַשִּׁבֳּלִים הַטֹּבוֹת וָאֹמַר אֶל־הַחַרְטֻמִּים וְאֵין מַגִּיד לִי: וַיֹּאמֶר
יוֹסֵף אֶל־פַּרְעֹה חֲלוֹם פַּרְעֹה אֶחָד הוּא אֵת אֲשֶׁר הָאֱלֹהִים עֹשֶׂה הִגִּיד לְפַרְעֹה:
כו שֶׁבַע פָּרֹת הַטֹּבֹת שֶׁבַע שָׁנִים הֵנָּה וְשֶׁבַע הַשִּׁבֳּלִים הַטֹּבֹת שֶׁבַע שָׁנִים הֵנָּה
כז חֲלוֹם אֶחָד הוּא: וְשֶׁבַע הַפָּרוֹת הָרַקּוֹת וְהָרָעֹת הָעֹלֹת אַחֲרֵיהֶן שֶׁבַע שָׁנִים
כח הֵנָּה וְשֶׁבַע הַשִּׁבֳּלִים הָרֵקוֹת שְׁדֻפוֹת הַקָּדִים יִהְיוּ שֶׁבַע שְׁנֵי רָעָב: הוּא הַדָּבָר
כט אֲשֶׁר דִּבַּרְתִּי אֶל־פַּרְעֹה אֲשֶׁר הָאֱלֹהִים עֹשֶׂה הֶרְאָה אֶת־פַּרְעֹה: הִנֵּה שֶׁבַע
ל שָׁנִים בָּאוֹת שָׂבָע גָּדוֹל בְּכָל־אֶרֶץ מִצְרָיִם: וְקָמוּ שֶׁבַע שְׁנֵי רָעָב אַחֲרֵיהֶן וְנִשְׁכַּח

רש״י

וְכָתוּב בְּנִמּוּסֵי מִצְרַיִם שֶׁאֵין עֶבֶד מוֹלֵךְ וְלֹא לוֹבֵשׁ בִּגְדֵי שָׂרִים: **אִישׁ כַּחֲלֹמוֹ.** לְפִי הַחֲלוֹם וְקָרוֹב לְעִנְיָנוֹ:

יג | **אֹתִי הֵשִׁיב עַל כַּנִּי.** פַּרְעֹה הַנִּזְכָּר לְמַעְלָה, כְּמוֹ שֶׁאָמַר: "פַּרְעֹה קָצַף עַל עֲבָדָיו" (לעיל פסוק י):

יד | **מִן הַבּוֹר.** מִן בֵּית הַסֹּהַר שֶׁהוּא עָשׂוּי כְּמִין גֻּמָּא, וְכֵן כָּל בּוֹר שֶׁבַּמִּקְרָא לְשׁוֹן גֻּמָּא הוּא, וְאַף אִם אֵין בּוֹ מַיִם קָרוּי בּוֹר, פוס"א בְּלַעַז: **וַיְגַלַּח.** מִפְּנֵי כְּבוֹד הַמַּלְכוּת:

טו | **תִּשְׁמַע חֲלוֹם לִפְתֹּר אֹתוֹ.** תַּאֲזִין וְתָבִין חֲלוֹם לִפְתֹּר אוֹתוֹ. "תִּשְׁמַע" – לְשׁוֹן הֲבָנָה וְהַאֲזָנָה, כְּמוֹ: "שֹׁמֵעַ יוֹסֵף" (להלן מב, כג), "אֲשֶׁר לֹא תִשְׁמַע לְשֹׁנוֹ" (דברים כח, מט), אנטנדר"א בְּלַעַז:

טז | **בִּלְעָדָי.** אֵין הַחָכְמָה מִשֶּׁלִּי, אֶלָּא "אֱלֹהִים יַעֲנֶה" – יִתֵּן עֲנִיָּה בְּפִי לִשְׁלוֹם פַּרְעֹה:

יט | **דַּלּוֹת.** כְּחוּשׁוֹת, כְּמוֹ: "מַדּוּעַ אַתָּה כָּכָה דַּל" (שמואל ב׳ יג, ד) דַּלְמָנוּן: **וְרַקּוֹת בָּשָׂר.** כָּל לְשׁוֹן 'רַקּוֹת' שֶׁבַּתּוֹרָה "חֲסִירָן בְּסַר", וּבְלַעַז בלוס"ש:

כג | **צְנֻמוֹת.** 'צוּנְמָא' בִּלְשׁוֹן אֲרַמִּי סֶלַע, הֲרֵי הֵן כְּעֵין בְּלִי לַחְלוּחַ, קָשׁוֹת כַּסֶּלַע; וְתַרְגּוּמוֹ 'נָצַן לָקְיָן'; 'נָצַן' – אֵין בָּהֶן אֶלָּא הַנֵּץ לְפִי שֶׁנִּתְרוֹקְנוּ מִן הַזֶּרַע:

כה-לב | **שֶׁבַע שָׁנִים וְשֶׁבַע שָׁנִים.** כֻּלָּן אֵינָן אֶלָּא שֶׁבַע, וַאֲשֶׁר נִשְׁנָה הַחֲלוֹם פַּעֲמַיִם לְפִי שֶׁהַדָּבָר

31 **The plenty shall not be known in the land due to that famine afterward, for it shall be very severe.** Here Joseph interprets Pharaoh's description of the fact that it was not apparent that the seven fat cows had come to the innards of the scrawny cows. He states that this is an indication that the bad years shall consume all the produce of the good years, of which nothing shall remain.

32 **With regard to the repetition of the dream to Pharaoh twice, it is because the matter is determined by God, and God hastens to perform it.** The two parts of the dream complement and clarify one another, as Joseph had explained, yet Pharaoh dreamed them separately. This reiteration is indicative of the finality of the matter and is a sign that the message expressed in the dream will come to pass in the near future. This is similar to a repeated cry at a time of danger.

33 **Now** that God has revealed the future to you and sent you a practical warning, **let Pharaoh look for an insightful** person, one who can anticipate forthcoming events from what he observes in the present, **and he must be a wise man,**[D] who has seen and heard much and accumulated knowledge,[3] **and install him over the land of Egypt.** Joseph stresses that this is a position that requires a man of exceptional qualities. Therefore, it is inadvisable for Pharaoh to appoint one of his current ministers.

34 **Pharaoh should proceed and appoint officials over the land, and he shall supply the land of Egypt during the seven years of plenty.**

35 **They will gather all the food of these coming good years and amass grain under the control of Pharaoh; they will collect food in the cities and they will preserve it.**

36 **The food shall be for a security for the land for the seven years of famine that shall be in the land of Egypt, and the land will not perish in the famine.**

37 **The matter was worthy in the eyes of Pharaoh.** The interpretation was accepted by Pharaoh, as each of its details matched a feature of his dream. He liked Joseph's advice because it had great economic potential for the country, and it would concentrate power in Pharaoh's hands during the years of famine. **And the matter was likewise worthy in the eyes of all his servants,** perhaps because each of them separately thought that he would

be selected as the insightful, wise man who would manage the Egyptian economy in the forthcoming years.

38 **Pharaoh said to his servants: Can we find someone like this, a man in whom there is the spirit of God?**

39 **Pharaoh said to Joseph: After God has disclosed all this to**
Third aliya **you, there is no one as insightful and wise as you.** Pharaoh was deeply impressed by Joseph. Perhaps Joseph's appearance contributed to this, as he appeared in civilian clothes and presumably, by that point, spoke fluent Egyptian. Like most of those who had encountered Joseph, Pharaoh recognized his wisdom and potential, and he realized that Joseph merited even divinely inspired insight.

40 Consequently, Pharaoh authorized Joseph to act in accordance with his interpretation and suggestions: **You will be in charge of my house, and all my people shall be sustained [*yishak*] at your directive.**[4] Alternatively, this may be interpreted to mean that the people would be able to bear arms only at Joseph's directive.[5] Yet another interpretation is that all would come to kiss him,[6] as everyone would honor and admire Joseph and would be subservient to him. These latter interpretations are based on different meanings of the root *nun-shin-kuf*, which can mean "weapon" or "kiss." Pharaoh further states: Although your authority is limited to a specific matter, due to its vital nature, **only the throne will I make too great for you.** I shall not relinquish the throne, but I will empower you to as great an extent as possible.

41 **Pharaoh said to Joseph: See, I have set you over the entire land of Egypt.** You are in charge of all of Egypt with regard to these matters.

42 **Pharaoh removed his signet ring from upon his hand.** Since the signet ring contained an official seal, its transfer to Joseph was a significant step in his empowerment. **And he placed it upon Joseph's hand;** once Joseph was granted his position of authority, **he dressed him in garments of linen, and he placed a gold chain**[D] **on his neck.**

Gold chain

DISCUSSION

41:33 | Now, let Pharaoh look for an insightful and wise man: Joseph, the Hebrew slave, is not one of Pharaoh's wise men or advisors and was merely asked to interpret a dream. Yet he dares to go beyond his given task and counsel Pharaoh on how to proceed given the information provided in his dream. It is possible

that Joseph was motivated by his understanding of the dream. He sensed that the very fact that he had been called upon to interpret the dream was significant and indicated that he had been called upon to play a role in the unfolding events. One can similarly explain his request from the chief butler to remember him: Since

the butler had shared his dream with him and asked him to interpret it, Joseph concluded that he himself was part of the story of the dream and its resolution. In the case of Pharaoh's dream, this conclusion is even more apparent in light of the nearly impossible set of circumstances that preceded it: An imprisoned slave ◀◀

לא כָּל־הַשָּׂבָע בְּאֶרֶץ מִצְרָיִם וְכִלָּה הָרָעָב אֶת־הָאָרֶץ: וְלֹא־יִוָּדַע הַשָּׂבָע בָּאָרֶץ
לב מִפְּנֵי הָרָעָב הַהוּא אַחֲרֵי־כֵן כִּי־כָבֵד הוּא מְאֹד: וְעַל הִשָּׁנוֹת הַחֲלוֹם אֶל־פַּרְעֹה
לג פַּעֲמָיִם כִּי־נָכוֹן הַדָּבָר מֵעִם הָאֱלֹהִים וּמְמַהֵר הָאֱלֹהִים לַעֲשֹׂתוֹ: וְעַתָּה יֵרֶא
לד פַרְעֹה אִישׁ נָבוֹן וְחָכָם וִישִׁיתֵהוּ עַל־אֶרֶץ מִצְרָיִם: יַעֲשֶׂה פַרְעֹה וְיַפְקֵד פְּקִדִים
לה עַל־הָאָרֶץ וְחִמֵּשׁ אֶת־אֶרֶץ מִצְרַיִם בְּשֶׁבַע שְׁנֵי הַשָּׂבָע: וְיִקְבְּצוּ אֶת־כָּל־אֹכֶל
הַשָּׁנִים הַטֹּבֹת הַבָּאֹת הָאֵלֶּה וְיִצְבְּרוּ־בָר תַּחַת יַד־פַּרְעֹה אֹכֶל בֶּעָרִים וְשָׁמָרוּ:
לו וְהָיָה הָאֹכֶל לְפִקָּדוֹן לָאָרֶץ לְשֶׁבַע שְׁנֵי הָרָעָב אֲשֶׁר תִּהְיֶיןָ בְּאֶרֶץ מִצְרָיִם וְלֹא־
לז לח תִכָּרֵת הָאָרֶץ בָּרָעָב: וַיִּיטַב הַדָּבָר בְּעֵינֵי פַרְעֹה וּבְעֵינֵי כָּל־עֲבָדָיו: וַיֹּאמֶר פַּרְעֹה לז
לט אֶל־עֲבָדָיו הֲנִמְצָא כָזֶה אִישׁ אֲשֶׁר רוּחַ אֱלֹהִים בּוֹ: וַיֹּאמֶר פַּרְעֹה אֶל־יוֹסֵף שלישי
מ אַחֲרֵי הוֹדִיעַ אֱלֹהִים אוֹתְךָ אֶת־כָּל־זֹאת אֵין־נָבוֹן וְחָכָם כָּמוֹךָ: אַתָּה תִּהְיֶה
מא עַל־בֵּיתִי וְעַל־פִּיךָ יִשַּׁק כָּל־עַמִּי רַק הַכִּסֵּא אֶגְדַּל מִמֶּךָּ: וַיֹּאמֶר פַּרְעֹה אֶל־יוֹסֵף
מב רְאֵה נָתַתִּי אֹתְךָ עַל כָּל־אֶרֶץ מִצְרָיִם: וַיָּסַר פַּרְעֹה אֶת־טַבַּעְתּוֹ מֵעַל יָדוֹ וַיִּתֵּן
אֹתָהּ עַל־יַד יוֹסֵף וַיַּלְבֵּשׁ אֹתוֹ בִּגְדֵי־שֵׁשׁ וַיָּשֶׂם רְבִד הַזָּהָב עַל־צַוָּארוֹ:

רש"י

מְזֻמָּן, כְּמוֹ שֶׁפֵּרַשׁ לוֹ בַּסּוֹף: "וְעַל הִשָּׁנוֹת הַחֲלוֹם" וְגוֹ': **וְנִשְׁכַּח כָּל הַשָּׂבָע.** הוּא פִּתְרוֹן הַבְּלִיעָה: **וְלֹא יִוָּדַע הַשָּׂבָע.** הוּא פִּתְרוֹן "וְלֹא נוֹדַע כִּי בָאוּ אֶל קִרְבֶּנָה" (לעיל פסוק כא): **נָכוֹן.** מְזֻמָּן. בְּשֶׁבַע שָׁנִים הַטּוֹבוֹת נֶאֱמַר: "הִגִּיד לְפַרְעֹה" (פסוק כה), לְפִי שֶׁהָיָה סָמוּךְ, וּבְשֶׁבַע שְׁנֵי רָעָב נֶאֱמַר: "הֶרְאָה אֶת פַּרְעֹה" (פסוק כח), לְפִי שֶׁהָיָה הַדָּבָר מֻפְלָג וְרִחוּק נוֹפֵל בּוֹ לְשׁוֹן מַרְאֶה:

לד| **וְחִמֵּשׁ.** כְּתַרְגּוּמוֹ: "וִיזָרְזוּן", וְכֵן: "וַחֲמֻשִׁים" (שמות יג, יח):

לה| **אֶת כָּל אֹכֶל.** שֵׁם דָּבָר הוּא, לְפִיכָךְ טַעְמוֹ בָּאָלֶ"ף וְנָקוּד בְּפַתָּח קָטָן (סגול). וְ'אוֹכֵל' שֶׁהוּא פּוֹעֵל, כְּגוֹן: "כִּי כָּל אֹכֵל חֵלֶב" (ויקרא ז, כה), טַעְמוֹ לְמַטָּה בַּכָּ"ף וְנָקוּד קָמָץ (צירי): **תַּחַת יַד פַּרְעֹה.** בִּרְשׁוּתוֹ וּבְאוֹצְרוֹתָיו:

לו| **וְהָיָה הָאֹכֶל.** הַצָּבוּר בִּשְׁאָר פִּקָּדוֹן גָּנוּז לְקִיּוּם הָאָרֶץ:

לח| **הֲנִמְצָא כָזֶה.** "הֲנַשְׁכַּח כְּדֵין", אִם נֵלֵךְ וּנְבַקְשֶׁנּוּ הֲנִמְצָא כָּמוֹהוּ? 'הֲנִמְצָא' לְשׁוֹן תְּמִיהָה, וְכֵן כָּל הֵ"א הַמְשַׁמֶּשֶׁת בְּרֹאשׁ תֵּבָה וּנְקוּדָה בַּחֲטַף פַּתָּח:

לט| **אֵין נָבוֹן וְחָכָם כָּמוֹךָ.** לְבַקֵּשׁ "אִישׁ נָבוֹן וְחָכָם" שֶׁאָמַרְתָּ (לעיל פסוק לג), לֹא נִמְצָא כָּמוֹךָ:

מ| **יִשַּׁק.** "יִתְזַן", יִתְפַּרְנֵס; כָּל צָרְכֵי עַמִּי יִהְיוּ נַעֲשִׂים עַל יָדְךָ, כְּמוֹ: "וּבֶן מֶשֶׁק בֵּיתִי" (לעיל טו, ב), וּכְמוֹ: "נַשְּׁקוּ בַר" (תהלים ב, יב), גרניסו"ן בְּלַעַז: **רַק הַכִּסֵּא.** שֶׁיִּהְיוּ קוֹרִין לִי מֶלֶךְ: **כִּסֵּא.** לְשׁוֹן שֵׁם הַמְּלוּכָה, כְּמוֹ: "וִיגַדֵּל אֶת כִּסְאוֹ מִכִּסֵּא אֲדֹנִי הַמֶּלֶךְ" (מלכים א' א, לז):

מא| **נָתַתִּי אֹתְךָ.** "מַנֵּיתִי יָתָךְ"; וְאַף עַל פִּי כֵן לְשׁוֹן נְתִינָה הוּא, כְּמוֹ: "וּלְתִתְּךָ עֶלְיוֹן" (דברים כו, יט). בֵּין לִגְדֻלָּה בֵּין לְשִׁפְלוּת נוֹפֵל לְשׁוֹן נְתִינָה עָלָיו, כְּמוֹ: "נָתַתִּי אֶתְכֶם נִבְזִים וּשְׁפָלִים" (מלאכי ב, ט):

מב| **וַיָּסַר פַּרְעֹה אֶת טַבַּעְתּוֹ.** נְתִינַת טַבַּעַת הַמֶּלֶךְ הִיא אוֹת לְמִי שֶׁנּוֹתְנָהּ לוֹ לִהְיוֹת שֵׁנִי לוֹ לִגְדֻלָּה: **בִּגְדֵי שֵׁשׁ.** דְּבַר חֲשִׁיבוּת הוּא בְּמִצְרַיִם: **רְבִד.** עֲנָק, וְעַל שֶׁהוּא רָצוּף בְּטַבָּעוֹת קָרוּי 'רָבִיד'; וְכֵן: "רָבַדְתִּי עַרְשִׂי" (משלי ז, טז), רִפַּדְתִּי עַרְשִׂי מַרְצָפוֹת. וּבִלְשׁוֹן מִשְׁנָה: "מֻקָּף רוֹבְדִין שֶׁל אֶבֶן" (מדות א, ח), "עַל הָרֹבֶד שֶׁבָּעֲזָרָה" (יומא מג ע"ב), וְהִיא רִצְפָּה:

DISCUSSION

was brought to advise Pharaoh on a matter that his wise men and advisors were unable to resolve. Joseph therefore infers that he has been granted special power by God. For this reason he does not merely interpret the dream, he also advises Pharaoh on how to exploit the harvest of the good years in order to soften the blow of the subsequent period of famine.

41:42| **A gold chain [*revid*]:** One can see in Egyptian engravings a kind of golden collar placed on the necks of kings and nobles as a sign of their lofty status. In Rambam's Commentary on the Mishna, he writes that a king's *revid* is a type of ring hung around the neck (Rambam, Mishna, *Kelim* 12:1).

43 **He had him ride in the alternate chariot that he had,** the chariot he would use when the king's regular chariot was unavailable. Pharaoh kept his personal chariot exclusively for himself. **And they cried before him: Kneel.**[7] When Joseph traveled in his chariot, all were obliged to kneel before him. **And he was set over the entire land of Egypt.** Pharaoh formally and publicly announced that Joseph was in charge of all of Egypt.

44 **Pharaoh** summarized the matter and **said to Joseph: I am Pharaoh,** descendant of the gods, ruler and governor, **and yet,** beyond that, **without you no man shall lift his hand or his foot in the entire land of Egypt.** You have full authority over everything that is done in the land.

45 **Pharaoh called Joseph's name Tzafenat Paneah;**[BD] and as Joseph was now an important figure, Pharaoh arranged for him to be married: **He gave him Asenat, daughter of Poti Fera,**[D] **priest of On,**[B] **as a wife. Joseph came out over the land of Egypt;** he traversed the land as its ruler and began to organize its internal affairs.

46 **Joseph was thirty years old as he stood before Pharaoh king of Egypt.** Thirteen years had passed since his original dreams, due to which he was sold and exiled from his land (37:2). Since that time his status had changed beyond recognition. **Joseph came out from before Pharaoh, and he passed through the entire land of Egypt** in order to put into practice his advice to Pharaoh.

47 **The earth produced, during the seven years of plenty, in abundance [*kematzim*].** The grains of a single stalk amounted to a handful [*kometz*], or several handfuls.[8] Alternatively, some explain that this means that the earth produced enough to fill the storehouses.[9] In any event, the verse expresses the fact that the yield of the land was extensive.

48 He, **Joseph, gathered all the food of the seven years that was in the land of Egypt and placed food in the cities;** he placed the food of the fields that was around the city in it. In every city Joseph stored the produce that grew in its environs, both in order to keep the produce in the local climate to which it

was accustomed, and also because each city could estimate accurately the amount of produce required for its inhabitants.

49 **Joseph amassed grain like the sand of the sea,**[D] **very much, until one stopped counting as it was without number.** An enormous amount of produce grew each year. It is possible that this verse should be understood literally: At first they tried keeping records, but eventually they gave up, overwhelmed by the sheer mass of produce.

Fresco, Tomb of Nakht, 1400–1390 BCE

50 **Two sons were born to Joseph** during the years of plenty **before the advent of the year of the famine, who were born to him by Asenat, daughter of Poti Fera, priest of On.**

51 **Joseph called the name of the firstborn Manasseh, as** he felt: **God has made me forget [*nashani*] all my toil,** my suffering and hardship, **and** the trouble of **my father's entire house,** from which I suffered for many years, as I am now a new person.

52 **He called the name of the second** son **Efraim, as** he said: Not only have I forgotten my suffering, but now **God has made me fruitful [*hifrani*]** in that I have become successful and risen to prominence **in the land of my affliction.**

Fourth 53 **The seven years of plenty that was in the land of Egypt**
aliya **concluded.**

54 **The seven years of famine began to come, as Joseph had said.** In Egypt, which is mainly dependent not on rainfall but on an irrigation system whose source is the Nile, this transition was sharp. If for whatever reason the water level in the Nile falls lower than required, the land does not produce, resulting in famine. Furthermore, this was not merely a local problem in

---

DISCUSSION

41:45 | Tzafenat Paneah: Some have explained this as a descriptive term in Hebrew meaning "interpreter of secrets" (*Targum Yonatan*; Rashi). However, as this is the only instance of the root *peh-ayin-nun-het* in the Bible, it is likely that this is in fact an Egyptian name given to Joseph by Pharaoh (Rashbam). There are other Israelites with Egyptian names in the Torah, e.g., Pinehas. Joseph's new name is a title of honor commensurate to his lofty position.

Asenat, daughter of Poti Fera: Despite the similarity in name, this was apparently not the daughter of Potifar (Rashbam), although there is a midrash which claims that Potifar and Poti Fera are one and the same (see *Sota* 13b). Joseph's father-in-law was not an executioner like Potifar, but the head priest in the capital city of On, where there was a temple. By arranging this marriage, Pharaoh not only acted generously toward Joseph but also strengthened his position: Since priests in Egypt were influential

members of society, Pharaoh wanted Joseph to have direct ties with this other source of power of the ruling classes.

41:49 | Grain like the sand of the sea: For a very long time, until nearly two thousand years ago, Egypt was the leading country in grain production. It grew enough for all its needs and even exported a significant amount of produce to lands near and far. During the period of Roman rule, Egypt served as the granary of Rome (see Isaiah 23:3).

מג וַיַּרְכֵּב אֹתוֹ בְּמִרְכֶּבֶת הַמִּשְׁנֶה אֲשֶׁר־לוֹ וַיִּקְרְאוּ לְפָנָיו אַבְרֵךְ וְנָתוֹן אֹתוֹ עַל
מד כָּל־אֶרֶץ מִצְרָיִם: וַיֹּאמֶר פַּרְעֹה אֶל־יוֹסֵף אֲנִי פַרְעֹה וּבִלְעָדֶיךָ לֹא־יָרִים אִישׁ
מה אֶת־יָדוֹ וְאֶת־רַגְלוֹ בְּכָל־אֶרֶץ מִצְרָיִם: וַיִּקְרָא פַרְעֹה שֵׁם־יוֹסֵף צָפְנַת פַּעְנֵחַ
וַיִּתֶּן־לוֹ אֶת־אָסְנַת בַּת־פּוֹטִי פֶרַע כֹּהֵן אֹן לְאִשָּׁה וַיֵּצֵא יוֹסֵף עַל־אֶרֶץ מִצְרָיִם:
מו וְיוֹסֵף בֶּן־שְׁלֹשִׁים שָׁנָה בְּעָמְדוֹ לִפְנֵי פַּרְעֹה מֶלֶךְ־מִצְרָיִם וַיֵּצֵא יוֹסֵף מִלִּפְנֵי
מז פַרְעֹה וַיַּעֲבֹר בְּכָל־אֶרֶץ מִצְרָיִם: וַתַּעַשׂ הָאָרֶץ בְּשֶׁבַע שְׁנֵי הַשָּׂבָע לִקְמָצִים:
מח וַיִּקְבֹּץ אֶת־כָּל־אֹכֶל ׀ שֶׁבַע שָׁנִים אֲשֶׁר הָיוּ בְּאֶרֶץ מִצְרַיִם וַיִּתֶּן־אֹכֶל בֶּעָרִים
מט אֹכֶל שְׂדֵה־הָעִיר אֲשֶׁר סְבִיבֹתֶיהָ נָתַן בְּתוֹכָהּ: וַיִּצְבֹּר יוֹסֵף בָּר כְּחוֹל הַיָּם הַרְבֵּה
נ מְאֹד עַד כִּי־חָדַל לִסְפֹּר כִּי־אֵין מִסְפָּר: וּלְיוֹסֵף יֻלַּד שְׁנֵי בָנִים בְּטֶרֶם תָּבוֹא שְׁנַת
נא הָרָעָב אֲשֶׁר יָלְדָה־לּוֹ אָסְנַת בַּת־פּוֹטִי פֶרַע כֹּהֵן אוֹן: וַיִּקְרָא יוֹסֵף אֶת־שֵׁם
נב הַבְּכוֹר מְנַשֶּׁה כִּי־נַשַּׁנִי אֱלֹהִים אֶת־כָּל־עֲמָלִי וְאֵת כָּל־בֵּית אָבִי: וְאֵת שֵׁם הַשֵּׁנִי
נג קָרָא אֶפְרָיִם כִּי־הִפְרַנִי אֱלֹהִים בְּאֶרֶץ עָנְיִי: וַתִּכְלֶינָה שֶׁבַע שְׁנֵי הַשָּׂבָע אֲשֶׁר רביעי
נד הָיָה בְּאֶרֶץ מִצְרָיִם: וַתְּחִלֶּינָה שֶׁבַע שְׁנֵי הָרָעָב לָבוֹא כַּאֲשֶׁר אָמַר יוֹסֵף וַיְהִי

רש"י

מג | **במרכבת המשנה.** השניה למרכבתו, המהלכת אצל שלו: **אברך.** כתרגומו: "דין אבא למלכא", 'רך' בלשון ארמי מלך, ב'השותפין': "לא ריכא ולא בר ריכא" (בבא בתרא ד ע"א). ובדברי אגדה, דרש רבי יהודה: "אברך" זה יוסף, שהוא אב בחכמה ורך בשנים. אמר לו רבי יוסי בן דורמסקית: ברבי, עד מתי אתה מעוות עלינו את הכתובים? אין 'אברך' אלא לשון ברכים, שהכל יהיו נכנסין ויוצאין תחת ידו, כענין שנאמר: "ונתון אתו" וגו':

מד | **אני פרעה.** שיש יכלת בידי לגזר גזרות על מלכותי, ואני גוזר שלא ירים איש את ידו בלעדיך, שלא ברשותך. דבר אחר, "אני פרעה", אני אהיה מלך, "ובלעדיך" וגו', זו דגמת "רק הכסא אגדל ממך" (לעיל פסוק מ) אלא שהצרך לפרש לו בשעת נתינת הטבעת: **את ידו ואת רגלו.** כתרגומו:

מה | **צפנת פענח.** מפרש הצפונות, ואין לפענח דמיון במקרא: **פוטי פרע.** הוא פוטיפר, ונקרא פוטיפרע על שנסתרס מאליו, לפי שלקח את יוסף למשכב זכור:

מז | **ותעש הארץ.** כתרגומו, ואין הלשון נעקר מלשון עשיה: **לקמצים.** קמץ על קמץ, יד על יד היו אוצרין:

מח | **אכל שדה העיר... נתן בתוכה.** שכל ארץ וארץ מעמדת פרותיה, ונותנין בתבואה מעפר המקום ומעמיד את התבואה מלרקב:

מט | **עד כי חדל לספר.** עד אשר חדל לו הסופר לספר, והרי זה מקרא קצר: **כי אין מספר.** לפי שאין מספר, והרי 'כי' משמש בלשון 'דהא':

BACKGROUND

41:45 | Tzafenat Paneah: The suffix represented here by the letters *ayin-nun-ḥet*, typically spelled "ankh" in English, denotes life in Egyptian. This suffix was added to the names of important individuals, e.g., the pharaoh Tutankhamun, whose name is a fusion of the words *tut*, *ankh*, and *amun*. One can see in Egyptian engravings the ankh symbol, an object that represents the life force, borne by gods and nobles. Some maintain that its shape is meant to be reminiscent of the Nile, which was the source of all life for Egypt.

On: The ancient capital of Egypt, located in the southern tip of the Nile Delta. On served as an important religious center for the sun god Aten. Upon the Hellenist conquest of Egypt, its name was changed to the Greek Heliopolis, which means City of the Sun (see commentary on Isaiah 19:18).

the mountains of Africa, which failed to provide enough water. Rather, **there was famine in all lands,** due to climate changes. **But in all of the land of Egypt there was bread.**

55 After private stores of food ran out and it became clear that the summer harvest produced a meager yield, **all of the land of Egypt was hungry, and the people cried to Pharaoh for bread.** The citizens' direct and indirect complaints were directed at Pharaoh not only because he was their ruler, but also because they attributed divine qualities to him. **Pharaoh said to all the Egyptians: Go to Joseph,** as he is in charge of dealing with your sustenance; **what he says to you, you shall do.** Pharaoh sought to spare himself, his ministers, and his close confidants the pressure of handling this problem. As soon as

it became necessary to start distributing food in an organized manner, he directed all complaints to Joseph.

56 **The famine was on the entire face of the earth,** outside Egypt as well, and therefore it was impossible to import food. **And Joseph opened all that was in them,** the storehouses, **and sold grain to the Egyptians.**[D] It is unclear whether in the first stage Joseph bought the produce or whether he collected it as a tax. In any case, at this point he sells it. **The famine was intensified in the land of Egypt,** as the people had nothing to eat apart from the produce in Joseph's granaries.

57 **All the land,** neighboring countries, **came to Egypt to purchase grain from Joseph, for the famine was severe in all the land.** Up to this point Joseph's interpretation of Pharaoh's dream had come to pass in full.

The First Descent of Joseph's Brothers to Egypt
GENESIS 42:1–28

When Joseph interpreted Pharaoh's dream, planned a solution to the grave problems posed by his interpretation, and put these ideas into practice, he unknowingly, through hidden divine providence, has prepared the way for his reencounter with his brothers. The famine, which affects the entire region, reaches the land of Canaan as well, and the family of Jacob seeks to assuage its hunger by purchasing some of the produce that Joseph has stored in Egypt.

42 1 **Jacob saw that there was grain in Egypt,** as Joseph sold produce not only to citizens of Egypt but to foreigners as well. Since Jacob and his sons were mainly shepherds, their distress was less immediate and apparent than that of their neighboring farmers. **And** therefore **Jacob said to his sons: Why are you presenting yourselves?** Do not display yourselves as exceptions to the general plight, lest hungry individuals surrounding us become envious of us or even attack us.

2 **He said: Behold, I have heard that there is grain in Egypt. Go down there and acquire grain for us from there that we will live and not die.**

3 **Ten of Joseph's brothers went down to acquire grain from Egypt.** The more men who went down, the more produce they could carry back with them.

4 **But Benjamin, Joseph's brother** on his mother's side as well, **Jacob did not send**[D] **with his** other **brothers, as he said: Lest disaster befall him.**

5 **The sons of Israel,** Jacob, **came to acquire grain among those** others **who came** from Canaan to acquire grain in Egypt, **as the famine was in the land of Canaan.**

6 **Joseph was the ruler over the land; he was the provider of grain to all the people of the land.** Joseph did not deal merely with the actual sale of food; he was also responsible for providing oversight of the entire process. This meant that he had to take political considerations into account when supplying produce in order to ensure that foreigners would not endanger the security of the country. **Joseph's brothers came, and** when they saw the powerful minister they **prostrated themselves to him, faces to the earth,** like all the other purchasers.

7 **Joseph saw his brothers, and he recognized them.** Although he had not seen them for over twenty years and their appearances had certainly changed, Joseph had no difficulty recognizing them, as they had all arrived together and wore their customary garments. **But he acted as** though he were a **stranger to them and spoke harshly to them.** Joseph used his authority in order to cause them difficulties. **He said to them: From where did you come? They said,** in complete innocence: **From the land of Canaan to acquire food.**

DISCUSSION

41:56 | Joseph opened all that was in them and sold grain to the Egyptians: Joseph was interested not only in selling the produce but also in regulating its distribution. As Pharaoh's representative he sought to establish a system that would enable him to oversee the people's

sustenance. On the one hand, this was not a free distribution of bread; on the other hand, the trade in grain was not conducted as a free market system. Joseph's aim was to regulate the sale of grain in order to ensure that no one in Egypt would die of hunger.

42:4 | But Benjamin, Joseph's brother, Jacob did not send: Jacob was especially close to Benjamin for two reasons: He was the only surviving child of Jacob's beloved wife, and he therefore served as a reminder of her; and he also reminded Jacob of his favorite son, Joseph.

נה רָעָב בְּכָל־הָאֲרָצוֹת וּבְכָל־אֶרֶץ מִצְרַיִם הָיָה לָחֶם: וַתִּרְעַב כָּל־אֶרֶץ מִצְרַיִם
וַיִּצְעַק הָעָם אֶל־פַּרְעֹה לַלָּחֶם וַיֹּאמֶר פַּרְעֹה לְכָל־מִצְרַיִם לְכוּ אֶל־יוֹסֵף אֲשֶׁר־
נו יֹאמַר לָכֶם תַּעֲשׂוּ: וְהָרָעָב הָיָה עַל כָּל־פְּנֵי הָאָרֶץ וַיִּפְתַּח יוֹסֵף אֶת־כָּל־אֲשֶׁר
נז בָּהֶם וַיִּשְׁבֹּר לְמִצְרַיִם וַיֶּחֱזַק הָרָעָב בְּאֶרֶץ מִצְרָיִם: וְכָל־הָאָרֶץ בָּאוּ מִצְרַיְמָה
מב א לִשְׁבֹּר אֶל־יוֹסֵף כִּי־חָזַק הָרָעָב בְּכָל־הָאָרֶץ: וַיַּרְא יַעֲקֹב כִּי יֶשׁ־שֶׁבֶר בְּמִצְרָיִם
ב וַיֹּאמֶר יַעֲקֹב לְבָנָיו לָמָּה תִּתְרָאוּ: וַיֹּאמֶר הִנֵּה שָׁמַעְתִּי כִּי יֶשׁ־שֶׁבֶר בְּמִצְרָיִם
ג רְדוּ־שָׁמָּה וְשִׁבְרוּ־לָנוּ מִשָּׁם וְנִחְיֶה וְלֹא נָמוּת: וַיֵּרְדוּ אֲחֵי־יוֹסֵף עֲשָׂרָה לִשְׁבֹּר
ד בָּר מִמִּצְרָיִם: וְאֶת־בִּנְיָמִין אֲחִי יוֹסֵף לֹא־שָׁלַח יַעֲקֹב אֶת־אֶחָיו כִּי אָמַר פֶּן־
ה יִקְרָאֶנּוּ אָסוֹן: וַיָּבֹאוּ בְּנֵי יִשְׂרָאֵל לִשְׁבֹּר בְּתוֹךְ הַבָּאִים כִּי־הָיָה הָרָעָב בְּאֶרֶץ
ו כְּנָעַן: וְיוֹסֵף הוּא הַשַּׁלִּיט עַל־הָאָרֶץ הוּא הַמַּשְׁבִּיר לְכָל־עַם הָאָרֶץ וַיָּבֹאוּ אֲחֵי
ז יוֹסֵף וַיִּשְׁתַּחֲווּ־לוֹ אַפַּיִם אָרְצָה: וַיַּרְא יוֹסֵף אֶת־אֶחָיו וַיַּכִּרֵם וַיִּתְנַכֵּר אֲלֵיהֶם
וַיְדַבֵּר אִתָּם קָשׁוֹת וַיֹּאמֶר אֲלֵהֶם מֵאַיִן בָּאתֶם וַיֹּאמְרוּ מֵאֶרֶץ כְּנַעַן לִשְׁבָּר־

רש״י

נ| **בטרם תבוא שנת הרעב.** מכאן שאדם אסור לשמש מטתו בשני רעבון:

נה| **ותרעב כל ארץ מצרים.** שהרקיבה תבואתם שאצרו, חוץ משל יוסף: **אשר יאמר לכם תעשו.** לפי שהיה יוסף אומר להם שימולו, וכשבאו אצל פרעה ואומרים: כך הוא אומר לנו, אמר להם: ולמה לא צברתם בר, והלא הכריז לכם ששני הרעב באים? אמרו לו: אספנו הרבה והרקיבה. אמר להם: אם כן, "אשר יאמר לכם תעשו"! הרי גזר על התבואה והרקיבה, מה אם יגזור עלינו ונמות?

נו| **על כל פני הארץ.** מי הם "פני הארץ"? אלו העשירים: **את כל אשר בהם.** כתרגומו: "די בהון עבורא": **וישבר למצרים.** 'שבר' לשון מכר ולשון קנין הוא, כאן משמש לשון מכר; "שברו לנו מעט אכל" (להלן מג, ב) – לשון קנין. ואל תאמר, אינו כי אם בתבואה, שאף ביין וחלב מצינו: "ולכו שברו בלוא כסף ובלוא מחיר יין וחלב" (ישעיה נה, א):

נז| **וכל הארץ באו מצרימה.** אל יוסף לשבר. ואם תדרשהו כסדרו, היה צריך לכתב: 'לשבר מן יוסף':

פרק מב

א| **וירא יעקב כי יש שבר במצרים.** ומהיכן ראה? והלא לא ראה אלא שמע, שנאמר: "הנה שמעתי" וגו' (להלן פסוק ב)! ומהו "וירא"? ראה באספקלריא של קדש שיש לו שבר עוד במצרים, ולא היתה נבואה ממש להודיעו בפרוש שזה יוסף: **למה תתראו.** אל תראו עצמכם בפני בני ישמעאל ובני עשו כאלו אתם שבעים; באותה שעה עדין היה להם תבואה. ומפי אחרים שמעתי, שהוא לשון כחישה: למה תהיו כחושים ברעב? ודומה לו: "ומרוה גם הוא יורא" (משלי יא, כה); ואין הדבר נכון בעיני:

ב| **רדו שמה.** ולא אמר 'לכו'! רמז למאתים ועשר שנים שנשתעבדו למצרים, כמנין רד"ו:

ג| **וירדו אחי יוסף.** ולא כתב 'בני יעקב'! מלמד שהיו מתחרטים במכירתו, ונתנו לבם להתנהג עמו באחוה ולפדותו בכל ממון שיפסקו עליהם: **עשרה.** מה תלמוד לומר? והלא כתיב: "ואת בנימין אחי יוסף לא שלח" (להלן פסוק ד)! אלא לענין האחוה היו חלוקין לעשרה, שלא היתה אהבת כלם ושנאת כלם שוה לו, אבל לענין "לשבר בר" כלם לב אחד להם. בראשית רבה (צא, ב):

ד| **פן יקראנו אסון.** ובבית לא יקראנו?! אמר רבי אליעזר בן יעקב: מכאן שהשטן מקטרג בשעת הסכנה:

ה| **בתוך הבאים.** מטמינין עצמן שלא יכירום, לפי שצוה אביהם שלא יתראו שלא תשלט בהם עין רעה, שכלם נאים וכלם גבורים:

ו| **וישתחוו לו אפים.** נשתטחו לו על פניהם, וכן כל השתחואה פשוט ידים ורגלים הוא:

ז| **ויתנכר אליהם.** נעשה להם כנכרי בדברים לדבר קשות:

DISCUSSION

→ As full brothers, it can also be assumed that there was a certain physical resemblance between Joseph and Benjamin. For these reasons, and also because Benjamin was his youngest son, Jacob was especially concerned for Benjamin's welfare. This was compounded by yet another factor: It was Jacob who had sent Joseph on a mission, after which all traces of him were lost. Perhaps for this reason too he was reluctant to send Benjamin now (see 44:27–29).

8 **Joseph recognized** each of **his brothers,**[10] **but they did not recognize him,** as he was older, his clothing had changed, his beard had grown, his hair was presumably cut in the Egyptian style, and everyone called him Tzafenat Paneah. Above all, the brothers presumably thought he had died, and they certainly did not expect him to have risen to a position of such prominence.

9 **Joseph remembered the dreams that he had dreamed about them,** as well as all the events that had followed those dreams, **and he said to them:** You are not mere purchasers of grain, but **you are spies;**[D] **to see the nakedness of the land you have come.** You are foreign agents who have been sent to discover Egypt's weaknesses.

10 **They said to him,** in all honesty: **No, my lord, but your servants have come to acquire food.**

11 **We are all the sons of one man.** Yes, we came as a group, but that is due to the fact that we are brothers, not because we are spies. **We are sincere; your servants have not been spies.** We are simple, honest folk who have never been involved in espionage.

12 **He said to them: No,** I do not believe you, **but the nakedness of the land you came to see.** Your story sounds suspicious to me.

13 The brothers, simple shepherds, were unsure how to defend themselves from the accusation of the Egyptian viceroy, who was responsible for the security of the entire realm. In their distress, they could do nothing other than tell the truth about themselves, even if the facts they offered had nothing to do with the matter at hand. **They said: We, your servants, are twelve brothers,**[D] **sons of one man in the land of Canaan; and behold, the youngest is with our father today, and one is absent.**

14 **Joseph said to them: That is what I spoke to you, saying: You are spies.** Your detailed presentation is very convincing, but those very details may be used to expose you as skilled liars and cunning spies.

15 **With this you shall be put to the test: By Pharaoh's life, you shall not depart from here unless your youngest brother comes here.** Swearing on the life of Pharaoh is the most severe oath an Egyptian can utter. Joseph declared that they would not leave until their brother came; only in that way could he confirm their account.

16 **Dispatch one of you, and he will take your brother** from his land, **and you shall be incarcerated, that your statements will be verified, whether there is truth with you; and if not, by Pharaoh's life, you are spies.** Joseph's suggestion is based on the reasonable assumption that when spies are captured, those who sent them might try to rescue them, but not by sending an additional agent to directly confront their captors. Therefore, the arrival of their youngest brother would attest to their family ties and refute the charge of military espionage.

17 **He gathered them into custody,** where they remained **for three days.**

18 **Joseph said to them on the third day: Do this and live,** as **I fear God.** I am a fair man, and so far I cannot prove my suspicions.

19 *Fifth aliya* **If you are sincere** and your story is true, **one of your brothers shall be incarcerated** as a guarantee **in the place of your custody, and** the rest of **you, go bring grain for the hunger of your houses.** If you indeed came to purchase food, your absence will not only be a source of sorrow for your families but will bring disaster upon them, as they will have no food.

20 Joseph expresses toward his brothers a measure of compassion tempered by caution: In his compassion he will permit them to return home, but in case they are spies he demands: **Bring your youngest brother to me** upon your next visit, **and your statements will** thereby **be verified, and you shall not die** from hunger or at the hand of my messengers.[11] **They did so.** Joseph's orders were followed: The brothers were given food like all other customers and were granted permission to leave.

21 Up to this point, the Torah has cited Joseph's statements and his brothers' replies; it has not related any conversations between the brothers themselves. Perhaps Joseph had them incarcerated in separate cells, and only now did they have the opportunity to talk to one another. Faced with such a baseless accusation, they felt pangs of conscience due to the trauma they remembered so well from years ago, when they sold their brother. **They said one to another: But we are** indeed **guilty with regard to our**

DISCUSSION

42:9 | **You are spies:** It seems that at the time Canaan was subservient to Egyptian authority. Although no real enemies of Egypt lived in Canaan itself, certain kingdoms north of Canaan were at war with Egypt. The Egyptians were therefore always wary of possible spies sent from Canaan by a hostile state. Consequently, there was some basis for Joseph's accusations that his brothers were spying.

As a pretext for his accusation, Joseph may have cited the fact that his brothers did not appear to be private buyers of food, as they arrived as an organized group and were probably all dressed in a similar manner. Such a group of young men close in age would look more like military men than ordinary citizens seeking food.

42:13 | **We, your servants, are twelve brothers:** It is clear from the brothers' report to Jacob (43:7) that Joseph interrogated them at great length, and that they related all they could about themselves, their father, and their families in order to demonstrate their integrity.

ח ט אֹכֶל: וַיַּכֵּר יוֹסֵף אֶת־אֶחָיו וְהֵם לֹא הִכִּרֻהוּ: וַיִּזְכֹּר יוֹסֵף אֵת הַחֲלֹמוֹת אֲשֶׁר חָלַם
י לָהֶם וַיֹּאמֶר אֲלֵהֶם מְרַגְּלִים אַתֶּם לִרְאוֹת אֶת־עֶרְוַת הָאָרֶץ בָּאתֶם: וַיֹּאמְרוּ
יא אֵלָיו לֹא אֲדֹנִי וַעֲבָדֶיךָ בָּאוּ לִשְׁבָּר־אֹכֶל: כֻּלָּנוּ בְּנֵי אִישׁ־אֶחָד נָחְנוּ כֵּנִים אֲנַחְנוּ
יב לֹא־הָיוּ עֲבָדֶיךָ מְרַגְּלִים: וַיֹּאמֶר אֲלֵהֶם לֹא כִּי־עֶרְוַת הָאָרֶץ בָּאתֶם לִרְאוֹת:
יג וַיֹּאמְרוּ שְׁנֵים עָשָׂר עֲבָדֶיךָ אַחִים | אֲנַחְנוּ בְּנֵי אִישׁ־אֶחָד בְּאֶרֶץ כְּנָעַן וְהִנֵּה
יד הַקָּטֹן אֶת־אָבִינוּ הַיּוֹם וְהָאֶחָד אֵינֶנּוּ: וַיֹּאמֶר אֲלֵהֶם יוֹסֵף הוּא אֲשֶׁר דִּבַּרְתִּי
טו אֲלֵכֶם לֵאמֹר מְרַגְּלִים אַתֶּם: בְּזֹאת תִּבָּחֵנוּ חֵי פַרְעֹה אִם־תֵּצְאוּ מִזֶּה כִּי אִם־
טז בְּבוֹא אֲחִיכֶם הַקָּטֹן הֵנָּה: שִׁלְחוּ מִכֶּם אֶחָד וְיִקַּח אֶת־אֲחִיכֶם וְאַתֶּם הֵאָסְרוּ
יז וְיִבָּחֲנוּ דִּבְרֵיכֶם הַאֱמֶת אִתְּכֶם וְאִם־לֹא חֵי פַרְעֹה כִּי מְרַגְּלִים אַתֶּם: וַיֶּאֱסֹף אֹתָם
יח אֶל־מִשְׁמָר שְׁלֹשֶׁת יָמִים: וַיֹּאמֶר אֲלֵהֶם יוֹסֵף בַּיּוֹם הַשְּׁלִישִׁי זֹאת עֲשׂוּ וִחְיוּ לח
יט אֶת־הָאֱלֹהִים אֲנִי יָרֵא: אִם־כֵּנִים אַתֶּם אֲחִיכֶם אֶחָד יֵאָסֵר בְּבֵית מִשְׁמַרְכֶם חמישי
כ וְאַתֶּם לְכוּ הָבִיאוּ שֶׁבֶר רַעֲבוֹן בָּתֵּיכֶם: וְאֶת־אֲחִיכֶם הַקָּטֹן תָּבִיאוּ אֵלַי וְיֵאָמְנוּ
כא דִבְרֵיכֶם וְלֹא תָמוּתוּ וַיַּעֲשׂוּ־כֵן: וַיֹּאמְרוּ אִישׁ אֶל־אָחִיו אֲבָל אֲשֵׁמִים | אֲנַחְנוּ
עַל־אָחִינוּ אֲשֶׁר רָאִינוּ צָרַת נַפְשׁוֹ בְּהִתְחַנְנוֹ אֵלֵינוּ וְלֹא שָׁמָעְנוּ עַל־כֵּן בָּאָה

רש"י

ח| **וַיַּכֵּר יוֹסֵף וְגוֹ׳.** לְפִי שֶׁהִנִּיחָם חֲתוּמֵי זָקָן: **וְהֵם לֹא הִכִּרֻהוּ.** שֶׁיָּצָא מֵאֶצְלָם בְּלֹא חֲתִימַת זָקָן וְעַכְשָׁיו בָּא בַּחֲתִימַת זָקָן. וּמִדְרַשׁ אַגָּדָה, "וַיַּכֵּר יוֹסֵף אֶת אֶחָיו", כְּשֶׁנִּמְסְרוּ בְּיָדוֹ הִכִּיר שֶׁהֵם אֶחָיו וְרִחֵם עֲלֵיהֶם, "וְהֵם לֹא הִכִּרֻהוּ" כְּשֶׁנָּפַל בְּיָדָם לִנְהֹג בּוֹ אַחֲוָה:

ט| **אֲשֶׁר חָלַם לָהֶם.** עֲלֵיהֶם, וְיָדַע שֶׁנִּתְקַיְּמוּ, שֶׁהֲרֵי הִשְׁתַּחֲווּ לוֹ: **עֶרְוַת הָאָרֶץ.** גִּלּוּי הָאָרֶץ, מֵהֵיכָן הִיא נוֹחָה לִכָּבֵשׁ, כְּמוֹ: "אֶת מְקֹרָהּ הֶעֱרָה" (ויקרא כ, יח), וּכְמוֹ: "עֵרֹם וְעֶרְיָה" (יחזקאל טז, ז), וְכֵן כָּל עֶרְוָה שֶׁבַּמִּקְרָא לְשׁוֹן גִּלּוּי. וְאוּנְקְלוֹס תִּרְגֵּם: "בִּדְקָא דְאַרְעָא", כְּמוֹ: "בֶּדֶק הַבַּיִת" (מלכים ב׳ יב, ו) – רְעוּעַ הַבַּיִת, אֲבָל לֹא דִּקְדֵּק לְפָרְשׁוֹ אַחַר לְשׁוֹן הַמִּקְרָא:

י| **לֹא אֲדֹנִי.** לֹא תֹאמַר כֵּן, וַהֲרֵי "עֲבָדֶיךָ בָּאוּ לִשְׁבָּר אֹכֶל":

יא| **כֻּלָּנוּ בְּנֵי אִישׁ אֶחָד נָחְנוּ.** נִצְנְצָה בָהֶם רוּחַ הַקֹּדֶשׁ וְכָלְלוּהוּ עִמָּהֶם, שֶׁאַף הוּא בֶּן אֲבִיהֶם: **כֵּנִים.** אֲמִתִּיִּים, כְּמוֹ: "כֵּן דִּבַּרְתָּ" (שמות י, כט), "כֵּן בְּנוֹת צְלָפְחָד דֹּבְרֹת" (במדבר כז, ז), "וְעֶבְרָתוֹ לֹא כֵן בַּדָּיו" (ישעיה טז, ו):

יב| **כִּי עֶרְוַת הָאָרֶץ בָּאתֶם לִרְאוֹת.** שֶׁהֲרֵי נִכְנַסְתֶּם בַּעֲשָׂרָה שַׁעֲרֵי הָעִיר, לָמָּה לֹא נִכְנַסְתֶּם בְּשַׁעַר אֶחָד?:

יג| **וַיֹּאמְרוּ שְׁנֵים עָשָׂר עֲבָדֶיךָ וְגוֹ׳.** וּבִשְׁבִיל אוֹתוֹ אֶחָד שֶׁאֵינֶנּוּ, נִתְפַּזַּרְנוּ בָּעִיר לְבַקְּשׁוֹ:

יד| **הוּא אֲשֶׁר דִּבַּרְתִּי.** הַדָּבָר אֲשֶׁר דִּבַּרְתִּי שֶׁאַתֶּם מְרַגְּלִים הוּא הָאֱמֶת וְהַנָּכוֹן, זֶהוּ לְפִי פְּשׁוּטוֹ. וּמִדְרָשׁוֹ, אָמַר לָהֶם: וְאִלּוּ מְצָאתֶם אוֹתוֹ וְיִפְסְקוּ עֲלֵיכֶם מָמוֹן הַרְבֵּה, תִּפְדּוּהוּ? אָמְרוּ לוֹ: הֵן. אָמַר לָהֶם: וְאִם יֹאמְרוּ לָכֶם שֶׁלֹּא יַחֲזִירוּהוּ בְּשׁוּם מָמוֹן, מַה תַּעֲשׂוּ? אָמְרוּ: לְכָךְ בָּאנוּ, לַהֲרֹג אוֹ לֵהָרֵג! אָמַר לָהֶם: "הוּא אֲשֶׁר דִּבַּרְתִּי אֲלֵכֶם", לַהֲרֹג בְּנֵי הָעִיר בָּאתֶם, מְנַחֵשׁ אֲנִי בַּגָּבִיעַ שֶׁלִּי שֶׁשְּׁנַיִם מִכֶּם הֶחֱרִיבוּ כְּרַךְ גָּדוֹל שֶׁל שְׁכֶם:

טו| **חֵי פַרְעֹה.** אִם יִחְיֶה פַרְעֹה. כְּשֶׁהָיָה נִשְׁבָּע לַשֶּׁקֶר הָיָה נִשְׁבָּע בְּחַיֵּי פַרְעֹה: **אִם תֵּצְאוּ מִזֶּה.** מִן הַמָּקוֹם הַזֶּה:

טז| **הַאֱמֶת אִתְּכֶם.** אִם אֱמֶת אִתְּכֶם, לְפִיכָךְ הֵ"א נָקוּד פַּתָּח, שֶׁהוּא כְּמוֹ בִּלְשׁוֹן תֵּמַהּ. "וְאִם לֹא" תְּבִיאוּהוּ – "חֵי פַרְעֹה כִּי מְרַגְּלִים אַתֶּם":

יז| **מִשְׁמָר.** בֵּית הָאֲסוּרִים:

יט| **בְּבֵית מִשְׁמַרְכֶם.** שֶׁאַתֶּם אֲסוּרִים בּוֹ עַכְשָׁיו: **וְאַתֶּם לְכוּ הָבִיאוּ.** לְבֵית אֲבִיכֶם: **שֶׁבֶר רַעֲבוֹן בָּתֵּיכֶם.** מַה שֶּׁקְּנִיתֶם לְרַעֲבוֹן אַנְשֵׁי בָּתֵּיכֶם:

כ| **וְיֵאָמְנוּ דִבְרֵיכֶם.** יִתְאַמְּתוּ וְיִתְקַיְּמוּ, כְּמוֹ: "אָמֵן אָמֵן" (במדבר ה, כב), וּכְמוֹ: "יֵאָמֶן נָא דְּבָרְךָ" (מלכים א׳ ח, כו):

כא| **אֲבָל.** כְּתַרְגּוּמוֹ: "בְּקוּשְׁטָא". וְרָאִיתִי בִּבְרֵאשִׁית רַבָּה (צא, ח): לְשׁוֹן דָּרוֹמָאָה הוּא, "אֲבָל" – בְּרַם: **בָּאָה אֵלֵינוּ.** טַעְמוֹ בַּבֵּי"ת לְפִי שֶׁהוּא בִּלְשׁוֹן עָבָר, שֶׁכְּבָר בָּאָה, וְתַרְגּוּמוֹ: "אֲתַת לָנָא":

brother, that we saw the anguish of his soul as he pleaded with us and we did not heed. We were all partners in Joseph's sale. Benjamin, who was too young at the time, is not with us now either. Having been thrown into the prison dungeon by a force beyond their control, as a result of an unjust accusation, the brothers had a similar experience to that which they had inflicted upon Joseph. They now sensed that they were being punished for their sin, and they declared: For that, this anguish has befallen us as a punishment from Heaven.

22 Reuben responded to them, saying: Didn't I say this to you at the time, saying: Do not sin against the child; and you did not heed my words? Now, behold, there is a divine reckoning for his blood. We caused his death, and now we are receiving our punishment.

23 They did not know that Joseph understood. Although Joseph was standing there while they were talking, it did not occur to them they he might understand what they were saying. To them he was an Egyptian unfamiliar with their language, as the interpreter was between them and had been interpreting all their conversations with Joseph.

24 He, Joseph, turned from them and wept[D] profusely. And he then returned to them, back in his customary role as the Egyptian leader; he spoke to them, took Simeon from them, and incarcerated him before their eyes. They saw that Joseph's commands were fulfilled. Simeon's imprisonment would not be of short duration, since even if the brothers were to return without delay, the journey to Canaan and back would take a considerable time.

25 Joseph commanded his men that they fill their, his brothers', vessels with grain, and restore each man's silver to his sack. Due to his position of authority, Joseph could issue instructions that their payment for the produce should be placed in their sacks. And he gave orders to give them provisions for the way; and he, one of his attendants, did so for them. It is possible that they were not given food when they were incarcerated and had consumed some of their provisions. Joseph therefore provided them with new provisions.

26 They loaded their grain that they had purchased onto their donkeys and went from there.

27 On their way back to Canaan, one of them opened his sack to give feed to his donkey at the lodging place. He saw his silver, and behold, it was in the opening of his sack.

28 He said to his brothers: My silver that I paid for the produce was returned, and behold, it is in my sack. Their hearts sank in shock, and they trembled one with another, saying: What is this that God has done to us? They could not understand how this had happened, and they sensed that the strange and unusual events had befallen them as a punishment for their sins.

Between the First and Second Journeys to Egypt
GENESIS 42:29–43:14

The return of Jacob's sons to their homes is marred by the difficulties they faced in Egypt: The demand of the Egyptian ruler that they bring their younger brother, whom their father had refused to send, in order to substantiate their claims; the incarceration of Simeon as a hostage in Egypt; and finally, the mystery of the money restored to one of their sacks.

The tension between Jacob and his sons rises. They were already separated by the dark secret that his sons shared with regard to Joseph's fate, and now they are driven further apart by the strange events they experienced in Egypt, with all the accusations and the mistreatment they suffered while their father waited for them in Canaan. Neither Jacob nor his sons understand the meaning of what has happened, but there is a significant difference between the direct experience of those who have been falsely accused and mistreated and one who has merely heard the report of these events, even if he hears it from his own sons.

Just as Reuben and Judah tried to mitigate their brothers' designs in the fateful encounter with Joseph in Dotan, here too the pair acts responsibly in order to soften their father's objections to sending Benjamin back with them to Egypt. Eventually, it is the famine that will compel Jacob to comply with the Egyptian viceroy's request, as the future of the family depends on their ability to purchase food.

29 They came to their father, Jacob, to the land of Canaan, and they told him all that had befallen them, saying:

30 The man, lord of the land, spoke harshly with us and accused us as spies of the land.

31 For our part, we were honest, and we said to him: We are sincere; we have not been spies at any point in our lives.

32 We are twelve brothers, sons of our father; one is absent, and the youngest is today with our father in the land of Canaan. This is what we said to the man.

33 The man, lord of the land, said to us: With this I shall know that you are sincere: One of your brothers leave with me, and take grain for the hunger of your households, and go.

34 Yet you must bring your youngest brother to me, and I shall thereby know that you are not spies, that you are sincere. I will then give you your brother, who is currently incarcerated, and you shall trade in the land. You will be permitted to buy grain and engage in business dealings in Egypt, like all other foreigners who bring commodities from their lands to sell them or exchange them for food. The brothers stressed to their father that Joseph had agreed to grant them full rights once they would be cleared of any suspicion.

35 It was as they were emptying the grain from their sacks, and behold, they discovered that the money which one of them had found earlier was not an exceptional occurrence, as each

כב אֵלֵינוּ הַצָּרָה הַזֹּאת: וַיַּעַן רְאוּבֵן אֹתָם לֵאמֹר הֲלוֹא אָמַרְתִּי אֲלֵיכֶם | לֵאמֹר
כג אַל־תֶּחֶטְאוּ בַיֶּלֶד וְלֹא שְׁמַעְתֶּם וְגַם־דָּמוֹ הִנֵּה נִדְרָשׁ: וְהֵם לֹא יָדְעוּ כִּי שֹׁמֵעַ
כד יוֹסֵף כִּי הַמֵּלִיץ בֵּינֹתָם: וַיִּסֹּב מֵעֲלֵיהֶם וַיֵּבְךְּ וַיָּשָׁב אֲלֵהֶם וַיְדַבֵּר אֲלֵהֶם וַיִּקַּח
כה מֵאִתָּם אֶת־שִׁמְעוֹן וַיֶּאֱסֹר אֹתוֹ לְעֵינֵיהֶם: וַיְצַו יוֹסֵף וַיְמַלְאוּ אֶת־כְּלֵיהֶם בָּר
כו וּלְהָשִׁיב כַּסְפֵּיהֶם אִישׁ אֶל־שַׂקּוֹ וְלָתֵת לָהֶם צֵדָה לַדָּרֶךְ וַיַּעַשׂ לָהֶם כֵּן: וַיִּשְׂאוּ
כז אֶת־שִׁבְרָם עַל־חֲמֹרֵיהֶם וַיֵּלְכוּ מִשָּׁם: וַיִּפְתַּח הָאֶחָד אֶת־שַׂקּוֹ לָתֵת מִסְפּוֹא
כח לַחֲמֹרוֹ בַּמָּלוֹן וַיַּרְא אֶת־כַּסְפּוֹ וְהִנֵּה־הוּא בְּפִי אַמְתַּחְתּוֹ: וַיֹּאמֶר אֶל־אֶחָיו הוּשַׁב
כַּסְפִּי וְגַם הִנֵּה בְאַמְתַּחְתִּי וַיֵּצֵא לִבָּם וַיֶּחֶרְדוּ אִישׁ אֶל־אָחִיו לֵאמֹר מַה־זֹּאת
כט עָשָׂה אֱלֹהִים לָנוּ: וַיָּבֹאוּ אֶל־יַעֲקֹב אֲבִיהֶם אַרְצָה כְּנָעַן וַיַּגִּידוּ לוֹ אֵת כָּל־הַקֹּרֹת
ל אֹתָם לֵאמֹר: דִּבֶּר הָאִישׁ אֲדֹנֵי הָאָרֶץ אִתָּנוּ קָשׁוֹת וַיִּתֵּן אֹתָנוּ כִּמְרַגְּלִים אֶת־
לא לב הָאָרֶץ: וַנֹּאמֶר אֵלָיו כֵּנִים אֲנָחְנוּ לֹא הָיִינוּ מְרַגְּלִים: שְׁנֵים־עָשָׂר אֲנַחְנוּ אַחִים
לג בְּנֵי אָבִינוּ הָאֶחָד אֵינֶנּוּ וְהַקָּטֹן הַיּוֹם אֶת־אָבִינוּ בְּאֶרֶץ כְּנָעַן: וַיֹּאמֶר אֵלֵינוּ
הָאִישׁ אֲדֹנֵי הָאָרֶץ בְּזֹאת אֵדַע כִּי כֵנִים אַתֶּם אֲחִיכֶם הָאֶחָד הַנִּיחוּ אִתִּי וְאֶת־
לד רַעֲבוֹן בָּתֵּיכֶם קְחוּ וָלֵכוּ: וְהָבִיאוּ אֶת־אֲחִיכֶם הַקָּטֹן אֵלַי וְאֵדְעָה כִּי לֹא מְרַגְּלִים
לה אַתֶּם כִּי כֵנִים אַתֶּם אֶת־אֲחִיכֶם אֶתֵּן לָכֶם וְאֶת־הָאָרֶץ תִּסְחָרוּ: וַיְהִי הֵם מְרִיקִים

רש"י

כב| **וְגַם דָּמוֹ.** אִיתִין וְגַמִּין רִבּוּיִין – דָּמוֹ וְגַם דַּם הַזָּקֵן:

כג| **וְהֵם לֹא יָדְעוּ כִּי שֹׁמֵעַ יוֹסֵף.** מֵבִין לְשׁוֹנָם, וּבְפָנָיו הָיוּ מְדַבְּרִים כֵּן: **כִּי הַמֵּלִיץ בֵּינֹתָם.** כִּי כְּשֶׁהָיוּ מְדַבְּרִים עִמּוֹ הָיָה הַמֵּלִיץ בֵּינֵיהֶם הַיּוֹדֵעַ לָשׁוֹן עִבְרִית וְלָשׁוֹן מִצְרִית, וְהָיָה מֵלִיץ דִּבְרֵיהֶם לְיוֹסֵף וְדִבְרֵי יוֹסֵף לָהֶם, לְכָךְ הָיוּ סְבוּרִים שֶׁאֵין יוֹסֵף מַכִּיר בְּלָשׁוֹן עִבְרִית: **הַמֵּלִיץ.** זֶה מְנַשֶּׁה:

כד| **וַיִּסֹּב מֵעֲלֵיהֶם.** נִתְרַחֵק מֵעֲלֵיהֶם שֶׁלֹּא יִרְאוּהוּ בוֹכֶה: **וַיֵּבְךְּ.** לְפִי שֶׁשָּׁמַע שֶׁהָיוּ מִתְחָרְטִין: **אֶת שִׁמְעוֹן.** הוּא הִשְׁלִיכוֹ לַבּוֹר, הוּא שֶׁאָמַר לְלֵוִי: "הִנֵּה בַּעַל הַחֲלֹמוֹת הַלָּזֶה בָּא" (לעיל לז, יט). דָּבָר אַחֵר, נִתְכַּוֵּן יוֹסֵף לְהַפְרִידוֹ מִלֵּוִי, שֶׁמָּא יִתְיָעֲצוּ שְׁנֵיהֶם לַהֲרֹג אוֹתוֹ: **וַיֶּאֱסֹר אֹתוֹ לְעֵינֵיהֶם.** לֹא אֲסָרוֹ אֶלָּא לְעֵינֵיהֶם, וְכֵיוָן שֶׁיָּצְאוּ הוֹצִיאוֹ וְהֶאֱכִילוֹ וְהִשְׁקָהוּ:

כז| **וַיִּפְתַּח הָאֶחָד.** הוּא לֵוִי שֶׁנִּשְׁאַר יָחִיד מִשִּׁמְעוֹן בֶּן זוּגוֹ: **בַּמָּלוֹן.** בַּמָּקוֹם שֶׁלָּנוּ בַּלַּיְלָה: **אַמְתַּחְתּוֹ.** הוּא שַׂק:

כח| **וְגַם הִנֵּה בְאַמְתַּחְתִּי.** גַּם הַכֶּסֶף בּוֹ עִם הַתְּבוּאָה: **מַה זֹּאת עָשָׂה אֱלֹהִים לָנוּ.** לַהֲבִיאֵנוּ לִידֵי עֲלִילָה זוֹ, שֶׁלֹּא הוּשַׁב אֶלָּא לְהִתְעוֹלֵל עָלֵינוּ:

לד| **וְאֶת הָאָרֶץ תִּסְחָרוּ.** תְּסוֹבְבוּ, וְכָל לְשׁוֹן 'סוֹחֲרִים' וּ'סְחוֹרָה' עַל שֵׁם שֶׁמְּחַזְּרִים וְסוֹבְבִים אַחַר הַפְּרַקְמַטְיָא:

DISCUSSION

42:24| **And wept:** Joseph's tendency to weep would be evident on several occasions (43:30, 45:2, 14–15, 46:29, 50:17). Here he weeps both due to the memory of the painful experience of his sale and because this is his first indication of how his brothers felt after they sold him. When they threw him into the pit they were indifferent to his suffering and simply sat down to eat. Now Joseph discovers that his brothers are still tormented by the wrong they inflicted upon him, and that they feel they deserve to be punished for their actions.

man's packet of silver was in his sack. **They and their father saw their packets of silver** that had been returned to them, **and they were afraid.**

36 **Jacob their father said to them: You have bereaved me.** Although their father is unaware of the truth about their sale of Joseph, he hurls a general accusation at them: **Joseph is not, and** now **Simeon is** also **not,** as he is incarcerated, **and Benjamin you will take.** You want me to send Benjamin with you as well? I am still pained by Joseph's disappearance. **All of these are upon me.** It is true that you too are affected by these misfortunes, but you are unable to share my grief fully, as these troubles fall chiefly upon me, their father.

37 **Reuben,** the firstborn, **said to his father** as the spokesman for all the sons, **saying:** Take my two sons as a guarantee until I bring Benjamin back to you, and **kill my two sons if I do not bring him to you; place him,** Benjamin, **in my charge, and I will return him to you.** I accept the responsibility of bringing him home safely.

38 Presumably all of the brothers likewise made offers to guarantee Benjamin's return, as they all wished to return to Egypt to free Simeon and to make matters right with the Egyptians, but Jacob resisted. **He said: My** youngest **son shall not go down with you, for** as you know, **his brother is dead, and only he is left** from his mother; **and if disaster befalls him on the path on which you will go,** then **you will cause my old age to descend in sorrow to the grave.** I will die from the terrible knowledge that Rachel's two sons have been lost. Therefore, I will not let Benjamin leave my side.

43 1 Jacob does not suggest how Simeon might be freed, nor how the family might find food. He simply expresses his fears and prefers to let matters stand as they are rather than accept the risks proposed by his sons. However, **the famine was severe in the land.**

2 **It was when they finished the grain that they had brought from Egypt; their father said to them: Return** to Egypt and **acquire a little** more **food for us.**

3 Although Judah was only the fourth son, his leadership qualities had already come to the fore at the time of the sale of Joseph.[12] Since his status is comparable to that of a firstborn, Judah now addresses his father. **Judah said to him, saying: The man** in charge of the land explicitly **forewarned us, saying: You shall not see my face,** and you will not be permitted to buy anything here, **unless your brother is with you.**

4 Consequently, **if you send our brother with us, we will go down** to Egypt **and acquire food for you.**

5 **But if you do not send him, we will not go down, for the man said to us: You shall not see my face unless your brother is with you.**

6 **Israel,** Jacob, once again **said: Why have you harmed me, to tell the man that you have another brother?** What possible reason could there have been for you to have even mentioned your younger brother? Your unnecessary comment brought about all this trouble.

7 **They said: The man asked with regard to us and with regard to our provenance.** He did not start by asking about our brother. First he engaged us in a general conversation about our background. However, during the ensuing investigation he approached the topic, **saying: Is your father still alive?** Although Joseph had his own reasons for this line of inquiry, from the brothers' perspective it was a natural question, after they had told him that they were all brothers of a single father. He subsequently asked: **Do you have** another **brother? We told him with regard to those matters,** answering his questions honestly. **Could we know that he would say: Bring your brother down?** Had we suspected that he would issue such a demand, we would certainly have acted with greater caution.

8 **Judah said** once again **to Israel, his father,** more firmly this time: **Send the lad with me, and we will arise and go, and we will live and not die, both we, and you, and our children.** Our plight is serious.

9 Finally, Judah promises his father: **I will guarantee him**[D] and his safe return. **From me you may solicit him; if I do not bring him to you and present him before you, I will have sinned to you forever,** a blot that will never be wiped clean, neither in my lifetime nor after my death.

10 **Since, had we not tarried** until now because you were unwilling to send Benjamin and we did not pressure you to do so, **we would** by **now have** traveled to Egypt and **returned twice.**

DISCUSSION

43:9 | I will guarantee him: The fact that Jacob accepted Judah's offer is somewhat puzzling, as it is a lesser commitment than that of Reuben, who had earlier declared: "Kill my two sons if I do not bring him to you" (42:37). Apparently, Jacob was not willing to rely on Reuben; even if his promise was motivated by heartfelt goodwill, Reuben was not as strong a personality as Judah, and Jacob feared that Reuben would be unable to keep his word.

שַׂקֵּיהֶם וְהִנֵּה־אִישׁ צְרוֹר־כַּסְפּוֹ בְּשַׂקּוֹ וַיִּרְאוּ אֶת־צְרֹרוֹת כַּסְפֵּיהֶם הֵמָּה וַאֲבִיהֶם
לו וַיִּירָאוּ: וַיֹּאמֶר אֲלֵהֶם יַעֲקֹב אֲבִיהֶם אֹתִי שִׁכַּלְתֶּם יוֹסֵף אֵינֶנּוּ וְשִׁמְעוֹן אֵינֶנּוּ
לז וְאֶת־בִּנְיָמִן תִּקָּחוּ עָלַי הָיוּ כֻלָּנָה: וַיֹּאמֶר רְאוּבֵן אֶל־אָבִיו לֵאמֹר אֶת־שְׁנֵי בָנַי
לח תָּמִית אִם־לֹא אֲבִיאֶנּוּ אֵלֶיךָ תְּנָה אֹתוֹ עַל־יָדִי וַאֲנִי אֲשִׁיבֶנּוּ אֵלֶיךָ: וַיֹּאמֶר
לֹא־יֵרֵד בְּנִי עִמָּכֶם כִּי־אָחִיו מֵת וְהוּא לְבַדּוֹ נִשְׁאָר וּקְרָאָהוּ אָסוֹן בַּדֶּרֶךְ אֲשֶׁר
א ב תֵּלְכוּ־בָהּ וְהוֹרַדְתֶּם אֶת־שֵׂיבָתִי בְּיָגוֹן שְׁאוֹלָה: וְהָרָעָב כָּבֵד בָּאָרֶץ: וַיְהִי כַּאֲשֶׁר
כִּלּוּ לֶאֱכֹל אֶת־הַשֶּׁבֶר אֲשֶׁר הֵבִיאוּ מִמִּצְרָיִם וַיֹּאמֶר אֲלֵיהֶם אֲבִיהֶם שֻׁבוּ שִׁבְרוּ־
ג לָנוּ מְעַט־אֹכֶל: וַיֹּאמֶר אֵלָיו יְהוּדָה לֵאמֹר הָעֵד הֵעִד בָּנוּ הָאִישׁ לֵאמֹר לֹא־
ד תִרְאוּ פָנַי בִּלְתִּי אֲחִיכֶם אִתְּכֶם: אִם־יֶשְׁךָ מְשַׁלֵּחַ אֶת־אָחִינוּ אִתָּנוּ נֵרְדָה
ה וְנִשְׁבְּרָה לְךָ אֹכֶל: וְאִם־אֵינְךָ מְשַׁלֵּחַ לֹא נֵרֵד כִּי־הָאִישׁ אָמַר אֵלֵינוּ לֹא־תִרְאוּ
ו פָנַי בִּלְתִּי אֲחִיכֶם אִתְּכֶם: וַיֹּאמֶר יִשְׂרָאֵל לָמָה הֲרֵעֹתֶם לִי לְהַגִּיד לָאִישׁ הַעוֹד
ז לָכֶם אָח: וַיֹּאמְרוּ שָׁאוֹל שָׁאַל־הָאִישׁ לָנוּ וּלְמוֹלַדְתֵּנוּ לֵאמֹר הַעוֹד אֲבִיכֶם חַי
הֲיֵשׁ לָכֶם אָח וַנַּגֶּד־לוֹ עַל־פִּי הַדְּבָרִים הָאֵלֶּה הֲיָדוֹעַ נֵדַע כִּי יֹאמַר הוֹרִידוּ אֶת־
ח אֲחִיכֶם: וַיֹּאמֶר יְהוּדָה אֶל־יִשְׂרָאֵל אָבִיו שִׁלְחָה הַנַּעַר אִתִּי וְנָקוּמָה וְנֵלֵכָה
ט וְנִחְיֶה וְלֹא נָמוּת גַּם־אֲנַחְנוּ גַם־אַתָּה גַּם־טַפֵּנוּ: אָנֹכִי אֶעֶרְבֶנּוּ מִיָּדִי תְּבַקְשֶׁנּוּ
י אִם־לֹא הֲבִיאֹתִיו אֵלֶיךָ וְהִצַּגְתִּיו לְפָנֶיךָ וְחָטָאתִי לְךָ כָּל־הַיָּמִים: כִּי לוּלֵא

רש"י

לה| **צְרוֹר כַּסְפּוֹ.** קֶשֶׁר כַּסְפּוֹ:

לו| **אֹתִי שִׁכַּלְתֶּם.** מְלַמֵּד שֶׁחֲשָׁדָן שֶׁמָּא הֲרָגוּהוּ אוֹ מְכָרוּהוּ כְּיוֹסֵף: שִׁכַּלְתֶּם. כָּל מִי שֶׁבָּנָיו אֲבוּדִים קָרוּי 'שַׁכּוּל':

לח| **לֹא יֵרֵד בְּנִי עִמָּכֶם.** לֹא קִבֵּל דְּבָרָיו שֶׁל רְאוּבֵן, אָמַר: בְּכוֹר שׁוֹטֶה הוּא זֶה! הוּא אוֹמֵר לְהָמִית בָּנָיו, וְכִי בָּנָיו הֵם וְלֹא בָּנַי?!:

פרק מג

ב| **כַּאֲשֶׁר כִּלּוּ לֶאֱכֹל.** יְהוּדָה אָמַר לָהֶם: הַמְתִּינוּ לַזָּקֵן עַד שֶׁתִּכְלֶה פַּת מִן הַבַּיִת: **כַּאֲשֶׁר כִּלּוּ.** "כַּד שֵׁיצִיאוּ", וְהַמְתַרְגֵּם 'כַּד סְפִיקוּ' טוֹעֶה. "כַּאֲשֶׁר כִּלּוּ הַגְּמַלִּים לִשְׁתּוֹת" (לעיל כד, כב) מְתֻרְגָּם "כַּד סְפִיקוּ", כְּשֶׁשָּׁתוּ דַּי סִפּוּקָם הוּא גְּמַר שְׁתִיָּתָם; אֲבָל זֶה, "כַּאֲשֶׁר כִּלּוּ לֶאֱכֹל", כַּאֲשֶׁר תַּם הָאֹכֶל הוּא, וּמְתַרְגְּמִינַן: "כַּד שֵׁיצִיאוּ":

ג| **הָעֵד הֵעִד.** לְשׁוֹן הַתְרָאָה, שֶׁסְּתָם הַתְרָאָה מַתְרֶה בּוֹ בִּפְנֵי עֵדִים, וְכֵן: "הַעִדֹתִי בַּאֲבוֹתֵיכֶם" (ירמיה יא, ז), "רֵד הָעֵד בָּעָם" (שמות יט, כא): **לֹא תִרְאוּ פָנַי בִּלְתִּי אֲחִיכֶם אִתְּכֶם.** לֹא תִרְאוּנִי בְּלֹא אֲחִיכֶם אִתְּכֶם. וְאוּנְקְלוֹס תִּרְגֵּם: "אֱלָהֵן כַּד אֲחוּכוֹן עִמְּכוֹן", יִשֵּׁב הַדָּבָר עַל אָפְנוֹ וְלֹא דִקְדֵּק לְתַרְגֵּם אַחַר לְשׁוֹן הַמִּקְרָא:

ז| **לָנוּ וּלְמוֹלַדְתֵּנוּ.** לְמִשְׁפְּחוֹתֵינוּ. וּמִדְרָשׁוֹ, אֲפִלּוּ עֲצֵי עֲרִיסוֹתֵינוּ גִּלָּה לָנוּ: **וַנַּגֶּד לוֹ.** שֶׁיֵּשׁ לָנוּ אָב וָאָח: **עַל פִּי הַדְּבָרִים הָאֵלֶּה.** עַל פִּי שְׁאֵלוֹתָיו אֲשֶׁר שָׁאַל הֻזְקַקְנוּ לְהַגִּיד: **כִּי יֹאמַר.** אֲשֶׁר יֹאמַר; 'כִּי' מְשַׁמֵּשׁ בִּלְשׁוֹן 'אִם' וְ'אִם' מְשַׁמֵּשׁ בִּלְשׁוֹן 'אֲשֶׁר', הֲרֵי זֶה שִׁמּוּשׁ אַחַת מֵאַרְבַּע לְשׁוֹנוֹתָיו, 'אִי', שֶׁהֲרֵי 'כִּי' זֶה כְּמוֹ 'אִם', כְּמוֹ: "עַד אִם דִּבַּרְתִּי דְּבָרָי" (לעיל כד, לג):

ח| **וְנִחְיֶה.** נִתְנַבֵּא בּוֹ רוּחַ הַקֹּדֶשׁ, עַל יְדֵי הֲלִיכָה זוֹ תְּחִי רוּחֲךָ, שֶׁנֶּאֱמַר: "וַתְּחִי רוּחַ יַעֲקֹב אֲבִיהֶם" (להלן מה, כז): **וְלֹא נָמוּת.** בָּרָעָב; בִּנְיָמִין סָפֵק יִתָּפֵשׂ סָפֵק לֹא יִתָּפֵשׂ, וַאֲנוּ כֻּלָּנוּ מֵתִים בָּרָעָב אִם לֹא נֵלֵךְ, מוּטָב שֶׁתַּנִּיחַ אֶת הַסָּפֵק וְתִתְפֹּשׂ אֶת הַוַּדַּאי:

ט| **וְהִצַּגְתִּיו לְפָנֶיךָ.** שֶׁלֹּא אֲבִיאֶנּוּ אֵלֶיךָ מֵת כִּי אִם חַי: **וְחָטָאתִי לְךָ כָּל הַיָּמִים.** לָעוֹלָם הַבָּא:

י| **לוּלֵא הִתְמַהְמָהְנוּ.** עַל יָדְךָ, כְּבָר הָיִינוּ שָׁבִים עִם שִׁמְעוֹן, וְלֹא נִצְטַעַרְתָּ כָּל הַיָּמִים הַלָּלוּ:

11 **Their father Israel said to them: If so, then** since there is no alternative, **do this: Take of the choice produce of the land in your vessels and take a gift down to the man.** A gift can soften even the hearts of nobles. Jacob suggests that they take superior produce that grows in Canaan but not in Egypt: **a little balm,** used for perfume or medicine that at the time was produced almost exclusively in the Jordan valley; **a little honey; spices**[13] [***nekhot***],[B] alternatively, some other luxury product;[14] **labdanum,** a type of cosmetic; as well as **pistachio nuts and almonds;**

12 **take double the** amount of **silver in your hand, and the silver that was returned in the opening of your sacks return in your hand.** Do not forget it, as they might remember it when you arrive and demand payment. **Perhaps it was an oversight,** and instead of putting your money away they accidentally placed it in your sacks together with the grain you purchased.

13 **And take your brother,** Benjamin, **and arise and return to the man.**

14 **May God Almighty grant you mercy before the man, and he will send with you your other brother,** Simeon, **and Benjamin; and me, as I am bereaved, I am bereaved.** If I experience another tragedy, so be it, as I am accustomed to tragedy.

Milk vetch

Joseph's Brothers Descend Once Again to Purchase Grain

GENESIS 43:15–34

When Joseph accused his brothers of being spies during their first visit to Egypt, he caused them great consternation. When they come a second time, the brothers are once again confronted with perplexing events. Their treatment as distinguished guests only increases their astonishment. Furthermore, their discomfort is likely increased by a troublesome, subconscious thought: Although they are dealing with the viceroy of Egypt, they have a vague sense that he is familiar to them from somewhere. Yet, the idea that they have met Pharaoh's viceroy on some past occasion seems logically untenable.

15 **The men took that gift, and they took in their hand double the silver and Benjamin; they arose and went down to Egypt, and they stood before Joseph.**

16 **Joseph saw Benjamin with them.** Perhaps Joseph recognized his maternal brother, and even if his features had changed greatly over the years, he could safely have assumed that the new arrival was their younger brother. **And he,** Joseph, who had his own palace, complete with attendants and servants, **said to the one in charge of his house: Bring the men** to me **to the house, and slaughter** animals **and prepare, as the men shall dine with me at noon.** They will be my guests. Since Joseph's Egyptian family was small, when a large group of guests arrived it was necessary to take them into account when planning the meal.

Sixth aliya

17 **The man did as Joseph said, and the man brought the men to Joseph's house.**

18 **The men were afraid because they were brought to Joseph's house.** Naturally, they wondered why they were being brought to the viceroy's palace when they had come to buy food. **They said: We have been brought on the matter of the silver that was restored to our sacks.** The viceroy is certainly plotting **to falsely accuse us, attack us,** and eventually **take us as slaves, and our donkeys.**

19 Therefore, **they approached the man in charge of Joseph's house, and they spoke to him at the entrance of the house** before entering.

20 **They said: Please, my lord,**[15] **we initially descended to acquire food.**

21 **It was when we came to the lodging place and we opened our sacks; behold, each man's silver was at the opening of his sack, our silver in its full weight; and we returned it in our hand.** First we wish to return the money, which was no doubt placed in our sacks by mistake.

BACKGROUND

43:11| **Spices [*nekhot*]:** According to ancient translations, this is resin. *Nekhot* has been identified with milkvetch, *Astragalus*, a low shrub that grows mainly in the desert regions of Israel. A medicinal resin is produced from its branches. Alternatively, the Sages translate *nekhot* as wax (*Bereshit Rabba* 91:13).

יא התמהמהנו כי־עתה שבנו זה פעמים: ויאמר אלהם ישראל אביהם אם־כן |
אפוא זאת עשו קחו מזמרת הארץ בכליכם והורידו לאיש מנחה מעט צרי
יב ומעט דבש נכאת ולט בטנים ושקדים: וכסף משנה קחו בידכם ואת־הכסף
יג המושב בפי אמתחתיכם תשיבו בידכם אולי משגה הוא: ואת־אחיכם קחו
יד וקומו שובו אל־האיש: ואל שדי יתן לכם רחמים לפני האיש ושלח לכם את־ לט
טו אחיכם אחר ואת־בנימין ואני כאשר שכלתי שכלתי: ויקחו האנשים את־
המנחה הזאת ומשנה־כסף לקחו בידם ואת־בנימן ויקמו וירדו מצרים ויעמדו
טז לפני יוסף: וירא יוסף אתם את־בנימין ויאמר לאשר על־ביתו הבא את־ ששי
יז האנשים הביתה וטבח טבח והכן כי אתי יאכלו האנשים בצהרים: ויעש
יח האיש כאשר אמר יוסף ויבא האיש את־האנשים ביתה יוסף: וייראו האנשים
כי הובאו בית יוסף ויאמרו על־דבר הכסף השב באמתחתינו בתחלה אנחנו
מובאים להתגלל עלינו ולהתנפל עלינו ולקחת אתנו לעבדים ואת־חמרינו:
יט כ ויגשו אל־האיש אשר על־בית יוסף וידברו אליו פתח הבית: ויאמרו בי אדני
כא ירד ירדנו בתחלה לשבר־אכל: ויהי כי־באנו אל־המלון ונפתחה את־
אמתחתינו והנה כסף־איש בפי אמתחתו כספנו במשקלו ונשב אתו בידנו:

רש״י

יא| **אפוא.** לשון יתר הוא לתקן מלה בלשון עברי: אם כן אזדקק לעשות שאשלחנו עמכם, צריך אני לחזור ולבקש איה פה תקנה ועצה להשיאכם, ואומר אני: "זאת עשו": **מזמרת הארץ.** כתרגומו "מדמשבח בארעא", שהכל מזמרים עליו כשהוא בא לעולם: **נכאת.** שעוה. בראשית רבה (צא, יא): **בטנים.** לא ידעתי מה הם. ובפירושי א״ב של רבי מכיר ראיתי פסטיקא״ס, ודומה לי שהן אפרסקים:

יב| **וכסף משנה.** פי שנים כראשון: **קחו בידכם.** לשבר אכל, שמא הוקר השער: **אולי משגה הוא.** שמא הממנה על הבית שכחו שוגג:

יד| **ואל שדי.** מעתה אינכם חסרים כלום אלא תפלה, הריני מתפלל עליכם: אל שיש די בנתינת רחמיו וכדי היכלת בידו לתן, "יתן לכם רחמים", זהו פשוטו. ומדרשו, מי שאמר לעולם די יאמר די לצרותי, שלא שקטתי מנעורי: צרת לבן, צרת עשו, צרת רחל, צרת דינה, צרת יוסף, צרת שמעון, צרת בנימין: **ושלח לכם.** "ויפטר לכון", כתרגומו, יפטרנו מאסוריו, לשון "לחפשי ישלחנו" (שמות כא, כו). ואין נופל בתרגומו לשון 'וישלח', שהרי לשם הם הולכים אצלו: **את אחיכם.** זה שמעון: **אחר.** רוח הקדש נזרקה בו, לרבות יוסף: **ואני.** עד שובכם אהיה שכול מספק: **כאשר שכלתי.** מיוסף ומשמעון: **שכלתי.** מבנימין:

טו| **ואת בנימן.** מתרגמינן "ודברו ית בנימין", לפי שאין לקיחת הכסף ולקיחת האדם שוה בלשון ארמי; בדבר הנקח ביד מתרגמינן: "ונסיב", ודבר הנקח בהנהגת דברים מתרגמינן: "ודבר":

טז| **וטבח טבח והכן.** כמו: 'ולטבח טבח ולהכן'. ואין 'וטבח' לשון צווי, שהיה לו לומר 'וטבח': **בצהרים.** זה מתרגם "בשירותא" שהוא לשון סעודה ראשונה בלשון ארמי, ובלעז דיסנ״ר, ויש הרבה בתלמוד: "שדא לכלבא שירותיה" (תענית יח ע״ב), "בצע אכלא שירותיה" (ברכות לט ע״ב). אבל כל תרגום של 'צהרים' – טיהרא:

יח| **וייראו האנשים.** כתוב הוא בשני יודי״ן, ותרגומו: "ודחילו": **כי הובאו בית יוסף.** ואין דרך שאר הבאים לשבר בר ללון בבית יוסף כי אם בפונדקאות שבעיר. "וייראו" שאין זה אלא לאספם אל משמר: **אנחנו מובאים.** אל תוך הבית הזה: **להתגלל.** להיות מתגלגלת עלינו עלילת הכסף ולהיותה נופלת עלינו. ואונקלוס שתרגם: "ולאסתקפא עלנא" הוא לשון 'להתעולל', כדמתרגמינן "עלילת דברים" (דברים כב, יד) – "תסקופי מלין", ולא תרגמו אחר לשון המקרא. ו"להתגלל" שתרגם "לאתרברבא" הוא לשון: "גלת הזהב" (קהלת יב, ו), "והצב גלתה העלתה" (נחום ב, ח), שהוא לשון מלכות:

כ| **בי אדני.** לשון בעיה ותחנונים הוא, ובלשון ארמי: "בייא בייא" (יומא סט ע״ב): **ירד ירדנו.** ירידה היא לנו, רגילים היינו לפרנס אחרים, עכשיו אנו צריכים לך:

22 Additionally, **we brought down other silver in our hand to acquire food. We do not know who placed our silver in our sacks.** It is not our fault, and we do not know how it happened, but we will certainly pay for everything.

23 **He,** the steward, **said** to them: **Peace be with you, fear not; your God and the God of your father, gave you hidden treasure in your sacks; your silver came to me.** The money you are obliged to pay has already reached me. It is possible that Joseph, an organized, honest man, had instructed that the payment for the brothers' food be placed in the royal treasury, which meant that he had placed a gift in their sacks at his own expense. **And he,** the steward, **brought Simeon out to them,** presumably in accordance with instructions he had received.

24 **The man brought the men to Joseph's house** as the viceroy's guests. **He gave them water** after their long, tiring journey, **and they washed their feet, and he gave feed to their donkeys.** He took care of all their needs.

25 **They,** the brothers, **prepared the gift** Jacob had sent with them, which up to that point had remained wrapped up on the donkey. They arranged it in a presentable manner **until Joseph's arrival at noon, because they heard that they would eat bread there.** Since they had heard from the man that they would be staying to eat with Joseph, they knew that they would have the opportunity to present him with their gift.

26 **Joseph came home, and they brought him the gift that was in their hand to the house, and they prostrated themselves to him to the earth.** This is the fulfillment of Joseph's first dream: His eleven brothers, who now seek grain and are waiting to eat at Joseph's table, were depicted in the dream as sheaves gathered around and prostrating to his sheaf (37:7).

27 Their friendly welcome continues, as Joseph himself acts in a friendly manner toward his brothers. **He asked them with regard to their wellbeing, and he** also **said: Is all well with your elderly father whom you mentioned; is he still alive?**

28 **They said: All is well with your servant, with our father, he is still alive; they bowed, and they prostrated themselves** as a mark of respect and gratitude to the viceroy who had bestowed honor upon them by inquiring into their welfare and asking about their father's health.

29 **He lifted his eyes and saw his brother Benjamin, his mother's son, and he said: Is this your youngest brother whom you mentioned to me** that you would bring here? **He,** Joseph, then **said: God be gracious to you, my son.** Due to Benjamin's youth, Joseph addressed him as a son.

30 *Seventh aliya* **Joseph hurried, because his mercy was aroused toward his brother,** whom he had not seen for many years, **and he sought to weep;** therefore, **he** quickly **entered the chamber,** his private room, **and wept there.**

31 **He washed his face** to hide the fact that he had been weeping **and emerged, and he restrained himself and said** to his attendants: **Serve bread.**

32 **They served** bread **for him by himself, and for them by themselves, and for the Egyptians who were eating with him by themselves.** His Egyptian associates and household members had their own table. This was yet another cause of confusion for the brothers: Although he was to all appearances Egyptian, the viceroy chose not to eat with the other Egyptians. The separation between the Egyptians and the Hebrews was **because the Egyptians may not eat bread with the Hebrews,**[D] **as it is an abomination for the Egyptians.** The religion of the Egyptians prohibited them from dining with Hebrews.

33 As their host, Joseph seated his brothers around the table. **They sat before him** in the places assigned by Joseph, **the firstborn according to his seniority and the younger according to his youth,** in age order. **And the men wondered to one another.** Since the differences in age between Jacob's sons were not great, an outsider would not be able to tell the age order of these grown men.

34 **He gave them gifts from before him, and Benjamin's gift was five times greater than the gifts of all of them,** the other brothers. **They drank and became inebriated with him.**[D] The meal took on a friendly, even celebratory tone.

DISCUSSION

43:32| **The Egyptians may not eat bread with the Hebrews:** It can be inferred from various sources that the ancient Egyptians were a conceited, racist nation, who treated the Semites from the north with contempt. The meals of Semites were considered an abomination for Egyptians, who refrained from eating animal meat and tended toward vegetarianism. Due to the great difference in menus, and the manner of eating of Egyptians and Hebrews, they would not dine together (see Onkelos and *Ḥizkuni*). The Greek historian Herodotus, writing in the fifth century BCE, attests to the Egyptians' hatred of strangers, whom they considered impure. He further states that Egyptians do not eat from vessels of foreigners and refrained from consuming beef (*The Histories* II:41).

43:34| **They drank and became inebriated with him:** Joseph acted in a manner that suited his own purposes, but he took pains to ensure that his behavior would appear reasonable to his brothers as well. The honor he bestowed upon them at this point appeared to be a gesture of reconciliation for suspecting the dignified representatives of a small tribe in Canaan of spying. It would be thought that this was the reason for his invitation to his home, his including them in a great feast, and his providing them with gifts. There is also a logical explanation for Benjamin's preferential treatment, as in contrast to the other brothers, who willingly came to Egypt, Benjamin was forced to come, and therefore he was entitled to compensation.

From Joseph's perspective, it would appear that his behavior was meant to repay his brothers by giving them an increasingly difficult, yet edifying, punishment. He gradually increased the pressure on his brothers and manipulated

כב וְכֶסֶף אַחֵר הוֹרַדְנוּ בְיָדֵנוּ לִשְׁבׇּר־אֹכֶל לֹא יָדַעְנוּ מִי־שָׂם כַּסְפֵּנוּ בְּאַמְתְּחֹתֵינוּ:
כג וַיֹּאמֶר שָׁלוֹם לָכֶם אַל־תִּירָאוּ אֱלֹהֵיכֶם וֵאלֹהֵי אֲבִיכֶם נָתַן לָכֶם מַטְמוֹן
כד בְּאַמְתְּחֹתֵיכֶם כַּסְפְּכֶם בָּא אֵלָי וַיּוֹצֵא אֲלֵהֶם אֶת־שִׁמְעוֹן: וַיָּבֵא הָאִישׁ אֶת־
כה הָאֲנָשִׁים בֵּיתָה יוֹסֵף וַיִּתֶּן־מַיִם וַיִּרְחֲצוּ רַגְלֵיהֶם וַיִּתֵּן מִסְפּוֹא לַחֲמֹרֵיהֶם: וַיָּכִינוּ
כו אֶת־הַמִּנְחָה עַד־בּוֹא יוֹסֵף בַּצׇּהֳרָיִם כִּי שָׁמְעוּ כִּי־שָׁם יֹאכְלוּ לָחֶם: וַיָּבֹא יוֹסֵף
כז הַבַּיְתָה וַיָּבִיאוּ לוֹ אֶת־הַמִּנְחָה אֲשֶׁר־בְּיָדָם הַבָּיְתָה וַיִּשְׁתַּחֲווּ־לוֹ אָרְצָה: וַיִּשְׁאַל
כח לָהֶם לְשָׁלוֹם וַיֹּאמֶר הֲשָׁלוֹם אֲבִיכֶם הַזָּקֵן אֲשֶׁר אֲמַרְתֶּם הַעוֹדֶנּוּ חָי: וַיֹּאמְרוּ
כט שָׁלוֹם לְעַבְדְּךָ לְאָבִינוּ עוֹדֶנּוּ חָי וַיִּקְּדוּ וַיִּשְׁתַּחֲוּ: וַיִּשָּׂא עֵינָיו וַיַּרְא אֶת־בִּנְיָמִין
אָחִיו בֶּן־אִמּוֹ וַיֹּאמֶר הֲזֶה אֲחִיכֶם הַקָּטֹן אֲשֶׁר אֲמַרְתֶּם אֵלָי וַיֹּאמַר אֱלֹהִים יׇחְנְךָ
ל בְּנִי: וַיְמַהֵר יוֹסֵף כִּי־נִכְמְרוּ רַחֲמָיו אֶל־אָחִיו וַיְבַקֵּשׁ לִבְכּוֹת וַיָּבֹא הַחַדְרָה וַיֵּבְךְּ שביעי
לא לב שָׁמָּה: וַיִּרְחַץ פָּנָיו וַיֵּצֵא וַיִּתְאַפַּק וַיֹּאמֶר שִׂימוּ לָחֶם: וַיָּשִׂימוּ לוֹ לְבַדּוֹ וְלָהֶם
לְבַדָּם וְלַמִּצְרִים הָאֹכְלִים אִתּוֹ לְבַדָּם כִּי לֹא יוּכְלוּן הַמִּצְרִים לֶאֱכֹל אֶת־הָעִבְרִים
לג לֶחֶם כִּי־תוֹעֵבָה הִוא לְמִצְרָיִם: וַיֵּשְׁבוּ לְפָנָיו הַבְּכֹר כִּבְכֹרָתוֹ וְהַצָּעִיר כִּצְעִרָתוֹ
לד וַיִּתְמְהוּ הָאֲנָשִׁים אִישׁ אֶל־רֵעֵהוּ: וַיִּשָּׂא מַשְׂאֹת מֵאֵת פָּנָיו אֲלֵהֶם וַתֵּרֶב מַשְׂאַת

רש"י

כג| **אֱלֹהֵיכֶם.** בִּזְכוּתְכֶם; וְאִם אֵין זְכוּתְכֶם כְּדַאי, "אֱלֹהֵי אֲבִיכֶם" – בִּזְכוּת אֲבִיכֶם "נָתַן לָכֶם מַטְמוֹן":

כד| **וַיָּבֵא הָאִישׁ.** הֲבָאָה אַחַר הֲבָאָה, לְפִי שֶׁהָיוּ דּוֹחֲפִים אוֹתוֹ חוּץ עַד שֶׁדִּבְּרוּ אֵלָיו פֶּתַח הַבַּיִת, וּמִשֶּׁאָמַר לָהֶם "שָׁלוֹם לָכֶם" (לעיל פסוק כג) נִמְשְׁכוּ וּבָאוּ אַחֲרָיו:

כה| **וַיָּכִינוּ.** הִזְמִינוּ, עִטְּרוּהָ בְּכֵלִים נָאִים:

כו| **הַבַּיְתָה.** מִפְּרוֹזְדוֹר לִטְרַקְלִין:

כח| **וַיִּקְּדוּ וַיִּשְׁתַּחֲוּ.** עַל שְׁאֵלַת שָׁלוֹם. קִדָּה – כְּפִיפַת קָדְקֹד, הִשְׁתַּחֲוָאָה – מִשְׁתַּטֵּחַ לָאָרֶץ:

כט| **אֱלֹהִים יָחְנְךָ בְּנִי.** בִּשְׁאָר שְׁבָטִים שָׁמַעְנוּ חֲנִינָה: "אֲשֶׁר חָנַן אֱלֹהִים אֶת עַבְדֶּךָ" (לעיל לג, ה), וּבִנְיָמִין עֲדַיִן לֹא נוֹלַד, לְכָךְ בֵּרְכוֹ יוֹסֵף בַּחֲנִינָה:

ל| **כִּי נִכְמְרוּ רַחֲמָיו.** שְׁאָלוֹ: יֵשׁ לְךָ אָח מֵאֵם? אָמַר לוֹ: אָח הָיָה לִי וְאֵינִי יוֹדֵעַ הֵיכָן הוּא. יֵשׁ לְךָ בָּנִים? אָמַר לוֹ: יֵשׁ לִי עֲשָׂרָה. אָמַר לוֹ: וּמַה שְּׁמָם? אָמַר לוֹ: בֶּלַע וָבֶכֶר וְגוֹ' (להלן מו, כא). אָמַר לוֹ: מַה טִּיבָן שֶׁל שֵׁמוֹת הַלָּלוּ? אָמַר לוֹ: כֻּלָּם עַל שֵׁם אָחִי וְהַצָּרוֹת שֶׁמְּצָאוּהוּ, כִּדְאִיתָא בְּמַסֶּכֶת סוֹטָה (דף לו ע"ב); מִיָּד נִכְמְרוּ רַחֲמָיו: **נִכְמְרוּ.** נִתְחַמְּמוּ, וּבִלְשׁוֹן מִשְׁנָה: "עַל הַכֹּמֶר שֶׁל זֵיתִים" (ב"מ מ"ע"א עד ע"א), וּבִלְשׁוֹן אֲרַמִּי: "מִכְמַר בִּשְׂרָא" (פסחים נח ע"א), וּבַמִּקְרָא: "עוֹרֵנוּ כְּתַנּוּר נִכְמָרוּ" (איכה ה, י) – נִתְחַמְּמוּ וְנִקְמְטוּ קְמָטִים קְמָטִים, "מִפְּנֵי זַלְעֲפוֹת רָעָב". כֵּן דֶּרֶךְ כָּל עוֹר, כְּשֶׁמְּחַמְּמִין אוֹתוֹ מְאֹד – נִקְמָט וְנִכְוָץ:

לא| **וַיִּתְאַפַּק.** נִתְאַמֵּץ, וְהוּא לְשׁוֹן "אֲפִיקֵי מָגִנִּים" (איוב מא, ז), חֹזֶק. וְכֵן: "וּמְזִיחַ אֲפִיקִים רִפָּה" (שם יב, כא):

לב| **כִּי תוֹעֵבָה הִוא.** דָּבָר שָׂנאוּי הוּא לְמִצְרִים "לֶאֱכֹל אֶת הָעִבְרִים", וְאוּנְקְלוֹס נָתַן טַעַם לַדָּבָר:

לג| **הַבְּכֹר כִּבְכֹרָתוֹ.** מַכֶּה בַּגָּבִיעַ וְקוֹרֵא: רְאוּבֵן שִׁמְעוֹן לֵוִי וִיהוּדָה יִשָּׂשכָר וּזְבוּלֻן בְּנֵי אֵם אַחַת, הָסֵבּוּ כַּסֵּדֶר הַזֶּה שֶׁהוּא תּוֹלְדוֹתֵיכֶם, וְכֵן כֻּלָּם. כֵּיוָן שֶׁהִגִּיעַ לְבִנְיָמִין, אָמַר: זֶה אֵין לוֹ אֵם וַאֲנִי אֵין לִי אֵם, יֵשֵׁב אֶצְלִי:

לד| **מַשְׂאֹת.** מָנוֹת: **חָמֵשׁ יָדוֹת.** חֶלְקוֹ עִם אֶחָיו, וּמַשְׂאַת

DISCUSSION

events in order to put them to a test that was as similar as possible to the situation in which they had sold him. Just as Joseph was his father's young, favored son, now Benjamin was his father's most beloved son, whom he kept at his side and refused to allow to travel on a long journey. The many gifts that Benjamin, son of Rachel, received from the viceroy of Egypt were designed to increase the tension among the brothers and highlight any lingering feelings of jealousy the brothers may have harbored toward Benjamin. The performance continues, and the brothers' confusion and distress intensify until the dramatic climax, planned by Joseph to the last detail.

Joseph's Increased Antagonism toward His Brothers and His Eventual Revelation

GENESIS 44:1–45:24

Here the brothers' distress reaches its climax as Joseph's fresh accusations center on none other than Benjamin, after their father expressed his fears for his youngest son's fate in such a powerful and poignant manner.

In the customary division of weekly Torah readings, this passage is interrupted in the middle. This heightens the drama even further just before Judah's eloquent speech, which will profoundly move Joseph. Similarly, with regard to the ancient division of chapters in Torah scrolls, indicated by a space between each passage, the portion of *Miketz* is unusual in that it does not contain any breaks at all until there is a break at the conclusion of the portion. It is as though the entire chain of events, with the gradual increase of drama and tension, should be read in a single breath, and right at the pinnacle of the brothers' woes the story pauses.

44 1 **He commanded the one in charge of his house, saying: Fill the men's sacks with food, as much as** the sacks **are able to carry, and place each man's silver at the opening of his sack,** as on the previous occasion,

2 However, this time Joseph added another instruction: **Place my** special **goblet, the silver goblet, at the opening of the sack of the youngest** brother. In ancient Egypt, silver was occasionally even more valuable than gold, as there were gold deposits in East Africa and other places near Egypt, whereas silver was mostly imported from Asia. Joseph continued: **And** also insert into the sacks **the silver of his purchase of the grain. He,** Joseph's servant, **did in accordance with the statement that Joseph had spoken.**

3 It is likely that the brothers had arrived in the afternoon and stayed overnight in Joseph's house. The next **morning broke, and the men were dispatched, they and their donkeys.**

4 **They left the city; they had not gone far, and Joseph said to the one in charge of his house: Arise** now and **pursue the men and overtake them, and say to them: Why have you repaid evil for good?** Joseph accused his brothers of theft.

5 **Isn't this** goblet that you stole from Joseph's house **that in which my lord drinks, and** moreover, isn't it the goblet **with which he divines?** It is no ordinary goblet, but the one with which he performs his divinations. **You have done evil in what you did.** By stealing the goblet from your host, you have displayed both ingratitude and stupidity, as naturally your theft was discovered immediately.

6 **He overtook them, and he spoke to them those words.**

7 **They said to him: Why would my lord speak words like those? Heaven forfend for your servants to act in that manner.** It is utterly absurd to suspect us of such a deed, as proven by our actions:

8 **Behold,** the **silver that we found in the opening of our sacks we returned to you from the land of Canaan.** Although the steward in charge of Joseph's house informed us that we owe nothing, and that the money we found was our treasure, we had brought it with us all the way from Canaan due to the possibility that we owed this money. **How would we steal from the house of your lord silver or gold?**

9 Since they were fully confident that none of them had stolen anything, the brothers declared: **With whomever of your servants it,** the goblet, **is found, he shall die, and we too,** all of us, **will be slaves to my lord.**

10 **He said: Now too, it should be in accordance with your words:** The criminal deserves the death sentence, and the rest of you, as his accomplices, should become slaves. Nevertheless, I have a more generous offer: **He with whom it shall be found shall be a slave to me.** I have no intention of putting him to death, but I will take him as a slave; **and** the rest of **you shall be exonerated.** Since you did not commit the crime, you will be spared all punishment.[16]

11 **Each man hurried and lowered his sack to the ground, and each man opened his sack** for inspection.

12 **He,** the steward, **searched; he began with the eldest, and with the youngest he concluded.** He proceeded in this manner both out of politeness and because if he had gone straight to Benjamin's sack and found the goblet immediately, it would have looked suspicious. He therefore conducted the search in accordance with the brothers' ages. **The goblet was found in Benjamin's sack.**

13 **They rent their garments** in shock, shame, helplessness, and terror at the implications of this discovery. The act of rending was also a mark of mourning. **Each man loaded** his sack onto **his donkey, and they returned to the city.**

14 *Maftir* **Judah and his brethren came to Joseph's house, and he,** Joseph, **was still there.** Joseph had, of course, good reason to remain in his house. Once again **they fell before him to the ground.**

15 **Joseph said to them,** in the manner of an important minister: **What is this deed that you have done? Don't you know that a man who is like me will practice divination?** By now you are aware of my wisdom and greatness. Did you not fear that

א בִּנְיָמִן מִמַּשְׂאֹת כֻּלָּם חָמֵשׁ יָדוֹת וַיִּשְׁתּוּ וַיִּשְׁכְּרוּ עִמּוֹ: וַיְצַו אֶת־אֲשֶׁר עַל־בֵּיתוֹ
לֵאמֹר מַלֵּא אֶת־אַמְתְּחֹת הָאֲנָשִׁים אֹכֶל כַּאֲשֶׁר יוּכְלוּן שְׂאֵת וְשִׂים כֶּסֶף־אִישׁ
ב בְּפִי אַמְתַּחְתּוֹ: וְאֶת־גְּבִיעִי גְּבִיעַ הַכֶּסֶף תָּשִׂים בְּפִי אַמְתַּחַת הַקָּטֹן וְאֵת כֶּסֶף
ג שִׁבְרוֹ וַיַּעַשׂ כִּדְבַר יוֹסֵף אֲשֶׁר דִּבֵּר: הַבֹּקֶר אוֹר וְהָאֲנָשִׁים שֻׁלְּחוּ הֵמָּה וַחֲמֹרֵיהֶם:
ד הֵם יָצְאוּ אֶת־הָעִיר לֹא הִרְחִיקוּ וְיוֹסֵף אָמַר לַאֲשֶׁר עַל־בֵּיתוֹ קוּם רְדֹף אַחֲרֵי
ה הָאֲנָשִׁים וְהִשַּׂגְתָּם וְאָמַרְתָּ אֲלֵהֶם לָמָּה שִׁלַּמְתֶּם רָעָה תַּחַת טוֹבָה: הֲלוֹא זֶה
ו אֲשֶׁר יִשְׁתֶּה אֲדֹנִי בּוֹ וְהוּא נַחֵשׁ יְנַחֵשׁ בּוֹ הֲרֵעֹתֶם אֲשֶׁר עֲשִׂיתֶם: וַיַּשִּׂגֵם וַיְדַבֵּר
ז אֲלֵהֶם אֶת־הַדְּבָרִים הָאֵלֶּה: וַיֹּאמְרוּ אֵלָיו לָמָּה יְדַבֵּר אֲדֹנִי כַּדְּבָרִים הָאֵלֶּה
ח חָלִילָה לַעֲבָדֶיךָ מֵעֲשׂוֹת כַּדָּבָר הַזֶּה: הֵן כֶּסֶף אֲשֶׁר מָצָאנוּ בְּפִי אַמְתְּחֹתֵינוּ
ט הֱשִׁיבֹנוּ אֵלֶיךָ מֵאֶרֶץ כְּנָעַן וְאֵיךְ נִגְנֹב מִבֵּית אֲדֹנֶיךָ כֶּסֶף אוֹ זָהָב: אֲשֶׁר יִמָּצֵא
י אִתּוֹ מֵעֲבָדֶיךָ וָמֵת וְגַם־אֲנַחְנוּ נִהְיֶה לַאדֹנִי לַעֲבָדִים: וַיֹּאמֶר גַּם־עַתָּה כְדִבְרֵיכֶם
יא כֶּן־הוּא אֲשֶׁר יִמָּצֵא אִתּוֹ יִהְיֶה־לִּי עָבֶד וְאַתֶּם תִּהְיוּ נְקִיִּם: וַיְמַהֲרוּ וַיּוֹרִדוּ אִישׁ
יב אֶת־אַמְתַּחְתּוֹ אָרְצָה וַיִּפְתְּחוּ אִישׁ אַמְתַּחְתּוֹ: וַיְחַפֵּשׂ בַּגָּדוֹל הֵחֵל וּבַקָּטֹן כִּלָּה
יג וַיִּמָּצֵא הַגָּבִיעַ בְּאַמְתַּחַת בִּנְיָמִן: וַיִּקְרְעוּ שִׂמְלֹתָם וַיַּעֲמֹס אִישׁ עַל־חֲמֹרוֹ וַיָּשֻׁבוּ
יד הָעִירָה: וַיָּבֹא יְהוּדָה וְאֶחָיו בֵּיתָה יוֹסֵף וְהוּא עוֹדֶנּוּ שָׁם וַיִּפְּלוּ לְפָנָיו אָרְצָה: מפטיר
טו וַיֹּאמֶר לָהֶם יוֹסֵף מָה־הַמַּעֲשֶׂה הַזֶּה אֲשֶׁר עֲשִׂיתֶם הֲלוֹא יְדַעְתֶּם כִּי־נַחֵשׁ יְנַחֵשׁ

רש״י

יוֹסֵף וְאָסְנַת וּמְנַשֶּׁה וְאֶפְרַיִם: וַיִּשְׁכְּרוּ עִמּוֹ. וּמִיּוֹם שֶׁמְּכָרוּהוּ לֹא שָׁתוּ יַיִן וְלֹא הוּא שָׁתָה יַיִן, וְאוֹתוֹ הַיּוֹם שָׁתוּ:

פרק מד

ב| גְּבִיעִי. כּוֹס אָרֹךְ וְקוֹרִין לוֹ מדירנ״ו:

ז| חָלִילָה לַעֲבָדֶיךָ. חוּלִין הוּא לָנוּ, לְשׁוֹן גְּנַאי. וְתַרְגּוּם: ״חַס לְעַבְדָּךְ״, חָס מֵאֵת הַקָּדוֹשׁ בָּרוּךְ הוּא יְהֵא עָלֵינוּ מֵעֲשׂוֹת זֹאת. וְהַרְבֵּה יֵשׁ בַּתַּלְמוּד ״חַס וְשָׁלוֹם״:

ח| הֵן כֶּסֶף אֲשֶׁר מָצָאנוּ. זֶה אֶחָד מֵעֲשָׂרָה קַל וָחֹמֶר הָאֲמוּרִים בַּתּוֹרָה, וְכֻלָּן מְנוּיִין בִּבְרֵאשִׁית רַבָּה (צב, ז):

י| גַּם עַתָּה. אַף זוֹ מִן הַדִּין אֱמֶת ״כְדִבְרֵיכֶם כֶּן הוּא״ שֶׁכֻּלְּכֶם חַיָּבִים בַּדָּבָר; עֲשָׂרָה שֶׁנִּמְצֵאת גְּנֵבָה בְּיַד אֶחָד מֵהֶם כֻּלָּם נִתְפָּשִׂים, אֲבָל אֲנִי אֶעֱשֶׂה לָכֶם לִפְנִים מִשּׁוּרַת הַדִּין: ״אֲשֶׁר יִמָּצֵא אִתּוֹ יִהְיֶה לִּי עָבֶד״ וְגוֹ׳:

יב| בַּגָּדוֹל הֵחֵל. שֶׁלֹּא יַרְגִּישׁוּ שֶׁהָיָה יוֹדֵעַ הֵיכָן הוּא:

יג| וַיַּעֲמֹס אִישׁ עַל חֲמֹרוֹ. בַּעֲלֵי זְרוֹעַ הָיוּ, וְלֹא הֻצְרְכוּ לְסַיֵּעַ זֶה אֶת זֶה לִטְעֹן: וַיָּשֻׁבוּ הָעִירָה. מֶטְרוֹפּוֹלִין הָיְתָה וְהוּא אוֹמֵר ״הָעִירָה״, הָעִיר כָּל שֶׁהִיא?! אֶלָּא שֶׁלֹּא הָיְתָה חֲשׁוּבָה בְּעֵינֵיהֶם אֶלָּא כְּעִיר בֵּינוֹנִית שֶׁל עֲשָׂרָה בְּנֵי אָדָם לְעִנְיַן הַמִּלְחָמָה:

יד| עוֹדֶנּוּ שָׁם. שֶׁהָיָה מַמְתִּין לָהֶם:

I would discover what had happened to my goblet? I cannot comprehend the reason for this foolish act.[17]

16 **Judah said: What shall we say to my lord, what shall we speak, and how shall we justify ourselves?** After all, the goblet was found in our possession. **God has revealed the iniquity of your servants.**[D] We cannot account for this matter; it was arranged by Heaven. **Behold, we are my lord's slaves, both**

we and he in whose possession the goblet was found. Since we came as a single group, take us all as slaves.

17 **He,** Joseph, **said: Heaven forfend that I should do so.** I will not act unjustly. **The man in whose hand the goblet was found, he shall be my slave** as a punishment; **and** as for the rest of **you,** who presumably knew nothing about the offense, I have no claim against you. Therefore, **go up in peace to your father.**

Maftir on Hanukkah is read from the respective day's portion in Numbers, chap. 7.

DISCUSSION

44:16 | God has revealed the iniquity of your servants: Judah and his brothers doubted that there had actually been a theft. First, they knew each other well and were certain that none of them would commit such an act. Additionally, they could not fathom any possible motive that Benjamin had to steal the goblet. What would

he do with it? Furthermore, they had experienced a chain of strange events involving the Egyptian viceroy, including accusations and reprimands, returned money, demonstrations of love and respect, the bestowal of gifts, and now a fresh round of accusations. They had certainly seen the restored money on this occasion

as well, when their sacks were opened, even if they had not had an opportunity to reflect on the matter. It is likely that Judah is alluding to the mysterious nature of these occurrences in his statement: "God has revealed the iniquity of your servants" (see Rashi).

Parashat
Vayigash

Judah's Plea and Joseph's Revelation
GENESIS 44:18–45:24

Parashat Vayigash continues where *Parashat Miketz* left off, with Joseph's threat to separate Benjamin from his brothers. Now Judah makes an impassioned plea for the sake of their father, causing Joseph to finally reveal his true identity.

18 **Judah approached him,** Joseph. Judah stands out here from the rest of the brothers as their leader, who takes responsibility for dealing with the situation. **And** Judah **said: Please, my lord, may your servant speak a word in my lord's ears?** I do not wish simply to accept or reject your suggestion, but to explain to you the series of events that led us to this confrontation, as I understand them. **Do not become incensed with your servant** if I repeat in my own style some information that you already know, **as to us you are like Pharaoh.** You are the most

distinguished person in this place, and therefore I will not fail to address you with reverence and honor; nevertheless, I ask permission to speak my mind.

19 In our previous encounter, among other questions, **my lord asked his servants** the following, **saying: Do you have a father or a brother?**

20 **We said to my lord: We have an elderly father, and a** relatively **young son of his old age; his brother,** the brother of this young son, **is dead, and he alone remains from his mother.**

טז אִישׁ אֲשֶׁר כָּמֹנִי: וַיֹּאמֶר יְהוּדָה מַה־נֹּאמַר לַאדֹנִי מַה־נְּדַבֵּר וּמַה־נִּצְטַדָּק
הָאֱלֹהִים מָצָא אֶת־עֲוֹן עֲבָדֶיךָ הִנֶּנּוּ עֲבָדִים לַאדֹנִי גַּם־אֲנַחְנוּ גַּם אֲשֶׁר־נִמְצָא
יז הַגָּבִיעַ בְּיָדוֹ: וַיֹּאמֶר חָלִילָה לִּי מֵעֲשׂוֹת זֹאת הָאִישׁ אֲשֶׁר נִמְצָא הַגָּבִיעַ בְּיָדוֹ
הוּא יִהְיֶה־לִּי עָבֶד וְאַתֶּם עֲלוּ לְשָׁלוֹם אֶל־אֲבִיכֶם: מ

רש"י

טז] הָאֱלֹהִים מָצָא. יוֹדְעִים אָנוּ שֶׁלֹּא סָרַחְנוּ, אֲבָל מֵאֵת הַמָּקוֹם נִהְיְתָה לְהָבִיא לָנוּ זֹאת, מָצָא בַּעַל חוֹב מָקוֹם לִגְבּוֹת שְׁטַר חוֹבוֹ: וּמַה נִּצְטַדָּק. לְשׁוֹן צֶדֶק, וְכֵן כָּל תֵּבָה שֶׁתְּחִלַּת יְסוֹדָהּ צָ"דִי וְהִיא בָּאָה לְדַבֵּר בִּלְשׁוֹן מִתְפַּעֵל אוֹ נִתְפַּעֵל, נוֹתֵן טֵי"ת בִּמְקוֹם תָּ"ו, וְאֵינוֹ נוֹתְנָהּ לִפְנֵי אוֹת רִאשׁוֹנָה שֶׁל יְסוֹד הַתֵּבָה אֶלָּא בְּאֶמְצַע אוֹתִיּוֹת הָעִקָּר, כְּגוֹן "נִצְטַדָּק", "יִצְטַבַּע" (דניאל ד, יב) מִגִּזְרַת "צֶבַע", "וַיִּצְטַיָּרוּ" (יהושע ט, ד) מִגִּזְרַת "צִיר אֱמוּנִים מַרְפֵּא" (משלי יג, יז), "הִצְטַיַּדְנוּ אֹתוֹ מִבָּתֵּינוּ" (יהושע ט, יב) מִגִּזְרַת "צֵדָה לַדָּרֶךְ" (לעיל מב, כה). וְתֵבָה שֶׁתְּחִלָּתָהּ סָמֶ"ךְ, כְּשֶׁהִיא מִתְפַּעֶלֶת מַפְרִיד תָּ"ו אֶת אוֹתִיּוֹת הָעִקָּר, כְּגוֹן: "וְיִסְתַּבֵּל הֶחָגָב" (קהלת יב, ה), "מִסְתַּכַּל הֲוֵית בְּקַרְנַיָּא" (דניאל ז, ח), "וְיִשְׁתַּמֵּר חֻקּוֹת עָמְרִי" (מיכה ו, טז), "וְסָר מֵרָע מִשְׁתּוֹלֵל" (ישעיה נט, טו) מִגִּזְרַת "מוֹלִיךְ יוֹעֲצִים שׁוֹלָל" (איוב יב, יז), "עוֹדְךָ מִסְתּוֹלֵל בְּעַמִּי" (שמות ט, יז) מִגִּזְרַת "דֶּרֶךְ לֹא סְלוּלָה" (ירמיה יח, טו).

פרשת
ויגש

יח וַיִּגַּשׁ אֵלָיו יְהוּדָה וַיֹּאמֶר בִּי אֲדֹנִי יְדַבֶּר־נָא עַבְדְּךָ דָבָר בְּאָזְנֵי אֲדֹנִי וְאַל־יִחַר
יט אַפְּךָ בְּעַבְדֶּךָ כִּי כָמוֹךָ כְּפַרְעֹה: אֲדֹנִי שָׁאַל אֶת־עֲבָדָיו לֵאמֹר הֲיֵשׁ־לָכֶם אָב
כ אוֹ־אָח: וַנֹּאמֶר אֶל־אֲדֹנִי יֶשׁ־לָנוּ אָב זָקֵן וְיֶלֶד זְקֻנִים קָטָן וְאָחִיו מֵת וַיִּוָּתֵר

רש"י

יח] וַיִּגַּשׁ אֵלָיו. דַּבֵּר בְּאָזְנֵי אֲדֹנִי. יִכָּנְסוּ דְּבָרַי בְּאָזְנֶיךָ: וְאַל יִחַר אַפְּךָ. מִכָּאן אַתָּה לָמֵד שֶׁדִּבֵּר אֵלָיו קָשׁוֹת: כִּי כָמוֹךָ כְּפַרְעֹה. חָשׁוּב אַתָּה בְּעֵינַי כְּמֶלֶךְ, זֶהוּ פְּשׁוּטוֹ. וּמִדְרָשׁוֹ, סוֹפְךָ לִלְקוֹת עָלָיו בְּצָרַעַת כְּמוֹ שֶׁלָּקָה פַרְעֹה עַל יְדֵי זְקֶנְתִּי שָׂרָה עַל לַיְלָה אַחַת שֶׁעֲכָבָהּ. דָּבָר אַחֵר, מָה פַרְעֹה גּוֹזֵר וְאֵינוֹ מְקַיֵּם מַבְטִיחַ וְאֵינוֹ עוֹשֶׂה, אַף אַתָּה כֵּן. וְכִי זוֹ הִיא שִׂימַת עַיִן שֶׁאָמַרְתָּ לָשׂוּם עֵינְךָ עָלָיו?! דָּבָר אַחֵר, "כִּי כָמוֹךָ כְּפַרְעֹה", אִם תַּקְנִיטֵנִי אֶהֱרֹג אוֹתְךָ וְאֶת אֲדוֹנֶיךָ:

יט-כ] אֲדֹנִי שָׁאַל אֶת עֲבָדָיו. מִתְּחִלָּה בַּעֲלִילָה בָּאתָ עָלֵינוּ, לָמָּה הָיָה לְךָ לִשְׁאֹל כָּל אֵלֶּה? בִּתְּךָ הָיִינוּ מְבַקְשִׁים אוֹ אֲחוֹתֵנוּ אַתָּה מְבַקֵּשׁ? וְאַף עַל פִּי כֵן: "וַנֹּאמֶר אֶל אֲדֹנִי", לֹא כִחַדְנוּ מִמְּךָ דָּבָר: וְאָחִיו מֵת. מִפְּנֵי הַיִּרְאָה

He is the lone surviving son of his mother, **and** in addition to these bare facts, **his father loves him** above all.
21 **You said to your servants: Bring him down to me, and I will set my eye upon him.** I will treat him well and pay special attention to him.
22 **We said to my lord: The lad cannot leave his father;** for **if he leaves his father,** then **he,** the father, **would die.**
23 **You said to your servants:** Nevertheless, **if your youngest brother does not come down with you, you shall not see my face again.**
24 **It was when we went up to your servant, my father, that we told him the words of my lord.**
25 Eventually, **our father said: Return, acquire us a little food.**
26 **We said: We cannot go down** to Egypt in the same manner as before; **if our youngest brother is with us, we will go down, for we cannot see the man's face unless our youngest brother is with us.**
27 **Your servant, my father, said to us: You know that my wife bore me two sons;**[D]
28 **the one departed from me, and I said** in conjecture: **Surely he was mauled.** Jacob could not be certain of this claim, as Joseph's body had not been found; however, there was circumstantial evidence that this was Joseph's fate. **And I have not seen him since;**
29 **and** if **you will take this one too from my presence, and a disaster will befall him, you will** thereby **cause my old age to descend in woe to the grave.** My old age will be even worse than it currently is, and I will be overcome with misery when I pass on from the world.
30 Until this point, Judah has been recounting previous events. He now begins to offer his own thoughts: **Now, when I come** home **to your servant, my father, and the lad is not with us, and his,** my father's, **soul is bound with his** son's **soul,**
31 **it will be when he sees that the lad is not with us; he will die**
Second aliya from excessive grief. **Your servants will cause the old age of your servant, my father, to descend in sorrow to the grave.** We will have caused our father's death.
32 Judah now explains why he is the one speaking on behalf of his brothers: **For your servant** personally **guaranteed the lad to my father, saying: If I do not bring him to you, I will have sinned to my father forever,** and my transgression will accompany me always.
33 **Now, please,** as it is my responsibility to ensure that Benjamin returns home at whatever cost, I suggest the following: **Your servant will remain in place of the lad** as **a slave to my lord.**[D] Take me for a slave in his place; **and the lad shall go up,** return home, **with his brothers.**
34 **For how will I go up to my father, and the lad is not with me? I cannot go, lest I see the woe that shall find my father.** I am unable to bear the thought of my father's reaction, and I will do anything to avoid witnessing it with my own eyes. Of course Jacob would not be pleased even if a different brother had to remain as a slave in Egypt, but due to his exceptional love for Benjamin, his loss would be far worse if Joseph's demand were accepted.

45 1 **Joseph could not restrain** from revealing **himself,** but he nevertheless held back **before all those standing before him** so as not to embarrass his brothers publicly by disclosing to the servants and guards that were present the fact that they had sold him to Egypt.[1] **And he called: Remove every man from before me. No** other **man stood with him when Joseph revealed himself to his brothers.**[D] Another explanation for Joseph's instructions is that his servants supported Judah's proposal and attempted to convince Joseph to accept it, as the lost goblet had been found. Furthermore, Judah's noble offer had left a profound impression on them. Joseph therefore requested that they exit the room.[2]
2 **He raised his voice in weeping.** Joseph had wept previously, but now he was able to cry openly in his brothers' presence and did not have to exit the room to do so.[3] **The Egyptians heard, and the house of Pharaoh heard.** Although the Egyptians who had been present had moved to another room or left the house entirely, they could still hear the sound of his weeping.

DISCUSSION

44:27| **My wife bore me two sons:** Clearly, Jacob had no qualms in describing Rachel as his primary wife even to the children of his other wives (see Ramban). Many generations later, during a ceremony arranged by Boaz, of Bethlehem and the tribe of Judah, the other residents of Bethlehem declared: "The Lord should make the woman that is coming into your house like Rachel and like Leah" (Ruth 4:11; *Midrash Tanḥuma, Vayetze* 15; Ramban). This shows that the tribe of Judah accepted this order, as they mentioned Rachel before their mother, Leah (see also Rabbi Meir ben Shimon, Jeremiah 31:14).

44:33| **Your servant will remain in place of the lad a slave to my lord:** Since Judah was older than Benjamin, he could offer himself as a slave of greater value. His implicit message is that this is not a just sentence of a thief punished for his crime, but a capricious decision imposed by the ruler of his own accord. Consequently, as the ruler demanded that one of the brothers must remain, Judah proposed himself as a permanent slave instead of Benjamin. Judah is subtly accusing Joseph of plotting against them. However, due to his fear of the powerful ruler, he did not explicitly state this allegation.

45:1| **When Joseph revealed himself to his brothers:** Joseph revealed himself to his brothers as soon as it became clear to him that they had successfully passed his test. One of the aims of the drama he had orchestrated was to assess how much his brothers had changed since selling him, and whether the trials and tribulations to which he was subjecting them would influence them at all. Gradually, the situation in

כא הוּא לְבַדּוֹ לְאִמּוֹ וְאָבִיו אֲהֵבוֹ: וַתֹּאמֶר אֶל־עֲבָדֶיךָ הוֹרִדֻהוּ אֵלָי וְאָשִׂימָה עֵינִי

כב עָלָיו: וַנֹּאמֶר אֶל־אֲדֹנִי לֹא־יוּכַל הַנַּעַר לַעֲזֹב אֶת־אָבִיו וְעָזַב אֶת־אָבִיו וָמֵת:

כג וַתֹּאמֶר אֶל־עֲבָדֶיךָ אִם־לֹא יֵרֵד אֲחִיכֶם הַקָּטֹן אִתְּכֶם לֹא תֹסִפוּן לִרְאוֹת פָּנָי:

כד וַיְהִי כִּי עָלִינוּ אֶל־עַבְדְּךָ אָבִי וַנַּגֶּד־לוֹ אֵת דִּבְרֵי אֲדֹנִי: וַיֹּאמֶר אָבִינוּ שֻׁבוּ שִׁבְרוּ־

כה לָנוּ מְעַט־אֹכֶל: וַנֹּאמֶר לֹא נוּכַל לָרֶדֶת אִם־יֵשׁ אָחִינוּ הַקָּטֹן אִתָּנוּ וְיָרַדְנוּ

כו כִּי־לֹא נוּכַל לִרְאוֹת פְּנֵי הָאִישׁ וְאָחִינוּ הַקָּטֹן אֵינֶנּוּ אִתָּנוּ: וַיֹּאמֶר עַבְדְּךָ אָבִי

כז אֵלֵינוּ אַתֶּם יְדַעְתֶּם כִּי שְׁנַיִם יָלְדָה־לִּי אִשְׁתִּי: וַיֵּצֵא הָאֶחָד מֵאִתִּי וָאֹמַר אַךְ

כח טָרֹף טֹרָף וְלֹא רְאִיתִיו עַד־הֵנָּה: וּלְקַחְתֶּם גַּם־אֶת־זֶה מֵעִם פָּנַי וְקָרָהוּ אָסוֹן

כט וְהוֹרַדְתֶּם אֶת־שֵׂיבָתִי בְּרָעָה שְׁאֹלָה: וְעַתָּה כְּבֹאִי אֶל־עַבְדְּךָ אָבִי וְהַנַּעַר אֵינֶנּוּ

ל אִתָּנוּ וְנַפְשׁוֹ קְשׁוּרָה בְנַפְשׁוֹ: וְהָיָה כִּרְאוֹתוֹ כִּי־אֵין הַנַּעַר וָמֵת וְהוֹרִידוּ עֲבָדֶיךָ שני

לא אֶת־שֵׂיבַת עַבְדְּךָ אָבִינוּ בְּיָגוֹן שְׁאֹלָה: כִּי עַבְדְּךָ עָרַב אֶת־הַנַּעַר מֵעִם אָבִי

לב לֵאמֹר אִם־לֹא אֲבִיאֶנּוּ אֵלֶיךָ וְחָטָאתִי לְאָבִי כָּל־הַיָּמִים: וְעַתָּה יֵשֶׁב־נָא עַבְדְּךָ

לג תַּחַת הַנַּעַר עֶבֶד לַאדֹנִי וְהַנַּעַר יַעַל עִם־אֶחָיו: כִּי־אֵיךְ אֶעֱלֶה אֶל־אָבִי וְהַנַּעַר

לד אֵינֶנּוּ אִתִּי פֶּן אֶרְאֶה בָרָע אֲשֶׁר יִמְצָא אֶת־אָבִי: וְלֹא־יָכֹל יוֹסֵף לְהִתְאַפֵּק

ה   לְכֹל הַנִּצָּבִים עָלָיו וַיִּקְרָא הוֹצִיאוּ כָל־אִישׁ מֵעָלָי וְלֹא־עָמַד אִישׁ אִתּוֹ בְּהִתְוַדַּע

ב   יוֹסֵף אֶל־אֶחָיו: וַיִּתֵּן אֶת־קֹלוֹ בִּבְכִי וַיִּשְׁמְעוּ מִצְרַיִם וַיִּשְׁמַע בֵּית פַּרְעֹה:

רש"י

הָיָה מוֹצִיא דָּבָר שֶׁקֶּר מִפִּיו, אָמַר: אִם הוּא אֹמֵר לוֹ שֶׁהוּא קַיָּם, יֹאמַר: הֲבִיאֵהוּ אֶצְלִי. לְבַדּוֹ לְאִמּוֹ. מֵאוֹתָהּ הָאֵם אֵין לוֹ עוֹד אָח:

כב. וְעָזַב אֶת־אָבִיו וָמֵת. אִם יַעֲזֹב אֶת אָבִיו דּוֹאֲגִים אָנוּ שֶׁמָּא יָמוּת בַּדֶּרֶךְ, שֶׁהֲרֵי אִמּוֹ בַּדֶּרֶךְ מֵתָה:

כט. וְקָרָהוּ אָסוֹן. שֶׁהַשָּׂטָן מְקַטְרֵג בִּשְׁעַת הַסַּכָּנָה. וְהוֹרַדְתֶּם אֶת שֵׂיבָתִי וְגו'. עַכְשָׁיו כְּשֶׁהוּא אֶצְלִי אֲנִי

מִתְנַחֵם בּוֹ עַל אִמּוֹ וְעַל אָחִיו, וְאִם יָמוּת זֶה, דּוֹמֶה עָלַי שֶׁשְּׁלָשְׁתָּן מֵתוּ בְּיוֹם אֶחָד:

לא. וְהָיָה כִּרְאוֹתוֹ כִּי אֵין הַנַּעַר וָמֵת. אָבִיו מִצַּעֲרוֹ:

לב. כִּי עַבְדְּךָ עָרַב אֶת הַנַּעַר. וְאִם תֹּאמַר, לָמָּה אֲנִי נִכְנָס לְתִגָּר יוֹתֵר מִשְּׁאָר אַחַי? הֵם כֻּלָּם מִבַּחוּץ, וַאֲנִי נִתְקַשַּׁרְתִּי בְּקֶשֶׁר חָזָק לִהְיוֹת מְנֻדֶּה בִּשְׁנֵי עוֹלָמוֹת:

לג. יֵשֶׁב נָא עַבְדְּךָ וְגו'. לְכָל דָּבָר אֲנִי מְעֻלֶּה מִמֶּנּוּ, לִגְבוּרָה וּלְמִלְחָמָה וּלְשַׁמֵּשׁ:

פרק מה

א. לְהִתְאַפֵּק לְכֹל הַנִּצָּבִים. לֹא יָכוֹל לִסְבֹּל שֶׁיִּהְיוּ מִצְרִים נִצָּבִים עָלָיו וְשׁוֹמְעִין שֶׁאֶחָיו מִתְבַּיְּשִׁין בְּהִוָּדְעוֹ לָהֶם:

ב. וַיִּשְׁמַע בֵּית פַּרְעֹה. בֵּיתוֹ שֶׁל פַּרְעֹה, כְּלוֹמַר אֲנָשָׁיו וְעַבְדָּיו:

DISCUSSION

➡ which the brothers were placed became more and more similar to that of Joseph many years earlier, and they slowly began to feel the distress of one whose fate has been placed in the hands of a powerful figure. However, just when it might appear that their younger brother, the son of Rachel, has sinned, they do not reject or abandon him, but struggle on his behalf and refuse to let him remain in Egypt under any circumstances. This transformation of the brothers reaches its climax with Judah's offer, as he is prepared to give his life for Benjamin. After this gesture, which serves as a kind of atonement for the sale of Joseph, Joseph cannot restrain himself any longer. Indeed, there is no more need to do so, and he finally discloses his identity to his brothers.

3 **Joseph said to his brothers: I am Joseph,** and then immediately asked: **Does my father still live?**[D] **And his brothers could not answer him because they were alarmed before him.** Joseph, of course, knew who they were the entire time, but the brothers were overcome by confusion and fear over the sudden revelation. Until now, they considered Joseph to be lost, even if they may have dreamt that one day they would discover him as a slave somewhere and possibly even free him. However, now he is present before them as an eminent personality, their apparent antagonist, the ruler in whose hands their fate rests.

4 **Joseph said to his brothers: Please approach me, and they approached** silently, as they were not yet able to speak. **He said** again: **I am Joseph your brother whom you sold to Egypt.** In this repetition he is no longer revealing his identity; rather, Joseph is emphasizing that he is still their brother.

5 However, **now** all that is in the past; **do not be sad, and do not become incensed with yourselves that you sold me here; it was for sustenance that God sent me before you.** If you wish, you can consider the entire matter from a different perspective. Look at all that transpired in the wake of the sale. Because I was taken to Egypt, I am now capable of supporting our family.

6 **For these** past **two years the famine is in the midst of the land, and there are an additional five years during which there shall be neither plowing nor harvest,** in accordance with Pharaoh's dream.

7 **God sent me before you to establish for you a remnant in the land,** as I will support you, **and to sustain you for a great deliverance.**

8 Joseph continues to placate his brothers: **Now,** you should know that **it was not you who sent me here, but God,** as you were simply the intermediaries for this great mission. **He made me into a father to Pharaoh,** a guardian of his kingdom, **and into a lord for all his house, and ruler over the entire land of Egypt.**

Third aliya

9 **Hurry and go up to my father and say to him: So said your son Joseph: God has made me lord for all Egypt.** Now, **come down to me**[D] **to Egypt; do not tarry.**

10 **You will live in the land of Goshen,**[D] which is on the eastern border of Egypt, near the land of Canaan, **and you will be near to me, you, and your children, and your children's children,**

and your flocks, and your cattle, and everything that you have.

11 **I will sustain you there,** as the Egyptian harvest was more stable than that of Canaan. Even if the produce of this harvest

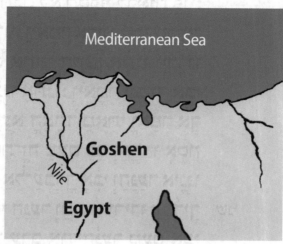

Goshen

does not suffice, I will make sure to provide you with all of your needs. **For there are an additional five years of famine; lest you become impoverished, you, and your household, and everything that you have.** If you have to continue to purchase food from Egypt, you will eventually be forced to sell all your property.

12 **Behold, your eyes see, and the eyes of my brother Benjamin, that it is my mouth that is speaking to you** in your language.[4] Prior to this point, Joseph had spoken in Egyptian, and the dialogue with the brothers had proceeded with the assistance of an interpreter. In addition to his change of language, here he soothes his brothers by equating them to Benjamin, his maternal brother, who did not participate in the plot against him.

13 **You shall tell my father all my glory in Egypt, and all that you have seen** with regard to my capabilities as a ruler; **hurry and bring my father down here.**[D]

— DISCUSSION —

45:3 | **Does my father still live?:** This question is difficult to understand, as the brothers had already told Joseph several times that Jacob was alive (see, e.g., 43:28 and 44:20). Perhaps he asked again due to the emotion of the moment, especially in light of Judah's moving plea. If so, it was not a calculated question (see Sforno). Since

he had not had a close, loving relationship with his brothers, whereas he did love his father, in his current emotional state he wondered again about his father's well-being. Moreover, now he could finally refer to him in the appropriate manner as "my father," rather than "your father" (see 43:27). Alternatively, perhaps his inquiry

stemmed from suspicion that his father had actually died and that the brothers had lied to him to support their claims and arouse his mercy. Consequently, Joseph sought to resolve the uncertainty that plagued him (see *Keli Yakar*).

ג וַיֹּאמֶר יוֹסֵף אֶל־אֶחָיו אֲנִי יוֹסֵף הַעוֹד אָבִי חָי וְלֹא־יָכְלוּ אֶחָיו לַעֲנוֹת אֹתוֹ כִּי
ד נִבְהֲלוּ מִפָּנָיו: וַיֹּאמֶר יוֹסֵף אֶל־אֶחָיו גְּשׁוּ־נָא אֵלַי וַיִּגָּשׁוּ וַיֹּאמֶר אֲנִי יוֹסֵף אֲחִיכֶם
ה אֲשֶׁר־מְכַרְתֶּם אֹתִי מִצְרָיְמָה: וְעַתָּה אַל־תֵּעָצְבוּ וְאַל־יִחַר בְּעֵינֵיכֶם כִּי־מְכַרְתֶּם
ו אֹתִי הֵנָּה כִּי לְמִחְיָה שְׁלָחַנִי אֱלֹהִים לִפְנֵיכֶם: כִּי־זֶה שְׁנָתַיִם הָרָעָב בְּקֶרֶב הָאָרֶץ
ז וְעוֹד חָמֵשׁ שָׁנִים אֲשֶׁר אֵין־חָרִישׁ וְקָצִיר: וַיִּשְׁלָחֵנִי אֱלֹהִים לִפְנֵיכֶם לָשׂוּם לָכֶם
ח שְׁאֵרִית בָּאָרֶץ וּלְהַחֲיוֹת לָכֶם לִפְלֵיטָה גְּדֹלָה: וְעַתָּה לֹא־אַתֶּם שְׁלַחְתֶּם אֹתִי שלישי
הֵנָּה כִּי הָאֱלֹהִים וַיְשִׂימֵנִי לְאָב לְפַרְעֹה וּלְאָדוֹן לְכָל־בֵּיתוֹ וּמֹשֵׁל בְּכָל־אֶרֶץ
ט מִצְרָיִם: מַהֲרוּ וַעֲלוּ אֶל־אָבִי וַאֲמַרְתֶּם אֵלָיו כֹּה אָמַר בִּנְךָ יוֹסֵף שָׂמַנִי אֱלֹהִים
י לְאָדוֹן לְכָל־מִצְרָיִם רְדָה אֵלַי אַל־תַּעֲמֹד: וְיָשַׁבְתָּ בְאֶרֶץ־גֹּשֶׁן וְהָיִיתָ קָרוֹב אֵלַי
יא אַתָּה וּבָנֶיךָ וּבְנֵי בָנֶיךָ וְצֹאנְךָ וּבְקָרְךָ וְכָל־אֲשֶׁר־לָךְ: וְכִלְכַּלְתִּי אֹתְךָ שָׁם כִּי־עוֹד
יב חָמֵשׁ שָׁנִים רָעָב פֶּן־תִּוָּרֵשׁ אַתָּה וּבֵיתְךָ וְכָל־אֲשֶׁר־לָךְ: וְהִנֵּה עֵינֵיכֶם רֹאוֹת
יג וְעֵינֵי אָחִי בִנְיָמִין כִּי־פִי הַמְדַבֵּר אֲלֵיכֶם: וְהִגַּדְתֶּם לְאָבִי אֶת־כָּל־כְּבוֹדִי בְּמִצְרַיִם

רש״י

וּבְנֵי בֵּיתוֹ, וְאֵין זֶה לְשׁוֹן בַּיִת מַמָּשׁ, אֶלָּא כְּמוֹ ״בֵּית יִשְׂרָאֵל״, ״בֵּית יְהוּדָה״, מֵישְׁנִיד״א בְּלַעַז:

ג| **כִּי נִבְהֲלוּ.** מִפְּנֵי הַבּוּשָׁה:

ד| **גְּשׁוּ נָא אֵלַי.** רָאָה אוֹתָם נְסוֹגִים לְאָחוֹר, אָמַר, עַכְשָׁיו אַחַי נִכְלָמִים, קָרָא לָהֶם בְּלָשׁוֹן רַכָּה וְתַחֲנוּנִים וְהֶרְאָה לָהֶם שֶׁהוּא מָהוּל:

ה| **לְמִחְיָה.** לִהְיוֹת לָכֶם לְמִחְיָה:

ו| **כִּי זֶה שְׁנָתַיִם הָרָעָב.** עָבְרוּ מִשְּׁנֵי הָרָעָב:

ח| **לְאָב.** חָבֵר וּפַטְרוֹן:

ט| **וַעֲלוּ אֶל אָבִי.** אֶרֶץ יִשְׂרָאֵל גְּבוֹהָה מִכָּל הָאֲרָצוֹת:

יא| **פֶּן תִּוָּרֵשׁ.** ״דִּלְמָא תִתְמַסְכַּן״, לְשׁוֹן: ״מוֹרִישׁ וּמַעֲשִׁיר״ (שמואל א׳ ב, ז):

יב| **וְהִנֵּה עֵינֵיכֶם רֹאוֹת.** בִּכְבוֹדִי, וְשֶׁאֲנִי אֲחִיכֶם שֶׁאֲנִי מָהוּל, וְעוֹד, ״כִּי פִי הַמְדַבֵּר אֲלֵיכֶם״ בִּלְשׁוֹן הַקֹּדֶשׁ: **וְעֵינֵי אָחִי בִנְיָמִין.** הִשְׁוָה אֶת כֻּלָּם יַחַד, לוֹמַר כְּשֵׁם שֶׁאֵין בְּלִבִּי שִׂנְאָה לְבִנְיָמִין אָחִי, שֶׁלֹּא הָיָה בִּמְכִירָתִי, כָּךְ אֵין בְּלִבִּי עֲלֵיכֶם:

BACKGROUND

45:10| **Goshen:** The majority of historians identify Goshen with the northeastern delta of the Nile River, spanning from the Lake of Manzala in the north to Wadi Tumilat in the south, and from the lakes in the east to the Nile in the west. This is an area that receives some of the most abundant rainfall in all Egypt, and therefore it has high-quality arable land. This conjecture is supported by the archaeological discovery of the Papyrus Anastasi VI from the thirteenth century BCE, which describes this area as agriculturally fertile. Furthermore, in this area there were several locations with Semitic rather than Egyptian names, such as Migdol, Baal Tzefon, and Sukot.

DISCUSSION

45:9| **Come down to me:** Joseph's suggestion was both reasonable and practical. It can be assumed that this was not a spontaneous idea but a plan that he had already formulated earlier. Due to Joseph's exalted position in Egypt and the fact that the famine had reached Canaan as well, it would only be natural for him to have considered how he could support his father and family. However, in order to bring the plan to fruition the entire family had to move to Egypt.

14 **He fell upon the neck of his brother Benjamin,** which he was finally able to do freely, **and wept** over his reuniting with his maternal brother; **and Benjamin wept upon his neck,**[D] following his elder brother's example.

15 **He** then **kissed all his brothers**[D] **and wept upon them.** As mentioned previously, although Joseph was a powerful ruler he could quickly become emotional.[5] The brothers' shock at the discovery that the ruler of the land was none other than Joseph was replaced by their concern that he might take revenge upon them, a worry that had not abated even many years after they had sold him. They knew that if he sought to punish them, justice would be on his side. **And** only **afterward,** upon hearing his statement and seeing his tears and emotion as he approached them, their fears were assuaged, and **his brothers spoke with him.**

16 **The news was heard in Pharaoh's house.** The men who had been sent outside and were now stationed in the courtyard could hear Joseph crying. Presumably, some had listened through the window or in some similar manner. Consequently, the members of Pharaoh's household heard the news, **saying: Joseph's brothers have come.** Although they could not understand the language that was spoken, they grasped the essence of what had transpired. **And it was good in the eyes of Pharaoh and the eyes of his servants.** Until now, Pharaoh and the Egyptians had considered Joseph no more than a slave, who presumably came from a family of slaves. Despite his proficiency and success, it was still a disgrace for them to have a slave as their ruler. Therefore, they were pleased to hear that Joseph in fact came from a distinguished family and had originally been a free man.

17 **Pharaoh said to Joseph: Say to your brothers: Do this: Load your animals, and go, and come to the land of Canaan.** This suggestion is similar to Joseph's. Pharaoh might have thought of it independently or heard about the idea from Joseph; either way, he agreed to the plan.

18 **Take your father and** the members of **your households** from Canaan, **and come to me** and remain in my care in Egypt; **I will give you the finest of the land of Egypt, and eat the fat of the land.** As Joseph's brothers and family, you will enjoy all of the benefits that I can offer to those with connections to the royal palace.

19 *Fourth aliya* To Joseph, Pharaoh said: **You are commanded, do this: Take wagons from the land of Egypt.** Wagons were rare in Canaan, as they were generally used in cultures more developed than that of shepherds such as the family of Jacob. Use these wagons **for your children and for your wives,** so that they not experience discomfort on their journey to Egypt. As for the males, they can ride on animals. **And** in this manner, **convey your father and come.**

20 **Your eye should not spare your vessels.** Do not be concerned about any possessions that might be damaged on your journey, or about items that you are forced to leave at home. In addition, do not travel slowly due to worry over losing your property, **for the bounty of the entire land of Egypt is yours,** and all your requirements will be met at my expense.

21 **The sons of Israel did so** and prepared to return home. **Joseph gave them wagons by Pharaoh's order, and he gave them provisions for the journey.** The use of wagons together with strong animals allowed them to take plenty of food, as well as other items.

22 **To all of them he gave each man changes of garments** for the journey, **and to Benjamin he gave three hundred pieces of silver,** as a special gift to his beloved brother, **and five changes of garments.**

23 **To his father he sent** a gift **as follows: Ten donkeys laden with the bounty of Egypt,** including clothing, vessels, and preserved foods, **and ten female donkeys laden with grain, and bread, and food for his father for the journey.** During their trip to Canaan, the brothers would certainly endeavor to minimize the amount of food they consumed and to reach their destination as fast as possible. In contrast, the family's journey to Egypt with the elderly Jacob, their wives, children, and all of their possessions would take significantly longer. Therefore, that journey required far more provisions.

24 **He sent his brothers** back to their home, **and they went.** Following their shocking experience in Egypt, the brothers were liable to blame each other for the selling of Joseph during the trip home. Reuben and Judah both had a certain amount

DISCUSSION

45:13 | **And bring my father down here:** Joseph's speech expressed his strong faith in God and his understanding of his role in these events. The names he gave to his sons also indicate that he interprets his rise to power as due to the hand of God (41:51–52). Moreover, in his new role as ruler of Egypt, he saw the dreams of his youth fulfilled, not only when his brothers prostrated themselves before him, but also in his rise to the highest level of leadership possible in the land, second only to Pharaoh himself. Those dreams, which could have been dismissed as childish fantasies or delusions of grandeur, ultimately symbolized his true mission in life and his destiny. Joseph did not credit the development of events to his own personal talents but to divine providence. Without God's assistance, he would have remained a servant of Potifar, and even if he had eventually been freed from slavery, the chances of him becoming an important personage in Egypt were minute. Only a higher power was capable of taking the young son of Jacob, who dwelled in the land of Canaan, and transforming him into the ruler over the entire land of Egypt.

This perspective caused Joseph to consider his brothers' actions in a new light. It is possible that initially, when he still longed to return

יד וְאֵת כָּל־אֲשֶׁר רְאִיתֶם וּמִהַרְתֶּם וְהוֹרַדְתֶּם אֶת־אָבִי הֵנָּה: וַיִּפֹּל עַל־צַוְּארֵי

טו בִנְיָמִן־אָחִיו וַיֵּבְךְּ וּבִנְיָמִן בָּכָה עַל־צַוָּארָיו: וַיְנַשֵּׁק לְכָל־אֶחָיו וַיֵּבְךְּ עֲלֵהֶם וְאַחֲרֵי

טז כֵן דִּבְּרוּ אֶחָיו אִתּוֹ: וְהַקֹּל נִשְׁמַע בֵּית פַּרְעֹה לֵאמֹר בָּאוּ אֲחֵי יוֹסֵף וַיִּיטַב בְּעֵינֵי

יז פַרְעֹה וּבְעֵינֵי עֲבָדָיו: וַיֹּאמֶר פַּרְעֹה אֶל־יוֹסֵף אֱמֹר אֶל־אַחֶיךָ זֹאת עֲשׂוּ טַעֲנוּ

יח אֶת־בְּעִירְכֶם וּלְכוּ־בֹאוּ אַרְצָה כְּנָעַן: וּקְחוּ אֶת־אֲבִיכֶם וְאֶת־בָּתֵּיכֶם וּבֹאוּ אֵלָי

יט וְאֶתְּנָה לָכֶם אֶת־טוּב אֶרֶץ מִצְרַיִם וְאִכְלוּ אֶת־חֵלֶב הָאָרֶץ: וְאַתָּה צֻוֵּיתָה זֹאת **רביעי**

עֲשׂוּ קְחוּ־לָכֶם מֵאֶרֶץ מִצְרַיִם עֲגָלוֹת לְטַפְּכֶם וְלִנְשֵׁיכֶם וּנְשָׂאתֶם אֶת־אֲבִיכֶם

כ וּבָאתֶם: וְעֵינְכֶם אַל־תָּחֹס עַל־כְּלֵיכֶם כִּי־טוּב כָּל־אֶרֶץ מִצְרַיִם לָכֶם הוּא:

כא וַיַּעֲשׂוּ־כֵן בְּנֵי יִשְׂרָאֵל וַיִּתֵּן לָהֶם יוֹסֵף עֲגָלוֹת עַל־פִּי פַרְעֹה וַיִּתֵּן לָהֶם צֵדָה לַדָּרֶךְ:

כב לְכֻלָּם נָתַן לָאִישׁ חֲלִפוֹת שְׂמָלֹת וּלְבִנְיָמִן נָתַן שְׁלֹשׁ מֵאוֹת כֶּסֶף וְחָמֵשׁ חֲלִפֹת

כג שְׂמָלֹת: וּלְאָבִיו שָׁלַח כְּזֹאת עֲשָׂרָה חֲמֹרִים נֹשְׂאִים מִטּוּב מִצְרָיִם וְעֶשֶׂר אֲתֹנֹת

כד נֹשְׂאֹת בָּר וָלֶחֶם וּמָזוֹן לְאָבִיו לַדָּרֶךְ: וַיְשַׁלַּח אֶת־אֶחָיו וַיֵּלֵכוּ וַיֹּאמֶר אֲלֵהֶם

רש"י

יד וַיִּפֹּל עַל צַוָּארֵי בִנְיָמִן אָחִיו וַיֵּבְךְּ. עַל שְׁנֵי מִקְדָּשׁוֹת שֶׁעֲתִידִין לִהְיוֹת בְּחֶלְקוֹ שֶׁל בִּנְיָמִין וְסוֹפָן לַחֱרַב: וּבִנְיָמִן בָּכָה עַל צַוָּארָיו. עַל מִשְׁכָּן שִׁילֹה שֶׁעֲתִיד לִהְיוֹת בְּחֶלְקוֹ שֶׁל יוֹסֵף וְסוֹפוֹ לַחֱרַב:

טו וְאַחֲרֵי כֵן. מֵאַחַר שֶׁרְאָהוּ בּוֹכֶה וְלִבּוֹ שָׁלֵם עִמָּהֶם, "דִּבְּרוּ אֶחָיו אִתּוֹ", שֶׁמִּתְּחִלָּה הָיוּ בּוֹשִׁים מִמֶּנּוּ:

טז וְהַקֹּל נִשְׁמַע בֵּית פַּרְעֹה. כְּמוֹ בְּבֵית פַּרְעֹה, וְזֶהוּ לְשׁוֹן בֵּית מַמָּשׁ:

יז טַעֲנוּ אֶת בְּעִירְכֶם. תְּבוּאָה:

יח אֶת טוּב אֶרֶץ מִצְרַיִם. אֶרֶץ גֹּשֶׁן. נִבֵּא וְאֵינוֹ יוֹדֵעַ מַה נִבֵּא, סוֹפָם לַעֲשׂוֹתָהּ כִּמְצוּלָה שֶׁאֵין בָּהּ דָּגִים: חֵלֶב הָאָרֶץ. כָּל "חֵלֶב" לְשׁוֹן מֵיטַב הוּא:

יט וְאַתָּה צֻוֵּיתָה. מִפִּי לוֹמַר לָהֶם: "זֹאת עֲשׂוּ", כָּךְ אֱמֹר לָהֶם שֶׁבִּרְשׁוּתִי הוּא:

כג שָׁלַח כְּזֹאת. כְּחֶשְׁבּוֹן הַזֶּה. וּמַה הוּא הַחֶשְׁבּוֹן? "עֲשָׂרָה חֲמֹרִים" וְגוֹ': מִטּוּב מִצְרָיִם. מָצִינוּ בַּתַּלְמוּד שֶׁשָּׁלַח לוֹ יַיִן יָשָׁן, שֶׁדַּעַת זְקֵנִים נוֹחָה הֵימֶנּוּ. וּמִדְרַשׁ אַגָּדָה, גְּרִיסִין שֶׁל פּוֹל: בָּר וָלֶחֶם. כְּתַרְגּוּמוֹ: וּמָזוֹן. לִפְתָּן:

DISCUSSION

↝ to his father's home, he was angry with them. However, over time it became clear to him that God was directing his life and watching over him. He therefore interpreted the difficulties he had to overcome not only as the required path for the actualization of his dreams and his personal rise to greatness, but also as a process preparing him for the fulfillment of his mission in life. In his speech here, he does not embellish the past, nor does he express forgiveness to his brothers; that occurred only several years later, following the death of his father, when they specifically requested his pardon (see 50:15–20). Instead, he presented to them his interpretation

of events, that regardless of the morality of their conduct, both he and they were messengers of God, and he encouraged them to view their history in a similar manner. Since they were all directed by a higher power, it would be wrong to quarrel over the past. Rather, they should focus on fulfilling their duties from this point onward, while attending to the well-being of Jacob's family.

45:14 | And Benjamin wept upon his neck: Benjamin's yearning for Joseph is reflected in the names he gave to his sons, through which he sought to remember his lost brother (see 46:21, *Sota* 36b, and Rashi, 43:30).

45:15 | He kissed all his brothers: The act of Joseph kissing his brothers is reminiscent of Esau kissing Jacob after an absence of twenty years (33:4). In both instances, the kiss of the injured brother indicates that he did not bear any grudge against those who harmed him, and that there was no purpose in arousing an old conflict. However, in both cases, a one-time encounter would not suffice to resolve the conflict. With regard to Esau and Jacob, there remained a permanent distance between the pair, and here too, the brothers were still concerned after the death of Jacob that Joseph might harbor enmity against them (50:15).

of mercy on their brother and attempted to delay or foil the attempt to kill him, but it is unclear how many of the other brothers, aside from Judah (see 37:26), were active participants in the sale and how many merely refrained from preventing it. Apparently, until now they considered themselves active participants. Now, when it became evident that Joseph was alive and his status was more powerful than theirs, they might use the journey to rehash past events.[6] Consequently, **he said to them: Do not quarrel on the way.**

The Brothers Return to Jacob
GENESIS 45:25–28

For many years, Jacob's mourning for his son differed from that of one whose loved one died under ordinary circumstances. Generally, the deceased is slowly forgotten over time, whereas Jacob refused to be consoled even as the years passed, perhaps due to some small hope that Joseph may not have died. It is unknown how much this mourning affected his physical and mental capabilities and whether it impaired his daily functioning. However, from his statement in the continuation of the narrative (47:9), it can be inferred that Jacob's later years were more difficult than those of his ancestors.

25 **They went up from Egypt, and they came to the land of Canaan, to Jacob their father.**

26 **They told him, saying: Joseph still lives, and he is ruler over the entire land of Egypt.** It is difficult to ascertain whether they presented their father with all the details of the story, or whether they preferred not to mention the events for which they themselves were responsible. It is also unknown whether Jacob ever discovered what had actually happened to Joseph.[7] **His heart was faint;** it ceased to beat, and perhaps he fainted out of shock, **because he did not believe them,** as he was not prepared for this astonishing news. Alternatively, he did not trust them and suspected that they had invented the story for some personal benefit.

27 Due to Jacob's reaction, **they spoke to him** in detail **all the words of Joseph that he had said to them, and he saw the wagons that Joseph sent to convey him.** The presence of the Egyptian wagons, which generally were used for military functions and were not easily transported out of Egypt, corroborated their story. **And the spirit of Jacob their father was revived** from his faintness, as he gradually became convinced that the report was indeed true. The knowledge that Joseph was alive shocked him, but also revived him.

28 **Israel said:** It is **enough** that **Joseph my son is still alive;** I need no more than this.[8] **I will go and see him**[D] **before I die.** Jacob's transformation is expressed in the change of his name back to Israel, the name given to him by God (35:10).

Fifth aliya

Jacob and His Family Descend to Egypt
GENESIS 46:1–27

Somewhat spontaneously, Jacob decides to leave the land of Canaan to see his beloved son. His decision to descend to Egypt without delay attests to his determination to see the son for whom he had mourned so many years.

Many years earlier, Jacob was forced to leave the land of Canaan and travel to Aram out of fear of his brother Esau. He now chooses to leave the land of his own accord in order to see his son. This departure will certainly be accompanied with serious reservations, such as his uncertainty with regard to whether, and when, he will return, and whether his family will be able to preserve their unique character. Although the Torah does not describe his concerns about the journey, they can be inferred from the calming statements of God, who reveals Himself to Jacob at this juncture.

46 1 **Israel and everything that he had traveled.**[D] He likely departed from Hebron, where he lived, **and he came to Beersheba,** which was located in the south, on the road to Egypt. Apparently, he specifically chose to pass this important landmark, where both Abraham and Isaac had constructed altars, just as he had on his initial journey to Haran (28:10). **And there he slaughtered offerings to the God of his father Isaac.**[D]

2 **God spoke to Israel in the visions of the night,** either a dream or a vision similar to a dream, **and said: Jacob, Jacob; and he said: Here I am.**

3 Since Jacob did not see an image but merely heard a voice, God explicitly states that He is the one speaking. **He said: I am the God, the God of your father; do not fear to go down to Egypt, as I will make you a great nation there.** This promise, that the family of Jacob would be transformed into a nation in Egypt, addressed the concern that they might assimilate into the society of this foreign land.

4 **I will go down with you to Egypt** and help you there; **and I will also take you up again** from Egypt, though not necessarily in your lifetime. You will merit seeing your beloved son, **and** furthermore, **Joseph shall place his hand over your eyes,** as he will care for you when you die. It is likely that the act of a son placing his hand over his father's eyes was part of the preparation ceremony for burial. This final contact of son and father was an expression of closeness and honor. To this day there is a custom among some communities to perform this action upon the death of a father, based on this verse.

5 **Jacob arose from Beersheba.** It was easier for him to leave the land of Canaan with God's approval and His promise to accompany him to a foreign land. **And the sons of Israel conveyed**

כה אל־תרגזו בדרך: ויעלו ממצרים ויבאו ארץ כנען אל־יעקב אביהם:
כו ויגדו לו לאמר עוד יוסף חי וכי־הוא משל בכל־ארץ מצרים ויפג לבו כי לא־
האמין להם: וידברו אליו את כל־דברי יוסף אשר דבר אלהם וירא את־
העגלות אשר־שלח יוסף לשאת אתו ותחי רוח יעקב אביהם: ויאמר ישראל חמישי
רב עוד־יוסף בני חי אלכה ואראנו בטרם אמות: ויסע ישראל וכל־אשר־לו
ויבא בארה שבע ויזבח זבחים לאלהי אביו יצחק: ויאמר אלהים | לישראל
במראת הלילה ויאמר יעקב | יעקב ויאמר הנני: ויאמר אנכי האל אלהי
אביך אל־תירא מרדה מצרימה כי־לגוי גדול אשימך שם: אנכי ארד עמך
מצרימה ואנכי אעלך גם־עלה ויוסף ישית ידו על־עיניך: ויקם יעקב מבאר
שבע וישאו בני־ישראל את־יעקב אביהם ואת־טפם ואת־נשיהם בעגלות

(Margin markers printed beside the lines above, top to bottom: כה, כו, כז, כח, ו א, ב, ג, ד, ה.)

רש"י

כד| **אל תרגזו בדרך.** אל תתעסקו בדבר הלכה שלא תרגז עליכם הדרך. דבר אחר, אל תפסיעו פסיעה גסה, והכניסו חמה לעיר. ולפי פשוטו של מקרא יש לומר, לפי שהיו נכלמים היה דואג שמא יריבו בדרך על דבר מכירתו להתווכח זה עם זה ולומר: על ידך נמכר, אתה ספרת לשון הרע עליו וגרמת לנו לשנאתו:

כו| **וכי הוא משל.** ואשר הוא מושל: **ויפג לבו.** נחלף לבו והלך מלהאמין, לא היה לבו פונה אל הדברים, לשון 'מפיגין טעמן' בלשון משנה, וכמו: "מאין הפגות" (איכה ג, מט), "וריחו לא נמר" (ירמיה מח, יא) מתרגמינן: "וריחיה לא פג":

כז| **את כל דברי יוסף.** סימן מסר להם במה היה עוסק כשפירש ממנו, בפרשת עגלה ערופה, וזהו שאמר: "וירא את העגלות אשר שלח יוסף" ולא נאמר: 'אשר שלח פרעה': **ותחי רוח יעקב.** שרתה עליו שכינה שפירשה ממנו:

כח| **רב.** רב לי עוד שמחה וחדוה הואיל ו"עוד יוסף בני חי":

פרק מו

א| **בארה שבע.** כמו לבאר שבע, ה"א בסוף תיבה במקום למ"ד בתחלתה: **לאלהי אביו יצחק.** חייב אדם בכבוד אביו יותר מבכבוד זקנו, לפיכך תלה ביצחק ולא באברהם:

ב| **יעקב יעקב.** לשון חבה:

ג| **אל תירא מרדה מצרימה.** לפי שהיה מצר על שנזקק לצאת לחוצה לארץ:

ד| **ואנכי אעלך.** הבטיחו להיות נקבר בארץ:

Jacob their father, and their children, and their wives, in the wagons that Pharaoh had sent to convey him. The sons rode on the animals, while the elderly and frail Jacob sat in the wagons together with the wives and children.

DISCUSSION

45:28| **Joseph my son is still alive; I will go and see him:** One of the reasons that Joseph invited his father to Egypt was that the ruler was apparently not permitted to travel to Canaan even for a visit. Jacob understood that Joseph had to remain where he was. Therefore, when he received the invitation he did not delay and did not analyze the long-term consequences for his family of descending to Egypt. Earlier, he had prevented the brothers from traveling to Egypt; now he enthusiastically accepted the opportunity to see his beloved son.

46:1| **Traveled:** Here and in many later verses, Jacob is referred to as Israel, a name that signifies greatness and authority. The change of names between Israel and Jacob in these passages is significant (see Ramban, verse 2).

And he slaughtered offerings to the God of his father Isaac: It is interesting that the Torah here refers to God specifically as the God of Isaac, the one patriarch who did not leave the land of Canaan (see 24:8, 26:2–3). Perhaps the mention of Isaac is indicative of Jacob's desire to elicit a response from God about the rightness of this trip (see Radak and Sforno). Indeed, God answers this request and reveals Himself to Jacob.

6 **They took their livestock,** which as shepherds was their primary possession, **and their** movable **property that they had acquired in the land of Canaan, and they came to Egypt: Jacob, and all his descendants with him.**

7 **His sons and his sons' sons** came **with him, his daughters,** his daughter and daughters-in-law, as the Torah mentions only one daughter born to Jacob: Dina, **and his sons' daughters,** his granddaughter and the wives of his grandsons, as in the following verses only one granddaughter is mentioned: Serah[9] (see 46:17). **And all his descendants he brought with him to Egypt.**

8 **And these are the names of the children of Israel,** the children of Jacob, who ultimately became the heads of families of the Jewish people, **who were coming to Egypt, Jacob and his sons: the firstborn of Jacob, Reuben.**

9 **And the sons of Reuben: Hanokh, Palu, Hetzron, and Karmi.**

10 **The sons of Simeon: Jemuel, Yamin, Ohad, Yakhin, Tzohar, and Shaul, son of the Canaanite woman.**[D] This unusual mention of a Canaanite woman might serve to emphasize that none of the other children were the offspring of Canaanites.[10]

11 **The sons of Levi: Gershon, Kehat, and Merari.**

12 **The sons of Judah: Er, Onan,**[D] **Shela,** who were born to him from the daughter of Shua, **Peretz and Zerah,** from Tamar; **Er and Onan died in the land of Canaan. And the sons of Peretz,** who married at a young age and therefore had children prior to the descent to Egypt, **were Hetzron and Hamul.**

13 **The sons of Issachar: Tola, Puva, Yov, and Shimron.**

14 **The sons of Zebulun: Sered, Elon, and Yahle'el.**

15 The list of Jacob's children is arranged by the maternal line. **These are the sons of Leah, whom she bore to Jacob in Padan Aram, with his daughter Dina; all the people, his sons and his daughters, thirty-three.**[D]

16 **The sons of Gad: Ziphion, Hagi, Shuni, Etzbon, Eri, Arodi, and Areli.**

17 **The sons of Asher: Yimna, Yishva, Yishvi, Beria, and Serah their sister.** Perhaps this granddaughter is mentioned because she was the only one born in Canaan. Alternatively, there were other unidentified granddaughters as well, but Serah had a unique personality. The Sages relate that she was very close to Jacob and that she merited numerous blessings, including exceptional longevity.[11] **And the sons of Beria: Hever and Malkiel.**

18 **These are the sons of Zilpa, whom Laban gave to Leah his daughter; she bore these to Jacob, sixteen souls.** The sons of Zilpa form the second largest group, almost half the size of the group of the sons of Leah.

19 **The sons of Rachel, Jacob's wife: Joseph and Benjamin.** Although Joseph did not travel with his brothers to Egypt, he is included in the list of the children of Israel who were there after they all arrived.

20 **To Joseph in the land of Egypt were born, whom Asenat, daughter of Poti Fera, priest of On, bore to him, Manasseh and Ephraim.** These three, Joseph and his two sons, are members of the house of Jacob who were already in Egypt. They are mentioned separately again at the conclusion of the count (verse 27).

21 **The sons of Benjamin:**[D] **Bela, Bekher, Ashbel, Gera, Naaman, Ehi, Rosh, Mupim, Hupim, and Ard.**

22 **These are the sons of Rachel, who were born to Jacob; all the people** of the descendants of Rachel, including Joseph and his two sons, **were fourteen.**

23 **The sons of Dan: Hushim.** Although Hushim, who is also called Shuham,[12] was the only son of Dan, he is referred to here as "the sons of Dan," probably due to his numerous descendants, the family of Shuham. For similar usage of the plural terminology, see Numbers 26:8 and II Samuel 23:32.

24 **The sons of Naphtali: Yahtze'el, Guni, Yetzer, and Shilem.**

25 **These are the sons of Bilha, whom Laban gave to Rachel his daughter, and these she bore to Jacob; all the people were seven.** As in the case of Zilpa and Leah, the descendants of Bilha numbered half of those of her mistress, Rachel.

DISCUSSION

46:10 | Son of the Canaanite woman: Unlike their father, the sons of Jacob did not travel great distances in order to search for wives. Nevertheless, they might have been aware of a general directive transmitted as a family tradition that they should not marry Canaanite women. This tradition was not an absolute prohibition; it was more a recommendation to endeavor to marry women from other local nations.

46:12 | The sons of Judah: Er, Onan: Er and Onan are also mentioned in other genealogical lists, despite the fact that they died childless (see Numbers 26:19; I Chronicles 2:3). This illustrates the principle that even children who died are not erased from memory, as they too imprint their legacy on the family history. Moreover, the incident of Judah and Tamar and the concept of levirate marriage allude to the idea that the souls of the dead can appear once again among the living. In this sense, Peretz and Zerah can be considered a kind of replacement for Er and Onan (see Ramban, verse 2).

46:15 | Thirty-three: Many commentaries note that this list contains only thirty-two offspring, not thirty-three. This peculiarity serves as the source for the Sages' statement that an additional daughter was born to Levi upon their entrance into Egypt. This daughter, Yokheved, ↤

ו אֲשֶׁר־שָׁלַח פַּרְעֹה לָשֵׂאת אֹתוֹ: וַיִּקְחוּ אֶת־מִקְנֵיהֶם וְאֶת־רְכוּשָׁם אֲשֶׁר רָכְשׁוּ
ז בְּאֶרֶץ כְּנַעַן וַיָּבֹאוּ מִצְרָיְמָה יַעֲקֹב וְכָל־זַרְעוֹ אִתּוֹ: בָּנָיו וּבְנֵי בָנָיו אִתּוֹ בְּנֹתָיו
ח וּבְנוֹת בָּנָיו וְכָל־זַרְעוֹ הֵבִיא אִתּוֹ מִצְרָיְמָה: וְאֵלֶּה שְׁמוֹת בְּנֵי־יִשְׂרָאֵל
ט הַבָּאִים מִצְרַיְמָה יַעֲקֹב וּבָנָיו בְּכֹר יַעֲקֹב רְאוּבֵן: וּבְנֵי רְאוּבֵן חֲנוֹךְ וּפַלּוּא וְחֶצְרֹן
י יא וְכַרְמִי: וּבְנֵי שִׁמְעוֹן יְמוּאֵל וְיָמִין וְאֹהַד וְיָכִין וְצֹחַר וְשָׁאוּל בֶּן־הַכְּנַעֲנִית: וּבְנֵי
יב לֵוִי גֵּרְשׁוֹן קְהָת וּמְרָרִי: וּבְנֵי יְהוּדָה עֵר וְאוֹנָן וְשֵׁלָה וָפֶרֶץ וָזָרַח וַיָּמָת עֵר וְאוֹנָן
יג בְּאֶרֶץ כְּנַעַן וַיִּהְיוּ בְנֵי־פֶרֶץ חֶצְרֹן וְחָמוּל: וּבְנֵי יִשָּׂשכָר תּוֹלָע וּפֻוָּה וְיוֹב וְשִׁמְרֹן:
יד טו וּבְנֵי זְבֻלוּן סֶרֶד וְאֵלוֹן וְיַחְלְאֵל: אֵלֶּה ׀ בְּנֵי לֵאָה אֲשֶׁר יָלְדָה לְיַעֲקֹב בְּפַדַּן אֲרָם
טז וְאֵת דִּינָה בִתּוֹ כָּל־נֶפֶשׁ בָּנָיו וּבְנוֹתָיו שְׁלֹשִׁים וְשָׁלֹשׁ: וּבְנֵי גָד צִפְיוֹן וְחַגִּי שׁוּנִי
יז וְאֶצְבֹּן עֵרִי וַאֲרוֹדִי וְאַרְאֵלִי: וּבְנֵי אָשֵׁר יִמְנָה וְיִשְׁוָה וְיִשְׁוִי וּבְרִיעָה וְשֶׂרַח אֲחֹתָם
יח וּבְנֵי בְרִיעָה חֶבֶר וּמַלְכִּיאֵל: אֵלֶּה בְּנֵי זִלְפָּה אֲשֶׁר־נָתַן לָבָן לְלֵאָה בִתּוֹ וַתֵּלֶד
יט כ אֶת־אֵלֶּה לְיַעֲקֹב שֵׁשׁ עֶשְׂרֵה נָפֶשׁ: בְּנֵי רָחֵל אֵשֶׁת יַעֲקֹב יוֹסֵף וּבִנְיָמִן: וַיִּוָּלֵד
לְיוֹסֵף בְּאֶרֶץ מִצְרַיִם אֲשֶׁר יָלְדָה־לּוֹ אָסְנַת בַּת־פּוֹטִי פֶרַע כֹּהֵן אֹן אֶת־מְנַשֶּׁה
כא וְאֶת־אֶפְרָיִם: וּבְנֵי בִנְיָמִן בֶּלַע וָבֶכֶר וְאַשְׁבֵּל גֵּרָא וְנַעֲמָן אֵחִי וָרֹאשׁ מֻפִּים וְחֻפִּים
כב כג וָאָרְדְּ: אֵלֶּה בְּנֵי רָחֵל אֲשֶׁר יֻלַּד לְיַעֲקֹב כָּל־נֶפֶשׁ אַרְבָּעָה עָשָׂר: וּבְנֵי־דָן חֻשִׁים:
כד כה וּבְנֵי נַפְתָּלִי יַחְצְאֵל וְגוּנִי וְיֵצֶר וְשִׁלֵּם: אֵלֶּה בְּנֵי בִלְהָה אֲשֶׁר־נָתַן לָבָן לְרָחֵל בִּתּוֹ

רש״י

ו| אֲשֶׁר רָכְשׁוּ בְּאֶרֶץ כְּנַעַן. אֲבָל מַה שֶּׁרָכַשׁ בְּפַדַּן אֲרָם נָתַן הַכֹּל לְעֵשָׂו בִּשְׁבִיל חֶלְקוֹ בִּמְעָרַת הַמַּכְפֵּלָה, אָמַר: נִכְסֵי חוּצָה לָאָרֶץ אֵינָן כְּדַאי לִי, וְזֶהוּ ״אֲשֶׁר כָּרִיתִי לִי״ (להלן נ, ה), הֶעֱמִיד לוֹ צִבּוּרִין שֶׁל זָהָב וָכֶסֶף כְּמִין כְּרִי, וְאָמַר לוֹ: טֹל אֶת אֵלּוּ:

ז| וּבְנוֹת בָּנָיו. סֶרַח בַּת אָשֵׁר וְיוֹכֶבֶד בַּת לֵוִי:

ח| הַבָּאִים מִצְרַיְמָה. עַל שֵׁם הַשָּׁעָה קוֹרֵא לָהֶם הַכָּתוּב ׳בָּאִים׳, וְאֵין לִתְמֹהַּ עַל אֲשֶׁר לֹא כָתַב ׳אֲשֶׁר בָּאוּ׳:

י| בֶּן הַכְּנַעֲנִית. בֶּן דִּינָה שֶׁנִּבְעֲלָה לִכְנַעֲנִי; כְּשֶׁהָרְגוּ אֶת שְׁכֶם לֹא הָיְתָה דִּינָה רוֹצָה לָצֵאת עַד שֶׁנִּשְׁבַּע לָהּ שִׁמְעוֹן שֶׁיִּשָּׂאֶנָּה. בִּרֵאשִׁית רַבָּה (פ, יא):

טו| אֵלֶּה בְּנֵי לֵאָה... וְאֵת דִּינָה בִתּוֹ. הַזְּכָרִים תָּלָה בְּלֵאָה וְהַנְּקֵבוֹת תָּלָה בְּיַעֲקֹב, לְלַמֶּדְךָ, אִשָּׁה מַזְרַעַת תְּחִלָּה יוֹלֶדֶת זָכָר, אִישׁ מַזְרִיעַ תְּחִלָּה יוֹלֶדֶת נְקֵבָה: שְׁלֹשִׁים וְשָׁלֹשׁ. וּבִפְרָטָן אִי אַתָּה מוֹצֵא אֶלָּא שְׁלֹשִׁים וּשְׁנַיִם, אֶלָּא זוֹ יוֹכֶבֶד שֶׁנּוֹלְדָה בֵּין הַחוֹמוֹת בִּכְנִיסָתָן לָעִיר, שֶׁנֶּאֱמַר: ״אֲשֶׁר יָלְדָה אֹתָהּ לְלֵוִי בְּמִצְרָיִם״ (במדבר כו, נט) – לֵדָתָהּ בְּמִצְרַיִם וְאֵין הוֹרָתָהּ בְּמִצְרַיִם:

יט| בְּנֵי רָחֵל אֵשֶׁת יַעֲקֹב. וּבְכֻלָּן לֹא נֶאֱמַר כֵּן! אֶלָּא שֶׁהָיְתָה עִקָּרוֹ שֶׁל בַּיִת:

DISCUSSION

46:21| **The sons of Benjamin:** The Sages interpret all ten of these names as allusions to Benjamin's lost maternal brother, Joseph (*Sota* 36b; Rashi, 43:30).

eventually became the mother of Moses (*Bava Batra* 123b; Rashi). Consequently, she is not included in the list of names of those who journeyed from Canaan, but she is added to the total sum of the children of Leah. Another explanation is that this number includes Jacob himself (Ibn Ezra, verse 23), as indicated by the phrase "all the people."

26 **All the people who were coming with Jacob to Egypt, the products of his loins, aside from the wives of Jacob's sons, all the people were sixty-six.**

27 **The sons of Joseph, who were born to him in Egypt, were two people.** If these are counted together with Joseph, and

Jacob is also included, then **all the people of the house of Jacob, who came to Egypt, were seventy.**[13] Alternatively, the number seventy is rounded up from sixty-nine.[14]

The Reunion between Jacob and Joseph, and the Settlement of the Family in Goshen
GENESIS 46:28–47:12

Joseph's plan is to settle his family in the land of Goshen. In order to accomplish this goal, he prepares them for their initial meeting with Pharaoh by stressing that they should present themselves as shepherds, not farmers. The Egyptian economy was based primarily on farming and the Egyptians tended to look down on shepherds.

This made it likely that Pharaoh would agree to settle them in the peripheral land of Goshen, which was suitable for tending flocks. Settling the family in a separate region with governmental approval would give them the opportunity to grow and develop without interference. It also suited Joseph's plans for the reorganization of the Egyptian economy, which will be recounted subsequently.

28 **He,** Jacob, **sent Judah,** who in their encounter with Joseph had
Sixth
aliya become the brothers' representative, **before him to Joseph, to guide him to Goshen.** Judah was to show them how precisely to get to Goshen, where they would live, in accordance with Joseph's plan (45:10). **And they** subsequently **came to the land of Goshen.**

29 **Joseph harnessed his chariot and went up toward Israel his father to Goshen, and he,** Joseph, **appeared to him,** Jacob, **fell upon his neck,** hugging his father, **and** in his overwhelming emotion, **wept on his neck prodigiously.**

30 **Israel said to Joseph: I can die now** in peace **after my seeing your face, for you are still alive,** as I myself have witnessed. I traveled here to see you, and now that we have reunited, I have received all that I could wish for and I lack nothing in life.

31 **Joseph said to his brothers and to his father's household: I will go up** to the capital city **and tell Pharaoh** the news, **and I will say to him: My brothers, and my father's household who were in the land of Canaan, came to me.**

32 **The men** of my family **are shepherds, as they are people of livestock,** which has always been their profession; **and they have brought their flocks, and their cattle, and everything that they have.** I will tell this to Pharaoh, as he might want to meet you personally.

33 **It shall be when Pharaoh shall call you and say: What is your occupation?**

34 **You shall say: Your servants have been people of livestock from our youth until now, both we and our fathers; so that you may live in the land of Goshen, for every shepherd is an abomination for the Egyptians.**[D] The Egyptians despised shepherding, as it involved the killing of animals, which was against their religion and considered an affront to its believers.

47 1 **Joseph went and told Pharaoh and said: My father and my brothers, and their flocks, and their cattle, and everything that they have, have come from the land of Canaan, and behold, they are in the land of Goshen.** It is possible that there was a general regulation in Egypt that shepherds must dwell in Goshen. If so, Joseph reported to Pharaoh that the directive was carried out in this case.

2 **From among his brothers he took five men, and he presented them before Pharaoh.** Perhaps Joseph did not deem it appropriate to present all of his eleven brothers, and therefore he selected a few to represent the group. The Sages suggest that Joseph specifically chose those who did not appear particularly strong, to avoid the possibility that Pharaoh would draft them into the Egyptian army.[15] Both Joseph and the brothers were interested in maintaining peaceful relations with Pharaoh so that they could remain in Goshen and pursue their livelihoods untroubled.

3 As Joseph expected, **Pharaoh said to his brothers: What is your occupation? They said to Pharaoh,** in accordance with

---

DISCUSSION

46:34 | **For every shepherd is an abomination for the Egyptians:** It can be inferred from several sources that the Egyptians refrained from eating the meat of sheep and cattle. Their attitude toward livestock was similar to that of the Hindus to cows. Therefore, shepherds, who not only use sheep wool but also eat sheep,

were denigrated by Egyptians. This is also the reason why the Egyptians would refuse to dine together with those who eat meat (43:32).

Joseph advised his brothers to tell Pharaoh that their ancestors had also been shepherds. They would thereby be indicating that they did not sin by choosing this profession themselves;

rather, this had been part of their culture and heritage for generations. Pharaoh certainly recognized that there were shepherds in the world, and he was aware that other nations did not necessarily accept the tenets of his faith.

כו וַתֵּלֶד אֶת־אֵלֶּה לְיַעֲקֹב כָּל־נֶפֶשׁ שִׁבְעָה: כָּל־הַנֶּפֶשׁ הַבָּאָה לְיַעֲקֹב מִצְרַיְמָה
כז יֹצְאֵי יְרֵכוֹ מִלְּבַד נְשֵׁי בְנֵי־יַעֲקֹב כָּל־נֶפֶשׁ שִׁשִּׁים וָשֵׁשׁ: וּבְנֵי יוֹסֵף אֲשֶׁר־יֻלַּד־לוֹ
בְמִצְרַיִם נֶפֶשׁ שְׁנָיִם כָּל־הַנֶּפֶשׁ לְבֵית־יַעֲקֹב הַבָּאָה מִצְרַיְמָה שִׁבְעִים:
כח כט וְאֶת־יְהוּדָה שָׁלַח לְפָנָיו אֶל־יוֹסֵף לְהוֹרֹת לְפָנָיו גֹּשְׁנָה וַיָּבֹאוּ אַרְצָה גֹּשֶׁן: וַיֶּאְסֹר מא ששי
יוֹסֵף מֶרְכַּבְתּוֹ וַיַּעַל לִקְרַאת־יִשְׂרָאֵל אָבִיו גֹּשְׁנָה וַיֵּרָא אֵלָיו וַיִּפֹּל עַל־צַוָּארָיו
ל וַיֵּבְךְּ עַל־צַוָּארָיו עוֹד: וַיֹּאמֶר יִשְׂרָאֵל אֶל־יוֹסֵף אָמוּתָה הַפָּעַם אַחֲרֵי רְאוֹתִי
לא אֶת־פָּנֶיךָ כִּי עוֹדְךָ חָי: וַיֹּאמֶר יוֹסֵף אֶל־אֶחָיו וְאֶל־בֵּית אָבִיו אֶעֱלֶה וְאַגִּידָה
לב לְפַרְעֹה וְאֹמְרָה אֵלָיו אַחַי וּבֵית־אָבִי אֲשֶׁר בְּאֶרֶץ־כְּנַעַן בָּאוּ אֵלָי: וְהָאֲנָשִׁים
לג רֹעֵי צֹאן כִּי־אַנְשֵׁי מִקְנֶה הָיוּ וְצֹאנָם וּבְקָרָם וְכָל־אֲשֶׁר לָהֶם הֵבִיאוּ: וְהָיָה כִּי־
לד יִקְרָא לָכֶם פַּרְעֹה וְאָמַר מַה־מַּעֲשֵׂיכֶם: וַאֲמַרְתֶּם אַנְשֵׁי מִקְנֶה הָיוּ עֲבָדֶיךָ
מִנְּעוּרֵינוּ וְעַד־עַתָּה גַּם־אֲנַחְנוּ גַּם־אֲבֹתֵינוּ בַּעֲבוּר תֵּשְׁבוּ בְּאֶרֶץ גֹּשֶׁן כִּי־תוֹעֲבַת
ז א מִצְרַיִם כָּל־רֹעֵה צֹאן: וַיָּבֹא יוֹסֵף וַיַּגֵּד לְפַרְעֹה וַיֹּאמֶר אָבִי וְאַחַי וְצֹאנָם וּבְקָרָם
ב וְכָל־אֲשֶׁר לָהֶם בָּאוּ מֵאֶרֶץ כְּנָעַן וְהִנָּם בְּאֶרֶץ גֹּשֶׁן: וּמִקְצֵה אֶחָיו לָקַח חֲמִשָּׁה
ג אֲנָשִׁים וַיַּצִּגֵם לִפְנֵי פַרְעֹה: וַיֹּאמֶר פַּרְעֹה אֶל־אֶחָיו מַה־מַּעֲשֵׂיכֶם וַיֹּאמְרוּ אֶל־

רש"י

כו-כז | **כל הנפש הבאה ליעקב.** שיצאו מארץ כנען לבא למצרים, ואין 'הבאה' זו לשון עבר אלא לשון הוה, כמו: "בערב היא באה" (אסתר ב, יד), וכמו: "והנה רחל בתו באה עם הצאן" (לעיל כט, ו), לפיכך טעמו למטה באל"ף, לפי שכשיצאו לבוא מארץ כנען לא היו אלא ששים ושש. והשני, "כל הנפש לבית יעקב הבאה מצרימה שבעים" הוא לשון עבר, לפיכך טעמו למעלה בבי"ת, לפי שמשבאו שם היו שבעים, שמצאו שם יוסף ושני בניו, ונתוספה להם יוכבד בין החומות. ולדברי האומר תאומות נולדו עם השבטים צריכים אנו לומר שמתו לפני ירידתן למצרים, שהרי לא נמנו כאן. מצאתי בויקרא רבה (ד, ו): עשו שש נפשות היו לו והכתוב קורא אותן 'נפשות ביתו' (לעיל לו, ו) לשון רבים, לפי שהיו עובדין לאלהות הרבה; יעקב שבעים היו לו והכתוב קורא אותן 'נפש', לפי שהיו עובדין לאל אחד:

כח | **להורת לפניו.** כתרגומו, לפנות לו מקום ולהורות היאך יתישב בה: **לפניו.** קדם שיגיע לשם. ומדרש אגדה, "להורת לפניו", לתקן לו בית תלמוד שמשם תצא הוראה:

כט | **ויאסר יוסף מרכבתו.** הוא עצמו אסר את הסוסים למרכבה להזדרז לכבוד אביו: **וירא אליו.** יוסף נראה אל אביו: **ויבך על צואריו עוד.** לשון הרבות בכיה, וכן: "כי לא על איש ישים עוד" (איוב לד, כג) לשון רבוי הוא, אינו שם עליו עלילות נוספות על חטאיו, אף כאן, הרבה והוסיף בבכי יותר על הרגיל. אבל יעקב לא נפל על צוארי יוסף ולא נשקו, ואמרו רבותינו שהיה קורא את שמע:

ל | **אמותה הפעם.** פשוטו כתרגומו. ומדרשו, סבור הייתי למות שתי מיתות, בעולם הזה ולעולם הבא, שנסתלקה ממני שכינה, והייתי אומר שיתבעני הקדוש ברוך הוא מיתתך. עכשיו שעודך חי, לא אמות אלא פעם אחת:

לא-לב | **ואמרה אליו אחי וגו'.** ועוד אמר לו: "והאנשים רעי צאן" וגו':

לד | **בעבור תשבו בארץ גשן.** והיא צריכה לכם, שהיא ארץ מרעה, וכשתאמרו לו שאין אתם בקיאין במלאכה אחרת ירחיקכם מעליו ויושיבכם שם: **כי תועבת מצרים כל רעה צאן.** לפי שהם להם אלהות:

פרק מז

ב | **ומקצה אחיו.** מן הפחותים שבהם לגבורה שאין נראים גבורים, שאם יראה אותם גבורים יעשה אותם אנשי מלחמתו. ואלה הם: ראובן, שמעון, לוי, יששכר ובנימין, אותן שלא כפל משה שמותם כשברכן. אבל שמות הגבורים כפל: "וזאת ליהודה... שמע ה' קול יהודה" (דברים לג, ז); "ולגד אמר ברוך מרחיב גד" (שם פסוק כ); "ולנפתלי אמר נפתלי" (שם פסוק כג); "ולדן אמר דן" (שם פסוק כב); וכן לזבולן (שם פסוק יח) וכן לאשר (שם פסוק כד), זהו לשון בראשית רבה (צה, ד) שהיא אגדת ארץ ישראל. אבל בתלמוד בבלי שלנו מצינו שאותן שכפל משה שמותן הם החלשים ואותן הביא לפני פרעה, ויהודה שהכפל שמו לא הכפל משום חלשות, אלא טעם יש בדבר, כדאיתא בבבא קמא (דף צב ע"א). ובברייתא דספרי שנינו בה כ'וזאת הברכה' (שנד) כמו תלמוד שלנו:

Joseph's advice: **Your servants are shepherds, both we and our fathers.**
4 **They** further **said to Pharaoh: We have come to reside** temporarily **in the land,** not to settle permanently, **because there is no pasture for your servants' flocks, as the famine is severe in the land of Canaan. Now, please,** if this is acceptable, **may your servants live in the land of Goshen?**
5 After hearing the brothers' suggestion, Pharaoh chose not to continue the conversation with them, but turned to Joseph instead. **Pharaoh spoke to Joseph, saying: Your father and your brothers have come to you.**
6 **The land of Egypt is before you,** at your disposal; **settle your father and your brothers in the best of the land,** as I accept their request; **they shall live in the land of Goshen,** as this is indeed the appropriate location, **and if you know any capable** and successful **men among them, set them chief herders over that which is mine.** Although the Egyptians were not shepherds, they did possess some livestock, which was designated not for consumption but for wool, milk, and other such purposes.
7 **Joseph brought Jacob his father, and stood him before Pharaoh.** Due to Jacob's status, his meeting and exchange with Pharaoh differed from that of the brothers. **And Jacob blessed Pharaoh.** This was probably an accepted formal blessing bestowed upon a king when one enters into an audience with him.
8 **Pharaoh said to Jacob: How many are the days of the years of your life?** Jacob appeared exceptionally old to Pharaoh, who inquired into his age out of curiosity or possibly due to etiquette.
9 **Jacob said to Pharaoh: The days of the years of my residing** in this world, the years of his life, which he considered a temporary period of wandering, **are one hundred and thirty years; few and unfavorable**[D] **have been the days of the years of my life.** Although I have lived longer than many others, I am not exceptionally old. Rather, I appear older than my actual age due to my sufferings.[16] **And** yet **they,** my years, **have not reached the days of the years of the life of my fathers in the days of their residing,** as Abraham and Isaac lived much longer than I have.
10 **Jacob blessed Pharaoh**[D] **and departed from the presence of Pharaoh.**
11 *Seventh aliya* **Joseph settled his father and his brothers and gave them a portion in the land of Egypt, in the best of the land, in the land of Rameses, in Goshen, as Pharaoh commanded.**
12 **Joseph provided for his father, his brothers, and his father's entire household, with bread into the mouths of the children.** Despite the lack of a large quantity of food, Joseph was able to provide for the needs of his entire family.[17]

Joseph Manages the Economy of Egypt

GENESIS 47:13–27

Following the reunification of Jacob's family and its settlement in Goshen, the Torah momentarily leaves them aside and turns its focus to the repercussions of the ongoing famine.

It is evident from this account that Joseph's earlier interpretation of Pharaoh's dreams coincides with what actually occurred. Here the chapter describes how Joseph deals with the task entrusted to him. On the one hand, he increases Pharaoh's absolute authority by means of the taxes paid to him by the Egyptians. On the other hand, he provides them with reasonable living conditions to ensure that they have no reason to rebel against their king.

13 **There was no bread in all the land, as the famine was very severe, and the land of Egypt and the land of Canaan languished due to the famine.**
14 Since he had amassed grain in Pharaoh's emergency storehouses, **Joseph** proceeded to sell it, and thereby **collected all the silver that was found in the land of Egypt and in the land of Canaan for the grain which they,** the people, **were purchasing. Joseph,** a faithful agent, **brought the** large amount of **silver to Pharaoh's house.**
15 After the majority of the population had exhausted the remainder of their produce and had also spent all their savings, **the silver was exhausted in the land of Egypt and in the land of Canaan; all the Egyptians came to Joseph, saying: Give us bread** to eat; **and why should we die in your presence because** any **silver** with which we could purchase food **has run out?**
16 **Joseph said: Give your livestock,**[D] **and I will give you** food in exchange **for your livestock, if silver has run out.**

DISCUSSION

47:9 | **Few and unfavorable:** Jacob aged prematurely due to the events of his life. His many travails, including his flight due to the threats of his brother Esau, the years of hard labor for Laban, the death of his beloved wife in the prime of her life, the tragic saga of Dina, and the extended period of mourning for his son, all took their toll on his appearance.

47:10 | **Jacob blessed Pharaoh:** Joseph had presumably described to Pharaoh the greatness of his father. Now, when this distinguished man, who appeared very elderly, came before him, it was expected that he would bless the king in addition to the standard greeting (verse 7). Although the content of the blessing

ד פַּרְעֹה רֹעֵה צֹאן עֲבָדֶיךָ גַּם־אֲנַחְנוּ גַּם־אֲבוֹתֵינוּ: וַיֹּאמְרוּ אֶל־פַּרְעֹה לָגוּר בָּאָרֶץ
בָּאנוּ כִּי־אֵין מִרְעֶה לַצֹּאן אֲשֶׁר לַעֲבָדֶיךָ כִּי־כָבֵד הָרָעָב בְּאֶרֶץ כְּנָעַן וְעַתָּה
ה יֵשְׁבוּ־נָא עֲבָדֶיךָ בְּאֶרֶץ גֹּשֶׁן: וַיֹּאמֶר פַּרְעֹה אֶל־יוֹסֵף לֵאמֹר אָבִיךָ וְאַחֶיךָ בָּאוּ
ו אֵלֶיךָ: אֶרֶץ מִצְרַיִם לְפָנֶיךָ הִוא בְּמֵיטַב הָאָרֶץ הוֹשֵׁב אֶת־אָבִיךָ וְאֶת־אַחֶיךָ
יֵשְׁבוּ בְּאֶרֶץ גֹּשֶׁן וְאִם־יָדַעְתָּ וְיֶשׁ־בָּם אַנְשֵׁי־חַיִל וְשַׂמְתָּם שָׂרֵי מִקְנֶה עַל־אֲשֶׁר־
ז לִי: וַיָּבֵא יוֹסֵף אֶת־יַעֲקֹב אָבִיו וַיַּעֲמִדֵהוּ לִפְנֵי פַרְעֹה וַיְבָרֶךְ יַעֲקֹב אֶת־פַּרְעֹה:
ח ט וַיֹּאמֶר פַּרְעֹה אֶל־יַעֲקֹב כַּמָּה יְמֵי שְׁנֵי חַיֶּיךָ: וַיֹּאמֶר יַעֲקֹב אֶל־פַּרְעֹה יְמֵי שְׁנֵי
מְגוּרַי שְׁלֹשִׁים וּמְאַת שָׁנָה מְעַט וְרָעִים הָיוּ יְמֵי שְׁנֵי חַיַּי וְלֹא הִשִּׂיגוּ אֶת־יְמֵי
י שְׁנֵי חַיֵּי אֲבֹתַי בִּימֵי מְגוּרֵיהֶם: וַיְבָרֶךְ יַעֲקֹב אֶת־פַּרְעֹה וַיֵּצֵא מִלִּפְנֵי פַרְעֹה:
יא וַיּוֹשֵׁב יוֹסֵף אֶת־אָבִיו וְאֶת־אֶחָיו וַיִּתֵּן לָהֶם אֲחֻזָּה בְּאֶרֶץ מִצְרַיִם בְּמֵיטַב הָאָרֶץ שביעי
יב בְּאֶרֶץ רַעְמְסֵס כַּאֲשֶׁר צִוָּה פַרְעֹה: וַיְכַלְכֵּל יוֹסֵף אֶת־אָבִיו וְאֶת־אֶחָיו וְאֵת כָּל־
יג בֵּית אָבִיו לֶחֶם לְפִי הַטָּף: וְלֶחֶם אֵין בְּכָל־הָאָרֶץ כִּי־כָבֵד הָרָעָב מְאֹד וַתֵּלַהּ
יד אֶרֶץ מִצְרַיִם וְאֶרֶץ כְּנַעַן מִפְּנֵי הָרָעָב: וַיְלַקֵּט יוֹסֵף אֶת־כָּל־הַכֶּסֶף הַנִּמְצָא
בְאֶרֶץ־מִצְרַיִם וּבְאֶרֶץ כְּנַעַן בַּשֶּׁבֶר אֲשֶׁר־הֵם שֹׁבְרִים וַיָּבֵא יוֹסֵף אֶת־הַכֶּסֶף
טו בֵּיתָה פַרְעֹה: וַיִּתֹּם הַכֶּסֶף מֵאֶרֶץ מִצְרַיִם וּמֵאֶרֶץ כְּנַעַן וַיָּבֹאוּ כָל־מִצְרַיִם אֶל־
טז יוֹסֵף לֵאמֹר הָבָה־לָּנוּ לֶחֶם וְלָמָּה נָמוּת נֶגְדֶּךָ כִּי אָפֵס כָּסֶף: וַיֹּאמֶר יוֹסֵף הָבוּ

רש״י

ו| **אַנְשֵׁי חַיִל.** בְּקִיאִין בְּאֻמָּנוּתָן לִרְעוֹת צֹאן: **עַל אֲשֶׁר לִי.** עַל צֹאן שֶׁלִּי:

ז| **וַיְבָרֶךְ יַעֲקֹב.** הִיא שְׁאֵלַת שָׁלוֹם כְּדֶרֶךְ כָּל הַנִּרְאִים לִפְנֵי הַמְּלָכִים לִפְרָקִים, סלודי״ר בְּלַעַ״ז:

ט| **שְׁנֵי מְגוּרַי.** יְמֵי גֵּרוּתִי, כָּל יָמַי הָיִיתִי גֵּר בָּאָרֶץ: **וְלֹא הִשִּׂיגוּ.** בַּטּוֹבָה:

י| **וַיְבָרֶךְ יַעֲקֹב.** כְּדֶרֶךְ כָּל הַנִּפְטָרִים מִלִּפְנֵי שָׂרִים, מְבָרְכִים אוֹתָם וְנוֹטְלִים רְשׁוּת. וּמַה בְּרָכָה בֵּרְכוֹ? שֶׁיַּעֲלֶה נִילוּס לְרַגְלָיו, לְפִי שֶׁאֵין מִצְרַיִם שׁוֹתָה מֵי גְּשָׁמִים, אֶלָּא נִילוּס עוֹלֶה וּמַשְׁקָה, וּמִבִּרְכָתוֹ שֶׁל יַעֲקֹב וָאֵילָךְ הָיָה פַּרְעֹה בָּא עַל נִילוּס וְהוּא עוֹלֶה לִקְרָאתוֹ וּמַשְׁקֶה אֶת הָאָרֶץ. תַּנְחוּמָא (נשא כו):

יא| **רַעְמְסֵס.** מֵאֶרֶץ גֹּשֶׁן הִיא:

יב| **לְפִי הַטָּף.** לְפִי הַצָּרִיךְ לְכָל בְּנֵי בֵיתָם:

יג| **וְלֶחֶם אֵין בְּכָל הָאָרֶץ.** חוֹזֵר לָעִנְיָן הָרִאשׁוֹן לִתְחִלַּת שְׁנֵי הָרָעָב: **וַתֵּלַהּ.** כְּמוֹ וַתִּלְאֶה, לְשׁוֹן עֲיֵפוּת כְּתַרְגּוּמוֹ, וְדוֹמֶה לוֹ: ״כְּמִתְלַהְלֵהַּ הַיֹּרֶה זִקִּים״ (משלי כו, יח):

יד| **בַּשֶּׁבֶר אֲשֶׁר הֵם שֹׁבְרִים.** נוֹתְנִין לוֹ אֶת הַכֶּסֶף:

טו| **אָפֵס.** כְּתַרְגּוּמוֹ, ״שְׁלִים״:

DISCUSSION

→ is not specified here, the Sages state that Jacob blessed Pharaoh that evil cease in his land, that he have much success, or that the waters of the Nile River ascend to greet him and irrigate the land (*Sifrei*, Deuteronomy 38; *Bemidbar Rabba* 12:2; Rashi).

47:16 | **Give your livestock:** Since the Egyptians could not farm the land during the drought, they had little use for livestock. Until this point,

17 **They brought their livestock to Joseph; Joseph gave them bread for the horses, for the livestock of flocks, for the livestock of cattle, and for the donkeys;** in exchange **for all their livestock he provided them with bread during that year,** the second year of the famine.

18 **That year concluded, and they came to him in the second year,** the next year,[18] **and said to him: We will not conceal from my lord how our silver and the herds of cattle are spent to my lord; nothing remains** of our movable property **before my lord, except for our bodies and our lands.**

19 **Why shall we die before your eyes, both we and our land,** if it becomes barren? **Purchase us and our land with bread, and we and our land will be slaves to Pharaoh.** In essence, the people were suggesting that their status be changed from Egyptian citizens and independent farmers into Pharaoh's serfs. **Give seed**[D] **that we will live and will not die, and the land will not become desolate.**

20 **Joseph purchased all the land of Egypt for Pharaoh because each Egyptian sold his field, for the famine was severe upon them. The land became Pharaoh's.** Once Pharaoh acquired the land, it became his personal property. Likewise, when he purchased the citizens of Egypt, all the farmers became his slaves.

21 **The people, he transferred them to the cities, from one end of the Egyptian border to its other end.**[D] The aim of this population transfer was to highlight the fact that the people no longer owned any land and were considered slaves. A person who lives on a particular plot of land, even if he does not possess complete legal ownership of it, still feels that it belongs to him to a certain extent. Joseph transferred and scattered the people in order to uproot their sense that they were living in

their homeland, and to eradicate their feelings of ownership and attachment to the soil. They are now sent to work in unfamiliar locations as slaves, with no say in the matter.

22 The verse notes exception to the above rule: **Only the land of the priests he,** Joseph, **did not buy, for there was an** exact **allotment** of food designated **for the priests from Pharaoh, and they ate their allotment that Pharaoh gave them; therefore, they did not sell their land.** Since the Egyptian priests did not starve, they were not compelled to sell themselves or their land.

23 **Joseph said to the people: Behold, I have purchased you today and your land for Pharaoh. Here is seed for you, and you shall sow the land.** Since Pharaoh was now the owner of the land, it was in his best interest to invest in its development by providing the people with seeds. It is evident from this verse that the famine had become more moderate in Egypt. However, in more distant lands, such as Canaan, it was still causing significant damage, which was preventing any substantial recovery. The residents of these lands were incapable of planting anything, as all the seeds had been consumed. The famine continued in this manner for several years until the populace was able to recover.

24 In contrast to the situation in other lands, Joseph offered the residents of Egypt seeds to plant, but he also demanded something in return: **It shall be at the harvests,** after the crops sprout, that **you shall give one-fifth** of the crop **to Pharaoh,**[D] **and four parts,** the four-fifths that will remain in your possession, **shall be yours, for seed of the field, and for your food, and for those in your households, and to be eaten by your children.**

DISCUSSION

the people had sought to retain ownership over their animals, as a source of labor and potential merchandise and as security for their livelihood. However, due to the severe economic crisis, they eventually become incapable of feeding them. Joseph gathered all of the livestock and placed them under Pharaoh's control, just as he had done for the produce. He chose not to slaughter them and sell the meat. Perhaps his reasoning was that if he were to do so, there would not be sufficient livestock for labor in the fields available during the years following the famine. Instead, Joseph had the animals brought to him, and he kept them fed and maintained in national farms. It is logical that during the years of plenty Joseph had amassed not only human food, but also

animal fodder, in large enough quantities to be used for such a purpose.

47:19 | Give seed: It would appear that the Egyptians had previously lacked sufficient water to irrigate their fields and therefore they had no reason to plant at all, even if they had possessed seeds. Apparently the drought had abated somewhat, and there was now a small amount of water available. However, no one had crops to plant, as all of the produce had been used for food. Therefore, they sought to purchase seeds from Joseph (*Bereshit Rabba* 89:9; Rashi).

47:21 | The people, he transferred them to the cities, from one end of the Egyptian border to its other end: Joseph's actions here

greatly exceeded his description to Pharaoh in his interpretation of the dreams. His original suggestion, that someone should amass the produce in storehouses, was designed to support the Egyptian population during the years of the famine, as otherwise the food would be wasted and people would die of starvation. This proposal would also enhance the status of Pharaoh over the Egyptian populace. At this point Joseph exploits the conditions to alter the entire national structure of the country. Purchasing the animals, land, and bodies of the majority of Egyptian citizens transformed Pharaoh from the king of Egypt, which itself was an exalted status, to a full-fledged dictator, a ruler with absolute power. Joseph thereby granted

יז מִקְנֵיכֶם וְאֶתְּנָה לָכֶם בְּמִקְנֵיכֶם אִם־אָפֵס כָּסֶף: וַיָּבִיאוּ אֶת־מִקְנֵיהֶם אֶל־יוֹסֵף וַיִּתֵּן לָהֶם יוֹסֵף לֶחֶם בַּסּוּסִים וּבְמִקְנֵה הַצֹּאן וּבְמִקְנֵה הַבָּקָר וּבַחֲמֹרִים וַיְנַהֲלֵם בַּלֶּחֶם בְּכָל־מִקְנֵהֶם בַּשָּׁנָה הַהִוא: יח וַתִּתֹּם הַשָּׁנָה הַהִוא וַיָּבֹאוּ אֵלָיו בַּשָּׁנָה הַשֵּׁנִית וַיֹּאמְרוּ לוֹ לֹא־נְכַחֵד מֵאֲדֹנִי כִּי אִם־תַּם הַכֶּסֶף וּמִקְנֵה הַבְּהֵמָה אֶל־אֲדֹנִי לֹא נִשְׁאַר לִפְנֵי אֲדֹנִי בִּלְתִּי אִם־גְּוִיָּתֵנוּ וְאַדְמָתֵנוּ: יט לָמָּה נָמוּת לְעֵינֶיךָ גַּם־אֲנַחְנוּ גַּם־אַדְמָתֵנוּ קְנֵה־אֹתָנוּ וְאֶת־אַדְמָתֵנוּ בַּלָּחֶם וְנִהְיֶה אֲנַחְנוּ וְאַדְמָתֵנוּ עֲבָדִים לְפַרְעֹה וְתֶן־זֶרַע וְנִחְיֶה וְלֹא נָמוּת וְהָאֲדָמָה לֹא תֵשָׁם: כ וַיִּקֶן יוֹסֵף אֶת־כָּל־אַדְמַת מִצְרַיִם לְפַרְעֹה כִּי־מָכְרוּ מִצְרַיִם אִישׁ שָׂדֵהוּ כִּי־חָזַק עֲלֵהֶם הָרָעָב וַתְּהִי הָאָרֶץ לְפַרְעֹה: כא וְאֶת־הָעָם הֶעֱבִיר אֹתוֹ לֶעָרִים מִקְצֵה גְבוּל־מִצְרַיִם וְעַד־קָצֵהוּ: כב רַק אַדְמַת הַכֹּהֲנִים לֹא קָנָה כִּי חֹק לַכֹּהֲנִים מֵאֵת פַּרְעֹה וְאָכְלוּ אֶת־חֻקָּם אֲשֶׁר נָתַן לָהֶם פַּרְעֹה עַל־כֵּן לֹא מָכְרוּ אֶת־אַדְמָתָם: כג וַיֹּאמֶר יוֹסֵף אֶל־הָעָם הֵן קָנִיתִי אֶתְכֶם הַיּוֹם וְאֶת־אַדְמַתְכֶם לְפַרְעֹה הֵא־לָכֶם זֶרַע וּזְרַעְתֶּם אֶת־הָאֲדָמָה: כד וְהָיָה בַּתְּבוּאֹת וּנְתַתֶּם חֲמִישִׁית לְפַרְעֹה וְאַרְבַּע הַיָּדֹת יִהְיֶה לָכֶם לְזֶרַע הַשָּׂדֶה

רש״י

יז וַיְנַהֲלֵם. כְּמוֹ וַיְנַהֲגֵם, וְדוֹמֶה לוֹ: ״אֵין מְנַהֵל לָהּ״ (ישעיה נא, יח), ״עַל מֵי מְנֻחוֹת יְנַהֲלֵנִי״ (תהלים כג, ב).

יח בַּשָּׁנָה הַשֵּׁנִית. לִשְׁנֵי הָרָעָב. כִּי אֲשֶׁר תַּם הַכֶּסֶף וְהַמִּקְנֶה וּבָא הַכֹּל אֶל יְדֵי אֲדֹנִי: בִּלְתִּי אִם־גְּוִיָּתֵנוּ. כְּמוֹ אִם לֹא גְוִיָּתֵנוּ.

יט וְתֶן זֶרַע. לִזְרוֹעַ הָאֲדָמָה. וְאַף עַל פִּי שֶׁאָמַר יוֹסֵף ״וְעוֹד חָמֵשׁ שָׁנִים אֲשֶׁר אֵין חָרִישׁ וְקָצִיר״ (לעיל מה, ו), מִכֵּיוָן שֶׁבָּא יַעֲקֹב לְמִצְרַיִם בָּאָה בְּרָכָה לְרַגְלָיו וְהִתְחִילוּ

לִזְרוֹעַ, וְכָלָה הָרָעָב. וְכֵן שָׁנִינוּ בַּתּוֹסֶפְתָּא דְּסוֹטָה (י, ג): לֹא תֵשָׁם. לֹא תְּהֵא שְׁמָמָה, ״לָא תְבוּר״, לְשׁוֹן שָׂדֶה בּוּר, שֶׁאֵינוֹ חָרוּשׁ:

כ וַתְּהִי הָאָרֶץ לְפַרְעֹה. קְנוּיָה לוֹ:

כא וְאֶת הָעָם הֶעֱבִיר. יוֹסֵף מֵעִיר לְעִיר לְזִכָּרוֹן שֶׁאֵין לָהֶם עוֹד חֵלֶק בָּאָרֶץ, וְהוֹשִׁיב שֶׁל עִיר זוֹ בַּחֲבֶרְתָּהּ. וְלֹא הִצְרַךְ הַכָּתוּב לִכְתּוֹב זֹאת, אֶלָּא לְהוֹדִיעֲךָ שִׁבְחוֹ שֶׁל יוֹסֵף שֶׁנִּתְכַּוֵּן לְהָסִיר חֶרְפָּה מֵעַל אֶחָיו, שֶׁלֹּא יִהְיוּ קוֹרִין אוֹתָם

גּוֹלִים: מִקְצֵה גְבוּל מִצְרַיִם וְגוֹ׳. כֵּן עָשָׂה לְכָל הֶעָרִים אֲשֶׁר בְּמַלְכוּת מִצְרַיִם, מִקְצֵה גְבוּלָהּ וְעַד קְצֵה גְבוּלָהּ:

כב הַכֹּהֲנִים. כּוֹמְרִים. כָּל לְשׁוֹן ״כֹּהֵן״ מְשָׁרֵת לֶאֱלֹהוּת הוּא, חוּץ מֵאוֹתָן שֶׁהֵם לְשׁוֹן גְּדֻלָּה, כְּמוֹ: ״כֹּהֵן מִדְיָן״ (שמות כ, טז), ״כֹּהֵן אֹן״ (לעיל מא, מה): חֹק לַכֹּהֲנִים. חֹק כָּךְ וְכָךְ לֶחֶם לַיּוֹם:

כג הֵא. כְּמוֹ הִנֵּה:

כד לְזֶרַע הַשָּׂדֶה. שֶׁבְּכָל שָׁנָה: וְלַאֲשֶׁר בְּבָתֵּיכֶם. וְלֶאֱכֹל

DISCUSSION

Pharaoh far greater power and authority than he ever had before. From this point onward, the land and the country belonged to Pharaoh not only as their king, but also as their owner. This radical political and economic revolution transformed Egypt into a country of slaves, all subject to Pharaoh, except for the temples and the priests, as stated in the next verse.

47:24 | You shall give one-fifth to Pharaoh: A tax of 20 percent is not considered an exceedingly large sum even today. Furthermore, it is likely that this was lower than the tax imposed on serf farmers in other countries at the time. It is also logical to assume that the Egyptians had paid a similar percentage of tax before this episode. Once they were transformed into slaves, they likely anticipated a division of opposite proportions, such that Pharaoh would receive the large majority of the crop while they would be allowed to keep only enough to sustain themselves.

25 **They said: You have saved our lives. Let us find favor in the eyes of my lord.** Please do as you suggested, as this is a generous offer. In their satisfaction, they willingly added: **And we will be slaves to Pharaoh.**

26 **Joseph instituted it,** his condition, **as a statute to this day with regard to the land of Egypt: One-fifth** of the land was **for Pharaoh; only the land of the priests alone did not become Pharaoh's.** As was previously mentioned, the priests,

who received support directly from the king, did not sell their land or themselves (verse 22).

27 **Israel,** which is used here for the first time as the title of the entire tribe, rather than the individual name of Jacob, **lived in the land of Egypt, in the land of Goshen; they settled there.** Jacob and his family lived in comfortable conditions, without worries. They dealt with their occupations, while Joseph provided their sustenance. **And** consequently, **they were fruitful and multiplied exceedingly.**

Parashat
Vayhi

Jacob's Farewell to His Family and His Passing
GENESIS 47:28–49:33

Jacob takes gradual leave of his family in several stages, in which he gives instructions for his burial and provides spiritual directives for his descendants' future. This section begins with Jacob asking Joseph not to bury him in Egypt, and it concludes with his request from his sons to ensure that he is buried in the cave of Makhpela in Canaan. Between these two stages, Jacob delivers poetic, prophetic blessings. These too are initially bestowed specifically upon Joseph and his sons Ephraim and Manasseh, who accompanied him on a special visit to Jacob. Afterward, Jacob blesses all of his sons, including Joseph once again.

28 **Jacob lived in the land of Egypt seventeen years.** During this time, the economic reforms described in the previous section (verses 14–26) were instituted, and the famine ceased. **The days of Jacob, the years of his life, were seven years and one hundred atnd forty years.**

29 **The time for Israel to die approached,** as he sensed that he would soon pass away. **And he called his son, Joseph,** both because he was his favorite son, and because he was the ruler of Egypt, **and he said to him: Please, if I have found favor**

in your eyes,[D] **please place your hand under my thigh and** swear to me (see 24:2) that you will **perform kindness and truth with me; please do not bury me in Egypt.** Jacob felt the need to administer an oath to Joseph, since this was not a simple request, as will be seen below.

30 **I shall lie with my fathers** after my death, **and you will convey me from Egypt and bury me in their,** my ancestors', **grave. He,** Joseph, **said: I will do in accordance with your words.**

DISCUSSION

47:29 | Please, if I have found favor in your eyes: This expression is generally employed by an individual of lower status when addressing one to whom he is submissive, such as a

servant speaking to his master, or a son to his father. Here, however, Jacob spoke in this manner to his son because Joseph was an important and powerful government official. During this

conversation, Jacob must balance expressions of paternal authority with his need for his son's good will.

כה ולאכלכם ולאשר בבתיכם ולאכל לטפכם: ויאמרו החיתנו נמצא־חן בעיני מפטיר
כו אדני והיינו עבדים לפרעה: וישם אתה יוסף לחק עד־היום הזה על־אדמת
כז מצרים לפרעה לחמש רק אדמת הכהנים לבדם לא היתה לפרעה: וישב
ישראל בארץ מצרים בארץ גשן ויאחזו בה ויפרו וירבו מאד:

רש״י

העבדים והשפחות חשר בביתיכם: טפכם. בנים קטנים:

כה| נמצא חן. לעשות לנו זאת כמו שאמרת: והיינו עבדים לפרעה. להעלות לו המס הזה בכל שנה:

כו| לחק. שלא יעבר:

כז| וישב ישראל בארץ מצרים. והיכן? ״בארץ גשן״, שהוא מארץ מצרים:

פרשת

ויחי

כח ויחי יעקב בארץ מצרים שבע עשרה שנה ויהי ימי־יעקב שני חייו שבע שנים
כט וארבעים ומאת שנה: ויקרבו ימי־ישראל למות ויקרא | לבנו ליוסף ויאמר לו
אם־נא מצאתי חן בעיניך שים־נא ידך תחת ירכי ועשית עמדי חסד ואמת
ל אל־נא תקברני במצרים: ושכבתי עם־אבתי ונשאתני ממצרים וקברתני

רש״י

כח| ויחי יעקב. למה פרשה זו סתומה? לפי שכיון שנפטר יעקב אבינו, נסתמו עיניהם ולבם של ישראל מצרת השעבוד, שהתחילו לשעבדם. דבר אחר, שבקש לגלות את הקץ לבניו ונסתם ממנו. בבראשית רבה (צו, א):

כט| ויקרבו ימי ישראל למות. כל מי שנאמרה בו קריבה למות לא הגיע לימי אבותיו: ויקרא לבנו ליוסף. למי שהיה יכלת בידו לעשות: שים נא ידך. והשבע: חסד ואמת. חסד שעושין עם המתים הוא חסד של אמת, שאינו מצפה לתשלום גמול: אל נא תקברני במצרים. סופה להיות עפרה כנים, ושאין מתי חוצה לארץ חיים אלא בצער גלגול מחלות, ושלא יעשוני מצרים עבודה זרה:

ל| ושכבתי עם אבתי. וי״ו זה מחבר למעלה לתחלת המקרא: ״שים נא ידך תחת ירכי״ והשבע לי, ואני סופי לשכב עם אבותי ואתה תשאני ממצרים. ואין לומר ״ושכבתי עם אבתי״ – השכיבני עם אבותי במערה, שהרי כתיב אחריו: ״ונשאתני ממצרים וקברתני בקברתם״; ועוד, מצינו בכל מקום לשון שכיבה עם אבותיו היא הגויעה ולא הקבורה, ״וישכב דוד עם אבתיו ויקבר בעיר דוד״ (מלכים א׳ ב, י):

31 **He,** Jacob, **said: Take an oath to me,**[D] as a declaration of intent alone is insufficient. **And he,** Joseph, **took an oath to him. Israel prostrated himself**[D] as a sign of gratitude **at the head of the bed.** He did not prostrate himself on the ground, in the customary manner, as he was ill and confined to bed.

48 1 **It was after these matters that one,** an unnamed person, **said to Joseph: Behold, your father is ill.** In the previous episode, Jacob had sensed that he was going to die soon; at this point, he became very ill. **He,** Joseph, **took his two sons, Manasseh and Ephraim, with him.**

2 **One told Jacob and said: Behold, your son Joseph is coming to you.** Joseph likely lived in the capital city, which was far from Goshen, and therefore he could not visit his father frequently. When he was notified that Joseph was coming to visit, **Israel exerted himself, and he sat upon the bed** instead of lying on it, as he wanted to greet the viceroy in a dignified manner. In addition, perhaps sitting was the more appropriate position for the nature of the conversation that Jacob wished to conduct with his son.

3 **Jacob said to Joseph: God Almighty appeared to me in Luz,** also known as Beit El, **in the land of Canaan, and He blessed me.**

4 **He said to me: Behold, I will make you fruitful and multiply you, and I will render you an assembly of peoples, and I will give this land to your descendants after you as an eternal portion.** Jacob received these two promises in his dream at Beit El on his way to Haran (28:12–15) and in his prophetic vision in the same location many years later, upon his return to Canaan (35:9–12). Although the greatness he was promised had yet to materialize, the assurance gave him the strength and authority to deliver blessings that would shape the future of his family and their land, as though God's promises had already come to pass at that time.

5 **And now,** based on the aforementioned promises, **your two sons, who were born to you in the land of Egypt before my coming to you to Egypt, they are mine;** I am adopting them

as though they were my children. **Ephraim and Manasseh, like Reuben and Simeon they shall be for me.** Your first and second sons, my grandsons, will be elevated to equivalent status as that of my own first and second sons.

6 Manasseh and Ephraim were Joseph's older sons, born before the onset of the years of famine. Even if no children had been born to Joseph during the famine, as the Sages maintain, he likely had others after those difficult years. However, as they were still young at this point, the matter that Jacob is discussing does not apply to them. **And** therefore, **your progeny that you beget after them,**[D] after Manasseh and Ephraim, **they shall be yours** and considered part of your immediate family, not as my adopted sons. This means that **they shall be called after the name of their brothers in their inheritance.** When the inheritance is divided among the sons of Jacob, those sons shall be considered part of the tribe of Ephraim or of Manasseh.

7 **And I, when coming** back **from Padan** Aram, your mother **Rachel died on me in the land of Canaan on the road, while still some distance to arrive at Efrat,** not in an inhabited area. **And** therefore **I buried her there on the road to Efrat, which is** another name for **Bethlehem.** Since it was impractical to bring her to the family burial plot in Hebron, I buried her where she died.[1] Indeed, to this day the tombstone assumed to mark Rachel's grave is located outside the city of Bethlehem. In the past, it was presumably even farther outside of the city than it is currently.[2]

8 **Israel saw Joseph's sons, and he said: Who are these?** Perhaps due to the distance between Joseph's and Jacob's places of residence, Jacob did not see his grandchildren very often, and therefore he did not recognize them. Although he had met them a few years earlier, their appearances had certainly changed in the meantime. Moreover, Jacob's vision had deteriorated (verse 10), which may be why he did not immediately identify his grandsons.

9 **Joseph said to his father: They are my sons,** Ephraim and Manasseh, whom you mentioned previously, **whom God has**

DISCUSSION

47:31 | He said: Take an oath to me: Jacob's statement combines weakness and strength. Since he was elderly and ill, he was forced to rely on the kindness of Joseph in order to be buried in Canaan. In addition, he felt the need to explain apologetically to Joseph why he was requesting to be buried together with the other patriarchs and matriarchs, despite the fact that he was unable to do the same for Joseph's mother Rachel (see *Targum Yonatan*; Ibn Ezra). Yet at the same time Jacob is strengthened by

the family legacy he bears and his capacity to deliver the blessing of God to his descendants as an inheritance and for the establishment of a powerful kingdom.

Israel prostrated himself: This action is possibly the fulfillment of Joseph's second dream, in which his father, symbolized by the sun, prostrated himself to him. If so, Jacob prostrated himself as a sign of deference (Rashbam). However, it is more likely that this gesture was an expression of Jacob's gratitude to God (see, e.g., 24:26, 52; Ibn Ezra).

Aside from his wish to return to the Land of Israel after his death, Jacob did not set any other goals or desires for himself. He also realized that he would be unable to return to Canaan during his lifetime. Therefore, upon hearing Joseph's oath confirming that he would facilitate his request, Jacob gave thanks to God for enabling him to complete his life in tranquility.

48:6 | And your progeny that you beget after them: These other sons of Joseph are not identified in the Torah (see Ramban, verse 15).

◄●

לא בקברתם ויאמר אנכי אעשה כדברך: ויאמר השבעה לי וישבע לו וישתחו
ישראל על־ראש המטה:
מח א ויהי אחרי הדברים האלה ויאמר ליוסף הנה אביך חלה ויקח את־שני בניו מב
ב עמו את־מנשה ואת־אפרים: ויגד ליעקב ויאמר הנה בנך יוסף בא אליך
ג ויתחזק ישראל וישב על־המטה: ויאמר יעקב אל־יוסף אל שדי נראה־אלי
ד בלוז בארץ כנען ויברך אתי: ויאמר אלי הנני מפרך והרביתך ונתתיך לקהל
ה עמים ונתתי את־הארץ הזאת לזרעך אחריך אחזת עולם: ועתה שני־בניך
הנולדים לך בארץ מצרים עד־באי אליך מצרימה לי־הם אפרים ומנשה
ו כראובן ושמעון יהיו־לי: ומולדתך אשר־הולדת אחריהם לך יהיו על שם
ז אחיהם יקראו בנחלתם: ואני | בבאי מפדן מתה עלי רחל בארץ כנען בדרך
בעוד כברת־ארץ לבא אפרתה ואקברה שם בדרך אפרת הוא בית לחם:
ח ט וירא ישראל את־בני יוסף ויאמר מי־אלה: ויאמר יוסף אל־אביו בני הם

רש״י

לא| **וישתחו ישראל.** תעלא בעדניה סגיד ליה: **על ראש המטה.** הפך עצמו לצד השכינה; מכאן אמרו שהשכינה למעלה מראשותיו של חולה. דבר אחר, "על ראש המטה", על שהיתה מטתו שלמה ולא היה בה רשע, שהרי יוסף מלך הוא, ועוד שנשבה לבין הגוים, והרי הוא עומד בצדקו:

פרק מח

א| **ויאמר ליוסף.** אחד מן המגידים, והרי זה מקרא קצר. ויש אומרים, אפרים היה רגיל לפני יעקב בתלמוד, וכשחלה יעקב בארץ גשן הלך אפרים אצל אביו למצרים להגיד לו: **ויקח את שני בניו עמו.** כדי שיברכם יעקב לפני מותו:

ב| **ויגד.** המגיד "ליעקב" ולא פרש מי, והרבה מקראות קצרי לשון: **ויתחזק ישראל.** אמר, אף על פי שהוא בני, מלך הוא, אחלק לו כבוד; מכאן שחולקים כבוד למלכות. וכן משה חלק כבוד למלכות: "וירדו כל עבדיך אלה אלי" (שמות יא, ח). וכן אליהו: "וישנס מתניו" וגו' (מלכים א' יח, מו):

ד| **ונתתיך לקהל עמים.** בשרני שעתידים לצאת ממני עוד קהל ועמים. ואף על פי שאמר לי: "גוי וקהל גוים" (לעיל לה, יא)! 'גוי' אמר לי על בנימין, 'קהל גוים' הרי שנים לבד מבנימין, ושוב לא נולד לי בן; למדני שעתיד אחד משבטי לחלק, ועתה אותה מתנה אני נותן לך:

ה| **הנולדים לך... עד באי אליך.** לפני בואי אליך, כלומר, שנולדו משפרשת ממני עד שבאתי אצלך: **לי הם.** בחשבון שאר בני הם, לטול חלק בארץ איש כנגדו:

ו| **ומולדתך.** אם תוליד עוד לא יהיו במנין בני, אלא בתוך שבטי אפרים ומנשה יהיו נכללים, ולא יהא להם שם בשבטים לענין הנחלה. ואף על פי שנחלקה הארץ למנין גלגלותם, כדכתיב: "לרב תרבה נחלתו" (במדבר כו, נד), וכל איש ואיש נטל בשוה חוץ מן הבכורות, מכל מקום לא נקראו שבטים אלא אלו:

ז| **ואני בבאי מפדן וגו'.** ואף על פי שאני מטריח עליך להוליכני לקבר בארץ כנען, לא כך עשיתי לאמך, שהרי מתה סמוך לבית לחם: **כברת ארץ.** מדת ארץ, והם אלפים אמה כמדת תחום שבת, כדברי רבי משה הדרשן. ולא תאמר שעכבו עלי גשמים מלהוליכה ולקברה בחברון, עת הגריד היה שהארץ חלולה ומנקבת ככברה: **ואקברה שם.** ולא הולכתיה אפילו לבית לחם להכניסה לארץ, וידעתי שיש בלבך עלי; אבל דע לך שעל פי הדבור קברתיה שם, שתהא לעזרה לבניה, כשיגלם נבוזראדן והיו עוברים דרך שם, יצאת רחל על קברה ובוכה ומבקשת עליהם רחמים, שנאמר: "קול ברמה נשמע" וגו' (ירמיה לא, יד). ואונקלוס תרגם: "כרוב ארעא", כדי שעור חרישת יום; ואומר אני שהיה להם קצב שהיו קורין אותו כדי מחרשה אחת, קרואיד"א בלעז, כדאמרינן: "כרוב ותני" (בבא מציעא קז ע"א), "כמה דמסיק תעלא מבי כרבא" (יומא מג ע"ב):

ח| **וירא ישראל את בני יוסף.** בקש לברכם ונסתלקה שכינה ממנו, לפי שעתיד ירבעם ואחאב לצאת מאפרים, ויהוא ובניו ממנשה: **ויאמר מי אלה.** מהיכן יצאו אלו שאינן ראוין לברכה?

DISCUSSION

However, some commentaries suggest that Bekher and Tahan, who are mentioned below as the sons of Ephraim (Numbers 26:35) but do not appear in the list in I Chronicles (7:20), are actually other sons of Joseph, who were ultimately incorporated into the tribe of Ephraim (*Sefer HaParshiyot*).

given me here. Jacob subsequently remembers and identifies the boys. Despite his physical impairment, his mental capacities were still fully intact. Therefore, **he said** decisively: **Please take them to me, and I will bless them.**[D]

10 *Second aliya* **And the eyes of Israel were heavy with age.** At that time there was no way to cure the degeneration of vision in old age. Once one's vision became cloudy, one could distinguish only between light and darkness. Therefore, **he was unable to see** anything other than shadows. **He,** Joseph, **had them approach him and he,** Jacob, **kissed them, and he embraced them.**

11 **Israel said to Joseph: I did not expect**[D] **to see your face** after so many years, as I did not believe it was possible, **and behold,** not only has this occurred, but **God has shown me your offspring as well.** Before bestowing his blessing, Jacob strengthens himself through this expression of amazement and praise.

12 Manasseh and Ephraim, who were still young at the time, had been standing between Joseph's knees. **Joseph took them out from between his knees, and he prostrated himself on his face to the earth.** Joseph bowed not to Jacob, but to God, in preparation for the upcoming revelation.[3]

13 **Joseph took the two of them:** He brought **Ephraim,** his younger son, **in his right hand,** so that he would be **to the left of Israel,** who was opposite him, with the younger son on his father's left side, in the customary manner. **And** he took **Manasseh,** his older son, **in his left hand, to the right of Israel, and he had them approach him.**

14 Contrary to Joseph's expectation that Jacob would extend his hands directly across onto his sons' heads, **Israel extended his right hand,** which was opposite Manasseh, **and laid it upon the head of Ephraim, who was the younger** brother, **and his left hand** he extended **upon the head of Manasseh, deliberately placing his hands,**[4] **as** he was aware that **Manasseh was the firstborn.**[5] Alternatively, the verse means: Although Manasseh was the firstborn.[6]

15 **He,** Jacob, **blessed Joseph and said: The God before whom my fathers, Abraham and Isaac, walked, the God who shepherds,** directs, **me from my beginnings until this day.** Although the blessing was bestowed upon Joseph's children, a blessing given to children is also automatically a blessing for their father as well.[7]

16 **May the angel,** a messenger of God, **who delivers me from all evil** and who has protected me until now, **bless the lads,** as the representative of God, its sender. **And** the first blessing is: **Let my name and the name of my fathers, Abraham and Isaac, be called upon them,** these two children, as well. Having previously adopted them as his own sons, Jacob adds that they shall continue his and his forebears' legacy. Just as God guided Jacob and his fathers throughout their lives, so too He will lead his grandchildren. The second blessing is: **May they proliferate like fish in the midst of the earth.**[8]

17 *Third aliya* While Jacob was reciting the blessing, **Joseph saw that his father** had switched his hands, as he **would lay his right hand upon the head of Ephraim, and it displeased him.** Joseph expected Jacob to give preference to Manasseh, the firstborn, by placing his right hand upon him. Since his father's vision was impaired, Joseph surmised that he had erred. Perhaps Joseph was displeased because he felt that Jacob thought that Joseph himself had mistakenly placed his sons on the wrong sides. In order to rectify what Joseph perceived as an error, **he supported his father's hand** from below, **to remove it from the head of Ephraim to the head of Manasseh.**

18 **Joseph** also **said** explicitly **to his father: Not so, my father, as this** one, Manasseh, **is the firstborn; place your right hand upon his head.**

19 **His father refused and said: I know, my son, I know** which is the firstborn, despite my impaired vision. I am not withholding my blessing from the firstborn, Manasseh, as **he too shall become a people, and he too shall be great. However, his younger brother** Ephraim **shall be greater than he**[D] with regard to the number of his descendants and their power, **and his descendants shall be the plenitude of nations,** as they will fill the world.

DISCUSSION

48:9| **And I will bless them:** Jacob plans to bless his grandchildren with everything at his disposal. He is offering them not merely good wishes, but a prophetic blessing, similar to the one which Isaac bestowed upon his children (chap. 27). Although Jacob was elderly, ill, and suffering from various travails, the strength of his blessing would not be affected, as it stemmed from his power as a prophet.

48:11| **I did not expect [*fillalti*]:** Some commentaries associate this term with *tefilla*, prayer, understanding the phrase to mean: I did not even pray for such a possibility. When I thought that you had been killed by a wild animal, I did not imagine that I would ever see you again (see Radak; *Ḥizkuni*).

48:19| **His younger brother shall be greater than he:** Jacob's prophetic blessing refers to Joshua, who was a member of the tribe of Ephraim. He became the leader of the Jewish people, and his reputation and influence were known throughout the world. Moreover, many years later the tribe of Ephraim still retained a more senior status, although at times it was smaller than Manasseh. Approximately 450 years after the time of Joshua, when the kingdom of Israel was divided, Ephraim was the primary tribe in which the independent dominion for the kingdom of Israel, which broke away from the kingdom of Judah, began (see I Kings, chap. 11). Furthermore, even in the generations when individuals from other tribes ruled over the kingdom of Israel, its capital city was Samaria, which was located within the tribal portion of

י אֲשֶׁר־נָתַן־לִי אֱלֹהִים בָּזֶה וַיֹּאמַר קָחֶם־נָא אֵלַי וַאֲבָרְכֵם: וְעֵינֵי יִשְׂרָאֵל כָּבְדוּ שני
יא מִזֹּקֶן לֹא יוּכַל לִרְאוֹת וַיַּגֵּשׁ אֹתָם אֵלָיו וַיִּשַּׁק לָהֶם וַיְחַבֵּק לָהֶם: וַיֹּאמֶר יִשְׂרָאֵל
יב אֶל־יוֹסֵף רְאֹה פָנֶיךָ לֹא פִלָּלְתִּי וְהִנֵּה הֶרְאָה אֹתִי אֱלֹהִים גַּם אֶת־זַרְעֶךָ: וַיּוֹצֵא
יג יוֹסֵף אֹתָם מֵעִם בִּרְכָּיו וַיִּשְׁתַּחוּ לְאַפָּיו אָרְצָה: וַיִּקַּח יוֹסֵף אֶת־שְׁנֵיהֶם אֶת־
אֶפְרַיִם בִּימִינוֹ מִשְּׂמֹאל יִשְׂרָאֵל וְאֶת־מְנַשֶּׁה בִשְׂמֹאלוֹ מִימִין יִשְׂרָאֵל וַיַּגֵּשׁ אֵלָיו:
יד וַיִּשְׁלַח יִשְׂרָאֵל אֶת־יְמִינוֹ וַיָּשֶׁת עַל־רֹאשׁ אֶפְרַיִם וְהוּא הַצָּעִיר וְאֶת־שְׂמֹאלוֹ
טו עַל־רֹאשׁ מְנַשֶּׁה שִׂכֵּל אֶת־יָדָיו כִּי מְנַשֶּׁה הַבְּכוֹר: וַיְבָרֶךְ אֶת־יוֹסֵף וַיֹּאמַר
הָאֱלֹהִים אֲשֶׁר הִתְהַלְּכוּ אֲבֹתַי לְפָנָיו אַבְרָהָם וְיִצְחָק הָאֱלֹהִים הָרֹעֶה אֹתִי מֵעוֹדִי
טז עַד־הַיּוֹם הַזֶּה: הַמַּלְאָךְ הַגֹּאֵל אֹתִי מִכָּל־רָע יְבָרֵךְ אֶת־הַנְּעָרִים וְיִקָּרֵא בָהֶם
יז שְׁמִי וְשֵׁם אֲבֹתַי אַבְרָהָם וְיִצְחָק וְיִדְגּוּ לָרֹב בְּקֶרֶב הָאָרֶץ: וַיַּרְא יוֹסֵף כִּי־יָשִׁית שלישי
אָבִיו יַד־יְמִינוֹ עַל־רֹאשׁ אֶפְרַיִם וַיֵּרַע בְּעֵינָיו וַיִּתְמֹךְ יַד־אָבִיו לְהָסִיר אֹתָהּ מֵעַל
יח רֹאשׁ־אֶפְרַיִם עַל־רֹאשׁ מְנַשֶּׁה: וַיֹּאמֶר יוֹסֵף אֶל־אָבִיו לֹא־כֵן אָבִי כִּי־זֶה הַבְּכֹר
יט שִׂים יְמִינְךָ עַל־רֹאשׁוֹ: וַיְמָאֵן אָבִיו וַיֹּאמֶר יָדַעְתִּי בְנִי יָדַעְתִּי גַּם־הוּא יִהְיֶה־
לְּעָם וְגַם־הוּא יִגְדָּל וְאוּלָם אָחִיו הַקָּטֹן יִגְדַּל מִמֶּנּוּ וְזַרְעוֹ יִהְיֶה מְלֹא־הַגּוֹיִם:

רש"י

ט| **בזה.** הראה לו שטר אירוסין ושטר כתובה, ובקש יוסף רחמים על הדבר, ונחה עליו רוח הקדש: **ויאמר קחם נא אלי ואברכם.** זהו שאמר הכתוב: "ואנכי תרגלתי לאפרים קחם על זרועותיו" (הושע יא, ג), תרגלתי רוחי ביעקב בשביל אפרים עד שלקחם על זרועותיו:

יא| **לא פללתי.** לא מלאני לבי לחשב מחשבה שאראה פניך עוד. 'פללתי' לשון מחשבה, כמו: "הביאי עצה עשו פלילה" (ישעיה טז, ג):

יב| **ויוצא יוסף אתם.** לאחר שנשקם הוציאם יוסף מעם ברכיו, כדי לישבם זה לימין וזה לשמאל לסמוך ידיו עליהם ולברכם: **וישתחו לאפיו.** כשחזר לאחוריו מלפני אביו:

יג| **את אפרים בימינו משמאל ישראל.** הבא לקראת חברו ימינו כנגד שמאל חברו, וכון שיהא הבכור מיומן לברכה:

יד| **שכל את ידיו.** כתרגומו "אחכמינון", בהשכל וחכמה השכיל את ידיו לכך ומדעת, כי יודע היה כי מנשה הבכור ואף על פי כן לא שת ימינו עליו:

טז| **המלאך הגאל אותי.** מלאך הרגיל להשתלח אלי בצרתי, כענין שנאמר: "ויאמר אלי מלאך האלהים בחלום יעקב וגו', אנכי האל בית אל" (לעיל לא, יא-יג): **יברך את הנערים.** מנשה ואפרים: **וידגו.** כדגים הללו שפרים ורבים ואין עין הרע שולטת בהם:

יז| **ויתמך יד אביו.** הרימה מעל ראש בנו ותמכה בידו:

יט| **ידעתי בני ידעתי.** שהוא הבכור, וגם הוא יהיה לעם ויגדל – עתיד גדעון לצאת ממנו, שהקדוש ברוך הוא עושה נס על ידו: **ואולם אחיו הקטן יגדל ממנו.** שעתיד יהושע לצאת ממנו, שינחיל את הארץ וילמד תורה לישראל: **וזרעו יהיה מלא הגוים.** כל העולם יתמלא בצאת שמעו ושמו, כשיעמיד חמה בגבעון וירח בעמק אילון:

DISCUSSION

→ Ephraim. On a different note, the golden calf that Yorovam established in the city of Beit El, in the portion of Ephraim (see I Kings, chap. 12; Judges 4:5; Jeremiah 31:8), alludes to the family symbol of Joseph, who is likened by Moses to an ox (see Deuteronomy 33:17). It should be noted that the golden calves were not initially intended to serve as objects of idolatry but as substitutes for the Temple, located in the tribe of Judah, where the symbol of Judah, a lion (see 49:9), was commonly found.

20 **He blessed them that day, saying: By you shall Israel bless**[D] their children, **saying: May God make you like Ephraim and like Manasseh,**[D] **and he placed Ephraim before Manasseh** in the text of the blessing.[9] In practice as well, Manasseh was given secondary status, despite the fact that he was the firstborn.

21 **Israel said to Joseph: Behold, I am dying** and will not return to the land of Canaan while I am alive. Although nothing was preventing his children from returning there at that time, Jacob knew prophetically that they would not return there in the near future. Nevertheless, he declared to his son: **God will be with you, and He will** eventually **restore you to the land of your fathers.**

22 Consequently, in my capacity as father and the transmitter of the inheritance, **I have given to you one portion [*shekhem*]** of an inheritance as a gift **beyond** that of **your brothers.** Instead of receiving one inheritance, your children will inherit two portions. This is the primary ramification of Ephraim and Manasseh being granted the status of Jacob's adopted children, on the same level as the other tribes of Israel. This is the portion **which I took from the hand of the Emorite with my sword and with my bow.**[D] The reference to *shekhem* here may mean that Jacob gave the city of Shekhem, to Joseph. Indeed, this city was included in the inheritance of his sons, and Joseph himself was buried there.[10]

49 1 **Jacob called to his sons, and he said: Gather and I will tell you that which shall befall you at the end of days.**[D]

Fourth aliya

2 **Assemble and hear, sons of Jacob, and heed Israel your father.**

3 Jacob's first few blessings follow his sons' order of age. **Reuben, you are my firstborn, my strength and the first of my potency;** as the eldest, you were born when my strength was at its greatest. Therefore, you should have merited **greater honor and greater power** and ruled over your brothers.[11]

4 However, because you were **impetuous as water, you shall not excel,**[D] as you lost your precedence **because you mounted your father's bed,** the bed of your father' wife, which is the prime example of your impetuousness. **Then you desecrated he who ascended my couch,** yourself.[12] Alternatively, this is referring to the Divine Presence that resides there.[13] Others explain that the phrase "he who ascended [*ala*]" means "removed."[14] In other words, from that day the couch, or Jacob's honor, was removed, as he was forced to separate from Bilha due to this incident. Yet another explanation is that Jacob is saying to Reuben: You desecrated my bed and marital activities, which should have been above [*lema'ala*] and beyond your concerns; therefore, you forfeited your status as firstborn.

5 **Simeon and Levi are brothers.** These two brothers were apparently very close. They acted together, and Jacob likewise addresses them together. **Weapons of villainy are their heritage.**[15] They grew up using weapons from a young age.

6 **My self shall not come in their company**[D] **[*sodam*].**[16] Alternatively, this is referring to their secret [*sod*] actions. **With their assembly may my glory not be associated; for in their**

DISCUSSION

48:20 | **By you shall Israel bless:** At this point, Israel the individual becomes identified with Israel the people, due to his prophecy. Jacob's prophecy was not merely ecstatic. Rather, he transcended his temporal existence, perceiving simultaneously his own present and future generations of the Jewish people. His prophecy has indeed come to pass and continues to be fulfilled to this day, as Jewish parents bless their children with Jacob's formulation every Friday night.

May God make you like Ephraim and like Manasseh: Jacob's blessing to his grandchildren Ephraim and Manasseh and to their father Joseph was that future generations should cite them as models of ideal individuals. This is similar to the blessing that God gave to Abraham: "And you shall be a blessing, and all of the families of the earth shall be blessed in you" (12:2–3, and Ramban ad loc.). In other words, Abraham himself will be a symbol of a blessing, as people will be blessed in his name.

48:22 | **Which I took from the hand of the Emorite with my sword and with my bow:** Although it is unknown how Jacob took possession of the city of Shekhem from the Emorites, it is possible that in the wake of the slaughter perpetrated by his sons there (see chap. 34), a war erupted between Jacob's family and the nations of Canaan. There are several recorded accounts of such battles (see *Bereshit Rabba* 80:10; *Tzava'at HaShevatim*, *Tzava'at Yehuda*, chaps. 4–5). Jacob, who was unable to prevent the outbreak of that war, defended himself and fought those nations. As a result, or perhaps in order to prevent a widespread war, Jacob conquered and took possession of Shekhem. If so, the city had been destroyed and abandoned many years before, and Jacob had no connection with it at this stage; nevertheless, the place remained in his possession, and here he bequeathed this inheritance to Joseph and his descendants.

49:1 | **And I will tell you that which shall befall you at the end of days:** The expression "end of days" does not necessarily refer to the end of time or even to thousands of years in the future, but can be referring to anytime in the somewhat distant future. In this case, some of Jacob's blessings deal with the nature of the inheritances of each tribe in the land of Canaan, which would be divided hundreds of years later, and occasionally he seems to reference points later in history. According to the Sages, Jacob wanted to issue a detailed prophecy with regard to the actual end of days. However, he was prevented by Heaven from doing so; perhaps not all his sons were worthy of such a prophecy (*Pesaḥim* 56a; *Targum Yonatan*; Rashi; Ramban).

Jacob's statements, which consist partially of blessings, partially of prophecies, and partially of rebuke, were delivered in a poetic style. As is customary for biblical poetry, almost every verse contains linguistic and thematic parallelisms.

49:4 | **Impetuous as water, you shall not exceed:** As mentioned earlier (35:22), Reuben ascended the bed of Bilha, whom he may have

כ ויברכם ביום ההוא לאמור בך יברך ישראל לאמר ישמך אלהים כאפרים
כא וכמנשה וישם את־אפרים לפני מנשה: ויאמר ישראל אל־יוסף הנה אנכי
כב מת והיה אלהים עמכם והשיב אתכם אל־ארץ אבתיכם: ואני נתתי לך שכם
אחד על־אחיך אשר לקחתי מיד האמרי בחרבי ובקשתי:
מט א ויקרא יעקב אל־בניו ויאמר האספו ואגידה לכם את אשר־יקרא אתכם מג רביעי
ב ג באחרית הימים: הקבצו ושמעו בני יעקב ושמעו אל־ישראל אביכם: ראובן
ד בכרי אתה כחי וראשית אוני יתר שאת ויתר עז: פחז כמים אל־תותר כי
עלית משכבי אביך אז חללת יצועי עלה:
ה ו שמעון ולוי אחים כלי חמס מכרתיהם: בסדם אל־תבא נפשי בקהלם אל־

רש"י

כ| **בך יברך ישראל.** הבא לברך את בניו יברכם בברכתם, ויאמר איש לבנו: "ישמך אלהים כאפרים וכמנשה": **וישם את אפרים.** בברכתו "לפני מנשה", להקדימו בדגלים ובחנוכת הנשיאים:

כב| **ואני נתתי לך.** לפי שאתה טורח להתעסק בקבורתי, וגם "אני נתתי לך" נחלה שתקבר בה, ואי זו? זו שכם, שנאמר: "ואת עצמות יוסף אשר העלו בני ישראל ממצרים קברו בשכם" (יהושע כד, לב): **שכם אחד על אחיך.** שכם ממש, היא תהיה לך חלק אחד יתרה על אחיך: **בחרבי ובקשתי.** כשהרגו שמעון ולוי את אנשי שכם נתכנסו כל סביבותיהם להזדוג להם, וחגר יעקב כלי מלחמה כנגדן. דבר אחר, "שכם אחד", היא הבכורה, שיטלו בניו שני חלקים, ו'שכם' לשון חלק הוא, והרבה יש לו דומים במקרא: "אחלקה שכם" (תהלים ס, ח); "כי תשיתמו שכם" (שם כא, יג), תשית שונאי לפני לחלקים; "דרך ירצחו שכמה" (הושע ו, ט), איש חלקו; "לעבדו שכם אחד" (צפניה ג, ט). "אשר לקחתי מיד האמרי" – מיד עשו שעושה מעשה אמורי. דבר אחר, שהיה צד אביו באמרי פיו. "בחרבי ובקשתי" – היא חכמתו ותפלתו:

פרק מט

א| **ואגידה לכם.** בקש לגלות את הקץ ונסתלקה ממנו שכינה, והתחיל אומר דברים אחרים:

ג-ד| **וראשית אוני.** היא טפה ראשונה לו, שלא ראה קרי מימיו: **אוני.** כחי, כמו: "מצאתי און לי" (הושע יב, ט), "מרב אונים" (ישעיה מ, כו), "ולאין אונים" (שם כט): **יתר שאת.** ראוי היית להיות יתר על אחיך בכהנה, לשון נשיאות כפים: **ויתר עז.** במלכות, כמו: "ויתן עז למלכו" (שמואל א' ב, י), ומי גרם לך להפסיד? "פחז כמים" – הפחז והבהלה אשר מהרת להראות כעסך כמים הללו הממהרים למרוצתם, לכך "אל תותר" – אל תרבה לטול כל היתרות הללו שהיו ראויות לך. ומהו הפחז אשר פחזת? "כי עלית משכבי אביך", אז חללת אותו שעלה על יצועי, שם שכינה שדרכו להיות עולה על יצועי: **פחז.** שם דבר הוא, לפיכך טעמו למעלה וכלו נקוד פתח. ואלו היה לשון עבר, היה נקוד חציו קמץ וחציו פתח וטעמו למטה: **יצועי.** לשון משכב, על שם שמציעים אותו על ידי לבדין וסדינין. והרבה דומים לו: "אם אעלה על ערש יצועי" (תהלים קלב, ג), "אם זכרתיך על יצועי" (שם סג, ז):

ה| **שמעון ולוי אחים.** בעצה אחת על שכם ועל יוסף: "ויאמרו איש אל אחיו וגו' ועתה לכו ונהרגהו" (לעיל לז, יט-כ). מי הם? אם תאמר ראובן או יהודה, הרי לא הסכימו בהריגתו. אם תאמר בני השפחות, הרי לא היתה שנאתן שלמה, שנאמר: "והוא נער את בני בלהה ואת בני זלפה" (לעיל לז, ב). יששכר וזבולון לא היו מדברים בפני אחיהם הגדולים מהם. על כרחך שמעון ולוי הם שקראם אביהם 'אחים': **כלי חמס.** אמנות זו של רציחה חמס הוא בידיהם, מברכת עשו היא זו, אמנות שלו היא, ואתם חמסתם אותה הימנו: **מכרתיהם.** לשון כלי זין, הסיף בלשון יוני מכי"ר. תנחומא (שם ט). דבר אחר, "מכרתיהם", בארץ מגורתם נהגו עצמן בכלי חמס, כמו: "מכרתיך ומלדתיך" (יחזקאל טז, ג), וזה תרגום של אונקלוס:

ו| **בסדם אל תבא נפשי.** זה מעשה זמרי, כשנתקבצו שבטו של שמעון להביא את המדינית לפני משה, ואמרו לו: זו אסורה או מתרת? אם תאמר אסורה, בת יתרו מי התירה לך? – אל יזכר שמי בדבר, "זמרי בן סלוא נשיא בית אב לשמעני" (במדבר כה, יד), ולא כתב 'בן יעקב': **בקהלם.** כשיקהיל קרח שהוא משבטו של לוי

DISCUSSION

considered a concubine. Whether or not he actually engaged in intercourse with her, physical desire on his part may have also been a motivating factor in his actions, as Reuben was still a young man at the time, and Bilha was presumably also relatively youthful. The Sages explain that Reuben sought to protest against the fact that even after Rachel's death, Jacob still did not treat Leah as his primary wife. At the time of the incident, Jacob's reaction is not described by the Torah; only now, close to his death, does he reprimand his firstborn son for his deed.

49:6| **My self shall not come in their company:** After the slaughter Simeon and Levi perpetrated in Shekhem, Jacob did not rebuke them personally; he reacted only to the practical consequences of their actions. However, as he did with Reuben, Jacob takes this opportunity to censure Simeon and Levi because they did not merely take revenge against the one who attacked their sister, but they killed his entire family and all of the males in the city, and harmed their animals as well (see chap. 34; see also *Tzeror Hamor*; Abravanel).

anger they killed men, the inhabitants of Shekhem, **and with their will they hamstrung oxen,** they cut the legs of the oxen of those inhabitants, so that they no longer would be usable.

7 **Cursed be their anger, as it is** unacceptably **fierce,**[17] **and their wrath, as it is** too **harsh; I will divide them in Jacob, and I will disperse them in Israel.**[D] They will continue to be identified as two tribes, but they will be scattered and will not inherit a permanent portion of land as their brothers will. It should be noted that Jacob did not curse Simeon and Levi themselves, but only their anger.

8 The Sages state that when Judah heard Jacob's harsh comments to his three older brothers, he was concerned that his father would rebuke him as well,[18] as he too had sinned in the past. Indeed, he began to retreat in hesitation, but his father called him back: **Judah,** not only are you not inferior to the others, but **you, your brothers shall acknowledge you** and give you honor; since **your hand shall be at the neck of your enemies,** as you will subjugate them. In addition, **your father's sons shall prostrate themselves to you,** for you will rule over your brothers.

9 Judah is the first of many of the sons to be compared to an animal. **Judah is a lion cub; from prey, my son, you rose up.** Like a predatory lion, you emerge from each battle with the upper hand. Alternatively, this is possibly an allusion to the sale of Joseph. Jacob, who by now was likely aware of the details of the story, states that Judah saved Joseph and prevented his death.[19] **He crouched, lay like a lion; and like a great cat, who shall rouse him?** Just as no one would challenge a rising lion, so too the tribe of Judah shall be full of warriors, and its fear shall be upon the surrounding region.

10 In addition to the fact that Judah will remain a tribe of warriors, **the scepter shall not depart from Judah, nor the ruler's staff,** a writing tool with which the king writes laws, **from between his feet,** as his descendants shall continue to rule and legislate the law; **until Shilo,** the redeemer, the king to whom everything belongs [*shelo*], **arrives. To him, nations shall assemble.** The tribe of Judah shall continue to lead the people until the coming of the Messiah.[20]

11 Jacob now grants Judah an economic blessing: **He shall bind his foal to the vine** and will not be concerned about its possible destruction, as grape vines will abound in his inheritance; **and to the branch of the vine** he shall bind **his jenny's foal. He launders his garments in wine.** Due to the abundance of wine flowing from his grapes, he could use it not only for drinking, but also for laundering instead of water. **And in the blood of grapes,** wine, he shall launder **his clothes.**

12 **Red-eyed from** drinking much **wine,**[D] **and white-toothed from milk.**

13 At this point, Jacob deviates from his sons' birth order by placing the sons of Leah before those of the maidservants. He also changes the internal order of the sons of Leah, as Zebulun is blessed before the older Issachar. **Zebulun shall dwell at the shore of seas;**[D] **he shall be a shore for ships,** as his inheritance will be on the shore of the Mediterranean Sea, **and his border will be upon Sidon,** as his portion was located in the north. Sidon was always a center of maritime commercial trade. It is possible that the tribe of Zebulun, located in close proximity to Sidon, had significant commercial ties to that city. Zebulun's border might also have extended to the Sea of Galilee, but the reference here to the shore of seas, and a harbor for ships, refers specifically to the Mediterranean.[21]

DISCUSSION

49:7 | I will divide them in Jacob, and I will disperse them in Israel: Simeon remained a small tribe, whose inheritance in the Land of Israel was surrounded by the territory of the tribe of Judah. From the little that is known about his descendants, many of them apparently mingled with the other tribes, and the tribe became almost entirely assimilated into the others (see Joshua 19:1–9 and commentaries there; *Bereshit Rabba* 98:5, 99:7). Levi, by contrast, developed into a distinguished tribe, which served in the Temple, but it too did not have its own land and was dispersed among the other tribes

(see Deuteronomy 18:1–2; *Bereshit Rabba* 99:7; *Targum Yonatan*; Rashi; Ibn Ezra).

Simeon and Levi's actions demonstrated their destructive potential, especially when they joined forces. As a punishment and a corrective measure for this tendency, they were divided and dispersed, to prevent them from causing further damage (see Rabbi Samson Raphael Hirsch).

49:12 | Red-eyed from wine: Judah's blessing indeed materialized during the course of history, as Judah proved to be a great and powerful tribe from which the Davidic royal dynasty emerged. Jacob's promise refers mainly to the distant

future, to the days of David, Solomon, and even later. The blessing of wine and milk also accurately describes the inheritance of Judah. In the Judean mountains there are no grain fields; therefore, raising sheep and cultivating vineyards are the primary source of livelihood.

49:13 | Zebulun shall dwell at the shore of seas: Zebulun's placement before Issachar, which is also the case in Moses' blessing (Deuteronomy 33:18), is possibly due to the fact that Zebulun facilitated Issachar's spiritual achievements by providing him with physical sustenance (see Abravanel; *Bereshit Rabba* 72:5; Deuteronomy 33:18).

ז תֵּחַד כְּבֹדִי כִּי בְאַפָּם הָרְגוּ אִישׁ וּבִרְצֹנָם עִקְּרוּ־שׁוֹר: אָרוּר אַפָּם כִּי עָז וְעֶבְרָתָם
כִּי קָשָׁתָה אֲחַלְּקֵם בְּיַעֲקֹב וַאֲפִיצֵם בְּיִשְׂרָאֵל:
ח ט יְהוּדָה אַתָּה יוֹדוּךָ אַחֶיךָ יָדְךָ בְּעֹרֶף אֹיְבֶיךָ יִשְׁתַּחֲווּ לְךָ בְּנֵי אָבִיךָ: גּוּר אַרְיֵה
י יְהוּדָה מִטֶּרֶף בְּנִי עָלִיתָ כָּרַע רָבַץ כְּאַרְיֵה וּכְלָבִיא מִי יְקִימֶנּוּ: לֹא־יָסוּר שֵׁבֶט
יא מִיהוּדָה וּמְחֹקֵק מִבֵּין רַגְלָיו עַד כִּי־יָבֹא שִׁילֹה וְלוֹ יִקְּהַת עַמִּים: אֹסְרִי לַגֶּפֶן
יב עִירֹה וְלַשֹּׂרֵקָה בְּנִי אֲתֹנוֹ כִּבֵּס בַּיַּיִן לְבֻשׁוֹ וּבְדַם־עֲנָבִים סוּתֹה: חַכְלִילִי עֵינַיִם
מִיָּיִן וּלְבֶן־שִׁנַּיִם מֵחָלָב:
יג זְבוּלֻן לְחוֹף יַמִּים יִשְׁכֹּן וְהוּא לְחוֹף אֳנִיֹּת וְיַרְכָתוֹ עַל־צִידֹן:

רש"י

את כל העדה על משה ועל אהרן, "אל תחד כבדי" שם, אל יתיחד עמהם שמי, שנאמר: "קרח בן יצהר בן קהת בן לוי" (במדבר טז, א), ולא נאמר 'בן יעקב'. אבל בדברי הימים (א׳ ו, כב-כג) כשנתיחסו בני קרח על הדוכן, נאמר: "בן קרח בן יצהר בן קהת בן לוי בן ישראל": אל תחד כבדי. כבוד לשון זכר הוא, ועל כרחך אתה צריך לפרש כמדבר אל הכבוד ואומר: אתה כבודי, אל תתיחד עמהם. כמו: "לא תחד אתם בקבורה" (ישעיה יד, כ): **כי באפם הרגו איש.** אלו חמור ואנשי שכם, ואינן חשובין כלם אלא כאיש אחד. וכן הוא אומר בגדעון: "והכית את מדין כאיש אחד" (שופטים ו, טז). וכן במצרים: "סוס ורכבו רמה בים" (שמות טו, א). זהו מדרשו. ופשוטו: אנשים הרבה קורא 'איש', כל אחד לעצמו, באפם הרגו כל איש שכעסו עליו, וכן: "וילמד לטרף טרף אדם אכל" (יחזקאל יט, ג): **וברצנם עקרו שור.** רצו לעקר את יוסף שנקרא שור, שנאמר: "בכור שורו הדר לו" (דברים לג, יז). "עקרו" אשיירטי״ר בלעז, לשון: "את סוסיהם תעקר" (יהושע יא, ו):

ז| **ארור אפם.** אפילו בשעת תוכחה לא קלל אלא אפם, וזהו שאמר בלעם: "מה אקב לא קבה אל" (במדבר כג, ח): **אחלקם ביעקב.** אפרידם זה מזה, שלא יהא לוי במנין השבטים, והרי הם חלוקים. דבר אחר, אין לך עניים סופרים ומלמדי תינוקות אלא משמעון, כדי שיהיו נפוצים, ושבטו של לוי עשאו מחזר על הגרנות לתרומות ולמעשרות, נתן לו תפוצתו דרך כבוד:

ח| **יהודה אתה יודוך אחיך.** לפי שהוכיח את הראשונים בקנטורים, התחיל יהודה נסוג לאחוריו, וקראו יעקב בדברי רצוי: לא אתה כמותם: **ידך בערף איביך.** בימי דוד, "ואיבי תתה לי ערף" (שמואל ב׳ כב, מא): **בני אביך.** על שם שהיו מנשים הרבה לא אמר 'בני אמך' כדרך שאמר יצחק (לעיל כז, כט):

ט| **גור אריה.** על דוד נתנבא. בתחלה "גור", "בהיות שאול מלך עלינו אתה... המוציא והמביא את ישראל" (שמואל ב׳ ה, ב), ולבסוף "אריה" כשהמליכוהו עליהם. וזהו שתרגם אונקלוס: "שלטון יהא בשרויה", בתחלתו: **מטרף.** ממה שחשדתיך ב"טרף טרף יוסף", "חיה רעה אכלתהו" (לעיל לז, לג), וזהו יהודה שנמשל לאריה – "בני עלית", סלקת את עצמך ואמרת: "מה בצע" וגו׳ (לעיל לז, כו), וכן מהריגת תמר שהודה "צדקה ממני" (לעיל לח, כו), לפיכך "כרע רבץ" וגו׳, בימי שלמה "איש תחת גפנו" וגו׳ (מלכים א׳ ה, ה):

י| **לא יסור שבט מיהודה.** מדוד ואילך, אלו ראשי גליות שבבבל שרודים את העם בשבט, שממנים על פי המלכות: **ומחקק מבין רגליו.** תלמידים, אלו נשיאי ארץ ישראל: **עד כי יבא שילה.** מלך המשיח שהמלוכה שלו. וכן תרגמו אונקלוס. ומדרש אגדה, "שילה", שי לו, שנאמר: "יובילו שי למורא" (תהלים עו, יב): **ולו יקהת עמים.** אסיפת העמים; שהיו״ד עקר היא ביסוד, כמו "יפעתך" (יחזקאל כח, ז; יז), ופעמים שנופלת ממנו. וכמה אותיות משמשות בלשון זה והם נקראים עקר נופל, כגון נו״ן של 'נוגף' ושל 'נושך', ואל״ף שב"אחותי באזניכם" (איוב יג, יז) ושב"אבחת חרב" (יחזקאל כא, כ) "אסוך שמן" (מלכים ב׳ ד, ב); אף זה, "יקהת עמים", אסיפת עמים, שנאמר: "אליו גוים ידרשו" (ישעיה יא, י), ודומה לו: "עין תלעג לאב ותבוז ליקהת אם" (משלי ל, יז), לקבוץ קמטים שבפניה מפני זקנתה. ובתלמוד: "דיתבי ומקהו אקהתא בשוקי דנהרדעא" במסכת יבמות (דף קי ע״ב). ויכול היה לומר: 'קהית עמים':

יא| **אסרי לגפן עירה.** נתנבא על ארץ יהודה שתהא מושכת יין כמעין, איש יהודה יאסר לגפן עיר אחד ויטעננו מגפן אחת, ומשרק אחד בן אתון אחד: **שרקה.** זמורה ארכה, קורייד״א בלעז: **כבס ביין.** כל זה לשון רבוי יין: **סותה.** לשון מין בגד הוא, ואין לו דמיון במקרא: **אסרי.** כמו אוסר, דגמת: "מקימי מעפר דל" (תהלים קיג, ז), "הישבי בשמים" (שם קכג, א), וכן "בני אתנו" כענין זה. ואונקלוס תרגם במלך המשיח: "גפן" הם ישראל, "עירה" זו ירושלים, "שרקה" – ישראל, "ואנכי נטעתיך שורק" (ירמיה ב, כא), "בני אתנו" – "יבנון היכליה", לשון "שער האיתון" בספר יחזקאל (מ, טו). ועוד תרגמו בפנים אחרים: "גפן" אלו צדיקים, "בני אתנו" – "עבדי אוריתא באולפן", על שם "רכבי אתנות צחרות" (שופטים ה, י), "כבס ביין" – "יהא ארגון טב לבושוהי", שצבעו דומה ליין. "ובעונין" הוא לשון "סותה", שהאשה לובשתן ומסיתה בהן את הזכר לתן עיניו בה. ואף רבותינו פרשו בתלמוד לשון הסתת שכרות, במסכת כתבות (דף קיא ע״ב): ועל היין שמא תאמר אינו מרוה, תלמוד לומר: "סותה":

יב| **חכלילי.** לשון אדם, כתרגומו. וכן: "למי חכללות עינים" (משלי כג, כט), שכן דרך שותי יין עיניהם מאדימין: **מחלב.** מרב חלב, שיהא בארצו מרעה טוב לעדרי צאן, וכן פרוש המקרא: אדם עינים יהא מרב יין, ולבן שנים יהא מרב חלב. ולפי תרגומו: "עינים" לשון הרים, שמשם צופים למרחוק. ועוד תרגמו בפנים אחרים, לשון מעינות וקלוח היקבים: "נעווהי", יקבים שלו, ולשון ארמי הוא במסכת עבודה זרה (דף עד ע״ב): "נעוה אדתאו". "יחורן בקעתיה" – תרגום "שנים", לשון "שני הסלעים" (שמואל א׳ יד, ד):

יג| **לחוף ימים.** על חוף ימים תהיה ארצו. "חוף" כתרגומו "ספר", מרק״א בלעז. והוא יהיה מצוי תדיר אל חוף אניות, במקום הנמל שאניות מביאות שם פרקמטיא, שהיה זבולון עוסק בפרקמטיא וממציא מזון לשבט יששכר, והם עוסקים בתורה. הוא שאמר משה: "שמח זבולן בצאתך ויששכר באהליך" (דברים לג, יח), זבולון יוצא בפרקמטיא ויששכר עוסק בתורה באהלים: **וירכתו על**

14 **Issachar is a strong-boned donkey, lying between the sheep folds,** places of pasture. Issachar is depicted here as a donkey lying tranquilly. There is nothing negative in this choice of animal, even though the word for donkey [*hamor*] was the name of the prince of Shekhem (see 34:2).

15 **He saw rest that it was good, and the land that it was pleasant.** Issachar will find blessing and enjoyment by living peacefully in his own land. Generally, he will not participate in major battles of conquest but will be satisfied with his portion. **He bowed his shoulder to bear** burdens like a donkey, as his tribe would engage in agriculture as a livelihood. **And he became an indentured servant.** Some explain that the Canaanites left in his inheritance would pay him a tax.[22]

16 After addressing the sons of Leah, Jacob turns to the firstborn of Bilha, Rachel's maidservant: **Dan shall avenge his people,**[23] **as one of the tribes of Israel.** His status will not be lower than the other tribes.[24] Jacob is emphasizing that the sons of his wives and the sons of the maidservants are equal in his eyes. Some explain that this prophetic blessing is referring not to the entire tribe but to the lone hero known from this tribe, Samson.[25]

17 **Dan shall be a serpent on the road, a viper**[B] **on the path, that bites a horse's heels and his rider falls backward.** In this scenario, the horse cannot remain standing, and when it falls, the rider falls with it. This depiction of a biting snake alludes to Samson, who did not engage in a military war and was not the head of an army, but acted alone and killed his enemies in unusual ways.[26]

Viper

18 **For your salvation I await, Lord.** When Jacob saw this terrifying snake in his vision that symbolized Dan, he turned to God and requested salvation from Him. Alternatively, following the explanation that the snake symbolizes Samson, Jacob perceived the suffering and tribulations that accompanied Samson's heroic actions, and he therefore prayed for his salvation.[27]

19 *Fifth aliya* After the firstborn son of Bilha, Jacob addresses the firstborn of Zilpa, the maidservant of Leah: **Gad, a troop,** his troops, **shall slash his enemies, and he shall slash their heel.**[D] Here and elsewhere, Gad is depicted as a tribe of warriors.[28]

20 Jacob blesses Zilpa's second son: **From Asher, his bread is fat,**[D] **and he shall provide royal delicacies.** His fertile land will produce choice foods.

21 Jacob blesses Bilha's second son, Naphtali: **Naphtali is a doe let loose** to run freely, **who provides pleasant sayings,**[D] fine and praiseworthy statements. Alternatively, this means that from his inheritance good tidings will come. One who returns from the portion of Naphtali will say: I have seen beautiful flowers, good fruits, and the like.[29]

22 The majority of descriptions in Jacob's blessings involve animals, but in the case of Joseph, the son of Rachel, his father uses imagery of vegetation. **Joseph is a fruitful tree,**[30] **a fruitful tree** growing tranquilly **alongside a spring,** as his needs are provided for him; **branches run over the wall.** Some explain that this means: Girls shall stroll over the wall.[31] The tribe shall live in tranquility, so that instead of soldiers patrolling the wall, girls will stroll over it.

23 Jacob describes Joseph's difficult experiences: **They embittered him** through their hatred and by selling him, **and shot him,**[32] **and archers hated him.**

BACKGROUND

49:17 | **Viper [*shefifon*]:** This name can refer onomatopoeically to any of three different types of snakes that emit hissing sounds. It is generally identified as the poisonous snake *Pseudocerestes fieldi*, which is yellowish in color, with a row of light spots on its skin and a bright underbelly. It also has hornlike indentations above its eyes. It is noteworthy that the names of many snakes in the Bible, e.g., *tzefa*, *tzifoni*, *ef'eh*, *shefifon*, and *sharaf*, contain letters such as *tzadi*, *shin*, or *peh*, which are reminiscent of a hissing sound.

DISCUSSION

49:19 | **Gad, a troop shall slash his enemies, and he shall slash their heel:** This is a highly alliterative blessing, which reads in the Hebrew: *Gad gedud yegudenu vehu yagud akev*. Jacob uses words with similar sounds but very different meanings.

49:20 | **Asher, his bread is fat:** The inheritance of Asher was located in a particularly fertile area, the western section of the upper Galilee (see Joshua 19:24–31).

49:21 | **Who provides pleasant sayings:** This blessing may allude to the song of Deborah, recorded in Judges, chap. 5 (Rashi; Ibn Ezra). Although Deborah was not herself a member of this tribe, she sang this victory song together with Barak, who was a member of Naphtali, following the battle in which his tribe changed the political landscape of the Land of Israel.

יד טו יִשָּׂשכָר חֲמֹר גָּרֶם רֹבֵץ בֵּין הַמִּשְׁפְּתָיִם: וַיַּרְא מְנֻחָה כִּי טוֹב וְאֶת־הָאָרֶץ כִּי
טז נָעֵמָה וַיֵּט שִׁכְמוֹ לִסְבֹּל וַיְהִי לְמַס־עֹבֵד: דָּן יָדִין עַמּוֹ כְּאַחַד
יז שִׁבְטֵי יִשְׂרָאֵל: יְהִי־דָן נָחָשׁ עֲלֵי־דֶרֶךְ שְׁפִיפֹן עֲלֵי־אֹרַח הַנֹּשֵׁךְ עִקְּבֵי־סוּס וַיִּפֹּל
יח יט רֹכְבוֹ אָחוֹר: לִישׁוּעָתְךָ קִוִּיתִי יְהוָה: גָּד גְּדוּד יְגוּדֶנּוּ וְהוּא יָגֻד חמישי
כ עָקֵב: מֵאָשֵׁר שְׁמֵנָה לַחְמוֹ וְהוּא יִתֵּן מַעֲדַנֵּי־מֶלֶךְ:
כא כב נַפְתָּלִי אַיָּלָה שְׁלֻחָה הַנֹּתֵן אִמְרֵי־שָׁפֶר: בֵּן פֹּרָת יוֹסֵף בֵּן
כג פֹּרָת עֲלֵי־עָיִן בָּנוֹת צָעֲדָה עֲלֵי־שׁוּר: וַיְמָרֲרֻהוּ וָרֹבּוּ וַיִּשְׂטְמֻהוּ בַּעֲלֵי חִצִּים:

רש"י

צידן. סוף גבולו יהיה סמוך לצידון. "וירכתו" – סופו, כמו: "ולירכתי המשכן" (שמות כו, כב):

יד | **יששכר חמר גרם.** חמור בעל עצמות, סובל עול תורה כחמור חזק שמטעינין אותו משא כבד: **רבץ בין המשפתים.** כחמור המהלך ביום ובלילה ואין לו לינה בבית, וכשהוא רוצה לנוח רובץ בין התחומין, בתחומי העירות שמוליך שם חבילות של פרקמטיא:

טו | **וירא מנחה כי טוב.** ראה לחלקו ארץ מבורכת וטובה להוציא פירות: **ויט שכמו לסבל.** עול תורה: **ויהי.** לכל אחיו ישראל "למס עבד" – לספק להם הוראות של תורה וסדרי עיבורין, שנאמר: "ומבני יששכר יודעי בינה לעתים לדעת מה יעשה ישראל, ראשיהם מאתים", מאתים ראשי סנהדראות העמיד, "וכל אחיהם על פיהם" (דברי הימים א' יב, לג): **ויט שכמו.** השפיל שכמו, כמו: "ויט שמים" (שמואל ב' כב, י), "הטו אזנכם" (תהלים עח, א). ואונקלוס תרגמו בפנים אחרים: ויט שכמו לסבל מלחמות ולכבש מחוזות, שהם יושבים על הספר, ויהי האויב כבוש תחתיו למס עבד:

טז | **דן ידין עמו.** ינקום נקמת עמו מפלשתים, כמו: "כי ידין ה' עמו" (דברים לב, לו): **כאחד שבטי ישראל.** כל ישראל יהיו כאחד עמו ואת כלם ידין, ועל שמשון נבא נבואה זו. ועוד יש לפרש, "כאחד שבטי ישראל", כמיוחד שבשבטים, הוא דוד שבא מיהודה:

יז | **שפיפן.** הוא נחש, ואומר אני שקרוי כן על שם שהוא נושף, "ואתה תשופנו עקב" (לעיל ג, טו): **הנשך עקבי סוס.** כך דרכו של נחש. ודמהו לנחש "הנשך עקבי סוס ויפל רכבו אחור", שלא נגע בו, ודוגמתו מצינו בשמשון: "וילפת וגו' את שני עמודי התוך" וגו' (שופטים טז, כט), ושעל הגג מתו. ואונקלוס תרגם: "כחוי חורמן", שם מין נחש שאין רפואה לנשיכתו והוא צפעוני, וקרוי חורמן על שם שעושה הכל חרם, "וכפתנא" כמו פתן, "יכמון" – יארב:

יח | **לישועתך קויתי ה'.** נתנבא שינקרו פלשתים את עיניו, וסופו לומר: "זכרני נא וחזקני נא אך הפעם" וגו' (שם טז, כח):

יט | **גד גדוד יגודנו.** גדודים יגודו הימנו, שיעברו את הירדן עם אחיהם למלחמה כל חלוץ עד ונכבשה הארץ (עיין במדבר פרק לב): **והוא יגד עקב.** כל גדודיו ישובו על עקבם לנחלתם שלקחו בעבר הירדן, ולא יפקד מהם איש: **עקב.** בדרכם ובמסלותם שהלכו ישובו, כמו: "ועקבותיך לא נדעו" (תהלים עז, כ), וכן: "בעקבי הצאן" (שיר השירים א, ח), בלשון לעז טראצי"ש:

כ | **מאשר שמנה לחמו.** מאכל הבא מחלקו של אשר יהא שמן, שיהיו זיתים מרובים בחלקו והוא מושך שמן כמעין. וכן ברכו משה: "וטבל בשמן רגלו" (דברים לג, כד), כמו ששנינו במנחות: פעם אחת נצטרכו אנשי לודקיא לשמן וכו':

כא | **אילה שלחה.** זו בקעת גנוסר, שהיא קלה לבשל פירותיה כאילה זו שהיא קלה לרוץ. "אילה שלחה" – אילה משולחת לרוץ: **הנתן אמרי שפר.** כתרגומו. דבר אחר, על מלחמת סיסרא נתנבא: "ולקחת עמך עשרת אלפים איש מבני נפתלי" וגו' (שופטים ד, ו) והלכו שם בזריזות. וכן נאמר שם לשון שלוח: "בעמק שלח ברגליו" (שם ה, טו). "הנתן אמרי שפר" – על ידם שרו דבורה וברק שירה. ורבותינו דרשוהו על יום קבורת יעקב, כשערער עשו על המערה, במסכת סוטה (דף יג ע"א). ותרגומו: "יתרמי עדביה", יפול חבלו, והוא יודה על חלקו אמרים נאים ושבח:

כב | **בן פרת.** בן חן. והוא לשון ארמי: "אפרין נמטייה לרבי שמעון" בסוף בבא מציעא (דף קיט ע"א): **בן פרת עלי עין.** חנו נטוי על העין הרואה אותו: **בנות צעדה עלי שור.** בנות מצרים היו צועדות על החומה להסתכל ביפיו. "בנות" הרבה "צעדה" כל אחת ואחת במקום שתוכל לראותו משם. דבר אחר, "עלי שור", על ראייתו, כמו: "אשורנו ולא קרוב" (במדבר כד, יז). ומדרשי אגדה יש רבים, וזה נוטה לישוב המקרא: **פרת.** תי"ו שבו הוא תיקון הלשון, כמו: "על דברת בני האדם" (קהלת ג, יח): **שור.** כמו לשור, "עלי שור" – בשביל לשור. ותרגום של אונקלוס "בנות צעדה עלי שור" – "תרין שבטין יפקון מבנוהי" וכו', וכתב 'בנות' על שם בנות מנשה בנות צלפחד שנטלו חלק בשני עברי הירדן. "ברי דיסגי יוסף" – 'פרת' לשון פריה ורביה. ויש מדרשי אגדה המתישבים על הלשון: בשעה שבא עשו לקראת יעקב, בכלן קדמו האמהות ללכת לפני בניהן להשתחוות, וברחל כתיב: "נגש יוסף ורחל וישתחוו" (לעיל לג, ז). אמר יוסף: הרשע הזה עינו רמה, שמא יתן עיניו באמי. יצא לפניה ושרבב קומתו לכסותה. והוא שברכו אביו: "בן פרת", הגדלת עצמך "יוסף, עלי עין" של עשו, לפיכך זכית לגדלה. "בנות צעדה עלי שור", להסתכל בך בצאתך על מצרים. ועוד דרשוהו לענין שלא ישלט בזרעו עין הרע. ואף כשברך מנשה ואפרים ברכם כדגים שאין עין הרע שולטת בהם:

כג | **וימררהו ורבו.** וימררוהו אחיו, וימררוהו פוטיפר ואשתו לאסרו, לשון: "וימררו את חייהם" (שמות א, יד): **ורבו.** נעשו לו אחיו אנשי ריב. ואין הלשון הזה לשון פעלו, שאם כן היה לו לנקד 'ורבו', כמו: "המה מי מריבה אשר רבו" וגו' (במדבר כ, יג), ואף אם לשון רבית חצים הוא, כן היה לו לנקד; ואינו אלא לשון פעלו, כמו: "שמו שמים" (ירמיה ב, יב) שהוא לשון הושמו, וכן: "רומו מעט" (איוב כד, כד) שהוא לשון הורמו, אלא שלשון הורמו והושמו על ידי אחרים, ולשון שמו, רמו, רבו – מאליהם הוא, משוממים את עצמם, נתרוממו מעצמם, נעשו אנשי ריב. וכן: "דמו ישבי אי" (ישעיה כג, ב) כמו נדמו. וכן תרגם אונקלוס: "ונקמוהי": **בעלי חצים.** שלשונם כחץ, ותרגומו לשון "ותהי המחנה" (במדבר לא, לו), אותן שהיו ראויים לחלק עמו נחלה:

24 However, Joseph did not respond in kind. Rather, **his bow sat firm** without moving,[33] **and the arms of his hands were golden.** His hands held the bow tightly, prepared to shoot if necessary.[34] All this ability comes to him **by the hands of the Mighty One of Jacob,**[35] **from there, from** the strength of **the Shepherd of the stone of Israel.** Israel is considered as strong as a stone.[36] Alternatively, this stone refers to God, in emphasis of His strength, similar to the more common expression "Rock of Israel."[37]

25 **From the God of your father, and He shall help you, and the Almighty, and He shall bless you.** Not only did God's blessings save you in your most difficult times in the past, but they shall continue to shower you and your descendants with abundance and success: With **blessings of heaven above,** e.g., rain, and **blessings of the depths lying beneath,** as the land of your inheritance shall be fertile and moist, as well as **blessings** of fertility, **of breasts and of womb.**

26 **The blessings of your father** that I am bestowing upon you **surpass the blessings of my parents**[D] to me, as I am blessing you with strength, courage, and constant support from Heaven, **until the edge of the eternal hills,** until the end of the world.[38] This is akin to saying: All of the days of the existence of the world.[39] **They,** these blessings, **shall** all **be** like a crown **on the head of Joseph,** placed **on the head of the elect among his brothers,** as their king.[40]

27 **Benjamin is a wolf that mauls; in the morning he devours**
Sixth aliya
prey, and in the evening he divides the spoils of the morning capture. Jacob blesses Benjamin, which is a tribe of warriors, with success in both earlier and later eras of Jewish history: The first king, Saul, came from Benjamin, while the delivery of the Jews from the evil Haman, toward the end of the biblical period, came about through Mordekhai, also a descendant of this tribe.[41]

28 **All these are the tribes of Israel, twelve, and this is that which their father spoke to them, and he blessed them; each man in accordance with his blessing he blessed them.** This seems inaccurate, as apparently some of the sons did not receive any blessings but only rebuke. However, it stands to reason that Jacob also gave each of his sons a separate personal blessing, in the manner of a father prior to his death, and that is the blessing referred to in this verse.[42]

29 **He instructed them and said to them: I am** about **to** die and **be gathered to my people; bury me with my ancestors**[D] **in the cave that is in the field of Efron the Hitite,**

30 **in the cave that is in the field of Makhpela, that is opposite Mamre in the land of Canaan, which Abraham had bought with the field from Efron the Hitite as a burial portion.**

31 **There they buried Abraham and Sarah, his wife; there they buried Isaac and Rebecca, his wife; and there I buried Leah.** My father, mother, grandfather, and grandmother are all

DISCUSSION

49:26 | **The blessings of your father surpass the blessings of my parents:** Joseph merited senior status among the brothers, and he also received the greatest blessings of them all. In Messianic times, the tribes of Joseph will once again be leaders of the Jewish people.

49:29 | **Bury me with my ancestors:** Jacob had initially requested specifically of Joseph to make sure that he would be buried in Canaan, not in Egypt, as Joseph had the authority to fulfill this petition. At this point he turned to his other sons with the same appeal. Presumably, he wanted all of the brothers to work together in this regard, since even if the others did not have the same status as Joseph, they could still assist him. In addition, it is possible that Jacob was concerned that his other sons might be reluctant to bury him far from where they were living. When the patriarch of the family is buried in close proximity to its surviving members, it often serves as a unifying factor, drawing them closer together.

כד וַתֵּשֶׁב בְּאֵיתָן קַשְׁתּוֹ וַיָּפֹזּוּ זְרֹעֵי יָדָיו מִידֵי אֲבִיר יַעֲקֹב מִשָּׁם רֹעֶה אֶבֶן יִשְׂרָאֵל׃
כה מֵאֵל אָבִיךָ וְיַעְזְרֶךָּ וְאֵת שַׁדַּי וִיבָרְכֶךָּ בִּרְכֹת שָׁמַיִם מֵעָל בִּרְכֹת תְּהוֹם רֹבֶצֶת
כו תָּחַת בִּרְכֹת שָׁדַיִם וָרָחַם׃ בִּרְכֹת אָבִיךָ גָּבְרוּ עַל־בִּרְכֹת הוֹרַי עַד־תַּאֲוַת גִּבְעֹת
עוֹלָם תִּהְיֶיןָ לְרֹאשׁ יוֹסֵף וּלְקָדְקֹד נְזִיר אֶחָיו׃
כז כח בִּנְיָמִין זְאֵב יִטְרָף בַּבֹּקֶר יֹאכַל עַד וְלָעֶרֶב יְחַלֵּק שָׁלָל׃ כָּל־אֵלֶּה שִׁבְטֵי יִשְׂרָאֵל ששי
שְׁנֵים עָשָׂר וְזֹאת אֲשֶׁר־דִּבֶּר לָהֶם אֲבִיהֶם וַיְבָרֶךְ אוֹתָם אִישׁ אֲשֶׁר כְּבִרְכָתוֹ
כט בֵּרַךְ אֹתָם׃ וַיְצַו אוֹתָם וַיֹּאמֶר אֲלֵהֶם אֲנִי נֶאֱסָף אֶל־עַמִּי קִבְרוּ אֹתִי אֶל־אֲבֹתָי
ל אֶל־הַמְּעָרָה אֲשֶׁר בִּשְׂדֵה עֶפְרוֹן הַחִתִּי׃ בַּמְּעָרָה אֲשֶׁר בִּשְׂדֵה הַמַּכְפֵּלָה אֲשֶׁר־
עַל־פְּנֵי מַמְרֵא בְּאֶרֶץ כְּנָעַן אֲשֶׁר קָנָה אַבְרָהָם אֶת־הַשָּׂדֶה מֵאֵת עֶפְרֹן הַחִתִּי
לא לַאֲחֻזַּת־קָבֶר׃ שָׁמָּה קָבְרוּ אֶת־אַבְרָהָם וְאֵת שָׂרָה אִשְׁתּוֹ שָׁמָּה קָבְרוּ אֶת־יִצְחָק

רש"י

כד| **ותשב באיתן קשתו.** נתישבה בחוזק: **קשתו.** חזקו: **ויפזו זרעי ידיו.** זו היא נתינת טבעת על ידו, לשון: "זהב מופז" (מלכים א׳ י, יח), זאת היתה לו מידי הקדוש ברוך הוא שהוא "אביר יעקב", ומשם עלה להיות "רעה אבן ישראל", עיקרן של ישראל, לשון: "האבן הראשה" (זכריה ד, ז), לשון מלכות. ואונקלוס אף הוא כך תרגמו: "ותשב" – "ותבת בהון נביאותיה", החלומות אשר חלם להם. "על דקיים אורייתא בסתרא" – תוספת הוא ולא מלשון עברי שבמקרא. "ושוי תקפא רוחצניה" – תרגום של "באיתן קשתו". וכך לשון התרגום על העברי: ותשב נבואתו בשביל שאיתנו של הקדוש ברוך הוא היתה לו לקשת ולמבטח, "בכן אתרמא דהב" – לכך "ויפזו זרעי ידיו", לשון 'פז': **אבן ישראל.** לשון נוטריקון, אב ובן, "אבהן ובנין", יעקב ובניו:

כה| **מאל אביך.** היתה לך זאת, והוא יעזרך: **ואת שדי.** ועם הקדוש ברוך הוא היה לבך כשלא שמעת לדברי אדונתך, והוא יברכך: **ברכת שדים ורחם.** "בריכתא דאבוך ודאמך", כלומר יתברכו המולידים והיולדות, שיהיו הזכרים מזריעים טפה הראויה להריון, והנקבות לא ישכלו את רחם שלהן להפיל עובריהן: **שדים.** "ירה יירה" (שמות יט, יג) מתרגמינן: "אשתדאה ישתדי", אף שדים כאן על שם שהזרע יורה כחץ:

כו| **ברכת אביך גברו וגו׳.** הברכות שברכני הקדוש ברוך הוא גברו על הברכות שברך את הורי: **עד תאות גבעת עולם.** לפי שהברכות שלי גברו והלכו עד סוף גבולי גבעות עולם, שנתן לי ברכה פרוצה בלי מצרים מגעת עד ארבע קצות העולם, שנאמר: "ופרצת ימה וקדמה" וגו׳ (לעיל כח, יד), מה שלא אמר לאברהם אבינו וליצחק. לאברהם אמר לו: "שא נא עיניך וראה... צפנה וגו׳ כי את כל הארץ אשר אתה ראה לך אתננה" (לעיל יג, יד-טו), ולא הראהו אלא ארץ ישראל בלבד. ליצחק אמר לו: "כי לך ולזרעך אתן את כל הארצת האל והקמתי את השבעה" וגו׳ (לעיל כו, ג). וזהו שאמר ישעיה: "והאכלתיך נחלת יעקב אביך" (ישעיה נח, יד) ולא אמר 'נחלת אברהם': **הורי.** לשון הריון, שהורוני במעי אמי, כמו "הרה גבר" (איוב ג, ג): **תאות.** אשמול"ץ, כך חברו מנחם בן סרוק: **עד תאות.** עד קצות, כמו: "והתאויתם לכם לגבול קדמה" (במדבר לד, י), "תתאו לבא חמת" (שם פסוק ח): **תהיין.** כלם "לראש יוסף": **נזיר אחיו.** "פרישא דאחוהי", שנבדל מאחיו, כמו: "וינזרו מקדשי בני ישראל" (ויקרא כב, ב), "נזרו אחור" (ישעיה א, ד). ורבותינו דרשו "ותשב באיתן קשתו" על כבישת יצרו באשת אדניו, וקורהו 'קשת' על שם שהזרע יורה כחץ. "ויפזו זרעי ידיו", כמו ויפוצו, שיצא הזרע מבין אצבעות ידיו. "מידי אביר יעקב", שנראתה לו דמות דיוקנו של אביו בחלון וכו׳, כדאיתא במסכת סוטה (דף לו ע״ב). ואונקלוס תרגם "תאות גבעת עולם" לשון תאוה וחמדה, 'וגבעות' לשון "מצקי ארץ" (שמואל א׳ ב, ח) שחמדתן אמו והזקיקתו לקבלם:

כז| **בנימין זאב יטרף.** זאב הוא אשר יטרף, נבא על שהיו עתידין להיות חטפנין, "וחטפתם לכם איש אשתו" בפילגש בגבעה (שופטים כא, כא). ונבא על שאול שהיה נוצח באויביו סביב, שנאמר: "ושאול לכד המלוכה... וילחם... במואב... ובאדום וגו׳ ובכל אשר יפנה ירשיע" (שמואל א׳ יד, מז): **בבקר יאכל עד.** לשון בזה ושלל המתרגם: 'עדאה'. ועוד יש לו דומה בלשון עברית: "אז חלק עד שלל" (ישעיה לג, כג), ועל שאול הוא אומר, שעמד בתחלת בקרן וזריחתן של ישראל: **ולערב יחלק שלל.** אף משתשקע שמשן של ישראל על ידי נבוכדנצר שיגלם לבבל, "יחלק שלל" – מרדכי ואסתר שהם מבנימין יחלקו את שלל המן, שנאמר: "הנה בית המן נתתי לאסתר" (אסתר ח, ז). ואונקלוס תרגמו על שלל הכהנים בקדשי המקדש:

כח| **וזאת אשר דבר להם אביהם ויברך אותם.** והלא יש מהם שלא ברכם אלא קנטרן? אלא כך פרושו: "וזאת אשר דבר להם אביהם", מה שאמור בענין. יכול שלא ברך לראובן שמעון ולוי? תלמוד לומר: "ויברך אותם", כלם במשמע: **אשר כברכתו.** ברכה העתידה לבא על כל אחד ואחד "ברך אתם". לא היה לו לומר אלא 'איש אשר כברכתו ברך אותו', מה תלמוד לומר: "ברך אתם"? לפי שנתן ליהודה גבורת ארי ולבנימין חטיפתו של זאב ולנפתלי קלותו של איל, יכול שלא כללן כלם בכל הברכות? תלמוד לומר: "ברך אתם":

כט| **נאסף אל עמי.** על שם שמכניסין הנפשות אל מקום גניזתן, שיש אסיפות בלשון עברית שהן לשון הכנסה, כגון: "ואין איש מאסף אותי הביתה" (שופטים יט, יח), "ואספתו אל תוך ביתך" (דברים כב, ב), "באספכם את תבואת הארץ" (ויקרא כג, לט) – הכנסתה לבית מפני הגשמים, "באספך את מעשיך" (שמות כג, טז), וכל אסיפה האמורה במיתה אף היא לשון הכנסה: **אל אבתי.** עם אבותי:

interred there, as well as my wife Leah. I wish to be buried there as well.

32 **The purchase of the field and the cave that is in it,**[D] the familial burial plot, **was** acquired by my grandfather **from the children of Het.**

33 **Jacob concluded instructing his sons.** Although he was ill, he spoke while sitting up on the bed. When he sensed he was about to die, **he drew his feet to the bed, and** in this state **he expired, and he was gathered to his people.**

After Jacob's Death

GENESIS 50:1–21

The death of Jacob, the elderly patriarch of the family, is followed by several official mourning ceremonies and emotional responses. Even the Egyptians pay their final respects to Joseph's father.

50 1 **Joseph,** the most eminent of the brothers, **fell upon his father's face, wept upon him, and kissed him.**

2 **Joseph commanded his servants, the physicians, to embalm his father.** Joseph had physicians under his jurisdiction who were responsible for embalming the dead, among other duties. This process involved removing the body's inner organs and filling the body with preservatives, so that its physical form would be preserved. **The physicians** then **embalmed Israel.**

Embalming the dead: Final stages of embalming, from a fresco found at Thebes, thirteenth century BCE

3 **Forty days** following his death **were completed for him, as so are the days of embalming completed.** This was the standard period necessary for this process, as preserving the form of the deceased is delicate work that takes an extensive amount of time. **Egypt wept for him seventy days.** The official mourning began only after Jacob's body was embalmed and placed in a coffin. In accordance with Egyptian custom, the period of weeping lasted for seventy days. Alternatively, these seventy days include the forty days of embalming, while the remaining thirty days of weeping correspond to the standard Jewish custom of a thirty-day mourning period.[43]

4 **The days of his weeping passed, and Joseph spoke to Pharaoh's household.** Joseph did not approach Pharaoh directly, perhaps because he was worried that he might receive a negative response. Rather, he first sent messengers to Pharaoh's household, **saying: Please, if I have found favor in your eyes, please, speak** in my name **in the ears of Pharaoh, saying:**

5 **My father administered an oath to me, saying: Behold, I am dying; in my grave that I dug for me in the land of Canaan, bury me there.** Joseph asks of Pharaoh: **I will go up** to the land of Canaan **now and bury my father** in the location he requested, **and** afterward **I will return**[D] to you.

6 **Pharaoh said: Go up and bury your father, in accordance with the oath he administered to you.**

7 **Joseph went up to bury his father, and all the servants of Pharaoh, the elders of his house, and all the elders of the land of Egypt went up with him,**

8 **and all of Joseph's household, and his brothers, and his father's household. They left only their children, their flocks, and their cattle in the land of Goshen.**

9 **He took up with him both chariots and horsemen,**[D] possibly sent by Pharaoh to ensure that Joseph would return to Egypt; **and the camp was very substantial.**

10 **They came to the threshing floor of Atad,**[B] which might have been given this name because it was surrounded by thorny *atad*, or *Lycium* bushes.[44] **That** threshing floor **is beyond the Jordan,** located on their route to Canaan. It is possible that they preferred

DISCUSSION

49:32 | **The purchase of the field and the cave that is in it:** The purchase of this burial plot and its use in practice are mentioned several times in the book of Genesis (see 25:9, 50:13). Jacob's request for burial in this ancestral plot serves as an anchor and provides hope to the rest of the family, who are currently in exile, reminding them that their stay in Egypt is only temporary. Their legacy is firmly planted in the land of Canaan, where they will eventually return.

50:5 | **I will go up…and I will return:** From the formulation of Joseph's request and the continuation of the narrative, it is understandable why he had never visited his family in Canaan. Although Joseph possessed a significant measure of authority in Egypt, he is clearly subordinate to Pharaoh. Despite his display of loyalty, Pharaoh may have wished to ensure that there was no risk in allowing him to leave the country. Pharaoh could have suspected that as a former resident of Canaan, Joseph might seek to return there and use the power he had amassed in Egypt to establish an independent empire. Aware of this potential concern, Joseph therefore clarifies to Pharaoh that he is leaving Egypt only due to his father's oath. Additionally, Joseph commits to returning to Egypt immediately following the burial.

לב וְאֶת רִבְקָה אִשְׁתּוֹ וְשָׁמָּה קָבַרְתִּי אֶת־לֵאָה: מִקְנֵה הַשָּׂדֶה וְהַמְּעָרָה אֲשֶׁר־בּוֹ
לג מֵאֵת בְּנֵי־חֵת: וַיְכַל יַעֲקֹב לְצַוֹּת אֶת־בָּנָיו וַיֶּאֱסֹף רַגְלָיו אֶל־הַמִּטָּה וַיִּגְוַע וַיֵּאָסֶף
נ א ב אֶל־עַמָּיו: וַיִּפֹּל יוֹסֵף עַל־פְּנֵי אָבִיו וַיֵּבְךְּ עָלָיו וַיִּשַּׁק־לוֹ: וַיְצַו יוֹסֵף אֶת־עֲבָדָיו
ג אֶת־הָרֹפְאִים לַחֲנֹט אֶת־אָבִיו וַיַּחַנְטוּ הָרֹפְאִים אֶת־יִשְׂרָאֵל: וַיִּמְלְאוּ־לוֹ אַרְבָּעִים
ד יוֹם כִּי כֵּן יִמְלְאוּ יְמֵי הַחֲנֻטִים וַיִּבְכּוּ אֹתוֹ מִצְרַיִם שִׁבְעִים יוֹם: וַיַּעַבְרוּ יְמֵי בְכִיתוֹ
וַיְדַבֵּר יוֹסֵף אֶל־בֵּית פַּרְעֹה לֵאמֹר אִם־נָא מָצָאתִי חֵן בְּעֵינֵיכֶם דַּבְּרוּ־נָא
ה בְּאָזְנֵי פַרְעֹה לֵאמֹר: אָבִי הִשְׁבִּיעַנִי לֵאמֹר הִנֵּה אָנֹכִי מֵת בְּקִבְרִי אֲשֶׁר כָּרִיתִי
לִי בְּאֶרֶץ כְּנַעַן שָׁמָּה תִּקְבְּרֵנִי וְעַתָּה אֶעֱלֶה־נָּא וְאֶקְבְּרָה אֶת־אָבִי וְאָשׁוּבָה:
ו ז וַיֹּאמֶר פַּרְעֹה עֲלֵה וּקְבֹר אֶת־אָבִיךָ כַּאֲשֶׁר הִשְׁבִּיעֶךָ: וַיַּעַל יוֹסֵף לִקְבֹּר אֶת־אָבִיו
ח וַיַּעֲלוּ אִתּוֹ כָּל־עַבְדֵי פַרְעֹה זִקְנֵי בֵיתוֹ וְכֹל זִקְנֵי אֶרֶץ־מִצְרָיִם: וְכֹל בֵּית יוֹסֵף
ט וְאֶחָיו וּבֵית אָבִיו רַק טַפָּם וְצֹאנָם וּבְקָרָם עָזְבוּ בְּאֶרֶץ גֹּשֶׁן: וַיַּעַל עִמּוֹ גַּם־רֶכֶב
י גַּם־פָּרָשִׁים וַיְהִי הַמַּחֲנֶה כָּבֵד מְאֹד: וַיָּבֹאוּ עַד־גֹּרֶן הָאָטָד אֲשֶׁר בְּעֵבֶר הַיַּרְדֵּן

רש״י

לג| וַיֶּאֱסֹף רַגְלָיו. הִכְנִיס רַגְלָיו: וַיִּגְוַע וַיֵּאָסֶף. וּמִיתָה לֹא נֶאֶמְרָה בּוֹ, וְאָמְרוּ רַבּוֹתֵינוּ: יַעֲקֹב אָבִינוּ לֹא מֵת:

פרק נ

ב| לַחֲנֹט אֶת אָבִיו. עִנְיַן מִרְקַחַת בְּשָׂמִים הוּא:

ג| וַיִּמְלְאוּ לוֹ. הִשְׁלִימוּ לוֹ יְמֵי חֲנִיטָתוֹ עַד שֶׁמָּלְאוּ לוֹ אַרְבָּעִים יוֹם: וַיִּבְכּוּ אֹתוֹ מִצְרַיִם שִׁבְעִים יוֹם. אַרְבָּעִים לַחֲנִיטָה וּשְׁלֹשִׁים לִבְכִי, לְפִי שֶׁבָּאָה לָהֶם בְּרָכָה לְרַגְלוֹ, שֶׁכָּלָה הָרָעָב וְהָיוּ מֵי נִילוּס מִתְבָּרְכִין:

ה| אֲשֶׁר כָּרִיתִי לִי. כִּפְשׁוּטוֹ, כְּמוֹ: "כִּי יִכְרֶה אִישׁ" (שמות כא, לג). וּמִדְרָשׁוֹ עוֹד מִתְיַשֵּׁב עַל הַלָּשׁוֹן, כְּמוֹ אֲשֶׁר קָנִיתִי. אָמַר רַבִּי עֲקִיבָא: כְּשֶׁהָלַכְתִּי לִכְרַכֵּי הַיָּם הָיוּ קוֹרִין לִמְכִירָה 'כִּירָה'. וְעוֹד מִדְרָשׁוֹ לְשׁוֹן כְּרִי, דְּגוֹר; שֶׁנָּטַל יַעֲקֹב כָּל כֶּסֶף וְזָהָב שֶׁהֵבִיא מִבֵּית לָבָן וְעָשָׂה אוֹתוֹ כְּרִי, וְאָמַר לְעֵשָׂו: טֹל זֶה בִּשְׁבִיל חֶלְקְךָ בַּמְּעָרָה:

ו| כַּאֲשֶׁר הִשְׁבִּיעֶךָ. וְאִם לֹא בִּשְׁבִיל הַשְּׁבוּעָה לֹא הָיִיתִי מַנִּיחֲךָ. אֲבָל יָרֵא לוֹמַר: עֲבֹר עַל הַשְּׁבוּעָה, שֶׁלֹּא יֹאמַר: אִם כֵּן, אֶעֱבֹר עַל הַשְּׁבוּעָה שֶׁנִּשְׁבַּעְתִּי לְךָ שֶׁלֹּא אֲגַלֶּה עַל לְשׁוֹן הַקֹּדֶשׁ שֶׁאֲנִי מַכִּיר עוֹדֵף עַל שִׁבְעִים לָשׁוֹן וְאַתָּה אֵינְךָ מַכִּיר בּוֹ, כִּדְאִיתָא בְּמַסֶּכֶת סוֹטָה (דף לו ע״ב):

י| גֹּרֶן הָאָטָד. מֻקָּף אֲטָדִין הָיָה. וְרַבּוֹתֵינוּ דָּרְשׁוּ עַל שֵׁם הַמְּאֹרָע, שֶׁבָּאוּ כָּל מַלְכֵי כְנַעַן וּנְשִׂיאֵי יִשְׁמָעֵאל לַמִּלְחָמָה, וְכֵיוָן שֶׁרָאוּ כִּתְרוֹ שֶׁל יוֹסֵף תָּלוּי בַּאֲרוֹנוֹ שֶׁל יַעֲקֹב, עָמְדוּ

BACKGROUND

50:10| **The threshing floor of Atad:** A threshing floor was a round, sometimes rocky area in which grain was gathered, and which often served as a meeting spot for people as well. In order to protect the grain there, a stone fence or a hedge of thorns, such as *atad* bushes, was occasionally constructed around it (see *Sota* 13a). Some have identified the threshing floor of Atad with Beit Hogla, located in close proximity to Jericho. Others claim it is Tall al-Ajjul, on the northern banks of the HaBesor Stream, south of Gaza. According to this suggestion, the verse's expression "beyond the Jordan" refers to the entire western portion of the land of Canaan.

DISCUSSION

50:9| **Both chariots and horsemen:** The large Egyptian entourage that accompanied Joseph served two purposes, which demonstrates the complex relationship between Pharaoh and Joseph. The elders of Pharaoh and Egypt accompanied Jacob's coffin to pay him last respects as the father of Joseph, the king's viceroy. Furthermore, they might have considered Jacob a god of sorts, as can also be inferred from the encounter between him and Pharaoh (47:7–10). However, at the same time the addition of the chariots and horsemen to the delegation indicate that beneath the expressions of honor toward Joseph and his father lies a political motivation, as Pharaoh uses them to ensure his viceroy's return.

to travel by this longer path, past the eastern side of the Jordan River, rather than the shorter route, which traverses the land of the Philistines, in order to avoid powerful foreign nations, which might have perceived the large Egyptian convoy as a threat. **And they eulogized a very great and substantial eulogy, and** Joseph **observed mourning for his father seven days.**

11 **The inhabitants of the land, the Canaanites,** who were unaware of the reason for this great convoy, **saw the mourning at the threshing floor of Atad, and they said: This is a substantial mourning [*evel*] for Egypt [*mitzrayim*]. Therefore, it was called,** either the entire inhabited area or this specific location which subsequently became a city, **Avel Mitzrayim, which is beyond the Jordan.**

12 **His,** Jacob's, **sons did to him just as he had commanded them.**

13 **His sons conveyed him to the land of Canaan, and buried him in the cave of the field of Makhpela, which Abraham had bought with the field, as a burial portion, from Efron the Hitite, opposite Mamre.**

14 **Joseph returned to Egypt, he, and his brothers, and all who went up with him to bury his father, after he** had **buried his father.**

15 **Joseph's brothers saw that their father had died, and they said: Perhaps**[45] **Joseph will hate us**[D] **and will repay us for all the evil that we did to him.**

16 **They instructed** messengers **to tell Joseph,** as they were too frightened to confront him directly,[46] **saying: Your father instructed before his death, saying:**

17 **So say to Joseph: Please, forgive the transgression of your brothers and their sin, as they did evil to you.** The brothers' message continues: **And now, please** fulfill your father's wishes and **forgive the transgression of the servants of the God of your father.** Whether Jacob indeed had issued such a request, or whether it was fabricated by the brothers,[47] they emphasize in his name that Joseph should forgive them, as they are all sons of one father who share a common faith. **Joseph wept as they spoke to him.**

18 Since Joseph did not respond to their request, the brothers were concerned that they had reminded him of the suffering they caused him all those years ago. Therefore, **his brothers too went** themselves **and fell before him,** Joseph, **and they said: Behold, we are your slaves.**

19 **Joseph said to them: Fear not, for am I in place of God?** Only God can grant atonement for your sin; I cannot punish you in His place.

20 **You intended me harm; God intended it for good, in order to engender, as it is today,** to bring about the outcome we see today, **to keep many people alive.** I do not bear any grudge against you, as it was due to your harmful intentions that I ascended to greatness, and it was ultimately because of your scheme that I became capable of sustaining you.

21 *Seventh aliya* **And now, fear not; I will sustain you and your children. He comforted them and spoke to their heart** reassuring statements of this kind.

DISCUSSION

50:15 | **Perhaps Joseph will hate us:** As long as Jacob was alive, the brothers were certain that Joseph would not harm them. At this point, following their father's death, they were concerned that he might take revenge for their actions. Although Joseph's fate was far better than they could have imagined, and although he himself had previously stated that God had sent him to Egypt to sustain the population during the years of famine (45:5–7), from their perspective they felt that their actions had not effected any positive result.

יא וַיִּסְפְּדוּ־שָׁם מִסְפֵּד גָּדוֹל וְכָבֵד מְאֹד וַיַּעַשׂ לְאָבִיו אֵבֶל שִׁבְעַת יָמִים: וַיַּרְא יוֹשֵׁב
הָאָרֶץ הַכְּנַעֲנִי אֶת־הָאֵבֶל בְּגֹרֶן הָאָטָד וַיֹּאמְרוּ אֵבֶל־כָּבֵד זֶה לְמִצְרָיִם עַל־כֵּן
יב קָרָא שְׁמָהּ אָבֵל מִצְרַיִם אֲשֶׁר בְּעֵבֶר הַיַּרְדֵּן: וַיַּעֲשׂוּ בָנָיו לוֹ כֵּן כַּאֲשֶׁר צִוָּם:
יג וַיִּשְׂאוּ אֹתוֹ בָנָיו אַרְצָה כְּנַעַן וַיִּקְבְּרוּ אֹתוֹ בִּמְעָרַת שְׂדֵה הַמַּכְפֵּלָה אֲשֶׁר קָנָה
יד אַבְרָהָם אֶת־הַשָּׂדֶה לַאֲחֻזַּת־קֶבֶר מֵאֵת עֶפְרֹן הַחִתִּי עַל־פְּנֵי מַמְרֵא: וַיָּשָׁב
יוֹסֵף מִצְרַיְמָה הוּא וְאֶחָיו וְכָל־הָעֹלִים אִתּוֹ לִקְבֹּר אֶת־אָבִיו אַחֲרֵי קָבְרוֹ אֶת־
טו אָבִיו: וַיִּרְאוּ אֲחֵי־יוֹסֵף כִּי־מֵת אֲבִיהֶם וַיֹּאמְרוּ לוּ יִשְׂטְמֵנוּ יוֹסֵף וְהָשֵׁב יָשִׁיב
טז לָנוּ אֵת כָּל־הָרָעָה אֲשֶׁר גָּמַלְנוּ אֹתוֹ: וַיְצַוּוּ אֶל־יוֹסֵף לֵאמֹר אָבִיךָ צִוָּה לִפְנֵי
יז מוֹתוֹ לֵאמֹר: כֹּה־תֹאמְרוּ לְיוֹסֵף אָנָּא שָׂא נָא פֶּשַׁע אַחֶיךָ וְחַטָּאתָם כִּי־רָעָה
יח גְמָלוּךָ וְעַתָּה שָׂא נָא לְפֶשַׁע עַבְדֵי אֱלֹהֵי אָבִיךָ וַיֵּבְךְּ יוֹסֵף בְּדַבְּרָם אֵלָיו: וַיֵּלְכוּ
יט גַּם־אֶחָיו וַיִּפְּלוּ לְפָנָיו וַיֹּאמְרוּ הִנֶּנּוּ לְךָ לַעֲבָדִים: וַיֹּאמֶר אֲלֵהֶם יוֹסֵף אַל־תִּירָאוּ
כ כִּי הֲתַחַת אֱלֹהִים אָנִי: וְאַתֶּם חֲשַׁבְתֶּם עָלַי רָעָה אֱלֹהִים חֲשָׁבָהּ לְטֹבָה לְמַעַן
כא עֲשֹׂה כַּיּוֹם הַזֶּה לְהַחֲיֹת עַם־רָב: וְעַתָּה אַל־תִּירָאוּ אָנֹכִי אֲכַלְכֵּל אֶתְכֶם וְאֶת־ שביעי

רש״י

כֻּלָּן וְתָלוּ בוֹ כִּתְרֵיהֶם, וְהִקִּיפוּהוּ כְּתָרִים כְּגֹרֶן הַמֻּקָּף סְיָג שֶׁל קוֹצִים:

יב-יג | **כַּאֲשֶׁר צִוָּם.** מַהוּ אֲשֶׁר צִוָּם? "וַיִּשְׂאוּ אֹתוֹ בָנָיו" וְלֹא בְּנֵי בָנָיו, שֶׁכָּךְ צִוָּם: אַל יִשְּׂאוּ מִטָּתִי לֹא אִישׁ מִצְרִי וְלֹא אֶחָד מִבְּנֵיכֶם, שֶׁהֵם מִבְּנוֹת כְּנַעַן, אֶלָּא אַתֶּם. וְקָבַע לָהֶם מָקוֹם, שְׁלֹשָׁה לַמִּזְרָח, וְכֵן לְאַרְבַּע רוּחוֹת, וּכְסִדְרָן לְמַסַּע מַחֲנֶה שֶׁל דְּגָלִים נִקְבְּעוּ כָּאן; לֵוִי לֹא יִשָּׂא, שֶׁהוּא עָתִיד לָשֵׂאת אֶת הָאָרוֹן, וְיוֹסֵף לֹא יִשָּׂא, שֶׁהוּא מֶלֶךְ, מְנַשֶּׁה וְאֶפְרַיִם יִהְיוּ תַּחְתֵּיהֶם. וְזֶהוּ "אִישׁ עַל דִּגְלוֹ בְאֹתֹת" (במדבר ב, ב) – בָּאוֹת שֶׁמָּסַר לָהֶם אֲבִיהֶם לָשֵׂאת מִטָּתוֹ:

יד | **הוּא וְאֶחָיו וְכָל הָעֹלִים אִתּוֹ.** בַּחֲזָרָתָן כָּאן הִקְדִּים אֶחָיו לַמִּצְרִים הָעוֹלִים אִתּוֹ, וּבַהֲלִיכָתָן הִקְדִּים מִצְרִים לְאֶחָיו, שֶׁנֶּאֱמַר: "וַיַּעֲלוּ אִתּוֹ כָּל עַבְדֵי פַרְעֹה" וְגוֹ' וְאַחַר כָּךְ: "וְכֹל בֵּית יוֹסֵף וְאֶחָיו" (לעיל פסוק ז-ח)! אֶלָּא לְפִי שֶׁרָאוּ כָּבוֹד שֶׁעָשׂוּ מַלְכֵי כְנַעַן, שֶׁתָּלוּ כִּתְרֵיהֶם בַּאֲרוֹנוֹ שֶׁל יַעֲקֹב, נָהֲגוּ בָהֶם כָּבוֹד:

טו | **וַיִּרְאוּ אֲחֵי יוֹסֵף כִּי מֵת אֲבִיהֶם.** מַהוּ "וַיִּרְאוּ"? הִכִּירוּ בְּמִיתָתוֹ אֵצֶל יוֹסֵף, שֶׁהָיוּ רְגִילִים לִסְעֹד עַל שֻׁלְחָנוֹ שֶׁל יוֹסֵף וְהָיָה מְקָרְבָן בִּשְׁבִיל כְּבוֹד אָבִיו, וּמִשֶּׁמֵּת יַעֲקֹב לֹא קֵרְבָן: **לוּ יִשְׂטְמֵנוּ.** שֶׁמָּא יִשְׂטְמֵנוּ. 'לוּ' מִתְחַלֵּק לְעִנְיָנִים הַרְבֵּה: יֵשׁ 'לוּ' מְשַׁמֵּשׁ בִּלְשׁוֹן בַּקָּשָׁה וּלְשׁוֹן הַלְוַאי, כְּגוֹן: "לוּ יְהִי כִדְבָרֶךָ" (לעיל ל, לד), "לוּ שְׁמָעֵנִי" (לעיל כג, יג), "וְלוּ הוֹאַלְנוּ" (יהושע ז, ז), "לוּ מַתְנוּ" (במדבר יד, ב); וְיֵשׁ 'לוּ' מְשַׁמֵּשׁ בִּלְשׁוֹן אִם וְאוּלַי, כְּגוֹן: "לוּ חָכְמוּ" (דברים לב, כט), "לוּ הִקְשַׁבְתָּ לְמִצְוֹתָי" (ישעיה מח, יח), "וְלוּ אָנֹכִי שֹׁקֵל עַל כַּפַּי" (שמואל ב׳ יח, יב); וְיֵשׁ 'לוּ' מְשַׁמֵּשׁ בִּלְשׁוֹן שֶׁמָּא: "לוּ יִשְׂטְמֵנוּ" וְאֵין לוֹ עוֹד דּוֹמֶה בַּמִּקְרָא, וְהוּא לְשׁוֹן אוּלַי, כְּמוֹ: "אֻלַי לֹא תֵלֵךְ הָאִשָּׁה אַחֲרָי" (לעיל כד, לט), לְשׁוֹן שֶׁמָּא הוּא. וְיֵשׁ 'אוּלַי' לְשׁוֹן בַּקָּשָׁה, כְּגוֹן: "אוּלַי יִרְאֶה ה׳ בְּעֵינִי" (שמואל ב׳ טז, יב), "אוּלַי ה׳ אוֹתִי" (יהושע יד, יב), הֲרֵי הוּא כְּמוֹ: "לוּ יְהִי כִדְבָרֶךָ" (לעיל ל, לד); וְיֵשׁ 'אוּלַי' לְשׁוֹן אִם: "אוּלַי יֵשׁ חֲמִשִּׁים צַדִּיקִם" (לעיל יח, כד):

טז | **וַיְצַוּוּ אֶל יוֹסֵף.** כְּמוֹ: "וַיְצַוֵּם אֶל בְּנֵי יִשְׂרָאֵל" (שמות ו, יג), צִוָּה לְמֹשֶׁה וּלְאַהֲרֹן לִהְיוֹת שְׁלוּחִים אֶל בְּנֵי יִשְׂרָאֵל, אַף זֶה, וַיְצַוּוּ אֶל שְׁלוּחָם לִהְיוֹת שָׁלִיחַ אֶל יוֹסֵף לוֹמַר לוֹ כֵּן. וְאֶת מִי צִוּוּ? אֶת בְּנֵי בִלְהָה שֶׁהָיוּ רְגִילִין אֶצְלוֹ, שֶׁנֶּאֱמַר: "וְהוּא נַעַר אֶת בְּנֵי בִלְהָה" (לעיל לז, ב): **אָבִיךָ צִוָּה.** שִׁנּוּ בַּדָּבָר מִפְּנֵי הַשָּׁלוֹם, כִּי לֹא צִוָּה יַעֲקֹב כֵּן, שֶׁלֹּא נֶחְשַׁד יוֹסֵף בְּעֵינָיו:

יז | **שָׂא נָא לְפֶשַׁע עַבְדֵי אֱלֹהֵי אָבִיךָ.** אִם אָבִיךָ מֵת, אֱלֹהָיו קַיָּם וְהֵם עֲבָדָיו:

יח | **וַיֵּלְכוּ גַּם אֶחָיו.** מוֹסִף עַל הַשְּׁלִיחוּת:

יט | **כִּי הֲתַחַת אֱלֹהִים אָנִי.** שֶׁמָּא בִּמְקוֹמוֹ אֲנִי? בִּתְמִיָּה. אִם הָיִיתִי רוֹצֶה לְהָרַע לָכֶם, כְּלוּם אֲנִי יָכוֹל? וַהֲלֹא אַתֶּם כֻּלְּכֶם חֲשַׁבְתֶּם עָלַי רָעָה וְהַקָּדוֹשׁ בָּרוּךְ הוּא חֲשָׁבָהּ לְטוֹבָה, וְהֵיאַךְ אֲנִי לְבַדִּי יָכוֹל לְהָרַע לָכֶם?:

כא | **וַיְדַבֵּר עַל לִבָּם.** דְּבָרִים הַמִּתְקַבְּלִים עַל הַלֵּב: עַד שֶׁלֹּא יְרַדְתֶּם לְכָאן הָיוּ מְרַנְּנִים עָלַי שֶׁאֲנִי עֶבֶד, וְעַל יְדֵיכֶם נוֹדַע שֶׁאֲנִי בֶּן חוֹרִין, וַאֲנִי הוֹרֵג אֶתְכֶם?! מָה הַבְּרִיּוֹת אוֹמְרוֹת? כַּת שֶׁל בַּחוּרִים רָאָה וְנִשְׁתַּבַּח בָּהֶם וְאָמַר: אַחַי הֵם, וּלְבַסּוֹף הֲרָגָם. יֵשׁ לְךָ אָח שֶׁהוֹרֵג אֶת אֶחָיו? דָּבָר אַחֵר, עֲשָׂרָה נֵרוֹת לֹא יָכְלוּ לְכַבּוֹת נֵר אֶחָד וְכוּ׳ (מגילה טז ע״ב):

Joseph's Death

GENESIS 50:22–26

Joseph, who is an Egyptian in many respects, still feels a bond to the land of Canaan. Therefore, he does not wish to remain buried in Egypt. Many years after his father administered an oath to him and his brothers not to bury him in Egypt, Joseph also requests from his brothers not to be left buried in Egyptian soil. In Jacob's case it was relatively easy to facilitate his burial in the land of Canaan, due to Joseph's position. In contrast, Joseph's brothers do not have the authority to fulfill his request immediately.

22 **Joseph lived in Egypt, he and his father's household; Joseph lived one hundred and ten years.**

23 **Joseph saw great-grandchildren from Ephraim; also the** *Maftir* **children of Makhir son of Manasseh were born at Joseph's knees.** Joseph was blessed with a relatively long life, and he lived to see great-grandchildren from both of his sons.

24 Before his death, **Joseph said to his brothers: I am dying, and God will remember you and bring you up from this land to the land about which He took an oath to Abraham, to Isaac,** **and to Jacob** to give to them. I do not know when this will occur, but I am certain that God will take you out of this land.

25 **Joseph administered an oath to the children of Israel, saying: God will remember you,**[D] **and** when that occurs **you shall carry up my bones from there,**[D] Egypt.

26 **Joseph died at the age of one hundred and ten years. They embalmed him,** in accordance with the local custom, **and he was placed in a coffin in Egypt.**

DISCUSSION

50:25 | **God will remember you:** It is difficult to ascertain whether Joseph's brothers wanted to return to Canaan, and if they did wish to return, why they did not do so. They presumably did not remain in Egypt against their will. Perhaps Pharaoh initially sought to prevent them from departing so that they would not take Joseph with them back to Canaan. However, it is likely that Joseph did not continue to serve in the same governmental position for his entire life,

as at some point his unique services were no longer required. Yet he and his expanding family remained in Egypt. When Joseph saw at the end of his life that his family was remaining in Egypt, he reiterated his father's prophecy to them, certain that the day would come when God would remember them and they would return to their homeland.

You shall carry up my bones from there: Joseph's final request was to be buried in the

land of Canaan, although he did not specify exactly where he wished to be buried. He was presumably aware that there were no remaining plots in the cave of Makhpela. Perhaps he wanted to be buried in his tribal inheritance in Shekhem (see 48:22; Joshua 24:32). As the Sages state with regard to Joseph: From Shekhem he was kidnapped, and to Shekhem they returned him (*Sota* 13b).

כב טַפְּכֶ֑ם וַיְנַחֵ֣ם אוֹתָ֔ם וַיְדַבֵּ֖ר עַל־לִבָּֽם׃ וַיֵּ֤שֶׁב יוֹסֵף֙ בְּמִצְרַ֔יִם ה֖וּא וּבֵ֣ית אָבִ֑יו
כג וַיְחִ֣י יוֹסֵ֔ף מֵאָ֥ה וָעֶ֖שֶׂר שָׁנִֽים׃ וַיַּ֤רְא יוֹסֵף֙ לְאֶפְרַ֔יִם בְּנֵ֖י שִׁלֵּשִׁ֑ים גַּ֗ם בְּנֵ֤י מָכִיר֙ מפטיר
כד בֶּן־מְנַשֶּׁ֔ה יֻלְּד֖וּ עַל־בִּרְכֵּ֥י יוֹסֵֽף׃ וַיֹּ֤אמֶר יוֹסֵף֙ אֶל־אֶחָ֔יו אָנֹכִ֖י מֵ֑ת וֵֽאלֹהִ֞ים פָּקֹ֧ד
יִפְקֹ֣ד אֶתְכֶ֗ם וְהֶעֱלָ֤ה אֶתְכֶם֙ מִן־הָאָ֣רֶץ הַזֹּ֔את אֶל־הָאָ֕רֶץ אֲשֶׁ֥ר נִשְׁבַּ֛ע לְאַבְרָהָ֖ם
כה לְיִצְחָ֥ק וּֽלְיַעֲקֹֽב׃ וַיַּשְׁבַּ֣ע יוֹסֵ֔ף אֶת־בְּנֵ֥י יִשְׂרָאֵ֖ל לֵאמֹ֑ר פָּקֹ֨ד יִפְקֹ֤ד אֱלֹהִים֙ אֶתְכֶ֔ם
כו וְהַעֲלִתֶ֥ם אֶת־עַצְמֹתַ֖י מִזֶּֽה׃ וַיָּ֣מָת יוֹסֵ֔ף בֶּן־מֵאָ֥ה וָעֶ֖שֶׂר שָׁנִ֑ים וַיַּחַנְט֣וּ אֹת֔וֹ וַיִּ֥ישֶׂם
בָּאָר֖וֹן בְּמִצְרָֽיִם׃
חזק

רש"י

כג| עַל בִּרְכֵּי יוֹסֵף. כְּתַרְגּוּמוֹ, גִּדְּלָן בֵּין בִּרְכָּיו:

Book of
Exodus

EXODUS

This book is dedicated in loving memory to

Louis Weisfeld *z"l*

who observed God's work,
who strove to emulate His ways and to walk along His path.

והיאך היא הדרך לאהבתו ויראתו?
בשעה שיתבונן האדם במעשיו וברואיו הנפלאים הגדולים....

רמב״ם ספר המדע, הלכות יסודי התורה ב:ב

What is the way that leads to the love of Him and to
reverence for Him? … a person who contemplates
His great and wondrous acts and creations….

Mishne Torah, Sefer HaMadda, Hilkhot Yesodei HaTorah 2:2

Gabi Weisfeld

Shemot

INTRODUCTION TO EXODUS

Exodus is the book of redemption and revelation. Its main events occur over a period of approximately two years, from when Moses is assigned the task of redeeming Israel, about a year before the exodus from Egypt, until the establishment of the Tabernacle, roughly a year afterward. The book consists of four parts of unequal lengths, each of which has its place of importance both in the book itself as well as in the collective national memory over the generations.

The first and shortest section describes the exile in Egypt, with the enslavement and suffering that this difficult period entailed.

The second section recounts the redemption from Egypt, including the series of terrible punishments that God inflicted upon Egypt and everything it possessed, from the ten plagues to the Egyptians' final downfall at the splitting of the Red Sea.

The redemption from Egypt was not simply another historical revolution; rather, it was a direct display of the greatness of God's power in the world. In this sense, the story of the exodus leads thematically into the third section, the revelation at Mount Sinai, in which God reveals Himself to His people and gives them His Torah.

The final part of the book, which details the construction of the Tabernacle with all its particulars, is a continuation of the events at Mount Sinai. The climactic, historically unique revelation just related is transformed, by means of this Tent of Meeting, into a continuous encounter between God and Moses, together with His people, Israel.

The main human figure at the center of the book of Exodus, as well as in the subsequent books of the Torah, is Moses our teacher. The book of Exodus describes the early years of Moses' life and his emergence as a prophet. Later, his character will be revealed in all its strength and majesty. Although the story of Moses' life does not approach a full biographical account, he is the figure in the Bible depicted in the greatest detail, starting from his birth and childhood, through the main episodes of his life, until his death.

The story of the revelation in Exodus draws attention to various aspects of the election of Israel. Although the plagues of Egypt and the splitting of the Red Sea are punishments for Egypt's sins, they also vividly demonstrates God's special affection for His chosen people, which leads Him to grant them His unique patronage. The Torah does not provide justification for the election of Israel, other than God's loyalty to the covenant He enacted with the patriarchs. In Egypt, the Israelites did not display any special signs of holiness or exemplary qualities, and even so, the text stresses again and again God's decision to differentiate between them and the nation in whose midst they dwelled. This is the case, despite the fact that Israel itself had not yet internalized the idea that it had been chosen by God. See, for example, the harsh but lyrical descriptions of the nation at that time in the book of Ezekiel, chapters 16 and 20. When summarizing the exodus, the verse states that on that day "all the hosts of the Lord departed from the land of Egypt" (12:41), but the Israelites had not yet come to see themselves as "hosts of the Lord."

There is no doubt that the revelation at Sinai is the climax of the entire Torah. Already in the book of Genesis, God revealed Himself to a few select individuals, and such rare encounters recur in the other books of the Bible as well. However, these instances are comparable to looking up through an open window, as those who merited such visions saw an image of God, as it were, in the place where He remained seated above. In contrast, the revelation at Sinai symbolizes the descent of God to earth below, onto Mount Sinai. From the start, this encounter depended on the agreement of Israel, and subsequently led to the enactment of a covenant between the entire people and God. The revelation signifies not only a connection with transcendence, but also the possibility of clear communication with the presence of God, with the Divine Immanence resident in the world.

A more permanent form of the revelation is provided by the Tabernacle, which served as the home for the Tablets of the Covenant that Moses brought down to Israel from Mount Sinai; it is therefore called the "Tabernacle of the Testimony" (38:21). The Tabernacle was also a center for the service of God, for prayer, and for the special revelation of God's word to Moses. However, in its essence, it represented the Divine Presence that resides on earth. The verse therefore states about the Tabernacle: "They shall make for Me a sanctuary, and I will dwell among them,"[1] rather than "I will dwell in it," as this structure clearly and recognizably expresses the continuous, experiential, and daily presence of God among His people everywhere.

Parashat
Shemot

Beginnings of the Enslavement in Egypt
EXODUS 1:1–22

The book of Exodus is not a direct continuation of the narrative of Genesis. Although it does begin from approximately the same point where Genesis ended, a few of the topics that were related in Genesis are repeated at the beginning of Exodus, due to their relevance to the events that will follow.

The final chapters of Genesis describe the exile of Jacob's family from Canaan to Egypt, where they will multiply and become a nation. With the regime change in Egypt, their geographic dislocation will turn into a painful exile marked by oppressive bondage and cruel decrees.

1 1 These are the names of the children of Israel, who came to Egypt with Jacob; each man came with his household.
2 Reuben, Simeon, Levi, and Judah;
3 Issachar, Zebulun, and Benjamin;
4 Dan and Naphtali, Gad and Asher.
5 All the people who emerged from Jacob's loins were seventy souls;[D] and this number includes Joseph, who was already in Egypt.
6 Joseph died, as was described in the final verse of Genesis, and then all of his brothers and all of that generation, Jacob's children and their children who were born while the family was still in Canaan, also died.
7 The children of Israel, who were now developing from a family of seventy people into a tribe, were fruitful and propagated[D] and increased and grew exceedingly mighty; they became a powerful presence in the land. In a short time, the children of Israel grew into a large tribe. And the land was filled with them. From the continuation of the narrative it will become apparent that not all the children of Israel remained in Goshen in seclusion from the Egyptians. Rather, some of them migrated to other regions, living in close proximity to the Egyptians.[1]
8 A new king,[B] from a new dynasty,[2] arose over Egypt, who did not know[D] Joseph. It is likely that this king was aware of

Joseph, his roots, and the revolutionary changes he brought about in Egypt. Nevertheless, he remained indifferent to Joseph's legacy and unconcerned with the fate of his people.
9 He, the king, said to his people: Behold, the people of the children of Israel are more numerous and mightier than we. As they continue to multiply exceedingly quickly, they are becoming a demographic threat to our existence.
10 Let us be cunning with it; we must employ sophisticated methods to limit their growth, lest it increase, and it shall be that if a war will occur on the northern border, it too will join our enemies[D] and wage war against us, and they will then go up from the land, leaving our country with a labor shortage.[3] Alternatively, Pharaoh was speaking euphemistically: If there will be a war, the children of Israel will join our enemies and we will go up from the land; we will be expelled.[4]
11 They, the Egyptians, appointed overseers over it,[D] in order to afflict it with their burdens. The centralized government of Egypt was administered by Pharaoh himself. Pharaoh installed overseers and conscripted many members of Israel into a labor force for public works for the benefit of Egypt. He hoped that the difficult life of servitude would cause the Hebrews to diminish in number, and that it would break their spirit. It, the

---
DISCUSSION

1:5 | **Seventy souls:** Jacob himself is also included in the count of seventy souls (*Bekhor Shor; Adderet Eliyahu;* Rashbam and Ibn Ezra, Genesis 46:27). Alternatively, if the verse refers specifically to "the people who emerged from Jacob's loins," perhaps the number seventy represents a rounding of the exact count of sixty-nine (see Radak, Judges 9:5).

1:7 | **And propagated:** The Hebrew term *vayishretzu* is suited more for describing the breeding of animals than humans. This is the basis for the tradition that the Hebrew women

in Egypt would miraculously give birth to several infants at once (*Shemot Rabba* 1:8; Rashi; Ibn Ezra).

1:8 | **Who did not know [*yada*]:** The root yod-dalet-ayin expresses not only an awareness but an intimate connection between two entities (see Genesis 4:1; Exodus 33:12–13; *Ha'amek Davar*).

1:10 | **Lest it increase, and it shall be that if a war will occur, it too will join our enemies:** Although Egypt was not faced with any significant military threats at that time, the king was

concerned that during some future confrontation, the children of Israel could easily act as a fifth column that could help topple the Egyptian regime from within. Even though the children of Israel had resided peacefully in Egypt for many years, the king viewed them as a threat and sought to restrain them, simply because of their numerical strength. This suspicion and distrust toward the children of Israel even before they became an actual nation may be seen as the first historical account of anti-Semitism.

פרשת

שמות

וְאֵ֗לֶּה שְׁמוֹת֙ בְּנֵ֣י יִשְׂרָאֵ֔ל הַבָּאִ֖ים מִצְרָ֑יְמָה אֵ֣ת יַעֲקֹ֔ב אִ֥ישׁ וּבֵית֖וֹ בָּֽאוּ: רְאוּבֵ֣ן

שִׁמְע֔וֹן לֵוִ֖י וִֽיהוּדָֽה: יִשָּׂשכָ֥ר זְבוּלֻ֖ן וּבִנְיָמִֽן: דָּ֥ן וְנַפְתָּלִ֖י גָּ֥ד וְאָשֵֽׁר: וַֽיְהִ֗י כָּל־נֶ֛פֶשׁ

יֹצְאֵ֥י יֶֽרֶךְ־יַעֲקֹ֖ב שִׁבְעִ֣ים נָ֑פֶשׁ וְיוֹסֵ֖ף הָיָ֥ה בְמִצְרָֽיִם: וַיָּ֤מָת יוֹסֵף֙ וְכָל־אֶחָ֔יו וְכֹ֖ל

הַדּ֥וֹר הַהֽוּא: וּבְנֵ֣י יִשְׂרָאֵ֗ל פָּר֧וּ וַֽיִּשְׁרְצ֛וּ וַיִּרְבּ֥וּ וַיַּֽעַצְמ֖וּ בִּמְאֹ֣ד מְאֹ֑ד וַתִּמָּלֵ֥א הָאָ֖רֶץ

אֹתָֽם:

וַיָּ֥קָם מֶֽלֶךְ־חָדָ֖שׁ עַל־מִצְרָ֑יִם אֲשֶׁ֥ר לֹֽא־יָדַ֖ע אֶת־יוֹסֵֽף: וַיֹּ֖אמֶר אֶל־עַמּ֑וֹ הִנֵּ֗ה עַ֚ם

בְּנֵ֣י יִשְׂרָאֵ֔ל רַ֥ב וְעָצ֖וּם מִמֶּֽנּוּ: הָ֚בָה נִֽתְחַכְּמָ֣ה ל֑וֹ פֶּן־יִרְבֶּ֗ה וְהָיָ֞ה כִּֽי־תִקְרֶ֤אנָה

מִלְחָמָה֙ וְנוֹסַ֤ף גַּם־הוּא֙ עַל־שֹׂ֣נְאֵ֔ינוּ וְנִלְחַם־בָּ֖נוּ וְעָלָ֥ה מִן־הָאָֽרֶץ: וַיָּשִׂ֤ימוּ עָלָיו֙

שָׂרֵ֣י מִסִּ֔ים לְמַ֥עַן עַנֹּת֖וֹ בְּסִבְלֹתָ֑ם וַיִּ֜בֶן עָרֵ֤י מִסְכְּנוֹת֙ לְפַרְעֹ֔ה אֶת־פִּתֹ֖ם וְאֶת־

רש"י

אא] וְאֵלֶּה שְׁמוֹת בְּנֵי יִשְׂרָאֵל. אַף עַל פִּי שֶׁמְּנָאָם בְּחַיֵּיהֶם בִּשְׁמוֹתָם חָזַר וּמְנָאָם בְּמִיתָתָם, לְהוֹדִיעַ חִבָּתָם שֶׁנִּמְשְׁלוּ לַכּוֹכָבִים שֶׁמּוֹצִיאָם וּמַכְנִיסָם בְּמִסְפָּר וּבִשְׁמוֹתָם, שֶׁנֶּאֱמַר: "הַמּוֹצִיא בְמִסְפָּר צְבָאָם לְכֻלָּם בְּשֵׁם יִקְרָא" (ישעיה מ, כו):

הה] וְיוֹסֵף הָיָה בְמִצְרָיִם. וַהֲלֹא הוּא וּבָנָיו הָיוּ בִּכְלַל שִׁבְעִים, וּמַה בָּא לְלַמְּדֵנוּ? וְכִי לֹא הָיִינוּ יוֹדְעִים שֶׁהוּא הָיָה בְמִצְרַיִם? אֶלָּא לְהוֹדִיעֲךָ צִדְקָתוֹ שֶׁל יוֹסֵף, הוּא יוֹסֵף הָרוֹעֶה אֶת צֹאן אָבִיו, הוּא יוֹסֵף שֶׁהָיָה בְמִצְרַיִם וְנַעֲשָׂה מֶלֶךְ, וְעוֹמֵד בְּצִדְקוֹ: †

זז] וַיִּשְׁרְצוּ. שֶׁהָיוּ יוֹלְדוֹת שִׁשָּׁה בְּכֶרֶס אֶחָד:

חח] וַיָּקָם מֶלֶךְ חָדָשׁ. רַב וּשְׁמוּאֵל, חַד אָמַר חָדָשׁ מַמָּשׁ, וְחַד אָמַר שֶׁנִּתְחַדְּשׁוּ גְּזֵרוֹתָיו: **אֲשֶׁר לֹא יָדַע.** שֶׁעָשָׂה עַצְמוֹ כְּאִלּוּ לֹא יָדַע:

יי] הָבָה נִתְחַכְּמָה לוֹ. כָּל 'הָבָה' לְשׁוֹן הַכָנָה וְהַזְמָנָה לְדָבָר הוּא, הָכִינוּ עַצְמְכֶם לְכָךְ: **נִתְחַכְּמָה לוֹ.** לָעָם, נִתְחַכֵּם מַה לַעֲשׂוֹת לוֹ. וְרַבּוֹתֵינוּ דָּרְשׁוּ, נִתְחַכֵּם לְמוֹשִׁיעָן שֶׁל יִשְׂרָאֵל לְדוּנָם בַּמַּיִם, שֶׁכְּבָר נִשְׁבַּע שֶׁלֹּא יָבִיא מַבּוּל לָעוֹלָם: **וְעָלָה**

מִן הָאָרֶץ. עַל כָּרְחֵנוּ. וְרַבּוֹתֵינוּ דָּרְשׁוּ, כְּאָדָם שֶׁמְּקַלֵּל עַצְמוֹ וְתוֹלֶה קִלְלָתוֹ בַּחֲבֵרוֹ, וַהֲרֵי הוּא כְּאִלּוּ כָּתַב: וְעָלִינוּ מִן הָאָרֶץ, וְהֵם יִירָשׁוּהָ:

יאא] עָלָיו. עַל הָעָם: **מִסִּים.** לְשׁוֹן מַס, שָׂרִים שֶׁגּוֹבִין מֵהֶם הַמַּס. וּמַהוּ הַמַּס? שֶׁיִּבְנוּ עָרֵי מִסְכְּנוֹת לְפַרְעֹה: **לְמַעַן עַנֹּתוֹ בְּסִבְלֹתָם.** שֶׁל מִצְרַיִם: **עָרֵי מִסְכְּנוֹת.** כְּתַרְגּוּמוֹ. וְכֵן: "לֶךְ בֹּא אֶל הַסֹּכֵן הַזֶּה" (ישעיה כב, טו) – גִּזְבָּר הַמְמֻנֶּה עַל הָאוֹצָרוֹת: **אֶת פִּתֹם וְאֶת רַעְמְסֵס.** שֶׁלֹּא הָיוּ רְאוּיוֹת מִתְּחִלָּה לְכָךְ וַעֲשָׂאוּם חֲזָקוֹת וּבְצוּרוֹת לְאוֹצָר:

BACKGROUND

1:8 | A new king: The identity of the Pharaoh referred to in this verse is uncertain. Some identify him as Thutmose III (1479–1425 BCE), one of the greatest Pharaohs of the Eighteenth Dynasty; others claim it was Rameses II of the Nineteenth Dynasty (1279–1213 BCE), who was perhaps the greatest of all the Pharaohs in Egyptian history. He initiated several large building projects during his reign, including the city of Pi-Rameses, meaning House of Rameses, in Lower Egypt. It should be noted that the name Rameses does not appear in any archaeological or historical data preceding the thirteenth century BCE, nor were any Pharaohs known by that name before this time.

DISCUSSION

1:11 | They appointed overseers over it: Since the time of Joseph, all residents of Egypt were officially classified as slaves to the throne (see Genesis 47:16–26). Thus, the children of Israel were also considered the slaves of Pharaoh, and as foreigners, it was easier to subjugate them. At first, Pharaoh used the children of Israel as a cheap labor force, even though he did not actually require their labor. Egypt was already a developed kingdom with many cities and buildings, in addition to the royal memorials and monumental structures known to us from historical and archaeological records. However, Egypt was in a state of constant development, which provided Pharaoh a prime opportunity and a convincing excuse to subjugate the foreigners, even though he did not require a tremendous amount of new laborers.

Israelite nation, **built storehouse cities for Pharaoh: Pitom and Rameses.**

12 **But as they would afflict it, so it would increase and so it would proliferate.** Although the lives of the Israelites became more difficult, they continued to grow. Since the children of Israel were not confined to a particular area of Egypt, the Egyptians witnessed this surge in population, and **they were revolted by the children of Israel.**

13 The population growth that the Egyptians sought to suppress through conscription for labor was ineffective; on the contrary, the children of Israel only grew in number. **The Egyptians** therefore sought to worsen the plight of Israel, so they **coerced the children of Israel to work with travail,** forcing them to perform hard labor that would break them. It is possible that in an effort to break their spirits, the children of Israel were denied access to technologies and tools that were already in use in Egypt at that time.

14 **They embittered their lives with hard work, with mortar and with bricks.** The monumental structures of Egypt were built with ashlar stones quarried primarily in the south of the country. Simple utilitarian structures, such as homes and warehouses, were constructed from bricks, as there was an abundance of earth in Egypt with which to produce them. **And** in addition to the royal construction projects, they also worked **with all work in the field,** both in the service of the king and in private fields, in order to provide food for themselves or for others. They did all this together **with all their work with which they worked for them,** the Egyptians, **with travail.** The repeated emphasis on harsh labor hints to the tremendous time pressure that was imposed on the children of Israel, or to the imposition of tasks that were not appropriate for the strength or skills of the specific workers. All of these cruelties were designed to break their bodies and spirits.[5]

15 Even hard labor and the embitterment of their lives did not have the desired effect upon the children of Israel; their numbers continued to rise. So **the king of Egypt said to the Hebrew midwives,**[D] **of whom the name of one was Shifra, and the name of the other, Pua.** The names of the midwives are mentioned by the verse since it will become apparent that they were not mere vessels in the hands of Pharaoh, but independent personalities who acted according to their own discretion.

Working with bricks. Fresco from the tomb of Thutmose III, Valley of the Kings, Luxor, fifteenth century BCE.

16 **He said: When you deliver the Hebrew women, and you look upon the birthstool,**[B] **if it is a son** that was born, **you shall kill him;**[D] **but if it is a daughter, she shall live.** Pharaoh assumed that without a sufficient population of Hebrew males, the females would assimilate among the Egyptians, and Israel would cease to maintain an independent identity.

17 **The midwives feared God, and** therefore, they **did not do as the king of Egypt commanded them, and** instead, **they kept the children alive.** Not only did they deliver the children, but they also cared for those who were in danger.[6]

18 **The king of Egypt summoned the midwives, and he said**

Second aliya **to them: Why did you do this thing, and you kept the children alive?** As I have not received reports of large-scale infant fatalities among the Hebrews, it is clear to me that you have not carried out my instructions.

19 The midwives were unable to make the argument to Pharaoh that his instructions were immoral or illegal. They therefore offered an excuse: **The midwives said to Pharaoh:** We were unable to carry out your instructions **because the Hebrew women are not like the Egyptian women** with whom you are familiar, **as they are vigorous** and remain alert throughout the birthing process, as opposed to the pampered and weak Egyptian women, who would frequently tire and enter a semi-conscious state during childbirth. As such, **before the midwife comes to them, they have** already **given birth,** and the midwife is therefore unable to interfere. The newborns are given to the midwives only after their mothers have already seen them.

20 In ancient Egypt, the Pharaoh was far more than just a king. He was viewed as a deity or demigod, even while still alive. Accordingly, disobeying the king was an exceptional act. As a reward for their extraordinary courage, **God favored the**

DISCUSSION

1:15| **To the Hebrew midwives:** Shifra and Pua could not have been the only midwives; a nation of many thousands of people requires more than just two (Ibn Ezra). It seems that these two women were the leaders of some sort of union of midwives. Pharaoh directed his command at them, as they were the leaders of the Hebrew midwives.

Most of the commentaries understand the expression "Hebrew midwives" to mean the Hebrew women who were responsible for delivering babies and caring for the mothers and the newborns (*Sota* 11b; Rashi; Ibn Ezra). However, others understand it as a reference to Egyptian midwives who delivered the babies of Hebrew mothers. This latter interpretation does not fit with the fact that the names Shifra and Pua sound Semitic and not Egyptian (see *Bekhor Shor*; *Keli Yakar*). Indeed, similar names appear in ancient Semitic documents found in various places in the Middle East.

1:16| **If it is a son, you shall kill him:** It seems that at this point, Pharaoh was incapable of, or uninterested in, issuing a public decree to kill

יב יג רַעַמְסֵס: וְכַאֲשֶׁר יְעַנּוּ אֹתוֹ כֵּן יִרְבֶּה וְכֵן יִפְרֹץ וַיָּקֻצוּ מִפְּנֵי בְּנֵי יִשְׂרָאֵל: וַיַּעֲבִדוּ
יד מִצְרַיִם אֶת־בְּנֵי יִשְׂרָאֵל בְּפָרֶךְ: וַיְמָרְרוּ אֶת־חַיֵּיהֶם בַּעֲבֹדָה קָשָׁה בְּחֹמֶר
טו וּבִלְבֵנִים וּבְכָל־עֲבֹדָה בַּשָּׂדֶה אֵת כָּל־עֲבֹדָתָם אֲשֶׁר־עָבְדוּ בָהֶם בְּפָרֶךְ: וַיֹּאמֶר
מֶלֶךְ מִצְרַיִם לַמְיַלְּדֹת הָעִבְרִיֹּת אֲשֶׁר שֵׁם הָאַחַת שִׁפְרָה וְשֵׁם הַשֵּׁנִית פּוּעָה:
טז וַיֹּאמֶר בְּיַלֶּדְכֶן אֶת־הָעִבְרִיּוֹת וּרְאִיתֶן עַל־הָאָבְנָיִם אִם־בֵּן הוּא וַהֲמִתֶּן אֹתוֹ
יז וְאִם־בַּת הִוא וָחָיָה: וַתִּירֶאןָ הַמְיַלְּדֹת אֶת־הָאֱלֹהִים וְלֹא עָשׂוּ כַּאֲשֶׁר דִּבֶּר
יח אֲלֵיהֶן מֶלֶךְ מִצְרָיִם וַתְּחַיֶּיןָ אֶת־הַיְלָדִים: וַיִּקְרָא מֶלֶךְ־מִצְרַיִם לַמְיַלְּדֹת שני
יט וַיֹּאמֶר לָהֶן מַדּוּעַ עֲשִׂיתֶן הַדָּבָר הַזֶּה וַתְּחַיֶּיןָ אֶת־הַיְלָדִים: וַתֹּאמַרְןָ הַמְיַלְּדֹת
אֶל־פַּרְעֹה כִּי לֹא כַנָּשִׁים הַמִּצְרִיֹּת הָעִבְרִיֹּת כִּי־חָיוֹת הֵנָּה בְּטֶרֶם תָּבוֹא
כ אֲלֵהֶן הַמְיַלֶּדֶת וְיָלָדוּ: וַיֵּיטֶב אֱלֹהִים לַמְיַלְּדֹת וַיִּרֶב הָעָם וַיַּעַצְמוּ מְאֹד:

רש"י

יב | **וְכַאֲשֶׁר יְעַנּוּ אֹתוֹ.** בְּכָל מַה שֶּׁהֵם נוֹתְנִין לֵב לְעַנּוֹת כֵּן לֵב הַקָּדוֹשׁ בָּרוּךְ הוּא לְהַרְבּוֹת וּלְהַפְרִין: **כֵּן יִרְבֶּה.** כֵּן רָבָה וְכֵן פּוֹרֵץ. וּמִדְרָשׁוֹ, רוּחַ הַקֹּדֶשׁ אוֹמֶרֶת כֵּן: אַתֶּם אוֹמְרִים "פֶּן יִרְבֶּה" וַאֲנִי אוֹמֵר "כֵּן יִרְבֶּה": **וַיָּקֻצוּ.** קָצוּ בְּחַיֵּיהֶם. וְרַבּוֹתֵינוּ דָּרְשׁוּ, כְּקוֹצִים הָיוּ בְּעֵינֵיהֶם:

יג | **בְּפָרֶךְ.** בַּעֲבוֹדָה קָשָׁה הַמְפָרֶכֶת וּמְשַׁבֶּרֶת אֶת הַגּוּף:

טו | **לַמְיַלְּדֹת.** הוּא לְשׁוֹן מוֹלִידוֹת, אֶלָּא שֶׁיֵּשׁ לָשׁוֹן קַל וְיֵשׁ לָשׁוֹן כָּבֵד, כְּמוֹ: שׁוֹבֵר וּמְשַׁבֵּר, דּוֹבֵר וּמְדַבֵּר, כָּךְ מוֹלִיד וּמְיַלֵּד: **שִׁפְרָה.** יוֹכֶבֶד, עַל שֵׁם שֶׁמְּשַׁפֶּרֶת אֶת הַוָּלָד: **פּוּעָה.** מִרְיָם, שֶׁפּוֹעָה וּמְדַבֶּרֶת וְהוֹגָה לַוָּלָד כְּדֶרֶךְ הַנָּשִׁים הַמְפַיְּסוֹת תִּינוֹק הַבּוֹכֶה. "פּוֹעָה" – לְשׁוֹן צְעָקָה, כְּמוֹ: "כַּיּוֹלֵדָה אֶפְעֶה" (ישעיה מב, יד):

טז | **בְּיַלֶּדְכֶן.** כְּמוֹ בְּהוֹלִידְכֶן: **עַל הָאָבְנָיִם.** מוֹשַׁב הָאִשָּׁה הַיּוֹלֶדֶת, וּבְמָקוֹם אַחֵר קוֹרְאוֹ 'מַשְׁבֵּר' (שם לז, ג), וְכָמוֹהוּ: "עֹשֶׂה מְלָאכָה עַל הָאָבְנָיִם" (ירמיה יח, ג) – מוֹשַׁב כְּלִי אֻמָּנוּת יוֹצֵר חֶרֶשׂ: **אִם בֵּן הוּא וְגוֹ'.** לֹא הָיָה מַקְפִּיד אֶלָּא עַל הַזְּכָרִים, שֶׁאָמְרוּ לוֹ אִצְטַגְנִינָיו שֶׁעֲתִידוֹת לֵילֵד בֵּן הַמּוֹשִׁיעַ אוֹתָם: **וָחָיָה.** וְתִחְיֶה:

יז | **וַתְּחַיֶּיןָ אֶת הַיְלָדִים.** מְסַפְּקוֹת לָהֶם מָזוֹן. תַּרְגּוּם הָרִאשׁוֹן "וְקַיָּימָא" וְהַשֵּׁנִי (בפסוק הבא) "וְקַיֵּמְתִּין". לְפִי שֶׁלָּשׁוֹן עָבָר לִנְקֵבוֹת רַבּוֹת, תֵּבָה זוֹ וְכַיּוֹצֵא בָּהּ מְשַׁמֶּשֶׁת לְשׁוֹן פָּעֲלוּ וּלְשׁוֹן פְּעַלְתֶּן, כְּגוֹן: "וַתֹּאמַרְןָ אִישׁ מִצְרִי" (להלן ב, יט) לְשׁוֹן עָבָר, כְּמוֹ 'וַיֹּאמְרוּ' לִזְכָרִים. "וַתְּדַבֵּרְנָה בְּפִיכֶם" (ירמיה מד, כה) לְשׁוֹן דִּבַּרְתֶּם כְּמוֹ 'וַתְּדַבְּרוּ' לִזְכָרִים. וְכֵן: "וַתְּחַלֶּלְנָה אֹתִי אֶל עַמִּי" (יחזקאל יג, יט) לְשׁוֹן עָבָר, חִלַּלְתֶּן, כְּמוֹ 'וַתְּחַלְּלוּ' לִזְכָרִים:

יט | **כִּי חָיוֹת הֵנָּה.** בְּקִיאוֹת כִּמְיַלְּדוֹת, תַּרְגּוּם מְיַלְּדוֹת 'חָיָתָא'. וְרַבּוֹתֵינוּ דָּרְשׁוּ, הֲרֵי הֵן מְשׁוּלוֹת כְּחַיּוֹת הַשָּׂדֶה שֶׁאֵינָן צְרִיכוֹת מְיַלֶּדֶת: "גּוּר אַרְיֵה" (בראשית מט, ט), "זְאֵב יִטְרָף" (שם פסוק כז), "בְּכוֹר שׁוֹרוֹ" (דברים לג, יז), "אַיָּלָה שְׁלֻחָה" (בראשית מט, כא). וּמִי שֶׁלֹּא נִכְתַּב בּוֹ, הֲרֵי הַכָּתוּב כּוֹלְלָן: "מָה אִמְּךָ לְבִיָּא" (יחזקאל יט, ב):

כ-כא | **וַיֵּיטֶב.** הֵיטִיב לָהֶן. וְזֶה חִלּוּק בְּתֵבָה שֶׁיְּסוֹדָהּ שְׁתֵּי אוֹתִיּוֹת וְנָתַן לָהּ וָי"ו יוּ"ד בְּרֹאשָׁהּ, כְּשֶׁהִיא בָּאָה לְדַבֵּר לְשׁוֹן וַיַּפְעִיל הוּא נוֹקֵד אֶת הַיּוּ"ד בְּצֵירֵי שֶׁהוּא קָמַץ קָטָן, כְּגוֹן: "וַיֵּיטֶב אֱלֹהִים לַמְיַלְּדֹת"; "וַיֶּרֶב בְּבַת יְהוּדָה" (איכה ב, ה), הִרְבָּה תַּאֲנִיָּה; וְכֵן "וַיֶּגֶל הַשְּׁאֵרִית" (דברי הימים ב' לו, כ) דִּנְבוּזַרְאֲדָן, הֶגְלָה אֶת הַשְּׁאֵרִית; "וַיֶּפֶן זָנָב אֶל זָנָב" (שופטים טו, ד) – הִפְנָה הַזְּנָבוֹת זוֹ לָזוֹ. כָּל אֵלּוּ לְשׁוֹן הִפְעִיל אֶת אֲחֵרִים. וּכְשֶׁהוּא מְדַבֵּר בִּלְשׁוֹן וַיִּפְעַל

DISCUSSION

the babies. Instead, he sufficed with a command to the midwives to do so (Ibn Ezra).

Pharaoh directed his command to the midwives because he assumed that in their capacity, they would be the first to see the newborns, and it would therefore be easy for them to carry out his plot. From their response in verse 19, it is implied that Pharaoh refrained from commanding the midwives to openly kill the newborn boys; rather, he commanded the midwives to kill the babies in a way that would not be detected (*Bekhor Shor*; *Akedat Yitzḥak*).

BACKGROUND

1:16| **The birthstool:** The literal meaning of this term is "two stones." Indeed, ancient Egyptian and Babylonian accounts describe a birthing practice in which a woman would give birth while squatting between two stones or large bricks, which provided support for the woman during the delivery. An archaeological finding from the Upper Egyptian city of Dendera includes a relief depicting a special birthing chair. Later, from the period of the Mishna, there are references to a special type of birthing chair known as the travailing chair (*Kelim* 23:4), whose seat was particularly narrow, or which had some sort of hole in it that enabled the midwife to assist in delivering the child.

midwives and the people increased and became very mighty. The population of Israel was not suppressed; on the contrary, it continued to grow.

21 **It was, because the midwives feared God, He established households for them.**[D] Their families grew and became honored and distinguished.[7]

22 Since he was unable to carry out his intentions through the midwives, **Pharaoh commanded all his people** directly,

saying: Every son who is born to the Hebrews, **into the Nile you shall cast him, but every daughter you shall keep alive.**[D] Whether this order became official Egyptian policy to be enforced by the government, or it was a command directed at any Egyptian citizen who found a Hebrew child, every newborn Hebrew boy was sentenced to be drowned in the river.

The Early Life of Moses
EXODUS 2:1–22

Against the backdrop of the deteriorating condition of the children of Israel to the point of state-sanctioned murder of their sons, the Torah describes the early life of the individual destined to become their savior.

Moses was born as a result of his parents' decision to bring a child into the world despite the very difficult circumstances. Paradoxically, the redeemer of Israel would grow up in the household of the very oppressor who sought their destruction. Perhaps Moses would draw the strength to save his brethren from his upbringing, as he was raised a freeman, or from his own personality as a sensitive individual who expressed compassion and empathy for the oppressed and downtrodden.

2 1 **A man from the house,** the tribe, **of Levi went and took a daughter of** the head of the tribe of **Levi.**[D]

2 **The woman conceived and bore a son; she saw him that he was good;** it was immediately apparent that he was special,[8] **and she concealed him for three months** because of the murderous decree upon all newborn Hebrew boys.

3 After some time passed, **she could no longer conceal him** because his voice became stronger as he grew, leading to the possibility that he would be discovered by the king's agents or other informants. The woman refused to capitulate to the king's decree, so she took drastic action, and **she took a wicker**[B] **basket for him and coated it with clay** on the inside **and with pitch** on the outside,[9] to make it waterproof; **she placed the child in it and placed it among the reeds** growing **on the bank of the Nile.**

4 **His** older **sister,** Miriam (see 15:20), who was herself quite young, **stationed herself at a distance, to know what would be done to him.** Although she could not protect him from the decree, she watched from a distance to see what would be his fate. Perhaps because the child was noticeably special, they expected great things to come from him; she therefore wanted to see if these expectations would be fulfilled.

5 At that moment, **Pharaoh's daughter went down** from her palace **to bathe in the Nile, and her maidens,** her servants, **walked alongside the Nile** to bathe as well, or to accompany

Reeds

and serve the princess. **She,** the princess, **saw the basket among the reeds, and** since it seemed unusual, she **sent her maidservant and she took it.**

6 **She opened it and she saw the child, and behold, a boy was crying.**[D] **She had compassion for him,**[D] **and she said: This is from the children of the Hebrews.** Perhaps she concluded that an Egyptian woman would not have abandoned a child in such a manner, or perhaps she was able to identify him as a Hebrew due to his skin color or facial features.

DISCUSSION

1:21 | He established households for them: This phrase led the Sages to identify Shifra and Pua with two well-known women: Yokheved, mother of Moses, and Miriam, sister of Moses (*Sota* 11b). Yokheved was the progenitor of the

house of the priesthood through her son Aaron, and Miriam was an ancestress of the leaders of the tribe of Judah, from whom descended the royal house of King David.

1:22 | Pharaoh commanded all his people, saying: Every son who is born, into the Nile you shall cast him: According to Ramban (1:10), this command was not an explicit policy to kill the newborn Hebrew babies, and it was

◀▶

כא כב וַיְהִי כִּי־יָרְאוּ הַמְיַלְּדֹת אֶת־הָאֱלֹהִים וַיַּעַשׂ לָהֶם בָּתִּים: וַיְצַו פַּרְעֹה לְכָל־עַמּוֹ
לֵאמֹר כָּל־הַבֵּן הַיִּלּוֹד הַיְאֹרָה תַּשְׁלִיכֻהוּ וְכָל־הַבַּת תְּחַיּוּן:
א ב וַיֵּלֶךְ אִישׁ מִבֵּית לֵוִי וַיִּקַּח אֶת־בַּת־לֵוִי: וַתַּהַר הָאִשָּׁה וַתֵּלֶד בֵּן וַתֵּרֶא אֹתוֹ כִּי־
ג טוֹב הוּא וַתִּצְפְּנֵהוּ שְׁלֹשָׁה יְרָחִים: וְלֹא־יָכְלָה עוֹד הַצְּפִינוֹ וַתִּקַּח־לוֹ תֵּבַת גֹּמֶא
וַתַּחְמְרָה בַחֵמָר וּבַזָּפֶת וַתָּשֶׂם בָּהּ אֶת־הַיֶּלֶד וַתָּשֶׂם בַּסּוּף עַל־שְׂפַת הַיְאֹר:
ד ה וַתֵּתַצַּב אֲחֹתוֹ מֵרָחֹק לְדֵעָה מַה־יֵּעָשֶׂה לוֹ: וַתֵּרֶד בַּת־פַּרְעֹה לִרְחֹץ עַל־הַיְאֹר
וְנַעֲרֹתֶיהָ הֹלְכֹת עַל־יַד הַיְאֹר וַתֵּרֶא אֶת־הַתֵּבָה בְּתוֹךְ הַסּוּף וַתִּשְׁלַח אֶת־אֲמָתָהּ
ו וַתִּקָּחֶהָ: וַתִּפְתַּח וַתִּרְאֵהוּ אֶת־הַיֶּלֶד וְהִנֵּה־נַעַר בֹּכֶה וַתַּחְמֹל עָלָיו וַתֹּאמֶר מִיַּלְדֵי

רש״י

הוא נוקד היו״ד בחיריק, כגון: ״וייטב בעיניו״ (ויקרא י, כ) – לשון הוטב; וכן ״וירב העם״ (להלן פסוק כ) – רבה העם; ״ויגל יהודה״ (מלכים ב׳ כה, כא) – גלה יהודה; ״ויפן כה וכה״ (להלן ב, יב) – פנה לכאן ולכאן. ואל תשיבני: וילך, וישב, וירד, ויצא, לפי שאינן מגזרתן של אלו, שהרי היו״ד יסוד בהן: ירד, יצא, ילך, ישב, היו״ד אות שלישית בו: וייטב אלהים למילדת. מהו הטובה? ״ויעש להם בתים״ – בתי כהונה ולויה ומלכות, שקרויין בתים: ״לבנות את בית ה׳ ואת בית המלך״ (מלכים א׳ ט, א); כהונה ולויה מיוכבד, ומלכות ממרים, כדאיתא במסכת סוטה (דף יא ע״ב):

כב| לכל עמו. אף עליהם גזר. יום שנולד משה אמרו לו אצטגניניו: היום נולד ואין אנו יודעים אם ממצרים אם מישראל, ורואין אנו שסופו ללקות במים, לפיכך גזר אותו היום אף על המצרים, שנאמר: ״כל הבן הילוד״ ולא נאמר ׳הילוד לעברים׳. והם לא היו יודעים שסופו ללקות על מי מריבה:

פרק ב

א| ויקח את בת לוי. פרוש היה ממנה מפני גזרת פרעה והחזירה ועשה בה לקוחין שניים. ואף היא נהפכה להיות נערה. ובת מאה ושלשים שנה היתה; שנולדה בבואם למצרים בין החומות, ומאתים ועשר נשתהו שם, וכשיצאו היה משה בן שמונים שנה – כשנתעברה ממנו היתה בת מאה ושלשים, וקורא אותה ׳בת לוי׳:

ב| כי טוב הוא. כשנולד נתמלא הבית כלו אורה:

ג| ולא יכלה עוד הצפינו. שמנו לה המצרים מיום שהחזירה, והיא ילדתו לששה חדשים ויום אחד, שהיולדת לשבעה יולדת למקוטעין, והם בדקו אחריה לסוף תשעה: גמא. גמי בלשון משנה, ובלעז יונ״ק, ודבר רך הוא ועומד בפני רך ובפני קשה: בחמר ובזפת. זפת מבחוץ וטיט מבפנים, כדי שלא יריח אותו צדיק ריח רע של זפת: ותשם בסוף. הוא לשון אגם, רוזי״ל בלעז, ודומה לו: ״קנה וסוף קמלו״ (ישעיה יט, ו):

ה| לרחץ על היאר. סרס המקרא ופרשהו, ותרד בת פרעה על היאור לרחוץ בו: על יד היאר. אצל היאור, כמו: ״ראו חלקת יואב אל ידי״ (שמואל ב׳ יד, ל), והוא לשון יד ממש, שיד האדם סמוכה לו. ורבותינו אמרו, ״הלכת״ לשון מיתה, הולכות למות לפי שמיחו בה. והכתוב מסייען, כי למה לנו לכתב: ״ונערתיה הלכת״?: את אמתה. את שפחתה. ורבותינו דרשו לשון יד, אבל לפי דקדוק לשון הקדש היה לו להנקד ׳אמתה׳ מ״ם דגושה, והם דרשו ״את אמתה״ – את ידה, ונשתרבבה אמתה אמות הרבה:

ו| ותפתח ותראהו. את מי ראתה? ״את הילד״, זהו פשוטו. ומדרשו, שראתה עמו שכינה: והנה נער בכה. קולו כנער:

DISCUSSION

therefore addressed specifically to the citizens of Egypt and not his military or police forces. Pharaoh instructed the Egyptian people that if they find a newborn Hebrew boy, they may murder him, and if the father will accuse one of them of murder, the authorities will demand that he provide witnesses to attest to the crime.

2:1| **A man from the house of Levi went and took a daughter of Levi:** Later on, the verse will identify these individuals as Amram and Yokheved, Amram's aunt. After the giving of the Torah, a union between a man and his aunt was prohibited. Since the focus of this passage is the birth of Moses, the verse makes no mention of the children born to Amram and Yokheved prior to the birth of Moses (see 6:20; see also Ibn Ezra).

2:6| **A boy was crying:** The use of the term "boy" [*na'ar*] instead of "child" [*yeled*] may indicate that he looked or sounded older than he actually was (see *Sota* 12b; Ramban; Rabbi Yehuda HaḤasid).

She had compassion for him: The text does not indicate how old Pharaoh's daughter was at that time, but presumably she was an adult. Perhaps her exhibition of mercy

BACKGROUND

2:3| **Wicker:** This refers to *Cyperus papyrus*, a type of reed that grows on the banks of rivers. It can reach 4–5 m in height. It was commonly used for weaving baskets and mats, and producing ropes, sandals, and small boats.

7 Presumably, the discovery of the child caused a stir. Miriam, who until now was standing at a distance, noticed the gathering of maidens around the baby and approached them: **His sister said to Pharaoh's daughter: Shall I go and call a wet nurse for you from the Hebrews, and she will nurse the child for you?** It would seem that Pharaoh's daughter picked up the crying child, but was unable to calm him. The child was too young to eat food, and she could not nurse him; if she wanted to keep the child, she needed a wet nurse. Miriam suggested a Hebrew wet nurse, not necessarily because the child was himself a Hebrew, but because Hebrew women were a source of cheap labor, especially in light of the fact that many of their babies were murdered by the Egyptians. These women would certainly be delighted to receive such employment.

8 Pharaoh's daughter was indifferent regarding the ethnicity of the wet nurse: **Pharaoh's daughter said to her: Go. The girl went, and summoned the child's mother.** This was obviously the preferable scenario, as the mother could now nurse her own child, and Pharaoh's daughter would be unaware that the wet nurse was in fact his biological mother.

9 **Pharaoh's daughter said to her: Take this child and nurse him for me, and I will pay your wages.** Since Pharaoh's daughter took an interest in the well-being of the child, he could safely be reunited with his mother. Now, the child's mother would care for him just as before, and would even receive payment for nursing him. **The woman took the child and nursed him.**

10 **The child grew, and** once he was weaned, he could be cared for by a woman who was not a wet nurse. So **she brought him to Pharaoh's daughter, and he was a son to her.** Pharaoh's daughter adopted the child, and **she called his name Moses [*Moshe*], and she said:** I named him thus **because I drew him from the water [*meshitihu*].**[D]

11 *Third aliya* Despite being raised by Pharaoh's daughter as a son of the Egyptian aristocracy, Moses was aware of his Hebrew ethnicity: **It was in those days, Moses grew** to adulthood,[10] **and he went out to his brethren**[D] to familiarize himself with them. Until now, because the lowly Hebrews did not enter the court of Pharaoh, Moses was unfamiliar with them. **And he saw their burdens, and he saw an Egyptian man beating a Hebrew man**[D] **from his brethren.** At this point, Moses felt a solidarity with the Hebrews.

12 **He,** Moses, **turned this way and that, and he saw that there was no one** in the vicinity. The area appeared secluded, although it seems that Moses did not look very carefully, as will become clear later on. **He smote the Egyptian,** killing him in a miraculous manner, or thanks to his strength of body and spirit, which Moses maintained until the age of 120 years.[11] **And** Moses then **hid him** by burying the body **in the sand,**[D] and he assumed that this was the conclusion of this incident.

13 Still not entirely familiar with the Hebrews, but feeling a familial bond to them, **he,** Moses, **emerged** to see them again **on the second day, and behold, two Hebrew men were fighting.** Apparently, the two men did not merely exchange insults; at least one of them physically assaulted the other. **And he,** Moses, **said to the wicked one,** the one who struck the other: **Why do you strike your neighbor?**

DISCUSSION

toward the child stemmed from an awareness of the decree against all male Hebrew babies. Although, as noted above, the decree was not an official law or public proclamation, it is possible that she knew of it. It is also possible that precisely because she was a princess and lived a sheltered life in the palace, she was unaware of the events taking place outside. In any case, it seems that she had enough of an awareness of the situation to recognize that the crying baby in the basket was a Hebrew, and that he was in mortal danger. Recognizing this, she felt compassion toward him. Alternatively, perhaps the unusual circumstances which led to her discovery of the child made a deep impression on her, regardless of the child's ethnicity, leading her to conclude that he was sent to her intentionally from Heaven.

The sons of Bitya daughter of Pharaoh, are listed in a verse in I Chronicles (4:18). The Sages identify Bitya as the daughter of Pharaoh mentioned here, and praise her (*Megilla* 13a). Even if the daughter of Pharaoh had other children, it is uncertain what type of relationship she had with them. It is clear, however, that she had a special relationship with this child. Regardless of the greatness he would exhibit later in life, she felt that he was an innately miraculous child.

2:10| **She called his name Moses [*Moshe*], and she said: Because I drew him from the water [*meshitihu*]:** Presumably, Moses was given another name at birth; nevertheless, throughout his life he was known by the name that Pharaoh's daughter gave him (see *Megilla* 13a; *Vayikra Rabba* 1:3).

It seems odd that Pharaoh's daughter gave him a Hebrew name. Moreover, it would appear that she explains the basis for this name as deriving from a Hebrew term, *meshitihu*. For this reason, some have suggested that the name *Moshe* is actually the Hebrew form of an Egyptian name that means water, or that she called him by a name whose root is *Moshe*, but which means child of the water, or offspring of the river. That is, she referred to him as a child of the Nile, which was considered sacred and a source of life by the Egyptians. It would seem, then, that a wordplay exists in both Hebrew and Egyptian, except that in Hebrew, *Moshe* is related to the term *meshitihu*, the act of drawing, while in the original Egyptian, Pharaoh's daughter called him *Moshe* because of the water itself, "Because I drew him from the water."

2:11| **Moses grew and he went out to his brethren:** Ironically, Pharaoh, who tried to eradicate all the Hebrew boys, ended up raising one

ז הָעִבְרִים זֶה: וַתֹּאמֶר אֲחֹתוֹ אֶל־בַּת־פַּרְעֹה הַאֵלֵךְ וְקָרָאתִי לָךְ אִשָּׁה מֵינֶקֶת
ח מִן הָעִבְרִיֹּת וְתֵינִק לָךְ אֶת־הַיָּלֶד: וַתֹּאמֶר־לָהּ בַּת־פַּרְעֹה לֵכִי וַתֵּלֶךְ הָעַלְמָה
ט וַתִּקְרָא אֶת־אֵם הַיָּלֶד: וַתֹּאמֶר לָהּ בַּת־פַּרְעֹה הֵילִיכִי אֶת־הַיֶּלֶד הַזֶּה וְהֵינִקִהוּ
י לִי וַאֲנִי אֶתֵּן אֶת־שְׂכָרֵךְ וַתִּקַּח הָאִשָּׁה הַיֶּלֶד וַתְּנִיקֵהוּ: וַיִּגְדַּל הַיֶּלֶד וַתְּבִאֵהוּ
לְבַת־פַּרְעֹה וַיְהִי־לָהּ לְבֵן וַתִּקְרָא שְׁמוֹ מֹשֶׁה וַתֹּאמֶר כִּי מִן־הַמַּיִם מְשִׁיתִהוּ:
יא וַיְהִי ׀ בַּיָּמִים הָהֵם וַיִּגְדַּל מֹשֶׁה וַיֵּצֵא אֶל־אֶחָיו וַיַּרְא בְּסִבְלֹתָם וַיַּרְא אִישׁ שלישי
יב מִצְרִי מַכֶּה אִישׁ־עִבְרִי מֵאֶחָיו: וַיִּפֶן כֹּה וָכֹה וַיַּרְא כִּי אֵין אִישׁ וַיַּךְ אֶת־הַמִּצְרִי
יג וַיִּטְמְנֵהוּ בַּחוֹל: וַיֵּצֵא בַּיּוֹם הַשֵּׁנִי וְהִנֵּה שְׁנֵי־אֲנָשִׁים עִבְרִים נִצִּים וַיֹּאמֶר לָרָשָׁע

רש״י

ז | **מִן הָעִבְרִיּוֹת.** שֶׁהֶחֱזִירַתּוּ עַל מִצְרִיּוֹת הַרְבֵּה לִינֹק וְלֹא יָנַק, לְפִי שֶׁהָיָה עָתִיד לְדַבֵּר עִם הַשְּׁכִינָה:

ח | **וַתֵּלֶךְ הָעַלְמָה.** הָלְכָה בִּזְרִיזוּת וְעַלְמוּת כְּעֶלֶם:

ט | **הֵילִיכִי.** נִתְנַבְּאָה וְלֹא יָדְעָה מַה נִּתְנַבְּאָה, הֵי שֶׁלִּיכִי:

י | **מְשִׁיתִהוּ.** "שְׁלִתִּיהּ", הוּא לְשׁוֹן הוֹצָאָה בְּלָשׁוֹן אֲרַמִּי: "כְּמִשְׁחַל בִּינִיתָא מֵחֲלָבָא" (ברכות ח ע״א). וּבְלָשׁוֹן עִבְרִי "מְשִׁיתִהוּ" לְשׁוֹן הֲסִירוֹתִיו, כְּמוֹ: "לֹא יָמוּשׁ" (יהושע א, ח), "לֹא מָשׁוּ" (במדבר יד, מד); כָּךְ חִבְּרוֹ מְנַחֵם. וַאֲנִי אוֹמֵר שֶׁאֵינוֹ מִמַּחְבֶּרֶת מָשׁ וְיָמוּשׁ, אֶלָּא מִגִּזְרַת מָשָׁה, וּלְשׁוֹן הוֹצָאָה הוּא; וְכֵן: "יַמְשֵׁנִי מִמַּיִם רַבִּים" (שמואל ב׳ כב, יז). שֶׁאִלּוּ הָיָה מִמַּחְבֶּרֶת מָשׁ, לֹא יִתָּכֵן לוֹמַר 'מְשִׁיתִיהוּ', אֶלָּא 'הֲמִישׁוֹתִיהוּ', כַּאֲשֶׁר יֵאָמֵר מִן קָם 'הֲקִימוֹתִי', וּמִן שָׁב 'הֲשִׁיבוֹתִי', וּמִן בָּא 'הֲבִיאוֹתִי'; אוֹ 'מַשְׁתִּיהוּ', כְּמוֹ: "וּמַשְׁתִּי אֶת עֲוֹן הָאָרֶץ" (זכריה ג, ט). אֲבָל 'מָשִׁיתִי' אֵינוֹ אֶלָּא מִגִּזְרַת תֵּבָה שֶׁפֹּעַל שֶׁלָּהּ מְיֻסָּד בְּהֵ״א בְּסוֹף הַתֵּבָה, כְּגוֹן: מָשָׁה, בָּנָה, עָשָׂה, צִוָּה, פָּנָה, כְּשֶׁיָּבוֹא לוֹמַר בָּהֶם פָּעַלְתִּי תָּבֹא הַיּוּ״ד בִּמְקוֹם הֵ״א, כְּמוֹ: עָשִׂיתִי, בָּנִיתִי, פָּנִיתִי, צִוִּיתִי:

יא | **וַיִּגְדַּל מֹשֶׁה.** וַהֲלֹא כְּבָר כָּתַב (לעיל פסוק י) "וַיִּגְדַּל הַיֶּלֶד"? אָמַר רַבִּי יְהוּדָה בְּרַבִּי אִלְעַאי, הָרִאשׁוֹן לְקוֹמָה וְהַשֵּׁנִי לִגְדֻלָּה, שֶׁמִּנָּהוּ פַּרְעֹה עַל בֵּיתוֹ: **וַיַּרְא בְּסִבְלֹתָם.** נָתַן עֵינָיו וְלִבּוֹ לִהְיוֹת מֵצֵר עֲלֵיהֶם: **אִישׁ מִצְרִי.** נוֹגֵשׂ הָיָה, מְמֻנֶּה עַל שׁוֹטְרֵי יִשְׂרָאֵל, וְהָיָה מַעֲמִידָם מִקְּרוֹת הַגֶּבֶר לִמְלַאכְתָּם: **מַכֶּה אִישׁ עִבְרִי.** מַלְקֵהוּ וְרוֹדֵהוּ; וּבַעְלָהּ שֶׁל שְׁלוֹמִית בַּת דִּבְרִי הָיָה, וְנָתַן עֵינָיו בָּהּ, וּבַלַּיְלָה הֶעֱמִידוֹ וְהוֹצִיאוֹ מִבֵּיתוֹ וְהוּא חָזַר וְנִכְנַס לַבַּיִת וּבָא עַל אִשְׁתּוֹ, כִּסְבוּרָה שֶׁהוּא בַּעְלָהּ. וְחָזַר הָאִישׁ לְבֵיתוֹ וְהִרְגִּישׁ בַּדָּבָר, וּכְשֶׁרָאָה אוֹתוֹ מִצְרִי שֶׁהִרְגִּישׁ בַּדָּבָר הָיָה מַכֵּהוּ וְרוֹדֵהוּ כָּל הַיּוֹם:

יב | **וַיִּפֶן כֹּה וָכֹה.** רָאָה מֶה עָשָׂה לוֹ בַּבַּיִת וּמֶה עָשָׂה לוֹ בַּשָּׂדֶה. וּלְפִי פְּשׁוּטוֹ כְּמַשְׁמָעוֹ: **וַיַּרְא כִּי אֵין אִישׁ.** עָתִיד לָצֵאת מִמֶּנּוּ שֶׁיִּתְגַּיֵּר:

יג | **שְׁנֵי אֲנָשִׁים עִבְרִים.** דָּתָן וַאֲבִירָם, הֵם שֶׁהוֹתִירוּ מִן

DISCUSSION

of them in his own home. This child, who grew up as a member of the royal household, did not know who his real family was. Perhaps he had some vague memories from when his mother cared for him as a small child. Even if his mother managed to maintain some connection with him while he lived in Pharaoh's home, she did not reveal to him that she was his mother. Moses needed to discover his true identity on his own. In this sense, Moses experienced, perhaps in a more dramatic fashion, the experience of all adolescents: Identity formation.

In the style of biblical prose, the text does not describe the emotions felt by Moses at this time. Nevertheless, the narrative reveals that despite his upbringing among the Egyptian royalty, Moses felt a deep connection to his brethren outside. Although he was unacquainted with their lifestyle and barely spoke their language, perhaps recalling only a few terms from when he was nursed by his mother, he felt that these people were his brethren.

An Egyptian man beating a Hebrew man: According to one midrash (see *Shemot Rabba* 1:28; Rashi), this beating occurred after the Egyptian man raped the wife of the Hebrew man. In truth, it is unnecessary to seek a reason for why the Egyptian struck the Hebrew man. As an enslaved people, the Hebrews were considered fair game for the Egyptians, and they were abused with complete impunity. The abuse was so terrible that the Hebrew man did not even attempt to defend himself.

2:12| **He smote the Egyptian and hid him in the sand:** The actions of Moses are characteristic of his personality. Being raised in the palace of the king led him to feel authorized to take such action. Furthermore, this incident demonstrated Moses' deep sensitivity for justice. His aversion to injustice, which will present itself throughout the remainder of his life, makes its first appearance here: The Egyptian's arbitrary abuse of the Hebrew man infuriated Moses, leading him to act. Nevertheless, Moses did not act impulsively. He was aware that in Egypt, an attack against a Hebrew man was not a punishable offense, and he therefore took pains to conceal his actions.

14 **He,** the assailant, **said: Who appointed you to be a leader and a judge over us,** that you see fit to judge me? Since you hold no position of judicial authority, what can you do to me? Indeed, I am aware of your use of force; **do you propose to kill me, as you killed the Egyptian? Moses was frightened,** because he knew he had broken the law, **and he said: Indeed,** although I thought my actions went unseen, **the matter is known.**^D

15 **Pharaoh heard this matter.** Perhaps the Hebrew man ceased to strike his colleague, but he did not remain silent, and the matter reached the ears of Pharaoh. It is unknown how Pharaoh related to the abandoned child his daughter brought home years earlier. Perhaps he only tolerated his presence, much as a parent might tolerate an abandoned kitten that his child rescued from the street, **and** therefore, once he became aware of what Moses had done, **he sought to kill Moses,** just as a parent might react toward his child's pet after learning that the animal began to cause damage. **Moses fled from Pharaoh, and he settled in the land of Midyan,**^{BD} **and** since he was a total stranger, **he sat beside the well,** which was an informal meeting place.

16 **The priest of Midyan had seven daughters,** who shepherded his flock, since he was not a wealthy man. **They came** to the well, **drew water, and filled the troughs** in order **to give their father's flock to drink.**

17 **The shepherds came and drove them away; Moses stood and rescued them.** Once again, Moses demonstrated his extreme sensitivity to injustice. Despite being completely unfamiliar with these girls, he responded to the injustice occurring before him.¹² **And** not only did he save them, but **he** also **gave their flock to drink.** Although he was a total stranger, he sought to assist them in any way possible.

18 The girls did not engage Moses in lengthy conversation: **They came to Re'uel,**^D **their father, and he said: Why were you so quick to come today?** This question makes it clear that the girls were regularly driven away from the water by the

Trough

other shepherds. Normally, they would return home late, as they needed to wait until the other shepherds finished giving their flocks to drink. It seems that their father was unable to offer much help to his daughters.

19 **They said: An Egyptian man rescued us from the shepherds, and he also drew water for us and gave the flock to drink.** Apparently, Moses spoke to them in Egyptian, or perhaps he was dressed in Egyptian garb. The Midyanite girls were unattuned to the differences between Moses, a Hebrew, and the native Egyptians.

20 **He,** Re'uel, **said to his daughters: And where is he?** After this stranger intervened on your behalf and assisted you with giving water to the flock, **why did you leave the man?** He must be waiting by the well for someone to strike up a conversation with him. At the very least, **call him, and let him eat bread** with us.

21 **Moses decided,**¹³ or desired,¹⁴ **to live with the man,** due to the pleasant manner in which he was accepted, and perhaps due to the personalities of his hosts;¹⁵ **and he gave his daughter**

DISCUSSION

2:14 | Moses was frightened and he said: Indeed, the matter is known: Although Moses turned this way and that and saw that there was no man, perhaps there were others in the vicinity who hid when they saw the Egyptian striking the Hebrew, in order to see what would transpire. Alternatively, even if there were no other witnesses, the Hebrew man who was saved by Moses bore witness to the entire incident, and he may have related to others the events that transpired (see *Akedat Yitzḥak; Abravanel*). Presumably, this man would have related the miraculous appearance of the Hebrew-Egyptian

savior from the royal palace with excitement and good intentions. Such a story would undoubtedly spread easily and quickly among the community of downtrodden slaves, and would thus have reached the ears of the Hebrew assailant. This violent individual, however, does not react to the incident with any measure of excitement, respect, or admiration toward Moses.

Perhaps Moses was frightened because he suddenly became aware of another reality: If on the first day, Moses saved a beaten and downtrodden Hebrew from a violent Egyptian, now Moses was faced with a dispute between

two Hebrews. It became clear to Moses that the Hebrews themselves were not completely free of violence and crime. This was a difficult reality for him to discover. Moses could also deduce this from the manner in which the Hebrew assailant responded to him. The question "do you propose to kill me, as you killed the Egyptian?" may contain an implied threat: You cannot kill me; someone will witness your crimes and will take care to report you (see *Shemot Rabba* 1:30).

2:15 | And he settled in the land of Midyan: The Midyanites were a collection of ←●

יד לָמָּה תַכֶּה רֵעֶךָ: וַיֹּאמֶר מִי שָׂמְךָ לְאִישׁ שַׂר וְשֹׁפֵט עָלֵינוּ הַלְהָרְגֵנִי אַתָּה אֹמֵר

טו כַּאֲשֶׁר הָרַגְתָּ אֶת־הַמִּצְרִי וַיִּירָא מֹשֶׁה וַיֹּאמַר אָכֵן נוֹדַע הַדָּבָר: וַיִּשְׁמַע פַּרְעֹה

אֶת־הַדָּבָר הַזֶּה וַיְבַקֵּשׁ לַהֲרֹג אֶת־מֹשֶׁה וַיִּבְרַח מֹשֶׁה מִפְּנֵי פַרְעֹה וַיֵּשֶׁב בְּאֶרֶץ־

טז מִדְיָן וַיֵּשֶׁב עַל־הַבְּאֵר: וּלְכֹהֵן מִדְיָן שֶׁבַע בָּנוֹת וַתָּבֹאנָה וַתִּדְלֶנָה וַתְּמַלֶּאנָה

יז אֶת־הָרְהָטִים לְהַשְׁקוֹת צֹאן אֲבִיהֶן: וַיָּבֹאוּ הָרֹעִים וַיְגָרְשׁוּם וַיָּקָם מֹשֶׁה וַיּוֹשִׁעָן

יח וַיַּשְׁקְ אֶת־צֹאנָם: וַתָּבֹאנָה אֶל־רְעוּאֵל אֲבִיהֶן וַיֹּאמֶר מַדּוּעַ מִהַרְתֶּן בֹּא הַיּוֹם:

יט וַתֹּאמַרְןָ אִישׁ מִצְרִי הִצִּילָנוּ מִיַּד הָרֹעִים וְגַם־דָּלֹה דָלָה לָנוּ וַיַּשְׁקְ אֶת־הַצֹּאן:

כ וַיֹּאמֶר אֶל־בְּנֹתָיו וְאַיּוֹ לָמָּה זֶּה עֲזַבְתֶּן אֶת־הָאִישׁ קִרְאֶן לוֹ וְיֹאכַל לָחֶם: וַיּוֹאֶל

רש"י

הַמָּן. נִצִּים. מְרִיבִים. לָמָּה תַכֶּה. אַף עַל פִּי שֶׁלֹּא הִכָּהוּ נִקְרָא רָשָׁע בַּהֲרָמַת יָד: רֵעֶךָ. רָשָׁע כְּמוֹתְךָ:

יד| מִי שָׂמְךָ לְאִישׁ. וַהֲרֵי עוֹדְךָ נַעַר: הַלְהָרְגֵנִי אַתָּה אֹמֵר. מִכָּאן חָנוּ לְמֵדִים שֶׁהֲרָגוֹ בַּשֵּׁם הַמְפֹרָשׁ: וַיִּירָא מֹשֶׁה. כִּפְשׁוּטוֹ. וּמִדְרָשׁוֹ, דָּאַג לוֹ עַל שֶׁרָאָה בְּיִשְׂרָאֵל רְשָׁעִים דֵּילָטוֹרִין. אָמַר, מֵעַתָּה שֶׁמָּא אֵינָם רְאוּיִין לְהִגָּאֵל: אָכֵן נוֹדַע הַדָּבָר. כְּמַשְׁמָעוֹ. וּמִדְרָשׁוֹ, נוֹדַע לִי הַדָּבָר שֶׁהָיִיתִי תָּמֵהַּ עָלָיו, מֶה חָטְאוּ יִשְׂרָאֵל מִכָּל שִׁבְעִים

טו| וַיִּשְׁמַע פַּרְעֹה. הֵם הִלְשִׁינוּ עָלָיו: וַיְבַקֵּשׁ לַהֲרֹג אֶת מֹשֶׁה. מְסָרוֹ לְקוּסְטִינֵר לְהָרְגוֹ, וְלֹא שָׁלְטָה בּוֹ הַחֶרֶב, הוּא שֶׁאָמַר מֹשֶׁה: "וַיַּצִּילֵנִי מֵחֶרֶב פַּרְעֹה" (להלן יח, ד): וַיֵּשֶׁב עַל הַבְּאֵר. לָמַד מִיַּעֲקֹב שֶׁנִּזְדַּוֵּג לוֹ זִוּוּגוֹ מִן הַבְּאֵר:

טז| וּלְכֹהֵן מִדְיָן. רַב שֶׁבָּהֶן, וּפֵרַשׁ לוֹ מֵעֲבוֹדָה זָרָה

וְנִדּוּהוּ מֵאֶצְלָם: אֶת הָרְהָטִים. אֶת בְּרֵכוֹת מְרוּצוֹת הַמַּיִם הָעֲשׂוּיוֹת בָּאָרֶץ:

יז| וַיְגָרְשׁוּם. מִפְּנֵי הַנִּדּוּי:

כ| לָמָּה זֶּה עֲזַבְתֶּן. הִכִּיר בּוֹ שֶׁהוּא מִזַּרְעוֹ שֶׁל יַעֲקֹב, שֶׁהַמַּיִם עוֹלִים לִקְרָאתוֹ: וְיֹאכַל לָחֶם. שֶׁמָּא יִשָּׂא אַחַת מִכֶּם, כְּמָה דְּאַתְּ אָמַר: "כִּי אִם הַלֶּחֶם אֲשֶׁר הוּא אוֹכֵל" (בראשית לט, ו):

כא| וַיּוֹאֶל. כְּתַרְגּוּמוֹ. וְדוֹמֶה לוֹ: "הוֹאֶל נָא וְלִין" (שופטים

BACKGROUND

2:15 | The land of Midyan: The precise borders of this land are uncertain. Some place Midyan in the entire southern part of the Negev desert, north of Eilat, and in the mountains east of the Arava Valley. Others claim that Midyan was located in the northern part of the Hejaz, a region on the western side of the Arabian Peninsula.

DISCUSSION

→ seminomadic tribes who lived in desert settlements either east or south of Canaan. As a fugitive fleeing from the Egyptian authorities, Moses sought refuge among these desert nomads, who did not assign much value to the law, even that of their own leaders.

It would seem that a significant amount of time passed between the time that Moses fled from Egypt and his arrival in Midyan. Various midrashic sources recount legends of the events of Moses' life during this period.

2:18 | Re'uel: Some identify Re'uel with Yitro, father-in-law of Moses and priest of Midyan (see 3:1, 4:18; *Mekhilta, Yitro* 1; *Shemot Rabba* 1:32). If so, the various names of Yitro reflect different periods of his life. Others explain that Re'uel was in fact the father of Yitro and thus the grandfather of these girls (see *Targum Yonatan*; Ibn Ezra; Ramban; Rashbam). Indeed, the *Sifrei* (*Behaalotekha* 20)

states regarding this matter: This indicates that children refer to their grandfather as father.

Although the name Re'uel seems to be Semitic, this alone is not sufficient evidence with which to reach a decisive conclusion regarding the man's ethnicity. Given that the Midyanites were descendants of Abraham (see Genesis 25:2), there were presumably similarities between Midyanite and Hebrew names (see Genesis 25:4).

Some have suggested that Re'uel, priest of Midyan, was the political leader of Midyan as well. However, the events described in the preceding verses would seem to indicate that he was not a very powerful man. The Sages have suggested that his religious beliefs deviated from those of his community, or that he may have ceased to function as priest after rejecting the prevailing Midyanite beliefs (see *Shemot Rabba* 1:32; Rashi). Such a priest would have been unwelcome in his town. Consequently, instead of earning a livelihood through

Tzipora to Moses. It would thus appear that Re'uel had additional motivations for accepting Moses into his home.

22 **She bore a son, and he called his name Gershom, as he said: I was a stranger [*ger*] in a foreign land,** over there [*sham*].[16]

Israel's Cries Bring about Redemption

EXODUS 2:23–25

Moses fled from Egypt when he was young, and would return there by divine command as a mature adult. Other than the incident at the well in Midyan and his marriage to Tzipora, the Bible does not relate any details about his life or wanderings during this lengthy period of time.

At the same time, the verse spares only a few verses to describe the worsening situation of Moses' brethren in Egypt. This brief passage describes their cries of suffering, which will spark the beginning of their redemption.

23 **It was during those many days; the king of Egypt died.** Presumably, this was the same king whose daughter raised Moses. Since the children of Israel were slaves of the government and labored on its behalf, the death of the king could have kindled hope for some measure of respite. However, the opposite occurred:[17] **The children of Israel sighed due to the work, and they cried out, and their plea rose**[D] **to God from the work.**

24 **God heard their groan and God remembered His covenant with Abraham, with Isaac, and with Jacob,** their forefathers.

25 **God saw the children of Israel, and God knew;** God connected Himself to them (see commentary on 1:8).

The Revelation at the Burning Bush

EXODUS 3:1–4:17

Moses, who was raised in the royal palace of Egypt, and who, according to some midrashic accounts, even ruled over other countries, ended up marrying a shepherdess and becoming himself a shepherd. In the solitude of the desert, Moses merited his first divine revelation, in which God called upon him to emerge from this solitude and return to his people. This time, Moses will not merely see their suffering but will become their leader and savior. He must return to Egypt not as a private individual, or even a personal emissary to Pharaoh, but as the representative of his people, to lead them out of Egypt. For the children of Israel, the path to freedom would ultimately require a long and tortuous journey, meant, among other things, to demonstrate God's power before the nations.

3 1 **Moses was herding the sheep of Yitro, his father-in-law,**
Fourth aliya **priest of Midyan.** It seems that Moses enjoyed this occupation, as it provided him opportunities to contemplate, pray, and connect to God. **He led the flock far into the** ownerless territory of the **wilderness;**[D] that way, there would be no concern that the flock might cause damage to another's property. Additionally, this reduced the chances of an enemy attack. **And** Moses **came to the mountain of God, to Horev.**[D]

2 **An angel of the Lord appeared to him in a flame of fire from inside the bush,**[B] the angel revealed itself as a flame of fire; **and he saw, and behold, the bush was burning in the fire,**[D] **but the bush was not consumed.**

3 **Moses said** to himself: **I will turn now, and** I will **see this great** and mysterious **sight.**[D] Normally, a flame would have consumed a flammable object such as the bush; this must not be an ordinary fire. Although Moses did not see the angel, he recognized that this was an extraordinary scene, so he sought to understand: **Why will the bush not burn?**

Bramble bush

DISCUSSION

the position of the priesthood, he did so through his sheep, like the rest of the nomadic Midyanites (see *Ḥizkuni*).

2:23 | **The king of Egypt died. The children of Israel sighed…and their plea rose:** As long as the king was alive, although the children of Israel were beaten and forced to perform hard labor, there was nevertheless some degree of order in their suffering. There were judges and law enforcement officials, some of whom were themselves Hebrews, and they had a certain degree of internal autonomy. Although they suffered, they accepted their difficult lot. After the death of the king, however, their suffering crossed a threshold they could no longer tolerate. For the first time, they began to cry and pray, and this is what ultimately brought about their salvation.

3:1 | **He led [*vayinhag*] the flock far into the wilderness [*midbar*]:** A *midbar* is a region in which there is not enough water to sustain agriculture, but which receives enough rainfall to provide pasture. An arid, desert region is known as a *tzia* or *yeshimon*. Among other meanings, the root *dalet-beit-reish* refers to leading or directing. Indeed, *Targum Yonatan* translates the word *vayinhag* as *udevar* (see also Ibn Ezra,

כב מֹשֶׁה לָשֶׁבֶת אֶת־הָאִישׁ וַיִּתֵּן אֶת־צִפֹּרָה בִתּוֹ לְמֹשֶׁה: וַתֵּלֶד בֵּן וַיִּקְרָא אֶת־שְׁמוֹ
גֵּרְשֹׁם כִּי אָמַר גֵּר הָיִיתִי בְּאֶרֶץ נָכְרִיָּה:
כג וַיְהִי בַיָּמִים הָרַבִּים הָהֵם וַיָּמָת מֶלֶךְ מִצְרַיִם וַיֵּאָנְחוּ בְנֵי־יִשְׂרָאֵל מִן־הָעֲבֹדָה
כד וַיִּזְעָקוּ וַתַּעַל שַׁוְעָתָם אֶל־הָאֱלֹהִים מִן־הָעֲבֹדָה: וַיִּשְׁמַע אֱלֹהִים אֶת־נַאֲקָתָם
כה וַיִּזְכֹּר אֱלֹהִים אֶת־בְּרִיתוֹ אֶת־אַבְרָהָם אֶת־יִצְחָק וְאֶת־יַעֲקֹב: וַיַּרְא אֱלֹהִים
ג א אֶת־בְּנֵי יִשְׂרָאֵל וַיֵּדַע אֱלֹהִים: וּמֹשֶׁה הָיָה רֹעֶה אֶת־צֹאן יִתְרוֹ ב רביעי
חֹתְנוֹ כֹּהֵן מִדְיָן וַיִּנְהַג אֶת־הַצֹּאן אַחַר הַמִּדְבָּר וַיָּבֹא אֶל־הַר הָאֱלֹהִים חֹרֵבָה:
ב וַיֵּרָא מַלְאַךְ יְהוָה אֵלָיו בְּלַבַּת־אֵשׁ מִתּוֹךְ הַסְּנֶה וַיַּרְא וְהִנֵּה הַסְּנֶה בֹּעֵר בָּאֵשׁ
ג וְהַסְּנֶה אֵינֶנּוּ אֻכָּל: וַיֹּאמֶר מֹשֶׁה אָסֻרָה־נָּא וְאֶרְאֶה אֶת־הַמַּרְאֶה הַגָּדֹל הַזֶּה

רש"י

יט, ו), "וְלֹא הוֹאַלְנוּ" (יהושע ז, ז), "הוֹאַלְתִּי לְדַבֵּר" (בראשית יח, לא). וּמִדְרָשׁוֹ, לְשׁוֹן אָלָה, נִשְׁבַּע לוֹ שֶׁלֹּא יָזוּז מִמִּדְיָן כִּי אִם בִּרְשׁוּתוֹ:

כג וַיָּמָת מֶלֶךְ מִצְרַיִם. נִצְטָרַע, וְהָיָה שׁוֹחֵט תִּינוֹקוֹת יִשְׂרָאֵל וְרוֹחֵץ בְּדָמָם:

כד נַאֲקָתָם. צַעֲקָתָם, וְכֵן: "מֵעִיר מְתִים יִנְאָקוּ" (איוב כד, יב): אֶת בְּרִיתוֹ אֶת אַבְרָהָם. עִם אַבְרָהָם:

כה וַיֵּדַע אֱלֹהִים. נָתַן עֲלֵיהֶם לֵב וְלֹא הֶעֱלִים עֵינָיו:

פרק ג

א אַחַר הַמִּדְבָּר. לְהִתְרַחֵק מִן הַגָּזֵל שֶׁלֹּא יִרְעוּ בִּשְׂדוֹת אֲחֵרִים: אֶל הַר הָאֱלֹהִים. עַל שֵׁם הֶעָתִיד:

ב בְּלַבַּת אֵשׁ. בְּשַׁלְהֶבֶת אֵשׁ, לִבּוֹ שֶׁל אֵשׁ, כְּמוֹ: "לֵב הַשָּׁמַיִם" (דברים ד, יא), "בְּלֵב הָאֵלָה" (שמואל ב' יח, יד). וְאַל תִּתְמַהּ עַל הַתָּי"ו, יֵשׁ לָנוּ כַּיּוֹצֵא בוֹ: "מָה אֲמֻלָה לִבָּתֵךְ" (יחזקאל טז, ל): מִתּוֹךְ הַסְּנֶה. וְלֹא אִילָן אַחֵר, מִשּׁוּם "עִמּוֹ אָנֹכִי בְצָרָה" (תהלים צא, טו): אֻכָּל. נֶאֱכָל, כְּמוֹ "לֹא עֻבַּד בָּהּ" (דברים כא, ג), "אֲשֶׁר לֻקַּח מִשָּׁם" (בראשית ג, כג):

ג אָסֻרָה. מִכָּאן לְהִתְקָרֵב שָׁם:

DISCUSSION

Psalms 47:4). Accordingly, *midbar* denotes an area to which one leads his flock to graze (see Malbim, Hosea 2:5, Psalms 8:40).

To the mountain of God, to Horev: This is Mount Sinai, the mountain upon which God will later reveal Himself to the children of Israel. It is possible that the names mountain of God and Horev are used anachronistically, and that they were given to this mountain at a later time (see *Shemot Rabba* 2:4; Rashi; see also Ibn Ezra; *Pirkei deRabbi Eliezer* 41; Responsa of Rav Avraham ben HaRambam 36). Many cultures depict Mount Sinai as an extraordinarily tall mountain, and have attempted to identify the historic Mount Sinai accordingly. Rabbinic tradition, however, describes the mountain as a small hill that barely deserves to be called a mountain (see *Bemidbar Rabba* 13:3). Indeed, the verses here seem to describe a hill that was suitable for a flock to graze upon.

3:2| **And behold, the bush was burning in the fire:** Although brush fires may occasionally break out spontaneously in the wilderness due to some object that concentrates the strong rays of the sun, it is a rare occurrence, especially in the case of a fire starting in a bush. This event was miraculous, however, as the flame did not consume the bush.

3:3| **This great sight:** It should be noted that fire is a feature in other prophetic visions as well (see Numbers 9:15–16; Ezekiel 1:27, 8:2).

BACKGROUND

3:2| **Bush:** This bush is typically identified as one of several low thorny trees, such as the acacia or the *Ziziphus spina-christi*, which grow in the streambeds of the Sinai desert, or as a plant whose fruits or flowers are red or orange, such as the acacia strap flower, *Loranthus acaciae*, the Maltese mushroom, *Cynomorium coccineum*, or the desert broomrape, *Cistanche tubulosa*. The Aramaic translations and midrashic sources seem to identify it as the holy bramble, *Rubus sanguineus*, a thorny plant with red fruit that grows in the streambeds of the Sinai desert (see *Shemot Rabba* 2:9; *Shabbat* 67a; Rav Se'adya Gaon).

4 **The Lord saw that he turned** and approached the bush in order **to see** it, **and God called to him from within the bush, and He said: Moses, Moses.** Although Moses did not know who was calling him, **he said: Here I am.**

5 **He said: Do not approach here; remove your shoes from your feet, as the place upon which you are standing is sacred ground.**[D] Because the Divine Presence rests in this place, you must stand in it with proper awe and respect, and you must therefore remove your shoes.

6 Moses removed his shoes and approached the bush, and then he heard the voice of God identify Himself: **He said: I am the God of your father,** Amram, and also **the God of Abraham, the God of Isaac, and the God of Jacob. Moses hid his face, as he was afraid to look at God.** Once Moses became aware that God was revealing Himself in the flame in the bush, he ceased to gaze at the flame out of reverence for God.[18] Alternatively, Moses feared that he would die.[19] Indeed, in similar instances, the revelation of an angel caused individuals to fear that this vision was to be their last, after which they would die.[20]

7 **The Lord said: I have seen the affliction of My people that is in Egypt, and I have heard their outcry because of its taskmasters,** who abuse the people; **as I know its pain.**[D]

8 **I have descended** and revealed Myself in the world both in order **to rescue it,** the nation, **from the hand of Egypt, and to bring it up from that land,** Egypt, **to a good and expansive land, to a land flowing with milk and honey.** They will not merely be rescued from the dire situation in Egypt, but they will also be brought to a far better place, namely **to the place of the Canaanites and the Hitites and the Emorites and the Perizites and the Hivites and the Yevusites.**

9 **And now, behold, the outcry of the children of Israel has come to Me, and I have also seen the oppression that the Egyptians are oppressing them.**

10 I intend to rescue My people, but I require a messenger: **Now, go and I will send you to Pharaoh and take My people, the children of Israel, out of Egypt.**

11 **Moses said to God: Who am I,**[D] **that I should go to Pharaoh and that I should take the children of Israel out of Egypt?**

12 **He,** God, **said: Because I will be with you.** I am not asking you to act on your own strength; you are merely a messenger. **And this is your sign**[D] **that I sent you: When you take the people out of Egypt, you will serve God upon this mountain.**[D] Although Moses would later be provided with additional signs, the primary sign of his appointment was that in just a short time, Moses would return to this mountain with the children of Israel, and God would reveal Himself to the entire nation. At that moment, the entire nation would be prepared to serve God.

13 **Moses said to God: Behold, I come to the children of Israel, and I will say to them: The God of your fathers sent me to you, and they will say to me: What is His name?**[D] **What shall I say to them?**

DISCUSSION

3:5 | **Sacred ground:** In the Temple as well, there were many requisite gestures of respect. Among them was the requirement to remove one's shoes when entering the area of the Temple Mount (see *Berakhot* 54a).

3:7 | **As I know its pain:** Not only does God hear the people's cries caused by their public oppression at the hands of the taskmasters, but He is also aware of the suffering they endure in private. The people's enslavement, which was not governed by established laws and guidelines, caused an upheaval of the family unit, namely the separation of man from his wife and parents from their children.

3:11 | **Who am I:** Many have pointed out that Divine Providence arranged the circumstances of Moses' childhood in such a way that he would not internalize any aspect of the enslavement of the children of Israel. In fact, of the entire nation of Israel at that time, he was the only one who grew up as a freeman. Being raised free in the house of the king of Egypt is precisely what emboldened Moses to fight for justice and freedom. Nevertheless, Moses did not attribute any measure of prominence to himself. Indeed, the Torah will later testify that Moses was "very humble, more than any person on the face of the earth" (Numbers 12:3). Moses always felt a deep sense of obligation to his people and to God, so much so that he is referred to as the servant of God throughout the Bible (see, e.g., Deuteronomy 34:5; Joshua 1:1; II Kings 18:12; see also Isaiah 63:11). Nevertheless, his humility prompted him to ask "Who am I," as he felt unworthy of such a lofty role as leader or representative.

3:12 | **And this is your sign:** The prophetic vision uproots an individual from his usual state of mind and transfers him to what seems like another place. It is impossible to describe the intensity of this experience, but it remains an undeniably real one. Nevertheless, this vision is not necessarily objective, as it may sometimes be related to the individual's emotional state or to a dream. For this reason, a sign is sometimes necessary to authenticate a prophetic experience.

When you take the people out of Egypt, you will serve God upon this mountain: Unlike most signs, which typically appear before the beginning of a mission, this sign is unique in that it will occur only when Moses completes his task. God tells Moses that the sign by which he may be certain of his divine appointment will be none other than his success in carrying out this mission. At the same time, unlike the other prophets, who were tasked with conveying a certain divine message without the assurance that they would succeed in their mission, Moses was assured from the outset that his message would be received and that he would succeed in fulfilling his task. From the moment of his appointment as God's messenger, he was assured that the entire nation would stand with him at Mount Sinai to serve God.

ד מַדּ֫וּעַ לֹא־יִבְעַר הַסְּנֶה: וַיַּרְא יהוה כִּי סָר לִרְאוֹת וַיִּקְרָא אֵלָיו אֱלֹהִים מִתּוֹךְ
ה הַסְּנֶה וַיֹּאמֶר מֹשֶׁה מֹשֶׁה וַיֹּאמֶר הִנֵּנִי: וַיֹּאמֶר אַל־תִּקְרַב הֲלֹם שַׁל־נְעָלֶיךָ
ו מֵעַל רַגְלֶיךָ כִּי הַמָּקוֹם אֲשֶׁר אַתָּה עוֹמֵד עָלָיו אַדְמַת־קֹדֶשׁ הוּא: וַיֹּאמֶר
אָנֹכִי אֱלֹהֵי אָבִיךָ אֱלֹהֵי אַבְרָהָם אֱלֹהֵי יִצְחָק וֵאלֹהֵי יַעֲקֹב וַיַּסְתֵּר מֹשֶׁה פָּנָיו
ז כִּי יָרֵא מֵהַבִּיט אֶל־הָאֱלֹהִים: וַיֹּאמֶר יהוה רָאֹה רָאִיתִי אֶת־עֳנִי עַמִּי אֲשֶׁר
ח בְּמִצְרָיִם וְאֶת־צַעֲקָתָם שָׁמַעְתִּי מִפְּנֵי נֹגְשָׂיו כִּי יָדַעְתִּי אֶת־מַכְאֹבָיו: וָאֵרֵד
לְהַצִּילוֹ מִיַּד מִצְרַיִם וּלְהַעֲלֹתוֹ מִן־הָאָרֶץ הַהִוא אֶל־אֶרֶץ טוֹבָה וּרְחָבָה
אֶל־אֶרֶץ זָבַת חָלָב וּדְבָשׁ אֶל־מְקוֹם הַכְּנַעֲנִי וְהַחִתִּי וְהָאֱמֹרִי וְהַפְּרִזִּי וְהַחִוִּי
ט וְהַיְבוּסִי: וְעַתָּה הִנֵּה צַעֲקַת בְּנֵי־יִשְׂרָאֵל בָּאָה אֵלָי וְגַם־רָאִיתִי אֶת־הַלַּחַץ
י אֲשֶׁר מִצְרַיִם לֹחֲצִים אֹתָם: וְעַתָּה לְכָה וְאֶשְׁלָחֲךָ אֶל־פַּרְעֹה וְהוֹצֵא אֶת־עַמִּי
יא בְנֵי־יִשְׂרָאֵל מִמִּצְרָיִם: וַיֹּאמֶר מֹשֶׁה אֶל־הָאֱלֹהִים מִי אָנֹכִי כִּי אֵלֵךְ אֶל־פַּרְעֹה
יב וְכִי אוֹצִיא אֶת־בְּנֵי יִשְׂרָאֵל מִמִּצְרָיִם: וַיֹּאמֶר כִּי־אֶהְיֶה עִמָּךְ וְזֶה־לְּךָ הָאוֹת
כִּי אָנֹכִי שְׁלַחְתִּיךָ בְּהוֹצִיאֲךָ אֶת־הָעָם מִמִּצְרַיִם תַּעַבְדוּן אֶת־הָאֱלֹהִים עַל
יג הָהָר הַזֶּה: וַיֹּאמֶר מֹשֶׁה אֶל־הָאֱלֹהִים הִנֵּה אָנֹכִי בָא אֶל־בְּנֵי יִשְׂרָאֵל וְאָמַרְתִּי
לָהֶם אֱלֹהֵי אֲבוֹתֵיכֶם שְׁלָחַנִי אֲלֵיכֶם וְאָמְרוּ־לִי מַה־שְּׁמוֹ מָה אֹמַר אֲלֵהֶם:

רש״י

ה| **שַׁל.** שְׁלֹף וְהוֹצֵא, כְּמוֹ: "וְנָשַׁל הַבַּרְזֶל" (דברים יט, ה), "כִּי יִשַּׁל זֵיתֶךָ" (דברים כח, מ): **אַדְמַת קֹדֶשׁ הוּא.** הַמָּקוֹם:

י| **וְעַתָּה לְכָה וְאֶשְׁלָחֲךָ אֶל פַּרְעֹה.** וְאִם תֹּאמַר, מַה תּוֹעִיל? "וְהוֹצֵא אֶת עַמִּי", יוֹעִילוּ דְּבָרֶיךָ וְתוֹצִיאֵם:

יא| **מִי אָנֹכִי.** מָה אֲנִי חָשׁוּב לְדַבֵּר עִם הַמְּלָכִים?: **וְכִי אוֹצִיא אֶת בְּנֵי יִשְׂרָאֵל.** וְאַף אִם חָשׁוּב אֲנִי, מַה זָּכוּ יִשְׂרָאֵל שֶׁיֵּעָשֶׂה לָהֶם נֵס וְאוֹצִיאֵם מִמִּצְרַיִם?:

יב| **וַיֹּאמֶר כִּי אֶהְיֶה עִמָּךְ.** הֱשִׁיבוֹ עַל רִאשׁוֹן רִאשׁוֹן וְעַל אַחֲרוֹן אַחֲרוֹן: שֶׁאָמַרְתָּ "מִי אָנֹכִי כִּי אֵלֵךְ אֶל פַּרְעֹה" – לֹא שֶׁלְּךָ הִיא כִּי אִם מִשֶּׁלִּי, "כִּי אֶהְיֶה עִמָּךְ"; "וְזֶה" הַמַּרְאָה אֲשֶׁר רָאִיתָ בַּסְּנֶה, "לְךָ הָאוֹת כִּי אָנֹכִי שְׁלַחְתִּיךָ" וּכְדַאי אֲנִי לְהַצִּיל, כַּאֲשֶׁר רָאִיתָ הַסְּנֶה עוֹשֶׂה שְׁלִיחוּתִי וְאֵינֶנּוּ אֻכָּל כָּךְ תֵּלֵךְ בִּשְׁלִיחוּתִי וְאֵינְךָ נִזּוֹק. וְשֶׁשָּׁאַלְתָּ: מַה זְּכוּת יֵשׁ לְיִשְׂרָאֵל שֶׁיֵּצְאוּ מִמִּצְרַיִם? דָּבָר גָּדוֹל יֵשׁ לִי עַל הוֹצָאָה זוֹ, שֶׁהֲרֵי עֲתִידִים לְקַבֵּל הַתּוֹרָה עַל הָהָר הַזֶּה לְסוֹף שְׁלֹשָׁה חֳדָשִׁים. דָּבָר אַחֵר, "כִּי אֶהְיֶה עִמָּךְ", "וְזֶה" שֶׁתַּצְלִיחַ בִּשְׁלִיחוּתְךָ, "לְךָ הָאוֹת" עַל הַבְטָחָה אַחֶרֶת שֶׁאֲנִי מַבְטִיחֲךָ, שֶׁכְּשֶׁתּוֹצִיאֵם מִמִּצְרַיִם תַּעַבְדוּן אוֹתִי עַל הָהָר הַזֶּה, שֶׁתְּקַבְּלוּ הַתּוֹרָה עָלָיו, וְהִיא הַזְּכוּת הָעוֹמֶדֶת לְיִשְׂרָאֵל. וּדְגְמַת לָשׁוֹן זֶה מָצִינוּ בִּישַׁעְיָה (לז, ל): "וְזֶה לְּךָ הָאוֹת אָכוֹל הַשָּׁנָה סָפִיחַ" וְגוֹ', מַפֶּלֶת סַנְחֵרִיב תִּהְיֶה לְךָ אוֹת עַל הַבְטָחָה אַחֶרֶת, שֶׁאַרְצְכֶם חֲרֵבָה מִפֵּרוֹת וַאֲנִי אֲבָרֵךְ הַסְּפִיחִים:

DISCUSSION

3:13| **What is His name:** This is not merely a technical question whose answer would allow Moses to communicate with the children of Israel. Even if the people succeeded in preserving their language and some traditional customs (see *Shemot Rabba* 1:28), hundreds of years of exile and enslavement in Egypt eroded the people's memory of their heritage. Perhaps they truly were unacquainted even with the name of the God of their ancestors. Still, it seems unlikely that this would be the first question asked by a nation of oppressed slaves upon hearing of their imminent salvation. Perhaps Moses personally felt that this question was of the utmost significance. Although he would not require this information to assume his role as leader of the children of Israel, he desired to know God's name.

14 **God said to Moses: I Will Be As I Will Be.** This response may be understood as a rejection of the question itself, indicating there is no significance to the knowledge of God's name;[21] as a promise that God will always be with them;[22] or that this is in fact God's name.[23] **And He,** God, **said:** When you speak to the children of Israel, do not begin with the frightening declaration: I Will Be As I Will Be. Although this statement contains the assurance that God will always be with them, this promise may itself seem threatening, as the appearance of God is not always a harbinger of respite. Therefore, **so shall you say to the children of Israel: I Will Be**[D] **sent me to you.** Here it is clear that "I Will Be" is God's name. Whereas God's first response: I Will Be As I Will Be, refers to the fact that God is present in all places and at all times, His second response: I Will Be, relates specifically to His eternal existence.

15 God reveals another divine name to Moses: **God again said to Moses: So you shall say to the children of Israel: The Lord,**[D] **God of your fathers, God of Abraham, God of Isaac, and God of Jacob** is the One who **sent me to you. This** special name **is My name forever and this is My appellation for all generations.** This is the name you shall use from now on; it is the most sacred of the divine names.

Fifth aliya 16 After responding to Moses' question "What shall I say to them?" God now instructs Moses: **Go and gather the elders** of Israel and say to them: The Lord, God of your forefathers, God of Abraham, Isaac, and Jacob, appeared to me, saying: I have remembered you, and I have also considered what is being done to you in Egypt, your suffering.

17 I said: I will take you up out of the affliction of Egypt, to the land of the Canaanites and the Hitites and the Emorites and the Perizites and the Hivites and the Yevusites, to a land flowing with milk and honey.

18 God saw that Moses was hesitant, so He assured Moses: **They will listen to your voice and you shall go, you and the elders of Israel, to the king of Egypt and you shall say to him: The Lord, God of the Hebrews, happened upon us,** He has revealed Himself to us and given us a message. **Now, please, let us go a journey of three days in the wilderness and we will sacrifice to the Lord our God.**[D]

19 **And I know that the king of Egypt will not allow you to go, except** if I force him to do so **with a powerful**[24] **hand.**[D]

20 **I will send forth My hand, and smite Egypt with all My wonders that I will perform in its midst;**[D] **and thereafter,** that is, after smiting Egypt with all My plagues, **he will send you forth.**

21 **I will give favor for this people in the eyes of Egypt.**[D] And therefore, **it shall be** that **when you go** out of Egypt, **you will not go empty-handed.**

DISCUSSION

3:14| I Will Be: In Biblical Hebrew, the future tense of a word may also refer to a continuous presence (see Rashi, Genesis 24:45, Numbers 9:15, and Job 1:5). Thus, the name "I Will Be" indicates not only that God will exist in the future, but that His existence and His presence are eternal (see *Bekhor Shor*). Although some commentaries do not consider the term "I Will Be" to be a name of God (see Rambam, *Sefer HaMadda, Hilkhot Yesodei HaTorah* 6:1–2, and *Kesef Mishne* ad loc.), in all kabbalistic literature it is treated as a divine name (see *Zohar* 3:11a; see also *Shevuot* 35a).

Many of God's names refer to a particular aspect of His Being. For example, the name *Elohim* refers to God's power and authority over all existence. I Will Be, however, is unique, as it is not limited to denoting any one facet or expression of God. Simply put, this name means: I am the essence of existence itself. Moses was commanded to bring the children of Israel to an understanding of God's Oneness, namely, that God is not merely the supreme deity in a pantheon of gods, nor is He simply the Creator and Judge of the universe. Rather, the God of their forefathers is the essence of all existence (see Rambam, *Guide of the Perplexed* 1:63; *Gevurot Hashem* 25).

3:15| The Lord: This name, spelled: *Yod-heh-vav-heh,* commonly known as the Tetragrammaton, shares a root with the previous divine name, *Ehyeh,* "I Will Be." The transition to this name from *Ehyeh* may be seen as a transition from first person narrative to third person, as if the term here was *Yihyeh,* "He Will Be" (see Ibn Ezra, long commentary on Exodus; Rashbam). Indeed, the replacement of the letter *yod* with the letter *vav* is a recurring phenomenon in the Bible (see Rashi, Genesis 3:20; Radak, II Samuel 6:23). Accordingly, when God speaks, He refers to Himself in the first person: I Will Be, while when others refer to Him, they do so in the third person: He Will Be.

Many commentaries debate the precise meaning of the Tetragrammaton. Some explain that the name emphasizes God's absolute and eternal existence. Others claim that it refers to God's role as Creator. Despite the numerous attempts to uncover the profound meanings hidden in this name, the Tetragrammaton remains shrouded in mystery.

3:18| Please, let us go a journey of three days in the wilderness and we will sacrifice to the Lord our God: Although Moses' mission was to lead the people out of Egypt, he was instructed to initially present Pharaoh with a more modest request. Pharaoh will eventually refuse to grant even this request; even when he subsequently agrees, he places excessive restrictions on such a journey. Ultimately, when Pharaoh capitulates, he will do so unconditionally, without any knowledge of where the children of Israel will go, or whether they will ever return.

One might ask: Was this modest request merely a ploy designed to conceal the true intention of Israel, namely to escape from Egypt? This is not necessarily the case. A journey of three days into the wilderness would have placed the people outside the territory of Egypt. Furthermore, the stated purpose of the journey, to sacrifice to God, constitutes a declaration of religious independence, as well as an assertion that the children of Israel are no longer subjects of the king of Egypt; rather, they are leaving Egypt to encounter their God, and they will subject themselves to His authority alone. If He shall instruct the people to continue their journey in the wilderness, they will obey and not return to Egypt (see *Or HaḤayyim*; Rabbeinu Baḥya; Rashbam, 3:11; *Derashot HaRan* 11).

יד וַיֹּאמֶר אֱלֹהִים אֶל־מֹשֶׁה אֶהְיֶה אֲשֶׁר אֶהְיֶה וַיֹּאמֶר כֹּה תֹאמַר לִבְנֵי יִשְׂרָאֵל
טו אֶהְיֶה שְׁלָחַנִי אֲלֵיכֶם: וַיֹּאמֶר עוֹד אֱלֹהִים אֶל־מֹשֶׁה כֹּה־תֹאמַר אֶל־בְּנֵי יִשְׂרָאֵל
יְהֹוָה אֱלֹהֵי אֲבֹתֵיכֶם אֱלֹהֵי אַבְרָהָם אֱלֹהֵי יִצְחָק וֵאלֹהֵי יַעֲקֹב שְׁלָחַנִי אֲלֵיכֶם
טז זֶה־שְּׁמִי לְעֹלָם וְזֶה זִכְרִי לְדֹר דֹּר: לֵךְ וְאָסַפְתָּ אֶת־זִקְנֵי יִשְׂרָאֵל וְאָמַרְתָּ אֲלֵהֶם חמישי
יְהֹוָה אֱלֹהֵי אֲבֹתֵיכֶם נִרְאָה אֵלַי אֱלֹהֵי אַבְרָהָם יִצְחָק וְיַעֲקֹב לֵאמֹר פָּקֹד
יז פָּקַדְתִּי אֶתְכֶם וְאֶת־הֶעָשׂוּי לָכֶם בְּמִצְרָיִם: וָאֹמַר אַעֲלֶה אֶתְכֶם מֵעֳנִי מִצְרַיִם
אֶל־אֶרֶץ הַכְּנַעֲנִי וְהַחִתִּי וְהָאֱמֹרִי וְהַפְּרִזִּי וְהַחִוִּי וְהַיְבוּסִי אֶל־אֶרֶץ זָבַת חָלָב
יח וּדְבָשׁ: וְשָׁמְעוּ לְקֹלֶךָ וּבָאתָ אַתָּה וְזִקְנֵי יִשְׂרָאֵל אֶל־מֶלֶךְ מִצְרַיִם וַאֲמַרְתֶּם אֵלָיו
יְהֹוָה אֱלֹהֵי הָעִבְרִיִּים נִקְרָה עָלֵינוּ וְעַתָּה נֵלְכָה־נָּא דֶּרֶךְ שְׁלֹשֶׁת יָמִים בַּמִּדְבָּר
יט וְנִזְבְּחָה לַיהֹוָה אֱלֹהֵינוּ: וַאֲנִי יָדַעְתִּי כִּי לֹא־יִתֵּן אֶתְכֶם מֶלֶךְ מִצְרַיִם לַהֲלֹךְ וְלֹא
כ בְּיָד חֲזָקָה: וְשָׁלַחְתִּי אֶת־יָדִי וְהִכֵּיתִי אֶת־מִצְרַיִם בְּכֹל נִפְלְאֹתַי אֲשֶׁר אֶעֱשֶׂה
כא בְּקִרְבּוֹ וְאַחֲרֵי־כֵן יְשַׁלַּח אֶתְכֶם: וְנָתַתִּי אֶת־חֵן הָעָם־הַזֶּה בְּעֵינֵי מִצְרָיִם וְהָיָה

רש"י

יד-טו | אֶהְיֶה אֲשֶׁר אֶהְיֶה. "אֶהְיֶה" עִמָּם בְּצָרָה זוֹ, "אֲשֶׁר אֶהְיֶה" עִמָּם בְּשִׁעְבּוּד שְׁאָר מַלְכֻיּוֹת. אָמַר לְפָנָיו: רִבּוֹנוֹ שֶׁל עוֹלָם, מָה אֲנִי מַזְכִּיר לָהֶם צָרָה אַחֶרֶת? דַּיָּם בְּצָרָה זוֹ! אָמַר לוֹ: יָפֶה אָמַרְתָּ, "כֹּה תֹאמַר" וְגוֹ': זֶה שְּׁמִי לְעֹלָם. חָסֵר וָי"ו, לוֹמַר הַעֲלִימֵהוּ שֶׁלֹּא יִקָּרֵא כִּכְתָבוֹ: וְזֶה זִכְרִי. לִמְּדוֹ הֵיאַךְ נִקְרָא. וְכֵן דָּוִד הוּא אוֹמֵר: "ה' שִׁמְךָ לְעוֹלָם ה' זִכְרְךָ לְדֹר וָדֹר" (תהלים קלה, יג):

טז | אֶת זִקְנֵי יִשְׂרָאֵל. מְיֻחָדִים לִישִׁיבָה. וְאִם תֹּאמַר זְקֵנִים סְתָם, הֵיאַךְ אֶפְשָׁר לוֹ לֶאֱסֹף זְקֵנִים שֶׁל שִׁשִּׁים רִבּוֹא?:

יח | וְשָׁמְעוּ לְקֹלֶךָ. מִכֵּיוָן שֶׁתֹּאמַר לָהֶם לָשׁוֹן זֶה יִשְׁמְעוּ לְקוֹלְךָ, שֶׁכְּבָר סִימָן זֶה מָסוּר בְּיָדָם מִיַּעֲקֹב וּמִיּוֹסֵף שֶׁבְּלָשׁוֹן זֶה הֵם נִגְאָלִים; יַעֲקֹב אָמַר לָהֶם: "וֵאלֹהִים פָּקֹד יִפְקֹד אֶתְכֶם" (בראשית נ, כד), יוֹסֵף אָמַר לָהֶם: "פָּקֹד יִפְקֹד אֱלֹהִים אֶתְכֶם" (שם פסוק כה): נִקְרָה עָלֵינוּ. לְשׁוֹן מִקְרֶה, וְכֵן: "וַיִּקָּר אֱלֹהִים" (במדבר כג, ד); "וְאָנֹכִי אִקָּרֶה כֹּה" (שם פסוק טו) – אֲהֵא נִקְרֶה מֵאִתּוֹ הֲלֹם:

יט | לֹא יִתֵּן אֶתְכֶם מֶלֶךְ מִצְרַיִם לַהֲלֹךְ. אִם אֵין אֲנִי מַרְאֶה לוֹ יָדִי הַחֲזָקָה; כְּלוֹמַר, כָּל עוֹד שֶׁאֵין אֲנִי מוֹדִיעוֹ יָדִי הַחֲזָקָה לֹא יִתֵּן אֶתְכֶם לַהֲלֹךְ: לֹא יִתֵּן. "לָא יִשְׁבּוֹק", כְּמוֹ: "עַל כֵּן לֹא נְתַתִּיךָ" (בראשית כ, ו), "וְלֹא נְתָנוֹ אֱלֹהִים לְהָרַע עִמָּדִי" (שם לא, ז), וְכֻלָּן לְשׁוֹן נְתִינָה הֵם. וְיֵשׁ מְפָרְשִׁים, "וְלֹא בְּיָד חֲזָקָה", וְלֹא בִּשְׁבִיל שֶׁיָּדוֹ חֲזָקָה, כִּי מֵאָז אֶשְׁלַח אֶת יָדִי "וְהִכֵּיתִי אֶת מִצְרַיִם" וְגוֹ' (פסוק כ), וּמְתַרְגְּמִין אוֹתוֹ: "וְלָא מִן קֳדָם דְּחֵילֵיהּ תַּקִּיף". מִשְּׁמוֹ שֶׁל רַבִּי יַעֲקֹב בְּרַבִּי מְנַחֵם נֶאֱמַר לִי:

DISCUSSION

3:19| **Except with a powerful hand:** A literal translation of this phrase would be: And not with a powerful hand. Accordingly, the verse could mean: The king of Egypt will not allow you to go, and this will not be due to his strong hand. Rather, even when I exert pressure on him with My strong hand, he will be unable to release you until I decide that he will do so. Alternatively, the verse means: And your hand will not be strong enough to secure your release without My direct involvement.

3:20| **With all My wonders that I will perform in its midst:** The plagues were not intended merely to force Pharaoh to comply with God's command; had that been the case, it would have been sufficient for God to strike Pharaoh alone. Rather, the plagues were to be the medium through which God would reveal Himself and His absolute power, both to Israel and to the Egyptians (see 7:5, 10:1–2). Pharaoh's refusal to release the children of Israel was simply God's pretense for this revelation.

The wonders performed in Egypt are not just matters of Israel's historical record; they are an integral part of the collective memory of Israel and a foundation of its faith. As such, these wonders are recalled, alongside the exodus itself, in the Great Hallel (Psalms 136) as well as in various other psalms (see Psalms 78:43–51, 105:26–38).

3:21| **I will give favor for this people in the eyes of Egypt:** It is clear from a number of references in the narratives about Joseph that the Egyptians loathed the Hebrews for both cultural and religious reasons (see, e.g., Genesis 43:32). Evidence of this condescending attitude toward the Hebrews is also found in a number

22 **Each woman will borrow,**[25] **or take**[26] **silver vessels and gold vessels and garments from her neighbor and from the resident of her house.**[D] By lending or giving these items to the women, the Egyptians will thereby demonstrate the respect toward the children of Israel foreordained in the previous verse. **And you shall place them,** all that you receive from the Egyptians, **upon your sons and upon your daughters, and you will** thereby **despoil the Egyptians,** in fulfillment of God's promise to Abraham: "And afterward, they will emerge with great property."[27]

4 1 Moses remained hesitant: **Moses answered and he said: But behold,** or perhaps,[28] **they will neither believe me, nor will they heed my voice, as they will say: The Lord did not appear to you.**

2 **The Lord said to him: What is that in your hand? And he said: A staff.**

3 **He,** God **said:** Take the staff and **cast it on the ground. He cast it on the ground and it became a serpent. Moses fled from it.**

4 **The Lord said to Moses: Send forth your arm and grasp its tail. He sent forth his arm and he seized it and it became a staff in his hand.**

5 God explained: You may show this sign to the people **so that they will believe that the Lord, God of their fathers, God of Abraham, God of Isaac, and God of Jacob, appeared to you.**

6 **The Lord said to him further: Bring your hand** under your garment, **into your bosom. He brought his hand into his bosom and he withdrew it, and behold, his hand was leprous, like snow.**

7 **He,** God, **said: Return your hand into your bosom. He returned his hand into his bosom and he withdrew it from his bosom, and behold, it recovered like his flesh:** that is, his flesh returned to its healthy state and the leprosy disappeared.

8 God said: **It shall be, if they do not believe you, and do not heed the voice of the first sign,** the sign of the staff turning into a snake and then reverting back into a staff, **they will believe the voice of the latter sign,** the hand that turns leprous and then miraculously heals.

9 **And it shall be if they will not believe even these two signs, and they will not heed your voice, you shall take water from the Nile and you shall pour it on the dry land and the water that you take from the Nile will become blood on the dry land.** Although there was no water in the wilderness with which to demonstrate this third sign, God promised Moses that it would indeed materialize if the situation required it.

10 Moses remained unsure of himself and lacked confidence in his ability to carry out his mission: **Moses said to the Lord: Please, my Lord, I am not a man of words.** I have never been able to express myself eloquently, **neither yesterday nor the day before, nor since You have spoken to Your servant.** Had

---

DISCUSSION

of ancient Egyptian documents. Undoubtedly, once the children of Israel were enslaved, their hatred of Israel reached more extreme proportions, as there was no need for an explicit directive to beat and abuse the enslaved nation. Now, God declares that when He smites the Egyptians, the tables will be turned and their attitude toward Israel will change. Their arrogant sense of superiority will turn into fear; ultimately, they will come to see Israel as the chosen

people. This powerful idea, that a lowly group of slaves, hardly considered a nation, can develop and grow until it ultimately becomes the mighty ruler, also appears in a slightly different form in Isaiah (see, e.g., Isaiah 52).

3:22| **From her neighbor and from the resident of her house:** This verse would seem to indicate that, at least in some areas of Egypt, the children of Israel were neighbors of Egyptian

families, and at times even shared houses. Presumably, the men of Israel, who labored a great distance from their homes, did not develop much of a relationship with their Egyptian neighbors. The women, however, remained in close proximity to their homes and thus developed some connection to their neighbors.

כב כִּי תֵלֵכוּן לֹא תֵלְכוּ רֵיקָם׃ וְשָׁאֲלָה אִשָּׁה מִשְּׁכֶנְתָּהּ וּמִגָּרַת בֵּיתָהּ כְּלֵי־כֶסֶף וּכְלֵי
ד א זָהָב וּשְׂמָלֹת וְשַׂמְתֶּם עַל־בְּנֵיכֶם וְעַל־בְּנֹתֵיכֶם וְנִצַּלְתֶּם אֶת־מִצְרָיִם׃ וַיַּעַן מֹשֶׁה
וַיֹּאמֶר וְהֵן לֹא־יַאֲמִינוּ לִי וְלֹא יִשְׁמְעוּ בְּקֹלִי כִּי יֹאמְרוּ לֹא־נִרְאָה אֵלֶיךָ יְהוָה׃
ב ג וַיֹּאמֶר אֵלָיו יְהוָה מַזֶּה בְיָדֶךָ וַיֹּאמֶר מַטֶּה׃ וַיֹּאמֶר הַשְׁלִיכֵהוּ אַרְצָה וַיַּשְׁלִכֵהוּ
ד אַרְצָה וַיְהִי לְנָחָשׁ וַיָּנָס מֹשֶׁה מִפָּנָיו׃ וַיֹּאמֶר יְהוָה אֶל־מֹשֶׁה שְׁלַח יָדְךָ וֶאֱחֹז
ה בִּזְנָבוֹ וַיִּשְׁלַח יָדוֹ וַיַּחֲזֶק־בּוֹ וַיְהִי לְמַטֶּה בְּכַפּוֹ׃ לְמַעַן יַאֲמִינוּ כִּי־נִרְאָה אֵלֶיךָ
ו יְהוָה אֱלֹהֵי אֲבֹתָם אֱלֹהֵי אַבְרָהָם אֱלֹהֵי יִצְחָק וֵאלֹהֵי יַעֲקֹב׃ וַיֹּאמֶר יְהוָה לוֹ
עוֹד הָבֵא־נָא יָדְךָ בְּחֵיקֶךָ וַיָּבֵא יָדוֹ בְּחֵיקוֹ וַיּוֹצִאָהּ וְהִנֵּה יָדוֹ מְצֹרַעַת כַּשָּׁלֶג׃
ז וַיֹּאמֶר הָשֵׁב יָדְךָ אֶל־חֵיקֶךָ וַיָּשֶׁב יָדוֹ אֶל־חֵיקוֹ וַיּוֹצִאָהּ מֵחֵיקוֹ וְהִנֵּה־שָׁבָה
ח כִּבְשָׂרוֹ׃ וְהָיָה אִם־לֹא יַאֲמִינוּ לָךְ וְלֹא יִשְׁמְעוּ לְקֹל הָאֹת הָרִאשׁוֹן וְהֶאֱמִינוּ
ט לְקֹל הָאֹת הָאַחֲרוֹן׃ וְהָיָה אִם־לֹא יַאֲמִינוּ גַּם לִשְׁנֵי הָאֹתוֹת הָאֵלֶּה וְלֹא יִשְׁמְעוּן
לְקֹלֶךָ וְלָקַחְתָּ מִמֵּימֵי הַיְאֹר וְשָׁפַכְתָּ הַיַּבָּשָׁה וְהָיוּ הַמַּיִם אֲשֶׁר תִּקַּח מִן־הַיְאֹר
י וְהָיוּ לְדָם בַּיַּבָּשֶׁת׃ וַיֹּאמֶר מֹשֶׁה אֶל־יְהוָה בִּי אֲדֹנָי לֹא אִישׁ דְּבָרִים אָנֹכִי גַּם

רש״י

כב | **וּמִגָּרַת בֵּיתָהּ.** מֵאוֹתָהּ שֶׁהִיא גָּרָה אִתָּהּ בַּבַּיִת: **וְנִצַּלְתֶּם.** כְּתַרְגּוּמוֹ: "וּתְרוֹקְנוּן", וְכֵן: "וַיְנַצְּלוּ אֶת מִצְרָיִם" (להלן יב, לו), "וַיִּתְנַצְּלוּ בְנֵי יִשְׂרָאֵל אֶת עֶדְיָם" (להלן לג, ו), וְהַנּוּ"ן בּוֹ יְסוֹד. וּמְנַחֵם חִבְּרוֹ בְּמַחְבֶּרֶת צָדִ"י עִם "וַיַּצֵּל אֱלֹהִים אֶת מִקְנֵה אֲבִיכֶם" (בראשית לא, ט), "אֲשֶׁר הִצִּיל אֱלֹהִים מֵאָבִינוּ" (שם טז), וְלֹא יֶאֶמְנוּ דְּבָרָיו, כִּי אִם לֹא הָיְתָה הַנּוּ"ן יְסוֹד וְהִיא נְקוּדָה בְּחִירִק, לֹא תְהֵא מְשַׁמֶּשֶׁת בִּלְשׁוֹן וּפְעַלְתֶּם אֶלָּא בִּלְשׁוֹן וְנִפְעַלְתֶּם, כְּמוֹ: "וְנִסַּחְתֶּם מֵעַל הָאֲדָמָה" (דברים כח, סג), "וְנִתַּתֶּם בְּיַד אוֹיֵב" (ויקרא כו, כה), "וְנִגַּפְתֶּם לִפְנֵי אֹיְבֵיכֶם" (שם פסוק יז), "וְנִתַּכְתֶּם בְּתוֹכָהּ" (יחזקאל כב, כא), "וַאֲמַרְתֶּם נִצַּלְנוּ" (ירמיה ז, י), לְשׁוֹן נִפְעַלְנוּ. וְכָל נוּ"ן שֶׁהִיא בָּאָה בְּתֵבָה לִפְרָקִים וְנוֹפֶלֶת מִמֶּנָּה, כְּנוּ"ן שֶׁל נוֹגֵף, נוֹשֵׂא, נוֹתֵן, נוֹשֵׁךְ, כְּשֶׁהִיא מְדַבֶּרֶת לְשׁוֹן וּפְעַלְתֶּם תִּנָּקֵד בִּשְׁבָא בַּחֲטָף, כְּגוֹן: "וּנְשָׂאתֶם אֶת אֲבִיכֶם" (בראשית מה, יט), "וּנְתַתֶּם לָהֶם אֶת אֶרֶץ הַגִּלְעָד" (במדבר לב, כט), "וּנְמַלְתֶּם אֵת בְּשַׂר עָרְלַתְכֶם" (בראשית יז, יא). לָכֵן אֲנִי אוֹמֵר שֶׁזֹּאת, הַנְּקוּדָה בְּחִירִק, מִן הַיְסוֹד הִיא, וִיסוֹד שֵׁם דָּבָר 'נִצּוּל', וְהוּא מִן הַלְּשׁוֹנוֹת הַכְּבֵדִים, כְּמוֹ דִּבּוּר, כִּפּוּר, לִמּוּד, כְּשֶׁיְּדַבֵּר בִּלְשׁוֹן וּפְעַלְתֶּם יִנָּקֵד בְּחִירִק, כְּמוֹ: "וְדִבַּרְתֶּם אֶל הַסֶּלַע" (במדבר כ, ח), "וְכִפַּרְתֶּם אֶת הַבַּיִת" (יחזקאל מה, כ), "וְלִמַּדְתֶּם אֹתָם אֶת בְּנֵיכֶם" (דברים יא, יט):

פרק ד

ב | **מַזֶּה בְיָדֶךָ.** לְכָךְ נִכְתַּב תֵּבָה אַחַת, לִדְרֹשׁ: מִזֶּה שֶׁבְּיָדְךָ אַתָּה חַיָּב לִלְקוֹת, שֶׁחָשַׁדְתָּ בִּכְשֵׁרִים. וּפְשׁוּטוֹ, כְּאָדָם שֶׁאוֹמֵר לַחֲבֵרוֹ: מוֹדֶה אַתָּה שֶׁזּוֹ שֶׁלְּפָנֶיךָ אֶבֶן הִיא? אָמַר לוֹ: הֵן. אָמַר לוֹ: הֲרֵינִי עוֹשֶׂה אוֹתָהּ עֵץ:

ג | **וַיְהִי לְנָחָשׁ.** רָמַז לוֹ שֶׁסִּפֵּר לָשׁוֹן הָרָע עַל יִשְׂרָאֵל וְתָפַשׂ אֻמָּנוּתוֹ שֶׁל נָחָשׁ:

ד | **וַיַּחֲזֶק בּוֹ.** לְשׁוֹן אֲחִיזָה הוּא, וְהַרְבֵּה יֵשׁ בַּמִּקְרָא: "וַיַּחֲזִיקוּ הָאֲנָשִׁים בְּיָדוֹ" (בראשית יט, טז), "וְהֶחֱזִיקָה בִּמְבֻשָׁיו" (דברים כה, יא), "וְהֶחֱזַקְתִּי בִּזְקָנוֹ" (שמואל א' יז, לה), כָּל לְשׁוֹן חִזּוּק הַדָּבוּק לְבֵי"ת לְשׁוֹן אֲחִיזָה הוּא:

ו | **מְצֹרַעַת כַּשָּׁלֶג.** דֶּרֶךְ צָרַעַת לִהְיוֹת לְבָנָה, "אִם בַּהֶרֶת לְבָנָה הִוא" (ויקרא יג, ד). אַף בְּאוֹת זֶה רָמַז לוֹ שֶׁלָּשׁוֹן הָרָע סִפֵּר בְּאָמְרוֹ: "לֹא יַאֲמִינוּ לִי" (לעיל פסוק א), לְפִיכָךְ הִלְקָהוּ בְּצָרַעַת, כְּמוֹ שֶׁלָּקְתָה מִרְיָם עַל לָשׁוֹן הָרָע:

ז | **וַיּוֹצִאָהּ מֵחֵיקוֹ וְהִנֵּה שָׁבָה כִּבְשָׂרוֹ.** מִכָּאן שֶׁמִּדָּה טוֹבָה מְמַהֶרֶת לָבֹא מִמִּדַּת פֻּרְעָנוּת, שֶׁהֲרֵי בָּרִאשׁוֹנָה לֹא נֶאֱמַר 'מֵחֵיקוֹ':

ח | **וְהֶאֱמִינוּ לְקֹל הָאֹת הָאַחֲרוֹן.** מִשֶּׁתֹּאמַר לָהֶם: בִּשְׁבִילְכֶם לָקִיתִי עַל שֶׁסִּפַּרְתִּי עֲלֵיכֶם לָשׁוֹן הָרָע, יַאֲמִינוּ לָךְ, שֶׁכְּבָר לָמְדוּ בְּכָךְ שֶׁהַמִּזְדַּוְּגִים לָהֶם לוֹקִים בִּנְגָעִים, כְּגוֹן פַּרְעֹה וַאֲבִימֶלֶךְ בִּשְׁבִיל שָׂרָה:

ט | **וְהָיוּ הַמַּיִם וְגוֹ'.** וְהָיוּ וְהָיוּ, שְׁתֵּי פְעָמִים. נִרְאֶה בְּעֵינַי, אִלּוּ נֶאֱמַר: 'וְהָיוּ הַמַּיִם אֲשֶׁר תִּקַּח מִן הַיְאֹר לְדָם בַּיַּבֶּשֶׁת' שׁוֹמֵעַ אֲנִי שֶׁבְּיָדוֹ הֵם נֶהְפָּכִים לְדָם, וְאַף כְּשֶׁיְּהִיוּ לָאָרֶץ יִהְיוּ בַּהֲוָיָתָן, אֲבָל עַכְשָׁיו מְלַמְּדֵנוּ שֶׁלֹּא יִהְיוּ דָם עַד שֶׁיִּהְיוּ בַּיַּבָּשֶׁת:

י | **גַּם מִתְּמוֹל וְגוֹ'.** לָמַדְנוּ שֶׁשִּׁבְעַת יָמִים הָיָה הַקָּדוֹשׁ בָּרוּךְ הוּא מְפַתֶּה אֶת מֹשֶׁה בַּסְּנֶה לֵילֵךְ בִּשְׁלִיחוּתוֹ: מִתְּמוֹל, שִׁלְשֹׁם, מֵאָז דַּבֶּרְךָ – הֲרֵי שְׁלֹשָׁה, וּשְׁלֹשָׁה גַּמִּין רִבּוּיִין הֵם הֲרֵי שִׁשָּׁה, וְהוּא הָיָה עוֹמֵד בַּיּוֹם הַשְּׁבִיעִי כְּשֶׁאָמַר לוֹ זֹאת עַד "שְׁלַח נָא בְּיַד תִּשְׁלָח" (להלן פסוק יג), עַד שֶׁחָרָה בּוֹ וְקִבֵּל עָלָיו. וְכָל זֶה, שֶׁלֹּא הָיָה רוֹצֶה לִטֹּל גְּדֻלָּה עַל אַהֲרֹן אָחִיו שֶׁהָיָה גָּדוֹל הֵימֶנּוּ, וְנָבִיא הָיָה, שֶׁנֶּאֱמַר: "הֲנִגְלֹה נִגְלֵיתִי אֶל בֵּית אָבִיךָ בִּהְיוֹתָם בְּמִצְרַיִם"

You effected any change in me that would enable me to speak clearly from this point onward, perhaps I would be suitable for the task. However, even after revealing Yourself to me, I remain inarticulate.[29] I am unfit for this mission, **as I am cumbrous of speech and cumbrous of tongue.** It is unclear whether Moses suffered from a stutter, or an inability to correctly pronounce certain consonants, or some other speech impediment that inhibited his ability to communicate effectively.[30]

11 **The Lord said to him: Who gives a mouth to a person? Or who renders one mute or deaf, or sighted or blind? Is it not I, the Lord?** Since a person's abilities and characteristics are entirely within My control, you need not be concerned with your speech impediment. If you should need to speak, I will give you the ability to do so.

12 **Now, go, and I will be with your mouth, and I will instruct you that which you shall say.** I will guide you throughout your mission.

13 Despite all the assurances of God, Moses did not want to accept his task: **He said: Please, my Lord, please send by means of** anyone else **whom You will send.**

14 **The wrath of the Lord was enflamed against Moses and He said: Is not Aaron the Levite your brother? I know that he can speak,** and that he has the qualities of a leader. **And also, here he is going out to meet you;** I will ensure that he will go out to greet you, **and he will see you,** his younger brother, upon whom the mantle of leadership has been placed, **and** not only will he act courteously toward you, but **he will** also **rejoice in his heart** over the greatness bestowed upon you.

15 In order to overcome the limitations caused by your speech impediment, you will receive instructions from Me and convey them to Aaron, and he will be your spokesman: **You shall speak to him, and you shall place the words in his mouth; and I will be with your mouth and with his mouth, and I will instruct you that which you shall do.**

16 **He shall speak to the people for you,**[D] **and he shall be a mouth** to speak **for you, and you shall be a leader for him,** as he will transmit only that which you instruct him to say.

17 **And this staff you shall take in your hand, with which you will perform the signs,** the sign of the snake that I have already shown you, and all the signs that I will command you to perform in the future.

Moses Leaves Midyan and Returns to Egypt
EXODUS 4:18–26

Faced with the command of God, Moses is ultimately unable to remain steadfast in his refusal to lead the children of Israel.

His journey from Midyan to Egypt is bracketed by two conversations, the first with his father-in-law, in which he requests permission to return to Egypt, and the second with Aaron, who is to assist him in bringing the word of God to Pharaoh and to the children of Israel. Along the way, while encamped with his family for the night, a crisis occurs. A grave danger threatens the life of Moses, from which he is saved due to his wife's swift action.

Before Moses departs from Midyan, God reveals to him the difficult confrontation that looms ahead. God describes the struggle with Egypt as a struggle over a firstborn son: God seeks to redeem His firstborn son, Israel, through the agency of Moses, but Pharaoh stubbornly refuses to allow their departure from Egypt. As a result, Pharaoh's own firstborn son will be killed together with all the firstborns of Egypt. It is interesting to note that the crisis that threatened Moses and his family also involved the relationship between father and son.

18 **Moses went and returned to Yeter his father-in-law, and he**
Sixth
aliya **said to him:** Many years have passed since I fled from Egypt. **Please, let me go and return to my brethren who are in Egypt and see if they are still alive.** In explaining his return to Egypt, Moses offered personal reasons instead of revealing anything to Yitro regarding his divine mission to redeem his people. Perhaps Moses was hesitant to reveal his mission before he could successfully carry it out, or maybe he was concerned that Yitro would not believe him. **Yitro said to Moses: Go in peace.**

19 Moses originally fled from Egypt as a fugitive accused of murder. With regard to Moses' delay in returning to Egypt due to this accusation, **the Lord said to Moses,** while he was still with Yitro **in Midyan: Go, return to Egypt, as all the men who seek your life have died.** The situation in Egypt has changed, and you can now return to Egypt without worry.

20 **Moses took his wife and his sons and mounted them on the donkey, and they returned to the land of Egypt.** Presumably, Moses walked alongside the donkey. **Moses** also **took the staff of God in his hand.**

מִתְּמוֹל גַּם מִשִּׁלְשֹׁם גַּם מֵאָז דַּבֶּרְךָ אֶל־עַבְדֶּךָ כִּי כְבַד־פֶּה וּכְבַד לָשׁוֹן אָנֹכִי׃
יא וַיֹּאמֶר יְהוָה אֵלָיו מִי שָׂם פֶּה לָאָדָם אוֹ מִי־יָשׂוּם אִלֵּם אוֹ חֵרֵשׁ אוֹ פִקֵּחַ אוֹ
יב עִוֵּר הֲלֹא אָנֹכִי יְהוָה׃ וְעַתָּה לֵךְ וְאָנֹכִי אֶהְיֶה עִם־פִּיךָ וְהוֹרֵיתִיךָ אֲשֶׁר תְּדַבֵּר׃
יג יד וַיֹּאמֶר בִּי אֲדֹנָי שְׁלַח־נָא בְּיַד־תִּשְׁלָח׃ וַיִּחַר־אַף יְהוָה בְּמֹשֶׁה וַיֹּאמֶר הֲלֹא אַהֲרֹן
אָחִיךָ הַלֵּוִי יָדַעְתִּי כִּי־דַבֵּר יְדַבֵּר הוּא וְגַם הִנֵּה־הוּא יֹצֵא לִקְרָאתֶךָ וְרָאֲךָ וְשָׂמַח
טו בְּלִבּוֹ׃ וְדִבַּרְתָּ אֵלָיו וְשַׂמְתָּ אֶת־הַדְּבָרִים בְּפִיו וְאָנֹכִי אֶהְיֶה עִם־פִּיךָ וְעִם־פִּיהוּ
טז וְהוֹרֵיתִי אֶתְכֶם אֵת אֲשֶׁר תַּעֲשׂוּן׃ וְדִבֶּר־הוּא לְךָ אֶל־הָעָם וְהָיָה הוּא יִהְיֶה־לְּךָ
יז לְפֶה וְאַתָּה תִּהְיֶה־לּוֹ לֵאלֹהִים׃ וְאֶת־הַמַּטֶּה הַזֶּה תִּקַּח בְּיָדֶךָ אֲשֶׁר תַּעֲשֶׂה־בּוֹ
אֶת־הָאֹתֹת׃

יח וַיֵּלֶךְ מֹשֶׁה וַיָּשָׁב ׀ אֶל־יֶתֶר חֹתְנוֹ וַיֹּאמֶר לוֹ אֵלְכָה־נָּא וְאָשׁוּבָה אֶל־אַחַי אֲשֶׁר־ ג ששי
יט בְּמִצְרַיִם וְאֶרְאֶה הַעוֹדָם חַיִּים וַיֹּאמֶר יִתְרוֹ לְמֹשֶׁה לֵךְ לְשָׁלוֹם׃ וַיֹּאמֶר יְהוָה
אֶל־מֹשֶׁה בְּמִדְיָן לֵךְ שֻׁב מִצְרָיִם כִּי־מֵתוּ כָּל־הָאֲנָשִׁים הַמְבַקְשִׁים אֶת־נַפְשֶׁךָ׃
כ וַיִּקַּח מֹשֶׁה אֶת־אִשְׁתּוֹ וְאֶת־בָּנָיו וַיַּרְכִּבֵם עַל־הַחֲמֹר וַיָּשָׁב אַרְצָה מִצְרָיִם וַיִּקַּח

רש״י

(שמואל א׳ ב, כז), הוא אהרן. וכן ביחזקאל: "ואודע להם בארץ מצרים וגו׳ ואמר אלהם איש שקוצי עיניו השליכו" (יחזקאל כ, ה-ז), ואותה נבואה לאהרן נאמרה: כבד פה. בכבדות אני מדבר, ובלשון לעז בלב"א:

יא| מי שם פה וגו׳. מי למדך לדבר כשהיית נדון לפני פרעה על המצרי? או מי ישום אלם. מי עשה פרעה אלם שלא נתאמץ במצות הריגתך, ואת משרתיו חרשים שלא שמעו בצוותו עליך, ולאספקלטורין ההורגים מי עשאם עורים שלא ראו כשברחת מן הבימה ונמלטת? הלא אנכי. ששמי "ה׳", עשיתי כל זאת:

יג| ביד תשלח. ביד מי שאתה רגיל לשלח, והוא אהרן. דבר אחר, ביד אחר שתרצה לשלח, אין סופי להכניסם לארץ ולהיות גואלם לעתיד, יש לך שלוחים הרבה:

יד| ויחר אף. רבי יהושע בן קרחה אומר: כל חרון אף שבתורה עושה רשם, וזה לא נאמר בו רשם, ולא מצינו שבא עונש על ידי אותו חרון. אמר לו רבי יוסי: אף בזו נאמר בו רשם: "הלא אהרן אחיך הלוי", שהיה עתיד להיות לוי ולא כהן, והכהונה הייתי אומר לצאת ממך, מעתה לא יהיה כן, אלא הוא יהיה כהן ואתה לוי, שנאמר: "ומשה איש האלהים בניו יקראו על שבט הלוי" (דברי הימים א׳ כג, יד): הנה הוא יצא לקראתך. כשתלך למצרים: וראך ושמח בלבו. לא כשאתה סבור שיהא מקפיד עליך שאתה עולה לגדלה. ומשם זכה אהרן לעדי החשן הנתון על הלב:

טז| ודבר הוא לך. בשבילך ידבר אל העם. וזה יוכיח על כל לך ולי ולו ולכם ולהם הסמוכים לדבור, שכלם לשון עליך הם: יהיה לך לפה. למליץ, לפי שאתה כבד פה: לאלהים. לרב ולשר:

יח| וישב אל יתר חתנו. לטל רשות, שהרי נשבע לו. ושבעה שמות היו לו: רעואל, יתר, יתרו, קיני, חובב, חבר, פוטיאל:

יט| כי מתו כל האנשים. מי הם? דתן ואבירם; חיים היו, אלא שירדו מנכסיהם, והעני חשוב כמת:

כ| על החמר. חמור המיחד. הוא החמור שחבש אברהם לעקדת יצחק, והוא שעתיד מלך המשיח להגלות עליו, שנאמר: "עני ורכב על חמור" (זכריה ט, ט): וישב ארצה מצרים ויקח משה את מטה. אין מקדם ומאחר מדקדקים במקרא:

DISCUSSION

4:16| **And he shall speak to the people for you:** Moses' hesitation to accept his role exemplifies his humility as the Torah recounts elsewhere: "The man Moses was very humble, more than any person on the face of the earth" (Numbers 12:3). Since Moses had no desire for grandeur, he wished that someone else would accept the task set for him. Another expression of Moses's humility was his hesitation to speak directly to the people; rather, Aaron spoke to the people on his behalf. In this sense, the word of Moses was similar to the word of God, as both were transmitted to the people through the agency of a prophet (see Ibn Ezra, Exodus 7:1).

21 **The Lord said to Moses: When you go to return to Egypt, see all the wonders that I have placed in your hand,** the various signs you have been provided, **and perform them before Pharaoh.** That is, these signs are not meant solely for the children of Israel, but for Pharaoh as well. **And** be aware that **I will harden his heart, and he will not send forth the people,** despite your rhetoric and these miraculous signs.

22 **You shall say to Pharaoh: So said the Lord: My firstborn son is Israel.**

23 **And I say to you: Send forth My son, and he will serve Me** in the wilderness, **and if you refuse to send him forth, behold, I will slay your firstborn son**[D] in retribution for your refusal to free My firstborn.

24 **It was on the way, in the lodging,** where Moses and his family rested on their way to Egypt, an angel of **the Lord encountered him and sought to kill him.** Moses was in critical condition, and may have appeared to be dying.

25 **Tzipora,** wife of Moses, was certain that this experience was due to some flaw in their behavior. Therefore, she **took a flint**[B] **and she cut her son's foreskin,**[D] **and touched it to his feet,** Tzipora placed the foreskin beside the angel's feet, or Moses', or her son's;[31] **and she said** to the child: **For you are a bridegroom of blood to me.** That is, now that I have circumcised you, there is a new connection between us. Alternatively, Tzipora said to Moses: You are a bridegroom of blood to me, as the merit of this circumcision saved you from death and atoned for your transgression, thus renewing the covenant between us.[32]

Flint

26 After Tzipora circumcised the child, **he,** the angel, **released him,** Moses. **Then she said: A bridegroom of blood because of circumcision.**[D]

Moses and Aaron Confront Pharaoh and the Children of Israel

EXODUS 4:27–6:1

Moses now begins to carry out his divine mission with the accompaniment and assistance of Aaron. They must face three sets of officials: the elders of Israel; Pharaoh; and the foremen of the children of Israel, who were the first to suffer as a result of the demands presented by Moses and Aaron.

At the end of this passage, Moses and Aaron will direct the harsh criticisms issued by the foremen toward God. God will respond to them, and He will promise them that the people's suffering will soon end; until then, however, the people needed to remain patient.

27 **The Lord said to Aaron: Go toward Moses to the wilderness. He went and he met him at the mountain of God,**[D] **and** Aaron greeted Moses with love and **he kissed him.**

28 **Moses told Aaron all the words of the Lord: That He sent him, and all the signs that He commanded him,** since they would now be required to carry out the mission together.

29 **Moses and Aaron went, and they assembled all the elders,** the leaders, **of the children of Israel.**

30 **Aaron,** who was a skilled orator and was known to the people, **spoke all the words that the Lord spoke to Moses, and he,** Aaron, **performed the signs** that Moses received in order to validate his prophecy, **in the sight of the people.**

DISCUSSION

4:23 | **Behold, I will slay your firstborn son:** This statement refers to the final plague with which God will strike the Egyptians. Thus, the culmination of the story of the plagues is foretold at the outset (Rashi).

4:25 | **Her son's foreskin:** Perhaps the child was until now uncircumcised because he was too small, or because Moses and Tzipora were concerned about bringing a newly circumcised and sick child on the journey to Egypt (*Nedarim* 31b; Rashi). Perhaps Moses reached an agreement with Yitro that some of his sons would be circumcised, in accordance with the tradition of the Hebrews, while the others would remain uncircumcised, in accordance with the tradition of Yitro (*Targum Yonatan*).

4:26 | **A bridegroom [*ḥatan*] of blood because of circumcision:** A circumcision is a joyous occasion that entails entry into a covenant, similar to a marriage. Thus, due to the circumcision, the child, or Moses, is referred to as a *ḥatan*, bridegroom. In a similar manner, when the children of Israel would later leave Egypt, they would conduct a mass circumcision of all males, including slaves and converts, in preparation for the sacrifice of the paschal lamb. There as well, the circumcision will represent a form of redemption and renewed covenant with the Lord (see 12:43–50).

4:27 | **At the mountain of God:** The verse would seem to indicate that the mountain of Horev, Mount Sinai, is situated between Midyan and Egypt (Ibn Ezra; Ramban; see *Bekhor Shor*). However, the precise location of Midyan is itself subject to debate (see commentary on 2:15).

כא מֹשֶׁה אֶת־מַטֵּה הָאֱלֹהִים בְּיָדוֹ: וַיֹּאמֶר יהוה אֶל־מֹשֶׁה בְּלֶכְתְּךָ לָשׁוּב מִצְרַיְמָה רְאֵה כָּל־הַמֹּפְתִים אֲשֶׁר־שַׂמְתִּי בְיָדֶךָ וַעֲשִׂיתָם לִפְנֵי פַרְעֹה וַאֲנִי אֲחַזֵּק אֶת־לִבּוֹ

כב וְלֹא יְשַׁלַּח אֶת־הָעָם: וְאָמַרְתָּ אֶל־פַּרְעֹה כֹּה אָמַר יהוה בְּנִי בְכֹרִי יִשְׂרָאֵל: וָאֹמַר

כג אֵלֶיךָ שַׁלַּח אֶת־בְּנִי וְיַעַבְדֵנִי וַתְּמָאֵן לְשַׁלְּחוֹ הִנֵּה אָנֹכִי הֹרֵג אֶת־בִּנְךָ בְּכֹרֶךָ:

כד וַיְהִי בַדֶּרֶךְ בַּמָּלוֹן וַיִּפְגְּשֵׁהוּ יהוה וַיְבַקֵּשׁ הֲמִיתוֹ: וַתִּקַּח צִפֹּרָה צֹר וַתִּכְרֹת אֶת־

כה עָרְלַת בְּנָהּ וַתַּגַּע לְרַגְלָיו וַתֹּאמֶר כִּי חֲתַן־דָּמִים אַתָּה לִי: וַיִּרֶף מִמֶּנּוּ אָז אָמְרָה

כו חֲתַן דָּמִים לַמּוּלֹת:

כז וַיֹּאמֶר יהוה אֶל־אַהֲרֹן לֵךְ לִקְרַאת מֹשֶׁה הַמִּדְבָּרָה וַיֵּלֶךְ וַיִּפְגְּשֵׁהוּ בְּהַר

כח הָאֱלֹהִים וַיִּשַּׁק־לוֹ: וַיַּגֵּד מֹשֶׁה לְאַהֲרֹן אֵת כָּל־דִּבְרֵי יהוה אֲשֶׁר שְׁלָחוֹ וְאֵת כָּל־

כט הָאֹתֹת אֲשֶׁר צִוָּהוּ: וַיֵּלֶךְ מֹשֶׁה וְאַהֲרֹן וַיַּאַסְפוּ אֶת־כָּל־זִקְנֵי בְּנֵי יִשְׂרָאֵל: וַיְדַבֵּר

ל אַהֲרֹן אֵת כָּל־הַדְּבָרִים אֲשֶׁר־דִּבֶּר יהוה אֶל־מֹשֶׁה וַיַּעַשׂ הָאֹתֹת לְעֵינֵי הָעָם:

רש"י

כא בְּלֶכְתְּךָ לָשׁוּב מִצְרַיְמָה וְגו'. דַּע שֶׁעַל מְנָת כֵּן תֵּלֵךְ, שֶׁתְּהֵא גִבּוֹר בִּשְׁלִיחוּתִי לַעֲשׂוֹת כָּל מוֹפְתַי לִפְנֵי פַרְעֹה וְלֹא תִירָא מִמֶּנּוּ: אֲשֶׁר־שַׂמְתִּי בְיָדֶךָ. לֹא עַל שֶׁלֹּשׁ אוֹתוֹת הָאֲמוּרוֹת לְמַעְלָה, שֶׁהֲרֵי לֹא לִפְנֵי פַרְעֹה עָשָׂה לַעֲשׂוֹתָם אֶלָּא לִפְנֵי יִשְׂרָאֵל שֶׁיַּאֲמִינוּ לוֹ, וְלֹא מָצִינוּ שֶׁעֲשָׂאָם לְפָנָיו, אֶלָּא מוֹפְתִים שֶׁאֲנִי עָתִיד לָשׂוּם בְּיָדְךָ בְּמִצְרַיִם, כְּמוֹ: "כִּי יְדַבֵּר אֲלֵכֶם פַּרְעֹה" וְגו' (להלן ז, ט), וְאַל תִּתְמַהּ עַל אֲשֶׁר כָּתַב: "אֲשֶׁר שַׂמְתִּי", שֶׁכֵּן מַשְׁמָעוֹ: כְּשֶׁתְּדַבֵּר עִמּוֹ כְּבָר שַׂמְתִּים בְּיָדְךָ:

כב וְאָמַרְתָּ אֶל־פַּרְעֹה. כְּשֶׁתִּשְׁמַע שֶׁלִּבּוֹ חָזֵק וִימָאֵן לְהָשִׁיב, אֱמֹר לוֹ כֵּן: בְּנִי בְכֹרִי. לְשׁוֹן גְּדֻלָּה, כְּמוֹ: "אַף אָנִי בְּכוֹר אֶתְּנֵהוּ" (תהלים פט, כח) זֶהוּ פְּשׁוּטוֹ, וּמִדְרָשׁוֹ, כָּאן חָתַם הַקָּדוֹשׁ בָּרוּךְ הוּא עַל מְכִירַת הַבְּכוֹרָה שֶׁלָּקַח יַעֲקֹב מֵעֵשָׂו:

כג וָאֹמַר אֵלֶיךָ. בִּשְׁלִיחוּתוֹ שֶׁל מָקוֹם: "שַׁלַּח אֶת־בְּנִי הִנֵּה אָנֹכִי הֹרֵג וְגו'. הִיא מַכָּה אַחֲרוֹנָה, וּבָהּ הִתְרָהוּ תְּחִלָּה מִפְּנֵי שֶׁהִיא קָשָׁה. וְזֶה הוּא שֶׁאָמַר אִיּוֹב: "הֶן אֵל יַשְׂגִּיב בְּכֹחוֹ" (איוב לו, כב), לְפִיכָךְ: "מִי כָמוֹהוּ מוֹרֶה" – בָּשָׂר וָדָם הַמְבַקֵּשׁ לְהִנָּקֵם מֵחֲבֵרוֹ מַעְלִים אֶת דְּבָרָיו, שֶׁלֹּא יְבַקֵּשׁ הַצָּלָה. אֲבָל הַקָּדוֹשׁ בָּרוּךְ הוּא יַצְדִּיק בְּכֹחוֹ וְאֵין יָכֹל לְהִמָּלֵט מִיָּדוֹ כִּי אִם בְּשׁוּבוֹ אֵלָיו, לְפִיכָךְ הוּא מוֹרֶהוּ וּמַתְרֶה בּוֹ לָשׁוּב:

כד וַיְהִי. מֹשֶׁה, בַדֶּרֶךְ בַּמָּלוֹן: וַיְבַקֵּשׁ הֲמִיתוֹ. לְמִי שֶׁלֹּא מָל אֶת אֱלִיעֶזֶר בְּנוֹ, וְעַל שֶׁנִּתְרַשֵּׁל נֶעֱנַשׁ מִיתָה. תַּנְיָא, אָמַר רַבִּי יוֹסֵי: חַס וְשָׁלוֹם, לֹא נִתְרַשֵּׁל, אֶלָּא אָמַר: אֶמּוֹל וְאֵצֵא לַדֶּרֶךְ – סַכָּנָה הִיא לַתִּינוֹק עַד שְׁלֹשָׁה יָמִים! אֶמּוֹל וְאֶשְׁהֶה שְׁלֹשָׁה יָמִים – הַקָּדוֹשׁ בָּרוּךְ הוּא צִוַּנִי: "לֵךְ שׁוּב מִצְרָיִם"! וּמִפְּנֵי מָה נֶעֱנַשׁ? לְפִי שֶׁנִּתְעַסֵּק בַּמָּלוֹן תְּחִלָּה.

בְּמַסֶּכֶת נְדָרִים (דף לב ע"ב). וְהָיָה הַמַּלְאָךְ נַעֲשָׂה כְּמִין נָחָשׁ וּבוֹלְעוֹ מֵרֹאשׁוֹ וְעַד יְרֵכָיו וְחוֹזֵר וּבוֹלְעוֹ מֵרַגְלָיו וְעַד אוֹתוֹ מָקוֹם, הֵבִינָה צִפּוֹרָה שֶׁבִּשְׁבִיל הַמִּילָה הוּא:

כה וַתַּגַּע לְרַגְלָיו. הִשְׁלִיכַתּוּ לִפְנֵי רַגְלָיו שֶׁל מֹשֶׁה: וַתֹּאמֶר. עַל בְּנָהּ: "כִּי חֲתַן דָּמִים אַתָּה לִי" – אַתָּה הָיִיתָ גוֹרֵם לִהְיוֹת הֶחָתָן שֶׁלִּי נִרְצָח עָלֶיךָ, הוֹרֵג אִישִׁי אַתָּה לִי:

כו וַיִּרֶף. הַמַּלְאָךְ "מִמֶּנּוּ", "אָז הֵבִינָה שֶׁעַל הַמִּילָה בָּא לְהָרְגוֹ: אָמְרָה. חֲתַן דָּמִים לַמּוּלֹת. חֲתָנִי הָיָה נִרְצָח עַל דְּבַר הַמִּילָה: לַמּוּלֹת. עַל דְּבַר הַמּוּלוֹת, שֵׁם דָּבָר הוּא, וְהַלָּמֶ"ד מְשַׁמֶּשֶׁת בִּלְשׁוֹן עַל, כְּמוֹ: "וָאֹמַר פַּרְעֹה לִבְנֵי יִשְׂרָאֵל" (להלן יד, ג), וְאוּנְקְלוֹס תִּרְגֵּם "דָּמִים", עַל דַּם הַמִּילָה:

BACKGROUND

4:25 | **Flint:** A hard stone with a glassy appearance, composed of silicon dioxide and commonly found in the Negev. In ancient times, it was common to sharpen these stones and use them as knives, as can be seen here and in the book of Joshua (5:3): "Joshua made for flint knives for himself, and circumcised the children of Israel at the Hill of the Foreskins."

31 **The people trusted and heard that the Lord remembered the children of Israel and that He saw their affliction.** Moses' concern that the people would react toward this declaration with skepticism was thus confuted. Although they were not personally acquainted with Moses, they believed him because of his personality, or because of the signs. **And they bowed and prostrated themselves** to God in gratitude for the news that the time for their redemption had arrived.

5 1 Then, once **Moses and Aaron** earned the people's trust and the

Seventh aliya recognition of their leaders, they felt empowered to continue their mission, and they **came and said to Pharaoh: So says the Lord, God of Israel: Send forth My people, and they will celebrate for Me in the wilderness.**

2 **Pharaoh said: Who is the Lord,**[D] **that I should heed His voice to send forth Israel?** I do not recognize the name of this deity; I have never heard of him. **I do not know the Lord, and I also will not send forth Israel,** as you have fabricated these claims.

3 **They,** Moses and Aaron, **said:** Since you do not recognize His name, we will tell you who the Lord is: **The Lord is the God of the Hebrews,** and He **has called upon us** and commanded us to leave Egypt to worship Him. Therefore, **please, let us go a three-day journey into the wilderness and we will sacrifice to the Lord our God, lest He strike us with pestilence, or with the sword.** The threat of punishment for failure to heed the voice of God was added by Moses and Aaron of their own accord (see 3:18).

4 **The king of Egypt said to them: Why, Moses and Aaron, do you disturb the people from its tasks**[D] by implanting in their minds these strange notions? **Go to your burdens.** Do not offer any more suggestions and do not involve yourselves in politics.

5 **Pharaoh said: Behold, the people of the land,** the children of Israel, **are now many, and** with your declarations **you will cause them to desist from their burdens.** Egypt requires their labor; there is no time for festivals or celebrations.

6 Pharaoh now takes steps to extinguish the people's hopes: **Pharaoh commanded the taskmasters of the people,** who were appointed by Pharaoh to oversee the labor of the children of Israel, **that day and their foremen,** the supervisors from the children of Israel, **saying:**

7 **You shall not continue to give straw to the people to produce bricks,**[B] **as previously. They will go and gather straw for themselves** from the fields.

Straw   Bricks containing straw

8 Despite the fact that they must now dedicate some of their time to gathering straw, they may not diminish their quota: **But you shall** continue to **impose upon them the total of the bricks that they produced previously; you shall not diminish from it, because they are indolent. Therefore, they cry out, saying: We will go and we will sacrifice to our God.** Since Pharaoh was unacquainted with the God of Israel, and since the children of Israel had hitherto not worshipped Him, he saw the demands of Moses and Aaron as nothing but a futile diversion that distracted the lazy slaves and deterred them from their labor.

9 By demanding the same quota of bricks without providing the necessary straw, **let the work become weighty upon the people,**[D] **and they will engage in it and they will not** have the time to **be occupied with false matters.**

10 **The taskmasters of the people and their foremen went out, and they said to the people, saying: So said Pharaoh: I am not giving you straw.**

DISCUSSION

5:2 | Who is the Lord: According to the Midrash (*Tanḥuma, Va'era* 5), Pharaoh searched through a book containing the names of all known pagan deities. When he could not find the name of the Lord, he said: I have searched through all my writings, and the name of your god does not appear.

5:4 | Why, Moses and Aaron, do you disturb the people from its tasks: Pharaoh rebuked Moses and Aaron, but he did not threaten them,

although this was certainly within his means. Perhaps he treated them with a degree of respect and reverence due to their advanced ages (see Ramban).

5:9 | Let the work become weighty upon the people: One might ask: Why did Pharaoh choose to stop providing straw instead of simply increasing their quota of bricks? Perhaps he wanted to avoid the hassle of collecting the straw for them. Additionally, since the bricks

were produced for the sake of building projects, the quantity of bricks needed to fit the pace of the construction workers. A surplus of bricks might have caused other difficulties in construction, e.g., issues of storage. Since Pharaoh was interested only in increasing the pressure on the Hebrew slaves in order to subdue them and break their spirit, he chose to increase their workload by forcing them to gather their own straw.

לא ויאמן העם וישמעו כי־פקד יהוה את־בני ישראל וכי ראה את־ענים ויקדו
א וישתחוו: ואחר באו משה ואהרן ויאמרו אל־פרעה כה־אמר יהוה אלהי שביעי
ב ישראל שלח את־עמי ויחגו לי במדבר: ויאמר פרעה מי יהוה אשר אשמע
בקלו לשלח את־ישראל לא ידעתי את־יהוה וגם את־ישראל לא אשלח:
ג ויאמרו אלהי העברים נקרא עלינו נלכה־נא דרך שלשת ימים במדבר ונזבחה
ד ליהוה אלהינו פן־יפגענו בדבר או בחרב: ויאמר אלהם מלך מצרים למה
ה משה ואהרן תפריעו את־העם ממעשיו לכו לסבלתיכם: ויאמר פרעה הן־
ו רבים עתה עם הארץ והשבתם אתם מסבלתם: ויצו פרעה ביום ההוא את־
ז הנגשים בעם ואת־שטריו לאמר: לא תאספון לתת תבן לעם ללבן הלבנים
ח כתמול שלשם הם ילכו וקששו להם תבן: ואת־מתכנת הלבנים אשר הם
עשים תמול שלשם תשימו עליהם לא תגרעו ממנו כי־נרפים הם על־כן הם
ט צעקים לאמר נלכה נזבחה לאלהינו: תכבד העבדה על־האנשים ויעשו־בה
י ואל־ישעו בדברי־שקר: ויצאו נגשי העם ושטריו ויאמרו אל־העם לאמר כה

רש"י

פרק ה

א] **ואחר באו משה ואהרן וגו'.** אבל הזקנים נשמטו אחד אחד מאחר משה ואהרן עד שנשמטו כלם קדם שהגיעו לפלטין, לפי שיראו ללכת. ובסיני נפרע להם: "ונגש משה לבדו והם לא יגשו" (להלן כד, ב), החזירם לאחוריהם.

ג] **פן יפגענו.** 'פן יפגעך' היה להם לומר, אלא שחלקו כבוד למלכות. פגיעה זו לשון מקרה מות הוא.

ד] **תפריעו את העם ממעשיו.** תבדילו ותרחיקו אותם ממלאכתם, שומעין לכם וסבורים לנוח מן המלאכה. וכן: "פרעהו אל תעבר בו" (משלי ד, טו) – רחקהו; וכן: "ותפרעו כל עצתי" (שם א, כה); "כי פרע הוא" (להלן לב, כה) – נרחק ונתעב: **לכו לסבלתיכם.** לכו למלאכתכם שיש לכם לעשות בבתיכם. אבל מלאכת שעבוד מצרים לא היתה על שבטו של לוי, ותדע לך, שהרי משה ואהרן יוצאים ובאים:

ה] **הן רבים עתה עם הארץ.** שהעבודה מטלת עליהם, ואתם משביתים אותם מסבלותם, הפסד גדול הוא זה:

ו] **הנגשים.** מצריים היו והשוטרים היו ישראל. הנוגש ממנה על כמה שוטרים, והשוטר ממנה לרדות בעושי המלאכה:

ז] **תבן.** אשטובל"א, היו גובלין אותו עם הטיט: **לבנים.** טיוול"ש, שעושים מטיט ומיבשין אותן בחמה, ויש ששורפין אותן בכבשן: **כתמול שלשם.** כאשר הייתם עושים עד הנה: **וקששו.** ולקטו:

ח] **ואת מתכנת הלבנים.** סכום חשבון הלבנים שהיה כל אחד עושה ליום כשהיה התבן נתן להם, אותו סכום "תשימו עליהם" גם עתה, למען תכבד העבודה עליהם: **כי נרפים.** מן העבודה הם, לכך לבם פונה אל הבטלה ו"צעקים לאמר נלכה" וגו': **מתכנת.** "ותכן לבנים" (להלן פסוק יח), "ולו נתכנו עללות" (שמואל א' ב, ג), ו"את הכסף המתכן" (מלכים ב' יב, יב), כלם לשון חשבון הם: **נרפים.** המלאכה רפויה בידם ועזובה מהם והם נרפים ממנה, רטריי"ש בלעז:

ט] **ואל ישעו בדברי שקר.** ואל יהגו וידברו תמיד בדברי רוח לאמר: "נלכה נזבחה". ודומה לו: "ואשעה בחקיך תמיד" (תהלים קיט, קיז); "למשל ולשנינה" (דברים כח, לז) – "ולשועי", "ויספר" (להלן יח, ח) – "ואשתעי".

BACKGROUND

5:7| Straw to the people to produce bricks: Bricks were produced from clay, with straw mixed into the clay in order to manufacture a stronger product. After being shaped, the clay would be baked or dried in order to harden it into bricks. Straw, the leftover stalks that remain in the field after harvesting grains, was a crucial ingredient in the production of bricks. Since it was readily available and inexpensive, it was provided to the slaves for use in preparing the bricks. Now, Pharaoh decreed that the straw would no longer be given to the slaves.

11 **You, go take straw for yourselves from what you find, for nothing will be diminished from your work;** your quota will remain the same.
12 **The people scattered** throughout the fields **in the entire land of Egypt to gather stalks** to cut up **for straw.**
13 **The taskmasters goaded them** to work faster,[33] **saying: Complete your task, each day's portion on its day, as when there was straw.** The taskmasters demanded that they work faster in order to produce the same yield as before.
14 **The foremen of the children of Israel, whom Pharaoh's taskmasters appointed over them, were beaten.** The foremen were men of stature from among the children of Israel who were appointed as low-level supervisors of the labor.[34] Although these foremen did not have any real authority, they were held accountable by the taskmasters for the productivity of the slaves. Thus, when the quota was not reached, the foremen were beaten, **saying: Why did you not complete your quota to produce bricks as previously, both yesterday and today?**
15 **The foremen of the children of Israel came and cried out to Pharaoh, saying: Why will you do this to your servants?**
16 On the one hand, **straw is not given to your servants, and** on the other hand, **they say to us: Produce bricks and behold,** we **your servants are beaten, and it is a sin to your people.** Ultimately, the reduction in productivity will affect your people; you gain nothing from your harsh decree.
17 Although the foremen were in no way rebelling against Pharaoh, the king suspected that their petition was driven by the hopes that Moses and Aaron planted in the minds of the people. Since Pharaoh attributed the endurance of these hopes to idleness, he decided to further increase the people's burdens. **He said: You are indolent, indolent. Therefore you say: Let us go and sacrifice to the Lord.**
18 **Now, go work, and straw will not be given to you, and the total of bricks, you will provide.**
19 **The foremen of the children of Israel saw them,** themselves, **in distress, saying: Do not diminish from your bricks, each day's portion on its day.** There was no escape from their predicament; they would be beaten for missing their quotas, despite the impossible demands placed on them.
20 **They,** the foremen, **encountered Moses and Aaron, standing toward them as they came out from before Pharaoh.**
21 **They,** the foremen, **said to them: May the Lord look upon you and judge** you, **because you have** damaged our reputations and **rendered us putrid in the eyes of Pharaoh and in the eyes of his servants;** now, they have an excuse **to put a sword in their hand to kill us.** The foremen understood that their increased burdens did not stem from Pharaoh's actual economic needs, but that Pharaoh sought to suppress the new ideas of rebellion that were introduced by Moses and Aaron.
22 For the first time, Moses initiates a dialogue with God: **Moses**
Maftir **returned to the Lord and he said: My Lord, why did You harm this people? Why did you send me?**
23 **Since I came to Pharaoh to speak in Your name, he has harmed this people, and You did not save Your people.** Although I returned to Egypt to redeem the children of Israel, I have brought only more suffering upon them.[D]

DISCUSSION

Moses' Protest of God's Treatment of the Children of Israel: In their initial dialogue at the burning bush, in the course of God's recruiting Moses to lead His people out of Egypt, He cautions Moses: "And I know that the king of Egypt will not allow you to go, except with a powerful hand" (3:19). It is, therefore, difficult to understand Moses' reaction to the setback after his initial encounter with Pharaoh: "Since I came to Pharaoh to speak in Your name, he has harmed this people, and You did not save Your people" (5:23). Why was Moses' reaction one of despair? Didn't God warn him that the process would be an extended one and that Pharaoh would not immediately comply with Moses' demands?

The Abravanel explains that the primary focus of Moses' protest was not the fact that God did not yet save His people. He protested the harm that the children of Israel were compelled to endure. His mention of the fact that the people had not yet been redeemed is merely as a consequence of that suffering. God reassures him: "Now you will see what I will do to Pharaoh; for with a powerful hand he will send them forth and with a powerful hand he will drive them from his land" (6:1); the duration of that suffering would be brief.

The Torah continues: "God spoke to Moses and He said to him: I am the Lord. I appeared to Abraham, to Isaac, and to Jacob as God Almighty, but with My name, the Lord, I was not known to them" (6:2–3). According to Rashi, God waxes nostalgic and says: I made several commitments to the patriarchs. Although those promises were not fulfilled in their lifetimes, as God employed his attribute of *El Shaddai*, and not the attribute represented by the Tetragrammaton, which connotes His reliability to fulfill promises, they never questioned Him. He rebukes Moses for his failure to accept God's commitment without question.

Ramban explains that God is not rebuking Moses, on the contrary, He is addressing his concern and encouraging him. God says: I performed miracles for the patriarchs, they were always miracles performed within the framework of nature, e.g., Sarah gave birth to Isaac at an advanced age, but it was not a virgin birth. He reassures Moses that in taking the children of Israel out of Egypt, He will no longer restrict himself and remain within the framework of nature; rather, he will free himself from the shackles of nature and perform supernatural miracles. The divine name, *El Shaddai*, like the name *Elokim*, represents the attribute of justice, through which God adheres to the laws of nature. The Tetragrammaton represents the attribute of mercy, through which God is not restricted by the laws of nature.

יא אָמַר פַּרְעֹה אֵינֶנִּי נֹתֵן לָכֶם תֶּבֶן׃ אַתֶּם לְכוּ קְחוּ לָכֶם תֶּבֶן מֵאֲשֶׁר תִּמְצָאוּ כִּי
יב אֵין נִגְרָע מֵעֲבֹדַתְכֶם דָּבָר׃ וַיָּפֶץ הָעָם בְּכָל־אֶרֶץ מִצְרָיִם לְקֹשֵׁשׁ קַשׁ לַתֶּבֶן׃
יג יד וְהַנֹּגְשִׂים אָצִים לֵאמֹר כַּלּוּ מַעֲשֵׂיכֶם דְּבַר־יוֹם בְּיוֹמוֹ כַּאֲשֶׁר בִּהְיוֹת הַתֶּבֶן׃ וַיֻּכּוּ
שֹׁטְרֵי בְּנֵי יִשְׂרָאֵל אֲשֶׁר־שָׂמוּ עֲלֵהֶם נֹגְשֵׂי פַרְעֹה לֵאמֹר מַדּוּעַ לֹא כִלִּיתֶם חָקְכֶם
טו לִלְבֹּן כִּתְמוֹל שִׁלְשֹׁם גַּם־תְּמוֹל גַּם־הַיּוֹם׃ וַיָּבֹאוּ שֹׁטְרֵי בְּנֵי יִשְׂרָאֵל וַיִּצְעֲקוּ אֶל־
טז פַּרְעֹה לֵאמֹר לָמָּה תַעֲשֶׂה כֹה לַעֲבָדֶיךָ׃ תֶּבֶן אֵין נִתָּן לַעֲבָדֶיךָ וּלְבֵנִים אֹמְרִים
יז לָנוּ עֲשׂוּ וְהִנֵּה עֲבָדֶיךָ מֻכִּים וְחָטָאת עַמֶּךָ׃ וַיֹּאמֶר נִרְפִּים אַתֶּם נִרְפִּים עַל־כֵּן
יח אַתֶּם אֹמְרִים נֵלְכָה נִזְבְּחָה לַיהוָה׃ וְעַתָּה לְכוּ עִבְדוּ וְתֶבֶן לֹא־יִנָּתֵן לָכֶם וְתֹכֶן
יט לְבֵנִים תִּתֵּנוּ׃ וַיִּרְאוּ שֹׁטְרֵי בְנֵי־יִשְׂרָאֵל אֹתָם בְּרָע לֵאמֹר לֹא־תִגְרְעוּ מִלִּבְנֵיכֶם
כ דְּבַר־יוֹם בְּיוֹמוֹ׃ וַיִּפְגְּעוּ אֶת־מֹשֶׁה וְאֶת־אַהֲרֹן נִצָּבִים לִקְרָאתָם בְּצֵאתָם מֵאֵת
כא פַּרְעֹה׃ וַיֹּאמְרוּ אֲלֵהֶם יֵרֶא יְהוָה עֲלֵיכֶם וְיִשְׁפֹּט אֲשֶׁר הִבְאַשְׁתֶּם אֶת־רֵיחֵנוּ בְּעֵינֵי
כב פַרְעֹה וּבְעֵינֵי עֲבָדָיו לָתֶת־חֶרֶב בְּיָדָם לְהָרְגֵנוּ׃ וַיָּשָׁב מֹשֶׁה אֶל־יְהוָה וַיֹּאמַר מפטיר
כג אֲדֹנָי לָמָה הֲרֵעֹתָה לָעָם הַזֶּה לָמָּה זֶּה שְׁלַחְתָּנִי׃ וּמֵאָז בָּאתִי אֶל־פַּרְעֹה לְדַבֵּר

רש"י

ואי אפשר לומר 'ישעו' לשון "וישע ה' אל הבל... ואל קין ואל מנחתו לא שעה" (בראשית ד, ד-ה) ולפרש 'אל ישעו' – אל יפנו, שאם כן היה לו לכתב: 'ואל ישעו אל דברי שקר' או 'לדברי שקר' כי כן גזרת כלם: "ישעה האדם על עשהו" (ישעיה יז, ז), "ולא שעו על קדוש ישראל" (שם לא, א), "ולא ישעה אל המזבחות" (שם יז, ח), ולא מצאתי שמוש של בי"ת סמוכה לאחריהם. אבל אחר לשון דבור כמתעסק לדבר בדבר נופל לשון שמוש בי"ת, כגון: "הנדברים בך" (יחזקאל לג, ל), "ותדבר מרים ואהרן במשה" (במדבר יב, א), "המלאך הדבר בי" (זכריה ד, א), "לדבר בם" (דברים יא, יט), "ואדברה בעדתיך" (תהלים קיט, מו). אף כאן, "אל ישעו בדברי שקר" – אל יהיו נדברים בדברי שוא והבאי:

יא| **אתם לכו קחו לכם תבן.** וצריכים אתם לילך בזריזות "כי אין נגרע" דבר מכל סכום לבנים שהייתם עושים ליום בהיות התבן נתן לכם מזמן מבית המלך:

יב| **לקשש קש לתבן.** לאסף אסיפה, ללקט לקט לצורך תבן הטיט: **קש.** לשון לקוט, על שם שדבר המתפזר הוא וצריך לקוששו הוא קרוי 'קש' באחר מקומות:

יג| **אצים.** דוחקים: **דבר יום ביומו.** חשבון של כל יום כלו ביומו, כאשר עשיתם בהיות התבן מוכן:

יד| **ויכו שטרי בני ישראל.** השוטרים ישראל היו וחסים על חבריהם מלדחקם, וכשהיו משלימים הלבנים לנוגשים שהם מצריים והיה חסר מן הסכום, היו מלקין אותם על שלא דחקו את עושי המלאכה. לפיכך זכו אותן שוטרים להיות סנהדרין ונאצל מן הרוח אשר על משה והושם עליהם, שנאמר "אספה לי שבעים איש מזקני ישראל", מאותן שידעת הטובה שעשו במצרים "כי הם זקני העם ושטריו" (במדבר יא, טז): **ויכו שטרי בני ישראל.** אשר שמו נגשי פרעה אותם לשוטרים עליהם: **לאמר מדוע וגו'.** למה "ויכו"? שהיו אומרים להם: מדוע לא כליתם גם תמול גם היום חק הקצוב עליכם ללבן כתמול השלישי, שהוא יום שלפני אתמול, והוא היה בהיות התבן נתן להם: **ויכו.** לשון ויפעלו, הכו מיד אחרים, הנוגשים הכום:

טז| **ולבנים אומרים לנו.** הנוגשים, "עשו" כמנין הראשון: **וחטאת עמך.** אלו היה נקוד פתח הייתי אומר שהוא דבוק – ודבר זה חטאת עמך הוא. עכשיו שהוא קמץ, שם דבר הוא, וכך פרושו, ודבר זה מביא חטאת על עמך, כאלו כתוב: 'וחטאת לעמך', כמו: "כבואנה בית לחם" (רות א, יט) שהוא כמו לבית לחם, וכן הרבה:

יח| **ותכן לבנים.** חשבון הלבנים, וכן: "את הכסף המתכן" (מלכים ב' יב, יב) המנוי, כמו שאמור בענין: "ויצרו וימנו את הכסף" (שם פסוק יא):

יט| **ויראו שטרי בני ישראל.** את חבריהם הנרדים על ידם, "ברע" – ראו אותם ברעה וצרה המוצאת אותם בהכבידם העבודה עליהם "לאמר: לא תגרעו" וגו':

כ| **ויפגעו.** אנשים מישראל, "את משה ואת אהרן" וגו'. ורבותינו אמרו, כל 'נצים' ו'נצבים' דתן ואבירם היו, שנאמר בהם: "יצאו נצבים" (במדבר טז, כז):

כב| **למה הרעתה לעם הזה.** ואם תאמר, מה אכפת לך? קובל אני על ששלחתני:

6 **1** God did not criticize Moses for his sharp claims, as they were said from genuine pain:[35] **The Lord said to Moses: Now you will see what I will do to Pharaoh; for** not only will he allow them to leave Egypt, but **with a powerful hand he will send them forth, and with a powerful hand he will drive them from his land,** he will demand that they leave Egypt.[36]

Parashat
Va'era

The Renewal of the Mission in Egypt
EXODUS 6:2–7:7

In the previous passage, God responded to Moses' poignant claim that when he attempted to carry out his mission, the plight of the children of Israel had immediately worsened. In the following section, God initiates the dialogue with Moses, as in His first revelation to him at the burning bush. Now, in Egypt, God repeats the central message of that encounter, and again commands Moses about his mission, which involves both the children of Israel and Pharaoh. God also emphasizes the grand implications of the coming events.

The narrative is interrupted by a partial genealogical list, which positions Moses and Aaron in the budding nation of Israel. Following this list, the chapter repeats God's directive to Moses, the subsequent concerns Moses raised, and God's complex response to those misgivings, again stressing that Aaron will aid Moses in his mission. Nevertheless, God does not conceal from him the difficult road that lies ahead, as the brothers will have to face a stubborn Pharaoh.

2 **God spoke to Moses, and He said to him: I am the Lord,** who appeared to you at the burning bush.

3 **I appeared to Abraham, to Isaac, and to Jacob,**[D] although not in the manner that I appeared to you. To them I made Myself known **as God Almighty,**[D] and that is what they called Me; **but with My name, the Lord,** the Tetragrammaton, **I was not known to them.** In other words, I did not reveal Myself to them to the same degree as to you, Moses.[1] Although the Tetragrammaton is written in Genesis, it is possible that it was unknown to the patriarchs, and it appears in the verse because it was revealed at a later time.[2]

4 Yet **I have also established My covenant with them,** as I pledged, **to give them the land of Canaan, the land of their residence, in which they resided.**

5 **And I also have heard the groans of the children of Israel,**

DISCUSSION

6:3 | I appeared to Abraham, to Isaac, and to Jacob: God mentions the patriarchs not simply to recall His covenant with them, but also to critique Moses: The patriarchs, who were promised the land of Canaan, did not question Me when My promise was not fulfilled in their lifetimes, despite the fact that My revelation to them was less powerful than the one you received. Will you, then, challenge Me simply because your mission was not an immediate success? (*Shemot Rabba* 6:4).

ו א בְּשִׁמְךָ הָרַע לָעָם הַזֶּה וְהַצֵּל לֹא־הִצַּלְתָּ אֶת־עַמֶּךָ: וַיֹּאמֶר יְהוָה אֶל־מֹשֶׁה עַתָּה תִרְאֶה אֲשֶׁר אֶעֱשֶׂה לְפַרְעֹה כִּי בְיָד חֲזָקָה יְשַׁלְּחֵם וּבְיָד חֲזָקָה יְגָרְשֵׁם מֵאַרְצוֹ:

רש״י

כג הָרַע. לְשׁוֹן הִפְעִיל הוּא, הִרְבָּה רָעָה עֲלֵיהֶם, וְתַרְגּוּמוֹ "אַבְאֵשׁ":

פרק ו

א עַתָּה תִרְאֶה וְגוֹ׳. הִרְהַרְתָּ עַל מִדּוֹתַי, לֹא כְּאַבְרָהָם

שֶׁאָמַרְתִּי לוֹ: "כִּי בְיִצְחָק יִקָּרֵא לְךָ זָרַע" (בראשית כא, יב) וְאַחַר כָּךְ אָמַרְתִּי לוֹ: "הַעֲלֵהוּ... לְעֹלָה" (שם כב, ב) וְלֹא הִרְהֵר אַחֲרַי. לְפִיכָךְ – "עַתָּה תִרְאֶה", הָעָשׂוּי לְפַרְעֹה תִרְאֶה, וְלֹא הָעָשׂוּי לְמַלְכֵי שִׁבְעָה אֻמּוֹת כְּשֶׁאֲבִיאֵם לְאָרֶץ:

כִּי בְיָד חֲזָקָה יְשַׁלְּחֵם. מִפְּנֵי יָדִי שֶׁתֶּחֱזַק עָלָיו יְשַׁלְּחֵם: וּבְיָד חֲזָקָה יְגָרְשֵׁם מֵאַרְצוֹ. עַל כָּרְחָם שֶׁל יִשְׂרָאֵל יְגָרְשֵׁם וְלֹא יַסְפִּיקוּ לַעֲשׂוֹת לָהֶם צֵדָה, וְכֵן הוּא אוֹמֵר: "וַתֶּחֱזַק מִצְרַיִם עַל הָעָם" (להלן יב, לג) וְגוֹ׳:

פרשת

וארא

ב ג וַיְדַבֵּר אֱלֹהִים אֶל־מֹשֶׁה וַיֹּאמֶר אֵלָיו אֲנִי יְהוָה: וָאֵרָא אֶל־אַבְרָהָם אֶל־יִצְחָק ד וְאֶל־יַעֲקֹב בְּאֵל שַׁדָּי וּשְׁמִי יְהוָה לֹא נוֹדַעְתִּי לָהֶם: וְגַם הֲקִמֹתִי אֶת־בְּרִיתִי אִתָּם ה לָתֵת לָהֶם אֶת־אֶרֶץ כְּנָעַן אֵת אֶרֶץ מְגֻרֵיהֶם אֲשֶׁר־גָּרוּ בָהּ: וְגַם ׀ אֲנִי שָׁמַעְתִּי

רש״י

ב וַיְדַבֵּר אֱלֹהִים אֶל־מֹשֶׁה. דִּבֶּר אִתּוֹ מִשְׁפָּט עַל שֶׁהִקְשָׁה לְדַבֵּר וְלוֹמַר: "לָמָה הֲרֵעֹתָה לָעָם הַזֶּה" (לעיל ה, כג): וַיֹּאמֶר אֵלָיו אֲנִי ה׳. נֶאֱמָן לְשַׁלֵּם שָׂכָר טוֹב לַמִּתְהַלְּכִים לְפָנַי. וְלֹא לְחִנָּם שְׁלַחְתִּיךָ, כִּי אִם לְקַיֵּם דְּבָרַי הָרִאשׁוֹנִים. וּבַלָּשׁוֹן הַזֶּה מָצִינוּ שֶׁהוּא נִדְרָשׁ בְּכַמָּה מְקוֹמוֹת: "אֲנִי ה׳" נֶאֱמָן לְפָרֵעַ, כְּשֶׁהוּא אֵצֶל עֹנֶשׁ כְּגוֹן: "וְחִלַּלְתָּ אֶת שֵׁם אֱלֹהֶיךָ אֲנִי ה׳" (ויקרא יט, יב): וּכְשֶׁהוּא אֵצֶל קִיּוּם מִצְוֹת כְּגוֹן: "וּשְׁמַרְתֶּם מִצְוֹתַי וַעֲשִׂיתֶם אֹתָם אֲנִי ה׳" (שם כב, לא) נֶאֱמָן לִתֵּן שָׂכָר:

ג וָאֵרָא. אֶל הָאָבוֹת: בְּאֵל שַׁדָּי. הִבְטַחְתִּים הַבְטָחוֹת

וּבְכֻלָּן אָמַרְתִּי לָהֶם: "אֲנִי אֵל שַׁדָּי": וּשְׁמִי ה׳ לֹא נוֹדַעְתִּי לָהֶם. "לֹא הוֹדַעְתִּי" אֵין כְּתִיב כָּאן אֶלָּא "לֹא נוֹדַעְתִּי", לֹא נִכַּרְתִּי לָהֶם בְּמִדַּת אֲמִתּוּת שֶׁלִּי שֶׁעָלֶיהָ נִקְרָא שְׁמִי ה׳, נֶאֱמָן לְאַמֵּת דְּבָרַי, שֶׁהֲרֵי הִבְטַחְתִּים וְלֹא קִיַּמְתִּי:

ד וְגַם הֲקִמֹתִי אֶת בְּרִיתִי וְגוֹ׳. וְגַם כְּשֶׁנִּרְאֵיתִי לָהֶם בְּאֵל שַׁדַּי הִצַּבְתִּי וְהֶעֱמַדְתִּי בְּרִיתִי בֵּינִי וּבֵינֵיהֶם: לָתֵת לָהֶם אֶת אֶרֶץ כְּנָעַן. לְאַבְרָהָם בְּפָרָשַׁת מִילָה נֶאֱמַר: "אֲנִי אֵל שַׁדַּי וְגוֹ׳ וְנָתַתִּי לְךָ וּלְזַרְעֲךָ אַחֲרֶיךָ אֵת אֶרֶץ מְגֻרֶיךָ" (בראשית יז, א, ח-ח): לְיִצְחָק: "כִּי לְךָ וּלְזַרְעֲךָ אֶתֵּן אֶת כָּל הָאֲרָצֹת הָאֵל וַהֲקִמֹתִי אֶת הַשְּׁבֻעָה אֲשֶׁר נִשְׁבַּעְתִּי

לְאַבְרָהָם" (שם כו, ג) וְאוֹתָהּ שְׁבוּעָה שֶׁנִּשְׁבַּעְתִּי לְאַבְרָהָם בְּאֵל שַׁדַּי אָמַרְתִּי; לְיַעֲקֹב: "אֲנִי אֵל שַׁדַּי פְּרֵה וּרְבֵה וְגוֹ׳ וְאֶת הָאָרֶץ אֲשֶׁר וְגוֹ׳" (שם לה, יא-יב), הֲרֵי שֶׁנָּדַרְתִּי לָהֶם וְלֹא קִיַּמְתִּי:

ה וְגַם אֲנִי. כְּמוֹ שֶׁהִצַּבְתִּי וְהֶעֱמַדְתִּי הַבְּרִית יֵשׁ עָלַי לְקַיֵּם. לְפִיכָךְ "שָׁמַעְתִּי אֶת נַאֲקַת בְּנֵי יִשְׂרָאֵל הַנֶּאֱנָקִים "אֲשֶׁר מִצְרַיִם מַעֲבִדִים אֹתָם", וְזָכַרְתִּי אוֹתָהּ הַבְּרִית, כִּי בִּבְרִית בֵּין הַבְּתָרִים אָמַרְתִּי לוֹ: "וְגַם אֶת הַגּוֹי אֲשֶׁר יַעֲבֹדוּ דָּן אָנֹכִי" (שם טו, יד):

DISCUSSION

➧ **I appeared to Abraham, to Isaac, and to Jacob as God Almighty:** God revealed Himself to Abraham and to Jacob as God Almighty (Genesis 17:1, 35:11). Isaac refers to God as God Almighty when he blesses Jacob (Genesis 28:3). Jacob also refers to God in this manner in an address to his children (Genesis 43:14) and to Joseph (Genesis 48:3), and in his blessing of Joseph (Genesis 49:25).

whom the Egyptians are coercing to work and I have remembered My covenant with the patriarchs.

Slave being punished in Egypt, mural, sixteenth to fifteenth century BCE

6 **Therefore, say to the children of Israel: I am the Lord.** I am the Source of all existence, and Master of all strengths, **and** therefore I can guarantee that **I will take you out from under the burdens of Egypt and I will deliver you from their work,** so that you will no longer be slaves. **And** not only that, but **I will** also **redeem you** from Egypt **with an outstretched arm,** with great strength, **and with great punishments** that will be exacted upon the Egyptians. The redemption process will be so powerful that it will be clear to all.

7 **I will take you for Me as** My **people,**[D] **and I will be God for you and you will know that I am the Lord your God, who takes you out from under the burdens of Egypt.** The nation of Israel was not established through natural processes, nor does it operate under such laws. When the Israelites will emerge united from under the burden of Egypt, all will know that the Lord has chosen them as His people.

8 **I will bring you to the land with regard to which I raised My hand**[D] as a sign of My oath **to give it to Abraham, to Isaac, and to Jacob, and I will give it you as** an eternal **heritage: I am the Lord.**

9 **Moses** carried out the directive of God. He **spoke so to the children of Israel, but they did not heed Moses,**[D] they remained unaffected by his statements, **because of lack of patience, and because of hard work.**

10 This verse introduces a new prophecy,[3] although it repeats certain elements from the revelation at the burning bush. **The Lord spoke to Moses, saying:**

11 **Come** and **speak** again **to Pharaoh king of Egypt and he will send forth the children of Israel from his land.**

12 **Moses spoke before the Lord, saying: Behold, the children of Israel did not heed me** despite the fact that I conveyed good tidings to them. **And how,** then, **will Pharaoh heed me** when I come with demands? **And I am one whose lips are obstructed;** I do not speak well (see 4:10), so how can I successfully persuade him to obey?

13 God does not directly address the issues raised by Moses. Rather, He again includes Aaron in the mission, as He did at the end of the revelation at the burning bush. **The Lord spoke to Moses and to Aaron and He commanded them** to speak **to the children of Israel, and to Pharaoh king of Egypt.** The aim of both missions was **to take the children of Israel out of the land of Egypt.**

14 Thus far, the Torah has depicted the events of Moses' life that prepared him for his mission: his birth and upbringing; his stay in Midyan; and his appointment by God at the burning bush and again in Egypt. Before describing Moses' fulfillment of his mission, the Torah presents a genealogical summary of his place among the children of Israel, the family that became a nation in Egypt. **These are the heads of their patrilineal houses** in Egypt: This list, which follows the order of birth of the sons of Jacob, is only partial and concludes with the descendants of Levi, the tribe of Moses and Aaron. It parallels, to a certain extent, the list of Jacob's descendants in Genesis 46:8–11. **The sons of Reuben, firstborn of Israel: Hanokh and Palu, Hetzron and Karmi; these are the families of Reuben.**

Second aliya

DISCUSSION

6:7 | **I will take you for Me as My people:** Until now, Moses' task was simply to free the children of Israel from their bondage. This verse introduces an additional aspect to his mission: Redeeming Israel will fulfill God's promise to the patriarchs, and will serve as proof that God has chosen Israel as His people. This does not contradict the fact that God is Ruler of the entire Universe, and all nations are subservient to Him. Nevertheless, God confers His name specifically upon Israel, His chosen nation. This privileged status is the source of their unique responsibility to God, in the form of the numerous mitzvot they must fulfill.

6:8 | **With regard to which I raised my hand:** In many societies, one would raise his hand as a sign of taking an oath. Clearly, the phrase cannot be understood in its literal sense here, as it is spoken by God (see Onkelos; Rashi; Ibn Ezra, long commentary on Exodus; see also Deuteronomy 32:40; Isaiah 62:8; Ezekiel 20:15, 42).

6:9 | **But they did not heed Moses:** As an enslaved people, the children of Israel did not have a clear internal national identity. Rather, they perceived themselves as a collective tied by familial bonds on the one hand, and the harsh decrees of Pharaoh on the other. The redemption envisioned by Moses appeared too distant from their current reality. The burden of their enslavement weighed so heavily on their spirit that they lacked the strength to attend to these seemingly fantastical images of their national destiny.

ו את־נאקת בני ישראל אשר מצרים מעבדים אתם ואזכר את־בריתי: לכן אמר
לבני־ישראל אני יהוה והוצאתי אתכם מתחת סבלת מצרים והצלתי אתכם
ז מעבדתם וגאלתי אתכם בזרוע נטויה ובשפטים גדלים: ולקחתי אתכם לי
לעם והייתי לכם לאלהים וידעתם כי אני יהוה אלהיכם המוציא אתכם מתחת
ח סבלות מצרים: והבאתי אתכם אל־הארץ אשר נשאתי את־ידי לתת אתה
ט לאברהם ליצחק וליעקב ונתתי אתה לכם מורשה אני יהוה: וידבר משה כן
אל־בני ישראל ולא שמעו אל־משה מקצר רוח ומעבדה קשה:
י יא וידבר יהוה אל־משה לאמר: בא דבר אל־פרעה מלך מצרים וישלח את־
יב בני־ישראל מארצו: וידבר משה לפני יהוה לאמר הן בני־ישראל לא־שמעו
אלי ואיך ישמעני פרעה ואני ערל שפתים:
יג וידבר יהוה אל־משה ואל־אהרן ויצום אל־בני ישראל ואל־פרעה מלך
יד מצרים להוציא את־בני־ישראל מארץ מצרים:
אלה ראשי שני
בית־אבתם בני ראובן בכר ישראל חנוך ופלוא חצרן וכרמי אלה משפחת

רש"י

ו| **לכן.** על פי אותה השבועה: **אמר לבני ישראל אני ה'.** הנאמן בהבטחתי: **והוצאתי אתכם.** כי כן הבטחתי: "ואחרי כן יצאו ברכש גדול" (שם): **סבלת.** טורח משא מצרים:

ח| **נשאתי את ידי.** הרימותיה לשבע בכסאי:

ט| **ולא שמעו אל משה.** לא קבלו תנחומין: **מקצר רוח.** כל מי שהוא מצר, רוחו ונשימתו קצרה ואינו יכול להאריך בנשימתו.

קרוב לענין זה שמעתי בפרשה זו מרבי ברוך ברבי אליעזר, והביא לי ראיה ממקרא זה: "בפעם הזאת אודיעם את ידי ואת גבורתי וידעו כי שמי ה'" (ירמיה טז, כא); למדנו כשהקדוש ברוך הוא מאמן את דבריו, אפלו לפרענות, מודיע ששמו ה', וכל שכן האמנה לטובה. ורבותינו דרשוהו לענין של מעלה שאמר משה: "למה הרעתה" (לעיל ה, כב), אמר לו הקדוש ברוך הוא: חבל על דאבדין ולא משתכחין! יש לי להתאונן על מיתת האבות, הרבה פעמים נגליתי עליהם באל שדי ולא אמרו לי מה שמך, ואתה אמרת: "מה שמו, מה אמר אליהם" (לעיל ג, יג): **וגם הקמתי וגו'.** וכשבקש אברהם לקבר את שרה לא מצא קבר עד שקנה בדמים מרבים; וכן יצחק – עוררו עליו על הבארות אשר חפר; וכן יעקב – "ויקן את חלקת השדה" (בראשית לג, יט) לנטות אהלו; ולא הרהרו אחר מדותי, ואתה אמרת: "למה הרעתה". ואין המדרש מתישב אחר המקרא מפני כמה דברים: אחת, שלא נאמר: 'ושמי ה' לא שאלו לי'. ואם תאמר, לא הודיעם שכך שמו; הרי תחלה כשנגלה לאברהם בין הבתרים נאמר: "אני ה' אשר הוצאתיך מאור כשדים" (שם טו, ז)! ועוד, היאך הסמיכה נמשכת בדברים שהוא סומך לכאן: "וגם אני שמעתי וגו', לכן אמר לבני ישראל"? לכך אני אומר יתישב המקרא על פשוטו דבור על אפניו והדרשה תדרש, שנאמר: "הלוא כה דברי כאש נאם ה' וכפטיש יפצץ סלע" (ירמיה כג, כט), מתחלק לכמה ניצוצות:

יב| **ערל שפתים.** אטום שפתים. וכן כל לשון ערלה אני אומר שהוא אטם: "ערלה אזנם" (שם ו, י) – אטומה משמע; "ערלי לב" (שם ט, כה) – אטומים מהבין; "שתה גם אתה והערל" (חבקוק ב, טז) – והאטם משכרות כוס הקללה; "ערלת בשר", שהגיד אטום ומכסה בה; "וערלתם ערלתו" (ויקרא יט, כג) – עשו לו אטם וכסוי איסור שיבדיל בפני אכילתו; "שלש שנים יהיה לכם ערלים" (שם) – אטום ומכסה ומבדל מלאכלו: **ואיך ישמעני פרעה.** זה אחד מעשרה קל וחמר שבתורה:

יג| **וידבר ה' אל משה ואל אהרן.** לפי שאמר משה: "ואני ערל שפתים" צרף הקדוש ברוך הוא את אהרן עמו להיות לו למליץ: **ויצום אל בני ישראל.** צום עליהם להנהיגם בנחת ולסבל אותם: **ואל פרעה מלך מצרים.** צום עליו לחלק לו כבוד בדבריהם, זה מדרשו. ופשוטו, צום על דבר ישראל ועל שליחותו אל פרעה. ודבר הצווי מהו, מפרש בפרשה שניה לאחר סדר היחס (להלן פסוק כט), אלא מתוך שהזכיר משה ואהרן, הפסיק הענין ב"אלה ראשי בית אבתם" ללמדנו היאך נולדו משה ואהרן ובמי נתיחסו:

יד| **אלה ראשי בית אבתם.** מתוך שהזקק ליחס שבטו של לוי עד משה ואהרן בשביל משה ואהרן, התחיל ליחסם דרך תולדותם מראובן. ובפסיקתא הגדולה (פסיקתא ז) ראיתי, לפי שקנתרם יעקב אביהם לשלשה שבטים הללו בשעת מותו, חזר הכתוב ליחסם כאן לבדם, לומר שחשובים הם:

15 The sons of Simeon: Yemuel, Yamin, Ohad, Yakhin, Tzohar, and Shaul, who was apparently anomalous in that he was **the son of a Canaanite woman; these are the families of Simeon.**

16 The genealogical list becomes more detailed as it nears Moses. **These are the names of the sons of Levi by their descendants: Gershon, Kehat, and Merari.** Since the chapter's focus is on the tribe of Levi, it relates information about him that did not appear with regard to the previous sons of Jacob: **And the years of the life of Levi were one hundred and thirty-seven years.** From among all the sons of Israel, the verse relates only the life spans of Joseph,[4] who was their leader in Egypt, and Levi, who was the forefather of the family of Moses and Aaron.

17 The sons of Gershon: Livni and Shimi, according to their families.

18 The sons of Kehat: Amram, Yitzhar, Hevron, and Uziel; and **the years of the life of Kehat,** which are mentioned because he was the grandfather of Moses and Aaron, **were one hundred and thirty-three years.**

19 The sons of Merari: Mahli and Mushi; these are the families of the Levites by their descendants.

20 Amram took Yokheved his aunt, Levi's daughter, **as his wife,** which was permitted before the giving of the Torah. **And she bore him Aaron and Moses** and their eldest child, Miriam. The verse does not mention her because it is dealing with the lineages of tribes and households, which are determined by patrilineal descent. **And** like Levi, **the years of the life of Amram were one hundred and thirty-seven years.**

21 Once the births of Moses and Aaron have been mentioned, the genealogical list refers only to those closely related to them. **The sons of Yitzhar** son of Kehat: **Korah,** who will later be revealed as a troublesome individual,[5] **Nefeg, and Zikhri.**

22 The sons of Uziel, son of Kehat: Mishael and Eltzafan, who will appear later in the Torah as well,[6] and Sitri.

23 Aaron took Elisheva, daughter of Aminadav, sister of Nahshon, for his wife. Nahshon is later listed as the prince of the tribe of Judah.[7] The fact that he married the sister of a prince of Israel indicates that Aaron was already considered an esteemed member of Israel. **And she,** Elisheva, **bore him Nadav and Avihu, Elazar and Itamar.**

24 The sons of Korah: Asir, Elkana, and Aviasaf; these are the families of the Korahites.[D]

25 Elazar son of Aaron took from the daughters of Putiel, an otherwise unknown person, **for his wife.** Some identify Putiel

as Yitro, who had many names; others say he was a member of the family of Joseph.[8] **And she bore him Pinhas,** who will later perform an important task.[9] It may be assumed that Itamar married as well, but the verse omits this fact because his marriage has no implications for future events. **These are the heads of the house of the fathers of the Levites by their families.**

26 The verse returns to the main story involving Moses and Aaron, listed above as the sons of Amram: These were **that** same

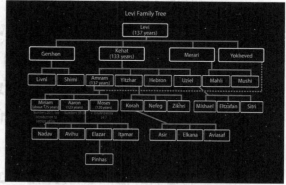

Family tree of Levi

Aaron and Moses, to whom the Lord said: Take out the children of Israel from the land of Egypt with their hosts, not only particular individuals or sections of the people, but the entire nation.

27 It is they who speak to Pharaoh king of Egypt to take the children of Israel out from Egypt: that Moses and Aaron.

28 After interrupting the narrative to present the tribal and familial background of Moses and Aaron, the verse reiterates the end of the earlier dialogue between God and Moses (6:11–12). It was on the day that the Lord spoke to Moses in the land of Egypt.

29 The Lord spoke to Moses, saying: I am the Lord; speak to Pharaoh king of Egypt everything that I speak to you.

30 Moses said before the Lord: Behold, I am one whose lips are obstructed and how will Pharaoh heed me?

7 1 The Lord said to Moses: See, I have put you as a god, meaning an angel[10] or a powerful figure,[11] for Pharaoh, and Aaron your brother will be your prophet, serving as your agent.

Third aliya

DISCUSSION

6:24 | These are the families of the Korahites: The Torah later relates that despite the abnormal death of Korah due to his disgraceful behavior, his sons were spared and they perpetuated the families of the Korahites (Numbers 26:11). In fact, some of the Levites who recited songs in the Temple were known to be from this family (see Psalms 42:1; II Chronicles 20:19).

טו וּבְנֵי שִׁמְעוֹן יְמוּאֵל וְיָמִין וְאֹהַד וְיָכִין וְצֹחַר וְשָׁאוּל בֶּן־הַכְּנַעֲנִית אֵלֶּה

טז מִשְׁפְּחֹת שִׁמְעוֹן: וְאֵלֶּה שְׁמוֹת בְּנֵי־לֵוִי לְתֹלְדֹתָם גֵּרְשׁוֹן וּקְהָת וּמְרָרִי וּשְׁנֵי חַיֵּי

יז לֵוִי שֶׁבַע וּשְׁלֹשִׁים וּמְאַת שָׁנָה: בְּנֵי גֵרְשׁוֹן לִבְנִי וְשִׁמְעִי לְמִשְׁפְּחֹתָם: וּבְנֵי קְהָת

יח עַמְרָם וְיִצְהָר וְחֶבְרוֹן וְעֻזִּיאֵל וּשְׁנֵי חַיֵּי קְהָת שָׁלֹשׁ וּשְׁלֹשִׁים וּמְאַת שָׁנָה: וּבְנֵי

יט מְרָרִי מַחְלִי וּמוּשִׁי אֵלֶּה מִשְׁפְּחֹת הַלֵּוִי לְתֹלְדֹתָם: וַיִּקַּח עַמְרָם אֶת־יוֹכֶבֶד דֹּדָתוֹ

כ לוֹ לְאִשָּׁה וַתֵּלֶד לוֹ אֶת־אַהֲרֹן וְאֶת־מֹשֶׁה וּשְׁנֵי חַיֵּי עַמְרָם שֶׁבַע וּשְׁלֹשִׁים וּמְאַת

כא/כב/כג שָׁנָה: וּבְנֵי יִצְהָר קֹרַח וָנֶפֶג וְזִכְרִי: וּבְנֵי עֻזִּיאֵל מִישָׁאֵל וְאֶלְצָפָן וְסִתְרִי: וַיִּקַּח

אַהֲרֹן אֶת־אֱלִישֶׁבַע בַּת־עַמִּינָדָב אֲחוֹת נַחְשׁוֹן לוֹ לְאִשָּׁה וַתֵּלֶד לוֹ אֶת־נָדָב

כד וְאֶת־אֲבִיהוּא אֶת־אֶלְעָזָר וְאֶת־אִיתָמָר: וּבְנֵי קֹרַח אַסִּיר וְאֶלְקָנָה וַאֲבִיאָסָף

כה אֵלֶּה מִשְׁפְּחֹת הַקָּרְחִי: וְאֶלְעָזָר בֶּן־אַהֲרֹן לָקַח־לוֹ מִבְּנוֹת פּוּטִיאֵל לוֹ לְאִשָּׁה

כו וַתֵּלֶד לוֹ אֶת־פִּינְחָס אֵלֶּה רָאשֵׁי אֲבוֹת הַלְוִיִּם לְמִשְׁפְּחֹתָם: הוּא אַהֲרֹן וּמֹשֶׁה

אֲשֶׁר אָמַר יְהוָה לָהֶם הוֹצִיאוּ אֶת־בְּנֵי יִשְׂרָאֵל מֵאֶרֶץ מִצְרַיִם עַל־צִבְאֹתָם:

כז הֵם הַמְדַבְּרִים אֶל־פַּרְעֹה מֶלֶךְ־מִצְרַיִם לְהוֹצִיא אֶת־בְּנֵי־יִשְׂרָאֵל מִמִּצְרָיִם הוּא

כח/כט מֹשֶׁה וְאַהֲרֹן: וַיְהִי בְּיוֹם דִּבֶּר יְהוָה אֶל־מֹשֶׁה בְּאֶרֶץ מִצְרָיִם: **שלישי** וַיְדַבֵּר

יְהוָה אֶל־מֹשֶׁה לֵּאמֹר אֲנִי יְהוָה דַּבֵּר אֶל־פַּרְעֹה מֶלֶךְ מִצְרַיִם אֵת כָּל־אֲשֶׁר אֲנִי

ל דֹּבֵר אֵלֶיךָ: וַיֹּאמֶר מֹשֶׁה לִפְנֵי יְהוָה הֵן אֲנִי עֲרַל שְׂפָתַיִם וְאֵיךְ יִשְׁמַע אֵלַי פַּרְעֹה:

ז א וַיֹּאמֶר יְהוָה אֶל־מֹשֶׁה רְאֵה נְתַתִּיךָ אֱלֹהִים לְפַרְעֹה וְאַהֲרֹן אָחִיךָ יִהְיֶה נְבִיאֶךָ:

רש"י

טז **וּשְׁנֵי חַיֵּי לֵוִי וְגוֹ'.** לָמָּה נִמְנוּ שְׁנוֹתָיו שֶׁל לֵוִי? לְהוֹדִיעַ כַּמָּה יְמֵי הַשִּׁעְבּוּד, שֶׁכָּל זְמַן שֶׁאֶחָד מִן הַשְּׁבָטִים קַיָּם לֹא הָיָה שִׁעְבּוּד, שֶׁנֶּאֱמַר: "וַיָּמָת יוֹסֵף וְכָל אֶחָיו" (לעיל א,) וְאַחַר כָּךְ: "וַיָּקָם מֶלֶךְ חָדָשׁ" (שם פסוק ח), וְלֵוִי הֶאֱרִיךְ יָמִים עַל כֻּלָּם:

יח **וּשְׁנֵי חַיֵּי קְהָת... וּשְׁנֵי חַיֵּי עַמְרָם וְגוֹ'.** מֵחֶשְׁבּוֹן זֶה אָנוּ לְמֵדִים עַל מוֹשַׁב בְּנֵי יִשְׂרָאֵל אַרְבַּע מֵאוֹת שָׁנָה שֶׁאָמַר הַכָּתוּב (בראשית טו, יג), וְעַיֵּן לְהַלָּן יב, מ), שֶׁלֹּא בְּאֶרֶץ מִצְרַיִם לְבַדָּהּ הָיוּ, אֶלָּא מִיּוֹם שֶׁנּוֹלַד יִצְחָק, שֶׁהֲרֵי קְהָת מִיּוֹלְדֵי מִצְרַיִם הָיָה, חֲשׁוֹב כָּל שְׁנוֹתָיו וְכָל שְׁנוֹת עַמְרָם וּשְׁמוֹנִים שֶׁל מֹשֶׁה, לֹא תִמְצָאֵם אַרְבַּע מֵאוֹת שָׁנָה, וְהַרְבֵּה שָׁנִים נִבְלָעִים לַבָּנִים בִּשְׁנֵי הָאָבוֹת:

כ **יוֹכֶבֶד דֹּדָתוֹ.** "אֲחוֹת אֲבִיוֹ", בַּת לֵוִי, אֲחוֹת קְהָת:

כה **מִבְּנוֹת פּוּטִיאֵל.** מִזֶּרַע יִתְרוֹ שֶׁפִּטֵּם עֲגָלִים לַעֲבוֹדָה זָרָה, וּמִזֶּרַע יוֹסֵף שֶׁפִּטְפֵּט בְּיִצְרוֹ:

כו **הוּא אַהֲרֹן וּמֹשֶׁה.** אֵלּוּ שֶׁהֻזְכְּרוּ לְמַעְלָה שֶׁיָּלְדָה יוֹכֶבֶד לְעַמְרָם, "הוּא אַהֲרֹן וּמֹשֶׁה אֲשֶׁר אָמַר ה'" וְגוֹ'. יֵשׁ מְקוֹמוֹת שֶׁמַּקְדִּים אַהֲרֹן לְמֹשֶׁה וְיֵשׁ מְקוֹמוֹת שֶׁמַּקְדִּים מֹשֶׁה לְאַהֲרֹן, לוֹמַר שֶׁשְּׁקוּלִים כְּאֶחָד: **עַל צִבְאֹתָם.** בְּצִבְאוֹתָם, כָּל צְבָאָם לְשִׁבְטֵיהֶם. יֵשׁ "עַל" שֶׁאֵינוֹ אֶלָּא בִּמְקוֹם אוֹת אַחַת "וְעַל חַרְבְּךָ תִחְיֶה" (בראשית כז, מ), כְּמוֹ בְּחַרְבֶּךָ; "עֲמַדְתֶּם עַל חַרְבְּכֶם" (יחזקאל לג, כו) בְּחַרְבְּכֶם:

כז **הֵם הַמְדַבְּרִים וְגוֹ'.** הֵם שֶׁנִּצְטַוּוּ הֵם שֶׁקִּיְּמוּ. הוּא מֹשֶׁה וְאַהֲרֹן. הֵם בִּשְׁלִיחוּתָם וּבְצִדְקָתָם מִתְּחִלָּה וְעַד סוֹף:

כח **וַיְהִי בְּיוֹם דִּבֶּר וְגוֹ'.** מְחֻבָּר לַמִּקְרָא שֶׁלְּאַחֲרָיו:

כט **וַיְדַבֵּר ה'.** הוּא הַדִּבּוּר עַצְמוֹ הָאָמוּר לְמַעְלָה, אֲנִי ה' דַּבֵּר אֶל פַּרְעֹה מֶלֶךְ מִצְרַיִם, אֶלָּא מִתּוֹךְ שֶׁהִפְסִיק הָעִנְיָן בִּשְׁבִיל לְיַחֲסָם, חָזַר עָלָיו לְהַתְחִיל בּוֹ: **אֲנִי ה'.** כְּדַאי אֲנִי לְשָׁלְחֲךָ וּלְקַיֵּם דִּבְרֵי שְׁלִיחוּתִי:

פרק ז

א **נְתַתִּיךָ אֱלֹהִים לְפַרְעֹה.** שׁוֹפֵט וְרוֹדֶה לִרְדּוֹתוֹ בְּמַכּוֹת וְיִסּוּרִין: **יִהְיֶה נְבִיאֶךָ.** כְּתַרְגּוּמוֹ: "מְתֻרְגְּמָנָךְ", וְכֵן כָּל לְשׁוֹן נְבוּאָה, אָדָם הַמַּכְרִיז וּמַשְׁמִיעַ לָעָם דִּבְרֵי תּוֹכָחוֹת, וְהוּא

2 **You shall speak all that I will command you, and Aaron your brother will speak to Pharaoh and** ultimately **he will send forth the children of Israel from his land.**

3 **But** beforehand, **I will harden Pharaoh's heart** and enable him to withstand severe punishments, **and I will increase My signs and My wonders in the land of Egypt,** through which My might will be revealed to the world.

4 **Pharaoh will not heed you and** therefore **I will put My** stern **hand upon Egypt,** bringing many plagues and punishments upon this land; **and I will take out My hosts, My people, the children of Israel, from the land of Egypt, with great punishments.**

5 **The Egyptians will know that I am the Lord when I extend My hand over Egypt** to strike it, **and I will take out the children of Israel from their midst.**

6 **Moses and Aaron did** exactly **as the Lord had commanded them; so they did.** From this point forward, Moses and Aaron typically did not initiate actions themselves; they accepted the directives of God and carried them out dutifully as His agents.

7 Here the verse provides a biographical note: **Moses was eighty years old and Aaron was eighty-three years old when they spoke to Pharaoh.** Even though the average human lifespan was longer in those days, Moses and Aaron were by no means young. They began their public service at an age when the active years of most other people would be coming to an end. As the verse in Psalms states: "The days of our lives are seventy years, or if in might, eighty years."[12] Indeed, this verse is ascribed to Moses himself.[13]

The Miraculous Sign before the Plagues
EXODUS 7:8–13

Before God afflicts Pharaoh and Egypt with plagues, He provides Moses and Aaron with a miraculous sign that they should present before Pharaoh. It is in some ways similar to the first sign that God produced for Moses at the burning bush.

Fourth aliya 8 **The Lord spoke to Moses and to Aaron, saying:**

9 **When** you come before **Pharaoh and he will speak to you, saying: Provide you a wonder,** to prove that you are indeed God's messengers, **you shall say to Aaron: Take your staff and cast it before Pharaoh, and it will become a crocodile.**[D]

10 **Moses and Aaron came to Pharaoh and they did so, as the Lord had commanded; Aaron cast his staff before Pharaoh and before his servants and it became a crocodile.**

11 **Pharaoh,** mimicking Moses' instruction to Aaron to produce a miraculous sign,[14] **also summoned the wise men and the** sorcerers of his court; **and they, the magicians of Egypt, also did so with their artifices,** by sleight of hand.[15]

12 **The** magicians followed suit, as **each man cast his staff, and they became crocodiles; and Aaron's staff,** in the form of a crocodile, **swallowed their staffs,**[D] which had turned into crocodiles.

13 **But** the miraculous sign did not impress Pharaoh, perhaps because his sorcerers were able to produce the same result. Rather, **Pharaoh's heart hardened,**[D] **and he did not heed them, as the Lord had spoken** from the outset, saying that Pharaoh would not easily capitulate.

The Plague of Blood
EXODUS 7:14–24

After the minor, private sign produced by Moses and Aaron before Pharaoh and his court, a series of widespread plagues are now inflicted upon all Egypt. Each plague serves a dual purpose: To confirm God's power over the laws of nature, and to deal a severe blow to the Egyptian people, in order to pressure them and their king into releasing Israel from bondage.

The first plague, blood, alters not only the appearance of all the waters of Egypt, but their very chemical makeup. The water is, in every sense, turned to blood. The ruin of the Nile, the life source of Egypt, is a particularly severe disaster that has cultural, economic, political, and religious implications.

14 It is uncertain whether Pharaoh expressly rejected the demands of Moses and Aaron, or if he merely avoided addressing their requests in a direct manner. God therefore clarifies the matter.

The Lord said to Moses: Pharaoh's heart is stubborn and he will not listen; **he refused to send forth the people.**

DISCUSSION

7:9 | The miracle of the staff: Although this sign is apparently very similar to the one produced for Moses at the burning bush (4:3), there are a number of differences between them. The sign at the burning bush was produced with the staff of Moses, whereas here Aaron's staff was used. Additionally, the earlier sign was intended to persuade the skeptics among the people of Israel; this marvel was to be performed before Pharaoh. Furthermore, Moses' staff, which was transformed in the desert, turned into a *naḥash*, a snake, whereas Aaron's staff, whose transformation occurred in Egypt, near the Nile, became a *tannin*, translated here as a crocodile. Perhaps the staff of Aaron was transformed into a *tannin* ◂●

ב אַתָּה תְדַבֵּר אֵת כָּל־אֲשֶׁר אֲצַוֶּךָּ וְאַהֲרֹן אָחִיךָ יְדַבֵּר אֶל־פַּרְעֹה וְשִׁלַּח אֶת־בְּנֵי־
ג יִשְׂרָאֵל מֵאַרְצוֹ: וַאֲנִי אַקְשֶׁה אֶת־לֵב פַּרְעֹה וְהִרְבֵּיתִי אֶת־אֹתֹתַי וְאֶת־מוֹפְתַי
ד בְּאֶרֶץ מִצְרָיִם: וְלֹא־יִשְׁמַע אֲלֵכֶם פַּרְעֹה וְנָתַתִּי אֶת־יָדִי בְּמִצְרָיִם וְהוֹצֵאתִי
ה אֶת־צִבְאֹתַי אֶת־עַמִּי בְנֵי־יִשְׂרָאֵל מֵאֶרֶץ מִצְרַיִם בִּשְׁפָטִים גְּדֹלִים: וְיָדְעוּ מִצְרַיִם
כִּי־אֲנִי יהוה בִּנְטֹתִי אֶת־יָדִי עַל־מִצְרָיִם וְהוֹצֵאתִי אֶת־בְּנֵי־יִשְׂרָאֵל מִתּוֹכָם:
ו ז וַיַּעַשׂ מֹשֶׁה וְאַהֲרֹן כַּאֲשֶׁר צִוָּה יהוה אֹתָם כֵּן עָשׂוּ: וּמֹשֶׁה בֶּן־שְׁמֹנִים שָׁנָה
וְאַהֲרֹן בֶּן־שָׁלֹשׁ וּשְׁמֹנִים שָׁנָה בְּדַבְּרָם אֶל־פַּרְעֹה:
ח ט וַיֹּאמֶר יהוה אֶל־מֹשֶׁה וְאֶל־אַהֲרֹן לֵאמֹר: כִּי יְדַבֵּר אֲלֵכֶם פַּרְעֹה לֵאמֹר תְּנוּ לָכֶם ה רביעי
י מוֹפֵת וְאָמַרְתָּ אֶל־אַהֲרֹן קַח אֶת־מַטְּךָ וְהַשְׁלֵךְ לִפְנֵי־פַרְעֹה יְהִי לְתַנִּין: וַיָּבֹא
מֹשֶׁה וְאַהֲרֹן אֶל־פַּרְעֹה וַיַּעֲשׂוּ כֵן כַּאֲשֶׁר צִוָּה יהוה וַיַּשְׁלֵךְ אַהֲרֹן אֶת־מַטֵּהוּ
יא לִפְנֵי פַרְעֹה וְלִפְנֵי עֲבָדָיו וַיְהִי לְתַנִּין: וַיִּקְרָא גַּם־פַּרְעֹה לַחֲכָמִים וְלַמְכַשְּׁפִים
יב וַיַּעֲשׂוּ גַם־הֵם חַרְטֻמֵּי מִצְרַיִם בְּלַהֲטֵיהֶם כֵּן: וַיַּשְׁלִיכוּ אִישׁ מַטֵּהוּ וַיִּהְיוּ לְתַנִּינִם
יג וַיִּבְלַע מַטֵּה־אַהֲרֹן אֶת־מַטֹּתָם: וַיֶּחֱזַק לֵב פַּרְעֹה וְלֹא שָׁמַע אֲלֵהֶם כַּאֲשֶׁר דִּבֶּר
יד יהוה: וַיֹּאמֶר יהוה אֶל־מֹשֶׁה כָּבֵד לֵב פַּרְעֹה מֵאֵן לְשַׁלַּח הָעָם:

רש"י

מגזרת "ניב שפתים" (ישעיה נז, יט), "ינוב חכמה" (משלי י, לא), "ויכל מהתנבות" דשמואל (שמואל א' י, יג), ובלעז קורחין לו פרידיג"ר:

ב| **אתה תדבר.** פעם אחת כל שליחות ושליחות לפי ששמעת מפי, ואהרן אחיך ימליצנו ויטעימנו באזני פרעה:

ג| **ואני אקשה.** מאחר שהרשיע והתריס כנגדי, וגלוי לפני שאין נחת רוח באומות לתת לב שלם לשוב, טוב לי שיתקשה לבו למען הרבות בו אותותי ותכירו אתם גבורותי. וכן מדתו של הקדוש ברוך הוא, מביא פורענות על האומות כדי שישמעו ישראל וייראו, שנאמר: "הכרתי גוים נשמו פנותם... אמרתי אך תיראי אותי תקחי מוסר" (צפניה ג, ו-ז). ואף על פי כן, בחמש מכות הראשונות לא נאמר: 'ויחזק ה' את לב פרעה', אלא: "ויחזק לב פרעה":

ד| **את ידי.** יד ממש, להכות בהם:

ט| **מופת.** אות, להודיע שיש צורך במי ששולח אתכם.
לתנין. נחש:

יא| **בלהטיהם.** "בלחשיהון", ואין לו דמיון במקרא. ויש לדמות לו: "להט החרב המתהפכת" (בראשית ג, כד), דומה שהיא מתהפכת על ידי לחש:

יב| **ויבלע מטה אהרן.** מאחר שחזר ונעשה מטה בלע את כלן:

יד| **כבד.** תרגומו "יקיר" ולא 'איתיקר', מפני שהוא שם דבר, כמו: "כי כבד ממך הדבר" (להלן יח, יח):

DISCUSSION

rather than a *naḥash* because Pharaoh considered himself "the great crocodile [*tannim*] that lies in the midst of his rivers, that has said: My river is my own, and I made it for myself" (Ezekiel 29:3). Alternatively, *tannin* is synonymous with *naḥash* (Rashi; see Onkelos; *Targum Yonatan*; see also Ibn Ezra, long commentary on Exodus, verse 10), or *tannin* denotes a particularly large *naḥash* (see Deuteronomy 32:33, and Rashi ad loc.; Psalms 91:13, and *Metzudat Zion* ad loc.; Isaiah 27:1).

7:12| **And Aaron's staff swallowed their staffs:** The Midrash (*Shemot Rabba* 9:7), cited by Rashi, interprets the verse literally: After each crocodile turned back into a staff, Aaron's staff swallowed the staffs of Pharaoh's sorcerers.

7:13| **But Pharaoh's heart hardened:** At the time of the Pharaohs, sorcery was regarded much like the natural sciences in the

15 Therefore, **go to Pharaoh in the morning: Behold, he goes out to the water** to bathe, relieve himself, relax, or worship. **And you shall stand facing him on the bank of the Nile; and the staff that was transformed into a serpent, take in your hand.**

16 **You shall say to him: The Lord, God of the Hebrews, sent me to you, saying: Send forth My people and they will serve Me in the wilderness; and behold, you have not heeded until now.**

17 **So says the Lord: With this you will know that I am the Lord: Behold, I will strike with the staff that is in my hand on the water that is in the Nile, and it will be transformed into blood.**

18 Consequently, **the fish that are in the Nile will die,** as they will be unable to survive in the river of blood, **and the Nile will reek** from the many dead fish. **And Egypt will be unable to drink water from the Nile;** the stench alone will prevent them from doing so.

19 **The Lord said to Moses: Say to Aaron,** your agent who will implement this plague: **Take your staff and extend your hand over the water of Egypt.** By raising your hand in the direction of the water, you will express the intent that the staff should affect all the waters of Egypt. **Over their rivers, over their canals** that bear water from the Nile, **and over their lakes and over all their pools of water, and they will** all **become blood; and there will be blood in the entire land of Egypt, in the wood and in the stones.** Even the water in the gardens, which is near wood and stone, will turn to blood.[16] Alternatively, even water inside wooden and stone vessels will become blood.[17] In sum, the plague of blood will not harm the Nile alone, but will affect all water located on Egyptian terrain.

20 **Moses and Aaron did so, as the Lord had commanded; and**

Irrigation system in Egypt

he, Aaron, **raised the staff and struck the water that was in the Nile before the eyes of Pharaoh and before the eyes of his servants and all the water that was in the Nile was transformed into blood.**

21 **The fish that were in the Nile died, and the Nile reeked; the Egyptians were unable to drink water from the Nile; the blood was** in every water source **in the entire land of Egypt.**

22 **The magicians of Egypt** in Pharaoh's court **did so;**[D] they turned water to blood **with their artifices, and** as a result, **Pharaoh's heart hardened and he did not heed them, as the Lord had spoken.**

23 **Pharaoh turned** from the Nile **and came to his house and he did not pay attention to this either.**[D]

24 **All of Egypt dug around the Nile,** searching **for clean water to drink, as they were unable to drink from the water of the Nile.**

The Plague of Frogs
EXODUS 7:25–8:11

The plague of frogs is particularly harmful and unpleasant. The sounds these creatures emit render it impossible for the Egyptians to direct their attention elsewhere. Nevertheless, it is not a deadly plague, and it does not endanger the physical well-being of the Egyptian people.

25 **Seven days were completed after the Lord struck the Nile.** In other words, the plague lasted seven days.[18] Nevertheless, Pharaoh did not relent.

DISCUSSION

modern era: A body of knowledge whose mastery allows one to manipulate the forces of nature. Consequently, no supernatural or divine sign would be sufficient to sway Pharaoh. Even if Moses and Aaron had produced a more magnificent sign than Pharaoh's sorcerers, he could simply have attributed this to trickery or powerful magic employed by them, rather than as proof that they were messengers of God.

7:22 | **And the magicians of Egypt did so:** From where did the magicians find water, if it had all turned into blood? One answer is that only the waters on the surface turned to blood during the plague; subterranean water was unaffected. Therefore, the magicians were able to draw water from underground (Ibn Ezra). Alternatively, the waters of Egypt were turned to blood only momentarily. Nevertheless, this was

sufficient to kill all the fish and render the waters of Egypt undrinkable (*Bekhor Shor*).

7:23 | **Pharaoh turned and came to his house and he did not pay attention to this either:** It is possible that Pharaoh was unimpressed by the plague because he personally was unaffected by it; perhaps he was able to allocate water for himself from surrounding areas. Alternatively, he dismissed the miracle because his magicians were able to produce a similar effect.

טו לֵךְ אֶל־פַּרְעֹה בַּבֹּקֶר הִנֵּה יֹצֵא הַמַּיְמָה וְנִצַּבְתָּ לִקְרָאתוֹ עַל־שְׂפַת הַיְאֹר וְהַמַּטֶּה
טז אֲשֶׁר־נֶהְפַּךְ לְנָחָשׁ תִּקַּח בְּיָדֶךָ׃ וְאָמַרְתָּ אֵלָיו יְהוָה אֱלֹהֵי הָעִבְרִים שְׁלָחַנִי אֵלֶיךָ
יז לֵאמֹר שַׁלַּח אֶת־עַמִּי וְיַעַבְדֻנִי בַּמִּדְבָּר וְהִנֵּה לֹא־שָׁמַעְתָּ עַד־כֹּה׃ כֹּה אָמַר
יְהוָה בְּזֹאת תֵּדַע כִּי אֲנִי יְהוָה הִנֵּה אָנֹכִי מַכֶּה ׀ בַּמַּטֶּה אֲשֶׁר־בְּיָדִי עַל־הַמַּיִם
יח אֲשֶׁר בַּיְאֹר וְנֶהֶפְכוּ לְדָם׃ וְהַדָּגָה אֲשֶׁר־בַּיְאֹר תָּמוּת וּבָאַשׁ הַיְאֹר וְנִלְאוּ מִצְרַיִם
יט לִשְׁתּוֹת מַיִם מִן־הַיְאֹר׃ וַיֹּאמֶר יְהוָה אֶל־מֹשֶׁה אֱמֹר אֶל־אַהֲרֹן
קַח מַטְּךָ וּנְטֵה־יָדְךָ עַל־מֵימֵי מִצְרַיִם עַל־נַהֲרֹתָם ׀ עַל־יְאֹרֵיהֶם וְעַל־אַגְמֵיהֶם
וְעַל כָּל־מִקְוֵה מֵימֵיהֶם וְיִהְיוּ־דָם וְהָיָה דָם בְּכָל־אֶרֶץ מִצְרַיִם וּבָעֵצִים וּבָאֲבָנִים׃
כ וַיַּעֲשׂוּ־כֵן מֹשֶׁה וְאַהֲרֹן כַּאֲשֶׁר ׀ צִוָּה יְהוָה וַיָּרֶם בַּמַּטֶּה וַיַּךְ אֶת־הַמַּיִם אֲשֶׁר
כא בַּיְאֹר לְעֵינֵי פַרְעֹה וּלְעֵינֵי עֲבָדָיו וַיֵּהָפְכוּ כָּל־הַמַּיִם אֲשֶׁר־בַּיְאֹר לְדָם׃ וְהַדָּגָה
אֲשֶׁר־בַּיְאֹר מֵתָה וַיִּבְאַשׁ הַיְאֹר וְלֹא־יָכְלוּ מִצְרַיִם לִשְׁתּוֹת מַיִם מִן־הַיְאֹר וַיְהִי
כב הַדָּם בְּכָל־אֶרֶץ מִצְרָיִם׃ וַיַּעֲשׂוּ־כֵן חַרְטֻמֵּי מִצְרַיִם בְּלָטֵיהֶם וַיֶּחֱזַק לֵב־פַּרְעֹה
כג וְלֹא־שָׁמַע אֲלֵהֶם כַּאֲשֶׁר דִּבֶּר יְהוָה׃ וַיִּפֶן פַּרְעֹה וַיָּבֹא אֶל־בֵּיתוֹ וְלֹא־שָׁת לִבּוֹ
כד גַּם־לָזֹאת׃ וַיַּחְפְּרוּ כָל־מִצְרַיִם סְבִיבֹת הַיְאֹר מַיִם לִשְׁתּוֹת כִּי לֹא יָכְלוּ לִשְׁתֹּת
כה מִמֵּימֵי הַיְאֹר׃ וַיִּמָּלֵא שִׁבְעַת יָמִים אַחֲרֵי הַכּוֹת־יְהוָה אֶת־הַיְאֹר׃

רש״י

טו | **הִנֵּה יֹצֵא הַמַּיְמָה.** לִנְקָבָיו, שֶׁהָיָה עוֹשֶׂה עַצְמוֹ אֱלוֹהַּ וְאוֹמֵר שֶׁאֵינוֹ צָרִיךְ לִנְקָבָיו, וּמַשְׁכִּים וְיוֹצֵא לַנִּילוּס וְעוֹשֶׂה שָׁם צְרָכָיו:

טז | **עַד כֹּה.** עַד הֵנָּה. וּמִדְרָשׁוֹ, עַד שֶׁתִּשְׁמַע מִמֶּנִּי מַכַּת בְּכוֹרוֹת שֶׁאֶפְתַּח בָּהּ בְּ"כֹה אָמַר ה׳ כַּחֲצֹת הַלַּיְלָה" וְגוֹ׳ (להלן יא, ד):

יז | **וְנֶהֶפְכוּ לְדָם.** לְפִי שֶׁאֵין גְּשָׁמִים יוֹרְדִים בְּמִצְרַיִם וְנִילוּס עוֹלֶה וּמַשְׁקֶה אֶת הָאָרֶץ וּמִצְרַיִם עוֹבְדִים לַנִּילוּס, לְפִיכָךְ הִלְקָה אֶת יִרְאָתָם וְאַחַר כָּךְ הִלְקָה אוֹתָם:

יח | **וְנִלְאוּ מִצְרַיִם.** לְבַקֵּשׁ רְפוּאָה לְמֵי הַיְאוֹר שֶׁיִּהְיוּ רְאוּיִין לִשְׁתוֹת:

יט | **אֱמֹר אֶל אַהֲרֹן.** לְפִי שֶׁהֵגֵן הַיְאוֹר עַל מֹשֶׁה כְּשֶׁנִּשְׁלַךְ לְתוֹכוֹ, לְפִיכָךְ לֹא לָקָה עַל יָדוֹ לֹא בַּדָּם וְלֹא בַּצְפַרְדְּעִים, וְלָקָה עַל יְדֵי אַהֲרֹן: **נַהֲרֹתָם.** הֵם נְהָרוֹת הַמּוֹשְׁכִים כְּעֵין נְהָרוֹת שֶׁלָּנוּ: **יְאֹרֵיהֶם.** הֵם נְגָרִים וּבְרֵכוֹת הָעֲשׂוּיִם בִּידֵי אָדָם מִשְּׂפַת הַנָּהָר לַשָּׂדוֹת, וְנִילוּס מֵימָיו מִתְבָּרְכִים וְעוֹלֶה דֶּרֶךְ הַיְאוֹרִים וּמַשְׁקֶה הַשָּׂדוֹת: **אַגְמֵיהֶם.** קְווּצַת מַיִם שֶׁאֵינָן נוֹבְעִין וְאֵין מוֹשְׁכִין אֶלָּא עוֹמְדִין בְּמָקוֹם אֶחָד, וְקוֹרִין לוֹ אשטנ"ק: **בְּכָל אֶרֶץ מִצְרַיִם.** אַף בַּמֶּרְחֲצָאוֹת וּבָאַמְבַּטְאוֹת שֶׁבַּבָּתִּים: **וּבָעֵצִים וּבָאֲבָנִים.** מַיִם שֶׁבִּכְלֵי עֵץ וּבִכְלֵי אֶבֶן:

כב | **בְּלָטֵיהֶם.** לַחַשׁ שֶׁאוֹמְרִין אוֹתוֹ בַּלָּט וּבַחֲשַׁאי. רַבּוֹתֵינוּ אָמְרוּ: 'בְּלָטֵיהֶם' – מַעֲשֵׂה שֵׁדִים, 'בְּלַהֲטֵיהֶם' – מַעֲשֵׂה כְשָׁפִים: **וַיֶּחֱזַק לֵב פַּרְעֹה.** לוֹמַר עַל יְדֵי מְכַשְּׁפוּת אַתֶּם עוֹשִׂים כֵּן; תֶּבֶן אַתֶּם מַכְנִיסִים לְעָפְרַיִם, עִיר שֶׁכֻּלָּהּ תֶּבֶן?! אַף אַתֶּם מְבִיאִין מְכַשְּׁפוּת לְמִצְרַיִם שֶׁכֻּלָּהּ כְּשָׁפִים?!:

כג | **גַּם לָזֹאת.** לְמוֹפֵת הַמַּטֶּה שֶׁנֶּהְפַּךְ לְתַנִּין, וְלֹא לָזֶה שֶׁל דָּם:

כה | **וַיִּמָּלֵא.** מִנְיַן שִׁבְעַת יָמִים שֶׁלֹּא שָׁב הַיְאוֹר לְקַדְמוּתוֹ, שֶׁהָיְתָה הַמַּכָּה מְשַׁמֶּשֶׁת רְבִיעַ חֹדֶשׁ, וּשְׁלֹשָׁה חֲלָקִים הָיָה מֵעִיד וּמַתְרֶה בָּהֶם:

26 **The Lord said to Moses: Go to Pharaoh and** once again **say to him: So said the Lord: Send forth My people and they will serve Me.**[D]

27 **If you refuse**[19] **to send them forth,** alternatively, this phrase may be translated to mean if you are a defiant person, one who refuses to send them forth,[20] **behold, I will afflict all your borders with frogs.**

28 **The Nile will swarm with frogs.** Since there will be so many frogs, they will not stay in the river, but will spread throughout the entire land: **And they will arise and come into your house and** once there, they will not remain confined to one location; rather, they will enter **into your bedroom, and upon your bed, and into the house of your servants and your people, and into your ovens and into your kneading bowls.**

29 Not only will the frogs enter people's houses, foods, and vessels, but **upon you, upon your people, and** also **upon all your servants the frogs will arise.** They will even enter people's mouths.[21] In sum, the frogs will know no boundaries.

8 1 **The Lord said to Moses: Say to Aaron: Extend your hand with your staff over the rivers, over the canals, and over the lakes, and** through this action, you will **raise the frogs upon the land of Egypt.**

2 **Aaron extended his hand over the water of Egypt, and the frogs arose and,** in their abundance, **covered the** entire **land of Egypt.**

3 **The magicians did the same with their artifices and they raised the frogs upon the land of Egypt.** This was rather unhelpful to Pharaoh, as instead of ridding Egypt of its frog infestation, they caused more frogs to ascend upon the land.

4 **Pharaoh summoned Moses and Aaron, and he said: Plead with the Lord that He remove the frogs from me and from my people, and I will send forth the people, and they will sacrifice to the Lord.** For the first time, Pharaoh expresses some measure of submission to Moses and Aaron.

5 **Moses said to Pharaoh: Challenge me,** you have the opportunity to glorify yourself in victory over me[22] by requesting a matter that you consider beyond my reach: **For when shall I plead for you and for your servants and for your people, to excise the frogs from you and from your houses?** Set a time when the frogs will be destroyed or removed, and from that moment **only in the Nile will they remain.** Moses wanted to show Pharaoh who was in control of this plague. The ability of Moses and Aaron to remove the frogs at will would increase Pharaoh's fear of them and further demonstrate God's power.

6 **He,** Pharaoh, **said: Tomorrow,**[D] **and he,** Moses, **said:** It shall be **as your word, so that you will know that there is none like the Lord our God.**

7 Tomorrow, **the frogs will depart from you and from your houses, and from your servants and from your people; only in the Nile will they remain.** They will not harm anyone there, but will serve as a constant reminder and a threat that might be visited upon Egypt at any time.

Fifth aliya

8 **Moses and Aaron left Pharaoh's presence and Moses cried out to the Lord over the matter of the frogs that He had inflicted upon Pharaoh.** Moses cried out in prayer before God because the removal of a plague at a specific time required a special request.

9 **The Lord did in accordance with the word of Moses, and the frogs died from the houses, from the courtyards and from the fields.**

10 **They piled them into heaps, and the land reeked** from the smell of the dead frogs.

11 However, **Pharaoh saw that there was respite,** as the frogs had gone, **and he made his heart stubborn and he did not heed them,** despite the fact that on this occasion he had asked Moses to plead on his behalf. This change of heart was **as the Lord had spoken.**

DISCUSSION

7:26 | Send forth My people and they will serve Me: It is clear from the repeated demand: "Send forth My people and they will serve Me," that the ultimate purpose of the redemption was not merely to free a people from slavery; it was so that the children of Israel would be free to serve God. This point is as important for the children of Israel to understand as it is for Pharaoh. The children of Israel must realize that God alone, not the Egyptians, will free them from Egypt, and that God is redeeming them in order that they should serve Him.

8:6 | Tomorrow: Why didn't Pharaoh request the immediate removal of the frogs? It is likely that Pharaoh outsmarted himself here. He wanted to test whether the plague of frogs was indeed due to the power of Moses and Aaron, or if they were simply experts at forecasting natural events, which remained completely beyond their control. He assumed that Moses made this offer on the day on which he forecast that the plague would naturally subside, thinking that Pharaoh would desire their immediate removal. In order to test whether Moses and Aaron were truly in control, Pharaoh stubbornly requested the removal of the plague only on the next day (see Ibn Ezra; Ramban).

כו ויאמר יהוה אל־משה בא אל־פרעה ואמרת אליו כה אמר יהוה שלח את־עמי
כז כח ויעבדני: ואם־מאן אתה לשלח הנה אנכי נגף את־כל־גבולך בצפרדעים: ושרץ
היאר צפרדעים ועלו ובאו בביתך ובחדר משכבך ועל־מטתך ובבית עבדיך
כט ובעמך ובתנוריך ובמשארותיך: ובכה ובעמך ובכל־עבדיך יעלו הצפרדעים:
ח א ויאמר יהוה אל־משה אמר אל־אהרן נטה את־ידך במטך על־הנהרת על־
ב היארים ועל־האגמים והעל את־הצפרדעים על־ארץ מצרים: ויט אהרן
ג את־ידו על מימי מצרים ותעל הצפרדע ותכס את־ארץ מצרים: ויעשו־כן
ד החרטמים בלטיהם ויעלו את־הצפרדעים על־ארץ מצרים: ויקרא פרעה
למשה ולאהרן ויאמר העתירו אל־יהוה ויסר הצפרדעים ממני ומעמי ואשלחה
ה את־העם ויזבחו ליהוה: ויאמר משה לפרעה התפאר עלי למתי | אעתיר לך
ו ולעבדיך ולעמך להכרית הצפרדעים ממך ומבתיך רק ביאר תשארנה: ויאמר
ז למחר ויאמר כדברך למען תדע כי־אין כיהוה אלהינו: וסרו הצפרדעים ממך חמישי
ח ומבתיך ומעבדיך ומעמך רק ביאר תשארנה: ויצא משה ואהרן מעם פרעה
ט ויצעק משה אל־יהוה על־דבר הצפרדעים אשר־שם לפרעה: ויעש יהוה כדבר
י משה וימתו הצפרדעים מן־הבתים מן־החצרת ומן־השדת: ויצברו אתם
יא חמרם חמרם ותבאש הארץ: וירא פרעה כי היתה הרוחה והכבד את־לבו

רש"י

כז | **ואם מאן אתה.** ואם סרבן אתה. 'מאן' כמו ממאן, מסרב, אלא כנוי האדם על שם המפעל, כמו: "שלו" (איוב טז, יב), "ושקט" (ירמיה מח, יא), "סר וזעף" (מלכים א' כ, מג): **נגף את כל גבולך.** מכה. וכן כל לשון מגפה אינו לשון מיתה אלא לשון מכה, וכן: "ונגפו אשה הרה" (להלן כא, כב) אינו מיתה, וכן: "ובטרם יתנגפו רגליכם" (ירמיה יג, טז), "פן תגף באבן רגלך" (תהלים צא, יב), "ולאבן נגף" (ישעיה ח, יד):

כח | **ועלו.** מן היאור: **בביתך.** ואחר כך "בבית עבדיך", הוא התחיל בעצה תחלה – "ויאמר אל עמו" (לעיל א, ט) וממנו התחילה הפרענות:

כט | **ובכה ובעמך.** בתוך מעיהם נכנסין ומקרקרין:

פרק ח

ב | **ותעל הצפרדע.** צפרדע אחת היתה והיו מכין אותה והיא מתזת נחילים נחילים, זהו מדרשו. ופשוטו יש לומר, שרוץ הצפרדעים קורא לשון יחידות. וכן: "ותהי הכנם" (להלן פסוק יד) הרחישה, פדוליר"א בלעז, ואף "ותעל הצפרדע" גרינוליי"רא בלעז:

ה | **התפאר עלי.** כמו: "היתפאר הגרזן על החצב בו" (ישעיה י, טו), משתבח לומר: אני גדול ממך. ונטי"ר בלעז. וכן "התפאר עלי", השתבח להתחכם ולשאול דבר גדול ולומר שלא אוכל לעשותו: **למתי אעתיר לך.** את אשר אעתיר לך היום על הכרתת הצפרדעים, למתי תרצה שיכרתו, ותראה אם אשלים דברי למועד שתקבע לי. אלו נאמר 'מתי אעתיר', היה משמע: מתי אתפלל? עכשיו שנאמר 'למתי', אני היום אתפלל עליך שיכרתו הצפרדעים לזמן שתקבע לי, אמור לאיזה יום תרצה שיכרתו. "אעתיר", "העתירו", "והעתרתי", ולא נאמר: 'אעתר', 'עתרו', 'ועתרתי', מפני שכל לשון 'עתר' הרבות פלל הוא, וכאשר יאמר: הרבו, ארבה, והרביתי, לשון מפעיל, כן יאמר: העתירו, אעתיר, אעתיר דברים, ואף לכלם: "והעתרתם עלי דבריכם" (יחזקאל לה, יג), הרביתם:

ו | **ויאמר למחר.** התפלל היום שיכרתו למחר:

ח | **ויצא... ויצעק.** מיד, שיכרתו למחר:

י | **חמרם חמרם.** צבורים צבורים, כתרגומו "דגורין", גלין:

יא | **והכבד את לבו.** לשון פעול הוא, "הלך הלוך" (ירמיה

The Plague of Lice

EXODUS 8:12–15

Like the previous plague, the plague of lice does not pose a mortal danger, but causes discomfort and even pain.

12 **The Lord said to Moses: Say to Aaron: Extend your staff and strike the dust of the earth, and it will become lice**[B] **in the entire land of Egypt.**
13 **They,** Moses and Aaron, **did so. Aaron extended his hand with his staff and struck the dust of the earth, and the lice were upon man and upon animal; all the dust of the earth was lice in the entire land of Egypt.**
14 **The magicians** in Pharaoh's court **did so with their artifices:** They attempted **to draw out the lice,** to mimic the plague by producing their own lice,[23] in order to mitigate the influence of the wonder produced by Moses and Aaron by showing that this, too, was within their capabilities, **but they could not.** Alternatively, they attempted to remove the lice but could not;[24] **the lice infested man and animal.**
15 **The magicians said to Pharaoh: It is the finger of God.** In other words, this infestation was not caused by an act of magic. Nevertheless, it is not a sign of divine intervention, as it is still within the bounds of natural occurrences.[25] Pharaoh accepted the magicians' claim, and refused to be swayed by the fact that they were incapable of producing or removing the lice. Perhaps he thought that their failure was due to a lack of skill, whereas a more expert magician might have been successful. In any case, **Pharaoh's heart hardened and he did not heed them,** and he refused to release the children of Israel, **as the Lord had spoken.**

Magnified image of a louse

The Plague of Wild Beasts

EXODUS 8:16–28

In the two previous plagues, Egypt was struck by particular species, frogs and lice. Both of these creatures are rather small, more of a nuisance than an actual danger. The next plague, however, is terrifying: Animals of many sizes and from many species roam throughout the cities of Egypt. Whether or not these animals are natural predators, they pose a threat to the Egyptians, and some of them are even capable of killing humans.

16 **The Lord said to Moses: Arise early in the morning and stand before Pharaoh; behold, he goes out to the water** to bathe, relieve himself, relax, or worship (see 7:15). **And you shall say to him: So said the Lord: Send forth My people and they will serve Me.**
17 **For if you do not send forth My people, I will cast the swarm** of wild beasts[26] **among you, among your servants, among your people, and in your houses; the houses of Egyptians will be filled with the swarm, as well as the ground on which they are.**
18 **I will distinguish on that day the land of Goshen upon which My people stands, so that a swarm will not be there.** Although Goshen is not far from here, it will remain unaffected by this plague. This will occur **so that you will know that I am the Lord in the midst of the land.** This differentiation between the Israelite and Egyptian population centers will demonstrate that God watches over and controls earthly events, as it will prove that the plague is intended solely for Pharaoh and his people.
19 **I will set a division**[27] **between My people and your people; tomorrow this sign will come to be.** Alternatively, this means: I will save My people while bringing the plague upon your people.[28] Some commentaries combine the two interpretations, explaining that the distinction between the peoples will be the salvation of the children of Israel.[29]

Sixth aliya

20 **The Lord did so** the next day, **and a heavy swarm** of wild beasts **came upon the house of Pharaoh and** from there it spread to **the house of his servants; in the entire land of Egypt the land was destroyed because of the swarm.** The beasts roamed unrestrained, wreaking havoc and sowing fear throughout the land.
21 After the first three plagues yielded no change in Pharaoh's behavior, the plague of wild beasts is apparently a turning point, as Pharaoh agrees to negotiate with Moses and Aaron. **Pharaoh summoned Moses and Aaron and he said: Go, sacrifice to**

יב וְלֹא שָׁמַע אֲלֵהֶם כַּאֲשֶׁר דִּבֶּר יהוה: וַיֹּאמֶר יהוה אֶל־מֹשֶׁה אֱמֹר
אֶל־אַהֲרֹן נְטֵה אֶת־מַטְּךָ וְהַךְ אֶת־עֲפַר הָאָרֶץ וְהָיָה לְכִנִּם בְּכָל־אֶרֶץ מִצְרָיִם:
יג וַיַּעֲשׂוּ־כֵן וַיֵּט אַהֲרֹן אֶת־יָדוֹ בְמַטֵּהוּ וַיַּךְ אֶת־עֲפַר הָאָרֶץ וַתְּהִי הַכִּנָּם בָּאָדָם
יד וּבַבְּהֵמָה כָּל־עֲפַר הָאָרֶץ הָיָה כִנִּים בְּכָל־אֶרֶץ מִצְרָיִם: וַיַּעֲשׂוּ־כֵן הַחַרְטֻמִּים
טו בְּלָטֵיהֶם לְהוֹצִיא אֶת־הַכִּנִּים וְלֹא יָכֹלוּ וַתְּהִי הַכִּנָּם בָּאָדָם וּבַבְּהֵמָה: וַיֹּאמְרוּ
הַחַרְטֻמִּם אֶל־פַּרְעֹה אֶצְבַּע אֱלֹהִים הִוא וַיֶּחֱזַק לֵב־פַּרְעֹה וְלֹא־שָׁמַע אֲלֵהֶם
טז כַּאֲשֶׁר דִּבֶּר יהוה: וַיֹּאמֶר יהוה אֶל־מֹשֶׁה הַשְׁכֵּם בַּבֹּקֶר וְהִתְיַצֵּב
לִפְנֵי פַרְעֹה הִנֵּה יוֹצֵא הַמָּיְמָה וְאָמַרְתָּ אֵלָיו כֹּה אָמַר יהוה שַׁלַּח עַמִּי וְיַעַבְדֻנִי:
יז כִּי אִם־אֵינְךָ מְשַׁלֵּחַ אֶת־עַמִּי הִנְנִי מַשְׁלִיחַ בְּךָ וּבַעֲבָדֶיךָ וּבְעַמְּךָ וּבְבָתֶּיךָ אֶת־
יח הֶעָרֹב וּמָלְאוּ בָּתֵּי מִצְרַיִם אֶת־הֶעָרֹב וְגַם הָאֲדָמָה אֲשֶׁר־הֵם עָלֶיהָ: וְהִפְלֵיתִי
בַיּוֹם הַהוּא אֶת־אֶרֶץ גֹּשֶׁן אֲשֶׁר עַמִּי עֹמֵד עָלֶיהָ לְבִלְתִּי הֱיוֹת־שָׁם עָרֹב לְמַעַן
יט תֵּדַע כִּי אֲנִי יהוה בְּקֶרֶב הָאָרֶץ: וְשַׂמְתִּי פְדֻת בֵּין עַמִּי וּבֵין עַמֶּךָ לְמָחָר יִהְיֶה ששי
כ הָאֹת הַזֶּה: וַיַּעַשׂ יהוה כֵּן וַיָּבֹא עָרֹב כָּבֵד בֵּיתָה פַרְעֹה וּבֵית עֲבָדָיו וּבְכָל־אֶרֶץ
כא מִצְרַיִם תִּשָּׁחֵת הָאָרֶץ מִפְּנֵי הֶעָרֹב: וַיִּקְרָא פַרְעֹה אֶל־מֹשֶׁה וּלְאַהֲרֹן וַיֹּאמֶר לְכוּ

רש"י

מח, ו), וכן: "והכות את מואב" (מלכים ב' ג, כד), "ואחול לו באלהים" (שמואל א' כב, יג), "הכה ופצע" (מלכים א' כ, לז): כאשר דבר ה'. והיכן דבר? "ולא ישמע אלכם פרעה" (לעיל ז, ד):

יב | אמר אל אהרן. לא היה העפר כדי ללקות על ידי משה, לפי שהגן עליו כשהרג את המצרי ויטמנהו בחול (לעיל ב, יב), ולקה על ידי אהרן:

יג | ותהי הכנם. הרחישה, פדולייר"א בלע"ז:

יד | להוציא את הכנים. לבראתם ממקום אחר: ולא יכלו. שאין השד שולט על בריה פחותה מכשעורה:

טו | אצבע אלהים הוא. מכה זו אינה על ידי כשפים, מאת המקום היא: כאשר דבר ה'. "ולא ישמע אלכם פרעה" (לעיל ז, ד):

יז | משליח בך. מגרה בך, וכן: "ושן בהמות אשלח בם" (דברים לב, כד) לשון שסוי, אינצטיצי"ר בלע"ז: את הערב. כל מיני חיות רעות ונחשים ועקרבים בערבוביא, והיו משחיתים בהם. ויש טעם בדבר באגדה בכל מכה ומכה למה זו ולמה זו: בטכסיסי מלחמות מלכים בא עליהם, כסדר מלכות כשצרה על עיר; בתחלה מקלקל מעינותיה, ואחר כך תוקע עליהם ומריעים בשופרות ליראם ולבהלם, וכן הצפרדעים מקרקרים והומים וכו', כדאיתא במדרש רבי תנחומא (בא ד):

יח | והפליתי. והפרשתי, וכן: "והפלה ה'" (להלן ט, ד), וכן: "לא נפלאת הוא ממך" (דברים ל, יא), לא מבדלת ומפרשת היא ממך: למען תדע כי אני ה' בקרב הארץ. אף על פי ששכינתי בשמים גזרתי מתקימת בתחתונים:

יט | ושמתי פדת. שיבדיל "בין עמי ובין עמך":

כ | תשחת הארץ. נשחתת הארץ, "אתחבלת ארעא":

BACKGROUND

8:12 | **Lice** [*kinnim*]: Although *kinnim* is generally translated as lice, it is likely that here it is actually referring to an insect that lives in the dust. Some maintain that *kinnim* means mosquitoes, whose eggs are often laid in organic materials in or near moisture. Others explain that the meaning is sand flies, whose bite can transfer single-celled parasites. Yet others contend that it refers to some species of tick. Perhaps *kinnim* is a general term for many species of insects (*Bekhor Shor*).

your God in the land. He granted them the freedom to perform their religious worship inside Egypt.

22 **Moses said** to Pharaoh: **It is not proper to do so, as we will be sacrificing the abomination**[D] **of Egypt to the Lord our God. Behold, will we sacrifice the abomination of Egypt before their eyes, and they not stone us?** If we desecrate the honor of an Egyptian deity, they will certainly respond by stoning us.

23 Rather, **we will** distance ourselves from the Egyptians and we will **go on a three-day journey into the wilderness and we will sacrifice to the Lord our God, as He will tell us,** in accordance with His command.

24 **Pharaoh said: I will send you forth, and you will sacrifice to the Lord your God in the wilderness; just do not go very far; plead for me** that the wild beasts will be removed from the land.

25 **Moses said: Behold, I am departing from your presence and I will plead with the Lord and** as a result, **the swarm will depart from Pharaoh, from his servants, and from his people tomorrow. Just, Pharaoh must not continue provoking by not sending forth the people to sacrifice to the Lord.** Since Pharaoh had already reneged on his previous commitment to release the children of Israel (8:4, 11), Moses warns him to keep his word this time.

26 **Moses departed from Pharaoh's presence and he pleaded with the Lord.** He did not pray in Pharaoh's palace, as it was an unfit location for supplication.

27 **The Lord did in accordance with the word of Moses and the swarm departed from Pharaoh, from his servants and from his people; not one remained.**

28 **Pharaoh made his heart stubborn this time as well**[D] **and he did not send forth the people,** notwithstanding his earlier pledge to release them.

The Plague of Pestilence

EXODUS 9:1–7

After striking Egypt's cities with a swarm of wild beasts that injured people and destroyed property, God now strikes their domesticated animals. Moses and Aaron are commanded to warn Pharaoh of the impending occurrence. As in the previous case, however, they are not actively involved in the onset of the plague.

9 1 **The Lord said to Moses: Go to Pharaoh and speak to him: So said the Lord, God of the Hebrews: Send forth My people and they will serve Me.**

2 **For if you refuse to send them forth, and continue to hold them,**

3 **behold, the** mighty **hand of the Lord,** which is capable of inflicting harm, **is**[D] already **on your livestock that is in the field, on the horses, on the donkeys, on the camels, on the cattle, and on the flocks: A very severe pestilence.**[B]

4 **And the Lord will distinguish between the livestock of Israel and the livestock of Egypt, and nothing of all** the livestock **that belongs to the children of Israel will die.**

5 To make matters clear, Moses added that **the Lord set an appointed time, saying: Tomorrow, the Lord will perform this matter in the land.** Moses warned Pharaoh of the impending epidemic, but did not wait for a response from him, as he expected Pharaoh to persist in his refusal to release the children of Israel.

6 **The Lord did this thing on the next day and all the livestock of Egypt died, but from the livestock of the children of Israel not one died.**

7 **Pharaoh sent** inspectors, **and, behold, from the livestock of Israel not even one died.** One would think that this was indisputable evidence that the plagues were brought upon Egypt by

DISCUSSION

8:22 | **The abomination:** To avoid showing respect to the false gods of Egypt, or even mentioning them by name, a verse will often refer to them in a derogatory manner, e.g., abominations, false gods, or disgusting, detestable things (see, e.g., Deuteronomy 29:16; II Kings 23:13; Ezekiel 7:20).

8:28 | **Pharaoh made his heart stubborn this time as well:** In the wake of the plague of wild beasts, Pharaoh felt threatened by Moses. He therefore attempted to placate him, but only in a half-hearted manner. Pharaoh used any means possible, including deceit, to defer the release of the children of Israel until the plague affecting his kingdom had passed. Even under the threat of wild beasts, Pharaoh failed to internalize Moses' perspective, and he did not accept upon himself the authority of the God of Israel.

9:3 | **Is [*hoya*]:** The unusual term *hoya* brings to mind the exclamations *hoy*, *oya*, which are expressions of mourning and tragedy (see, e.g., I Kings 13:30; Isaiah 1:4; Psalms 120:5).

זִבְחוּ לֵאלֹהֵיכֶם בָּאָרֶץ: וַיֹּאמֶר מֹשֶׁה לֹא נָכוֹן לַעֲשׂוֹת כֵּן כִּי תּוֹעֲבַת מִצְרַיִם כב

נִזְבַּח לַיהוָה אֱלֹהֵינוּ הֵן נִזְבַּח אֶת־תּוֹעֲבַת מִצְרַיִם לְעֵינֵיהֶם וְלֹא יִסְקְלֻנוּ: דֶּרֶךְ כג

שְׁלֹשֶׁת יָמִים נֵלֵךְ בַּמִּדְבָּר וְזָבַחְנוּ לַיהוָה אֱלֹהֵינוּ כַּאֲשֶׁר יֹאמַר אֵלֵינוּ: וַיֹּאמֶר כד

פַּרְעֹה אָנֹכִי אֲשַׁלַּח אֶתְכֶם וּזְבַחְתֶּם לַיהוָה אֱלֹהֵיכֶם בַּמִּדְבָּר רַק הַרְחֵק לֹא־

תַרְחִיקוּ לָלֶכֶת הַעְתִּירוּ בַּעֲדִי: וַיֹּאמֶר מֹשֶׁה הִנֵּה אָנֹכִי יוֹצֵא מֵעִמָּךְ וְהַעְתַּרְתִּי כה

אֶל־יְהוָה וְסָר הֶעָרֹב מִפַּרְעֹה מֵעֲבָדָיו וּמֵעַמּוֹ מָחָר רַק אַל־יֹסֵף פַּרְעֹה הָתֵל

לְבִלְתִּי שַׁלַּח אֶת־הָעָם לִזְבֹּחַ לַיהוָה: וַיֵּצֵא מֹשֶׁה מֵעִם פַּרְעֹה וַיֶּעְתַּר אֶל־יְהוָה: כו

וַיַּעַשׂ יְהוָה כִּדְבַר מֹשֶׁה וַיָּסַר הֶעָרֹב מִפַּרְעֹה מֵעֲבָדָיו וּמֵעַמּוֹ לֹא נִשְׁאַר אֶחָד: כז

וַיַּכְבֵּד פַּרְעֹה אֶת־לִבּוֹ גַּם בַּפַּעַם הַזֹּאת וְלֹא שִׁלַּח אֶת־הָעָם: כח

וַיֹּאמֶר יְהוָה אֶל־מֹשֶׁה בֹּא אֶל־פַּרְעֹה וְדִבַּרְתָּ אֵלָיו כֹּה־אָמַר יְהוָה אֱלֹהֵי א

הָעִבְרִים שַׁלַּח אֶת־עַמִּי וְיַעַבְדֻנִי: כִּי אִם־מָאֵן אַתָּה לְשַׁלֵּחַ וְעוֹדְךָ מַחֲזִיק בָּם: ב

הִנֵּה יַד־יְהוָה הוֹיָה בְּמִקְנְךָ אֲשֶׁר בַּשָּׂדֶה בַּסּוּסִים בַּחֲמֹרִים בַּגְּמַלִּים בַּבָּקָר וּבַצֹּאן ג

דֶּבֶר כָּבֵד מְאֹד: וְהִפְלָה יְהוָה בֵּין מִקְנֵה יִשְׂרָאֵל וּבֵין מִקְנֵה מִצְרָיִם וְלֹא יָמוּת ד

מִכָּל־לִבְנֵי יִשְׂרָאֵל דָּבָר: וַיָּשֶׂם יְהוָה מוֹעֵד לֵאמֹר מָחָר יַעֲשֶׂה יְהוָה הַדָּבָר הַזֶּה ה

בָּאָרֶץ: וַיַּעַשׂ יְהוָה אֶת־הַדָּבָר הַזֶּה מִמָּחֳרָת וַיָּמָת כֹּל מִקְנֵה מִצְרָיִם וּמִמִּקְנֵה ו

בְנֵי־יִשְׂרָאֵל לֹא־מֵת אֶחָד: וַיִּשְׁלַח פַּרְעֹה וְהִנֵּה לֹא־מֵת מִמִּקְנֵה יִשְׂרָאֵל עַד־ ז

רש״י

כא| זִבְחוּ לֵאלֹהֵיכֶם בָּאָרֶץ. בִּמְקוֹמְכֶם, וְלֹא תֵלְכוּ בַּמִּדְבָּר:

כב| תּוֹעֲבַת מִצְרַיִם. יִרְאַת מִצְרַיִם, כְּמוֹ: "וּלְמִלְכֹּם תּוֹעֲבַת בְּנֵי עַמּוֹן" (מלכים ב' כג, יג), וְאֵצֶל יִשְׂרָאֵל קוֹרֵא אוֹתָהּ תּוֹעֵבָה. וְעוֹד יֵשׁ לוֹמַר בְּלָשׁוֹן אַחֵר, "תּוֹעֲבַת מִצְרַיִם", דָּבָר שָׂנאוּי הוּא לְמִצְרַיִם זְבִיחָה שֶׁאָנוּ זוֹבְחִים, שֶׁהֲרֵי יִרְאָתָם אָנוּ זוֹבְחִים. **וְלֹא יִסְקְלֻנוּ.** בִּתְמִיהַּ:

כה| הָתֵל. כְּמוֹ לְהָתֵל:

כו-כז| וַיָּסַר הֶעָרֹב. וְלֹא מֵתוּ כְּמוֹ שֶׁמֵּתוּ הַצְפַרְדְּעִים, שֶׁאִם מֵתוּ הָיָה לָהֶם הֲנָאָה בְּעוֹרוֹתָם: **וַיֶּעְתַּר אֶל ה'.** נִתְאַמֵּץ בִּתְפִלָּה, וְכֵן אִם בָּא לוֹמַר "וַיַּעְתִּיר" הָיָה יָכוֹל לוֹמַר, וּמַשְׁמַע וַיַּרְבֶּה תְפִלָּה, וּכְשֶׁהוּא אוֹמֵר בְּלָשׁוֹן וַיִּפְעַל מַשְׁמַע וַיַּרְבֶּה לְהִתְפַּלֵּל:

כח| גַּם בַּפַּעַם הַזֹּאת. אַף עַל פִּי שֶׁאָמַר "אָנֹכִי אֲשַׁלַּח אֶתְכֶם" (לעיל פסוק כד) לֹא קִיֵּם הַבְטָחָתוֹ:

פרק ט

ב| מַחֲזִיק בָּם. אוֹחֵז בָּם, כְּמוֹ: "וְהֶחֱזִיקָה בִּמְבֻשָׁיו" (דברים כה, יא):

ג| הִנֵּה יַד ה' הוֹיָה. לְשׁוֹן הֹוֶה, כִּי כֵן יֹאמַר בִּלְשׁוֹן נְקֵבָה עַל שֶׁעָבַר "הָיְתָה", וְעַל הֶעָתִיד "תִּהְיֶה", וְעַל הָעוֹמֵד "הוֹיָה", כְּמוֹ: עוֹשָׂה, רוֹצָה, רוֹעָה:

ד| וְהִפְלָה. וְהִבְדִּיל:

BACKGROUND

9:3 | Pestilence [dever]: According to some opinions, *dever* is anthrax, which is especially harmful to livestock. The prophets Jeremiah and Ezekiel indicate that the three most terrible atrocities that can befall mankind are *dever*, war, and starvation. It is possible that in the Bible and rabbinic literature, *dever* is a generic term that refers to numerous ailments, or to any disease of epidemic proportions (see *Ta'anit* 19a).

God, and were not naturally occurring events. But **Pharaoh's heart became stubborn and he did not send forth the people.** Presumably, Pharaoh insisted that this too was the product of sorcery.

The Plague of Rash

EXODUS 9:8–12

The sixth plague, *shekhin*, usually translated as boils but more likely referring to a skin rash, is brought upon the Egyptians without forewarning, like the third and ninth plagues of lice and darkness. Thus, the plagues can be arranged in sequential sets, each consisting of three plagues. Alternatively, they may be viewed as two sets of five plagues each: After each of the first five plagues, Pharaoh hardens his own heart and refuses to allow the Israelites to leave Egypt. In contrast, following most of the last five plagues, starting with the rash, God hardens Pharaoh's heart against his will. It is possible that if Pharaoh had the ability to decide, he would relent and release the children of Israel; however, the privilege of choice is removed from him at this stage.

8 **The Lord said to Moses and Aaron: Take for yourselves** two **handfuls of soot** each, **of a furnace,** with your hands placed together, **and Moses shall throw it heavenward before the eyes of Pharaoh.**

9 **It will become** fine **dust over the entire land of Egypt.** Generally, when one spreads a handful of soot over even a small area, it quickly dissipates. In this case, however, it will spread throughout Egypt, **and it will become a rash**[B] of the skin, **erupting in blisters on man and on animal in the entire land of Egypt.**

10 **They took soot of the furnace, they stood before Pharaoh, and Moses threw it heavenward; it became a rash erupting in blisters on man and on animal.**

11 Not only were **the magicians** unable to produce a similar effect, but they **could not** even **stand before Moses because of the rash, as the rash was on the magicians,** and they were ashamed of their appearance or were experiencing extreme discomfort due to the rash; **and** the rash was also **on all the Egyptians.**

12 Pharaoh saw the magicians suffering, and perhaps even he too was afflicted by the rash. It is possible that he would have acquiesced, for he lacked the strength to persist in his stubborn stance, but **the Lord hardened Pharaoh's heart and he did not heed them, as the Lord had spoken to Moses.**

The Plague of Hail

EXODUS 9:13–35

In the warning that precedes the plague of hail, God stresses that the main aim of the plagues is not to pressure Pharaoh into releasing the children of Israel from slavery. Rather, their primary purpose is to instill in Pharaoh, his servants, and his people a recognition of God's omnipotence.

The hail that is brought upon Egypt is especially destructive; Pharaoh even cries out to Moses and admits guilt as a result. Perhaps this deviation from past behavior may be attributed to the fact that a hailstorm of such magnitude is entirely inconsistent with normal weather patterns in Egypt, as even rainfall is an uncommon occurrence.

13 **The Lord said to Moses: Arise early in the morning, stand before Pharaoh, and say to him: So said the Lord, God of the Hebrews: Send forth My people and they will serve Me.**

14 **For this time, I will send all My strokes to your heart and against your servants and against your people, so that you will know that there is none like Me on the entire earth.**

15 **For I could have sent My hand now and smitten you and your people with pestilence and you would have been eradicated from the earth.** The pestilence could easily have spread to the citizens of Egypt, and in that case there would have been no one left to oppose the release of Israel from Egypt, but also no one to recognize God's kingship.

16 **However, for this I have sustained you: In order to show you My power and in order to promulgate My name,** My kingship, **in the entire earth.**

17 Yet **you continue to abuse My people, in not sending them forth.** Although you have expressed willingness to release them in principle, you have repeatedly failed to do so.

Seventh aliya

18 **Behold, at this time tomorrow I will rain down a very heavy hail,**[B] **that there has not been like it in Egypt from the day of its founding until now.**

Hail

BACKGROUND

9:9 | **Rash [*sheḥin*]:** In most Semitic languages, the root *shin-ḥet-nun* refers to a fever. Researchers identify *sheḥin* with a number of skin diseases that cause heat and severe itching, such as urticaria, or hives, which appears as a sudden inflammation of itchy red spots on one's skin; smallpox, whose symptoms include high fever and small blisters filled with clear fluid; or bilharzia, a disease prevalent in Africa which causes an

אֶחָד וַיִּכְבַּד לֵב פַּרְעֹה וְלֹא שִׁלַּח אֶת־הָעָם:
ח וַיֹּאמֶר יְהוָה אֶל־מֹשֶׁה וְאֶל־אַהֲרֹן קְחוּ לָכֶם מְלֹא חָפְנֵיכֶם פִּיחַ כִּבְשָׁן וּזְרָקוֹ
ט מֹשֶׁה הַשָּׁמַיְמָה לְעֵינֵי פַרְעֹה: וְהָיָה לְאָבָק עַל כָּל־אֶרֶץ מִצְרָיִם וְהָיָה עַל־הָאָדָם
י וְעַל־הַבְּהֵמָה לִשְׁחִין פֹּרֵחַ אֲבַעְבֻּעֹת בְּכָל־אֶרֶץ מִצְרָיִם: וַיִּקְחוּ אֶת־פִּיחַ הַכִּבְשָׁן
וַיַּעַמְדוּ לִפְנֵי פַרְעֹה וַיִּזְרֹק אֹתוֹ מֹשֶׁה הַשָּׁמָיְמָה וַיְהִי שְׁחִין אֲבַעְבֻּעֹת פֹּרֵחַ
יא בָּאָדָם וּבַבְּהֵמָה: וְלֹא־יָכְלוּ הַחַרְטֻמִּים לַעֲמֹד לִפְנֵי מֹשֶׁה מִפְּנֵי הַשְּׁחִין כִּי־הָיָה
יב הַשְּׁחִין בַּחַרְטֻמִּם וּבְכָל־מִצְרָיִם: וַיְחַזֵּק יְהוָה אֶת־לֵב פַּרְעֹה וְלֹא שָׁמַע אֲלֵהֶם
יג כַּאֲשֶׁר דִּבֶּר יְהוָה אֶל־מֹשֶׁה: וַיֹּאמֶר יְהוָה אֶל־מֹשֶׁה הַשְׁכֵּם בַּבֹּקֶר
וְהִתְיַצֵּב לִפְנֵי פַרְעֹה וְאָמַרְתָּ אֵלָיו כֹּה־אָמַר יְהוָה אֱלֹהֵי הָעִבְרִים שַׁלַּח אֶת־
יד עַמִּי וְיַעַבְדֻנִי: כִּי ׀ בַּפַּעַם הַזֹּאת אֲנִי שֹׁלֵחַ אֶת־כָּל־מַגֵּפֹתַי אֶל־לִבְּךָ וּבַעֲבָדֶיךָ
טו וּבְעַמֶּךָ בַּעֲבוּר תֵּדַע כִּי אֵין כָּמֹנִי בְּכָל־הָאָרֶץ: כִּי עַתָּה שָׁלַחְתִּי אֶת־יָדִי וָאַךְ
טז אוֹתְךָ וְאֶת־עַמְּךָ בַּדָּבֶר וַתִּכָּחֵד מִן־הָאָרֶץ: וְאוּלָם בַּעֲבוּר זֹאת הֶעֱמַדְתִּיךָ
יז בַּעֲבוּר הַרְאֹתְךָ אֶת־כֹּחִי וּלְמַעַן סַפֵּר שְׁמִי בְּכָל־הָאָרֶץ: עוֹדְךָ מִסְתּוֹלֵל בְּעַמִּי שביעי
יח לְבִלְתִּי שַׁלְּחָם: הִנְנִי מַמְטִיר כָּעֵת מָחָר בָּרָד כָּבֵד מְאֹד אֲשֶׁר לֹא־הָיָה כָמֹהוּ

רש"י

ח | מלא חפניכם. ילוני"ש בלעז: פיח כבשן. דבר הנפח מן הגחלים עמומים הנשרפים בכבשן, ובלעז חולב"ש. 'פיח' לשון הפחה, שהרוח מפיחן ומפריחן: וזרקו משה. וכל דבר הנזרק בכח אינו נזרק אלא ביד אחת, הרי נסים הרבה: אחד, שהחזיק קמצו של משה מלא חפנים שלו ושל אהרן; ואחד, שהלך האבק על כל ארץ מצרים:

ט | פרח אבעבעת. כתרגומו: "לשחין סגי אבעבועין" שעל ידו צומחין בהן בועות: שחין. לשון חמימות, והרבה יש בלשון משנה: "שנה שחונה" (יומא נג ע"ב):

י | באדם ובבהמה. ואם תאמר, מאין היו להם הבהמות, והלא כבר נאמר: "וימת כל מקנה מצרים" (לעיל פסוק ו)? לא נגזרה גזרה אלא על אותן שבשדות בלבד, שנאמר: "במקנך אשר בשדה" (לעיל פסוק ג), והירא את דבר ה' הכניס את מקנהו אל הבתים. וכן שנויה במכילתא אצל "ויקח שש מאות רכב בחור" (להלן יד, ז):

יד | את כל מגפתי. למדנו מכאן שמכת בכורות שקולה כנגד כל המכות:

טו | כי עתה שלחתי את ידי וגו'. כי אלו רציתי כשהיתה ידי במקנך שהכיתים בדבר, שלחתיה והכיתי אותך ואת עמך עם הבהמות ונכחדתם מן הארץ, אבל "בעבור זאת העמדתיך" וגו':

יז | עודך מסתולל בעמי. כתרגומו: "כבישת ביה בעמי" והוא מגזרת 'מסלה' (במדבר כ, יט) דמתרגמינן: "אורח כבישא", ובלעז קלקי"ר. וכבר פרשתי בסוף ויהי מקץ (בראשית מד, טז), כל תבה שתחלת יסודה סמ"ך והיא באה לדבר בלשון מתפעל נותן התי"ו של שמוש באמצע אותיות של עקר, כגון זו, וכגון: "ויסתבל החגב" (קהלת יב, ה) מגזרת 'סבל' (מלכים א' ה, כט); "כי תשתרר עלינו" (במדבר טז, יג) מגזרת 'שר ונגיד' (דברי הימים ב' לב, כא); "משתכל הוית" (דניאל ז, ח):

יח | כעת מחר. כעת הזאת למחר. שרט לו שריטה בכתל, למחר כשתגיע חמה לכאן ירד הברד: הוסדה. שנתיסדה.

BACKGROUND

inflammation of the skin and is followed by a high fever.

9:18| **Hail:** In the desert climate of Egypt, the average temperature in winter does not drop below 15°C, while average annual rainfall ranges from 100 to 180 mm. It is not uncommon for several years to pass without any rainfall at all. The formation of hail requires a combination of several factors: Rain clouds, known as cumulonimbus clouds, humidity, and temperatures approaching freezing. None of these conditions are normally present in Egypt. Nevertheless, the country is on rare occasions affected by a weather system known as Active Red Sea Trough, which causes dramatic drops in temperature and the formation of clouds, thunderstorms, and hail.

19 **And now, send and collect your livestock** that survived the pestilence, or which was imported from an unaffected area, e.g., Goshen, where the children of Israel had settled because it provided good pasture,[30] **and everything that is yours in the field; every man and animal that will be found in the field and will not be gathered into the house, the hail will fall upon them and they will die.** The force of the hail will kill any man or beast struck by it. Moses was interested only in the display of the awesome power of God, not the deaths of Egyptian civilians. He therefore advised the Egyptians to go indoors and bring in their animals as well.

20 **He who feared the word of the Lord among the servants of Pharaoh drove his servants and his livestock into the houses.** Some of Pharaoh's servants heeded Moses' warning and thereby expressed a measure of fear of God.

21 **But he who did not pay attention to the word of the Lord, he left his servants and his livestock in the field.**

22 **The Lord said to Moses: Extend your hand at the heavens and there will be hail**[D] **in the entire land of Egypt, on man and on animals and on all the vegetation of the field in the land of Egypt.**

23 **Moses extended his staff at the heavens, and the Lord provided thunder and hail and,** due to the lightning that accompanied the hail, **fire descended to the earth; the Lord rained hail on the land of Egypt.**

24 **There was hail and fire igniting amid the hail: Very heavy, that there had not been like it in the entire land of Egypt since it became a nation.** Even though Egypt was an ancient civilization, no hail of this kind had been recorded in its history.

25 **The hail struck in the entire land of Egypt everything that was in the field, from man to animal, and the hail struck all the vegetation of the field and broke every tree of the field.**

26 **Only in the land of Goshen, where the children of Israel were, was there no hail.**

27 **Pharaoh sent and summoned Moses and Aaron.** Perhaps Pharaoh was especially frightened on this occasion because the hail descended from above, or due to the powerful thunder. Evidently Pharaoh had not heard such sounds in his life, certainly not accompanied by such a deadly hailstorm. **And he said to them: I sinned this time; the Lord is the righteous and I and my people are the wicked.**

28 **Plead with the Lord; there has been too much thunder of God and hail. I will send you forth and you will not continue to abide.**

29 **Moses said to him: Upon my leaving the city, I will spread my hands** in prayer **to the Lord,** as Moses would not pray in the midst of Pharaoh's kingdom. **The thunder will cease and the hail will be no longer, so that you will know that the earth is the Lord's.**

30 **And as for you and your servants, I know that you do not yet fear the Lord God,** as your admission of guilt was insincere.

31 **The flax and the barley** in the fields **were struck** by the hail, **as the barley was just ripened and the flax was in stalk.** Their stems had already emerged and they were no longer soft sprouts. As a result, they were damaged by the hail.

32 **But the wheat and the spelt were not struck, as they are late ripening.** Since they sprout later in the year, they were soft at the time and were not broken by the hail. The fact that some of

---

DISCUSSION

9:22 | **Extend your hand at the heavens and there will be hail:** Apparently, Moses performed these symbolic acts which started the plagues, e.g., stretching out his hand or his staff, in the presence of Pharaoh. Later prophets used symbolic actions in a similar manner, to signal the beginning of a wonder (see II Kings 13:16–17; Jeremiah 51:63). The aim of these actions is to connect the material world to the metaphysical world beyond (see Ramban, Genesis 12:6).

יט בְּמִצְרַיִם לְמִן־הַיּוֹם הִוָּסְדָה וְעַד־עָתָּה: וְעַתָּה שְׁלַח הָעֵז אֶת־מִקְנְךָ וְאֵת כָּל־
אֲשֶׁר לְךָ בַּשָּׂדֶה כָּל־הָאָדָם וְהַבְּהֵמָה אֲשֶׁר־יִמָּצֵא בַשָּׂדֶה וְלֹא יֵאָסֵף הַבַּיְתָה

כ וְיָרַד עֲלֵהֶם הַבָּרָד וָמֵתוּ: הַיָּרֵא אֶת־דְּבַר יְהוָה מֵעַבְדֵי פַּרְעֹה הֵנִיס אֶת־עֲבָדָיו

כא וְאֶת־מִקְנֵהוּ אֶל־הַבָּתִּים: וַאֲשֶׁר לֹא־שָׂם לִבּוֹ אֶל־דְּבַר יְהוָה וַיַּעֲזֹב אֶת־עֲבָדָיו
וְאֶת־מִקְנֵהוּ בַּשָּׂדֶה:

כב וַיֹּאמֶר יְהוָה אֶל־מֹשֶׁה נְטֵה אֶת־יָדְךָ עַל־הַשָּׁמַיִם וִיהִי בָרָד בְּכָל־אֶרֶץ מִצְרָיִם

כג עַל־הָאָדָם וְעַל־הַבְּהֵמָה וְעַל כָּל־עֵשֶׂב הַשָּׂדֶה בְּאֶרֶץ מִצְרָיִם: וַיֵּט מֹשֶׁה אֶת־
מַטֵּהוּ עַל־הַשָּׁמַיִם וַיהוָה נָתַן קֹלֹת וּבָרָד וַתִּהֲלַךְ־אֵשׁ אָרְצָה וַיַּמְטֵר יְהוָה בָּרָד

כד עַל־אֶרֶץ מִצְרָיִם: וַיְהִי בָרָד וְאֵשׁ מִתְלַקַּחַת בְּתוֹךְ הַבָּרָד כָּבֵד מְאֹד אֲשֶׁר לֹא־

כה הָיָה כָמֹהוּ בְּכָל־אֶרֶץ מִצְרַיִם מֵאָז הָיְתָה לְגוֹי: וַיַּךְ הַבָּרָד בְּכָל־אֶרֶץ מִצְרַיִם
אֵת כָּל־אֲשֶׁר בַּשָּׂדֶה מֵאָדָם וְעַד־בְּהֵמָה וְאֵת כָּל־עֵשֶׂב הַשָּׂדֶה הִכָּה הַבָּרָד

כו וְאֶת־כָּל־עֵץ הַשָּׂדֶה שִׁבֵּר: רַק בְּאֶרֶץ גֹּשֶׁן אֲשֶׁר־שָׁם בְּנֵי יִשְׂרָאֵל לֹא הָיָה

כז בָּרָד: וַיִּשְׁלַח פַּרְעֹה וַיִּקְרָא לְמֹשֶׁה וּלְאַהֲרֹן וַיֹּאמֶר אֲלֵהֶם חָטָאתִי הַפָּעַם יְהוָה

כח הַצַּדִּיק וַאֲנִי וְעַמִּי הָרְשָׁעִים: הַעְתִּירוּ אֶל־יְהוָה וְרַב מִהְיֹת קֹלֹת אֱלֹהִים וּבָרָד

כט וַאֲשַׁלְּחָה אֶתְכֶם וְלֹא תֹסִפוּן לַעֲמֹד: וַיֹּאמֶר אֵלָיו מֹשֶׁה כְּצֵאתִי אֶת־הָעִיר אֶפְרֹשׂ
אֶת־כַּפַּי אֶל־יְהוָה הַקֹּלוֹת יֶחְדָּלוּן וְהַבָּרָד לֹא יִהְיֶה־עוֹד לְמַעַן תֵּדַע כִּי לַיהוָה

ל הָאָרֶץ: וְאַתָּה וַעֲבָדֶיךָ יָדַעְתִּי כִּי טֶרֶם תִּירְאוּן מִפְּנֵי יְהוָה אֱלֹהִים: וְהַפִּשְׁתָּה

לא וְהַשְּׂעֹרָה נֻכָּתָה כִּי הַשְּׂעֹרָה אָבִיב וְהַפִּשְׁתָּה גִּבְעֹל: וְהַחִטָּה וְהַכֻּסֶּמֶת לֹא נֻכּוּ

לב

רש"י

וְכָל תֵּבָה שֶׁתְּחִלַּת יְסוֹדָהּ יוֹ"ד כְּגוֹן: יָסַד, יֵלֵד, יָדַע, יָסַר,
כְּשֶׁהִיא מִתְפַּעֶלֶת תָּבֹא הַוָּי"ו בִּמְקוֹם הַיּוֹ"ד כְּמוֹ: "הִוָּסְדָה",
"הִוָּלְדָהּ" (הושע ב, ה), "וַיִּוָּדַע" (אסתר ב, כב), "וַיִּוָּלֶד לְיוֹסֵף"
(בראשית מו, כ), "בְּדְבָרִים לֹא יִוָּסֶר עָבֶד" (משלי כט, יט):

יט שְׁלַח הָעֵז. כְּתַרְגּוּמוֹ: "שְׁלַח כְּנוֹשׁ". וְכֵן: "יֹשְׁבֵי הַגִּבִּים
הָעִיזוּ" (ישעיה י, לא), "הָעִזוּ בְּנֵי בִנְיָמִן" (ירמיה ו, א) וְלֹא
יֵאָסֵף הַבַּיְתָה. לְשׁוֹן הַכְנָסָה הוּא:

כו הֵנִיס. הִבְרִיחַ:

כב עַל הַשָּׁמַיִם. לְצַד הַשָּׁמַיִם. וּמִדְרַשׁ אַגָּדָה, הִגְבִּיהוֹ
הַקָּדוֹשׁ בָּרוּךְ הוּא לְמֹשֶׁה לְמַעְלָה מִן הַשָּׁמַיִם:

כד מִתְלַקַּחַת בְּתוֹךְ הַבָּרָד. נֵס בְּתוֹךְ נֵס, הָאֵשׁ וְהַבָּרָד
מְעֹרָבִין, וְהַבָּרָד מַיִם הוּא, וְלַעֲשׂוֹת רְצוֹן קוֹנָם עָשׂוּ שָׁלוֹם
בֵּינֵיהֶם:

כח וְרַב. דַּי לוֹ בְּמָה שֶׁהוֹרִיד כְּבָר:

כט כְּצֵאתִי אֶת הָעִיר. מִן הָעִיר. אֲבָל בְּתוֹךְ הָעִיר לֹא
הִתְפַּלֵּל לְפִי שֶׁהָיְתָה מְלֵאָה גִּלּוּלִים:

ל טֶרֶם תִּירְאוּן. עֲדַיִן לֹא תִירְאוּן. וְכֵן כָּל טֶרֶם
שֶׁבַּמִּקְרָא עֲדַיִן לֹא הוּא וְאֵינוֹ לְשׁוֹן קֹדֶם. "טֶרֶם יִשְׁכָּבוּ"
(בראשית יט, ד) – "עַד לֹא שְׁכִיבוּ", "טֶרֶם יִצְמָח" (שם ב,

ה) – "עַד לֹא צָמַח". אַף זֶה כֵּן הוּא, יָדַעְתִּי כִּי עֲדַיִן
אֵינְכֶם יְרֵאִים, וּמִשֶּׁהָיְה הָרְוָחָה תַּעַמְדוּ בְּקִלְקוּלְכֶם:

לא וְהַפִּשְׁתָּה וְהַשְּׂעֹרָה נֻכָּתָה. נִשְׁבְּרָה, לְשׁוֹן "פַּרְעֹה
נְכֹה" (מלכים ב כג, כט), "נְכָאִים" (ישעיה טז, ז), וְכֵן "לֹא
נֻכּוּ" (להלן פסוק לב). וְלֹא יִתָּכֵן לְפָרְשֵׁם לְשׁוֹן הַכָּאָה, שֶׁאֵין
עַיִ"ן בַּמִּקּוֹם הֵ"א לְפָרֵשׁ "נֻכְּתָה" כְּמוֹ "הֻכְּתָה", "נֻכּוּ" כְּמוֹ
"הֻכּוּ", אֶלָּא הָעַיִ"ן שֹׁרֶשׁ בַּתֵּבָה, וַהֲרֵי הוּא מִגִּזְרַת "וְשֻׁפּוּ
עַצְמוֹתָיו" (איוב לג, כא). כִּי הַשְּׂעֹרָה אָבִיב. כְּבָר בִּכְּרָה
וְעוֹמֶדֶת בְּקָשֶׁיהָ וְנִשְׁבְּרוּ וְנָפָלוּ. וְכֵן הַפִּשְׁתָּה גְּדֵלָה כְּבָר
וְהֻקְשָׁה לַעֲמֹד בִּגְבָעוֹלֶיהָ. הַשְּׂעֹרָה אָבִיב. עָמְדָה בְּאִבֶּיהָ,
לְשׁוֹן "בְּאִבֵּי הַנָּחַל" (שיר השירים ו, יא):

the crops were not destroyed is important, as these were left to be damaged by the next plague.

33 **Moses emerged from Pharaoh's presence, from the city,**
Maftir **and spread his hands to the Lord; the thunders and hail ceased and rain did not pour onto the earth.**

34 **Pharaoh saw that the rain, the hail, and the thunders ceased, and he continued to sin; he made his heart stubborn, he and**

his servants. Following the respite from the plague, Pharaoh reassured himself by rationalizing that the hail was nothing more than a passing natural phenomenon.

35 **Pharaoh's heart was hardened and he did not send forth the children of Israel, as the Lord had spoken at the hand of Moses.**

Parashat
Bo

The Plague of Locusts
EXODUS 10:1–20

At the eighth plague, locusts, the confrontation between Moses and Pharaoh intensifies. Moses reports God's message and leaves the palace without attempting to listen to Pharaoh's response. Due to Moses' forceful action, the content of his warning, or perhaps the unbearable suffering of the Egyptians, Pharaoh's servants muster the audacity to raise their objections to their ruler and demand the release of the Hebrew slaves from Egypt. For the first time, Pharaoh summons Moses and Aaron to negotiate even before the plague has arrived; however, this negotiation does not bear fruit.

10 1 **The Lord said to Moses: Come to Pharaoh for I made his heart and the heart of his servants stubborn,** in their continuous refusal to let the Israelites go, **so that I might place these signs of Mine in his midst,** and thereby display My power;

2 **and so that you may relate, in the ears of your son and the son of your son,**[D] how I have harried Egypt. I did not strike them with the ultimate plague of death at the outset, but repeatedly with other plagues, all the while strengthening Pharaoh's

heart. **And** you will retell **My signs that I placed among them; and you will know that I am the Lord.**

3 **Moses and Aaron came to Pharaoh and said to him: So said the Lord, God of the Hebrews: How long will you refuse to submit before Me** and refuse to accept My authority? **Send forth My people, and they will serve Me.**

4 **For if you refuse to send forth My people, behold, tomorrow I will bring locusts**[B] **into your border.**

BACKGROUND

10:4 | **Locusts:** These are *Schistocerca gregaria*, flying insects from East Africa. These grasshoppers are ordinarily solitary creatures, but under certain conditions they will reproduce at tremen-

DISCUSSION

10:2 | **So that you may relate, in the ears of your son and the son of your son:** The plagues of Egypt will become part of the Jewish people's collective memory. The main message to be

internalized by the recollection of the plagues is that God exerts His power in the world, and it is expressed in a series of signs which have both direction and purpose. It is for this reason that

לג כִּי אֲפִילֹת הֵנָּה: וַיֵּצֵא מֹשֶׁה מֵעִם פַּרְעֹה אֶת־הָעִיר וַיִּפְרֹשׂ כַּפָּיו אֶל־יהוה וַיַּחְדְּלוּ מפטיר
לד הַקֹּלוֹת וְהַבָּרָד וּמָטָר לֹא־נִתַּךְ אָרְצָה: וַיַּרְא פַּרְעֹה כִּי־חָדַל הַמָּטָר וְהַבָּרָד
לה וְהַקֹּלֹת וַיֹּסֶף לַחֲטֹא וַיַּכְבֵּד לִבּוֹ הוּא וַעֲבָדָיו: וַיֶּחֱזַק לֵב פַּרְעֹה וְלֹא שִׁלַּח אֶת־
בְּנֵי יִשְׂרָאֵל כַּאֲשֶׁר דִּבֶּר יהוה בְּיַד־מֹשֶׁה:

רש״י

לב] כִּי אֲפִילֹת הֵנָּה. מְאֻחָרוֹת, וַעֲדַיִן הָיוּ רַכּוֹת וִיכוֹלוֹת לַעֲמֹד בִּפְנֵי קָשֶׁה. וְאַף עַל פִּי שֶׁנֶּאֱמַר: "וְאֵת כָּל עֵשֶׂב הַשָּׂדֶה הִכָּה הַבָּרָד" (לעיל פסוק כה), יֵשׁ לְיַשֵּׁב פְּשׁוּטוֹ שֶׁל מִקְרָא בַּעֲשָׂבִים הָעוֹמְדִים בְּקַלְחָם הָרְאוּיִם לִלְקוֹת בְּבָרָד. וּמִדְרַשׁ רַבִּי תַּנְחוּמָא (ו) יֵשׁ מְרַבּוֹתֵינוּ שֶׁנֶּחְלְקוּ עַל זֹאת, וְדָרְשׁוּ "כִּי אֲפִילֹת", פִּלְאֵי פְלָאוֹת נַעֲשׂוּ לָהֶם שֶׁלֹּא לָקוּ:

לג] לֹא נִתַּךְ. לֹא הִגִּיעַ, וְאַף אוֹתָן שֶׁהָיוּ בָּאֲוִיר לֹא הִגִּיעוּ לָאָרֶץ. וְדוֹמֶה לוֹ: "וַתִּתַּךְ עָלֵינוּ הָאָלָה וְהַשְּׁבֻעָה" דְּעֶזְרָא (דניאל ט, יא), וַתַּגִּיעַ עָלֵינוּ. וּמְנַחֵם בֶּן סָרוּק חִבְּרוֹ בְּחֵלֶק "כְּהִתּוּךְ כֶּסֶף" (יחזקאל כב, כב), לְשׁוֹן יְצִיקַת מַתֶּכֶת, וְרוֹאֶה אֲנִי אֶת דְּבָרָיו; כְּתַרְגּוּמוֹ "וַיִּצֹּק" – "וְאַתִּיךְ" (להלן לח, ה), "לָצֶקֶת" (שם פסוק כז) – "לְאַתָּכָא". אַף זֶה "לֹא נִתַּךְ", לֹא הוּצַק לָאָרֶץ:

פרשת

בא

א וַיֹּאמֶר יהוה אֶל־מֹשֶׁה בֹּא אֶל־פַּרְעֹה כִּי־אֲנִי הִכְבַּדְתִּי אֶת־לִבּוֹ וְאֶת־לֵב עֲבָדָיו ז
ב לְמַעַן שִׁתִי אֹתֹתַי אֵלֶּה בְּקִרְבּוֹ: וּלְמַעַן תְּסַפֵּר בְּאָזְנֵי בִנְךָ וּבֶן־בִּנְךָ אֵת אֲשֶׁר
ג הִתְעַלַּלְתִּי בְּמִצְרַיִם וְאֶת־אֹתֹתַי אֲשֶׁר־שַׂמְתִּי בָם וִידַעְתֶּם כִּי־אֲנִי יהוה: וַיָּבֹא
מֹשֶׁה וְאַהֲרֹן אֶל־פַּרְעֹה וַיֹּאמְרוּ אֵלָיו כֹּה־אָמַר יהוה אֱלֹהֵי הָעִבְרִים עַד־מָתַי
ד מֵאַנְתָּ לֵעָנֹת מִפָּנָי שַׁלַּח עַמִּי וְיַעַבְדֻנִי: כִּי אִם־מָאֵן אַתָּה לְשַׁלֵּחַ אֶת־עַמִּי הִנְנִי

רש״י

א] וַיֹּאמֶר ה' אֶל מֹשֶׁה בֹּא אֶל פַּרְעֹה. וְהַתְרֵה בּוֹ: שִׁתִי. שׂוּמִי, שֶׁאָשִׁית אֲנִי:

ב] הִתְעַלַּלְתִּי. שִׂחַקְתִּי, כְּמוֹ: "כִּי הִתְעַלַּלְתְּ בִּי" (במדבר כב, כט), "הֲלוֹא כַּאֲשֶׁר הִתְעַלֵּל בָּהֶם" (שמואל א' ו, ו) הָאָמוּר בְּמִצְרַיִם. וְאֵינוֹ לְשׁוֹן פֹּעַל וּמַעֲלָלִים, שֶׁאִם כֵּן הָיָה לוֹ לִכְתֹּב 'עוֹלַלְתִּי', כְּמוֹ: "וְעוֹלֵל לָמוֹ כַּאֲשֶׁר עוֹלַלְתָּ לִי" (איכה א, כב), "אֲשֶׁר עוֹלַל לִי" (שם פסוק יב):

ג] לֵעָנֹת. כְּתַרְגּוּמוֹ: "לְאִתְכְּנָעָא", וְהוּא מִגִּזְרַת 'עָנִי', מֵאַנְתָּ לִהְיוֹת עָנִי וְשָׁפָל מִפָּנָי:

5 **They,** the great swarm of locusts, **will cover the face of the earth, that one will be unable to see the earth, and they will devour the rest of that which was saved that remains for you from the hail,** the young plants that survived the hail (9:32), **and they will devour all the trees that grow for you from the field,** since not all the trees were completely destroyed by the earlier hail. Anything remaining will be eaten by the locusts.

Locust

6 **They will fill your houses and the houses of all your servants and the houses of all Egypt, as your fathers and the fathers of your fathers did not see from the day that they were upon the earth until this day. He turned and departed from Pharaoh's presence,** without waiting for a response. Moses' dramatic exit from Pharaoh is an act of defiance, marking a turning point in their relationship.

7 **Pharaoh's servants said to him: Until when will this** man, Moses, **be a snare for us?** He is constantly bringing upon us fresh troubles. **Send forth the people that they may serve the Lord their God; do you not yet know that Egypt is lost?** While you sit in your comfortable palace, we move among the people. The kingdom is suffering from plague after plague, and the population cannot bear it anymore.

8 **Moses and Aaron were returned to Pharaoh;** messengers were sent to bring them back to the ruler, **and he said to them: Go, serve the Lord your God.** After expressing his agreement in principle, Pharaoh seeks to clarify the details: **Who are those who are going?**

9 **Moses said: With our youth and with our elders we will go, with our sons and with our daughters, with our flocks and with our cattle we will go.** We will not leave anyone or anything here, young or old, male or female, human or animal, **because it is a festival of the Lord for us.** Moses is alluding to the fact that Israel's exit will signal its independence, and he does not promise their return.

10 **He,** Pharaoh, **said to them,** angrily and with derision: **So may the Lord be with you when I will send forth you and your children.** In a mocking tone, Pharaoh makes it clear that he has no intention of allowing this to occur. **See that evil faces you.** You do not wish to go out to celebrate a religious holiday, but to seek trouble for yourselves.

11 **Not so!** Pharaoh continued. You do not get to decide. **Rather, let the men go now and serve the Lord; as that,** a one-time gathering to worship the Lord, **is what you seek.** The women and children, and certainly the flocks, are not required for such a purpose. **He banished them from Pharaoh's presence.**ᴰ

12 **The Lord said to Moses: Extend your hand over the land of Egypt for the locusts,** meaning, in order to begin the plague of locusts.²²Alternatively, God commands Moses: Extend your hand while grasping a locust, or tie a locust to the end of your staff, as a symbolic action marking the plague that is about to occur.³³**And they shall go up upon the land of Egypt and eat all the vegetation of the land, everything that the hail left.**

Second aliya

13 **Moses extended his staff over the land of Egypt and the Lord directed an east wind in the land all that day and all the night; it was morning and the east wind carried the locusts.**

14 **The locusts went up upon the entire land of Egypt and settled within the entire border of Egypt; it was very severe; before them there were no locusts like them, and there will never be so after them.**ᴰ

—— BACKGROUND ——

dous rates and undergo physiological transformations of color and size, growing to as much as 7 cm in length. When this occurs, their behavior also changes, and they gather into swarms and are called locusts. Aided by the wind, swarms of locusts can travel vast distances in search of food, from southern Sudan and Ethiopia to neighboring countries along the Red Sea and even to the Sinai Peninsula and the Land of Israel. Along the way, these locust swarms can cover hundreds of square miles of land and destroy all agricultural produce growing there.

—— DISCUSSION ——

the Israelites' enslavement in Egypt and their suffering in exile were not resolved through a single miraculous demonstration of divine power.

10:11 | He banished them from Pharaoh's presence: Moses and Aaron would have left Pharaoh regardless, as no further negotiations were forthcoming. They had no intention of accepting Pharaoh's offer, nor were they authorized by God to do so. Their active banishment by Pharaoh was a deliberate expression of his disdain of Moses and Aaron, in retaliation against Moses' earlier demonstrative departure from the court.

10:14 | Before them there were no locusts like them, and there will never be so after them: The prophet Joel describes a terrible infestation of

locusts in the Land of Israel in the following terms: "It will be a day of darkness and gloom, a day of cloud and fog; it will be like dawn spread over the mountains, a numerous and mighty people; there has never been its like and there will not be more until the years of generation upon generation" (Joel 2:2). This apparently contradicts the claim of exclusivity of this verse for the plague in Egypt. Some commentaries explain that the locust infestation described by Joel was in fact greater than the one depicted here, but it consisted of several different species of locust, whereas the locust plague in Egypt was the worst ever of a single species. Alternatively, the description here is referring specifically to Egypt; Joel is speaking of the worst ever to afflict the Land of Israel.

ה מֵבִיא מָחָר אַרְבֶּה בִּגְבֻלֶךָ: וְכִסָּה אֶת־עֵין הָאָרֶץ וְלֹא יוּכַל לִרְאֹת אֶת־הָאָרֶץ
וְאָכַל ׀ אֶת־יֶתֶר הַפְּלֵטָה הַנִּשְׁאֶרֶת לָכֶם מִן־הַבָּרָד וְאָכַל אֶת־כָּל־הָעֵץ הַצֹּמֵחַ
ו לָכֶם מִן־הַשָּׂדֶה: וּמָלְאוּ בָתֶּיךָ וּבָתֵּי כָל־עֲבָדֶיךָ וּבָתֵּי כָל־מִצְרַיִם אֲשֶׁר לֹא־
רָאוּ אֲבֹתֶיךָ וַאֲבוֹת אֲבֹתֶיךָ מִיּוֹם הֱיוֹתָם עַל־הָאֲדָמָה עַד הַיּוֹם הַזֶּה וַיִּפֶן וַיֵּצֵא
ז מֵעִם פַּרְעֹה: וַיֹּאמְרוּ עַבְדֵי פַרְעֹה אֵלָיו עַד־מָתַי יִהְיֶה זֶה לָנוּ לְמוֹקֵשׁ שַׁלַּח
ח אֶת־הָאֲנָשִׁים וְיַעַבְדוּ אֶת־יְהוָה אֱלֹהֵיהֶם הֲטֶרֶם תֵּדַע כִּי אָבְדָה מִצְרָיִם: וַיּוּשַׁב
אֶת־מֹשֶׁה וְאֶת־אַהֲרֹן אֶל־פַּרְעֹה וַיֹּאמֶר אֲלֵהֶם לְכוּ עִבְדוּ אֶת־יְהוָה אֱלֹהֵיכֶם
ט מִי וָמִי הַהֹלְכִים: וַיֹּאמֶר מֹשֶׁה בִּנְעָרֵינוּ וּבִזְקֵנֵינוּ נֵלֵךְ בְּבָנֵינוּ וּבִבְנוֹתֵנוּ בְּצֹאנֵנוּ
י וּבִבְקָרֵנוּ נֵלֵךְ כִּי חַג־יְהוָה לָנוּ: וַיֹּאמֶר אֲלֵהֶם יְהִי כֵן יְהוָה עִמָּכֶם כַּאֲשֶׁר אֲשַׁלַּח
יא אֶתְכֶם וְאֶת־טַפְּכֶם רְאוּ כִּי רָעָה נֶגֶד פְּנֵיכֶם: לֹא כֵן לְכוּ־נָא הַגְּבָרִים וְעִבְדוּ
יב אֶת־יְהוָה כִּי אֹתָהּ אַתֶּם מְבַקְשִׁים וַיְגָרֶשׁ אֹתָם מֵאֵת פְּנֵי פַרְעֹה: וַיֹּאמֶר יְהוָה שני
אֶל־מֹשֶׁה נְטֵה יָדְךָ עַל־אֶרֶץ מִצְרַיִם בָּאַרְבֶּה וְיַעַל עַל־אֶרֶץ מִצְרָיִם וְיֹאכַל אֶת־
יג כָּל־עֵשֶׂב הָאָרֶץ אֵת כָּל־אֲשֶׁר הִשְׁאִיר הַבָּרָד: וַיֵּט מֹשֶׁה אֶת־מַטֵּהוּ עַל־אֶרֶץ
מִצְרַיִם וַיהוָה נִהַג רוּחַ־קָדִים בָּאָרֶץ כָּל־הַיּוֹם הַהוּא וְכָל־הַלָּיְלָה הַבֹּקֶר הָיָה
יד וְרוּחַ הַקָּדִים נָשָׂא אֶת־הָאַרְבֶּה: וַיַּעַל הָאַרְבֶּה עַל כָּל־אֶרֶץ מִצְרַיִם וַיָּנַח בְּכֹל
גְּבוּל מִצְרָיִם כָּבֵד מְאֹד לְפָנָיו לֹא־הָיָה כֵן אַרְבֶּה כָּמֹהוּ וְאַחֲרָיו לֹא יִהְיֶה־כֵּן:

רש״י

ה| **אֶת עֵין הָאָרֶץ.** אֶת מַרְאֵה הָאָרֶץ: **וְלֹא יוּכַל.** הָרוֹאֶה ״לִרְאוֹת אֶת הָאָרֶץ״, וְלָשׁוֹן קְצָרָה דִּבֵּר:

ז| **הֲטֶרֶם תֵּדַע.** הַעוֹד לֹא יָדַעְתָּ ״כִּי אָבְדָה מִצְרָיִם״:

ח| **וַיּוּשַׁב.** הוּשְׁבוּ עַל יְדֵי שָׁלִיחַ, שֶׁשָּׁלְחוּ אַחֲרֵיהֶם וֶהֱשִׁיבוּם אֶל פַּרְעֹה:

י| **כַּאֲשֶׁר אֲשַׁלַּח אֶתְכֶם וְאֶת טַפְּכֶם.** אַף כִּי אֲשַׁלַּח גַּם אֶת הַצֹּאן וְאֶת הַבָּקָר כַּאֲשֶׁר אֲמַרְתֶּם: **רְאוּ כִּי רָעָה נֶגֶד פְּנֵיכֶם.** כְּתַרְגּוּמוֹ. וּמִדְרַשׁ אַגָּדָה שָׁמַעְתִּי, כּוֹכָב אֶחָד יֵשׁ שֶׁשְּׁמוֹ רָעָה, אָמַר לָהֶם פַּרְעֹה: רוֹאֶה אֲנִי בְּאִיצְטַגְנִינוּת שֶׁלִּי אוֹתוֹ כּוֹכָב עוֹלֶה לִקְרַאתְכֶם בַּמִּדְבָּר וְהוּא סִימָן דָּם וַהֲרִיגָה. וּכְשֶׁחָטְאוּ יִשְׂרָאֵל בָּעֵגֶל וּבִקֵּשׁ הַקָּדוֹשׁ בָּרוּךְ הוּא לְהָרְגָם, אָמַר מֹשֶׁה בִּתְפִלָּתוֹ: ״לָמָּה יֹאמְרוּ מִצְרַיִם לֵאמֹר בְּרָעָה הוֹצִיאָם״ (להלן לב, יב), זוֹ הִיא שֶׁאָמַר לָהֶם: ״רְאוּ כִּי רָעָה נֶגֶד פְּנֵיכֶם״. מִיָּד – ״וַיִּנָּחֶם ה׳ עַל הָרָעָה״ (שם פסוק יד) וְהָפַךְ אֶת הַדָּם לְדַם מִילָה שֶׁמָּל יְהוֹשֻׁעַ אוֹתָם. וְזֶהוּ שֶׁנֶּאֱמַר: ״הַיּוֹם גַּלּוֹתִי אֶת חֶרְפַּת מִצְרַיִם מֵעֲלֵיכֶם״ (יהושע ה, ט) שֶׁהָיוּ אוֹמְרִים לָכֶם: דָּם אָנוּ רוֹאִין עֲלֵיכֶם בַּמִּדְבָּר:

יא| **לֹא כֵן.** כַּאֲשֶׁר אֲמַרְתֶּם לְהוֹלִיךְ הַטַּף עִמָּכֶם, אֶלָּא לְכוּ הַגְּבָרִים וְעִבְדוּ אֶת ה׳ כִּי אוֹתָהּ בִּקַּשְׁתֶּם עַד הֵנָּה, ״נִזְבְּחָה לֵאלֹהֵינוּ״ (לעיל ה, ח), וְאֵין דֶּרֶךְ הַטַּף לִזְבֹּחַ: **וַיְגָרֶשׁ אֹתָם.** הֲרֵי זֶה לָשׁוֹן קָצָר וְלֹא פֵּרֵשׁ מִי הַמְגָרֵשׁ:

יב| **בָּאַרְבֶּה.** בִּשְׁבִיל מַכַּת הָאַרְבֶּה:

יד| **וְאַחֲרָיו לֹא יִהְיֶה כֵּן.** וְאוֹתוֹ שֶׁהָיָה בִּימֵי יוֹאֵל שֶׁנֶּאֱמַר: ״כָּמֹהוּ לֹא נִהְיָה מִן הָעוֹלָם״ (יואל ב, ב) לָמַדְנוּ שֶׁהָיָה כָּבֵד מִשֶּׁל מֹשֶׁה – עַל יְדֵי מִינִין הַרְבֵּה שֶׁהָיוּ יַחַד: אַרְבֶּה, יֶלֶק, חָסִיל, גָּזָם; אֲבָל שֶׁל מֹשֶׁה מִין אֶחָד, וְכָמוֹהוּ לֹא נִהְיָה וְלֹא יִהְיֶה:

15 **They covered the face of the entire land, and the land was darkened,** as it was covered with locusts.[44] Alternatively, the shadow of the flying swarm of locusts cast a giant shadow over the surface of the earth.[55] **And they consumed all the vegetation of the land and all the fruit of the trees that the hail left, and no greenery remained on the tree or in the vegetation of the field, in the entire land of Egypt.**

16 **Pharaoh hastened to summon Moses and Aaron, and he said: I have sinned to the Lord your God and to you.** This time he explicitly apologized for his rude behavior and for banishing them from his presence.

17 **Now, please bear my sin just this time and plead with the Lord your God that He will remove from me just this death.** Since it consumes all agricultural produce, the plague of locusts could kill us all.

18 **He,** Moses, **departed from Pharaoh's presence, and pleaded with the Lord** to remove the locusts.

19 Countering the east wind that brought the locusts to Egypt, **the Lord changed it to a very powerful west wind, and it carried the locusts and cast them into the Red Sea; not one locust remained within the entire border of Egypt.**

20 However, after Pharaoh's admission that he had sinned, his apology and his realization beyond a shadow of a doubt that Moses was capable of controlling these dramatic events, **the Lord hardened Pharaoh's heart and he did not send forth the children of Israel.**

The Plague of Darkness

EXODUS 10:21–29

The land of Egypt had already been darkened during the plague of locusts. The ninth plague consists of a deep, palpable darkness that prevents the Egyptians from even moving about. This foreshadows the ultimate plague, the death of the firstborn, for without the ability to see or move, the Egyptians experienced, to a certain degree, the taste of death.

21 **The Lord said to Moses: Extend your hand at the heavens and let there be darkness over the land of Egypt, and the darkness will be** a **palpable,**[D] tangible entity, not merely the absence of light.[66] Alternatively, the verse means that the darkness will move, arriving from elsewhere.[77]

22 **Moses extended his hand at the heavens and there was pitch darkness,** an absolute blackness, **in the entire land of Egypt for three days.**

23 **They did not see one another, nor did anyone rise from his place, for three days.** Due to the intensity of the darkness, they could not move around. **But all the children of Israel had light in their dwellings.** The darkness did not reach their vicinity. The Sages teach that the Israelites were accompanied by light wherever they went.[88]

24 **Pharaoh summoned Moses and he said:** All of you, **go, serve the Lord; only your flocks and your cattle will remain** as security for your return; **also your children will go with you.** This time I am allowing all the people, including men, women, and children, to depart.

Third aliya

25 **Moses said:** We have no intention of leaving our herds and flocks behind. On the contrary, **you too will put in our hand peace offerings and burnt offerings, and we will sacrifice to the Lord our God.**

26 **Our livestock will also go with us; a hoof** from our animals **shall not remain, as we will take from it,** our herds and flocks, **to serve the Lord our God, and we will not know with what we will serve the Lord until we come there.** We do not know how, in what quantity, and which kinds of animals will be required as offerings until we reach the wilderness and God reveals Himself and instructs us in His worship.

27 **The Lord hardened Pharaoh's heart, and he did not assent to send them forth,** despite the fearful darkness.

28 **Pharaoh said to him,** Moses: **Go from my presence; beware, do not continue to see my face, because on the day that you see my face you shall die.** Once again, Pharaoh banished Moses, but this time he threatened his life if he dared approach him again.

29 Since Moses had already heard from God what would happen, as recounted in the following section, he knew that he would not need to initiate another meeting with Pharaoh at the palace. Therefore, he confirmed Pharaoh's statement. **And Moses said: You have spoken truly; I will not continue to see your face anymore.**

DISCUSSION

10:21 | **The darkness will be palpable:** It has been noted that even nowadays there are types of darkness that are virtually tangible, such as smog, which can be impenetrable to artificial lighting. Accordingly, some have speculated that the historical occurrence that gave rise to this darkness was a volcanic eruption somewhere in the Mediterranean. A cloud of ash and dust, which was carried by the winds to Egypt, darkened the land for several days (see Shaul Hon, *Kings and Potsherds,* Tel Aviv: Golan Publishers, 1994 [Hebrew]).

טו וַיְכַס אֶת־עֵין כָּל־הָאָרֶץ וַתֶּחְשַׁךְ הָאָרֶץ וַיֹּאכַל אֶת־כָּל־עֵשֶׂב הָאָרֶץ וְאֵת כָּל־
פְּרִי הָעֵץ אֲשֶׁר הוֹתִיר הַבָּרָד וְלֹא־נוֹתַר כָּל־יֶרֶק בָּעֵץ וּבְעֵשֶׂב הַשָּׂדֶה בְּכָל־אֶרֶץ
טז מִצְרָיִם׃ וַיְמַהֵר פַּרְעֹה לִקְרֹא לְמֹשֶׁה וּלְאַהֲרֹן וַיֹּאמֶר חָטָאתִי לַיהוה אֱלֹהֵיכֶם
יז וְלָכֶם׃ וְעַתָּה שָׂא נָא חַטָּאתִי אַךְ הַפַּעַם וְהַעְתִּירוּ לַיהוה אֱלֹהֵיכֶם וְיָסֵר מֵעָלַי
יח יט רַק אֶת־הַמָּוֶת הַזֶּה׃ וַיֵּצֵא מֵעִם פַּרְעֹה וַיֶּעְתַּר אֶל־יהוה׃ וַיַּהֲפֹךְ יהוה רוּחַ־יָם
חָזָק מְאֹד וַיִּשָּׂא אֶת־הָאַרְבֶּה וַיִּתְקָעֵהוּ יָמָּה סּוּף לֹא נִשְׁאַר אַרְבֶּה אֶחָד בְּכֹל
כ גְּבוּל מִצְרָיִם׃ וַיְחַזֵּק יהוה אֶת־לֵב פַּרְעֹה וְלֹא שִׁלַּח אֶת־בְּנֵי יִשְׂרָאֵל׃
כא וַיֹּאמֶר יהוה אֶל־מֹשֶׁה נְטֵה יָדְךָ עַל־הַשָּׁמַיִם וִיהִי חֹשֶׁךְ עַל־אֶרֶץ מִצְרָיִם וְיָמֵשׁ
כב חֹשֶׁךְ׃ וַיֵּט מֹשֶׁה אֶת־יָדוֹ עַל־הַשָּׁמָיִם וַיְהִי חֹשֶׁךְ־אֲפֵלָה בְּכָל־אֶרֶץ מִצְרַיִם
כג שְׁלֹשֶׁת יָמִים׃ לֹא־רָאוּ אִישׁ אֶת־אָחִיו וְלֹא־קָמוּ אִישׁ מִתַּחְתָּיו שְׁלֹשֶׁת יָמִים
כד וּלְכָל־בְּנֵי יִשְׂרָאֵל הָיָה אוֹר בְּמוֹשְׁבֹתָם׃ וַיִּקְרָא פַרְעֹה אֶל־מֹשֶׁה וַיֹּאמֶר לְכוּ
כה עִבְדוּ אֶת־יהוה רַק צֹאנְכֶם וּבְקַרְכֶם יֻצָּג גַּם־טַפְּכֶם יֵלֵךְ עִמָּכֶם׃ וַיֹּאמֶר מֹשֶׁה
כו גַּם־אַתָּה תִּתֵּן בְּיָדֵנוּ זְבָחִים וְעֹלֹת וְעָשִׂינוּ לַיהוה אֱלֹהֵינוּ׃ וְגַם־מִקְנֵנוּ יֵלֵךְ
עִמָּנוּ לֹא תִשָּׁאֵר פַּרְסָה כִּי מִמֶּנּוּ נִקַּח לַעֲבֹד אֶת־יהוה אֱלֹהֵינוּ וַאֲנַחְנוּ לֹא־נֵדַע
כז מַה־נַּעֲבֹד אֶת־יהוה עַד־בֹּאֵנוּ שָׁמָּה׃ וַיְחַזֵּק יהוה אֶת־לֵב פַּרְעֹה וְלֹא אָבָה
כח לְשַׁלְּחָם׃ וַיֹּאמֶר־לוֹ פַרְעֹה לֵךְ מֵעָלָי הִשָּׁמֶר לְךָ אַל־תֹּסֶף רְאוֹת פָּנַי כִּי בְּיוֹם
כט רְאֹתְךָ פָנַי תָּמוּת׃ וַיֹּאמֶר מֹשֶׁה כֵּן דִּבַּרְתָּ לֹא־אֹסִף עוֹד רְאוֹת פָּנֶיךָ׃

רש"י

טו | כָּל יֶרֶק. עָלֶה יָרֹק, ויירדור"א בְּלַעַז:

יט | לֹא נִשְׁאַר אַרְבֶּה אֶחָד. אַף הַמְּלוּחִים שֶׁמָּלְחוּ מֵהֶן:

כא | וְיָמֵשׁ חֹשֶׁךְ. וְיַחְשִׁיךְ עֲלֵיהֶם חֹשֶׁךְ יוֹתֵר מֵחֶשְׁכּוֹ שֶׁל לַיְלָה, וְחֹשֶׁךְ שֶׁל לַיְלָה יַאֲמִישׁ וְיַחֲשִׁיךְ עוֹד: וְיָמֵשׁ. כְּמוֹ 'וְיַאֲמֵשׁ'. יֵשׁ לָנוּ תֵּבוֹת הַרְבֵּה חֲסֵרוֹת אָלֶ"ף, לְפִי שֶׁאֵין הֲבָרַת הָאָלֶ"ף נִכֶּרֶת כָּל כָּךְ אֵין הַכָּתוּב מַקְפִּיד עַל חֶסְרוֹנָהּ, כְּגוֹן: "וְלֹא יַהֵל שָׁם עֲרָבִי" (ישעיה יג, כ) כְּמוֹ 'לֹא יַאֲהֵל', לֹא יַטֶּה אָהֳלוֹ. וְכֵן: "וַתַּזְרֵנִי חַיִל" (שמואל ב' כב, מ) כְּמוֹ 'וַתְּאַזְּרֵנִי'. וְאוּנְקְלוֹס תִּרְגֵּם לְשׁוֹן הֲסָרָה, כְּמוֹ: "לֹא יָמִישׁ" (להלן יג, כב) – "בָּתַר דְּיִעְדֵּי קְבַל לֵילְיָא", כְּשֶׁיַּגִּיעַ סָמוּךְ לְאוֹר הַיּוֹם. אֲבָל אֵין הַדִּבּוּר מְיֻשָּׁב עַל הַוָּי"ו שֶׁל 'וְיָמֵשׁ', לְפִי שֶׁהוּא כָּתוּב אַחַר "וִיהִי חֹשֶׁךְ". וּמִדְרַשׁ אַגָּדָה פּוֹתְרוֹ לְשׁוֹן "מְמַשֵּׁשׁ בַּצָּהֳרַיִם" (דברים כח, כט), שֶׁהָיָה כָּפוּל וּמְכֻפָּל וְעָב עַד שֶׁהָיָה בּוֹ מַמָּשׁ:

כב | שְׁלֹשֶׁת יָמִים. שִׁלּוּשׁ שֶׁל יָמִים, טרציין"א בְּלַעַז. וְכֵן 'שִׁבְעַת יָמִים' בְּכָל מָקוֹם, סטיין"א שֶׁל יָמִים: וַיְהִי חֹשֶׁךְ אֲפֵלָה... שְׁלֹשֶׁת יָמִים. חֹשֶׁךְ שֶׁל אֹפֶל שֶׁ"לֹּא רָאוּ אִישׁ אֶת אָחִיו" אוֹתָן שְׁלֹשֶׁת יָמִים, וְעוֹד שְׁלֹשֶׁת יָמִים אֲחֵרִים חֹשֶׁךְ מְכֻפָּל עַל זֶה שֶׁ"לֹּא קָמוּ אִישׁ מִתַּחְתָּיו", יוֹשֵׁב אֵין יָכוֹל לַעֲמֹד וְעוֹמֵד אֵין יָכוֹל לֵישֵׁב. וְלָמָּה הֵבִיא עֲלֵיהֶם חֹשֶׁךְ? שֶׁהָיוּ בְּיִשְׂרָאֵל בְּאוֹתוֹ הַדּוֹר רְשָׁעִים וְלֹא הָיוּ רוֹצִים לָצֵאת, וּמֵתוּ בִּשְׁלֹשֶׁת יְמֵי אֲפֵלָה, כְּדֵי שֶׁלֹּא יִרְאוּ מִצְרִים בְּמַפָּלָתָם וְיֹאמְרוּ: אַף הֵם לוֹקִים כָּמוֹנוּ. וְעוֹד, שֶׁחִפְּשׂוּ יִשְׂרָאֵל וְרָאוּ אֶת כְּלֵיהֶם, וּכְשֶׁיָּצְאוּ וְהָיוּ שׁוֹאֲלִים מֵהֶן וְהָיוּ אוֹמְרִים: אֵין בְּיָדֵינוּ כְּלוּם, אוֹמֵר לוֹ: אֲנִי רְאִיתִיו בְּבֵיתְךָ וּבְמָקוֹם פְּלוֹנִי הוּא:

כד | יֻצָּג. יְהֵא מֻצָּג בִּמְקוֹמוֹ:

כה | גַּם אַתָּה תִּתֵּן. לֹא דַּיְּךָ שֶׁמִּקְנֵנוּ יֵלֵךְ עִמָּנוּ, אֶלָּא אַף מִשֶּׁלְּךָ תִּתֵּן:

כו | פַּרְסָה. פַּרְסַת רֶגֶל, פלנט"א בְּלַעַז: לֹא נֵדַע מַה נַּעֲבֹד. כַּמָּה תִּכְבַּד הָעֲבוֹדָה, שֶׁמָּא יִשְׁאַל יוֹתֵר מִמַּה שֶּׁיֵּשׁ בְּיָדֵינוּ:

כט | כֵּן דִּבַּרְתָּ. יָפֶה דִּבַּרְתָּ וּבִזְמַנּוֹ דִּבַּרְתָּ, אֱמֶת שֶׁ"לֹּא אֹסִף עוֹד רְאוֹת פָּנֶיךָ":

The Impending Plague of the Firstborn and an Interim Summary

EXODUS 11:1–10

Moses has not yet left Pharaoh's presence, and their conversation will continue in a few verses. Before Moses' latest confrontation with Pharaoh, God had already informed him that there would be one more plague before Israel would leave Egypt. That instruction was not recorded in its chronological place so that Pharaoh's response to the plague of darkness would appear immediately after the description of the plague. The verses below account for the fact that Moses has the confidence to say to Pharaoh: "You have spoken truly; I will not continue to see your face anymore" (10:29).

11 1 **The Lord said to Moses,** after the plague of darkness: **One more blow I will bring upon Pharaoh and upon Egypt; afterwards, he will send you forth from here; when he sends you forth, he will completely expel you from here.**

2 Therefore, the Israelites must prepare for the upcoming events: **Speak now in the ears of the people, and they shall ask each man from his neighbor, and each woman from her neighbor, silver vessels and gold vessels.** Although the Israelites were enslaved, they remained part of Egyptian society and maintained relationships with their neighbors. God commanded them, or perhaps merely requested, that they should borrow valuable objects from their Egyptian acquaintances.

3 One might have thought that the Egyptians would resent the Israelites after the plagues they had suffered on their account. However, **the Lord granted the people favor in the eyes of Egypt.** Initially victims of oppression and censure, the Israelites were now treated favorably by the Egyptians, who had become aware that a Great Power stood behind Israel. The social standing of the all the Israelites improved, **while the man Moses** was no longer looked upon as a stranger, but **was very great in the land of Egypt, in the eyes of Pharaoh's servants, and in the eyes of the people.**

4 After the above interlude, the Torah narrates the conclusion of the confrontation between Moses and Pharaoh in the palace. *Fourth aliya* Although he has been banished by Pharaoh, Moses continues to speak before he leaves. **Moses said: So said the Lord: About midnight,** or: At midnight,[99] **I will emerge in the midst of Egypt** and strike the Egyptians.

5 **Every firstborn in the land of Egypt will die, from the firstborn of Pharaoh,** the highest and most important in the land, **who sits on his throne, to the firstborn of the maidservant, who** possesses the lowest social status, as his mother performs the menial task of grinding grain while she **is** standing **behind the mill, and all firstborn animals.**

6 **There will be a great outcry in the entire land of Egypt that there has not been like it, nor will there be like it again.** The disaster will strike the entire land, as death will reach every household.

7 **But for all the children of Israel, a dog will not extend his tongue** at anyone, **from man to beast.** The dogs will not dare to so much as bark at the children of Israel or even at their animals, **so that you will know that the Lord distinguishes between Egypt and Israel.**

8 **All these servants of yours,** who surround you here, **will descend to me**[D] **and prostrate themselves to me, saying: Leave, you and all the people that follow you;**[1010] **and thereafter I will leave** Egypt. **He departed from Pharaoh's presence in enflamed wrath,** visibly angry.

9 This and the following verse conclude the account of the plagues, except for the very last and worst plague. The final plague is separated from the others both due to its severity and because of the commandments which will be given to the Israelites to be performed at the same time, as related in the next section. **The Lord** had **said to Moses** already: **Pharaoh will not heed you,** despite the threat against his own firstborn, **in order to increase My wonders in the land of Egypt.** This was stated before the onset of the plagues, in 7:4: "Pharaoh will not heed you."[1111]

10 **Moses and Aaron performed all these wonders before Pharaoh, and the Lord hardened Pharaoh's heart, and he did not send forth the children of Israel**[D] **from his land.**

DISCUSSION

11:8 | **All these servants of yours will descend to me:** The Sages note that Moses actually meant that Pharaoh himself would come to him to beg for their departure, as in fact occurred (12:31). However, despite Pharaoh's sins Moses addresses the king politely, ascribing the future humiliation to his servants (*Zevaḥim* 102a; *Shemot Rabba* 7:3).

11:10 | **The children of Israel:** The precise status of the Israelites during the plagues is unknown. Did their Egyptian masters continue to oppress them, or was it a period of anarchy in Egypt during which their enslavement and oppression were suspended (see *Rosh HaShana* 11a, and *Tosafot* ad loc.)? Either way, the plagues undoubtedly weakened the authority of the Egyptian monarchy, while in parallel the prestige of Israel increased in the eyes of the Egyptian people.

א וַיֹּאמֶר יְהוָה אֶל־מֹשֶׁה עוֹד נֶגַע אֶחָד אָבִיא עַל־פַּרְעֹה וְעַל־מִצְרַיִם אַחֲרֵי־ ח

ב כֵן יְשַׁלַּח אֶתְכֶם מִזֶּה כְּשַׁלְּחוֹ כָּלָה גָּרֵשׁ יְגָרֵשׁ אֶתְכֶם מִזֶּה: דַּבֶּר־נָא בְּאָזְנֵי

הָעָם וְיִשְׁאֲלוּ אִישׁ ׀ מֵאֵת רֵעֵהוּ וְאִשָּׁה מֵאֵת רְעוּתָהּ כְּלֵי־כֶסֶף וּכְלֵי זָהָב:

ג וַיִּתֵּן יְהוָה אֶת־חֵן הָעָם בְּעֵינֵי מִצְרָיִם גַּם ׀ הָאִישׁ מֹשֶׁה גָּדוֹל מְאֹד בְּאֶרֶץ

ד מִצְרַיִם בְּעֵינֵי עַבְדֵי־פַרְעֹה וּבְעֵינֵי הָעָם: וַיֹּאמֶר מֹשֶׁה כֹּה אָמַר יְהוָה כַּחֲצֹת רביעי

ה הַלַּיְלָה אֲנִי יוֹצֵא בְּתוֹךְ מִצְרָיִם: וּמֵת כָּל־בְּכוֹר בְּאֶרֶץ מִצְרַיִם מִבְּכוֹר פַּרְעֹה

הַיֹּשֵׁב עַל־כִּסְאוֹ עַד בְּכוֹר הַשִּׁפְחָה אֲשֶׁר אַחַר הָרֵחָיִם וְכֹל בְּכוֹר בְּהֵמָה:

ו וְהָיְתָה צְעָקָה גְדֹלָה בְּכָל־אֶרֶץ מִצְרָיִם אֲשֶׁר כָּמֹהוּ לֹא נִהְיָתָה וְכָמֹהוּ לֹא

ז תֹסִף: וּלְכֹל ׀ בְּנֵי יִשְׂרָאֵל לֹא יֶחֱרַץ־כֶּלֶב לְשֹׁנוֹ לְמֵאִישׁ וְעַד־בְּהֵמָה לְמַעַן

ח תֵּדְעוּן אֲשֶׁר יַפְלֶה יְהוָה בֵּין מִצְרַיִם וּבֵין יִשְׂרָאֵל: וְיָרְדוּ כָל־עֲבָדֶיךָ אֵלֶּה אֵלַי

וְהִשְׁתַּחֲווּ־לִי לֵאמֹר צֵא אַתָּה וְכָל־הָעָם אֲשֶׁר־בְּרַגְלֶיךָ וְאַחֲרֵי־כֵן אֵצֵא וַיֵּצֵא

ט מֵעִם־פַּרְעֹה בָּחֳרִי־אָף: וַיֹּאמֶר יְהוָה אֶל־מֹשֶׁה לֹא־יִשְׁמַע אֲלֵיכֶם פַּרְעֹה לְמַעַן

י רְבוֹת מוֹפְתַי בְּאֶרֶץ מִצְרָיִם: וּמֹשֶׁה וְאַהֲרֹן עָשׂוּ אֶת־כָּל־הַמֹּפְתִים הָאֵלֶּה

לִפְנֵי פַרְעֹה וַיְחַזֵּק יְהוָה אֶת־לֵב פַּרְעֹה וְלֹא־שִׁלַּח אֶת־בְּנֵי־יִשְׂרָאֵל מֵאַרְצוֹ:

רש"י

פרק יא

א] כָּלָה. "גְּמִירָא", כָּלִיל, כֻּלְּכֶם יְשֻׁלַּח:

ב] דַּבֶּר נָא. אֵין נָא אֶלָּא לְשׁוֹן בַּקָּשָׁה, בְּבַקָּשָׁה מִמְּךָ הַזְהִירֵם עַל כָּךְ, שֶׁלֹּא יֹאמַר אוֹתוֹ צַדִּיק, אַבְרָהָם, "וַעֲבָדוּם וְעִנּוּ אֹתָם" (בראשית טו, יג), קִיֵּם בָּהֶם, "וְאַחֲרֵי כֵן יֵצְאוּ בִּרְכֻשׁ גָּדוֹל" (שם פסוק יד) לֹא קִיֵּם בָּהֶם:

ד] וַיֹּאמֶר מֹשֶׁה כֹּה אָמַר ה'. בְּעָמְדוֹ לִפְנֵי פַרְעֹה נֶאֶמְרָה לוֹ, שֶׁהֲרֵי מִשֶּׁיָּצָא מִלְּפָנָיו לֹא הוֹסִיף רְאוֹת פָּנָיו: **כַּחֲצֹת הַלַּיְלָה.** כְּהֵחָלֵק הַלַּיְלָה. כַּחֲצֹת כְּמוֹ: "כַּעֲלוֹת" (יהושע ה, יח, ועוד), "כְּכַלֹּת" (דברים כ, ט, ועוד) "בַּחֲרוֹת חַמֵּם כַּפֵּס בְּנִי" (תהלים קכד, ב). זֶהוּ פְשׁוּטוֹ לְיַשְּׁבוֹ עַל אָפְנָיו, שֶׁאֵין "חֲצוֹת" שֵׁם דָּבָר שֶׁל חֵצִי. וְרַבּוֹתֵינוּ דְּרָשׁוּהוּ כְּמוֹ "כַּחֲצִי הַלַּיְלָה", וְאָמְרוּ שֶׁאָמַר מֹשֶׁה "כַּחֲצֹת" דְּמַשְׁמַע סָמוּךְ לוֹ לְפָנָיו אוֹ לְאַחֲרָיו, וְלֹא אָמַר "בַּחֲצֹת" שֶׁמָּא יִטְעוּ אִצְטַגְנִינֵי פַרְעֹה וְיֹאמְרוּ: מֹשֶׁה בַּדַּאי הוּא:

ה] עַד בְּכוֹר הַשְּׁבִי (להלן יב, כט). לָמָּה לָקוּ הַשְּׁבוּיִים? כְּדֵי שֶׁלֹּא יֹאמְרוּ, יִרְאָתָם תָּבְעָה עֶלְבּוֹנָם וְהֵבִיאָה פֻּרְעָנוּת עַל מִצְרַיִם: **מִבְּכוֹר פַּרְעֹה... עַד בְּכוֹר הַשִּׁפְחָה.** כָּל הַפְּחוּתִים מִבְּכוֹר פַּרְעֹה וַחֲשׁוּבִים מִבְּכוֹר הַשִּׁפְחָה הָיוּ בִכְלָל. וְלָמָּה לָקוּ בְנֵי הַשְּׁפָחוֹת? שֶׁאַף הֵם הָיוּ מִשְׁתַּעְבְּדִים בָּהֶם וּשְׂמֵחִים בְּצָרָתָם, וְכֹל בְּכוֹר בְּהֵמָה. לְפִי שֶׁהָיוּ עוֹבְדִין לָהּ — כְּשֶׁהַקָּדוֹשׁ בָּרוּךְ הוּא נִפְרָע מִן הָאֻמָּה נִפְרָע מֵאֱלֹהֶיהָ:

ז] לֹא יֶחֱרַץ כֶּלֶב לְשֹׁנוֹ. אוֹמֵר אֲנִי שֶׁהוּא לְשׁוֹן שִׁנּוּן, לֹא יְשַׁנֵּן. וְכֵן: "לֹא חָרַץ לִבְנֵי יִשְׂרָאֵל לְאִישׁ אֶת לְשֹׁנוֹ" (יהושע י, כח) — לֹא שִׁנֵּן, "חָז תְּחֱרָךְ" (שמואל ב' ה, כד) — תִּשְׁתַּנֵּן, "לִמְגוּג חָרוּץ" (ישעיה מא, טו), "מַחֲשְׁבוֹת חָרוּץ" (משלי כא, ה) — אָדָם חָרִיף וְשָׁנוּן, "יָד חָרוּצִים תַּעֲשִׁיר" (משלי י, ד) — חָרִיפִים, סוֹחֲרִים שְׁנוּנִים: **אֲשֶׁר יַפְלֶה.** יַבְדִּיל:

ח] וְיָרְדוּ כָל עֲבָדֶיךָ. חָלַק כָּבוֹד לַמַּלְכוּת, שֶׁהֲרֵי סוֹף שֶׁיָּרַד פַּרְעֹה בְּעַצְמוֹ אֵלָיו בַּלַּיְלָה, "וַיֹּאמֶר קוּמוּ צְּאוּ מִתּוֹךְ עַמִּי" (להלן יב, לא), וְלֹא אָמַר לוֹ מֹשֶׁה מִתְּחִלָּה: **וְיָרַדְתָ חֵלִי וְהִשְׁתַּחֲווּ לִי:** **אֲשֶׁר בְּרַגְלֶיךָ.** הַהוֹלְכִים אַחַר עֲצָתְךָ וְהִלּוּכְךָ: **וְאַחֲרֵי כֵן אֵצֵא.** עִם כָּל הָעָם מֵאַרְצְךָ: **וַיֵּצֵא מֵעִם פַּרְעֹה.** כְּשֶׁגָּמַר דְּבָרָיו יָצָא מִלְּפָנָיו: **בָּחֳרִי אָף.** עַל שֶׁאָמַר לוֹ: "אַל תֹּסֶף רְאוֹת פָּנַי" (לעיל י, כח):

ט] לְמַעַן רְבוֹת מוֹפְתַי. מַכַּת בְּכוֹרוֹת וּקְרִיעַת יַם סוּף וּלְנַעֵר אֶת מִצְרַיִם:

י] וּמֹשֶׁה וְאַהֲרֹן עָשׂוּ וְגו'. כְּבָר כָּתַב לָנוּ זֹאת בְּכָל הַמּוֹפְתִים, וְלֹא שְׁנָאָהּ כָּאן אֶלָּא בִּשְׁבִיל לְסָמְכָהּ לַפָּרָשָׁה שֶׁל אַחֲרֶיהָ: **וַיֹּאמֶר ה' אֶל מֹשֶׁה וְאֶל אַהֲרֹן,** שֶׁבִּשְׁבִיל שֶׁהֵם עָשׂוּ אֶת הַמּוֹפְתִים כְּמֹשֶׁה, חָלַק לוֹ כָּבוֹד זֶה בְּמִצְוָה רִאשׁוֹנָה שֶׁנִּכְלְלוּ עִם מֹשֶׁה בַּדִּבּוּר:

Commandments Associated with the Exodus

EXODUS 12:1–28

Up to this point, the Torah has recounted the events leading up to the exodus: The birth of Moses and the early events of his life, including his appointment as God's agent to lead the people. This was followed by a detailed account of the plagues that God inflicted upon Egypt, and Moses' ongoing confrontation with Pharaoh. The following section is the first passage which is law rather than narrative.

12 1 **The Lord spoke to Moses and Aaron in the land of Egypt, saying:**

2 **This** current **month,** Nisan, **is for you the beginning of months;**ᴰ **it is first for you of the months of the year.**

3 The commandment of the beginning of months was given solely to Moses and Aaron because as heads of the judicial system, they were in charge of establishing the calendar and determining the months and years.¹²¹²The other commandments that God gave to Moses at this juncture had to be communicated to the people. **Speak to the entire congregation of Israel, saying: On the tenth** day **of this month they shall take for themselves, each one, a lamb,** a young sheep or goat, **for each house of the fathers, a lamb for the household.**

4 **If the household will be too few for a lamb,** as the family is too small to eat an entire lamb, **then he and his neighbor who is near his house shall take** one lamb together, **according to the number of people; each according to** the estimated amount of **his eating you shall account,** by setting the number of those appointed **for** eating **the lamb.** Since the lamb is an offering that must be eaten, only those who can actually consume some minimal amount may be numbered among those who will partake of it. The elderly, sick, or very young, who are unable to eat a minimal amount, are excluded from the tally for each particular lamb.¹³¹³

5 **An unblemished lamb, a male in the first year** of its life **it shall be for you; you shall take it from the sheep or from the goats.**

6 After setting the lamb aside on the tenth of the month, **it shall be for you for safekeeping until the fourteenth day of this month and the entire assembly of the congregation of Israel shall slaughter it** as an offering **in the afternoon.**ᴰ

Placing the blood on the doorposts and on the lintel

7 **They shall take from the blood**ᴰ of the slaughtered lamb, **and put it on the two doorposts** of the entryway to the house **and on the lintel, on the houses in which they will eat it.** If more

---

DISCUSSION

12:2 | This month is for you the beginning of months: The two halves of this verse express their related ideas, in the poetic form of a parallel couplet. This verse teaches that the Jewish calendar begins with the month of Nisan (see Mishna *Rosh HaShana* 1:1, and the Talmud ad loc., 10b–11a).

The Sages interpret the first appearance in the verse of the word *ḥodesh*, "month," as referring to the monthly renewal of the moon. This follows the Biblical usage of the term in various other places (see Numbers 29:6; I Samuel 20:34; II Kings 4:23; commentary on Exodus 19:1). This exposition is based on the fact that the moon itself, at least at the time of its renewal, *ḥidusho*, can be called *ḥodesh*, just as the sun, whose presence defines the daytime, is sometimes called "day." Accordingly, in Rabbinic Hebrew *ḥodesh*

often refers to the new moon (see, e.g., Mishna *Rosh HaShana* 1:7). If so, the word "this" is not referring to the specific month, but to an object that was visible to Moses and Aaron: This new moon (*Tanḥuma Shemini* 11; Rashi). This is the basis for the idea that God showed Moses and Aaron a new moon as an example of what must be seen for the court to consecrate the months in the future. The Sages derive from here that the beginning of each month is established in accordance with the sighting of the new moon.

12:6 | In the afternoon [bein ha'arbayim]: This is a special plural form that indicates a matching pair. The term could be rendered literally as between the evenings. Some commentaries note that the word for evening, *erev*, is related to the word for west, *ma'arav*, the direction of the setting sun. Accordingly, *bein ha'arbayim* is

the period of time from when the sun begins to enter the western part of the sky until it sets, which is the afternoon (see *Shabbat* 34b; Rashi; Ibn Ezra; Ramban).

12:7 | They shall take from the blood: The paschal lamb must be consumed by those who bring it, similar to what will come to be known as a peace offering. In the Temple, the blood of the paschal offering was poured onto the altar, and certain portions of the animal were burnt upon it. Here, however, the entire animal was eaten by its owners. For this reason, the sprinkling of the blood on the doorposts is of special significance, as it is the only indication that this is an offering. For the time being, the Israelites had no Temple, no consecrated objects, and no altar, and therefore their homes served as a kind of substitute for the altar (see *Pesaḥim* 66a).

ב א ב וַיֹּאמֶר יְהוָה אֶל־מֹשֶׁה וְאֶל־אַהֲרֹן בְּאֶרֶץ מִצְרַיִם לֵאמֹר: הַחֹדֶשׁ הַזֶּה לָכֶם
ג רֹאשׁ חֳדָשִׁים רִאשׁוֹן הוּא לָכֶם לְחָדְשֵׁי הַשָּׁנָה: דַּבְּרוּ אֶל־כָּל־עֲדַת יִשְׂרָאֵל
לֵאמֹר בֶּעָשֹׂר לַחֹדֶשׁ הַזֶּה וְיִקְחוּ לָהֶם אִישׁ שֶׂה לְבֵית־אָבֹת שֶׂה לַבָּיִת:
ד וְאִם־יִמְעַט הַבַּיִת מִהְיֹת מִשֶּׂה וְלָקַח הוּא וּשְׁכֵנוֹ הַקָּרֹב אֶל־בֵּיתוֹ בְּמִכְסַת
ה נְפָשֹׁת אִישׁ לְפִי אָכְלוֹ תָּכֹסּוּ עַל־הַשֶּׂה: שֶׂה תָמִים זָכָר בֶּן־שָׁנָה יִהְיֶה לָכֶם
ו מִן־הַכְּבָשִׂים וּמִן־הָעִזִּים תִּקָּחוּ: וְהָיָה לָכֶם לְמִשְׁמֶרֶת עַד אַרְבָּעָה עָשָׂר יוֹם
ז לַחֹדֶשׁ הַזֶּה וְשָׁחֲטוּ אֹתוֹ כֹּל קְהַל עֲדַת־יִשְׂרָאֵל בֵּין הָעַרְבָּיִם: וְלָקְחוּ מִן־
הַדָּם וְנָתְנוּ עַל־שְׁתֵּי הַמְּזוּזֹת וְעַל־הַמַּשְׁקוֹף עַל הַבָּתִּים אֲשֶׁר־יֹאכְלוּ אֹתוֹ
ח בָּהֶם: וְאָכְלוּ אֶת־הַבָּשָׂר בַּלַּיְלָה הַזֶּה צְלִי־אֵשׁ וּמַצּוֹת עַל־מְרֹרִים יֹאכְלֻהוּ:

רש"י

פרק יב

א| **בארץ מצרים.** חוץ לכרך. או אינו אלא בתוך הכרך? תלמוד לומר: "כצאתי את העיר" וגו' (לעיל ט, כט). ומה תפלה קלה לא התפלל בתוך הכרך, דבור חמור לא כל שכן? ומפני מה לא נדבר עמו בתוך הכרך? לפי שהיתה מלאה גלולים:

ב| **החדש הזה.** הראהו לבנה בחדושה ואמר לו: כשהירח מתחדש יהיה לך ראש חדש. ואין מקרא יוצא מידי פשוטו, על חדש ניסן אמר לו, זה יהיה ראש לסדר מנין החדשים, שיהא אייר קרוי שני, סיון שלישי: **הזה.** נתקשה משה על מולד הלבנה באיזו שעור תראה ותהיה ראויה לקדש, והראה לו באצבע את הלבנה ברקיע ואמר לו: כזה ראה וקדש. וכיצד הראהו? והלא לא היה נדבר עמו אלא ביום, שנאמר: "ויהי ביום דבר ה'" (לעיל ו, כח), "ביום צותו" (ויקרא ז, לח), "מן היום אשר צוה ה' והלאה" (במדבר טו, כג)? אלא סמוך לשקיעת החמה נאמרה לו פרשה זו והראהו עם חשכה:

ג| **דברו אל כל עדת.** וכי אהרן מדבר? והלא כבר נאמר: "אתה תדבר" (לעיל ז, ב)! אלא חולקין כבוד זה לזה ואומרים זה לזה: למדני, והדבור יוצא מבין שניהם כאלו שניהם מדברים: **דברו אל כל עדת ישראל לאמר בעשר לחדש.** דברו היום בראש חדש שיקחוהו בעשור לחדש: **הזה.** פסח מצרים מקחו בעשור ולא פסח דורות: **שה לבית אבת.** למשפחה אחת. הרי שהיו מרבין יכול שה אחד לכלן? תלמוד לומר: "שה לבית":

ד| **ואם ימעט הבית מהיות משה.** ואם יהיו מועטין מהיות משה אחד, שאין יכולין לאכלו ויבא לידי נותר – "ולקח הוא ושכנו" וגו', זהו משמעו לפשוטו. ועוד יש בו מדרש, ללמד שאחר שנמנו עליו יכולין להתמעט ולמשוך ידיהם הימנו ולהמנות על שה אחר, אך אם באו למשוך ידיהם ולהתמעט – "מהיות משה" יתמעטו, בעוד השה קים, בהיותו בחיים, ולא משנשחט: **במכסת.** חשבון, וכן: "מכסת הערכך" (ויקרא כז, כג): **לפי אכלו.** הראוי לאכילה, פרט לחולה ולזקן שאינו יכול לאכול כזית: **תכסו.** "תתמנון":

ה| **תמים.** בלא מום: **בן שנה.** כל שנתו קרוי 'בן שנה', כלומר שנולד בשנה זו: **מן הכבשים ומן העזים.** או מזה או מזה, שאף עז קרוי 'שה', שנאמר: "ושה עזים" (דברים יד, ד):

ו| **והיה לכם למשמרת.** זהו לשון בקור, שטעון בקור ממום ארבעה ימים קדם שחיטה. ומפני מה הקדים לקיחתו לשחיטתו ארבעה ימים, מה שלא צוה כן בפסח דורות? היה רבי מתיא בן חרש אומר: הרי הוא אומר: "ואעבר עליך ואראך והנה עתך עת דדים" (יחזקאל טז, ח), הגיעה שבועה שנשבעתי לאברהם שאגאל את בניו, ולא היו בידם מצוות להתעסק בהם כדי שיגאלו, שנאמר: "ואת ערם ועריה" (שם פסוק ז), ונתן להם שתי מצוות, דם פסח ודם מילה, שמלו באותו הלילה, שנאמר: "מתבוססת בדמיך" (שם פסוק ו) בשני דמים, ואומר: "גם את בדם בריתך שלחתי אסיריך מבור אין מים בו" (זכריה ט, יא); ושהיו שטופים בעבודה זרה, אמר להם: "משכו וקחו לכם" (להלן פסוק כא), משכו ידיכם מעבודה זרה וקחו לכם צאן של מצוה: **ושחטו אתו וגו'.** וכי כלן שוחטין? אלא מכאן ששלוחו של אדם כמותו: **קהל עדת ישראל.** קהל ועדה וישראל. מכאן אמרו: פסחי צבור נשחטים בשלש כתות זו אחר זו. נכנסה כת ראשונה ננעלו דלתות העזרה וכו', כדאיתא בפסחים (דף סד ע"א): **בין הערבים.** משש שעות ולמעלה קרוי 'בין הערבים', שהשמש נוטה לבית מבואו לערב. ולשון 'בין הערבים' נראה בעיני, אותן שעות שבין עריבת היום לעריבת הלילה, עריבת היום בתחלת שבע שעות מכי ינטו צללי ערב, ועריבת הלילה בתחלת הלילה. 'ערב' לשון נשף וחשך, כמו: "ערבה כל שמחה" (ישעיה כד, יא):

ז| **ולקחו מן הדם.** זו קבלת הדם. יכול ביד? תלמוד לומר: "אשר בסף" (להלן פסוק כב): **המזוזת.** הם הזקופות, אחת מכאן לפתח ואחת מכאן: **המשקוף.** הוא העליון, שהדלת שוקף עליו כשסוגרין אותו, לינט"ל בלע"ז. ולשון 'שקיפה' – חבטה, כמו: "קול עלה נדף" (ויקרא כו, לו) – "דשקיף". "חבורה" (להלן כא, כה) – משקופי: **על הבתים אשר יאכלו אתו בהם.** ולא על משקוף ומזוזות שבבית התבן ובית הבקר, שאין דרין בתוכו:

ח| **את הבשר.** ולא גידים ועצמות: **על מררים.** כל עשב מר נקרא 'מרור'. וצוה לאכל מר זכר ל"וימררו את חייהם" (לעיל א, יד):

than one family eats in one house, or if a single family eats two lambs as separate groups in two houses, the blood must be sprinkled on each house in which the eating takes place.[1414]

8 **They shall eat the meat on that night, roasted over fire, and they shall** also **eat it with unleavened bread, with** either the leaves or stalks of **bitter herbs.**

9 **You shall not eat from it half cooked, nor cooked in water, only roasted over fire, its head with its legs and with its innards.** The entire lamb must be roasted as a single unit.

10 **You shall not leave anything from it until morning,**[D] as it must be wholly consumed that night. **And** if this nevertheless occurs, **that which remains until morning you shall burn with fire.**

11 As well as the requirement that it be eaten in the manner of liberated people, there is a further significance to the consumption of the lamb. **So you shall eat it: Your loins girded, your shoes on your feet.** Many people, especially simple farm workers, would ordinarily go barefoot. The donning of shoes signifies that they are about to depart on a journey. **And** eat it with **your** walking **staff in your hand; you shall eat it in haste, it is the paschal lamb to the Lord.**[D]

12 God informs Israel of the forthcoming events: **I will pass through the land of Egypt on that night and I will smite all** the firstborn in the land of Egypt, from man to animal, and against all the gods of Egypt I will administer great **punishments: I am the Lord.**

13 **The blood** that you will place on the doorways **shall be a sign for you on the houses where you are and I will see the blood; I will pass over you,** or: I will have mercy upon you, that you will not be struck. **And there shall not be a stroke against you to destroy, when I smite the land of Egypt.**

14 Up to this point, the Israelites have been commanded only with regard to the next few days, until the fourteenth of Nisan of the current year. Now God instructs them to commemorate this date in the future as well: **This day shall be a remembrance for you, and you shall celebrate it as a festival to the Lord; for your generations, you shall celebrate it as an eternal statute.**

15 These days shall be commemorated each year in the following manner: **Seven days you shall eat unleavened bread.**[D] At this

---
DISCUSSION

12:10 | **You shall not leave anything from it until morning:** As an expression of their liberation, the Israelites are commanded to eat the roasted paschal lamb whole, in the manner of free hunters. The prohibition to leave over any meat until the morning, the commandment that it must be roasted, and the instruction to eat it with bitter herbs all typify the practices of free people who are their own masters. A person of limited means would prefer to cook meat in liquid, as he can save some for later and thereby maximize the meals that he can derive from one animal, whereas nobles and princes

would eat their meat roasted. Similarly, eating the meat with bitter herbs as a condiment is a sort of luxurious behavior (see Ibn Ezra). The commandment not to break the bones of the paschal lamb (verse 46), without concern for maximizing the extraction of as much meat as possible from the animal (see *Sefer HaḤinnukh* 16), is a further expression of the largesse associated with the offering.

12:11 | **It is the paschal lamb [pesaḥ] to the Lord:** It is difficult to establish the precise meaning of the term *pesaḥ* from the appearances

of the word in the Bible. Some commentaries interpret it as skipping or passing over (Rashi; *Bekhor Shor*; see Isaiah 35:6; I Kings 18:21). If so, the paschal lamb is an offering that evokes the salvation wrought when God passed over the Israelites and spared them the punishments and plagues He brought upon Egypt. Others explain that *pesaḥ* means a gift, aid, or grace (*Targum Yonatan*; Onkelos, verse 13; see Isaiah 31:5; Ibn Janaḥ, I Kings 18:21, 26). The two interpretations, despite the linguistic difference between them, do not contradict one another, and both fit the context well.

The Commandments Involving the Paschal Lamb that Apply for All Generations

Two positive commandments	Seven negative commandments
"The entire assembly of the congregation of Israel shall slaughter it in the afternoon" (verse 6)	"You shall not eat from it half cooked, nor cooked in water" (verse 9)
"They shall eat the meat on that night, roasted over fire, and they shall eat it with unleavened bread with bitter herbs" (verse 8)	"You shall not leave anything from it until morning" (verse 10)
	"No foreigner shall eat from it" (verse 43)
	"A resident alien and a hired laborer shall not eat from it" (verse 45)
	"You shall not remove any of the meat from the house to the outside" (verse 46)
	"You shall not break a bone of it" (verse 46)
	"But all uncircumcised persons shall not eat from it" (verse 48), including uncircumcised Jews

ט אַל־תֹּאכְלוּ מִמֶּנּוּ נָא וּבָשֵׁל מְבֻשָּׁל בַּמָּיִם כִּי אִם־צְלִי־אֵשׁ רֹאשׁוֹ עַל־כְּרָעָיו
י וְעַל־קִרְבּוֹ׃ וְלֹא־תוֹתִירוּ מִמֶּנּוּ עַד־בֹּקֶר וְהַנֹּתָר מִמֶּנּוּ עַד־בֹּקֶר בָּאֵשׁ תִּשְׂרֹפוּ׃
יא וְכָכָה תֹּאכְלוּ אֹתוֹ מָתְנֵיכֶם חֲגֻרִים נַעֲלֵיכֶם בְּרַגְלֵיכֶם וּמַקֶּלְכֶם בְּיֶדְכֶם וַאֲכַלְתֶּם
יב אֹתוֹ בְּחִפָּזוֹן פֶּסַח הוּא לַיהוָה׃ וְעָבַרְתִּי בְאֶרֶץ־מִצְרַיִם בַּלַּיְלָה הַזֶּה וְהִכֵּיתִי כָל־
בְּכוֹר בְּאֶרֶץ מִצְרַיִם מֵאָדָם וְעַד־בְּהֵמָה וּבְכָל־אֱלֹהֵי מִצְרַיִם אֶעֱשֶׂה שְׁפָטִים
יג אֲנִי יְהוָה׃ וְהָיָה הַדָּם לָכֶם לְאֹת עַל הַבָּתִּים אֲשֶׁר אַתֶּם שָׁם וְרָאִיתִי אֶת־הַדָּם
יד וּפָסַחְתִּי עֲלֵכֶם וְלֹא־יִהְיֶה בָכֶם נֶגֶף לְמַשְׁחִית בְּהַכֹּתִי בְּאֶרֶץ מִצְרָיִם׃ וְהָיָה הַיּוֹם
טו הַזֶּה לָכֶם לְזִכָּרוֹן וְחַגֹּתֶם אֹתוֹ חַג לַיהוָה לְדֹרֹתֵיכֶם חֻקַּת עוֹלָם תְּחָגֻּהוּ׃ שִׁבְעַת
יָמִים מַצּוֹת תֹּאכֵלוּ אַךְ בַּיּוֹם הָרִאשׁוֹן תַּשְׁבִּיתוּ שְּׂאֹר מִבָּתֵּיכֶם כִּי ׀ כָּל־אֹכֵל חָמֵץ

רש״י

ט | **אַל תֹּאכְלוּ מִמֶּנּוּ נָא.** שֶׁאֵינוֹ צָלוּי כָּל צָרְכּוֹ קוֹרְאוֹ 'נָא' בְּלָשׁוֹן עֲרָבִי: **וּבָשֵׁל מְבֻשָּׁל.** כָּל זֶה בְּאַזְהָרַת "אַל תֹּאכְלוּ": **בַּמָּיִם.** מִנַּיִן לִשְׁאָר מַשְׁקִים? תַּלְמוּד לוֹמַר: "וּבָשֵׁל מְבֻשָּׁל" מִכָּל מָקוֹם: **כִּי אִם צְלִי אֵשׁ.** לְמַעְלָה גָּזַר עָלָיו בְּמִצְוַת עֲשֵׂה, וְכָאן הוֹסִיף עָלָיו לֹא תַעֲשֶׂה: "אַל תֹּאכְלוּ מִמֶּנּוּ... כִּי אִם צְלִי אֵשׁ": **רֹאשׁוֹ עַל כְּרָעָיו.** צוֹלֵהוּ כֻּלּוֹ כְּאֶחָד עִם רֹאשׁוֹ וְעִם כְּרָעָיו וְעִם קִרְבּוֹ, וּבְנֵי מֵעָיו נוֹתֵן לְתוֹכוֹ לְאַחַר הֲדָחָתָן. וּלְשׁוֹן: "עַל כְּרָעָיו וְעַל קִרְבּוֹ" כִּלְשׁוֹן "עַל צִבְאֹתָם" (לעיל ו, כו) כְּמוֹ בְּצִבְאֹתָם, כְּמוֹת שֶׁהֵן, אַף זֶה כְּמוֹת שֶׁהוּא, כָּל בְּשָׂרוֹ מֻשְׁלָם:

י | **וְהַנֹּתָר מִמֶּנּוּ עַד בֹּקֶר.** מַה תַּלְמוּד לוֹמַר "עַד בֹּקֶר" פַּעַם שְׁנִיָּה? לִתֵּן בֹּקֶר עַל בֹּקֶר, שֶׁהַבֹּקֶר מַשְׁמָעוֹ הָנֵץ הַחַמָּה, וּבָא הַכָּתוּב לְהַקְדִּים שֶׁאָסוּר בַּאֲכִילָה מֵעֲלוֹת הַשַּׁחַר; זֶהוּ לְפִי מַשְׁמָעוֹ. וְעוֹד מִדְרָשׁ אַחֵר, לִמֵּד שֶׁאֵינוֹ נִשְׂרָף בְּיוֹם טוֹב אֶלָּא מִמָּחֳרָת, וְכָךְ תִּדְרְשֶׁנּוּ: "וְהַנּוֹתָר מִמֶּנּוּ" בְּבֹקֶר רִאשׁוֹן "עַד בֹּקֶר" שֵׁנִי תַּעֲמֹד וְתִשְׂרְפֶנּוּ:

יא | **מָתְנֵיכֶם חֲגֻרִים.** מְזֻמָּנִים לַדֶּרֶךְ: **בְּחִפָּזוֹן.** לְשׁוֹן בֶּהָלָה וּמְהִירוּת, כְּמוֹ: "וַיְהִי דָוִד נֶחְפָּז לָלֶכֶת" (שמואל א' כג, כו), "אֲשֶׁר הִשְׁלִיכוּ אֲרָם בְּחָפְזָם" (מלכים ב' ז, טו): **פֶּסַח הוּא לַה'.** הַקָּרְבָּן קָרוּי 'פֶּסַח' עַל שֵׁם הַפְּסִיחָה, וְאַתֶּם עֲשׂוּ כָּל עֲבוֹדוֹתָיו לְשֵׁם שָׁמַיִם:

יב | **וְעָבַרְתִּי.** כְּמֶלֶךְ הָעוֹבֵר מִמָּקוֹם לְמָקוֹם וּבְהַעֲבָרָה אַחַת וּבְרֶגַע אֶחָד כֻּלָּן לוֹקִין: **כָּל בְּכוֹר בְּאֶרֶץ מִצְרַיִם.** אַף בְּכוֹרוֹת אֲחֵרִים וְהֵם בְּמִצְרַיִם. וּמִנַּיִן אַף בְּכוֹרֵי מִצְרַיִם שֶׁבִּמְקוֹמוֹת אֲחֵרִים? תַּלְמוּד לוֹמַר: "לְמַכֵּה מִצְרַיִם בִּבְכוֹרֵיהֶם" (תהלים קלו, י): **מֵאָדָם וְעַד בְּהֵמָה.** מִי שֶׁהִתְחִיל בַּעֲבֵרָה תְּחִלָּה מִמֶּנּוּ מַתְחֶלֶת הַפֻּרְעָנוּת: **וּבְכָל אֱלֹהֵי מִצְרַיִם.** שֶׁל עֵץ נִרְקֶבֶת וְשֶׁל מַתֶּכֶת נִמֶּסֶת וְנִתֶּכֶת לָאָרֶץ: **אֶעֱשֶׂה שְׁפָטִים אֲנִי ה'.** אֲנִי בְּעַצְמִי וְלֹא עַל יְדֵי שָׁלִיחַ:

יג | **וְהָיָה הַדָּם לָכֶם לְאֹת.** לָכֶם לְאוֹת וְלֹא לַאֲחֵרִים לְאוֹת. מִכָּאן שֶׁלֹּא נָתְנוּ הַדָּם אֶלָּא מִבִּפְנִים: **וְרָאִיתִי אֶת הַדָּם.** הַכֹּל גָּלוּי לְפָנָיו, אֶלָּא אָמַר הַקָּדוֹשׁ בָּרוּךְ הוּא: נוֹתֵן אֲנִי אֶת עֵינַי לִרְאוֹת שֶׁאַתֶּם עֲסוּקִים בְּמִצְוֹתַי וּפוֹסֵחַ אֲנִי עֲלֵיכֶם: **וּפָסַחְתִּי.** וְחָמַלְתִּי, וְדוֹמֶה לוֹ: "פָּסוֹחַ וְהִמְלִיט" (ישעיה לא, ה). וַאֲנִי אוֹמֵר כָּל פְּסִיחָה לְשׁוֹן דִּלּוּג וּקְפִיצָה, "וּפָסַחְתִּי" – מְדַלֵּג הָיָה מִבָּתֵּי יִשְׂרָאֵל לְבָתֵּי מִצְרַיִם, שֶׁהָיוּ שְׁרוּיִם זֶה בְּתוֹךְ זֶה. וְכֵן: "פֹּסְחִים עַל שְׁתֵּי הַסְּעִפִּים" (מלכים א' יח, כא). וְכֵן כָּל הַפִּסְחִים הוֹלְכִים כְּקוֹפְצִים. וְכֵן: "פָּסוֹחַ וְהִמְלִיט", מְדַלְּגוֹ וּמְמַלְּטוֹ מִבֵּין הַמּוּמָתִים: **וְלֹא יִהְיֶה בָכֶם נֶגֶף.** אֲבָל הֹוֶה הוּא בַּמִּצְרִים. הֲרֵי שֶׁהָיָה מִצְרִי בְּבֵיתוֹ שֶׁל יִשְׂרָאֵל, יָכוֹל יִמָּלֵט? תַּלְמוּד לוֹמַר: "וְלֹא יִהְיֶה בָכֶם נֶגֶף", אֲבָל הֹוֶה בַּמִּצְרִים שֶׁבְּבָתֵּיכֶם. הֲרֵי שֶׁהָיָה יִשְׂרָאֵל בְּבֵיתוֹ שֶׁל מִצְרִי, שׁוֹמֵעַ אֲנִי יִלְקֶה כְּמוֹתוֹ? תַּלְמוּד לוֹמַר: "וְלֹא יִהְיֶה בָכֶם נֶגֶף":

יד | **לְזִכָּרוֹן.** לְדוֹרוֹת: **וְחַגֹּתֶם אֹתוֹ.** יוֹם שֶׁהוּא לְךָ לְזִכָּרוֹן אַתָּה חוֹגְגוֹ. וַעֲדַיִן לֹא שָׁמַעְנוּ אֵי זֶהוּ יוֹם הַזִּכָּרוֹן, תַּלְמוּד לוֹמַר: "זָכוֹר אֶת הַיּוֹם הַזֶּה אֲשֶׁר יְצָאתֶם" (להלן יג, ג), לָמַדְנוּ שֶׁיּוֹם הַיְּצִיאָה הוּא יוֹם שֶׁל זִכָּרוֹן. וְאֵי זֶה יוֹם יָצְאוּ? תַּלְמוּד לוֹמַר: "מִמָּחֳרַת הַפֶּסַח יָצְאוּ" (במדבר לג, ג), הֱוֵי אוֹמֵר יוֹם חֲמִשָּׁה עָשָׂר בְּנִיסָן הוּא שֶׁל יוֹם טוֹב, שֶׁהֲרֵי לֵיל חֲמִשָּׁה עָשָׂר אָכְלוּ אֶת הַפֶּסַח וְלַבֹּקֶר יָצְאוּ: **לְדֹרֹתֵיכֶם.** שׁוֹמֵעַ אֲנִי מִעוּט דּוֹרוֹת שְׁנַיִם, תַּלְמוּד לוֹמַר: "חֻקַּת עוֹלָם תְּחָגֻּהוּ":

טו | **שִׁבְעַת יָמִים.** שְׁטַיי"א שֶׁל יָמִים: **שִׁבְעַת יָמִים מַצּוֹת תֹּאכֵלוּ.** וּבְמָקוֹם אַחֵר הוּא אוֹמֵר: "שֵׁשֶׁת יָמִים תֹּאכַל מַצּוֹת" (דברים טז, ח), לִמְּדָנוּ עַל שְׁבִיעִי שֶׁאֵינוֹ חוֹבָה לֶאֱכֹל מַצָּה, וּבִלְבַד שֶׁלֹּא יֹאכַל חָמֵץ. מִנַּיִן אַף שִׁשָּׁה רְשׁוּת? זוֹ מִדָּה בַּתּוֹרָה: דָּבָר שֶׁהָיָה בִּכְלָל וְיָצָא מִן הַכְּלָל לְלַמֵּד, לֹא לְלַמֵּד עַל עַצְמוֹ בִּלְבַד יָצָא אֶלָּא לְלַמֵּד עַל הַכְּלָל כֻּלּוֹ יָצָא, מַה שְּׁבִיעִי רְשׁוּת אַף שִׁשָּׁה רְשׁוּת. יָכוֹל אַף לַיְלָה הָרִאשׁוֹן רְשׁוּת? תַּלְמוּד לוֹמַר: "בָּעֶרֶב תֹּאכְלוּ מַצֹּת" (להלן פסוק יח), הַכָּתוּב קְבָעוֹ חוֹבָה: **אַךְ בַּיּוֹם הָרִאשׁוֹן תַּשְׁבִּיתוּ שְׂאֹר.** מֵעֶרֶב יוֹם טוֹב, וְקָרוּי רִאשׁוֹן שֶׁהוּא

DISCUSSION

12:15 | You shall eat unleavened bread: Leavened bread is considered more sophisticated and tastier, as well as easier to digest, than its unleavened counterpart. Furthermore, leavened bread represents culture and civilization, as its preparation, involving the addition of yeast or some other rising agent, is relatively complex. Unleavened bread, by contrast, is a basic food, made from mere flour and water. The festival of Passover celebrates the birth of a people, and the simplicity and the foundational nature of that experience are represented by unleavened bread. Almost all meal offerings, which will later be brought in the Tabernacle and the Temple, must consist of unleavened bread. Apparently, as in the festival of Passover, unleavened bread in the Temple symbolizes fundamental simplicity.

point no explanation is given for this command. **However, on the first day you shall eliminate leaven from your houses. For anyone who eats leavened bread from the first day until the** conclusion of the **seventh day** of the festival, **that person shall be excised from Israel.**

16 **It shall be for you a holy convocation,** a gathering devoted to holiness,[1515] **on the first day** of the festival that will be celebrated in subsequent years, **and a holy convocation on the seventh day.** In addition, **no labor shall be performed on them,**[D] ex-cept labor required in the preparation **for that which shall be eaten for each person,** such as slaughtering, cooking, and bak-ing; **it alone may be performed for you.** The types of labor permitted on festivals are called by the Sages the labors neces-sary for preparing food.[1616]

17 **You shall guard the unleavened bread,** to ensure that it shall not become leavened at all; **because on this very day** of the festival, **I brought your hosts,** camps, **out of the land of Egypt; and you shall observe this day for your generations, an eternal statute.** The significance of these events will remain important in your future as well.

18 **In the first** month, Nisan, **on the fourteenth day of the month, in the evening,** after nightfall, **you shall eat unleav-ened bread** with the offering that was slaughtered earlier that day in the afternoon, **until the twenty-first day of the month in the evening.**

19 Not only must you eat unleavened bread and refrain from eating leavened bread, but for these **seven days, leaven,** the sourdough used to leaven other dough, **shall not be found in your houses; as anyone who eats leavening,** sourdough, **that person shall be excised from the congregation of Israel, whether he is a stranger or a native of the land.**

20 **You shall not eat anything leavened, or containing** leaven-ing;[17] **in all your dwellings you shall eat unleavened bread** during the festival of Passover.

21 The above commands were issued by God to Moses. **Moses** then **summoned all the elders of Israel and said to them that** they must prepare themselves: **Select and take for yourselves lambs for your families and slaughter the paschal lamb.**

Fifth aliya

22 **You shall take a bunch of hyssop,**[B] **and dip it in the blood that is in the basin,**[1818]**and you shall touch the lin-tel and the two doorposts with the blood that is in the basin, and no man shall emerge from the entrance of his house until morning,** as destruction shall be inflict-ed upon Egypt on this night.

Common hyssop plant

DISCUSSION

The Commandments of Leavened Bread and Unleavened Bread

Two positive commandments	Four negative commandments
"However, on the first day you shall eliminate leaven from your houses" (verse 15)	"Seven days, leaven shall not be found in your houses" (verse 19)
"In the first, on the fourteenth day of the month in the evening, you shall eat unleavened bread" (verse 18)	"You shall not eat anything leavened" (verse 20)
	"Leavened bread may not be eaten" (13:3)
	"Neither leavened bread shall be seen with you, nor shall leaven be seen with you, within your entire border" (13:7)

12:16 | No labor shall be performed on them: Every religion has holy convocations: public assemblies which include ceremonies, prayers, and celebrations. In the cultural context of the ancient world, the Torah's innovation is the rest from labor; from all organized and structured action.

טז וְנִכְרְתָה הַנֶּפֶשׁ הַהִוא מִיִּשְׂרָאֵל מִיּוֹם הָרִאשֹׁן עַד־יוֹם הַשְּׁבִעִי: וּבַיּוֹם הָרִאשׁוֹן
מִקְרָא־קֹדֶשׁ וּבַיּוֹם הַשְּׁבִיעִי מִקְרָא־קֹדֶשׁ יִהְיֶה לָכֶם כָּל־מְלָאכָה לֹא־יֵעָשֶׂה
בָהֶם אַךְ אֲשֶׁר יֵאָכֵל לְכָל־נֶפֶשׁ הוּא לְבַדּוֹ יֵעָשֶׂה לָכֶם: יז וּשְׁמַרְתֶּם אֶת־הַמַּצּוֹת
כִּי בְּעֶצֶם הַיּוֹם הַזֶּה הוֹצֵאתִי אֶת־צִבְאוֹתֵיכֶם מֵאֶרֶץ מִצְרָיִם וּשְׁמַרְתֶּם אֶת־
הַיּוֹם הַזֶּה לְדֹרֹתֵיכֶם חֻקַּת עוֹלָם: יח בָּרִאשֹׁן בְּאַרְבָּעָה עָשָׂר יוֹם לַחֹדֶשׁ בָּעֶרֶב
תֹּאכְלוּ מַצֹּת עַד יוֹם הָאֶחָד וְעֶשְׂרִים לַחֹדֶשׁ בָּעָרֶב: יט שִׁבְעַת יָמִים שְׂאֹר לֹא
יִמָּצֵא בְּבָתֵּיכֶם כִּי ׀ כָּל־אֹכֵל מַחְמֶצֶת וְנִכְרְתָה הַנֶּפֶשׁ הַהִוא מֵעֲדַת יִשְׂרָאֵל
בַּגֵּר וּבְאֶזְרַח הָאָרֶץ: כ כָּל־מַחְמֶצֶת לֹא תֹאכֵלוּ בְּכֹל מוֹשְׁבֹתֵיכֶם תֹּאכְלוּ מַצּוֹת:
כא וַיִּקְרָא מֹשֶׁה לְכָל־זִקְנֵי יִשְׂרָאֵל וַיֹּאמֶר אֲלֵהֶם מִשְׁכוּ וּקְחוּ לָכֶם צֹאן לְמִשְׁפְּחֹתֵיכֶם   חמישי
וְשַׁחֲטוּ הַפָּסַח: כב וּלְקַחְתֶּם אֲגֻדַּת אֵזוֹב וּטְבַלְתֶּם בַּדָּם אֲשֶׁר־בַּסַּף וְהִגַּעְתֶּם אֶל־
הַמַּשְׁקוֹף וְאֶל־שְׁתֵּי הַמְּזוּזֹת מִן־הַדָּם אֲשֶׁר בַּסָּף וְאַתֶּם לֹא תֵצְאוּ אִישׁ מִפֶּתַח־

לִפְנֵי הַשְּׁבִיעָה, וּמֵעֵינוֹ מִקְדָּם קָרֵי רַאשׁוֹן, "הָרִאשׁוֹן חָדָם תִּוָּלֵד" (איוב טו, ז), הֲלִפְנֵי אָדָם נוֹלַדְתָּ. אוֹ אֵינוֹ חֶלָּא רִאשׁוֹן שֶׁל שְׁבִיעָה? תַּלְמוּד לוֹמַר: "לֹא תִשְׁחַט עַל חָמֵץ" (שמות לד, כה), לֹא תִשְׁחַט הַפֶּסַח וַעֲדַיִן חָמֵץ קַיָּם: הַנֶּפֶשׁ הַהִוא. כְּשֶׁהִיא בְנַפְשָׁהּ וּבְדַעְתָּהּ, פְּרָט לְאָנוּס: מִיִּשְׂרָאֵל. שׁוֹמֵעַ אֲנִי תִּכָּרֵת מִיִּשְׂרָאֵל וְתֵלֵךְ לָהּ לְעַם אַחֵר? תַּלְמוּד לוֹמַר בְּמָקוֹם אַחֵר: "מִלְּפָנַי" (ויקרא כב, ג), בְּכָל מָקוֹם שֶׁהוּא רְשׁוּתִי:

טז מִקְרָא קֹדֶשׁ. "מִקְרָא" שֵׁם דָּבָר, קְרָא אוֹתוֹ קֹדֶשׁ לַאֲכִילָה וּשְׁתִיָּה וּכְסוּת: לֹא יֵעָשֶׂה בָהֶם. אֲפִלּוּ עַל יְדֵי אֲחֵרִים. הוּא לְבַדּוֹ. הוּא וְלֹא מַכְשִׁירָיו שֶׁאֶפְשָׁר לַעֲשׂוֹתָן מֵעֶרֶב יוֹם טוֹב: לְכָל נֶפֶשׁ. אַף לִבְהֵמָה, יָכוֹל אַף לְגוֹיִם? תַּלְמוּד לוֹמַר: "אַךְ":

יז וּשְׁמַרְתֶּם אֶת הַמַּצּוֹת. שֶׁלֹּא יָבֹאוּ לִידֵי חִמּוּץ. מִכָּאן אָמְרוּ: תָּפַח, תִּלְטֹשׁ בְּצוֹנֵן. רַבִּי יֹאשִׁיָּה אוֹמֵר: אַל תְּהִי קוֹרֵא "אֶת הַמַּצּוֹת" אֶלָּא "אֶת הַמִּצְוֹת", כְּדֶרֶךְ שֶׁאֵין מַחְמִיצִין אֶת הַמַּצָּה כָּךְ אֵין מַחְמִיצִין אֶת הַמִּצְוָה, אֶלָּא

חֵם בָּאָה לְיָדְךָ עֲשֵׂה אוֹתָהּ מִיָּד: וּשְׁמַרְתֶּם אֶת הַיּוֹם הַזֶּה. מִמְּלָאכָה: לְדֹרֹתֵיכֶם חֻקַּת עוֹלָם. לְפִי שֶׁלֹּא נֶאֱמַר "דּוֹרוֹת" וְ"חֻקַּת עוֹלָם" עַל הַמְּלָאכָה אֶלָּא עַל הַחֲגִיגָה (לעיל פסוק יד), לְכָךְ חָזַר וּשְׁנָאוֹ כָּאן, שֶׁלֹּא תֹאמַר: אַזְהָרַת "כָּל מְלָאכָה לֹא יֵעָשֶׂה" (לעיל פסוק טז) לֹא לְדוֹרוֹת נֶאֶמְרָה אֶלָּא לְאוֹתוֹ הַדּוֹר:

יח עַד יוֹם הָאֶחָד וְעֶשְׂרִים. לָמָּה נֶאֱמַר? וַהֲלֹא כְבָר נֶאֱמַר: "שִׁבְעַת יָמִים" (לעיל פסוק טו)? לְפִי שֶׁנֶּאֱמַר "יָמִים", לֵילוֹת מִנַּיִן? תַּלְמוּד לוֹמַר: "עַד יוֹם הָאֶחָד וְעֶשְׂרִים" וְגוֹ':

יט לֹא יִמָּצֵא בְּבָתֵּיכֶם. מִנַּיִן לַגְּבוּלִין? תַּלְמוּד לוֹמַר: "בְּכָל גְּבֻלְךָ" (להלן יג, ז). מַה תַּלְמוּד לוֹמַר בְּבָתֵּיכֶם? מַה בֵּיתְךָ בִּרְשׁוּתְךָ אַף גְּבוּלְךָ שֶׁבִּרְשׁוּתְךָ, יָצָא חֲמֵצוֹ שֶׁל נָכְרִי שֶׁהוּא אֵצֶל יִשְׂרָאֵל וְלֹא קִבֵּל עָלָיו אַחֲרָיוּת: כִּי כָל אֹכֵל מַחְמֶצֶת. לַעֲנֹשׁ כָּרֵת עַל הַשְּׂאוֹר, וַהֲלֹא כְבָר עָנַשׁ עַל הֶחָמֵץ? אֶלָּא שֶׁלֹּא תֹאמַר: חָמֵץ שֶׁרָאוּי לַאֲכִילָה עָנַשׁ עָלָיו, שְׂאוֹר שֶׁאֵין רָאוּי לַאֲכִילָה לֹא יֵעָנֵשׁ עָלָיו, וְאִם עָנַשׁ עַל הַשְּׂאוֹר וְלֹא עָנַשׁ עַל הֶחָמֵץ, הָיִיתִי אוֹמֵר: שְׂאוֹר שֶׁהוּא

מְחַמֵּץ אֲחֵרִים עָנַשׁ עָלָיו, חָמֵץ שֶׁאֵינוֹ מְחַמֵּץ אֲחֵרִים לֹא יֵעָנַשׁ עָלָיו - לְכָךְ נֶאֶמְרוּ שְׁנַיִם: בַּגֵּר וּבְאֶזְרַח הָאָרֶץ. לְפִי שֶׁהַנֵּס נַעֲשָׂה לְיִשְׂרָאֵל הֻצְרַךְ לְרַבּוֹת אֶת הַגֵּרִים:

כ מַחְמֶצֶת לֹא תֹאכֵלוּ. אַזְהָרָה עַל אֲכִילַת שְׂאוֹר: כָּל מַחְמֶצֶת. לְהָבִיא אֶת תַּעֲרָבְתּוֹ: בְּכֹל מוֹשְׁבֹתֵיכֶם תֹּאכְלוּ מַצּוֹת. זֶה בָא לְלַמֵּד שֶׁתְּהֵא רְאוּיָה לְהֵאָכֵל בְּכָל מוֹשְׁבוֹתֵיכֶם, פְּרָט לְמַעֲשֵׂר שֵׁנִי וְחַלּוֹת תּוֹדָה:

כא מִשְׁכוּ. מִי שֶׁיֵּשׁ לוֹ צֹאן יִמְשֹׁךְ מִשֶּׁלּוֹ: וּקְחוּ. מִי שֶׁאֵין לוֹ יִקַּח מִן הַשּׁוּק: לְמִשְׁפְּחֹתֵיכֶם. שֶׂה לְבֵית אָבוֹת (לעיל פסוק ג):

כב אֵזוֹב. מִין יָרָק שֶׁיֵּשׁ לוֹ גִּבְעוֹלִין: אֲגֻדַּת אֵזוֹב. שְׁלֹשָׁה קְלָחִין קְרוּיִין אֲגֻדָּה: אֲשֶׁר בַּסַּף. בַּכְּלִי, כְּמוֹ: "סִפּוֹת כֶּסֶף" (מלכים ב' יב, יד): מִן הַדָּם אֲשֶׁר בַּסַּף. לָמָּה חָזַר וּשְׁנָאוֹ? שֶׁלֹּא תֹאמַר טְבִילָה אַחַת לִשְׁלֹשׁ הַמַּתָּנוֹת, לְכָךְ נֶאֱמַר עוֹד: "אֲשֶׁר בַּסַּף", שֶׁתְּהֵא כָל נְתִינָה וּנְתִינָה "מִן הַדָּם אֲשֶׁר בַּסַּף", עַל כָּל הַגָּעָה טְבִילָה: וְאַתֶּם לֹא תֵצְאוּ וְגוֹ'. מַגִּיד

12:22 | Hyssop [ezov]: From various descriptions it appears that this is the common hyssop plant, *Majorana syriaca (L)* The hyssop is a fragrant plant that grows to a height of 50–100 cm. The plant spreads out from its base into rigid wooden branches, which annually produce straight stems that dry out and die in winter. The white flowers of the plant are found in crowded bunches on the ends of its branches. This plant grows in rocky terrain throughout the Middle East, and is considered to have healing properties. Dried hyssop leaves are used in the spice *za'atar*. In the Bible it is used in the purification rites of lepers, and of those who have come into contact with a corpse. It is also considered a symbol of humility (I Kings 5:13).

23 **The Lord will pass to strike the Egyptians, and when He sees the blood on the lintel and on the two doorposts, the Lord will pass over the entrance** of your houses, **and He will not allow the destroyer to come to your houses to strike.**[D]
24 **You shall observe this matter as a statute for you and for your children forever.** Some of the details mentioned here, such as the requirement to eat the paschal lamb with girded loins and shoes on one's feet, applied only to the original Passover when Israel left Egypt. However, the festival itself must be observed in future generations.
25 **It shall be when you come to the land that the Lord will give you, as He spoke** and promised, **you shall observe this service.** You are required to observe the laws of Passover in the future as well.
26 **It shall be when your children will say to you: What is this service to you?** For what purpose are you performing these complicated rites?
27 **You shall say: It is the paschal offering to the Lord, who passed over the houses of the children of Israel in Egypt when He struck Egypt, and our households He saved.** From that time onward, we celebrate our salvation with this offering. **The people bowed their heads** upon hearing this message, **and prostrated themselves.** They thereby indicated their willingness to follow these instructions. This response also expressed their gratitude at the tidings of their imminent release from bondage, as until now they had not been given a specific date on which they would be free.[1919]
28 **The children of Israel went and did; as the Lord had commanded Moses and Aaron, so they did,** in compliance with all the details of the commandment.

The Plague of the Firstborn and Israel's Expulsion from Egypt

EXODUS 12:29–42

On the night of the plague of the firstborn all the previous events come to a climax. Striking the firstborn dead was a divine blow to every household in Egypt, while the Israelites stayed protected in their houses, each family eating its paschal lamb. This catastrophe in the depths of the night terrified the Egyptians and led to their frantic need to expel Israel. After the long, slow process of intensifying enslavement, followed by an extended series of plagues, all the events of this fateful night occur one after the other in abrupt succession.

Following a detailed description of the happenings of this night, the Torah provides a summary of Israel's time in Egypt and its conclusion with the exodus.

29 **It was at midnight, and the Lord smote every firstborn in**
Sixth aliya **the land of Egypt, from the** exalted **firstborn of Pharaoh,** the prince, **who was sitting on his throne, to the** lowliest **firstborn of the captive who was in the dungeon, and every firstborn animal.**
30 **Pharaoh arose during the night, he, and all his servants, and all Egypt, and there was a great outcry in Egypt.** The cries of anguish filled the land **because there was no house in which there were no dead.**
31 **He summoned Moses and Aaron at** the middle of the **night and said: Rise and go out from among my people, both you and the children of Israel, and go serve the Lord as you have spoken.**
32 **Take both your flocks and your cattle, as you have spoken, and go and bless me too.**[D] I can do nothing but ask that you include me in your prayers.
33 **The Egyptians urged the people, to hasten to send them forth from the land.** The Egyptians realized that they had been stricken because they forced the Israelites to stay in their land. Now, in terror of death, they urged them to leave immediately. **As they said: We are all dying.**[D]

DISCUSSION

12:23| **He will not allow the destroyer to come to your houses to strike:** The destroying force that will pass through Egypt that night can be described as blind, to a certain extent. It is God alone who distinguishes between those who are to be harmed and those who will be saved, between the firstborn and those who are not firstborn. Only God prevents the destroyer from harming the children of Israel (see *Bekhor Shor* on verse 7; *Ḥizkuni*).

12:32| **Bless me too:** Some commentaries claim that Pharaoh himself was a firstborn, and this request is due to his fear for his life (Rashi). Alternatively, Pharaoh is seeking to take advantage of his position. Fully aware of Egypt's suffering from the plagues, which came as a result of his own obstinacy, he asks Moses and Aaron to pray for him, since he ultimately agreed to allow Israel to go.

12:33| **As they said: We are all dying:** Apparently, the Egyptians did not yet understand that the tenth plague had struck only the firstborn. Presumably there were households with more than one firstborn, for instance, if the father was also a firstborn. It is also possible that the category of firstborn included those born first to one parent but not the other. Perhaps the plague was not limited to those who were born first in a family but included the most important member of every household (*Mekhilta deRashbi* 12:33; Rashi).

כג בֵּיתוֹ עַד־בֹּקֶר: וְעָבַר יְהוָה לִנְגֹּף אֶת־מִצְרַיִם וְרָאָה אֶת־הַדָּם עַל־הַמַּשְׁקוֹף
וְעַל שְׁתֵּי הַמְּזוּזֹת וּפָסַח יְהוָה עַל־הַפֶּתַח וְלֹא יִתֵּן הַמַּשְׁחִית לָבֹא אֶל־בָּתֵּיכֶם
כד כה לִנְגֹּף: וּשְׁמַרְתֶּם אֶת־הַדָּבָר הַזֶּה לְחָק־לְךָ וּלְבָנֶיךָ עַד־עוֹלָם: וְהָיָה כִּי־תָבֹאוּ
אֶל־הָאָרֶץ אֲשֶׁר יִתֵּן יְהוָה לָכֶם כַּאֲשֶׁר דִּבֵּר וּשְׁמַרְתֶּם אֶת־הָעֲבֹדָה הַזֹּאת:
כו כז וְהָיָה כִּי־יֹאמְרוּ אֲלֵיכֶם בְּנֵיכֶם מָה הָעֲבֹדָה הַזֹּאת לָכֶם: וַאֲמַרְתֶּם זֶבַח־פֶּסַח
הוּא לַיהוָה אֲשֶׁר פָּסַח עַל־בָּתֵּי בְנֵי־יִשְׂרָאֵל בְּמִצְרַיִם בְּנָגְפּוֹ אֶת־מִצְרַיִם וְאֶת־
כח בָּתֵּינוּ הִצִּיל וַיִּקֹּד הָעָם וַיִּשְׁתַּחֲווּ: וַיֵּלְכוּ וַיַּעֲשׂוּ בְּנֵי יִשְׂרָאֵל כַּאֲשֶׁר צִוָּה יְהוָה
כט אֶת־מֹשֶׁה וְאַהֲרֹן כֵּן עָשׂוּ: וַיְהִי בַּחֲצִי הַלַּיְלָה וַיהוָה הִכָּה כָל־בְּכוֹר בְּאֶרֶץ ט ששי
מִצְרַיִם מִבְּכֹר פַּרְעֹה הַיֹּשֵׁב עַל־כִּסְאוֹ עַד בְּכוֹר הַשְּׁבִי אֲשֶׁר בְּבֵית הַבּוֹר וְכֹל
ל בְּכוֹר בְּהֵמָה: וַיָּקָם פַּרְעֹה לַיְלָה הוּא וְכָל־עֲבָדָיו וְכָל־מִצְרַיִם וַתְּהִי צְעָקָה
לא גְדֹלָה בְּמִצְרָיִם כִּי־אֵין בַּיִת אֲשֶׁר אֵין־שָׁם מֵת: וַיִּקְרָא לְמֹשֶׁה וּלְאַהֲרֹן לַיְלָה
וַיֹּאמֶר קוּמוּ צְּאוּ מִתּוֹךְ עַמִּי גַּם־אַתֶּם גַּם־בְּנֵי יִשְׂרָאֵל וּלְכוּ עִבְדוּ אֶת־יְהוָה
לב כְּדַבֶּרְכֶם: גַּם־צֹאנְכֶם גַּם־בְּקַרְכֶם קְחוּ כַּאֲשֶׁר דִּבַּרְתֶּם וָלֵכוּ וּבֵרַכְתֶּם גַּם־אֹתִי:
לג וַתֶּחֱזַק מִצְרַיִם עַל־הָעָם לְמַהֵר לְשַׁלְּחָם מִן־הָאָרֶץ כִּי אָמְרוּ כֻּלָּנוּ מֵתִים:

רש"י

שֶׁמֵּאַחַר שֶׁנִּתְּנָה רְשׁוּת לַמַּשְׁחִית לְחַבֵּל אֵינוֹ מַבְחִין בֵּין צַדִּיק לְרָשָׁע. וְלַיְלָה רְשׁוּת לַמְחַבְּלִים הוּא, שֶׁנֶּאֱמַר: "בּוֹ תִרְמֹשׂ כָּל חַיְתוֹ יָעַר" (תהלים קד, כ):

כג| וּפָסַח. וְחָמַל, וְיֵשׁ לוֹמַר, וְדִלֵּג: וְלֹא יִתֵּן הַמַּשְׁחִית. וְלֹא יִתֵּן לוֹ יְכֹלֶת לָבֹא, כְּמוֹ: "וְלֹא נְתָנוֹ אֱלֹהִים לְהָרַע עִמָּדִי" (בראשית לא, ז):

כה| כַּאֲשֶׁר דִּבֵּר. וְהֵיכָן דִּבֵּר? "וְהֵבֵאתִי אֶתְכֶם אֶל הָאָרֶץ" וְגוֹ' (לעיל ו, ח):

כז| וַיִּקֹּד הָעָם. עַל בְּשׂוֹרַת הַגְּאֻלָּה וּבִיאַת הָאָרֶץ וּבְשׂוֹרַת הַבָּנִים שֶׁיִּהְיוּ לָהֶם וְיִשְׁאֲלוּם:

כח| וַיֵּלְכוּ וַיַּעֲשׂוּ בְּנֵי יִשְׂרָאֵל. וְכִי כְּבָר עָשׂוּ? וַהֲלֹא מֵרֹאשׁ חֹדֶשׁ נֶאֱמַר לָהֶם! אֶלָּא מִכֵּיוָן שֶׁקִּבְּלוּ עֲלֵיהֶם מַעֲלֶה עֲלֵיהֶם הַכָּתוּב כְּאִלּוּ עָשׂוּ: וַיֵּלְכוּ וַיַּעֲשׂוּ. אַף הַהֲלִיכָה מָנָה הַכָּתוּב, לִתֵּן שָׂכָר לַהֲלִיכָה וְשָׂכָר לַעֲשִׂיָּה: כַּאֲשֶׁר צִוָּה ה' אֶת מֹשֶׁה וְאַהֲרֹן. לְהַגִּיד שִׁבְחָן שֶׁל יִשְׂרָאֵל שֶׁלֹּא הִפִּילוּ דָּבָר מִכָּל מִצְוַת מֹשֶׁה וְאַהֲרֹן. וּמַהוּ "כֵּן עָשׂוּ"? אַף מֹשֶׁה וְאַהֲרֹן כֵּן עָשׂוּ:

כט| וַה'. כָּל מָקוֹם שֶׁנֶּאֱמַר "וַה'" – הוּא וּבֵית דִּינוֹ, שֶׁהַוָּי"ו לְשׁוֹן תּוֹסֶפֶת הוּא, כְּמוֹ: פְּלוֹנִי וּפְלוֹנִי: הִכָּה כָל בְּכוֹר. אַף שֶׁל אֻמָּה אַחֶרֶת וְהוּא בְּמִצְרַיִם: מִבְּכֹר פַּרְעֹה. אַף פַּרְעֹה בְּכוֹר הָיָה וְנִשְׁתַּיֵּר מִן הַבְּכוֹרוֹת, וְעָלָיו הוּא אוֹמֵר: "בַּעֲבוּר הַרְאֹתְךָ אֶת כֹּחִי" (לעיל ט, טז) – בְּיַם סוּף: עַד בְּכוֹר הַשְּׁבִי. שֶׁהָיוּ שְׂמֵחִין לְאֵידָם שֶׁל יִשְׂרָאֵל. וְעוֹד, שֶׁלֹּא יֹאמְרוּ: יִרְאָתֵנוּ הֵבִיאָה הַפֻּרְעָנוּת. וּבְכוֹר הַשִּׁפְחָה בִּכְלָל הָיָה, שֶׁהֲרֵי מָנָה מִן הֶחָשׁוּב שֶׁבְּכֻלָּן עַד הַפָּחוּת, וּבְכוֹר הַשִּׁפְחָה חָשׁוּב מִבְּכוֹר הַשְּׁבִי:

ל| וַיָּקָם פַּרְעֹה. מִמִּטָּתוֹ: לַיְלָה. וְלֹא כְּדֶרֶךְ הַמְּלָכִים בְּשָׁלֹשׁ שָׁעוֹת בַּיּוֹם: הוּא. תְּחִלָּה וְאַחַר כָּךְ "עֲבָדָיו", מְלַמֵּד שֶׁהָיָה הוּא מְחַזֵּר עַל בָּתֵּי עֲבָדָיו וּמַעֲמִידָן: כִּי אֵין בַּיִת אֲשֶׁר אֵין שָׁם מֵת. יֵשׁ שָׁם בְּכוֹר – מֵת, אֵין שָׁם בְּכוֹר – גָּדוֹל שֶׁבַּבַּיִת קָרוּי בְּכוֹר, שֶׁנֶּאֱמַר "אַף אָנִי בְּכוֹר אֶתְּנֵהוּ" (תהלים פט, כח). דָּבָר אַחֵר, מִצְרִיּוֹת מְזַנּוֹת תַּחַת בַּעְלֵיהֶן וְיוֹלְדוֹת מֵרַוָּקִים פְּנוּיִים וְהָיוּ לָהֶם בְּכוֹרוֹת הַרְבֵּה, פְּעָמִים הֵם חֲמִשָּׁה לְאִשָּׁה אַחַת, כָּל אֶחָד בְּכוֹר לְאָבִיו:

לא-לב| וַיִּקְרָא לְמֹשֶׁה וּלְאַהֲרֹן לַיְלָה. מַגִּיד שֶׁהָיָה מְחַזֵּר עַל פִּתְחֵי הָעִיר וְצוֹעֵק: הֵיכָן מֹשֶׁה שָׁרוּי? הֵיכָן אַהֲרֹן שָׁרוּי?: גַּם אַתֶּם. הַגְּבָרִים: גַּם בְּנֵי יִשְׂרָאֵל. הַטָּף: וּלְכוּ עִבְדוּ אֶת ה' כְּדַבֶּרְכֶם. הַכֹּל כְּמוֹ שֶׁאֲמַרְתֶּם וְלֹא כְּמוֹ שֶׁאָמַרְתִּי אֲנִי. בָּטֵל "לֹא אֲשַׁלֵּחַ" (לעיל ה, ב), בָּטֵל "מִי וָמִי הַהֹלְכִים" (לעיל י, ח), בָּטֵל "רַק צֹאנְכֶם וּבְקַרְכֶם יֻצָּג" (לעיל י, כד) – "גַּם צֹאנְכֶם גַּם בְּקַרְכֶם קְחוּ"; וּמַהוּ "כַּאֲשֶׁר דִּבַּרְתֶּם"? "גַּם אַתָּה תִּתֵּן בְּיָדֵנוּ זְבָחִים וְעֹלֹת" (לעיל י, כה) – "קְחוּ כַּאֲשֶׁר דִּבַּרְתֶּם": וּבֵרַכְתֶּם גַּם אֹתִי. הִתְפַּלְּלוּ עָלַי שֶׁלֹּא אָמוּת, שֶׁאֲנִי בְּכוֹר:

לג| כֻּלָּנוּ מֵתִים. אָמְרוּ: לֹא כִּגְזֵרַת מֹשֶׁה הוּא, שֶׁהֲרֵי אָמַר: "וּמֵת כָּל בְּכוֹר" (לעיל יא, ה) וְכָאן אַף הַפְּשׁוּטִים מֵתִים, חֲמִשָּׁה אוֹ עֲשָׂרָה בְּבַיִת אֶחָד:

34 In their haste, **the people carried their dough before it became leavened; their kneading bowls,** in which they prepared the dough, were **bound in their garments on their shoulders.** They did not have time to let the dough rise, and as the kneading bowls were full of dough they could not be packed up with the rest of their belongings. Therefore, they carried those bowls separately.

35 Beforehand, **the children of Israel acted in accordance with the word of Moses, and they requested silver vessels, gold vessels, and garments from Egypt.**

36 **The Lord granted the people favor in the eyes of Egypt, and they acceded to their request, and they stripped Egypt,** taking everything they could.

37 **The children of Israel traveled from Rameses,** the place with the greatest concentration of Israelites, where the Egyptians built large cities, **to** a place called **Sukot.** The Israelites numbered **some six hundred thousand men on foot, besides children,** women, and the elderly.[2020]

38 **A mixed multitude** of other peoples **came up with them.**[D] Once the possibility of leaving Egypt became available, the Egyptians lost control of their borders and many others took advantage of the opportunity and joined Israel. **And** the Israelites took with them the **flocks and cattle** that they owned, **very considerable livestock.**

39 **They baked the dough that they took out from Egypt into unleavened cakes, as it was not leavened, because they were** banished from Egypt and could not linger and wait for the dough to rise. Although they knew about the exodus in advance, the events unfolded at an unexpectedly rapid pace. Moreover, they had only a limited time to prepare both the paschal lamb and the unleavened bread they ate the night before. **And** due to these pressing circumstances, **they also did not prepare** the requisite **provisions** of a long journey **for themselves.**

40 The Torah provides a historical summary: **The dwelling of the children of Israel that they dwelled in Egypt was thirty years and four hundred years.**[D]

41 **It was at the end of thirty years and four hundred years; it was on that very day** mentioned above, the first day of Passover, **that all the hosts of the Lord departed from the land of Egypt.** The people who left Egypt were not a random group but a nation that would serve as the hosts of the Lord. This role will be clarified in greater detail in the account of the giving of the Torah.

42 **It is a night of vigilance of the Lord.** God had waited with anticipation for this night,[2121] **to bring them out of the land of Egypt; it is this night for the Lord.** This is not only the night on which Israel was saved. God designated this night ahead of time and imbued it with a significance that goes beyond the events of that period.[2222] This night will become one of **vigilance for all the children of Israel for their generations.** Israel will always remember and celebrate this night and pass on the commemoration of these events to future generations.

DISCUSSION

12:38| A mixed multitude came up with them: It is clear that there were other slaves in Egypt besides the Israelites. The Torah states explicitly that "the firstborn of the maidservant, who is behind the mill" (11:5) was subject to the plague of the firstborn. Such slaves, presumably from other nations, seized this opportunity to escape as well. The phenomenon of various groups taking advantage of a rebellion or mass migration for their own purposes is well documented. A different possibility is that the mixed multitude were not slaves but free people who chose to join their fate to Israel's upon witnessing the creation of a fresh nation with a new culture, which they envisioned might benefit them as well.

12:40| The dwelling of the children of Israel that they dwelled in Egypt was thirty years and four hundred years: Kehat, son of Levi, was one of the original seventy descendants of Jacob who came to Egypt (Genesis 46:11). The number of the years that Kehat, Amram his son, and Moses his grandson lived are all explicitly stated in the Torah (6:18, 20; Deuteronomy 34:7). The sum of these lifetimes is less than four hundred years, even without taking into consideration the time that Kehat lived before going to Egypt, or the forty years that Moses led the children of Israel after leaving Egypt, or the overlap of time between fathers and sons. Due to this discrepancy, the Sages explain that the four hundred and thirty years mentioned here are the number of years since the Covenant between the Parts, when Abraham was informed of the future enslavement of his descendants and their ultimate redemption (Rashi; *Targum Yonatan*). Others maintain that the count starts slightly earlier, from when Abraham left Ḥaran (*Bekhor Shor*). Although they were not in Egypt, nor were they enslaved for many of those years, Abraham and his descendants were considered foreigners for most of this time, and the period as a whole was characterized by frequent wandering and upheavals.

לד וַיִּשָּׂא הָעָם אֶת־בְּצֵקוֹ טֶרֶם יֶחְמָץ מִשְׁאֲרֹתָם צְרֻרֹת בְּשִׂמְלֹתָם עַל־שִׁכְמָם:
לה וּבְנֵי־יִשְׂרָאֵל עָשׂוּ כִּדְבַר מֹשֶׁה וַיִּשְׁאֲלוּ מִמִּצְרַיִם כְּלֵי־כֶסֶף וּכְלֵי זָהָב וּשְׂמָלֹת:
לו וַיהוה נָתַן אֶת־חֵן הָעָם בְּעֵינֵי מִצְרַיִם וַיַּשְׁאִלוּם וַיְנַצְּלוּ אֶת־מִצְרָיִם:
לז וַיִּסְעוּ בְנֵי־יִשְׂרָאֵל מֵרַעְמְסֵס סֻכֹּתָה כְּשֵׁשׁ־מֵאוֹת אֶלֶף רַגְלִי הַגְּבָרִים לְבַד מִטָּף:
לח לט וְגַם־עֵרֶב רַב עָלָה אִתָּם וְצֹאן וּבָקָר מִקְנֶה כָּבֵד מְאֹד: וַיֹּאפוּ אֶת־הַבָּצֵק אֲשֶׁר
הוֹצִיאוּ מִמִּצְרַיִם עֻגֹת מַצּוֹת כִּי לֹא חָמֵץ כִּי־גֹרְשׁוּ מִמִּצְרַיִם וְלֹא יָכְלוּ לְהִתְמַהְמֵהַּ
מ וְגַם־צֵדָה לֹא־עָשׂוּ לָהֶם: וּמוֹשַׁב בְּנֵי יִשְׂרָאֵל אֲשֶׁר יָשְׁבוּ בְּמִצְרָיִם שְׁלֹשִׁים שָׁנָה
מא וְאַרְבַּע מֵאוֹת שָׁנָה: וַיְהִי מִקֵּץ שְׁלֹשִׁים שָׁנָה וְאַרְבַּע מֵאוֹת שָׁנָה וַיְהִי בְּעֶצֶם הַיּוֹם
מב הַזֶּה יָצְאוּ כָּל־צִבְאוֹת יהוה מֵאֶרֶץ מִצְרָיִם: לֵיל שִׁמֻּרִים הוּא לַיהוה לְהוֹצִיאָם
מֵאֶרֶץ מִצְרָיִם הוּא־הַלַּיְלָה הַזֶּה לַיהוה שִׁמֻּרִים לְכָל־בְּנֵי יִשְׂרָאֵל לְדֹרֹתָם:

רש"י

לד| **טֶרֶם יֶחְמָץ.** הַמִּצְרִים לֹא הִנִּיחוּם לִשְׁהוֹת כְּדֵי חִמּוּץ: **מִשְׁאֲרֹתָם.** שְׁיָרֵי מַצָּה וּמָרוֹר: **עַל שִׁכְמָם.** אַף עַל פִּי שֶׁבְּהֵמוֹת הַרְבֵּה הוֹלִיכוּ עִמָּהֶם, מְחַבְּבִין הָיוּ אֶת הַמִּצְוָה:

לה| **כִּדְבַר מֹשֶׁה.** שֶׁאָמַר לָהֶם בְּמִצְרַיִם: "וְיִשְׁאֲלוּ אִישׁ מֵאֵת רֵעֵהוּ" (לעיל יא, ב): **וּשְׂמָלֹת.** אַף הֵן הָיוּ חֲשׁוּבוֹת לָהֶם מִן הַכֶּסֶף וּמִן הַזָּהָב, וְהַמְאֻחָר בַּפָּסוּק חָשׁוּב:

לו| **וַיַּשְׁאִלוּם.** אַף מַה שֶּׁלֹּא הָיוּ שׁוֹאֲלִים מֵהֶם הָיוּ נוֹתְנִים לָהֶם, אַתָּה אוֹמֵר אֶחָד, טֹל שְׁנַיִם וָלֵךְ: **וַיְנַצְּלוּ.** "וְרוֹקִינוּ":

לז| **מֵרַעְמְסֵס סֻכֹּתָה.** מֵאָה וְעֶשְׂרִים מִיל הָיוּ, וּבָאוּ שָׁם לְפִי שָׁעָה, שֶׁנֶּאֱמַר: "וָאֶשָּׂא אֶתְכֶם עַל כַּנְפֵי נְשָׁרִים" (להלן יט, ד): **הַגְּבָרִים.** מִבֶּן עֶשְׂרִים וָמַעְלָה:

לח| **עֵרֶב רַב.** תַּעֲרֹבֶת אֻמּוֹת שֶׁל גֵּרִים:

לט| **עֻגֹת מַצּוֹת.** חֲרָרָה שֶׁל מַצָּה. בָּצֵק שֶׁלֹּא הֶחֱמִיץ קָרוּי מַצָּה: **וְגַם צֵדָה לֹא עָשׂוּ לָהֶם.** לַדֶּרֶךְ. מַגִּיד שִׁבְחָן שֶׁל יִשְׂרָאֵל, שֶׁלֹּא אָמְרוּ: הֵיאַךְ נֵצֵא לַמִּדְבָּר בְּלֹא צֵדָה? אֶלָּא הֶאֱמִינוּ וְהָלְכוּ. הוּא שֶׁמְּפֹרָשׁ בַּקַּבָּלָה: "זָכַרְתִּי לָךְ חֶסֶד נְעוּרַיִךְ אַהֲבַת כְּלוּלֹתָיִךְ לֶכְתֵּךְ אַחֲרַי בַּמִּדְבָּר בְּאֶרֶץ לֹא זְרוּעָה" (ירמיה ב, ב), מַה שָּׂכָר מְפֹרָשׁ אַחֲרָיו? "קֹדֶשׁ יִשְׂרָאֵל לַה'" וְגוֹ' (שם פסוק ג):

מ| **אֲשֶׁר יָשְׁבוּ בְּמִצְרָיִם.** אַחַר שְׁאָר הַיְשִׁיבוֹת שֶׁיָּשְׁבוּ גֵּרִים בְּאֶרֶץ לֹא לָהֶם: **שְׁלֹשִׁים שָׁנָה וְאַרְבַּע מֵאוֹת שָׁנָה.** בֵּין הַכֹּל, מִשֶּׁנּוֹלַד יִצְחָק עַד עַכְשָׁיו הָיוּ אַרְבַּע מֵאוֹת שָׁנָה. מִשֶּׁהָיָה לוֹ זֶרַע לְאַבְרָהָם נִתְקַיֵּם: "כִּי גֵר יִהְיֶה זַרְעֲךָ" (בראשית טו, יג), וּשְׁלֹשִׁים שָׁנָה הָיוּ מִשֶּׁנִּגְזְרָה גְּזֵרַת בֵּין הַבְּתָרִים עַד שֶׁנּוֹלַד יִצְחָק. וְאִי אֶפְשָׁר לוֹמַר בְּאֶרֶץ מִצְרַיִם לְבַדָּהּ, שֶׁהֲרֵי קְהָת מִן הַבָּאִים עִם יַעֲקֹב הָיָה, צֵא וַחֲשֹׁב כָּל שְׁנוֹתָיו וְכָל שְׁנוֹת עַמְרָם בְּנוֹ וּשְׁמוֹנִים שֶׁל מֹשֶׁה, לֹא תִמְצָאֵם כָּל כָּךְ. וְעַל כָּרְחֲךָ הַרְבֵּה שָׁנִים הָיוּ לִקְהָת עַד שֶׁלֹּא יָרַד לְמִצְרַיִם, וְהַרְבֵּה מִשְּׁנוֹת עַמְרָם נִבְלָעִים בִּשְׁנוֹת קְהָת, וְהַרְבֵּה מִשְּׁמוֹנִים שֶׁל מֹשֶׁה נִבְלָעִים בִּשְׁנוֹת עַמְרָם, הֲרֵי שֶׁלֹּא תִמְצָא אַרְבַּע מֵאוֹת לְבִיאַת מִצְרַיִם; וְהֻזְקַקְתָּ לוֹמַר עַל כָּרְחֲךָ שֶׁאַף שְׁאָר הַיְשִׁיבוֹת נִקְרְאוּ גֵּרוּת, וַאֲפִלּוּ בְּחֶבְרוֹן, שֶׁנֶּאֱמַר: "אֲשֶׁר גָּר שָׁם אַבְרָהָם וְיִצְחָק" (בראשית לה, כז), וְאוֹמֵר: "אֵת אֶרֶץ מְגֻרֵיהֶם אֲשֶׁר גָּרוּ בָהּ" (לעיל ו, ד). לְפִיכָךְ אַתָּה צָרִיךְ לוֹמַר "כִּי גֵר יִהְיֶה זַרְעֲךָ" – מִשֶּׁהָיָה לוֹ זֶרַע. וּכְשֶׁתִּמְנֶה אַרְבַּע מֵאוֹת שָׁנָה מִשֶּׁנּוֹלַד יִצְחָק, תִּמְצָא מִבִּיאָתָן לְמִצְרַיִם עַד יְצִיאָתָן מָאתַיִם וָעֶשֶׂר שָׁנִים. וְזֶה אֶחָד מִן הַדְּבָרִים שֶׁשִּׁנּוּ לְתַלְמַי הַמֶּלֶךְ:

מא| **וַיְהִי מִקֵּץ שְׁלֹשִׁים שָׁנָה... וַיְהִי בְּעֶצֶם הַיּוֹם הַזֶּה.** מַגִּיד שֶׁכֵּיוָן שֶׁהִגִּיעַ הַקֵּץ לֹא עִכְּבָן הַמָּקוֹם כְּהֶרֶף עַיִן. בַּחֲמִשָּׁה עָשָׂר בְּנִיסָן בָּאוּ מַלְאֲכֵי הַשָּׁרֵת אֵצֶל אַבְרָהָם לְבַשְּׂרוֹ, בַּחֲמִשָּׁה עָשָׂר בְּנִיסָן נוֹלַד יִצְחָק, בַּחֲמִשָּׁה עָשָׂר בְּנִיסָן נִגְזְרָה גְּזֵרַת בֵּין הַבְּתָרִים:

מב| **לֵיל שִׁמֻּרִים.** שֶׁהָיָה הַקָּדוֹשׁ בָּרוּךְ הוּא שׁוֹמֵר וּמְצַפֶּה לוֹ לְקַיֵּם הַבְטָחָתוֹ "לְהוֹצִיאָם מֵאֶרֶץ מִצְרַיִם": **הוּא הַלַּיְלָה הַזֶּה לַה'.** הוּא הַלַּיְלָה שֶׁאָמַר לְאַבְרָהָם: בַּלַּיְלָה הַזֶּה אֲנִי גוֹאֵל אֶת בָּנֶיךָ: **שִׁמֻּרִים לְכָל בְּנֵי יִשְׂרָאֵל לְדֹרֹתָם.** מְשֻׁמָּר וּבָא מִן הַמַּזִּיקִין, כְּעִנְיָן שֶׁנֶּאֱמַר: "וְלֹא יִתֵּן הַמַּשְׁחִית" וְגוֹ' (לעיל פסוק כג):

Laws for Future Generations, in Memory of the Exodus

EXODUS 12:43–13:16

The laws that Israel will observe in future generations for the purpose of preserving the memory of the dramatic event of the exodus are called testimonies [*edot*]. These include the yearly paschal offering, the celebration of the festival of Passover, and the commandment to recount the exodus verbally. Also included is the consecration of both firstborn animals and firstborn male children, as well as the commemoration of the redemption in writing inside phylacteries.

In addition to the commandments that were relevant to the night of the redemption itself, the laws of the festival of Passover for future generations were given before the plague of the firstborn, and it is possible that all of these commemorative commandments were also given then to Moses and Aaron.

Perhaps the giving of commandments involving the commemoration of events before they actually occurred was meant to assure the children of Israel of the certainty of the exodus, and also to generate in them the consciousness that they were participating in events of great historical significance. Furthermore, the service of God was thereby indelibly associated with their actual departure from Egypt. They are listed here, after the account of the events, in order to not interrupt the narrative flow.

43 **The Lord said to Moses and Aaron: This is the statute of the paschal lamb.** In addition to the practical instructions stated above, which apply only to the paschal lambs in Egypt, the following general commands relate to all paschal offerings in the future: **No foreigner** from another nation **shall eat from it,** despite the fact that a mixed multitude also left Egypt at the exodus.

44 **Any man's slave, purchased with silver: You shall circumcise him, then he shall eat from it.** Only the circumcised may partake of the paschal offering. The Sages debate whether the last clause of this verse is referring to the slaves themselves or to their master, who also may not eat from the offering if a male of his household is uncircumcised.[2323]

45 **A resident alien,** a non-Jew who lives among you, **and a** gentile **hired laborer**[2424]**shall not eat from it,** even though they are considered part of the household.

46 **It,** the paschal lamb, **shall be eaten in one house; you shall not remove any of the meat from the house to the outside.** It is entirely consecrated as an offering and must be eaten in a designated space. **And you shall not break a bone of it,** as you must consume it in the manner of kings.[2525]

47 **The entire congregation of Israel shall do it.**

48 **When a stranger resides with you,** not a temporary resident or a hired hand, but someone who wishes to convert and join the nation of Israel and worship God, **and** he **performs the paschal offering to the Lord,** before he may do so, one must **circumcise every male of his.** One of the necessary conditions of conversion is that all the male members of the household who wish to convert must enter into the covenant of circumcision. **And then he shall approach to perform it,** to offer the paschal lamb, **and he shall be like a native of the land; but all uncircumcised persons shall not eat from it,** including one who was born an Israelite but is not circumcised.

49 In this matter, **there shall be one law for the native and for the stranger who resides among you.**

50 **The children of Israel did as the Lord had commanded Moses and Aaron, so they did.** They followed his instructions precisely on the night of the redemption, when they partook of the paschal lamb.[2626]

51 **It was on that very day,** following the night when they ate the paschal lamb, that **the Lord brought the children of Israel out of the land of Egypt by their hosts.**

13 1 *Seventh aliya* The Torah presents commandments that relate to commemorating the exodus of the Israelites from Egypt on the same night that God struck down the firstborn of Egypt. **The Lord spoke to Moses, saying:**

2 **Sanctify to Me every firstborn; the first issue of any womb**[D] **among the children of Israel, from man and animal, is Mine.** Its sanctification expresses the fact that it belongs to God.

3 Before mentioning the matter of the firstborn, the command he received from God in the previous verse, Moses addresses other matters. **Moses said to the people: Remember this day, on which you departed from Egypt, from the house of bondage,** the place where you were slaves. You did not have to flee from there, **for with strength of hand,** by force, **the Lord took you out from this; and leavened bread may not be eaten** during the exodus itself and on the dates set aside to commemorate the exodus in future generations.

4 **This day,** in this season,[2727]**you depart, in the month of the ripening.** This is not only a description of the season when Israel left Egypt. It is also a normative instruction, as the festival of Passover must always occur in the spring.[2828]

5 The festival of Passover is relevant not only for the present. **It shall be when the Lord shall bring you to the land of the Canaanites, the Hitites, the Emorites, the Hivites, and the Yevusites, that He took an oath to your forefathers to give**

מג וַיֹּאמֶר יְהוָה אֶל־מֹשֶׁה וְאַהֲרֹן זֹאת חֻקַּת הַפָּסַח כָּל־בֶּן־נֵכָר לֹא־יֹאכַל בּוֹ:
מד מה וְכָל־עֶבֶד אִישׁ מִקְנַת־כָּסֶף וּמַלְתָּה אֹתוֹ אָז יֹאכַל בּוֹ: תּוֹשָׁב וְשָׂכִיר לֹא־יֹאכַל
מו בּוֹ: בְּבַיִת אֶחָד יֵאָכֵל לֹא־תוֹצִיא מִן־הַבַּיִת מִן־הַבָּשָׂר חוּצָה וְעֶצֶם לֹא תִשְׁבְּרוּ־
מז מח בוֹ: כָּל־עֲדַת יִשְׂרָאֵל יַעֲשׂוּ אֹתוֹ: וְכִי־יָגוּר אִתְּךָ גֵּר וְעָשָׂה פֶסַח לַיהוָה הִמּוֹל לוֹ
מט כָל־זָכָר וְאָז יִקְרַב לַעֲשֹׂתוֹ וְהָיָה כְּאֶזְרַח הָאָרֶץ וְכָל־עָרֵל לֹא־יֹאכַל בּוֹ: תּוֹרָה
נ אַחַת יִהְיֶה לָאֶזְרָח וְלַגֵּר הַגָּר בְּתוֹכְכֶם: וַיַּעֲשׂוּ כָּל־בְּנֵי יִשְׂרָאֵל כַּאֲשֶׁר צִוָּה יְהוָה
נא אֶת־מֹשֶׁה וְאֶת־אַהֲרֹן כֵּן עָשׂוּ: וַיְהִי בְּעֶצֶם הַיּוֹם הַזֶּה הוֹצִיא יְהוָה אֶת־בְּנֵי
יִשְׂרָאֵל מֵאֶרֶץ מִצְרַיִם עַל־צִבְאֹתָם:

ג
א ב וַיְדַבֵּר יְהוָה אֶל־מֹשֶׁה לֵּאמֹר: קַדֶּשׁ־לִי כָל־בְּכוֹר פֶּטֶר כָּל־רֶחֶם בִּבְנֵי יִשְׂרָאֵל שביעי
ג בָּאָדָם וּבַבְּהֵמָה לִי הוּא: וַיֹּאמֶר מֹשֶׁה אֶל־הָעָם זָכוֹר אֶת־הַיּוֹם הַזֶּה אֲשֶׁר
יְצָאתֶם מִמִּצְרַיִם מִבֵּית עֲבָדִים כִּי בְּחֹזֶק יָד הוֹצִיא יְהוָה אֶתְכֶם מִזֶּה וְלֹא
ד ה יֵאָכֵל חָמֵץ: הַיּוֹם אַתֶּם יֹצְאִים בְּחֹדֶשׁ הָאָבִיב: וְהָיָה כִי־יְבִיאֲךָ יְהוָה אֶל־אֶרֶץ

רש"י

מג | **זאת חקת הפסח.** בארבעה עשר בניסן נאמרה להם פרשה זו: **כל בן נכר.** שנתנכרו מעשיו לאביו שבשמים, ואחד הגוי ואחד ישראל משומד במשמע:

מד | **ומלתה אתו אז יאכל בו.** רבו; מגיד שמילת עבדיו מעכבתו מלאכול בפסח, דברי רבי יהושע. רבי אליעזר אומר: אין מילת עבדיו מעכבתו מלאכול בפסח, אם כן מה תלמוד לומר: "אז יאכל בו"? העבד:

מה | **תושב.** זה גר תושב: **ושכיר.** זה הגוי. ומה תלמוד לומר? והלא ערלים הם, ונאמר: "וכל ערל לא יאכל בו" (להלן פסוק מח)! אלא כגון ערבי מהול וגבעוני מהול והוא תושב או שכיר:

מו | **בבית אחד יאכל.** בחבורה אחת, שלא יעשו הנמנין עליו שתי חבורות ויחלקוהו. אתה אומר בחבורה אחת, או אינו אלא "בבית אחד" כמשמעו, וללמד שאם התחילו והיו אוכלים בחצר וירדו גשמים שלא יכנסו לבית? תלמוד לומר: "על הבתים אשר יאכלו אתו בהם" (לעיל פסוק ז), מכאן שהאוכל אוכל בשני מקומות: **לא תוציא מן הבית.** מן החבורה: **ועצם לא תשברו בו.** הראוי לאכילה, כגון שיש עליו כזית בשר, יש בו משום שבירת עצם, אין עליו כזית בשר אין בו משום שבירת עצם:

מז | **כל עדת ישראל יעשו אתו.** למה נאמר? לפי שהוא אומר בפסח מצרים: "שה לבית אבת" (לעיל פסוק ג) שנמנו עליו למשפחות, יכול אף פסח דורות כן? תלמוד לומר: "כל עדת ישראל יעשו אתו":

מח | **ועשה פסח.** יכול כל המתגייר יעשה פסח מיד? תלמוד לומר: "והיה כאזרח הארץ", מה אזרח בארבעה עשר אף גר בארבעה עשר: **וכל ערל לא יאכל בו.** להביא את שמתו אחיו מחמת מילה, שאינו משומד לערלות ואינו למד מ"בן נכר לא יאכל בו" (לעיל פסוק מג):

מט | **תורה אחת וגו'.** להשוות גר לאזרח אף לשאר מצות שבתורה:

פרק יג

ב | **פטר כל רחם.** שפתח את הרחם תחלה, כמו: "פוטר מים ראשית מדון" (משלי יז, יד), וכן: "יפטירו בשפה" (תהלים כב, ח) – יפתחו שפתים: **לי הוא.** לעצמי קניתים על ידי שהכיתי בכורי מצרים:

ג | **זכור את היום הזה.** למד שמזכירין יציאת מצרים בכל יום:

ד | **בחדש האביב.** וכי לא היינו יודעין באי זה חדש? אלא כך אמר להם: ראו חסד שגמלכם, שהוציא אתכם בחדש שהוא כשר לצאת, לא חמה ולא צנה ולא גשמים. וכן הוא אומר: "מוציא אסירים בכושרות" (תהלים סח, ז), חדש שהוא כשר לצאת:

ה | **אל ארץ הכנעני וגו'.** אף על פי שלא מנה אלא

DISCUSSION

13:2| **The first issue of any womb:** This phrase indicates that the first offspring of every female is categorized a firstborn, a definition that applies both to humans and animals. The Sages discuss various cases of miscarriages, stillbirths, and births by caesarian section, where it is unclear whether a subsequent birth is regarded as the first issue of a womb. In practice, this biological question is not the only consideration in determining whether a newly born person or animal is consecrated as a firstborn (see *Mekhilta deRashbi* 13:12; *Bekhorot* 19a; Rambam, *Sefer Korbanot*, *Hilkhot Bekhorot* 11:14–16).

to you, which is **a land flowing with milk and honey, you shall perform this service** that you observed in Egypt, of the paschal offering, **in this month**[D] of spring.

6 **Seven days you shall eat unleavened bread; and on the seventh day is a festival to the Lord.**

7 Only **unleavened bread shall be eaten for the seven days.** You are not obligated to eat unleavened bread for all seven days, as might have been inferred from the previous verse. Rather, if one wishes to eat bread during these seven days, it must be unleavened.[2929]Not only is consuming leavened bread prohibited, but **neither leavened bread shall be seen with you, nor shall leaven be seen with you, within your entire border.**

8 **You shall tell your son**[D] **on that day,** when you commemorate the exodus, **saying: It is because of this,** in order that I will preserve the memory of these events and perform the commandments, **that the Lord did this,** all the signs and wonders, **for me upon my exodus from Egypt.**

9 **It,** the story of the exodus, **shall be a sign for you on your hand and a remembrance between your eyes.**[D] You must write a reference to this story on an object that you will attach to your arm and between your eyes, **so that the law of the Lord will be in your mouth, because** you must remember that **with a powerful hand the Lord took you out of Egypt.**

10 In addition to the various means of commemorating the exodus throughout the entire year, **you shall observe this statute,** the paschal lamb, **at its appointed time, from year to year.**

11 Up to this point, Moses has detailed the various rituals dedicated to the remembrance of the exodus: Eating unleavened bread and refraining from consuming leavened bread on the festival of Passover; establishing that festival in the spring; eliminating leaven from one's possession for this festival; telling the story of the exodus; and binding a written sign to one's arm and head.

He now returns to the command that God had earlier instructed him to give to Israel: **It shall be when the Lord will take you to the land of the Canaanite, as He took an oath to you and to your forefathers, and He shall give it to you,**

12 **you shall transfer to the Lord each first issue of the womb;**[D] **and of each first issue discharged** from the body **of an animal that you will have, the males** are sanctified and **are the Lord's.**

The beheading of a donkey in Egypt, etching from the tenth century BCE

13 **Every first issue of a donkey you shall redeem with a lamb.** The firstborn of a donkey is sacred but it may not be used in its consecrated state. Instead, it must be exchanged for a lamb, which is given to the priests, as is explained later.[3030]**And if you do not redeem it,** the firstborn donkey, **then you shall behead it.**[D] It is not clear why someone would refuse to redeem his donkey. Perhaps he is angry with his local priest or he cannot get hold of a lamb for whatever reason. **And all the firstborn of man among your sons,** who of course may not be offered upon the altar either, **you shall redeem.**

14 **It shall be when your son asks you tomorrow, saying: What** *Maftir* **is this?** Why do you redeem the human firstborn and the firstborn of a donkey, and consecrate the firstborn of sheep, goats

---

DISCUSSION

13:5 | You shall perform this service in this month: The Jewish calendar was created on the basis of this instruction, which will be explained further below (23:15). Although primarily a lunar calendar, it also takes into account the solar year in order to ensure that the month of the exodus always occurs in the spring (see *Rosh HaShana* 21a; Ibn Ezra). In order to synchronize the lunar calendar with the solar year, it is necessary to add an additional month seven times in each cycle of nineteen years. The tradition is to add a second Adar, which is the last month of the year starting from Nisan.

13:8 | You shall tell your son: This obligation, to preserve the memory of the exodus and to pass it on to the next generation by relating the story of the redemption to one's children, is the basis of the Passover Haggada.

13:9 | It shall be a sign for you on your hand and a remembrance between your eyes: These expressions recur below (verse 16) as well as in other places in the Torah (Deuteronomy 6:8, 11:18). Some understand them figuratively, that these matters must be impressed upon one's consciousness as though they were attached to one's hand or placed between one's eyes. Certain commentators vigorously object to this interpretation. They argue that as a general principle the Torah does not speak figuratively but gives specific instructions to perform particular actions (see Rashbam; Ibn Ezra, long commentary on Exodus; Rashi). In any case, the commandment to don phylacteries is derived from here and the aforementioned similar verses. Phylacteries are bound on the arm and the head, while the details of their shape, contents,

and construction are passed down by tradition. They serve as a sign and reminder of the exodus.

13:12 | You shall transfer to the Lord each first issue of the womb: The Torah does not explain here how this command is to be carried out in practice. At a later stage firstborn animals will be given to the priests, but as yet there is no Tabernacle or hereditary priesthood, and the firstborn sons functioned as priests at the time.

13:13 | If you do not redeem it, then you shall behead it: The Torah does not explain why, out of all non-kosher animals, only the firstborn of a donkey requires redemption. The donkey was not one of the animals revered by the Egyptians as gods, although it did represent Set, a god of the desert, darkness, and destruction, who was an object of fear for the Egyptians. In any case,

↤

הַכְּנַעֲנִי וְהַחִתִּי וְהָאֱמֹרִי וְהַחִוִּי וְהַיְבוּסִי אֲשֶׁר נִשְׁבַּע לַאֲבֹתֶיךָ לָתֶת לָךְ אֶרֶץ

ו זָבַת חָלָב וּדְבָשׁ וְעָבַדְתָּ אֶת־הָעֲבֹדָה הַזֹּאת בַּחֹדֶשׁ הַזֶּה: שִׁבְעַת יָמִים תֹּאכַל

ז מַצֹּת וּבַיּוֹם הַשְּׁבִיעִי חַג לַיהוה: מַצּוֹת יֵאָכֵל אֵת שִׁבְעַת הַיָּמִים וְלֹא־יֵרָאֶה לְךָ

ח חָמֵץ וְלֹא־יֵרָאֶה לְךָ שְׂאֹר בְּכָל־גְּבֻלֶךָ: וְהִגַּדְתָּ לְבִנְךָ בַּיּוֹם הַהוּא לֵאמֹר בַּעֲבוּר

ט זֶה עָשָׂה יהוה לִי בְּצֵאתִי מִמִּצְרָיִם: וְהָיָה לְךָ לְאוֹת עַל־יָדְךָ וּלְזִכָּרוֹן בֵּין עֵינֶיךָ

י לְמַעַן תִּהְיֶה תּוֹרַת יהוה בְּפִיךָ כִּי בְּיָד חֲזָקָה הוֹצִאֲךָ יהוה מִמִּצְרָיִם: וְשָׁמַרְתָּ

אֶת־הַחֻקָּה הַזֹּאת לְמוֹעֲדָהּ מִיָּמִים יָמִימָה:

יא וְהָיָה כִּי־יְבִאֲךָ יהוה אֶל־אֶרֶץ הַכְּנַעֲנִי כַּאֲשֶׁר נִשְׁבַּע לְךָ וְלַאֲבֹתֶיךָ וּנְתָנָהּ לָךְ:

יב וְהַעֲבַרְתָּ כָל־פֶּטֶר־רֶחֶם לַיהוה וְכָל־פֶּטֶר ׀ שֶׁגֶר בְּהֵמָה אֲשֶׁר יִהְיֶה לְךָ הַזְּכָרִים

יג לַיהוה: וְכָל־פֶּטֶר חֲמֹר תִּפְדֶּה בְשֶׂה וְאִם־לֹא תִפְדֶּה וַעֲרַפְתּוֹ וְכֹל בְּכוֹר אָדָם

יד בְּבָנֶיךָ תִּפְדֶּה: וְהָיָה כִּי־יִשְׁאָלְךָ בִנְךָ מָחָר לֵאמֹר מַה־זֹּאת וְאָמַרְתָּ אֵלָיו בְּחֹזֶק מפטיר

רש"י

חֲמִשָּׁה עֲמָמִים, כָּל שִׁבְעָה גּוֹיִם בַּמַּשְׁמָע שֶׁכֻּלָּן בִּכְלַל כְּנַעֲנִי הֵם, וְאַחַת מִמִּשְׁפְּחוֹת כְּנַעַן שֶׁלֹּא נִקְרָא לָהּ שֵׁם אֶלָּא כְּנַעֲנִי: **נִשְׁבַּע לַאֲבֹתֶיךָ**. בְּאַבְרָהָם הוּא אוֹמֵר: "בַּיּוֹם הַהוּא כָּרַת ה' אֶת אַבְרָם" וְגו' (בראשית טו, יח), וּבְיִצְחָק הוּא אוֹמֵר: "גּוּר בָּאָרֶץ הַזֹּאת" וְגו' (שם כו, ג), וּבְיַעֲקֹב הוּא אוֹמֵר: "הָאָרֶץ אֲשֶׁר אַתָּה שֹׁכֵב עָלֶיהָ" וְגו' (שם כח, יג): **זָבַת חָלָב וּדְבָשׁ**. חָלָב זָב מִן הָעִזִּים, וְהַדְּבַשׁ זָב מִן הַתְּאֵנִים וּמִן הַתְּמָרִים: **אֶת הָעֲבֹדָה הַזֹּאת**. שֶׁל פֶּסַח. וַהֲלֹא כְּבַר נֶאֱמַר לְמַעְלָה: "וְהָיָה כִּי תָבֹאוּ אֶל הָאָרֶץ" וְגו' (לעיל יב, כה), וְלָמָּה חָזַר וּשְׁנָאָהּ? בִּשְׁבִיל דָּבָר שֶׁנִּתְחַדֵּשׁ בָּהּ. בְּפָרָשָׁה רִאשׁוֹנָה נֶאֱמַר: "וְהָיָה כִּי יֹאמְרוּ אֲלֵיכֶם בְּנֵיכֶם מָה הָעֲבֹדָה הַזֹּאת לָכֶם" (שם פסוק כו), בְּבֵן רָשָׁע הַכָּתוּב מְדַבֵּר שֶׁהוֹצִיא עַצְמוֹ מִן הַכְּלָל, וְכָאן: "וְהִגַּדְתָּ לְבִנְךָ" (להלן פסוק ח), בְּבֵן שֶׁאֵינוֹ יוֹדֵעַ לִשְׁאֹל, וְהַכָּתוּב מְלַמֶּדְךָ שֶׁתִּפְתַּח לוֹ אַתָּה בְּדִבְרֵי אַגָּדָה הַמּוֹשְׁכִין אֶת הַלֵּב:

ח | בַּעֲבוּר זֶה. בַּעֲבוּר שֶׁאֲקַיֵּם מִצְו‍ֹתָיו כְּגוֹן פֶּסַח מַצָּה וּמָרוֹר הַלָּלוּ: **עָשָׂה ה' לִי**. רֶמֶז תְּשׁוּבָה לְבֵן רָשָׁע, לוֹמַר: "עָשָׂה ה' לִי", וְלֹא לְךָ, שֶׁאִלּוּ הָיִיתָ שָׁם לֹא הָיִיתָ כְּדַאי לִגָּאֵל:

ט | וְהָיָה לְךָ לְאוֹת. יְצִיאַת מִצְרַיִם תִּהְיֶה לְךָ לְאוֹת עַל יָדְךָ וּבֵין עֵינֶיךָ, שֶׁתִּכְתֹּב פָּרָשִׁיּוֹת הַלָּלוּ וְתִקְשְׁרֵם בָּרֹאשׁ וּבַזְּרוֹעַ: **עַל יָדְךָ**. יָד שְׂמֹאל, לְפִיכָךְ "יָדְכָה" מָלֵא בְּפָרָשָׁה שְׁנִיָּה (להלן פסוק טז) לִדְרֹשׁ בּוֹ, יָד שֶׁהִוא כֵּהָה:

י | מִיָּמִים יָמִימָה. מִשָּׁנָה לְשָׁנָה:

יא | נִשְׁבַּע לְךָ. וְהֵיכָן נִשְׁבַּע לְךָ? "וְהֵבֵאתִי אֶתְכֶם אֶל הָאָרֶץ אֲשֶׁר נָשָׂאתִי" וְגו' (לעיל ו, ח). **וּנְתָנָהּ לָךְ**. תְּהֵא בְעֵינֶיךָ כְּאִלּוּ נְתָנָהּ לָךְ בּוֹ בַיּוֹם וְאַל תְּהִי בְעֵינֶיךָ כִּירֻשַּׁת אָבוֹת:

יב | וְהַעֲבַרְתָּ. אֵין "וְהַעֲבַרְתָּ" אֶלָּא לְשׁוֹן הַפְרָשָׁה, וְכֵן הוּא אוֹמֵר: "וְהַעֲבַרְתֶּם אֶת נַחֲלָתוֹ לְבִתּוֹ" (במדבר כז, ח): **שֶׁגֶר בְּהֵמָה**. נֵפֶל שֶׁשִּׁגְּרַתּוּ אִמּוֹ וְשִׁלְּחַתּוֹ בְּלֹא עִתּוֹ, וּלְמֶדְךָ הַכָּתוּב שֶׁהוּא קָדוֹשׁ בִּבְכוֹרָה לִפְטֹר אֶת הַבָּא אַחֲרָיו. וְאַף שֶׁאֵינוֹ נֵפֶל קָרוּי שֶׁגֶר, כְּמוֹ: "שֶׁגַר אֲלָפֶיךָ" (דברים ז, יג), אֲבָל זֶה לֹא בָא לְלַמֵּד עַל הַנֵּפֶל, שֶׁהֲרֵי כְּבַר כָּתַב "כָּל פֶּטֶר רֶחֶם", וְאִם תֹּאמַר, אַף בְּכוֹר בְּהֵמָה טְמֵאָה בַּמַּשְׁמָע, בָּא וְגִלָּה בְּמָקוֹם אַחֵר: "בִּבְקָרְךָ וּבְצֹאנֶךָ" (שם טו, יט). לָשׁוֹן אַחֵר יֵשׁ לְפָרֵשׁ, "וְהַעֲבַרְתָּ כָל פֶּטֶר רֶחֶם" – בִּבְכוֹר אָדָם הַכָּתוּב מְדַבֵּר:

יג | פֶּטֶר חֲמֹר. וְלֹא פֶּטֶר שְׁאָר בְּהֵמָה טְמֵאָה, וּגְזֵרַת הַכָּתוּב הִיא, לְפִי שֶׁנִּמְשְׁלוּ בְּכוֹרֵי מִצְרַיִם לַחֲמוֹרִים. וְעוֹד, שֶׁסִּיְּעוּ אֶת יִשְׂרָאֵל בִּיצִיאָתָן מִמִּצְרַיִם, שֶׁאֵין לְךָ אֶחָד מִיִּשְׂרָאֵל שֶׁלֹּא נָטַל עִמּוֹ הַרְבֵּה חֲמוֹרִים טְעוּנִים מִכַּסְפָּהּ וּמִזְּהָבָהּ שֶׁל מִצְרַיִם: **תִּפְדֶּה בְשֶׂה**. נוֹתֵן שֶׂה לַכֹּהֵן וּפֶטֶר חֲמוֹר מֻתָּר בַּהֲנָאָה, וְהַשֶּׂה חֻלִּין בְּיַד כֹּהֵן: **וַעֲרַפְתּוֹ**. עוֹרְפוֹ בְּקוֹפִיץ מֵאֲחוֹרָיו וְהוֹרְגוֹ. הוּא הִפְסִיד מָמוֹנוֹ שֶׁל כֹּהֵן לְפִיכָךְ יֻפְסַד מָמוֹנוֹ: **וְכֹל בְּכוֹר אָדָם בְּבָנֶיךָ תִּפְדֶּה**. חָמֵשׁ סְלָעִים פִּדְיוֹנוֹ קָצוּב בְּמָקוֹם אַחֵר (במדבר יח, טז):

יד | כִּי יִשְׁאָלְךָ בִנְךָ מָחָר. יֵשׁ "מָחָר" שֶׁהוּא עַכְשָׁיו וְיֵשׁ "מָחָר" שֶׁהוּא לְאַחַר זְמָן, כְּגוֹן זֶה וּכְגוֹן: "מָחָר יֹאמְרוּ בְנֵיכֶם לְבָנֵינוּ" (יהושע כב, כד) דִּבְנֵי גָד וּבְנֵי רְאוּבֵן: **מַה זֹּאת**. זֶה תִּינוֹק טִפֵּשׁ שֶׁאֵינוֹ יוֹדֵעַ לְהַעֲמִיק שְׁאֵלָתוֹ וְסוֹתֵם וְשׁוֹאֵל: "מַה זֹּאת". וּבְמָקוֹם אַחֵר הוּא אוֹמֵר: "מָה הָעֵדֹת וְהַחֻקִּים וְהַמִּשְׁפָּטִים" וְגו' (דברים ו, כ), הֲרֵי זֹאת שְׁאֵלַת בֵּן חָכָם. דִּבְּרָה תוֹרָה כְּנֶגֶד אַרְבָּעָה בָנִים: רָשָׁע, וְשֶׁאֵינוֹ יוֹדֵעַ לִשְׁאֹל, וְהַשּׁוֹאֵל דֶּרֶךְ סְתוּמָה, וְהַשּׁוֹאֵל דֶּרֶךְ חָכְמָה:

DISCUSSION

↦ the text indicates that redemption is the preferred alternative and beheading should be performed only if one refuses to redeem his firstborn donkey (see Mishna *Bekhorot* 1:7).

and cattle? **You shall say to him: With strength of hand,** power and force, **the Lord took us out from Egypt, from the house of bondage.**

15 **It was when Pharaoh hesitated to send us forth, the Lord killed all the firstborn in the land of Egypt, from the firstborn man to the firstborn animal,** and only such measures persuaded Pharaoh to let us go. Consequently, God took all the firstborn as His possession. **Therefore, I sacrifice to the Lord every first issue of the womb, the males; and all the firstborn of my sons I will redeem.** I give to God the firstborn that He selected for Himself.

16 **It,** the sanctity of the firstborn, in addition to the story of the exodus (13:9), **shall be a sign upon your arm,**[D] **and an ornament between your eyes;**[D] **for with strength of hand the Lord took us out of Egypt.** He chose us and wants us to be His people. This is commemorated both by the giving of the firstborn to God and through the donning of phylacteries, which symbolize the unique bond between Israel and God.

DISCUSSION

13:16| **It shall be a sign upon your arm:** The significance of phylacteries is not only in the writing that is placed in the boxes; they are not simply a means of remembering the exodus. Rather, they are a sign of nobility and royalty, an ornamental symbol designed to inspire respect. Surprisingly, the crown of Pharaoh himself included an element that resembles the phylactery placed on the head. The phylactery of the head represents a kind of crown granted to Israel, indicating its princely status as the firstborn son of God (4:22). The phylactery bound on the arm also bears symbolic meaning. It signifies both the power of action (see *Berakhot* 6a), and one's subordination to the Holy One, Blessed be He, as this phylactery is tilted toward the heart.

The final passages of this section, both of which mention phylacteries (verses 1–10 and 11–16), are two of the four passages that are written on parchment and placed in the boxes of the phylacteries.

And an ornament [*totafot*] between your eyes: The precise meaning of the word *totafot* is unclear. It is possible that it is borrowed from a different language. The Sages understood *totafot* as referring to an ornament placed on the head (see *Shabbat* 57b). According to the Oral Torah, the sign upon your arm and the *totafot* between your eyes are phylacteries (see *Sanhedrin* 4b; *Bekhor Shor*; Ramban).

טו יָד הוֹצִיאָנוּ יְהוָה מִמִּצְרַיִם מִבֵּית עֲבָדִים: וַיְהִי כִּי־הִקְשָׁה פַרְעֹה לְשַׁלְּחֵנוּ וַיַּהֲרֹג
יְהוָה כָּל־בְּכוֹר בְּאֶרֶץ מִצְרַיִם מִבְּכֹר אָדָם וְעַד־בְּכוֹר בְּהֵמָה עַל־כֵּן אֲנִי זֹבֵחַ
טז לַיהוָה כָּל־פֶּטֶר רֶחֶם הַזְּכָרִים וְכָל־בְּכוֹר בָּנַי אֶפְדֶּה: וְהָיָה לְאוֹת עַל־יָדְכָה
וּלְטוֹטָפֹת בֵּין עֵינֶיךָ כִּי בְּחֹזֶק יָד הוֹצִיאָנוּ יְהוָה מִמִּצְרָיִם:

רש״י

טז] וּלְטוֹטָפֹת. תְּפִלִּין, וְעַל שֵׁם שֶׁהֵם אַרְבָּעָה בָּתִּים קְרוּיִים 'טוֹטָפֹת', 'טַט' בְּכַתְפֵי שְׁתַּיִם 'פַּת' בְּאַפְרִיקֵי שְׁתַּיִם. וּמְנַחֵם חִבְּרוֹ עִם "וְהַטֵּף אֶל דָּרוֹם" (יחזקאל כא, ב), "אַל תַּטִּפוּ" (מיכה ב, ו), לְשׁוֹן דִּבּוּר, כְּמוֹ: "וּלְזִכָּרוֹן בֵּין עֵינֶיךָ" (לעיל פסוק ט), שֶׁהָרוֹאֶה אוֹתָם קְשׁוּרִים בֵּין הָעֵינַיִם יִזְכֹּר הַנֵּס וִידַבֵּר בּוֹ:

Parashat
Beshalah

The Beginning of the Journey in the Wilderness

EXODUS 13:17–22

Certain commandments were enumerated before and after the account of the plague of the firstborn and the exodus from Egypt, in order to imprint the memory of these great events on the consciousness of the Jewish people for all time. The Torah now returns to the story of the children of Israel, describing the beginning of their journey into the wilderness. Here, the people's first campsites are briefly enumerated, as well as certain matters concerning their general route and manner of travel. The Torah also notes the fulfillment of the promise made to Joseph, that his bones would be returned from Egypt.

17 **It was, in Pharaoh's sending forth the people, that God did not guide them via the land of the Philistines,** along the Mediterranean coast, **although it was near, for God said: Lest the people reconsider when they see war.** Although the Philistines were not a large nation, they were militarily powerful. Passing through their land risked a war which might have caused the Israelites to reverse course **and return to Egypt.**

18 **God led the people circuitously, via the wilderness of the Red Sea.** Instead of turning northward, toward the Mediterranean coastline, God led them southeast. **And the children of Israel came up armed from the land of Egypt,** as they assumed that they would eventually be forced to fight.[2] God decided that they were not yet ready to stand in battle, and He therefore guided them on a path that would avoid direct confrontation with the Philistines.

19 **Moses took the bones of Joseph with him, for he,** Joseph, **had administered an oath to the children of Israel,** the children of Jacob,[3] or the Israelites in general, **saying: God will remember** and redeem **you; and** when this occurs, I request that

you shall bring my bones up from here, from Egypt, **with you.**

20 **They,** the Israelites, **traveled from** a place called **Sukot;** alternatively, from a place where there were booths [*sukkot*], **and they encamped in Etam, at the edge of the wilderness.** Until this point, the Israelites traveled in fertile areas that were part of Egypt or Goshen. Now, they begin to travel in uninhabited areas.

21 So that they could navigate the desert, an angel of **the Lord**[D] **was going before them by day in a pillar of cloud to guide them on the way.** They followed the cloud, which represented the glory of God. **And by night** He would go with them **in a pillar of fire to illuminate for them, to go day and night.** It is unclear whether the Israelites actually traveled by night. In any event, the pillar of fire gave them the ability to do so.[4]

22 **The pillar of cloud by day and the pillar of fire by night would not move from before the people.** The Israelites did not know where they were traveling; these two pillars represented God's guiding hand in the wilderness.

The Israelites at the Red Sea

EXODUS 14:1–31

When God struck Egypt with the plagues, the Israelites remained on the periphery. They stayed in their dwellings, and they did not witness with their own eyes the wonders that Moses performed in God's name. Only at the Red Sea do Israel witness these miraculous events to their full dramatic extent. Furthermore, unlike the plagues that descended on Egypt within their borders, the occurrences described here come with sudden, quick intensity. This is also a defining moment for Moses in his capacity as leader and redeemer in the eyes of the people.

14 1 **The Lord spoke to Moses, saying:**

2 **Speak to the children of Israel, that they return** in the direction of Egypt **and encamp before Pi HaHirot,**[B] a famous place

at the time. The name Pi is Egyptian. It is located **between Migdol and the Red Sea, before** the pagan god **Baal Tzefon.**[BD] **Opposite it you shall encamp, by the sea.** On their way to

---

DISCUSSION

13:21 | **The Lord:** God appears in the world by way of angels or messengers (see Rashi; Rashbam; Ramban; *Ḥizkuni*; *Bekhor Shor* 14:19). The verse below (14:19) describes the

movements of this pillar, and there it is referred to as an angel.

14:2 | **Baal Tzefon:** This may be a reference to Set, Egyptian god of the desert, darkness, and

destruction. Over the course of many generations the Egyptians did not know how to relate to the God of Israel, and where to place Him within their pantheon. They saw Him as a local

פרשת בשלח

יז וַיְהִי בְּשַׁלַּח פַּרְעֹה אֶת־הָעָם וְלֹא־נָחָם אֱלֹהִים דֶּרֶךְ אֶרֶץ פְּלִשְׁתִּים כִּי קָרוֹב הוּא

יח כִּי | אָמַר אֱלֹהִים פֶּן־יִנָּחֵם הָעָם בִּרְאֹתָם מִלְחָמָה וְשָׁבוּ מִצְרָיְמָה: וַיַּסֵּב אֱלֹהִים |

יט אֶת־הָעָם דֶּרֶךְ הַמִּדְבָּר יַם־סוּף וַחֲמֻשִׁים עָלוּ בְנֵי־יִשְׂרָאֵל מֵאֶרֶץ מִצְרָיִם: וַיִּקַּח

מֹשֶׁה אֶת־עַצְמוֹת יוֹסֵף עִמּוֹ כִּי הַשְׁבֵּעַ הִשְׁבִּיעַ אֶת־בְּנֵי יִשְׂרָאֵל לֵאמֹר פָּקֹד

כ יִפְקֹד אֱלֹהִים אֶתְכֶם וְהַעֲלִיתֶם אֶת־עַצְמֹתַי מִזֶּה אִתְּכֶם: וַיִּסְעוּ מִסֻּכֹּת וַיַּחֲנוּ

כא בְאֵתָם בִּקְצֵה הַמִּדְבָּר: וַיהוה הֹלֵךְ לִפְנֵיהֶם יוֹמָם בְּעַמּוּד עָנָן לַנְחֹתָם הַדֶּרֶךְ

כב וְלַיְלָה בְּעַמּוּד אֵשׁ לְהָאִיר לָהֶם לָלֶכֶת יוֹמָם וָלָיְלָה: לֹא־יָמִישׁ עַמּוּד הֶעָנָן יוֹמָם

וְעַמּוּד הָאֵשׁ לָיְלָה לִפְנֵי הָעָם:

א ב וַיְדַבֵּר יהוה אֶל־מֹשֶׁה לֵּאמֹר: דַּבֵּר אֶל־בְּנֵי יִשְׂרָאֵל וְיָשֻׁבוּ וְיַחֲנוּ לִפְנֵי פִּי הַחִירֹת

רש״י

יז | **וַיְהִי בְּשַׁלַּח פַּרְעֹה. וְלֹא נָחָם.** נְהָגָם, כְּמוֹ: ״לֵךְ נְחֵה אֶת הָעָם״ (להלן לב, לד), ״בְּהִתְהַלֶּכְךָ תַּנְחֶה אֹתָךְ״ (משלי ו, כב): **כִּי קָרוֹב הוּא.** וְנוֹחַ לָשׁוּב בְּאוֹתוֹ הַדֶּרֶךְ לְמִצְרַיִם. וּמִדְרְשֵׁי אַגָּדָה יֵשׁ הַרְבֵּה: **בִּרְאֹתָם מִלְחָמָה.** כְּגוֹן מִלְחֶמֶת ״וַיֵּרֶד הָעֲמָלֵקִי וְהַכְּנַעֲנִי״ וְגוֹ׳ (במדבר יד, מה), אִם הָלְכוּ דֶּרֶךְ יָשָׁר הָיוּ חוֹזְרִים. מָה אִם כְּשֶׁהִקִּיפָם דֶּרֶךְ מְעֻקָּם אָמְרוּ: ״נִתְּנָה רֹאשׁ וְנָשׁוּבָה מִצְרָיְמָה״ (שם פסוק ד), אִם הוֹלִיכָם בִּפְשׁוּטָה עַל אַחַת כַּמָּה וְכַמָּה: **פֶּן יִנָּחֵם.** יַחְשְׁבוּ מַחֲשָׁבָה עַל שֶׁיָּצְאוּ וְיִתְּנוּ לֵב לָשׁוּב:

יח | **וַיַּסֵּב.** הֱסִבָּם מִן הַדֶּרֶךְ הַפְּשׁוּטָה לַדֶּרֶךְ הָעֲקֻמָּה: **יַם סוּף.** כְּמוֹ לְיַם סוּף. וְ׳סוּף׳ הוּא לְשׁוֹן אֲגַם שֶׁגְּדֵלִים בּוֹ קָנִים, וְכֵן: ״וַתָּשֶׂם בַּסּוּף״ (לעיל ב, ג), ״קָנֶה וָסוּף קָמֵלוּ״ (ישעיה יט, ו): **וַחֲמֻשִׁים.** אֵין ׳חֲמֻשִׁים׳ אֶלָּא מְזֻיָּנִים, וְכֵן הוּא אוֹמֵר: ״וְאַתֶּם תַּעַבְרוּ חֲמֻשִׁים״ (יהושע א, יד). וְכֵן תִּרְגֵּם אוּנְקְלוֹס ״מְזָרְזִין״, כְּמוֹ: ״וַיָּרֶק אֶת חֲנִיכָיו״ (בראשית יד, יד), ״וְזָרֵיז״. דָּבָר אַחֵר, ״וַחֲמֻשִׁים״, מְחֻמָּשִׁים, אֶחָד מֵחֲמִשָּׁה יָצְאוּ וְאַרְבָּעָה חֲלָקִים מֵתוּ בִּשְׁלֹשֶׁת יְמֵי אֲפֵלָה:

יט | **הַשְׁבֵּעַ הִשְׁבִּיעַ.** הִשְׁבִּיעָם שֶׁיַּשְׁבִּיעוּ לִבְנֵיהֶם. וְלָמָּה לֹא הִשְׁבִּיעַ לְבָנָיו שֶׁיִּשָּׂאוּהוּ לְאֶרֶץ כְּנַעַן מִיָּד כְּמוֹ שֶׁהִשְׁבִּיעַ יַעֲקֹב? אָמַר יוֹסֵף: אֲנִי שַׁלִּיט הָיִיתִי בְּמִצְרַיִם וְהָיָה סִפֵּק בְּיָדִי לַעֲשׂוֹת, אֲבָל בָּנַי לֹא יַנִּיחוּם מִצְרִים לַעֲשׂוֹת, לְכָךְ הִשְׁבִּיעָם לִכְשֶׁיִּגָּאֲלוּ וְיֵצְאוּ מִשָּׁם שֶׁיִּשָּׂאוּהוּ: **וְהַעֲלִיתֶם אֶת עַצְמֹתַי מִזֶּה אִתְּכֶם.** לְאֶחָיו הִשְׁבִּיעַ כֵּן, לָמַדְנוּ שֶׁאַף עַצְמוֹת כָּל הַשְּׁבָטִים הֶעֱלוּ עִמָּהֶם, שֶׁנֶּאֱמַר ״אִתְּכֶם״:

כ | **וַיִּסְעוּ מִסֻּכֹּת.** בַּיּוֹם הַשֵּׁנִי, שֶׁהֲרֵי בָּרִאשׁוֹן בָּאוּ מֵרַעְמְסֵס לְסֻכּוֹת (לעיל יב, לז):

כא | **לַנְחֹתָם הַדֶּרֶךְ.** נָקוּד פַּתָּח, שֶׁהוּא כְּמוֹ לְהַנְחוֹתָם, כְּמוֹ: ״לַרְאֹתְכֶם בַּדֶּרֶךְ אֲשֶׁר תֵּלְכוּ בָהּ״ (דברים א, לג) שֶׁהוּא כְּמוֹ לְהַרְאוֹתְכֶם, אַף כָּאן לְהַנְחוֹתָם עַל יְדֵי שָׁלִיחַ. וּמִי הוּא הַשָּׁלִיחַ? עַמּוּד הֶעָנָן, וְהַקָּדוֹשׁ בָּרוּךְ הוּא בִּכְבוֹדוֹ מוֹלִיכוֹ לִפְנֵיהֶם, וּמִכָּל מָקוֹם אֶת עַמּוּד הֶעָנָן הֵכִין לְהַנְחוֹתָם עַל יָדוֹ, שֶׁהֲרֵי עַל יְדֵי עַמּוּד הֶעָנָן הֵם הוֹלְכִים. עַמּוּד הֶעָנָן אֵינוֹ לְאוֹרָה אֶלָּא לְהוֹרוֹתָם הַדֶּרֶךְ:

כב | **לֹא יָמִישׁ.** הַקָּדוֹשׁ בָּרוּךְ הוּא אֶת ״עַמּוּד הֶעָנָן יוֹמָם וְעַמּוּד הָאֵשׁ לָיְלָה״, מַגִּיד שֶׁעַמּוּד הֶעָנָן מַשְׁלִים לְעַמּוּד הָאֵשׁ וְעַמּוּד הָאֵשׁ מַשְׁלִים לְעַמּוּד הֶעָנָן, שֶׁעַד שֶׁלֹּא יִשְׁקַע זֶה עוֹלֶה זֶה:

פרק יד

ב | **וְיָשֻׁבוּ.** לַאֲחוֹרֵיהֶם, לְצַד מִצְרַיִם הָיוּ מְקָרְבִין כָּל יוֹם הַשְּׁלִישִׁי, כְּדֵי לְהַטְעוֹת אֶת פַּרְעֹה שֶׁיֹּאמַר תּוֹעִים הֵם בַּדֶּרֶךְ, כְּמוֹ שֶׁנֶּאֱמַר: ״וְאָמַר פַּרְעֹה לִבְנֵי יִשְׂרָאֵל״ וְגוֹ׳ (להלן פסוק ג): **וְיַחֲנוּ לִפְנֵי פִּי הַחִירֹת.** הִיא פִּיתוֹם, וְעַכְשָׁיו נִקְרֵאת ׳פִּי

BACKGROUND

14:2 | **Pi HaHirot:** *Pi* means temple in Egyptian and appears in names of other Egyptian places, such as Pitom and Pi Beset. It is possible that Hirot is a reference to Hathor, an Egyptian goddess, or to Hirot, a Syrian goddess attested to in Syrian and Egyptian inscriptions, whom the Egyptians worshipped. Despite the theory that Pi HaHirot refers to the location of a temple, the location is not known today.

A different view suggests that the name Pi HaHirot is of Semitic origin and signifies a canal or gulf (the word *khiritu* means canal in Ugaritic and Akkadian). Accordingly, this name could refer to two possible areas: The city known as Suez (Jebel Attaka), on the coast of the Gulf of Suez, a branch of the Red Sea, or near the source of one of the branches of the Nile, perhaps the eastern (Pelusian) branch, called Shihor (Isaiah 23:3) after the Egyptian god Hor.

Baal Tzefon: Baal Tzefon is the name of a Canaanite god mentioned in an Egyptian contract

Canaan, the Israelites did not need to cross the Red Sea. From the eastern bank of the Nile, their way was open toward the Land of Israel, even if the Red Sea once extended further north than it does today. Still, God instructed Moses to turn from their route and camp by the sea.

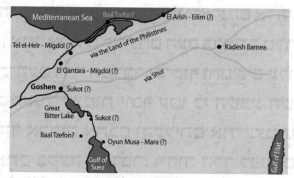

Possible locations of Sukot, Migdol, and Baal Tzefon

3 **Pharaoh will** then **say of the children of Israel: They are astray in the land.** They have lost their way, and are doubling back. **The wilderness has closed in on them,** allowing them to travel no further.

4 **I will harden Pharaoh's heart.** After the plagues, the ruin, and the destruction inflicted upon Egypt, Pharaoh's heart will be hardened one last time, **and he will pursue them; and I will be exalted through Pharaoh, and through his entire army, and the Egyptians will know that I am the Lord,** for something will occur now more miraculous than the plagues of Egypt. **And they,** the Israelites, **did so.**

5 Meanwhile, **it was told to the king of Egypt that the people had fled.**D The three days originally agreed upon (see 8:23–24) had passed, and the Israelites did not seem bound for any particular destination. **The heart of Pharaoh and his servants was transformed with regard to the people, and they said: What is this that we have done, that we have sent Israel from our servitude?** This nation of slaves filled an important

economic function for us, and was part of our way of life. We did not mean to set them free, only to allow them a respite.

6 **He harnessed his chariot.** Pharaoh commanded that his horses be harnessed to his personal chariot. **And** he **took his people,** his soldiers, **with him.**

7 **He took six hundred select chariots,** the best he had. These were the elite forces of Egypt, whose size is comparable to that of a modern armored division. **And** he took as well **all the chariots of Egypt; chariots played** a dominant role in Egypt's military. **And there were auxiliaries with all of them.**D In addition to the driver, who held the reins, and the warrior, who held a weapon, usually a bow, as seen in ancient Egyptian drawings, Pharaoh added an officer over each chariot.

Mural of Egyptian warriors on chariots laying siege, found in Rameses II's temple in Thebes, thirteenth century BCE

8 **The Lord hardened the heart of Pharaoh, king of Egypt, and he pursued the children of Israel; the children of Israel went out with a high hand,** not as escapees.

9 **Egypt pursued them; all the horses and chariots of Pharaoh and his horsemen and his army caught up with them encamped by the sea, by Pi HaHirot, before Baal Tzefon.**

Second aliya

10 **Pharaoh approached** the Israelite encampment; **the children of Israel lifted their eyes and behold,** the forces of **the**

── DISCUSSION ──

deity associated only with Israel, and despite the plagues, they retained their pagan beliefs. The encampment of the Israelites before Baal Tzefon was likely to suggest to Pharaoh that the Israelites worshipped a god of desolation and ruin, and that this cruel, capricious god might perhaps abandon them in favor of the Egyptians (see *Mekhilta*).

14:5 | It was told to the king of Egypt that the people had fled: Pharaoh almost certainly

sent men to accompany the Israelites, either officially or as undercover spies, in order to gather information about their activities. He therefore learned that the people did not go out like slaves on a temporary break from labor, but as victorious free men (see *Mekhilta*).

14:7 | And there were auxiliaries with all of them: The ancient Egyptians harnessed their horses by the neck, as they had not yet developed methods of harnessing the horse's body,

which would have allowed them to fully benefit from the horse's strength. The addition of an auxiliary to the chariot would slow it considerably, and was not necessarily appropriate for a military maneuver. Still, the additional soldier would make the chariot appear more imposing. This suggests that Pharaoh did not intend to engage the Israelites in open battle. Rather, he wished to frighten the Israelites into returning, and in this regard he nearly succeeded.

ג בֵּין מִגְדֹּל וּבֵין הַיָּם לִפְנֵי בַּעַל צְפֹן נִכְחוֹ תַחֲנוּ עַל־הַיָּם: וְאָמַר פַּרְעֹה לִבְנֵי
ד יִשְׂרָאֵל נְבֻכִים הֵם בָּאָרֶץ סָגַר עֲלֵיהֶם הַמִּדְבָּר: וְחִזַּקְתִּי אֶת־לֵב־פַּרְעֹה וְרָדַף
אַחֲרֵיהֶם וְאִכָּבְדָה בְּפַרְעֹה וּבְכָל־חֵילוֹ וְיָדְעוּ מִצְרַיִם כִּי־אֲנִי יהוה וַיַּעֲשׂוּ־כֵן:
ה וַיֻּגַּד לְמֶלֶךְ מִצְרַיִם כִּי בָרַח הָעָם וַיֵּהָפֵךְ לְבַב פַּרְעֹה וַעֲבָדָיו אֶל־הָעָם וַיֹּאמְרוּ
ו מַה־זֹּאת עָשִׂינוּ כִּי־שִׁלַּחְנוּ אֶת־יִשְׂרָאֵל מֵעָבְדֵנוּ: וַיֶּאְסֹר אֶת־רִכְבּוֹ וְאֶת־עַמּוֹ
ז לָקַח עִמּוֹ: וַיִּקַּח שֵׁשׁ־מֵאוֹת רֶכֶב בָּחוּר וְכֹל רֶכֶב מִצְרָיִם וְשָׁלִשִׁם עַל־כֻּלּוֹ:
ח וַיְחַזֵּק יהוה אֶת־לֵב פַּרְעֹה מֶלֶךְ מִצְרַיִם וַיִּרְדֹּף אַחֲרֵי בְּנֵי יִשְׂרָאֵל וּבְנֵי יִשְׂרָאֵל
ט יֹצְאִים בְּיָד רָמָה: וַיִּרְדְּפוּ מִצְרַיִם אַחֲרֵיהֶם וַיַּשִּׂיגוּ אוֹתָם חֹנִים עַל־הַיָּם כָּל־סוּס שני
י רֶכֶב פַּרְעֹה וּפָרָשָׁיו וְחֵילוֹ עַל־פִּי הַחִירֹת לִפְנֵי בַּעַל צְפֹן: וּפַרְעֹה הִקְרִיב וַיִּשְׂאוּ

רש"י

הַחִירֹת עַל שֵׁם שֶׁנַּעֲשׂוּ שָׁם בְּנֵי חוֹרִין. וְהֵם שְׁנֵי סְלָעִים גְּבוֹהִים זְקוּפִים, וְהַגַּיְא שֶׁבֵּינֵיהֶם קָרוּי פִּי הַסְּלָעִים: לִפְנֵי בַּעַל צְפֹן. הוּא נִשְׁאַר מִכָּל אֱלֹהֵי מִצְרַיִם כְּדֵי לְהַטְעוֹתָן שֶׁיֹּאמְרוּ: קָשָׁה יִרְאָתָן. וְעָלָיו פֵּרֵשׁ אִיּוֹב: "מַשְׂגִּיא לַגּוֹיִם וַיְאַבְּדֵם" (איוב יב, כג):

ג| וְאָמַר פַּרְעֹה. כְּשֶׁיִּשְׁמַע שֶׁהֵם שָׁבִים לַאֲחוֹרֵיהֶם: לִבְנֵי יִשְׂרָאֵל. עַל בְּנֵי יִשְׂרָאֵל. וְכֵן: "ה' יִלָּחֵם לָכֶם" (להלן פסוק יד) – עֲלֵיכֶם; "אִמְרִי לִי אָחִי הוּא" (בראשית כ, יג) – אִמְרִי עָלַי: נְבֻכִים הֵם. כְּלוּאִים וּמְשֻׁקָּעִים, וּבְלַעַז שירי"ר. כְּמוֹ: "נִבְכֵי יָם" (איוב לח, טז), "בְּעֵמֶק הַבָּכָא" (תהלים פד, ז), "מִבְּכִי נְהָרוֹת" (איוב כח, יא). "נְבֻכִים הֵם" – כְּלוּאִים הֵם בַּמִּדְבָּר, שֶׁאֵינָן יוֹדְעִין לָצֵאת מִמֶּנּוּ וּלְהֵיכָן יֵלְכוּ:

ד| וְאִכָּבְדָה בְּפַרְעֹה. כְּשֶׁהַקָּדוֹשׁ בָּרוּךְ הוּא מִתְנַקֵּם בָּרְשָׁעִים שְׁמוֹ מִתְגַּדֵּל וּמִתְכַּבֵּד. וְכֵן הוּא אוֹמֵר: "וְנִשְׁפַּטְתִּי אִתּוֹ" וְגוֹ' וְאַחַר כָּךְ: "וְהִתְגַּדִּלְתִּי וְהִתְקַדִּשְׁתִּי וְנוֹדַעְתִּי" וְגוֹ' (יחזקאל לח, כב-כג), וְאוֹמֵר: "שָׁמָּה שִׁבַּר רִשְׁפֵי קָשֶׁת" וְאַחַר כָּךְ: "נוֹדָע בִּיהוּדָה אֱלֹהִים" (תהלים עו, ב-ד), וְאוֹמֵר: "נוֹדַע ה' מִשְׁפָּט עָשָׂה" (שם ט, יז): בְּפַרְעֹה וּבְכָל חֵילוֹ. הוּא הִתְחִיל בָּעֲבֵרָה וּמִמֶּנּוּ הִתְחִילָה הַפֻּרְעָנוּת: וַיַּעֲשׂוּ כֵן. לְהַגִּיד שִׁבְחָן שֶׁשָּׁמְעוּ לְקוֹל מֹשֶׁה, וְלֹא אָמְרוּ: הֵיאַךְ נִתְקָרֵב אֶל רוֹדְפֵינוּ? אָנוּ צְרִיכִים לִבְרֹחַ! אֶלָּא אָמְרוּ: אֵין לָנוּ אֶלָּא דִּבְרֵי בֶּן עַמְרָם:

ה| וַיֻּגַּד לְמֶלֶךְ מִצְרַיִם. אִיקְטוֹרִין שָׁלַח עִמָּהֶם, וְכֵיוָן שֶׁהִגִּיעוּ לִשְׁלֹשֶׁת יָמִים שֶׁקָּבְעוּ לֵילֵךְ וְלָשׁוּב וְרָאוּ שֶׁאֵינָן חוֹזְרִין לְמִצְרַיִם, בָּאוּ וְהִגִּידוּ לְפַרְעֹה בַּיּוֹם הָרְבִיעִי. וּבַחֲמִישִׁי וּבַשִּׁשִּׁי רָדְפוּ אַחֲרֵיהֶם, לֵיל שְׁבִיעִי יָרְדוּ לַיָּם, בְּשַׁחֲרִית אָמְרוּ שִׁירָה, וְהוּא יוֹם שְׁבִיעִי שֶׁל פֶּסַח. לְכָךְ אָנוּ קוֹרִין הַשִּׁירָה בַּיּוֹם הַשְּׁבִיעִי: וַיֵּהָפֵךְ. נֶהְפַּךְ מִמַּה שֶּׁהָיָה, שֶׁהֲרֵי אָמַר לָהֶם: "קוּמוּ צְּאוּ מִתּוֹךְ עַמִּי" (לעיל יב, לא), וְנֶהְפַּךְ לֵב עֲבָדָיו, שֶׁהֲרֵי לְשֶׁעָבַר הָיוּ אוֹמְרִים לוֹ: "עַד מָתַי יִהְיֶה זֶה לָנוּ לְמוֹקֵשׁ" (לעיל י, ז) וְעַכְשָׁיו נֶהֶפְכוּ לִרְדֹּף אַחֲרֵיהֶם בִּשְׁבִיל מָמוֹנָם שֶׁהִשְׁאִילוּם: מֵעָבְדֵנוּ. מֵעֲבֹד אוֹתָנוּ:

ו| וַיֶּאְסֹר אֶת רִכְבּוֹ. הוּא בְּעַצְמוֹ: וְאֶת עַמּוֹ לָקַח עִמּוֹ. מְשָׁכָם בִּדְבָרִים: לָקִינוּ וְנָטְלוּ מָמוֹנֵנוּ וְשִׁלַּחְנוּם; בּוֹאוּ עִמִּי וַאֲנִי לֹא אֶתְנַהֵג עִמָּכֶם כִּשְׁאָר מְלָכִים, דֶּרֶךְ מְלָכִים עֲבָדָיו קוֹדְמִין לוֹ בַּמִּלְחָמָה, וַאֲנִי אֶקְדִּים לִפְנֵיכֶם, שֶׁנֶּאֱמַר: "וּפַרְעֹה הִקְרִיב" (להלן פסוק י), הִקְרִיב עַצְמוֹ וּמִהֵר לִפְנֵי חֵילוֹתָיו; דֶּרֶךְ מְלָכִים לִטֹּל בִּזָּה בָּרֹאשׁ כְּמוֹ שֶׁיִּבְחַר, אֲנִי אֶשְׁוֶה עִמָּכֶם בַּחֵלֶק, שֶׁנֶּאֱמַר: "אֲחַלֵּק שָׁלָל" (להלן טו, ט):

ז| בָּחוּר. נִבְחָרִים. 'בָּחוּר' לְשׁוֹן יָחִיד, כָּל רֶכֶב וְרֶכֶב שֶׁבְּמִנְיָן זֶה הָיָה בָּחוּר: וְכֹל רֶכֶב מִצְרָיִם. וְעִמָּהֶם כָּל שְׁאָר הָרֶכֶב. וּמֵהֵיכָן הָיוּ הַבְּהֵמוֹת הַלָּלוּ? אִם תֹּאמַר מִשֶּׁל מִצְרַיִם, הֲרֵי נֶאֱמַר: "וַיָּמָת כֹּל מִקְנֵה מִצְרָיִם" (לעיל ט, ו)! וְאִם מִשֶּׁל יִשְׂרָאֵל, וַהֲלֹא נֶאֱמַר: "וְגַם מִקְנֵנוּ יֵלֵךְ עִמָּנוּ" (לעיל י, כו)! מִשֶּׁל מִי הָיוּ? מֵ"הַיָּרֵא אֶת דְּבַר ה'" (לעיל ט, כ). מִכָּאן הָיָה רַבִּי שִׁמְעוֹן אוֹמֵר: כָּשֵׁר שֶׁבַּגּוֹיִם הֲרֹג, טוֹב שֶׁבַּנְּחָשִׁים רְצֹץ אֶת מֹחוֹ: וְשָׁלִשִׁם עַל כֻּלּוֹ. שָׂרֵי צְבָאוֹת, כְּתַרְגּוּמוֹ:

ח| וַיְחַזֵּק ה' אֶת לֵב פַּרְעֹה. שֶׁהָיָה תּוֹלֶה אִם לִרְדֹּף אִם לָאו, וְחִזֵּק אֶת לִבּוֹ לִרְדֹּף: בְּיָד רָמָה. בִּגְבוּרָה גְּבוֹהָה וּמְפֻרְסֶמֶת:

י| וּפַרְעֹה הִקְרִיב. הָיָה לוֹ לִכְתֹּב: 'וּפַרְעֹה קָרַב', מַהוּ

BACKGROUND

from the sixth century BCE along with the gods of Tahpanhes. It is also the name of the ancient temple built to this god, on Jebel Aqra in Lebanon, near Ugarit. Some have hypothesized, without archaeological evidence, that the Baal Tzefon mentioned here is a temple similar to that in Jebel Aqra that stood on Casius Mons, near Lake Bardawil, which historical records (Strabo) indicate was built by Phoenician seafarers to Baal. However, one must take into account the phenomenon of multiple places called by the same name: Names of places close to the Egyptian border, such as Sukot and Goshen, also appear as the names of places in the Land of Israel and northward.

Egyptians were traveling after them, and they were very frightened.[D] They were startled to see an entire army advancing on them. Despite all the losses that the Egyptian army suffered during the plagues, they had enough animals left to mount a campaign. **The children of Israel cried out to the Lord.**

11 After crying out to God, **they said to Moses: Is it due to the lack of graves in Egypt that you took us to die in the wilderness?** If we are to die now, we might as well have died in Egypt, without going through the trouble of traveling through the desert. **What is this that you have done to us, to take us out of Egypt?** They, as much as Pharaoh, were filled with regret at their release (see above, 14:5).

12 **Is this not the matter of which we spoke to you in Egypt,**[D] **saying: Let us be;** stop tempting us with the unrealistic prospect of leaving Egypt for a good and spacious land, **and we will serve Egypt? For serving Egypt is preferable to us to dying in the wilderness.** Already in Egypt we told you to leave us to our work and not to fill our heads with unattainable dreams; now you see that your dreams were for nothing.

13 **Moses said to the people: Fear not; stand and see the salvation of the Lord that He will perform for you today; for as you saw the Egyptians today, you shall not see them ever again.** God's salvation will ensure that they never threaten you again.

14 **The Lord will make war for you, and** you will not need to do anything; rather, **you will be silent.**[D]

15 **The Lord said to Moses: For what are you crying out to Me?**

Third aliya This is no time for lengthy prayers; you need to act.[5] **Speak to the children of Israel that they will travel.** It seemed as though the Israelites had no means of escape. They could not retreat, since that would send them into the arms of the Egyptian army. Perhaps they could have run to one side or another, but it is nearly certain that the Egyptians would have quickly caught them. God instead ordered them to march forward, into the sea.

16 **And you, raise your staff, and extend your hand over the sea, and** you will thereby **split it; and the children of Israel will go into the sea on dry land.** That is, they will march into the sea, and it will turn into dry land.

17 **As for me, behold, I am hardening the heart of Egypt, and they will come after them.** Were the Egyptians to act rationally, they would not choose to enter the sea in pursuit of the Israelites, since they had already been stricken by plagues that targeted them selectively. But because I am hardening their hearts, they will enter the sea. **And I will be exalted through** the demise of **Pharaoh and through his entire army, through his chariots and through his horsemen.**

18 **Egypt will know that I am the Lord, when I am exalted through Pharaoh, through his chariots, and through his horsemen.** All the power of Egypt is concentrated here. When I break that power, My honor will grow in the eyes of those Egyptians left alive who will hear of these events.

19 **The angel of God, who was going before the camp of Israel, traveled and went behind them; and the pillar of cloud,** which during the day embodied the angel of God and was always in front of the camp, **traveled from before them and stood behind them,** at the back of the camp.

20 **It,** the cloud, **came between the camp of Egypt and the camp of Israel and there was the cloud and the darkness** in the space between the camps, **and it illuminated the night.**[D] Perhaps the pillar of fire shone from within the cloud, or the pillar of cloud turned to fire, and thus lit up the night. On the Egyptian side, the cloud and darkness hid the Israelites from the view of the Egyptians; on the Israelite side, the fire illuminated

DISCUSSION

14:10| **And they were very frightened:** The Israelite population was far superior in number to the Egyptian army. Even according to the most conservative calculations, the number of adult Israelite males was several times that of the Egyptian soldiers. The Israelites, however, were simple workers with no military experience. Furthermore, being slaves from birth, descended from parents and grandparents who were slaves, they experienced the encounter with Pharaoh's army from the point of view of slaves. The appearance of their former masters filled them with alarm and terror (Ibn Ezra; *Ḥizkuni*). One must remember that the Egyptian cohorts appeared proud, impressive, and imposing. Isaiah (30:7) would later refer to Egypt as Rahav, a name connoting pride and haughtiness, and Jeremiah (46:20) referred to them as a beautiful heifer. Pitted against the mighty Egyptian cavalry and chariots, the Israelites felt helpless. They may not even have known how to use the weapons with which they had armed themselves.

14:12| **Is this not the matter of which we spoke to you in Egypt:** The Torah does not relate any such discussions in the chapters that describe the events that transpired in Egypt, but apparently there were individuals who presented this argument at that time. The preference of a life of slavery over death, expressed here, is the opposite of the attitude of the residents of Masada, as related by Josephus, who preferred taking their own lives rather than submitting to the Roman legions and becoming slaves. The Israelites were used to a life of slavery and reverted to a submissive state. The challenges involved in freedom intimidated them.

14:14| **The Lord will make war for you and you will be silent:** The verses imply that different groups within the Israelite camp responded in various ways to the impending crisis. There were those who immediately began arguing with Moses. As the Egyptian army approached, their response was to assign blame to Moses for leading them out of Egypt and toward catastrophe, despite their previous objections back in Egypt. Others apparently began to cry out to God in fervent prayer. Some may have stood

בְּנֵי־יִשְׂרָאֵל אֶת־עֵינֵיהֶם וְהִנֵּה מִצְרַיִם ׀ נֹסֵעַ אַחֲרֵיהֶם וַיִּירְאוּ מְאֹד וַיִּצְעֲקוּ בְנֵי־

יא יִשְׂרָאֵל אֶל־יְהוָה: וַיֹּאמְרוּ אֶל־מֹשֶׁה הֲמִבְּלִי אֵין־קְבָרִים בְּמִצְרַיִם לְקַחְתָּנוּ

יב לָמוּת בַּמִּדְבָּר מַה־זֹּאת עָשִׂיתָ לָּנוּ לְהוֹצִיאָנוּ מִמִּצְרָיִם: הֲלֹא־זֶה הַדָּבָר אֲשֶׁר

דִּבַּרְנוּ אֵלֶיךָ בְמִצְרַיִם לֵאמֹר חֲדַל מִמֶּנּוּ וְנַעַבְדָה אֶת־מִצְרָיִם כִּי טוֹב לָנוּ עֲבֹד

יג אֶת־מִצְרַיִם מִמֻּתֵנוּ בַּמִּדְבָּר: וַיֹּאמֶר מֹשֶׁה אֶל־הָעָם אַל־תִּירָאוּ הִתְיַצְּבוּ וּרְאוּ

אֶת־יְשׁוּעַת יְהוָה אֲשֶׁר־יַעֲשֶׂה לָכֶם הַיּוֹם כִּי אֲשֶׁר רְאִיתֶם אֶת־מִצְרַיִם הַיּוֹם

יד לֹא תֹסִפוּ לִרְאֹתָם עוֹד עַד־עוֹלָם: יְהוָה יִלָּחֵם לָכֶם וְאַתֶּם תַּחֲרִשׁוּן:

טו וַיֹּאמֶר יְהוָה אֶל־מֹשֶׁה מַה־תִּצְעַק אֵלָי דַּבֵּר אֶל־בְּנֵי־יִשְׂרָאֵל וְיִסָּעוּ: וְאַתָּה הָרֵם   **יא שלישי**

טז אֶת־מַטְּךָ וּנְטֵה אֶת־יָדְךָ עַל־הַיָּם וּבְקָעֵהוּ וְיָבֹאוּ בְנֵי־יִשְׂרָאֵל בְּתוֹךְ הַיָּם בַּיַּבָּשָׁה:

יז וַאֲנִי הִנְנִי מְחַזֵּק אֶת־לֵב מִצְרַיִם וְיָבֹאוּ אַחֲרֵיהֶם וְאִכָּבְדָה בְּפַרְעֹה וּבְכָל־חֵילוֹ

יח בְּרִכְבּוֹ וּבְפָרָשָׁיו: וְיָדְעוּ מִצְרַיִם כִּי־אֲנִי יְהוָה בְּהִכָּבְדִי בְּפַרְעֹה בְּרִכְבּוֹ וּבְפָרָשָׁיו:

יט וַיִּסַּע מַלְאַךְ הָאֱלֹהִים הַהֹלֵךְ לִפְנֵי מַחֲנֵה יִשְׂרָאֵל וַיֵּלֶךְ מֵאַחֲרֵיהֶם וַיִּסַּע עַמּוּד

כ הֶעָנָן מִפְּנֵיהֶם וַיַּעֲמֹד מֵאַחֲרֵיהֶם: וַיָּבֹא בֵּין ׀ מַחֲנֵה מִצְרַיִם וּבֵין מַחֲנֵה יִשְׂרָאֵל

רש"י

"הִקְרִיב"? הִקְרִיב עַצְמוֹ וְנִתְחַזֵּק לִקְדֹּם לְתַעֲנִית כְּמוֹ שֶׁהִתְוַדָּה עֲמָם: נֹסֵעַ אַחֲרֵיהֶם. בְּלֵב אֶחָד כְּאִישׁ אֶחָד. דָּבָר אַחֵר, וְהִנֵּה מִצְרַיִם נֹסֵעַ אַחֲרֵיהֶם, רָאוּ שַׂר שֶׁל מִצְרַיִם נֹסֵעַ מִן הַשָּׁמַיִם לַעֲזֹר לְמִצְרַיִם. תַּנְחוּמָא (יא): וַיִּצְעָקוּ. תָּפְשׂוּ אֻמָּנוּת אֲבוֹתָם, בְּאַבְרָהָם הוּא אוֹמֵר: "אֶל הַמָּקוֹם אֲשֶׁר עָמַד שָׁם" (בראשית יט, כז), בְּיִצְחָק: "לָשׂוּחַ בַּשָּׂדֶה" (שם כד, סג), בְּיַעֲקֹב: "וַיִּפְגַּע בַּמָּקוֹם" (שם כח, יא):

יא הֲמִבְּלִי אֵין קְבָרִים. וְכִי מֵחֲמַת חֶסְרוֹן קְבָרִים, שֶׁאֵין קְבָרִים בְּמִצְרַיִם לִקְבֹּר שָׁם, לְקַחְתָּנוּ מִשָּׁם? שי"ט פלונ"ד דינו"ן פושיי"ן בְּלַעַז:

יב אֲשֶׁר דִּבַּרְנוּ אֵלֶיךָ בְמִצְרָיִם. וְהֵיכָן דִּבְּרוּ? "יֵרֶא ה' עֲלֵיכֶם וְיִשְׁפֹּט" (לעיל ה, כא): מִמֻּתֵנוּ. מֵאֲשֶׁר נָמוּת. וְאִם הָיָה נָקוּד מֵלָאפֻ"ם הָיָה נִבְאָר 'מִמִּיתָתֵנוּ', עַכְשָׁו שֶׁנָּקוּד

בְּשׁוּרֻ"ק נִבְאָר 'מֵאֲשֶׁר נָמוּת'. וְכֵן: "מִי יִתֵּן מוּתֵנוּ" (להלן טז, ג), שֶׁנָּמוּת. וְכֵן: "מִי יִתֵּן מוּתֵנוּ" (שמואל ב' יח, לג), שֶׁאָמֵנוּ, כְּמוֹ: "לֵיוֹם קוּמִי לְעַד" (צפניה ג, ח), "עַד שׁוּבִי בְשָׁלוֹם" (דברי הימים ב' יח, כו), שֶׁאָקוּם, שֶׁאָשׁוּב:

יג כִּי אֲשֶׁר רְאִיתֶם אֶת מִצְרַיִם וְגוֹ'. מַה שֶּׁרְאִיתֶם אוֹתָם אֵינוֹ אֶלָּא הַיּוֹם, הַיּוֹם הוּא שֶׁרְאִיתֶם אוֹתָם וְלֹא תֹסִיפוּ עוֹד:

יד יִלָּחֵם לָכֶם. בִּשְׁבִילְכֶם. וְכֵן: "כִּי ה' נִלְחָם לָהֶם" (להלן פסוק כה), וְכֵן: "אִם לָאֵל תְּרִיבוּן" (איוב יג, ח), וְכֵן: "וַאֲשֶׁר דִּבֶּר לִי" (בראשית כד, ז), וְכֵן: "הַחֲתָם תְּרִיבוּן לַבַּעַל" (שופטים ו, לא):

טו מַה תִּצְעַק אֵלָי. לִמְּדֵנוּ שֶׁהָיָה מֹשֶׁה עוֹמֵד וּמִתְפַּלֵּל, אָמַר לוֹ הַקָּדוֹשׁ בָּרוּךְ הוּא: לֹא עֵת עַתָּה לְהַאֲרִיךְ

שֶׁיִּשְׂרָאֵל נְתוּנִין בְּצָרָה. דָּבָר אַחֵר, "מַה תִּצְעַק אֵלָי", עָלַי הַדָּבָר וְלֹא עָלֶיךָ, כְּמוֹ שֶׁנֶּאֱמַר לְהַלָּן: "עַל בָּנַי וְעַל פֹּעַל יָדַי תְּצַוֻּנִי" (ישעיה מה, יא): דַּבֵּר אֶל בְּנֵי יִשְׂרָאֵל וְיִסָּעוּ. אֵין לָהֶם אֶלָּא לִסַּע, שֶׁאֵין הַיָּם עוֹמֵד בִּפְנֵיהֶם, כְּדַאי זְכוּת אֲבוֹתֵיהֶם וְהֵם וְהָאֱמָנָה שֶׁהֶאֱמִינוּ בִּי וְיָצְאוּ, לִקְרֹעַ לָהֶם אֶת הַיָּם:

יט-כ וַיֵּלֶךְ מֵאַחֲרֵיהֶם. לְהַבְדִּיל בֵּין מַחֲנֵה מִצְרַיִם וּבֵין מַחֲנֵה יִשְׂרָאֵל וּלְקַבֵּל חִצִּים וּבַלִּיסְטְרָאוֹת שֶׁל מִצְרַיִם. בְּכָל מָקוֹם הוּא אוֹמֵר: "מַלְאַךְ ה'", וְכָאן: "מַלְאַךְ הָאֱלֹהִים", אֵין 'אֱלֹהִים' בְּכָל מָקוֹם אֶלָּא דִּין, מְלַמֵּד שֶׁהָיוּ יִשְׂרָאֵל נְתוּנִין בְּדִין בְּאוֹתָהּ שָׁעָה אִם לְהִנָּצֵל אִם לְהֵאָבֵד עִם מִצְרַיִם: וַיָּבֹא בֵּין מַחֲנֵה מִצְרַיִם. מָשָׁל לִמְהַלֵּךְ בַּדֶּרֶךְ וּבְנוֹ מְהַלֵּךְ לְפָנָיו. בָּאוּ לִסְטִים לְשָׁבוֹתוֹ, נְטָלוֹ מִלְּפָנָיו נְתָנוֹ לְאַחֲרָיו, בָּא זְאֵב מֵאַחֲרָיו, נְתָנוֹ לְפָנָיו, בָּאוּ

DISCUSSION

around passively, not knowing what to do. Very possibly, others tried to begin organizing a military resistance to the Egyptian army. However, at this stage, shortly after being set free from a life of slavery, they had no chance of mounting

an effective defense against the advancing Egyptians (see *Mekhilta, Beshalah* 2; *Targum Yonatan*; Ramban).

14:20 | And it illuminated [*vaya'er*] the night: See *Targum Yonatan*. According to many opinions,

the verb *vaya'er* should be understood contrary to its usual meaning, i.e., that it darkened, rather than illuminated, the night (Menahem ben Saruq; Ibn Janah; *Bekhor Shor*; Rashi, Psalms 139:11; see Ibn Ezra; Joshua 24:7).

the night. **And one,** the Egyptian camp, **did not approach the other,** the Israelite camp, **the entire night,** due to the thick fog separating them.

21 **Moses extended his hand**[D] **over the sea, and the Lord moved the sea with a powerful east wind the entire night, and it rendered the sea dry land, and the water split.**

22 **The children of Israel came into the sea,** but **on dry land; and the water was a wall for them on their right and on their left.** The sea did not disappear entirely. Rather, a path, or perhaps several paths, took shape, through which the Israelites could pass. Although dry strips of land may naturally appear in the water during low tide, here the water stood up like walls on either side of the Israelites.

23 **Egypt pursued and came after them.** It is probable that as morning approached, the pillars of fire and cloud disappeared, and the Egyptians caught sight of the Israelites marching into the sea and gave chase. **All Pharaoh's horses, his chariots, and his horsemen** pursued them **into the sea.**

24 **It was at the morning watch,**[D] the final third of the night, **and the Lord looked down at the camp of Egypt** and struck at them **with a pillar of fire and cloud** that approached the camp, **and** the Lord **confounded the camp of Egypt.**

25 **He removed the wheels of its chariots and caused them to drive with difficulty.** The pillars of fire and cloud caused the wheels to separate from their chariots. Even if only some of the wheels fell off, it caused the chariots to lose their balance, so that the horses could not pull them. This caused panic in the camp. The Egyptians could not move, let alone fight, so **Egypt said: I will flee from before Israel, as the Lord is making war for them against Egypt.** Now there can be no doubt that some supreme power is aiding them. This place is strange and dangerous; we would do well to flee.

26 **The Lord said to Moses: Extend your hand over the sea**
Fourth
aliya
again, so **that the water will return** to its place, **upon Egypt, upon its chariots, and upon its horsemen.**

27 **Moses extended his hand over the sea** that had turned in just a few hours into dry land, **and the sea returned to its** original **vigor before morning,** as morning approached.[6] The waters previously stood as walls on either side of the dry path; they now came crashing down into the Egyptians' path as they fled toward the shore. **And thus, Egypt was fleeing toward it,** the water that came crashing down between them and the shore, **and the Lord shook up the Egyptians in the sea.**

28 **The water returned** to its normal state, **and it covered the chariots and the horsemen, all the army of Pharaoh that came after them into the sea.** The walls of water collapsed onto the Egyptians so forcefully that they wiped out their entire army. **Not one of them remained.** The chariots, horsemen, and infantry disappeared; all of them drowned in the supernaturally stormy waters.

29 While the Egyptians drowned in the water, **the children of Israel walked on the dry land in the sea;**[BD] **and the water was a wall for them on their right and on their left.** It seems that these walls guided their route through the sea.

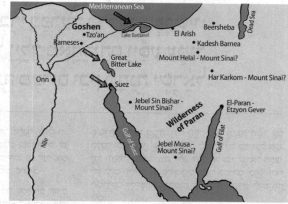

Main opinions on where the Israelites crossed the Red Sea, indicated by arrows

---

DISCUSSION

14:21 | **Moses extended his hand:** This verse, along with the two verses preceding it, describes the beginning of the Israelites' miraculous journey. Although they relate events that occurred before the splitting of the Red Sea, according to ancient tradition, these verses conceal within them God's great name. Seventy-two letters comprise each of these verses. These letters, when properly arranged, spell the sacred name of God consisting of seventy-two secret words, also hinted at in prayers from the Second Temple period. This unique, esoteric name is hidden within the story of the parting of the sea (see *Sukka* 45a, and Rashi ad loc.; *Sekhel Tov*).

14:24 | **It was at the morning watch:** The night is divided into three parts. The last part of the night is thus called the morning watch (see Rashi; *Berakhot* 3b).

14:29 | **The children of Israel walked on the dry land in the sea:** It is not clear from the verses whether the children of Israel actually crossed the sea from west to east. There is a tradition that states that they did not cross the sea, but actually returned to shore on the same side of the sea as they had entered (see *Tosafot*, *Arakhin* 15a; Radak, Judges 11:16).

כא ויהי הענן והחשך ויאר את־הלילה ולא־קרב זה אל־זה כל־הלילה: ויט משה
את־ידו על־הים ויולך יהוה | את־הים ברוח קדים עזה כל־הלילה וישם את־
כב הים לחרבה ויבקעו המים: ויבאו בני־ישראל בתוך הים ביבשה והמים להם
כג חומה מימינם ומשמאלם: וירדפו מצרים ויבאו אחריהם כל סוס פרעה רכבו
כד ופרשיו אל־תוך הים: ויהי באשמרת הבקר וישקף יהוה אל־מחנה מצרים
כה בעמוד אש וענן ויהם את מחנה מצרים: ויסר את אפן מרכבתיו וינהגהו
בכבדת ויאמר מצרים אנוסה מפני ישראל כי יהוה נלחם להם במצרים:
כו רביעי ויאמר יהוה אל־משה נטה את־ידך על־הים וישבו המים על־מצרים על־רכבו
כז ועל־פרשיו: ויט משה את־ידו על־הים וישב הים לפנות בקר לאיתנו ומצרים
כח נסים לקראתו וינער יהוה את־מצרים בתוך הים: וישבו המים ויכסו את־הרכב
ואת־הפרשים לכל חיל פרעה הבאים אחריהם בים לא־נשאר בהם עד־אחד:
כט ובני ישראל הלכו ביבשה בתוך הים והמים להם חמה מימינם ומשמאלם:

רש"י

לסטים לפניו וזאבים מאחריו, נתנו על זרועו ונלחם בהם. כך: "ואנכי תרגלתי לאפרים קחם על זרועתיו" (הושע יא, ג): ויסע עמוד הענן. כשחשכה והשלים עמוד הענן את המחנה לעמוד האש, לא נסתלק הענן כמו שהיה רגיל להסתלק ערבית לגמרי, אלא נסע והלך לו מאחריהם להחשיך למצרים: ויהי הענן והחשך. למצרים: ויאר. עמוד האש "את הלילה" לישראל, והולך לפניהם כדרכו ללכת כל הלילה. והחשך של ערפל לצד מצרים: ולא קרב זה אל זה. מחנה אל מחנה:

כא| ברוח קדים עזה. ברוח קדים שהיא עזה שברוחות, היא הרוח שהקדוש ברוך הוא נפרע בה מן הרשעים, שנאמר: "כרוח קדים אפיצם" (ירמיה יח, יז), "יבוא קדים רוח ה'" (הושע יג, טו), "רוח הקדים שברך בלב ימים" (יחזקאל כז, כו), "הגה ברוחו הקשה ביום קדים" (ישעיה כז, ח): ויבקעו המים. כל מים שבעולם:

כג| כל סוס פרעה. וכי סוס אחד היה?! מגיד שאין כלם חשובין לפני המקום אלא כסוס אחד:

כד| באשמרת הבקר. שלשת חלקי הלילה קרויין אשמרת, ואותה שלפני היום קורא "אשמרת הבקר". ואומר אני, שהוא חלוק למשמרות שיר מלאכי השרת כת אחר כת לשלשה חלקים, לכך קרוי אשמרת, וזהו שתרגם אונקלוס: "מטרת": וישקף. ויבט, כלומר פנה אליהם להשחיתם. ותרגומו: "ואסתכי" אף הוא לשון הבטה, כמו: "שדה צפים" (במדבר כג, יד), "אקל סכותא": בעמוד אש וענן. עמוד ענן יורד ועושה אותו כטיט, ועמוד אש מרתיחו, וטלפי סוסיהם משתמטות: ויהם. לשון מהומה, אשטורד"יסון בלעז. ערבבם, נטל סגניות שלהם. ושנינו בפרקי רבי אליעזר בנו של רבי יוסי הגלילי, כל מקום שנאמר 'מהומה' הרעשת קול הוא, וזה אב לכלן: "וירעם ה' בקול גדול... על פלשתים ויהמם" (שמואל א' ז, י):

כה| ויסר את אפן מרכבתיו. מכח האש נשרפו הגלגלים, והמרכבות נגררות, והיושבים בהם נעים ואבריהן מתפרקים: וינהגהו בכבדת. בהנהגה שהיא כבדה וקשה להם. במדה שמדדו, "ויכבד לבו הוא ועבדיו" (לעיל ט, לד), אף כאן, "וינהגהו בכבדת": נלחם להם במצרים. במצריים. דבר אחר "במצרים", בארץ מצרים; שכשם שאלו לוקים על הים כך לוקים אותם שנשארו במצרים:

כו| וישבו המים. שזקופים ועומדים כחומה, ישובו למקומם ויכסו "על מצרים":

כז| לפנות בקר. לעת שהבקר פונה לבא: לאיתנו. לתקפו הראשון: נסים לקראתו. שהיו מהממים ומטרפים ורצין לקראת המים: וינער ה'. כאדם שמנער את הקדרה והופך העליון למטה והתחתון למעלה, כך היו עולין ויורדין ומשתברין בים. ונתן הקדוש ברוך הוא בהם חיות לקבל היסורין. "ונער", הוא לשון טרוף בלשון ארמי, והרבה יש במדרשי אגדה:

כח| ויכסו את הרכב... לכל חיל פרעה. כן דרך המקראות לכתב למ"ד יתרה, כמו: "לכל כליו תעשה נחשת" (להלן כז, ג), וכן: "לכל כלי המשכן בכל עבדתו" (שם פסוק יט), "ויתדתם ומיתריהם לכל כליהם" (במדבר ד, לב), ואינה אלא תקון לשון:

BACKGROUND

14:29| **The children of Israel walked on the dry land in the sea:** There are various theories as to the Israelites' route. According to one theory, the Israelites followed a northern route and the splitting of the sea occurred at Lake Bardawil. They continued in the direction of present-day El Arish before turning southward toward Mount Sinai. Another theory has the Israelites crossing the sea in the region of the Great Bitter Lake and

30 **The Lord saved Israel on that day from the hand of Egypt, and Israel saw the Egyptians dead**[D] **on the seashore.** Dead bodies in the sea usually wash up on the shore; the Israelites thus saw a tremendous number of dead Egyptian soldiers on the beach.

31 **Israel saw the great power that the Lord wielded against Egypt.** God's ability to perform miracles was established beyond all doubt to the Israelites when they witnessed the unnatural behavior of the sea, the fate of the Egyptians, and their own salvation. **And the people feared the Lord and believed in the Lord and in Moses, His servant.** They saw with their own eyes that Moses acted according to the will of God, and that God had suspended the laws of nature in response to Moses' actions.[D]

Splitting of the Red Sea, fresco from Dura-Europos synagogue, third century BCE

The Song by the Sea

EXODUS 15:1–21

The song recited after the miraculous splitting of the Red Sea closes a chapter in the history of the Jewish people. The drowning of Pharaoh's army lowers the curtain on a centuries-long period in which the Israelites dwelled among the Egyptians and were influenced by them. Now, with their newfound independence, and with their revolutionary message, they may finally assert their own voice. As they open their mouths in the collective, creative song, they are unified into a true people.

This song has the appearance of the quintessential victory hymn, containing elements of joy, triumph, the demise of enemies, and even a vision of the future, which would have been quickly fulfilled if not for the long wandering that was decreed upon the Israelites.[7] However, when compared to other well-known victory songs, which glorify human heroes who battled fearlessly, the Song by the Sea presents men as passive, extras in a play, as it were, where the only hero is God. Before entering the sea, Moses said: "The Lord will make war for you, and you will be silent" (14:14). Here, Moses and the Israelites acknowledge that this is exactly what occurred: God was the warrior who defeated the Egyptians; He deserves honor and glory, and it is to Him that the Israelites express their gratitude.

Ancient literary forms found only rarely in biblical prose surface repeatedly in poetry, including expanded forms of nouns, adjectives, and verbs. For example, in the Song by the Sea, one can find the letters *yod* and *vav* attached to the ends of many words, even though they do not alter their meaning.

The Song by the Sea is the first great song in the Torah. Aside from focusing on the events at the Red Sea, there are allusions to other events beyond the place and time of this great miracle.

15 1 **Then Moses and the children of Israel sang this song to the Lord.** It seems that Moses led the people in song; he would sing a verse, and they would repeat it after him. The Talmud presents other opinions regarding the recitation of this song.[8] **And they said, saying: I will sing to the Lord, as He is** highly **exalted;** He has exalted Himself by displaying His power, for **the horse and its rider He cast into the sea.**

2 **The Lord is my strength and song.** The meaning of this Hebrew phrase is uncertain, though it occurs elsewhere in the Bible.[9] Other interpretations have been suggested: The strength and song of God; a song of praise for God's strength; strength

DISCUSSION

14:30| **Israel saw the Egyptians dead:** This phrase literally means that Israel saw that Egypt was dead. It is possible that this is a reference to the Egyptian leadership, which represented the entire nation (see verse 10). Alternatively, since the army had been destroyed, Egypt had lost all its power and it was as though the entire nation of Egypt had died (see 3:20; Numbers 20:18, and Ramban ad loc.).

14:31| **Commemoration of the splitting of the sea in an ancient synagogue:** In the ancient synagogue of Dura-Europos in Syria (third century CE), there is a wall painting that portrays scenes from the events surrounding the splitting of the sea. On the right, Moses extends his hand over the sea, and the Egyptians drown. At left, Moses leads the Song by the Sea. The Israelites are near him, with the first row of people holding weapons (see above, 13:18; "The children of Israel came up armed from the land of Egypt"). Twelve individuals situated above the first row are holding flags. At the bottom of the picture there are fish in the sea, which has returned to its former state. The horizontal lines behind Moses represent the paths along which the Israelites traveled through the sea (see *Mekhilta, Beshalah* 3; *Avot deRabbi Natan* 33).

The two hands that appear at the top of each part of the picture represent the power of God as reflected through His judgment of the Egyptians and His mercy toward the Israelites, as stated in the Midrash: The Israelites said to the Holy One, blessed be He: Peace upon Your two hands; one

ל וַיּוֹשַׁע יְהוָה בַּיּוֹם הַהוּא אֶת־יִשְׂרָאֵל מִיַּד מִצְרָיִם וַיַּרְא יִשְׂרָאֵל אֶת־מִצְרַיִם מֵת
לא עַל־שְׂפַת הַיָּם: וַיַּרְא יִשְׂרָאֵל אֶת־הַיָּד הַגְּדֹלָה אֲשֶׁר עָשָׂה יְהוָה בְּמִצְרַיִם וַיִּירְאוּ
הָעָם אֶת־יְהוָה וַיַּאֲמִינוּ בַּיהוָה וּבְמֹשֶׁה עַבְדּוֹ:

א אָז יָשִׁיר־מֹשֶׁה וּבְנֵי יִשְׂרָאֵל אֶת־הַשִּׁירָה הַזֹּאת לַיהוָה וַיֹּאמְרוּ לֵאמֹר אָשִׁירָה
לַיהוָה כִּי־גָאֹה גָּאָה סוּס
ב וְרֹכְבוֹ רָמָה בַיָּם: עָזִּי וְזִמְרָת יָהּ וַיְהִי־לִי
לִישׁוּעָה זֶה אֵלִי וְאַנְוֵהוּ אֱלֹהֵי

רש"י

ל| **וירא ישראל את מצרים מת.** שפלטן הים על שפתו, כדי שלא יאמרו ישראל: כשם שאנו עולים מצד זה כך הם עולין מצד אחר רחוק ממנו וירדפו אחרינו:

לא| **את היד הגדלה.** את הגבורה הגדולה שעשתה ידו של הקדוש ברוך הוא. והרבה לשונות נופלין על לשון 'יד' וכלן לשון יד ממש הן, והמפרש יתקן הלשון אחר ענין הדבור:

פרק טו

א| **אז ישיר משה.** אז כשראה הנס עלה בלבו שישיר שירה. וכן: "אז ידבר יהושע" (יהושע י, יב), וכן: "ובית יעשה לבת פרעה" (מלכים א' ז, ח), חשב בלבו שיעשה לה, אף כאן, "ישיר", אמר לו לבו שישיר, וכן עשה: "ויאמרו לאמר אשירה לה'". וכן ביהושע כשראה הנס אמר לו לבו שידבר, וכן עשה: "ויאמר לעיני ישראל" (יהושע שם). וכן שירת הבאר שפתח בה: "אז ישיר ישראל", פרש אחריו: "עלי באר ענו לה" (במדבר כא, יז); "אז יבנה שלמה במה" (מלכים א' יא, ז) פרשו בו חכמי ישראל שבקש לבנות ולא בנה. למדנו שהיו"ד על שם המחשבה נאמרה. זהו ליישב פשוטו. אבל מדרשו, אמרו רבותינו זכרונם לברכה, מכאן רמז לתחית המתים מן התורה, וכן בכלן, חוץ משל שלמה שפרשוהו בקש לבנות ולא בנה. ואין לומר וליישב לשון הזה כשאר דברים הנכתבים בלשון עתיד והן מיד, כגון: "ככה יעשה איוב" (איוב א, ה), "על פי ה' יחנו" (במדבר ט, כ), "ויש אשר יהיה הענן" (שם), לפי שהן דבר ההוה תמיד ונופל בו בין לשון עתיד בין לשון עבר, אבל זה שלא היה אלא לשעה אינו יכול ליישבו בלשון הזה: **כי גאה גאה.** כתרגומו. דבר אחר, "כי גאה גאה", על כל השירות וכל מה שאקלס בו עוד יש נוספות, ולא כמדת מלך בשר ודם שמקלסין אותו ואין בו: **סוס ורכבו.** שניהם קשורים זה בזה, והמים מעלין אותן לרום ויורדין לעמק ואינן נפרדין: **רמה.** השליך, וכן: "ורמיו לגוא אתון נורא" (דניאל ג, כא). ומדרש אגדה, כתוב אחד אומר "רמה" וכתוב אחד אומר "ירה", מלמד שהיו עולין לרום ויורדין לתהום, כמו: "מי ירה אבן פנתה" (איוב לח, ו) מלמעלה למטה:

ב| **עזי וזמרת יה.** אונקלוס תרגם "עזי" כמו 'עזי', "וזמרת" כמו 'וזמרתי'. ואני תמה על לשון המקרא, שאין לך כמוהו בנקדתו במקרא אלא בשלשה מקומות שהוא סמוך אצל "וזמרת", וכל שאר מקומות נקוד שורק, "ה' עזי ומעזי" (ירמיה טז, יט), "עזו אליך אשמרה" (תהלים נט, י). וכן כל תבה בת שתי אותיות הנקודה מלאפום, כשהיא מאריכת באות שלישית ואין השנית בשבא בחטף, הראשונה נקודה בשורק, כגון: עז עזי, רק רקי, חק חקי, על עלו, "יסור... עלו" (ישעיה יד, כה), כל כלו, "ושלשם על כלו" (לעיל יד, ז). ואלו שלשה "עזי וזמרת" של כאן ושל ישעיה (יב, ב) ושל תהלים (קיח, יד) נקודים בחטף קמץ; ועוד, אין באחד מהם כתוב 'וזמרתי' אלא "וזמרת", וכלם סמוך להם: "ויהי לי לישועה". לכך אני אומר ליישב לשון המקרא, שאין "עזי" כמו 'עזי' ולא "וזמרת" כמו 'וזמרתי', אלא "עזי" שם דבר הוא, כמו: "הישבי בשמים" (שם קכג, א), "שכני בחגוי סלע" (עובדיה א, ג), "שכני סנה" (דברים לג, טז). וזהו השבח: עז וזמרת יה הוא היה לי לישועה. ו"זמרת" דבוק הוא לתבת ה', כמו "לעזרת ה'" (שופטים ה, כג), "כעברת ה'" (ישעיה ט, יח), "על דברת בני האדם" (קהלת ג, יח). ולשון "וזמרת" לשון "לא תזמר" (ויקרא כה, ד), "זמיר עריצים" (ישעיה כה, ה), כסוח וכריתה, עזו ונקמתו של אלהינו היה לנו לישועה. ואל תתמה על לשון "ויהי" שלא נאמר 'היה', שיש לנו מקראות מדברים בלשון זה, וזה דגמתו: "את קירות הבית סביב להיכל ולדביר ויעש צלעות סביב" (מלכים א' ו, ה), היה לו לומר: 'עשה צלעות סביב'; וכן בדברי הימים (ב' י, יז): "ובני ישראל הישבים בערי יהודה וימלך עליהם רחבעם", היה לו לומר: 'מלך עליהם רחבעם'; "מבלתי יכלת ה' וגו' וישחטם" (במדבר יד, טז), היה לו לומר: 'שחטם'; "והאנשים אשר שלח משה... וימתו" (שם פסוקים לו-לז), 'מתו' היה לו לומר; "ואשר לא שם לבו אל דבר ה' ויעזב" (לעיל ט, כא), היה לו לומר: 'עזב': **זה אלי.** בכבודו נגלה עליהם והיו מראין אותו באצבע, ראתה שפחה על הים מה שלא ראו נביאים: **ואנוהו.** אונקלוס תרגם לשון נוה, "נוה שאנן" (ישעיה לג, כ), "לנוה צאן" (שם סה, י). דבר אחר, "ואנוהו", לשון נוי, אספר נויו ושבחו לבאי עולם, כגון: "מה דודך מדוד" (שיר השירים ה, ט), "דודי צח ואדום" (שם פסוק י) וכל הענין: **אלהי אבי.** הוא זה, "וארממנהו": **אלהי אבי.** לא אני תחלת

DISCUSSION

that saved us at the sea, and one that drowned the Egyptians, as it is stated (15:6): "Your right hand, Lord, is glorious in power; Your right hand, Lord, shatters an enemy" (*Shemot Rabba* 22:2).

BACKGROUND

crossing through the central Sinai by the biblical way of Shur, known today as the Darb Al-Hajj, the Muslim pilgrimage route to Mecca. According to a third theory, the Israelites crossed the sea south of the present-day city of Suez, and traveled through the southern part of the Sinai. According to all of these theories, the Israelites could have continued to travel on dry land without entering the sea.

expressed by God cutting down His foes;[10] my strength is God's and my song is directed to Him.[11] **And He has become my salvation; this is my God, and I will glorify Him.**[12] Some would translate this as: I will enshrine him;[13] **my father's God, and I will exalt Him.**

3 **The Lord** acted like He **is a warrior** by doing battle for us. **The Lord is His name.**[D] He fought and no other, and in doing so revealed His name.

4 **Pharaoh's chariots and his army He cast in the sea, and the elite of his officers were drowned in the Red Sea.**

Golden chariot of Pharaoh Tutankhamun

5 **The deep covers them,** Pharaoh's army. **They descended into the depths** of the sea **like a stone.** One infers from the song that the Egyptians sank in stormy waters, which overcame them with tremendous force. They were tossed and thrown about in the waves.

6 **Your right hand, Lord, is glorious in power,** Your power is enormous;[14] **Your right hand, Lord, shatters an enemy.** Alternatively: Your right hand, Lord, glorious in power, shall shatter the enemy.[15]

7 **In the abundance of Your majesty You overthrow those who rise against You,** Your enemies; **You send forth Your wrath,** which is sometimes likened to fire;[16] **it consumes them like** flames consume **straw.**

8 **With the blast of Your nostrils,** the strong east wind that blew through the night (14:21), **the water was piled.**[17] Some translate this: The water became intelligent, behaved unnaturally.[18] **Fluids stood like a mound; the deep was congealed**[19] **in the heart of the sea.**

9 **The enemy said: I will pursue, I will overtake** the Israelites, **I will divide the spoils** after I defeat them. The Egyptians did not expect to engage in battle, but assumed they would easily overtake and capture the Israelites and plunder their possessions.

DISCUSSION

15:3 | The Lord is a warrior; the Lord is His name: God's name connotes strength, triumph, and even destruction, among other attributes. Usually, the four-letter name of God, *Yod-heh-vav-heh*, is associated with being or eternity. However, the root *heh-vav-heh* can also connote the opposite, for example: "Calamity [*hova*] will come upon calamity" (Ezekiel 7:26). Accordingly, God's name also evokes images of calamity and war for His enemies.

ג אָבִי וַאֲרֹמְמֶנְהוּ׃ יְהוָה אִישׁ מִלְחָמָה יְהוָה

ד שְׁמוֹ׃ מַרְכְּבֹת פַּרְעֹה וְחֵילוֹ יָרָה בַיָּם וּמִבְחַר

ה שָׁלִשָׁיו טֻבְּעוּ בְיַם־סוּף׃ תְּהֹמֹת יְכַסְיֻמוּ יָרְדוּ בִמְצוֹלֹת כְּמוֹ־אָבֶן׃

ו יְמִינְךָ יְהוָה נֶאְדָּרִי בַּכֹּחַ יְמִינְךָ

ז יְהוָה תִּרְעַץ אוֹיֵב׃ וּבְרֹב גְּאוֹנְךָ תַּהֲרֹס

ח קָמֶיךָ תְּשַׁלַּח חֲרֹנְךָ יֹאכְלֵמוֹ כַּקַּשׁ׃ וּבְרוּחַ

אַפֶּיךָ נֶעֶרְמוּ מַיִם נִצְּבוּ כְמוֹ־נֵד

ט נֹזְלִים קָפְאוּ תְהֹמֹת בְּלֶב־יָם׃ אָמַר

אוֹיֵב אֶרְדֹּף אַשִּׂיג אֲחַלֵּק שָׁלָל תִּמְלָאֵמוֹ

רש"י

הקדשה, מחזקת ועומדת לי הקדשה ואלהותו עלי מימי אבותי:

ג| **ה׳ איש מלחמה.** בעל מלחמות, כמו: "איש נעמי" (רות א, ג), וכל 'איש' ו'אישך' מתרגמין בעל. וכן: "וחזקת והיית לאיש" (מלכים א׳ ב, ב), לגבור: **ה׳ שמו.** מלחמותיו לא בכלי זין אלא בשמו הוא נלחם, "ואנכי בא אליך בשם ה׳ צבאות" (שמואל א׳ יז, מה). דבר אחר, "ה׳ שמו", אף בשעה שהוא נלחם ונוקם מאויביו, אוחז הוא במדתו לרחם על קרואיו ולזון את כל באי עולם, ולא כמדת מלכי אדמה כשהוא עסוק במלחמה פונה עצמו מכל עסקים ואין בו כח לעשות זו וזו:

ד| **ירה בים.** "שדי בימא", "שדי" לשון יריה. וכן הוא אומר: "או ירה יירה" (להלן יט, יג), "או אשתדאה ישתדי", והתי"ו משמשת באלו במקום יתפעל: **ומבחר.** שם דבר, כמו: "מרכב" (ויקרא טו, ט), "משכב" (שם פסוק ד), "מקרא קדש" (לעיל יב, טז): **טבעו.** אין טביעה אלא במקום טיט, כמו: "טבעתי ביון מצולה" (תהלים סט, ג), "ויטבע ירמיהו בטיט" (ירמיה לח, ו), מלמד שנעשה הים טיט, לגמול להם כמדתם ששעבדו את ישראל בחמר ובלבנים:

ה| **יכסימו.** כמו 'יכסום'. והיו"ד האמצעית יתרה בו ודרך המקראות בכך, כמו: "ובקרך וצאנך ירבין" (דברים ח, יג), "ירוין מדשן ביתך" (תהלים לו, ט), והיו"ד ראשונה שמשמעה לשון עתיד, כך פרשהו: טבעו בים סוף כדי שיחזרו המים ויכסו אותן. "יכסימו" אין דומה לו במקרא בנקדתו, ודרכו להיות נקוד 'יכסימו' מלאפום: **כמו אבן.** ובמקום אחר "צללו כעופרת" (להלן פסוק י), ובמקום אחר "יאכלמו כקש" (להלן פסוק ז). הרשעים כקש הולכים ומטרפין עולין ויורדין, בינונים כאבן, והכשרים כעופרת שנחו מיד:

ו| **ימינך ימינך.** שתי פעמים, כשישראל עושין רצונו של מקום השמאל נעשית ימין: **ימינך ה׳ נאדרי בכח.** להציל את ישראל, וימינך השנית "תרעץ אויב": **נאדרי.** כמו: "רבתי עם" (איכה א, א), "שרתי במדינות" (שם), "גנבתי יום" (בראשית לא, לט): **תרעץ אויב.** תמיד היא רוצצת ומשברת האויב, ודומה לו: "וירעצו וירצצו את בני ישראל", בשופטים (י, ח):

ז| **תהרס קמיך.** תמיד אתה הורס קמיך הקמים נגדך. ומי הם הקמים כנגדו? אלו הקמים על ישראל. וכן הוא אומר: "כי הנה אויביך יהמיון" (תהלים פג, ג), ומה היא ההמיה? "על עמך יערימו סוד" (שם פסוק ד), ועל זה קורא אותם אויביו:

ח| **וברוח אפיך.** היוצא משני נחירים של אף. דבר הכתוב כביכול בשכינה דגמת מלך בשר ודם, כדי להשמיע אוזן הבריות כפי ההוה שיוכלו להבין דבר. כשאדם כועס יוצא רוח מנחיריו, וכן: "עלה עשן באפו" (שם יח, ט), וכן: "ומרוח אפו יכלו" (איוב ד, ט). וזהו שאמר: "למען שמי אאריך אפי" (ישעיה מח, ט), כשזעפו נחה נשימתו ארוכה וכשהוא כועס נשימתו קצרה, "ותהלתי אחטם לך" (שם), ולמען תהלתי אשים חטם באפי לסתם נחירי בפני האף והרוח שלא יצאו "לך", בשבילך. "אחטם" כמו 'נאקה בחטם' במסכת שבת (דף נא ע"ב), כך נראה בעיני. וכל אף וחרון שבמקרא אני אומר כן: "חרה אף" (ישעיה ה, כה) כמו: "ועצמי חרה מני חרב" (איוב ל, ל) לשון שרפה ומוקד, שהנחירים מתחממים ונחרים בעת הקצף, וחרון מגזרת חרה כמו רצון מגזרת רצה, וכן חמה לשון חמימות, על כן הוא אומר: "וחמתו בערה בו" (אסתר א, יב), ובנוח החמה אומר: "נתקררה דעתו" (יבמות סג ע"א): **נערמו מים.** אונקלוס תרגם לשון ערמימות. ולשון צחות המקרא כמו: "ערמת חטים" (שיר השירים ז, ג), ו"נצבו כמו נד" יוכיח: **נערמו.** ממוקד רוח שיצא מאפך יבשו המים והם נעשו כמין גלים וכריות של ערמה שהם גבוהים: **כמו נד.** כתרגומו, "כשור", כחומה: **נד.** לשון צבור וכנוס, כמו: "נד קציר ביום נחלה" (ישעיה יז, יא), "כנס כנד" (תהלים לג, ז), לא כתב 'כנס כנאד' אלא "כנד", ואלו היה "כנד" כמו 'כנאד' ו'כנס' לשון הכנסה, היה לו לכתב 'מכניס כבנאד מי הים'. אלא 'כנס' לשון אוסף וצובר הוא, וכן: "קמו נד אחד" (יהושע ג, טז), "ויעמדו נד אחד" (שם פסוק יג), ואין לשון קימה ועמידה בנאדות אלא בחומות וצבורים. ולא מצינו 'נאד' נקוד אלא במלאפום, כמו: "שימה דמעתי בנאדך" (תהלים נו, ט), "את נאוד החלב" (שופטים ד, יט): **קפאו.** כמו: "וכגבינה תקפיאני" (איוב י, י), שהקשו ונעשו כאבנים, והמים זורקים את המצרים על האבן בכח ונלחמים בם בכל מיני קשי: **בלב ים.** בחזק הים. ודרך המקראות לדבר כן: "עד לב השמים" (דברים ד, יא), "בלב האלה" (שמואל ב׳ יח, יד), לשון עקרו ותקפו של דבר:

ט| **אמר אויב.** לעמו כשפתם בדברים, ארדף ואשיגם ואחלק שלל עם שרי ועבדי: **תמלאמו.** תמלא מהם: **נפשי.** רוחי ורצוני. ואל תתמה על תבה המדברת בשתים, "תמלאמו" תמלא מהם, יש הרבה בלשון הזה: "כי ארץ הנגב נתתני" (שופטים א, טו) כמו נתת לי; "ולא יכלו דברו לשלם" (בראשית לז, ד) כמו דבר עמו; "בני יצאני" (ירמיה י, כ) כמו יצאו ממני; "מספר צעדי אגידנו" (איוב לא, לז) כמו אגיד לו; אף כאן "תמלאמו" תמלא נפשי מהם: **אריק חרבי.** אשלף. ועל שם שהוא מריק את התער בשליפתו ונשאר ריק נופל בו לשון הריקה, כמו: "מריקים שקיהם" (בראשית מב, לה), "וכליו יריקו" (ירמיה מח, יב). ואל

My desire shall be sated upon them, I will devour them; **I will draw my sword, my hand will dispossess them.**[D]
10 But **You blew with Your wind,** and **the sea covered them; they sank like lead**[D] in the **mighty water.**
11 **Who is like You among the powers, Lord? Who is like You, mighty in sanctity, awesome in praise,** exalted in praise, **performer of wonders?**
12 One of the wonders You just performed: **You extended Your right hand** against the enemy and **the earth swallowed them.**
13 Until now, the song addressed the defeat of the enemies and their demise at sea. Now it turns in a new, softer direction: **You guided with Your kindness, this people You redeemed; You directed them with Your strength to** reach their ultimate goal, **Your holy abode,** the Land of Israel. Alternatively, this is a prophecy for the future: You will direct them with Your strength until they reach Your holy abode, the Land of Israel.
14 Since the song refers to the march to the Land of Israel, it addresses the dramatic impact of the exodus and the parting of the Red Sea on the surrounding nations: **Nations,** when they **heard, they were agitated; trembling has gripped the inhabitants of Philistia.** The Philistines feared the Israelites would pass through their land.
15 **Then the chieftains of Edom were alarmed,** lest the Israelites cross their borders; **trembling gripped the powers,**[D] the leaders, **of Moav; all the inhabitants of Canaan have dissipated,** as they knew that the Israelites were marching toward their land.
16 **May dread and fear fall over them; with** the display of **the greatness of Your arm may they be stilled as a stone** from fear; **until Your people will pass** to their destination, **Lord, until this people whom You have acquired will pass.**
17 Eventually, **You will bring them,** the Israelites, **and plant them in the mountain of Your inheritance, the place You fashioned for Your dwelling, Lord, the Sanctuary, my Lord, that Your hands** have already **established.** This is the intended goal toward which the Israelites are directed: They will enter Canaan, settle it, and build the Temple of God.
18 **The Lord shall reign forever and ever.**[D]
19 The verse provides a prose summary of the song: **For the horses of Pharaoh came with his chariots and with his**

DISCUSSION

15:9| **My hand will dispossess them [*torishemo*]:** The verb *horish* often means to destroy or dispossess (e.g., Numbers 33:52). Alternatively: My hand shall impoverish [*teroshesh*] them (Rashi).

15:10| **They sank like lead:** Lead was the heaviest readily available metal in biblical times. Although gold is heavier than lead, the Israelites did not wish to compare the Egyptians to gold. It is possible that the soldiers and cavalrymen, and certainly the charioteers, were heavily armored, and their equipment caused them to sink faster into the sea.

15:15| **Powers [*eilei*]:** The word *eilei* is the plural form of the word *ayil*, ram. The use of this word as a reference to the leaders of Moav derives from the ram's role in leading a flock of sheep. In a similar manner, the chiefs of Edom are referred to as *alufei Edom*; an *aluf* refers to a bull or cow. Some identify the word *eilei* as deriving from the word *eyal*, meaning strength, power, and courage (see Psalms 22:20).

15:18| **The Lord shall reign forever and ever:** The Song by the Sea does not focus only on the defeat of the Egyptians at the Red Sea. News of the exodus, the parting of the sea, and the Egyptians' downfall echoed far and wide. Reports of these events struck fear in the hearts of the surrounding nations for generations (e.g., Joshua 2:9–10, 9:9; I Samuel 4:8, 6:6), and their memory was embedded deep into the Israelite consciousness. Since the impact of the miracles of the exodus extended beyond those who experienced it firsthand, the song includes statements that transcend time, and even visions for the future.

י נַפְשִׁי אָרִיק חַרְבִּי תּוֹרִישֵׁמוֹ יָדִי: נָשַׁפְתָּ
בְרוּחֲךָ כִּסָּמוֹ יָם צָלֲלוּ כַּעוֹפֶרֶת בְּמַיִם
יא אַדִּירִים: מִי־כָמֹכָה בָּאֵלִם יְהוָה מִי
כָּמֹכָה נֶאְדָּר בַּקֹּדֶשׁ נוֹרָא תְהִלֹּת עֹשֵׂה
יב יג פֶלֶא: נָטִיתָ יְמִינְךָ תִּבְלָעֵמוֹ אָרֶץ: נָחִיתָ
בְחַסְדְּךָ עַם־זוּ גָּאָלְתָּ נֵהַלְתָּ בְעָזְּךָ אֶל־נְוֵה
יד קָדְשֶׁךָ: שָׁמְעוּ עַמִּים יִרְגָּזוּן חִיל
טו אָחַז יֹשְׁבֵי פְּלָשֶׁת: אָז נִבְהֲלוּ אַלּוּפֵי
אֱדוֹם אֵילֵי מוֹאָב יֹאחֲזֵמוֹ רָעַד נָמֹגוּ
טז כֹּל יֹשְׁבֵי כְנָעַן: תִּפֹּל עֲלֵיהֶם אֵימָתָה
וָפַחַד בִּגְדֹל זְרוֹעֲךָ יִדְּמוּ כָּאָבֶן עַד־
יַעֲבֹר עַמְּךָ יְהוָה עַד־יַעֲבֹר עַם־זוּ
יז קָנִיתָ: תְּבִאֵמוֹ וְתִטָּעֵמוֹ בְּהַר נַחֲלָתְךָ מָכוֹן
לְשִׁבְתְּךָ פָּעַלְתָּ יְהוָה מִקְּדָשׁ אֲדֹנָי כּוֹנְנוּ
יח יט יָדֶיךָ: יְהוָה ׀ יִמְלֹךְ לְעֹלָם וָעֶד: כִּי

רש״י

תֹּאמַר, אֵין לְשׁוֹן רֵיקוּת נוֹפֵל עַל הַיּוֹצֵא אֶלָּא עַל הַתִּיק וְעַל הַשַּׂק וְעַל הַכְּלִי שֶׁיָּצָא מִמֶּנּוּ, אֲבָל לֹא עַל הַחֶרֶב וְעַל הַיַּיִן, וְלִדְחֹק וּלְפָרֵשׁ ״אָרִיק חַרְבִּי״ כִּלְשׁוֹן ״וַיָּרֶק אֶת חֲנִיכָיו״ (בראשית יד, יד), אֶזְדַּיֵּן בְּחַרְבִּי – מָצִינוּ הַלָּשׁוֹן מוּסָב אַף עַל הַיּוֹצֵא, ״שֶׁמֶן תּוּרַק״ (שיר השירים א, ג), ״וְלֹא הוּרַק מִכְּלִי אֶל כֶּלִי״ (ירמיה מח, יא), ׳לֹא הוּרַק הַכְּלִי׳ אֵין כָּתוּב כָּאן אֶלָּא ״לֹא הוּרַק הַיַּיִן מִכְּלִי אֶל כְּלִי״, מָצִינוּ הַלָּשׁוֹן מוּסָב עַל הַיַּיִן, וְכֵן: ״וְהֵרִיקוּ חַרְבוֹתָם עַל יְפִי חָכְמָתֶךָ״ (יחזקאל כח, ז) דִּבְּרָם: תּוֹרִישֵׁמוֹ. לְשׁוֹן רִישׁוּת וְדַלּוּת, כְּמוֹ: ״מוֹרִישׁ וּמַעֲשִׁיר״ (שמואל א׳ ב, ז):

י | נָשַׁפְתָּ. לְשׁוֹן הֲפָחָה, וְכֵן ״וְגַם נָשַׁף בָּהֶם״ (ישעיה מ, כד): צָלֲלוּ. שָׁקְעוּ, עָמְקוּ, לְשׁוֹן ״מְצוּלָה״: כַּעוֹפֶרֶת. אֲבָר, פלו״ם בְּלַעַז:

יא | בָּאֵלִם. בַּחֲזָקִים, כְּמוֹ: ״וְאֶת אֵילֵי הָאָרֶץ לָקָח״ (יחזקאל יז, יג), ״אֱיָלוּתִי לְעֶזְרָתִי חוּשָׁה״ (תהלים כב, כ): נוֹרָא תְהִלֹּת. יָרֵאוּי מִלְּהַגִּיד תְּהִלּוֹתֶיךָ פֶּן יִמְעֲטוּ, עַל כֵּן: ״לְךָ דֻמִיָּה תְהִלָּה״ (שם סה, ב):

יב | נָטִיתָ יְמִינְךָ. כְּשֶׁהַקָּדוֹשׁ בָּרוּךְ הוּא נוֹטֶה יָדוֹ הָרְשָׁעִים כָּלִים וְנוֹפְלִים, לְפִי שֶׁהַכֹּל נָתוּן בְּיָדוֹ וְנוֹפְלִים בְּהַטָּיָתָהּ, וְכֵן הוּא אוֹמֵר: ״וַה׳ יַטֶּה יָדוֹ וְכָשַׁל עוֹזֵר וְנָפַל עָזֻר״ (ישעיה לא, ג). מָשָׁל לִכְלֵי זְכוּכִית הַנְּתוּנִים בְּיַד אָדָם, מַטֶּה יָדוֹ מְעַט וְהֵם נוֹפְלִים וּמִשְׁתַּבְּרִים: תִּבְלָעֵמוֹ אָרֶץ. מִכָּאן שֶׁזָּכוּ לִקְבוּרָה, בִּשְׂכַר שֶׁאָמְרוּ: ״ה׳ הַצַּדִּיק״ (לעיל ט, כז):

יג | נֵהַלְתָּ. לְשׁוֹן מְנַהֵל. וְאוּנְקְלוֹס תִּרְגֵּם לְשׁוֹן נוֹשֵׂא וְסוֹבֵל, וְלֹא דִּקְדֵּק לְפָרֵשׁ אַחַר לְשׁוֹן הָעִבְרִית:

יד | יִרְגָּזוּן. מִתְרַגְּזִין: יֹשְׁבֵי פְּלָשֶׁת. מִפְּנֵי שֶׁהָרְגוּ אֶת בְּנֵי אֶפְרַיִם שֶׁמִּהֲרוּ אֶת הַקֵּץ וְיָצְאוּ בְּחָזְקָה, כַּמְפֹרָשׁ בְּדִבְרֵי הַיָּמִים (א׳ ז, כא): ״וַהֲרָגוּם אַנְשֵׁי גַת״:

טו | אַלּוּפֵי אֱדוֹם אֵילֵי מוֹאָב. וַהֲלֹא לֹא הָיָה לָהֶם לִירֹא כְּלוּם, שֶׁהֲרֵי לֹא עֲלֵיהֶם הוֹלְכִים? אֶלָּא מִפְּנֵי אֲנִינוּת שֶׁהָיוּ מִתְאוֹנְנִים וּמִצְטַעֲרִים עַל כְּבוֹדָם שֶׁל יִשְׂרָאֵל: נָמֹגוּ. נָמַסּוּ, כְּמוֹ: ״בִּרְבִיבִים תְּמֹגְגֶנָּה״ (תהלים סה, יא), אָמְרוּ: עָלֵינוּ הֵם בָּאִים לְכַלּוֹתֵנוּ וְלִירַשׁ אֶת אַרְצֵנוּ:

טז | תִּפֹּל עֲלֵיהֶם אֵימָתָה. עַל הָרְחוֹקִים: וָפַחַד. עַל הַקְּרוֹבִים, כְּעִנְיָן שֶׁנֶּאֱמַר: ״כִּי שָׁמַעְנוּ אֵת אֲשֶׁר הוֹבִישׁ״ וְגוֹ׳ (יהושע ב, י): עַד יַעֲבֹר... עַד יַעֲבֹר. כְּתַרְגּוּמוֹ: קָנִיתָ. חִבַּבְתָּ מִשְּׁאָר אֻמּוֹת, כְּחֵפֶץ הַקָּנוּי בְּדָמִים יְקָרִים שֶׁחָבִיב עַל הָאָדָם:

יז-יח | תְּבִאֵמוֹ. נִתְנַבֵּא מֹשֶׁה שֶׁלֹּא יִכָּנֵס לָאָרֶץ, לְכָךְ לֹא נֶאֱמַר ׳תְּבִיאֵנוּ׳: מָכוֹן לְשִׁבְתְּךָ. מִקְדָּשׁ שֶׁל מַטָּה מְכֻוָּן כְּנֶגֶד כִּסֵּא שֶׁל מַעְלָה אֲשֶׁר ״פָּעַלְתָּ״: מִקְּדָשׁ. הַטַּעַם עָלָיו זָקֵף גָּדוֹל לְהַפְרִידוֹ מִתֵּבַת הַשֵּׁם שֶׁלְּאַחֲרָיו, הַמִּקְדָּשׁ אֲשֶׁר כּוֹנְנוּ יָדֶיךָ ה׳. חָבִיב בֵּית הַמִּקְדָּשׁ, שֶׁהָעוֹלָם נִבְרָא בְּיָד אַחַת, שֶׁנֶּאֱמַר ״אַף יָדִי יָסְדָה אֶרֶץ״ (ישעיה מח, יג), וּמִקְדָּשׁ בִּשְׁתֵּי יָדַיִם. וְאֵימָתַי יִבָּנֶה בִּשְׁתֵּי יָדַיִם? בִּזְמַן שֶׁ״ה׳ יִמְלֹךְ לְעֹלָם וָעֶד״, לֶעָתִיד לָבֹא שֶׁכָּל הַמְּלוּכָה שֶׁלּוֹ, וּ״לְעֹלָם וָעֶד״ לְשׁוֹן עוֹלָמִית הוּא וְהַוָּי״ו בּוֹ יְסוֹד, לְפִיכָךְ הִיא פְּתוּחָה, אֲבָל ״וְאָנֹכִי הַיּוֹדֵעַ וָעֵד״ (ירמיה כט, כג) שֶׁהַוָּי״ו בּוֹ שִׁמּוּשׁ, קְמוּצָה הִיא:

horsemen into the sea, and the Lord returned the water of the sea upon them to drown them; **and the children of Israel walked on dry land in the sea.** The Israelites did not walk on land that had historically been sea but had become shallow and fordable. Rather, the area of their passage turned miraculously from sea into dry land at God's command so that the Israelites could pass.

20 **Miriam the prophetess, sister of Aaron,**[D] **took the drum in her hand, and all the women came out after her with drums and in dance.** Alternatively: With tambourines and with hollow [*ḥalul*], or round, instruments.[20]

21 As the women sang and danced, **Miriam called** and sang **to them** the first verse of the Song by the Sea: **Sing to the Lord, as He is** highly **exalted, the horse and its rider He cast into the sea;** and all the women followed Miriam in song.

The Initial Travels after the Red Sea: The Wilderness of Shur, Mara, and Eilim
EXODUS 15:22–27

It was to be expected that the Israelites would encounter physical hardships in the wilderness, including difficulty in finding water and food. At this stage, the Israelites encounter the trial of thirst and receive some of God's laws.

22 **Moses led Israel from the Red Sea, and they went out to the wilderness of Shur**[B] on the western edge of the Sinai. From the fact that the wilderness of Shur is mentioned in the story of Hagar's wanderings,[21] it is apparent that this wilderness is not very far from Canaan. **They walked three days in the wilderness, and did not find water** to drink.

23 **They came to Mara,** perhaps adjacent to one of the saltwater lakes near the Nile, **and they could not drink** the **water from Mara, as it is bitter. Therefore, its name is called Mara,**[B] meaning bitter.

24 **The people complained against Moses, saying: What will we drink?** For three days we have found no water in the wilderness. Now that we have finally reached a body of water, it is undrinkable.

25 **He,** Moses, **cried out to the Lord, and the Lord indicated** the natural properties of **a certain tree to him, and he cast it into the waters, and the waters sweetened**[D] from their contact with the tree. Apparently, the Israelites stayed for a time at Mara, for **there He,** God, **instituted for it statutes and ordinances.** Until now, the Israelites were largely commanded to observe laws connected specifically to the exodus and the paschal offering. Now, however, they were ready to receive new laws and commandments. At Mara, the Israelites received a few ritual commandments and civil laws; the Sages identify these based on oral tradition.[22] **And there He tested it,** Israel, by the bitter waters. In this case, the Israelites passed the test and became stronger for it.

26 God **said: If you heed the voice of the Lord your God and will perform that which is right in His eyes and listen to His commandments and observe all His statutes, all of the diseases that I placed on Egypt I will not place upon you, as I am the Lord your healer,** and I will protect you from sickness.

27 The Israelites traveled from Mara and **they came to Eilim,**[B] **and**
Fifth aliya
there were **twelve springs of water and seventy palm trees;**[D]

BACKGROUND

15:22 | **The wilderness of Shur:** This is the wilderness adjacent to Egypt to the east, as indicated in other verses (Genesis 25:18; I Samuel 15:7). A road (see Genesis 16:7) crossed through this wilderness, from Beersheba through Kadesh Barnea, to the central Sinai, in the area of the Bitter Lakes. The word *shur* also means wall or fortification in biblical Hebrew (see Genesis 49:22), as well as in Aramaic. It is possible that the wilderness of Shur was called by that name due to the chain of Egyptian fortresses that defended against invasion from the Sinai. The term *shur* may also imply looking out over an area (see Song of Songs 4:8), as the wilderness and the road that passed through it could be seen from the mountain peaks.

DISCUSSION

15:20 | **Miriam the prophetess, sister of Aaron:** In certain instances, women are referred to as the sister of the eldest brother in the family (see Genesis 28:9; Exodus 6:23; see also Rashbam; *Bekhor Shor*; Ramban). Sometimes a man will also be referred to in this manner (see I Chronicles 2:42).

15:25 | **And the Lord indicated a tree to him, and he cast it into the waters, and the waters sweetened:** Sweetening water by means of a tree seems like a miracle. However, the language of the verse appears to indicate that the identity of the tree in question was important, such that the water would not have become sweet if not for some property it possessed. Moses was not an expert in botany, so God taught him about this tree and its powers in order to make the water drinkable for the Israelites (see Ramban; *Ha'amek Davar*; *Bekhor Shor* here and 9:10).

15:27 | **Twelve springs of water and seventy palm trees:** The number of springs and trees are mentioned because they carried symbolic significance for the Israelites. The twelve springs of water corresponded to the twelve tribes, and the seventy palm trees corresponded to the number of children of Israel who originally went down to Egypt (*Mekhilta*; see *Bereshit Rabba* 49:2; see also Rashi).

בָּא סוּס פַּרְעֹה בְּרִכְבּוֹ וּבְפָרָשָׁיו בַּיָּם וַיָּשֶׁב יהוה עֲלֵהֶם אֶת־מֵי הַיָּם וּבְנֵי יִשְׂרָאֵל הָלְכוּ בַיַּבָּשָׁה בְּתוֹךְ הַיָּם:

כ וַתִּקַּח מִרְיָם הַנְּבִיאָה אֲחוֹת אַהֲרֹן אֶת־הַתֹּף בְּיָדָהּ וַתֵּצֶאןָ כָל־הַנָּשִׁים אַחֲרֶיהָ כא בְּתֻפִּים וּבִמְחֹלֹת: וַתַּעַן לָהֶם מִרְיָם שִׁירוּ לַיהוה כִּי־גָאֹה גָּאָה סוּס וְרֹכְבוֹ רָמָה כב בַיָּם: וַיַּסַּע מֹשֶׁה אֶת־יִשְׂרָאֵל מִיַּם־סוּף וַיֵּצְאוּ אֶל־מִדְבַּר־שׁוּר וַיֵּלְכוּ כג שְׁלֹשֶׁת־יָמִים בַּמִּדְבָּר וְלֹא־מָצְאוּ מָיִם: וַיָּבֹאוּ מָרָתָה וְלֹא יָכְלוּ לִשְׁתֹּת מַיִם מִמָּרָה כד כִּי מָרִים הֵם עַל־כֵּן קָרָא־שְׁמָהּ מָרָה: וַיִּלֹּנוּ הָעָם עַל־מֹשֶׁה לֵּאמֹר מַה־נִּשְׁתֶּה: כה וַיִּצְעַק אֶל־יהוה וַיּוֹרֵהוּ יהוה עֵץ וַיַּשְׁלֵךְ אֶל־הַמַּיִם וַיִּמְתְּקוּ הַמָּיִם שָׁם שָׂם לוֹ חֹק וּמִשְׁפָּט וְשָׁם נִסָּהוּ: וַיֹּאמֶר אִם־שָׁמוֹעַ תִּשְׁמַע לְקוֹל | יהוה אֱלֹהֶיךָ וְהַיָּשָׁר כו בְּעֵינָיו תַּעֲשֶׂה וְהַאֲזַנְתָּ לְמִצְוֹתָיו וְשָׁמַרְתָּ כָּל־חֻקָּיו כָּל־הַמַּחֲלָה אֲשֶׁר־שַׂמְתִּי כז בְמִצְרַיִם לֹא־אָשִׂים עָלֶיךָ כִּי אֲנִי יהוה רֹפְאֶךָ: וַיָּבֹאוּ אֵילִמָה וְשָׁם חמישי

רש"י

יט | כִּי בָא סוּס פַּרְעֹה. כַּאֲשֶׁר בָּא סוּס פַּרְעֹה וְגו':

כ | וַתִּקַּח מִרְיָם הַנְּבִיאָה. הֵיכָן נִתְנַבְּאָה? כְּשֶׁהָיְתָה אֲחוֹת אַהֲרֹן קֹדֶם שֶׁנּוֹלַד מֹשֶׁה. אָמְרָה: עֲתִידָה אִמִּי שֶׁתֵּלֵד בֵּן וְכו', כִּדְאִיתָא בְּסוֹטָה (דף יב ע"ב). דָּבָר אַחֵר: "אֲחוֹת אַהֲרֹן", לְפִי שֶׁמָּסַר נַפְשׁוֹ עָלֶיהָ כְּשֶׁנִּצְטָרְעָה נִקְרֵאת עַל שְׁמוֹ: **אֶת הַתֹּף.** כְּלִי שֶׁל מִין זֶמֶר: **בְּתֻפִּים וּבִמְחֹלֹת.** מֻבְטָחוֹת הָיוּ צַדְקָנִיּוֹת שֶׁבַּדּוֹר שֶׁהַקָּדוֹשׁ בָּרוּךְ הוּא עוֹשֶׂה לָהֶם נִסִּים, וְהוֹצִיאוּ תֻפִּים מִמִּצְרַיִם:

כא | וַתַּעַן לָהֶם מִרְיָם. מֹשֶׁה אָמַר שִׁירָה לָאֲנָשִׁים, הוּא אוֹמֵר וְהֵם עוֹנִין אַחֲרָיו, וּמִרְיָם אָמְרָה שִׁירָה לַנָּשִׁים:

כב | וַיַּסַּע מֹשֶׁה. הִסִּיעָן בְּעַל כָּרְחָם, שֶׁעִטְּרוּ מִצְרַיִם אֶת סוּסֵיהֶם בְּתַכְשִׁיטֵי זָהָב וָכֶסֶף וַאֲבָנִים טוֹבוֹת, וְהָיוּ יִשְׂרָאֵל מוֹצְאִין אוֹתָן בַּיָּם. וּגְדוֹלָה הָיְתָה בִּזַּת הַיָּם מִבִּזַּת מִצְרַיִם, שֶׁנֶּאֱמַר: "תּוֹרֵי זָהָב נַעֲשֶׂה לָּךְ עִם נְקֻדּוֹת הַכָּסֶף" (שיר השירים א, יא), לְפִיכָךְ הֻצְרַךְ לְהַסִּיעָן בְּעַל כָּרְחָם:

כג | וַיָּבֹאוּ מָרָתָה. כְּמוֹ "לְמָרָה", ה"א בְּסוֹף תֵּבָה בִּמְקוֹם לָמֶ"ד בִּתְחִלָּתָהּ, וְהָתַי"ו הִיא בִּמְקוֹם ה"א הַנִּשְׁרֶשֶׁת בְּתֵבַת מָרָה, וּבִסְמִיכָתָהּ, כְּשֶׁהִיא מִדֶּבֶּקֶת לַה"א שֶׁהוּא מוֹסִיף בִּמְקוֹם הַלָּמֶ"ד, תֵּהָפֵךְ הַה"א שֶׁל שֹׁרֶשׁ לְתָי"ו. וְכֵן כָּל ה"א שֶׁהִיא בִּנְקֻדָּה תֵּהָפֵךְ לְתָי"ו בִּסְמִיכָתָהּ, כְּמוֹ: "חֵמָה אֵין לִי" (ישעיה כז, ד), "וַחֲמָתוֹ בַּעֲרָה בוֹ" (אסתר א, יב), הֲרֵי ה"א שֶׁל שֹׁרֶשׁ נֶהְפֶּכֶת לְתָי"ו מִפְּנֵי שֶׁנִּסְמְכָה עַל הַוָּי"ו הָנּוֹסֶפֶת. וְכֵן: "עֶבֶד וְאָמָה" (ויקרא כה, מד), "הִנֵּה חֲמַת מַלְכָּה" (כדרכֵּהֶם), "לְנַפְשָׁה חַיָּה" (בראשית ב, ז), "פֵּן הֲרֵמָה" (איוב לג, כד); "פֵּן הֲרֵמָה" (שופטים ה, ה), "יִתְשׁוּעֲתוֹ הַדָּמָתָה" (שמואל א' ז, יז):

כד | וַיִּלֹּנוּ. לְשׁוֹן נִפְעַל הוּא. וְכֵן הַתַּרְגּוּם לְשׁוֹן נִפְעַל הוּא "וְאִתְרַעֲמוּ". וְכֵן דֶּרֶךְ לְשׁוֹן תְּלֻנָּה לְהָסֵב הַדִּבּוּר אֶל הָאָדָם: מִתְלוֹנֵן, מִתְרָעֵם, וְלֹא יֹאמַר: לוֹנֵן, רוֹעֵם. וְכֵן יֹאמַר הַלֹּעֵז דְּקוֹמפְּלַיינְטְ שֶׁ"יְ, מַסֵב הַדִּבּוּר אֵלָיו בְּאָמְרוֹ שֶׁ"יְ:

כה | שָׁם שָׂם לוֹ. בְּמָרָה נָתַן לָהֶם מִקְצָת פָּרָשִׁיּוֹת שֶׁל תּוֹרָה שֶׁיִּתְעַסְּקוּ בָהֶם: שַׁבָּת וּפָרָה אֲדֻמָּה וְדִינִין: וְשָׁם נִסָּהוּ. לָעָם. וְרָאָה קְשִׁי עָרְפָּן שֶׁלֹּא נִמְלְכוּ בְּמֹשֶׁה בְּלָשׁוֹן יָפָה: בַּקֵּשׁ עָלֵינוּ שֶׁיִּהְיוּ לָנוּ מַיִם לִשְׁתּוֹת, אֶלָּא נִתְלוֹנְנוּ:

כו | אִם שָׁמוֹעַ תִּשְׁמַע. זוֹ קַבָּלָה, שֶׁיְּקַבְּלוּ עֲלֵיהֶם: הַיָּשָׁר בְּעֵינָיו עָשָׂה. הִיא: וְהַאֲזַנְתָּ. תַּטֶּה אָזְנַיִם לְדַקְדֵּק בָּהֶם: כָּל חֻקָּיו. דְּבָרִים שֶׁאֵינָן אֶלָּא גְּזֵרַת מֶלֶךְ בְּלֹא שׁוּם טַעַם, וְיֵצֶר הָרַע מְקַנְטֵר עֲלֵיהֶם, מָה אִסּוּר בְּאֵלּוּ? לָמָּה נֶאֶסְרוּ? כְּגוֹן לְבִישַׁת כִּלְאַיִם, וַאֲכִילַת חֲזִיר וּפָרָה אֲדֻמָּה וְכַיּוֹצֵא בָהֶם: לֹא אָשִׂים עָלֶיךָ. וְאִם אָשִׂים הֲרֵי הוּא כְּלֹא הוּשְׂמָה, "כִּי אֲנִי ה' רֹפְאֶךָ". זֶהוּ לְפִי פְּשׁוּטוֹ. וּלְפִי מִדְרָשׁוֹ, "כִּי אֲנִי ה' רֹפְאֶךָ", הַמְלַמֶּדְךָ תּוֹרָה וּמִצְוֹת לְמַעַן תִּנָּצֵל מֵהֶם, כָּרוֹפֵא הַזֶּה הָאוֹמֵר לָאָדָם: אַל תֹּאכַל דָּבָר זֶה פֶּן יְבִיאֲךָ לִידֵי חֳלִי זֶה. וְכֵן הוּא אוֹמֵר: "רִפְאוּת תְּהִי לְשָׁרֶּךָ" (משלי ג, ח):

BACKGROUND

15:23 | Mara: There are two known springs of bitter water that have high levels of sulfur: the springs southeast of the city of Suez, known as Bir al Murrah, perhaps derived from the name Mara, located about 14 km southeast of the city of Suez; and the springs of Ein Hawarah, south of Wadi Amra, about 70 km southeast of Suez and 80 km north of Ein Arandal.

15:27 | Eilim: Scholars have suggested four sites that may be identified as Eilim: Ein Moussa, a desert oasis of about 700 sq m, 8 km south of Suez; Ein Gerendal, the largest desert oasis in the Sinai, located about 110 km south of Suez; and two locations further north, El Arish and Abu Agila.

they encamped there by the water after their wearying journey.

The Quail and the Manna

EXODUS 16:1–36

The Israelites' encampment at Eilim was comfortable. When the people reached the twelve springs and seventy palm trees, they felt as if the place had been waiting for them. Their next destination, the wilderness of Tzin, would challenge them with hunger. The miraculous manna, which first appears here, would nourish them for the rest of their journeys in the wilderness.

In addition to the gift of the manna, the Israelites would also receive here the gift of the Sabbath.

16 **1** **They traveled from Eilim, and the entire congregation of the children of Israel came to the wilderness of Tzin,**[B] **which is between Eilim and Sinai, on the fifteenth day of the second month since their exodus from the land of Egypt,** the month of Iyyar.

Possible locations of the wilderness of Tzin

2 **The entire congregation of the children of Israel complained against Moses and against Aaron in the wilderness.**

Mara and Eilim

The Israelites likely still had some grain and livestock. However, a whole month had passed since they left Egypt, and they had exhausted much of their food supply.

3 **The children of Israel said to them: If only our death had been at the hand of the Lord in the land of Egypt, when we sat by the fleshpots, when we ate bread until satiation.**[D] Then, at least, we had food to eat. **For you have taken us out into this wilderness to kill this entire assembly through famine.**

4 **The Lord said to Moses: Behold, I am raining** a miraculous form of **food for you from the heavens; and the people shall go out and gather each day's portion on its day, so that I may test them,** to see **whether they will follow My law,** and gather only one portion each day, **or not.**

5 **It shall be on the sixth day, that they will prepare that which they will bring, and it will be twice what they gather each day.** As will be explained, the Sabbath is a day of rest, and it is therefore prohibited for the Israelites to gather the manna, or cook or bake it, on that day. To ensure they have enough food for the Sabbath, God will provide a double portion of manna on the sixth day for them to gather.

6 **Moses and Aaron said to the entire children of Israel: In the evening you will know that the Lord took you out of the land of Egypt.** God listens to you and attends to your needs.

7 **And in the morning you will see the glory of the Lord, because He has heard your complaints against the Lord. And as for us, why do you bring complaints against us?** We make

— DISCUSSION —

16:3| When we sat by the fleshpots, when we ate bread until satiation: It seems unlikely that a people subjugated to backbreaking labor would have enjoyed the economic prosperity described here. Rather, the Israelites are expressing their feelings of insecurity. In a short span of time, they have managed to construct a nostalgic memory of their conditions in Egypt, one that did not match the reality they experienced there.

א שְׁתֵּים עֶשְׂרֵה עֵינֹת מַיִם וְשִׁבְעִים תְּמָרִים וַיַּחֲנוּ־שָׁם עַל־הַמָּיִם: וַיִּסְעוּ מֵאֵילִם
וַיָּבֹאוּ כָּל־עֲדַת בְּנֵי־יִשְׂרָאֵל אֶל־מִדְבַּר־סִין אֲשֶׁר בֵּין־אֵילִם וּבֵין סִינָי בַּחֲמִשָּׁה
ב עָשָׂר יוֹם לַחֹדֶשׁ הַשֵּׁנִי לְצֵאתָם מֵאֶרֶץ מִצְרָיִם: וַיִּלִּינוּ כָּל־עֲדַת בְּנֵי־יִשְׂרָאֵל עַל־ וילונו
ג מֹשֶׁה וְעַל־אַהֲרֹן בַּמִּדְבָּר: וַיֹּאמְרוּ אֲלֵהֶם בְּנֵי יִשְׂרָאֵל מִי־יִתֵּן מוּתֵנוּ בְיַד־יְהוָה
בְּאֶרֶץ מִצְרַיִם בְּשִׁבְתֵּנוּ עַל־סִיר הַבָּשָׂר בְּאָכְלֵנוּ לֶחֶם לָשֹׂבַע כִּי־הוֹצֵאתֶם אֹתָנוּ
ד אֶל־הַמִּדְבָּר הַזֶּה לְהָמִית אֶת־כָּל־הַקָּהָל הַזֶּה בָּרָעָב: וַיֹּאמֶר יב
יְהוָה אֶל־מֹשֶׁה הִנְנִי מַמְטִיר לָכֶם לֶחֶם מִן־הַשָּׁמָיִם וְיָצָא הָעָם וְלָקְטוּ דְּבַר־יוֹם
ה בְּיוֹמוֹ לְמַעַן אֲנַסֶּנּוּ הֲיֵלֵךְ בְּתוֹרָתִי אִם־לֹא: וְהָיָה בַּיּוֹם הַשִּׁשִּׁי וְהֵכִינוּ אֵת אֲשֶׁר־
ו יָבִיאוּ וְהָיָה מִשְׁנֶה עַל אֲשֶׁר־יִלְקְטוּ יוֹם ׀ יוֹם: וַיֹּאמֶר מֹשֶׁה וְאַהֲרֹן אֶל־כָּל־בְּנֵי
ז יִשְׂרָאֵל עֶרֶב וִידַעְתֶּם כִּי יְהוָה הוֹצִיא אֶתְכֶם מֵאֶרֶץ מִצְרָיִם: וּבֹקֶר וּרְאִיתֶם
אֶת־כְּבוֹד יְהוָה בְּשָׁמְעוֹ אֶת־תְּלֻנֹּתֵיכֶם עַל־יְהוָה וְנַחְנוּ מָה כִּי תלונו עָלֵינוּ: תלינו

רש״י

כז| **שְׁתֵּים עֶשְׂרֵה עֵינֹת מַיִם.** כְּנֶגֶד שְׁנֵים עָשָׂר שְׁבָטִים נִזְדַּמְּנוּ לָהֶם: **וְשִׁבְעִים תְּמָרִים.** כְּנֶגֶד שִׁבְעִים זְקֵנִים:

פרק טז

א| **בַּחֲמִשָּׁה עָשָׂר יוֹם.** נִתְפָּרֵשׁ הַיּוֹם שֶׁל חֲנִיָּה זוֹ לְפִי שֶׁבּוֹ בַּיּוֹם כָּלְתָה הַחֲרָרָה שֶׁהוֹצִיאוּ מִמִּצְרַיִם וְהֻצְרְכוּ לַמָּן, לְלַמְּדֵנוּ שֶׁאָכְלוּ מִשְּׁיָרֵי הַבָּצֵק שִׁשִּׁים וְאַחַת סְעוּדוֹת, וְיָרַד לָהֶם מָן בְּשִׁשָּׁה עָשָׂר בְּאִיָּר, וְיוֹם אֶחָד בְּשַׁבָּת הָיָה, כִּדְאִיתָא בְּמַסֶּכֶת שַׁבָּת (דף פז ע״ב):

ב| **וַיִּלּוֹנוּ.** לְפִי שֶׁכָּלָה הַלֶּחֶם:

ג| **מִי יִתֵּן מוּתֵנוּ.** שֶׁנָּמוּת. וְאֵינוֹ שֵׁם דָּבָר כְּמוֹ ׳מוֹתֵנוּ׳, אֶלָּא כְּמוֹ: עֲשׂוֹתֵנוּ, חֲנוֹתֵנוּ, שׁוּבֵנוּ – לַעֲשׂוֹת אֲנַחְנוּ, לַחֲנוֹת אֲנַחְנוּ, לָמוּת אֲנַחְנוּ. ״לְוַי דְּמִיתְנָא״ – לוּ מַתְנוּ, הַלְוַאי וְהָיִינוּ מֵתִים:

ד| **דְּבַר יוֹם בְּיוֹמוֹ.** צֹרֶךְ אֲכִילַת יוֹם יִלְקְטוּ בְּיוֹמוֹ, וְלֹא יִלְקְטוּ הַיּוֹם לְצֹרֶךְ מָחָר: **לְמַעַן אֲנַסֶּנּוּ.** כִּי אֲנַסֶּנּוּ ״הֲיֵלֵךְ בְּתוֹרָתִי״, אִם יִשְׁמְרוּ מִצְוֹת הַתְּלוּיוֹת בּוֹ, שֶׁלֹּא יוֹתִירוּ מִמֶּנּוּ וְלֹא יֵצְאוּ בְּשַׁבָּת לִלְקֹט:

ה| **וְהָיָה מִשְׁנֶה.** לַיּוֹם וְלַמָּחֳרָת: **מִשְׁנֶה.** עַל שֶׁהָיוּ רְגִילִים לִלְקֹט יוֹם יוֹם שֶׁל שְׁאָר יְמוֹת הַשָּׁבוּעַ:

ו| **עֶרֶב.** כְּמוֹ לָעֶרֶב: **וִידַעְתֶּם כִּי ה׳ הוֹצִיא אֶתְכֶם מֵאֶרֶץ מִצְרָיִם.** לְפִי שֶׁאֲמַרְתֶּם לָנוּ: ״כִּי הוֹצֵאתֶם אֹתָנוּ״ (לעיל פסוק ג), תֵּדְעוּ כִּי לֹא אֲנַחְנוּ הַמּוֹצִיאִים אֶלָּא ה׳ הוֹצִיא אֶתְכֶם, שֶׁיָּגִיז לָכֶם אֶת הַשְּׂלָו:

ז| **וּבֹקֶר וּרְאִיתֶם.** לֹא עַל הַכָּבוֹד שֶׁנֶּאֱמַר: ״וְהִנֵּה כְּבוֹד ה׳ נִרְאָה בֶּעָנָן״ (להלן פסוק י) נֶאֱמַר, אֶלָּא כָּךְ אָמַר לָהֶם: עֶרֶב וִידַעְתֶּם כִּי הַיְכֹלֶת בְּיָדוֹ לִתֵּן תַּאֲוַתְכֶם, וּבָשָׂר יִתֵּן, אַךְ לֹא בְּפָנִים מְאִירוֹת יִתְּנֶנָּה לָכֶם, כִּי שֶׁלֹּא כַּהֹגֶן שְׁאַלְתֶּם אוֹתוֹ, וּמִכָּרֵס מְלֵאָה. וְהַלֶּחֶם שֶׁשְּׁאַלְתֶּם לְצֹרֶךְ, בִּירִידָתוֹ לַבֹּקֶר תִּרְאוּ אֶת כְּבוֹד אוֹר פָּנָיו, שֶׁיּוֹרִידֵהוּ לָכֶם דֶּרֶךְ חִבָּה בַּבֹּקֶר שֶׁיֵּשׁ שָׁהוּת לַהֲכִינוֹ, וְטַל מִלְמַעְלָה וְטַל מִלְמַטָּה כְּמֻנָּח בְּקֻפְסָא: **אֶת תְּלֻנֹּתֵיכֶם עַל ה׳.** כְּמוֹ אֲשֶׁר עַל ה׳: **וְנַחְנוּ מָה.** מָה אֲנַחְנוּ חֲשׁוּבִין: **כִּי תַלִּינוּ עָלֵינוּ.** שֶׁתַּרְעִימוּ עָלֵינוּ אֶת הַכֹּל, אֶת בְּנֵיכֶם וּנְשֵׁיכֶם וּבְנוֹתֵיכֶם וְעֵרֶב רַב. וְעַל כָּרְחִי אֲנִי זָקוּק לְפָרֵשׁ ״תַּלִּינוּ״ בִּלְשׁוֹן תַּפְעִילוּ, מִפְּנֵי דְּגֵשׁוּתוֹ וּקְרִיָּתוֹ. שֶׁאִלּוּ הָיָה רָפֶה הָיִיתִי מְפָרְשׁוֹ בִּלְשׁוֹן תִּפְעֲלוּ, כְּמוֹ: ״וַיָּלֶן הָעָם עַל מֹשֶׁה״ (להלן יז, ג), אוֹ אִם הָיָה דָּגוּשׁ וְאֵין בּוֹ יוּ״ד וְנִקְרָא ׳תִּלּוֹנוּ׳, הָיִיתִי מְפָרְשׁוֹ לְשׁוֹן תִּתְלוֹנְנוּ. עַכְשָׁיו הוּא מַשְׁמָע תַּלִּינוּ אֶת אֲחֵרִים, כְּמוֹ בַּמְרַגְּלִים: ״וַיַּלִּינוּ עָלָיו אֶת כָּל הָעֵדָה״ (במדבר יד, לו):

BACKGROUND

16:1 | **The wilderness of Tzin:** This is described here as being located between Eilim and Sinai, and elsewhere it is associated with Kadesh Barnea (see Numbers 20:1). Some scholars place it in the eastern part of the Sinai Peninsula, north of Ein Qudeirat (Kadesh Barnea). Some claim it is located between Aqaba and Wadi Jariah, in the southeastern part of Jebel El Tih. Some say it is north of Arava, perhaps even in the territory of Edom, based on a verse in Joshua (15:1). It is possible that the name Tzin refers to the tip of palm branches, in which case the name alludes to desert oases in which there were palm trees, similar to those in Eilim and Kadesh Barnea.

no decisions on our own; we are only messengers of God, and you are subject to His direct supervision.

8 **Moses said:** You will be convinced of God's providence **with the Lord giving you meat to eat in the evening**ᴰ **and bread in the morning to be satiated, with the Lord hearing your complaints that you bring against Him, then what are we? Your complaints are not against us, but against the Lord.**

9 **Moses said to Aaron: Say to the entire congregation of the children of Israel: Approach before the Lord, as He has heard your complaints.**

10 **And it was, as Aaron spoke to the entire congregation of the children of Israel, that they turned toward the wilderness, and behold, the glory of the Lord appeared in a cloud.**

Sixth 11 **The Lord spoke to Moses, saying:**
aliya

12 **I have heard the complaints of the children of Israel. Speak to them, saying: In the afternoon you shall eat meat, and in the morning you shall be sated with bread, and you shall know that I am the Lord your God.**

13 Indeed, **it was in the evening that the quails**ᴮ **came up and covered the camp, and in the morning there was a layer of dew around the camp.** In springtime in the desert, formation of a layer of dew around the camp at night is a natural phenomenon.

14 When the morning sun warmed the air, **the layer of dew lifted and behold,** the Israelites found that **on the surface of the wilderness**

Quail

there lay **a fine, grainy substance;** alternatively, this may be translated to mean that it was a fine substance that dissolved easily.²³ It was **fine as the frost on the earth,** but it was clear that this was not frost.

15 **The children of Israel saw it, and they said one to another: What [*man*] is it?**²⁴ Others would translate: It is food,²⁵ or: It is

a portion.²⁶ **As they did not know what it was, Moses said to them: It is the bread that the Lord has given you for eating** throughout your journey.

16 **This is the matter that the Lord has commanded: Gather from it, each man according to his eating; an omer,** a dry measure greater than two liters, **for a person, according to the number of your people, you shall each take for whomever is in his tent.** God will provide every person the same measure.

17 **The children of Israel did so,** and **they gathered** the manna that was scattered on the surface of the ground; **some** diligent or greedy people took **more, and some,** who were slower or less interested, took **less.**

18 But **they measured it with an omer** measure after gathering it in all their different vessels, **and** they found that **he who took more did not have excess, and he who took less did not lack;** all their different vessels held the same measure per person. **Each gathered according to his eating.** Already from the gathering of this food, it became apparent that it was an unnatural substance.

19 **Moses said to them:** The manna collected in the morning is meant to be consumed throughout the day, but no later. Therefore, **no man may leave from it until morning.**

20 **But they did not heed Moses; people left from it until the morning.** As can be found in any large group, there were some who were averse to any authority imposed upon them. Perhaps it was these individuals who refused to heed the instructions of Moses. However, it is possible that people left some of their manna overnight because they were not told that the manna would fall again the next day; they were therefore worried they would have no food. **And it,** the manna, **became infested with worms and reeked; and Moses became angry with them** for disregarding his instructions, and in the process, disgracing the manna, a miraculous gift from God. Here, yet another extraordinary property of the manna was revealed. Normally, worms do not appear in food within a matter of hours, and the process of decomposition takes longer.²⁷

BACKGROUND

16:13 | Quails: The common quail, *Coturnix coturnix,* is a small bird from the pheasant family. Its body is small and round, reaching a length of up to 18 cm and a weight of about 100 g. At the end of the summer this species engages in a mass migration from central and eastern Europe, via the coast of Turkey, to the northern Sinai Peninsula and east-
ern Egypt, traveling about 750 km in a single night. They arrive exhausted from this long flight, and can be gathered easily by hand. The appearance of the quail was not in itself miraculous; the miracle was in the precise timing of this natural phenomenon in a manner that allowed for an immediate fulfillment of a promise to the children of Israel.

DISCUSSION

16:8 | With the Lord giving you meat to eat in the evening: God was not quoted above as promising meat, but Moses would not have introduced such a promise on his own. Rather, God revealed to Moses more than what is reported in the Torah. In general, whenever the Torah states: And the Lord spoke to Moses, the Torah does not record the entirety of God's statement to Moses. Rather, it records only the content intended to be written. God said much to Moses that is not written explicitly in the Torah, some of which was transmitted orally by Moses afterward.

ח וַיֹּאמֶר מֹשֶׁה בְּתֵת יְהוָה לָכֶם בָּעֶרֶב בָּשָׂר לֶאֱכֹל וְלֶחֶם בַּבֹּקֶר לִשְׂבֹּעַ בִּשְׁמֹעַ יְהוָה אֶת־תְּלֻנֹּתֵיכֶם אֲשֶׁר־אַתֶּם מַלִּינִם עָלָיו וְנַחְנוּ מָה לֹא־עָלֵינוּ תְלֻנֹּתֵיכֶם כִּי עַל־יְהוָה: ט וַיֹּאמֶר מֹשֶׁה אֶל־אַהֲרֹן אֱמֹר אֶל־כָּל־עֲדַת בְּנֵי יִשְׂרָאֵל קִרְבוּ לִפְנֵי יְהוָה כִּי שָׁמַע אֵת תְּלֻנֹּתֵיכֶם: י וַיְהִי כְּדַבֵּר אַהֲרֹן אֶל־כָּל־עֲדַת בְּנֵי־יִשְׂרָאֵל וַיִּפְנוּ אֶל־הַמִּדְבָּר וְהִנֵּה כְּבוֹד יְהוָה נִרְאָה בֶּעָנָן:

יא וַיְדַבֵּר יְהוָה אֶל־מֹשֶׁה לֵּאמֹר: שָׁמַעְתִּי אֶת־תְּלוּנֹת בְּנֵי יִשְׂרָאֵל דַּבֵּר אֲלֵהֶם שׁשׁי לֵאמֹר בֵּין הָעַרְבַּיִם תֹּאכְלוּ בָשָׂר וּבַבֹּקֶר תִּשְׂבְּעוּ־לָחֶם וִידַעְתֶּם כִּי אֲנִי יְהוָה אֱלֹהֵיכֶם: יג וַיְהִי בָעֶרֶב וַתַּעַל הַשְּׂלָו וַתְּכַס אֶת־הַמַּחֲנֶה וּבַבֹּקֶר הָיְתָה שִׁכְבַת הַטָּל סָבִיב לַמַּחֲנֶה: יד וַתַּעַל שִׁכְבַת הַטָּל וְהִנֵּה עַל־פְּנֵי הַמִּדְבָּר דַּק מְחֻסְפָּס דַּק כַּכְּפֹר עַל־הָאָרֶץ: טו וַיִּרְאוּ בְנֵי־יִשְׂרָאֵל וַיֹּאמְרוּ אִישׁ אֶל־אָחִיו מָן הוּא כִּי לֹא יָדְעוּ מַה־הוּא וַיֹּאמֶר מֹשֶׁה אֲלֵהֶם הוּא הַלֶּחֶם אֲשֶׁר נָתַן יְהוָה לָכֶם לְאָכְלָה:

טז זֶה הַדָּבָר אֲשֶׁר צִוָּה יְהוָה לִקְטוּ מִמֶּנּוּ אִישׁ לְפִי אָכְלוֹ עֹמֶר לַגֻּלְגֹּלֶת מִסְפַּר נַפְשֹׁתֵיכֶם אִישׁ לַאֲשֶׁר בְּאָהֳלוֹ תִּקָּחוּ: יז וַיַּעֲשׂוּ־כֵן בְּנֵי יִשְׂרָאֵל וַיִּלְקְטוּ הַמַּרְבֶּה וְהַמַּמְעִיט: יח וַיָּמֹדּוּ בָעֹמֶר וְלֹא הֶעְדִּיף הַמַּרְבֶּה וְהַמַּמְעִיט לֹא הֶחְסִיר אִישׁ לְפִי־אָכְלוֹ לָקָטוּ: יט וַיֹּאמֶר מֹשֶׁה אֲלֵהֶם אִישׁ אַל־יוֹתֵר מִמֶּנּוּ עַד־בֹּקֶר: וְלֹא־שָׁמְעוּ אֶל־מֹשֶׁה וַיּוֹתִרוּ אֲנָשִׁים מִמֶּנּוּ עַד־בֹּקֶר וַיָּרֻם תּוֹלָעִים וַיִּבְאַשׁ וַיִּקְצֹף עֲלֵהֶם מֹשֶׁה:

רש"י

ח] בְּשָׂר לֶאֱכֹל. וְלֹא לִשְׂבֹּעַ, לִמְּדָה תוֹרָה דֶּרֶךְ אֶרֶץ שֶׁאֵין אוֹכְלִין בָּשָׂר לָשֹׂבַע. וּמַה רָאָה לְהוֹרִיד לֶחֶם בַּבֹּקֶר וּבָשָׂר בָּעֶרֶב? לְפִי שֶׁהַלֶּחֶם שָׁאֲלוּ כַּהֹגֶן, שֶׁאִי אֶפְשָׁר לוֹ לָאָדָם בְּלֹא לֶחֶם, אֲבָל בָּשָׂר שָׁאֲלוּ שֶׁלֹּא כַהֹגֶן, שֶׁהַרְבֵּה בְּהֵמוֹת הָיוּ לָהֶם, וְעוֹד שֶׁהָיָה אֶפְשָׁר לָהֶם בְּלֹא בָשָׂר, לְפִיכָךְ נָתַן לָהֶם בִּשְׁעַת טֹרַח שֶׁלֹּא כַהֹגֶן. אֵת הָאֲחֵרִים הַשּׁוֹמְעִים אֶתְכֶם חַתֶּם מִתְלוֹנְנִים:

ט] קְרְבוּ. לַמָּקוֹם שֶׁהֶעָנָן יֵרֵד:

יג] הַשְּׂלָו. מִין עוֹף שָׁמֵן מְאֹד: הָיְתָה שִׁכְבַת הַטָּל. הַטַּל שׁוֹכֵב עַל הַמָּן, וּבְמָקוֹם אַחֵר חוֹמֵר: וּבְרֶדֶת הַטַּל וְגוֹ' (במדבר יח, ט), הַטַּל יוֹרֵד עַל הָאָרֶץ וְהַמָּן יוֹרֵד עָלָיו וְחוֹזֵר וְיוֹרֵד טַל עָלָיו, וַהֲרֵי הוּא כְּמֻנָּח בְּקֻפְסָא:

יד] וַתַּעַל שִׁכְבַת הַטָּל. כְּשֶׁהַחַמָּה זוֹרַחַת עוֹלֶה הַטַּל שֶׁעַל הַמָּן לִקְרַאת הַחַמָּה כְּדֶרֶךְ טַל עוֹלֶה לִקְרַאת חַמָּה, אַף

חֵם תְּמַלֵּא שְׁפוֹפֶרֶת שֶׁל בֵּיצָה טַל וְתִסְתֹּם אֶת פִּיהָ וְתַנִּיחֶנָּה בַּחַמָּה, הִיא עוֹלָה מֵאֵלֶיהָ בָּאֲוִיר. וְרַבּוֹתֵינוּ דָּרְשׁוּ שֶׁהַטַּל עוֹלֶה מִן הָאָרֶץ, וְכַעֲלוֹת שִׁכְבַת הַטַּל נִתְגַּלֶּה הַמָּן, וְרָאוּ וְהִנֵּה עַל פְּנֵי הַמִּדְבָּר דָּבָר דַּק, מְחֻסְפָּס, וְחֵן דּוֹמֶה לוֹ בַּמִּקְרָא. יֵשׁ לוֹמַר "מְחֻסְפָּס" לְשׁוֹן "חֲסִיסָה וּדְלוּסְקְמָא" שֶׁבַּלְּשׁוֹן מִשְׁנָה; כְּשֶׁנִּתְגַּלָּה מִשִּׁכְבַת הַטַּל רָאוּ שֶׁהָיָה דָבָר דַּק מְחֻסְפָּס בְּתוֹכוֹ בֵּין שְׁתֵּי שִׁכְבוֹת הַטַּל. וְאוּנְקְלוֹס תִּרְגֵּם: "מְקֻלַּף", לְשׁוֹן "מַחְשׂף הַלָּבָן" (בראשית ל, לז): כַּכְּפֹר. כָּפוֹר – גלויד"א בְּלַעַז, "הַעֲדָה בֶגֶד" (ישעיה כו, ט), "כְּרָבְבַךְ גָּר" (ישעיה כו, ט), וְהוּא מִין נֶגַע שָׁחוֹר לַח כְּדַאֲמְרִינַן גַּבֵּי כִסּוּי הַדָּם: "הַצִּיר וְהַזַּרְנִיךְ" (חולין פח ע"ב), "דָּק כִּגְּלִיד כְּלְגְלַלְחָא עַל הָאָרֶץ, דַּק הָיָה כְּגִּיר וְשׁוֹכֵב מְגֻלָּד כְּקֶרַח עַל הָאָרֶץ, וְכֵן פֵּרוּשׁוֹ: דַּק כַּכְּפֹר, שָׁטוּחַ קָלוּשׁ וּמְחֻבָּר כְּגָּלִיד. "דַּק" טינוא"ש בְּלַעַז, שֶׁהָיָה מְגֻלָּד גֶּלֶד דַּק מִלְמַעְלָה. וְכַגִּיר" שֶׁתַּרְגֵּם אוּנְקְלוֹס תּוֹסֶפֶת הוּא עַל לְשׁוֹן הָעִבְרִי וְאֵין לוֹ תֵּבָה בַּמִּקְרָא:

טו] מָן הוּא. הֲכָנַת מָזוֹן הוּא, כְּמוֹ: "וַיְמַן לָהֶם הַמֶּלֶךְ" (דניאל א, ה): כִּי לֹא יָדְעוּ מַה הוּא. שֶׁיִּקְרָאוּהוּ בִּשְׁמוֹ:

טז] עֹמֶר. שֵׁם מִדָּה: מִסְפַּר נַפְשֹׁתֵיכֶם. כְּפִי מִנְיַן נְפָשׁוֹת שֶׁיֵּשׁ לְאִישׁ בְּאָהֳלוֹ תִּקָּחוּ עֹמֶר לְכָל גֻּלְגֹּלֶת:

יז] הַמַּרְבֶּה וְהַמַּמְעִיט. יֵשׁ שֶׁלָּקְטוּ מְעַט, וּכְשֶׁבָּאוּ לְבֵיתָם מָדְדוּ בְּעֹמֶר אִישׁ אִישׁ מַה שֶּׁלָּקְטוּ, וּמָצְאוּ שֶׁהַמַּרְבֶּה לִלְקֹט לֹא הֶעְדִּיף עַל עֹמֶר לַגֻּלְגֹּלֶת אֲשֶׁר בְּאָהֳלוֹ, וְהַמַּמְעִיט לִלְקֹט לֹא מָצָא חָסֵר מֵעֹמֶר לַגֻּלְגֹּלֶת, וְזֶהוּ נֵס גָּדוֹל שֶׁנַּעֲשָׂה בּוֹ:

כ] וַיּוֹתִרוּ אֲנָשִׁים. דָּתָן וַאֲבִירָם: וַיָּרֻם תּוֹלָעִים. לְשׁוֹן רִמָּה: וַיִּבְאַשׁ. הֲרֵי זֶה מִקְרָא הָסוּף, שֶׁבַּתְּחִלָּה הִבְאִישׁ וּלְבַסּוֹף הִתְלִיעַ, כָּעִנְיָן שֶׁנֶּאֱמַר: "וְלֹא הִבְאִישׁ וְרִמָּה לֹא הָיְתָה בּוֹ" (להלן פסוק כד), וְכֵן דֶּרֶךְ כָּל הַמַּתְלִיעִים:

21 **They gathered it each morning,** just as the dew evaporated, **each** man **according to his eating,** as much as he needed to eat,[28] or according to the size of his household;[29] **and then the sun grew hot and it melted.**

22 **It was on the sixth day that they gathered double the bread, two omer for each one.** As always, the amount they gathered was independent, miraculously, of their efforts. On the sixth day, everyone found they had gathered two omers per person, rather than one. **And all the princes,** leaders, **of the congregation came and told Moses** about this anomaly.

23 **He said to them: It is what the Lord said:**[D] **Tomorrow is a day of rest, a holy Sabbath to the Lord.** Tomorrow is the holy day of which we spoke at Mara,[30] whose laws were not explained until now. Perhaps this is the first time he used the word Sabbath. **That which you would bake, bake, and that which you would cook, cook** today, on the sixth day; **and all that remains, set aside for safekeeping until morning.** You cannot eat the extra food today; set it aside for tomorrow.

24 **They set it aside until the morning, as Moses had commanded; and,** unlike what had occurred on the previous days, **it,** the manna gathered on the sixth day, **did not reek** on the seventh, **and there were no maggots in it.**

25 **Moses said: Eat it today, for today is** a **Sabbath of the Lord; today you will not find it in the field.** God Himself rests today, as it were, and does not produce manna.

26 This will be the arrangement from now on: **Six days you shall gather it, and on the seventh day it is Sabbath; there will be none on it.** No manna will fall on the seventh day.

27 Indeed, **it was on the seventh day,** and **some of the people** who did not believe Moses and wanted to see for themselves, or who were greedy, **went out to gather and they did not find** any manna.

28 **The Lord said to Moses: Until when do you** continue to **refuse to observe My commandments and My laws?** I gave very few restrictions, but already some people are beginning to flout them.

29 **See that the Lord has given you the Sabbath;**[D] **therefore, He gives you on the sixth day bread for two days. Remain each man where he is; no man shall leave his place on the seventh day.**[D]

30 The majority of **the people**[31] **rested on the seventh day.**

31 **The house of Israel called it manna,** after their initial response to it (above, verse 15). For want of another name, this word endured. **And** this is a description of the manna: **It was like** a **white coriander seed,** meaning that it was perfectly round, like coriander, but white, unlike coriander, which is brown; **and its** natural **taste was like a cake with honey.**

Coriander seeds

32 The following passage was actually stated at a later point; however, it is brought here since it relates to the manna:[32] **Moses said: This is the matter that the Lord has commanded: An omerful from it,** the manna, **is** to be kept **for safekeeping for your generations, so that they,** your descendants, **will see the bread that I fed you in the wilderness when I took you out of the land of Egypt.** It shall be kept as a reminder of these events.

33 **Moses said to Aaron: Take one jar and put there an omerful of manna and set it before the Lord for safekeeping for your generations.**

DISCUSSION

16:23 | **It is what the Lord said:** Some commentaries explain, as per the *Mekhilta*, that this refers to God's command that they should gather a double portion on the sixth day (16:5), and that Moses did not relay this statement to the Israelites until now (see Rashi; Rashbam).

16:29 | **See that the Lord has given you the Sabbath:** Although the Sabbath is described in the story of Creation (Genesis 2), the Torah relates there that only God Himself rested. The Torah makes no explicit mention of the Sabbath as a part of the Israelite consciousness until now. Rabbinic tradition teaches that the patriarchs were familiar with the Sabbath and observed it (*Yoma* 28b; *Kiddushin* 82a), but it is unclear in what manner. The Sages also mention observance of this holy day in Egypt (*Shemot Rabba* 1:28), even though some details pertaining to it were given only at Mara (see *Sanhedrin* 56b). Here, as the Torah tells the story of God's gift of manna to the Israelites, the Sabbath is mentioned for the first time as being a divine gift to Israel.

No man shall leave his place on the seventh day: This verse is accepted as the first commandment with regard to the laws of the Sabbath that would apply for all time. It is the source for the prohibition of traveling beyond a certain city limit on the Sabbath (see *Eiruvin* 17b, 51b). It would seem that when the verse refers to one's place, it does not mean the small space in which an individual stands or sits, but the area in which one generally conducts himself on a daily basis. God commands the Israelites not to travel from this area on the Sabbath, as the Sabbath is to be a day on which one turns inward and rests, rather than journeying far away.

כא וַיִּלְקְטוּ אֹתוֹ בַּבֹּקֶר בַּבֹּקֶר אִישׁ כְּפִי אָכְלוֹ וְחַם הַשֶּׁמֶשׁ וְנָמָס: וַיְהִי ׀ בַּיּוֹם הַשִּׁשִּׁי

לָקְטוּ לֶחֶם מִשְׁנֶה שְׁנֵי הָעֹמֶר לָאֶחָד וַיָּבֹאוּ כָּל־נְשִׂיאֵי הָעֵדָה וַיַּגִּידוּ לְמֹשֶׁה:

כג וַיֹּאמֶר אֲלֵהֶם הוּא אֲשֶׁר דִּבֶּר יְהוָה שַׁבָּתוֹן שַׁבַּת־קֹדֶשׁ לַיהוָה מָחָר אֵת אֲשֶׁר־

תֹּאפוּ אֵפוּ וְאֵת אֲשֶׁר־תְּבַשְּׁלוּ בַּשֵּׁלוּ וְאֵת כָּל־הָעֹדֵף הַנִּיחוּ לָכֶם לְמִשְׁמֶרֶת

כד עַד־הַבֹּקֶר: וַיַּנִּיחוּ אֹתוֹ עַד־הַבֹּקֶר כַּאֲשֶׁר צִוָּה מֹשֶׁה וְלֹא הִבְאִישׁ וְרִמָּה לֹא־

כה הָיְתָה־בּוֹ: וַיֹּאמֶר מֹשֶׁה אִכְלֻהוּ הַיּוֹם כִּי־שַׁבָּת הַיּוֹם לַיהוָה הַיּוֹם לֹא תִמְצָאֻהוּ

כו בַּשָּׂדֶה: שֵׁשֶׁת יָמִים תִּלְקְטֻהוּ וּבַיּוֹם הַשְּׁבִיעִי שַׁבָּת לֹא יִהְיֶה־בּוֹ: וַיְהִי בַּיּוֹם

כז הַשְּׁבִיעִי יָצְאוּ מִן־הָעָם לִלְקֹט וְלֹא מָצָאוּ: וַיֹּאמֶר יְהוָה אֶל־מֹשֶׁה יג

כח עַד־אָנָה מֵאַנְתֶּם לִשְׁמֹר מִצְוֹתַי וְתוֹרֹתָי: רְאוּ כִּי־יְהוָה נָתַן לָכֶם הַשַּׁבָּת עַל־כֵּן

כט הוּא נֹתֵן לָכֶם בַּיּוֹם הַשִּׁשִּׁי לֶחֶם יוֹמָיִם שְׁבוּ ׀ אִישׁ תַּחְתָּיו אַל־יֵצֵא אִישׁ מִמְּקֹמוֹ

ל בַּיּוֹם הַשְּׁבִיעִי: וַיִּשְׁבְּתוּ הָעָם בַּיּוֹם הַשְּׁבִעִי: וַיִּקְרְאוּ בֵית־יִשְׂרָאֵל אֶת־שְׁמוֹ מָן

לא וְהוּא כְּזֶרַע גַּד לָבָן וְטַעְמוֹ כְּצַפִּיחִת בִּדְבָשׁ: וַיֹּאמֶר מֹשֶׁה זֶה הַדָּבָר אֲשֶׁר צִוָּה

לב יְהוָה מְלֹא הָעֹמֶר מִמֶּנּוּ לְמִשְׁמֶרֶת לְדֹרֹתֵיכֶם לְמַעַן ׀ יִרְאוּ אֶת־הַלֶּחֶם אֲשֶׁר

לג הֶאֱכַלְתִּי אֶתְכֶם בַּמִּדְבָּר בְּהוֹצִיאִי אֶתְכֶם מֵאֶרֶץ מִצְרָיִם: וַיֹּאמֶר מֹשֶׁה אֶל־אַהֲרֹן

קַח צִנְצֶנֶת אַחַת וְתֶן־שָׁמָּה מְלֹא־הָעֹמֶר מָן וְהַנַּח אֹתוֹ לִפְנֵי יְהוָה לְמִשְׁמֶרֶת

רש״י

כא| וְחַם הַשֶּׁמֶשׁ וְנָמָס. הַנִּשְׁאָר בַּשָּׂדֶה נַעֲשֶׂה נְחָלִים וְשׁוֹתִין מִמֶּנּוּ חַיָּלִים וּגְדָיִים, וְאֻמּוֹת הָעוֹלָם צָדִין מֵהֶם וְטוֹעֲמִים בָּהֶם טַעַם מָן וְיוֹדְעִים מַה שִּׁבְחָן שֶׁל יִשְׂרָאֵל. "וְחַם" (אונקלוס), לְשׁוֹן פּוֹשְׁרִין, עַל יְדֵי הַשֶּׁמֶשׁ מִתְחַמֵּם וּמַפְשִׁיר: וְנָמָס. דִּסְטמַפ״רי. וְהִנְמְעוּ בַּסַּנְהֶדְרִין בְּסוֹף אַרְבַּע מִיתוֹת (דף סז ע״ב):

כב| לָקְטוּ לֶחֶם מִשְׁנֶה. כְּשֶׁמָּדְדוּ אֶת לִקְטָתָם בְּאָהֳלֵיהֶם מָצְאוּ כִפְלַיִם, "שְׁנֵי הָעֹמֶר לָאֶחָד". וּמִדְרַשׁ אַגָּדָה, "לֶחֶם מִשְׁנֶה" מְשֻׁנֶּה, אוֹתוֹ הַיּוֹם נִשְׁתַּנָּה לְשֶׁבַח בְּרֵיחוֹ וְטַעֲמוֹ: וַיַּגִּידוּ לְמֹשֶׁה. שָׁאֲלוּהוּ מַה הַיּוֹם מִיּוֹמַיִם? וּמִכָּאן יֵשׁ לִלְמֹד שֶׁעֲדַיִן לֹא הִגִּיד לָהֶם מֹשֶׁה פָּרָשַׁת שַׁבָּת שֶׁנִּצְטַוָּה לוֹמַר לָהֶם: "וְהָיָה בַּיּוֹם הַשִּׁשִּׁי וְהֵכִינוּ" וְגו' (לעיל פסוק ה), עַד שֶׁשָּׁאֲלוּ אֶת זֹאת. אָמַר לָהֶם: "הוּא אֲשֶׁר דִּבֶּר ה'" (בפסוק הבא), שֶׁנִּצְטַוֵּיתִי לוֹמַר לָכֶם. וּלְכָךְ עָנְשׁוֹ הַכָּתוּב, שֶׁאָמַר לוֹ: "עַד אָנָה מֵאַנְתֶּם" (להלן פסוק כח) וְלֹא הוֹצִיאוֹ מִן הַכְּלָל:

כג| אֵת אֲשֶׁר תֹּאפוּ אֵפוּ. מַה שֶּׁאַתֶּם רוֹצִים לֶאֱפוֹת בַּתַּנּוּר,

"תֹּאפוּ" הַיּוֹם הַכֹּל לִשְׁנֵי יָמִים. וּמַה שֶּׁאַתֶּם צְרִיכִים לְבַשֵּׁל מִמֶּנּוּ בַּמַּיִם, "בַּשֵּׁלוּ" הַיּוֹם. לְשׁוֹן חֲיָיא נוֹפֵל בְּלָשׁוֹן וּלְשׁוֹן בִּשּׁוּל בְּתַבְשִׁיל: לְמִשְׁמֶרֶת. לִגְנִיזָה:

כה| וַיֹּאמֶר מֹשֶׁה אִכְלֻהוּ הַיּוֹם. שַׁחֲרִית שֶׁהָיָה רְגִילִים לָצֵאת וְלִלְקֹט, בָּאוּ לִשְׁאֹל הֵם נֵצֵא אִם לָאו, אָמַר לָהֶם: אֶת שֶׁבְּיֶדְכֶם אִכְלוּ. לָעֶרֶב חָזְרוּ לִפְנָיו: מַהוּ לָצֵאת? אָמַר לָהֶם: "שַׁבָּת הַיּוֹם". רָאָה אוֹתָם דּוֹאֲגִים שֶׁמָּא פָּסַק הַמָּן וְלֹא יֵרֵד עוֹד, אָמַר לָהֶם: "הַיּוֹם לֹא תִמְצָאֻהוּ". מַה תַּלְמוּד לוֹמַר "הַיּוֹם"? הַיּוֹם לֹא תִמְצָאֻהוּ אֲבָל מָחָר תִּמְצָאֻהוּ:

כו| וּבַיּוֹם הַשְּׁבִיעִי שַׁבָּת. "שַׁבָּת" הוּא, "לֹא יִהְיֶה־בּוֹ". וְלֹא בָא הַכָּתוּב אֶלָּא לְרַבּוֹת יוֹם הַכִּפּוּרִים וְיָמִים טוֹבִים:

כח| עַד אָנָה מֵאַנְתֶּם. מָשָׁל הֶדְיוֹט הוּא, בַּהֲדֵי הוּצָא לָקֵי כַּרְבָּא, עַל יְדֵי הָרְשָׁעִים מִתְגַּנִּין הַכְּשֵׁרִים:

כט| רְאוּ. בְּעֵינֵיכֶם כִּי ה' בִּכְבוֹדוֹ מַזְהִיר אֶתְכֶם עַל הַשַּׁבָּת, שֶׁהֲרֵי נֵס נַעֲשֶׂה בְּכָל עֶרֶב שַׁבָּת לָתֵת לָכֶם לֶחֶם יוֹמָיִם: שְׁבוּ אִישׁ תַּחְתָּיו. מִכָּאן סָמְכוּ חֲכָמִים אַרְבַּע אַמּוֹת לַיּוֹצֵא

חוּץ לַתְּחוּם: אַל יֵצֵא אִישׁ מִמְּקֹמוֹ. אֵלּוּ אַלְפַּיִם אַמָּה, וְלֹא בִמְפֹרָשׁ, שֶׁאֵין תְּחוּמִין אֶלָּא מִדִּבְרֵי סוֹפְרִים, וְעִקָּרוֹ שֶׁל מִקְרָא עַל לוֹקְטֵי הַמָּן נֶאֱמַר:

לא| וְהוּא כְּזֶרַע גַּד. עֵשֶׂב שֶׁשְּׁמוֹ אליי״נדרי, וְזֶרַע שֶׁלּוֹ עָגֹל וְאֵינוֹ לָבָן, וְהַמָּן הָיָה לָבָן, וְאֵינוֹ נִמְשָׁל לַגַּד אֶלָּא לְעִנְיַן הָעִגּוּל, "כְּזֶרַע גַּד" הָיָה וְהוּא "לָבָן": כְּצַפִּיחִת. בְּצֵק שֶׁמְּטַגְּנִין אוֹתוֹ בִּדְבַשׁ, וְקוֹרִין לוֹ "אסקריטין" בְּלָשׁוֹן מִשְׁנָה (חלה פ״א, ד, פסחים לז ע״א), וְהוּא תַרְגּוּם שֶׁל אֻנְקְלוֹס:

לב| לְמִשְׁמֶרֶת. לִגְנִיזָה: לְדֹרֹתֵיכֶם. בִּימֵי יִרְמְיָהוּ, כְּשֶׁהָיָה יִרְמְיָהוּ מוֹכִיחָם: לָמָּה אֵין אַתֶּם עוֹסְקִים בַּתּוֹרָה? וְהֵם אוֹמְרִים: נַנִּיחַ מְלַאכְתֵּנוּ וְנַעֲסֹק בַּתּוֹרָה, מֵהֵיכָן נִתְפַּרְנֵס? הוֹצִיא לָהֶם צִנְצֶנֶת הַמָּן, אָמַר לָהֶם: "הֲדוֹר אַתֶּם רְאוּ דְבַר ה'" (ירמיה ב, לא), "שִׁמְעוּ" לֹא נֶאֱמַר אֶלָּא "רְאוּ", בָּזֶה נִתְפַּרְנְסוּ אֲבוֹתֵיכֶם, הַרְבֵּה שְׁלוּחִין יֵשׁ לוֹ לַמָּקוֹם לְהָכִין מָזוֹן לִירֵאָיו:

לג| צִנְצֶנֶת. צְלוֹחִית שֶׁל חֶרֶס, כְּתַרְגּוּמוֹ: וְהַנַּח אֹתוֹ לִפְנֵי

34 **As the Lord had commanded Moses** to place the manna before the Lord, **Aaron set it before** the Ark of **the Testimony**[D] in the Tabernacle, **for safekeeping,** as a reminder of the miracles that God performed for the Israelites in the wilderness.

35 **The children of Israel ate the manna** for **forty years, until they came to an inhabited land; they ate the manna until**

they came to the border of the land of Canaan. When Joshua eventually led the Israelites across the Jordan River, the manna ceased to fall.

36 The Torah notes: **And the omer is one-tenth of an ephah,**[B] another dry measure.

Masa and Meriva

EXODUS 17:1–7

Not a long time passed since the first appearance of the manna before the Israelites became accustomed to it. Soon they took the miraculous provision of food for granted, to the point that they began to complain again, despite the sustenance of heavenly bread provided them on a daily basis.

17 **1** **The entire congregation of the children of Israel traveled**
Seventh **from the wilderness of Tzin on their travels, at the word of**
aliya **the Lord,** by the guidance of the pillar of cloud; **they encamped in Refidim,**[B] and here again, **there was no water for the people to drink.**

2 **The people quarreled with Moses and said: Give us water that we may drink. Moses said to them: Why do you quarrel with me?** You know that these matters are not in my control. And furthermore, **why do you try the Lord,** rather than trusting Him? In the meantime, there is no need to complain, for perhaps tomorrow we will be commanded to travel elsewhere.

3 They remained there, and the request turned into a complaint. **The people thirsted there for water, and the people complained against Moses and said: Why did you bring us up from Egypt, to kill me and my children and my livestock with thirst?** Their language was becoming belligerent and confrontational.

4 **Moses cried out to the Lord, saying: What shall I do for this people? A moment more and they will stone me.** Moses was

afraid that the complaints would increase in intensity until they led to a riot.

5 **The Lord said to Moses: Pass before the people** ceremoniously, **and take with you some of the elders of Israel, and take in your hand your staff with which you struck the Nile,**[D] **and go.** This procession of Moses with his staff and the elders was meant to remind everyone that he was acting as the messenger of God.

6 **Behold, I am standing before you there upon the rock at Horev,** Mount Sinai; you will feel My presence there; and **you shall strike the rock, and** when you do so **water will emerge from it, and the people will drink. Moses did so before the eyes of the elders of Israel.** The elders saw with their own eyes the water flow from the rock as Moses struck it.

7 Pursuant to this, **he called the place Masa,** trial, and **Meriva,** quarrel, **due to the quarrel of the children of Israel, and due to their trying of the Lord, saying: Is the Lord among us, or not?** At first, the Israelites expressed doubts as to whether God cared for them, as He sent them to a place without water. These doubts then evolved into a quarrel with Moses.

DISCUSSION

16:34| Aaron set it before the Ark of the Testimony: Clearly, this must have occurred at least a year after the first appearance of the manna, since at the point that the manna was first given, the Tabernacle had not yet been erected, nor had the ark been built. God's command to Moses to have the manna placed before the Ark of the Testimony would therefore have been unintelligible if given then.

The falling of manna from heaven was exceptionally miraculous. Whereas all the other wonders that God performed during and after the exodus were short-lived, the manna fell every morning for years with no natural explanation. God provided His people with ready food that required no labor to grow. The Sages relate that the manna was a perfectly nutritious food that produced no waste by-products (*Sifrei; Yoma* 75b; Rashi, Numbers 21:5).

17:5| And take in your hand your staff with which you struck the Nile: This is the staff with which Moses and Aaron turned the waters of Egypt to blood, the dust of Egypt to lice, and the Red Sea to dry land. It would now produce water from a rock to quench the people's thirst.

לד לְדֹרֹתֵיכֶם: כַּאֲשֶׁר צִוָּה יהוה אֶל־מֹשֶׁה וַיַּנִּיחֵהוּ אַהֲרֹן לִפְנֵי הָעֵדֻת לְמִשְׁמָרֶת:
לה וּבְנֵי יִשְׂרָאֵל אָכְלוּ אֶת־הַמָּן אַרְבָּעִים שָׁנָה עַד־בֹּאָם אֶל־אֶרֶץ נוֹשָׁבֶת אֶת־הַמָּן
לו אָכְלוּ עַד־בֹּאָם אֶל־קְצֵה אֶרֶץ כְּנָעַן: וְהָעֹמֶר עֲשִׂרִית הָאֵיפָה הוּא:
יז א וַיִּסְעוּ כָּל־עֲדַת בְּנֵי־יִשְׂרָאֵל מִמִּדְבַּר־סִין לְמַסְעֵיהֶם עַל־פִּי יהוה וַיַּחֲנוּ בִּרְפִידִים שביעי
ב וְאֵין מַיִם לִשְׁתֹּת הָעָם: וַיָּרֶב הָעָם עִם־מֹשֶׁה וַיֹּאמְרוּ תְּנוּ־לָנוּ מַיִם וְנִשְׁתֶּה וַיֹּאמֶר
ג לָהֶם מֹשֶׁה מַה־תְּרִיבוּן עִמָּדִי מַה־תְּנַסּוּן אֶת־יהוה: וַיִּצְמָא שָׁם הָעָם לַמַּיִם וַיָּלֶן
הָעָם עַל־מֹשֶׁה וַיֹּאמֶר לָמָּה זֶּה הֶעֱלִיתָנוּ מִמִּצְרַיִם לְהָמִית אֹתִי וְאֶת־בָּנַי וְאֶת־
ד מִקְנַי בַּצָּמָא: וַיִּצְעַק מֹשֶׁה אֶל־יהוה לֵאמֹר מָה אֶעֱשֶׂה לָעָם הַזֶּה עוֹד מְעַט
ה וּסְקָלֻנִי: וַיֹּאמֶר יהוה אֶל־מֹשֶׁה עֲבֹר לִפְנֵי הָעָם וְקַח אִתְּךָ מִזִּקְנֵי יִשְׂרָאֵל וּמַטְּךָ
ו אֲשֶׁר הִכִּיתָ בּוֹ אֶת־הַיְאֹר קַח בְּיָדְךָ וְהָלָכְתָּ: הִנְנִי עֹמֵד לְפָנֶיךָ שָּׁם | עַל־הַצּוּר
בְּחֹרֵב וְהִכִּיתָ בַצּוּר וְיָצְאוּ מִמֶּנּוּ מַיִם וְשָׁתָה הָעָם וַיַּעַשׂ כֵּן מֹשֶׁה לְעֵינֵי זִקְנֵי
ז יִשְׂרָאֵל: וַיִּקְרָא שֵׁם הַמָּקוֹם מַסָּה וּמְרִיבָה עַל־רִיב | בְּנֵי יִשְׂרָאֵל וְעַל נַסֹּתָם
אֶת־יהוה לֵאמֹר הֲיֵשׁ יהוה בְּקִרְבֵּנוּ אִם־אָיִן:

רש"י

ה'. לִפְנֵי הָאָרוֹן. וְלֹא נֶאֱמַר מִקְרָא זֶה עַד שֶׁנִּבְנָה אֹהֶל מוֹעֵד, אֶלָּא שֶׁנִּכְתַּב כָּאן בְּפָרָשַׁת הַמָּן:

לה| **אַרְבָּעִים שָׁנָה.** וַהֲלֹא חָסֵר שְׁלֹשִׁים יוֹם, שֶׁהֲרֵי בַּחֲמִשָּׁה עָשָׂר בְּאִיָּר יָרַד לָהֶם הַמָּן תְּחִלָּה וּבַחֲמִשָּׁה עָשָׂר בְּנִיסָן פָּסַק, שֶׁנֶּאֱמַר: "וַיִּשְׁבֹּת הַמָּן מִמָּחֳרָת" (יהושע ה, יב)? אֶלָּא מַגִּיד שֶׁהָעוּגוֹת שֶׁהוֹצִיאוּ יִשְׂרָאֵל מִמִּצְרַיִם טָעֲמוּ בָּהֶם טַעַם מָן: **אֶל אֶרֶץ נוֹשָׁבֶת.** לְאַחַר שֶׁעָבְרוּ אֶת הַיַּרְדֵּן: **אֶל קְצֵה אֶרֶץ כְּנָעַן.** בִּתְחִלַּת הַגְּבוּל קֹדֶם שֶׁעָבְרוּ אֶת הַיַּרְדֵּן, וְהֵם עַרְבוֹת מוֹאָב. נִמְצְאוּ מַכְחִישִׁין זֶה אֶת זֶה! אֶלָּא בְּעַרְבוֹת מוֹאָב כְּשֶׁמֵּת מֹשֶׁה בְּשִׁבְעָה בַּאֲדָר פָּסַק הַמָּן מִלֵּרֵד, וְנִסְתַּפְּקוּ מִמָּן שֶׁלָּקְטוּ בּוֹ בַּיּוֹם עַד שֶׁהִקְרִיבוּ הָעֹמֶר בְּשִׁשָּׁה עָשָׂר בְּנִיסָן, שֶׁנֶּאֱמַר: "וַיֹּאכְלוּ מֵעֲבוּר הָאָרֶץ מִמָּחֳרַת הַפֶּסַח" (יהושע ה, יא):

לו| **עֲשִׂרִית הָאֵיפָה.** הָאֵיפָה שָׁלֹשׁ סְאִין, וְהַסְּאָה שֵׁשֶׁת קַבִּין, וְהַקַּב אַרְבָּעָה לֻגִּין, וְהַלֹּג שֵׁשׁ בֵּיצִים; נִמְצָא עֲשִׂירִית הָאֵיפָה אַרְבָּעִים וְשָׁלֹשׁ בֵּיצִים וְחֹמֶשׁ בֵּיצָה, וְהוּא שִׁעוּר לַחַלָּה וְלַמְּנָחוֹת:

פרק יז

ב| **מַה תְּנַסּוּן.** לוֹמַר, הֲיוּכַל לָתֵת מַיִם בְּאֶרֶץ צִיָּה:

ד| **עוֹד מְעַט.** אִם אַמְתִּין "עוֹד מְעַט, וּסְקָלֻנִי":

ה| **עֲבֹר לִפְנֵי הָעָם.** וּרְאֵה אִם יִסְקְלוּךָ, לָמָּה הוֹצֵאתָ לַעַז עַל בָּנַי? **וְקַח אִתְּךָ מִזִּקְנֵי יִשְׂרָאֵל.** לְעֵדוּת, שֶׁיִּרְאוּ שֶׁעַל יָדְךָ הַמַּיִם יוֹצְאִים מִן הַצּוּר, וְלֹא יֹאמְרוּ: מַעְיָנוֹת הָיוּ שָׁם מִימֵי קֶדֶם: **וּמַטְּךָ אֲשֶׁר הִכִּיתָ בּוֹ אֶת הַיְאֹר.** מַה תַּלְמוּד לוֹמַר: "אֲשֶׁר הִכִּיתָ בּוֹ אֶת הַיְאֹר"? אֶלָּא שֶׁהָיוּ יִשְׂרָאֵל אוֹמְרִים עַל הַמַּטֶּה שֶׁאֵינוֹ מוּכָן אֶלָּא לְפֻרְעָנוּת, בּוֹ לָקָה פַּרְעֹה וּמִצְרַיִם כַּמָּה מַכּוֹת בְּמִצְרַיִם וְעַל הַיָּם, לְכָךְ נֶאֱמַר: "אֲשֶׁר הִכִּיתָ בּוֹ אֶת הַיְאֹר" וְהֵם אוֹמְרִים עָלָיו שֶׁאֵינוֹ אֶלָּא לְפֻרְעָנוּת, יִרְאוּ עַתָּה שֶׁאַף לְטוֹבָה הוּא מוּכָן:

ו| **וְהִכִּיתָ בַצּוּר.** 'עַל הַצּוּר' לֹא נֶאֱמַר אֶלָּא "בַּצּוּר", מִכָּאן שֶׁהַמַּטֶּה הָיָה שֶׁל מִין דָּבָר חָזָק וּשְׁמוֹ סַנְפִּירִינוֹן, וְהַצּוּר נִבְקַע מִפָּנָיו:

BACKGROUND

16:36| **Ephah:** The ephah is an ancient measure of volume. According to the most widely accepted view, it is equivalent to approximately 24 L. Scholars speculate that the name derives from the Egyptian word *afat*, which means counting.

17:1| **Refidim:** This is a location close to Mount Sinai, as indicated by the verse: "They traveled from Refidim and came to the wilderness of Sinai" (19:2). Just as there are numerous opinions as to the identification of Mount Sinai, the same is true of Refidim. Some identify it with the entrance of Wadi Sudr, east of Ein Moussa in Wadi Feiran; some identify it with Ein Karkom, about 7 km north of Mount Karkom, or with Wadi Raphid, southeast of El Arish.

The War with Amalek

EXODUS 17:8–16

Although God provided miraculous food from heaven for Israel every day, the Israelites doubted that He would provide them with water as well. In their thirst, they even cast doubt as to whether God was among them at all. Perhaps it was this spiritual weakness that brought the confrontation with Amalek upon them.

8 **Amalek**[B] **came** from its territory, **and made war with Israel**[D] **in Refidim,** in the wilderness. There is no indication that Amalek was a particularly large or strong nation, yet it nevertheless had the courage to leave its own territory and attack the Israelites, who were already great in number. It seems that Amalek dared attack the Israelites because the Israelites had not yet organized themselves militarily into effective fighting units, making them vulnerable.[33]

9 **Moses said to Joshua,**[D] his servant: **Choose men for us** who are capable of fighting, as most of the people are simple slaves with no combat experience, **and go out and fight with Amalek; tomorrow,** during the battle, **I will be standing on top of the hill and the staff of God will be in my hand.** It will symbolize God's support for you.

10 **Joshua did as Moses said to him and fought with Amalek; and Moses, Aaron** his brother, **and Hur**[D] **ascended to the top of the hill.**

11 So **it was that when Moses raised his hand, Israel prevailed** in battle; **and when he** tired and **lowered his hand, Amalek prevailed.**

12 **Moses' hands,**[D] held up continuously, perhaps holding the staff,[34] **were heavy** as the battle went on; **and they took a stone**

and they placed it beneath him, and he sat on it, and Aaron and Hur supported his hands without having to lift their own, as Moses was seated, **one of them on this side, and the other on that side, and his hands were steady,**[35] or raised in prayer,[36] **until the setting of the sun.**

13 **Joshua defeated Amalek and its people by sword.**

14 **The Lord said to Moses: Write** down **this** episode of Amalek *Maftir* **as a remembrance** for all time **in the book, and set it in the ears of Joshua**[D] as a lesson for the future: **For** I promise that **I will expunge the memory of Amalek from under the heavens.** Because of its intrinsic hatred for Israel, there can be no co-existence with Amalek. It will fight Israel as long as it survives.

15 **Moses built an altar** out of gratitude to God, **and he called it: The Lord is my standard.**[D]

16 **He said: Because a hand is on the throne of the Lord.** Raising one's hand expresses an oath,[37] as does holding a sacred object.[38] The image of a hand gripping God's throne, which symbolizes His kingship, signifies that God vows on His very kingship that **the Lord's war with Amalek is from generation to generation,** until all descendants of Amalek have been wiped out.

DISCUSSION

17:8 | Amalek came and made war with Israel: There was no clear motive behind Amalek's attack on the Israelites. The Egyptians' hostility toward Israel had stemmed from fear of them, and this was also the case for the Canaanite nations that the Israelites would conquer and dispossess. Amalek, on the other hand, did not inhabit Canaan, nor did they live along the assumed route of the Israelites. They did not attack, therefore, as a preemptive defensive measure. They may only have been interested in looting the Israelites' property, but this too is unlikely, as they had no way of knowing what possessions the people were carrying with them.

Amalek did not intend to wipe out the Israelites, as there were too many of them, but merely to damage them or drive them away. They acted out of pointless, arbitrary hatred. This is why the memory of Amalek in the Jewish consciousness symbolizes hostility and opposition to the Jews as such. They are the archetype for anti-Semitism throughout the ages, which, even if it sometimes finds specific claims, real or

imagined, against the Jews, is in truth rooted in baseless hatred of Israel itself.

The tribes of Amalek seem to have lived in several places. Some were in the Negev (see Numbers 13:29, 14:45). Those that came to wage war against Israel in the wilderness came from Mount Se'ir, i.e., Edom (*Mekhilta*; see Genesis 14:7). The Midrash cites one opinion that states that the Amalekites had left their ancestral homeland of Se'ir and settled on the borders of Canaan, bringing them into contact with the Israelites (see *Bemidbar Rabba* 16:18).

17:9 | Joshua: Joshua has not been mentioned until now. It seems he was a young man from a distinguished family. His grandfather was the prince of the tribe of Ephraim (see I Chronicles 7:26–27). Further on in Exodus, Joshua will become Moses' most loyal servant (33:11). The verse makes no mention of Joshua's previous military experience. Perhaps Moses simply felt that Joshua's personality was appropriate for military command, and so he chose him to lead the people in their first battle.

17:10 | Hur: Hur is mentioned later, also in connection with Aaron (24:14). According to tradition, Hur was the son of Miriam (see *Sota* 11b–12a, and Rashi ad loc.). This theory is supported by the text here, since it was customary in biblical times that a chief or leader would surround himself primarily with close confidants, and even family. It is therefore expected that Moses would stand next to his brother and nephew.

17:12 | Moses' hands: According to the Mishna (*Rosh HaShana* 3:8), Moses' hands themselves did not make any difference in the outcome of the battle, but rather served as inspiration for the people. Moses himself possibly never participated in any battle until the war against Sihon and Og years later (see *Devarim Rabba* 1:24; *Targum Yonatan*, Numbers 21:34). At this point, however, he stood on the hill, while Joshua directed the battle. Even when Moses was not on the front lines, his heart was with the people, and his hands served as a powerful symbol.

17:14 | Write this as a remembrance in the book and set it in the ears of Joshua: This is ←•

ח ט וַיָּבֹא עֲמָלֵק וַיִּלָּחֶם עִם־יִשְׂרָאֵל בִּרְפִידִם: וַיֹּאמֶר מֹשֶׁה אֶל־יְהוֹשֻׁעַ בְּחַר־לָנוּ
אֲנָשִׁים וְצֵא הִלָּחֵם בַּעֲמָלֵק מָחָר אָנֹכִי נִצָּב עַל־רֹאשׁ הַגִּבְעָה וּמַטֵּה הָאֱלֹהִים
י בְּיָדִי: וַיַּעַשׂ יְהוֹשֻׁעַ כַּאֲשֶׁר אָמַר־לוֹ מֹשֶׁה לְהִלָּחֵם בַּעֲמָלֵק וּמֹשֶׁה אַהֲרֹן וְחוּר
יא עָלוּ רֹאשׁ הַגִּבְעָה: וְהָיָה כַּאֲשֶׁר יָרִים מֹשֶׁה יָדוֹ וְגָבַר יִשְׂרָאֵל וְכַאֲשֶׁר יָנִיחַ יָדוֹ
יב וְגָבַר עֲמָלֵק: וִידֵי מֹשֶׁה כְּבֵדִים וַיִּקְחוּ־אֶבֶן וַיָּשִׂימוּ תַחְתָּיו וַיֵּשֶׁב עָלֶיהָ וְאַהֲרֹן
יג וְחוּר תָּמְכוּ בְיָדָיו מִזֶּה אֶחָד וּמִזֶּה אֶחָד וַיְהִי יָדָיו אֱמוּנָה עַד־בֹּא הַשָּׁמֶשׁ: וַיַּחֲלֹשׁ
יְהוֹשֻׁעַ אֶת־עֲמָלֵק וְאֶת־עַמּוֹ לְפִי־חָרֶב:
יד וַיֹּאמֶר יהוה אֶל־מֹשֶׁה כְּתֹב זֹאת זִכָּרוֹן בַּסֵּפֶר וְשִׂים בְּאָזְנֵי יְהוֹשֻׁעַ כִּי־מָחֹה מפטיר
טו אֶמְחֶה אֶת־זֵכֶר עֲמָלֵק מִתַּחַת הַשָּׁמָיִם: וַיִּבֶן מֹשֶׁה מִזְבֵּחַ וַיִּקְרָא שְׁמוֹ יהוה
טז נִסִּי: וַיֹּאמֶר כִּי־יָד עַל־כֵּס יָהּ מִלְחָמָה לַיהוה בַּעֲמָלֵק מִדֹּר דֹּר:

רש"י

ח| **ויבא עמלק.** סמך פרשה זו למקרא זה, לומר, תמיד אני ביניכם ומזומן לכל צרכיכם, ואתם אומרים: "היש ה' בקרבנו אם אין" (לעיל פסוק ז)?! חייכם שהכלב בא ונושך אתכם ואתם צועקים לי ותדעו היכן אני. משל לאדם שהרכיב בנו על כתפו ויצא לדרך, היה אותו הבן רואה חפץ ואומר: אבא, טול חפץ זה ותן לי! והוא נותן לו, וכן שניה וכן שלישית. פגעו באדם אחד, אמר לו אותו הבן: ראית את אבא? אמר לו אביו: אינך יודע היכן אני?! השליכו מעליו, ובא הכלב ונשכו:

ט| **בחר לנו.** לי ולך, השווהו לו. מכאן אמרו: "יהי כבוד תלמידך חביב עליך כשלך" (אבות ד, טו). כבוד חברך כמורא רבך, מנין? "ויאמר אהרן אל משה בי אדני" (במדבר יב, יא), והלא גדול האחין היה, ועשה את חברו כרבו. ו"מורא רבך כמורא שמים", שנאמר: "אדני משה כלאם" (שם יא, כח), כלם מן העולם, חייבין הם כליה המורדים בך כאלו פשעו בהקדוש ברוך הוא: **וצא הלחם.** צא מן הענן והלחם בו: **מחר.** בעת המלחמה "אנכי נצב": **בחר לנו אנשים.** גבורים ויראי חטא, שתהא זכותן מסייעתן. דבר אחר, בחר לנו אנשים שיודעין לבטל כשפים, לפי שבני עמלק מכשפים היו:

י| **ומשה אהרן וחור.** מכאן לתענית שצריכים שלשה לעבור לפני התבה, שבתענית היו שרויים: **חור.** בנה של מרים היה:

יא| **כאשר ירים משה ידו.** וכי ידיו של משה נוצחות היו המלחמה? וכו', כדאיתא בראש השנה (דף כט ע"א):

יב| **וידי משה כבדים.** בשביל שנתעצל במצוה ומנה אחר תחתיו, נתיקרו ידיו: **ויקחו.** אהרן וחור "אבן, וישימו תחתיו", ולא ישב לו על כר וכסת, אמר: ישראל שרויין בצער, אף אני אהיה עמהם בצער: **ויהי ידיו אמונה.** ויהי משה ידיו באמונה פרושות השמים בתפלה נאמנה ונכונה: **עד בא השמש.** שהיו עמלקים מחשבין את השעות באסטרולוגיאה באיזו שעה הם נוצחים, והעמיד להם משה חמה ועירבב את השעות:

יג| **ויחלש יהושע.** חתך ראשי גבוריו ולא השאיר אלא חלשים שבהם, ולא הרגם כלם. מכאן אנו למדים שעשו על פי הדבור של שכינה:

יד| **כתב זאת זכרון.** שבא עמלק להזדווג לישראל קודם לכל האמות: **ושים באזני יהושע.** המכניס את ישראל לארץ, שיצוה את ישראל לשלם לו את גמולו. כאן נרמז לו למשה שיהושע מכניס את ישראל לארץ: **כי מחה אמחה.** לכך אני מזהירך כן, כי חפץ אני למחותו:

טו| **ויקרא שמו.** של מזבח "ה' נסי" – הקדוש ברוך הוא עשה לנו כאן נס. לא שהמזבח קרוי ה', אלא המזכיר שמו של מזבח זוכר את הנס שעשה המקום, ה' הוא נס שלנו:

טז| **ויאמר.** משה "כי יד על כס יה" – ידו של הקדוש ברוך הוא הורמה לשבע בכסאו להיות לו מלחמה ואיבה בעמלק עולמית. ומהו "כס" ולא נאמר 'כסא', ואף השם נחלק לחציו? נשבע הקדוש ברוך הוא שאין שמו שלם ואין כסאו שלם עד שימחה שמו של עשו כלו, וכשימחה שמו יהיה השם שלם והכסא שלם, שנאמר: "האויב תמו חרבות לנצח" (תהלים ט, ז) זהו עשו שכתוב בו: "ועברתו שמרה נצח" (עמוס א, יא), "וערים נתשת אבד זכרם המה" (תהלים שם), מהו אומר אחריו? "וה' לעולם ישב" (שם פסוק ח), הרי השם שלם, "כונן למשפט כסאו" (שם), הרי הכסא שלם:

DISCUSSION

the beginning of the dual transmission of Torah through both the Written and Oral Law. God commands Moses to record the incident, both in writing and through verbal transmission to Joshua, his successor.

17:15| **Moses built an altar and called it: The Lord is my standard:** This altar is similar to those the patriarchs built as memorials for events in which God showed His greatness (e.g., Genesis 12:7, 26:25). Sometimes these altars were called by particular names (Genesis 33:20, 35:7). It is nevertheless unclear whether they were actually used for sacrifice.

BACKGROUND

17:8| **Amalek:** Amalek, progenitor of the nation that bore his name, was a grandson of Esau (Genesis 36:12). The nation of Amalek was a nomadic people who lived in the Negev, the area of Kadesh Barnea, extending toward the wilderness of Shur (Genesis 14:7; Numbers 13:29; I Samuel 27:8). It derived its sustenance from raising livestock and from raiding settlements, its reach extending to the highlands of Ephraim (Judges 5:14).

Parashat
Yitro

Yitro's Arrival and His Advice
EXODUS 18:1–27

It is unclear whether Moses' father-in-law, Yitro, arrived at this point in the chronology of events just after the war with Amalek or whether he arrived at some later point. There are indications in the narrative that this visit in fact occurred after the giving of the Torah, which is described in chapters 19 and 20 below. Whereas the Israelites' journey from Refidim, where the war with Amalek was waged, is described below (19:2), Yitro joins the people when they are already encamped at the mountain of God (18:5). Furthermore, Yitro gives Moses advice with regard to judicial administration and legal instructions, when he sees his son-in-law engaged in the dispensation of justice from morning until night. This discussion would appear to correspond more closely to the scene subsequent to the giving of the Torah, rather than beforehand. Traditional commentators are divided on this issue. Some commentaries, reluctant to accept that the chronology of some stories differs from their historical order unless compelled to do so, prefer to struggle with the above arguments and preserve the textual order as chronological. Conversely, others contend that the order of passages in the Torah does not always reflect their actual order of occurrence, and whenever the verses deviate from the chronological sequence of events, they are designed to create a different thematic flow that has its own significance.

18 1 **Yitro, priest of Midyan, father-in-law of Moses, heard all that God had done to Moses, and to Israel His people, that the Lord took Israel out of Egypt.** Due to the exceptional nature of the events, news of the ten plagues and the exodus of an entire nation from Egypt had reached Midyan, despite the fact that it was not located in close proximity to Egypt. Indeed, reports of the miraculous events spread to even more distant places.[1] Yitro now realizes that Moses did not return to Egypt merely to visit his family.

2 **Yitro, father-in-law of Moses, took Tzipora, wife of Moses, after she had been sent away,** after Moses had sent her to her father's house.[2] Moses had not arranged for Tzipora's return or even contacted her, but nevertheless Yitro felt that the time had come to bring Moses his wife.

3 **And her two sons, of whom one was named Gershom, as he,** Moses, **said: I was a stranger in a foreign land.** The name Gershom is composed of two Hebrew words: stranger [*ger*] and there [*sham*].[3]

4 **And the name of the other was Eliezer,** derived from the following statement of Moses: **For the God of my father was my assistance, and He delivered me from the sword of Pharaoh.** The name Eliezer contains the two Hebrew words: my God [*Eli*], and my help [*ezri*]. It is possible that Eliezer was born after the death of the Pharaoh who sought to kill Moses (2:15), which is how he was certain that he had been saved from Pharaoh.[4] In naming his sons, Moses referred to critical events in his own life, indicating that he did not consider them the

unwanted progeny of a brief visit in a foreign land. Yitro thus understood that it was important to reunite Moses with his sons.

5 **Yitro, father-in-law of Moses, came with his sons and his,** Moses', **wife to Moses, to the wilderness where he was encamped,** which is the place of **the mountain of God.**[D]

6 **He,** Yitro, **said to Moses,** by means of a messenger he had sent ahead: **I, your father-in-law Yitro, am coming to you, and** I bring **your wife and her two sons with her.**

7 **Moses went out toward his father-in-law, and prostrated himself and kissed him.** Although it is unclear from the Hebrew text who prostrated himself, it was likely Moses who prostrated himself in honor of his father-in-law. Although he may have been no older than Moses, Yitro was a dignitary in his own region. Despite the fact that Moses himself had become the leader of a large nation since his marriage, he continued to act deferentially toward his father-in-law, as was his practice in the past.[5] **And each** man **greeted the other, and they came into the tent** of Moses.

8 **Moses related to his father-in-law everything that the Lord had done to Pharaoh and to the Egyptians on behalf of Israel.** Until this point, Yitro had gleaned information merely from passing travelers; now he heard firsthand how the events had actually transpired. Moses also described to him **all the adversity that encountered them on the way, and** how the **Lord delivered them** from Pharaoh and his pursuing army, as well as from other dangers along the way.

DISCUSSION

18:5 | **The mountain of God:** Even if this episode took place before the giving of the Torah, the reference to a known mountain of God is not surprising, as Moses was familiar with Mount Sinai. An angel of God had appeared to him there in the vision of the burning bush (3:1–12) and had informed him that the Israelites would return there to worship God.

פרשת

יתרו

א וַיִּשְׁמַע יִתְרוֹ כֹהֵן מִדְיָן חֹתֵן מֹשֶׁה אֵת כָּל־אֲשֶׁר עָשָׂה אֱלֹהִים לְמֹשֶׁה וּלְיִשְׂרָאֵל יד
ב עַמּוֹ כִּי־הוֹצִיא יְהוָה אֶת־יִשְׂרָאֵל מִמִּצְרָיִם: וַיִּקַּח יִתְרוֹ חֹתֵן מֹשֶׁה אֶת־צִפֹּרָה
ג אֵשֶׁת מֹשֶׁה אַחַר שִׁלּוּחֶיהָ: וְאֵת שְׁנֵי בָנֶיהָ אֲשֶׁר שֵׁם הָאֶחָד גֵּרְשֹׁם כִּי אָמַר גֵּר
ד הָיִיתִי בְּאֶרֶץ נָכְרִיָּה: וְשֵׁם הָאֶחָד אֱלִיעֶזֶר כִּי־אֱלֹהֵי אָבִי בְּעֶזְרִי וַיַּצִּלֵנִי מֵחֶרֶב
ה פַּרְעֹה: וַיָּבֹא יִתְרוֹ חֹתֵן מֹשֶׁה וּבָנָיו וְאִשְׁתּוֹ אֶל־מֹשֶׁה אֶל־הַמִּדְבָּר אֲשֶׁר־הוּא
ו חֹנֶה שָׁם הַר הָאֱלֹהִים: וַיֹּאמֶר אֶל־מֹשֶׁה אֲנִי חֹתֶנְךָ יִתְרוֹ בָּא אֵלֶיךָ וְאִשְׁתְּךָ וּשְׁנֵי
ז בָנֶיהָ עִמָּהּ: וַיֵּצֵא מֹשֶׁה לִקְרַאת חֹתְנוֹ וַיִּשְׁתַּחוּ וַיִּשַּׁק־לוֹ וַיִּשְׁאֲלוּ אִישׁ־לְרֵעֵהוּ
ח לְשָׁלוֹם וַיָּבֹאוּ הָאֹהֱלָה: וַיְסַפֵּר מֹשֶׁה לְחֹתְנוֹ אֵת כָּל־אֲשֶׁר עָשָׂה יְהוָה לְפַרְעֹה
וּלְמִצְרַיִם עַל אוֹדֹת יִשְׂרָאֵל אֵת כָּל־הַתְּלָאָה אֲשֶׁר מְצָאָתַם בַּדֶּרֶךְ וַיַּצִּלֵם יְהוָה:

א| **וַיִּשְׁמַע יִתְרוֹ.** מַה שְּׁמוּעָה שָׁמַע? קְרִיעַת יַם סוּף וּמִלְחֶמֶת עֲמָלֵק: **יִתְרוֹ.** שִׁבְעָה שֵׁמוֹת נִקְרְאוּ לוֹ: רְעוּאֵל, יֶתֶר, יִתְרוֹ, חוֹבָב, חֶבֶר, קֵינִי, פּוּטִיאֵל. יֶתֶר, עַל שֵׁם שֶׁיִּתֵּר פָּרָשָׁה אַחַת בַּתּוֹרָה: "וְאַתָּה תֶחֱזֶה" (להלן פסוק כא); יִתְרוֹ, כְּשֶׁנִּתְגַּיֵּר וְקִיֵּם הַמִּצְוֹת הוֹסִיפוּ לוֹ אוֹת; חוֹבָב, שֶׁחִבֵּב אֶת הַתּוֹרָה, וְחוֹבָב הוּא יִתְרוֹ, שֶׁנֶּאֱמַר: "מִבְּנֵי חֹבָב חֹתֵן מֹשֶׁה" (שופטים ד, יא). וְיֵשׁ אוֹמְרִים: רְעוּאֵל אָבִיו שֶׁל יִתְרוֹ הָיָה, וּמַהוּ אוֹמֵר: "וַתָּבֹאנָה אֶל רְעוּאֵל אֲבִיהֶן" (לעיל ב, יח)? שֶׁהַתִּינוֹקוֹת קוֹרִין לַאֲבִי אֲבִיהֶן אַבָּא. בְּסִפְרֵי (בהעלותך עח): **חֹתֵן מֹשֶׁה.** כָּאן הָיָה יִתְרוֹ מִתְכַּבֵּד בְּמֹשֶׁה: אֲנִי חוֹתֵן הַמֶּלֶךְ, וּלְשֶׁעָבַר הָיָה מֹשֶׁה תּוֹלֶה הַגְּדֻלָּה בְּחָמִיו, שֶׁנֶּאֱמַר: "וַיָּשָׁב אֶל יֶתֶר חֹתְנוֹ" (לעיל ד, יח): **לְמֹשֶׁה וּלְיִשְׂרָאֵל.** שָׁקַל מֹשֶׁה כְּנֶגֶד כָּל יִשְׂרָאֵל: **אֵת כָּל אֲשֶׁר עָשָׂה.** לָהֶם בִּירִידַת הַמָּן וּבַבְּאֵר וּבַעֲמָלֵק: **כִּי הוֹצִיא ה' וְגוֹ'.** זוֹ גְּדוֹלָה עַל כֻּלָּם:

ב| **אַחַר שִׁלּוּחֶיהָ.** כְּשֶׁאָמַר לוֹ הַקָּדוֹשׁ בָּרוּךְ הוּא בְּמִדְיָן: "לֵךְ שֻׁב מִצְרָיִם", "וַיִּקַּח מֹשֶׁה אֶת אִשְׁתּוֹ וְאֶת בָּנָיו" וְגוֹ' (לעיל ד, יט-כ), וְיָצָא אַהֲרֹן לִקְרָאתוֹ "וַיִּפְגְּשֵׁהוּ בְּהַר הָאֱלֹהִים" (שם פסוק כז); אָמַר לוֹ: מִי הֵם הַלָּלוּ? אָמַר לוֹ: זוֹ אִשְׁתִּי שֶׁנָּשָׂאתִי בְּמִדְיָן וְאֵלּוּ בָּנַי. אָמַר לוֹ: וְהֵיכָן אַתָּה מוֹלִיכָן? אָמַר לוֹ: לְמִצְרַיִם. אָמַר לוֹ: עַל הָרִאשׁוֹנִים אָנוּ מִצְטַעֲרִים וְאַתָּה בָּא לְהוֹסִיף עֲלֵיהֶם? אָמַר לָהּ: לְכִי לְבֵית אָבִיךְ. נָטְלָה שְׁנֵי בָנֶיהָ וְהָלְכָה לָהּ:

ד| **וַיַּצִּלֵנִי מֵחֶרֶב פַּרְעֹה.** כְּשֶׁגִּלּוּ דָּתָן וַאֲבִירָם עַל דְּבַר הַמִּצְרִי וּבִקֵּשׁ לַהֲרֹג אֶת מֹשֶׁה, נַעֲשָׂה צַוָּארוֹ כְּעַמּוּד שֶׁל שַׁיִשׁ:

ה| **אֶל הַמִּדְבָּר.** אַף אָנוּ יוֹדְעִים שֶׁבַּמִּדְבָּר הָיוּ, אֶלָּא בְּשִׁבְחוֹ שֶׁל יִתְרוֹ דִּבֶּר הַכָּתוּב, שֶׁהָיָה יוֹשֵׁב בִּכְבוֹדוֹ שֶׁל עוֹלָם, וְנָדְבוֹ לִבּוֹ לָצֵאת אֶל הַמִּדְבָּר מְקוֹם תֹּהוּ לִשְׁמֹעַ דִּבְרֵי תּוֹרָה:

ו| **וַיֹּאמֶר אֶל מֹשֶׁה.** עַל יְדֵי שָׁלִיחַ: **אֲנִי חֹתֶנְךָ יִתְרוֹ וְגוֹ'.** אִם אֵין אַתָּה יוֹצֵא בִּגְלָלִי צֵא בִּגְלַל אִשְׁתְּךָ, וְאִם אֵין אַתָּה יוֹצֵא בִּגְלַל אִשְׁתְּךָ צֵא בִּגְלַל שְׁנֵי בָנֶיהָ:

ז| **וַיֵּצֵא מֹשֶׁה.** כָּבוֹד גָּדוֹל נִתְכַּבֵּד יִתְרוֹ בְּאוֹתָהּ שָׁעָה; כֵּיוָן שֶׁיָּצָא מֹשֶׁה יָצָא אַהֲרֹן נָדָב וַאֲבִיהוּא, וּמִי הוּא שֶׁרָאָה אֶת אֵלּוּ יוֹצְאִין וְלֹא יָצָא?: **וַיִּשְׁתַּחוּ וַיִּשַּׁק לוֹ.** אֵינִי יוֹדֵעַ מִי הִשְׁתַּחֲוָה לְמִי, כְּשֶׁהוּא אוֹמֵר: "אִישׁ לְרֵעֵהוּ", מִי הַקָּרוּי "אִישׁ"? זֶה מֹשֶׁה (ראה במדבר יב, ג):

ח| **וַיְסַפֵּר מֹשֶׁה לְחֹתְנוֹ.** לִמְשֹׁךְ אֶת לִבּוֹ לְקָרְבוֹ לַתּוֹרָה: **אֵת כָּל הַתְּלָאָה.** שֶׁעַל הַיָּם וְשֶׁל עֲמָלֵק: **הַתְּלָאָה.** לָמֶ"ד אָלֶ"ף מִן הַיְסוֹד שֶׁל תֵּבָה, וְהַתָּי"ו הוּא תִּקּוּן וִיסוֹד הַנּוֹפֵל מִמֶּנּוּ לִפְרָקִים. וְכֵן: תְּרוּמָה, תְּנוּפָה, תְּקוּמָה, תְּנוּאָה:

9 **Yitro rejoiced over all the good that the Lord had done to Israel,**[D] **that He had delivered it from the hand of Egypt.**

10 **Yitro said: Blessed is the Lord, who delivered you from the hand of Egypt and from the hand of Pharaoh;** and not just you, or a small band of individuals, but **who delivered the** entire **people from under the hand of Egypt.**

11 **Now I know that the Lord is greater than all the gods, as** God saved the Israelites and punished the Egyptians **in,** through, **the** very **matter that they,** the Egyptians, **conspired against them.** Yitro considered the drowning of the Egyptians in the Red Sea as divine retribution for their decree to cast all newborn Israelite males into the Nile (1:22). Since the Egyptians drowned Israelite children in the Nile, they themselves were drowned. This was not merely an impressive miracle that brought salvation to the Israelites, but a demonstration of God's execution of the appropriate punishment, measure for measure, for their crime.[6]

12 **Yitro, father-in-law of Moses, took a burnt offering and feast offerings to God.** The custom of sacrificing offerings predated the giving of the Torah. **Aaron,** Moses' brother, **and all the elders,** dignitaries **of Israel, came to break bread** in the ritual consumption of the offerings **with the father-in-law of Moses before God.**

13 **It was the next day that Moses sat,** as was his custom, **to judge**
Second aliya **the people** and to administer communal affairs, **and the people stood over Moses from the morning until the evening.**

14 **The father-in-law of Moses saw everything that he,** Moses, **was doing with the people.** Yitro saw the disarray surrounding Moses, as a huge number of people were gathered around his tent, all waiting to hear direct instructions from their leader. **And he said: What is it that you are doing with the people? Why are you sitting by yourself and all the people stand over you,** waiting for you **from morning until evening?**

15 **Moses said to his father-in-law: Because the people come to me to seek God,** as I am their prophet and know God's laws. Even if this encounter transpired before the giving of the Torah, it is still logical that they turned to him, as Moses was the most senior figure, and inquiries of judicial matters were naturally directed to him.[7]

16 **When they have a matter** that requires judgment, **it comes before me; and I adjudicate between one man and another,** including those who are not quarreling but simply seeking general advice with regard to proper conduct, **and I communicate the statutes of God and His laws.**

17 **The father-in-law of Moses said to him: It is not a good thing that you are doing.**

18 **You will wither away,** like a plant that lacks the requisite conditions for growth. **Both you and this people that is with you** cannot maintain the current practice, **as the matter is too arduous for you; you cannot do it by yourself.** The large nation will only become more numerous, and you will not be able to attend to every individual case. Furthermore, the people are also suffering from the lack of a formal arrangement, as they are forced to wait long hours to speak to you.

19 **Now heed my voice, let me advise you, and may God be with you,** to help you execute this plan. **You will be** the representative **for the people before God, and you will bring the matters to God.** When weighty matters arise, which must be resolved, you shall present them before God.

DISCUSSION

18:9| **Yitro rejoiced over all the good that the Lord had done to Israel:** Yitro felt an affinity for the Israelites due to his familial ties to Moses. In addition, perhaps there was another reason for his joy: The Midyanites were related to the Israelites; they may even have descended from Abraham (see Genesis 25:2).

ט וַיִּחַדְּ יִתְרוֹ עַל כָּל־הַטּוֹבָה אֲשֶׁר־עָשָׂה יהוה לְיִשְׂרָאֵל אֲשֶׁר הִצִּילוֹ מִיַּד מִצְרָיִם׃
י וַיֹּאמֶר יִתְרוֹ בָּרוּךְ יהוה אֲשֶׁר הִצִּיל אֶתְכֶם מִיַּד מִצְרַיִם וּמִיַּד פַּרְעֹה אֲשֶׁר הִצִּיל
יא אֶת־הָעָם מִתַּחַת יַד־מִצְרָיִם׃ עַתָּה יָדַעְתִּי כִּי־גָדוֹל יהוה מִכָּל־הָאֱלֹהִים כִּי
יב בַדָּבָר אֲשֶׁר זָדוּ עֲלֵיהֶם׃ וַיִּקַּח יִתְרוֹ חֹתֵן מֹשֶׁה עֹלָה וּזְבָחִים לֵאלֹהִים וַיָּבֹא אַהֲרֹן
יג וְכֹל ׀ זִקְנֵי יִשְׂרָאֵל לֶאֱכָל־לֶחֶם עִם־חֹתֵן מֹשֶׁה לִפְנֵי הָאֱלֹהִים׃ וַיְהִי מִמָּחֳרָת שני
יד וַיֵּשֶׁב מֹשֶׁה לִשְׁפֹּט אֶת־הָעָם וַיַּעֲמֹד הָעָם עַל־מֹשֶׁה מִן־הַבֹּקֶר עַד־הָעָרֶב׃ וַיַּרְא
חֹתֵן מֹשֶׁה אֵת כָּל־אֲשֶׁר־הוּא עֹשֶׂה לָעָם וַיֹּאמֶר מָה־הַדָּבָר הַזֶּה אֲשֶׁר אַתָּה
עֹשֶׂה לָעָם מַדּוּעַ אַתָּה יוֹשֵׁב לְבַדֶּךָ וְכָל־הָעָם נִצָּב עָלֶיךָ מִן־בֹּקֶר עַד־עָרֶב׃
טו טז וַיֹּאמֶר מֹשֶׁה לְחֹתְנוֹ כִּי־יָבֹא אֵלַי הָעָם לִדְרֹשׁ אֱלֹהִים׃ כִּי־יִהְיֶה לָהֶם דָּבָר בָּא
אֵלַי וְשָׁפַטְתִּי בֵּין אִישׁ וּבֵין רֵעֵהוּ וְהוֹדַעְתִּי אֶת־חֻקֵּי הָאֱלֹהִים וְאֶת־תּוֹרֹתָיו׃
יז יח וַיֹּאמֶר חֹתֵן מֹשֶׁה אֵלָיו לֹא־טוֹב הַדָּבָר אֲשֶׁר אַתָּה עֹשֶׂה׃ נָבֹל תִּבֹּל גַּם־אַתָּה
יט גַּם־הָעָם הַזֶּה אֲשֶׁר עִמָּךְ כִּי־כָבֵד מִמְּךָ הַדָּבָר לֹא־תוּכַל עֲשֹׂהוּ לְבַדֶּךָ׃ עַתָּה
שְׁמַע בְּקֹלִי אִיעָצְךָ וִיהִי אֱלֹהִים עִמָּךְ הֱיֵה אַתָּה לָעָם מוּל הָאֱלֹהִים וְהֵבֵאתָ

רש״י

ט | **וַיִּחַדְּ יִתְרוֹ.** וַיִּשְׂמַח יִתְרוֹ, זֶהוּ פְּשׁוּטוֹ. וּמִדְרָשׁוֹ, נַעֲשָׂה בְשָׂרוֹ חִדּוּדִין חִדּוּדִין, מֵצֵר עַל אִבּוּד מִצְרַיִם. ״הַיְנוּ דְּאָמְרֵי אֱנָשֵׁי: גִּיּוֹרָא, עַד עַשְׂרָה דָּרֵי לָא תְּבַזֵּי אֲרַמָּאָה בְּאַפֵּיהּ״ (סנהדרין צד ע״א): **עַל כָּל הַטּוֹבָה.** טוֹבַת הַמָּן וְהַבְּאֵר וְהַתּוֹרָה. וְעַל כֻּלָּן ״אֲשֶׁר הִצִּילוֹ מִיַּד מִצְרָיִם״, עַד עַכְשָׁיו לֹא הָיָה עֶבֶד יָכוֹל לִבְרֹחַ מִמִּצְרַיִם, שֶׁהָיְתָה הָאָרֶץ מְסֻגֶּרֶת, וְאֵלּוּ יָצְאוּ שִׁשִּׁים רִבּוֹא:

י | **אֲשֶׁר הִצִּיל אֶתְכֶם מִיַּד מִצְרַיִם.** אֻמָּה קָשָׁה: **וּמִיַּד פַּרְעֹה.** מֶלֶךְ קָשֶׁה: **מִתַּחַת יַד מִצְרָיִם.** כְּתַרְגּוּמוֹ, לְשׁוֹן רִדּוּי וּמָרוּת הַיָּד שֶׁהָיוּ מַכְבִּידִים עֲלֵיהֶם, הִיא הָעֲבוֹדָה:

יא | **עַתָּה יָדַעְתִּי.** מַכִּירוֹ הָיִיתִי לְשֶׁעָבַר, וְעַכְשָׁיו בְּיוֹתֵר: **מִכָּל הָאֱלֹהִים.** מְלַמֵּד שֶׁהָיָה מַכִּיר בְּכָל עֲבוֹדָה זָרָה שֶׁבָּעוֹלָם, שֶׁלֹּא הִנִּיחַ עֲבוֹדָה זָרָה שֶׁלֹּא עֲבָדָהּ: **כִּי בַדָּבָר אֲשֶׁר זָדוּ עֲלֵיהֶם.** כְּתַרְגּוּמוֹ, בַּמַּיִם דִּמּוּ לְאַבְּדָם וְהֵם נֶאֶבְדוּ בַמַּיִם: **אֲשֶׁר זָדוּ.** אֲשֶׁר הִרְשִׁיעוּ. וְרַבּוֹתֵינוּ דְּרָשׁוּהוּ לְשׁוֹן: ״וַיָּזֶד יַעֲקֹב נָזִיד״ (בראשית כה, כט), בַּקְּדֵרָה שֶׁבִּשְּׁלוּ בָּהּ נִתְבַּשְּׁלוּ:

יב | **עֹלָה.** כְּמַשְׁמָעָהּ, שֶׁהִיא כֻלָּהּ כָּלִיל: **וּזְבָחִים.** שְׁלָמִים: **וַיָּבֹא אַהֲרֹן וְגוֹ׳.** וּמֹשֶׁה הֵיכָן הָלַךְ? וַהֲלֹא הוּא שֶׁיָּצָא לִקְרָאתוֹ וְגָרַם לוֹ אֶת כָּל הַכָּבוֹד? אֶלָּא שֶׁהָיָה עוֹמֵד וּמְשַׁמֵּשׁ לִפְנֵיהֶם: **לִפְנֵי הָאֱלֹהִים.** מִכָּאן שֶׁהַנֶּהֱנֶה מִסְּעוּדָה שֶׁתַּלְמִידֵי חֲכָמִים מְסֻבִּין בָּהּ כְּאִלּוּ נֶהֱנֶה מִזִּיו הַשְּׁכִינָה:

יג | **וַיְהִי מִמָּחֳרָת.** מוֹצָאֵי יוֹם הַכִּפּוּרִים הָיָה, כָּךְ שָׁנִינוּ בְּסִפְרֵי (ראה מכילתא יתרו, עמלק א). וּמַהוּ ״מִמָּחֳרָת״? לְמָחֳרַת רִדְתּוֹ מִן הָהָר. וְעַל כָּרְחֲךָ אִי אֶפְשָׁר לוֹמַר אֶלָּא מִמָּחֳרַת יוֹם הַכִּפּוּרִים, שֶׁהֲרֵי קֹדֶם מַתַּן תּוֹרָה אִי אֶפְשָׁר לוֹמַר ״וְהוֹדַעְתִּי אֶת חֻקֵּי״ וְגוֹ׳ (להלן פסוק טז), וּמִשֶּׁנִּתְּנָה תּוֹרָה עַד יוֹם הַכִּפּוּרִים לֹא יָשַׁב מֹשֶׁה לִשְׁפֹּט אֶת הָעָם, שֶׁהֲרֵי בְּשִׁבְעָה עָשָׂר בְּתַמּוּז יָרַד וְשִׁבֵּר אֶת הַלּוּחוֹת, וּלְמָחָר עָלָה בְּהַשְׁכָּמָה וְשָׁהָה שְׁמוֹנִים יוֹם וְיָרַד בְּיוֹם הַכִּפּוּרִים. וְאֵין פָּרָשָׁה זוֹ כְּתוּבָה כַּסֵּדֶר, שֶׁלֹּא נֶאֱמַר: ״וַיְהִי מִמָּחֳרָת״ עַד שָׁנָה שְׁנִיָּה. אַף לְדִבְרֵי הָאוֹמֵר יִתְרוֹ קֹדֶם מַתַּן תּוֹרָה בָּא, שִׁלּוּחוֹ אֶל אַרְצוֹ לֹא הָיָה אֶלָּא עַד שָׁנָה שְׁנִיָּה, שֶׁהֲרֵי נֶאֱמַר כָּאן: ״וַיְשַׁלַּח מֹשֶׁה אֶת חֹתְנוֹ״ (להלן פסוק כז), וּמָצִינוּ בְּמַסַּע הַדְּגָלִים שֶׁאָמַר לוֹ מֹשֶׁה: ״נֹסְעִים אֲנַחְנוּ אֶל הַמָּקוֹם וְגוֹ׳ אַל נָא תַּעֲזֹב אוֹתָנוּ״ (במדבר י, כט-לא), וְאִם זֶה קֹדֶם מַתַּן תּוֹרָה, מִשֶּׁשִּׁלְּחוֹ וְהָלַךְ הֵיכָן מָצִינוּ שֶׁחָזַר? וְאִם תֹּאמַר, שָׁם לֹא נֶאֱמַר יִתְרוֹ אֶלָּא חוֹבָב, וּבְנוֹ שֶׁל יִתְרוֹ הָיָה – הוּא חוֹבָב הוּא יִתְרוֹ, שֶׁהֲרֵי כָּתוּב: ״מִבְּנֵי חֹבָב חֹתֵן מֹשֶׁה״ (שופטים ד, יא): **וַיֵּשֶׁב מֹשֶׁה... וַיַּעֲמֹד הָעָם.** יוֹשֵׁב כְּמֶלֶךְ וְכֻלָּן עוֹמְדִים, וְהֻקְשָׁה הַדָּבָר לְיִתְרוֹ שֶׁהָיָה מְזַלְזֵל בִּכְבוֹדָן שֶׁל יִשְׂרָאֵל וְהוֹכִיחוֹ עַל כָּךְ, שֶׁנֶּאֱמַר: ״מַדּוּעַ אַתָּה יוֹשֵׁב לְבַדֶּךָ״ וְכֻלָּם נִצָּבִים: **מִן הַבֹּקֶר עַד הָעָרֶב.** אֶפְשָׁר לוֹמַר כֵּן?! אֶלָּא כָּל דַּיָּן שֶׁדָּן דִּין אֱמֶת לַאֲמִתּוֹ אֲפִלּוּ שָׁעָה אַחַת מַעֲלֶה עָלָיו הַכָּתוּב כְּאִלּוּ עוֹסֵק בַּתּוֹרָה כָּל הַיּוֹם, וּכְאִלּוּ נַעֲשָׂה שֻׁתָּף לְהַקָּדוֹשׁ בָּרוּךְ הוּא בְּמַעֲשֵׂה בְרֵאשִׁית שֶׁנֶּאֱמַר בּוֹ: ״וַיְהִי עֶרֶב וַיְהִי בֹקֶר יוֹם אֶחָד״ (בראשית א, ה):

טו | **כִּי יָבֹא.** כִּי בָא, לְשׁוֹן הוֹוֶה, ״לְמִתְבַּע אֻלְפָן״, לִשְׁאֹל תַּלְמוּד מִפִּי הַגְּבוּרָה:

טז | **כִּי יִהְיֶה לָהֶם דָּבָר.** מִי שֶׁיִּהְיֶה לוֹ דָּבָר בָּא אֵלַי:

יז | **וַיֹּאמֶר חֹתֵן מֹשֶׁה.** דֶּרֶךְ כָּבוֹד קוֹרֵהוּ הַכָּתוּב, חוֹתְנוֹ שֶׁל מֶלֶךְ:

יח | **נָבֹל תִּבֹּל.** כְּתַרְגּוּמוֹ. וּלְשׁוֹנוֹ לְשׁוֹן כְּמִישָׁה, פלייסטר״א בְּלַעַז, כְּמוֹ: ״וְהֶעָלֶה נָבֵל״ (ירמיה ח, יג), ״כִּנְבֹל עָלֶה מִגֶּפֶן״ (ישעיה לד, ד), שֶׁהוּא כָּמוּשׁ עַל יְדֵי חַמָּה וְעַל יְדֵי קֶרַח וְכָחוֹ תָּשׁ וְנִלְאֶה: **גַּם אַתָּה.** לְרַבּוֹת אַהֲרֹן וְחוּר וְשִׁבְעִים זְקֵנִים: **כִּי כָבֵד מִמְּךָ.** כָּבְדּוֹ רַב יוֹתֵר מִכֹּחֲךָ:

יט | **אִיעָצְךָ וִיהִי אֱלֹהִים עִמָּךְ.** בְּעֵצָה, אָמַר לוֹ: צֵא הִמָּלֵךְ בַּגְּבוּרָה: **הֱיֵה אַתָּה לָעָם מוּל הָאֱלֹהִים.** שָׁלִיחַ וּמֵלִיץ

20 **You shall caution them of the statutes and the laws**[D] that you receive from God, **and shall communicate to them the path in which they should walk and the actions that they should perform** by providing general guidelines for them to follow.[8]

21 In addition, **you shall identify from all the people capable men,** accomplished in various fields, who are courageous individuals with leadership qualities. From this group, you shall select those who are also **fearers of God** as well as **men of truth, haters of ill-gotten gain.**[D] These are the essential characteristics of a good judge.[9] **Set** these judges **over them,** the people, in a hierarchy as **leaders of thousands, leaders of hundreds, leaders of fifties, and leaders of tens.**[D]

22 **They shall judge the people at all times; it shall be that every major matter,** which has ramifications for the entire nation, **they shall bring to you, and every minor matter,** for which they do not require your ruling, **they shall adjudicate themselves. It will ease the burden** of leadership **from upon you, and they will bear** it together **with you.**

23 **If you do this thing, and God commands you** to act accordingly, as I know that you will not follow this plan without receiving confirmation from God, then **you will be able to endure; and also this entire people,** who are currently suffering

from a lack of order and sufficient leaders, **will come to their place in peace.**

Third aliya 24 **Moses heeded the voice of his father-in-law**[D] and did everything that he said.

25 **Moses selected capable men from all Israel.** No mention is made, however, of the other qualities outlined by Yitro above. Perhaps Moses was unable to find enough leaders with all of those qualities, and those who were capable had to suffice.[10] **And he set them to be heads over the people, leaders of thousands, leaders of hundreds, leaders of fifties, and leaders of tens.** Moses established the hierarchy according to their merit, despite the fact that all the candidates were fundamentally qualified for the positions.

26 **They would judge the people at all times.** Since there were now many judges, they could handle all small matters, and the litigants no longer had a long wait. **The difficult matter they would bring to Moses,**[D] **and any minor matter they would adjudicate themselves.**

27 **Moses sent forth his father-in-law, and he went to his land.**[D] Although this occurred at a later time than the previous narrative,[11] it is mentioned here because it concludes the account of Yitro's visit.

DISCUSSION

18:20 | The statutes and the laws: This is referring not only to the Written Law, but also to the Oral Law. The Oral Law includes elucidations of the statements of the Torah, which were transmitted word-for-word to Moses and require elaboration. It also incorporates general principles of morality and other aspects of human conduct that were not included as specific laws.

18:21 | Haters of ill-gotten gain: Some maintain that this is referring not only to men who are disgusted by illegitimately obtained money, but to those for whom the entire enterprise of accumulating wealth is foreign (Rabbi Elazar HaModa'i in the *Mekhilta*; see Ramban; Radak, I Samuel 8:3, and Isaiah 33:15). The Rambam explains similarly that the phrase "haters of ill-gotten gain" refers to those who are not attached even to their own possessions, and they are not motivated to pursue wealth (Rambam, *Sefer Shofetim, Hilkhot Sanhedrin* 2:7).

Leaders of thousands, leaders of hundreds, leaders of fifties, and leaders of tens: These can be understood as precise designations, e.g., a leader of ten will be in charge of ten people. However, it is likely that these titles actually indicate the status of the judge, similar to a rank in the army or a position in modern judicial systems. If so, a leader of tens is a judge appointed over a small, local group, while a leader of thousands is granted responsibility for a larger group of people (see I Samuel 17:18, and Rashi ad loc.).

18:24 | Moses heeded the voice of his father-in-law: Even in those days, Egypt maintained an organized hierarchy and a large bureaucracy. Why then was Moses, who grew up in the Egyptian royal palace, apparently unaware of the need for such organization himself, such that his father-in-law, who may also have served in Pharaoh's court at one point (see *Pirkei de-Rabbi Eliezer* 39; *Sota* 11a), felt compelled to suggest it to him? It should have been obvious to

Moses that the leader of several million people, including women and children, cannot mediate every argument between two neighbors over a goat or each minor quarrel between a husband and wife.

It is likely that Moses was unsure whether he was permitted to establish governmental institutions similar to those of other countries, not only due to his humility, but for other reasons as well: Since Israel is not an ordinary people but the chosen nation of God, perhaps its forms of leadership must also be different. Perhaps, just as God is available at any time to all who seek Him, so too must the leader of Israel always be accessible and available to everyone.

Nevertheless, Yitro urged his son-in-law to change the structure of government and the judicial system. He understood that there was no way for Moses, even with the greatest kindness and devotion, to listen to everyone in need. When Moses heard his father-in-law's ◄●

כ אַתָּה אֶת־הַדְּבָרִים אֶל־הָאֱלֹהִים: וְהִזְהַרְתָּה אֶתְהֶם אֶת־הַחֻקִּים וְאֶת־הַתּוֹרֹת
כא וְהוֹדַעְתָּ לָהֶם אֶת־הַדֶּרֶךְ יֵלְכוּ בָהּ וְאֶת־הַמַּעֲשֶׂה אֲשֶׁר יַעֲשׂוּן: וְאַתָּה תֶחֱזֶה
מִכָּל־הָעָם אַנְשֵׁי־חַיִל יִרְאֵי אֱלֹהִים אַנְשֵׁי אֱמֶת שֹׂנְאֵי בָצַע וְשַׂמְתָּ עֲלֵהֶם שָׂרֵי
כב אֲלָפִים שָׂרֵי מֵאוֹת שָׂרֵי חֲמִשִּׁים וְשָׂרֵי עֲשָׂרֹת: וְשָׁפְטוּ אֶת־הָעָם בְּכָל־עֵת וְהָיָה
כָּל־הַדָּבָר הַגָּדֹל יָבִיאוּ אֵלֶיךָ וְכָל־הַדָּבָר הַקָּטֹן יִשְׁפְּטוּ־הֵם וְהָקֵל מֵעָלֶיךָ וְנָשְׂאוּ
כג אִתָּךְ: אִם אֶת־הַדָּבָר הַזֶּה תַּעֲשֶׂה וְצִוְּךָ אֱלֹהִים וְיָכָלְתָּ עֲמֹד וְגַם כָּל־הָעָם הַזֶּה
כד כה עַל־מְקֹמוֹ יָבֹא בְשָׁלוֹם: וַיִּשְׁמַע מֹשֶׁה לְקוֹל חֹתְנוֹ וַיַּעַשׂ כֹּל אֲשֶׁר אָמָר: וַיִּבְחַר שלישי
מֹשֶׁה אַנְשֵׁי־חַיִל מִכָּל־יִשְׂרָאֵל וַיִּתֵּן אֹתָם רָאשִׁים עַל־הָעָם שָׂרֵי אֲלָפִים שָׂרֵי
כו מֵאוֹת שָׂרֵי חֲמִשִּׁים וְשָׂרֵי עֲשָׂרֹת: וְשָׁפְטוּ אֶת־הָעָם בְּכָל־עֵת אֶת־הַדָּבָר הַקָּשֶׁה
כז יְבִיאוּן אֶל־מֹשֶׁה וְכָל־הַדָּבָר הַקָּטֹן יִשְׁפּוּטוּ הֵם: וַיְשַׁלַּח מֹשֶׁה אֶת־חֹתְנוֹ וַיֵּלֶךְ
לוֹ אֶל־אַרְצוֹ:

רש״י

בֵּינוֹתָם לַמָּקוֹם וְשׁוֹאֵל מִשְׁפָּטִים מֵאִתּוֹ: **אֶת הַדְּבָרִים.** דִּבְרֵי רִיבוֹתָם:

כא | **וְאַתָּה תֶחֱזֶה.** בְּרוּחַ הַקֹּדֶשׁ שֶׁעָלֶיךָ: **אַנְשֵׁי חַיִל.** עֲשִׁירִים, שֶׁאֵין צְרִיכִין לְהַחֲנִיף וּלְהַכִּיר פָּנִים: **אַנְשֵׁי אֱמֶת.** אֵלּוּ בַּעֲלֵי הַבְטָחָה שֶׁהֵם כְּדַאי לִסְמֹךְ עַל דִּבְרֵיהֶם, שֶׁעַל יְדֵי כָךְ יִהְיוּ דִּבְרֵיהֶם נִשְׁמָעִין: **שֹׂנְאֵי בָצַע.** שֶׁשּׂוֹנְאִים אֶת מָמוֹנָם בַּדִּין, כְּהַהִיא דַּאֲמְרִינַן: כָּל דַּיָּנָא דְּמַפְּקִין מָמוֹנָא מִנֵּיהּ בְּדִינָא לָאו דַּיָּנָא הוּא: **שָׂרֵי אֲלָפִים.** הֵם הָיוּ שֵׁשׁ מֵאוֹת שָׂרִים לְשֵׁשׁ מֵאוֹת אֶלֶף: **שָׂרֵי מֵאוֹת.** שֵׁשֶׁת אֲלָפִים הָיוּ: **שָׂרֵי חֲמִשִּׁים.** שְׁנֵים עָשָׂר אֶלֶף: **וְשָׂרֵי עֲשָׂרֹת.** שִׁשִּׁים אֶלֶף:

כב | **וְשָׁפְטוּ.** "וִידוּנוּן", לְשׁוֹן צִוּוּי: **וְהָקֵל מֵעָלֶיךָ.** דָּבָר זֶה לְהָקֵל מֵעָלֶיךָ. "וְהָקֵל" כְּמוֹ: "וְהַכְבֵּד אֶת לִבּוֹ" (לעיל ח, יא), "וְהַכּוֹת אֶת מוֹאָב" (מלכים ב׳ ג, כד), לְשׁוֹן הֹוֶה:

כג | **וְצִוְּךָ אֱלֹהִים וְיָכָלְתָּ עֲמֹד.** הִמָּלֵךְ בַּגְּבוּרָה, אִם מְצַוֶּה אוֹתְךָ לַעֲשׂוֹת כֵּן – תּוּכַל לַעֲמֹד, וְאִם יְעַכֵּב עַל יָדְךָ – לֹא תּוּכַל לַעֲמֹד: **וְגַם כָּל הָעָם הַזֶּה.** אַהֲרֹן נָדָב וַאֲבִיהוּא וְשִׁבְעִים זְקֵנִים הַנִּלְוִים עַתָּה עִמָּךְ:

כו | **וְשָׁפְטוּ.** "וְדָיְנִין יָת עַמָּא": **יְבִיאוּן.** "מַיְתַן": **יִשְׁפּוּטוּ הֵם.** כְּמוֹ יִשְׁפְּטוּ. וְכֵן: "לֹא תַעֲבוּרִי" (רות ב, ח) כְּמוֹ לֹא תַעַבְרִי. וְתַרְגּוּמוֹ: "דָּיְנִין אִנּוּן". מִקְרָאוֹת הָעֶלְיוֹנִים (לעיל פסוק כב) הָיוּ לְשׁוֹן צִוּוּי, לְכָךְ מְתֻרְגָּמִין: וִידוּנוּן, יֵיתוֹן, יְדוּנוּן, וּמִקְרָאוֹת הַלָּלוּ לְשׁוֹן עֲשִׂיָּה:

כז | **וַיֵּלֶךְ לוֹ אֶל אַרְצוֹ.** לְגַיֵּר בְּנֵי מִשְׁפַּחְתּוֹ:

DISCUSSION

suggestion, which he may have considered himself previously, he reacted enthusiastically, as he trusted his advice as one who was on the one hand, an objective outsider, and on the other, a person who had affection for Moses and cared for his welfare. Presumably Moses also subsequently received divine sanction for his father-in-law's plan (see Rashi and commentary on Deuteronomy 1:9).

18:26| **The difficult matter they would bring to Moses:** Even centuries later, after the details of the Oral Torah have become more established, not everything is sufficiently clear, and a question must often be taken to a higher authority. This was true even more so at the outset, when the Torah had just been given, and the Oral Torah was chiefly a general framework which had to be fleshed out during the years in the wilderness and thereafter. Therefore, all the difficult inquiries were brought to Moses, who would turn directly to God if he did not know how to resolve them himself.

18:27| **Moses sent forth his father-in-law, and he went to his land:** This happened a considerable time after the giving of the Torah. It is unclear whether following his return Yitro remained in his home in Midyan or if he subsequently returned to the wilderness and joined the Israelite camp (see Numbers 10:29–32), as it is related that Yitro's descendants resided with the Israelites in the Land of Israel several generations later (see Judges 1:16). It is possible that Moses' father-in-law intended to join the Israelite nation, but in order to do so he first had to return home to make the necessary arrangements for his conversion.

The Giving of the Torah at Mount Sinai

EXODUS 19:1–25

Prior to the momentous event in which God reveals Himself to His people, Moses ascends the mountain and returns to the people with several messages. In addition to the practical stages of their preparation, such as the command to keep their distance from the place of the revelation and the commandment to sanctify themselves for it, God instructs Moses to speak to the people as a collective unit in anticipation of their first covenant with God. This covenant includes the special destiny of the nation on the one hand, and their obligation to obey the will of God, on the other.

19 1 **In the third month,** the month of Sivan, **from the exodus of the children of Israel from the land of Egypt, on that day,** the first of the month,[12] **they came to the wilderness of Sinai.**

Fourth aliya

2 **They traveled from Refidim and came to the wilderness of Sinai and encamped in the wilderness; Israel encamped there next to the** same **mountain**[D] familiar to Moses from his first revelation, when God informed him that the people would worship Him there (3:12).

3 **Moses ascended** the mountain **to God; the Lord summoned him from the mountain, saying: So you shall say to the house of Jacob and tell to the children of Israel:**[D]

4 **You saw what I did to Egypt,** all the signs and the miracles, **and I bore you on the wings of eagles.** You arrived here in a wondrous fashion. Such a long journey for a large nation, including all of the families and baggage, is no simple matter. **And I brought you to Me,** to this place, where the entire people will experience a direct encounter with God, an unprecedented event in history.

5 Here God summarizes the significance of the forthcoming revelation: **Now, if you will heed My voice, and observe My covenant,** then **you shall be distinguished,** a special treasure **for Me from among all the peoples,** not only the nations of the region, **as all the earth is Mine.** Until now God has revealed His love for the Israelites and has aided them in their plight. Here, for the first time, He establishes a covenant with them, which includes mutual obligations.

6 **You shall be for Me a kingdom of priests,**[D] a people who serve as priests for all humanity, **and a holy nation.** Matters that are considered reasonable by others are not necessarily normal for you.[13] The destiny that Israel will be a kingdom of priests and a holy nation is not merely a promise of a lofty status; it entails a serious commitment, as explained below. **These are the words that you shall speak to the children of Israel.** If the Israelites accept this role upon themselves, they will be given detailed instructions through the Ten Precepts and all of the 613 commandments. However, before this special covenant between God and the people can take effect, they must accept the basic obligations: To listen to His commands, to observe the covenant, and to be His holy people.

7 **Moses came and summoned the elders of the people,** in the presence of the entire people, **and he set before them all these matters that the Lord had commanded him.**

Fifth aliya

8 **All the people answered together and said: Everything that the Lord has spoken we will perform.** We accept upon ourselves the terms of the covenant with God, to be a kingdom of priests and a holy nation, and we will obey His commands. **Moses returned the statement of the people to the Lord.** Since Moses was sent to relay the statement of God to the people, it is proper etiquette for him to return to God, either in body or perhaps just spiritually,[14] with their response, despite the fact that God was of course aware of what they had said.[15]

9 **The Lord said to Moses: Behold, I am coming** to reveal Myself **to you in a thickness of the cloud.**[16] The cloud serves as a kind of physical intermediary, allowing My presence to be grasped by humans, **so that the people will hear while I speak with you.** In contrast to all other prophecies, which God conveys to the soul and mind of a single prophet, this revelation through a cloud will enable His word to be heard in public. **And they will believe also in you forever,**[D] with a stronger faith.

DISCUSSION

19:2| **Next to the mountain:** Despite common depictions of Mount Sinai as towering, it can be inferred from the continuation of the chapter that this was not a particularly tall mountain. This is also the tradition of the Sages (see *Sota* 5a).

19:3| **So you shall say to the house of Jacob and tell to the children of Israel:** The parallel structure of this introduction, which is written in the style of poetic passages in the Bible, is fitting for the celebratory tone of the declaration. There is a tradition that the expression "house of Jacob" refers to the women, while "the children of Israel" refers to the men (see *Targum Yonatan* and Rashi; *Shemot Rabba* 22:8). In any case, the statement is addressed to the entire people.

19:6| **A kingdom of priests:** All humans are commanded to believe in God and observe His basic commandments. However, the nation of Israel, as an entire people of priests, possesses an additional level of obligation in their service of God. This idea is reiterated in Isaiah's prophecies of the future: "Strangers will stand and herd your flocks and foreigners will be your farmers and your vineyard workers; and you will be called priests of the Lord; servants of our God will be said of you; you will eat the wealth of the nations, and in their glory will you revel" (Isaiah 61:5–6). The gentiles will deal with necessary labors, while you will serve as the priests of God on behalf of the entire world. Later the Torah will describe the selection of another level of priesthood from among the nation of Israel itself. The descendants of Aaron will be granted the status of priests, with special obligations and services beyond those of the rest of the Israelites (28:41–29:30; Leviticus 21:8).

יט א בַּחֹדֶשׁ הַשְּׁלִישִׁי לְצֵאת בְּנֵי־יִשְׂרָאֵל מֵאֶרֶץ מִצְרָיִם בַּיּוֹם הַזֶּה בָּאוּ מִדְבַּר סִינָי: רביעי
ב וַיִּסְעוּ מֵרְפִידִים וַיָּבֹאוּ מִדְבַּר סִינַי וַיַּחֲנוּ בַּמִּדְבָּר וַיִּחַן־שָׁם יִשְׂרָאֵל נֶגֶד הָהָר:
ג וּמֹשֶׁה עָלָה אֶל־הָאֱלֹהִים וַיִּקְרָא אֵלָיו יהוה מִן־הָהָר לֵאמֹר כֹּה תֹאמַר לְבֵית
ד יַעֲקֹב וְתַגֵּיד לִבְנֵי יִשְׂרָאֵל: אַתֶּם רְאִיתֶם אֲשֶׁר עָשִׂיתִי לְמִצְרָיִם וָאֶשָּׂא אֶתְכֶם
ה עַל־כַּנְפֵי נְשָׁרִים וָאָבִא אֶתְכֶם אֵלָי: וְעַתָּה אִם־שָׁמוֹעַ תִּשְׁמְעוּ בְּקֹלִי וּשְׁמַרְתֶּם
ו אֶת־בְּרִיתִי וִהְיִיתֶם לִי סְגֻלָּה מִכָּל־הָעַמִּים כִּי־לִי כָּל־הָאָרֶץ: וְאַתֶּם תִּהְיוּ־לִי טו
ז מַמְלֶכֶת כֹּהֲנִים וְגוֹי קָדוֹשׁ אֵלֶּה הַדְּבָרִים אֲשֶׁר תְּדַבֵּר אֶל־בְּנֵי יִשְׂרָאֵל: וַיָּבֹא חמישי
מֹשֶׁה וַיִּקְרָא לְזִקְנֵי הָעָם וַיָּשֶׂם לִפְנֵיהֶם אֵת כָּל־הַדְּבָרִים הָאֵלֶּה אֲשֶׁר צִוָּהוּ
ח יהוה: וַיַּעֲנוּ כָל־הָעָם יַחְדָּו וַיֹּאמְרוּ כֹּל אֲשֶׁר־דִּבֶּר יהוה נַעֲשֶׂה וַיָּשֶׁב מֹשֶׁה אֶת־
ט דִּבְרֵי הָעָם אֶל־יהוה: וַיֹּאמֶר יהוה אֶל־מֹשֶׁה הִנֵּה אָנֹכִי בָּא אֵלֶיךָ בְּעַב הֶעָנָן
בַּעֲבוּר יִשְׁמַע הָעָם בְּדַבְּרִי עִמָּךְ וְגַם־בְּךָ יַאֲמִינוּ לְעוֹלָם וַיַּגֵּד מֹשֶׁה אֶת־דִּבְרֵי

רש״י

פרק יט

א| **ביום הזה.** בראש חדש. לא היה צריך לכתב אלא ׳ביום ההוא׳, מהו ״ביום הזה״? שיהיו דברי תורה חדשים עליך כאלו היום נתנו:

ב| **ויסעו מרפידים.** מה תלמוד לומר לחזור ולפרש מהיכן נסעו? והלא כבר כתב שברפידים היו חונים (לעיל יז, א), בידוע שמשם נסעו! אלא להקיש נסיעתן מרפידים לביאתן למדבר סיני; מה ביאתן למדבר סיני בתשובה אף נסיעתן מרפידים בתשובה: **ויחן שם ישראל.** כאיש אחד בלב אחד, אבל שאר כל החניות בתרעמת ובמחלקת: **נגד ההר.** למזרחו, וכל מקום שאתה מוצא ׳נגד׳ – פנים למזרח:

ג| **ומשה עלה.** ביום השני, וכל עליותיו בהשכמה היו, שנאמר: ״וישכם משה בבקר״ (להלן לד, ד): **כה תאמר.** בלשון הזה וכסדר הזה: **לבית יעקב.** אלו הנשים, תאמר להן בלשון רכה: **ותגיד לבני ישראל.** עונשין ודקדוקין פרש לזכרים, דברים הקשין כגידין:

ד| **אתם ראיתם.** ולא מסרת היא בידכם בדברים אשר עשיתי במצרים, על כמה עברות היו חיבין לי קדם שנזדוגו לכם, ולא נפרעתי מהם אלא על ידכם: **ואשא אתכם.** זה יום שבאו ישראל לרעמסס, שהיו ישראל מפזרין בכל ארץ גשן, ולשעה קלה כשבאו לסע ולצאת נקבצו כלם לרעמסס. ואונקלוס תרגם ״ואשא״ כמו ואסיע אתכם: ״ואטלית יתכון״, תקן את הדבור דרך כבוד למעלה: **על כנפי נשרים.** כנשר הנושא גוזליו על כנפיו, שכל שאר העופות נותנים את בניהם בין רגליהם, לפי שמתיראין מעוף אחר שפורח על גביהם, אבל הנשר הזה אינו מתירא אלא מן האדם שמא יזרק בו חץ, לפי שאין עוף פורח על גביו, לכך נותנו על כנפיו, אומר: מוטב יכנס החץ בי ולא בבני. אף אני עשיתי כן: ״ויסע מלאך האלהים וגו׳ ויבא בין מחנה מצרים וגו׳ (לעיל יד, יט-כ), והיו מצרים זורקים חצים ואבני בליסטראות והענן מקבלם: **ואבא אתכם אלי.** כתרגומו:

ה| **ועתה.** אם עתה תקבלו עליכם יערב לכם מכאן ואילך, שכל התחלות קשות: **ושמרתם את בריתי.** שאכרת עמכם על שמירת התורה: **סגלה.** אוצר חביב, כמו: ״וסגלת מלכים״ (קהלת ב, ח), כלי יקר ואבנים טובות שהמלכים גונזים אותם, כך אתם לי סגלה משאר אמות. ולא תאמרו, אתם לבדכם שלי ואין לי אחרים עמכם, ומה יש לי עוד שתהא חבתכם נכרת? – ״כי לי כל הארץ״, והם בעיני ולפני לכלום:

ו| **ואתם תהיו לי ממלכת כהנים.** שרים, כמה דאת אמר: ״ובני דוד כהנים היו״ (שמואל ב׳ ח, יח): **אלה הדברים.** לא פחות ולא יותר:

ח| **וישב משה את דברי העם וגו׳.** ביום המחרת שהוא שלישי, שהרי בהשכמה עלה. וכי צריך היה משה להשיב? אלא בא הכתוב ללמדך דרך ארץ ממשה, שלא אמר: הואיל ויודע מי ששלחני, איני צריך להשיב:

ט| **בעב הענן.** במעבה הענן, וזהו ערפל: **וגם בך.** גם בנביאים הבאים אחריך: **ויגד משה את דברי וגו׳.** ביום המחרת שהוא רביעי לחדש: **את דברי העם וגו׳.** תשובה על דבר זה שמעתי מהם, שרצונם לשמע ממך, אינו דומה השומע מפי שליח לשומע מפי המלך, רצוננו לראות את מלכנו:

DISCUSSION

19:9| **And they will believe also in you forever:** Apparently, the earlier wonders performed by Moses were not sufficient to implant firm roots of faith within the people. The acceptance of prophetic statements can be due to the miracles the prophet performs or his

Moses related the statement of the people to the Lord, that they had agreed enthusiastically.[17]

10 **The Lord said to Moses: Go to the people and sanctify,** summon, and prepare **them,**[18] **today and tomorrow** for the revelation; **and they shall wash their garments** as part of the purification process that would become the accepted one in Israel.

11 **They shall be ready for the third day, as on the third day the Lord will descend before the eyes of all the people on Mount Sinai.**

12 In addition, **you shall restrict the people all around, saying:** This border shall signify the location of the forbidden area. **Beware of ascending the mountain or** even **touching its edge,** as **anyone who touches the mountain,** thereby entering the sanctified area, **shall be** punished by being **put to death.**

13 However, **no hand shall touch him,** that person who enters the forbidden place, **for** if others chase after him to catch him, they too will enter the demarcated area.[19] Therefore, **he shall be stoned** from afar **or shot** with arrows; **whether** it is an **animal** that wandered inside **or man, it will not live.** Only later, **with the extended blast of the shofar,** or alternatively, when that sound ceases, which is the signal for the cessation of the event, **they,** anyone who wishes, **shall** be permitted to **ascend the mountain.**[D]

14 **Moses descended from the mountain to the people. He sanctified the people and they washed their garments.**

15 **He said to the people:** As part of your sanctification process, **be prepared in three days; do not approach a woman.** Refrain from sexual relations during these three days in order to focus your minds and prepare for the encounter.

16 **It was on the third day, when it was morning, and there was thunder and lightning and a thick cloud on the mountain, and the blast of a shofar** was **extremely powerful, and all the people who were in the camp trembled.**

17 **Moses took the people out of the camp toward God.** Despite the warning against approaching too close to the central area of the event, it was appropriate for the people to advance as close as they could within the permitted area. **And they stood at the foot of the mountain.**

18 **Mount Sinai was all smoke, because the Lord descended upon it in fire. Its** thick, concentrated **smoke ascended like the smoke of a furnace,** which is produced by a large fire in a small area. **And the entire mountain trembled greatly.**

19 **The** loud **blast of the shofar,** which was initially heard together with the other noises, **grew continuously stronger.** As this occurred, **Moses would speak, and God would answer him with a voice.** The people heard this conversation between Moses and God.

20 **The Lord descended upon Mount Sinai to the top of the**
Sixth aliya **mountain; the Lord summoned Moses to the top of the mountain,** while all the people listened in order to hear the exchange between them, **and Moses ascended.**

DISCUSSION

charismatic personality, but in such cases, the belief in the prophecy itself is limited. The public revelation at Sinai, in contrast, was designed to lead to a profound, permanent belief. The nation of Israel would see and hear God without an intermediary, and directly perceive the prophecy given to Moses and witness the truth of his mission (see Rambam, *Sefer HaMadda, Hilkhot Yesodei HaTorah* 8:1).

19:13 | **With the extended blast of the shofar, they shall ascend the mountain:** Undoubtedly, the descent of God to a particular spot is of theological significance. The giving of the Torah and the establishment of the covenant with the people of Israel will occur within the boundaries of that location and therefore any approach to that area must be restricted. Nevertheless, the sanctity of Mount Sinai was merely temporary, as it was solely due to the momentous encounter about to take place there. In the Jewish tradition, the mountain is a site of historical memory, but it does not retain any measure of holiness. Consequently, no pilgrimages were undertaken to Mount Sinai, and even its precise location has not been preserved.

Not only is the place of the revelation unknown, but its exact date is not specified in the Torah either. In contrast to many other events, whose exact dates are recorded, here the date is mentioned only in a general manner: In the third month, a few days after the first of the month. According to the tradition, which accords with a straightforward reading of the verses, the revelation occurred on the sixth or the seventh of the month of Sivan (see *Shabbat* 86b). This unresolved issue further increases the mystery surrounding the event, which occurred outside conventional boundaries, in an unidentified place and time. Momentarily, the Jewish people entered a different, unfamiliar state where they encountered their God, and that state faded away after the revelation. No similar event, where an entire nation of men, women, and children encounter God beyond the boundaries of time and space, occurred prior to this one, and there will be nothing comparable in the future (see Rambam, *Guide of the Perplexed* 1:40, 2:33).

י הָעָם אֶל־יְהוָה: וַיֹּאמֶר יְהוָה אֶל־מֹשֶׁה לֵךְ אֶל־הָעָם וְקִדַּשְׁתָּם הַיּוֹם וּמָחָר
יא וְכִבְּסוּ שִׂמְלֹתָם: וְהָיוּ נְכֹנִים לַיּוֹם הַשְּׁלִישִׁי כִּי בַּיּוֹם הַשְּׁלִשִׁי יֵרֵד יְהוָה לְעֵינֵי
יב כָל־הָעָם עַל־הַר סִינָי: וְהִגְבַּלְתָּ אֶת־הָעָם סָבִיב לֵאמֹר הִשָּׁמְרוּ לָכֶם עֲלוֹת בָּהָר
יג וּנְגֹעַ בְּקָצֵהוּ כָּל־הַנֹּגֵעַ בָּהָר מוֹת יוּמָת: לֹא־תִגַּע בּוֹ יָד כִּי־סָקוֹל יִסָּקֵל אוֹ־יָרֹה
יד יִיָּרֶה אִם־בְּהֵמָה אִם־אִישׁ לֹא יִחְיֶה בִּמְשֹׁךְ הַיֹּבֵל הֵמָּה יַעֲלוּ בָהָר: וַיֵּרֶד מֹשֶׁה
טו מִן־הָהָר אֶל־הָעָם וַיְקַדֵּשׁ אֶת־הָעָם וַיְכַבְּסוּ שִׂמְלֹתָם: וַיֹּאמֶר אֶל־הָעָם הֱיוּ
טז נְכֹנִים לִשְׁלֹשֶׁת יָמִים אַל־תִּגְּשׁוּ אֶל־אִשָּׁה: וַיְהִי בַיּוֹם הַשְּׁלִישִׁי בִּהְיֹת הַבֹּקֶר
וַיְהִי קֹלֹת וּבְרָקִים וְעָנָן כָּבֵד עַל־הָהָר וְקֹל שֹׁפָר חָזָק מְאֹד וַיֶּחֱרַד כָּל־הָעָם
יז אֲשֶׁר בַּמַּחֲנֶה: וַיּוֹצֵא מֹשֶׁה אֶת־הָעָם לִקְרַאת הָאֱלֹהִים מִן־הַמַּחֲנֶה וַיִּתְיַצְּבוּ
יח בְּתַחְתִּית הָהָר: וְהַר סִינַי עָשַׁן כֻּלּוֹ מִפְּנֵי אֲשֶׁר יָרַד עָלָיו יְהוָה בָּאֵשׁ וַיַּעַל עֲשָׁנוֹ
יט כְּעֶשֶׁן הַכִּבְשָׁן וַיֶּחֱרַד כָּל־הָהָר מְאֹד: וַיְהִי קוֹל הַשֹּׁפָר הוֹלֵךְ וְחָזֵק מְאֹד מֹשֶׁה
כ יְדַבֵּר וְהָאֱלֹהִים יַעֲנֶנּוּ בְקוֹל: וַיֵּרֶד יְהוָה עַל־הַר סִינַי אֶל־רֹאשׁ הָהָר וַיִּקְרָא ששי

רש"י

י | וְקִדַּשְׁתָּם. וְזִמַּנְתָּם, שֶׁיָּכִינוּ עַצְמָם "הַיּוֹם וּמָחָר":

יא | וְהָיוּ נְכֹנִים. מֵאִשָּׁה: לַיּוֹם הַשְּׁלִישִׁי. שֶׁהוּא שִׁשָּׁה בַּחֹדֶשׁ, וּבַחֲמִישִׁי בָּנָה מֹשֶׁה אֶת הַמִּזְבֵּחַ תַּחַת הָהָר וּשְׁתֵּים עֶשְׂרֵה מַצֵּבָה, כָּל הָעִנְיָן הָאָמוּר בְּפָרָשַׁת וְאֵלֶּה הַמִּשְׁפָּטִים (להלן פרק כד), וְאֵין מֻקְדָּם וּמְאֻחָר בַּתּוֹרָה: לְעֵינֵי כָל הָעָם. מְלַמֵּד שֶׁלֹּא הָיָה בָּהֶם סוּמָא, שֶׁנִּתְרַפְּאוּ כֻּלָּם:

יב | וְהִגְבַּלְתָּ. קְבַע לָהֶם תְּחוּמִין לְסִימָן, שֶׁלֹּא יִקְרְבוּ מִן הַגְּבוּל וָהָלְאָה: לֵאמֹר. הַגְּבוּל אוֹמֵר לָהֶם: הִשָּׁמְרוּ מֵעֲלוֹת מִכָּאן וּלְהַלָּן, וְאַתָּה הַזְהִירֵם עַל כָּךְ: וּנְגֹעַ בְּקָצֵהוּ. אֲפִלּוּ בְּקָצֵהוּ:

יג | יָרֹה יִיָּרֶה. מִכָּאן לַנִּסְקָלִין שֶׁהֵם נִדְחִין לְמַטָּה מִבֵּית הַסְּקִילָה, שֶׁהָיָה גָבוֹהַּ שְׁתֵּי קוֹמוֹת: יִיָּרֶה. יֻשְׁלַךְ לְמַטָּה לָאָרֶץ, כְּמוֹ: "יָרָה בַיָּם" (לעיל טו, ד): בִּמְשֹׁךְ הַיֹּבֵל. כְּשֶׁיִּמְשֹׁךְ הַיּוֹבֵל קוֹל אָרֹךְ, הוּא סִימָן סִלּוּק שְׁכִינָה וְהַפְסָקַת הַקּוֹל, וְכֵיוָן שֶׁנִּסְתַּלֵּק הֵם רַשָּׁאִין לַעֲלוֹת: הַיֹּבֵל. הוּא שׁוֹפָר שֶׁל אַיִל, שֶׁכֵּן בַּעֲרַבְיָא קוֹרִין לְדִכְרָא 'יוּבְלָא', וְשׁוֹפָר שֶׁל אֵילוֹ שֶׁל יִצְחָק הָיָה:

יד | מִן הָהָר אֶל הָעָם. מְלַמֵּד שֶׁלֹּא הָיָה מֹשֶׁה פּוֹנֶה לַעֲסָקָיו, אֶלָּא מִן הָהָר אֶל הָעָם:

טו | הֱיוּ נְכֹנִים לִשְׁלֹשֶׁת יָמִים. לְסוֹף שְׁלֹשֶׁת יָמִים, הוּא יוֹם רְבִיעִי, שֶׁהוֹסִיף מֹשֶׁה יוֹם אֶחָד מִדַּעְתּוֹ, כְּדִבְרֵי רַבִּי יוֹסֵי. וּלְדִבְרֵי הָאוֹמֵר בְּשִׁשָּׁה בַּחֹדֶשׁ נִתְּנוּ עֲשֶׂרֶת הַדִּבְּרוֹת, לֹא הוֹסִיף מֹשֶׁה כְּלוּם, וְ"לִשְׁלֹשֶׁת יָמִים" כְּמוֹ 'לַיּוֹם הַשְּׁלִישִׁי': אַל תִּגְּשׁוּ אֶל אִשָּׁה. כָּל שְׁלֹשֶׁת יָמִים הַלָּלוּ, כְּדֵי שֶׁיִּהְיוּ הַנָּשִׁים טוֹבְלוֹת לַיּוֹם הַשְּׁלִישִׁי וְיִהְיוּ טְהוֹרוֹת לְקַבֵּל תּוֹרָה, שֶׁאִם יְשַׁמְּשׁוּ תּוֹךְ שְׁלֹשָׁה שֶׁמָּא תִּפְלֹט הָאִשָּׁה שִׁכְבַת זֶרַע לְאַחַר טְבִילָתָהּ וְתַחֲזֹר וְתִטְמָא, אֲבָל מִשֶּׁשָּׁהֲתָה שְׁלֹשָׁה יָמִים כְּבָר הַזֶּרַע מַסְרִיחַ וְאֵינוֹ רָאוּי לְהַזְרִיעַ, וְטָהוֹר מִלְּטַמֵּא אֶת הַפּוֹלֶטֶת:

טז | בִּהְיֹת הַבֹּקֶר. מְלַמֵּד שֶׁהִקְדִּים עַל יָדָם, מַה שֶּׁאֵין דֶּרֶךְ בָּשָׂר וָדָם לַעֲשׂוֹת כֵּן שֶׁיְּהֵא הָרַב מַמְתִּין לַתַּלְמִיד. וְכֵן מָצִינוּ בִּיחֶזְקֵאל: "קוּם צֵא אֶל הַבִּקְעָה... וָאָקוּם וָאֵצֵא אֶל הַבִּקְעָה וְהִנֵּה שָׁם כְּבוֹד ה' עֹמֵד" (יחזקאל ג, כב-כג):

יז | לִקְרַאת הָאֱלֹהִים. מַגִּיד שֶׁהָיְתָה שְׁכִינָה יוֹצְאָה לִקְרָאתָם כְּחָתָן הַיּוֹצֵא לִקְרַאת כַּלָּה, וְזֶהוּ שֶׁנֶּאֱמַר: "ה' מִסִּינַי בָּא" (דברים לג, ב) וְלֹא נֶאֱמַר: 'לְסִינַי בָּא': בְּתַחְתִּית הָהָר. לְפִי פְּשׁוּטוֹ בְּרַגְלֵי הָהָר. וּמִדְרָשׁוֹ, שֶׁנִּתְלַשׁ הָהָר מִמְּקוֹמוֹ וְנִכְפָּה עֲלֵיהֶם כְּגִיגִית:

יח | עָשַׁן כֻּלּוֹ. אֵין 'עָשַׁן' זֶה שֵׁם דָּבָר, שֶׁהֲרֵי נָקוּד הַשִּׁי"ן פַּתָּח, אֶלָּא לְשׁוֹן פָּעַל, כְּמוֹ אָמַר, שָׁמַר, שָׁמַע. לְכָךְ תַּרְגּוּמוֹ: "תְּנַן כֻּלֵּיהּ" וְלֹא תִּרְגֵּם 'תְּנָנָא'. וְכָל 'עָשָׁן' שֶׁבַּמִּקְרָא נְקוּדִים קָמַץ, מִפְּנֵי שֶׁהֵם שֵׁם דָּבָר: הַכִּבְשָׁן. שֶׁל סִיד. יָכוֹל כְּכִבְשָׁן זֶה וְלֹא יוֹתֵר? תַּלְמוּד לוֹמַר: "בֹּעֵר בָּאֵשׁ עַד לֵב הַשָּׁמַיִם" (דברים ד, יא). וּמַה תַּלְמוּד לוֹמַר: "כִּבְשָׁן"? לְשַׁבֵּר אֶת הָאֹזֶן מַה שֶּׁהִיא יְכוֹלָה לִשְׁמֹעַ, נוֹתֵן לַבְּרִיּוֹת סִימָן הַנִּכָּר לָהֶם. כַּיּוֹצֵא בּוֹ: "כְּאַרְיֵה יִשְׁאָג" (הושע יא, י), וְכִי מִי נָתַן כֹּחַ בָּאֲרִי אֶלָּא הוּא, וְהַכָּתוּב מוֹשְׁלוֹ כָּאַרְיֵה? אֶלָּא אָנוּ מְכַנִּין וּמְדַמִּין אוֹתוֹ לִבְרִיּוֹתָיו כְּדֵי לְשַׁבֵּר אֶת הָאֹזֶן מַה שֶּׁיְּכוֹלָה לִשְׁמֹעַ. כַּיּוֹצֵא בּוֹ: "וְקוֹלוֹ כְּקוֹל מַיִם רַבִּים" (יחזקאל מג, ב), וְכִי מִי נָתַן קוֹל לַמַּיִם אֶלָּא הוּא, וְאַתָּה מְכַנֶּה אוֹתוֹ לְדַמּוֹתוֹ לִבְרִיּוֹתָיו, כְּדֵי לְשַׁבֵּר אֶת הָאֹזֶן:

יט | הוֹלֵךְ וְחָזֵק מְאֹד. מִנְהַג הֶדְיוֹט כָּל זְמַן שֶׁהוּא מַאֲרִיךְ לִתְקֹעַ קוֹלוֹ מַחֲלִישׁ וְכוֹהֶה, אֲבָל כָּאן "הוֹלֵךְ וְחָזֵק מְאֹד". וְלָמָּה כָּךְ מִתְּחִלָּה? לְשַׁבֵּר אָזְנֵיהֶם מַה שֶּׁיְּכוֹלִין לִשְׁמֹעַ: מֹשֶׁה יְדַבֵּר. כְּשֶׁהָיָה מֹשֶׁה מְדַבֵּר וּמַשְׁמִיעַ הַדִּבְּרוֹת לְיִשְׂרָאֵל, שֶׁהֲרֵי לֹא שָׁמְעוּ מִפִּי הַגְּבוּרָה אֶלָּא "אָנֹכִי" וְ"לֹא יִהְיֶה לְךָ", וְהַקָּדוֹשׁ בָּרוּךְ הוּא מְסַיְּעוֹ לָתֵת בּוֹ כֹּחַ לִהְיוֹת קוֹלוֹ מַגְבִּיר וְנִשְׁמָע: יַעֲנֶנּוּ בְקוֹל. יַעֲנֶנּוּ עַל דְּבַר הַקּוֹל, כְּמוֹ: "אֲשֶׁר יַעֲנֶה בָאֵשׁ" (מלכים א' יח, כד), עַל דְּבַר הָאֵשׁ לְהוֹרִידוֹ:

כ | וַיֵּרֶד ה' עַל הַר סִינַי. יָכוֹל יָרַד עָלָיו מַמָּשׁ? תַּלְמוּד לוֹמַר: "כִּי מִן הַשָּׁמַיִם דִּבַּרְתִּי עִמָּכֶם" (להלן כ, יט)! מְלַמֵּד שֶׁהִרְכִּין שָׁמַיִם הַתַּחְתּוֹנִים וְהָעֶלְיוֹנִים וְהִצִּיעָן עַל גַּבֵּי הָהָר כְּמַצָּע עַל הַמִּטָּה, וְיָרַד כִּסֵּא הַכָּבוֹד עֲלֵיהֶם:

21 **The Lord said to Moses: Descend,** and again **warn the people, lest they break through to the Lord to see.** When they realize that this is no ordinary fire, the smoke is unusual, and the shofar is unlike any other shofar they have heard, they might be drawn to the place out of curiosity and yearning for God. **And if they do come near, many of them will fall,** either because there are guards stationed there, instructed to stop anyone who attempts to approach, or due to divine retribution for this infraction.

22 **Also the priests,**[D] those who perform the sanctified rites and **who approach the Lord** and stand in front of the people at the foot of the mountain,[20] **shall sanctify themselves, lest the Lord burst out against them.**

23 **Moses said to the Lord:** Why do I need to warn them a second time? After all, **the people will not be able to ascend Mount Sinai, as you have** already **warned us, saying: Demarcate the mountain, and sanctify it.**

24 **The Lord said to him: Go, descend,**[D] **and you shall ascend, and Aaron with you.** Your brother shall accompany you part of the way. It is evident from the verses below that even those close to Moses, who were permitted to ascend higher than the rest of the people, were not permitted to reach the spot of the encounter itself, where Moses alone ascended (see 20:18). God again warns: **But the priests and the people shall not advance** and break through **to ascend to the Lord, lest He burst out against them.**

25 **Moses descended to the people, and said** God's repeated warning **to them.** Apparently, he then ascended the mountain again.[21]

The Ten Precepts
EXODUS 20:1–14

The Torah lists Ten Precepts spoken by God on Mount Sinai, which He later wrote on stone tablets. The familiar term "Ten Commandments" is translated here as "Ten Precepts." In three places the Torah recounts the writing of the ten *devarim* on the Tablets of the Covenant.[22] *Devarim* is best translated as statements or precepts, not commandments. Furthermore, the passages in which these are stated[23] can readily be divided up into ten precepts, while it is difficult to divide them into ten commandments.

It should be noted that the precise division of the revelation into ten sections is a matter of dispute. These precepts, which include matters between man and God as well as those involving relationships between man and his fellow man, are at the foundation of the Judaic religious structure and the Jewish approach to life. In large part, they are also the source of universal values. Most of them are prohibitions relating to actions, but there are also some positive commands, as well as matters relating to one's emotional and psychological states.

There is a distinction between the first five precepts, which focus on the relationship between God and man – including the honoring of one's parents, as this precept is also within the rubric of honoring God – and the last five precepts, which consist of interpersonal prohibitions. In fact, the name of God does not appear in the second section at all.

All the precepts are addressed to the individual, in a direct, personal manner. However, in the early precepts, which focus on the belief in God, God is referred to in the first person, as the Speaker, whereas in the other precepts God is referred to in the third person.

20 1 **God spoke all these matters, saying:** It is unclear from the continuation of the account whether the entire people heard all the precepts directly.[24] In any case, they certainly heard the first section from God.

2 **I am the Lord your God,**[D] **who took you out of the land of Egypt, from the house of bondage.** According to some commentaries, this is not a separate command, but the Speaker presenting Himself, since without the acceptance of this basic identification of God there is no meaning to the commands that follow.[25] Others maintain that this is a command to believe in God and to know Him.[26]

3 The previous declaration leads to the demand for exclusivity: **You shall have no other gods before Me,** together with Me. There is no other god but Me.

─────────────────────────── DISCUSSION ───────────────────────────

19:22 | The priests: The identity of the priests at the time is uncertain. According to tradition, the firstborn sons of each family served as priests. The special status of the firstborn can be seen, for example, in the story of Esau's sale of his birthright to Jacob (Genesis 25:31–34; see also Exodus 4:22–23). After the sin of the Golden Calf, when the Tabernacle was built, Aaron's descendants were appointed priests (*Zevaḥim* 112b; *Bemidbar Rabba* 3:5; Ibn Ezra; *Bekhor Shor*; see Numbers 3:13, and *Bekhor Shor* ad loc.).

19:24 | The Lord said to him: Go, descend: Some commentaries interpret the phrase "Go, descend" as an explanation for why a repeat of the earlier warning is necessary. Although Moses was certain that no one would disobey the command and ascend the mountain, God told him that if he were to go down and examine the people's nature, he would realize the need to warn them again at this juncture, due to the great danger and the temptation to draw close to God (see *Ohev Yisrael, Likkutim Ḥadashim, Yitro*).

20:2 | I am the Lord your God: The first of the Ten Precepts appears in a positive and negative formulation relating to the presence of God. This matter must necessarily precede all the

כא יהוה למשה אל־ראש ההר ויעל משה: ויאמר יהוה אל־משה רד העד בעם
כב פן־יהרסו אל־יהוה לראות ונפל ממנו רב: וגם הכהנים הנגשים אל־יהוה
כג יתקדשו פן־יפרץ בהם יהוה: ויאמר משה אל־יהוה לא־יוכל העם לעלת
כד אל־הר סיני כי־אתה העדתה בנו לאמר הגבל את־ההר וקדשתו: ויאמר
אליו יהוה לך־רד ועלית אתה ואהרן עמך והכהנים והעם אל־יהרסו לעלת
כה כ א אל־יהוה פן־יפרץ־בם: וירד משה אל־העם ויאמר אלהם: וידבר
ב אלהים את כל־הדברים האלה לאמר: אנכי יהוה אלהיך אשר
ג הוצאתיך מארץ מצרים מבית עבדים: לא־יהיה לך אלהים אחרים על־פני:

רש"י

כא| **העד בעם.** התרה בהם שלא לעלות בהר: **פן יהרסו וגו'.** שלא יהרסו את מצבם על ידי שתאותם "אל ה' לראות" ויקרבו לצד ההר: **ונפל ממנו רב.** כל מה שיפול מהם, ואפילו הוא יחידי, חשוב לפני רב: **פן יהרסו.** כל הריסה מפרדת אסיפת הבנין, אף הנפרדין ממצב אנשים הורסים את המצב:

כב| **וגם הכהנים.** אף הבכורות שהעבודה בהם: **הנגשים אל ה'.** להקריב קרבנות, אף הם אל יסמכו על חשיבותם לעלות: **יתקדשו.** יהיו מזמנים להתיצב על עמדן: **פן יפרץ.** לשון פרצה, יהרג בהם ויעשה בהם פרצה:

כג| **לא יוכל העם.** איני צריך להעיד בהם, שהרי מתרין ועומדין הם היום שלשה ימים, ולא יוכלו לעלות, שאין להם רשות:

כד| **לך רד.** והעד בהם שנית, שמזרזין את האדם קודם מעשה וחוזרין ומזרזין אותו בשעת מעשה: **ועלית אתה ואהרן עמך והכהנים.** יכול אף הם "עמך"? תלמוד לומר: "ועלית אתה". אמור מעתה, אתה מחיצה לעצמך, ואהרן מחיצה לעצמו; משה נגש יותר מאהרן ואהרן יותר מן הכהנים, "והעם" כל עקר "אל יהרסו" את מצבם "לעלת אל ה'": **פן יפרץ בם.** אף על פי שהוא נקוד חטף קמץ אינו זז מגזרתו. כך דרך כל תבה שנקדתה מלאפום, כשהיא סמוכה במקף משתנה הנקוד לחטף קמץ:

כה| **ויאמר אלהם.** התראה זו:

פרק כ

א| **וידבר אלהים.** אין "אלהים" אלא דין, לפי שיש פרשיות בתורה שאם עשאן אדם מקבל שכר ואם לאו אינו מקבל עליהם פרענות, יכול אף עשרת הדברות כן? תלמוד לומר: "וידבר אלהים", דין לפרע: **את כל הדברים האלה.** מלמד שאמר הקדוש ברוך הוא עשרת הדברות בדבור אחד, מה שאי אפשר לאדם לומר כן. אם כן מה תלמוד לומר עוד "אנכי" ו"לא יהיה לך"? שחזר ופרש על כל דבור ודבור בפני עצמו: **לאמר.** מלמד שהיו עונין על הן – הן, ועל לאו – לאו:

ב| **אשר הוצאתיך מארץ מצרים.** כדאי היא ההוצאה שתהיו משעבדים לי. דבר אחר, לפי שנגלה בים כגבור מלחמה ונגלה כאן כזקן מלא רחמים, שנאמר: "ותחת רגליו כמעשה לבנת הספיר" (להלן כד, י), זו היתה לפניו בשעת השעבוד, "וכעצם השמים" (שם) משנגאלו, הואיל ואני משתנה במראות, אל תאמרו שתי רשויות הן! אנכי הוא אשר הוצאתיך ממצרים ועל הים. דבר אחר, לפי שהיו שומעין קולות הרבה, שנאמר "את הקולת" (להלן פסוק טו), קולות באין מארבע רוחות ומן השמים ומן הארץ, אל תאמרו רשויות הרבה הן! ולמה אמר לשון יחיד, "אלהיך"? לתן פתחון פה למשה ללמד סניגוריא במעשה העגל, וזה הוא שאמר: "למה ה' יחרה אפך בעמך" (להלן לב, יא), לא להם צוית "לא יהיה לכם אלהים אחרים", אלא לי לבדי: **מבית עבדים.** מבית פרעה שהייתם עבדים לו. או אינו אומר אלא "מבית עבדים" שהיו עבדים לעבדים? תלמוד לומר: "ויפדך מבית עבדים מיד פרעה מלך מצרים" (דברים ז, ח), אמור מעתה, עבדים למלך היו ולא עבדים לעבדים:

ג| **לא יהיה לך.** למה נאמר? לפי שנאמר: "לא תעשה לך", אין לי אלא שלא יעשה, העשוי כבר מנין שלא יקים? תלמוד לומר: "לא יהיה לך": **אלהים אחרים.** שאינן אלהות, אלא אחרים עשאום אלהים עליהם. ולא יתכן לפרש "אלהים אחרים" זולתי, שגנאי הוא כלפי מעלה לקרותם אלהות אצלו. דבר אחר, "אלהים אחרים", שהם אחרים לעובדיהם, צועקים אליהם ואינן עונין אותם, ודומה כאלו הוא אחר שאינו מכירו מעולם: **על פני.** כל זמן שאני קים, שלא תאמר, לא נצטוו על עבודה זרה אלא אותו הדור:

DISCUSSION

others, as the practical precepts mentioned below are based on the existence of a Commander. Although some of those also have social value, their importance is not due merely to their usefulness within daily life. Rather, the precepts given on this lofty occasion mainly serve to establish values of good and evil. Furthermore, the opening declaration: "I am the Lord your God" identifies the Giver of the Torah as the One who saved Israel from Egypt, which provides the legal force for the ensuing commands. These are not statutes that must be fulfilled out of awe of judgment or fear of the police, but rather due to their independent, absolute value.

4 Furthermore, faith alone is not enough. **You shall not make for you an idol** to worship, **nor any** item that is an **image of that which is in the heavens above, or that which is on the earth below, or that which is in the water beneath the earth,** anywhere on earth. The phrase "that which is in the water beneath the earth" might also allude to large, primeval sea creatures, which were considered powerful beings that people would worship.

5 **You shall not prostrate yourselves to them, and you shall not worship them, because I am the Lord your God, a zealous God,**ᴰ and cannot stand another god to be worshipped together with Me. I am He **who reckons the iniquity of the fathers against the children, against the third generation,** grandchildren, **and against the fourth generation,** great-grandchildren, **to My enemies.** I recall transgressions and even punish one's descendants to the fourth generation, in accordance with the wicked deeds of the fathers, if the descendants continue on their evil path. For a lengthy description of this principle, see Ezekiel 18 and *Berakhot* 7a. Some maintain that this principle applies only to the severe transgression of idolatry, whose worshippers are called "My enemies."²⁷

6 **And** conversely, I am also a God **who engages in kindness for the thousands** of generations, as in the verse: "Who maintains the covenant and the kindness to those who love Him and those who observe His commandments, for one thousand generations."²⁸ God's loving-kindness extends far beyond the four generations that apply in the case of a sinner. This kindness is **for those who love Me and observe My commandments.** God's zealousness, which demands exclusivity, entails both the negation of all competitors as well as a great love for the faithful.

7 The previous precept of not worshipping other gods leads to the requirement to honor and fear God: **You shall not take the name of the Lord your God in vain,**ᴰ by swearing falsely or mentioning it for no reason. This is a severe prohibition, as the person who does so disrespects the honor of the one Ruler of the entire world. **As the Lord will not absolve one who takes His name in vain.** It is difficult to achieve atonement for the

desecration of God's name. In general, the Ten Precepts deal with the laws themselves, not the punishments for those who violate them. The desecration of the name of God is an exception in this regard, as the punishment for the violator cannot always be administered by the court or society, and it is far more serious than other sins. Not even Yom Kippur and suffering can atone for the damage to one's very relationship with God.²⁹ The Sages have said that if there is any remedy for the desecration of God's name, it is through the opposite type of act, of increasing the sanctification of the name of God.³⁰

8 The next precept is one that creates the basic framework for Jewish life: **Remember the Sabbath day, to keep it holy.**ᴰ The Sabbath was already given to the Israelites (16:23–30), but here it is granted the lofty status of a uniquely holy day. One of the ways in which this precept is fulfilled is through the recitation of Kiddush, the blessing of Sanctification, on the Sabbath, in which the day is praised and its special value underscored. In the Kiddush of Friday night, one welcomes the holy day.³¹ The remembrance of the Sabbath day and its sanctification are also fulfilled through other customs and *halakhot*, such as the choice food one eats and the wearing of fine garments.³²

9 **Six days you shall work and perform all your labor.** The six weekdays are for people to work and accomplish all their necessary tasks.

10 **The seventh day is Sabbath for the Lord your God.** On this day God rested, as related at the beginning of the Torah.³³ **You,** too, Israel, who are entering a covenant with God, **shall not perform any labor**ᴰ on this day. This applies not only to **you** personally, but also to the members of your extended household: **And your son, and your daughter, your slave, and your maidservant, and your animal, and your stranger who is within your gates.** Since the Sabbath belongs to the entire nation, all are prohibited from performing labor on this day,

11 **because in six days the Lord made the heavens and the earth, the sea and everything that is in them, and He rested on the seventh day; therefore, the Lord blessed the Sabbath day,** as the day on which the labor of creation was completed. **And** furthermore, **He** set aside the Sabbath and **sanctified it**ᴰ

DISCUSSION

20:5 | A zealous [*kanna*] God: The root *kuf-nun-alef* can be translated as zealous or jealous. The zealousness described here is not based on desire but on love, similar to the verse: "As love is as intense as death, jealousy [*kina*] is as cruel as the grave" (Song of Songs 8:6). This zealousness is characterized by the demand for complete, exclusive ownership. Both here and in its human, social manifestation, jealousy is

expressed not merely through a lack of patience with the closeness of others to the beloved, but is accompanied by a desire for vengeance and a combative spirit (see *Bekhor Shor*). Indeed, the expressions of zealousness attributed to God in the Bible appear invariably in the context of idolatry, which is essentially the betrayal of God (based on Ramban).

20:7 | You shall not take the name of the Lord your God in vain: This verse teaches that the very name of God must be treated with respect. In addition, it is derived from this verse that there are limitations on mentioning the ineffable name of God for no purpose or in a negative context. God's name is usually replaced by various other appellations such as *Hashem*, which literally means "The Name," in order to ◄●

ד לֹא־תַעֲשֶׂה לְךָ פֶסֶל וְכָל־תְּמוּנָה אֲשֶׁר בַּשָּׁמַיִם מִמַּעַל וַאֲשֶׁר בָּאָרֶץ מִתָּחַת
ה וַאֲשֶׁר בַּמַּיִם מִתַּחַת לָאָרֶץ: לֹא־תִשְׁתַּחֲוֶה לָהֶם וְלֹא תָעָבְדֵם כִּי אָנֹכִי יהוה
אֱלֹהֶיךָ אֵל קַנָּא פֹּקֵד עֲוֺן אָבֹת עַל־בָּנִים עַל־שִׁלֵּשִׁים וְעַל־רִבֵּעִים לְשֹׂנְאָי:
ו ז וְעֹשֶׂה חֶסֶד לַאֲלָפִים לְאֹהֲבַי וּלְשֹׁמְרֵי מִצְוֺתָי: לֹא תִשָּׂא אֶת־שֵׁם־
יהוה אֱלֹהֶיךָ לַשָּׁוְא כִּי לֹא יְנַקֶּה יהוה אֵת אֲשֶׁר־יִשָּׂא אֶת־שְׁמוֹ לַשָּׁוְא:
ח ט זָכוֹר אֶת־יוֹם הַשַּׁבָּת לְקַדְּשׁוֹ: שֵׁשֶׁת יָמִים תַּעֲבֹד וְעָשִׂיתָ כָּל־מְלַאכְתֶּךָ: וְיוֹם
י הַשְּׁבִיעִי שַׁבָּת לַיהוה אֱלֹהֶיךָ לֹא־תַעֲשֶׂה כָל־מְלָאכָה אַתָּה וּבִנְךָ וּבִתֶּךָ עַבְדְּךָ
יא וַאֲמָתְךָ וּבְהֶמְתֶּךָ וְגֵרְךָ אֲשֶׁר בִּשְׁעָרֶיךָ: כִּי שֵׁשֶׁת־יָמִים עָשָׂה יהוה אֶת־הַשָּׁמַיִם
וְאֶת־הָאָרֶץ אֶת־הַיָּם וְאֶת־כָּל־אֲשֶׁר־בָּם וַיָּנַח בַּיּוֹם הַשְּׁבִיעִי עַל־כֵּן בֵּרַךְ יהוה

רש"י

ד | פסל. על שם שנפסל. כל תמונת דבר "אשר בשמים" וגו':

ה-ו | אל קנא. מקנא לפרע ואינו עובר על מדתו למחול על עבודה זרה. כל לשון 'קנא' אנפרינמנ"ט בלעז, נותן לב לפרע: לשנאי. כתרגומו, כשאוחזין מעשה אבותיהם בידיהם. ונצר חסד שאדם עושה, לשלם שכר עד לאלפים דור. נמצאת מדה טובה יתרה על מדת פרענות אחת על חמש מאות, שזו לארבעה דורות וזו לאלפים:

ז | לשוא. חנם, להבל. ואי זהו שבועת שוא? נשבע לשנות את הידוע, על עמוד של אבן שהוא של זהב:

ח | "זכור" ו"שמור" בדבור אחד נאמרו. וכן: "מחלליה מות יומת" (להלן לא, יד), "וביום השבת שני כבשים" (במדבר כח, ט); וכן: "לא תלבש שעטנז", "גדלים תעשה לך" (דברים כב, יא-יב); וכן: "ערות אשת אחיך" (ויקרא יח, טז), "יבמה יבא עליה" (דברים כה, ה); הוא שנאמר: "אחת דבר אלהים שתים זו שמעתי" (תהלים סב, יב). "זכור" לשון פעול הוא, כמו: "אכול ושתו" (ישעיה כב, יג), "הלוך ובכה" (שמואל ב' ג, טז), וכן פתרונו: תנו לב לזכר תמיד את יום השבת, שאם נזדמן לך חפץ יפה תהא מזמינו לשבת:

ט | ועשית כל מלאכתך. כשתבא שבת יהא בעיניך כאלו כל מלאכתך עשויה, שלא תהרהר אחר מלאכה:

י | אתה ובנך ובתך. אלו קטנים. או אינו אלא גדולים? אמרת, הרי כבר מוזהרין הם, אלא לא בא אלא להזהיר הגדולים על שביתת הקטנים, וזהו ששנינו: קטן שבא לכבות אין שומעין לו, מפני ששביתתו עליך:

יא | וינח ביום השביעי. כביכול הכתיב בעצמו מנוחה,

DISCUSSION

safeguard people from using the actual name of God in an unseemly manner.

This command is also interpreted as a reference to the desecration of the honor of God in other ways. Since over the course of time the nation of Israel became identified as the people of God, any clearly negative behavior on their part in the presence of strangers serves to desecrate the name of God. Due to the impact of their actions, they do not merely desecrate their own good names and the honor of their families and their nation, but even the name of God Himself (see, e.g., *Pesikta Rabbati* 22; *Sha'arei Teshuva* 2:45; see also Leviticus 19:12; *Yoma* 86a).

20:8| **Remember the Sabbath day, to keep it holy:** In addition to one's actions on the Sabbath itself, one also fulfills this command through his everyday speech. In Hebrew, unlike most other languages, there are no names for the days of the week; they are simply called first day, second day, and so on. They are numbered in relation to the Sabbath, which is the only one whose name is not relative to the other days of the week (see Ramban; *Bekhor Shor*; *Mekhilta deRashbi* 20:8).

20:10| **You shall not perform any labor:** The revelation at Mount Sinai does not include the details of the prohibitions or the positive commandments of the Sabbath. Clearly, the demand to rest does not mean that the Jews must sit motionless for the entire day. Rather, the prohibition involves the performance of labor, which is a defined act not necessarily synonymous with hard work. Work refers to a physical action, whereas labor in this context is a creative, deliberate act.

20:11| **Therefore, the Lord blessed the Sabbath day, and He sanctified it:** The Sabbath is not merely a day of prohibitions and restrictions, on which one refrains from labor in commemoration of God's cessation of work at the completion of the creation of the world. Rather, it is also God's weekly celebration, which is why it is not only a day of rest, but a holy day as well. This feature of the day links the Sabbath to the preceding precepts, which deal with one's exclusive faith in God. Since the people of Israel are now entering into a covenant with God, He instructs them to participate in His private holiday. For this reason, remembering the Sabbath

from the beginning of creation.[34]
12 **Honor your father and your mother.**[D] Honoring one's parents does not involve a ritual act, but is a requirement of daily life, **so that your days will be extended on the land that the Lord your God gives you.** The reward for one who honors his parents is a long life in this world.[35] In addition, in a society where the elderly generation is respected, there will be long life, as aging parents will be confident that they can rely on the younger generation, and they will be valued as important members of the family and the wider society.[36]
13 **You shall not murder.**[D] **You shall not commit adultery.**[D] This prohibition of adultery is defined by Jewish law and the traditional commentaries as pertaining to the relationship of a married woman with a man other than her husband.[37] The commands against taking the life of another and damaging his family structure are followed by a prohibition against taking his property: **You shall not steal.**[D] Following the absolute prohibitions that define the basic behavior required toward one's fellow man, such as murder, adultery, and theft, the Torah presents a command that is seemingly less severe than the previous ones, but which refers to a common social situation: **You shall not bear false witness against your neighbor.**[D] The halakhic definition of this prohibition is the submission of untrue or invalid testimony over the course of a trial in court. Such testimony undermines the trust between people.
14 **You shall not covet**[D] **your neighbor's house; you shall not covet your neighbor's wife, or his slave, or his maidservant, or his ox, or his ass, or anything that is your neighbor's.** This coveting is the notorious, unshakable sin of envy, which has not disappeared in more than three thousand years since the Torah was given.

The Experience of the People during the Revelation at Sinai

EXODUS 20:15–18

The precepts that God pronounces to His people at Sinai were the verbal and intellectual features of the revelation. However, they were accompanied by an unprecedented sensory and suprasensory experience. As a result, the nation felt that it was unable to cope with the force of the vision. The same individuals who before the giving of the Torah had apparently yearned to ascend the mountain en masse, and who had required several warnings not to approach it, now recoiled in terror from the direct encounter between man and the Eternal.

15 **All the people were seeing the thunder, and the** lights that
Seventh aliya glowed like **flames, and the blast of the shofar, and the mountain smoking;**[D] **the people saw** these phenomena **and trembled,** instinctively recoiling, **and stood at a distance.**

DISCUSSION

is the first practical commandment of regular Jewish life.

20:12 | **Honor your father and your mother:** Although this precept was not explicitly mentioned previously, it was already a basic value one thousand years before the giving of the Torah, as indicated in the story of Noah's sons (see Genesis 9:20–23).

Honoring one's parents is now presented as a fundamental principle of the Torah. It is not presented here as part of the obligation to respect one's elders, alongside the commandment: "You shall rise before the graybeard, and show deference before the elderly" (Leviticus 19:32). Instead, it appears as one of the Ten Precepts, which detail the basic principles of worshipping God, as one's attitude toward his parents should parallel his attitude toward God. The first precept connected the people of Israel to God by virtue of the fact that He fashioned them as a nation: "Who took you out of the land of Egypt, from the house of bondage" (verse 2). The precept to observe the Sabbath, which appears just before this one, is associated with God's creation of the entire world. The duty to honor one's parents extends this theme in that it is not dependent upon the individual personalities of the parents, but on the fact that they, like God, are the source of a person's existence (see Ramban; *Kiddushin* 30b).

20:13 | **You shall not murder:** The basis for social coexistence is the security of each individual and the confidence that others will not kill him. In a society where murder is permitted, humanity in general, and each individual in particular, is in a constant state of peril. Even in the animal kingdom, in many species, animals in a pack do not attack one another. However, in the Ten Precepts this fundamental prohibition is imbued with meaning that goes beyond its social utility, as evident from the fact that it is formulated in the future tense: You shall not murder [*lo tirtzaḥ*], rather than the command form: Do not murder [*al tirtzaḥ*]. In effect, the Torah is saying: There shall be no murder, as acts of this kind shall not be part of your world. This style is repeated in the subsequent precepts as well.

You shall not commit adultery: Other sexual prohibitions, e.g., incest and forbidden relations that stem from the elevated status of Jews or of certain segments of the Jewish people, are not included in this precept. This is true despite the fact that they are no less severe than adultery, and the punishment for some of them is in fact more severe. The reason adultery appears here is because it shatters the most basic social unit, the family. In addition, it harms a relationship that goes back to the beginning of the Creation: "Therefore, a man shall leave his father and his mother, and he shall cleave to his wife, and they shall become one flesh" (Genesis 2:24). Likewise, the prohibition against murder relates to a verse in the first part of Genesis (9:6): "One who sheds the blood of man, by man shall his blood be shed, as He made man in the image of God."

You shall not steal: The Sages maintain, based on the context, that this precept is referring to stealing people, kidnapping, whereas the prohibition against taking another's property appears in Leviticus 19:11 (see *Sanhedrin* 86a; see

→

יב אֶת־יוֹם הַשַּׁבָּת וַיְקַדְּשֵׁהוּ׃ כַּבֵּד אֶת־אָבִיךָ וְאֶת־אִמֶּךָ לְמַעַן יַאֲרִכוּן
יג יָמֶיךָ עַל הָאֲדָמָה אֲשֶׁר־יְהוָה אֱלֹהֶיךָ נֹתֵן לָךְ׃ לֹא
תִּרְצָח לֹא
תִּנְאָף לֹא תִּגְנֹב לֹא
יד תַעֲנֶה בְרֵעֲךָ עֵד שָׁקֶר׃ לֹא
תַחְמֹד בֵּית רֵעֶךָ לֹא
תַחְמֹד אֵשֶׁת רֵעֶךָ וְעַבְדּוֹ וַאֲמָתוֹ וְשׁוֹרוֹ וַחֲמֹרוֹ וְכֹל אֲשֶׁר לְרֵעֶךָ׃
טו וְכָל־הָעָם רֹאִים אֶת־הַקּוֹלֹת וְאֶת־הַלַּפִּידִם וְאֵת קוֹל הַשֹּׁפָר וְאֶת־הָהָר עָשֵׁן וַיַּרְא שביעי

רש״י

לִלְמֹד הֵימֶנּוּ קַל וָחֹמֶר לָאָדָם שֶׁמְּלַאכְתּוֹ בְּעָמָל וִיגִיעָה שֶׁיְּהֵא נָח בַּשַּׁבָּת: בֵּרַךְ... וַיְקַדְּשֵׁהוּ. בֵּרְכוֹ בַּמָּן, לִכְפְלוֹ בַּשִּׁשִּׁי לֶחֶם מִשְׁנֶה, וְקִדְּשׁוֹ בַּמָּן, שֶׁלֹּא הָיָה יוֹרֵד בּוֹ:

יב | לְמַעַן יַאֲרִכוּן יָמֶיךָ. אִם תְּכַבֵּד – יַאֲרִיכוּן, וְאִם לָאו – יִקְצְרוּן, שֶׁדִּבְרֵי תוֹרָה נוֹטָרִיקוֹן הֵם נִדְרָשִׁים, מִכְּלָל הֵן לָאו וּמִכְּלָל לָאו הֵן:

יג | לֹא תִנְאָף. אֵין נִאוּף אֶלָּא בְּאֵשֶׁת אִישׁ, שֶׁנֶּאֱמַר: "מוֹת יוּמַת הַנֹּאֵף וְהַנֹּאָפֶת" (ויקרא כ, י), וְאוֹמֵר: "הָאִשָּׁה הַמְנָאֶפֶת תַּחַת אִישָׁהּ תִּקַּח אֶת זָרִים" (יחזקאל טז, לב): לֹא תִגְנֹב. בְּגוֹנֵב נְפָשׁוֹת הַכָּתוּב מְדַבֵּר. "לֹא תִגְנֹבוּ" (ויקרא יט, יא) בְּגוֹנֵב מָמוֹן. אוֹ אֵינוֹ אֶלָּא זֶה בְּגוֹנֵב מָמוֹן וּלְהַלָּן בְּגוֹנֵב נְפָשׁוֹת? אָמַרְתָּ, דָּבָר לָמֵד מֵעִנְיָנוֹ, "לֹא תִרְצָח, לֹא תִנְאָף" מִיתַת בֵּית דִּין, אַף "לֹא תִגְנֹב" דָּבָר שֶׁחַיָּבִין עָלָיו מִיתַת בֵּית דִּין:

טו | וְכָל הָעָם רֹאִים. מְלַמֵּד שֶׁלֹּא הָיָה בָּהֶם אֶחָד סוּמָא. וּמִנַּיִן שֶׁלֹּא הָיָה בָּהֶם אִלֵּם? תַּלְמוּד לוֹמַר: "וַיַּעֲנוּ כָל הָעָם" (לעיל יט, ח). וּמִנַּיִן שֶׁלֹּא הָיָה בָּהֶם חֵרֵשׁ? תַּלְמוּד לוֹמַר: "נַעֲשֶׂה וְנִשְׁמָע" (להלן כד, ז): רֹאִים אֶת הַקּוֹלֹת. רוֹאִים אֶת הַנִּשְׁמָע, שֶׁאִי אֶפְשָׁר לִרְאוֹת בְּמָקוֹם אַחֵר:

DISCUSSION

also 21:16; Rav Se'adya Gaon; and Ibn Ezra, long commentary on Exodus).

You shall not bear false witness against your neighbor: This precept may include a broad range of situations where one speaks falsely about another (see *Bekhor Shor*, 23:1). If people would refrain from speaking falsehoods entirely, everyone could rely on others, not only due to the knowledge that his life, family, and property are secure, as required by the previous precepts, but in full confidence that the statements he hears are spoken in good faith.

20:14| **You shall not covet:** Ostensibly, a prohibition of this kind has no place in a legal system, as legal codes regulate actions rather than people's thoughts and desires. God alone can command people not to want something and set limits to the hidden desires in the heart of man.

Due to the singular nature of this prohibition among the other precepts, most of which apply to actions and words, the Sages interpreted this prohibition in a more limited manner, as prohibiting taking action to deprive another of an item that belongs to him (see Rambam, *Sefer HaMitzvot*, negative commandment 265). Consequently, it is prohibited to apply pressure or other forms of manipulation in order to gain possession of another individual's property, or to acquire another person's wife, even if the acquisition itself is performed legally. This manifestation of coveting is somewhat akin to the villainy identified as the sin of the generation of the flood (Genesis 6:11–13), as it too was motivated by lust for the property of another. Accordingly, this final precept serves to prohibit practical planning and scheming for the purpose of appropriating that which belongs to someone else.

However, it should be noted that this limited interpretation does not negate the simple meaning of the term. Indeed, in the parallel account of the Ten Precepts in Deuteronomy (5:17), the word "covet" is replaced by "desire," which refers to a passion that does not necessarily have any practical effect (see Rambam, *Sefer Nezikin*, *Hilkhot Gezeila* 1:9–12).

20:15| **Were seeing the thunder, and the flames, and the blast of the shofar, and the mountain smoking:** Although the verse states that the people saw the thunder and the blast of the shofar, some commentaries explain that this means they saw the visual sources from where such sounds came (Rashbam; Rabbeinu Baḥya). However, the attribution of seeing to auditory phenomena can be understood as a precise description of an experience beyond the realm of ordinary human senses (see Rashi). The speech of God cannot be recorded by any device, nor can its waves be measured. One's senses do not play a central role in the absorption of the word of God, as His statements penetrate directly into the consciousness (Ibn Ezra). A prophecy is the transfer of content from the consciousness of God, as it were, to human consciousness, without the use of external aids, such as pictures or

They had formerly recognized the prophet as God's spokesperson, but now, for the first time, they were granted a taste of the process of hearing and receiving a prophecy, and they felt its accompanying terror.

16 Therefore, **they,** the people, **said to Moses:**[D] **You speak with us and we will hear, and God should not speak with us, lest we die.**[D]

17 **Moses said to the people: Do not fear;** God will not continue to speak to you in this manner every day,[38] **as it is in order to test [*nasot*] you that God has come.** You are being tested to see whether you can withstand the experience and accept the word of God. The term for test [*nes*] can also mean a banner,

as one who passes the test is elevated like a banner, since he has survived the direct encounter with the Divine and successfully heard the voice of God.[39] **And He has also come so that His fear will be on your faces,** so **that you will not sin.** One who has personally heard the voice of God and remembers the unmediated event will find it more difficult to sin.

18 Ultimately, **the people stood at a distance,** as they retreated further back, **and Moses approached** closer to the place of the lightning and smoke, **to the fog where God was.** Certainly Moses was afraid as well, but his desire to come close to God and the knowledge that he was representing the entire people helped him overcome his fears.

Additional Commands
EXODUS 20:19–23

Following the giving of the Torah, God conveys to Moses certain restrictions involving the practical worship of God. These commands are introduced by a declaration emphasizing the intangible source of the revelation at Sinai.

19 **The Lord said to Moses: So you shall say to the children of**
Maftir **Israel: You saw that from the heavens,** from an abstract place, **I spoke with you.**[D]

20 Since you did not see any sort of image in your encounter with Me, **You shall not make with Me,** or for Me, any physical image or bodily form; **gods of silver or gods of gold**[D] **you shall not make for yourselves.** It is permitted to worship God through a ritual that involves physical objects, but only if these fulfill specific conditions:

21 **You shall make for Me an altar of earth and shall slaughter upon it**[D] **your burnt offerings and your peace offerings, your sheep and your oxen; in every place where I mention My name,** every place where I choose to rest My Presence, which will lead you to mention My name,[40] **I will come to you and I will bless you.** Alternatively, the verse can be explained as follows: When you, man, pray to Me and serve Me, I in turn will be present and mention My name. This is similar to the saying of the Sages that the Divine Presence rests upon every group of ten individuals of Israel.[41] Indeed, this is

---

DISCUSSION

sounds, which could be seen or heard by a nonprophet. Rather, a prophecy takes the form of an internal vision or voice (see *Responsa of the Rashba* 4:234). Consequently, there is no meaning to the question of whether this experience was seen by the people with their eyes or heard with their ears. However, it is impossible to describe this experience with making metaphorical use of sensory perception. Here the description draws on sight and hearing, and the Sages added the sense of smell, saying that with every statement uttered by God a fragrance was released to perfume the world (*Shabbat* 88b).

20:16 | **They said to Moses:** The people's address to Moses during the revelation indicates that despite his greater closeness to God, he was not located on top of the mountain at the time.

When God spoke to His nation, everyone stood together equally. Nevertheless, the people felt that their status differed from that of Moses, as he was accustomed to hearing the word of God (see Deuteronomy 5:5; Ibn Ezra, 19:17; Ramban, 19:9).

And God should not speak with us, lest we die: Some prophets would fall to the ground and lose control of their senses when they received a prophecy (see Genesis 15:12, 17:3; Numbers 24:4; Daniel 10:7–9). Since the prophecy described here is on a higher level than other prophecies, the people feared that they might die.

It is unclear when the people issued this statement to Moses. Most likely, the Israelites reacted after they began to hear the precepts, before their completion. However, since the Torah lists the Ten Precepts without interruption, this

request is only recorded afterward. The Sages say that only the precepts: "I am the Lord your God..." (20:2) and: "You shall have no other gods before Me..." (20:3) were heard by the entire nation directly from God (*Makkot* 24a), as these precepts alone are formulated in the first person, whereas God is mentioned in the third person in the rest of the precepts (*Bekhor Shor,* verse 1, citing Rav Yosef Kara; *Or Hashem*).

20:19 | **From the heavens I spoke with you:** Since the voice of God did not emanate from any material source or physical intermediary, the point of this phrase is not to express the direction from which the sound emanated but rather the intangible source of the sound. The sound itself was abstract, because its divine source has ◀◀

טז הָעָם וַיָּנֻעוּ וַיַּעַמְדוּ מֵרָחֹק: וַיֹּאמְרוּ אֶל־מֹשֶׁה דַּבֵּר־אַתָּה עִמָּנוּ וְנִשְׁמָעָה וְאַל־
יז יְדַבֵּר עִמָּנוּ אֱלֹהִים פֶּן־נָמוּת: וַיֹּאמֶר מֹשֶׁה אֶל־הָעָם אַל־תִּירָאוּ כִּי לְבַעֲבוּר נַסּוֹת
יח אֶתְכֶם בָּא הָאֱלֹהִים וּבַעֲבוּר תִּהְיֶה יִרְאָתוֹ עַל־פְּנֵיכֶם לְבִלְתִּי תֶחֱטָאוּ: וַיַּעֲמֹד
הָעָם מֵרָחֹק וּמֹשֶׁה נִגַּשׁ אֶל־הָעֲרָפֶל אֲשֶׁר־שָׁם הָאֱלֹהִים:
יט וַיֹּאמֶר יהוה אֶל־מֹשֶׁה כֹּה תֹאמַר אֶל־בְּנֵי יִשְׂרָאֵל אַתֶּם רְאִיתֶם כִּי מִן־ מפטיר
כ הַשָּׁמַיִם דִּבַּרְתִּי עִמָּכֶם: לֹא תַעֲשׂוּן אִתִּי אֱלֹהֵי כֶסֶף וֵאלֹהֵי זָהָב לֹא תַעֲשׂוּ
כא לָכֶם: מִזְבַּח אֲדָמָה תַּעֲשֶׂה־לִּי וְזָבַחְתָּ עָלָיו אֶת־עֹלֹתֶיךָ וְאֶת־שְׁלָמֶיךָ אֶת־
צֹאנְךָ וְאֶת־בְּקָרֶךָ בְּכָל־הַמָּקוֹם אֲשֶׁר אַזְכִּיר אֶת־שְׁמִי אָבוֹא אֵלֶיךָ וּבֵרַכְתִּיךָ:

רש"י

את הקולות. היוצאין מפי הגבורה: **וינעו.** אין 'נוע' אלא זיע: **ויעמדו מרחק.** היו נרתעין לאחוריהם שנים עשר מיל כאורך מחניהם, ומלאכי השרת באין ומסייעין אותן להחזירם, שנאמר: "מלכי צבאות ידדון ידדון" (תהלים סח, יג):

יז| **לבעבור נסות אתכם.** לגדל אתכם בעולם, שיצא לכם שם באומות שהוא בכבודו נגלה עליכם: **נסות.** לשון הרמה וגדלה, כמו: "הרימו נס" (ישעיה סב, י), "ארים נסי" (שם מט, כב), "וכנס על הגבעה" (שם ל, יז) שהוא זקוף: **ובעבור תהיה יראתו.** על ידי שראיתם אותו יראוי ומאוים, תדעו כי אין זולתו ותיראו מפניו:

יח| **נגש אל הערפל.** לפנים משלש מחיצות: חשך, ענן וערפל, שנאמר: "וההר בער באש עד לב השמים חשך ענן וערפל" (דברים ד, יא). ערפל הוא עב הענן, שאמר לו: "הנה אנכי בא אליך בעב הענן" (לעיל יט, ט):

יט| **כה תאמר.** בלשון הזה: **אתם ראיתם.** יש הפרש בין מה שאדם רואה למה שאחרים מסיחין לו, שמה שאחרים מסיחין לו פעמים שלבו חלוק מלהאמין: **כי מן השמים דברתי.** וכתוב אחד אומר: "וירד ה' על הר סיני" (לעיל יט, כ)! בא הכתוב השלישי והכריע ביניהם: "מן השמים השמיעך את קלו ליסרך ועל הארץ הראך את אשו הגדולה" (דברים ד, לו), כבודו בשמים ואשו וגבורתו על הארץ. דבר אחר, הרכין שמים ושמי שמים והציען על ההר, וכן הוא אומר: "ויט שמים וירד" (שמואל ב' כב, י):

כ| **לא תעשון אתי.** לא תעשון דמות שמשי המשמשים לפני במרום: **אלהי כסף.** בא להזהיר על הכרובים שאתה עושה לעמוד אתי שלא יהיו של כסף, שאם שניתם לעשותם של כסף הרי הן לפני כאלהות: **ואלהי זהב.** בא להזהיר שלא יוסיף על שנים, שאם עשית ארבעה הרי הן לפני כאלהי זהב: **לא תעשו לכם.** שלא תאמר, הריני עושה כרובים בבתי כנסיות ובבתי מדרשות כדרך שאני עושה בבית עולמים, לכך נאמר: "לא תעשו לכם":

כא| **מזבח אדמה.** מחבר באדמה, שלא יבננו על גבי עמודים או על גבי כיפים. דבר אחר, שהיה ממלא את חלל מזבח הנחשת אדמה בשעת חנייתן: **תעשה לי.** שתהא תחלת עשייתו לשמי: **וזבחת עליו.** אצלו, כמו: "ועליו מטה מנשה" (במדבר ב, כ). או אינו אלא עליו ממש? תלמוד לומר: "הבשר והדם על מזבח ה' אלהיך" (דברים יב, כז), ואין שחיטה בראש המזבח: **את עלתיך ואת שלמיך.** אשר מצאנך ומבקרך. "את צאנך ואת בקרך" פירוש ל"את עלתיך ואת שלמיך": **בכל המקום אשר אזכיר את שמי.** אשר אתן לך רשות להזכיר שם המפורש שלי, שם "אבוא אליך", אשרה את שכינתי, "וברכתיך". מכאן אתה למד שלא נתן רשות להזכיר שם המפורש אלא במקום שהשכינה באה שם, וזהו בית הבחירה, שם נתן רשות לכהנים להזכיר שם המפורש בנשיאות כפים ולברך את העם:

DISCUSSION

no body or physical image (see commentary on Genesis 1:8)

20:20| **You shall not make with Me gods of silver or gods of gold:** Unlike the earlier precept that prohibited the fashioning of an idol or any image (20:4), which refers to the worship of other gods, this verse refers to the physical representation of God by means of silver or gold images.

20:21| **And shall slaughter upon it:** The use of an altar does not depend on the presence of the Tabernacle or the Temple, as is evident from the Talmud in *Shevuot* 16b, which states: One may sacrifice offerings even though there is no Temple standing. In fact, some of the Sages' statements indicate that animal sacrifice continued for some years after the destruction of the Temple. Moreover, there were earlier periods when there was no central place of worship, during which it was permitted to sacrifice on personal altars (see *Zevaḥim* 112b). For this reason, the command to establish an altar precedes the instructions of the building of the Tabernacle, and altars remained in use even in the absence of the Tabernacle or Temple. Furthermore, the sacrifice of offerings on altars was performed in earlier periods of history, beginning in the second generation of humanity with Cain and Abel (Genesis 4:3–4), generations before the giving of the Torah.

a general declaration with regard to prayer and the mention of God's name, which are not restricted to any particular place, just as the presence of God and His blessing are not limited to a specific place.

22 **If you make Me an altar of stone,** rather than the altar of earth mentioned in the previous verse, which will be built for the Tabernacle **you shall not build it of hewn stones;**[D] **for you wielded your sword upon it and profaned it.** The traditional explanation of this verse is that the Torah prohibits such stones because it does not want any destructive iron tool to be used in the preparation of the altar, which provides atonement and

brings peace.[42] This is supported by the verse: "You shall build there an altar to the Lord your God, an altar of stones; you shall not wield iron upon them."[43]

23 **You shall not ascend on stairs to My altar, so that your nakedness will not be exposed upon it.**[D] At that time, people wore gowns or robes of various lengths, and undergarments were not worn at all. Consequently, when one climbed stairs, parts of the body were liable to be exposed. Even if no part of the body of a priest was actually visible due to the trousers worn by the priests under their robes (28:42), the very act of climbing stairs may have appeared to be immodest.[44]

DISCUSSION

20:22 | You shall not build it of hewn stones: Elsewhere the Torah commands: "Whole stones you shall build the altar of the Lord your God" (Deuteronomy 27:6). The Torah objects to the construction of the altar using any metal implement, despite the fact that these are convenient for working stone; this is apparently because the altar must be built in a simple manner. Consequently, if the altar is not fashioned from shapeless earth but from stones, they must be in their natural state, neither hewn nor altered in any other manner. In contrast, the use of tools in fashioning the stones renders the altar

a complex structure that is consider a newly created form. Some explain that the Torah prohibits the building of a sophisticated altar in order to distance the Jewish people from the types of altars customarily used for idolatry (see Rambam, *Guide of the Perplexed* 2:45; Sforno ad loc. and on verse 21).

Due to this prohibition, the altars built by Joshua and by Solomon for the First Temple were constructed of unhewn stones (*Targum Yonatan*; Rashi; *Middot* 3:4; see Joshua 8:30–31; I Kings 6:7). The stone altar in the Temple was smooth, as it had to be a perfect square, but

this was not because the stones were hewn, but because it was molded. The stones themselves were unaltered and after they were put into place they were covered with plaster (see *Zevaḥim* 54a; *Ḥullin* 18a; Rambam, *Sefer Avoda, Hilkhot Beit HaBeḥira* 2:16).

20:23 | Your nakedness will not be exposed upon it: Some altars were built to match the height of an average person, while others were far taller. The height of the altar in the Temple was approximately 5 m, more than twice the height of a person. In order to reach the top of

---

כב וְאִם־מִזְבַּח אֲבָנִים֙ תַּֽעֲשֶׂה־לִּ֔י לֹֽא־תִבְנֶ֥ה אֶתְהֶ֖ן גָּזִ֑ית כִּ֧י חַרְבְּךָ֛ הֵנַ֥פְתָּ עָלֶ֖יהָ
כג וַתְּחַלְלֶֽהָ׃ וְלֹֽא־תַעֲלֶ֥ה בְמַעֲלֹ֖ת עַֽל־מִזְבְּחִ֑י אֲשֶׁ֛ר לֹֽא־תִגָּלֶ֥ה עֶרְוָתְךָ֖ עָלָֽיו׃

רש״י

כב | **וְאִם מִזְבַּח אֲבָנִים.** רַבִּי יִשְׁמָעֵאל אוֹמֵר: כָּל אִם וְאִם שֶׁבַּתּוֹרָה רְשׁוּת חוּץ מִשְּׁלֹשָׁה: "וְאִם מִזְבַּח אֲבָנִים תַּעֲשֶׂה לִּי", הֲרֵי 'אִם' זֶה מְשַׁמֵּשׁ בִּלְשׁוֹן 'כַּאֲשֶׁר', וְכַאֲשֶׁר תַּעֲשֶׂה לִּי מִזְבַּח אֲבָנִים "לֹא תִבְנֶה אֶתְהֶן גָּזִית", שֶׁהֲרֵי חוֹבָה עָלֶיךָ לִבְנוֹת מִזְבַּח אֲבָנִים, שֶׁנֶּאֱמַר: "אֲבָנִים שְׁלֵמוֹת תִּבְנֶה" (דברים כז, ו). וְכֵן: "אִם כֶּסֶף תַּלְוֶה" (להלן כב, כד) חוֹבָה הוּא, שֶׁנֶּאֱמַר: "וְהַעֲבֵט תַּעֲבִיטֶנּוּ" (דברים טו, ח), וְאַף זֶה מְשַׁמֵּשׁ בִּלְשׁוֹן 'כַּאֲשֶׁר'. וְכֵן: "וְאִם תַּקְרִיב מִנְחַת בִּכּוּרִים" (ויקרא ב, יד), זוֹ מִנְחַת הָעֹמֶר שֶׁהִיא חוֹבָה. וְעַל כָּרְחֲךָ אֵין 'אִם' הַלָּלוּ תְּלוּיִין אֶלָּא וַדַּאי, וּבִלְשׁוֹן 'כַּאֲשֶׁר' הֵם מְשַׁמְּשִׁים: **גָּזִית.** לְשׁוֹן גְּזִיזָה, שֶׁפּוֹסְלָן וּמְכַתְּתָן בְּבַרְזֶל: **כִּי חַרְבְּךָ הֵנַפְתָּ עָלֶיהָ.** הֲרֵי "כִּי" זֶה מְשַׁמֵּשׁ בִּלְשׁוֹן 'פֶּן' שֶׁהוּא 'דִּלְמָא', פֶּן תָּנִיף חַרְבְּךָ עָלֶיהָ: **וַתְּחַלְלֶהָ.** הָא לָמַדְתָּ שֶׁאִם הֵנַפְתָּ עָלֶיהָ בַּרְזֶל – חִלַּלְתָּ, שֶׁהַמִּזְבֵּחַ נִבְרָא לְהַאֲרִיךְ יָמָיו שֶׁל אָדָם וְהַבַּרְזֶל נִבְרָא לְקַצֵּר יָמָיו שֶׁל אָדָם, אֵין זֶה בְּדִין שֶׁיּוּנַף הַמְקַצֵּר עַל הַמַּאֲרִיךְ. וְעוֹד, שֶׁהַמִּזְבֵּחַ מַטִּיל שָׁלוֹם בֵּין יִשְׂרָאֵל לַאֲבִיהֶם שֶׁבַּשָּׁמַיִם, לְפִיכָךְ לֹא יָבֹא עָלָיו כּוֹרֵת וּמְחַבֵּל. וַהֲרֵי דְּבָרִים קַל וָחֹמֶר: וּמָה אֲבָנִים שֶׁאֵינָן רוֹאוֹת וְלֹא שׁוֹמְעוֹת וְלֹא מְדַבְּרוֹת, עַל יְדֵי שֶׁמַּטִּילוֹת שָׁלוֹם אָמְרָה תּוֹרָה: "לֹא תָנִיף עֲלֵיהֶם בַּרְזֶל" (דברים כז, ה), הַמַּטִּיל שָׁלוֹם בֵּין אִישׁ לְאִשְׁתּוֹ, בֵּין מִשְׁפָּחָה לְמִשְׁפָּחָה, בֵּין אָדָם לַחֲבֵרוֹ, עַל אַחַת כַּמָּה וְכַמָּה שֶׁלֹּא תְבוֹאֵהוּ פֻּרְעָנוּת:

כג | **וְלֹא תַעֲלֶה בְמַעֲלֹת.** כְּשֶׁאַתָּה בּוֹנֶה כֶּבֶשׁ לַמִּזְבֵּחַ לֹא תַעֲשֵׂהוּ מַעֲלוֹת מַעֲלוֹת, אשקלונ"ש בְּלַעַז, אֶלָּא חָלָק יְהֵא וּמְשֻׁפָּע: **אֲשֶׁר לֹא תִגָּלֶה עֶרְוָתְךָ.** שֶׁעַל יְדֵי הַמַּעֲלוֹת אַתָּה צָרִיךְ לְהַרְחִיב פְּסִיעוֹתֶיךָ. וְאַף עַל פִּי שֶׁאֵינוֹ גִּלּוּי עֶרְוָה מַמָּשׁ, שֶׁהֲרֵי כְּתִיב: "וַעֲשֵׂה לָהֶם מִכְנְסֵי בָד" (להלן כח, מב), מִכָּל מָקוֹם הַרְחָבַת הַפְּסִיעוֹת קָרוֹב לְגִלּוּי עֶרְוָה הוּא, וְאַתָּה נוֹהֵג בָּם מִנְהַג בִּזָּיוֹן. וַהֲרֵי דְּבָרִים קַל וָחֹמֶר: וּמָה אֲבָנִים הַלָּלוּ שֶׁאֵין בָּהֶם דַּעַת לְהַקְפִּיד עַל בִּזְיוֹנָן, אָמְרָה תּוֹרָה: הוֹאִיל וְיֵשׁ בָּהֶם צֹרֶךְ לֹא תִנְהַג בָּהֶם מִנְהַג בִּזָּיוֹן, חֲבֵרְךָ שֶׁהוּא בִּדְמוּת יוֹצֶרְךָ וּמַקְפִּיד עַל בִּזְיוֹנוֹ, עַל אַחַת כַּמָּה וְכַמָּה:

DISCUSSION

this altar without the use of stairs or a ladder, the priests would walk up a sloped ramp, which prevented any unsuitable exposure of the body. In addition to preserving the modesty of the person going onto the altar, the lack of stairs contributed to the modesty and simplicity of the altar itself. The prohibition against climbing stairs and the need for a ramp also served to limit the height of the altar, preventing it from becoming a structure of huge dimensions.

Parashat
Mishpatim

Laws and Statutes
EXODUS 21:1–23:19

This section contains the first major compilation of positive and negative commandments in the Torah. It is not always obvious how the subject matter discussed in one verse is related to the preceding law; at times the transition from one subject to another is puzzling. Consequently, it is difficult to ascertain any general structure in this section. However, there are parallels between some of the laws mentioned here and those presented in a more succinct form in the Ten Precepts.

The laws in this section are relevant to all generations, and not just the generation that left Egypt. Nevertheless, it stands to reason that such matters involving the structure and functioning of civil society were a preoccupation of the people and judges of this new nation of former slaves that had become free only a few months earlier and was taking its first steps as an independent unit. Presumably, separate socioeconomic strata were already being formed. Some individuals owned livestock, others engaged in commerce, there were masters and servants, and naturally there were also lenders and borrowers, bailees and businessmen. It is fair to assume that cases of damage caused by a goring ox, theft, and physical assault could all occur in their daily lives.

21 1 **These are the ordinances**[D] pertaining to the establishment of a properly functioning society **that you shall place before them.** It is likely that Moses transmitted these laws to the people immediately after the giving of the Torah, before he ascended to Mount Sinai for an extended period of time (24:15–18). He did so because the overall structure of society, which is the crux of the laws in this section, is more pressing than other matters.[1]

2 **If you acquire a Hebrew slave,**[D] **six years he shall work.** His servitude is for a limited period, and he does not become the personal property of his master. The Hebrew slave is an Israelite who finds himself in such difficult financial straits that he cannot support himself, and has to sell himself as a slave in order to survive. Alternatively, he is an Israelite who stole an item that he cannot repay and is therefore sold by the court (see 22:2) in order to compensate the victim of the theft. According to a tradition of the Sages, the six-year term applies only to a slave who was sold by the court rather than one who sells himself.[2] However, a simple reading of the text supports the possibility

that the law applies to any Israelite slave.[3] **And in the seventh year he shall go free,**[D] **without charge.** He does not have to redeem himself at the conclusion of his term of servitude. Furthermore, the master is required to give his Hebrew slave gifts upon his release.[4]

3 **If he shall come** into his term of servitude **by himself,** without a wife and children, **he shall leave** when he completes his period of servitude **by himself. If he is the husband of a wife**[D] when he becomes a slave, upon his release **his wife shall leave with him.**

4 However, **if his master shall give him a** gentile maidservant as a **wife, and she bears him sons or daughters, the wife and her children shall belong to her master**[D] and he, the Hebrew slave, **shall leave by himself.**

5 **But if,** after six years in which the Hebrew slave has had children with the woman he received from his master, it is possible that when it is time for him to go free, **the slave shall say: I love my master,** as I have lived with him as a member of his family,

DISCUSSION

21:1 | **These are the ordinances:** The Torah does not draw a sharp distinction between civil law and criminal law, or even between these two legal fields and ritual law. Consequently, all three categories are covered by the term "ordinances." Although the laws in this section focus mainly on interpersonal relations, there are exceptions that are from other areas of Jewish law.

21:2 | **If you acquire a Hebrew slave:** The case of a Hebrew slave is the first law of this section probably due to the recent redemption of the children of Israel from slavery in Egypt. After many long years of servitude, the nation is finally

taking its first steps toward independence. In the emerging society it is inevitable that certain individuals will become wealthy while others will be poor, with some experiencing such severe financial distress that they will be compelled to become slaves. Consequently, the first law in this section establishes the unique status of a Hebrew slave among his brethren. Due to the fraternal connection between him and the rest of the children of Israel, the rights of the Hebrew slave are protected by law. This is in stark contrast to the status of a slave in other societies of that era, which often related to them as animals who could speak. The relationship

between a Hebrew slave and his master is not inherently different from that of a hired laborer, albeit with a longer than usual length of service. Indeed, there are indications in various sources that laborers were often hired for periods lasting three years, although one could also be hired for a shorter term (see Deuteronomy 15:18; Isaiah 16:14; *Shabbat* 127b; *Kiddushin* 17a and *Tosafot* ad loc.). If so, the Hebrew slave is essentially a hired laborer for double the average length of service. The slave and his master are bound by a structure of mutual obligations. Moreover, the fact that someone has become a slave does ◄◄

משפטים

א ב וְאֵ֙לֶּה֙ הַמִּשְׁפָּטִ֔ים אֲשֶׁ֥ר תָּשִׂ֖ים לִפְנֵיהֶֽם: כִּ֤י תִקְנֶה֙ עֶ֣בֶד עִבְרִ֔י שֵׁ֥שׁ שָׁנִ֖ים יַעֲבֹ֑ד טז

ג וּבַ֨שְּׁבִעִ֔ת יֵצֵ֥א לַֽחָפְשִׁ֖י חִנָּֽם: אִם־בְּגַפּ֣וֹ יָבֹ֔א בְּגַפּ֖וֹ יֵצֵ֑א אִם־בַּ֤עַל אִשָּׁה֙ ה֔וּא וְיָצְאָ֥ה

ד אִשְׁתּ֖וֹ עִמּֽוֹ: אִם־אֲדֹנָיו֙ יִתֶּן־ל֣וֹ אִשָּׁ֔ה וְיָלְדָה־ל֥וֹ בָנִ֖ים א֣וֹ בָנ֑וֹת הָאִשָּׁ֣ה וִילָדֶ֗יהָ

ה תִּֽהְיֶה֙ לַֽאדֹנֶ֔יהָ וְה֖וּא יֵצֵ֥א בְגַפּֽוֹ: וְאִם־אָמֹ֤ר יֹאמַר֙ הָעֶ֔בֶד אָהַ֙בְתִּי֙ אֶת־אֲדֹנִ֔י אֶת־

רש״י

א| וְאֵלֶּה הַמִּשְׁפָּטִים. כָּל מָקוֹם שֶׁנֶּאֱמַר "אֵלֶּה" – פָּסַל אֶת הָרִאשׁוֹנִים, "וְאֵלֶּה" – מוֹסִיף עַל הָרִאשׁוֹנִים, מַה הָרִאשׁוֹנִים מִסִּינַי, אַף אֵלּוּ מִסִּינַי. וְלָמָּה נִסְמְכָה פָּרָשַׁת דִּינִין לְפָרָשַׁת מִזְבֵּחַ? לוֹמַר לְךָ שֶׁתָּשִׂים סַנְהֶדְרִין אֵצֶל הַמִּקְדָּשׁ: **אֲשֶׁר תָּשִׂים לִפְנֵיהֶם.** לֹא תַעֲלֶה עַל דַּעְתְּךָ לוֹמַר אֶשְׁנֶה לָהֶם הַפֶּרֶק וְהַהֲלָכָה שְׁנַיִם אוֹ שְׁלֹשָׁה פְעָמִים עַד שֶׁתְּהֵא סְדוּרָה בְּפִיהֶם כְּמִשְׁנָתָהּ, וְאֵינִי מַטְרִיחַ עַצְמִי לַהֲבִינָם טַעֲמֵי הַדָּבָר וּפֵרוּשׁוֹ, לְכָךְ נֶאֱמַר: "אֲשֶׁר תָּשִׂים לִפְנֵיהֶם", כְּשֻׁלְחָן הֶעָרוּךְ וּמוּכָן לֶאֱכֹל לִפְנֵי הָאָדָם: **לִפְנֵיהֶם.** וְלֹא לִפְנֵי גוֹיִם, וַאֲפִילּוּ יָדַעְתָּ בְּדִין אֶחָד שֶׁהֵם דָּנִין אוֹתוֹ כְּדִינֵי יִשְׂרָאֵל אַל תְּבִיאֵהוּ בְּעַרְכָּאוֹת שֶׁלָּהֶם, שֶׁהַמֵּבִיא דִּינֵי יִשְׂרָאֵל לִפְנֵי גוֹיִם מְחַלֵּל אֶת הַשֵּׁם וּמְיַקֵּר שֵׁם עֲבוֹדָה זָרָה לְהַחֲשִׁיבָהּ, שֶׁנֶּאֱמַר: "כִּי לֹא כְצוּרֵנוּ צוּרָם

וְאֹיְבֵינוּ פְּלִילִים" (דברים לב, לא), כְּשֶׁאוֹיְבֵינוּ פְּלִילִים זֶהוּ עֵדוּת לְעִלּוּי יִרְאָתָם:

ב| כִּי תִקְנֶה עֶבֶד עִבְרִי. עֶבֶד שֶׁהוּא עִבְרִי. אוֹ אֵינוֹ אֶלָּא עַבְדּוֹ שֶׁל עִבְרִי, עֶבֶד כְּנַעֲנִי שֶׁלְּקָחְתּוֹ מִיִּשְׂרָאֵל, וְעָלָיו הוּא אוֹמֵר: "שֵׁשׁ שָׁנִים יַעֲבֹד", וּמָה אֲנִי מְקַיֵּם "וְהִתְנַחַלְתֶּם אֹתָם" (ויקרא כה, מו) – בַּלְּקוּחִין מִן הַגּוֹי, אֲבָל בְּלָקוּחַ מִיִּשְׂרָאֵל יֵצֵא בְּשֵׁשׁ? תַּלְמוּד לוֹמַר: "כִּי יִמָּכֵר לְךָ אָחִיךָ הָעִבְרִי" (דברים טו, יב), לֹא אָמַרְתִּי אֶלָּא בְּאָחִיךָ: **כִּי תִקְנֶה.** מִיַּד בֵּית דִּין שֶׁמְּכָרוּהוּ בִּגְנֵבָתוֹ, כְּמוֹ שֶׁנֶּאֱמַר: "אִם אֵין לוֹ וְנִמְכַּר בִּגְנֵבָתוֹ" (להלן כב, ב). אוֹ אֵינוֹ אֶלָּא בְּמוֹכֵר עַצְמוֹ מִפְּנֵי דָחְקוֹ, אֲבָל מְכָרוּהוּ בֵית דִּין לֹא יֵצֵא בְּשֵׁשׁ? כְּשֶׁהוּא אוֹמֵר: "וְכִי יָמוּךְ אָחִיךָ עִמָּךְ וְנִמְכַּר לָךְ" (ויקרא כה, לט) הֲרֵי מוֹכֵר עַצְמוֹ מִפְּנֵי דָחְקוֹ אָמוּר, וּמָה אֲנִי מְקַיֵּם "כִּי תִקְנֶה"? בְּנִמְכָּר בְּבֵית דִּין: **לַחָפְשִׁי.** לַחֵרוּת:

ג| אִם בְּגַפּוֹ יָבֹא. שֶׁלֹּא הָיָה נָשׂוּי אִשָּׁה, כְּתַרְגּוּמוֹ: "אִם בִּלְחוֹדוֹהִי". וּלְשׁוֹן "בְּגַפּוֹ", בִּכְנָפוֹ, שֶׁלֹּא בָא חֶלֶק כְּמוֹת שֶׁהוּא יְחִידִי בְּתוֹךְ לְבוּשׁוֹ, בִּכְנַף בִּגְדוֹ: **בְּגַפּוֹ יֵצֵא.** מַגִּיד שֶׁאִם לֹא הָיָה נָשׂוּי מִתְּחִלָּה, אֵין רַבּוֹ מוֹסֵר לוֹ שִׁפְחָה כְנַעֲנִית לְהוֹלִיד מִמֶּנָּה עֲבָדִים: **אִם בַּעַל אִשָּׁה הוּא.** יִשְׂרְאֵלִית: **וְיָצְאָה אִשְׁתּוֹ עִמּוֹ.** וְכִי מִי הִכְנִיסָהּ שֶׁתֵּצֵא? אֶלָּא מַגִּיד הַכָּתוּב שֶׁהַקּוֹנֶה עֶבֶד עִבְרִי חַיָּב בִּמְזוֹנוֹת אִשְׁתּוֹ וּבָנָיו:

ד| אִם אֲדֹנָיו יִתֶּן לוֹ אִשָּׁה. מִכָּאן שֶׁהָרְשׁוּת בְּיַד רַבּוֹ לִמְסוֹר לוֹ שִׁפְחָה כְנַעֲנִית לְהוֹלִיד מִמֶּנָּה עֲבָדִים. אוֹ אֵינוֹ אֶלָּא בְיִשְׂרְאֵלִית? תַּלְמוּד לוֹמַר: "הָאִשָּׁה וִילָדֶיהָ תִּהְיֶה לַאדֹנֶיהָ", הָא אֵינוֹ מְדַבֵּר אֶלָּא בִכְנַעֲנִית, שֶׁהֲרֵי הָעִבְרִיָּה אַף הִיא יוֹצְאָה בְּשֵׁשׁ, וַאֲפִילּוּ לִפְנֵי שֵׁשׁ אִם הֵבִיאָה סִימָנִין יוֹצְאָה, שֶׁנֶּאֱמַר: "אָחִיךָ הָעִבְרִי אוֹ הָעִבְרִיָּה" (דברים טו, יב), מְלַמֵּד שֶׁאַף הָעִבְרִיָּה יוֹצְאָה בְּשֵׁשׁ:

DISCUSSION

➡ not eliminate his religious obligations as a Jew (*Kiddushin* 22a).

This is an important principle in defining the nation of Israel as a distinct unit. Elsewhere God says: "For to Me the children of Israel are slaves; they are My slaves whom I took out of the land of Egypt: I am the Lord your God." Therefore, Hebrew slaves cannot choose to become completely subservient to another master (Leviticus 25:55; see also the preceding verses there). In this respect, this opening ordinance is connected to the first of the Ten Precepts.

Six years he shall work, and in the seventh he shall go free: The structure of the Hebrew slave's six years of labor, followed by his emancipation in the seventh year, parallels other patterns in time, such as six days of work followed

by a day of rest (see 23:10–12), and six years of agricultural labor that precede the Sabbatical Year, during which agricultural labor is prohibited and the land must be left fallow (Leviticus 25). In the case of the Hebrew slave, the years are counted from when he becomes a slave and are not connected to the cycle of the Sabbatical Year. However, elsewhere the duration of a Hebrew slave's servitude is further constrained. Every Hebrew slave goes free in the Jubilee Year, which is the fiftieth year after seven Sabbatical cycles of seven years each (see, e.g., Leviticus 25; Deuteronomy 15; see also *Bekhor Shor* here and verse 11, 21:14).

21:3 | If he is the husband of a wife: His master has presumably benefited from his wife's labor. She may have helped the master with

various chores in return for his support, despite the fact that she is not legally required to do so, as the master is her sole means of support. It is also possible that her work might have been an express condition of the master's original purchase of the Hebrew slave (see *Bekhor Shor*).

21:4 | The wife and her children shall belong to her master: It is clear from the context that this is not referring to an Israelite woman whom the master arranged for his slave to marry, but to a gentile maidservant belonging to the master, whom he gave to his Hebrew slave for his slave's benefit or in order to produce more slaves for his own profit (see *Mekhilta, Masekhta deNezikin* 2; Rashi; Ibn Ezra; Ramban).

This law is one of the first references to the status of children born to Jewish and non-Jewish

as well as **my wife,** whom I received from my master, **and my children** that she has born to me. Consequently, **I will not go free;** I prefer to remain here as a Hebrew slave, despite the inherent limitations of that status.

6 Then **his master shall** ceremoniously **bring him**[D] **to the judges;**[D] **he shall bring him to the door** at the entrance to the house, **or to the doorpost,** the structure that frames the door on both sides, **and his master shall perforate his ear with an awl,** as a sign that he has relinquished his freedom,[5] **and he shall serve him forever.**[D] According to rabbinic tradition, this means that the slave serves his master until the Jubilee Year.[6] The word "forever" in the Bible can mean a very long time; it should not always be understood literally.[7]

7 **If an Israelite man sells his** minor **daughter as a maidservant, she shall not leave like** gentile **slaves' leaving.** The status of a Hebrew maidservant is higher than that of a gentile maidservant, just as a Hebrew slave is superior in status to a gentile slave.

8 **If she is displeasing in the eyes of her master, to whom she was designated, he shall facilitate her redemption.** Upon purchasing a Hebrew maidservant, the master must take into account that he is commanded to marry her, or have her marry one of his sons. If she is displeasing to him, she can be redeemed in the following manner: The sum of her purchase is divided by six, which determines the value of each year of her servitude, and if she is willing to compensate him for the remaining years of her service, he must accept the payment and she returns home.[8] Alternatively, he must allow this compensation to be paid by someone else if the maidservant is interested in that individual's patronage. In any case, **he shall not presume to sell her to a foreign people,** another family,[9] **in his betrayal of her.**[D] She entered his household under the assumption that she would marry one of the family members. If this marriage does not come to fruition, which is a form of betrayal, the master may not sell the rights to the maidservant to anyone else. Rather, he must allow her to go free.[10]

9 **If he designates her for his son** in marriage, he and his son may not consider her as their property. Rather, **he shall treat her as is the practice of the daughters**. From a legal perspective, the purchase of the Hebrew maidservant is considered the first step toward marriage, similar to betrothal.[11] Although this marriage was not established in the conventional method, it is considered like a regular marriage and she must be treated in the same manner as any other Israelite woman.

10 Consequently, **if he,** the son **takes another** wife **for himself,** after marrying the Hebrew maidservant, the rights of the former maidservant remain protected. He is required to fulfill all his marital obligations toward his first wife, and therefore **he shall not diminish her food, her garments, or her conjugal rights.**[12]

11 **If he does not perform** one of **these three for her,** in that he does not marry her, have her marry his son, or facilitate her redemption,[13] **she shall leave without charge;**[D] **there is no payment,** and all her obligations to the master are canceled.[14]

12 **One who strikes a man** in any fashion, **and he dies** as a result

---

DISCUSSION

parents. The gentile maidservant lives with the Jewish people and has a certain connection to them, which is why a Hebrew slave is permitted to cohabit with her. However, their relationship is not defined as full marriage. Although family and tribal identity are based upon paternal lineage, in this case, where there is no legally recognized family unit and the mother is not fully Jewish, the status of the children follows the status of their mother (see *Kiddushin* 66b, 68b; *Yevamot* 23a).

21:6 | His master shall bring him: The Sages explain that in order to perform this procedure, the master and slave must both agree to the slave's continued servitude. If the slave's love for his master is not reciprocated, the slave cannot force the master to keep him in servitude

(*Kiddushin* 22a). Since the slave has become a member of his master's household, it is possible that both sides will want to maintain that arrangement, but in any case the slave's refusal to go free requires formal approval. In keeping with the serious nature of this decision, master and slave are required to appear together before the rabbinical court, which must approve the agreement. Occasionally, the judges would use their authority and recommend that the two parties do not go ahead with their plan (see Deuteronomy 25:8; *Yevamot* 44a).

Judges [*elohim*]: This word has various meanings. In many contexts it refers to God. At other times it can denote a range of authority figures: a master, ruler, judge, officer, or king (see

22:8, 27). It is interesting to note that there are other languages, such as Japanese, where a single term is used for authority figures of varying levels that range from feudal lords to gods.

And his master shall perforate his ear with an awl, and he shall serve him forever: It is evident from this ceremony that the Torah has grave reservations regarding an individual's choice to relinquish his personal freedom, regardless of the reason for this decision. A Jew should remain free and independent if it is in his power to do so. The Jewish people never had a genuine aristocracy or any system of set social classes. Each individual is meant to have equal rights, and the Torah is critical of one who voluntarily relinquishes this status.

ו אשתי ואת־בני לא אצא חפשי: והגישו אדניו אל־האלהים והגישו אל־הדלת
ז או אל־המזוזה ורצע אדניו את־אזנו במרצע ועבדו לעלם: וכי־
ח ימכר איש את־בתו לאמה לא תצא כצאת העבדים: אם־רעה בעיני אדניה
ט אשר־לא יעדה והפדה לעם נכרי לא־ימשל למכרה בבגדו־בה: ואם־לבנו
י ייעדנה כמשפט הבנות יעשה־לה: אם־אחרת יקח־לו שארה כסותה ועונתה
יא יב לא יגרע: ואם־שלש־אלה לא יעשה לה ויצאה חנם אין כסף: מכה

רש״י

ה| **את אשתי.** השפחה:

ו| **אל האלהים.** לבית דין, צריך שימלך במוכריו שמכרוהו לו: **אל הדלת או אל המזוזה.** יכול שתהא המזוזה כשרה לרצע עליה? תלמוד לומר: "ונתתה באזנו ובדלת" (דברים טו, יז), בדלת ולא במזוזה, הא מה תלמוד לומר: "או אל המזוזה"? הקיש דלת למזוזה, מה מזוזה מעומד אף דלת מעומד. רבי שמעון היה דורש מקרא זה כמין חומר: מה נשתנו דלת ומזוזה מכל כלים שבבית? אמר הקדוש ברוך הוא: דלת ומזוזה שהיו עדי במצרים כשפסחתי על המשקוף ועל שתי המזוזות, ואמרתי: "כי לי בני ישראל עבדים" (ויקרא כה, נה), ולא עבדים לעבדים, והלך זה וקנה אדון לעצמו, ירצע בפניהם: **ורצע אדניו את אזנו.** הימנית. או אינו אלא של שמאל? תלמוד לומר: 'אזן' 'אזן' לגזרה שוה, שנאמר במצרע: "תנוך אזן המטהר הימנית" (ויקרא יד, יד). ומה ראית אזן לרצע מכל האברים? אמר רבן יוחנן בן זכאי: אזן ששמעה בסיני: "לא תגנב" (לעיל כ, יג) והלך וגנב, תרצע. ואם מוכר עצמו הוא, אזן ששמעה "כי לי בני ישראל עבדים" (ויקרא כה, נה) והלך וקנה אדון לעצמו, תרצע: **ועבדו לעלם.** עד היובל. או אינו אלא 'לעולם' כמשמעו? תלמוד לומר: "ואיש אל משפחתו תשבו" (ויקרא כה, י), מגיד שחמשים שנה קרויים 'עולם'. ולא שיהא עובדו כל חמשים שנה, אלא עובדו עד היובל, בין סמוך בין מופלג:

ז| **וכי ימכר איש את בתו לאמה.** בקטנה הכתוב מדבר. יכול אפילו הביאה סימנים? אמרת, קל וחומר: ומה מכורה קודם לכן יוצאה בסימנין, כמו שכתוב: "ויצאה חנם אין כסף" (להלן פסוק יא) שאנו דורשים אותו לסימני נערות, שאינה מכורה אינו דין שלא תמכר?: **לא תצא כצאת העבדים.** כיציאת עבדים כנענים שיוצאים בשן ועין, אבל זו לא תצא בשן ועין אלא עובדת שש, או עד היובל, או עד שתביא סימנין, וכל הקודם קודם לחירותה, ונותן לה דמי עינה או דמי שנה. או אינו אלא "לא תצא כצאת העבדים" בשש וביובל? תלמוד לומר: "כי ימכר לך אחיך העברי או העבריה" (דברים טו, יב), מקיש עבריה לעברי לכל יציאותיו: מה עברי יוצא בשש וביובל, אף עבריה יוצאה בשש וביובל. ומהו "לא תצא כצאת העבדים"? לא תצא בראשי אברים כעבדים כנענים. יכול העברי יוצא בראשי אברים? תלמוד לומר: "העברי או העבריה", מקיש עברי לעבריה, מה העבריה אינה יוצאה בראשי אברים, אף הוא אינו יוצא בראשי אברים:

ח| **אם רעה בעיני אדניה.** שלא נשאה חן בעיניו לכנסה: **אשר לא יעדה.** שהיה לו ליעדה ולהכניסה לו לאשה, וכסף קנינה הוא כסף קידושיה. וכאן רמז לך הכתוב שמצוה ביעוד, ורמז לך שאינה צריכה קידושין אחרים: **והפדה.** יתן לה מקום להפדות ולצאת, שאף הוא מסייע בפדיונה. ומה הוא מקום שנותן לה? שמגרע מפדיונה במספר השנים שעשתה אצלו, כאלו היא שכורה אצלו. כיצד? הרי שקנאה במנה ועשתה אצלו שתי שנים, אומרים לו, יודע היית שעתידה לצאת לסוף שש, נמצא שקנית עבודת כל שנה ושנה בששית המנה, ועשתה אצלך שתי שנים, הרי שלישית המנה. טול שני שלישי מנה ותצא מאצלך: **לעם נכרי לא ימשל למכרה.** אינו רשאי למכרה לאחר, לא האדון ולא האב: **בבגדו בה.** אם בא לבגד בה שלא לקיים בה מצות יעוד. וכן אביה, מאחר שבגד בה ומכרה לזה:

ט| **ואם לבנו ייעדנה.** האדון, מלמד שאף בנו קם תחתיו ליעדה אם ירצה אביו, ואינו צריך לקדשה קידושין אחרים, אלא אומר לה: הרי את מיועדת לי בכסף שקבל אביך בדמיך: **כמשפט הבנות.** שאר כסות ועונה:

י| **אם אחרת יקח לו.** עליה: **שארה כסותה וענתה לא יגרע.** מן האמה שיעד לו כבר: **שארה.** מזונות: **כסותה.** כמשמעו: **ענתה.** תשמיש:

יא| **ואם שלש אלה לא יעשה לה.** אם אחת משלש אלה לא יעשה לה. ומה הן השלש? ייעדנה לו, או לבנו, או יגרע מפדיונה ותצא, וזה לא יעדה לא לו ולא לבנו, והיא לא היה בידה לפדות את עצמה: **ויצאה חנם.** רבה לה יציאה לזו יותר ממה שרבה לעבדים. ומה היא היציאה? למדך שתצא בסימנים – תשהא עמו עד שתצא בסימנים. ואם הגיעו שש שנים קודם סימנים, כבר למדנו שתצא, שנאמר: "העברי או העבריה ועבדך שש שנים" (דברים טו, יב), ומהו האמור כאן: "ויצאה חנם"? שאם קדמו סימנים לשש שנים תצא בהן. או אינו אומר שתצא אלא בבגרות? תלמוד לומר: "אין כסף" לרבות יציאת בגרות. ואם לא נאמרו שניהם, הייתי אומר: "ויצאה חנם" זו בגרות, לכך נאמרו שניהם, שלא לתן פתחון פה לבעל הדין לחלק:

יב| **מכה איש ומת.** כמה כתובים נאמרו בפרשת רוצחין,

DISCUSSION

21:8| **He shall not presume to sell her to a foreign people in his betrayal of her:** According to the Sages, this phrase applies to the Hebrew maidservant's father as well as her master. Once her father has sold her and she has been redeemed and returned to his house, he is not permitted to sell her a second time (see *Kiddushin* 18a–b; Rashi).

21:11| **She shall leave without charge:** Although the verse does not specify when the Hebrew maidservant goes free, the Sages explain that she is emancipated when she turns twelve and displays signs of physical maturity, even if she has not served her full term of six years (see *Kiddushin* 4a).

of his wounds, **shall be put to death.** The murderer is liable to receive the death penalty.

13 **But for one who** killed another but **did not have intent** to kill him, **and God caused it to come to his hand** through some accident, he is not liable to receive the death penalty. Rather, **I will provide you a place where he shall flee,** as explained in detail elsewhere.[15]

14 **If a man shall act intentionally against his neighbor to kill him cunningly,** he is liable to receive the death penalty. Consequently, **you shall take him** even **from My altar to die.** There indeed were cases of individuals who grabbed hold of the corners of the altar in an attempt to seek refuge, under God's protection, from the rule of law.[16] However, the altar does not protect one from his rightful punishment. Although he is not actually killed at the altar, and in this sense it does provide him with temporary protection, he must be removed from the Temple compound to the court, where he is judged and sentenced.[17]

15 Similar to the preceding laws involving murder, the following laws are also related to the Ten Precepts. **One who strikes his father or his mother,** even if he does not kill them, has violated a severe prohibition, as he has acted in a manner that is diametrically opposed to the commandment to honor one's parents. Consequently, he **shall be put to death.**

16 In the case of **one who abducts a man and he sells him** as a slave, **or he,** the kidnapped man, **is found in his,** the abductor's, **possession** before he could be sold,[18] **he,** the kidnapper, **shall be put to death.** The Sages contend that the prohibition of stealing listed in the Ten Precepts applies specifically to kidnapping, which is punishable by the death penalty.[19]

17 **One who curses his father or his mother shall be put to death.** Although the biblical term for "curse" may apply to any expression of derision or contempt,[20] cursing one's parent is punishable by death only in particularly harsh expressions of wishing evil upon one's parent. Merely contemptuous remarks addressed to a parent are the subject of a different verse: "Cursed is one who demeans his father or his mother."[21]

18 **If men quarrel, and** in the course of their argument **one strikes the other with a stone or with a fist,** forcefully enough to cause death, **and he does not die but collapses into bed** due to his injuries,

19 **if he,** the injured person, **arises and walks outside on his** walking **cane,**[22] as he is healing and is able walk without assistance from others, then **the assailant shall be absolved** of the death penalty, which would have applied had the victim died. **He shall give only his loss of livelihood, and he shall provide healing.**[D] The assailant must compensate his victim for the wages he lost while he was unable to work due to his injuries. The assailant must also pay for the medical treatment the victim required to recover from his wounds.

20 **If a man strikes his** gentile **slave or his** gentile **maidservant,** whose status is lower than that of a Hebrew slave or maidservant,[23] **with a staff, and he,** the slave or maidservant, **dies under his hand,** from the master's blows, **he shall be avenged.**[D] The

Second aliya

DISCUSSION

21:19| **And he shall provide healing:** This is the Torah's first notable acknowledgment of the role of doctors as part of the ideal world order. The Sages derive from this verse that doctors have the right to engage in medical practice (see *Berakhot* 60a).

21:20| **He shall be avenged:** The phrase "he shall be avenged" means death by the sword, which is the form of execution of murderers (see *Targum Yonatan*; Rashi; *Sanhedrin* 52a).

יג אִישׁ וָמֵת מוֹת יוּמָת: וַאֲשֶׁר לֹא צָדָה וְהָאֱלֹהִים אִנָּה לְיָדוֹ וְשַׂמְתִּי לְךָ מָקוֹם
יד אֲשֶׁר יָנוּס שָׁמָּה: וְכִי־יָזִד אִישׁ עַל־רֵעֵהוּ לְהָרְגוֹ בְעָרְמָה
טו מֵעִם מִזְבְּחִי תִּקָּחֶנּוּ לָמוּת: וּמַכֵּה אָבִיו וְאִמּוֹ מוֹת יוּמָת:
טז יז וְגֹנֵב אִישׁ וּמְכָרוֹ וְנִמְצָא בְיָדוֹ מוֹת יוּמָת: וּמְקַלֵּל אָבִיו וְאִמּוֹ מוֹת
יח יוּמָת: וְכִי־יְרִיבֻן אֲנָשִׁים וְהִכָּה־אִישׁ אֶת־רֵעֵהוּ בְּאֶבֶן אוֹ בְאֶגְרֹף
יט וְלֹא יָמוּת וְנָפַל לְמִשְׁכָּב: אִם־יָקוּם וְהִתְהַלֵּךְ בַּחוּץ עַל־מִשְׁעַנְתּוֹ וְנִקָּה הַמַּכֶּה
כ רַק שִׁבְתּוֹ יִתֵּן וְרַפֹּא יְרַפֵּא: וְכִי־יַכֶּה אִישׁ אֶת־עַבְדּוֹ אוֹ אֶת־אֲמָתוֹ שני

רש"י

ומה שבידי לפרש למה באו כלם אפרש: **מכה איש ומת.** למה נאמר? לפי שנאמר: "ואיש כי יכה כל נפש אדם מות יומת" (ויקרא כד, יז), שומע אני הכאה בלא מיתה? תלמוד לומר: "מכה איש ומת", אינו חייב אלא בהכאה של מיתה. ואם נאמר "מכה איש" ולא נאמר "ואיש כי יכה", הייתי אומר אינו חייב עד שיכה איש, הכה את האשה ואת הקטן מנין? תלמוד לומר: "כי יכה כל נפש אדם", אפילו קטן ואפילו אשה. ועוד, אלו נאמר "מכה איש" שומע אני אפילו קטן שהכה והרג יהא חייב? תלמוד לומר: "ואיש כי יכה", ולא קטן שהכה. ועוד, "כי יכה כל נפש אדם" אפילו נפלים במשמע, תלמוד לומר: "מכה איש", עד שיכה בן קיימא הראוי להיות איש:

יג | **ואשר לא צדה.** לא ארב לו ולא נתכון. 'צדה' לשון ארב, וכן הוא אומר: "ואתה צדה את נפשי לקחתה" (שמואל א' כד, יא). ולא יתכן לומר 'צדה' לשון "הצד ציד" (בראשית כז, לג), שצידת חיות אין נופל ה"א בפעל שלה, ושם דבר בה 'ציד', וזה שם דבר בו 'צדיה', ופעל שלו 'צודה', וזה פעל שלו 'צד'. ואומר אני, פתרונו כתרגומו: "ודלא כמן ליה". ומנחם חברו בחלק 'צד ציד', ואין אני מודה לו. ואם יש לחברו באחת ממחלקת של 'צד', נחברנו בחלק "על צד תנשאו" (ישעיה סו, יב), "צדה אורה" (שמואל א' כ, כ), "ומלין לצד עלאה ימלל" (דניאל ז, כה), אף כאן "אשר לא צדה" לא צדד למצוא לו שום צד מיתה. ואף זה יש להרהר עליו, מכל מקום לשון אורב הוא: **והאלהים אנה לידו.** זמן לידו. לשון: "לא תאנה אליך רעה" (תהלים צא, י), "לא יאנה לצדיק כל און" (משלי יב, כא), "מתאנה הוא לי" (מלכים ב' ה, ז) – מזדמן למצוא לי עלה: **והאלהים אנה לידו.** ולמה תצא זאת מלפניו? הוא שאמר דוד: "כאשר יאמר משל הקדמני מרשעים יצא רשע" (שמואל א' כד, יג) ומשל הקדמוני היא התורה שהיא משל הקדוש ברוך הוא שהוא קדמונו של עולם. והיכן אמרה תורה: "מרשעים יצא רשע"? – "והאלהים אנה לידו". במה הכתוב מדבר? בשני בני אדם, אחד הרג שוגג ואחד הרג מזיד, ולא היו עדים בדבר שיעידו, זה לא נהרג וזה לא גלה. הקדוש ברוך הוא מזמנן לפונדק אחד, זה שהרג שוגג עולה בסלם ונופל על זה שהרג מזיד והורגו, ועדים מעידים עליו ומחייבים אותו לגלות. נמצא זה שהרג שוגג גולה וזה שהרג מזיד נהרג: **ושמתי לך מקום.** אף במדבר, שינוס שמה. ואי זה מקום קולטו? זה מחנה לויה:

יד | **וכי יזד.** למה נאמר? לפי שנאמר: "מכה איש" וגו' (לעיל פסוק יב), שומע אני אפילו גוי, והרופא שהמית, ושליח בית דין שהמית במלקות ארבעים, והאב המכה את בנו, והרב הרודה את תלמידו, והשוגג? תלמוד לומר: "וכי יזד" ולא שוגג, "על רעהו" ולא על גוי, "להרגו בערמה" ולא שליח בית דין והרופא והרודה בנו ותלמידו, שאף על פי שהם מזידין אין מערימין: **מעם מזבחי.** אם היה כהן ורוצה לעבד עבודה, "תקחנו למות":

טו | **ומכה אביו ואמו.** לפי שלמדנו על החובל בחברו שהוא בתשלומין ולא במיתה, הצרך לומר על החובל באביו שהוא במיתה. ואינו חייב אלא בהכאה שיש בה חבורה: **אביו ואמו.** או זה או זה: **מות יומת.** בחנק:

טז | **וגנב איש ומכרו.** למה נאמר? לפי שנאמר: "כי ימצא איש גנב נפש מאחיו" (דברים כד, ז), אין לי אלא איש שגנב נפש, אשה או טומטום או אנדרוגינוס שגנבו מנין? תלמוד לומר: "וגנב איש ומכרו". ולפי שנאמר כאן: "וגנב איש", אין לי אלא גונב איש, גונב אשה מנין? תלמוד לומר: "גנב נפש". לכך הצרכו שניהם, מה שחסר זה גלה זה: **ונמצא בידו.** שראוהו עדים שגנבו ומכרו, "ונמצא" כבר קדם המכירה: **מות יומת.** בחנק. כל מיתה האמורה בתורה סתם חנק היא:

יז | **ומקלל אביו ואמו.** למה נאמר? לפי שהוא אומר: "איש איש אשר יקלל את אביו" (ויקרא כ, ט), אין לי אלא איש שקלל את אביו, אשה שקללה את אביה מנין? תלמוד לומר: "ומקלל אביו ואמו", סתם, בין איש ובין אשה. אם כן למה נאמר: "איש אשר יקלל"? להוציא את הקטן: **מות יומת.** בסקילה, וכל מקום שנאמר 'דמיו בו', בסקילה, ובנין אב לכלם: "באבן ירגמו אתם דמיהם בם" (ויקרא כ, כז), ובמקלל אביו נאמר: "דמיו בו" (שם פסוק ט):

יח | **וכי יריבן אנשים.** למה נאמר? לפי שנאמר: "עין תחת עין" (להלן פסוק כד), לא למדנו אלא דמי אבריו, אבל שבת ורפוי לא למדנו, לכך נאמרה פרשה זו: **ונפל למשכב.** כתרגומו: "ויפול לבוטלן", לחלי שמבטלו ממלאכתו:

יט | **על משענתו.** על בוריו וכחו: **ונקה המכה.** וכי תעלה על דעתך שיהרג זה שלא הרג?! אלא למדך כאן שחובשים אותו עד שנראה אם יתרפא זה. וכן משמעו: כשקם זה והולך על משענתו אז נקה המכה, אבל עד שלא יקום זה לא נקה המכה: **רק שבתו.** בטול מלאכתו מחמת החלי. אם קטע ידו או רגלו רואין בטול מלאכתו מחמת החלי כאלו הוא שומר קשואין, שהרי אף לאחר החלי אינו ראוי למלאכת יד ורגל, והוא כבר נתן לו מחמת נזקו דמי ידו ורגלו, שנאמר: "יד תחת יד רגל תחת רגל" (להלן פסוק כד): **ורפא ירפא.** כתרגומו, ישלם שכר הרופא:

כ | **וכי יכה איש את עבדו או את אמתו.** בעבד כנעני הכתוב מדבר. או אינו אלא בעברי? תלמוד לומר: "כי כספו הוא", מה כספו קנוי לו עולמית, אף עבד הקנוי לו עולמית. והרי היה בכלל "מכה איש ומת" (לעיל פסוק יב), אלא בא הכתוב והוציאו מן הכלל להיות נדון בדין יום או יומים, שאם לא מת תחת ידו ושהה מעת

master is liable to receive the death penalty for killing a human being, regardless of the fact that he was a gentile slave.

21 However, **if he,** the slave, **shall survive a day or two days,** despite his grave injuries, **he shall not be avenged.** The master is not liable to receive the death penalty, **as he,** the slave, **is his property.** The master is less accountable for the outcome of his aggression than others, due to the fact that he struck him in the regular manner in which masters discipline their slaves. Conversely, if one strikes someone who is not a gentile slave and the victim dies, one is liable to receive the death penalty even if the victim does not die immediately.[24]

22 **If men fight, and** as they struggle, **they** accidentally **strike** a bystander who is **a pregnant woman and her children are miscarried, but there is no fatality** of the woman herself,[25] **he,** the individual who struck the woman, **shall be fined, as the husband of the woman shall impose upon him.** The woman's husband may sue him for the loss of the offspring, **and** if they fail to reach an agreement with regard to the compensation, **he shall give in court,** in accordance with the determination of the judges.

23 **But if there will be a fatality,** the woman died, then **you shall give a life for a life.** From the context it can be inferred that this is referring to monetary payment rather than the death penalty, as this is not a case of premeditated murder but an accidental killing due to negligence.[26]

24 Similarly, if one caused permanent bodily damage to another, whether in the course of a fight or in some other manner, he must pay **an eye for an eye;**[D] **a tooth for a tooth; a hand for a hand; a foot for a foot;**

25 **a burn for a burn;** an open **wound for a wound; an injury,** without breaking the skin, **for an injury.**

26 The Torah states another law involving physical injury: **If a man shall strike the eye of his** gentile **slave,**[D] **or the eye of his** gentile **maidservant, and he** thereby **destroys it,** by rendering it permanently unusable, **he shall send him to freedom** in compensation **for his eye.**

27 Furthermore, even **if he,** the master, **shall** merely **dislodge the tooth of his slave or the tooth of his maidservant, he shall** be penalized by having to **send him to freedom for his tooth.**

28 Up to this point, with the exception of Hebrew slaves and maidservants, all of the laws in this section are cases of criminal law, illegal acts such as murder and inflicting bodily harm, as well as acting disrespectfully toward one's parents, which is a crime in Jewish law. When there was a criminal justice system that functioned in accordance with Jewish law, capital punishment could be meted out for certain infractions of criminal law. Criminals were judged by a special rabbinical court of twenty-three judges. From this verse onward, the focus is mainly on civil law. **If an ox** belonging to someone **gores a man or a woman and he shall die, the ox shall be stoned,**[D] **and its meat shall not be eaten.** As soon as the ox is sentenced to stoning its meat is rendered forbidden for consumption.[27] **And the owner of the ox is absolved** from personal responsibility for the victim's death, and he is not punished beyond the loss of his ox.

29 **But if** this is not the first occurrence of such a terrible event, as **the ox was wont to gore** people and endanger them **previously,**[28] **and** witnesses had testified to these events in the presence of the owner, and **its owner was warned** by the court that this is a dangerous ox, **but** nevertheless he **did not guard it and it killed a man or a woman,** then **the ox shall be stoned** for killing a person, **and its owner too shall die** [*yumat*]. The wording "and its owner too shall die" is formulated in an unusual

---

DISCUSSION

21:24 | An eye for an eye: These punishments have never been carried out in accordance with a literal reading of the verse. The Sages present a long list of reasons why one should not be punished for inflicting a wound on another by having the same injury inflicted on himself. They also infer from the Torah that a perpetrator receives a measure-for-measure punishment only in the case of murder, whereas one who causes physical injury is subject to monetary payment alone (see Numbers 35:31; *Bava Kamma* 83b–84a). The reason the verse expresses this monetary punishment figuratively in the form of physical injury to the perpetrator is in order to emphasize the gravity of the sin, as though to say that it would be fitting to inflict bodily injury on the perpetrator, although in practice he provides monetary compensation instead.

Since monetary payment is the only punishment that can be applied to one who inflicts these physical injuries, even if the perpetrator claims that he cannot afford the payment and would prefer to suffer physical injury, the court does not inflict injury upon him, but he remains liable for the monetary compensation until he has the means to pay (based on *Bava Kamma* 83b; Ibn Ezra, long commentary on Exodus; see also verses 29–30).

21:26 | If a man shall strike the eye of his slave: One who inflicts injury upon a free person must pay a defined monetary compensation. Since a gentile slave is considered the property of his owner, one might have thought that the master may employ harsh methods of discipline. However, the Torah penalizes the master for inflicting serious physical injuries upon his

slave by forcing him to set him free, in order to discourage masters from such callous types of chastisement (Ibn Ezra).

According to rabbinic tradition, the eye and tooth are merely examples, as a gentile slave is also set free if his master severs any visible limb that will not grow back, such as a finger or nose (see *Kiddushin* 24a; Rashi).

21:28 | The ox shall be stoned: The law of an ox that gored a person is based on a principle stated at the beginning of the Torah: "But I will demand your blood of your lives; from every beast I will demand it" (Genesis 9:5). An animal that kills a human being is considered to have subverted the natural order of the universe and is therefore subject to ritual execution (see Mishna *Sanhedrin* 1:4).

כא בַּשֵּׁבֶט וּמֵת תַּחַת יָדוֹ נָקֹם יִנָּקֵם: אַךְ אִם־יוֹם אוֹ יוֹמַיִם יַעֲמֹד לֹא יֻקַּם כִּי כַסְפּוֹ
כב הוּא: וְכִי־יִנָּצוּ אֲנָשִׁים וְנָגְפוּ אִשָּׁה הָרָה וְיָצְאוּ יְלָדֶיהָ וְלֹא יִהְיֶה
כג אָסוֹן עָנוֹשׁ יֵעָנֵשׁ כַּאֲשֶׁר יָשִׁית עָלָיו בַּעַל הָאִשָּׁה וְנָתַן בִּפְלִלִים: וְאִם־אָסוֹן יִהְיֶה
כד וְנָתַתָּה נֶפֶשׁ תַּחַת נָפֶשׁ: עַיִן תַּחַת עַיִן שֵׁן תַּחַת שֵׁן יָד תַּחַת יָד רֶגֶל תַּחַת רָגֶל:
כה כו כְּוִיָּה תַּחַת כְּוִיָּה פֶּצַע תַּחַת פָּצַע חַבּוּרָה תַּחַת חַבּוּרָה: וְכִי־יַכֶּה
אִישׁ אֶת־עֵין עַבְדּוֹ אוֹ־אֶת־עֵין אֲמָתוֹ וְשִׁחֲתָהּ לַחָפְשִׁי יְשַׁלְּחֶנּוּ תַּחַת עֵינוֹ:
כז וְאִם־שֵׁן עַבְדּוֹ אוֹ־שֵׁן אֲמָתוֹ יַפִּיל לַחָפְשִׁי יְשַׁלְּחֶנּוּ תַּחַת שִׁנּוֹ:
כח וְכִי־יִגַּח שׁוֹר אֶת־אִישׁ אוֹ אֶת־אִשָּׁה וָמֵת סָקוֹל יִסָּקֵל הַשּׁוֹר וְלֹא יֵאָכֵל
כט אֶת־בְּשָׂרוֹ וּבַעַל הַשּׁוֹר נָקִי: וְאִם שׁוֹר נַגָּח הוּא מִתְּמֹל שִׁלְשֹׁם וְהוּעַד
בִּבְעָלָיו וְלֹא יִשְׁמְרֶנּוּ וְהֵמִית אִישׁ אוֹ אִשָּׁה הַשּׁוֹר יִסָּקֵל וְגַם־בְּעָלָיו יוּמָת:

רש"י

לְעֵת - פָּטוּר: **בַּשֵּׁבֶט.** כְּשֶׁיֵּשׁ בּוֹ כְּדֵי לְהָמִית הַכָּתוּב מְדַבֵּר. אוֹ אֲפִלּוּ אֵין בּוֹ כְּדֵי לְהָמִית? תַּלְמוּד לוֹמַר בְּיִשְׂרָאֵל: "וְאִם בְּאֶבֶן יָד אֲשֶׁר יָמוּת בָּהּ הִכָּהוּ" (במדבר לה, יז), וַהֲלֹא דְּבָרִים קַל וָחֹמֶר: וּמַה יִּשְׂרָאֵל חָמוּר, אֵין חַיָּב עָלָיו אֶלָּא אִם כֵּן הִכָּהוּ בְּדָבָר שֶׁיֵּשׁ בּוֹ כְּדֵי לְהָמִית וְעַל אֵבֶר שֶׁהוּא כְּדֵי לָמוּת בְּהַכָּאָה זוֹ, עֶבֶד הַקַּל לֹא כָּל שֶׁכֵּן?: **נָקֹם יִנָּקֵם.** מִיתַת סַיִף. וְכֵן הוּא אוֹמֵר: "חֶרֶב נֹקֶמֶת נְקַם בְּרִית" (ויקרא כו, כה):

כא | **אַךְ אִם יוֹם אוֹ יוֹמַיִם יַעֲמֹד לֹא יֻקַּם.** אִם עַל יוֹם אֶחָד הוּא פָּטוּר עַל יוֹמַיִם לֹא כָּל שֶׁכֵּן?! אֶלָּא יוֹם שֶׁהוּא כְּיוֹמַיִם, וְאֵי זֶה זֶהוּ? זֶה מֵעֵת לְעֵת: **לֹא יֻקַּם כִּי כַסְפּוֹ הוּא.** הָא אַחֵר שֶׁהִכָּהוּ, אַף עַל פִּי שֶׁשָּׁהָה מֵעֵת לְעֵת קֹדֶם שֶׁמֵּת, חַיָּב:

כב | **וְכִי יִנָּצוּ אֲנָשִׁים.** זֶה עִם זֶה, וְנִתְכַּוֵּן לְהַכּוֹת אֶת חֲבֵרוֹ וְהִכָּה אֶת הָאִשָּׁה: **וְנָגְפוּ.** אֵין נְגִיפָה אֶלָּא לְשׁוֹן דְּחִיפָה וְהַכָּאָה, כְּמוֹ: "פֶּן תִּגֹּף בָּאֶבֶן רַגְלֶךָ" (תהלים צא, יב), "וּבְטֶרֶם יִתְנַגְּפוּ רַגְלֵיכֶם" (ירמיה יג, טז), "וּלְאֶבֶן נֶגֶף" (ישעיה ח, יד): **וְלֹא יִהְיֶה אָסוֹן.** בָּאִשָּׁה: **עָנוֹשׁ יֵעָנֵשׁ.** לְשַׁלֵּם דְּמֵי וְלָדוֹת לַבַּעַל. שָׁמִין אוֹתָהּ כַּמָּה הָיְתָה רְאוּיָה לִמָּכֵר בַּשּׁוּק לְהַעֲלוֹת בְּדָמֶיהָ בִּשְׁבִיל הֶרְיוֹנָהּ: **עָנוֹשׁ יֵעָנֵשׁ.** יִגְבּוּ מָמוֹן מִמֶּנּוּ, כְּמוֹ: "וְעָנְשׁוּ אֹתוֹ מֵאָה כֶסֶף" (דברים כב, יט): **כַּאֲשֶׁר יָשִׁית עָלָיו וְגוֹ'.** כְּשֶׁיִּתְבָּעֶנּוּ הַבַּעַל בְּבֵית דִּין לְהָשִׁית עָלָיו עֹנֶשׁ עַל כָּךְ: **וְנָתַן.** הַמַּכֶּה דְּמֵי וְלָדוֹת: **בִּפְלִלִים.** עַל פִּי הַדַּיָּנִים:

כג | **וְאִם אָסוֹן יִהְיֶה.** בָּאִשָּׁה: **וְנָתַתָּה נֶפֶשׁ תַּחַת נָפֶשׁ.** רַבּוֹתֵינוּ חוֹלְקִים בַּדָּבָר: יֵשׁ אוֹמְרִים נֶפֶשׁ מַמָּשׁ, וְיֵשׁ אוֹמְרִים מָמוֹן, אֲבָל לֹא נֶפֶשׁ מַמָּשׁ, שֶׁהַמִּתְכַּוֵּן לַהֲרֹג אֶת זֶה וְהָרַג אֶת זֶה פָּטוּר מִמִּיתָה, וּמְשַׁלֵּם לְיוֹרְשָׁיו דָּמָיו כְּמוֹ שֶׁהָיָה נִמְכָּר בַּשּׁוּק:

כד | **עַיִן תַּחַת עַיִן.** סִמֵּא עֵין חֲבֵרוֹ נוֹתֵן לוֹ דְּמֵי עֵינוֹ כַּמָּה שֶׁפָּחֲתוּ דָּמָיו לִמָּכֵר בַּשּׁוּק, וְכֵן כֻּלָּם, וְלֹא נְטִילַת אֵבֶר מַמָּשׁ, כְּמוֹ שֶׁדָּרְשׁוּ רַבּוֹתֵינוּ בְּפֶרֶק 'הַחוֹבֵל' (בבא קמא פג ע"ב - פד ע"א):

כה | **כְּוִיָּה תַּחַת כְּוִיָּה.** מִכְוַת אֵשׁ. וְעַד עַכְשָׁיו דִּבֵּר בַּחֲבָלָה שֶׁיֵּשׁ בָּהּ פְּחַת דָּמִים, וְעַכְשָׁיו בְּשֶׁאֵין בָּהּ פְּחַת דָּמִים אֶלָּא צַעַר, כְּגוֹן כְּוָאוֹ בִּשְׁפוּד עַל צִפָּרְנוֹ, אוֹמְדִים כַּמָּה אָדָם כַּיּוֹצֵא בָּזֶה רוֹצֶה לִטֹּל לִהְיוֹת מִצְטַעֵר כָּךְ: **פֶּצַע.** הִיא מַכָּה הַמּוֹצִיאָה דָּם, שֶׁפָּצַע אֶת בְּשָׂרוֹ, נבררור"א בְּלַעַ"ז. הַכֹּל לְפִי מַה שֶּׁהוּא, אִם יֵשׁ בּוֹ פְּחַת דָּמִים נוֹתֵן נֶזֶק, וְאִם נָפַל לְמִשְׁכָּב נוֹתֵן שֶׁבֶת וְרִפּוּי וּבֹשֶׁת וְצַעַר. וּמִקְרָא זֶה יָתֵר הוּא, וּבְ'הַחוֹבֵל' דְּרָשׁוּהוּ רַבּוֹתֵינוּ לְחַיֵּב עַל הַצַּעַר אֲפִלּוּ בִּמְקוֹם נֶזֶק, שֶׁאַף עַל פִּי שֶׁנּוֹתֵן לוֹ דְּמֵי יָדוֹ אֵין פּוֹטְרִין אוֹתוֹ מִן הַצַּעַר, לוֹמַר הוֹאִיל וְקָנָה יָדוֹ יֵשׁ עָלָיו לַחְתְּכָהּ בְּכָל מַה שֶּׁיִּרְצֶה, אֶלָּא אוֹמְרִים יֵשׁ לוֹ לַחְתְּכָהּ בְּסַם שֶׁאֵינוֹ מִצְטַעֵר כָּל כָּךְ, וְזֶה חֲתָכָהּ בְּבַרְזֶל וְצִעֲרוֹ: **חַבּוּרָה.** הִיא מַכָּה שֶׁהַדָּם נִצְרָר בָּהּ וְאֵינוֹ יוֹצֵא אֶלָּא שֶׁמַּאֲדִים הַבָּשָׂר כְּנֶגְדּוֹ. וּלְשׁוֹן חַבּוּרָה טק"א בְּלַעַז, כְּמוֹ: "וְנָמֵר חֲבַרְבֻּרֹתָיו" (ירמיה יג, כג), וְתַרְגּוּמוֹ "מַשְׁקוּפֵי", לְשׁוֹן חֲבָטָה, בטדור"א בְּלַעַז, וְכֵן: "שְׁדֻפוֹת קָדִים" (בראשית מא, כג), "שְׁקִיפָן קִדּוּם", חֲבוּטוֹת בָּרוּחַ. וְכֵן: "עַל הַמַּשְׁקוֹף" (לעיל יב, ז), עַל שֵׁם שֶׁהַדֶּלֶת נוֹקֵשׁ עָלָיו:

כו | **אֶת עֵין עַבְדּוֹ.** כְּנַעֲנִי, אֲבָל עִבְרִי אֵינוֹ יוֹצֵא בְּשֵׁן וָעַיִן, כְּמוֹ שֶׁאָמַרְנוּ אֵצֶל "לֹא תֵצֵא כְּצֵאת הָעֲבָדִים" (לעיל פסוק ז): **תַּחַת עֵינוֹ.** וְכֵן בְּעֶשְׂרִים וְאַרְבָּעָה רָאשֵׁי אֵבָרִים: אֶצְבְּעוֹת הַיָּדַיִם וְהָרַגְלַיִם וּשְׁתֵּי אָזְנַיִם וְהַחֹטֶם וְרֹאשׁ הַגְּוִיָּה שֶׁהוּא גִּיד הָאַמָּה. וְלָמָּה נֶאֶמְרוּ שֵׁן וָעַיִן? שֶׁאִם נֶאֱמַר עַיִן וְלֹא נֶאֱמַר שֵׁן, הָיִיתִי אוֹמֵר, מָה עַיִן שֶׁנִּבְרְאָה עִמּוֹ אַף כָּל שֶׁנִּבְרָא עִמּוֹ, וַהֲרֵי שֵׁן לֹא נִבְרָא עִמּוֹ. וְאִם נֶאֱמַר שֵׁן וְלֹא נֶאֱמַר עַיִן, הָיִיתִי אוֹמֵר, אֲפִלּוּ שֵׁן תִּינוֹק שֶׁיֵּשׁ לָהּ חֲלִיפִין, לְכָךְ נֶאֱמַר עָיִן:

כח | **וְכִי יִגַּח שׁוֹר.** אֶחָד שׁוֹר וְאֶחָד כָּל בְּהֵמָה וְחַיָּה וָעוֹף, אֶלָּא שֶׁדִּבֵּר הַכָּתוּב בַּהֹוֶה: **וְלֹא יֵאָכֵל אֶת בְּשָׂרוֹ.** מִמַּשְׁמַע שֶׁנֶּאֱמַר: "סָקוֹל יִסָּקֵל הַשּׁוֹר" אֵינִי יוֹדֵעַ שֶׁהוּא נְבֵלָה וּנְבֵלָה אֲסוּרָה בַּאֲכִילָה? אֶלָּא מַה תַּלְמוּד לוֹמַר: "וְלֹא יֵאָכֵל אֶת בְּשָׂרוֹ"? שֶׁאֲפִלּוּ שְׁחָטוֹ לְאַחַר שֶׁנִּגְמַר דִּינוֹ אָסוּר בַּאֲכִילָה. בַּהֲנָאָה מִנַּיִן? תַּלְמוּד לוֹמַר: "וּבַעַל הַשּׁוֹר נָקִי", כְּאָדָם הָאוֹמֵר לַחֲבֵרוֹ: יָצָא פְּלוֹנִי נָקִי מִנְּכָסָיו וְאֵין לוֹ בָּהֶם הֲנָאָה שֶׁל כְּלוּם. זֶהוּ מִדְרָשׁוֹ. וּפְשׁוּטוֹ כְּמַשְׁמָעוֹ, לְפִי שֶׁנֶּאֱמַר בְּמוּעָד: "וְגַם בְּעָלָיו יוּמָת", הֻצְרַךְ לוֹמַר בְּתָם: "וּבַעַל הַשּׁוֹר נָקִי":

כט | **מִתְּמֹל שִׁלְשֹׁם.** הֲרֵי שָׁלֹשׁ נְגִיחוֹת: **וְהוּעַד בִּבְעָלָיו.** לְשׁוֹן הַתְרָאָה בְּעֵדִים, כְּמוֹ: "הָעֵד הֵעִד בָּנוּ הָאִישׁ" (בראשית מג, ג): **וְהֵמִית אִישׁ וְגוֹ'.** לְפִי שֶׁנֶּאֱמַר: "וְכִי יִגַּח" (לעיל פסוק כח), אֵין לִי אֶלָּא שֶׁהֱמִיתוֹ בִּנְגִיחָה, הֱמִיתוֹ בִּנְשִׁיכָה דְּחִיפָה בְּעִיטָה מִנַּיִן? תַּלְמוּד לוֹמַר: "וְהֵמִית": **וְגַם בְּעָלָיו יוּמָת.** בִּידֵי שָׁמַיִם. יָכוֹל בִּידֵי אָדָם? תַּלְמוּד לוֹמַר: "מוֹת יוּמַת הַמַּכֶּה רֹצֵחַ הוּא" (במדבר לה, כא), עַל רְצִיחָתוֹ אַתָּה הוֹרְגוֹ וְאִי אַתָּה הוֹרְגוֹ עַל רְצִיחַת שׁוֹרוֹ:

manner. It differs from the double formulation [*mot yumat*] that appears in many other verses (see, e.g., verse 16). The reason for this distinction is that although the owner of the ox may be worthy of death for his negligence, he is not liable to receive the death penalty by the court.[29]

30 Instead, **when** a monetary **ransom is imposed upon him,**[D] the owner of the ox, then **he shall give ransom of his life, in accordance with all that will be imposed upon him** by the court. Instead of being executed, he pays the value of his life as ransom. Some Sages explain that the ransom is the value of his victim's life. The amount to be paid is determined by objective criteria used for assessing the value of a person.[30]

31 **Whether it shall gore a son or it shall gore a daughter,** even if it gores a minor, **in accordance with this ordinance shall be done to him.** These laws do not depend upon the victim's age.

32 **If the ox shall gore a** gentile **slave or a** gentile **maidservant,** who do not have the status of full citizens, **he,** the owner of the ox, **shall give thirty silver shekels to his,** the slave's, **master, and the ox shall be stoned,** like any case where an animal causes the death of a human being.

33 The Torah states another case involving civil law and injury: **If a man shall uncover a pit** that had previously been covered up properly, **or if a man shall dig a pit** himself **and he does not cover it, and an ox or a donkey** or any other living creature[31] **falls there,**

34 **the owner of the pit,** the one who dug the pit or uncovered it[32] is responsible for the damage and he **shall pay. He shall compensate its owner with silver and the carcass shall be his.** Once the individual responsible for the pit has paid the owner of the animal, he has the right to take the dead animal, which still has some value. The owner of the animal has no rights to the carcass because he has been compensated for the full value of his animal.[33] Alternatively, this verse teaches the opposite, that the dead animal remains the property of its original owner. The owner of the pit, after returning the carcass to its owner, may subtract the value of the carcass from the value of the live animal that he must pay in compensation.[34]

35 **If the ox of a man shall strike** and injure **the ox of his neighbor** in any manner, such as by pushing or goring it,[35] **and it dies, they shall sell the living ox** that caused the damage **and divide its value,** the price received for its sale, **and they shall divide** the price for which they can sell **the carcass too.**[D] In this manner, the owner of the ox that caused the injury compensates the other owner for half the damage, as he pays the value of half of his ox minus half the value of the carcass. The sale mentioned in the verse represents the share of the live ox that is granted to the owner of the dead ox.

36 **Or if**[36] **it became known** to the court **that it is an ox wont to gore previously,** and this is at least the third or fourth time that it has gored[37] **and** yet **its owners would not** take the necessary steps to **guard it** properly, **he shall pay** a live **ox** in exchange **for** the dead **ox, and the carcass shall be his** own, as the owner of the dead ox has received full compensation for his loss (see verse 34).

37 **If a man steals an ox or a sheep,**[D] **and slaughters it or sells it,** this is not a simple case of greed, where the offender succumbed to a momentary temptation, but a crime committed over an extended period of time and which eventually leads to the loss of the stolen item. Therefore, **he shall pay five oxen for the ox, and four sheep for the sheep.** The thief pays four or five times the value of the animal he stole, unlike standard cases of theft where one pays only double the value of the item he stole (see 22:3).

22 1 **If the thief is found while excavating** in order to break in

DISCUSSION

21:30| **When [*im*] ransom is imposed upon him:** The Sages have a tradition that although the word *im* generally refers to a conditional, and would be translated "if," in this instance the ransom is not conditional. Rather, the court is obligated to impose this ransom payment upon the owner of the ox. There are several other cases in the Torah where the term *im* is attached to an obligation (see Rashi). The reason that the obligation is phrased in this manner is to emphasize that the owner of the ox has in essence forfeited his life by his negligence, and were it not for the ransom he ought to be put to death. In practice, he is not subject to the death penalty even if he fails to pay. This is similar to the law that a father must ransom his firstborn son by giving money to a priest (see Numbers 3:45–51; 18:16). Even if the father does not pay, the priests do not own the child or have any rights over him.

Since the ransom payment serves as an act of atonement for the negligence of the owner of the ox, some maintain that the court does not force him to pay or appropriate his property, as it would for a regular monetary debt. Accordingly, it has been suggested that the word *im* alludes to the idea that this is not a regular monetary obligation but a religious obligation incumbent upon the owner (see Ramban; see also *Bekhor Shor*; *Adderet Eliyahu*).

21:35| **They shall sell the living ox and divide its value, and they shall divide the carcass too:** This calculation is applicable when there are two oxen of equal worth. However, it does not make sense to follow this procedure when the oxen are unequal in value. This law has been the subject of many disputes and discussions over the generations (see, e.g., *Bava Kamma* 33a, 34a; Rashi). The principle that is accepted by all is that the owner of an ox which has not been established as one that gores habitually is not liable to pay the full value of the damage caused by his ox's unusual behavior. If the ox that caused damage was worth less than half the damage it caused, the owner pays only the full value of his ox; if it was worth more than half the damage, the owner pays half the damage. In other words, the individual who suffered the damage is never entitled to more than the value of the ox that caused the damage, and he does not receive more than half of the damage he suffered.

ל לא אִם־כֹּפֶר יוּשַׁת עָלָיו וְנָתַן פִּדְיֹן נַפְשׁוֹ כְּכֹל אֲשֶׁר־יוּשַׁת עָלָיו׃ אוֹ־בֵן יִגָּח אוֹ־בַת
לב יִגָּח כַּמִּשְׁפָּט הַזֶּה יֵעָשֶׂה לּוֹ׃ אִם־עֶבֶד יִגַּח הַשּׁוֹר אוֹ אָמָה כֶּסֶף ׀ שְׁלֹשִׁים שְׁקָלִים
לג יִתֵּן לַאדֹנָיו וְהַשּׁוֹר יִסָּקֵל׃ וְכִי־יִפְתַּח אִישׁ בּוֹר אוֹ כִּי־יִכְרֶה
לד אִישׁ בֹּר וְלֹא יְכַסֶּנּוּ וְנָפַל־שָׁמָּה שּׁוֹר אוֹ חֲמוֹר׃ בַּעַל הַבּוֹר יְשַׁלֵּם כֶּסֶף יָשִׁיב
לה לִבְעָלָיו וְהַמֵּת יִהְיֶה־לּוֹ׃ וְכִי־יִגֹּף שׁוֹר־אִישׁ אֶת־שׁוֹר רֵעֵהוּ
לו וָמֵת וּמָכְרוּ אֶת־הַשּׁוֹר הַחַי וְחָצוּ אֶת־כַּסְפּוֹ וְגַם אֶת־הַמֵּת יֶחֱצוּן׃ אוֹ נוֹדַע כִּי
שׁוֹר נַגָּח הוּא מִתְּמוֹל שִׁלְשֹׁם וְלֹא יִשְׁמְרֶנּוּ בְּעָלָיו שַׁלֵּם יְשַׁלֵּם שׁוֹר תַּחַת הַשּׁוֹר
לז וְהַמֵּת יִהְיֶה־לּוֹ׃ כִּי יִגְנֹב־אִישׁ שׁוֹר אוֹ־שֶׂה וּטְבָחוֹ אוֹ מְכָרוֹ חֲמִשָּׁה
כב א בָקָר יְשַׁלֵּם תַּחַת הַשּׁוֹר וְאַרְבַּע־צֹאן תַּחַת הַשֶּׂה׃ אִם־בַּמַּחְתֶּרֶת יִמָּצֵא הַגַּנָּב

רש"י

ל| **אם כפר יושת עליו.** 'אם' זה אינו תלוי, והרי הוא כמו: "אם כסף תלוה" (להלן כב, כד), לשון 'אשר', זה משפטו שישיתו עליו בית דין כפר: **ונתן פדין נפשו.** דמי נזק, דברי רבי ישמעאל. רבי עקיבא אומר: דמי מזיק:

לא| **או בן יגח.** בן שהוא קטן: **או בת.** שהיא קטנה. לפי שנאמר: "והמית איש או אשה" (לעיל פסוק כט), יכול אינו חייב אלא על הגדולים? תלמוד לומר: "או בן יגח" וגו', לחייב על הקטנים כגדולים:

לב| **אם עבד או אמה.** כנעניים: **שלשים שקלים יתן.** גזרת הכתוב הוא, בין שהוא שוה אלף זוז בין שאינו שוה אלא דינר והשקל משקלו ארבעה זהובים שהם חצי אונקיא למשקל הישר של קולוניא:

לג| **וכי יפתח איש בור.** שהיה מכסה וגלהו: **או כי יכרה.** למה נאמר? אם על הפתיחה חייב על הכריה לא כל שכן?! אלא להביא כורה אחר כורה שהוא חייב: **ולא יכסנו.** הא אם כסהו פטור, ובחופר ברשות הרבים דבר הכתוב: **שור או חמור.** הוא הדין לכל בהמה וחיה, שבכל מקום שנאמר שור וחמור אנו למדין אותו 'שור' 'שור' משבת, שנאמר: "למען ינוח שורך וחמרך" (להלן כג, יב), מה להלן כל בהמה וחיה כשור, שהרי נאמר במקום אחר: "וכל בהמתך" (דברים ה, יד), אף כאן כל בהמה וחיה כשור, ולא נאמר שור וחמור אלא 'שור' ולא אדם, 'חמור' ולא כלים:

לד| **בעל הבור.** בעל התקלה, אף על פי שאין הבור שלו, שעשאו ברשות הרבים, עשאו הכתוב בעליו להתחייב בנזקיו: **כסף ישיב לבעליו.** "ישיב" לרבות שוה כסף ואפילו סבין: **והמת יהיה לו.** לנזק. שמין את הנבלה ונוטלה בדמים, ומשלם לו המזיק עליה תשלומי נזקו:

לה| **וכי יגף.** ידחף, בין בקרניו בין בגופו בין ברגליו בין שנשכו בשניו כלן בכלל נגיפה הם, שאין נגיפה אלא לשון מכה: **שור איש.** שור של איש: **ומכרו את השור וגו'.** בשוים הכתוב מדבר, שור שוה מאתים שהמית שור שוה מאתים, בין שהנבלה שוה הרבה בין שהיא שוה מעט, כשנוטל זה חצי החי וחצי המת וזה חצי החי וחצי המת נמצא כל אחד מפסיד חצי נזק שהזיקה המיתה. למדנו שהתם משלם חצי נזק, שמן השוין אתה למד לשאינן שוין כי דין התם לשלם חצי נזק, לא פחות ולא יותר. או יכול אף כשאינן שוין בדמיהן כשהן חיים אמר הכתוב: וחצו את שניהם? אם אמרת כן, פעמים שהמזיק משתכר הרבה, כשהנבלה שוה למכר לגוים הרבה יותר מדמי שור המזיק, ואי אפשר שיאמר הכתוב שיהא המזיק נשכר. או פעמים שהנזק נוטל הרבה יותר מדמי נזק שלם, שחצי דמי שור המזיק שוין יותר מכל דמי שור הנזק, ואם אמרת כן, הרי תם חמור ממועד. על כרחך לא דבר הכתוב אלא בשוין, ולמדך שהתם משלם חצי נזק, ומן השוין תלמד לשאינן שוין, שהמשתלם חצי נזקו שמין לו את הנבלה, ומה שפחתו דמיו בשביל המיתה, נוטל חצי הפחת והולך. ולמה אמר הכתוב בלשון הזה, ולא אמר: 'ישלם חציו'? ללמד שאין התם משלם אלא מגופו, ואם נגח ומת אין הנזק נוטל אלא הנבלה, ואם אינה מגעת לחצי נזקו יפסיד. או שור שוה מנה שנגח שור שוה חמש מאות זוז אינו נוטל אלא את השור, שלא נתחייב התם לחייב את בעליו לשלם מן העליה:

לו| **או נודע.** או לא היה תם, אלא "נודע כי שור נגח הוא" היום ומתמול שלשם, הרי שלש נגיחות: **שלם ישלם שור.** נזק שלם: **והמת יהיה לו.** לנזק, ועליו ישלים המזיק עד שישתלם נזק כל נזקו:

לז| **חמשה בקר וגו'.** אמר רבן יוחנן בן זכאי: חס המקום על כבודן של בריות, שור שהולך ברגליו ולא נתבזה בו הגנב לנשאו על כתפו – משלם חמשה; שה שנושאו על כתפו – משלם ארבעה הואיל ונתבזה בו. אמר רבי מאיר: בא וראה כמה גדולה כחה של מלאכה, שור שבטלו ממלאכתו – חמשה, שה שלא בטלו ממלאכתו – ארבעה: **תחת השור... תחת השה.** שנאן הכתוב, לומר שאין מדת תשלומי ארבעה וחמשה נוהגת אלא בשור ושה בלבד:

פרק כב

א| **אם במחתרת.** כשהיה חותר את הבית: **אין לו דמים.** אין זו רציחה, הרי הוא כמת מעיקרו. כאן למדתך תורה:

DISCUSSION

21:37| **If a man steals an ox or a sheep:** Since in this particular case an ox is distinguished from a sheep, it is clear that this is a unique ordinance which does not apply to other animals. One who steals and sells a donkey or camel pays only double, like one who steals any other item (see *Bava Kamma* 62b; Rashi).

through a tunnel **and he is struck** by the homeowner or someone else **and he dies, there is no bloodguilt for him.** The person who kills him is not liable for his death. A burglar is treated more stringently than an ordinary thief because, under certain circumstances, he is suspected of being prepared to kill anyone who stands in his way or attempts to stop him. Consequently, if the homeowner attempts to prevent the theft and ends up killing the burglar, he is exempt from punishment because he is considered to have acted in self-defense.[38]

2 **If the sun shone upon him,**[D] the burglar, meaning that he broke into the house during the day[39] or he emerged from his tunnel to the sunlight,[40] it is assumed that he is only attempting to steal but is not prepared to kill anyone, as he assumes that the homeowner is not at home. In contrast, one who breaks in at night knows that the homeowner will be present and will attempt to defend his property. Consequently, the burglar by day is not considered a potential murderer but a simple thief, which means that if one kills him **there is bloodguilt for him,** the thief, and the killer is liable for murder. If this burglar steals property, **he shall pay; if he has nothing** with which to pay, then **he shall be sold** as a Hebrew slave (see 21:2–4), and the price of his purchase is used to pay **for his theft.**

3 **If the theft shall be found alive in his possession, whether an ox, or a donkey, or a sheep** or any other animal, **he shall pay double.** He must return the stolen item and also pay a sum of money equivalent to its value. This law applies to any stolen item, not just to animals (see verse 6).

4 **If a man grazes an animal in a field or a vineyard,**[41] **and dispatched his animal,** either intentionally or through failing to take the necessary precautions to keep it enclosed, **and it grazes in another's field, he shall pay the best of his field and the best of his vineyard.** This means that in a case where the individual responsible for the damage chooses to compensate the damaged party with land, he must give his highest quality field or vineyard.[42]

Third aliya

5 **If a fire spreads** from the spot where it was started **and encounters thorns, and** as a result **a grain pile or standing grain or a field is consumed, the one who ignited the fire shall pay** for all of the damages.

6 **If a man gives silver or vessels to his neighbor to safeguard and it is stolen from the man's house, if the thief is found, he shall pay double.** The rule that a thief must pay back double the value of the item he stole applies to any stolen article, not only live animals, as might have been inferred from verse 3.

7 **If the thief is not found,** and the bailee with whom the object was safeguarded claims that the item disappeared without his knowledge, the question arises as to whether it was really stolen by a third party at all. Therefore, **the householder,** meaning the bailee, **shall be brought to the judges** to swear **that he did not extend his hand to the property of his neighbor.**

8 **For every matter of transgression,** where the bailee claims that the item he was safeguarding was lost and he is accused of having taken it himself, **whether for an ox, for a donkey, for a sheep, for a garment, or for any lost item, with regard to which he,** the owner of the item, **shall say: This is it,** as the item is one that he could point to if it were present and claim that it is his, **the statement of both parties shall come to the judges** for a ruling. **Whomever,** any bailee, whom **the judges shall condemn shall pay double to his neighbor,** the individual who entrusted his item in his care.[43]

9 **If a man shall give his neighbor**[D] **a donkey, or an ox, or a sheep, or any animal to safeguard, and it dies, or is injured,** e.g., it breaks a leg, **or is captured, and there is no onlooker** who witnessed the event,

DISCUSSION

22:2| **If the sun shone upon him:** The Sages understood this phrase as a metaphor meaning that it is clear that the burglar does not intend to kill (see *Sanhedrin* 72a; Rashi). This certainty is not dependent on the fact that it is daytime; the same applies if the burglar is unarmed, or the homeowner knows him and can be sure that the intruder would not kill him.

22:9| **If a man shall give his neighbor:** The two groups of verses (6–8, 9–12) refer to a bailee. However, there is a significant difference between the two passages with regard to a situation where the bailee claims that the item was stolen. In the first case, the bailee takes an oath and is exempt from payment, whereas in the second case he is liable to pay for the item. One might suppose that the difference is due to the different categories of items mentioned in each group of verses. In the first case, the bailee was asked to guard money or articles, whereas in the second case he agreed to watch over someone's animals. However, the Sages explain that the difference is not due to the type of item that the bailee is guarding. Rather, each passage refers to a different type of bailee. In the first passage, the Torah is referring to an unpaid bailee, who accepts responsibility for the item as a favor to the owner. The unpaid bailee is liable only if he was negligent, not if the item was stolen from him. The second passage refers to a paid bailee, who receives payment or some other form of compensation in exchange for safeguarding the item. Consequently, his level of responsibility is higher, and he must compensate the owner even if the item was stolen from him. A paid bailee is exempt only if the item was lost as a result of some unavoidable accident, for example, if the animal he was guarding was killed by a wild animal.

The reason for the use of different examples in each passage is that generally one will agree to guard another's silver or vessels as a favor, because these items do not require any upkeep. One who watches another's animals will typically do so only for a fee, as animals need constant care. Nevertheless, these are merely examples; an unpaid bailee is liable only for criminal negligence regardless of whether he was guarding objects or animals. Similarly, a paid bailee is liable even if it was not a living animal, and he is exempt only if the damage occurred in a manner

ב וְהֻכָּה וָמֵת אֵין לוֹ דָּמִים׃ אִם־זָרְחָה הַשֶּׁמֶשׁ עָלָיו דָּמִים לוֹ שַׁלֵּם יְשַׁלֵּם אִם־אֵין
ג לוֹ וְנִמְכַּר בִּגְנֵבָתוֹ׃ אִם־הִמָּצֵא תִמָּצֵא בְיָדוֹ הַגְּנֵבָה מִשּׁוֹר עַד־חֲמוֹר עַד־שֶׂה
ד חַיִּים שְׁנַיִם יְשַׁלֵּם׃ כִּי יַבְעֶר־אִישׁ שָׂדֶה אוֹ־כֶרֶם וְשִׁלַּח אֶת־בְּעִירֹה שלישי
ה וּבִעֵר בִּשְׂדֵה אַחֵר מֵיטַב שָׂדֵהוּ וּמֵיטַב כַּרְמוֹ יְשַׁלֵּם׃ כִּי־תֵצֵא
אֵשׁ וּמָצְאָה קֹצִים וְנֶאֱכַל גָּדִישׁ אוֹ הַקָּמָה אוֹ הַשָּׂדֶה שַׁלֵּם יְשַׁלֵּם הַמַּבְעִר אֶת־
ו הַבְּעֵרָה׃ כִּי־יִתֵּן אִישׁ אֶל־רֵעֵהוּ כֶּסֶף אוֹ־כֵלִים לִשְׁמֹר וְגֻנַּב מִבֵּית
ז הָאִישׁ אִם־יִמָּצֵא הַגַּנָּב יְשַׁלֵּם שְׁנָיִם׃ אִם־לֹא יִמָּצֵא הַגַּנָּב וְנִקְרַב בַּעַל־הַבַּיִת אֶל־
ח הָאֱלֹהִים אִם־לֹא שָׁלַח יָדוֹ בִּמְלֶאכֶת רֵעֵהוּ׃ עַל־כָּל־דְּבַר־פֶּשַׁע עַל־שׁוֹר עַל־
חֲמוֹר עַל־שֶׂה עַל־שַׂלְמָה עַל־כָּל־אֲבֵדָה אֲשֶׁר יֹאמַר כִּי־הוּא זֶה עַד הָאֱלֹהִים
ט יָבֹא דְּבַר־שְׁנֵיהֶם אֲשֶׁר יַרְשִׁיעֻן אֱלֹהִים יְשַׁלֵּם שְׁנַיִם לְרֵעֵהוּ׃ כִּי־יִתֵּן
אִישׁ אֶל־רֵעֵהוּ חֲמוֹר אוֹ־שׁוֹר אוֹ־שֶׂה וְכָל־בְּהֵמָה לִשְׁמֹר וּמֵת אוֹ־נִשְׁבַּר אוֹ־

אם בא להרגך השכם להרגו, וזה להרגך בא, שהרי יודע הוא שאין אדם מעמיד עצמו ורואה שנוטלין ממונו בפניו ושותק, לפיכך על מנת כן בא שאם יעמוד בעל הממון כנגדו יהרגנו:

ב| **אם זרחה השמש עליו.** אין זה אלא כמין משל, אם ברור לך הדבר שיש לו שלום עמך, כשמש הזה שהוא שלום בעולם, כך פשוט לך שאינו בא להרוג אפילו יעמוד בעל הממון כנגדו, כגון אב החותר לגנוב ממון הבן, בידוע שרחמי האב על הבן ואינו בא על עסקי נפשות: **דמים לו.** כחי הוא חשוב, ורציחה היא אם יהרגנו בעל הבית: **שלם ישלם.** הגנב ממון שגנב ואינו חייב מיתה. ואונקלוס שתרגם: "אם עינא דסהדיא נפלת עלוהי" לקח לו שטה אחרת, לומר שאם מצאוהו עדים קודם שבא בעל הבית וכשבא בעל הבית נגדו התרו בו שלא יהרגהו, "דמים לו", חייב עליו אם הרגו, שמאחר שיש רואים להם אין הגנב הזה בא על עסקי נפשות, ולא יהרג את בעל הממון:

ג| **אם המצא תמצא בידו.** ברשותו, שלא טבח ולא מכר: **משור עד חמור.** כל דבר בכלל תשלומי כפל, בין שיש בו רוח חיים בין שאין בו רוח חיים, שהרי נאמר מקרא אחר: "על שה על שלמה על כל אבדה וגו' ישלם שנים לרעהו" (להלן פסוק ח): **חיים שנים ישלם.** ולא ישלם לו מתים, אלא חיים או דמי חיים:

ד| **כי יבער... את בעירה ובער.** כלם לשון בהמה, כמו: "אנחנו ובעירנו" (במדבר כ, ד): **כי יבער.** יוליך בהמותיו בשדה וכרם של חברו ויזיק אותה באחת משתי אלו: או בשלוח בעירה או בבעור. ופרשו רבותינו: 'שלוח' הוא נזקי מדרך כף רגל, "ובער" הוא נזקי השן האוכלת ומבערת: **בשדה אחר.** בשדה של איש אחר: **מיטב שדהו ... ישלם.** שמין את הנזק, ואם בא לשלם לו קרקע דמי נזקו ישלם לו ממיטב שדותיו, אם היה נזקו סלע יתן לו שוה סלע מעדית שיש לו. למדך הכתוב שהניזקין שמין להם בעדית:

ה| **כי תצא אש.** אפילו מעצמה: **ומצאה קצים.** קרדונ"ש בלעז: **ונאכל גדיש.** שלחכה בקוצים עד שהגיעה לגדיש או לקמה המחוברת לקרקע: **או השדה.** שלחכה את נירו וצריך לניר אותה פעם שניה: **שלם ישלם המבער.** אף על פי שהדליק בתוך שלו והיא יצאה מעצמה על ידי קוצים שמצאה, חייב לשלם, לפי שלא שמר את גחלתו שלא תצא ותזיק:

ו| **וגנב מבית האיש.** לפי דבריו: **אם ימצא הגנב.** ישלם הגנב שנים לבעלים:

ז| **אם לא ימצא הגנב.** ובא השומר הזה שהוא בעל הבית: **ונקרב.** אל הדיינין לדון עם זה ולשבע לו שלא שלח ידו בשלו:

ח| **על כל דבר פשע.** שימצא שקרן בשבועתו, שיעידו עדים שהוא עצמו גנבו, וירשיעוהו אלהים על פי העדים: **ישלם שנים לרעהו.** למדך הכתוב שהטוען בפקדון לומר נגנב הימנו, ונמצא שהוא עצמו גנבו, משלם תשלומי כפל. ואימתי? בזמן שנשבע ואחר כך באו עדים, שכך דרשו רבותינו: "ונקרב בעל הבית אל האלהים", קריבה זו שבועה היא. אתה אומר לשבועה או אינו אלא לדין, שכיון שבא לדין וכפר לומר נגנבה, מיד יתחייב כפל אם באו עדים שהוא בידו? נאמר כאן שליחות יד ונאמר למטה שליחות יד: "שבעת ה' תהיה בין שניהם אם לא שלח ידו" (להלן פסוק י), מה להלן שבועה אף כאן שבועה: **אשר יאמר כי הוא זה.** לפי פשוטו, אשר יאמר העד: "כי הוא זה" שנשבעת עליו הרי הוא אצלך, עד הדיינין "יבא דבר שניהם" ויחקרו את העדות, ואם כשרים הם וירשיעוהו לשומר זה – "ישלם שנים", ואם ירשיעו את העדים שנמצאו זוממין, ישלמו הם שנים לשומר. ורבותינו זכרונם לברכה דרשו: "כי הוא זה" ללמד שאין מחייבין אותו שבועה אלא אם כן הודה במקצת, לומר: כך וכך אני חייב לך והמותר נגנב ממני:

ט-י| **כי יתן איש אל רעהו חמור או שור.** פרשה ראשונה נאמרה בשומר חנם, לפיכך פטר בו את הגנבה, כמו שכתוב: "וגנב מבית האיש... אם לא ימצא הגנב ונקרב בעל הבית" (לעיל פסוקים ו-ז) לשבועה, למדת שפוטר

10 **the oath of the Lord shall be between the two of them.** Since the bailee claims that the item was lost in a manner that does not render him liable, he must take an oath. The content of his oath is **that he has not extended his hand to the property of his neighbor** in order to use it without permission. **And its owner shall accept it,** the oath.[44] Alternatively, he shall accept, or receive, from the bailee the carcass of the animal, or the pieces of the broken item.[45] **And he,** the bailee who took the oath, **shall not pay.**

11 **But if it is stolen from him,** from the bailee, who was charged with guarding it, **he shall pay to its owner,** as he was obligated to watch over it and prevent its theft.

12 **If it is mauled** by a wild animal, **he shall bring** what remains of **it,** such as a thigh or a piece of its ear[46] **as evidence** that it was mauled. In such a case, **he shall not pay for the mauled animal.**

13 **If a man borrows** an item **from his neighbor, and it,** if it is an animal, **is injured or dies,** and likewise if an object breaks, while **its owner is not with it, he,** the borrower, **shall pay.** Since the borrower received the right to use the item as a favor, his liability is greater than that of a bailee. He must compensate the owner for the loss even if the item was harmed due to an unavoidable accident.

14 **If its,** the animal's or object's, **owner is with it, he,** the borrower, **shall not pay,**[D] as the presence of the owner is a determining factor in establishing that the borrower did not use the item in an inappropriate manner.[47] **If he is a renter,**[D] and the item was not lent as a favor but in exchange for a rental fee, then **it,** the loss incurred by the owner, **goes for his rent.** Because he pays for the right to use the item, the renter is not liable for damages to the same extent as a borrower.[48]

15 The Torah introduces a new topic: **If a man seduces**[D] **a virgin who was not betrothed and lies with her, he shall pay the bride price for her to be a wife for him.** The man's punishment for seducing the woman is that he is required to marry her.[49] However, she or her father may object to the marriage.

16 **If her father shall refuse to give her to him,**[D] then the seducer shall not marry her; however, **he shall weigh out silver,** pay money,[50] **according to the bride price of virgins,** the amount one would commonly pay when marrying a virgin.

17 **You shall not keep a witch alive.** Rather, you shall kill her. Witchcraft is considered a very severe transgression due to its association with idolatry, which is a fundamental prohibition of the Torah.[51]

18 **Anyone who lies with an animal shall be put to death,** whether man or woman, and whether the person is active or passive.[52]

19 **One who sacrifices to gods shall be destroyed, except to the Lord alone.** It is permitted to bring offerings only to God; one who sacrifices to anything else, whether an idol of wood or stone or an intangible power such as an angel,[53] is liable to receive the death penalty.[54]

DISCUSSION

entirely beyond his control. It should be noted that in any case where a bailee is exempt from payment, he must take an oath in court confirming his version of events (based on *Mekhilta, Masekhta deNezikin* 15–16; *Bava Metzia* 93a–95a; Rashi; see also *Bekhor Shor; Meshekh Ḥokhma*).

22:14| **If its owner is with it, he shall not pay:** The Sages maintain that it does not matter whether the owner was physically with the borrower at the time when his animal or object was damaged. Rather, if the owner was working for the borrower when he lent him his item, whether he was hired by the borrower or was working for him as a favor, the borrower is exempt from liability for the item he borrowed (see *Bava Metzia* 94b–97a; Rashi).

If he is a renter: In the case of a borrowed item, the owner does not gain anything from lending it; the borrower receives all the benefit from the arrangement, which is why his level of liability is so high. In the case of a rental, the owner benefits from the rental fee, and therefore the renter has a lower level of liability than a borrower. Some Sages equate the renter's liability to that of an unpaid bailee. Others argued that as the renter also benefits from the rental, his liability should be like that of the paid bailee. This second opinion is accepted in practice, and therefore a renter is liable if the object was lost or stolen, but is exempt if it was ruined due to an unavoidable accident (*Bava Metzia* 80b; Rashi).

The following table outlines the laws of the four types of guardians according to the tradition of the Sages:

	Negligence	Theft (loss)	Unavoidable accident
Unpaid bailee	Liable	Exempt	Exempt
Paid bailee	Liable	Liable	Exempt
Borrower	Liable	Liable	Liable
Renter	Liable	Ruling disputed	Exempt

י נִשְׁבָּה אֵין רֹאֶה: שְׁבֻעַת יְהוָה תִּהְיֶה בֵּין שְׁנֵיהֶם אִם־לֹא שָׁלַח יָדוֹ בִּמְלֶאכֶת
יא יב רֵעֵהוּ וְלָקַח בְּעָלָיו וְלֹא יְשַׁלֵּם: וְאִם־גָּנֹב יִגָּנֵב מֵעִמּוֹ יְשַׁלֵּם לִבְעָלָיו: אִם־טָרֹף
יִטָּרֵף יְבִאֵהוּ עֵד הַטְּרֵפָה לֹא יְשַׁלֵּם:
יג יד וְכִי־יִשְׁאַל אִישׁ מֵעִם רֵעֵהוּ וְנִשְׁבַּר אוֹ־מֵת בְּעָלָיו אֵין־עִמּוֹ שַׁלֵּם יְשַׁלֵּם: אִם־
טו בְּעָלָיו עִמּוֹ לֹא יְשַׁלֵּם אִם־שָׂכִיר הוּא בָּא בִּשְׂכָרוֹ: וְכִי־יְפַתֶּה אִישׁ
טז בְּתוּלָה אֲשֶׁר לֹא־אֹרָשָׂה וְשָׁכַב עִמָּהּ מָהֹר יִמְהָרֶנָּה לּוֹ לְאִשָּׁה: אִם־מָאֵן יְמָאֵן
יז אָבִיהָ לְתִתָּהּ לוֹ כֶּסֶף יִשְׁקֹל כְּמֹהַר הַבְּתוּלֹת: מְכַשֵּׁפָה לֹא תְחַיֶּה:
יח יט כָּל־שֹׁכֵב עִם־בְּהֵמָה מוֹת יוּמָת: זֹבֵחַ לָאֱלֹהִים יָחֳרָם בִּלְתִּי לַיהוָה

רש״י

עַצְמוֹ בִּשְׁבוּעָה זוֹ; וּפָרָשָׁה זוֹ אֲמוּרָה בְּשׁוֹמֵר שָׂכָר, לְפִיכָךְ אֵינוֹ פָּטוּר אִם נִגְנְבָה, כְּמוֹ שֶׁכָּתוּב: "אִם גָּנֹב יִגָּנֵב מֵעִמּוֹ יְשַׁלֵּם" (להלן פסוק יא). אֲבָל עַל הָאֹנֶס, כְּמוֹ "מֵת" מֵעַצְמוֹ "אוֹ נִשְׁבַּר אוֹ נִשְׁבָּה" בְּחָזְקָה עַל יְדֵי לִסְטִים, וְ"אֵין רֹאֶה" שֶׁיָּעִיד בַּדָּבָר – "שְׁבֻעַת ה' תִּהְיֶה", יִשָּׁבַע שֶׁכֵּן הוּא כִּדְבָרָיו, וְהוּא לֹא שָׁלַח בָּהּ יָד לְהִשְׁתַּמֵּשׁ בָּהּ לְעַצְמוֹ, שֶׁאִם שָׁלַח בָּהּ יָד וְאַחַר כָּךְ נֶאֶנְסָה חַיָּב בְּאָנְסֶיהָ: וְלָקַח בְּעָלָיו. הַשְּׁבוּעָה: וְלֹא יְשַׁלֵּם. לוֹ הַשּׁוֹמֵר כְּלוּם:

יב | אִם טָרֹף יִטָּרֵף. עַל יְדֵי חַיָּה רָעָה: יְבִאֵהוּ עֵד. יָבִיא עֵדִים שֶׁנִּטְרְפָה בְּאֹנֶס וּפָטוּר: הַטְּרֵפָה לֹא יְשַׁלֵּם. אֵינוֹ אוֹמֵר 'טְרֵפָה לֹא יְשַׁלֵּם' אֶלָּא "הַטְּרֵפָה", יֵשׁ טְרֵפָה שֶׁהוּא מְשַׁלֵּם וְיֵשׁ טְרֵפָה שֶׁאֵינוֹ מְשַׁלֵּם: טְרֵפַת חָתוּל וְשׁוּעָל וּנְמִיָּה מְשַׁלֵּם; טְרֵפַת זְאֵב אֲרִי וְדֹב וְנָחָשׁ אֵינוֹ מְשַׁלֵּם. וּמִי לִחְשְׁךָ לָדוּן כֵּן? שֶׁהֲרֵי כָּתוּב: "וּמֵת אוֹ נִשְׁבַּר אוֹ נִשְׁבָּה", מַה מִּיתָה שֶׁאֵין יָכוֹל לְהַצִּיל, אַף שֶׁבֶר וְשִׁבְיָה שֶׁאֵין יָכוֹל לְהַצִּיל:

יג | וְכִי יִשְׁאַל. בָּא לְלַמֵּד עַל הַשּׁוֹאֵל שֶׁחַיָּב בָּאֳנָסִין: בְּעָלָיו אֵין עִמּוֹ. אִם בְּעָלָיו שֶׁל שׁוֹר אֵינוֹ עִם הַשּׁוֹאֵל בִּמְלַאכְתּוֹ:

יד | אִם בְּעָלָיו עִמּוֹ. בֵּין שֶׁהוּא בְּאוֹתָהּ מְלָאכָה בֵּין שֶׁהוּא בִּמְלָאכָה אַחֶרֶת. הָיָה עִמּוֹ בִּשְׁעַת שְׁאֵלָה אֵינוֹ צָרִיךְ לִהְיוֹת עִמּוֹ בִּשְׁעַת שְׁבִירָה וּמִיתָה: אִם שָׂכִיר הוּא. אִם הַשּׁוֹר אֵינוֹ שָׁאוּל אֶלָּא שָׂכוּר, "בָּא בִּשְׂכָרוֹ" לְיַד הַשּׂוֹכֵר הַזֶּה וְלֹא בִּשְׁאֵלָה, וְאֵין כָּל הֲנָאָה שֶׁלּוֹ שֶׁהֲרֵי עַל יְדֵי שְׂכָרוֹ נִשְׁתַּמֵּשׁ, וְאֵין לוֹ מִשְׁפַּט שׁוֹאֵל לְהִתְחַיֵּב בָּאֳנָסִין. וְלֹא פֵּרַשׁ מַה דִּינוֹ אִם כְּשׁוֹמֵר חִנָּם אוֹ כְּשׁוֹמֵר שָׂכָר, לְפִיכָךְ נֶחְלְקוּ בוֹ חַכְמֵי יִשְׂרָאֵל: שׂוֹכֵר כֵּיצַד מְשַׁלֵּם? רַבִּי מֵאִיר אוֹמֵר: כְּשׁוֹמֵר חִנָּם, רַבִּי יְהוּדָה אוֹמֵר: כְּשׁוֹמֵר שָׂכָר:

טו | וְכִי יְפַתֶּה. מְדַבֵּר עַל לִבָּהּ עַד שֶׁשּׁוֹמַעַת לוֹ, וְכֵן תַּרְגּוּמוֹ: "וַאֲרֵי יְשַׁדֵּל". שִׁדּוּל בִּלְשׁוֹן אֲרַמִּי כְּפִתּוּי בִּלְשׁוֹן עִבְרִי: מָהֹר יִמְהָרֶנָּה. יִפְסֹק לָהּ מֹהַר כְּמִשְׁפַּט אִישׁ לְאִשְׁתּוֹ, שֶׁכּוֹתֵב לָהּ כְּתֻבָּה וְיִשָּׂאֶנָּה:

טז | כְּמֹהַר הַבְּתוּלֹת. שֶׁהוּא קָצוּב חֲמִשִּׁים כֶּסֶף אֵצֶל הַתּוֹפֵס אֶת הַבְּתוּלָה וְשׁוֹכֵב עִמָּהּ בְּאֹנֶס, שֶׁנֶּאֱמַר: "וְנָתַן הָאִישׁ הַשֹּׁכֵב עִמָּהּ לַאֲבִי הַנַּעֲרָ חֲמִשִּׁים כָּסֶף" (דברים כב, כט):

יז | מְכַשֵּׁפָה לֹא תְחַיֶּה. אֶלָּא תּוּמַת בְּבֵית דִּין. וְאֶחָד זְכָרִים וְאֶחָד נְקֵבוֹת, אֶלָּא שֶׁדִּבֵּר הַכָּתוּב בַּהוֹוֶה, שֶׁהַנָּשִׁים מְצוּיוֹת בִּכְשָׁפִים:

יח | כָּל שֹׁכֵב עִם בְּהֵמָה מוֹת יוּמָת. בִּסְקִילָה, רוֹבֵעַ כְּנִרְבַּעַת, שֶׁכָּתוּב בָּהֶם: "דְּמֵיהֶם בָּם" (ויקרא כ, טז):

יט | לָאֱלֹהִים. לַעֲבוֹדָה זָרָה. אִלּוּ הָיָה נָקוּד 'לֵאלֹהִים', הָיָה צָרִיךְ לְפָרֵשׁ וְלִכְתֹּב 'אֲחֵרִים', עַכְשָׁיו שֶׁאָמַר: "לָאֱלֹהִים" אֵין צָרִיךְ לְפָרֵשׁ 'אֲחֵרִים'; שֶׁכָּל לָמֶ"ד וּבֵי"ת הַמְשַׁמֶּשֶׁת בְּרֹאשׁ הַתֵּבָה, אִם נְקוּדָה בַּחֲטַף, כְּגוֹן: לְמֶלֶךְ, לְמִדְבָּר, לְעִיר, צָרִיךְ לְפָרֵשׁ לְאֵיזֶה מֶלֶךְ, לְאֵיזֶה מִדְבָּר, לְאֵיזֶה עִיר. וְכֵן: לִמְלָכִים, לִרְגָלִים צָרִיךְ לְפָרֵשׁ לְאֵיזֶה, וְאִם אֵינוֹ מְפָרֵשׁ, כָּל מְלָכִים בְּמַשְׁמָע. וְכֵן 'לֵאלֹהִים' כָּל אֱלֹהִים בְּמַשְׁמָע, אֲפִלּוּ קֹדֶשׁ. אֲבָל כְּשֶׁהִיא נְקוּדָה פַּתָּח, כְּמוֹ: לַמֶּלֶךְ, לַמִּדְבָּר, לָעִיר, נוֹדַע בְּאֵיזֶה מֶלֶךְ מְדַבֵּר, וְכֵן 'לָעִיר' נוֹדַע בְּאֵיזֶה עִיר מְדַבֵּר, וְכֵן "לָאֱלֹהִים", לְאוֹתָן שֶׁהֻזְהַרְתֶּם עֲלֵיהֶם בְּמָקוֹם אַחֵר. כַּיּוֹצֵא בוֹ: "אֵין כָּמוֹךָ בָאֱלֹהִים" (תהלים פו, ח), לְפִי שֶׁלֹּא פֵּרַשׁ הֻצְרַךְ לִנָּקֵד פַּתָּח: יָחֳרָם. יוּמַת. וְלָמָּה נֶאֱמַר "יָחֳרָם"? וַהֲלֹא כְּבָר נֶאֶמְרָה בוֹ מִיתָה בְּמָקוֹם אַחֵר: "וְהוֹצֵאתָ אֶת הָאִישׁ הַהוּא אוֹ אֶת הָאִשָּׁה הַהִיא" וְגוֹ' (דברים יז, ה), אֶלָּא לְפִי שֶׁלֹּא פֵּרַשׁ עַל אֵיזוֹ עֲבוֹדָה חַיָּב מִיתָה, שֶׁלֹּא תֹּאמַר כָּל עֲבוֹדוֹת בְּמִיתָה, בָּא וּפֵרַשׁ לְךָ כָּאן: "זֹבֵחַ לָאֱלֹהִים", מַה זְּבִיחָה עֲבוֹדָה הַנַּעֲשֵׂית בִּפְנִים לַשָּׁמַיִם, אַף אֲנִי מְרַבֶּה הַמְקַטֵּר וְהַמְנַסֵּךְ שֶׁהֵן עֲבוֹדָה בִּפְנִים, וְחַיָּבִים עֲלֵיהֶם לְכָל עֲבוֹדָה

DISCUSSION

22:15 | **If a man seduces:** The Sages explain that this is referring to the seduction of a girl younger than twelve and a half, which is why the marriage requires her father's consent. In the case of an adult woman, the man is no more at fault than the woman herself. The seducer's obligation to marry his victim is meant to deter people from taking advantage of young girls and subsequently abandoning them (see *Ketubot* 38a; Ramban).

22:16 | **If her father shall refuse to give her to him:** The Sages add that the girl herself has the right to refuse the marriage (see *Ketubot* 39b).

20 **You shall not mistreat a stranger,**[D] **and you shall not oppress him.** It is prohibited to cheat or mislead a stranger, or to cause him any sort of harm.[55] **For you were strangers in the land of Egypt,** and you know from personal experience how difficult it is to be strangers in a foreign land. Consequently, it is incumbent upon you to be careful not to persecute the foreigners living among you.

21 Similarly, **you shall not afflict any widow or orphan,** as they are also more vulnerable than other members of society.

22 **If you afflict him, then when he cries out to Me, I will hear his cry.** Since they do not have any other protection, I am the "Father of the orphans and Judge of the widows."[56]

23 When I hear their cries, **My wrath will be enflamed, and I will kill you with the sword; and your wives will be widows, and your children orphans,** measure for measure, due to your mistreatment of widows and orphans.

24 **If you shall lend silver to** any of **My people,** especially **to the poor who is with you, you shall not be as a creditor to him.** This law applies to every member of the nation but the transgression is particularly severe when one mistreats the poor. One may not act in the manner of a creditor who applies pressure upon the borrower to repay his loan.[57] Additionally, **you shall not impose upon him interest.**[D]

25 **If you take your neighbor's garment as collateral, you shall return it to him by the setting of the sun.**

26 **For that alone is his covering; it is his garment for his skin; in what shall he lie?** If the borrower has to offer an essential object as collateral, clearly he does not have many items to give. In such a case, the indigent borrower will inevitably suffer. During the day he can make do with the garments he is wearing, but if at night he requires his other garment for a blanket and he does not have it, he will be unable to cover himself. **It shall be** that **when he cries out to Me** in distress,[58] **I will hear, as I am gracious.** Although the lender has the right to take collateral, the borrower's situation cries out for mercy. Consequently, the lender must return the collateral at night.

27 **You shall not curse judges, and a prince among your people you shall not imprecate.**[D] It is prohibited to curse anyone.[59] Perhaps the Torah imposes an additional prohibition against cursing judges because it is tempting for one who loses a court case to curse the judge who ruled against him.[60] Similarly, rulers are likely to become the targets of those who feel they have been mistreated by the establishment.

Fourth aliya

28 **The surfeit of your crops and the outpouring of your juices you shall not delay.** This is referring to agricultural produce, both food and beverage, which must be given to God in the form of *teruma* and tithes.[61] In addition to the basic requirement to separate tithes, this verse teaches that one must do so at the proper time. **The firstborn of your sons you shall give to Me.** As explained earlier, one does not actually give his firstborn son, but redeems him for money.[62]

29 **So you shall do to your cattle and to your flock,** as the sanctity of the firstborn is not limited to people.[63] However, in the case of an animal, **seven days it shall be with its mother; on the eighth day, you shall give it to Me** as an offering. One must leave a young calf or lamb with its mother for at least one week.

30 **You shall be holy people to Me;** and one of the ramifications of this holy state is that **you shall not eat meat of a mauled animal in the field**[D] that has been injured by a predator. However, you are permitted to derive other forms of benefit

DISCUSSION

22:20 | **You shall not mistreat a stranger:** The Torah repeatedly warns against the persecution of foreigners. Of course, it is prohibited to wrong or oppress anyone, but extra care is required when dealing with strangers, as they are more vulnerable than those living in their native land.

22:24 | **You shall not impose upon him interest:** The prohibition against charging interest is limited to loans between Jews. The Torah does not state that charging interest is inherently immoral; rather, it is improper for Jews to charge interest from each other just as it would be inappropriate for parents to charge interest from their children or vice versa. With regard to people outside the family unit, charging interest is a fair practice. However, within the nation, which is considered like one family, it is prohibited.

22:27 | **And a prince among your people you shall not imprecate:** The prohibition against cursing a ruler is stated in an absolute manner. Nevertheless, the Sages maintain that it is limited to rulers who act properly. They explain that the phrase "a prince among your people" is referring specifically to a ruler who acts in the manner of your people (see *Bava Batra* 4a). There is no requirement to honor a ruler who does not act in accordance with Jewish laws and values.

According to the Rambam (*Sefer Shofetim, Hilkhot Sanhedrin* 26:1; see also *Sefer HaMitzvot*, negative commandment 316), the ruler mentioned in this verse is a king or the head of the Sanhedrin. Some maintain that it includes other leaders as well (see *Minḥat Ḥinnukh* 71).

22:30 | **You shall not eat meat of a mauled animal in the field:** The Sages explain that this is a typical case of an animal that was mortally wounded. As in the case of bailees (see verse 9), the verse mentions a familiar situation, but the same law applies even when the details of the case are different (Rashi). Irrespective of how it came to be that way, the meat of an animal with a mortal defect is forbidden. All the laws of a *tereifa*, an animal with a condition that will cause it to die within twelve months, are based on this verse. Even if the animal was ritually slaughtered, it is forbidden to consume its meat (see *Ḥullin* 42a).

כ כא לְבַדּוֹ: וְגֵר לֹא־תוֹנֶה וְלֹא תִלְחָצֶנּוּ כִּי־גֵרִים הֱיִיתֶם בְּאֶרֶץ מִצְרָיִם: כָּל־אַלְמָנָה
כב וְיָתוֹם לֹא תְעַנּוּן: אִם־עַנֵּה תְעַנֶּה אֹתוֹ כִּי אִם־צָעֹק יִצְעַק אֵלַי שָׁמֹעַ אֶשְׁמַע
כג צַעֲקָתוֹ: וְחָרָה אַפִּי וְהָרַגְתִּי אֶתְכֶם בֶּחָרֶב וְהָיוּ נְשֵׁיכֶם אַלְמָנוֹת וּבְנֵיכֶם יְתֹמִים:
כד אִם־כֶּסֶף ׀ תַּלְוֶה אֶת־עַמִּי אֶת־הֶעָנִי עִמָּךְ לֹא־תִהְיֶה לוֹ כְּנֹשֶׁה לֹא־תְשִׂימוּן עָלָיו
כה כו נֶשֶׁךְ: אִם־חָבֹל תַּחְבֹּל שַׂלְמַת רֵעֶךָ עַד־בֹּא הַשֶּׁמֶשׁ תְּשִׁיבֶנּוּ לוֹ: כִּי הִוא כְסוּתֹה
לְבַדָּהּ הִוא שִׂמְלָתוֹ לְעֹרוֹ בַּמֶּה יִשְׁכָּב וְהָיָה כִּי־יִצְעַק אֵלַי וְשָׁמַעְתִּי כִּי־חַנּוּן
כז כח אָנִי: אֱלֹהִים לֹא תְקַלֵּל וְנָשִׂיא בְעַמְּךָ לֹא תָאֹר: מְלֵאָתְךָ וְדִמְעֲךָ רביעי
כט לֹא תְאַחֵר בְּכוֹר בָּנֶיךָ תִּתֶּן־לִי: כֵּן־תַּעֲשֶׂה לְשֹׁרְךָ לְצֹאנֶךָ שִׁבְעַת יָמִים יִהְיֶה
ל עִם־אִמּוֹ בַּיּוֹם הַשְּׁמִינִי תִּתְּנוֹ־לִי: וְאַנְשֵׁי־קֹדֶשׁ תִּהְיוּן לִי וּבָשָׂר בַּשָּׂדֶה טְרֵפָה

רש״י

זָרָה, בֵּין שֶׁדַּרְכָּהּ לְעָבְדָהּ כָּכָה בֵּין שֶׁאֵין דַּרְכָּהּ לְעָבְדָהּ כָּכָה. אֲבָל שְׁאָר עֲבוֹדוֹת, כְּגוֹן: הַמְכַבֵּד וְהַמְרַבֵּץ וְהַמְגַפֵּף וְהַמְנַשֵּׁק, אֵינָן בְּמִיתָה:

כ| **וגר לא תונה.** אוֹנָאַת דְּבָרִים, קונטרליי״ר בְּלַעַז, כְּמוֹ: "וְהַאֲכַלְתִּי אֶת מוֹנַיִךְ אֶת בְּשָׂרָם" (ישעיה מט, כו): **ולא תלחצנו.** בִּגְזֵלַת מָמוֹן: **כי גרים הייתם.** אִם הוֹנֵיתוֹ אַף הוּא יָכוֹל לְהוֹנוֹתְךָ וְלוֹמַר לְךָ: אַף אַתָּה מִגֵּרִים בָּאתָ. מוּם שֶׁבְּךָ אַל תֹּאמַר לַחֲבֵרְךָ. כָּל לְשׁוֹן 'גֵּר' אָדָם שֶׁלֹּא נוֹלַד בְּאוֹתָהּ מְדִינָה, אֶלָּא בָּא מִמְּדִינָה אַחֶרֶת לָגוּר שָׁם:

כא| **כל אלמנה ויתום לא תענון.** הוּא הַדִּין לְכָל אָדָם, אֶלָּא שֶׁדִּבֵּר הַכָּתוּב בַּהֹוֶה, לְפִי שֶׁהֵם תְּשׁוּשֵׁי כֹּחַ וְדָבָר מָצוּי לְעַנּוֹתָם:

כב| **אם ענה תענה אתו.** הֲרֵי זֶה מִקְרָא קָצָר. גִּזֵּם וְלֹא פֵּרֵשׁ עָנְשׁוֹ, כְּמוֹ: "לָכֵן כָּל הֹרֵג קַיִן" (בראשית ד, טו), וְלֹא פֵּרֵשׁ עָנְשׁוֹ. אַף כָּאן: "אִם עַנֵּה תְעַנֶּה אֹתוֹ" לְשׁוֹן גִּזּוּם, כְּלוֹמַר, סוֹפְךָ לִטֹּל אֶת שֶׁלְּךָ, לָמָּה? "כִּי אִם צָעֹק יִצְעַק אֵלַי" וְגוֹ':

כג| **והיו נשיכם אלמנות.** מִמַּשְׁמָע שֶׁנֶּאֱמַר: "וְהָרַגְתִּי אֶתְכֶם" אֵינִי יוֹדֵעַ שֶׁ"נְּשֵׁיכֶם אַלְמָנוֹת וּבְנֵיכֶם יְתֹמִים"? אֶלָּא הֲרֵי זוֹ קְלָלָה אַחֶרֶת, שֶׁיִּהְיוּ הַנָּשִׁים צְרוּרוֹת כְּאַלְמְנוּת חַיּוּת, שֶׁלֹּא יִהְיוּ עֵדִים לְמִיתַת בַּעְלֵיהֶן וְתִהְיֶינָה אֲסוּרוֹת לְהִנָּשֵׂא, וְהַבָּנִים יִהְיוּ יְתוֹמִים, שֶׁלֹּא יַנִּיחוּם בֵּית דִּין לֵירֵד לְנִכְסֵי אֲבִיהֶם, לְפִי שֶׁאֵין יוֹדְעִים אִם מֵתוּ אִם נִשְׁבּוּ:

כד| **אם כסף תלוה את עמי.** רַבִּי יִשְׁמָעֵאל אוֹמֵר: כָּל 'אִם' וְ'אִם' שֶׁבַּתּוֹרָה רְשׁוּת חוּץ מִשְּׁלֹשָׁה, וְזֶה אֶחָד מֵהֶן: **את עמי.** עַמִּי וְגוֹי, עַמִּי קוֹדֵם. עָנִי וְעָשִׁיר, עָנִי קוֹדֵם. עֲנִיֵּי עִירְךָ וַעֲנִיֵּי עִיר אַחֶרֶת, עֲנִיֵּי עִירְךָ קוֹדְמִין. וְזֶה מַשְׁמָעוֹ: "אִם כֶּסֶף תַּלְוֶה, אֶת עַמִּי" תַּלְוֵהוּ, וְלֹא לַגּוֹי. וּלְאֵיזֶה מֵעַמִּי? "אֶת הֶעָנִי". וּלְאֵיזֶה עָנִי? לְאוֹתוֹ שֶׁ"עִמָּךְ". דָּבָר אַחֵר "אֶת עַמִּי", שֶׁלֹּא תִנְהַג בּוֹ מִנְהַג בִּזָּיוֹן בְּהַלְוָאָה, שֶׁהוּא עַמִּי: **את העני עמך.** הֱוֵי מִסְתַּכֵּל בְּעַצְמְךָ כְּאִלּוּ אַתָּה עָנִי: **לא תהיה לו כנשה.** לֹא תִתְבָּעֶנּוּ בְּחָזְקָה. אִם אַתָּה יוֹדֵעַ שֶׁאֵין לוֹ, אַל תְּהִי דוֹמֶה עָלָיו כְּאִלּוּ הִלְוִיתוֹ אֶלָּא כְּאִלּוּ לֹא הִלְוִיתוֹ, כְּלוֹמַר לֹא תַכְלִימֵהוּ: **נשך.** רִבִּית, שֶׁהוּא כִּנְשִׁיכַת נָחָשׁ, שֶׁנּוֹשֵׁךְ חַבּוּרָה קְטַנָּה בְּרַגְלוֹ וְאֵינוֹ מַרְגִּישׁ, וּפִתְאוֹם הוּא מַבְצִבֵּץ וְנוֹפֵחַ עַד קָדְקֳדוֹ, כָּךְ רִבִּית אֵינוֹ מַרְגִּישׁ וְאֵינוֹ נִכָּר, עַד שֶׁהָרִבִּית עוֹלָה וּמְחַסְּרוֹ מָמוֹן הַרְבֵּה:

כה| **אם חבל תחבל.** כָּל לְשׁוֹן חֲבָלָה אֵינוֹ מַשְׁכּוֹן בִּשְׁעַת הַלְוָאָה, אֶלָּא שֶׁמְּמַשְׁכְּנִין אֶת הַלֹּוֶה כְּשֶׁמַּגִּיעַ הַזְּמַן וְאֵינוֹ פּוֹרֵעַ. "חָבֹל תַּחְבֹּל", כָּפַל לְךָ בַּחֲבָלָה עַד כַּמָּה פְּעָמִים, אָמַר הַקָּדוֹשׁ בָּרוּךְ הוּא, כַּמָּה אַתָּה חַיָּב לִי, וַהֲרֵי נַפְשְׁךָ עוֹלָה אֶצְלִי בְּכָל לַיְלָה וְלַיְלָה נוֹתֶנֶת דִּין וְחֶשְׁבּוֹן וּמִתְחַיֶּבֶת לְפָנַי וַאֲנִי מַחֲזִירָהּ לְךָ, אַף אַתָּה טֹל וְהָשֵׁב וְהָשֵׁב: **עד בא השמש תשיבנו לו.** כָּל הַיּוֹם תְּשִׁיבֶנּוּ לוֹ עַד בֹּא הַשֶּׁמֶשׁ, וּכְבוֹא הַשֶּׁמֶשׁ תַּחֲזֹר וְתִטְּלֶנּוּ עַד שֶׁיָּבֹא בֹּקֶר שֶׁל מָחָר. וּבִכְסוּת יוֹם הַכָּתוּב מְדַבֵּר, שֶׁאֵין צָרִיךְ לָהּ בַּלַּיְלָה:

כו| **כי הוא כסותה.** זוֹ טַלִּית: **שמלתו.** זוֹ חָלוּק: **במה ישכב.** לְרַבּוֹת אֶת הַמַּצָּע:

כז| **אלהים לא תקלל.** הֲרֵי זוֹ אַזְהָרָה לְבִרְכַּת הַשֵּׁם, וְאַזְהָרָה לְקִלְלַת דַּיָּן:

כח| **מלאתך.** חוֹבָה הַמֻּטֶּלֶת עָלֶיךָ כְּשֶׁתִּתְמַלֵּא תְּבוּאָתְךָ לְהִתְבַּשֵּׁל, וְהֵם בִּכּוּרִים: **ודמעך.** הִיא תְּרוּמָה, וְאֵינִי יוֹדֵעַ מַהוּ לְשׁוֹן דֶּמַע: **לא תאחר.** לֹא תְשַׁנֶּה סֵדֶר הַפְרָשָׁתָן לְאַחֵר אֶת הַמֻּקְדָּם וּלְהַקְדִּים אֶת הַמְאֻחָר, שֶׁלֹּא יַקְדִּים תְּרוּמָה לְבִכּוּרִים וּמַעֲשֵׂר לִתְרוּמָה: **בכור בניך תתן לי.** לִפְדּוֹתוֹ חָמֵשׁ סְלָעִים מִן הַכֹּהֵן. וַהֲלֹא כְּבָר צִוָּה עָלָיו בְּמָקוֹם אַחֵר (במדבר יח, טז)? אֶלָּא כְּדֵי לִסְמֹךְ לוֹ: "כֵּן תַּעֲשֶׂה לְשֹׁרְךָ", מַה בְּכוֹר אָדָם לְאַחַר שְׁלֹשִׁים יוֹם פּוֹדֵהוּ, שֶׁנֶּאֱמַר: "וּפְדוּיָו מִבֶּן חֹדֶשׁ תִּפְדֶּה" (שם), אַף בְּכוֹר בְּהֵמָה גַּסָּה מְטַפֵּל בּוֹ שְׁלֹשִׁים יוֹם וְאַחַר כָּךְ נוֹתְנוֹ לַכֹּהֵן:

כט| **שבעת ימים יהיה עם אמו.** זוֹ אַזְהָרָה לַכֹּהֵן, שֶׁאִם בָּא לְמַהֵר הַקְרָבָתוֹ לֹא יְמַהֵר קֹדֶם שְׁמוֹנָה, לְפִי שֶׁהוּא מְחֻסַּר זְמָן: **ביום השמיני תתנו לי.** יָכוֹל יְהֵא חוֹבָה לְבוֹ בַּיּוֹם? נֶאֱמַר כָּאן: "שְׁמִינִי" וְנֶאֱמַר לְהַלָּן: "וּמִיּוֹם הַשְּׁמִינִי וָהָלְאָה יֵרָצֶה" (ויקרא כב, כז), מַה שְּׁמִינִי הָאָמוּר לְהַלָּן לְהַכְשִׁיר מִשְּׁמִינִי וּלְהַלָּן, אַף שְׁמִינִי הָאָמוּר כָּאן לְהַכְשִׁיר מִשְּׁמִינִי וּלְהַלָּן. וְכֵן מַשְׁמָעוֹ: וּבַיּוֹם הַשְּׁמִינִי אַתָּה רַשַּׁאי לִתְּנוֹ לִי:

ל| **ואנשי קדש תהיון לי.** אִם אַתֶּם קְדוֹשִׁים וּפְרוּשִׁים מִשִּׁקּוּצֵי נְבֵלוֹת וּטְרֵפוֹת הֲרֵי אַתֶּם שֶׁלִּי, וְאִם לָאו אֵינְכֶם שֶׁלִּי: **ובשר בשדה טרפה.** אַף בַּבַּיִת כֵּן, אֶלָּא שֶׁדִּבֶּר הַכָּתוּב בַּהֹוֶה, מָקוֹם שֶׁדֶּרֶךְ בְּהֵמוֹת לִטָּרֵף. וְכֵן: "כִּי בַשָּׂדֶה מְצָאָהּ" (דברים כב, כז). וְכֵן: "אֲשֶׁר לֹא יִהְיֶה טָהוֹר מִקְרֵה לָיְלָה" (שם כג, יא), הוּא הַדִּין לְמִקְרֵה יוֹם, אֶלָּא שֶׁדִּבֶּר הַכָּתוּב בַּהֹוֶה. "וּבָשָׂר תָּלוּשׁ מִן חֵיוָא חַיָּא", בָּשָׂר שֶׁנִּתְלַשׁ עַל יְדֵי טְרֵפַת זְאֵב אוֹ אֲרִי מִן חַיָּה כְּשֵׁרָה אוֹ

from the carcass, and therefore **you shall cast it to the dog** for it to eat.

23 1 A collection of laws involving the court and the execution of justice is now presented. The first command is addressed to judges: **You shall not accept a false report,** testimony that is false or which is stated for no practical purpose other than to tarnish someone's reputation.[64] **Do not place your hand with the wicked to be a corrupt witness.**[D] Do not collaborate with a wicked person to submit testimony even if you know that the testimony is true. Additionally, one may not join false witnesses even if their testimony would be admitted regardless of your participation.[65] This is an elaboration of one of the Ten Precepts: "You shall not bear false witness against your neighbor."[66]

2 **You shall not follow the majority for evil.** Do not be influenced by the actions or opinions of the majority if you do not agree with them. This statement is always applicable, but is particularly important for a judge, who is obligated to reach a just verdict. It is absolutely prohibited for him to rely on the majority opinion and to ratify their ruling against his better judgment.[67] **And you shall not respond in a dispute to distort** justice, by **inclining after the majority.**[D]

3 **You shall not favor a poor man in his** legal **dispute.**[D] This law, which is addressed to a judge, refers to the tendency to have mercy for the weaker litigant. A judge must issue a just verdict, even if a pitiful individual will thereby suffer.

4 **If you encounter the ox of your enemy or his donkey** lost and **wandering, you shall return it to him.** Not only is it prohibited to harm your enemy by injuring his animal, you must take positive action to return the animal to its owner.

5 **If you see the donkey of your enemy**[D] **crouching under its burden,** because it was laden with an overly heavy load and will not stand until part of the burden is removed, **shall you refrain**[68] **from assisting him,** its owner? Not so; rather, **you shall assist with him.** You must help the owner to lighten the donkey's burden.

6 **You shall not distort the judgment of your poor in his dispute.** In the earlier prohibition against favoring the poor (verse 3), the Torah warned the judge not to follow blindly his noble instinct in order to help those who are disadvantaged. It is no less common for judges to favor wealthy, powerful litigants to the disadvantage of the poor, whose ability to protest injustice is more limited.

Fifth aliya

7 **You shall distance yourself from falsehood.**[D] From the context it appears that this instruction is also directed at judges. When they receive the impression that one of the litigants is presenting a false claim, even if their suspicion cannot be proven, they should rely on their intuition and reject that claim. **And you shall not kill the innocent and the righteous.** If a judge thinks that an innocent person is being accused of a crime based upon false testimony he should not convict him, **as I will not vindicate the wicked**[D] who kill innocent people.

DISCUSSION

23:1 | **Do not place your hand with the wicked to be a corrupt witness:** A false witness cannot absolve himself of responsibility by arguing that he is merely a small cog in a vast system and he is not the one handing down the verdict. He also cannot claim in his defense that he derived no personal gain from his testimony. The fact that he participated in a false testimony is itself considered an injustice. Although the witness did not actually steal anything from the victim, he improperly facilitated the forceful confiscation of property, and one who does so earns the harsh title of a corrupt witness.

23:2 | **And you shall not respond in a dispute to distort, inclining after the majority:** The plain meaning of the verse is that it is prohibited to reinforce the opinion of the majority when one does not think it is correct. The Sages infer from here that in cases of unresolved disagreement, where both sides present worthy arguments, the fact that one opinion is held by the majority is significant. The principle of following the majority opinion can be inferred from the very law that constrains it by prohibiting the judge from allowing himself to be influenced by irrelevant social pressures. The verse implies that when the opinion of the majority is not for evil and will not pervert justice, it should be accepted. In order to expound the verse in accordance with this conclusion, the Sages isolated the phrase "inclining after the majority" and interpreted it as a positive principle. As explained, this accords with the overall meaning of the verse, despite the fact that the words themselves bear almost the opposite meaning in this context (*Bava Metzia* 59b; *Sanhedrin* 2a; *Ḥullin* 11a; see Rashi and Ibn Ezra here). This general principle that one follows the majority applies not only to judicial decision-making but also to other areas of law.

23:3 | **You shall not favor a poor man in his dispute:** Laws prohibiting a judge from bias toward wealthy and powerful litigants appear in practically every book of laws in the world. Conversely, this prohibition against favoring the poor is unusual. It is directed at judges whose weakness stems from mercy. It warns those who wish to assist the downtrodden that they must find the right balance between the inclination to help, which is a generally positive tendency, and justice, which they must implement in their role as judges.

23:5 | **The donkey of your enemy:** Although the last two cases refer to an animal belonging to one's enemy, it is obvious that they apply equally to the animals of other people. The Torah requires one to help unburden an animal even when its owner is present. This obligation stems, first and foremost, from the general requirement to help anyone in distress, but it is also based upon the concern one must have for the suffering of animals. In addition to these two elements, the demand that one must help his enemy unload his animal is partly based on the Torah's expectation that by taking this initiative one will overcome whatever personal enmity he might have toward the other person (see *Bava Metzia* 32b).

כג א לֹא תֹאכֵלוּ לַכֶּלֶב תַּשְׁלִכוּן אֹתוֹ: לֹא תִשָּׂא שֵׁמַע שָׁוְא אַל־תָּשֶׁת
ב יָדְךָ עִם־רָשָׁע לִהְיֹת עֵד חָמָס: לֹא־תִהְיֶה אַחֲרֵי־רַבִּים לְרָעֹת וְלֹא־תַעֲנֶה עַל־
ג ד רִב לִנְטֹת אַחֲרֵי רַבִּים לְהַטֹּת: וְדָל לֹא תֶהְדַּר בְּרִיבוֹ: כִּי תִפְגַּע
ה שׁוֹר אֹיִבְךָ אוֹ חֲמֹרוֹ תֹּעֶה הָשֵׁב תְּשִׁיבֶנּוּ לוֹ: כִּי־תִרְאֶה חֲמוֹר
ו שֹׂנַאֲךָ רֹבֵץ תַּחַת מַשָּׂאוֹ וְחָדַלְתָּ מֵעֲזֹב לוֹ עָזֹב תַּעֲזֹב עִמּוֹ: לֹא חמישי
ז תַטֶּה מִשְׁפַּט אֶבְיֹנְךָ בְּרִיבוֹ: מִדְּבַר־שֶׁקֶר תִּרְחָק וְנָקִי וְצַדִּיק אַל־תַּהֲרֹג כִּי לֹא־

רש"י

בהמה כשרה בחייה: לכלב תשלכון אתו. אף הגוי ככלב. או אינו אלא כלב כמשמעו, תלמוד לומר בנבלה: "או מכר לנכרי" (שם יד, כא), קל וחומר לטרפה שמותרת בכל הנאות. אם כן מה תלמוד לומר: "לכלב"? למדך שהכלב מכבד מן הגוי שהנבלה לגוי והטרפה לכלב. וללמדך שאין הקדוש ברוך הוא מקפח שכר כל בריה, שנאמר: "ולכל בני ישראל לא יחרץ כלב לשנו" (לעיל יא, ז), אמר הקדוש ברוך הוא: תנו לו שכרו:

פרק כג

א| לא תשא שמע שוא. כתרגומו, "לא תקבל שמע דשקר", אזהרה למקבל לשון הרע ולדין שלא ישמע דברי בעל דין עד שיבוא בעל דין חברו: אל תשת ידך עם רשע. הטוען את חברו תביעת שקר, שמבטיחהו להיות לו עד חמס:

ב| לא תהיה אחרי רבים לרעת. יש במקרא זה מדרשי חכמי ישראל, אבל אין לשון המקרא מיושב בהן על אפניו. מכאן דרשו שאין מטין לחובה בהכרעת דיין אחד. וסוף המקרא דרשו: "אחרי רבים להטת", שאם יש שנים במחייבין יותר על המזכין, הטה הדין על פיהם לחובה, ובדיני נפשות הכתוב מדבר. ואמצע המקרא דרשו: "ולא תענה על רב", על רב, שאין חולקין על מפלא שבבית דין, לפיכך מתחילין בדיני נפשות מן הצד, לקטנים שבהם שואלין תחלה שיאמרו את דעתם. ולפי דברי רבותינו כך פתרון המקרא: "לא תהיה אחרי רבים לרעת", לחייב מיתה בשביל דיין אחד שירבו מחייבין על המזכין; ולא תענה על הרב לנטות מדבריו, ולפי שהוא חסר יו"ד דרשו בו כן; "אחרי רבים להטת", ויש רבים שאתה נוטה אחריהם, ואימתי? בזמן שהן שנים המכריעין במחייבין יותר מן המזכין, וממשמע שנאמר: "לא תהיה אחרי רבים לרעת" שומע אני: אבל היה עמהם לטובה, מכאן אמרו: דיני נפשות מטין על פי אחד לזכות ועל פי שנים לחובה. ואונקלוס תרגם: "לא תתמנע מלאלפא מה דבעינך על דינא", ולשון העברי לפי התרגום כך הוא נדרש: "לא תענה על רב לנטות", אם ישאלך דבר למשפט לא תענה לנטות לצד אחד ולסלק עצמך מן הריב, אלא הוי דן אותו לאמתו. ואני אומר ליישבו על אפניו כפשוטו כך פתרונו: "לא תהיה אחרי רבים לרעת" – אם ראית רשעים מטין משפט, לא תאמר: הואיל ורבים הם הנני נוטה אחריהם. "ולא תענה על רב לנטות" וגו' – ואם ישאלך הנדון על אותו המשפט, אל תענהו על הריב דבר הנוטה אחרי אותן רבים להטות את המשפט מאמתו, אלא אמור את המשפט כאשר הוא, והקולר יהא תלוי בצואר הרבים:

ג| לא תהדר. לא תחלק לו כבוד לזכותו בדין, ולומר: דל הוא, אזכנו ואכבדנו:

ה| כי תראה חמור שנאך וגו'. הרי "כי" משמש לשון 'דלמא', שהוא מארבע לשונות של שמושי 'כי'. וכה פתרונו: שמא תראה חמורו "רבץ תחת משאו, וחדלת מעזב לו", בתמיה; "עזב תעזב עמו" – עזיבה זו לשון עזרה, וכן: "עצור ועזוב" (דברים לב, לו), וכן: "ויעזבו ירושלם עד החומה" (נחמיה ג, ח), מלאוה עפר לעזר ולסייע את חוזק החומה. כיוצא בו: "כי תאמר בלבבך רבים הגוים האלה ממני" וגו' (דברים ז, יז), שמא תאמר כן, בתמיה – "לא תירא מהם" (שם פסוק יח). ומדרשו, כך דרשו רבותינו: "כי תראה וחדלת", פעמים שאתה חודל ופעמים שאתה עוזר. הא כיצד? זקן ואינה לפי כבודו – "וחדלת", או בהמת גוי ומשאו של ישראל – "וחדלת": עזב תעזב עמו. לפרק המשא. "מלמשקל ליה", מלטול משאו ממנו:

ו| אבינך. לשון אובה, שהוא מדלדל ותאב לכל טובה:

ז| ונקי וצדיק אל תהרג. מנין ליוצא מבית דין חייב, ואמר אחד: יש לי ללמד עליו זכות, שמחזירין אותו? תלמוד לומר: "ונקי אל תהרג", ואף על פי שאינו "צדיק", שלא נצטדק בבית דין, מכל מקום "נקי" הוא מדין מיתה, שהרי יש לך לזכותו. ומנין ליוצא מבית דין זכאי, ואמר אחד: יש לי ללמד עליו חובה, שאין מחזירין אותו לבית דין? תלמוד לומר: "וצדיק אל תהרג", וזה צדיק הוא שנצטדק בבית דין: כי לא אצדיק רשע. אין עליך

DISCUSSION

23:7| You shall distance yourself from falsehood: On the one hand, the context indicates that this prohibition is limited to matters of monetary law and the judicial process; it is not a general prohibition against lying. On the other hand, the opposition to falsehood is expressed in rather extreme terms; not only may one not lie, but he should actively distance himself from false matters, as though they are ritually impure.

And you shall not kill the innocent and the righteous, as I will not vindicate the wicked: The combination of innocent and righteous in this verse has been interpreted as referring to two types of defendants, the innocent but not righteous (acquitted in court) and the righteous but not innocent. The innocent but not righteous is someone who was wrongly convicted by the court. In a case where a judge considers this to be the case, he must reexamine the verdict instead of carrying out the sentence. The righteous but not innocent is an individual who was acquitted and declared righteous by the court, but the judges have become convinced that he is in fact guilty and deserving of the death penalty. This individual is not be punished by the court either. Once the court has judged the case and has issued an acquittal, the judges should rely on God to perform justice and to punish the wrongdoer if they erred in their judgment (*Sanhedrin* 33b; Rashi; *Targum Yonatan*).

8 **You shall not take a bribe,**[D] a gift or any form of benefit from one of the litigants; **as a bribe will blind the perceptive** from recognition of the truth, **and corrupt the words of the righteous.**

9 **You shall not oppress a stranger.** Do not harm him, discriminate against him, or issue demands that he cannot fulfill. As a defenseless foreigner, the Torah specifically warns against persecuting him. For **you** Israelites **know the soul of a stranger, as you were strangers in the land of Egypt.**

10 The following law will become relevant only when the children of Israel enter the land of Israel: **Six years you shall sow your land,** perform other agricultural labors, **and gather its produce.**

11 **But the seventh year you shall leave it fallow and relinquish it.**[D] You must cease your agricultural activities and consider the field as though it does not belong to you. You shall render your field ownerless so **that the poor of your people may eat** its produce, **and their leftovers, the beast of the field shall eat. So you shall do to your vineyard,** and **to your olive grove.** This command is not limited to grain, as it applies to all forms of agricultural produce.

12 Similarly, **six days you shall perform your activities, and on the seventh day you shall rest,**[D] **so that your ox and your donkey will** also **rest, and the son of your maidservant,** even if he is young and does not get tired from his work, **and the stranger** who works as a hired laborer **will be invigorated.** The Sages explain that this "stranger" is a gentile who resides in the Land of Israel and observes the Noahide laws. He too must be given leave to relax on Shabbat, despite the fact that he is not obligated to keep Shabbat, unlike gentile slaves owned by Jews.[69]

13 **You shall observe everything that I have said to you.** This general command comes toward the end of a series of laws that touched upon a wide range of topics. It serves to preclude the notion that one can fulfill his obligations by keeping only some or even most of the Torah's commandments. God's instructions are not recommendations but a system of laws that is obligatory in its entirety. **You shall not mention the name of other gods;**[D] **they shall not be heard from your mouth.** This law serves to ensure that one keep his distance from anything related to idolatry.

14 **Three times in the year you shall hold a festival**[D] **to Me.**

15 **You shall observe the Festival of Unleavened Bread; seven days you shall eat unleavened bread, as I commanded you** when I took you out of Egypt (12:15). The consumption of unleavened bread is one of the defining characteristics of the festival of Passover. This festival shall be observed **at the appointed time in the month of the ripening,**[D] **for during it you came out from Egypt; they shall not appear before Me empty-handed.** You shall express respect toward Me and My Sanctuary by bringing offerings.

16 **The festival of the** wheat **harvest,** Shavuot, will be with your harvesting **the first fruits of your handiwork that you sow in the field; and the festival of the ingathering,** Sukkot, **at the end of the year,**[D] **when you gather your handiwork,** the grain and most of the summer fruit, **from the field.**

DISCUSSION

23:8| **You shall not take a bribe:** Although the term "bribery" in many legal codes refers to a gift given to a judge in exchange for a favorable ruling, here the term is employed in a much broader sense, as it includes a present given with the stipulation that the judge will rule in accordance with his conscience. This is clear from the language of the verse, which would not refer to the blinding of the wise if the judge had explicitly agreed to issue a favorable ruling. The verse is speaking of a far more delicate process in which the gift causes the judge to become appreciative of the giver. This response subconsciously influences his reasoning process and does not allow him to assess the case objectively and recognize the liability or shortcomings of the individual who benefited him (see *Mekhilta*; Rashi; *Ketubot* 106a).

23:11| **But the seventh year you shall leave it fallow and relinquish it:** During the seventh year, not only does an individual owner lose possession of the land. All human ownership is suspended. Once every seven years the land returns virtually to the state of the Garden of Eden, where all creatures, man and animal alike, had equal rights to its fruit (see the Jerusalem Talmud, *Pe'a* 6:1; *Tosafot* and Rashash, *Rosh HaShana* 9b; *Ḥazon Ish, Shevi'it* 14:4).

23:12| **And on the seventh day you shall rest:** Just like the seventh year, the weekly day of rest expresses one's freedom from the yoke of human activity. Shabbat is God's day, and therefore it applies equally to all; it must be shared even by one's animals.

23:13| **You shall observe everything that I have said to you; you shall not mention the name of other gods:** What is the connection between the general directive to keep all of God's instructions and the specific requirement that one must keep his distance from idolatry by avoiding the very mention of the names of other gods? This can be understood in the context of the first of the Ten Precepts, God's demand for exclusivity in religious worship. This in turn leads to the requirement for absolute fealty to all of God's commands together with the complete denial of any other deity.

23:14| **You shall hold a festival [*taḥog*]:** The word *ḥag*, which means festival, is related to *ḥug*, a circle. This is because the festivals are celebrated annually in accordance with a cyclical yearly calendar. It is also related to the circle dances with which festivals would typically be celebrated.

אַצַדִּיק רָשָׁע: וְשֹׁחַד לֹא תִקָּח כִּי הַשֹּׁחַד יְעַוֵּר פִּקְחִים וִיסַלֵּף דִּבְרֵי צַדִּיקִים: וְגֵר ח

לֹא תִלְחָץ וְאַתֶּם יְדַעְתֶּם אֶת־נֶפֶשׁ הַגֵּר כִּי־גֵרִים הֱיִיתֶם בְּאֶרֶץ מִצְרָיִם: וְשֵׁשׁ י

שָׁנִים תִּזְרַע אֶת־אַרְצֶךָ וְאָסַפְתָּ אֶת־תְּבוּאָתָהּ: וְהַשְּׁבִיעִת תִּשְׁמְטֶנָּה וּנְטַשְׁתָּהּ יא

וְאָכְלוּ אֶבְיֹנֵי עַמֶּךָ וְיִתְרָם תֹּאכַל חַיַּת הַשָּׂדֶה כֵּן־תַּעֲשֶׂה לְכַרְמְךָ לְזֵיתֶךָ: שֵׁשֶׁת יב

יָמִים תַּעֲשֶׂה מַעֲשֶׂיךָ וּבַיּוֹם הַשְּׁבִיעִי תִּשְׁבֹּת לְמַעַן יָנוּחַ שׁוֹרְךָ וַחֲמֹרֶךָ וְיִנָּפֵשׁ

בֶּן־אֲמָתְךָ וְהַגֵּר: וּבְכֹל אֲשֶׁר־אָמַרְתִּי אֲלֵיכֶם תִּשָּׁמֵרוּ וְשֵׁם אֱלֹהִים אֲחֵרִים יג

לֹא תַזְכִּירוּ לֹא יִשָּׁמַע עַל־פִּיךָ: שָׁלֹשׁ רְגָלִים תָּחֹג לִי בַּשָּׁנָה: אֶת־חַג הַמַּצּוֹת יד טו

תִּשְׁמֹר שִׁבְעַת יָמִים תֹּאכַל מַצּוֹת כַּאֲשֶׁר צִוִּיתִךָ לְמוֹעֵד חֹדֶשׁ הָאָבִיב כִּי־בוֹ

יָצָאתָ מִמִּצְרָיִם וְלֹא־יֵרָאוּ פָנַי רֵיקָם: וְחַג הַקָּצִיר בִּכּוּרֵי מַעֲשֶׂיךָ אֲשֶׁר תִּזְרַע טז

רש"י

לְהַחְזִירוֹ, כִּי חֲנֵי לֹא תַחֲזִירֵנּוּ בְּדִינֵי, אִם יֵצֵא מִיָּדְךָ זַכַּאי יֵשׁ לִי שְׁלוּחִים הַרְבֵּה לַהֲמִיתוֹ בַּמִּיתָה שֶׁנִּתְחַיֵּב בָּהּ:

ח| וְשֹׁחַד לֹא תִקָּח. אֲפִלּוּ לִשְׁפֹּט אֱמֶת, וְכָל שֶׁכֵּן כְּדֵי לְהַטּוֹת הַדִּין, שֶׁהֲרֵי כְּדֵי לְהַטּוֹת אֶת הַדִּין כְּבָר נֶאֱמַר "לֹא תַטֶּה מִשְׁפָּט" (לְעֵיל פסוק ו): יְעַוֵּר פִּקְחִים. אֲפִלּוּ חָכָם בַּתּוֹרָה וְנוֹטֵל שֹׁחַד, סוֹף שֶׁתִּטָּרֵף דַּעְתּוֹ עָלָיו, וְיִשְׁתַּכַּח תַּלְמוּדוֹ וְיִכְהֶה מְאוֹר עֵינָיו: וִיסַלֵּף. כְּתַרְגּוּמוֹ "וּמְקַלְקֵל": דִּבְרֵי צַדִּיקִים. דְּבָרִים הַמְצֻדָּקִים, מִשְׁפְּטֵי אֱמֶת, כְּתַרְגּוּמוֹ "פִּתְגָמִין תְּרִיצִין", יְשָׁרִים:

ט| וְגֵר לֹא תִלְחָץ. בְּהַרְבֵּה מְקוֹמוֹת הִזְהִירָה תּוֹרָה עַל הַגֵּר, מִפְּנֵי שֶׁסּוּרוֹ רָע: אֶת נֶפֶשׁ הַגֵּר. כַּמָּה קָשֶׁה לוֹ כְּשֶׁלּוֹחֲצִין אוֹתוֹ:

י| וְאָסַפְתָּ אֶת תְּבוּאָתָהּ. לְשׁוֹן הַכְנָסָה לַבַּיִת, כְּמוֹ "וַאֲסַפְתּוֹ אֶל תּוֹךְ בֵּיתֶךָ" (דברים כב, ב):

יא| תִּשְׁמְטֶנָּה. מֵעֲבוֹדָה: וּנְטַשְׁתָּהּ. מֵאֲכִילָה אַחַר זְמַן

הַבִּעוּר. דָּבָר אַחֵר, "תִּשְׁמְטֶנָּה" מֵעֲבוֹדָה גְמוּרָה, כְּגוֹן חֲרִישָׁה וּזְרִיעָה. "וּנְטַשְׁתָּהּ" מִלְּזַבֵּל וּמִלְּקַשְׁקֵשׁ: וְיִתְרָם תֹּאכַל חַיַּת הַשָּׂדֶה. לְהַקִּישׁ מַאֲכַל אֶבְיוֹן לְמַאֲכַל חַיָּה, מַה חַיָּה אוֹכֶלֶת בְּלֹא מַעֲשֵׂר אַף חֲכֵינוֹנִים אוֹכְלִים בְּלֹא מַעֲשֵׂר, מִכָּאן אָמְרוּ: אֵין מַעֲשֵׂר בַּשְּׁבִיעִית: כֵּן תַּעֲשֶׂה לְכַרְמְךָ. וּתְחִלַּת הַמִּקְרָא מְדַבֵּר בִּשְׂדֵה הַלָּבָן, כְּמוֹ שֶׁאָמוּר לְמַעְלָה הֵימֶנּוּ: "תִּזְרַע אֶת אַרְצֶךָ" (בפסוק הקודם):

יב| וּבַיּוֹם הַשְּׁבִיעִי תִּשְׁבֹּת. אַף בַּשָּׁנָה הַשְּׁבִיעִית לֹא תֵעָקֵר שַׁבַּת בְּרֵאשִׁית מִמְּקוֹמָהּ, שֶׁלֹּא תֹּאמַר: הוֹאִיל וְכָל הַשָּׁנָה קְרוּיָה שַׁבָּת לֹא תִנְהַג בָּהּ שַׁבַּת בְּרֵאשִׁית: לְמַעַן יָנוּחַ שׁוֹרְךָ וַחֲמֹרֶךָ. תֵּן לוֹ נִיחַ, לְהַתִּיר שֶׁיְּהֵא תוֹלֵשׁ וְאוֹכֵל עֲשָׂבִים מִן הַקַּרְקַע, אוֹ אֵינוֹ אֶלָּא יַחְבְּשֶׁנּוּ בְּתוֹךְ הַבַּיִת? אָמַרְתָּ, אֵין זֶה נִיחַ אֶלָּא צַעַר: בֶּן אֲמָתְךָ. בְּעֶבֶד עָרֵל הַכָּתוּב מְדַבֵּר: וְהַגֵּר. זֶה גֵּר תּוֹשָׁב:

יג| וּבְכֹל אֲשֶׁר אָמַרְתִּי אֲלֵיכֶם תִּשָּׁמֵרוּ. לַעֲשׂוֹת כָּל מִצְוֹת עֲשֵׂה בְּאַזְהָרָה, שֶׁכָּל שְׁמִירָה שֶׁבַּתּוֹרָה אַזְהָרָה

הִיא בִּמְקוֹם לָאו: לֹא תַזְכִּירוּ. שֶׁלֹּא יֹאמַר לוֹ: שְׁמֹר לִי בְּצַד עֲבוֹדָה זָרָה פְּלוֹנִית, אוֹ תַעֲמֹד עִמִּי בְּיוֹם עֲבוֹדָה זָרָה פְּלוֹנִית. דָּבָר אַחֵר, "וּבְכֹל אֲשֶׁר אָמַרְתִּי אֲלֵיכֶם תִּשָּׁמֵרוּ וְשֵׁם אֱלֹהִים אֲחֵרִים לֹא תַזְכִּירוּ", לְלַמֶּדְךָ שֶׁשְּׁקוּלָה עֲבוֹדָה זָרָה כְּנֶגֶד כָּל הַמִּצְוֹת כֻּלָּן, וְהַנִּזְהָר בָּהּ כְּשׁוֹמֵר אֶת כֻּלָּן: לֹא יִשָּׁמַע. מִן הַגּוֹי: עַל פִּיךָ. שֶׁלֹּא תַעֲשֶׂה שֻׁתָּפוּת עִם הַגּוֹי וְיִשָּׁבַע לְךָ בַּעֲבוֹדָה זָרָה שֶׁלּוֹ, נִמְצֵאתָ שֶׁאַתָּה גוֹרֵם שֶׁיִּזָּכֵר עַל יָדְךָ:

יד| רְגָלִים. פְּעָמִים, וְכֵן "כִּי הִכִּיתַנִי זֶה שָׁלֹשׁ רְגָלִים" (במדבר כב, כח):

טו| חֹדֶשׁ הָאָבִיב. שֶׁהַתְּבוּאָה מִתְמַלֵּאת בּוֹ בְּאִבֶּיהָ. לְשׁוֹן אַחֵר, "אָבִיב", לְשׁוֹן אָב, בְּכוֹר וְרִאשׁוֹן לְבַשֵּׁל פֵּרוֹת: וְלֹא יֵרָאוּ פָנַי רֵיקָם. כְּשֶׁתָּבֹאוּ לֵרָאוֹת פָּנַי בָּרְגָלִים, הָבִיאוּ לִי עוֹלוֹת:

טז| וְחַג הַקָּצִיר. הוּא חַג שָׁבוּעוֹת: בִּכּוּרֵי מַעֲשֶׂיךָ. שֶׁהוּא זְמַן הֲבָאַת בִּכּוּרִים, שֶׁשְּׁתֵּי הַלֶּחֶם הַבָּאִין בַּעֲצֶרֶת הָיוּ

DISCUSSION

23:15 | At the appointed time in the month of the ripening: It is inferred from this phrase that the festival of Passover must always be celebrated during the spring (see also Deuteronomy 16:1). In a yearly calendar comprised of a cycle of twelve lunar months, each date will occur earlier in the solar cycle than it did the previous year, which renders it impossible for a fixed festival to remain in the spring. Consequently, it became

necessary to institute the system of leap years that is characteristic of the Jewish calendar. This system serves to reconcile the lunar calendar with the solar cycle so that Passover always occurs in the season when the children of Israel left Egypt.

23:16 | And the festival of the ingathering, at the end of the year: In addition to the yearly cycle of months beginning in Nisan, when the

children of Israel left Egypt (see 12:2, and commentary ad loc.), the year exists as an independent unit of time based upon the agricultural cycle. This year starts with the rainy season when farmers plant their crops and ends with the ingathering of the crops (see also commentary on 34:22 and Leviticus 23:26).

17 **Three times during the year,** on Passover, Shavuot, and Sukkot, **all your males shall appear**[D] **before the Master, the Lord.** On these three major festivals, which have agricultural significance, the men must appear in the Temple in the manner of subjects before their master.
18 **You shall not slaughter the blood of My offering with leavened bread.** In addition to the general prohibition against owning leavened bread on Passover, there is a further requirement to destroy all one's leavened bread by the time one's paschal lamb is offered. The Sages disagree with regard to the precise application of this prohibition.[70] **And the fat of My offering** that must be burned on the altar **shall not remain overnight until morning.** The sacrificial rites of the paschal lamb and the festival peace offering brought on the eve of Passover must be completed on that day, rather than left until the following day.[71]
19 **You shall bring the choicest of the first fruits of your land to the house of the Lord your God.** This can mean the best first fruits or simply the first fruits.[72] This commandment does not have to be performed specifically on a festival; it can be fulfilled any time from the beginning of the harvest until the gathering of the crops, which is between Shavuot and Sukkot. The bringing of the first fruits is presented in greater detail in Deuteronomy (26:1–15). **You shall not cook a kid in its mother's milk.**[D] Cooking a kid in the very milk from which it should have gained its sustenance is considered cruel.[73] The tradition of the Sages extends this prohibition to cooking any milk and meat together, as well as eating meat and milk that were cooked together.[74] It is possible that these extensions of this law are based on the fact that one who buys meat and milk from the marketplace cannot be certain that they have no original connection to each other.[75] Nonetheless, in practice the prohibition applies even when it is known with certainty that the milk is not from the mother of that kid.

God's Promise and Demand Pertaining to the Journey to Israel and Living in the Land

EXODUS 23:20–33

At this point the Torah turns from timeless laws and ordinances to matters involving the historical events of the moment: the travels of the Jewish people through the wilderness and their entry into the Land of Israel. God promises them protection from the dangers of travel and the military confrontations that await them upon entering the land. At the same time, He warns them about the spiritual dangers inherent in living near the Canaanite nations.

The basic prohibition of idolatry, which appears in the Ten Precepts and is repeated in the previous series of laws, is expressed here, for the first of many times, in relation to a particular historical situation: The Jewish people are about to enter a land that has already been settled by others, and there is a danger that they might assimilate into the surrounding peoples and cultures. It is incumbent upon them to be careful to avoid the influence of the depraved Canaanite culture.

20 **Behold, I am sending an angel** as a messenger **before you to protect you along the way, and to take you to the place that I have prepared.** God's angel represents His presence in the midst of the Jewish people.

Sixth aliya

21 **Beware of him and heed his voice; do not defy him, for he will not forgive your transgression,** since God alone can pardon; His messenger cannot do so independently. Nonetheless, you must listen to him, **for My name,** God's manifestation in the world, **is in him.**
22 **For if you heed his voice and perform all that I say** through him, **then I,** God, **will be an enemy to your enemies and I will be hostile to those who are hostile to you.**
23 **For My angel shall go before you and he will take you to the Emorites, the Hitites, the Perizites, the Canaanites, the Hivites, and the Yevusites, and I will annihilate them.**
24 In addition to these general warnings, the Torah reiterates a prohibition: **You shall not prostrate yourselves to their gods,** and **you shall not serve them** in any manner, **and you shall not act in accordance with their actions** in their religious rites; **rather, you shall** actively **destroy them and smash their monuments** and all their places of religious worship.
25 **You shall serve the Lord your God and He will bless your bread and your water, and I will remove illness from your midst.**

DISCUSSION

23:17 | **All your males shall appear:** The purpose of the pilgrimage on these festivals is to appear before God, to be seen rather than to see. By appearing as subjects before their master, the people express their acceptance of God's rule. This obligation applies specifically to males, who are comparable to soldiers appearing for roll call before their superior. Practically speaking, however, entire families would undertake the pilgrimage to Jerusalem for the festivals (see Deuteronomy 31:11–12, 12:5–12; I Samuel 1:1–7).

יז בַּשָּׂדֶה וְחַג הָאָסִף בְּצֵאת הַשָּׁנָה בְּאָסְפְּךָ אֶת־מַעֲשֶׂיךָ מִן־הַשָּׂדֶה: שָׁלֹשׁ פְּעָמִים

יח בַּשָּׁנָה יֵרָאֶה כָּל־זְכוּרְךָ אֶל־פְּנֵי הָאָדֹן ׀ יְהוָה: לֹא־תִזְבַּח עַל־חָמֵץ דַּם־זִבְחִי

יט וְלֹא־יָלִין חֵלֶב־חַגִּי עַד־בֹּקֶר: רֵאשִׁית בִּכּוּרֵי אַדְמָתְךָ תָּבִיא בֵּית יְהוָה אֱלֹהֶיךָ לֹא־תְבַשֵּׁל גְּדִי בַּחֲלֵב אִמּוֹ:

שישי כ הִנֵּה אָנֹכִי שֹׁלֵחַ מַלְאָךְ לְפָנֶיךָ לִשְׁמָרְךָ בַּדָּרֶךְ וְלַהֲבִיאֲךָ אֶל־הַמָּקוֹם אֲשֶׁר

כא הֲכִנֹתִי: הִשָּׁמֶר מִפָּנָיו וּשְׁמַע בְּקֹלוֹ אַל־תַּמֵּר בּוֹ כִּי לֹא יִשָּׂא לְפִשְׁעֲכֶם כִּי שְׁמִי

כב בְּקִרְבּוֹ: כִּי אִם־שָׁמוֹעַ תִּשְׁמַע בְּקֹלוֹ וְעָשִׂיתָ כֹּל אֲשֶׁר אֲדַבֵּר וְאָיַבְתִּי אֶת־אֹיְבֶיךָ

כג וְצַרְתִּי אֶת־צֹרְרֶיךָ: כִּי־יֵלֵךְ מַלְאָכִי לְפָנֶיךָ וֶהֱבִיאֲךָ אֶל־הָאֱמֹרִי וְהַחִתִּי וְהַפְּרִזִּי

כד וְהַכְּנַעֲנִי הַחִוִּי וְהַיְבוּסִי וְהִכְחַדְתִּיו: לֹא־תִשְׁתַּחֲוֶה לֵאלֹהֵיהֶם וְלֹא תָעָבְדֵם וְלֹא

כה תַעֲשֶׂה כְּמַעֲשֵׂיהֶם כִּי הָרֵס תְּהָרְסֵם וְשַׁבֵּר תְּשַׁבֵּר מַצֵּבֹתֵיהֶם: וַעֲבַדְתֶּם אֵת יְהוָה אֱלֹהֵיכֶם וּבֵרַךְ אֶת־לַחְמְךָ וְאֶת־מֵימֶיךָ וַהֲסִרֹתִי מַחֲלָה מִקִּרְבֶּךָ:

רש"י

מַתְחִילִין הֶחָדָשׁ לַמְּנָחוֹת וּלְהָבִיא בִּכּוּרִים לַמִּקְדָּשׁ, שֶׁנֶּאֱמַר "וּכְיוֹם הַבִּכּוּרִים" וְגוֹ' (במדבר כח, כו). **וְחַג הָאָסִף. הוּא חַג** הַסֻּכּוֹת. **בְּאָסְפְּךָ אֶת מַעֲשֶׂיךָ.** שֶׁכָּל יְמוֹת הַחַמָּה הַתְּבוּאָה מִתְבַּשֶּׁלֶת בַּשָּׂדוֹת, וּבֶחָג אוֹסְפִים אוֹתָהּ אֶל הַבַּיִת מִפְּנֵי הַגְּשָׁמִים:

יז שָׁלֹשׁ פְּעָמִים וְגוֹ'. לְפִי שֶׁהָעִנְיָן מְדַבֵּר בַּשְּׁבִיעִית, הֻצְרַךְ לוֹמַר שֶׁלֹּא יִסְתָּרְסוּ רְגָלִים מִמְּקוֹמָן. **כָּל זְכוּרְךָ.** הַזְּכָרִים שֶׁבָּךְ:

יח לֹא תִזְבַּח עַל חָמֵץ וְגוֹ'. לֹא תִשְׁחַט אֶת הַפֶּסַח בְּאַרְבָּעָה עָשָׂר בְּנִיסָן עַד שֶׁתְּבַעֵר הֶחָמֵץ: **וְלֹא יָלִין חֵלֶב** חַגִּי וְגוֹ'. חוּץ לַמִּזְבֵּחַ. **עַד בֹּקֶר.** יָכוֹל אַף עַל הַמַּעֲרָכָה יִפָּסֵל בְּלִינָה? תַּלְמוּד לוֹמַר: "עַל מוֹקְדָה עַל הַמִּזְבֵּחַ כָּל הַלַּיְלָה" (ויקרא ו, ב), אֵין לִינָה חֵלֶב בְּעַמּוּד הַשַּׁחַר, שֶׁנֶּאֱמַר: "עַד בֹּקֶר". אֲבָל כָּל הַלַּיְלָה יָכוֹל לְהַעֲלוֹתוֹ מִן הָרִצְפָּה לַמִּזְבֵּחַ:

יט רֵאשִׁית בִּכּוּרֵי אַדְמָתְךָ. אַף הַשְּׁבִיעִית חַיֶּבֶת בַּבִּכּוּרִים, לְכָךְ נֶאֱמַר אַף כָּאן: בִּכּוּרֵי אַדְמָתְךָ. כֵּיצַד? אָדָם נִכְנָס לְתוֹךְ שָׂדֵהוּ, רָאָה תְּאֵנָה שֶׁבִּכְּרָה, כּוֹרֵךְ עָלֶיהָ גֶּמִי לְסִימָן, וּמַקְדִּישָׁהּ. וְאֵין בִּכּוּרִים אֶלָּא מִשִּׁבְעַת הַמִּינִין הָאֲמוּרִים בַּמִּקְרָא: "אֶרֶץ חִטָּה וּשְׂעֹרָה" וְגוֹ' (דברים ח, ח). **לֹא תְבַשֵּׁל גְּדִי.** אַף עֵגֶל וְכֶבֶשׂ בִּכְלַל גְּדִי, שֶׁאֵין גְּדִי אֶלָּא לְשׁוֹן וָלָד רַךְ, מִמַּה שֶּׁאַתָּה מוֹצֵא בְּכַמָּה מְקוֹמוֹת בַּתּוֹרָה שֶׁכָּתוּב "גְּדִי" וְהֻצְרַךְ לְפָרֵשׁ אַחֲרָיו "עִזִּים", כְּגוֹן: "אָנֹכִי אֲשַׁלַּח גְּדִי עִזִּים" (בראשית לח, יז), "אֶת גְּדִי הָעִזִּים" (שם פסוק כ; שופטים יג, יט), "שְׁנֵי גְּדָיֵי עִזִּים" (בראשית כז, ט), לְלַמֶּדְךָ שֶׁכָּל מְקוֹם שֶׁנֶּאֱמַר "גְּדִי" סְתָם אַף עֵגֶל וְכֶבֶשׂ בַּמַּשְׁמָע, וּבִשְׁלֹשָׁה מְקוֹמוֹת נִכְתַּב בַּתּוֹרָה: אֶחָד לְאִסּוּר אֲכִילָה, וְאֶחָד לְאִסּוּר הֲנָאָה, וְאֶחָד לְאִסּוּר בִּשּׁוּל:

כ הִנֵּה אָנֹכִי שֹׁלֵחַ מַלְאָךְ. כָּאן נִתְבַּשְּׂרוּ שֶׁעֲתִידִין לַחֲטוֹא וּשְׁכִינָה אוֹמֶרֶת לָהֶם: "כִּי לֹא אֶעֱלֶה בְּקִרְבְּךָ" (להלן לג, ג):

אֲשֶׁר הֲכִנֹתִי. אֲשֶׁר זִמַּנְתִּי לָתֵת לָכֶם, זֶהוּ פְּשׁוּטוֹ. וּמִדְרָשׁוֹ, "אֶל הַמָּקוֹם אֲשֶׁר הֲכִנֹתִי", כְּבָר מְקוֹמִי נִכָּר כְּנֶגְדּוֹ. וְזֶה אֶחָד מִן הַמִּקְרָאוֹת שֶׁאוֹמְרִים שֶׁבֵּית הַמִּקְדָּשׁ שֶׁל מַעְלָה מְכֻוָּן כְּנֶגֶד בֵּית הַמִּקְדָּשׁ שֶׁל מַטָּה:

כא אַל תַּמֵּר בּוֹ. לְשׁוֹן הַמְרָאָה, "אֲשֶׁר יַמְרֶה אֶת פִּיךָ" (יהושע א, יח), "וַיַּמְרוּ בִי" (יחזקאל כ, ח). **כִּי לֹא יִשָּׂא לְפִשְׁעֲכֶם.** אֵינוֹ מְלֻמָּד בְּכָךְ, שֶׁהוּא מִן הַכַּת שֶׁאֵין חוֹטְאִין. וְעוֹד, שֶׁהוּא שָׁלִיחַ וְאֵינוֹ עוֹשֶׂה אֶלָּא שְׁלִיחוּתוֹ. **כִּי שְׁמִי בְּקִרְבּוֹ.** מְחֻבָּר לְרֹאשׁ הַמִּקְרָא, "הִשָּׁמֶר מִפָּנָיו כִּי שְׁמִי מְשֻׁתָּף בּוֹ", וְרַבּוֹתֵינוּ אָמְרוּ, זֶה מְטַטְרוֹן שֶׁשְּׁמוֹ כְּשֵׁם רַבּוֹ, מְטַטְרוֹן בְּגִימַטְרִיָּא שַׁדָּי:

כב וְצַרְתִּי. כְּתַרְגּוּמוֹ: "וְאָעִיק":

כד הַרֵס תְּהָרְסֵם. לְאוֹתָם אֱלֹהוֹת: **מַצֵּבֹתֵיהֶם.** אֲבָנִים שֶׁהֵם מַצִּיבִין לְהִשְׁתַּחֲווֹת לָהֶם:

DISCUSSION

23:19 | You shall not cook a kid in its mother's milk: This law appears three times in the Torah. In each case, the connection between the prohibition and the context is unclear (see 34:26; Deuteronomy 14:21). With regard to this verse, it can be suggested that some pagan groups would gather together on their holidays and perform idolatrous rituals that included meat and milk cooked together for consumption, or for pouring on young plants as a good omen (see Rambam, *Guide of the Perplexed* 3:48; Abravanel).

26 **There shall be no woman who miscarries**[D] **or is barren in**
Seventh aliya **your land; I will fill the number of your days;** you will merit long lives.

27 When you arrive in Israel, you will not have to rely solely on your own military power: **I will send My fear before you and I will stun,** unnerve and throw into panic, **all the people into whose midst you shall come** for war; **and I will** thereby **cause all your enemies to turn their backs to you** and flee from you.

28 **I will send the hornet before you** to join the attack, **and it shall expel the Hivites, the Canaanites, and the Hitites from before you.**

Oriental hornet

29 **I will not expel them from before you in one year, lest the land become desolate and the beasts of the field multiply against you.** The attack of the hornets will empty the land of its inhabitants slowly and gradually. Had the Canaanites been killed all at once, such as through a plague, the land would have become desolate, which would have made it difficult to repopulate.

30 **I will expel them from before you little by little,**[D] **until you increase and inherit the** entire **land.**

31 **I will set your border from the Red Sea to the sea of the Philistines,** the Mediterranean, much of whose southern coast had been settled by the Philistines, **and from the wilderness** of the Arabian Desert, on the eastern side of the Land of Israel, **to the** Euphrates **River, for I will deliver into your hand the inhabitants of the land and you shall expel them from before you** and take possession of the entire land.

32 **You shall not establish a covenant with them or with their gods.**

33 **They shall not live in your land lest they cause you to sin against Me.** You must entirely destroy them from your land lest you come to imitate their ways and be influenced by their culture. **For you will serve their gods, for they will be a snare for you.** You will be unable to ignore their deep roots in the land. A state of isolation is critical for the development and shaping of your new society.

The Covenant at Sinai

EXODUS 24:1–18

Unlike the revelation on Mount Sinai, when the children of Israel, with the exception of Moses, stood at the foot of the mountain and sought to further distance themselves from the divine revelation, here a mutual covenant is established between God and the children of Israel. Human beings are active parties in the establishment of this covenant: Moses builds an altar and sprinkles blood; representatives of the nation move closer to the place of the revelation, prostrate themselves, bring offerings, and partake of food and drink; and the entire nation declares its commitment not only to the commandments that they have already been given but also to those that God will issue in the future.

24 1 **To Moses, He said:**[D] **Ascend to the** place where the glory of the **Lord** had been present, and where the fire and cloud was seen on the mountain,[76] **you and Aaron, Nadav, and Avihu,** Aaron's older sons, **and seventy of the elders of Israel and prostrate yourselves,** but **from a distance.** Later, this group of seventy elders would become a fixed institution.[77]

2 **Moses alone shall approach the Lord, and they,** Aaron, Nadav, Avihu, and the elders, **shall not approach;** the rest of **the people shall not ascend with him.**

3 **Moses came and related to the people all the words of the Lord,** which was possibly a review of the Ten Precepts, **and all the ordinances** that God had commanded. **All the people answered in one voice,** in unanimous agreement, **and said: All the words that the Lord has spoken, we will perform.**

4 **Moses wrote all the words of the Lord,** the Ten Precepts and the ordinances he had transmitted to them. **And he arose early in the morning and built an altar at the foot of the mountain, and twelve** commemorative stones as **pillars,**[78] **for the twelve tribes of Israel,**[D] one for each tribe.

DISCUSSION

23:26| **There shall be no woman who miscarries:** The Canaanites believed that their gods had the power to provide sustenance and health. There was a concern that some Israelites might adopt these beliefs and would therefore be afraid of the negative consequences of destroying Canaanite places of worship. This verse comes to allay such fears.

23:30| **I will expel them from before you little by little:** When the children of Israel conquered the Land of Israel under Joshua's leadership, they did not take over the entire land. This was not only because they were not powerful enough but also due to the fact that they were able to settle the entire land only when they increased in number. As can be seen in the book of Joshua (see chap. 18), this situation was exacerbated by some of the tribes' lack of motivation to complete the conquest of the land.

24:1| **To Moses, He said:** The Sages disagree as to whether this passage appears in accordance with the chronological order of events or whether it describes events that occurred before the giving of the Torah (see *Yoma* 4a; *Mekhilta*; Rashi).

24:4| **For the twelve tribes of Israel:** The twelve tribes mentioned here are the descendants of each of the twelve sons of Jacob. Later the list of tribes will change: Joseph will generally be divided into two separate tribes, Manasseh and Ephraim, while the tribe of Levi will generally not be counted with the other tribes, as it did not inherit a portion of the Land of Israel.

כו כז לֹא תִהְיֶה מְשַׁכֵּלָה וַעֲקָרָה בְּאַרְצֶךָ אֶת־מִסְפַּר יָמֶיךָ אֲמַלֵּא: אֶת־אֵימָתִי אֲשַׁלַּח
לְפָנֶיךָ וְהַמֹּתִי אֶת־כָּל־הָעָם אֲשֶׁר תָּבֹא בָּהֶם וְנָתַתִּי אֶת־כָּל־אֹיְבֶיךָ אֵלֶיךָ עֹרֶף:
כח וְשָׁלַחְתִּי אֶת־הַצִּרְעָה לְפָנֶיךָ וְגֵרְשָׁה אֶת־הַחִוִּי אֶת־הַכְּנַעֲנִי וְאֶת־הַחִתִּי מִלְּפָנֶיךָ:
כט לֹא אֲגָרְשֶׁנּוּ מִפָּנֶיךָ בְּשָׁנָה אֶחָת פֶּן־תִּהְיֶה הָאָרֶץ שְׁמָמָה וְרַבָּה עָלֶיךָ חַיַּת
ל לא הַשָּׂדֶה: מְעַט מְעַט אֲגָרְשֶׁנּוּ מִפָּנֶיךָ עַד אֲשֶׁר תִּפְרֶה וְנָחַלְתָּ אֶת־הָאָרֶץ: וְשַׁתִּי
אֶת־גְּבֻלְךָ מִיַּם־סוּף וְעַד־יָם פְּלִשְׁתִּים וּמִמִּדְבָּר עַד־הַנָּהָר כִּי ׀ אֶתֵּן בְּיֶדְכֶם אֵת
לב לג יֹשְׁבֵי הָאָרֶץ וְגֵרַשְׁתָּמוֹ מִפָּנֶיךָ: לֹא־תִכְרֹת לָהֶם וְלֵאלֹהֵיהֶם בְּרִית: לֹא יֵשְׁבוּ
בְּאַרְצְךָ פֶּן־יַחֲטִיאוּ אֹתְךָ לִי כִּי תַעֲבֹד אֶת־אֱלֹהֵיהֶם כִּי־יִהְיֶה לְךָ לְמוֹקֵשׁ:
א וְאֶל־מֹשֶׁה אָמַר עֲלֵה אֶל־יְהוָה אַתָּה וְאַהֲרֹן נָדָב וַאֲבִיהוּא וְשִׁבְעִים מִזִּקְנֵי
ב יִשְׂרָאֵל וְהִשְׁתַּחֲוִיתֶם מֵרָחֹק: וְנִגַּשׁ מֹשֶׁה לְבַדּוֹ אֶל־יְהוָה וְהֵם לֹא יִגָּשׁוּ וְהָעָם
ג לֹא יַעֲלוּ עִמּוֹ: וַיָּבֹא מֹשֶׁה וַיְסַפֵּר לָעָם אֵת כָּל־דִּבְרֵי יְהוָה וְאֵת כָּל־הַמִּשְׁפָּטִים
ד וַיַּעַן כָּל־הָעָם קוֹל אֶחָד וַיֹּאמְרוּ כָּל־הַדְּבָרִים אֲשֶׁר־דִּבֶּר יְהוָה נַעֲשֶׂה: וַיִּכְתֹּב
מֹשֶׁה אֵת כָּל־דִּבְרֵי יְהוָה וַיַּשְׁכֵּם בַּבֹּקֶר וַיִּבֶן מִזְבֵּחַ תַּחַת הָהָר וּשְׁתֵּים עֶשְׂרֵה

רש״י

כו| **לֹא תִהְיֶה מְשַׁכֵּלָה.** אִם תַּעֲשֶׂה רְצוֹנִי: **מְשַׁכֵּלָה.** מַפֶּלֶת נְפָלִים אוֹ קוֹבֶרֶת אֶת בָּנֶיהָ קְרוּיָה מְשַׁכֵּלָה:

כז| **וְהַמֹּתִי.** כְּמוֹ וְהֲמַמְתִּי, וְתַרְגּוּמוֹ: "וַאֲשַׁגֵּשׁ". וְכֵן כָּל תֵּבָה שֶׁפָּעַל שֶׁלָּהּ בְּכֶפֶל אוֹת אַחֲרוֹנָה, כְּשֶׁתֵּהָפֵךְ לְדַבֵּר בִּלְשׁוֹן פָּעַלְתִּי יֵשׁ מְקוֹמוֹת שֶׁנּוֹטֵל אוֹת הַכְּפוּלָה וּמַדְגִּישׁ אֶת הָאוֹת וְנוֹקְדוֹ בְּמַלָּאפוּם, כְּגוֹן: "וְהַמֹּתִי" מִגִּזְרַת "וְהָמַם גַּלְגַּל עֶגְלָתוֹ" (ישעיה כח, כח); "וְסַבּוֹתִי" (קהלת ב, כ) מִגִּזְרַת "וְסָבַב בֵּית אֵל" (שמואל א׳ ז, טז); "דַּלּוֹתִי" (תהלים קטז, ו) מִגִּזְרַת "דָּלְלוּ וְחָרְבוּ" (ישעיה יט, ו); "עַל כַּפַּיִם חַקֹּתִיךְ" (שם מט, טז) מִגִּזְרַת "חִקְקֵי לֵב" (שופטים ה, טו); "אֶת מִי רַצּוֹתִי" (שמואל א׳ יב, ג) מִגִּזְרַת "רִצַּץ עָזַב דַּלִּים" (איוב כ, יט). וְהַמְתַרְגֵּם "וְהַמֹּתִי" - 'וְאֶקְטֵיל' טוֹעֶה הוּא, שֶׁאִלּוּ מִגִּזְרַת מִיתָה הָיָה, אֵין הֵ"א שֶׁלָּהּ בְּפַתָּח וְלֹא מֵ"ם שֶׁלָּהּ מְדֻגֶּשֶׁת וְלֹא נְקוּדָה מַלָּאפוּם, אֶלָּא 'וְהֵמַתִּי', כְּגוֹן: "וְהֵמַתָּה אֶת הָעָם הַזֶּה" (במדבר יד, טו), וְהַתָּי"ו מְדֻגֶּשֶׁת לְפִי שֶׁתָּבֹא בִּמְקוֹם שְׁתֵּי תָוִי"ן, הָאַחַת נִשְׁרֶשֶׁת, לְפִי שֶׁאֵין 'מִיתָה' בְּלֹא תָי"ו, וְהָאַחֶרֶת מְשַׁמֶּשֶׁת, כְּמוֹ: אָמַרְתִּי, חָטָאתִי, עָשִׂיתִי. וְכֵן 'וְנָתַתִּי' הַתָּי"ו מְדֻגֶּשֶׁת, שֶׁהִיא בָּאָה בִּמְקוֹם שְׁתַּיִם, לְפִי שֶׁהָיָה צָרִיךְ שָׁלֹשׁ תָּוִי"ן, שְׁתַּיִם לַיְסוֹד כְּמוֹ: "בְּיוֹם תֵּת ה׳" (יהושע י, יב), "מַתַּת אֱלֹהִים הִיא" (קהלת ג, יג), וְהַשְּׁלִישִׁית לְשִׁמּוּשׁ: **עֹרֶף.** שֶׁיָּנוּסוּ לְפָנֶיךָ וְיַהַפְכוּ לְךָ עָרְפָּם:

כח| **הַצִּרְעָה.** מִין שֶׁרֶץ הָעוֹף, וְהָיְתָה מַכָּה אוֹתָם בְּעֵינֵיהֶם וּמַטִּילָה בָּהֶם אֶרֶס וְהֵם מֵתִים. וְהַצִּרְעָה לֹא עָבְרָה אֶת הַיַּרְדֵּן. וְחִתִּי וּכְנַעֲנִי הֵם אֶרֶץ סִיחוֹן וְעוֹג, לְפִיכָךְ מִכָּל שֶׁבַע אֻמּוֹת לֹא מָנָה כָּאן אֶלָּא אֵלּוּ. וְחִוִּי, אַף עַל פִּי שֶׁהוּא מֵעֵבֶר הַיַּרְדֵּן וָהָלְאָה, שָׁנוּ רַבּוֹתֵינוּ בְּמַסֶּכֶת סוֹטָה (דף לו ע״א): עַל שְׂפַת הַיַּרְדֵּן עָמְדָה וְזָרְקָה בָּהֶם מָרָה:

כט| **שְׁמָמָה.** רֵיקָנִית מִבְּנֵי אָדָם, לְפִי שֶׁאַתֶּם מְעַט וְאֵין בָּכֶם כְּדֵי לְמַלֹּאת אוֹתָהּ: **וְרַבָּה עָלֶיךָ.** וְתִרְבֶּה עָלֶיךָ:

ל| **עַד אֲשֶׁר תִּפְרֶה.** תִּרְבֶּה, לְשׁוֹן פְּרִי, כְּמוֹ: "פְּרוּ וּרְבוּ" (בראשית א, כב):

לא| **וְשַׁתִּי.** לְשׁוֹן הֲשָׁתָה, וְהַתָּי"ו מְדֻגֶּשֶׁת מִפְּנֵי שֶׁבָּאָה תַּחַת שְׁתַּיִם, שֶׁאֵין שִׁיתָה בְּלֹא תָי"ו, וְהָאַחַת לְשִׁמּוּשׁ: **עַד הַנָּהָר.** פְּרָת: **וְגֵרַשְׁתָּמוֹ.** וּתְגָרְשֵׁם:

לג| **כִּי תַעֲבֹד וְגוֹ׳.** הֲרֵי אֵלּוּ "כִּי" מְשַׁמְּשִׁין בִּמְקוֹם 'אֲשֶׁר', וְכֵן בְּכַמָּה מְקוֹמוֹת. וְזֶהוּ לְשׁוֹן 'אִי', שֶׁהוּא אֶחָד מֵאַרְבָּעָה לְשׁוֹנוֹת שֶׁהַ'כִּי' מְשַׁמֵּשׁ. וְגַם מָצִינוּ בְּהַרְבֵּה מְקוֹמוֹת 'אִם' מְשַׁמֵּשׁ בִּלְשׁוֹן 'אֲשֶׁר', כְּמוֹ: "וְאִם תַּקְרִיב מִנְחַת בִּכּוּרִים" (ויקרא ב, יד) שֶׁהוּא חוֹבָה:

פרק כד

א| **וְאֶל מֹשֶׁה אָמַר.** פָּרָשָׁה זוֹ נֶאֶמְרָה קֹדֶם עֲשֶׂרֶת הַדִּבְּרוֹת, בְּאַרְבָּעָה בְּסִיוָן נֶאֱמַר לוֹ: "עֲלֵה":

ב| **וְנִגַּשׁ מֹשֶׁה לְבַדּוֹ.** אֶל הָעֲרָפֶל:

ג| **וַיָּבֹא מֹשֶׁה וַיְסַפֵּר לָעָם.** בּוֹ בַּיּוֹם: **אֵת כָּל דִּבְרֵי ה׳.** מִצְוֹת פְּרִישָׁה וְהַגְבָּלָה: **וְאֵת כָּל הַמִּשְׁפָּטִים.** שֶׁבַע מִצְוֹת שֶׁנִּצְטַוּוּ בְּנֵי נֹחַ, וְשַׁבָּת וְכִבּוּד אָב וָאֵם וּפָרָה אֲדֻמָּה וְדִינִין שֶׁנִּתְּנוּ לָהֶם בְּמָרָה:

ד| **וַיִּכְתֹּב מֹשֶׁה.** מִבְּרֵאשִׁית וְעַד מַתַּן תּוֹרָה, וְכָתַב מִצְוֹת שֶׁנִּצְטַוּוּ בְּמָרָה: **וַיַּשְׁכֵּם בַּבֹּקֶר.** בַּחֲמִשָּׁה בְּסִיוָן:

5 **He sent the young men**[79] **of the children of Israel.**[D]
Alternatively, this does not mean actual young men, but the
servants of God, and it is a reference to the firstborn, who at
that time served as priests.[80] **And they offered up burnt offerings and they slaughtered feast offerings of bulls to the
Lord.** Burnt offerings are burnt in their entirety upon the altar,
whereas peace offerings are mostly eaten by those who brought
them.
6 **Moses took half the blood** of the bulls, as atonement is
achieved by the rite of sprinkling the blood,[81] **and he placed
it in the basins,**[82] **and half the blood he sprinkled upon the
altar,** as would be done with the blood of regular offerings in
the future.
7 **He,** Moses, **took the book of the covenant**[D] containing the
words of God, which he had written earlier (see verse 4), **and
read** it **in the ears of the people.** Previously he had informed
them verbally of God's statements. Now he read it to them from
the book. **And they said: Everything that the Lord has spoken we will perform and we will heed.** In addition to their expressed agreement to obey what God had already commanded
(see 19:8, 24:3), they now declared their commitment to obey
His future instructions.[83] This commitment included not only
the actual fulfillment of God's commands in practice but also
their internal acceptance of His will.[84]
8 **Moses took the blood** that was in the basins **and sprinkled it
on the people, and he said: This is the blood of the covenant
that the Lord has established**[D] **with you with regard to all
these matters.**
9 **Moses and Aaron, Nadav, and Avihu, and seventy of the elders of Israel went up.**
10 **They saw the God of Israel**[D] in a prophetic vision; **and under
His feet was like a configuration of sapphire [*sappir*] brick
[*livnat*],**[D] a square[85] blue[86] stone. Alternatively, *livnat* indicates
a white [*lavan*] color,[87] in which case *sappir* is not referring to
sapphire but to a different gem. It can be inferred from elsewhere that *sappir* is white or almost white.[88] **And** it was **like the
very heavens in** terms of **purity.** This could also be a description of the color of the mysterious object that they saw under
the feet of the God of Israel.[89]
11 **Against the noblemen [*atzilei*] of the children of Israel,**
Aaron, Nadav, Avihu, and the elders, **He did not extend His
hand.**[D] God did not strike them down despite the fact that they
had approached the Divine Presence. The term *atzilei* refers to
individuals of elevated status but who have not entirely separated and detached themselves from society.[90] **And they beheld
God,**[D] to the extent that this is possible, **and ate** the peace offerings **and drank,**[D] as though sharing a meal with God.[91]
12 **The Lord said to Moses: Ascend** higher **to Me, to the mountaintop, and be there** for some time; **and** there **I will give you
the stone tablets,** which are described below (31:18, 32:15–16),
**and the law and the commandment that I have written, to
teach them.**

DISCUSSION

24:5| **The young men of the children of Israel:** The Talmud notes that in the Septuagint this phrase and the phrase below, "the noblemen of the children of Israel" (verse 11), are both translated as "the elect of the children of Israel" (see *Megilla* 9a, and *Tosafot* ad loc.; Ibn Ezra, short commentary on Exodus, verse 11). Some commentaries distinguish between the terms, and maintain that this verse is referring to young men whereas verse 11 refers to the elders (Ramban and Rashi, verse 11).

24:7| **The book of the covenant:** It would appear from a plain reading of the passage that this is a small book of uncertain scope, although it must have included part of the Torah. Some say that it contained the books of Genesis and Exodus up to that current point in time, or only the commandments the people had already received (Rashi; see *Mekhilta, Masekhta deBaḤodesh* 3).

24:8| **The blood of the covenant that the Lord has established [*karat*]:** A covenant differs from a contract in that it includes an element of unification between the parties. Consequently, the ceremony of establishing a covenant often involved a symbolic act of cutting or bloodletting, as in circumcision. The term *karat*, which can be translated as cut, alludes to this aspect of the covenant. Letting blood symbolizes the commitment and willingness to sacrifice each side is undertaking with regard to the other. Similarly, the Covenant between the Parts (see Genesis 15), which was enacted between God and Abraham, involved splitting animals into two parts, symbolizing that each side is incomplete without the other. This symbolism was also invoked during the reestablishment of the covenant in the time of King Tzidkiyahu (Jeremiah 34:18). In the covenant at Sinai described here, the blood was divided into two halves: One half was sprinkled on the altar to indicate God's participation in the covenant; the other half was sprinkled upon the Jewish people, symbolizing their participation (see *Bekhor Shor*; *Sefer HaIkkarim* 4:45; Abravanel, Jeremiah 34:18).

24:10| **They saw the God of Israel:** Isaiah also describes a prophetic vision in which he saw God (Isaiah 6:1–5), while a far more extensive vision of this type appears in Ezekiel in his account of the divine chariot (Ezekiel 1, 10). Like the vision here, Ezekiel describes seeing a kind of sapphire throne (Ezekiel 1:26, 10:1).

And under His feet was like a configuration of sapphire brick: There is a parallel to this imagery in the construction of the Tabernacle. The tablets upon which the Ten Precepts were written were made of stone, possibly sapphire (see *Tanḥuma, Ki Tisa* 29; *Yalkut Shimoni, Ekev* 854). They were placed in the ark beneath the cherubs, like a footstool under the feet of the Divine Presence (see also 25:22; I Samuel 4:4; II Samuel 22:10; Ezekiel 43:7).

ה מצבה לשנים עשר שבטי ישראל: וישלח את־נערי בני ישראל ויעלו עלת
ו ויזבחו זבחים שלמים ליהוה פרים: ויקח משה חצי הדם וישם באגנת וחצי
ז הדם זרק על־המזבח: ויקח ספר הברית ויקרא באזני העם ויאמרו כל אשר־
ח דבר יהוה נעשה ונשמע: ויקח משה את־הדם ויזרק על־העם ויאמר הנה
ט דם־הברית אשר כרת יהוה עמכם על כל־הדברים האלה: ויעל משה ואהרן
י נדב ואביהוא ושבעים מזקני ישראל: ויראו את אלהי ישראל ותחת רגליו
יא כמעשה לבנת הספיר וכעצם השמים לטהר: ואל־אצילי בני ישראל לא שלח
יב ידו ויחזו את־האלהים ויאכלו וישתו: ויאמר יהוה אל־משה
עלה אלי ההרה והיה־שם ואתנה לך את־לחת האבן והתורה והמצוה אשר

רש"י

ה| את נערי. הבכורות:

ו| ויקח משה חצי הדם. מי חלקו? מלאך בא וחלקו: באגנת. שתי אגנות, אחד לחצי דם עולה ואחד לחצי דם שלמים להזות אותם על העם. ומכאן למדו רבותינו שנכנסו אבותינו לברית במילה וטבילה והרצאת דמים; שאין הזאה בלא טבילה:

ז| ספר הברית. מבראשית ועד מתן תורה, ומצוות שנצטוו במרה:

ח| ויזרק. ענין הזאה, ותרגומו: "וזרק על מדבחא לכפרא על עמא":

י| ויראו את אלהי ישראל. נסתכלו והציצו ונתחייבו מיתה, אלא שלא רצה הקדוש ברוך הוא לערבב שמחת התורה, והמתין לנדב ואביהוא עד יום חנוכת המשכן, ולזקנים עד "ויהי העם כמתאננים... ותבער בם אש ה' ותאכל בקצה המחנה" (במדבר יא, א), בקצינים שבמחנה: כמעשה לבנת הספיר. היא היתה לפניו בשעת השעבוד, לזכור צרתן של ישראל שהיו משועבדים במעשה לבנים: וכעצם השמים לטהר. משנגאלו היה אור וחדוה לפניו: וכעצם. כתרגומו, לשון מראה: לטהר. לשון ברור וצלול:

יא| ואל אצילי. הם נדב ואביהוא והזקנים: לא שלח ידו. מכלל שהיו ראויים להשלחת יד: ויחזו את האלהים. היו מסתכלין בו בלב גס מתוך אכילה ושתיה, כך מדרש תנחומא. ואונקלוס לא תרגם כן; "אצילי" לשון גדולים, כמו: "ומאציליה קראתיך" (ישעיה מא, ט), "ויאצל מן הרוח" (במדבר יא, כה), "שש אמות אצילה" (יחזקאל מא, ח):

יב| ויאמר ה' אל משה. לאחר מתן תורה: עלה אלי ההרה והיה שם. ארבעים יום: את לחת האבן והתורה והמצוה אשר כתבתי להורתם. כל שש מאות ושלש עשרה מצוות בכלל עשרת הדברות הן. ורבנו סעדיה פירש באזהרות שיסד לכל דבור ודבור מצוות התלויות בו:

DISCUSSION

24:11| **And against the noblemen of the children of Israel He did not extend His hand:** After experiencing such a level of closeness to God, it cannot be taken for granted that the nobles would be able to return safely to an earthly existence. From other contexts it is clear that a divine revelation, even the sight of an angel, can endanger the life of the beholder (see 33:20; Judges 6:22–23, 13:22; Isaiah 6:5). Nevertheless, the nobles of the children of Israel were not harmed by their experience.

And they beheld [*vayeḥezu*] God: The verb beheld, whose root is *ḥet-zayin-heh*, is commonly used in Aramaic as a translation of the root *reish-alef-heh*, which is the standard Hebrew term for seeing. However, in the Bible these roots apparently have different meanings. The root *reish-alef-heh* refers to seeing a tangible object, whereas the root *ḥet-zayin-heh* or the related term *maḥazeh* applies to a prophetic vision that is imperceptible with one's regular senses (see Genesis 15:1; Exodus 18:21; I Samuel 3:1; Isaiah 47:13).

And ate and drank: There are several examples in the Torah where establishing a covenant is accompanied by a shared meal between the parties, e.g., the covenants between Isaac and Avimelekh (Genesis 26:26–30) and between Jacob and Laban (Genesis 31:43–54). It is possible that this meal was undertaken in celebration of the giving of the Torah (see the Ramban here and at the beginning of his sermon on Ecclesiastes). Some commentaries suggest that as the verse emphasizes that the nobles were not harmed, it teaches that they were worthy of punishment because they lacked the appropriate fear and trepidation when beholding God, as expressed by their eating and drinking (see *Tanḥuma*, *Aharei Mot* 7; Rashi; Rambam, *Guide of the Perplexed* 1:5). Others claim that the verse is saying that the experience of beholding God sustained them as though they had eaten and drank, even though they did not actually do so (Onkelos; *Targum Yonatan*).

13 **Moses and his servant Joshua rose.** Aaron, his sons, and the elders all returned to the people, while Joshua alone accompanied Moses. Joshua was Moses' personal attendant and was closer to him than anyone else, which is why he escorted Moses farther than the others. **And Moses** alone **ascended the mountain of God,** whereas Joshua remained somewhere along the route.

14 **To the elders, he,** Moses, had previously **said,** before he ascended the mountain: **Remain here for us until we will return to you; behold, Aaron and Hur are with you;**[D] **whoever has a matter,** a dispute with someone, **shall approach them** for mediation.

15 **Moses ascended to the mountaintop, and** after he began his ascent, **the cloud covered the mountain.**

16 *Maftir* **The glory of the Lord rested upon Mount Sinai, and the cloud covered it,** the mountain; or, the cloud covered him, Moses,[92] **for six days,** during which Moses sanctified himself to reach the requisite spiritual level. Then **He,** God, **called to Moses on the seventh day from the midst of the cloud.**[D]

17 **The appearance of the glory of the Lord was like devouring fire on the top of the mountain in the eyes of the children of Israel.** The revelation that the Jewish people were privileged to experience was similar to a cloud covering the mountain, with a consuming fire at its peak.

18 **Moses entered into the midst of the cloud, and went up to the mountaintop,** so that the cloud, which represented the Divine Presence, surrounded him. **Moses was on the mountaintop for forty days and forty nights.**[D]

Maftir on Shabbat Shekalim is read from Exodus 30:11–16.

DISCUSSION

24:14| **Behold, Aaron and Hur are with you:** Moses might not have known in advance how long he would remain on the mountain, and therefore he appointed Aaron and Hur as the nation's leaders until his return. Aaron and Hur are also mentioned together in the story of the war against Amalek (see 17:10–12). According to the Sages, Hur, from the tribe of Judah (see 31:2), was Miriam's son (*Pirkei deRabbi Eliezer* 44). This family connection is not surprising, as Aaron, Miriam's brother, likewise took a wife from the tribe of Judah (see 6:23). This verse is the last time that Hur is mentioned in the Torah (see *Tanḥuma*, *Tetzaveh* 10, with regard to his fate). Betzalel, Hur's grandson, would later be appointed to oversee the construction of the Tabernacle (see 31:2).

24:16| **And the cloud covered it for six days; He called to Moses on the seventh day from the midst of the cloud:** The Sages derive from here a general principle that one may not enter the place of the Divine Presence without appropriate preparation (see *Yoma* 3b–4a; Rashi).

24:18| **Moses was on the mountaintop for forty days and forty nights:** While he was on the mountain for forty days and nights in God's presence, Moses was removed from the limitations of the physical world. The Sages explain that in these unique conditions Moses lived an existence unbound by time or nature, and his awareness of whether it was day or night was based upon the topic that God taught him: When God would teach him the Written Torah, Moses knew it was day; when God would teach him the Oral Torah, he knew it was night (see *Tanḥuma, Ki Tisa* 36).

It is impossible to tell from the verses whether Moses informed the Jewish people how long he

יג כְּתַבְתִּי לְהוֹרֹתָם: וַיָּקָם מֹשֶׁה וִיהוֹשֻׁעַ מְשָׁרְתוֹ וַיַּעַל מֹשֶׁה אֶל־הַר הָאֱלֹהִים:
יד וְאֶל־הַזְּקֵנִים אָמַר שְׁבוּ־לָנוּ בָזֶה עַד אֲשֶׁר־נָשׁוּב אֲלֵיכֶם וְהִנֵּה אַהֲרֹן וְחוּר
טו עִמָּכֶם מִי־בַעַל דְּבָרִים יִגַּשׁ אֲלֵהֶם: וַיַּעַל מֹשֶׁה אֶל־הָהָר וַיְכַס הֶעָנָן אֶת־הָהָר: מפטיר
טז וַיִּשְׁכֹּן כְּבוֹד־יהוה עַל־הַר סִינַי וַיְכַסֵּהוּ הֶעָנָן שֵׁשֶׁת יָמִים וַיִּקְרָא אֶל־מֹשֶׁה בַּיּוֹם
יז הַשְּׁבִיעִי מִתּוֹךְ הֶעָנָן: וּמַרְאֵה כְּבוֹד יהוה כְּאֵשׁ אֹכֶלֶת בְּרֹאשׁ הָהָר לְעֵינֵי בְּנֵי
יח יִשְׂרָאֵל: וַיָּבֹא מֹשֶׁה בְּתוֹךְ הֶעָנָן וַיַּעַל אֶל־הָהָר וַיְהִי מֹשֶׁה בָּהָר אַרְבָּעִים יוֹם
וְאַרְבָּעִים לָיְלָה:

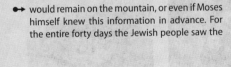

רש"י

יג| וַיָּקָם מֹשֶׁה וִיהוֹשֻׁעַ מְשָׁרְתוֹ. לֹא יָדַעְתִּי מַה טִּיבוֹ שֶׁל יְהוֹשֻׁעַ כָּאן. וְאוֹמֵר אֲנִי, שֶׁהָיָה הַתַּלְמִיד מְלַוֶּה לָרַב עַד מְקוֹם הַגְבָּלַת תְּחוּמֵי הָהָר, שֶׁאֵינוֹ רַשַּׁאי לֵילֵךְ מִשָּׁם וָהָלְאָה, וּמִשָּׁם "וַיַּעַל מֹשֶׁה" לְבַדּוֹ "אֶל הַר הָאֱלֹהִים", וִיהוֹשֻׁעַ נָטָה שָׁם אָהֳלוֹ וְנִתְעַכֵּב שָׁם כָּל אַרְבָּעִים יוֹם, שֶׁכֵּן מָצִינוּ כְּשֶׁיָּרַד מֹשֶׁה: "וַיִּשְׁמַע יְהוֹשֻׁעַ אֶת קוֹל הָעָם בְּרֵעֹה" (להלן לב, יז), לָמַדְנוּ שֶׁלֹּא הָיָה יְהוֹשֻׁעַ עִמָּהֶם:

יד| וְאֶל הַזְּקֵנִים אָמַר. בְּצֵאתוֹ מִן הַמַּחֲנֶה: שְׁבוּ לָנוּ בָזֶה. וְהִתְעַכְּבוּ כָּאן עִם שְׁאָר הָעָם בַּמַּחֲנֶה לִהְיוֹת נְכוֹנִים לִשְׁפֹּט לְכָל אִישׁ רִיבוֹ: חוּר. בְּנָהּ שֶׁל מִרְיָם הָיָה, וְאָבִיו כָּלֵב בֶּן יְפֻנֶּה, שֶׁנֶּאֱמַר: "וַיִּקַּח לוֹ כָלֵב אֶת אֶפְרָת וַתֵּלֶד לוֹ אֶת חוּר" (דברי הימים א' ב, יט), אֶפְרָת זוֹ מִרְיָם, כִּדְאִיתָא בְּסוֹטָה (דף יא ע"ב): מִי בַעַל דְּבָרִים. מִי שֶׁיֵּשׁ לוֹ דִּין:

טז| וַיְכַסֵּהוּ הֶעָנָן. רַבּוֹתֵינוּ חוֹלְקִים בַּדָּבָר: יֵשׁ מֵהֶם אוֹמְרִים, אֵלּוּ שִׁשָּׁה יָמִים שֶׁמֵּרֹאשׁ חֹדֶשׁ; "וַיְכַסֵּהוּ הֶעָנָן" לָהָר; "וַיִּקְרָא אֶל מֹשֶׁה בַּיּוֹם הַשְּׁבִיעִי" לוֹמַר עֲשֶׂרֶת הַדִּבְּרוֹת, וּמֹשֶׁה וְכָל בְּנֵי יִשְׂרָאֵל עוֹמְדִים, אֶלָּא שֶׁחָלַק הַכָּתוּב כָּבוֹד לְמֹשֶׁה. וְיֵשׁ אוֹמְרִים, "וַיְכַסֵּהוּ הֶעָנָן" לְמֹשֶׁה "שֵׁשֶׁת יָמִים" לְאַחַר עֲשֶׂרֶת הַדִּבְּרוֹת, וְהֵם הָיוּ בִּתְחִלַּת אַרְבָּעִים יוֹם שֶׁעָלָה מֹשֶׁה לְקַבֵּל הַלּוּחוֹת, וְלִמֶּדְךָ שֶׁכָּל הַנִּכְנָס לְמַחֲנֵה שְׁכִינָה טָעוּן פְּרִישָׁה שִׁשָּׁה יָמִים:

יח| בְּתוֹךְ הֶעָנָן. עָנָן זֶה כְּמִין עָשָׁן הוּא, וְעָשָׂה לוֹ הַקָּדוֹשׁ בָּרוּךְ הוּא לְמֹשֶׁה שְׁבִיל בְּתוֹכוֹ:

DISCUSSION

would remain on the mountain, or even if Moses himself knew this information in advance. For the entire forty days the Jewish people saw the cloud covering the mountain, with the devouring fire at its top. No one knew what was happening to Moses, who was enveloped by fog in the place of the Divine Presence.

Parashat
Teruma

The Commandments to Construct and Consecrate the Tabernacle and Its Utensils

This *parasha* and the following one, *Parashat Tetzaveh*, are part of one extended speech in which God instructs Moses in detail how to construct the Tabernacle and its various utensils, and how to consecrate Aaron and his sons as priests to serve therein. These instructions were given to Moses during the forty days and forty nights that he was on Mount Sinai, as was stated in the last verse of the previous *parasha*.

The Tabernacle is the site of divine revelation and is constructed in the form of a human home. The vessels of the Tabernacle correspond to the basic furniture of a home: a bed or chair, a lamp, and a table. The ark corresponds to a bed or chair; the table represents a table for eating, as the showbread was placed on it; and the candelabrum serves as a lamp that provides light inside.

The Call for Donations

EXODUS 25:1–9

The construction of the Tabernacle entailed using a wide range of both expensive and inexpensive materials. Each Israelite was asked to donate some material on the list, in accordance with his means and personal level of generosity. Although some of the expenses for the construction of the Tabernacle were collected in equal amounts from all Israelites in the form of a tax, this was not the primary source of funding for the construction. For the most part, the Tabernacle was constructed using donations that were given freely, through the goodwill of the people.

25 1 **The Lord spoke to Moses, saying:**[D]

2 **Speak to the children of Israel**[D] **and** command them that **they shall collect for Me,** on My behalf,[1] **a gift; from every man whose heart pledges you shall collect My gift.** This is a donation, not a tax, and the specific amount that is donated depends on the generosity of the individual.

3 **This is the gift that you shall collect from them.** Since the donations were to be used for the construction of the Tabernacle, only certain metals could be donated: **gold, silver, and bronze.** Other metals that the children of Israel possessed in the wilderness were not needed.[2]

4 **And** fabrics: **sky-blue** wool,[B] colored a deep blue with dye extracted from the blood of a certain species of snail; and wool dyed **purple**[B] or some reddish color. The dye used to make this color, which was also extracted from various snails, was very expensive, and in many places symbolized nobility. **And**

Murex trunculus, source of sky-blue dye

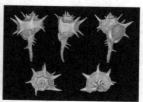

Murex brandaris, source of purple dye

scarlet wool,[B] colored bright red with a dye extracted from certain insects. And in addition to threads of dyed sheep's wool, the people should take fine, clean **linen** [*shesh*], a word derived from Egyptian, **and** thicker, woven **goat hair.**

5 **And** materials for the roofs and the walls: **rams' hides** from which the hair has been removed and **dyed red,** and *taḥash*[B] **hides, and** boards of **acacia wood,**[B]

Ram

Gum arabic tree

Dugong

6 **oil** suitable **for the lighting** of the candelabrum, **spices** used **for the anointing oil and for the incense of the spices.**

פרשת

תרומה

א ב וַיְדַבֵּר יְהוָה אֶל־מֹשֶׁה לֵּאמֹר: דַּבֵּר אֶל־בְּנֵי יִשְׂרָאֵל וְיִקְחוּ־לִי תְּרוּמָה מֵאֵת
ג כָּל־אִישׁ אֲשֶׁר יִדְּבֶנּוּ לִבּוֹ תִּקְחוּ אֶת־תְּרוּמָתִי: וְזֹאת הַתְּרוּמָה אֲשֶׁר תִּקְחוּ
ד ה מֵאִתָּם זָהָב וָכֶסֶף וּנְחֹשֶׁת: וּתְכֵלֶת וְאַרְגָּמָן וְתוֹלַעַת שָׁנִי וְשֵׁשׁ וְעִזִּים: וְעֹרֹת
ו אֵילִם מְאָדָּמִים וְעֹרֹת תְּחָשִׁים וַעֲצֵי שִׁטִּים: שֶׁמֶן לַמָּאֹר בְּשָׂמִים לְשֶׁמֶן הַמִּשְׁחָה

רש"י

ב | וְיִקְחוּ לִי תְּרוּמָה. "לִי" – לִשְׁמִי: תְּרוּמָה. הַפְרָשָׁה, יַפְרִישׁוּ לִי מִמָּמוֹנָם נְדָבָה: יִדְּבֶנּוּ לִבּוֹ. לְשׁוֹן נְדָבָה, וְהוּא לְשׁוֹן רָצוֹן טוֹב, פייסנ"ט בְּלַעַז: תִּקְחוּ אֶת תְּרוּמָתִי. אָמְרוּ רַבּוֹתֵינוּ, שָׁלֹשׁ תְּרוּמוֹת אֲמוּרוֹת כָּאן: אַחַת תְּרוּמַת בֶּקַע לַגֻּלְגֹּלֶת שֶׁנַּעֲשׂוּ מֵהֶם הָאֲדָנִים, כְּמוֹ שֶׁמְּפֹרָשׁ בְּ'אֵלֶּה פְקוּדֵי' (להלן לח, כו-כז); וְאַחַת תְּרוּמַת הַמִּזְבֵּחַ בֶּקַע לַגֻּלְגֹּלֶת, לַקֻּפּוֹת לִקְנוֹת מֵהֶן קָרְבְּנוֹת צִבּוּר; וְאַחַת תְּרוּמַת הַמִּשְׁכָּן נִדְבַת כָּל אֶחָד וְאֶחָד שֶׁהִתְנַדְּבוּ. שְׁלֹשָׁה עָשָׂר דְּבָרִים הָאֲמוּרִים בָּעִנְיָן כֻּלָּם הֻצְרְכוּ לִמְלֶאכֶת הַמִּשְׁכָּן אוֹ לְבִגְדֵי כְהֻנָּה כְּשֶׁתְּדַקְדֵּק בָּהֶם:

ג | זָהָב וָכֶסֶף וּנְחֹשֶׁת וְגוֹ'. כֻּלָּם בָּאוּ בִּנְדָבָה אִישׁ אִישׁ מַה שֶּׁנְּדָבוֹ לִבּוֹ, חוּץ מִן הַכֶּסֶף שֶׁבָּא בְּשָׁוֶה, מַחֲצִית הַשֶּׁקֶל לְכָל אֶחָד. וְלֹא מָצִינוּ בְּכָל מְלֶאכֶת הַמִּשְׁכָּן שֶׁהֻצְרַךְ שָׁם כֶּסֶף יוֹתֵר, שֶׁנֶּאֱמַר: "וְכֶסֶף פְּקוּדֵי הָעֵדָה וְגוֹ' בֶּקַע לַגֻּלְגֹּלֶת" וְגוֹ' (להלן לח, כה-כו). וּשְׁאָר הַכֶּסֶף הַבָּא שָׁם בִּנְדָבָה (להלן לה, כד) עֲשָׂאוּהוּ לִכְלֵי שָׁרֵת:

ד | וּתְכֵלֶת. צֶמֶר צָבוּעַ בְּדַם חִלָּזוֹן, וְצִבְעוֹ יָרֹק: וְאַרְגָּמָן. צֶמֶר צָבוּעַ מִמִּין צֶבַע שֶׁשְּׁמוֹ אַרְגָּמָן: וְשֵׁשׁ. הוּא פִשְׁתָּן: וְעִזִּים. נוֹצָה שֶׁל עִזִּים, לְכָךְ תִּרְגֵּם אוּנְקְלוֹס: "וּמַעְזֵי", דָּבָר הַבָּא מִן הָעִזִּים וְלֹא עִזִּים עַצְמָן, שֶׁתַּרְגּוּם שֶׁל עִזִּים 'עִזַּיָּא':

ה | מְאָדָּמִים. צְבוּעוֹת הָיוּ אָדֹם לְאַחַר עֲבּוּדָן: תְּחָשִׁים. מִין חַיָּה, וְלֹא הָיְתָה אֶלָּא לְשָׁעָה, וְהַרְבֵּה גְּוָנִים הָיוּ לָהּ, לְכָךְ מְתֻרְגָּם "סַסְגּוֹנָא", שֶׁשָּׂשׂ וּמִתְפָּאֵר בִּגְוָנִין שֶׁלּוֹ: וַעֲצֵי שִׁטִּים. וּמֵאַיִן הָיוּ לָהֶם בַּמִּדְבָּר? פֵּרֵשׁ רַבִּי תַּנְחוּמָא, יַעֲקֹב אָבִינוּ צָפָה בְּרוּחַ הַקֹּדֶשׁ שֶׁעֲתִידִין יִשְׂרָאֵל לִבְנוֹת מִשְׁכָּן בַּמִּדְבָּר, וְהֵבִיא אֲרָזִים לְמִצְרַיִם וּנְטָעָם, וְצִוָּה לְבָנָיו לִטְּלָם עִמָּהֶם כְּשֶׁיֵּצְאוּ מִמִּצְרַיִם:

ו | שֶׁמֶן לַמָּאֹר. שֶׁמֶן זַיִת זָךְ לְהַעֲלוֹת נֵר תָּמִיד: בְּשָׂמִים לְשֶׁמֶן הַמִּשְׁחָה. שֶׁנַּעֲשָׂה לִמְשֹׁחַ כְּלֵי הַמִּשְׁכָּן וְהַמִּשְׁכָּן לְקַדְּשׁוֹ, וְהֻצְרְכוּ לוֹ בְּשָׂמִים, כְּמוֹ שֶׁמְּפֹרָשׁ בְּ'כִי תִשָּׂא' (להלן

DISCUSSION

25:1 | The Lord spoke to Moses saying [*lemor*]: This is the most frequently repeated verse in the Torah. The simplest explanation of the word *lemor* is that it performs the same function as the colon in modern-day punctuation. Others explain that it means "to say," denoting a command by God to Moses to repeat to others what he will now hear (see Ramban, 6:10).

25:2 | Speak to the children of Israel: Although "speaking" [*dibbur*], the word used here, and "saying" [*amira*] are roughly synonymous, the former denotes a firmer instruction than the latter (see *Bereshit Rabba* 44:6; Rashi, Numbers 12:1).

BACKGROUND

25:4 | Sky-blue [*tekhelet*] wool: This refers to a deep blue dye, bordering on purple, and the word also refers to wool dyed that color. Many today identify *tekhelet* as the dye extracted from the banded dye-murex, *Murex trunculus*, a species of sea snail. This blue dye was used in the distinguished priestly garments and other royal clothes (see Esther 8:15).

Purple [*argaman*]: This reddish-purple dye is extracted from the spiny dye-murex, *Murex brandaris*, another kind of sea snail. Early documents indicate that wool dyed with this substance was four times more expensive than other dyed wool. In addition to being frequently mentioned in the Bible together with the sky-blue dye used in the construction of the Tabernacle, it is also mentioned as being used in the covers of the Tabernacle's accoutrements and the vestments of the High Priest. The *argaman* dye is also mentioned in external sources dating from the fourteenth century BCE. In the Roman period, purple dye was used mainly by priests, kings, and ministers, and due to its importance and high price, production of the dye was monitored and trade in it was controlled.

Scarlet [*tola'at shani*] wool: This is a bright red dye produced from a certain species of insect (see Isaiah 1:18). It was used extensively in dyeing wool and expensive fabrics, as well as for the ritual purification of lepers and those who had become impure from contact with a corpse (see Leviticus 14:4–6; Numbers 19:6). In the description of the building of the Temple in II Chronicles (2:6–13), the word *karmil* is used to refer to this insect instead of *tola'at shani* (see Rav Se'adya Gaon; Rashi; Radak). *Karmil* is a type of insect known as *kermes* in Arabic, and similar names for *tola'at shani* exist in many European languages, such as "carmine" in English.

Current research suggests that *tola'at shani* is the scale insect *Kermes echinatus*, which feeds on the sap of evergreen trees and is found in Israel; this accords with the description in the Midrash (*Pesikta Rabbati* 20). The dye is extracted by drying the insects and then grinding and cooking them.

25:5 | *Taḥash*: *Taḥash* is mentioned in the book of Ezekiel as an expensive material used for making shoes: "I clothed you in embroidery and shod you with *taḥash*,

7 Precious stones: **Onyx stones,**[B] usually yellowish-brown, **and**
stones for setting.[3] The onyx stones were used **for the ephod,**
and the stones to be set were **for** affixing in **the breast piece.**
8 **They,** the children of Israel, **shall make for Me a sanctuary,**
and through it **I will dwell among them.**[D]
9 **In accordance with everything that I show you,** Moses, **the**
configuration of the Tabernacle and the configuration of all
its vessels, as detailed below, **so you shall** later **make it,** in fulfillment of My command.

The Command to Build the Ark

EXODUS 25:10–22

The first vessel that God commands the Israelites to build is the Ark of the Testimony, the most sacred vessel in the Tabernacle. The Tabernacle as a whole is called the Tabernacle of Testimony, after the two tablets, which served as testimony to the covenant between God and Israel. The Tabernacle can be described as an earthly home for the heavenly tablets. The order in which the vessels are described in this section does not necessarily imply the order in which they were eventually constructed or how they were arranged inside the Tabernacle, but it might reflect their relative importance.

Although the Torah's description of the Tabernacle and its vessels is detailed and exact, many descriptive elements are missing. Despite all that is revealed about this sacred place, the Tabernacle remains shrouded in mystery.

10 **They shall make an ark**[D] **of acacia wood: Its length shall be**
two and a half cubits, its width one and a half cubits, and its
height one and a half cubits. A cubit is the distance between a
man's elbow and the end of his fingers. The length of this rectangular box is greater than its height, indicating that it was placed
lengthwise, not upright.
11 **You shall plate it,** the acacia wood, **with pure gold, within**
and without you shall plate it. The verse does not state precisely how this should be done, nor does it specify the thickness
or shape of the plating. The Sages explain that this was not a
coating painted directly on the wood, but separate objects covering its inner and outer surfaces: A golden box inserted into
the wooden one, which was in turn inserted into another, larger
golden box.[4] **And you shall make a gold rim [*zer*] upon it all**
around. The size and exact appearance of this *zer* is not detailed. Due to the similarity between the word *zer*, a gold rim,
and *nezer*, a crown, and since both words apparently denote
objects that surround or encircle from above, one can conclude
that the *zer* was a kind of crown for the ark, similar to the one
on the table in the Sanctuary (see verse 24).
12 **You shall cast four rings of gold for it,** the ark, **and place**
them on its four corners [*pa'amotav*].[5] Ibn Ezra interprets
pa'amotav as referring to legs, even though the Torah never explicitly dictates that the ark should have legs. **Two rings** shall be
on its one side, and two rings shall be **on its second side.**
13 **You shall make staves of acacia wood and** you shall **plate**
them too **with gold.**
14 **You shall insert the staves into the rings on the sides of the**
ark, to carry the ark with them. The Tabernacle and its vessels
must be portable. If the staves had been made of pure gold, a
soft metal, they could not have borne such a heavy weight.
15 **In the rings of the ark the staves shall be; they shall not be**
removed from it. The staves of the ark are not merely a means
for carrying it, they are an integral part of the ark. Consequently,
they may not be removed from the rings even when they are not
needed for transporting the ark.

BACKGROUND

and I wrapped you with linen and covered you with silk" (Ezekiel 16:10). Some maintain that *taḥash* is the name of a color; according to Rabbi Yehuda in the Jerusalem Talmud, it is purple (Shabbat 2:3). Onkelos and Targum Yonatan translate it simply as a colorful hide. In addition, researchers note the similarity between the word *taḥash* and *tah-si-a*, which is mentioned in the Nuzi tablets (fourteenth century BCE) and denotes a yellow or pink hide.

Others hold that the *taḥash* is an animal, although there has never been any consensus as to which kind. The Talmud identifies the *taḥash* as an extinct unicorn (Shabbat 28b).

Yet others posit that the *taḥash* is a dolphin or some other sea mammal. In light of the Arabic cognate, it may be the dugong, a type of aquatic mammal that can be found in the Red Sea and whose skin is sometimes used by Bedouin in shoemaking. Some have identified the *taḥash* as the narwhal, a species of arctic whale that travels in small groups and can grow up to 6 m in length. The narwhal is primarily light yellow in color, with dark spots, and is the only spotted cetacean. A twisted tooth, which can reach 3 m in length, grows out of one side of its mouth, and throughout history its horn has been mistaken for that of the unicorn.

Acacia wood: Acacia wood is strong and resistant to worms and rot, and various types are found in the Middle East. Some remains have been found in furniture and ships in archaeological finds in Egypt. One especially sturdy variety of acacia wood is from the gum arabic tree, *Vachellia nilotica*, although the boards from this tree, at 3 m long, are too short to have been the acacia boards used in the Tabernacle. Some scholars identify the acacia wood here as *Faidherbia albida*, also known as the ana tree. This tree's branches are long and straight, and it can reach a height of 20 m. Although the ana tree typically grows in environments that have a good deal of water and not in desert-like

ז ח וְלִקְטֹרֶת הַסַּמִּים: אַבְנֵי־שֹׁהַם וְאַבְנֵי מִלֻּאִים לָאֵפֹד וְלַחֹשֶׁן: וְעָשׂוּ לִי מִקְדָּשׁ
ט וְשָׁכַנְתִּי בְּתוֹכָם: כְּכֹל אֲשֶׁר אֲנִי מַרְאֶה אוֹתְךָ אֵת תַּבְנִית הַמִּשְׁכָּן וְאֵת תַּבְנִית
י כָּל־כֵּלָיו וְכֵן תַּעֲשׂוּ: וְעָשׂוּ אֲרוֹן עֲצֵי שִׁטִּים אַמָּתַיִם וָחֵצִי אָרְכּוֹ
יא וְאַמָּה וָחֵצִי רָחְבּוֹ וְאַמָּה וָחֵצִי קֹמָתוֹ: וְצִפִּיתָ אֹתוֹ זָהָב טָהוֹר מִבַּיִת וּמִחוּץ
יב תְּצַפֶּנּוּ וְעָשִׂיתָ עָלָיו זֵר זָהָב סָבִיב: וְיָצַקְתָּ לּוֹ אַרְבַּע טַבְּעֹת זָהָב וְנָתַתָּה עַל
אַרְבַּע פַּעֲמֹתָיו וּשְׁתֵּי טַבָּעֹת עַל־צַלְעוֹ הָאֶחָת וּשְׁתֵּי טַבָּעֹת עַל־צַלְעוֹ הַשֵּׁנִית:
יג יד וְעָשִׂיתָ בַדֵּי עֲצֵי שִׁטִּים וְצִפִּיתָ אֹתָם זָהָב: וְהֵבֵאתָ אֶת־הַבַּדִּים בַּטַּבָּעֹת עַל
טו צַלְעֹת הָאָרֹן לָשֵׂאת אֶת־הָאָרֹן בָּהֶם: בְּטַבְּעֹת הָאָרֹן יִהְיוּ הַבַּדִּים לֹא יָסֻרוּ מִמֶּנּוּ:

רש״י

ל, כג-כה): **וְלִקְטֹרֶת הַסַּמִּים.** שֶׁהָיוּ מַקְטִירִין בְּכָל בֹּקֶר וָעֶרֶב, כְּמוֹ שֶׁמְּפֹרָשׁ בִּ׳וְאַתָּה תְּצַוֶּה׳ (להלן ל, ז-ח). וּלְשׁוֹן קְטֹרֶת, הַעֲלָאַת קִיטוֹר וְתִימְרוֹת עָשָׁן:

ז | **אַבְנֵי שֹׁהַם.** שְׁתַּיִם הֻצְרְכוּ שָׁם לְצֹרֶךְ הָאֵפוֹד הָאָמוּר בִּ׳וְאַתָּה תְּצַוֶּה׳ (שם כח, ט-יב): **מִלֻּאִים.** עַל שֵׁם שֶׁעוֹשִׂין לָהֶם בַּזָּהָב מוֹשָׁב כְּמִין גּוּמָא וְנוֹתְנִין הָאֶבֶן שָׁם לְמַלֹּאות הַגּוּמָא, קְרוּיִים ״אַבְנֵי מִלּוּאִים״, וּמְקוֹם הַמּוֹשָׁב קָרוּי מִשְׁבֶּצֶת: **לָאֵפֹד וְלַחֹשֶׁן.** הַשֹּׁהַם לָאֵפוֹד וְאַבְנֵי הַמִּלּוּאִים לַחֹשֶׁן. וְחֹשֶׁן וְאֵפוֹד מְפֹרָשִׁים בִּ׳וְאַתָּה תְּצַוֶּה׳ (שם כח, ו-ל), וְהֵם מִינֵי תַּכְשִׁיט:

ח | **וְעָשׂוּ לִי מִקְדָּשׁ.** וְעָשׂוּ לִשְׁמִי בֵּית קְדֻשָּׁה:

ט | **כְּכֹל אֲשֶׁר אֲנִי מַרְאֶה אוֹתְךָ.** כָּאן ״אֵת תַּבְנִית הַמִּשְׁכָּן״. הַמִּקְרָא הַזֶּה מְחֻבָּר לַמִּקְרָא שֶׁלְּמַעְלָה הֵימֶנּוּ: ״וְעָשׂוּ לִי מִקְדָּשׁ... כְּכֹל אֲשֶׁר אֲנִי מַרְאֶה אוֹתְךָ... וְכֵן תַּעֲשׂוּ״ לְדוֹרוֹת, אִם יֹאבַד אֶחָד מִן הַכֵּלִים, אוֹ כְּשֶׁתַּעֲשׂוּ לִי כְּלֵי בֵּית עוֹלָמִים כְּגוֹן שֻׁלְחָנוֹת וּמְנוֹרוֹת וְכִיּוֹרוֹת וּמְכוֹנוֹת שֶׁעָשָׂה שְׁלֹמֹה, כְּתַבְנִית אֵלּוּ תַּעֲשׂוּ אוֹתָם. וְאִם לֹא הָיָה הַמִּקְרָא מְחֻבָּר לְמַעְלָה הֵימֶנּוּ, לֹא הָיָה לוֹ לִכְתֹּב: ״וְכֵן תַּעֲשׂוּ״ אֶלָּא ״כֵּן תַּעֲשׂוּ״, וְהָיָה מְדַבֵּר עַל עֲשִׂיַּת אֹהֶל מוֹעֵד וְכֵלָיו:

י | **וְעָשׂוּ אֲרוֹן.** כְּמִין אֲרוֹנוֹת שֶׁעוֹשִׂים בְּלֹא רַגְלַיִם עֲשׂוּיִם כְּמִין אַרְגָּז שֶׁקּוֹרִין אשקרי״ן, יוֹשֵׁב עַל שׁוּלָיו:

יא | **מִבַּיִת וּמִחוּץ תְּצַפֶּנּוּ.** שְׁלֹשָׁה אֲרוֹנוֹת עָשָׂה בְּצַלְאֵל, שְׁנַיִם שֶׁל זָהָב וְאֶחָד שֶׁל עֵץ, אַרְבָּעָה כְּתָלִים וְשׁוּלַיִם לְכָל אֶחָד, וּפְתוּחִים מִלְמַעְלָה. נָתַן שֶׁל עֵץ בְּתוֹךְ שֶׁל זָהָב, וְשֶׁל זָהָב בְּתוֹךְ שֶׁל עֵץ, וְחִפָּה שְׂפָתוֹ הָעֶלְיוֹנָה בְּזָהָב, נִמְצָא מְצֻפֶּה מִבַּיִת וּמִחוּץ: **זֵר זָהָב.** כְּמִין כֶּתֶר מַקִּיף לוֹ סָבִיב לְמַעְלָה מִשְּׂפָתוֹ, שֶׁעָשָׂה הָאָרוֹן הַחִיצוֹן גָּבוֹהַּ מִן הַפְּנִימִי עַד שֶׁעָלָה לְמוּל עֳבִי הַכַּפֹּרֶת וּלְמַעְלָה הֵימֶנּוּ מַשֶּׁהוּ, וּכְשֶׁהַכַּפֹּרֶת שׁוֹכֵב עַל עֳבִי הַכְּתָלִים עוֹלֶה הַזֵּר לְמַעְלָה מִכָּל עֳבִי הַכַּפֹּרֶת כָּל שֶׁהוּא, וְהוּא סִימָן לְכֶתֶר תּוֹרָה:

יב | **וְיָצַקְתָּ.** לְשׁוֹן הַתָּכָה, כְּתַרְגּוּמוֹ: **פַּעֲמֹתָיו.** כְּתַרְגּוּמוֹ: ״זָוְיָתֵיהּ״. וּבַזָּוִיּוֹת הָעֶלְיוֹנוֹת סָמוּךְ לַכַּפֹּרֶת הָיוּ נְתוּנוֹת, שְׁתַּיִם מִכָּאן וּשְׁתַּיִם מִכָּאן לְרָחְבּוֹ שֶׁל אָרוֹן, וְהַבַּדִּים נְתוּנִים בָּהֶם, וְאָרְכּוֹ שֶׁל אָרוֹן מַפְסִיק בֵּין הַבַּדִּים אַמָּתַיִם וָחֵצִי בֵּין בַּד לְבַד, שֶׁיִּהְיוּ שְׁנֵי בְּנֵי אָדָם הַנּוֹשְׂאִים אֶת הָאָרוֹן מְהַלְּכִין בֵּינֵיהֶם, וְכֵן מְפֹרָשׁ בִּמְנָחוֹת בְּפֶרֶק ׳שְׁתֵּי הַלֶּחֶם׳ (דף צח ע״ב): **וּשְׁתֵּי טַבָּעֹת עַל צַלְעוֹ הָאֶחָת.** הֵן הֵן אַרְבַּע טַבָּעוֹת שֶׁבִּתְחִלַּת הַמִּקְרָא, וּפֵרֵשׁ לְךָ הֵיכָן הָיוּ. וְהַוָּי״ו זוֹ יְתֵרָה הִיא, וּפִתְרוֹנוֹ כְּמוֹ שְׁתֵּי טַבָּעֹת. וְיֵשׁ לְךָ לְיַשְּׁבָהּ כֵּן: וּשְׁתַּיִם מִן הַטַּבָּעוֹת הָאֵלּוּ עַל צַלְעוֹ הָאֶחָת: **צַלְעוֹ.** צִדּוֹ:

יג | **בַּדֵּי.** מוֹטוֹת:

טו | **לֹא יָסֻרוּ מִמֶּנּוּ.** לְעוֹלָם:

BACKGROUND

conditions, many of the materials used for the Tabernacle were not found in the desert but brought from elsewhere.

According to the Talmud (*Rosh HaShana* 23a), the wood mentioned here is not acacia wood, but *tornita*, a type of cedar. Some commentaries maintain that it is a kind of pine, genus *Pinus* (Rashi; Rashbam).

25:7 | **Onyx stones:** The translation of *avnei shoham* follows the opinion of those who claim that *shoham* is onyx or sardonyx, a soft quartz stone typically brownish-red in color. These precious stones apparently came from the area of Sudan, as the Torah states they were found in the land of Havila (Genesis 2:11–12), now identified with modern-day Sudan.

From the command, "You shall take two onyx stones and engrave on them the names of the children of Israel" (Exodus 28:9), one can infer that these stones were suited to engraving. In the ancient world onyx was used for seals, rings, necklaces, and other ornaments. The word for onyx in Ethiopian is *samu*, which is similar to *shoham*.

DISCUSSION

25:8 | **I will dwell among them:** The commentaries stress that the verse does not state "I will dwell in it," but "I will dwell among them" (see Alsheikh). In other words, the Tabernacle was not built as a place in which God would reside, but rather to symbolize God's closeness to the people and to act as a sign that the Divine Presence dwells among the children of Israel.

25:10 | **They shall make an ark:** Whereas the measurements of the Tabernacle and its other vessels are multiples of whole cubits, all three dimensions of the ark are multiples of half-cubits. Some commentaries homiletically infer from this that the nature of the ark cannot be grasped, measured, or known with precision.

16 **You shall place in the ark** the Tablets of **the Testimony,**^D the two tablets of the covenant, **that I will give you.**

17 **You shall make an ark cover**^D **of pure gold.** Its size should match that of the ark itself. **Its length shall be two and a half cubits and its width a cubit and a half.**

Second aliya

18 **You shall make two cherubs of gold,** in the likeness of heavenly beings.⁶ **Hammered you shall make them, at the two ends of the ark cover.** The cherubs and the ark cover were formed from one contiguous piece of solid gold. This could have been achieved by casting the gold in a mold, but the word hammered indicates that the cherubs were made by beating and striking a large gold block.⁷ This must have been a highly complicated and difficult process.

19 **And make one cherub from this end** of the ark cover **and one cherub from that end; from the ark cover you shall make the cherubs from its two ends.**

20 **The cherubs shall have wings spread from above, shielding with their wings over the ark cover, and their faces one to another; toward the ark cover the faces of the cherubs**^D **shall be.** Though they should face each other, their gaze is to be directed downward, toward the ark cover.

21 **You shall place the ark cover upon the ark from above; and in the ark you shall place** the Tablets of **the Testimony that I shall give you.**

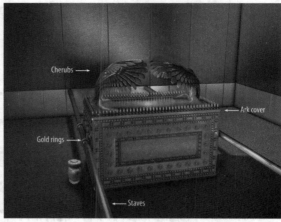

Ark of the Testimony

22 **I will meet with you there, and I will tell you, from upon the ark cover, from between the two cherubs**^D **that are upon the Ark of the Testimony, everything that I will command you to the children of Israel.** This would be the place of God's revelation to Moses.

The Command to Build the Table

EXODUS 25:23–30

After giving the command to construct the ark, which will be the only item located inside the Holy of Holies, God tells Moses how to build the table and the candelabrum, both of which will be situated within the Sanctuary. Since the ark contained the Tablets of the Covenant, engraved with the word of God, the decoration surrounding the ark's rim is known as the crown of the Torah. However, the table enjoys more visibility, and holds the showbread, symbolizing the material bounty bestowed by God upon His world. The gold rim around the table is therefore known as the crown of kingship, as it is the king who cares for the physical needs of the people.

23 **You shall make a table of acacia wood: Its length shall be two cubits, and its width one cubit, and its height one and a half cubits.**

24 **You shall plate it with pure gold, and you shall make for it**

a rim of gold all around. Like the ark (verse 11), the table was adorned with a kind of crown.

25 **You shall make for it a border of one handbreadth all around** in height, **and you shall make** the aforementioned **rim of gold for its border all around.**

DISCUSSION

25:16 | You shall place in the ark the Testimony: This is why the ark is called the Ark of the Testimony. A straightforward reading of the verses indicates that the ark contained nothing apart from the tablets, but certain Sages maintain that at a later point a Torah scroll was also placed there (*Bava Batra* 14a; see Deuteronomy 31:26; *Tosafot, Eiruvin* 83b).

25:17 | Ark cover: The ark, which was an open box, was fitted with a cover of pure gold. This cover must have been extremely heavy,

especially given the tradition that it was one handbreadth thick (*Sukka* 4b).

25:20 | Cherubs: The verse does not state how many wings were on each cherub. Clearly, one pair of wings was raised upward, stretching over the ark cover, but it is possible that each creature possessed six wings, like the cherubs in the vision of the prophet Isaiah (Isaiah 6:2). One can infer from the verses that each of the cherubs had a body, wings, and face.

Although their appearance is never described in detail, cherubs are mentioned elsewhere in the

Bible as angels. They first appear keeping watch over the Garden of Eden to bar Adam's return (Genesis 3:24). When the prophet Ezekiel, who as a priest had seen the Temple before its destruction, saw heavenly beings in his vision, he knew they were cherubs due to their similarity to the cherubs above the ark (see Ezekiel 10:20).

The Sages state, based on a tradition and the Aramaic root of the word, that the cherubs had the faces of children (*Sukka* 5b) and that the pair were male and female in appearance (*Yoma* 54a).

טז וְנָתַתָּ אֶל־הָאָרֹן אֵת הָעֵדֻת אֲשֶׁר אֶתֵּן אֵלֶיךָ: וְעָשִׂיתָ כַפֹּרֶת זָהָב טָהוֹר אַמָּתַיִם שני

יז וָחֵצִי אָרְכָּהּ וְאַמָּה וָחֵצִי רָחְבָּהּ: וְעָשִׂיתָ שְׁנַיִם כְּרֻבִים זָהָב מִקְשָׁה תַּעֲשֶׂה אֹתָם

יח מִשְּׁנֵי קְצוֹת הַכַּפֹּרֶת: וַעֲשֵׂה כְּרוּב אֶחָד מִקָּצָה מִזֶּה וּכְרוּב־אֶחָד מִקָּצָה מִזֶּה

יט מִן־הַכַּפֹּרֶת תַּעֲשׂוּ אֶת־הַכְּרֻבִים עַל־שְׁנֵי קְצוֹתָיו: וְהָיוּ הַכְּרֻבִים פֹּרְשֵׂי כְנָפַיִם

כ לְמַעְלָה סֹכְכִים בְּכַנְפֵיהֶם עַל־הַכַּפֹּרֶת וּפְנֵיהֶם אִישׁ אֶל־אָחִיו אֶל־הַכַּפֹּרֶת יִהְיוּ

כא פְּנֵי הַכְּרֻבִים: וְנָתַתָּ אֶת־הַכַּפֹּרֶת עַל־הָאָרֹן מִלְמָעְלָה וְאֶל־הָאָרֹן תִּתֵּן אֶת־

כב הָעֵדֻת אֲשֶׁר אֶתֵּן אֵלֶיךָ: וְנוֹעַדְתִּי לְךָ שָׁם וְדִבַּרְתִּי אִתְּךָ מֵעַל הַכַּפֹּרֶת מִבֵּין שְׁנֵי

הַכְּרֻבִים אֲשֶׁר עַל־אֲרֹן הָעֵדֻת אֵת כָּל־אֲשֶׁר אֲצַוֶּה אוֹתְךָ אֶל־בְּנֵי יִשְׂרָאֵל:

כג וְעָשִׂיתָ שֻׁלְחָן עֲצֵי שִׁטִּים אַמָּתַיִם אָרְכּוֹ וְאַמָּה רָחְבּוֹ וְאַמָּה וָחֵצִי קֹמָתוֹ: וְצִפִּיתָ

כד אֹתוֹ זָהָב טָהוֹר וְעָשִׂיתָ לּוֹ זֵר זָהָב סָבִיב: וְעָשִׂיתָ לּוֹ מִסְגֶּרֶת טֹפַח סָבִיב וְעָשִׂיתָ

כה

רש"י

טז וְנָתַתָּ אֶל הָאָרֹן. כְּמוֹ בָּאָרֹן: הָעֵדֻת. הַתּוֹרָה שֶׁהִיא לְעֵדוּת בֵּינִי וּבֵינֵיכֶם שֶׁצִּוִּיתִי אֶתְכֶם מִצְוֹת הַכְּתוּבוֹת בָּהּ:

יז כַּפֹּרֶת. כִּסּוּי עַל הָאָרוֹן, שֶׁהָיָה פָּתוּחַ מִלְמָעְלָה וּמַנִּיחוֹ עָלָיו כְּמִין דַּף: אַמָּתַיִם וָחֵצִי אָרְכָּהּ. כְּאָרְכּוֹ שֶׁל אָרוֹן, וְרָחְבּוֹ כְּרָחְבּוֹ שֶׁל אָרוֹן, וּמֻנַּחַת עַל שְׁנֵי עֳבָיֵי הַכְּתָלִים. וְאַף עַל פִּי שֶׁלֹּא נָתַן שִׁעוּר לְעָבְיָהּ, פֵּרְשׁוּ רַבּוֹתֵינוּ שֶׁהָיְתָה עָבְיָהּ טֶפַח:

יח כְּרֻבִים. דְּמוּת פַּרְצוּף תִּינוֹק לָהֶם: מִקְשָׁה תַּעֲשֶׂה אֹתָם. שֶׁלֹּא תַעֲשֵׂם בִּפְנֵי עַצְמָם וּתְחַבְּרֵם בְּרָאשֵׁי הַכַּפֹּרֶת לְאַחַר עֲשִׂיָּתָם כְּמַעֲשֵׂה צוֹרְפִים שֶׁקּוֹרִין שולדור"י, אֶלָּא הַטֵּל זָהָב הַרְבֵּה בִּתְחִלַּת עֲשִׂיַּת הַכַּפֹּרֶת, וְהַכֵּה בַּפַּטִּישׁ וּבְקֻרְנָס בְּאֶמְצַע וְרָאשִׁין בּוֹלְטִין לְמַעְלָה, וְצַיֵּר הַכְּרוּבִים בִּבְלִיטַת קְצוֹתָיו: מִקְשָׁה. בטדי"ץ בְּלַעַז. כְּמוֹ "דָּא לְדָא נָקְשָׁן" (דניאל ה, ו): קְצוֹת הַכַּפֹּרֶת. רָאשֵׁי הַכַּפֹּרֶת:

יט וַעֲשֵׂה כְּרוּב אֶחָד מִקָּצָה. שֶׁלֹּא תֹאמַר שְׁנַיִם כְּרֻבִים לְכָל קָצֶה וְקָצֶה, לְכָךְ הֻצְרַךְ לְפָרֵשׁ "כְּרוּב אֶחָד מִקָּצָה מִזֶּה": מִן הַכַּפֹּרֶת. עַצְמָהּ, "תַּעֲשׂוּ אֶת הַכְּרֻבִים". זֶהוּ

פֵּרוּשׁוֹ שֶׁל "מִקְשָׁה תַּעֲשֶׂה אֹתָם", שֶׁלֹּא תַעֲשֵׂם בִּפְנֵי עַצְמָם וּתְחַבְּרֵם לַכַּפֹּרֶת:

כ פֹּרְשֵׂי כְנָפַיִם. שֶׁלֹּא תַעֲשֶׂה כַנְפֵיהֶם שׁוֹכְבִים, אֶלָּא פְּרוּשִׂים וּגְבוֹהִים לְמַעְלָה אֵצֶל רָאשֵׁיהֶם, שֶׁיְּהֵא עֲשָׂרָה טְפָחִים בַּחֲלָל שֶׁבֵּין הַכְּנָפַיִם לַכַּפֹּרֶת, כִּדְאִיתָא בְּסֻכָּה (דף ה ע"ב):

כא וְאֶל הָאָרֹן תִּתֵּן אֶת הָעֵדֻת. לֹא יָדַעְתִּי לָמָּה נִכְפַּל, שֶׁהֲרֵי כְּבָר נֶאֱמַר "וְנָתַתָּ אֶל הָאָרֹן אֵת הָעֵדֻת" (לְעֵיל פסוק טז)? וְיֵשׁ לוֹמַר, שֶׁבָּא לְלַמֵּד שֶׁבְּעוֹדוֹ אָרוֹן לְבַדּוֹ בְּלֹא כַפֹּרֶת יִתֵּן תְּחִלָּה הָעֵדוּת לְתוֹכוֹ, וְאַחַר כָּךְ יִתֵּן אֶת הַכַּפֹּרֶת עָלָיו, וְכֵן מָצִינוּ כְּשֶׁהֵקִים אֶת הַמִּשְׁכָּן, נֶאֱמַר: "וַיִּתֵּן אֶת הָעֵדֻת אֶל הָאָרֹן", וְאַחַר כָּךְ: "וַיִּתֵּן אֶת הַכַּפֹּרֶת עַל הָאָרֹן מִלְמָעְלָה" (לְהַלָּן מ, כ):

כב וְנוֹעַדְתִּי. כְּשֶׁאֶקְבַּע מוֹעֵד לְךָ לְדַבֵּר עִמְּךָ, אוֹתוֹ מָקוֹם אֶקְבָּע לַמּוֹעֵד, שֶׁאָבֹא שָׁם לְדַבֵּר אֵלֶיךָ: וְדִבַּרְתִּי אִתְּךָ מֵעַל הַכַּפֹּרֶת. וּבְמָקוֹם אַחֵר הוּא אוֹמֵר: "וַיְדַבֵּר ה' אֵלָיו מֵאֹהֶל מוֹעֵד לֵאמֹר" (ויקרא א, א), זֶה הַמִּשְׁכָּן מִחוּץ

לַפָּרֹכֶת, נִמְצְאוּ שְׁנֵי כְתוּבִים מַכְחִישִׁים זֶה אֶת זֶה! בָּא הַכָּתוּב הַשְּׁלִישִׁי וְהִכְרִיעַ בֵּינֵיהֶם: "וּבְבֹא מֹשֶׁה אֶל אֹהֶל מוֹעֵד... וַיִּשְׁמַע אֶת הַקּוֹל מִדַּבֵּר אֵלָיו מֵעַל הַכַּפֹּרֶת וְגו'" (במדבר ז, פט), מֹשֶׁה הָיָה נִכְנָס לַמִּשְׁכָּן, וְכֵיוָן שֶׁבָּא בְּתוֹךְ הַפֶּתַח קוֹל יוֹרֵד מִן הַשָּׁמַיִם לְבֵין הַכְּרוּבִים, וּמִשָּׁם יוֹצֵא וְנִשְׁמָע לְמֹשֶׁה בְּאֹהֶל מוֹעֵד: וְאֵת כָּל אֲשֶׁר אֲצַוֶּה אוֹתְךָ אֶל בְּנֵי יִשְׂרָאֵל. הֲרֵי וָי"ו זוֹ יְתֵרָה וּטְפֵלָה, וְכָמוֹהוּ הַרְבֵּה בַּמִּקְרָא, וְכֹה תִּפְתֹּר, וְאֵת כָּל אֲשֶׁר אֲדַבֵּר עִמְּךָ שָׁם "אֵת" כָּל אֲשֶׁר חַוֶּה אוֹתְךָ אֶל בְּנֵי יִשְׂרָאֵל הוּא:

כג קֹמָתוֹ. גֹּבַהּ רַגְלָיו עִם עֳבִי הַשֻּׁלְחָן:

כד זֵר זָהָב. סִימָן לְכֶתֶר מַלְכוּת, שֶׁהַשֻּׁלְחָן שֵׁם עֹשֶׁר וּגְדֻלָּה, כְּמוֹ שֶׁאוֹמְרִין שֻׁלְחָן מְלָכִים:

כה מִסְגֶּרֶת. כְּתַרְגּוּמוֹ "גְּדַנְפָא". וְנֶחְלְקוּ חַכְמֵי יִשְׂרָאֵל בַּדָּבָר, יֵשׁ אוֹמְרִים לְמַעְלָה הָיְתָה סָבִיב לַשֻּׁלְחָן, כְּמוֹ לְבִזְבְּזִין שֶׁבִּשְׂפַת שֻׁלְחָן שָׂרִים, וְיֵשׁ אוֹמְרִים לְמַטָּה הָיְתָה תְּקוּעָה מֵרֶגֶל לְרֶגֶל בְּאַרְבַּע רוּחוֹת הַשֻּׁלְחָן, וְדַף הַשֻּׁלְחָן

DISCUSSION

25:22 | **I will tell you, from upon the ark cover, from between the two cherubs:** The outstretched wings of the cherubs sheltered the Throne of Glory upon which God sits, as it were, while the Tablets of the Covenant in the Ark served as a footstool for His legs. For this reason, God is depicted in the Bible as sitting with the cherubs (I Samuel 4:4; Psalms 80:2). This recalls the vision of Moses, Aaron, Nadav and Avihu, and the seventy elders: "They saw the God of Israel, and under His feet was like a configuration of sapphire brick" (Exodus 24:10).

This sapphire footstool refers to the Tablets of the Covenant, which were made of stone, perhaps sapphire (see *Tanḥuma, Ki Tisa* 29; Rashi, Exodus 34:1), and which were stored in the ark.

26 You shall make for it four rings of gold, and you shall place the rings on the four corners that are on its, the table's, **four legs.**

27 Adjacent to the border the rings shall be, and they shall be used **as housings for the staves** that are used **to carry the table.**

28 You shall make the staves of acacia wood and you shall plate them with gold, and the table will be carried with them. Like the ark, the table should be carried from place to place by its staves.[8]

29 You shall also **make** accoutrements for the table: **Its bowls** to hold flour or dough; **and its spoons** for the frankincense;[9] **and its tubes [*uksotav*],** which formed a layered frame above the table on which to place the bread.[10] Some interpret this word to mean bowls in which the dough was kneaded.[11] **And its supports [*umnakiyotav*],** two posts on either side of the table, which would hold the layers of the frame like drawers.[12] These are the accoutrements **with which it,** the table, **shall be covered.** Others interpret *umnakiyotav* as denoting tools used for cleaning the oven. **From pure gold you shall make** all of **them.**

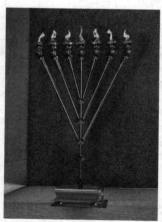

Spoon for frankincense

Table with the showbread

30 You shall place showbread [*leḥem panim*], literally "bread with a front," **upon the table,**[D] **before Me always.**

The Command to Fashion the Candelabrum

EXODUS 25:31–40

In addition to the ark, which represents the throne of God, and the table, God's "residence" also contained a candelabrum, corresponding to the light source an individual would have in his house.

31 You shall make a candelabrum of pure gold; the candelabrum shall be made hammered. Like the ark cover and its cherubs, the candelabrum was not fashioned by casting or by joining separate pieces, but by beating a single block of gold. **Its base**[D] **and its shaft,** its main trunk, or all its shafts: **its cups, its knobs, and its flowers,** decorations, the position of which are detailed below, **shall** all **be** fashioned **from it,** the same block of gold.

The candelabrum

32 Six branches shall emerge from its sides, three branches of the candelabrum from its one side and three branches of the candelabrum from its second side.

33 These are the decorations on the branches: **Three finely crafted [*meshukadim*] cups,**[13] or, according to another interpretation, cups that are made to look like almond blossoms, **on the one branch,** and also **a knob,** of a form unknown today, **and** an ornament in the shape of **a flower. And three finely crafted cups on the next branch, a knob and a flower;** and **so** forth **for the six branches that emerge from the candelabrum.** All the branches of the candelabrum were made of gold and had identical decorations of cups, knobs, and flowers.

DISCUSSION

25:30| You shall place showbread upon the table: The showbread was changed once a week (Leviticus 24:5–9). The Torah explains neither how the bread was to be prepared nor its precise shape. The Sages dispute whether the showbread was shaped like a box, open

כו זֵר־זָהָב לְמִסְגַּרְתּוֹ סָבִיב׃ וְעָשִׂיתָ לּוֹ אַרְבַּע טַבְּעֹת זָהָב וְנָתַתָּ אֶת־הַטַּבָּעֹת עַל
כז אַרְבַּע הַפֵּאֹת אֲשֶׁר לְאַרְבַּע רַגְלָיו׃ לְעֻמַּת הַמִּסְגֶּרֶת תִּהְיֶיןָ הַטַּבָּעֹת לְבָתִּים
כח לְבַדִּים לָשֵׂאת אֶת־הַשֻּׁלְחָן׃ וְעָשִׂיתָ אֶת־הַבַּדִּים עֲצֵי שִׁטִּים וְצִפִּיתָ אֹתָם זָהָב
כט וְנִשָּׂא־בָם אֶת־הַשֻּׁלְחָן׃ וְעָשִׂיתָ קְּעָרֹתָיו וְכַפֹּתָיו וּקְשׂוֹתָיו וּמְנַקִּיֹּתָיו אֲשֶׁר יֻסַּךְ
ל בָּהֵן זָהָב טָהוֹר תַּעֲשֶׂה אֹתָם׃ וְנָתַתָּ עַל־הַשֻּׁלְחָן לֶחֶם פָּנִים לְפָנַי תָּמִיד׃
לא וְעָשִׂיתָ מְנֹרַת זָהָב טָהוֹר מִקְשָׁה תֵּיעָשֶׂה הַמְּנוֹרָה יְרֵכָהּ וְקָנָהּ גְּבִיעֶיהָ כַּפְתֹּרֶיהָ
לב וּפְרָחֶיהָ מִמֶּנָּה יִהְיוּ׃ וְשִׁשָּׁה קָנִים יֹצְאִים מִצִּדֶּיהָ שְׁלֹשָׁה ׀ קְנֵי מְנֹרָה מִצִּדָּהּ הָאֶחָד
לג וּשְׁלֹשָׁה קְנֵי מְנֹרָה מִצִּדָּהּ הַשֵּׁנִי׃ שְׁלֹשָׁה גְבִעִים מְשֻׁקָּדִים בַּקָּנֶה הָאֶחָד כַּפְתֹּר
וָפֶרַח וּשְׁלֹשָׁה גְבִעִים מְשֻׁקָּדִים בַּקָּנֶה הָאֶחָד כַּפְתֹּר וָפָרַח כֵּן לְשֵׁשֶׁת הַקָּנִים

רש"י

סובב על אותה מסגרת: **ועשית זר זהב למסגרתו.** הוא זר האמור למעלה, ופרש לך כאן שעל המסגרת היה:

כז| **לעמת המסגרת תהיין הטבעות.** ברגלים תקועות כנגד ראשי המסגרת: **לבתים לבדים.** אותן הטבעות יהיו בתים להכנס בהן הבדים: **לבתים.** לצרך בתים: **לבדים.** כתרגומו: "לאתרא לאריחיא":

כח| **ונשא בם.** לשון נפעל, יהיה נשא בם את השלחן:

כט| **ועשית קערתיו וכפותיו.** קערותיו זה דפוס, שהיה עשוי כדפוס הלחם. והלחם היה עשוי כמין תבה פרוצה משתי רוחותיה, שולים לו למטה, וקופל מכאן ומכאן כלפי מעלה כמין כתלים. ולכך קרוי לחם הפנים, שיש לו פנים רואים לכאן ולכאן לצדי הבית מזה ומזה. ונותן ארכו לרחבו של שלחן, וכתליו זקופים כנגד שפת השלחן. והיה עשוי לו דפוס זהב ודפוס ברזל; בשל ברזל הוא נאפה, וכשמוציאו מן התנור נותנו בשל זהב עד למחר, בשבת, שמסדרו על השלחן, ואותו דפוס קרוי קערה: **וכפתיו.** בזיכין שנותנין בהם לבונה, שתים היו לשני קמצי לבונה שנותנין על שתי המערכות, שנאמר: "ונתת על המערכת לבנה זכה" (ויקרא כד, ז): **וקשותיו.** הן כמין חצאי קנים חלולים הנסדקין לארכן, דוגמתן עושה של זהב ומסדר שלשה על ראש כל לחם, שישב לחם האחד על גבי אותן הקנים, ומבדילין בין לחם ללחם כדי שתכנס הרוח ביניהם ולא יתעפשו. ובלשון ערבי כל דבר חלול קרוי קסו"א: **ומנקיתיו.** תרגומו "ומכילתיה", הן סניפין כמין יתדות זהב עומדין בארץ וגבוהין עד למעלה מן השלחן הרבה כנגד גבה מערכת הלחם, ומפצלים ששה פצולים, זה למעלה מזה, וראשי הקנים שבין לחם ללחם סמוכין על אותן פצולין, כדי שלא יכבד משא הלחם העליונים על התחתונים וישברו. ולשון "מכילתיה" סובלותיו, כמו: "נלאיתי הכיל" (ירמיה ו, יא). אבל לשון 'מנקית' איני יודע איך נופל על סניפין. ויש מחכמי ישראל אומרים, "קשותיו" אלו סניפין, שמקשין אותו ומחזיקים אותו שלא ישבר, "ומנקיתיו" אלו הקנים, שמנקין אותו שלא יתעפש. אבל אונקלוס שתרגם: "ומכילתיה" היה שונה כדברי האומר מנקיות הן סניפין: **אשר יסך בהן.** אשר יכסה בהן. ועל קשותיו הוא אומר: "אשר יסך", שהיו עליו כמין סכך וכסוי, וכן במקום אחר הוא אומר: "ואת קשות הנסך" (במדבר ד, ז). וזה וזה, 'יסך' ו'הנסך', לשון סכך וכסוי הם:

ל| **לחם פנים.** שהיו לו פנים כמו שפרשתי. ומנין הלחם וסדר מערכותיו מפרשים ב'אמר אל הכהנים' (ויקרא כד, ה-ט):

לא| **מקשה תיעשה המנורה.** שלא יעשנה חליות, ולא יעשה קניה ונרותיה אברים אברים ואחר כך ידביקם כדרך הצורפים שקורין סולדי"ן, אלא כלה באה מחתיכה אחת, ומקיש בקורנס וחותך בכלי האומנות ומפריד הקנים אילך ואילך. תרגומו של "מקשה": "נגיד", לשון המשכה, שממשיך האברים מן העשת לכאן ולכאן בהקשת הקורנס. ולשון "מקשה" מכת קורנס, בטדי"ן בלעז: **תיעשה המנורה.** מאליה, לפי שהיה משה מתקשה בה, אמר לו הקדוש ברוך הוא: השלך את הככר לאור והיא נעשית מאליה. לכך לא נכתב 'תעשה': **ירכה.** הוא הרגל שלמטה העשוי כמין תבה, ושלשת הרגלים יוצאין הימנה מטה: **וקנה.** הקנה האמצעי שלה העולה באמצע הירך זקוף כלפי מעלה, ועליו נר האמצעי עשוי כמין בזך לצוק השמן לתוכו ולתת הפתילה: **גביעיה.** הן כמין כוסות שעושין מזכוכית ארכים וקצרים, וקורין להם מדרינ"ש, ואלו עשויין של זהב ובולטין ויוצאין מכל קנה וקנה כמנין שנתן בהם הכתוב, ולא היו בה אלא לנוי: **כפתריה.** כמין תפוחים היו עגולין סביב, בולטין סביבות הקנה האמצעי, כדרך שעושין למנורות שלפני השרים וקורין להם פומיל"ש, ומנין שלהם כתוב בפרשה, כמה כפתורים בולטין ממנה וכמה חלק בין כפתור לכפתור: **ופרחיה.** ציורין עשויין בה כמין פרחים: **ממנה יהיו.** הכל מקשה יוצא מתוך חתיכת העשת, ולא יעשם לבדם וידביקם:

לב| **יצאים מצדיה.** לכאן ולכאן באלכסון, נמשכים ועולין עד כנגד גבהה של מנורה שהוא קנה האמצעי, ויוצאים מתוך קנה האמצעי זה למעלה מזה, התחתון ארוך ושל מעלה קצר הימנו והעליון קצר הימנו, לפי שהיה גבה ראשיהן שוה לגבהו של קנה האמצעי השביעי שממנו יוצאים הששה:

לג| **משקדים.** כתרגומו, מציירים היו כדרך שעושין לכלי כסף וזהב שקורין נייל"ר: **שלשה גבעים.** בולטין מכל קנה וקנה: **כפתר ופרח.** היה לכל קנה וקנה:

DISCUSSION

from two sides, or like a boat with a sloped hull (*Menaḥot* 94b).

25:31| **Its base:** According to rabbinic tradition, the base of the candelabrum had legs (see *Menaḥot* 28b). This does not match the image of the candelabrum on the Arch of Titus.

34 **On** the body of **the candelabrum,** meaning its central shaft, **four finely crafted [*meshukadim*] cups, with its knobs, and its flowers.** The special craftsmanship, possibly in the shape of almond blossom, may apply to the knobs and flowers as well. The Sages include this in a list of five cases in the Torah where the reference of a modifier is ambiguous.[14]

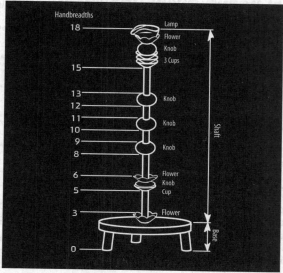

Parts of the shaft of the candelabrum

35 There shall be **a knob under the** first set of **two branches extending from it,** the body of the candelabrum, **and a knob under the** second set of **two branches extending from it, and a knob under the** third set of **two branches extending from**

it, so it shall be **for the six branches emerging from the candelabrum.** There was an ornamental knob at each point where the branches were joined to the central shaft.

36 The Torah reiterates: **Their knobs,** meaning the knobs of the branches, **and their branches,** meaning the branches themselves, **shall be** made **from it,** from the candelabrum itself; **all of it,** including its branches and ornamentation, **hammered of pure gold.**[D]

37 **You shall make its lamps,** receptacles for the oil and the wicks located on top of the branches, **seven,** six above the branches that extend on the sides and one on the main shaft of the candelabrum. **And he shall kindle** the wicks in **its lamps**[15] **so that it will illuminate toward its front.** All the flames were turned toward the central shaft or toward the area directly in front of it.[16]

38 **Its tongs,** used for handling the wicks, **and its pans,** small, spoon-like receptacles with flat bottoms that were open at the front, with which the burnt wicks and ash were removed from the lamps; these **shall be of pure gold.**

39 **He shall make it of a talent of pure gold with,** including in the total weight, **all these vessels.** The total weight of the candelabrum and its vessels shall be one talent of pure gold. Modern estimates of a talent range between 30 and 50 kg.

40 **See and craft**[D] the candelabrum and the other vessels **in their form, as you are shown on the mountain.** Despite the lengthy passage dealing with the candelabrum, it is difficult to describe such complex and detailed forms in words. Therefore, God showed Moses an image of the vessels in order to enable him to guide the craftsmen in their proper construction. Moses saw the heavenly Tabernacle, with all the forms of the vessels inside, and this vision filled in the details missing from the verses, allowing the artisans to recreate the vessels faithfully in the earthly Tabernacle.

DISCUSSION

25:36| Hammered of pure gold: Notwithstanding the great detail provided by the verses, many aspects of the construction of the candelabrum remain shrouded in mystery. The Torah does not specify whether the branches were curved or straight. The word used for "branch," *kaneh,* is indicative of a long, straight object, like a reed; however, in certain archaeological findings from the Second Temple period and later, as well as on the Arch of Titus, the branches of the candelabrum are depicted as curved. It should be noted that there are other significant differences between the candelabrum depicted on

the arch and the one in the Temple, and it is possible that the engraving there is the work of an artist who never saw the candelabrum. By contrast, in a painting of the candelabrum found in the ancient Dura-Europos synagogue in Syria (circa third century CE), the oldest known representation of the candelabrum from a communal Jewish institution, the branches are straight. Likewise, the sketch drawn by the Rambam features straight branches extending diagonally from the central shaft. Perhaps there were various candelabra in the First and Second Temples, of diverse forms.

In addition, the Torah does not state whether the branches turned in different directions or whether they were all on a single plane, nor does it specify the height of the candelabrum, only its great weight. According to rabbinic tradition it was three cubits tall, roughly 1.5 m (*Menaḥot* 28b). The volume of one talent of pure gold (see verse 39) is about 1,500 cubic cm, and one can therefore deduce mathematically that the branches of the candelabrum must have been thin.

לד הַיֹּצְאִים מִן־הַמְּנֹרָה׃ וּבַמְּנֹרָה אַרְבָּעָה גְבִעִים מְשֻׁקָּדִים כַּפְתֹּרֶיהָ וּפְרָחֶיהָ׃
לה וְכַפְתֹּר תַּחַת שְׁנֵי הַקָּנִים מִמֶּנָּה וְכַפְתֹּר תַּחַת שְׁנֵי הַקָּנִים מִמֶּנָּה וְכַפְתֹּר תַּחַת־
לו שְׁנֵי הַקָּנִים מִמֶּנָּה לְשֵׁשֶׁת הַקָּנִים הַיֹּצְאִים מִן־הַמְּנֹרָה׃ כַּפְתֹּרֵיהֶם וּקְנֹתָם
לז מִמֶּנָּה יִהְיוּ כֻּלָּהּ מִקְשָׁה אַחַת זָהָב טָהוֹר׃ וְעָשִׂיתָ אֶת־נֵרֹתֶיהָ שִׁבְעָה וְהֶעֱלָה
לח לט אֶת־נֵרֹתֶיהָ וְהֵאִיר עַל־עֵבֶר פָּנֶיהָ׃ וּמַלְקָחֶיהָ וּמַחְתֹּתֶיהָ זָהָב טָהוֹר׃ כִּכָּר זָהָב
מ טָהוֹר יַעֲשֶׂה אֹתָהּ אֵת כָּל־הַכֵּלִים הָאֵלֶּה׃ וּרְאֵה וַעֲשֵׂה בְּתַבְנִיתָם אֲשֶׁר־אַתָּה

רש"י

לד | **ובמנרה ארבעה גבעים.** בגופה של מנורה היו ארבעה גביעים, אחד בולט בה למטה מן הקנים, והשלשה למעלה מן יציאת הקנים היוצאים מצדיה: **משקדים כפתריה ופרחיה.** זה אחד מחמשה מקראות שאין להם הכרע, אין ידוע אם "גבעים משקדים" או "משקדים כפתריה ופרחיה":

לה | **וכפתר תחת שני הקנים.** מתוך הכפתור היו הקנים נמשכים משני צדיה אילך ואילך. כך שנינו במלאכת המשכן: גבהה של מנורה שמונה עשר טפחים. הרגלים והפרח שלשה טפחים, הוא הפרח האמור בירך, שנאמר: "עד ירכה עד פרחה" (במדבר ח, ד), וטפחים חלק, וטפח שבו גביע מהארבעה גביעים וכפתור ופרח משני כפתורים ושני פרחים האמורים במנורה עצמה, שנאמר: "משקדים כפתריה ופרחיה" (בפסוק הקודם), למדנו שהיו בקנה שני כפתורים ושני פרחים לבד מן השלשה כפתורים שהקנים נמשכין מתוכן, שנאמר: "וכפתר תחת שני הקנים" וגו', וטפחים חלק, וטפח כפתור, ושני קנים יוצאים ממנו אילך ואילך נמשכים ועולים כנגד גבהה של מנורה, וטפח חלק, וטפח כפתור, ושני קנים יוצאים ממנו, וטפח חלק, וטפח כפתור, ושני קנים יוצאים ממנו, וטפחים חלק, נשתיירו שם שלשה טפחים, שבהם שלשה גביעים וכפתור ופרח. נמצאו גביעים שנים ועשרים, שמונה עשרה לששה קנים שלשה לכל אחד ואחד, וארבעה בגופה של מנורה; ואחד עשר כפתורים, ששה בששת הקנים, ושלשה בגופה של מנורה שהקנים יוצאים מהם, ושנים עוד במנורה שנאמר: "משקדים כפתריה" ומעוט כפתורים שנים, האחד למטה אצל הירך והאחד בשלשה טפחים העליונים עם השלשה גביעים. ותשעה פרחים היו לה, ששה לששת הקנים, שנאמר: "בקנה האחד כפתר ופרח" (לעיל פסוק לג), ושלשה למנורה, שנאמר: "משקדים כפתריה ופרחיה" (בפסוק הקודם) ומעוט פרחים שנים, ואחד האמור בפרשת 'בהעלתך' (במדבר ח, ד) "עד ירכה עד פרחה". ואם תדקדק במשנה זו הכתובה למעלה תמצאם כמנינם איש איש במקומו:

לז | **את נרתיה.** כמין בזיכין שנותנין בתוכם השמן והפתילות: **והאיר על עבר פניה.** עשה פי ששת הנרות שבראשי הקנים היוצאים מצדיה מסבים כלפי האמצעי, כדי שיהיו הנרות כשתדליקם מאירים "אל עבר פניה", מוסב אורם אל צד פני הקנה האמצעי שהוא גוף המנורה:

לח | **ומלקחיה.** הם הצבתים העשוין ליקח בהם הפתילות מתוך השמן ליישבן ולמשכן בפי הנרות, ועל שם שלוקחים בהם קרויים מלקחים, ו"צבתהא" שתרגם אונקלוס, לשון צבת, טנייל"ש בלעז: **ומחתתיה.** הם כמין בזיכין קטנים שחותה בהן את האפר שבנר בבקר בבקר, כשהוא מטיב את הנרות מאפר הפתילות שדלקו הלילה וכבו. ולשון מחתה פושידור"א בלעז, כמו: "לחתות אש מיקוד" (ישעיה ל, יד):

לט | **ככר זהב טהור.** שלא יהיה משקלה עם כל כליה אלא ככר, לא פחות ולא יותר. והככר של חול ששים מנה, ושל קדש היה כפול, מאה ועשרים מנה, והמנה היא ליטרא ששוקלין בה כסף למשקל קולוניא, והם מאה זהובים, עשרים וחמשה סלעים, והסלע ארבעה זהובים:

מ | **וראה ועשה.** ראה כאן בהר תבנית שאני מראה אותך, מגיד שנתקשה משה במעשה המנורה עד שהראה לו הקדוש ברוך הוא מנורה של אש: **אשר אתה מראה.** כתרגומו: "דאת מתחזי בטורא". אלו היה נקוד 'מראה' בפתח, היה פתרונו, אתה מראה לאחרים, עכשיו שנקוד חטף קמץ, פתרונו 'דאת מתחזי', שאחרים מראים לך:

DISCUSSION

25:40| **See and craft:** One feature of the Sanctuary is notably missing from the instructions in this *parasha*: The instructions for constructing the incense altar (see 30:1–10) are not given until after the description of the cloth coverings of the Tabernacle, the structure of the Tabernacle itself, the courtyard, the altar for offerings located in the courtyard, and the priestly vestments. Since the Tabernacle was to be constructed in the likeness of a house, with its main vessels corresponding to a bed or chair, a table, and a lamp, the altar for incense was a luxurious addition: Historically, the wealthy would burn incense in their homes to provide a pleasing fragrance, mainly during mealtimes. Perhaps the altar of the incense was therefore seen as an addendum rather than a crucial part of the Tabernacle (see Sforno; *Adderet Eliyahu*; *HaKetav VehaKabbala*).

The Command to Prepare the Sheets for the Roof of the Tabernacle

EXODUS 26:1–14

As stated above, the order of the instruction about the vessels of the Tabernacle and its parts does not necessarily reflect the order of their construction. The verses first dealt with the preparation of the vessels, and only now do they turn to the Tabernacle itself, despite the logical necessity of erecting the structure before furnishing it. Indeed, when the Torah later describes the fulfillment of these instructions, the building of the outer structure precedes the fashioning of the vessels. With regard to the structure itself, there is also a difference between the command and its fulfillment: Moses is first instructed concerning the sheets that will cover the Tabernacle, and only afterward does he receive instruction with regard to its walls and boundaries.

26 **1** **You shall make the Tabernacle of ten sheets** made **of spun**
Third **white linen,**[17] **and** dyed woolen threads shall be spun into it:
aliya **Threads of sky-blue, purple, and scarlet wool. With artfully worked** likenesses of **cherubs shall you make them,** the
sheets. High-level craftsmanship was required to render the
form of cherubs on every sheet. According to some opinions,
there was a different picture on each side of the fabric.[18]

2 **The length of each sheet shall be twenty-eight cubits and
the width** shall be **four cubits for each sheet; there shall be
one measure for all the sheets.**

3 **Five of the** ten **sheets shall be attached one to another:** They
must be sewn into a single unit; **and five sheets shall be attached one to another** in the same fashion.

4 **You shall make loops of sky-blue wool,** sewn **on the edge of
the sheet, at the extremity,** at the end **of the first array** of five
sheets; **and you shall do likewise,** making loops of dyed, sky-
blue wool, **at the edge of the outermost sheet** at the edge **of
the second array** of five sheets.

5 **Fifty loops shall you make in the one sheet, and fifty loops
you shall make at the extremity of the sheet that is in the
second array; the loops shall correspond one to another,**
fifty loops facing fifty loops.

6 **You shall make fifty hooks of gold and attach the sheets
one to another with the hooks.** Each pair of loops were
held together by a gold hook. All the Tabernacle's sheets were
thus to be joined together. **And the Tabernacle shall be one,**
a single unit. The Rashbam explains that the use of the word
"Tabernacle" here denotes only the sheets rather than the structure as a whole. His interpretation is supported in subsequent
verses.[19]

7 In addition to the first set of sheets, which were made of dyed
wool and linen, and can be considered part of the Tabernacle
itself, **you shall make sheets of goats' hair as a tent over the
Tabernacle,** a second layer over the aforementioned cover;
you shall make them eleven sheets.

8 **The length of each sheet shall be thirty cubits and the width
of each sheet four cubits; one measure for eleven sheets.**

9 **You shall attach five sheets alone and six sheets alone;**[D] five
of the sheets shall be one unit, while the other six shall form
a separate unit. **And** after the tent has been erected, **you shall
fold** half of the width of **the sixth sheet** (see verse 12) and let it
hang down over the roof's edge **at the front of the tent.**[20]

DISCUSSION

Are the details significant?: In reviewing
the descriptions of the various coverings of the
Tabernacle, the question arises: What is the significance of the specifications in each description,
e.g., ten sheets of linen and wool divided into two
arrays of five sheets; eleven sheets of goats' hair
divided into two arrays, one of five sheets and
one of six sheets, and so on.

The Rambam, in his *Guide of the Perplexed*, addressed similar examples of this phenomenon:

We cannot say why one offering should be
a lamb, while another is a ram; and why a fixed
number of them should be brought. Those who
trouble themselves to find a cause for any of these
detailed rules are in my eyes void of sense; they
do not remove any difficulties, but rather increase
them. Those who believe that these detailed rules
originate in a certain cause are as far from the
truth as those who assume that the whole law is

useless. You must know that divine wisdom demanded it or, if you prefer, say that circumstances
made it necessary… That it cannot be avoided
may be seen from the following instance. You
ask why a lamb must be sacrificed and not a ram.
But the same question would be asked, why a
ram had been commanded instead of a lamb, so
long as one particular kind is required. The same
is to be said as to the question why seven lambs
were sacrificed and not eight; the same question
might have been asked if there were eight, ten, or
twenty lambs, so long as some definite number
of lambs was sacrificed. (3:26)

The Rambam is saying that although divine
wisdom dictated these details, it is futile to ask
why, whether the details are of the numbers of
lambs and rams or in this case sheets of wool and
linen.

The *Or Haḥayyim* disagrees. He explains
that the ten sheets are an allusion to the ten
statements with which the world was created,
indicating that the Tabernacle parallels the world,
and through the Tabernacle, the children of Israel
draw merit for sustaining the world.

He continues by explaining that God commanded that all of the sheets be four cubits wide
as an allusion to the Tetragrammaton, the four-
letter name of God. The ten wool and linen sheets
allude to the letter *yod*, the first of the four letters.
The arrays of five sheets each of linen and wool
allude to the *heh*, the second letter. The sheets of
goats' hair were divided into an array of six sheets,
alluding to the letter *vav*, the third letter, and an
array of five sheets, alluding to the letter *heh*, the
fourth letter. The *Or Haḥayyim* continues with
explanations of further symbolism and parallels
reflected in the configuration of the Tabernacle.

כו א מַרְאֶה בָּהָר: וְאֶת־הַמִּשְׁכָּן תַּעֲשֶׂה עֶשֶׂר יְרִיעֹת שֵׁשׁ מָשְׁזָר וּתְכֵלֶת יט שלישי
ב וְאַרְגָּמָן וְתֹלַעַת שָׁנִי כְּרֻבִים מַעֲשֵׂה חֹשֵׁב תַּעֲשֶׂה אֹתָם: אֹרֶךְ ׀ הַיְרִיעָה הָאַחַת
שְׁמֹנֶה וְעֶשְׂרִים בָּאַמָּה וְרֹחַב אַרְבַּע בָּאַמָּה הַיְרִיעָה הָאֶחָת מִדָּה אַחַת לְכָל־
ג הַיְרִיעֹת: חֲמֵשׁ הַיְרִיעֹת תִּהְיֶיןָ חֹבְרֹת אִשָּׁה אֶל־אֲחֹתָהּ וְחָמֵשׁ יְרִיעֹת חֹבְרֹת
ד אִשָּׁה אֶל־אֲחֹתָהּ: וְעָשִׂיתָ לֻלְאֹת תְּכֵלֶת עַל שְׂפַת הַיְרִיעָה הָאֶחָת מִקָּצָה
ה בַּחֹבָרֶת וְכֵן תַּעֲשֶׂה בִּשְׂפַת הַיְרִיעָה הַקִּיצוֹנָה בַּמַּחְבֶּרֶת הַשֵּׁנִית: חֲמִשִּׁים לֻלָאֹת
תַּעֲשֶׂה בַּיְרִיעָה הָאֶחָת וַחֲמִשִּׁים לֻלָאֹת תַּעֲשֶׂה בִּקְצֵה הַיְרִיעָה אֲשֶׁר בַּמַּחְבֶּרֶת
ו הַשֵּׁנִית מַקְבִּילֹת הַלֻּלָאֹת אִשָּׁה אֶל־אֲחֹתָהּ: וְעָשִׂיתָ חֲמִשִּׁים קַרְסֵי זָהָב וְחִבַּרְתָּ
ז אֶת־הַיְרִיעֹת אִשָּׁה אֶל־אֲחֹתָהּ בַּקְּרָסִים וְהָיָה הַמִּשְׁכָּן אֶחָד: וְעָשִׂיתָ יְרִיעֹת
ח עִזִּים לְאֹהֶל עַל־הַמִּשְׁכָּן עַשְׁתֵּי־עֶשְׂרֵה יְרִיעֹת תַּעֲשֶׂה אֹתָם: אֹרֶךְ ׀ הַיְרִיעָה
הָאַחַת שְׁלֹשִׁים בָּאַמָּה וְרֹחַב אַרְבַּע בָּאַמָּה הַיְרִיעָה הָאֶחָת מִדָּה אַחַת לְעַשְׁתֵּי
ט עֶשְׂרֵה יְרִיעֹת: וְחִבַּרְתָּ אֶת־חֲמֵשׁ הַיְרִיעֹת לְבָד וְאֶת־שֵׁשׁ הַיְרִיעֹת לְבָד וְכָפַלְתָּ

רש״י

פרק כו

א| **וְאֶת הַמִּשְׁכָּן תַּעֲשֶׂה עֶשֶׂר יְרִיעֹת.** לִהְיוֹת לוֹ לְגַג וְלִמְחִצּוֹת מִחוּץ לַקְּרָשִׁים, שֶׁהַיְרִיעוֹת תְּלוּיוֹת מֵאֲחוֹרֵיהֶן לְכַסּוֹתָן: **שֵׁשׁ מָשְׁזָר וּתְכֵלֶת וְאַרְגָּמָן וְתֹלַעַת שָׁנִי.** הֲרֵי אַרְבָּעָה מִינִין בְּכָל חוּט וְחוּט, אֶחָד שֶׁל פִּשְׁתִּים וּשְׁלֹשָׁה שֶׁל צֶמֶר, וְכָל מִין וּמִין חוּטוֹ כָּפוּל שִׁשָּׁה, הֲרֵי אַרְבָּעָה מִינִין כְּשֶׁהֵן שְׁזוּרִין יַחַד עֶשְׂרִים וְאַרְבָּעָה כְּפָלִים לַחוּט: **כְּרֻבִים מַעֲשֵׂה חֹשֵׁב.** כְּרוּבִים הָיוּ מְצֻיָּרִין בָּהֶם בַּאֲרִיגָתָן, וְלֹא בִּרְקִימָה שֶׁהוּא מַעֲשֵׂה מַחַט, אֶלָּא בַּאֲרִיגָה בִּשְׁנֵי כְּתָלִים, פַּרְצוּף אֶחָד מִכָּאן וּפַרְצוּף אֶחָד מִכָּאן, אֲרִי מִצַּד זֶה וְנֶשֶׁר מִצַּד זֶה, כְּמוֹ שֶׁאוֹרְגִין חֲגוֹרוֹת שֶׁל מֶשִׁי שֶׁקּוֹרִין בְּלַעַז פיישׁ״שׂ:

ג| **תִּהְיֶיןָ חֹבְרֹת.** תּוֹפְרָן בְּמַחַט זוֹ בְּצַד זוֹ, חָמֵשׁ לְבַד וְחָמֵשׁ לְבַד: **אִשָּׁה אֶל אֲחֹתָהּ.** כָּךְ דֶּרֶךְ הַמִּקְרָא לְדַבֵּר בְּדָבָר שֶׁהוּא לְשׁוֹן נְקֵבָה; וּבְדָבָר שֶׁהוּא לְשׁוֹן זָכָר אוֹמֵר: 'אִישׁ אֶל אָחִיו', כְּמוֹ שֶׁנֶּאֱמַר בַּכְּרוּבִים: "וּפְנֵיהֶם אִישׁ אֶל אָחִיו" (לעיל כה, כ):

ד| **לֻלְאֹת.** לַצוּל״שׂ בְּלַעַז, וְכֵן תִּרְגֵּם אוּנְקְלוֹס: "עֲנוּבִין", לְשׁוֹן עֲנִיבָה: **מִקָּצָה בַּחֹבָרֶת.** בְּאוֹתָהּ יְרִיעָה שֶׁבְּסוֹף הַחִבּוּר, קְבוּצַת חֲמֵשֶׁת הַיְרִיעוֹת קְרוּיָה חוֹבֶרֶת: **וְכֵן תַּעֲשֶׂה בִּשְׂפַת הַיְרִיעָה הַקִּיצוֹנָה בַּמַּחְבֶּרֶת הַשֵּׁנִית.** בְּאוֹתָהּ יְרִיעָה שֶׁהִיא קִיצוֹנָה, לְשׁוֹן קָצֶה, כְּלוֹמַר לְסוֹף הַחוֹבֶרֶת:

ה| **מַקְבִּילֹת הַלֻּלָאֹת אִשָּׁה אֶל אֲחֹתָהּ.** שְׁמֹר שֶׁתַּעֲשֶׂה הַלּוּלָאוֹת מְכֻוָּנוֹת בְּמִדָּה אַחַת הַבְדָּלָתָן זוֹ מִזּוֹ, וּכְמִדָּתָן בִּירִיעָה זוֹ כֵּן יְהֵא בַּחֲבֶרְתָּהּ, כְּשֶׁתִּפְרֹשׂ חוֹבֶרֶת אֵצֶל חוֹבֶרֶת יִהְיוּ הַלּוּלָאוֹת שֶׁל יְרִיעָה זוֹ מְכֻוָּנוֹת כְּנֶגֶד לוּלָאוֹת שֶׁל זוֹ. וְזֶהוּ לְשׁוֹן 'מַקְבִּילֹת', זוֹ כְּנֶגֶד זוֹ, תַּרְגּוּמוֹ שֶׁל 'נֶגֶד' (לעיל י, י) – 'לָקֳבֵל'. הַיְרִיעוֹת אָרְכָּן עֶשְׂרִים וּשְׁמוֹנֶה וְרָחְבָּן אַרְבַּע, וּכְשֶׁחִבֵּר חָמֵשׁ יְרִיעוֹת יַחַד נִמְצָא רָחְבָּן עֶשְׂרִים, וְכֵן הַחוֹבֶרֶת הַשֵּׁנִית. וְהַמִּשְׁכָּן אָרְכּוֹ שְׁלֹשִׁים מִן הַמִּזְרָח לַמַּעֲרָב, שֶׁנֶּאֱמַר: "עֶשְׂרִים קְרָשִׁים לִפְאַת נֶגְבָּה תֵימָנָה" (להלן לו, כג; כעין זה להלן פסוק יח), וְכֵן לַצָּפוֹן (להלן פסוק כ), וְכָל קֶרֶשׁ אַמָּה וַחֲצִי הָאַמָּה (להלן פסוק טז), הֲרֵי שְׁלֹשִׁים מִן הַמִּזְרָח לַמַּעֲרָב. רֹחַב הַמִּשְׁכָּן מִן הַצָּפוֹן לַדָּרוֹם עֶשֶׂר אַמּוֹת, שֶׁנֶּאֱמַר: "וּלְיַרְכְּתֵי הַמִּשְׁכָּן יָמָּה וְגוֹ' וּשְׁנֵי קְרָשִׁים... לִמְקֻצְעֹת" (להלן פסוקים כב-כג) הֲרֵי עֶשֶׂר, וּבִמְקוֹמָם אֲפָרְשֵׁם לַמִּקְרָאוֹת הַלָּלוּ. נוֹתֵן הַיְרִיעוֹת אָרְכָּן לְרָחְבּוֹ שֶׁל מִשְׁכָּן, עֶשֶׂר אַמּוֹת הָאֶמְצָעִיּוֹת לְגַג חֲלַל רֹחַב הַמִּשְׁכָּן, וְאַמָּה מִכָּאן וְאַמָּה מִכָּאן לְעֳבִי רָאשֵׁי הַקְּרָשִׁים, שֶׁעָבְיָן אַמָּה, נִשְׁתַּיְּרוּ שֵׁשׁ עֶשְׂרֵה אַמָּה, שְׁמוֹנֶה לַצָּפוֹן וּשְׁמוֹנֶה לַדָּרוֹם, מְכַסּוֹת קוֹמַת הַקְּרָשִׁים שֶׁגָּבְהָן עֶשֶׂר, נִמְצְאוּ שְׁתֵּי אַמּוֹת הַתַּחְתּוֹנוֹת מְגֻלּוֹת. רָחְבָּן שֶׁל יְרִיעוֹת אַרְבָּעִים אַמָּה כְּשֶׁהֵן מְחֻבָּרוֹת, עֶשְׂרִים אַמָּה לְחוֹבֶרֶת. שְׁלֹשִׁים מֵהֶן לְגַג חֲלַל הַמִּשְׁכָּן לְאָרְכּוֹ, וְאַמָּה כְּנֶגֶד עֳבִי רָאשֵׁי הַקְּרָשִׁים שֶׁבַּמַּעֲרָב, וְאַמָּה לְכַסּוֹת עֳבִי הָעַמּוּדִים שֶׁבַּמִּזְרָח, שֶׁלֹּא הָיוּ קְרָשִׁים בַּמִּזְרָח אֶלָּא אַרְבָּעָה עַמּוּדִים שֶׁהַמָּסָךְ פָּרוּשׂ וְתָלוּי בָּוִין שֶׁבָּהֶן כְּמִין וִילוֹן, נִשְׁתַּיְּרוּ שְׁמוֹנֶה אַמּוֹת הַתְּלוּיִין עַל אֲחוֹרֵי הַמִּשְׁכָּן שֶׁבַּמַּעֲרָב, וּשְׁתֵּי אַמּוֹת הַתַּחְתּוֹנוֹת מְגֻלּוֹת. זוֹ מָצָאתִי בַּבָּרַיְתָא דְּאַרְבָּעִים וָתֵשַׁע מִדּוֹת. אֲבָל בְּמַסֶּכֶת שַׁבָּת (דף צח ע״ב) אֵין הַיְרִיעוֹת מְכַסּוֹת אֶת עַמּוּדֵי הַמִּזְרָח, וְתֵשַׁע אַמּוֹת תְּלוּיוֹת אֲחוֹרֵי הַמִּשְׁכָּן, וְהַכָּתוּב מְסַיְּעֵנוּ: "וְנָתַתָּה אֶת הַפָּרֹכֶת תַּחַת הַקְּרָסִים" (להלן פסוק לג), וְאִם כְּדִבְרֵי הַבָּרַיְתָא הַזֹּאת, נִמְצֵאת פָּרֹכֶת מְשׁוּכָה מִן הַקְּרָסִים וְלַמַּעֲרָב אַמָּה:

ו| **קַרְסֵי זָהָב.** פירמיל״ש בְּלַעַז, וּמַכְנִיסִין רֹאשָׁן אֶחָד בַּלּוּלָאוֹת שֶׁבְּחוֹבֶרֶת זוֹ וְרֹאשָׁן אֶחָד בַּלּוּלָאוֹת שֶׁבְּחוֹבֶרֶת זוֹ וּמְחַבְּרָן בָּהֶן:

ז| **יְרִיעֹת עִזִּים.** מִנּוֹצָה שֶׁל עִזִּים: **לְאֹהֶל עַל הַמִּשְׁכָּן.** לִפְרֹשׂ אוֹתָן עַל הַיְרִיעוֹת הַתַּחְתּוֹנוֹת:

ח| **שְׁלֹשִׁים בָּאַמָּה.** שֶׁכְּשֶׁנּוֹתֵן אָרְכָּן לְרֹחַב הַמִּשְׁכָּן כְּמוֹ שֶׁנָּתַן אֶת הָרִאשׁוֹנוֹת, נִמְצְאוּ אֵלּוּ עוֹדְפוֹת אַמָּה מִכָּאן וְאַמָּה מִכָּאן, לְכַסּוֹת אַחַת מֵהַשְּׁתַּיִם אַמּוֹת שֶׁנִּשְׁאֲרוּ מְגֻלּוֹת בַּקְּרָשִׁים. וְהָאַמָּה הַתַּחְתּוֹנָה שֶׁל קֶרֶשׁ שֶׁאֵין הַיְרִיעָה מְכַסָּה אוֹתוֹ, הִיא הָאַמָּה הַתְּחוּבָה בְּנֶקֶב הָאֶדֶן, שֶׁהָאֲדָנִים גָּבְהָן אַמָּה:

ט| **וְכָפַלְתָּ אֶת הַיְרִיעָה הַשִּׁשִּׁית.** שֶׁעוֹדֶפֶת בְּאֵלּוּ הָעֶלְיוֹנוֹת יוֹתֵר מִן הַתַּחְתּוֹנוֹת: **אֶל מוּל פְּנֵי הָאֹהֶל.** חֲצִי רָחְבָּהּ הָיָה תָּלוּי וְכָפוּל עַל הַמָּסָךְ שֶׁבַּמִּזְרָח כְּנֶגֶד הַפֶּתַח, דּוֹמֶה לְכַלָּה צְנוּעָה הַמְכֻסָּה בְּצָעִיף עַל פָּנֶיהָ:

10 **You shall make fifty loops on the edge of the one sheet, the outermost of the first array, and fifty loops on the edge of the** outermost **sheet of the second array.**

11 **You shall make fifty hooks of bronze, and you shall place the hooks into the loops and attach the tent, and it shall be one.**[D] Together these sheets formed a tent, which was laid over the wool and linen sheets that served as the roof of the Tabernacle.

12 As there was one extra sheet of goats' hair over and above the length of the tent itself, and only half of it was hung over the front of the tent (verse 9), half a length of a sheet remained. **The overhang that remains of the sheets of the tent, half the sheet that remains shall hang over** the ground at **the back of the Tabernacle,** where there is no entrance.

13 The cover of goats' hair was larger than the linen and wool cover of the Tabernacle not only in its length, which comprised the widths of each section, but also in its breadth, which corresponded to each section's length. The length of each sheet of goats' hair was 30 cubits, while that of the cloth sheets of the Tabernacle was 28 cubits. With regard to these two extra cubits, **the cubit on this side and the cubit on that side, from that which remains of the length of the sheets of the tent, shall hang over the sides of the Tabernacle on this side and on that side, to cover it.** These sheets hung over the boards of the Tabernacle, which served as its walls.

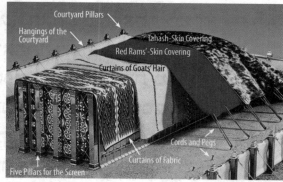

Cutaway view of the tent covers

14 **You shall make a cover for the** goats' hair **tent.** This covering shall be **of rams' hides dyed red and** a fourth layer, **a cover of *tahash* hides over the top.**[21] According to some opinions, there were only three layers, and the outermost one was made half of rams' hides and half of *tahash* hides.[22]

The Command to Build the Walls of the Tabernacle

EXODUS 26:15–37

The sheets of wool and skins that covered the Tabernacle and hung down over its outer edges were described above. Now God instructs Moses with regard to the boards of the Tabernacle; its outer walls and inner partitions. Some of these were made of hard materials such as acacia wood or metals, while others were made from embroidered textiles.

15 **You shall make the boards for the Tabernacle of** sanded boards of **acacia wood.**[23] The boards must be constructed **standing upright,** oriented in the manner that the trees grow.[24] Some understand this as an instruction that the boards should be sturdy.[25]

Fourth aliya

16 **Ten cubits shall be the length of a board,** of each one. Because the boards were positioned upright, this was also the height of the Tabernacle. **And one and a half cubits** shall be **the width of each board.**

17 **Two tenons,** pegs, **for each board** will protrude from the edges, **parallel one to another.**[D] Due to their height, the boards needed to be supported. To accomplish this, protruding pegs were placed in each board opposite corresponding sockets in the next board. The boards were placed side by side, so that the protruding tenons fit into the sockets. **So you shall make for all the boards of the Tabernacle.**

18 **You shall make the boards for the Tabernacle. Twenty boards** shall be constructed **for** placement on **the southern side.**

19 **You shall make forty silver sockets**[D] **under the twenty boards: Two sockets under the one board for its two tenons,** protrusions at the bottom of the boards, **and two sockets**

DISCUSSION

26:11| **And attach the tent, and it shall be one:** The Tabernacle was constructed from many parts that were subsequently joined together. The lower layer of sheets, which was woven by craftsmen and was visible to those inside the Tabernacle, was made into a single unit by attaching the sheets together with the sky-blue loops and clasps of gold. The second layer, which faced outward, was made of sheets woven of goats' hair that attached by loops and clasps of bronze.

26:17| **Parallel one to another:** The translation here follows the interpretation of Rabbi Neḥemya, as explained by the Rambam, that the tenons extended from the edges of the boards to be inserted in the neighboring boards. Others maintain that the protrusions were at the bottom of the boards for insertion in the sockets, as detailed in the following verses.

י אֶת־הַיְרִיעָה הַשִּׁשִּׁית אֶל־מוּל פְּנֵי הָאֹהֶל: וְעָשִׂיתָ חֲמִשִּׁים לֻלָאֹת עַל שְׂפַת
הַיְרִיעָה הָאֶחָת הַקִּיצֹנָה בַּחֹבָרֶת וַחֲמִשִּׁים לֻלָאֹת עַל שְׂפַת הַיְרִיעָה הַחֹבֶרֶת
יא הַשֵּׁנִית: וְעָשִׂיתָ קַרְסֵי נְחֹשֶׁת חֲמִשִּׁים וְהֵבֵאתָ אֶת־הַקְּרָסִים בַּלֻּלָאֹת וְחִבַּרְתָּ
יב אֶת־הָאֹהֶל וְהָיָה אֶחָד: וְסֶרַח הָעֹדֵף בִּירִיעֹת הָאֹהֶל חֲצִי הַיְרִיעָה הָעֹדֶפֶת תִּסְרַח
יג עַל אֲחֹרֵי הַמִּשְׁכָּן: וְהָאַמָּה מִזֶּה וְהָאַמָּה מִזֶּה בָּעֹדֵף בְּאֹרֶךְ יְרִיעֹת הָאֹהֶל יִהְיֶה
יד סָרוּחַ עַל־צִדֵּי הַמִּשְׁכָּן מִזֶּה וּמִזֶּה לְכַסֹּתוֹ: וְעָשִׂיתָ מִכְסֶה לָאֹהֶל עֹרֹת אֵילִם
מְאָדָּמִים וּמִכְסֵה עֹרֹת תְּחָשִׁים מִלְמָעְלָה:
טו טז וְעָשִׂיתָ אֶת־הַקְּרָשִׁים לַמִּשְׁכָּן עֲצֵי שִׁטִּים עֹמְדִים: עֶשֶׂר אַמּוֹת אֹרֶךְ הַקָּרֶשׁ רביעי
יז וְאַמָּה וַחֲצִי הָאַמָּה רֹחַב הַקֶּרֶשׁ הָאֶחָד: שְׁתֵּי יָדוֹת לַקֶּרֶשׁ הָאֶחָד מְשֻׁלָּבֹת
יח אִשָּׁה אֶל־אֲחֹתָהּ כֵּן תַּעֲשֶׂה לְכֹל קַרְשֵׁי הַמִּשְׁכָּן: וְעָשִׂיתָ אֶת־הַקְּרָשִׁים לַמִּשְׁכָּן
יט עֶשְׂרִים קֶרֶשׁ לִפְאַת נֶגְבָּה תֵימָנָה: וְאַרְבָּעִים אַדְנֵי־כֶסֶף תַּעֲשֶׂה תַּחַת עֶשְׂרִים

רש״י

יב-יג | **וסרח העדף ביריעת האהל.** על יריעות המשכן. ׳יריעת האהל׳ הן העליונות של עזים שקרויים אהל, כמו שאמור בהן: ״לאהל על המשכן״ (לעיל פסוק ז), וכל אהל האמור בהן אינו אלא לשון גג, שמאהילות ומסככות על התחתונות. והן היו עודפות על התחתונות חצי היריעה למערב, שהחצי של יריעה אחת עשרה היתרה היה נכפל אל מול פני האהל, נשארו שתי אמות רוחב יריעה עודף על רוחב התחתונות: **תסרח על אחרי המשכן.** לכסות שתי אמות שהיו מגלות בקרשים: **והאמה מזה והאמה מזה.** לצפון ולדרום: **בעדף בארך יריעת האהל.** שהן עודפות על אורך יריעות המשכן שתי אמות: **יהיה סרוח על צדי המשכן.** לצפון ולדרום, כמו שפירשתי למעלה. למדה תורה דרך ארץ, שיהא אדם חס על היפה: **אחרי המשכן.** הוא צד המערב, לפי שהפתח במזרח שהן פניו, וצפון ודרום קרויין צדדין לימין ולשמאל:

יד | **מכסה לאהל.** לאותו גג של יריעות עזים, עשה עוד מכסה אחד של ״ערת אילם מאדמים״, ועוד למעלה ממנו ״מכסה ערת תחשים״, ואותן מכסאות לא היו מכסין אלא את הגג, ארכן שלשים ורחבן עשר, אלו דברי רבי נחמיה. ולדברי רבי יהודה מכסה אחד היה, חציו של עורות אילים מאדמים וחציו של עורות תחשים:

טו | **ועשית את הקרשים.** היה לו לומר: ׳ועשית קרשים׳, כמו שנאמר בכל דבר ודבר. מהו ״הקרשים״? מאותן העומדין ומיוחדין לכך; יעקב אבינו נטע ארזים במצרים, וכשמת צוה לבניו להעלותם עמהם כשיצאו ממצרים, ואמר להם שעתיד הקדוש ברוך הוא לצוות אותן לעשות משכן במדבר מעצי שטים, ראו שיהיו מזומנים בידכם. הוא שיסד הבבלי בפיוט שלו: ״טס מטע מזרזים, קורות בתינו ארזים״ (יוצר ליום ראשון של פסח), שנזדרזו להיות מוכנים בידם מקודם לכן: **עצי שטים עמדים.** אישטנטיב״ש בלעז, שיהא אורך הקרשים זקוף למעלה בקירות המשכן, ולא תעשה הכתלים בקרשים שוכבים להיות רוחב הקרשים לגובה הכתלים קרש על קרש:

טז | **עשר אמות ארך הקרש.** למדנו גבהו של משכן עשר אמות: **ואמה וחצי האמה רחב.** למדנו ארכו של משכן לעשרים קרשים שהיו בצפון ובדרום מן המזרח למערב, שלשים אמה:

יז | **שתי ידות לקרש האחד.** היה חורץ את הקרש מלמטה באמצעו בגובה אמה, מניח רביע רחבו מכאן ורביע רחבו מכאן והן הן הידות, והחריץ חצי רוחב הקרש באמצע. ואותן הידות מכניס באדנים שהיו חלולים, והאדנים גבהן אמה ויושבים רצופים ארבעים זה אצל זה. וידות הקרש הנכנסות בחלל האדנים חרוצות משלשת צדיהן, רוחב החריץ כעובי שפת האדן, שיכסה הקרש את כל ראש האדן, שאם לא כן נמצא ריוח בין קרש לקרש כעובי שפת שני האדנים שיפסיקו ביניהם, וזהו שנאמר: ״ויהיו תאמם מלמטה״ (להלן פסוק כד), שיחרוץ את צדי הידות כדי שיתחברו הקרשים זה אצל זה: **משלבת.** עשויות כמין שליבות סולם מובדלות זו מזו, ומשופין ראשיהם ליכנס בתוך חלל האדן כשליבה הנכנסת בנקב עמודי הסולם: **אשה אל אחתה.** מכוונות זו כנגד זו, שיהיו אריעיהם שוים זו כמדת זו, כדי שלא יהיו שתי ידות זו משוכה לצד פנים וזו משוכה לצד חוץ בעובי הקרש שהוא אמה. ותרגום של ״ידות״ – ״צירין״, לפי שדומות לצירי הדלת הנכנסים בחורי המפתן:

יח | **לפאת נגבה תימנה.** אין ׳פאה׳ זו לשון מקצוע, אלא כל הרוח קרויה פאה. כתרגומו: ״לרוח עבר דרומא״:

DISCUSSION

26:19| **Forty silver sockets:** The weight of each socket was one talent of silver (see 38:27), which means that two sockets weighed roughly 60 kg. Metal pieces of this weight were able to stabilize the large, heavy boards.

under the one board for its two tenons. These protruding tenons were inserted into the hollow sockets below them, which held the boards in place.

Socket and tenons

20 **For the second side of the Tabernacle, for the north side: twenty boards,**
21 **and their forty sockets of silver: two sockets under the one board and two sockets under the one board.** The arrangements of boards and sockets on the southern and northern sides of the Tabernacle were identical.
22 **For the side of the Tabernacle on the west,**[D] **you shall make** only **six boards,** as the Tabernacle's length and width were unequal.
23 **And you shall make two** additional **boards for the corners of the Tabernacle on the sides.** The aforementioned six boards spanned the western side of the Tabernacle from the inside. However, an additional two boards were required on either side to cover the width of the northern and southern walls.[26]
24 **They,** the boards, **shall be even at the bottom,** at the level of the sockets, and matching along their entire length.[27] **And they shall meet together at its top,** at **its one ring,** a ring at the top of each pair of boards which will bind them together. **So it shall** also **be for two of them,** the two extra planks mentioned above; **they shall be for the two corners.**
25 **There shall be** on the west side a total of **eight boards, and their silver sockets: sixteen sockets, two sockets under the one board and two sockets under the one board.** This is how the overall structure of the Tabernacle was built, on the western, northern, and southern sides.
26 **You shall make bars of acacia wood** to hold the boards together: **Five for the boards of the one side of the Tabernacle,**
27 **and five bs for the boards of the second side of the Tabernacle, and five bars for the boards of the side of the**

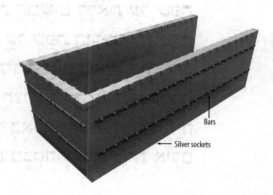

Structure of the Tabernacle

Tabernacle, for the side to the west. Four of these bars extended from each board on the outside, two on its right side and two on its left, on the upper and lower parts of the boards. Each spanned half the width of the board, and they met in the middle.
28 **And the** fifth, **central bar shall be inside the boards.** A hole was made through the width of the boards, and through it ran the fifth board, **from the end to the end.** Unlike the other four bars, the fifth bar spanned the entire width of the board.[28]
29 **You shall plate the boards with gold, and their rings,** which join them together, **you shall make of gold.** These rings shall be **housings for the bars. And you shall plate the bars with gold** as well.

Board and bars

DISCUSSION

26:22| **On the west:** According to many traditions, the direction east is considered sacred. However, the descriptions of the Tabernacle indicate that its west side possessed greater sanctity. In contemporary Judaism, emphasis is often placed on the east, since the Land of Israel was historically east of the Jews living in Europe, who therefore would always pray eastward. However, both in the Tabernacle in the wilderness and in the Temple in Jerusalem, the Holy of Holies was located in the west, while the east served as the entrance for worshippers facing westward toward the divine abode (*Bava Batra* 25a; *Shemot Rabba* 2:2).

הַקָּרֶשׁ שְׁנֵי אֲדָנִים תַּחַת־הַקֶּרֶשׁ הָאֶחָד לִשְׁתֵּי יְדֹתָיו וּשְׁנֵי אֲדָנִים תַּחַת־הַקֶּרֶשׁ
כ כא הָאֶחָד לִשְׁתֵּי יְדֹתָיו׃ וּלְצֶלַע הַמִּשְׁכָּן הַשֵּׁנִית לִפְאַת צָפוֹן עֶשְׂרִים קָרֶשׁ׃ וְאַרְבָּעִים
אַדְנֵיהֶם כָּסֶף שְׁנֵי אֲדָנִים תַּחַת הַקֶּרֶשׁ הָאֶחָד וּשְׁנֵי אֲדָנִים תַּחַת הַקֶּרֶשׁ הָאֶחָד׃
כב כג וּלְיַרְכְּתֵי הַמִּשְׁכָּן יָמָּה תַּעֲשֶׂה שִׁשָּׁה קְרָשִׁים׃ וּשְׁנֵי קְרָשִׁים תַּעֲשֶׂה לִמְקֻצְעֹת
כד הַמִּשְׁכָּן בַּיַּרְכָתָיִם׃ וְיִהְיוּ תֹאֲמִם מִלְּמַטָּה וְיַחְדָּו יִהְיוּ תַמִּים עַל־רֹאשׁוֹ אֶל־
כה הַטַּבַּעַת הָאֶחָת כֵּן יִהְיֶה לִשְׁנֵיהֶם לִשְׁנֵי הַמִּקְצֹעֹת יִהְיוּ׃ וְהָיוּ שְׁמֹנָה קְרָשִׁים
וְאַדְנֵיהֶם כֶּסֶף שִׁשָּׁה עָשָׂר אֲדָנִים שְׁנֵי אֲדָנִים תַּחַת הַקֶּרֶשׁ הָאֶחָד וּשְׁנֵי אֲדָנִים
כו תַּחַת הַקֶּרֶשׁ הָאֶחָד׃ וְעָשִׂיתָ בְרִיחִם עֲצֵי שִׁטִּים חֲמִשָּׁה לְקַרְשֵׁי צֶלַע־הַמִּשְׁכָּן
כז הָאֶחָד׃ וַחֲמִשָּׁה בְרִיחִם לְקַרְשֵׁי צֶלַע־הַמִּשְׁכָּן הַשֵּׁנִית וַחֲמִשָּׁה בְרִיחִם לְקַרְשֵׁי
כח צֶלַע הַמִּשְׁכָּן לַיַּרְכָתַיִם יָמָּה׃ וְהַבְּרִיחַ הַתִּיכֹן בְּתוֹךְ הַקְּרָשִׁים מַבְרִחַ מִן־הַקָּצֶה
כט אֶל־הַקָּצֶה׃ וְאֶת־הַקְּרָשִׁים תְּצַפֶּה זָהָב וְאֶת־טַבְּעֹתֵיהֶם תַּעֲשֶׂה זָהָב בָּתִּים

רש"י

כב| **וּלְיַרְכְּתֵי.** לְשׁוֹן סוֹף, כְּתַרְגּוּמוֹ: "וְלִסְיָפֵי". וּלְפִי שֶׁהַפֶּתַח בַּמִּזְרָח, קָרוּי מִזְרָח פָּנִים וְהַמַּעֲרָב אֲחוֹרַיִם, וְזֶהוּ סוֹף, שֶׁהַפָּנִים הֵן הָרֹאשׁ: **תַּעֲשֶׂה שִׁשָּׁה קְרָשִׁים.** הֲרֵי תֵּשַׁע אַמּוֹת רֹחַב:

כג| **וּשְׁנֵי קְרָשִׁים תַּעֲשֶׂה לִמְקֻצְעֹת.** אֶחָד לְמִקְצוֹעַ צְפוֹנִית מַעֲרָבִית וְאֶחָד לְמַעֲרָבִית דְּרוֹמִית. כָּל שְׁמֹנָה קְרָשִׁים בְּסֵדֶר אֶחָד הֵן, אֶלָּא שֶׁאֵלּוּ הַשְּׁתַּיִם אֵינָן בַּחֲלַל הַמִּשְׁכָּן, אֶלָּא חֲצִי אַמָּה מִזּוֹ וַחֲצִי אַמָּה מִזּוֹ נִרְאוֹת בֶּחָלָל, לְהַשְׁלִים רָחְבּוֹ לְעֶשֶׂר, וְהָאַמָּה מִזֶּה וְהָאַמָּה מִזֶּה בָּאוֹת כְּנֶגֶד אַמַּת עֳבִי קַרְשֵׁי הַמִּשְׁכָּן הַצָּפוֹן וְהַדָּרוֹם, כְּדֵי שֶׁיְּהֵא הַמִּקְצוֹעַ מִבַּחוּץ שָׁוֶה:

כד| **וְיִהְיוּ.** כָּל הַקְּרָשִׁים "תֹּאֲמִם" זֶה לָזֶה "מִלְּמַטָּה", שֶׁלֹּא יַפְסִיק עֳבִי שְׂפַת שְׁנֵי הָאֲדָנִים בֵּינֵיהֶם לְהַרְחִיקָם זוֹ מִזּוֹ. זֶהוּ שֶׁפֵּרַשְׁתִּי שֶׁיִּהְיוּ צִדֵּי הַיָּדוֹת חֲרוּצִים מִצִּדֵּיהֶן, שֶׁיְּהֵא רֹחַב הַקֶּרֶשׁ בּוֹלֵט לְצִדָּיו חוּץ לִידֵי הַקֶּרֶשׁ לְכַסּוֹת אֶת שְׂפַת הָאֶדֶן, וְכֵן הַקֶּרֶשׁ שֶׁאֶצְלוֹ, וְנִמְצְאוּ תּוֹאֲמִים זֶה לָזֶה. וְקֶרֶשׁ הַמִּקְצוֹעַ שֶׁבְּסֵדֶר הַמַּעֲרָב חָרוּץ לְרָחְבּוֹ בְּעָבְיוֹ, כְּנֶגֶד חֲרִיץ שֶׁל צַד קֶרֶשׁ הַצְּפוֹנִי וְהַדְּרוֹמִי, כְּדֵי שֶׁלֹּא יַפְרִידוּ הָאֲדָנִים בֵּינֵיהֶם: **וְיַחְדָּו יִהְיוּ תַמִּים.** כְּמוֹ "תֹּאֲמִם": **עַל רֹאשׁוֹ.** שֶׁל קֶרֶשׁ: **אֶל הַטַּבַּעַת הָאֶחָת.** כָּל קֶרֶשׁ וָקֶרֶשׁ הָיָה חָרוּץ לְמַעְלָה בְּרָחְבּוֹ שְׁנֵי חֲרִיצִין בִּשְׁנֵי צִדָּיו כְּדֵי עֳבִי טַבַּעַת, וּמַכְנִיסוֹ בְּטַבַּעַת אַחַת, נִמְצָא מַתְאִים לַקֶּרֶשׁ שֶׁאֶצְלוֹ. אֲבָל אוֹתָן טַבָּעוֹת לֹא יָדַעְתִּי אִם קְבוּעוֹת הֵן אִם מְטֻלְטָלוֹת. וּבַקֶּרֶשׁ שֶׁבַּמִּקְצוֹעַ הָיָה טַבַּעַת בְּעֳבִי הַקֶּרֶשׁ הַדְּרוֹמִי וְהַצְּפוֹנִי וְרֹאשׁ קֶרֶשׁ הַמִּקְצוֹעַ שֶׁבְּסֵדֶר מַעֲרָב נִכְנָס לְתוֹכוֹ, נִמְצְאוּ שְׁנֵי הַכְּתָלִים מְחֻבָּרִים: **כֵּן יִהְיֶה לִשְׁנֵיהֶם.** הַקְּרָשִׁים שֶׁבַּמִּקְצוֹעַ, לַקֶּרֶשׁ שֶׁבְּסוֹף צָפוֹן וְלַקֶּרֶשׁ הַמַּעֲרָבִי. וְכֵן "לִשְׁנֵי הַמִּקְצֹעֹת":

כה| **וְהָיוּ שְׁמֹנָה קְרָשִׁים.** הֵן הָאֲמוּרוֹת לְמַעְלָה: "תַּעֲשֶׂה שִׁשָּׁה קְרָשִׁים וּשְׁנֵי קְרָשִׁים תַּעֲשֶׂה לִמְקֻצְעֹת" (לעיל פסוקים כב-כג), נִמְצְאוּ שְׁמֹנָה קְרָשִׁים בְּסֵדֶר מַעֲרָבִי. כָּךְ שְׁנוּיָה בְּמִשְׁנַת מַעֲשֵׂה סֵדֶר הַקְּרָשִׁים בִּמְלֶאכֶת הַמִּשְׁכָּן (ברייתא דמלאכת המשכן, פרק א): הָיָה עוֹשֶׂה אֶת הָאֲדָנִים חֲלוּלִים, וְחוֹרֵץ אֶת הַקֶּרֶשׁ מִלְּמַטָּה רְבִיעַ מִכָּאן וּרְבִיעַ מִכָּאן וְהֶחָרִיץ חֶצְיוֹ בָּאֶמְצַע, וְעָשָׂה לוֹ שְׁתֵּי יָדוֹת כְּמִין שְׁנֵי חַמּוּקִין, וְלִי נִרְאֶה שֶׁהַגִּרְסָא: כְּמִין שְׁנֵי חֲוָקִין, כְּמִין שְׁתֵּי שְׁלִיבוֹת סֻלָּם הַמֻּבְדָּלוֹת זוֹ מִזּוֹ, וּמְשֻׁפּוֹת לִכָּנֵס בַּחֲלַל הָאֶדֶן כִּשְׁלִיבָה הַנִּכְנֶסֶת בְּנֶקֶב עַמּוּד הַסֻּלָּם, וְהוּא לְשׁוֹן "מְשֻׁלָּבֹת", עֲשׂוּיוֹת כְּמִין שְׁלִיבָה. וּמַכְנִיסָן לְתוֹךְ שְׁנֵי אֲדָנִים, שֶׁנֶּאֱמַר: "שְׁנֵי אֲדָנִים... וּשְׁנֵי אֲדָנִים" (לעיל פסוק יט). וְחוֹרֵץ אֶת הַקֶּרֶשׁ מִלְמַעְלָה אֶצְבַּע מִכָּאן וְאֶצְבַּע מִכָּאן וְנוֹתֵן לְתוֹךְ טַבַּעַת אַחַת שֶׁל זָהָב, כְּדֵי שֶׁלֹּא יִהְיוּ נִפְרָדִים זֶה מִזֶּה, שֶׁנֶּאֱמַר: "וְיִהְיוּ תֹאֲמִם מִלְּמַטָּה" וְגוֹ' (לעיל פסוק כד). כָּךְ הִיא הַמִּשְׁנָה, וְהַפֵּרוּשׁ שֶׁלָּהּ הִנַּעְתִּי לְמַעְלָה בְּסֵדֶר הַמִּקְרָאוֹת:

כו| **בְּרִיחִם.** כְּתַרְגּוּמוֹ "עַבְרִין", וּבְלַעַז אשפרי"ש:

חֲמִשָּׁה לְקַרְשֵׁי צֶלַע הַמִּשְׁכָּן. אֵלּוּ חֲמִשָּׁה שְׁלֹשָׁה הֵן, אֶלָּא שֶׁהַבְּרִיחַ הָעֶלְיוֹן וְהַתַּחְתּוֹן עָשׂוּי מִשְּׁתֵּי חֲתִיכוֹת, זֶה מַבְרִיחַ עַד חֲצִי הַכֹּתֶל וְזֶה מַבְרִיחַ עַד חֲצִי הַכֹּתֶל, זֶה נִכְנָס בַּטַּבַּעַת מִצַּד זֶה וְזֶה נִכְנָס בַּטַּבַּעַת מִצַּד זֶה עַד שֶׁמַּגִּיעִין זֶה לָזֶה, נִמְצְאוּ הָעֶלְיוֹן וְהַתַּחְתּוֹן שְׁנַיִם שֶׁהֵן אַרְבָּעָה. אֲבָל הָאֶמְצָעִי אָרְכּוֹ כְּנֶגֶד כָּל הַכֹּתֶל, וּמַבְרִיחַ מִקְּצֵה הַכֹּתֶל וְעַד קָצֵהוּ, שֶׁנֶּאֱמַר: "וְהַבְּרִיחַ הַתִּיכֹן וְגוֹ' מַבְרִחַ מִן הַקָּצֶה אֶל הַקָּצֶה" (להלן פסוק כח). שֶׁהָעֶלְיוֹנִים וְהַתַּחְתּוֹנִים הָיוּ לָהֶן טַבָּעוֹת בַּקְּרָשִׁים לִכָּנֵס לְתוֹכָן, שְׁתֵּי טַבָּעוֹת לְכָל קֶרֶשׁ, מְשֻׁלָּשִׁים בְּתוֹךְ עֶשֶׂר אַמּוֹת שֶׁל גֹּבַהּ הַקֶּרֶשׁ, חֵלֶק אֶחָד מִן הַטַּבַּעַת הָעֶלְיוֹנָה וּלְמַעְלָה וְחֵלֶק אֶחָד מִן הַתַּחְתּוֹנָה וּלְמַטָּה, וְכָל חֵלֶק הוּא רְבִיעַ אֹרֶךְ הַקֶּרֶשׁ, וּשְׁנֵי חֲלָקִים בֵּין טַבַּעַת לְטַבַּעַת, כְּדֵי שֶׁיִּהְיוּ כָּל הַטַּבָּעוֹת מְכֻוָּנִין זֶה כְּנֶגֶד זֶה. אֲבָל לַבְּרִיחַ הַתִּיכוֹן אֵין טַבָּעוֹת, אֶלָּא הַקְּרָשִׁים נְקוּבִין בְּעָבְיָן, וְהוּא נִכְנָס בָּהֶם דֶּרֶךְ הַנְּקָבִים שֶׁהֵם מְכֻוָּנִין זֶה מוּל זֶה, וְזֶהוּ שֶׁנֶּאֱמַר: "בְּתוֹךְ הַקְּרָשִׁים" (שם). הַבְּרִיחִים הָעֶלְיוֹנִים וְהַתַּחְתּוֹנִים שֶׁבַּצָּפוֹן וְשֶׁבַּדָּרוֹם אֹרֶךְ כָּל אֶחָד חָמֵשׁ עֶשְׂרֵה אַמָּה, וְהַתִּיכוֹן אָרְכּוֹ שְׁלֹשִׁים אַמָּה, וְזֶהוּ "מִן הַקָּצֶה אֶל הַקָּצֶה" (שם), מִן הַמִּזְרָח וְעַד הַמַּעֲרָב. וַחֲמִשָּׁה בְּרִיחִים שֶׁבַּמַּעֲרָב, אֹרֶךְ הָעֶלְיוֹנִים וְהַתַּחְתּוֹנִים שֵׁשׁ אַמּוֹת, וְהַתִּיכוֹן אָרְכּוֹ שְׁתֵּים עֶשְׂרֵה, כְּנֶגֶד רֹחַב שְׁמוֹנָה קְרָשִׁים. כָּךְ הִיא מְפֹרֶשֶׁת בִּמְלֶאכֶת הַמִּשְׁכָּן:

כט| **בָּתִּים לַבְּרִיחִם.** הַטַּבָּעוֹת שֶׁתַּעֲשֶׂה בָּהֶן יִהְיוּ בָּתִּים

30 **You shall establish the Tabernacle in accordance with its** proper **design, which you were shown on the mountain.**

31 **You shall make a curtain of sky-blue, purple, and scarlet**
Fifth **wool, and linen,** all of which must be **spun together; it shall**
aliya **be artfully made with** decorative **cherubs** on its back. The curtain was fashioned skillfully, such that the decorations could be seen on both sides.[29]

32 As the curtain will not be connected to any wall, **you shall place it on four acacia pillars plated with gold, their hooks of gold, upon four silver sockets.** The four pillars were likely evenly spaced, with the curtain hanging on their hooks.

33 **You shall place the curtain under the** gold **hooks** which connect the sets of overhanging sheets (see verse 6), **and you shall bring there the Ark of the Testimony behind the curtain, and the** opaque **curtain shall partition for you between the Sanctuary and the Holy of Holies.**

34 **You shall place the** golden **ark cover upon the Ark of the Testimony in the Holy of Holies.**

35 **You shall place the table outside the curtain,** in the Sanctuary, the larger space facing the entrance, **and the candelabrum opposite the table on the side of the Tabernacle to the south, and the table you shall place on the north side.**

36 At the eastern end of the Tent of Meeting, where the table and candelabrum will stand, **you shall make a screen for the entrance of the tent of sky-blue, purple and scarlet wool, and linen,** all of which shall be **spun together, the work of an embroiderer.** This task was simpler than the weaving required for the sheets of the Tabernacle and the curtain dividing the sanctuary, which were described above as the work of a craftsman (verse 31).

37 **You shall make five acacia pillars for the screen, and you shall plate them with gold; their hooks,** upon which the

screen is hung, **shall be of gold. You shall cast for them five bronze sockets.** The screen of the Tabernacle was hung on the five pillars inserted into bronze sockets and served as the Tabernacle's fourth wall.[D]

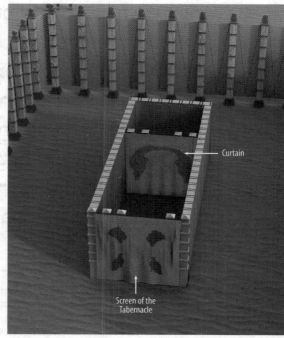

Curtain and screen

The Command to Build the Altar for Burnt Offerings

EXODUS 27:1–8

The Torah has dealt with the structure of the Tabernacle itself, the larger Sanctuary for the table and the candelabrum, and a smaller area, the Holy of Holies, for the ark alone. The Torah now turns to the space outside the Tabernacle.

27 1 **You shall make the altar,** where most offerings will be brought,
Sixth **of acacia wood, five cubits' length and five cubits' width;**
aliya

the altar shall be square.[D] **And three cubits shall be its height.**[D] The height of the altar was lower than that of an

---

DISCUSSION

26:37 | **The structure of the Tabernacle and the courtyard:** In summary, the Tabernacle was a single structure enclosed by outer walls and divided by inner partitions. Three of the four outer walls were comprised of boards made from acacia wood, while a screen of fabric bridged the walls on the fourth side. Inside the Tabernacle was another curtain, which divided the area between the Sanctuary, where the table and candelabrum were located, and the Holy of Holies, which housed the ark. The roof of the Tabernacle was made from sheets of cloth, which were themselves divided into two segments: One that covered the Sanctuary and another that covered the Holy of Holies and the rear wall. These were themselves covered with a second layer of sheets made of goats' hair, which enclosed all the boards of the Tabernacle, and draped slightly over its entrance. Additional layers of animal skin covered those sheets of goats' hair.

לַבְּרִיחִם וְצִפִּיתָ אֶת־הַבְּרִיחִם זָהָב: וַהֲקֵמֹתָ אֶת־הַמִּשְׁכָּן כְּמִשְׁפָּטוֹ אֲשֶׁר הָרְאֵיתָ
בָּהָר: לא וְעָשִׂיתָ פָרֹכֶת תְּכֵלֶת וְאַרְגָּמָן וְתוֹלַעַת שָׁנִי וְשֵׁשׁ מָשְׁזָר כ חמישי
לב מַעֲשֵׂה חֹשֵׁב יַעֲשֶׂה אֹתָהּ כְּרֻבִים: וְנָתַתָּה אֹתָהּ עַל־אַרְבָּעָה עַמּוּדֵי שִׁטִּים
לג מְצֻפִּים זָהָב וָוֵיהֶם זָהָב עַל־אַרְבָּעָה אַדְנֵי־כָסֶף: וְנָתַתָּה אֶת־הַפָּרֹכֶת תַּחַת
הַקְּרָסִים וְהֵבֵאתָ שָׁמָּה מִבֵּית לַפָּרֹכֶת אֵת אֲרוֹן הָעֵדוּת וְהִבְדִּילָה הַפָּרֹכֶת
לָכֶם בֵּין הַקֹּדֶשׁ וּבֵין קֹדֶשׁ הַקֳּדָשִׁים: לד וְנָתַתָּ אֶת־הַכַּפֹּרֶת עַל אֲרוֹן הָעֵדֻת בְּקֹדֶשׁ
הַקֳּדָשִׁים: לה וְשַׂמְתָּ אֶת־הַשֻּׁלְחָן מִחוּץ לַפָּרֹכֶת וְאֶת־הַמְּנֹרָה נֹכַח הַשֻּׁלְחָן עַל צֶלַע
הַמִּשְׁכָּן תֵּימָנָה וְהַשֻּׁלְחָן תִּתֵּן עַל־צֶלַע צָפוֹן: לו וְעָשִׂיתָ מָסָךְ לְפֶתַח הָאֹהֶל תְּכֵלֶת
וְאַרְגָּמָן וְתוֹלַעַת שָׁנִי וְשֵׁשׁ מָשְׁזָר מַעֲשֵׂה רֹקֵם: לז וְעָשִׂיתָ לַמָּסָךְ חֲמִשָּׁה עַמּוּדֵי
שִׁטִּים וְצִפִּיתָ אֹתָם זָהָב וָוֵיהֶם זָהָב וְיָצַקְתָּ לָהֶם חֲמִשָּׁה אַדְנֵי נְחֹשֶׁת:
א וְעָשִׂיתָ אֶת־הַמִּזְבֵּחַ עֲצֵי שִׁטִּים חָמֵשׁ אַמּוֹת אֹרֶךְ וְחָמֵשׁ אַמּוֹת רֹחַב רָבוּעַ שישי

רש"י

לְבָרְחָם בָּהֶן הַבְּרִיחִם: וְצִפִּיתָ אֶת הַבְּרִיחִם זָהָב. לֹא שֶׁהָיָה הַזָּהָב מְצֻפֶּה עַל הַבְּרִיחִם, שֶׁאֵין עֲלֵיהֶם שׁוּם צִפּוּי, אֶלָּא בַּקֶּרֶשׁ הָיָה קוֹבֵעַ כְּמִין שְׁנֵי פִּיפִיּוֹת שֶׁל זָהָב כְּמִין שְׁנֵי סְדָקֵי קָנֶה חָלוּק, וְקוֹבְעָן אֵצֶל חֲלַל הַטַּבָּעוֹת לַבְּרִיחַ וְלַקֶּרֶשׁ, חַרְכָּן מְמַלֵּא אֶת רֹחַב הַקֶּרֶשׁ מִן הַטַּבַּעַת וּמִמֶּנָּה לַטַּבַּעַת וּמִן הַטַּבַּעַת לַפֶּה הַשֵּׁנִי, וְנִכְנָס הַבְּרִיחַ לְתוֹכוֹ וּמִמֶּנּוּ לְטַבַּעַת וּמִן הַטַּבַּעַת לַפֶּה הַשֵּׁנִי, נִמְצְאוּ הַבְּרִיחִים מְצֻפִּים זָהָב כְּשֶׁהֵן תְּחוּבִין בַּקְּרָשִׁים. וְהַבְּרִיחִים הַלָּלוּ מִבַּחוּץ הָיוּ, בְּלִיטַת הַטַּבָּעוֹת וְהַפִּיפִיּוֹת לֹא הָיְתָה נִרְאֵית בְּתוֹךְ הַמִּשְׁכָּן, אֶלָּא כָּל הַכֹּתֶל חָלָק מִבִּפְנִים:

וַהֲקֵמֹתָ אֶת הַמִּשְׁכָּן. לְאַחַר שֶׁיִּגָּמֵר הֲקִימֵהוּ. הָרְאֵיתָ בָּהָר. קֹדֶם לָכֵן, שֶׁאֲנִי עָתִיד לְלַמֶּדְךָ וּלְהַרְאוֹתְךָ סֵדֶר הֲקָמָתוֹ:

לא) פָּרֹכֶת. לְשׁוֹן מְחִצָּה הוּא, וּבִלְשׁוֹן חֲכָמִים: פַּרְגּוֹד, דָּבָר הַמַּבְדִּיל בֵּין הַמֶּלֶךְ וּבֵין הָעָם: תְּכֵלֶת וְאַרְגָּמָן. כָּל מִין וָמִין הָיָה כָּפוּל, בְּכָל חוּט וָחוּט שִׁשָּׁה חוּטִין: מַעֲשֵׂה

חֹשֵׁב. כְּבָר פֵּרַשְׁתִּי שֶׁזּוֹ הִיא אֲרִיגָה שֶׁל שְׁתֵּי קִירוֹת, וְהַצּוּרִין שֶׁמִּשְּׁנֵי עֲבָרֶיהָ אֵינָן דּוֹמִין זֶה לָזֶה: כְּרֻבִים. צִיּוּרִין שֶׁל בְּרִיּוֹת יַעֲשֶׂה בָּהּ:

לב) אַרְבָּעָה עַמּוּדִים תְּקוּעִים בְּתוֹךְ אַרְבָּעָה אֲדָנִים, וְאֻנְקְלָיוֹת קְבוּעִין בָּהֶן עֲקוּמִין לְמַעְלָה, לְהוֹשִׁיב עֲלֵיהֶן כְּלוֹנָס שֶׁרֹאשׁ הַפָּרֹכֶת כָּרוּךְ בָּהּ, וְהָאֻנְקְלָיוֹת הֵן הַוָּוִין, שֶׁהֲרֵי כְּמִין וָוִין הֵן עֲשׂוּיִין: וְהִפְרִילַת הַפָּרֹכֶת עֶשֶׂר אַמּוֹת לְרָחְבּוֹ שֶׁל מִשְׁכָּן, וְרָחְבָּהּ עֶשֶׂר אַמּוֹת כְּנֶגְדָּן שֶׁל קְרָשִׁים, פְּרוּסָה בִּשְׁלִישׁוֹ שֶׁל מִשְׁכָּן, שֶׁיְּהֵא הֵימֶנָּה וְלַפְנִים עֶשֶׂר אַמּוֹת וְהֵימֶנָּה וְלַחוּץ עֶשְׂרִים אַמָּה. נִמְצָא בֵּית קֹדֶשׁ הַקֳּדָשִׁים עֶשֶׂר עַל עֶשֶׂר, שֶׁנֶּאֱמַר: "וְנָתַתָּה אֶת הַפָּרֹכֶת תַּחַת הַקְּרָסִים" (להלן פסוק לג) הַמְחַבְּרִים אֶת שְׁתֵּי חוֹבְרוֹת שֶׁל יְרִיעוֹת הַמִּשְׁכָּן, רֹחַב הַחוֹבֶרֶת עֶשְׂרִים אַמָּה. וּכְשֶׁפְּרָסָהּ עַל גַּג הַמִּשְׁכָּן מִן הַפֶּתַח לַמַּעֲרָב, כַּלְּתָה בִּשְׁנֵי שְׁלִישֵׁי הַמִּשְׁכָּן, וְהַחוֹבֶרֶת הַשֵּׁנִית כִּסְּתָה שְׁלִישׁוֹ שֶׁל מִשְׁכָּן, וְהַמּוֹתָר תָּלוּי לַאֲחוֹרָיו לְכַסּוֹת אֶת הַקְּרָשִׁים:

לה) וְשַׂמְתָּ אֶת הַשֻּׁלְחָן. שֻׁלְחָן בַּצָּפוֹן מָשׁוּךְ מִן הַכֹּתֶל הַצְּפוֹנִי שְׁתֵּי אַמּוֹת וּמֶחֱצָה, וּמְנוֹרָה בַּדָּרוֹם מְשׁוּכָה מִן הַכֹּתֶל הַדְּרוֹמִי שְׁתֵּי אַמּוֹת וּמֶחֱצָה, וּמִזְבַּח הַזָּהָב נָתוּן כְּנֶגֶד אֲוִיר שֶׁבֵּין שֻׁלְחָן לַמְּנוֹרָה מָשׁוּךְ קִמְעָא כְּלַפֵּי הַמִּזְרָח, וְכֻלָּם נְתוּנִים מִן חֲצִי הַמִּשְׁכָּן וְלִפְנִים. כֵּיצַד? אֹרֶךְ הַמִּשְׁכָּן מִן הַפֶּתַח לַפָּרֹכֶת עֶשְׂרִים אַמָּה, הַמִּזְבֵּחַ וְהַשֻּׁלְחָן וְהַמְּנוֹרָה מְשׁוּכִים מִן הַפֶּתַח לְצַד מַעֲרָב עֶשֶׂר אַמּוֹת:

לו) וְעָשִׂיתָ מָסָךְ. וִילוֹן שֶׁהוּא מָסָךְ כְּנֶגֶד הַפֶּתַח, כְּמוֹ: "שַׂכְתָּ בַעֲדוֹ" (איוב א, י), לְשׁוֹן מָגֵן: מַעֲשֵׂה רֹקֵם. הַצּוּרוֹת עֲשׂוּיוֹת בּוֹ מַעֲשֵׂה מַחַט, כַּדַּרְתּוֹף שֶׁל עֵבֶר זֶה כָּךְ פַּרְצוּף שֶׁל עֵבֶר זֶה. רֹקֵם. שֵׁם הָאֻמָּן וְלֹא שֵׁם הָאֻמָּנוּת, וְתַרְגּוּמוֹ: "עוֹבֵד צַיָּר" וְלֹא "עוֹבֵד עֵיּוּר". מִדַּת הַמָּסָךְ כְּמִדַּת הַפָּרֹכֶת, עֶשֶׂר אַמּוֹת עַל עֶשֶׂר אַמּוֹת:

פרק כז
א) וְעָשִׂיתָ אֶת הַמִּזְבֵּחַ וְגוֹ' וְשָׁלֹשׁ אַמּוֹת קֹמָתוֹ. דְּבָרִים

DISCUSSION

27:1 | The altar shall be square: Although it is clear from the measurements that the altar must be square, the verse reiterates this fact to teach that even if the measurements of the altar should change in the future permanent Temple, the square shape will still be a requirement.

As the Talmud states: "The horn, the ramp, the base, and [the requirement that the altar must be exactly] square are indispensable [in order for the altar to be fit for use]. The measurement of its length, the measurement of its width, and the measurement of its height are not indispensable" (Zevaḥim 62a; see HaKetav VehaKabbala; Meshekh Ḥokhma).

And three cubits shall be its height: According to the opinion that the three cubits begin from the ledge, the total height of the altar was 10 cubits (see Zevaḥim 59b). It is also

average person and disproportionate to its large area. Some Sages argue that the three cubits stated here do not refer to the entire height of the altar but only to the upper part of it, from the ledge on which the priests would walk to its top.

The altar for burnt offerings

2 **You shall make its horns on its four corners.** According to the tradition of the Sages, the horns of the altar were straight,

square blocks.[30] **Its horns shall be from it,** the altar. The horns were not made from separate material joined to the altar, but from the same wood as the altar itself. **And you shall plate it,** the entire altar, **with bronze.**[D]

3 **You shall make its pots to clear its ashes,** the soot and waste left from the offerings, **and its shovels,** for sweeping away the ashes, **and its basins,** for collecting the blood of offerings and sprinkling it upon the altar, **and its large forks,** used for placing pieces of meat upon the altar and turning them over, **and its pans,** for raking the coals and moving them around.[31] **All its vessels you shall make of bronze.**

4 **You shall make for it a grate, a work of bronze mesh,** laid over the bronze plating on the altar. **And you shall make on the mesh four bronze rings on its,** the altar's, **four corners,** to insert the poles for carrying it.

5 **You shall place it,** this grate, **under the surrounding ledge of the altar from below.**[D] The ledge was a protrusion that surrounded the outer wall of the altar. **And the mesh shall be up to the middle of the altar.** The upper edge of the grate should reach the ledge, which will be in the upper portion of the altar, and it should extend down to half the height of the altar.[32]

6 **You shall make staves for the altar, staves of acacia wood, and you shall plate them with bronze.**

7 **Its staves shall be inserted into the rings** which are on the grate, at the edges of the altar, **and the staves shall be on the two sides of the altar when carrying it** from place to place.

8 **You shall make it,** the altar, **hollow, out of planks,** with no bottom part closing it,[33] of wooden boards covered with bronze. When the altar was put in its place, it was filled with earth and was therefore called "an altar of earth" (see 20:21). When the Israelites traveled, the altar was emptied of its earth, and they carried only the framework by its staves. **As He showed you on the mountain so shall they,** the children of Israel, **make it.**

DISCUSSION

possible that these 3 cubits are only the minimum height for the altar (see Rambam, *Sefer Avoda, Hilkhot Beit HaBeḥira* 2:5; see also Rabbi Yitzchak Zev Soloveitchik, *Zevaḥim* 59b).

27:2 | **And you shall plate it with bronze:** Although bronze is not the ideal metal to use in close proximity to fire, it is appropriate for this altar's level of sanctity relative to the vessels located inside the Tabernacle, which were

plated with gold. Both the location of this altar, in the courtyard, and the material from which it was made, are indicative of its comparatively lesser sanctity. Bronze was also used for the Tabernacle's basin, located likewise in the courtyard, as well as for the sockets for the pillars standing at the entrance to the Tabernacle and the courtyard. The sockets for the boards of the Tabernacle itself, and those supporting

the pillars for the veil inside it, were made of silver.

27:5 | **Under the surrounding ledge [karkov] of the altar from below:** See *Targum Yonatan.* The Sages call this ledge the *sovev,* literally "surrounding," since it goes around the altar. According to another opinion, the *karkov* was not the ledge but a molded relief that served for decoration (see *Zevaḥim* 62a).

ב יִהְיֶה הַמִּזְבֵּחַ וְשָׁלֹשׁ אַמּוֹת קֹמָתוֹ׃ וְעָשִׂיתָ קַרְנֹתָיו עַל אַרְבַּע פִּנֹּתָיו מִמֶּנּוּ תִּהְיֶיןָ
ג קַרְנֹתָיו וְצִפִּיתָ אֹתוֹ נְחֹשֶׁת׃ וְעָשִׂיתָ סִּירֹתָיו לְדַשְּׁנוֹ וְיָעָיו וּמִזְרְקֹתָיו וּמִזְלְגֹתָיו
ד וּמַחְתֹּתָיו לְכָל־כֵּלָיו תַּעֲשֶׂה נְחֹשֶׁת׃ וְעָשִׂיתָ לּוֹ מִכְבָּר מַעֲשֵׂה רֶשֶׁת נְחֹשֶׁת
ה וְעָשִׂיתָ עַל־הָרֶשֶׁת אַרְבַּע טַבְּעֹת נְחֹשֶׁת עַל אַרְבַּע קְצוֹתָיו׃ וְנָתַתָּה אֹתָהּ
ו תַּחַת כַּרְכֹּב הַמִּזְבֵּחַ מִלְּמָטָּה וְהָיְתָה הָרֶשֶׁת עַד חֲצִי הַמִּזְבֵּחַ׃ וְעָשִׂיתָ בַדִּים
ז לַמִּזְבֵּחַ בַּדֵּי עֲצֵי שִׁטִּים וְצִפִּיתָ אֹתָם נְחֹשֶׁת׃ וְהוּבָא אֶת־בַּדָּיו בַּטַּבָּעֹת וְהָיוּ
ח הַבַּדִּים עַל־שְׁתֵּי צַלְעֹת הַמִּזְבֵּחַ בִּשְׂאֵת אֹתוֹ׃ נְבוּב לֻחֹת תַּעֲשֶׂה אֹתוֹ כַּאֲשֶׁר

רש"י

ככתבן, דברי רבי יהודה. רבי יוסי אומר: נאמר כאן "רבוע" ונאמר בפנימי "רבוע" (להלן ל, ב), מה להלן גבהו פי שנים כארכו, אף כאן גבהו פי שנים כארכו; ומה אני מקים "ושלש אמות קמתו"? משפת סובב ולמעלה:

ב| ממנו תהיין קרנתיו. שלא יעשם לבדם ויחברם בו: וצפית אתו נחשת. לכפר על עזות מצח, שנאמר: "ומצחך נחושה" (ישעיה מח, ד):

ג| סירתיו. כמין יורות: לדשנו. להסיר דשנו לתוכם; והוא שתרגם אונקלוס: "למספי קטמיה", לספות הדשן לתוכם. כי יש מלות בלשון עברית מלה אחת מתחלפת בפתרון לשמש בנין וסתירה, כמו "ותשרש שרשיה" (תהלים פ, י), "אויל משריש" (איוב ה, ג), וחלופו: "ובכל תבואתי תשרש" (שם לא, יב). וכמוהו: "בסעפיה פריה" (ישעיה יז, ו), וחלופו: "מסעף פארה" (שם י, לג), מפשח סעיפיה. וכמוהו: "וזה האחרון עצמו" (ירמיה נ, יז), שבר עצמותיו. וכמוהו: "ויסקלהו באבנים" (מלכים א׳ כא, יג), וחלופו: "סקלו מאבן" (ישעיה סב, י), הסירו אבניה, וכן: "ויעזקהו ויסקלהו" (שם ה, ב). אף כאן "לדשנו" להסיר דשנו, ובלעז אדשנדרי"ר: ויעיו. כתרגומו, מגרפות שנוטל בהם הדשן, והן כמין כסוי קדרה, והוא של מתכת דק ולו בית יד, ובלעז וודי"ל: ומזרקתיו. לקבל בהם דם הזבחים: ומזלגתיו. כמין אונקליות כפופין, ומכה בהן בבשר ונתחבין בו, ומהפכן בהן על גחלי המערכה שיהא ממהר שרפתן, ובלעז קרוצנ"ש, ובלשון חכמים: צנוריות: ומחתתיו. בית קבול יש להם לטול בהן גחלים מן המזבח לשאתם על מזבח הפנימי לקטרת. ועל שם חתיתן קרויים מחתות, כמו: "לחתות אש מיקוד" (ישעיה ל, יד), לשון שאיבת אש ממקומה, וכן: "היחתה איש אש בחיקו" (משלי ו, כז): לכל כליו. כמו כל כליו:

ד| מכבר. לשון כברה שקורין קריב"ל, כמין לבוש עשוי לו למזבח, עשוי חורין חורין כמין רשת. ומקרא זה מסרס וכה פתרונו: ועשית לו מכבר נחשת מעשה רשת:

ה| כרכב המזבח. סובב. כל דבר המקיף סביב בעגול קרוי כרכב, כמו ששנינו בהכל שוחטין: "אלו הן גלמי כלי עץ, כל שעתיד לשוף ולכרכב" (חולין כה ע"א), והוא שעושין חריצין עגולין בקרשי דפני התבות וספסלי העץ, אף למזבח עשה חרין סביבו בדפנו לנוי, והוא לסוף שש אמות של גבהו כדברי האומר (זבחים נט ע"ב – ס ע"א) מה אני מקים "ושלש אמות קמתו"? משפת סובב ולמעלה. אבל סובב להלוך הכהנים לא היה למזבח הנחשת אלא על ראשו לפנים מקרנותיו. וכן שנינו בזבחים (דף סב ע"א): איזהו כרכב? בין קרן לקרן, ולפנים מהן אמה של הלוך רגלי הכהנים, שתי אמות הללו קרויים כרכב. ודקדקנו שם: והכתיב: "תחת כרכבו מלמטה" (להלן לח, ד), למדנו שהכרכב בדפנו הוא ולבוש המכבר תחתיו! ותרץ המתרץ: תרי הוו, חד לנוי וחד לכהנים דלא נשתרקו; זה שבדפן לנוי היה, ומתחתיו הלבישו המכבר, והגיע רחבו עד חצי המזבח, והוא היה סימן לחצי גבהו להבדיל בין דמים העליונים לדמים התחתונים, וכנגדו עשו למזבח בית עולמים חוט הסקרא באמצעו (מדות ג, א). וכבש שהיו עולין בו, אף על פי שלא פרשו בענין זה, כבר שמענו בפרשת 'מזבח אדמה תעשה לי': "ולא תעלה במעלת" (לעיל כ, כב), לא תעשה לו מעלות בכבש שלו, אלא כבש חלק, למדנו שהיה לו כבש. כך שנינו במכילתא (בחדש פרשה יא). ו'מזבח אדמה' הוא מזבח הנחשת, שהיו ממלאין חללו אדמה במקום חנייתן. והכבש היה בדרום המזבח מבדל מן המזבח מלא חוט השערה, ורגליו מגיעין עד אמה סמוך לקלעי החצר שבדרום, כדברי האומר עשר אמות קומתו; ולדברי האומר דברים ככתבן "שלש אמות קמתו" (זבחים נט ע"ב), לא היה ארך הכבש אלא עשר אמות. כך מצאתי במשנת ארבעים ותשע מדות. וזה שהוא מבדל מן המזבח מלא החוט, במסכת זבחים (דף סב ע"ב) למדנוה מן המקרא:

ז| בטבעת. בארבע טבעות שנעשו למכבר:

ח| נבוב לחת. כתרגומו: "חליל לוחין", לוחות עצי שטים מכל צד והחלל באמצע, ולא יהא כלו עץ אחד שיהא עביו חמש אמות על חמש אמות כמין סדן:

The Command to Build the Courtyard

EXODUS 27:9–19

After describing the altar, the center of the service in the Tabernacle courtyard, the Torah moves on to describe the courtyard itself.

9 *Seventh aliya* **You shall make the courtyard of the Tabernacle: On the south side there shall be hangings for the courtyard,** the main function of which was to conceal the courtyard from view. The hangings shall be made **of spun linen** strings. According to tradition, each string was comprised of six thin, entwined threads.[34] The hangings shall be **one hundred cubits long for the one side.**

10 **Its pillars,** of the courtyard, **shall be twenty** in number. The hangings were draped over twenty pillars, with a gap of five cubits between each pillar. **And their,** the pillars', **sockets** for holding them in place shall also be **twenty** in number. The sockets themselves shall be made **of bronze,** unlike the silver sockets inside the Tabernacle (see 26:19). However, **the hooks of the pillars,** for the hangings, **and their bands,** the hoops which surrounded the pillars for decoration or to prevent them from cracking, **shall be of silver.**

11 **Likewise, on the north side, in length, there shall be hangings one hundred cubits long, their pillars twenty** in number **and their sockets twenty** in number, **of bronze. The hooks of the pillars and their bands shall be of silver.**

12 **The width of the courtyard on the west side shall be** enclosed by **hangings of fifty cubits, their pillars ten** in number **and their sockets ten** in number, by the same ratio.

13 **The width of the courtyard on the east side shall** also **be fifty cubits.**

14 Since the gate is located on the east side of the courtyard, only **fifteen cubits of hangings** shall be allocated **for the one side of the entrance, their pillars three** in number **and their sockets three** in number,

15 **and on the second side of the entrance** shall also be **fifteen** cubits' length of **hangings, their pillars three** in number **and their sockets three** in number.

16 In the middle, **for the gate of the courtyard,** there shall be **a** magnificent **screen of twenty cubits,** made **of sky-blue, purple, and scarlet wool, and linen,** all of which shall be **spun together,** all **the work of an embroiderer. Their pillars,** which hold the screen, **shall be four** in number, **and their sockets** shall be **four** in number. There was no heavy gate at the entrance to the courtyard, but merely a decorative screen, which was turned aside or rolled up to allow entry.

17 *Maftir* **All the pillars of the courtyard all around shall be banded** with loops of silver. **Their hooks shall be of silver, and their sockets** shall be **of bronze.**

18 **The length of the courtyard shall be one hundred cubits, and the width shall be fifty on each side,** a rectangle. **And the height** of the hangings of the courtyard **shall be five cubits,** and they shall be **of spun linen, and their sockets** shall be **of bronze.**

19 **All the vessels of the Tabernacle, for all its craftsmanship,** all the instruments required for its preparation, its assembly and dismantling, and its upkeep; **and all its pegs, and all the pegs of the courtyard,** which were required for holding the Tabernacle in place to prevent the sheets and hangings from blowing over in heavy winds,[35] **shall be bronze.**

Hangings of the courtyard

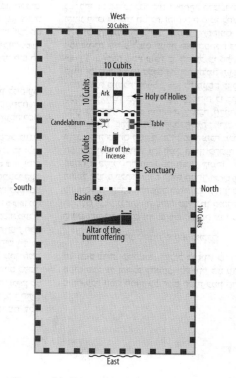

Diagram of the Tabernacle and courtyard

Maftir on Shabbat Shekalim is read from Exodus 30:11–16. Maftir on Shabbat Zakhor is read from Deuteronomy 25:17–19.

ט הָרְאָה אֹתְךָ בָּהָר כֵּן יַעֲשׂוּ׃ וְעָשִׂיתָ אֵת חֲצַר הַמִּשְׁכָּן לִפְאַת שביעי
י נֶגֶב־תֵּימָנָה קְלָעִים לֶחָצֵר שֵׁשׁ מָשְׁזָר מֵאָה בָאַמָּה אֹרֶךְ לַפֵּאָה הָאֶחָת׃ וְעַמֻּדָיו
יא עֶשְׂרִים וְאַדְנֵיהֶם עֶשְׂרִים נְחֹשֶׁת וָוֵי הָעַמֻּדִים וַחֲשֻׁקֵיהֶם כָּסֶף׃ וְכֵן לִפְאַת צָפוֹן
בָּאֹרֶךְ קְלָעִים מֵאָה אֹרֶךְ וְעַמֻּדָו עֶשְׂרִים וְאַדְנֵיהֶם עֶשְׂרִים נְחֹשֶׁת וָוֵי הָעַמֻּדִים
יב וַחֲשֻׁקֵיהֶם כָּסֶף׃ וְרֹחַב הֶחָצֵר לִפְאַת־יָם קְלָעִים חֲמִשִּׁים אַמָּה עַמֻּדֵיהֶם עֲשָׂרָה
יג יד וְאַדְנֵיהֶם עֲשָׂרָה׃ וְרֹחַב הֶחָצֵר לִפְאַת קֵדְמָה מִזְרָחָה חֲמִשִּׁים אַמָּה׃ וַחֲמֵשׁ
טו עֶשְׂרֵה אַמָּה קְלָעִים לַכָּתֵף עַמֻּדֵיהֶם שְׁלֹשָׁה וְאַדְנֵיהֶם שְׁלֹשָׁה׃ וְלַכָּתֵף הַשֵּׁנִית
טז חֲמֵשׁ עֶשְׂרֵה קְלָעִים עַמֻּדֵיהֶם שְׁלֹשָׁה וְאַדְנֵיהֶם שְׁלֹשָׁה׃ וּלְשַׁעַר הֶחָצֵר מָסָךְ ׀
עֶשְׂרִים אַמָּה תְּכֵלֶת וְאַרְגָּמָן וְתוֹלַעַת שָׁנִי וְשֵׁשׁ מָשְׁזָר מַעֲשֵׂה רֹקֵם עַמֻּדֵיהֶם
יז אַרְבָּעָה וְאַדְנֵיהֶם אַרְבָּעָה׃ כָּל־עַמּוּדֵי הֶחָצֵר סָבִיב מְחֻשָּׁקִים כֶּסֶף וָוֵיהֶם כָּסֶף מפטיר
יח וְאַדְנֵיהֶם נְחֹשֶׁת׃ אֹרֶךְ הֶחָצֵר מֵאָה בָאַמָּה וְרֹחַב ׀ חֲמִשִּׁים בַּחֲמִשִּׁים וְקֹמָה
יט חָמֵשׁ אַמּוֹת שֵׁשׁ מָשְׁזָר וְאַדְנֵיהֶם נְחֹשֶׁת׃ לְכֹל כְּלֵי הַמִּשְׁכָּן בְּכֹל עֲבֹדָתוֹ וְכָל־
יְתֵדֹתָיו וְכָל־יִתְדֹת הֶחָצֵר נְחֹשֶׁת׃

רש"י

ט| **קלעים.** עשוין כמין קלעי ספינה נקבים נקבים, מעשה קליעה ולא מעשה אורג. ותרגומו: "סרדין", כתרגומו של "מכבר" (לעיל פסוק ד) המתרגם: "סרדא", לפי שהן מנוקבין ככברה: **לפאה האחת.** כל הרוח קרוי פאה:

י| **ועמדיו עשרים.** חמש אמות בין עמוד לעמוד: **ואדניהם.** של העמודים "נחשת". האדנים יושבין על הארץ והעמודים תקועים לתוכן. והיה עושה כמין קנדסין שקורין פלא"ש ארכן ששה טפחים ורחבן שלשה, וטבעת נחשת קבועה בו באמצעו, וכורך שפת הקלע סביביו במיתרים כנגד כל עמוד ועמוד, ותולה הקנדס דרך טבעתו באנקלי שבעמוד, העשוי כמין וי"ו, ראשו זקוף למעלה וראשו אחד תקוע בעמוד, כאותן שעושין להציב דלתות שקורין גונזי"ש, ורחב הקלע תלוי מלמטה והיא קומת מחיצות החצר: **ווי העמדים.** הם האנקליות: **וחשקיהם.** מקפין היו העמודים בחוטי כסף סביב. ואיני יודע אם על פני כלם אם בראשם אם באמצעם, אך יודע אני ש'חשוק' לשון חגורה, שכך מצינו בפילגש בגבעה: "ועמו צמד חמורים חבושים" (שופטים יט, י), תרגומו: 'חשיקין':

יג| **לפאת קדמה מזרחה.** פני המזרח קרוי 'קדם', לשון פנים, 'אחור' לשון אחורים. לפיכך מזרח קרוי קדם שהוא פנים, ומערב קרוי אחור, כמא דאת אמר: "הים האחרון" (דברים יא, כד) – "ימא מערבאה" (אונקלוס שם): **חמשים אמה.** אותן חמשים אמה לא היו סתומים כלם בקלעים, לפי ששם הפתח, אלא חמש עשרה אמה קלעים לכתף הפתח מכאן וכן לכתף השנית, נשאר רחב חלל הפתח בינתים עשרים אמה, וזהו שנאמר: "ולשער החצר מסך עשרים אמה" (להלן פסוק טז), וילון להסך כנגד הפתח עשרים אמה ארך, כרחב הפתח:

יד| **עמדיהם שלשה.** חמש אמות בין עמוד לעמוד, בין עמוד שבראש הדרום העומד במקצוע דרומית מזרחית עד עמוד שהוא מן השלשה שבמזרח חמש אמות, וממנו לשני חמש אמות, ומן השני לשלישי חמש אמות, וכן לכתף השנית, וארבעה עמודים למסך. הרי עשרה עמודים למזרח כנגד עשרה למערב:

יז| **כל עמודי החצר סביב וגו'.** לפי שלא פרש ווין וחשוקים ואדני נחשת אלא לצפון ולדרום, אבל למזרח ולמערב לא נאמר ווין וחשוקים ואדני נחשת, לכך בא ולמד כאן:

יח| **ארך החצר.** הצפון והדרום שמן המזרח למערב "מאה באמה": **ורחב חמשים בחמשים.** חצר שבמזרח היתה מרבעת חמשים על חמשים, שהמשכן ארכו שלשים ורחבו עשר, העמיד מזרח פתחו בשפת חמשים החיצונים של ארך החצר, נמצא כלו בחמשים הפנימיים, וכלה ארכו לסוף שלשים, נמצאו עשרים אמה רוח לאחוריו בין הקלעים שבמערב ליריעות של אחורי המשכן. ורחב המשכן עשר אמות באמצע רחב החצר, נמצאו לו עשרים אמה רוח לצפון ולדרום מן קלעי החצר ליריעות המשכן, וכן למערב, וחמשים על חמשים חצר לפניו: **וקמה חמש אמות.** גבה מחיצות החצר, והוא רחב הקלעים: **ואדניהם נחשת.** להביא אדני המסך, שלא תאמר לא נאמרו אדני נחשת אלא לעמודי הקלעים, אבל אדני המסך של מין אחר. כך נראה בעיני שלכך חזר ושנאן:

יט| **לכל כלי המשכן.** שהיו צריכין להקמתו ולהורדתו, כגון מקבות לתקע יתדות ועמודים: **יתדות.** כמין נגרי נחשת עשוין ליריעות האהל ולקלעי החצר קשורים במיתרים סביב בשפוליהן כדי שלא תהא הרוח מגביהתן. ואיני יודע אם תחובין בארץ, או קשורין ותלויין וכבדן מכביד שפולי היריעות שלא ינועו ברוח. ואומר אני ששמן מוכיח עליהם שהם תקועים בארץ, לכך נקראו 'יתדות', ומקרא זה מסייעני: "אהל בל יצען בל יסע יתדתיו לנצח" (ישעיה לג, כ):

Parashat
Tetzaveh

The Command to Light the Eternal Flame

EXODUS 27:20–21

Olive oil for lighting the candelabrum is among the substances required in the Tabernacle. The commandment to bring oil for this purpose concludes the current list of the vessels in the Tabernacle. Following the instructions regarding the construction of the Tabernacle and the vessels contained therein, the Torah begins to delineate some of the requirements with regard to the service in the Tabernacle, specifically the lighting of the candelabrum and the priestly vestments used in the Tabernacle. Whereas the specifications of the Tabernacle's construction were only germane to the period before the building of the Temple in Jerusalem, the laws presented in this *parasha* continued to apply afterward. Later, the Torah will discuss additional vessels of the Tabernacle that were hitherto undiscussed: the incense altar and the basin. Perhaps they were not considered part of the central structure of the Tabernacle and were therefore mentioned separately.

20 **You,** Moses, **shall command the children of Israel, and they shall take for you pure virgin olive oil.** This refers to oil produced by pounding ripe olives. Such oil is of superior quality and purer than oil produced by crushing and grinding olives in a press.[1] This oil shall be **for the light, to kindle a lamp continually.**

21 **In the Tent of Meeting,** the Sanctuary, **outside the curtain which is** a cover **before the** Ark of the **Testimony, Aaron and his sons shall arrange it,** to burn **from evening to morning before the Lord.** The lamps shall be kindled in the evening, and they will remain lit throughout the night. **It is an eternal statute for their generations from the children of Israel.** The priests are commanded to light the lamps, while the children of Israel are required to provide the necessary oil.

The Command to Prepare Priestly Vestments for Aaron and His Sons

EXODUS 28:1–43

Until now, the priestly functions were the duty of the firstborn of each Israelite family. From here on, the priesthood is transferred to Moses' brother Aaron, and to his descendants. Perhaps this exchange is related to the construction of the Tabernacle, although it may be a consequence of the sin of the Golden Calf, in which the entire people participated with the exception of the tribe of Levi. Although the sin of the Golden Calf appears after the command to fashion the priestly vestments for Aaron and his sons, some of the Sages hold that this sin actually occurred before Moses was commanded to construct the Tabernacle. According to this opinion, it was because of this sin that it became necessary to establish a physical house of God in the midst of the Israelite encampment.

The first expression of the priests' new status will be their special garments. Here, the Torah will detail the vestments that must be worn by Aaron when he enters the Sanctuary, as well as the requisite vestments of any priest who performs the service. Later, the priests will be ceremonially dressed in their vestments as part of their initiation ritual.

28 1 **And you, have Aaron your brother approach you, and his sons**[D] **with him,** separately, and designate them **from among the children of Israel, to serve as priests to Me: Aaron, Nadav and Avihu, Elazar and Itamar, Aaron's sons.** The general designation of Aaron and his sons, followed by a specification of their names, indicates that each of Aaron's sons was worthy of appointment, independent of his relation to Aaron.

2 Moses is tasked with expressing this appointment in deed: **You shall make holy vestments for Aaron your brother,** who is to be the High Priest. These vestments are service garments, which must be donned when performing the sacred service in the Tabernacle, and they are also intended **for glory and for splendor,** to publicize the importance of the priestly role.

3 **You shall speak to all the wisehearted, whom I have filled with a spirit of wisdom** so that they may satisfy the unique requirements for manufacturing the priestly vestments; **and they shall make Aaron's vestments to sanctify him,** in order for him **to serve as a priest to Me.**[D] Donning these garments would itself sanctify Aaron as High Priest.

4 **These are the vestments that they shall make: a breast piece and an ephod,** a short, apron-like cloak; **and a robe and a quilted tunic; a mitre; and a** special **sash. And they shall make holy vestments for Aaron your brother and for his sons to serve as priests to Me.**

תצוה

כ וְאַתָּה תְּצַוֶּה ׀ אֶת־בְּנֵי יִשְׂרָאֵל וְיִקְחוּ אֵלֶיךָ שֶׁמֶן זַיִת זָךְ כָּתִית לַמָּאוֹר לְהַעֲלֹת כא
נֵר תָּמִיד: בְּאֹהֶל מוֹעֵד מִחוּץ לַפָּרֹכֶת אֲשֶׁר עַל־הָעֵדֻת יַעֲרֹךְ אֹתוֹ אַהֲרֹן וּבָנָיו
מֵעֶרֶב עַד־בֹּקֶר לִפְנֵי יְהוָה חֻקַּת עוֹלָם לְדֹרֹתָם מֵאֵת בְּנֵי יִשְׂרָאֵל:

א וְאַתָּה הַקְרֵב אֵלֶיךָ אֶת־אַהֲרֹן אָחִיךָ וְאֶת־בָּנָיו אִתּוֹ מִתּוֹךְ בְּנֵי יִשְׂרָאֵל לְכַהֲנוֹ־
ב לִי אַהֲרֹן נָדָב וַאֲבִיהוּא אֶלְעָזָר וְאִיתָמָר בְּנֵי אַהֲרֹן: וְעָשִׂיתָ בִגְדֵי־קֹדֶשׁ לְאַהֲרֹן
ג אָחִיךָ לְכָבוֹד וּלְתִפְאָרֶת: וְאַתָּה תְּדַבֵּר אֶל־כָּל־חַכְמֵי־לֵב אֲשֶׁר מִלֵּאתִיו רוּחַ
ד חָכְמָה וְעָשׂוּ אֶת־בִּגְדֵי אַהֲרֹן לְקַדְּשׁוֹ לְכַהֲנוֹ־לִי: וְאֵלֶּה הַבְּגָדִים אֲשֶׁר יַעֲשׂוּ
חֹשֶׁן וְאֵפוֹד וּמְעִיל וּכְתֹנֶת תַּשְׁבֵּץ מִצְנֶפֶת וְאַבְנֵט וְעָשׂוּ בִגְדֵי־קֹדֶשׁ לְאַהֲרֹן

רש״י

כ] וְאַתָּה תְּצַוֶּה. זָךְ. בְּלִי שְׁמָרִים, כְּמוֹ שֶׁשָּׁנִינוּ בִּמְנָחוֹת (דף
עט ע״א), מְגַרְגְּרוֹ בְּרֹאשׁ הַזַּיִת וְכוּ׳: כָּתִית. הַזֵּיתִים, כּוֹתֵשׁ
בַּמַּכְתֶּשֶׁת וְאֵינוֹ טוֹחֲנָן בָּרֵיחַיִם, כְּדֵי שֶׁלֹּא יְהוּ בּוֹ שְׁמָרִים,
וְאַחַר שֶׁהוֹצִיא טִפָּה רִאשׁוֹנָה מַכְנִיסָן לָרֵיחַיִם וְטוֹחֲנָן.
וְהַשֶּׁמֶן הַשֵּׁנִי פָּסוּל לַמְּנוֹרָה וְכָשֵׁר לַמְּנָחוֹת, שֶׁנֶּאֱמַר:
"כָּתִית לַמָּאוֹר", וְלֹא כָּתִית לַמְּנָחוֹת (שם): לְהַעֲלֹת נֵר
תָּמִיד. מַדְלִיק עַד שֶׁתְּהֵא שַׁלְהֶבֶת עוֹלָה מֵאֵלֶיהָ: תָּמִיד.
כָּל לַיְלָה וְלַיְלָה קָרוּי 'תָּמִיד', כְּמוֹ שֶׁאַתָּה אוֹמֵר: "עֹלַת
תָּמִיד" (להלן כט, מב; במדבר כח, ו), וְאֵינָהּ אֶלָּא מִיּוֹם לְיוֹם.
וְכֵן בְּמִנְחַת חֲבִתִּין: "תָּמִיד" (ויקרא ו, יג), וְאֵינָהּ אֶלָּא
מֵחֲצִיתָהּ בַּבֹּקֶר וּמַחֲצִיתָהּ בָּעֶרֶב. אֲבָל "תָּמִיד" הָאָמוּר
בְּלֶחֶם הַפָּנִים (לעיל כה, ל) מִשַּׁבָּת לְשַׁבָּת הוּא:

כא] מֵעֶרֶב עַד בֹּקֶר. תֵּן לָהּ מִדָּתָהּ שֶׁתְּהֵא דּוֹלֶקֶת מֵעֶרֶב
וְעַד בֹּקֶר. וְשִׁעֲרוּ חֲכָמִים חֲצִי לֹג לְלֵילֵי טֵבֵת הָאֲרֻכִּין,
וְכֵן לְכָל הַלֵּילוֹת, וְאִם יִתֵּר אֵין בְּכָךְ כְּלוּם:

פרק כח

א] וְאַתָּה הַקְרֵב אֵלֶיךָ. לְאַחַר שֶׁתִּגְמַר מְלֶאכֶת הַמִּשְׁכָּן.

ג] לְקַדְּשׁוֹ לְכַהֲנוֹ לִי. לְקַדְּשׁוֹ לְהַכְנִיסוֹ בִּכְהֻנָּה עַל
יְדֵי הַבְּגָדִים, שֶׁיְּהֵא כֹּהֵן לִי. וּלְשׁוֹן 'כְּהֻנָּה' שֵׁרוּת הוּא,
שיריינטרי״ה בְּלַעַז:

ד] חֹשֶׁן. תַּכְשִׁיט כְּנֶגֶד הַלֵּב: וְאֵפוֹד. לֹא שָׁמַעְתִּי
וְלֹא מָצָאתִי בַּבָּרַיְתָא פֵּרוּשׁ תַּבְנִיתוֹ, וְלִבִּי אוֹמֵר לִי
שֶׁהוּא חֲגוּרָה לוֹ מֵאַחֲרָיו, רָחָב כְּרֹחַב גַּב אִישׁ כְּמִין
סִינָר שֶׁקּוֹרִין רענ״ט שֶׁחוֹגְרוֹת הַשָּׂרוֹת כְּשֶׁרוֹכְבוֹת עַל
הַסּוּסִים, כָּךְ מַעֲשֵׂהוּ מִלְּמַטָּה, שֶׁנֶּאֱמַר: "וְזָרֵד חֵגוֹר אֵפוֹד
בָּד" (שמואל ב׳ ו, יד), לָמַדְנוּ שֶׁהָאֵפוֹד חֲגוֹרָה הִיא. וְאִי
אֶפְשָׁר לוֹמַר שֶׁאֵין בּוֹ אֶלָּא חֲגוֹרָה לְבַדָּהּ, שֶׁהֲרֵי נֶאֱמַר:
"וַיִּתֵּן עָלָיו אֶת הָאֵפֹד" (ויקרא ח, ז), וְאַחַר כָּךְ: "וַיַּחְגֹּר
אֹתוֹ בְּחֵשֶׁב הָאֵפֹד", וְתִרְגֵּם אוּנְקְלוֹס: "בְּהֶמְיַן אֵפוֹדָא",
לָמַדְנוּ שֶׁהַחֵשֶׁב הוּא הַחֲגוֹר, וְהָאֵפוֹד שֵׁם תַּכְשִׁיט לְבַדּוֹ.
וְאִי אֶפְשָׁר לוֹמַר שֶׁעַל שֵׁם שְׁתֵּי הַכְּתֵפוֹת שֶׁבּוֹ הוּא
קָרוּי אֵפוֹד, שֶׁהֲרֵי נֶאֱמַר: "שְׁתֵּי כִתְפוֹת הָאֵפוֹד" (להלן
פסוק כז), לָמַדְנוּ שֶׁהָאֵפוֹד שֵׁם לְבַד, וְהַכְּתֵפוֹת שֵׁם לְבַד,
וְהַחֵשֶׁב שֵׁם לְבַד. לְכָךְ אֲנִי אוֹמֵר שֶׁעַל שֵׁם הַסִּינָר שֶׁל
מַטָּה קָרוּי אֵפוֹד, עַל שֵׁם שֶׁאוֹפְדוֹ וּמְקַשְּׁטוֹ בּוֹ, כְּמוֹ
שֶׁנֶּאֱמַר: "וַיֶּאְפֹּד לוֹ בּוֹ" (ויקרא ח, ז), וְהַחֵשֶׁב הוּא חֲגוֹר

שֶׁלְּמַעְלָה הֵימֶנּוּ, וְהַכְּתֵפוֹת קְבוּעוֹת בּוֹ, וְעוֹד אוֹמֵר לִי
לִבִּי שֶׁיֵּשׁ רְאָיָה שֶׁהוּא מִין לְבוּשׁ, שֶׁתִּרְגֵּם יוֹנָתָן: "וְדָוִד
חָגוּר אֵפוֹד בָּד" (שמואל ב׳ ו, יד), - "כַּרְדּוּט דְּבוּץ",
וְתִרְגֵּם כְּמוֹ כֵן "מְעִילִים" - "כַּרְדּוּטִין" בְּמַעֲשֵׂה תָּמָר
אֲחוֹת אַבְשָׁלוֹם: "כִּי כֵן תִּלְבַּשְׁןָ בְנוֹת הַמֶּלֶךְ הַבְּתוּלֹת
מְעִילִים" (שם יג, יח): וּמְעִיל. הוּא כְּמִין חָלוּק, וְכֵן
הַכְּתֹנֶת, אֶלָּא שֶׁהַכְּתֹנֶת סָמוּךְ לִבְשָׂרוֹ, וּמְעִיל קָרוּי
חָלוּק הָעֶלְיוֹן: תַּשְׁבֵּץ. עֲשׂוּיִין מִשְׁבְּצוֹת לְנוֹי, וְהַמִּשְׁבְּצוֹת
הֵם כְּמִין גוּמּוֹת הָעֲשׂוּיִין בְּתַכְשִׁיטֵי זָהָב לְמוֹשַׁב קְבִיעַת
אֲבָנִים טוֹבוֹת וּמַרְגָּלִיּוֹת, כְּמוֹ שֶׁנֶּאֱמַר בְּאַבְנֵי הָאֵפוֹד:
"מֻסַבֹּת מִשְׁבְּצֹת זָהָב" (להלן פסוק יא), וּבְלַעַז קוֹרִין
אוֹתָן קשטונ״ש: מִצְנָפֶת. כְּמִין כִּפַּת כּוֹבַע שֶׁקּוֹרִין
קופי״א, שֶׁהֲרֵי בְּמָקוֹם אַחֵר קוֹרֵא לָהֶם "מִגְבָּעֹת" (להלן
כט, ט) וּמְתַרְגְּמִינַן: "כּוֹבָעִין": וְאַבְנֵט. הִיא חֲגוֹרָה עַל
הַכְּתֹנֶת, וְהָאֵפוֹד חֲגוֹרָה עַל הַמְּעִיל, כְּמוֹ שֶׁשָּׁנִינוּ בְּסֵדֶר
לְבִישָׁתָן: "וַיִּתֵּן עָלָיו אֶת הַכֻּתֹּנֶת וַיַּחְגֹּר אֹתוֹ בָּאַבְנֵט,
וַיַּלְבֵּשׁ אֹתוֹ אֶת הַמְּעִיל וַיִּתֵּן עָלָיו אֶת הָאֵפֹד" (ויקרא
ח, ז): בִּגְדֵי קֹדֶשׁ. מִתְּרוּמָה הַמֻּקְדֶּשֶׁת לִשְׁמִי יַעֲשׂוּ
אוֹתָם:

DISCUSSION

28:1 | Have Aaron your brother approach you, and his sons: It may be inferred from here that the sons already born to the four sons of Aaron did not merit appointment as priests. Indeed, Pinhas, son of Elazar, who was alive at

this time, was appointed to the priesthood only at a later stage, in reward for his zealous deed (see Numbers 25:13).

28:3 | And they shall make Aaron's vestments to sanctify him, to serve as a priest to

Me: In the Second Temple, when priests were no longer anointed with the anointing oil, High Priests were invested by being dressed in the vestments of the High Priest (see *Yoma* 5a, 12a).

5 **They,** the craftsmen, **shall take the gold and the sky-blue wool and the purple wool and the scarlet wool and the linen.** The priestly vestments will be fashioned from these materials alone.

6 **They shall make the** cloth of the **ephod of** the following materials: **gold, sky-blue wool and purple wool, scarlet wool,** all of them fine twined, **and spun linen, artfully crafted.** The priestly vestments must be produced by skilled artisans.

7 The ephod shall consist of several parts sewn together: **It shall have two shoulder pieces attached to its two ends,** on the

upper end of the apron, **and it,** the apron, **will be attached.** That is, the shoulder pieces will be attached to the apron after they have been fashioned.[2]

8 **The belt of his ephod,**ᴰ **which is on it, shall be of similar craftsmanship; it shall be from it:** That is, the belt is to be woven as an inseparable part of the apron, and from the same materials: **gold, sky-blue, purple, and scarlet wool, and linen,** all **spun together.**

9 **You shall take two onyx stones,**ᴰ **and engrave on them the names of the children of Israel,** the names of the twelve tribes. The stones must be large enough for this engraving, an indication that they are not of the most valuable gems.

10 **Six of their names shall be** engraved **on the one stone, and the names of the six that remain on the second stone, according to** the order of **their birth.**

Onyx stone

11 The engraving shall be done with **the craftsmanship of an engraver in stone,** like **the engravings of a signet,** a delicate and exact procedure. It is unclear whether the names should be embossed, as on a signet,[3] or if they are to be engraved on the stone. **You shall engrave the two stones with the names of the children of Israel; you shall make them surrounded with settings of gold,** which will secure them in place.

12 **You shall place the two stones on the** broad **shoulder pieces of the ephod; they are stones of remembrance for the children of Israel;**ᴰ **Aaron shall carry their names before the Lord on his two shoulders as a remembrance.**

Front of the ephod, according to Rashi

DISCUSSION

28:8 | His ephod: It is unclear whether the main part of the ephod itself, which is girded by the belt and joined to the shoulder pieces, is a woven cloth that is worn only on the back of the priest (see *Midrash HaGadol; Torah Shelema*), or only in the front, like an apron, or whether there are separate cloths in the front and back, or if these separate cloths are hemmed together to form a kind of skirt (Rashbam, verse 7).

28:9 | Onyx [*shoham*] stones: The *shoham* stones are most likely onyx, a stone that is not particularly expensive. Each stone needed to be large enough to engrave the names of six of the tribes (see verse 10); it would therefore seem likely that relatively inexpensive stones were used.

28:12 | Stones of remembrance for the children of Israel: The names of the tribes appear not only on the two onyx stones set on the shoulder pieces of the ephod but also on the stones of the breast piece worn by the High Priest over his heart (see verse 21 below). The vestments of the High Priest express his dual function, both as the servant of God who brings His word to the people, and as the messenger of the children of Israel who represents them before God.

ה אחיך ולבניו לכהנו־לי: והם יקחו את־הזהב ואת־התכלת ואת־הארגמן
ואת־תולעת השני ואת־השש:
ו ועשו את־האפד זהב תכלת וארגמן תולעת שני ושש משזר מעשה חשב:
ז ח שתי כתפת חברת יהיה־לו אל־שני קצותיו וחבר: וחשב אפדתו אשר עליו
ט כמעשהו ממנו יהיה זהב תכלת וארגמן ותולעת שני ושש משזר: ולקחת
י את־שתי אבני־שהם ופתחת עליהם שמות בני ישראל: ששה משמתם על
האבן האחת ואת־שמות הששה הנותרים על־האבן השנית כתולדתם:
יא מעשה חרש אבן פתוחי חתם תפתח את־שתי האבנים על־שמת בני ישראל
יב מסבת משבצות זהב תעשה אתם: ושמת את־שתי האבנים על כתפת האפד
אבני זכרן לבני ישראל ונשא אהרן את־שמותם לפני יהוה על־שתי כתפיו

רש"י

ה| **והם יקחו.** אותם חכמי לב שיעשו הבגדים יקבלו מן המתנדבים "את הזהב ואת התכלת" לעשות מהן את הבגדים:

ו| **ועשו את האפד.** אם באתי לפרש מעשה האפוד והחשן על סדר המקראות, הרי פרושן פרקים, ויטעה הקורא בצרופן. לכך אני כותב מעשיהם כמות שהוא למען ירוץ קורא בו, ואחר כך אפרש על סדר המקראות. האפוד עשוי כמין סינר של נשים רוכבות סוסים, וחוגר אותו מאחוריו כנגד לבו למטה מאציליו, רחבו כמדת רחב גבו של אדם ויותר, ומגיע עד עקביו. והחשב מחבר בראשו על פני רחבו מעשה אורג, ומאריך לכאן ולכאן כדי להקיף ולחגר בו. והכתפות מחברות בחשב, אחד לימין ואחד לשמאל, מאחורי הכהן לשני קצות רחבו של סינר, וכשזוקפן עומדות לו על שני כתפיו. והן כמין שתי רצועות עשויות ממין האפוד, ארוכות כדי שעור לזקפן אצל צוארו מכאן ומכאן, ונקפלות לפניו למטה מכתפיו מעט. ואבני השהם קבועות בהם, אחת על כתף ימין ואחת על כתף שמאל, והמשבצות נתונות בראשיהם לפני כתפיו, ושתי עבותות הזהב תחובות בשתי טבעות שבחשן בשני קצות רחבו העליון, אחת לימין ואחת לשמאל, ושני ראשי השרשרת תקועין במשבצות לימין, וכן שני ראשי השרשרת השמאלית תקועין במשבצת שבכתף שמאל, נמצא החשן תלוי במשבצות האפוד על לבו מלפניו. ועוד שתי טבעות בשני קצות החשן בתחתיתו, וכנגדם שתי טבעות בשתי כתפות האפוד מלמטה בראשו התחתון המחבר בחשב, טבעות החשן אל מול טבעות האפוד שוכבים זה על זה, ומרכסן בפתיל תכלת תחוב בטבעות האפוד והחשן, שיהא תחתית החשן דבוק לחשב האפוד, ולא יהא נד ונבדל הולך וחוזר: **זהב תכלת וארגמן תולעת שני ושש משזר.** חמשת מינים הללו שזורין בכל חוט וחוט. היו מרדדין את הזהב כמין טסים דקים וקוצצין פתילים מהם, וטווין אותן חוט של זהב עם ששה חוטין של תכלת, וחוט של זהב עם ששה חוטין של ארגמן, וכן בתולעת שני וכן בשש, שכל המינין חוטן כפול ששה וחוט של זהב עם כל אחד ואחד. ואחר כך שוזר את כלם כאחד, נמצא חוטן כפול עשרים ושמונה. וכן מפרש במסכת יומא (דף עב ע"א), ולמד מן המקרא הזה: "וירקעו את פחי הזהב וקצץ פתילם לעשות את פתילי הזהב "בתוך התכלת ובתוך הארגמן" וגו' (להלן לט, ג). למדנו שחוט של זהב שזור עם כל מין ומין: **מעשה חשב.** כבר פרשתי (רש"י לעיל כו, א) שהיא אריגת שתי קירות, שאין צורת שני עבריה דומות זו לזו:

ז| **שתי כתפת וגו'.** הסינר מלמטה, וחשב האפוד היא החגורה, ונמודה לו מלמעלה דגמת סינר הנשים. ומגבו של כהן היו מחברות בחשב שתי חתיכות כמין שתי רצועות רחבות, אחת כנגד כל כתף וכתף, וזוקפן על שתי כתפותיו עד שנקפלות לפניו כנגד החזה, ועל ידי חבורן לטבעות החשן נאחזין מלפניו כנגד לבו שאין נופלות, כמו שמפרש בענין, והיו זקופות והולכות כנגד כתפיו, ושתי אבני שהם קבועות בהן, אחת בכל אחת: **אל שני קצותיו.** אל רחבו של אפוד, שלא היה רחבו אלא כנגד גבו של כהן, וגבהו עד כנגד האצילים שקורין קודי"ש, שנאמר: "לא יחגרו ביזע" (יחזקאל מד, יח), אין חוגרין במקום זיעה, לא למעלה מאציליהם ולא למטה ממתניהם, אלא כנגד אציליהם: **וחבר.** האפוד עם אותן שתי כתפות האפוד, יחבר אותם במחט למטה בחשב, ולא יארגם עמו, אלא אורגם לבד ואחר כך מחברם:

ח| **וחשב אפדתו.** חגור שעל ידו הוא מאפדו ומתקנו לכהן ומקשטו: **אשר עליו.** למעלה בשפת הסינר, והיא החגורה: **כמעשהו.** כאריגת הסינר מעשה חושב ומחמשת מינים, כך אריגת החשב מעשה חושב ומחמשת מינים: **ממנו יהיה.** עמו יהיה ארוג, ולא יארגנו לבד ויחברנו:

י| **כתולדתם.** כסדר שנולדו: ראובן, שמעון, לוי, יהודה, דן, נפתלי על האחת; ועל השנית: גד, אשר, יששכר, זבולן, יוסף, בנימין מלא, שכן הוא כתוב במקום תולדתו (בראשית לה, יח), עשרים וחמש אותיות בכל אחת ואחת:

יא| **מעשה חרש אבן.** מעשה אמן של אבנים. 'חרש' זה, דבוק הוא לתבה שלאחריו ולפיכך הוא נקוד פתח בסופו, וכן: "חרש עצים נטה קו" (ישעיה מד, יג), חרש של עצים, וכן: "חרש ברזל מעצד" (שם פסוק יב), כל אלה דבוקים ופתוחים: **פתוחי חתם.** כתרגומו: "כתב מפרש כגלף דעזקא", חרוצות האותיות בתוכן כמו שחורצין חותמי טבעות שהם לחתם אגרות, כתב נכר ומפרש: **על שמת.** כמו בשמות: **מסבת משבצות.** מקפות האבנים במשבצות זהב, שעושה מושב האבן בזהב כמין גומא למדת האבן ומשקעה במשבצת, נמצאת המשבצת סובבת את האבן סביב, ומחבר המשבצת באפוד:

13 The verse returns to elaborate on the production of the settings
Second for the onyx stones. The process will have relevance for the
aliya breast piece as well: **You shall make settings of gold.** Perhaps
this command includes the other settings of gold, which were
placed on the breast piece.[4]

14 **And two chains of pure gold: You shall make them at the
edges of the settings; they shall be braided craftsmanship.**
After fashioning them, **you shall set the braided chains in the
settings.**

15 **You shall make** an ornamental **breast piece,**[D] which will be
utilized in the administration **of judgment;**[5] alternatively, the
breast piece will symbolize your status as a judge. It shall be
**artfully crafted; you shall make it like the craftsmanship of
the ephod,** in a similar manner and from the same materials:
gold, sky-blue, purple, and scarlet wool, and linen, all **spun
together you shall make it.**

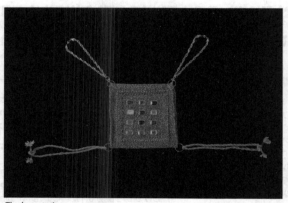

The breast piece

16 **It shall be square** in appearance, and yet it shall actually be
made from a rectangular cloth that has been **folded,** doubled
over. This will form a kind of pouch, in which the Urim and the
Tumim are most likely meant to be placed (see verse 30). **Its
length** shall be **a span [*zeret*]** after it is folded, **and its width
a span.** A *zeret* is approximately half a cubit, slightly more than
20 cm. It is roughly the distance between the tip of one's little
finger [*zeret*] and the tip of one's thumb when spreading out
fingers to their greatest extent.

17 **You shall set in it,** the breast piece, **a mounting of stone, four
rows of stone,** each of which shall contain three different precious stones. The identity of these stones is difficult to determine with absolute certainty: **A row of** *odem*, which is commonly identified as **a ruby,**[BD] **a peridot,**[B] **and an emerald;**[B] this
shall be **the first row.**

18 **And the second row: a carbuncle, a sapphire [*sappir*]** (see
24:10 above). The identity of the *sappir* stone is uncertain. **And
a clear quartz [*yahalom*].** Although in modern Hebrew, *yahalom* refers to a diamond, it is likely that *yahalom* once referred
to a different precious stone.

19 **And the third row: a jacinth, an agate, and an amethyst.**

20 **And the fourth row: a beryl, and an onyx, and a chalcedony;**[B]
they shall be set in gold in their mountings. Due to the difficulty in cutting and smoothing these precious stones, the enclosures must be made to suit the shapes of the stones that will
be set inside them, so that they will be held firmly.

21 **The stones**[D] **shall correspond to the names of the children
of Israel: Twelve, according to their names.** On each stone
the name of one tribe will be engraved. And they shall be engraved like the **engravings of a signet,**[D] each according to its
name, for the twelve tribes.**

22 The verse reiterates, this time in the context of the breast piece,
an earlier command with regard to the chains (see verse 14

DISCUSSION

28:15 | You shall make a breast piece: It is
possible that in ancient times, judges would
adorn themselves with a garment or ornament
similar to the High Priest's breast piece of judgment. It would appear that some type of ephod
was donned by others besides the High Priest
(see I Samuel 2:18, 22:18; II Samuel 6:14). Perhaps
articles similar to the priestly vestments, among
them the breast piece, were likewise worn by
individuals of authority.

28:17 | Ruby [*odem*]: The ruby is a very expen-
sive gem, and it is also one of the hardest stones.
The Torah will state later that each stone represents one of the tribes. If *odem* is indeed the

ruby, it is possible that since this was the stone
of Reuben, the eldest of the tribes, it was named
after him, and when this term was transmitted to
other languages it evolved into the term "ruby"
(see Rabbeinu Baḥya). Nevertheless, the true
identity of the *odem* stone remains uncertain.

28:21 | The stones: According to ancient tra-
dition, the color of the stone used for each
tribe became the color of its respective flag
(*Tanḥuma*, Bemidbar 12; see *Targum Yerushalmi*).

Engravings of a signet: Although archaeological digs have uncovered ancient tools that
were used to cut precious stones, the process
of actually inscribing words on such stones is

of such unparalleled difficulty that in modern
times it is performed only by means of lasers.
Sapphire and ruby, from the mineral corundum,
have a hardness of 9 on the Mohs scale, one
level below that of the hardest stone, diamond.
Consequently, there have been no discoveries of
letters etched on such stones that date from ancient periods. The Sages therefore explain that
the *shamir* worm, which may or may not have
been a naturally occurring creature, was used
for the engraving and writing of letters on the
breast-piece stones (see *Avot* 5:6; *Gittin* 68a; *Sota*
48b; Rashi and Radak, Ezekiel 3:9).

יג לְזִכָּרֹן: וְעָשִׂיתָ מִשְׁבְּצֹת זָהָב: וּשְׁתֵּי שַׁרְשְׁרֹת זָהָב טָהוֹר מִגְבָּלֹת שְׁנִי

יד תַּעֲשֶׂה אֹתָם מַעֲשֵׂה עֲבֹת וְנָתַתָּה אֶת־שַׁרְשְׁרֹת הָעֲבֹתֹת עַל־הַמִּשְׁבְּצֹת:

טו וְעָשִׂיתָ חֹשֶׁן מִשְׁפָּט מַעֲשֵׂה חֹשֵׁב כְּמַעֲשֵׂה אֵפֹד תַּעֲשֶׂנּוּ זָהָב תְּכֵלֶת וְאַרְגָּמָן

טז וְתוֹלַעַת שָׁנִי וְשֵׁשׁ מָשְׁזָר תַּעֲשֶׂה אֹתוֹ: רָבוּעַ יִהְיֶה כָּפוּל זֶרֶת אׇרְכּוֹ וְזֶרֶת רׇחְבּוֹ:

יז וּמִלֵּאתָ בוֹ מִלֻּאַת אֶבֶן אַרְבָּעָה טוּרִים אָבֶן טוּר אֹדֶם פִּטְדָה וּבָרֶקֶת הַטּוּר

יח הָאֶחָד: וְהַטּוּר הַשֵּׁנִי נֹפֶךְ סַפִּיר וְיָהֲלֹם: וְהַטּוּר הַשְּׁלִישִׁי לֶשֶׁם שְׁבוֹ וְאַחְלָמָה:

יט וְהַטּוּר הָרְבִיעִי תַּרְשִׁישׁ וְשֹׁהַם וְיָשְׁפֵה מְשֻׁבָּצִים זָהָב יִהְיוּ בְּמִלּוּאֹתָם: וְהָאֲבָנִים

כ תִּהְיֶיןָ עַל־שְׁמֹת בְּנֵי־יִשְׂרָאֵל שְׁתֵּים עֶשְׂרֵה עַל־שְׁמֹתָם פִּתּוּחֵי חוֹתָם אִישׁ

כא עַל־שְׁמוֹ תִּהְיֶיןָ לִשְׁנֵי עָשָׂר שָׁבֶט: וְעָשִׂיתָ עַל־הַחֹשֶׁן שַׁרְשֹׁת גַּבְלֻת מַעֲשֵׂה

כב

רש"י

יב לְזִכָּרֹן. שֶׁיִּרְאֶה הַקָּדוֹשׁ בָּרוּךְ הוּא שְׁבָטִים כְּתוּבִים לְפָנָיו וְיִזְכֹּר צִדְקָתָם:

יג וְעָשִׂיתָ מִשְׁבְּצֹת. מִעוּט "מִשְׁבְּצֹת" שְׁתַּיִם, וְלֹא פֵּרַשׁ לָךְ עַתָּה בְּפָרָשָׁה זוֹ חֵלֶק מִקְצָת צָרְכָּן, וּבְפָרָשַׁת הַחֹשֶׁן גּוֹמֵר לָךְ פֵּרוּשָׁן:

יד שַׁרְשְׁרֹת זָהָב. שַׁלְשְׁלָאוֹת: מִגְבָּלֹת. לְסוֹף גְּבוּל הַחֹשֶׁן תַּעֲשֶׂה אֹתָם: מַעֲשֵׂה עֲבֹת. מַעֲשֵׂה קְלִיעַת חוּטִין, וְלֹא מַעֲשֵׂה נְקָבִים וּכְפָלִים כְּאוֹתָן שֶׁעוֹשִׂין לְבוֹרוֹת, אֶלָּא כְּאוֹתָן שֶׁעוֹשִׂין לְעֲרֵדַּסְקָאוֹת שֶׁקּוֹרִין אנצינשיי"ר: וְנָתַתָּה אֶת שַׁרְשְׁרֹת. שֶׁל עֲבוֹתוֹת הָעֲשׂוּיוֹת מַעֲשֵׂה עֲבֹת, עַל מִשְׁבְּצֹת הַלָּלוּ. וְלֹא זֶה הוּא מְקוֹם אַחַת עֲשִׂיָּתָן שֶׁל שַׁרְשְׁרֹת וְלֹא עַל אֵלּוּ קְבִיעָתָן, וְכֵן "תַּעֲשֶׂה" חָמוּר כָּאן לָשׁוֹן צִוּוּי, וְכֵן "וְנָתַתָּה" חָמוּר כָּאן לָשׁוֹן צִוּוּי, אֶלָּא

לְשׁוֹן עֲתִידָה, כִּי בְּפָרָשַׁת הַחֹשֶׁן חוֹזֵר וּמְצַוֶּה עַל עֲשִׂיָּתָן וְעַל קְבִיעָתָן, וְלֹא נִכְתַּב כָּאן חֵלֶק לְהוֹדִיעַ מִקְצַת צֹרֶךְ הַמִּשְׁבְּצֹת שֶׁעָה לַעֲשׂוֹתָם עִם הָאֵפֹד, וְכָתַב לְךָ זֹאת לוֹמַר לְךָ, הַמִּשְׁבְּצֹת הַלָּלוּ יִזְקְקוּ לְךָ, לִכְשֶׁתַּעֲשֶׂה שַׁרְשְׁרֹת מִגְבָּלֹת עַל הַמִּשְׁבְּצֹת הַלָּלוּ:

טו חֹשֶׁן מִשְׁפָּט. שֶׁמְּכַפֵּר עַל קִלְקוּל הַדִּין. דָּבָר אַחֵר, "מִשְׁפָּט", שֶׁמְּבָרֵר דְּבָרָיו וְהַבְטָחָתוֹ אֱמֶת, דְּרִישׁנמנ"ט בְּלַעַז: שֶׁהַמִּשְׁפָּט מְשַׁמֵּשׁ שָׁלֹשׁ לְשׁוֹנוֹת: דִּבְרֵי בַּעֲלֵי הַדִּין, וְגֶמֶר הַדִּין, וְעֹנֶשׁ הַדִּין, אִם עֹנֶשׁ מִיתָה אִם עֹנֶשׁ מַכּוֹת אִם עֹנֶשׁ מָמוֹן. וְזֶה מְשַׁמֵּשׁ לָשׁוֹן בֵּרוּר דְּבָרִים, שֶׁמְּפָרֵשׁ וּמְכַרֵּר דְּבָרָיו: כְּמַעֲשֵׂה אֵפֹד. מַעֲשֵׂה חֹשֵׁב וּמֵחֲמֵשֶׁת מִינִין:

טז זֶרֶת אׇרְכּוֹ וְזֶרֶת רׇחְבּוֹ. כָּפוּל וּמֻטָּל לוֹ לְמָעְלָה כְּנֶגֶד לִבּוֹ, שֶׁנֶּאֱמַר: "וְהָיוּ עַל לֵב אַהֲרֹן" (להלן פסוק ל), תָּלוּי

בְּכְתָפוֹת הָאֵפוֹד הַבָּאוֹת מֵאֲחוֹרָיו עַל כְּתֵפָיו וְנִכְפָּלוֹת וְיוֹרְדוֹת לְפָנָיו מְעַט, וְהַחֹשֶׁן תָּלוּי בָּהֶן בְּשַׁרְשְׁרֹת וְטַבָּעוֹת, כְּמוֹ שֶׁמְּפֹרָשׁ בָּעִנְיָן:

יז וּמִלֵּאתָ בוֹ. עַל שֵׁם שֶׁהָאֲבָנִים מְמַלְּאוֹת גּוּמוֹת הַמִּשְׁבְּצוֹת הַמְּתֻקָּנוֹת לָהֶן, קוֹרֵא אוֹתָן בִּלְשׁוֹן מִלּוּאִים:

כ מְשֻׁבָּצִים זָהָב יִהְיוּ. הַטּוּרִים "בְּמִלּוּאֹתָם", מֻקְפִים מִשְׁבְּצוֹת זָהָב בְּעָמְקָן שִׁעוּר שֶׁיִּתְמַלֵּא בְּעָבְיָן שֶׁל אֶבֶן, זֶהוּ לְשׁוֹן "בְּמִלּוּאֹתָם", כְּשִׁעוּר מִלּוּי עׇבְיָן שֶׁל אֲבָנִים יִהְיֶה עֹמֶק הַמִּשְׁבְּצוֹת, לֹא פָּחוֹת וְלֹא יוֹתֵר:

כא אִישׁ עַל שְׁמוֹ. כְּסֵדֶר תּוֹלְדוֹתָם סֵדֶר הָאֲבָנִים, אֹדֶם לִרְאוּבֵן, פִּטְדָה לְשִׁמְעוֹן, וְכֵן כֻּלָּם:

כב עַל הַחֹשֶׁן. בִּשְׁבִיל הַחֹשֶׁן, לְקָבְעָם בְּטַבְּעוֹתָיו, כְּמוֹ

BACKGROUND

28:17 | Ruby [odem]: Researchers have attempted to identify the odem with stones whose names in other Semitic languages relate their reddish [adom] appearance, such as the samtu stone in Akkadian, or samkan in Aramaic (see Onkelos; Targum Yonatan). Others identify the odem stone as sardion, carnelian, which appears in Greek and Roman literature, or as red jasper, which was used in Egypt at the time. Rabbeinu Bahya identifies odem as the ruby, which he considers the choicest of the precious stones.

Peridot [pitda]: According to Onkelos, the pitda is the jade stone. However, a verse in Job (28:19) identifies the pitda as coming from Kush: "It cannot be valued like the pitda of Kush." This suggests an identification as peridot, which can be found in East Africa. The Septuagint translates pitda as "topazi[os]," a word originally derived from the island of Topazos in the Red Sea, now known as Zabargad, which features significant deposits of peridot. This translation has led to the misidentification of pitda as topaz in many translations.

Emerald [bareket]: This refers to a shiny [mavrika] stone. Based on the Sanskrit term marakata, some maintain that it is the green emerald. Others have identified bareket as either a dark red carbuncle; an agate, which is a striped quartz stone of various colors; or a precious stone with the appearance of fiery coal, e.g., a ruby.

28:20 | Chalcedony [yashfe]: The English word "chalcedony" derives from the name of the ancient town Chalcedon in Asia Minor. The Arabic yashb means jasper. In the Septuagint, yashfe is identified as the same stone as the kadkhod mentioned in Isaiah (54:12), a quartz stone of various colors. In Greek as well, there is the karchedon, probably named after the ancient city of Carthage, located in modern-day Tunisia, from where these stones were exported.

above). **You shall fix bordering chains**[D] **of braided crafts-manship on the breast piece of pure gold.** These will be placed on the edges of the breast piece.

23 **You shall fix two rings of gold upon** the upper part of **the breast piece, and you shall put the two rings on the two ends of the breast piece,** on the right and left.

24 **You shall put the two braids of gold on the two rings at the ends of the breast piece.**

25 The other **two ends of the two braids you shall put on the two settings** mentioned above with regard to the ephod, **and you shall place them,** the settings,[6] **on the shoulder pieces of the ephod, toward its front,** in the area of the neck. In this manner the breast piece shall hang over the chest.

26 **You shall make two** additional **rings of gold and you shall place them on the two ends of the breast piece, on its edge, that is toward the ephod on the inner side** of the folded breast piece, which faces the ephod.

27 **You shall make two** additional **rings of gold, and you shall put them on the two shoulder pieces of the ephod,**

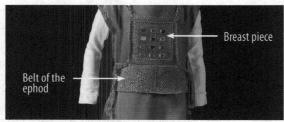

Breast piece

Belt of the ephod

The breast piece and the belt of the ephod

specifically **from below** those shoulder pieces, **toward its front,** on the backside of the ephod, **adjacent to its seam,** that is, the area where the shoulder pieces are sewn to the ephod,[7] **above the belt of the ephod.**

28 **They shall lace the breast piece from its rings,** namely those on the bottom of the breast piece, **to the rings** attached to the bottoms of the shoulder pieces **of the ephod, with a thread of sky-blue wool, to be on the belt of the ephod, and the breast piece shall not be detached from upon the ephod.** That is to say, there is a specific requirement that the breast piece will be attached to the ephod at all times.[8]

29 **Aaron shall bear the names of the children of Israel on the breast piece of judgment upon his heart upon his entry into the Sanctuary, as a constant remembrance before the Lord.** The stones of the breast piece are not mere ornaments meant for beauty; rather, they serve as a remembrance of Israel before God, just like the stones of the ephod.

30 **You shall place the Urim and the Tumim**[D] **in** the pouch between the folds of **the breast piece of judgment.** The nature of the Urim and the Tumim is shrouded in mystery and is not explained in the Bible. The Sages explain that they were sacred names that, when placed inside the fold, would cause the stones of the breast piece to shine in response to questions posed about the future.[9] According to Ibn Ezra (verse 6 above), the Urim and the Tumim are instruments for making astrological measurements. Others suggest that they contained a list of the borders and cities of each tribe.[10] **And they shall be upon Aaron's heart upon his entry before the Lord; and Aaron shall constantly bear the judgment,** meaning the ways and practices, **of the children of Israel on his heart,** inside the breast piece, **before the Lord.**

DISCUSSION

28:22 | Chains [*sharshot*]: A *sharsheret*, chain (see verse 14 above), is formed by attaching links one to another, and its root is perhaps derived from the word *she'ir*, meaning ring or bracelet (see *Shabbat* 51b). By contrast, *sharshot*, which also refers to some form of connecting, would seem to derive from the word *shoresh*, root, such as twisted or braided cords just like the roots of a tree, which fix the tree in the ground (see Rashi).

28:30 | The Urim and the Tumim: When Joshua son of Nun was appointed successor to Moses as

leader of Israel, the verse states: "Before Elazar the priest he shall stand, and he will inquire for him regarding the judgment of the Urim before the Lord" (Numbers 27:21). The Sages explain that when the High Priest was posed a question by one who was qualified to do so, such as Joshua, the Urim, which were in the pouch of the breast piece, caused certain stones or letters to light up, and the Tumim instructed the High Priest how to combine the bright letters into

meaningful sentences, which constituted God's response to the question (*Yoma* 73a).

Apparently, the Urim and the Tumim existed only in the Tabernacle and the First Temple, but not in the Second Temple (see *Yoma* 21b; *Sota* 48b; see also Rambam, *Sefer Avoda, Hilkhot Kelei HaMikdash* 10:10; Ra'avad on Rambam, *Sefer Avoda, Hilkhot Beit HaBeḥira* 4:1; Rashi). Consequently, the Sages themselves did not actually see the form of the Urim and the Tumim, nor did they observe them at work.

כג עֲבֹת זָהָב טָהוֹר׃ וְעָשִׂיתָ עַל־הַחֹשֶׁן שְׁתֵּי טַבְּעוֹת זָהָב וְנָתַתָּ אֶת־שְׁתֵּי הַטַּבָּעוֹת
כד עַל־שְׁנֵי קְצוֹת הַחֹשֶׁן׃ וְנָתַתָּה אֶת־שְׁתֵּי עֲבֹתֹת הַזָּהָב עַל־שְׁתֵּי הַטַּבָּעֹת אֶל־
כה קְצוֹת הַחֹשֶׁן׃ וְאֵת שְׁתֵּי קְצוֹת שְׁתֵּי הָעֲבֹתֹת תִּתֵּן עַל־שְׁתֵּי הַמִּשְׁבְּצוֹת וְנָתַתָּה
כו עַל־כִּתְפוֹת הָאֵפֹד אֶל־מוּל פָּנָיו׃ וְעָשִׂיתָ שְׁתֵּי טַבְּעוֹת זָהָב וְשַׂמְתָּ אֹתָם עַל־שְׁנֵי
כז קְצוֹת הַחֹשֶׁן עַל־שְׂפָתוֹ אֲשֶׁר אֶל־עֵבֶר הָאֵפוֹד בָּיְתָה׃ וְעָשִׂיתָ שְׁתֵּי טַבְּעוֹת
זָהָב וְנָתַתָּה אֹתָם עַל־שְׁתֵּי כִתְפוֹת הָאֵפוֹד מִלְּמַטָּה מִמּוּל פָּנָיו לְעֻמַּת מַחְבַּרְתּוֹ
כח מִמַּעַל לְחֵשֶׁב הָאֵפוֹד׃ וְיִרְכְּסוּ אֶת־הַחֹשֶׁן מִטַּבְּעֹתָו אֶל־טַבְּעֹת הָאֵפוֹד בִּפְתִיל
כט תְּכֵלֶת לִהְיוֹת עַל־חֵשֶׁב הָאֵפוֹד וְלֹא־יִזַּח הַחֹשֶׁן מֵעַל הָאֵפוֹד׃ וְנָשָׂא אַהֲרֹן
אֶת־שְׁמוֹת בְּנֵי־יִשְׂרָאֵל בְּחֹשֶׁן הַמִּשְׁפָּט עַל־לִבּוֹ בְּבֹאוֹ אֶל־הַקֹּדֶשׁ לְזִכָּרֹן לִפְנֵי־
ל יהוה תָּמִיד׃ וְנָתַתָּ אֶל־חֹשֶׁן הַמִּשְׁפָּט אֶת־הָאוּרִים וְאֶת־הַתֻּמִּים וְהָיוּ עַל־לֵב
אַהֲרֹן בְּבֹאוֹ לִפְנֵי יהוה וְנָשָׂא אַהֲרֹן אֶת־מִשְׁפַּט בְּנֵי־יִשְׂרָאֵל עַל־לִבּוֹ לִפְנֵי יהוה

רש"י

שֶׁמְּפֹרָשׁ לְמַטָּה בָּעִנְיָן: שַׁרְשֹׁת. לְשׁוֹן שָׁרְשֵׁי אִילָן שֶׁהֵן מַאֲחִזִין לָאִילָן לְהֵאָחֵז וּלְהִתָּקַע בָּאָרֶץ, אַף אֵלּוּ יִהְיוּ מַאֲחִיזִין לַחֹשֶׁן, שֶׁבָּהֶם יִהְיֶה תָּלוּי בָּאֵפוֹד, וְהֵן שְׁתֵּי שַׁרְשְׁרוֹת הָאֲמוּרוֹת לְמַעְלָה בְּעִנְיַן הַמִּשְׁבְּצוֹת (לעיל פסוק יד). וְאַף 'שַׁרְשְׁרוֹת' פָּתַר מְנַחֵם בֶּן סָרוּק לְשׁוֹן שָׁרָשִׁים, וְאָמַר שֶׁהָרֵי"שׁ יְתֵרָה כְּמוֹ מֵ"ם שֶׁבְּ'שִׁלְשׁוֹם' (בראשית לא, ב) וּמֵ"ם שֶׁבְּ'רֵיקָם' (שם פסוק מב). וְאֵינִי רוֹאֶה אֶת דְּבָרָיו, אֶלָּא 'שַׁרְשֶׁרֶת' בִּלְשׁוֹן עִבְרִית כְּ'שַׁלְשֶׁלֶת' בִּלְשׁוֹן מִשְׁנָה (כלים יד, ג): גַּבְלֻת. הוּא "מִגְבָּלֹת" הָאָמוּר לְמַעְלָה (לעיל פסוק יד), שֶׁתִּתְקָעֵם בַּטַּבָּעוֹת שֶׁיִּהְיוּ בִּגְבוּל הַחֹשֶׁן. וְכָל 'גְּבוּל' לְשׁוֹן קָצֶה, אשומי"ל בְּלַעַז: מַעֲשֵׂה עֲבֹת. מַעֲשֵׂה קְלִיעָה:

כג| עַל הַחֹשֶׁן. לְצֹרֶךְ הַחֹשֶׁן, כְּדֵי לְקָבְעָם בּוֹ. וְלֹא יִתָּכֵן לוֹמַר שֶׁתְּהֵא תְּחִלַּת עֲשִׂיָּתָן עָלָיו, שֶׁאִם כֵּן מַה הוּא שֶׁחוֹזֵר וְאוֹמֵר: "וְנָתַתָּ אֶת שְׁתֵּי הַטַּבָּעוֹת", וַהֲלֹא כְּבָר נְתוּנִים בּוֹ! הָיָה לוֹ לִכְתֹּב בִּתְחִלַּת הַמִּקְרָא: 'וְעָשִׂיתָ עַל קְצוֹת הַחֹשֶׁן שְׁתֵּי טַבְּעוֹת זָהָב'! וְאַף בַּשַּׁרְשְׁרוֹת צָרִיךְ אַתָּה לִפְתֹּר כֵּן: עַל שְׁנֵי קְצוֹת הַחֹשֶׁן. לִשְׁתֵּי פֵּאוֹת שֶׁכְּנֶגֶד הַצַּוָּאר, לַיְמָנִית וְלַשְּׂמָאלִית, הַבָּאִים מוּל כִּתְפוֹת הָאֵפוֹד:
כד| וְנָתַתָּה אֶת שְׁתֵּי עֲבֹתֹת הַזָּהָב. הֵן הֵן "שַׁרְשֹׁת גַּבְלֻת" הַכְּתוּבוֹת לְמַעְלָה (לעיל פסוק כב), וְלֹא פֵּרַשׁ מְקוֹם קְבִיעָתָן בַּחֹשֶׁן, עַכְשָׁיו מְפָרֵשׁ לְךָ שֶׁיְּהֵא תּוֹחֵב אוֹתָן בַּטַּבָּעוֹת. וְתֵדַע לְךָ שֶׁהֵן הֵן הָרִאשׁוֹנוֹת, שֶׁהֲרֵי בְּפָרָשַׁת 'אֵלֶּה פְקוּדֵי' לֹא הֻכְפְּלוּ:

כה| וְאֵת שְׁתֵּי קְצוֹת. שֶׁל "שְׁתֵּי הָעֲבֹתֹת", שְׁנֵי רָאשֵׁיהֶם שֶׁל כָּל אַחַת וְאַחַת: תִּתֵּן עַל שְׁתֵּי הַמִּשְׁבְּצוֹת. הֵן הֵן הַכְּתוּבוֹת לְמַעְלָה בֵּין פָּרָשַׁת הַחֹשֶׁן וּפָרָשַׁת הָאֵפוֹד, וְלֹא פֵּרַשׁ אֶת צָרְכָּן וְאֶת מְקוֹמָן, עַכְשָׁיו מְפָרֵשׁ שֶׁיִּתָּקַע בָּהֶן רָאשֵׁי הָעֲבוֹתוֹת הַתְּחוּבוֹת בְּטַבְּעוֹת הַחֹשֶׁן לְיָמִין וְלִשְׂמֹאל אֵצֶל הַצַּוָּאר, שְׁנֵי רָאשֵׁי שַׁרְשֶׁרֶת הַיְמָנִית תּוֹקֵעַ בְּמִשְׁבֶּצֶת שֶׁל יָמִין, וְכֵן בְּשֶׁל שְׂמֹאל שְׁנֵי רָאשֵׁי שַׁרְשֶׁרֶת הַשְּׂמָאלִית: וְנָתַתָּה. הַמִּשְׁבְּצוֹת "עַל כִּתְפוֹת הָאֵפוֹד". אַחַת בָּזוֹ וְאַחַת בָּזוֹ, נִמְצְאוּ כִּתְפוֹת הָאֵפוֹד מַחֲזִיקִין אֶת הַחֹשֶׁן שֶׁלֹּא יִפֹּל, וּבָהֶן הוּא תָּלוּי. וַעֲדַיִן שְׂפַת הַחֹשֶׁן הַתַּחְתּוֹנָה הוֹלֶכֶת וּבָאָה וְנוֹקֶשֶׁת עַל כְּרֵסוֹ וְאֵינָהּ דְּבוּקָה לוֹ יָפֶה, לְכָךְ הֻצְרַךְ עוֹד שְׁתֵּי טַבָּעוֹת לְתַחְתִּיתוֹ כְּמוֹ שֶׁמְּפָרֵשׁ וְהוֹלֵךְ: אֶל מוּל פָּנָיו. שֶׁל אֵפוֹד, שֶׁלֹּא יִתֵּן הַמִּשְׁבְּצוֹת בְּעֵבֶר הַכְּתֵפוֹת שֶׁכְּלַפֵּי הַמְּעִיל, אֶלָּא בָּעֵבֶר הָעֶלְיוֹן שֶׁכְּלַפֵּי הַחוּץ, וְהוּא קָרוּי 'מוּל פָּנָיו' שֶׁל אֵפוֹד, כִּי אוֹתוֹ עֵבֶר שֶׁאֵינוֹ נִרְאֶה אֵינוֹ קָרוּי פָּנִים:

כו| עַל שְׁנֵי קְצוֹת הַחֹשֶׁן. הֵן שְׁתֵּי פֵּאוֹתָיו הַתַּחְתּוֹנוֹת לְיָמִין וְלִשְׂמֹאל: עַל שְׂפָתוֹ אֲשֶׁר אֶל עֵבֶר הָאֵפוֹד בָּיְתָה. הֲרֵי לְךָ שְׁנֵי סִימָנִין: הָאֶחָד שֶׁיִּתְּנֵם בִּשְׁנֵי קְצָווֹת שֶׁל תַּחְתִּיתוֹ שֶׁהוּא כְּנֶגֶד הָאֵפוֹד, שֶׁעֶלְיוֹנוֹ אֵינוֹ כְּנֶגֶד הָאֵפוֹד, שֶׁהֲרֵי סָמוּךְ לַצַּוָּאר הוּא וְהָאֵפוֹד נָתוּן עַל מָתְנָיו. וְעוֹד נָתַן סִימָן, שֶׁלֹּא יִקְבָּעֵם בְּעֵבֶר הַחֹשֶׁן שֶׁכְּלַפֵּי הַחוּץ אֶלָּא בָּעֵבֶר שֶׁכְּלַפֵּי פְּנִים, שֶׁנֶּאֱמַר "בָּיְתָה", וְאוֹתוֹ הָעֵבֶר הוּא לְצַד הָאֵפוֹד, שֶׁחֵשֶׁב הָאֵפוֹד חוֹגְרוֹ לַכֹּהֵן וְנִקְפָּל הַסִּינָר לִפְנֵי הַכֹּהֵן עַל מָתְנָיו וּקְצָת כְּרֵסוֹ מִכָּאן וּמִכָּאן עַד כְּנֶגֶד קְצוֹת הַחֹשֶׁן, וּקְצוֹתָיו שׁוֹכְבִין עָלָיו:

כז| עַל שְׁתֵּי כִּתְפוֹת הָאֵפוֹד מִלְּמַטָּה. שֶׁהַמִּשְׁבְּצוֹת נְתוּנוֹת בְּרָאשֵׁי כִּתְפוֹת הָאֵפוֹד הָעֶלְיוֹנִים הַבָּאִים עַל כְּתֵפָיו כְּנֶגֶד גְּרוֹנוֹ וְנִקְפָּלוֹת וְיוֹרְדוֹת לְפָנָיו, וְהַטַּבָּעוֹת צִוָּה לִתֵּן בָּרֹאשׁ הַשֵּׁנִי שֶׁהוּא מְחֻבָּר לָאֵפוֹד, וְהוּא שֶׁנֶּאֱמַר: "לְעֻמַּת מַחְבַּרְתּוֹ", סָמוּךְ לִמְקוֹם חִבּוּרָן בָּאֵפוֹד לְמַעְלָה מִן הַחֲגוֹרָה מְעַט, שֶׁהַמַּחְבֶּרֶת לְעֻמַּת הַחֲגוֹרָה, וְאֵלּוּ נְתוּנִים מְעַט בְּגָבְהָהּ זְקִיפַת הַכְּתֵפוֹת, הוּא שֶׁנֶּאֱמַר: "מִמַּעַל לְחֵשֶׁב הָאֵפוֹד", וְהֵן כְּנֶגֶד סוֹף הַחֹשֶׁן. וְנוֹתֵן פְּתִיל תְּכֵלֶת בְּאוֹתָן הַטַּבָּעוֹת וּבְטַבְּעוֹת הַחֹשֶׁן, וְרוֹכְסָן בְּאוֹתוֹ פְּתִיל לְיָמִין וְלִשְׂמֹאל, שֶׁלֹּא יְהֵא תַּחְתִּית הַחֹשֶׁן הוֹלֵךְ לְפָנִים וְחוֹזֵר לְאָחוֹר וְנוֹקֵשׁ עַל כְּרֵסוֹ, וְנִמְצָא מְיֻשָּׁב עַל הַמְּעִיל יָפֶה: מִמּוּל פָּנָיו. בָּעֵבֶר הַחִיצוֹן:

כח| וְיִרְכְּסוּ. לְשׁוֹן חִבּוּר, וְכֵן: "מֵרֻכְסֵי אִישׁ" (תהלים לא, כא), חִבּוּרֵי חַבְלֵי רְשָׁעִים, וְכֵן: "וְהָרְכָסִים לְבִקְעָה" (ישעיה מ, ד), הָרִים הַסְּמוּכִים זֶה לָזֶה שֶׁאִי אֶפְשָׁר לֵירֵד לַגַּיְא שֶׁבֵּינֵיהֶם אֶלָּא בְּקֹשִׁי גָּדוֹל, שֶׁמִּתּוֹךְ סְמִיכָתָן הַגַּיְא זְקוּפָה וַעֲמֻקָּה, יִהְיוּ לְבִקְעַת מִישׁוֹר וְנוֹחָה לֵילֵךְ: לִהְיוֹת עַל חֵשֶׁב הָאֵפוֹד. לִהְיוֹת הַחֹשֶׁן דָּבוּק אֶל חֵשֶׁב הָאֵפוֹד: וְלֹא יִזַּח. לְשׁוֹן נִתּוּק, וּלְשׁוֹן עֲרָבִי הוּא, כְּדִבְרֵי דוּנַשׁ בֶּן לַבְרַט:

ל| אֶת הָאוּרִים וְאֶת הַתֻּמִּים. הוּא כְּתָב שֵׁם הַמְּפֹרָשׁ שֶׁהָיָה נוֹתְנוֹ בְּתוֹךְ כִּפְלֵי הַחֹשֶׁן, שֶׁעַל יָדוֹ הוּא מֵאִיר דְּבָרָיו וּמְתַמֵּם אֶת דְּבָרָיו. וּבְמִקְדָּשׁ שֵׁנִי הָיָה הַחֹשֶׁן, שֶׁאִי

31 **You shall make the robe of the ephod entirely of sky-blue** *Third aliya* **wool.** The ephod would be placed above the robe and would fasten it in place.[11] The High Priest's robe was somewhat similar to the modern robe. However, since the verse makes no mention of sleeves, it would seem that this robe resembled a cloak that covered the back and sides of one's body. In front, the robe was open from the neck downward; the ephod and its belt held its front parts together so that they would not spread too far apart.[12]

Alternative view of the robe, according to Rashi

Collar like the opening of a coat of mail

32 **The opening for his,** the High Priest's, **head shall be within it,** in its center. **There shall be a hem,**[13] **the craftsmanship of a weaver, around its opening, like the opening of a coat of mail it shall be for it,**[14] folded slightly inward so that it should not harm the wearer or obstruct him. This will ensure that **it,** the robe, **shall not be rent.**[15] Alternatively, this is an instruction, that it is prohibited to tear the robe.[16]

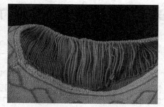

Bells and pomegranates

33 **You shall fix on its hem** ornaments in the shape of **pomegranates of sky-blue, purple, and scarlet wool,** and they shall be placed **all around its hem; there shall be bells of gold among them all around.**

34 They shall be placed as follows: a **golden bell and** then a **pomegranate, a golden bell and** then a **pomegranate,**[17] **on the hem of the robe all around.** Alternatively, a golden bell was placed inside each pomegranate.[18] According to tradition, there were seventy-two pomegranates on the High Priest's robe.[19]

35 **It,** the robe, **shall be on Aaron** when he comes **to serve, and its sound shall be heard upon his entry into the Sanctuary before the Lord and upon his emergence,**[D] **and he will not die.** Although gold is a relatively soft metal, such that the sound produced by a golden bell would be quite gentle, the large quantity of bells on the High Priest's robe ensured that a sound would be heard as he walked.

36 **You shall make a diadem of pure gold,** which will be positioned at the front of his head. This diadem is also called "the holy crown,"[20] and the Sages refer to it as the crown of the priesthood.[21] **And you shall engrave upon it the engravings of a signet,** in decorative and elegant writing, the phrase **Holy to the Lord.**[D]

37 **You shall place on it a thread of sky blue,** in order to tie the diadem, which did not extend around the whole head. **And it shall be upon the mitre,** adjacent to the mitre on the High Priest's forehead.[22] According to Rashi, threads were inserted into holes situated at the edges of the diadem and in the center of the diadem on top; the threads were wrapped around the head of the High Priest and over the mitre, and all of the threads were tied together in the back. **It,** the diadem, **shall be toward the forefront of the mitre.**

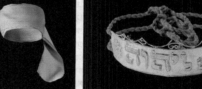

The mitre

The diadem

38 **It shall be on Aaron's forehead and Aaron shall bear,** atone for by means of the diadem, **the iniquity of the sacraments that the children of Israel shall consecrate, for all their sacraments.** This refers to ritually impure sacred gifts that were brought into the Sanctuary; the diadem and the words engraved upon it shall serve as an atonement for this transgression.[23] **It shall be on his forehead always, for propitiation for them,** the Israelites, **before the Lord.**

לא לב תָּמִיד: וְעָשִׂיתָ אֶת־מְעִיל הָאֵפוֹד כְּלִיל תְּכֵלֶת: וְהָיָה פִי־רֹאשׁוֹ בְּתוֹכוֹ שלישי
לג שָׂפָה יִהְיֶה לְפִיו סָבִיב מַעֲשֵׂה אֹרֵג כְּפִי תַחְרָא יִהְיֶה־לּוֹ לֹא יִקָּרֵעַ: וְעָשִׂיתָ עַל־
שׁוּלָיו רִמֹּנֵי תְּכֵלֶת וְאַרְגָּמָן וְתוֹלַעַת שָׁנִי עַל־שׁוּלָיו סָבִיב וּפַעֲמֹנֵי זָהָב בְּתוֹכָם
לד לה סָבִיב: פַּעֲמֹן זָהָב וְרִמּוֹן פַּעֲמֹן זָהָב וְרִמּוֹן עַל־שׁוּלֵי הַמְּעִיל סָבִיב: וְהָיָה עַל־
אַהֲרֹן לְשָׁרֵת וְנִשְׁמַע קוֹלוֹ בְּבֹאוֹ אֶל־הַקֹּדֶשׁ לִפְנֵי יְהוָה וּבְצֵאתוֹ וְלֹא
לו יָמוּת: וְעָשִׂיתָ צִּיץ זָהָב טָהוֹר וּפִתַּחְתָּ עָלָיו פִּתּוּחֵי חֹתָם קֹדֶשׁ לַיהוָה:
לז וְשַׂמְתָּ אֹתוֹ עַל־פְּתִיל תְּכֵלֶת וְהָיָה עַל־הַמִּצְנָפֶת אֶל־מוּל פְּנֵי־הַמִּצְנֶפֶת יִהְיֶה:
לח וְהָיָה עַל־מֵצַח אַהֲרֹן וְנָשָׂא אַהֲרֹן אֶת־עֲוֹן הַקֳּדָשִׁים אֲשֶׁר יַקְדִּישׁוּ בְּנֵי יִשְׂרָאֵל
לְכָל־מַתְּנֹת קָדְשֵׁיהֶם וְהָיָה עַל־מִצְחוֹ תָּמִיד לְרָצוֹן לָהֶם לִפְנֵי יְהוָה:

רש״י

אֶפְשָׁר לְכֹהֵן גָּדוֹל לִהְיוֹת מְחֻסַּר בְּגָדִים, אֲבָל אוֹתוֹ הַשֵּׁם לֹא הָיָה בְּתוֹכוֹ. וְעַל שֵׁם אוֹתוֹ הַכְּתָב הוּא קָרוּי ׳מִשְׁפָּט׳, שֶׁנֶּאֱמַר: ״וְשָׁאַל לוֹ בְּמִשְׁפַּט הָאוּרִים״ (במדבר כז, כא): **אֶת מִשְׁפַּט בְּנֵי יִשְׂרָאֵל.** דָּבָר שֶׁהֵם נִשְׁפָּטִים וְנוֹכָחִים עַל יָדוֹ אִם לַעֲשׂוֹת דָּבָר אוֹ לֹא לַעֲשׂוֹת. וּלְפִי מִדְרַשׁ אַגָּדָה שֶׁהַחֹשֶׁן מְכַפֵּר עַל מְעֻוְּתֵי הַדִּין, נִקְרָא ״מִשְׁפָּט״ עַל שֵׁם סְלִיחַת הַמִּשְׁפָּט:

לא| **אֶת מְעִיל הָאֵפוֹד.** שֶׁהָאֵפוֹד נָתוּן עָלָיו לַחֲגוֹרָה: **כְּלִיל תְּכֵלֶת.** כֻּלּוֹ תְּכֵלֶת, שֶׁאֵין מִין אַחֵר מְעֹרָב בּוֹ:

לב| **וְהָיָה פִי רֹאשׁוֹ.** פִּי הַמְּעִיל שֶׁבְּגָבְהוֹ, הוּא פְּתִיחַת בֵּית הַצַּוָּאר: **בְּתוֹכוֹ.** כְּתַרְגּוּמוֹ: ״כְּפִיל לְגַוֵּהּ״, כָּפוּל לְתוֹכוֹ לִהְיוֹת לוֹ לְשָׂפָה כְּפִילָתוֹ. וְהָיָה מַעֲשֵׂה אוֹרֵג וְלֹא בְּמַחַט: **כְּפִי תַחְרָא.** לָמַדְנוּ שֶׁהַשִּׁרְיוֹנִים שֶׁלָּהֶם פִּיהֶם כָּפוּל: **לֹא יִקָּרֵעַ.** כְּדֵי שֶׁלֹּא יִקָּרֵעַ. וְהַקּוֹרְעוֹ עוֹבֵר בְּלָאו, שֶׁזֶּה מִמִּנְיַן לָאוִין שֶׁבַּתּוֹרָה. וְכֵן: ״וְלֹא יִזַּח הַחֹשֶׁן״ (לעיל פסוק כח), וְכֵן: ״לֹא יָסֻרוּ מִמֶּנּוּ״ (לעיל כה, טו) הַנֶּאֱמַר בְּבַדֵּי הָאָרוֹן:

לג| **רִמֹּנֵי.** עֲגֻלִּים וַחֲלוּלִים הָיוּ, כְּמִין רִמּוֹנִים הָעֲשׂוּיִים כְּבֵיצַת תַּרְנְגֹלֶת: **וּפַעֲמֹנֵי זָהָב.** זוּגִים עִם עִנְבָּלִים שֶׁבְּתוֹכָם: **בְּתוֹכָם סָבִיב.** בֵּינֵיהֶם סָבִיב, בֵּין שְׁנֵי רִמּוֹנִים פַּעֲמוֹן אֶחָד דָּבוּק וְתָלוּי בְּשׁוּלֵי הַמְּעִיל:

לד| **פַּעֲמֹן זָהָב וְרִמּוֹן.** אֶצְלוֹ: פַּעֲמֹן זָהָב וְרִמּוֹן. אֶצְלוֹ:

לה| **וְלֹא יָמוּת.** מִכְּלָל לָאו אַתָּה שׁוֹמֵעַ הֵן: אִם יִהְיוּ לֹא יִתְחַיֵּב מִיתָה, הָא אִם יִכָּנֵס מְחֻסַּר אֶחָד מִן הַבְּגָדִים הַלָּלוּ חַיָּב מִיתָה בִּידֵי שָׁמַיִם:

לו| **צִיץ.** כְּמִין טַס שֶׁל זָהָב הָיָה, רֹחַב שְׁתֵּי אֶצְבָּעוֹת, מַקִּיף עַל הַמֵּצַח מֵאֹזֶן לְאֹזֶן:

לז| **עַל פְּתִיל תְּכֵלֶת.** וּבְמָקוֹם אַחֵר הוּא אוֹמֵר: ״וַיִּתְּנוּ עָלָיו פְּתִיל תְּכֵלֶת״ (להלן לט, לא), וְעוֹד, כְּתִיב כָּאן: ״וְהָיָה עַל הַמִּצְנֶפֶת״, וּלְמַטָּה הוּא אוֹמֵר: ״וְהָיָה עַל מֵצַח אַהֲרֹן״ (בפסוק הבא), וּבִשְׁחִיטַת קָדָשִׁים שָׁנִינוּ: ״שְׂעָרוֹ הָיָה נִרְאֶה בֵּין צִיץ לְמִצְנֶפֶת שֶׁשָּׁם מַנִּיחַ תְּפִלִּין״ (זבחים יט ע״א), לָמַדְנוּ שֶׁהַמִּצְנֶפֶת לְמַעְלָה בְּגֹבַהּ הָרֹאשׁ וְאֵינָהּ עֲמֻקָּה לִכָּנֵס בָּהּ כָּל הָרֹאשׁ עַד הַמֵּצַח, וְהַצִּיץ מִלְּמַטָּה, וְהַפְּתִילִים הָיוּ נְקוּבִין וְתְלוּיִין בּוֹ בִּשְׁנֵי רָאשִׁים וּבְאֶמְצָעִיתוֹ, שִׁשָּׁה בִּשְׁלֹשָׁה מְקוֹמוֹת הַלָּלוּ, פְּתִיל מִלְמַעְלָה – אֶחָד מִבַּחוּץ וְאֶחָד מִבִּפְנִים כְּנֶגְדּוֹ, וְקוֹשֵׁר רָאשֵׁי הַפְּתִילִים מֵאֲחוֹרֵי הָעֹרֶף שְׁלָשְׁתָּן, וְנִמְצְאוּ בֵּין אֹרֶךְ הַטַּס וּפְתִילֵי רָאשָׁיו מַקִּיפִין אֶת הַקָּדְקֹד; וְהַפְּתִיל הָאֶמְצָעִי, כְּשֶׁרֹאשׁוֹ קָשׁוּר עִם רָאשֵׁי הַשְּׁנַיִם, הוֹלֵךְ עַל פְּנֵי רֹחַב הָרֹאשׁ מִלְמַעְלָה, וְנִמְצָא עָשׂוּי כְּמִין כּוֹבַע. וְעַל פְּתִיל הָאֶמְצָעִי הוּא אוֹמֵר: ״וְהָיָה עַל הַמִּצְנֶפֶת״, וְהָיָה נוֹתֵן הַצִּיץ עַל רֹאשׁוֹ כְּמִין כּוֹבַע עַל הַמִּצְנֶפֶת, וְהַפְּתִיל הָאֶמְצָעִי מַחֲזִיקוֹ שֶׁאֵינוֹ נוֹפֵל, וְהַטַּס תָּלוּי כְּנֶגֶד מִצְחוֹ. וְנִתְקַיְּמוּ כָּל הַמִּקְרָאוֹת: פְּתִיל עַל הַצִּיץ, וְצִיץ עַל הַפְּתִיל, וּפְתִיל עַל הַמִּצְנֶפֶת מִלְמַעְלָה:

לח| **וְנָשָׂא אַהֲרֹן.** לְשׁוֹן סְלִיחָה, וְאַף עַל פִּי כֵן אֵינוֹ זָז מִמַּשְׁמָעוֹ, אַהֲרֹן נוֹשֵׂא אֶת הַמַּשָּׂא שֶׁל עָוֹן, נִמְצָא מְסַלֵּק הֶעָוֹן מִן הַקֳּדָשִׁים: **אֶת עֲוֹן הַקֳּדָשִׁים.** לְרַצּוֹת עַל הַדָּם וְעַל הַחֵלֶב שֶׁקָּרְבוּ בְּטֻמְאָה, כְּמוֹ שֶׁשָּׁנִינוּ: אֵי זֶה עָוֹן הוּא נוֹשֵׂא? אִם עֲוֹן פִּגּוּל, הֲרֵי כְּבָר נֶאֱמַר וְכוּ׳. וְאֵין לוֹמַר שֶׁיְּכַפֵּר עַל הַכֹּהֵן שֶׁהִקְרִיבָם טָמֵא, שֶׁהֲרֵי ״עֲוֹן הַקֳּדָשִׁים״ נֶאֱמַר וְלֹא עֲוֹן הַמַּקְרִיב! אֵינוֹ מְרַצֶּה אֶלָּא לְהַכְשִׁיר הַקָּרְבָּן: **וְהָיָה עַל מִצְחוֹ תָּמִיד.** אִי אֶפְשָׁר לוֹמַר שֶׁיְּהֵא עַל מִצְחוֹ תָּמִיד, שֶׁהֲרֵי אֵינוֹ עָלָיו אֶלָּא בִּשְׁעַת הָעֲבוֹדָה! אֶלָּא ״תָּמִיד לְרָצוֹן לָהֶם״, אֲפִלּוּ אֵינוֹ עַל מִצְחוֹ, שֶׁלֹּא הָיָה כֹּהֵן גָּדוֹל עוֹבֵד בְּאוֹתָהּ שָׁעָה. וּלְדִבְרֵי הָאוֹמֵר עוֹדֵהוּ עַל מִצְחוֹ מְכַפֵּר וּמְרַצֶּה וְאִם לָאו אֵינוֹ מְרַצֶּה, נִדְרָשׁ ״עַל מִצְחוֹ תָּמִיד״ לְלַמֵּד שֶׁיְּמַשְׁמֵשׁ בּוֹ בְּעוֹדוֹ עַל מִצְחוֹ, שֶׁלֹּא יַסִּיחַ דַּעְתּוֹ מִמֶּנּוּ:

DISCUSSION

28:35| **And its sound shall be heard upon his entry into the Sanctuary before the Lord and upon his emergence:** There is no door at the entrance of the Sanctuary upon which one can knock. Instead, the chimes of the High Priest's robe as he walks declare his arrival. Even a king's closest advisor does not enter the king's presence unannounced; likewise, the High Priest must not enter the Sanctuary unannounced. Aside from promoting proper etiquette, the chimes of the bells serve as a reminder to the High Priest that he is in a sacred place, so that he may prepare himself to act with appropriate solemnity and dignity (see *Midrash HaGadol*; Rabbeinu Baḥya; *HaKetav VehaKabbala*).

28:36| **Holy to the Lord:** The Sages teach that this phrase was written on two lines. On the first line, the name of God was written, while below it, perhaps to the side and in the form of a step below the name of God, were the words "Holy to the" (see *Shabbat* 63b, and Rashba, Ritva, Meiri ad loc.; see also Rambam, *Sefer Avoda*, *Hilkhot Kelei HaMikdash* 9:1).

39 The Torah turns to the less complex of the High Priest's vestments, which are similar to those worn by the other priests: **You shall quilt the linen tunic.** The tunic, which is worn against the body, is woven with quilted patterns. **And you shall make a mitre of linen,** a long piece of linen cloth to be wrapped around the head. **And you shall make a sash, the craftsmanship of an embroiderer,** which will be tied around the tunic. The Sages teach that the sash was 32 cubits long, or 15–19 m.[24] The materials from which the sash shall be made are discussed below (39:29).

Sash

40 The sacred vestments of Aaron's sons were fewer and simpler than those worn by Aaron and the High Priests who followed him: **You shall make tunics for the sons of Aaron and you shall make for them sashes, and** tall, brimless **headdresses**[D] **you shall make for them,**[25] **for glory and for splendor.** These special uniforms will distinguish them from the rest of the people.

41 **You shall dress them** with these garments, **Aaron your brother and his sons with him; you shall anoint them** with the anointing oil (see 29:21) **and you shall invest them,**[D] **and you shall sanctify them, and they shall** be fit to **serve as priests for Me.**

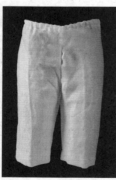

42 **Make them linen trousers,**[D] which will serve as an undergarment **to cover the flesh of their nakedness.** These trousers are not listed together with the other garments listed in verse 40 since they are not visible, and their purpose is entirely practical, neither for splendor nor for beauty.[26] Indeed, when the Torah describes the donning of the priestly vestments below, the trousers are not mentioned. **They shall be** worn **from waist to thighs,** until the knee, or perhaps to some other point along the thigh.

Trousers

43 **They,** the trousers,[27] or all the priestly vestments,[28] **shall be on Aaron and on his sons, upon their entry into the Tent of Meeting, or upon their approach to the altar to serve in sanctity, that they will not bear iniquity and die. It,** the donning of the garments, **is an eternal statute for him and for his descendants after him.** It is prohibited for a priest who is not wearing these garments to serve in the Sanctuary.

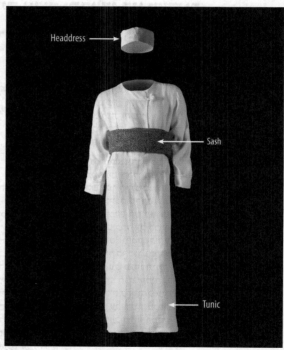

Vestments of a common priest

DISCUSSION

28:40 | **And headdresses:** Whereas all common priests wore ordinary headdresses, the High Priest alone donned a splendid mitre. It is possible that the mitre was a long piece of fabric wrapped around the head in the manner of a crown or turban, as found in various cultures (see Ra'avad on Rambam, *Sefer Avoda, Hilkhot Kelei HaMikdash* 8:2). Josephus Flavius, who was himself a priest, reported on the appearance of the High Priest, and compared the mitre to a stylized form of the golden henbane plant.

28:41 | **And you shall invest them:** That is, install them as priests. This expression literally means: You shall fill their hands. Rashi suggests a possible link between this phrase and an old European custom of giving a glove to someone at the time of his appointment to a position of authority.

28:42 | **Make them linen trousers:** It should be noted that trousers were not generally worn at

לט מ ושבצת הכתנת שש ועשית מצנפת שש ואבנט תעשה מעשה רקם: ולבני
אהרן תעשה כתנת ועשית להם אבנטים ומגבעות תעשה להם לכבוד
מא ולתפארת: והלבשת אתם את־אהרן אחיך ואת־בניו אתו ומשחת אתם
מב ומלאת את־ידם וקדשת אתם וכהנו־לי: ועשה להם מכנסי־בד לכסות בשר
מג ערוה ממתנים ועד־ירכים יהיו: והיו על־אהרן ועל־בניו בבאם | אל־אהל
מועד או בגשתם אל־המזבח לשרת בקדש ולא־ישאו עון ומתו חקת עולם
א לו ולזרעו אחריו: וזה הדבר אשר תעשה להם לקדש אתם לכהן כב רביעי
ב לקח פר אחד בן־בקר ואילם שנים תמימים: ולחם מצות וחלת מצת בלולת

רש"י

לט | ושבצת. עשה אותה משבצות, והכל של שש:

מ | ולבני אהרן תעשה. ארבעה בגדים הללו ולא יותר: כתנת, ואבנט, ומגבעות היא מצנפת, ומכנסים כתובים למטה בפרשה (להלן פסוק מב):

מא | והלבשת אתם את אהרן. אותם האמורים באהרן: "חשן ואפוד ומעיל וכתנת תשבץ מצנפת ואבנט" (לעיל פסוק ד), וציץ, ומכנסים כתובים למטה בכלם: ואת בניו אתו. אותם הכתובים בהם: ומשחת אתם. את אהרן ואת בניו בשמן המשחה: ומלאת את ידם. כל מלוי ידים לשון חנוך, כשהוא נכנס לדבר להיות מחזק בו מאותו יום והלאה הוא, ובלשון לעז כשממנין אדם על פקדת דבר, נותן השליט בידו בית יד של עור שקורין גואנ"ט, ועל ידו הוא מחזיקו בדבר, וקורין לאותה מסירה רוויסטי"ר, והוא מלוי ידים:

מב | ועשה להם. לאהרן ולבניו: מכנסי בד. הרי שמונה בגדים לכהן גדול וארבעה לכהן הדיוט:

מג | והיו. כל הבגדים האלה, "על אהרן" הראויים לו, "ועל בניו" האמורים בהם: בבאם אל אהל מועד. להיכל, וכן למשכן: ומתו. הא למדת שהמשמש מחסר בגדים – במיתה: חקת עולם לו. כל מקום שנאמר 'חקה' לעכב:

פרק כט

א | לקח. כמו קח. ושתי גזרות הן, אחת של קיחה ואחת של לקיחה, ולהן פתרון אחד: פר אחד. לכפר על מעשה העגל שהוא פר:

ב | ולחם מצות וחלת מצת... ורקיקי מצות. הרי אלו

The Command to Sacrifice Offerings of Investiture

EXODUS 29:1–37

Until this point, the Torah has described the structure of the Tabernacle and its vessels, as well as the priestly vestments to be worn by Aaron and his sons when they perform the service. Now, the Torah begins to discuss the instructions with regard to the seven days of investiture, during which Moses will sanctify the Tabernacle by means of special offerings, and will appoint the priests to their service by washing, dressing, and anointing them, as well as through other actions that will tie them to their new positions. The consecration of the Tabernacle and the sanctification of the priests are connected to one another.

The details of this ceremony are specific to the dedication of the Tabernacle, and they would not be repeated in the regular service of either the Tabernacle or the Temple.

29 1 **This is the thing that you shall do to them,** Aaron and his
Fourth sons, **to sanctify them to serve as priests to Me: Take one**
aliya **young bull,**[D] a bull in its third year, **and two rams;** the bull and the rams must be **unblemished.** Later, the Torah will delineate the blemishes that disqualify an animal from sacrifice.[29]

2 **And** you shall bring **unleavened bread.** The Sages understand

DISCUSSION

the time. Most people would don a tunic alone, without undergarments. Priests, by contrast, were obligated to wear trousers for greater modesty, dignity, and sanctity.

29:1 | **One young bull:** This phrase is comprised of two contradictory terms: *par*, an adult bull, and *ben bakar*, a young calf. Thus, the entire phrase is taken to mean an animal that is no longer a young calf but not yet an adult bull, such as a young bull in its third year (see *Sifra*; *Rosh HaShana* 10a).

that bread was first boiled in water, then baked, and then fried in oil.[30] This bread is also known as "oil bread,"[31] since it is more saturated with oil than the regular unleavened loaves and wafers.[32] **And unleavened loaves,** baked loaves with a particular shape,[33] **mixed with oil, and unleavened wafers anointed with oil.** These are the various types of unleavened breads that will be offered; **you shall make them of high-quality wheat flour.**

3 **You shall place them,** these baked items, **in one basket, and bring them near in the basket, with the bull and the two rams.** Later, Moses will be instructed what to do with each of these items.

4 **You shall have Aaron and his sons approach the entrance of the Tent of Meeting and you shall wash them in water,** immerse them.[34]

5 **You shall take the vestments and dress Aaron in the tunic and** above it **the robe of the ephod, and the ephod,** tied around the robe, **and the breast piece, and gird him with the belt of the ephod.**

6 **You shall place the mitre on his head and you shall place the crown of sanctity,** the diadem, **on the mitre.**

7 Before placing the mitre on his head,[35] **you shall take the anointing oil, and you shall pour it** directly **on his head and anoint him.**[D]

8 **And his sons you shall bring near and you shall dress them in tunics.**

9 **You shall gird them with a sash, Aaron and his sons.** Aaron was not yet girded with a sash, but with the belt of the ephod (verse 5). **And you shall wrap the headdresses on them,** Aaron's sons,[36] **and the priesthood shall be for them as an eternal statute,** for all generations. The actions described here, namely the dressing and anointing of the priests, will sanctify Aaron's sons as well as their future descendants for all generations. **And** in this manner **you shall invest Aaron and his sons** and thereby appoint them to the priesthood.

10 **You shall bring the bull before the Tent of Meeting, and Aaron and his sons shall place their hands** forcefully **on the head of the bull,** specifically between its horns.[37]

11 **You shall slaughter the bull before the Lord, at the entrance of the Tent of Meeting.**

12 **You shall take from the blood of the bull, and you shall place it on** each of **the horns of the** large **altar** that will stand in the courtyard of the Tabernacle, **with your finger; and you shall pour all the** remaining **blood** that is in the vessel **at the base of the altar.**

13 **You shall take all the fat**[B] **that covers the innards** of the bull, **and the diaphragm above the liver, and the two kidneys and the fat that is on them, and burn them on the altar.** These portions of the offering, which were consumed upon the altar, are referred to by the Sages as the *imurim*.

14 **You shall burn the flesh of the bull, its hide, and its dung** found in the intestines, which are cleaned out after slaughter, **in fire outside the camp; it is a sin offering.** Like a regular sin offering, the bull's blood was placed upon the outer altar. However, unlike other sin offerings whose rites were performed on the outer altar, its meat was not to be consumed at all. All that remained of the bull, aside from those portions burned on the altar, was to be burned outside the camp.

15 **You shall take the one ram, and Aaron and his sons shall place their hands on the head of the ram.**

16 **You shall slaughter the ram and you shall take its blood and you shall cast it around the altar.** Like all burnt offerings, the blood was not smeared with a finger, as is done with the blood of sin offerings. Rather, it was collected in a bowl, from which it was tossed over the corners of the altar, such that it reached all of its sides.[38]

17 **You shall cut the ram into its pieces, and you shall wash its innards,** after they have been removed from the body, **and its legs, and you shall put them with its pieces and with its head,** which was previously severed from the body.

DISCUSSION

29:7 | **And anoint him:** According to tradition, the oil was placed on the head of the priests in a manner resembling the Greek letter *chi*, X (see *Menaḥot* 75a; Rashi; see also Ramban).

BACKGROUND

29:13 | **The fat:** This refers to the layer of fat that covers the abdominal muscles. This fat serves to protect the inner organs and regulate body temperature and is involved in hormonal activity. It also allows the animal to store energy for times when other sources of nutrition are unavailable.

ג בשמן ורקיקי מצות משחים בשמן סלת חטים תעשה אתם: ונתת אותם
ד על־סל אחד והקרבת אתם בסל ואת־הפר ואת שני האילם: ואת־אהרן
ה ואת־בניו תקריב אל־פתח אהל מועד ורחצת אתם במים: ולקחת את־הבגדים
והלבשת את־אהרן את־הכתנת ואת מעיל האפד ואת־האפד ואת־החשן
ו ואפדת לו בחשב האפד: ושמת המצנפת על־ראשו ונתת את־נזר הקדש
ז על־המצנפת: ולקחת את־שמן המשחה ויצקת על־ראשו ומשחת אתו:
ח ט ואת־בניו תקריב והלבשתם כתנת: וחגרת אתם אבנט אהרן ובניו וחבשת
להם מגבעת והיתה להם כהנה לחקת עולם ומלאת יד־אהרן ויד־בניו:
י והקרבת את־הפר לפני אהל מועד וסמך אהרן ובניו את־ידיהם על־ראש
יא יב הפר: ושחטת את־הפר לפני יהוה פתח אהל מועד: ולקחת מדם הפר ונתתה
יג על־קרנת המזבח באצבעך ואת־כל־הדם תשפך אל־יסוד המזבח: ולקחת
את־כל־החלב המכסה את־הקרב ואת היתרת על־הכבד ואת שתי הכלית
יד ואת־החלב אשר עליהן והקטרת המזבחה: ואת־בשר הפר ואת־ערו ואת־
טו פרשו תשרף באש מחוץ למחנה חטאת הוא: ואת־האיל האחד תקח וסמכו
טז אהרן ובניו את־ידיהם על־ראש האיל: ושחטת את־האיל ולקחת את־דמו
יז וזרקת על־המזבח סביב: ואת־האיל תנתח לנתחיו ורחצת קרבו וכרעיו

רש״י

שלשה מינין: רבוכה וחלות ורקיקין. "לחם מצות" הוא הקרויה למטה בענין: "חלת לחם שמן" (להלן פסוק כג), על שם שנותן שמן ברבוכה כנגד החלות והרקיקין. וכל המינין באים עשר עשר חלות: בלולת בשמן. כשהן קמח יוצק בהן שמן ובוללן: משחים בשמן. אחר אפייתן מושחן כמין כ״י, כ״ף יונית, שהיא עשויה כנו״ן שלנו:

ג| והקרבת אתם. אל חצר המשכן ביום הקמתו:

ד| ורחצת. טבילת כל הגוף:

ה| ואפדת. קשט ותקן החגורה והסינר סביבותיו:

ו| נזר הקדש. זה הציץ: על המצנפת. כמו שפרשתי למעלה (לעיל כח, לז), על ידי הפתיל האמצעי ושני פתילין שבראשו הקשורין שלשתן מאחורי העורף, הוא נותנו על המצנפת כמין כובע:

ז| ומשחת אתו. אף משיחה זו כמין כ״י, נותן שמן על ראשו ובין ריסי עיניו ומחברן באצבעו:

ט| והיתה להם. מלוי ידים זה לכהנת עולם: ומלאת. על ידי הדברים האלה: יד אהרן ויד בניו. במלוי ופקדת הכהנה:

יא| פתח אהל מועד. בחצר המשכן שלפני הפתח:

יב| על קרנת. למעלה בקרנות ממש: ואת כל הדם. שירי הדם: אל יסוד המזבח. כמין בליטת בית קבול עשוי לו סביב סביב לאחר שעלה אמה מן הארץ:

יג| החלב המכסה את הקרב. הוא הקרום שעל הכרס שקורין טיל״א: ואת היתרת. הוא טרפשא דכבדא שקורין איבל״ש: על הכבד. אף מן הכבד יטל עמה:

יד| תשרף באש. לא מצינו חטאת חיצונה נשרפת אלא זו:

טז| וזרקת. בכלי, אוחז במזרק וזורק כנגד הקרן, כדי שיראה לכאן ולכאן. ואין קרבן טעון מתנה באצבע אלא חטאת בלבד, אבל שאר זבחים אינן טעונין קרן ולא אצבע, שמתן דמם מחצי המזבח ולמטה, ואינו עולה בכבש אלא עומד בארץ וזורק: סביב. כך מפרש בשחיטת קדשים (זבחים נג ע״ב), שאין "סביב" אלא שתי מתנות שהן ארבע, האחת בקרן זוית זו והאחת בשכנגדה באלכסון, וכל מתנה נראית בשני צדי הקרן אילך ואילך, נמצא הדם נתון בארבע רוחות סביב, לכך קרוי סביב:

יז| על נתחיו. עם נתחיו, מוסף על שאר הנתחים:

18 **You shall burn the entire ram on the altar; it is a burnt offering to the Lord.** Unlike the sin offering, the entire burnt offering is offered to God. After its hide has been removed, it is cut into parts in a manner prescribed by the Sages,[39] and the entire offering is burned upon the altar. It is **a pleasing aroma,**[D] **a fire offering to the Lord.**

19 **You shall take the second ram, and Aaron and his sons shall place their hands on the head of the ram.**

Fifth aliya

20 **You shall slaughter the ram,** collect its blood in a vessel, **take** from **its blood, and you shall place it,** some of the blood, **on the tip**[D] **of Aaron's right ear and on the tip of the right ear of his sons**[D] **and on the thumb of their right hand and on the big toe of their right foot and you shall** then **cast the** remaining **blood around the altar.**

21 **You shall take from the blood that is on the altar and from the anointing oil, and you shall sprinkle it on Aaron and on his vestments and on his sons and on the vestments of his sons with him; and he and his vestments shall be sanctified, and his sons and the vestments of his sons with him.**

22 **You shall take the fat from the ram and the fat tail,** which most breeds of sheep have, **and the fat that covers the innards, and the diaphragm above the liver, and the two kidneys and the fat that is on them, and the right haunch, as it is a ram of consecration,** that is, a one-time offering intended for the appointment of the priests.

23 **And** you shall also take **one cake of bread** from the unleavened bread, **and one loaf of oil bread,**[40] **and** take **one wafer from the basket of unleavened bread that is before the Lord.** The different types of bread are listed above (verse 2).

24 **You shall place everything,** all the parts of the offering and the unleavened breads, **on the palms of Aaron and on the palms of his sons and you shall wave them,** that is, lift up their hands,[41] **as a wave offering before the Lord.**

25 **You shall take them,** the parts of the ram and the unleavened breads, **from their hands and you shall burn them on the altar with,** in addition to, **the burnt offering,** the first ram, **for a pleasing aroma before the Lord; it is a fire offering to the Lord.**

26 **You shall take the breast from the ram of investiture that is Aaron's and you shall wave it as a wave offering before the Lord, and it,** the breast, **shall be a portion for you,**[D] Moses' portion. This ram is a peace offering.

27 **You shall sanctify,** set aside, **the breast of the wave offering and the gift haunch that was waved and that was lifted from the ram of investiture.** In the particular case of this offering of investiture, the breast of the wave offering is given to Moses while the gift haunch shall be burned on the altar. In general, however, the breast and haunch of a peace offering are considered **from that of Aaron and from that of his sons,** and they are to be given to the priests.

28 From this point forward, **it,** the breast and haunch, **shall be for Aaron and for his sons as an eternal portion from the children of Israel. For it is a gift** [*teruma*], a portion separated [*muram*] from the offering; **and it shall be a gift from the children of Israel** to be set aside **from their peace offerings** and given to the priests for consumption, **their gift to the Lord.** The offering to God is expressed in giving the breast and haunch to His ministers, the priests.

DISCUSSION

29:18 | **A pleasing aroma:** Although the smell of burning flesh and fats is rather unpleasant for humans, God considers it a pleasing aroma, as it signifies that one has sacrificed the offering in accordance with His will (*Sifrei, Shelah* 107; Rashi).

29:20 | **On the tip [*tenukh*]:** The exact location of the *tenukh* is the subject of debate among the Sages. Some maintain that the *tenukh* is the hard part of the ear, while others hold that it is the earlobe. Still others maintain that it is the midsection of the ear (see *Sifra, Metzora* 3:5; Rambam's Commentary on the Mishna, *Nega'im* 14:9; Rashi; Ibn Ezra; Ibn Janaḥ; Radak).

And you shall place it on the tip of Aaron's right ear and on the tip of the right ear of his sons: Perhaps these actions symbolize the consecration of the priest's limbs for their special role. The priests must perform the service without anything separating their hands from the offering, nor with anything between their feet and the floor. As for the ear, it symbolizes the need to attend to the additional commandments incumbent upon the priests. Note that with regard to the placing of the blood on the thumbs and toes, the verse includes Aaron together with his sons, while they are stated separately with regard to the ear. Perhaps this alludes to the fact that there are even more commandments incumbent upon the High Priest than ordinary priests (see *Sifrei, Korah* 14; *Meshekh Ḥokhma*).

29:26 | **And it shall be a portion for you:** In contrast to the burnt offering, which is burned in its entirety upon the altar, the breast and thigh of a peace offering are given to the priest, and the rest of the meat is consumed by the person who brings the offering. Since during this transitional stage the sanctification of the priests has not yet been completed, Moses serves temporarily as the priest and therefore receives the breast of the peace offering (see Jerusalem Talmud, *Yoma* 1:1; Rashi, verse 24). Once Aaron and his sons were invested as priests, Moses no longer functioned as a priest.

Moses filled all the leadership roles of Israel. He was their political leader, effectively their king; he was their prophet; and for a limited period, he also served as priest. Over the generations these functions would be divided among different people, but Moses, as the conduit through which holiness and greatness flowed to the Israelites, filled all of these roles.

יח וְנָתַתָּ עַל־נְתָחָיו וְעַל־רֹאשׁוֹ׃ וְהִקְטַרְתָּ אֶת־כָּל־הָאַיִל הַמִּזְבֵּחָה עֹלָה הוּא

יט לַיהוָה רֵיחַ נִיחוֹחַ אִשֶּׁה לַיהוָה הוּא׃ וְלָקַחְתָּ אֵת הָאַיִל הַשֵּׁנִי וְסָמַךְ אַהֲרֹן וּבָנָיו חמישי

כ אֶת־יְדֵיהֶם עַל־רֹאשׁ הָאָיִל׃ וְשָׁחַטְתָּ אֶת־הָאַיִל וְלָקַחְתָּ מִדָּמוֹ וְנָתַתָּה עַל־תְּנוּךְ

אֹזֶן אַהֲרֹן וְעַל־תְּנוּךְ אֹזֶן בָּנָיו הַיְמָנִית וְעַל־בֹּהֶן יָדָם הַיְמָנִית וְעַל־בֹּהֶן רַגְלָם

כא הַיְמָנִית וְזָרַקְתָּ אֶת־הַדָּם עַל־הַמִּזְבֵּחַ סָבִיב׃ וְלָקַחְתָּ מִן־הַדָּם אֲשֶׁר עַל־הַמִּזְבֵּחַ

וּמִשֶּׁמֶן הַמִּשְׁחָה וְהִזֵּיתָ עַל־אַהֲרֹן וְעַל־בְּגָדָיו וְעַל־בָּנָיו וְעַל־בִּגְדֵי בָנָיו אִתּוֹ

כב וְקָדַשׁ הוּא וּבְגָדָיו וּבָנָיו וּבִגְדֵי בָנָיו אִתּוֹ׃ וְלָקַחְתָּ מִן־הָאַיִל הַחֵלֶב וְהָאַלְיָה

וְאֶת־הַחֵלֶב ׀ הַמְכַסֶּה אֶת־הַקֶּרֶב וְאֵת יֹתֶרֶת הַכָּבֵד וְאֵת ׀ שְׁתֵּי הַכְּלָיֹת וְאֶת־

כג הַחֵלֶב אֲשֶׁר עֲלֵיהֶן וְאֵת שׁוֹק הַיָּמִין כִּי אֵיל מִלֻּאִים הוּא׃ וְכִכַּר לֶחֶם אַחַת וְחַלַּת

כד לֶחֶם שֶׁמֶן אַחַת וְרָקִיק אֶחָד מִסַּל הַמַּצּוֹת אֲשֶׁר לִפְנֵי יְהוָה׃ וְשַׂמְתָּ הַכֹּל עַל

כה כַּפֵּי אַהֲרֹן וְעַל כַּפֵּי בָנָיו וְהֵנַפְתָּ אֹתָם תְּנוּפָה לִפְנֵי יְהוָה׃ וְלָקַחְתָּ אֹתָם מִיָּדָם

כו וְהִקְטַרְתָּ הַמִּזְבֵּחָה עַל־הָעֹלָה לְרֵיחַ נִיחוֹחַ לִפְנֵי יְהוָה אִשֶּׁה הוּא לַיהוָה׃ וְלָקַחְתָּ

אֶת־הֶחָזֶה מֵאֵיל הַמִּלֻּאִים אֲשֶׁר לְאַהֲרֹן וְהֵנַפְתָּ אֹתוֹ תְּנוּפָה לִפְנֵי יְהוָה וְהָיָה

כז לְךָ לְמָנָה׃ וְקִדַּשְׁתָּ אֵת ׀ חֲזֵה הַתְּנוּפָה וְאֵת שׁוֹק הַתְּרוּמָה אֲשֶׁר הוּנַף וַאֲשֶׁר

כח הוּרָם מֵאֵיל הַמִּלֻּאִים מֵאֲשֶׁר לְאַהֲרֹן וּמֵאֲשֶׁר לְבָנָיו׃ וְהָיָה לְאַהֲרֹן וּלְבָנָיו לְחָק־

עוֹלָם מֵאֵת בְּנֵי יִשְׂרָאֵל כִּי תְרוּמָה הוּא וּתְרוּמָה יִהְיֶה מֵאֵת בְּנֵי־יִשְׂרָאֵל מִזִּבְחֵי

רש״י

יח | רֵיחַ נִיחוֹחַ. נַחַת רוּחַ לְפָנַי שֶׁאָמַרְתִּי וְנַעֲשָׂה רְצוֹנִי: אִשֶּׁה. לְשׁוֹן אֵשׁ, וְהִיא הַקְטָרַת אֵבָרִים שֶׁעַל הָאֵשׁ:

כ | תְּנוּךְ. הוּא הַסְּחוּס הָאֶמְצָעִי שֶׁבְּתוֹךְ הָאֹזֶן שֶׁקּוֹרִין טנרו״ס: בֹּהֶן יָדָם. הַגּוּדָל, וּבַפֶּרֶק הָאֶמְצָעִי:

כב | הַחֵלֶב. זֶה חֵלֶב הַדַּקִּים אוֹ הַקֵּבָה: וְהָאַלְיָה. מִן הַכְּלָיוֹת וּלְמַטָּה, כְּמוֹ שֶׁמְּפֹרָשׁ בְּ״וַיִּקְרָא״ (ג, ט), שֶׁנֶּאֱמַר: ״לְעֻמַּת הֶעָצֶה יְסִירֶנָּה״, מָקוֹם שֶׁהַכְּלָיוֹת יוֹעֲצוֹת. וּבְאֵמוּרֵי הַפָּר לֹא נֶאֱמַר אַלְיָה, שֶׁאֵין אַלְיָה קְרֵבָה אֶלָּא בְּכֶבֶשׂ וּבְכִבְשָׂה וְאַיִל, אֲבָל שׁוֹר וָעֵז אֵין טְעוּנִים אַלְיָה: וְאֵת שׁוֹק הַיָּמִין. לֹא מָצִינוּ הַקְטָרָה בְּשׁוֹק הַיָּמִין עִם הָאֵמוּרִים אֶלָּא זוֹ בִּלְבַד: כִּי אֵיל מִלֻּאִים הוּא. שְׁלָמִים, לְשׁוֹן שְׁלֵמוּת, שֶׁמֻּשְׁלָם בַּכֹּל. מַגִּיד הַכָּתוּב שֶׁהַמִּלּוּאִים שְׁלָמִים, שָׁלוֹם לַמִּזְבֵּחַ וּלְעוֹבֵד הָעֲבוֹדָה וְלַבְּעָלִים, לְכָךְ אֲנִי מַצְרִיכוֹ הֶחָזֶה לִהְיוֹת לְעוֹבֵד הָעֲבוֹדָה לְמָנָה, וְזֶהוּ מֹשֶׁה שֶׁשִּׁמֵּשׁ בַּמִּלּוּאִים, וְהַשְּׁאָר אֲכָלוּהוּ אַהֲרֹן וּבָנָיו שֶׁהֵם בְּעָלִים כַּמְפֹרָשׁ בָּעִנְיָן:

כג | וְכִכַּר לֶחֶם. מִן הַחַלּוֹת: וְחַלַּת לֶחֶם שֶׁמֶן. מִמִּין הָרְבוּכָה: וְרָקִיק. מִן הָרְקִיקִין, אֶחָד מֵעֲשָׂרָה שֶׁבְּכָל מִין וָמִין. וְלֹא מָצִינוּ תְּרוּמַת לֶחֶם הַבָּא עִם זֶבַח נִקְטֶרֶת אֶלָּא זוֹ בִּלְבַד, שֶׁתְּרוּמַת לַחְמֵי תוֹדָה וְאֵיל נָזִיר נְתוּנָה לַכֹּהֲנִים עִם חָזֶה וָשׁוֹק, וּמִזֶּה לֹא הָיָה לְמֹשֶׁה לְמָנָה אֶלָּא חָזֶה בִּלְבַד:

כד | עַל כַּפֵּי אַהֲרֹן... וְהֵנַפְתָּ. שְׁנֵיהֶם עֲסוּקִין בַּתְּנוּפָה, הַבְּעָלִים וְהַכֹּהֵן; הָא כֵּיצַד? כֹּהֵן מַנִּיחַ יָדוֹ תַּחַת יַד הַבְּעָלִים וּמֵנִיף, וּבָזֶה הָיוּ אַהֲרֹן וּבָנָיו בְּעָלִים וּמֹשֶׁה כֹּהֵן: תְּנוּפָה. מוֹלִיךְ וּמֵבִיא, לְמִי שֶׁאַרְבַּע רוּחוֹת הָעוֹלָם שֶׁלּוֹ, וּתְנוּפָה מְעַכֶּבֶת וּמְבַטֶּלֶת פֻּרְעָנֻיּוֹת רוּחוֹת רָעוֹת. וּמַעֲלֶה וּמוֹרִיד, לְמִי שֶׁהַשָּׁמַיִם וְהָאָרֶץ שֶׁלּוֹ, וּמְעַכֶּבֶת טְלָלִים רָעִים:

כה | עַל הָעֹלָה. עַל הָאַיִל הָרִאשׁוֹן שֶׁהֶעֱלֵיתָ עוֹלָה: לְרֵיחַ נִיחֹחַ. לְנַחַת רוּחַ לְמִי שֶׁאָמַר וְנַעֲשָׂה רְצוֹנוֹ: אִשֶּׁה. לָאֵשׁ נִתַּן: לַה׳. לִשְׁמוֹ שֶׁל מָקוֹם:

כז-כח | וְקִדַּשְׁתָּ אֵת חֲזֵה הַתְּנוּפָה וְאֵת שׁוֹק הַתְּרוּמָה וְגוֹ׳. קַדְּשֵׁם לְדוֹרוֹת לִהְיוֹת נוֹהֶגֶת תְּרוּמָתָם וַהֲנָפָתָם בְּחָזֶה וָשׁוֹק שֶׁל שְׁלָמִים, אֲבָל לֹא לְהַקְטָרָה, אֶלָּא ״וְהָיָה לְאַהֲרֹן וּלְבָנָיו״ לֶאֱכֹל: לְחָק עוֹלָם מֵאֵת בְּנֵי יִשְׂרָאֵל. שֶׁהַשְּׁלָמִים לַבְּעָלִים, וְאֶת הֶחָזֶה וְהַשּׁוֹק יִתְּנוּ לַכֹּהֵן: תְּנוּפָה. לְשׁוֹן הוֹלָכָה וַהֲבָאָה, ונטלי״ר בְּלַעַז: הוּרָם. לְשׁוֹן מַעֲלֶה וּמוֹרִיד: כִּי תְרוּמָה הוּא. הֶחָזֶה וְהַשּׁוֹק הַזֶּה:

29 The holy vestments of Aaron shall be for his sons after him, for prominence through them,[42] and with them to invest them. That is, one becomes High Priest by the donning of the priestly vestments.[43]

30 For **seven days the priest from** among **his,** Aaron's, **sons who will be** serving **in his stead, who will come into the Tent of Meeting to serve in the Sanctuary, shall don them,** the vestments of the High Priest. Before a High Priest may enter the holy place, the Holy of Holies, he must wear these garments and perform the service for seven days.[44]

31 You shall take the ram of investiture and you shall cook its meat in a holy place, in the courtyard of the Tent of Meeting.

32 **Aaron and his sons shall eat the meat of the ram and the bread that is** left **in the basket at the entrance of the Tent of Meeting.** In the future, this portion of a peace offering will be eaten by the owner of the offering; in this particular instance, the priests are considered the owners and therefore they shall consume it.

33 They who have been atoned through them shall eat them, to invest them and to sanctify them. Through their consumption of these portions, the priests shall be elevated from all depravity.[45] **But a stranger shall not eat** from these portions, **because they are sacred.**

34 **If there remains** anything **from the meat of the investiture, or from the bread** that is to be eaten by the priests, and it is left over **until the morning, then you shall burn the leftover in the fire; it shall not be eaten, as it is sacred.** The requirement to burn the leftover meat of an offering is repeated in several instances in the Torah.[46]

35 **You shall do so to Aaron and to his sons, in accordance with everything that I commanded you; seven days you shall invest them.**

36 **You shall sacrifice a bull for a sin offering each day;** on each of the days of investiture you shall sacrifice a bull as a sin offering in the manner described above (29:10–14), and it shall be **for atonement; and you shall cleanse the altar**[47] by your act of **atoning for it,**[D] by placing the blood of the bull upon it; **and you shall anoint it to sanctify it.** In this manner it will be sanctified.

37 **Seven days you shall atone for the altar and sanctify it;** therefore, **the altar shall be,** from then on, **a sacred sacrament. Anything that** is fit to be sacrificed as an offering and **touches the altar,** as in, ascends upon it, **shall be holy**[D] and must be burned there.[48]

The Command to Sacrifice the Daily Offering

EXODUS 29:38–46

The bringing of offerings plays an integral part of the sanctification of the Tabernacle and the altar, as well as the investiture of Aaron and his sons. In addition to the sin offering, burnt offering, and peace offering described above, Moses is now commanded to bring two additional offerings on each of the days of investiture, namely the daily offerings. These offerings will, from this point forward, be the foundation of the daily service in the Tabernacle and the Temple, throughout the generations.

All the efforts and rituals performed until now, whether for the construction of the Tabernacle, the preparation of the priests, or the bringing of the offerings, will be of no meaning if God's presence does not dwell in the Tabernacle to sanctify it. God therefore informs Moses that He will meet with His people and His messengers in this Tent, and that His presence will be felt there.

38 **This is that which you shall offer upon the altar** as a fixed offering: **Two lambs in the first year** of their lives,[49] **for each day** **continually.**

Sixth
aliya

39 **The one lamb you shall offer in the morning and the second lamb you shall offer in the afternoon,**

40 **and** together with the lamb you shall bring a meal offering: **One-tenth of an ephah,** a dry measure slightly larger than the equivalent of two liters, **of high-quality flour mixed with one-fourth of a hin of virgin** olive **oil** (see 27:20). The hin is a liquid measure equal to twelve *log*, approximately 4 L. **And you shall also bring a libation of one-fourth of a hin of wine for the one lamb.**

DISCUSSION

29:36 | And you shall cleanse the altar by your atoning for it: Some commentaries explain that atonement is required in case someone donated a stolen item toward the construction of the Tabernacle and the altar.

29:37 | Anything that touches the altar shall be holy: The Sages explain that this refers to consecrated items that were fit for sacrifice. If they ascend upon the altar they may not descend from it, even if they were subsequently disqualified (see *Zevaḥim* 83a).

כט שַׁלְמֵיהֶם תְּרוּמָתָם לַיהוָה: וּבִגְדֵי הַקֹּדֶשׁ אֲשֶׁר לְאַהֲרֹן יִהְיוּ לְבָנָיו אַחֲרָיו לְמָשְׁחָה
ל בָהֶם וּלְמַלֵּא־בָם אֶת־יָדָם: שִׁבְעַת יָמִים יִלְבָּשָׁם הַכֹּהֵן תַּחְתָּיו מִבָּנָיו אֲשֶׁר יָבֹא
לא אֶל־אֹהֶל מוֹעֵד לְשָׁרֵת בַּקֹּדֶשׁ: וְאֵת אֵיל הַמִּלֻּאִים תִּקָּח וּבִשַּׁלְתָּ אֶת־בְּשָׂרוֹ
לב בְּמָקֹם קָדֹשׁ: וְאָכַל אַהֲרֹן וּבָנָיו אֶת־בְּשַׂר הָאַיִל וְאֶת־הַלֶּחֶם אֲשֶׁר בַּסָּל פֶּתַח
לג אֹהֶל מוֹעֵד: וְאָכְלוּ אֹתָם אֲשֶׁר כֻּפַּר בָּהֶם לְמַלֵּא אֶת־יָדָם לְקַדֵּשׁ אֹתָם וְזָר לֹא־
לד יֹאכַל כִּי־קֹדֶשׁ הֵם: וְאִם־יִוָּתֵר מִבְּשַׂר הַמִּלֻּאִים וּמִן־הַלֶּחֶם עַד־הַבֹּקֶר וְשָׂרַפְתָּ
לה אֶת־הַנּוֹתָר בָּאֵשׁ לֹא יֵאָכֵל כִּי־קֹדֶשׁ הוּא: וְעָשִׂיתָ לְאַהֲרֹן וּלְבָנָיו כָּכָה כְּכֹל
לו אֲשֶׁר־צִוִּיתִי אֹתָכָה שִׁבְעַת יָמִים תְּמַלֵּא יָדָם: וּפַר חַטָּאת תַּעֲשֶׂה לַיּוֹם עַל־
לז הַכִּפֻּרִים וְחִטֵּאתָ עַל־הַמִּזְבֵּחַ בְּכַפֶּרְךָ עָלָיו וּמָשַׁחְתָּ אֹתוֹ לְקַדְּשׁוֹ: שִׁבְעַת יָמִים
תְּכַפֵּר עַל־הַמִּזְבֵּחַ וְקִדַּשְׁתָּ אֹתוֹ וְהָיָה הַמִּזְבֵּחַ קֹדֶשׁ קָדָשִׁים כָּל־הַנֹּגֵעַ בַּמִּזְבֵּחַ
לח יִקְדָּשׁ: וְזֶה אֲשֶׁר תַּעֲשֶׂה עַל־הַמִּזְבֵּחַ כְּבָשִׂים בְּנֵי־שָׁנָה שְׁנַיִם לַיּוֹם ששי
לט תָּמִיד: אֶת־הַכֶּבֶשׂ הָאֶחָד תַּעֲשֶׂה בַבֹּקֶר וְאֵת הַכֶּבֶשׂ הַשֵּׁנִי תַּעֲשֶׂה בֵּין הָעַרְבָּיִם:
מ וְעִשָּׂרֹן סֹלֶת בָּלוּל בְּשֶׁמֶן כָּתִית רֶבַע הַהִין וְנֵסֶךְ רְבִיעִת הַהִין יָיִן לַכֶּבֶשׂ הָאֶחָד:

רש״י

כט | **יִהְיוּ לְבָנָיו אַחֲרָיו.** לְמִי שֶׁבָּא בִּגְדֻלָּה אַחֲרָיו: **לְמָשְׁחָה.** לְהִתְגַּדֵּל בָּהֶם, שֶׁיֵּשׁ מְשִׁיחָה שֶׁהִיא לְשׁוֹן שְׂרָרָה, כְּמוֹ: "לְךָ נְתַתִּים לְמָשְׁחָה" (במדבר יח, ח), "אַל תִּגְּעוּ בִמְשִׁיחָי" (תהלים קה, טו): **וּלְמַלֵּא בָם אֶת יָדָם.** עַל יְדֵי הַבְּגָדִים הוּא מִתְלַבֵּשׁ בִּכְהֻנָּה גְּדוֹלָה:

ל | **שִׁבְעַת יָמִים.** רְצוּפִין: **יִלְבָּשָׁם הַכֹּהֵן.** אֲשֶׁר יָקוּם מִבָּנָיו תַּחְתָּיו לִכְהֻנָּה גְּדוֹלָה, כְּשֶׁיְּמַנּוּהוּ לִהְיוֹת כֹּהֵן גָּדוֹל: **אֲשֶׁר יָבֹא אֶל אֹהֶל מוֹעֵד.** אוֹתוֹ כֹּהֵן הַמּוּכָן לִכָּנֵס לִפְנַי וְלִפְנִים בְּיוֹם הַכִּפּוּרִים, וְזֶהוּ כֹּהֵן גָּדוֹל, שֶׁאֵין עֲבוֹדַת יוֹם הַכִּפּוּרִים כְּשֵׁרָה אֶלָּא בּוֹ: **תַּחְתָּיו מִבָּנָיו.** מְלַמֵּד שֶׁאִם יֵשׁ לוֹ לְכֹהֵן גָּדוֹל בֵּן מְמַלֵּא אֶת מְקוֹמוֹ, יְמַנּוּהוּ כֹּהֵן גָּדוֹל תַּחְתָּיו:

לא | **בְּמָקֹם קָדֹשׁ.** בַּחֲצַר אֹהֶל מוֹעֵד, שֶׁהַשְּׁלָמִים הַלָּלוּ קָדְשֵׁי קָדָשִׁים הָיוּ:

לב | **פֶּתַח אֹהֶל מוֹעֵד.** כָּל הֶחָצֵר קָרוּי כֵּן:

לג | **וְאָכְלוּ אֹתָם.** אַהֲרֹן וּבָנָיו, לְפִי שֶׁהֵם בַּעֲלֵיהֶם: **אֲשֶׁר כֻּפַּר בָּהֶם.** לָהֶם כָּל זָרוּת וְתִעוּב: **לְמַלֵּא אֶת יָדָם.** בְּאַיִל וָלֶחֶם הַלָּלוּ: **לְקַדֵּשׁ אֹתָם.** שֶׁעַל יְדֵי הַמִּלּוּאִים הַלָּלוּ נִתְמַלְּאוּ יְדֵיהֶם וְנִתְקַדְּשׁוּ לִכְהֻנָּה: **כִּי קֹדֶשׁ הֵם.** קָדְשֵׁי קָדָשִׁים. וּמִכָּאן לָמַדְנוּ אַזְהָרָה לְזָר הָאוֹכֵל קָדְשֵׁי קָדָשִׁים (מכות יח ע"א), שֶׁנָּתַן הַמִּקְרָא טַעַם לַדָּבָר מִשּׁוּם דְּ"קֹדֶשׁ הֵם":

לה | **וְעָשִׂיתָ לְאַהֲרֹן וּלְבָנָיו כָּכָה.** שָׁנָה הַכָּתוּב וְכָפַל לְעַכֵּב, שֶׁאִם חִסֵּר דָּבָר אֶחָד מִכָּל הָאָמוּר בָּעִנְיָן, לֹא נִתְמַלְּאוּ יְדֵיהֶם לִהְיוֹת כֹּהֲנִים וַעֲבוֹדָתָם פְּסוּלָה: **אֹתָכָה.** כְּמוֹ אוֹתְךָ: **שִׁבְעַת יָמִים תְּמַלֵּא.** בָּעִנְיָן הַזֶּה וּבַקָּרְבָּנוֹת הַלָּלוּ בְּכָל יוֹם:

לו | **עַל הַכִּפֻּרִים.** בִּשְׁבִיל הַכִּפּוּרִים, לְכַפֵּר עַל הַמִּזְבֵּחַ מִכָּל זָרוּת וְתִעוּב. וּלְפִי שֶׁנֶּאֱמַר: "שִׁבְעַת יָמִים תְּמַלֵּא יָדָם" (בפסוק הקודם), אֵין לִי אֶלָּא דָּבָר הַבָּא בִּשְׁבִילָם, כְּגוֹן הָאֵילִים וְהַלֶּחֶם, אֲבָל הַבָּא בִּשְׁבִיל הַמִּזְבֵּחַ, כְּגוֹן פַּר שֶׁהוּא לְחִטּוּי הַמִּזְבֵּחַ, לֹא שָׁמַעְנוּ, לְכָךְ הֻצְרַךְ מִקְרָא זֶה. וּמִדְרַשׁ תּוֹרַת כֹּהֲנִים (ויקרא ח, יד מלואים טו) אוֹמֵר: כַּפָּרַת הַמִּזְבֵּחַ הֻצְרְכָה שֶׁמָּא הִתְנַדֵּב אִישׁ מִיִּשְׂרָאֵל דְּבַר גָּזֵל בִּמְלֶאכֶת הַמִּשְׁכָּן וְהַמִּזְבֵּחַ: **וְחִטֵּאתָ.** "וּתְדַכֵּי", לְשׁוֹן מַתְּנַת דָּמִים הַנְּתוּנִים בְּאֶצְבַּע קָרוּי חִטּוּי: **וּמָשַׁחְתָּ אֹתוֹ.** בְּשֶׁמֶן הַמִּשְׁחָה. וְכָל הַמְּשִׁיחוֹת כְּמִין כ"י:

לז | **וְהָיָה הַמִּזְבֵּחַ קֹדֶשׁ.** וּמַה הִיא קְדֻשָּׁתוֹ? "כָּל הַנֹּגֵעַ בַּמִּזְבֵּחַ יִקְדָּשׁ", אֲפִלּוּ קָרְבָּן פָּסוּל שֶׁעָלָה עָלָיו, קִדְּשׁוֹ הַמִּזְבֵּחַ לְהַכְשִׁירוֹ שֶׁלֹּא יֵרֵד. מִתּוֹךְ שֶׁנֶּאֱמַר: "כָּל הַנֹּגֵעַ... יִקְדָּשׁ", שׁוֹמֵעַ אֲנִי בֵּין רָאוּי בֵּין שֶׁאֵינוֹ רָאוּי, כְּגוֹן דָּבָר שֶׁלֹּא הָיָה פְּסוּלוֹ בַּקֹּדֶשׁ, כְּגוֹן הָרוֹבֵעַ וְהַנִּרְבָּע וּמֻקְצֶה וְנֶעֱבָד וְהַטְּרֵפָה וְכַיּוֹצֵא בָּהֶן, תַּלְמוּד לוֹמַר: "וְזֶה אֲשֶׁר תַּעֲשֶׂה" הַסָּמוּךְ אַחֲרָיו, מָה עוֹלָה רְאוּיָה אַף כָּל רָאוּי, שֶׁנִּרְאָה לוֹ כְּבָר וְנִפְסַל מִשֶּׁבָּא לָעֲזָרָה, כְּגוֹן הַלָּן וְהַיּוֹצֵא וְהַטָּמֵא וְשֶׁנִּשְׁחַט בְּמַחֲשֶׁבֶת חוּץ לִזְמַנּוֹ וְחוּץ לִמְקוֹמוֹ וְכַיּוֹצֵא בָּהֶן:

מ | **וְעִשָּׂרֹן סֹלֶת.** עֲשִׂירִית הָאֵיפָה, אַרְבָּעִים וְשָׁלֹשׁ בֵּיצִים וְחֹמֶשׁ בֵּיצָה: **בְּשֶׁמֶן כָּתִית.** לֹא לְחוֹבָה נֶאֱמַר 'כָּתִית' אֶלָּא לְהַכְשִׁיר, לְפִי שֶׁנֶּאֱמַר: "כָּתִית לַמָּאוֹר" (לעיל כז, כ) וּמַשְׁמַע לַמָּאוֹר וְלֹא לַמְּנָחוֹת, יָכוֹל לְפָסְלוֹ לַמְּנָחוֹת? תַּלְמוּד לוֹמַר כָּאן: "כָּתִית", וְלֹא נֶאֱמַר: "כָּתִית לַמָּאוֹר" אֶלָּא לְמַעֵט מְנָחוֹת שֶׁאֵין צָרִיךְ כָּתִית, שֶׁאַף הַטָּחוּן בְּרֵיחַיִם כָּשֵׁר בָּהֶן: **רֶבַע הַהִין.** שְׁלֹשָׁה לֻגִּין: **וְנֵסֶךְ.** לַסְּפָלִים, כְּמוֹ שֶׁשָּׁנִינוּ בְּמַסֶּכֶת סֻכָּה (דף מח ע"א): שְׁנֵי סְפָלִים שֶׁל כֶּסֶף הָיוּ בְּרֹאשׁ הַמִּזְבֵּחַ וּמְנֻקָּבִים כְּמִין שְׁנֵי חֳטָמִין דַּקִּים, נוֹתֵן הַיַּיִן לְתוֹכוֹ וְהוּא מְקַלֵּחַ וְיוֹצֵא דֶּרֶךְ הַחֹטֶם וְנוֹפֵל עַל גַּג הַמִּזְבֵּחַ, וּמִשָּׁם יוֹרֵד לַשִּׁיתִין בְּמִזְבַּח בֵּית עוֹלָמִים, וּבְמִזְבַּח הַנְּחֹשֶׁת יוֹרֵד מִן הַמִּזְבֵּחַ לָאָרֶץ:

41 **The second lamb you shall sacrifice in the afternoon, like the meal offering** of flour and oil **of the morning and like its libation for a pleasing aroma, a fire offering to the Lord.** The daily offerings are burnt offerings, to be consumed in their entirety upon the altar.

42 **A continual burnt offering for your generations,** which you shall sacrifice **at the entrance of the Tent of Meeting before the Lord, where I will meet with you,** the people, through your representatives, the priests. Moreover, this shall be the Tent where I meet with you, Moses, **to speak to you there.**

43 **I will meet there with the children of Israel; and it,** the Tent, **shall be sanctified with My glory.** Even after the performance of all the rituals of appointing the priests and atoning for the altar, the Tabernacle is consecrated only through the presence of the glory of God.

44 **I will sanctify the Tent of Meeting and the altar, and Aaron and his sons I will sanctify, to serve as priests to Me.**

45 **I will dwell among the children of Israel,** in the Tabernacle and afterward in the Temple, where the Divine Presence will reside and be revealed, **and I will be their God.**

46 **They will know that I am the Lord their God who brought them out from the land of Egypt to dwell among them.** Not only did God redeem the Israelites in the past, His presence will continuously rest among them in the Tabernacle. **I am the Lord their God.**

The Command to Build the Incense Altar

EXODUS 30:1–10

The celebratory tone of the previous verses might give the impression that the commands regarding the preparation of the Tabernacle have been concluded. However, there remain two vessels which have yet to be discussed: the incense altar and the basin. The command to construct the incense altar, which will be positioned with the table and the candelabrum in the Tent of Meeting, is described here, while the command to construct the basin, which will be placed near the outer altar in the courtyard, will appear after a brief interlude in the following *parasha* (see verses 17–21).

30 **1** In addition to the altar for offerings, **you shall make an altar for burning incense; of acacia wood you shall make it.**

Seventh aliya **2** **One cubit shall be its length and one cubit its width; it,** the altar, **shall be square, and two cubits shall be its height.** This is a very small altar, resembling a meter-high stand. **From it shall be its horns.** Like the large altar, this altar shall have horns, made from the same substance as the altar itself, and perhaps included in the measure of its height.

3 **You shall plate it with pure gold, its top and its sides all around and its horns, and you shall make for it** an ornamental **rim of gold**[D] **all around.**

4 **You shall make two gold rings for it under its rim; on its two corners you shall make them on its two sides,** at opposing corners; **and they,** the rings, **shall be as housings for staves with which to carry it,** the altar.

5 **You shall make the staves of acacia wood and you shall plate them with gold.**

6 **You shall put it before,** outside, **the curtain,** which separates the Sanctuary from the Holy of Holies, **that is upon the Ark of the Testimony, before the ark cover that is over** the Ark **of the Testimony,** opposite the ark cover, **where I will meet with you.** On the north-south axis, the altar shall be situated between the table and the candelabrum, opposite the ark in the Holy of Holies. On the east-west axis it will be closer to the entrance of the Sanctuary.[50]

The incense altar

7 **Aaron shall burn on it incense of spices;** early[51] **every morning when he cleans the lamps,** he cleans out the old wicks and the accumulated soot and prepares new wicks and oil for them,[52] **he shall burn it.**

8 Likewise, **when Aaron**
Maftir **kindles the lamps in the afternoon, he shall burn it,** the incense. The burning of the incense shall be performed adjacent to the lighting of the lamps. It shall be **a daily incense before the Lord for your generations.**

DISCUSSION

30:3 | **A rim of gold:** The altar of incense is the third vessel coated with gold and decorated with a crown of gold, following the ark and the table. The Sages consider these vessels to symbolize, respectively, the crowns of priesthood, Torah, and kingship (see *Shemot Rabba* 34:2; *Avot* 4:13).

מא וְאֵת הַכֶּבֶשׂ הַשֵּׁנִי תַּעֲשֶׂה בֵּין הָעַרְבָּיִם כְּמִנְחַת הַבֹּקֶר וּכְנִסְכָּהּ תַּעֲשֶׂה־לָּהּ לְרֵיחַ
מב נִיחֹחַ אִשֶּׁה לַיהוָה: עֹלַת תָּמִיד לְדֹרֹתֵיכֶם פֶּתַח אֹהֶל־מוֹעֵד לִפְנֵי יְהוָה אֲשֶׁר
מג אִוָּעֵד לָכֶם שָׁמָּה לְדַבֵּר אֵלֶיךָ שָׁם: וְנֹעַדְתִּי שָׁמָּה לִבְנֵי יִשְׂרָאֵל וְנִקְדַּשׁ בִּכְבֹדִי:
מד וְקִדַּשְׁתִּי אֶת־אֹהֶל מוֹעֵד וְאֶת־הַמִּזְבֵּחַ וְאֶת־אַהֲרֹן וְאֶת־בָּנָיו אֲקַדֵּשׁ לְכַהֵן לִי:
מה מו וְשָׁכַנְתִּי בְּתוֹךְ בְּנֵי יִשְׂרָאֵל וְהָיִיתִי לָהֶם לֵאלֹהִים: וְיָדְעוּ כִּי אֲנִי יְהוָה אֱלֹהֵיהֶם
אֲשֶׁר הוֹצֵאתִי אֹתָם מֵאֶרֶץ מִצְרַיִם לְשָׁכְנִי בְתוֹכָם אֲנִי יְהוָה אֱלֹהֵיהֶם:
א ב וְעָשִׂיתָ מִזְבֵּחַ מִקְטַר קְטֹרֶת עֲצֵי שִׁטִּים תַּעֲשֶׂה אֹתוֹ: אַמָּה אָרְכּוֹ וְאַמָּה רָחְבּוֹ כג שביעי
ג רָבוּעַ יִהְיֶה וְאַמָּתַיִם קֹמָתוֹ מִמֶּנּוּ קַרְנֹתָיו: וְצִפִּיתָ אֹתוֹ זָהָב טָהוֹר אֶת־גַּגּוֹ
ד וְאֶת־קִירֹתָיו סָבִיב וְאֶת־קַרְנֹתָיו וְעָשִׂיתָ לּוֹ זֵר זָהָב סָבִיב: וּשְׁתֵּי טַבְּעֹת זָהָב
תַּעֲשֶׂה־לּוֹ ׀ מִתַּחַת לְזֵרוֹ עַל שְׁתֵּי צַלְעֹתָיו תַּעֲשֶׂה עַל־שְׁנֵי צִדָּיו וְהָיָה לְבָתִּים
ה לְבַדִּים לָשֵׂאת אֹתוֹ בָּהֵמָּה: וְעָשִׂיתָ אֶת־הַבַּדִּים עֲצֵי שִׁטִּים וְצִפִּיתָ אֹתָם זָהָב:
ו וְנָתַתָּה אֹתוֹ לִפְנֵי הַפָּרֹכֶת אֲשֶׁר עַל־אֲרֹן הָעֵדֻת לִפְנֵי הַכַּפֹּרֶת אֲשֶׁר עַל־הָעֵדֻת
ז אֲשֶׁר אִוָּעֵד לְךָ שָׁמָּה: וְהִקְטִיר עָלָיו אַהֲרֹן קְטֹרֶת סַמִּים בַּבֹּקֶר בַּבֹּקֶר בְּהֵיטִיבוֹ
ח אֶת־הַנֵּרֹת יַקְטִירֶנָּה: וּבְהַעֲלֹת אַהֲרֹן אֶת־הַנֵּרֹת בֵּין הָעַרְבַּיִם יַקְטִירֶנָּה קְטֹרֶת מפטיר

רש״י

מא| **לְרֵיחַ נִיחֹחַ.** עַל הַמִּנְחָה נֶאֱמַר, שֶׁמִּנְחַת נְסָכִים כֻּלָּהּ כָּלִיל. וְסֵדֶר הַקְרָבָתָם, הָאֵבָרִים בַּתְּחִלָּה וְאַחַר כָּךְ הַמִּנְחָה, שֶׁנֶּאֱמַר: "עֹלָה וּמִנְחָה" (ויקרא כג, לז):

מב| **תָּמִיד.** מִיּוֹם אֶל יוֹם, לֹא יַפְסִיק יוֹם בֵּינְתַיִם: **אֲשֶׁר אִוָּעֵד לָכֶם.** כְּשֶׁאֶקְבַּע מוֹעֵד לְדַבֵּר אֵלֶיךָ, שָׁם אֶקְבָּעֶנּוּ לָבֹא. וְיֵשׁ מֵרַבּוֹתֵינוּ לְמֵדִים מִכָּאן שֶׁמֵּעַל מִזְבַּח הַנְּחֹשֶׁת הָיָה הַקָּדוֹשׁ בָּרוּךְ הוּא מְדַבֵּר עִם מֹשֶׁה מִשֶּׁהוּקַם הַמִּשְׁכָּן. וְיֵשׁ אוֹמְרִים מֵעַל הַכַּפֹּרֶת, כְּמוֹ שֶׁנֶּאֱמַר: "וְדִבַּרְתִּי אִתְּךָ מֵעַל הַכַּפֹּרֶת" (לעיל כה, כב), וַ"אֲשֶׁר אִוָּעֵד לָכֶם" הָאָמוּר כָּאן אֵינוֹ אָמוּר עַל הַמִּזְבֵּחַ, אֶלָּא עַל "אֹהֶל מוֹעֵד" הַנִּזְכָּר בַּמִּקְרָא:

מג| **וְנֹעַדְתִּי שָׁמָּה.** אֶתְוַעֵד עִמָּם בְּדִבּוּר, כְּמֶלֶךְ הַקּוֹבֵעַ מְקוֹם מוֹעֵד לְדַבֵּר עִם עֲבָדָיו שָׁם: **וְנִקְדַּשׁ.** הַמִּשְׁכָּן "בִּכְבֹדִי", שֶׁתִּשְׁרֶה שְׁכִינָתִי בוֹ. וּמִדְרַשׁ אַגָּדָה, אַל תִּקְרֵי 'בִּכְבֹדִי' אֶלָּא 'בִּכְבוּדַי', בַּמְּכֻבָּדִים שֶׁלִּי, כָּאן רָמַז לוֹ מִיתַת בְּנֵי אַהֲרֹן בְּיוֹם הֲקָמָתוֹ, וְזֶהוּ שֶׁאָמַר מֹשֶׁה: "הוּא אֲשֶׁר דִּבֶּר ה' לֵאמֹר בִּקְרֹבַי אֶקָּדֵשׁ" (ויקרא י, ג), וְהֵיכָן דִּבֶּר? "וְנִקְדַּשׁ בִּכְבֹדִי":

מו| **לְשָׁכְנִי בְתוֹכָם.** עַל מְנָת לִשְׁכֹּן אֲנִי בְּתוֹכָם:

פרק ל

א| **מִקְטַר קְטֹרֶת.** לְהַעֲלוֹת עָלָיו קִטּוּר עֲשַׁן סַמִּים:

ג| **אֶת גַּגּוֹ.** זֶה הָיָה לוֹ גַּג, אֲבָל מִזְבַּח הָעוֹלָה לֹא הָיָה לוֹ גַּג, אֶלָּא מְמַלְּאִים חֲלָלוֹ אֲדָמָה בְּכָל חֲנִיָּתָן: **זֵר זָהָב.** סִימָן לְכֶתֶר כְּהֻנָּה:

ד| **צַלְעֹתָיו.** כָּאן הוּא לְשׁוֹן זָוִיּוֹת, כְּתַרְגּוּמוֹ, לְפִי שֶׁנֶּאֱמַר: "עַל שְׁנֵי צִדָּיו", שְׁתֵּי זָוִיּוֹתָיו שֶׁבִּשְׁנֵי צִדָּיו: **וְהָיָה.** מַעֲשֵׂה הַטַּבָּעוֹת הָאֵלֶּה "לְבָתִּים לְבַדִּים", בַּיִת תִּהְיֶה הַטַּבַּעַת לַבַּד:

ו| **לִפְנֵי הַפָּרֹכֶת.** שֶׁמָּא תֹּאמַר מָשׁוּךְ מִכְּנֶגֶד הָאָרוֹן לַצָּפוֹן אוֹ לַדָּרוֹם? תַּלְמוּד לוֹמַר: "לִפְנֵי הַכַּפֹּרֶת", מְכֻוָּן כְּנֶגֶד הָאָרוֹן מִבַּחוּץ:

ז-ח| **בְּהֵיטִיבוֹ.** לְשׁוֹן נִקּוּי הַבָּזִיכִין שֶׁל הַמְּנוֹרָה מִדֶּשֶׁן הַפְּתִילוֹת שֶׁנִּשְׂרְפוּ בַּלַּיְלָה, וְהָיָה מְטִיבָן בְּכָל בֹּקֶר וּבֹקֶר: **הַנֵּרֹת.** לוּמִי"שׁ בְּלַעַז, וְכֵן כָּל נֵרוֹת הָאֲמוּרוֹת בַּמְּנוֹרָה, חוּץ מִמָּקוֹם שֶׁנֶּאֱמַר שָׁם הַעֲלָאָה, שֶׁהוּא לְשׁוֹן הַדְלָקָה: **וּבְהַעֲלֹת.** כְּשֶׁיַּדְלִיקֵם לְהַעֲלוֹת לַהַבְתָּן "יַקְטִירֶנָּה". בְּכָל יוֹם מַקְטִיר פְּרָס שַׁחֲרִית וּפְרָס בֵּין הָעַרְבַּיִם:

9 **You shall not offer up on it strange incense,** incense not commanded by the Torah, **or** any type of offering, including animal offerings such as **a burnt offering or a meal offering** of produce; **and you shall not pour a libation** of wine **on it.**

10 Only once a year is the altar used for a service other than the burning of the incense: **Aaron shall atone,** purify, or remove

sin from **on its horns, with the blood of the sin offering of atonement,** which the High Priest offers on the outer altar, **once in the year,** on Yom Kippur; **once in the year he shall atone for it for your generations,** by placing some of the blood of the sin offering on the incense altar in a manner described elsewhere;[53] **it is a sacred sacrament to the Lord.**

Maftir on Shabbat Zakhor is read from Deuteronomy 25:17–19.

Parashat
Ki Tisa

The Commandment to Give the Half Shekel
EXODUS 30:11–16

Although this passage does not directly focus on the building of the Tabernacle, it addresses a related matter, the method of collecting the necessary resources for its construction. The half shekels collected during the national census that was carried out shortly before the construction of the Tabernacle were melted down and used for the silver sockets into which the boards of the Tabernacle were placed. The half shekels of subsequent collections would be used to purchase communal offerings.[1] Some say that there was no census at that time and that this command is for future occasions.[2]

11 **The Lord spoke to Moses, saying:**

12 **When you take a census of the children of Israel, according to their count** of men enlisted in the army, and excluding women, children, and members of the mixed multitude with them, then **each man shall give a ransom for himself to the**

Lord upon their counting, and there will not be a plague against them[D] **upon their counting.**

13 **This is what everyone who passes among the counted,** all those that are counted, **shall give: One half shekel in the sacred shekel.** The Talmud states that the sacred shekel weighed twice as much as the standard shekel.[3] **Twenty gera**[B] **is the**

DISCUSSION

30:12 | And there will not be a plague against them: One possible explanation for the danger in conducting a census of the Jewish people is as follows: The Torah states: "The Lord your God has multiplied you, and, behold, you are today as the stars of the heavens in abundance. The Lord, God of your fathers, shall add to you one thousand times as you are, and He will bless

you, as He spoke to you" (Deuteronomy 1:10–11). If one were to count the stars, each star, which is an entire world, would appear insignificant when counted as merely one of many. Similarly, reducing individuals to mere numbers obscures the unique personality of each of them. Consequently, when King David conducted a census of the nation by counting the people

rather than collecting half shekels, a severe plague broke out (II Samuel 24). The collection of the monetary ransom serves a twofold purpose: It transforms the census from a direct counting of the people to an indirect one conducted by counting the half shekels. In addition, the ransom atones for the act of conducting the census, protecting the people from divine punishment.

תָּמִיד לִפְנֵי יְהוָה לְדֹרֹתֵיכֶם׃ לֹא־תַעֲלוּ עָלָיו קְטֹרֶת זָרָה וְעֹלָה וּמִנְחָה וְנֶסֶךְ לֹא ט
תִסְּכוּ עָלָיו׃ וְכִפֶּר אַהֲרֹן עַל־קַרְנֹתָיו אַחַת בַּשָּׁנָה מִדַּם חַטַּאת הַכִּפֻּרִים אַחַת י
בַּשָּׁנָה יְכַפֵּר עָלָיו לְדֹרֹתֵיכֶם קֹדֶשׁ־קָדָשִׁים הוּא לַיהוָה׃

רש"י

ט | לא תעלו עליו. על מזבח זה: קטרת זרה. שום קטרת של נדבה, כלן זרות לו חוץ מזו: ועלה ומנחה. ולא עולה ומנחה. עולה של בהמה ועוף, מנחה היא של מין לחם:

י | וכפר אהרן. מתן דמים "על קרנתיו": אחת בשנה. ביום הכפורים, הוא שנאמר באחרי מות: "ויצא אל המזבח אשר לפני ה' וכפר עליו" (ויקרא טז, יח): חטאת הכפרים. הם פר ושעיר של יום הכפורים המכפרים על טומאת מקדש וקדשיו: קדש קדשים הוא. המזבח מקדש לדברים הללו בלבד ולא לעבודה אחרת:

פרשת

כי תשא

וַיְדַבֵּר יְהוָה אֶל־מֹשֶׁה לֵּאמֹר׃ כִּי תִשָּׂא אֶת־רֹאשׁ בְּנֵי־יִשְׂרָאֵל לִפְקֻדֵיהֶם וְנָתְנוּ יא יב
אִישׁ כֹּפֶר נַפְשׁוֹ לַיהוָה בִּפְקֹד אֹתָם וְלֹא־יִהְיֶה בָהֶם נֶגֶף בִּפְקֹד אֹתָם׃ זֶה | יִתְּנוּ יג
כָּל־הָעֹבֵר עַל־הַפְּקֻדִים מַחֲצִית הַשֶּׁקֶל בְּשֶׁקֶל הַקֹּדֶשׁ עֶשְׂרִים גֵּרָה הַשֶּׁקֶל

רש"י

יב | כי תשא. לשון קבלה, כתרגומו. כשתחפץ לקבל סכום מנינם לדעת כמה הם, אל תמנם לגלגלת, אלא יתנו כל אחד מחצית השקל, ותמנה את השקלים ותדע מנינם: ולא יהיה בהם נגף. שהמנין שולט בו עין הרע והדבר בא עליהם, כמו שמצינו בימי דוד (שמואל ב' כד, א-י):

יג | זה יתנו. הראה לו כמין מטבע של אש ומשקלה מחצית השקל, ואמר לו: כזה יתנו: העבר על הפקדים. דרך המונין מעבירין את הנמנין זה אחר זה, וכן: "כל אשר יעבר תחת השבט" (ויקרא כז, לב), וכן: "תעברנה הצאן על ידי מונה" (ירמיה לג, יג): מחצית השקל בשקל הקדש. במשקל השקל שקצבתי לך לשקל בו שקלי הקדש, כגון שקלים האמורין בפרשת ערכין (ויקרא כז, א-ח) ושדה אחזה (שם פסוק טז-יט): עשרים גרה השקל. עכשיו פירש לך כמה הוא: גרה. לשון מעה, וכן בשמואל: "יבוא להשתחוות לו לאגורת כסף וככר לחם" (שמואל א' ב, לו): עשרים גרה השקל. הסלע, שהשקל ארבעה זוזים, והזוז מתחלתו חמש מעות, אלא בא והוסיפו עליו שתות והעלוהו לשש מעה כסף, ומחצית השקל הזה שאמרתי לך יתנו תרומה לה':

BACKGROUND

30:13 | **Gera:** The word gera, which refers to a small measure of weight, is derived from *gargir*, meaning a seed. It is similar to the term karat, which is still used in the sale of gold and diamonds, and which originally meant a carob seed (see Ibn Ezra, long commentary on Exodus). Its use stems from the ancient practice of using the seeds of grains or fruit as a measurement for small weights (see Ruth 3:15). The word *agora*, which appears in I Samuel (2:36), is also derived from gera: "It will be that all who remain of your house will come to prostrate themselves to him for a gera of silver and a loaf of bread." The word gera also appears in an inscription from the sixth century BCE, on a potshard found in Kadesh Barnea. In the Talmud, the gera is referred to as a *ma'a*, which also originally meant a seed.

shekel; **one half shekel** shall be given **as a gift to the Lord.**

Half-shekel coin from the time of the Great Revolt prior to the destruction of the Second Temple. On one side of the coin the inscription reads: Holy Jerusalem, while the other side states: Half a shekel

14 **Everyone who passes among the counted, from twenty years old and above, shall give the gift of the Lord.**

15 **The wealthy shall not add and the poor shall not subtract from the half shekel.** The fixed amount is due to the practical purpose of the census, **to give the gift of the Lord, to atone for your souls**, and to protect you all from any danger entailed by the census.[4]

16 **You shall take the silver of the atonement from the children of Israel and you shall allocate it for the service of the Tent of Meeting,** so that it will be used for the needs of the Tabernacle. The Torah states (38:27) that the silver collected through the census before the construction of the Tabernacle was used to fashion the sockets in which the boards were inserted. **And it,** the silver used in the work for the Tabernacle, **shall be for the children of Israel as a remembrance before the Lord, to atone for your souls.**

The Commandment to Fashion the Basin

EXODUS 30:17–21

The commandment to fashion the basin is appended to the main body of instructions for the Tabernacle vessels. It is likely, at the reason it does not appear earlier is that it is not one of the actual service vessels. It serves merely as a source of water with which the priests washed their hands and feet before they commenced their service in the Tabernacle. A different vessel could be used for the same purpose.

17 **The Lord spoke to Moses, saying:**

18 **You shall make a basin of bronze,**[D] **and its base** also **of bronze, for** the purpose of **washing; and you shall place it** in the Tabernacle courtyard, **between the Tent of Meeting and the altar, and you shall put water** in there.

19 **Aaron and his sons,** the priests, **shall wash their hands and their feet from** the water in **it.**

20 **Before their entry into the Tent of Meeting, they shall wash with water, and they will not die; or before their approach to the altar to serve, to burn a fire offering to the Lord.**

21 **They shall wash their hands**[D] **and their feet and not die, and it shall be for them an eternal statute, for him and for his descendants for their generations.** This statute does not depend on the circumstances; it applies forever.

Replica of the basin

── DISCUSSION ──

30:18 | Basin of bronze: Since the basin is not one of the service vessels, and it stands outside the Sanctuary, it is made of bronze rather than gold. Nevertheless, it is essential to the Tabernacle service, as any priest who performs the divine service without first washing his hands and feet in water from the basin is liable to receive the death penalty by the hand of Heaven. The Torah does not describe the size or exact form of the basin,

and indeed, the basins used in the Tabernacle, the First Temple, and the Second Temple all differed.

30:21 | They shall wash their hands: Anyone who enters the Tabernacle is required to purify himself beforehand by immersing his entire body in a ritual bath. In addition, the priests who perform the sacred service must wash their hands and feet as an expression of their higher degree of purity. The importance of the cleanliness of one's

hands appears several times in the Bible, often in a symbolic or allegorical sense. Isaiah admonishes the people whose "hands are full of blood" (Isaiah 1:15), and the psalmist declares: "I wash my hands in purity" (Psalms 26:6). Similarly, if a body is discovered and his murderer is unknown, the elders of the city nearest to the corpse must wash their hands as part of the ceremony of the heifer whose neck is broken (see Deuteronomy 21:6).

יד מַחֲצִית הַשֶּׁקֶל תְּרוּמָה לַיהוָה: כֹּל הָעֹבֵר עַל־הַפְּקֻדִים מִבֶּן עֶשְׂרִים שָׁנָה
טו וָמָעְלָה יִתֵּן תְּרוּמַת יהוה: הֶעָשִׁיר לֹא־יַרְבֶּה וְהַדַּל לֹא יַמְעִיט מִמַּחֲצִית הַשָּׁקֶל
טז לָתֵת אֶת־תְּרוּמַת יהוה לְכַפֵּר עַל־נַפְשֹׁתֵיכֶם: וְלָקַחְתָּ אֶת־כֶּסֶף הַכִּפֻּרִים מֵאֵת
בְּנֵי יִשְׂרָאֵל וְנָתַתָּ אֹתוֹ עַל־עֲבֹדַת אֹהֶל מוֹעֵד וְהָיָה לִבְנֵי יִשְׂרָאֵל לְזִכָּרוֹן לִפְנֵי
יהוה לְכַפֵּר עַל־נַפְשֹׁתֵיכֶם:
יז יח וַיְדַבֵּר יהוה אֶל־מֹשֶׁה לֵּאמֹר: וְעָשִׂיתָ כִּיּוֹר נְחֹשֶׁת וְכַנּוֹ נְחֹשֶׁת לְרָחְצָה וְנָתַתָּ
יט אֹתוֹ בֵּין־אֹהֶל מוֹעֵד וּבֵין הַמִּזְבֵּחַ וְנָתַתָּ שָׁמָּה מָיִם: וְרָחֲצוּ אַהֲרֹן וּבָנָיו מִמֶּנּוּ
כ אֶת־יְדֵיהֶם וְאֶת־רַגְלֵיהֶם: בְּבֹאָם אֶל־אֹהֶל מוֹעֵד יִרְחֲצוּ־מַיִם וְלֹא יָמֻתוּ אוֹ
כא בְגִשְׁתָּם אֶל־הַמִּזְבֵּחַ לְשָׁרֵת לְהַקְטִיר אִשֶּׁה לַיהוָה: וְרָחֲצוּ יְדֵיהֶם וְרַגְלֵיהֶם וְלֹא
יָמֻתוּ וְהָיְתָה לָהֶם חָק־עוֹלָם לוֹ וּלְזַרְעוֹ לְדֹרֹתָם:

רש"י

יד | **מִבֶּן עֶשְׂרִים שָׁנָה וָמָעְלָה.** לִמֶּדְךָ כָּאן שֶׁאֵין פָּחוּת מִבֶּן עֶשְׂרִים יוֹצֵא לַצָּבָא וְנִמְנֶה בִּכְלַל אֲנָשִׁים:

טו | **לְכַפֵּר עַל נַפְשֹׁתֵיכֶם.** שֶׁלֹּא תִּנָּגְפוּ עַל יְדֵי מִנְיָן. דָּבָר אַחֵר, "לְכַפֵּר עַל נַפְשֹׁתֵיכֶם", לְפִי שֶׁרָמַז לָהֶם כָּאן שָׁלֹשׁ תְּרוּמוֹת, שֶׁנִּכְתַּב כָּאן "תְּרוּמַת ה'" שָׁלֹשׁ פְּעָמִים: אַחַת תְּרוּמַת אֲדָנִים, שֶׁמְּנָאָן כְּשֶׁהִתְחִילוּ בִּנְדְבַת הַמִּשְׁכָּן, שֶׁנָּתְנוּ כָּל אֶחָד וְאֶחָד מַחֲצִית הַשֶּׁקֶל וְעָלָה לִמְאַת הַכִּכָּר, שֶׁנֶּאֱמַר: "וְכֶסֶף פְּקוּדֵי הָעֵדָה מְאַת כִּכָּר" (להלן לח, כה), וּמֵהֶם נַעֲשׂוּ הָאֲדָנִים, שֶׁנֶּאֱמַר: "וַיְהִי מְאַת כִּכַּר הַכֶּסֶף" וְגוֹ' (שם פסוק כז); וְהַשֵּׁנִית אַף הִיא עַל יְדֵי מִנְיָן שֶׁמְּנָאָן מִשֶּׁהוּקַם הַמִּשְׁכָּן, הוּא הַמִּנְיָן הָאָמוּר בִּתְחִלַּת חוּמַשׁ הַפְּקוּדִים "בְּאֶחָד לַחֹדֶשׁ הַשֵּׁנִי בַּשָּׁנָה הַשֵּׁנִית" (במדבר א, א), וְנָתְנוּ כָּל אֶחָד מַחֲצִית הַשֶּׁקֶל, וְהֵן לִקְנוֹת מֵהֶן קָרְבְּנוֹת צִבּוּר שֶׁל כָּל שָׁנָה וְשָׁנָה, וְהֻשְׁווּ בָּהֶם עֲנִיִּים וַעֲשִׁירִים, וְעַל אוֹתָהּ תְּרוּמָה נֶאֱמַר: "לְכַפֵּר עַל נַפְשֹׁתֵיכֶם", שֶׁהַקָּרְבָּנוֹת לְכַפָּרָה הֵם בָּאִים; וְהַשְּׁלִישִׁית הִיא תְּרוּמַת הַמִּשְׁכָּן, כְּמוֹ שֶׁנֶּאֱמַר: "כָּל מֵרִים תְּרוּמַת כֶּסֶף וּנְחֹשֶׁת" (להלן לה, כד), וְלֹא הָיְתָה יַד כֻּלָּם שָׁוָה בָּהּ, אֶלָּא אִישׁ מַה שֶּׁנְּדָבוֹ לִבּוֹ:

טז | **וְנָתַתָּ אֹתוֹ עַל עֲבֹדַת אֹהֶל מוֹעֵד.** לָמַדְתָּ שֶׁנִּצְטַוָּה לִמְנוֹתָם בִּתְחִלַּת נִדְבַת הַמִּשְׁכָּן אַחַר מַעֲשֵׂה הָעֵגֶל, מִפְּנֵי שֶׁנִּתְּנָה בָּהֶם מַגֵּפָה, כְּמוֹ שֶׁנֶּאֱמַר: "וַיִּגֹּף ה' אֶת הָעָם" (להלן לב, לה). מָשָׁל לְצֹאן הַחֲבִיבָה עַל בְּעָלֶיהָ שֶׁנָּפַל בָּהּ דֶּבֶר, וּמִשֶּׁפָּסַק אָמַר לוֹ לָרוֹעֶה: בְּבַקָּשָׁה מִמְּךָ, מְנֵה אֶת צֹאנִי וְדַע כַּמָּה נוֹתְרוּ בָּהּ, לְהוֹדִיעוֹ שֶׁהִיא חֲבִיבָה עָלָיו. וְאִי אֶפְשָׁר לוֹמַר שֶׁהַמִּנְיָן הַזֶּה הוּא הָאָמוּר בְּחוּמַשׁ הַפְּקוּדִים, שֶׁהֲרֵי נֶאֱמַר בּוֹ: "בְּאֶחָד לַחֹדֶשׁ הַשֵּׁנִי" (במדבר א, א), וְהַמִּשְׁכָּן הוּקַם בְּאֶחָד לַחֹדֶשׁ הָרִאשׁוֹן, שֶׁנֶּאֱמַר: "בְּיוֹם הַחֹדֶשׁ הָרִאשׁוֹן בְּאֶחָד לַחֹדֶשׁ תָּקִים" וְגוֹ' (להלן מ, ב), וּמֵהַמִּנְיָן הַזֶּה נַעֲשׂוּ הָאֲדָנִים מִשְּׁקָלִים שֶׁלּוֹ, שֶׁנֶּאֱמַר: "וַיְהִי מְאַת כִּכַּר הַכֶּסֶף לָצֶקֶת" וְגוֹ' (להלן לח, כז), הָא לָמַדְתָּ שְׁנַיִם הָיוּ: אֶחָד בִּתְחִלַּת נִדְבָתָן אַחַר יוֹם הַכִּפּוּרִים בְּשָׁנָה רִאשׁוֹנָה, וְאֶחָד בְּשָׁנָה שְׁנִיָּה בְּאִיָּר מִשֶּׁהוּקַם הַמִּשְׁכָּן. וְאִם תֹּאמַר, וְכִי אֶפְשָׁר שֶׁבִּשְׁנֵיהֶם הָיוּ יִשְׂרָאֵל שָׁוִים שֵׁשׁ מֵאוֹת אֶלֶף וּשְׁלֹשֶׁת אֲלָפִים וַחֲמֵשׁ מֵאוֹת וַחֲמִשִּׁים? שֶׁהֲרֵי בְּכֶסֶף פְּקוּדֵי הָעֵדָה נֶאֱמַר כֵּן (להלן לח, כו), וּבְחוּמַשׁ הַפְּקוּדִים אַף בּוֹ נֶאֱמַר כֵּן: "וַיִּהְיוּ כָּל הַפְּקֻדִים שֵׁשׁ מֵאוֹת אֶלֶף וּשְׁלֹשֶׁת אֲלָפִים וַחֲמֵשׁ מֵאוֹת וַחֲמִשִּׁים" (במדבר א, מו), וַהֲלֹא בִּשְׁתֵּי שָׁנִים הָיוּ, וְאִי אֶפְשָׁר שֶׁלֹּא הָיוּ בִּשְׁעַת מִנְיָן הָרִאשׁוֹן בְּנֵי תְּשַׁע עֶשְׂרֵה שָׁנָה שֶׁלֹּא נִמְנוּ וּבַשְּׁנִיָּה נַעֲשׂוּ בְּנֵי עֶשְׂרִים! תְּשׁוּבָה לַדָּבָר, אֵצֶל שְׁנוֹת הָאֲנָשִׁים בְּשָׁנָה אַחַת נִמְנוּ, אֲבָל לְמִנְיַן יְצִיאַת מִצְרַיִם הָיוּ שְׁתֵּי שָׁנִים, לְפִי שֶׁלִּיצִיאַת מִצְרַיִם מוֹנִין מִנִּיסָן, כְּמוֹ שֶׁשָּׁנִינוּ בְּמַסֶּכֶת רֹאשׁ הַשָּׁנָה (דף ב ע"ב), וְנִבְנָה הַמִּשְׁכָּן בָּרִאשׁוֹנָה וְהוּקַם בַּשְּׁנִיָּה, שֶׁנִּתְחַדְּשָׁה שָׁנָה בְּאֶחָד בְּנִיסָן, אֲבָל שְׁנוֹת הָאֲנָשִׁים מְנוּיִין לְמִנְיַן שְׁנוֹת עוֹלָם הַמַּתְחִילִין מִתִּשְׁרֵי, נִמְצְאוּ שְׁנֵיהֶם הַמִּנְיָנִים בְּשָׁנָה אַחַת, הַמִּנְיָן הָאֶחָד הָיָה בְּתִשְׁרֵי לְאַחַר יוֹם הַכִּפּוּרִים, שֶׁנִּתְרַצָּה הַמָּקוֹם לְיִשְׂרָאֵל לִסְלֹחַ לָהֶם וְנִצְטַוּוּ עַל הַמִּשְׁכָּן, וְהַשֵּׁנִי בְּאֶחָד בְּאִיָּר: **עַל עֲבֹדַת אֹהֶל מוֹעֵד.** הֵן הָאֲדָנִים שֶׁנַּעֲשׂוּ בּוֹ:

יח | **כִּיּוֹר.** כְּמִין דּוּד גְּדוֹלָה וְלָהּ דַּדִּים הַמְרִיקִים בְּפִיהֶם מַיִם: **וְכַנּוֹ.** כְּתַרְגּוּמוֹ: "בְּסִיסֵיהּ", מוֹשָׁב מְתֻקָּן לַכִּיּוֹר: **לְרָחְצָה.** מוּסָב עַל הַכִּיּוֹר: **וּבֵין הַמִּזְבֵּחַ.** מִזְבַּח הָעוֹלָה, שֶׁכָּתוּב בּוֹ שֶׁהוּא לִפְנֵי פֶּתַח מִשְׁכַּן אֹהֶל מוֹעֵד (להלן מ, כט), וְהָיָה הַכִּיּוֹר מָשׁוּךְ קִמְעָא וְעוֹמֵד כְּנֶגֶד הָאֲוִיר שֶׁבֵּין הַמִּזְבֵּחַ וְהַמִּשְׁכָּן וְאֵינוֹ מַפְסִיק כְּלָל בֵּינְתַיִם, מִשּׁוּם שֶׁנֶּאֱמַר: "וְאֵת מִזְבַּח הָעֹלָה שָׂם פֶּתַח מִשְׁכַּן אֹהֶל מוֹעֵד" (שם), כְּלוֹמַר, מִזְבֵּחַ לִפְנֵי אֹהֶל מוֹעֵד וְאֵין כִּיּוֹר לִפְנֵי אֹהֶל מוֹעֵד, הָא כֵּיצַד? מָשׁוּךְ קִמְעָא כְּלַפֵּי הַדָּרוֹם. כָּךְ שְׁנוּיָה בִּזְבָחִים (דף נט ע"א):

יט | **אֶת יְדֵיהֶם וְאֶת רַגְלֵיהֶם.** בְּבַת אַחַת הָיָה מְקַדֵּשׁ יָדָיו וְרַגְלָיו. וְכָךְ שָׁנִינוּ בִּזְבָחִים (דף יט ע"ב): כֵּיצַד קִדּוּשׁ יָדַיִם וְרַגְלַיִם? מַנִּיחַ יָדוֹ הַיְמָנִית עַל גַּבֵּי רַגְלוֹ הַיְמָנִית, וְיָדוֹ הַשְּׂמָאלִית עַל גַּבֵּי רַגְלוֹ הַשְּׂמָאלִית, וּמְקַדֵּשׁ:

כ | **בְּבֹאָם אֶל אֹהֶל מוֹעֵד.** לְהַקְטִיר שַׁחֲרִית וּבֵין הָעַרְבַּיִם קְטֹרֶת, אוֹ לְהַזּוֹת מִדַּם פַּר כֹּהֵן הַמָּשִׁיחַ וּשְׂעִירֵי עֲבוֹדָה זָרָה: **וְלֹא יָמֻתוּ.** הָא אִם לֹא יִרְחֲצוּ – יָמוּתוּ, שֶׁבַּתּוֹרָה נֶאֶמְרוּ כְּלָלוֹת, וּמִכְּלַל לָאו אַתָּה שׁוֹמֵעַ הֵן: **אֶל הַמִּזְבֵּחַ.** הַחִיצוֹן, שֶׁאֵין כָּאן בִּיאַת אֹהֶל מוֹעֵד אֶלָּא בֶּחָצֵר:

כא | **וְלֹא יָמֻתוּ.** לְחַיֵּב מִיתָה עַל הַמְשַׁמֵּשׁ בַּמִּזְבֵּחַ וְאֵינוֹ רָחוּץ יָדַיִם וְרַגְלַיִם, שֶׁהַמִּיתָה הָרִאשׁוֹנָה לֹא שָׁמַעְנוּ אֶלָּא עַל הַנִּכְנָס לַהֵיכָל:

The Commandments to Prepare the Anointing Oil and the Incense

EXODUS 30:22–38

The anointing oil and the incense, which are prepared from various plants, are also required for the Tabernacle service. Although both were mentioned earlier (25:6, 29:7, 30:7–8), here the Torah explains the manner of their preparation in greater detail.

22 **The Lord spoke to Moses, saying:**

23 **You shall take for yourself high-quality spices:**[5] **Pure,** unadulterated[6] **myrrh** weighing **five hundred shekels,**[D] **and fragrant cinnamon,**[B] **half of it two hundred and fifty** shekels. The reason the cinnamon was divided into two halves that were weighed separately may have been in order to lower the margin of error.[7] **And** you shall also take **fragrant cane,**[B] possibly a type of aromatic grain, weighing **two hundred and fifty** shekels.

Cinnamon

Iris

24 **And** you shall also take **cassia** [***kidda***][B] weighing **five hundred** shekels **in the sacred shekel, and olive oil** in the amount of **one hin,** a liquid measure (see 29:40).

25 **You shall make it an oil of sacred anointment,** for anointing and thereby sanctifying the Tabernacle and its vessels.[8] It shall be **a blend mixture** compounded with great care and precision, the **craftsmanship of a blender;**[D] **an oil of sacred anointment it shall be.**

26 **You shall anoint with it,** the anointing oil, **the Tent of Meeting, the Ark of the Testimony,**

27 **the table and all its vessels, the candelabrum and its vessels, the altar of incense,**

28 **the altar of the burnt offering and all its vessels, and the basin and its base.**

29 **You shall sanctify them,** all of these vessels, **and they shall be a sacred sacrament; anything** fit to be placed in one of them **that touches them,** that is, placed in one them, **shall become sanctified** with the inherent sanctity of an offering.[9] Some explain that the latter clause of this verse teaches that one must purify himself before touching these vessels.[10]

30 **You shall** also **anoint Aaron and his sons** with the anointing oil, **and you shall sanctify them to serve as priests to Me.** Just as the service vessels become sacred when they are anointed, Aaron and his sons are anointed and are thereby sanctified as priests.

31 **You shall speak to the children of Israel, saying: This shall be oil of sacred anointment for Me, for your generations.**

32 **It shall not be poured on a person's flesh,** if that person is not fit to be anointed with it, **and you shall not make** any substance **like it according to its formula; it is sacred, and it shall be sacred to you.**

33 **Anyone who shall blend** any oil **like it** for use outside the Temple, **or who shall put of it,** the anointing oil, **on a non-priest, shall be excised from his people.**

DISCUSSION

30:23 | **Five hundred shekels:** This was a significant amount, approximately equivalent to 8.3 kg.

30:25 | **Craftsmanship of a blender:** The Sages disagree over the manner in which the anointing oil was blended. According to one opinion it was prepared by boiling the ingredients in a pot of water and then pouring oil onto the contents of the pot, so that the oil would absorb the fragrance of the various ingredients. According to another opinion, the spices were boiled in the oil without water. However, as the specified amount of oil was insufficient even to spread over the ingredients, and was certainly not enough to boil them, this method required a miracle (*Horayot* 11b; Jerusalem Talmud, *Shekalim* 6:1).

BACKGROUND

30:23 | **Fragrant cinnamon [*kinnamon*]:** Many commentaries identify this as the bark of the cinnamon tree. This tree is from the Lauraceae family, found in tropical regions, including India. It grows abundantly in the isles near Indonesia, and it was regularly imported to the Middle East in antiquity. The tree, which grows to a height of up to 10 m, was well known in the Land of Israel in the mishnaic period. The Ramban claims that *kinnamon* is a fragrant plant from the Graminae family, *Andropogon nardus*. This plant grows in eastern Asia, but there are similar, albeit rare, species that grow in Israel.

Fragrant cane [*kaneh*]: Some claim that this is the inner bark of the cinnamon tree, which is called *kaneh*, as it curls up and has the appearance of a stick [*kaneh*] during its drying

כב כג וַיְדַבֵּר יְהוָה אֶל־מֹשֶׁה לֵּאמֹר׃ וְאַתָּה קַח־לְךָ בְּשָׂמִים רֹאשׁ מָר־דְּרוֹר חֲמֵשׁ
מֵאוֹת וְקִנְּמָן־בֶּשֶׂם מַחֲצִיתוֹ חֲמִשִּׁים וּמָאתָיִם וּקְנֵה־בֹשֶׂם חֲמִשִּׁים וּמָאתָיִם׃
כד כה וְקִדָּה חֲמֵשׁ מֵאוֹת בְּשֶׁקֶל הַקֹּדֶשׁ וְשֶׁמֶן זַיִת הִין׃ וְעָשִׂיתָ אֹתוֹ שֶׁמֶן מִשְׁחַת־
כו קֹדֶשׁ רֹקַח מִרְקַחַת מַעֲשֵׂה רֹקֵחַ שֶׁמֶן מִשְׁחַת־קֹדֶשׁ יִהְיֶה׃ וּמָשַׁחְתָּ בוֹ אֶת־אֹהֶל
כז מוֹעֵד וְאֵת אֲרוֹן הָעֵדֻת׃ וְאֶת־הַשֻּׁלְחָן וְאֶת־כָּל־כֵּלָיו וְאֶת־הַמְּנֹרָה וְאֶת־כֵּלֶיהָ
כח וְאֵת מִזְבַּח הַקְּטֹרֶת׃ וְאֶת־מִזְבַּח הָעֹלָה וְאֶת־כָּל־כֵּלָיו וְאֶת־הַכִּיֹּר וְאֶת־כַּנּוֹ׃
כט ל וְקִדַּשְׁתָּ אֹתָם וְהָיוּ קֹדֶשׁ קָדָשִׁים כָּל־הַנֹּגֵעַ בָּהֶם יִקְדָּשׁ׃ וְאֶת־אַהֲרֹן וְאֶת־בָּנָיו
לא תִּמְשָׁח וְקִדַּשְׁתָּ אֹתָם לְכַהֵן לִי׃ וְאֶל־בְּנֵי יִשְׂרָאֵל תְּדַבֵּר לֵאמֹר שֶׁמֶן מִשְׁחַת־
לב קֹדֶשׁ יִהְיֶה זֶה לִי לְדֹרֹתֵיכֶם׃ עַל־בְּשַׂר אָדָם לֹא יִיסָךְ וּבְמַתְכֻּנְתּוֹ לֹא תַעֲשׂוּ
לג כָּמֹהוּ קֹדֶשׁ הוּא קֹדֶשׁ יִהְיֶה לָכֶם׃ אִישׁ אֲשֶׁר יִרְקַח כָּמֹהוּ וַאֲשֶׁר יִתֵּן מִמֶּנּוּ

רש"י

כג | **בְּשָׂמִים רֹאשׁ.** חֲשׁוּבִים: **וְקִנְּמָן בֶּשֶׂם.** לְפִי שֶׁהַקִּנָּמוֹן קְלִפַּת עֵץ הוּא, יֵשׁ שֶׁהוּא טוֹב וְיֵשׁ בּוֹ רֵיחַ טוֹב וָטַעַם, וְיֵשׁ שֶׁאֵינוֹ אֶלָּא כְּעֵץ, לְכָךְ הֻצְרַךְ לוֹמַר "קִנְּמָן בֶּשֶׂם", מִן הַטּוֹב: **מַחֲצִיתוֹ חֲמִשִּׁים וּמָאתָיִם.** מַחֲצִית הֲבָאָתוֹ תְּהֵא "חֲמִשִּׁים וּמָאתָיִם", נִמְצָא כֻּלּוֹ חֲמֵשׁ מֵאוֹת, כְּמוֹ שִׁעוּר מָר דְּרוֹר. אִם כֵּן לָמָּה נֶאֱמַר בּוֹ חֲצָאִין? גְּזֵרַת הַכָּתוּב הִיא לַהֲבִיאוֹ לַחֲצָאִין, לְהַרְבּוֹת בּוֹ שְׁנֵי הֶכְרֵעוֹת, שֶׁאֵין שׁוֹקְלִין עַיִן בְּעַיִן. וְכָךְ שְׁנוּיָה בִּכְרֵיתוֹת (דף ה ע"א): **וּקְנֵה בֹשֶׂם.** קָנֶה שֶׁל בֹּשֶׂם, לְפִי שֶׁיֵּשׁ קָנִים שֶׁאֵינָן שֶׁל בֹּשֶׂם הֻצְרַךְ לוֹמַר: "בֹּשֶׂם": **חֲמִשִּׁים וּמָאתָיִם.** סַךְ מִשְׁקַל כֻּלּוֹ:

כד | **וְקִדָּה.** שֵׁם שֹׁרֶשׁ עֵשֶׂב, וּבִלְשׁוֹן חֲכָמִים 'קְצִיעָה': **הִין.** שְׁנֵים עָשָׂר לֻגִּין. וְנֶחְלְקוּ בּוֹ חַכְמֵי יִשְׂרָאֵל: רַבִּי מֵאִיר אוֹמֵר: בּוֹ שָׁלְקוּ אֶת הָעִקָּרִין. אָמַר לוֹ רַבִּי יְהוּדָה: וַהֲלֹא לָסוּךְ אֶת הָעִקָּרִין אֵינוֹ סִפֵּק, אֶלָּא שְׁרָאוּם בְּמַיִם שֶׁלֹּא יִבְלְעוּ אֶת הַשֶּׁמֶן, וְאַחַר כָּךְ הֵצִיף עֲלֵיהֶם הַשֶּׁמֶן עַד שֶׁקָּלַט הָרֵיחַ, וְקִפְּחוֹ לַשֶּׁמֶן מֵעַל הָעִקָּרִין:

כה | **רֹקַח מִרְקַחַת.** 'רֹקַח' שֵׁם דָּבָר הוּא, וְהַטַּעַם מוֹכִיחַ, שֶׁהוּא לְמַעְלָה. וַהֲרֵי הוּא כְּמוֹ 'רֶקַח' (שיר השירים ח, ב), 'רֶגַע' (להלן לג, ה), וְאֵינוֹ כְּמוֹ "רֹגַע הַיָּם" (ישעיה נא, טו) וּכְמוֹ "רֹקַע הָאָרֶץ" (שם מב, ה) שֶׁהַטַּעַם לְמַטָּה. וְכָל דָּבָר הַמְעֹרָב בַּחֲבֵרוֹ עַד שֶׁזֶּה קוֹפֵחַ מִזֶּה אוֹ רֵיחַ אוֹ טַעַם, קָרוּי 'מִרְקַחַת': **רֹקַח מִרְקַחַת.** רֹקַח הֶעָשׂוּי עַל יְדֵי אֻמָּנוּת וְתַעֲרֹבֶת: **מַעֲשֵׂה רֹקֵחַ.** שֵׁם הָאֻמָּן בַּדָּבָר:

כו | **וּמָשַׁחְתָּ בוֹ.** כָּל הַמְּשִׁיחוֹת כְּמִין כ"י, חוּץ מִשֶּׁל מְלָכִים שֶׁהֵן כְּמִין נֵזֶר:

כט | **וְקִדַּשְׁתָּ אֹתָם.** מְשִׁיחָה זוֹ מְקַדַּשְׁתָּם לִהְיוֹת קֹדֶשׁ קָדָשִׁים. וּמַה הִיא קְדֻשָּׁתָם? "כָּל הַנֹּגֵעַ" וְגוֹ' – כָּל הָרָאוּי לִכְלִי שָׁרֵת מִשֶּׁנִּכְנַס לְתוֹכוֹ, קָדוֹשׁ קְדֻשַּׁת הַגּוּף לִפָּסֵל בְּיוֹצֵא וּלִינָה וּטְבוּל יוֹם, וְאֵינוֹ נִפְדֶּה לָצֵאת לְחֻלִּין, אֲבָל דָּבָר שֶׁאֵינוֹ רָאוּי לָהֶם אֵין מְקַדְּשִׁין. וּשְׁנוּיָה הִיא מִשְׁנָה שְׁלֵמָה אֵצֶל מִזְבֵּחַ: מִתּוֹךְ שֶׁנֶּאֱמַר: "כָּל הַנֹּגֵעַ בַּמִּזְבֵּחַ יִקְדָּשׁ" (לעיל כט, לז), שׁוֹמֵעַ אֲנִי בֵּין רָאוּי בֵּין שֶׁאֵינוֹ רָאוּי, תַּלְמוּד לוֹמַר: "כְּבָשִׂים", מַה כְּבָשִׂים רְאוּיִים אַף כָּל רָאוּי (זבחים פג ע"ב). כָּל מְשִׁיחַת מִשְׁכָּן וְכֹהֲנִים וּמְלָכִים מְתֻרְגָּם לְשׁוֹן 'רִבּוּי', לְפִי שֶׁאֵין דֶּרֶךְ מְשִׁיחָתָן אֶלָּא לִגְדֻלָּה, כִּי כֵן יִסַּד הַמֶּלֶךְ שֶׁזֶּה חִנּוּךְ גְּדֻלָּתָן. וּשְׁאָר מְשִׁיחוֹת, כְּגוֹן 'רְקִיקִין מְשׁוּחִין', "וְרֵאשִׁית שְׁמָנִים יִמְשָׁחוּ" (עמוס ו, ו) לְשׁוֹן אֲרַמִּית הֵן כִּלְשׁוֹן עִבְרִית:

לא | **לְדֹרֹתֵיכֶם.** מִכָּאן לָמְדוּ רַבּוֹתֵינוּ לוֹמַר שֶׁכֻּלּוֹ קַיָּם לֶעָתִיד לָבוֹא, "זֶה" בְּגִימַטְרִיָּא תְּרֵיסַר לֻגִּין הֲווּ:

לב | **לֹא יִיסָךְ.** בִּשְׁנֵי יוּדִי"ן, לְשׁוֹן לֹא יִפָּעֵל, כְּמוֹ: "לְמַעַן יִיטַב לָךְ" (דברים ו, יח): **עַל בְּשַׂר אָדָם לֹא יִיסָךְ.** מִן הַשֶּׁמֶן הַזֶּה עַצְמוֹ: **וּבְמַתְכֻּנְתּוֹ לֹא תַעֲשׂוּ כָּמֹהוּ.** בְּסִכּוּם סַמָּנָיו לֹא תַעֲשׂוּ אַחֵר כָּמֹהוּ בְּמִשְׁקַל סַמָּנִין הַלָּלוּ לְפִי מִדַּת הִין שֶׁמֶן, אֲבָל אִם פִּחֵת אוֹ רִבָּה סַמָּנִין לְפִי מִדַּת הִין שֶׁמֶן – מֻתָּר. וְאַף הֶעָשׂוּי כְּמַתְכֻּנְתּוֹ שֶׁל זֶה, אֵין הַסָּךְ מִמֶּנּוּ חַיָּב, אֶלָּא הָרוֹקְחוֹ: **וּבְמַתְכֻּנְתּוֹ.** לְשׁוֹן חֶשְׁבּוֹן, כְּמוֹ "מַתְכֹּנֶת הַלְּבֵנִים" (לעיל ה, ח), וְכֵן "בְּמַתְכֻּנְתָּהּ" (להלן פסוק לז) שֶׁל קְטֹרֶת:

לג | **וַאֲשֶׁר יִתֵּן מִמֶּנּוּ.** מֵאוֹתוֹ שֶׁל מֹשֶׁה: **עַל זָר.** שֶׁאֵינוֹ צֹרֶךְ כְּהֻנָּה וּמַלְכוּת:

BACKGROUND

→ process. Others identify it with calamus, which is a variety of *Cymbopogon*, or lemongrass, originating from India, whose leaves contain aromatic oils. Some scholars claim that it is *Acorus calamus*, also called sweet flag, a plant of the Acoraceae family that has fragrant roots (Yehuda Felix, *The World of Biblical Plants*. Ramat Gan: Masada, 1968 [Hebrew], 268–69).

30:24 | **Cassia [*kidda*]**: In the Septuagint, *kidda* is translated as cassia, which accords with Onkelos and the commentaries on the Torah. This probably refers to *Cinnamomum cassia*, a tall tree whose height extends up to 10 m. It is native to East Asia, where it is grown for its bark, its flower buds, and the oil extracted from it. The Ramban identifies it as *Aquilaria agallocha*, a tall tree, native to India, with a wide trunk that contains highly fragrant sap. Josephus writes that it is the iris. A species of iris identified today as *Iris florentina* was used to produce perfume.

34 **The Lord said to Moses: Take for yourself spices:**ᴰ **Stacte,**ᴮ **onycha,**ᴮ **and galbanum,**ᴮ a plant with a strong and unpleasant odor,¹¹ which nevertheless contributed to the overall pleasant aroma of the incense. You should also add other **spices and pure frankincense;**ᴮ **each part shall be equal.**

Galbanum plant   Frankincense tree

35 **You shall make incense of it,** with the aforementioned components **blended, the craftsmanship of** an expert **blender.** It must be **well mixed [*memulaḥ*].**¹² Others explain that a small

amount of salt [*melaḥ*] must be added to the incense, as is done for every offering.¹³ The incense must be **pure** and **sacred.**

36 **You shall grind some of it finely, and you shall put some of it before** the Ark of **the Testimony in the Tent of Meeting, where I shall meet with you,** and you shall burn it there. **It shall be a sacred sacrament for you.**

37 **The incense that you shall make, you shall not make for yourselves according to its formula.** A similar command appeared above (30:32) with regard to the anointing oil. One may not prepare this precise combination of spices, in the same quantities as for the incense, for any other purpose, because the scent of the incense must be preserved exclusively for the Tabernacle and the Temple. **It shall be sacred for you to the Lord.** It is prohibited to copy any element of the Temple service outside the Temple.

38 As with regard to the anointing oil, the commandment of the incense concludes by reiterating the severity of the prohibition against using it for improper purposes: **Anyone who makes** incense **like it for it to serve as perfume** for himself, rather than for the Temple service, **shall be excised from his people.**

The Craftsmen for the Tabernacle

EXODUS 31:1–11

Although the instructions for building the Tabernacle and fashioning its vessels were given to Moses, he is not to build the Tabernacle by himself. Instead, God informs Moses of the identity of the craftsmen who will construct the Tabernacle and its vessels. This role requires knowledge, insight, the ability to concretize abstract descriptions, and organizational talent. Therefore, God Himself selects the appropriate individuals for this important task.

31 1 **The Lord spoke to Moses, saying:**

2 **See, I have called by name,** appointed, out of esteem and appreciation,¹⁴ **Betzalel, son of Uri, son of Hur, of the tribe of Judah.** Hur was one of Moses' closest associates (see 17:10, 24:14). According to the Sages, he was Moses' nephew.¹⁵

3 **I have filled him with a divine spirit:**ᴰ **with wisdom, with understanding, with knowledge, and with all craftsmanship.** Betzalel had to be both a skilled craftsman and a capable manager, capable of overseeing the entire task.

4 He is able **to implement** complex **designs,** thereby actualizing the instructions for the Tabernacle (see 35:33),

---
DISCUSSION

30:34 | Take for yourself spices: In addition to the four spices mentioned explicitly in the verse, seven additional spices were used for the incense, making a total of eleven. The presence of additional ingredients is derived from the mention of the general term spices among the ingredients of the incense (*Karetot* 6b). The amount of each of the other components was far less than the amount of each of the spices expressly mentioned in the verse, and together those additional components approximately equaled the amount of one of the specified components. Some explain that the additional fragrant spices were selected by the Sages due to their mention in Song of Songs 4:14 (Ramban).

31:3 | I have filled him with a divine spirit: The Sages infer from this verse that Betzalel was endowed with a form of prophetic ability, which allowed him to extrapolate the necessary details of the construction from the directions he was given (see *Berakhot* 55a). When he heard instructions from Moses he could visualize the form of the artifacts that were shown to Moses upon Mount Sinai. This concept of a divine spirit can also be interpreted as an expression of respect toward the craftsman who fashions an object. Not only is the designer of something new deserving of honor, but also the craftsman, who forms the object from physical materials. The ability to create is a manifestation of divine inspiration.

BACKGROUND

30:34 | Stacte [*nataf*]: According to rabbinic tradition, *nataf* is derived from the resin that drips from a certain type of tree. Many scholars identify *nataf* as balsam (see Genesis 43:11 and Ezekiel 27:17), which is *Commiphora opobalsamum*, a bush or short tree, 3–5 m high. The tree has extremely thin branches, complex leaves, and small white flowers. The perfume is generally extracted by boiling the branches, leaving a sticky residue of balsam resin. Balsam was utilized for medicinal purposes in antiquity, in addition to its use as incense and as fragrant oil (see *Yoma* 39a). During the Second Temple period, the finest balsam grew in the Jordan Valley, near the Dead Sea, and the perfume was as expensive, by weight, as gold.

לד עַל־זָר וְנִכְרַת מֵעַמָּיו: וַיֹּאמֶר יְהוָה אֶל־מֹשֶׁה קַח־לְךָ סַמִּים נָטָף ׀
לה וּשְׁחֵלֶת וְחֶלְבְּנָה סַמִּים וּלְבֹנָה זַכָּה בַּד בְּבַד יִהְיֶה: וְעָשִׂיתָ אֹתָהּ קְטֹרֶת רֹקַח
לו מַעֲשֵׂה רוֹקֵחַ מְמֻלָּח טָהוֹר קֹדֶשׁ: וְשָׁחַקְתָּ מִמֶּנָּה הָדֵק וְנָתַתָּה מִמֶּנָּה לִפְנֵי
לז הָעֵדֻת בְּאֹהֶל מוֹעֵד אֲשֶׁר אִוָּעֵד לְךָ שָׁמָּה קֹדֶשׁ קָדָשִׁים תִּהְיֶה לָכֶם: וְהַקְּטֹרֶת
לח אֲשֶׁר תַּעֲשֶׂה בְּמַתְכֻּנְתָּהּ לֹא תַעֲשׂוּ לָכֶם קֹדֶשׁ תִּהְיֶה לְךָ לַיהוָה: אִישׁ אֲשֶׁר־
א יַעֲשֶׂה כָמוֹהָ לְהָרִיחַ בָּהּ וְנִכְרַת מֵעַמָּיו: וַיְדַבֵּר יְהוָה אֶל־מֹשֶׁה כד
ב ג לֵּאמֹר: רְאֵה קָרָאתִי בְשֵׁם בְּצַלְאֵל בֶּן־אוּרִי בֶן־חוּר לְמַטֵּה יְהוּדָה: וָאֲמַלֵּא
ד אֹתוֹ רוּחַ אֱלֹהִים בְּחָכְמָה וּבִתְבוּנָה וּבְדַעַת וּבְכָל־מְלָאכָה: לַחְשֹׁב מַחֲשָׁבֹת

רש"י

לד| **נטף.** הוא צרי. ועל שאינו אלא שרף הנוטף מעצי הקטף קרוי 'נטף', ובלעז גומ"א, והצרי קורין לו טריאק"ה: **ושחלת.** שרש בשם חלק ומאהיר כצפרן, ובלשון המשנה קרוי צפרן, וזהו שתרגם אונקלוס: "וטופרא": **וחלבנה.** בשם שריחו רע וקורין לו גלבנ"א. ומנאה הכתוב בין סממני הקטרת, ללמדנו שלא יקל בעינינו לצרף עמנו באגדת תעניותינו ותפלותינו את פושעי ישראל שיהיו נמנין עמנו: **סמים.** אחרים: **ולבנה זכה.** מכאן למדו רבותינו אחד עשר סממנין נאמרו לו למשה בסיני: מעוט "סמים" שנים, "נטף ושחלת וחלבנה" שלשה, הרי חמשה. "סמים", לרבות עוד כמו אלו, הרי עשרה. "ולבנה", הרי אחד עשר. ואלו הן: הצרי והצפרן, החלבנה והלבונה, מור וקציעה, שבלת נרד וכרכם, הרי שמונה, שהשבלת ונרד אחד, שהנרד דומה לשבלת; הקשט והקלופה והקנמון, הרי אחד עשר. בורית כרשינה אינו נקטר, אלא בו שפין את הצפרן ללבנה שתהא נאה: **בד בבד יהיה.** אלו האחד עשר הנזכרים כאן יהיו שוין משקל במשקל, כמשקלו של זה כך משקלו של זה, וכן שנינו: "הצרי והצפרן החלבנה והלבונה משקל שבעים שבעים מנה" (כריתות ו ע"א), ולשון "בד" נראה בעיני שהוא לשון 'יחיד', אחד באחד יהיו, זה כמות זה:

לה| **ממלח.** כתרגומו, "מערב", שיערב שחיקתן יפה יפה זה עם זה. ואומר אני שדומה לו: "וייראו המלחים" (יונה א, ה), "מלחיך וחבליך" (יחזקאל כז, כז), על שם שמהפכין את המים במשוטות כשמנהיגים את הספינה, כאדם המהפך בכף ביצים טרופות לערבן עם המים, וכל דבר שאדם רוצה לערב יפה יפה מהפכו באצבע או בכף: **ממלח טהור קדש.** ממלח יהיה, וטהור יהיה, וקדש יהיה:

לו| **ונתתה ממנה וגו'.** היא קטרת שבכל יום ויום שעל מזבח הפנימי, שהוא "באהל מועד": **אשר אועד לך שמה.** כל מועדי דבור שאקבע לך, אני קובעם לאותו מקום:

לז| **במתכנתה.** במנין סממניה: **קדש תהיה לך לה'.** שלא תעשנה אלא לשמי:

לח| **להריח בה.** אבל עושה אתה במתכנתה משלך כדי למסרה לצבור:

פרק לא

ב| **קראתי בשם.** לעשות מלאכתי, את בצלאל:

ג| **בחכמה.** מה שאדם שומע מאחרים ולמד: **ובתבונה.** מבין דבר מלבו מתוך דברים שלמד: **ובדעת.** רוח הקדש:

BACKGROUND

Onycha [*shekhelet*]: *Shekhelet* is a fragrant spice, and there are various opinions as to its identification. The term *shekhelet* is possibly related to the Assyrian *seheltu*, meaning thorn (Zohar Amar, *Shekhelet-Tziporen*, *Al Atar* vol. 3, *Tishrei* 5758), and is also mentioned in an Ugaritic document from the fourteenth century BCE. According to the Aramaic translations and the interpretations of early commentaries (Rav Se'adya Gaon; Rashi; Rambam), *shekhelet* is the same as *tziporen*, which appears in a list of the components of the incense cited in the Talmud (*Karetot* 6a), and which the Talmud describes as a type of plant. This *tziporen* should not be confused with the herb *Eugenia caryophyllata*, or clove, which is called *tziporen* in modern Hebrew. However, modern research supports the opinion of the Ramban, who identifies it with a species of sea snail with a shiny shell resembling a fingernail, the Hebrew for which is also *tziporen*. This creature inhabits the Red Sea and emits a pleasant odor.

Galbanum: Galbanum is a resin prepared from several species of the ferula plant, from the Apiaceae family. Specifically, it is derived from *Ferula galbaniufla*, which grows in and to the north of Syria. This resin, which is sometimes used for medicinal purposes, has an unpleasant odor, similar to asafetida. Nevertheless, it was an essential component of the incense, and was also used in the production of perfumes, to strengthen and complement other components. Likewise, in the modern manufacture of perfumes, substances with a disagreeable odor are sometimes incorporated into perfumes in order to strengthen certain scents or to enhance the fragrance as a whole.

Frankincense: Frankincense, which is still used for perfumes and incense today, is a fragrant whitish-yellow resin produced from the frankincense or olibanum tree, *Boswellia sacra*, from the Burseraceae family. The frankincense tree is modest in height, reaching up to 7 m high, with narrow leaves and whitish-pink flowers. It is found in the region of Somalia and Ethiopia, as well as in the southern Arabian Peninsula. The resin is extracted by means of an incision in the tree's bark, from which the resin drips and is collected into a vessel. The liquid resin then slowly coagulates into pellets.

and **to work with gold, with silver, and with bronze,** as an expert in metalwork.

5 He is also skilled **in the cutting of** precious **stone for setting,** which was the only stonework involved in the building of the Tabernacle and its vessels, **and in the carving of wood;** he has the ability **to perform all** forms of **craftsmanship.**

6 **And I, behold, have appointed with him** as his deputy **Oholiav, son of Ahisamakh, of the tribe of Dan,** who is also expert in these crafts (see 35:34–35). **And in the hearts of all the wise-hearted** men, the craftsmen, **I have** also **put wisdom,** as the building of the Tabernacle involves more than technical expert craftsmanship. **And they shall make everything that I have commanded you:**

7 **The Tent of Meeting and the Ark** of the testimony, both of which are intended **for** the placement of **the Testimony,** the tablets of stone, which is the reason they are called the

Tabernacle of the Testimony and the Ark of the Testimony respectively, **and the Ark cover that is upon it, and all the** other **vessels of the Tent:**

8 **The table and its vessels, the pure candelabrum**[D] **and all its vessels, the altar of incense,**

9 **the altar of the burnt offering and all its vessels, the basin and its base,**

10 and **the woven fabrics,** the materials woven like nets, which were used to cover the Tabernacle, as well as to cover the service vessels when the people traveled.[16] **And they shall fabricate the sacred vestments for Aaron the priest, and the vestments of his sons, to serve as priests.**

11 **And** they shall prepare **the anointing oil and the incense of the spices for the Sanctuary,** each of which requires specific expertise; **in accordance with everything that I commanded you, they shall do.**

The Commandment to Observe the Sabbath

EXODUS 31:12–17

Once again the Torah reiterates the commandment to observe the Sabbath, in this case in connection with the building of the Tabernacle. This instruction begins with the restrictive term "however," which indicates that it is linked to the previous section. The Sages derive from this term that even labor performed for the sake of Heaven, such as constructing a Tabernacle for His presence, must not be performed on the seventh day. The labors of building the Tabernacle are sacred, but the Sabbath has even greater sanctity.

12 **The Lord spoke to Moses, saying:**

13 **And you, speak to the children of Israel, saying:** It is fitting to perform the labors of preparing the Tabernacle as swiftly and efficiently as possible; **however, you shall observe My Sabbaths.** The Sabbath is not merely a day of rest for the Jewish people, but a day dedicated to God. The sanctity of the Sabbath overrides the commandment to build the Tabernacle, **as it is a sign between Me and you** of the closeness of the Jewish people to God, as you are the only nation to be commanded to observe God's holy day. The Sabbath is not a festival that commemorates Jewish history. Rather, it is a gift that I have given to you **for your generations, to know that I am the Lord, your Sanctifier.** The sanctity of the Sabbath and its rest are a gift for you, My chosen people.

14 **You shall observe the Sabbath, as it is sacred for you;** its

desecrators shall be put to death by the court. Elsewhere, the Torah relates an instance where this punishment was put into practice.[17] **For anyone who performs labor on it,** if for whatever reason he is not punished by the court, **that person shall be excised from among his people,** as God will put him to death.

15 **Six days labor shall be performed, and on the seventh day shall be a sabbatical rest,**[D] **sacred to the Lord. Anyone who performs** creative **labor on the Sabbath day,** irrespective of the effort exerted, **shall be put to death.**

16 **The children of Israel shall keep the Sabbath, to observe the Sabbath for their generations,** preserving its sanctity and keeping its commandments,[18] **an eternal covenant.**

17 **Between Me and the children of Israel,**[D] it is a sign of the covenant **forever. For** this sign indicates that **in six days the**

── DISCUSSION ──

31:8 | The pure [*tehora*] candelabrum: The candelabrum is described as pure in several places (Exodus 39:37; Leviticus 24:4). Since all the service vessels must be ritually pure, this term clearly has an additional meaning. It is possible that the root tet-heh-reish is related to the root tzadi-heh-reish, which refers to an object that is shiny and sparkling. If so, the verse means that the candelabrum shined, both due to the light

emitted by its flames and because it was fashioned from pure gold. Of all the Temple's service vessels, only the candelabrum was fashioned entirely from gold (see Rashi; *Adderet Eliyahu; Bekhor Shor,* 39:37).

31:15 | A sabbatical rest: The term sabbath, which refers to the cessation of labor, also appears in the Torah in reference to the festivals. However, the phrase "a sabbatical rest"

is stated only in connection to the Sabbath and Yom Kippur, as it indicates that all labor is prohibited, even those actions necessary for the preparation of food, e.g., cooking and baking, which are permitted on festivals (see 12:16; Leviticus 16:31, 23:26–32).

31:17 | Between Me and the children of Israel: The sanctity of the Sabbath encompasses others who are in the close circles of influence

ה לַעֲשׂוֹת בַּזָּהָב וּבַכֶּסֶף וּבַנְּחֹשֶׁת: וּבַחֲרֹשֶׁת אֶבֶן לְמַלֹּאת וּבַחֲרֹשֶׁת עֵץ לַעֲשׂוֹת

ו בְּכָל־מְלָאכָה: וַאֲנִי הִנֵּה נָתַתִּי אִתּוֹ אֵת אָהֳלִיאָב בֶּן־אֲחִיסָמָךְ לְמַטֵּה־דָן

ז וּבְלֵב כָּל־חֲכַם־לֵב נָתַתִּי חָכְמָה וְעָשׂוּ אֵת כָּל־אֲשֶׁר צִוִּיתִךָ: אֵת ׀ אֹהֶל מוֹעֵד

ח וְאֶת־הָאָרֹן לָעֵדֻת וְאֶת־הַכַּפֹּרֶת אֲשֶׁר עָלָיו וְאֵת כָּל־כְּלֵי הָאֹהֶל: וְאֶת־הַשֻּׁלְחָן

ט וְאֶת־כֵּלָיו וְאֶת־הַמְּנֹרָה הַטְּהֹרָה וְאֶת־כָּל־כֵּלֶיהָ וְאֵת מִזְבַּח הַקְּטֹרֶת: וְאֶת־

י מִזְבַּח הָעֹלָה וְאֶת־כָּל־כֵּלָיו וְאֶת־הַכִּיּוֹר וְאֶת־כַּנּוֹ: וְאֵת בִּגְדֵי הַשְּׂרָד וְאֶת־בִּגְדֵי

יא הַקֹּדֶשׁ לְאַהֲרֹן הַכֹּהֵן וְאֶת־בִּגְדֵי בָנָיו לְכַהֵן: וְאֵת שֶׁמֶן הַמִּשְׁחָה וְאֶת־קְטֹרֶת

הַסַּמִּים לַקֹּדֶשׁ כְּכֹל אֲשֶׁר־צִוִּיתִךָ יַעֲשׂוּ:

יב וַיֹּאמֶר יְהוָה אֶל־מֹשֶׁה לֵּאמֹר: וְאַתָּה דַּבֵּר אֶל־בְּנֵי יִשְׂרָאֵל לֵאמֹר אַךְ אֶת־

יג שַׁבְּתֹתַי תִּשְׁמֹרוּ כִּי אוֹת הִוא בֵּינִי וּבֵינֵיכֶם לְדֹרֹתֵיכֶם לָדַעַת כִּי אֲנִי יְהוָה

יד מְקַדִּשְׁכֶם: וּשְׁמַרְתֶּם אֶת־הַשַּׁבָּת כִּי קֹדֶשׁ הִוא לָכֶם מְחַלְלֶיהָ מוֹת יוּמָת כִּי

טו כָּל־הָעֹשֶׂה בָהּ מְלָאכָה וְנִכְרְתָה הַנֶּפֶשׁ הַהִוא מִקֶּרֶב עַמֶּיהָ: שֵׁשֶׁת יָמִים יֵעָשֶׂה

מְלָאכָה וּבַיּוֹם הַשְּׁבִיעִי שַׁבַּת שַׁבָּתוֹן קֹדֶשׁ לַיהוָה כָּל־הָעֹשֶׂה מְלָאכָה בְּיוֹם

טז הַשַּׁבָּת מוֹת יוּמָת: וְשָׁמְרוּ בְנֵי־יִשְׂרָאֵל אֶת־הַשַּׁבָּת לַעֲשׂוֹת אֶת־הַשַּׁבָּת לְדֹרֹתָם

יז בְּרִית עוֹלָם: בֵּינִי וּבֵין בְּנֵי יִשְׂרָאֵל אוֹת הִוא לְעֹלָם כִּי־שֵׁשֶׁת יָמִים עָשָׂה יְהוָה

רש"י

ד לַחְשֹׁב מַחֲשָׁבֹת. אֲרִיגַת מַעֲשֵׂה חוֹשֵׁב:

ה וּבַחֲרֹשֶׁת. לְשׁוֹן אֻמָּנוּת, כְּמוֹ: "חָרַשׁ חָכָם" (ישעיה מ, כ). וְאוּנְקְלוֹס פֵּרַשׁ וְשִׁנָּה בְּפֵרוּשָׁן, שֶׁאֻמָּן חֲכָמִים קָרוּי 'אֻמָּן' וְחָכָם עֵץ קָרוּי 'נַגָּר': לְמַלֹּאת. לְהוֹשִׁיבָהּ בַּמִּשְׁבֶּצֶת שֶׁלָּהּ בְּמִלּוּאָהּ, לַעֲשׂוֹת הַמִּשְׁבֶּצֶת לְמִדַּת מוֹשַׁב הָאֶבֶן וְעָבְיָהּ:

ו וּבְלֵב כָּל־חֲכַם־לֵב וְגוֹ'. וְעוֹד שְׁאָר חַכְמֵי לֵב יֵשׁ בָּכֶם, וְכָל אֲשֶׁר נָתַתִּי בּוֹ חָכְמָה, "וְעָשׂוּ אֵת כָּל אֲשֶׁר צִוִּיתִךָ":

ז וְאֶת־הָאָרֹן לָעֵדֻת. לְצֹרֶךְ לוּחוֹת הָעֵדוּת:

ח הַטְּהֹרָה. עַל שֵׁם זָהָב טָהוֹר:

י וְאֵת בִּגְדֵי הַשְּׂרָד. אוֹמֵר אֲנִי לְפִי פְּשׁוּטוֹ שֶׁל מִקְרָא שֶׁאִי אֶפְשָׁר לוֹמַר שֶׁבְּבִגְדֵי כְהֻנָּה מְדַבֵּר, לְפִי שֶׁנֶּאֱמַר אֶצְלָם: "וְאֵת בִּגְדֵי הַקֹּדֶשׁ לְאַהֲרֹן הַכֹּהֵן וְאֵת בִּגְדֵי בָנָיו

לְכַהֵן", חָלָּא אֵלּוּ בִּגְדֵי הַשְּׂרָד הֵם בִּגְדֵי הַתְּכֵלֶת וְהָאַרְגָּמָן וְתוֹלַעַת שָׁנִי הָאֲמוּרִים בְּפָרָשַׁת מַסָּעוֹת: וְנָתְנוּ עָלָיו בֶּגֶד תְּכֵלֶת (עיין במדבר ד, ז). וְנָתְנוּ עָלָיו בֶּגֶד אַרְגָּמָן (שם פסוק ח). וְנָתְנוּ עֲלֵיהֶם בֶּגֶד תּוֹלַעַת שָׁנִי (שם פסוק ח). וְנִרְאִין דְּבָרַי, שֶׁנֶּאֱמַר: "וּמִן הַתְּכֵלֶת וְהָאַרְגָּמָן וְתוֹלַעַת הַשָּׁנִי עָשׂוּ בִגְדֵי שְׂרָד לְשָׁרֵת בַּקֹּדֶשׁ" (להלן לט, א), וְלֹא הֻזְכַּר שֵׁשׁ עִמָּהֶם, וְאִם בְּבִגְדֵי כְהֻנָּה מְדַבֵּר, לֹא מָצִינוּ בְּאֶחָד מֵהֶם אַרְגָּמָן אוֹ תוֹלַעַת שָׁנִי בְּלֹא שֵׁשׁ: בִּגְדֵי הַשְּׂרָד. יֵשׁ מְפָרְשִׁים לְשׁוֹן עֲבוֹדָה וְשֵׁרוּת, כְּתַרְגּוּמוֹ: "לְבוּשֵׁי שִׁמּוּשָׁא", וְאֵין לוֹ דִּמְיוֹן בַּמִּקְרָא. וַאֲנִי אוֹמֵר שֶׁהוּא לְשׁוֹן אֲרַמִּי כְּתַרְגּוּמוֹ שֶׁל "קְלָעִים" (לעיל כז, ט) וְתַרְגּוּם שֶׁל "מִכְבָּר" (שם פסוק ד) שֶׁהָיוּ אֲרוּגִים בְּמַחַט, עֲשׂוּיִים נְקָבִים נְקָבִים, לייד"ץ בְּלַעַז:

יא וְאֵת קְטֹרֶת הַסַּמִּים לַקֹּדֶשׁ. לְצֹרֶךְ הַקְּטָרַת הֵיכָל שֶׁהוּא קֹדֶשׁ:

יג וְאַתָּה דַּבֵּר אֶל־בְּנֵי יִשְׂרָאֵל. וְאַתָּה, אַף עַל פִּי שֶׁהִפְקַדְתִּיךָ לְצַוּוֹתָם עַל מְלֶאכֶת הַמִּשְׁכָּן, אַל יֵקַל בְּעֵינֶיךָ לִדְחוֹת אֶת הַשַּׁבָּת מִפְּנֵי אוֹתָהּ מְלָאכָה: אַךְ אֶת שַׁבְּתֹתַי תִּשְׁמֹרוּ. אַף עַל פִּי שֶׁתִּהְיוּ רְדוּפִין וּזְרִיזִין בִּזְרִיזוּת הַמְּלָאכָה, שַׁבָּת אַל תִּדְחֶה מִפָּנֶיהָ. כָּל אַכִין וְרַקִּין מִעוּטִין, לְמַעֵט שַׁבָּת מִמְּלֶאכֶת הַמִּשְׁכָּן: כִּי אוֹת הִוא בֵּינִי וּבֵינֵיכֶם. אוֹת גְּדֻלָּה הִיא בֵּינֵינוּ שֶׁבָּחַרְתִּי בָּכֶם, בְּהַנְחִילִי לָכֶם אֶת יוֹם מְנוּחָתִי לִמְנוּחָה: לָדַעַת. הָאֻמּוֹת בָּהּ "כִּי אֲנִי ה' מְקַדִּשְׁכֶם":

יד מוֹת יוּמָת. אִם יֵשׁ עֵדִים וְהַתְרָאָה: וְנִכְרְתָה. בְּלֹא הַתְרָאָה: מְחַלְלֶיהָ. הַנּוֹהֵג בָּהּ חֹל בִּקְדֻשָּׁתָהּ:

טו שַׁבַּת שַׁבָּתוֹן. מְנוּחַת מַרְגּוֹעַ וְלֹא מְנוּחַת עֲרַאי לַה'. שְׁמִירַת קְדֻשָּׁתָהּ לִשְׁמִי וּבְמִצְוָתִי:

481

Lord made the heaven and the earth, and on the seventh day He rested and was invigorated. When the Jewish people pause from their labors and rest on the Sabbath, they participate in the divine cessation from work, and thereby testify to the relationship and covenant between them and God.

The Sin of the Golden Calf and Its Aftermath
EXODUS 31:18–33:17

The numerous instructions for the preparation of the Tabernacle, its vessels, and the priestly vestments concluded with the commandment of the Sabbath. These instructions were all given to Moses while he was alone on Mount Sinai. The Sages state that during this period God taught Moses not only the aforementioned commandments, but the entire Written Law and the Oral Law, including every idea that would be derived by Sages in future generations.

Toward the end of Moses' time on Mount Sinai, while he was still receiving the Torah and forging the divine covenant with the Jewish people, the people broke that covenant by fashioning a golden calf and worshipping it. This sin, so soon after God had given them the Torah, brought terrible shame upon the nation, to be remembered by all future generations.

18 **At the conclusion of His speaking with him on Mount Sinai,**
Second **He,** God, **gave to Moses the two Tablets of Testimony.** These
aliya tablets testify to the covenant between God and the Jewish people.[19] They were **tablets of stone,** created by God and **written with the finger of God.**[D]

32 1 Although Moses may have told the people that he would return at the end of forty days, there could have been a misunderstanding with regard to the precise counting of those days.[20] **The people saw that Moses tarried in descending from the mountain, and the people assembled around Aaron,** whom they knew as Moses' spokesman from when they were in Egypt (7:1). **And they said to him: Rise, make us a god that will go before us,**[D] **because this man Moses, who brought us up from the land of Egypt, we do not know what became of him.**

2 **Aaron said to them:** If this is your wish, you must do it in the proper manner. **Remove the gold rings that are in the ears of your wives,**[D] **your sons, and your daughters,** as their jewelry is an easily available source of gold, **and bring them to me.**

3 **All the people removed the gold rings that were in their ears, and they brought them to Aaron.**

4 **He took them,** the gold rings, **from their hands, and, fashioning it with a graving tool**[D] used by goldsmiths,[21] **he made a cast figure of a calf.**[22] They, all those present, **said: This is your god, Israel, who brought you up from the land of Egypt.**[D]

Goldsmith using graving tool, from the Tomb of Nebamun, Egypt, fourteenth century BCE

DISCUSSION

of those resting on the holy day. The Jewish people figuratively resemble God's household, and therefore they must cease from labor on God's day of rest. Likewise, Jews must enable the members of their household, including their slaves, maidservants, and even animals, to rest (20:9; 23:12).

31:18| Tablets of stone, written with the finger of God: The previous passages detailed the building of the Tabernacle. Moses now receives the tablets of stone that will become the focal point of the Tabernacle. Whereas the service vessels were sanctified due to their role in the sacred service, the tablets were not used in any of the rites of the Tabernacle. Rather, they had inherent sanctity, and the Tabernacle was designed around them. According to the plain reading of the text

only the Ten Precepts were written upon the tablets, but the Sages state that the entire Torah was written on them in various forms (*Kohelet Rabba* 1:29). The miraculous writing on the tablets appears together with the tablets themselves in the list of items that were fashioned at the end of the six days of Creation, at twilight of the Sabbath eve (*Avot* 5:6).

32:1| Make us a god [*elohim*] that will go before us: The people did not know the eventual outcome of Moses' encounter with God. Many commentaries explain that they did not actually seek another god, but they felt abandoned in the wilderness and feared that their leader would not return. Seeking a replacement who would be similar to Moses (see Ramban; Rav Eliyahu Mizraḥi), they turned to Aaron, Moses'

brother and representative, as the most capable substitute, or the one who could choose a new leader for them (see *Bekhor Shor* 32:4). The word *elohim* is sometimes used to refer to a leader or figure of authority (see 4:16, 7:1, 22:27).

32:2| Aaron said to them, remove the gold rings that are in the ears of your wives: The Sages explain that Aaron was employing a delaying tactic. He expected that the men would have substantial difficulty in bringing their wives' and children's jewelry, and he hoped that Moses would return in the meantime (see *Bemidbar Rabba* 21:10; Rashi; *Bekhor Shor*).

32:4| And fashioning it with a graving tool: Here too, Aaron was likely trying to stall by engraving and embellishing the gold, as he anticipated Moses' arrival.

יח אֶת־הַשָּׁמַיִם וְאֶת־הָאָרֶץ וּבַיּוֹם הַשְּׁבִיעִי שָׁבַת וַיִּנָּפַשׁ: וַיִּתֵּן שני
אֶל־מֹשֶׁה כְּכַלֹּתוֹ לְדַבֵּר אִתּוֹ בְּהַר סִינַי שְׁנֵי לֻחֹת הָעֵדֻת לֻחֹת אֶבֶן כְּתֻבִים
א בְּאֶצְבַּע אֱלֹהִים: וַיַּרְא הָעָם כִּי־בֹשֵׁשׁ מֹשֶׁה לָרֶדֶת מִן־הָהָר וַיִּקָּהֵל הָעָם עַל־
אַהֲרֹן וַיֹּאמְרוּ אֵלָיו קוּם | עֲשֵׂה־לָנוּ אֱלֹהִים אֲשֶׁר יֵלְכוּ לְפָנֵינוּ כִּי־זֶה | מֹשֶׁה הָאִישׁ
ב אֲשֶׁר הֶעֱלָנוּ מֵאֶרֶץ מִצְרַיִם לֹא יָדַעְנוּ מֶה־הָיָה לוֹ: וַיֹּאמֶר אֲלֵהֶם אַהֲרֹן פָּרְקוּ
ג נִזְמֵי הַזָּהָב אֲשֶׁר בְּאָזְנֵי נְשֵׁיכֶם בְּנֵיכֶם וּבְנֹתֵיכֶם וְהָבִיאוּ אֵלָי: וַיִּתְפָּרְקוּ כָּל־הָעָם
ד אֶת־נִזְמֵי הַזָּהָב אֲשֶׁר בְּאָזְנֵיהֶם וַיָּבִיאוּ אֶל־אַהֲרֹן: וַיִּקַּח מִיָּדָם וַיָּצַר אֹתוֹ בַּחֶרֶט
וַיַּעֲשֵׂהוּ עֵגֶל מַסֵּכָה וַיֹּאמְרוּ אֵלֶּה אֱלֹהֶיךָ יִשְׂרָאֵל אֲשֶׁר הֶעֱלוּךָ מֵאֶרֶץ מִצְרָיִם:

רש"י

יז | **וינפש.** כתרגומו "ונח". וכל לשון 'נפש' הוא לשון נפש, שמשיב נפשו ונשימתו בהרגיעו מטורח המלאכה. ומי שכתוב בו: "לא ייעף ולא ייגע" (ישעיה מ, כח) וכל פעלו במאמר, הכתיב מנוחה בעצמו, לשבר האוזן מה שהיא יכולה לשמוע:

יח | **ויתן אל משה וגו'.** אין מוקדם ומאוחר בתורה. מעשה העגל קודם לצווי מלאכת המשכן ימים רבים היה, שהרי בשבעה עשר בתמוז נשתברו הלוחות וביום הכפורים נתרצה הקדוש ברוך הוא לישראל, ולמחרת התחילו בנדבת המשכן והוקם באחד בניסן: **ככלתו.** 'ככלתו' כתיב חסר, שנמסרה לו תורה במתנה ככלה לחתן, שלא היה יכול ללמוד כלה בזמן מועט כזה. דבר אחר, מה כלה מתקשטת בעשרים וארבעה קישוטין, הן האמורים בספר ישעיה (ג, יח-כד), אף תלמיד חכם צריך להיות בקי בעשרים וארבעה ספרים: **לדבר אתו.** החקים והמשפטים שב'ואלה המשפטים': **לדבר אתו.** מלמד שהיה משה שומע מפי הגבורה וחוזרין ושונין את ההלכה שניהם יחד: **לחת.** 'לחת' כתיב, שהיו שתיהן שוות:

פרק לב

א | **כי בשש משה.** כתרגומו לשון איחור, וכן: "בשש רכבו" (שופטים ה, כח), "ויחילו עד בוש" (שם ג, כה). כי כשעלה משה להר אמר להם: לסוף ארבעים יום אני בא בתוך שש שעות. כסבורים הם שאותו יום שעלה מן המנין הוא, והוא אמר להם שלמים, ארבעים יום ולילו עמו, ויום עלייתו אין לילו עמו. בשבעה בסיון עלה, נמצא יום ארבעים בשבעה עשר בתמוז. בששה עשר בא שטן ועירבב את העולם והראה דמות חשך ואפלה וערבוביא, לומר ודאי מת משה לכך בא ערבוביא לעולם. אמר להם: מת משה, שכבר באו שש שעות ולא בא וכו', כדאיתא במסכת שבת (דף פט ע"א). ואי אפשר לומר שלא טעו אלא ביום המעונן בין קודם חצות בין לאחר חצות, שהרי לא ירד משה עד יום המחרת, שנאמר: "וישכימו ממחרת ויעלו עלת" (להלן פסוק ו): **אשר ילכו לפנינו.** אלהות הרבה אוו להם: **כי זה משה האיש.** כמין דמות משה הראה להם השטן שנושאים אותו באויר רקיע השמים: **אשר העלנו מארץ מצרים.** והיה מורה לנו דרך אשר נעלה בה, עתה צריכין אנו לאלהות "אשר ילכו לפנינו":

ב | **באזני נשיכם.** אמר אהרן בלבו: הנשים והילדים חסים על תכשיטיהן, שמא יתעכב הדבר ובתוך כך יבא משה. והם לא המתינו ופרקו מעל עצמן: **פרקו.** לשון צווי מגזרת 'פרק' ליחיד, כמו 'ברכו' מגזרת 'ברך':

ג | **ויתפרקו.** לשון פריקת משא, כשנטלום מאזניהם נמצאו הם מפורקים מנזמיהם, דישקרייר בלעז: **את נזמי.** כמו מנזמי. כמו: "כצאתי את העיר" (לעיל ט, כט) – מן העיר:

ד | **ויצר אותו בחרט.** יש לתרגמו בשני פנים: האחד – "ויצר" לשון קשירה, "בחרט" לשון סודר, כמו "והמטפחות והחריטים" (ישעיה ג, כב), "ויצר ככרים כסף בשני חרטים" (מלכים ב' ה, כג). והשני – "ויצר" לשון צורה, "בחרט" כלי אומנות הצורפין שחורצין וחורטין בו צורות בזהב כעט סופר החורט אותיות בלוחות ופנקסין, כמו: "וכתב עליו בחרט אנוש" (ישעיה ח, א), וזהו שתרגם אונקלוס: "וצר יתיה בזיפא" לשון זיוף, הוא כלי אומנות שחורצין בו בזהב אותיות ושקודים שקורין בלעז ניי"ל, ומזייפין על ידו חותמות: **עגל מסכה.** כיון שהשליכו לאור בכור, באו מכשפי ערב רב שעלו עמהם ממצרים ועשאוהו בכשפים. ויש אומרים: מיכה היה שם, שיצא מתוך דמוסי בנין שנתמכמך בו במצרים, והיה בידו שם וטס שכתב בו משה: "עלה שור עלה שור" להעלות ארונו של יוסף מתוך נילוס, והשליכו לתוך הכור ויצא העגל: **מסכה.** לשון מתכת. דבר אחר, מאה ועשרים וחמשה קנטרין זהב היו בו כגימטריא של מסכה: **אלה אלהיך.** ולא נאמר 'אלה אלהינו', מכאן שערב רב שעלו ממצרים הם שנקהלו על אהרן והם שעשאוהו, ואחר כך הטעו את ישראל אחריו:

DISCUSSION

And they said, this is your god Israel, who brought you up from the land of Egypt: The people had seen the divine glory and experienced God's miracles. It is therefore impossible that they imagined that a recently fashioned golden calf had taken them out of Egypt. They may have believed that the idol was infused with the spirit of Moses, the agent who had taken them out of Egypt. If so, the worship of the golden calf was not idolatrous in the strict sense of the term, as they did not view it as a replacement for God but as a replacement for Moses. Here the term "your god" is used as a reference to one who holds a position of leadership and authority, as the verse states with regard to Moses: "See, I have placed you as a god for Pharaoh" (7:1; *Bekhor Shor*).

5 **Aaron saw, and he built an altar before it; and Aaron proclaimed and said: A festival for the Lord tomorrow.** He emphasized that the festival would be in God's honor.

6 **They,** the entire people, **arose early the next day, and they offered up burnt offerings and brought peace offerings; and
the people sat to eat and drink,** typical practices for a festival,
and they also **rose to frolic,**D to engage in activities of a com-
petitive or sexual nature.[23]

7 At that moment, **the Lord spoke to Moses: Go, descend**
from the mountaintop. Alternatively: Descend from your
greatness;[24] while you have been in My presence, at the highest
spiritual level of any human, matters have occurred below that
require you to descend from your level of sanctity. **For your
people, whom you brought up from the land of Egypt, have
acted corruptly.**

8 **They quickly deviated from the path that I have commanded them; they made for themselves a cast figure of a calf;**D
they prostrated themselves before it and slaughtered animals **to it and said: This is your god, Israel, who brought you
up from the land of Egypt.**

9 **The Lord said to Moses: I have seen this people, and behold, it is a stiff-necked,** stubborn, **people.** Due to their obstinacy, they were deaf to My explicit prohibitions.

10 **Now,** therefore, **allow Me,**D **and My wrath will be enflamed
against them, and I will destroy them; and I will make you
into a great nation.** The children of Israel will be destroyed,
and your children alone shall become My chosen people.
God's covenant with Abraham, Isaac, and Jacob would not be
rescinded, as Moses is their descendant.

11 **Moses implored [*vayeḥal*] the Lord his God,** perhaps even
to the extent that he became sick [*ḥoleh*],[25] **and he said: Lord,
why shall Your wrath be enflamed against Your people, that
You took out of the land of Egypt**D **with great power and
with a mighty hand?**

12 Moses justifies his request: **Why shall the Egyptians say, saying: He took them out for evil, to kill them in the mountains and to destroy them from upon the face of the earth?**
If You destroy the people at this juncture, the Egyptians will
assume that You were angry with them from the outset and sent
them to the wilderness to kill them there. Consequently, **relent
from Your enflamed wrath and reconsider with regard to
the evil for Your people.**

13 Furthermore, **remember Abraham, Isaac, and Israel, Your
servants, to whom You swore,** not through mention of some
fleeting item that will pass from the world but **by Yourself.
And** in your oath You **spoke to them** and said: **I will multiply
your offspring like the stars of the heavens, and this entire
land that I said I will give to your descendants, they shall
inherit it forever.** Your oath to the forefathers that You would
have mercy upon their descendants was unconditional.

14 **The Lord reconsidered the evil that He had spoken of doing
to His people.** He changed His mind, as it were.

15 **Moses turned and descended from the mountaintop, and
the two Tablets of Testimony were in his hand. The tablets**
were miraculously **inscribed on both their sides; from this
side and from that side they were inscribed.**

DISCUSSION

32:6 | And they rose to frolic: The Jewish
people had only recently been slaves, subject
to the surrounding cultural influences. Their
neighbors may have sacrificed offerings at the
beginning of their pagan festivals. With their
emotions aroused, the worshippers would engage in feasting and drinking, which eventually
deteriorated into extravagant orgies. When the
Israelites felt that they had found a replacement
for Moses that would unite the nation, they
wanted to celebrate the occasion in the manner
that was familiar to them, without considering
the consequences.

**32:8 | They quickly deviated from the path
that I have commanded them; they made
for themselves a cast figure of a calf:** There
are many differences between the worship of
God taught by the Torah and the idolatrous
practices of the pagans. Some of these are easily

discernable, but more subtle, differences are also
manifest in the manner in which the people worshipped the golden calf. Both the Israelites and
pagans sacrificed offerings. In the holiest place
in the Tabernacle there were even the sculpted
figures of the cherubs. However, the cherubs,
which were created at God's command, and the
sapphire brick perceived by the elders at Sinai did
not represent God Himself. They rather served
as the resting place for the divine Glory. In contrast, the golden calf was an expression of human
ideas and imagination. The revelers who danced
around it did not perceive it as a mere vehicle for
the manifestation of the Divine Presence or as an
emissary of God. Even if the golden calf was initially fashioned as an embodiment of the spirit of
Moses, God's messenger, the people's old habits
of worship caused them to degenerate and engage in actual idolatry.

32:10 | Now allow Me: The Sages explain that
Moses was too shocked by God's statement to
respond. God therefore intimated that Moses
had the opportunity to defend the people. The
request to let Him act was effectively an
invitation to argue on the people's behalf, as
though God was saying to Moses: If you do not
intervene, I will destroy them immediately (see
Berakhot 32a; *Shemot Rabba* 42:9; Rashi).

**32:11 | Why shall Your wrath be enflamed
against Your people, that You took out of
the land of Egypt:** In His previous statement,
God called the Israelites Moses' people (verse 7).
Moses responded that they are not his people,
but God's own people; it was not Moses who
took them out of Egypt, but God Himself (see
Rashbam).

ה ו וַיַּרְא אַהֲרֹן וַיִּבֶן מִזְבֵּחַ לְפָנָיו וַיִּקְרָא אַהֲרֹן וַיֹּאמַר חַג לַיהוה מָחָר: וַיַּשְׁכִּימוּ
מִמָּחֳרָת וַיַּעֲלוּ עֹלֹת וַיַּגִּשׁוּ שְׁלָמִים וַיֵּשֶׁב הָעָם לֶאֱכֹל וְשָׁתוֹ וַיָּקֻמוּ לְצַחֵק:
ז ח וַיְדַבֵּר יהוה אֶל־מֹשֶׁה לֶךְ־רֵד כִּי שִׁחֵת עַמְּךָ אֲשֶׁר הֶעֱלֵיתָ מֵאֶרֶץ מִצְרָיִם: סָרוּ
מַהֵר מִן־הַדֶּרֶךְ אֲשֶׁר צִוִּיתִם עָשׂוּ לָהֶם עֵגֶל מַסֵּכָה וַיִּשְׁתַּחֲווּ־לוֹ וַיִּזְבְּחוּ־לוֹ
ט וַיֹּאמְרוּ אֵלֶּה אֱלֹהֶיךָ יִשְׂרָאֵל אֲשֶׁר הֶעֱלוּךָ מֵאֶרֶץ מִצְרָיִם: וַיֹּאמֶר יהוה אֶל־מֹשֶׁה
י רָאִיתִי אֶת־הָעָם הַזֶּה וְהִנֵּה עַם־קְשֵׁה־עֹרֶף הוּא: וְעַתָּה הַנִּיחָה לִּי וְיִחַר־אַפִּי בָהֶם
יא וַאֲכַלֵּם וְאֶעֱשֶׂה אוֹתְךָ לְגוֹי גָּדוֹל: וַיְחַל מֹשֶׁה אֶת־פְּנֵי יהוה אֱלֹהָיו וַיֹּאמֶר לָמָה
יהוה יֶחֱרֶה אַפְּךָ בְּעַמֶּךָ אֲשֶׁר הוֹצֵאתָ מֵאֶרֶץ מִצְרַיִם בְּכֹחַ גָּדוֹל וּבְיָד חֲזָקָה:
יב לָמָּה יֹאמְרוּ מִצְרַיִם לֵאמֹר בְּרָעָה הוֹצִיאָם לַהֲרֹג אֹתָם בֶּהָרִים וּלְכַלֹּתָם מֵעַל
יג פְּנֵי הָאֲדָמָה שׁוּב מֵחֲרוֹן אַפֶּךָ וְהִנָּחֵם עַל־הָרָעָה לְעַמֶּךָ: זְכֹר לְאַבְרָהָם לְיִצְחָק
וּלְיִשְׂרָאֵל עֲבָדֶיךָ אֲשֶׁר נִשְׁבַּעְתָּ לָהֶם בָּךְ וַתְּדַבֵּר אֲלֵהֶם אַרְבֶּה אֶת־זַרְעֲכֶם
כְּכוֹכְבֵי הַשָּׁמָיִם וְכָל־הָאָרֶץ הַזֹּאת אֲשֶׁר אָמַרְתִּי אֶתֵּן לְזַרְעֲכֶם וְנָחֲלוּ לְעֹלָם:
יד וַיִּנָּחֶם יהוה עַל־הָרָעָה אֲשֶׁר דִּבֶּר לַעֲשׂוֹת לְעַמּוֹ:
טו וַיִּפֶן וַיֵּרֶד מֹשֶׁה מִן־הָהָר וּשְׁנֵי לֻחֹת הָעֵדֻת בְּיָדוֹ לֻחֹת כְּתֻבִים מִשְּׁנֵי עֶבְרֵיהֶם כה

רש״י

ה| וַיַּרְא אַהֲרֹן. שֶׁהָיָה בּוֹ רוּחַ חַיִּים, שֶׁנֶּאֱמַר: ״בְּתַבְנִית שׁוֹר אֹכֵל עֵשֶׂב״ (תהלים קו, כ), וְרָאָה שֶׁהִצְלִיחַ מַעֲשֵׂה שָׂטָן, וְלֹא הָיָה לוֹ פֶּה לְדָחוֹתָם לְגַמְרֵי: וַיִּבֶן מִזְבֵּחַ. לְדָחוֹתָם: וַיִּקְרָא... חַג לַה׳ מָחָר. וְלֹא הַיּוֹם, שֶׁמָּא יָבֹא מֹשֶׁה קֹדֶם שֶׁיַּעַבְדוּהוּ, זֶהוּ פְּשׁוּטוֹ. וּמִדְרָשׁוֹ בְּוַיִּקְרָא רַבָּה (י, ג): דְּבָרִים הַרְבֵּה רָאָה אַהֲרֹן; רָאָה חוּר בֶּן אֲחוֹתוֹ שֶׁהָיָה מוֹכִיחָם וַהֲרָגוּהוּ, וְזֶהוּ ״וַיִּבֶן מִזְבֵּחַ לְפָנָיו״, וַיָּבֶן מִזָּבוּחַ לְפָנָיו; וְעוֹד רָאָה וְאָמַר, מוּטָב שֶׁיִּתָּלֶה בִּי הַסִּרְחוֹן וְלֹא בָּהֶם; וְעוֹד רָאָה וְאָמַר, אִם הֵם בּוֹנִים אוֹתוֹ הַמִּזְבֵּחַ, זֶה מֵבִיא צְרוֹר וְזֶה מֵבִיא אֶבֶן וְנִמְצֵאת מְלַאכְתָּן בְּבַת אַחַת, מִתּוֹךְ שֶׁאֲנִי בּוֹנֶה אוֹתוֹ אֲנִי מִתְעַצֵּל בִּמְלַאכְתִּי, וּבֵין כָּךְ וּבֵין כָּךְ מֹשֶׁה בָּא. חַג לַה׳. בְּלִבּוֹ הָיָה לַשָּׁמַיִם, בָּטוּחַ הָיָה שֶׁיָּבֹא מֹשֶׁה וְיַעַבְדוּ אֶת הַמָּקוֹם:

ו| וַיַּשְׁכִּימוּ. הַשָּׂטָן זֵרְזָם כְּדֵי שֶׁיֶּחֶטְאוּ: לְצַחֵק. יֵשׁ בַּמַּשְׁמָע הַזֶּה גִּלּוּי עֲרָיוֹת, כְּמוֹ שֶׁנֶּאֱמַר: ״לְצַחֶק בִּי״ (בראשית לט, יז), וּשְׁפִיכוּת דָּמִים, כְּמוֹ שֶׁנֶּאֱמַר: ״יָקוּמוּ נָא הַנְּעָרִים וִישַׂחֲקוּ לְפָנֵינוּ״ (שמואל ב׳ ב, יד), אַף כָּאן נֶהֱרַג חוּר:

ז| וַיְדַבֵּר. לְשׁוֹן קֹשִׁי הוּא, כְּמוֹ: ״וַיְדַבֵּר אִתָּם קָשׁוֹת״ (בראשית מב, ז): לֶךְ רֵד. מִגְּדֻלָּתְךָ, לֹא נָתַתִּי לְךָ גְּדֻלָּה אֶלָּא בִּשְׁבִילָם. בְּאוֹתָהּ שָׁעָה נִתְנַדָּה מֹשֶׁה מִפִּי בֵּית דִּין שֶׁלְּמַעְלָה: שִׁחֵת עַמְּךָ. ״שִׁחֵת הָעָם״ לֹא נֶאֱמַר, אֶלָּא ״עַמְּךָ״, עֵרֶב רַב שֶׁקִּבַּלְתָּ מֵעַצְמְךָ וְגִיַּרְתָּם וְלֹא נִמְלַכְתָּ בִּי, וְאָמַרְתָּ: טוֹב שֶׁיִּדָּבְקוּ גֵּרִים בַּשְּׁכִינָה – הֵם שִׁחֲתוּ וְהִשְׁחִיתוּ:

ט| קְשֵׁה עֹרֶף. מַחֲזִירִין קֹשִׁי עָרְפָּם לְנֶגֶד מוֹכִיחֵיהֶם וּמְמָאֲנִים לִשְׁמֹעַ:

י| הַנִּיחָה לִּי. עֲדַיִן לֹא שָׁמַעְנוּ שֶׁהִתְפַּלֵּל מֹשֶׁה עֲלֵיהֶם, וְהוּא אוֹמֵר ״הַנִּיחָה לִּי״? אֶלָּא כָּאן פָּתַח לוֹ פֶּתַח וְהוֹדִיעוֹ שֶׁהַדָּבָר תָּלוּי בּוֹ, שֶׁאִם יִתְפַּלֵּל עֲלֵיהֶם לֹא יְכַלֵּם:

יא| לָמָה ה׳ יֶחֱרֶה אַפְּךָ. כְּלוּם מִתְקַנֵּא אֶלָּא חָכָם בְּחָכָם גִּבּוֹר בְּגִבּוֹר:

יב| וְהִנָּחֵם. הִתְעַשֵּׁת לָהֶם מַחֲשָׁבָה אַחֶרֶת לְהֵיטִיב: עַל הָרָעָה. אֲשֶׁר חָשַׁבְתָּ לָהֶם:

יג| זְכֹר לְאַבְרָהָם. אִם עָבְרוּ עַל עֲשֶׂרֶת הַדִּבְּרוֹת, אַבְרָהָם אֲבִיהֶם נִתְנַסָּה בְּעֶשֶׂר נִסְיוֹנוֹת וַעֲדַיִן לֹא קִבֵּל שְׂכָרוֹ, תְּנֵהוּ לוֹ, וְיֵצְאוּ עֶשֶׂר בְּעֶשֶׂר: לְאַבְרָהָם לְיִצְחָק וּלְיִשְׂרָאֵל. וְאִם אֵינָן נִצּוֹלִין בִּזְכוּתָן, מָה אַתָּה אוֹמֵר לִי: ״וְאֶעֱשֶׂה אוֹתְךָ לְגוֹי גָּדוֹל״? אִם כִּסֵּא שֶׁל שָׁלֹשׁ רַגְלַיִם אֵינוֹ עוֹמֵד לְפָנֶיךָ, קַל וָחֹמֶר לְכִסֵּא שֶׁל רֶגֶל אֶחָד: אֲשֶׁר נִשְׁבַּעְתָּ לָהֶם בָּךְ. לֹא נִשְׁבַּעְתָּ לָהֶם בְּדָבָר שֶׁהוּא כָּלֶה, לֹא בַּשָּׁמַיִם וְלֹא בָּאָרֶץ, לֹא בֶּהָרִים וְלֹא בַּגְּבָעוֹת, אֶלָּא בְּךָ שֶׁאַתָּה קַיָּם וְכֵן שְׁבוּעָתְךָ תִּתְקַיֵּם, שֶׁנֶּאֱמַר: ״בִּי נִשְׁבַּעְתִּי נְאֻם ה׳״ (בראשית כב, טז), וּלְיִצְחָק נֶאֱמַר: ״וַהֲקִמֹתִי אֶת הַשְּׁבֻעָה אֲשֶׁר נִשְׁבַּעְתִּי לְאַבְרָהָם אָבִיךָ״ (שם כו, ג), וּלְיַעֲקֹב נֶאֱמַר: ״אֲנִי אֵל שַׁדַּי פְּרֵה וּרְבֵה״ (שם לה, יא), נִשְׁבַּע לוֹ בְּאֵל שַׁדַּי:

טו| מִשְּׁנֵי עֶבְרֵיהֶם. הָיוּ הָאוֹתִיּוֹת נִקְרָאוֹת, וּמַעֲשֵׂה נִסִּים הוּא:

16 **The tablets** were not fashioned by human hands, but **were the work of God; and the writing was the writing of God, engraved** by Him **on the tablets.**
17 When Moses ascended Mount Sinai, Joshua had accompanied him to the base of the mountain. However, Joshua was prohibited from passing some point, and he waited there until Moses' return (24:13). When Moses descended from the mountain, Joshua was the one he met first. **Joshua heard the sound of the people in its uproar, and he said to Moses: There is the sound of battle in the camp.** The shouting and commotion sounded to him like the cries of battle.
18 **He,** Moses, **said** to Joshua: **There is not the sound of a cry of valor, and there is not the sound of a cry of weakness,** and therefore your characterization of the sounds is inaccurate. If the people were engaged in battle, one would hear both the sound of the victors shouting out in triumph and the wail of the defeated. Yet I hear neither of these; merely **the sound of a cry I hear.**[26] Others explain that Moses was arguing that they could hear the sound of singing and rejoicing.
19 **It was when he approached the camp; he saw the calf and** the **dancing** around it. **Moses' wrath was enflamed, and he cast the tablets from his hands, and he shattered them**[D] upon the stones **at the foot of the mountain.**
20 **He took the calf that they** had **made, and he burned it in the fire**[D] **and ground it into powder,** completely destroying it. **And he scattered it,** the powder, **on the surface of the water and gave** the solution to **the children of Israel to drink,**[D] to debase it and to shame the people, as though saying to them: This is your god; eat it, drink it, and later you will excrete it.[27]
21 **Moses said to Aaron: What did this people do to you** that forced you to act in such a manner[28] **that you brought great sin upon them?** Others explain: Did you hate the people so much that you sought to bring about their complete annihilation?[29]
22 **Aaron,** whose intentions had been pure, was greatly alarmed both by the people's actions and Moses' reproach. He **said: Let the wrath of my lord not be enflamed; you have known the people, that it is in an evil state.**
23 **They said to me: Make us a god that will go before us, because this man Moses, who brought us up from the land of Egypt, we do not know what became of him.**
24 **I said to them: Who has** any **gold?** If you do, **remove it. They gave it,** their jewelry, **to me, and I cast it into the fire; and** without any intention on my part of creating any form, **this calf emerged.** Some say that others intervened and fashioned the form of the calf,[30] possibly through witchcraft.[31]
25 **Moses saw the people, that it was unsettled.** The festivities that had surrounded the golden calf, Moses' descent, and the

Statue of calf depicting the Egyptian god Apis, sixth century BCE

DISCUSSION

32:19| **Moses' wrath was enflamed, and he cast the tablets from his hands, and he shattered them:** Earlier, the Torah mentioned God's anger toward the people. Here the Torah describes Moses' rage upon witnessing the scene below and observing all the ugly details that God had refrained from telling him. Moses saw that the people had not merely fashioned a golden calf, but had let loose their base impulses without restraint (see Sforno; Alsheikh; Rabbi Samson Raphael Hirsch).

Beyond expressing Moses' wrath (see Ramban), the breaking of the tablets had additional meaning. The writing on the tablets represented the covenant between God and Israel. When the people broke the covenant, they could no longer keep its physical manifestation. The Sages compare this to a bridegroom who, upon coming to give his bride her marriage contract, discovers that she is consorting with another man. Under such circumstances it would be a farce to give her the marriage contract. By breaking the tablets, Moses demonstrated that the covenant was void (see *Tanḥuma* 30; *Avot deRabbi Natan* 2:3; Rashi, 34:1).

32:20| **He took the calf that they had made, and he burned it in the fire:** Apparently no one objected to Moses' burning of the golden calf. This is a further indication that the calf was not designed to be an object of worship, but only as a substitute for the leader. When Moses returned, the golden calf lost its significance in the eyes of the people (see Ramban, 32:1).

And gave the children of Israel to drink: The act of administering the people a drink made of water mixed with the ashes of the golden calf is reminiscent of the ritual in which a woman suspected by her husband of having been unfaithful to him [*sota*] is made to drink water mixed with dust from the earth of the Tabernacle. The water serves to test whether or not the woman was indeed unfaithful (Numbers 5:17–24). Some commentaries explain that Moses caused the people to drink the water with the ashes of the golden calf in order to determine who had sinned and was liable to be punished, and who was innocent (see *Avoda Zara* 44a; Rashi; Rashbam).

32:24| **And this calf emerged:** Perhaps the Israelites worshipped the image of a calf because it was one with which they were familiar, as the Egyptian god Apis was depicted as a bull.

When Moses ascended Mount Sinai he left both Aaron and Hur in charge (24:14). However, Hur is not mentioned again. The Sages explain that Hur objected to the people's demand to make them a god, and they killed him (see *Sanhedrin* 7a; *Targum Yonatan* and Rashi, 32:5). The reason this incident is not mentioned is that the Torah does not want to emphasize the fact that the incident of the golden calf involved murder, in addition to idolatry and forbidden sexual relations. One might have assumed that Hur is not mentioned again because he also participated in the sin of the golden calf. However, when God appoints Betzalel to be in charge of building the Tabernacle, the Torah

טז מִזֶּה וּמִזֶּה הֵם כְּתֻבִים: וְהַלֻּחֹת מַעֲשֵׂה אֱלֹהִים הֵמָּה וְהַמִּכְתָּב מִכְתַּב אֱלֹהִים
יז הוּא חָרוּת עַל־הַלֻּחֹת: וַיִּשְׁמַע יְהוֹשֻׁעַ אֶת־קוֹל הָעָם בְּרֵעֹה וַיֹּאמֶר אֶל־מֹשֶׁה
יח קוֹל מִלְחָמָה בַּמַּחֲנֶה: וַיֹּאמֶר אֵין קוֹל עֲנוֹת גְּבוּרָה וְאֵין קוֹל עֲנוֹת חֲלוּשָׁה קוֹל
יט עַנּוֹת אָנֹכִי שֹׁמֵעַ: וַיְהִי כַּאֲשֶׁר קָרַב אֶל־הַמַּחֲנֶה וַיַּרְא אֶת־הָעֵגֶל וּמְחֹלֹת וַיִּחַר־
כ אַף מֹשֶׁה וַיַּשְׁלֵךְ מִיָּדָו אֶת־הַלֻּחֹת וַיְשַׁבֵּר אֹתָם תַּחַת הָהָר: וַיִּקַּח אֶת־הָעֵגֶל
אֲשֶׁר עָשׂוּ וַיִּשְׂרֹף בָּאֵשׁ וַיִּטְחַן עַד אֲשֶׁר־דָּק וַיִּזֶר עַל־פְּנֵי הַמַּיִם וַיַּשְׁקְ אֶת־בְּנֵי
כא יִשְׂרָאֵל: וַיֹּאמֶר מֹשֶׁה אֶל־אַהֲרֹן מֶה־עָשָׂה לְךָ הָעָם הַזֶּה כִּי־הֵבֵאתָ עָלָיו חֲטָאָה
כב גְדֹלָה: וַיֹּאמֶר אַהֲרֹן אַל־יִחַר אַף אֲדֹנִי אַתָּה יָדַעְתָּ אֶת־הָעָם כִּי בְרָע הוּא:
כג וַיֹּאמְרוּ לִי עֲשֵׂה־לָנוּ אֱלֹהִים אֲשֶׁר יֵלְכוּ לְפָנֵינוּ כִּי־זֶה ׀ מֹשֶׁה הָאִישׁ אֲשֶׁר הֶעֱלָנוּ
כד מֵאֶרֶץ מִצְרַיִם לֹא יָדַעְנוּ מֶה־הָיָה לוֹ: וָאֹמַר לָהֶם לְמִי זָהָב הִתְפָּרָקוּ וַיִּתְּנוּ־לִי
כה וָאַשְׁלִכֵהוּ בָאֵשׁ וַיֵּצֵא הָעֵגֶל הַזֶּה: וַיַּרְא מֹשֶׁה אֶת־הָעָם כִּי פָרֻעַ הוּא כִּי־פְרָעֹה

רש״י

טז | **מַעֲשֵׂה אֱלֹהִים הֵמָּה.** כְּמַשְׁמָעוֹ, הוּא בִּכְבוֹדוֹ עֲשָׂאָן. דָּבָר אַחֵר, כְּאָדָם הָאוֹמֵר לַחֲבֵרוֹ: כָּל עֲסָקָיו שֶׁל פְּלוֹנִי בִּמְלָאכָה פְּלוֹנִית, כָּךְ כָּל שַׁעֲשׁוּעָיו שֶׁל הַקָּדוֹשׁ בָּרוּךְ הוּא בַּתּוֹרָה: **חָרוּת.** לְשׁוֹן ׳חֶרֶט׳ וְ׳חָרוּת׳ אֶחָד הוּא, שְׁנֵיהֶם לְשׁוֹן חִקּוּק, אנטליי״ר בְּלַעַז:

יז | **בְּרֵעֹה.** בַּהֲרִיעוֹ, שֶׁהָיוּ מְרִיעִים וּשְׂמֵחִים וְצוֹחֲקִים:

יח | **אֵין קוֹל עֲנוֹת גְּבוּרָה.** אֵין קוֹל הַזֶּה נִרְאֶה קוֹל עֲנִיַּת גִּבּוֹרִים הַצּוֹעֲקִים ׳נִצָּחוֹן׳, וְלֹא קוֹל חַלָּשִׁים הַצּוֹעֲקִים ׳וַי׳ אוֹ ׳נִיסָה׳: **קוֹל עַנּוֹת.** קוֹל חֵרוּפִין וְגִדּוּפִין הַמְעַנִּין אֶת נֶפֶשׁ שׁוֹמְעָן כְּשֶׁנֶּאֱמָרִין לוֹ:

יט | **וַיַּשְׁלֵךְ מִיָּדָו וְגוֹ׳.** אָמַר: מָה פֶּסַח שֶׁהוּא אַחַת מִן הַמִּצְוֹת, אָמְרָה תּוֹרָה: ״כָּל בֶּן נֵכָר לֹא יֹאכַל בּוֹ״ (לעיל יב, מג), הַתּוֹרָה כֻּלָּהּ כָּאן וְכֻלָּם מְשֻׁמָּדִים, וְאֶתְּנֶנָּה לָהֶם?!: **תַּחַת הָהָר.** לְרַגְלֵי הָהָר:

כ | **וַיִּזֶר.** לְשׁוֹן נִפּוּץ, וְכֵן: ״יְזֹרֶה עַל נָוֵהוּ גָפְרִית״ (איוב יח, טו), וְכֵן: ״כִּי חִנָּם מְזֹרָה הָרָשֶׁת״ (משלי א, יז) שֶׁזּוֹרִין בָּהּ דָּגָן וְקִטְנִית: **וַיַּשְׁקְ אֶת בְּנֵי יִשְׂרָאֵל.** נִתְכַּוֵּן לְבָדְקָן כְּסוֹטוֹת. שָׁלֹשׁ מִיתוֹת נִדּוֹנוּ שָׁם: אִם יֵשׁ עֵדִים וְהַתְרָאָה, בְּסַיִף, כְּמִשְׁפַּט אַנְשֵׁי עִיר הַנִּדַּחַת שֶׁהֵן מְרֻבִּין; עֵדִים בְּלֹא הַתְרָאָה, בְּמַגֵּפָה, שֶׁנֶּאֱמַר: ״וַיִּגֹּף ה׳ אֶת הָעָם״ (להלן פסוק לה); לֹא עֵדִים וְלֹא הַתְרָאָה, בְּהַדְרוֹקָן, שֶׁבְּדָקוּם הַמַּיִם וְצָבוּ בִּטְנֵיהֶם:

כא | **מֶה עָשָׂה לְךָ הָעָם הַזֶּה.** כַּמָּה יִסּוּרִים סָבַלְתָּ שֶׁיִּסְּרוּךְ עַד שֶׁלֹּא תָּבִיא עֲלֵיהֶם חֵטְא זֶה:

כב | **כִּי בְרָע הוּא.** בְּדֶרֶךְ רַע הֵם הוֹלְכִין תָּמִיד וּבְנִסְיוֹנוֹת לִפְנֵי הַמָּקוֹם:

כד | **וָאֹמַר לָהֶם.** דָּבָר אֶחָד, וְהֵם מִהֲרוּ וְ״הִתְפָּרְקוּ״: **וָאַשְׁלִכֵהוּ בָאֵשׁ.** וְלֹא יָדַעְתִּי שֶׁיֵּצֵא הָעֵגֶל הַזֶּה, ״וַיֵּצֵא״:

כה | **פָּרֻעַ.** מְגֻלֶּה, נִתְגַּלָּה שִׁמְצוֹ וְקְלוֹנוֹ, כְּמוֹ: ״וּפָרַע אֶת

DISCUSSION

explicitly states that he is Hur's grandson (31:2), and it would not mention Hur in such a laudable context if he had become a sinner.

Despite Aaron's involvement in the fashioning of the golden calf, God appoints him as the High Priest. The Sages state that in light of the incident of the golden calf, Aaron's appointment caused him embarrassment, and he hesitated to commence his duties as High Priest (see *Sifra, Tzav, Mekhilta deMilluim*; Rashi, Leviticus 9:7, 23). In a sense, Aaron's appointment could itself be considered a punishment of sorts, as it was a constant reminder that he nearly became a priest to idolatry. The death of Aaron's two sons on the day that the Tabernacle was inaugurated might also be related to the sin of the golden calf (see *Tanḥuma, Tetzaveh* 10; Rashi, Deuteronomy 9:20). In a similar vein, the Sages state that the High Priest did not wear his golden vestments when he entered the Holy of Holies on Yom Kippur, in order to avoid any association with the sin of the golden calf.

There may be a different connection between Aaron's involvement in the sin of the golden calf and his appointment as High Priest. As High Priest, Aaron was required to intercede on behalf of the Jewish people and to bring peace between God and His nation. Indeed, Aaron's actions here demonstrate the very qualities that rendered him fit to serve in the capacity of High Priest. He listened to the people, loved and cared for them, and endeavored to ensure their welfare (see Malachi 2:5–7; *Avot* 1:12; *Avot deRabbi Natan*, 12). Although these traits led to unwanted consequences in the case of the golden calf, those same traits made him the best candidate for the role of High Priest.

subsequent destruction of the calf had all sown confusion among the people. **For Aaron had exposed them to ignominy on the part of those who would rise** up **against them.**[D] The Jewish people's transgression of idolatry is a constant source of shame, especially their worship of the golden calf. Some translate the latter part of the verse to mean that Aaron had revealed their shame before their enemies.[32] Others interpret this to mean that he had caused their disorder and confusion.[33]

26 When Moses saw the people's wild idolatrous worship and accompanying orgies, he realized that he had to reunite them and strengthen their faith in God. **Moses** therefore **stood at the gate of the camp and said: Whoever is for the Lord,** faithful to God and willing to fight for Him, come **to me. And all the sons of Levi,** Moses' own tribe, **gathered to him,** either due to their kinship with Moses, or because they opposed the worship of the golden calf.

27 **He said to them: So said the Lord, God of Israel: Each man, place his sword upon his thigh,** in preparation for battle or forceful punitive action. **Pass to and fro from gate to gate in the camp, and slay each** one who stands against you, even each man **his brother,**[D] **and each his neighbor, and each his relative.** Uncontrollable and immoral behavior had spread quickly throughout the camp. The Levites were therefore instructed to kill all who opposed them, without hesitation.

28 **The sons of Levi acted in accordance with the word of Moses, and some three thousand men fell from the people on that day.** Although the tribe of Levi was not large, the worshippers of the golden calf did not actively resist them. Despondent and all too aware of their severe sin and its consequences, they no longer saw meaning in the golden calf or a reason to worship it.[34] The Levites' actions were not an attempt to punish everyone who had sinned. Rather, they were an affirmation of their loyalty to God and to the Torah.

29 **Moses said: Dedicate yourselves today to** be appointed to serve **the Lord, as each man** of you **is** even **against his son and against his brother,** disregarding considerations of sentiment. Your deeds were not wicked, nor were they merely an expression of faith. They were imperative, of the utmost importance, **and so He may bestow upon you a blessing this day.**[D] You will receive a blessing for your deeds.

30 **It was on the next day; Moses said to the people: You have sinned a great sin, and now I will ascend to the Lord** to plead on your behalf; **perhaps I will atone for your sin.**

31 **Moses returned to the Lord, and he said: Please, this people has sinned a great sin, and they made themselves a god of gold.** Although the people as a whole have sinned, not all are guilty to the same extent. Some participated reluctantly, others merely wanted to find a substitute for Moses, and yet others rejoiced at the opportunity to relapse into their idolatrous habits.

32 **Now,** I implore You: **If You will bear their sin…, and if not, erase me please**[D] **from Your book,** the book of life,[35] **that You have written.**[D] Moses is asking God to kill him if He does not forgive the people. Alternatively, this book is the Torah. Moses is saying that if God now considers the giving of the Torah an unsuccessful attempt, then he himself failed as well, and should be erased from the Torah.

33 **The Lord said to Moses:** I will not remove you from the book. **Whoever sinned against Me, I shall erase him** alone **from My book** of life, and he shall be blotted out from the course of history.

34 **Now,** I have accepted your plea; therefore, **go, lead the people to where I have spoken to you.** Take the nation to the land of Canaan, in accordance with the original purpose of the exodus. But **behold,** henceforth **My angel will go before you.** The Jewish people will now be subject to an angel, whom God will appoint as His intermediary to ensure their well-being, in the manner that He rules over other nations.[36] **And on the day of My reckoning,** when judgment will be meted out,[37] **I will reckon their sin upon them.** Many of the people sinned actively, others transgressed by encouraging the sinners, and yet others were guilty for failure to act or for their indifference. Retribution for the sin of the golden calf will be meted out in small doses, but the punishment will not bring about full atonement for the sin until the End of Days.[38]

DISCUSSION

32:25 | To ignominy on the part of those who would rise against them: Many generations later, the Egyptian ruler al-Ḥākim bi-Amr Allāh (985–1021), the sixth caliph of the Fatimid dynasty, decreed that Jews must wear a wooden calf necklace as a mark of shame.

32:27 | And slay each his brother: These killings are not to be understood as a full punishment for the sin of the golden calf, which was such a severe sin that the people could not achieve complete atonement for it in a single stage (see *Sanhedrin* 102a; Rashi, verse 34). They could not be punished immediately in accordance with the severity of their actions, as they did not yet comprehend the implications of their behavior. Nonetheless, the consequences of their actions would accompany them for the rest of their lives. This may be likened to a child who causes a permanent scar to his own face or body; although he does not fully understand what he is doing and cannot be held accountable, he will bear the scar forever. In the meantime, Moses attempted to cleanse the moral pollution of the people, by eradicating those who had been especially culpable.

32:29 | And so He may bestow upon you a blessing this day: When Moses blessed the tribes before his death, he mentioned the ◄●

כו אַהֲרֹן לְשִׁמְצָה בְּקָמֵיהֶם׃ וַיַּעֲמֹד מֹשֶׁה בְּשַׁעַר הַמַּחֲנֶה וַיֹּאמֶר מִי לַיהוָה אֵלָי
כז וַיֵּאָסְפוּ אֵלָיו כָּל־בְּנֵי לֵוִי׃ וַיֹּאמֶר לָהֶם כֹּה־אָמַר יְהוָה אֱלֹהֵי יִשְׂרָאֵל שִׂימוּ אִישׁ־
חַרְבּוֹ עַל־יְרֵכוֹ עִבְרוּ וָשׁוּבוּ מִשַּׁעַר לָשַׁעַר בַּמַּחֲנֶה וְהִרְגוּ אִישׁ־אֶת־אָחִיו וְאִישׁ
כח אֶת־רֵעֵהוּ וְאִישׁ אֶת־קְרֹבוֹ׃ וַיַּעֲשׂוּ בְנֵי־לֵוִי כִּדְבַר מֹשֶׁה וַיִּפֹּל מִן־הָעָם בַּיּוֹם הַהוּא
כט כִּשְׁלֹשֶׁת אַלְפֵי אִישׁ׃ וַיֹּאמֶר מֹשֶׁה מִלְאוּ יֶדְכֶם הַיּוֹם לַיהוָה כִּי אִישׁ בִּבְנוֹ וּבְאָחִיו
ל וְלָתֵת עֲלֵיכֶם הַיּוֹם בְּרָכָה׃ וַיְהִי מִמָּחֳרָת וַיֹּאמֶר מֹשֶׁה אֶל־הָעָם אַתֶּם חֲטָאתֶם
לא חֲטָאָה גְדֹלָה וְעַתָּה אֶעֱלֶה אֶל־יְהוָה אוּלַי אֲכַפְּרָה בְּעַד חַטַּאתְכֶם׃ וַיָּשָׁב מֹשֶׁה
אֶל־יְהוָה וַיֹּאמַר אָנָּא חָטָא הָעָם הַזֶּה חֲטָאָה גְדֹלָה וַיַּעֲשׂוּ לָהֶם אֱלֹהֵי זָהָב׃
לב לג וְעַתָּה אִם־תִּשָּׂא חַטָּאתָם וְאִם־אַיִן מְחֵנִי נָא מִסִּפְרְךָ אֲשֶׁר כָּתָבְתָּ׃ וַיֹּאמֶר יְהוָה
לד אֶל־מֹשֶׁה מִי אֲשֶׁר חָטָא־לִי אֶמְחֶנּוּ מִסִּפְרִי׃ וְעַתָּה לֵךְ נְחֵה אֶת־הָעָם אֶל
אֲשֶׁר־דִּבַּרְתִּי לָךְ הִנֵּה מַלְאָכִי יֵלֵךְ לְפָנֶיךָ וּבְיוֹם פָּקְדִי וּפָקַדְתִּי עֲלֵיהֶם חַטָּאתָם׃

רש"י

"רֹאשׁ הָאִשָּׁה" (במדבר ה, יח): לְשִׁמְצָה בְּקָמֵיהֶם. לִהְיוֹת לָהֶם הַדָּבָר הַזֶּה לִגְנוּת בְּפִי כָּל הַקָּמִים עֲלֵיהֶם:

כו| מִי לַה' אֵלָי. יָבֹא אֵלַי: כָּל בְּנֵי לֵוִי. מִכָּאן שֶׁכָּל הַשֵּׁבֶט כָּשֵׁר:

כז| כֹּה אָמַר וְגוֹ'. וְהֵיכָן אָמַר? "זֹבֵחַ לָאֱלֹהִים יָחֳרָם" (לעיל כב, יט), כָּךְ שְׁנוּיָה בַּמְּכִילְתָּא: אָחִיו. מֵאִמּוֹ, וְהוּא יִשְׂרָאֵל:

כט| מִלְאוּ יֶדְכֶם. אַתֶּם הַהוֹרְגִים אוֹתָם, בְּדָבָר זֶה תִּתְחַנְּכוּ לִהְיוֹת כֹּהֲנִים לַמָּקוֹם: כִּי אִישׁ. מִכֶּם, יְמַלֵּא יָדוֹ "בִּבְנוֹ וּבְאָחִיו":

ל| אֲכַפְּרָה בְּעַד חַטַּאתְכֶם. אָשִׂים כֹּפֶר וְקִנּוּחַ וּסְתִימָה לְנֶגֶד חַטַּאתְכֶם, לְהַבְדִּיל בֵּינֵיכֶם וּבֵין הַחֵטְא:

לא| אֱלֹהֵי זָהָב. אַתָּה הוּא שֶׁגָּרַמְתָּ לָהֶם, שֶׁהִשְׁפַּעְתָּ לָהֶם זָהָב וְכָל חֶפְצָם, מַה יַּעֲשׂוּ שֶׁלֹּא יֶחֶטְאוּ? מָשָׁל לְמֶלֶךְ שֶׁהָיָה מַאֲכִיל וּמַשְׁקֶה אֶת בְּנוֹ וּמְקַשְּׁטוֹ, וְתוֹלֶה לוֹ כִּיס בְּצַוָּארוֹ, וּמַעֲמִידוֹ בְּפֶתַח בֵּית זוֹנוֹת, מַה יַּעֲשֶׂה הַבֵּן שֶׁלֹּא יֶחֱטָא?

לב| וְעַתָּה אִם תִּשָּׂא חַטָּאתָם. הֲרֵי טוֹב, אֵינִי אוֹמֵר לְךָ מְחֵנִי, "וְאִם אַיִן – מְחֵנִי", וְזֶה מִקְרָא קָצָר, וְכֵן הַרְבֵּה: מִסִּפְרְךָ. מִכָּל הַתּוֹרָה כֻּלָּהּ, שֶׁלֹּא יֹאמְרוּ עָלַי שֶׁלֹּא הָיִיתִי כְדַאי לְבַקֵּשׁ עֲלֵיהֶם רַחֲמִים:

לד| אֶל אֲשֶׁר דִּבַּרְתִּי לָךְ. יֵשׁ כָּאן "לָךְ" אֵצֶל דִּבּוּר בִּמְקוֹם 'אֵלֶיךָ', וְכֵן: "לְדַבֵּר לוֹ עַל אֲדֹנִיָּהוּ" (מלכים א' ב, יט): הִנֵּה מַלְאָכִי. וְלֹא אֲנִי: וּבְיוֹם פָּקְדִי וְגוֹ'. עַתָּה שָׁמַעְתִּי אֵלֶיךָ מִלְּכַלּוֹתָם יַחַד, וְתָמִיד תָּמִיד כְּשֶׁאֶפְקֹד עֲלֵיהֶם עֲוֹנוֹתֵיהֶם, "וּפָקַדְתִּי עֲלֵיהֶם" מְעַט מִן הֶעָוֹן הַזֶּה עִם שְׁאָר הָעֲוֹנוֹת. וְאֵין פֻּרְעָנוּת בָּאָה עַל יִשְׂרָאֵל שֶׁאֵין בָּהּ קְצָת מִפִּרְעוֹן עֲוֹן הָעֵגֶל:

DISCUSSION

Levites' act of devotion in his prophetic blessing: "Who said of his father and of his mother: I did not see him, and his brothers he did not recognize, and his children he did not know, because they observed Your saying, and Your covenant they upheld" (Deuteronomy 33:9; see *Bekhor Shor*).

32:32| **If You will bear their sin…, and if not, erase me please:** This is the continuation of Moses' response to God's proposal to destroy the people and to create a new nation from Moses' descendants. Moses replies that the Torah is intended for ordinary people, with weaknesses and imperfections. If the Jewish people cannot adhere to the Torah, there is no reason to think that Moses' descendants would be more successful. Consequently, if God does not want human beings as His people, and will not forgive their faults, then even Moses is fit to be wiped out together with the rest of humanity.

From Your book that You have written: This obscure reference to a book is probably the source of the idea that there is a book of life and a book of death open before God (see *Rosh HaShana* 16b; Ramban; Rambam, *Guide of the Perplexed* 2:47).

35 **The Lord** immediately initiated the sinners' punishment; He **afflicted the people**[D] and killed many of them with a plague, **because they made the calf that Aaron** had **made.**

33 **1** **The Lord spoke to Moses: Set out,** and **go up from here, you and the people whom you brought up from the land of Egypt, to the land about which I took an oath to Abraham, to Isaac and to Jacob, saying: I will give it to your descendants.** Although the people have sinned and will be held accountable in the future for their transgression, the journey to the Promised Land will continue for now.

2 **I will send an angel before you**[D] **and expel the Canaanites, the Emorites, the Hitites, the Perizites, the Hivites, and the Yevusites.**

3 The angel will bring you **to a land flowing with milk and honey, as I will not go up** with you by residing **in your midst** Myself, **because you are a stiff-necked people, lest I destroy you**[39] **on the way.** You might sin again, and if you do so while My presence is in your midst, your sin will be greater and your punishment more severe.

4 **The people heard this evil tiding,** that God did not wish to continue residing among them, and that they would lose their unique relationship with Him, **and they mourned. And each** man **did not place his ornament on himself.** The people had adorned themselves in honor of receiving the Torah. Having lost their elevated status, some of the people now removed their ornaments (see 33:6). According to a midrashic tradition, at the time of the giving of the Torah God had adorned the Jewish people with crowns or symbolic ornaments.[40]

5 **The Lord said to Moses: Say to the children of Israel: You are a stiff-necked people; if for one moment I would go up in your midst, I would destroy you. Now, remove your ornament from you,** as you realize yourselves that you are no longer fit to wear the ornaments, **and I will know what I will do to you** as you progress from here.

6 After receiving this instruction to remove their ornaments, **the children of Israel were stripped of their ornament,** which they had received **from Mount Horev.**[41]

7 **Moses would take the tent,** his tent, **and pitch it outside the camp, far from the camp.** Moses' tent had formerly been located in the center of the camp, as in the description of the people's encampment.[42] When God stated that He would not reside among the people, Moses emulated Him and removed his tent from the camp.[43] **And he called it the Tent of Meeting,** a place where people could meet and talk to him.[44] **It was the** practice **that anyone who sought the Lord would go out to the Tent of Meeting, which was outside the camp.** Although Moses had departed from the camp, he did not detach himself from the nation entirely. Anyone who wished to study Torah could meet him in the isolation of his tent.

8 Moses continued to sleep in his family tent inside the camp. Every day he would leave that tent and pass through the camp to the Tent of Meeting outside. **It would be, upon Moses' going out to the tent, that all the people would rise, and each would stand at his tent's entrance; they would gaze after Moses until he went into the tent.**

9 **It would be upon Moses' entry into the Tent** of Meeting, **that the pillar of cloud,** which was a manifestation of the Divine Presence, **would descend and stand at the entrance of the tent; and He,** God, **would speak with Moses,** while no one else heard. During this period, Moses lived only partially in the camp, and the Divine Presence was with Moses; it did not dwell among the people.

10 **The entire people would see the pillar of cloud standing at the entrance of the tent, and the entire people would rise and prostrate themselves, each man at the entrance of his tent.**

DISCUSSION

32:35 | The Lord afflicted the people: Not even the plague atoned sufficiently for the sin of the golden calf. The worship of the calf brought lasting shame upon Israel for their failure to comprehend their new status as God's nation. They were unable to maintain their elevated status even for a short period, as they engaged in idolatrous worship so soon after receiving the Torah. The Sages express this idea in the following manner: Insolent is the bride who is promiscuous under her wedding canopy (*Shabbat* 88b).

33:2 | I will send an angel before you: The book of Daniel indicates that each nation has a guardian angel (Daniel 10:13–21). Although Daniel describes the angel of the Jewish people as "Mikhael, the great prince" (Daniel 12:1), he is not necessarily the angel referred to here. As a result of the sin of the golden calf, the people were demoted to a status similar to that of the other nations. When God Himself governs the people without the agency of an angel, walking among His people, as it were (see Leviticus 26:12), this expresses the unique status of the Jews as God's chosen nation. Nevertheless, as indicated by the next verse, such closeness to God can be perilous (*Shemot Rabba* 18:5).

לה וַיִּגֹּף יְהוָה אֶת־הָעָם עַל אֲשֶׁר עָשׂוּ אֶת־הָעֵגֶל אֲשֶׁר עָשָׂה אַהֲרֹן׃
א וַיְדַבֵּר יְהוָה אֶל־מֹשֶׁה לֵךְ עֲלֵה מִזֶּה אַתָּה וְהָעָם אֲשֶׁר הֶעֱלִיתָ מֵאֶרֶץ מִצְרָיִם
אֶל־הָאָרֶץ אֲשֶׁר נִשְׁבַּעְתִּי לְאַבְרָהָם לְיִצְחָק וּלְיַעֲקֹב לֵאמֹר לְזַרְעֲךָ אֶתְּנֶנָּה׃
ב וְשָׁלַחְתִּי לְפָנֶיךָ מַלְאָךְ וְגֵרַשְׁתִּי אֶת־הַכְּנַעֲנִי הָאֱמֹרִי וְהַחִתִּי וְהַפְּרִזִּי הַחִוִּי וְהַיְבוּסִי׃
ג אֶל־אֶרֶץ זָבַת חָלָב וּדְבָשׁ כִּי לֹא אֶעֱלֶה בְּקִרְבְּךָ כִּי עַם־קְשֵׁה־עֹרֶף אַתָּה פֶּן־
ד אֲכֶלְךָ בַּדָּרֶךְ׃ וַיִּשְׁמַע הָעָם אֶת־הַדָּבָר הָרָע הַזֶּה וַיִּתְאַבָּלוּ וְלֹא־שָׁתוּ אִישׁ עֶדְיוֹ
ה עָלָיו׃ וַיֹּאמֶר יְהוָה אֶל־מֹשֶׁה אֱמֹר אֶל־בְּנֵי־יִשְׂרָאֵל אַתֶּם עַם־קְשֵׁה־עֹרֶף רֶגַע
אֶחָד אֶעֱלֶה בְקִרְבְּךָ וְכִלִּיתִיךָ וְעַתָּה הוֹרֵד עֶדְיְךָ מֵעָלֶיךָ וְאֵדְעָה מָה אֶעֱשֶׂה־לָּךְ׃
ו ז וַיִּתְנַצְּלוּ בְנֵי־יִשְׂרָאֵל אֶת־עֶדְיָם מֵהַר חוֹרֵב׃ וּמֹשֶׁה יִקַּח אֶת־הָאֹהֶל וְנָטָה־לוֹ
מִחוּץ לַמַּחֲנֶה הַרְחֵק מִן־הַמַּחֲנֶה וְקָרָא לוֹ אֹהֶל מוֹעֵד וְהָיָה כָּל־מְבַקֵּשׁ יְהוָה
ח יֵצֵא אֶל־אֹהֶל מוֹעֵד אֲשֶׁר מִחוּץ לַמַּחֲנֶה׃ וְהָיָה כְּצֵאת מֹשֶׁה אֶל־הָאֹהֶל יָקוּמוּ
ט כָּל־הָעָם וְנִצְּבוּ אִישׁ פֶּתַח אָהֳלוֹ וְהִבִּיטוּ אַחֲרֵי מֹשֶׁה עַד־בֹּאוֹ הָאֹהֱלָה׃ וְהָיָה
י כְּבֹא מֹשֶׁה הָאֹהֱלָה יֵרֵד עַמּוּד הֶעָנָן וְעָמַד פֶּתַח הָאֹהֶל וְדִבֶּר עִם־מֹשֶׁה׃ וְרָאָה
כָל־הָעָם אֶת־עַמּוּד הֶעָנָן עֹמֵד פֶּתַח הָאֹהֶל וְקָם כָּל־הָעָם וְהִשְׁתַּחֲווּ אִישׁ פֶּתַח

רש״י

לה| **ויגף ה׳ את העם.** מיתה בידי שמים לעדים בלא התראה:

פרק לג

א| **לך עלה מזה.** ארץ ישראל גבוהה מכל הארצות, לכך נאמר "עלה". דבר אחר, כלפי שאמר לו בשעת הכעס: "לך רד" (לעיל לב, ז), אמר לו בשעת רצון: "לך עלה": **אתה והעם.** כאן לא נאמר 'ועמך':

ב| **וגרשתי את הכנעני וגו׳.** שש אמות הן, והגרגשי עמד ופנה מפניהם מאליו:

ג| **אל ארץ זבת חלב ודבש.** אני אומר לך להעלותם: **כי לא אעלה בקרבך.** לכך אני אומר לך: "ושלחתי לפניך מלאך": **כי עם קשה ערף אתה.** וכששכינתי בקרבכם ואתם ממרים בי מרבה אני עליכם זעם: **אכלך.** לשון כליון:

ד| **הדבר הרע.** שאין השכינה שורה ומהלכת עמם: **איש עדיו.** כתרים שנתנו להם בחורב כשאמרו: "נעשה ונשמע" (לעיל כד, ז):

ה| **רגע אחד אעלה בקרבך וכליתיך.** אם אעלה בקרבך ואתם ממרים בי בקשיות ערפכם, אזעם עליכם רגע אחד – שהוא שיעור זעמו, שנאמר: "חבי כמעט רגע עד יעבר זעם" (ישעיה כו, כ) – ואכלה אתכם, לפיכך טוב לכם שאשלח מלאך: **ועתה.** פורענות זו תלקו מיד, שתורידו עדיכם מעליכם: **ואדעה מה אעשה לך.** כפקדת אחר העון אני יודע מה בלבי לעשות:

ו| **את עדים מהר חורב.** את העדי שהיה בידם מהר חורב:

ז| **ומשה.** מאותו ענין והלאה "יקח את האהל", לשון הוה הוא, לוקח אהלו ונוטהו מחוץ למחנה, אמר: מנודה לרב מנודה לתלמיד: **הרחק.** אלפים אמה, כענין שנאמר: "אך רחוק יהיה ביניכם וביניו כאלפים אמה במדה" (יהושע ג, ד): **וקרא לו.** והיה קורא לו "אהל מועד", הוא בית ועד למבקשי תורה: **כל מבקש ה׳.** מכאן למבקש פני זקן כמקבל פני שכינה: **יצא אל אהל מועד.** כמו 'יוצא'. דבר אחר, "והיה כל מבקש ה׳", אפילו מלאכי השרת כשהיו שואלים מקום שכינה, חבריהם אומרים להם הרי הוא באהלו של משה:

ח| **והיה.** לשון הוה: **כצאת משה מן המחנה.** ללכת אל האהל: **יקומו כל העם.** עומדים מפניו, ואין יושבין עד שנתכסה מהם: **והביטו אחרי משה.** לשבח: אשרי ילוד אשה שכך מובטח שהשכינה תכנס אחריו לפתח אהלו:

ט| **ודבר עם משה.** כמו ומדבר עם משה, ותרגומו: "ומתמלל עם משה" שהוא כבוד שכינה, כמו: "וישמע את הקול מדבר אליו" (במדבר ז, פט), ואינו קורא 'מדבר' אליו; כשהוא קורא 'מדבר' פתרונו, הקול מדבר בינו לבין עצמו וההדיוט שומע מאליו, וכשהוא קורא 'מדבר' משמע שהמלך מדבר עם ההדיוט:

י| **והשתחוו.** לשכינה:

11 **The Lord would speak to Moses face-to-face as a man speaks** intimately **to his neighbor.** This contrasts sharply with the fear and disorientation which other prophets would experience in prophecy.[45] Furthermore, Moses could address questions directly to God.[46] **And** after God spoke to him, **he would return to** his personal tent in **the camp. But** even when Moses returned to that tent, **his servant Joshua, son of Nun, a lad,**[D] **would not move from within the Tent**[D] of Meeting.

12 After describing the ramifications of the divine decree that God's presence would not reside with the people, the Torah relates the continuation of the dialogue between Moses and God. **Moses said to the Lord: See, You say to me: Take this people up, but You did not inform me whom You will send with me.** Although You said that You will send an angel, You did not explain how this would occur. **And You said: I know you by name, and you have also found favor in My eyes.** Although the expression "I know you by name" does not appear previously, it is clear that Moses was chosen by God and enjoyed a uniquely close relationship with Him (see, e.g., chaps. 3–4; 32:10).

Third aliya

13 **Now, if I have found favor now in Your eyes, inform me, please, of Your ways.** Just as You know me intimately, I too wish to comprehend Your ways, **and I,** as Your chosen one, **will know You** with greater understanding, **so that I will find favor in Your eyes.** Moses requested a deeper relationship with God than he had attained thus far. Until this point, he had mainly received instructions. Now Moses desired the secret knowledge that would enable him to achieve communion with God, as one's closeness to God is related to the extent of his knowledge of the Divine.[47] **And see that this nation is Your people.**[D]

14 **He,** God, **said,** in acceptance of Moses' request: Instead of an angel, **My presence will go** with you, **and I will** thereby **give you rest.**[48]

15 **He,** Moses, **said to Him: If Your presence does not go** with us, **do not bring us up from here.** Without God's presence among us, there is no purpose in continuing our journey.[49]

16 **How then will it be known that I have found favor in Your eyes, I and Your people? Is it not by Your going with us** Yourself? There is no value to our inheriting the land of Canaan if Your presence is not among us. Furthermore, **we will be distinct, I and Your people, from every people that is on the face of the earth,** as Your chosen nation.

17 **The Lord said to Moses: This matter that you have spoken, I will do as well,** to distinguish you and the people, **as you have found favor in My eyes, and I have known you by name.** I have honored you by revealing Myself to you and teaching you My name.[50]

Fourth aliya

The Revelation in the Rock Crevice and the Renewal of the Covenant

EXODUS 33:18–34:26

God accepted Moses' request to keep His presence among the people and accompany them on their journey Himself, rather than to guide them by means of an angel. Moses seeks to attain greater closeness to God, and he indeed experiences a unique personal revelation unparalleled by that of any other person. This divine revelation is both a visual revelation and a verbal communication through which Moses learns God's ways. God subsequently instructs Moses with regard to certain commandments, most of which had been taught previously.

Moses' vision in the rock crevice can be considered a small-scale repetition of the major revelation at Mount Sinai, which took place a short time earlier. The entire nation had experienced that revelation, and forty days later they were supposed to have received the tablets in a public ceremony. With the nation's sin now forgiven, the second tablets are given in very different fashion, in a far more intimate setting, with Moses alone placed in a rocky crevice on Mount Sinai while God passes before him.

The content of this revelation is possibly related to God's statement that He Himself would go with the nation. So that the people are not subject to treatment in accordance with God's attribute of strict justice, which could lead to their destruction (see 33:2–3), it is necessary for God to reveal His higher attributes of mercy.

18 **He,** Moses, **said: Please show me Your glory.** Moses previously asked to know God's hidden ways. Now his request is even more far-reaching; he desires to see God's glory, to attain a true understanding of the Divine, beyond that which is required for his prophetic mission.[51]

19 **He, God, said: I will pass all My goodness before you,**

DISCUSSION

33:11 | **A lad:** This designation refers to one serving as an apprentice or assistant, irrespective of his actual age. At this time, Joshua was actually fifty-six years old (see Ibn Ezra; Ramban).

But his servant, Joshua, son of Nun, a lad, would not move from within the tent: As Moses' assistant, Joshua remained with him even when the Divine Presence spoke with Moses. Although the Divine Presence was manifest in the pillar of cloud outside the tent, while Joshua remained inside, nevertheless, Joshua was spiritually elevated by his unique closeness to Moses and the Divine Presence. When Moses died, he was succeeded as leader not by his son, but by Joshua, who had constantly remained in his tent (see Numbers 27:15–23; Joshua 1:1).

33:13 | **And see that this nation is Your people:** Moses had previously requested of God that the Jewish people maintain their elevated status and receive unique divine guidance. He did not abandon this request. Upon hearing that the people

יא אהלו: וידבר יהוה אל־משה פנים אל־פנים כאשר ידבר איש אל־רעהו ושב
אל־המחנה ומשרתו יהושע בן־נון נער לא ימיש מתוך האהל:
יב ויאמר משה אל־יהוה ראה אתה אמר אלי העל את־העם הזה ואתה לא שלישי
הודעתני את אשר־תשלח עמי ואתה אמרת ידעתיך בשם וגם־מצאת חן
יג בעיני: ועתה אם־נא מצאתי חן בעיניך הודעני נא את־דרכך ואדעך למען
יד טו אמצא־חן בעיניך וראה כי עמך הגוי הזה: ויאמר פני ילכו והנחתי לך: ויאמר
טז אליו אם־אין פניך הלכים אל־תעלנו מזה: ובמה | יודע אפוא כי־מצאתי חן
בעיניך אני ועמך הלוא בלכתך עמנו ונפלינו אני ועמך מכל־העם אשר על־
פני האדמה:
יז ויאמר יהוה אל־משה גם את־הדבר הזה אשר דברת אעשה כי־מצאת חן רביעי
יח יט בעיני ואדעך בשם: ויאמר הראני נא את־כבדך: ויאמר אני אעביר כל־טובי

רש"י

יא | **ודבר ה' אל משה פנים אל פנים.** ומתמלל עם משה: **ושב אל המחנה.** לאחר שנדבר עמו היה משה שב אל המחנה ומלמד לזקנים מה שלמד. והדבר הזה נהג משה מיום הכפורים עד שהוקם המשכן ולא יותר, שהרי בשבעה עשר בתמוז נשתברו הלוחות, ובשמונה עשר שרף את העגל ודן את החוטאים, ובתשעה עשר עלה, שנאמר: "ויהי ממחרת ויאמר משה אל העם" וגו' (לעיל לב, ל), עשה שם ארבעים יום ובקש רחמים, שנאמר: "ואתנפל לפני ה'" וגו' (דברים ט, יח), ובראש חדש אלול נאמר לו: "ועלית בבקר אל הר סיני" (להלן לד, ב) לקבל לוחות האחרונות, ועשה שם ארבעים יום, שנאמר בהם: "ואנכי עמדתי בהר כימים הראשנים" וגו' (דברים י, י), מה הראשונים ברצון אף האחרונים ברצון, אמור מעתה אמצעיים היו בכעס. בעשרה בתשרי נתרצה הקדוש ברוך הוא לישראל בשמחה ובלב שלם, ואמר לו למשה: סלחתי כדברך, ומסר לו לוחות אחרונות, וירד, והתחיל לצוותם על מלאכת המשכן, ועשאוהו עד אחד בניסן, ומשהוקם לא נדבר עמו עוד אלא מאהל מועד: **ושב אל המחנה.** תרגומו: "ותאיב למשריתא" לפי שהוא לשון הוה, וכן כל הענין: "וראה כל העם" (לעיל פסוק י) – "וחזן", "ונצבו" (לעיל פסוק ח) – "וקימין", "והביטו" (שם) – "ומסתכלין", "והשתחוו" (לעיל פסוק י) – "וסגדין". ומדרשו: "ודבר ה' אל משה" שישוב אל המחנה, אמר לו: אני בכעס ואתה בכעס, אם כן מי יקרבם?

יב | **ראה אתה אמר אלי.** ראה, תן עיניך ולבך על דבריך: אתה אומר אלי וגו' ואתה לא הודעתני וגו'. שאמרת לי: "הנה אנכי שלח מלאך" (לעיל כג, כ), אין זו הודעה, שאיני חפץ בו: **ואתה אמרת.** הכרתיך משאר בני אדם בשם חשיבות, שהרי אמרת לי: "הנה אנכי בא אליך בעב הענן" וגו' וגם בך יאמינו לעולם" (לעיל יט, ט):

יג | **ועתה.** אם אמת שמצאתי חן בעיניך: **הודעני נא את דרכך.** מה שכר אתה נותן למוצאי חן בעיניך: **ואדעך למען אמצא חן בעיניך.** ואדע בזו מדת תגמולך, מה היא מציאת חן שמצאתי בעיניך. ופתרון "למען אמצא חן" – למען אכיר כמה שכר מציאת החן: **וראה כי עמך הגוי הזה.** שלא תאמר: "ואעשה אותך לגוי גדול" (לעיל לב, י) ואת אלה תעזב, ראה כי עמך הם מקדם, ואם בהם תמאס, איני סומך על היוצאים מחלצי שיתקיימו; ואת תשלום השכר שלי בעם הזה תודיעני. ורבותינו דרשוהו במסכת ברכות (דף ז ע"א), ואני ליישב המקראות על אפניהם ועל סדרם באתי:

יד | **ויאמר פני ילכו.** כתרגומו. לא אשלח עוד מלאך, אני בעצמי אלך, כמו: "ופניך הלכים בקרב" (שמואל ב' יז, יא):

טו | **ויאמר אליו.** בזו אני חפץ, כי על ידי מלאך "אל תעלנו מזה":

טז | **ובמה יודע אפוא.** ידע מציאת החן, "הלוא בלכתך עמנו". ועוד דבר אחר אני שואל ממך, שלא תשרה שכינתך עוד על אמות העולם: **ונפלינו אני ועמך.** ונהיה מבדלים בדבר הזה "מכל העם", כמו: "והפלה ה' בין מקנה ישראל" וגו' (לעיל ט, ד):

יז | **גם את הדבר הזה.** שלא תשרה שכינתי עוד על אמות העולם, "אעשה". ואין דבריו של בלעם על ידי שרית שכינה, אלא "נפל וגלוי עינים" (במדבר כד, ד), כגון: "ואלי דבר יגנב" (איוב ד, יב), שומעין על ידי שליח:

יח | **ויאמר הראני נא את כבדך.** ראה משה שהיה עת רצון ודבריו מקבלים, והוסיף לשאל להראותו מראית כבודו:

יט | **ויאמר אני אעביר וגו'.** הגיעה שעה שתראה בכבודי מה שארשה אותך לראות, לפי שאני רוצה וצריך ללמדך

DISCUSSION

would continue to the land of Canaan under the auspices of an angel, Moses realized that this meant that they would cease to be the chosen nation and would inherit Canaan only as fulfillment of God's covenant with their forefathers. Refusing to accept this, Moses stressed that the people were not merely the descendants of the patriarchs; they were themselves God's people, and Moses wished to know God's ways for their sake.

and furthermore **I will call with the name of the Lord,** the Tetragrammaton, **before you.** What you hear will enable you to comprehend a higher aspect of My being, **and** from this aspect **I will favor whom I will favor and I will have mercy on whom I will have mercy.** You shall experience not only the attribute of justice, which is the external form of My governance, but also the essence of My providence, the attribute of immeasurable and unlimited loving-kindness and mercy.

20 **He,** God, further **said** to Moses: **You will not be able to see My face,**[D] the essence of My being, as you requested, **as man shall not see Me and** still **live.** Only when one departs from the world can he experience a direct encounter with God.[52]

21 **The Lord** therefore **said: Behold, there is a place with Me.** I will provide you with a spot from which you can see as much of My presence as you are able without ceasing to exist. **And you shall stand on the rock.**

22 **It shall be** during the revelation, **with the passage of My glory,** that **I will** take you from your place upon the rock and **place you in the crevice of the rock; and I will cover My hand upon you** and protect you **until My passage.** Although Moses will not actually see God's face, he will stand so close that he will require divine protection in order to remain alive.

23 Then **I will remove My hand, and you will** witness the revelation of some of My presence, as you will **see My back,** the external aspects of My presence. **But My face,** the essence of My being, **will not be seen.** Moses alone will witness the greatest level of divine revelation that a human is capable of experiencing, the Divine Presence viewed from behind. This idea of seeing God from behind perhaps represents Moses' comprehension of how the world operates in accordance with the divine will.[53] Any greater closeness would cause one to merge with the spiritual realm, which would mean that he would cease to exist as an individual.

34 1 **The Lord said to Moses: Carve for yourself two tablets of**
Fifth **stone like the first,** similar in form to the first tablets. **And I**
aliya **will write on the tablets the words that were on the first**

tablets, which you shattered. Whereas the first tablets were made by God (32:16), Moses is commanded to fashion the second tablets, upon which God will write His commandments.

2 **Be prepared for the morning; you shall ascend in the morning to Mount Sinai, and you shall stand there** ready **for Me on top of the mountain.**

3 **No man shall ascend with you, and no man shall be seen on the entire mountain; the flocks and the cattle shall not graze before that mountain.** Just as at the time of the giving of the Torah, Moses ascends Mount Sinai alone.

4 **He,** Moses, **carved two tablets of stone like** the form of **the first** tablets; **Moses arose early in the morning and ascended to the top of Mount Sinai, as the Lord** had **commanded him, and he took in his hand** the **two tablets of stone** that he had prepared.

5 **The Lord descended in the cloud and stood with him there, and** He **called with the name of the Lord,**[D] thereby teaching Moses how to call Him.

6 **The Lord passed before him,** and a small measure of the Divine Presence was thereby revealed to Moses, in fulfillment of his request to see God's glory (33:18). **And** God **called:**[D] **The Lord, the Lord, God, merciful and gracious, slow to anger, and abounding in kindness and truth.**

7 **He maintains kindness to the thousands** of generations, **bearing iniquity and transgression and sin.** This phrase literally means: He bears the burden of sins. **And He will not exonerate.** Although one can achieve atonement, he is not entirely cleansed of his sin. **Reckoning the iniquity of the fathers upon the children and upon the children's children, upon the third and upon the fourth generation.** God is exceedingly merciful, and does not eternally punish one's descendants for their forefathers' sins, but only until the fourth generation. Furthermore, if the children do not evoke the memory of their father's sin by following in their footsteps, they are not punished for those sins at all.[54]

DISCUSSION

33:20 | You will not be able to see My face: Although the Torah states that God spoke to Moses "face-to-face" (verse 11), this is a figurative expression, which means that He talked to Moses directly. However, Moses did not actually see God's face, as even he could not comprehend God's limitless essence.

34:5 | And called with the name of the Lord: The syntax of the verse, as well as the subsequent verses, indicate that it was God who

proclaimed His name, not Moses (see Rashbam; Ibn Ezra, long commentary on Exodus; Sforno; *Gur Arye; Targum Yonatan*).

34:6 | The Lord passed before him and called: According to tradition, verses 6–7 contain the thirteen divine attributes of mercy, although there are different opinions with regard to the exact method of counting them. These two verses serve as the focal point of the *Seliḥot* service, which is recited during the days prior

to Rosh HaShana, between Rosh HaShana and Yom Kippur, and on fast days. It should be noted that in this service the biblical phrase "and He will not exonerate [*venakeh lo yenakeh*]" is truncated, and it is read as "and He will exonerate [*venakeh*]." This is because the last two Hebrew words, which turn the phrase into a negative statement, are not part of the attributes of mercy (see *Rosh HaShana* 17b, and commentaries ad loc.; *Yoma* 86a).

עַל־פָּנֶיךָ וְקָרָאתִי בְשֵׁם יְהוָֹה לְפָנֶיךָ וְחַנֹּתִי אֶת־אֲשֶׁר אָחֹן וְרִחַמְתִּי אֶת־אֲשֶׁר

כ אֲרַחֵם: וַיֹּאמֶר לֹא תוּכַל לִרְאֹת אֶת־פָּנָי כִּי לֹא־יִרְאַנִי הָאָדָם וָחָי: וַיֹּאמֶר יְהוָֹה

כא הִנֵּה מָקוֹם אִתִּי וְנִצַּבְתָּ עַל־הַצּוּר: וְהָיָה בַּעֲבֹר כְּבֹדִי וְשַׂמְתִּיךָ בְּנִקְרַת הַצּוּר

כב וְשַׂכֹּתִי כַפִּי עָלֶיךָ עַד־עָבְרִי: וַהֲסִרֹתִי אֶת־כַּפִּי וְרָאִיתָ אֶת־אֲחֹרָי וּפָנַי לֹא יֵרָאוּ:

חמישי א וַיֹּאמֶר יְהוָֹה אֶל־מֹשֶׁה פְּסָל־לְךָ שְׁנֵי־לֻחֹת אֲבָנִים כָּרִאשֹׁנִים וְכָתַבְתִּי עַל־הַלֻּחֹת

ב אֶת־הַדְּבָרִים אֲשֶׁר הָיוּ עַל־הַלֻּחֹת הָרִאשֹׁנִים אֲשֶׁר שִׁבַּרְתָּ: וֶהְיֵה נָכוֹן לַבֹּקֶר

ג וְעָלִיתָ בַבֹּקֶר אֶל־הַר סִינַי וְנִצַּבְתָּ לִי שָׁם עַל־רֹאשׁ הָהָר: וְאִישׁ לֹא־יַעֲלֶה עִמָּךְ

וְגַם־אִישׁ אַל־יֵרָא בְּכָל־הָהָר גַּם־הַצֹּאן וְהַבָּקָר אַל־יִרְעוּ אֶל־מוּל הָהָר הַהוּא:

ד וַיִּפְסֹל שְׁנֵי־לֻחֹת אֲבָנִים כָּרִאשֹׁנִים וַיַּשְׁכֵּם מֹשֶׁה בַבֹּקֶר וַיַּעַל אֶל־הַר סִינַי כַּאֲשֶׁר

ה צִוָּה יְהוָֹה אֹתוֹ וַיִּקַּח בְּיָדוֹ שְׁנֵי לֻחֹת אֲבָנִים: וַיֵּרֶד יְהוָֹה בֶּעָנָן וַיִּתְיַצֵּב עִמּוֹ שָׁם

ו וַיִּקְרָא בְשֵׁם יְהוָֹה: וַיַּעֲבֹר יְהוָֹה ׀ עַל־פָּנָיו וַיִּקְרָא יְהוָֹה ׀ יְהוָֹה אֵל רַחוּם וְחַנּוּן

ז אֶרֶךְ אַפַּיִם וְרַב־חֶסֶד וֶאֱמֶת: נֹצֵר חֶסֶד לָאֲלָפִים נֹשֵׂא עָוֹן וָפֶשַׁע וְחַטָּאָה וְנַקֵּה

סֵדֶר תְּפִלָּה, שֶׁכְּשֶׁנִּצְרַכְתָּ לְבַקֵּשׁ רַחֲמִים עַל יִשְׂרָאֵל הִזְכַּרְתָּ לִי זְכוּת אָבוֹת, כִּסְבוּר אַתָּה שֶׁאִם תַּמָּה זְכוּת אָבוֹת אֵין עוֹד תִּקְוָה, אֲנִי מַעֲבִיר כָּל מִדַּת טוּבִי לְפָנֶיךָ עַל הַצּוּר וְאַתָּה נָתוּן בַּמְּעָרָה. "וְקָרָאתִי בְשֵׁם ה' לְפָנֶיךָ", לְלַמֶּדְךָ סֵדֶר בַּקָּשַׁת רַחֲמִים אַף אִם תִּכְלֶה זְכוּת אָבוֹת. וּכְסֵדֶר זֶה שֶׁאַתָּה רוֹאֶה אוֹתִי מְעֻטָּף וְקוֹרֵא שְׁלֹשׁ עֶשְׂרֵה מִדּוֹת הֱוֵי מְלַמֵּד אֶת יִשְׂרָאֵל לַעֲשׂוֹת כֵּן, וְעַל יְדֵי שֶׁיַּזְכִּירוּ לְפָנַי "רַחוּם וְחַנּוּן" יִהְיוּ נַעֲנִים, כִּי רַחֲמַי לֹא כָלִים: וְחַנֹּתִי אֶת־אֲשֶׁר אָחֹן. אוֹתָן פְּעָמִים שֶׁאֶרְצֶה לָחֹן. וְרִחַמְתִּי. עֵת שֶׁאֶחְפֹּץ לְרַחֵם. עַד כָּאן לֹא הִבְטִיחוֹ אֶלָּא עִתִּים מֵעֲנֶה עִתִּים לֹא מֵעֲנֶה, אֲבָל בִּשְׁעַת מַעֲשֶׂה אָמַר לוֹ: "הִנֵּה אָנֹכִי כֹּרֵת בְּרִית" (להלן לה, י), הִבְטִיחוֹ שֶׁאֵינָן חוֹזְרִין רֵיקָם:

כב וַיֹּאמֶר לֹא תוּכַל וְגו'. אַף כְּשֶׁאַעֲבִיר כָּל טוּבִי עַל פָּנֶיךָ, אֵינִי נוֹתֵן לְךָ רְשׁוּת לִרְאוֹת אֶת פָּנָי:

כא הִנֵּה מָקוֹם אִתִּי. בָּהָר אֲשֶׁר אֲנִי מְדַבֵּר עִמְּךָ תָּמִיד, יֵשׁ מָקוֹם מוּכָן לִי לְצָרְכְּךָ שֶׁאַטְמִינְךָ שָׁם שֶׁלֹּא תִזֹּק, וּמִשָּׁם תִּרְאֶה מַה שֶּׁתִּרְאֶה, זֶהוּ פְשׁוּטוֹ. וּמִדְרָשׁוֹ, עַל מָקוֹם שֶׁהַשְּׁכִינָה שָׁם מְדַבֵּר, וְאוֹמֵר "הַמָּקוֹם אִתִּי", וְאֵינִי אוֹמֵר אֲנִי בַּמָּקוֹם, שֶׁהַקָּדוֹשׁ בָּרוּךְ הוּא מְקוֹמוֹ שֶׁל עוֹלָם וְאֵין עוֹלָמוֹ מְקוֹמוֹ:

כב בַּעֲבֹר כְּבֹדִי. כְּשֶׁאֶעֱבֹר לְפָנֶיךָ. בְּנִקְרַת הַצּוּר. כְּמוֹ

"הָעֵינֵי הָאֲנָשִׁים הָהֵם תְּנַקֵּר" (במדבר טז, יד), "יִקְּרוּהָ עֹרְבֵי נַחַל" (משלי ל, יז), "אֲנִי קַרְתִּי וְשָׁתִיתִי מָיִם" (ישעיה לז, כה), גְּזֵרָה אַחַת לָהֶם: נִקְרַת הַצּוּר. כְּרִיַּת הַטּוּר. וְשַׂכֹּתִי כַפִּי. מִכָּאן שֶׁנִּתְּנָה רְשׁוּת לַמְחַבְּלִים לְחַבֵּל, וְתַרְגּוּמוֹ: "וְאָגֵן בְּמֵימְרִי", כִּנּוּי הוּא לִכְבוֹד שֶׁל מַעְלָה, שֶׁאֵינוֹ צָרִיךְ לִסְכּוֹךְ עָלָיו בְּכַף מַמָּשׁ:

כג וַהֲסִרֹתִי אֶת־כַּפִּי. "וְאַעְדֵּי יָת דְּבָרַת יְקָרִי", כְּשֶׁאֲסַלֵּק הַנְהָגַת כְּבוֹדִי מִכְּנֶגֶד פָּנֶיךָ לָלֶכֶת מִשָּׁם וּלְהַלָּן: וְרָאִיתָ אֶת־אֲחֹרָי. הֶרְאָהוּ קֶשֶׁר שֶׁל תְּפִלִּין:

פרק לד

א פְּסָל־לְךָ. הֶרְאָהוּ מַחְצַב סַנְפִּירִינוֹן מִתּוֹךְ אָהֳלוֹ, וְאָמַר לוֹ: הַפְּסֹלֶת יִהְיֶה שֶׁלְּךָ, וּמִשָּׁם נִתְעַשֵּׁר מֹשֶׁה הַרְבֵּה: פְּסָל־לְךָ. אַתָּה שִׁבַּרְתָּ הָרִאשֹׁנוֹת, אַתָּה פְּסָל־לְךָ אֲחֵרוֹת. מָשָׁל לְמֶלֶךְ שֶׁהָלַךְ לִמְדִינַת הַיָּם וְהִנִּיחַ אֲרוּסָתוֹ עִם הַשְּׁפָחוֹת. מִתּוֹךְ קִלְקוּל הַשְּׁפָחוֹת יָצָא עָלֶיהָ שֵׁם רָע, עָמַד שׁוֹשְׁבִינָהּ וְקָרַע כְּתֻבָּתָהּ, אָמַר: אִם יֹאמַר הַמֶּלֶךְ לְהָרְגָהּ, אֹמַר לוֹ: עֲדַיִן אֵינָהּ אִשְׁתֶּךָ. בָּדַק הַמֶּלֶךְ וּמָצָא שֶׁלֹּא הָיָה הַקִּלְקוּל אֶלָּא מִן הַשְּׁפָחוֹת, נִתְרַצָּה לָהּ. אָמַר לוֹ שׁוֹשְׁבִינָהּ: כְּתֹב לָהּ כְּתֻבָּה אַחֶרֶת, שֶׁנִּקְרְעָה הָרִאשׁוֹנָה. אָמַר לוֹ הַמֶּלֶךְ: אַתָּה קָרַעְתָּ אוֹתָהּ, אַתָּה קְנֵה לָהּ נְיָר אַחֵר וַאֲנִי אֶכְתֹּב לָהּ בְּיָדִי. כָּךְ הַמֶּלֶךְ זֶה הַקָּדוֹשׁ

בָּרוּךְ הוּא, הַשְּׁפָחוֹת אֵלּוּ עֵרֶב רַב, וְהַשּׁוֹשְׁבִין זֶה מֹשֶׁה, לְכָךְ נֶאֱמַר: "פְּסָל־לְךָ":

ב נָכוֹן. מְזֻמָּן:

ג וְאִישׁ לֹא־יַעֲלֶה עִמָּךְ. הָרִאשֹׁנוֹת עַל יְדֵי שֶׁהָיוּ בִּתְשׁוּאוֹת וְקוֹלוֹת וּקְהִלָּה, שָׁלְטָה בָהֶן עַיִן רָעָה, אֵין לְךָ יָפֶה מִן הַצְּנִיעוּת:

ה וַיִּקְרָא בְשֵׁם ה'. מְתַרְגְּמִינָן: "וּקְרָא בִשְׁמָא דַּה'":

ו ה' ה'. הוּא מִדַּת רַחֲמִים, אַחַת קֹדֶם שֶׁיֶּחֱטָא וְאַחַת לְאַחַר שֶׁיֶּחֱטָא וְיָשׁוּב: אֵל. אַף זוֹ מִדַּת רַחֲמִים, וְכֵן הוּא אוֹמֵר: "אֵלִי אֵלִי לָמָה עֲזַבְתָּנִי" (תהלים כב, ב), וְאֵין לוֹמַר לְמִדַּת הַדִּין: "לָמָה עֲזַבְתָּנִי". כָּךְ מָצָאתִי בִּמְכִילְתָּא (סדרה ג, ט): אֶרֶךְ אַפַּיִם. מַאֲרִיךְ אַפּוֹ וְאֵינוֹ מְמַהֵר לִפָּרַע, שֶׁמָּא יַעֲשֶׂה תְשׁוּבָה: וְרַב חֶסֶד. לִצְרִיכֵי חֶסֶד, שֶׁאֵין לָהֶם זְכֻיּוֹת כָּל כָּךְ: וֶאֱמֶת. לְשַׁלֵּם שָׂכָר טוֹב לְעוֹשֵׂי רְצוֹנוֹ:

ז נֹצֵר חֶסֶד. שֶׁהָאָדָם עוֹשֶׂה לְפָנָיו: לָאֲלָפִים. לִשְׁנֵי אֲלָפִים דּוֹרוֹת: עָוֹן. אֵלּוּ הַזְּדוֹנוֹת, "פְּשָׁעִים" אֵלּוּ הַמְּרָדִים שֶׁאָדָם עוֹשֶׂה לְהַכְעִיס: וְחַטָּאָה. אֵלּוּ הַשְּׁגָגוֹת: וְנַקֵּה לֹא יְנַקֶּה. לְפִי פְשׁוּטוֹ מַשְׁמָע מְיַתֵּר עַל הָעָוֹן אֵינוֹ לְגַמְרֵי, אֶלָּא נִפְרָע מִמֶּנּוּ מְעַט מְעַט. וְרַבּוֹתֵינוּ דָּרְשׁוּ, "מְנַקֶּה" הוּא לַשָּׁבִים "וְלֹא יְנַקֶּה"

---

8 As soon as he heard God's declaration, **Moses hastened and bowed to the ground and prostrated himself,** in awe of the divine revelation and the accompanying proclamation.

9 **He,** Moses, **said: If now I have found favor in Your eyes, my Lord, may my Lord please go in our midst.** Once Moses has heard the divine attributes of mercy, he no longer fears that the people might be punished solely in accordance with the strict attribute of justice.[55] He therefore reiterates his request that God Himself go with the people. Interestingly, Moses employs the same reason in his request that God used to explain why He would not go with the people:[56] **As it is a stiff-necked people,** and it is therefore possible that they would sin again. Nevertheless, You are merciful and gracious, and You forgive iniquity and transgression, and therefore **may You forgive our iniquity and our sin and be our inheritance.** A stubborn nation can survive the judgment of the merciful and gracious God, but not that of an angel, who can rule only in accordance with the attribute of justice.

10 **He,** God, **said** to Moses: **Behold, I am establishing a covenant.** In the future, when you conquer the land of Canaan, **before your entire people I will perform wonders that have not been created in the entire earth and in all the nations; the entire people, with you in their midst, will see the work of the Lord, that it is awesome what I am doing with you.**

Sixth aliya

11 The people will soon continue their journey to the land of Canaan. God therefore reiterates His commands with regard to the nations that currently dwell in Canaan: **Mark for yourself that which I am commanding you today; behold,** for My part I promise you that **I am expelling from before you the Emorites, the Canaanites, the Hitites, the Perizites, the Hivites, and the Yevusites.**

12 And you in turn, **beware, lest you establish a covenant with the inhabitant of the land into which you are entering, lest he be a snare in your midst.** The inhabitants of Canaan are apt to corrupt your behavior.

13 **Rather, you shall smash their altars, and shatter their monuments, and chop down their sacred trees,** those used as part of idolatrous rites. You must completely destroy all objects of idol worship, including their accessories and symbolic artifacts.

14 **For you shall not prostrate yourself to another god, as the Lord, His name is Zealous,**[D] **He is a zealous God.** God is not tolerant toward faith in idols, even if they are worshipped in conjunction with Him. God's jealousy is not envy; rather, it is the jealousy of love that stems from an exclusive relationship, which leaves no room for a third party.

15 Pay heed, **lest you establish a covenant with the inhabitants of the land, and they,** those inhabitants, continue to **stray**[D] **after their gods and slaughter to their gods. And** if you maintain neighborly relations with them, **they will call you** to participate in their religious festivities, **and you will** be likely to accept their invitation and **eat from their slaughter.**

16 Your relationship with the inhabitants will subsequently become closer, beyond mutual visits, as **you will take from their daughters for your sons.**[D] **And** even if you rule over the inhabitants, if you intermarry with them, **their daughters will stray after their gods, and they will cause your sons to stray after their gods.**

17 The Torah briefly reiterates several commandments that were already stated, some of them related to the exodus from Egypt. They are repeated here in the context of the renewal of the covenant. **You shall not make for yourself gods of cast figures.**

18 **You shall observe the Festival of Unleavened Bread,** Passover. On this festival, for **seven days you shall eat unleavened bread, as I commanded you** (12:15–20; 13:3, 7; 23:15), **at the appointed time of the month of ripening,** the month of Nisan, **as in the month of ripening you emerged from Egypt.** Not only must the date itself be preserved, but equally important is that it occur in the spring.[57]

19 **Every first issue of the womb,** the firstborn animal, **is Mine; from all your livestock you shall take the males,**[58] when they are **the first issue of a bull and a sheep.** You shall sacrifice the firstborn male animals as offerings, as you were commanded at the time of the exodus from Egypt (13:2, 12).

20 **The first issue of a donkey you shall redeem with a lamb,** as stated earlier (13:13); **and if you do not redeem it, you shall behead it.** Furthermore, **every firstborn of your sons you shall redeem,** as stated earlier as well (13:2, 15). **And they,** people who ascend to the Temple, **shall not appear** there **before Me empty-handed.**

21 **Six days you shall perform labor, and on the seventh day**

DISCUSSION

34:14 | You shall not prostrate yourself to another god, as the Lord, His name is Zealous: This is the antithesis of the polytheistic belief system prevalent at that time. One fundamental distinction between the nation of Israel and other nations was that Israel's belief system would not compromise by integrating with other faiths.

34:15 | They stray: The Hebrew word translated as "stray" comes from the root *zayin-nun-heh,* meaning to behave licentiously. The use of this verb here indicates an association, either symbolic or practical, between idolatry and licentious behavior.

34:16 | You will take from their daughters for your sons: This is the first time the Torah mentions the prohibition against intermarriage. According to this verse, the prohibition of a marriage between a Jewish man and a gentile woman is of greater severity than that of a match between a Jewish woman and a gentile man. According to *halakha,* the status of the offspring of a mixed marriage is determined by the status of the mother (see Malachi 2:11; Ezra 9:2, 10:2–14).

לֹא יְנַקֶּה פֹּקֵד ׀ עֲוֺן אָבוֹת עַל־בָּנִים וְעַל־בְּנֵי בָנִים עַל־שִׁלֵּשִׁים וְעַל־רִבֵּעִים:

ח ט וַיְמַהֵר מֹשֶׁה וַיִּקֹּד אַרְצָה וַיִּשְׁתָּחוּ: וַיֹּאמֶר אִם־נָא מָצָאתִי חֵן בְּעֵינֶיךָ אֲדֹנָי יֵלֶךְ־

נָא אֲדֹנָי בְּקִרְבֵּנוּ כִּי עַם־קְשֵׁה־עֹרֶף הוּא וְסָלַחְתָּ לַעֲוֺנֵנוּ וּלְחַטָּאתֵנוּ וּנְחַלְתָּנוּ:

י וַיֹּאמֶר הִנֵּה אָנֹכִי כֹּרֵת בְּרִית נֶגֶד כָּל־עַמְּךָ אֶעֱשֶׂה נִפְלָאֹת אֲשֶׁר לֹא־נִבְרְאוּ ששי

בְכָל־הָאָרֶץ וּבְכָל־הַגּוֹיִם וְרָאָה כָל־הָעָם אֲשֶׁר־אַתָּה בְקִרְבּוֹ אֶת־מַעֲשֵׂה יהוה

יא כִּי־נוֹרָא הוּא אֲשֶׁר אֲנִי עֹשֶׂה עִמָּךְ: שְׁמָר־לְךָ אֵת אֲשֶׁר אָנֹכִי מְצַוְּךָ הַיּוֹם הִנְנִי

יב גֹרֵשׁ מִפָּנֶיךָ אֶת־הָאֱמֹרִי וְהַכְּנַעֲנִי וְהַחִתִּי וְהַפְּרִזִּי וְהַחִוִּי וְהַיְבוּסִי: הִשָּׁמֶר לְךָ

פֶּן־תִּכְרֹת בְּרִית לְיוֹשֵׁב הָאָרֶץ אֲשֶׁר אַתָּה בָּא עָלֶיהָ פֶּן־יִהְיֶה לְמוֹקֵשׁ בְּקִרְבֶּךָ:

יג יד כִּי אֶת־מִזְבְּחֹתָם תִּתֹּצוּן וְאֶת־מַצֵּבֹתָם תְּשַׁבֵּרוּן וְאֶת־אֲשֵׁרָיו תִּכְרֹתוּן: כִּי לֹא

טו תִשְׁתַּחֲוֶה לְאֵל אַחֵר כִּי יהוה קַנָּא שְׁמוֹ אֵל קַנָּא הוּא: פֶּן־תִּכְרֹת בְּרִית לְיוֹשֵׁב

טז הָאָרֶץ וְזָנוּ ׀ אַחֲרֵי אֱלֹהֵיהֶם וְזָבְחוּ לֵאלֹהֵיהֶם וְקָרָא לְךָ וְאָכַלְתָּ מִזִּבְחוֹ: וְלָקַחְתָּ

יז מִבְּנֹתָיו לְבָנֶיךָ וְזָנוּ בְנֹתָיו אַחֲרֵי אֱלֹהֵיהֶן וְהִזְנוּ אֶת־בָּנֶיךָ אַחֲרֵי אֱלֹהֵיהֶן: אֱלֹהֵי

יח מַסֵּכָה לֹא תַעֲשֶׂה־לָּךְ: אֶת־חַג הַמַּצּוֹת תִּשְׁמֹר שִׁבְעַת יָמִים תֹּאכַל מַצּוֹת אֲשֶׁר

יט צִוִּיתִךָ לְמוֹעֵד חֹדֶשׁ הָאָבִיב כִּי בְּחֹדֶשׁ הָאָבִיב יָצָאתָ מִמִּצְרָיִם: כָּל־פֶּטֶר רֶחֶם

כ לִי וְכָל־מִקְנְךָ תִּזָּכָר פֶּטֶר שׁוֹר וָשֶׂה: וּפֶטֶר חֲמוֹר תִּפְדֶּה בְשֶׂה וְאִם־לֹא תִפְדֶּה

כא וַעֲרַפְתּוֹ כֹּל בְּכוֹר בָּנֶיךָ תִּפְדֶּה וְלֹא־יֵרָאוּ פָנַי רֵיקָם: שֵׁשֶׁת יָמִים תַּעֲבֹד וּבַיּוֹם

רש״י

לשאינן שבים: **פקד עון אבות על בנים.** כשאוחזים מעשה אבותיהם בידיהם, שכבר פרש במקרא אחר "לשנאי" (לעיל כ, ה): **ועל רבעים.** דור רביעי. נמצאת מדה טובה מרבה על מדת פרענות אחת לחמש מאות, שבמדה טובה הוא אומר: "נצר חסד לאלפים":

ח| **וימהר משה.** כשראה משה שכינה עוברת ושמע קול הקריאה, מיד "וישתחו":

ט| **ילך נא ה׳ בקרבנו.** כמו שהבטחת, מאחר שאתה נושא עון, ואם "עם קשה ערף הוא" ויאמרו כך ואמרת על זאת: "פן אכלך בדרך" (לעיל לג, ג) – אתה תסלח "לעוננו" וגו׳. יש ׳כי׳ במקום ׳אם׳: **ונחלתנו.** ותתננו לך לנחלה מיוחדת. זו היא בקשת "ונפלינו אני ועמך" (שם פסוק טז), שלא תשרה שכינתך על האמות:

י| **כרת ברית.** על זאת: **אעשה נפלאת.** לשון "ונפלינו", שתהיו מובדלים בזו מכל האמות, שלא תשרה שכינתי עליהם:

יא| **את האמרי וגו׳.** שש אמות יש כאן, כי הגרגשי עמד ופנה מפניהם:

יג| **אשריו.** הוא אילן שעובדים אותו:

יד| **קנא שמו.** מקנא לפרע ואינו מותר, וזהו כל לשון קנאה, אוחז בנצחונו ופורע מעוזביו:

טו-טז| **ואכלת מזבחו.** כסבור אתה שאין ענש באכילתו, ואני מעלה עליך כמודה בעבודתם, שמתוך כך אתה בא ולוקח "מבנתיו לבניך":

יח| **חדש האביב.** חדש הבכיר, שהתבואה מבכרת בבשולה:

יט| **כל פטר רחם לי.** באדם: **וכל מקנך תזכר וגו׳.** וכל מקנך אשר תזכר בפטר שור ושה, אשר יפטר זכר את רחמה. ׳פטר׳ לשון פתיחה, וכן: "פוטר מים ראשית מדון" (משלי יז, יד). תי"ו של "תזכר" לשון נקבה היא, מוסב על היולדת:

כ| **ופטר חמור.** ולא שאר בהמה טמאה: **תפדה בשה.** נותן שה לכהן והוא חלין ביד כהן, ופטר חמור מתר בעבודה לבעלים: **וערפתו.** עורפו בקופיץ. הוא הפסיד ממון כהן, לפיכך יפסד ממונו: **כל בכור בניך תפדה.** חמשה סלעים פדיונו קצוב, שנאמר: "ופדויו מבן חדש תפדה" וגו׳ (במדבר יח, טז): **ולא יראו פני ריקם.** לפי פשוטו של מקרא דבר בפני עצמו הוא ואינו מוסב על הבכור, שאין במצות בכור ראיית פנים, אלא אזהרה אחרת היא: וכשתעלו לרגל לראות "לא יראו פני ריקם", מצוה עליכם להביא עולת ראיית פנים. ולפי מדרש ברייתא, מקרא יתר הוא ומפנה לגזרה שוה, ללמד על

you shall rest; from plowing and from harvest you shall rest. One may not perform even tasks that are essential for one's livelihood.[59]

22 **You shall hold the Festival of Weeks,** Shavuot, fifty days after the start of Passover, **with the** ripening of the **first fruits of the wheat harvest. And** lastly, you shall observe **the Festival of the Ingathering of the Crops,** Sukkot, **at the turn of the year,**[D] when the new year commences, in the autumn.

23 **Three times in the year,** on Passover, Shavuot, and Sukkot, **all your males shall appear,** like soldiers in a roll call, **before the Master, the Lord, God of Israel.**

24 The Torah reassures the Jewish people about a potential worry with regard to the duty to ascend to Jerusalem on the pilgrimage festivals: **For I will expel nations before you, and I will expand your borders, and** consequently, although you will all leave your homes to ascend for the pilgrimage, **no man will covet your land when you go up to appear**[D] **before the Lord your God three times in the year.**

25 **You shall not slaughter with leavened bread the blood of My offering.** This applies specifically to the paschal lamb, and prohibits one from owning any leavened bread at the time one's paschal lamb is slaughtered.[60] **And the feast of the Paschal Festival,** the meat of the paschal lamb, **shall not lie until the morning.** It must be eaten on the first night of Passover, and anything that remains the next day is burned (12:10).

26 **You shall bring the choicest** of the **first fruits of your land**[D] **to the house of the Lord your God.**[61] **You shall not cook a kid in its mother's milk.**[D] Both of these commandments were stated previously in the exact same formulation (23:19).

The Covenant Is Recorded and Brought to the People

EXODUS 34:27–35

While Moses was on Mount Sinai, two separate documents attesting to the covenant with God were written. First, Moses wrote down, as instructed, the commandments stated in the previous section, many of which define the national character of Israel as a nation dwelling in its own land. Second, God wrote the Ten Precepts again, this time upon the tablets which Moses had fashioned.

The people's reaction to Moses' second descent with the stone tablets contrasts sharply with their previous response. Earlier, Moses came down the mountain to find the people dancing around the golden calf. This time, the people are cautious and fearful. They are even afraid of a direct encounter with Moses' shining countenance, and their leader has to cover his face. The unique closeness to God that Moses attained while in the rock crevice may have necessitated a certain degree of detachment from the people.

27 **The Lord said to Moses: Write for yourself these matters,**
Seventh aliya this short Book of the Covenant**, as according to these matters I established a covenant with you and with Israel.** The commandments stated in the previous section will form the foundation of the national life of the Jewish people,[62] and this is the basis of the covenant between us.

DISCUSSION

34:22 | **And the Festival of the Ingathering of the Crops at the turn of the year:** For many purposes, the calendar year begins with the month of Nisan, when the exodus took place. The counting of the months themselves and the years of a Jewish king's rule start from Nisan. Additionally, communal offerings in the Temple would be funded from the new year's half-shekel donations beginning in Nisan. Nevertheless, there are certain matters with regard to which the year begins with the month of Tishrei, in the autumn. For example, with regard to the laws of tithes, the Sabbatical Year, and counting the years of *orla*, the year commences in Tishrei (see 23:16; Leviticus 23:26, and commentary ad loc.; *Rosh HaShana* 4b). According to the tradition of the Sages, the festival of Sukkot must fall at the turn of the year, i.e., in the autumn, specifically when the day and night are roughly equal in length. This parallels the requirement that Passover must occur in the spring (*Sanhedrin* 12b–13a).

34:24 | **And no man will covet your land when you go up to appear:** When the Jewish nation dwelt in the wilderness, visiting the Tabernacle did not pose any difficulty, as they all lived in close proximity to the holy site. However, once the people settled throughout the Land of Israel, some places were far away from the Temple and close to the border. The neighboring nations were aware of the fact that the Jews would ascend to Jerusalem on specific dates, and they could attempt to exploit this fact to plunder or conquer those territories. God promises the nation that this will not occur.

34:26 | **The choicest of the first fruits of your land:** Several commandments were reiterated after the sin of the golden calf, in the same order that they were originally taught to the Jewish people; see table on facing page.

You shall not cook a kid in its mother's milk: The commentaries discuss the reason that this prohibition appears here. Some suggest that the cooking of a kid in its mother's milk would be performed as a fertility ritual aimed at causing the land to give forth bountiful produce. This prohibition is therefore mentioned in juxtaposition with the commandment to bring the first fruits, to emphasize that it is the observance of God's commandments, not an idolatrous fertility ritual, that brings a blessing upon the land (Sforno; see commentary on 23:19).

כב הַשְּׁבִיעִי תִּשְׁבֹּת בֶּחָרִישׁ וּבַקָּצִיר תִּשְׁבֹּת: וְחַג שָׁבֻעֹת תַּעֲשֶׂה לְךָ בִּכּוּרֵי קְצִיר
כג חִטִּים וְחַג הָאָסִיף תְּקוּפַת הַשָּׁנָה: שָׁלֹשׁ פְּעָמִים בַּשָּׁנָה יֵרָאֶה כָּל־זְכוּרְךָ אֶת־
כד פְּנֵי הָאָדֹן | יהוה אֱלֹהֵי יִשְׂרָאֵל: כִּי־אוֹרִישׁ גּוֹיִם מִפָּנֶיךָ וְהִרְחַבְתִּי אֶת־גְּבֻלֶךָ
וְלֹא־יַחְמֹד אִישׁ אֶת־אַרְצְךָ בַּעֲלֹתְךָ לֵרָאוֹת אֶת־פְּנֵי יהוה אֱלֹהֶיךָ שָׁלֹשׁ פְּעָמִים
כה כו בַּשָּׁנָה: לֹא־תִשְׁחַט עַל־חָמֵץ דַּם־זִבְחִי וְלֹא־יָלִין לַבֹּקֶר זֶבַח חַג הַפָּסַח: רֵאשִׁית
בִּכּוּרֵי אַדְמָתְךָ תָּבִיא בֵּית יהוה אֱלֹהֶיךָ לֹא־תְבַשֵּׁל גְּדִי בַּחֲלֵב אִמּוֹ:
כז וַיֹּאמֶר יהוה אֶל־מֹשֶׁה כְּתָב־לְךָ אֶת־הַדְּבָרִים הָאֵלֶּה כִּי עַל־פִּי | הַדְּבָרִים הָאֵלֶּה כו שביעי

רש"י

הַעֲנָקָתוֹ שֶׁל עֶבֶד עִבְרִי שֶׁהוּא חֲמִשָּׁה סְלָעִים מִכָּל מִין וָמִין כְּפִדְיוֹן בְּכוֹר. בְּמַסֶּכֶת קִדּוּשִׁין (דף יז ע"א):

כא| **בֶּחָרִישׁ וּבַקָּצִיר תִּשְׁבֹּת.** לָמָּה נִזְכַּר חָרִישׁ וְקָצִיר? יֵשׁ מֵרַבּוֹתֵינוּ אוֹמְרִים: עַל חָרִישׁ שֶׁל עֶרֶב שְׁבִיעִית הַנִּכְנָס לִשְׁבִיעִית וְקָצִיר שֶׁל שְׁבִיעִית הַיּוֹצֵא לְמוֹצָאֵי שְׁבִיעִית, לְלַמֶּדְךָ שֶׁמּוֹסִיפִין מֵחֹל עַל הַקֹּדֶשׁ. וְכָךְ מַשְׁמָעוֹ: "שֵׁשֶׁת יָמִים תַּעֲבֹד וּבַיּוֹם הַשְּׁבִיעִי תִּשְׁבֹּת", וַעֲבוֹדַת שֵׁשֶׁת הַיָּמִים שֶׁהִתַּרְתִּי לְךָ, יֵשׁ שָׁנָה שֶׁהֶחָרִישׁ וְהַקָּצִיר אָסוּר. וְאֵין צָרִיךְ לוֹמַר חָרִישׁ וְקָצִיר שֶׁל שְׁבִיעִית, שֶׁהֲרֵי כְּבָר נֶאֱמַר: "שָׂדְךָ לֹא תִזְרָע" וְגוֹ' (ויקרא כה, ד). וְיֵשׁ מֵהֶם אוֹמְרִים: אֵינוֹ מְדַבֵּר אֶלָּא בְּשַׁבָּת, וְחָרִישׁ וְקָצִיר שֶׁהֻזְכַּר בּוֹ לוֹמַר לְךָ, מַה חָרִישׁ רְשׁוּת אַף קָצִיר רְשׁוּת, יָצָא קְצִיר הָעֹמֶר שֶׁהוּא מִצְוָה וְדוֹחֶה אֶת הַשַּׁבָּת:

כב| **בִּכּוּרֵי קְצִיר חִטִּים.** שֶׁאַתָּה מֵבִיא בּוֹ שְׁתֵּי הַלֶּחֶם מִן הַחִטִּים בִּכּוּרִים, שֶׁהִיא מִנְחָה רִאשׁוֹנָה הַבָּאָה מִן הֶחָדָשׁ חִטִּים לַמִּקְדָּשׁ, כִּי מִנְחַת הָעֹמֶר הַבָּאָה בַּפֶּסַח, מִן הַשְּׂעוֹרִים הִיא: **וְחַג הָאָסִיף.** בִּזְמַן שֶׁאַתָּה אוֹסֵף תְּבוּאָתְךָ מִן הַשָּׂדֶה לַבַּיִת. אֲסִיפָה זוֹ לְשׁוֹן הַכְנָסָה לַבַּיִת, כְּמוֹ: "וַאֲסַפְתּוֹ אֶל תּוֹךְ בֵּיתֶךָ" (דברים כב, ב): **תְּקוּפַת הַשָּׁנָה.** שֶׁהִיא בַּחֲזָרַת הַשָּׁנָה, בִּתְחִלַּת הַשָּׁנָה הַבָּאָה: **תְּקוּפַת.** לְשׁוֹן מְסִבָּה וְהַקָּפָה:

כג| **כָּל זְכוּרְךָ.** כָּל הַזְּכָרִים שֶׁבְּךָ. הַרְבֵּה מִצְוֹת בַּתּוֹרָה נֶאֶמְרוּ וְנִכְפְּלוּ, וְיֵשׁ מֵהֶם שָׁלֹשׁ פְּעָמִים וְאַרְבַּע, לְחַיֵּב וְלַעֲנֹשׁ עַל מִנְיַן לָאוִין שֶׁבָּהֶם וְעַל מִנְיַן עֲשֵׂה שֶׁבָּהֶם:

כד| **אוֹרִישׁ.** כְּתַרְגּוּמוֹ: "אֲתָרֵיךְ", וְכֵן: "הָאֵל רָשׁ" (דברים ב, לא), וְכֵן: "וַיּוֹרֶשׁ אֶת הָאֱמֹרִי" (במדבר כא, לב), לְשׁוֹן גֵּרוּשִׁין: **וְהִרְחַבְתִּי אֶת גְּבֻלֶךָ.** וְאַתָּה רָחוֹק מִבֵּית הַבְּחִירָה וְאֵינְךָ יָכוֹל לֵרָאוֹת לְפָנַי תָּמִיד, לְכָךְ אֲנִי קוֹבֵעַ לְךָ שָׁלֹשׁ רְגָלִים הַלָּלוּ:

כה| **לֹא תִשְׁחַט וְגוֹ'.** לֹא תִּשְׁחַט אֶת הַפֶּסַח וַעֲדַיִן חָמֵץ קַיָּם, אַזְהָרָה לַשּׁוֹחֵט אוֹ לַזּוֹרֵק אוֹ לְאֶחָד מִבְּנֵי חֲבוּרָה: **וְלֹא יָלִין.** כְּתַרְגּוּמוֹ. אֵין לִינָה מוֹעֶלֶת בְּרֹאשׁ הַמִּזְבֵּחַ, וְאֵין לִינָה אֶלָּא בְּעַמּוּד הַשַּׁחַר: **זֶבַח חַג הַפָּסַח.** אֵמוּרָיו, וּמִכָּאן אַתָּה לָמֵד לְכָל הֶקְטֵר חֲלָבִים וְאֵבָרִים:

כו| **רֵאשִׁית בִּכּוּרֵי אַדְמָתְךָ.** מִשִּׁבְעַת הַמִּינִין הָאֲמוּרִים בְּשֶׁבַח אַרְצְךָ: "אֶרֶץ חִטָּה וּשְׂעֹרָה וְגֶפֶן" וְגוֹ' (דברים ח, ח) "וּדְבָשׁ" – הֵן תְּמָרִים: **לֹא תְבַשֵּׁל גְּדִי.** אַזְהָרָה לְבָשָׂר בְּחָלָב. וּשְׁלֹשָׁה פְּעָמִים כָּתוּב בַּתּוֹרָה: אֶחָד לַאֲכִילָה, וְאֶחָד לַהֲנָאָה, וְאֶחָד לְאִסּוּר בִּשּׁוּל: **גְּדִי.** כָּל וָלָד רַךְ בְּמַשְׁמָע וְאַף עֵגֶל וָכֶבֶשׂ, מִמַּה שֶּׁהֻצְרַךְ לְפָרֵשׁ בְּכַמָּה מְקוֹמוֹת: 'גְּדִי עִזִּים' (בראשית לח, יז, ועוד) לָמַדְתָּ שֶׁ'גְּדִי' סְתָם כָּל יוֹנְקִים בְּמַשְׁמָע: **בַּחֲלֵב אִמּוֹ.** פְּרָט לְעוֹף, שֶׁאֵין לוֹ חֲלֵב אֵם, שֶׁאֵין אִסּוּרוֹ מִן הַתּוֹרָה אֶלָּא מִדִּבְרֵי סוֹפְרִים:

כז| **אֶת הַדְּבָרִים הָאֵלֶּה.** וְלֹא אַתָּה רַשַּׁאי לִכְתֹּב תּוֹרָה שֶׁבְּעַל פֶּה:

Commandment	Place where the people first received the commandment
Observance of the festival of Passover	Egypt (12:18)
Consecration of a woman's firstborn son and the male firstborn of a kosher animal or a donkey	Egypt (13:2, 12–13)
Cessation of labor on the Sabbath	Mara and Mount Sinai (16:23; 20:10)
Observance of the festivals of Shavuot and Sukkot	Mount Sinai (23:15–16)
Appearing in the Temple before God on the three pilgrimage festivals	Mount Sinai (23:17)
Prohibition against slaughtering the paschal offering with leavened bread	Mount Sinai (23:18)
Bringing the first fruits to the Temple	Mount Sinai (23:19)
Prohibition against mixing meat and milk	Mount Sinai (23:19)

28 **He,** Moses, **was there with the Lord forty days and forty nights,** in addition to the previous forty days; **he did not eat bread, and he did not drink water. He,** God,[63] **wrote upon the tablets the words of the covenant, the Ten Precepts.**

29 **It was upon Moses' descent from Testimonyinai; the two Tablets of the Testimony**[D] **were in the hand of Moses upon his descent from the mountain, and Moses did not know that the skin of his face was radiant upon His speaking with him,** as a result of God speaking to him face-to-face.

The Ten Precepts on the two Tablets of the Testimony

30 **Aaron and all the children of Israel saw Moses** from afar, **and behold, the skin of his face was radiant; and they feared approaching him,** due to his shining countenance, as he appeared to them like an angelic being who emits light.

31 **Moses** therefore **called to them, and** only then **Aaron and all the princes in the congregation,** i.e., the princes of the tribes,[64] **returned to him; and Moses spoke to them** the words of the covenant.[65]

32 **Thereafter,** at a later stage, once the people saw that Moses spoke with the princes of the congregation and they remained unharmed,[66] or alternatively, after they had undergone a type of purification ritual, **all the children of Israel approached** Moses. **And he commanded them everything that the Lord spoke with him on Mount Sinai.**

33 **Moses concluded speaking with them and put a mask on**
Maftir **his face.** Moses did not deem it appropriate to engage in other activities while his face shone. He may have considered his shining countenance as a valuable gift from God that should be displayed only at special times, i.e., when he was teaching Torah to the people.

34 **Upon the coming of Moses before the Lord to speak with Him, he would remove the mask until his emergence,** so that there would be no obstruction between him and the Divine Presence. **He would emerge and** would not immediately replace the mask. Rather, he would first **speak to the children of Israel that which he would be commanded.**

35 When Moses exited the Tent of Meeting **the children of Israel saw the face of Moses,** and they noticed **that the skin of Moses' face was radiant.** Moses did not cover his face while transmitting the words of God to the people, so that the divine light upon his countenance would accompany the Torah that he taught the Jewish people. **And** yet at other times **Moses replaced the mask on his face, until his entering to speak with Him,** as it was unfitting that his shining, awe-inspiring countenance be seen without proper cause.

Maftir on Shabbat Para is read from Numbers 19:1–22.

DISCUSSION

34:29| **The two Tablets of the Testimony:** The Torah does not describe the shape of the tablets. Since they always remained in the Ark of the Covenant, few people ever saw the tablets, and their exact shape is unknown. The Sages describe them as two rectangular stone tablets that were not attached to each other. Their length was six handbreadths, about 48–60 cm, their width was six handbreadths, and their depth three handbreadths (*Bava Batra* 14a). There is no known source for the common depiction of the tablets as two attached stone tablets with rounded tops. This is not an authentic depiction but merely the product of an artist's imagination

כח כָּרַתִּי אִתְּךָ בְּרִית וְאֶת־יִשְׂרָאֵל: וַיְהִי־שָׁם עִם־יהוה אַרְבָּעִים יוֹם וְאַרְבָּעִים
לַיְלָה לֶחֶם לֹא אָכַל וּמַיִם לֹא שָׁתָה וַיִּכְתֹּב עַל־הַלֻּחֹת אֵת דִּבְרֵי הַבְּרִית עֲשֶׂרֶת
כט הַדְּבָרִים: וַיְהִי בְּרֶדֶת מֹשֶׁה מֵהַר סִינַי וּשְׁנֵי לֻחֹת הָעֵדֻת בְּיַד־מֹשֶׁה בְּרִדְתּוֹ מִן־
ל הָהָר וּמֹשֶׁה לֹא־יָדַע כִּי קָרַן עוֹר פָּנָיו בְּדַבְּרוֹ אִתּוֹ: וַיַּרְא אַהֲרֹן וְכָל־בְּנֵי יִשְׂרָאֵל
לא אֶת־מֹשֶׁה וְהִנֵּה קָרַן עוֹר פָּנָיו וַיִּירְאוּ מִגֶּשֶׁת אֵלָיו: וַיִּקְרָא אֲלֵהֶם מֹשֶׁה וַיָּשֻׁבוּ
לב אֵלָיו אַהֲרֹן וְכָל־הַנְּשִׂאִים בָּעֵדָה וַיְדַבֵּר מֹשֶׁה אֲלֵהֶם: וְאַחֲרֵי־כֵן נִגְּשׁוּ כָּל־בְּנֵי
לג יִשְׂרָאֵל וַיְצַוֵּם אֵת כָּל־אֲשֶׁר דִּבֶּר יהוה אִתּוֹ בְּהַר סִינָי: וַיְכַל מֹשֶׁה מִדַּבֵּר אִתָּם מפטיר
לד וַיִּתֵּן עַל־פָּנָיו מַסְוֶה: וּבְבֹא מֹשֶׁה לִפְנֵי יהוה לְדַבֵּר אִתּוֹ יָסִיר אֶת־הַמַּסְוֶה עַד־
לה צֵאתוֹ וְיָצָא וְדִבֶּר אֶל־בְּנֵי יִשְׂרָאֵל אֵת אֲשֶׁר יְצֻוֶּה: וְרָאוּ בְנֵי־יִשְׂרָאֵל אֶת־פְּנֵי
מֹשֶׁה כִּי קָרַן עוֹר פְּנֵי מֹשֶׁה וְהֵשִׁיב מֹשֶׁה אֶת־הַמַּסְוֶה עַל־פָּנָיו עַד־בֹּאוֹ לְדַבֵּר
אִתּוֹ:

רש"י

כט| **וַיְהִי בְּרֶדֶת מֹשֶׁה.** כְּשֶׁהֵבִיא לוּחוֹת אַחֲרוֹנוֹת בְּיוֹם הַכִּפּוּרִים: **כִּי קָרַן.** לְשׁוֹן קַרְנַיִם, שֶׁהָאוֹר מַבְהִיק וּבוֹלֵט כְּמִין קֶרֶן. וּמֵהֵיכָן זָכָה מֹשֶׁה לְקַרְנֵי הַהוֹד? רַבּוֹתֵינוּ אָמְרוּ: מִן הַמְּעָרָה, שֶׁנָּתַן הַקָּדוֹשׁ בָּרוּךְ הוּא יָדוֹ עַל פָּנָיו, שֶׁנֶּאֱמַר: "וְשַׂכֹּתִי כַפִּי" (לעיל לג, כב):

ל| **וַיִּירְאוּ מִגֶּשֶׁת אֵלָיו.** בֹּא וּרְאֵה כַּמָּה גָּדוֹל כֹּחָהּ שֶׁל עֲבֵרָה, שֶׁעַד שֶׁלֹּא פָּשְׁטוּ יְדֵיהֶם בַּעֲבֵרָה מַהוּ אוֹמֵר? "וּמַרְאֵה כְּבוֹד ה' כְּאֵשׁ אֹכֶלֶת בְּרֹאשׁ הָהָר לְעֵינֵי בְּנֵי יִשְׂרָאֵל" (לעיל כד, יז), וְלֹא יְרֵאִים וְלֹא מִזְדַּעְזְעִים; וּמִשֶּׁעָשׂוּ אֶת הָעֵגֶל, אַף מִקַּרְנֵי הוֹדוֹ שֶׁל מֹשֶׁה הָיוּ מִרְתָּעִים וּמִזְדַּעְזְעִים:

לא| **הַנְּשִׂאִים בָּעֵדָה.** כְּמוֹ נְשִׂיאֵי הָעֵדָה: **וַיְדַבֵּר מֹשֶׁה אֲלֵהֶם.** שְׁלִיחוּתוֹ שֶׁל מָקוֹם. וּלְשׁוֹן הֹוֶה הוּא כָּל הָעִנְיָן הַזֶּה:

לב| **וְאַחֲרֵי כֵן נִגְּשׁוּ.** אַחַר שֶׁלִּמֵּד לַזְּקֵנִים חוֹזֵר וּמְלַמֵּד הַפָּרָשָׁה אוֹ הַהֲלָכָה לְיִשְׂרָאֵל. תָּנוּ רַבָּנָן: כֵּיצַד סֵדֶר הַמִּשְׁנָה? מֹשֶׁה הָיָה לָמֵד מִפִּי הַגְּבוּרָה. נִכְנַס אַהֲרֹן, שָׁנָה לוֹ מֹשֶׁה פִּרְקוֹ, נִסְתַּלֵּק אַהֲרֹן וְיָשַׁב לוֹ לִשְׂמֹאל מֹשֶׁה. נִכְנְסוּ בָּנָיו, שָׁנָה לָהֶם מֹשֶׁה פִּרְקָם, נִסְתַּלְּקוּ הֵם, יָשַׁב אֶלְעָזָר לִימִין מֹשֶׁה וְאִיתָמָר לִשְׂמֹאל אַהֲרֹן. נִכְנְסוּ זְקֵנִים, שָׁנָה לָהֶם מֹשֶׁה פִּרְקָם, נִסְתַּלְּקוּ זְקֵנִים, יָשְׁבוּ לַצְּדָדִין. נִכְנְסוּ כָּל הָעָם, שָׁנָה לָהֶם מֹשֶׁה פִּרְקָם. נִמְצָא בְּיַד כָּל הָעָם אֶחָד, בְּיַד הַזְּקֵנִים שְׁנַיִם, בְּיַד בְּנֵי אַהֲרֹן שְׁלֹשָׁה, בְּיַד אַהֲרֹן אַרְבָּעָה וְכוּ', כִּדְאִיתָא בְּעֵרוּבִין (דף נד ע"ב):

לג-לה| **וַיִּתֵּן עַל פָּנָיו מַסְוֶה.** כְּתַרְגּוּמוֹ: "בֵּית אַפֵּי", לְשׁוֹן אֲרַמִּי הוּא בַּתַּלְמוּד (כתובות סב ע"ב): "סְוִי לְבַּהּ", וְעוֹד בִּכְתֻבּוֹת (דף ס ע"א): "הֲוָה קָא מַסְוֵי לְאַפַּהּ", לְשׁוֹן הַבָּטָה, הָיָה מִסְתַּכֵּל בָּהּ. אַף כָּאן "מַסְוֶה", בֶּגֶד הַנִּתָּן כְּנֶגֶד הַפַּרְצוּף וּבֵית הָעֵינַיִם. וְלִכְבוֹד קַרְנֵי הַהוֹד שֶׁלֹּא יָזוֹנוּ הַכֹּל מֵהֶם הָיָה נוֹתֵן הַמַּסְוֶה כְּנֶגְדָּן, וְנוֹטְלוֹ בְּשָׁעָה שֶׁהָיָה מְדַבֵּר עִם יִשְׂרָאֵל, וּבְשָׁעָה שֶׁהַמָּקוֹם נִדְבָּר עִמּוֹ "עַד צֵאתוֹ", וּבְצֵאתוֹ – "וְיָצָא" בְּלֹא מַסְוֶה "וְדִבֶּר אֶל בְּנֵי יִשְׂרָאֵל" וְרָאוּ קַרְנֵי הַהוֹד בְּפָנָיו. וּכְשֶׁהוּא מִסְתַּלֵּק מֵהֶם, "וְהֵשִׁיב... אֶת הַמַּסְוֶה עַל פָּנָיו עַד בֹּאוֹ לְדַבֵּר אִתּוֹ", וּכְשֶׁבָּא לְדַבֵּר אִתּוֹ – נוֹטְלוֹ מֵעַל פָּנָיו:

Parashat
Vayak'hel

The Law of the Sabbath

EXODUS 35:1–3

Once God has accepted Moses' prayer and given him the second set of tablets, Moses assembles the entire congregation to announce God's instructions concerning the Tabernacle. When God originally conveyed these instructions to Moses, He concluded with the instruction "However, you shall observe My Sabbaths" (31:13). Now, in addressing the people, Moses opens with this injunction, emphasizing that the Sabbath, which is the focal point of the sanctity of time, is not overridden by the construction of the Tabernacle, the focal point of the sanctity of place.

35 1 **Moses assembled the entire congregation of the children of Israel and said to them: These are the matters that the Lord commanded to perform them.**

2 **Six days shall** all **labor be performed,** including that of the Tabernacle, **and on the seventh day there shall be a sacrament for you, a day of sabbatical rest,** a full rest day on which all labor is prohibited (see 31:15), **to the Lord; anyone who**

performs any materially creative **labor on it,** whether it is hard to perform or easy, **shall be put to death.**

3 **You shall not kindle fire in all your dwellings**[D] **on the Sabbath day,** despite the fact that this labor, which is required for a large proportion of the labor in constructing the Tabernacle, involves little effort or toil.

Moses Calls for the Offering from the People

EXODUS 35:4–20

Moses asked the people to bring the requisite materials for the construction of the Tabernacle. He first listed the materials needed for the labor and requested volunteers to contribute their time and skill to help build a dwelling place for God. He then explained the purpose of the materials. Since the Israelites were so recently slaves, and were alone in the wilderness, their ability to purchase items was limited. This project therefore demanded much effort and generosity on their part.

4 **Moses said to the entire congregation of the children of Israel, saying: This is the matter that the Lord commanded, saying:**

5 **Take from among you a gift to the Lord; anyone who is generous of heart shall bring it** (see commentary on 25:2). Unlike the half shekel tax, which was imposed equally upon each member of the congregation, the construction of the Tabernacle depended on the generosity of the people. **The gift of the Lord** included many elements, e.g., the metals required for the Tabernacle: **gold, silver, and bronze.**

6 It also included fabrics: **sky-blue** wool, colored with a dye extracted from the blood of a type of snail, which was probably a deep, dark blue; highly expensive **purple** wool, extracted from a different snail; **and scarlet wool,** colored with a dye extracted from scale insects; in addition, **linen,** and woven **goats' hair.**

7 The materials for the roofs and the walls: **rams' hides,** from which the hair had been removed, and which had been **dyed red; taḥash hides,** possibly an extinct species, or a sea mammal of some kind, whose hide was apparently very valuable and used for shoes;[1] **and** beams of **acacia wood.**

8 Oil and spices: **oil for the lighting, and spices for the anointing oil and for the incense of the spices.**

9 Precious stones: **onyx stones,** typically yellowish brown, **and stones for setting.** The onyx stones were used **for the ephod, and** the stones to be set were **for** fixing in **the breast piece.**

10 In addition to offering the above materials, the Israelites were requested to contribute their time and skills: **Every wise-hearted man among you shall come and make everything that the Lord commanded:**

11 **The Tabernacle,** the linen and wool that served as the ceiling (see, e.g., 26:1); **its tent,** the goats' hides that served as a tent over the Tabernacle (see 26:7, 36:14), **and its covering** of hides above the tent (see 26:14, 36:19); **its hooks and its boards; its bars, its pillars, and its sockets.**

12 The vessels of the Tabernacle: **the ark and its staves, the ark cover, and the curtain for the screen;**

13 **the table** for the showbread **and its staves, all its vessels, and the showbread** [*leḥem hapanim*], bread [*leḥem*] that has a front [*panim*], which was placed on the table;

14 **the candelabrum of the light and its vessels,** the implements for cleaning it and for preparing the lighting, **and its lamps,** placed on the candelabrum, **and the lighting oil;**

15 **the altar of incense and its staves, the anointing oil,** and the **incense of the spices,** for the altar of incense. Since some of

פרשת
ויקהל

לה א וַיַּקְהֵל מֹשֶׁה אֶת־כָּל־עֲדַת בְּנֵי יִשְׂרָאֵל וַיֹּאמֶר אֲלֵהֶם אֵלֶּה הַדְּבָרִים אֲשֶׁר־
ב צִוָּה יְהוָה לַעֲשֹׂת אֹתָם: שֵׁשֶׁת יָמִים תֵּעָשֶׂה מְלָאכָה וּבַיּוֹם הַשְּׁבִיעִי יִהְיֶה לָכֶם
ג קֹדֶשׁ שַׁבַּת שַׁבָּתוֹן לַיהוָה כָּל־הָעֹשֶׂה בוֹ מְלָאכָה יוּמָת: לֹא־תְבַעֲרוּ אֵשׁ בְּכֹל
מֹשְׁבֹתֵיכֶם בְּיוֹם הַשַּׁבָּת:
ד וַיֹּאמֶר מֹשֶׁה אֶל־כָּל־עֲדַת בְּנֵי־יִשְׂרָאֵל לֵאמֹר זֶה הַדָּבָר אֲשֶׁר־צִוָּה יְהוָה לֵאמֹר:
ה קְחוּ מֵאִתְּכֶם תְּרוּמָה לַיהוָה כֹּל נְדִיב לִבּוֹ יְבִיאֶהָ אֵת תְּרוּמַת יְהוָה זָהָב וָכֶסֶף
ו ז וּנְחֹשֶׁת: וּתְכֵלֶת וְאַרְגָּמָן וְתוֹלַעַת שָׁנִי וְשֵׁשׁ וְעִזִּים: וְעֹרֹת אֵילִם מְאָדָּמִים וְעֹרֹת
ח תְּחָשִׁים וַעֲצֵי שִׁטִּים: וְשֶׁמֶן לַמָּאוֹר וּבְשָׂמִים לְשֶׁמֶן הַמִּשְׁחָה וְלִקְטֹרֶת הַסַּמִּים:
ט י וְאַבְנֵי־שֹׁהַם וְאַבְנֵי מִלֻּאִים לָאֵפוֹד וְלַחֹשֶׁן: וְכָל־חֲכַם־לֵב בָּכֶם יָבֹאוּ וְיַעֲשׂוּ אֵת
יא כָּל־אֲשֶׁר צִוָּה יְהוָה: אֶת־הַמִּשְׁכָּן אֶת־אָהֳלוֹ וְאֶת־מִכְסֵהוּ אֶת־קְרָסָיו וְאֶת־
יב קְרָשָׁיו אֶת־בְּרִיחָו אֶת־עַמֻּדָיו וְאֶת־אֲדָנָיו: אֶת־הָאָרֹן וְאֶת־בַּדָּיו אֶת־הַכַּפֹּרֶת
יג וְאֵת פָּרֹכֶת הַמָּסָךְ: אֶת־הַשֻּׁלְחָן וְאֶת־בַּדָּיו וְאֶת־כָּל־כֵּלָיו וְאֵת לֶחֶם הַפָּנִים:
יד טו וְאֶת־מְנֹרַת הַמָּאוֹר וְאֶת־כֵּלֶיהָ וְאֶת־נֵרֹתֶיהָ וְאֵת שֶׁמֶן הַמָּאוֹר: וְאֶת־מִזְבַּח

רש"י

א| וַיַּקְהֵל מֹשֶׁה. לְמָחֳרַת יוֹם הַכִּפּוּרִים כְּשֶׁיָּרַד מִן הָהָר. וְהוּא לְשׁוֹן הִפְעִיל, שֶׁאֵינוֹ אוֹסֵף אֲנָשִׁים בַּיָּדַיִם, אֶלָּא הֵן נֶאֱסָפִים עַל פִּי דִּבּוּרוֹ, וְתַרְגּוּמוֹ: "וְאַכְנֵישׁ":

ב| שֵׁשֶׁת יָמִים. הִקְדִּים לָהֶם אַזְהָרַת שַׁבָּת לְצִוּוּי מְלֶאכֶת הַמִּשְׁכָּן, לוֹמַר שֶׁאֵינוֹ דּוֹחֶה אֶת הַשַּׁבָּת:

ג| לֹא תְבַעֲרוּ אֵשׁ. יֵשׁ מֵרַבּוֹתֵינוּ אוֹמְרִים הַבְעָרָה לְלָאו יָצָאת, וְיֵשׁ אוֹמְרִים לַחֲלֵק יָצָאת:

ד| זֶה הַדָּבָר אֲשֶׁר צִוָּה ה'. לִי "לֵאמֹר" לָכֶם:

ה| נְדִיב לִבּוֹ. עַל שֵׁם שֶׁלִּבּוֹ נוֹדְבוֹ קָרוּי 'נְדִיב לֵב'. כְּבָר פֵּרַשְׁתִּי נִדְבַת הַמִּשְׁכָּן וּמְלַאכְתּוֹ בִּמְקוֹם צַוָּאָתָם:

יא| אֶת הַמִּשְׁכָּן. יְרִיעוֹת הַתַּחְתּוֹנוֹת הַנִּרְאוֹת בְּתוֹכוֹ קָרוּי 'מִשְׁכָּן': אֶת אָהֳלוֹ. הוּא אֹהֶל יְרִיעוֹת עִזִּים הֶעָשׂוּי לְגַג: וְאֶת מִכְסֵהוּ. מִכְסֵה עוֹרוֹת אֵילִים וְהַתְּחָשִׁים:

יב| וְאֵת פָּרֹכֶת הַמָּסָךְ. פָּרֹכֶת הַמְּחִצָּה. כָּל דָּבָר הַמֵּגֵן בֵּין מִלְמַעְלָה בֵּין מִכְּנֶגֶד קָרוּי 'מָסָךְ' וּ'סְכָךְ', וְכֵן: "שַׂכְתָּ בַעֲדוֹ" (איוב א, י), "הִנְנִי שָׂךְ אֶת דַּרְכֵּךְ" (הושע ב, ח):

יג| לֶחֶם הַפָּנִים. כְּבָר פֵּרַשְׁתִּי (לעיל כה, כט) עַל שֵׁם שֶׁהָיוּ לוֹ פָּנִים לְכָאן וּלְכָאן, שֶׁהָיָה עָשׂוּי כְּמִין תֵּבָה פְּרוּצָה:

יד| וְאֶת כֵּלֶיהָ. מֶלְקָחַיִם וּמַחְתּוֹת: נֵרֹתֶיהָ. לוּצִינִי"שׁ בְּלַעַ"ז, בָּזִיכִים שֶׁהַשֶּׁמֶן וְהַפְּתִילוֹת נְתוּנִין בָּהֶן: וְאֵת שֶׁמֶן הַמָּאוֹר. אַף הוּא צָרִיךְ חַכְמֵי לֵב, שֶׁהוּא מְשֻׁנֶּה מִשְּׁאָר שְׁמָנִים, כְּמוֹ שֶׁמְּפֹרָשׁ בִּמְנָחוֹת (דף פו ע"א): מְגַרְגְּרוֹ בְּרֹאשׁ הַזַּיִת, וְהוּא כָּתִית וָזָךְ:

DISCUSSION

35:3| **You shall not kindle fire in all your dwellings:** The act of lighting a fire was easy even in biblical times, not very different from igniting one nowadays. Furthermore, this category of labor includes the use of an existing fire to light a new one, which is certainly a simple act. Consequently, Moses issued a special warning with regard to the performance of this labor on the Sabbath (see *Bekhor Shor*; *Ḥizkuni*).

the ingredients of the incense were used in the preparation of the anointing oil, the oil and the incense are listed alongside one another. **And the screen of the entrance for the entrance of the Tabernacle.**

16 The vessels placed outside the Tabernacle: **the altar of the burnt offering, its bronze grate, its staves and all its vessels;** and **the basin and its base.**

17 Surrounding those vessels: **the hangings of the courtyard, its pillars and its sockets, and the screen of the gate of the courtyard;**

18 **the pegs of the Tabernacle,** by which the sheets are tied, **the pegs of the courtyard, and their cords,** the ropes that bind them;

19 **the woven fabrics to serve in the Sanctuary.** Included among the woven fabrics were the cloths used for wrapping the vessels while traveling.[2] Alternatively, this is a general name for all the various textiles involved in the service of the Tabernacle. If so, it also includes **the sacred vestments for Aaron the priest and the vestments of his sons, to serve as priests.**

20 **The entire congregation of the children of Israel departed from the presence of Moses.**

The Assembly of the Tabernacle and Consecration of the Priests

EXODUS 35:21–40:33

The detailed report of the execution of the instructions for building the Tabernacle matches the account of those instructions that was given in the previous *parashot*. The few small differences that can be found can be understood as simply stylistic differences. This repetition of all the technical details of the Tabernacle may be exhausting or boring to the reader and raises the question of why the repetition is necessary. In understanding this phenomenon, one must appreciate that the Tabernacle is not merely a symbol of the Divine Presence, but is the actual location in which the Divine Presence is revealed. Though the glory of the Lord fills the entire earth, His presence is concentrated in the Tabernacle and is mysteriously more substantial there than elsewhere: A cloud rests on the Tabernacle; there, fire comes down from heaven; and the word of God is communicated there to Moses. In commanding the building of the Tabernacle, God instructs Moses how to create a means of communication between material reality and the upper, heavenly reality. Like any complex apparatus, the Tabernacle is composed of different parts, all of which are necessary to its functioning, even if we do not necessarily understand the role each one plays. Only at the conclusion of the description of the assembly of the Tabernacle does the Torah provide us with an account of the Tabernacle operating as a completed entity.[3]

The process of building the Tabernacle can be compared to that of constructing a rocket that is meant to fly to the outer reaches of the solar system. For such a project, extreme precision and detailed work is required. The Tabernacle is also a system that contains enormous power, and any small error in its construction could give rise to disaster. The awesome device that Israel creates in the wilderness makes direct contact with the Sacred possible, but it is therefore also dangerous. As will become clear, behavior that does not include strict adherence to the procedures and rules of the Tabernacle will even cause fatalities.[4] Despite the fact that recounting all the technical details of the Tabernacle another time is likely to be uninteresting to the reader, it serves to emphasize the importance of absolute precision in the construction and operation of the Tabernacle in order for it to be able to fulfill its role.

Due to the repetitive nature of these passages, the commentary here will be brief. The reader interested in more elaborate explanations will find them in the parallel chapters that recount the commands to build the various parts of the Tabernacle.

The Response of the People

EXODUS 35:21–29

The entire people responded to Moses' call. Women and men, commoners and princes, all brought whatever was required for the construction of the Tabernacle.

21 *Second aliya* **Every man whose heart inspired him came,** with the uplifting realization that he had the opportunity to participate in the building of the Tabernacle for God, **and everyone whose spirit was generous brought the gift of the Lord for the labor of the Tent of Meeting, for all its service,** its requirements, **and for the sacred vestments.**

22 **The men came along with the women.** The women went first due to their great enthusiasm for the task. **Everyone generous of heart brought a bracelet,**[5] **earring, ring, or girdle,**[BD] **any gold vessel. And** in addition to those who brought these adornments and vessels, there came **every man who made a donation of** plain **gold to the Lord.** Those who brought gold would raise it aloft in order to display their generosity before all.[6]

23 **And every man with whom was found sky-blue, purple, and scarlet wool, linen, goats' hair, rams' hides dyed red, and taḥash hides, brought them** as well.

24 **Everyone who raised a gift of silver and bronze brought the gift of the Lord, and everyone with whom was found acacia wood**[D] of the appropriate size **for any labor of the service brought it.**[D]

הַקְּטֹרֶת וְאֶת־בַּדָּיו וְאֵת שֶׁמֶן הַמִּשְׁחָה וְאֵת קְטֹרֶת הַסַּמִּים וְאֶת־מָסַךְ הַפֶּתַח
טז לַפֶּתַח הַמִּשְׁכָּן: אֵת ׀ מִזְבַּח הָעֹלָה וְאֶת־מִכְבַּר הַנְּחֹשֶׁת אֲשֶׁר־לוֹ אֶת־בַּדָּיו
יז וְאֶת־כָּל־כֵּלָיו אֶת־הַכִּיֹּר וְאֶת־כַּנּוֹ: אֵת קַלְעֵי הֶחָצֵר אֶת־עַמֻּדָיו וְאֶת־אֲדָנֶיהָ
יח וְאֵת מָסַךְ שַׁעַר הֶחָצֵר: אֶת־יִתְדֹת הַמִּשְׁכָּן וְאֶת־יִתְדֹת הֶחָצֵר וְאֶת־מֵיתְרֵיהֶם:
יט אֶת־בִּגְדֵי הַשְּׂרָד לְשָׁרֵת בַּקֹּדֶשׁ אֶת־בִּגְדֵי הַקֹּדֶשׁ לְאַהֲרֹן הַכֹּהֵן וְאֶת־בִּגְדֵי בָנָיו
כ כא לְכַהֵן: וַיֵּצְאוּ כָּל־עֲדַת בְּנֵי־יִשְׂרָאֵל מִלִּפְנֵי מֹשֶׁה: וַיָּבֹאוּ כָּל־אִישׁ אֲשֶׁר־נְשָׂאוֹ שני
לִבּוֹ וְכֹל אֲשֶׁר נָדְבָה רוּחוֹ אֹתוֹ הֵבִיאוּ אֶת־תְּרוּמַת יְהוָה לִמְלֶאכֶת אֹהֶל מוֹעֵד
כב וּלְכָל־עֲבֹדָתוֹ וּלְבִגְדֵי הַקֹּדֶשׁ: וַיָּבֹאוּ הָאֲנָשִׁים עַל־הַנָּשִׁים כֹּל ׀ נְדִיב לֵב הֵבִיאוּ
חָח וָנֶזֶם וְטַבַּעַת וְכוּמָז כָּל־כְּלִי זָהָב וְכָל־אִישׁ אֲשֶׁר הֵנִיף תְּנוּפַת זָהָב לַיהוָה:
כג וְכָל־אִישׁ אֲשֶׁר־נִמְצָא אִתּוֹ תְּכֵלֶת וְאַרְגָּמָן וְתוֹלַעַת שָׁנִי וְשֵׁשׁ וְעִזִּים וְעֹרֹת אֵילִם
כד מְאָדָּמִים וְעֹרֹת תְּחָשִׁים הֵבִיאוּ: כָּל־מֵרִים תְּרוּמַת כֶּסֶף וּנְחֹשֶׁת הֵבִיאוּ אֵת

רש״י

טו| מָסַךְ הַפֶּתַח. וִילוֹן שֶׁלִּפְנֵי הַמִּזְרָח, שֶׁלֹּא הָיוּ שָׁם קְרָשִׁים וְלֹא יְרִיעוֹת.

יז| אֵת עַמֻּדָיו וְאֶת אֲדָנֶיהָ. הֲרֵי 'חָצֵר' קָרוּי כָּאן לְשׁוֹן זָכָר וּלְשׁוֹן נְקֵבָה, וְכֵן דְּבָרִים הַרְבֵּה: וְאֵת מָסַךְ שַׁעַר הֶחָצֵר. וִילוֹן פָּרוּשׂ לְצַד הַמִּזְרָח, עֶשְׂרִים אַמָּה הָאֶמְצָעִיּוֹת שֶׁל רֹחַב הֶחָצֵר, שֶׁהָיָה חֲמִשִּׁים רֹחַב, וּסְתוּמִין הֵימֶנּוּ לְצַד צָפוֹן חָמֵשׁ עֶשְׂרֵה אַמָּה וְכֵן לַדָּרוֹם, שֶׁנֶּאֱמַר: "וַחֲמֵשׁ עֶשְׂרֵה אַמָּה קְלָעִים לַכָּתֵף" (לעיל כז, יד)

יח| יִתְדֹת. לִתְקֹעַ וְלִקְשֹׁר בָּהֶם סוֹפֵי הַיְרִיעוֹת בָּאָרֶץ שֶׁלֹּא יָנוּעוּ בָּרוּחַ: מֵיתְרֵיהֶם. חֲבָלִים לִקְשֹׁר:

יט| בִּגְדֵי הַשְּׂרָד. לְכַסּוֹת הָאָרוֹן וְהַשֻּׁלְחָן וְהַמְּנוֹרָה וְהַמִּזְבְּחוֹת בִּשְׁעַת סִלּוּק הַמַּסָּעוֹת:

כב| עַל הַנָּשִׁים. עִם הַנָּשִׁים וּסְמוּכִין אֲלֵיהֶם: חָח. הוּא תַּכְשִׁיט שֶׁל זָהָב עָגֹל נָתוּן עַל הַזְּרוֹעַ וְהוּא הַצָּמִיד: וְכוּמָז. כְּלִי זָהָב הוּא נָתוּן כְּנֶגֶד אוֹתוֹ מָקוֹם לָאִשָּׁה, וְרַבּוֹתֵינוּ פֵּרְשׁוּ שֵׁם 'כּוּמָז': כָּאן מְקוֹם זִמָּה.

כג| וְכָל אִישׁ אֲשֶׁר נִמְצָא אִתּוֹ. תְּכֵלֶת אוֹ אַרְגָּמָן אוֹ תּוֹלַעַת שָׁנִי אוֹ עוֹרוֹת אֵילִים אוֹ תְּחָשִׁים, כֻּלָּם "הֵבִיאוּ".

BACKGROUND

35:22| **Girdle** [***kumaz***]: According to the Talmud (*Shabbat* 64a), the *kumaz* was an ornament in the shape of a womb, which covered the genitals. There is evidence of a similar ornament in Ugarit, from the fourteenth century BCE. Some maintain that the *kumaz* was a necklace made of small balls, as the Arabic *kumzat* means small ball.

DISCUSSION

35:22| **A bracelet, earring, ring, or girdle:** These are mainly ornaments used by women, although they are sometimes worn by men as well. This is another indication of the robust response of the women to the call for donations for the construction of the Tabernacle.

35:24| **And everyone with whom was found acacia wood:** Although it could not have been easy to find acacia wood of the requisite size in the wilderness, there were those who found it and carried it with them in the desert (see *Bekhor Shor*, 25:5). Since the Israelites were situated on international trade routes in the Sinai, they could import raw materials from Lebanon, from African countries such as Egypt, and from India. According to one midrash, the Israelites brought the acacia wood with them when leaving Egypt, as they possessed a tradition dating back to Jacob that they would need it (*Tanḥuma*, *Teruma* 9).

The lists of gifts: The building materials are listed from most to least expensive: first gold, then costly fabrics, plain metals, and finally wood. The command to fashion the priestly vestments followed a similar order: The most expensive garments appeared first, while the more basic ones were last (28:4–42).

25 **Every woman who was wise-hearted,** skilled in crafts, **spun with her hands.** The women volunteered for the service, **and they brought yarn: the sky-blue and the purple wool, the scarlet wool and the linen,** that is, the spun threads of dyed wool and linen.
26 **All women whose heart inspired them in wisdom,** the most talented craftswomen, **spun the goats' hair** to weave the sheets of the Tent and perhaps also to entwine the cords. This was complicated labor, which required particular expertise, as it is far more difficult to spin goats' hair than sheep's wool.[7]
27 **The princes,** who were wealthy, **brought the onyx stones and the stones for setting:** The onyx stones **for the ephod, and** the stones to be set **for the breast piece;**
28 **and the spice**[D] **and the oil, for the light, for the anointing oil, and for the incense of the spices.** These were also brought by the princes, as they were expensive at that time and place.
29 In sum, **any man or woman, whose heart was generous for them to bring** materials and skills **for all the labor that the Lord commanded to perform at the hand of Moses – the children of Israel brought** these **as a pledge to the Lord.**[D]

The Craftsmen and the Abundance of Donations

EXODUS 35:30–36:7

On the one hand, donation of the materials was not levied as a tax upon the people, but was given freely. On the other hand, Moses did not turn to a limited number of wealthy individuals or leaders, who could collect the necessary resources by themselves. Rather, he addressed all the people, with the aim that all the Israelites should participate in the construction of the Tabernacle. The enthusiastic response of the entire people and their efforts in building a place for God's residence thus reflects the great public desire to take part in this project. Unlike the Temples built by Solomon and Herod, which were projects of individuals, the Tabernacle was characterized by the nationwide contributions and the involvement of the whole people in its construction.

30 **Moses said to the children of Israel: See, the Lord has called**
Third aliya (Second aliya) **by name,** appointed out of honor and respect, **Betzalel, son of Uri, son of Hur, of the tribe of Judah.** God had already selected Betzalel to supervise the labor (31:2), but it was important for the Israelites to know that he had been appointed.
31 **He has filled him with the spirit of God, in wisdom, in understanding, and in** general **knowledge, and in all craftsmanship,**
32 **to devise designs;** to prepare plans **to work with gold, with silver, and with bronze;**
33 **and in stone-cutting for setting,** to polish the precious stones and insert them into the breast piece; **and in wood-carving; to perform all artful craftsmanship.**
34 Since Betzalel was to work with a team, he required not only the talent of an expert craftsman and the creativity to put into effect the plan shown to Moses on Mount Sinai, but also the ability to guide those working under his authority. Consequently, **He,** God, **has put in his,** Betzalel's, **heart to teach: He,** as the head, **and** with him **Oholiav, son of Ahisamakh, of the tribe of Dan.**
35 **He filled them with wisdom of heart, to perform all craft of the carver; and of the artisan; and of the embroiderer in sky-blue** wool, **and purple wool,** and **scarlet wool, and in linen; and of the weaver; performers of craftsmanship and devisers of designs.** They had to master the variety of crafts necessary for the different labors, in wood and textiles, each of which requires a separate type of expertise.
36 1 **Betzalel and Oholiav and every wise-hearted man, in whom the Lord has put wisdom and understanding to know** how **to perform all the labor of the service of the Sanctuary, shall perform everything that the Lord commanded.**
2 **Moses summoned Betzalel and Oholiav and every wise-hearted man, in whose heart the Lord put wisdom,** and he even called **everyone whose heart inspired him to approach the work to perform it.** The weighty task required one to have self-confidence that he would be capable of performing it properly.
3 The craftsmen invited by Moses began their volunteer labor. **They took from before Moses all the gifts that the children of Israel brought for the labor of the service of the**

DISCUSSION

35:28 | **And the spice:** Some of the materials for the spices were not found locally but were imported from distant places, e.g., deep in Africa, and even from India and Indonesia. These spices were acquired via international trade, which was certainly difficult at the time, and were consequently very expensive. Even simple oil was a rare commodity in such circumstances, as there are no sources for producing olive oil in the wilderness, and such materials were generally not produced in Egypt.

35:29 | **The children of Israel brought as a pledge to the Lord:** Some suggest that this repetition indicates that every individual brought some sort of gift for the Tabernacle (see *Alsheikh*).

תְּרוּמַת יְהוָה וְכֹל אֲשֶׁר נִמְצָא אִתּוֹ עֲצֵי שִׁטִּים לְכָל־מְלֶאכֶת הָעֲבֹדָה הֵבִיאוּ׃
כה וְכָל־אִשָּׁה חַכְמַת־לֵב בְּיָדֶיהָ טָווּ וַיָּבִיאוּ מַטְוֶה אֶת־הַתְּכֵלֶת וְאֶת־הָאַרְגָּמָן
כו אֶת־תּוֹלַעַת הַשָּׁנִי וְאֶת־הַשֵּׁשׁ׃ וְכָל־הַנָּשִׁים אֲשֶׁר נָשָׂא לִבָּן אֹתָנָה בְּחָכְמָה
כז טָווּ אֶת־הָעִזִּים׃ וְהַנְּשִׂאִם הֵבִיאוּ אֵת אַבְנֵי הַשֹּׁהַם וְאֵת אַבְנֵי הַמִּלֻּאִים לָאֵפוֹד
כח וְלַחֹשֶׁן׃ וְאֶת־הַבֹּשֶׂם וְאֶת־הַשָּׁמֶן לְמָאוֹר וּלְשֶׁמֶן הַמִּשְׁחָה וְלִקְטֹרֶת הַסַּמִּים׃
כט כָּל־אִישׁ וְאִשָּׁה אֲשֶׁר נָדַב לִבָּם אֹתָם לְהָבִיא לְכָל־הַמְּלָאכָה אֲשֶׁר צִוָּה יְהוָה
לַעֲשׂוֹת בְּיַד־מֹשֶׁה הֵבִיאוּ בְנֵי־יִשְׂרָאֵל נְדָבָה לַיהוָה׃
ל וַיֹּאמֶר מֹשֶׁה אֶל־בְּנֵי יִשְׂרָאֵל רְאוּ קָרָא יְהוָה בְּשֵׁם בְּצַלְאֵל בֶּן־אוּרִי בֶן־ שלישי /שני/
לא חוּר לְמַטֵּה יְהוּדָה׃ וַיְמַלֵּא אֹתוֹ רוּחַ אֱלֹהִים בְּחָכְמָה בִּתְבוּנָה וּבְדַעַת וּבְכָל־
לב לג מְלָאכָה׃ וְלַחְשֹׁב מַחֲשָׁבֹת לַעֲשֹׂת בַּזָּהָב וּבַכֶּסֶף וּבַנְּחֹשֶׁת׃ וּבַחֲרֹשֶׁת אֶבֶן
לד לְמַלֹּאת וּבַחֲרֹשֶׁת עֵץ לַעֲשׂוֹת בְּכָל־מְלֶאכֶת מַחֲשָׁבֶת׃ וּלְהוֹרֹת נָתַן בְּלִבּוֹ
לה הוּא וְאָהֳלִיאָב בֶּן־אֲחִיסָמָךְ לְמַטֵּה־דָן׃ מִלֵּא אֹתָם חָכְמַת־לֵב לַעֲשׂוֹת כָּל־
מְלֶאכֶת חָרָשׁ וְחֹשֵׁב וְרֹקֵם בַּתְּכֵלֶת וּבָאַרְגָּמָן בְּתוֹלַעַת הַשָּׁנִי וּבַשֵּׁשׁ וְאֹרֵג עֹשֵׂי
ו א כָּל־מְלָאכָה וְחֹשְׁבֵי מַחֲשָׁבֹת׃ וְעָשָׂה בְצַלְאֵל וְאָהֳלִיאָב וְכֹל אִישׁ חֲכַם־לֵב
אֲשֶׁר נָתַן יְהוָה חָכְמָה וּתְבוּנָה בָּהֵמָּה לָדַעַת לַעֲשֹׂת אֶת־כָּל־מְלֶאכֶת עֲבֹדַת
ב הַקֹּדֶשׁ לְכֹל אֲשֶׁר־צִוָּה יְהוָה׃ וַיִּקְרָא מֹשֶׁה אֶל־בְּצַלְאֵל וְאֶל־אָהֳלִיאָב וְאֶל
כָּל־אִישׁ חֲכַם־לֵב אֲשֶׁר נָתַן יְהוָה חָכְמָה בְּלִבּוֹ כֹּל אֲשֶׁר נְשָׂאוֹ לִבּוֹ לְקָרְבָה
ג אֶל־הַמְּלָאכָה לַעֲשֹׂת אֹתָהּ׃ וַיִּקְחוּ מִלִּפְנֵי מֹשֶׁה אֵת כָּל־הַתְּרוּמָה אֲשֶׁר הֵבִיאוּ
בְּנֵי יִשְׂרָאֵל לִמְלֶאכֶת עֲבֹדַת הַקֹּדֶשׁ לַעֲשֹׂת אֹתָהּ וְהֵם הֵבִיאוּ אֵלָיו עוֹד נְדָבָה

רש״י

כו| **טָווּ אֶת הָעִזִּים.** הִיא הָיְתָה אֻמָּנוּת יְתֵרָה, שֶׁמֵּעַל גַּבֵּי הָעִזִּים טָווִין אוֹתָם:

כז| **וְהַנְּשִׂאִם הֵבִיאוּ.** אָמַר רַבִּי נָתָן: מָה רָאוּ נְשִׂיאִים לְהִתְנַדֵּב בַּחֲנֻכַּת הַמִּזְבֵּחַ בַּתְּחִלָּה, וּבִמְלֶאכֶת הַמִּשְׁכָּן לֹא הִתְנַדְּבוּ בַּתְּחִלָּה? אֶלָּא כָּךְ אָמְרוּ נְשִׂיאִים: יִתְנַדְּבוּ צִבּוּר מַה שֶּׁמִּתְנַדְּבִין, וּמַה שֶּׁמְּחַסְּרִין – אָנוּ מַשְׁלִימִין אוֹתוֹ. כֵּיוָן שֶׁהִשְׁלִימוּ צִבּוּר אֶת הַכֹּל, שֶׁנֶּאֱמַר: ״וְהַמְּלָאכָה הָיְתָה דַיָּם״ (להלן לו, ז), אָמְרוּ נְשִׂיאִים: מֶה עָלֵינוּ לַעֲשׂוֹת? ״הֵבִיאוּ אֵת אַבְנֵי הַשֹּׁהַם״ וְגוֹ׳, לְכָךְ הִתְנַדְּבוּ בַּחֲנֻכַּת הַמִּזְבֵּחַ תְּחִלָּה. וּלְפִי שֶׁנִּתְעַצְּלוּ מִתְּחִלָּה נֶחְסְרָה אוֹת מִשְּׁמָם, ״וְהַנְּשִׂאִם״ כְּתִיב:

ל| **חוּר.** בְּנָהּ שֶׁל מִרְיָם הָיָה:

לד| **וְאָהֳלִיאָב.** מִשֵּׁבֶט דָּן, מִן הַיְרוּדִין שֶׁבַּשְּׁבָטִים, מִבְּנֵי הַשְּׁפָחוֹת, וְהִשְׁוָהוּ הַמָּקוֹם לִבְצַלְאֵל לִמְלֶאכֶת הַמִּשְׁכָּן וְהוּא מִגְּדוֹלֵי הַשְּׁבָטִים, לְקַיֵּם מַה שֶּׁנֶּאֱמַר: ״וְלֹא נִכַּר שׁוֹעַ לִפְנֵי דָל״ (איוב לד, יט):

Sanctuary, to perform it. They, the Israelites, **brought him more pledges morning after morning**. Some interpret the last phrase to mean that after Moses' request for donations for the Tabernacle, the people brought their gifts for a whole day and the following day.

4 **All the wise men,** the craftsmen **who performed all the craftsmanship of the Sanctuary, each one came from his craft that they were performing.** This was a large team, composed of experts in all types of craftsmanship and in the use of the various implements, who could cooperate in the required tasks.

5 **They said to Moses, saying: The people are bringing more than enough for the service of the labor that the Lord commanded to perform.** Based on a calculation of the requirements, they estimated that more material had already been received than needed.

6 **Moses commanded, and they circulated a proclamation in the camp, saying: Man or woman shall not perform any more labor**[D] **for the gifts of the Sanctuary; and the people ceased bringing** materials.

7 **And the labor,** the bringing of the donations or the donations themselves,[8] **was sufficient for all the labor to perform it, and beyond.** There was leftover material, which was not used.

The Preparation of the Sheets for the Roof of the Tabernacle

EXODUS 36:8–19

The sheets that covered the Tabernacle were prepared in accordance with the instructions given earlier. Apart from some minor details missing here, which do not concern the making of the sheets but the manner of their placement, all the information is identical to that which was stated to Moses, with slightly different wording. As stated elsewhere, the order of the commands did not determine the order of their performance, which is described here, and in fact, the commandment to construct the main vessels of the Tabernacle was written before the instruction to build the Tabernacle itself and its sheets. This was due to the importance of the ark, which was the focal point of the Divine Presence, and of the vessels placed nearby. Nevertheless, in performing the instructions, certain practical considerations had to be taken into account. For example, it was more reasonable to erect the structure first, and only afterward fashion the vessels that would be placed within it.

8 **All the wise-hearted among the performers of the labor made** the roof of **the Tabernacle,** which consisted of **ten** fabric **sheets,** made **of spun** white **linen and sky-blue, purple, and scarlet wool; with artfully crafted** forms of **cherubs they made them.** The sheets were woven in a complex manner, in which the form of cherubs appeared on every sheet, on both sides.

Fourth aliya

9 **The length of one sheet was twenty-eight cubits, and the width** was **four cubits for each sheet; there was one measure for all the sheets.**

10 **He attached five sheets** by sewing them **one to another,** into a single unit, **and** the other **five sheets**[D] **he attached one to another.**

11 **He made loops of sky-blue wool at the edge of the one sheet** located **at the extremity of the array** of five sheets sewn together, and **he did likewise at the edge of the outermost sheet in the second array** of five sheets.

12 **Fifty loops he made in the one sheet, and fifty loops he made at the extremity of the sheet that was in the second array,** along the entire length; **the loops corresponded one to another.** The loops were placed at equal intervals, so that the loops of the two sheets would correspond to one another.

13 **He made fifty hooks of gold and attached the sheets one to another with the hooks,** which each linked a pair of loops. In this manner the two units of sheets were joined, **and the Tabernacle was one,** as it became a single structure. Alternatively, the term "Tabernacle" here is referring to the sheets that cover the structure (see 36:14).

14 **He made sheets of goats' hair as a tent over the Tabernacle,** above the fabric sheets, which are considered part of the Tabernacle itself; **eleven sheets he made them.**

15 **The length of the one sheet was thirty cubits, and four cubits the width of the one sheet; there was one** uniform **measure for eleven sheets.**

16 **He attached five sheets by themselves and six sheets by themselves.** There were two separate units of sheets sewn together, one consisting of five sheets of goats' hair and the other of six sheets.

17 **He made fifty loops at the edge of the outermost sheet in the array, and he made fifty loops at the edge of the sheet in the second array.**

DISCUSSION

36:6 | **Shall not perform any more labor:** The term "labor" in this context can suggest that those who brought the gifts performed some work with them first. They would not bring dirty, damaged, or unfinished articles, but would prepare them appropriately for the Sanctuary.

36:10 | **He attached five sheets...and five sheets:** In addition to the allegoric and esoteric ideas derived from the attachment of the sheets,

ד בַּבֹּקֶר בַּבֹּקֶר: וַיָּבֹאוּ כָּל־הַחֲכָמִים הָעֹשִׂים אֵת כָּל־מְלֶאכֶת הַקֹּדֶשׁ אִישׁ אִישׁ
ה מִמְּלַאכְתּוֹ אֲשֶׁר־הֵמָּה עֹשִׂים: וַיֹּאמְרוּ אֶל־מֹשֶׁה לֵּאמֹר מַרְבִּים הָעָם לְהָבִיא
ו מִדֵּי הָעֲבֹדָה לַמְּלָאכָה אֲשֶׁר־צִוָּה יהוה לַעֲשֹׂת אֹתָהּ: וַיְצַו מֹשֶׁה וַיַּעֲבִירוּ קוֹל
בַּמַּחֲנֶה לֵאמֹר אִישׁ וְאִשָּׁה אַל־יַעֲשׂוּ־עוֹד מְלָאכָה לִתְרוּמַת הַקֹּדֶשׁ וַיִּכָּלֵא הָעָם
ז מֵהָבִיא: וְהַמְּלָאכָה הָיְתָה דַיָּם לְכָל־הַמְּלָאכָה לַעֲשׂוֹת אֹתָהּ וְהוֹתֵר:
ח וַיַּעֲשׂוּ כָל־חֲכַם־לֵב בְּעֹשֵׂי הַמְּלָאכָה אֶת־הַמִּשְׁכָּן עֶשֶׂר יְרִיעֹת שֵׁשׁ מָשְׁזָר וּתְכֵלֶת רביעי
ט וְאַרְגָּמָן וְתוֹלַעַת שָׁנִי כְּרֻבִים מַעֲשֵׂה חֹשֵׁב עָשָׂה אֹתָם: אֹרֶךְ הַיְרִיעָה הָאַחַת
שְׁמֹנֶה וְעֶשְׂרִים בָּאַמָּה וְרֹחַב אַרְבַּע בָּאַמָּה הַיְרִיעָה הָאֶחָת מִדָּה אַחַת לְכָל־
י הַיְרִיעֹת: וַיְחַבֵּר אֶת־חֲמֵשׁ הַיְרִיעֹת אַחַת אֶל־אֶחָת וְחָמֵשׁ יְרִיעֹת חִבַּר אַחַת
יא אֶל־אֶחָת: וַיַּעַשׂ לֻלְאֹת תְּכֵלֶת עַל שְׂפַת הַיְרִיעָה הָאֶחָת מִקָּצָה בַּמַּחְבָּרֶת כֵּן
יב עָשָׂה בִּשְׂפַת הַיְרִיעָה הַקִּיצוֹנָה בַּמַּחְבֶּרֶת הַשֵּׁנִית: חֲמִשִּׁים לֻלָאֹת עָשָׂה בַּיְרִיעָה
הָאֶחָת וַחֲמִשִּׁים לֻלָאֹת עָשָׂה בִּקְצֵה הַיְרִיעָה אֲשֶׁר בַּמַּחְבֶּרֶת הַשֵּׁנִית מַקְבִּילֹת
יג הַלֻּלָאֹת אַחַת אֶל־אֶחָת: וַיַּעַשׂ חֲמִשִּׁים קַרְסֵי זָהָב וַיְחַבֵּר אֶת־הַיְרִיעֹת אַחַת
אֶל־אַחַת בַּקְּרָסִים וַיְהִי הַמִּשְׁכָּן אֶחָד:
יד טו וַיַּעַשׂ יְרִיעֹת עִזִּים לְאֹהֶל עַל־הַמִּשְׁכָּן עַשְׁתֵּי־עֶשְׂרֵה יְרִיעֹת עָשָׂה אֹתָם: אֹרֶךְ
הַיְרִיעָה הָאַחַת שְׁלֹשִׁים בָּאַמָּה וְאַרְבַּע אַמּוֹת רֹחַב הַיְרִיעָה הָאֶחָת מִדָּה אַחַת
טז לְעַשְׁתֵּי עֶשְׂרֵה יְרִיעֹת: וַיְחַבֵּר אֶת־חֲמֵשׁ הַיְרִיעֹת לְבָד וְאֶת־שֵׁשׁ הַיְרִיעֹת לְבָד:
יז וַיַּעַשׂ לֻלָאֹת חֲמִשִּׁים עַל שְׂפַת הַיְרִיעָה הַקִּיצֹנָה בַּמַּחְבָּרֶת וַחֲמִשִּׁים לֻלָאֹת

רש״י

פרק לו

ה] מִדֵּי הָעֲבֹדָה. יוֹתֵר מִכְּדֵי צֹרֶךְ הָעֲבוֹדָה:

ו] וַיִּכָּלֵא. לְשׁוֹן מְנִיעָה:

ז] וְהַמְּלָאכָה הָיְתָה דַיָּם לְכָל הַמְּלָאכָה. וּמְלֶאכֶת הַהֲבָאָה "הָיְתָה דַיָּם" שֶׁל עוֹשֵׂי הַמִּשְׁכָּן, "לְכָל הַמְּלָאכָה" שֶׁל מִשְׁכָּן "לַעֲשׂוֹת אוֹתָהּ" וּלְהוֹתִיר: וְהוֹתֵר. כְּמוֹ: "וְהַכְבֵּד אֶת לִבּוֹ" (לעיל ח, יא), "וְהַכּוֹת אֶת מוֹאָב" (מלכים ב׳ ג, כד):

DISCUSSION

there is a simple, practical reason for their division into two separate units: Since the Tabernacle was required to be mobile, it was important for its sheets to be removable, so that they could be folded and carried easily. Had all the sheets been joined into one unit, they would have been too heavy and cumbersome. They were therefore sewn as two units, each roughly 10 m wide and 14 m long (*Bekhor Shor*, 26:5).

18 He made **fifty hooks of bronze**[D] to attach the tent, to be one.
19 He made **a cover for the tent** of goats' hides, **of rams' hides dyed red, and** a fourth **cover of taḥash hides above** it. Alternatively, this was all one covering, partly of rams' hides and

partly of *taḥash* hides, meaning that there were only three layers above the Tabernacle.[9]

The Construction of the Tabernacle Walls
EXODUS 36:20–38

Sheets of the Tabernacle

After detailing the coverings of the Tabernacle, the Torah explains the construction of the walls. This passage includes technical matters involving the erection of walls by means of sockets that held the boards together from below, rings that connected each pair of adjacent boards from above, four external bars, which joined together different sections of the boards, and a central bar that connected all the boards and steadied the entire structure.

Lastly, the Torah describes the two partitions that were made of fabric, rather than wood: The curtain, which divided the Sanctuary from the Holy of Holies, and the screen, at the entrance to the Tent.

20 **He made the boards for** the walls of **the Tabernacle of** smoothed boards of **acacia wood,**[10] **standing.** The boards were to be positioned upright, like their position when the trees grew.[11]
Fifth aliya
21 **Ten cubits was the length of a board** and the height of the Tabernacle, as the boards were placed standing, **and one cubit and a half** was **the width of each board.**
22 **Two tenons,** protrusions, **were for one board, parallel one to another.**[D] Due to the great height of the boards, across from the protrusions of each board corresponding indentations were made in the two adjacent boards, in order to join them together by having the protruding tenons enter the indentations. **So he did for all the boards of the Tabernacle.**
23 **He made the boards for the Tabernacle; twenty boards** were used **for the southern side.**
24 **He made forty silver sockets** placed **under the twenty boards,** as a base upon which the boards of the Tabernacle rested: **Two sockets under the one board for its two tenons,** the protrusions under the boards, **and two sockets under the one board for its two tenons.** The protruding tenons were inserted into the sockets, to hold the boards.
25 **For the second side of the Tabernacle, for the north side, he made twenty boards.**
26 **Their forty sockets were of silver: Two sockets under the one board and two sockets under the one board.** The arrangements of boards and sockets on the southern and northern sides of the Tabernacle were simple and identical to each other.
27 **For the side of the Tabernacle** that faced **to the west, he made six boards,** each one and a half cubits in width. Together they spanned nine cubits, the bulk of the western wall.
28 **He made two boards for the corners of the Tabernacle on the sides.** These boards helped stabilize the Tabernacle and also served an aesthetic purpose, as they filled in the empty corners.
29 **They,** all the boards, **were even** and adjacent to one another **at the bottom,** with no space between them, **and they each met**

the adjacent board **at its top for the one ring,** which was itself inserted into grooves in the top of each pair of boards, holding the ends together. **So he did for the two of them, for the two corners,** the northwestern and southwestern corners.
30 **There were** on the west side a total of **eight boards and their silver sockets: Sixteen sockets, two sockets under the one board.** Viewed externally, the western wall had two additional boards which were not part of the main, internal structure but which filled the corners on the outside.
31 **He made bars of acacia wood,** for holding the boards together: **Five for the boards of the one side of the Tabernacle,**
32 **and five bars for the boards of the second side of the Tabernacle, and five bars for the boards of the Tabernacle for the side to the west.** Four of these bars ran along the outer side of each wall. Two held the top half in place, each one spanning half the length of the wall, and the other two were similarly placed on the bottom half. Thus, the four bars joined the boards of each wall in two separate units, each constituting half of the wall.
33 In addition to the four outer bars, **he made the central bar,** the fifth bar, **to run inside the boards from end to end.**[D] He made a hole in the thickness of the boards through which this bar was inserted, to strengthen the boards from within, and join the entire wall together.
34 **He plated the boards with gold, and their rings,** which facilitated joining the boards together, **he made of gold.** The rings were made **as housings,** receptacles, **for the bars. He** also **plated the bars** themselves **with gold.**
35 **He made the curtain of sky-blue** wool, **purple** wool, **and scarlet wool, and linen,** all **spun together; he made it artfully crafted with cherubs.** The curtain was fashioned in a skilled manner so that the design could be seen on each side.[12]
36 **He made for it four acacia pillars and plated them with gold; their hooks were of gold. He cast for them four silver**

יח עָשָׂה עַל־שְׂפַת הַיְרִיעָה הַחֹבֶרֶת הַשֵּׁנִית: וַיַּעַשׂ קַרְסֵי נְחֹשֶׁת חֲמִשִּׁים לְחַבֵּר
יט אֶת־הָאֹהֶל לִהְיֹת אֶחָד: וַיַּעַשׂ מִכְסֶה לָאֹהֶל עֹרֹת אֵילִם מְאָדָּמִים וּמִכְסֵה עֹרֹת
כ תְּחָשִׁים מִלְמָעְלָה: וַיַּעַשׂ אֶת־הַקְּרָשִׁים לַמִּשְׁכָּן עֲצֵי שִׁטִּים חמישי
כא כב עֹמְדִים: עֶשֶׂר אַמֹּת אֹרֶךְ הַקָּרֶשׁ וְאַמָּה וַחֲצִי הָאַמָּה רֹחַב הַקֶּרֶשׁ הָאֶחָד: שְׁתֵּי
כג יָדֹת לַקֶּרֶשׁ הָאֶחָד מְשֻׁלָּבֹת אַחַת אֶל־אֶחָת כֵּן עָשָׂה לְכֹל קַרְשֵׁי הַמִּשְׁכָּן: וַיַּעַשׂ
כד אֶת־הַקְּרָשִׁים לַמִּשְׁכָּן עֶשְׂרִים קְרָשִׁים לִפְאַת נֶגֶב תֵּימָנָה: וְאַרְבָּעִים אַדְנֵי־כֶסֶף
עָשָׂה תַּחַת עֶשְׂרִים הַקְּרָשִׁים שְׁנֵי אֲדָנִים תַּחַת־הַקֶּרֶשׁ הָאֶחָד לִשְׁתֵּי יְדֹתָיו וּשְׁנֵי
כה אֲדָנִים תַּחַת־הַקֶּרֶשׁ הָאֶחָד לִשְׁתֵּי יְדֹתָיו: וּלְצֶלַע הַמִּשְׁכָּן הַשֵּׁנִית לִפְאַת צָפוֹן
כו עָשָׂה עֶשְׂרִים קְרָשִׁים: וְאַרְבָּעִים אַדְנֵיהֶם כָּסֶף שְׁנֵי אֲדָנִים תַּחַת הַקֶּרֶשׁ הָאֶחָד
כז וּשְׁנֵי אֲדָנִים תַּחַת הַקֶּרֶשׁ הָאֶחָד: וּלְיַרְכְּתֵי הַמִּשְׁכָּן יָמָּה עָשָׂה שִׁשָּׁה קְרָשִׁים:
כח כט וּשְׁנֵי קְרָשִׁים עָשָׂה לִמְקֻצְעֹת הַמִּשְׁכָּן בַּיַּרְכָתָיִם: וְהָיוּ תוֹאֲמִם מִלְּמַטָּה וְיַחְדָּו יִהְיוּ
ל תַמִּים אֶל־רֹאשׁוֹ אֶל־הַטַּבַּעַת הָאֶחָת כֵּן עָשָׂה לִשְׁנֵיהֶם לִשְׁנֵי הַמִּקְצֹעֹת: וְהָיוּ
שְׁמֹנָה קְרָשִׁים וְאַדְנֵיהֶם כֶּסֶף שִׁשָּׁה עָשָׂר אֲדָנִים שְׁנֵי אֲדָנִים שְׁנֵי אֲדָנִים תַּחַת
לא הַקֶּרֶשׁ הָאֶחָד: וַיַּעַשׂ בְּרִיחֵי עֲצֵי שִׁטִּים חֲמִשָּׁה לְקַרְשֵׁי צֶלַע־הַמִּשְׁכָּן הָאֶחָת:
לב וַחֲמִשָּׁה בְרִיחִם לְקַרְשֵׁי צֶלַע־הַמִּשְׁכָּן הַשֵּׁנִית וַחֲמִשָּׁה בְרִיחִם לְקַרְשֵׁי הַמִּשְׁכָּן
לג לַיַּרְכָתַיִם יָמָּה: וַיַּעַשׂ אֶת־הַבְּרִיחַ הַתִּיכֹן לִבְרֹחַ בְּתוֹךְ הַקְּרָשִׁים מִן־הַקָּצֶה
לד אֶל־הַקָּצֶה: וְאֶת־הַקְּרָשִׁים צִפָּה זָהָב וְאֶת־טַבְּעֹתָם עָשָׂה זָהָב בָּתִּים לַבְּרִיחִם
לה וַיְצַף אֶת־הַבְּרִיחִם זָהָב: וַיַּעַשׂ אֶת־הַפָּרֹכֶת תְּכֵלֶת וְאַרְגָּמָן וְתוֹלַעַת שָׁנִי וְשֵׁשׁ
לו מָשְׁזָר מַעֲשֵׂה חֹשֵׁב עָשָׂה אֹתָהּ כְּרֻבִים: וַיַּעַשׂ לָהּ אַרְבָּעָה עַמּוּדֵי שִׁטִּים וַיְצַפֵּם

DISCUSSION

36:18| **He made fifty hooks of bronze:** The inner layer, woven mainly out of dyed wool, was considered part of the Tabernacle itself and was visible from inside. The tent of goats' hair, the outer layer, was of secondary importance, and therefore it was made of cheaper material and was less complex. Furthermore, although its form was similar to that of the first layer, the hooks used to join the arrays together were made of bronze, not gold.

36:22| **Parallel one to another:** The commentary on the verse follows the opinion of Rabbi Neḥemya (*Shabbat* 98b), as explained by the Rambam. Others maintain that the indentations were on the bottom of the boards, for the sockets, which are described in the verses below.

36:33| **From end to end:** According to rabbinic tradition, the central bar miraculously bent around and passed through all three walls (see *Targum Yonatan*; *Shabbat* 98b).

sockets. The curtain was hung from the gold hooks placed on the pillars.

37 Instead of a fourth wall on the eastern side, **he made a screen for the entrance of the Tent, of sky-blue, purple, and scarlet wool, and linen,** all **spun together, the work of an embroiderer.** This task was simpler than the weaving required for the ceiling of the Tabernacle and for the curtain that partitioned off the Holy of Holies, which are described as "artfully crafted" (verses 8, 35).

38 **And** he made **its five pillars and their hooks,** upon which the screen was hung; **he plated their tops and their bands with gold. And their sockets were five,** made **of bronze.**

The Tabernacle and the courtyard

The Construction of the Ark

EXODUS 37:1–9

After the construction of the Tabernacle itself, the craftsmen fashioned its vessels, starting with the ark, the heart of the Tabernacle. In contrast to the verses where the command to build the ark appears, here the Torah refers only to the making of the wooden ark itself and its appurtenances, without addressing the ark's function as the container of the tablets and the place where God encounters His people.

37 1 **Betzalel made the ark of acacia wood; its length was two and a half cubits, and its width one cubit and a half, and its height a cubit and a half.**

2 **He plated it with pure gold within and without.** According to tradition, this was more than just plating but rather two gold boxes. The wooden ark was placed within the larger gold box, while the smaller gold box was placed inside it.[13] **And he made a rim of gold upon it, all around.**

3 **He cast for it four rings of gold, on its four corners,**[14] or legs:[15] **Two rings on its one side, and two rings on its second side.** Each ring was placed at the edge of the side.

4 **He made staves of acacia wood, and he plated them with gold.**

5 **He brought the staves into the rings on the sides of the ark, to carry the ark.**

6 **He made an ark cover of pure gold; its length was two and a half cubits,** corresponding to the length of the ark, **and its width one and a half cubits,** in accordance with the width of the ark.

7 **He made two cherubs,** figures of angels, heavenly beings,[16] **of gold,** hammered out of the same gold block as the ark cover.[17] **He made them hammered, at the two ends of the ark cover:**

8 **One cherub from this end** of the ark cover **and one cherub from that end – he made the cherubs** extend **from the ark cover at its two ends.**

9 **The cherubs had wings spread from above, shielding with their wings over the ark cover and their faces one to another; the faces of the cherubs were toward the ark cover.** The cherubs were not fully turned toward one another, but faced downward, to the ark cover.

The Construction of the Table

EXODUS 37:10–16

These verses, which describe the fashioning of the table, are similar to the instructions for building it, except that they do not describe the function of the table, namely, to hold the showbread.

10 **He made the table** for the showbread **of acacia wood; its length was two cubits, its width one cubit, and its height a cubit and a half.**

11 **He plated it with pure gold, and he made for it an** ornamental **rim of gold all around.**

12 **He made for it a border** the height **of one handbreadth** all **around, and he made** the aforementioned **rim of gold for its border all around.**

13 **He** also **cast for it four gold rings, and he put the rings on the four corners that were on its four legs.**

14 **The rings were adjacent to the border,** which was between the legs of the table or along the tabletop, and they were alongside the border and beneath it, on the four legs of the table, rather than on the border itself.[18] The rings were **housings for the staves,** or poles, used **to carry the table.**

15 **He made the staves of acacia wood, and he plated them with gold, to carry the table.**

16 **He made the vessels that were on the table** for the showbread: **its bowls,** for containing flour or dough; **its spoons,** for the frankincense; **its supports,** upright posts on the two sides of the table; **and the tubes,** which formed a lattice above the table, **with which it,** the bread, **was to be covered** layer by layer. All these he made **of pure gold.**

לז זָהָב וַיְצַ֥פּ זָהָ֖ב וַיִּצֹ֥ק לָהֶ֖ם אַרְבָּעָ֣ה אַדְנֵי־כָ֑סֶף: וַיַּ֤עַשׂ מָסָךְ֙ לְפֶ֣תַח הָאֹ֔הֶל תְּכֵ֖לֶת

לח וְאַרְגָּמָ֤ן וְתוֹלַ֨עַת֙ שָׁנִ֣י וְשֵׁ֣שׁ מָשְׁזָ֔ר מַעֲשֵׂ֖ה רֹקֵֽם: וְאֶת־עַמּוּדָ֤יו חֲמִשָּׁה֙ וְאֶת־וָוֵיהֶ֔ם

וְצִפָּ֧ה רָאשֵׁיהֶ֛ם וַחֲשֻׁקֵיהֶ֖ם זָהָ֑ב וְאַדְנֵיהֶ֥ם חֲמִשָּׁ֖ה נְחֹֽשֶׁת:

כז א וַיַּ֧עַשׂ בְּצַלְאֵ֛ל אֶת־הָאָרֹ֖ן עֲצֵ֣י שִׁטִּ֑ים אַמָּתַ֨יִם וָחֵ֜צִי אָרְכּ֗וֹ וְאַמָּ֤ה וָחֵ֨צִי֙ רָחְבּ֔וֹ

ב וְאַמָּ֥ה וָחֵ֖צִי קֹמָתֽוֹ: וַיְצַפֵּ֜הוּ זָהָ֣ב טָה֗וֹר מִבַּ֥יִת וּמִח֖וּץ וַיַּ֥עַשׂ ל֛וֹ זֵ֥ר זָהָ֖ב סָבִֽיב:

ג וַיִּצֹ֣ק ל֗וֹ אַרְבַּע֙ טַבְּעֹ֣ת זָהָ֔ב עַ֖ל אַרְבַּ֣ע פַּעֲמֹתָ֑יו וּשְׁתֵּ֣י טַבָּעֹ֗ת עַל־צַלְעוֹ֙ הָֽאֶחָ֔ת

ה וּשְׁתֵּ֣י טַבָּעֹ֔ת עַל־צַלְע֖וֹ הַשֵּׁנִֽית: וַיַּ֥עַשׂ בַּדֵּ֖י עֲצֵ֣י שִׁטִּ֑ים וַיְצַ֥ף אֹתָ֖ם זָהָֽב: וַיָּבֵ֤א

ו אֶת־הַבַּדִּים֙ בַּטַּבָּעֹ֔ת עַ֖ל צַלְעֹ֣ת הָאָרֹ֑ן לָשֵׂ֖את אֶת־הָאָרֹֽן: וַיַּ֥עַשׂ כַּפֹּ֖רֶת זָהָ֣ב

ז טָה֑וֹר אַמָּתַ֤יִם וָחֵ֨צִי֙ אָרְכָּ֔הּ וְאַמָּ֥ה וָחֵ֖צִי רָחְבָּֽהּ: וַיַּ֛עַשׂ שְׁנֵ֥י כְרֻבִ֖ים זָהָ֑ב מִקְשָׁה֙

ח עָשָׂ֣ה אֹתָ֔ם מִשְּׁנֵ֖י קְצ֥וֹת הַכַּפֹּֽרֶת: כְּרוּב־אֶחָ֤ד מִקָּצָה֙ מִזֶּ֔ה וּכְרוּב־אֶחָ֖ד מִקָּצָ֑ה

ט קְצוֹתָֽיו מִזֶּ֑ה מִן־הַכַּפֹּ֛רֶת עָשָׂ֥ה אֶת־הַכְּרֻבִ֖ים מִשְּׁנֵ֥י קְצוֹתָֽו: וַיִּהְי֣וּ הַכְּרֻבִים֩ פֹּרְשֵׂ֨י כְנָפַ֜יִם

לְמַ֗עְלָה סֹכְכִ֤ים בְּכַנְפֵיהֶם֙ עַל־הַכַּפֹּ֔רֶת וּפְנֵיהֶ֖ם אִ֣ישׁ אֶל־אָחִ֑יו אֶל־הַכַּפֹּ֔רֶת הָי֖וּ

פְּנֵ֥י הַכְּרֻבִֽים:

י וַיַּ֥עַשׂ אֶת־הַשֻּׁלְחָ֖ן עֲצֵ֣י שִׁטִּ֑ים אַמָּתַ֤יִם אָרְכּוֹ֙ וְאַמָּ֣ה רָחְבּ֔וֹ וְאַמָּ֥ה וָחֵ֖צִי קֹמָתֽוֹ:

יא יב וַיְצַ֥ף אֹת֖וֹ זָהָ֣ב טָה֑וֹר וַיַּ֥עַשׂ ל֛וֹ זֵ֥ר זָהָ֖ב סָבִֽיב: וַיַּ֨עַשׂ ל֤וֹ מִסְגֶּ֨רֶת֙ טֹ֔פַח סָבִ֖יב וַיַּ֥עַשׂ

יג זֵר־זָהָ֛ב לְמִסְגַּרְתּ֖וֹ סָבִֽיב: וַיִּצֹ֣ק ל֗וֹ אַרְבַּע֙ טַבְּעֹ֣ת זָהָ֔ב וַיִּתֵּן֙ אֶת־הַטַּבָּעֹ֔ת עַ֚ל

יד אַרְבַּ֣ע הַפֵּאֹ֔ת אֲשֶׁ֖ר לְאַרְבַּ֣ע רַגְלָֽיו: לְעֻמַּת֙ הַמִּסְגֶּ֔רֶת הָי֖וּ הַטַּבָּעֹ֑ת בָּתִּים֙ לַבַּדִּ֔ים

טו לָשֵׂ֖את אֶת־הַשֻּׁלְחָֽן: וַיַּ֤עַשׂ אֶת־הַבַּדִּים֙ עֲצֵ֣י שִׁטִּ֔ים וַיְצַ֥ף אֹתָ֖ם זָהָ֑ב לָשֵׂ֖את אֶת־

טז הַשֻּׁלְחָֽן: וַיַּ֜עַשׂ אֶֽת־הַכֵּלִ֣ים ׀ אֲשֶׁ֣ר עַל־הַשֻּׁלְחָ֗ן אֶת־קְעָרֹתָ֤יו וְאֶת־כַּפֹּתָיו֙ וְאֵ֣ת

מְנַקִּיֹּתָ֔יו וְאֶת־הַקְּשָׂוֺ֔ת אֲשֶׁ֥ר יֻסַּ֖ךְ בָּהֵ֑ן זָהָ֥ב טָהֽוֹר:

קְצוֹתָ֖יו

<hr/>

פרק לו

א] וַיַּ֥עַשׂ בְּצַלְאֵ֛ל. לְפִי שֶׁנָּתַן נַפְשׁוֹ עַל הַמְּלָאכָה יוֹתֵר מִשְּׁאָר חֲכָמִים, נִקְרֵאת עַל שְׁמוֹ:

The Fashioning of the Candelabrum

EXODUS 37:17–24

Here, too, the verses depict the making of the vessel in accordance with the earlier instructions. The description of the fashioning of the candelabrum repeats with precision the details in the command to make it, with the exception of its function to provide light.

17 **He made the candelabrum of pure gold; hammered he**
Sixth aliya (Third aliya) **made the candelabrum,** not by casting or by joining separate
pieces, but by beating a single block of gold. From the same
block he even made **its base and its** central **shaft,** or all its
shafts; and **its cups, its knobs, and its flowers,** various decorations. All of these **were from it,** they were all fashioned from
the same block of gold.
18 **Six branches emerged from its sides: Three branches of the**
candelabrum from its one side and three branches of the
candelabrum from its second side;
19 **three finely crafted [*meshukkadim*]** ornamental **cups,** finely
wrought, or made like almond blossoms [*shekedim*],[19] **were on**
the one branch. In addition to the cups there was **a knob and**
a flower on each branch. **And** there were **three finely crafted**
cups on the other branch, with a knob and a flower. So it was
for the six branches that emerged from the candelabrum.
20 **On** the body of **the candelabrum,** its central shaft, **were four**
finely crafted cups, with **its knobs and its flowers;**

Illustration of candelabrum with straight branches, made by the Rambam in his Commentary on the Mishna

Candelabrum with curved branches, from a mosaic dating to the Talmudic era, in a synagogue in Susya, south Hebron Hills

21 **and** there was **a knob under two of the branches from it, a**
knob under two of the branches from it, and a knob under
two of the branches from it, for the six branches emerg-
ing from it. There was an ornamental knob where each pair of
branches met the central shaft.
22 **Their knobs and their branches,** the branches of the candelabrum, **were from it,** of one piece, **all of it hammered of pure**
gold.

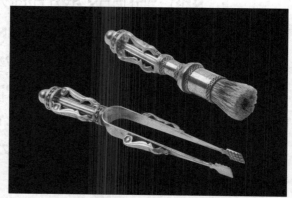

Tongs and brush for handling wicks and cleaning out oil lamps

23 **Fire-made its seven lamps,** receptacles atop the branches for
the oil and the wicks; **and its tongs,** for handling the wicks;
and its fire-pans, spoon-like receptacles for removing the
burnt wicks from the lamps and for cleaning the oil. These too
he made **of pure gold.**
24 **He made it and all its vessels of a talent of pure gold.** The
sum weight of the candelabrum and its vessels was one talent.
Modern estimates of a talent range from 30 to 50 kg.

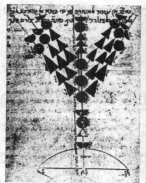

The Construction of the Incense Altar

EXODUS 37:25–29

The description of the fashioning of the vessels follows the order of their placement, from within the Sanctuary outward. Therefore, the incense altar appears immediately after the table for the showbread and the candelabrum, as like them it was located inside the Tent, but nearer to the entrance. This is followed by the preparation of the incense of sweet spices, which was burnt on this altar, as well as the anointing oil, which also required special knowledge for its preparation. As with the other vessels, the description here omits the function of these items, which was covered in the instructions (chaps. 25–30).

25 **He made the incense altar of acacia wood; its length was**
one cubit and its width one cubit, square, its height was two
cubits, and **its horns were from it.** The verse does not explain
the precise shape of the horns.[20]

ששי
/שלישי/

יז וַיַּעַשׂ אֶת־הַמְּנֹרָה זָהָב טָהוֹר מִקְשָׁה עָשָׂה אֶת־הַמְּנֹרָה יְרֵכָהּ וְקָנָהּ גְּבִיעֶיהָ
יח כַּפְתֹּרֶיהָ וּפְרָחֶיהָ מִמֶּנָּה הָיוּ: וְשִׁשָּׁה קָנִים יֹצְאִים מִצִּדֶּיהָ שְׁלֹשָׁה ׀ קְנֵי מְנֹרָה
יט מִצִּדָּהּ הָאֶחָד וּשְׁלֹשָׁה קְנֵי מְנֹרָה מִצִּדָּהּ הַשֵּׁנִי: שְׁלֹשָׁה גְבִעִים מְשֻׁקָּדִים בַּקָּנֶה
הָאֶחָד כַּפְתֹּר וָפֶרַח וּשְׁלֹשָׁה גְבִעִים מְשֻׁקָּדִים בְּקָנֶה אֶחָד כַּפְתֹּר וָפָרַח כֵּן לְשֵׁשֶׁת
כ הַקָּנִים הַיֹּצְאִים מִן־הַמְּנֹרָה: וּבַמְּנֹרָה אַרְבָּעָה גְבִעִים מְשֻׁקָּדִים כַּפְתֹּרֶיהָ וּפְרָחֶיהָ:
כא וְכַפְתֹּר תַּחַת שְׁנֵי הַקָּנִים מִמֶּנָּה וְכַפְתֹּר תַּחַת שְׁנֵי הַקָּנִים מִמֶּנָּה וְכַפְתֹּר תַּחַת־
כב שְׁנֵי הַקָּנִים מִמֶּנָּה לְשֵׁשֶׁת הַקָּנִים הַיֹּצְאִים מִמֶּנָּה: כַּפְתֹּרֵיהֶם וּקְנֹתָם מִמֶּנָּה הָיוּ
כג כֻּלָּהּ מִקְשָׁה אַחַת זָהָב טָהוֹר: וַיַּעַשׂ אֶת־נֵרֹתֶיהָ שִׁבְעָה וּמַלְקָחֶיהָ וּמַחְתֹּתֶיהָ
כד זָהָב טָהוֹר: כִּכָּר זָהָב טָהוֹר עָשָׂה אֹתָהּ וְאֵת כָּל־כֵּלֶיהָ:
כה וַיַּעַשׂ אֶת־מִזְבַּח הַקְּטֹרֶת עֲצֵי שִׁטִּים אַמָּה אָרְכּוֹ וְאַמָּה רָחְבּוֹ רָבוּעַ וְאַמָּתַיִם
כו קֹמָתוֹ מִמֶּנּוּ הָיוּ קַרְנֹתָיו: וַיְצַף אֹתוֹ זָהָב טָהוֹר אֶת־גַּגּוֹ וְאֶת־קִירֹתָיו סָבִיב וְאֶת־
כז קַרְנֹתָיו וַיַּעַשׂ לוֹ זֵר זָהָב סָבִיב: וּשְׁתֵּי טַבְּעֹת זָהָב עָשָׂה־לוֹ ׀ מִתַּחַת לְזֵרוֹ עַל
כח שְׁתֵּי צַלְעֹתָיו עַל שְׁנֵי צִדָּיו לְבָתִּים לְבַדִּים לָשֵׂאת אֹתוֹ בָּהֶם: וַיַּעַשׂ אֶת־הַבַּדִּים
כט עֲצֵי שִׁטִּים וַיְצַף אֹתָם זָהָב: וַיַּעַשׂ אֶת־שֶׁמֶן הַמִּשְׁחָה קֹדֶשׁ וְאֶת־קְטֹרֶת הַסַּמִּים

26 He plated it with pure gold: its top, its sides all around, and its horns; and he made a rim of gold upon it around, as he did for the ark and the table for the showbread.

27 He made two gold rings for it under its rim, on two of its corners and on two of its sides, on diagonally opposite corners, **as housings for** inserting **staves**, poles, **with which to carry it.** Since the incense altar was a small vessel, it did not require four rings, but only two.

28 He made the staves of acacia wood, and he plated them with gold.

29 He made the anointing oil in sanctity, taking care to preserve its sanctity and for the sake of anointing the sacred vessels and priests,[21] **and the incense of the spices, pure** of all waste and impurity.[22] Both were prepared with **the craftsmanship of a blender,** using precision and great care, like the work of an apothecary.

The Fashioning of the Altar of Burnt Offerings and Basin

EXODUS 38:1–8

Having detailed the building of the vessels that were placed inside the Sanctuary, the Torah describes the forming of the vessels situated nearby.

38
Seventh aliya
(Fourth aliya)

1 **He made the altar of the burnt offering** out **of acacia wood: Its length was five cubits and its width five cubits, square, and its height was three cubits** (see 27:1).

2 **He made its horns,** flat, square blocks,[23] **on its four corners: Its horns were from it,** not made from additional material joined to the altar; **and he plated it with bronze.**

3 **He made all the vessels of the altar: the pots; the shovels,** for removing the ashes; **the basins,** for collecting the blood of offerings and sprinkling it upon the altar; **the forks,** for placing pieces of meat upon the altar and turning them over; **and the pans,** for raking the coals and moving them from one place to another. **He made all its vessels of bronze.**

Basin for collecting the blood of an offering

4 **He made a grate for the altar,** made as **a work of bronze mesh. It was** placed **under its,** the altar's, **surrounding ledge from below, until its middle.**

5 **He cast four rings on the four ends for,** attached to, **the bronze grate as housings for the staves** for carrying the altar.

6 **He made the staves of acacia wood, and he plated them with bronze.**

7 **He brought the staves into the rings on the sides of the altar**

in order **to carry it with them; he made it hollow, out of planks.** The altar consisted of a wooden framework covered with bronze. Its hollow interior was filled with earth when the Israelites encamped.

Relative sizes of the golden altar, the ark, the table, the candelabrum, and the bronze altar, from left to right

8 **He made the basin of bronze and its base of bronze, with the mirrors of the assembled[D] women who assembled at the entrance of the Tent of Meeting.** These women brought their polished bronze mirrors to the Tabernacle as a gift, and the basin was fashioned from these mirrors.

The Formation of the Courtyard

EXODUS 38:9–20

After describing the building of the bronze altar and the basin and its base, which were located in the courtyard of the Tabernacle, the Torah describes the courtyard itself, which was a wide area surrounded by curtains.

9 **He made the courtyard; on the south side, the hangings of the courtyard were of spun linen,** and they were **one hundred cubits** in length, 50–60 m.

10 **Their pillars** for the hangings **were twenty,** placed at intervals of five cubits, **and their sockets,** for holding the pillars, were **twenty,** made **of bronze.** These sockets with their flat base held the pillars to prevent them from falling in the wind, in addition to the pegs, which were driven into the ground and tied down the hangings (see verse 20). **The hooks of the pillars,** to which the hangings were fastened, **and their bands,** which

surrounded the pillars for decoration or to prevent them from cracking,[24] **were** made of **silver.**

11 **On the north side, they,** the hangings, **were one hundred cubits,** and **their pillars** were **twenty and their sockets twenty, of bronze; the hooks of the pillars and their bands were silver.**

12 **On the west side,** along the breadth of the courtyard, where there was no entrance, **there were hangings of fifty cubits,** and **their pillars** were **ten and their sockets ten; the hooks of the pillars and their bands were** made of **silver.** Like the Tabernacle itself, the surrounding courtyard was rectangular.

שביעי
/רביעי/

א וַיַּעַשׂ אֶת־מִזְבַּח הָעֹלָה עֲצֵי שִׁטִּים חָמֵשׁ אַמּוֹת טָהוֹר מַעֲשֵׂה רֹקֵחַ:

ב אָרְכּוֹ וְחָמֵשׁ־אַמּוֹת רָחְבּוֹ רָבוּעַ וְשָׁלֹשׁ אַמּוֹת קֹמָתוֹ: וַיַּעַשׂ קַרְנֹתָיו עַל אַרְבַּע

ג פִּנֹּתָיו מִמֶּנּוּ הָיוּ קַרְנֹתָיו וַיְצַף אֹתוֹ נְחֹשֶׁת: וַיַּעַשׂ אֶת־כָּל־כְּלֵי הַמִּזְבֵּחַ אֶת־הַסִּירֹת וְאֶת־הַיָּעִים וְאֶת־הַמִּזְרָקֹת אֶת־הַמִּזְלָגֹת וְאֶת־הַמַּחְתֹּת כָּל־כֵּלָיו עָשָׂה נְחֹשֶׁת:

ד וַיַּעַשׂ לַמִּזְבֵּחַ מִכְבָּר מַעֲשֵׂה רֶשֶׁת נְחֹשֶׁת תַּחַת כַּרְכֻּבּוֹ מִלְּמַטָּה עַד־חֶצְיוֹ: וַיִּצֹק

ה אַרְבַּע טַבָּעֹת בְּאַרְבַּע הַקְּצָוֹת לְמִכְבַּר הַנְּחֹשֶׁת בָּתִּים לַבַּדִּים: וַיַּעַשׂ אֶת־הַבַּדִּים

ו עֲצֵי שִׁטִּים וַיְצַף אֹתָם נְחֹשֶׁת: וַיָּבֵא אֶת־הַבַּדִּים בַּטַּבָּעֹת עַל צַלְעֹת הַמִּזְבֵּחַ

ז לָשֵׂאת אֹתוֹ בָּהֶם נְבוּב לֻחֹת עָשָׂה אֹתוֹ: וַיַּעַשׂ אֵת הַכִּיּוֹר נְחֹשֶׁת וְאֵת

ח כַּנּוֹ נְחֹשֶׁת בְּמַרְאֹת הַצֹּבְאֹת אֲשֶׁר צָבְאוּ פֶּתַח אֹהֶל מוֹעֵד: וַיַּעַשׂ

ט אֶת־הֶחָצֵר לִפְאַת | נֶגֶב תֵּימָנָה קַלְעֵי הֶחָצֵר שֵׁשׁ מָשְׁזָר מֵאָה בָּאַמָּה: עַמּוּדֵיהֶם

י עֶשְׂרִים וְאַדְנֵיהֶם עֶשְׂרִים נְחֹשֶׁת וָוֵי הָעַמֻּדִים וַחֲשֻׁקֵיהֶם כָּסֶף: וְלִפְאַת צָפוֹן מֵאָה בָאַמָּה עַמּוּדֵיהֶם עֶשְׂרִים וְאַדְנֵיהֶם עֶשְׂרִים נְחֹשֶׁת וָוֵי הָעַמּוּדִים וַחֲשֻׁקֵיהֶם

יא כָּסֶף: וְלִפְאַת־יָם קְלָעִים חֲמִשִּׁים בָּאַמָּה עַמֻּדֵיהֶם עֲשָׂרָה וְאַדְנֵיהֶם עֲשָׂרָה

רש"י

פרק לח

ז **נבוב לחת.** נָבוּב הוּא חָלוּל, וְכֵן: "וַעֲבָיוֹ אַרְבַּע אֶצְבָּעוֹת נָבוּב" (ירמיה נ, כא). **נבוב לחת.** הַלּוּחוֹת שֶׁל עֲצֵי שִׁטִּים לְכָל רוּחַ, וְהֶחָלָל בָּאֶמְצַע:

ח **במראת הצבאת.** בְּנוֹת יִשְׂרָאֵל הָיוּ בְּיָדָן מַרְאוֹת שֶׁרוֹאוֹת בָּהֶן כְּשֶׁהֵן מִתְקַשְּׁטוֹת, וְאַף אוֹתָן לֹא עִכְּבוּ מִלְּהָבִיא לְנִדְבַת הַמִּשְׁכָּן, וְהָיָה מוֹאֵס מֹשֶׁה בָּהֶן מִפְּנֵי שֶׁעֲשׂוּיִים לְיֵצֶר הָרָע. אָמַר לוֹ הַקָּדוֹשׁ בָּרוּךְ הוּא: קַבֵּל,

כִּי אֵלּוּ חֲבִיבִין עָלַי מִן הַכֹּל, שֶׁעַל יְדֵיהֶם הֶעֱמִידוּ הַנָּשִׁים צְבָאוֹת רַבּוֹת בְּמִצְרַיִם. כְּשֶׁהָיוּ בַּעְלֵיהֶן יְגֵעִים בַּעֲבוֹדַת פֶּרֶךְ בַּשָּׂדֶה, הָיוּ הוֹלְכוֹת וּמוֹלִיכוֹת לָהֶם מַאֲכָל וּמִשְׁתֶּה וּמַאֲכִילוֹת אוֹתָם, וְנוֹטְלוֹת הַמַּרְאוֹת, וְכָל אַחַת רוֹאָה עַצְמָהּ עִם בַּעְלָהּ בַּמַּרְאָה, וּמְשַׁדַּלְתּוֹ בִּדְבָרִים: אֲנִי נָאָה מִמְּךָ, וּמִתּוֹךְ כָּךְ מְבִיאוֹת אוֹתָם לִידֵי תַּאֲוָה וְנִזְקָקוֹת לָהֶם וּמִתְעַבְּרוֹת וְיוֹלְדוֹת שָׁם, שֶׁנֶּאֱמַר: "תַּחַת הַתַּפּוּחַ עוֹרַרְתִּיךָ" (שיר השירים ח, ה), וְזֶהוּ שֶׁנֶּאֱמַר: "בְּמַרְאֹת הַצֹּבְאֹת". וְנַעֲשָׂה הַכִּיּוֹר מֵהֶם שֶׁהוּא לָשׂוּם שָׁלוֹם בֵּין

אִישׁ לְאִשְׁתּוֹ, לְהַשְׁקוֹת מִמַּיִם שֶׁבְּתוֹכוֹ אֶת שֶׁקִּנֵּא לָהּ בַּעְלָהּ. וְתֵדַע לְךָ שֶׁהֵן מַרְאוֹת מַמָּשׁ, שֶׁהֲרֵי נֶאֱמַר: "וּנְחֹשֶׁת הַתְּנוּפָה שִׁבְעִים כִּכָּר וְגוֹ' וַיַּעַשׂ בָּהּ" וְגוֹ' (להלן פסוקים כט-לא), וְכִיּוֹר וְכַנּוֹ לֹא הֻזְכַּר שָׁם, לְמַדְתָּ שֶׁלֹּא הָיָה נְחֹשֶׁת שֶׁל כִּיּוֹר מִנְּחֹשֶׁת הַתְּנוּפָה. כָּךְ דָּרַשׁ רַבִּי תַּנְחוּמָא (פקודי ט). וְכֵן תִּרְגֵּם אוּנְקְלוֹס: "בְּמֶחְזְיַת נְשַׁיָּא", וְהוּא תַּרְגּוּם שֶׁל 'מַרְאוֹת', מִירֹא"ש בְּלַעַז. וְכֵן מָצִינוּ בִּישַׁעְיָה: "וְהַגִּלְיֹנִים" (ג, כג) מְתַרְגְּמִינָן: "וּמֶחְזְיָתָא": **אשר צבאו.** לְהָבִיא נִדְבָתָן:

DISCUSSION

38:8 | Assembled: This is apparently referring to special women who permanently stationed themselves at the entrance to the Tent of Meeting. They may have dedicated themselves to a life of holiness, and they were habitually found near the place where God appeared. By donating to the Tabernacle their bronze mirrors, which were certainly objects of great sentimental value for them, they demonstrated their willingness to serve God with utmost dedication (see Onkelos; *Targum Yonatan*; Ibn Ezra, long commentary on Exodus; Ramban).

13 **On the east side,** where the entrance to the courtyard of the Tent of Meeting was located, the total width of the Tabernacle was **fifty cubits.**

14 This side had to accommodate the courtyard entrance in its center. It consisted of **hangings fifteen cubits** long **on the** one **side** of the entrance; **their pillars were three and their sockets three,** each pillar placed at intervals of five cubits.

15 The same number of hangings were positioned **on the second side** of the entrance; **from this side and from that side of the gate of the courtyard, the hangings were fifteen cubits; their pillars were three and their sockets three.** This left an entrance twenty cubits long in the middle.

16 **All the hangings of the courtyard all around were of spun linen.**

17 **The sockets for the pillars were bronze, the hooks of the pillars and their bands were silver, the plating of their tops was silver, and all the pillars of the courtyard were banded with silver.**

18 *Maftir* As stated above, the eastern side of the courtyard of the Tabernacle included fifteen cubits of hangings on each side of the gate, with twenty cubits occupied by the space of the gate itself. **The screen of the gate of the courtyard was the craftsmanship of an embroiderer.** The screen was more decorated than the hangings, and it was made **of sky-blue, purple, and scarlet wool, and linen,** all finely **spun together.** It was **twenty cubits** in **length, and standing at the width of five cubits, corresponding to the hangings of the courtyard,** the screen was between the hangings, on the same plane as them.

19 **Their pillars,**[D] the pillars for the screen, **were four and their sockets four, of bronze; their hooks were silver, and the plating of their tops and their bands were silver.** In contrast to the hangings, which were fixed to the pillars, the screen was tied only above, to enable it to be rolled up, permitting entry between the pillars.

20 **All the pegs of the Tabernacle and of the courtyard around,** with which the hangings were fixed in place, **were** made of **bronze.**

Maftir on Shabbat Shekalim is read from Exodus 30:11–16. Maftir on Shabbat Para is read from Numbers 19:1–22. Maftir on Shabbat HaHodesh is read from Exodus 12:1–20.

DISCUSSION

38:19 | **Their pillars:** The verse uses the plural form, "their pillars," even though it means the pillars for the single screen, to parallel similar expressions in adjacent verses. See the informative article in Hebrew by Meir ben Ori: "The Pillars of the Tabernacle Courtyard," *Beit Mikra*, vol. 85.

יג יד וָוֵי הָעַמֻּדִים וַחֲשׁוּקֵיהֶם כָּסֶף: וְלִפְאַת קֵדְמָה מִזְרָחָה חֲמִשִּׁים אַמָּה: קְלָעִים

טו חֲמֵשׁ־עֶשְׂרֵה אַמָּה אֶל־הַכָּתֵף עַמּוּדֵיהֶם שְׁלֹשָׁה וְאַדְנֵיהֶם שְׁלֹשָׁה: וְלַכָּתֵף

הַשֵּׁנִית מִזֶּה וּמִזֶּה לְשַׁעַר הֶחָצֵר קְלָעִים חֲמֵשׁ עֶשְׂרֵה אַמָּה עַמֻּדֵיהֶם שְׁלֹשָׁה

טז יז וְאַדְנֵיהֶם שְׁלֹשָׁה: כָּל־קַלְעֵי הֶחָצֵר סָבִיב שֵׁשׁ מָשְׁזָר: וְהָאֲדָנִים לָעַמֻּדִים נְחֹשֶׁת

וָוֵי הָעַמּוּדִים וַחֲשׁוּקֵיהֶם כֶּסֶף וְצִפּוּי רָאשֵׁיהֶם כָּסֶף וְהֵם מְחֻשָּׁקִים כֶּסֶף כֹּל עַמֻּדֵי

יח הֶחָצֵר: וּמָסַךְ שַׁעַר הֶחָצֵר מַעֲשֵׂה רֹקֵם תְּכֵלֶת וְאַרְגָּמָן וְתוֹלַעַת שָׁנִי וְשֵׁשׁ מָשְׁזָר מפטיר

יט וְעֶשְׂרִים אַמָּה אֹרֶךְ וְקוֹמָה בְרֹחַב חָמֵשׁ אַמּוֹת לְעֻמַּת קַלְעֵי הֶחָצֵר: וְעַמֻּדֵיהֶם

אַרְבָּעָה וְאַדְנֵיהֶם אַרְבָּעָה נְחֹשֶׁת וָוֵיהֶם כֶּסֶף וְצִפּוּי רָאשֵׁיהֶם וַחֲשֻׁקֵיהֶם כָּסֶף:

כ וְכָל־הַיְתֵדֹת לַמִּשְׁכָּן וְלֶחָצֵר סָבִיב נְחֹשֶׁת:

רש"י

יח | לְעֻמַּת קַלְעֵי הֶחָצֵר. כְּמִדַּת קַלְעֵי הֶחָצֵר:

Parashat
Pekudei

The Accounts of the Tabernacle
EXODUS 38:21–39:1

In this section the Torah provides an accounting of the materials used in the construction of the Tabernacle, its vessels and their accompanying implements. Perhaps the recording of these details is meant to stress the importance of transparency with regard to all matters involving donations and volunteer work, as the materials and labor for the Tabernacle were given freely by the people.

21 **These are the reckonings,** the details of the materials used in the construction **of the Tabernacle, the Tabernacle of the Testimony, as they were reckoned,** or instructed, **at the directive of Moses: The service of the Levites was in the hand of Itamar son of Aaron the priest.** Moses delivered these quantities of materials to the Levites, headed by Itamar.[1]

22 **Betzalel, son of Uri, son of Hur, of the tribe of Judah** was not only responsible for the entire project, but he also **made everything** himself, including the designs and perhaps all of the important vessels **that the Lord had commanded Moses.**[2]

23 **With him was Oholiav son of Ahisamakh, of the tribe of Dan,** who was **a carpenter and a craftsman,** one who could help design the vessels, **and an embroiderer in the sky-blue, purple, and scarlet wool, and in the linen.**

24 The accounting begins: **All the gold that was used for the work, in all the sacred work, the gold of the donation,** the gold raised as a gift offering (see above 35:22), **was twenty-nine talents and seven hundred and thirty shekels in the sacred shekel,** whose weight is double that of the regular shekel.[3] A talent is between 30 and 50 kg.

25 **The silver of those who were counted of the congregation was one hundred talents and one thousand seven hundred and seventy-five shekels, in the sacred shekel.**

26 **One beka** weight **was** donated **per head,** by each person; one *beka* is equal to **half** of **a shekel in the sacred shekel.**[D] A *beka* was given **for everyone who passed among the counted,**[D] who was included in the census, **from twenty years old and above, for six hundred thousand three thousand five hundred and fifty.**

27 **The one hundred talents of silver were to cast the sockets of the Sanctuary,** the central structure of the Tabernacle,[4] **and the sockets of the curtain.** Therefore there were **one hundred sockets for one hundred talents, one talent for a socket.**

28 **Of the** remaining **one thousand seven hundred and seventy-five** silver shekels, **he made hooks for the pillars and plated their tops and banded them.** Only a small amount of silver was required for decorating the pillars.

29 **The donated bronze was seventy talents and two thousand four hundred shekels.**

30 **He made with it,** with the bronze, **the sockets of the entrance of the Tent of Meeting, the bronze altar, its bronze grate, all the vessels of the altar,**

31 **the sockets of the courtyard around, the sockets of the gate of the courtyard, all the pegs of the Tabernacle, and all the pegs of the courtyard around.**

DISCUSSION

38:26 | **In the sacred shekel:** The talent is a unit of weight equivalent to sixty *maneh*. From here, and from other sources, it is derived that the weight of the *maneh* of the Sanctuary was fifty shekels. Accordingly, the weight of each talent was three thousand shekels, or six thousand half-shekels, and the six hundred thousand half-shekels collected from the people amounted to one hundred talents (see *Bekhorot* 5a; Rashbam, 38:25). A shekel of the Sanctuary is equal to approximately 20 grams.

For everyone who passed among the counted: In the Jerusalem Talmud (*Shekalim* 1:3) this phrase is interpreted as a reference to those who passed through the Red Sea. According to the plain meaning of the verse, it is possible that this phrase reflects the manner in which people or animals are counted, namely by having them pass through a narrow entrance (see Leviticus 27:32).

פרשת

פְקוּדֵי

כח אֵלֶּה פְקוּדֵי הַמִּשְׁכָּן מִשְׁכַּן הָעֵדֻת אֲשֶׁר פֻּקַּד עַל־פִּי מֹשֶׁה עֲבֹדַת הַלְוִיִּם בְּיַד

כב אִיתָמָר בֶּן־אַהֲרֹן הַכֹּהֵן: וּבְצַלְאֵל בֶּן־אוּרִי בֶן־חוּר לְמַטֵּה יְהוּדָה עָשָׂה אֵת

כג כָּל־אֲשֶׁר־צִוָּה יְהוָה אֶת־מֹשֶׁה: וְאִתּוֹ אָהֳלִיאָב בֶּן־אֲחִיסָמָךְ לְמַטֵּה־דָן חָרָשׁ

כד וְחֹשֵׁב וְרֹקֵם בַּתְּכֵלֶת וּבָאַרְגָּמָן וּבְתוֹלַעַת הַשָּׁנִי וּבַשֵּׁשׁ: כָּל־הַזָּהָב הֶעָשׂוּי לַמְּלָאכָה בְּכֹל מְלֶאכֶת הַקֹּדֶשׁ וַיְהִי ׀ זְהַב הַתְּנוּפָה תֵּשַׁע וְעֶשְׂרִים כִּכָּר

כה וּשְׁבַע מֵאוֹת וּשְׁלֹשִׁים שֶׁקֶל בְּשֶׁקֶל הַקֹּדֶשׁ: וְכֶסֶף פְּקוּדֵי הָעֵדָה מְאַת כִּכָּר וְאֶלֶף

כו וּשְׁבַע מֵאוֹת וַחֲמִשָּׁה וְשִׁבְעִים שֶׁקֶל בְּשֶׁקֶל הַקֹּדֶשׁ: בֶּקַע לַגֻּלְגֹּלֶת מַחֲצִית הַשֶּׁקֶל בְּשֶׁקֶל הַקֹּדֶשׁ לְכֹל הָעֹבֵר עַל־הַפְּקֻדִים מִבֶּן עֶשְׂרִים שָׁנָה וָמַעְלָה לְשֵׁשׁ־מֵאוֹת אֶלֶף וּשְׁלֹשֶׁת אֲלָפִים וַחֲמֵשׁ מֵאוֹת וַחֲמִשִּׁים:

כז וַיְהִי מְאַת כִּכַּר הַכֶּסֶף לָצֶקֶת אֵת אַדְנֵי הַקֹּדֶשׁ וְאֵת אַדְנֵי הַפָּרֹכֶת מְאַת אֲדָנִים לִמְאַת הַכִּכָּר כִּכָּר לָאָדֶן: וְאֶת־

כח הָאֶלֶף וּשְׁבַע הַמֵּאוֹת וַחֲמִשָּׁה וְשִׁבְעִים עָשָׂה וָוִים לָעַמּוּדִים וְצִפָּה רָאשֵׁיהֶם

כט וְחִשַּׁק אֹתָם: וּנְחֹשֶׁת הַתְּנוּפָה שִׁבְעִים כִּכָּר וְאַלְפַּיִם וְאַרְבַּע־מֵאוֹת שָׁקֶל:

ל וַיַּעַשׂ בָּהּ אֶת־אַדְנֵי פֶּתַח אֹהֶל מוֹעֵד וְאֵת מִזְבַּח הַנְּחֹשֶׁת וְאֶת־מִכְבַּר הַנְּחֹשֶׁת

לא אֲשֶׁר־לוֹ וְאֵת כָּל־כְּלֵי הַמִּזְבֵּחַ: וְאֶת־אַדְנֵי הֶחָצֵר סָבִיב וְאֶת־אַדְנֵי שַׁעַר הֶחָצֵר

רש״י

כא | **אֵלֶּה פְקוּדֵי.** בְּפָרָשָׁה זוֹ נִמְנוּ כָּל מִשְׁקְלֵי נִדְבַת הַמִּשְׁכָּן לַכֶּסֶף, לַזָּהָב וְלַנְּחֹשֶׁת, וְנִמְנוּ כָּל כֵּלָיו לְכָל עֲבוֹדָתוֹ: **הַמִּשְׁכָּן מִשְׁכַּן.** שְׁנֵי פְעָמִים, רֶמֶז לַמִּקְדָּשׁ שֶׁנִּתְמַשְׁכֵּן בִּשְׁנֵי חֻרְבָּנִין עַל עֲוֹנוֹתֵיהֶן שֶׁל יִשְׂרָאֵל: **מִשְׁכַּן הָעֵדֻת.** עֵדוּת לְיִשְׂרָאֵל שֶׁוִּתֵּר לָהֶם הַקָּדוֹשׁ בָּרוּךְ הוּא עַל מַעֲשֵׂה הָעֵגֶל, שֶׁהֲרֵי הִשְׁרָה שְׁכִינָתוֹ בֵּינֵיהֶם: **עֲבֹדַת הַלְוִיִּם.** פְּקוּדֵי הַמִּשְׁכָּן וְכֵלָיו הִיא עֲבוֹדָה הַמְּסוּרָה לַלְוִיִּם בַּמִּדְבָּר, לָשֵׂאת וּלְהוֹרִיד וּלְהָקִים אִישׁ אִישׁ לְמַשָּׂאוֹ הַמֻּפְקָד עָלָיו, כְּמוֹ שֶׁאָמוּר בְּפָרָשַׁת נָשֹׂא (במדבר ד): **בְּיַד אִיתָמָר.** הוּא הָיָה פָקוּד עֲלֵיהֶם, לִמְסֹר לְכָל בֵּית אָב עֲבוֹדָה שֶׁעָלָיו:

כב | **וּבְצַלְאֵל בֶּן־אוּרִי... עָשָׂה.** **אֵת** כָּל אֲשֶׁר עָשָׂה אֹתוֹ

כג | מֹשֶׁה אֵין כְּתִיב כָּאן אֶלָּא **אֵת** כָּל אֲשֶׁר עָשָׂה ה', אֵת מֹשֶׁה, אֲפִלּוּ דְּבָרִים שֶׁלֹּא אָמַר לוֹ רַבּוֹ הִסְכִּימָה דַּעְתּוֹ לְמַה שֶּׁנֶּאֱמַר לְמֹשֶׁה בְּסִינַי:

כד | **כִּכָּר.** שִׁשִּׁים מָנֶה. וּמָנֶה שֶׁל קֹדֶשׁ כָּפוּל הָיָה, הֲרֵי הַכִּכָּר מֵאָה וְעֶשְׂרִים מָנֶה, וְהַמָּנֶה עֶשְׂרִים וַחֲמִשָּׁה סְלָעִים, הֲרֵי כִּכָּר שֶׁל קֹדֶשׁ שְׁלֹשֶׁת אֲלָפִים שֵׁשׁ מֵאוֹת שְׁקָלִים, לְפִיכָךְ מָנֶה בִּפְרוֹטְרוֹט כָּל הַשְּׁקָלִים שֶׁפְּחִיתוּתָן בְּמִנְיָנָן מִשְּׁלֹשֶׁת אֲלָפִים שֶׁאֵין מַגִּיעִין לְכִכָּר:

כו | **בֶּקַע.** הוּא שֵׁם מִשְׁקָל שֶׁל מַחֲצִית הַשֶּׁקֶל: **לְשֵׁשׁ מֵאוֹת אֶלֶף וְגוֹ'.** כָּךְ הָיוּ יִשְׂרָאֵל, וְכָךְ עָלָה מִנְיָנָם אַחַר שֶׁהוּקַם הַמִּשְׁכָּן בְּסֵפֶר וַיְדַבֵּר (במדבר א, מו), וְאַף עַתָּה בְּנִדְבַת הַמִּשְׁכָּן כָּךְ הָיוּ. וּמִנְיַן חֲצָאֵי הַשְּׁקָלִים שֶׁל שֵׁשׁ

כו | מֵאוֹת אֶלֶף עוֹלֶה מְאַת כִּכָּר, כָּל אֶחָד שֶׁל שְׁלֹשֶׁת אֲלָפִים שְׁקָלִים. כֵּיצַד? שֵׁשׁ מֵאוֹת אֶלֶף חֲצָאִין, הֲרֵי הֵן שְׁלֹשׁ מֵאוֹת אֶלֶף שְׁלֵמִים, וְהִשְׁלֹשֶׁת אֲלָפִים וַחֲמֵשׁ מֵאוֹת וַחֲמִשִּׁים חֲצָאִין, עוֹלִין אֶלֶף וְשֶׁבַע מֵאוֹת וַחֲמִשָּׁה וְשִׁבְעִים שְׁקָלִים:

כו | **לָצֶקֶת.** "לַתְחָבֵך". שֶׁל קֹדֶשׁ הַמִּשְׁכָּן, שֶׁהֵם אַרְבָּעִים וּשְׁמוֹנֶה קְרָשִׁים וְלָהֶן תִּשְׁעִים וְשִׁשָּׁה אֲדָנִים, וְאַדְנֵי הַפָּרֹכֶת אַרְבָּעָה, הֲרֵי מֵאָה. וְכָל שְׁאָר הָאֲדָנִים נְחֹשֶׁת כָּתוּב בָּהֶם:

כח | **וְצִפָּה רָאשֵׁיהֶם.** שֶׁל עַמּוּדִים מֵהֶם, שֶׁבְּכֻלָּן כָּתוּב וְצִפָּה רָאשֵׁיהֶם וַחֲשׁוּקֵיהֶם כָּסֶף (עיין לעיל לח, יז):

39 1 **From the sky-blue, purple, and scarlet wool they made woven,** or mesh,[5] **fabrics for service in the Sanctuary.** This refers to the coverings of the Tabernacle, the screen of the gate of the Tabernacle, and the cloths that covered the vessels during the Israelites' travels. **They** also **made the sacred vestments for Aaron, as the Lord commanded Moses.**

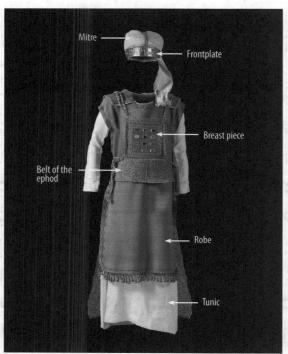

Vestments of the High Priest, front view

Mitre
Frontplate
Breast piece
Belt of the ephod
Robe
Tunic

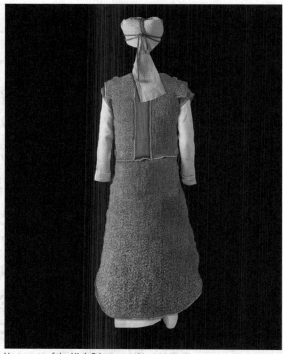

Vestments of the High Priest, rear view

The Making of the Priestly Vestments

EXODUS 39:2–31

After enumerating the materials used to construct the Tabernacle itself, the Torah turns to the other main use of the donated fabrics, metals, and precious stones: The production of the garments of the High Priest. It would seem that the ephod was considered the High Priest's principal garment, as the other garments are associated with it. The breast piece is tied to the ephod, and the robe is referred to as the "robe of the ephod" (see 28:31, 39:22). Following this, the Torah will describe the production of the vestments of the ordinary priests.

Second aliya (Fifth aliya) 2 **He made the ephod of gold,** and of **sky-blue, purple, and scarlet wool, and linen,** all **spun together.** It is difficult to combine gold threads with interwoven wool and linen threads. No earlier use of gold for a similar purpose is known.[6]

3 This may have been the first use of this complex technique: **They hammered out the sheets of gold, and then cut wires to work in,** to weave, **with the sky-blue wool, with the purple wool, with the scarlet wool, and with the linen.** This was **artfully crafted,** as it involved unique craftsmanship.

4 **They made shoulder pieces for it,** the ephod, and **attached** it; **it was attached at the two ends.** The ephod, which resembled an apron or a skirt, was held in place by the two shoulder pieces.

5 **The belt of his ephod that is on it is from it;** the belt was not fashioned separately, but was part of the woven fabric of the ephod; and therefore, the band was made **like its work,** in the same manner as the ephod: Of **gold,** and of **sky-blue, purple, and scarlet wool, and linen, spun together as the Lord had commanded Moses.**

6 **They made the onyx stones surrounded with settings of gold.** These stones were **engraved with the engravings of a signet.** Each was engraved with writing, like a seal, **with the names** of the tribes **of the children of Israel.**

7 **He placed them on the shoulder pieces of the ephod as stones of remembrance for the children of Israel,** as these

א וְאֵת כָּל־יִתְדֹת הַמִּשְׁכָּן וְאֶת־כָּל־יִתְדֹת הֶחָצֵר סָבִיב׃ וּמִן־הַתְּכֵלֶת וְהָאַרְגָּמָן
וְתוֹלַעַת הַשָּׁנִי עָשׂוּ בִגְדֵי־שְׂרָד לְשָׁרֵת בַּקֹּדֶשׁ וַיַּעֲשׂוּ אֶת־בִּגְדֵי הַקֹּדֶשׁ אֲשֶׁר
לְאַהֲרֹן כַּאֲשֶׁר צִוָּה יְהוָה אֶת־מֹשֶׁה׃
ב וַיַּעַשׂ אֶת־הָאֵפֹד זָהָב תְּכֵלֶת וְאַרְגָּמָן וְתוֹלַעַת שָׁנִי וְשֵׁשׁ מָשְׁזָר׃ וַיְרַקְּעוּ אֶת־ שני/חמישי/
ג פַּחֵי הַזָּהָב וְקִצֵּץ פְּתִילִם לַעֲשׂוֹת בְּתוֹךְ הַתְּכֵלֶת וּבְתוֹךְ הָאַרְגָּמָן וּבְתוֹךְ תּוֹלַעַת
ד הַשָּׁנִי וּבְתוֹךְ הַשֵּׁשׁ מַעֲשֵׂה חֹשֵׁב׃ כְּתֵפֹת עָשׂוּ־לוֹ חֹבְרֹת עַל־שְׁנֵי קצוותו חֻבָּר׃ קְצוֹתָיו
ה וְחֵשֶׁב אֲפֻדָּתוֹ אֲשֶׁר עָלָיו מִמֶּנּוּ הוּא כְּמַעֲשֵׂהוּ זָהָב תְּכֵלֶת וְאַרְגָּמָן וְתוֹלַעַת שָׁנִי
ו וְשֵׁשׁ מָשְׁזָר כַּאֲשֶׁר צִוָּה יְהוָה אֶת־מֹשֶׁה׃ וַיַּעֲשׂוּ אֶת־אַבְנֵי הַשֹּׁהַם
ז מֻסַבֹּת מִשְׁבְּצֹת זָהָב מְפֻתָּחֹת פִּתּוּחֵי חוֹתָם עַל־שְׁמוֹת בְּנֵי יִשְׂרָאֵל׃ וַיָּשֶׂם
אֹתָם עַל כִּתְפֹת הָאֵפֹד אַבְנֵי זִכָּרוֹן לִבְנֵי יִשְׂרָאֵל כַּאֲשֶׁר צִוָּה יְהוָה אֶת־מֹשֶׁה׃
ח וַיַּעַשׂ אֶת־הַחֹשֶׁן מַעֲשֵׂה חֹשֵׁב כְּמַעֲשֵׂה אֵפֹד זָהָב תְּכֵלֶת וְאַרְגָּמָן וְתוֹלַעַת שָׁנִי
ט וְשֵׁשׁ מָשְׁזָר׃ רָבוּעַ הָיָה כָּפוּל עָשׂוּ אֶת־הַחֹשֶׁן זֶרֶת אָרְכּוֹ וְזֶרֶת רָחְבּוֹ כָּפוּל׃
י יא וַיְמַלְאוּ־בוֹ אַרְבָּעָה טוּרֵי אָבֶן טוּר אֹדֶם פִּטְדָה וּבָרֶקֶת הַטּוּר הָאֶחָד׃ וְהַטּוּר
יב יג הַשֵּׁנִי נֹפֶךְ סַפִּיר וְיָהֲלֹם׃ וְהַטּוּר הַשְּׁלִישִׁי לֶשֶׁם שְׁבוֹ וְאַחְלָמָה׃ וְהַטּוּר הָרְבִיעִי

רש״י

פרק לט

א] וּמִן הַתְּכֵלֶת וְהָאַרְגָּמָן וְגוֹ׳. שֵׁשׁ לֹא נֶאֱמַר כָּאן; מִכָּאן אֲנִי אוֹמֵר שֶׁאֵין בִּגְדֵי שְׂרָד הַלָּלוּ בִּגְדֵי כְהֻנָּה, שֶׁבְּבִגְדֵי כְהֻנָּה הָיָה שֵׁשׁ, אֶלָּא הֵם בְּגָדִים שֶׁמְּכַסִּים בָּהֶם כְּלֵי הַקֹּדֶשׁ בִּשְׁעַת סִלּוּק מַסָּעוֹת, שֶׁלֹּא הָיָה בָהֶם שֵׁשׁ:

ג] וַיְרַקְּעוּ. כְּמוֹ: "לְרֹקַע הָאָרֶץ" (תהלים קלו, ו), כְּתַרְגּוּמוֹ "וְרַדִּידוּ". טַסִּין הָיוּ מְרַדְּדִין מִן הַזָּהָב, אשטנדר"א בְּלַעַז, טַסִּין דַּקּוֹת. כָּךְ הוּא מְלַמֶּדְךָ הֵיאַךְ הָיוּ טוֹוִין אֶת הַזָּהָב עִם הַחוּטִין: מְרַדְּדִין הַטַּסִּין דַּקִּין, וְקוֹצְצִין מֵהֶן פְּתִילִים לְאֹרֶךְ הַטַּס, לַעֲשׂוֹת אוֹתָן פְּתִילִים תַּעֲרֹבֶת עִם כָּל מִין וָמִין בַּחֹשֶׁן וְהָאֵפוֹד, שֶׁנֶּאֱמַר בָּהֶן "זָהָב" (לעיל כח, ו; טו), חוּט אֶחָד שֶׁל זָהָב עִם שִׁשָּׁה חוּטִין שֶׁל תְּכֵלֶת, וְכֵן עִם כָּל מִין וָמִין, שֶׁכָּל הַמִּינִים חוּטָן כָּפוּל שִׁשָּׁה, וְהַזָּהָב חוּט שְׁבִיעִי עִם כָּל אֶחָד וְאֶחָד:

stones bore their names, **as the Lord had commanded Moses.**

8 **He made the breast piece, artfully crafted, like the work of the ephod,** with the same materials: **Gold, and sky-blue, purple, and scarlet wool, and linen, spun together.**

9 **It was square; they made the breast piece folded,** such that it formed a pouch into which, according to tradition, holy names were inserted;[7] **its length a span and its width a span, folded.** A span [*zeret*] is approximately half a cubit, slightly more than 20 cm. It is roughly the distance between the tip of one's little finger [*zeret*] and the tip of one's thumb, when one spreads his fingers to their full extent.

10 **They mounted in it,** the breast piece, **four rows of stones: A row of a ruby, a peridot, and an emerald, the first row;**

11 **and the second row: a carbuncle, a sapphire, and a clear quartz;**

12 **and the third row: a jacinth, an agate and an amethyst;**

13 **and the fourth row: a beryl, an onyx, and a chalcedony; surrounded in settings of gold in their mountings.** Each

stone was placed in a gold setting, which held it in place in one of the rows.

14 **The stones** of the breast piece, like the onyx stones, **were according to the names of the children of Israel; they were twelve, according to their names, the engravings of a signet, each man according to his name, for the twelve tribes.** On each stone the name of one tribe was engraved.

15 **They crafted bordering chains on the breast piece, of braided craftsmanship,** they formed twined cords, not linked chains, made **of pure gold.**

16 **They crafted two settings of gold and two gold rings, and they put the two rings at the two ends of the breast piece.**

17 **They put the two braids,** cords, **of gold on the two rings at the ends of the breast piece.**

18 **The two ends of the two braids they put on the two settings,** and they put them, the settings, **on the shoulder pieces of the ephod, toward its front.**

19 **They made two** additional **gold rings and they put them on the two ends of the breast piece, on its edge that was toward the ephod, on the inner side.**

20 **They made** another **two gold rings and they put them on the two shoulder pieces of the ephod from below, toward its front, adjacent to its seam, above the belt of the ephod.**

21 **They attached the breast piece with its rings to the rings of the ephod with a thread of sky-blue wool, to be on the belt of the ephod.** The breast piece was tied to the shoulder pieces by its upper rings and to the ephod by its lower rings. In this manner it was ensured that **the breast piece would not be detached from the ephod, as the Lord had commanded Moses.** Alternatively, it was prohibited for the breast piece to be loosened from the ephod.[8]

Third aliya (Sixth aliya) 22 **He made the robe of the ephod,** the robe upon which the ephod is bound and which fastens it, **of woven work, entirely of sky-blue wool** threads.

23 **The opening of the robe was** made **within it;** the edge of the robe was folded over into the garment and hemmed, **like the opening of a coat of mail,**[9] which was also folded inward.

There was a stitched **hem for its opening around** so that **it would not be rent.** Alternatively, it was prohibited for the robe to be rent.[10]

24 **They made on the hem of the robe** ornaments in the shape of **pomegranates of sky-blue, purple, and scarlet wool,** all spun together.

25 **They made bells of pure gold, and they put the bells among the pomegranates on the hem of the robe around, among the pomegranates.** A golden bell was placed inside each pomegranate.[11] Alternatively, each bell was placed between two pomegranates.[12]

26 **A bell and a pomegranate, a bell and a pomegranate were on the hem of the robe around, to serve, as the Lord commanded Moses.** Previously, the verse states that the bell chimes of the High Priest's robe "shall be heard upon his entry into the Sanctuary before the Lord and upon his emergence" (28:35).

27 **They made the tunics of linen, woven work for Aaron and for his sons,** for all of the priests,

28 and they made **the mitre,** similar to a turban for the High Priest, **of linen, and the headdresses of linen** for the other priests, **and the linen trousers of spun linen** for all the priests.

29 They made **the sash worn by all priests**[13] **of spun linen, and sky-blue, purple, and scarlet wool, the work of an embroiderer, as the Lord had commanded Moses.** The linen tunics and headdresses were white; the sash wrapped around the tunic added color to the uniform of the ordinary priests.

30 The Torah returns to the description of the garments of the High Priest: **They made the diadem of the crown of sanctity,** a gold ornament positioned on the High Priest's forehead, **of pure gold, and they wrote upon it in the writing of the engraving of a signet: Holy to the Lord.** The crown of the priesthood signifies the High Priest's consecration to God as well as his lofty status as minister to God.

31 **They put upon it a thread of sky-blue wool, to put it,** fasten it, **on the mitre from above, as the Lord had commanded Moses.**

יד תַּרְשִׁישׁ שֹׁהַם וְיָשְׁפֵה מוּסַבֹּת מִשְׁבְּצֹת זָהָב בְּמִלֻּאֹתָם: וְהָאֲבָנִים עַל־שְׁמֹת
בְּנֵי־יִשְׂרָאֵל הֵנָּה שְׁתֵּים עֶשְׂרֵה עַל־שְׁמֹתָם פִּתּוּחֵי חֹתָם אִישׁ עַל־שְׁמוֹ לִשְׁנֵים
טו טז עָשָׂר שָׁבֶט: וַיַּעֲשׂוּ עַל־הַחֹשֶׁן שַׁרְשְׁרֹת גַּבְלֻת מַעֲשֵׂה עֲבֹת זָהָב טָהוֹר: וַיַּעֲשׂוּ
שְׁתֵּי מִשְׁבְּצֹת זָהָב וּשְׁתֵּי טַבְּעֹת זָהָב וַיִּתְּנוּ אֶת־שְׁתֵּי הַטַּבָּעֹת עַל־שְׁנֵי קְצוֹת
יז יח הַחֹשֶׁן: וַיִּתְּנוּ שְׁתֵּי הָעֲבֹתֹת הַזָּהָב עַל־שְׁתֵּי הַטַּבָּעֹת עַל־קְצוֹת הַחֹשֶׁן: וְאֵת
שְׁתֵּי קְצוֹת שְׁתֵּי הָעֲבֹתֹת נָתְנוּ עַל־שְׁתֵּי הַמִּשְׁבְּצֹת וַיִּתְּנֻם עַל־כִּתְפֹת הָאֵפֹד
יט אֶל־מוּל פָּנָיו: וַיַּעֲשׂוּ שְׁתֵּי טַבְּעֹת זָהָב וַיָּשִׂימוּ עַל־שְׁנֵי קְצוֹת הַחֹשֶׁן עַל־שְׂפָתוֹ
כ אֲשֶׁר אֶל־עֵבֶר הָאֵפֹד בָּיְתָה: וַיַּעֲשׂוּ שְׁתֵּי טַבְּעֹת זָהָב וַיִּתְּנֻם עַל־שְׁתֵּי כִתְפֹת
כא הָאֵפֹד מִלְּמַטָּה מִמּוּל פָּנָיו לְעֻמַּת מַחְבַּרְתּוֹ מִמַּעַל לְחֵשֶׁב הָאֵפֹד: וַיִּרְכְּסוּ אֶת־
הַחֹשֶׁן מִטַּבְּעֹתָיו אֶל־טַבְּעֹת הָאֵפֹד בִּפְתִיל תְּכֵלֶת לִהְיֹת עַל־חֵשֶׁב הָאֵפֹד
וְלֹא־יִזַּח הַחֹשֶׁן מֵעַל הָאֵפֹד כַּאֲשֶׁר צִוָּה יהוה אֶת־מֹשֶׁה:
כב כג וַיַּעַשׂ אֶת־מְעִיל הָאֵפֹד מַעֲשֵׂה אֹרֵג כְּלִיל תְּכֵלֶת: וּפִי־הַמְּעִיל בְּתוֹכוֹ כְּפִי תַחְרָא שלישי /ששי/
כד שָׂפָה לְפִיו סָבִיב לֹא יִקָּרֵעַ: וַיַּעֲשׂוּ עַל־שׁוּלֵי הַמְּעִיל רִמּוֹנֵי תְּכֵלֶת וְאַרְגָּמָן
כה וְתוֹלַעַת שָׁנִי מָשְׁזָר: וַיַּעֲשׂוּ פַעֲמֹנֵי זָהָב טָהוֹר וַיִּתְּנוּ אֶת־הַפַּעֲמֹנִים בְּתוֹךְ
כו הָרִמֹּנִים עַל־שׁוּלֵי הַמְּעִיל סָבִיב בְּתוֹךְ הָרִמֹּנִים: פַּעֲמֹן וְרִמֹּן פַּעֲמֹן וְרִמֹּן עַל־
כז שׁוּלֵי הַמְּעִיל סָבִיב לְשָׁרֵת כַּאֲשֶׁר צִוָּה יהוה אֶת־מֹשֶׁה: וַיַּעֲשׂוּ
כח אֶת־הַכֻּתְנֹת שֵׁשׁ מַעֲשֵׂה אֹרֵג לְאַהֲרֹן וּלְבָנָיו: וְאֵת הַמִּצְנֶפֶת שֵׁשׁ וְאֶת־פַּאֲרֵי
כט הַמִּגְבָּעֹת שֵׁשׁ וְאֶת־מִכְנְסֵי הַבָּד שֵׁשׁ מָשְׁזָר: וְאֶת־הָאַבְנֵט שֵׁשׁ מָשְׁזָר וּתְכֵלֶת
וְאַרְגָּמָן וְתוֹלַעַת שָׁנִי מַעֲשֵׂה רֹקֵם כַּאֲשֶׁר צִוָּה יהוה אֶת־מֹשֶׁה:
ל וַיַּעֲשׂוּ אֶת־צִיץ נֵזֶר־הַקֹּדֶשׁ זָהָב טָהוֹר וַיִּכְתְּבוּ עָלָיו מִכְתַּב פִּתּוּחֵי חוֹתָם קֹדֶשׁ
לא לַיהוה: וַיִּתְּנוּ עָלָיו פְּתִיל תְּכֵלֶת לָתֵת עַל־הַמִּצְנֶפֶת מִלְמָעְלָה כַּאֲשֶׁר צִוָּה יהוה

רש"י

כח| וְאֶת פַּאֲרֵי הַמִּגְבָּעֹת. תִּפְאֶרֶת הַמִּגְבָּעוֹת, הַמִּגְבָּעוֹת הַמְפֹאָרִין:

לא| לָתֵת עַל הַמִּצְנֶפֶת מִלְמָעְלָה. שֶׁעַל יְדֵי הַפְּתִילִים הָיָה מוֹשִׁיבוֹ עַל הַמִּצְנֶפֶת כְּמִין כֶּתֶר. וְאִי אֶפְשָׁר לוֹמַר הַצִּיץ עַל הַמִּצְנֶפֶת, שֶׁהֲרֵי בִּשְׁחִיטַת קָדָשִׁים שָׁנִינוּ: שְׂעָרוֹ הָיָה נִרְאֶה בֵּין צִיץ לַמִּצְנֶפֶת שֶׁשָּׁם מַנִּיחַ תְּפִלִּין (זבחים יט ע"א), וְהַצִּיץ הָיָה נָתוּן עַל הַמֵּצַח, הֲרֵי הַמִּצְנֶפֶת לְמַעְלָה וְהַצִּיץ לְמַטָּה, כָּאן הוּא אוֹמֵר: "וַיִּתְּנוּ עָלָיו פְּתִיל תְּכֵלֶת", וּבְעִנְיַן הַצַּוָּאָה הוּא אוֹמֵר: "וְשַׂמְתָּ אֹתוֹ עַל פְּתִיל תְּכֵלֶת"

The Completion of the Parts of the Tabernacle and Their Presentation before Moses

EXODUS 39:32–43

In this section the Torah relates the completion of the preparation work for the Tabernacle and the presentation of the completed items before Moses. Listed here are the parts of the Tent of Meeting and its partitions, the vessels, and the materials used in their service, such as the showbread that was placed on the table, the oil used for lighting the candelabrum, and the incense burned upon the golden altar.

32 **All the work of the Tabernacle of the Tent of Meeting was**
completed, and the children of Israel and their chief craftsmen **did in accordance with all that the Lord had com-**
manded Moses; so they did. They successfully constructed all
the parts of the Tabernacle, its vessels and their appurtenances,
and the priestly vestments, exactly as their design was shown to
Moses on Mount Sinai (see 25:9).
33 **They brought the Tabernacle,** the wool and linen coverings,
Fourth aliya **to Moses, with the tent,** the goats' hair sheets, **and all its ves-**
sels: its hooks, its boards, its bars, and its pillars, and its
sockets;
34 **and the covering of rams' hides dyed red, and the covering**
of taḥash hides, and the curtain of the screen;
35 **the Ark of the Testimony, and its staves, and the ark cover;**
36 **the table, all its vessels, and the showbread;**
37 **the pure candelabrum, its lamps, the lamps of the arrange-**
ment, and all its vessels, and the lighting oil;
38 **and the golden altar, and the anointing oil, and the incense**
of the spices, and the screen of the entrance of the tent;
39 **the bronze altar and its grate of bronze, its staves and all its**
vessels; the basin and its base;
40 **the hangings of the courtyard, its pillars, and its sockets,**
and the screen for the entrance of the courtyard, its, the
courtyard's, **cords,**[14] **and its pegs, and all the vessels of the**
service of the Tabernacle for the Tent of Meeting;
41 Likewise, they brought **the woven fabrics to serve in the holy**
place, the sacred vestments for Aaron the priest and the
vestments of his sons to serve as priests.
42 **In accordance with everything that the Lord had com-**
manded Moses, so did the children of Israel perform all
the work. They neither added nor subtracted. The work of the
many craftsmen was precisely in accordance with all that God
had commanded Moses. Given the scale of the operation and
the number of people involved, such precise execution of the
plans was a noteworthy achievement.
43 **Moses saw all the labor** that was brought before him for inspection, **and behold, they had performed it; as the Lord**
had commanded,[D] **so had they performed; and Moses**
blessed them.

Erecting the Tabernacle and Sanctifying the Priests

EXODUS 40:1–33

The Torah describes the Tabernacle and its vessels seven times: First, when God commands Moses to make these items and shows him their respective designs; second, when the roles of Betzalel and Oholiav are mentioned; third, when Moses requests from the people to bring the necessary materials; fourth, when the work is performed by all the wise-hearted individuals; fifth, when the Tabernacle and its vessels are brought before Moses. The sixth and seventh times appear here, when God commands Moses to erect the Tabernacle and the Torah then recounts its construction.

It would seem that these numerous reiterations, like other repetitions involving offerings and consecrated items, e.g., descriptions of the individual offerings, the offerings of the days of investiture, the offerings brought by the princes of Israel, and the additional offerings of the festivals, stem from God's affinity for sacred items and the centrality of the Sanctuary for Israel.

These repetitions also serve to emphasize that the Tabernacle is not merely a symbolic structure meant to honor God and to remind the Israelites of His presence among them, but also a means of creating a mutual connection between God and Israel. Its precise construction is necessary in order to actualize this connection between the eternal and the material.

The frequent repetition of the phrase "as the Lord had commanded Moses," in the second section of this passage, forms a kind of poetic rhythm that introduces an exalted theme into the account. Human actions parallel the divine command in a precise manner, and as a result the Tabernacle and its vessels indeed serve as a vehicle for the encounter between God and man.

40 1 **The Lord spoke to Moses, saying:**
Fifth aliya 2 **On the day of the first month, on the first of the month** of
(…nth aliya) Nisan, the month in which the Israelites were brought out of
Egypt and which was therefore established as the first month of
the year (see 12:2), **you shall erect the Tabernacle of the Tent**
of Meeting.

לב את־משה: ותכל כל־עבדת משכן אהל מועד ויעשו בני
ישראל ככל אשר צוה יהוה את־משה כן עשו:
לג ויביאו את־המשכן אל־משה את־האהל ואת־כל־כליו קרסיו קרשיו בריחו כט רביעי
לד ועמדיו ואדניו: ואת־מכסה עורת האילם המאדמים ואת־מכסה ערת התחשים
לה ואת פרכת המסך: את־ארון העדת ואת־בדיו ואת הכפרת: את־השלחן את־
לו
לז כל־כליו ואת לחם הפנים: את־המנרה הטהרה את־נרתיה נרת המערכה
לח ואת־כל־כליה ואת שמן המאור: ואת מזבח הזהב ואת שמן המשחה ואת
לט קטרת הסמים ואת מסך פתח האהל: את ׀ מזבח הנחשת ואת־מכבר הנחשת
מ אשר־לו את־בדיו ואת־כל־כליו את־הכיר ואת־כנו: את קלעי החצר את־
עמדיה ואת־אדניה ואת־המסך לשער החצר את־מיתריו ויתדתיה ואת
מא כל־כלי עבדת המשכן לאהל מועד: את־בגדי השרד לשרת בקדש את־בגדי
מב הקדש לאהרן הכהן ואת־בגדי בניו לכהן: ככל אשר־צוה יהוה את־משה
מג כן עשו בני ישראל את כל־העבדה: וירא משה את־כל־המלאכה והנה עשו
אתה כאשר צוה יהוה כן עשו ויברך אתם משה:
א וידבר יהוה אל־משה לאמר: ביום־החדש הראשון באחד לחדש תקים את־ חמישי
ב /שביעי/

רש"י

(לעיל כח, לז)? שני חוטין היו בכל קנה וקנה, אחד ממעל ואחד מתחת לצד מצחו, וכן באמצע, וקושר ראשיהם השנים כלם יחד מאחוריו למול ערפו, ומושיבו על המצנפת. ואל תתמה שלא נאמר 'פתילי תכלת' הואיל ומרבין הן, שהרי מצינו בחשן ואפוד: "וירכסו את החשן" וגו' (לעיל פסוק כא), ועל כרחך פתות משנים לא היו, שהרי בשני קצות החשן היו שתי טבעות החשן ובשתי כתפות האפוד היו טבעות האפוד שכנגדן, ולפי דרך קשירה ארבעה חוטין היו, ומכל מקום פחות משנים אי אפשר:

לב | ויעשו בני ישראל. את המלאכה, "ככל אשר צוה ה'" וגו':

לג | ויביאו את המשכן וגו'. שלא היו יכולין להקימו, ולפי שלא עשה משה שום מלאכה במשכן הניח לו הקדוש ברוך הוא הקמתו, שלא היה יכול להקימו שום אדם מחמת כבד הקרשים שאין כח באדם לזקפן, ומשה העמידו. אמר משה לפני הקדוש ברוך הוא: איך אפשר הקמתו על ידי אדם? אמר לו: עסוק אתה בידך נראה כמקימו, והוא נזקף וקם מאליו. וזהו שנאמר: "הוקם המשכן" (להלן מ, יז), הוקם מאליו. מדרש רבי תנחומא (פקודי יא):

מג | ויברך אתם משה. אמר להם: יהי רצון שתשרה שכינה במעשה ידיכם, "ויהי נעם ה' אלהינו עלינו" וגו' (תהלים צ, יז), והוא אחד מאחד עשר מזמורים שב'תפלה למשה' (תהלים צ-ק):

DISCUSSION

39:43 | And behold, they had performed it; as the Lord had commanded: The Sages see a parallel between the divine creation of heaven and earth and the construction of the Tabernacle. It is also interesting to note the similarities in terminology used in each respective case. In Genesis, the Torah states: "God saw everything that He had made, and behold, it was very good…. The heavens and the earth and their entire host were completed…. God blessed the seventh day" (Genesis 1:31–2:3). Here, the verse states: "All the work of the Tabernacle of the Tent of Meeting was completed…. Moses saw all the labor, and behold, they had performed it; as the Lord had commanded…and Moses blessed them."

3 After the framework of the Tabernacle has been erected, the placement of its vessels begins with the ark, the focal point of its holiness. The sanctity, and therefore the significance, of the entire structure stems from here. **You shall place there the Ark of the Testimony, and you shall screen the ark with the curtain,** which separates and conceals the Holy of Holies.

4 **You shall bring the table, and you shall arrange its arrangement,** the showbread; **you shall bring the candelabrum, and you shall kindle its lamps.** It is not enough to place the candelabrum in its spot; you must also kindle its lights.

5 **You shall put the golden altar for incense before the Ark of the Testimony.** Although the golden altar was further away from the Holy of Holies than the table and the candelabrum, it was positioned opposite the ark. **And you shall set in place the screen of the entrance of the Tabernacle,** of the Sanctuary, the structure in the center of the courtyard.

6 **You shall put the altar of the burnt offering before the entrance of the Tabernacle of the Tent of Meeting.** The large altar, upon which the offerings will be sacrificed, must be placed in the courtyard.

7 **You shall put the basin between the Tent of Meeting and the altar, and you shall put water there,** in the basin, so that it will be ready for the service.

8 **You shall place** the pillars, sockets, and hangings, which together form **the courtyard all around** the Tabernacle, **and you shall put the screen of the gate of the courtyard** in its appropriate place.

9 In order to sanctify the service vessels, it is not enough to simply place the vessels, appurtenances, and other materials in their respective locations in the Tabernacle. Rather, it is also necessary to perform an anointing ritual, which will sanctify the vessels: **You shall take the anointing oil,** which was also brought before you, **and anoint the Tabernacle and all that is in it; you shall sanctify it and all its vessels; it shall be holy.**

10 **You shall anoint the altar of the burnt offering and all its vessels; you shall sanctify the altar, and the altar shall be a sacred sacrament.**

11 **You shall anoint the basin and its base, and you shall sanctify it.**[D]

12 After the vessels have been constructed, set in place, and anointed, Moses is commanded to sanctify the priests as well: **You shall bring Aaron and his sons near to the entrance of the Tent of Meeting, and you shall wash them with water there.**

13 **You shall clothe Aaron with the sacred vestments; you shall anoint him; you shall** thereby **sanctify him, that he will serve as priest to Me.** From this point onward he shall be fit for the priesthood.

14 **You shall bring near his sons, and you shall clothe them in tunics.**

15 **You shall anoint them, as you anointed their father, that they may serve as priests to Me.** The High Priest undergoes a separate anointing ritual, as he is anointed in a different manner to that of the other priests.[15] **And their anointment shall be to them for an eternal priesthood.** This anointing ritual will not be repeated, as they will retain their status as priests **for their generations.** Aaron's sons did not inherit the priesthood from their father, as they were born before Aaron was sanctified with the priesthood. Consequently, like their father, they were required to undergo a sanctification ritual. However, any sons born to them from now on inherit the priesthood from their fathers.

16 **Moses did in accordance with everything that the Lord had commanded him** with regard to erecting the Tabernacle; **so he did.**

17 *Sixth aliya* **It was in the first month,** Nisan, **during** the beginning of **the second year** following the exodus of the Jewish people from Egypt, **on the first of the month, the Tabernacle was erected.**

18 **Moses** himself[16] **erected the Tabernacle;**[D] **he put its sockets,** the bases for the boards, **he placed its boards** upon the sockets, **he put in its bars** to hold up the walls, **and he erected its pillars** at the entrance to the Tabernacle.

19 **He spread the tent,** the tapestry of goat hair, **over the Tabernacle, and he placed the covering of the tent,** made of rams' skins dyed red and taḥash skins, **over it from above, as the Lord had commanded Moses.**

20 After the main structure of the Tabernacle was erected and covered, **he took the testimony,** the Tablets of the Covenant, which had been located in Moses' tent until now, **and put it into the ark.** This is the point of contact between worlds. With the placement of the tablets in their proper spot in the ark, they begin to serve as sources of strength and power. A resting place

DISCUSSION

40:11 | You shall anoint the basin, and its base and you shall sanctify it: Some of the service vessels and their appurtenances were fashioned like ordinary implements, such as the bowls and pans. Most, however, were distinctive objects. In addition to preparing the vessels in accordance with the requirements for the service of the Tabernacle, it was necessary to sanctify them through a ceremonious act using the anointing oil.

During the First Temple era, and throughout the entire Second Temple period, anointing oil was unavailable. Instead, the vessels were consecrated by means of their use in practice (*Yoma* 12b).

40:18 | Moses erected the Tabernacle: The difficult task of erecting the Tabernacle for the first time is attributed to Moses alone. This is because

ג מִשְׁכַּן אֹהֶל מוֹעֵד: וְשַׂמְתָּ שָׁם אֵת אֲרוֹן הָעֵדוּת וְסַכֹּתָ עַל־הָאָרֹן אֶת־הַפָּרֹכֶת:

ד וְהֵבֵאתָ אֶת־הַשֻּׁלְחָן וְעָרַכְתָּ אֶת־עֶרְכּוֹ וְהֵבֵאתָ אֶת־הַמְּנֹרָה וְהַעֲלֵיתָ אֶת־נֵרֹתֶיהָ:

ה וְנָתַתָּה אֶת־מִזְבַּח הַזָּהָב לִקְטֹרֶת לִפְנֵי אֲרוֹן הָעֵדֻת וְשַׂמְתָּ אֶת־מָסַךְ הַפֶּתַח

ו לַמִּשְׁכָּן: וְנָתַתָּה אֵת מִזְבַּח הָעֹלָה לִפְנֵי פֶּתַח מִשְׁכַּן אֹהֶל־מוֹעֵד: וְנָתַתָּ אֶת־

ז הַכִּיֹּר בֵּין־אֹהֶל מוֹעֵד וּבֵין הַמִּזְבֵּחַ וְנָתַתָּ שָׁם מָיִם: וְשַׂמְתָּ אֶת־הֶחָצֵר סָבִיב

ט וְנָתַתָּ אֶת־מָסַךְ שַׁעַר הֶחָצֵר: וְלָקַחְתָּ אֶת־שֶׁמֶן הַמִּשְׁחָה וּמָשַׁחְתָּ אֶת־הַמִּשְׁכָּן

י וְאֶת־כָּל־אֲשֶׁר־בּוֹ וְקִדַּשְׁתָּ אֹתוֹ וְאֶת־כָּל־כֵּלָיו וְהָיָה קֹדֶשׁ: וּמָשַׁחְתָּ אֶת־מִזְבַּח

יא הָעֹלָה וְאֶת־כָּל־כֵּלָיו וְקִדַּשְׁתָּ אֶת־הַמִּזְבֵּחַ וְהָיָה הַמִּזְבֵּחַ קֹדֶשׁ קָדָשִׁים: וּמָשַׁחְתָּ

יב אֶת־הַכִּיֹּר וְאֶת־כַּנּוֹ וְקִדַּשְׁתָּ אֹתוֹ: וְהִקְרַבְתָּ אֶת־אַהֲרֹן וְאֶת־בָּנָיו אֶל־פֶּתַח אֹהֶל

יג מוֹעֵד וְרָחַצְתָּ אֹתָם בַּמָּיִם: וְהִלְבַּשְׁתָּ אֶת־אַהֲרֹן אֵת בִּגְדֵי הַקֹּדֶשׁ וּמָשַׁחְתָּ אֹתוֹ

יד וְקִדַּשְׁתָּ אֹתוֹ וְכִהֵן לִי: וְאֶת־בָּנָיו תַּקְרִיב וְהִלְבַּשְׁתָּ אֹתָם כֻּתֳּנֹת: וּמָשַׁחְתָּ אֹתָם

טו כַּאֲשֶׁר מָשַׁחְתָּ אֶת־אֲבִיהֶם וְכִהֲנוּ לִי וְהָיְתָה לִהְיֹת לָהֶם מָשְׁחָתָם לִכְהֻנַּת

טז עוֹלָם לְדֹרֹתָם: וַיַּעַשׂ מֹשֶׁה כְּכֹל אֲשֶׁר צִוָּה יְהוָה אֹתוֹ כֵּן עָשָׂה:

יז שׁשׁי וַיְהִי בַּחֹדֶשׁ הָרִאשׁוֹן בַּשָּׁנָה הַשֵּׁנִית בְּאֶחָד לַחֹדֶשׁ הוּקַם הַמִּשְׁכָּן: וַיָּקֶם

יח מֹשֶׁה אֶת־הַמִּשְׁכָּן וַיִּתֵּן אֶת־אֲדָנָיו וַיָּשֶׂם אֶת־קְרָשָׁיו וַיִּתֵּן אֶת־בְּרִיחָיו וַיָּקֶם

יט אֶת־עַמּוּדָיו: וַיִּפְרֹשׂ אֶת־הָאֹהֶל עַל־הַמִּשְׁכָּן וַיָּשֶׂם אֶת־מִכְסֵה הָאֹהֶל עָלָיו

כ מִלְמָעְלָה כַּאֲשֶׁר צִוָּה יְהוָה אֶת־מֹשֶׁה: וַיִּקַּח וַיִּתֵּן אֶת־הָעֵדֻת

אֶל־הָאָרֹן וַיָּשֶׂם אֶת־הַבַּדִּים עַל־הָאָרֹן וַיִּתֵּן אֶת־הַכַּפֹּרֶת עַל־הָאָרֹן מִלְמָעְלָה:

רש״י

פרק מ

ג | וְסַכֹּתָ עַל הָאָרֹן. לְשׁוֹן הֲגָנָה, שֶׁהֲרֵי מְחִצָּה הָיָה:

ד | וְעָרַכְתָּ אֶת עֶרְכּוֹ. שְׁתֵּי מַעֲרָכוֹת שֶׁל לֶחֶם הַפָּנִים:

יט | וַיִּפְרֹשׂ אֶת הָאֹהֶל. הֵן יְרִיעוֹת הָעִזִּים:

כו | אֶת הָעֵדֻת. הַלּוּחוֹת:

DISCUSSION

the Tabernacle was not merely a physical structure, but a means of establishing a mutual bond between God and Israel, to enable communication between this world and the infinite. The elaborate preparations were necessary for the unique function of this structure. Only Moses was capable of arranging the Tabernacle for the first time in the precise manner. On subsequent occasions the work was performed by others, who were taught by Moses.

for the Tablets of Testimony that had descended from heaven
has now been built on earth. God's descent upon Mount Sinai
is no longer a singular event in the past; God has now acquired
a real, fixed resting place in the world. **And he,** Moses, **placed**
the staves on the ark, and he put the ark cover, with the cherubim upon it, **on the ark from above.**
21 **He brought the ark,** which contained the tablets, and over
which the ark cover with the cherubim was placed, **into the**
Tabernacle, and he placed the curtain of the screen, and he
screened the Ark of the Testimony, as the Lord had com-
manded Moses.
22 **He put the table in the Tent of Meeting, on the side of the**
Tabernacle to the north, outside the curtain, which divides
between the Sanctuary and the Holy of Holies.
23 **He arranged upon it an arrangement of bread before the**
Lord, as the Lord had commanded Moses.
24 **He put the candelabrum in the Tent of Meeting, opposite**
the table, on the side of the Tabernacle to the south.
25 **He kindled the lamps before the Lord, as the Lord had**
commanded Moses.
26 **He placed the golden altar in the Tent of Meeting before the**
curtain, between the table and the candelabrum, but slightly
closer to the entrance to the Sanctuary.
27 **He burned on it incense of the spices, as the Lord had com-**
manded Moses.
28 **He placed the screen of the entrance to the Tabernacle.**
Seventh aliya 29 **The altar of the burnt offering he placed at the entrance of**
the Tabernacle of the Tent of Meeting, and he offered up on
it the burnt offering and the meal offering, as the Lord had
commanded Moses.
30 **He placed the basin between the Tent of Meeting and the**
altar, and he put water there for washing.

The Sanctuary

31 **Moses and Aaron and his sons would wash their hands and**
their feet[D] **from it.** They would not wash their entire bodies.
32 **Upon their entry into the Tent of Meeting and upon their**
approach to the altar, they shall wash, as the Lord had com-
manded Moses.
33 **He erected the courtyard around the Tabernacle and the**
altar, and he put up the screen of the gate of the courtyard;
Moses concluded the labor.

The Glory of God Fills the Tabernacle

EXODUS 40:34–38

The book of Exodus concludes with the resting of the Divine Presence in the Tent of Meeting. The handiwork of the Israelites, which combined an outpouring of generous donations with a desire to obey in a precise manner all the details of the instructions given to Moses, receives God's approval, and the cloud of the glory of God covers the Tabernacle.

34 Then the connection was established: **The cloud covered**
Maftir **the Tent of Meeting, and the glory of the Lord filled**
the Tabernacle.[D] Although the cloud is a physical entity, it
embodies the glory of God and symbolizes the resting of the
Divine Presence.
35 **Moses was unable to enter the Tent of Meeting because the**

DISCUSSION

40:31 | **Their hands and their feet:** Some Sages maintain that the priests would wash their hands and feet simultaneously. It is difficult to know whether this was the precise manner of the ritual as performed in the Tabernacle, and if so, how exactly it was performed. According to Rabbi Yosei son of Rabbi Yehuda, the priest would lay his hands one on top of the other and lay them together on both his feet, themselves laid one on top of the other, and would sanctify them by pouring water over them. In order for the priest to maintain his balance, another priest would support him (*Zevaḥim* 19b).

It is known that the basin used in the Second Temple contained faucets, under which the

כא וַיָּבֵ֣א אֶת־הָֽאָרֹן֮ אֶל־הַמִּשְׁכָּן֒ וַיָּ֗שֶׂם אֵ֚ת פָּרֹ֣כֶת הַמָּסָ֔ךְ וַיָּ֕סֶךְ עַ֖ל אֲר֣וֹן הָעֵד֑וּת
כב כַּאֲשֶׁ֛ר צִוָּ֥ה יְהוָ֖ה אֶת־מֹשֶֽׁה׃ וַיִּתֵּ֤ן אֶת־הַשֻּׁלְחָן֙ בְּאֹ֣הֶל מוֹעֵ֔ד עַ֛ל
כג יֶ֥רֶךְ הַמִּשְׁכָּ֖ן צָפֹ֑נָה מִח֖וּץ לַפָּרֹֽכֶת׃ וַיַּעֲרֹ֥ךְ עָלָ֛יו עֵ֥רֶךְ לֶ֖חֶם לִפְנֵ֣י יְהוָ֑ה כַּאֲשֶׁ֛ר
כד צִוָּ֥ה יְהוָ֖ה אֶת־מֹשֶֽׁה׃ וַיָּ֤שֶׂם אֶת־הַמְּנֹרָה֙ בְּאֹ֣הֶל מוֹעֵ֔ד נֹ֖כַח
כה הַשֻּׁלְחָ֑ן עַ֛ל יֶ֥רֶךְ הַמִּשְׁכָּ֖ן נֶֽגְבָּה׃ וַיַּ֥עַל הַנֵּרֹ֖ת לִפְנֵ֣י יְהוָ֑ה כַּאֲשֶׁ֛ר צִוָּ֥ה יְהוָ֖ה אֶת־
כו כז מֹשֶֽׁה׃ וַיָּ֛שֶׂם אֶת־מִזְבַּ֥ח הַזָּהָ֖ב בְּאֹ֣הֶל מוֹעֵ֑ד לִפְנֵ֖י הַפָּרֹֽכֶת׃ וַיַּקְטֵ֥ר
כח עָלָ֖יו קְטֹ֣רֶת סַמִּ֑ים כַּאֲשֶׁ֛ר צִוָּ֥ה יְהוָ֖ה אֶת־מֹשֶֽׁה׃ וַיָּ֛שֶׂם אֶת־מָסַ֥ךְ שביעי
כט הַפֶּ֖תַח לַמִּשְׁכָּֽן׃ וְאֵת֙ מִזְבַּ֣ח הָֽעֹלָ֔ה שָׂ֕ם פֶּ֖תַח מִשְׁכַּ֣ן אֹֽהֶל־מוֹעֵ֑ד וַיַּ֣עַל עָלָ֗יו
ל אֶת־הָֽעֹלָה֙ וְאֶת־הַמִּנְחָ֔ה כַּאֲשֶׁ֛ר צִוָּ֥ה יְהוָ֖ה אֶת־מֹשֶֽׁה׃ וַיָּ֙שֶׂם֙
לא אֶת־הַכִּיֹּ֔ר בֵּֽין־אֹ֥הֶל מוֹעֵ֖ד וּבֵ֣ין הַמִּזְבֵּ֑חַ וַיִּתֵּ֥ן שָׁ֛מָּה מַ֖יִם לְרָחְצָֽה׃ וְרָחֲצ֣וּ מִמֶּ֔נּוּ
לב מֹשֶׁ֖ה וְאַהֲרֹ֣ן וּבָנָ֑יו אֶת־יְדֵיהֶ֖ם וְאֶת־רַגְלֵיהֶֽם׃ בְּבֹאָ֞ם אֶל־אֹ֣הֶל מוֹעֵ֗ד וּבְקָרְבָתָ֛ם
אֶל־הַמִּזְבֵּ֖חַ יִרְחָ֑צוּ כַּאֲשֶׁ֛ר צִוָּ֥ה יְהוָ֖ה אֶת־מֹשֶֽׁה׃
לג וַיָּ֣קֶם אֶת־הֶֽחָצֵ֗ר סָבִיב֙ לַמִּשְׁכָּ֣ן וְלַמִּזְבֵּ֔חַ וַיִּתֵּ֕ן אֶת־מָסַ֖ךְ שַׁ֣עַר הֶחָצֵ֑ר וַיְכַ֥ל מֹשֶׁ֖ה
אֶת־הַמְּלָאכָֽה׃
לד לה וַיְכַ֥ס הֶעָנָ֖ן אֶת־אֹ֣הֶל מוֹעֵ֑ד וּכְב֣וֹד יְהוָ֔ה מָלֵ֖א אֶת־הַמִּשְׁכָּֽן׃ וְלֹא־יָכֹ֣ל מֹשֶׁ֗ה לָב֙וֹא֙ מפטיר

רש״י

כב| עַל יֶרֶךְ הַמִּשְׁכָּן צָפֹנָה. בַּחֲצִי הַצְּפוֹנִי שֶׁל רֹחַב הַבַּיִת: יֶרֶךְ. כְּתַרְגּוּמוֹ: ״צִדָּא״, כַּיָּרֵךְ הַזֶּה שֶׁהוּא בְּצִדּוֹ שֶׁל אָדָם:

כז| וַיַּקְטֵר עָלָיו קְטֹרֶת. שַׁחֲרִית וְעַרְבִית, כְּמוֹ שֶׁנֶּאֱמַר: ״בַּבֹּקֶר בַּבֹּקֶר בְּהֵיטִיבוֹ אֶת הַנֵּרֹת וְגוֹ׳ וּבְהַעֲלֹת אַהֲרֹן״ וְגוֹ׳ (לעיל ל, ז-ח):

כט| אַף בַּיּוֹם הַשְּׁמִינִי לַמִּלּוּאִים שֶׁהוּא יוֹם הֲקָמַת הַמִּשְׁכָּן, שִׁמֵּשׁ מֹשֶׁה וְהִקְרִיב קָרְבְּנוֹת צִבּוּר, חוּץ מֵאוֹתָן שֶׁנִּצְטַוּוּ לְבוֹ בַּיּוֹם, שֶׁנֶּאֱמַר: ״קְרַב אֶל הַמִּזְבֵּחַ״ וְגוֹ׳ (ויקרא ט, ז): אֶת הָעֹלָה. עוֹלַת הַתָּמִיד: וְאֶת הַמִּנְחָה. מִנְחַת נְסָכִים שֶׁל תָּמִיד, כְּמוֹ שֶׁנֶּאֱמַר: ״וְעִשָּׂרֹן סֹלֶת בָּלוּל בְּשֶׁמֶן״ וְגוֹ׳ (לעיל כט, מ):

לא| וְרָחֲצוּ מִמֶּנּוּ מֹשֶׁה וְאַהֲרֹן וּבָנָיו. יוֹם שְׁמִינִי לַמִּלּוּאִים הֻשְׁווּ כֻּלָּם לִכְהֻנָּה, וְתַרְגּוּמוֹ: ״וּמְקַדְּשִׁין מִנֵּיהּ״, בּוֹ בַּיּוֹם קִדֵּשׁ מֹשֶׁה עִמָּהֶם:

לב| וּבְקָרְבָתָם. כְּמוֹ וּבְקָרְבָם, כְּשֶׁיִּקְרְבוּ:

לה| וְלֹא יָכֹל מֹשֶׁה לָבוֹא אֶל אֹהֶל מוֹעֵד. וְכָתוּב אֶחָד אוֹמֵר: ״וּבְבֹא מֹשֶׁה אֶל אֹהֶל מוֹעֵד״ (במדבר ז, פט), בָּא הַכָּתוּב הַשְּׁלִישִׁי וְהִכְרִיעַ בֵּינֵיהֶם: ״כִּי שָׁכַן עָלָיו הֶעָנָן״, אֱמֹר מֵעַתָּה, כָּל זְמַן שֶׁהָיָה הֶעָנָן עָלָיו לֹא הָיָה יָכוֹל לָבֹא, נִסְתַּלֵּק הֶעָנָן, נִכְנָס וּמְדַבֵּר עִמּוֹ:

DISCUSSION

→ priests would place their hands and feet, enabling the water to fall on the hands and feet together (see *Yoma* 37a).

40:34| **And the glory of the Lord filled the Tabernacle:** Similar descriptions appear with regard to Solomon's Temple when the cloud filled the Temple (I Kings 8:10–11), as well as in prophetic depictions of the future (see Isaiah 4:5 and Zechariah 2:9).

cloud rested upon it, and the glory of the Lord filled the
Tabernacle. Since the Tabernacle now stands consecrated for
God, Moses is permitted to enter only when God calls him, not
at any time of his choosing.[17]

36 Upon the ascent of the cloud over the Tabernacle, the children of Israel would travel on all their journeys. This is the
sign that they should continue on their travels.

37 But if the cloud would not ascend, they would not travel
until the day of its ascent. The cloud, which symbolizes the

Divine Presence, signals to the Israelites when they should set
up camp and when they should travel. They set out on their
journeys only in accordance with this nonverbal instruction.

38 For the cloud of the Lord was on the Tabernacle by day,
and fire would be in it by night. The pillar of cloud and the
pillar of fire, mentioned earlier (see 13:21–22), moved into the
Tabernacle: The cloud during the day and the fire during the
night would be before the eyes... of the entire house of Israel
on all their journeys.

Maftir on Shabbat Shekalim is read from Exodus 30:11–16. Maftir on Shabbat Para is read from Numbers 19:1–22. Maftir on Shabbat HaHodesh is read from Exodus 12:1–20.

לו אֶל־אֹ֣הֶל מוֹעֵ֔ד כִּֽי־שָׁכַ֥ן עָלָ֖יו הֶעָנָ֑ן וּכְב֣וֹד יְהוָ֔ה מָלֵ֖א אֶת־הַמִּשְׁכָּֽן׃ וּבְהֵעָל֤וֹת
לז הֶֽעָנָן֙ מֵעַ֣ל הַמִּשְׁכָּ֔ן יִסְע֖וּ בְּנֵ֣י יִשְׂרָאֵ֑ל בְּכֹ֖ל מַסְעֵיהֶֽם׃ וְאִם־לֹ֥א יֵעָלֶ֖ה הֶֽעָנָ֑ן וְלֹ֣א
לח יִסְע֔וּ עַד־י֖וֹם הֵעָלֹתֽוֹ׃ כִּי֩ עֲנַ֨ן יְהוָ֤ה עַל־הַמִּשְׁכָּן֙ יוֹמָ֔ם וְאֵ֕שׁ תִּהְיֶ֥ה לַ֖יְלָה בּ֑וֹ לְעֵינֵ֥י
כָל־בֵּֽית־יִשְׂרָאֵ֖ל בְּכָל־מַסְעֵיהֶֽם׃ חזק

רש"י

לח | לְעֵינֵי כָל בֵּית יִשְׂרָאֵל בְּכָל מַסְעֵיהֶם. בְּכָל מַסָּע שֶׁהָיוּ נוֹסְעִים, הָיָה הֶעָנָן שׁוֹכֵן בִּמְקוֹם אֲשֶׁר יַחֲנוּ שָׁם. מְקוֹם חֲנִיָּתָן אַף הוּא קָרוּי מַסָּע, וְכֵן: "וַיֵּלֶךְ לְמַסָּעָיו" (בראשית יג, ג), וְכֵן: "אֵלֶּה מַסְעֵי" (במדבר לג, א), לְפִי שֶׁמִּמְּקוֹם הַחֲנִיָּה חָזְרוּ וְנָסְעוּ, לְכָךְ נִקְרְאוּ כֻּלָּן מַסָּעוֹת:

Book of
Leviticus

LEVITICUS

This book is dedicated to

my parents and grandparents, and to their parents and grandparents, and those who came before.

It is they on whose shoulders I stand.
If it were not for them, their sacrifices and wisdom,
I would be but dust in the wind.

William A. Ackman

Vayikra

INTRODUCTION TO LEVITICUS

The book of Leviticus is referred to in ancient sources as the Priestly Code,[1] as a large part of the book deals with matters that concern the priests: The laws of the sacrificial offerings, the instructions pertaining to the priests' duties and the manner of their consecration, the commandments that apply specifically to priests, and the gifts that the people are commanded to give to the priests. Nevertheless, a significant number of the commandments included in this book are not limited to priests. Leviticus contains practically no narrative sections.

It is possible to find a common denominator for the wide range of commandments included in Leviticus, which is that they constitute a continuation, and perhaps expansion, of that which was stated in the book of Exodus. Exodus concluded with the construction of the Tabernacle, in which sanctity was given physical expression, bounded by time and space. In the book of Leviticus, sanctity is given more specific expression through the commandments; it is also expanded well beyond the Tabernacle or Temple, such that it eventually encompasses the entire world.

The covenant declared in Exodus (19:6): "You shall be for Me a kingdom of priests, and a holy nation," is applied in a detailed, practical manner in Leviticus. The commandments stated in Leviticus, which are more numerous than in any other book of the Torah, provide instruction as to the manner in which the Jewish people can become a holy nation, and teach that sanctity is not limited to a holy place and the rituals performed there, but rather applies to every facet of creation.

The sacrificial rites performed in the Temple express the manner in which man relates to the concept of sanctity. As the boundaries of sanctity are more clearly defined and man seeks to attain sanctity, the antitheses of sanctity, sin or impurity, also becomes clearly evident, and these concepts are dealt with extensively as part of the laws of the offerings. The Tabernacle is a symbolic microcosm of the universe, and the erection of the Tabernacle may be likened to a miniature reenactment of Creation. When God created the world, He not only created new beings; He also created distinctions between those beings. The creation of light necessarily created a separate reality of darkness. Similarly, the manifestation of divine sanctity in the world highlights and sharpens the distinction between the sacred and the profane.

The concept of sanctity, which characterizes the Temple and its sacrificial rites, and the concept of ritual purity are closely related. The implications of the various forms of impurity chiefly concern the Temple. Without the Temple, most of the laws concerning ritual purity become irrelevant. The book of Leviticus discusses the various forms of impurity in detail, and presents most of the laws pertaining to this topic. Where the light of the Temple's sanctity shines, the dark recesses of impurity are most evident.

As mentioned, the central message of Leviticus is that the concept of sanctity is not limited to the Temple, although the Temple is its focal point. Sanctity must be manifest in every facet of life, in every action. The commandment "You shall be holy, for I am holy," is reiterated several times in the book of Leviticus (see 11:44–45, 19:2, 20:26, 22:32). It appears in different contexts, in relation to the most intimate aspects of life as well as in relation to the communal aspects of life. The book of Leviticus includes a comprehensive list of those with whom it is forbidden to engage in sexual relations, as well as a set of prohibitions concerning types of food that are unfit for a holy nation; it also contains the social precepts fitting for a holy society, such as the prohibition of usury and the precept "you shall love your neighbor as yourself" (19:18).

The book of Leviticus teaches that the concept of sanctity is not an abstract concept or a concept manifest only within the confines of religious ritual. It is a concept with clear, practical implications, meant to be part and parcel of life itself. Sanctity, or the lack thereof, is manifest in the way one conducts business, in the way one behaves toward his relatives, and in the way one

behaves toward his fellow Jew. In every sphere of life there is room to distinguish between light and dark, virtuous behavior and transgression, and purity and impurity. Sanctity, whose source is in the upper, ethereal world of divine glory, is given concrete expression in this world, the world of human beings and other physical creatures, all of which become part of the spiritual order. The book of Leviticus is, therefore, the book of applied sanctity.

The Torah does not mention when the commandments appearing in Leviticus were given. Since there is no absolute chronological order in the Torah,[2] the juxtaposition of various passages does not necessarily indicate that they were taught at the same time. It is reasonable to assume, however, that the bulk of the commandments in Leviticus were stated before the inauguration of the Tabernacle, as most of the book is related to the rites performed therein.[3]

Parashat
Vayikra

The Burnt Offering
LEVITICUS 1:1–17

The first offering to be discussed in the book of Leviticus is the burnt offering. The burnt offering is primarily a voluntary offering that expresses the owner's desire to present a gift to God. While other offerings are eaten by the priests or the owners, with only part of the offering burned on the altar, the burnt offering is burned on the altar in its entirety. The few references to offerings in the previous books of the Torah, mainly in Genesis, indicate that in early generations the main type of offering presented in divine worship was the burnt offering.

The concept of sacrificial offerings is foreign to modern sensibilities, and the slaughter of animals as a ritual of divine service is not practiced. However, the offering is merely a symbolic expression of giving to God. The person who presents an offering understands that God does not literally partake of the offering, yet he feels as though he is presenting God with a gift, as he wholeheartedly relinquishes something that belongs to him, burning it on the altar and thereby destroying it. This act expresses the complete communion with God of one who is entirely consumed by his love or fear of Him. The offering allows one to symbolically give everything to God, leaving nothing for himself except, perhaps, some inconsequential remnants.

1 1 It is stated at the conclusion of Exodus (40:35) that Moses could not enter the Tabernacle due to the cloud of God's glory that filled it. Therefore, **the Lord called to Moses,** telling him to enter the Sanctuary. Similarly, at the time of the giving of the Torah, God called Moses to enter the cloud of glory upon Mount Sinai.[1] **And** the Lord **spoke to him from the Tent of Meeting,** which was designated from this point on as the place of divine revelation,[2] **saying:**

2 **Speak to the children of Israel, and say to them: When any man of you brings an offering**[D] **to the Lord,** if **you shall bring your offering from animals,** which is one of the items that may be brought as an offering, **from the cattle or from the flock you shall bring your offering.**

3 The Torah presents the laws of the burnt offering, which is one of the five types of offerings detailed in subsequent passages. **If his offering is a burnt offering from the cattle, an unblemished male he shall present it,** and the laws detailing what constitutes a blemish are detailed later in Leviticus (22:17–26). **To the entrance of the Tent of Meeting he shall present it,** as the burnt offering is offered upon the external altar, whether in the Tabernacle or in the Temple.[3] The obligation to bring the offering to the Tabernacle is incumbent upon the owner, not the priest.[4] The offering is brought by the owner **for his propitiation before the Lord,** in order to find favor in His eyes.[5] Alternatively, the verse does not refer to the desire of the person bringing the offering to propitiate God, but to the fact that he brings the offering of his own free will, as a gift offering rather than in fulfillment of an obligation.[6]

Cattle

4 **He shall lay his hand**[D] **upon the head of the burnt offering** and lean on it with all of his weight.[7] This is the first of the rites of the offering. **And it shall be accepted for him,** causing him to be accepted and to find favor in God's eyes, **to atone for him.**[D]

5 **He shall slaughter the young bull before the Lord.**[8] This may be performed by the owner or by any other Jew.[9] Ritual slaughter is required also in order to allow a non-sacred animal to be eaten. It is not considered an intrinsic part of the sacrificial

DISCUSSION

1:2| **When any man of you brings an offering**: The word order of the Hebrew verse is difficult, as it literally reads: "When any man brings, of you, an offering to the Lord." This alludes to the idea that when one brings an offering it is as though he sacrifices himself; the offering is "of you" (see Sforno; see also Ibn Ezra, *Od Yosef Ḥai*, and *Mei HaShiloaḥ*, for alternative allusions based on this phraseology).

1:4| **He shall lay his hand**: The Mishna and Gemara describe the manner in which this was performed during the Second Temple period. There is no reason to suppose that the procedure changed in any way over time, and it is therefore reasonable to assume that the Talmud describes the original method of performing this ritual. The owner placed both of his hands upon the head of the animal, between its horns, and leaned upon it with all his strength (see Ramban, Mishna *Yoma* 3:8, and *Menaḥot* 93a).

This rite is performed on almost every type of animal offering. Placing one's hands on the head of the animal symbolizes an exchange of the person for the animal. The animal is sacrificed as a substitute for the owner; through the sacrifice of the animal's flesh and blood, it is as though one sacrifices himself (see Ramban on verse 9). By leaning upon the animal the owner expresses his identification with the animal and symbolically transfers his identity to the animal, thereby allowing it to be sacrificed in his stead. It is for this reason that the verse states here that he achieves propitiation, even though the offering has not yet been brought upon the altar.

פרשת
וַיִּקְרָא

א

אב וַיִּקְרָא אֶל־מֹשֶׁה וַיְדַבֵּר יְהוָה אֵלָיו מֵאֹהֶל מוֹעֵד לֵאמֹר: דַּבֵּר אֶל־בְּנֵי יִשְׂרָאֵל
וְאָמַרְתָּ אֲלֵהֶם אָדָם כִּי־יַקְרִיב מִכֶּם קָרְבָּן לַיהוָה מִן־הַבְּהֵמָה מִן־הַבָּקָר
ג וּמִן־הַצֹּאן תַּקְרִיבוּ אֶת־קָרְבַּנְכֶם: אִם־עֹלָה קָרְבָּנוֹ מִן־הַבָּקָר זָכָר תָּמִים
ד יַקְרִיבֶנּוּ אֶל־פֶּתַח אֹהֶל מוֹעֵד יַקְרִיב אֹתוֹ לִרְצֹנוֹ לִפְנֵי יְהוָה: וְסָמַךְ יָדוֹ עַל
ה רֹאשׁ הָעֹלָה וְנִרְצָה לוֹ לְכַפֵּר עָלָיו: וְשָׁחַט אֶת־בֶּן הַבָּקָר לִפְנֵי יְהוָה וְהִקְרִיבוּ

רש"י

פרק א

א וַיִּקְרָא אֶל מֹשֶׁה. לְכָל דִּבְּרוֹת וּלְכָל אֲמִירוֹת וּלְכָל
צִוּוּיִים קָדְמָה קְרִיאָה, לְשׁוֹן חִבָּה, לְשׁוֹן שֶׁמַּלְאֲכֵי הַשָּׁרֵת
מִשְׁתַּמְּשִׁין בּוֹ, שֶׁנֶּאֱמַר: "וְקָרָא זֶה אֶל זֶה" (ישעיה ו, ג). אֲבָל
לִנְבִיאֵי אֻמּוֹת הָעוֹלָם נִגְלָה עֲלֵיהֶן בִּלְשׁוֹן עֲרָאִי, בִּלְשׁוֹן
טֻמְאָה, שֶׁנֶּאֱמַר: "וַיִּקָּר אֱלֹהִים אֶל בִּלְעָם" (במדבר כג, ד):
וַיִּקְרָא אֶל מֹשֶׁה. הַקּוֹל הוֹלֵךְ וּמַגִּיעַ לְאָזְנָיו וְכָל יִשְׂרָאֵל
לֹא שׁוֹמְעִין. יָכוֹל אַף לַהַפְסָקוֹת הָיְתָה קְרִיאָה? תַּלְמוּד
לוֹמַר: "וַיְדַבֵּר", לַדִּבּוּר הָיְתָה קְרִיאָה וְלֹא לַהַפְסָקוֹת.
וּמֶה הָיוּ הַפְסָקוֹת מְשַׁמְּשׁוֹת? לִתֵּן רֶוַח לְמֹשֶׁה לְהִתְבּוֹנֵן
בֵּין פָּרָשָׁה לְפָרָשָׁה וּבֵין עִנְיָן לְעִנְיָן, קַל וָחֹמֶר לְהֶדְיוֹט
הַלָּמֵד מִן הַהֶדְיוֹט: אֵלָיו. לְמַעֵט אֶת אַהֲרֹן. רַבִּי יְהוּדָה בֶּן
בְּתֵירָא אוֹמֵר: שְׁלֹשָׁה עָשָׂר דִּבְּרוֹת נֶאֶמְרוּ בַּתּוֹרָה לְמֹשֶׁה
וּלְאַהֲרֹן, וּכְנֶגְדָּן נֶאֶמְרוּ שְׁלֹשָׁה עָשָׂר מִעוּטִין, לְלַמֶּדְךָ,
שֶׁלֹּא לְאַהֲרֹן נֶאֶמְרוּ, אֶלָּא לְמֹשֶׁה שֶׁיֹּאמַר לְאַהֲרֹן. וְאֵלּוּ הֵן
שְׁלֹשָׁה עָשָׂר מִעוּטִין: "לְדַבֵּר אִתּוֹ" (במדבר ז, פט), "מִדַּבֵּר
אֵלָיו" (שם), "וַיְדַבֵּר אֵלָיו" (שם), "וְנוֹעַדְתִּי לְךָ" (שם), (שמות כה,
כב), כֻּלָּן בְּתוֹרַת כֹּהֲנִים (פרק א, כ). יָכוֹל יִשְׁמְעוּ אֶת קוֹל
הַקְּרִיאָה? תַּלְמוּד לוֹמַר: קוֹל לוֹ, קוֹל אֵלָיו, מֹשֶׁה שָׁמַע
וְכָל יִשְׂרָאֵל לֹא שָׁמְעוּ: מֵאֹהֶל מוֹעֵד. מְלַמֵּד שֶׁהָיָה הַקּוֹל
נִפְסָק וְלֹא הָיָה יוֹצֵא חוּץ לָאֹהֶל. יָכוֹל מִפְּנֵי שֶׁהַקּוֹל
נָמוּךְ? תַּלְמוּד לוֹמַר: "אֶת הַקּוֹל" (במדבר ז, פט), מַהוּ
"הַקּוֹל"? הוּא הַקּוֹל הַמְפֹרָשׁ בַּכְּתוּבִים: "קוֹל ה' בַּכֹּחַ,
קוֹל ה' בֶּהָדָר, קוֹל ה' שֹׁבֵר אֲרָזִים" (תהלים כט, ד-ה). אִם

כֵּן, לָמָּה נֶאֱמַר: "מֵאֹהֶל מוֹעֵד"? מְלַמֵּד שֶׁהָיָה הַקּוֹל
נִפְסָק. כַּיּוֹצֵא בּוֹ: "וְקוֹל כַּנְפֵי הַכְּרוּבִים נִשְׁמַע עַד הֶחָצֵר
הַחִיצֹנָה" (יחזקאל י, ה). יָכוֹל מִפְּנֵי שֶׁהַקּוֹל נָמוּךְ? תַּלְמוּד
לוֹמַר: "כְּקוֹל אֵל שַׁדַּי בְּדַבְּרוֹ" (שם). אִם כֵּן, לָמָּה נֶאֱמַר:
"עַד הֶחָצֵר הַחִיצֹנָה"? שֶׁכֵּיוָן שֶׁמַּגִּיעַ שָׁם הָיָה נִפְסָק:
מֵאֹהֶל מוֹעֵד לֵאמֹר (במדבר ז, פט). יָכוֹל מִכָּל הַבַּיִת? תַּלְמוּד
לוֹמַר: "מֵעַל הַכַּפֹּרֶת" (שם). יָכוֹל מֵעַל הַכַּפֹּרֶת כֻּלָּהּ?
תַּלְמוּד לוֹמַר: "מִבֵּין שְׁנֵי הַכְּרֻבִים" (שם): לֵאמֹר. צֵא וֶאֱמֹר
לָהֶם דִּבְרֵי כִבּוּשִׁין: בִּשְׁבִילְכֶם הוּא נִדְבָּר עִמִּי. שֶׁכֵּן מָצִינוּ,
שֶׁכָּל שְׁמוֹנֶה וּשְׁלֹשִׁים שָׁנָה שֶׁהָיוּ יִשְׂרָאֵל בַּמִּדְבָּר כַּמְנֻדִּים,
מִן הַמְרַגְּלִים וְאֵילָךְ, לֹא נִתְיַחֵד הַדִּבּוּר עִם מֹשֶׁה, שֶׁנֶּאֱמַר:
"וַיְהִי כַאֲשֶׁר תַּמּוּ כָל אַנְשֵׁי הַמִּלְחָמָה לָמוּת... וַיְדַבֵּר ה'
אֵלַי לֵאמֹר" (דברים ב, טז-יז). דָּבָר אַחֵר, צֵא וֶאֱמֹר לָהֶם
דְּבָרַי וַהֲשִׁיבֵנִי אִם יְקַבְּלוּם, כְּמוֹ שֶׁנֶּאֱמַר: "וַיָּשֶׁב מֹשֶׁה אֶת
דִּבְרֵי הָעָם וְגוֹ'" (שמות יט, ח):

ב אָדָם כִּי יַקְרִיב מִכֶּם. כְּשֶׁיַּקְרִיב, בְּקָרְבְּנוֹת נְדָבָה דִּבֵּר
הָעִנְיָן: אָדָם. לָמָּה נֶאֱמַר? מָה אָדָם הָרִאשׁוֹן לֹא הִקְרִיב
מִן הַגָּזֵל, שֶׁהַכֹּל הָיָה שֶׁלּוֹ, אַף אַתֶּם לֹא תַקְרִיבוּ מִן הַגָּזֵל:
הַבְּהֵמָה. יָכוֹל אַף חַיָּה בַּכְּלָל? תַּלְמוּד לוֹמַר: "בָּקָר וָצֹאן":
מִן הַבְּהֵמָה. וְלֹא כֻלָּהּ, לְהוֹצִיא אֶת הָרוֹבֵעַ וְאֶת הַנִּרְבָּע:
מִן הַבָּקָר. לְהוֹצִיא אֶת הַנֶּעֱבָד: מִן הַצֹּאן. לְהוֹצִיא אֶת
הַמֻּקְצֶה: וּמִן הַצֹּאן. לְהוֹצִיא אֶת הַנּוֹגֵחַ שֶׁהֵמִית. כְּשֶׁהוּא
אוֹמֵר לְמַטָּה מִן הָעִנְיָן: "מִן הַבָּקָר" (פסוק ג), שֶׁאֵין תַּלְמוּד
לוֹמַר – לְהוֹצִיא אֶת הַטְּרֵפָה: תַּקְרִיבוּ. מְלַמֵּד שֶׁשְּׁנַיִם

מִתְנַדְּבִים עוֹלָה בְּשֻׁתָּפוּת: קָרְבַּנְכֶם. מְלַמֵּד שֶׁהִיא בָּאָה
נִדְבַת צִבּוּר, הִיא הָיְתָה עוֹלַת קַיִן הַמִּזְבֵּחַ, הַבָּאָה מִן הַמּוֹתָרוֹת:

ג זָכָר. וְלֹא נְקֵבָה. כְּשֶׁהוּא אוֹמֵר: "זָכָר" לְמַטָּה (פסוק
י), שֶׁאֵין תַּלְמוּד לוֹמַר – זָכָר וְלֹא נְקֵבָה טֻמְטוּם וְאַנְדְּרוֹגִינוֹס:
תָּמִים. בְּלֹא מוּם: אֶל פֶּתַח אֹהֶל מוֹעֵד. מְטַפֵּל בַּהֲבָאָתוֹ
עַד הָעֲזָרָה. מַהוּ אוֹמֵר: "יַקְרִיב יַקְרִיב"? אֲפִלּוּ נִתְעָרְבָה
עוֹלַת רְאוּבֵן בְּעוֹלַת שִׁמְעוֹן, יַקְרִיב כָּל אַחַת לְשֵׁם מִי
שֶׁהוּא. וְכֵן עוֹלָה בְּחֻלִּין, יִמָּכְרוּ הַחֻלִּין לְצָרְכֵי עוֹלוֹת, וַהֲרֵי
הֵן כֻּלָּן עוֹלוֹת, וְתִקָּרֵב כָּל אַחַת לְשֵׁם מִי שֶׁהוּא. יָכוֹל
אֲפִלּוּ נִתְעָרְבָה בִּפְסוּלִין, אוֹ בְּשֶׁאֵינוֹ מִינוֹ? תַּלְמוּד לוֹמַר:
"יַקְרִיבֶנּוּ". מְלַמֵּד שֶׁסּוֹפְנִין אוֹתוֹ: יַקְרִיב אֹתוֹ. מְלַמֵּד שֶׁכּוֹפִין אוֹתוֹ עַד
כָּרְחוֹ. יָכוֹל בְּעַל כָּרְחוֹ? תַּלְמוּד לוֹמַר: "לִרְצֹנוֹ", הָא כֵּיצַד? כּוֹפִין אוֹתוֹ עַד
שֶׁיֹּאמַר: 'רוֹצֶה אֲנִי': לִפְנֵי ה'. וְסָמַךְ. אֵין סְמִיכָה בְּבָמָה:

ד עַל רֹאשׁ הָעֹלָה. לְהָבִיא עוֹלַת חוֹבָה לַסְּמִיכָה, וּלְהָבִיא
עוֹלַת הַצֹּאן: הָעֹלָה. פְּרָט לְעוֹלַת הָעוֹף: וְנִרְצָה לוֹ. עַל
מַה הוּא מְרַצֶּה לוֹ? אִם תֹּאמַר עַל כָּרֵתוֹת וּמִיתוֹת בֵּית
דִּין אוֹ מִיתָה בִּידֵי שָׁמַיִם אוֹ מַלְקוּת – הֲרֵי עָנְשָׁן אָמוּר,
הָא אֵינוֹ מְרַצֶּה אֶלָּא עַל עֲשֵׂה וְעַל לָאו שֶׁנִּתַּק לַעֲשֵׂה:

ה וְשָׁחַט... וְהִקְרִיבוּ. הַכֹּהֲנִים. מִקַּבָּלָה וָאֵילָךְ מִצְוַת
כְּהֻנָּה, לִמֵּד עַל הַשְּׁחִיטָה שֶׁכְּשֵׁרָה בְּזָר: לִפְנֵי ה'.
בָּעֲזָרָה: וְהִקְרִיבוּ. זוֹ קַבָּלָה שֶׁהִיא הָרִאשׁוֹנָה, וּמַשְׁמָעָהּ
לְשׁוֹן הוֹלָכָה, לָמְדוּ שְׁתֵּיהֶן: בְּנֵי אַהֲרֹן. יָכוֹל חֲלָלִים?
תַּלְמוּד לוֹמַר: "הַכֹּהֲנִים": אֶת הַדָּם וְזָרְקוּ אֶת הַדָּם.

DISCUSSION

In this respect, the story of the binding of Isaac (Genesis, chap. 22), in which an animal was sacrificed in lieu of a human being, can be seen as a model for all animal offerings. This can also explain the seemingly cryptic statement

that Isaac's ashes form a heap upon the altar (see, e.g., Jerusalem Talmud, *Ta'anit* 2:1). Isaac himself was never sacrificed, but since the ram took Isaac's place, it is as though he himself were burned upon the altar.

And it shall be accepted for him to atone for him: One is not required to bring a burnt offering in order to achieve atonement for any specific transgression. Nevertheless one may bring a burnt offering in the case of a transgression

ritual but rather a preparatory rite. **And Aaron's sons, the priests, shall present the blood,** which is the beginning of the priests' service. The priests collect the blood that flows out of the neck of the animal in a bowl,[10] convey it to the altar, **and cast the blood around the** external **altar that is at the entrance of the Tent of Meeting.** According to tradition the blood was not sprinkled around the entire perimeter of the altar, which would be somewhat difficult to perform. Rather, the blood was cast upon two opposite corners of the altar, so that it reached a section of all four of the altar's walls.[11]

6 **He shall** subsequently **flay the burnt offering,** as the hide is not burned on the altar, **and cut it into its pieces.**[D]

7 **The sons of Aaron the priest shall place fire upon the altar and arrange wood upon the fire.** This commandment is not directly related to the burnt offering or to any other offering.[12]

8 **Aaron's sons, the priests, shall arrange the pieces, the head, and the fats** of the inner organs[13] **on the wood that is on the fire that is on the altar.** Alternatively, the verse does not refer only to the fats, but also to various inner organs.[14]

9 **Its innards,** including the stomach and intestines, **and its legs he shall wash with water.** This may be performed either by a priest or by a non-priest.[15] The intestines are soiled with partially digested food and waste, and the legs are usually also soiled. They are therefore unfit to be burned on the altar before being cleansed. **The priest shall burn everything on the altar,** the head, the fats, the inner organs, and the rest of the flesh, **as a burnt offering, a fire offering of a pleasing aroma to the Lord.**[D] The offering is a unique gift that pleases God as one would be pleased by a pleasant aroma, as His will has been fulfilled.[16]

10 **If his offering is from the flock,**[D] rather than from cattle, **from the sheep or from the goats, as a burnt offering; an unblemished male he shall present it.** The term "flock" refers to small domesticated animals, sheep and goats, as opposed to cattle.

Sheep

Goat

11 **He shall slaughter it on the north side of the altar before the Lord; and Aaron's sons, the priests, shall cast its blood around the altar,** as stated above (verse 5) with regard to the bull burnt offering.

12 **He shall cut it,** the body of the animal, **into its pieces, and its head,** which is severed and not dissected like the rest of the body, **and its fats,** which are separated from the rest of the flesh. **And the priest shall arrange them,** the pieces, the head, and the fats, **on the wood that is on the fire that is upon the altar.**

13 **The innards and the legs he shall wash with water** to cleanse them. **And the priest shall present everything,** all the pieces of the offering, including the innards and the legs, **and burn it on the altar. It is a burnt offering, a fire offering of a pleasing aroma to the Lord.**

DISCUSSION

that does not require an atonement offering, e.g., the dereliction of a positive commandment (*Zevaḥim* 5a–7b; *Tosefta, Menaḥot* 10:12). If one neglected to perform a commandment and desires to completely atone for his sin and to attain divine favor, he may express his desire by bringing a voluntary burnt offering. The burnt offering also atones for immoral thoughts (Jerusalem Talmud, *Yoma* 8:7), as illustrated by the actions of Job: "It was when the cycle of days of their feasting was completed that Job would send and sanctify them, and he would rise early in the morning, and offer up burnt offerings corresponding to the number of them all. For Job would say: Perhaps my sons have sinned and blasphemed God in their hearts. So would Job do always" (Job 1:5). Immoral thoughts are not subject to external evaluation, but one may

bring a burnt offering as part of his self-improvement and as an expression of self-sacrifice. A burnt offering may also be brought in response to good tidings, and as a general atonement for unknown transgressions (see *Bekhor Shor; Bemidbar Rabba* 10:5).

1:6 | And cut it into its pieces: Some of the pieces into which the burnt offering is dissected are stated or indicated in the upcoming verses, e.g., the head and the legs. The Mishna contains a detailed description of the manner of dissection (see *Yoma* 7:2 and *Tamid* 4:2–3). The pieces needed to be respectable portions, large enough to be easily held, yet small enough to be carried (see *Ḥullin* 11a). One of the pieces of the bull burnt offering was the hind leg, which was too heavy for a single priest to carry, at least in the case of a large bull. Although the Gemara

relates a case where a particularly strong priest carried the hind legs alone (*Sukka* 52b), each piece of a bull burnt offering was usually carried to the altar by two or three priests. This might explain the difference between the language employed in verse 8, which states with regard to the bull burnt offering that the pieces shall be arranged by the priests, in the plural, and the language of verse 12, which refers to a single priest arranging the pieces of the sheep or goat burnt offering (see *Da'at Zekenim* and Ramban).

1:9 | Of a pleasing aroma to the Lord: The average person would not enjoy the smell of an offering being burned to ashes, which is quite different from the aroma of roasting meat. Furthermore, the process of sacrificing an offering includes slaughter, collecting the blood and sprinkling it on the altar, dissecting the carcass, ◂◂

בְּנֵי אַהֲרֹן הַכֹּהֲנִים אֶת־הַדָּם וְזָרְקוּ אֶת־הַדָּם עַל־הַמִּזְבֵּחַ סָבִיב אֲשֶׁר־פֶּתַח

אֹהֶל מוֹעֵד: וְהִפְשִׁיט אֶת־הָעֹלָה וְנִתַּח אֹתָהּ לִנְתָחֶיהָ: וְנָתְנוּ בְּנֵי אַהֲרֹן

הַכֹּהֵן אֵשׁ עַל־הַמִּזְבֵּחַ וְעָרְכוּ עֵצִים עַל־הָאֵשׁ: וְעָרְכוּ בְּנֵי אַהֲרֹן הַכֹּהֲנִים

אֵת הַנְּתָחִים אֶת־הָרֹאשׁ וְאֶת־הַפָּדֶר עַל־הָעֵצִים אֲשֶׁר עַל־הָאֵשׁ אֲשֶׁר עַל־

הַמִּזְבֵּחַ: וְקִרְבּוֹ וּכְרָעָיו יִרְחַץ בַּמָּיִם וְהִקְטִיר הַכֹּהֵן אֶת־הַכֹּל הַמִּזְבֵּחָה עֹלָה

אִשֵּׁה רֵיחַ־נִיחוֹחַ לַיהוָה: וְאִם־מִן־הַצֹּאן קָרְבָּנוֹ מִן־הַכְּשָׂבִים אוֹ

מִן־הָעִזִּים לְעֹלָה זָכָר תָּמִים יַקְרִיבֶנּוּ: וְשָׁחַט אֹתוֹ עַל יֶרֶךְ הַמִּזְבֵּחַ צָפֹנָה לִפְנֵי

יְהוָה וְזָרְקוּ בְּנֵי אַהֲרֹן הַכֹּהֲנִים אֶת־דָּמוֹ עַל־הַמִּזְבֵּחַ סָבִיב: וְנִתַּח אֹתוֹ לִנְתָחָיו

וְאֶת־רֹאשׁוֹ וְאֶת־פִּדְרוֹ וְעָרַךְ הַכֹּהֵן אֹתָם עַל־הָעֵצִים אֲשֶׁר עַל־הָאֵשׁ אֲשֶׁר

עַל־הַמִּזְבֵּחַ: וְהַקֶּרֶב וְהַכְּרָעַיִם יִרְחַץ בַּמָּיִם וְהִקְרִיב הַכֹּהֵן אֶת־הַכֹּל וְהִקְטִיר

הַמִּזְבֵּחָה עֹלָה הוּא אִשֵּׁה רֵיחַ נִיחֹחַ לַיהוָה:

רש״י

מַה תַּלְמוּד לוֹמַר: 'פָּס' שְׁתֵּי פְעָמִים? לְהָבִיא אֶת שֶׁנִּתְעָרֵב דָּמוֹ בְּשֶׁאֵינוֹ מִינוֹ, יָכוֹל אַף בִּפְסוּלִים, אוֹ בַּחַטָּאוֹת הַפְּנִימִיּוֹת אוֹ בַּחַטָּאוֹת הַחִיצוֹנִיּוֹת, שֶׁאֵלּוּ לְמַעְלָה וְהִיא לְמַטָּה? תַּלְמוּד לוֹמַר בְּמָקוֹם אַחֵר: 'דָּמוֹ' (להלן פסוק יא). זָרְקוּ. עוֹמֵד לְמַטָּה וְזוֹרֵק מִן הַכְּלִי לִכְתָלֵי הַמִּזְבֵּחַ לְמַטָּה מֵחוּט הַסִּקְרָא כְּנֶגֶד הַזָּוִית, לְכָךְ נֶאֱמַר: "סָבִיב", שֶׁיְּהֵא הַדָּם נָתוּן בְּאַרְבַּע רוּחוֹת הַמִּזְבֵּחַ. אוֹ יָכוֹל יַקִּיפֶנּוּ כְּחוּט? תַּלְמוּד לוֹמַר: "וְזָרְקוּ", וְאִי אֶפְשָׁר לְהַקִּיף בִּזְרִיקָה. אִי "וְזָרְקוּ", יָכוֹל בִּזְרִיקָה אַחַת? תַּלְמוּד לוֹמַר: "סָבִיב". הָא כֵּיצַד? נוֹתֵן שְׁתֵּי מַתָּנוֹת שֶׁהֵן אַרְבַּע: אֲשֶׁר פֶּתַח אֹהֶל מוֹעֵד. וְלֹא בִּזְמַן שֶׁהוּא מְפֹרָק:

ז) וְהִפְשִׁיט אֶת הָעֹלָה. מַה תַּלְמוּד לוֹמַר "הָעֹלָה"?

לְרַבּוֹת אֶת כָּל הָעוֹלוֹת לְהֶפְשֵׁט וְנִתּוּחַ: אֹתָהּ לִנְתָחֶיהָ. וְלֹא נְתָחֶיהָ לִנְתָחִים:

ז) וְנָתְנוּ אֵשׁ. אַף עַל פִּי שֶׁהָאֵשׁ יוֹרֶדֶת מִן הַשָּׁמַיִם, מִצְוָה לְהָבִיא מִן הַהֶדְיוֹט: בְּנֵי אַהֲרֹן הַכֹּהֵן. כְּשֶׁהוּא בְּכִהוּנוֹ, הָא אִם עָבַד בְּבִגְדֵי כֹּהֵן הֶדְיוֹט עֲבוֹדָתוֹ פְּסוּלָה:

ח) בְּנֵי אַהֲרֹן הַכֹּהֲנִים. כְּשֶׁהֵם בְּכִהוּנָם, הָא כֹּהֵן הֶדְיוֹט שֶׁעָבַד בִּשְׁמוֹנָה בְּגָדִים עֲבוֹדָתוֹ פְּסוּלָה: אֵת הַנְּתָחִים אֶת הָרֹאשׁ. לְפִי שֶׁאֵין הָרֹאשׁ בִּכְלַל הֶפְשֵׁט, שֶׁכְּבָר הֻתַּז בַּשְּׁחִיטָה, לְפִיכָךְ הֻצְרַךְ לִמְנוֹתוֹ לְעַצְמוֹ: וְאֶת הַפָּדֶר. לָמָּה נֶאֱמַר? לְלַמֶּדְךָ שֶׁמַּעֲלֵהוּ עִם הָרֹאשׁ וּמְכַסֶּה בּוֹ אֶת בֵּית

הַשְּׁחִיטָה, וְזֶהוּ דֶּרֶךְ כָּבוֹד שֶׁל מַעְלָה: אֲשֶׁר עַל הַמִּזְבֵּחַ. שֶׁלֹּא יִהְיוּ הַגִּזְרִין יוֹצְאִין חוּץ לַמַּעֲרָכָה:

ט) עֹלָה. לְשֵׁם עוֹלָה יַקְטִירֶנּוּ: אִשֵּׁה. כְּשֶׁיִּשְׁחֲטֶנּוּ יְהֵא שׁוֹחֲטוֹ לְשֵׁם הָאֵשׁ, וְכָל 'אִשֶּׁה' לְשׁוֹן אֵשׁ, פוֹאיד״א בְּלַעַז: נִיחוֹחַ. נַחַת רוּחַ לְפָנַי שֶׁאָמַרְתִּי וְנַעֲשָׂה רְצוֹנִי:

י) וְאִם מִן הַצֹּאן. וָי״ו מוּסָף עַל עִנְיָן רִאשׁוֹן. וְלָמָּה הִפְסִיק? לִתֵּן רֶוַח לְמֹשֶׁה לְהִתְבּוֹנֵן בֵּין פָּרָשָׁה לְפָרָשָׁה: מִן הַצֹּאן... מִן הַכְּשָׂבִים... מִן הָעִזִּים. הֲרֵי אֵלּוּ שְׁלֹשָׁה מִעוּטִין, פְּרָט לְזָקֵן לְחוֹלֶה וְלִמְזֹהָם:

יא) עַל יֶרֶךְ הַמִּזְבֵּחַ. צָפֹנָה לִפְנֵי ה'. וְאֵין עַמּוּן בַּכֶּבֶשׁ:

DISCUSSION

→ and removing the inner organs. It is fair to assume that many people would find this scene repulsive, and not only in modern times.

A person brings an offering of his own free will in order to achieve propitiation (see *Menaḥot* 110a and Rashi ad loc.). This involves a deep identification with the sacrificial process; in order for this process to be meaningful, he must be deeply emotionally engaged, to the point of ecstasy. Such a process can cause one to experience events in a drastically different

manner from the way he would usually experience them. Something that one might otherwise find repulsive may become pleasant and gratifying when he is deeply engaged in the process, identifies with it, and is exhilarated by it. This experience, which every person undergoes in different ways over the course of his lifetime, should occur while performing the rituals of an offering. Only then may one be considered to be presenting an offering which is of a pleasing aroma to God.

1:10 | And if his offering is from the flock: There are many similarities between the sacrificial rites described with regard to the different types of animals offered as burnt offerings. However, the Torah reiterates the many details in order to teach additional laws that were not stated previously, in accordance with the principle that was taught by the school of Rabbi Yishmael (*Sota* 3b): "Every passage in the Torah that was stated and repeated was repeated only for the novel element introduced therein." In

14 Apart from the burnt offerings from the cattle and flocks, there
Second is an additional type of burnt offering: **If his offering is from**
aliya **the birds, a burnt offering to the Lord, from turtledoves,** a type of wild bird, **or from young pigeons**[BD] **he shall bring** one as **his offering.**
15 **The priest shall bring it to the altar, shall pinch off its head,**[D] **and shall burn it,** the severed head, **on the altar** separately from the body.[17] Prior to burning the bird's head, **its blood shall be squeezed on the wall of the altar.** Both in the case of the animal burnt offering and in the case of the bird offering, the blood is first sprinkled upon the altar and then the body is burned on the altar. However, the blood of the bird offering is not cast upon the altar from a vessel as in the case of the animal burnt offering. Rather, the bird is pressed against the wall of the altar so that its blood is squeezed out.[18]

Pigeon

Turtledove

16 Before burning the bird on the altar, **he shall remove its crop,** the section of the gullet that enlarges to form a pocket, in which the food is stored before being transferred to the stomach, **with its feathers** that surround the crop. The priest shall cut out the crop, which is soiled with partially digested food, together with the feathers, **and cast it beside the altar to the east, to the place of the ashes,** where a portion of the ashes removed from the altar were placed (see 6:3).

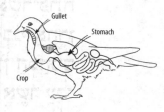

Digestive tract of a bird

17 After removing the crop, **he,** the priest, **shall split it by its wings but shall not separate** it into two completely detached parts. **The priest shall burn it on the altar, on the wood that is on the fire; it is a burnt offering, a fire offering of a pleasing aroma to the Lord.** The Torah has concluded its presentation of the three types of burnt offerings: The bull burnt offering, the burnt offering from the flock, and the bird burnt offering.

The Meal Offering

LEVITICUS 2:1–16

The previous section dealt with the burnt offering and discussed the various animals that may be brought as burnt offerings. In the upcoming section, the Torah discusses the meal offering, which is comprised entirely of vegetable matter and does not include any component derived from animals. The Hebrew term for a meal offering, *minḥa*, means a gift, usually one that is given in order to express the giver's appreciation of the recipient's kindness, or to express his subservience toward the recipient. The meal offering may be brought as a voluntary offering, but there are also meal offerings that are incumbent upon the individual and upon the community. The meal offering does not differ from the burnt offering only in its components; its sacrificial rites also differ, and they resemble those of the peace offering (see chap. 3) more than those of the burnt offering.

Although some of the details with regard to the meal offering are stated only later (see 6:7–16), the main laws concerning the manner of preparing the meal offering are stated here, as are the details of the different types of meal offerings.

Frankincense pellets

2 **1** **When a person brings a meal offering to the Lord, of high-quality flour**[D] **his offering shall be. He shall pour oil upon it and place frankincense**[B] **on it.**

DISCUSSION

this passage the Torah clarifies the location of the slaughter. Previously the Torah stated that the burnt offering is slaughtered before the Lord (see verse 5), that is, opposite or adjacent to the Tabernacle entrance. In this passage (see next verse), the Torah clarifies that the burnt offering must be slaughtered in the north of the Tabernacle courtyard. This applies to all burnt offerings, and this law applies also in the Temple: Any offerings of the most sacred order, e.g., burnt offerings, are slaughtered only in the north of the Temple courtyard (see Ramban).

1:14| **From turtledoves or from young pigeons**: Only mature turtledoves are fit to be brought as offerings. Conversely, only the young pigeons, the fledglings, may be offered (see *Ḥullin* 22b). The bird offering costs much less than even an offering from sheep or goats, and is certainly far cheaper than the bull offering. The cost of young pigeons is minimal, particularly if one takes into account that pigeons lay eggs nearly every month, and turtledoves are wild birds whose capture is not costly.

יד ואם מן־העוף עלה קרבנו ליהוה והקריב מן־התרים או מן־בני היונה את־ שני
טו קרבנו: והקריבו הכהן אל־המזבח ומלק את־ראשו והקטיר המזבחה ונמצה דמו
טז על קיר המזבח: והסיר את־מראתו בנצתה והשליך אתה אצל המזבח קדמה
יז אל־מקום הדשן: ושסע אתו בכנפיו לא יבדיל והקטיר אתו הכהן המזבחה על־
א העצים אשר על־האש עלה הוא אשה ריח ניחח ליהוה: ונפש כי־
תקריב קרבן מנחה ליהוה סלת יהיה קרבנו ויצק עליה שמן ונתן עליה לבנה:

רש"י

יד| **מן העוף.** ולא כל העוף, לפי שנאמר: "תמים זכר בבקר בכשבים ובעזים" (להלן כב, יט), תמות וזכרות בבהמה ואין תמות וזכרות בעופות, יכול אף מחסר אבר? תלמוד לומר: "מן העוף": **תרים.** גדולים ולא קטנים: **בני יונה.** קטנים ולא גדולים: **מן התרים או מן בני היונה.** פרט לתחלת הצהוב שבזה ושבזה שהוא פסול, שגדול הוא אצל בני יונה וקטן אצל תורים:

טו| **והקריבו.** אפילו פרידה אחת יביא: **הכהן ומלק.** אין מליקה בכלי אלא בעצמו של כהן, קוצץ בצפרנו ממול העורף, וחותך המפרקת עד שמגיע לסימנין וקוצצן: **ונמצה דמו.** לשון "ומיץ אפים" (משלי ל, לג), "כי אפס המץ" (ישעיה טז, ד). כובש בית השחיטה על קיר המזבח והדם מתמצה ויורד: **ומלק והקטיר ונמצה.** אפשר לומר כן, מאחר שהוא מקטיר הוא מוצה?! אלא, מה הקטרה הראש בעצמו והגוף בעצמו אף מליקה כן. ופשוטו של מקרא, מסרס הוא: "ומלק והקטיר", וקדם הקטרה "ונמצה דמו" כבר:

טז| **מראתו.** מקום הראי, זה הזפק: **בנצתה.** עם בני מעיה. ו'נוצה' לשון דבר המאוס, כמו: "כי נצו גם נעו" (איכה ד, טו), וזהו שתרגם אונקלוס: "באוכליה", וזהו מדרשו של אבא יוסי בן חנן, שאמר: נוטל את הקרקבן עמה. ורבותינו זכרונם לברכה אמרו: קודר סביב הזפק בסכין כעין ארבה, ונוטלו עם הנוצה שעל העור. בעולת בהמה שאינה אוכלת אלא באבוס בעליה, נאמר: "והקרב והכרעים ירחץ במים וגו' והקטיר" (לעיל פסוק יג), ובעוף שנזון מן הגזל, נאמר: "והשליך" את המעים שאכלו מן הגזל: **אצל המזבח קדמה.** במזרחו של כבש: **אל מקום הדשן.** מקום שנותנין שם תרומת הדשן בכל בקר ודשון מזבח הפנימי והמנורה, וכלם נבלעים שם במקומן:

יז| **ושסע.** אין שסוע אלא ביד, וכן הוא אומר בשמשון: "וישסעהו כשסע הגדי" (שופטים יד, ו): **בכנפיו.** עם כנפיו, אינו צריך למרט כנפי נוצתו: **בכנפיו.** נוצה ממש. והלא אין לך הדיוט שמריח ריח כנפים נשרפים ואין נפשו קצה עליו, ולמה אמר הכתוב יקריב? כדי שיהא המזבח שבע ומהדר בקרבנו של עני: **לא יבדיל.** אינו מפרקו לגמרי לשתי חתיכות, אלא קורעו מגבו. נאמר בעוף 'ריח ניחוח' ונאמר בבהמה 'ריח ניחוח' (לעיל פסוקים ט; יג), לומר לך, אחד המרבה ואחד הממעיט, ובלבד שיכון את לבו לשמים:

פרק ב

א| **ונפש כי תקריב.** לא נאמר 'נפש' בכל קרבנות נדבה אלא במנחה. מי דרכו להתנדב מנחה? עני. אמר הקדוש ברוך הוא: מעלה אני עליו כאלו הקריב נפשו: **סלת יהיה קרבנו.** האומר: 'הרי עלי מנחה' סתם, מביא מנחת סלת שהיא הראשונה שבמנחות, ונקמצת כשהיא סלת כמו שמפרש בענין. לפי שנאמרו כאן חמשה מיני מנחות וכלן באות אפויות קדם קמיצה חוץ מזו, לכך קרויה מנחת סלת: **סלת.** אין 'סלת' אלא מן החטין, שנאמר: "סלת חטים" (שמות כט, ב), ואין מנחה פחותה מעשרון, שנאמר: "ועשרון סלת... למנחה" (ויקרא יד, כא), עשרון לכל מנחה: **ויצק עליה שמן.** על כלה: **ונתן עליה לבנה.** על מקצתה, מניח קמץ לבונה עליה לצד אחד. ומה ראית לומר כן? שאין רבוי אחר רבוי בתורה אלא למעט. דבר אחר, שמן על כלה מפני שהוא נבלל עמה ונקמץ עמה, כמו שנאמר: "מסלתה ומשמנה" (פסוק ב), ולבונה על מקצתה, שאינה נבללת עמה ולא נקמצת עמה, שנאמר: "על כל לבנתה", שלאחר שקמץ מלקט את הלבונה כלה מעליה ומקטירה: **ויצק, ונתן, והביאה.** מלמד שיציקה ובלילה כשרים בזר:

BACKGROUND

1:14| **From turtledoves or from young pigeons**: These are two species of birds from the Columbidae family. The pigeon, *Columba livia*, has a stout body, short neck, and small, round head. The turtledove, *Streptopelia turtur*, is a migratory bird, which may be found in Israel during the spring and summer. It is smaller than the pigeon, with a slight body, shorter wings, and a long tail. Its color is grey or brown with a mark at the sides of the neck containing black and white stripes.

2:1| **Frankincense**: This is a fragrant whitish-yellow resin, also called olibanum, derived from the *Boswellia sacra* tree of the Burseraceae family. These trees grow in the vicinity of Somalia, Ethiopia, and the south of the Arabian Peninsula. Frankincense resin is extracted by making an incision in the tree's bark and then collecting the resin, which drips into a vessel. The liquid resin slowly coagulates into pellets, which can then be used.

DISCUSSION

1:15| **Shall pinch off its head**: According to tradition, the priest pinches off the head of the bird from the back of its neck with his thumbnail (see 5:8; *Zevaḥim* 64a–65b). This is different from slaughter, which is performed from the front of the throat. Pinching off the head in this manner is possible because these are small birds.

2:1| **High-quality flour**: When wheat is ground with a hand mill, there are large, hard particles from the center of the wheat kernel that are incompletely crushed. These coarsely ground particles, which resemble couscous, are referred to as high-quality flour, as they are considered the tastiest and most important part of the wheat. The more finely crushed part of the grain is referred to simply as flour, and it is considered of lesser quality.

2 **He shall bring it to Aaron's sons, the priests, and he,** the priest, **shall take from there his handful**[D] **from its high-quality flour and from its oil.** The flour and oil are mixed together, and the oil is absorbed by the flour,[19] and it is therefore possible to hold the oil in one's hand. The priest separates the handful of flour and oil from the meal offering, and the handful is taken together **with all its frankincense.**[20] **The priest shall burn its memorial portion,** which consists of the handful of flour and oil and all of the frankincense, **on the altar** as **a fire offering of a pleasing aroma to the Lord.**
3 **The remnant of the meal offering,** everything apart from the small portion that was burned on the altar, **shall be for Aaron and for his sons; it is a sacred sacrament from the fire offerings of the Lord.** Although this offering is not burned on the altar in its entirety like the burnt offering, it is an important offering, considered to be of the most sacred order, and its degree of sanctity is equivalent to that of the burnt offering.
4 Apart from the aforementioned type of meal offering, in which the flour and oil are mixed together to form a dough, there are additional types of meal offerings: **When you bring a meal offering baked in the oven** as a gift offering, **it shall be unleavened loaves of high-quality** wheat **flour mixed with oil,**[21] **or unleavened wafers smeared with oil.**[22]
5 There is another type of meal offering: **If your offering is a meal offering** fried in oil **on a flat pan,**[23] it shall also be made **of high-quality flour, mixed with oil,** and **it shall** also **be unleavened bread.**
6 **Break it into** small **pieces, and pour oil on it** a second time.[24] **It is a meal offering,** and this is the manner of preparing all meal offerings.[25]
7 **If your offering is a meal offering** deep-fried **in a deep pan,**[D]
Third aliya **it shall** also **be prepared of high-quality flour with oil.**
8 The rites of the aforementioned types of meal offerings are identical:[26] **You shall bring the meal offering that is prepared of these,** either just mixed with oil, baked in an oven, or fried, **to the Lord. He,** the individual bringing the offering, **shall bring it to the priest, and he,** the priest, **shall bring it to the altar.** As part of the ritual, the priest is required to bring the entire meal offering in its sacred vessel to the altar.
9 **The priest shall separate from the meal offering its memorial portion,** the handful and the frankincense, **and he shall burn it upon the altar, a fire offering of a pleasing aroma to the Lord.**
10 **The remnant of the meal offering shall be for Aaron and for his sons; it is** considered **a sacred sacrament from the fire offerings of the Lord,** even though it is eaten by the priests rather than being burned on the altar.
11 **All meal offerings that you shall bring to the Lord shall not be prepared as leavened bread, for all leaven and all honey,**[D] the sweet liquid that seeps out of various fruits,[27] **you shall not burn as a fire offering to the Lord.**[D]
12 Nevertheless, there are instances where leaven and honey are presented as offerings: **As an offering of first fruits you shall bring them to the Lord.** The two loaves brought on Shavuot, which constituted the first offering brought from the new crop of wheat, were baked as leavened bread (23:17), and the first fruits were brought near to the altar despite the fact that they contained fruit juice.[28] Apart from the first fruits, no fruit were brought to the Temple. These offerings shall be brought to the Temple, **but on the altar they shall not ascend for a pleasing aroma;** they are not burned on the altar.

DISCUSSION

2:2 | **And he shall take from there his handful**: According to tradition, this is not referring to a complete handful, but includes only the amount of flour that fits between the priest's three middle fingers when they are bent over the palm of the hand. The little finger and thumb are used to remove the extra flour that cannot be held by the three middle fingers (*Menaḥot* 11a).

2:7 | **A deep pan [*marḥeshet*]:** The term *marḥeshet* is apparently derived from the term *meraḥeshet*, which means to speak or to whisper, and refers to the sound made by a large quantity of boiling oil (see Rashi; Ibn Ezra; Mishna *Menaḥot* 5:8).

2:11 | **Honey**: The term honey refers most commonly in the Bible to the juice of sweet fruit, e.g., dates. However, it is sometimes also used as a reference to bee honey (see Judges 14:8), despite the fact that bee honey is quite different from honey derived from fruit in both appearance and taste.

For all leaven and all honey you shall not burn as a fire offering to the Lord: The prohibition of burning leavened bread as an offering is related to the prohibition of leaven during Passover. Leaven is an artificial addition to bread; the rudimentary bread is unleavened. Everything offered on the altar, as well as the altar itself (see Exodus 20:21), is characterized by its simplicity and by its elementary form. The meal offering is made as a rudimentary mixture of flour and oil, without either leaven, which changes the texture of the loaf, or honey, which improves its taste. Similarly, although the priestly vestments are designed for splendor and for beauty (see Exodus 28:2) they are essentially plain garments, fashioned from simple materials.

ב וֶהֱבִיאָהּ אֶל־בְּנֵי אַהֲרֹן הַכֹּהֲנִים וְקָמַץ מִשָּׁם מְלֹא קֻמְצוֹ מִסָּלְתָּהּ וּמִשַּׁמְנָהּ עַל כָּל־לְבֹנָתָהּ וְהִקְטִיר הַכֹּהֵן אֶת־אַזְכָּרָתָהּ הַמִּזְבֵּחָה אִשֵּׁה רֵיחַ נִיחֹחַ לַיהוָה:

ג וְהַנּוֹתֶרֶת מִן־הַמִּנְחָה לְאַהֲרֹן וּלְבָנָיו קֹדֶשׁ קָדָשִׁים מֵאִשֵּׁי יְהוָה:

ד וְכִי תַקְרִב קָרְבַּן מִנְחָה מַאֲפֵה תַנּוּר סֹלֶת חַלּוֹת מַצֹּת בְּלוּלֹת בַּשֶּׁמֶן וּרְקִיקֵי מַצּוֹת מְשֻׁחִים בַּשָּׁמֶן: ה וְאִם־מִנְחָה עַל־הַמַּחֲבַת קָרְבָּנֶךָ סֹלֶת בְּלוּלָה בַשֶּׁמֶן

מַצָּה תִהְיֶה: ו פָּתוֹת אֹתָהּ פִּתִּים וְיָצַקְתָּ עָלֶיהָ שָׁמֶן מִנְחָה הִוא:

ז וְאִם־מִנְחַת מַרְחֶשֶׁת קָרְבָּנֶךָ סֹלֶת בַּשֶּׁמֶן תֵּעָשֶׂה: וְהֵבֵאתָ אֶת־הַמִּנְחָה אֲשֶׁר שלישי

ח יֵעָשֶׂה מֵאֵלֶּה לַיהוָה וְהִקְרִיבָהּ אֶל־הַכֹּהֵן וְהִגִּישָׁהּ אֶל־הַמִּזְבֵּחַ: וְהֵרִים הַכֹּהֵן

ט מִן־הַמִּנְחָה אֶת־אַזְכָּרָתָהּ וְהִקְטִיר הַמִּזְבֵּחָה אִשֵּׁה רֵיחַ נִיחֹחַ לַיהוָה: וְהַנּוֹתֶרֶת

יא מִן־הַמִּנְחָה לְאַהֲרֹן וּלְבָנָיו קֹדֶשׁ קָדָשִׁים מֵאִשֵּׁי יְהוָה: כָּל־הַמִּנְחָה אֲשֶׁר תַּקְרִיבוּ לַיהוָה לֹא תֵעָשֶׂה חָמֵץ כִּי כָל־שְׂאֹר וְכָל־דְּבַשׁ לֹא־תַקְטִירוּ מִמֶּנּוּ אִשֶּׁה

יב לַיהוָה: קָרְבַּן רֵאשִׁית תַּקְרִיבוּ אֹתָם לַיהוָה וְאֶל־הַמִּזְבֵּחַ לֹא־יַעֲלוּ לְרֵיחַ נִיחֹחַ:

בּ] הַכֹּהֲנִים וְקָמַץ. מִקְּמִיצָה וָאֵילָךְ מִצְוַת כְּהֻנָּה: וְקָמַץ מִשָּׁם. מִמְּקוֹם שֶׁרַגְלֵי הַזָּר עוֹמְדוֹת, לְלַמֶּדְךָ שֶׁהַקְּמִיצָה כְּשֵׁרָה בְּכָל מָקוֹם בָּעֲזָרָה, אַף בְּאַחַד עָשָׂר אַמָּה שֶׁל מְקוֹם דְּרִיסַת רַגְלֵי יִשְׂרָאֵל: מְלֹא קֻמְצוֹ. יָכוֹל מְבֻרָץ, מְבַצְבֵּץ וְיוֹצֵא לְכָל צַד? תַּלְמוּד לוֹמַר (לְהַלָּן ו, ח): "בְּקֻמְצוֹ", לֹא יְהֵא כָּשֵׁר אֶלָּא מַה שֶּׁבְּתוֹךְ הַקֹּמֶץ. אִי "בְּקֻמְצוֹ", יָכוֹל חָסֵר? תַּלְמוּד לוֹמַר: "מְלֹא". הָא כֵיצַד? חוֹפֶה שָׁלֹשׁ אֶצְבְּעוֹתָיו עַל פַּס יָדוֹ, וְזֶהוּ "קֹמֶץ" בְּמַשְׁמַע לָשׁוֹן הָעִבְרִית: עַל כָּל־לְבֹנָתָהּ. לְבַד כָּל הַלְּבוֹנָה יְהֵא הַקֹּמֶץ מָלֵא: וְהִקְטִיר. אַף הַלְּבוֹנָה בַּהַקְטָרָה: מְלֹא קֻמְצוֹ מִסָּלְתָּהּ וּמִשַּׁמְנָהּ. הָא אִם קָמַץ וְעָלָה בְיָדוֹ גַּרְגִּיר מֶלַח אוֹ קֹרֶט לְבוֹנָה פְּסוּלָה: אַזְכָּרָתָהּ. הַקֹּמֶץ הָעוֹלֶה לַגָּבוֹהַּ הוּא זִכְרוֹן הַמִּנְחָה, שֶׁבּוֹ נִזְכָּר בְּעָלֶיהָ לְטוֹבָה וּלְנַחַת רוּחַ:

גּ] לְאַהֲרֹן וּלְבָנָיו. כֹּהֵן גָּדוֹל נוֹטֵל חֵלֶק בָּרֹאשׁ שֶׁלֹּא בְמַחֲלֹקֶת, וְהַהֶדְיוֹט בְּמַחֲלֹקֶת: קֹדֶשׁ קָדָשִׁים. הוּא לָהֶם: מֵאִשֵּׁי ה' – אֵין לָהֶם חֵלֶק בָּהּ אֶלָּא לְאַחַר מַתְּנוֹת הָאִשִּׁים:

דּ] וְכִי תַקְרִב וְגוֹ'. שֶׁנֶּאֱמַר: 'הֲרֵי עָלַי מִנְחַת מַאֲפֵה תַנּוּר', וְלִמֵּד הַכָּתוּב שֶׁיָּבִיא אוֹ חַלּוֹת אוֹ רְקִיקִין. הַחַלּוֹת בְּלוּלוֹת

וּרְקִיקִין מְשׁוּחִין. וְנֶחְלְקוּ רַבּוֹתֵינוּ בִּמְשִׁיחָתָן, יֵשׁ אוֹמְרִים: מוֹשְׁחָן וְחוֹזֵר וּמוֹשְׁחָן עַד שֶׁיִּכְלֶה כָּל הַשֶּׁמֶן שֶׁבַּלֹּג, שֶׁכָּל הַמְּנָחוֹת טְעוּנוֹת לֹג שֶׁמֶן. וְיֵשׁ אוֹמְרִים: מוֹשְׁחָן כְּמִין כִי, וּשְׁאָר הַשֶּׁמֶן נֶאֱכָל לַכֹּהֲנִים. מַה תַּלְמוּד לוֹמַר "בַּשֶּׁמֶן", "בַּשָּׁמֶן" שְׁתֵּי פְעָמִים? לְהַכְשִׁיר שֶׁמֶן שֵׁנִי וּשְׁלִישִׁי הַיּוֹצֵא מִן הַזֵּיתִים, וְאֵין צָרִיךְ שֶׁמֶן רִאשׁוֹן חַלָּה לַמְּנוֹרָה, שֶׁנֶּאֱמַר בּוֹ: "זָךְ" (שְׁמוֹת כז, כ). וְשָׁנִינוּ בִּמְנָחוֹת (דַּף עו ע"א): כָּל הַמְּנָחוֹת הָאֲפוּיוֹת לִפְנֵי קְמִיצָתָן וְנִקְמָצוֹת עַל יְדֵי פְּתִיתָה, כֻּלָּן בָּאוֹת עֶשֶׂר עֶשֶׂר חַלּוֹת, וְהָאָמוּר פֹּה "רְקִיקִין" בָּאָה עֶשֶׂר רְקִיקִין:

הּ] וְאִם מִנְחָה עַל הַמַּחֲבַת. שֶׁאָמַר: 'הֲרֵי עָלַי מִנְחַת מַחֲבַת'. וּכְלִי הוּא שֶׁהָיָה בַּמִּקְדָּשׁ שֶׁאוֹפִין בּוֹ מִנְחָה זוֹ עַל הָאוּר בַּשֶּׁמֶן, וְהַכְּלִי אֵינוֹ עָמֹק אֶלָּא צָף, וּמַעֲשֵׂי הַמִּנְחָה שֶׁבְּתוֹכוֹ קָשִׁין, שֶׁמִּתּוֹךְ שֶׁהִיא צָפָה הָאוּר שׂוֹרֵף אֶת הַשֶּׁמֶן. וְכֻלָּן טְעוּנוֹת שָׁלֹשׁ מַתְּנוֹת שֶׁמֶן: יְצִיקָה וּבְלִילָה וּמַתַּן שֶׁמֶן בַּכְּלִי קֹדֶם לַעֲשִׂיָּתָן: סֹלֶת בְּלוּלָה בַשֶּׁמֶן. מְלַמֵּד שֶׁבּוֹלְלָן בְּעוֹדָן סֹלֶת:

וּ] פָּתוֹת אֹתָהּ פִּתִּים. לְרַבּוֹת כָּל הַמְּנָחוֹת הָאֲפוּיוֹת קֹדֶם קְמִיצָה לִפְתִיתָה: וְיָצַקְתָּ עָלֶיהָ שָׁמֶן מִנְחָה הִוא. לְרַבּוֹת כָּל הַמְּנָחוֹת לִיצִיקָה. יָכוֹל אַף מִנְחַת מַחֲבַת כֵּן?

תַּלְמוּד לוֹמַר: "עָלֶיהָ". חַלּוֹת אֶת הַחַלּוֹת וְלֹא חוֹלֵל אֶת הָרְקִיקִין? תַּלְמוּד לוֹמַר: "הִוא":

זּ] מַרְחֶשֶׁת. כְּלִי הוּא שֶׁהָיָה בַּמִּקְדָּשׁ, עָמֹק, וּמִתּוֹךְ שֶׁהוּא עָמֹק שַׁמְנוֹ צָבוּר וְאֵין הָאוּר שׂוֹרְפוֹ, לְפִיכָךְ מַעֲשֵׂי מִנְחָה הָעֲשׂוּיִם לְתוֹכָהּ רוֹחֲשִׁין, כָּל דָּבָר רַךְ עַל יְדֵי מַשְׁקֶה נִרְאֶה כְּרוֹחֵשׁ וּמִתְנַעֲנֵעַ:

חּ] אֲשֶׁר יֵעָשֶׂה מֵאֵלֶּה. מֵאֶחָד מִן הַמִּינִים הַלָּלוּ: וְהִקְרִיבָהּ. בְּעָלֶיהָ "אֶל הַכֹּהֵן": וְהִגִּישָׁהּ. הַכֹּהֵן: אֶל הַמִּזְבֵּחַ. מַגִּישָׁהּ לְקֶרֶן דְּרוֹמִית מַעֲרָבִית שֶׁל מִזְבֵּחַ:

טּ] אֶת אַזְכָּרָתָהּ. הִיא הַקֹּמֶץ:

יא] וְכָל דְּבַשׁ. כָּל מְתִיקַת פְּרִי קְרוּיָה דְבַשׁ:

יב] קָרְבַּן רֵאשִׁית תַּקְרִיבוּ אֹתָם. מַה יֵּשׁ לְךָ לְהָבִיא מִן הַשְּׂאוֹר וּמִן הַדְּבַשׁ? קָרְבַּן רֵאשִׁית, שְׁתֵּי הַלֶּחֶם שֶׁל עֲצֶרֶת הַבָּאִים מִן הַשְּׂאוֹר, שֶׁנֶּאֱמַר (וַיִּקְרָא כג, יז): "חָמֵץ תֵּאָפֶינָה", וּבִכּוּרִים מִן הַדְּבַשׁ, כְּמוֹ בִכּוּרֵי תְאֵנִים וּתְמָרִים:

יג] מֶלַח בְּרִית. שֶׁהַבְּרִית כְּרוּתָה לַמֶּלַח מִשֵּׁשֶׁת יְמֵי בְרֵאשִׁית, שֶׁהֻבְטְחוּ הַמַּיִם הַתַּחְתּוֹנִים לִקָּרֵב בַּמִּזְבֵּחַ

13 **All your meal offerings you shall salt with salt; and you shall not withhold the salt of the covenant**[D] **of your God from upon your meal offering.** Moreover, **on all your offerings you shall bring salt,** not just on meal offerings.

14 **If,** or when, **you bring a meal offering of first fruits to the Lord,** it shall be made of **just-ripened** produce,[29] **roasted in fire, ground of a moist,** soft **kernel.** In this manner **you shall bring the meal offering of your first fruits.** According to the interpretation of the Sages, this is referring to the *omer* offering, the meal offering of barley brought on the sixteenth of Nissan, which is the first meal offering brought from the new crop of produce.[30]

15 **You shall put oil on it, and place frankincense on it. It is a meal offering,** and this is the manner of preparing a meal offering (see verse 6).

16 **The priest shall burn its memorial portion,** consisting of a handful **from its flour and from its oil, with all its frankincense; it is a fire offering to the Lord.**[31]

The Peace Offering
LEVITICUS 3:1–17

The peace offering was mentioned previously in Exodus (24:5). Like the burnt offering and the meal offering, it is usually brought as a voluntary offering. However, the peace offering differs from those offerings with regard to the manner in which it is consumed. The burnt offering is an offering that indicates one's full devotion to God and desire to give Him a gift, and it is therefore entirely consumed on the altar. The sin offering (see chap. 4) is partially burned on the altar and partially eaten by the priests, who receive their portion as a gift from God. In contrast, the peace offering is shared by all: Parts of the offering are burned on the altar, parts are consumed by the priests, and a significant part of the offering belongs to the individual who brought the offering.

The sacred feast in which the peace offering is consumed evokes a unique experience that differs from the experience of sacrificing a burnt offering or meal offering. The term peace offering points to the atmosphere of peace and harmony that is inspired by the offering. The Hebrew term for peace offering, *shelamim,* is derived from the root *shin-lamed-mem,* which denotes completeness.

The section concerning the peace offering concludes with the general prohibition of consuming forbidden fat or blood. These are the parts of the peace offering that are presented to God on the altar. Consequently, these parts of any animal are forbidden for human consumption.

3 1 **If his offering is a peace offering: If he brings it from cattle,**
Fourth **whether male or female, he shall offer it unblemished be-**
aliya **fore the Lord.** In contrast to the burnt offering, for which one may bring only a male animal, the peace offering may be either male or female. It must still be unblemished, as is the case with regard to all offerings.

2 **He,** the owner, **shall lay his hand on the head of his offering** as though to transfer his identity to the animal. **And he** shall **slaughter it at the entrance of the Tent of Meeting** in the Tabernacle courtyard, or, during the Temple period, in the Temple courtyard. The rite of slaughter is not considered one of the four proper sacrificial rites; rather, it is a preparatory rite and therefore may be performed by a non-priest. The priestly service commences with the rites involving the blood of the offering: **Aaron's sons, the priests, shall cast the blood around the altar.**

3 The peace offering is not burned in its entirety. Rather, **he shall present from the peace offering** a portion of the offering that will be burned on the altar as **a fire offering to the Lord: The** layer of **fat**[BD] **that covers the innards, and all the fat that is on the innards,** additional sections of fat that are adjacent to the internal organs.[32]

4 Also included in the portion of the offering burned on the altar are **the two kidneys, and the fat that is on them, that is on the flanks.** This refers to the fat of the animal's flanks, which lies on the kidneys and extends to the hindquarters.[33] Some understand the flanks to refer to the inner muscles of the haunches.[34] **And the diaphragm above the liver,** although not the liver itself,[35] **with the kidneys he shall remove it.**

5 **Aaron's sons shall burn it,** the above sections of the animal, which are burned as one unit,[36] **on the altar on the burnt**

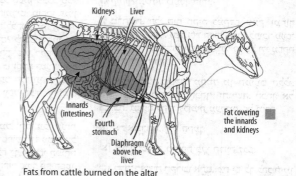

Kidneys · Liver

Innards (intestines)

Fourth stomach

Diaphragm above the liver

Fat covering the innards and kidneys

Fats from cattle burned on the altar

── BACKGROUND ──

3:3 | **The fat:** The *ḥelev* is a layer of fat that covers the muscles in order to protect the internal organs, to control body temperature, and to control hormonal activity. The *ḥelev* also serves as a food repository that is digested by the body when it lacks nourishment. This layer of fat exists in all animals, though its thickness varies from one type of animal to another.

יג וְכׇל־קׇרְבַּן מִנְחָתְךָ בַּמֶּלַח תִּמְלָח וְלֹא תַשְׁבִּית מֶלַח בְּרִית אֱלֹהֶיךָ מֵעַל מִנְחָתֶךָ
יד עַל כׇּל־קׇרְבָּנְךָ תַּקְרִיב מֶלַח׃ וְאִם־תַּקְרִיב מִנְחַת בִּכּוּרִים
טו לַיהוה אָבִיב קָלוּי בָּאֵשׁ גֶּרֶשׂ כַּרְמֶל תַּקְרִיב אֵת מִנְחַת בִּכּוּרֶיךָ׃ וְנָתַתָּ עָלֶיהָ
טז שֶׁמֶן וְשַׂמְתָּ עָלֶיהָ לְבֹנָה מִנְחָה הִוא׃ וְהִקְטִיר הַכֹּהֵן אֶת־אַזְכָּרָתָהּ מִגִּרְשָׂהּ
וּמִשַּׁמְנָהּ עַל כׇּל־לְבֹנָתָהּ אִשֶּׁה לַיהוה׃

א וְאִם־זֶבַח שְׁלָמִים קׇרְבָּנוֹ אִם מִן־הַבָּקָר הוּא מַקְרִיב אִם־זָכָר אִם־נְקֵבָה תָּמִים רביעי
ב יַקְרִיבֶנּוּ לִפְנֵי יהוה׃ וְסָמַךְ יָדוֹ עַל־רֹאשׁ קׇרְבָּנוֹ וּשְׁחָטוֹ פֶּתַח אֹהֶל מוֹעֵד וְזָרְקוּ
ג בְּנֵי אַהֲרֹן הַכֹּהֲנִים אֶת־הַדָּם עַל־הַמִּזְבֵּחַ סָבִיב׃ וְהִקְרִיב מִזֶּבַח הַשְּׁלָמִים אִשֶּׁה
ד לַיהוה אֶת־הַחֵלֶב הַמְכַסֶּה אֶת־הַקֶּרֶב וְאֵת כׇּל־הַחֵלֶב אֲשֶׁר עַל־הַקֶּרֶב׃ וְאֵת
שְׁתֵּי הַכְּלָיֹת וְאֶת־הַחֵלֶב אֲשֶׁר עֲלֵהֶן אֲשֶׁר עַל־הַכְּסָלִים וְאֶת־הַיֹּתֶרֶת עַל־
ה הַכָּבֵד עַל־הַכְּלָיוֹת יְסִירֶנָּה׃ וְהִקְטִירוּ אֹתוֹ בְנֵי־אַהֲרֹן הַמִּזְבֵּחָה עַל־הָעֹלָה

רש״י

בַּמֶּלַח, וְנִסּוּךְ הַמַּיִם בֶּחָג: עַל כׇּל קׇרְבָּנְךָ. עַל עוֹלַת בְּהֵמָה וְעוֹף וְאֵמוּרֵי כׇּל הַקֳּדָשִׁים כֻּלָּן:

יד| וְאִם תַּקְרִיב. הֲרֵי "אִם" מְשַׁמֵּשׁ בִּלְשׁוֹן 'כִּי', שֶׁהֲרֵי אֵין זֶה רְשׁוּת, שֶׁהֲרֵי בְּמִנְחַת הָעֹמֶר הַכָּתוּב מְדַבֵּר, שֶׁהִיא חוֹבָה. וְכֵן: "וְאִם יִהְיֶה הַיֹּבֵל" וְגוֹ' (במדבר לו, ד): מִנְחַת בִּכּוּרִים. בְּמִנְחַת הָעֹמֶר הַכָּתוּב מְדַבֵּר, שֶׁהִיא בָּאָה אָבִיב, בִּשְׁעַת בִּשּׁוּל הַתְּבוּאָה, וּמִן הַשְּׂעוֹרִים הִיא בָּאָה, נֶאֱמַר כָּאן: "אָבִיב" וְנֶאֱמַר לְהַלָּן: "כִּי הַשְּׂעֹרָה אָבִיב" (שמות ט, לא): קָלוּי בָּאֵשׁ. שֶׁמְּיַבְּשִׁין אוֹתָהּ עַל הָאוּר בְּאַבּוּב שֶׁל קָלָאִים, שֶׁאִלּוּלֵי כֵן אֵינָהּ נִטְחֶנֶת בָּרֵחַיִם, לְפִי שֶׁהִיא לַחָה: גֶּרֶשׂ כַּרְמֶל. גְּרוּסָה בְּעוֹדָהּ לַחָה: גֶּרֶשׂ. לְשׁוֹן שְׁבִירָה וּטְחִינָה גַּסָּה בָּרֵחַיִם שֶׁל גְּרוֹסוֹת, כְּמוֹ: "וַיַּגְרֵס בֶּחָצָץ" (איכה ג, טז), וְכֵן: "גָּרְסָה נַפְשִׁי" (תהלים קיט, כ): כַּרְמֶל. בְּעוֹד הַכַּר מָלֵא, שֶׁהַתְּבוּאָה לַחָה וּמְלֵאָה בְּקַשִּׁין שֶׁלָּהּ, וְעַל כֵּן נִקְרָאִים הַמְּלִילוֹת 'כַּרְמֶל', וְכֵן: "וְכַרְמֶל בְּצִקְלֹנוֹ" (מלכים ב' ד, מב):

פרק ג

א| שְׁלָמִים. שֶׁמַּטִּילִים שָׁלוֹם בָּעוֹלָם. "שְׁלָמִים" – שֶׁיֵּשׁ בָּהֶם שָׁלוֹם לַמִּזְבֵּחַ וְלַכֹּהֲנִים וְלַבְּעָלִים:

ג| וְאֵת כׇּל הַחֵלֶב וְגוֹ'. לְהָבִיא חֵלֶב שֶׁעַל הַקֵּבָה, דִּבְרֵי רַבִּי יִשְׁמָעֵאל. רַבִּי עֲקִיבָא אוֹמֵר: לְהָבִיא חֵלֶב שֶׁעַל הַדַּקִּין:

ד| הַכְּסָלִים. פלנק"ש בְּלַעַז, שֶׁהַחֵלֶב שֶׁעַל הַכְּלָיוֹת כְּשֶׁהַבְּהֵמָה חַיָּה הוּא בְּגֹבַהּ הַכְּסָלִים וְהֵם לְמַטָּה, וְזֶהוּ הַחֵלֶב שֶׁתַּחַת הַמָּתְנַיִם שֶׁקּוֹרִין בְּלַעַז לונביל"ש, לְכָךְ הַנִּרְאֶה לְמַעְלָה בְּגֹבַהּ הַכְּסָלִים, וּבְתַחְתִּיתוֹ הַבָּשָׂר חוֹפֵהוּ: הַיֹּתֶרֶת. הוּא דֹּפֶן הַמָּסָךְ שֶׁקּוֹרִין איבל"ש, וּבִלְשׁוֹן אֲרַמִּי "חַצְרָא": עַל הַכָּבֵד. שֶׁיִּטֹּל מִן הַכָּבֵד עִמָּהּ מְעַט, וּבְמָקוֹם אַחֵר הוּא אוֹמֵר: "וְאֶת הַיֹּתֶרֶת מִן הַכָּבֵד" (ויקרא ט, י): עַל הַכָּבֵד עַל הַכְּלָיוֹת. לְבַד מִן הַכָּבֵד וּלְבַד מִן הַכְּלָיוֹת "יְסִירֶנָּה" לָזוֹ:

ה| עַל הָעֹלָה. מִלְּבַד הָעוֹלָה, לִמְּדָנוּ שֶׁתִּקְדֹּם עוֹלַת תָּמִיד לְכׇל קׇרְבָּן עַל הַמַּעֲרָכָה:

DISCUSSION

2:13| **The salt of the covenant**: In the ancient world, covenants were made using items that symbolized endurance or by performing acts that symbolized the fate of one who breaks the covenant, e.g., slaughtering animals or melting wax. Salt was a substance that was essential for the preparation of food and for its preservation, and it was also used medicinally and as an antiseptic. These characteristics caused it to become a symbol of endurance, perpetuity, and purification. Conversely, salt can dry up the earth and destroy fertile land. For all these reasons, salt was commonly used to symbolize the sealing of a covenant. A person who partook of the bread and salt of another was considered to be close to him (see also Genesis 31:54, Numbers 18:19, and II Chronicles 13:5).

The offerings burned on the altar come from all of the three types of matter that comprise the physical world: Salt is inanimate matter, the meal offering is a form of vegetable life, and the animals and birds belong to the world of animal life. Salt, which is the most elementary of these items, is included in all of the offerings (see Rashi and Ramban).

3:3| **The fat**: The Torah distinguishes between two types of fat. The fat referred to as *ḥelev* is a fatty membrane, relatively firm and solid, which lies above the meat. Conversely, the fat that is integrated into the meat and the muscle tissue is known in rabbinic literature as *shuman*. It is not among the parts of a peace offering that are burned on the altar, and it is permitted for human consumption (see *Horayot* 2a; Ramban, verse 9).

offering that is placed **on the wood that is on the fire,** as stated above (1:7). The peace offering is burned on the altar either together with the burnt offering or after it.[37] Although there is no requirement for a burnt offering to always be burning on the altar, there is often a burnt offering burning there, as it is one of the offerings presented by the community at the beginning and end of each day. Furthermore, whenever there was no other offering to be burned on the altar, the priests would bring a communal burnt offering.[38] The aforementioned sections of the offering are **a fire offering of a pleasing aroma to the Lord.**

6 **If his offering is from the flock as a peace offering to the Lord,** rather than from cattle, then it may also be **male or female; unblemished he shall present it.** The rites of the peace offering are identical irrespective of the type of animal brought. The details are reiterated three times with slight differences. The necessity for this repetition is discussed in the halakhic midrash.[39]

7 **If he brings a lamb as his offering, he shall bring it before the Lord** to the Tabernacle's entrance.

8 **He shall lay his hand on the head of his offering, and slaughter it before the Tent of Meeting.** The Torah reiterates the rites of the peace offering: **Aaron's sons shall cast its blood around the altar.**

9 **He shall present from the peace offering a fire offering,** the part burned by fire, **to the Lord.** There is one difference with regard to the lamb peace offering, due to which the entire set of rites is reiterated: **Its fats** include **the** long, thick, and fatty **tail**[D] **in its entirety.**[40] **Opposite the** last vertebrae of the **backbone he shall remove it.** The tail must be removed at the lower end of the spine. The priest shall also present other fats, which are identical to those presented from the cattle: **The fat that covers the innards, all the fat that is on the innards,**

10 **the two kidneys, the fat that is on them, that is on the flanks, and the diaphragm above the liver, with the kidneys he shall remove it.**

11 **The priest shall burn it,** the aforementioned part of the offering, **on the altar; it is the food**[D] **of the fire offering to the Lord.**

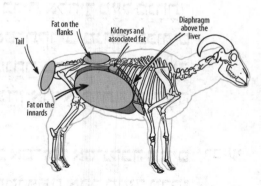

12 **If his offering is a goat, he shall bring it before the Lord.** The Torah again reiterates the details of the peace offering, in this case with regard to the sacrifice of a goat. Although sheep and goats are closely related, the sheep's tail is included in the portion of the peace offering burned on the altar, while the goat's tail is not. The laws of each are therefore presented separately.[41]

Sacrificial portions of a sheep

13 **He shall lay his hand upon its head, and slaughter it before the Tent of Meeting; the sons of Aaron shall cast its blood around the altar.**

14 **He shall present from it his offering, a fire offering to the Lord: The fat that covers the innards, all the fat that is on the innards,**

15 **the two kidneys, the fat that is on them that is on the flanks, and the diaphragm above the liver, with the kidneys he shall remove it.** The tail is not mentioned because the goat's tail, which is not as fatty as the tail of a sheep, is not burned on the altar.

16 **The priest shall burn them on the altar; it is the food of the fire offering for a pleasing aroma. All the fat** of the animal **is** burned on the altar as an offering **for the Lord.**

17 **It shall be an eternal statute for your generations,** irrespective of whether or not the Temple is standing and offerings can be sacrificed, **in all your dwellings,** both in the Land of Israel and outside the Land of Israel: **All fat and all blood you shall not eat.**[D]

DISCUSSION

3:9| **The tail**: The genus of sheep that was common in the Land of Israel and the surrounding areas during the Temple era had a long, thick, fatty tail. However, it is not common to all species of sheep, nor do goats or cattle have this kind of tail. This may be the reason why the Torah describes the sheep peace offering separately from the goat peace offering (see *Sifra*; *Pesaḥim* 96b). In the case of the burnt offering, the Torah does not differentiate between sheep and goats, as it is burned on the altar in its entirety (see 1:10).

3:11| **Food**: Literally, "the bread." The term bread is sometimes used in reference to any type of food that provides sustenance (see Numbers 15:19; I Kings 5:2). In this case it refers to those parts of the offering that are presented to God and are consumed by the fire on the altar.

3:17| **All fat and all blood you shall not eat**: The prohibition of eating the fat and blood of an animal is presented here as a *ḥok*, a divine statute without explanation (see *Bemidbar*

אֲשֶׁר עַל־הָעֵצִים אֲשֶׁר עַל־הָאֵשׁ אִשֵּׁה רֵיחַ נִיחֹחַ לַיהוה׃
ו וְאִם־מִן־הַצֹּאן קָרְבָּנוֹ לְזֶבַח שְׁלָמִים לַיהוה זָכָר אוֹ נְקֵבָה תָּמִים יַקְרִיבֶנּוּ׃
ז ח אִם־כֶּשֶׂב הוּא־מַקְרִיב אֶת־קָרְבָּנוֹ וְהִקְרִיב אֹתוֹ לִפְנֵי יהוה׃ וְסָמַךְ אֶת־יָדוֹ עַל־
רֹאשׁ קָרְבָּנוֹ וְשָׁחַט אֹתוֹ לִפְנֵי אֹהֶל מוֹעֵד וְזָרְקוּ בְּנֵי אַהֲרֹן אֶת־דָּמוֹ עַל־הַמִּזְבֵּחַ
ט סָבִיב׃ וְהִקְרִיב מִזֶּבַח הַשְּׁלָמִים אִשֶּׁה לַיהוה חֶלְבּוֹ הָאַלְיָה תְמִימָה לְעֻמַּת
הֶעָצֶה יְסִירֶנָּה וְאֶת־הַחֵלֶב הַמְכַסֶּה אֶת־הַקֶּרֶב וְאֵת כָּל־הַחֵלֶב אֲשֶׁר עַל־הַקֶּרֶב׃
י וְאֵת שְׁתֵּי הַכְּלָיֹת וְאֶת־הַחֵלֶב אֲשֶׁר עֲלֵהֶן אֲשֶׁר עַל־הַכְּסָלִים וְאֶת־הַיֹּתֶרֶת
יא עַל־הַכָּבֵד עַל־הַכְּלָיֹת יְסִירֶנָּה׃ וְהִקְטִירוֹ הַכֹּהֵן הַמִּזְבֵּחָה לֶחֶם אִשֶּׁה לַיהוה׃
יב יג וְאִם־עֵז קָרְבָּנוֹ וְהִקְרִיבוֹ לִפְנֵי יהוה׃ וְסָמַךְ אֶת־יָדוֹ עַל־רֹאשׁוֹ וְשָׁחַט אֹתוֹ לִפְנֵי
יד אֹהֶל מוֹעֵד וְזָרְקוּ בְּנֵי אַהֲרֹן אֶת־דָּמוֹ עַל־הַמִּזְבֵּחַ סָבִיב׃ וְהִקְרִיב מִמֶּנּוּ קָרְבָּנוֹ
אִשֶּׁה לַיהוה אֶת־הַחֵלֶב הַמְכַסֶּה אֶת־הַקֶּרֶב וְאֵת כָּל־הַחֵלֶב אֲשֶׁר עַל־הַקֶּרֶב׃
טו וְאֵת שְׁתֵּי הַכְּלָיֹת וְאֶת־הַחֵלֶב אֲשֶׁר עֲלֵהֶן אֲשֶׁר עַל־הַכְּסָלִים וְאֶת־הַיֹּתֶרֶת
טז עַל־הַכָּבֵד עַל־הַכְּלָיֹת יְסִירֶנָּה׃ וְהִקְטִירָם הַכֹּהֵן הַמִּזְבֵּחָה לֶחֶם אִשֶּׁה לְרֵיחַ
יז נִיחֹחַ כָּל־חֵלֶב לַיהוה׃ חֻקַּת עוֹלָם לְדֹרֹתֵיכֶם בְּכֹל מוֹשְׁבֹתֵיכֶם כָּל־חֵלֶב וְכָל־
דָּם לֹא תֹאכֵלוּ׃

רש"י

ז | **אִם כֶּשֶׂב.** לְפִי שֶׁיֵּשׁ בְּאֵמוּרֵי הַכֶּשֶׂב מַה שֶּׁאֵין בְּאֵמוּרֵי הָעֵז, שֶׁהַכֶּשֶׂב אַלְיָתוֹ קְרֵבָה, לְכָךְ נֶחְלְקוּ לִשְׁתֵּי פָרָשִׁיּוֹת.

ח | **וְזָרְקוּ.** שְׁתֵּי מַתָּנוֹת שֶׁהֵן אַרְבַּע, וְעַל יְדֵי הַכְּלִי הוּא זוֹרֵק, וְאֵינוֹ נוֹתֵן בָּאֶצְבַּע אֶלָּא חַטָּאת.

ט | **חֶלְבּוֹ.** הַמֻּבְחָר שֶׁבּוֹ, וּמַהוּ זֶה? "הָאַלְיָה תְמִימָה": לְעֻמַּת הֶעָצֶה. לְמַעְלָה מִן הַכְּלָיוֹת הַיּוֹעֲצוֹת.

יא | **לֶחֶם אִשֶּׁה לַה'.** לַחְמוֹ שֶׁל אֵשׁ לְשֵׁם גָּבוֹהַּ. לֶחֶם, לְשׁוֹן מַאֲכָל, וְכֵן: "נַשְׁחִיתָה עֵץ בְּלַחְמוֹ" (ירמיה יא, יט), "עֲבַד לְחֶם רַב" (דניאל ה, א), "לִשְׂחוֹק עֹשִׂים לֶחֶם" (קהלת י, יט).

DISCUSSION

Rabba 19:8), and it is not dependent upon the laws of sacrificial offerings. Nevertheless, there is a connection between them: Not all fat is forbidden fat [*ḥelev*]. Forbidden fat is, roughly, the sheets of fat tissue along the abdomen and surrounding the internal organs. This fat, along with blood that is discharged when the animal is slaughtered, is brought upon the altar as part of the sacrificial service, and it is prohibited for human consumption (see *Bekhor Shor* 11:2; *Meshekh Ḥokhma* 17:10; Ramban, *Hullin* 5b). The fat is considered the finest portion of the animal, and it is therefore the portion presented to God and burned on the altar. This is the meaning of the phrase: "All the fat is for the Lord" (see verse 16).

The fatty sheep's tail is the exception to this rule. The sheep's tail is burned as part of the offering but there is no prohibition against eating it, and in fact it is commonly eaten even nowadays. The Sages understood that only those fats burned on the altar in every offering are prohibited. Since neither goats nor cattle have fatty tails and their tails are not burned on the altar, even the sheep's tail is permitted for human consumption (see *Ḥullin* 117a; *Sifra*, verse 9; and Ra'avad ad loc.). The Karaites disputed this rabbinic tradition and considered the fat of the sheep's tail to be prohibited.

The Sin Offering

LEVITICUS 4:1–5:13

At this point, the Torah transitions from its discussion of voluntary gift offerings to its discussion of obligatory offerings. The passage below deals with different types of sin offerings. The sin offering is usually brought to atone for sins committed unwittingly due to forgetfulness or because one is not paying attention to what he is doing. The fact that one is obligated to bring a sin offering to atone for unwitting transgressions indicates that these transgressions cause a certain level of liability. Although such transgressions are not comparable to purposeful transgressions, neither are they comparable to transgressions committed with a total lack of consciousness, e.g., by one who is completely drunk or by one who never knew about the existence of such prohibitions.

In contrast to a sin committed unwittingly, one cannot atone for an intentional transgression by bringing an offering, since the sinner acted with full awareness of his actions and with evil intent. In some cases an intentional transgression is punishable by the court; in all cases, he is liable to punishment at the hands of Heaven. In any event, the intentional transgressor does not usually bring a sin offering as part of his process of repentance and achieving atonement. Moreover, if one sinned unwittingly, but would not have refrained from sinning even if he had remembered that it was prohibited, he does not bring an offering. The sin offering atones for those sins that were committed unwittingly and would not have been committed intentionally.

The first part of the following section details five types of sin offerings that apply to four categories of sinners respectively. They are the sin offering of the High Priest, the sin offering of the High Court, the sin offering of the ruler, and two types of sin offerings that may be brought by the common Jew. The sinners are not listed according to their social standing; rather, the order in which they are listed reflects the level of sanctity of the sinner and the extent of his moral responsibility. The list therefore begins with the High Priest, whose sanctity elevates him above the rest of the people. All of these sin offerings pertain only to severe transgressions that carry the punishment of excision from the World to Come when they are transgressed intentionally.

The second part of this section discusses sin offerings that are brought to atone for specific transgressions that do not incur the punishment of excision even when transgressed intentionally. In the case of these sin offerings, the type of sin offering that the sinner is required to bring is dependent on his financial ability.

4 **1** **The Lord spoke to Moses, saying:**

Fifth aliya **2** **Speak to the children of Israel, saying: When a person sins unwittingly with regard to any of the commandments of the Lord that may not be performed,**[D] **and he performs one of them,** he shall bring a sin offering in accordance with the laws set down below. An unwitting sin is a sin performed due to forgetfulness or by confusing a prohibited matter with a permitted matter. The transgression was not performed intentionally, but neither was it performed under duress or with complete lack of cognizance, as in the case of a transgression performed by one who was completely drunk.[42]

3 The laws of the sin offering vary depending on the identity of the transgressor. The Torah describes the first type of sin offering: **If the anointed priest,** the High Priest, who was appointed during most of the First Temple period by anointing with the anointing oil,[43] erroneously rules that a forbidden matter is permitted and subsequently follows that ruling, he thereby **sins to bring guilt on the people.** The transgression of the chosen individual, who was elevated from among all his brethren, is indicative of the guilt of the nation as a whole. This is not merely because the High Priest represents the people, but because his actions are a reflection of the spiritual level of the nation. Furthermore, the actions of the High Priest have far-reaching influence on the nation.[44] **He shall present for his sin that he sinned, an unblemished young bull, to the Lord as a sin offering.**

4 **He shall bring the bull to the** Tabernacle courtyard, opposite the **entrance of the Tent of Meeting before the Lord;**[45]**he** shall lay his hand on the head of the bull, and slaughter the bull before the Lord.

5 **The anointed priest shall take from the blood of the bull, and bring it to the Tent of Meeting.** In this unique case, the sinner and the priest who performs the service that brings him atonement are the same individual; the High Priest performs the rites on the offering brought for his own transgression. It is possible that the reason for this unusual policy is that the blood of this sin offering is sprinkled toward the Holy of Holies, and therefore the rite must be performed by the priest of the greatest sanctity. In a case where the rites were performed by another priest, there is a dispute among the Sages as to whether the offering is fit.[46]

6 **The priest shall dip his finger in the blood, and sprinkle from the blood seven times before the Lord, before the Curtain of the Sanctuary.** Whereas the blood of most offerings is cast or sprinkled only on the

External altar in the Tabernacle

א ב וַיְדַבֵּר יְהוָה אֶל־מֹשֶׁה לֵּאמֹר׃ דַּבֵּר אֶל־בְּנֵי יִשְׂרָאֵל לֵאמֹר נֶפֶשׁ כִּי־תֶחֱטָא ב חמישי
ג בִשְׁגָגָה מִכֹּל מִצְוֺת יְהוָה אֲשֶׁר לֹא תֵעָשֶׂינָה וְעָשָׂה מֵאַחַת מֵהֵנָּה׃ אִם הַכֹּהֵן
הַמָּשִׁיחַ יֶחֱטָא לְאַשְׁמַת הָעָם וְהִקְרִיב עַל חַטָּאתוֹ אֲשֶׁר חָטָא פַּר בֶּן־בָּקָר
ד תָּמִים לַיהוָה לְחַטָּאת׃ וְהֵבִיא אֶת־הַפָּר אֶל־פֶּתַח אֹהֶל מוֹעֵד לִפְנֵי יְהוָה וְסָמַךְ
ה אֶת־יָדוֹ עַל־רֹאשׁ הַפָּר וְשָׁחַט אֶת־הַפָּר לִפְנֵי יְהוָה׃ וְלָקַח הַכֹּהֵן הַמָּשִׁיחַ מִדַּם
ו הַפָּר וְהֵבִיא אֹתוֹ אֶל־אֹהֶל מוֹעֵד׃ וְטָבַל הַכֹּהֵן אֶת־אֶצְבָּעוֹ בַּדָּם וְהִזָּה מִן־הַדָּם
ז שֶׁבַע פְּעָמִים לִפְנֵי יְהוָה אֶת־פְּנֵי פָּרֹכֶת הַקֹּדֶשׁ׃ וְנָתַן הַכֹּהֵן מִן־הַדָּם עַל־קַרְנוֹת
מִזְבַּח קְטֹרֶת הַסַּמִּים לִפְנֵי יְהוָה אֲשֶׁר בְּאֹהֶל מוֹעֵד וְאֵת ׀ כָּל־דַּם הַפָּר יִשְׁפֹּךְ
ח אֶל־יְסוֹד מִזְבַּח הָעֹלָה אֲשֶׁר־פֶּתַח אֹהֶל מוֹעֵד׃ וְאֶת־כָּל־חֵלֶב פַּר הַחַטָּאת

רש״י

פרק ד

ב] מִכֹּל מִצְוֹת ה׳. פֵּרְשׁוּ רַבּוֹתֵינוּ: אֵין חַטָּאת בָּאָה אֶלָּא עַל דָּבָר שֶׁזְּדוֹנוֹ לָאו וְכָרֵת: מֵאַחַת מֵהֵנָּה. מִמִּקְצָת אַחַת מֵהֶן, כְּגוֹן הַכּוֹתֵב בְּשַׁבָּת ״שֵׁם״ מִ״שִּׁמְעוֹן״, ״נֹחַ״ מִ״נָּחוֹר״, ״דָּן״ מִ״דָּנִיֵּאל״:

ג] אִם הַכֹּהֵן הַמָּשִׁיחַ יֶחֱטָא לְאַשְׁמַת הָעָם. מִדְרָשׁוֹ, אֵינוֹ חַיָּב אֶלָּא בְּהֶעְלֵם דָּבָר עִם שִׁגְגַת מַעֲשֶׂה, כְּמוֹ שֶׁנֶּאֱמַר בְּאַשְׁמַת הָעָם: ״וְנֶעְלַם דָּבָר מֵעֵינֵי הַקָּהָל וְעָשׂוּ״ (להלן פסוק יג). וּפְשׁוּטוֹ לְפִי הַגָּדָה, כְּשֶׁכֹּהֵן גָּדוֹל חוֹטֵא ״אַשְׁמַת הָעָם״ הִיא, שֶׁזֶּה שֶׁהֵן תְּלוּיִין בּוֹ לְכַפֵּר עֲלֵיהֶם וּלְהִתְפַּלֵּל בַּעֲדָם נַעֲשָׂה מְקֻלְקָל: פַּר. יָכוֹל זָקֵן? תַּלְמוּד לוֹמַר: ״בֶּן״. אִי ״בֶּן״, יָכוֹל קָטָן? תַּלְמוּד לוֹמַר: ״פַּר״, הָא כֵּיצַד? זֶה פַּר בֶּן שָׁלֹשׁ:

ה] אֶל אֹהֶל מוֹעֵד. לַמִּשְׁכָּן, וּבְבֵית עוֹלָמִים – לַהֵיכָל:

ו] אֶת פְּנֵי פָּרֹכֶת הַקֹּדֶשׁ. כְּנֶגֶד מְקוֹם קְדֻשָּׁתָהּ, מְכֻוָּן כְּנֶגֶד בֵּין הַבַּדִּים, וְלֹא הָיוּ נוֹגְעִים דָּמִים בַּפָּרֹכֶת, וְאִם נָגְעוּ נָגְעוּ:

ז] וְאֵת כָּל דַּם. שְׁיָרֵי הַדָּם:

ח] וְאֶת כָּל חֵלֶב פַּר. ״חֶלְבּוֹ״ הָיָה לוֹ לוֹמַר, מַה תַּלְמוּד לוֹמַר: ״פַּר״? לְרַבּוֹת פַּר שֶׁל יוֹם הַכִּפּוּרִים לִכְלָיוֹת וְלַחֲלָבִים וְיוֹתֶרֶת: הַחַטָּאת. לְהָבִיא שְׂעִירֵי עֲבוֹדָה זָרָה

external altar, in this case the High Priest enters the Sanctuary and sprinkles the blood toward the Curtain that separates the Holy of Holies from the Sanctuary.

7 **The priest shall place from the blood on the horns of the altar of the incense of the spices, before the Lord, which is in the Tent of Meeting.** No offerings are burned on the incense altar, and generally, the blood of offerings is sprinkled on the incense altar only on the Day of Atonement.[47] Nevertheless, the High Priest uses his finger to place some of the blood of his sin offering on the incense altar. **All the blood of the bull** remaining in the bowl, which is fairly large, **he shall pour at the base of the altar of the burnt offering, which is at the entrance of the Tent of Meeting.** The blood is poured at the west side of the altar, which is the side facing the entrance to the Tent of Meeting.[48] The rites performed with the blood of offerings vary depending on the offering. The blood of burnt offerings and peace offerings are cast upon the external altar, whereas the blood of the High Priest's sin offering is sprinkled toward the Curtain and placed upon the incense altar.

8 However, with regard to the sacrificial portions of the offering, there is no difference between the peace offering and the sin offering: **All the fat of the bull of the sin offering he shall**

DISCUSSION

4:2| **With regard to any of the commandments of the Lord that may not be performed**: Despite the generic wording of this verse, the sin offering does not apply with regard to every unwitting transgression. According to tradition, one brings a sin offering only for unwittingly transgressing a severe prohibition that carries the punishment of excision from the World to Come for one who transgresses intentionally. For example, one who desecrated the Sabbath because he forgot that it was the Sabbath or was unaware that a certain labor was prohibited on the Sabbath is liable to bring a sin offering (see *Sifra*; Mishna *Karetot* 1:1–2; see also Numbers 15:27–31).

separate from it: **The fat that covers the innards, and all the fat that is on the innards;**

9 **and the two kidneys, and the fat that is on them that is on the flanks,** extending to the hindquarters; **and the diaphragm above the liver with the kidneys, he shall remove them,**

10 **as it,** the sacrificial portion consisting of the fat and internal organs, **is separated from the bull of the peace offering** to be burned on the altar (see 3:3); **the priest shall burn them on the altar of the burnt offering.**

11 Once the sacrificial portions have been separated from the offering, there remains the bulk of the animal, **and this includes the hide of the bull, and all its flesh, with its head, and with its legs, and its innards, and its dung.**

12 **He shall take the entire bull outside the camp,** outside the settled area, **to a pure place, to the place where the ashes** of all the offerings burned on the altar **are poured** (see 6:1–4). He shall **burn it on wood in the fire; on the place where the ashes are poured it shall be burned.** All the parts of the bull that are not burned on the altar are burned outside, not as an offering, but because it is not permitted to use these parts of the bull in any way.

13 The Torah now presents the second type of sin offering: **If the entire congregation of Israel errs unwittingly,** a sin offering must be brought. It is unlikely that the entire community would violate a prohibition due to forgetfulness. Consequently, this is explained as referring to a case where the High Court unwittingly issued an erroneous ruling permitting a certain aspect of a severe transgression.[49] The High Court is sometimes referred to as the congregation, since its members are the representatives of the community.[50] Due to the court's erroneous ruling **the matter is concealed from the eyes of the assembly, and they,** the community as a whole, **perform one of all the commandments of the Lord that may not be performed,** one of the severe prohibitions that incurs a sin offering.[51] The entire

community erred, as they adhered to the court's ruling,[52] **and they,** the court, **are guilty,** as they ruled erroneously due to lack of understanding or lack of knowledge.

14 When **the sin in which they sinned** subsequently **becomes known, the assembly shall present a young bull as a sin offering,**[D] **and bring it before the Tent of Meeting.**

15 **The elders of the congregation,** who bear the responsibility for the transgression, **shall lay their hands on the head of the bull before the Lord; and one shall slaughter the bull before the Lord.**

16 **The anointed priest shall bring from the blood of the bull to the Tent of Meeting.** As in the case of the High Priest's sin offering, it is the High Priest who brings the blood into the Sanctuary and sprinkles it, and not any other priest. In this regard these sin offerings differ from other offerings, whose blood may be sprinkled on the external altar by any priest.

17 **The priest shall dip his finger in the blood, and sprinkle it seven times before the Lord, before the Curtain.**

18 **From the blood, he shall** also **place** some **on the horns of the** incense **altar that is before the Lord, that is in the Tent of Meeting; and all the blood** remaining in the bowl **he shall pour at the base of the altar of the burnt offering, which is at the entrance of the Tent of Meeting.**

19 **All its fat he shall separate from it,** as explained above (verses 8–10), **and burn it on the altar.**

20 **He shall do to the bull as he did to the bull of the** High Priest's **sin offering; so shall he do to it; and the priest shall atone for them,** for the entire community, **and it shall be forgiven for them.**[D]

21 **He shall take the bull outside the camp, and burn it** in the same place and in the same manner **as he burned the first bull,** the bull of the anointed priest; **it is the sin offering of the assembly.**[D]

DISCUSSION

4:14 | The assembly shall present a young bull as a sin offering: In a case where the High Court issues an erroneous ruling, only the High Court itself has the authority to overturn that ruling. If the judges conclude that they were mistaken and that which they had deemed permitted is actually prohibited, they are required to bring a sin offering to atone for their unwitting transgression. The laws concerning an erroneous ruling of the High Court are detailed primarily in tractate *Horayot*, which discusses the subjects with regard to which an erroneous

ruling might be issued, as well as the manner in which such errors are viewed retroactively. In this passage the Torah presents only the laws of the High Court's sin offering, which is referred to in the Talmud as the bull offering for an unwitting communal sin (see, e.g., *Zevaḥim* 41a).

4:20 | And it shall be forgiven for them: The Ramban (verse 11) notes that in the case of the High Priest's transgression the verse does not state that he is forgiven. Due to the elevated status of the High Priest, it is possible that even once he has brought his sin offering his

transgression is not completely atoned for, and he must beseech God for forgiveness.

4:21 | As he burned the first bull; it is the sin offering of the assembly: Both the High Priest's transgression and the transgression of the High Court are considered to bring guilt on the people, as stated above (verse 3), and therefore both bring identical offerings. The Talmud refers to these offerings as the inner sin offerings, because their blood is brought into the Sanctuary to be sprinkled.

יָרִ֣ים מִמֶּ֑נּוּ אֶת־הַחֵ֙לֶב֙ הַֽמְכַסֶּ֣ה עַל־הַקֶּ֔רֶב וְאֵת֙ כָּל־הַחֵ֔לֶב אֲשֶׁ֖ר עַל־הַקֶּֽרֶב׃
ט וְאֵת֙ שְׁתֵּ֣י הַכְּלָיֹ֔ת וְאֶת־הַחֵ֙לֶב֙ אֲשֶׁ֣ר עֲלֵיהֶ֔ן אֲשֶׁ֖ר עַל־הַכְּסָלִ֑ים וְאֶת־הַיֹּתֶ֙רֶת֙
י עַל־הַכָּבֵ֔ד עַל־הַכְּלָי֖וֹת יְסִירֶֽנָּה׃ כַּאֲשֶׁ֣ר יוּרָ֔ם מִשּׁ֖וֹר זֶ֣בַח הַשְּׁלָמִ֑ים וְהִקְטִירָם֙
יא הַכֹּהֵ֔ן עַ֖ל מִזְבַּ֥ח הָעֹלָֽה׃ וְאֶת־ע֤וֹר הַפָּר֙ וְאֶת־כָּל־בְּשָׂר֔וֹ עַל־רֹאשׁ֖וֹ וְעַל־כְּרָעָ֑יו
יב וְקִרְבּ֖וֹ וּפִרְשֽׁוֹ׃ וְהוֹצִ֣יא אֶת־כָּל־הַ֠פָּר אֶל־מִח֨וּץ לַֽמַּחֲנֶ֜ה אֶל־מָק֤וֹם טָהוֹר֙ אֶל־
שֶׁ֣פֶךְ הַדֶּ֔שֶׁן וְשָׂרַ֥ף אֹת֛וֹ עַל־עֵצִ֖ים בָּאֵ֑שׁ עַל־שֶׁ֥פֶךְ הַדֶּ֖שֶׁן יִשָּׂרֵֽף׃
יג וְאִ֨ם כָּל־עֲדַ֤ת יִשְׂרָאֵל֙ יִשְׁגּ֔וּ וְנֶעְלַ֣ם דָּבָ֔ר מֵעֵינֵ֖י הַקָּהָ֑ל וְ֠עָשׂוּ אַחַ֨ת מִכָּל־מִצְוֺ֧ת
יד יְהוָ֛ה אֲשֶׁ֥ר לֹא־תֵעָשֶׂ֖ינָה וְאָשֵֽׁמוּ׃ וְנֽוֹדְעָה֙ הַֽחַטָּ֔את אֲשֶׁ֥ר חָטְא֖וּ עָלֶ֑יהָ וְהִקְרִ֨יבוּ
טו הַקָּהָ֜ל פַּ֤ר בֶּן־בָּקָר֙ לְחַטָּ֔את וְהֵבִ֣יאוּ אֹת֔וֹ לִפְנֵ֖י אֹ֥הֶל מוֹעֵֽד׃ וְ֠סָמְכוּ זִקְנֵ֨י הָעֵדָ֧ה
טז אֶת־יְדֵיהֶ֛ם עַל־רֹ֥אשׁ הַפָּ֖ר לִפְנֵ֣י יְהוָ֑ה וְשָׁחַ֥ט אֶת־הַפָּ֖ר לִפְנֵ֥י יְהוָֽה׃ וְהֵבִ֛יא הַכֹּהֵ֥ן
יז הַמָּשִׁ֖יחַ מִדַּ֣ם הַפָּ֑ר אֶל־אֹ֖הֶל מוֹעֵֽד׃ וְטָבַ֛ל הַכֹּהֵ֥ן אֶצְבָּע֖וֹ מִן־הַדָּ֑ם וְהִזָּ֞ה שֶׁ֤בַע
יח פְּעָמִים֙ לִפְנֵ֣י יְהוָ֔ה אֵ֖ת פְּנֵ֥י הַפָּרֹֽכֶת׃ וּמִן־הַדָּ֞ם יִתֵּ֣ן ׀ עַל־קַרְנֹ֣ת הַמִּזְבֵּ֗חַ אֲשֶׁר֙
לִפְנֵ֣י יְהוָ֔ה אֲשֶׁ֖ר בְּאֹ֣הֶל מוֹעֵ֑ד וְאֵ֣ת כָּל־הַדָּ֗ם יִשְׁפֹּךְ֙ אֶל־יְסוֹד֙ מִזְבַּ֣ח הָעֹלָ֔ה
יט כ אֲשֶׁר־פֶּ֖תַח אֹ֥הֶל מוֹעֵֽד׃ וְאֵ֥ת כָּל־חֶלְבּ֖וֹ יָרִ֣ים מִמֶּ֑נּוּ וְהִקְטִ֖יר הַמִּזְבֵּֽחָה׃ וְעָשָׂ֣ה
לַפָּ֔ר כַּאֲשֶׁ֤ר עָשָׂה֙ לְפַ֣ר הַֽחַטָּ֔את כֵּ֖ן יַעֲשֶׂה־לּ֑וֹ וְכִפֶּ֧ר עֲלֵהֶ֛ם הַכֹּהֵ֖ן וְנִסְלַ֥ח לָהֶֽם׃
כא וְהוֹצִ֣יא אֶת־הַפָּ֗ר אֶל־מִחוּץ֙ לַֽמַּחֲנֶ֔ה וְשָׂרַ֣ף אֹת֔וֹ כַּאֲשֶׁ֣ר שָׂרַ֔ף אֵ֖ת הַפָּ֣ר הָרִאשׁ֑וֹן
חַטַּ֥את הַקָּהָ֖ל הֽוּא׃

רש״י

לִכְלָיוֹת וְלַחֲלָבִים וְיוֹתֶרֶת: **יָרִים מִמֶּנּוּ.** מִן הַמְחֻבָּר, שֶׁלֹּא יְנַתְּחֶנּוּ קֹדֶם הֲסָרַת חֶלְבּוֹ. תּוֹרַת כֹּהֲנִים:

ט-יא| **כַּאֲשֶׁר יוּרָם.** כְּאוֹתָן אֵמוּרִין הַמְפֹרָשִׁין בְּשׁוֹר זֶבַח הַשְּׁלָמִים. וְכִי מַה פֵּרַשׁ בְּזֶבַח הַשְּׁלָמִים שֶׁלֹּא פֵּרַשׁ כָּאן? אֶלָּא לְהַקִּישׁוֹ לִשְׁלָמִים: מַה שְּׁלָמִים לִשְׁמָן, אַף זֶה לִשְׁמוֹ; וּמַה שְּׁלָמִים שָׁלוֹם לָעוֹלָם, אַף זֶה שָׁלוֹם לָעוֹלָם. וּבִשְׁחִיטַת קָדָשִׁים מַצְרִיכוֹ לִלְמֹד הֵימֶנּוּ שֶׁאֵין לְמֵדִין לָמֵד מִן הַלָּמֵד בְּקָדָשִׁים, בְּפֶרֶק 'אֵיזֶהוּ מְקוֹמָן' (זבחים מט ע״ב): עַל הַכָּבֵד, עַל הַכְּלָיוֹת, עַל רֹאשׁוֹ, וְעַל כְּרָעָיו. כֻּלָּן לְשׁוֹן תּוֹסֶפֶת הֵן, כְּמוֹ: 'מִלְּבַד':

יב| **אֶל מָקוֹם טָהוֹר.** לְפִי שֶׁיֵּשׁ מִחוּץ לָעִיר מָקוֹם מוּכָן לְטֻמְאָה, לְהַשְׁלִיךְ אֲבָנִים מְנֻגָּעוֹת וּלְבֵית הַקְּבָרוֹת, הֻצְרַךְ לוֹמַר בְּ"מִחוּץ לַמַּחֲנֶה" זֶה, שֶׁהוּא חוּץ לָעִיר, שֶׁיְּהֵא הַמָּקוֹם טָהוֹר: מִחוּץ לַמַּחֲנֶה. חוּץ לְשָׁלֹשׁ מַחֲנוֹת, וּבְבֵית עוֹלָמִים – חוּץ לָעִיר, כְּמוֹ שֶׁפֵּרְשׁוּהוּ רַבּוֹתֵינוּ בְּמַסֶּכֶת יוֹמָא (דף סח ע״א) וּבְסַנְהֶדְרִין (דף מב ע״ב): **אֶל שֶׁפֶךְ הַדֶּשֶׁן.** מָקוֹם שֶׁשּׁוֹפְכִין בּוֹ הַדֶּשֶׁן הַמְסֻלָּק מִן הַמִּזְבֵּחַ, כְּמוֹ שֶׁנֶּאֱמַר: "וְהוֹצִיא אֶת הַדֶּשֶׁן אֶל מִחוּץ לַמַּחֲנֶה" (להלן ו, ד): **עַל שֶׁפֶךְ הַדֶּשֶׁן יִשָּׂרֵף.** שֶׁאֵין תַּלְמוּד לוֹמַר, אֶלָּא לְלַמֵּד שֶׁאֲפִלּוּ אֵין שָׁם דֶּשֶׁן:

יג| **עֲדַת יִשְׂרָאֵל.** אֵלּוּ סַנְהֶדְרִין: **וְנֶעְלַם דָּבָר.** טָעוּ לְהוֹרוֹת בְּאַחַת מִכָּל כָּרֵתוֹת שֶׁבַּתּוֹרָה שֶׁהוּא מֻתָּר: **הַקָּהָל וְעָשׂוּ.** שֶׁעָשׂוּ הַצִּבּוּר עַל פִּיהֶם:

יז| **אֵת פְּנֵי הַפָּרֹכֶת.** וּלְמַעְלָה הוּא אוֹמֵר: "אֶת פְּנֵי פָּרֹכֶת הַקֹּדֶשׁ" (לעיל פסוק ו)! מָשָׁל לְמֶלֶךְ שֶׁסָּרְחָה עָלָיו מְדִינָה, אִם מִעוּטָהּ סָרְחָה – פָּמַלְיָא שֶׁלּוֹ מִתְקַיֶּמֶת, וְאִם כֻּלָּהּ סָרְחָה – אֵין פָּמַלְיָא שֶׁלּוֹ מִתְקַיֶּמֶת. אַף כָּאן, כְּשֶׁחָטָא כֹּהֵן מָשִׁיחַ עֲדַיִן שֵׁם קְדֻשַּׁת הַמָּקוֹם עַל הַמִּקְדָּשׁ, מִשֶּׁחָטְאוּ כֻּלָּם אִם וְשָׁלוֹם נִסְתַּלְּקָה הַקְּדֻשָּׁה:

יח| **יְסוֹד מִזְבַּח הָעֹלָה אֲשֶׁר פֶּתַח אֹהֶל מוֹעֵד.** זֶה יְסוֹד מַעֲרָבִי שֶׁהוּא כְּנֶגֶד הַפֶּתַח:

יט-כ| **וְאֵת כָּל חֶלְבּוֹ יָרִים.** אַף עַל פִּי שֶׁלֹּא פֵּרַשׁ כָּאן יוֹתֶרֶת וּשְׁתֵּי כְלָיוֹת, לְמֵדִין הֵם מִ"וְעָשָׂה לַפָּר כַּאֲשֶׁר עָשָׂה" וְגוֹ'. וּמִפְּנֵי מָה לֹא נִתְפָּרְשׁוּ בּוֹ? תָּנָא דְּבֵי רַבִּי יִשְׁמָעֵאל: מָשָׁל לְמֶלֶךְ שֶׁזָּעַם עַל אוֹהֲבוֹ, וּמִעֵט בְּסִרְחוֹנוֹ מִפְּנֵי חִבָּתוֹ: **וְעָשָׂה לַפָּר.** זֶה, "כַּאֲשֶׁר עָשָׂה לְפַר הַחַטָּאת", כְּמוֹ שֶׁמְּפֹרָשׁ בְּפַר כֹּהֵן מָשִׁיחַ, לְהָבִיא יוֹתֶרֶת וּשְׁתֵּי כְלָיוֹת שֶׁפֵּרַשׁ שָׁם (לעיל פסוק ט), שֶׁלֹּא פֵּרַשׁ כָּאן, וְלִכְפֹּל בְּמִצְוַת הָעֲבוֹדוֹת, לְלַמֵּד שֶׁאִם חִסֵּר אַחַת מִכָּל הַמַּתָּנוֹת – פָּסַל, לְפִי שֶׁמָּצִינוּ בַּנִּתָּנִין עַל הַמִּזְבֵּחַ הַחִיצוֹן שֶׁנְּתָנָן בְּמַתָּנָה אַחַת – כִּפֵּר, הֻצְרַךְ לוֹמַר כָּאן שֶׁמַּתָּנָה אַחַת מֵהֶן מְעַכֶּבֶת:

22 The Torah describes the third type of sin offering: **When a ruler,**[D] a king or whoever holds the most elevated position among the Jewish people,[53] **sins,**[D]**and** he **unwittingly performs one of all the commandments of the Lord his God that may not be performed, and he** subsequently recognizes that he **is guilty.**

23 **Or if his sin that he sinned becomes known to him** because he is informed of it by others,[54] **he shall bring his** unique **offering, an unblemished male goat,**[D] old enough to no longer be considered a young kid.

24 **He shall lay his hand on the head of the goat, and slaughter it in the place where he shall slaughter the burnt offering,** to the north of the altar (1:11), **before the Lord; it is a sin offering.**

25 **The priest shall take from the blood of the sin offering with his finger, and place it on the horns of the altar of the burnt offering.**[D] While the blood of other offerings is cast or poured upon the altar directly from the bowl, the blood of the sin offering is sprinkled or smeared by the priest on the altar with his finger. This is performed four times, once on each horn of the altar. Since the blood is smeared rather than cast, a large quantity of blood remains in the bowl, **and the** remainder of the **blood he shall pour at the base of the altar of the burnt offering.**

26 **All its fat he shall burn on the altar, like the fat of the peace offering;** the procedure is the same as with regard to the peace offering. **The priest shall atone for him for his sin, and it shall be forgiven for him.**

27 The Torah describes the fourth type of sin offering, the sin offer-
Sixth ing of the common person: **If one person from the common**
aliya **people sins unwittingly, in his performance of any of the commandments of the Lord that may not be performed, and is guilty,** he shall bring a sin offering. Although one cannot be prosecuted criminally for an unwitting transgression, there is nevertheless a certain level of guilt even for transgressions that were committed due to forgetfulness or because one is not paying attention to his actions. One is held responsible not only for his conscious actions and for his conscious thoughts, but also for actions that he performs subconsciously and for information that has receded into the subconscious realm of his mind.

28 **Or if his sin that he sinned becomes known to him** because he is informed of it by others (see verse 23), **he shall bring his offering, an unblemished female goat for his sin that he sinned.** Whereas the ruler brings a male goat, the common person brings a female goat.

29 **He shall lay his hand upon the head of the sin offering, and slaughter the sin offering in the place of the burnt offering.**

30 **The priest shall take from its blood with his finger, and place it on the horns of the altar of the burnt offering, and all** of the remainder of **its blood he shall pour at the base of the altar.**

31 **All its fat he shall remove, as the fat was removed from the peace offering; and the priest shall burn it upon the altar for a pleasing aroma to the Lord; and the priest shall atone for him, and it shall be forgiven for him.**

DISCUSSION

4:22| **Ruler [*nasi*]**: The Hebrew term *nasi*, a ruler or prince, literally means an individual whose status is elevated above that of others. Although the term *nasi* can refer to the head of a tribe or family, here it refers only to the supreme ruler. This is indicated by the phrase used in this verse, "the commandments of the Lord his God," which emphasizes the submission of the ruler to God, as opposed to the term "the commandments of the Lord," which appears with regard to the other sin offerings (see, e.g., verse 2). This indicates that the ruler under discussion is subject to none except God Himself. Nevertheless, the Talmud states that there could be two such rulers who reign concurrently. This was the case during most of the First Temple period, when the kingdom of Israel was divided. Both the king of Judah and the king of Israel were Jewish rulers, and neither was subject to the other (see *Horayot* 11).

The Torah elsewhere uses the term king to refer to the supreme ruler, as in Deuteronomy (17:14–20), where the Torah presents a detailed list of laws pertaining to the king. The kingship is an institution of government with clearly defined parameters, whereas the term *nasi* refers to the status of the individual. It is possible that the Torah here employs the term *nasi* due to the problematic nature of the institution of kingship. In the book of Ezekiel, the leader of the Jewish people is nearly always referred to as the *nasi* and not as the king (see Ezekiel 12:12, 45, 48:22; see also commentary on I Samuel 8:22 and on II Kings 20:5).

When [*asher*] a ruler sins: The Torah introduces each of the other types of sin offerings in this section by stating that "if" one sins, he must bring a sin offering (see, e.g., verses 3 and 13); however, in this verse the Torah states that "when" the ruler sins he must bring a sin offering. This may allude to the unfortunate fact of life that with regard to the ruler, in contrast to the High Priest, judges, or regular citizens, it is generally only a matter of time until he commits a transgression (see Sforno, verse 22). The Hebrew term *asher* is also interpreted by the Sages homiletically as deriving from the term *ashrei*, happy or fortunate. The good fortune is not in the fact that the ruler commits a transgression, but in the fact that his sin causes him to be plagued by guilt and to bring a sin offering. It is not uncommon that rulers are unable to admit error, and many leaders consider themselves to be above the law. If the king recognizes that he is subject to the laws of the Torah and endeavors to atone for his sin, his generation is indeed fortunate (see *Horayot* 10b; Rashi).

כב אֲשֶׁר נָשִׂיא יֶחֱטָא וְעָשָׂה אַחַת מִכָּל־מִצְוֺת יְהוָה אֱלֹהָיו אֲשֶׁר לֹא־תֵעָשֶׂינָה
כג בִּשְׁגָגָה וְאָשֵׁם׃ אוֹ־הוֹדַע אֵלָיו חַטָּאתוֹ אֲשֶׁר חָטָא בָּהּ וְהֵבִיא אֶת־קָרְבָּנוֹ שְׂעִיר
כד עִזִּים זָכָר תָּמִים׃ וְסָמַךְ יָדוֹ עַל־רֹאשׁ הַשָּׂעִיר וְשָׁחַט אֹתוֹ בִּמְקוֹם אֲשֶׁר־יִשְׁחַט
כה אֶת־הָעֹלָה לִפְנֵי יְהוָה חַטָּאת הוּא׃ וְלָקַח הַכֹּהֵן מִדַּם הַחַטָּאת בְּאֶצְבָּעוֹ וְנָתַן
כו עַל־קַרְנֹת מִזְבַּח הָעֹלָה וְאֶת־דָּמוֹ יִשְׁפֹּךְ אֶל־יְסוֹד מִזְבַּח הָעֹלָה׃ וְאֶת־כָּל־חֶלְבּוֹ
יַקְטִיר הַמִּזְבֵּחָה כְּחֵלֶב זֶבַח הַשְּׁלָמִים וְכִפֶּר עָלָיו הַכֹּהֵן מֵחַטָּאתוֹ וְנִסְלַח לוֹ׃
כז וְאִם־נֶפֶשׁ אַחַת תֶּחֱטָא בִשְׁגָגָה מֵעַם הָאָרֶץ בַּעֲשֹׂתָהּ אַחַת מִמִּצְוֺת יְהוָה אֲשֶׁר ששי
כח לֹא־תֵעָשֶׂינָה וְאָשֵׁם׃ אוֹ הוֹדַע אֵלָיו חַטָּאתוֹ אֲשֶׁר חָטָא וְהֵבִיא קָרְבָּנוֹ שְׂעִירַת
כט עִזִּים תְּמִימָה נְקֵבָה עַל־חַטָּאתוֹ אֲשֶׁר חָטָא׃ וְסָמַךְ אֶת־יָדוֹ עַל רֹאשׁ הַחַטָּאת
ל וְשָׁחַט אֶת־הַחַטָּאת בִּמְקוֹם הָעֹלָה׃ וְלָקַח הַכֹּהֵן מִדָּמָהּ בְּאֶצְבָּעוֹ וְנָתַן עַל־
לא קַרְנֹת מִזְבַּח הָעֹלָה וְאֶת־כָּל־דָּמָהּ יִשְׁפֹּךְ אֶל־יְסוֹד הַמִּזְבֵּחַ׃ וְאֶת־כָּל־חֶלְבָּהּ
יָסִיר כַּאֲשֶׁר הוּסַר חֵלֶב מֵעַל זֶבַח הַשְּׁלָמִים וְהִקְטִיר הַכֹּהֵן הַמִּזְבֵּחָה לְרֵיחַ
נִיחֹחַ לַיהוָה וְכִפֶּר עָלָיו הַכֹּהֵן וְנִסְלַח לוֹ׃

רש״י

כב | אֲשֶׁר נָשִׂיא יֶחֱטָא. לְשׁוֹן 'אַשְׁרֵי', אַשְׁרֵי הַדּוֹר שֶׁהַנָּשִׂיא שֶׁלּוֹ נוֹתֵן לֵב לְהָבִיא כַּפָּרָה עַל שִׁגְגָתוֹ, קַל וָחֹמֶר שֶׁמִּתְחָרֵט עַל זְדוֹנוֹתָיו:

כג | אוֹ הוֹדַע. כְּמוֹ: אִם הוֹדַע הַדָּבָר, הַרְבֵּה 'אוֹ' יֵשׁ מְשַׁמְּשִׁין בִּלְשׁוֹן 'אִם' וְ'אִם' בִּמְקוֹם 'אוֹ', וְכֵן: "אוֹ נוֹדַע כִּי שׁוֹר נַגָּח הוּא" (שמות כא, לו): הוֹדַע אֵלָיו. כְּשֶׁחָטָא הָיָה סָבוּר שֶׁהוּא הֶתֵּר, וּלְאַחַר מִכָּאן נוֹדַע לוֹ שֶׁאִסּוּר הָיָה:

כד | בִּמְקוֹם אֲשֶׁר יִשְׁחַט אֶת הָעֹלָה. בַּצָּפוֹן, שֶׁהוּא מְפֹרָשׁ בָּעוֹלָה (לעיל א, יא): חַטָּאת הוּא. לִשְׁמוֹ כָּשֵׁר, שֶׁלֹּא לִשְׁמוֹ פָּסוּל:

כה | וְאֶת דָּמוֹ. שְׁיָרֵי הַדָּם:

כו | כְּחֵלֶב זֶבַח הַשְּׁלָמִים. כְּאוֹתָן אֵמוּרִין הַמְפֹרָשִׁים בְּעֵז הָאָמוּר אֵצֶל שְׁלָמִים (לעיל ג, יד-טו):

לא | כַּאֲשֶׁר הוּסַר חֵלֶב מֵעַל זֶבַח הַשְּׁלָמִים. כְּאֵמוּרֵי עֵז הָאֲמוּרִים בִּשְׁלָמִים (לעיל שם):

DISCUSSION

4:23 | **An unblemished male goat** [*se'ir*]: The *Sifra* states that the ruler brings a male goat that is still within its first year (see Ibn Ezra, Numbers 15:27). The Mishna (*Para* 1:4) states that sin offerings must be at least one month old (see Rambam's Commentary on the Mishna, introduction to the Order of *Kodashim*; Rambam, *Sefer Avoda, Hilkhot Ma'aseh HaKorbanot* 1:14, and *Kesef Mishne* and *Mishne LaMelekh* ad loc.; *Ḥazon Ish*, *Para* 1:11). According to some versions of the Rambam's writings, the goat must be one year old. It seems that the Hebrew term *se'ir* refers to a somewhat mature goat that is no longer a kid. Nevertheless, if he brought a young kid he has fulfilled his obligation.

4:25 | **On the horns of the altar of the burnt offering**: In contrast to the blood of the High Priest's sin offering and the High Court's sin offering, which are placed on the inner altar, the blood of the ruler's sin offering is sprinkled on the external altar in the courtyard of the Tabernacle, in the same manner as the individual's sin offering. This difference is due to the fact that the High Priest and the High Court are spiritual leaders who are concerned with the inner, spiritual life of the nation, whereas the king is a political leader. Due to his elevated status, the ruler brings a unique offering, a male goat, rather than the female goat or lamb brought by the common individual. Nevertheless, his sin is essentially a personal matter, similar to the sin of any other individual (see *Bekhor Shor*, verse 3).

32 **And if he brings a lamb,** rather than a goat, **as his offering for a sin offering, an unblemished female he shall bring it.**

33 **He shall lay his hand on the head of the sin offering, and slaughter it as a sin offering in the place where he shall slaughter the burnt offering.**

34 **The priest shall take from the blood of the sin offering with his finger, and place it on the horns of the altar of the burnt offering, and all** the remainder of **its blood he shall pour at the base of the altar.**

35 **He shall remove all its fat, as the fat of the lamb is removed from the peace offering,** including the sheep's fatty tail.[55] **The priest shall burn them on the altar, on the fire offerings of the Lord; and the priest shall atone for his sin that he sinned,**[D] **and it shall be forgiven for him.** Alternatively, some interpret the verse as stating that the priest shall burn them on the altar, on the fires of the Lord,[56] rather than on the fire offerings of the Lord.[57]

5 1 In contrast to the sin offerings mentioned above, the offerings discussed below pertain to a number of specific transgressions that do not carry a punishment of excision from the World to Come when they are performed intentionally. Additionally, whereas the regular sin offering is fixed, the offerings discussed below are known as sliding-scale offerings,[58] as their value depends on the sinner's financial ability. Some commentaries explain that in the case of the three transgressions mentioned below, the sinner does not usually derive any benefit from the transgression. This is in contrast to the cases where one is liable to bring a fixed sin offering, in which the sin generally involves pleasure or personal benefit.[59] **If a person sins, in that he hears the voice of an oath** directed at him, **and he is a witness, who either saw** a certain occurrence **or knew** of a certain

matter, **if he does not tell** whatever he knows, **he shall bear his iniquity** and receive his punishment. The case described here is where a plaintiff claims that another individual has information supporting his case. The individual refuses to testify, denying under oath that he has information about the case. Since he lied, either intentionally or unwittingly, after an oath was administered to him requiring him to testify, he must bring an offering to atone for his sin.

2 **Or a person who touches any impure thing: The carcass of a non-pure beast, the carcass of a non-pure animal, or the carcass of an impure swarming animal, and it is hidden from him,** that is, he forgot that he is impure, **and he is impure, and he is guilty.** In such a case one must also bring a sin offering. Similar to most sin offerings, this sin offering is brought to atone for an unwitting transgression. The guilt referred to here is not because of the person's ritual impurity in itself, as there is no sin involved in being ritually impure, and although it is preferable to become ritually pure, one is not required to do so.[60] The person's guilt is because he acted in the manner of a ritually pure individual, either entering the Temple or partaking of sacrificial food, and in doing so he defiled the Temple or sacred items.[61]

3 **Or if he touches human impurity, in any impurity with which he will become impure, and it is hidden from him; and he knew, and he is guilty.** This law does not pertain to one who never knew that he was rendered impure, e.g., if one touched an impure object in the dark without realizing it; it applies only to one who knew that he had become impure and subsequently forgot.[62]

4 **Or,** lastly, a sin offering must be brought by **a person who takes an oath, to express with lips** an undertaking **to do harm** to himself by abstaining from a certain matter **or to do good** to

---

DISCUSSION

The Animal Sin Offerings (chap. 4)

	Inner sin offerings		External sin offerings	
	The High Priest's sin offering	The High Court's sin offering	The ruler's sin offering	The common person's sin offering
The species of animal brought	Bull	Bull	Male goat	Female goat or sheep
The priest who performs the rites of the offering	High Priest	High Priest	Any priest	Any priest
The place where the blood is sprinkled	Sprinkled toward the Curtain and placed on the horns of the inner incense altar	Sprinkled toward the Curtain and placed on the horns of the inner incense altar	Placed on the horns of the external altar	Placed on the horns of the external altar
The flesh and hide of the offering, apart from the fats that are burned on the altar	Burned outside the camp	Burned outside the camp	Given to the priests	Given to the priests

לב לג וְאִם־כֶּבֶשׂ יָבִיא קָרְבָּנוֹ לְחַטָּאת נְקֵבָה תְמִימָה יְבִיאֶנָּה: וְסָמַךְ אֶת־יָדוֹ עַל
לד רֹאשׁ הַחַטָּאת וְשָׁחַט אֹתָהּ לְחַטָּאת בִּמְקוֹם אֲשֶׁר יִשְׁחַט אֶת־הָעֹלָה: וְלָקַח
הַכֹּהֵן מִדַּם הַחַטָּאת בְּאֶצְבָּעוֹ וְנָתַן עַל־קַרְנֹת מִזְבַּח הָעֹלָה וְאֶת־כָּל־דָּמָהּ
לה יִשְׁפֹּךְ אֶל־יְסוֹד הַמִּזְבֵּחַ: וְאֶת־כָּל־חֶלְבָּהּ יָסִיר כַּאֲשֶׁר יוּסַר חֵלֶב־הַכֶּשֶׂב מִזֶּבַח
הַשְּׁלָמִים וְהִקְטִיר הַכֹּהֵן אֹתָם הַמִּזְבֵּחָה עַל אִשֵּׁי יהוה וְכִפֶּר עָלָיו הַכֹּהֵן עַל־
חַטָּאתוֹ אֲשֶׁר־חָטָא וְנִסְלַח לוֹ:

א וְנֶפֶשׁ כִּי־תֶחֱטָא וְשָׁמְעָה קוֹל אָלָה וְהוּא עֵד אוֹ רָאָה אוֹ יָדָע אִם־לוֹא יַגִּיד
ב וְנָשָׂא עֲוֺנוֹ: אוֹ נֶפֶשׁ אֲשֶׁר תִּגַּע בְּכָל־דָּבָר טָמֵא אוֹ בְנִבְלַת חַיָּה טְמֵאָה אוֹ
בְּנִבְלַת בְּהֵמָה טְמֵאָה אוֹ בְּנִבְלַת שֶׁרֶץ טָמֵא וְנֶעְלַם מִמֶּנּוּ וְהוּא טָמֵא וְאָשֵׁם:
ג אוֹ כִי יִגַּע בְּטֻמְאַת אָדָם לְכֹל טֻמְאָתוֹ אֲשֶׁר יִטְמָא בָּהּ וְנֶעְלַם מִמֶּנּוּ וְהוּא
ד יָדַע וְאָשֵׁם: אוֹ נֶפֶשׁ כִּי תִשָּׁבַע לְבַטֵּא בִשְׂפָתַיִם לְהָרַע אוֹ לְהֵיטִיב לְכֹל
אֲשֶׁר יְבַטֵּא הָאָדָם בִּשְׁבֻעָה וְנֶעְלַם מִמֶּנּוּ וְהוּא־יָדַע וְאָשֵׁם לְאַחַת מֵאֵלֶּה:

רש״י

לג| וְשָׁחַט אֹתָהּ לְחַטָּאת. שֶׁתְּהֵא שְׁחִיטָתָהּ לְשֵׁם חַטָּאת:

לה| כַּאֲשֶׁר יוּסַר חֵלֶב הַכֶּשֶׂב. שֶׁנִּתְרַבּוּ אֵמוּרִין בְּאַלְיָה, אַף חַטָּאת כְּשֶׁהִיא בָּאָה כִּבְשָׂה טְעוּנָה אַלְיָה עִם הָאֵמוּרִין: עַל אִשֵּׁי ה׳. עַל מְדוּרוֹת הָאֵשׁ הָעֲשׂוּיוֹת לַשֵּׁם, פוּאיילי״ש בְּלַעַז:

פרק ה

א| וְשָׁמְעָה קוֹל אָלָה. בְּדָבָר שֶׁהוּא עֵד בּוֹ, שֶׁהִשְׁבִּיעוּהוּ שְׁבוּעָה שֶׁאִם יוֹדֵעַ לוֹ בְּעֵדוּת שֶׁיָּעִיד לוֹ:

ב| אוֹ נֶפֶשׁ אֲשֶׁר תִּגַּע וְגוֹ׳. וּלְאַחַר הַטֻּמְאָה הַזּוֹ יֹאכַל קָדָשִׁים אוֹ יִכָּנֵס לַמִּקְדָּשׁ, שֶׁהוּא דָּבָר שֶׁזְּדוֹנוֹ כָּרֵת. בְּמַסֶּכֶת שְׁבוּעוֹת (דף ו ע״ב – ז ע״ב; יד ע״ב) נִדְרָשׁ כֵּן: וְנֶעְלַם מִמֶּנּוּ. הַטֻּמְאָה: וְאָשֵׁם. בַּאֲכִילַת קֹדֶשׁ אוֹ בְּבִיאַת מִקְדָּשׁ:

ג| בְּטֻמְאַת אָדָם. זוֹ טֻמְאַת מֵת: לְכֹל טֻמְאָתוֹ. לְרַבּוֹת טֻמְאַת מַגַּע זָבִין וְזָבוֹת: אֲשֶׁר יִטְמָא. לְרַבּוֹת הַנּוֹגֵעַ בְּבוֹעֵל נִדָּה: בָּהּ. לְרַבּוֹת בּוֹלֵעַ נִבְלַת עוֹף טָהוֹר, וְנֶעְלַם. וְלֹא יָדַע, שֶׁשָּׁכַח הַטֻּמְאָה: וְאָשֵׁם. בַּאֲכִילַת קֹדֶשׁ אוֹ בְּבִיאַת מִקְדָּשׁ:

ד| בִשְׂפָתַיִם. וְלֹא בַּלֵּב: לְהָרַע. לְעַצְמוֹ: אוֹ לְהֵיטִיב. לְעַצְמוֹ, כְּגוֹן אֹכַל וְלֹא אֹכַל, אִישַׁן וְלֹא אִישַׁן: לְכֹל אֲשֶׁר יְבַטֵּא. לְרַבּוֹת לְשֶׁעָבַר: וְנֶעְלַם מִמֶּנּוּ. וְעָבַר עַל שְׁבוּעָתוֹ. כָּל אֵלֶּה בְּקָרְבָּן עוֹלֶה וְיוֹרֵד כַּמְפֹרָשׁ כָּאן, אֲבָל שְׁבוּעָה שֶׁיֵּשׁ בָּהּ כְּפִירַת מָמוֹן אֵינָהּ בְּקָרְבָּן זֶה אֶלָּא בְּאָשָׁם (להלן פסוקים כ-כו):

himself by performing a certain matter, **for everything that a person shall express in an oath, and it was** subsequently **hidden from him,** as he forgot his oath. He violated his oath, **and he** subsequently **knew and he is guilty of** violating **one of these** oaths. While in the case of an oath of testimony (see verse 1) the oath was administered by another,[63] in this case one took an oath at his own initiative and subsequently forgot his oath and unwittingly violated it, either actively or by failing to perform his undertaking. This type of oath is known as an oath on an utterance.[64]

DISCUSSION

4:35| **The priest shall atone for his sin that he sinned**: With regard to the High Priest's sin offering and the High Court's sin offering, the Torah states that the flesh is taken out of the camp and burned in its entirety on the place of the ashes. The laws pertaining to the flesh of the ruler's sin offering and the common person's sin offering are not stated here. The Torah states below (6:19) that it is eaten, similar to the flesh of the peace offering. However, the sanctity of the sin offering is greater than that of the peace offering: It is eaten only by the priests, in a sacred place, and it must be consumed within a shorter time period than is allocated for the consumption of the peace offering.

5 Three transgressions were mentioned so far: One who refrained from testifying on behalf of another and swore falsely that he does not know of relevant information; one who entered the Temple or partook of sacrificial food while he was ritually impure; and one who took an oath to perform or to abstain from a particular activity and violated his oath. **It shall be when he is guilty of one of these** transgressions, **he shall confess**[D] **with regard to that which he sinned.** It is not sufficient that one is aware of his guilt. He must verbally confess his sin, and only then may he bring a sin offering.[65]

6 Once the sinner has confessed, he takes action to achieve atonement. **He shall bring his restitution,** his offering,[66] **to the Lord for his sin that he sinned.** Beyond the violation of specific prohibitions, there is an aspect of each of these actions that defines it as particularly improper behavior toward God. The sinner expresses his guilt by bringing **a female from the flock, a lamb or a goat, as a sin offering; and the priest shall atone for him for his sin,** performing the rites of the sin offering as described above (4:27–35).

7 **If his means do not suffice for** the purchase of **a lamb, he shall bring his restitution,** his offering, **for that which he sinned, two turtledoves or two young pigeons, to the Lord: One as a sin offering and one as a burnt offering.** Instead of an animal sin offering, a poor man may bring two birds, which are much cheaper, and only one of them is sacrificed as a sin offering.

8 **He shall bring them to the priest, and** the priest **shall offer that** bird **which is** intended **for the sin offering first. He shall pinch off its head adjacent to its nape** with his thumbnail, cutting the back of its neck below the cranium,[67] **but** the priest **shall not separate** the head from the body. The Mishna cites a dispute among the Sages with regard to whether the offering is fit in a case where the priest separated the head from the body.[68]

9 **He shall sprinkle from the blood of the sin offering,** from the cut in the bird's neck, **on the wall of the altar; and the remainder of the blood shall be squeezed at the base of the altar** by pressing the bird against the wall of the altar or by squeezing the bird's neck with his hand,[69] so that the remainder of the blood flows down to the base of the altar. **It is a sin offering.**

10 In contrast to the animal sin offering, there are no sacrificial portions burned on the altar from the bird sin offering. The sinner is therefore required to bring a burnt offering as well: **And the second** bird **he shall prepare as a burnt offering, in accordance with the procedure** stated above (1:14–17). The priest pinches off the bird's head, severing it from the body, squeezes out the blood on the wall of the altar, and burns the bird on the altar in its entirety, after removing its crop. **And the priest shall atone for him** with the two bird offerings **for his sin that he sinned, and it shall be forgiven for him.**

11 If he is so poor that **his means do not suffice** even **for two**
Seventh aliya **turtledoves or two young pigeons, he shall bring his offering for that which he sinned, one-tenth of an ephah of high-quality flour as a sin offering.** However, **he shall not place oil on it, nor shall he place frankincense on it, as it is a sin offering.** Whereas the gift meal offering is mixed with oil and brought together with frankincense, it is fitting for the meal offering of a sinner to be plain and modest.[70]

12 **He shall bring it to the priest, and the priest shall take his handful from it, his full handful,**[71] **its memorial portion, and** he shall **burn it on the altar, on the fire offerings of the Lord; it is a sin offering.**

13 **The priest shall atone for his sin that he sinned for one of these, and it shall be forgiven for him; and it,** the remainder of the meal offering of the sinner that is not burned, **shall be for the priest like the meal offering,** and he is commanded to eat it.

The Guilt Offering

LEVITICUS 5:14–26

The previous section detailed the laws of the sin offering, including the different types of fixed sin offering, which depend on the identity of the sinner, and the sliding-scale sin offering that is brought in the case of three specific transgressions. The following section details three cases in which a sinner is required to bring a guilt offering. Like the sin offering, the guilt offering is an obligatory offering. In this section the Torah details only the species of animal brought as a guilt offering and the transgressions for which one is required to bring a guilt offering. The laws pertaining to the rituals of the offering and to the manner of its consumption are detailed below (7:1–7).

The guilt offerings detailed here atone for transgressions that stem from indifference and a blurring of the boundaries between permitted and prohibited actions. This, together with a person's ambition for expanded activity and control, may lead one to perform one of the actions described below: Inadvertently misusing consecrated property; performing actions that leave one in doubt as to whether he violated a prohibition; and falsely denying under oath that he does not have the property of another individual in his possession.

14 **The Lord spoke to Moses, saying:**

15 **A person who commits a trespass, and sins unwittingly with regard to the sacred items of the Lord, he shall bring his restitution,** his offering, **to the Lord.** If one unwittingly derives personal benefit from consecrated property that belongs to the Temple treasury, or eats sacred food, and subsequently discovers that he derived benefit from these sacred items, he is required to make restitution. He shall bring **an**

ה ו וְהָיָה כִי־יֶאְשַׁם לְאַחַת מֵאֵלֶּה וְהִתְוַדָּה אֲשֶׁר חָטָא עָלֶיהָ: וְהֵבִיא אֶת־אֲשָׁמוֹ
לַיהוָה עַל חַטָּאתוֹ אֲשֶׁר חָטָא נְקֵבָה מִן־הַצֹּאן כִּשְׂבָּה אוֹ־שְׂעִירַת עִזִּים לְחַטָּאת
ז וְכִפֶּר עָלָיו הַכֹּהֵן מֵחַטָּאתוֹ: וְאִם־לֹא תַגִּיעַ יָדוֹ דֵּי שֶׂה וְהֵבִיא אֶת־אֲשָׁמוֹ אֲשֶׁר
ח חָטָא שְׁתֵּי תֹרִים אוֹ־שְׁנֵי בְנֵי־יוֹנָה לַיהוָה אֶחָד לְחַטָּאת וְאֶחָד לְעֹלָה: וְהֵבִיא
אֹתָם אֶל־הַכֹּהֵן וְהִקְרִיב אֶת־אֲשֶׁר לַחַטָּאת רִאשׁוֹנָה וּמָלַק אֶת־רֹאשׁוֹ מִמּוּל
ט עָרְפּוֹ וְלֹא יַבְדִּיל: וְהִזָּה מִדַּם הַחַטָּאת עַל־קִיר הַמִּזְבֵּחַ וְהַנִּשְׁאָר בַּדָּם יִמָּצֵה
י אֶל־יְסוֹד הַמִּזְבֵּחַ חַטָּאת הוּא: וְאֶת־הַשֵּׁנִי יַעֲשֶׂה עֹלָה כַּמִּשְׁפָּט וְכִפֶּר עָלָיו הַכֹּהֵן
יא מֵחַטָּאתוֹ אֲשֶׁר־חָטָא וְנִסְלַח לוֹ: וְאִם־לֹא תַשִּׂיג יָדוֹ לִשְׁתֵּי שביעי
תֹרִים אוֹ לִשְׁנֵי בְנֵי־יוֹנָה וְהֵבִיא אֶת־קָרְבָּנוֹ אֲשֶׁר חָטָא עֲשִׂירִת הָאֵפָה סֹלֶת
יב לְחַטָּאת לֹא־יָשִׂים עָלֶיהָ שֶׁמֶן וְלֹא־יִתֵּן עָלֶיהָ לְבֹנָה כִּי חַטָּאת הִוא: וֶהֱבִיאָהּ
אֶל־הַכֹּהֵן וְקָמַץ הַכֹּהֵן מִמֶּנָּה מְלוֹא קֻמְצוֹ אֶת־אַזְכָּרָתָהּ וְהִקְטִיר הַמִּזְבֵּחָה
יג עַל אִשֵּׁי יְהוָה חַטָּאת הִוא: וְכִפֶּר עָלָיו הַכֹּהֵן עַל־חַטָּאתוֹ אֲשֶׁר־חָטָא מֵאַחַת
יד מֵאֵלֶּה וְנִסְלַח לוֹ וְהָיְתָה לַכֹּהֵן כַּמִּנְחָה: וַיְדַבֵּר יְהוָה אֶל־מֹשֶׁה לֵּאמֹר:
טו נֶפֶשׁ כִּי־תִמְעֹל מַעַל וְחָטְאָה בִּשְׁגָגָה מִקָּדְשֵׁי יְהוָה וְהֵבִיא אֶת־אֲשָׁמוֹ לַיהוָה

רש"י

ח| **והקריב את אשר לחטאת ראשונה.** חטאת קודמת לעולה. למה הדבר דומה? לפרקליט שנכנס לרצות, רצה פרקליט, נכנס דורון אחריו: **ולא יבדיל.** אינו מולק אלא סימן אחד: **ערף.** הוא גובה הראש המשפע לצד הצואר. 'מול ערף' – מול הרואה את העורף, והוא אורך כל אחורי הצואר:

ט| **והזה מדם החטאת.** בעולה לא הטעין אלא מצוי (לעיל א, טו) ובחטאת הזאה ומצוי, אוחז בעוף ומתיז והדם נתז והולך למזבח: **חטאת הוא.** לשמה כשרה, שלא לשמה פסולה:

י| **כמשפט.** כדת האמורה בעולת העוף של נדבה בראש הפרשה:

יא| **כי חטאת הוא.** ואין בדין שיהא קרבנו מהודר:

יב| **חטאת הוא.** נקמצה ונקטרה לשמה כשרה, שלא לשמה פסולה:

יג| **על חטאתו אשר חטא.** כאן שנה הכתוב, שהרי בעשירות ובדלות נאמר: "מחטאתו" (לעיל פסוק ו ופסוק י), וכאן בדלי דלות נאמר: "על חטאתו", דקדקו רבותינו מכאן, שאם חטא כשהוא עשיר והפריש מעות לכשבה או שעירה והעני, יביא ממקצתן שתי תורים. הפריש מעות לשתי תורים והעני, יביא ממקצתן עשירית האיפה. הפריש מעות לעשירית האיפה והעשיר, יוסיף עליהן ויביא קרבן עשיר, לכך נאמר כאן: "על חטאתו": **מאחת מאלה.** מאחת משלש כפרות האמורות בענין: או בעשירות, או בדלות, או בדלי דלות. ומה תלמוד לומר? שיכול החמורים שבהם יהיו בכשבה או שעירה, והקלין יהיו בעוף, והקלין שבקלין יהיו בעשירית האיפה? תלמוד לומר: "מאחת מאלה", להשוות קלין לחמורין לכשבה ושעירה אם השיגה ידם, ואת החמורין לקלין לעשירית האיפה בדלי דלות: **והיתה לכהן כמנחה.** ללמד על מנחת חוטא שיהיו שיריה נאכלין, זהו לפי פשוטו. ורבותינו דרשו, "והיתה לכהן", ואם חוטא זה כהן הוא, תהא כשאר מנחת נדבת כהן, שהיא ב"כליל תהיה לא תאכל" (להלן ו, טז):

טו| **כי תמעל מעל.** אין מעילה בכל מקום אלא שנוי, וכן הוא אומר: "וימעלו באלהי אבותיהם ויזנו אחרי אלהי עמי הארץ" (דברי הימים א' ה, כה), וכן הוא אומר בסוטה: "ומעלה בו מעל" (במדבר ה, יב): **וחטאה בשגגה מקדשי ה'.** שנהנה מן ההקדש. והיכן הזהר? נאמר כאן 'חטא' ונאמר להלן 'חטא' בתרומה: "ולא ישאו עליו חטא" (להלן כב, ט), מה להלן הזהיר, אף כאן הזהיר. אי מה להלן

DISCUSSION

5:5| **He shall confess**: The Sages derived from this verse that a verbal confession is a prerequisite for any offering that is brought to atone for sin (see *Yoma* 36a; *Zevaḥim* 7b; *Karetot* 12a).

unblemished ram, a mature sheep, **from the flock, according to the valuation**[D] **of** at least two **silver shekels,**[D] **according to the sacred shekel, as a guilt offering.**[72] The sacred shekel, which was twice the weight of the ordinary shekel, was later known as a Tyrian *sela*, worth four dinars.[73]

16 In addition to bringing a guilt offering, **that which he sinned** by taking or benefiting **from the sacred** property **he shall pay, and one-fifth of it he shall add to it**[D] as a penalty, **and he shall give it to the priest; the priest shall atone for him with the ram of the guilt offering, and it shall be forgiven for him.** This offering is known as a guilt offering brought for misuse of consecrated property.[74]

17 The Torah discusses a second type of guilt offering: **And if a person sins and performs one of all the commandments of the Lord that shall not be performed, and he did not know** whether or not he committed a sin, **and he is guilty,**[D] **and he shall bear his iniquity,** and receive his punishment.[75]

18 **He shall bring an unblemished ram from the flock, according to the valuation** of at least two silver shekels (see verse 15), **as a guilt offering to the priest. The priest shall atone for him for the unwitting sin that he performed unwittingly, and he did not know**[D] at the time that he presented the offering whether or not he had committed a sin, **and it shall be forgiven for him.**

19 **It is a guilt offering.** Lest one think that he need not be overly concerned about uncertain transgression, the verse emphasizes that **he is guilty to the Lord.**[76]

20 **The Lord spoke to Moses, saying:**

21 The Torah introduces the third type of guilt offering: **A person who sins and commits a trespass against the Lord, and lies**[D]

DISCUSSION

5:15| **According to the valuation [*be'erkekha*]**: This term appears several times in this section, and again in chapter 27 and in Numbers 18:16. The *kaf* suffix of the Hebrew term *be'erkekha* appears to be the suffix indicating the second person singular, rendering the term "your valuation." Although some commentaries interpret the term in this manner (Rabbi Samson Raphael Hirsch), it seems more likely that this is merely an unusual form of the word *erekh*, valuation or value, in which the last consonant is repeated (see 27:23; Rashbam 27:3; Ibn Ezra 27:2). According to this interpretation the verse should be rendered: "He shall bring…an unblemished ram from the flock according to the valuation of silver shekels."

He shall bring his restitution to the Lord, an unblemished ram from the flock, according to the valuation of silver shekels: The sin offering does not have a fixed value. One may bring a small lamb as a sin offering, and in some cases even two bird offerings or a tenth of an ephah of high-quality flour (see verses 5–11). Conversely, the guilt offering has a set value: It must be worth no less than two silver shekels. A provisional guilt offering, brought by one who is uncertain as to whether he committed a transgression that requires a sin offering (see verses 17–18), is liable to cost more than the sin offering brought by one who is certain that he sinned. Apparently, when one is certain that he sinned, it is easier for him to feel regret for his actions; this regret, together with the sin offering, atones for his sin. However, when his guilt is uncertain, he is more likely to repress the thought of his possible guilt, and therefore a more costly offering is necessary in order to raise his awareness of his sin (see Ramban; *Zevaḥim* 48a; *Talmidei Rabbeinu Yona, Berakhot* 1b in Rif).

5:16| **And one-fifth of it he shall add to it**: The Sages explain that when the Torah refers to one-fifth of it, this means one-fifth of the total payment after the fine is added to the principal, which is equal to one-quarter of the value of the principal (*Sifra*; *Bava Metzia* 53b–54a).

5:17| **And he did not know and he is guilty**: The lack of knowledge in this case is necessarily different from that in the cases that require one to bring a sin offering, which have been detailed above. The Sages explained that this passage refers to one who has become aware of his actions, but is uncertain as to whether or not he committed a sin (see *Karetot* 19b). For example, one is uncertain whether he ate permitted fat or prohibited fat, or whether the Sabbath had concluded at the time that he performed a certain labor. The guilt offering brought in these cases in known as a provisional guilt offering (Mishna *Zevaḥim* 5:5) as it suspends punishment in the interim until one's guilt is determined. It serves to soothe one's conscience and lessen one's punishment during this period of uncertainty, as the sinner feels that he has done everything in his power to atone for his sin (see *Karetot* 23b, 25a; Rashi, *Ketubot* 22b; Rashi, *Ḥullin* 41b; *Tzidkat HaTzaddik* 57). If one subsequently becomes aware that he definitely sinned, he must bring the requisite sin offering. Conversely, if he finds out that he did not commit a sin, his provisional guilt offering is considered similar to a gift offering. According to one opinion, one may voluntarily bring a provisional guilt offering every day, even if there is no specific action that one suspects might have been a transgression. The Talmud relates that Bava ben Buta, a pious Sage who lived at the time of the Second Temple, would bring a provisional guilt offering every day except for the day following the Day of Atonement (see *Karetot* 25a).

5:18| **And he did not know**: This term contrasts with the terms used with regard to the sin offering: "And he knew" (verses 3–4), and: "If

טז אֵיל תָּמִים מִן־הַצֹּאן בְּעֶרְכְּךָ כֶּסֶף־שְׁקָלִים בְּשֶׁקֶל־הַקֹּדֶשׁ לְאָשָׁם: וְאֵת אֲשֶׁר
חָטָא מִן־הַקֹּדֶשׁ יְשַׁלֵּם וְאֶת־חֲמִישִׁתוֹ יוֹסֵף עָלָיו וְנָתַן אֹתוֹ לַכֹּהֵן וְהַכֹּהֵן יְכַפֵּר
עָלָיו בְּאֵיל הָאָשָׁם וְנִסְלַח לוֹ:
יז וְאִם־נֶפֶשׁ כִּי תֶחֱטָא וְעָשְׂתָה אַחַת מִכָּל־מִצְוֺת יהוה אֲשֶׁר לֹא תֵעָשֶׂינָה וְלֹא־
יח יָדַע וְאָשֵׁם וְנָשָׂא עֲוֺנוֹ: וְהֵבִיא אַיִל תָּמִים מִן־הַצֹּאן בְּעֶרְכְּךָ לְאָשָׁם אֶל־הַכֹּהֵן
יט וְכִפֶּר עָלָיו הַכֹּהֵן עַל שִׁגְגָתוֹ אֲשֶׁר־שָׁגָג וְהוּא לֹא־יָדַע וְנִסְלַח לוֹ: אָשָׁם הוּא
אָשֹׁם אָשַׁם לַיהוה:
כ כא וַיְדַבֵּר יהוה אֶל־מֹשֶׁה לֵּאמֹר: נֶפֶשׁ כִּי תֶחֱטָא וּמָעֲלָה מַעַל בַּיהוה

רש"י

לא הזהיר אלא על האוכל, אף כאן לא הזהיר אלא על האוכל? תלמוד לומר: "תמעול מעל", רבה: **מקדשי ה'.** המיוחדים לשם, יצאו קדשים קלים: **איל.** לשון 'קשה', כמו: "ואת אילי הארץ לקח" (יחזקאל יז, יג), אף כאן קשה, בן שתי שנים: **בערכך כסף שקלים.** שיהא שוה שתי סלעים:

טז| **ואת אשר חטא מן הקדש ישלם.** קרן וחומש להקדש:

יז| **ולא ידע ואשם והביא.** הענין הזה מדבר במי שבא ספק כרת לידו ולא ידע אם עבר עליו אם לאו, כגון חלב ושומן לפניו וכסבור ששתיהן היתר ואכל את האחת. אמרו לו: אחת של חלב היתה, ולא ידע אם זו של חלב אכל – הרי זה מביא אשם תלוי, ומגין עליו כל זמן שלא נודע לו שודאי חטא, ואם יודע לו לאחר זמן, יביא חטאת: **ולא ידע ואשם ונשא עונו.** רבי יוסי הגלילי אומר: הרי הכתוב ענש את מי שלא ידע, על אחת כמה וכמה שיענש את מי שידע. רבי יוסי אומר: אם נפשך לידע מתן שכרן של צדיקים, צא ולמד מאדם הראשון, שלא נצטוה אלא על מצות לא תעשה ועבר עליה, ראה כמה מיתות נקנסו עליו ולדורותיו. וכי איזו מדה מרבה, של טובה או של פרענות? הוי אומר מדה טובה. אם מדת פרענות מעטה, ראה כמה מיתות נקנסו לו ולדורותיו, מדה טובה המרבה, היושב לו מן הפגולין והנותרות והמתענה ביום הכפורים, על אחת כמה וכמה שיזכה לו ולדורותיו ולדורות דורותיו עד סוף כל הדורות. רבי עקיבא אומר: הרי הוא אומר: "על פי שנים עדים או שלשה" וגו' (דברים יז, ו), אם מתקימת העדות בשנים, למה פרט לך הכתוב שלשה, אלא להביא שלישי להחמיר עליו כאלו הועיל ולעשות דינו כיוצא באלו לענין ענש והזמה; אם כך ענש הכתוב לנטפל לעוברי עברה כעוברי עברה, על אחת כמה וכמה שישלם שכר טוב לנטפל לעושי מצוה כעושי מצוה. רבי אלעזר בן עזריה אומר: "כי תקצר קצירך בשדך ושכחת עמר בשדה" (דברים כד, יט), הרי הוא אומר: "למען יברכך" וגו' (שם), קבע הכתוב ברכה למי שבאת על ידו מצוה בלא ידע, אמר מעתה: היתה סלע צרורה בכנפיו ונפלה הימנו ומצאה העני ונתפרנס בה, הרי הקדוש ברוך הוא קובע לו ברכה:

יח| **בערכך לאשם.** בערך האמור למעלה (פסוק טו): **אשר שגג והוא לא ידע.** הא אם ידע לאחר זמן, לא נתכפר לו באשם זה, עד שיביא חטאת. הא למה זה דומה? לעגלה ערופה שנתערפה ואחר כך נמצא ההורג – הרי זה יהרג:

יט| **אשם הוא אשם אשם.** הראשון כלו קמוץ, שהוא שם דבר, והאחרון חציו קמץ וחציו פתח, שהוא לשון פעל. ואם תאמר, מקרא שלא לצרך הוא! כבר דרוש הוא בתורת כהנים (ג, ו): "אשם אשם" להביא אשם שפחה חרופה שיהא איל בן שתי שנים. יכול שאני מרבה אשם נזיר ואשם מצרע? תלמוד לומר: "הוא":

כא| **נפש כי תחטא.** אמר רבי עקיבא: מה תלמוד לומר: "ומעלה מעל בה'"? לפי שכל המלוה והלוה והנושא

DISCUSSION

his sin that he sinned becomes known to him" (4:23, 28). This indicates that while the sin offering is brought only when one becomes aware of his sin, the provisional guilt offering is brought when the person is uncertain as to whether or not he committed a sin.

5:21| **A person who shall sin and commit a trespass against the Lord, and lies to his counterpart**: One might think that these transgressions, which involve monetary misappropriation, would not be considered a direct offense against God, but only toward the other person.

to his counterpart with regard to a deposit, by using the other person's deposit for his own benefit and subsequently denying his actions; **or with regard to** money received as **a loan,** and he does not return the money; **or with regard to** open **robbery** that he denies having perpetrated; **or** he **exploited his counterpart,** e.g., by refusing to pay the wages due to him.[77]

22 **Or** the trespass occurs when one **finds a lost item, and** when the owner demands its return, the finder **lies in its regard,** claiming that he does not have it. **And** moreover, the sinner **takes a false oath about one of all that a person does to sin with regard to these.** In each of these cases the sinner has taken another's property, denied doing so, and taken a false oath to that effect.

23 **It shall be when he sins and is guilty, he shall restore** to its owner **the robbed item that he robbed, or the proceeds of the exploitation that he exploited, or the deposit that was deposited with him, or the lost item that he found,** whether it was money or other items.

24 *Maftir* **Or** in **any** similar case concerning an **item with regard to which he has taken a false oath, he shall repay its principal,** the value of whatever he stole or withheld, **and one-fifth of it he shall add to it** as a penalty. **To him to whom it belongs, he shall give it,** the total sum, **on the day** on which he recognizes the fact **of his guilt,** regrets his deed, and confesses.[78]

25 After he returns the money,[79] **his restitution,** his offering, **he shall bring to the Lord, an unblemished ram from the flock, according to the valuation** of at least two silver shekels (see verse 15), **as a guilt offering, to the priest.** This offering is known as the guilt offering for robbery.[80]

26 **The priest shall atone for him before the Lord,** performing the rites of the guilt offering as described below (7:1–5). **And it shall be forgiven for him, for one of all that he may perform to incur guilt.**

DISCUSSION

However, the Torah emphasizes that one who commits these transgressions is committing a trespass against God. When a person denies events that occurred without the presence of witnesses, he denies or ignores the fact that God sees everything. Furthermore, God, as it were, relies on man to act honestly and guarantees the honest behavior of one person toward another. When one lies to another person, he betrays not only that person's trust, but also the trust which God placed in him (see Rashi).

The Sin Offerings and Guilt Offerings Detailed in *Parashat Vayikra*:

	Fixed sin offering	Sliding-scale sin offering	Guilt offering
The transgression	Unwitting transgression of a prohibition that carries the punishment of excision when violated intentionally	1. Falsely taking an oath of testimony, denying knowledge that would enable one to testify on behalf of another 2. Unwittingly entering the Temple or partaking of sacrificial food while ritually impure 3. Unwittingly violating an oath	1. Unwitting misuse of consecrated property 2. Uncertainty about whether one committed a sin that requires a sin offering 3. Intentionally taking a false oath denying that one has in his possession the property of another individual
The required offering	Female sheep or goat	Depends on financial means: Female sheep or goat; two birds; or a meal offering	A ram that is worth two silver shekels

וְכִחֵשׁ בַּעֲמִיתוֹ בְּפִקָּדוֹן אוֹ־בִתְשׂוּמֶת יָד אוֹ בְגָזֵל אוֹ עָשַׁק אֶת־עֲמִיתוֹ׃
כב אוֹ־מָצָא אֲבֵדָה וְכִחֶשׁ בָּהּ וְנִשְׁבַּע עַל־שָׁקֶר עַל־אַחַת מִכֹּל אֲשֶׁר־יַעֲשֶׂה הָאָדָם
כג לַחֲטֹא בָהֵנָּה׃ וְהָיָה כִּי־יֶחֱטָא וְאָשֵׁם וְהֵשִׁיב אֶת־הַגְּזֵלָה אֲשֶׁר גָּזָל אוֹ אֶת־הָעֹשֶׁק
כד אֲשֶׁר עָשָׁק אוֹ אֶת־הַפִּקָּדוֹן אֲשֶׁר הָפְקַד אִתּוֹ אוֹ אֶת־הָאֲבֵדָה אֲשֶׁר מָצָא׃ אוֹ מפטיר
מִכֹּל אֲשֶׁר־יִשָּׁבַע עָלָיו לַשֶּׁקֶר וְשִׁלַּם אֹתוֹ בְּרֹאשׁוֹ וַחֲמִשִׁתָיו יֹסֵף עָלָיו לַאֲשֶׁר
כה הוּא לוֹ יִתְּנֶנּוּ בְּיוֹם אַשְׁמָתוֹ׃ וְאֶת־אֲשָׁמוֹ יָבִיא לַיהוָה אַיִל תָּמִים מִן־הַצֹּאן
כו בְּעֶרְכְּךָ לְאָשָׁם אֶל־הַכֹּהֵן׃ וְכִפֶּר עָלָיו הַכֹּהֵן לִפְנֵי יְהוָה וְנִסְלַח לוֹ עַל־אַחַת
מִכֹּל אֲשֶׁר־יַעֲשֶׂה לְאַשְׁמָה בָהּ׃

רש״י

וְהַנּוֹתֵן אֵינוֹ עוֹשֶׂה אֶלָּא בְּעֵדִים וּבִשְׁטָר, לְפִיכָךְ בִּזְמַן שֶׁהוּא מְכַחֵשׁ, מְכַחֵשׁ בָּעֵדִים וּבִשְׁטָר; אֲבָל הַמַּפְקִיד אֵצֶל חֲבֵרוֹ וְאֵינוֹ רוֹצֶה שֶׁתֵּדַע בּוֹ נְשָׁמָה אֶלָּא שְׁלִישִׁי שֶׁבֵּינֵיהֶם, לְפִיכָךְ בִּזְמַן שֶׁהוּא מְכַחֵשׁ מְכַחֵשׁ בַּשְּׁלִישִׁי שֶׁבֵּינֵיהֶם:

בִּתְשׂוּמֶת יָד. שֶׁשָּׂם בְּיָדוֹ מָמוֹן לְהִתְעַסֵּק אוֹ בְּמִלְוֶה: אוֹ בְגָזֵל. שֶׁגָּזַל מִיָּדוֹ כְּלוּם: אוֹ עָשַׁק. הוּא שְׂכַר שָׂכִיר:

כב| וְכִחֶשׁ בָּהּ. שֶׁכָּפַר עַל אַחַת מִכָּל אֵלֶּה "אֲשֶׁר יַעֲשֶׂה הָאָדָם", לַחֲטֹא וּלְהִשָּׁבַע עַל שֶׁקֶר לִכְפִירַת מָמוֹן:

כג| כִּי יֶחֱטָא וְאָשֵׁם. כְּשֶׁיַּכִּיר בְּעַצְמוֹ לָשׁוּב בִּתְשׁוּבָה וְלָדַעַת וּלְהוֹדוֹת כִּי חָטָא וְאָשֵׁם:

כד| בְּרֹאשׁוֹ. הוּא הַקֶּרֶן, רֹאשׁ הַמָּמוֹן: לַאֲשֶׁר הוּא לוֹ. לְמִי שֶׁהַמָּמוֹן שֶׁלּוֹ:

Parashat
Tzav

Sacrificial Laws Relevant to the Priests

LEVITICUS 6:1–7:38

In this section, the Torah delineates the protocols for each offering mentioned at the beginning of the book of Leviticus. God instructs Moses to teach Aaron and his sons the laws pertaining to each type of offering. Some of these laws have already been mentioned in previous contexts; here, however, the Torah provides additional information that completes the picture.

Until now, God's instructions regarding the offerings were addressed to the children of Israel as a whole. Although some of this content was relevant only to the priests, the classification of the offerings and the reasons for sacrificing them were relevant to the entire nation of Israel. At this point, the Torah addresses the service of the priests in particular, describing their role in supervising the offerings, as well as their rights and responsibilities with regard to the offerings. The Torah does not discuss the reason for sacrificing each offering; rather, it focuses on the laws specific to each one.

Here, the Torah discusses the offerings in an order different from that in their previous appearance: First the Torah addresses those offerings that have the greatest sanctity, offerings of the most sacred order. This includes burnt offerings, sin offerings, and guilt offerings. It then mentions offerings of lesser sanctity, individual peace offerings. The Torah also reiterates the prohibition against consuming forbidden fat as well as blood, this time adding the punishment for one who transgresses these prohibitions.

6 **1** **The Lord spoke to Moses, saying:**

2 **Command Aaron and his sons:** Since the following laws pertain to the priestly responsibilities and privileges, the command was directed specifically toward Aaron and his sons. **Saying: This is the law of the burnt offering.** Although the laws of the burnt offering were essentially delineated in the beginning of Leviticus (see chap. 1), an additional point is added by the verse here: **It is the burnt offering** that burns **on the pyre on the altar all night until the morning,**[D] **and the fire of the altar shall be kept burning on it.** Most of the Temple service was performed during the day, including the slaughter of the burnt offering and the sprinkling of its blood upon the altar.[1] The burning of the offering upon the altar, however, could be performed at night. When many offerings were sacrificed during the day, they would remain burning on the pyre throughout the night. The fire on the altar was especially intense, as the wood of the pyre was coupled with the fat of the portions of the animals that were burned on the altar. The burnt offering, which was burned in its entirety, burned slowly on the pyre relative to the other offerings, as its fat was covered by its flesh. It was also offered after all the other offerings had been sacrificed.[2] Consequently, it remained on the altar throughout the night.

3 At the end of the night, **the priest shall don his linen vestment [*middo*],** which is precisely fitted to his size [*midda*],[3] **and his linen trousers,** another basic article of the priestly garments, **he shall don on his flesh; and he shall separate** from the altar **the ashes of the burnt offering that the fire consumes on the altar, and he shall place it beside the altar.** The removal of these accumulated ashes from the altar was a daily ritual that could be likened to an offering itself.

4 **He,** the priest, **shall remove his vestments and don other** priestly **vestments** of lesser quality than the previous

vestments.[4] According to tradition, it was prohibited for the priestly vestments to be soiled or worn out;[5] consequently, the priest had to change his clothing when performing this particularly sullying rite. Aside from the symbolic, daily removal of the ashes that was performed after the completion of the day's rites and before the arrival of the new day, it was also necessary to remove ash from the altar when copious amounts accumulated on it. **And** in that case, **he shall take the ashes outside the camp.** [BD] In the wilderness, the ashes from the altar in the Tabernacle were placed outside the encampment of the Israelites, while the ashes from the altar in the Temple were placed outside the walls of Jerusalem. The Sages teach that the ashes were placed outside the northern part of the city.[6] These ashes shall be taken **to a pure place.** They are not of inferior status; rather,

Tel al-Masabin, north of Jerusalem, 1925, possibly the site where the ashes from the altar were poured out

וַיְדַבֵּ֥ר יְהוָ֖ה אֶל־מֹשֶׁ֥ה לֵּאמֹֽר: צַ֣ו אֶֽת־אַהֲרֹ֤ן וְאֶת־בָּנָיו֙ לֵאמֹ֔ר זֹ֥את תּוֹרַ֖ת הָעֹלָ֑ה
הִ֣וא הָעֹלָ֡ה עַל֩ מוֹקְדָ֨ה עַל־הַמִּזְבֵּ֤חַ כָּל־הַלַּ֙יְלָה֙ עַד־הַבֹּ֔קֶר וְאֵ֥שׁ הַמִּזְבֵּ֖חַ תּ֥וּקַד בּֽוֹ:
וְלָבַ֨שׁ הַכֹּהֵ֜ן מִדּ֣וֹ בַ֗ד וּמִֽכְנְסֵי־בַד֮ יִלְבַּ֣שׁ עַל־בְּשָׂרוֹ֒ וְהֵרִ֣ים אֶת־הַדֶּ֗שֶׁן אֲשֶׁ֨ר תֹּאכַ֥ל
הָאֵ֛שׁ אֶת־הָעֹלָ֖ה עַל־הַמִּזְבֵּ֑חַ וְשָׂמ֕וֹ אֵ֖צֶל הַמִּזְבֵּֽחַ: וּפָשַׁט֙ אֶת־בְּגָדָ֔יו וְלָבַ֖שׁ בְּגָדִ֣ים
אֲחֵרִ֑ים וְהוֹצִ֤יא אֶת־הַדֶּ֙שֶׁן֙ אֶל־מִח֣וּץ לַֽמַּחֲנֶ֔ה אֶל־מָק֖וֹם טָהֽוֹר: וְהָאֵ֨שׁ עַל־
הַמִּזְבֵּ֤חַ תּֽוּקַד־בּוֹ֙ לֹ֣א תִכְבֶּ֔ה וּבִעֵ֨ר עָלֶ֧יהָ הַכֹּהֵ֛ן עֵצִ֖ים בַּבֹּ֣קֶר בַּבֹּ֑קֶר וְעָרַ֤ךְ עָלֶ֙יהָ֙

ב] צַו אֶת אַהֲרֹן. אֵין 'צַו' אֶלָּא לְשׁוֹן זֵרוּז, מִיָּד וּלְדוֹרוֹת.
אָמַר רַבִּי שִׁמְעוֹן: בְּיוֹתֵר צָרִיךְ הַכָּתוּב לְזָרֵז בְּמָקוֹם שֶׁיֵּשׁ
בּוֹ חֶסְרוֹן כִּיס: **זֹאת תּוֹרַת הָעֹלָה וְגוֹ'.** הֲרֵי הָעִנְיָן הַזֶּה
בָּא לְלַמֵּד עַל הַקְטֵר חֲלָבִים וְאֵבָרִים, שֶׁיְּהֵא כָּשֵׁר כָּל
הַלַּיְלָה, וּלְלַמֵּד עַל הַפְּסוּלִין, אֵיזֶה אִם עָלָה יֵרֵד וְאֵיזֶה
אִם עָלָה לֹא יֵרֵד, שֶׁכָּל 'תּוֹרָה' לְרַבּוֹת הוּא בָא, לוֹמַר:
תּוֹרָה אַחַת לְכָל הָעוֹלִים וַאֲפִלּוּ פְּסוּלִין, שֶׁאִם עָלוּ לֹא
יֵרְדוּ: **הִוא הָעֹלָה.** מְעֵט אֵת הָרוֹבֵעַ וְאֵת הַנִּרְבָּע וְכַיּוֹצֵא
בָּהֶן, שֶׁלֹּא הָיָה פְסוּלָן בַּקֹּדֶשׁ, שֶׁנִּפְסְלוּ קֹדֶם שֶׁבָּאוּ לָעֲזָרָה:

ג] מִדּוֹ בַד. הִיא הַכְּתֹנֶת, וּמַה תַּלְמוּד לוֹמַר "מִדּוֹ"?

עַל בְּשָׂרוֹ. שֶׁלֹּא יְהֵא דָבָר חוֹצֵץ בֵּינְתַיִם:
וְהֵרִים אֶת הַדֶּשֶׁן. הָיָה חוֹתֶה מְלֹא הַמַּחְתָּה מִן
הַמְאֻכָּלוֹת הַפְּנִימִיּוֹת, וְנוֹתְנָן בְּמִזְרָחוֹ שֶׁל כֶּבֶשׁ: **הַדֶּשֶׁן
אֲשֶׁר תֹּאכַל הָאֵשׁ אֶת הָעֹלָה.** וַעֲשָׂאַתָּה דֶשֶׁן, מֵאוֹתוֹ דֶשֶׁן
יָרִים תְּרוּמָה וְשָׂמוֹ אֵצֶל הַמִּזְבֵּחַ:

ד] וּפָשַׁט אֶת בְּגָדָיו. אֵין זוֹ חוֹבָה אֶלָּא דֶרֶךְ אֶרֶץ, שֶׁלֹּא
יְלַכְלֵךְ בְּהוֹצָאַת הַדֶּשֶׁן בְּגָדִים שֶׁהוּא מְשַׁמֵּשׁ בָּהֶן תָּמִיד;
בְּגָדִים שֶׁבִּשֵּׁל בָּהֶן קְדֵרָה לְרַבּוֹ אַל יִמְזֹג בָּהֶן כּוֹס לְרַבּוֹ,
לְכָךְ: "וְלָבַשׁ בְּגָדִים אֲחֵרִים", פְּחוּתִין מֵהֶן: **וְהוֹצִיא אֶת
הַדֶּשֶׁן.** הַצָּבוּר בַּתַּפּוּחַ, כְּשֶׁהוּא רָבֶה וְאֵין מָקוֹם לַמַּעֲרָכָה

מוֹצִיאוֹ מִשָּׁם. וְאֵין זֶה חוֹבָה בְּכָל יוֹם, אֲבָל הַתְּרוּמָה
חוֹבָה בְּכָל יוֹם:

ה] וְהָאֵשׁ עַל הַמִּזְבֵּחַ תּוּקַד בּוֹ. רִבָּה כָאן יְקִידוֹת הַרְבֵּה:
"עַל מוֹקְדָה" (לְעֵיל פָּסוּק ב), "וְאֵשׁ הַמִּזְבֵּחַ תּוּקַד בּוֹ" (שם),
"וְהָאֵשׁ עַל הַמִּזְבֵּחַ תּוּקַד בּוֹ", "אֵשׁ תָּמִיד תּוּקַד עַל
הַמִּזְבֵּחַ" (לְהַלָּן פָּסוּק ו). כֻּלָּן נִדְרְשׁוּ בְּמַסֶּכֶת יוֹמָא (דף מה
ע"ב) שֶׁנֶּחְלְקוּ רַבּוֹתֵינוּ בְּמִנְיַן הַמַּעֲרָכוֹת שֶׁהָיוּ שָׁם: **וְעָרַךְ
עָלֶיהָ,** עוֹלָה תָּמִיד הִיא תִקְרַב: חֶלְבֵי הַשְּׁלָמִים.
"חֶם יַחְיוּ שָׁם שְׁלָמִים. וְרַבּוֹתֵינוּ לָמְדוּ מִכָּאן: "עָלֶיהָ",

---

they are removed because it is prohibited to make use of them. Accordingly, they must be taken to a pure place.[7]

5 **The fire on the altar shall be kept burning on it; it shall not be extinguished, and to that end, the priest shall kindle**

wood on it every morning. He shall arrange a new pyre on the altar every morning to feed the continuously burning fire. In addition, **he shall arrange the** pieces of the

---

6:4 | Outside the camp: As mentioned, in the Temple these ashes were taken outside what was the northern wall of Jerusalem in the Second Temple period. Today, north of the remains of the northern wall, near the graves of Shimon HaTzaddik and the kings of Adiabene, there is an ash mound, referred to in Arabic as *al masabin*. Due to the discovery there of ashes comingled with animal tissue, some have concluded that this was where ash was taken from the altar.

6:2 | It is the burnt offering on the pyre on the altar all night until the morning: The verse indicates that one is required to leave the limbs of the burnt offering on the pyre throughout the night to ensure that the altar never remain idle either during the day or the night (Bekhor Shor).

6:4 | And he shall take the ashes outside the camp: The elucidation of this verse in the commentary follows the rabbinic tradition. According to the plain meaning of the verse, before the priest removes the ashes from the altar, he dons priestly vestments and then ascends upon the altar. After removing the ashes from the altar, he dons fresh vestments and then proceeds to take those ashes outside the camp (Bekhor Shor).

burnt offering upon it, and he shall also **burn on it the fats of the peace offering.** Although the peace offering was not the only offering whose fats were burned on the altar, it seems that the Torah deliberately omits mention of the sin offering or guilt offering in this context. Accordingly, it mentions only the burnt offering, which is the first offering of the morning, and the peace offering.

6 The Torah reiterates what was mentioned in the previous verse, establishing a continuous obligation:[8] **A perpetual fire shall be kept burning upon the altar; it shall not be extinguished.** This concludes the laws of the burnt offering, although other laws were introduced in this passage as well: the removal of the ashes from the altar, their removal to a pure place outside the camp, the arrangement of the wood on the altar, and the requirement to maintain a perpetual fire upon the altar. This is because these laws are especially relevant to the daily burnt offerings, which were the first and last offerings to be sacrificed during the day.[9]

7 **This is the law of the meal offering.** A general overview of the meal offering already appears in the beginning of Leviticus (chap. 2). Here the Torah emphasizes the priestly obligations pertaining to the meal offering. **The sons of Aaron shall present it before the Lord to the front of the altar.**[10]

8 After the priest presents the meal offering at the foot of the altar, **he shall separate from it,** from the meal offering, **his handful,** by inserting his middle three fingers into the meal offering, **from the high-quality flour of the meal offering and from its oil.** The base of all meal offerings is flour; generally, a large measure of oil is mixed into the flour as well. **And he shall also remove all the frankincense that is on the meal offering.** The priest would sprinkle frankincense on the mixture of flour and oil. **He shall burn its memorial portion,** both the handful of flour and all the frankincense, **on the altar,** as a **pleasing aroma to the Lord.**[11]

9 **The remnant of it Aaron and his sons shall eat** in their role as priests in the Temple; **as unleavened bread it shall be eaten.** Leavened bread was hardly ever brought to the Temple (see 2:11). Here, the verse stresses that the remnants of the meal offering must also be consumed unleavened, and they are to be consumed **in a holy place;**[D] **in the courtyard of the Tent of Meeting they shall eat it.**

10 **It,** the meal offering, **shall not be baked leavened.** Aside from the general prohibition against allowing the meal offering to become leavened, there is an additional prohibition against baking it leavened.[12] **I have given it as their,** that is, the priests', **portion from My fire offerings; it,** the entire meal offering, **is a sacred sacrament like the sin offering and like the guilt offering.**

11 Because of the sacred nature of the meal offering, **every male among the children of Aaron shall eat it,** but other members of the priest's family could not partake of it. This is yet another indication that the consumption of the remnant by the priests is itself a sacrificial rite, which may be performed only by the priests themselves, in contrast to other sacred items that are given to the priests as gifts, which may be consumed by all members of the priest's family (see 22:11–13). It is **an eternal statute for your generations from the fire offerings of the Lord.** The verse now states an additional law: **Anything that touches them,** the meal offerings, **shall become sacred.** Since it is possible to consume meal offerings, sin offerings, and guilt offerings with other foods, the Torah states that anything that touches them and thereby absorbs their taste must be treated with their sanctity.

12 Following the previous verses, which discussed the laws of meal offerings in general, many of which pertained to their consumption by the priests, the Torah now discusses certain meal offerings that are brought only by the priests: **The Lord spoke to Moses, saying:**

Second aliya

13 **This is the offering of Aaron and of his sons that they shall present to the Lord on the day he is anointed,** on the first day that any priest performs the Temple service. This is known as the priestly meal offering of inauguration. Although the verse refers to any priest who enters the service, this same offering is to be brought by the High Priest every day. In that context, it is known as the griddle-cake offering of the High Priest:[13] **One-tenth of an ephah of high-quality flour as a perpetual meal offering, half of it in the morning, and half of it in the evening.** The Sages explain that this last clause applies only to the griddle-cake offering of the High Priest. The priestly meal offering of inauguration, however, was brought only once on the day of a priest's investiture.[14]

14 **On a pan it,** the meal offering, **shall be prepared with oil, fried; you shall bring it boiled.**[15] **You shall present the baked meal offering in pieces;** that is, it is boiled, then baked, and then fried.[16] The meal offering was prepared as one loaf and then broken into pieces.[17] All of it was burned on the altar as **a pleasing aroma to the Lord.**

15 As mentioned above (verse 13), this offering was brought not only by a priest when beginning his Temple service, but also, **the priest who is anointed in his stead from his sons,** the High Priest, who is descended from Aaron, **shall prepare it** every day as a fixed offering. **It is an eternal statute to the Lord; it shall be burned in its entirety** upon the altar.

16 Likewise, **every meal offering of the priest,** whether brought as a voluntary meal offering or in any other manner, **shall be offered in its entirety,** entirely burned on the altar; **it shall not be eaten.** This is in contrast to the meal offering of a non-priest, of which only a portion is burned on the altar, while the remainder is designated by God for the priests' consumption alone.

ו הָעֹלָה וְהִקְטִיר עָלֶיהָ חֶלְבֵי הַשְּׁלָמִים׃ אֵשׁ תָּמִיד תּוּקַד עַל־הַמִּזְבֵּחַ לֹא תִכְבֶּה׃
ז וְזֹאת תּוֹרַת הַמִּנְחָה הַקְרֵב אֹתָהּ בְּנֵי־אַהֲרֹן לִפְנֵי יְהוָה אֶל־פְּנֵי
ח הַמִּזְבֵּחַ׃ וְהֵרִים מִמֶּנּוּ בְּקֻמְצוֹ מִסֹּלֶת הַמִּנְחָה וּמִשַּׁמְנָהּ וְאֵת כָּל־הַלְּבֹנָה אֲשֶׁר
ט עַל־הַמִּנְחָה וְהִקְטִיר הַמִּזְבֵּחַ רֵיחַ נִיחֹחַ אַזְכָּרָתָהּ לַיהוָה׃ וְהַנּוֹתֶרֶת מִמֶּנָּה יֹאכְלוּ
י אַהֲרֹן וּבָנָיו מַצּוֹת תֵּאָכֵל בְּמָקוֹם קָדֹשׁ בַּחֲצַר אֹהֶל־מוֹעֵד יֹאכְלוּהָ׃ לֹא תֵאָפֶה
יא חָמֵץ חֶלְקָם נָתַתִּי אֹתָהּ מֵאִשָּׁי קֹדֶשׁ קָדָשִׁים הִוא כַּחַטָּאת וְכָאָשָׁם׃ כָּל־זָכָר
בִּבְנֵי אַהֲרֹן יֹאכְלֶנָּה חָק־עוֹלָם לְדֹרֹתֵיכֶם מֵאִשֵּׁי יְהוָה כֹּל אֲשֶׁר־יִגַּע בָּהֶם יִקְדָּשׁ׃
יב יג וַיְדַבֵּר יְהוָה אֶל־מֹשֶׁה לֵּאמֹר׃ זֶה קָרְבַּן אַהֲרֹן וּבָנָיו אֲשֶׁר־יַקְרִיבוּ לַיהוָה בְּיוֹם ג שני
הִמָּשַׁח אֹתוֹ עֲשִׂירִת הָאֵפָה סֹלֶת מִנְחָה תָּמִיד מַחֲצִיתָהּ בַּבֹּקֶר וּמַחֲצִיתָהּ בָּעָרֶב׃
יד עַל־מַחֲבַת בַּשֶּׁמֶן תֵּעָשֶׂה מֻרְבֶּכֶת תְּבִיאֶנָּה תֻּפִינֵי מִנְחַת פִּתִּים תַּקְרִיב רֵיחַ־נִיחֹחַ
טו לַיהוָה׃ וְהַכֹּהֵן הַמָּשִׁיחַ תַּחְתָּיו מִבָּנָיו יַעֲשֶׂה אֹתָהּ חָק־עוֹלָם לַיהוָה כָּלִיל תָּקְטָר׃
טז וְכָל־מִנְחַת כֹּהֵן כָּלִיל תִּהְיֶה לֹא תֵאָכֵל׃

רש״י

עַל עוֹלַת הַבֹּקֶר, הַשְׁלֵם כָּל הַקָּרְבָּנוֹת כֻּלָּם, מִכָּאן שֶׁלֹּא יְהֵא דָּבָר מְאֻחָר לְתָמִיד שֶׁל בֵּין הָעַרְבַּיִם:

ו| אֵשׁ תָּמִיד. אֵשׁ שֶׁנֶּאֱמַר בָּהּ "תָּמִיד", הִיא שֶׁמַּדְלִיקִין בָּהּ אֶת הַנֵּרוֹת, שֶׁנֶּאֱמַר בָּהּ: "לְהַעֲלֹת נֵר תָּמִיד" (שמות כז, כ), אַף הִיא מֵעַל הַמִּזְבֵּחַ הַחִיצוֹן תּוּקַד: לֹא תִכְבֶּה. הַמְכַבֶּה אֵשׁ עַל הַמִּזְבֵּחַ עוֹבֵר בִּשְׁנֵי לָאוִין:

ז| וְזֹאת תּוֹרַת הַמִּנְחָה. תּוֹרָה אַחַת לְכֻלָּן, לְהַטְעִינָן שֶׁמֶן וּלְבוֹנָה הָאֲמוּרִין בָּעִנְיָן, שֶׁיָּכוֹל אֵין לִי טְעוּנוֹת שֶׁמֶן וּלְבוֹנָה אֶלָּא מִנְחַת יִשְׂרָאֵל שֶׁהִיא נִקְמֶצֶת, מִנְחַת כֹּהֲנִים שֶׁהִיא כָּלִיל מִנַּיִן? תַּלְמוּד לוֹמַר: "תּוֹרַת": הַקְרֵב אֹתָהּ. הִיא הַגָּשָׁה בְּקֶרֶן דְּרוֹמִית מַעֲרָבִית: לִפְנֵי ה׳. הוּא מַעֲרָב, שֶׁהוּא לְצַד אֹהֶל מוֹעֵד: אֶל פְּנֵי הַמִּזְבֵּחַ. הוּא הַדָּרוֹם שֶׁהוּא פָּנָיו שֶׁל מִזְבֵּחַ, שֶׁהַכֶּבֶשׁ נָתוּן לְאוֹתוֹ הָרוּחַ:

ח| בְּקֻמְצוֹ. שֶׁלֹּא יַעֲשֶׂה מִדָּה לַקֹּמֶץ: מִסֹּלֶת הַמִּנְחָה וּמִשַּׁמְנָהּ. מִכָּאן שֶׁקּוֹמֵץ מִמָּקוֹם שֶׁנִּתְרַבָּה שַׁמְנָהּ: וְאֵת כָּל הַלְּבֹנָה אֲשֶׁר עַל הַמִּנְחָה וְהִקְטִיר. שֶׁמְּלַקֵּט אֶת לְבוֹנָתָהּ לְאַחַר קְמִיצָה וּמַקְטִירוֹ. וּלְפִי שֶׁלֹּא פֵּרַשׁ כֵּן אֶלָּא בְּאַחַת מִן הַמְּנָחוֹת בְּ"וַיִּקְרָא" (לעיל ב, ב), הֻצְרַךְ לִשְׁנוֹת פָּרָשָׁה זוֹ, לִכְלֹל כָּל הַמְּנָחוֹת כְּמִשְׁפָּטָן:

ט| בְּמָקוֹם קָדֹשׁ. וְאֵיזֶהוּ? "בַּחֲצַר אֹהֶל מוֹעֵד":

י| לֹא תֵאָפֶה חָמֵץ חֶלְקָם. אַף הַשְּׁיָרִים אֲסוּרִים בְּחָמֵץ: כַּחַטָּאת וְכָאָשָׁם. מִנְחַת חוֹטֵא הֲרֵי הִיא כַּחַטָּאת, לְפִיכָךְ קְמָצָהּ שֶׁלֹּא לִשְׁמָהּ פְּסוּלָה. מִנְחַת נְדָבָה הֲרֵי הִיא כָּאָשָׁם, לְפִיכָךְ קְמָצָהּ שֶׁלֹּא לִשְׁמָהּ כְּשֵׁרָה:

יא| כָּל זָכָר. אֲפִלּוּ בַּעַל מוּם. לָמָּה נֶאֱמַר? אִם לַאֲכִילָה, הֲרֵי כְּבָר אָמוּר: "לֶחֶם אֱלֹהָיו מִקָּדְשֵׁי הַקֳּדָשִׁים" וְגוֹ' (להלן כא, כב), אֶלָּא לְרַבּוֹת בַּעֲלֵי מוּמִין לְמַחֲלֹקֶת: כֹּל אֲשֶׁר יִגַּע וְגוֹ'. קָדָשִׁים קַלִּים אוֹ חֻלִּין שֶׁיִּגְּעוּ בָהּ וְיִבְלְעוּ מִמֶּנָּה: יִקְדָּשׁ. לִהְיוֹת כָּמוֹהָ, שֶׁאִם פְּסוּלָה יִפָּסְלוּ, וְאִם כְּשֵׁרָה יֵאָכְלוּ כְּחֹמֶר הַמִּנְחָה:

יג| זֶה קָרְבַּן אַהֲרֹן וּבָנָיו. אַף הַהֶדְיוֹטוֹת מַקְרִיבִין עֲשִׂירִית הָאֵיפָה בַּיּוֹם שֶׁהֵן מִתְחַנְּכִין לַעֲבוֹדָה, אֲבָל כֹּהֵן גָּדוֹל בְּכָל יוֹם, שֶׁנֶּאֱמַר: "מִנְחָה תָּמִיד... וְהַכֹּהֵן הַמָּשִׁיחַ תַּחְתָּיו מִבָּנָיו... חָק עוֹלָם":

DISCUSSION

6:9| The remnant of it Aaron and his sons shall eat; as unleavened bread it shall be eaten in a holy place: The fact that the priests must consume the remnant of the meal offering in a holy place indicates that the entire meal offering is sanctified. Moreover, the remnants are not given to the priests simply because they are left over from the sacrifice of the meal offering. Rather, their consumption is itself considered the performance of a rite, parallel, in a certain sense, to the burning of an offering upon the altar. Thus, a portion of the offering is consumed by the fire, while the remaining portion is consumed by the priests with a sense of purpose and service. As the Sages say: The priests eat and the owners attain atonement (see *Pesaḥim* 59b; Exodus 29:33).

Although the handful removed from the meal offering constitutes a very small portion of the whole, it is the flour remaining in the service vessel that the Torah deems "the remnant." Clearly, then, the principal acts of sacrifice of the meal offering are the removal of the handful and the burning of it upon the altar.

17 **The Lord spoke to Moses, saying:**
18 **Speak to Aaron and to his sons, saying: This is the law of the sin offering.** After previously stating the basic laws of the sin offering (see chaps. 4–5), the Torah elaborates: **In the place where the burnt offering is slaughtered,** on the north side of the altar (see 1:11), **the sin offering shall be slaughtered before the Lord; it is a sacred sacrament.** The difference between a sacred sacrament and an offering of lesser sanctity is not only conceptual; there are also practical differences with regard to the manner in which each type of offering is sacrificed. For example, since a burnt offering and sin offering are sacred sacraments, they must be slaughtered on the north side of the altar.
19 Furthermore, **the priest who presents it as a sin offering [*ha-meḥatei*]**[D] **shall eat it.**[18] The priest who engages in the sacrificial rite of the sin offering has the first right to consumption of its meat. However, as will be stated below (6:22), in practice this right is granted to all priests serving in the Tabernacle on that day. Additionally, since the consumption of the sin offering is itself a sacred act, **in a holy place it shall be eaten, in the courtyard of the Tent of Meeting.**
20 **Anyone who shall touch its flesh,** the flesh of the sin offering, **shall become holy.** It must be treated with sanctity, and, like the sin offering, it must be consumed in a holy place, by the priests, and within the allotted time in which the sin offering itself may be consumed.[19] **And if some of its blood is** accidentally **sprinkled on a garment** rather than the altar, then **that upon which it is sprinkled you shall wash in a holy place.** It may not be removed from the holy place, just like the blood itself.
21 Since the sin offering is consumed by the priests only after first cooking or roasting it, the status of the cooking implements must also be clarified: **An earthenware implement in which it,** the sin offering, **shall be cooked shall** subsequently **be broken,** as such a vessel absorbs some of the matter of the sin offering during the cooking process. This matter will remain absorbed in the implement beyond its allotted time for consumption; it will then be rendered unfit for consumption, at which point the matter must be destroyed.[20] As such, the implement must be destroyed after the elapse of that allotted time.[21] This is similar to the law that an earthenware implement is not purified through immersion in water or in any other manner, and so, when it becomes impure, it remains that way until it is broken (see 11:33). **If it is is cooked in a bronze implement, it shall be scoured,** scrubbed clean, then placed in boiling water to purge the absorbed matter **and rinsed in water.** It is then permitted subsequently to use such a vessel.[22]
22 It has already been stated that the priest who sacrifices the sin offering has the first right to its consumption. Nevertheless, **every male among the priests shall eat it,** that is, may partake of it, and their consumption is part of the atonement process. **It,** the entire sin offering, **is a sacred sacrament.**
23 Until now, this passage has discussed only the typical sin offering brought by an individual who unwittingly transgresses certain prohibitions. Earlier, however (chap. 4), the Torah mentioned several different types of sin offerings, in particular the sin offering of the High Priest and the sin offering brought for an unwitting communal sin, whose blood is not sprinkled on the outer altar, but inside the Sanctuary itself. These offerings are referred to by the Sages as the inner sin offerings[23] and are mentioned in this verse: **Any sin offering from which blood shall be brought to the Tent of Meeting** to sprinkle opposite the curtain and on the incense altar, **to atone in the holy place, shall not be eaten** at all; rather, **it shall be burned in fire.**[D] As stated above (4:1–21), certain portions of these sin offerings are burned on the altar, while the remainder is burned outside the encampment of Israel. Here, the Torah explicitly states that its consumption is prohibited.

7 1 **This is the law of the guilt offering.** The instances in which one brings a guilt offering have already been described above (5:14–26). The Torah now describes the manner of its sacrifice: **It is a sacred sacrament.** The guilt offering is considered an offering of the most sacred order, and its sanctity therefore demands greater stringency than an offering of lesser sanctity.[24]
2 Because a guilt offering is an offering of the most sacred order, **in the place where the burnt offering is slaughtered they shall slaughter the guilt offering,** on the north side of the altar (see 1:11). The equation of the guilt offering with the burnt offering is of great significance, as one might have otherwise assumed that the latter is of greater sanctity, since it is burned in its entirety on the altar. **And its blood he,** the priest, **shall cast** from the vessel into which the blood was received when the animal was slaughtered **around the altar,** like the blood of the burnt offering, and unlike the blood of the sin offering, which the priest places with his finger on the horns of the altar.
3 Although the guilt offering resembles the burnt offering with regard to the sprinkling of its blood, in other matters it is comparable to the sin offering: **All of its fat he shall offer from it: The fat tail** of the guilt offering, which may be either a ram or a lamb,[25] **and the** large layer of **fat that covers the innards,**
4 **and the two kidneys and the fat that is on them, which is on the flanks, and the diaphragm above the liver; he shall remove it with the kidneys** from the liver, which is not burned on the altar.
5 **The priest shall burn them on the altar as a fire offering to the Lord; it is a guilt offering.**

יז יח וַיְדַבֵּר יְהוָה אֶל־מֹשֶׁה לֵּאמֹר: דַּבֵּר אֶל־אַהֲרֹן וְאֶל־בָּנָיו לֵאמֹר זֹאת תּוֹרַת
הַחַטָּאת בִּמְקוֹם אֲשֶׁר תִּשָּׁחֵט הָעֹלָה תִּשָּׁחֵט הַחַטָּאת לִפְנֵי יְהוָה קֹדֶשׁ קָדָשִׁים
יט כ הִוא: הַכֹּהֵן הַמְחַטֵּא אֹתָהּ יֹאכְלֶנָּה בְּמָקוֹם קָדֹשׁ תֵּאָכֵל בַּחֲצַר אֹהֶל מוֹעֵד: כֹּל
אֲשֶׁר־יִגַּע בִּבְשָׂרָהּ יִקְדָּשׁ וַאֲשֶׁר יִזֶּה מִדָּמָהּ עַל־הַבֶּגֶד אֲשֶׁר יִזֶּה עָלֶיהָ תְּכַבֵּס
כא בְּמָקוֹם קָדֹשׁ: וּכְלִי־חֶרֶשׂ אֲשֶׁר תְּבֻשַּׁל־בּוֹ יִשָּׁבֵר וְאִם־בִּכְלִי נְחֹשֶׁת בֻּשָּׁלָה וּמֹרַק
כב כג וְשֻׁטַּף בַּמָּיִם: כָּל־זָכָר בַּכֹּהֲנִים יֹאכַל אֹתָהּ קֹדֶשׁ קָדָשִׁים הִוא: וְכָל־חַטָּאת אֲשֶׁר
יוּבָא מִדָּמָהּ אֶל־אֹהֶל מוֹעֵד לְכַפֵּר בַּקֹּדֶשׁ לֹא תֵאָכֵל בָּאֵשׁ תִּשָּׂרֵף:

ז א ב וְזֹאת תּוֹרַת הָאָשָׁם קֹדֶשׁ קָדָשִׁים הוּא: בִּמְקוֹם אֲשֶׁר יִשְׁחֲטוּ אֶת־הָעֹלָה
ג יִשְׁחֲטוּ אֶת־הָאָשָׁם וְאֶת־דָּמוֹ יִזְרֹק עַל־הַמִּזְבֵּחַ סָבִיב: וְאֵת כָּל־חֶלְבּוֹ
ד יַקְרִיב מִמֶּנּוּ אֵת הָאַלְיָה וְאֶת־הַחֵלֶב הַמְכַסֶּה אֶת־הַקֶּרֶב: וְאֵת שְׁתֵּי הַכְּלָיֹת
וְאֶת־הַחֵלֶב אֲשֶׁר עֲלֵיהֶן אֲשֶׁר עַל־הַכְּסָלִים וְאֶת־הַיֹּתֶרֶת עַל־הַכָּבֵד עַל־
ה הַכְּלָיֹת יְסִירֶנָּה: וְהִקְטִיר אֹתָם הַכֹּהֵן הַמִּזְבֵּחָה אִשֶּׁה לַיהוָה אָשָׁם הוּא:

רש"י

יד| **מרבכת.** חלוטה ברותחין כל צרכה: **תפיני.** אפויה אפיות הרבה: אחר חליטתה אופה בתנור וחוזר ומטגנה במחבת: **מנחת פתים.** מלמד שטעונה פתיתה:

טו-טז| **המשיח תחתיו מבניו.** המשיח מבניו תחתיו: **כליל תקטר.** אין נקמצת להיות שיריה נאכלין, אלא כולה כליל, וכן "כל מנחת כהן" של נדבה, "כליל תהיה": **כליל.** כולה שוה לגבוה:

יט| **המחטא אתה.** העובד עבודותיה, שהיא נעשית חטאת על ידו: **המחטא אתה יאכלנה.** הראוי לעבודה, יצא טמא בשעת זריקת דמים, שאינו חולק בבשר. ואי אפשר לומר שאוסר שאר כהנים באכילתה חוץ מן הזורק דמה, שהרי נאמר למטה: "כל זכר בכהנים יאכל אתה" (להלן פסוק כב):

כ| **כל אשר יגע בבשרה.** כל דבר אוכל אשר יגע ויבלע ממנה: **יקדש.** להיות כמוה, אם פסולה תפסל, ואם היא כשרה תאכל כחומר שבה: **ואשר יזה מדמה על הבגד.** ואם הזה מדמה על הבגד, אותו הבגד מקום הדם "אשר יזה עליה תכבס" בתוך העזרה: **אשר יזה.** יהא נזה, כמו: "ולא יטה לארץ מנלם" (איוב טו, כט), יהא נטוי:

כא| **ישבר.** לפי שהבליעה שנבלעת בו נעשית נותר, והוא הדין לכל הקדשים: **ומרק.** לשון "תמרוקי הנשים" (אסתר ב, יב), אישקור"מנט בלעז: **ומרק ושטף.** לפלוט את בליעתו. אבל כלי חרס למדך הכתוב כאן שאינו יוצא מידי דפיו לעולם:

כב| **כל זכר בכהנים יאכל אתה.** הא למדת שה"מחטא אותה" האמור למעלה (פסוק יט) לא להוציא שאר הכהנים, אלא להוציא את שאינו ראוי לחטוי:

כג| **וכל חטאת וגו'.** שאם הכניס מדם חטאת החיצונה לפנים פסולה:

פרק ז

א| **קדש קדשים הוא.** הוא קרב ואין תמורתו קרבה:

ג| **ואת כל חלבו וגו'.** עד כאן לא נתפרשו אמורין באשם, לכך הוצרך לפרשם כאן, אבל חטאת כבר נתפרש בה בפרשת ויקרא (לעיל פרק ד): **את האליה.** לפי שאשם אינו בא אלא איל או כבש, ואיל וכבש נתרבו באליה (לעיל ג, ט):

DISCUSSION

6:19| **The priest who presents it as a sin offering [*hameḥatei*]:** The term "sin offering" [*hatat*], like the word for the general concept of atonement [*kappara*], has a connotation of cleansing and purifying, as in the verse: "Purify me [*teḥate'eini*] with hyssop, and I will be clean" (Psalms 51:9). Therefore, the priest who sacrifices the sin offering is in essence the one who cleanses [*meḥatei*] the individual of the sin. Now the sin offering is not brought as payment, as it were, for transgressing a prohibition, as one does not bring a sin offering for the intentional transgression of a prohibition; one brings it only for an unwitting transgression. Rather, it cleanses the blemish that an unwitting transgression creates on one's soul (see Rashi; Rav Se'adya Gaon; Ibn Ezra).

6:23| **Shall not be eaten; it shall be burned in fire:** According to Rabbi Akiva, it is derived from this verse that any sin offering whose blood enters the Sanctuary is disqualified (*Zevaḥim* 81b–82a; see 10:18).

6 With regard to the flesh that is not consumed on the altar, **every male among the priests may eat it; in a holy place it shall be eaten: It is a sacred sacrament.** The requirement to consume the flesh of the guilt offering in a holy place, in the courtyard of the Tabernacle or Temple, stems from its status as an offering of the most sacred order. By contrast, it was permitted for offerings of lesser sanctity to be consumed anywhere in the Israelite camp surrounding the Tabernacle in the wilderness, or anywhere in Jerusalem during the time the Temple was in existence.

7 **Like the sin offering, so is the guilt offering; there is one law for them.** In both cases, **the priest that atones with it, it,** the flesh of the offering, **shall be his.** The right to consume the guilt offering is given to the priest that sacrifices it. He may choose to consume it himself or divide it among the other priests.

8 Similarly, in the case of **the priest who presents the burnt offering of a man,** although the flesh is burned in its entirety, **the hide of the burnt offering that he presents, it shall be for the priest,** not the individual who brings the offering. This law holds true for other offerings as well, with the exception of the peace offering.[26]

9 **Every meal offering that is baked in the oven, and any prepared** by frying **in a deep pan, or on a** shallow **pan, it shall be for the priest who presents it.**

10 **Every meal offering,** either **mixed with oil,** e.g., the voluntary meal offering of flour mixed with oil (see 2:1) **or dry,** e.g., the meal offering of a sinner, which does not contain any oil (see 5:11), **shall be for all the sons of Aaron,**[D] **one like another.**

11 This is the law of the peace offering that one presents to the

Third aliya

Lord. The peace offering, which is consumed in partnership, as it were, with God, has already been mentioned above (chap. 3). Here, the Torah discusses a particular type of peace offerings whose laws are unique.

12 **If he presents it for thanksgiving,** then although it is indeed a peace offering with regard to its sanctity and the manner in which it is sacrificed, there is an additional requirement: **He shall present with the thanks offering unleavened loaves mixed with oil, and unleavened wafers,** similar to pitas, **smeared with oil, and loaves of boiled high-quality flour,** flour that is first boiled and then baked into loaves,[27] **mixed with oil.**

13 Although leavened bread is generally forbidden as part of an offering (see 2:11), in this exceptional case, **with loaves of leavened bread he shall present his offering with the thanks offering of his peace offerings.**

14 **He shall present from it,** the loaves, **one of each offering,** one unleavened loaf mixed with oil, one unleavened wafer smeared with oil, one loaf of boiled fine flour mixed with oil, and one loaf of leavened bread, **as a gift to the Lord;**[D] **it shall be for the priest who sprinkles the blood of the peace offering.** The remaining loaves belong to the owner of the thanks offering.

15 **The flesh** that remains **of the thanks offering of his peace offerings,** after the removal of the portions intended for burning on the altar, **shall be eaten on the day of its offering.** In contrast to a typical peace offering, a thanks offering may be consumed only on the day it is offered; **he shall not leave any of it until the** next **morning.**[D]

16 In contrast to a thanks offering, which may be consumed only on the day of its offering and the following night, **if his offering is** brought in fulfillment of **a vow** to bring an offering, **or a pledge** to offer a specific animal, **on the day that he presents his offering it shall be eaten and** also **on the morrow, and that which remains of it** on the first day **may be eaten**[D] on the morrow as well. In all, a vow offering or a pledge offering may be consumed for two days and the evening between them.

DISCUSSION

7:9–10| It shall be for the priest who presents it...every meal offering...shall be for all the sons of Aaron: According to the plain meaning of the verse, it would appear that meal offerings whose preparation is relatively tedious, such as baked or fried meal offerings, are given to the priest who offers them, as is the case with regard to animal offerings. Other meal offerings, however, whose preparation is relatively simple, are divided among the priests. However, rabbinic tradition teaches that this is not in fact the case. Since it is impossible for one priest to perform all the sacrificial rites without the help of other priests, and since one priest's occupation with the rites of the meal offering

leaves the remaining Temple service to the other priests, all the members of the current priestly watch are effectively considered to have contributed to the sacrifice of the meal offering. Accordingly, each meal offering is divided among all the priests together with the one who actually offers it. The precise manner of their division depends on the type of offering as well as the various agreements between the priests (see *Sifra*; Rashi; *Bekhor Shor*; Ramban; Deuteronomy 18:8, and Rashi ad loc.; *Sukka* 55b–56a).

7:14| He shall present from it one of each offering as a gift to the Lord: The number of loaves, as well as the manner of their preparation, are not stated explicitly in the Torah. The

Sages, however, teach that ten units of each of the four types of loaves were to be brought with the thanks offering. One loaf from each type was given as a gift to the priest, similar to other gifts given to the priests or Levites, where they would receive one-tenth of the total (see *Menaḥot* 77b; Rashi, verse 12). As is typical of the Torah, the complete set of laws of sacrifice is not written in one place; as such, the precise laws pertaining to an offering are derived from a combination of all the relevant passages dispersed throughout the Torah.

7:15| Shall be eaten on the day of its offering; he shall not leave any of it until the morning: With regard to offerings, "the day of

◀●

ו ז כָּל־זָכָר בַּכֹּהֲנִים יֹאכְלֶנּוּ בְּמָקוֹם קָדוֹשׁ יֵאָכֵל קֹדֶשׁ קָדָשִׁים הוּא: כַּחַטָּאת כָּאָשָׁם
ח תּוֹרָה אַחַת לָהֶם הַכֹּהֵן אֲשֶׁר יְכַפֶּר־בּוֹ לוֹ יִהְיֶה: וְהַכֹּהֵן הַמַּקְרִיב אֶת־עֹלַת
ט אִישׁ עוֹר הָעֹלָה אֲשֶׁר הִקְרִיב לַכֹּהֵן לוֹ יִהְיֶה: וְכָל־מִנְחָה אֲשֶׁר תֵּאָפֶה בַּתַּנּוּר
י וְכָל־נַעֲשָׂה בַמַּרְחֶשֶׁת וְעַל־מַחֲבַת לַכֹּהֵן הַמַּקְרִיב אֹתָהּ לוֹ תִהְיֶה: וְכָל־מִנְחָה
בְלוּלָה־בַשֶּׁמֶן וַחֲרֵבָה לְכָל־בְּנֵי אַהֲרֹן תִּהְיֶה אִישׁ כְּאָחִיו:
יא יב וְזֹאת תּוֹרַת זֶבַח הַשְּׁלָמִים אֲשֶׁר יַקְרִיב לַיהוָה: אִם עַל־תּוֹדָה יַקְרִיבֶנּוּ וְהִקְרִיב | עַל־ שלישי
זֶבַח הַתּוֹדָה חַלּוֹת מַצּוֹת בְּלוּלֹת בַּשֶּׁמֶן וּרְקִיקֵי מַצּוֹת מְשֻׁחִים בַּשָּׁמֶן וְסֹלֶת מֻרְבֶּכֶת
יג חַלֹּת בְּלוּלֹת בַּשָּׁמֶן: עַל־חַלֹּת לֶחֶם חָמֵץ יַקְרִיב קָרְבָּנוֹ עַל־זֶבַח תּוֹדַת שְׁלָמָיו:
יד וְהִקְרִיב מִמֶּנּוּ אֶחָד מִכָּל־קָרְבָּן תְּרוּמָה לַיהוָה לַכֹּהֵן הַזֹּרֵק אֶת־דַּם הַשְּׁלָמִים
טו לוֹ יִהְיֶה: וּבְשַׂר זֶבַח תּוֹדַת שְׁלָמָיו בְּיוֹם קָרְבָּנוֹ יֵאָכֵל לֹא־יַנִּיחַ מִמֶּנּוּ עַד־בֹּקֶר:

רש״י

ה| **אשם הוא.** עד שינתק שמו ממנו, למד על אשם שמתו בעליו או שנתכפרו בעליו, אף על פי שעומד להיות דמיו עולה לקיץ המזבח, אם שחטו סתם אינו כשר לעולה קודם שניתק לרעיה. ואינו בא ללמד על האשם שיהא פסול שלא לשמו, כמו שדרשו "הוא" הכתוב בחטאת (לעיל ד, כד), לפי שאשם לא נאמר בו "אשם הוא" אלא לאחר הקטרת אמורין, והוא עצמו שלא הקטרו אמוריו כשר:

ו| **קדש קדשים הוא.** בתורת כהנים הוא נדרש:

ז| **תורה אחת להם.** בדבר זה: **הכהן אשר יכפר בו.** הראוי לכפרה חולק בו, פרט לטבול יום ומחוסר כפורים ואונן:

ח| **עור העלה אשר הקריב לכהן לו יהיה.** פרט לטבול יום ומחוסר כפורים ואונן, שאין חולקים בעורות:

ט| **לכהן המקריב אתה וגו׳.** יכול לו לבדו? תלמוד לומר: "לכל בני אהרן תהיה" (להלן פסוק י). יכול לכלן? תלמוד לומר: "לכהן המקריב", הא כיצד? לבית אב של יום שמקריבין אותה:

י| **בלולה בשמן.** זו מנחת נדבה: **וחרבה.** זו מנחת חוטא ומנחת קנאות שאין בהן שמן:

יב| **אם על תודה יקריבנו.** אם על דבר הודאה על נס שנעשה לו, כגון יורדי הים והולכי מדברות וחבושי בית האסורים וחולה שנתרפא שהן צריכין להודות, שכתוב בהן: "יודו לה׳ חסדו ונפלאותיו לבני אדם" (תהלים קז, ח ועוד), "ויזבחו זבחי תודה" (שם פסוק כב), אם על אחת מאלה נדר שלמים הללו, שלמי תודה הן, וטעונות לחם האמור בענין, ואינן נאכלין אלא ליום ולילה כמו שמפורש כאן (להלן פסוק טז): **והקריב על זבח התודה.** ארבעה מיני לחם: חלות ורקיקין ורבוכה – שלשה מיני מצה, וכתיב: "על חלת לחם חמץ" וגו׳ (להלן פסוק יג). וכל מין ומין עשר חלות, כך מפורש במנחות (דף עז ע״א), ושעורן חמש סאין ירושלמיות שהן שש מדבריות, עשרים עשרון: **מרבכת.** לחם חלוט ברותחין כל צרכו:

יג| **יקריב קרבנו על זבח.** מגיד שאין הלחם קדוש קדשת הגוף לפסל ביוצא וטבול יום ומלאכת לחלין בפדיון, עד שישחט הזבח:

יד| **אחד מכל קרבן.** לחם אחד מכל מין ומין יטול תרומה לכהן העובד עבודתה, והשאר נאכל לבעלים. ובשרה לבעלים חוץ מחזה ושוק שבה, כמו שמפורש למטה תנופת חזה ושוק בשלמים (להלן פסוקים כט-לד), והתודה קרויה שלמים:

טו| **ובשר זבח תודת שלמיו.** יש כאן רבויין הרבה, לרבות חטאת ואשם ואיל נזיר וחגיגת ארבעה עשר שיהיו נאכלין ליום ולילה: **ביום קרבנו יאכל.** וכזמן בשרה זמן לחמה: **לא יניח ממנו עד בקר.** אוכל הוא כל הלילה. אם כן, למה אמרו עד חצות? כדי להרחיק אדם מן העברה:

DISCUSSION

Consequently, it is permitted to consume the offering for two days and the evening between them. However, one may not partake of it during the second evening, despite the fact that any leftover flesh will be burned only on the third day (*Zevaḥim* 56b; *Pesaḥim* 3a; Ramban, based on 19:6).

7:16| **On the day that he presents his offering it shall be eaten and on the morrow and that which remains of it may be eaten:** Ramban, based on the *Sifra*, explains that the usage of the phrase "that which remains" indicates that there is a commandment to consume the offering on the day it is sacrificed. If, however, some of it remains, it may be consumed on the next day as well.

→ its offering" is defined as the day on which an offering is sacrificed and the night that follows it. Although with regard to other laws, the Torah defines a complete day as beginning with the night, in the case of sacrificing offerings it begins with the daytime. This is because the sacrificial rites are performed during the daytime, and its portions are then burned on the altar in the evening.

17 **That which remains of the flesh of the offering on** the morning of **the third day shall be burned in fire.**[D]

18 **If the flesh of his peace offerings shall be eaten on the third day, it shall not be accepted, nor shall it be credited to him that presents it;** rather, **it shall be a detestable thing.**[D] The Sages explain that the verse refers to a case where, at the time of an animal's sacrifice, an individual expresses intent to leave over some of the flesh until the third day, which disqualifies the offering. Although the leftover flesh does not appear different from other flesh, it is rendered detestable [*piggul*] by Torah law, and **the person who eats from it shall bear his iniquity.**

19 The Torah now states another law that resembles those of the leftover and detestable flesh, both of which disqualify an offering and render its consumption prohibited: **The flesh** of an offering **that shall touch any impure item shall not be eaten.** Leftover and detestable flesh are not impure by Torah law, although the Sages decreed that they transmit some measure of impurity.[28] Sacrificial meat that contracts ritual impurity may not be consumed, even if it is not leftover or detestable. Rather, **it shall be burned in fire; and with regard to the** ritually pure **flesh** of a peace offering, **every pure person may eat** the **flesh,** not only the owner of the offering.[29]

20 **The person who eats flesh of the peace offering that is to the Lord while his ritual impurity is upon him** receives a severe punishment: **That person shall be excised from his people.**

21 This holds true not only for ritual impurity that stems from the person himself, but also from impurity that comes from without: **When a person touches anything impure: the impurity of man,** that is, any one of the types of impurities that a person may contract,[30] **or a non-pure animal,** a non-kosher animal carcass, **or any impure, detestable thing,** a dead creeping animal (see 11:20–43), once an individual touches any of the aforementioned sources of impurity, he is rendered impure, **and** consequently, if he shall **eat of the flesh of the peace offering that is to the Lord, that person shall be excised from his people.**

22 Until now, the Torah has described three categories of disqualifications with regard to a peace offering, which are also applicable to all other offerings: leftover flesh, which results from inaction, that is, failure to consume an offering within its allotted time; detestable flesh, which is the result of prohibited intent; and ritual impurity, which is dependent on an action, contact with an impure item. The punishment for consuming any of these disqualified offerings is severe: excision from the people. The following law does not directly pertain to offerings, but it bears relation to the laws stated above: **The Lord spoke to Moses, saying:**

23 **Speak to the children of Israel, saying: All fat of a bull or a sheep or a goat you shall not eat.** One may not consume the fat of those types of animals that may be brought as an offering, even if they are not sacrificed in practice.

24 **The fat of an unslaughtered carcass** of a pure animal that died naturally, **and the fat of a mauled animal** or an animal with an equally severe injury or defect **may be used for all labor.** You may benefit from such fat in any manner,[31] **but you shall not eat it.**

25 **For anyone who eats fat from an animal that one could offer from it a fire offering to the Lord, the person eating shall be excised from his people.** In addition to the earlier prohibition against consuming the fat of an offering (3:17), the Torah states here that this prohibition applies even to animals that are not fit to be brought as offerings, such as an unslaughtered carcass and a mauled animal, and that one who consumes the fat of an animal is liable to excision.

26 Likewise, **all blood you shall not eat in any of your dwellings, of bird or of animal.** Since their blood is sacrificed as an offering to God on the altar, it may not be consumed by man (see 3:17). In contrast to the prohibition against consuming the fat of an offering, this prohibition extends even to the blood of birds, as there are bird offerings whose blood is placed on the altar as well.

DISCUSSION

7:17 | That which remains of the flesh of the offering on the third day shall be burned in fire: This law is referred to by the Sages as the law of *notar*, offerings that are left over. It states that an offering whose flesh was not completely consumed or whose portions were not burned in the allotted time is disqualified and must be burned during the day (see *Pesaḥim* 23b–24a;

Zevaḥim 28a–b). Therefore, in the case of an offering of the most sacred order, a thanks offering or a paschal lamb, which may be consumed only on the day it is sacrificed, any parts that remain by the next morning are considered leftover and must be burned. In the case of offerings of lesser sanctity, which may be consumed for an additional day, the offering is not

rendered leftover until its allotted time for consumption has passed. The consumption of an offering that has already been rendered leftover is considered a grave transgression, one that is also mentioned in the rebukes of some of the prophets (see Amos 4:4, and Rashi ad loc.).

טז וְאִם־נֶדֶר ׀ אוֹ נְדָבָה זֶבַח קָרְבָּנוֹ בְּיוֹם הַקְרִיבוֹ אֶת־זִבְחוֹ יֵאָכֵל וּמִמָּחֳרָת וְהַנּוֹתָר
יז יח מִמֶּנּוּ יֵאָכֵל׃ וְהַנּוֹתָר מִבְּשַׂר הַזָּבַח בַּיּוֹם הַשְּׁלִישִׁי בָּאֵשׁ יִשָּׂרֵף׃ וְאִם הֵאָכֹל
יֵאָכֵל מִבְּשַׂר־זֶבַח שְׁלָמָיו בַּיּוֹם הַשְּׁלִישִׁי לֹא יֵרָצֶה הַמַּקְרִיב אֹתוֹ לֹא יֵחָשֵׁב
יט לוֹ פִּגּוּל יִהְיֶה וְהַנֶּפֶשׁ הָאֹכֶלֶת מִמֶּנּוּ עֲוֺנָהּ תִּשָּׂא׃ וְהַבָּשָׂר אֲשֶׁר־יִגַּע בְּכָל־טָמֵא
כ לֹא יֵאָכֵל בָּאֵשׁ יִשָּׂרֵף וְהַבָּשָׂר כָּל־טָהוֹר יֹאכַל בָּשָׂר׃ וְהַנֶּפֶשׁ אֲשֶׁר־תֹּאכַל בָּשָׂר
מִזֶּבַח הַשְּׁלָמִים אֲשֶׁר לַיהוָה וְטֻמְאָתוֹ עָלָיו וְנִכְרְתָה הַנֶּפֶשׁ הַהִוא מֵעַמֶּיהָ׃
כא וְנֶפֶשׁ כִּי־תִגַּע בְּכָל־טָמֵא בְּטֻמְאַת אָדָם אוֹ ׀ בִּבְהֵמָה טְמֵאָה אוֹ בְּכָל־שֶׁקֶץ
טָמֵא וְאָכַל מִבְּשַׂר־זֶבַח הַשְּׁלָמִים אֲשֶׁר לַיהוָה וְנִכְרְתָה הַנֶּפֶשׁ הַהִוא מֵעַמֶּיהָ׃
כב כג וַיְדַבֵּר יְהוָה אֶל־מֹשֶׁה לֵּאמֹר׃ דַּבֵּר אֶל־בְּנֵי יִשְׂרָאֵל לֵאמֹר כָּל־חֵלֶב שׁוֹר וְכֶשֶׂב
כד וָעֵז לֹא תֹאכֵלוּ׃ וְחֵלֶב נְבֵלָה וְחֵלֶב טְרֵפָה יֵעָשֶׂה לְכָל־מְלָאכָה וְאָכֹל לֹא
כה תֹאכְלֻהוּ׃ כִּי כָּל־אֹכֵל חֵלֶב מִן־הַבְּהֵמָה אֲשֶׁר יַקְרִיב מִמֶּנָּה אִשֶּׁה לַיהוָה וְנִכְרְתָה
כו הַנֶּפֶשׁ הָאֹכֶלֶת מֵעַמֶּיהָ׃ וְכָל־דָּם לֹא תֹאכְלוּ בְּכֹל מוֹשְׁבֹתֵיכֶם לָעוֹף וְלַבְּהֵמָה׃

רש"י

טז | **ואם נדר או נדבה.** שלא הביאה על הודאה של נס, אינה טעונה לחם, ונאכלת לשני ימים, כמו שמפורש בענין: **וממחרת והנותר ממנו.** בראשון, יאכל. וי"ו זו יתרה היא, ויש כמוה הרבה במקרא, כגון: "ואלה בני צבעון ואיה וענה" (בראשית לו, כד), "תת וקדש וצבא מרמס" (דניאל ח, יג):

יח | **ואם האכל יאכל וגו'.** במחשב בשחיטה לאכלו בשלישי הכתוב מדבר. יכול אם אכל ממנו בשלישי יפסל למפרע? תלמוד לומר: "המקריב אתו לא יחשב", בשעת הקרבה הוא נפסל, ואינו נפסל בשלישי. וכן פרושו: בשעת הקרבתו לא תעלה זאת במחשבה, ואם חשב – "פגול יהיה": **והנפש האכלת ממנו.** אפילו בתוך הזמן, "עונה תשא":

יט | **והבשר.** של קדש שלמים "אשר יגע בכל טמא לא יאכל": **והבשר.** לרבות אבר שיצא מקצתו, שהפנימי מתר: **כל טהור יאכל בשר.** מה תלמוד לומר? לפי שנאמר: "ודם זבחיך ישפך... והבשר תאכל" (דברים יב, כז), יכול לא יאכלו שלמים אלא הבעלים? לכך נאמר: "כל טהור יאכל בשר":

כ | **וטמאתו עליו.** בטמאת הגוף הכתוב מדבר, אבל טהור שאכל את הטמא אינו ענוש כרת אלא באזהרה: "והבשר אשר יגע בכל טמא" וגו' (לעיל פסוק יט). ואזהרת טמא שאכל את הטהור אינה מפרשת בתורה, אלא חכמים למדוה בגזרה שוה: שלש כריתות אמורות באוכלי קדשים בטמאת הגוף, ודרשום רבותינו בשבועות (דף ז ע"א) אחת לכלל, ואחת לפרט, ואחת ללמד על קרבן עולה ויורד שלא נאמר אלא על טמאת מקדש וקדשיו:

כד | **יעשה לכל מלאכה.** בא ולמד על החלב שאינו מטמא טמאת נבלות: **ואכל לא תאכלהו.** אמרה תורה: יבוא אסור נבלה וטרפה ויחול על אסור חלב, שאם אכלו יתחיב אף על לאו של נבלה, ולא תאמר אין אסור חל על אסור:

כו | **לעוף ולבהמה.** פרט לדם דגים וחגבים: **בכל מושבתיכם.** לפי שהיא חובת הגוף ואינה חובת קרקע, נוהגת בכל מושבות, ובמסכת קדושין בפרק ראשון (דף לז ע"ב) מפרש למה הצרך לומר:

DISCUSSION

7:18 | **If the flesh of his peace offerings shall be eaten on the third day it shall not be accepted nor shall it be credited to him that presents it; it shall be a detestable thing:** The plain meaning of the verse would seem to indicate that if an individual sacrifices an offering in the proper manner, but consumes some of its flesh on the third day, the offering is retroactively disqualified. However, such a precedent of retroactive disqualification is not found anywhere else in the Torah. That which occurs after the incident in question cannot retroactively affect it, neither with regard to punishment nor with regard to anything else. Indeed, the Sages, who elaborate upon many halakhic details concerning this issue, interpret this verse in the manner described in the commentary (see *Zevaḥim* 29a; Ibn Ezra). On the other hand, an offering that is sacrificed with the intent to leave over some of its flesh is disqualified and does not effect atonement, as it stands in direct conflict with the laws of the Torah. Moreover, the flesh of the offering is rendered detestable, and its consumption constitutes a grave transgression, even if in practice none of the flesh remains by the third morning.

27 Moreover, **any person who eats any blood,** even the blood of an animal that may not be sacrificed as an offering, **that person shall be excised from his people,** though the Sages derived that this does not include the blood of smaller creatures such as fish or grasshoppers.[32] Although some of their laws differ from one another, the prohibitions against consuming fat and consuming blood are similar in that the basis for their prohibition is that both are sacrificed as offerings to God, as mentioned in the previous verse. In addition, both prohibitions apply to non-sacred animals in addition to sacrificial animals. However, while the prohibition with regard to fat applies only to species of animals that are fit to sacrifice as an offering, the prohibition with regard to blood applies to other creatures as well, albeit for another reason.[33]

28 The Torah now describes various details with regard to the peace offering that were previously unmentioned: **The Lord spoke to Moses, saying:**

29 **Speak to the children of Israel, saying: The one who presents his peace offering to the Lord shall** himself **bring his offering to the Lord from his peace offering.**[34]

30 **His own hands shall bring the fire offerings of the Lord; the fat on the breast he shall bring it.** The fat rests on the breast when they are presented in his hands, but only the fat will be burned on the altar, while with regard to **the breast,** he is **to wave it as a wave offering** to display it **before the Lord.**[35] However, it is not offered on the altar.

31 **The priest shall burn the fat on the altar; and the breast shall be for Aaron and for his sons.** The breast is the priestly portion of the peace offering. Aside from the breast and the fats, the majority of the offering is consumed by its owner in the Tabernacle. The consumption of the fat on the altar in close proximity to the owner's meal can be likened to a feast in which man and God partake together.

32 In addition to the breast, **the right haunch** of the offering **you shall give to the priest as a gift from your peace offerings.**

33 The Torah reiterates a principle that was mentioned previously (verses 8–10, 14): **The one who presents the blood of the peace offering and the fat from the sons of Aaron,** the priest who sacrifices the peace offering, and any priest who assists the priest directly or indirectly, **for him shall be the right haunch as a portion.**

34 **For I have taken the breast of waving and the haunch of lifting from the children of Israel, from their peace offerings, and have given them to Aaron the priest and to his sons as**

an eternal allotment from the children of Israel. Just as I have taken the fat and the portions to be burned on the altar, so too I have taken the breast and the right haunch from the peace offerings and given them to the priests. The Sages teach: The priests eat from the table of the Most High.[36] In other words, the owner of the offering does not give the breast and the right haunch to the priests. Rather, these portions are God's and should have been burned on the altar, but God gave them to the priests for consumption.

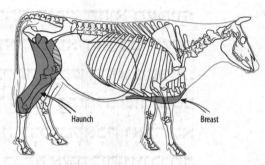

Breast of waving and haunch of lifting

35 **This is the portion** [*mishḥat*],[D] or, alternatively, the gift of splendor or greatness, **of Aaron, and the portion of his sons, from the fire offerings of the Lord, on the day that He brought them near to serve as priests to the Lord,**

36 **that the Lord commanded to give to them on the day He anointed them.** With their appointment to the priesthood, Aaron and his sons were granted certain rights **from the children of Israel.** Although this commandment was stated on the day of their anointment, the gifts of the priesthood shall be **an eternal statute for their generations,** and they shall be given to the priests in any generation in which offerings are brought.

37 In summary: **This is the law,** the statutes and ordinances, **for the burnt offering, for the meal offering, and for the sin offering, and for the guilt offering, and for the investiture offering,**[D] **and for the peace offering**

38 **that the Lord commanded Moses at Mount Sinai,** which perhaps refers to the Tent of Meeting, which was erected opposite Mount Sinai,[37] **on the day of His commanding the children of Israel to present their offerings to the Lord** in the Tabernacle,[38] **in the wilderness of Sinai.**

כז כָּל־נֶפֶשׁ אֲשֶׁר־תֹּאכַל כָּל־דָּם וְנִכְרְתָה הַנֶּפֶשׁ הַהִוא מֵעַמֶּיהָ:
כח כט וַיְדַבֵּר יְהוָה אֶל־מֹשֶׁה לֵּאמֹר: דַּבֵּר אֶל־בְּנֵי יִשְׂרָאֵל לֵאמֹר הַמַּקְרִיב אֶת־זֶבַח
ל שְׁלָמָיו לַיהוָה יָבִיא אֶת־קָרְבָּנוֹ לַיהוָה מִזֶּבַח שְׁלָמָיו: יָדָיו תְּבִיאֶינָה אֵת אִשֵּׁי
יְהוָה אֶת־הַחֵלֶב עַל־הֶחָזֶה יְבִיאֶנּוּ אֵת הֶחָזֶה לְהָנִיף אֹתוֹ תְּנוּפָה לִפְנֵי יְהוָה:
לא לב וְהִקְטִיר הַכֹּהֵן אֶת־הַחֵלֶב הַמִּזְבֵּחָה וְהָיָה הֶחָזֶה לְאַהֲרֹן וּלְבָנָיו: וְאֵת שׁוֹק
לג הַיָּמִין תִּתְּנוּ תְרוּמָה לַכֹּהֵן מִזִּבְחֵי שַׁלְמֵיכֶם: הַמַּקְרִיב אֶת־דַּם הַשְּׁלָמִים וְאֶת־
לד הַחֵלֶב מִבְּנֵי אַהֲרֹן לוֹ תִהְיֶה שׁוֹק הַיָּמִין לְמָנָה: כִּי אֶת־חֲזֵה הַתְּנוּפָה וְאֵת
שׁוֹק הַתְּרוּמָה לָקַחְתִּי מֵאֵת בְּנֵי־יִשְׂרָאֵל מִזִּבְחֵי שַׁלְמֵיהֶם וָאֶתֵּן אֹתָם לְאַהֲרֹן
לה הַכֹּהֵן וּלְבָנָיו לְחָק־עוֹלָם מֵאֵת בְּנֵי יִשְׂרָאֵל: זֹאת מִשְׁחַת אַהֲרֹן וּמִשְׁחַת בָּנָיו
לו מֵאִשֵּׁי יְהוָה בְּיוֹם הִקְרִיב אֹתָם לְכַהֵן לַיהוָה: אֲשֶׁר צִוָּה יְהוָה לָתֵת לָהֶם בְּיוֹם
לז מָשְׁחוֹ אֹתָם מֵאֵת בְּנֵי יִשְׂרָאֵל חֻקַּת עוֹלָם לְדֹרֹתָם: זֹאת הַתּוֹרָה לָעֹלָה לַמִּנְחָה
לח וְלַחַטָּאת וְלָאָשָׁם וְלַמִּלּוּאִים וּלְזֶבַח הַשְּׁלָמִים: אֲשֶׁר צִוָּה יְהוָה אֶת־מֹשֶׁה בְּהַר
סִינָי בְּיוֹם צַוֹּתוֹ אֶת־בְּנֵי יִשְׂרָאֵל לְהַקְרִיב אֶת־קָרְבְּנֵיהֶם לַיהוָה בְּמִדְבַּר סִינָי:

רש"י

ל| **יָדָיו תְּבִיאֶינָה וְגוֹ׳.** שֶׁתְּהֵא יַד הַבְּעָלִים מִלְמַעְלָה וְהַחֵלֶב וְהֶחָזוֹת נְתוּנִין בָּהּ, וְיַד כֹּהֵן מִלְמַטָּה וּמְנִיפָן: **אֵת אִשֵּׁי ה׳.** וּמַה הֵן הָאִשִּׁים? ״אֶת הַחֵלֶב עַל הֶחָזֶה יְבִיאֶנּוּ״, כְּשֶׁמְּבִיאוֹ מִבֵּית הַמִּטְבָּחַיִם נוֹתֵן חֵלֶב עַל הֶחָזֶה, וּכְשֶׁנּוֹתְנוֹ לְיַד הַמֵּנִיף נִמְצָא הֶחָזֶה לְמַעְלָה וְהַחֵלֶב לְמַטָּה, וְזֶהוּ הָאָמוּר בְּמָקוֹם אַחֵר: ״שׁוֹק הַתְּרוּמָה וַחֲזֵה הַתְּנוּפָה עַל אִשֵּׁי הַחֲלָבִים יָבִיאוּ לְהָנִיף״ וְגוֹ׳ (להלן י, טו), וּלְאַחַר הַתְּנוּפָה נוֹתְנוֹ לַכֹּהֵן הַמַּקְטִיר, וְנִמְצָא הֶחָזֶה לְמַטָּה, וְזֶהוּ שֶׁנֶּאֱמַר: ״וַיָּשִׂימוּ אֶת הַחֲלָבִים עַל הֶחָזוֹת וַיַּקְטֵר הַחֲלָבִים הַמִּזְבֵּחָה״ (להלן ט, כ). לָמַדְנוּ שֶׁשְּׁלֹשָׁה כֹּהֲנִים זְקוּקִין לָהּ, כָּךְ מְפֹרָשׁ בִּמְנָחוֹת (דף סב ע״א): **אֶת הַחֵלֶב עַל הֶחָזֶה יְבִיאֶנּוּ.** וְ״אֵת הֶחָזֶה״ לָמָּה מְבִיאוֹ? ״לְהָנִיף אֹתוֹ״ הוּא מְבִיאוֹ, וְלֹא שֶׁיְּהֵא הוּא מִן הָאִשִּׁים. לְפִי שֶׁנֶּאֱמַר: ״אֵת אִשֵּׁי ה׳ אֶת הַחֵלֶב עַל הֶחָזֶה״, יָכוֹל שֶׁיְּהֵא אַף הֶחָזֶה לָאִשִּׁים? לְכָךְ נֶאֱמַר: ״אֵת הֶחָזֶה לְהָנִיף״ וְגוֹ׳:

לא| **וְהִקְטִיר הַכֹּהֵן אֶת הַחֵלֶב.** וְאַחַר כָּךְ ״וְהָיָה הֶחָזֶה לְאַהֲרֹן״, לָמַדְנוּ שֶׁאֵין הַבָּשָׂר נֶאֱכָל בְּעוֹד הָאֵמוּרִים לְמַטָּה מִן הַמִּזְבֵּחַ:

לב| **שׁוֹק.** מִן הַפֶּרֶק שֶׁל אַרְכֻּבָּה הַנִּמְכֶּרֶת עִם הָרֹאשׁ עַד הַפֶּרֶק הָאֶמְצָעִי שֶׁהוּא סֹבֶךְ שֶׁל רֶגֶל:

לג| **הַמַּקְרִיב אֶת דַּם הַשְּׁלָמִים וְגוֹ׳.** מִי שֶׁהוּא רָאוּי לִזְרִיקָתוֹ וּלְהַקְטִיר חֲלָבָיו, יָצָא טָמֵא בִּשְׁעַת זְרִיקַת דָּמִים אוֹ בִּשְׁעַת הֶקְטֵר חֲלָבִים שֶׁאֵינוֹ חוֹלֵק בַּבָּשָׂר:

לד| **תְּנוּפָה, תְּרוּמָה.** מוֹלִיךְ וּמֵבִיא, מַעֲלֶה וּמוֹרִיד:

לז| **וְלַמִּלּוּאִים.** לְיוֹם חִנּוּךְ הַכְּהֻנָּה:

DISCUSSION

7:35| **This is the portion** [*mishḥat*]: Although the word "*mashaḥ*" is generally translated as "anointing," in this context it also refers to giving Aaron and his sons a special portion as well as the gift of splendor and greatness, as mentioned in the commentary (see *Zevaḥim* 28a; *Sifrei*, Numbers 18:8; *Ha'amek Davar*).

7:37| **And for the investiture offering:** This refers to the special offerings brought by Aaron and his sons during the seven days of the inauguration of the Tabernacle. Although the nature of these offerings has been described explicitly only in the book of Exodus (chap. 29; see *Bekhor Shor*), they are essentially no different from the other offerings mentioned in this verse. Alternatively, the verse refers to the meal offering brought by a priest on his first day of Temple service, which was indeed mentioned here (6:13; see Rashi).

Consecration of the Priests and the Tabernacle

LEVITICUS 8:1–36

Once Moses erects the Tabernacle and is taught the *halakhot* of the various offerings, he is commanded to initiate the consecration of the Tabernacle and its ministers, the priests. The Torah will describe the Israelites' role in this process, which includes the anointing of the priests, the Tabernacle, and its appurtenances with the anointing oil, as well as the sacrifice of the investiture offerings for seven days. During this time, Moses himself ministers in the Tabernacle as a priest and performs the investiture services described in the book of Exodus (chaps. 28–29, 40). The Sages discuss which garments Moses donned when performing the service during the seven days of investiture, as only the vestments of Aaron and his sons are mentioned explicitly in the Torah. They conclude that Moses served while donning a white linen robe. Moses has now effectively filled every leadership position: He is the prophet, chief justice, priest, and king of the children of Israel. Eventually, he transfers the priesthood to Aaron; until then, however, Moses serves as the messenger of God in all respects.

8 1 **The Lord spoke to Moses, saying:**

Fourth aliya 2 **Take Aaron and his sons with him, the vestments** that they are to don when they minister, **the anointing oil, the bull of the sin offering, the two rams, and the basket of unleavened bread,** all of which are necessary for appointing the priests. Moses was previously instructed with regard to the function of these items;[39] now God commands Moses to fulfill those commandments.

3 **Assemble the entire congregation**ᴰ **at the entrance of the Tent of Meeting,** so that they may witness these events. Even though they would not actively minister, they would participate in the consecration of the priests, which inaugurated the priests as both messengers of God and representatives of the nation of Israel.

4 **Moses did as the Lord had commanded him.** Moses took Aaron and his sons, and the items listed above, and instructed the congregation to assemble. **And the congregation was assembled at the entrance of the Tent of Meeting.**

5 **Moses said to the congregation: This is the matter that the Lord commanded to be done.** Moses stressed to the congregation that his actions were part of a sacred ceremony, and they must observe all the elements of the process.

6 **Moses brought Aaron and his sons near, and he washed them with water,** that is, he commanded Aaron and his sons to immerse.[40]

7 **He placed upon him,** Aaron, **the tunic and girded him with the belt and clothed him with the robe, and placed the ephod on him, and he girded him with the belt of the ephod and adorned him with it,** the ephod, which was placed above the other vestments.

8 **He placed the breast piece on him; and in the breast piece he placed the Urim and the Tumim,** whose nature is mysterious.[41]

9 **He placed the mitre on his,** Aaron's, **head; and he placed on the mitre, toward** the front of **his head, the golden frontplate, the sacred diadem,** the crown of the High Priest, **as the Lord had commanded Moses.**

10 **Moses took the anointing oil and anointed the Tabernacle and all that was in it, and he consecrated them** through this anointing.

11 **He sprinkled from it,** from the anointing oil, **on the altar seven times, and he anointed the altar and all its vessels, and the basin and its base, to consecrate them.**

12 **He poured from the anointing oil on Aaron's head and anointed him to consecrate him.**

13 **Moses brought Aaron's sons near, clothed them in tunics, girded them with a belt, and wrapped headdresses on them,** which were different from the mitre worn by the High Priest,[42] **as the Lord had commanded Moses.**

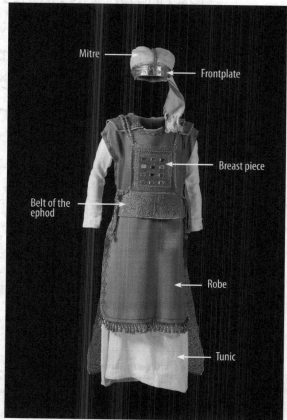

Mitre

Frontplate

Breast piece

Belt of the ephod

Robe

Tunic

Vestments of the High Priest

א ב וַיְדַבֵּר יְהוָה אֶל־מֹשֶׁה לֵּאמֹר: קַח אֶת־אַהֲרֹן וְאֶת־בָּנָיו אִתּוֹ וְאֵת הַבְּגָדִים ד רביעי
וְאֵת שֶׁמֶן הַמִּשְׁחָה וְאֵת | פַּר הַחַטָּאת וְאֵת שְׁנֵי הָאֵילִים וְאֵת סַל הַמַּצּוֹת:
ג ד וְאֵת כָּל־הָעֵדָה הַקְהֵל אֶל־פֶּתַח אֹהֶל מוֹעֵד: וַיַּעַשׂ מֹשֶׁה כַּאֲשֶׁר צִוָּה יְהוָה
ה אֹתוֹ וַתִּקָּהֵל הָעֵדָה אֶל־פֶּתַח אֹהֶל מוֹעֵד: וַיֹּאמֶר מֹשֶׁה אֶל־הָעֵדָה זֶה הַדָּבָר
ו אֲשֶׁר־צִוָּה יְהוָה לַעֲשׂוֹת: וַיַּקְרֵב מֹשֶׁה אֶת־אַהֲרֹן וְאֶת־בָּנָיו וַיִּרְחַץ אֹתָם
ז בַּמָּיִם: וַיִּתֵּן עָלָיו אֶת־הַכֻּתֹּנֶת וַיַּחְגֹּר אֹתוֹ בָּאַבְנֵט וַיַּלְבֵּשׁ אֹתוֹ אֶת־הַמְּעִיל
ח וַיִּתֵּן עָלָיו אֶת־הָאֵפֹד וַיַּחְגֹּר אֹתוֹ בְּחֵשֶׁב הָאֵפֹד וַיֶּאְפֹּד לוֹ בּוֹ: וַיָּשֶׂם עָלָיו
ט אֶת־הַחֹשֶׁן וַיִּתֵּן אֶל־הַחֹשֶׁן אֶת־הָאוּרִים וְאֶת־הַתֻּמִּים: וַיָּשֶׂם אֶת־הַמִּצְנֶפֶת
עַל־רֹאשׁוֹ וַיָּשֶׂם עַל־הַמִּצְנֶפֶת אֶל־מוּל פָּנָיו אֵת צִיץ הַזָּהָב נֵזֶר הַקֹּדֶשׁ כַּאֲשֶׁר
י צִוָּה יְהוָה אֶת־מֹשֶׁה: וַיִּקַּח מֹשֶׁה אֶת־שֶׁמֶן הַמִּשְׁחָה וַיִּמְשַׁח אֶת־הַמִּשְׁכָּן
יא וְאֶת־כָּל־אֲשֶׁר־בּוֹ וַיְקַדֵּשׁ אֹתָם: וַיַּז מִמֶּנּוּ עַל־הַמִּזְבֵּחַ שֶׁבַע פְּעָמִים וַיִּמְשַׁח
יב אֶת־הַמִּזְבֵּחַ וְאֶת־כָּל־כֵּלָיו וְאֶת־הַכִּיֹּר וְאֶת־כַּנּוֹ לְקַדְּשָׁם: וַיִּצֹק מִשֶּׁמֶן הַמִּשְׁחָה
יג עַל רֹאשׁ אַהֲרֹן וַיִּמְשַׁח אֹתוֹ לְקַדְּשׁוֹ: וַיַּקְרֵב מֹשֶׁה אֶת־בְּנֵי אַהֲרֹן וַיַּלְבִּשֵׁם
כֻּתֳּנֹת וַיַּחְגֹּר אֹתָם אַבְנֵט וַיַּחֲבֹשׁ לָהֶם מִגְבָּעוֹת כַּאֲשֶׁר צִוָּה יְהוָה אֶת־מֹשֶׁה:

רש״י

פרק ח

ב| **קַח אֶת אַהֲרֹן.** פָּרָשָׁה זוֹ נֶאֶמְרָה שִׁבְעַת יָמִים קֹדֶם הֲקָמַת הַמִּשְׁכָּן, שֶׁאֵין מֻקְדָּם וּמְאֻחָר בַּתּוֹרָה: **קַח אֶת אַהֲרֹן.** קָחֶנּוּ בִּדְבָרִים וּמָשְׁכֵהוּ: **וְאֵת פַּר הַחַטָּאת וְגוֹ׳.** אֵלּוּ הָאֲמוּרִים בְּעִנְיַן צַוָּאַת הַמִּלּוּאִים בִּ׳וְאַתָּה תְּצַוֶּה׳ (שמות כט), וְעַכְשָׁיו בְּיוֹם רִאשׁוֹן לַמִּלּוּאִים חָזַר וְזֵרְזוֹ בִּשְׁעַת מַעֲשֶׂה:

ג| **הַקְהֵל אֶל פֶּתַח אֹהֶל מוֹעֵד.** זֶה אֶחָד מִן הַמְּקוֹמוֹת שֶׁהֶחֱזִיק מוּעָט אֶת הַמְרֻבֶּה:

ה| **זֶה הַדָּבָר.** דְּבָרִים שֶׁתִּרְאוּ שֶׁאֲנִי עוֹשֶׂה לִפְנֵיכֶם צִוַּנִי הַקָּדוֹשׁ בָּרוּךְ הוּא לַעֲשׂוֹת, וְאַל תֹּאמְרוּ לִכְבוֹדִי וְלִכְבוֹד אָחִי אֲנִי עוֹשֶׂה. כָּל הָעִנְיָן הַזֶּה פֵּרַשְׁתִּי בִּ׳וְאַתָּה תְּצַוֶּה׳ (שמות כט, א-לז):

ח| **אֶת הָאוּרִים.** כְּתָב שֶׁל שֵׁם הַמְפֹרָשׁ:

ט| **וַיָּשֶׂם עַל הַמִּצְנֶפֶת.** פְּתִילֵי תְכֵלֶת הַקְּבוּעִים בַּצִּיץ נוֹתֵן עַל הַמִּצְנֶפֶת, נִמְצָא הַצִּיץ תָּלוּי בַּמִּצְנֶפֶת:

יא| **וַיַּז מִמֶּנּוּ עַל הַמִּזְבֵּחַ.** לֹא יָדַעְתִּי הֵיכָן נִצְטַוָּה בַּהַזָּאוֹת הַלָּלוּ:

יב| **וַיִּצֹק, וַיִּמְשַׁח.** בַּתְּחִלָּה יוֹצֵק עַל רֹאשׁוֹ, וְאַחַר כָּךְ נוֹתֵן בֵּין רִיסֵי עֵינָיו וּמוֹשֵׁךְ בְּאֶצְבָּעוֹ מִזֶּה לָזֶה:

יג| **וַיַּחֲבֹשׁ.** לְשׁוֹן קְשִׁירָה:

DISCUSSION

8:3| **The entire congregation [*eida*]:** Whereas the word "assembly" [*kahal*] refers to a wide audience, the word "congregation" [*eida*], generally refers to a select group of people that constitutes the leadership. Sometimes it refers to a small group of people, such as the members of the High Court or some other court (see Numbers 35:24–25; Joshua 20:6; *Sifra*, *Vayikra*, *Dibbura DeNedava* 4; *Sanhedrin* 16a). Other times it may refer to a larger group (see Exodus 12:3–6; Numbers 16:1–11; see also commentary on Leviticus 4:13), such as a legislative council (see Ibn Ezra).

14 Following the initial consecration of the Tabernacle and the
Fifth priests, Moses began the sacrificial service: **He brought for-**
aliya **ward the bull of the sin offering, and** just as any individual
who brings an offering lays his hands on his offering, **Aaron
and his sons laid their hands on the head of the bull of the
sin offering.**

15 **He,** Moses,[43] **slaughtered** the bull of the sin offering, **and Moses**
alone **took the blood, placed it all around on the horns of
the** outer **altar with his finger, and purified [*vayeḥate*] the
altar.**[44] Alternatively: And he performed the rites of the sin offering [*ḥatat*] on the altar. **He poured the blood at the base of
the altar, and he consecrated it to atone for it.** With the performance of this rite, the altar and the priests were consecrated
and purified. For the time being, however, the Tabernacle's rites
continued to be performed by Moses rather than the priests.

16 **He took all the fat that was on the innards, the diaphragm
of,** that is, above, **the liver, and the two kidneys, and their fat,
and Moses burned it on the altar.**

17 **The bull, its hide, its flesh, and its dung** that remained in its
intestines, **he burned in fire outside the camp, as the Lord
had commanded Moses.** Normally, only a sin offering whose
blood is sprinkled inside the Sanctuary is burned outside the
camp (see 4:13–21, 16:27). Nevertheless, God commanded
that this bull should be burned outside the camp as well, even
though its blood was sprinkled on the external altar, outside
the Sanctuary.

18 Following the sacrifice of the sin offering, whose purpose was
purification, the priests presented their burnt offering, brought
as a gift:[45] **He brought the ram of the burnt offering near,
and Aaron and his sons laid their hands on the head of the
ram,** as it was their offering.

19 **He slaughtered it, and Moses cast the blood around the altar,** according to the laws of the burnt offering.

20 **He cut the ram into its pieces, and Moses burned the head,
the pieces, and the fats.**

21 **The innards and the legs he washed with water,** according to
the laws of the burnt offering, **and Moses burned the entire
ram on the altar. It is a burnt offering for a pleasing aroma;
it is a fire offering to the Lord as the Lord had commanded
Moses.**

22 **He brought near the second ram, the ram of investiture,** the
Sixth ram brought specifically in honor of the investiture ceremony
aliya

in which the priests would be officially appointed to their position and invested to minister,[46] **and Aaron and his sons laid
their hands on the head of the ram.**

23 **He slaughtered, and Moses took from its blood and placed
it on the tip of Aaron's right ear,**[D] **and upon the thumb of his
right hand, and upon the big toe of his right foot.**

24 **He brought Aaron's sons near, and Moses placed the blood
on the tip of their right ear, and on the thumb of their right
hand, and on the big toe of their right foot; and Moses cast
the** remaining **blood around the altar.**

25 **He took the fat, the fat tail, and all the fat that was upon the
innards, and the diaphragm of,** that is, above, **the liver, and
the two kidneys, and their fat, and the right haunch,** and
brought all of them to the altar.

26 **From the basket of unleavened bread that was before the
Lord,** he took one unleavened loaf, one loaf of oil bread,
and one wafer, and he placed them on the fat and on the
right haunch.

27 **He placed it all,** the loaves and the sacrificial portions, **on the
palms of Aaron and on the palms of his sons, and** Moses
waved them, Aaron and his sons, or their palms, which held
the sacrificial parts,[47] **as a wave offering before the Lord.**

28 **Moses took them,** the loaves and sacrificial portions, **from on
their palms and burned them on the altar on,** that is, after,
**the burnt offering. They are an investiture offering for a
pleasing aroma; it is a fire offering to the Lord.**

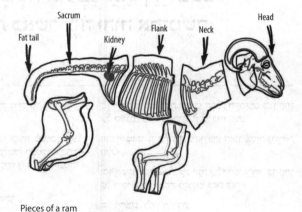

Pieces of a ram

─────────────────────────── DISCUSSION ───────────────────────────

8:23 | On the tip [*tenukh*] of Aaron's right ear:
The source of this word in uncertain. Nowadays
it refers to the earlobe. The Sages, however, do
not interpret the verse in this manner, although

it is certainly a plausible interpretation (see Rav
Se'adya Gaon and Ibn Ezra, Exodus 29:20; Ibn
Janaḥ; Radak). Some maintain that the *tenukh* is
the middle of the ear, while others claim that it is

the upper part (see *Sifra, Metzora* 3:5; Rambam's
Commentary on the Mishna, *Nega'im* 14:9).

חמישי

יד וַיַּגֵּשׁ אֵת פַּר הַחַטָּאת וַיִּסְמֹךְ אַהֲרֹן וּבָנָיו אֶת־יְדֵיהֶם עַל־רֹאשׁ פַּר הַחַטָּאת:
טו וַיִּשְׁחָט וַיִּקַּח מֹשֶׁה אֶת־הַדָּם וַיִּתֵּן עַל־קַרְנוֹת הַמִּזְבֵּחַ סָבִיב בְּאֶצְבָּעוֹ וַיְחַטֵּא
טז אֶת־הַמִּזְבֵּחַ וְאֶת־הַדָּם יָצַק אֶל־יְסוֹד הַמִּזְבֵּחַ וַיְקַדְּשֵׁהוּ לְכַפֵּר עָלָיו: וַיִּקַּח אֶת־
כָּל־הַחֵלֶב אֲשֶׁר עַל־הַקֶּרֶב וְאֵת יֹתֶרֶת הַכָּבֵד וְאֶת־שְׁתֵּי הַכְּלָיֹת וְאֶת־חֶלְבְּהֶן
יז וַיַּקְטֵר מֹשֶׁה הַמִּזְבֵּחָה: וְאֶת־הַפָּר וְאֶת־עֹרוֹ וְאֶת־בְּשָׂרוֹ וְאֶת־פִּרְשׁוֹ שָׂרַף בָּאֵשׁ
יח מִחוּץ לַמַּחֲנֶה כַּאֲשֶׁר צִוָּה יְהוָה אֶת־מֹשֶׁה: וַיַּקְרֵב אֵת אֵיל הָעֹלָה וַיִּסְמְכוּ אַהֲרֹן
יט וּבָנָיו אֶת־יְדֵיהֶם עַל־רֹאשׁ הָאָיִל: וַיִּשְׁחָט וַיִּזְרֹק מֹשֶׁה אֶת־הַדָּם עַל־הַמִּזְבֵּחַ
כ סָבִיב: וְאֶת־הָאַיִל נִתַּח לִנְתָחָיו וַיַּקְטֵר מֹשֶׁה אֶת־הָרֹאשׁ וְאֶת־הַנְּתָחִים וְאֶת־
כא הַפָּדֶר: וְאֶת־הַקֶּרֶב וְאֶת־הַכְּרָעַיִם רָחַץ בַּמָּיִם וַיַּקְטֵר מֹשֶׁה אֶת־כָּל־הָאַיִל
הַמִּזְבֵּחָה עֹלָה הוּא לְרֵיחַ־נִיחֹחַ אִשֶּׁה הוּא לַיהוָה כַּאֲשֶׁר צִוָּה יְהוָה אֶת־מֹשֶׁה:

ששי

כב וַיַּקְרֵב אֶת־הָאַיִל הַשֵּׁנִי אֵיל הַמִּלֻּאִים וַיִּסְמְכוּ אַהֲרֹן וּבָנָיו אֶת־יְדֵיהֶם עַל־רֹאשׁ
כג הָאָיִל: וַיִּשְׁחָט ׀ וַיִּקַּח מֹשֶׁה מִדָּמוֹ וַיִּתֵּן עַל־תְּנוּךְ אֹזֶן־אַהֲרֹן הַיְמָנִית וְעַל־בֹּהֶן
כד יָדוֹ הַיְמָנִית וְעַל־בֹּהֶן רַגְלוֹ הַיְמָנִית: וַיַּקְרֵב אֶת־בְּנֵי אַהֲרֹן וַיִּתֵּן מֹשֶׁה מִן־הַדָּם
עַל־תְּנוּךְ אָזְנָם הַיְמָנִית וְעַל־בֹּהֶן יָדָם הַיְמָנִית וְעַל־בֹּהֶן רַגְלָם הַיְמָנִית וַיִּזְרֹק
כה מֹשֶׁה אֶת־הַדָּם עַל־הַמִּזְבֵּחַ סָבִיב: וַיִּקַּח אֶת־הַחֵלֶב וְאֶת־הָאַלְיָה וְאֶת־כָּל־
הַחֵלֶב אֲשֶׁר עַל־הַקֶּרֶב וְאֵת יֹתֶרֶת הַכָּבֵד וְאֶת־שְׁתֵּי הַכְּלָיֹת וְאֶת־חֶלְבְּהֶן וְאֵת
כו שׁוֹק הַיָּמִין: וּמִסַּל הַמַּצּוֹת אֲשֶׁר ׀ לִפְנֵי יְהוָה לָקַח חַלַּת מַצָּה אַחַת וְחַלַּת לֶחֶם
כז שֶׁמֶן אַחַת וְרָקִיק אֶחָד וַיָּשֶׂם עַל־הַחֲלָבִים וְעַל שׁוֹק הַיָּמִין: וַיִּתֵּן אֶת־הַכֹּל עַל
כח כַּפֵּי אַהֲרֹן וְעַל כַּפֵּי בָנָיו וַיָּנֶף אֹתָם תְּנוּפָה לִפְנֵי יְהוָה: וַיִּקַּח מֹשֶׁה אֹתָם מֵעַל
כַּפֵּיהֶם וַיַּקְטֵר הַמִּזְבֵּחָה עַל־הָעֹלָה מִלֻּאִים הֵם לְרֵיחַ נִיחֹחַ אִשֶּׁה הוּא לַיהוָה:

רש"י

טו] וַיְחַטֵּא אֶת הַמִּזְבֵּחַ. חִטְּאוֹ וְטִהֲרוֹ מִזָּרוּת לִכָּנֵס לִקְדֻשָּׁה: וַיְקַדְּשֵׁהוּ. בַּעֲבוֹדָה זוֹ, "לְכַפֵּר עָלָיו" מֵעַתָּה כָּל הַכַּפָּרוֹת.

טז] "עַל הַכָּבֵד" (שמות כט, יג), לְבַד הַכָּבֵד, שֶׁהָיָה נוֹטֵל מְעַט מִן הַכָּבֵד עִמָּהּ.

כב] אֵיל הַמִּלֻּאִים. אֵיל הַשְּׁלָמִים, שֶׁ'מִּלּוּאִים' לְשׁוֹן שְׁלָמִים, שֶׁמְּמַלְּאִין וּמַשְׁלִימִין אֶת הַכֹּהֲנִים בִּכְהֻנָּתָם.

כו] וְחַלַּת לֶחֶם שֶׁמֶן. הִיא רְבוּכָה, שֶׁהָיָה מַרְבֶּה בָּהּ שֶׁמֶן כְּנֶגֶד הַחַלּוֹת וְהָרְקִיקִין, כָּךְ מְפֹרָשׁ בִּמְנָחוֹת (דף עח ע"א).

כח] וַיַּקְטֵר הַמִּזְבֵּחָה. מֹשֶׁה שִׁמֵּשׁ כָּל שִׁבְעַת יְמֵי הַמִּלּוּאִים בְּחָלוּק לָבָן: עַל הָעֹלָה. אַחַר הָעֹלָה, וְלֹא מָצִינוּ שׁוֹק שֶׁל שְׁלָמִים קָרֵב בְּכָל מָקוֹם חוּץ מִזֶּה.

29 **Moses took the breast** as well **and waved it as a wave offering before the Lord; it,** the breast, **was the portion for Moses from the ram of investiture, as the Lord had commanded Moses.**

30 **Moses took from the anointing oil and from the blood that**
Seventh aliya **was** placed **on the altar, and he sprinkled it on Aaron, on his vestments, and on his sons, and on the vestments of his sons with him, and he** again **consecrated Aaron and his vestments, and his sons and the vestments of his sons with him.**

31 **Moses said to Aaron and to his sons: Cook the flesh** that remains of the ram of investiture **at the entrance of the Tent of Meeting, and there you shall eat it and the bread that is in the basket of investiture, as I commanded, saying: Aaron and his sons shall eat it.** The ram and its loaves are considered offerings of the most sacred order; as such, they may not leave the Tabernacle.

32 If the flesh and the bread are not consumed in their entirety by the next morning,[48] **that which remains of the flesh and of the bread you shall burn in fire.**

33 **From the entrance of the Tent of Meeting you shall not**
Maftir **emerge seven days, until the day of completion of the days of your investiture** as priests; **as for seven days He shall invest you.**

34 **As he did on this day,** referring to all the sprinkling of blood and offerings, **the Lord commanded to do, to atone for you.**

35 **At the entrance of the Tent of Meeting you shall remain day and night,** for all **seven days** of the investiture, **and** you shall serve as an honorary guard and **keep the commission of the Lord, that you shall not die, for so I was commanded.** Presumably, the priests did not go an entire week without sleep. Rather, the verse means that there shall be a rotation of priests standing watch at the entrance to the Tent of Meeting.[49]

36 **Aaron and his sons did all the things that the Lord commanded at the hand of Moses.**

Maftir on Shabbat Zakhor is read from Deuteronomy 25:17–19. Maftir on Shabbat Para is read from Numbers 19:1–22.

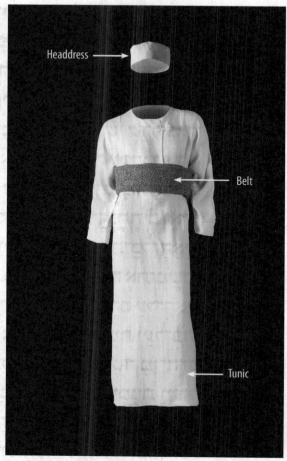

Belt
Tunic

Vestments of an ordinary priest

כט וַיִּקַּ֨ח מֹשֶׁ֤ה אֶת־הֶֽחָזֶה֙ וַיְנִיפֵ֤הוּ תְנוּפָה֙ לִפְנֵ֣י יְהֹוָ֔ה מֵאֵ֥יל הַמִּלֻּאִ֖ים לְמֹשֶׁ֣ה הָיָ֣ה

ל לְמָנָ֔ה כַּאֲשֶׁ֛ר צִוָּ֥ה יְהֹוָ֖ה אֶת־מֹשֶֽׁה׃ וַיִּקַּ֨ח מֹשֶׁ֜ה מִשֶּׁ֣מֶן הַמִּשְׁחָ֗ה וּמִן־הַדָּם֮ אֲשֶׁ֣ר   שביעי

עַל־הַמִּזְבֵּ֒חַ֒ וַיַּ֤ז עַל־אַהֲרֹן֙ עַל־בְּגָדָ֔יו וְעַל־בָּנָ֛יו וְעַל־בִּגְדֵ֥י בָנָ֖יו אִתּ֑וֹ וַיְקַדֵּ֤שׁ

לא אֶֽת־אַהֲרֹן֙ אֶת־בְּגָדָ֔יו וְאֶת־בָּנָ֛יו וְאֶת־בִּגְדֵ֥י בָנָ֖יו אִתּֽוֹ׃ וַיֹּ֨אמֶר מֹשֶׁ֜ה אֶל־אַהֲרֹ֣ן

וְאֶל־בָּנָ֗יו בַּשְּׁל֤וּ אֶת־הַבָּשָׂר֙ פֶּ֚תַח אֹ֣הֶל מוֹעֵ֔ד וְשָׁם֙ תֹּאכְל֣וּ אֹת֔וֹ וְאֶ֨ת־הַלֶּ֔חֶם

לב אֲשֶׁ֖ר בְּסַ֣ל הַמִּלֻּאִ֑ים כַּאֲשֶׁ֤ר צִוֵּ֙יתִי֙ לֵאמֹ֔ר אַהֲרֹ֥ן וּבָנָ֖יו יֹֽאכְלֻֽהוּ׃ וְהַנּוֹתָ֥ר בַּבָּשָׂ֖ר

לג וּבַלָּ֑חֶם בָּאֵ֖שׁ תִּשְׂרֹֽפוּ׃ וּמִפֶּ֩תַח֩ אֹ֨הֶל מוֹעֵ֜ד לֹ֤א תֵֽצְאוּ֙ שִׁבְעַ֣ת יָמִ֔ים עַ֚ד י֣וֹם   מפטיר

לד מְלֹ֔את יְמֵ֖י מִלֻּאֵיכֶ֑ם כִּ֚י שִׁבְעַ֣ת יָמִ֔ים יְמַלֵּ֖א אֶת־יֶדְכֶֽם׃ כַּאֲשֶׁ֥ר עָשָׂ֖ה בַּיּ֣וֹם הַזֶּ֑ה

לה צִוָּ֧ה יְהֹוָ֛ה לַעֲשֹׂ֖ת לְכַפֵּ֥ר עֲלֵיכֶֽם׃ וּפֶ֩תַח֩ אֹ֨הֶל מוֹעֵ֜ד תֵּשְׁב֣וּ יוֹמָ֣ם וָלַ֗יְלָה שִׁבְעַ֣ת

לו יָמִ֔ים וּשְׁמַרְתֶּ֛ם אֶת־מִשְׁמֶ֥רֶת יְהֹוָ֖ה וְלֹ֣א תָמ֑וּתוּ כִּי־כֵ֖ן צֻוֵּ֑יתִי׃ וַיַּ֤עַשׂ אַהֲרֹן֙ וּבָנָ֔יו

אֵ֚ת כָּל־הַדְּבָרִ֔ים אֲשֶׁר־צִוָּ֥ה יְהֹוָ֖ה בְּיַד־מֹשֶֽׁה׃

רש״י

לד] צִוָּה ה' לַעֲשֹׂת. כָּל שִׁבְעַת הַיָּמִים. וְרַבּוֹתֵינוּ דָּרְשׁוּ: "לַעֲשֹׂת" – זֶה מַעֲשֵׂה פָרָה, "לְכַפֵּר" – זֶה מַעֲשֵׂה יוֹם הַכִּפּוּרִים, וּלְלַמֵּד שֶׁכֹּהֵן גָּדוֹל טָעוּן פְּרִישָׁה קֹדֶם יוֹם

הַכִּפּוּרִים שִׁבְעַת יָמִים, וְכֵן הַכֹּהֵן הַשּׂוֹרֵף אֶת הַפָּרָה:

לה] וְלֹא תָמוּתוּ. הָא אִם לֹא תַעֲשׂוּ כֵן הֲרֵי אַתֶּם חַיָּבִים מִיתָה:

לו] וַיַּעַשׂ אַהֲרֹן וּבָנָיו. לְהַגִּיד שִׁבְחָן, שֶׁלֹּא הִטּוּ יָמִין וּשְׂמֹאל:

Parashat **Shemini**

The Eighth Day
LEVITICUS 9:1–24

The previous chapter dealt with the rites of the seven days of inauguration of the Tabernacle. These seven days witnessed the actualization of the Tabernacle service, as well as the anointing of the priests to serve in the Tabernacle. These were days of preparation, during which Moses, Aaron, and Aaron's sons practiced rites that would be performed in the Tabernacle. Aaron and his sons served as a ceremonial guard over the Tabernacle, while Moses ministered as the priest. The time has now come for Aaron and his sons to take their place as ministers.

The construction of the Tabernacle was a work of particular complexity and precision. Consequently, the instructions regarding its construction, as well as the execution of those instructions, are described repeatedly in the book of Exodus. The ceremony of the Tabernacle's inauguration is the climax, and perhaps the test, of all the preceding stages: Will the Tabernacle indeed serve as an intermediary between the nation of Israel and God? As the moment that will determine the worth of this massive undertaking approaches, the people seek a sign that will indicate the success of their endeavor. Such a sign is indeed provided.

The date of the eighth day of the inauguration is uncertain. According to one opinion, the days of the inauguration began on the first day of the first month, on the first day of Nisan, so that the eighth day fell on the eighth of Nisan. Others maintain that the eighth day itself fell on the first of Nisan. In any case, the intensive work of building the Tabernacle, in which the entire people participated, took roughly half a year. It is possible that the preparation of the Tabernacle and its vessels was completed relatively quickly, and that the people waited for the command to begin constructing the Tabernacle.

9 1 **It was on the eighth day** of the days of inauguration, that **Moses summoned Aaron and his sons and the elders of Israel.** On this day, the inauguration of the Tabernacle was completed. It was this pivotal ceremony, the transition from preparing the Tabernacle to ministering in it, that constituted its inauguration.

2 **He,** Moses, **said to Aaron: Take for yourself a young calf as a sin offering and a ram as a burnt offering, unblemished, and present them before the Lord.** This is the first day on which Aaron ministers as a priest.

3 Aaron must also command the people with regard to their offerings: **Speak to the children of Israel, saying: Take a goat as a sin offering and a calf and a lamb, one year old, unblemished, as a burnt offering,**

4 **and a bull and a ram as peace offerings, to slaughter before the Lord, and a meal offering** of flour **mixed with oil. For today the Lord appears to you** in the Tabernacle.

5 **They took that which Moses commanded before the Tent of Meeting, and the entire congregation approached and stood before the Lord.**

6 **Moses said: This is the matter that the Lord commanded that you shall do, and the glory of the Lord will appear to you.** If you obey my commands precisely, God will reveal Himself to you.

7 **Moses said to Aaron: Approach the altar and perform your sin offering and your burnt offering, and atone for yourself and** then atone **for the people; perform the offering of the people and atone for them, as the Lord commanded.** Until now, Aaron was like any other member of Israel whose offerings were sacrificed on his behalf. Until this point, he was considered an apprentice; now he must perform the sacred service himself.

8 **Aaron approached the altar** in the courtyard of the Tabernacle, **and he slaughtered the calf of the sin offering that was for him,** that is, that belonged to him,[1] and that was to atone for him so that he should enter the priesthood in a state of spiritual purity.[2]

9 **The sons of Aaron,** who were newly inaugurated to the priesthood and were also required to learn the procedures of the service, **presented the blood** in a vessel **to him,** their father. Aaron **dipped his finger in the blood, and he placed it on the horns of the altar,** according to the laws of the sin offering, **and he poured** the remainder of **the blood at the base of the altar.**

10 **The fat, the kidneys, and the diaphragm above the liver of the sin offering he burned on the altar, as the Lord had commanded Moses.**

11 **The flesh and the skin he burned in fire outside the camp.**[D] Unlike the flesh of ordinary sin offerings, which was eaten by the priests, the flesh of this sin offering was burned.

Calf

Goat

פרשת שמיני

א ב וַיְהִי בַּיּוֹם הַשְּׁמִינִי קָרָא מֹשֶׁה לְאַהֲרֹן וּלְבָנָיו וּלְזִקְנֵי יִשְׂרָאֵל: וַיֹּאמֶר אֶל־
אַהֲרֹן קַח־לְךָ עֵגֶל בֶּן־בָּקָר לְחַטָּאת וְאַיִל לְעֹלָה תְּמִימִם וְהַקְרֵב לִפְנֵי יְהוָה:
ג וְאֶל־בְּנֵי יִשְׂרָאֵל תְּדַבֵּר לֵאמֹר קְחוּ שְׂעִיר־עִזִּים לְחַטָּאת וְעֵגֶל וָכֶבֶשׂ בְּנֵי־
ד שָׁנָה תְּמִימִם לְעֹלָה: וְשׁוֹר וָאַיִל לִשְׁלָמִים לִזְבֹּחַ לִפְנֵי יְהוָה וּמִנְחָה בְּלוּלָה
ה בַשָּׁמֶן כִּי הַיּוֹם יְהוָה נִרְאָה אֲלֵיכֶם: וַיִּקְחוּ אֵת אֲשֶׁר צִוָּה מֹשֶׁה אֶל־פְּנֵי אֹהֶל
ו מוֹעֵד וַיִּקְרְבוּ כָּל־הָעֵדָה וַיַּעַמְדוּ לִפְנֵי יְהוָה: וַיֹּאמֶר מֹשֶׁה זֶה הַדָּבָר אֲשֶׁר־
ז צִוָּה יְהוָה תַּעֲשׂוּ וְיֵרָא אֲלֵיכֶם כְּבוֹד יְהוָה: וַיֹּאמֶר מֹשֶׁה אֶל־אַהֲרֹן קְרַב אֶל־
הַמִּזְבֵּחַ וַעֲשֵׂה אֶת־חַטָּאתְךָ וְאֶת־עֹלָתֶךָ וְכַפֵּר בַּעַדְךָ וּבְעַד הָעָם וַעֲשֵׂה אֶת־
ח קָרְבַּן הָעָם וְכַפֵּר בַּעֲדָם כַּאֲשֶׁר צִוָּה יְהוָה: וַיִּקְרַב אַהֲרֹן אֶל־הַמִּזְבֵּחַ וַיִּשְׁחַט
ט אֶת־עֵגֶל הַחַטָּאת אֲשֶׁר־לוֹ: וַיַּקְרִבוּ בְּנֵי אַהֲרֹן אֶת־הַדָּם אֵלָיו וַיִּטְבֹּל אֶצְבָּעוֹ
י בַּדָּם וַיִּתֵּן עַל־קַרְנוֹת הַמִּזְבֵּחַ וְאֶת־הַדָּם יָצַק אֶל־יְסוֹד הַמִּזְבֵּחַ: וְאֶת־הַחֵלֶב
וְאֶת־הַכְּלָיֹת וְאֶת־הַיֹּתֶרֶת מִן־הַכָּבֵד מִן־הַחַטָּאת הִקְטִיר הַמִּזְבֵּחָה כַּאֲשֶׁר
יא צִוָּה יְהוָה אֶת־מֹשֶׁה: וְאֶת־הַבָּשָׂר וְאֶת־הָעוֹר שָׂרַף בָּאֵשׁ מִחוּץ לַמַּחֲנֶה:

רש"י

א| וַיְהִי בַּיּוֹם הַשְּׁמִינִי. לַמִּלּוּאִים, הוּא רֹאשׁ חֹדֶשׁ נִיסָן, שֶׁהוּקַם הַמִּשְׁכָּן בּוֹ בַּיּוֹם, וְנָטַל עֶשֶׂר עֲטָרוֹת הַשְּׁנוּיוֹת בְּסֵדֶר עוֹלָם: וּלְזִקְנֵי יִשְׂרָאֵל. לְהַשְׁמִיעָם שֶׁעַל פִּי הַדִּבּוּר אַהֲרֹן נִכְנָס וּמְשַׁמֵּשׁ בִּכְהֻנָּה גְּדוֹלָה, וְלֹא יֹאמְרוּ: מֵאֵלָיו נִכְנָס:

ב| קַח לְךָ עֵגֶל. לְהוֹדִיעַ שֶׁמְּכַפֵּר לוֹ הַקָּדוֹשׁ בָּרוּךְ הוּא עַל יְדֵי עֵגֶל זֶה עַל מַעֲשֵׂה הָעֵגֶל שֶׁעָשָׂה:

ד| כִּי הַיּוֹם ה' נִרְאָה אֲלֵיכֶם. לְהַשְׁרוֹת שְׁכִינָתוֹ בְּמַעֲשֵׂה יְדֵיכֶם, לְכָךְ קָרְבָּנוֹת הַלָּלוּ בָּאִין חוֹבָה לְיוֹם זֶה:

ז| קְרַב אֶל הַמִּזְבֵּחַ. שֶׁהָיָה אַהֲרֹן בּוֹשׁ וְיָרֵא לָגֶשֶׁת, אָמַר לוֹ מֹשֶׁה: לָמָּה אַתָּה בּוֹשׁ? לְכָךְ נִבְחַרְתָּ: אֶת חַטָּאתְךָ. עֵגֶל בֶּן בָּקָר: וְאֶת עֹלָתֶךָ. אַיִל: קָרְבַּן הָעָם. שְׂעִיר עִזִּים וְעֵגֶל וָכֶבֶשׂ. כָּל מָקוֹם שֶׁנֶּאֱמַר 'עֵגֶל' בֶּן שָׁנָה הוּא, וּמִכָּאן אַתָּה לָמֵד:

יא| וְאֶת הַבָּשָׂר וְאֶת הָעוֹר וְגוֹ'. לֹא מָצִינוּ חַטָּאת חִיצוֹנָה נִשְׂרֶפֶת אֶלָּא זוֹ וְשֶׁל מִלּוּאִים (שמות כט, יד), וְכֻלָּן עַל פִּי הַדִּבּוּר:

DISCUSSION

9:11| He burned in fire outside the camp: Like many offerings brought as part of the ceremony marking the beginning of the service, this sin offering is treated like a sin offering whose blood is brought inside the Sanctuary, even though it was sacrificed on the outer altar. Such a sin offering is not consumed at all; rather, its fat is burned upon the altar while the rest of the animal is burned outside the camp (see Rashi; *Ḥizkuni*). It is possible that this sin offering was not consumed because the priests were not yet completely inaugurated, and there was therefore no one fit to consume its flesh.

12 After the sin offering, **he slaughtered the burnt offering; and Aaron's sons** stretched out their hands and **passed the blood to him, and he cast it around the altar** by means of a vessel, in accordance with the laws of the burnt offering (see 1:5).

13 **They passed the burnt offering to him in its pieces, and the head.** For seven days, Aaron's sons had practiced the various sacrificial rites. They had watched Moses perform them and learned how to properly carry out their priestly duties. Now they cut the offering into its pieces in the proper manner and brought its parts to their father, **and he burned them,** the pieces and the head, **on the altar.**

14 **He washed the innards and the legs and burned them on the** pieces of **the burnt offering** that he had placed **on the altar.**

15 After sacrificing his sin offering and burnt offering, **he, Aaron, brought the people's offering near,** as the priest must first offer his own atonement before offering that of another.[3] **He took the goat of the sin offering that was for the people and slaughtered it and presented it as a sin offering like the first,** like Aaron's first sin offering. That is, its blood was placed with a finger on the corners of the altar, and its sacrificial portions were placed upon the altar for burning. Perhaps the remaining flesh was burned as well, like that of Aaron's sin offering.[4] Some say that the flesh of the people's sin offering was eaten.[5]

16 **He brought the burnt offering near, and he performed it in accordance with the procedure** stated with regard to the burnt offering (see chap. 1).

17 **He brought the meal offering near, and he filled his palm**
Second aliya **from it,** he removed a handful, **and burned it on the altar, in addition to the morning burnt offering.** The morning burnt offering is part of the daily service; it is not one of the special offerings of the inauguration.

18 **He slaughtered the bull and the ram, the peace offerings that were for the people; and Aaron's sons passed the blood**

to him, and he cast it around the altar, in accordance with the laws of the peace offering (3:2).

19 They passed him **the fats from the bull and from the ram, the fat tail** of the ram, **and those that cover,** the fats of the bull and the ram that cover various parts of the animal, **and the kidneys, and the diaphragm above the liver.**

20 **They placed the fats upon the breasts, and he burned the fats on the altar.**

21 **Aaron waved the breasts and the right haunch as a wave offering before the Lord, as Moses had commanded.**

22 **Aaron raised his hands toward the people and blessed them.** Although the formula of this blessing does not appear in the verse, it appears later in the Torah[6] as the priestly blessing that is part of the daily service.[7] **And he descended from** the altar after performing the sin offering, the burnt offering, and the peace offerings.

23 **Moses and Aaron came into the Tent of Meeting.** Until this point, the entire service was performed in the courtyard of the Tabernacle, where the outer altar, upon which all the offerings were sacrificed, was situated. Now Moses and Aaron entered the Sanctuary, the tent covered with tapestries and hides, presumably in order to pray.[8] **And they emerged and blessed the people;**[D] **and then the glory of the Lord appeared to the entire people.** This revelation did not occur during the sacrifice of the offerings or even after the priestly blessing. Rather, the pivotal moment followed the blessing of Moses and Aaron.

24 **Fire emerged from before the Lord and consumed upon**
Third aliya **the altar the burnt offering and the fats; all the people saw it,** the fire consuming the offerings, which was a sign that God accepted their service and their prayers, **and sang praise,** or shouted,[9] **and fell upon their faces** due to this revelation.[10] Now the people knew that the Tabernacle was properly constructed and that the presence of God dwelled within it.

The Deaths of Holy Individuals and the Ensuing Instructions
LEVITICUS 10:1–20

The inauguration of the Tabernacle reached its pinnacle when fire descended from Heaven and the glory of God was revealed to the people. This was proof that the work of the Tabernacle was indeed complete. Suddenly, an unexpected disaster occurs: Two of the five priests who were just inaugurated die.

10 1 **Each of the** two eldest **sons of Aaron, Nadav and Avihu, took his fire-pan and placed in it** coals of **fire, and placed incense**

upon the fire, **and they offered before the Lord strange fire that He had not commanded them.**[D]

DISCUSSION

9:23 | And blessed the people: According to the Sages, Moses and Aaron said: "May the graciousness of the Lord our God be upon us, making firm the work of our hands for us; indeed, making firm the work of our hands" (Psalms 90:17). The Sages explain the verse as follows: We have done what we can; now let it be Your will

that the graciousness of God be revealed upon us (*Sifrei, Matot* 143; Rashi). Indeed, the psalm in which this blessing appears begins with "A prayer of Moses."

10:1 | And they offered before the Lord strange fire that He had not commanded

them: Perhaps Nadav and Avihu were close in age, possibly even twins, and they acted together. During the inauguration ceremony they felt a strong desire to volunteer an additional offering, perhaps as a consequence of the excitement in the atmosphere, or because they were slightly drunk or at least not entirely

יב וַיִּשְׁחַט אֶת־הָעֹלָה וַיַּמְצִאוּ בְּנֵי אַהֲרֹן אֵלָיו אֶת־הַדָּם וַיִּזְרְקֵהוּ עַל־הַמִּזְבֵּחַ
יג סָבִיב׃ וְאֶת־הָעֹלָה הִמְצִיאוּ אֵלָיו לִנְתָחֶיהָ וְאֶת־הָרֹאשׁ וַיַּקְטֵר עַל־הַמִּזְבֵּחַ׃
יד טו וַיִּרְחַץ אֶת־הַקֶּרֶב וְאֶת־הַכְּרָעָיִם וַיַּקְטֵר עַל־הָעֹלָה הַמִּזְבֵּחָה׃ וַיַּקְרֵב אֵת קָרְבַּן
טז הָעָם וַיִּקַּח אֶת־שְׂעִיר הַחַטָּאת אֲשֶׁר לָעָם וַיִּשְׁחָטֵהוּ וַיְחַטְּאֵהוּ כָּרִאשׁוֹן׃ וַיַּקְרֵב
יז אֶת־הָעֹלָה וַיַּעֲשֶׂהָ כַּמִּשְׁפָּט׃ וַיַּקְרֵב אֶת־הַמִּנְחָה וַיְמַלֵּא כַפּוֹ מִמֶּנָּה וַיַּקְטֵר שני
יח עַל־הַמִּזְבֵּחַ מִלְּבַד עֹלַת הַבֹּקֶר׃ וַיִּשְׁחַט אֶת־הַשּׁוֹר וְאֶת־הָאַיִל זֶבַח הַשְּׁלָמִים
יט אֲשֶׁר לָעָם וַיַּמְצִאוּ בְּנֵי אַהֲרֹן אֶת־הַדָּם אֵלָיו וַיִּזְרְקֵהוּ עַל־הַמִּזְבֵּחַ סָבִיב׃ וְאֶת־
כ הַחֲלָבִים מִן־הַשּׁוֹר וּמִן־הָאַיִל הָאַלְיָה וְהַמְכַסֶּה וְהַכְּלָיֹת וְיֹתֶרֶת הַכָּבֵד׃ וַיָּשִׂימוּ
כא אֶת־הַחֲלָבִים עַל־הֶחָזוֹת וַיַּקְטֵר הַחֲלָבִים הַמִּזְבֵּחָה׃ וְאֵת הֶחָזוֹת וְאֵת שׁוֹק
כב הַיָּמִין הֵנִיף אַהֲרֹן תְּנוּפָה לִפְנֵי יהוה כַּאֲשֶׁר צִוָּה מֹשֶׁה׃ וַיִּשָּׂא אַהֲרֹן אֶת־יָדָו
כג אֶל־הָעָם וַיְבָרְכֵם וַיֵּרֶד מֵעֲשֹׂת הַחַטָּאת וְהָעֹלָה וְהַשְּׁלָמִים׃ וַיָּבֹא מֹשֶׁה וְאַהֲרֹן
כד אֶל־אֹהֶל מוֹעֵד וַיֵּצְאוּ וַיְבָרְכוּ אֶת־הָעָם וַיֵּרָא כְבוֹד־יהוה אֶל־כָּל־הָעָם׃ וַתֵּצֵא שלישי
אֵשׁ מִלִּפְנֵי יהוה וַתֹּאכַל עַל־הַמִּזְבֵּחַ אֶת־הָעֹלָה וְאֶת־הַחֲלָבִים וַיַּרְא כָּל־הָעָם
א וַיָּרֹנּוּ וַיִּפְּלוּ עַל־פְּנֵיהֶם׃ וַיִּקְחוּ בְנֵי־אַהֲרֹן נָדָב וַאֲבִיהוּא אִישׁ מַחְתָּתוֹ וַיִּתְּנוּ
בָהֵן אֵשׁ וַיָּשִׂימוּ עָלֶיהָ קְטֹרֶת וַיַּקְרִיבוּ לִפְנֵי יהוה אֵשׁ זָרָה אֲשֶׁר לֹא צִוָּה אֹתָם׃

רש"י

יב | **וימצאו.** לשון הושטה והזמנה:

טו | **ויחטאהו.** עשהו כמשפט חטאת: **כראשון.** כעגל שלו:

טז | **ויעשה כמשפט.** המפורש בעולת נדבה ב"ויקרא" (לעיל פרק א):

יז | **וימלא כפו.** היא קמיצה: **מלבד עלת הבקר.** כל אלה עשה אחר עולת התמיד:

יט | **והמכסה.** חלב המכסה את הקרב:

כ | **וישימו את החלבים על החזות.** לאחר התנופה נתנן כהן המניף לכהן אחר להקטירם, נמצאו העליונים למטה:

כב | **ויברכם.** ברכת כהנים: יברכך, יאר, ישא: **וירד.** מעל המזבח:

כג | **ויבא משה ואהרן.** למה נכנסו? מצאתי בפרשת מלואים בברייתא הנוספת על תורת כהנים שלנו (מכילתא דמלואים, פרשתא א, ל): למה נכנס משה עם אהרן? ללמדו על מעשה הקטרת. או לא נכנס אלא לדבר אחר? הריני דן: ירידה וביאה טעונות ברכה, מה ירידה מעין עבודה, אף ביאה מעין עבודה, הא למדת, למה נכנס משה עם אהרן – ללמדו על מעשה הקטרת. דבר אחר, כיון שראה אהרן שקרבו כל הקרבנות ונעשו כל המעשים ולא ירדה שכינה לישראל, היה מצטער ואומר: יודע אני שכעס הקדוש ברוך הוא עלי ובשבילי לא ירדה שכינה לישראל. אמר לו למשה: משה אחי, כך עשית לי, שנכנסתי ונתביישתי; מיד נכנס משה עמו ובקשו רחמים וירדה שכינה לישראל: **ויצאו ויברכו את העם.** אמרו: "ויהי נעם ה' אלהינו עלינו" (תהלים צ, יז), יהי רצון שתשרה שכינה במעשה ידיכם; לפי שכל שבעת ימי המלואים שהעמידו משה למשכן ושמש בו ופרקו בכל יום, לא שרתה בו שכינה, והיו ישראל נכלמים ואומרים למשה: משה רבנו, כל הטורח שטרחנו שתשרה שכינה בינינו ונדע שנתכפר לנו עון העגל, לכך אמר להם: "זה הדבר אשר צוה ה' תעשו וירא אליכם כבוד ה'" (לעיל פסוק ו), אהרן אחי כדאי וחשוב ממני, שעל ידי קרבנותיו ועבודתו תשרה שכינה בכם, ותדעו שהמקום בחר בו:

כד | **וירנו.** כתרגומו:

פרק י

ב | **ותצא אש.** רבי אליעזר אומר: לא מתו בני אהרן אלא על ידי שהורו הלכה בפני משה רבן. רבי ישמעאל

2 **Fire emerged from before the Lord and consumed them.** It is uncertain from where this fire emerged.[11] **And they died before the Lord,** inside the Sanctuary. As will soon be made evident, although the fire killed them, their bodies were not burned, as would have been the case in a regular fire. Rather, their deaths resembled a death by electrocution or by lightning strike, as their bodies remained physically intact.[12]

3 **Moses said to Aaron: This** incident **is that** about **which the Lord spoke, saying: Through those who are near to Me I will be sanctified.**[D] That is, My sanctity will be manifest among those who are close to Me, **and** then **before all the people I will be glorified; and Aaron was silent.** It is possible that before this statement, Aaron cried in shock at the sudden deaths of his sons,[13] but upon hearing Moses' statement he voiced no complaints and remained silent. There is no doubt that Aaron's silence stemmed not from indifference, but from his acceptance of this divine decree.

4 **Moses called Mishael and Eltzafan, the sons of Uzziel,** an **uncle of Aaron.** They were Levites and family members. **And** Moses **said to them: Approach, carry your brethren,** your cousins, **from inside the Sanctuary to outside the camp.**

5 **They approached and carried them by their tunics to outside the camp,** for the dead were not left inside the camp, **as Moses had spoken.** It is clear from the verse that Aaron's sons were not burned in an ordinary manner, as they were carried out in their garments, indicating that the garments were whole and durable enough to pull their wearers with them.[14]

6 **Moses said to Aaron, and to Elazar and to Itamar, his,** Aaron's, other **sons:** Despite the tragedy that has occurred, **you shall not grow out the hair of your heads.** Do not allow your hair to grow wild during the mourning period,[15] **and you shall**

not rend your garments in the manner of mourners, **that you will not die.** If you observe the usual customs of mourning, you will be liable to death, **and** not only will you be punished, but **He will rage against all the congregation,** as you are now their priests.[16] **And your brethren, the entire house of Israel, shall weep** over **the burning that the Lord has burned.** Mourning and weeping are of course a natural response to death. However, you have been consecrated, and you must remain in your posts within the confines of the Tabernacle. Consequently, you must not let their deaths affect you.

7 **From the entrance of the Tent of Meeting you shall not emerge**[D] for the entire period that you are obligated to be within the sacred area, so **that you not die, as the anointing oil of the Lord is upon you.** Since you have been anointed and consecrated for the service, you are no longer private citizens who may act according to their own discretion. **They acted in accordance with the word of Moses,** that is, Aaron and his surviving sons did not display any signs of mourning and they remained in the Tabernacle.

8 **The Lord spoke to Aaron, saying:**[D]

9 **You shall not drink wine or** any **intoxicating drink,**[17] **neither you nor your sons with you, upon your entry into the Tent of Meeting, that you not die;**[D] this is **an eternal statute for your generations.** This prohibition is not restricted to the unique occasion of the inauguration ceremony. Rather, it remains in force for all generations in which the priestly service is performed.

10 The eternal prohibition against intoxicated priests performing the Temple service is not due merely to their presence in the Tent of Meeting. In addition to performing sacrificial rites, the priests must fulfill other functions: **To distinguish** for the

---

DISCUSSION

levelheaded (see verse 9; Rashi, verse 2; *Vayikra Rabba* 12:1). For whatever reason, they brought incense at their own initiative, most likely into the Sanctuary. The Tabernacle service, however, had to be performed in an orderly and highly methodical fashion; there was no place whatsoever for spontaneity. The service did not represent the personal desires of Moses or Aaron to serve; rather, it was based entirely on adherence to commands. Every aspect of the service had to be executed as a precise combination of sacred vessels, the appropriate functionaries, and a meticulous performance of the respective rites. It is through this alone that the Tabernacle was transformed into an effective mechanism. Consequently, even if the fire brought by Aaron's eldest sons was brought out of good intentions, it was nevertheless a strange fire, as it was

estranged from the essential nature of the occasion and even violated its spirit.

10:3 | Through those who are near to Me I will be sanctified: Nadav and Avihu crossed a line, perhaps due to their heightened enthusiasm, and they were swiftly and severely punished as a result. Had this incident involved individuals of unremarkable stature, it would not have left such a mark on the people. The dramatic effect of their deaths on this festive day was made all the more powerful by their closeness to God, as they were next in line of succession to replace Aaron as High Priest. The tragic deaths of Nadav and Avihu displayed the sanctity of God, as holiness always contains a measure of distance and exaltedness; the danger inherent in the blurring of these boundaries was clearly demonstrated before the entire people. Faced with the deaths

of these two holy brothers, the people expressed awe toward the Tabernacle. The sight of the divine fire consuming Aaron's two sons on the celebratory occasion of inaugurating the Tabernacle demonstrated to the people, beyond a shadow of a doubt, that great caution must be exercised with regard to the Temple of God and the services performed therein (see Rashi).

10:7 | From the entrance of the Tent of Meeting you shall not emerge: Although an ordinary priest observes the laws of mourning for immediate relatives that have passed away, the status of Elazar and Itamar on the day of their anointment was similar to that of their father, Aaron the High Priest, who was prohibited from becoming ritually impure for any of his relatives. The verse states that the High Priest must not contract ritual impurity, "as the crown

ב ג ותצא אש מלפני יהוה ותאכל אותם וימתו לפני יהוה: ויאמר משה אל-
אהרן הוא אשר-דבר יהוה | לאמר בקרבי אקדש ועל-פני כל-העם אכבד
ד וידם אהרן: ויקרא משה אל-מישאל ואל אלצפן בני עזיאל דד אהרן ויאמר
ה אלהם קרבו שאו את-אחיכם מאת פני-הקדש אל-מחוץ למחנה: ויקרבו
ו וישאם בכתנתם אל-מחוץ למחנה כאשר דבר משה: ויאמר משה אל-אהרן
ולאלעזר ולאיתמר | בניו ראשיכם אל-תפרעו | ובגדיכם לא-תפרמו ולא תמתו
ועל כל-העדה יקצף ואחיכם כל-בית ישראל יבכו את-השרפה אשר שרף
ז יהוה: ומפתח אהל מועד לא תצאו פן-תמתו כי-שמן משחת יהוה עליכם
ויעשו כדבר משה:
ח ט וידבר יהוה אל-אהרן לאמר: יין ושכר אל-תשת | אתה | ובניך אתך בבאכם
י אל-אהל מועד ולא תמתו חקת עולם לדרתיכם: ולהבדיל בין הקדש ובין

רש״י

אומר: שתויי יין נכנסו למקדש; תדע, שאחר מיתתן הזהיר הנותרים שלא יכנסו שתויי יין למקדש. משל למלך שהיה לו בן בית וכו׳ [נאמן, מצאו עומד על פתח חנויות והתיז את ראשו בשתיקה, ומינה בן בית אחר תחתיו, ואין אנו יודעים מפני מה הרג את הראשון, אלא ממה שמצוה את השני ואמר לא תכנס בפתח חנויות, אנו יודעין שמתוך כך הרג הראשון], כדאיתא בויקרא רבה (יב, א):

ג | הוא אשר דבר וגו׳. היכן דבר? "ונעדתי שמה לבני ישראל ונקדש בכבדי" (שמות כט, מג), אל תקרי 'בכבדי' אלא 'בכבודי'. אמר לו משה לאהרן: אהרן אחי, יודע הייתי שיתקדש הבית במיודעיו של מקום, והייתי סבור או בי או בך, עכשיו רואה אני שהם גדולים ממני וממך: וידם אהרן. וקבל שכר על שתיקתו, ומה שכר קבל? שנתיחד עמו הדבור, שנאמרה לו לבדו פרשת שתויי יין: בקרבי. בבחירי: ועל פני כל העם אכבד. כשהקדוש ברוך הוא עושה דין בצדיקים, מתירא ומתעלה ומתקלס; אם כן באלו, כל שכן ברשעים. וכן הוא אומר: "נורא אלהים ממקדשיך" (תהלים סח, לו), אל תקרי 'ממקדשיך', אלא 'ממקדשיך':

ד | דד אהרן. עוזיאל אחי עמרם היה, שנאמר: "ובני קהת" וגו׳ (שמות ו, יח): שאו את אחיכם וגו׳. כאדם האומר לחברו: העבר את המת מלפני הכלה, שלא לערבב את השמחה:

ה | בכתנתם. של מתים, מלמד שלא נשרפו בגדיהם אלא נשמתם, כמין שני חוטין של אש נכנסו לתוך חטמיהם:

ו | אל תפרעו. אל תגדלו שער, מכאן שאבל אסור בתספרת, אבל אתם אל תערבבו שמחתו של מקום: ולא תמתו. הא אם תעשו – תמותו: ואחיכם כל בית ישראל. מכאן שצרתן של תלמידי חכמים מוטלת על הכל להתאבל בה:

ט | יין ושכר. יין דרך שכרותו: בבאכם אל אהל מועד. אין לי אלא בבאכם להיכל. בגשתם למזבח מנין? נאמר כאן ביאת אהל מועד ונאמר בקדוש ידים ורגלים ביאת אהל מועד (שמות ל, כ), מה להלן עשה גישת מזבח כביאת אהל מועד, אף כאן עשה גישת מזבח כביאת אהל מועד:

י | ולהבדיל. כדי שתבדילו בין עבודה קדושה למחללת. הא למדת שאם עבד – עבודתו פסולה:

DISCUSSION

of the anointing oil of his God is on him" (21:12). Aaron's sons were anointed as well (Rashbam; *Bekhor Shor*; see Rambam, *Sefer Avoda*, *Hilkhot Biat HaMikdash* 2:5, and Ra'avad ad loc.).

10:8| **The Lord spoke to Aaron, saying**: This is an unusual address, as God generally issued His commands to Moses, who then disseminated them. The commentaries discuss whether this prophecy was actually given to Moses, who then repeated it to Aaron, or if this was an exceptional case of a direct revelation to Aaron himself (see Ibn Ezra).

Some explain that Aaron merited this prophecy in reward for his silence. Although it would have been natural for Aaron to weep, emerge from the Tabernacle, or tear his clothes, this would have been inappropriate for his elevated status as High Priest. Since Aaron overcame his inclinations and obeyed Moses' commands to the last detail, God granted him a personal address and a private message (see *Vayikra Rabba* 12:2; Rashi, verse 3).

10:9| **That you not die**: Although not stated explicitly, the fact that this command immediately follows the deaths of Aaron's sons alludes

people **between the sacred and the profane, and between the impure and the pure,**

11 **and to teach the children of Israel all the statutes that the Lord spoke to them at the hand of Moses.** The roles of instructing the people and teaching them to distinguish between the sacred and the profane demands that the priests avoid drunkenness, as this can easily lead to error and confusion.[18]

12 While the tragic incident of the deaths of Nadav and Avihu was
Fourth still resonating in the consciousness of all those present, espe-
aliya cially in the minds of Aaron, Elazar, and Itamar, Moses returns Aaron and his surviving sons to the ceremony of the consecration of the Tabernacle and to their inauguration as priests: **Moses spoke to Aaron, and to Elazar and to Itamar, his surviving sons: Take the meal offering that remains from the fire offerings of the Lord,** after its handful has been sacrificed, **and eat it unleavened beside the altar,** in the Tabernacle courtyard, **as it is a sacred sacrament.**

13 **You shall eat it in a holy place, as it is your allotment,** Aaron, **and the allotment of your sons from the fire offerings of the Lord,** as the majority of meal offerings are eaten by the priests, and it is their sustenance. **For so I was commanded.** This is not a voluntary consumption or a personal gift that I am bestowing upon you; rather, God has commanded that you must eat the meal offering.

14 **You shall eat the breast of waving and the haunch of lifting in a pure place,** not necessarily inside the Sanctuary. This command is more inclusive: **You and your sons and your daughters with you**[D] may partake of this portion, **as they are given as your allotment and the allotments of your sons from the peace offerings of the children of Israel.**

15 **The haunch of lifting and the breast of waving they shall bring** to the altar **with the fire offerings of the fats,** not for burning on the fire like the fats, but **to wave it for a wave offering before the Lord; and it shall be for you and for your sons with you** a gift from the altar, as it were, **as an eternal allotment, as the Lord commanded.**

16 **Moses inquired about the goat of the sin offering,** which
Fifth was supposed to have been eaten by the priests as part of their
aliya service, after the removal of the portions designated for burning on the altar. **And** Moses discovered that **behold, it was burned; and he was angry with Elazar and with Itamar, the surviving sons of Aaron.** Perhaps Moses did not express his anger toward Aaron out of respect for his older brother, or because he held Aaron's sons responsible, since they performed this part of the service.[19] Therefore, Moses addressed Elazar and Itamar, **saying:**

17 **Why didn't you eat the sin offering in the holy place, as it is a sacred sacrament,** and it should have been eaten there? Furthermore, while the breast and haunch are gifts bestowed upon the priests as ministers of the Tabernacle that may be consumed by the members of their households, the sin offering is consumed because **He gave it you to bear the iniquity of the congregation, to atone for them before the Lord.** The consumption of the sin offering by the priests is part of the atonement process, together with the sprinkling of the blood and the sacrifice of the offering. Since its consumption is a part of the service and does not depend on your wishes or your appetite, why have you not eaten the sin offering?

18 **Behold, its blood was not brought to the Sanctuary within.** Moses already taught that the flesh of a sin offering whose blood is brought inside the Sanctuary may not be eaten; rather, it is burned (6:23). In this case, however, the blood was not brought inside the Sanctuary. Therefore, **you should have eaten it in the holy place, as I commanded.** Since I instructed you to eat the sin offering, why did you burn it?

DISCUSSION

to a connection between the prohibition and the circumstances of their demise (Rashi, verse 2; *Vayikra Rabba* 12:1; see commentary on verse 1). In any event, this prohibition applies in a general manner to the sanctity of the Temple.

10:14| **You and your sons and your daughters with you**: The breast and haunch may be eaten by the priests, their wives, their children, and their slaves (*Zevaḥim* 55a). Although these portions must be eaten in sanctity, they are considered the property of the priest to a certain extent, and the priest therefore has a measure of discretion in their consumption. They are not offerings of the most sacred order, and there is no obligation to eat them in a sacred place, as demonstrated by the fact that the wives of the priests may partake of them, even though they are not found inside the Temple.

יא הַחֹל וּבֵין הַטָּמֵא וּבֵין הַטָּהוֹר: וּלְהוֹרֹת אֶת־בְּנֵי יִשְׂרָאֵל אֵת כׇּל־הַחֻקִּים אֲשֶׁר
דִּבֶּר יהוה אֲלֵיהֶם בְּיַד־מֹשֶׁה:
יב וַיְדַבֵּר מֹשֶׁה אֶל־אַהֲרֹן וְאֶל אֶלְעָזָר וְאֶל־אִיתָמָר | בָּנָיו הַנּוֹתָרִים קְחוּ אֶת־ רביעי
הַמִּנְחָה הַנּוֹתֶרֶת מֵאִשֵּׁי יהוה וְאִכְלוּהָ מַצּוֹת אֵצֶל הַמִּזְבֵּחַ כִּי קֹדֶשׁ קׇדָשִׁים
יג הִוא: וַאֲכַלְתֶּם אֹתָהּ בְּמָקוֹם קָדוֹשׁ כִּי חׇקְךָ וְחׇק־בָּנֶיךָ הִוא מֵאִשֵּׁי יהוה כִּי־כֵן
יד צֻוֵּיתִי: וְאֵת חֲזֵה הַתְּנוּפָה וְאֵת | שׁוֹק הַתְּרוּמָה תֹּאכְלוּ בְּמָקוֹם טָהוֹר אַתָּה
טו וּבָנֶיךָ וּבְנֹתֶיךָ אִתָּךְ כִּי־חׇקְךָ וְחׇק־בָּנֶיךָ נִתְּנוּ מִזִּבְחֵי שַׁלְמֵי בְּנֵי יִשְׂרָאֵל: שׁוֹק
הַתְּרוּמָה וַחֲזֵה הַתְּנוּפָה עַל אִשֵּׁי הַחֲלָבִים יָבִיאוּ לְהָנִיף תְּנוּפָה לִפְנֵי יהוה
טז וְהָיָה לְךָ וּלְבָנֶיךָ אִתְּךָ לְחׇק־עוֹלָם כַּאֲשֶׁר צִוָּה יהוה: וְאֵת | שְׂעִיר הַחַטָּאת חמישי
דָּרֹשׁ דָּרַשׁ מֹשֶׁה וְהִנֵּה שֹׂרָף וַיִּקְצֹף עַל־אֶלְעָזָר וְעַל־אִיתָמָר בְּנֵי אַהֲרֹן הַנּוֹתָרִם
יז לֵאמֹר: מַדּוּעַ לֹא־אֲכַלְתֶּם אֶת־הַחַטָּאת בִּמְקוֹם הַקֹּדֶשׁ כִּי קֹדֶשׁ קׇדָשִׁים הִוא
יח וְאֹתָהּ | נָתַן לָכֶם לָשֵׂאת אֶת־עֲוֺן הָעֵדָה לְכַפֵּר עֲלֵיהֶם לִפְנֵי יהוה: הֵן לֹא־
הוּבָא אֶת־דָּמָהּ אֶל־הַקֹּדֶשׁ פְּנִימָה אָכוֹל תֹּאכְלוּ אֹתָהּ בַּקֹּדֶשׁ כַּאֲשֶׁר צִוֵּיתִי:

רש"י

יא| **ולהורת.** למד שאסור שכור בהוראה. יכול יהא חייב מיתה? תלמוד לומר: "אתה ובניך אתך... ולא תמתו" (לעיל פסוק ט), כהנים בעבודתם במיתה ואין חכמים בהוראתם במיתה:

יב| **הנותרים.** מן המיתה, מלמד שאף עליהן נקנסה מיתה על עון העגל, הוא שנאמר: "ובאהרן התאנף ה' מאד להשמידו" (דברים ט, כ), ואין השמד אלא כלוי בנים, שנאמר: "ואשמיד פריו ממעל" (עמוס ב, ט), ותפלתו של משה בטלה מחצה, שנאמר: "ואתפלל גם בעד אהרן בעת ההיא" (דברים שם): **קחו את המנחה.** אף על פי שאתם אוננין ואף על פי שהקדשים אסורים לאונן: **את המנחה.** זו מנחת שמיני ומנחת נחשון (במדבר ז, ג): **ואכלוה מצות.** מה תלמוד לומר? לפי שהיא מנחת צבור ומנחת שעה ואין כיוצא בה לדורות, הצרך לפרש בה דין שאר מנחות:

יג| **וחק בניך.** אין לבנות חק בקדשים: **כי כן צויתי.** באנינות יאכלוה:

יד| **ואת חזה התנופה.** של שלמי צבור: **תאכלו במקום טהור.** וכי את הראשונים אכלו במקום טמא?! אלא הראשונים שהם קדשי קדשים הזקקה אכילתם במקום קדוש, אבל אלו אין צריכים תוך הקלעים, אבל צריכים הם לאכל תוך מחנה ישראל, שהוא טהור מלהכנס שם מצרעים. מכאן שקדשים קלים נאכלין בכל העיר: **אתה ובניך ובנתיך.** אתה ובניך בחלק, אבל בנותיך לא בחלק, אלא אם תתנו להם מתנות רשאות הן לאכל בחזה ושוק. או אינו אלא אף הבנות בחלק? תלמוד לומר: "כי חקך וחק בניך נתנו", חק לבנים ואין חק לבנות:

טו| **על אשי החלבים.** מכאן שהחלבים למטן בשעת תנופה. ויישוב המקראות שלא יכחישו זה את זה, כבר פרשתי שלשתן ב'צו את אהרן' (לעיל ז, ל):

טז| **שעיר החטאת.** שעיר מוספי ראש חדש. ושלשה שעירי חטאות קרבו בו ביום: "קחו שעיר עזים" (לעיל ט, ג), ושעיר נחשון, ושעיר ראש חדש. ומכלן לא נשרף אלא זה. ונחלקו בדבר חכמי ישראל: יש אומרים מפני טמאה שנגעה בו נשרף, ויש אומרים מפני אנינות נשרף, לפי שהוא קדשי דורות, אבל בקדשי שעה סמכו על משה שאמר להם במנחה: "ואכלוה מצות" (לעיל פסוק יב):

דרש דרש. שתי דרישות – מפני מה נשרף זה, ומפני מה נאכלו אלו. כך היא בתורת כהנים (פרק ב, ב): **על אלעזר ועל איתמר.** בשביל כבודו של אהרן, הפך פניו כנגד הבנים וכעס: **לאמר.** אמר להם: השיבוני על דברי:

יז| **מדוע לא אכלתם את החטאת במקום הקדש.** וכי חוץ לקדש אכלוה?! והלא שרפוה! ומהו אומר "במקום הקדש"? אלא אמר להם: שמא חוץ לקלעים יצאה ונפסלה?: **כי קדש קדשים הוא.** ונפסלת ביוצא. והם אמרו לו: לאו. אמר להם: הואיל ובמקום הקדש היתה, מדוע לא אכלתם אותה?: **ואתה נתן לכם לשאת וגו'.** שהכהנים אוכלים ובעלים מתכפרים: **לשאת את עון העדה.** מכאן למדנו ששעיר ראש חדש היה, שהוא מכפר על עון טמאת מקדש וקדשיו, שחטאת שמיני וחטאת נחשון לא לכפרה באו:

יח| **הן לא הובא וגו'.** שאלו הובא היה לכם לשרפה, כמו שנאמר: "וכל חטאת אשר יובא מדמה" וגו' (לעיל ו, כג): **אכול תאכלו אתה.** היה לכם לאכלה אף על פי שאתם אוננים: **כאשר צויתי.** לכם במנחה (לעיל פסוק יב):

19 **Aaron spoke to Moses.** Out of respect for his brother, Moses rebuked Aaron's sons rather than Aaron himself. It is clear, however, that Aaron was involved in this incident, and it is even likely that his sons acted on instructions from him. Consequently, Aaron accepted responsibility for their actions and replied to Moses:[20] **Indeed, today they offered their sin offering and their burnt offering before the Lord, and** such tragedies as **these have befallen me, that had I eaten the sin offering today,** when I am in a state of mourning, **would it have been satisfactory in the eyes of the Lord?**[D] Although I accepted your instructions to remain in the Temple and to refrain from displaying any visible signs of mourning, I am still hurting from my loss. Is it really permitted for me and my sons, whose brothers died today, to partake of sacrificial meat in such a state? The very fact that its consumption is a sacred service is why we should not perform it at such a time, as the service of God must be performed wholly and happily.[21]

20 **Moses heard; it was satisfactory in his eyes.** Although Moses did not instruct Aaron in this manner, he agreed that Aaron and his sons acted properly, which means that their behavior was satisfactory in the eyes of the Lord as well.

Purity and Impurity with Regard to Animals

LEVITICUS 11:1–47

After detailing the laws of the offerings, which are consumed on the altar, the Torah elaborates on the laws of animals that may be consumed by the children of Israel. Additionally, after the completion of the consecration of the Tabernacle, its vessels, and its ministers, it becomes necessary to distinguish between the ritually impure, which is far removed from the sacred, and the ritually pure.

In a broad sense, the concept of impurity refers to that which should be rejected and abhorred to some degree. In the following passages, this concept is used in two respects: An impure animal is a non-kosher animal whose consumption is prohibited to Israel. An item is also described as impure when its impurity can be transmitted to other items, foodstuffs, or people. Impurity of this kind is usually the one discussed in the book of Leviticus. The implications for this latter category of impurity are far greater than for the former, because this type of impurity can be transmitted to other items and because of its relevance to the laws of consecrated items and the Temple, as it is prohibited for an impure item to be found in the Temple or for it to come into contact with consecrated items. Therefore, while the prohibitions stated here relating to the consumption of animals apply to all of Israel, the category of impurity that requires purification, which is also mentioned in these passages, is relevant mainly to the Temple and belongs to the purview of the priests. Perhaps this explains the juxtaposition of these passages to the inauguration of the Temple and also accounts for the fact that these commandments are addressed to Aaron in addition to Moses.

With regard to the commandments contained in these passages, some are perhaps comprehensible to a certain degree, while others must remain categorized as divine decrees beyond human comprehension.

11 1 **The Lord spoke to Moses and to Aaron, saying to them.**

Sixth aliya God addresses Aaron as well as Moses, whether due to the connection between purity and impurity and the matters of the Temple and its consecrated items, or due to the fact that the priests are to be the teachers of Torah to the people.[22]

Hooves that are not split

Split hooves

2 **Speak to the children of Israel, saying: These are the living creatures that you may eat from all the animals**[D] **that are on the earth,** i.e., land animals:

3 **Anything that has hooves,** as opposed to paws, e.g., dogs, cats, and bears,[23] **and** specifically, if **the hooves are split,** like those of sheep, goats, and cows, **and** if, in addition to this, it **brings up the cud,**[B] it regurgitates its food and chews it a second time, **among the animals, that you may eat.**[B]

4 **However, these you shall not eat from those that bring up**

DISCUSSION

10:19 | **Would it have been satisfactory in the eyes of the Lord**: Aaron's reasoning, that he and his sons must refrain from partaking of offerings during the mourning period, is incorporated into the laws of the Temple. Even the High Priest, who is prohibited from emerging from the Temple upon the death of an immediate relative (21:10–12), is prohibited from consuming sacrificial flesh when in a period of mourning (see *Zevaḥim* 15b–16b, 101a; Rashi).

The presentation of this incident sheds an interesting light on the nature of the sacred and the service of the Temple, as well as on the individuals involved in it. Certain spontaneous deviations from the ordained service are considered a strange fire, a breach of the sacred for which one is severely punished, while other deviations, no less personally motivated, are granted divine

יט וידבר אהרן אל־משה הן היום הקריבו את־חטאתם ואת־עלתם לפני יהוה
כ ותקראנה אתי כאלה ואכלתי חטאת היום הייטב בעיני יהוה: וישמע משה
וייטב בעיניו:
א ב וידבר יהוה אל־משה ואל־אהרן לאמר אלהם: דברו אל־בני ישראל לאמר זאת ששי
ג החיה אשר תאכלו מכל־הבהמה אשר על־הארץ: כל ׀ מפרסת פרסה ושסעת
ד שסע פרסת מעלת גרה בבהמה אתה תאכלו: אך את־זה לא תאכלו ממעלי

רש"י

יט | **וידבר אהרן.** אין לשון 'דבור' אלא לשון עז, שנאמר: "וידבר העם" וגו' (במדבר כא, ה). אפשר משה קצף על אלעזר ועל איתמר ואהרן מדבר? הא ידעת שלא היתה אלא מדת כבוד, אמרו: אינו בדין שיהא אבינו יושב ואנו מדברים לפניו, ואינו בדין שיהא תלמיד משיב את רבו. יכול מפני שלא היה באלעזר להשיב? תלמוד לומר: "ויאמר אלעזר הכהן אל אנשי הצבא" וגו' (שם לא, כא), הרי כשרצה דבר לפני משה ולפני הנשיאים. זו מצאתי בספרי של פנים שני (ספרי זוטא לא, כא): **הן היום הקריבו.** מהו אומר? אלא אמר להם משה: שמא זרקתם דמה אוננים, שאונן שעבד חלל? אמר לו אהרן: וכי הם הקריבו שהם הדיוטות? אני הקרבתי, שאני כהן גדול ומקריב אונן: **ותקראנה אתי כאלה.** אפילו לא היו המתים בני, אלא שאר קרובים שאני חייב להיות אונן עליהם כאלו, כגון כל האמורים בפרשת כהנים (להלן כא, ב-ג) שהכהן מטמא להם: **ואכלתי חטאת.** ואם אכלתי, "הייטב" וגו'?: **היום.** אבל אנינות לילה מותר, שאין אונן אלא יום קבורה: **הייטב בעיני ה'.** אם שמעת בקדשי שעה, אין לך להקל בקדשי דורות:

כ | **וייטב בעיניו.** הודה, ולא בוש לומר: לא שמעתי:

פרק יא

א | **אל משה ואל אהרן.** למשה אמר שיאמר לאהרן: **לאמר אלהם.** אמר שיאמר לאלעזר ולאיתמר. או אינו אלא לאמר לישראל? כשהוא אומר: "דברו אל בני ישראל", הרי דבור אמור לישראל, הא מה אני מקיים "לאמר אלהם"? לבנים, לאלעזר ולאיתמר:

ב | **דברו אל בני ישראל.** את כלם השוה להיות שלוחים בדבור זה, לפי ששוו בדמימה וקבלו עליהם גזרת המקום מאהבה: **זאת החיה.** לשון חיים, לפי שישראל דבוקים במקום וראויין להיות חיים, לפיכך הבדילם מן הטמאה וגזר עליהם מצות, ולאמות לא אסר כלום. משל לרופא שנכנס לבקר את החולה וכו', כדאיתא במדרש רבי תנחומא (ו) [משל למה הדבר דומה? לרופא שהלך לבקר שני חולים, ראה אחד מהם שהיה בסכנה, אמר לבני ביתו: תנו לו כל מאכל שהוא מבקש. ראה האחד שעתיד לחיות, אמר להם: כך וכך מאכל יאכל, כך וכך לא יאכל. אמרו לרופא: מה זה, לזה אתה אומר יאכל כל מאכל שהוא מבקש, ולאחר אמרת לא יאכל כך וכך? אמר להם הרופא: לזה שהוא לחיים אמרתי לו זה אכול וזה לא תאכל, אבל אותו שהוא למיתה אמרתי להם כל מה שהוא מבקש תנו לו, שאינו לחיים]: **זאת החיה.** מלמד שהיה משה אוחז בחיה ומראה אותה לישראל: זאת תאכלו וזאת לא תאכלו. "את זה תאכלו" וגו' (להלן פסוק ט) – אף בשרצי המים אוחז מכל מין ומין ומראה להם, וכן בעוף: "ואת אלה תשקצו מן העוף" (להלן פסוק יג), וכן בשרצים: "וזה לכם הטמא" (להלן פסוק כט): **זאת החיה... מכל הבהמה.** מלמד שהבהמה בכלל חיה:

ג | **מפרסת.** כתרגומו: "סדיקא": **פרסה.** פלנט"א בלעז: **ושסעת שסע.** שמבדלת מלמעלה ומלמטה בשתי צפרנים, כתרגומו: "ומטלפן טלפין", שיש שפרסותיו סדוקות מלמעלה ואין שסועות ומבדלות לגמרי, שמלמטה מחברות: **מעלת גרה.** מעלה ומקיאה האכל ממעיה ומחזרת אותו לתוך פיה לכתשו ולטחנו הדק: **גרה.** כך שמו, ויתכן לתתו מגזרת: "מים הנגרים" (שמואל ב' יד, יד), שהוא נגרר אחר הפה. ותרגומו: "פשרא", שעל ידי הגרה האכל נפשר ונמוח: **בבהמה.** תבה יתרה היא לדרשה, להתיר את השליל הנמצא במעי אמו: **אתה תאכלו.** ולא בהמה טמאה. והלא באזהרה היא (להלן פסוק ח)? אלא לעבר עליה בעשה ולא תעשה:

DISCUSSION

approval. Specifically, Aaron's strong intuition that it would be inappropriate for him and his sons to partake of the sacrificial flesh, despite the lack of any divine instruction to that end, is granted divine approval and ultimately established as permanent law. This incident offers insight into the balance between the requirement to fulfill all divine commands, in all their details, and the need for people to sincerely address new realities and respond appropriately to them.

11:2 | **These are the living creatures [*hayya*] that you may eat from all the animals [*behema*]:** In later generations, a *behema* was defined as a domesticated animal, while a *ḥayya* was defined as an undomesticated animal. In the Bible, however, these two terms sometimes overlap or are similar to one another, and they have a broader meaning. This verse indicates that a domesticated animal may also be included in the category of *ḥayya*. *Ḥayya* even includes creeping animals and birds (see Genesis 1:28, 8:1). On the other hand, the verse indicates that *behema* is a broad term that includes all living creatures, in particular the various species of mammal (see Deuteronomy 14:4–5, 32:24; Proverbs 30:30; *Ḥullin* 70b–71a).

BACKGROUND

11:3 | **Brings up the cud:** This refers to a ruminant animal, an animal with four stomachs. Such an animal swallows its food for the first time after little or no chewing, and it descends into the first and second stomachs, the rumen and the reticulum, where it ferments and is broken down. The food is then regurgitated by the animal and chewed for a second time, after which it descends to the third and fourth stomachs, the omasum and the abomasum.

Anything that has hooves, and the hooves are split, and brings up the cud among the animals, that you may eat: These animals belong to the order Artiodactyla, and are also known as even-toed ungulates. The majority of the animals of this order are permitted for consumption.

the cud, and from those that have hooves, that is, they fulfill one criterion or the other, but not both: **The camel, because it brings up the cud, but it does not have hooves; it is impure to you,** and its consumption is prohibited.

5 The hyrax,[B] which lives in rocky terrain in Israel and other regions, you may not consume, **because it brings up the cud but it does not have hooves.** Although the hyrax does not have four stomachs like ruminant animals, it chews in a manner that makes it appear as if it chews its cud. With regard to its feet, while there are nails that resemble hooves at the ends of its toes, it does not have one hoof that includes multiple toes, and consequently **it is impure to you.**

6 **The hare,**[B] **because it** appears as if it **brings up the cud but it does not have hooves,** and **it is** therefore **impure to you.**

7 **And the pig,**[B] **because it has hooves, and its hoof is split,** like those of kosher animals, **but it does not chew the cud** at all. Consequently, **it is impure to you.**

8 **From their flesh you shall not eat, and their carcasses you shall not touch.**[D] The Sages derive from other verses that the latter prohibition applies only to one who wishes to enter the Temple or handle consecrated items, e.g., during a festival pilgrimage,[24] since one may do so only when ritually pure. **They are impure to you**[D] in both senses of the term. Their consumption is prohibited, and their carcasses impart ritual impurity upon contact.

9 **This you may eat from everything that is in the water: All things that have fins**[B] **and scales**[BD] **in the water,** even if they

fall off when the creature is removed from the water.[25] Whether such a creature is **in the seas, or in the rivers, those you may eat.**

Signs of a kosher fish

10 **And all things that do not have fins and scales in the seas and in the rivers, of all** small **creatures that swarm** slowly **in the waters, and of all the living creatures that are in the water,** whether they are fish, such as eels and most cartilaginous fish, or whether they are not fish, e.g., marine mammals such as whales or dolphins, with regard to all these creatures that do not have scales, whether they ascend upon land or not, **they are a destable thing to you.**

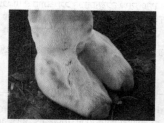

Foot of a camel

Hyrax

Hare

Wild boar

DISCUSSION

11:8 | From their flesh you shall not eat, and their carcasses you shall not touch: Although the Sages explain that this prohibition applies only to one who wishes to handle consecrated items (see *Rosh HaShana* 16b; Rashi; Ba'al HaTurim; see also *Sifra Shemini*, 10:4; Ibn Ezra), the plain meaning of the verse seems to prohibit

touching the carcasses of non-kosher animals altogether. This discrepancy can be understood in light of the fact that the Israelites did not eat non-sacred meat while in the wilderness (see Deuteronomy 12:20–21, and Rashi ad loc.). Rather, they had to sacrifice an animal in the Tabernacle and consume its flesh as sacrificial

meat. It is understandable, then, that in the context of consuming meat, the prohibition against coming into contact with an impure carcass was stated to the generation of the wilderness with regard to all impure carcasses (see 15:31, 17:16).

They are impure to you: Until now, the chapter has dealt mainly with mammals that either have

↤

הַגֵּרָה וּמִמַּפְרִיסֵי הַפַּרְסָה אֶת־הַגָּמָל כִּי־מַעֲלֵה גֵרָה הוּא וּפַרְסָה אֵינֶנּוּ מַפְרִיס

ה טָמֵא הוּא לָכֶם: וְאֶת־הַשָּׁפָן כִּי־מַעֲלֵה גֵרָה הוּא וּפַרְסָה לֹא יַפְרִיס טָמֵא הוּא

ו לָכֶם: וְאֶת־הָאַרְנֶבֶת כִּי־מַעֲלַת גֵּרָה הִוא וּפַרְסָה לֹא הִפְרִיסָה טְמֵאָה הִוא

ז לָכֶם: וְאֶת־הַחֲזִיר כִּי־מַפְרִיס פַּרְסָה הוּא וְשֹׁסַע שֶׁסַע פַּרְסָה וְהוּא גֵּרָה לֹא־

ח יִגָּר טָמֵא הוּא לָכֶם: מִבְּשָׂרָם לֹא תֹאכֵלוּ וּבְנִבְלָתָם לֹא תִגָּעוּ טְמֵאִים הֵם

ט לָכֶם: אֶת־זֶה תֹּאכְלוּ מִכֹּל אֲשֶׁר בַּמָּיִם כֹּל אֲשֶׁר־לוֹ סְנַפִּיר וְקַשְׂקֶשֶׂת בַּמַּיִם

בַּיַּמִּים וּבַנְּחָלִים אֹתָם תֹּאכֵלוּ: וְכֹל אֲשֶׁר אֵין־לוֹ סְנַפִּיר וְקַשְׂקֶשֶׂת בַּיַּמִּים

וּבַנְּחָלִים מִכֹּל שֶׁרֶץ הַמַּיִם וּמִכֹּל נֶפֶשׁ הַחַיָּה אֲשֶׁר בַּמָּיִם שֶׁקֶץ הֵם לָכֶם:

ח | מִבְּשָׂרָם לֹא תֹאכֵלוּ. אֵין לִי אֶלָּא אֵלּוּ, שְׁאָר בְּהֵמָה טְמֵאָה שֶׁאֵין לָהּ סִימָן טָהֳרָה, מִנַּיִן? אָמַרְתָּ קַל וָחֹמֶר: וּמָה אֵלּוּ שֶׁיֵּשׁ בָּהֶן קְצָת סִימָנֵי טָהֳרָה אֲסוּרוֹת וְכוּ': מִבְּשָׂרָם. עַל בְּשָׂרָם בְּאַזְהָרָה, וְלֹא עַל עֲצָמוֹת וְגִידִין וְקַרְנַיִם וּטְלָפַיִם. וּבְנִבְלָתָם לֹא תִגָּעוּ. יָכוֹל יְהוּ יִשְׂרָאֵל מֻזְהָרִים עַל מַגַּע נְבֵלָה? תַּלְמוּד לוֹמַר: "אֱמֹר אֶל הַכֹּהֲנִים" וְגוֹ' (להלן כא, א), כֹּהֲנִים מֻזְהָרִין וְאֵין יִשְׂרָאֵל מֻזְהָרִין. קַל וָחֹמֶר מֵעַתָּה: וּמָה טֻמְאָה קַלָּה מֵהֶן הִזְהִיר בָּהּ חֵלֶק הַכֹּהֵן, טֻמְאַת מֵת חֲמוּרָה לֹא הִזְהִיר בָּהּ חֵלֶק הַכֹּהֵן, טֻמְאַת נְבֵלָה לֹא כָל שֶׁכֵּן? וּמַה תַּלְמוּד לוֹמַר "לֹא תִגָּעוּ"? בָּרֶגֶל.

ט | סְנַפִּיר. אֵלּוּ שֶׁשָּׁט בָּהֶם: קַשְׂקֶשֶׂת. אֵלּוּ קְלָפִין הַקְּבוּעִים בּוֹ, כְּמוֹ שֶׁנֶּאֱמַר: "וְשִׁרְיוֹן קַשְׂקַשִּׂים הוּא לָבוּשׁ" (שמואל א' יז, ה).

י | שֶׁרֶץ. בְּכָל מָקוֹם מַשְׁמָעוֹ דָּבָר נָמוּךְ שֶׁרוֹחֵשׁ וְנָד עַל הָאָרֶץ.

DISCUSSION

➡ hooves or chew the cud. Animals that do not have hooves but walk on their paws, a category that includes most mammals, are prohibited for consumption. Below (verse 27), the Torah states that their carcasses also impart ritual impurity through contact.

11:9 | This you may eat from everything that is in the water: All things that have fins and scales: The two criteria put forward in the verse, fins and scales, are unique, among all sea creatures, to the superclass of bony fish, Osteichthyes (see *Avoda Zara* 39a, 40a; Rambam, *Sefer Kedusha, Hilkhot Ma'akhalot Assurot* 2:12). A fish that does not have scales at all, or whose scales are not actual scales, e.g., the shark, whose skin is covered in placoid scales, which are hard, tooth-like structures that cannot be peeled from the skin itself, is non-kosher (see *Ḥullin* 66). The classification of certain kinds of fish is uncertain, and these fish have been the subject of discussion and debate over the generations.

BACKGROUND

11:5 | Hyrax [*shafan*]: Because this creature is mentioned in Psalms (104:18) and Proverbs (30:26) as an animal that lives in rocky terrain, it is therefore accepted to identify the *shafan* as the rock hyrax, *Procavia capensis syriaca*, which can be found in the cliffs of Israel. The rock hyrax is roughly 50 cm in length and weighs between 4 and 5 kg. Although it looks somewhat like a giant rodent, the rock hyrax actually belongs to a family of animals related to elephants. Some have misidentified the *shafan* as as the rabbit, but no rabbits are native to the Middle East.

11:6 | Hare: The hare, *Lepus capensis*, is the most common rodent mammal in Israel. It grows to a length of about 50 cm, weighs 4–5 kg, and has long ears. The reddish-brown and gray color of its fur allows it to camouflage itself to blend in with the ground. Like the hyrax, the hare moves its mouth in a manner that makes it appear as if it chews its cud (see Rabbi David Zvi Hoffman).

11:7 | Pig: This refers to the wild boar, *Sus scrofa*, a large animal from the pig family. It can grow up to 1.5 m long and 1 m tall. Its body is hairy and covered with stiff bristles. The wild boar is omnivorous and will eat almost anything, including vegetation, birds' eggs, chicks, small rodents, and even carcasses. Unlike ruminants, it has a single stomach. The wild boar is common in northern and central Israel, in marshes, thickets, and agricultural areas. Remainders of pig bones have been uncovered in almost all non-Israelite settlements in Israel.

11:9 | Fins: A bony protrusion on the side of a fish's stomach, which it uses to glide in the water. On the back and tail of a fish there are also fins that do not move.

Scales: Flat protrusions on the skin of a fish that overlap like tiles, with their edges angled toward the tail. There are fish whose scales waste away, as they are weakly connected to the body, and fall off with age.

11 **They shall be a detestable thing to you; you shall not eat from their flesh, and their carcasses you shall detest**. There is an opinion that the requirement to detest their carcasses indicates a prohibition against commercial activity involving creatures prohibited for consumption.[26]

12 The verse reiterates: **Anything that does not have fins and scales in the water,** which includes most water creatures, **is a detestable thing to you.**

13 **And these you shall detest** and distance yourselves from them, **among the fowls;**[D] **they shall not be eaten, they are a detestable thing: the griffon vulture,**[B] **the bearded vulture,**[B] **and the lappet-faced vulture.**[BD]

14 **And the kite,**[B] **and the buzzard**[B] **after its kind.** The prohibition against consuming the buzzard does not apply to a specific bird but to a group of birds of similar or identical species. The Talmud states: There are one hundred non-kosher birds in the east, and they are all species of *ayya*.[27]

15 **Every raven after its kind.** Most species of raven are easily identified, due to their similarity in appearance. There are, however, some birds whose identity as ravens is disputed.[28]

16 And **the ostrich,**[B] a large flightless bird found mainly in desert climates, and **the swift,**[B] **the seagull,**[B]

Griffon vulture

Lappet-faced vulture

Black kite

European honey buzzard

Ostrich

Swift

Common kestrel

Seagull

DISCUSSION

11:13 | And these you shall detest among the fowls: Unlike the Torah's instructions with regard to mammals and fish, the Torah does not provide definitive signs of a kosher bird. Rather, the Torah presents a list of non-kosher birds that constitutes only a minority of all birds (see *Ḥullin* 63b). In general, birds of prey, whether large or small, are prohibited for consumption (see *Ḥullin* 59a, 61a).

The Sages sought to uncover general principles in order to establish definitive signs for differentiating between kosher and non-kosher birds, but these signs are incomplete. It can be assumed that birds that possess some of the signs mentioned by the Sages are kosher, but this does not mean that every bird that lacks these signs is non-kosher. The only birds that are certainly non-kosher are the ones listed in the Torah, and even here there is a measure of uncertainty, as tradition has not definitively identified all the birds mentioned in the Torah's list. This problem was exacerbated by the exile, since different parts of the world have different species of animals and birds, and those who have sought to identify a species were not necessarily familiar with the species living in the Land of Israel.

The griffon vulture [*nesher*], the bearded vulture [*peres*], and the lappet-faced vulture [*ozniyya*]: The precise identifications of the *peres* and the *ozniyya* were already unknown in the period of the Mishna, and opinions are divided with regard to the identity of the *nesher* as well (see *Ḥullin* 61a, 63a; *Tosafot* ad loc.).

BACKGROUND

11:13 | Griffon vulture [*nesher*]: Some identify the *nesher* as the griffon vulture, a large bird that builds its nest and soars at noticeably high altitudes, allowing it to swiftly glide toward its food (see Jeremiah 48:8; Obadiah 1:4; Job 39:27–28; Micah 1:16). Its wingspan stretches to 2.5 m, and it weighs roughly 10 kg. Its head and neck are bare of feathers, as if they were plucked [*nashar*]; perhaps for this reason the vulture is known as the *nesher*. Some opinions identify the *nesher* with the eagle, which was an important Roman symbol, while others maintain that *nesher* is a general term for several different birds of prey. It should be noted that the vulture, or a bird resembling one, was a royal symbol in Egypt and Assyria.

Bearded vulture [*peres*]: In modern times, it has become accepted to identify the *peres* as the bearded vulture, which is known to drop its prey from high altitudes in order to shatter [*pores*] its bones. In Arabic it is known as *kasr al-'itham*, which means bonebreaker. In the nineteenth century this vulture nested in all rocky areas of Israel. The bearded vulture is roughly 100–115 cm in length, with a wingspan of 265–280 cm, and weighs between ←

596

יא יב וְשֶׁקֶץ יִהְיוּ לָכֶם מִבְּשָׂרָם לֹא תֹאכֵלוּ וְאֶת־נִבְלָתָם תְּשַׁקֵּצוּ: כֹּל אֲשֶׁר אֵין־לוֹ
יג סְנַפִּיר וְקַשְׂקֶשֶׂת בַּמָּיִם שֶׁקֶץ הוּא לָכֶם: וְאֶת־אֵלֶּה תְּשַׁקְּצוּ מִן־הָעוֹף לֹא
יד יֵאָכְלוּ שֶׁקֶץ הֵם | אֶת־הַנֶּשֶׁר וְאֶת־הַפֶּרֶס וְאֵת הָעָזְנִיָּה: וְאֶת־הַדָּאָה וְאֶת־הָאַיָּה
טו טז לְמִינָהּ: אֵת כָּל־עֹרֵב לְמִינוֹ: וְאֵת בַּת הַיַּעֲנָה וְאֶת־הַתַּחְמָס וְאֶת־הַשָּׁחַף

רש"י

יא| וְשֶׁקֶץ יִהְיוּ. לֶאֱסֹר אֶת עֵרוּבֵיהֶם, אִם יֵשׁ בּוֹ בְּנוֹתֵן טַעַם: מִבְּשָׂרָם. אֵינוֹ מֻזְהָר עַל הַסְּנַפִּירִים וְעַל הָעֲצָמוֹת: וְאֶת נִבְלָתָם תְּשַׁקֵּצוּ. לְרַבּוֹת יַבְחוּשִׁין שֶׁסִּנְנָן. יַבְחוּשִׁין מוישרונ"ש בְּלַעַז:

יב| כֹּל אֲשֶׁר אֵין לוֹ וְגוֹ'. מַה תַּלְמוּד לוֹמַר? שֶׁיָּכוֹל אֵין לִי שֶׁיְּהֵא מֻתָּר אֶלָּא הַמַּעֲלֶה סִימָנִין שֶׁלּוֹ לַיַּבָּשָׁה, הִשִּׁירָן בַּמַּיִם מִנַּיִן? תַּלְמוּד לוֹמַר: "כֹּל אֲשֶׁר אֵין לוֹ סְנַפִּיר וְקַשְׂקֶשֶׂת בַּמָּיִם" – הָא אִם הָיוּ לוֹ בַּמַּיִם, אַף עַל פִּי שֶׁהִשִּׁירָן בָּעֲלִיָּתוֹ, מֻתָּר:

יג| לֹא יֵאָכְלוּ. לְחַיֵּב אֶת הַמַּאֲכִילָן לִקְטַנִּים, שֶׁכָּךְ מַשְׁמָעוֹ: לֹא יְהוּ נֶאֱכָלִין עַל יָדְךָ. אוֹ אֵינוֹ אֶלָּא לְאָסְרָן בַּהֲנָאָה? תַּלְמוּד לוֹמַר: "לֹא תֹאכְלוּ" (דברים יד, יב), בַּאֲכִילָה אֲסוּרִין, בַּהֲנָאָה מֻתָּרִין. כָּל עוֹף שֶׁנֶּאֱמַר בּוֹ 'לְמִינָהּ', 'לְמִינוֹ', 'לְמִינֵהוּ', יֵשׁ בְּאוֹתוֹ הַמִּין שֶׁאֵין דּוֹמִין זֶה לָזֶה לֹא בְּמַרְאֵיהֶם וְלֹא בִּשְׁמוֹתֵיהֶם, וְכֻלָּן מִין אֶחָד:

טז| הַנֵּץ. אושטוי"ר:

BACKGROUND

4.5 and 8 kg. It has sharp-edged wings and a wedge-shaped tail.

11:13| **Lappet-faced vulture** [*ozniyya*]: Different identities and etymologies have been suggested for this bird. According to Radak, the word derives from the root *ayin-zayin-zayin*, denoting might. The Mishna refers to this bird as the *oz* (*Kelim* 17:14). According to the Sages, the *ozniyya* is solitary and does not live near settlements (*Ḥullin* 62a). The Septuagint translates *ozniyya* as the white-tailed eagle, *Haliaeetus albicilla*, which is rarely sighted in Israel. As such, it is commonly accepted to identify the *ozniyya* with the lappet-faced vulture, *Torgos tracheliotus*, from the order Accipitriformes. The lappet-faced vulture's neck and head are bald and pink, it has a wingspan of 3 m, and it can weigh as much as 14 kg. It has a large, powerful beak that can tear through the skin of animals and break bones. Some opinions maintain that the *ozniyya* is the cinereous vulture, *Aegypius monachus*, which passes through Israel but is rarely sighted there nowadays (see *Encyclopaedia Biblica*).

11:14| **Kite** [*da'a*]: The Sages consider *da'a* and *ayya* as general terms for various birds with similar characteristics (*Ḥullin* 63). The *da'a* is also known as the *dayya* (see Onkelos). It is depicted as a desert bird that gathers in groups to sleep and eat (see Isaiah 34:15) and is commonly identified as the black kite, *Milvus migrans*, a scavenger bird from the family Accipitridae, which can be found in Israel. The black kite weighs from 600 to 1,000 g, is 55–60 cm in length, and has a wingspan of between 135 and 150 cm. It hunts mice, medium-size birds, and chicks, but it feeds from carrion and trash as well and will occasionally snatch food that has been abandoned or left in the open. It nests in trees or on rocks.

Buzzard [*ayya*]: The *ayya* is described in Job (28:7) as a bird that can see across great distances. Some identify it as the common buzzard, *Buteo buteo*, a nomadic bird of prey from the family Accipitridae, whose wingspan is about 120 cm and can weigh up to 900 g. Alternatively, it is identified as the European honey buzzard, *Pernis apivorus*, also a nomadic bird of prey from the family Accipitridae, which may be found in Israel. It is of medium size, weighing from 460 to 800 g, with a body length of 53–58 cm and a wingspan of 145 cm.

11:16| **Ostrich** [*bat haya'ana*]: The identity of this bird, like that of many others listed here, is uncertain. The term is mentioned elsewhere in the Bible among desert animals and birds (Isaiah 34:13; Jeremiah 50:9; Micah 1:8). Its name probably stems from the root *vav-ayin-nun* or *yod-ayin-nun*, which means "greedy" in Syriac Aramaic. Alternatively, it comes from the root *ayin-nun-yod* or *ayin-nun-heh*, which refers to the screeching sound [*anot*] it makes. Some opinions, based on *Targum Onkelos* and *Targum Yonatan*, identify the *bat haya'ana* as the ostrich, *Struthio camelus* (Rav Se'adya Gaon; Malbim). The ostrich once populated the deserts of Syria, Iraq, the Arabian Peninsula, and the Negev. Ostriches reach a height of approximately 2.5 m and a weight of 150 kg. Others, however, note that the *bat haya'ana* is listed in the verse together with nocturnal birds of prey from the owl family, and therefore identify it as the pharaoh eagle-owl, *Bubo ascalaphus*, which is approximately 40 cm long, weighs about 2 kg, and emits a howling sound.

Swift [*taḥmas*]: Based on the root of its name, *ḥet-mem-samekh*, which denotes robbery, commentaries and researchers alike maintain that the *taḥmas* is a bird that is characterized by snatching or theft. Indeed, *Targum Yonatan* translates *taḥmas* as "thief," while Onkelos translates it as *tzitza*, the swift, *Apus apus*, which is noted for the manner in which it snatches flying insects during its flight. Some identify the *taḥmas* with nightjars, *Caprimulgus*, small nocturnal birds of prey, which are also known by this name in modern Hebrew. The nightjar weighs roughly 80 g and is also known for preying on flying insects. Others suggest that the *taḥmas* is the common kestrel, *Falco tinnunculus*, or *baz* in modern Hebrew, whose name also refers to looting [*biza*] or stealing. The common kestrel is a brown, speedy bird of prey that can be found throughout Israel. It is the size of a large pigeon, with a wingspan of 70–80 cm and a weight of roughly 150 g; it feeds on birds, rodents, and insects.

Seagull [*shaḥaf*]: Following the Septuagint, which translates *shaḥaf* as λάρονα, *laron*, some identify it with the seagull, *Larus*, called *shaḥaf* in modern Hebrew. Several species of seagull may be found near water sources in Israel. Its size ranges from 25 to 70 cm, its wings are long and sharp, and it has three webbed toes. It feeds on fish, carrion, and trash.

and the sparrow hawk[B] **after its kind.**

17 **The little owl,**[B] **the fish owl,**[B] a coastal bird that snatches fish from the sea,[29] **and the short-eared owl.**[B]

18 **The barn owl,**[B] **the eagle-owl,**[B] **and the roller.**[B]

19 **The stork [ḥasida].**[B] Although *ḥasida* refers to the stork in modern Hebrew, the true identity of the *ḥasida* was a matter of disagreement among Jews in the Middle Ages. Jews living in central and eastern Europe considered the stork a non-kosher bird, while the Jews of Spain considered it kosher.[30] And **the heron,**[B] a bird similar to the *ḥasida,* **after its kind, the hoopoe,**[B]

and the bat.[B] The bat is a mammal, not a bird. It is listed here among the fowl because the Torah does not use modern zoological categories. The Hebrew for fowl, *of* is literally rendered flying creatures, which include the bat.

20 **Every flying swarming creature that walks on all fours,** flying insects that have four legs and two additional limbs, which are not feet but are used for walking, e.g., ants, each of these creatures **is a detestable thing to you.**

21 **However, this you may eat from all flying swarming**

Eurasian sparrow hawk

Little owl

Short-eared owl

Barn owl

Brown fish owl

Eagle-owl

Roller

Egyptian vulture

Heron

Hoopoe

Bat

BACKGROUND

Sparrow hawk [*netz*]: Based on the translation appearing in the Septuagint, *ieraka*, the *netz* has been identified as the Eurasian sparrow hawk, *Accipiter nisus*, one of the most common and noticeable birds of prey in Israel (see Rashi here and *Ḥullin* 63a). The Eurasian sparrow hawk is 30–40 cm in length, while its wingspan reaches up to 65 cm. Its back is brownish-gray, and it has a striped tail. It would seem that the phrase "the sparrow hawk [*netz*] after its kind" includes other types of birds of prey of similar size that are found in Israel, such as the peregrine falcon, *Falco peregrinus*; the Eurasian hobby, *Falco subbuteo*; the lanner falcon, *Falco biarmicus*; and the saker falcon, *Falco cherrug*. The Midrash refers to

the fact that the *netz* is a bird hunter, as it states: To what was Israel comparable at that hour? To a pigeon fleeing from a *netz* (*Mekhilta, Beshalah, Masekhta deVayehi* 2).

11:17 | Little owl [*kos*]: The *kos* is depicted in Psalms (102:7) as a solitary desert bird that inhabits wastelands and ruins. Aramaic translations, the Septuagint, and the majority of commentaries and researchers identify the *kos* as the little owl, *Athene noctua saharae*, a small nocturnal bird of prey from the owl family. The little owl measures up to 21 cm, with a wingspan of approximately 60 cm; the weight of an adult can reach up to 150 g. The little owl is commonly found in open areas and dwells among ruins and

in rocky terrain. Some claim that the *kos* is a water bird, e.g., the pelican, due to the fact that it is listed alongside the *shalakh*.

Fish owl [*shalakh*]: According to the Sages and the Septuagint, the *shalakh* snatches fish from the sea (*Ḥullin* 63a). Some claim that it is the osprey, *Pandion haliaetus*, which almost entirely feeds off fish. According to the Septuagint, it is the cormorant, which dives into the sea to catch fish and is found near large bodies of water in Israel. Researchers suggest other possibilities: the pelican; the white-throated kingfisher, *Halcyon smyrnensis*; and the pied kingfisher, *Ceryle rudis*. Due to the mention of this bird alongside the *yanshuf*, some maintain that it is the brown

↢

598

יז יח וְאֶת־הַנֵּץ לְמִינֵהוּ: וְאֶת־הַכּוֹס וְאֶת־הַשָּׁלָךְ וְאֶת־הַיַּנְשׁוּף: וְאֶת־הַתִּנְשֶׁמֶת
יט וְאֶת־הַקָּאָת וְאֶת־הָרָחָם: וְאֵת הַחֲסִידָה הָאֲנָפָה לְמִינָהּ וְאֶת־הַדּוּכִיפַת וְאֶת־
כ כא הָעֲטַלֵּף: כֹּל שֶׁרֶץ הָעוֹף הַהֹלֵךְ עַל־אַרְבַּע שֶׁקֶץ הוּא לָכֶם: אַךְ אֶת־זֶה תֹּאכְלוּ

רש״י

יז | שָׁלָךְ. פֵּרְשׁוּ רַבּוֹתֵינוּ, זֶה הַשּׁוֹלֶה דָּגִים מִן הַיָּם, וְזֶהוּ שֶׁתִּרְגֵּם אוּנְקְלוֹס: "וְשָׁלֵינוּנָא": כּוֹס וְיַנְשׁוּף. הֵם צוֹאִיטוּ״ש הַצּוֹעֲקִים בַּלַּיְלָה, וְיֵשׁ לָהֶם לְסָתוֹת כְּאָדָם. וְעוֹד אַחֵר דּוֹמֶה לוֹ שֶׁקּוֹרִין ייב״ן:

יח | תִּנְשֶׁמֶת. הִיא קלב״א שורי״ץ, וְדוֹמָה לְעַכְבָּר, וּפוֹרַחַת בַּלַּיְלָה, וְ'תִנְשֶׁמֶת' הָאֲמוּרָה בַּשְּׁרָצִים הִיא דּוֹמָה לָהּ, וְאֵין לָהּ עֵינַיִם, וְקוֹרִין לָהּ טלפ״א:

יט | הַחֲסִידָה. זוֹ דַּיָּה לְבָנָה, ציגוני״א, וְלָמָּה נִקְרָא שְׁמָהּ 'חֲסִידָה'? שֶׁעוֹשָׂה חֲסִידוּת עִם חַבְרוֹתֶיהָ בִּמְזוֹנוֹת: הָאֲנָפָה. הִיא דַּיָּה רַגְזָנִית, וְנִרְאֶה לִי, שֶׁהוּא שֶׁקּוֹרִין הײרו״ן: הַדּוּכִיפַת. תַּרְנְגוֹל הַבָּר, וְכַרְבָּלְתּוֹ כְּפוּלָה, וּבְלַעַז הרופ״א, וְלָמָּה נִקְרָא שְׁמוֹ 'דּוּכִיפַת'? שֶׁהוֹדוֹ כָּפוּת, וְזוֹ הִיא כַּרְבָּלְתּוֹ, וְ'נַגַּר טוּרָא' נִקְרָא עַל שֵׁם מַעֲשָׂיו, כְּמוֹ שֶׁפֵּרְשׁוּ רַבּוֹתֵינוּ בְּמַסֶּכֶת גִּטִּין בְּפֶרֶק 'מִי שֶׁאֲחָזוֹ' (דף סח ע״ב):

כ | שֶׁרֶץ הָעוֹף. הֵם הַדַּקִּים הַנְּמוּכִים הָרוֹחֲשִׁין עַל הָאָרֶץ, כְּגוֹן זְבוּבִים וּצְרָעִין וְיַתּוּשִׁין וַחֲגָבִים:

BACKGROUND

fish owl, *Ketupa zeylonensis*, a small nocturnal bird of prey from the owl family, which also hunts fish.

Short-eared owl [*yanshuf*]: According to Isaiah (34:10–11), the *yanshuf* is a bird that lives in ruins and wastelands. The commentaries maintain that it is a nocturnal bird whose name is derived from the noun *neshef*, meaning "night" (Ibn Ezra; Radak), or from the sounds it emits when exhaling [*neshifa*]. Onkelos and the Talmud (*Nidda* 23a) identify it by the Aramaic term *kifofa*, a bird that is similar in appearance to a monkey [*kof*], in that its eyes are situated at the front of its head. This description fits the nocturnal birds of prey from the owl family. Nowadays, this is indeed the accepted identification of the *yanshuf*. Two species of owl are found in Israel: the long-eared owl, *Asio otus*, and the short-eared owl, *Asio flammeus*. Their length can reach up to 40 cm, their wingspans are about 1 m, and they weigh up to 300 g.

11:18| **Barn owl [*tinshemet*]**: The barn owl, *Tyto alba*, is a common nocturnal bird from the owl family. Onkelos calls it *baveta*, while the Talmud refers to it as *ba'ut* (*Ḥullin* 63a). Its length is 34 cm, and it is recognizable by the heart-shaped feathers around its eyes. The barn owl lives in pits, ruins, and caves and hunts field mice and small birds.

Eagle-owl [*ka'at*]: The *ka'at* lives in wastelands and desolated areas (Isaiah 34:11; Zephaniah 2:14; Psalms 102:7). Its name alludes to its habit of vomiting [*haka'a*] undigested food pellets, something done primarily by nocturnal birds of prey. Some identify the *ka'at* with the eagle-owl, a desert owl, since the *ka'at* is mentioned in the verse alongside other nocturnal birds of prey. Others suggest that it is the houbara bustard, *Chlamydotis undulata*, a large land bird with long legs and an elongated neck. Its length extends up to 65 cm, with a wingspan of 150 cm.

Roller [*raḥam*]: The translation of *raḥam* as the roller follows the Talmud (*Ḥullin* 63a), *Targum Yonatan*, and the meaning of a similar Arabic term. The roller gets its name from the aerial acrobatics some of these birds perform during courtship or territorial flights. Rollers resemble crows in size and build but are colored blue, pink, or brown. Rashi explains that its name derives from the fact that its arrival signals the coming rainfalls, which are called *raḥamim*, mercy. Rav Se'adya Gaon identifies the *raḥam* as the Egyptian vulture, *Neophron percnopterus*, based on the fact that this is its name in Arabic. The Egyptian vulture is approximately 60 cm in length, with a wingspan of 150–170 cm, and it weighs up to about 2 kg. Some commentaries contend that the *raḥam* is a nocturnal bird of prey, since it is mentioned alongside the *ka'at* and the *tinshemet*.

11:19| **Stork [*hasida*]**: The *ḥasida* is mentioned in the Bible as a migratory bird that nests in juniper trees (Jeremiah 8:7; Zechariah 5:9; Psalms 104:17; Job 39:13). *Targum Yonatan* and the Talmud identify it as the white *dayya*, which Rashi understands to be the stork, which is from the order Ciconiiformes, or a related species. The Septuagint and the Vulgate identify it in a similar fashion. The stork commonly lives near swamps or on riverbanks and subsists on a diet of frogs, insects, young birds, lizards, and rodents. Ancient cultures viewed the stork as a symbol of dedication and respect for one's parents. The Talmud describes it as a bird that performs acts of kindness [*ḥesed*] with its young and others of its kind (*Ḥullin* 63a).

Heron [*anafa*]: According to the Talmud (*Ḥullin* 63a), the *anafa* is similar to the *ḥasida* in appearance and in its flight. It is accepted to identify the *anafa* with the heron, an aquatic bird from the family Ardeidae, which resembles the *ḥasida* (see Rashi). Several species of heron are found in Israel. While these species differ in size, herons all possess long legs, a long neck, and a long beak.

Hoopoe [*dukhifat*]: According to the Talmud (*Ḥullin* 63a), this is referring to a bird whose comb appears bent [*hodo kafut*]. The Aramaic translations refer to it as *naggar tura*, which the Talmud (*Gittin* 68a) identifies as a wild rooster. According to the Septuagint, as well as the Latin translations, the *dukhifat* is identified as the hoopoe, *Upupa epops*, a bird with a distinctive colorful comb on its head consisting of feathers that appear either folded over or spread out. Its length is roughly 28 cm, with a wingspan of about 44 cm, and its weight ranges from 46 to 70 g.

Bat [*atalef*]: From the order Chiroptera, the bat is a flying mammal that lives in trees and caves. It is a nocturnal creature and sustains itself on insects and fruit. There are dozens of species of bats in Israel.

creatures that walk on all fours: those that have jointed legs above their feet, to leap with them upon the earth. Some insects from the grasshopper family have, in addition to four legs for walking, another two large and tall legs with which they hop from place to place. These species are permitted for consumption, although here, too, the identities and classification of the species of grasshopper have not been sufficiently clarified. It should be noted that many North African and Yemenite Jews consume grasshoppers, based on traditions they have maintained.

22 These of them you may eat: the locust after its kind, the bald locust after its kind, the cricket after its kind, and the grasshopper after its kind. In summary, flying swarming creatures are generally prohibited for consumption, with the exception of a few permitted species.

23 But all flying swarming creatures that have four feet are a detestable thing to you.

24 By these creatures that will be enumerated below you shall become impure. Not only is their consumption prohibited, but also anyone who touches their carcasses shall be impure until the evening.

25 And furthermore, anyone who carries some of their carcasses, even without touching them,[31] e.g., one who carries their carcasses inside a sack, shall wash his garments, and be

impure until the evening. The act of carrying them renders him and his garments ritually impure.

26 In addition, with regard to any animal that has hooves, but they are not split, e.g., a horse, which has round hooves that are not split, or it does not bring up the cud, it is impure to you. Their carcasses also impart impurity through contact and through carrying; anyone who touches their carcasses shall become impure.

27 And likewise, anything that walks on its paws, that does not have hooves, among all beasts that walk on all fours, a category that includes most mammals, they are impure to you; anyone who touches their carcasses shall be impure until the evening.

28 And similarly, one who carries their carcasses shall wash his garments and shall be impure until the evening; they are impure to you.

29 And this is impure to you among the swarming creatures that teem upon the earth. These are small creatures that do not necessarily belong to the same zoological category: the marten,[B] the mouse, and the spiny-tailed lizard[B] after its kind. Although some opinions maintain that *tzav* refers to a turtle, as it does in modern Hebrew, many commentaries understand that the verse is referring to a different creature.[32]

30 The shrew,[B] the monitor,[B] the lizard, the skink,[B] and the

Grasshopper with jointed leg

Marten

Leech

Egyptian spiny-tailed lizard

Desert monitor

Skink

Shrew

BACKGROUND

11:29| Marten [*ḥoled*]: According to the *Sifra* (*Shemini* 5:4) and Onkelos, this is a rat, genus *Rattus*. However, many commentaries and researchers identify the *ḥoled* as the Middle East mole-rat, *Spalax ehrenbergi*, referred to as *ishut* in the Mishna. This is a tailless rodent with very short legs, a member of the Spalacidae family, that is

commonly found throughout Israel. It is 12–25 cm in length, with a cylindrical, ungainly body, and is covered with velvety gray fur. Its eyes are atrophied and sunken beneath its skin. The mole-rat lives in underground tunnels, is sustained by roots and tubers, and is harmful to agriculture. Other scholars identify the *ḥoled* as a member of

the weasel family, the *ḥulda* of the Mishna. Based on the fact that it is described as eating both bread and fowl, it is probably the stone marten. Professor Mordechai Kislev contends that *ḥoled* is a general term for all rodents larger than a mouse.

Spiny-tailed lizard [*tzav*]: According to the Sages (*Sifra* 6:7; *Ḥullin* 127a) and the Aramaic

מִכֹּל שֶׁרֶץ הָעוֹף הַהֹלֵךְ עַל־אַרְבַּע אֲשֶׁר־לא כְרָעַיִם מִמַּעַל לְרַגְלָיו לְנַתֵּר בָּהֵן לוֹ
כב עַל־הָאָרֶץ: אֶת־אֵלֶּה מֵהֶם תֹּאכֵלוּ אֶת־הָאַרְבֶּה לְמִינוֹ וְאֶת־הַסָּלְעָם לְמִינֵהוּ
כג וְאֶת־הַחַרְגֹּל לְמִינֵהוּ וְאֶת־הֶחָגָב לְמִינֵהוּ: וְכֹל שֶׁרֶץ הָעוֹף אֲשֶׁר־לוֹ אַרְבַּע רַגְלָיִם
כד כה שֶׁקֶץ הוּא לָכֶם: וּלְאֵלֶּה תִּטַּמָּאוּ כָּל־הַנֹּגֵעַ בְּנִבְלָתָם יִטְמָא עַד־הָעָרֶב: וְכָל־
כו הַנֹּשֵׂא מִנִּבְלָתָם יְכַבֵּס בְּגָדָיו וְטָמֵא עַד־הָעָרֶב: לְכָל־הַבְּהֵמָה אֲשֶׁר הִוא מַפְרֶסֶת
פַּרְסָה וְשֶׁסַע ׀ אֵינֶנָּה שֹׁסַעַת וְגֵרָה אֵינֶנָּה מַעֲלָה טְמֵאִים הֵם לָכֶם כָּל־הַנֹּגֵעַ
כז בָּהֶם יִטְמָא: וְכֹל ׀ הוֹלֵךְ עַל־כַּפָּיו בְּכָל־הַחַיָּה הַהֹלֶכֶת עַל־אַרְבַּע טְמֵאִים הֵם
כח לָכֶם כָּל־הַנֹּגֵעַ בְּנִבְלָתָם יִטְמָא עַד־הָעָרֶב: וְהַנֹּשֵׂא אֶת־נִבְלָתָם יְכַבֵּס בְּגָדָיו
כט וְטָמֵא עַד־הָעָרֶב טְמֵאִים הֵמָּה לָכֶם: וְזֶה לָכֶם הַטָּמֵא בַּשֶּׁרֶץ הַשֹּׁרֵץ
ל עַל־הָאָרֶץ הַחֹלֶד וְהָעַכְבָּר וְהַצָּב לְמִינֵהוּ: וְהָאֲנָקָה וְהַכֹּחַ וְהַלְּטָאָה וְהַחֹמֶט

רש"י

כא| **על ארבע.** ארבע רגלים: **ממעל לרגליו.** סמוך לצוארו יש לו כמין שתי רגלים לבד ארבע רגליו, וכשרוצה לעוף ולקפוץ מן הארץ מתחזק באותן שתי כרעים ופורח. ויש מהן הרבה באותן שקורין לנגוסט"א, אבל אין אנו בקיאין בהן, שארבעה סימני טהרה נאמרו בהם: ארבע רגלים וארבע כנפים וקרסלין – אלו הכתובים כאן, וכנפיו חופין את רובו. וכל סימנים הללו מצוים באותן שבינותינו, אבל יש שראשן ארוך, ויש שאין להם זנב, וצריך שיהא שמו 'חגב', ובזה אין אנו יודעים להבדיל ביניהן:

כג| **וכל שרץ העוף וגו'.** בא ולמד שאם יש לו חמש טהור:

כד| **ולאלה.** העתידין להאמר בענין למטה: **תטמאו.** כלומר, בנגיעתם יש טומאה:

כה| **וכל הנשא מנבלתם.** כל מקום שנאמרה טומאת משא, חמורה מטומאת מגע, שהיא טעונה כבוס בגדים:

כו| **מפרסת פרסה ושסע איננה שסעת.** כגון גמל, שפרסתו סדוקה למעלה אבל למטה היא מחוברת. כאן למדך שנבלת בהמה טמאה מטמאה, ובענין שבסוף הפרשה (להלן פסוקים לט-מ) פרש על בהמה טהורה:

כז| **על כפיו.** כגון כלב ודב וחתול: **טמאים הם לכם.** למגע:

כט| **וזה לכם הטמא.** כל טומאות הללו אינן לאסור אכילה, אלא לטומאה ממש להיות טמא במגען, ונאסר לאכול תרומה וקדשים וליכנס למקדש: **החלד.** מוסטיל"א: **והצב.** פרויי"ט שדומה לצפרדע:

ל| **אנקה.** הריצו"ן: **הלטאה.** לויסרד"א: **חמט.** לימצ"א:

BACKGROUND

translations (*Targum Yonatan*; *HaShomroni*; *HaPeshitata*) the *tzav* is a type of lizard. The Septuagint and the Latin translation of the Bible identify the *tzav* as the crocodile. Researchers maintain that it is the Egyptian spiny-tailed lizard, *Uromastyx aegyptia*, a large lizard from the Agamidae family commonly found in the Negev. Its length is approximately 75 cm, and it weighs up to 3 kg.

11:30| **Shrew [*anaka*]**: Onkelos identifies this as the *yala*. Based on the description in the Talmud (*Bava Batra* 4a), the *yala* is a hedgehog, perhaps the southern white-breasted hedgehog, *Erinaceus concolor*. This is the opinion of Rashi as well. According to the Septuagint and the Latin translation, the *anaka* is the shrew, *Crocidura*, a small, mouse-like mammal. Some researchers argue that the creature's name indicates that it emits the sound of a groan [*anaka*], and they therefore identify it as a type of lizard that produces sounds, e.g., the Mediterranean house gecko, the fan-fingered gecko, *Ptyodactylus hasselquistii guttatus*, or the common chameleon, *Chamaeleon vulgaris*. According to the *Arukh*, the *anaka* is the leech, subclass Hirudinea, a parasitic worm that obtains its nourishment by sucking the blood of animals.

Monitor [*ko'aḥ*]: According to the Septuagint and the Latin translation, the *ko'aḥ* is the chameleon. Nowadays, it is accepted to identify the *ko'aḥ* as the desert monitor, *Varanus griseus*. The longest lizard in Israel, it can reach a length of up to 1.5 m and weigh up to 3 kg. The desert monitor's skin appears yellowish-gray, and it is found primarily in the Negev desert.

Skink [*ḥomet*]: According to the Septuagint and the Latin translation of the Bible, *ḥomet* is a general term for a lizard. Some claim that it is a specific lizard. Rav Se'adya Gaon translates it to Arabic as *al ḥarba'*, a chameleon. Researchers identify the *ḥomet* as a skink, e.g., the wedge-snouted skink, *Trachylepis acutilabris*, from the Scincidae family. Skinks are lizards that resemble snakes; they have very short legs and tough, stretched skin. Rashi and other commentaries identify the *ḥomet* as a type of snail (see *Tosafot Rid*, *Ḥagiga* 11b).

chameleon [**tinshamet**].^B The *tinshemet* that appears above in the list of non-kosher birds is different from the swarming creature of the same name listed here, whose identity is uncertain. Some explain that it is called the *tinshemet* due to the sound of its breathing [*neshima*].

31 **These are those that are impure to you among all the swarming creatures,** in the sense that **anyone who touches them when they are dead shall be impure until the evening.** In addition to the prohibition against eating these creatures, which is due to their lack of kosher signs, they also impart ritual impurity to one who touches their carcasses. Since these swarming creatures are commonly found in human habitations, especially in rural areas, the impurity due to swarming creatures is particularly widespread.

32 **And** not only is a person who touches them rendered ritually impure, but **anything upon which some of** these swarming creatures **may fall when they are dead shall become impure.** The verse specifies: **From any wooden implement, or garment, or leather, or sackcloth, any** fashioned **item with which work is done,** which is designed to be used for work, not raw material or a vessel that is still being processed,³³ **it shall be brought into water,** immersed, **and it shall be impure until the evening; and** then it will **be purified.**

33 **And any earthenware vessel into which any of them falls, anything that is** found **in it shall become impure,** even if the dead swarming creature did not come into contact with it. The airspace inside an earthenware vessel is rendered impure, in contrast to other types of impure vessels, which become impure and impart impurity only through contact. Another difference between earthenware vessels and other items is that other items may be purified by immersion in a ritual bath, **and it,** the earthenware vessel, **you shall break,**^D as it cannot be purified; rather, it remains ritually impure for as long as it is categorized as a vessel.

Seventh aliya

34 In addition to people and vessels, which may be rendered impure on account of dead swarming creatures and the like, **any food that may be eaten upon which water comes shall become impure,**^D shall become susceptible to contracting ritual impurity. That is, solid food is susceptible to impurity only if water has touched it. **And** conversely, **any liquid that may be drunk,** that is fit for drinking,³⁴ **in any vessel shall become impure;** namely, it is automatically susceptible to impurity.³⁵

35 **And anything upon which shall fall some of their carcasses,** of swarming creatures, **shall become impure.** For example, if a dead swarming creature falls into **an oven or stove,**^B which are earthenware vessels, then they **shall be shattered,** as they **are impure,** despite the fact that they are attached to the ground, **and shall be impure to you,** as there is no way to purify them.

Biblical-era pot on a stove

36 **However, a spring or cistern, a gathering of water, shall be pure.**^D Water in a spring or collected in the ground remains pure. **But** even so, **one who touches their carcasses,** of swarming creatures, **shall become impure.** If a swarming creature falls into a gathering of water, it remains impure and transmits impurity to one who touches it.³⁶ Nevertheless, the collection of water itself remains pure.

37 **And if some of their carcasses,** of the swarming creatures or of the other animals mentioned above, **shall fall upon any sown seed that shall be sown,** that is not prepared as food, **it is pure.**

DISCUSSION

11:33 | And it you shall break: It should be noted that there is no obligation to purify one's impure vessels or to break an earthenware vessel that has become impure. Although any item placed in that vessel from that point onward will become impure, one is permitted to leave vessels in a state of impurity if one wishes to do so (see Rashi, verse 35; see also commentary on verse 8 and 17:16).

11:34 | Any food that may be eaten upon which water comes shall become impure: Before a fruit or vegetable is picked, it is not susceptible to ritual impurity since it is not yet considered food. After it has been picked, it is susceptible to ritual impurity only if water has fallen on it. Presumably, this is true only if the water was intended for some beneficial purpose. At this stage it is rendered susceptible to impurity (see, e.g., *Makhshirin* 1:1; *Tosefta, Teharot* 10:4; *Kiddushin* 59b). For example, if rain fell on fruit that was spread on the ground, the fruit is not rendered susceptible to impurity, as it was not intentionally wet by a human being (see *Makhshirin*, chap. 1; Rambam, *Sefer Tahara, Hilkhot Tumat Okhalin*, chap. 12).

11:36 | A gathering [mikveh] of water shall be pure: This is the source of the name *mikveh* for a ritual bath designed for ritual purification.

The conditions for such a ritual bath and its measurements are complex, detailed topics. In general, a ritual bath must be large enough to hold an entire human body (see *Ḥagiga* 11a). Other gatherings of water, e.g., water that has collected in a puddle, can be used for purification in certain cases, but they cannot serve as ritual baths for people, both due to their small size and because they are not stable and fixed (see *Mikvaot* 1:1–7).

The phrase "however, a spring or cistern, a gathering of water, shall be pure" is somewhat puzzling. On the one hand, it was stated above that if water comes into contact with foodstuffs, it renders them susceptible to ritual impurity. ←→

לא וְהַתִּנְשָׁמֶת: אֵלֶּה הַטְּמֵאִים לָכֶם בְּכָל־הַשָּׁרֶץ כָּל־הַנֹּגֵעַ בָּהֶם בְּמֹתָם יִטְמָא
לב עַד־הָעָרֶב: וְכֹל אֲשֶׁר־יִפֹּל עָלָיו מֵהֶם ׀ בְּמֹתָם יִטְמָא מִכָּל־כְּלִי־עֵץ אוֹ בֶגֶד אוֹ־
עוֹר אוֹ שָׂק כָּל־כְּלִי אֲשֶׁר־יֵעָשֶׂה מְלָאכָה בָּהֶם בַּמַּיִם יוּבָא וְטָמֵא עַד־הָעֶרֶב
לג וְטָהֵר: וְכָל־כְּלִי־חֶרֶשׂ אֲשֶׁר־יִפֹּל מֵהֶם אֶל־תּוֹכוֹ כֹּל אֲשֶׁר בְּתוֹכוֹ יִטְמָא וְאֹתוֹ שביעי
לד תִשְׁבֹּרוּ: מִכָּל־הָאֹכֶל אֲשֶׁר יֵאָכֵל אֲשֶׁר יָבוֹא עָלָיו מַיִם יִטְמָא וְכָל־מַשְׁקֶה אֲשֶׁר
לה יִשָּׁתֶה בְּכָל־כְּלִי יִטְמָא: וְכֹל אֲשֶׁר־יִפֹּל מִנִּבְלָתָם ׀ עָלָיו יִטְמָא תַּנּוּר וְכִירַיִם יֻתָּץ
לו טְמֵאִים הֵם וּטְמֵאִים יִהְיוּ לָכֶם: אַךְ מַעְיָן וּבוֹר מִקְוֵה־מַיִם יִהְיֶה טָהוֹר וְנֹגֵעַ
לז בְּנִבְלָתָם יִטְמָא: וְכִי יִפֹּל מִנִּבְלָתָם עַל־כָּל־זֶרַע זֵרוּעַ אֲשֶׁר יִזָּרֵעַ טָהוֹר הוּא:

רש״י

תִּנְשָׁמֶת. טלפ״א:

לב| **בַּמַּיִם יוּבָא.** וְאַף לְאַחַר טְבִילָתוֹ טָמֵא הוּא לִתְרוּמָה "עַד הָעֶרֶב", וְאַחַר כָּךְ "וְטָהֵר" בְּהַעֲרֵב שֶׁמֶשׁ:

לג| **אֶל תּוֹכוֹ.** אֵין כְּלִי חֶרֶס מִטַּמֵּא אֶלָּא מֵאֲוִירוֹ: **כֹּל אֲשֶׁר בְּתוֹכוֹ יִטְמָא.** הַכְּלִי חוֹזֵר וּמְטַמֵּא מַה שֶּׁבַּאֲוִירוֹ: **וְאֹתוֹ תִשְׁבֹּרוּ.** לִמֵּד שֶׁאֵין לוֹ טָהֳרָה בְּמִקְוֶה:

לד| **מִכָּל הָאֹכֶל אֲשֶׁר יֵאָכֵל.** מוּסָב עַל מִקְרָא הָעֶלְיוֹן: כֹּל אֲשֶׁר בְּתוֹכוֹ יִטְמָא, מִכָּל הָאֹכֶל אֲשֶׁר יֵאָכֵל אֲשֶׁר בָּאוּ עָלָיו מַיִם, וְהוּא בְּתוֹךְ כְּלִי חֶרֶס הַטָּמֵא, יִטְמָא. לָמַדְנוּ מִכָּאן דְּבָרִים הַרְבֵּה: לָמַדְנוּ שֶׁאֵין אֹכֶל מֻכְשָׁר וּמְתֻקָּן לְקַבֵּל טֻמְאָה עַד שֶׁיָּבוֹאוּ עָלָיו מַיִם פַּעַם אַחַת, וּמִשֶּׁבָּאוּ עָלָיו מַיִם פַּעַם אַחַת מְקַבֵּל טֻמְאָה לְעוֹלָם וַאֲפִלּוּ נָגוּב; וְהַיַּיִן וְהַשֶּׁמֶן וְכָל הַנִּקְרָא מַשְׁקֶה מַכְשִׁיר זְרָעִים לְטֻמְאָה כַּמַּיִם, שֶׁכָּךְ יֵשׁ לִדְרֹשׁ הַמִּקְרָא: "אֲשֶׁר יָבוֹא עָלָיו מַיִם" אוֹ "כָל מַשְׁקֶה אֲשֶׁר יִשָּׁתֶה בְּכָל כְּלִי, יִטְמָא" הָאֹכֶל. וְעוֹד לָמְדוּ רַבּוֹתֵינוּ מִכָּאן שֶׁאֵין וְלַד הַטֻּמְאָה מְטַמֵּא כֵּלִים, שֶׁכָּךְ שָׁנִינוּ: יָכוֹל יְהוּ כָּל הַכֵּלִים מִטַּמְּאִין מֵאֲוִיר כְּלִי חֶרֶס? תַּלְמוּד לוֹמַר: "כֹּל אֲשֶׁר בְּתוֹכוֹ יִטְמָא... מִכָּל הָאֹכֶל" – אֹכֶל וּמַשְׁקֶה מִטַּמֵּא מֵאֲוִיר כְּלִי חֶרֶס, וְאֵין כָּל הַכֵּלִים מִטַּמְּאִין מֵאֲוִיר כְּלִי חֶרֶס; לְפִי שֶׁהַשֶּׁרֶץ אַב הַטֻּמְאָה וְהַכְּלִי שֶׁנִּטְמָא מִמֶּנּוּ וְלַד הַטֻּמְאָה, לְפִיכָךְ אֵינוֹ חוֹזֵר וּמְטַמֵּא כֵּלִים שֶׁבְּתוֹכוֹ. וְלָמַדְנוּ עוֹד, שֶׁהַשֶּׁרֶץ שֶׁנָּפַל לַאֲוִיר תַּנּוּר וְהַפַּת בְּתוֹכוֹ, וְלֹא נָגַע הַשֶּׁרֶץ בַּפַּת, הַתַּנּוּר רִאשׁוֹן וְהַפַּת שְׁנִיָּה, וְלֹא נֹאמַר רוֹאִין אֶת הַתַּנּוּר כְּאִלּוּ מָלֵא טֻמְאָה וּתְהֵא הַפַּת תְּחִלָּה, שֶׁאִם אַתָּה אוֹמֵר כֵּן, לֹא נִתְמַעֲטוּ כָּל הַכֵּלִים מִלִּטַּמֵּא מֵאֲוִיר כְּלִי חֶרֶס, שֶׁהֲרֵי טֻמְאָה עַצְמָהּ נָגְעָה בָּהֶן מִגַּבָּן. וְלָמַדְנוּ עוֹד עַל בִּיאַת מַיִם שֶׁאֵינָהּ מַכְשֶׁרֶת זְרָעִים אֶלָּא אִם כֵּן נָפְלוּ עֲלֵיהֶן מִשֶּׁנִּתְלְשׁוּ, שֶׁאִם אַתָּה אוֹמֵר מְקַבְּלִין הֶכְשֵׁר בִּמְחֻבָּר, אֵין לְךָ שֶׁלֹּא בָּאוּ עָלָיו מַיִם, וּמַהוּ אוֹמֵר: "אֲשֶׁר יָבוֹא עָלָיו מַיִם"? וְלָמַדְנוּ עוֹד שֶׁאֵין אֹכֶל מְטַמֵּא אֲחֵרִים אֶלָּא אִם כֵּן יֵשׁ בּוֹ כַּבֵּיצָה, שֶׁנֶּאֱמַר: "אֲשֶׁר יֵאָכֵל" – אֹכֶל הַנֶּאֱכָל בְּבַת אַחַת, וְשִׁעֲרוּ חֲכָמִים אֵין בֵּית הַבְּלִיעָה מַחֲזִיק יוֹתֵר מִבֵּיצַת תַּרְנְגֹלֶת:

לה| **תַּנּוּר וְכִירַיִם.** כֵּלִים הַמִּטַּלְטְלִין הֵן, וְהֵן שֶׁל חֶרֶס וְיֵשׁ לָהֶן תּוֹךְ, וְשׁוֹפֵת עַל נֶקֶב הֶחָלָל אֶת הַקְּדֵרָה, וּשְׁנֵיהֶם פִּיהֶם לְמַעְלָה: **יֻתָּץ.** שֶׁאֵין לִכְלִי חֶרֶס טָהֳרָה בִּטְבִילָה: **וּטְמֵאִים יִהְיוּ לָכֶם.** שֶׁלֹּא תֹּאמַר מְצֻוֶּה אֲנִי לְנָתְצָם, תַּלְמוּד לוֹמַר: "וּטְמֵאִים יִהְיוּ לָכֶם", אִם רָצָה לְקַיְּמָן בְּטֻמְאָתָן – רַשַּׁאי:

לו| **אַךְ מַעְיָן וּבוֹר מִקְוֵה מַיִם.** הַמְחֻבָּרִים לַקַּרְקַע, אֵין מְקַבְּלִין טֻמְאָה. וְעוֹד יֵשׁ לְךָ לִלְמֹד, "יִהְיֶה טָהוֹר" הַטּוֹבֵל בָּהֶם מִטֻּמְאָתוֹ: **וְנֹגֵעַ בְּנִבְלָתָם יִטְמָא.** אֲפִלּוּ הוּא בְּתוֹךְ מַעְיָן וּבוֹר וְנוֹגֵעַ בְּטֻמְאָתָם – יִטְמָא, שֶׁלֹּא תֹּאמַר קַל וָחֹמֶר: אִם מְטַהֵר אֶת הַטְּמֵאִים מִטֻּמְאָתָם, קַל וָחֹמֶר שֶׁיַּצִּיל אֶת הַטָּהוֹר מִלִּטַּמֵּא, לְכָךְ נֶאֱמַר: "וְנֹגֵעַ בְּנִבְלָתָם יִטְמָא":

לז| **זֶרַע זֵרוּעַ.** זְרִיעָה שֶׁל מִינֵי זֵרְעוֹנִין. 'זֵרוּעַ' שֵׁם דָּבָר הוּא, כְּמוֹ: "וְיִתְּנוּ לָנוּ מִן הַזֵּרֹעִים" (דניאל א, יב): **טָהוֹר הוּא.** לִמֶּדְךָ הַכָּתוּב שֶׁלֹּא הֻכְשַׁר וְנִתְקַן לִקְרוֹת אֹכֶל לְקַבֵּל טֻמְאָה עַד שֶׁיָּבוֹאוּ עָלָיו מַיִם:

DISCUSSION

➞ Water itself is also in the category of "any liquid that may be drunk in any vessel," which is automatically susceptible to impurity. On the other hand, people and vessels are purified by immersion in water, in accordance with the verse: "It shall be brought into water" (11:32, 15:5–11). The question therefore arises: Does the water purify or transmit impurity?

Apparently, there is a difference between collected water that has not yet been harnessed by human hands and water drawn for use by people. Water transfers impurity when drawn in a vessel or otherwise used. Water that has gathered in a reservoir, such as a spring or cistern, but has not been drawn can neither become impure nor impart impurity. A reservoir of collected ground or rainwater is essentially pure, such that when a person or vessel enters it they are purified. This distinction is alluded to by the superfluous phrase "any liquid that may be drunk in any vessel" (see *Sifra*; Ramban).

BACKGROUND

11:30| **Chameleon [*tinshamet*]:** The Aramaic translations identify this creature as the chameleon. Others claim that the name is indicative of its breathing [*neshima*] and exhalation sounds, and they therefore maintain that it is a creature that emits sounds when it breathes, e.g., the gecko, or the common chameleon, *Chamaeleon vulgaris*. Alternatively, the name is based on the creature's unusual appearance, which causes astonishment [*hishtomemut*] (Ibn Ezra). Yet others contend that it is a mole (Rashi) or the monitor lizard.

11:35| **Stove:** Unlike the modern stove, this refers to a device shaped like a basin. One places pots either into the device or on its rim (see Zechariah 12:6; *Shabbat* 38b).

38 **But if water shall** intentionally **be placed on the seed, and some of their carcasses,** of these swarming creatures, **shall fall on it, it is impure to you,** as was already stated above with regard to food in general. Unlike vessels, which are fashioned and completed by people, seeds and other foods must first be rendered susceptible to ritual impurity by means of water or one of six other types of liquids.[37] If one of these liquids comes into contact with a seed or some other food, with human intentionality, the food is susceptible to impurity from that point onward.

39 **And if any animal that is for your consumption,** that comes from a species whose consumption is permitted, **shall die, one who touches its carcass shall be impure until the evening.**

40 **One who eats of its carcass shall wash his garments and be impure until the evening; and one who carries its carcass,** even without touching it, **shall wash his garments and be impure until the evening.** Although these animals would have been considered kosher while still alive, not only are their carcasses prohibited for consumption, but they also impart impurity through contact or carrying. It should be noted that the Sages derive several laws from the verse's mention of the two cases of eating and carrying.[38]

41 **And any swarming creature that swarms upon the earth,** small creatures not included in the list of swarming creatures whose carcasses impart impurity through contact (11:29–30), **is a detestable thing; it shall not be eaten.**

42 Consequently, **any** creature **that crawls upon the belly,** e.g., snakes and worms, **and any** creature **that walks on four** legs, whether mammals or other creatures, such as scorpions,[39] **up to any** creature **that has numerous feet among all swarming creatures that swarm on the earth,** not only those that walk on four legs, **you shall not eat them, as they are a detestable thing.**

43 **You shall not render yourselves detestable with any swarming creature that swarms, and you shall not be rendered impure by them, and become impure through them.**[D]

44 **For I am the Lord your God; you shall sanctify yourselves and be holy, for I am holy.** One of the ways to sanctify yourselves and draw closer to Me is by refraining from eating certain foods. **And** therefore **you shall not render yourselves impure with any swarming creature that creeps upon the earth.**

45 **For I am the Lord who brought you up from the land of**
Maftir **Egypt to be your God; you shall be holy,**[D] **as I am holy.** These commandments do not apply to mankind in general, but specifically to the people of God. Since the nation of Israel was chosen by God to be "a kingdom of priests, and a holy nation,"[40] they must avoid eating or coming into contact with all creatures defined as impure.

46 In summation: **This is the law of the animals, and of the birds, and of every living creature that creeps in the water, and of every creature that swarms on the earth.**

47 With regard to all of these, it is necessary **to distinguish between the impure and the pure,** the various aspects of impurity and purity mentioned above, beginning with impurity that results from death, where one must avoid contact and the like, e.g., the impurity of animal carcasses, and including other aspects of impurity and purity, non-kosher and kosher animals (see, e.g., 20:25, 27:27), **and between the living creature that may be eaten and the living creature that may not be eaten.**

Maftir on Shabbat Para is read from Numbers 19:1–22. Maftir on Shabbat HaḤodesh is read from Exodus 12:1–20.

DISCUSSION

11:43 | **And become impure [*venitmetem*] through them:** The absence of the *alef* from the word *venitmetem* alludes to the idea that the verse refers not only to ritual impurity, but to *timtum*, covering or sealing. By consuming these creatures, one becomes dense, coarse, and stupefied (*Yoma* 39a). These creatures are harmful both to body and soul. This is an important principle with regard to all prohibited foods: The verse does not claim that the hare is worse than the sheep, or that kosher birds are essentially better than non-kosher ones. Rather, the verse teaches that the consumption of such creatures has a deleterious effect on a person.

11:45 | **You shall be holy:** None of the many attempts to explain or justify these prohibitions are valid. Perhaps the foundation for these prohibitions is the general rationale provided by this verse, namely that the essence and nature of Israel differs from that of other nations (see Abravanel; Rabbi Samson Raphael Hirsch). One allusion to this is the phrase "they are a detestable thing to you" (11:10): They are a detestable thing to you, but they are not inherently detestable.

לח לט וְכִי יֻתַּן־מַיִם עַל־זֶרַע וְנָפַל מִנִּבְלָתָם עָלָיו טָמֵא הוּא לָכֶם׃ וְכִי
יָמוּת מִן־הַבְּהֵמָה אֲשֶׁר־הִיא לָכֶם לְאָכְלָה הַנֹּגֵעַ בְּנִבְלָתָהּ יִטְמָא עַד־הָעָרֶב׃
מ וְהָאֹכֵל מִנִּבְלָתָהּ יְכַבֵּס בְּגָדָיו וְטָמֵא עַד־הָעָרֶב וְהַנֹּשֵׂא אֶת־נִבְלָתָהּ יְכַבֵּס
מא בְּגָדָיו וְטָמֵא עַד־הָעָרֶב׃ וְכָל־הַשֶּׁרֶץ הַשֹּׁרֵץ עַל־הָאָרֶץ שֶׁקֶץ הוּא לֹא יֵאָכֵל׃
מב כֹּל הוֹלֵךְ עַל־גָּחוֹן וְכֹל ׀ הוֹלֵךְ עַל־אַרְבַּע עַד כָּל־מַרְבֵּה רַגְלַיִם לְכָל־הַשֶּׁרֶץ
מג הַשֹּׁרֵץ עַל־הָאָרֶץ לֹא תֹאכְלוּם כִּי־שֶׁקֶץ הֵם׃ אַל־תְּשַׁקְּצוּ אֶת־נַפְשֹׁתֵיכֶם
מד בְּכָל־הַשֶּׁרֶץ הַשֹּׁרֵץ וְלֹא תִטַּמְּאוּ בָּהֶם וְנִטְמֵתֶם בָּם׃ כִּי אֲנִי יְהוָה אֱלֹהֵיכֶם
וְהִתְקַדִּשְׁתֶּם וִהְיִיתֶם קְדֹשִׁים כִּי קָדוֹשׁ אָנִי וְלֹא תְטַמְּאוּ אֶת־נַפְשֹׁתֵיכֶם בְּכָל־
מה הַשֶּׁרֶץ הָרֹמֵשׂ עַל־הָאָרֶץ׃ כִּי ׀ אֲנִי יְהוָה הַמַּעֲלֶה אֶתְכֶם מֵאֶרֶץ מִצְרַיִם לִהְיֹת מפטיר
מו לָכֶם לֵאלֹהִים וִהְיִיתֶם קְדֹשִׁים כִּי קָדוֹשׁ אָנִי׃ זֹאת תּוֹרַת הַבְּהֵמָה וְהָעוֹף וְכֹל
מז נֶפֶשׁ הַחַיָּה הָרֹמֶשֶׂת בַּמָּיִם וּלְכָל־נֶפֶשׁ הַשֹּׁרֶצֶת עַל־הָאָרֶץ׃ לְהַבְדִּיל בֵּין הַטָּמֵא
וּבֵין הַטָּהֹר וּבֵין הַחַיָּה הַנֶּאֱכֶלֶת וּבֵין הַחַיָּה אֲשֶׁר לֹא תֵאָכֵל׃

רש"י

לח| **וכי יתן מים על זרע.** לאחר שנתלש, שאם תאמר יש הכשר במחובר, אין לך זרע שלא הוכשר: **מים על זרע.** בין מים בין שאר משקין, בין הם על הזרע בין זרע נופל לתוכן, הכל נדרש בתורת כהנים (פרק יא, ו, ט): **ונפל מנבלתם עליו.** אף משנגב מן המים, שלא הקפידה תורה אלא להיות עליו שם אוכל, ומשירד לו הכשר קבלת טומאה פעם אחת, שוב אינו נעקר הימנו:

לט| **בנבלתה.** ולא בעצמות וגידים ולא בקרנים וטלפים ולא בעור:

מ| **והנשא את נבלתה.** חמורה טומאת משא מטומאת מגע, שהנושא מטמא בגדים, והנוגע אין בגדיו טמאין, שלא נאמר בו: "יכבס בגדיו": **והאכל מנבלתה.** יכול תטמאנו אכילתו? כשהוא אומר בנבלת עוף טהור: "לא יאכל לטמאה בה" (להלן כב, ח), בה אתה מטמא בגדים באכילתה, ואין נבלת בהמה מטמאה בגדים באכילתה בלא מגע או בלא משא, כגון אם תחבה לו חברו בבית הבליעה. אם כן, מה תלמוד לומר: "האכל"? ליתן שיעור לנושא ולנוגע כדי אכילה, והוא כזית: **וטמא עד הערב.** אף על פי שטבל, צריך הערב שמש:

מא| **השרץ על הארץ.** להוציא את היתושין שבכליסין ושבפולין ואת הזיזין שבעדשים, שהרי לא שרצו על הארץ אלא בתוך האוכל, אבל משיצאו לאויר ושרצו הרי נאסרו: **לא יאכל.** לחייב על המאכיל כאוכל. ואין קרוי שרץ אלא דבר נמוך קצר רגלים שאינו נראה אלא כרוחש ונד:

מב| **הולך על גחון.** זה נחש, ולשון 'גחון' – שחייה, שהולך שח ונופל על מעיו: **וכל הולך.** להביא השלשולין ואת הדומה לדומה: **הולך על ארבע.** זה עקרב: **כל.** להביא את החפושית, אשקרבו"ט בלעז, ואת הדומה לדומה: **מרבה רגלים.** זה נדל, שרץ שיש לו רגלים מראשו ועד זנבו לכאן ולכאן, וקורין ענטפיד"ש:

מג| **אל תשקצו.** באכילתן, שהרי כתיב: "נפשתיכם", ואין שקוץ נפש במגע, וכן: אל תטמאו באכילתן: **ונטמתם בם.** אם אתם מטמאין בהם בארץ, אף אני מטמא אתכם בעולם הבא ובישיבת מעלה:

מד| **כי אני ה' אלהיכם.** כשם שאני קדוש שאני ה' אלהיכם, כך "והתקדשתם", קדשו עצמכם למטה: **והייתם קדשים.** לפני, שאני אקדש אתכם למעלה ובעולם הבא: **ולא תטמאו וגו'.** לעבור עליהם בלאוין הרבה, וכל לאו – מלקות. וזהו שאמרנו בתלמוד: אכל פוטיתא לוקה ארבע, נמלה לוקה חמש, צרעה לוקה שש:

מה| **כי אני ה' המעלה אתכם.** על מנת שתקבלו מצותי העליתי אתכם:

מז| **להבדיל.** לא בלבד השונה, אלא שתהא יודע ומכיר ובקי בהן: **בין הטמא ובין הטהר.** צריך לומר בין חמור לפרה? והלא כבר מפורשים הם! אלא בין טמאה לך לטהורה לך, בין נשחט חציו של קנה לנשחט רובו: **ובין החיה הנאכלת וגו'.** צריך לומר בין צבי לערוד? והלא כבר מפורשים הם! אלא בין שנולד בה סימני טרפה כשרה לנולד בה סימני טרפה פסולה:

Parashat **Tazria**

The Purification of a Woman Who Has Given Birth

LEVITICUS 12:1–8

The book of Leviticus has focused on matters of sacrificial offerings. It has also listed the permitted and forbidden foods of animal origin, as well as those living creatures whose carcasses impart ritual impurity. Unlike other living creatures, which can impart ritual impurity only after they have died, humans can generate impurity while alive as a result of certain physiological processes or changes. This section, which begins a new unit in the book that deals with the *halakhot* of ritual purity and impurity pertaining to humans, addresses the ritual impurity of a woman who has given birth. This impurity is linked to bringing life into the world. Despite the rationalizations that have been suggested for these *halakhot*, the statutes of ritual purity and impurity are essentially without reason, and the hygienic explanations that have been put forward have no real basis.

12 1 **The Lord spoke to Moses, saying:**
2 **Speak to the children of Israel, saying: If a woman conceives and bears a male child, she shall be impure seven days; like the days,** the duration, **of her menstrual [*niddat*] suffering,**[D] the pain that comes with her blood of menstruation,[11] so **she** who gives birth to a male child **shall be impure.** Some commentaries associate *niddat* with *nadad*, wander, and *nidui*, excommunication, her separation during her sickness.
3 Since the text is dealing with a woman who has given birth to a male child, it adds in passing the *halakha* that was already stated in the book of Genesis (17:12), which applies after the seven days mentioned here: **On the eighth day, the flesh of his foreskin shall be circumcised.**[D]
4 After the seven days of impurity, for **thirty days and three days she shall abide in the blood of purity.**[D] Although it is possible that she might continue to bleed even after the first week, this blood is considered blood of purity. In other words, for the next thirty-three days, until a total of forty days have passed since the birth, she is no longer governed by the *halakhot* that distance a menstruating woman or a woman who gave birth from her husband. Nevertheless, **she shall not touch any consecrated item, and she shall not enter the sanctuary until the completion of the days of her purity.** Only after forty days will she become fully purified from the impurity connected to childbirth.
5 **If she bears a female child, then she shall be impure two weeks as during her menstruation,**[D] when she must separate herself from her husband and from any items they wish to preserve in a state of ritual purity. **And sixty days and six days she shall abide in the blood of purity.** The days of impurity and purity that follow the birth of a female are double the amount of days that come after the birth of a male.
6 **With the completion of the days of her purity,** the end of the forty-day period **for a son or** the eighty-day period **for a daughter,** in order to purify herself fully, **she** or an agent on her behalf **shall bring** to the Temple **a lamb in its first year as a burnt offering, and** either **a young pigeon or a turtledove as a sin offering, to the entrance of the Tent of Meeting to the priest.**
7 **He,** the priest, **shall offer it,** the pair of offerings, **before the Lord,** in accordance with the rites of a burnt offering and a sin offering, **and** he shall thereby **atone for her; and she shall be purified**[D] **from the source of her blood.** Only then is she purified from her bleeding, which after an ordinary birth would

DISCUSSION

12:2| **Like the days of her menstrual suffering:** The Torah has not yet presented the *halakhot* of a menstruating woman; these appear below (15:19; 18:19). The ritual impurity of a menstruating woman is severe; she may not approach the Temple or consecrated items, and she also imparts impurity to others. Furthermore, she is prohibited from all sexual contact, which is a ban that is unrelated to the Temple and consecrated items; it applies in all places and at all times while she is impure.

12:3| **On the eighth day, the flesh of his foreskin shall be circumcised:** The connection between the impurity resulting from birth and circumcision is not clear. This may be an instance where the midrashic interpretation of the text is not far from the plain meaning of the text. According to the Midrash, for seven days the woman is withdrawn, as she is ritually impure and forbidden to her husband. Only on the eighth day, when, in principle, she becomes pure, can the parents celebrate the circumcision of their son together (see *Nidda* 31b; see also Rabbi Samson Raphael Hirsch; Malbim).

12:4| **Thirty days and three days she shall abide in the blood of purity:** In practice, any woman who experiences vaginal bleeding must count, once the bleeding has ceased, seven clean days during which there is no bleeding whatsoever. After seven clean days pass she must immerse in a ritual bath, at which point she is purified. This *halakha* applies both to a woman after childbirth and to ordinary days of menstruation (see *Nidda* 37a, and Rosh ad loc.; *Shulḥan Arukh*, *Yoreh De'a* 194:1; *Encyclopedia Talmudit* 7:503–504).

פרשת
תזריע

א ב וַיְדַבֵּר יְהוָה אֶל־מֹשֶׁה לֵּאמֹר: דַּבֵּר אֶל־בְּנֵי יִשְׂרָאֵל לֵאמֹר אִשָּׁה כִּי תַזְרִיעַ וְיָלְדָה
ג זָכָר וְטָמְאָה שִׁבְעַת יָמִים כִּימֵי נִדַּת דְּוֺתָהּ תִּטְמָא: וּבַיּוֹם הַשְּׁמִינִי יִמּוֹל בְּשַׂר
ד עָרְלָתוֹ: וּשְׁלֹשִׁים יוֹם וּשְׁלֹשֶׁת יָמִים תֵּשֵׁב בִּדְמֵי טָהֳרָה בְּכָל־קֹדֶשׁ לֹא־תִגָּע
ה וְאֶל־הַמִּקְדָּשׁ לֹא תָבֹא עַד־מְלֹאת יְמֵי טָהֳרָהּ: וְאִם־נְקֵבָה תֵלֵד וְטָמְאָה שְׁבֻעַיִם
ו כְּנִדָּתָהּ וְשִׁשִּׁים יוֹם וְשֵׁשֶׁת יָמִים תֵּשֵׁב עַל־דְּמֵי טָהֳרָה: וּבִמְלֹאת ׀ יְמֵי טָהֳרָהּ
לְבֵן אוֹ לְבַת תָּבִיא כֶּבֶשׂ בֶּן־שְׁנָתוֹ לְעֹלָה וּבֶן־יוֹנָה אוֹ־תֹר לְחַטָּאת אֶל־פֶּתַח
ז אֹהֶל־מוֹעֵד אֶל־הַכֹּהֵן: וְהִקְרִיבוֹ לִפְנֵי יְהוָה וְכִפֶּר עָלֶיהָ וְטָהֲרָה מִמְּקֹר דָּמֶיהָ

רש״י

ב | **אִשָּׁה כִּי תַזְרִיעַ.** אָמַר רַבִּי שִׂמְלַאי: כְּשֵׁם שֶׁיְּצִירָתוֹ שֶׁל אָדָם אַחַר כָּל בְּהֵמָה חַיָּה וָעוֹף בְּמַעֲשֵׂה בְרֵאשִׁית, כָּךְ תּוֹרָתוֹ נִתְפָּרְשָׁה אַחַר תּוֹרַת בְּהֵמָה חַיָּה וָעוֹף: **כִּי תַזְרִיעַ.** לְרַבּוֹת שֶׁאֲפִלּוּ יְלָדַתּוּ מָחוּי, שֶׁנִּמְחָה וְנַעֲשָׂה כְּעֵין זֶרַע, אִמּוֹ טְמֵאָה לֵדָה: **כִּימֵי נִדַּת דְּוֺתָהּ תִּטְמָא.** כְּסֵדֶר כָּל טֻמְאָה הָאֲמוּרָה בְּנִדָּה מִטַּמְּאָה בְּטֻמְאַת לֵדָה, וַאֲפִלּוּ נִפְתַּח הַקֶּבֶר בְּלֹא דָם: **דְּוֺתָהּ.** לְשׁוֹן דָּבָר הַזָּב מִגּוּפָהּ. לָשׁוֹן אַחֵר, לְשׁוֹן מַדְוֶה וְחֹלִי, שֶׁאֵין אִשָּׁה רוֹאָה דָם שֶׁלֹּא תֶּחֱלֶה, וְרֹאשָׁהּ וְאֵבָרֶיהָ כְּבֵדִין עָלֶיהָ:

ד | **תֵּשֵׁב.** אֵין 'תֵּשֵׁב' אֶלָּא לְשׁוֹן עַכָּבָה, כְּמוֹ: "וַתֵּשְׁבוּ בְקָדֵשׁ" (דברים א, מו), "וַיֵּשֶׁב בְּאֵלֹנֵי מַמְרֵא" (בראשית יג, יח): **בִּדְמֵי טָהֳרָה.** אַף עַל פִּי שֶׁרוֹאָה דָם, טְהוֹרָה: **בִּדְמֵי טָהֳרָה.** לֹא מַפִּיק הֵ״א, וְהוּא שֵׁם דָּבָר, כְּמוֹ 'טֹהַר': **יְמֵי טָהֳרָהּ.** מַפִּיק הֵ״א, יְמֵי טֹהַר שֶׁלָּהּ: **לֹא תִגָּע.** אַזְהָרָה לָאוֹכֵל, כְּמוֹ שֶׁשְּׁנוּיָה בִּיבָמוֹת (דף עה ע״א): **בְּכָל קֹדֶשׁ** וְגוֹ'. לְרַבּוֹת אֶת הַתְּרוּמָה, לְפִי שֶׁזּוֹ טְבוּלַת יוֹם אָרֹךְ, שֶׁטָּבְלָה לְסוֹף שִׁבְעָה, וְאֵין שִׁמְשָׁהּ מַעֲרִיב לְטַהֲרָהּ עַד שְׁקִיעַת הַחַמָּה שֶׁל יוֹם אַרְבָּעִים, שֶׁלְּמָחָר תָּבִיא אֶת כַּפָּרַת טָהֳרָתָהּ:

ז | **וְהִקְרִיבוֹ.** לִמֶּדְךָ שֶׁאֵין מְעַכְּבָהּ לֶאֱכֹל בְּקָדָשִׁים אֶלָּא אֶחָד מֵהֶם, וְאֵי זֶה הוּא? זֶה חַטָּאת, שֶׁנֶּאֱמַר: "וְכִפֶּר עָלֶיהָ הַכֹּהֵן וְטָהֵרָה" (להלן פסוק ח), מִי שֶׁהוּא בָּא לְכַפֵּר, בּוֹ הַטָּהֳרָה תְּלוּיָה: **וְטָהֲרָה.** מִכְּלָל שֶׁעַד כָּאן קְרוּיָה טְמֵאָה:

DISCUSSION

12:5| **If she bears a female child, then she shall be impure two weeks as during her menstruation:** Although one cannot know for certain the reason for the difference between the cycle of impurity and purity in the case of the birth of a son and the corresponding cycle in the birth of a daughter, one explanation is as follows: The cycle of impurity and purity of a woman who has given birth is connected to the subjugation and freedom of her body in relation to the traumatic event that it experienced. As mentioned above, on the eighth day following the birth of a male child, the father brings him into the covenant of Abraham by means of circumcision. The circumcision serves as a transitional point between the days of the woman's impurity and the process of her purification. Symbolizing the body's liberation from its primal, impulsive nature to moral freedom in keeping with God's will, the circumcision cuts the woman's cycle of impurity and purity in half (see Rabbi Samson Raphael Hirsch).

Another explanation of the disparity in the duration of a woman's impurity following the birth of a boy and a girl is that there is a difference between the curses of the male and female, which were pronounced upon Adam and Eve after they ate from the tree of the knowledge of good and evil. Adam was told: "In suffering shall you eat of it all the days of your life" (Genesis 3:17), whereas Eve was cursed doubly: "I will increase your suffering and your pregnancy; in pain you shall give birth to children" (Genesis 3:16; see *Tzeror HaMor*).

12:7| **He shall offer it before the Lord and atone for her; and she shall be purified:** Several types of impurity require the one who is impure to sacrifice an offering as part of his or her process of purification. Individuals who contract these types of impurity include: a *zav*, a man who experienced a gonorrhea-like discharge; a *zava*, a woman who experienced an irregular discharge of blood from the uterus; an individual who suffered from leprosy; and a woman following childbirth. The Sages labeled such people, whose time for purification has arrived but whose offerings have not yet been brought, as "those who lack atonement," because they still require further steps to reach atonement (see *Zevaḥim* 19b; *Karetot* 8b).

One can readily understand why the woman brings a burnt offering, as this is an expression of gratitude for a birth that went smoothly (see Abravanel), but what does her offering have to do with atonement? What sin has she committed? The Sages suggest, though not necessarily

have ceased much earlier. **This is the law of the woman after childbirth of a male child or of a female child.**

8 A burnt offering is generally a voluntary offering, and as stated earlier, there are several types: a large bull, a smaller lamb, or a bird (see chap. 1). A woman who has given birth does not bring her burnt offering voluntarily; rather, it is an obligation following childbirth. Therefore, the Torah provides allowances for a poor woman in this situation: **If her means do not suffice**

for buying **a lamb** for her burnt offering, **she shall take two turtledoves, or two young pigeons,** referred to by the Sages as a nest of birds,[12] **one bird as a burnt offering** in place of the lamb, **and one as a sin offering,** which all such women must bring (see verse 6); **and the priest shall atone for her** by sacrificing them, **and she shall be purified** for all purposes. At this stage she is permitted to enter the Temple and partake of consecrated foods.

Leprosy of People
LEVITICUS 13:1–46

The following passages deal with a complex, lengthy aspect of the *halakhot* of impurity: The plague of leprosy [*tzara'at*]. In addition to rendering a person or object ritually impure, leprosy also bears a message. Based on the descriptions of the Torah and the statements of the Sages, *tzara'at* is not the same as the illness known today as leprosy, nor is it identical to any other skin disease. It does not appear to be a recognized physical illness; rather, it is a miraculous disease, a sign from Heaven that something is amiss, on account of which the afflicted person must remove himself from the community. Therefore, this leprosy was treated not by a doctor but by one who deals with sacred matters, a priest. Both the descriptions of the affliction and the *halakhot* governing it, which are unlike those of a clinical illness, indicate that leprosy is not a natural skin disease.

The Sages sought to clarify the moral defects which might lead to leprosy. The lepers mentioned in the Bible are not simple people, but people of repute, leaders, or patriots. Leprosy is likely to strike the arrogant and those who, through their statements or actions, invaded a sphere where they do not belong, especially the realm of the sacred. Sometimes leprosy strikes one who brings false accusations against another, or one whose relationship with society is otherwise impaired.

13 1 **The Lord spoke to Moses and to Aaron.** Since the priests play an active role in matters of leprosy, God also addresses Aaron, who is the representative of all priests throughout the generations,[13] **saying:**

2 **A man** or a woman, whether an adult or a child,[14] **when he shall have in the skin of his flesh a spot, or a scab, or a bright spot,** which are various types of skin discolorations,[15] **and it shall become in the skin of his flesh a mark of leprosy, he shall be brought** to Aaron the priest, or to one of his sons the priests,[D] who are the ruling authorities on matters of leprosy.

3 **The priest shall examine the mark,** which is like a white spot **on the skin of the flesh. If hair in the mark turned white,** which shows that the mark is not superficial but reaches the roots of the hair, so that even the hair turns white as a result,[16] **and** in addition **the appearance of the mark is deeper than the skin of his flesh,** although the mark is on the skin, its color or some other quality causes it to appear as though it were sunk deep into the skin,[17] these facts indicate that **it is the mark of**

leprosy in all aspects. Therefore, **the priest shall see it and pronounce it impure,** a declaration that establishes this person as a leper.

4 On the other hand, **if it is a bright white spot on the skin of his flesh**[D] but there are no other symptoms, **and its appearance is not deeper than the skin, and its hair did not turn white, the priest shall** issue a ruling to **quarantine** the person with **the mark for seven days**[D] for a follow-up examination.[8] Some maintain that the priest first marks the boundaries of the initial discoloration.

5 **The priest shall examine it,** the mark, once again **on the seventh day** of the quarantine; **and behold,** if **the mark maintained its** previous **appearance, and the mark did not spread on the skin** and grow beyond its original size, then **the priest shall quarantine** the person with **it seven days again.**

6 **The priest shall examine it on the seventh day again,** for the third time; **and behold, the mark has faded,** as its whiteness has waned, **or** at least **the mark did not spread on the skin,**[19]

Second aliya

DISCUSSION

based on the plain meaning of the verses, that the woman might have committed sins or entertained evil thoughts in the wake of the pregnancy or childbirth. In her pain and suffering she might have expressed herself inappropriately, and she must therefore bring an offering for atonement after a period of time has passed,

during which she would have come to regret her actions (see *Nidda* 31b; Ibn Ezra, and *Keli Yakar* here).

13:2 | He shall be brought to Aaron the priest, or to one of his sons the priests: The priests have full authority over halachic decision-making in these matters. This is not necessarily

because they are the foremost experts in the field, although presumably they were knowledgeable on the subject. See, for example, the story of a priest who wished to leave Israel and taught his wife how to examine skin spots (*Midrash Tanhuma, Tazria* 6). Rather, the reason priests must fulfill this role is because it involves

◄►

ח זֹאת תּוֹרַת הַיֹּלֶדֶת לַזָּכָר אוֹ לַנְּקֵבָה: וְאִם־לֹא תִמְצָא יָדָהּ דֵּי שֶׂה וְלָקְחָה שְׁתֵּי־
תֹרִים אוֹ שְׁנֵי בְּנֵי יוֹנָה אֶחָד לְעֹלָה וְאֶחָד לְחַטָּאת וְכִפֶּר עָלֶיהָ הַכֹּהֵן וְטָהֵרָה:
יג א ב וַיְדַבֵּר יְהוָה אֶל־מֹשֶׁה וְאֶל־אַהֲרֹן לֵאמֹר: אָדָם כִּי־יִהְיֶה בְעוֹר־בְּשָׂרוֹ שְׂאֵת
אוֹ־סַפַּחַת אוֹ בַהֶרֶת וְהָיָה בְעוֹר־בְּשָׂרוֹ לְנֶגַע צָרָעַת וְהוּבָא אֶל־אַהֲרֹן הַכֹּהֵן
ג אוֹ אֶל־אַחַד מִבָּנָיו הַכֹּהֲנִים: וְרָאָה הַכֹּהֵן אֶת־הַנֶּגַע בְּעוֹר־הַבָּשָׂר וְשֵׂעָר בַּנֶּגַע
הָפַךְ ׀ לָבָן וּמַרְאֵה הַנֶּגַע עָמֹק מֵעוֹר בְּשָׂרוֹ נֶגַע צָרַעַת הוּא וְרָאָהוּ הַכֹּהֵן וְטִמֵּא
ד אֹתוֹ: וְאִם־בַּהֶרֶת לְבָנָה הִוא בְּעוֹר בְּשָׂרוֹ וְעָמֹק אֵין־מַרְאֶהָ מִן־הָעוֹר וּשְׂעָרָה
ה לֹא־הָפַךְ לָבָן וְהִסְגִּיר הַכֹּהֵן אֶת־הַנֶּגַע שִׁבְעַת יָמִים: וְרָאָהוּ הַכֹּהֵן בַּיּוֹם הַשְּׁבִיעִי
וְהִנֵּה הַנֶּגַע עָמַד בְּעֵינָיו לֹא־פָשָׂה הַנֶּגַע בָּעוֹר וְהִסְגִּירוֹ הַכֹּהֵן שִׁבְעַת יָמִים שֵׁנִית:
ו וְרָאָה הַכֹּהֵן אֹתוֹ בַּיּוֹם הַשְּׁבִיעִי שֵׁנִית וְהִנֵּה כֵּהָה הַנֶּגַע וְלֹא־פָשָׂה הַנֶּגַע בָּעוֹר שני

רש״י

ח| אֶחָד לְעֹלָה וְאֶחָד לְחַטָּאת. לֹא הִקְדִּימָהּ הַכָּתוּב אֶלָּא לְמִקְרָאָהּ, אֲבָל לְהַקְרָבָה חַטָּאת קוֹדֶם לְעוֹלָה. כָּךְ שָׁנִינוּ בִּזְבָחִים בְּפֶרֶק ׳כָּל הַתָּדִיר׳ (דף צ ע״א):

פרק יג

ב| שְׂאֵת אוֹ סַפַּחַת וגו׳. שְׁמוֹת נְגָעִים הֵם, וּלְבָנוֹת זוֹ מִזּוֹ: בַּהֶרֶת. חֲבַרְבּוּרוֹת, טיי״ח בְּלַעַז, וְכֵן: ״בָּהִיר הוּא בַּשְּׁחָקִים״ (איוב לז, כא): אֶל אַהֲרֹן וגו׳. גְּזֵרַת הַכָּתוּב הִיא שֶׁאֵין טֻמְאַת נְגָעִים וְטָהֳרָתָן אֶלָּא עַל פִּי כֹּהֵן:

ג| הָפַךְ לָבָן. מִתְּחִלָּה שָׁחוֹר וְהָפַךְ לְלָבָן בְּתוֹךְ הַנֶּגַע. וּמִעוּט שֵׂעָר – שְׁנַיִם: עָמֹק מֵעוֹר בְּשָׂרוֹ. כָּל מַרְאֵה לָבָן עָמֹק הוּא, כְּמַרְאֵה חַמָּה עֲמֻקָּה מִן הַצֵּל: וְטִמֵּא אֹתוֹ. יֹאמַר לוֹ: ׳טָמֵא אַתָּה׳, שֶׁשֵּׂעָר לָבָן סִימַן טֻמְאָה הוּא גְּזֵרַת הַכָּתוּב:

ד| וְעָמֹק אֵין מַרְאֶהָ. לֹא יָדַעְתִּי פֵּרוּשׁוֹ: וְהִסְגִּיר. יַסְגִּירֶנּוּ בְּבַיִת אֶחָד וְלֹא יֵרָאֶה עַד סוֹף הַשָּׁבוּעַ, וְיוֹכִיחוּ סִימָנִים עָלָיו:

ה| בְּעֵינָיו. בְּמַרְאֵהוּ וּבְשִׁעוּרוֹ הָרִאשׁוֹן: וְהִסְגִּירוֹ שֵׁנִית. הָא אִם פָּשָׂה בַּשָּׁבוּעַ רִאשׁוֹן – טָמֵא מֻחְלָט (נגעים ג, ג):

ו| כֵּהָה. הָכְהָה מִמַּרְאִיתוֹ. הָא אִם עָמַד בְּמַרְאִיתוֹ אוֹ פָּשָׂה – טָמֵא: מִסְפַּחַת. שֵׁם נֶגַע טָהוֹר: וְכִבֶּס בְּגָדָיו וְטָהֵר. הוֹאִיל וְנִזְקַק לְהֶסְגֵּר נִקְרָא טָמֵא וְצָרִיךְ טְבִילָה:

DISCUSSION

more than mere counseling; it bears essential and ritual significance. The priest's declaration is an example of a performative utterance in that it changes the reality it describes: It causes the individual to become impure. Therefore, although a non-priest who is learned and an expert in the details of the *halakhot* of leprosy can advise a priest whether to render a spot pure or impure, ultimately it is only the declaration of the priest that determines the spot's halakhic status (see *Sifra*, end of chap. 9; *Nega'im* 3:1; *Arakhin* 3a, and *Tosafot* ad loc.).

13:4| **If it is a bright white spot on the skin of his flesh:** The appearance of a mark on one's skin depends, among other factors, on his skin color. The Sages discuss this issue and explain that the natural skin color of the ancient Israelites was not white but a shade of light brown similar to the color of the wood of the box tree, *Buxus* (see *Nega'im* 2:1). A white mark will not stand out against light-colored skin, nor will it appear to be deeper than that skin; conversely, it will be highly prominent against a background of brownish skin.

The priest shall quarantine the mark seven days: A quarantined leper is kept in isolation, as a leper must be sent out of the camp (see *Megilla* 8b, Rashi, and *Tur* ad loc.; Rashi and Tosafot, *Moed Katan* 7a). However, some explain that this term does not denote physical isolation but rather represents a purely legal determination of the mark as requiring further clarification (see *Mishne LaMelekh*, Rambam, *Sefer Tahara, Hilkhot Tumat Tzara'at* 14:5). Alternatively, some explain that it is the act of drawing an outline around the mark (see *Tur*, citing Rosh).

13:6| **Scab [*mispaḥat*]:** Unlike the *sappaḥat* mentioned in verse 2 as an impure mark, which the Sages understood to mean a secondary mark to a spot or a bright spot, a *mispaḥat* is not a ritually impure mark. Alternatively, a *mispaḥat* and a *sappaḥat* are one and the same, but such a mark is impure only if it spreads (see *Bekhor Shor*, verse 2).

And he shall wash his garments, and he shall be purified: This individual, who bore a quasi-impurity (see Rashi; *Bekhor Shor*), is designated by the Sages as a quarantined leper (*Megilla* 1:7). Although he did not contract the severe impurity of an absolute leper, he must still wash his garments when his period of quarantine ends.

the priest shall pronounce it pure: It is a scab,[D] a mere skin disease that does not entail ritual impurity; **and he,** the person who had been quarantined, **shall wash his garments, and he shall be purified.**[D]

7 **But if the scab spread on the skin,** the affected area grew, **after he was shown to the priest** at the end of the first quarantine **for** the sake of **his purification, he shall be examined again by the priest.**

8 **The priest shall examine; and behold, the scab spread on the skin, the priest shall pronounce him impure: It is leprosy.**

9 It has been established that in order for the priest to determine that a mark is leprosy, he must find one of two indications: Either white hair, or the spreading of the mark during the days of quarantine. The Torah now presents another sign: **A mark of leprosy, when it is on a person, he shall be brought to the priest.**

10 **The priest shall examine; and behold, if there be a white spot**[D] **on the skin, and it** changed its appearance and **turned** the **hair** found in it **white, or there is a growth**[D] **of raw flesh in the spot,** meaning that on the affected area there appears tissue that looks altogether healthy,[20]

11 **it is an old,** extended **leprosy in the skin of his flesh; the priest shall pronounce him impure.** The growth of healthy flesh does not render the mark pure; on the contrary, it is an indication that it is old leprosy. **He,** the priest, **shall not quarantine him,** since this is unnecessary, **as he,** the afflicted individual, **is** immediately declared **impure.**

12 There is a case which contrasts with the previous instances of impurity: **And if the leprosy shall erupt,** as the discoloration grows larger and larger **on the skin, and the leprosy shall cover all the skin of the mark from his head to his feet, for the entire view of the eyes of the priest,** meaning that all of the skin exposed to the priest became lighter in color, like the shade of the mark,

13 **the priest shall examine; and behold, the leprosy covered all his flesh,** as no exposed portion remains unaffected; **he shall pronounce the mark pure.** Since **it turned white in its entirety, it is pure.** A single spot on a person's skin renders him ritually impure, but if the leprosy erupts over his entire body, he is pure.

14 **But on the day that raw flesh appears on him,** and some of his flesh regains its natural appearance, only then **he shall be impure.**

15 **The priest shall examine the raw flesh and pronounce it impure; the raw flesh is impure: It is leprosy.** Paradoxically, if one's entire body is covered by leprosy, he is pure, but if only part of his body is affected, he is impure.

16 **Or if** some raw flesh appears, so that he is rendered impure, and then **the raw flesh is restored and turns white, he shall come to the priest.**

17 **The priest shall examine him; and behold, the** skin affected by the **mark turned white, the priest shall pronounce the mark to be pure: It is** once again **pure.**

18 The section so far has dealt with a mark that appears on healthy
Third aliya skin. However, a leprous mark can also appear in a different manner: **Flesh, when there is in its skin a rash**[D] **that is healed,**

19 **on the place of the rash,** where the skin has not yet fully mended,[21] **there is a white spot, or a white-red bright spot.** This new form of leprosy, which is red and white in color, is referred to by the Sages as a *patukh*.[22] **It shall be shown to the priest.**

20 **The priest shall examine; and behold, its appearance,** the appearance of the bright spot,[23] **is lower than the skin, and its hair turned white,** which, as stated above (verse 3), is one of the indications of impurity, **the priest shall pronounce it impure: It is a mark of leprosy,** as **it erupted in the** place where there had earlier been a **rash.**

21 **But if the priest shall examine it, and behold, there is no white hair in it, and it is not lower than the skin, and it is faded,** meaning that its whiteness is relatively weak, and therefore it does not appear to be lower than the skin,[24] and some explain that the word "not" applies to both clauses, for it is neither

DISCUSSION

13:10 | **White spot [*se'et*]:** This word is understood to be derived from the root *nun-sin-alef* meaning raise. The spot appears to be raised above the surrounding skin, even if it is not actually raised (see *Targum Yonatan*; *She'iltot deRav Aḥai* 104; Ramban, and *Ha'amek Davar*, verse 3; Ra'avad, based on Rambam, *Sefer Tahara, Hilkhot Tumat Tzara'at* 1:6). Others explain that the *se'et* appears raised in relation to the bright spot, not in relation to the surrounding skin.

Or there is a growth [*miḥyat*]: The word *miḥyat* is derived from the root *ḥet-yod-heh*, which indicates healing. Some maintain that it is from the root *mem-ḥet-heh*, meaning melting and softening, and that the mark contains raw flesh that emits moisture (Abravanel).

13:18 | **Rash [*sheḥin*]:** *Sheḥin* is a skin disease, likely inflammatory. According to the Sages, *sheḥin* is a disease connected to excessive heat, a type of burn that is not inflicted by an external force. The root *shin-ḥet-nun* refers to the quality of being hot and sometimes also dry (see *Sifra*; *Nega'im* 9:1; *Ḥullin* 8a, and Rashi ad loc.; see also *Ta'anit* 24b, and Rashi ad loc.; Rashi, Exodus 9:9; *Tosafot, Bava Kama* 101b; Ritva, *Sukka* 40a; *Tashbetz Katan* 131).

ז וְטִהֲרוֹ הַכֹּהֵן מִסְפַּחַת הִוא וְכִבֶּס בְּגָדָיו וְטָהֵר: וְאִם־פָּשֹׂה תִפְשֶׂה הַמִּסְפַּחַת

ח בָּעוֹר אַחֲרֵי הֵרָאֹתוֹ אֶל־הַכֹּהֵן לְטָהֳרָתוֹ וְנִרְאָה שֵׁנִית אֶל־הַכֹּהֵן: וְרָאָה הַכֹּהֵן

וְהִנֵּה פָּשְׂתָה הַמִּסְפַּחַת בָּעוֹר וְטִמְּאוֹ הַכֹּהֵן צָרַעַת הִוא:

ט נֶגַע צָרַעַת כִּי תִהְיֶה בְּאָדָם וְהוּבָא אֶל־הַכֹּהֵן: וְרָאָה הַכֹּהֵן וְהִנֵּה שְׂאֵת־לְבָנָה

יא בָעוֹר וְהִיא הָפְכָה שֵׂעָר לָבָן וּמִחְיַת בָּשָׂר חַי בַּשְׂאֵת: צָרַעַת נוֹשֶׁנֶת הִוא בְּעוֹר

בְּשָׂרוֹ וְטִמְּאוֹ הַכֹּהֵן לֹא יַסְגִּרֶנּוּ כִּי טָמֵא הוּא: וְאִם־פָּרוֹחַ תִּפְרַח הַצָּרַעַת בָּעוֹר

וְכִסְּתָה הַצָּרַעַת אֵת כָּל־עוֹר הַנֶּגַע מֵרֹאשׁוֹ וְעַד־רַגְלָיו לְכָל־מַרְאֵה עֵינֵי הַכֹּהֵן:

יג וְרָאָה הַכֹּהֵן וְהִנֵּה כִסְּתָה הַצָּרַעַת אֶת־כָּל־בְּשָׂרוֹ וְטִהַר אֶת־הַנָּגַע כֻּלּוֹ הָפַךְ לָבָן

יד טָהוֹר הוּא: וּבְיוֹם הֵרָאוֹת בּוֹ בָּשָׂר חַי יִטְמָא: וְרָאָה הַכֹּהֵן אֶת־הַבָּשָׂר הַחַי

טז וְטִמְּאוֹ הַבָּשָׂר הַחַי טָמֵא הוּא צָרַעַת הוּא: אוֹ כִי יָשׁוּב הַבָּשָׂר הַחַי וְנֶהְפַּךְ לְלָבָן

יז וּבָא אֶל־הַכֹּהֵן: וְרָאָהוּ הַכֹּהֵן וְהִנֵּה נֶהְפַּךְ הַנֶּגַע לְלָבָן וְטִהַר הַכֹּהֵן אֶת־הַנֶּגַע

טָהוֹר הוּא:

יח וּבָשָׂר כִּי־יִהְיֶה בוֹ־בְעֹרוֹ שְׁחִין וְנִרְפָּא: וְהָיָה בִּמְקוֹם הַשְּׁחִין שְׂאֵת לְבָנָה אוֹ **שלישי**

כ בַהֶרֶת לְבָנָה אֲדַמְדָּמֶת וְנִרְאָה אֶל־הַכֹּהֵן: וְרָאָה הַכֹּהֵן וְהִנֵּה מַרְאֶהָ שָׁפָל

מִן־הָעוֹר וּשְׂעָרָהּ הָפַךְ לָבָן וְטִמְּאוֹ הַכֹּהֵן נֶגַע־צָרַעַת הִוא בַּשְּׁחִין פָּרָחָה:

כא וְאִם ׀ יִרְאֶנָּה הַכֹּהֵן וְהִנֵּה אֵין־בָּהּ שֵׂעָר לָבָן וּשְׁפָלָה אֵינֶנָּה מִן־הָעוֹר וְהִיא כֵהָה

רש"י

ח] וְטִמְּאוֹ הַכֹּהֵן. וּמִשֶּׁטִּמְּאוֹ הֲרֵי הוּא מֻחְלָט, וְזָקוּק
לְצִפֳּרִים וּלְתִגְלַחַת וּלְקָרְבָּן הָאָמוּר בְּפָרָשַׁת "זֹאת תִּהְיֶה"
(לְהַלָּן יד, ח-לב): הַמִּסְפַּחַת הַזֹּאת. צָרַעַת
לְשׁוֹן נְקֵבָה, "נֶגַע" לְשׁוֹן זָכָר:

יא] וּמִחְיַת. שיינ"ט בְּלַעַז, שֶׁנֶּהְפַּךְ מִקְצַת הַלֹּבֶן
שֶׁבְּתוֹךְ הַשְּׂאֵת לְמַרְאֵה בָּשָׂר, אַף הוּא סִימָן טֻמְאָה,
שֵׂעָר לָבָן בְּלֹא מִחְיָה, וּמִחְיָה בְּלֹא שֵׂעָר לָבָן, וְחַד עַל
פִּי שֶׁלֹּא נֶאֶמְרָה מִחְיָה חֶלְּא בַּשְׂאֵת, אַף בְּכָל הַמַּרְאוֹת
וְתוֹלְדוֹתֵיהֶן הוּא סִימָן טֻמְאָה:

יא] צָרַעַת נוֹשֶׁנֶת הִוא. מַכָּה יְשָׁנָה הִיא תַּחַת הַמִּחְיָה,
וַחֲבוּרָה זוֹ נִרְאֵית בְּרִיאָה מִלְמַעְלָה וּמִתַּחְתֶּיהָ מְלֵאָה לֵחָה,
שֶׁלֹּא תֹּאמַר הוֹאִיל וְעָלְתָה מִחְיָה מְטַהֲרֶנָּה:

יב] מֵרֹאשׁוֹ. שֶׁל אָדָם "וְעַד רַגְלָיו": לְכָל מַרְאֵה עֵינֵי
הַכֹּהֵן. פְּרָט לְכֹהֵן שֶׁחָשַׁךְ מְאוֹרוֹ:

יד] וּבְיוֹם הֵרָאוֹת בּוֹ בָּשָׂר חַי. אִם צָמְחָה בּוֹ מִחְיָה הֲרֵי
כְּבָר פֵּרַשׁ שֶׁהַמִּחְיָה סִימָן טֻמְאָה, אֶלָּא הֲרֵי שֶׁהָיָה הַנֶּגַע
בְּאֶחָד מֵאֵיבָרִים וַחֲבוּרָה רָאשֵׁי אֵבָרִים מְטַמְּאִין
מִשּׁוּם מִחְיָה, לְפִי שֶׁאֵין נִרְאֶה כֻּלּוֹ כְּאֶחָד שֶׁשּׁוֹפְעִין
אֵילָךְ וְאֵילָךְ, וְחַד לֹא אָמַר הַכָּתוּב שֶׁפִּיעוּנוֹ עַל יְדֵי
שָׁמֶן, כְּגוֹן שֶׁהֶעֱבִיר רֹחַב וְנַעֲשָׂה רָחָב מִן הַמִּחְיָה,
לְמָדְנוּ הַכָּתוּב שֶׁתְּטַמֵּא. וּבְיוֹם. מַה תַּלְמוּד לוֹמַר? יֵשׁ יוֹם
שֶׁאַתָּה רוֹאֶה בּוֹ וְיֵשׁ יוֹם שֶׁאֵין אַתָּה רוֹאֶה בּוֹ: מִכָּאן אָמְרוּ,
חָתָן נוֹתְנִין לוֹ כָּל שִׁבְעַת יְמֵי הַמִּשְׁתֶּה לוֹ וּלְאִצְטְלִיתוֹ
וּלְכִסּוּתוֹ, וְכֵן בָּרֶגֶל נוֹתְנִין לוֹ כָּל יְמֵי הָרֶגֶל:

טו] צָרַעַת הוּא. הַבָּשָׂר הַהוּא, "בָּשָׂר" לְשׁוֹן זָכָר:

יז] שְׁחִין. לְשׁוֹן חִמּוּם, שֶׁנִּתְחַמֵּם הַבָּשָׂר בְּלִקּוּי
הַבָּא לוֹ מֵחֲמַת מַכָּה שֶׁלֹּא מֵחֲמַת הָאוּר: וְנִרְפָּא.
הַשְּׁחִין הֶעֱלָה אֲרוּכָה, וּבִמְקוֹמוֹ הֶעֱלָה נֶגַע
אַחֵר:

יט] אוֹ בַהֶרֶת לְבָנָה אֲדַמְדָּמֶת. שֶׁאֵין הַנֶּגַע לָבָן חֶלֶק
אֶלָּא פָּתוּךְ וּמְעֹרָב בִּשְׁתֵּי מַרְאוֹת - לָבָן וְאָדֹם:

כ] מַרְאֶהָ שָׁפָל. וְאֵין מַמָּשָׁהּ שָׁפָל, אֶלָּא מִתּוֹךְ לַבְנוּנִיתוֹ
הוּא נִרְאֶה שָׁפָל וְעָמֹק, כְּמַרְאֵה חַמָּה עֲמֻקָּה מִן הַצֵּל:

lower nor faded,[25] then **the priest shall quarantine him** in a
specific place (see verse 4) for **seven days.**
22 After seven days he is examined once again, **and if it shall
spread on the skin, the priest shall pronounce him impure:
It is a mark.**
23 **But if the bright spot shall remain in place,** meaning that it
stays the same size, and **it did not spread, it is a scar of the
rash.** It is merely the natural consequence of an inflammation
and has no significance with regard to ritual purity or impurity,
and therefore **the priest shall pronounce him pure.**
24 The verse states a similar case: **Or flesh, when there is on its**
Fourth aliya **skin a burn by fire, and the healed flesh of the burn became**
(Second aliya) **a bright spot, reddish white, or white,**
25 **the priest shall examine it; and behold, hair in the bright
spot turned white, and its appearance is deeper than the
skin, it is leprosy that erupted in** the spot of **the burn; the
priest shall pronounce him impure: It is a mark of leprosy.**
26 **But if the priest shall examine it, and behold, there is no
white hair in the bright spot, and it is no lower than the
skin, and it is faded** (see verse 21), **the priest shall quarantine
him seven days.**
27 **The priest shall examine him on the seventh day; if** the bright
spot has **spread on the skin, the priest shall pronounce him
impure,** because **it is a mark of leprosy.**
28 **But if the bright spot remains in** its **place and has not spread
on the skin,[D] and it is faded,** it is not as bright as it was at the
outset, **it is the spot of the burn; the priest shall pronounce
him pure,[D] as it is the scar of the burn.**
29 The section has discussed marks found on exposed skin,
Fifth aliya whether it is hairy or smooth; it now shifts to marks found
on areas with a high concentration of hair. **A man or woman,
when there shall be a mark on a head or on a beard,**
30 **the priest shall examine the mark,** which might be the symp-
tom of an illness, the result of an accident, or perhaps a sign
of leprosy.[26] **And behold, its appearance is deeper than the
skin, and there is yellow, thin hair[D] in it. The priest shall
pronounce it impure: It is a scall;[D] it is leprosy of the head
or of the beard.**
31 **When the priest examines the mark of the scall, and behold,
its appearance is not deeper than the skin, and** yet **there is
no black hair in it,** as would be found on a healthy head, since
black is the most common hair color among Jews, **the priest
shall quarantine the mark of the scall seven days.**
32 **The priest shall examine the mark on the seventh day; and
behold, the scall did not spread, and there is no yellow hair
in it, and the appearance of the scall is not deeper than the
skin.**
33 In this case the mark must be re-examined. **He,** the quarantined
leper, **shall be shaved,** one must shave the hair surrounding the
mark,[27] **but** the hair growing in **the scall** itself or along its edges
he shall not shave.[28] This enables the priest to examine the
edges of the mark and follow its progress. **And the priest shall
quarantine the scall seven days again,** a kind of intermediate
stage between impurity and purity.
34 **The priest shall examine the scall** once again **on the seventh
day; and behold, the scall did not spread in the skin, and
its appearance is not deeper than the skin, the priest shall
pronounce it pure; and he shall wash his garments and be
purified.**
35 **But if the scall** did not spread during the period that the leper
was quarantined, and yet it **shall spread on the skin after his
purification,**

DISCUSSION

13:28 | **But if the bright spot remains in place and has not spread on the skin:** According to the plain meaning of the text, there are two conditions for pronouncing the mark pure: It did not spread and it faded. However, the *halakha* is that one of these conditions is enough: The mark is declared pure either if it did not spread or if it faded below the four levels of whiteness that characterize marks of leprosy. Rabbi Samson Raphael Hirsch explains that the phrase "and it is faded" means: Even if it faded slightly, e.g., the shade of a bright spot turned into the shade of a slightly fainter spot, it is pure, provided that it did not spread. Others maintain, as in verse 21, that the word "not" refers to both conditions, and the verse is saying: If it did not spread on the skin and it is not faded, as it retained its strong whiteness, it is pure (*Ḥizkuni*).

The priest shall pronounce him pure: The *halakhot* of leprosy of an inflammation or a burn are very similar to those of leprosy of the flesh. There too, the mark's status is determined by whether or not the hair turned white and whether the mark spread on the skin. It can be inferred from the verses that there are two differences between these cases: With regard to inflammations and burns, if signs of impurity were not seen after a week of quarantine, the mark is pure, as the skin was already damaged. By contrast, in the case of leprosy of the flesh, a further week of quarantine is necessary to determine the matter. Another difference is that only two signs of impurity are mentioned for inflammations and burns, while the third sign of impurity for leprosy of the flesh, that is, the healing of the flesh, is absent here (see Mishna *Nega'im* 3:3–4, 9:1).

13:30 | **Yellow thin [*dak*] hair:** Unlike the forms of leprosy discussed earlier, these hairs are not white, but they are also not their natural color. Their appearance is unusual in another way as well; *tannai'im* disagree whether the word *dak* means thin or short (see *Nega'im* 10:1).

Scall [*netek*]: Some interpret this term as an unexplained detachment [*nituk*] of hair from a particular area, even if is not accompanied by a change in the appearance of the skin (see Rambam, *Sefer Tahara*, *Hilkhot Tumat Tzara'at* 8:1, and Ra'avad ad loc.).

כב וְהִסְגִּירוֹ הַכֹּהֵן שִׁבְעַת יָמִים: וְאִם־פָּשֹׂה תִפְשֶׂה בָּעוֹר וְטִמֵּא הַכֹּהֵן אֹתוֹ נֶגַע
כג הִוא: וְאִם־תַּחְתֶּיהָ תַּעֲמֹד הַבַּהֶרֶת לֹא פָשָׂתָה צָרֶבֶת הַשְּׁחִין הִוא וְטִהֲרוֹ
כד הַכֹּהֵן: אוֹ בָשָׂר כִּי־יִהְיֶה בְעֹרוֹ מִכְוַת־אֵשׁ וְהָיְתָה מִחְיַת הַמִּכְוָה רביעי /שני/
כה בַּהֶרֶת לְבָנָה אֲדַמְדֶּמֶת אוֹ לְבָנָה: וְרָאָה אֹתָהּ הַכֹּהֵן וְהִנֵּה נֶהְפַּךְ שֵׂעָר לָבָן
בַּבַּהֶרֶת וּמַרְאֶהָ עָמֹק מִן־הָעוֹר צָרַעַת הִוא בַּמִּכְוָה פָּרָחָה וְטִמֵּא אֹתוֹ הַכֹּהֵן
כו נֶגַע צָרַעַת הִוא: וְאִם ׀ יִרְאֶנָּה הַכֹּהֵן וְהִנֵּה אֵין־בַּבַּהֶרֶת שֵׂעָר לָבָן וּשְׁפָלָה אֵינֶנָּה
כז מִן־הָעוֹר וְהִוא כֵהָה וְהִסְגִּירוֹ הַכֹּהֵן שִׁבְעַת יָמִים: וְרָאָהוּ הַכֹּהֵן בַּיּוֹם הַשְּׁבִיעִי
כח אִם־פָּשֹׂה תִפְשֶׂה בָּעוֹר וְטִמֵּא הַכֹּהֵן אֹתוֹ נֶגַע צָרַעַת הִוא: וְאִם־תַּחְתֶּיהָ תַעֲמֹד
הַבַּהֶרֶת לֹא־פָשְׂתָה בָעוֹר וְהִוא כֵהָה שְׂאֵת הַמִּכְוָה הִוא וְטִהֲרוֹ הַכֹּהֵן כִּי־צָרֶבֶת
הַמִּכְוָה הִוא:
כט ל וְאִישׁ אוֹ אִשָּׁה כִּי־יִהְיֶה בוֹ נָגַע בְּרֹאשׁ אוֹ בְזָקָן: וְרָאָה הַכֹּהֵן אֶת־הַנֶּגַע וְהִנֵּה ח חמישי
מַרְאֵהוּ עָמֹק מִן־הָעוֹר וּבוֹ שֵׂעָר צָהֹב דָּק וְטִמֵּא אֹתוֹ הַכֹּהֵן נֶתֶק הוּא צָרַעַת
לא הָרֹאשׁ אוֹ הַזָּקָן הוּא: וְכִי־יִרְאֶה הַכֹּהֵן אֶת־נֶגַע הַנֶּתֶק וְהִנֵּה אֵין־מַרְאֵהוּ עָמֹק
מִן־הָעוֹר וְשֵׂעָר שָׁחֹר אֵין בּוֹ וְהִסְגִּיר הַכֹּהֵן אֶת־נֶגַע הַנֶּתֶק שִׁבְעַת יָמִים:
לב וְרָאָה הַכֹּהֵן אֶת־הַנֶּגַע בַּיּוֹם הַשְּׁבִיעִי וְהִנֵּה לֹא־פָשָׂה הַנֶּתֶק וְלֹא־הָיָה בוֹ
לג שֵׂעָר צָהֹב וּמַרְאֵה הַנֶּתֶק אֵין עָמֹק מִן־הָעוֹר: וְהִתְגַּלָּח וְאֶת־הַנֶּתֶק לֹא יְגַלֵּחַ
לד וְהִסְגִּיר הַכֹּהֵן אֶת־הַנֶּתֶק שִׁבְעַת יָמִים שֵׁנִית: וְרָאָה הַכֹּהֵן אֶת־הַנֶּתֶק בַּיּוֹם
הַשְּׁבִיעִי וְהִנֵּה לֹא־פָשָׂה הַנֶּתֶק בָּעוֹר וּמַרְאֵהוּ אֵינֶנּוּ עָמֹק מִן־הָעוֹר וְטִהַר
לה אֹתוֹ הַכֹּהֵן וְכִבֶּס בְּגָדָיו וְטָהֵר: וְאִם־פָּשֹׂה יִפְשֶׂה הַנֶּתֶק בָּעוֹר אַחֲרֵי טָהֳרָתוֹ:

רש״י

כב | **נֶגַע הוּא.** הַשְּׂאֵת הַזֹּאת אוֹ הַבַּהֶרֶת:

כג | **תַּחְתֶּיהָ.** בִּמְקוֹמָהּ: **צָרֶבֶת הַשְּׁחִין.** כְּתַרְגּוּמוֹ: "רֹשֶׁם שִׁחְנָא", אֵינוֹ אֶלָּא רֹשֶׁם הַחִמּוּם הַנִּכָּר בַּבָּשָׂר. כָּל 'צָרֶבֶת' לְשׁוֹן רְגִיעַת עוֹר הַנִּרְגָּע מֵחֲמַת חִמּוּם, כְּמוֹ: "וְנִצְרְבוּ בָהּ כָּל פָּנִים" (יחזקאל כא, ג), רייטרי"ר בְּלַעַז: **צָרֶבֶת.** רטריחמנ"ט בְּלַעַז:

כד | **מִחְיַת הַמִּכְוָה.** סנמנ"ט, כְּשֶׁחָיְתָה הַמִּכְוָה, נֶהֶפְכָה לְבַהֶרֶת פְּתוּכָה אוֹ לְבָנָה חֲלָקָה:

כט | **בְּרֹאשׁ אוֹ בְזָקָן.** בָּא הַכָּתוּב לְחַלֵּק בֵּין נֶגַע שֶׁבִּמְקוֹם שֵׂעָר לְנֶגַע שֶׁבִּמְקוֹם בָּשָׂר, שֶׁזֶּה סִימָנוֹ בְּשֵׂעָר לָבָן וְזֶה סִימָנוֹ בְּשֵׂעָר צָהֹב:

ל | **וּבוֹ שֵׂעָר צָהֹב.** שֶׁנֶּהֱפַךְ שֵׂעָר שָׁחוֹר שֶׁבּוֹ לְצָהֹב: **נֶתֶק הוּא.** כָּךְ שְׁמוֹ שֶׁל נֶגַע שֶׁבִּמְקוֹם שֵׂעָר:

לא | **וְשֵׂעָר שָׁחֹר אֵין בּוֹ.** הָא אִם הָיָה בּוֹ שֵׂעָר שָׁחוֹר – טָהוֹר וְאֵין צָרִיךְ לְהֶסְגֵּר, שֶׁשֵּׂעָר שָׁחוֹר סִימַן טָהֳרָה הוּא בִּנְתָקִים, כְּמוֹ שֶׁנֶּאֱמַר: "וְשֵׂעָר שָׁחֹר צָמַח בּוֹ" וְגוֹ' (להלן פסוק לז):

לב | **וְהִנֵּה לֹא פָשָׂה וְגוֹ'.** הָא אִם פָּשָׂה אוֹ הָיָה בּוֹ שֵׂעָר צָהֹב – טָמֵא:

לג | **וְהִתְגַּלָּח.** סְבִיבוֹת הַנֶּתֶק: **וְאֶת הַנֶּתֶק לֹא יְגַלֵּחַ.** מַנִּיחַ שְׁתֵּי שְׂעָרוֹת סָמוּךְ לוֹ סָבִיב, כְּדֵי שֶׁיְּהֵא נִכָּר אִם פָּשָׂה, שֶׁאִם יִפְשֶׂה יַעֲבֹר הַשְּׂעָרוֹת וְיֵצֵא לִמְקוֹם הַגִּלּוּחַ:

לה | **אַחֲרֵי טָהֳרָתוֹ.** אֵין לִי אֶלָּא פּוֹשֶׂה לְאַחַר הַפְּטוּר. מִנַּיִן אַף בְּסוֹף שָׁבוּעַ רִאשׁוֹן וּבְסוֹף שָׁבוּעַ שֵׁנִי? תַּלְמוּד לוֹמַר: "פָּשֹׂה יִפְשֶׂה":

36 the priest shall examine him; and behold, the scall spread on the skin, and therefore **the priest shall not** have to **inspect for the yellow hair** and see whether or not there is any yellow hair in it, as in any case **it is impure.** The spread of the scall alone is confirmation of the impurity of the mark.

37 **But if the scall maintained its appearance** after the quarantine, **and black hair grew in it,**[D] it is a sign that **the scall** has **healed, it is pure. The priest shall pronounce it pure.** Although the scall healed and there is no longer any reason for it to be impure, the priest must declare and establish its purity.

38 Next, the Torah deals with a case similar to that of a scall with black hair in it, which is not an impure mark: **A man or a woman, if there will be in the skin of their flesh bright spots, bright white spots,**

39 **the priest shall examine; and behold, the bright spots in the skin of their flesh are faded white,** whitish but not pure white, **it is a tetter,** a certain skin disease, **that erupted on the skin,** and therefore **it is pure.**

40 Having presented the *halakhot* of marks on the flesh and marks on the hairy part of the head, the Torah adds: **A man, if the hair of his head falls out** for any reason, **he is** merely **bald; he is pure,** as baldness in itself has no significance with respect to the *halakhot* of ritual impurity. Since baldness is more common among men, the verse refers to a man.[29]

Sixth aliya
(Third aliya)

41 **And** likewise, **if on the** front **side of his face the hair of his head falls,**[30] **he is frontally bald;** this too is a natural phenomenon, and therefore **he is pure.**

42 But when there is on the bald head, or the bald forehead, a reddish-white mark, a white mark with a reddish hue, it is leprosy erupting on his bald head or on his bald forehead.

43 **The priest shall examine it; and behold, if the spot of the mark is reddish white on his bald head, or on his bald forehead,** and it is **like the appearance of** ordinary **leprosy in the skin of the flesh,**

44 **he is a leprous man, he is impure; the priest shall pronounce him impure: His mark is on his head.** This is like the ordinary leprosy of the skin, except for the fact that it lacks the sign of impurity which stems from the color of the hair, as it appears on a bald spot of the head. Even if a small amount of white hair grew on the mark in the bald area, it would not necessarily be a sign of impurity.[21]

45 After explaining the various appearances of leprous marks, the Torah addresses the *halakhot* governing the leper himself: **And the leper in whom the mark is,** and whom the priest has pronounced as a leper, **his garments shall be rent.** He must tear his garments, among other reasons, as a sign of mourning.[22] **And the hair of his head shall be grown out.**[D] Some explain that this means that his hair shall be uncovered.[23] **And he shall cover** his mouth and **his upper lip**[D] with his outer garment **and shall cry: Impure, impure,** thereby informing others of his ritually impure status.

46 **All the days that the mark is on him he shall be impure; he is impure; he shall live alone; outside the camp is his dwelling,**[D] where he is cut off almost entirely from human society.

Leprosy of Clothing

LEVITICUS 13:47–59

After dealing with the *halakhot* of leprosy that appears on the human body, the Torah discusses an even stranger phenomenon: Leprosy of clothing, a ball of thread, or a leather implement. This phenomenon, which is unique to the Jewish people, is likewise perceived as a sign from Heaven. The list of specific materials that are subject to this impurity, which is repeated in almost every verse in the passage, perhaps serves to emphasize the wondrous nature of the plague.

The *halakhot* of leprosy of clothing differ from those of leprosy of the body both with regard to the signs of purity and impurity and with regard to the eventual obligation to burn the impure garment. Nevertheless, there is a certain similarity between the cases: In both instances the suspicious mark must be brought to a priest for examination, and it is he who determines whether there is indeed cause for concern and whether the mark must be left under observation. A week later he examines it again. If the mark grew in size, it is confirmed leprosy, which imparts impurity. If it did not grow, he continues to track the progress of the mark, by additional quarantine in the case of a human body, or by laundering in the case of clothing.

47 **The garment, if there shall be in it a mark of leprosy, whether in a woolen garment, or in a linen garment.** This verse is not referring to a spot caused by some external factor or one that can easily be removed through rinsing and the like, but to an abnormal mark growing on the garment through no apparent cause.

DISCUSSION

13:37 | But if the scall maintained its appearance and black hair grew in it: It is unclear from the verse whether both conditions are necessary for purity or if one suffices. The Sages interpret the text in a lenient fashion (*Bekhor Shor; Ḥizkuni*; see *Nega'im* 10:3).

13:45 | His garments shall be rent and the hair of his head shall be grown out: Leprosy is a relatively severe form of ritual impurity, similar to the impurity imparted by a corpse. It is considered like the penetration of death into a living body. Although this infiltration occurs only at the surface, on the skin, nevertheless it symbolizes that the leper is a walking corpse, as it were, and that he is cut off from human society (see Numbers 12:12; *Nedarim* 64b). This might be the reason that the leper observes certain mourning practices, as though he were

↤↦

וְרָאָהוּ הַכֹּהֵן וְהִנֵּה פָּשָׂה הַנֶּתֶק בָּעוֹר לֹא־יְבַקֵּר הַכֹּהֵן לַשֵּׂעָר הַצָּהֹב טָמֵא הוּא: לז

וְאִם־בְּעֵינָיו עָמַד הַנֶּתֶק וְשֵׂעָר שָׁחֹר צָמַח־בּוֹ נִרְפָּא הַנֶּתֶק טָהוֹר הוּא וְטִהֲרוֹ הַכֹּהֵן: לז

וְאִישׁ אוֹ־אִשָּׁה כִּי־יִהְיֶה בְעוֹר־בְּשָׂרָם בֶּהָרֹת בֶּהָרֹת לְבָנֹת: לח

וְרָאָה הַכֹּהֵן וְהִנֵּה בְעוֹר־בְּשָׂרָם בֶּהָרֹת כֵּהוֹת לְבָנֹת בֹּהַק הוּא פָּרַח בָּעוֹר טָהוֹר הוּא: לט

וְאִישׁ כִּי יִמָּרֵט רֹאשׁוֹ קֵרֵחַ הוּא טָהוֹר הוּא: וְאִם מִפְּאַת פָּנָיו מ

יִמָּרֵט רֹאשׁוֹ גִּבֵּחַ הוּא טָהוֹר הוּא: וְכִי־יִהְיֶה בַקָּרַחַת אוֹ בַגַּבַּחַת נֶגַע לָבָן אֲדַמְדָּם מא

צָרַעַת פֹּרַחַת הִוא בְּקָרַחְתּוֹ אוֹ בְגַבַּחְתּוֹ: וְרָאָה אֹתוֹ הַכֹּהֵן וְהִנֵּה שְׂאֵת־הַנֶּגַע מב

לְבָנָה אֲדַמְדֶּמֶת בְּקָרַחְתּוֹ אוֹ בְגַבַּחְתּוֹ כְּמַרְאֵה צָרַעַת עוֹר בָּשָׂר: אִישׁ־צָרוּעַ הוּא מג

טָמֵא הוּא טַמֵּא יְטַמְּאֶנּוּ הַכֹּהֵן בְּרֹאשׁוֹ נִגְעוֹ: וְהַצָּרוּעַ אֲשֶׁר־בּוֹ הַנֶּגַע בְּגָדָיו יִהְיוּ מד

פְרֻמִים וְרֹאשׁוֹ יִהְיֶה פָרוּעַ וְעַל־שָׂפָם יַעְטֶה וְטָמֵא | טָמֵא יִקְרָא: כָּל־יְמֵי אֲשֶׁר מה

הַנֶּגַע בּוֹ יִטְמָא טָמֵא הוּא בָּדָד יֵשֵׁב מִחוּץ לַמַּחֲנֶה מוֹשָׁבוֹ: מו

כִּי־יִהְיֶה בוֹ נֶגַע צָרַעַת בְּבֶגֶד צֶמֶר אוֹ בְּבֶגֶד פִּשְׁתִּים: אוֹ בִשְׁתִי אוֹ בְעֵרֶב מז

שישי
/שלישי/

מז וְהַבֶּגֶד

לז | וְשֵׂעָר שָׁחֹר. מִנַּיִן אַף הַיָּרֹק וְהָאָדֹם שֶׁאֵינוֹ צָהֹב? תַּלְמוּד לוֹמַר: "וְשֵׂעָר", וְלָמָּה זֶה דוֹמֶה? לְתַבְנִית הַזָּהָב. טָהוֹר הוּא וְטִהֲרוֹ הַכֹּהֵן. הָא טָמֵא שֶׁטִּהֲרוֹ הַכֹּהֵן לֹא טָהֵר:

לח | בֶּהָרֹת. חֲבַרְבֻּרוֹת:

לט | כֵּהוֹת לְבָנֹת. שֶׁאֵין לֹבֶן שֶׁלָּהֶן עַז אֶלָּא כֵּהֶה: בֹּהַק. כְּמִין לֹבֶן הַנִּרְאֶה בִּבְשַׂר אָדָם שֶׁבֵּין חֲבַרְבֻּרוֹת הַדְּמִימִיּוֹת, קָרוּי בֹּהַק, כְּאָדָם עַדָשָׁן, שֶׁבֵּין עֲדָשָׁה לַעֲדָשָׁה מַבְהִיק הַבָּשָׂר בְּלֹבֶן עַז:

מ | קֵרֵחַ הוּא טָהוֹר הוּא. מִטֻּמְאַת נְתָקִין, שֶׁאֵין נִדּוֹן בְּסִימָנֵי רֹאשׁ וְזָקָן שֶׁהֵם מְקוֹם שֵׂעָר, אֶלָּא בְּסִימָנֵי נֶגַע עוֹר בָּשָׂר – מִחְיָה וּפִשְׂיוֹן:

מא | וְאִם מִפְּאַת פָּנָיו. מִשִּׁפּוּעַ קָדְקֹד כְּלַפֵּי פָנָיו קָרוּי גִּבֵּחַ, וְאַף הַצְּדָעִין שֶׁמִּכָּאן וּמִכָּאן בַּכְּלָל, וּמִשִּׁפּוּעַ קָדְקֹד כְּלַפֵּי אֲחוֹרָיו קָרוּי קָרַחַת:

מב | נֶגַע לָבָן אֲדַמְדָּם. פָּתוּךְ. מִנַּיִן שְׁאָר הַמַּרְאוֹת? תַּלְמוּד לוֹמַר: "נֶגַע":

מג | כְּמַרְאֵה צָרַעַת עוֹר בָּשָׂר. כְּמַרְאֵה הַצָּרַעַת הָאָמוּר בְּפָרָשַׁת עוֹר בָּשָׂר: "אָדָם כִּי יִהְיֶה בְעוֹר בְּשָׂרוֹ" (לְעֵיל פָּסוּק ב), וּמַה אָמוּר בּוֹ? שֶׁמְּטַמֵּא בְּאַרְבָּעָה מַרְאוֹת, וְנִדּוֹן בִּשְׁנֵי שָׁבוּעוֹת, וְלֹא כְמַרְאֵה צָרַעַת הָאָמוּר בִּשְׁחִין וּמִכְוָה שֶׁהוּא נִדּוֹן בְּשָׁבוּעַ אֶחָד, וְלֹא כְמַרְאֵה נְתָקִים שֶׁל מְקוֹם שֵׂעָר שֶׁאֵין מְטַמְּאִין בְּאַרְבַּע מַרְאוֹת:

מד | בְּרֹאשׁוֹ נִגְעוֹ. אֵין לִי אֶלָּא נְתָקִין. מִנַּיִן לְרַבּוֹת

שְׁאָר הַמְנֻגָּעִים? תַּלְמוּד לוֹמַר: "טַמֵּא יְטַמְּאֶנּוּ", לְרַבּוֹת אֶת כֻּלָּן, עַל כֻּלָּן הוּא אוֹמֵר: "בְּגָדָיו יִהְיוּ פְרֻמִים" וְגוֹ' (לְהַלָּן פָּסוּק מה):

מה | פְרֻמִים. קְרוּעִים: פָרוּעַ. מְגֻדַּל שֵׂעָר: וְעַל שָׂפָם יַעְטֶה. כְּאָבֵל: שָׂפָם. שֵׂעָר הַשְּׂפָתַיִם, גרנו"ן בְּלַעַ"ז: וְטָמֵא טָמֵא יִקְרָא. מַשְׁמִיעַ שֶׁהוּא טָמֵא וְיִפְרְשׁוּ מִמֶּנּוּ:

מו | בָּדָד יֵשֵׁב. שֶׁלֹּא יִהְיוּ טְמֵאִים יוֹשְׁבִים עִמּוֹ. וְאָמְרוּ רַבּוֹתֵינוּ: מַה נִּשְׁתַּנָּה מִשְּׁאָר טְמֵאִים לֵשֵׁב בָּדָד? הוֹאִיל וְהוּא הִבְדִּיל בְּלָשׁוֹן הָרָע בֵּין אִישׁ לְאִשְׁתּוֹ, בֵּין אִישׁ לְרֵעֵהוּ, אַף הוּא יִבָּדֵל: מִחוּץ לַמַּחֲנֶה. חוּץ לְשָׁלֹשׁ מַחֲנוֹת:

DISCUSSION

⟶ mourning his own death in his lifetime. The Midrash of Rabbi Pineḥas ben Ya'ir notes additional parallels between a leper and a corpse with regard to their *halakhot* and processes of purification (Eisenstein, *Otzar Midrashim*, 482).

And he shall cover his upper lip: It was customary to wear a large linen or woolen cloth in the biblical period. It was easy to wrap one's body and face with such a garment. Covering

one's face was a standard mourning practice (see II Samuel 15:30, 19:5), along with rending one's garments and growing the hair long (see 10:6).

13:46 | He shall live alone; outside the camp is his dwelling: This description refers to the camp of the Israelites in the wilderness, which had boundaries outside of which a leper could dwell. Lepers in the Land of Israel lived alone

outside the city walls (see II Kings 7:3, 15:5; Kelim 1:7).

In principle, this isolation could last the leper's entire lifetime. This fate befell Uzia, king of Judah, who was afflicted with leprosy and had to live in "a house set apart," an isolated place outside the city, for many years until his death (II Chronicles 26:21).

48 Such a mark might be found not only on a woven garment: **Or in the warp,** the threads that runs lengthwise in a woven fabric, **or in the woof,** the threads that run crosswise in such a fabric, at right angles to the warp threads, **for linen or for wool, or in leather,**^D used for clothing or as an implement, e.g., a jacket or rug made from the hide of an animal without further processing.[24] The verse concludes the list of materials: **Or in anything made of leather,** an implement made from, among other materials, leather pieces or strips.[25]

49 **If the mark was deep green or deep red,**^D an unnatural appearance which is a certain indication that it emerged from the garment itself, and such a spot is found **in the garment, or in the leather, or in the warp, or in the woof, or in any implement of leather, it is a mark of leprosy and shall be shown to the priest.**

50 **The priest shall examine the mark, and he shall quarantine the mark seven days** for observation.

51 Unlike leprosy of the body, leprosy of clothing cannot be confirmed upon the priest's first examination, but only after re-examination. **He shall examine the mark on the seventh day: If the mark spread in the garment, or in the warp, or in the woof, or in the leather, for any labor that leather is utilized, the mark is a malignant**^D **leprosy,** it depletes and impairs the item and has no remedy. **It is impure,** as this is a sign from Heaven that the garment is banned.

52 Therefore, **he shall burn the garment, or the warp, or the woof, of wool or of linen, or any leather implement in which there is a mark;** the garment or implement is entirely impure, **as it is a malignant leprosy; it shall be burned in fire.**

53 **If the priest shall examine** the garment or implement at the end of the seven days, **and behold, the mark did not spread in the garment, or in the warp, or in the woof, or in any implement of leather,**

54 **the priest shall command, and** in accordance with his instructions **they shall wash that in which there is a mark** with certain cleansing agents,[26] **and he shall quarantine it seven days again.**

55 **The priest shall examine after the mark has been washed,**^D **and behold, the mark has not changed its appearance,** its hue remains as it was, **and** even if **the mark did not spread, it is** nevertheless **impure.** Therefore, **you shall burn it in fire; it is a depression,** a deficiency, a loss,[27] or a cavity.[28] This is the designation of leprosy of clothing,[29] whether it is **in its back or its front.**^D Similar terms appear with regard to a person's head (verses 40–41), where they refer to the back of the skull and its front. In contrast to leprosy of the body, where a person can never become a confirmed leper without the appearance of at least one sign of impurity, in the case leprosy of clothing this is possible, if it retains its appearance after having been washed.

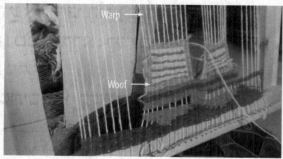

Seventh aliya (Fourth aliya)

Warp and woof on a loom

56 **And if the priest examines, and behold, the** color of the **mark has faded after it has been washed, he shall rip it,** the affected area, **from the garment, or from the leather, or from the warp, or from the woof.**

DISCUSSION

13:48 | For linen or for wool, or in leather: Some authorities maintain that even a hide that has not been tanned at all is subject to the impurity of leprosy, like the warp and the woof, which contract no ritual impurity other than the impurity of leprosy (see Rashi; *Bekhor Shor*).

13:49 | Deep green [*yerakrak*] or deep red [*adamdam*]: Over the course of the generations, the Sages have disputed the meaning of the terms *yerakrak* and *adamdam*. The change in form from *yarok*, green, and *adom*, red, clearly expresses a quality of the color. However, it is unclear whether this indicates a deepening of the color or its weakening. In modern Hebrew the word *yerakrak* means slightly green, but it is likely that in the Bible it means very green, and *adamdam* accordingly means heavily red (see *Sifra*; Rashi; Ibn Ezra; *Nega'im* 11:4–5, and Vilna Gaon ad loc.; Jerusalem Talmud, *Sukka* 3:6; Rambam, *Sefer Tahara, Hilkhot Tumat Tzara'at* 12:1; *Responsa Ḥavvat Ya'ir* 1).

13:51 | Malignant [*mam'eret*]: Some associate *mam'eret* with *me'era*, curse or deficiency; others explain that it means piercing and painful (see Rashi; Ibn Ezra; Rashbam; Ramban; Rashi, Radak, and Rabbi Eliezer of Beaugency, Ezekiel 28:24).

13:55 | After the mark has been washed: A confirmed determination that a mark on the body has the ritual impurity of leprosy depends on the signs of impurity: If signs of impurity appear on the body one is impure, even after only the first examination, and if signs of impurity did not appear on the body he is pure, even if the mark remains permanently. In contrast, in the case leprosy of clothing, the element of time is decisive. Although on the one hand there is no immediate confirmation, as at least a week must pass from the initial examination, on the other hand, after a certain amount of time has passed

מט לַפִּשְׁתִּים וְלַצָּמֶר אוֹ בָעוֹר אוֹ בְּכָל־מְלֶאכֶת עוֹר: וְהָיָה הַנֶּגַע יְרַקְרַק | אוֹ אֲדַמְדָּם
בַּבֶּגֶד אוֹ בָעוֹר אוֹ־בַשְּׁתִי אוֹ־בָעֵרֶב אוֹ בְכָל־כְּלִי־עוֹר נֶגַע צָרַעַת הוּא וְהָרְאָה
נ נא אֶת־הַכֹּהֵן: וְרָאָה הַכֹּהֵן אֶת־הַנָּגַע וְהִסְגִּיר אֶת־הַנֶּגַע שִׁבְעַת יָמִים: וְרָאָה אֶת־
הַנֶּגַע בַּיּוֹם הַשְּׁבִיעִי כִּי־פָשָׂה הַנֶּגַע בַּבֶּגֶד אוֹ־בַשְּׁתִי אוֹ־בָעֵרֶב אוֹ בָעוֹר לְכֹל
נב אֲשֶׁר־יֵעָשֶׂה הָעוֹר לִמְלָאכָה צָרַעַת מַמְאֶרֶת הַנֶּגַע טָמֵא הוּא: וְשָׂרַף אֶת־הַבֶּגֶד
אוֹ אֶת־הַשְּׁתִי | אוֹ אֶת־הָעֵרֶב בַּצֶּמֶר אוֹ בַפִּשְׁתִּים אוֹ אֶת־כָּל־כְּלִי הָעוֹר אֲשֶׁר־
נג יִהְיֶה בוֹ הַנָּגַע כִּי־צָרַעַת מַמְאֶרֶת הִוא בָּאֵשׁ תִּשָּׂרֵף: וְאִם יִרְאֶה הַכֹּהֵן וְהִנֵּה
נד לֹא־פָשָׂה הַנֶּגַע בַּבֶּגֶד אוֹ בַשְּׁתִי אוֹ בָעֵרֶב אוֹ בְּכָל־כְּלִי־עוֹר: וְצִוָּה הַכֹּהֵן וְכִבְּסוּ
נה אֵת אֲשֶׁר־בּוֹ הַנָּגַע וְהִסְגִּירוֹ שִׁבְעַת־יָמִים שֵׁנִית: וְרָאָה הַכֹּהֵן אַחֲרֵי | הֻכַּבֵּס שביעי /רביעי/
אֶת־הַנֶּגַע וְהִנֵּה לֹא־הָפַךְ הַנֶּגַע אֶת־עֵינוֹ וְהַנֶּגַע לֹא־פָשָׂה טָמֵא הוּא בָּאֵשׁ
נו תִּשְׂרְפֶנּוּ פְּחֶתֶת הִוא בְּקָרַחְתּוֹ אוֹ בְגַבַּחְתּוֹ: וְאִם רָאָה הַכֹּהֵן וְהִנֵּה כֵּהָה הַנֶּגַע
אַחֲרֵי הֻכַּבֵּס אֹתוֹ וְקָרַע אֹתוֹ מִן־הַבֶּגֶד אוֹ מִן־הָעוֹר אוֹ מִן־הַשְּׁתִי אוֹ מִן־הָעֵרֶב:

רש"י

מח | **לפשתים ולצמר.** של פשתים או של צמר: **או בעור.** זה עור שלא נעשה בו מלאכה: **או בכל מלאכת עור.** עור שנעשה בו מלאכה:

מט | **ירקרק.** ירוק שבירוקין: **אדמדם.** אדום שבאדומים:

נא | **צרעת ממארת.** לשון "סלון ממאיר" (יחזקאל כח, כד), פוינ"ט בלעז. ומדרשו, תן בו מארה, שלא תהנה הימנו:

נב | **בצמר או בפשתים.** של צמר או של פשתים, זהו פשוטו. ומדרשו, יכול יביא גזי צמר ואניצי פשתן וישרפם עמו? תלמוד לומר: "הוא באש תשרף", אינה צריכה דבר אחר עמה. אם כן מה תלמוד לומר: "בצמר או בפשתים"? להוציא את האמריות שבו שהן ממין אחר. 'אמריות' לשון שפה, כמו: 'אמרא':

נד | **את אשר בו הנגע.** יכול מקום הנגע בלבד? תלמוד לומר: "את אשר בו הנגע". יכול כל הבגד כלו טעון כבוס? תלמוד לומר: "הנגע". הא כיצד? יכבס מן הבגד עמו:

נה | **אחרי הכבס.** לשון העשות: **לא הפך הנגע את עינו.** לא הכהה ממראיתו: **והנגע לא פשה.** שמענו שאם לא הפך ולא פשה טמא, ואין צריך לומר לא הפך ופשה. הפך ולא פשה איני יודע מה יעשה לו? תלמוד לומר: "והסגיר את הנגע", מכל מקום, דברי רבי יהודה. וחכמים אומרים וכו', כדאיתא בתורת כהנים (פרק טו, ז), ורמזתיה כאן ליישב המקרא על אפניו: **פחתת הוא.** לשון גומא, כמו: "באחת הפחתים" (שמואל ב' יז, ט), כלומר שפלה היא, נגע שמראיו שוקעין: **בקרחתו** **או בגבחתו.** כתרגומו: "בשחיקותיה או בחדתותיה": קרחתו. שחקים, ישנים. ומפני המדרש שהצרך לגזרה שוה: מנין לפריחה בבגדים שהיא טהורה? נאמרה קרחת וגבחת באדם (לעיל פסוק מב) ונאמרה קרחת וגבחת בבגדים, מה להלן פרח בכלו טהור (לעיל פסוק יג), אף כאן פרח בכלו טהור – לכך אחז הכתוב לשון קרחת וגבחת. ולענין פרושו ותרגומו זהו משמעו, קרחת לשון ישנים וגבחת לשון חדשים, כאלו נכתב: 'באחריתו או בקדמותו', שהקרחת לשון אחורים והגבחת לשון פנים, כמו שכתוב: "ואם מפאת פניו" וגו' (לעיל פסוק מא), והקרחת כל ששופע ויורד מן הקדקד ולאחריו. כך מפרש בתורת כהנים (פרק טו, ט):

נו | **וקרע אתו.** יקרע מקום הנגע מן הבגד וישרפנו:

DISCUSSION

→ the garment is declared definitely impure, even if no additional signs of impurity have appeared.

In its back or its front: There are other explanations of these unusual terms: Worn out or new; a smooth garment or one with protruding wool fibers which raise the mark (see *Sifra*; *Pesikta Zutrati*; Rambam, *Sefer Tahara*, *Hilkhot Tzara'at* 12:9; Rambam's commentary, Mishna *Nega'im* 11:11).

57 **If it,** the mark, **shall be seen again in the garment, or in the**
Maftir **warp, or in the woof, or in any leather implement,** although one cut off and removed the affected area, the mark nevertheless appeared once again in the garment or the leather, **it is erupting** leprosy, and therefore **you shall burn in fire that in which the mark is.**
58 **The garment, or the warp, or the woof, or any leather implement, that you shall wash and the mark leaves them,** that is, if due to the laundering, the mark disappears and does not return, **it shall be washed again,** this time by immersion in a ritual bath,[30] **and it shall be purified** from its impurity.
59 **This is the law of the mark of leprosy of the woolen or the linen garment, or the warp, the woof, or any leather implement, to pronounce it pure or to pronounce it impure.**

Maftir on Shabbat HaHodesh is read from Exodus 12:1-20.

Parashat
Metzora

The Leper's Purification
LEVITICUS 14:1–32

The previous chapter concluded with a discussion of leprosy of a garment; however, the treatment of the matter addressed prior to that, the law of the leprous person, has yet to be completed. That section discussed the ways in which one becomes ritually impure with leprosy, as well as the required comportment while impure. This chapter concludes the topic of the leprosy of a person with a detailed description of his purification process, which consists of a series of different actions. No other procedure in the Torah contains as many stages and details as the ritual purification of the leper.

14 1 **The Lord spoke to Moses, saying:**
2 **This shall be the law of the leper on the day,** at the time, **of his purification,** his healing: **He shall be brought to the priest.** The leper must return to the priest, as he has the exclusive authority to deal with leprosy.
3 **The priest shall go outside the camp,** and the leper shall come before him for examination.[1] **And the priest shall examine, and behold, the mark of leprosy has been healed from the leper,** that is, it disappeared or signs of purification appeared (see 13:13, 37).
4 **The priest shall command, and one,** that is, any person, **shall take for the one being purified two living, pure birds.** When the Torah mentions an unspecified bird, the reference is to a sparrow or to another small, chirping bird.[2] **And cedar**[B] **wood,** which by tradition is a wooden beam that is not particularly large,[3] **and scarlet wool,**[B] **and hyssop.**[B]
5 **The priest shall command, and one shall slaughter the one bird** of the two, **in an earthenware vessel,** so that its blood will be poured **over spring water** that is already in the vessel.

Cedar

Kermes insects on an oak tree

Hyssop

מפטיר נז וְאִם־תֵּרָאֶה עוֹד בַּבֶּגֶד אוֹ־בַשְּׁתִי אוֹ־בָעֵרֶב אוֹ בְכָל־כְּלִי־עוֹר פֹּרַחַת הִוא בָּאֵשׁ

נח תִּשְׂרְפֶנּוּ אֵת אֲשֶׁר־בּוֹ הַנָּגַע: וְהַבֶּגֶד אוֹ־הַשְּׁתִי אוֹ־הָעֵרֶב אוֹ־כָל־כְּלִי הָעוֹר

נט אֲשֶׁר תְּכַבֵּס וְסָר מֵהֶם הַנָּגַע וְכֻבַּס שֵׁנִית וְטָהֵר: זֹאת תּוֹרַת נֶגַע־צָרַעַת בֶּגֶד

הַצֶּמֶר אוֹ הַפִּשְׁתִּים אוֹ הַשְּׁתִי אוֹ הָעֵרֶב אוֹ כָּל־כְּלִי־עוֹר לְטַהֲרוֹ אוֹ לְטַמְּאוֹ:

רש"י

נו פֹּרַחַת הִוא. דָּבָר הַחוֹזֵר וְצוֹמֵחַ: בָּאֵשׁ תִּשְׂרְפֶנּוּ. אֶת כָּל הַבֶּגֶד:

נח וְסָר מֵהֶם הַנָּגַע. אִם כְּשֶׁכִּבְּסוֹהוּ בַּתְּחִלָּה עַל פִּי כֹהֵן סָר מִמֶּנּוּ הַנֶּגַע לְגַמְרֵי: וְכֻבַּס שֵׁנִית. לְשׁוֹן טְבִילָה. תַּרְגּוּם שֶׁל כִּבּוּסִין שֶׁבְּפָרָשָׁה זוֹ לְשׁוֹן לִבּוּן, "וְיִתְחַוַּר",

חוּץ מִזֶּה שֶׁאֵינוֹ לְלִבּוּן אֶלָּא לְטִבּוּל, לְכָךְ תַּרְגּוּמוֹ "וְיִצְטַבַּע". וְכֵן כָּל כִּבּוּסֵי בְגָדִים שֶׁהֵן לִטְבִילָה מִתְרַגְּמִין "וְיִצְטַבַּע":

פָּרָשַׁת

מְצֹרָע

ט א וַיְדַבֵּר יהוה אֶל־מֹשֶׁה לֵּאמֹר: זֹאת תִּהְיֶה תּוֹרַת הַמְּצֹרָע בְּיוֹם טָהֳרָתוֹ וְהוּבָא ב

אֶל־הַכֹּהֵן: וְיָצָא הַכֹּהֵן אֶל־מִחוּץ לַמַּחֲנֶה וְרָאָה הַכֹּהֵן וְהִנֵּה נִרְפָּא נֶגַע־הַצָּרַעַת ג

מִן־הַצָּרוּעַ: וְצִוָּה הַכֹּהֵן וְלָקַח לַמִּטַּהֵר שְׁתֵּי־צִפֳּרִים חַיּוֹת טְהֹרוֹת וְעֵץ אֶרֶז וּשְׁנִי ד

תוֹלַעַת וְאֵזֹב: וְצִוָּה הַכֹּהֵן וְשָׁחַט אֶת־הַצִּפּוֹר הָאֶחָת אֶל־כְּלִי־חֶרֶשׂ עַל־מַיִם: ה

רש"י

ב זֹאת תִּהְיֶה תּוֹרַת הַמְּצֹרָע בְּיוֹם טָהֳרָתוֹ. מְלַמֵּד שֶׁאֵין מְטַהֲרִין אוֹתוֹ בַּלַּיְלָה:

ג אֶל־מִחוּץ לַמַּחֲנֶה. חוּץ לְשָׁלֹשׁ מַחֲנוֹת שֶׁנִּשְׁתַּלַּח שָׁם בִּימֵי חִלּוּטוֹ:

ד חַיּוֹת. פְּרָט לִטְרֵפוֹת: טְהֹרוֹת. פְּרָט לְעוֹף טָמֵא. לְפִי שֶׁהַנְּגָעִים בָּאִין עַל לְשׁוֹן הָרַע שֶׁהוּא מַעֲשֵׂה פִּטְפּוּטֵי דְבָרִים, לְפִיכָךְ הֻזְקְקוּ לְטָהֳרָתוֹ צִפֳּרִים, שֶׁמְּפַטְפְּטִין תָּמִיד בְּצִפְצוּף קוֹל: וְעֵץ אֶרֶז. לְפִי שֶׁהַנְּגָעִים בָּאִין עַל גַּסּוּת הָרוּחַ: וּשְׁנִי תוֹלַעַת וְאֵזֹב. מַה תַּקָּנָתוֹ וְיִתְרַפֵּא?

יַשְׁפִּיל עַצְמוֹ מִגַּאֲוָתוֹ כְּתוֹלַעַת וּכְאֵזוֹב: עֵץ אֶרֶז. מַקֵּל שֶׁל אֶרֶז: וּשְׁנִי תוֹלַעַת. לָשׁוֹן שֶׁל צֶמֶר צָבוּעַ זְהוֹרִית:

ה עַל מַיִם חַיִּים. נוֹתֵן אוֹתָם תְּחִלָּה בַּכְּלִי כְּדֵי שֶׁיְּהֵא דַּם צִפּוֹר נִכָּר בָּהֶם, וְכַמָּה הֵם? רְבִיעִית:

BACKGROUND

14:4 | Cedar: The cedar, *Cedrus*, a coniferous tree from the Pinaceae family, is an impressive tree in both height and appearance. It can grow to a height of 30 m, and its trunk can reach 3 m in diameter. It grows in cold, elevated regions, notably in Lebanon. Due to its durability and its straight, long branches, cedar wood was utilized in biblical times in construction, especially in public structures and palaces. It also serves as a symbol of strength and resilience.

Scarlet wool: This appears to refer to a red dye produced from the aphid called *qirmiz* in Arabic, and is consistent with the explanation given by many commentaries (Rav Se'adya Gaon; Rashi; Radak; see Sifra). Current research identifies it as a scale insect known as the *Kermes echinatus*, which exists on oak trees and from which a bright red-orange dye is produced through drying the aphid, grinding it, and cooking it.

Hyssop: This appears to refer to the common hyssop, *Majorana syriaca* L. The hyssop is an aromatic bush from the Lamiaceae family of plants; it grows approximately 40 cm high and branches out from its base into hard and woody branches. Erect stems grow from these branches annually and then dry out and wither each winter. White flowers cluster at the ends of the branches of the bush. The plant grows in rocky terrain of limestone and chalk and in undergrowth throughout the Middle East. Dried hyssop leaves are used as a spice, and they are one of the primary ingredients in the well-known spice mixture *za'atar* (Numbers 19:6). In addition, they are considered to have medicinal properties. Hyssop, together with the ashes of the red heifer and scarlet wool, is also used in the purification ritual of those impure with impurity imparted by a corpse. It serves as a symbol for lowliness and baseness (I Kings 5:13).

6 **The living bird, he shall take it, and** separately **the cedar wood, and the scarlet wool, and the hyssop** bound together,[5] **and he shall dip them and the living bird,** by the ends of its limbs and its tail, adjacent to its body.[6] In this manner, the bird's wings remain out of the blood, so that they will not adhere to its body, thereby enabling it to fly over the field at a later point. He shall dip them **in the blood of the slaughtered bird** that is **over** the **spring water.**

7 **He shall sprinkle** from this mixture of the blood of the slaughtered bird and the spring water into which the aforementioned items were dipped, **on the one being purified from the leprosy seven times, and** he **shall** then be able to **pronounce him pure,**[7] **and shall dispatch the living bird over the field,**[D] set it free, concluding its role in this ritual. This completes the first stage of the leper's purification, which is performed in the field, outside the camp.

8 In the next stage, **the one being purified shall wash,** immerse, **his garments,** as they too were rendered ritually impure by his wearing them, **shave all his hair, bathe,** immerse[8] **in water, and be purified; and then he shall enter the camp, and shall dwell outside his tent seven days.** Although he is now inside the Israelite camp, or the city, he remains somewhat in isolation, as he may not enter his house and must remain apart from his wife.[9] According to rabbinic tradition, he renders people and vessels impure through contact.[10]

9 **It shall be on the seventh day; he shall** again **shave all his hair, his head and his beard and his eyebrows; all his hair he shall shave** from his entire body, or alternatively, only from hairy places.[11] There is an opinion that by Torah law he is required to shave only those parts of his body where the hair is visible, and by rabbinic law he must shave all his hair.[12] **And he shall wash his garments** a second time, **bathe his flesh in water, and be purified.**

10 Although the leper is ritually purified, his status is that of one who lacks atonement; he must bring the requisite offerings in order to be rendered fit to enter the Temple and partake of consecrated food. Therefore, **on the eighth day he shall take two unblemished** male **lambs, and one unblemished ewe in its first year, and three-tenths of an ephah of high-quality flour mixed with oil as a meal offering.** In current measures, three-tenths of an ephah equals more than 7 L; and there is an opinion that it equals 12.8 L. **And one log of oil,** which according to the conventional opinion is about 0.33 L, and according to the other opinion, approximately 0.6 L.

11 **The priest who purifies shall position the man who is being purified and them,** the lambs, **before the Lord, at the entrance of the Tent of Meeting.**[D]

12 **The priest shall take one of the lambs and present it as a guilt offering, and** likewise he shall present **the log of oil** brought by the one who is being purified, **and wave them,** the living sheep with the *log*, **as a wave offering before the Lord.** If he waved each separately, he fulfills his obligation.[13]

13 **He shall slaughter the lamb in the** same **place where one**
Second aliya **slaughters the sin offering and the burnt offering, in the holy place,** on the north side of the altar (1:11, 6:18), and unlike offerings of lesser sanctity, it may not be slaughtered anywhere else in the Tabernacle courtyard. **Since like the sin offering, the guilt offering is for the priest,** they are similar with regard to all matters involving the service of the priest,[14] or in that both are given solely to the priest.[15] This is an indication that **it is a sacred sacrament,** an offering of the most sacred order.

14 **The priest shall take from the blood of the** slaughtered **guilt offering, and the priest shall place** some of the blood **on the tip**[16] **of the right ear of the one being purified, and on the thumb of his right hand, and on the big toe of his right foot.**

15 **The priest shall take** with his right hand **from the log of oil** brought by the one undergoing purification, **and pour it on the** cupped **left palm of the priest,** either a different priest or on his own palm.[17]

16 **The priest shall dip his right finger from,** into, **the oil that** is accumulated **on his left palm, and he shall sprinkle**[D] **from the oil with his finger seven times before the Lord,** toward the Sanctuary.

DISCUSSION

14:7 | **And shall dispatch the living bird over the field:** Although the Torah does not explain the mystery of leprosy and its purification process, there are some things we can intuit from the details of the rite. Perhaps the release of the bird alludes to the removal of the ritual impurity from the individual, as well as his release from a state of social isolation (see *Bekhor Shor*; Rabbeinu Baḥya; Rabbi Samson Raphael Hirsch).

14:11 | **The priest who purifies shall position the man who is being purified and them before the Lord, at the entrance of the Tent of Meeting:** Since this is not merely a process of atonement, but a process of purification as well, the Sages discuss how it was permitted for the leper to enter the Temple for performance of this rite, in light of the fact that it is prohibited for ritually impure individuals to enter the holy place. They explain that in the course of his purification, the leper stands outside the courtyard at the Nicanor Gate, an area that was not sanctified with the sanctity that exists in the courtyard of the Temple and the Tabernacle. His participation in the purification process is accomplished though extending the various parts of his body, e.g., ear, thumb, big toe, into the courtyard (see Rashi, *Nega'im* 14:8–9; *Tosefta Nega'im* 8:9–10).

14:16 | **The priest shall dip his right finger from the oil that is on his left palm, and he shall sprinkle:** This is a clear illustration of the halakhic principle that the priests must perform the primary rites of the Temple service with the right hand (see *Zevaḥim* 25a). In fact, left-handed priests were not permitted to perform the Temple service (see *Bekhorot* 45b).

ו חַיִּים: אֶת־הַצִּפֹּר הַחַיָּה יִקַּח אֹתָהּ וְאֶת־עֵץ הָאֶרֶז וְאֶת־שְׁנִי הַתּוֹלַעַת וְאֶת־הָאֵזֹב
ז וְטָבַל אוֹתָם וְאֵת ׀ הַצִּפֹּר הַחַיָּה בְּדַם הַצִּפֹּר הַשְּׁחֻטָה עַל הַמַּיִם הַחַיִּים: וְהִזָּה
עַל הַמִּטַּהֵר מִן־הַצָּרַעַת שֶׁבַע פְּעָמִים וְטִהֲרוֹ וְשִׁלַּח אֶת־הַצִּפֹּר הַחַיָּה עַל־
ח פְּנֵי הַשָּׂדֶה: וְכִבֶּס הַמִּטַּהֵר אֶת־בְּגָדָיו וְגִלַּח אֶת־כָּל־שְׂעָרוֹ וְרָחַץ בַּמַּיִם וְטָהֵר
ט וְאַחַר יָבוֹא אֶל־הַמַּחֲנֶה וְיָשַׁב מִחוּץ לְאָהֳלוֹ שִׁבְעַת יָמִים: וְהָיָה בַיּוֹם הַשְּׁבִיעִי
יְגַלַּח אֶת־כָּל־שְׂעָרוֹ אֶת־רֹאשׁוֹ וְאֶת־זְקָנוֹ וְאֵת גַּבֹּת עֵינָיו וְאֶת־כָּל־שְׂעָרוֹ יְגַלֵּחַ
י וְכִבֶּס אֶת־בְּגָדָיו וְרָחַץ אֶת־בְּשָׂרוֹ בַּמַּיִם וְטָהֵר: וּבַיּוֹם הַשְּׁמִינִי יִקַּח שְׁנֵי־כְבָשִׂים
תְּמִימִם וְכַבְשָׂה אַחַת בַּת־שְׁנָתָהּ תְּמִימָה וּשְׁלֹשָׁה עֶשְׂרֹנִים סֹלֶת מִנְחָה בְּלוּלָה
יא בַשֶּׁמֶן וְלֹג אֶחָד שָׁמֶן: וְהֶעֱמִיד הַכֹּהֵן הַמְטַהֵר אֵת הָאִישׁ הַמִּטַּהֵר וְאֹתָם לִפְנֵי
יב יְהוָה פֶּתַח אֹהֶל מוֹעֵד: וְלָקַח הַכֹּהֵן אֶת־הַכֶּבֶשׂ הָאֶחָד וְהִקְרִיב אֹתוֹ לְאָשָׁם
יג וְאֶת־לֹג הַשָּׁמֶן וְהֵנִיף אֹתָם תְּנוּפָה לִפְנֵי יְהוָה: וְשָׁחַט אֶת־הַכֶּבֶשׂ בִּמְקוֹם אֲשֶׁר שני
יִשְׁחַט אֶת־הַחַטָּאת וְאֶת־הָעֹלָה בִּמְקוֹם הַקֹּדֶשׁ כִּי כַּחַטָּאת הָאָשָׁם הוּא לַכֹּהֵן
יד קֹדֶשׁ קָדָשִׁים הוּא: וְלָקַח הַכֹּהֵן מִדַּם הָאָשָׁם וְנָתַן הַכֹּהֵן עַל־תְּנוּךְ אֹזֶן הַמִּטַּהֵר
טו הַיְמָנִית וְעַל־בֹּהֶן יָדוֹ הַיְמָנִית וְעַל־בֹּהֶן רַגְלוֹ הַיְמָנִית: וְלָקַח הַכֹּהֵן מִלֹּג הַשָּׁמֶן
טז וְיָצַק עַל־כַּף הַכֹּהֵן הַשְּׂמָאלִית: וְטָבַל הַכֹּהֵן אֶת־אֶצְבָּעוֹ הַיְמָנִית מִן־הַשֶּׁמֶן
אֲשֶׁר עַל־כַּפּוֹ הַשְּׂמָאלִית וְהִזָּה מִן־הַשֶּׁמֶן בְּאֶצְבָּעוֹ שֶׁבַע פְּעָמִים לִפְנֵי יְהוָה:

רש״י

ו| **אֶת הַצִּפֹּר הַחַיָּה יִקַּח אֹתָהּ.** מְלַמֵּד שֶׁאֵינוֹ אוֹגְדָהּ עִמָּהֶם, אֶלָּא מַפְרִישָׁהּ לְעַצְמָהּ, אֲבָל הָעֵץ וְהָאֵזוֹב כְּרוּכִין יַחַד בִּלְשׁוֹן הַזְּהוֹרִית, כָּעִנְיָן שֶׁנֶּאֱמַר: "וְאֶת עֵץ הָאֶרֶז וְאֶת שְׁנִי הַתּוֹלַעַת וְאֶת הָאֵזֹב", קִיחָה אַחַת לִשְׁלָשְׁתָּן. יָכוֹל כְּשֵׁם שֶׁאֵינָהּ בִּכְלַל אֲגֻדָּה כָּךְ לֹא תִּהְיֶה בִּכְלַל טְבִילָה? תַּלְמוּד לוֹמַר: "וְטָבַל אוֹתָם וְאֵת הַצִּפֹּר הַחַיָּה", הֶחֱזִיר אֶת הַצִּפּוֹר לִכְלַל טְבִילָה:

ח| **וְיָשַׁב מִחוּץ לְאָהֳלוֹ.** מְלַמֵּד שֶׁאָסוּר בְּתַשְׁמִישׁ הַמִּטָּה:

ט| **אֶת כָּל שְׂעָרוֹ וְגוֹ׳.** כְּלָל וּפְרָט וּכְלָל, לְהָבִיא כָּל מְקוֹם כִּנּוּס שֵׂעָר וְנִרְאֶה:

י| **וְכַבְשָׂה אַחַת.** לְחַטָּאת: **וּשְׁלֹשָׁה עֶשְׂרֹנִים.** לְנִסְכֵּי שְׁלֹשָׁה כְּבָשִׂים הַלָּלוּ, שֶׁחַטָּאתוֹ וַאֲשָׁמוֹ שֶׁל מְצֹרָע טְעוּנִין נְסָכִים: **וְלֹג אֶחָד שָׁמֶן.** לְהַזּוֹת עָלָיו שֶׁבַע וְלִתֵּן מִמֶּנּוּ עַל תְּנוּךְ אָזְנוֹ וּמַתַּן בְּהוֹנוֹת:

יא| **לִפְנֵי ה׳.** בְּשַׁעַר נִיקָנוֹר וְלֹא בָּעֲזָרָה עַצְמָהּ, לְפִי שֶׁהוּא מְחֻסַּר כִּפּוּרִים:

יב| **וְהִקְרִיב אֹתוֹ לְאָשָׁם.** יַקְרִיבֶנּוּ לְתוֹךְ הָעֲזָרָה לְשֵׁם אָשָׁם: **וְהֵנִיף.** שֶׁהוּא טָעוּן תְּנוּפָה חַי: **וְהֵנִיף אֹתָם.** אֶת הָאָשָׁם וְאֶת הַלֹּג:

יג| **בִּמְקוֹם אֲשֶׁר יִשְׁחַט וְגוֹ׳.** עַל יֶרֶךְ הַמִּזְבֵּחַ בַּצָּפוֹן. וּמַה תַּלְמוּד לוֹמַר? וַהֲלֹא כְּבָר נֶאֱמַר בְּתוֹרַת אָשָׁם בְּפָרָשַׁת "צַו אֶת אַהֲרֹן" שֶׁהָאָשָׁם טָעוּן שְׁחִיטָה בַּצָּפוֹן (לעיל ז, ב)? לְפִי שֶׁיָּצָא זֶה מִכְּלַל אֲשָׁמוֹת לִדּוֹן בְּהַעֲמָדָה, יָכוֹל תְּהֵא שְׁחִיטָתוֹ בִּמְקוֹם הַעֲמָדָתוֹ? לְכָךְ נֶאֱמַר: "וְשָׁחַט בִּמְקוֹם אֲשֶׁר יִשְׁחַט" וְגוֹ׳: **כִּי כַּחַטָּאת.** כִּי כְּכָל הַחַטָּאוֹת הָאָשָׁם הַזֶּה הוּא לַכֹּהֵן, בְּכָל עֲבוֹדוֹת הַתְּלוּיוֹת בַּכֹּהֵן הֻשְׁוָה אָשָׁם זֶה לְחַטָּאת, שֶׁלֹּא תֹּאמַר הוֹאִיל וְיָצָא דָּמוֹ מִכְּלַל שְׁאָר אֲשָׁמוֹת לִנָּתֵן עַל תְּנוּךְ וּבְהוֹנוֹת, לֹא יְהֵא טָעוּן מַתַּן דָּמִים וְאֵמוּרִים לְגַבֵּי מִזְבֵּחַ, לְכָךְ נֶאֱמַר: "כִּי כַּחַטָּאת הָאָשָׁם הוּא לַכֹּהֵן". יָכוֹל יְהֵא דָּמוֹ נִתָּן לְמַעְלָה כְּחַטָּאת? תַּלְמוּד לוֹמַר וְכוּ׳. בְּתוֹרַת כֹּהֲנִים (פרק ג, ח):

יד| **תְּנוּךְ.** גֵּדֶר אֶמְצָעִי שֶׁבָּאֹזֶן, וּלְשׁוֹן 'תְּנוּךְ' לֹא נוֹדַע לִי, וְהַפּוֹתְרִים קוֹרִים לוֹ טנדרו״ס: **בֹּהֶן.** גּוּדָל:

טז| **לִפְנֵי ה׳.** כְּנֶגֶד בֵּית קָדְשֵׁי הַקֳּדָשִׁים:

17 **And from the rest of the oil that is** inevitably left **on his palm, the priest shall place** some **on the tip of the right ear of the one being purified, and on the thumb of his right hand, and on the big toe of his right foot, on the blood of the guilt offering,** which he previously placed on those spots.

18 Even after placing the three drops on the parts of the leper's body, oil will remain on the priest's palm. **The remainder of the oil that is on the priest's palm, he,** the priest, **shall place,** that is, spread, **on the head of the one being purified; and the priest shall** thereby **atone for him before the Lord.**

19 **The priest shall perform** the service of the ewe of **the sin offering** that was brought by the one undergoing purification **and atone for the one being purified from his impurity; and then he shall slaughter** the sheep of **the burnt offering.**[D]

20 **The priest shall offer up the burnt offering and the meal offering,** consisting of the three-tenths of an ephah of fine flour that was brought by the purifying leper, **on the altar; and the priest shall atone for him** through these rites, **and he shall become pure.**

21 If the leper **is impoverished,**[D] **and his means do not suffice** for all the above offerings, **he shall take one lamb as a guilt offering for waving, to atone for him** as would the offering of a wealthy individual, **and only one-tenth,** not three-tenths, **of an ephah of high-quality flour mixed with oil as a meal offering, and a log of oil.**

Third aliya (Fifth aliya)

22 **And** instead of bringing the ewe of the sin offering and the sheep of the burnt offering, the poor leper shall bring **two turtledoves or two young pigeons, for which his means suffice,** that he can afford; **one** of them **shall be a sin offering and the** other **one a burnt offering.**

23 **He shall bring them,** the sheep and the two birds, **on the eighth day of his purification to the priest, to the entrance of the Tent of Meeting, before the Lord.**

24 **The priest shall take the lamb of the guilt offering and the log of oil, and the priest shall wave them as a wave offering before the Lord.**

25 **He shall slaughter the lamb of the guilt offering, and the priest shall take from the blood of the guilt offering, and place it on the tip of the right ear of the one being purified, and on the thumb of his right hand, and on the big toe of his right foot.**

26 **The priest shall pour from the oil on the left palm of the priest.**

27 **The priest shall sprinkle with his right finger from the oil that is on his left palm seven times before the Lord.**

28 **The priest shall place from the oil that is on his palm on the tip of the right ear of the one being purified, and on the thumb of his right hand, and on the big toe of his right foot, on the place of the blood of the guilt offering.**

29 **The remainder of the oil that is on the priest's palm he shall place on the head of the one being purified, to atone for him before the Lord.**

30 **He shall offer one of the turtledoves or** one **of the young pigeons, from that which his means suffice.** Turtledoves are birds that exist in the wild and are at times easy to acquire without payment. In contrast, pigeons were more plentiful in the Land of Israel; however, their acquisition often involved payment or greater exertion.

31 The priest shall sacrifice **that for which his means suffice, one as a sin offering and one as a burnt offering, with,** in addition to, **the meal offering;**[D] **the priest shall** thereby **atone for the one being purified before the Lord.**

32 **This is the law of one in whom there is a mark of leprosy, whose means do not suffice in his purification.**

DISCUSSION

14:19 | And then he shall slaughter the burnt offering: The sin offering [*ḥatat*] is brought in order to cleanse oneself [*lehitḥatei*] from sin and to ask forgiveness. The burnt offering is in essence a voluntary offering, brought "of his own free will" (1:3, 22:19), and it is therefore characterized by the Sages as a gift. Accordingly, the leper must present the sin offering first, and only after he has requested forgiveness and atonement, and, he hopes, God has granted his request and forgiven him, is his gift offering appropriate (see *Zevaḥim* 7b).

14:21 | If the leper is impoverished: All the actions in the purification process of a poor leper are performed in the same manner as they are performed in the process of a wealthy person. In the following verses, the entire process is described again. In fact, the Torah could have sufficed with: "The priest shall perform as he performed with the wealthy leper." Perhaps the repetition serves to emphasize that there is no difference between the purification of a rich leper and that of a poor leper. Although the offering of the poor person appears inferior and the priests derive less benefit from it, the series of actions and the result are identical.

14:31 | The meal offering: A meal offering always accompanies animal offerings but not bird offerings. In addition, it always accompanies burnt offerings and peace offerings, but not sin offerings or guilt offerings (see Numbers 15:11–12). The sin offering and guilt offering of a leper are exceptions to this principle, as a meal offering is sacrificed with them. Therefore, a wealthy leper, who brings animals for his sin offering and guilt offering, brings one-tenth of an ephah for each sheep as a meal offering. Since a poor leper sacrifices only one sheep, as a guilt offering, and his sin offering and burnt offering are birds, he brings only one-tenth of an ephah as his meal offering (see *Menaḥot* 90b).

יז וּמִיֶּ֨תֶר הַשֶּׁ֜מֶן אֲשֶׁ֣ר עַל־כַּפּ֗וֹ יִתֵּ֤ן הַכֹּהֵן֙ עַל־תְּנ֞וּךְ אֹ֤זֶן הַמִּטַּהֵר֙ הַיְמָנִ֔ית וְעַל־בֹּ֤הֶן

יח יָדוֹ֙ הַיְמָנִ֔ית וְעַל־בֹּ֥הֶן רַגְל֖וֹ הַיְמָנִ֑ית עַ֖ל דַּ֥ם הָאָשָֽׁם׃ וְהַנּוֹתָ֗ר בַּשֶּׁ֙מֶן֙ אֲשֶׁר֙ עַל־כַּ֣ף

יט הַכֹּהֵ֔ן יִתֵּ֖ן עַל־רֹ֣אשׁ הַמִּטַּהֵ֑ר וְכִפֶּ֥ר עָלָ֛יו הַכֹּהֵ֖ן לִפְנֵ֥י יְהֹוָֽה׃ וְעָשָׂ֤ה הַכֹּהֵן֙ אֶת־

כ הַֽחַטָּ֔את וְכִפֶּ֕ר עַֽל־הַמִּטַּהֵ֖ר מִטֻּמְאָת֑וֹ וְאַחַ֖ר יִשְׁחַ֥ט אֶת־הָעֹלָֽה׃ וְהֶעֱלָ֧ה הַכֹּהֵ֛ן

כא אֶת־הָעֹלָ֥ה וְאֶת־הַמִּנְחָ֖ה הַמִּזְבֵּ֑חָה וְכִפֶּ֥ר עָלָ֛יו הַכֹּהֵ֖ן וְטָהֵֽר׃ וְאִם־דַּ֣ל

שלישי /חמישי/

ה֗וּא וְאֵ֣ין יָדוֹ֮ מַשֶּׂ֒גֶת֒ וְ֠לָקַ֠ח כֶּ֣בֶשׂ אֶחָ֥ד אָשָׁ֛ם לִתְנוּפָ֖ה לְכַפֵּ֣ר עָלָ֑יו וְעִשָּׂר֨וֹן סֹ֜לֶת

כב אֶחָ֨ד בָּל֥וּל בַּשֶּׁ֛מֶן לְמִנְחָ֖ה וְלֹ֥ג שָֽׁמֶן׃ וּשְׁתֵּ֣י תֹרִ֗ים א֤וֹ שְׁנֵי֙ בְּנֵ֣י יוֹנָ֔ה אֲשֶׁ֥ר תַּשִּׂ֖יג יָד֑וֹ

כג וְהָיָ֤ה אֶחָד֙ חַטָּ֔את וְהָאֶחָ֖ד עֹלָֽה׃ וְהֵבִ֨יא אֹתָ֜ם בַּיּ֧וֹם הַשְּׁמִינִ֛י לְטׇהֳרָת֖וֹ אֶל־הַכֹּהֵ֑ן

כד אֶל־פֶּ֥תַח אֹֽהֶל־מוֹעֵ֖ד לִפְנֵ֥י יְהֹוָֽה׃ וְלָקַ֧ח הַכֹּהֵ֛ן אֶת־כֶּ֥בֶשׂ הָאָשָׁ֖ם וְאֶת־לֹ֣ג הַשָּׁ֑מֶן

כה וְהֵנִ֨יף אֹתָ֧ם הַכֹּהֵ֛ן תְּנוּפָ֖ה לִפְנֵ֥י יְהֹוָֽה׃ וְשָׁחַט֮ אֶת־כֶּ֣בֶשׂ הָֽאָשָׁם֒ וְלָקַ֤ח הַכֹּהֵן֙ מִדַּ֣ם

הָֽאָשָׁ֔ם וְנָתַ֛ן עַל־תְּנ֥וּךְ אֹֽזֶן־הַמִּטַּהֵ֖ר הַיְמָנִ֑ית וְעַל־בֹּ֤הֶן יָדוֹ֙ הַיְמָנִ֔ית וְעַל־בֹּ֥הֶן רַגְל֖וֹ

כו הַיְמָנִֽית׃ וּמִן־הַשֶּׁ֖מֶן יִצֹ֣ק הַכֹּהֵ֑ן עַל־כַּ֥ף הַכֹּהֵ֖ן הַשְּׂמָאלִֽית׃ וְהִזָּ֤ה הַכֹּהֵן֙ בְּאֶצְבָּע֣וֹ

כז הַיְמָנִ֔ית מִן־הַשֶּׁ֕מֶן אֲשֶׁ֥ר עַל־כַּפּ֖וֹ הַשְּׂמָאלִ֑ית שֶׁ֥בַע פְּעָמִ֖ים לִפְנֵ֥י יְהֹוָֽה׃ וְנָתַ֨ן

כח הַכֹּהֵ֜ן מִן־הַשֶּׁ֗מֶן ׀ אֲשֶׁ֣ר עַל־כַּפּ֘וֹ עַל־תְּנ֤וּךְ אֹ֤זֶן הַמִּטַּהֵר֙ הַיְמָנִ֔ית וְעַל־בֹּ֤הֶן יָדוֹ֙

כט הַיְמָנִ֔ית וְעַל־בֹּ֥הֶן רַגְל֖וֹ הַיְמָנִ֑ית עַל־מְק֖וֹם דַּ֥ם הָאָשָֽׁם׃ וְהַנּוֹתָ֗ר מִן־הַשֶּׁ֙מֶן֙ אֲשֶׁר֙

ל עַל־כַּ֣ף הַכֹּהֵ֔ן יִתֵּ֖ן עַל־רֹ֣אשׁ הַמִּטַּהֵ֑ר לְכַפֵּ֥ר עָלָ֖יו לִפְנֵ֥י יְהֹוָֽה׃ וְעָשָׂ֤ה אֶת־הָֽאֶחָד֙

לא מִן־הַתֹּרִ֔ים א֖וֹ מִן־בְּנֵ֣י הַיּוֹנָ֑ה מֵאֲשֶׁ֥ר תַּשִּׂ֖יג יָד֑וֹ׃ אֵ֣ת אֲשֶׁר־תַּשִּׂ֣יג יָד֗וֹ אֶת־הָאֶחָ֤ד

לב חַטָּאת֙ וְאֶת־הָאֶחָ֣ד עֹלָ֔ה עַל־הַמִּנְחָ֑ה וְכִפֶּ֧ר הַכֹּהֵ֛ן עַ֥ל הַמִּטַּהֵ֖ר לִפְנֵ֥י יְהֹוָֽה׃ זֹ֤את

תּוֹרַ֔ת אֲשֶׁר־בּ֖וֹ נֶ֣גַע צָרָ֑עַת אֲשֶׁ֛ר לֹֽא־תַשִּׂ֥יג יָד֖וֹ בְּטׇהֳרָתֽוֹ׃

כו] וְאֶת־הַמִּנְחָה. מִנְחַת נְסָכִים שֶׁל בְּהֵמָה:

כא] וְעִשָּׂרוֹן סֹלֶת אֶחָד. לְכֶבֶשׂ זֶה שֶׁהוּא אֶחָד, יָבִיא עִשָּׂרוֹן אֶחָד לְנִסְכָּיו: וְלֹג שָׁמֶן. לָתֵת מִמֶּנּוּ עַל הַבְּהוֹנוֹת. וְשֶׁמֶן שֶׁל נִסְכֵּי הַמִּנְחָה לֹא הֻזְקַק הַכָּתוּב לְפָרֵשׁ:

כג] בַּיּוֹם הַשְּׁמִינִי לְטׇהֳרָתוֹ. שְׁמִינִי לְצִפֳּרִים וּלְהַזָּאַת עֵץ אֶרֶז וְאֵזוֹב וּשְׁנִי תוֹלַעַת:

כח] עַל מְקוֹם דַּם הָאָשָׁם. אֲפִלּוּ נִתְקַנַּח הַדָּם. לִמֵּד שֶׁאֵין הַדָּם גּוֹרֵם אֶלָּא הַמָּקוֹם גּוֹרֵם:

623

Leprosy of Houses
LEVITICUS 14:33–57

Leprosy is a form of nonverbal divine revelation, whereby God intimates to a person in a supernatural manner that his matters are not being conducted properly. Just as leprosy of the body and leprosy of the garment are not natural diseases, the same is true with regard to leprosy of a house, which is the next stage that afflicts a person after his skin and his garments. This leprosy too, is not a natural phenomenon, like dampness, but a heavenly sign. The green mark, the red mark, or both together, are miraculous indicators that the house is not ritually pure. Their appearance necessitates treatment of the afflicted part of the house, and at times, its total demolition. It should be noted that there were Sages who asserted that there was never an actual case of leprosy of the house, while others stated that there were cases, albeit rare, of leprosy of the house.[18]

Following its treatment of leprosy of the house, the Torah proceeds to address another form of ritual impurity, the impurity of one who experiences a discharge. Although such a condition is primarily an illness, it also contains an element of impurity, and its treatment, as addressed in detail by the Torah, reflects this fact. However, the process of purification from leprosy is longer and far more intricate than that of purification from discharge. That difference underscores the fact that leprosy in the Torah is not an illness, but a wondrous sign.

Fourth aliya **33** **The Lord spoke to Moses and to Aaron, saying:**
(Sixth aliya) **34** **When you come to the land of Canaan,**[D] **which I give to you as a portion, if I shall place a mark of leprosy on a house,** that is, **on one of the houses, in the land of your ancestral portion.** Although the various forms of leprosy are somewhat similar in that they involve the appearance of a mark and are all included in the general framework of the laws of leprosy, it is obvious that a mark on one's skin is very different from a spot found on a garment or on stones.[19]

35 **He to whom the house belongs shall come and tell to the priest, saying: Something like a mark seems to me to be on the house.** He cannot attest to the fact that it is leprosy, as he is not authorized to make that determination. Until a priest diagnoses the plague, the owner of the house can only assert his suspicion that there is leprosy in his house.[20]

36 The directive in this verse does not relate to treatment of the leprosy; rather, it relates to another aspect of this matter. **The priest shall command and they shall empty the house** of any vessels, **before the priest shall come to see the mark, so that all that is in the house shall not become impure;**[D] **and afterward the priest shall come to see the house.**

37 **He,** the priest, **shall examine the mark** after entering the house, **and behold, the mark is,** or appears to be, **recessed** [*sheka'arurot*] **in the walls of the house,** similar to the shape of a bowl [*ke'ara*], giving the impression of **deep green or deep reddish recesses, and their appearance is lower than the wall.** Due to their color, they appear to be sunken relative to the wall, although that is not the case.

38 **The priest shall exit the house** and proceed **to the entrance of the house, and he shall quarantine the house,** he shall issue an instruction to seal the house[21] for **seven days.**

39 **The priest shall return on the seventh day, and shall examine it; and behold, the mark has spread on the walls of the**
house. The mark that was on one wall has now relocated to other walls, or it has become enlarged.

40 **The priest shall command, and they shall remove the stones on which there is a mark.** The stone house described in the verse was apparently not compactly constructed; therefore, it was possible to remove an individual stone from the wall. **And they shall dispose of them,** as they are ritually impure, **in an impure place outside the city.** Although not all places outside the city are impure, there were certain areas designated for the disposal of impure objects, perhaps in places where there were garbage heaps or graves, locations not frequented by those carrying ritually pure items.[22]

41 **And** as for **the house,** in which there are holes, **he shall scrape**[B] and remove the layer of plaster[23] **from inside all around.** According to the *Sifra*, cited by Rashi, he would scrape only the plaster immediately around the mark.[24] **And they shall pour out the plaster that they scraped outside the city in an impure place.**

42 **They shall take other stones, and they shall bring them in the place of the stones** that they removed from the wall; **and he shall take other plaster, and** then **he shall plaster the house,** at which point it may once again serve as a residence.

Stones and plaster in the walls of a house

BACKGROUND

14:41 And the house, he shall scrape: To this day it is the practice in Middle Eastern countries to build with stones or bricks coated with earth or clay, in order to smooth the walls and seal gaps and cracks. Occasionally, the walls are built of two layers of stone, with a filling of earth between them, in order to construct a thicker wall and provide insulation.

לג וַיְדַבֵּ֣ר יְהֹוָ֔ה אֶל־מֹשֶׁ֥ה וְאֶֽל־אַהֲרֹ֖ן לֵאמֹֽר׃ כִּ֤י תָבֹ֙אוּ֙ אֶל־אֶ֣רֶץ כְּנַ֔עַן אֲשֶׁ֥ר אֲנִ֛י ‏ רביעי /שישי

לד נֹתֵ֥ן לָכֶ֖ם לַאֲחֻזָּ֑ה וְנָתַתִּי֙ נֶ֣גַע צָרַ֔עַת בְּבֵ֖ית אֶ֣רֶץ אֲחֻזַּתְכֶֽם׃ וּבָ֢א אֲשֶׁר־ל֣וֹ הַבַּ֗יִת

לה וְהִגִּ֣יד לַכֹּהֵ֣ן לֵאמֹ֑ר כְּנֶ֕גַע נִרְאָ֥ה לִ֖י בַּבָּֽיִת׃ וְצִוָּ֣ה הַכֹּהֵ֗ן וּפִנּ֤וּ אֶת־הַבַּ֙יִת֙ בְּטֶ֜רֶם

לו יָבֹ֤א הַכֹּהֵן֙ לִרְא֣וֹת אֶת־הַנֶּ֔גַע וְלֹ֥א יִטְמָ֖א כׇּל־אֲשֶׁ֣ר בַּבָּ֑יִת וְאַ֣חַר כֵּ֔ן יָבֹ֥א הַכֹּהֵ֖ן

לז לִרְא֣וֹת אֶת־הַבָּֽיִת׃ וְרָאָ֣ה אֶת־הַנֶּ֗גַע וְהִנֵּ֤ה הַנֶּ֙גַע֙ בְּקִירֹ֣ת הַבַּ֔יִת שְׁקַֽעֲרוּרֹת֙

יְרַקְרַקֹּ֔ת א֖וֹ אֲדַמְדַּמֹּ֑ת וּמַרְאֵיהֶ֥ן שָׁפָ֖ל מִן־הַקִּֽיר׃ וְיָצָ֧א הַכֹּהֵ֛ן מִן־הַבַּ֖יִת אֶל־פֶּ֣תַח

לח הַבָּ֑יִת וְהִסְגִּ֥יר אֶת־הַבַּ֖יִת שִׁבְעַ֥ת יָמִֽים׃ וְשָׁ֧ב הַכֹּהֵ֛ן בַּיּ֥וֹם הַשְּׁבִיעִ֖י וְרָאָ֑ה וְהִנֵּ֛ה

לט פָּשָׂ֥ה הַנֶּ֖גַע בְּקִירֹ֥ת הַבָּֽיִת׃ וְצִוָּ֣ה הַכֹּהֵ֗ן וְחִלְּצוּ֙ אֶת־הָ֣אֲבָנִ֔ים אֲשֶׁ֥ר בָּהֵ֖ן הַנָּ֑גַע

מ וְהִשְׁלִ֤יכוּ אֶתְהֶן֙ אֶל־מִח֣וּץ לָעִ֔יר אֶל־מָק֖וֹם טָמֵֽא׃ וְאֶת־הַבַּ֣יִת יַקְצִ֔עַ מִבַּ֖יִת

מא סָבִ֑יב וְשָׁפְכ֗וּ אֶת־הֶֽעָפָר֙ אֲשֶׁ֣ר הִקְצ֔וּ אֶל־מִח֣וּץ לָעִ֔יר אֶל־מָק֖וֹם טָמֵֽא׃ וְלָֽקְחוּ֙

מב אֲבָנִ֣ים אֲחֵר֔וֹת וְהֵבִ֖יאוּ אֶל־תַּ֣חַת הָאֲבָנִ֑ים וְעָפָ֥ר אַחֵ֛ר יִקַּ֖ח וְטָ֥ח אֶת־הַבָּֽיִת׃

רש״י

לד | וְנָתַתִּ֣י נֶ֣גַע צָרַ֔עַת. בְּשׂוֹרָה הִיא לָהֶם שֶׁהַנְּגָעִים בָּאִים עֲלֵיהֶם, לְפִי שֶׁהִטְמִינוּ אֱמוֹרִיִּים מַטְמוֹנִיּוֹת שֶׁל זָהָב בְּקִירוֹת בָּתֵּיהֶם כָּל אַרְבָּעִים שָׁנָה שֶׁהָיוּ יִשְׂרָאֵל בַּמִּדְבָּר, וְעַל יְדֵי הַנֶּגַע נוֹתֵץ הַבַּיִת וּמוֹצְאָן׃

לה | כְּנֶ֕גַע נִרְאָ֥ה לִ֖י בַּבָּֽיִת. שֶׁאֲפִלּוּ הוּא חָכָם וְיוֹדֵעַ שֶׁהוּא נֶגַע וַדַּאי, לֹא יִפְסֹק דָּבָר בָּרוּר לוֹמַר: ״נֶגַע נִרְאָה לִי״, אֶלָּא: ״כְּנֶגַע נִרְאָה לִי״׃

לו | בְּטֶ֜רֶם יָבֹ֤א הַכֹּהֵן֙ וְגוֹ׳. שֶׁכָּל זְמַן שֶׁאֵין כֹּהֵן נִזְקָק לוֹ אֵין שָׁם תּוֹרַת טֻמְאָה. **וְלֹ֥א יִטְמָ֖א כׇּל־אֲשֶׁ֣ר בַּבָּֽיִת.** שֶׁאִם לֹא יְפַנֵּהוּ וְיָבֹא הַכֹּהֵן וְיִרְאֶה הַנֶּגַע, נִזְקָק לְהִסָּגֵר, וְכָל מַה שֶּׁבְּתוֹכוֹ יִטְמָא. וְעַל מַה חָסָה תּוֹרָה? אִם עַל כְּלֵי שֶׁטֶף, יַטְבִּילֵם וְיִטְהָרוּ, וְאִם עַל אֳכָלִין וּמַשְׁקִין, יֹאכְלֵם בִּימֵי טֻמְאָתוֹ, הָא לֹא חָסָה תּוֹרָה אֶלָּא עַל כְּלֵי חֶרֶס שֶׁאֵין לָהֶם טׇהֳרָה בְּמִקְוֶה׃

לז | שְׁקַֽעֲרוּרֹת. שׁוֹקְעוֹת בְּמַרְאֵיהֶן׃

מ | וְחִלְּצוּ֙ אֶת־הָ֣אֲבָנִ֔ים. כְּתַרְגּוּמוֹ ״וְיִשַׁלְּפוּן״, יְטוֹלוּם מִשָּׁם, כְּמוֹ ״וְחָלְצָה נַעֲלוֹ״ (דברים כה, ט), לְשׁוֹן הֲסָרָה. **אֶל מָקוֹם טָמֵא.** מְקוֹם שֶׁאֵין טׇהֳרוֹת מִשְׁתַּמְּשׁוֹת שָׁם. לִמֵּד הַכָּתוּב שֶׁהָאֲבָנִים הַלָּלוּ מְטַמְּאוֹת מְקוֹמָן בְּעוֹדָן בּוֹ׃

מא | יַקְצִ֔עַ. רְדוֹיִי״ר בְּלַעַז, וּבִלְשׁוֹן מִשְׁנָה יֵשׁ הַרְבֵּה. **מִבַּיִת.** מִבִּפְנִים. **סָבִיב.** סְבִיבוֹת הַנֶּגַע, בְּתוֹרַת כֹּהֲנִים דָּרַשׁ כֵּן (פרק ה, ה), שֶׁיְּקַלֵּף הַטִּיחַ שֶׁסָּבִיב אַבְנֵי הַנֶּגַע. **הִקְצוּ.** לְשׁוֹן קָצֶה, אֲשֶׁר קָצוּ בִּקְצוֹת הַנֶּגַע סָבִיב׃

DISCUSSION

14:34 | When you come to the land of Canaan: The laws of leprosy of the house are recorded in the Torah after those of leprosy of the body and leprosy of the garment, and after the laws of their purification. Perhaps this is because leprosy of the body and of the garments was already relevant at the time the Torah was given, whereas leprosy of the house would only be applicable in the future (based on *Or HaHayyim*).

14:36 | The priest shall command and they shall empty the house, before the priest shall come to see the mark, so all that is in the house shall not become impure: Clearing the house is not a component of the purification process. Rather, its primary purpose is to spare the owner unnecessary exertion and financial loss, as the moment that the priest enters the house and declares it ritually impure, all the vessels inside the house are rendered impure. Accordingly, earthenware vessels, which are not subject to purification, must be broken, while the other vessels require immersion. The Torah commands the priest to be considerate vis-à-vis the owner and minimize the damage to his property. Therefore, the priest urges him to remove from the house any item susceptible to impurity (see *Sifra*; Rashi; *Nega'im* 12:5, and commentaries ad loc.).

According to one tannaitic opinion in the Mishna (*Nega'im* 12:5), one must remove even bundles of wood and straw from the house, even though such objects are not susceptible to ritual impurity. Some commentaries understand this position as incompatible with the above reasoning, since leaving these items in the house would cause no inconvenience to the owner. Rather, these *tanna'im* apparently hold that clearing the house entirely is a biblically mandated obligation for other reasons. This appears to be the position of the Rambam as well (Rambam, *Sefer Tahara, Hilkhot Tumat Tzara'at* 14:4).

43 **If** these actions are ineffective, and **the mark returns and erupts in the house, after removing the stones, and after scraping the house and after plastering** it,

44 **the priest shall come and examine; and** if **behold, the mark has spread** again either in the same place or elsewhere **in the house, it is a malignant leprosy,** a leprosy accompanied by a curse (see 13:51), **in the house,** which does not affect only those particular stones, but the entire house, and **it is impure.**

45 **He,** that is, anyone, **shall demolish the** entire **house, its stones, and its timber, and all the plaster of the house; and he shall take it,** all these, **outside the city to an impure place.**

46 Special laws of impurity apply to a leprous house: **One who comes into the house all the days that it is quarantined shall be impure**[D] **until the evening.**

47 **One who** remains and **sleeps in the house shall wash his garments** that he is wearing; **and one who eats in the house,** even if he did not sleep there but remained there long enough to eat,[25] **shall wash his garments.** These laws of ritual impurity apply to this house during the quarantine period, at which point it is uncertain whether the house will be purified.

48 Until this point, the reference has been to a case where the leprosy returned after the removal of the stones and the scraping of the plaster. The Torah now proceeds to address the alternative case. **If the priest shall come and examine, and behold, the mark did not spread in the house after the plastering of the house, the priest shall pronounce the house pure, because the mark was healed.**

49 **He shall take, to cleanse,** purify, **the house, two birds, cedar wood, scarlet wool, and hyssop.**

50 **He shall slaughter one of the birds in an earthenware vessel over spring water.**

51 **He shall take the cedar wood, and the hyssop, and the scarlet wool, and the living bird, and dip them in the blood of the slaughtered bird and in the spring water, and he shall sprinkle on the house seven times.** This entire process parallels the purification process of a leprous individual; however, in this case, one sprinkles on the leprous house rather than on a leprous person.

52 **He shall** thereby **cleanse the house with the blood of the bird, and with the spring water, and with the living bird, and with the cedar wood, and with the hyssop, and with the scarlet wool.**

53 **He shall dispatch the living bird outside the city out on the field; and he shall atone for the house,** eliminate its punishment, **and it shall be purified.**

54 **This is the law for any leprous mark,** which appears primarily on the skin, **and for a scall,** leprosy of the head or the beard;

Fifth aliya

55 **and for leprosy of the garment, and of the house;**

56 **and** for the following marks specifically: **for the spot, and for the scab, and for the bright spot.**

57 **To teach on which day it is impure,** when one must declare the afflicted house impure, **and on which day it is pure; this is the law of leprosy.**

רש״י

מג | **הִקְצוֹת.** לְשׁוֹן הֲעָשׂוֹת, וְכֵן "הִטּוֹחַ", אֲבָל "חִלֵּץ אֶת הָאֲבָנִים" מוּסָב הַלָּשׁוֹן אֶל הָאָדָם שֶׁחִלְּצָן, וְהוּא מִשְׁקַל לָשׁוֹן כָּבֵד, כְּמוֹ 'כִּפֵּר', 'דִּבֵּר': **וְאִם יָשׁוּב הַנֶּגַע וְגוֹ'.** יָכוֹל חָזַר בּוֹ בַּיּוֹם יְהֵא טָמֵא? תַּלְמוּד לוֹמַר: "וְשָׁב הַכֹּהֵן", "וְאִם יָשׁוּב", מַה 'שִׁיבָה' הָאֲמוּרָה לְהַלָּן בְּסוֹף שָׁבוּעַ, אַף 'שִׁיבָה' הָאֲמוּרָה כָּאן בְּסוֹף שָׁבוּעַ:

מד | **וּבָא הַכֹּהֵן וְרָאָה וְהִנֵּה פָּשָׂה.** יָכוֹל לֹא יְהֵא הַחוֹזֵר טָמֵא אֶלָּא אִם כֵּן פָּשָׂה? נֶאֱמַר: "צָרַעַת מַמְאֶרֶת" בְּבָתִּים, וְנֶאֱמַר: "צָרַעַת מַמְאֶרֶת" בִּבְגָדִים (לעיל יג, נא-נב), מַה לְּהַלָּן טִמֵּא אֶת הַחוֹזֵר אַף עַל פִּי שֶׁאֵינוֹ פוֹשֶׂה, אַף כָּאן טִמֵּא אֶת הַחוֹזֵר אַף עַל פִּי שֶׁאֵינוֹ פוֹשֶׂה. אִם כֵּן, מַה תַּלְמוּד לוֹמַר: "וְהִנֵּה פָּשָׂה"? אֵין כָּאן מְקוֹמוֹ שֶׁל מִקְרָא זֶה, אֶלָּא: "וְנָתַץ אֶת הַבַּיִת" הָיָה לוֹ לִכְתֹּב אַחַר: "וְאִם יָשׁוּב הַנֶּגַע", "וְרָאָה וְהִנֵּה פָּשָׂה" הָא לֹא בָּא לְלַמֵּד אֶלָּא עַל נֶגַע הָעוֹמֵד בְּעֵינָיו בְּשָׁבוּעַ רִאשׁוֹן, וּבָא בְּסוֹף שָׁבוּעַ שֵׁנִי וּמְצָאוֹ שֶׁפָּשָׂה, שֶׁלֹּא פֵּרֵשׁ בּוֹ הַכָּתוּב לְמַעְלָה (לעיל פסוק לט) כְּלוּם בְּעוֹמֵד בְּעֵינָיו בְּשָׁבוּעַ רִאשׁוֹן, וּלְמֶדְךָ כָּאן בְּפִשְׂיוֹן זֶה, שֶׁאֵינוֹ מְדַבֵּר אֶלָּא בְּעוֹמֵד בָּרִאשׁוֹן וּפָשָׂה בַּשֵּׁנִי. וּמַה יֵּעָשֶׂה לוֹ? יָכוֹל יִתְּצֶנּוּ כְּמוֹ שֶׁסָּמַךְ לוֹ: "וְנָתַץ אֶת הַבַּיִת"? תַּלְמוּד לוֹמַר: "וְשָׁב הַכֹּהֵן" (לעיל פסוק לט) "וּבָא הַכֹּהֵן", נִלְמַד בִּיאָה מִשִּׁיבָה, מַה שִּׁיבָה חוֹלֵץ וְקוֹצֶה וְטָח וְנוֹתֵן לוֹ שָׁבוּעַ, אַף בִּיאָה חוֹלֵץ וְקוֹצֶה וְטָח וְנוֹתֵן לוֹ שָׁבוּעַ, וְאִם חוֹזֵר – נוֹתֵץ, לֹא חָזַר – טָהוֹר. וּמִנַּיִן שֶׁאִם עָמַד בָּזֶה וּבָזֶה חוֹלֵץ וְקוֹצֶה וְטָח וְנוֹתֵן לוֹ שָׁבוּעַ?

DISCUSSION

14:46| **One who comes into the house all the days that it is quarantined shall be impure:** This exceptional form of ritual impurity is similar to the impurity imparted by a corpse in a tent (Numbers 19:14). In both cases, all items under the same roof are rendered impure, even if they did not come into direct contact with the source of impurity (see *Tosefta Megilla* 1:12). As stated earlier, the impurity of leprosy is to a certain extent considered a microcosm of death (see commentary on 13:45).

מג ואם־ישוב הנגע ופרח בבית אחר חלץ את־האבנים ואחרי הקצות את־הבית
מד ואחרי הטוח: ובא הכהן וראה והנה פשה הנגע בבית צרעת ממארת הוא
מה בבית טמא הוא: ונתץ את־הבית את־אבניו ואת־עציו ואת כל־עפר הבית
מו והוציא אל־מחוץ לעיר אל־מקום טמא: והבא אל־הבית כל־ימי הסגיר
מז אתו יטמא עד־הערב: והשכב בבית יכבס את־בגדיו והאכל בבית יכבס
מח את־בגדיו: ואם־בא יבא הכהן וראה והנה לא־פשה הנגע בבית אחרי הטח
מט את־הבית וטהר הכהן את־הבית כי נרפא הנגע: ולקח לחטא את־הבית
נ שתי צפרים ועץ ארז ושני תולעת ואזב: ושחט את־הצפר האחת אל־כלי
נא חרש על־מים חיים: ולקח את־עץ־הארז ואת־האזב ואת ׀ שני התולעת ואת
הצפר החיה וטבל אתם בדם הצפר השחוטה ובמים החיים והזה אל־הבית
נב שבע פעמים: וחטא את־הבית בדם הצפור ובמים החיים ובצפר החיה ובעץ
נג הארז ובאזב ובשני התולעת: ושלח את־הצפר החיה אל־מחוץ לעיר אל־פני
נד נה השדה וכפר על־הבית וטהר: זאת התורה לכל־נגע הצרעת ולנתק: ולצרעת חמישי
נו נז הבגד ולבית: ולשאת ולספחת ולבהרת: להורת ביום הטמא וביום הטהר
זאת תורת הצרעת:

רש"י

תלמוד לומר: "ובא" "ואם בא יבא" (להלן פסוק מח), במה הכתוב מדבר? אם בפושה בראשון – הרי כבר אמור, אם בפושה בשני – הרי כבר אמור, הא אינו אומר "ובא" "ואם בא יבא" אלא את שבא בסוף שבוע ראשון ובא בסוף שבוע שני "וראה והנה לא פשה". זה העומד – מה יעשה לו? יכול יפטר וילך, כמו שכתוב כאן: "וטהר את הבית"? תלמוד לומר: "כי נרפא הנגע", לא טהרתי אלא את הרפוי. מה יעשה לו? ביאה אמורה למעלה וביאה אמורה למטה (להלן פסוק מח), מה בעליונה חולץ וקוצה וטח ונותן לו שבוע, דגמר לה זהו שיבה זהו ביאה, אף בתחתונה כן וכו', כדאיתא בתורת כהנים (פרשתא ז, ד-ט). גמרו של דבר, אין נתיצה אלא בנגע החוזר אחר חליצה וקצוי וטיחה, ואין החוזר צריך פשיון. וסדר המקראות כך הוא, "ואם ישוב" (מג), "ונתץ" (מה), "והבא אל הבית" (מו), "והאכל בבית" (מז), "ובא הכהן וראה והנה פשה" (מד), ודבר הכתוב בעומד בראשון שנותן לו שבוע שני להסגרו, ובסוף שבוע שני להסגרו בא וראהו שפשה, ומה יעשה לו? חולץ וקוצה וטח ונותן לו שבוע. חזר – נותץ, לא חזר – טעון צפרים, שאין בנגעים יותר משלשה שבועות. "ואם בא יבא" (מח) לסוף שבוע שני, "וראה והנה לא פשה", מקרא זה בא ללמד בעומד בעיניו בראשון ובשני. ומה יעשה לו? יכול יטהרנו כמשמעו של מקרא "וטהר הכהן את הבית"? תלמוד לומר: "כי נרפא הנגע", לא טהרתי אלא את הרפוי, ואין רפוי אלא הבית שהקצה והוטח ולא חזר הנגע, אבל זה טעון חליצה וקצוי וטיחה ושבוע שלישי. וכן המקרא נדרש: "ואם בא יבא" בשני "וראה והנה לא פשה", יטיחנו, ואין טיחה בלא חלוץ וקצוי. ו"אחרי הטח את הבית, וטהר הכהן את הבית" אם לא חזר לסוף השבוע, "כי נרפא הנגע", ואם חזר, כבר פרש על החוזר שטעון נתיצה:

מו | **כל ימי הסגיר אתו.** ולא ימים שקלף את נגעו. יכול שאני מוציא המחלט שקלף את נגעו? תלמוד לומר: "כל ימי": **יטמא עד הערב.** מלמד שאין מטמא בגדים. יכול אפלו שהה כדי אכילת פרס? תלמוד לומר: "והאכל בבית יכבס את בגדיו" (להלן פסוק מז), אין לי אלא אוכל, שוכב מנין? תלמוד לומר: "והשכב". אין לי אלא אוכל ושוכב, לא אוכל ולא שוכב מנין? תלמוד לומר: "יכבס" "יכבס" רבה. אם כן למה נאמר: 'אוכל' ו'שוכב'? לתן שעור לשוכב כדי אכילת פרס:

נז | **להורת ביום הטמא וגו'.** איזה יום מטהרו ואיזה יום מטמאו:

Bodily Impurities Due to Emissions
LEVITICUS 15:1–33

After a lengthy discussion of the ritual impurity of leprosy, the Torah turns to other forms of impurity, mainly various types of *ziva*, emissions from the reproductive organs. Unlike leprosy, *ziva* is still recognized as a malady today. Male *ziva*, or gonorrhea, is essentially an infectious sexual disease, which cannot be entirely eradicated, even by antibiotics.

This topic concludes the *halakhot* of ritual impurity and purity in Leviticus. Although these matters are mentioned elsewhere in the Torah, the majority of their *halakhot* appear here.

15 1 **The Lord spoke to Moses and to Aaron, saying:**

2 **Speak to the children of Israel, and say to them: Any man, when he has a discharge from his flesh,**[D] the member, **his discharge is impure.**

3 **This shall be his impurity with his discharge: Whether his flesh,** member, **emits his discharge** of fluid, **or his flesh is blocked from his discharge,** due to the fact that the discharge is thick and blocks the orifice,[26] either way **it is his impurity.**

4 **Any bedding** or article of furniture designed for reclining, **on which the one who has a discharge lies, shall be impure; and any item on which he sits,** any object fashioned for sitting, **shall be impure.** In other words, any object designed for reclining, e.g., a bed or chair, is rendered impure by the use of the one who had the discharge, even if he did not touch the object with an exposed part of his body.

5 **A man who will touch his bedding shall wash his garments and bathe in water, and he is impure until the evening.** The seats and bedding rendered impure by a *zav* have a severe level of impurity; in the terminology of the Sages, they are referred to as a primary source of ritual impurity. Like the *zav* himself, they transmit impurity to people with whom they come in contact and to the garments those people are wearing at the time.

6 Furthermore, **one who sits on an article on which the one who has a discharge sat,** even if neither he nor the *zav* touched it directly with an exposed part of the body, he too **shall wash his garments and bathe in water, and he is impure until the evening.**

7 In addition to the impurity of vessels and items upon which the *zav* has leaned, there is also the impurity of his own body: **One who touches the flesh,** any part of the body, **of the one who has a discharge shall wash his garments and bathe in water, and he is impure until the evening.**

8 **If the one who has a discharge shall spit on one who is pure,** that individual who was pure **shall wash his garments and bathe in water, and he is impure until the evening.** Not only does the discharge of the *zav* itself, and his body, transmit impurity, but his spittle is also impure and imparts impurity. This category includes other emissions, the so-called founts of a *zav*, in the terminology of the Sages,[27] which also render one who touches them ritually impure.

9 **Any saddle**[D] **on which the one who has a discharge shall ride shall be impure.** Similar to items used for lying and sitting, articles on which a *zav* rides, such as a saddle, are rendered impure even without direct contact with his body.

10 **Anyone who touches any item that was underneath him,** the *zav*, such as the aforementioned articles used for bedding, sitting, and riding,[28] **shall be impure until the evening,** as stated above. The verse adds: **And one who carries them,** one of these articles, even if he does not touch it, **shall wash his garments and bathe in water, and he is impure until the evening.** The two ways in which one can contract this impurity are direct contact with one of those objects upon which the *zav* leaned, or by carrying and leaning without direct contact, e.g., the sitting mentioned in verse 6.[29]

11 **Anyone whom the one who has a discharge shall touch when he,** the *zav*, **did not rinse his hands in water,** if the *zav* has yet to immerse himself from his impurity,[30] **he shall wash his garments and bathe in water, and he is impure until the evening.**[D] The touch of a *zav* transmits impurity even if the flow of his emission has ceased until he immerses for his purification.

12 **And an earthenware vessel,** which cannot be purified while it remains whole (see 11:33), **that the one who has a discharge shall touch, shall be broken; and every wooden implement,** and likewise vessels made from other materials, such as metal[31] **shall be rinsed in water,** it is immersed in a ritual bath and is thereby purified.

Ancient wooden vessel

Earthenware vessel

אַ וַיְדַבֵּ֣ר יְהֹוָ֔ה אֶל־מֹשֶׁ֥ה וְאֶֽל־אַהֲרֹ֖ן לֵאמֹֽר: דַּבְּר֙וּ֙ אֶל־בְּנֵ֣י יִשְׂרָאֵ֔ל וַאֲמַרְתֶּ֖ם אֲלֵהֶ֑ם

בַּ אִ֤ישׁ אִישׁ֙ כִּ֤י יִהְיֶה֙ זָ֣ב מִבְּשָׂר֔וֹ זוֹב֖וֹ טָמֵ֥א הֽוּא:

גַּ וְזֹ֛את תִּהְיֶ֥ה טֻמְאָת֖וֹ בְּזוֹב֑וֹ רָ֣ר בְּשָׂר֞וֹ אֶת־זוֹב֗וֹ אֽוֹ־הֶחְתִּ֤ים בְּשָׂרוֹ֙ מִזּוֹב֔וֹ טֻמְאָת֖וֹ הִֽוא: כׇּל־הַמִּשְׁכָּ֗ב אֲשֶׁ֨ר יִשְׁכַּ֥ב

דַ עָלָ֛יו הַזָּ֖ב יִטְמָ֑א וְכׇֽל־הַכְּלִ֛י אֲשֶׁר־יֵשֵׁ֥ב עָלָ֖יו יִטְמָֽא: וְאִ֕ישׁ אֲשֶׁ֥ר יִגַּ֖ע בְּמִשְׁכָּב֑וֹ

הַ יְכַבֵּ֧ס בְּגָדָ֛יו וְרָחַ֥ץ בַּמַּ֖יִם וְטָמֵ֥א עַד־הָעָֽרֶב: וְהַיֹּשֵׁב֙ עַֽל־הַכְּלִ֔י אֲשֶׁר־יֵשֵׁ֥ב עָלָ֖יו הַזָּ֑ב

וַ יְכַבֵּ֧ס בְּגָדָ֛יו וְרָחַ֥ץ בַּמַּ֖יִם וְטָמֵ֥א עַד־הָעָֽרֶב: וְהַנֹּגֵ֖עַ בִּבְשַׂ֣ר הַזָּ֑ב יְכַבֵּ֧ס בְּגָדָ֛יו וְרָחַ֥ץ

זַ בַּמַּ֖יִם וְטָמֵ֥א עַד־הָעָֽרֶב: וְכִֽי־יָרֹ֥ק הַזָּ֖ב בַּטָּה֑וֹר וְכִבֶּ֧ס בְּגָדָ֛יו וְרָחַ֥ץ בַּמַּ֖יִם וְטָמֵ֥א

חַ עַד־הָעָֽרֶב: וְכׇל־הַמֶּרְכָּ֗ב אֲשֶׁ֨ר יִרְכַּ֥ב עָלָ֛יו הַזָּ֖ב יִטְמָֽא: וְכׇל־הַנֹּגֵ֗עַ בְּכֹל֙ אֲשֶׁ֣ר

טַ יִהְיֶ֣ה תַחְתָּ֔יו יִטְמָ֖א עַד־הָעָ֑רֶב וְהַנּוֹשֵׂ֣א אוֹתָ֔ם יְכַבֵּ֧ס בְּגָדָ֛יו וְרָחַ֥ץ בַּמַּ֖יִם וְטָמֵ֥א

יַ עַד־הָעָֽרֶב: וְכֹ֨ל אֲשֶׁ֤ר יִגַּע־בּוֹ֙ הַזָּ֔ב וְיָדָ֖יו לֹא־שָׁטַ֣ף בַּמָּ֑יִם וְכִבֶּ֧ס בְּגָדָ֛יו וְרָחַ֥ץ בַּמָּ֖יִם

יא וְטָמֵ֥א עַד־הָעָֽרֶב: וּכְלִי־חֶ֛רֶשׂ אֲשֶׁר־יִגַּע־בּ֥וֹ הַזָּ֖ב יִשָּׁבֵ֑ר וְכׇ֨ל־כְּלִי־עֵ֔ץ יִשָּׁטֵ֖ף בַּמָּֽיִם:

רש"י

פרק טו ב) **כִּי יִהְיֶה זָב.** יָכוֹל זָב מִכָּל מָקוֹם יְהֵא טָמֵא? תַּלְמוּד לוֹמַר: "מִבְּשָׂרוֹ", וְלֹא כָּל בְּשָׂרוֹ. אַחַר שֶׁחִלֵּק הַכָּתוּב בֵּין בָּשָׂר לְבָשָׂר, זָכִיתִי לַדִּין: טָמֵא בְּזָב וְטָמֵא בְּזָבָה, מַה זֶּה מִמָּקוֹם שֶׁהוּא מְטַמֵּא טֻמְאָה קַלָּה – נִדָּה, מְטַמֵּא טֻמְאָה חֲמוּרָה – זִיבָה, אַף זֶה מִמָּקוֹם שֶׁהוּא מְטַמֵּא טֻמְאָה קַלָּה – קֶרִי, מְטַמֵּא טֻמְאָה חֲמוּרָה – זִיבָה. **זוֹבוֹ טָמֵא.** לַמֵּד עַל הַטִּפָּה שֶׁהִיא מְטַמְּאָה. זוֹב דּוֹמֶה לְמֵי בָצֵק שֶׁל שְׂעוֹרִין, וְדִחוּי, וְדוֹמֶה לְלֹבֶן בֵּיצָה הַמּוּזֶרֶת. שִׁכְבַת זֶרַע, קָשׁוּר כְּלֹבֶן בֵּיצָה שֶׁאֵינָהּ מוּזֶרֶת:

ג) **רָר.** לְשׁוֹן רִיר, שֶׁזָּב בְּשָׂרוֹ "אֶת זוֹבוֹ", כְּמוֹ רִיר שֶׁזָּב זוֹבוֹ צָלוּל. **אוֹ הֶחְתִּים.** שֶׁיּוֹצֵא עָב וְסוֹתֵם אֶת פִּי הָאַמָּה, וְנִסְתָּם בְּשָׂרוֹ מִטִּפַּת זוֹבוֹ, זֶהוּ פְּשׁוּטוֹ. וּמִדְרָשׁוֹ, מָנָה הַכָּתוּב הָרִאשׁוֹן לִרְאִיּוֹת שְׁתַּיִם וּקְרָאוֹ טָמֵא, שֶׁנֶּאֱמַר: "זָב מִבְּשָׂרוֹ זוֹבוֹ טָמֵא הוּא", וּמָנָה הַכָּתוּב הַשֵּׁנִי לִרְאִיּוֹת שָׁלֹשׁ וּקְרָאוֹ טָמֵא, שֶׁנֶּאֱמַר: "טֻמְאָתוֹ בְּזוֹבוֹ רָר בְּשָׂרוֹ אֶת זוֹבוֹ אוֹ הֶחְתִּים בְּשָׂרוֹ מִזּוֹבוֹ טֻמְאָתוֹ הִיא"

הוּא. הָא כֵּיצַד? שְׁתַּיִם לְטֻמְאָה וְהַשְּׁלִישִׁית מַזְקִיקָתוֹ לְקָרְבָּן:

ד) **כָּל הַמִּשְׁכָּב.** הָרָאוּי לְמִשְׁכָּב. יָכוֹל אֲפִלּוּ מְיֻחָד לִמְלָאכָה אַחֶרֶת? תַּלְמוּד לוֹמַר: "אֲשֶׁר יִשְׁכַּב", "אֲשֶׁר שָׁכַב" לֹא נֶאֱמַר, אֶלָּא "אֲשֶׁר יִשְׁכַּב", הַמְיֻחָד תָּמִיד לְכָךְ, יָצָא זֶה שֶׁאוֹמְרִים לוֹ: עֲמֹד וְנַעֲשֶׂה מְלַאכְתֵּנוּ. **אֲשֶׁר יֵשֵׁב.** "יֵשֵׁב" לֹא נֶאֱמַר, אֶלָּא "אֲשֶׁר יֵשֵׁב עָלָיו הַזָּב", בַּמְיֻחָד תָּמִיד לְכָךְ:

ה) **וְאִישׁ אֲשֶׁר יִגַּע בְּמִשְׁכָּבוֹ.** לַמֵּד עַל הַמִּשְׁכָּב שֶׁחָמוּר מִן הַמַּגָּע, שֶׁזֶּה נַעֲשֶׂה אַב הַטֻּמְאָה לְטַמֵּא אָדָם לְטַמֵּא בְּגָדִים, וְהַמַּגָּע שֶׁאֵינוֹ מִשְׁכָּב אֵינוֹ אֶלָּא וְלַד הַטֻּמְאָה, וְאֵינוֹ מְטַמֵּא אֶלָּא אֳכָלִין וּמַשְׁקִין:

ו) **וְהַיֹּשֵׁב עַל הַכְּלִי.** אֲפִלּוּ לֹא נָגַע. אֲפִלּוּ עֲשָׂרָה כֵּלִים זֶה עַל זֶה כֻּלָּן מְטַמְּאִין מִשּׁוּם מוֹשָׁב, וְכֵן בְּמִשְׁכָּב:

ח) **וְכִי יָרֹק הַזָּב בְּטָהוֹר.** וְנָגַע בּוֹ אוֹ נְשָׂאוֹ, שֶׁהָרֹק מְטַמֵּא בְּמַשָּׂא:

טו) **וְכָל הַמֶּרְכָּב.** אַף עַל פִּי שֶׁלֹּא יָשַׁב עָלָיו, כְּגוֹן הַתְּפוּס שֶׁל סֶרֶג שֶׁקּוֹרִין ארצו"ן, טָמֵא מִשּׁוּם מֶרְכָּב, וְהָאֻכָּף שֶׁקּוֹרִין אלוו"ש טָמֵא טֻמְאַת מוֹשָׁב:

י) **וְכָל הַנֹּגֵעַ בְּכֹל אֲשֶׁר יִהְיֶה תַחְתָּיו.** שֶׁל זָב, וְלֹא. וְלַמֵּד עַל הַמֶּרְכָּב שֶׁיְּהֵא הַנּוֹגֵעַ בּוֹ טָמֵא, וְאֵין טָעוּן כִּבּוּס בְּגָדִים, וְהוּא חֹמֶר בַּמִּשְׁכָּב מִבַּמֶּרְכָּב. **וְהַנּוֹשֵׂא אוֹתָם.** כָּל הָאָמוּר בָּעִנְיָן הַזָּב, זוֹבוֹ וְרִיקוֹ וְשִׁכְבַת זַרְעוֹ וּמֵימֵי רַגְלָיו וְהַמִּשְׁכָּב וְהַמֶּרְכָּב, מַשָּׂאָן מְטַמֵּא אָדָם לְטַמֵּא בְּגָדִים:

יא) **וְיָדָיו לֹא שָׁטַף בַּמָּיִם.** בְּעוֹד שֶׁלֹּא טָבַל מִטֻּמְאָתוֹ, וַאֲפִלּוּ פָּסַק מִזּוֹבוֹ וְסָפַר שִׁבְעָה וּמְחֻסָּר טְבִילָה, מְטַמֵּא בְּכָל טֻמְאוֹתָיו. **וְיָדָיו לֹא שָׁטַף.** זֶה שֶׁהוֹצִיא הַכָּתוּב טְבִילַת גּוּפוֹ שֶׁל זָב בִּלְשׁוֹן שְׁטִיפַת יָדַיִם, לְלַמֶּדְךָ שֶׁאֵין בֵּית הַסְּתָרִים טָעוּן בִּיאַת מַיִם, אֶלָּא אֵיבָר הַגָּלוּי כְּמוֹ הַיָּדַיִם:

יב) **וּכְלִי חֶרֶשׂ אֲשֶׁר יִגַּע בּוֹ הַזָּב.** יָכוֹל אֲפִלּוּ לֹא נָגַע. כְּדִלְחִתָּא בְּרֹאשׁ לַקָּנֶה (פסחתא ג, ה-ב), עַד חַיְזְהוּ מַגָּעוֹ שֶׁהוּא בְכֻלּוֹ, הֱוֵי אוֹמֵר זֶה הֶסֵּטוֹ:

DISCUSSION

15:2 | From his flesh: In this chapter, the recurring mention of "flesh" has two meanings. Here it is a euphemism for the male reproductive organ (see also, e.g., Genesis 17:13; Exodus 28:42; Ezekiel 44:7). Elsewhere in the chapter, it bears the more common meaning of one's entire body (see, e.g., verse 7).

15:9 | Saddle: There is an opinion that a regular saddle is in the category of articles fashioned for sitting. Instead, the reference here is to an article on which the rider leans but does not sit (see Kelim 23:2 and commentaries ad loc.; Kelim 1:2; Sifra).

15:11 | Anyone whom the one who has a discharge shall touch when he did not rinse his hands in water, he shall wash his garments and bathe in water, and he is impure until the evening: This verse is apparently superfluous, as it is already stated above: "One who touches the flesh of the one who has a

13 The chapter turns to the purification of the *zav*. **When the one who has a discharge shall be cleansed from his discharge,** after he is healed, **he shall count for himself seven days from his cleansing.** These are the so-called seven clean days, in the terminology of the Sages, seven days on which one examined himself and did not find an emission. **And he shall wash,** immerse in water, **his garments,** those he wore when he was a *zav*, **and he shall bathe his flesh in spring water,** water connected to its source.[32] The requirement of spring water for ritual immersion is stated only with regard to a *zav*; in all other cases, the impure individual may immerse in a different type of ritual bath. **And he is** thereby **purified.**

14 **On the eighth day, he shall take for himself two turtledoves or two young pigeons, and come before the Lord to the entrance of the Tent of Meeting, and he shall give them to the priest.**

15 **The priest shall offer them, one as a sin offering, and one as a burnt offering; and the priest shall atone for him before the Lord from his discharge.**[D]

16 The chapter mentions another type of impurity, which is somewhat similar to *ziva*: **And a man, when semen is emitted from him,**[D] **shall bathe,** immerse **all his flesh in water, and he is impure until the evening.** The emission of semen from a man is a light category of impurity, which is unconnected to a disease, unlike the impurity of a *zav*.

Sixth aliya

(Seventh aliya)

17 **Every garment and any leather skin, upon which there shall be semen, shall be washed in water, and it is impure until the evening.**

18 **And a woman with whom a man shall lie with the emission of semen,** as both the man and woman participated in the act, **they shall bathe in water, and they are impure until the evening.**

19 **A woman, if she has a discharge,** not like the *ziva* of a man, but **her discharge from her flesh being blood,**[D] referring not to an illness but to the blood of the menstrual cycle,[33] **seven days she shall be in** the ritual impurity of **her menstrual state.** This severe form of impurity lasts for seven days, regardless of the duration of the blood flow during that period. **Anyone who touches her** on those days **shall be impure until the evening.**

20 **Anything on which she lies in her menstrual state shall be impure; and anything on which she sits shall be impure,** whether or not she touches them directly. In this regard, the impurity of a menstruating woman parallels that of a *zav*.

21 **Anyone who touches her bedding shall wash his garments and bathe in water, and he is impure until the evening.**

22 **Anyone who touches any article on which she sits shall wash his garments and bathe in water, and he is impure until the evening.**

23 **If he,** a ritually pure person,[34] or a pure vessel,[35] or the aforementioned blood[36] **is on the bedding, or on any article on which she sits, in touching it he shall be impure until the evening.**

24 **If a man lies with her,** during her menstrual period or afterward, before she has immersed, **then** the impurity of **her menstrual status shall be upon him,** due to contact with a menstruating woman, he has the same level of impurity as she does, but she does not actually transmit menstrual impurity to him.[37] **And he shall be impure seven days; and** also **any bedding on which he lies shall be impure.**[D]

25 Although menstruation usually occurs at regular intervals, with regard to both its appearance and its duration, a woman occasionally can bleed in a similar manner at other times. **And** consequently, with regard to **a woman, if her discharge of blood**

— DISCUSSION —

discharge shall wash his garments and bathe in water, and he is impure until the evening" (verse 7). The Sages derive from here that there is an additional method of contracting impurity, known as impurity through movement [*heset*]: If a *zav* moves a person or vessel without touching it, this is considered as if actual contact had occurred. This transfer of impurity is unique to a *zav* (see *Nidda* 43a; *Shabbat* 83b).

15:15 | From his discharge: In summary, the ritual impurity of the *zav* includes impurity transferred by contact, carrying, and the impurity of vessels usually found under his body weight, called by the Sages the impurity of

touching [*midras*]. In addition, the severity of the impurity of a *zav* is expressed in various special *halakhot*: Those items upon which he lies or sits become a primary source of ritual impurity, like the *zav* himself; he must immerse in spring water, as gathered water is insufficient for his purification; and only a *zav* transmits impurity by moving an item [*heset*], even without touching it (see *Shabbat* 83b). The details of the *halakhot* of a *zav* are discussed extensively in tractate *Zavim*.

Although from a medical perspective, *ziva*, or gonorrhea, is a sexual disease that afflicts both men and women, halakhically speaking it

applies to men alone, since a woman who has gonorrhea is not ritually impure.

15:16 | And a man, when semen is emitted from him: The emission of a *zav* is not semen. This fact, of which the Sages were aware, became widespread knowledge only about 1,500 years ago. The Sages conducted empirical tests to differentiate between the emission of a *zav* and semen (*Tosefta, Zavim* 2:4; see *Nidda* 35b).

15:19 | If she has a discharge, her discharge from her flesh being blood: In a general sense, the laws of ritual impurity are linked to death. Although semen is essential for the start of life, it also involves the death of cells, as whether it ◄►

יג וְכִֽי־יִטְהַ֤ר הַזָּב֙ מִזּוֹב֔וֹ וְסָ֨פַר ל֜וֹ שִׁבְעַ֥ת יָמִ֛ים לְטׇהֳרָת֖וֹ וְכִבֶּ֣ס בְּגָדָ֑יו וְרָחַ֥ץ בְּשָׂר֛וֹ
יד בְּמַ֥יִם חַיִּ֖ים וְטָהֵֽר׃ וּבַיּ֣וֹם הַשְּׁמִינִ֗י יִֽקַּֽח־לוֹ֙ שְׁתֵּ֣י תֹרִ֔ים א֥וֹ שְׁנֵ֖י בְּנֵ֣י יוֹנָ֑ה וּבָ֣א ׀ לִפְנֵ֣י
טו יהוה אֶל־פֶּ֙תַח֙ אֹ֣הֶל מוֹעֵ֔ד וּנְתָנָ֖ם אֶל־הַכֹּהֵֽן׃ וְעָשָׂ֤ה אֹתָם֙ הַכֹּהֵ֔ן אֶחָ֣ד חַטָּ֔את
טז וְהָאֶחָ֖ד עֹלָ֑ה וְכִפֶּ֨ר עָלָ֧יו הַכֹּהֵ֛ן לִפְנֵ֥י יהוה מִזּוֹבֽוֹ׃ וְאִ֕ישׁ כִּֽי־תֵצֵ֥א מִמֶּ֖נּוּ ששי /שביעי/
יז שִׁכְבַת־זָ֑רַע וְרָחַ֥ץ בַּמַּ֛יִם אֶת־כׇּל־בְּשָׂר֖וֹ וְטָמֵ֥א עַד־הָעָֽרֶב׃ וְכׇל־בֶּ֣גֶד וְכׇל־ע֔וֹר
יח אֲשֶׁר־יִהְיֶ֥ה עָלָ֖יו שִׁכְבַת־זָ֑רַע וְכֻבַּ֥ס בַּמַּ֖יִם וְטָמֵ֥א עַד־הָעָֽרֶב׃ וְאִשָּׁ֕ה אֲשֶׁ֨ר יִשְׁכַּ֥ב
אִ֛ישׁ אֹתָ֖הּ שִׁכְבַת־זָ֑רַע וְרָחֲצ֣וּ בַמַּ֔יִם וְטָמְא֖וּ עַד־הָעָֽרֶב׃
יט וְאִשָּׁ֞ה כִּֽי־תִהְיֶ֣ה זָבָ֗ה דָּ֛ם יִהְיֶ֥ה זֹבָ֖הּ בִּבְשָׂרָ֑הּ שִׁבְעַ֤ת יָמִים֙ תִּהְיֶ֣ה בְנִדָּתָ֔הּ וְכׇל־הַנֹּגֵ֥עַ
כ בָּ֖הּ יִטְמָ֥א עַד־הָעָֽרֶב׃ וְכֹל֩ אֲשֶׁ֨ר תִּשְׁכַּ֥ב עָלָ֛יו בְּנִדָּתָ֖הּ יִטְמָ֑א וְכֹ֛ל אֲשֶׁר־תֵּשֵׁ֥ב
כא עָלָ֖יו יִטְמָֽא׃ וְכׇל־הַנֹּגֵ֖עַ בְּמִשְׁכָּבָ֑הּ יְכַבֵּ֧ס בְּגָדָ֛יו וְרָחַ֥ץ בַּמַּ֖יִם וְטָמֵ֥א עַד־הָעָֽרֶב׃
כב וְכׇל־הַנֹּגֵ֔עַ בְּכׇל־כְּלִ֖י אֲשֶׁר־תֵּשֵׁ֣ב עָלָ֑יו יְכַבֵּ֧ס בְּגָדָ֛יו וְרָחַ֥ץ בַּמַּ֖יִם וְטָמֵ֥א עַד־הָעָֽרֶב׃
כג וְאִ֨ם עַֽל־הַמִּשְׁכָּ֜ב ה֗וּא א֛וֹ עַֽל־הַכְּלִ֛י אֲשֶׁר־הִ֥וא יֹשֶֽׁבֶת־עָלָ֖יו בְּנׇגְעוֹ־ב֑וֹ יִטְמָ֖א
כד עַד־הָעָֽרֶב׃ וְאִ֡ם שָׁכֹ֨ב יִשְׁכַּ֥ב אִ֜ישׁ אֹתָ֗הּ וּתְהִ֤י נִדָּתָהּ֙ עָלָ֔יו וְטָמֵ֖א שִׁבְעַ֣ת יָמִ֑ים
כה וְכׇל־הַמִּשְׁכָּ֛ב אֲשֶׁר־יִשְׁכַּ֥ב עָלָ֖יו יִטְמָֽא׃ וְאִשָּׁ֡ה כִּֽי־יָז֨וּב ז֜וֹב דָּמָ֗הּ יב

רש"י

יג] וְכִי יִטְהַר. כְּשֶׁיִּפְסֹק: שִׁבְעַת יָמִים לְטׇהֳרָתוֹ. שִׁבְעַת יָמִים טְהוֹרִים מִטֻּמְאַת זִיבָה שֶׁלֹּא יִרְאֶה זוֹב, וְכֻלָּן רְצוּפִין:

יח] וְרָחֲצוּ בַמַּיִם. גְּזֵרַת מֶלֶךְ הִיא שֶׁתִּטְמָא הָאִשָּׁה בְּבִיאָה, וְאֵין הַטַּעַם מִשּׁוּם נוֹגֵעַ בְּשִׁכְבַת זֶרַע, שֶׁהֲרֵי מַגַּע בֵּית הַסְּתָרִים הוּא:

יט] כִּי תִהְיֶה זָבָה. יָכוֹל מֵאֶחָד מִכׇּל אֵיבָרֶיהָ? תַּלְמוּד לוֹמַר "וְהִוא גִּלְּתָה אֶת מְקוֹר דָּמֶיהָ" (להלן כ, יח), אֵין דָּם מְטַמֵּא אֶלָּא הַבָּא מִן הַמָּקוֹר: דָּם יִהְיֶה זֹבָהּ בִּבְשָׂרָהּ. אֵין זוֹבָהּ קָרוּי זוֹב לְטַמֵּא אֶלָּא אִם כֵּן הוּא אָדֹם: בְּנִדָּתָהּ. כְּמוֹ "וּמְנֻדַּל יְנִדֻּהוּ" (איוב יח, יח), שֶׁהִיא מְנֻדָּה מִמַּגַּע כׇּל אָדָם: תִּהְיֶה בְנִדָּתָהּ. אֲפִלּוּ לֹא רָאֲתָה אֶלָּא רְאִיָּה רִאשׁוֹנָה:

כג] וְאִם עַל הַמִּשְׁכָּב הוּא. הַשּׁוֹכֵב אוֹ הַיּוֹשֵׁב עַל מִשְׁכָּבָהּ אוֹ עַל מוֹשָׁבָהּ, אֲפִלּוּ לֹא נָגַע בּוֹ, אַף הוּא בְּדַת טֻמְאָה הָאֲמוּרָה בַּמִּקְרָא הָעֶלְיוֹן, שֶׁטָּעוּן כִּבּוּס בְּגָדִים: עַל הַכְּלִי. לְרַבּוֹת אֶת הַמֶּרְכָּב: בְּנׇגְעוֹ בוֹ יִטְמָא. אֵינוֹ מְדַבֵּר אֶלָּא עַל הַמֶּרְכָּב שֶׁנִּתְרַבָּה מֵ"עַל הַכְּלִי": בְּנׇגְעוֹ בוֹ יִטְמָא. וְאֵינוֹ טָעוּן כִּבּוּס בְּגָדִים, שֶׁהַמֶּרְכָּב אֵין מַגָּעוֹ מְטַמֵּא אָדָם לְטַמֵּא בְּגָדִים:

כד] וּתְהִי נִדָּתָהּ עָלָיו. יָכוֹל יַעֲלֶה לְרַגְלָהּ, שֶׁאִם בָּא עָלֶיהָ בַּחֲמִישִׁי לְנִדָּתָהּ לֹא יִטְמָא אֶלָּא שְׁלֹשָׁה יָמִים כְּמוֹתָהּ? תַּלְמוּד לוֹמַר: "וְטָמֵא שִׁבְעַת יָמִים". וּמָה תַּלְמוּד לוֹמַר "וּתְהִי נִדָּתָהּ עָלָיו"? מָה הִיא מְטַמְּאָה אָדָם וּכְלִי חֶרֶס, אַף הוּא מְטַמֵּא אָדָם וּכְלִי חֶרֶס:

DISCUSSION

is produced as a nocturnal emission or as part of sexual intercourse, the vast majority of semen goes to waste. Since each sperm has the potential for life, when it does not bring life to the world but dies, impurity is created. This impurity is unrelated to whether the seminal emission is considered a transgression, but to the fact that a small element of death is present. Likewise, a woman's menstrual cycle involves the death of cells: A woman's period begins when the ovum dies, and the blood that flows includes other tissues that have undergone a process of erosion and death (see *Kuzari* 2:60; Ramban, verse 17). It is possible that the impurity of a woman after childbirth is also related to death, due to the detachment of the life that was in her body, or because of the life-threatening situation she faced while giving birth.

15:24 | **And any bedding on which he lies shall be impure:** This verse does not say that the bedding of one who lies with a menstruating woman transmits impurity to another person by contact and carrying, as is stated with regard to a menstruating woman herself. Rather, the Sages derive that the impurity of his bedding is of a lesser severity, as it is not a primary source of ritual impurity, which imparts impurity

shall flow many days not at the time of her menstruation; or alternatively, **if it shall flow beyond,** in addition to **her menstruation,** if the blood of her menstruation flows beyond its usual time. In such cases, **for all the days of the discharge of her impurity she shall be like during the days of her menstruation; she is impure.** This bleeding is considered a type of sickness, and it is ritually impure. Such a woman is referred to by the Sages as a *zava*.

26 Consequently, **any bedding on which she lies all the days of her discharge shall be for her like the bedding of her menstruation** with regard to ritual impurity, **and any article on which she shall sit,** including bedsheets, **shall be impure, like the impurity of her menstruation.**

27 **And anyone who touches them,** the vessels, furniture, or bedsheets on which she had sat or lain, **shall become impure, and he shall wash his garments and bathe in water, and he is impure until the evening.**

28 **But if she was cleansed from her discharge,** when the blood flow ends, **she shall count for herself seven days, and then she shall be pure.** The counting of seven clean days applies by Torah law only to a *zav* and a *zava*, whose bleeding is considered a form of illness, unlike regular menstrual bleeding, as stated previously in the commentary (see verse 19).

29 Furthermore, like the *zav*, the *zava* must bring offerings to atone for herself and permit her to enter the Temple: **And on the eighth day,** after seven days clean without bleeding, **she shall take for herself two turtledoves or two young pigeons, and she shall bring them to the priest, to the entrance of the Tent of Meeting.**

Seventh aliya

30 **The priest shall perform one as a sin offering, and one as a burnt offering; and the priest shall atone for her before the Lord for the discharge of her impurity.**[D]

31 **You shall separate,** distance,[38] **the children of Israel from their impurity, that they shall not die in their impurity, by their rendering My Tabernacle that is in their midst impure.**[D]

Maftir

32 The chapter concludes: **This is the law of the one who has a discharge, and of one from whom semen will be emitted, to become impure through it;**

33 and **the law of she who is suffering**[D] **with her menstruation,** at the time of her period, **and** the law for **one who has a discharge, for a man or for a woman; and** likewise **for one who lies with an impure woman,** whether she is a menstruating woman, a *zava*, or has given birth.[39]

DISCUSSION

to people and other vessels. Rather, it transmits impurity to food and drink alone, in the manner of a secondary source of ritual impurity (see *Kelim* 1:3; *Nidda* 33a; *Yoma* 6a).

15:30 | For the discharge of her impurity: The impurity of a menstruating woman differs from that of a *zava* by Torah law, but not in terms in practical *halakha* as observed today. By Torah law, a menstruating woman counts seven days of impurity from the beginning of her bleeding, although in most normal cases the blood flow of menstruation does not last that long. The time frame of the bleeding is highly variable, not only with regard to different women, but also with regard to the same woman at different stages in her life, as noted by the Sages. Although the menstruation period is generally determined by an independent hormonal cycle, there are certain factors that can affect the hormonal system and change or disrupt regular patterns of menstruation. Likewise, the cause of a blood flow need not be a specific illness; blood flow can

also be the result of physiological or psychosomatic complications (see *Sota* 20b; *Nidda* 20b).

The impurity of *ziva*, by contrast, occurs whenever a woman experiences a flow of blood not at the time of her menstruation. In this case, her purification depends on her counting of seven clean days (*Nidda* 35b). However, nowadays no method exists for clearly differentiating between normal menstrual blood and the blood of *ziva* or other types of blood. Therefore, a woman counts seven clean days after every kind of bleeding, as was already the practice in the talmudic period (*Berakhot* 31a; *Nidda* 66a).

Unlike menstruation, which is a natural process, the blood flow of *ziva* is indicative of a sickness. It is true that a natural occurrence can also cause ritual impurity; after all, death itself is part of the normal course of events, and yet it leads to a severe level of impurity. Nevertheless, there is no need for atonement following an impurity due to a regular event. Consequently, menstruation, the emission of semen, and the impurity of

a corpse do not render one liable to bring an offering, whereas the diseases of leprosy and *ziva*, both that of a man and of a woman, require the sacrifice of an atonement offering (see Ramban and Sforno, verse 19).

15:31 | By their rendering My Tabernacle that is in their midst impure: It is evident from this verse that the laws of impurity are an extension of the regulations surrounding the Temple. In general, ritual impurity is undesirable, but is not intrinsically prohibited. The problem with impurity, and the need to avoid it, arises in practice when one wishes to enter the Temple or handle consecrated items (see commentary on 11:8; Rambam, *Guide of the Perplexed* 3:47; *Sefer HaḤinnukh* 159; *Bekhor Shor*, 11:8).

15:33 | She who is suffering [*hadava*]: This translation follows the Ibn Ezra on 20:18. Alternatively, the word may mean flowing, similar to the word *ziva* (see commentary on 20:18).

יָמִים רַבִּים בְּלֹא עֶת־נִדָּתָהּ אוֹ כִי־תָזוּב עַל־נִדָּתָהּ כָּל־יְמֵי זוֹב טֻמְאָתָהּ כִּימֵי
כו נִדָּתָהּ תִּהְיֶה טְמֵאָה הִוא: כָּל־הַמִּשְׁכָּב אֲשֶׁר תִּשְׁכַּב עָלָיו כָּל־יְמֵי זוֹבָהּ כְּמִשְׁכַּב
כז נִדָּתָהּ יִהְיֶה־לָּהּ וְכָל־הַכְּלִי אֲשֶׁר תֵּשֵׁב עָלָיו טָמֵא יִהְיֶה כְּטֻמְאַת נִדָּתָהּ: וְכָל־
כח הַנּוֹגֵעַ בָּם יִטְמָא וְכִבֶּס בְּגָדָיו וְרָחַץ בַּמַּיִם וְטָמֵא עַד־הָעָרֶב: וְאִם־טָהֲרָה מִזּוֹבָהּ
כט וְסָפְרָה־לָּהּ שִׁבְעַת יָמִים וְאַחַר תִּטְהָר: וּבַיּוֹם הַשְּׁמִינִי תִּקַּח־לָהּ שְׁתֵּי תֹרִים אוֹ שביעי
ל שְׁנֵי בְּנֵי יוֹנָה וְהֵבִיאָה אוֹתָם אֶל־הַכֹּהֵן אֶל־פֶּתַח אֹהֶל מוֹעֵד: וְעָשָׂה הַכֹּהֵן אֶת־
הָאֶחָד חַטָּאת וְאֶת־הָאֶחָד עֹלָה וְכִפֶּר עָלֶיהָ הַכֹּהֵן לִפְנֵי יְהוָה מִזּוֹב טֻמְאָתָהּ:
לא וְהִזַּרְתֶּם אֶת־בְּנֵי־יִשְׂרָאֵל מִטֻּמְאָתָם וְלֹא יָמֻתוּ בְּטֻמְאָתָם בְּטַמְּאָם אֶת־מִשְׁכָּנִי מפטיר
לב אֲשֶׁר בְּתוֹכָם: זֹאת תּוֹרַת הַזָּב וַאֲשֶׁר תֵּצֵא מִמֶּנּוּ שִׁכְבַת־זֶרַע לְטָמְאָה־בָהּ:
לג וְהַדָּוָה בְּנִדָּתָהּ וְהַזָּב אֶת־זוֹבוֹ לַזָּכָר וְלַנְּקֵבָה וּלְאִישׁ אֲשֶׁר יִשְׁכַּב עִם־טְמֵאָה:

רש"י

כה] **יָמִים רַבִּים.** שְׁלֹשָׁה יָמִים: **בְּלֹא עֵת נִדָּתָהּ.** אַחַר שֶׁיָּצְאוּ שִׁבְעַת יְמֵי נִדָּתָהּ: **אוֹ כִי תָזוּב.** אֶת שְׁלֹשֶׁת הַיָּמִים הַלָּלוּ: **עַל נִדָּתָהּ.** מֻפְלָג מִנִּדָּתָהּ יוֹם אֶחָד, זוֹ הִיא זָבָה, וּמִשְׁפָּטָהּ חָרוּץ בְּפָרָשָׁה זוֹ, וְלֹא כְּדַת הַנִּדָּה, שֶׁזּוֹ טְעוּנָה סְפִירַת שִׁבְעָה נְקִיִּים וְקָרְבָּן, וְהַנִּדָּה אֵינָהּ טְעוּנָה סְפִירַת שִׁבְעָה נְקִיִּים, אֶלָּא "שִׁבְעַת יָמִים תִּהְיֶה בְנִדָּתָהּ" (לעיל פסוק יט), בֵּין רוֹאָה בֵּין שֶׁאֵינָהּ רוֹאָה. וְדָרְשׁוּ בְּפָרָשָׁה זוֹ אַחַד עָשָׂר יוֹם שֶׁבֵּין סוֹף נִדָּה לִתְחִלַּת נִדָּה, שֶׁכָּל שְׁלֹשָׁה רְצוּפִין שֶׁתִּרְאֶה בְּאַחַד עָשָׂר יוֹם הַלָּלוּ תְּהֵא זָבָה.

לא] **וְהִזַּרְתֶּם.** אֵין נְזִירָה אֶלָּא פְּרִישָׁה, וְכֵן "נָזֹרוּ אָחוֹר" (ישעיה א, ד), וְכֵן "נְזִיר אֶחָיו" (בראשית מט, כו): **וְלֹא יָמֻתוּ בְּטֻמְאָתָם.** הֲרֵי הַכָּרֵת שֶׁל מְטַמֵּא מִקְדָּשׁ קָרוּי מִיתָה:

לב] **זֹאת תּוֹרַת הַזָּב.** בַּעַל רְאִיָּה אַחַת, וּמַהוּ תּוֹרָתוֹ? **וַאֲשֶׁר תֵּצֵא מִמֶּנּוּ שִׁכְבַת זֶרַע.** הֲרֵי הוּא כְּבַעַל קֶרִי, טָמֵא טֻמְאַת עֶרֶב:

לג] **וְהַזָּב אֶת זוֹבוֹ.** בַּעַל שְׁתֵּי רְאִיּוֹת וּבַעַל שָׁלֹשׁ רְאִיּוֹת, שֶׁתּוֹרָתָן מְפֹרֶשֶׁת לְמַעְלָה:

Parashat
Aharei Mot

The High Priest's Entrance to the Holy of Holies
LEVITICUS 16:1–34

The previous sections dealt with the sanctity of the children of Israel as expressed in the laws of forbidden foods and the laws of ritual purity and impurity. The following passage returns to the laws that apply specifically to priests.

Not only are the ritually impure mandated to keep their distance from the Sanctuary, but even the ritually pure are prohibited from entering the Sanctum as they please. Furthermore, even Aaron the High Priest is not permitted to enter the Holy of Holies except to perform a particular ritual on a specific date. He is not allowed to enter empty-handed; rather, his entrance has to be accompanied by the burning of incense and the sprinkling of the blood of sin offerings to atone for any ritual impurity or sin on behalf of the entire nation. In other words, if any individual, priest or non-priest alike, would approach the sanctified areas or touch consecrated items while in a state of ritual impurity, they would achieve atonement once a year, through the High Priest's entrance into the innermost sanctum on Yom Kippur.

On this day, in addition to receiving atonement for transgressions related to ritual impurity, the nation would also receive absolution for all other sins accumulated over the course of the year. The transgressions would be banished, as it were, to an otherworldly realm.

16 1 **The Lord spoke to Moses after the death of the two sons of Aaron, when they approached before the Lord and they died.** There are different allusions in the Torah as to the reason why Aaron's sons died.[1] The explanation suggested here is that Aaron's sons came too close to God's Presence without receiving His permission.[2]

2 **The Lord said to Moses: Speak to Aaron, your brother, that he shall not come at all times into the Sanctum** that is **within,** behind, **the curtain, before the cover that is upon the ark, and he shall not die, for it is in the cloud that I will** always **be seen upon the cover,** that is, the Divine Presence is found on the cover.[3] This command alludes to the deaths of Aaron's sons Nadav and Avihu, who died because they had approached the Sanctuary in an unfit manner. Although Aaron was the High Priest, not even he was permitted to enter the inner sanctum whenever he pleased.

3 **With this shall Aaron,** or any High Priest of his descendants, **come into the Sanctum: with a young bull as a sin offering and a ram as a burnt offering.** The verse explains that the only permissible way to enter the Holy of Holies is by bringing offerings and following the procedures described in the verses that follow. Even so, it is clear from the continuation of the passage that the High Priest may not enter the Holy of Holies whenever he wants, even to perform this procedure; rather, he can enter only one day a year, on Yom Kippur.[4] Some commentaries, however, hold that Aaron was uniquely permitted to enter the Holy of Holies on any day of the year by following the procedure described here.[5]

4 When entering the Holy of Holies, the High Priest is not to wear his standard vestments, which were fashioned from sky-blue and purple wool and gold threads and contained precious gems. Rather, **he shall don a sacred linen tunic, and linen trousers shall be on his flesh, and he shall gird himself with**

a linen belt,[D] **and he shall wear a linen mitre.** These four simple garments were worn by common priests as well, and the entire outfit was made from white linen. Most Sages maintain that the only difference between the High Priest's vestments described in this verse and those of the common priest was in the mitre, which differed from the headdress worn by all other priests. Although they are simple, **they are sacred vestments; and** therefore **he shall bathe his flesh in water, and** only then shall he **don them.**

5 The High Priest's entry into the Holy of Holies is not a private matter; he represents all the children of Israel. Consequently, it is not sufficient for him to sacrifice the bull and ram mentioned above, as these are personal offerings. **From the congregation of the children of Israel he shall take two** identical **goats as a sin offering**[6] **and one ram as a burnt offering.** These offerings are brought on behalf of all the children of Israel.

6 **Aaron shall present the bull of the sin offering that is for him,** which he purchased with his own private funds, **and** place his hands on the bull and recite a confession,[7] and thereby **atone for himself and for his household.** The term "household" refers either to his private family or to the broader household of Aaron, all priests.[8]

7 After confessing his own transgressions and those of his family, the High Priest performs the rite of atonement on behalf of the nation. **He shall take the two goats** that were set aside for the people, **and he shall set them before the Lord at the entrance of the Tent of Meeting.**

8 **Aaron shall place lots on the two goats,**[D] as the destiny of each of these identical goats will be determined by the lots. **One lot** shall contain the words **for the Lord,** or, according to another interpretation, simply, Lord, **and on the other lot** shall be written the phrase **for Azazel.**

פרשת
אחרי מות

א וַיְדַבֵּר יְהוָה אֶל־מֹשֶׁה אַחֲרֵי מוֹת שְׁנֵי בְּנֵי אַהֲרֹן בְּקָרְבָתָם לִפְנֵי־יְהוָה וַיָּמֻתוּ:
ב וַיֹּאמֶר יְהוָה אֶל־מֹשֶׁה דַּבֵּר אֶל־אַהֲרֹן אָחִיךָ וְאַל־יָבֹא בְכָל־עֵת אֶל־הַקֹּדֶשׁ מִבֵּית לַפָּרֹכֶת אֶל־פְּנֵי הַכַּפֹּרֶת אֲשֶׁר עַל־הָאָרֹן וְלֹא יָמוּת כִּי בֶּעָנָן אֵרָאֶה עַל־הַכַּפֹּרֶת:
ג בְּזֹאת יָבֹא אַהֲרֹן אֶל־הַקֹּדֶשׁ בְּפַר בֶּן־בָּקָר לְחַטָּאת וְאַיִל לְעֹלָה: ד כְּתֹנֶת־בַּד קֹדֶשׁ יִלְבָּשׁ וּמִכְנְסֵי־בַד יִהְיוּ עַל־בְּשָׂרוֹ וּבְאַבְנֵט בַּד יַחְגֹּר וּבְמִצְנֶפֶת בַּד יִצְנֹף בִּגְדֵי־קֹדֶשׁ הֵם וְרָחַץ בַּמַּיִם אֶת־בְּשָׂרוֹ וּלְבֵשָׁם: ה וּמֵאֵת עֲדַת בְּנֵי יִשְׂרָאֵל יִקַּח שְׁנֵי־שְׂעִירֵי עִזִּים לְחַטָּאת וְאַיִל אֶחָד לְעֹלָה: ו וְהִקְרִיב אַהֲרֹן אֶת־פַּר הַחַטָּאת אֲשֶׁר־לוֹ וְכִפֶּר בַּעֲדוֹ וּבְעַד בֵּיתוֹ: ז וְלָקַח אֶת־שְׁנֵי הַשְּׂעִירִם וְהֶעֱמִיד אֹתָם לִפְנֵי יְהוָה פֶּתַח אֹהֶל מוֹעֵד: ח וְנָתַן אַהֲרֹן עַל־שְׁנֵי הַשְּׂעִירִם גֹּרָלוֹת גּוֹרָל אֶחָד לַיהוָה וְגוֹרָל אֶחָד לַעֲזָאזֵל:

רש"י

א] וַיְדַבֵּר ה' אֶל מֹשֶׁה אַחֲרֵי מוֹת שְׁנֵי בְּנֵי אַהֲרֹן וְגו'. מַה תַּלְמוּד לוֹמַר? הָיָה רַבִּי אֶלְעָזָר בֶּן עֲזַרְיָה מוֹשְׁלוֹ מָשָׁל, לְחוֹלֶה שֶׁנִּכְנַס אֶצְלוֹ רוֹפֵא, אָמַר לוֹ: אַל תֹּאכַל צוֹנֵן וְאַל תִּשְׁכַּב בַּטַּחַב. בָּא אַחֵר וְאָמַר לוֹ: אַל תֹּאכַל צוֹנֵן וְאַל תִּשְׁכַּב בַּטַּחַב, שֶׁלֹּא תָמוּת כְּדֶרֶךְ שֶׁמֵּת פְּלוֹנִי. זֶה זֵרְזוֹ יוֹתֵר מִן הָרִאשׁוֹן, לְכָךְ נֶאֱמַר: "אַחֲרֵי מוֹת שְׁנֵי בְּנֵי אַהֲרֹן":

ב] וַיֹּאמֶר ה' אֶל מֹשֶׁה דַּבֵּר אֶל אַהֲרֹן אָחִיךָ וְאַל יָבֹא. שֶׁלֹּא יָמוּת כְּדֶרֶךְ שֶׁמֵּתוּ בָנָיו: וְלֹא יָמוּת. שֶׁאִם בָּא, הוּא מֵת: כִּי בֶּעָנָן אֵרָאֶה. כִּי תָמִיד אֲנִי נִרְאֶה שָׁם עִם עַמּוּד עֲנָנִי, וּלְפִי שֶׁגִּלּוּי שְׁכִינָתִי שָׁם, יִזָּהֵר שֶׁלֹּא יַרְגִּיל לָבֹא, זֶהוּ פְשׁוּטוֹ. וּמִדְרָשׁוֹ, אַל יָבֹא כִּי אִם בַּעֲנַן הַקְּטֹרֶת בְּיוֹם הַכִּפּוּרִים:

ג] בְּזֹאת. גִּימַטְרִיָּא שֶׁלּוֹ אַרְבַּע מֵאוֹת וְעֶשֶׂר, רֶמֶז לְבַיִת רִאשׁוֹן: בְּזֹאת יָבֹא אַהֲרֹן וְגו'. וְאַף זוֹ לֹא בְּכָל עֵת, כִּי אִם בְּיוֹם הַכִּפּוּרִים, כְּמוֹ שֶׁמְּפֹרָשׁ בְּסוֹף הַפָּרָשָׁה: "בַּחֹדֶשׁ הַשְּׁבִיעִי בֶּעָשׂוֹר לַחֹדֶשׁ" (להלן פסוק כט):

ד] כְּתֹנֶת בַּד וְגו'. מַגִּיד שֶׁאֵינוֹ מְשַׁמֵּשׁ לִפְנִים בִּשְׁמוֹנָה בְּגָדִים שֶׁהוּא מְשַׁמֵּשׁ בָּהֶן בַּחוּץ, שֶׁיֵּשׁ בָּהֶן זָהָב, לְפִי שֶׁאֵין קַטֵּגוֹר נַעֲשֶׂה סָנֵגוֹר, אֶלָּא בְּאַרְבָּעָה כְּכֹהֵן הֶדְיוֹט, וְכֻלָּן שֶׁל בּוּץ: קֹדֶשׁ יִלְבָּשׁ. שֶׁיִּהְיוּ מִשֶּׁל הֶקְדֵּשׁ: יִצְנֹף. כְּתַרְגּוּמוֹ "יָחֵית בְּרֵישֵׁיהּ", יַנִּיחַ בְּרֹאשׁוֹ, כְּמוֹ: "וַתַּנַּח בִּגְדוֹ" (בראשית לט, טז), "אַחְתִּיתֵיהּ": וְרָחַץ בַּמַּיִם. אוֹתוֹ הַיּוֹם טָעוּן טְבִילָה בְּכָל חֲלִיפוֹתָיו, וְחָמֵשׁ פְּעָמִים הָיָה מַחֲלִיף מֵעֲבוֹדַת פְּנִים לַעֲבוֹדַת חוּץ וּמִחוּץ לִפְנִים, וּמְשַׁנֶּה מִבִּגְדֵי זָהָב לְבִגְדֵי

לָבָן וּמִבִּגְדֵי לָבָן לְבִגְדֵי זָהָב, וּבְכָל חֲלִיפָה טָעוּן טְבִילָה וּשְׁנֵי קִדּוּשׁ יָדַיִם וְרַגְלַיִם מִן הַכִּיּוֹר:

ו] אֶת פַּר הַחַטָּאת אֲשֶׁר לוֹ. הָאָמוּר לְמַעְלָה (פסוק ג), וְלִמֶּדְךָ כָּאן שֶׁמִּשֶּׁלּוֹ הוּא בָא וְלֹא מִשֶּׁל צִבּוּר: וְכִפֶּר בַּעֲדוֹ וּבְעַד בֵּיתוֹ. מִתְוַדֶּה עָלָיו עֲוֹנוֹתָיו וַעֲוֹנוֹת בֵּיתוֹ:

ח] וְנָתַן אַהֲרֹן עַל שְׁנֵי הַשְּׂעִירִים גֹּרָלוֹת. מַעֲמִיד אֶחָד לְיָמִין וְאֶחָד לִשְׂמֹאל, וְנוֹתֵן שְׁתֵּי יָדָיו בַּקַּלְפִּי, וְנוֹטֵל גּוֹרָל בְּיָמִין וַחֲבֵרוֹ בִּשְׂמֹאל, וְנוֹתֵן עֲלֵיהֶם, אֶת שֶׁכָּתוּב בּוֹ לַשֵּׁם הוּא לַשֵּׁם, וְאֶת שֶׁכָּתוּב בּוֹ לַעֲזָאזֵל מִשְׁתַּלֵּחַ לַעֲזָאזֵל: עֲזָאזֵל. הוּא הַר עַז וְקָשֶׁה, צוּק גָּבוֹהַּ, שֶׁנֶּאֱמַר: "אֶרֶץ גְּזֵרָה" (להלן פסוק כב), חֲתוּכָה:

DISCUSSION

16:4 | And he shall gird himself with a linen belt: There is an opinion among the tanna'im and amora'im that the belt worn by common priests was made of linen interwoven with colorful wool (Yoma 12a). If so, the belt worn by the High Priest on Yom Kippur, which was fashioned solely from white linen, was, in fact, simpler than the belt worn by all other priests.

16:8 | Aaron shall place lots on the two goats: According to the personal testimony of various Sages as to what actually took place in the Temple, these two lots were initially fashioned from wood and later from gold. They were placed in a wooden box specially constructed for this purpose. The High Priest would mix the lots, insert both hands into the box, and then simultaneously remove both lots, one in each hand. He would place the lot that he had removed with his right hand upon the goat to his right and the lot in his left hand upon the goat to his left (see Yoma 39a, and Rashi ad loc.; Jerusalem Talmud, Yoma 4:1).

9 **Aaron shall present the goat on which fell the lot for the Lord and render it a sin offering** by consecrating it for this purpose.[9] Alternatively, the verse means that the lot itself renders the goat a sin offering.[10]

10 **The** second **goat, on which fell the lot for Azazel, shall be set alive before the Lord, to atone with it** by placing his hands upon it and reciting a confession, and afterward, **to dispatch it to Azazel to the wilderness.**[D]

11 Once the High Priest has designated the goats on behalf of the nation, he returns to his own sin offering: **Aaron shall present the bull of the sin offering that is for him, and he shall atone for himself and for his household** by placing his hands on the bull and confessing his own sins and those of all the priests;[11] **and he shall slaughter the bull of the sin offering that is for him.**

12 After the High Priest has confessed, slaughtered the bull as a sin offering, and received its blood in a vessel, but before he sprinkles its blood in the Holy of Holies, he must leave the sin offering aside. **He shall take a fire-pan,** a small shovel used for scooping and transporting embers, **full of smoldering coals**[12] taken **from upon the** outer **altar, from before the Lord, and his hands full of finely ground fragrant incense,** as much incense as he can hold in his two hands cupped together, **and bring it** in a vessel **within the curtain,** to the Holy of Holies.

13 **He shall place the incense on the fire,** on the smoldering coals in the fire-pan, **before the Lord,**[D] **and the cloud of the incense shall obscure the cover that is upon the testimony, and he shall not die.** While the incense itself is considered an offering, the cloud it produces also serves as a screen to protect the High Priest from death, as though concealing the revelation of God. Aaron's sons died upon entering the Holy of Holies, because one may not enter and look upon the inner sanctum as he pleases. Even their father, Aaron the High Priest, was not permitted to be exposed to God's Presence.[13] Moses, however, according to some opinions, was permitted to enter the Holy of Holies unprotected and speak with God there at any time.[14]

14 After the Holy of Holies is filled with smoke, the High Priest returns to the bull that has been slaughtered as a sin offering (verse 11). **He shall take the** vessel that contains the **blood of the bull** he had slaughtered previously, enter the Holy of Holies, **and sprinkle it with his finger upon the cover toward the east,** toward the eastern side of the cover; **and** after that, **before the cover he shall sprinkle from the blood with his finger seven times.** The Sages describe this procedure as sprinkling once upward and seven times downward.[15]

15 After sprinkling the blood of his bull, the High Priest does the same with the offering that is brought on behalf of the nation (see also 9:15). **He shall** go to the Tabernacle courtyard and **slaughter the goat of the sin offering that is for the people, and he shall bring its blood** in a vessel[17] **within the curtain,** to the Holy of Holies, **and he shall do with its blood as he did with the blood of the bull, and sprinkle it upon the cover and before the cover.**

16 By entering the Holy of Holies and sprinkling the blood of the offerings there, **he shall atone for the Sanctum from the impurity of the children of Israel,** which marred its sanctity, **and from their transgressions, for** the general impurity of **all their sins;**[18] **and so shall he do for the Tent of Meeting that dwells with them in the midst of their impurity,** by sprinkling the blood of the offerings again in the same manner.[19]

17 The Torah adds a general comment: **No** other **man,** including priests, who are usually permitted to enter the Tabernacle,[20] **shall be in the Tent of Meeting from** the time of **his entry to atone** by performing the rites of the incense and the sprinkling of the blood **in the Sanctum until his emergence,**[21] **and he,** the High Priest, **shall** thereby **atone for himself, for his household, and for the entire assembly of Israel.**

18 This completes the Yom Kippur service in the Holy of
Second Holies, but there are other rites that the High Priest must
aliya perform in the Sanctuary with the sin offerings. **He shall go out** of the Holy of Holies **to the altar that is before the Lord,** the golden, inner altar, **and he shall atone for it,** purify it of the people's sins, in the following manner:

DISCUSSION

16:10 | **To dispatch it to Azazel to the wilderness:** The Sages and commentaries discuss the meaning of the term Azazel, as they analyze in depth the significance of this mysterious rite (see Ramban, verse 8; Rambam, *Guide of the Perplexed* 3:46). Apparently, Azazel is a term for evil or the forces of impurity, which are also known as *sitra aḥara*, "the other side," that which is dark, desolate, and fierce. These forces are symbolized by the uninhabitable wilderness. The goat is not slaughtered and is not classified as an offering; rather, it is sent to Azazel, which, whether it is a place name or a state of being, is in the wilderness.

16:13 | **He shall place the incense on the fire before the Lord:** The Sages emphasize that, as indicated by the order of the verses, the High Priest must place the incense on the coals only after entering the Holy of Holies, despite the fact that he enters a rather dark room. They fiercely rejected the opposing interpretation of heretics, who claimed that the incense was placed on the

ט והקריב אהרן את־השעיר אשר עלה עליו הגורל ליהוה ועשהו חטאת:
י והשעיר אשר עלה עליו הגורל לעזאזל יעמד־חי לפני יהוה לכפר עליו לשלח
יא אתו לעזאזל המדברה: והקריב אהרן את־פר החטאת אשר־לו וכפר בעדו
יב ובעד ביתו ושחט את־פר החטאת אשר־לו: ולקח מלא־המחתה גחלי־אש
מעל המזבח מלפני יהוה ומלא חפניו קטרת סמים דקה והביא מבית לפרכת:
יג ונתן את־הקטרת על־האש לפני יהוה וכסה | ענן הקטרת את־הכפרת אשר
יד על־העדות ולא ימות: ולקח מדם הפר והזה באצבעו על־פני הכפרת קדמה
טו ולפני הכפרת יזה שבע־פעמים מן־הדם באצבעו: ושחט את־שעיר החטאת
אשר לעם והביא את־דמו אל־מבית לפרכת ועשה את־דמו כאשר עשה לדם
טז הפר והזה אתו על־הכפרת ולפני הכפרת: וכפר על־הקדש מטמאת בני ישראל
ומפשעיהם לכל־חטאתם וכן יעשה לאהל מועד השכן אתם בתוך טמאתם:
יז וכל־אדם לא־יהיה | באהל מועד בבאו לכפר בקדש עד־צאתו וכפר בעדו
יח ובעד ביתו ובעד כל־קהל ישראל: ויצא אל־המזבח אשר לפני־יהוה וכפר עליו שני

רש"י

ט| **ועשהו חטאת.** כשמניח הגורל עליו קורא לו שם ואומר: 'לה' חטאת':

י| **יעמד חי.** כמו 'יעמד חי', על ידי אחרים, ותרגומו: "יתקם כד חי". מה תלמוד לומר? לפי שנאמר: "לשלח אתו לעזאזל", ואיני יודע שלוחו אם למיתה אם לחיים, לכך נאמר: "יעמד חי", עמידתו חי עד שישתלח, מכאן ששלוחו למיתה: **לכפר עליו.** שיתודה עליו, כדכתיב: "והתודה עליו" וגו' (להלן פסוק כא):

יא| **וכפר בעדו וגו'.** ודוי שני, עליו ועל אחיו הכהנים, שהם כלם קרויים 'ביתו', שנאמר: "בית אהרן ברכו את ה'" וגו' (תהלים קלה, יט), מכאן שהכהנים מתכפרים בו. וכל כפרתן אינה אלא על טמאת מקדש וקדשיו, כמו שנאמר: "וכפר על הקדש מטמאת" וגו' (להלן פסוק טז):

יב| **מעל המזבח.** החיצון: **מלפני ה'.** מצד שלפני הפתח, והוא צד מערבי: **דקה.** מה תלמוד לומר "דקה"? והלא כל הקטרת דקה היא, שנאמר: "ושחקת ממנה הדק" (שמות ל, לו)! אלא שתהא דקה מן הדקה, שבערב יום הכפורים היה מחזירה למכתשת:

יג| **על האש.** שבתוך המחתה: **ולא ימות.** הא אם לא עשאה כתקנה חיב מיתה:

יד| **והזה באצבעו.** הזאה אחת במשמע: **ולפני הכפרת יזה שבע.** הרי אחת למעלה ושבע למטה:

טו| **אשר לעם.** מה שהפר מכפר על הכהנים, מכפר השעיר על ישראל, והוא השעיר שעלה עליו הגורל לשם: **כאשר עשה לדם הפר.** אחת למעלה ושבע למטה:

טז| **מטמאת בני ישראל.** על הנכנסין למקדש בטמאה ולא נודע להם בסוף, שנאמר: "לכל חטאתם", וחטאת היא שוגג: **ומפשעיהם.** אף הנכנסין מזיד בטמאה: **וכן יעשה לאהל מועד.** כשם שהזה משניהם בפנים אחת למעלה ושבע למטה, כך מזה על הפרכת מבחוץ משניהם אחת למעלה ושבע למטה: **השכן אתם בתוך טמאתם.** אף על פי שהם טמאים, שכינה ביניהם:

יח| **אל המזבח אשר לפני ה'.** זה מזבח הזהב שהוא לפני ה' בהיכל. ומה תלמוד לומר "ויצא"? לפי שהזה ההזאות על הפרכת ועמד מן המזבח ולפנים והזה, ובמתנות המזבח הזקיקו לצאת מן המזבח ולחוץ ויתחיל מקרן מזרחית צפונית: **וכפר עליו.** ומה היא כפרתו? "ולקח מדם הפר ומדם השעיר" – מערבין זה לתוך זה:

DISCUSSION

coals before the High Priest entered the Holy of Holies (*Sifra*; *Yoma* 53a).

The verses do not clearly state where the High Priest should place the fire-pan. In the First Temple period, when the ark was in the Holy of Holies, he would put it on the ground, between the staves of the ark. Since there was no ark in the Holy of Holies in the Second Temple, the priest would place the fire-pan on the ground, on the spot that would have been between the staves of the ark had it been present. According to tradition, the High Priest would set it on a rock known as the foundation rock, which was slightly raised from the ground of the Holy of Holies (*Yoma* 52b, 53b).

He shall take from the blood of the bull of his own sin offering **and from the blood of the goat**[D] of the people's sin offering **and place it on the horns of the altar all around.**
19 After placing the blood on the corners of the golden altar, **he,** the High Priest, **shall sprinkle from the blood on it,** the golden altar, **with his finger seven times, and he shall purify it and sanctify it from the impurity of the children of Israel.** Although this altar is generally used only for incense, the blood of certain uncommon sin offerings is sprinkled on it as well.[22]
20 **He shall conclude atoning**[D] **for the Sanctum,** by means of the sacrificial rites he performs there, **and for the Tent of Meeting, and the altar, and he shall present the living goat,** which is ready to be sent to the wilderness.
21 **Aaron shall lay both his hands on the head of the living goat, and he shall confess over it all the iniquities of the children of Israel, and all their transgressions, for all their sins; and he shall place** those transgressions and sins **upon the head of the goat, and he shall dispatch it in the hand of a designated man**[23] **to the wilderness.**[D] Obviously, it is impossible for the High Priest to specify all the sins of the children of Israel; instead, he refers generally to the sins committed by the nation over the course of the year. The High Priest's earlier confessions are made in a similar manner.
22 **The goat shall bear upon it all their iniquities to a precipitous land,** mountainous, uneven terrain, such as a rocky cliff;[24] **and he shall dispatch the goat into the wilderness.** Alternatively, the verse can be understood as referring to a desolate land, bereft of all good qualities, and not necessarily to precipitous terrain.[25]
23 After confessing and sending the goat into the wilderness, **Aaron shall come into the Tent of Meeting and remove the linen vestments that he donned with his entry into the Sanctum, and he shall leave them there.** The Sages explain that these vestments may not be used again, but must be buried.[26]
24 **He shall bathe his flesh in water in a holy place,** in a ritual bath in the Temple compound, **and don his vestments,** the eight vestments generally worn by the High Priest to perform the Temple service, which are the four basic white garments and four additional special garments.[27] **And he shall emerge and perform his burnt offering and the burnt offering of the people, and atone for himself and for the people.**
Third aliya (Second aliya)
25 **The fat of the** aforementioned **sin offering,** the bull and goat, **he shall burn on the altar.**[D]
26 Because the dispatching of the goat to Azazel involves some degree of contact with impure forces, **the one who dispatches the goat to Azazel shall wash his garments and bathe his flesh in water, and** only **afterward shall he come into the camp.**

DISCUSSION

16:18 | He shall take from the blood of the bull and from the blood of the goat: The Sages dispute whether the blood of each of these offerings must be separately placed on the corners of the golden altar or whether the High Priest should mix the blood of the two offerings together and smear the mixture of blood on the corners (see *Yoma* 57b–58a; Rambam, *Sefer Avoda, Hilkhot Ma'aseh HaKorbanot* 5:12). All agree, however, that before the sprinkling of the blood that is described in the next verse, the blood of the two animals must be mixed together, as that verse states: "He shall sprinkle from the blood on it with his finger seven times." This indicates that the blood must be sprinkled only seven times rather than fourteen (Jerusalem Talmud, *Yoma* 5:4; *Tosafot, Yoma* 58a).

16:20 | He shall conclude atoning: The Sages learn from here that alacrity in the proper performance of the commandments leads to cleanliness (Jerusalem Talmud, *Shabbat* 1:3, and *Korban HaEda* ad loc.). This idea is derived from the fact that the High Priest does not pause to rest between the stages of the Temple service, despite the fact that he is fasting; rather, he immediately continues the service by sending away the goat, in order to cleanse the people of sin without delay (*Aleh Yona* 306).

16:21 | And he shall dispatch it in the hand of a designated man to the wilderness: The Temple was located a significant distance from the wilderness. The Mishna describes how the goat was led through the wilderness, on foot, over a distance of approximately 12 km, or 7 mi (*Yoma* 6:4–5). At this point, the goat was not simply released into the wilderness; rather, it was pushed off a cliff and became dismembered as it rolled down the slope (Mishna, *Yoma* 6:6). The Torah does not specify that the goat must be killed, and therefore there was no problem if it escaped from the designated man. However, it usually died by falling from the cliff onto the rocks below.

The Sages state that the commandment has been performed once the goat reaches the wilderness (see *Yoma* 68b; Rashbam, verse 10). By placing his hands on the offering and confessing on behalf of the nation, the High Priest symbolically places all the sins of the children of Israel onto the animal. Releasing this goat into the wilderness, the place that represents the source of all sin (see commentary on verse 10) symbolically returns the sins to their place of origin, where they are swallowed up and disappear (see also Rambam, *Guide of the Perplexed* 3:46; Ibn Ezra; Ramban).

16:25 | The fat of the sin offering he shall burn on the altar: The Yom Kippur service in the Temple included stages that are not mentioned in this chapter. Regular services, such as the preparation of the altar, the daily offerings, the burning of the incense, and the kindling of the lamp were also performed on Yom Kippur. In addition, there was the sacrifice of special festive offerings, the additional offerings, as detailed in Numbers (chap. 29). These services, like most sacrificial services throughout the year, were performed by the High Priest in his eight ornamental garments, which, woven with sky-blue,

יח ולקח מדם הפר ומדם השעיר ונתן על־קרנות המזבח סביב: והזה עליו
יט מן־הדם באצבעו שבע פעמים וטהרו וקדשו מטמאת בני ישראל: וכלה
כ מכפר את־הקדש ואת־אהל מועד ואת־המזבח והקריב את־השעיר החי:
כא וסמך אהרן את־שתי ידו על־ראש השעיר החי והתודה עליו את־כל־עונת
בני ישראל ואת־כל־פשעיהם לכל־חטאתם ונתן אתם על־ראש השעיר
כב ושלח ביד־איש עתי המדברה: ונשא השעיר עליו את־כל־עונתם אל־ארץ
כג גזרה ושלח את־השעיר במדבר: ובא אהרן אל־אהל מועד ופשט את־
כד בגדי הבד אשר לבש בבאו אל־הקדש והניחם שם: ורחץ את־בשרו במים
במקום קדוש ולבש את־בגדיו ויצא ועשה את־עלתו ואת־עלת העם וכפר
כה כו בעדו ובעד העם: ואת חלב החטאת יקטיר המזבחה: והמשלח את־השעיר שלישי /שני/
לעזאזל יכבס בגדיו ורחץ את־בשרו במים ואחרי־כן יבוא אל־המחנה:

רש"י

יט | **והזה עליו מן הדם.** אחר שנתן מתנות באצבעו על קרנותיו, מזה שבע הזאות על גגו: **וטהרו.** ממה שעבר: **וקדשו.** לעתיד לבא:

כא | **איש עתי.** המוכן לכך מיום אתמול:

כג | **ובא אהרן אל אהל מועד.** אמרו רבותינו שאין זה מקומו של מקרא זה, ונתנו טעם לדבריהם במסכת יומא (דף לב ע"א) ואמרו, כל הפרשה כלה נאמרה על הסדר חוץ מביאה זו, שהיא אחר עשית עולתו ועולת העם והקטרת אמורי פר ושעיר שנעשים בחוץ בבגדי זהב, וטובל ומקדש ופושטן ולובש בגדי לבן, ובא אל אהל מועד להוציא את הכף ואת המחתה שהקטיר בה הקטרת לפני ולפנים: **ופשט את בגדי הבד.** אחר שהוציאם, ולובש בגדי זהב לתמיד של בין הערבים. וזהו סדר העבודות: תמיד של שחר בבגדי זהב, ועבודת פר ושעיר הפנימיים וקטרת של מחתה בבגדי לבן, ואילו ואיל העם ומקצת המוספין בבגדי זהב, והוצאת כף ומחתה בבגדי לבן, ושירי המוספין ותמיד של בין הערבים וקטרת ההיכל שעל מזבח הפנימי בבגדי זהב. וסדר המקראות לפי סדר העבודות כך הוא: "ושלח את השעיר במדבר" (לעיל פסוק כב), "ורחץ את בשרו במים וגו', ויצא ועשה את עלתו וגו', ואת חלב החטאת" וגו', וכל הפרשה עד "ואחרי כן יבוא אל המחנה" (להלן פסוקים כד-כח), ואחר כך "ובא אהרן" (פסוק כג): **והניחם שם.** מלמד שטעונין גניזה, ולא ישתמש באותן ארבעה בגדים ליום כפורים אחר:

כד | **ורחץ את בשרו וגו'.** למעלה למדנו מ"ורחץ... את בשרו ולבשם" (לעיל פסוק ד) שכשהוא משנה מבגדי זהב לבגדי לבן טעון טבילה, שבאותה טבילה פשט בגדי זהב שעבד בהן עבודת תמיד של שחר ולבש בגדי לבן לעבודת היום, וכאן למדנו שכשהוא משנה מבגדי לבן לבגדי זהב טעון טבילה: **במקום קדוש.** המקדש בקדשת עזרה, והיא היתה בגג בית הפרוה, וכן ארבע טבילות הבאות חובה ליום, אבל הראשונה היתה בחל: **ולבש את בגדיו.** שמונה בגדים שהוא עובד בהן כל ימות השנה: **ויצא.** מן ההיכל אל החצר, שמזבח העולה שם: **ועשה את עלתו.** איל לעולה האמור למעלה, "בזאת יבא אהרן" וגו' (לעיל פסוק ג): **ואת עלת העם.** "ואיל אחד לעלה" האמור למעלה: "ומאת עדת בני ישראל" וגו' (לעיל פסוק ה):

כה | **ואת חלב החטאת.** אמורי פר ושעיר: **יקטיר המזבחה.** על מזבח החיצון, דאלו בפנימי כתיב: "לא תעלו עליו קטרת זרה ועלה ומנחה" (שמות ל, ט):

DISCUSSION

→ purple, and gold thread, represented the splendor of humanity. For the services detailed in this chapter, which involved entry into the Holy of Holies, the High Priest assumed a more humble and subdued pose, wearing white linen garments symbolizing simplicity and self-negation and evoking the purity of the angels.

According to tradition, whenever the High Priest donned a different set of garments, he first had to immerse his entire body in water. Furthermore, each donning and disrobing of priestly vestments required the sanctification of hands and feet, which was done by washing them in the basin that stood in the Temple courtyard. Altogether, on Yom Kippur the High Priest immersed on five occasions and washed his hands and feet a total of ten times.

27 **The** carcass of the **bull of the sin offering** of Aaron **and the goat of the sin offering** of the nation, the goat not sent to Azazel, **whose blood was brought in to atone in the Sanctum, he shall take outside the camp; and they shall burn in fire their hides, their flesh, and their dung.** This was stated in earlier chapters with regard to all inner sin offerings, the blood of which is sprinkled on the inner, golden altar rather than on the outer altar. Such offerings are not eaten but are entirely burned outside settled areas (4:1–21, 6:23).

28 **The one who burns them shall wash his garments and bathe his flesh in water, and afterward he shall come into the camp.** Because he has been dealing with the remnants of a consecrated item whose level of sanctity has been reduced, he must afterward be purified.

29 As stated at the beginning of this passage, the entire ceremony prescribed here had to be performed when Aaron wanted to enter the Holy of Holies. This verse adds that Aaron was not permitted to enter the Holy of Holies whenever he wished; rather, there was a set time when he was permitted to do so. **It shall be for you an eternal statute: During the seventh month,** which later became known as Tishrei, **on the tenth of the month,** Yom Kippur, **you shall afflict yourselves.** This is not a command to cause oneself unnecessary suffering; rather, "afflict yourselves" is a technical term meaning that one must refrain from eating, drinking, and other specific forms of physical pleasure.[28] Furthermore, **you shall not perform all labor, the native and the stranger that resides among you,** that is, converts who have joined the children of Israel.

DISCUSSION

The table below presents the full order of the Yom Kippur services. It is based on the Sages' derivations of the verses and is in accordance with the opinion of the Rambam. Daily services not unique to Yom Kippur are marked with an asterisk (*).

Yom Kippur Service of the High Priest

Garments	Services	Offerings
Gold	Removal of the ashes at about midnight; arrangement of wood on the altar; removal of the ashes from the inner altar* Slaughter of the daily offering at the first light in the eastern sky and sprinkling of the daily offering's blood* Burning of the sacrificial portions of the daily offering, daily meal offering, daily griddle-cake offering, and wine libation* Sacrifice of the majority of the additional offerings (Numbers 29:8)	One lamb, burnt offering* One bull and seven lambs, burnt offerings
White	High Priest's personal confession and confession for his family, said while placing his hands on the bull (verse 6) Placing of lots on the goats (verse 8) High Priest's second confession, for both his own sins and those of his family, while placing his hands on his bull; slaughter of the bull and receiving its blood (verse 11) Burning of the incense in the Holy of Holies (verse 13); a short prayer in the Sanctuary; sprinkling the blood of his personal bull in the Holy of Holies (verse 14) Slaughter of the goat designated by lot as "for the Lord" and the sprinkling of its blood in the Holy of Holies (verse 15) Sprinklings in the Sanctuary from the blood of the inner sin offerings, the bull and the goat (verses 18–19) Confession on behalf of the children of Israel, said while placing his hands on the goat designated by lot as "for Azazel" (verses 20–21) Sending of the goat to the wilderness (verses 21–22); handing over the flesh of the inner sin offering to be burned outside the settled area; reading from the Torah and reciting eight blessings	One bull, inner sin offering One goat, inner sin offering
Gold	Completion of the additional offerings and the other offerings of the day (verse 24; Numbers 29:11) Burning of the sacrificial portions of the inner sin offering, the bull and goat (verse 25) Sacrifice of the daily afternoon offering*	One goat, outer sin offering High Priest's ram, burnt offering Ram of the people, burnt offering One lamb, burnt offering*
White	Removal of the fire-pan and the spoon from the Holy of Holies (verse 23; see Rashi). Some say that this removal is performed before the sacrifice of the daily afternoon offering	
Gold	Burning of the afternoon incense Kindling of the lamp*	

כז וְאֵת֩ פַּ֨ר הַחַטָּ֜את וְאֵ֣ת ׀ שְׂעִ֣יר הַחַטָּ֗את אֲשֶׁ֨ר הוּבָ֤א אֶת־דָּמָם֙ לְכַפֵּ֣ר בַּקֹּ֔דֶשׁ יוֹצִ֖יא אֶל־מִח֣וּץ לַמַּֽחֲנֶ֑ה וְשָׂרְפ֣וּ בָאֵ֔שׁ אֶת־עֹרֹתָ֥ם וְאֶת־בְּשָׂרָ֖ם וְאֶת־פִּרְשָֽׁם:

כח וְהַשֹּׂרֵ֣ף אֹתָ֔ם יְכַבֵּ֣ס בְּגָדָ֔יו וְרָחַ֥ץ אֶת־בְּשָׂר֖וֹ בַּמָּ֑יִם וְאַֽחֲרֵי־כֵ֖ן יָב֥וֹא אֶל־הַֽמַּֽחֲנֶֽה:

כט וְהָֽיְתָ֥ה לָכֶ֖ם לְחֻקַּ֣ת עוֹלָ֑ם בַּחֹ֣דֶשׁ הַשְּׁבִיעִ֣י בֶּֽעָשׂ֣וֹר לַחֹ֗דֶשׁ תְּעַנּ֣וּ אֶת־נַפְשֹֽׁתֵיכֶ֗ם

ל וְכָל־מְלָאכָה֙ לֹ֣א תַֽעֲשׂ֔וּ הָֽאֶזְרָ֔ח וְהַגֵּ֖ר הַגָּ֥ר בְּתֽוֹכְכֶֽם: כִּֽי־בַיּ֥וֹם הַזֶּ֛ה יְכַפֵּ֥ר עֲלֵיכֶ֖ם לְטַהֵ֣ר אֶתְכֶ֑ם מִכֹּל֙ חַטֹּ֣אתֵיכֶ֔ם לִפְנֵ֥י יְהֹוָ֖ה תִּטְהָֽרוּ:

לא שַׁבַּ֨ת שַׁבָּת֥וֹן הִיא֙ לָכֶ֔ם וְעִנִּיתֶ֖ם אֶת־נַפְשֹֽׁתֵיכֶ֑ם חֻקַּ֖ת עוֹלָֽם:

לב וְכִפֶּ֨ר הַכֹּהֵ֜ן אֲשֶׁר־יִמְשַׁ֣ח אֹת֗וֹ וַֽאֲשֶׁ֤ר יְמַלֵּא֙ אֶת־יָד֔וֹ לְכַהֵ֖ן תַּ֣חַת אָבִ֑יו וְלָבַ֛שׁ אֶת־בִּגְדֵ֥י הַבָּ֖ד בִּגְדֵ֥י הַקֹּֽדֶשׁ:

לג וְכִפֶּר֙ אֶת־מִקְדַּ֣שׁ הַקֹּ֔דֶשׁ וְאֶת־אֹ֧הֶל מוֹעֵ֛ד וְאֶת־הַמִּזְבֵּ֖חַ יְכַפֵּ֑ר וְעַ֧ל הַכֹּֽהֲנִ֛ים וְעַל־כָּל־עַ֥ם הַקָּהָ֖ל יְכַפֵּֽר:

רש״י

כז אֲשֶׁ֣ר הוּבָ֣א אֶת־דָּמָם. לַהֵיכָל וְלִפְנַי וְלִפְנִים:

לב וְכִפֶּ֣ר הַכֹּהֵ֣ן אֲשֶׁ֣ר יִמְשַׁ֣ח וְגוֹ׳. כַּפָּרָה זוֹ שֶׁל יוֹם הַכִּפּוּרִים אֵינָהּ כְּשֵׁרָה אֶלָּא בְּכֹהֵן גָּדוֹל, לְפִי שֶׁנֶּאֶמְרָה כָל הַפָּרָשָׁה בְּאַהֲרֹן, הֻצְרַךְ לוֹמַר כֹּהֵן גָּדוֹל הַבָּא אַחֲרָיו שֶׁיְּהֵא כָמוֹהוּ: וַֽאֲשֶׁ֣ר יְמַלֵּ֣א אֶת־יָד֣וֹ. אֵין לִי אֶלָּא הַמָּשׁוּחַ בְּשֶׁמֶן הַמִּשְׁחָה, מְרֻבֶּה בְגָדִים מִנַּיִן? תַּלְמוּד לוֹמַר: ״וַֽאֲשֶׁ֣ר יְמַלֵּ֣א אֶת־יָד֣וֹ וְגוֹ׳, וְהֵם כָּל הַכֹּֽהֲנִים הַגְּדוֹלִים שֶׁעָֽמְדוּ מִיֹּאשִׁיָּהוּ וָאֵילָךְ, שֶׁבִּימָיו נִגְנְזָה צְלוֹחִית שֶׁל שֶׁמֶן הַמִּשְׁחָה: לְכַהֵ֣ן תַּ֣חַת אָבִֽיו. לְלַמֵּד שֶׁאִם שָׁם בְּנוֹ מְמַלֵּא אֶת מְקוֹמוֹ הוּא קוֹדֵם לְכָל אָדָם:

---

30 For on this day he shall atone for you, to purify you; from all your sins before the Lord you shall be purified. On this day the children of Israel are granted atonement and are forgiven for their sins. This is achieved both through the offerings whose blood is sprinkled in the Holy of Holies and the Sanctuary and by means of the goat sent to Azazel, as well as through the inherent sanctity of the day.[29] The children of Israel, for their part, must prepare themselves for this atonement by abstaining from eating, drinking, and the other physical pleasures.

31 It is a sabbatical rest for you.[D] This is a day of rest like the Sabbath itself, when prohibited labors are completely forbidden, and, unlike on the festivals, none of the labors prohibited on the Sabbath may be performed for the sake of food preparation.[30] **And you shall afflict yourselves.** Yom Kippur is a day of cessation not only from prohibited labor, but also from attending to one's general physical needs. **It is an eternal statute.**

Even when there is no Temple or High Priest, atonement will always be granted on this day.[31] The sanctity of Yom Kippur and its attendant commandments do not depend upon the High Priest's entry into the Holy of Holies or his performance of the sacrificial rites.

32 The Torah now returns to the discussion of the High Priest's service in the Temple: **The priest who shall be anointed and who shall be ordained to serve in his father's stead** as the High Priest, which is an office that is mainly inherited from father to son, **shall atone and shall don linen vestments, the sacred vestments.**

33 He shall atone for the sacred Sanctum, for the most sacred part of the Temple, the Holy of Holies, **and for the Tent of Meeting and for the altar he shall atone; and for the priests and for all the people of the assembly he shall atone.**

DISCUSSION

16:31 | It is a sabbatical rest for you: There are two parallel aspects to this day: On the one hand, it is a sabbatical rest, a day of purity that is absolutely holy and on which God forgives the children of Israel for all of their sins. Accordingly, the children of Israel fast and desist from prohibited labors, as the theme of the day is abstention and withdrawal. On the other hand, it is the only day on which the High Priest, who is himself fasting, is permitted to enter the most sacred place, the Holy of Holies, as the representative of the children of Israel. From this perspective, Israel's encounter with holiness is a central theme of the day.

It is interesting to note that in this context, the day is referred to only by its calendar date and is not identified by its name, Yom HaKippurim, which it is called when the Torah lists the festivals systematically (see Numbers 29:7–11).

34 **This shall be an eternal statute for you, to atone for the children of Israel for all their sins once in the year.**ᴰ When Yom Kippur came, **he,** Aaron, **did as the Lord** had **commanded Moses.**[32]

Laws Pertaining to Eating Meat
LEVITICUS 17:1–16

This passage deals primarily with the slaughter of animals, as well as related commandments.

17 1 **The Lord spoke to Moses, saying:**

Fourth aliya 2 **Speak to Aaron, to his sons, and to all the children of Israel,** as the upcoming passage is somewhat related to the Tabernacle but most of it applies to the entire nation, **and say to them: This is the matter that the Lord has commanded, saying:**

3 **Any man from the house of Israel who shall slaughter a bull or a sheep or a goat in the camp,** as the Israelite camp in the wilderness was large and it is reasonable to assume that those who lived in the inner part of the camp did not wish to trouble themselves with leaving the camp to slaughter animals, **or who slaughters it,** such an animal, **outside the camp,** e.g., in a field used as pasture for the flock,

4 **and to the entrance of the Tent of Meeting he did not bring it, to present an offering to the Lord**ᴰ **before the Tabernacle of the Lord, it will be accounted as blood for that man; he has shed blood, and that man shall be excised from among his people.** All animals must be slaughtered in the Tabernacle courtyard as offerings. One who slaughters an animal in the wilderness, outside the Tabernacle area, is punished with excision. Excision is a punishment that is administered by God rather than an earthly court. There are various opinions regarding the precise meaning of the word "excision," including untimely death or the cutting off of the soul in the World to Come.

5 **So that the children of Israel shall bring their slaughtered animals that they** currently **slaughter in the open field, and they shall bring them to the Lord, to the entrance of the Tent of Meeting, to the priest, and they shall slaughter peace offerings to the Lord.** They may no longer slaughter animals wherever they wish.

6 **The priest shall cast the blood on the altar of the Lord** that is **at the entrance of the Tent of Meeting and burn the fat for a pleasing aroma to the Lord.** During their time in the wilderness, the children of Israel were not permitted to slaughter unconsecrated animals for their meat, as explained above. Instead, they were required to consecrate the animals whose meat they wanted to consume as a peace offering. The blood and fats of a peace offering, which may not be eaten even in the case of a non-sacred animal, are burned on the altar. The breast and thigh are given to the priest, and the rest of the animal is eaten by the individual who has brought the offering (see 7:28–36).

7 **That they shall no longer slaughter their offerings to the satyrs, after whom they go astray.**ᴰ This phrase constitutes an independent commandment and provides the reason for the prohibition against slaughtering animals outside the Tabernacle.[33] **This** prohibition against bringing offerings to satyrs **shall be an eternal statute for them, for their generations.**

DISCUSSION

16:34 | To atone for the children of Israel for all their sins once in the year: In essence, Yom Kippur as a day of atonement is a gift from God. In contrast to ordinary repentance, which stems from human initiative, atonement on this holiest of days is an act of divine grace. Still, the people must prepare themselves for atonement by abstaining from eating, drinking, and other prohibited physical pleasures (see *Meshekh Ḥokhma,* verse 1). If atonement depended solely upon the willingness of the people to properly repent, their sins would gradually accumulate from year to year, and their great weight would soon become unbearable. Consequently, God pardons all of the year's sins on one day and cleanses the children of Israel proactively (see *Sefer HaḤinnukh* 185).

17:4 | And to the entrance of the Tent of Meeting he did not bring it, to present an offering to the Lord: The Sages dispute the meaning of this commandment (see *Ḥullin* 16b–17a). The translation here follows the opinion of Rabbi Yishmael (see Ramban; *Bekhor Shor*). According to Rabbi Akiva, however, when the children of Israel were in the wilderness, they were permitted to eat unconsecrated meat even without ritually slaughtering the animal. This became prohibited only when they entered the Land of Israel. The commandment here is that the act of slaughtering must be performed in the Tabernacle; some say that this commandment refers only to animals being brought as offerings, while others maintain that it applies to the slaughter of non-sacred animals as well

(see Ramban; Rambam, *Sefer Kedusha, Hilkhot Sheḥita* 4:17).

In any case, this commandment applied specifically in the wilderness, when eating meat simply to satisfy one's physical appetite was prohibited, but this became permissible when the children of Israel entered the Land of Israel (see Deuteronomy 12:20). However, some hold that this prohibition remained in force even after the children of Israel entered the land, during periods when it was permissible to worship on a personal altar in any location and the presentation of offerings was not limited to the Temple (see Rav Yosef Kara's commentary on I Samuel 14:32).

The effect of this prohibition was that while the children of Israel were in the wilderness all ⬌

לד וְהָיְתָה־זֹּאת לָכֶם לְחֻקַּת עוֹלָם לְכַפֵּר עַל־בְּנֵי יִשְׂרָאֵל מִכָּל־חַטֹּאתָם אַחַת בַּשָּׁנָה וַיַּעַשׂ כַּאֲשֶׁר צִוָּה יְהוָה אֶת־מֹשֶׁה:

א וַיְדַבֵּר יְהוָה אֶל־מֹשֶׁה לֵּאמֹר: ב דַּבֵּר אֶל־אַהֲרֹן וְאֶל־בָּנָיו וְאֶל כָּל־בְּנֵי יִשְׂרָאֵל **יג** רביעי

ג וְאָמַרְתָּ אֲלֵיהֶם זֶה הַדָּבָר אֲשֶׁר־צִוָּה יְהוָה לֵאמֹר: אִישׁ אִישׁ מִבֵּית יִשְׂרָאֵל אֲשֶׁר

ד יִשְׁחַט שׁוֹר אוֹ־כֶשֶׂב אוֹ־עֵז בַּמַּחֲנֶה אוֹ אֲשֶׁר יִשְׁחַט מִחוּץ לַמַּחֲנֶה: וְאֶל־פֶּתַח

אֹהֶל מוֹעֵד לֹא הֱבִיאוֹ לְהַקְרִיב קָרְבָּן לַיהוָה לִפְנֵי מִשְׁכַּן יְהוָה דָּם יֵחָשֵׁב לָאִישׁ

ה הַהוּא דָּם שָׁפָךְ וְנִכְרַת הָאִישׁ הַהוּא מִקֶּרֶב עַמּוֹ: לְמַעַן אֲשֶׁר יָבִיאוּ בְּנֵי יִשְׂרָאֵל

אֶת־זִבְחֵיהֶם אֲשֶׁר הֵם זֹבְחִים עַל־פְּנֵי הַשָּׂדֶה וֶהֱבִיאֻם לַיהוָה אֶל־פֶּתַח אֹהֶל מוֹעֵד

אֶל־הַכֹּהֵן וְזָבְחוּ זִבְחֵי שְׁלָמִים לַיהוָה אוֹתָם: ו וְזָרַק הַכֹּהֵן אֶת־הַדָּם עַל־מִזְבַּח

יְהוָה פֶּתַח אֹהֶל מוֹעֵד וְהִקְטִיר הַחֵלֶב לְרֵיחַ נִיחֹחַ לַיהוָה: ז וְלֹא־יִזְבְּחוּ עוֹד אֶת־

זִבְחֵיהֶם לַשְּׂעִירִם אֲשֶׁר הֵם זֹנִים אַחֲרֵיהֶם חֻקַּת עוֹלָם תִּהְיֶה־זֹּאת לָהֶם לְדֹרֹתָם:

רש"י

לד| וַיַּעַשׂ כַּאֲשֶׁר צִוָּה ה' וְגו'. כְּשֶׁהִגִּיעַ יוֹם הַכִּפּוּרִים
עָשָׂה כַּסֵּדֶר הַזֶּה, וּלְהַגִּיד שִׁבְחוֹ שֶׁל אַהֲרֹן, שֶׁלֹּא הָיָה
לוֹבְשָׁן לִגְדֻלָּתוֹ, אֶלָּא כִּמְקַיֵּם גְּזֵרַת הַמֶּלֶךְ:

פרק יז
ג| אֲשֶׁר יִשְׁחַט שׁוֹר אוֹ כֶשֶׂב. בִּמְקֻדָּשִׁין הַכָּתוּב מְדַבֵּר,
שֶׁנֶּאֱמַר: "לְהַקְרִיב קָרְבָּן": בַּמַּחֲנֶה. חוּץ לָעֲזָרָה:

ד| דָּם יֵחָשֵׁב. כְּשׁוֹפֵךְ דַּם הָאָדָם, שֶׁמִּתְחַיֵּב בְּנַפְשׁוֹ: דָּם
שָׁפָךְ. לְרַבּוֹת אֶת הַזּוֹרֵק דָּמִים בַּחוּץ:

ה| אֲשֶׁר הֵם זֹבְחִים. אֲשֶׁר הֵם רְגִילִים לִזְבּוֹחַ:

ז| לַשְּׂעִירִם. לַשֵּׁדִים, כְּמוֹ: "וּשְׂעִירִים יְרַקְּדוּ שָׁם" (ישעיה יג, כא):

DISCUSSION

consumption of meat was limited to the context of a sacrificial offering. Instead of slaughtering animals merely to satisfy their physical desire to eat meat, an action that this verse compares to murder, the children of Israel would slaughter animals as offerings, turning the slaughter into a holy act.

There are various limitations to the consumption of sacrificial meat: One must be ritually pure, and the meat may be consumed only in certain times and places. These restrictions further advance the sanctity and purity of the Jewish people. Even after the people had settled throughout the Land of Israel and it had become permissible to slaughter unconsecrated animals in order to eat the meat, the Sages

recommended numerous spiritual and moral practices in this regard. For example, they said that an ignoramus should not eat meat (*Pesaḥim* 49b) and that one should not eat meat regularly or consume it to one's full satiation (see *Ḥullin* 84a; see also *Sifra*).

17:7 | That they shall no longer slaughter their offerings to the satyrs, after whom they go astray: This mention of the practice of sacrificing offerings to satyrs indicates that it was a well-known phenomenon. The verse refers to demons that supposedly traverse the world, including areas of human habitation (see Rashi; Ramban; Onkelos; *Vayikra Rabba* 22; Rambam, *Guide of the Perplexed* 3:46). In those times,

and for many generations afterward, it was a common practice among various peoples, and sometimes even Jews, for animal slaughter to be accompanied by the dedication of part of the slaughtered animal to demonic or other supernatural beings. The aim of this rite was to pacify supernatural forces so that they would not harm the person who had slaughtered the animal or to request their assistance. Occasionally, people would dig a hole in the ground, and the blood that had been consecrated to the supernatural beings would be poured into it. Even when the slaughter was not originally performed as a religious ritual, part of a slaughtered animal, typically its blood, was sometimes consecrated to satyrs. This is considered a type of idolatrous rite.

8 Following the commandment that in the wilderness animals may be slaughtered only for the purpose of bringing offerings, the verse adds a detail that applies for all generations: **And to them,** the children of Israel, **you shall** also **say** the following: **Any man from the house of Israel, or from the strangers who reside among them, who offers up a burnt offering,** which is entirely consumed on the altar, **or a feast offering,**[D] much of which is eaten by people,

Fifth aliya (Third aliya)

9 **and to the entrance of the Tent of Meeting does not bring it to present it to the Lord, that man shall be excised from his people.** Presenting an offering outside the Tabernacle or the Temple is a serious transgression that renders one liable to the severe punishment of excision.

10 This verse provides an additional prohibition concerning the slaughter of animals for food. **Any man from the house of Israel, or from the stranger who resides among them, who eats any blood, I will direct My attention to the person who eats the blood,** in the form of retribution, **and I will excise him from the midst of his people.**

11 **For the life,** the life force, **of the flesh is in the blood, and I have given it to you** only to sacrifice **on the altar to atone for your souls, as it is the blood that shall atone for the life.** The blood, upon which life depends, may be used only to atone for the soul of the individual who slaughters the animal as an offering to God. One is permitted to eat meat, the dead flesh of the animal; however, blood, which represents the life force of that creature, is for God only and may not be consumed.[34]

12 **Therefore I said to the children of Israel: Every person among you shall not eat blood, and the stranger who resides among you shall not eat blood.** This broad prohibition applies to all the children of Israel, including gentiles who join them. The Sages interpret the phrase "every person among you" as including even minors, thereby indicating that adults are required to ensure that children do not eat blood.[35]

13 A related commandment: **Any man from the children of Israel, or from the strangers that reside among them, who shall hunt game of a beast or a bird that may be eaten,** according to the criteria specified elsewhere,[36] **he shall pour out its blood and cover it with dirt.**[D] Not only is blood prohibited from being eaten, but it may not be left exposed. Beasts, meaning undomesticated animals, and most birds may not be brought as offerings. This commandment to cover the blood applies to undomesticated animals and birds, which are generally hunted; it does not apply to domesticated animals.[37]

14 **For the life of all flesh, its blood is with its life; therefore I said to the children of Israel: The blood of all flesh you shall not eat, because the life of all flesh is its blood.** To symbolize the limits of human power over life, **anyone who eats it shall be excised.**

15 Up to this point, the verses have introduced various commandments pertaining to the killing of animals. These include the prohibition against eating meat from an animal that was not brought as an offering, which applied only while the children of Israel were in the wilderness; the prohibition against bringing offerings outside the Tabernacle or Temple; the prohibition against eating blood; and the obligation to cover the blood of an undomesticated animal or bird that has been slaughtered. The next commandment refers to animals that were not necessarily killed by human beings: **Any person who shall eat an unslaughtered carcass or a mauled animal** that has suffered a fatal injury,[38] **whether he is native or stranger, he shall wash his garments and bathe in water, and he is impure until the evening, and he shall be purified.** Not only is it prohibited to eat such animals, but having direct physical contact with their carcasses, or even moving their carcasses indirectly, renders a person impure (see 11:27–28, 39–40). However, since this verse specifically refers to eating the carcass, the Sages explain that it refers to a unique type of impurity, contracted specifically from the carcass of a kosher bird, and not through contact or by being moved, but only when it is swallowed.[39]

16 **But if he does not wash and he does not bathe his flesh, he shall bear his iniquity.** An impure person is not required to purify himself immediately, as there is no prohibition against being ritually impure. He violates a prohibition only if he touches consecrated food items or enters the Temple. Priests generally did not own land and could not grow their own produce, and so this prohibition was undoubtedly an important concern of theirs, since consecrated food items comprised a significant portion of their diet. The same prohibition also applied to the entire nation while they were in the wilderness, during which time they were permitted to eat meat only if the animal had been brought as an offering; however, even after it became permissible to eat unconsecrated meat, one who was impure could still come into contact with consecrated food. Because this is a severe prohibition, the verse emphasizes the importance of maintaining ritual purity.[40]

ח וַאֲלֵהֶם תֹּאמַר אִישׁ אִישׁ מִבֵּית יִשְׂרָאֵל וּמִן־הַגֵּר אֲשֶׁר־יָגוּר בְּתוֹכָם אֲשֶׁר־יַעֲלֶה חמישי /שלישי/
ט עֹלָה אוֹ־זָבַח: וְאֶל־פֶּתַח אֹהֶל מוֹעֵד לֹא יְבִיאֶנּוּ לַעֲשׂוֹת אֹתוֹ לַיהוָה וְנִכְרַת
י הָאִישׁ הַהוּא מֵעַמָּיו: וְאִישׁ אִישׁ מִבֵּית יִשְׂרָאֵל וּמִן־הַגֵּר הַגָּר בְּתוֹכָם אֲשֶׁר
יֹאכַל כָּל־דָּם וְנָתַתִּי פָנַי בַּנֶּפֶשׁ הָאֹכֶלֶת אֶת־הַדָּם וְהִכְרַתִּי אֹתָהּ מִקֶּרֶב עַמָּהּ:
יא כִּי־נֶפֶשׁ הַבָּשָׂר בַּדָּם הִוא וַאֲנִי נְתַתִּיו לָכֶם עַל־הַמִּזְבֵּחַ לְכַפֵּר עַל־נַפְשֹׁתֵיכֶם כִּי־
יב הַדָּם הוּא בַּנֶּפֶשׁ יְכַפֵּר: עַל־כֵּן אָמַרְתִּי לִבְנֵי יִשְׂרָאֵל כָּל־נֶפֶשׁ מִכֶּם לֹא־תֹאכַל
יג דָּם וְהַגֵּר הַגָּר בְּתוֹכְכֶם לֹא־יֹאכַל דָּם: וְאִישׁ אִישׁ מִבְּנֵי יִשְׂרָאֵל וּמִן־הַגֵּר הַגָּר
בְּתוֹכָם אֲשֶׁר יָצוּד צֵיד חַיָּה אוֹ־עוֹף אֲשֶׁר יֵאָכֵל וְשָׁפַךְ אֶת־דָּמוֹ וְכִסָּהוּ בֶּעָפָר:
יד כִּי־נֶפֶשׁ כָּל־בָּשָׂר דָּמוֹ בְנַפְשׁוֹ הוּא וָאֹמַר לִבְנֵי יִשְׂרָאֵל דַּם כָּל־בָּשָׂר לֹא תֹאכֵלוּ
טו כִּי נֶפֶשׁ כָּל־בָּשָׂר דָּמוֹ הִוא כָּל־אֹכְלָיו יִכָּרֵת: וְכָל־נֶפֶשׁ אֲשֶׁר תֹּאכַל נְבֵלָה וּטְרֵפָה
טז בָּאֶזְרָח וּבַגֵּר וְכִבֶּס בְּגָדָיו וְרָחַץ בַּמַּיִם וְטָמֵא עַד־הָעֶרֶב וְטָהֵר: וְאִם לֹא יְכַבֵּס
וּבְשָׂרוֹ לֹא יִרְחָץ וְנָשָׂא עֲוֺנוֹ:

רש"י

ח| **אֲשֶׁר יַעֲלֶה עֹלָה.** לְחַיֵּב עַל הַמַּקְטִיר אֵיבָרִים בַּחוּץ כְּשׁוֹחֵט בַּחוּץ, שֶׁאִם שָׁחַט אֶחָד וְהֶעֱלָה חֲבֵרוֹ שְׁנֵיהֶן חַיָּבִין:

ט| **וְנִכְרַת.** זַרְעוֹ נִכְרָת וְיָמָיו נִכְרָתִין:

י| **כָּל דָּם.** לְפִי שֶׁנֶּאֱמַר: "בַּנֶּפֶשׁ יְכַפֵּר" (פסוק יא), יָכוֹל לֹא יְהֵא חַיָּב אֶלָּא עַל דַּם הַמֻּקְדָּשִׁים? תַּלְמוּד לוֹמַר: "כָּל דָּם": **וְנָתַתִּי פָנַי.** פְּנַאי שֶׁלִּי, פּוֹנֶה אֲנִי מִכָּל עֲסָקַי וְעוֹסֵק בּוֹ:

יא| **כִּי נֶפֶשׁ הַבָּשָׂר.** שֶׁל כָּל בְּרִיָּה "בַּדָּם הִיא" תְּלוּיָה, וּלְפִיכָךְ נְתַתִּיו עַל הַמִּזְבֵּחַ לְכַפֵּר עַל נֶפֶשׁ הָאָדָם, תָּבוֹא נֶפֶשׁ וּתְכַפֵּר עַל הַנֶּפֶשׁ:

יב| **כָּל נֶפֶשׁ מִכֶּם.** לְהַזְהִיר גְּדוֹלִים עַל הַקְּטַנִּים:

יג| **אֲשֶׁר יָצוּד.** אֵין לִי אֶלָּא צַיִד, אַוָּזִין וְתַרְנְגוֹלִין מִנַּיִן? תַּלְמוּד לוֹמַר "צֵיד" – מִכָּל מָקוֹם. אִם כֵּן לָמָּה נֶאֱמַר "אֲשֶׁר יָצוּד"? שֶׁלֹּא יֹאכַל בָּשָׂר אֶלָּא בַּהַזְמָנָה הַזֹּאת: **אֲשֶׁר יֵאָכֵל.** פְּרָט לִטְמֵאִים:

יד| **דָּמוֹ בְנַפְשׁוֹ הוּא.** דָּמוֹ הוּא לוֹ בִּמְקוֹם הַנֶּפֶשׁ, שֶׁהַנֶּפֶשׁ תְּלוּיָה בּוֹ: **כִּי נֶפֶשׁ כָּל בָּשָׂר דָּמוֹ הִוא.** הַנֶּפֶשׁ הִיא הַדָּם. 'דָּם' וּ'בָשָׂר' – לְשׁוֹן זָכָר, 'נֶפֶשׁ' – לְשׁוֹן נְקֵבָה:

טו| **אֲשֶׁר תֹּאכַל נְבֵלָה וּטְרֵפָה.** בְּנִבְלַת עוֹף טָהוֹר דִּבֵּר הַכָּתוּב, שֶׁאֵין לָהּ טֻמְאָה אֶלָּא בְּשָׁעָה שֶׁנִּבְלַעַת בְּבֵית הַבְּלִיעָה, וְלִמֶּדְךָ כָּאן שֶׁמְּטַמְּאָה בַּאֲכִילָתָהּ. וּטְרֵפָה הָאֲמוּרָה כָּאן לֹא נִכְתַּב אֶלָּא לִדְרֹשׁ, וְכֵן שָׁנִינוּ: יָכוֹל תְּהֵא נִבְלַת עוֹף טָמֵא מְטַמְּאָה בְּבֵית הַבְּלִיעָה? תַּלְמוּד לוֹמַר: "טְרֵפָה", מִי שֶׁיֵּשׁ בְּמִינוֹ טְרֵפָה, יָצָא עוֹף טָמֵא שֶׁאֵין בְּמִינוֹ טְרֵפָה:

טז| **וְנָשָׂא עֲוֹנוֹ.** אִם יֹאכַל קֹדֶשׁ אוֹ יִכָּנֵס לַמִּקְדָּשׁ, חַיָּב עַל טֻמְאָה זוֹ כְּכָל שְׁאָר טֻמְאוֹת: **וּבְשָׂרוֹ לֹא יִרְחַץ וְנָשָׂא עֲוֹנוֹ.** עַל רְחִיצַת גּוּפוֹ עָנוּשׁ כָּרֵת, וְעַל כִּבּוּס בְּגָדִים בְּמַלְקוּת:

DISCUSSION

17:8| **Who offers up a burnt offering or a feast offering:** This refers to the prohibition against presenting offerings outside of the Temple courtyard (see *Nedarim* 78a). For a thousand years after the giving of the Torah, the slaughter of offerings outside the Temple was an ongoing problem for the children of Israel. There were certain periods when, under specific conditions, it was permissible to bring some offerings to God on personal altars. At other times, when there was a central, operational Temple, it was prohibited to bring offerings in other locations, even for the sake of Heaven (see *Zevaḥim*, chap. 14).

17:13| **He shall pour out its blood and cover it with dirt:** Puddles or holes filled with blood were common features in idolatrous rituals. Some commentaries suggest that the covering of the blood is a kind of apology to God or a way of downplaying the fact that human beings consume other living creatures (see Ba'al HaTurim). Alternatively, this commandment, which remains in effect today, alludes to burial. Just as the burial of a human corpse is an expression of honor for the deceased, so too covering the blood of a beast or bird grants a measure of dignity to these creatures (see *Kohelet Rabba* 3:19).

The Prohibitions against Sexual Immorality and Other Abominations

LEVITICUS 18:1–30

Thus far, the book of Leviticus has focused primarily on matters that concern the Temple and the priests, either directly or indirectly. These include a discussion of sacrificial offerings and the laws of ritual purity and impurity, which limit one's ability to touch or handle sanctified items. Here, however, is a section that is not related to the Temple, sacred items, or ritual purity and impurity. Instead, it provides a separate set of commandments.

Like the previous passage, this one focuses on one narrow topic, in this case, forbidden sexual relations. The verses mainly deal with the various prohibited sexual relations, not the punishments for which offenders are liable or other ramifications of violating the prohibitions. These are addressed separately, in a different section. The topic is bookended by long, unique introductory and concluding sections.

18 1 **The Lord spoke to Moses, saying:**

2 **Speak to the children of Israel and say to them: I am the Lord your God.**^D

3 **You shall not follow the practices of the land of Egypt in which you lived, and you shall not follow the practices of the land of Canaan, where I am bringing you,**^D **and you shall not follow their statutes,** their ways. You shall not follow their mores or their prescribed laws.[41]

4 Rather, **My ordinances you shall perform, and My statutes you shall observe,**^D **to follow them; I am the Lord your God.**

5 **You shall observe My statutes and My ordinances, which a man shall perform and live by them.** The commandments concerning the standards of sexual morality, which mandate the distinctiveness and sanctity of the children of Israel, shape the proper way to lead one's life. **I am the Lord,** I live forever.

6 **Any man of you shall not approach his kin to uncover nakedness,** to engage in sexual relations; **I am the Lord.** This general declaration serves to underline the basic principle of this passage that sexual relations with all close blood relatives are prohibited.

Sixth aliya

7 **The nakedness of your father and the nakedness of your mother you shall not uncover. She is your mother; you shall not uncover her nakedness.** In practically all societies, sexual relations between a mother and son are proscribed. Although this prohibition applies directly to a mother, in any normal family the shame and embarrassment caused by such an act would impact both parents. Consequently, the verse first mentions both the father and mother.[42]

8 **The nakedness of your father's wife,** even if she is not your mother, **you shall not uncover; it is your father's nakedness**

[*erva*]. The narrow meaning of the word *erva* is nakedness, as it has been explained here, or it can specifically refer to the sexual organs. However, it can also be used in the sense of shame or embarrassment.[43] Consequently, one possible interpretation of this verse is that sexual relations with one's father's wife would cause the father shame and embarrassment.

9 **The nakedness of your sister, the daughter of your father or the daughter of your mother,** and all the more so if she is the daughter of both your father and your mother, although this case is not explicitly mentioned in the verse,[44] whether she is **born into the household or born outside** of wedlock,[45] **you shall not uncover their nakedness,** as they are your relatives.

10 **The nakedness of the daughter of your son, or of the daughter of your daughter,** and certainly of your daughter herself, although she is not mentioned in the verse,[46] **you shall not uncover their nakedness, for it is your nakedness.** One's relationship with one's own children is even closer than one's relationship with other relatives; sexual relations with one's child would constitute the parent's own personal nakedness or shame.

11 **The nakedness of the daughter of your father's wife,** who was **born to your father** and not necessarily to your mother, **she is your sister;** therefore, **you shall not uncover her nakedness.** There is overlap between this verse and the prohibition of verse 9. Consequently, sexual relations with the daughter of one's father who is also the daughter of the father's wife is prohibited by two commandments.[47] However, if one does not share either parent with the daughter of his father's wife, he is not considered her relative at all, and she is not forbidden to

---

DISCUSSION

18:2 | **I am the Lord your God:** This phrase indicates that the prohibitions listed in the upcoming passage are a direct result of the chosen status of the children of Israel. The expression "I am the Lord your God" appears both at the beginning of this passage and at its conclusion (verse

30). It does not mean merely I am the Ruler, the Master, and the Judge, but also, since you belong to Me, there are rules and limitations that apply to you that are not relevant to all other peoples (see *Sifra*).

18:3 | **You shall not follow the practices of the land of Egypt in which you lived, and you shall not follow the practices of the land of Canaan, where I am bringing you:** The pagan cultures of Egypt and Canaan differed from each other; however, regarding the topic of this

↤

א ב וַיְדַבֵּר יְהוָה אֶל־מֹשֶׁה לֵּאמֹר: דַּבֵּר אֶל־בְּנֵי יִשְׂרָאֵל וְאָמַרְתָּ אֲלֵהֶם אֲנִי יְהוָה יד
ג אֱלֹהֵיכֶם: כְּמַעֲשֵׂה אֶרֶץ־מִצְרַיִם אֲשֶׁר יְשַׁבְתֶּם־בָּהּ לֹא תַעֲשׂוּ וּכְמַעֲשֵׂה אֶרֶץ־
ד כְּנַעַן אֲשֶׁר אֲנִי מֵבִיא אֶתְכֶם שָׁמָּה לֹא תַעֲשׂוּ וּבְחֻקֹּתֵיהֶם לֹא תֵלֵכוּ: אֶת־מִשְׁפָּטַי
ה תַּעֲשׂוּ וְאֶת־חֻקֹּתַי תִּשְׁמְרוּ לָלֶכֶת בָּהֶם אֲנִי יְהוָה אֱלֹהֵיכֶם: וּשְׁמַרְתֶּם אֶת־חֻקֹּתַי
ו וְאֶת־מִשְׁפָּטַי אֲשֶׁר יַעֲשֶׂה אֹתָם הָאָדָם וָחַי בָּהֶם אֲנִי יְהוָה: אִישׁ ששי
ז אִישׁ אֶל־כָּל־שְׁאֵר בְּשָׂרוֹ לֹא תִקְרְבוּ לְגַלּוֹת עֶרְוָה אֲנִי יְהוָה: עֶרְוַת
ח אָבִיךָ וְעֶרְוַת אִמְּךָ לֹא תְגַלֵּה אִמְּךָ הִוא לֹא תְגַלֶּה עֶרְוָתָהּ: עֶרְוַת
ט אֵשֶׁת־אָבִיךָ לֹא תְגַלֵּה עֶרְוַת אָבִיךָ הִוא: עֶרְוַת אֲחוֹתְךָ בַת־אָבִיךָ
י אוֹ בַת־אִמֶּךָ מוֹלֶדֶת בַּיִת אוֹ מוֹלֶדֶת חוּץ לֹא תְגַלֶּה עֶרְוָתָן: עֶרְוַת
יא בַּת־בִּנְךָ אוֹ בַת־בִּתְּךָ לֹא תְגַלֶּה עֶרְוָתָן כִּי עֶרְוָתְךָ הֵנָּה: עֶרְוַת

רש״י

פרק יח

ב| **אני ה' אלהיכם.** אני הוא שאמרתי בסיני: "אנכי ה' אלהיך" (שמות כ, ב), וקבלתם עליכם מלכותי, מעתה קבלו גזרותי. רבי אומר: גלוי וידוע לפניו שסופן לנתק בעריות בימי עזרא, לפיכך בא עליהם בגזרה: "אני ה' אלהיכם", דעו מי גוזר עליכם, דין לפרע ונאמן לשלם שכר:

ג| **כמעשה ארץ מצרים.** מגיד שמעשיהם של מצריים ושל כנעניים מקולקלים מכל האומות, ואותו מקום שישבו בו ישראל מקולקל מן הכל: **אשר אני מביא אתכם שמה.** מגיד שאותן עממין שכבשו ישראל, מקולקלים יותר מכלם: **ובחקתיהם לא תלכו.** מה הניח הכתוב שלא אמר? אלא אלו נימוסות שלהן, דברים החקוקין להם, כגון טרטיאות ואצטדיאות. רבי מאיר אומר, אלו דרכי האמורי שמנו חכמים:

ד| **את משפטי תעשו.** אלו דברים האמורים בתורה במשפט, שאלו לא נאמרו היו כדאי לאמרן: **ואת חקתי תשמרו.** דברים שהם גזרת המלך, שיצר הרע משיב עליהם למה לנו לשמרן, ואומות העולם משיבין עליהם, כגון אכילת חזיר ולבישת שעטנז וטהרת מי חטאת, לכך נאמר: "אני ה'" – גזרתי עליכם, אי אתה רשאי להפטר: **ללכת בהם.** אל תפטר מתוכם, שלא תאמר: למדתי חכמת ישראל, אלך ואלמד חכמת האומות:

ה| **ושמרתם את חקתי וגו'.** לרבות שאר דקדוקי הפרשה, שלא פרט הכתוב בהם. דבר אחר, לתן שמירה ועשיה לחקים ושמירה ועשיה למשפטים, לפי שלא נתן אלא עשיה למשפטים ושמירה לחקים (לעיל פסוק ד): **וחי בהם.** לעולם הבא, שאם תאמר בעולם הזה, והלא סופו הוא מת: **אני ה'.** נאמן לשלם שכר:

ו| **לא תקרבו.** להזהיר הנקבה כזכר, לכך נאמר לשון רבים: **אני ה'.** נאמן לשלם שכר:

ז| **ערות אביך.** זו אשת אביך. או אינו אלא כמשמעו? נאמר כאן: "ערות אביך", ונאמר להלן: "ערות אביו גלה" (ויקרא כ, יא), מה להלן אשת אביו, אף כאן אשת אביו: **וערות אמך.** להביא אמו שאינה אשת אביו:

ח| **ערות אשת אביך.** לרבות לאחר מיתה:

ט| **בת אביך.** אף בת אנוסה במשמע: **מולדת בית או מולדת חוץ.** בין שאומרים לו לאביך קיים את אמה, ובין שאומרים לו הוצא את אמה, כגון ממזרת או נתינה:

י| **ערות בת בנך וגו'.** בבתו מאנוסתו הכתוב מדבר, ובתו ובת בתו מאשתו אנו למדין מערות אשה ובתה, שנאמר בהן: "לא תגלה" (להלן פסוק יז) בין שהיא ממנו בין שהיא מאיש אחר: **ערות בת בנך.** קל וחמר לבתך, אלא לפי שאין מזהירין מן הדין, למדוה מגזרה שוה במסכת יבמות (דף ג ע"א):

יא| **ערות בת אשת אביך.** למד שאינו חיב על אחותו

DISCUSSION

→ passage, sexual morality, there were very few, if any, injunctions observed by either of these two cultures. Rampant promiscuity was characteristic of both Canaan and Egypt. As the children of Israel moved from Egypt to Canaan, they needed to be warned to observe the boundaries of sexual morality.

18:4| **My ordinances you shall perform, and My statutes you shall observe:** The emphasis on obedience to God's ordinances expressed in this verse contradicts the apologetic explanations of the sexual prohibitions as eugenic limitations for the purpose of improving the gene pool. These prohibitions are not based on the idea that incestuous relationships can lead to hereditary diseases and other health problems. One cannot say that they are designed to benefit a particular human society; rather, they should be understood as laws that have been prescribed by divine decree (see Ramban, verse 6; *Sifra*, *Kedoshim* 20:26).

18:6| **To uncover nakedness:** This is a euphemistic expression for sexual relations. The Bible

him.[48] Indeed, there are historical precedents of men marrying their stepsisters.[49]

12 **The nakedness of your father's sister you shall not uncover; she is your father's kin,** or flesh.[50]

13 **The nakedness of your mother's sister you shall not uncover, as she is your mother's kin.**

14 The aunts mentioned in the previous two verses are blood relatives from the side of each parent. This verse adds that even an aunt who is not a blood relative is prohibited. **The nakedness of your father's brother you shall not uncover; you shall not approach his wife; she is your aunt.**[D] Since she is married to your uncle, she should be considered as much your aunt as the sister of your father or mother.

15 The Torah lists further prohibitions involving relatives through marriage. **The nakedness of your daughter-in-law you shall not uncover; she is your son's wife.** Therefore, **you shall not uncover her nakedness.**

16 **The nakedness of your brother's wife you shall not uncover; it is your brother's nakedness.**

17 The list of forbidden relations began with close blood relatives, e.g., parents, children, and siblings, before continuing with those who are relatives through marriage. In contrast, the next two prohibitions do not involve a familial relationship between the man and woman but rather focus on a preexisting relationship with a female relative of the woman. **The nakedness of a woman and her daughter you shall not uncover.** It is prohibited for a man to have relations with a mother and her daughter. This applies not only to her actual daughter, as even **her son's daughter or her daughter's daughter you shall not take to uncover her nakedness. They are kin; it is lewdness [*zima*].** Alternatively, *zima* means the thought process of sinners and is similar to the word *mezima*, plot.[51] Although a man is permitted to wed either woman, he may not marry one of them once he has already been married to the other. Such a marriage would ruin the mother-daughter relationship.[52] An additional negative consequence of such a marriage is that the husband is more liable to think of one woman while he is with the other, as there is often a resemblance between mother and daughter.

18 Similarly, **a woman with her sister you shall not take to be rivals to uncover her nakedness through her in her lifetime.** It is prohibited to marry two sisters. The verse clearly states that a man may not marry his wife's sister if his wife is still alive, even if she is no longer his wife and he has divorced her. The prohibition against marrying two sisters is similar to the prohibition against marrying a mother and her daughter. However, the permissibility of marrying the sister of one's wife after the wife's death is a unique feature of this case that does not apply to the prohibition of marrying a mother and her daughter or to any of the other forbidden relations. The prohibition is in effect only during the lifetime of the sister one marries first.

19 The following forbidden sexual relationships are not prohibited due to familial connections of any kind between the participants. **To a woman in her state of menstrual impurity you shall not approach to uncover her nakedness.** It is prohibited to engage in sexual relations with a woman when she is in a state of menstrual impurity. Furthermore, one may not even approach to uncover her nakedness, which is a broader prohibition than refraining from actual sexual relations. It is prohibited for a man to engage in all forms of close contact with a woman in a state of menstrual impurity, and it makes no difference whether she is not related to him or if she is his own wife.[53]

20 **And with the wife of your counterpart,**[D] another Jewish man,[54] **you shall not engage in sexual relations, to defile yourself with her.**

21 The Torah now turns to a different type of prohibition: **You shall not give from your offspring to pass** him as a symbolic or an actual offering **to Molekh,**[DB] which is the name of a particular idol or cult that was widespread at the time.[55] **And you shall not profane the name of your God; I am the Lord.** According to the alternative opinion that Molekh is not the name of any particular idol, this might mean that one may not worship God by sacrificing children, as in the Molekh ritual, since this is a degenerate practice that profanes the name of God. This interpretation also fits the verses in Deuteronomy that discuss the topic of burning one's sons or daughters.[56]

DISCUSSION

often prefers to employ euphemistic terminology, and certainly uses it with regard to sexual relations (see commentary on Genesis 9:21–22; *Pesaḥim* 3a).

18:14 | **You shall not approach his wife; she is your aunt:** This idea that the wife of an uncle related by blood is considered like a blood relation herself is one of the sources for the halakhic principle that the marriage bond causes

husband and wife to be considered virtually like a single entity. In the words of the Sage: One wife is like his own flesh (see *Sanhedrin* 28b; *Berakhot* 24a). This concept has ramifications in many areas of Jewish law.

18:20 | **With the wife of your counterpart:** Although the prohibition of adultery is one of the Ten Precepts (Exodus 20:12), it is mentioned here again in the context of the other forbidden

sexual relations. Traditional Jewish sources include the prohibition of adultery together with incest in the general category of forbidden sexual relations (e.g., see *Yevamot* 91a).

18:21 | **You shall not give from your offspring to pass to Molekh:** Why is the prohibition of Molekh worship mentioned in the context of forbidden sexual relations? The Molekh cult was not directly related to sexual impropriety, but ←●

יב בַּת־אֵשֶׁת אָבִיךָ מוֹלֶדֶת אָבִיךָ אֲחוֹתְךָ הִוא לֹא תְגַלֶּה עֶרְוָתָהּ׃ עֶרְוַת
יג אֲחוֹת־אָבִיךָ לֹא תְגַלֵּה שְׁאֵר אָבִיךָ הִוא׃ עֶרְוַת אֲחוֹת־אִמְּךָ
יד לֹא תְגַלֵּה כִּי־שְׁאֵר אִמְּךָ הִוא׃ עֶרְוַת אֲחִי־אָבִיךָ לֹא תְגַלֵּה אֶל־
טו אִשְׁתּוֹ לֹא תִקְרָב דֹּדָתְךָ הִוא׃ עֶרְוַת כַּלָּתְךָ לֹא תְגַלֵּה אֵשֶׁת בִּנְךָ
טז הִוא לֹא תְגַלֶּה עֶרְוָתָהּ׃ עֶרְוַת אֵשֶׁת־אָחִיךָ לֹא תְגַלֵּה עֶרְוַת אָחִיךָ
יז הִוא׃ עֶרְוַת אִשָּׁה וּבִתָּהּ לֹא תְגַלֵּה אֶת־בַּת־בְּנָהּ וְאֶת־בַּת־בִּתָּהּ
יח לֹא תִקַּח לְגַלּוֹת עֶרְוָתָהּ שַׁאֲרָה הֵנָּה זִמָּה הִוא׃ וְאִשָּׁה אֶל־אֲחֹתָהּ לֹא תִקָּח
יט לִצְרֹר לְגַלּוֹת עֶרְוָתָהּ עָלֶיהָ בְּחַיֶּיהָ׃ וְאֶל־אִשָּׁה בְּנִדַּת טֻמְאָתָהּ לֹא תִקְרַב
כ לְגַלּוֹת עֶרְוָתָהּ׃ וְאֶל־אֵשֶׁת עֲמִיתְךָ לֹא־תִתֵּן שְׁכָבְתְּךָ לְזָרַע לְטָמְאָה־בָהּ׃
כא וּמִזַּרְעֲךָ לֹא־תִתֵּן לְהַעֲבִיר לַמֹּלֶךְ וְלֹא תְחַלֵּל אֶת־שֵׁם אֱלֹהֶיךָ אֲנִי יְהוָה׃

רש״י

מִשְׁפָּחָה וְנָכְרִית, לְכָךְ נֶאֱמַר: "בַּת אֵשֶׁת אָבִיךָ", בִּרְאוּיָה לְקִדּוּשִׁין:

יד | **עֶרְוַת אֲחִי אָבִיךָ לֹא תְגַלֵּה.** וּמַה הִיא עֶרְוָתוֹ? "אֶל אִשְׁתּוֹ לֹא תִקְרָב":

טו | **אֵשֶׁת בִּנְךָ הִוא.** לֹא אָמַרְתִּי אֶלָּא בְּשֶׁיֵּשׁ לְבִנְךָ אִישׁוּת בָּהּ, פְּרָט לַאֲנוּסָה וְשִׁפְחָה וְנָכְרִית:

יז | **עֶרְוַת אִשָּׁה וּבִתָּהּ.** לֹא אָסַר הַכָּתוּב אֶלָּא עַל יְדֵי נִשּׂוּאֵי הָרִאשׁוֹנָה, לְכָךְ נֶאֱמַר: "לֹא תִקַּח", לְשׁוֹן קִיחָה. וְכֵן לְעִנְיַן הָעֹנֶשׁ: "אֲשֶׁר יִקַּח אֶת אִשָּׁה וְאֶת אִמָּהּ" (להלן כ, יד), לְשׁוֹן קִיחָה, אֲבָל אָנַס אִשָּׁה, מֻתָּר לִשָּׂא בִּתָּהּ: **שַׁאֲרָה הֵנָּה.** קְרוֹבוֹת זוֹ לָזוֹ: **זִמָּה.** עֵצָה, כְּתַרְגּוּמוֹ: "עֵצַת חַטָּאִין", שֶׁיִּצְרְךָ יוֹעֶצְךָ לַחֲטֹא:

יח | **אֶל אֲחֹתָהּ.** שְׁתֵּיהֶן כְּאַחַת: **לִצְרֹר.** לְשׁוֹן צָרָה, לַעֲשׂוֹת אֶת זוֹ צָרָה לָזוֹ: **בְּחַיֶּיהָ.** לִמֶּדְךָ שֶׁאִם גֵּרְשָׁהּ, לֹא יִשָּׂא אֶת אֲחוֹתָהּ כָּל זְמַן שֶׁהִיא בַּחַיִּים:

כא | **לַמֹּלֶךְ.** עֲבוֹדָה זָרָה הִיא שֶׁשְּׁמָהּ 'מֹלֶךְ', וְזוֹ הִיא עֲבוֹדָתָהּ, שֶׁמּוֹסֵר בְּנוֹ לַכְּמָרִים, וְעוֹשִׂין שְׁתֵּי מְדוּרוֹת גְּדוֹלוֹת, וּמַעֲבִירִין אֶת הַבֵּן בְּרַגְלָיו בֵּין שְׁתֵּי מְדוּרוֹת הָאֵשׁ: **לֹא תִתֵּן.** זוֹ הִיא מְסִירָתוֹ לַכְּמָרִים: **לְהַעֲבִיר לַמֹּלֶךְ.** זוֹ הַעֲבָרַת הָאֵשׁ:

BACKGROUND

18:21 | **To pass to Molekh:** This was an idolatrous ritual in which one would bring his children as an offering by burning them in fire (see Deuteronomy 12:31; Jeremiah 7:31; Ezekiel 23:39). It was a common practice among some of the nations in the region, such as the Phoenicians. Alternatively, this might refer to a ritual in which children were ceremoniously passed through fire without actually being burned (see commentary on Isaiah 57:5).

It is possible that Molekh was not the real name of this god, but a Hebrew appellation for the Amonite god Milkom, as the children of Israel would distort the names of foreign deities (see I Kings 11:7, 33). It is also possible that its original name was Melekh, meaning "king," as in the verse "and the Sefarvites burned their children in the fire to Adramelekh and Anamelekh, the gods of Sefarvaim" (II Kings 17:31; see Ramban, verse 21). One of the common ways in which names were altered in this regard was to take the two syllables of the principle name and vocalize it with a stressed *o* and an unstressed *e* sound, as in the name Boshet (e.g., see Hosea 9:10; see also *Avoda Zara* 45a).

DISCUSSION

➞ worship of Molekh expresses a corrupt conception of parental authority. Children and other subordinate members of the family are not under the absolute control of the head of the family, to be used sexually or as ritual offerings. This sort of exploitation is a profanation of the name of God, as the verse states.

It is also possible that the appearance of this prohibition in the context of the forbidden sexual acts reflects the existence of a fertility cult in which children were slaughtered in the hope of ensuring the fertility of the land or the family (see Sforno; Rambam, *Guide of the Perplexed* 3:37).

22 This verse adds another prohibition to the list of forbidden sexual relations that are not due to familial ties, in addition to adultery and relations with a menstruating woman: **You shall not lie with a male in the manner of lying with a woman;**[D] **it is an abomination.** Homosexual relations between two men is not considered a normal sexual act; it is an abomination.

Seventh aliya (Fourth aliya)

23 **You shall not engage sexually with any animal to defile yourself with it.** The defilement of this deed is due to its nature as a purely sexual act, with no possibility of mutual human attachment or procreation. Up to this point, the forbidden sexual acts have been stated as prohibitions for males, though it is clear from context and parallel sources that these prohibitions apply equally to females.[57] The verses have been addressed to men because the man is generally the more active party in these acts. Here the verse addresses a situation where no man is involved at all: **And a woman shall not stand before an animal for it to copulate with her; it is a perversion.** The verse insists that bestiality is a perversion, though it appears to not have been unheard of in Canaanite culture.

24 To conclude the section, the verse adds that transgressions in the area of forbidden sexual relations are not only legally proscribed, but also cause moral and spiritual debasement. Therefore, **do not defile yourselves in any of these; for in all these were defiled the nations that I am sending forth from before you.** Various types of forbidden sexual relations, including adultery, homosexuality, and bestiality, were a central feature of ancient Canaanite culture.

25 **The land was defiled, and I visited its iniquity upon it.** These acts are not merely private, personal transgressions. When they become accepted and normative they defile the land itself. Severe sexual transgressions contaminate not only the individual who commits them, but one's surroundings as well, and they cause punishment to be inflicted on the entire land.[58] **And**

the land spewed out its inhabitants, by conquest at the hands of other nations or through natural disasters.

26 In contrast to those nations, **you,** the children of Israel, **shall observe My statutes,** which determine what is considered a familial relationship, although these definitions are not predicated on human logic, **and My ordinances,** laws with discernible logical or practical underpinnings.[59] **You shall not perform any of these abominations, the native and the stranger who resides among you,** as these restrictions apply to anyone who resides in the land.[60]

27 **For all these abominations were performed by the people of the land, who were** living there **before you,** the Canaanites, **and the land was defiled** through these acts.

28 If you do not sin, the result will be that **the land will not expel you by your defiling it, as it spewed out the nation that was before you.** The Land of Israel in particular cannot tolerate moral debasement, and it spews out the sinners who defile it.[61]

29 **For anyone who shall perform any of these abominations** listed above, as opposed to other, less severe prohibitions involving sexual relations that are not mentioned here,[62] **the people who perform them shall be excised from among their people.** Even prior to the involvement of a human court in the case of one who violates these prohibitions, those who transgress these prohibitions are liable to excision at the hands of Heaven.[63]

Maftir

30 **You shall keep My commission to refrain from performing any of the abominable practices that were performed before you** in the land of Canaan, **and you shall not defile yourselves through** performing **them; I am the Lord your God.** The phrase "you shall keep My commission" may also be rendered as: You shall establish a safeguard for My commission. The Sages interpreted this as a mandate to enact protective measures to prevent people from performing transgressions.[64]

DISCUSSION

18:22 | **You shall not lie with a male in the manner of lying with a woman:** This law also distinguished the children of Israel from the culture of the surrounding societies at the time, for whom homosexual relations was considered perfectly acceptable.

כב וְאֶת־זָכָר לֹא תִשְׁכַּב מִשְׁכְּבֵי אִשָּׁה תּוֹעֵבָה הִוא: וּבְכָל־בְּהֵמָה לֹא־תִתֵּן שְׁכָבְתְּךָ   שביעי

כג לְטָמְאָה־בָהּ וְאִשָּׁה לֹא־תַעֲמֹד לִפְנֵי בְהֵמָה לְרִבְעָהּ תֶּבֶל הוּא: אַל־תִּטַּמְּאוּ   /רביעי/

כד בְּכָל־אֵלֶּה כִּי בְכָל־אֵלֶּה נִטְמְאוּ הַגּוֹיִם אֲשֶׁר־אֲנִי מְשַׁלֵּחַ מִפְּנֵיכֶם: וַתִּטְמָא

כה הָאָרֶץ וָאֶפְקֹד עֲוֹנָהּ עָלֶיהָ וַתָּקִא הָאָרֶץ אֶת־יֹשְׁבֶיהָ: וּשְׁמַרְתֶּם אַתֶּם אֶת־חֻקֹּתַי

כו וְאֶת־מִשְׁפָּטַי וְלֹא תַעֲשׂוּ מִכֹּל הַתּוֹעֵבֹת הָאֵלֶּה הָאֶזְרָח וְהַגֵּר הַגָּר בְּתוֹכְכֶם: כִּי

כז אֶת־כָּל־הַתּוֹעֵבֹת הָאֵל עָשׂוּ אַנְשֵׁי־הָאָרֶץ אֲשֶׁר לִפְנֵיכֶם וַתִּטְמָא הָאָרֶץ: וְלֹא־   מפטיר

כח תָקִיא הָאָרֶץ אֶתְכֶם בְּטַמַּאֲכֶם אֹתָהּ כַּאֲשֶׁר קָאָה אֶת־הַגּוֹי אֲשֶׁר לִפְנֵיכֶם: כִּי

כט כָּל־אֲשֶׁר יַעֲשֶׂה מִכֹּל הַתּוֹעֵבֹת הָאֵלֶּה וְנִכְרְתוּ הַנְּפָשׁוֹת הָעֹשֹׂת מִקֶּרֶב עַמָּם:

ל וּשְׁמַרְתֶּם אֶת־מִשְׁמַרְתִּי לְבִלְתִּי עֲשׂוֹת מֵחֻקּוֹת הַתּוֹעֵבֹת אֲשֶׁר נַעֲשׂוּ לִפְנֵיכֶם

וְלֹא תִטַּמְּאוּ בָּהֶם אֲנִי יְהוָה אֱלֹהֵיכֶם:

רש"י

כג| תֶּבֶל הוּא. לְשׁוֹן קֹדֶשׁ וְעֶרְוָה וְנִאוּף, וְכֵן: "וְחֵפִי
עַל תַּבְלִיתָם" (ישעיה י, כה). דָּבָר אַחֵר, "תֶּבֶל הוּא" –
לְשׁוֹן בְּלִילָה וְעִרְבּוּב, זֶרַע אָדָם וְזֶרַע בְּהֵמָה:

כח| וְלֹא תָקִיא הָאָרֶץ אֶתְכֶם. מָשָׁל לְבֶן מֶלֶךְ

שֶׁהֶאֱכִילוּהוּ דָּבָר מָאוּס, שֶׁאֵין עוֹמֵד בְּמֵעָיו אֶלָּא מְקִיאוֹ,
כָּךְ אֶרֶץ יִשְׂרָאֵל אֵינָהּ מְקַיֶּמֶת עוֹבְרֵי עֲבֵרָה. וְתַרְגּוּמוֹ:
"וְלָא תְרוֹקֵן", לְשׁוֹן רִקּוּן, מְרִיקָה עַצְמָהּ מֵהֶם:

כט| הַנְּפָשׁוֹת הָעֹשֹׂת. הַזָּכָר וְהַנְּקֵבָה בְּמַשְׁמָע:

ל| וּשְׁמַרְתֶּם אֶת מִשְׁמַרְתִּי. לְהַזְהִיר בֵּית דִּין עַל כָּךְ:
וְלֹא תִטַּמְּאוּ בָּהֶם אֲנִי ה' אֱלֹהֵיכֶם. הָא אִם תִּטַּמְּאוּ
אֵינִי אֱלֹהֵיכֶם וְאַתֶּם נִפְסָלִים מֵאַחֲרַי, וּמַה הֲנָאָה יֵשׁ
לִי בָּכֶם וְאַתֶּם מִתְחַיְּבִים כְּלָיָה, לְכָךְ נֶאֱמַר: "אֲנִי ה'
אֱלֹהֵיכֶם":

Parashat
Kedoshim

The Command to Be Holy
LEVITICUS 19:1–20:27

Until this point, the book of Leviticus has addressed specific topics of Jewish Law: offerings, forbidden foods, ritual impurity, etc.[1] The issue it now addresses, holiness, constitutes an entire way of life not restricted to any one area.

Commentaries note that the set of laws presented below echoes the Ten Precepts. Here, the contents of the Ten Precepts are expanded and deepened, taking on new meanings.[2] Still, it is difficult to clearly discern the organizing principle behind this section's structure and the order of its contents.[3]

Fear of One's Parents, the Sabbath, Idol Worship, and Observing the Laws of Offerings
LEVITICUS 19:1–8

19 1 **The Lord spoke to Moses, saying:**

2 **Speak to the entire congregation of the children of Israel,**[D] **and say to them: You shall be holy, for I, the Lord your God, am holy.** Before giving the Torah to the children of Israel, God declares and demands that they "shall be for Me a kingdom of priests and a holy nation."[4] Now it is time for the people to actualize this declaration: Their holiness must express itself in deed. Holiness is not the performance of a specific deed, ritual, or initiation. Rather, the holiness of the children of Israel is due to their special relationship with God, and the ramifications of this relationship include a tremendous collection of requisite actions.

3 **Each of you shall fear his mother and his father and you shall observe My Sabbaths:**[D] **I am the Lord your God.** Some explain that the juxtaposition of these two laws indicates that although one must take great care to fear one's parents and obey them, the obligation to observe the Sabbath takes precedence over this commandment; one is not obligated to obey one's

parents when their instructions involve a transgression of the Sabbath or other commandments.[5]

4 **Do not turn to the false gods,**[D] **and do not fashion for yourselves cast gods,** because you are holy and **I am the Lord your God.**

5 **And when you slaughter a peace offering to the Lord, for your propitiation you shall offer it,** of your own goodwill,[6] or in order to find favor in God's eyes.[7]

6 To this end, you must observe the laws of the offering:[8] **On the day of your slaughter it shall be eaten and on the next day,** in accordance with that which was stated previously (7:16); **and the leftover until the third day, it shall be burned in fire.**

7 **And if it,** the offering, **is eaten on the third day, it is detestable [*piggul*].** According to rabbinic tradition, sacrificial meat that was left until the third day is considered leftover [*notar*]. *Piggul* refers to an offering that was initially offered with intent to consume its flesh on the third day.[9] Although it is prohibited to eat *notar*, the offering itself is accepted so long as it was offered with proper intent; it is not disqualified retroactively. *Piggul*, however, since **it** is offered with improper intent, **shall not be accepted** by God at all, no matter when its flesh is consumed in practice.

8 **And he who eats it shall bear** responsibility for **his iniquity, because he profaned that which is sacred to the Lord; and that person shall be excised from his people.**[D]

DISCUSSION

19:2 | **Speak to the entire congregation of the children of Israel:** This introductory phrase differs from the standard phrase: "Speak to the children of Israel," which introduces the previous chapter dealing with forbidden relationships (18:2), as well as from the other forms of introductions appearing in Leviticus. Here, the address is to the entire congregation, rather than to any particular assembly, as this passage presents a general perspective which expresses itself in numerous details. Thus, the chapter is delivered to the entire congregation, as it does not refer to specific issues or sins (see *Sifra*).

19:3 | **Each of you shall fear his mother and his father and you shall observe My Sabbaths:** The requirements to honor one's parents and to observe the Sabbath appear adjacent in the Ten Precepts as well (Exodus 20:8–11). It would seem that their juxtaposition serves to express two opposite extremes: On the one hand, the special status accorded to parents, and to elders in general, is a fundamental feature of human society, and is not specifically related to the sanctity of Israel. For generations, people have honored their elders, and it is this show of respect that is perceived as an example

of humanity's moral superiority over all other living creatures, whose elders are left to die alone. Here, man is commanded to fear one's parents in addition to honoring them. This commandment addresses both young children who may still be punished by their parents, as well as adults whose parents can no longer control their child's actions. Therefore, fear of one's parents is not based on force or power, but on acknowledgment of their elevated status. On the other hand, the commandment to observe the Sabbath contains an emphasis on the fact that they are "My Sabbaths," and the Sabbath is God's

פרשת
קדושים

א וַיְדַבֵּ֥ר יְהוָ֖ה אֶל־מֹשֶׁ֥ה לֵּאמֹֽר: דַּבֵּ֞ר אֶל־כָּל־עֲדַ֧ת בְּנֵֽי־יִשְׂרָאֵ֛ל וְאָמַרְתָּ֥ טו

ב אֲלֵהֶ֖ם קְדֹשִׁ֣ים תִּֽהְי֑וּ כִּ֣י קָד֔וֹשׁ אֲנִ֖י יְהוָ֥ה אֱלֹֽהֵיכֶֽם: אִ֣ישׁ אִמּ֤וֹ וְאָבִיו֙ תִּירָ֔אוּ

ג וְאֶת־שַׁבְּתֹתַ֖י תִּשְׁמֹ֑רוּ אֲנִ֖י יְהוָ֥ה אֱלֹֽהֵיכֶֽם: אַל־תִּפְנוּ֙ אֶל־הָ֣אֱלִילִ֔ם וֵֽאלֹהֵי֙

ד מַסֵּכָ֔ה לֹ֥א תַעֲשׂ֖וּ לָכֶ֑ם אֲנִ֖י יְהוָ֥ה אֱלֹֽהֵיכֶֽם: וְכִ֧י תִזְבְּח֛וּ זֶ֥בַח שְׁלָמִ֖ים לַֽיהוָ֑ה

ה לִֽרְצֹנְכֶ֖ם תִּזְבָּחֻֽהוּ: בְּי֧וֹם זִבְחֲכֶ֛ם יֵֽאָכֵ֖ל וּמִֽמָּחֳרָ֑ת וְהַנּוֹתָ֕ר עַד־י֥וֹם הַשְּׁלִישִׁ֖י

ו בָּאֵ֥שׁ יִשָּׂרֵֽף: וְאִ֛ם הֵֽאָכֹ֥ל יֵֽאָכֵ֖ל בַּיּ֣וֹם הַשְּׁלִישִׁ֑י פִּגּ֥וּל ה֖וּא לֹ֥א יֵֽרָצֶֽה:

ז וְאֹֽכְלָיו֙ עֲוֹנ֣וֹ יִשָּׂ֔א כִּֽי־אֶת־קֹ֥דֶשׁ יְהוָ֖ה חִלֵּ֑ל וְנִכְרְתָ֛ה הַנֶּ֥פֶשׁ הַהִ֖וא מֵֽעַמֶּֽיהָ:

רש"י

ב דַּבֵּר אֶל כָּל עֲדַת בְּנֵי יִשְׂרָאֵל. מְלַמֵּד שֶׁנֶּאֶמְרָה פָרָשָׁה זוֹ בְּהַקְהֵל, מִפְּנֵי שֶׁרֹב גּוּפֵי תוֹרָה תְּלוּיִין בָּהּ: **קְדֹשִׁים תִּהְיוּ.** הֱווּ פְרוּשִׁים מִן הָעֲרָיוֹת וּמִן הָעֲבֵרָה, שֶׁכָּל מָקוֹם שֶׁאַתָּה מוֹצֵא גֶדֶר עֶרְוָה אַתָּה מוֹצֵא קְדֻשָּׁה: "אִשָּׁה זֹנָה וַחֲלָלָה" וְגוֹ', "אֲנִי ה' מְקַדִּשְׁכֶם" (ויקרא כא, ז-ח), "וְלֹא יְחַלֵּל זַרְעוֹ... אֲנִי ה' מְקַדְּשׁוֹ" (שם פסוק טו), "קְדֹשִׁים יִהְיוּ", "אִשָּׁה זֹנָה וַחֲלָלָה" וְגוֹ' (שם פסוקים ו-ז):

ג אִישׁ אִמּוֹ וְאָבִיו תִּירָאוּ. כָּל אֶחָד מִכֶּם תִּירְאוּ אָבִיו וְאִמּוֹ, זֶהוּ פְשׁוּטוֹ. וּמִדְרָשׁוֹ, אֵין לִי אֶלָּא אִישׁ, אִשָּׁה מִנַּיִן? כְּשֶׁהוּא אוֹמֵר "תִּירָאוּ" הֲרֵי כָאן שְׁנַיִם. אִם כֵּן לָמָּה נֶאֱמַר "אִישׁ"? שֶׁהָאִישׁ סִפֵּק בְּיָדוֹ לַעֲשׂוֹת, אֲבָל אִשָּׁה - רְשׁוּת אֲחֵרִים עָלֶיהָ: **אִמּוֹ וְאָבִיו תִּירָאוּ.** כָּאן הִקְדִּים אֵם לְאָב, לְפִי שֶׁגָּלוּי לְפָנָיו שֶׁהַבֵּן יָרֵא אֶת אָבִיו יוֹתֵר מֵאִמּוֹ, וּבִכְבוֹד הִקְדִּים אָב לְאֵם, לְפִי שֶׁגָּלוּי לְפָנָיו שֶׁהַבֵּן מְכַבֵּד אֶת אִמּוֹ יוֹתֵר מֵאָבִיו, מִפְּנֵי שֶׁמְּשַׁדַּלְתּוֹ בִּדְבָרִים: **וְאֶת שַׁבְּתֹתַי תִּשְׁמֹרוּ.** סָמַךְ שְׁמִירַת שַׁבָּת לְמוֹרָא אָב, לוֹמַר, אַף עַל פִּי שֶׁהִזְהַרְתִּיךָ עַל מוֹרָא אָב, אִם יֹאמַר לְךָ חַלֵּל אֶת

הַשַּׁבָּת, אַל תִּשְׁמַע לוֹ, וְכֵן בִּשְׁאָר כָּל הַמִּצְוֹת: **אֲנִי ה' אֱלֹהֵיכֶם.** אַתָּה וְאָבִיךָ חַיָּבִים בִּכְבוֹדִי, לְפִיכָךְ לֹא תִשְׁמַע לוֹ לְבַטֵּל אֶת דְּבָרַי. אֵיזֶהוּ מוֹרָא? לֹא יֵשֵׁב בִּמְקוֹמוֹ וְלֹא יְדַבֵּר בִּמְקוֹמוֹ וְלֹא יִסְתֹּר אֶת דְּבָרָיו. וְאֵיזֶהוּ כָבוּד? מַאֲכִיל וּמַשְׁקֶה, מַלְבִּישׁ וּמַנְעִיל, מַכְנִיס וּמוֹצִיא:

ד אַל תִּפְנוּ אֶל הָאֱלִילִם. לְעָבְדָם. "אֱלִילִם" לְשׁוֹן "אַל", כְּלֹא הוּא חָשׁוּב: **וֵאלֹהֵי מַסֵּכָה.** תְּחִלָּתָן אֱלִילִים הֵם, וְאִם אַתָּה פוֹנֶה אַחֲרֵיהֶם סוֹף אַתָּה עוֹשָׂן אֱלֹהוֹת: **לֹא תַעֲשׂוּ לָכֶם.** לֹא תַעֲשׂוּ לַאֲחֵרִים וְלֹא אֲחֵרִים לָכֶם, וְאִם תֹּאמַר לֹא תַעֲשׂוּ לַעֲנַגְמְכֶם אֲבָל אֲחֵרִים עוֹשִׂין לָכֶם, הֲרֵי כְבָר נֶאֱמַר: "לֹא יִהְיֶה לְךָ" (שמות כ, ג), לֹא שֶׁלְּךָ וְלֹא שֶׁל אֲחֵרִים:

ה וְכִי תִזְבְּחוּ וְגוֹ'. לֹא נֶאֶמְרָה פָרָשָׁה זוֹ אֶלָּא לְלַמֵּד שֶׁלֹּא תְהֵא זְבִיחָתָן אֶלָּא עַל מְנָת לְהֵאָכֵל בְּתוֹךְ הַזְּמַן הַזֶּה, שֶׁאִם לִקְבֹּעַ לָהֶם זְמַן אֲכִילָה, הֲרֵי כְבָר נֶאֱמַר: "וְאִם נֶדֶר אוֹ נְדָבָה זֶבַח קָרְבָּנוֹ" וְגוֹ' (לעיל ז, טז): **לִרְצֹנְכֶם תִּזְבָּחֻהוּ.** תְּחִלַּת זְבִיחָתוֹ תְּהֵא עַל מְנָת נַחַת רוּחַ שֶׁיְּהֵא לָכֶם לְרָצוֹן,

שֶׁאִם תַּחְשְׁבוּ עָלָיו מַחֲשֶׁבֶת פְּסוּל לֹא יֵרָצֶה עֲלֵיכֶם לְפָנַי: **לִרְצֹנְכֶם.** אפיימינ"ט, זֶהוּ לְפִי פְשׁוּטוֹ. וְרַבּוֹתֵינוּ לָמְדוּ מִכָּאן לַמִּתְעַסֵּק בְּקָדָשִׁים שֶׁפָּסוּל, שֶׁצָּרִיךְ שֶׁיִּתְכַּוֵּן לִשְׁחֹט:

ו בְּיוֹם זִבְחֲכֶם יֵאָכֵל. כְּשֶׁתִּזְבָּחוּהוּ, תִּשְׁחֲטוּהוּ עַל מְנָת זְמַן זֶה שֶׁקָּבַעְתִּי לָכֶם כְּבָר:

ז וְאִם הֵאָכֹל יֵאָכֵל וְגוֹ'. אִם אֵינוֹ עִנְיָן לַחוּץ לִזְמַנּוֹ, שֶׁהֲרֵי כְבָר נֶאֱמַר: "וְאִם הֵאָכֹל יֵאָכֵל מִבְּשַׂר זֶבַח שְׁלָמָיו" וְגוֹ' (לעיל ז, יח), תְּנֵהוּ עִנְיָן לַחוּץ לִמְקוֹמוֹ. יָכוֹל יִהְיוּ חַיָּבִים כָּרֵת עַל אֲכִילָתוֹ? תַּלְמוּד לוֹמַר: "וְהַנֶּפֶשׁ הָאֹכֶלֶת מִמֶּנּוּ עֲוֹנָהּ תִּשָּׂא" (לעיל ז, יח), מִמֶּנּוּ וְלֹא מֵחֲבֵרוֹ, יָצָא הַנִּשְׁחָט בְּמַחֲשֶׁבֶת חוּץ לִמְקוֹמוֹ: **פִּגּוּל.** מְתֹעָב, כְּמוֹ: "וּמְרַק פִּגֻּלִים כְּלֵיהֶם" (ישעיה סה, ד):

ח וְאֹכְלָיו עֲוֹנוֹ יִשָּׂא. בְּנוֹתָר גָּמוּר הַכָּתוּב מְדַבֵּר, וְאֵינוֹ עָנוּשׁ כָּרֵת עַל הַנִּשְׁחָט חוּץ לִמְקוֹמוֹ, שֶׁכְּבָר מִעֲטוֹ הַכָּתוּב, וְזֶה בְנוֹתָר גָּמוּר מְדַבֵּר. וּבְמַסֶּכֶת כְּרֵתוֹת (דף ה ע"א) לְמָדוּהוּ מִגְּזֵרָה שָׁוָה:

DISCUSSION

→ special festive day (see Genesis 2:2–3; Exodus 20:9, 31:13–17; Deuteronomy 5:14). Furthermore, unlike the festivals, which bear some connection to seasonal events in nature, the Sabbath is unrelated to the material world. Thus, the commandments to fear one's parents and to observe the Sabbath contain the notion of elevating those who are deserving of it, albeit in opposite realms: the realm of interpersonal relationships, and the abstract realm of ritual. Each of these domains must find a place in the holy society.

19:4 | Do not turn to the false gods [elilim]: The term *elilim*, which appears for the first time here, has clear undertones of mockery and ridicule (see Sifra). The repetition of the *lamed* transforms *elilim* into a diminished form of *el*, God, just as the additions of *lamed* and *beit* to the word *kelev*, dog, transform it into the word *kelavlav*, a term that denotes a puppy. Thus, the verse does not stress one's abandonment of God, but the fact that one turns to lesser gods, as it were.

19:8 | And he who eats it shall bear his iniquity, because he profaned that which is sacred to the Lord; and that person shall be excised from his people: The prophets also accused the children of Israel of partaking of offerings on the third day, in the Temples at Beit El and Dan (Amos 4:4). It seems puzzling, however, that such a transgression should incur such severe punishment and rebuke. Why is the consumption of an offering the day after its allotted time punishable by excision? Granted,

Gifts for the Poor, Honesty, and Brotherhood

LEVITICUS 19:9–18

After addressing the preservation of holiness in purely spiritual or ritualistic matters – the Sabbath, idol worship, and sacrificial offerings – the chapter turns to other facets of holiness relating to the daily lives of individuals. The Torah's concept of holiness is not limited to an isolated realm detached from the mundane aspects of life. Rather, all areas of life fall under the purview of this holiness, and its implications express themselves in a myriad of ways in the private and public domains. Therefore, the virtue of holiness demands both small and large obligations in interpersonal relationships.

9 **When you reap the harvest of your land, you shall not finish reaping the corner of your field;** do not harvest it. **And the gleanings of your harvest,** the sheaves that fall from the sickle during the harvest, **you shall not gather;** rather, you must leave them in the field.

Ancient Egyptian fresco depicting a harvest, thirteenth century BCE

10 **Your vineyard you shall not harvest completely [*te'olel*],** do not gather the small, incompletely formed clusters of grapes [*olelot*], **and the fallen fruit of your vineyard,** the grapes that have separated and fallen off the cluster, **you shall not gather.** All this produce, meaning the the corner of your field, the gleanings of your harvest, the incomplete clusters, and the fallen grapes, you may not gather from your field. Rather, **for the poor and for the stranger,** who is financially unstable, **you shall leave them: I am the Lord your God.**[D]

11 In addition to charity, the following prohibitions, some of which are designed to prevent social injustices, are important for the establishment of a holy congregation: **You shall not steal; nor shall you falsely deny a claim** that you owe another money, **nor shall you lie to one another.**

12 **You shall not take an oath in My name falsely, as you will profane the name of your God** by using it for wrongdoing: **I am the Lord,** and invoking My name among your falsehoods is doubly wrong.

13 **You shall not** use your power, status, or authority to **exploit your neighbor,** that is, you shall not prevent him from receiving that which he rightfully deserves.[10] Such exploitation might occur during business negotiations or during disagreements, or may relate to the hiring of workers.[11] **And you shall not rob** someone of that which belongs to him; **you shall not keep the wages of a hired laborer with you overnight**[D] **until morning.** You must pay your employees without delay. In particular, if you employ a day laborer who is to receive his wages after each day's work, you must pay him during the same evening in which he completes his labor.

14 **You shall not curse a deaf person;**[D] **you shall not place an obstacle before the blind.**[D] Upon these prohibitions, the Torah adds the warning: **You shall fear your God: I am the Lord.** In many instances, an injured person is unaware of who harmed him, and an offender can easily escape responsibility, especially if his victim is deaf, blind, or otherwise helpless with no one to argue on his behalf. Moreover, one may harm another in a discrete manner, unnoticeable even to those surrounding the victim. Therefore, the verse stresses that even when one has no reason to fear the reactions of the victim or society, he must fear God, before whom all actions and intentions are revealed.[12]

DISCUSSION

one chooses of one's own goodwill to bring a peace offering, in order to partake of its flesh before God. Part of the offering is burned upon the altar, and a portion of the offering is given to the priests, while most of the flesh goes to the owner. Since all three parties participate in the offering, it engenders an atmosphere of peace and tranquility, hence the name "peace offering" (*Sifra, Dibbura DeNedava* 13; Rashi, 4:10). However, a peace offering is a sacred item,

and its consumption is not meant to be a personal celebratory feast of which only a portion is designated for God. If the consumption of the offering is treated merely as a large family meal, its sanctity is marred. Consequently, one who consumes it on the third day, or intends to do so, without care for when or where he consumes the offering, profanes a sacred item of God. Therefore, the severe penalty incurred by this transgression does not stem from the

temptation to actually consume an offering beyond its appropriate time; rather, it results from the desecration of a sacred item and its transformation into a non-sacred one (see *Bekhor Shor*; commentary on 22:31).

19:10 | I am the Lord your God: This declaration, repeated on ten occasions in *Parashat Kedoshim,* serves to emphasize that these actions are not merely decent human behavior. Behind each of these commands stands the ◄•

ט וּבְקֻצְרְכֶם֙ אֶת־קְצִ֣יר אַרְצְכֶ֔ם לֹ֧א תְכַלֶּ֛ה פְּאַ֥ת שָׂדְךָ֖ לִקְצֹ֑ר וְלֶ֥קֶט קְצִירְךָ֖
י לֹ֥א תְלַקֵּֽט׃ וְכַרְמְךָ֙ לֹ֣א תְעוֹלֵ֔ל וּפֶ֥רֶט כַּרְמְךָ֖ לֹ֣א תְלַקֵּ֑ט לֶֽעָנִ֤י וְלַגֵּר֙ תַּעֲזֹ֣ב
יא אֹתָ֔ם אֲנִ֖י יְהוָ֥ה אֱלֹהֵיכֶֽם׃ לֹ֖א תִּגְנֹ֑בוּ וְלֹֽא־תְכַחֲשׁ֥וּ וְלֹֽא־תְשַׁקְּר֖וּ אִ֥ישׁ
יב בַּעֲמִיתֽוֹ׃ וְלֹֽא־תִשָּׁבְע֥וּ בִשְׁמִ֖י לַשָּׁ֑קֶר וְחִלַּלְתָּ֛ אֶת־שֵׁ֥ם אֱלֹהֶ֖יךָ אֲנִ֥י יְהוָֽה׃
יג לֹֽא־תַעֲשֹׁ֥ק אֶת־רֵֽעֲךָ֖ וְלֹ֣א תִגְזֹ֑ל לֹֽא־תָלִ֞ין פְּעֻלַּ֥ת שָׂכִ֛יר אִתְּךָ֖ עַד־בֹּֽקֶר׃
יד לֹא־תְקַלֵּ֣ל חֵרֵ֔שׁ וְלִפְנֵ֣י עִוֵּ֔ר לֹ֥א תִתֵּ֖ן מִכְשֹׁ֑ל וְיָרֵ֥אתָ מֵּאֱלֹהֶ֖יךָ אֲנִ֥י יְהוָֽה׃

רש"י

ט| **לֹא תְכַלֶּה פְּאַת שָׂדְךָ.** שֶׁיַּנִּיחַ פֵּאָה בְּסוֹף שָׂדֵהוּ: **וְלֶקֶט קְצִירְךָ.** שִׁבֳּלִים הַנּוֹשְׁרִים בִּשְׁעַת קְצִירָה אַחַת אוֹ שְׁתַּיִם, אֲבָל שָׁלֹשׁ אֵינָן לֶקֶט (פאה ו, ה):

י| **לֹא תְעוֹלֵל.** לֹא תִטֹּל עוֹלֵלוֹת שֶׁבָּהּ, וְהֵן נִכָּרוֹת. אֵיזֶהוּ עוֹלֵלוֹת? כָּל שֶׁאֵין לָהּ לֹא כָּתֵף וְלֹא נָטֵף: **וּפֶרֶט כַּרְמְךָ.** גַּרְגְּרֵי עֲנָבִים הַנּוֹשְׁרִים בִּשְׁעַת בְּצִירָה: **אֲנִי ה' אֱלֹהֵיכֶם.** דַּיָּן לִפָּרַע, וְאֵינִי גּוֹבֶה מִכֶּם אֶלָּא נְפָשׁוֹת, שֶׁנֶּאֱמַר: "אַל תִּגְזָל דָּל" וְגוֹ' "כִּי ה' יָרִיב רִיבָם" וְגוֹ' (משלי כב, כב-כג):

יא| **לֹא תִּגְנֹבוּ.** אַזְהָרָה לְגוֹנֵב מָמוֹן, אֲבָל "לֹא תִּגְנֹב" שֶׁבַּעֲשֶׂרֶת הַדִּבְּרוֹת אַזְהָרָה לְגוֹנֵב נְפָשׁוֹת, דָּבָר הַלָּמֵד מֵעִנְיָנוֹ, דָּבָר שֶׁחַיָּבִין עָלָיו מִיתַת בֵּית דִּין: **וְלֹא תְכַחֲשׁוּ.** לְפִי שֶׁנֶּאֱמַר: "וְכִחֶשׁ בָּהּ" – מְשַׁלֵּם קֶרֶן וָחֹמֶשׁ (לעיל ה, כב-כד), לָמַדְנוּ עֹנֶשׁ, אַזְהָרָה מִנַּיִן? תַּלְמוּד לוֹמַר: "וְלֹא תְכַחֲשׁוּ": **וְלֹא תְשַׁקְּרוּ.** לְפִי שֶׁנֶּאֱמַר: "וְנִשְׁבַּע עַל שָׁקֶר" – יְשַׁלֵּם קֶרֶן וָחֹמֶשׁ (לעיל ה, כב-כד), לָמַדְנוּ עֹנֶשׁ, אַזְהָרָה מִנַּיִן? תַּלְמוּד לוֹמַר "וְלֹא תְשַׁקְּרוּ": **לֹא תִּגְנֹבוּ וְלֹא תְכַחֲשׁוּ וְלֹא תְשַׁקְּרוּ... וְלֹא תִשָּׁבְעוּ.** אִם גָּנַבְתָּ סוֹפְךָ לְכַחֵשׁ, סוֹפְךָ לְשַׁקֵּר, סוֹפְךָ לְהִשָּׁבַע לַשָּׁקֶר:

יב| **וְלֹא תִשָּׁבְעוּ בִשְׁמִי.** לָמָּה נֶאֱמַר? לְפִי שֶׁנֶּאֱמַר: "לֹא תִשָּׂא אֶת שֵׁם ה' אֱלֹהֶיךָ לַשָּׁוְא" (שמות כ, ז), יָכוֹל לֹא יְהֵא חַיָּב אֶלָּא עַל שֵׁם הַמְיֻחָד, מִנַּיִן לְרַבּוֹת כָּל הַכִּנּוּיִין? תַּלְמוּד לוֹמַר: "וְלֹא תִשָּׁבְעוּ בִשְׁמִי לַשָּׁקֶר", כָּל שֵׁם שֶׁיֵּשׁ לִי:

יג| **לֹא תַעֲשֹׁק.** זֶה הַכּוֹבֵשׁ שְׂכַר שָׂכִיר: **לֹא תָלִין.** לְשׁוֹן נְקֵבָה, מוּסָב עַל הַפְּעֻלָּה: **עַד בֹּקֶר.** בְּשָׂכִיר יוֹם הַכָּתוּב מְדַבֵּר, שֶׁיְּצִיאָתוֹ מִשֶּׁשָּׁקְעָה הַחַמָּה, לְפִיכָךְ זְמַן גְּבוּי שְׂכָרוֹ כָּל הַלַּיְלָה. וּבְמָקוֹם אַחֵר הוּא אוֹמֵר: "וְלֹא תָבוֹא עָלָיו הַשֶּׁמֶשׁ" (דברים כד, טו), מְדַבֵּר בִּשְׂכִיר לַיְלָה, שֶׁהַשְׁלָמַת פְּעֻלָּתוֹ מִשֶּׁיַּעֲלֶה עַמּוּד הַשַּׁחַר, לְפִיכָךְ זְמַן גְּבוּי שְׂכָרוֹ כָּל הַיּוֹם, לְפִי שֶׁנָּתְנָה תוֹרָה זְמַן לְבַעַל הַבַּיִת עוֹנָה לְבַקֵּשׁ מָעוֹת:

יד| **לֹא תְקַלֵּל חֵרֵשׁ.** אֵין לִי אֶלָּא חֵרֵשׁ, מִנַּיִן לְרַבּוֹת כָּל אָדָם? תַּלְמוּד לוֹמַר: "בְּעַמְּךָ לֹא תָאֹר" (שמות כב, כז), אִם כֵּן, לָמָּה נֶאֱמַר "חֵרֵשׁ"? מָה חֵרֵשׁ מְיֻחָד שֶׁהוּא בַּחַיִּים, אַף כָּל שֶׁהוּא בַּחַיִּים, יָצָא הַמֵּת שֶׁאֵינוֹ בַּחַיִּים: **וְלִפְנֵי עִוֵּר לֹא תִתֵּן מִכְשֹׁל.** לִפְנֵי הַסּוּמָא בַּדָּבָר לֹא תִתֵּן עֵצָה שֶׁאֵינָהּ הוֹגֶנֶת לוֹ, אַל תֹּאמַר מְכֹר שָׂדְךָ וְקַח לְךָ חֲמוֹר, וְאַתָּה עוֹקֵף עָלָיו וְנוֹטְלָהּ הֵימֶנּוּ: **וְיָרֵאתָ מֵּאֱלֹהֶיךָ.** לְפִי שֶׁהַדָּבָר הַזֶּה אֵינוֹ מָסוּר לַבְּרִיּוֹת לֵידַע אִם

DISCUSSION

sanctity of the Lawgiver, the Creator of all existence. Just as it is the holiness of God that stands behind the prohibitions against turning to false gods or fashioning cast gods (verse 4), so too it is His sanctity that serves as the source for the obligation to leave a portion of one's property for the poor, the strangers, and the needy. In this manner, holiness permeates the fabric of daily life far more than through the performance of ritualistic acts.

19:13| **You shall not keep the wages of a hired laborer with you overnight:** In a developed economy, it might be financially advantageous for an employer to delay paying his employees, or it might simply be a matter of convenience for the employer. Regardless, the Torah obligates the timely payment of wages in order to prevent abuse and to establish labor relations on a foundation of honesty.

The hired laborer mentioned in the Torah is one who is in need of his wages. As such, it is prohibited to delay payment for his labor. Nevertheless, even if the situation were reversed, and the employer required the services of a particular laborer while the laborer had several job offers, it is still prohibited to delay payment of wages.

19:14| **You shall not curse a deaf person:** Although it is prohibited to curse anyone (see *Sifra*; Rashi; Ramban; *Sanhedrin* 66a; *Shevuot* 36a), the Torah specifies a deaf person in order to highlight the damage caused by the statement itself, even when the target of the curse cannot hear it. Clearly, one who curses or demeans a deaf person in the presence of others harms him, despite the fact that the individual himself is unaware of the damage inflicted. Perhaps it is due to ignorance of this fact that people justify such behavior (see Ramban; Rabbeinu Baḥya). Even if nobody hears the curse and no tangible damage will be inflicted upon the deaf person, it is still prohibited to curse him, as such speech has a deleterious effect on the soul of the speaker (see *Derashot HaRan* 12).

Although there are specific parameters regarding this prohibition, it is clear from several places that a curse as mentioned in the Bible is not merely the expression of ill will from one to another, but also involves a statement of belittlement or mockery (see Deuteronomy 21:23, 25:3; I Samuel 3:13, and Rashi ad loc.; II Samuel 6:22; *Targum Yonatan*, Leviticus 24:11; Rashi and Ramban, Deuteronomy 21:22).

You shall not place an obstacle block before the blind: The Sages understand this prohibition to extend far beyond its literal meaning. That is, anyone who lacks knowledge in a certain field, or is unaware of all sides of a matter, is considered blind with regard to that matter. Any statement that might lead such an individual to fail or to follow the wrong course of action, or cause him to sin, is included in this prohibition (see Rashi; *Sifra*, *Kedoshim* 2:2; *Pesaḥim* 22b).

15 **You shall not perform injustice in judgment.** This is a general demand for honesty in judgment. Furthermore, not only is it prohibited to discriminate against those on the margins of society, but **you shall not favor the impoverished** as well, and conversely, **you shall not defer to the great;**[D] do not favor either of the litigants. **With righteousness you shall judge your counterpart,** regardless of his identity or status.

Second aliya (Fifth aliya)

16 **You shall not go as a gossip**[D] **among your people**: Do not recount in one place certain rumors or private matters that you heard or witnessed in another place.[13] Additionally, when you see a member of Israel in danger or distress, **you shall not stand by the blood of your neighbor.**[D] That is, one must attempt to come to his aid if he is in distress. This is true even if the matter is not actually one of life and death.[14] **I am the Lord,** and My commands must be obeyed. Furthermore, given that one might easily shirk this responsibility by claiming that he was unaware of his neighbor's distress, that he was in a hurry or was busy, that he did not think his assistance was critical, or that the situation was too dangerous to intervene in, God declares: I am the Lord, and I know the truth.[15]

17 **You shall not hate your brother in your heart.** Although this would seem to be a general commandment, its practical ramifications are limited. The verse does not refer to actions that express hatred, but to the harboring of negative feelings in one's heart. Indeed, the verse instructs an alternative course of action: **You shall rebuke your neighbor,**[D] **and** thereby **you shall not bear a sin because of him.**[16] If you keep these matters in your heart and do not reprove him, this will be considered a sin.[17]

18 **You shall not take vengeance** upon someone who has wronged you or withheld some benefit from you; do not treat him as he treated you. Now, there are some who will refrain from seeking actual vengeance, but will harbor anger in their hearts. To counter this, the verse states: **You shall not** even **bear any grudge**[D] in your heart. Although taking vengeance or bearing a grudge may be legitimate courses of action against foreign enemies, it is prohibited to do so **against members of your people.**[18] **You shall love your neighbor as yourself:**[D] **I am the Lord.**[D] As above, the declaration "I am the Lord" serves to emphasize two points: On the one hand, although it is morally appropriate and even socially beneficial to love one's neighbor, these are not the motivations for this commandment. Rather, you must love your neighbor as yourself because God has commanded it. On the other hand, since God alone can judge the relationship between one's deeds and emotions, it is crucial to remind the people that this commandment, which pertains to the inner feelings of the individual, comes from God, and He can see what hides in one's heart.[19]

DISCUSSION

19:15 | **You shall not favor the impoverished; you shall not defer to the great:** All legal systems contain some sort of prohibition against favoring the rich, the powerful, or the strong. However, prohibiting a judge from pitying the poor is an anomaly.

Additionally, the "great" individual referred to in the verse is not only one who is wealthy or of noble status, as opposed to a pauper or one on the margins of society. The verse may also refer to a spiritually great person: a sage or important rabbi (see Exodus 11:3).

19:16 | **You shall not go as a gossip [*rakhil*]:** This expression borrows from the behavior of the wandering peddler [*rakhil*]. The root *reish-khaf-lamed* is similar to the root *reish-gimmel-lamed*, meaning "foot" (see Rashi), as both involve movement from place to place. The root *reish-gimmel-lamed* also has a negative connotation relating to movement and the passing on of information, namely in the term *meragel*, a spy, who uses his feet and ability to walk in order to pass on information.

The Torah prohibits one from revealing the private matters of another. This does not refer to spreading lies, nor does it refer specifically to revealing shameful or embarrassing episodes, but to the very exposure of private matters, which is today considered the duty of the press. Granted, certain matters must be revealed for specific purposes. However, there are many matters that people are accustomed to revealing, even though their revelation has no positive value. For example, a reliable account of a quarrel between a husband and wife does not involve a criminal offense, but such a report is likely to increase the tension in that relationship. A gossip who hears rumors or stories and goes off to tell them to another, creates undesirable situations through the very transmission of this information, and he violates a Torah prohibition.

You shall not go as a gossip among your people; you shall not stand by the blood of your neighbor: These two prohibitions appear adjacent to one another due to their similarity: The gossip seeks to witness deplorable acts, perhaps even ones that involve an element of danger. Not only does he not intervene to provide assistance and save that individual, but he takes pleasure in the event and enjoys passing on the details of it to others (see Ibn Ezra; *Bekhor Shor*; Rambam, *Sefer HaMadda, Hilkhot Deot* 7:1).

19:17 | **You shall not hate your brother in your heart; you shall rebuke your neighbor:** Generally, one comes to hate another individual due to some unscrupulous behavior on the latter's part. One's performance of a good deed might arouse jealousy, but not hatred. Some people will quarrel with an individual they have observed acting in an improper manner, especially when they are personally affected, while others, who generally refrain from interfering in the affairs of others, will remain silent even if the improper behavior arouses feelings of hatred. If left unresolved, this hatred may not subside, and might even intensify. Therefore, one is commanded to rebuke his neighbor and inform him of his feelings. Oftentimes an individual is unaware that he has done something wrong;

טו לֹא־תַעֲשׂוּ עָוֶל בַּמִּשְׁפָּט לֹא־תִשָּׂא פְנֵי־דָל וְלֹא תֶהְדַּר פְּנֵי גָדוֹל בְּצֶדֶק שני
טז תִּשְׁפֹּט עֲמִיתֶךָ: לֹא־תֵלֵךְ רָכִיל בְּעַמֶּיךָ לֹא תַעֲמֹד עַל־דַּם רֵעֶךָ אֲנִי יְהוָה: /חמישי/
יז לֹא־תִשְׂנָא אֶת־אָחִיךָ בִּלְבָבֶךָ הוֹכֵחַ תּוֹכִיחַ אֶת־עֲמִיתֶךָ וְלֹא־תִשָּׂא עָלָיו
יח חֵטְא: לֹא־תִקֹּם וְלֹא־תִטֹּר אֶת־בְּנֵי עַמֶּךָ וְאָהַבְתָּ לְרֵעֲךָ כָּמוֹךָ אֲנִי יְהוָה:

רש״י

דַּעְתּוֹ שֶׁל זֶה לְטוֹבָה אוֹ לְרָעָה, וְיָכוֹל לְהִשָּׁמֵט וְלוֹמַר: לְטוֹבָה נִתְכַּוַּנְתִּי, לְפִיכָךְ נֶאֱמַר בּוֹ: "וְיָרֵאתָ מֵאֱלֹהֶיךָ", הַמַּכִּיר מַחְשְׁבוֹתֶיךָ. וְכֵן כָּל דָּבָר הַמָּסוּר לְלִבּוֹ שֶׁל אָדָם הָעוֹשֵׂהוּ, וְאֵין אַחֵר הַבְּרִיּוֹת מַכִּירוֹת בּוֹ, נֶאֱמַר בּוֹ: "וְיָרֵאתָ מֵאֱלֹהֶיךָ":

טו | **לֹא תַעֲשׂוּ עָוֶל בַּמִּשְׁפָּט.** מְלַמֵּד שֶׁהַדַּיָּן הַמְקַלְקֵל אֶת הַדִּין קָרוּי עַוָּל, שָׂנוּי וּמְשֻׁקָּץ, חֵרֶם וְתוֹעֵבָה, שֶׁהָעָוֶל קָרוּי תוֹעֵבָה, שֶׁנֶּאֱמַר: "כִּי תוֹעֲבַת ה' וְגוֹ' כֹּל עֹשֵׂה עָוֶל" (דברים כה, טז), וְהַתּוֹעֵבָה קְרוּיָה שֶׁקֶץ וְחֵרֶם, שֶׁנֶּאֱמַר: "וְלֹא תָבִיא תוֹעֵבָה אֶל בֵּיתֶךָ וְהָיִיתָ חֵרֶם כָּמֹהוּ שַׁקֵּץ תְּשַׁקְּצֶנּוּ" וְגוֹ' (שם ז, כו): **לֹא תִשָּׂא פְנֵי דָל.** שֶׁלֹּא תֹאמַר, עָנִי הוּא זֶה וְהֶעָשִׁיר חַיָּב לְפַרְנְסוֹ, אֲזַכֶּנּוּ בַּדִּין וְנִמְצָא מִתְפַּרְנֵס בִּנְקִיּוּת: **וְלֹא תֶהְדַּר פְּנֵי גָדוֹל.** שֶׁלֹּא תֹאמַר, עָשִׁיר הוּא זֶה, בֶּן גְּדוֹלִים הוּא זֶה, הֵיאַךְ אֲבַיְּשֶׁנּוּ וְאֶרְאֶה בְּבָשְׁתּוֹ? עֹנֶשׁ יֵשׁ בַּדָּבָר! לְכָךְ נֶאֱמַר: "וְלֹא תֶהְדַּר פְּנֵי גָדוֹל": **בְּצֶדֶק תִּשְׁפֹּט עֲמִיתֶךָ.** כְּמַשְׁמָעוֹ. דָּבָר אַחֵר, הֱוֵי דָן אֶת חֲבֵרְךָ לְכַף זְכוּת:

טז | **לֹא תֵלֵךְ רָכִיל.** אֲנִי אוֹמֵר עַל שֵׁם שֶׁכָּל מְשַׁלְּחֵי מְדָנִים וּמְסַפְּרֵי לָשׁוֹן הָרָע הוֹלְכִים בְּבָתֵּי רֵעֵיהֶם לְרַגֵּל מַה יִּרְאוּ רָע אוֹ מַה יִּשְׁמְעוּ רָע לְסַפֵּר בַּשּׁוּק, נִקְרָאִים הוֹלְכֵי רָכִיל, הוֹלְכֵי רְגִילָה, אשפיימינ"ט בְּלַעַ"ז. וּרְאָיָה לִדְבָרַי, שֶׁלֹּא מָצִינוּ רְכִילוּת שֶׁאֵין כָּתוּב בִּלְשׁוֹן הֲלִיכָה, "לֹא תֵלֵךְ רָכִיל", "הֹלְכֵי רָכִיל נְחֹשֶׁת וּבַרְזֶל" (ירמיה ו, כח). וּשְׁאָר לָשׁוֹן הָרָע אֵין כָּתוּב בּוֹ הֲלִיכָה, "מְלָשְׁנִי בַסֵּתֶר רֵעֵהוּ" (תהלים קא, ה), "לָשׁוֹן רְמִיָּה" (שם קכ, ב-ג), "לָשׁוֹן מְדַבֶּרֶת גְּדֹלוֹת" (שם יב, ד). לְכָךְ אֲנִי אוֹמֵר שֶׁהַלָּשׁוֹן "רָכִיל" לְשׁוֹן הוֹלֵךְ וּמְרַגֵּל, שֶׁהַכָּ"ף נֶחְלֶפֶת בְּגִימֶ"ל, שֶׁכָּל הָאוֹתִיּוֹת שֶׁמּוֹצָאֵיהֶן מִמָּקוֹם אֶחָד מִתְחַלְּפוֹת זוֹ בָּזוֹ: בֵּי"ת בְּפֵ"א, וְגִימֶ"ל בְּכָ"ף, וְקוּ"ף בְּכָ"ף, וְנוּ"ן בְּלָמֶ"ד, וְזַיִ"ן בְּצַדִּ"י. וְכֵן: "וַיְרַגֵּל בְּעַבְדְּךָ" (שמואל ב' יט, כח), רִגֵּל בְּמִרְמָה לֵאמֹר עָלַי רָעָה, וְכֵן: "לֹא רָגַל עַל לְשֹׁנוֹ" (תהלים טו, ג), וְכֵן רוֹכֵל, הַסּוֹחֵר וּמְרַגֵּל אַחַר כָּל סְחוֹרָה, וְכָל הַמּוֹכֵר בְּשָׂמִים לְהִתְקַשֵּׁט בָּהֶם הַנָּשִׁים, עַל שֵׁם שֶׁמְּחַזֵּר תָּמִיד בָּעֲיָרוֹת נִקְרָא רוֹכֵל, לְשׁוֹן רוֹגֵל. וְתַרְגּוּמוֹ: "לָא תֵיכוֹל קוּרְצִין", כְּמוֹ "וַאֲכַלוּ קַרְצֵיהוֹן דִּי יְהוּדָיֵא" (דניאל ג, ח), "אֲכַל בֵּיהּ קֻרְצָא בֵּי מַלְכָּא" (ברכות נח ע"א), נִרְאֶה בְּעֵינַי שֶׁהָיָה מִשְׁפָּטָם לֶאֱכֹל בְּבֵית הַמְקַבֵּל דִּבְרֵיהֶם שׁוּם הַלְעָטָה, וְהוּא גְּמַר חִזּוּק שֶׁדְּבָרָיו מְקֻיָּמִים וּמַעֲמִידָם עַל הָאֱמֶת, וְאוֹתָהּ הַלְעָטָה נִקְרֵאת 'אֲכִילַת קוּרְצִין', לְשׁוֹן: "קֹרֵץ בְּעֵינָו" (משלי ו, יג), שֶׁכֵּן דֶּרֶךְ כָּל הוֹלְכֵי רָכִיל לִקְרֹץ בְּעֵינֵיהֶם וְלִרְמֹז דִּבְרֵי רְכִילוּתָן, שֶׁלֹּא יָבִינוּ שְׁאָר הַשּׁוֹמְעִים: **לֹא תַעֲמֹד עַל דַּם רֵעֶךָ.** לִרְאוֹת בְּמִיתָתוֹ וְאַתָּה יָכוֹל לְהַצִּילוֹ, כְּגוֹן טוֹבֵעַ בַּנָּהָר וְחַיָּה אוֹ לִסְטִים בָּאִים עָלָיו: **אֲנִי ה'.** נֶאֱמָן לְשַׁלֵּם שָׂכָר, וְנֶאֱמָן לְפָּרַע:

יז | **וְלֹא תִשָּׂא עָלָיו חֵטְא.** לֹא תַלְבִּין אֶת פָּנָיו בָּרַבִּים:

יח | **לֹא תִקֹּם.** אָמַר לוֹ: הַשְׁאִילֵנִי מַגָּלְךָ, אָמַר לוֹ: לָאו. לְמָחָר אָמַר לוֹ: הַשְׁאִילֵנִי קַרְדֻּמְךָ, אָמַר לוֹ: אֵינִי מַשְׁאִילְךָ כְּדֶרֶךְ שֶׁלֹּא הִשְׁאַלְתַּנִי, זוֹ הִיא נְקִימָה. וְאֵיזוֹ הִיא נְטִירָה? אָמַר לוֹ: הַשְׁאִילֵנִי קַרְדֻּמְךָ, אָמַר לוֹ: לָאו. לְמָחָר אָמַר לוֹ: הַשְׁאִילֵנִי מַגָּלְךָ, אָמַר לוֹ: הֵא לְךָ, וְאֵינִי כְּמוֹתְךָ שֶׁלֹּא הִשְׁאַלְתַּנִי, זוֹ הִיא נְטִירָה, שֶׁנּוֹטֵר הָאֵיבָה בְּלִבּוֹ, אַף עַל פִּי שֶׁאֵינוֹ נוֹקֵם: **וְאָהַבְתָּ לְרֵעֲךָ כָּמוֹךָ.** אָמַר רַבִּי עֲקִיבָא: זֶה כְּלָל גָּדוֹל בַּתּוֹרָה:

DISCUSSION

rebuking him might lead him to mend his ways and thus resolve the issue (see Rashbam; Ramban; Abravanel; *Sefer Yere'im* 39). In any case, the verse does not demand a public expression of disapproval, but a direct address of one's neighbor in order to help him mend his ways. In this sense, this commandment is similar to the previous one: "You shall not stand by the blood of your neighbor."

19:18| **You shall not take vengeance; you shall not bear any grudge:** These prohibitions are related to the commandments of the previous verse. Even if one does not actually hate his neighbor, he may still harbor a grudge toward him. Perhaps had he rebuked his neighbor, he would not have come even to this.

You shall love your neighbor as yourself: A statement of Hillel the Elder seems to indicate that this commandment is the basis of the entire Torah; indeed, Rabbi Akiva says so explicitly (see *Shabbat* 31a; *Bereshit Rabba* 24; Rashi). Love is not merely positive interaction with another individual, but is also an emotional attitude. The commandment to love one's neighbor demands this emotional component as well. Nevertheless, from a legal perspective, it is impossible to demand these emotions from a person. Therefore, it seems that this commandment requires that an individual reflect on how to properly interact with his friend: to be sensitive and to keep his friend's best interests at heart, just as he would for himself, and to refrain from doing anything to another that he would himself consider painful, unpleasant, uncomfortable, or distasteful. Hillel the Elder interpreted the verse as follows: That which is hated by you, do not do to your friend (*Targum Yonatan*; *Shabbat* 31a). This formulation constitutes the minimal requirement of the verse to treat another as oneself (see *Bekhor Shor*; Ramban).

You shall love your neighbor as yourself, I am the Lord: The various commandments governing interpersonal relationships present a standard of behavior by which each individual is required to treat others as he himself wishes to be treated. Although the Torah does not offer a reason for this standard, it would seem that the basis for these commandments is the acknowledgment of the divine spark in each person. For this reason, the Sages explain that the command: "You shall love your neighbor as yourself," finds broader expression in the verse: "This is the book of the legacy of Adam…in the likeness of God He made him" (Genesis 5:1; Jerusalem Talmud, *Nedarim* 9:4; *Bereshit Rabba* 24:7).

Diverse Kinds, the Designated Maidservant, and Orla

LEVITICUS 19:19–25

After stating commandments which may be classified as ordinances, namely laws governing social norms and expectations, the verse lists several statutes, commandments that are divine decrees. Some of these statutes may be understood as aimed at preserving the established framework of the natural world.

19 **You shall observe My statutes; you shall not breed your animal with diverse kinds,** you shall not crossbreed them. The verse does not state that such diverse kinds are unpleasant, harmful, or otherwise dangerous. This prohibition is a divine decree for which there is no utilitarian explanation. Likewise, **you shall not sow your field with diverse kinds** of seeds; **and a garment that is a mixture**[D] **of diverse kinds,** of wool and linen, **shall not be put on by you.**

20 **A man, if he lies sexually with a woman, and she is a maidservant, designated for a man,**[D] **and she was not redeemed** with money, **or full freedom was not granted her,**[20] **there shall be an inspection.**[D] If she was a willing participant, she receives a punishment. However, **they shall not be put to death,** unlike in the case of a married woman, **because she,** the maidservant, **was not freed.** This transgression is not a capital offense. So long as she has not been fully freed, her bond to a man has an intermediate status, and she is not considered a married woman.

21 Nevertheless, since he has sinned, **he shall bring his guilt offering**[D] **to the Lord, to the entrance of the Tent of Meeting, a ram of a guilt offering.** Although he is not subject to formal punishment, his act must be remedied, and to that end he brings a ram as an offering.

22 **The priest shall atone for him with the ram of the guilt offering before the Lord for his sin that he has sinned; and he shall be forgiven for his sin that he has sinned.**

23 The following law is also built on a foundation of behavioral
Third
aliya
restraint and moderation: **When you come into the land and plant any food tree, then you shall seal [*araltem*] its fruit.** The first fruit must be treated as *orla.* The term *orla* appears elsewhere in reference to the foreskin which is removed in circumcision, as well as in the expressions: sealed lips, sealed ears, and sealed heart.[21] In all these cases, *orla* refers to a seal or covering that is unusable and must be removed.[22] For the first **three years it,** the food tree, **shall be sealed for you; it,** its fruit, **shall not be eaten.**

24 **And in the fourth year, all its fruit shall be sacred for praise to the Lord.** Fourth-year produce maintains a level of sanctity. According to tradition, it is not completely sacred, not completely set aside from the needs of people. Rather, its sanctity is expressed in the obligation to eat it in the environment of the Temple in an atmosphere of holiness and praise.[23]

25 **And in the fifth year, you may eat of its fruit,** as the tree is now considered ordinary. Not only may you eat of its fruit, but I will also cause the tree **to increase its yield for you,** as reward for observing My commandments: **I am the Lord your God.** This declaration is repeated here due to the difficulty in observing these commandments. It is difficult for one who has invested in a tree to refrain from eating its fruit day after day, year after year. In order for one to successfully do so, he must remember who commanded him to act in this manner.[24]

DISCUSSION

19:19 | A mixture [*sha'atnez*]: The source of this word is unknown, and its exact meaning is also unclear. According to the verse in Deuteronomy (22:11), it may be concluded that *sha'atnez* denotes a mixture of wool and linen (see *Shabbat* 26b). Perhaps this term comes from a foreign language, as it is not used in any other context, and it is one of the only words in the Bible with a five-letter root (see *Nidda* 61b; Ibn Ezra; Ramban).

19:20 | Designated for a man: The translation follows Onkelos, *Targum Yonatan,* and Rashi. Some, based on a similar Arabic term, render the phrase as follows: And she is a maidservant who was turned away from acquisition as a slave to betrothal to a man (Ibn Janaḥ; Rambam, *Guide of the Perplexed* 1:39). The verse does not refer to a Hebrew maidservant, but to a female slave from a foreign nation. Slaves in the households of Israel have the status of quasi-members of Israel. They are granted special rights and

privileges, and are even partially obligated in the commandments. The female slave described in the verse is not actually married, but lives with a Hebrew slave, in accordance with the verse in Exodus, which states that a master may give a female slave to his Hebrew slave, and their children will belong to the master (see Exodus 21:4; *Kiddushin* 15a).

There shall be an inspection [*bikkoret*]: Although in modern times *bikkoret* denotes an examination or inspection, it is clear from the ◄◄

יט אֶת־חֻקֹּתַי֮ תִּשְׁמֹרוּ֒ בְּהֶמְתְּךָ֙ לֹא־תַרְבִּ֣יעַ כִּלְאַ֔יִם שָׂדְךָ֖ לֹא־תִזְרַ֣ע כִּלְאָ֑יִם וּבֶ֤גֶד

כ כִּלְאַ֨יִם֙ שַֽׁעַטְנֵ֔ז לֹ֥א יַעֲלֶ֖ה עָלֶֽיךָ: וְ֠אִישׁ כִּֽי־יִשְׁכַּ֨ב אֶת־אִשָּׁ֜ה שִׁכְבַת־זֶ֗רַע וְהִ֤וא

שִׁפְחָה֙ נֶחֱרֶ֣פֶת לְאִ֔ישׁ וְהָפְדֵּה֙ לֹ֣א נִפְדָּ֔תָה א֥וֹ חֻפְשָׁ֖ה לֹ֣א נִתַּן־לָ֑הּ בִּקֹּ֧רֶת תִּהְיֶ֛ה

כא לֹ֥א יוּמְת֖וּ כִּי־לֹ֥א חֻפָּֽשָׁה: וְהֵבִ֤יא אֶת־אֲשָׁמוֹ֙ לַֽיהוָ֔ה אֶל־פֶּ֖תַח אֹ֣הֶל מוֹעֵ֑ד אֵ֖יל

כב אָשָֽׁם: וְכִפֶּר֩ עָלָ֨יו הַכֹּהֵ֜ן בְּאֵ֤יל הָֽאָשָׁם֙ לִפְנֵ֣י יְהוָ֔ה עַל־חַטָּאת֖וֹ אֲשֶׁ֣ר חָטָ֑א וְנִסְלַ֣ח

ל֔וֹ מֵֽחַטָּאת֖וֹ אֲשֶׁ֥ר חָטָֽא:

כג וְכִֽי־תָבֹ֣אוּ אֶל־הָאָ֗רֶץ וּנְטַעְתֶּם֙ כָּל־עֵ֣ץ מַֽאֲכָ֔ל וַֽעֲרַלְתֶּ֥ם עָרְלָת֖וֹ אֶת־פִּרְי֑וֹ שָׁלֹ֣שׁ **טז שלישי**

כד שָׁנִ֗ים יִהְיֶ֥ה לָכֶ֛ם עֲרֵלִ֖ים לֹ֣א יֵֽאָכֵֽל: וּבַשָּׁנָה֙ הָֽרְבִיעִ֔ת יִהְיֶ֖ה כָּל־פִּרְי֑וֹ קֹ֥דֶשׁ הִלּוּלִ֖ים

כה לַֽיהוָֽה: וּבַשָּׁנָ֣ה הַֽחֲמִישִׁ֗ת תֹּֽאכְלוּ֙ אֶת־פִּרְי֔וֹ לְהוֹסִ֥יף לָכֶ֖ם תְּבֽוּאָת֑וֹ אֲנִ֖י יְהוָ֥ה

רש"י

יט אֶת חֻקֹּתַי תִּשְׁמֹרוּ. וְאֵלּוּ הֵן: "בְּהֶמְתְּךָ לֹא תַרְבִּיעַ כִּלְאַיִם" וְגוֹ'. חֻקִּים אֵלּוּ גְּזֵרַת מֶלֶךְ, שֶׁאֵין טַעַם לַדָּבָר: וּבֶגֶד כִּלְאַיִם וְגוֹ'. לָמָּה נֶאֱמַר? לְפִי שֶׁנֶּאֱמַר: "לֹא תִלְבַּשׁ שַׁעַטְנֵז צֶמֶר וּפִשְׁתִּים יַחְדָּו" (דברים כב, יא), יָכוֹל לֹא יִלְבַּשׁ גִּזֵּי צֶמֶר וַאֲנִיצֵי פִשְׁתָּן? תַּלְמוּד לוֹמַר: "בֶּגֶד". מִנַּיִן לְרַבּוֹת הַלְּבָדִים? תַּלְמוּד לוֹמַר: "שַׁעַטְנֵז", דָּבָר שֶׁהוּא שׁוּעַ טָווּי וְנוּז. וְאוֹמֵר אֲנִי, "נוּז" לְשׁוֹן דָּבָר הַנִּמְלָל וְשָׁזוּר זֶה עִם זֶה לְחַבְּרוֹ, מֵיסְטְי"ר בְּלַעַ"ז, כְּמוֹ "חֲזַי לְנָחֲזֵי דְּחִית פְּהוֹן" (מועד קטן יב ע"ב), שֶׁאָנוּ מְפָרְשִׁין לְשׁוֹן כְּמוּשׁ, פייללוטרי"א. וּלְשׁוֹן "שַׁעַטְנֵז" פֵּרֵשׁ מְנַחֵם, מַחֲבֶרֶת צֶמֶר וּפִשְׁתִּים:

כ נֶחֱרֶפֶת לְאִישׁ. מְיֻעֶדֶת וּמְיֻחֶדֶת לְאִישׁ, וְאֵינִי יוֹדֵעַ לוֹ דִּמְיוֹן בַּמִּקְרָא, וּבְשִׁפְחָה כְנַעֲנִית שֶׁחֶצְיָהּ שִׁפְחָה וְחֶצְיָהּ בַּת חוֹרִין הַמְאֹרֶסֶת לְעֶבֶד עִבְרִי שֶׁמֻּתָּר בְּשִׁפְחָה הַכָּתוּב מְדַבֵּר: וְהָפְדֵּה לֹא

נִפְדָּתָה. פְּדוּיָה וְאֵינָהּ פְּדוּיָה, וּסְתַם פִּדְיוֹן בְּכֶסֶף, אוֹ חֻפְשָׁה. בִּשְׁטָר: בִּקֹּרֶת תִּהְיֶה. הִיא לוֹקָה וְלֹא הוּא. יֵשׁ עַל בֵּית דִּין לְבַקֵּר אֶת הַדָּבָר שֶׁלֹּא לְחַיְּבוֹ מִיתָה, "כִּי לֹא חֻפָּשָׁה" וְאֵין קִדּוּשֶׁיהָ קִדּוּשִׁין גְּמוּרִין. וְרַבּוֹתֵינוּ לָמְדוּ מִכָּאן, שֶׁמִּי שֶׁהוּא בְּמַלְקוּת – תְּהֵא בַקֹּרֶת, שֶׁהַדַּיָּנִים הַמַּלְקִין קוֹרִין עַל הַלּוֹקֶה: "אִם לֹא תִשְׁמֹר לַעֲשׂוֹת וְגוֹ' וְהִפְלָא ה' אֶת מַכֹּתְךָ" וְגוֹ' (דברים כח נח-נט): כִּי לֹא חֻפָּשָׁה. לְפִיכָךְ אֵין חַיָּב עָלֶיהָ מִיתָה, שֶׁאֵין קִדּוּשֶׁיהָ קִדּוּשִׁין, הָא חֻפָּשָׁה קִדּוּשֶׁיהָ קִדּוּשִׁין וְחַיָּב מִיתָה:

כא וְנִסְלַח לוֹ מֵחַטָּאתוֹ אֲשֶׁר חָטָא. לְרַבּוֹת אֶת הַמֵּזִיד כַּשּׁוֹגֵג:

כג וַעֲרַלְתֶּם עָרְלָתוֹ. וַאֲטַמְתֶּם אֲטִימָתוֹ, יְהֵא אָטוּם וְנִסְתָּם מִלֵּהָנוֹת מִמֶּנּוּ: שָׁלֹשׁ שָׁנִים יִהְיֶה לָכֶם עֲרֵלִים. מֵאֵימָתַי מוֹנֶה לוֹ? מִשְּׁעַת נְטִיעָתוֹ. יָכוֹל אִם הִצְנִיעוֹ

לְאַחַר שָׁלֹשׁ שָׁנִים יְהֵא מֻתָּר? תַּלְמוּד לוֹמַר: "יִהְיֶה", בַּהֲוָיָתוֹ יְהֵא:

כד יִהְיֶה כָּל פִּרְיוֹ קֹדֶשׁ. כְּמַעֲשֵׂר שֵׁנִי שֶׁכָּתוּב בּוֹ: "וְכָל מַעְשַׂר הָאָרֶץ וְגוֹ' קֹדֶשׁ לַה'" (ויקרא כז, ל), מָה מַעֲשֵׂר שֵׁנִי אֵינוֹ נֶאֱכָל חוּץ לְחוֹמַת יְרוּשָׁלַיִם אֶלָּא בְּפִדְיוֹן, אַף זֶה כֵּן. וְדָבָר זֶה "הִלּוּלִים לַה'" הוּא, שֶׁנּוֹשְׂאוֹ שָׁם לְשַׁבֵּחַ וּלְהַלֵּל לַשָּׁמָיִם:

כה לְהוֹסִיף לָכֶם תְּבוּאָתוֹ. הַמִּצְוָה הַזֹּאת שֶׁתִּשְׁמְרוּ תִּהְיֶה "לְהוֹסִיף לָכֶם תְּבוּאָתוֹ", שֶׁבִּשְׂכָרָהּ אֲנִי מְבָרֵךְ לָכֶם פֵּרוֹת הַנְּטִיעוֹת. הָיָה רַבִּי עֲקִיבָא אוֹמֵר: דִּבְּרָה תוֹרָה כְּנֶגֶד יֵצֶר הָרַע, שֶׁלֹּא יֹאמַר אָדָם, הֲרֵי אַרְבַּע שָׁנִים אֲנִי מִצְטַעֵר בּוֹ חִנָּם, לְפִיכָךְ נֶאֱמַר: "לְהוֹסִיף לָכֶם תְּבוּאָתוֹ": אֲנִי ה'. אֲנִי ה' הַמַּבְטִיחַ עַל כָּךְ, וְנֶאֱמָן לִשְׁמֹר הַבְטָחָתִי:

DISCUSSION

➤ context of the verse that this is not its meaning here. According to the Sages, the word *bikkoret* is related to *bakkar* cow; *keri'ah*, reading; and *bikkur*, inspection. Thus, the word *bikkoret* alludes to the punishment of lashes, which is administered with strips of cowhide and is accompanied by the recitation of verses. It is also preceded by a detailed inspection of the sentenced party, to determine the degree to which he can tolerate the punishment of lashes

(see *Keritut* 11a; *Pesikta Zutreta*; Ibn Ezra; see also *Adderet Eliyahu*, Exodus 21:3).

19:21 | He shall bring his guilt offering: This offering, known by the Sages as the guilt offering of the designated maidservant (*Zevaḥim* 54b), is brought by the man who lay with the maidservant. Although no punishment is specified for the woman, this relationship is certainly prohibited to both parties. According to rabbinic tradition, if the act was consensual, the woman

is flogged (*Keritut* 10b–11a). The man does not receive one of the standard punishments for transgressing a Torah prohibition, due to the intermediate status of the maidservant, as explained above. In this regard, this law resembles the laws of diverse kinds: After mentioning various problematic mixtures of animals, seeds, and threads, the verse discusses a prohibition involving a sort of mixture of people, namely the relationship between a freeman and a female slave (see Ibn Ezra, verse 20).

Eating over the Blood, Customs of Idolatry, Lewdness, Sabbath, Reverence for the Temple, and Honoring the Elderly
LEVITICUS 19:26–32

Some of the following laws are likely associated with idolatrous practices.

26 **You shall not eat over,** alongside, **the blood.**[D] It seems that this prohibition relates to the gentile custom of pouring the blood of animals and eating nearby, either as some form of an offering or based on a popular belief that the blood is offered to the dead, or to demons and the like.[25] **You shall not practice divination.** It is prohibited to perform an action that involves divination through the use of appurtenances or various rituals. **And you shall not practice soothsaying** in order to discern the future by looking at the shapes of clouds or by attributing certain qualities to seasons or times. For example, it is prohibited for one to say: Today is a propitious day for going away on a journey; tomorrow is propitious for purchasing successfully.[26] Such actions are prohibited because they involve an aspect of idolatry, if not actual idol worship.

27 **You shall not round the edge of your head,** the hairs that grow on the sides of your head. It is prohibited for one to shear all the hair around his head in an equal manner; rather, the hairs between one's ears and eyes must be left to grow. **And you shall not mar the edge of your beard.**[D] It is prohibited to completely shave off the hairs of one's beard.

Detail from the Black Obelisk of Shalmaneser III depicting bearded Israelites offering tribute together

28 **You shall not make a laceration for the dead in your flesh.** In ancient times, it was customary for mourners to lacerate their flesh as a sign of mourning. This prohibition constitutes one of the limitations imposed by the Torah on customs of mourning.[27] **And the imprint of a tattoo you shall not place upon you.**[D] Once again, the verse reiterates: **I am the Lord,** the ultimate authority, and I do not want you to practice such customs.

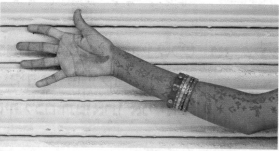

Tattoo

29 **Do not profane your daughter to pander her as a harlot.** That is, do not hand over your daughter to prostitution. To a certain degree, the requirement to guard a daughter's modesty is connected to her father's honor. Nevertheless, even if a father forgoes his honor and permits his daughter, or even encourages her, to engage in harlotry, the practice is entirely prohibited. **And** on a broader scale, **the land shall not become licentious, and the land will be filled with lewdness.** Casual sexual relationships between unmarried individuals are also forbidden. Although this is not explicitly formulated in the verse as a distinct prohibition, the verse stresses that sexual relations must be clearly defined, organized, and sanctified. When these relations are treated with abandon, the land is filled with licentiousness and even becomes impure.[28]

30 **You shall observe My Sabbaths**[D] **and you shall revere My Sanctuary:**[D] **I am the Lord.**

31 **Do not turn to mediums,** who communicate with the dead, **or to necromancers,**[D] magicians or witches who claim to communicate with the dead and acquire important information from them. **Do not seek to be defiled by them: I am the Lord your God.**

DISCUSSION

19:26 | You shall not eat over the blood: The elucidation follows one of the five or six interpretations offered by the Sages regarding this commandment. This prohibition is an example of what the Sages call a general prohibition: A single negative commandment that encompasses a variety of different cases (*Sanhedrin* 63a; see *Berakhot* 10b; *Vayikra Rabba* 25:8).

19:27 | You shall not round the edge of your head and you shall not mar the edge of your beard: The juxtaposition of these two prohibitions indicates that just as the latter prohibition

↤

כו כז אֱלֹהֵיכֶם׃ לֹא תֹאכְלוּ עַל־הַדָּם לֹא תְנַחֲשׁוּ וְלֹא תְעוֹנֵנוּ׃ לֹא תַקִּפוּ פְּאַת רֹאשְׁכֶם
כח וְלֹא תַשְׁחִית אֵת פְּאַת זְקָנֶךָ׃ וְשֶׂרֶט לָנֶפֶשׁ לֹא תִתְּנוּ בִּבְשַׂרְכֶם וּכְתֹבֶת קַעֲקַע
כט לֹא תִתְּנוּ בָּכֶם אֲנִי יְהוָה׃ אַל־תְּחַלֵּל אֶת־בִּתְּךָ לְהַזְנוֹתָהּ וְלֹא־תִזְנֶה הָאָרֶץ
ל לא וּמָלְאָה הָאָרֶץ זִמָּה׃ אֶת־שַׁבְּתֹתַי תִּשְׁמֹרוּ וּמִקְדָּשִׁי תִּירָאוּ אֲנִי יְהוָה׃ אַל־תִּפְנוּ
אֶל־הָאֹבֹת וְאֶל־הַיִּדְּעֹנִים אַל־תְּבַקְשׁוּ לְטָמְאָה בָהֶם אֲנִי יְהוָה אֱלֹהֵיכֶם׃

רש"י

כו| **לא תאכלו על הדם.** להרבה פנים נדרש בסנהדרין (דף סג ע"א), אזהרה שלא יאכל מבשר קדשים לפני זריקת דמים, ואזהרה לאוכל מבהמת חולין טרם שתצא נפשה, ועוד הרבה: **לא תנחשו.** כגון אלו המנחשין בחלדה ובעופות, פתו נפלה מפיו, צבי הפסיקו בדרך: **ולא תעוננו.** לשון עונות ושעות, שאומר, יום פלוני יפה להתחיל מלאכה, שעה פלונית קשה לצאת:

כז| **לא תקפו פאת ראשכם.** זה המשוה צדעיו לאחורי אזנו ולפדחתו, ונמצא הקף ראשו עגול סביב, שעל אחורי אזניו עקרי שערו למעלה מצדעיו הרבה: **פאת זקנך.** סוף הזקן וגבוליו, והן חמש: שתים בכל לחי ולחי למעלה אצל הראש, שהוא רחב ויש בו שתי פאות, ואחת למטה בסנטרו, מקום חבור שני הלחיים יחד:

כח| **ושרט לנפש.** כן דרכן של אמוריים להיות משרטין בשרם כשמת להם מת: **וכתבת קעקע.** כתב המחקה ושקוע שאינו נמחק לעולם, שמקעקעו במחט והוא משחיר לעולם: **קעקע.** לשון "והוקע אותם" (במדבר כה, ד), "והוקענום" (שמואל ב' כא, ו), תוחבין עץ בארץ ותולין אותם עליהם ונמצאו מחקין ותחובין בקרקע, פורפוינ"ט בלע"ז:

כט| **אל תחלל את בתך להזנותה.** במוסר בתו פנויה לביאה שלא לשם קדושין: **ולא תזנה הארץ.** אם אתה עושה כן, הארץ מזנה את פירותיה לעשותן במקום אחר ולא בארצכם, וכן הוא אומר "וימנעו רבבים" וגו' (ירמיה ג, ג):

ל| **ומקדשי תיראו.** לא יכנס לו במקלו ובמנעלו ובאפנדתו ובאבק שעל רגליו. ואף על פי שאני מזהירכם על המקדש, "את שבתתי תשמרו", אין בנין בית המקדש דוחה שבת:

לא| **אל תפנו אל האבת.** אזהרה לבעל אוב וידעוני. בעל אוב זה פיתום המדבר משחיו, וידעוני – המכניס עצם חיה ששמה 'ידוע' לתוך פיו והעצם מדבר: **אל תבקשו.** להיות עסוקים בם, שאם תעסקו בם אתם

DISCUSSION

applies only to men, so too the limitations on rounding the edges of one's head apply only to men. There is no such limitation with regard to the haircuts of women (*Kiddushin* 35b). Additionally, based on a comparison between this verse and other verses that discuss the shaving of one's beard, it is derived that the prohibition to shave one's beard applies only to shaving with a razor, but not to shaving with scissors and the like (see 14:9, 21:5; Isaiah 7:20; *Kiddushin* 35b).

There is no doubt that for generations it was customary for Jewish men to grow beards. Even in ancient depictions dating from the First Temple period, all Israelite males are depicted as bearded, although their beards were not long.

19:28| **And the imprint of a tattoo [*ketovet ka'aka*] you shall not place upon you**: Many opinions maintain that although any sort of tattoo is prohibited, the severe Torah prohibition applies specifically to imprinting the names of idols, and perhaps also their symbols (see *Makkot* 21a). The word *ka'aka* is unique, and its root and precise meaning are unclear. However, its appearance next to the prohibition against lacerating one's skin indicates that *ka'aka* refers to writing on one's flesh in a manner that the dye remains permanently, a tattoo (see Ibn Ezra).

19:30| **You shall observe My Sabbaths:** The commandment to observe the Sabbath also appears alongside commandments pertaining to the construction of the Tabernacle (see Exodus 35). Essentially, the verse seems to indicate that the commandment of the Sabbath is superior to the commandments of the Temple, as they follow the Sabbath in the verse (see *Yevamot* 6a).

And you shall revere My Sanctuary: Many practical ramifications stem from this obligation to revere the sacred environment of the Temple. For example, people would walk in the Temple and its surrounding areas without shoes, and when they would leave the Temple, they would walk backward so as not to turn their backs on the Temple (see *Berakhot* 54a; *Yoma* 53a).

19:31| **Do not turn to mediums or to necromancers:** Although the appeal to mediums and necromancers is not itself an act of idolatry, it is similar to idol worship, as it involves one's subjugation to dark forces, a false belief in the power of the dead, and a reverent attitude toward death (see *Responsa of Rav Avraham ben HaRambam* 20). As mentioned above, it is one's interaction with the dead that causes ritual impurity (see commentary on 14:45, 15:24). Death is outside the boundary of mankind, and people should avoid dealing with it. Of course, it is appropriate to honor the deceased, and there is no prohibition against visiting a cemetery. Nevertheless, since death, evil, and deprivation are all connected, it is absolutely prohibited to try communicating with the dead, either through the performance of some rite or through intermediaries.

32 **You shall rise** out of respect **before the graybeard,**[D] an old person, **and show deference before the elderly,**[D] a distinguished individual. Since an encounter with such distinguished individuals might occur outside the public eye, or even in a manner such that the distinguished individual is unaware of the encounter, one could avoid the elder or simply neglect to accord him due respect.[29] Therefore, the verse warns: **You shall fear your God;** the reverence of these individuals is closely related to the reverence of God. **I am the Lord.**

The Equation of the Stranger and the Native, and the Importance of Honesty in Business Dealings

LEVITICUS 19:33–37

33 **If a stranger,** someone of foreign origin, **resides with you in your land, you shall not mistreat him.** Do not cause him distress through hurtful comments, by cheating him, or in any other manner.[30] Obviously, it is prohibited to mistreat any person; however, since a stranger is unprotected and unfamiliar with local customs, there is greater opportunity, or even temptation, to upset, mock, or otherwise demean him.

Fourth aliya (Sixth aliya)

34 **Like a native of your own shall be for you the stranger that resides with you.**[D] You must treat him like one of your own, **and you shall love him as yourself, since you were strangers in the land of Egypt: I am the Lord your God,** that is, both your God and his. Alternatively, the verse means: Your fear of God will be confirmed through your respect and love for the stranger.

35 **You shall do no injustice in judgment.**[D] It is prohibited to deviate from the truth and from proper balance in judgment. Similarly, there may be no injustice or deviation **in measure,** measurements of area or volume, **in weight, or in** liquid **volume.** Likewise, it is prohibited to tamper with measuring implements.

36 The verse elaborates: **Accurate scales, accurate weights, an accurate dry measure, and an accurate liquid measure, you shall have.** You must take care to ensure that all such measuring implements are precise. **I am the Lord your God, who took you out of the land of Egypt.**

37 **You shall observe all My statutes, and all My ordinances,** namely My instructions for how to interact with others and with the world at large, **and perform them: I am the Lord.**[D]

The Punishments for Severe Transgressions Involving Illicit Familial Relationships

LEVITICUS 20:1–21

The Torah now returns to the laws pertaining to forbidden sexual relations discussed at the end of *Parashat Aḥarei Mot*. There, the Torah delineates the various prohibited relationships, but the punishment for their transgression is listed only as excision at the hands of Heaven. Here, the Torah describes other forms of punishment as well, in particular punishments to be administered by the courts.

20 1 **The Lord spoke to Moses, saying:**

Fifth aliya

2 **And to the children of Israel you shall say: Each man from the children of Israel, or from the strangers that reside in Israel, who gives of his offspring to** the worship of **Molekh,**[31] **he shall be put to death; the people of the land,** the community, **shall stone him with stones.**[32]

DISCUSSION

19:32 | **You shall rise before the graybeard:** The rabbinic definition of a graybeard depends on age. One who is seventy years old is considered to have reached this status (see *Avot* 5:21; *Tikkunei Zohar* 21; Rosh, *Kiddushin* 1:53; *Shulḥan Arukh, Yoreh De'a* 244:1).

The purpose of rising before the graybeard is not to vacate a seat for him, but to express respect toward the elder, specifically toward the years he has lived and his accumulated life experience (see *Kiddushin* 33a).

And show deference before the elderly [*zaken*]: The term *zaken* does not refer specifically to one who is old; it is often used as an indication of a special status. For instance, the expressions "the elders [*ziknei*] of the assembly" or "the elders of the people" refer primarily to the leaders or wise men of Israel, although it is often the case that such individuals are advanced in years (see 4:15; Exodus 3:16, 19:7; *Kiddushin* 32b–33a). In many other languages and cultures as well, communal leaders are known as elders.

19:34 | **Like a native of your own shall be for you the stranger that resides with you:** According to many commentaries, the verse refers specifically to a convert (see Onkelos; *Targum Yonatan*; Rashi on 19:23; *Yevamot* 46b). A convert has no family, has uprooted himself from his home, and has limited protection in society. However, the comparison of the stranger to the children of Israel in Egypt would seem to indicate that the verse refers to all foreigners (see Deuteronomy 23:16, and *Sifrei* ad loc.; *Gerim* 3:2; Jerusalem Talmud, *Yevamot* 8:1; Ibn

לב לג מִפְּנֵי שֵׂיבָה תָּקוּם וְהָדַרְתָּ פְּנֵי זָקֵן וְיָרֵאתָ מֵּאֱלֹהֶיךָ אֲנִי יהוה: וְכִי־יָגוּר רביעי /ששי/
לד אִתְּךָ גֵּר בְּאַרְצְכֶם לֹא תוֹנוּ אֹתוֹ: כְּאֶזְרָח מִכֶּם יִהְיֶה לָכֶם הַגֵּר | הַגָּר אִתְּכֶם
לה וְאָהַבְתָּ לוֹ כָּמוֹךָ כִּי־גֵרִים הֱיִיתֶם בְּאֶרֶץ מִצְרָיִם אֲנִי יהוה אֱלֹהֵיכֶם: לֹא־תַעֲשׂוּ
לו עָוֶל בַּמִּשְׁפָּט בַּמִּדָּה בַּמִּשְׁקָל וּבַמְּשׂוּרָה: מֹאזְנֵי צֶדֶק אַבְנֵי־צֶדֶק אֵיפַת צֶדֶק
וְהִין צֶדֶק יִהְיֶה לָכֶם אֲנִי יהוה אֱלֹהֵיכֶם אֲשֶׁר־הוֹצֵאתִי אֶתְכֶם מֵאֶרֶץ מִצְרָיִם:
לז וּשְׁמַרְתֶּם אֶת־כָּל־חֻקֹּתַי וְאֶת־כָּל־מִשְׁפָּטַי וַעֲשִׂיתֶם אֹתָם אֲנִי יהוה:
א ב וַיְדַבֵּר יהוה אֶל־מֹשֶׁה לֵּאמֹר: וְאֶל־בְּנֵי יִשְׂרָאֵל תֹּאמַר אִישׁ אִישׁ מִבְּנֵי יִשְׂרָאֵל וּמִן־ חמישי
הַגֵּר | הַגָּר בְּיִשְׂרָאֵל אֲשֶׁר יִתֵּן מִזַּרְעוֹ לַמֹּלֶךְ מוֹת יוּמָת עַם הָאָרֶץ יִרְגְּמֻהוּ בָאָבֶן:

רש״י

מטמאין לפני ואני מתעב אתכם: **אני ה׳ אלהיכם.** דעו את מי אתם מחליפין במי:

לב| **מפני שיבה תקום.** יכול זקן אשמאי? תלמוד לומר: "זקן", אין זקן אלא שקנה חכמה: **והדרת פני זקן.** איזהו הדור? לא ישב במקומו ולא ידבר במקומו ולא יסתר את דבריו. יכול יעצים עיניו כמי שלא ראהו? לכך נאמר: "ויראת מאלהיך", שהרי דבר זה מסור ללבו של עושהו, שאין מכיר בו אלא הוא, וכל דבר המסור ללב נאמר בו: "ויראת מאלהיך":

לג| **לא תונו.** אונאת דברים, לא תאמר לו, אמש היית עובד עבודה זרה ועכשיו אתה בא ללמד תורה שנתנה מפי הגבורה:

לד| **כי גרים הייתם.** מום שבך אל תאמר לחברך: **אני ה׳ אלהיכם.** אלהיך ואלהיו אני: ה לה| **לא תעשו עול במשפט.** אם לדין, הרי כבר נאמר: "לא תעשו עול במשפט" (לעיל פסוק טו), ומהו "משפט" השנוי כאן? הוא המדה והמשקל והמשורה, מלמד שהמודד נקרא דין, שאם שקר במדה הרי הוא כמקלקל את הדין, וקרוי עול שנוי ומשקץ חרם ותועבה, וגורם לחמשה דברים האמורים בדין: מטמא את הארץ, ומחלל את השם, ומסלק את השכינה, ומפיל את ישראל בחרב, ומגלה אותם מארצם: **במדה.** זו מדת הארץ: **במשקל.** כמשמעו: **ובמשורה.** היא מדת הלח והיבש:

לו| **אבני צדק.** הם המשקולות ששוקלין כנגדן: **איפה.** היא מדת היבש: **הין.** זו היא מדת הלח: **אשר הוצאתי אתכם.** על מנת כן. דבר אחר, אני הבחנתי במצרים בין טפה של בכור לטפה שאינה של בכור, ואני הנאמן לפרע ממי שטומן משקלותיו במלח להונות את הבריות שאין מכירים בהם:

פרק כ

ב| **ואל בני ישראל תאמר.** עונשין על האזהרות: **מות יומת.** בבית דין. ואם אין כח בבית דין, "עם הארץ" מסייעין אותן: **עם הארץ.** שבגינו נבראת הארץ, שעתידין לירש את הארץ על ידי מצוות הללו:

ג| **אתן את פני.** פנאי שלי, פונה אני מכל עסקי ועוסק בו: **באיש.** ולא בצבור, שאין כל הצבור נכרתין: **כי מזרעו נתן למלך.** לפי שנאמר: "מעביר בנו ובתו באש" (דברים יח, י), בן בנו ובן בתו מנין? תלמוד לומר: "כי מזרעו נתן למלך". זרע פסול מנין? תלמוד לומר: "בתתו מזרעו למלך" (להלן פסוק ד): **למען טמא את מקדשי.** את כנסת ישראל שהיא מקדשת לי, כלשון: "ולא יחלל את מקדשי" (להלן כא, כג):

DISCUSSION

Ezra, Exodus 23:9). In any case, the verse states: Since you, the children of Israel, were yourselves strangers for many years, "you know the soul of a stranger" (Exodus 23:9), you are familiar with the experience of an exile in a foreign land.

19:35 | **You shall do no injustice in judgment:** Although this prohibition was already mentioned above (19:15), the verse here does not refer only to formal adjudication. Rather, it includes any erroneous judgment of another, even when such assessments are nonbinding. The temptation to judge others unfairly can ultimately lead one to make unjust decisions. The verse therefore warns against all unjust assessments of others (see *Sifra*).

19:36–37 | **I am the Lord your God, who took you out of the land of Egypt…I am the Lord:** Elsewhere, the verse states that God took the children of Israel out of Egypt to be His servants (25:55). That is, their redemption was for His honor and so that they would serve as His legion. God brought them out of Egypt in order for them to become a special nation that follows its own unique system of law, whether in interpersonal matters or those between man and God.

The meaning of the phrase "I am the Lord" is that God is Commander, and God is all-knowing, and one must act with an awareness of this truth. Aside from this, the declaration "I am the Lord your God" refers to God's particular authority over Israel as their King. In general, the phrase "I am the Lord" is applied to matters of ethics or intrapersonal behavior, whereas the phrase "I am the Lord your God" emphasizes the establishment of particular laws and statutes. It is interesting to note that each of these expressions appears ten times in *Parashat Kedoshim*.

3 Meanwhile,[33] **I shall direct My attention to that man and will excise him from the midst of his people, because he gave of his offspring to Molekh, in order to defile My Sanctuary, and to profane My sacred name.** Aside from the actual sin of idol worship, this act constitutes a severe desecration of God's name.

4 **If the people of the land avert their eyes from that man, when he gives of his offspring to Molekh, and do not put him to death;** that is, if they do not fulfill their duty to execute him, such as in a case where the judges share the same false beliefs as those on trial,

5 **I will direct My attention to that man and to his family, and I will excise him**[D] **and everyone who strays after him,**[D] **to stray after Molekh, from the midst of their people.**

6 **The person who turns to the mediums or to the necromancers,** who communicate with the dead,[34] **to stray after them** by seeking their council, **I will direct My attention to that person**[D] **and will excise him from the midst of his people.** The verse does not state that such individuals are punished by the court; rather, they are punished by God.[35] Other early commentaries maintain that one who turns to a medium is not punished by excision, but has indeed transgressed a prohibition.[36]

7 In general, **you shall sanctify yourselves, and you shall be holy.** This statement refers both to the previous verses and the following ones. Some of these statutes apply specifically to the children of Israel and are not universal, while others are universally considered repulsive. In any case, the main focus of this passage is the special level of sanctity that the nation of Israel must uphold. **For I am the Lord your God,** and therefore you must be committed to this sanctity.

8 **You shall observe My statutes and perform them: I am the Lord who sanctifies you.** I am the One who bestows upon you a unique status, and therefore you must observe My commandments, both the simple, understandable ones, and those which may appear to you as the arbitrary decrees of a King.

Sixth aliya (Seventh aliya)

9 **For each man who curses his father or his mother,** even if he does not harm them in any other way, **shall be put to death; he cursed his father or his mother; his blood is upon him,** on his hands. He is guilty and shall be punished for his transgression in this world. The obligation to honor one's parents also appears in the Ten Precepts.[37] Here, however, the verse emphasizes the severity of dishonoring one's parents and the accompanying punishment. In other cultures as well, it is considered inappropriate to curse another, let alone one's parents. However, in the framework of the sanctity of Israel such behavior is absolutely intolerable. One who curses his parents is therefore sentenced to death.

10 **A man who commits adultery with the wife of a man,** that is, **who commits adultery with the wife of his neighbor, the adulterer and the adulteress shall be put to death.** The repetitive language of the verse points to the dual aspects of the crime of adultery: Transgression of a prohibition, as well as injury to one's neighbor. The prohibition against adultery with the wife of a man points to the religious aspect, while the prohibition against committing adultery with the wife of one's neighbor points to its social aspect. Not all prohibitions of a sexual nature directly affect a third party, but the adulterer sins against both God and his fellow man.

11 **The man that lies with his father's wife, he has uncovered his father's nakedness,** the act is shameful and disgraceful to his father; **both of them shall be put to death; their blood is upon them.**[D]

12 **If a man lies with his daughter-in-law, both of them shall be put to death; they have performed a perversion; their blood is upon them.** Alternatively, the verse means: Father and son have mixed up one woman between them.[38] This prohibition parallels the previous one, as lying with the wife of one's father and lying with one's daughter-in-law are two sides of the same coin. However, in the instance of lying with one's father's wife, there is an aspect of shaming one's father, while in the instance of lying with one's daughter-in-law, the verse stresses the repulsive intermingling and partnering.

13 **A man who lies with a male, in the manner that one lies with a woman,** willingly and with consent, **both of them have performed an abomination.** Just as in the cases involving relations between a man and a woman, this prohibition applies equally to both the active and passive participants. **They shall be put to death** by stoning; **their blood is upon them.**

DISCUSSION

20:5| **And I will excise him:** There are several explanations of the nature of *karet*, excision, including an untimely death, and the even more severe penalty of excision of one's soul from the world (see commentary on 22:9). When one is penalized in this world, the punishment serves to atone for his sins and remove their record; this is why such punishments are prevalent in the Torah. By contrast, if a person is not reprimanded in this world but only in another, his punishment is more severe, more permanent, and affects his very existence.

Everyone who strays after him: The word *zonim*, meaning stray, is derived from the word *zona*, meaning prostitute. Worship of false gods is understood as a kind of prostituting of oneself.

ג וַאֲנִי אֶתֵּן אֶת־פָּנַי בָּאִישׁ הַהוּא וְהִכְרַתִּי אֹתוֹ מִקֶּרֶב עַמּוֹ כִּי מִזַּרְעוֹ נָתַן לַמֹּלֶךְ

ד לְמַעַן טַמֵּא אֶת־מִקְדָּשִׁי וּלְחַלֵּל אֶת־שֵׁם קָדְשִׁי: וְאִם הַעְלֵם יַעְלִימוּ עַם הָאָרֶץ אֶת־עֵינֵיהֶם מִן־הָאִישׁ הַהוּא בְּתִתּוֹ מִזַּרְעוֹ לַמֹּלֶךְ לְבִלְתִּי הָמִית אֹתוֹ:

ה וְשַׂמְתִּי אֲנִי אֶת־פָּנַי בָּאִישׁ הַהוּא וּבְמִשְׁפַּחְתּוֹ וְהִכְרַתִּי אֹתוֹ וְאֵת ׀ כָּל־הַזֹּנִים

ו אַחֲרָיו לִזְנוֹת אַחֲרֵי הַמֹּלֶךְ מִקֶּרֶב עַמָּם: וְהַנֶּפֶשׁ אֲשֶׁר תִּפְנֶה אֶל־הָאֹבֹת וְאֶל־הַיִּדְּעֹנִים לִזְנֹת אַחֲרֵיהֶם וְנָתַתִּי אֶת־פָּנַי בַּנֶּפֶשׁ הַהִוא וְהִכְרַתִּי אֹתוֹ מִקֶּרֶב

ז עַמּוֹ: וְהִתְקַדִּשְׁתֶּם וִהְיִיתֶם קְדֹשִׁים כִּי אֲנִי יְהוָה אֱלֹהֵיכֶם: וּשְׁמַרְתֶּם אֶת־

ח חֻקֹּתַי וַעֲשִׂיתֶם אֹתָם אֲנִי יְהוָה מְקַדִּשְׁכֶם: כִּי־אִישׁ אִישׁ אֲשֶׁר יְקַלֵּל אֶת־אָבִיו

י וְאֶת־אִמּוֹ מוֹת יוּמָת אָבִיו וְאִמּוֹ קִלֵּל דָּמָיו בּוֹ: וְאִישׁ אֲשֶׁר יִנְאַף אֶת־אֵשֶׁת

יא אִישׁ אֲשֶׁר יִנְאַף אֶת־אֵשֶׁת רֵעֵהוּ מוֹת־יוּמַת הַנֹּאֵף וְהַנֹּאָפֶת: וְאִישׁ אֲשֶׁר

יב יִשְׁכַּב אֶת־אֵשֶׁת אָבִיו עֶרְוַת אָבִיו גִּלָּה מוֹת־יוּמְתוּ שְׁנֵיהֶם דְּמֵיהֶם בָּם: וְאִישׁ

יג אֲשֶׁר יִשְׁכַּב אֶת־כַּלָּתוֹ מוֹת יוּמְתוּ שְׁנֵיהֶם תֶּבֶל עָשׂוּ דְּמֵיהֶם בָּם: וְאִישׁ אֲשֶׁר יִשְׁכַּב אֶת־זָכָר מִשְׁכְּבֵי אִשָּׁה תּוֹעֵבָה עָשׂוּ שְׁנֵיהֶם מוֹת יוּמָתוּ דְּמֵיהֶם בָּם:

שׁשׁי /שׁביעי/

ד וְאִם הַעְלֵם יַעְלִימוּ. אִם הֶעְלִימוּ בְּדָבָר אֶחָד סוֹף שֶׁיַּעְלִימוּ בִּדְבָרִים הַרְבֵּה, אִם הֶעְלִימוּ סַנְהֶדְרֵי קְטַנָּה סוֹף שֶׁיַּעְלִימוּ סַנְהֶדְרֵי גְדוֹלָה:

ה וּבְמִשְׁפַּחְתּוֹ. אָמַר רַבִּי שִׁמְעוֹן: וְכִי מִשְׁפָּחָה מֶה חָטְאָה? אֶלָּא לְלַמֶּדְךָ שֶׁאֵין לְךָ מִשְׁפָּחָה שֶׁיֵּשׁ בָּהּ מוֹכֵס שֶׁאֵין כֻּלָּם מוֹכְסִין, שֶׁכֻּלָּן מְחַפִּין עָלָיו: וְהִכְרַתִּי אֹתוֹ. לָמָּה נֶאֱמַר? לְפִי שֶׁנֶּאֱמַר: "וּבְמִשְׁפַּחְתּוֹ", יָכוֹל יִהְיוּ כָּל הַמִּשְׁפָּחָה בְּהִכָּרֵת? תַּלְמוּד לוֹמַר: "אֹתוֹ", אוֹתוֹ בְּהִכָּרֵת וְלֹא כָל הַמִּשְׁפָּחָה בְּהִכָּרֵת אֶלָּא בְּיִסּוּרִין: לִזְנוֹת אַחֲרֵי

הַמֹּלֶךְ. לְרַבּוֹת שְׁאָר עֲבוֹדָה זָרָה שֶׁעֲבָדָהּ בְּכָךְ, וַחֲפָלוּ אֵין זוֹ עֲבוֹדָתָהּ:

ו וְהִתְקַדִּשְׁתֶּם. זוֹ פְּרִישׁוּת עֲבוֹדָה זָרָה:

ט אָבִיו וְאִמּוֹ קִלֵּל. לְרַבּוֹת לְאַחַר מִיתָה: דָּמָיו בּוֹ. זוֹ סְקִילָה, וְכֵן כָּל מָקוֹם שֶׁנֶּאֱמַר: "דָּמָיו בּוֹ", "דְּמֵיהֶם בָּם". וּלְמַדְנוּ מֵאוֹב וְיִדְּעוֹנִי שֶׁנֶּאֱמַר בָּהֶם: "בָּאֶבֶן יִרְגְּמוּ אֹתָם דְּמֵיהֶם בָּם" (להלן פסוק כז). וּפְשׁוּטוֹ שֶׁל מִקְרָא: "דָּמוֹ בְרֹאשׁוֹ" (יהושע ב, יט), אֵין נֶעֱנָשׁ עַל מִיתָתוֹ אֶלָּא הוּא שֶׁהוּא גָּרַם לְעַצְמוֹ שֶׁיֵּהָרֵג:

י וְאִישׁ. פְּרָט לְקָטָן: אֲשֶׁר יִנְאַף אֶת אֵשֶׁת אִישׁ. פְּרָט לְאֵשֶׁת קָטָן, לִמְּדָנוּ שֶׁאֵין לְקָטָן קִדּוּשִׁין. וְעַל אֵיזוֹ אֵשֶׁת אִישׁ חִיַּבְתִּי לְךָ? "אֲשֶׁר יִנְאַף אֶת אֵשֶׁת רֵעֵהוּ", פְּרָט לְאֵשֶׁת גּוֹי, לִמְּדָנוּ שֶׁאֵין קִדּוּשִׁין לְגוֹי: מוֹת יוּמַת הַנֹּאֵף וְהַנֹּאָפֶת. כָּל מִיתָה הָאֲמוּרָה בַּתּוֹרָה סְתָם אֵינָהּ אֶלָּא חֶנֶק:

יב תֶּבֶל עָשׂוּ. גְּנַאי. לָשׁוֹן אַחֵר, מְבַלְבְּלִין זֶרַע הָאָב בְּזֶרַע הַבֵּן:

יג מִשְׁכְּבֵי אִשָּׁה. מַכְנִיס כְּמִכְחוֹל בִּשְׁפוֹפֶרֶת:

DISCUSSION

20:6 | The person who turns to the mediums or to the necromancers to stray after them, I will direct My attention to that person: King Saul consulted a medium (I Samuel 28:3–20),

and the book of Chronicles states explicitly that this was one of the causes of his untimely death (I Chronicles 10:13).

20:11 | Their blood is upon them: According to tradition, the phrase "their blood is upon them" alludes to the punishment of death by stoning (see Rashi, verse 9; *Sanhedrin* 54a).

14 **A man who takes a woman and her mother,** or a woman and her daughter, as the order makes no difference, **it is lewdness.**[39] While the case where two male relatives have relations with one woman is described by the verse as a perversion, the case where one man has relations with two related women is described as lewdness. This lewdness stems from the fact that both women are intermingled in his thoughts, his imagination, and his life. **He and they shall be burned in fire,**[D] **and there shall be no lewdness among you.**

15 **A man who copulates with an animal, he shall be put to death; and the animal you shall kill.** Obviously, an animal does not possess mental competence and cannot be considered guilty of a transgression. Nevertheless, it is put to death due to the shame that was brought upon the children of Israel through it, and because it was a stumbling block for people.[40] In other words, the man is put to death for his transgression, while the animal is killed because it was used in the performance of the transgression, just as vegetation or vessels used for idol worship must be destroyed.[41]

16 Similarly, **a woman who approaches any animal** in order for it **to copulate with her, you shall kill the woman and the animal. They shall be put to death** by stoning; **their blood is upon them.**

17 The verse now turns to prohibitions for which a punishment to be administered by the courts is not prescribed; rather, one who transgresses these prohibitions is liable to receive excision: **A man who takes his sister, daughter of his father or daughter of his mother,** meaning even if she is his half-sister, **and he sees her nakedness, and she sees his nakedness, it is a disgrace [*ḥesed*].** *Ḥesed* resembles the Aramaic term *ḥisuda,* disgrace. Note that *ḥesed,* which usually means kindness in Hebrew, is a contronym, a word with two opposite meanings. **And they shall be excised in the sight of the members of their people; he has uncovered his sister's nakedness; he shall bear his iniquity.** By describing a scenario in which each sibling sees the nakedness of the other, the verse makes it clear that it does not refer to a case where a young sister falls victim to incestuous rape by her older brother, but to a mutual act in which two consenting adults are aware of their actions and proceed deliberately.[42]

18 **A man who lies with a menstruating**[D] **woman, and he uncovered her nakedness, he has probed,** specifically in a negative, sexual sense, **her source** of blood, **and she has exposed the source of her blood.** Once again, the verse stresses the participation of each side, as it is possible for this act to occur at the hands of the man alone, e.g., in the case of a man who forces himself on his wife who is menstruating.[43] If the woman uncovers her nakedness knowingly and willingly, then **both of them shall be excised** by the hand of Heaven **from the midst of their people.**

19 **The nakedness of the sister of your mother and the sister of your father you shall not uncover; for he exposed his kin,** as they are blood relatives; **they shall** both **bear their iniquity.**[D]

20 **A man who lies with his aunt,** the wife of his father's brother or mother's brother, **he exposed his uncle's nakedness, they shall bear their sin; they shall die childless.**

21 **A man who takes his brother's wife** as a wife for himself, even if she is no longer married to the brother, e.g., they divorced or the brother died, **it is an abhorrent**[D] act;[44] **he exposed his brother's nakedness; they shall be childless.**

DISCUSSION

20:14| **He and they shall be burned in fire:** Most of the punishments prescribed by the Torah are not described in detail. According to tradition, the punishment of death by burning is not actual burning but death caused indirectly by fire, specifically by pouring molten lead down the throat of the condemned (see *Sanhedrin* 52a).

The Sages have a tradition, and derive from the verses, that capital punishment as prescribed by the Torah is administered only if the offender was forewarned at the time of the act, and only if he explicitly acknowledged the warning and indicated that he is performing the deed with full knowledge of the punishment it entails. Consequently, it is easy to surmise that the death penalty was rarely imposed in practice, and that when it was administered, it was only to those who acted brazenly, as a blatant declaration of rebellion against God (see *Sanhedrin* 40–41; *Makkot* 7a; Rosh, *Moed Katan*, chap. 3).

20:18| **Menstruating [*dava*]:** The word *dava,* implying suffering, alludes to menstruation, which is usually accompanied by some discomfort (see Deuteronomy 7:15). Perhaps there is a connection between *dava* and the root *dalet-va-v-beit,* which refers to flowing, as one who suffers sheds tears. In this sense, *dava* is related to *zava,* a woman who experiences a discharge of uterine blood after her menstrual period, and to *nidda,* a menstruating woman, in terms of their literal meanings (see Ralbag, II Samuel 10:4).

20:19| **They shall bear their iniquity:** The punishment for one who lies with the sister of his father or mother is not stated explicitly in the verse, unlike the previous prohibitions, for which the verse clearly states: "Both of them shall be excised," or: "They shall be put to death," and the like. Perhaps this is in order to preserve the honor of Moses, leader of Israel, who was born to Amram and Yokheved, the sister of Amram's father. Although some of these laws are not included in the seven Noahide laws and

יד וְאִ֗ישׁ אֲשֶׁ֨ר יִקַּ֧ח אֶת־אִשָּׁ֛ה וְאֶת־אִמָּ֖הּ זִמָּ֣ה הִ֑וא בָּאֵ֞שׁ יִשְׂרְפ֣וּ אֹתוֹ֙ וְאֶתְהֶ֔ן וְלֹא־
טו תִהְיֶ֥ה זִמָּ֖ה בְּתוֹכְכֶֽם׃ וְאִ֗ישׁ אֲשֶׁ֨ר יִתֵּ֧ן שְׁכׇבְתּ֛וֹ בִּבְהֵמָ֖ה מ֣וֹת יוּמָ֑ת וְאֶת־הַבְּהֵמָ֖ה
טז תַּהֲרֹֽגוּ׃ וְאִשָּׁ֗ה אֲשֶׁ֨ר תִּקְרַ֤ב אֶל־כׇּל־בְּהֵמָה֙ לְרִבְעָ֣ה אֹתָ֔הּ וְהָרַגְתָּ֥ אֶת־הָאִשָּׁ֖ה
יז וְאֶת־הַבְּהֵמָ֑ה מ֥וֹת יוּמָ֖תוּ דְּמֵיהֶ֥ם בָּֽם׃ וְאִ֣ישׁ אֲשֶׁר־יִקַּ֣ח אֶת־אֲחֹת֡וֹ בַּת־אָבִ֣יו א֣וֹ
בַת־אִ֠מּ֠וֹ וְרָאָ֨ה אֶת־עֶרְוָתָ֜הּ וְהִֽיא־תִרְאֶ֤ה אֶת־עֶרְוָתוֹ֙ חֶ֣סֶד ה֔וּא וְנִ֨כְרְת֔וּ לְעֵינֵ֖י
יח בְּנֵ֣י עַמָּ֑ם עֶרְוַ֧ת אֲחֹת֛וֹ גִּלָּ֖ה עֲוֺנ֥וֹ יִשָּֽׂא׃ וְ֠אִ֠ישׁ אֲשֶׁר־יִשְׁכַּ֨ב אֶת־אִשָּׁ֜ה דָּוָ֗ה וְגִלָּ֤ה
אֶת־עֶרְוָתָהּ֙ אֶת־מְקֹרָ֣הּ הֶֽעֱרָ֔ה וְהִ֕וא גִּלְּתָ֖ה אֶת־מְק֣וֹר דָּמֶ֑יהָ וְנִכְרְת֥וּ שְׁנֵיהֶ֖ם
יט מִקֶּ֥רֶב עַמָּֽם׃ וְעֶרְוַ֨ת אֲח֧וֹת אִמְּךָ֛ וַאֲח֥וֹת אָבִ֖יךָ לֹ֣א תְגַלֵּ֑ה כִּ֧י אֶת־שְׁאֵר֛וֹ הֶעֱרָ֖ה
כ עֲוֺנָ֥ם יִשָּֽׂאוּ׃ וְאִ֗ישׁ אֲשֶׁ֤ר יִשְׁכַּב֙ אֶת־דֹּ֣דָת֔וֹ עֶרְוַ֥ת דֹּד֖וֹ גִּלָּ֑ה חֶטְאָ֥ם יִשָּׂ֖אוּ עֲרִירִ֥ים
כא יָמֻֽתוּ׃ וְאִ֗ישׁ אֲשֶׁ֥ר יִקַּ֛ח אֶת־אֵ֥שֶׁת אָחִ֖יו נִדָּ֣ה הִ֑וא עֶרְוַ֥ת אָחִ֛יו גִּלָּ֖ה עֲרִירִ֥ים יִהְיֽוּ׃

רש"י

יד| **יִשְׂרְפוּ אֹתוֹ וְאֶתְהֶן.** אִי אַתָּה יָכוֹל לוֹמַר אִשְׁתּוֹ הָרִאשׁוֹנָה יִשְׂרְפוּ, שֶׁהֲרֵי נְשָׂאָהּ בְּהֶתֵּר וְלֹא נֶאֶסְרָה עָלָיו, אֶלָּא "אִשָּׁה וְאִמָּהּ" הַכְּתוּבִין כָּאן שְׁתֵּיהֶן לְאִסּוּר, שֶׁנָּשָׂא חֲמוֹתוֹ וְאִמָּהּ. וְיֵשׁ מֵרַבּוֹתֵינוּ שֶׁאוֹמְרִים, אֵין כָּאן אֶלָּא חֲמוֹתוֹ, וּמַהוּ "אֶתְהֶן"? אֶת אַחַת מֵהֶן, וּלְשׁוֹן יְוָנִי הוּא: 'הֵן' – אַחַת:

טו| **וְאֶת הַבְּהֵמָה תַּהֲרֹגוּ.** אִם אָדָם חָטָא, בְּהֵמָה מֶה חָטְאָה? אֶלָּא מִפְּנֵי שֶׁבָּאָה לָאָדָם תַּקָּלָה עַל יָדָהּ לְפִיכָךְ אָמַר הַכָּתוּב תִּסָּקֵל, קַל וָחֹמֶר לָאָדָם שֶׁיּוֹדֵעַ לְהַבְחִין בֵּין טוֹב לְרָע וְגוֹרֵם רָעָה לַחֲבֵרוֹ לַעֲבֹר עֲבֵרָה. כַּיּוֹצֵא בַּדָּבָר אַתָּה אוֹמֵר: "אַבֵּד תְּאַבְּדוּן אֶת כָּל הַמְּקֹמוֹת" (דברים יב, ב), הֲרֵי דְּבָרִים קַל וָחֹמֶר: וּמָה אִילָנוֹת שֶׁאֵינָן רוֹאִין וְאֵינָן שׁוֹמְעִין, עַל שֶׁבָּאת תַּקָּלָה עַל יָדָם אָמְרָה תּוֹרָה הַשְׁחֵת גַּדֵּעַ וְכַלֵּה, הַמַּטֶּה אֶת חֲבֵרוֹ מִדֶּרֶךְ חַיִּים לְדַרְכֵי מִיתָה עַל אַחַת כַּמָּה וְכַמָּה:

יז| **חֶסֶד הוּא.** לָשׁוֹן אֲרַמִּי "חֶרְפָּה" (בראשית לד, יד) – 'חִסּוּדָא'. וּמִדְרָשׁוֹ: אִם תֹּאמַר, קַיִן נָשָׂא אֲחוֹתוֹ! חֶסֶד עָשָׂה הַמָּקוֹם לִבְנוֹת עוֹלָמוֹ מִמֶּנּוּ, שֶׁנֶּאֱמַר: "עוֹלָם חֶסֶד יִבָּנֶה" (תהלים פט, ג):

יח| **הֶעֱרָה.** גִּלָּה, וְכֵן כָּל לְשׁוֹן 'עֶרְוָה' גִּלּוּי הוּא, וְהַוָּי"ו יוֹרֶדֶת בַּתֵּבָה לְשֵׁם דָּבָר, כְּמוֹ 'זַעֲוָה' (דברים כח, כה) מִגִּזְרַת "וְלֹא קָם וְלֹא זָע" (אסתר ה, ט), וְכֵן 'אַחֲוָה' (זכריה יא, יד) מִגִּזְרַת 'אָח'. וְהַעֲרָאָה זוֹ נֶחְלְקוּ בָּהּ רַבּוֹתֵינוּ: יֵשׁ אוֹמְרִים זוֹ נְשִׁיקַת שַׁמָּשׁ, וְיֵשׁ אוֹמְרִים זוֹ הַכְנָסַת עֲטָרָה:

יט| **וְעֶרְוַת אֲחוֹת אִמְּךָ.** שָׁנָה הַכָּתוּב בְּאַזְהָרָתָן, לוֹמַר שֶׁהִזְהִיר עֲלֵיהֶן בֵּין עַל אֲחוֹת אָבִיו וְאִמּוֹ מִן הָאָב בֵּין עַל אַחְיוֹתֵיהֶן מִן הָאֵם, אֲבָל עַל עֶרְוַת אֵשֶׁת אֲחִי אָבִיו לֹא הִזְהִיר אֶלָּא עַל אֵשֶׁת אֲחִי אָבִיו מִן הָאָב:

כ| **אֲשֶׁר יִשְׁכַּב אֶת דֹּדָתוֹ.** הַמִּקְרָא הַזֶּה בָּא לְלַמֵּד עַל כָּרֵת הָאָמוּר לְמַעְלָה, שֶׁהוּא בְּעֹנֶשׁ הֲלִיכַת עֲרִירִי: **עֲרִירִים.** כְּתַרְגּוּמוֹ, בְּלֹא וָלָד, וְדוֹמֶה לוֹ "וְאָנֹכִי הוֹלֵךְ עֲרִירִי" (בראשית טו, ב). יֵשׁ לוֹ בָּנִים – קוֹבְרָן, אֵין לוֹ בָּנִים – מֵת בְּלֹא בָנִים. לְכָךְ שִׁנָּה בִּשְׁנֵי מִקְרָאוֹת אֵלּוּ, "עֲרִירִים יָמֻתוּ" "עֲרִירִים יִהְיוּ" (להלן פסוק כא), "עֲרִירִים יָמֻתוּ" – אִם יִהְיוּ לוֹ בִּשְׁעַת עֲבֵרָה לֹא יִהְיוּ לוֹ כְּשֶׁיָּמוּת לְפִי שֶׁקּוֹבְרָן בְּחַיָּיו, "עֲרִירִים יִהְיוּ" – שֶׁאִם אֵין לוֹ בִּשְׁעַת עֲבֵרָה יִהְיֶה כָּל יָמָיו כְּמוֹ שֶׁהוּא עַכְשָׁיו:

כא| **נִדָּה הִוא.** הַשְּׁכִיבָה הַזֹּאת מְנֻדָּה הִיא וּמְאוּסָה. וְרַבּוֹתֵינוּ דָּרְשׁוּ, לֶאֱסֹר הַעֲרָאָה בָּהּ כְּנִדָּה שֶׁהַעֲרָאָה מְפֹרֶשֶׁת בָּהּ: "אֶת מְקֹרָהּ הֶעֱרָה" (לעיל פסוק יח):

DISCUSSION

do not apply to anyone except the children of Israel after they received the Torah at Sinai, in which case Amram was not in violation of any prohibition, the Torah nevertheless saw fit to use a polite and vague formulation out of respect for Moses (see Ibn Ezra, based on Exodus 6:20).

20:21| **A man who takes his brother's wife, it is abhorrent [*nidda*]:** The verse does not mention the law of levirate marriage, namely the obligation of a brother to marry the wife of his brother who died childless. It seems that the verse refers specifically to a case where the deceased brother was not childless, or where the law of levirate marriage did not apply for some other reason; in such a case, the act is prohibited and abhorred. The Sages note a connection between this prohibition and the prohibition of lying with a *nidda*, menstruating woman: Just as the prohibition against lying with a menstruating woman no longer applies after a given time, when the same woman is no longer menstruating, so too the prohibition of marrying the wife of one's brother ceases to apply in certain circumstances, such as in the case of levirate marriage (see Ibn Ezra; *Yevamot* 54b).

A Closing Statement on the Topic of Holiness, Separation between the Impure and the Pure, the Punishment for a Medium and a Necromancer

LEVITICUS 20:22–27

22 The chapter concludes with a general commandment: **You shall observe all My statutes,** My commandments that are not subject to human judgment, **and all My ordinances,** namely, the instructions to the courts, stated in this passage and the previous one; **and you shall perform them, and the land to which I am bringing you to live there will not spew you out.** It may be inferred that if you do not observe My statutes and ordinances, you will indeed be spewed out of the land.
23 **And you shall not follow the practices of the nation, which**
Seventh aliya **I am sending forth from before you; as they,** those nations, **did all these** prohibited acts, **and I abhorred them.**
24 **I said to you: You shall inherit their land, and I will give it to you to inherit it, a land flowing with milk and honey.** Your inheritance of the land serves a dual purpose: On the one hand, it is the fulfillment of My promise to you; on the other hand, I will thereby expel the sinful nations who are unworthy of residing in the land. **I am the Lord,** who has the authority to perform these actions, and I am also **your God, who has distinguished you from the peoples.** The inhabitants of the Land of Israel are guilty of transgressing the prohibitions enumerated above; in response, God has rejected them and will remove them from the land. Some of these prohibitions, however, apply only to the children of Israel, due to their distinction from the peoples.
25 On account of your special and revered status, **you shall dis-**
Maftir **tinguish between the pure animal,** that which is permitted for consumption, **and the non-pure,** which may not be eaten, **and between the non-pure birds and the pure.** The list of pure and non-pure animals and birds appears in an earlier chapter (11:1–31). They are referenced here in the context of the distinction between Israel and the other nations, even though these prohibitions are less severe than the forbidden sexual relations. **And you shall not render yourselves detestable by means of** consuming **the animals,**[D] **or the birds, or by** consuming **any creature that creeps on the ground, which I have distinguished for you to deem non-pure.** The soul of a member of Israel is polluted in some manner by consuming non-kosher animals.
26 **You shall be holy to Me,** and distinguished in various ways, **for I, the Lord, am holy.** The holy is that which is situated beyond the boundary. To be holy, then, means to separate oneself. **And I have distinguished you from the peoples to be Mine.**
27 The concluding verse of this chapter seems quite puzzling. Perhaps it is related to the concept of the exclusivity of the unique bond between God and Israel: **A man or a woman, if there is among them a medium or a necromancer,**[D] **they shall be put to death; with stones they shall stone them; their blood is upon them.** The verse is not referring to those who seek the council of such individuals (see 19:31), but to the mediums and necromancers themselves.

DISCUSSION

20:25 | **And you shall not render yourselves detestable by means of the animals:** Jewish tradition does not relate to these prohibited animals in a neutral manner; rather, these creatures have traditionally been considered detestable. For many generations, Jews not only refrained from the consumption of, e.g., oysters and pigs, but also considered them revolting creatures. This repulsion may be likened to the abhorrence with which the majority of Western society views the consumption of cats and dogs, even if their consumption is not legally prohibited.

20:27 | **If there is among them [*bahem*] a medium or a necromancer:** This phrase could alternatively be translated: If they are a medium for a ghost or a wraith. Often, such individuals claim that some force enters their bodies, namely, that the dead or a spirit speaks from within them. For this reason the verse uses the word *bahem*, literally, within them, specifically targeting those who claim to channel spirits. These actions might be a result of madness, but in most cases, the individual subjugates himself, as it were, to something that lies outside the divinely permitted realm of interaction (see *Sifra*, *Kedoshim* 3:7).

According to *Sefer HaḤinnukh* (208), at that time people were fervent followers of this cult behavior. Therefore a separate prohibition was enumerated with regard to these practices, in addition to the general warning not to engage in idol worship.

כב וּשְׁמַרְתֶּם אֶת־כָּל־חֻקֹּתַי וְאֶת־כָּל־מִשְׁפָּטַי וַעֲשִׂיתֶם אֹתָם וְלֹא־תָקִיא אֶתְכֶם
כג הָאָרֶץ אֲשֶׁר אֲנִי מֵבִיא אֶתְכֶם שָׁמָּה לָשֶׁבֶת בָּהּ: וְלֹא תֵלְכוּ בְּחֻקֹּת הַגּוֹי אֲשֶׁר־ שביעי
כד אֲנִי מְשַׁלֵּחַ מִפְּנֵיכֶם כִּי אֶת־כָּל־אֵלֶּה עָשׂוּ וָאָקֻץ בָּם: וָאֹמַר לָכֶם אַתֶּם תִּירְשׁוּ
אֶת־אַדְמָתָם וַאֲנִי אֶתְּנֶנָּה לָכֶם לָרֶשֶׁת אֹתָהּ אֶרֶץ זָבַת חָלָב וּדְבָשׁ אֲנִי יְהוָה
כה אֱלֹהֵיכֶם אֲשֶׁר־הִבְדַּלְתִּי אֶתְכֶם מִן־הָעַמִּים: וְהִבְדַּלְתֶּם בֵּין־הַבְּהֵמָה הַטְּהֹרָה מפטיר
לַטְּמֵאָה וּבֵין־הָעוֹף הַטָּמֵא לַטָּהֹר וְלֹא־תְשַׁקְּצוּ אֶת־נַפְשֹׁתֵיכֶם בַּבְּהֵמָה וּבָעוֹף
כו וּבְכֹל אֲשֶׁר תִּרְמֹשׂ הָאֲדָמָה אֲשֶׁר־הִבְדַּלְתִּי לָכֶם לְטַמֵּא: וִהְיִיתֶם לִי קְדֹשִׁים כִּי
כז קָדוֹשׁ אֲנִי יְהוָה וָאַבְדִּל אֶתְכֶם מִן־הָעַמִּים לִהְיוֹת לִי: וְאִישׁ אוֹ־אִשָּׁה כִּי־יִהְיֶה
בָהֶם אוֹב אוֹ יִדְּעֹנִי מוֹת יוּמָתוּ בָּאֶבֶן יִרְגְּמוּ אֹתָם דְּמֵיהֶם בָּם:

רש״י

כג] וָאָקֻץ. לְשׁוֹן מִאוּס, כְּמוֹ: "קַצְתִּי בְּחַיַּי" (בראשית כז, מו), כְּאָדָם שֶׁהוּא קָץ בִּמְזוֹנוֹ:

כה] וְהִבְדַּלְתֶּם בֵּין הַבְּהֵמָה הַטְּהֹרָה לַטְּמֵאָה. אֵין צָרִיךְ לוֹמַר בֵּין פָּרָה לַחֲמוֹר, שֶׁהֲרֵי מֻבְדָּלִין וְנִכָּרִין הֵם, אֶלָּא בֵּין טְהוֹרָה לְךָ לִטְמֵאָה לְךָ, בֵּין שֶׁנִּשְׁחַט רֻבּוֹ שֶׁל סִימָן לְנִשְׁחַט חֶצְיוֹ. וְכַמָּה בֵּין רֻבּוֹ לְחֶצְיוֹ? מְלֹא שְׂעָרָה: אֲשֶׁר הִבְדַּלְתִּי לָכֶם לְטַמֵּא. לֶאֱסֹר:

כו] וָאַבְדִּל אֶתְכֶם מִן הָעַמִּים לִהְיוֹת לִי. אִם אַתֶּם מֻבְדָּלִים מֵהֶם הֲרֵי אַתֶּם שֶׁלִּי, וְאִם לָאו הֲרֵי אַתֶּם שֶׁל נְבוּכַדְנֶצַּר וַחֲבֵרָיו. רַבִּי אֶלְעָזָר בֶּן עֲזַרְיָה אוֹמֵר, מִנַּיִן שֶׁלֹּא יֹאמַר אָדָם: נַפְשִׁי קָצָה בִּבְשַׂר חֲזִיר, אִי אֶפְשִׁי לִלְבֹּשׁ כִּלְאַיִם, אֲבָל יֹאמַר: אֶפְשִׁי, וּמָה אֶעֱשֶׂה וְאָבִי שֶׁבַּשָּׁמַיִם גָּזַר עָלַי? – תַּלְמוּד לוֹמַר: "וָאַבְדִּל אֶתְכֶם מִן הָעַמִּים לִהְיוֹת לִי", שֶׁתְּהֵא הַבְדָּלַתְכֶם מֵהֶם לִשְׁמִי, פּוֹרֵשׁ מִן הָעֲבֵרָה וּמְקַבֵּל עָלָיו עֹל מַלְכוּת שָׁמַיִם:

כז] כִּי יִהְיֶה בָהֶם אוֹב וגו׳. כָּאן נֶאֱמַר בָּהֶם מִיתָה, וּלְמַעְלָה (לעיל פסוק ו) כָּרֵת! – עֵדִים וְהַתְרָאָה בִּסְקִילָה, מֵזִיד בְּלֹא הַתְרָאָה בְּהִכָּרֵת, וְשִׁגְגָתָם חַטָּאת. וְכֵן בְּכָל חַיָּבֵי מִיתוֹת שֶׁנֶּאֱמַר בָּהֶם כָּרֵת:

Parashat
Emor

The Commandments Relating to the Sanctity of the Priests and the Offerings

LEVITICUS 21:1–22:33

Although the entire Jewish people is holy, the priests have additional aspects of sanctity. Their sanctity is expressed in a unique set of laws that restrict the priests more than the rest of the Jewish people. The previous sections discussed the commandments that express the sanctity of the Jewish people as a whole. The following section details the commandments that pertain to the sanctity of the priests, as well as certain commandments that pertain to the sanctity of the offerings.

The Sanctity of the Priests

LEVITICUS 21:1–9

The Temple and the sacrificial food must not be defiled by any form of ritual impurity. The following passage prohibits priests specifically from coming into contact with the impurity imparted by a corpse, irrespective of whether or not they are engaged in the Temple service.

21 **1** **The Lord said to Moses: Speak to the priests, sons of Aaron.**[D] Since the following commandments concern the priests, they should be addressed mainly to them. **And say to them: He,** a priest, **shall not become impure from a corpse**[D] **among his people.**[D] It is prohibited for a priest to come into contact with the ritual impurity imparted by a corpse, even outside the Temple.

2 The verse lists the exceptions to the aforementioned prohibition. The priest may become impure **only for his** deceased **kin, who is close to him:**[D] **for his mother, for his father, for his son, for his daughter,** and **for his brother,** all of whom are first-degree blood relations.

3 The priest may also become impure **for his virgin sister, who is close to him, who has not been with a man,** neither married nor betrothed to one; **for her, he may become impure.**

4 The priest is **an important man among his people;** therefore, he **shall not become impure, to profane himself.**[1] Alternatively, the verse means that a priest may not become impure for an important individual;[2] that a husband may not become impure for a wife who profanes him, that is, in a case where he married a woman prohibited to him;[3] or that a priest may not become impure for more distant relatives.[4] The list of relatives for whom a priest may become impure includes only

first-degree relatives; it is far shorter than the list of relatives with whom sexual relations are prohibited (18:6–18).

5 **They shall not create a bald spot on their head** by tearing out their hair, **and the corner of their beard they shall not shave, and in their flesh they shall not make a laceration.** In the surrounding heathen societies, mourners would tear out their hair and lacerate themselves as an expression of sorrow or due to some other overwhelming emotion.[5] The prohibition against shaving the corner of one's beard is stated above with regard to all Jews[6] and is reiterated here with regard to the priests in the context of mourning.[7]

6 **They shall be holy to their God, and they shall not profane the name of their God** due to their sanctity, **for the fire offerings of the Lord, the food of their God, they offer; they shall be holy.** Due to their unique status as ministers of God, certain restrictions apply to priests that do not apply to the rest of the people. These include the requirement to distance themselves from the dead and the additional prohibitions against disfiguring their bodies.

7 In addition to these prohibitions, the priests are also restricted with regard to whom they may marry: **A licentious woman,** one who engaged in prohibited sexual relations, **or a profaned woman,**[D] a woman profaned because of sexual relations, **they,** the priests, **shall not marry.**

DISCUSSION

21:1 | Speak to the priests, sons of Aaron: Although the commandments detailed in this section chiefly concern the priesthood, Moses subsequently teaches these commandments to the entire people (verse 24), as they are required to ensure that the priests maintain their sanctity.

Speak to the priests…. He shall not become impure from a corpse: This law emphasizes the attitude of the Jewish people toward the duties of the priests and the priests' noninvolvement with the dead. In Judaism, the priests serve in the Temple of the Living God, where death has

no place. This is in contrast to the prevalent custom in many religions, where the priests accompany the dead and are often occupied with those who have passed away.

Shall not become impure from a corpse among his people: The Sages derive from the

◄◄

פרשת
אמור

א וַיֹּאמֶר יְהוָה אֶל־מֹשֶׁה אֱמֹר אֶל־הַכֹּהֲנִים בְּנֵי אַהֲרֹן וְאָמַרְתָּ אֲלֵהֶם לְנֶפֶשׁ לֹא־ יז
ב יִטַּמָּא בְּעַמָּיו: כִּי אִם־לִשְׁאֵרוֹ הַקָּרֹב אֵלָיו לְאִמּוֹ וּלְאָבִיו וְלִבְנוֹ וּלְבִתּוֹ וּלְאָחִיו:
ג ד וְלַאֲחֹתוֹ הַבְּתוּלָה הַקְּרוֹבָה אֵלָיו אֲשֶׁר לֹא־הָיְתָה לְאִישׁ לָהּ יִטַּמָּא: לֹא יִטַּמָּא
ה בַּעַל בְּעַמָּיו לְהֵחַלּוֹ: לֹא־יקרחה קָרְחָה בְּרֹאשָׁם וּפְאַת זְקָנָם לֹא יְגַלֵּחוּ וּבִבְשָׂרָם יִקְרְחוּ
ו לֹא יִשְׂרְטוּ שָׂרָטֶת: קְדֹשִׁים יִהְיוּ לֵאלֹהֵיהֶם וְלֹא יְחַלְּלוּ שֵׁם אֱלֹהֵיהֶם כִּי אֶת־
ז אִשֵּׁי יְהוָה לֶחֶם אֱלֹהֵיהֶם הֵם מַקְרִיבִם וְהָיוּ קֹדֶשׁ: אִשָּׁה זֹנָה וַחֲלָלָה לֹא יִקָּחוּ

רש"י

א| **אמר אל הכהנים.** "אמר" "ואמרת", להזהיר גדולים על הקטנים: **בני אהרן.** יכול חללים? תלמוד לומר: "הכהנים": **בני אהרן.** אף בעלי מומין במשמע: **בני אהרן.** ולא בנות אהרן: **לא יטמא בעמיו.** בעוד שהמת בתוך עמיו, יצא מת מצוה:

ב| **כי אם לשארו.** אין "שארו" אלא אשתו:

ג| **הקרובה.** לרבות את הארוסה: **אשר לא היתה לאיש.** למשכב: **לה יטמא.** מצוה:

ד| **לא יטמא בעל בעמיו להחלו.** לא יטמא לאשתו פסולה שהוא מחולל בה בעודה עמו, וכן פשוטו של מקרא: "לא יטמא בעל" בשארו בעוד שהיא בתוך עמיו, שיש לה קוברין שאינה מת מצוה. ובאיזה שאר אמרתי? באותו שהיא "להחלו", להתחלל הוא מכהונתו:

ה| **לא יקרחה קרחה.** על מת. והלא אף ישראל הוזהרו על כך? אלא לפי שנאמר בישראל: "בין עיניכם" (דברים יד, א), יכול לא יהא חייב על כל הראש? תלמוד לומר: "בראשם". וילמדו ישראל מכהנים בגזרה שוה: נאמר כאן "קרחה" ונאמר להלן בישראל "קרחה" (שם), מה כאן כל הראש אף להלן כל הראש במשמע, כל מקום שיקרח בראש. ומה להלן על מת, אף כאן על מת: **ופאת זקנם לא יגלחו.** לפי שנאמר בישראל: "ולא תשחית" (לעיל יט, כז), יכול לקטו במלקט ורהיטני יהא חייב? לכך נאמר: "לא יגלחו", שאינו חייב אלא על דבר הקרוי גלוח ויש בו השחתה, וזהו תער: **ובבשרם לא ישרטו שרטת.** לפי שנאמר בישראל: "ושרט לנפש לא תתנו" (לעיל יט, כח), יכול שרט חמש שריטות לא יהא חייב אלא אחת? תלמוד לומר: "לא ישרטו שרטת", לחייב על כל שריטה ושריטה, שתיבה זו יתרה היא לדרש, שהיה לו לכתב "לא ישרטו" ואני יודע שהיא "שרטת":

ו| **קדשים יהיו.** על כרחם יקדישום בית דין בכך:

ז| **זנה.** שנבעלה בעילת ישראל האסור לה, כגון חייבי כריתות או נתין או ממזר: **חללה.** שנולדה מן הפסולים שבכהנה, כגון בת אלמנה מכהן גדול או בת גרושה מכהן הדיוט, וכן שנתחללה מן הכהנה על ידי ביאת אחד מן הפסולים לכהנה:

DISCUSSION

phrase "among his people" that in a case where there is no one to tend to the burial of the dead, even a priest must do so (see *Sifra*; *Nazir* 43b; *Berakhot* 19b).

21:2| **For his kin, who is close to him:** Although all of the relatives mentioned here explicitly are blood relations, a priest may also become ritually impure for his dead wife, as one's wife is considered even closer to him than these relatives (see Genesis 2:23–24). Furthermore, it may even be a positive commandment to do so. The phrase "his kin, who is close to him" may be interpreted, not as a generalization that is followed by the details, but as the first in a list of relatives. According to this reading, the phrase alludes to one's closest kin, his wife (see *Yevamot* 22b; *Sifrei*; *Targum Yonatan*; Rashi; *Adderet Eliyahu*; Rabbi Samson Raphael Hirsch). The Sages similarly interpret an analogous expression with regard to the laws of inheritance: "His next of kin, from his family" (Numbers 27:11; see *Bava Batra* 111b). The law that one's wife is included among those relatives from whom one may become impure may also be derived from the following verse, which states that one may become impure from his dead sister only if she was unmarried. When a woman marries she departs to a certain extent from her former circle of immediate relatives and becomes part of her husband's family. Her status is therefore akin to that of her husband's blood relations.

21:7| **A licentious woman [*zona*] or a profaned woman:** According to the tradition of the Sages, and as indicated by the context, the term "*zona*" does not refer to a woman who engages in prostitution, despite the fact that the term is used in this sense elsewhere (see Genesis 38:15; Joshua 2:1; Judges 16:1). Rather, a licentious woman is one whose legal status was impaired by engaging in adulterous or incestuous relations, irrespective of whether she was a willing or unwilling partner to the act (see *Sifra*; Rashi; *Yevamot* 66a). The licentious woman may not be morally flawed; she might be an innocent victim. However, the fact that she was involved in a prohibited sexual act renders her legal status flawed with regard to marriage to priests.

A profaned woman is one with whom a priest engaged in prohibited sexual relations, or a woman born from those relations (see Rashi; Rashbam; *Kiddushin* 77a). A profaned woman is permitted to marry any non-priest, as her status is impaired only due to the violation of the prohibitions of the priesthood.

And a woman divorced from her husband they shall not marry,[D] **for he,** the priest, **is holy to his God.**

8 The Torah now addresses all Jews, or at least the courts that are responsible for the enforcement of the commandments, and instructs them: **You shall sanctify him,** the priest, treating him with reverence and ensuring that he maintains his sanctity, **for he presents the food of your God.** Not only are the priests themselves required to maintain their sanctity by adhering to the aforementioned commandments, but the rest of the people are also required to sanctify them. These commandments are not for the priests' self-aggrandizement and glorification. They are obligations imposed upon the entire community to uphold the sanctity of the priests, so that they will be worthy of their noble function.[8] **He shall be holy to you, for I, the Lord your sanctifier, am holy.** Due to the priests' closeness to God, they must maintain a greater state of sanctity, which involves the observance of certain prohibitions.

9 The verse presents another law that stems from the priests' state of sanctity: **The** married **daughter of a man who is a priest, if she shall profane herself by acting licentiously,**[9] **she profanes her father; she shall be burned in fire.** Even if she were not the daughter of a priest, she would be liable to receive the death penalty. However, the particular method of execution, burning, is more severe than the death penalty meted out to other women who committed the same sin, and this emphasizes the severity of her offense as the daughter of a priest.[10]

The Sanctity of the High Priest

LEVITICUS 21:10–15

The Jewish people are a holy nation. The priests are distinguished from the rest of the Jewish people and sanctified to a greater extent. Similarly, there is one priest, the High Priest, who is distinguished from among his priestly brethren and elevated to an even greater degree of sanctity.

10 **The priest who is greater than his brethren, that the anointing oil will be poured on his head,** in order to appoint him as the High Priest, **and who is ordained to don the** unique **vestments**[D] of the High Priest, since he is sanctified to a greater extent than the other priests, **he shall not grow out the hair of his head** during a period of mourning, **and he shall not rend his garments.**[D]

11 **He shall not go near any dead people.** He is prohibited from coming into contact with a corpse under any circumstances. **He shall not become impure** even **for his father and for his mother,** and certainly not for other relatives, whom he is under no obligation to honor.[11]

12 **He shall not emerge from the Sanctuary**[D] to accompany the dead or for other matters concerned with mourning the deceased.[12] This is so **that he not profane the Sanctuary of his God** by deviating from the prohibitions that sanctify him. He must maintain his sanctity, **for the crown of the anointing oil of his God,** his unique appointment, **is on him. I am the Lord,** and it is I who confer a unique role and elevated status upon the High Priest.

13 The High Priest is also restricted to a greater extent in the matter of marriage: **He shall marry** only **a woman with her virginity** intact.

14 **A widow, or a divorcée, or a profaned woman, or a licentious woman, these he shall not marry.** Three of these four women are prohibited to common priests (see verse 7). In addition to these, the High Priest is also prohibited from marrying a divorcée. He may not marry a woman who has had relations with a man: **Only a virgin from his people he shall take as a wife.**

15 **He shall not profane his offspring**[D] **among his people, for I am the Lord, his sanctifier.**

The Ban on Service for a Blemished Priest

LEVITICUS 21:16–24

The previous section set down prohibitions that pertain to the priests' conduct. These prohibitions sanctify the priests, setting them apart from the rest of the people. The following section lists physical blemishes that prevent priests from serving in the Temple.

Second aliya 16 **The Lord spoke to Moses, saying:**

17 **Speak to Aaron.** The following matter is addressed to Aaron, as it introduces an additional aspect of his priesthood. You shall speak to him, **saying: Any man from your descendants,** the

DISCUSSION

A woman divorced from her husband they shall not marry: The matter of divorce is not dealt with in the Torah in great detail. Although in certain instances a man divorces his wife due to some failing he finds in her (see Deuteronomy 24:1), this law would appear to be unrelated to any flaw in the divorcée's character. Divorce does, however, cause a change in the woman's legal status. Due to the sanctity of the priest, he may not marry a woman whose legal status is less than pristine, even if it comes through no fault of her own. Similarly, a priest is prohibited from marrying a woman born of a prohibited relationship, even though the circumstances of her birth need not have any bearing on her character.

21:10| And who is ordained to don the vestments: The common priest serves in the Temple

ח ואשה גרושה מאישה לא יקחו כי־קדש הוא לאלהיו: וקדשתו כי־את־לחם
ט אלהיך הוא מקריב קדש יהיה־לך כי קדוש אני יהוה מקדשכם: ובת איש
י כהן כי תחל לזנות את־אביה היא מחללת באש תשרף: והכהן
הגדול מאחיו אשר־יוצק על־ראשו | שמן המשחה ומלא את־ידו ללבש
יא את־הבגדים את־ראשו לא יפרע ובגדיו לא יפרם: ועל כל־נפשת מת לא
יב יבא לאביו ולאמו לא יטמא: ומן־המקדש לא יצא ולא יחלל את מקדש
יג אלהיו כי נזר שמן משחת אלהיו עליו אני יהוה: והוא אשה בבתוליה יקח:
יד אלמנה וגרושה וחללה זנה את־אלה לא יקח כי אם־בתולה מעמיו יקח
טו טז אשה: ולא־יחלל זרעו בעמיו כי אני יהוה מקדשו: שני וידבר
יז יהוה אל־משה לאמר: דבר אל־אהרן לאמר איש מזרעך לדרתם

רש״י

ח | וְקִדַּשְׁתּוֹ. עַל כָּרְחוֹ, שֶׁאִם לֹא רָצָה לְגָרֵשׁ הַלְקֵהוּ וְיַסְּרֵהוּ עַד שֶׁיְּגָרֵשׁ: קָדֹשׁ יִהְיֶה לָּךְ. נְהֹג בּוֹ קְדֻשָּׁה לִפְתֹּחַ רִאשׁוֹן בְּכָל דָּבָר וּלְבָרֵךְ רִאשׁוֹן בִּסְעוּדָה:

ט | כִּי תֵחֵל לִזְנוֹת. כְּשֶׁתִּתְחַלֵּל עַל יְדֵי זְנוּת, שֶׁהָיְתָה בָּהּ זִיקַת בַּעַל וְזִנְּתָה אוֹ מִן הָאֵרוּסִין אוֹ מִן הַנִּשּׂוּאִין. וְרַבּוֹתֵינוּ נֶחְלְקוּ בַּדָּבָר, וְהַכֹּל מוֹדִים שֶׁלֹּא דִבֵּר הַכָּתוּב בִּפְנוּיָה: אֶת אָבִיהָ הִיא מְחַלֶּלֶת. חִלְּלָה וּבִזְּתָה אֶת כְּבוֹדוֹ, שֶׁאוֹמְרִים עָלָיו: אָרוּר שֶׁזּוֹ יָלַד, אָרוּר שֶׁזּוֹ גִּדֵּל:

י | לֹא יִפְרָע. לֹא יְגַדֵּל פֶּרַע עַל אֵבֶל, וְאֵיזֶהוּ גִּדּוּל פֶּרַע? יוֹתֵר מִשְּׁלֹשִׁים יוֹם:

יא | וְעַל כָּל נַפְשֹׁת מֵת. בְּאֹהֶל הַמֵּת: נַפְשֹׁת מֵת. לְהָבִיא רְבִיעִית דָּם מִן הַמֵּת שֶׁמְּטַמֵּא בְּאֹהֶל: לְאָבִיו וּלְאִמּוֹ לֹא יִטַּמָּא. לֹא בָא אֶלָּא לְהַתִּיר לוֹ מֵת מִצְוָה:

יב | וּמִן הַמִּקְדָּשׁ לֹא יֵצֵא. אֵינוֹ הוֹלֵךְ אַחַר הַמִּטָּה. וְעוֹד, מִכָּאן לָמְדוּ רַבּוֹתֵינוּ שֶׁכֹּהֵן גָּדוֹל מַקְרִיב אוֹנֵן, וְכֵן מַשְׁמָעוֹ: אֲפִלּוּ אִם מֵתוּ אָבִיו וְאִמּוֹ אֵינוֹ צָרִיךְ לָצֵאת מִן הַמִּקְדָּשׁ, אֶלָּא עוֹבֵד עֲבוֹדָה: וְלֹא יְחַלֵּל אֵת מִקְדַּשׁ. שֶׁאֵינוֹ מְחַלֵּל בְּכָךְ אֶת הָעֲבוֹדָה, שֶׁהִתִּיר לוֹ הַכָּתוּב, הָא כֹּהֵן הֶדְיוֹט שֶׁעָבַד אוֹנֵן חִלֵּל:

יד | וַחֲלָלָה. שֶׁנּוֹלְדָה מִפְּסוּלֵי כְהֻנָּה:

טו | וְלֹא יְחַלֵּל זַרְעוֹ. הָא אִם נָשָׂא אַחַת מִן הַפְּסוּלוֹת, זַרְעוֹ הֵימֶנָּה חָלָל מִדִּין קְדֻשַּׁת כְּהֻנָּה:

DISCUSSION

wearing four priestly vestments, whereas the High Priest wears eight. Part of the ceremony by which a High Priest is appointed involves wearing the High Priest's vestments for the first time. However, it is evident that merely putting on the vestments does not change his status if the priest was not appointed for this role. In the Second Temple, when priests were no longer anointed with the anointing oil, High Priests were invested by being dressed in the vestments of the High Priest (see Exodus 29:29; *Horayot* 11b–12a).

He shall not grow out the hair of his head, and he shall not rend his garments: These prohibitions pertain only to the High Priest. The Sages derived from this that an ordinary person must let his hair grow during a period of mourning. He is prohibited to shave, and likewise he must rend his garments (see *Moed Katan* 14b; *Horayot* 12b; see also 10:6).

21:12| **He shall not emerge from the Sanctuary:** The verse should not be interpreted literally, as requiring the High Priest to remain in the Temple at all times and never leave it. Rather, this prohibition is related to the prohibition against becoming ritually impure even for a close family relative. There is a dispute between the Sages of the Mishna with regard to whether the High Priest does not participate in the funeral procession at all, or whether he participates while keeping his distance (see *Sanhedrin* 18a–19a).

21:15| **He shall not profane his offspring:** This law applies not only in the case of a High Priest who marries a woman prohibited to him, but in the case of any priest who marries a woman prohibited to him, due to the sanctity of the priesthood. The offspring of a priest from a woman prohibited to him are known as *halalim*, profaned ones. They do not have the status of priests, despite the fact that they are Aaron's descendants. They are profaned from the sanctity of the priesthood and are considered ordinary Israelites (Rashi; *Kiddushin* 77b). The daughters born from such marriages may not marry priests, as stated above (verse 7). However, they are not prohibited from marrying Jews who are non-priests, as these prohibitions do not apply to common Jews.

priests, **throughout their generations, in whom there shall be a blemish shall not approach to offer the food of his God,**[D] to perform the divine service.

18 **For any man in whom there is a blemish** at present **shall not approach** the Sanctuary. He is unfit to perform the sacred service, even if the blemish is only temporary.[13] The Torah lists those blemishes that render a priest unfit: **a blind man, or lame, or with a sunken nose.** A sunken nose is an overtly visible blemish, even though it does not impair one's abilities.[14] The list of blemishes continues: **or** a man **with a protruding limb,** the opposite of a sunken nose,[15]

19 **or a man with a broken foot or a broken hand** that has not yet healed,

20 **or a hunchback,**[D] **or a dwarf,**[D] **or** a man **with a cataract in his eye,** a white spot that covers part of the eye, usually without causing blindness,[18] **or scabbed, or with a skin eruption,** certain forms of skin diseases,[19] **or with crushed testicles.** The Sages dispute the precise nature of this last blemish.[20] Some of these blemishes do not bother the individual in question, but nevertheless are conspicuous to an observer.

21 **Any man in whom there is a blemish from the descendants of Aaron the priest**[D] **shall not approach to present the fire offerings of the Lord; he has a blemish,** and **the food of his God he shall not approach to offer.** The verse twice states the prohibition that a blemished priest "shall not approach" to present offerings. The Sages derive from the repetition that other physical blemishes that are noticeably abnormal also prohibit a priest from serving in the Temple.

22 **The food of his God from the sacred sacraments and from the sacraments** of lesser sanctity[21] **he may eat.** Although a blemished priest is unfit to present offerings on the altar, the blemishes do not mar the priest's character and do not disqualify him from the sanctity of the priesthood. He therefore does not forfeit his right to partake of the sacrificial food.

23 **However, he shall not come to** the inner sanctum, behind **the curtain,** as the High Priest does on the Day of Atonement, **and he may not approach the altar,** in the manner of all priests, **because there is a blemish in him. And he shall not profane My Sanctuary.** This teaches that if a blemished priest performs the rites of an offering, the offering is profaned and disqualified,[22] **for I am the Lord, their sanctifier.**[23]

24 **Moses spoke to Aaron and to his sons,** to whom this passage is specifically addressed, **and to all the children of Israel.** These commandments do not pertain only to the priests, as all Jews are commanded to ensure that the priests observe these commandments meticulously.[242]

Those Fit to Partake of the Sacred Food

LEVITICUS 22:1–16

The requirement to preserve the sanctity of the offerings, as well as the sanctity of the portion of the crop designated for the priest, is incumbent upon all Jews. Although the priests serve in the Temple and their lives revolve around holiness, they are also warned to be meticulous in their adherence to the laws concerning the sanctity of the priestly gifts that they receive. The sanctity of these gifts is not merely a matter of sentiment, but is inherent to these items.

22 1 **The Lord spoke to Moses, saying:**

2 **Speak to Aaron and to his sons, that** in the cases stated below **they shall refrain from** approaching **the sacred items of the children of Israel that they consecrate to Me,**[25] **and they shall not profane My holy name. I am the Lord.** Some of the sacred items that are consecrated to God are subsequently given to the priests. The priests must therefore treat those gifts with the necessary sanctity and reverence.

3 The Torah presents the practical details deriving from the sanctity of these items: **Say to them: Throughout your generations, any man from all your descendants who approaches** to eat[26] **the sacred items that the children of Israel**

DISCUSSION

21:17 | **Any man from your descendants throughout their generations in whom there shall be a blemish shall not approach to offer the food of his God:** Physical blemishes do not impair one's status in other contexts, and do not necessarily prevent one from engaging in the occupation of his choice. However, for priests to serve in the Temple they must physically be whole. Their status as God's ministers must be reflected not only in their characters and moral qualities, but also in their physical appearance. As keepers of the charge of the sacred (see Numbers 18:1–7; Ezekiel 44:15; Nehemiah 12; *Ta'anit* 26a) who serve in their King's Sanctuary, even their bodies must be as perfect as possible.

21:20 | **A hunchback:** The exact definition of this blemish is unclear, as it may appear in various forms (Rav Se'adya Gaon). In some cases, it is the result of a congenital defect; in others, it is merely a person who walks with a very bent back (see *Ḥizkuni*). Alternatively, the Sages explain that the verse is referring to one whose eyebrows are overly thick or attached to one another, or to a similar blemish (see Rashi; Ramban; *Bekhorot* 43b). According to these interpretations, the term "in his eye" refers to all of the blemishes mentioned up to this point in the verse (Ramban).

Or a dwarf: Instead of a dwarf (Ibn Ezra; *Ḥizkuni*), the verse may be referring to one who has a membrane or blots on his eye (see Ramban; *Bekhorot* 38a–39a, 44a; see also commentary on Deuteronomy 28:27) or a defect of his eyelids (see Rashi, *Bekhorot* 16a).

21:21 | **Any man in whom there is a blemish from the descendants of Aaron the priest:**

יח אֲשֶׁר יִהְיֶה בוֹ מוּם לֹא יִקְרָב לְהַקְרִיב לֶחֶם אֱלֹהָיו: כִּי כָל־אִישׁ אֲשֶׁר־בּוֹ מוּם

יט לֹא יִקְרָב אִישׁ עִוֵּר אוֹ פִסֵּחַ אוֹ חָרֻם אוֹ שָׂרוּעַ: אוֹ אִישׁ אֲשֶׁר־יִהְיֶה בוֹ שֶׁבֶר

כ רֶגֶל אוֹ שֶׁבֶר יָד: אוֹ־גִבֵּן אוֹ־דַק אוֹ תְּבַלֻּל בְּעֵינוֹ אוֹ גָרָב אוֹ יַלֶּפֶת אוֹ מְרוֹחַ

כא אָשֶׁךְ: כָּל־אִישׁ אֲשֶׁר־בּוֹ מוּם מִזֶּרַע אַהֲרֹן הַכֹּהֵן לֹא יִגַּשׁ לְהַקְרִיב אֶת־אִשֵּׁי

כב יְהוָה מוּם בּוֹ אֵת לֶחֶם אֱלֹהָיו לֹא יִגַּשׁ לְהַקְרִיב: לֶחֶם אֱלֹהָיו מִקָּדְשֵׁי הַקֳּדָשִׁים

כג וּמִן־הַקֳּדָשִׁים יֹאכֵל: אַךְ אֶל־הַפָּרֹכֶת לֹא יָבֹא וְאֶל־הַמִּזְבֵּחַ לֹא יִגַּשׁ כִּי־מוּם בּוֹ

כד וְלֹא יְחַלֵּל אֶת־מִקְדָּשַׁי כִּי אֲנִי יְהוָה מְקַדְּשָׁם: וַיְדַבֵּר מֹשֶׁה אֶל־אַהֲרֹן וְאֶל־בָּנָיו וְאֶל־כָּל־בְּנֵי יִשְׂרָאֵל:

ב א וַיְדַבֵּר יְהוָה אֶל־מֹשֶׁה לֵּאמֹר: דַּבֵּר אֶל־אַהֲרֹן וְאֶל־בָּנָיו וְיִנָּזְרוּ מִקָּדְשֵׁי בְּנֵי

ג יִשְׂרָאֵל וְלֹא יְחַלְּלוּ אֶת־שֵׁם קָדְשִׁי אֲשֶׁר הֵם מַקְדִּשִׁים לִי אֲנִי יְהוָה: אֱמֹר אֲלֵהֶם

רש"י

יז] **לֶחֶם אֱלֹהָיו.** מַאֲכַל אֱלֹהָיו. כָּל סְעוּדָה קְרוּיָה לֶחֶם, כְּמוֹ: "עֲבַד לֶחֶם רַב" (דניאל ה, א):

יח] **כִּי כָל אִישׁ אֲשֶׁר בּוֹ מוּם לֹא יִקְרָב.** אֵינוֹ דִין שֶׁיִּקְרַב, כְּמוֹ: "הַקְרִיבֵהוּ נָא לְפֶחָתֶךָ" (מלאכי א, ח): **חָרֻם.** שֶׁחָטְמוֹ שָׁקוּעַ בֵּין שְׁתֵּי הָעֵינַיִם, שֶׁכּוֹחֵל שְׁתֵּי עֵינָיו כְּאַחַת: **שָׂרוּעַ.** שֶׁאֶחָד מֵאֵבָרָיו גָּדוֹל מֵחֲבֵרוֹ, עֵינוֹ אַחַת גְּדוֹלָה וְעֵינוֹ אַחַת קְטַנָּה, אוֹ שׁוֹקוֹ אַחַת אֲרֻכָּה מֵחֲבֶרְתָּהּ:

כ] **אוֹ גִבֵּן.** שורצילו"ש בְּלַעַז, שֶׁגְּבִינֵי עֵינָיו שְׂעָרָן אָרֹךְ וְשׁוֹכֵב: **אוֹ דַק.** שֶׁיֵּשׁ לוֹ בְּעֵינָיו דֹק שֶׁקּוֹרִין טיי"לא, כְּמוֹ "הַנּוֹטֶה כַדֹּק" (ישעיה מ, כב): **אוֹ תְבַלֻּל.** דָּבָר הַמְבַלְבֵּל אֶת הָעַיִן, כְּגוֹן חוּט לָבָן הַנִּמְשָׁךְ מִן הַלָּבָן וּפוֹסֵק בַּסִּירָא, שֶׁהוּא עִגּוּל הַמַּקִּיף אֶת הַשָּׁחוֹר שֶׁקּוֹרְחִים פרונ"ילא, וְהַחוּט הַזֶּה פּוֹסֵק אֶת הָעִגּוּל וְנִכְנָס בַּשָּׁחוֹר. וְתַרְגּוּם "תְּבַלֻּל" "חִלְיוֹן", לְשׁוֹן חִלָּזוֹן, שֶׁהוּא דוֹמֶה לְתוֹלַעַת — אוֹתוֹ הַחוּט, וְכֵן כִּנּוּהוּ חַכְמֵי יִשְׂרָאֵל בְּמוּמֵי הַבְּכוֹר, חִלָּזוֹן נָחָשׁ עֵנָב: **גָרָב אוֹ יַלֶּפֶת.** מִינֵי שְׁחִין הֵם. "גָרָב" זוֹ הַחֶרֶס, שְׁחִין

הַיָּבֵשׁ מִבִּפְנִים וּמִבַּחוּץ. "יַלֶּפֶת" הִיא חַזָּזִית הַמִּצְרִית, וְלָמָּה נִקְרֵאת "יַלֶּפֶת"? שֶׁמְּלַפֶּפֶת וְהוֹלֶכֶת עַד יוֹם הַמִּיתָה, וְהוּא לַח מִבַּחוּץ וְיָבֵשׁ מִבִּפְנִים. וּבְמָקוֹם אַחֵר קוֹרֵא לְגָרָב שְׁחִין הַלַּח מִבַּחוּץ וְיָבֵשׁ מִבִּפְנִים, שֶׁנֶּאֱמַר: "וּבַגָּרָב וּבֶחָרֶס" (דברים כח, כז), כְּשֶׁסָּמַךְ גָּרָב אֵצֶל חֶרֶס קוֹרֵא לַיַּלֶּפֶת "גָּרָב", וּכְשֶׁהוּא אֵצֶל יַלֶּפֶת קוֹרֵא לַחֶרֶס "גָּרָב", כָּךְ מְפֹרָשׁ בִּבְכוֹרוֹת (דף מא ע"א): **מְרוֹחַ אָשֶׁךְ.** לְפִי הַתַּרְגּוּם "מְרִיס פַּחֲדִין", שְׁפָחֲדָיו מְרֻסָּסִין, שֶׁבֵּיצִים שֶׁלּוֹ כְּתוּתִין. "פַּחֲדִין" כְּמוֹ: "גִּידֵי פַחֲדָו יְשׂרָגוּ" (איוב מ, יז):

כא] **כָּל אִישׁ אֲשֶׁר בּוֹ מוּם.** לְרַבּוֹת שְׁאָר מוּמִין: **מוּם בּוֹ.** בְּעוֹד מוּמוֹ בּוֹ פָּסוּל, הָא אִם עָבַר מוּמוֹ — כָּשֵׁר: **לֶחֶם אֱלֹהָיו.** כָּל מַאֲכָל קָרוּי לֶחֶם:

כב] **מִקָּדְשֵׁי הַקֳּדָשִׁים.** אֵלּוּ קָדְשֵׁי הַקֳּדָשִׁים: **וּמִן הַקֳּדָשִׁים יֹאכֵל.** אֵלּוּ קָדָשִׁים קַלִּים. וְאִם נֶאֶמְרוּ קָדְשֵׁי הַקֳּדָשִׁים לָמָּה נֶאֱמַר קָדָשִׁים קַלִּים? אִם לֹא נֶאֱמַר הָיִיתִי

חוֹמֵר, בְּקָדְשֵׁי הַקֳּדָשִׁים יֹאכַל בַּעַל מוּם, שֶׁמָּצִינוּ שֶׁהֻתְּרוּ לְזָר, שֶׁאָכַל מֹשֶׁה בְּשַׂר הַמִּלּוּאִים, אֲבָל בְּחָזֶה וָשׁוֹק שֶׁל קָדָשִׁים קַלִּים לֹא יֹאכַל, שֶׁלֹּא מָצִינוּ זָר חוֹלֵק בָּהֶן, לְכָךְ נֶאֶמְרוּ קָדָשִׁים קַלִּים: כָּךְ מְפֹרָשׁ בַּזְּבָחִים (דף קא ע"ב):

כג] **אַךְ אֶל הַפָּרֹכֶת.** לְהַזּוֹת שֶׁבַע הַזָּאוֹת שֶׁעַל הַפָּרֹכֶת: **וְאֶל הַמִּזְבֵּחַ.** הַחִיצוֹן, וּשְׁנֵיהֶם הֻצְרְכוּ לִכְתֹּב, וּמְפֹרָשׁ בְּתוֹרַת כֹּהֲנִים (פרק ג, י): **וְלֹא יְחַלֵּל אֶת מִקְדָּשַׁי.** שֶׁאִם עָבַד, עֲבוֹדָתוֹ מְחֻלֶּלֶת לִפָּסֵל:

כד] **וַיְדַבֵּר מֹשֶׁה.** הַמִּצְוָה הַזֹּאת: **אֶל אַהֲרֹן וְגו' וְאֶל כָּל בְּנֵי יִשְׂרָאֵל.** לְהַזְהִיר בֵּית דִּין עַל הַכֹּהֲנִים:

פרק כב

ב] **וְיִנָּזְרוּ.** אֵין נְזִירָה אֶלָּא פְּרִישָׁה, וְכֵן הוּא אוֹמֵר "וְיֵּאוֹר מֵאַחֲרַי" (יחזקאל יד, ז), "נָזֹרוּ אָחוֹר" (ישעיהו א, ד), יִפְרְשׁוּ מִן הַקֳּדָשִׁים בִּימֵי טֻמְאָתָן: **וְיִנָּזְרוּ מִקָּדְשֵׁי בְנֵי יִשְׂרָאֵל, אֲשֶׁר הֵם מַקְדִּשִׁים לִי וְלֹא יְחַלְּלוּ אֶת שֵׁם קָדְשִׁי.** וְכָל פָּרָשָׁה שֶׁל מִקְרָא קֹדֶשׁ וְדַרְשָׁהּ: **אֲשֶׁר הֵם מַקְדִּשִׁים לִי.** לְרַבּוֹת קָדְשֵׁי כֹּהֲנִים עַצְמָן:

DISCUSSION

This verse is interpreted as hinting at an additional set of blemishes, aside from those set out explicitly above, which render the priest "unequal among the seed of Aaron" (Bekhorot 43b). These blemishes are deemed less severe than those blemishes that are explicitly stated in the Torah. If a priest deemed "unequal among the seed of Aaron" serves in the Temple, the service is not disqualified. Furthermore, unlike those blemishes that are stated explicitly, only a priest suffering from unusual physical features is deemed unfit to serve in the Temple, but an animal with these unusual physical features is still fit to be presented as an offering. In addition to these blemishes, there are other physical imperfections that are not considered blemishes by Torah law, but nevertheless priests who suffer from them may not serve in the Temple, as they have the appearance of a blemish, e.g., one whose eyelashes or teeth have fallen out (see Bekhorot 43a–b).

consecrate to the Lord with his impurity upon him, that person shall be excised from before Me. I am the Lord. A person often becomes ritually impure due to common occurrences. The consecrated gifts of the priesthood, which include the portions of the offerings given to the priests, as well as the portions of produce given to the priests, may not be consumed in a state of ritual impurity. Although any impure individual is prohibited from drawing near to the sacred, the Torah commands the priests specifically, as they are the ones who most frequently consume and have contact with consecrated foods.

4 The Torah lists the different forms of ritual impurity: **Any man from the descendants of Aaron who is a leper**[D] **or has a** gonorrhea-like **discharge, he shall not partake of the sacred items until he is purified,** even if he remains impure for many years. **And** the following individuals are also ritually impure and may not partake of consecrated food: **one who touches anyone** or anything rendered **impure from a corpse,** and all the more so one who himself comes into contact with a corpse, **or a man from whom semen has been emitted,**

5 **or a man who touches any** dead **swarming creature that renders him impure,** of those listed above (11:29–31), **or** who shall touch **a man that renders him impure, whatever his impurity,** including all forms of impurity not mentioned here.

6 **A person who touches him,** the impure person, **shall be impure until the evening.** This is in contrast to those impure individuals whose impurity is of a greater degree of severity: a leper, one who experiences a gonorrhea-like discharge, and one who comes into contact with a corpse, as in those cases a lengthier process of purification is required. **And** yet, although this person's impurity is of a lesser degree, **he shall not partake of the sacred items, unless he bathes his flesh in water,** immersing in a ritual bath.

7 After he immerses he must wait until **the sun shall set, and** only then **he shall be purified.**[D] Then he may once again **partake of the sacred items, because it is his food.** The sacred food constitutes an important part of the priest's sustenance. He is therefore permitted to partake of it as soon as nighttime has commenced and a new day has begun (see 23:32), and he is not required to wait until the following morning.

8 The Torah presents a related prohibition: **He shall not eat an unslaughtered carcass or a mauled animal,**[D] one that suffered a fatal injury,[27] **to render himself impure with it.**[D] **I am the Lord.**

9 **They,** the priests, **shall keep My commission,** keeping charge of the sacred food that is given to them.[28] The verse may also be referring to the charge of the Temple's sanctity.[29] If they maintain the sanctity of their charge, **they shall not bear sin for it and die on its account.**[D] However, if they do not maintain the sanctity of their charge and partake of the sacred food in a state of ritual impurity, they will be punished by death at the hands of Heaven, **because they profane it.** The desecration of consecrated items is a severe transgression punishable by death at the hands of Heaven. This applies to a ritually impure person who partakes of the sacred portion of the produce given to the priests.[30] **I am the Lord their sanctifier.**

10 The Torah continues to detail the restrictions on the consumption of sacred foods: **No non-priest shall partake of sacred items.** The Sages interpret this verse too as referring to the sacred portion of the produce given to the priests. The prohibition applies not only to one who is entirely unaffiliated with the priesthood, but also to **one who resides** for a lengthy period **with a priest or** to a priest's **hired laborer,**[D] even if he was hired for several years. They **shall not partake of sacred items,** despite the fact that they are *de facto* members of the priest's household.

DISCUSSION

22:4 | Any man from the descendants of Aaron who is a leper: The various forms of ritual impurity are not listed according to their severity, but according to the frequency in which they usually occur. First the verse lists individuals afflicted with leprosy or with a gonorrhea-like discharge, which are rare occurrences; then impurity imparted by the dead, with whom anyone might come into contact; and finally impurity due to a seminal emission, which is part of marital life and, in contrast to a gonorrhea-like discharge, is not caused by sickness. The subsequent verse lists impurity imparted by dead swarming creatures, which is a common

occurrence particularly in rural areas and is usually unanticipated.

22:7 | The sun shall set, and he shall be purified: In some of the cases of impurity listed here, e.g., a leper and one who experienced a gonorrhea-like discharge, the impure individual is required to bring an offering after his purification. If he is a priest, he is not permitted to partake of sacrificial food until he has presented his atonement offering. In contrast, the priests are permitted to partake of the sacred portion of the produce that is given to them as soon as night falls. It is this portion, referred to in the Talmud

as *teruma*, that the Torah refers to in this verse (see *Yevamot* 74a).

22:8 | Or a mauled animal: There are certain cases where a mauled animal transmits the impurity of an unslaughtered carcass even before it dies, while it is still twitching (see *Ḥullin* 21a; Rambam, *Sefer Kedusha, Hilkhot Sheḥita* 3:19).

To render himself impure with it: In addition to the general prohibition against eating an unslaughtered carcass or one mauled by an animal, which applies to all Jews, this verse teaches that these items also impart ritual impurity (see 5:2). A priest is prohibited from becoming ritually

לדרתיכם כל־איש אשר־יקרב מכל־זרעכם אל־הקדשים אשר יקדישו בני־
ד ישראל ליהוה וטמאתו עליו ונכרתה הנפש ההוא מלפני אני יהוה: איש איש
מזרע אהרן והוא צרוע או זב בקדשים לא יאכל עד אשר יטהר והנגע בכל־
ה טמא־נפש או איש אשר־תצא ממנו שכבת־זרע: או־איש אשר יגע בכל־שרץ
ו אשר יטמא־לו או באדם אשר יטמא־לו לכל טמאתו: נפש אשר תגע־בו
ז וטמאה עד־הערב ולא יאכל מן־הקדשים כי אם־רחץ בשרו במים: ובא השמש
ח וטהר ואחר יאכל מן־הקדשים כי לחמו הוא: נבלה וטרפה לא יאכל לטמאה־
ט בה אני יהוה: ושמרו את־משמרתי ולא־ישאו עליו חטא ומתו בו כי יחללהו
י אני יהוה מקדשם: וכל־זר לא־יאכל קדש תושב כהן ושכיר לא־יאכל קדש:

רש"י

ג | **כל איש אשר יקרב.** אין קריבה זו אלא אכילה, וכן מצינו שנאמרה אזהרת אכילת קדשים בטומאה בלשון נגיעה: "בכל קדש לא תגע" (ויקרא יב, ד) אזהרה לאוכל, ולמדוה רבותינו מגזרה שוה. ואי אפשר לומר שחייב על הנגיעה, שהרי נאמר כרת על האכילה בצו את אהרן, שתי כריתות זו אצל זו (לעיל ז, כ-כא), ואם על הנגיעה חייב, לא הוצרך לחייבו על האכילה. וכן נדרש בתורת כהנים (פרשתא ד, ז): וכי יש נוגע חייב? אם כן מה תלמוד לומר: "יקרב"? משיכשר ליקרב, שאין חייבין עליו משום טומאה אלא אם כן קרבו מתיריו. ואם תאמר, שלש כריתות בטומאת כהנים למה? כבר נדרשו במסכת שבועות (דף ז ע"א), אחת לכלל ואחת לפרט וכו': **וטמאתו עליו.** וטומאת האדם עליו. יכול בבשר הכתוב מדבר, וטומאתו של בשר עליו, ובטהור שאכל את הטמא הכתוב מדבר? על כרחך ממשמעו אתה למד, במי שטומאתו פורחת ממנו הכתוב מדבר, וזהו האדם שיש לו טהרה בטבילה: ונכרתה וגו'. יכול מצד זה לצד זה, יכרת ממקומו ויתישב במקום אחר? תלמוד לומר: "אני ה'", בכל מקום אני:

ד | **בכל טמא נפש.** במי שנטמא במת:

ה | **בכל שרץ אשר יטמא לו.** בשיעור הראוי לטמא, בכעדשה: **או באדם.** במת: **אשר יטמא לו.** בשיעורו לטמא, וזהו כזית: **לכל טמאתו.** לרבות נוגע בזב וזבה נדה ויולדת:

ו | **נפש אשר תגע בו.** באחד מן הטמאים הללו:

ז | **ואחר יאכל מן הקדשים.** נדרש ביבמות (דף עד ע"ב) בתרומה, שמותר לאכלה בהערב השמש: **מן הקדשים.** ולא כל הקדשים:

ח | **נבלה וטרפה לא יאכל לטמאה בה.** לענין הטומאה הזהיר כאן, שאם אכל נבלת עוף טהור שאין לה טומאת מגע ומשא אלא טומאת אכילה בבית הבליעה, אסור לאכול בקדשים. וצריך לומר: "וטרפה" – מי שיש במינו טרפה, יצא נבלת עוף טמא שאין במינו טרפה:

ט | **ושמרו את משמרתי.** מלאכול תרומה בטומאת הגוף: **ומתו בו.** למדנו שהיא מיתה בידי שמים:

י | **לא יאכל קדש.** בתרומה הכתוב מדבר, שכל הענין דבר בה: **תושב כהן ושכיר.** תושבו של כהן ושכירו, לפיכך "תושב" זה נקוד פתח, לפי שהוא דבוק. ואיזהו תושב? זה נרצע שהוא קנוי לו עד היובל; ואיזהו שכיר? זה קנוי קנין שנים שיוצא בשש, בא הכתוב ולמדך כאן שאין גופו קנוי לאדוניו לאכול בתרומתו:

DISCUSSION

→ impure in this manner (see Rashi, 11:8; see also Rashi; *Eiruvin* 31a; *Yoma* 80b; *Ḥullin* 35a). Some commentaries maintain that the intent of the verse, according to its plain meaning, is to reiterate specifically with regard to the priests the prohibition against consuming an unslaughtered carcass or one mauled by an animal (see Abravanel; Radak, Ezekiel 4:14).

22:9| **And die on its account:** This applies to a ritually impure person who partakes of the sacred portion of the produce given to the priests. Partaking of offerings in a state of ritual impurity is punishable by excision, as stated above (7:20–21), which is a more severe punishment than death at the hands of Heaven. Excision may refer to an untimely death at a younger age than death at the hands of Heaven. It may also refer to dying childless, or even to excision from the World to Come (see *Shevuot* 13a; Rashi and *Tosafot, Keritut* 2a; *Tosafot, Shabbat* 25a; *Tosafot, Yevamot* 2a; *Moed Katan* 28a; Jerusalem Talmud, *Bikkurim* 2:1; Rambam, *Sefer HaMadda, Hilkhot Teshuva* 8:1; Ramban, Leviticus 11:29; *Torat HaAdam, Sha'ar HaGemul*).

22:10| **One who resides with a priest or a hired laborer:** The Sages explain that "hired laborer" refers to a Hebrew slave who is acquired for a period of six years, after which he is set free. Similarly, "one who resides with a priest" refers to a Hebrew slave who did not wish to terminate his servitude at the conclusion of the six-year period and underwent a ceremony in which his ear was pierced with an awl. In this case the Hebrew slave is obligated to serve his master until the Jubilee Year (see Exodus 21:1–6; Rav Se'adya Gaon; *Yevamot* 70b).

11 But conversely, **if a priest acquires a person,** a Canaanite slave, as **an acquisition of his silver,**[D] **he may partake of it.** Since the Canaanite slave becomes the priest's possession, he may partake of the priest's sacred food. **And** similarly, with regard to **one born into his household,** Canaanite slaves born in the priest's possession, **they may partake of his** sacred **food.**
12 **If the daughter of a priest is married,** or even betrothed, **to a non-priest, she shall not partake from that which is separated of the sacred items,** the sacred portion separated from the produce. Alternatively, the verse may be referring to the portion separated from the offerings and given to the priests, which may be eaten by the members of the priest's household.[31] Once she becomes the wife of a non-priest, she is no longer considered a member of the priestly family, and she may no longer partake of the priest's sacred food.
13 **But if a priest's daughter,** who married a non-priest, **is a widow or a divorcée, and she has no offspring** from that husband, **and she returns to her father's house, as in her youth,** before she married, **from the** sacred **food of her father she may partake.**[D] Since she has no child from her marriage, her former status as a member of her father's priestly household is reinstated, and she may again eat the sacred portions given to the priest from the produce and offerings. **But no non-priest may partake of it.** If she gave birth to a child from her Israelite husband, since that child is a non-priest, neither she nor her offspring may eat from the sacred food.[32]
14 **If a man,** a non-priest, **shall eat a sacred item unwittingly, he shall add its one-fifth to it,** as a fine, **and he shall give to the priest the sacred item.**[D] The sacred portion separated from the crop is not brought to the Temple, but given to a priest anywhere in the Land of Israel. Since it bears no sign of its consecrated status, a non-priest might unwittingly partake of it, in which case he must give the value of the sacred food to a priest, together with an additional 25 percent, which is one-fifth of the total amount repaid.
15 **They shall not profane the sacraments of the children of Israel that they separate for the Lord.** This commandment applies to all Jews, although it is addressed to the priests. Not only are the offerings presented upon the altar sacred, the portion given to priests from the produce is also sacred. Its sanctity must be maintained by ensuring that it is not eaten by non-priests or in a state of ritual impurity.
16 **They will cause them,** the priests will cause themselves,[33] **to bear the iniquity of guilt,** if they are negligent **when they eat their sacred items; for I am the Lord, their sanctifier.**

Blemished Offerings

LEVITICUS 22:17–25

Third aliya 17 **The Lord spoke to Moses, saying:**
18 **Speak to Aaron, and to his sons, and to all the children of Israel.** The passage is addressed to both the priests and the nation as a whole, as the laws that appear below pertain both to the consecration of offerings by all Jews and to their acceptance as offerings by the priests. **And say to them:** The following laws pertain to **any man**[D] **from the house of Israel or from the strangers in Israel,** the converts who join the Jewish people, **who presents his offering.** This refers to an offering presented **for** the fulfillment of **any of their vows,** when one vowed to bring an offering, **or for any of their pledges,**[D] when one pledged a specific animal as a voluntary offering, **that they shall bring to the Lord as a burnt offering.**
19 The offering must be brought **for your propitiation,**[D] in order for you to find favor in God's eyes. Alternatively, the verse is not referring to the desire of the person bringing the offering to propitiate God, but to the fact that he brings the offering as a gift offering rather than in fulfillment of an obligation. It must be **an unblemished male of cattle, of sheep, or of goats.**

DISCUSSION

22:11 | **But if a priest acquires a person, an acquisition of his silver:** Although this verse refers primarily to the acquisition of human slaves (see *Yevamot* 66b; Rashi), it may also be interpreted as alluding to the purchase of animals. According to the Sages, a priest's animals may be fed with the sacred portion of the produce given to the priests (see *Sifra, Emor* 5). The priest's animals would not be fed with food fit for human consumption but with produce that was designated as animal fodder. A non-priest may not eat the priest's sacred food, irrespective of how important he is or how close he is to the priest. The priest's animals, however, may partake of his sacred food.

22:13 | **From the food of her father she may partake:** The widowed or divorced daughter of a priest might well return to dwell in her father's house, even if she bore children from her non-priest husband, in which case her non-priest offspring would also dwell in the priest's house. Legally, however, as long as she has a child from her non-priest husband she is considered a member of a non-priest family, and she is prohibited from partaking of the priest's sacred food. Although not stated explicitly, the same principle applies in the reverse case: The daughter of a non-priest who married a priest is considered a member of the priesthood and may partake of the sacred food even after her

יא וכהן כי־יקנה נפש קנין כספו הוא יאכל בו ויליד ביתו הם יאכלו בלחמו:
יב יג ובת־כהן כי תהיה לאיש זר הוא בתרומת הקדשים לא תאכל: ובת־כהן כי
תהיה אלמנה וגרושה וזרע אין לה ושבה אל־בית אביה כנעוריה מלחם אביה
יד תאכל וכל־זר לא־יאכל בו: ואיש כי־יאכל קדש בשגגה ויסף חמשיתו עליו
טו ונתן לכהן את־הקדש: ולא יחללו את־קדשי בני ישראל את אשר־ירימו
טז ליהוה: והשיאו אותם עון אשמה באכלם את־קדשיהם כי אני יהוה מקדשם:
יז יח וידבר יהוה אל־משה לאמר: דבר אל־אהרן ואל־בניו ואל כל־בני ישראל יח שלישי
ואמרת אלהם איש איש מבית ישראל ומן־הגר בישראל אשר יקריב
יט קרבנו לכל־נדריהם ולכל־נדבותם אשר־יקריבו ליהוה לעלה: לרצנכם

רש"י

יא| וכהן כי יקנה נפש. עבד כנעני שקנוי לגופו: ויליד ביתו. אלו בני השפחות. ואשת כהן אוכלת בתרומה מן המקרא הזה, שאף היא קנין כספו, ועוד למד ממקרא אחר: "כל טהור בביתך" וגו' (במדבר יח, יא), בספרי (קרח קיז):

יב| לאיש זר. ללוי וישראל:

יג| אלמנה וגרושה. מן האיש הזר: וזרע אין לה. ממנו: ושבה. הא אם יש לה זרע ממנו, אסורה בתרומה כל זמן שהזרע קיים: וכל זר לא יאכל בו. לא בא אלא להוציא את האונן שמותר בתרומה, זרות אמרתי לך ולא אנינות:

יד| כי יאכל קדש. תרומה: ונתן לכהן את הקדש. דבר הראוי להיות קדש, שאינו פורע לו מעות אלא פרות של חולין, והן נעשין תרומה:

טו| ולא יחללו וגו'. להאכילם לזרים:

טז| והשיאו אותם. את עצמם יטעינו עון, "באכלם את קדשיהם" שהבדלו לשם תרומה וקדשו, ונאסרו עליהן: והשיאו אותם. זה אחד משלשה אתים שהיה רבי ישמעאל דורש בתורה שמדברים באדם עצמו, וכן: "ביום מלאת ימי נזרו יביא אתו" (במדבר ו, יג) – הוא יביא את עצמו, וכן: "ויקבר אתו בגי" (דברים לד, ו) – הוא קבר את עצמו. כך נדרש בספרי (נשא לב):

יח| נדריהם. הרי עלי: נדבותם. הרי זו:

יט| לרצנכם. הביאו דבר הראוי לרצות אתכם לפני

DISCUSSION

husband's death, provided that she has a child from him (see Ibn Ezra; *Yevamot* 86b–87a).

22:14| **And he shall give to the priest the sacred item:** The Sages derive from the words "the sacred item" that the transgressor must give the priest an item fit to become sacred, produce in lieu of the consumed produce. The produce returned to the priest then receives the status of the original sacred produce designated for the priest (see Mishna *Terumot*, chap. 7; *Bava Metzia* 54a).

22:18| **Any man:** The Sages derive from these words that burnt offerings may be brought even by gentiles, either as vow offerings or as voluntary offerings (see *Menahot* 73b). From time to time gentiles from various nations did indeed come to the Temple, seeking to present offerings to God.

For any of their vows or for any of their pledges: The Mishna elaborates: Which is the case of a vow offering? It is where one says, without designating a specific animal: It is incumbent upon me to bring a burnt offering. And which is the case of a voluntary offering, brought due to a pledge? It is where one says: This animal is a burnt offering. What is the difference between vow offerings and voluntary offerings? The difference is only that in the case of vow offerings, if the animals died or were stolen one bears the responsibility of replacing them, as one's vow is not fulfilled until he presents the offering. However, in the case of voluntary offerings, if the animals died or were stolen, one does not bear responsibility to replace them, as the undertaking to present an offering pertained only to that specific animal (*Kinnim* 1:1).

22:19| **For your propitiation:** Although certain burnt offerings are obligatory (see 12:6, 16:3), it is usually brought as a voluntary offering that expresses the owner's desire to present an offering to God. The Talmud expresses this as follows: I did not say to you to present offerings to Me so that you will say: I will do His will and He will do my will. You are not presenting offerings to fulfill My will, for My benefit, as I do not wish to burden you with offerings that you do not wish to present. Rather, you are presenting offerings for your own benefit, in order to achieve atonement for your sins by observing My commandments (*Menahot* 101a, and Rashi ad loc.).

20 **Any** animal **in which there is a blemish you shall not offer, as it shall not be accepted for you.** God will not accept a blemished offering, and it will not enable you to achieve propitiation.[34]

21 The previous verses dealt with the presentation of a burnt offering. The Torah now refers to the presentation of a peace offering, which is not burned in its entirety upon the altar. Rather, portions of it are eaten by the priests and by the owners. **If a man shall present a peace offering to the Lord, to fulfill a vow,** or to consecrate as a vow offering,[35] **or as a pledge,** in a case where a specific animal was designated as an offering, **of the cattle or of the flock, it shall be an unblemished** male or female animal **to be accepted. No blemish shall be in it.**

22 For example, the following blemishes render an animal unfit to be presented as an offering: a **blind** animal, even in one eye;[36] **or an animal with a broken** limb; **or maimed,** with a cracked or damaged limb;[37] **or an animal with a cyst.** According to the tradition of the Sages, this refers to a cyst that contains a bone, and to certain cysts in the eye, but not to a small protrusion of flesh that may commonly be found on an animal's body.[38] The list of blemishes continues: **or a scabbed** animal **or one with a skin eruption,** types of boils on the animal's skin;[39] **you shall not offer these to the Lord, and you shall not place them as a fire offering upon the altar to the Lord.**

23 **A bull or a sheep with an extended limb or a truncated limb,**[D] **as a pledge** to the Temple treasury **you may present**[40] it to be sold so that the proceeds may be used for the Temple maintenance.[41] **But as a vow** offering or as a voluntary offering **it shall not be accepted.**

24 **Those** animals, the testicles of **which are bruised, or crushed, or torn, or cut, you shall not present to the Lord.**[42] An animal that has been castrated in any form is considered blemished and unfit to be presented as an offering, **and** furthermore, **you shall not do so in your land.**[D] It is prohibited to castrate any animal.[43] This is a distinct prohibition, which does not apply solely to animals designated as offerings.

25 This applies not only to offerings brought by the Jewish people, but also **from the hand of a foreigner you shall not present the food of your God from any of these, because their defect is in them, a blemish is in them;**[D] **they shall not be accepted for you.** It is not prohibited for a gentile to castrate animals. Nevertheless, it is deemed unfitting to do so, and a castrated animal may not be accepted as an offering even from gentiles.

Additional Laws Concerning Animals and the Presentation of Offerings
LEVITICUS 22:26–33

The following section lists further restrictions with regard to the presentation of offerings.

26 **The Lord spoke to Moses, saying:**

27 **An ox or a sheep or a goat, when it is born, shall be seven days under its mother.** It is prohibited to slaughter it for any purpose during this time. Only **from the eighth day on, it shall be accepted as a fire offering to the Lord.**[D]

28 **An ox or a sheep, it and its offspring you shall not slaughter on one day,**[D] for any purpose, not only as offerings.

29 **When you slaughter a thanks offering,**[D] as an expression of

---

DISCUSSION

22:23 | A truncated limb: Alternatively, the verse may be referring to a bull or sheep whose hooves are closed like those of a donkey, rather than split (see Rashi; *Bekhorot* 40a). In any event, this is only an example of a physical abnormality that results in a deformed body.

22:24 | And you shall not do so in your land: The prohibition against presenting a blemished animal pertains even to naturally occurring blemishes, e.g., blindness. The castration of an animal, however, is likely to be intentionally inflicted by man, as a castrated animal can be easier to use for labor. The prohibition against presenting a castrated animal as an offering

stems from the honor due to the divine service. Conversely, the prohibition against castration expresses the ethical perception that it is immoral to remove the animal's reproductive capabilities.

22:25 | A blemish is in them: A blemish does not disqualify animals for all purposes. A blemished animal is not deemed impure, and in some cases it may be fit for consumption by Jews. However, due to the significance of offerings, an imperfect animal may not be presented in the Temple. Furthermore, an offering must be presented as a respectable gift to God. The Sages therefore expanded the categories of blemishes

to include additional cases that are deemed unfit. This idea finds prominent expression in the book of Malachi, where the prophet castigates those who bring unfit offerings for their insufficient respect of the divine service. He sharply criticizes people who present as an offering an animal that they would not dream of presenting as a gift to a person of importance (Malachi 1:8).

22:27 | From the eighth day on, it shall be accepted as a fire offering to the Lord: The Torah does not usually provide reasons for the commandments. Nevertheless, the commentaries suggest two reasons for this prohibition. First, during the first days of the animal's life its

←●

כ תְּמִימִ֥ם זָכָ֛ר בַּבָּקָ֖ר בַּכְּשָׂבִ֣ים וּבָֽעִזִּ֑ים כֹּ֛ל אֲשֶׁר־בּ֥וֹ מ֖וּם לֹ֥א תַקְרִ֑יבוּ כִּי־לֹ֥א לְרָצ֖וֹן

כא יִהְיֶ֥ה לָכֶֽם: וְאִ֗ישׁ כִּֽי־יַקְרִ֤יב זֶֽבַח־שְׁלָמִים֙ לַֽיהֹוָ֔ה לְפַלֵּא־נֶ֙דֶר֙ א֣וֹ לִנְדָבָ֔ה בַּבָּקָ֖ר

כב א֣וֹ בַצֹּ֑אן תָּמִ֤ים יִֽהְיֶה֙ לְרָצ֔וֹן כָּל־מ֖וּם לֹ֥א יִֽהְיֶה־בּֽוֹ: עַוֶּ֩רֶת֩ א֨וֹ שָׁב֜וּר אֽוֹ־חָר֣וּץ אֽוֹ־יַבֶּ֗לֶת א֤וֹ גָרָב֙ א֣וֹ יַלֶּ֔פֶת לֹֽא־תַקְרִ֥יבוּ אֵ֖לֶּה לַֽיהֹוָ֑ה וְאִשֶּׁ֗ה לֹֽא־תִתְּנ֥וּ מֵהֶ֛ם עַל־

כג הַמִּזְבֵּ֖חַ לַֽיהֹוָֽה: וְשׁ֣וֹר וָשֶׂ֗ה שָׂר֤וּעַ וְקָלוּט֙ נְדָבָ֣ה תַּֽעֲשֶׂ֣ה אֹת֔וֹ וּלְנֵ֖דֶר לֹ֥א יֵֽרָצֶֽה:

כד וּמָע֤וּךְ וְכָתוּת֙ וְנָת֣וּק וְכָר֔וּת לֹ֥א תַקְרִ֖יבוּ לַֽיהֹוָ֑ה וּבְאַרְצְכֶ֖ם לֹ֥א תַֽעֲשֽׂוּ: וּמִיַּ֣ד בֶּן־

כה נֵכָ֗ר לֹ֥א תַקְרִ֛יבוּ אֶת־לֶ֥חֶם אֱלֹֽהֵיכֶ֖ם מִכָּל־אֵ֑לֶּה כִּ֣י מָשְׁחָתָ֤ם בָּהֶם֙ מ֣וּם בָּ֔ם לֹ֥א

כו יֵֽרָצ֖וּ לָכֶֽם: וַיְדַבֵּ֥ר יְהֹוָ֖ה אֶל־מֹשֶׁ֥ה לֵּאמֹֽר: שׁ֣וֹר אוֹ־כֶ֤שֶׂב אוֹ־עֵז֙ כִּ֣י

כז יִוָּלֵ֔ד וְהָיָ֛ה שִׁבְעַ֥ת יָמִ֖ים תַּ֣חַת אִמּ֑וֹ וּמִיּ֤וֹם הַשְּׁמִינִי֙ וָהָ֔לְאָה יֵֽרָצֶ֔ה לְקָרְבַּ֥ן אִשֶּׁ֖ה

רש"י

שֶׁיְּהֵא לָכֶם לְרָצוֹן, חֲפֵיאמֵינ"ט בְּלַעַ. וְאֵיזֶהוּ הָרָצוּי לְרָצוֹן? "תְּמִים זָכָר בַּבָּקָר בַּכְּשָׂבִים וּבָעִזִּים". אֲבָל בְּעוֹלַת הָעוֹף אֵין צָרִיךְ תַּמּוּת זְכָרוּת, וְאֵינוֹ נִפְסָל בְּמוּם אֶלָּא בַּחֲסָרוֹן אֵיבֶר.

כא לְפַלֵּא נֶדֶר. לְהַפְרִישׁ בְּדִבּוּרוֹ.

כב עַוֶּרֶת. שֵׁם דָּבָר שֶׁל מוּם עִוָּרוֹן בִּלְשׁוֹן נְקֵבָה, שֶׁלֹּא יְהֵא בּוֹ מוּם שֶׁל עַוֶּרֶת. אוֹ שָׁבוּר. לֹא יְהֵא. חָרוּץ. רִיס שֶׁל עַיִן שֶׁנִּסְדַּק אוֹ שֶׁנִּפְגַּם, וְכֵן שְׂפָתוֹ שֶׁנִּסְדְּקָה אוֹ נִפְגְּמָה. יַבֶּלֶת. ורוא"ה בְּלַעַ. גָּרָב. מִין חֲזָזִית, וְכֵן יַלֶּפֶת. וּלְשׁוֹן "יַלֶּפֶת" כְּמוֹ "וַיִּלְפֹּת שִׁמְשׁוֹן" (שופטים טז, כט), שֶׁאֲחוּזָה בּוֹ עַד יוֹם מִיתָה, שֶׁאֵין לָהּ רְפוּאָה. לֹא תַקְרִיבוּ. שָׁלֹשׁ פְּעָמִים (פסוקים כ, כב, כד), לְהַזְהִיר עַל הַקְדָּשָׁתָן וְעַל שְׁחִיטָתָן וְעַל זְרִיקַת דָּמָן. וְאִשֶּׁה לֹא תִתְּנוּ. אַזְהָרַת הַקְטָרָתָן.

כג שָׂרוּעַ. אֵיבָר גָּדוֹל מֵחֲבֵרוֹ. וְקָלוּט. פַּרְסוֹתָיו קְלוּטוֹת. נְדָבָה תַּעֲשֶׂה אֹתוֹ. לְבֶדֶק הַבַּיִת. וּלְנֵדֶר. לְמִזְבֵּחַ. לֹא יֵרָצֶה. אֵי זֶה הֶקְדֵּשׁ בָּא לְרָצוֹי? הֱוֵי אוֹמֵר זֶה הֶקְדֵּשׁ הַמִּזְבֵּחַ.

כד וּמָעוּךְ וְכָתוּת וְנָתוּק וְכָרוּת. בַּבֵּיצִים אוֹ בַגִּיד. מָעוּךְ. בֵּיצִין מְעוּכִין בְּיָד. כָּתוּת. כְּתוּשִׁים יוֹתֵר מִמְּעוּךְ. נָתוּק. תְּלוּשִׁין בְּיָד עַד שֶׁנִּפְסְקוּ חוּטִים שֶׁתְּלוּיִים בָּהֶן, אֲבָל נְתוּנִים הֵם בְּתוֹךְ הַכִּיס, וְהַכִּיס לֹא נִתְלַשׁ. וְכָרוּת. כְּרוּתִין בִּכְלִי וְעוֹדָן בַּכִּיס, שֶׁלֹּא יְהֵא כִּמְחֻסַּר אֵיבֶר. וּמָעוּךְ. תַּרְגּוּמְרִים "וְדִימְרִיס" זֶהוּ לְשׁוֹן וַחֲלַחְמַת, לְשׁוֹן חֶרְטָהּ. וְכָתוּת. תַּרְגּוּמוֹ "וּדְרִיסִין", כְּמוֹ "הַבַּיִת הַגָּדוֹל רְסִיסִים" (עמוס ו, יא), בְּקִיעוֹת דַּקּוֹת, וְכֵן "קְנֵה הַמְרֻסָּס" (סבת פ עב) כָּתוּשׁ כְּתִיתִין. וּבְאַרְצְכֶם לֹא תַעֲשׂוּ. דָּבָר זֶה, לְסָרֵס שׁוּם בְּהֵמָה וְחַיָּה וַאֲפִלּוּ טְמֵאָה, לְכָךְ נֶאֱמַר "בְּאַרְצְכֶם", לְרַבּוֹת כָּל אֲשֶׁר בְּאַרְצְכֶם, שֶׁאִי אֶפְשַׁר לוֹמַר לֹא נִצְטַוּוּ עַל הַסֵּרוּס

חֵלֶף בָּאָרֶץ, שֶׁהֲרֵי סֵרוּס חוֹבַת הַגּוּף הוּא, וְכָל חוֹבַת הַגּוּף נוֹהֶגֶת בֵּין בָּאָרֶץ בֵּין בְּחוּצָה לָאָרֶץ:

כה וּמִיַּד בֶּן נֵכָר. גּוֹי שֶׁהֵבִיא קָרְבָּן בְּיַד כֹּהֵן לְהַקְרִיבוֹ לַשָּׁמַיִם, לֹא תַקְרִיבוּ לוֹ בַעַל מוּם. וְאַף עַל פִּי שֶׁלֹּא נֶאֶסְרוּ בַּעֲלֵי מוּמִין לְקָרְבַּן בְּנֵי נֹחַ אֶלָּא אִם כֵּן מְחֻסְּרֵי אֵיבֶר, זֹאת נוֹהֶגֶת בַּבָּמָה שֶׁבַּשָּׂדוֹת, אֲבָל עַל הַמִּזְבֵּחַ שֶׁבַּמִּשְׁכָּן לֹא תַקְרִיבוּ, אֲבָל תְּמִימָה תְּקַבְּלוּ מֵהֶם, לְכָךְ נֶאֱמַר לְמַעְלָה "אִישׁ אִישׁ" (פסוק יח), לְרַבּוֹת אֶת הַגּוֹיִם, שֶׁעֹלָרִים נְדָרִים וּנְדָבוֹת כְּיִשְׂרָאֵל. מָשְׁחָתָם. חִבּוּלְהוֹן. לֹא יֵרָצוּ לָכֶם. לְכַפֵּר עֲלֵיכֶם.

כו כִּי יִוָּלֵד. פְּרָט לְיוֹצֵא דֹפֶן.

כז אֹתוֹ וְאֶת בְּנוֹ. נוֹהֵג בַּנְּקֵבָה, שֶׁאָסוּר לִשְׁחוֹט הָאֵם וְהַבֵּן אוֹ הַבַּת, וְאֵינוֹ נוֹהֵג בַּזְּכָרִים, וּמֻתָּר לִשְׁחוֹט הָאָב וְאֶת הַבֵּן. אֹתוֹ וְאֶת בְּנוֹ. אַף בְּנוֹ וְאוֹתוֹ בַּמַּשְׁמַע.

DISCUSSION

viability is still uncertain, and offering an animal that might not survive is prohibited. After eight days it can be established with a high degree of probability that the animal will survive. In the case of humans, the Sages determined that a child is considered viable after thirty days (see *Targum Yonatan*; *Shabbat* 135b; *Bekhor Shor*; Rambam, *Guide of the Perplexed* 3:49). Second, even an animal designated as an offering is given a week of grace to remain with its mother, as it is considered cruel to act otherwise. This explanation relates to the law stated subsequently as well (see Abravanel; *Meshekh Hokhma*).

22:28 | **It and its offspring you shall not slaughter on one day:** There is a humane rationale for this commandment, as the act is considered somewhat cruel. According to the accepted opinion among the Sages, the verse refers specifically to female cows, sheep, and goats, as the mother's parenthood is evident while the father's is often difficult to determine (see Onkelos; Rashi; *Bekhor Shor*; *Hullin* 78b–79a). Nevertheless, the Talmud does cite a dissenting opinion, which maintains that the prohibition applies to both male and female animals (see *Hullin* 78a; Ibn Ezra; *Hizkuni*).

22:29 | **A thanks offering:** Psalm 107 details four instances where a thanks offering should be brought: in the case of one who traveled a long distance, one who returned after traveling over the ocean, one who recovered from a serious illness, and one who was released from prison (see Psalms 107:4, 10, 20, 23; *Berakhot* 54b; Rashi, 7:12; on the nature of the obligation to show gratitude by presenting an offering, and the source for this obligation, see Rashi and *Shita Mekubbetzet*, *Menahot* 79b; *Tosefot Rid*, *Rosh HaShana* 5b; *Peri Megadim*, *Orah Hayyim* 219).

gratitude **to the Lord, for your propitiation you shall slaughter it.** Alternatively, the verse means that the thanks offering is not an obligatory offering. Rather, you shall slaughter it of your own free will, out of a personal desire to show appreciation for God's assistance, e.g., for deliverance at a time of need.

30 **On that day** on which it is slaughtered **it shall be eaten; you shall not leave from it until morning.**[D] The thanks offering is eaten by its owner, presumably in a comfortable family setting. The verse therefore stresses that in the case of this offering too the time for its consumption is limited to a single day. **I am the Lord.**

31 The passage concludes with a general commandment: **You,** priests and non-priests alike, **shall observe My commandments and perform them. I am the Lord.**

32 Moreover, **you shall not profane My holy name** by committing transgressions or by performing the service in an inappropriate manner. **And I shall be sanctified among the children of Israel.**[D] The verse restates the general concept that is conveyed by the many laws that define the practical concept of sanctity: One does not stand before God merely as an individual. The obligation to observe the commandments is not just the personal right or duty of a particular person. Rather, it is due to God's choice of the Jewish people and their sanctification. **I am the Lord your sanctifier.** The sanctity does not stem from your desire to perform the service, but from Me.

33 I am the Lord **who took you out of the land of Egypt to be your God.** I sanctify you and I am your savior. **I am the Lord.** You belong to Me, and this relationship obligates you to maintain your sanctity.

The Festivals

LEVITICUS 23:1–44

The previous sections dealt with laws concerning the sanctity of the priests and the sanctity of the Temple service. Having discussed the sanctity inherent to certain people and to a certain place, the following section turns to discuss the sanctity inherent to certain days of the year, the festivals. Furthermore, this section is related to the previous sections, as it deals with the specific offerings that must be presented on the festivals. Some of the festival offerings are presented in this section in detail, while others are only alluded to here and their details appear elsewhere.[44] These offerings are known as additional offerings, as they are brought in addition to the daily offerings that are presented every day.

23 1 **The Lord spoke to Moses, saying:**

Fourth aliya 2 **Speak to the children of Israel, and say to them: The appointed times of the Lord that you shall proclaim as holy convocations,**[D] gatherings,[45] **these are My appointed times.**

3 The Sabbath precedes the festivals:[46] **Six days labor shall be performed,** both by man and by his animals. The passive form indicates that engaging in labor during the six days of the week is permitted but is not an obligation. **And on the seventh day, a sabbatical rest,** a complete rest from all types of labor, in contrast to the festivals mentioned below, during which certain types of labor are permitted. It is **a holy convocation,** a sacred gathering for the acceptance of the sanctity of the Sabbath and to mark the day.[47] **You shall not perform any labor. It is** the **Sabbath to the Lord in all your dwellings,** wherever you are. In contrast to the festivals, the sanctity of the Sabbath is not determined by the Jewish people. Whereas the days of the festivals are determined by the nation,[48] the day of the Sabbath is predetermined by God as part of the order of Creation. The Jewish people accept the Sabbath and observe its sanctity, but in essence it is not a festival day of the Jewish people, but the day of God, commemorating His creation of the world. The character of the Sabbath is therefore the same everywhere.[49]

4 **These are the appointed times of the Lord, holy convocations, that you shall proclaim at their appointed time.** This verse introduces the subsequent list of festival days. While these festivals are "the appointed times of the Lord," their dates are determined by the Jewish people. The order of this list of festivals follows the order of the months of the year.

5 **During the first month,** Nisan, which was established as the first month because the exodus from Egypt took place during

DISCUSSION

22:30 | **You shall not leave from it until morning:** This restriction with regard to the thanks offering was already mentioned above (7:15) and is reiterated here at the conclusion of the laws concerning offerings. It emphasizes that the thanks offering cannot be turned into a family event lasting several days. The repeated emphasis on the innate significance of the offerings links the time restriction on the consumption of the thanks offering to the previously stated laws. One might desire to present an offering for any number of reasons that originate from one's personal life and experiences. Nevertheless, when one presents a thanks offering he must remember that the focal point of the offering is the sanctity inherent in the sacrificial rites and not the social value of the family gathering. Similarly, the prohibitions against presenting blemished animals as offerings serve to maintain the honor and respect necessary to the divine service (see also commentary on 19:8).

22:32 | **And I shall be sanctified among the children of Israel:** The Sages derive from this verse that if gentiles order a Jew to commit a

כח כט לַיהוָה׃ וְשׁוֹר אוֹ־שֶׂה אֹתוֹ וְאֶת־בְּנוֹ לֹא תִשְׁחֲטוּ בְּיוֹם אֶחָד׃ וְכִי־תִזְבְּחוּ זֶבַח־תּוֹדָה
ל לַיהוָה לִרְצֹנְכֶם תִּזְבָּחוּ׃ בַּיּוֹם הַהוּא יֵאָכֵל לֹא־תוֹתִירוּ מִמֶּנּוּ עַד־בֹּקֶר אֲנִי יְהוָה׃
לא לב וּשְׁמַרְתֶּם מִצְוֹתַי וַעֲשִׂיתֶם אֹתָם אֲנִי יְהוָה׃ וְלֹא תְחַלְּלוּ אֶת־שֵׁם קָדְשִׁי וְנִקְדַּשְׁתִּי
לג בְּתוֹךְ בְּנֵי יִשְׂרָאֵל אֲנִי יְהוָה מְקַדִּשְׁכֶם׃ הַמּוֹצִיא אֶתְכֶם מֵאֶרֶץ מִצְרַיִם לִהְיוֹת
לָכֶם לֵאלֹהִים אֲנִי יְהוָה׃
א ב וַיְדַבֵּר יְהוָה אֶל־מֹשֶׁה לֵּאמֹר׃ דַּבֵּר אֶל־בְּנֵי יִשְׂרָאֵל וְאָמַרְתָּ אֲלֵהֶם מוֹעֲדֵי יְהוָה רביעי
ג אֲשֶׁר־תִּקְרְאוּ אֹתָם מִקְרָאֵי קֹדֶשׁ אֵלֶּה הֵם מוֹעֲדָי׃ שֵׁשֶׁת יָמִים תֵּעָשֶׂה מְלָאכָה
וּבַיּוֹם הַשְּׁבִיעִי שַׁבַּת שַׁבָּתוֹן מִקְרָא־קֹדֶשׁ כָּל־מְלָאכָה לֹא תַעֲשׂוּ שַׁבָּת הִוא
לַיהוָה בְּכֹל מוֹשְׁבֹתֵיכֶם׃

רש"י

כט| **לרצנכם תזבחו.** תחלת זביחתכם הזהרו שתהא לרצון לכם. ומהו הרצון? "ביום ההוא יאכל" (להלן פסוק ל), לא בא להזהיר אלא שתהא שחיטה על מנת כן, אל תשחטוהו על מנת לאכלו למחר, שאם תחשבו בו מחשבת פסול לא יהא לכם לרצון. דבר אחר "לרצנכם", לדעתכם, מכאן למתעסק שפסול בשחיטת קדשים. ואף על פי שפרט בנאכלים לשני ימים, חזר ופרט בנאכלין ליום אחד, שתהא זביחתן על מנת לאכלן בזמנן:

ל| **ביום ההוא יאכל.** לא בא להזהיר אלא שתהא שחיטה על מנת כן, שאם לקבוע לה זמן אכילה, כבר כתוב: "ובשר זבח תודת שלמיו" וגו' (לעיל ז, טו): **אני ה'.** דע מי גזר על הדבר ואל יקל בעיניך:

לא| **ושמרתם.** זו המשנה: **ועשיתם.** זה המעשה:

לב| **ולא תחללו.** לעבר על דברי מזידין. ממשמע שנאמר: "ולא תחללו את שם קדשי", מה תלמוד לומר: "ונקדשתי"? מסר עצמך וקדש שמי. יכול ביחיד? תלמוד לומר: "בתוך בני ישראל". וכשהוא מוסר עצמו ימסר עצמו על מנת למות, שכל המוסר עצמו על מנת הנס אין עושין לו נס, שכן מצינו בחנניה מישאל ועזריה שלא מסרו עצמן על מנת הנס, שנאמר: "והן לא, ידיע להוא לך מלכא" וגו' (דניאל ג, יח), מציל ולא מציל, "ידיע להוא לך" וגו':

לג| **המוציא אתכם.** על מנת כן: **אני ה'.** נאמן לשלם שכר:

פרק כג

ב| **דבר אל בני ישראל וגו' מועדי ה'.** עשה מועדות שיהיו ישראל מלמדין בהם, שמעברים את השנה על גליות שנעקרו ממקומן לעלות לרגל ועדין לא הגיעו לירושלים:

ג| **ששת ימים.** מה ענין שבת אצל מועדות, ללמדך שכל המחלל את המועדות מעלין עליו כאלו חלל את השבתות, וכל המקים את המועדות מעלין עליו כאלו קים את השבתות:

ד| **אלה מועדי ה'.** למעלה מדבר בעבור שנה, וכאן מדבר בקדוש החדש:

DISCUSSION

transgression in public, even if they threaten him with death he must sanctify God's name by allowing himself to be killed rather than commit a transgression (see *Sanhedrin* 74a–b; Rambam, *Sefer HaMadda*, *Hilkhot Yesodei HaTorah*, chap. 5).

23:2| **Holy convocations:** This expression appears many times in the verses below and may also be translated as holy occasions (see Onkelos; *Targum Yonatan*). The Jewish people proclaim these days as holy days when the High Court, as the nation's representatives, sanctify the New Moon, declaring it to be the first of the month and thereby determining the ensuing day of the festival. Furthermore, the communal gatherings on the festivals proclaim their sanctity (see Ramban). The festivals are not only gatherings of the people; they are also the occasions of a meeting between the Jewish people and God.

this month,[50] **on the fourteenth of the month in the afternoon,**[D] **there is** the Festival of **a Paschal Lamb to the Lord.**[D] The paschal lamb is mentioned here only as the name of the festival on which it is offered.[51] The laws of Passover were discussed in Exodus (chap. 12), and will be discussed again in Numbers (28:16–25). Since Leviticus focuses on the offerings, the festivals are defined in this section chiefly by the offerings presented on those days.[52]

6 **On the fifteenth day of that month it is the Festival of Unleavened Bread to the Lord; seven days you shall eat unleavened bread.** Two festivals take place one after the other: The fourteenth of Nisan is the Festival of the Paschal Lamb, which is immediately followed on the fifteenth of Nisan by the Festival of Unleavened Bread, Passover, which lasts for seven days.

7 **On the first day** of the seven days of Passover, **it shall be a holy convocation for you,** a time to gather together and concern yourselves with sacred matters. **You shall not perform any toilsome labor,**[D] labor that is not required for the immediate preparation of food.

8 **You shall present a fire offering to the Lord seven days. On the seventh day** too it shall be **a holy convocation; you shall not perform any toilsome labor.** Of the seven days of Passover, labor is prohibited only on the first and seventh days. The intermediate days of the festival are known as *Ḥol HaMoed,* the non-sacred days of the festival. Although they are part of the festival, in some aspects they are similar to weekdays.

9 **The Lord spoke to Moses, saying:**

10 **Speak to the children of Israel, and say to them: When you come to the land that I am giving to you,** as this commandment does not apply outside the Land of Israel, **and you will reap its harvest, then you shall bring a sheaf** of barley, from which one can extract one-tenth of an ephah of fine flour,[53] **of the first of your** grain **harvest to the priest.** This is the barley harvest, as at the time of Passover the wheat has not yet ripened.[54]

11 **He,** the priest, **shall wave the sheaf before the Lord, for your propitiation [*lirtzonekhem*],** in order to find favor in God's eyes. Additionally, the word *lirtzonekhem* connotes that the offering is a gift freely given out of devotion to God.[55] **On the day after the sabbath,**[D] which refers here to the first day of Passover,[56] **the priest shall wave it.**

12 **You shall present on the day of your waving of the sheaf an unblemished lamb in its first year, as a burnt offering to the Lord.**

13 **Its** accompanying **meal offering is two-tenths of an ephah of high-quality flour,**[D] a dry measure of volume corresponding to around 5 L, **mixed with oil.** The offering is brought **as a fire offering to the Lord for a pleasing aroma, and its libation is wine, one-fourth of a hin,** a liquid measure equivalent to three *log,* which is approximately 1 L according to the standard opinion. This is the same amount of wine as is brought as a libation with a burnt offering or peace offering.

14 Before you bring the sheaf offering you shall not eat **bread, roasted grain**[57] or flour made from it,[58] **or fresh kernels,** raw grain that has not yet dried.[59] **You shall not eat** the new produce in any form **until that very day,** the day after the sabbath, **until your bringing of the** sheaf

---

DISCUSSION

23:5 | In the afternoon [*bein ha'arbayim*]: The literal meaning of this phrase is "between the evenings" (see also Exodus 29:39, 30:7–8). Some explain that it refers to the period between the time when the sun begins to progress toward evening, just after midday when it begins to point in a westerly direction, and the time when the sun sets, as these two times define the end of the day (see *Shabbat* 34b; *Zevaḥim* 11b; Rashi, Ibn Ezra, and Ramban, Exodus 12:6). One must offer the paschal lamb during this time.

A Paschal Lamb to the Lord: The term *Pesaḥ,* which is derived from the term *pasaḥ,* to pass over (see Exodus 12:27), is used in the Torah in reference to the paschal lamb, and by extension to the day on which the paschal lamb is offered, the fourteenth of Nisan. The festival of Passover, commencing on the fifteenth of Nisan, is referred to as the Festival of Unleavened Bread. In contrast, in talmudic and modern Hebrew, the term *Pesaḥ* refers to the festival of Passover itself. There is support also for this terminology in the Bible (see *Ḥizkuni*; Ezekiel 45:21–23; commentary on Joshua 4:11).

23:7 | You shall not perform any toilsome labor: The phrase "toilsome labor" appears here in contrast to the term that appears above with regard to the Sabbath: "You shall not perform any labor" (verse 3). The general term "labor" includes any form of creative activity, regardless of its extent or the exertion involved in its performance. Kindling a fire, which is explicitly singled out in this regard (Exodus 35:3), or the writing of a simple note, both constitute forms of labor. Conversely, toilsome labor refers to the type of labor generally performed for one's livelihood, whether the toil of a hired worker or the toil involved in maintaining one's own property. On festival days there are many types of labor that may be performed in order to prepare food for the holy day, whereas on the Sabbath even labor required for the preparation of food is prohibited. It should be noted that labors such as plowing and weaving are prohibited even on a festival, as they are categorized as toilsome labor. However, there is no prohibition against cooking, baking, and the like (see Ramban; *Minḥa Belula*; Exodus 12:16).

23:11 | On the day after the sabbath: According to the Sages' tradition, the sheaf must be waved on the second day of Passover. The term "sabbath," therefore, refers here to the first day of Passover, which is a sacred day of rest (see verse 7). If "sabbath" were to be understood

◄●

ד ה אלה מועדי יהוה מקראי קדש אשר־תקראו אתם במועדם: בחדש הראשון
ו בארבעה עשר לחדש בין הערבים פסח ליהוה: ובחמשה עשר יום לחדש
ז הזה חג המצות ליהוה שבעת ימים מצות תאכלו: ביום הראשון מקרא־קדש
ח יהיה לכם כל־מלאכת עבדה לא תעשו: והקרבתם אשה ליהוה שבעת ימים
ביום השביעי מקרא־קדש כל־מלאכת עבדה לא תעשו:
ט י וידבר יהוה אל־משה לאמר: דבר אל־בני ישראל ואמרת אלהם כי־תבאו
אל־הארץ אשר אני נתן לכם וקצרתם את־קצירה והבאתם את־עמר ראשית
יא קצירכם אל־הכהן: והניף את־העמר לפני יהוה לרצנכם ממחרת השבת יניפנו
יב הכהן: ועשיתם ביום הניפכם את־העמר כבש תמים בן־שנתו לעלה ליהוה:
יג ומנחתו שני עשרנים סלת בלולה בשמן אשה ליהוה ריח ניחח ונסכה יין רביעת

רש״י

ה | בין הערבים. משש שעות ולמעלה: פסח לה׳. הקרבת קרבן ששמו פסח:

ח | והקרבתם אשה וגו׳. הם המוספין האמורים בפרשת פינחס. ולמה נאמרו כאן? לומר לך שאין המוספין מעכבין זה את זה: "והקרבתם אשה לה׳" – מכל מקום, אם אין פרים הבא אילים, ואם אין פרים ואילים הבא כבשים: שבעת ימים. כל מקום שנאמר ׳שבעת׳ שם דבר הוא, שבוע של ימים, סטיי״נ בלעז. וכן כל לשון שמנת, ששת, חמשת, שלשת: מלאכת עבדה. אפלו מלאכות החשובות לכם עבודה וצורך, שיש חסרון כיס בבטלה שלהן, כגון דבר האבד. כך הבנתי מתורת כהנים (פרשתא יב, ח), דקתני: יכול אף חלו של מועד יהא אסור במלאכת עבודה? וכו׳:

י | ראשית קצירכם. שתהא ראשונה לקציר: עמר. עשירית האיפה, כך היה שמה, כמו: "וימדו בעמר" (שמות טז, יח):

יא | והניף. כל תנופה מוליך ומביא מעלה ומוריד, מוליך ומביא לעצור רוחות רעות, מעלה ומוריד לעצור טללים רעים: לרצנכם. אם תקריבו כמשפט הזה יהיה לרצון לכם: ממחרת השבת. ממחרת יום טוב הראשון של פסח, שאם אתה אומר שבת בראשית, אי אתה יודע איזהו:

יב | ועשיתם... כבש. חובה לעמר הוא בא:

יג | ומנחתו. מנחת נסכיו: שני עשרנים. כפולה היתה: ונסכה יין רביעת ההין. אף על פי שמנחתו כפולה, אין נסכיו כפולים:

יד | וקלי. קמח עשוי מכרמל רך שמיבשין אותו בתנור: וכרמל. הן קליות שקורין גרניי״ש:

DISCUSSION

here as referring to the seventh day of the week, the strange result would be that one might wave the sheaf on any Sunday of the year, and there would be no fixed date for this obligation. Furthermore, since the order of this section follows the yearly calendar, it may be inferred from the location of this commandment in relation to the other festivals that it is connected to Passover. The Sages state that it is a hermeneutical principle that a verse does not come to make matters obscure but to clarify them (see Rashi, Genesis 10:25, 21:34). One may therefore infer that the term "sabbath" here refers to the aforementioned festival, as the festivals are also referred to as days of rest (see, e.g., verse 39).

The exact relationship between the festival and the Sabbath mentioned here was the subject of acrimonious disputes. Both the Sadducees and later, the Karaites, rejected the Sages' interpretation and interpreted the term "sabbath" as referring to either the Sabbath following Passover or to the Sabbath that occurs during Passover (see Ibn Ezra; Rabbi David Tzvi Hoffman; *Menaḥot* 65a–b; *Sefer HaKuzari* 3:41). In the Beta Israel community, this expression was also interpreted as referring to the festival, but they would commence counting the days of the omer after the seventh day of Passover.

Rabbi Samson Raphael Hirsch suggests that perhaps the Torah refers to the first day of Passover as a sabbath due to the fact that harvesting and consuming the new produce is prohibited until the day on which the sheaf offering is presented. The term "sabbath," therefore, also alludes to the resting of the land (see 25:2).

23:13 | **Two-tenths of an ephah of high-quality flour:** This is twice the amount of flour usually brought as a lamb's accompanying meal offering (*Menaḥot* 89b). It is possible that the second tenth of an ephah is the meal offering of the sheaf mentioned previously (see *Bekhor Shor*; *Ḥizkuni*).

offering of your God. It is an eternal statute for your generations in all your dwellings. One may not partake of the new produce until the day upon which the sheaf offering would be presented in the Temple.

To the left: fresh wheat kernels; to the right: dry wheat kernels

15 **You shall count for yourselves from the day after the sabbath, from the day of your bringing of the sheaf of the waving, seven weeks; they shall be complete.**[D]

16 **Until the day after the seventh week, you shall count** up to **fifty days,**[D] not including the fiftieth day. Seven weeks are forty-nine days, and **then,** on the fiftieth day, **you shall present a new meal offering,** a meal offering from the new produce, **to the Lord.**

17 **From your dwellings you shall bring two loaves of waving,**[D] two meal offerings,[60] **from two-tenths of an ephah,** one-tenth of an ephah for each loaf. Of **high-quality** wheat **flour,** ground and sifted[61] **they shall be, baked as leavened bread,** unlike other meal offerings, which must be baked as unleavened bread (see 2:11), **a first offering to the Lord.**

18 **You shall offer with the bread seven unblemished lambs in their first year, and one young bull, and two rams. They shall** all **be a burnt offering to the Lord, and their meal offering and their libations** shall be in accordance with the quantities stated elsewhere in the Torah, which depend on the species of animal brought as an offering.[62] They shall be **a fire offering of a pleasing aroma to the Lord.**

19 **You shall** also **present one goat as a sin offering.**[D] A communal sin offering is presented on all of the festivals and New Moons. The Sages teach that these sin offerings atone for cases in which a ritually impure person defiled the Temple's sanctity. **And** a unique offering of **two lambs in the first year** shall be presented **as a peace offering.** Unlike all other peace offerings, which are presented by individuals, these lambs are presented as a communal peace offering.

20 **The priest shall wave them,** the lambs, **with the loaves of the first offering as a wave offering before the Lord.** He shall wave them **with,** or alongside, **the two lambs.**[D] **They shall be sacred to the Lord,** and their flesh shall be given as a portion **for the priest,** that is, God acquired the offering and gave it to the priest.[63]

21 The fiftieth day is not only the day on which the two loaves are presented; it is also a festival: **You shall proclaim on that very day, a holy convocation it shall be for you; you shall not perform any toilsome labor; it is an eternal statute in all your dwellings for your generations.**[D]

22 Since the Torah mentioned the first harvest, the following law is addressed to the owners of fields: **When you reap the harvest of your land, you shall not finish the corner of your**

DISCUSSION

23:15| **Seven weeks; they shall be complete:** These seven weeks must be complete, whole weeks; one does not mark the passing of any particular day of the week. This contradicts the interpretation of those sects that claimed that the obligation is to count the Sabbaths.

23:16| **Until the day after the seventh week, you shall count fifty days:** The commandment to count seven weeks from the bringing of the sheaf is known as the counting of the sheaf, or the counting of the omer. At the conclusion of this period, on the fiftieth day, the Festival of Weeks, Shavuot, is celebrated, and a unique offering is presented. It is called the Festival of Weeks due to the fact that it is celebrated seven weeks after the sheaf offering is brought (Exodus 34:22; Deuteronomy 16:10, 16; II Chronicles 8:13; see also Numbers 28:26). It is also called the Festival of Reaping (Exodus 23:16) and the Day of the First Fruits (Numbers 28:26). The Festival of Weeks does not occur on a fixed date; it is celebrated at the culmination of the period of counting (see Deuteronomy 16:9–10). During the Temple period, when there was no fixed calendar, the Festival of Weeks could fall on either the fifth, sixth, or seventh day of the month of Sivan (see *Shabbat* 86b–87a; *Rosh HaShana* 6b).

23:17| **You shall bring two loaves of waving:** The fifty days between the bringing of the sheaf offering and the bringing of the two loaves of waving correlate to the period between the ripening of barley and the ripening of wheat. The sheaf offering consists of one-tenth of an ephah of roasted barley grains from the new produce (2:14), whereas the two loaves of waving are baked from wheat flour of the new produce. The two loaves were very large, and according to the tradition of the Sages they were molded in a special, decorative shape, as they were considered a unique gift presented to God on this festival (see *Menaḥot* 96a).

23:19| **One goat as a sin offering:** The Talmud states that the communal sin offerings presented on festivals and New Moons atone in the case of one who unwittingly entered the Temple while ritually impure or partook of the sacrificial food while ritually impure (see *Shevuot* 2a).

23:20| **With the two lambs:** There are different opinions among the Sages with regard to the precise manner in which this offering is waved (see *Menaḥot* 62a). In any case, only the two loaves and the lambs were waved, and not the other offerings, even though they were also brought "with the bread" (verse 18). For this reason the verse reiterates that "the priest shall wave them" and that the loaves are waved "with the two lambs." Rav Se'adya Gaon translates the

יד ההין: ולחם וקלי וכרמל לא תאכלו עד־עצם היום הזה עד הביאכם את־קרבן יט
טו אלהיכם חקת עולם לדרתיכם בכל משבתיכם: וספרתם
לכם ממחרת השבת מיום הביאכם את־עמר התנופה שבע שבתות תמימת
טז תהיינה: עד ממחרת השבת השביעת תספרו חמשים יום והקרבתם מנחה
יז חדשה ליהוה: ממושבתיכם תביאו | לחם תנופה שתים שני עשרנים סלת
יח תהיינה חמץ תאפינה בכורים ליהוה: והקרבתם על־הלחם שבעת כבשים
תמימם בני שנה ופר בן־בקר אחד ואילם שנים יהיו עלה ליהוה ומנחתם
יט ונסכיהם אשה ריח־ניחח ליהוה: ועשיתם שעיר־עזים אחד לחטאת ושני
כ כבשים בני שנה לזבח שלמים: והניף הכהן | אתם על לחם הבכרים תנופה
כא לפני יהוה על־שני כבשים קדש יהיו ליהוה לכהן: וקראתם בעצם | היום
הזה מקרא־קדש יהיה לכם כל־מלאכת עבדה לא תעשו חקת עולם בכל־

רש"י

בכל משבתיכם. נחלקו בו חכמי ישראל, יש שלמדו מכאן שהחדש נוהג בחוצה לארץ, ויש אומרים, לא בא אלא ללמד שלא נצטוו על החדש אלא לאחר ירשה וישיבה משכבשו וחלקו:

טו | **ממחרת השבת.** ממחרת יום טוב: **תמימת תהיינה.** מלמד שמתחיל ומונה מבערב, שאם לא כן אינן תמימות:

טז | **השבת השביעת.** כתרגומו: "שבועתא שביעתא": **עד ממחרת השבת השביעת תספרו.** ולא עד בכלל, והן ארבעים ותשעה יום: **חמשים יום והקרבתם מנחה חדשה לה'.** ביום החמשים תקריבוה. ואומר אני, זהו מדרשו, אבל פשוטו: "עד ממחרת השבת השביעת שהוא יום חמשים תספרו", ומקרא מסרס הוא: **מנחה חדשה.** היא המנחה הראשונה שהובאה מן החדש. ואם תאמר, הרי קרבה מנחת העמר? אינה כשאר כל המנחות, שהיא באה מן השעורים:

יז | **ממושבתיכם.** ולא מחוצה לארץ: **לחם תנופה.** לחם תרומה המורם לשם גבוה, וזו היא המנחה החדשה האמורה למעלה: **בכורים.** ראשונה לכל המנחות, אף למנחת קנאות הבאה מן השעורים, לא תקרב מן החדש קדם לשתי הלחם:

יח | **על הלחם.** בגלל הלחם, חובה ללחם: **ומנחתם ונסכיהם.** כמשפט מנחה ונסכים המפרשים בכל בהמה בפרשת נסכים (במדבר טו, ח-טז): שלשה עשרנים לפר ושני עשרנים לאיל ועשרון לכבש – זו היא המנחה. והנסכים: חצי ההין לפר ושלישית ההין לאיל ורביעית ההין לכבש:

יט | **ועשיתם שעיר עזים.** יכול שבעת הכבשים והשעיר האמורים כאן הם שבעת הכבשים והשעיר האמורים בחומש הפקודים (שם כח, כז, ל)? כשאתה מגיע אצל פרים ואילים אינן הם, אמור מעתה, אלו לעצמן ואלו לעצמן, אלו קרבו בגלל הלחם ואלו למוספין:

כ | **והניף הכהן אתם... תנופה.** מלמד שטעונין תנופה חיים. יכול כלם? תלמוד לומר: "על שני כבשים": **קדש יהיו.** לפי ששלמי יחיד קדשים קלים, הזקק לומר בשלמי צבור שהם קדשי קדשים:

כב | **ובקצרכם.** חזר ושנה לעבר עליהם בשני לאוין. אמר רבי אבדימי ברבי יוסף, מה ראה הכתוב לתנה באמצע הרגלים, פסח ועצרת מכאן וראש השנה ויום הכפורים מכאן? ללמדך שכל הנותן לקט שכחה ופאה לעני כראוי, מעלין עליו כאלו בנה בית המקדש והקריב עליו קרבנותיו בתוכו: **תעזב.** הנח לפניהם והם ילקטו, ואין לך לסיע לאחד מהם: **אני ה' אלהיכם.** נאמן לשלם שכר:

DISCUSSION

verse: "The priest shall wave of them with the loaves," and explains that only the breast, thigh, and fats of the lambs are waved (see also Rabbi Samson Raphael Hirsch).

23:21| **An eternal statute in all your dwellings for your generations:** The verse perhaps alludes to the fact that the offerings would not always be presented in the Temple. The Jewish people were exiled, and the Temple destroyed. Nevertheless, the significance of the fiftieth day always remains, and it is observed as a festival by Jews everywhere (see Ramban, verse 16). The Talmud and the prayer liturgy link the Festival of Weeks to the day of the giving of the Torah, as it may be derived from the verses that the giving of the Torah took place fifty days after the exodus from Egypt (see *Shabbat* 86b–87a; *Pesaḥim* 68b; *Megilla* 31a).

field in your reaping; rather, you shall leave an unharvested area. **And the gleanings of your harvest,** the sheaves that fall during the harvest, **you shall not gather. For the poor and for the stranger you shall leave them,** both the unharvested area and the fallen sheaves. **I am the Lord your God.**

23 The Torah continues the list of festivals, which are presented *Fifth aliya* according to the order in which they occur during the calendar year: **The Lord spoke to Moses, saying:**

24 **Speak to the children of Israel, saying: In the seventh month,** Tishrei, **on the first day of the month,**[D] **shall be a** day of **rest for you, a remembrance by means of an alarm blast.** On this day you will remember your duties to God, and you will be remembered by Him, through the blast of the shofar.[64] This day is also **a holy convocation.**

25 **You shall not perform any toilsome labor, and you shall present a fire offering to the Lord,** as detailed elsewhere.[65]

26 **The Lord spoke to Moses, saying:**

27 In general, the festivals are times of feasting and rejoicing. **However, on the tenth day of this seventh month,** Tishrei, **is the Day of Atonement**[D] for the Jewish people, which is a different kind of festival.[66] **A holy convocation it shall be for you. And you shall afflict yourselves.** The form of this affliction is not explained here. However, it seems that the verse is not instructing one to inflict upon himself any possible form of suffering, but to abstain from food, drink, and other common forms of physical pleasure. These are referred to here literally as "afflictions of the soul."[67] **And you shall bring a fire offering to the Lord,** the offerings unique to this day.[68]

28 In addition to the commandment to afflict oneself, there is another distinction between the Day of Atonement and the other festivals: **You shall not perform any labor on that very day.** In contrast to the festivals, on which only toilsome labor is prohibited, on the Day of Atonement all forms of labor are prohibited, just as they are prohibited on the Sabbath. This prohibition is not dependent on the presenting of the day's offerings. It is due to the sanctity of the day itself, **as it is a day of atonement, to atone for you before the Lord your God.**

29 **For any person who is not afflicted on that very day shall be excised from his people.**

30 **And any person who performs any labor on that very day, I shall destroy that person from among his people.** The transgression of performing labor on the Day of Atonement is no less severe than the sin of not fasting. One who violates either commandment is liable to the punishment of excision.[697]

31 **You shall not perform any labor; it is an eternal statute for your generations in all your dwellings.**

32 **It,** the Day of Atonement, **is a sabbatical rest for you, and you shall afflict yourselves** on it. **On the ninth of the month,** at the conclusion of the day, **in the evening** following that day, **from evening to evening,**[D] **you shall rest on your sabbath.**

Sixth aliya 33 **The Lord spoke to Moses, saying:**

34 **Speak to the children of Israel, saying: On the fifteenth day of this seventh month is the Festival of Tabernacles** for **seven days to the Lord.**

35 **On the first day is a holy convocation; you shall not perform any toilsome labor.**

36 For **seven days you shall present a fire offering to the Lord** each day, as detailed elsewhere.[70] **On the eighth day shall be a holy convocation for you, and you shall bring a fire offering to the Lord. It is an assembly,**[D] a general gathering for God and the Jewish people. **You shall not perform any toilsome labor** on this day.

37 The Torah concludes: **These are the appointed times of the Lord, which you shall proclaim** and observe as **holy convocations, to present a fire offering to the Lord: a burnt offering and a meal offering, a feast offering and libations, each day's matter on its day.** On each festival day one must present the offerings prescribed for that day. On some of these days toilsome labor is prohibited, and with regard to some of these days the Torah sets down specific commandments.

DISCUSSION

23:24| **In the seventh month, on the first day of the month:** Virtually nothing is stated in the Written Torah about the character of this festival, other than that it is "a remembrance by means of an alarm blast" and "a day of sounding the alarm" (Numbers 29:1). The Talmud gives this festival the name Rosh HaShana, the New Year, despite the fact that it occurs on the first day of the seventh month. The fact that the New Year does not occur in the first month is due to the merging of two calendar systems into one (see commentary on Exodus 22:16, 34:22).

23:27| **The Day of Atonement:** The Torah does not associate this day with any historical occurrence. Nevertheless, the Talmud links the date of the Day of Atonement, the tenth of Tishrei, to the giving of the second tablets of stone, which signified God's forgiveness for the sin of the Golden Calf (see *Ta'anit* 30b).

23:32| **From evening to evening:** According to the Torah, a day is a time unit that commences in the evening and concludes with nightfall the following day. Since the Day of Atonement occurs on the tenth of Tishrei, it commences at the conclusion of the ninth of Tishrei, in the evening. The concept of a day commencing with nightfall is already alluded to in Genesis (1:5; see commentary ad loc.).

23:36| **An assembly:** Unlike Passover, when the seventh day is a holy convocation, it is the eighth day that is celebrated on the Festival of Tabernacles. The Bible uses the term "*atzeret*," assembly, only with regard to the eighth day of the Festival of Tabernacles (see also Numbers 29:35; Nehemiah 8:18) and the seventh day of Passover (Deuteronomy 16:8), while the Sages use the term *atzeret* in reference to the Festival of Weeks, Shavuot. In order to differentiate between the Festival of Weeks and the eighth day of Tabernacles, the Sages refer to the eighth day of Tabernacles as *Shemini Atzeret*, the Eighth Day of Assembly.

כב מוֹשְׁבֹתֵיכֶם לְדֹרֹתֵיכֶם: וּבְקֻצְרְכֶם אֶת־קְצִיר אַרְצְכֶם לֹא־תְכַלֶּה פְּאַת שָׂדְךָ
בְּקֻצְרֶךָ וְלֶקֶט קְצִירְךָ לֹא תְלַקֵּט לֶעָנִי וְלַגֵּר תַּעֲזֹב אֹתָם אֲנִי יהוה אֱלֹהֵיכֶם:
כג כד וַיְדַבֵּר יהוה אֶל־מֹשֶׁה לֵּאמֹר: דַּבֵּר אֶל־בְּנֵי יִשְׂרָאֵל לֵאמֹר בַּחֹדֶשׁ הַשְּׁבִיעִי חמישי
כה בְּאֶחָד לַחֹדֶשׁ יִהְיֶה לָכֶם שַׁבָּתוֹן זִכְרוֹן תְּרוּעָה מִקְרָא־קֹדֶשׁ: כָּל־מְלֶאכֶת
כו עֲבֹדָה לֹא תַעֲשׂוּ וְהִקְרַבְתֶּם אִשֶּׁה לַיהוה: וַיְדַבֵּר יהוה אֶל־
כז מֹשֶׁה לֵּאמֹר: אַךְ בֶּעָשׂוֹר לַחֹדֶשׁ הַשְּׁבִיעִי הַזֶּה יוֹם הַכִּפֻּרִים הוּא מִקְרָא־קֹדֶשׁ
כח יִהְיֶה לָכֶם וְעִנִּיתֶם אֶת־נַפְשֹׁתֵיכֶם וְהִקְרַבְתֶּם אִשֶּׁה לַיהוה: וְכָל־מְלָאכָה לֹא
תַעֲשׂוּ בְּעֶצֶם הַיּוֹם הַזֶּה כִּי יוֹם כִּפֻּרִים הוּא לְכַפֵּר עֲלֵיכֶם לִפְנֵי יהוה אֱלֹהֵיכֶם:
כט ל כִּי כָל־הַנֶּפֶשׁ אֲשֶׁר לֹא־תְעֻנֶּה בְּעֶצֶם הַיּוֹם הַזֶּה וְנִכְרְתָה מֵעַמֶּיהָ: וְכָל־הַנֶּפֶשׁ
אֲשֶׁר תַּעֲשֶׂה כָּל־מְלָאכָה בְּעֶצֶם הַיּוֹם הַזֶּה וְהַאֲבַדְתִּי אֶת־הַנֶּפֶשׁ הַהִוא מִקֶּרֶב
לא לב עַמָּהּ: כָּל־מְלָאכָה לֹא תַעֲשׂוּ חֻקַּת עוֹלָם לְדֹרֹתֵיכֶם בְּכֹל מֹשְׁבֹתֵיכֶם: שַׁבַּת
שַׁבָּתוֹן הוּא לָכֶם וְעִנִּיתֶם אֶת־נַפְשֹׁתֵיכֶם בְּתִשְׁעָה לַחֹדֶשׁ בָּעֶרֶב מֵעֶרֶב עַד־
עֶרֶב תִּשְׁבְּתוּ שַׁבַּתְּכֶם:
לג לד וַיְדַבֵּר יהוה אֶל־מֹשֶׁה לֵּאמֹר: דַּבֵּר אֶל־בְּנֵי יִשְׂרָאֵל לֵאמֹר בַּחֲמִשָּׁה עָשָׂר ששי
לה יוֹם לַחֹדֶשׁ הַשְּׁבִיעִי הַזֶּה חַג הַסֻּכּוֹת שִׁבְעַת יָמִים לַיהוה: בַּיּוֹם הָרִאשׁוֹן
לו מִקְרָא־קֹדֶשׁ כָּל־מְלֶאכֶת עֲבֹדָה לֹא תַעֲשׂוּ: שִׁבְעַת יָמִים תַּקְרִיבוּ אִשֶּׁה
לַיהוה בַּיּוֹם הַשְּׁמִינִי מִקְרָא־קֹדֶשׁ יִהְיֶה לָכֶם וְהִקְרַבְתֶּם אִשֶּׁה לַיהוה עֲצֶרֶת
לז הוּא כָּל־מְלֶאכֶת עֲבֹדָה לֹא תַעֲשׂוּ: אֵלֶּה מוֹעֲדֵי יהוה אֲשֶׁר־תִּקְרְאוּ אֹתָם

רש״י

כד| **זִכְרוֹן תְּרוּעָה.** זִכְרוֹן פְּסוּקֵי זִכְרוֹנוֹת וּפְסוּקֵי שׁוֹפָרוֹת, לִזְכֹּר לָכֶם עֲקֵדַת יִצְחָק שֶׁקָּרַב תַּחְתָּיו אַיִל:

כה| **וְהִקְרַבְתֶּם אִשֶּׁה.** הַמּוּסָפִים הָאֲמוּרִים בְּחוּמַשׁ הַפְּקֻדִים (במדבר כט, א-ו):

כז| **אַךְ.** כָּל אַכִין וְרַקִּין שֶׁבַּתּוֹרָה מִעוּטִין, מְכַפֵּר הוּא לַשָּׁבִין וְאֵינוֹ מְכַפֵּר עַל שֶׁאֵינָם שָׁבִין:

ל| **וְהַאֲבַדְתִּי.** לְפִי שֶׁהוּא אוֹמֵר כָּרֵת בְּכָל מָקוֹם וְאֵינִי יוֹדֵעַ מַה הוּא, כְּשֶׁהוּא אוֹמֵר: "וְהַאֲבַדְתִּי", לִמֵּד עַל הַכָּרֵת שֶׁאֵינוֹ אֶלָּא אֲבָדוֹן:

לא| **כָּל מְלָאכָה וְגוֹ׳.** לַעֲבֹר עָלָיו בְּלָאוִין הַרְבֵּה, אוֹ לְהַזְהִיר עַל מְלֶאכֶת לַיְלָה כִּמְלֶאכֶת יוֹם: "מִקְרָא קֹדֶשׁ" (לעיל פסוק כז) – קַדְּשֵׁהוּ בִּכְסוּת נְקִיָּה וּבִתְפִלָּה, וְכָל שְׁאָר יָמִים טוֹבִים – בְּמַאֲכָל וּבְמִשְׁתֶּה וּבִכְסוּת נְקִיָּה וּבִתְפִלָּה:

לו| **עֲצֶרֶת הִוא.** עָצַרְתִּי אֶתְכֶם אֶצְלִי, כְּמֶלֶךְ שֶׁזִּמֵּן אֶת בָּנָיו לִסְעוּדָה לְכָךְ וְכָךְ יָמִים, כֵּיוָן שֶׁהִגִּיעַ זְמַנָּן לִפָּטֵר אָמַר: בָּנַי בְּבַקָּשָׁה מִכֶּם, עַכְּבוּ עִמִּי עוֹד יוֹם אֶחָד, קָשָׁה עָלַי פְּרִישַׁתְכֶם: **כָּל מְלֶאכֶת עֲבֹדָה.** אֲפִלּוּ מְלָאכָה שֶׁהִיא עֲבוֹדָה לָכֶם, שֶׁאִם לֹא תַעֲשׂוּהָ יֵשׁ חֶסְרוֹן כִּיס בַּדָּבָר: **לֹא תַעֲשׂוּ.** יָכוֹל אַף חֻלּוֹ שֶׁל מוֹעֵד יְהֵא אָסוּר בִּמְלֶאכֶת עֲבוֹדָה? תַּלְמוּד לוֹמַר: "הִוא":

לז| **עֹלָה וּמִנְחָה.** מִנְחַת נְסָכִים הַקְּרֵבָה עִם הָעוֹלָה: **דְּבַר יוֹם בְּיוֹמוֹ.** חֹק הַכָּתוּב בְּחוּמַשׁ הַפְּקוּדִים (במדבר כח-כט): **דְּבַר יוֹם בְּיוֹמוֹ.** הָא אִם עָבַר יוֹמוֹ בָּטֵל קָרְבָּנוֹ:

Myrtle, "bough of a leafy tree"

Citron, "the fruit of a pleasant tree"

"Willows of the brook"

Lulav, "branches of date palms"

38 The festival offerings are **besides** the offerings of **the Sabbaths of the Lord,** which are detailed elsewhere,[71] **and besides your gifts** to the Temple, **and besides all your vows,** offerings that one vowed to bring to the Temple, **and besides all your pledges,** specific animals that one pledged to bring as an offering (see 22:21). The offerings presented on the festivals are besides those offerings **that you give to the Lord** even at other times of year.

39 **However,** in addition to the characteristics common to all of the festival days, the offerings and the prohibition of toilsome labor, the Festival of Tabernacles has unique characteristics,[72] which pertain to the timing of the festival, during the rejoicing over the gathering of one's produce:[73] **On the fifteenth day of the seventh month, when you gather the produce of the land, you shall celebrate the Festival of the Lord seven days,** presenting the festival offerings. **On the first day** there shall be **a day of rest, and on the eighth day** there shall be **a day of rest.** These are the holy convocations mentioned above (23:35–36).

40 **You shall take for you on the first day the fruit of a pleasant tree,**[B] identified by tradition as the citron, an *etrog*;[74] **branches of date palms,**[B] identified by tradition as the *lulav*, a young branch of a date palm, the leaves of which have yet to separate and are still bound to the branch's spine;[75] **a bough of a leafy tree,**[B] a myrtle branch;[76] **and** branches of **willows of the brook,**[B] a species of tree that typically grows next to streams.[77] **You shall rejoice** with these four species **before the Lord your God,** in the Temple, **seven days.**[78] The taking of these four species together expresses the celebration and joy of these days. The Jewish people go forth with these plants in their hands, which they wave like flags.

41 **You shall celebrate it** as **a festival to the Lord seven days in the year, an eternal statute for your generations; in the seventh month you shall celebrate it.**

42 There is another commandment that is unique to the Festival of Tabernacles: **You shall live in booths seven days.** The Torah does not describe the precise manner in which these booths, or *sukkot*, must be constructed. Some of the laws concerning these booths are derived from verses, while others are part of the Sages' oral tradition.[79] **Every native,** every permanent resident,[80] **in Israel shall live in booths.** This excludes gentiles who reside in the Land of Israel. Even if they reside there permanently and observe the Noahide commandments, they are not defined as "natives."

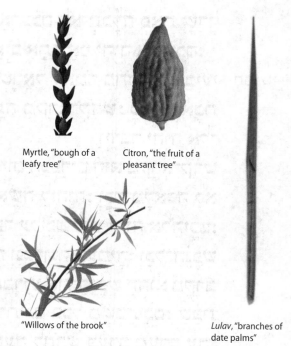

43 You shall dwell in booths **so that your generations will know that I had the children of Israel live in booths**[D] **when I took them out of the land of Egypt. I am the Lord your God.** The dwelling in booths is intended to recall the exodus from Egypt. By dwelling in a booth, one places himself in a similar environment to that of the Israelites who wandered in the wilderness. While the people dwelt in the wilderness they lacked fixed accommodations, whereas previously, in Egypt, and subsequently, when they entered the land of Canaan, they dwelt in houses. Apparently, during their journey in the wilderness, the Israelites did not dwell in tents but took cover in the shade of booths, temporary dwellings constructed from any available material.

44 **Moses spoke to the children of Israel the appointed times of the Lord.** He told them all the aforementioned festivals, which comprise all of the festivals that appear in the Torah.

DISCUSSION

23:43 | **That I had the children of Israel dwell in booths:** There is a certain romantic aspect to living in a booth. Even once the people have already settled in their land, when the gathering of produce from the fields has been completed, the Jewish people return to their origins and dwell like nomads who wander in the wilderness. By reverting to their former status, they recall the first love between the Jewish people and God: "So said the Lord: I have remembered for you the kindness of your youth, the love of your nuptials; your following Me in the wilderness, in a land not sown" (Jeremiah 2:2). Although the nation was at that point homeless, the lack of commitments that accompanied their rootlessness allowed them to forge a deeper relationship with God (see Rashbam; *Keli Yakar*).

מִקְרָאֵי קֹדֶשׁ לְהַקְרִיב אִשֶּׁה לַיהוָה עֹלָה וּמִנְחָה זֶבַח וּנְסָכִים דְּבַר־יוֹם בְּיוֹמוֹ׃
לח מִלְּבַד שַׁבְּתֹת יְהוָה וּמִלְּבַד מַתְּנוֹתֵיכֶם וּמִלְּבַד כָּל־נִדְרֵיכֶם וּמִלְּבַד כָּל־נִדְבֹתֵיכֶם
לט אֲשֶׁר תִּתְּנוּ לַיהוָה׃ אַךְ בַּחֲמִשָּׁה עָשָׂר יוֹם לַחֹדֶשׁ הַשְּׁבִיעִי בְּאָסְפְּכֶם אֶת־תְּבוּאַת
הָאָרֶץ תָּחֹגּוּ אֶת־חַג־יְהוָה שִׁבְעַת יָמִים בַּיּוֹם הָרִאשׁוֹן שַׁבָּתוֹן וּבַיּוֹם הַשְּׁמִינִי
מ שַׁבָּתוֹן׃ וּלְקַחְתֶּם לָכֶם בַּיּוֹם הָרִאשׁוֹן פְּרִי עֵץ הָדָר כַּפֹּת תְּמָרִים וַעֲנַף עֵץ־עָבֹת
מא וְעַרְבֵי־נָחַל וּשְׂמַחְתֶּם לִפְנֵי יְהוָה אֱלֹהֵיכֶם שִׁבְעַת יָמִים׃ וְחַגֹּתֶם אֹתוֹ חַג לַיהוָה
מב שִׁבְעַת יָמִים בַּשָּׁנָה חֻקַּת עוֹלָם לְדֹרֹתֵיכֶם בַּחֹדֶשׁ הַשְּׁבִיעִי תָּחֹגּוּ אֹתוֹ׃ בַּסֻּכֹּת
מג תֵּשְׁבוּ שִׁבְעַת יָמִים כָּל־הָאֶזְרָח בְּיִשְׂרָאֵל יֵשְׁבוּ בַּסֻּכֹּת׃ לְמַעַן יֵדְעוּ דֹרֹתֵיכֶם
כִּי בַסֻּכּוֹת הוֹשַׁבְתִּי אֶת־בְּנֵי יִשְׂרָאֵל בְּהוֹצִיאִי אוֹתָם מֵאֶרֶץ מִצְרָיִם אֲנִי יְהוָה

רש"י

לט | **אַךְ בַּחֲמִשָּׁה עָשָׂר יוֹם... תָּחֹגּוּ.** קָרְבַּן שְׁלָמִים לַחֲגִיגָה. יָכוֹל תִּדְחֶה אֶת הַשַּׁבָּת? תַּלְמוּד לוֹמַר "אַךְ", הוֹאִיל וְיֵשׁ לָהּ תַּשְׁלוּמִין כָּל שִׁבְעָה: **בְּאָסְפְּכֶם אֶת תְּבוּאַת הָאָרֶץ.** שֶׁיְּהֵא חֹדֶשׁ שְׁבִיעִי זֶה בָּא בִּזְמַן אֲסִיפָה, מִכָּאן שֶׁנִּצְטַוּוּ לְעַבֵּר אֶת הַשָּׁנִים, שֶׁאִם אֵין הָעִבּוּר, פְּעָמִים שֶׁהוּא בְּאֶמְצַע הַקַּיִץ אוֹ הַחֹרֶף: **תָּחֹגּוּ.** שַׁלְמֵי חֲגִיגָה: **שִׁבְעַת יָמִים.** אִם לֹא הֵבִיא בָּזֶה יָבִיא בָּזֶה. יָכוֹל יְהֵא מֵבִיא כָּל שִׁבְעָה? תַּלְמוּד לוֹמַר: "וְחַגֹּתֶם אֹתוֹ", יוֹם אֶחָד בְּמַשְׁמָע וְלֹא יוֹתֵר. וְלָמָּה נֶאֱמַר שִׁבְעָה? לְתַשְׁלוּמִין:

מ | **פְּרִי עֵץ הָדָר.** עֵץ שֶׁטַּעַם עֵצוֹ וּפִרְיוֹ שָׁוֶה: **הָדָר.** הַדָּר בְּאִילָנוֹ מִשָּׁנָה לְשָׁנָה, וְזֶהוּ אֶתְרוֹג: **כַּפֹּת תְּמָרִים.** חָסֵר וָי"ו, לְלַמֵּד שֶׁאֵינָהּ אֶלָּא אַחַת: **וַעֲנַף עֵץ עָבֹת.** שֶׁעֲנָפָיו קְלוּעִים כַּעֲבוֹתוֹת וְכַחֲבָלִים, וְזֶהוּ הֲדַס הֶעָשׂוּי כְּמִין קְלִיעָה:

מב | **הָאֶזְרָח.** זֶה אֶזְרָח: **בְּיִשְׂרָאֵל.** לְרַבּוֹת אֶת הַגֵּרִים:

מג | **כִּי בַסֻּכּוֹת הוֹשַׁבְתִּי.** עַנְנֵי כָבוֹד:

BACKGROUND

23:40 | **The fruit of a pleasant tree:** The citron, or *etrog*, is the fruit of the citron tree, *Citrus madicia*. The citron tree is a small tree, of the Rutaceae family, which originates in Southeast Asia. It has short, hard thorns, and its fruit are egg-shaped or elongated. The fruit was well known in the region of the Land of Israel during the biblical period. Murals of fruit resembling citrons were found in a tomb in Karnak, Egypt, dated 1500 BCE. Furthermore, remains of citron seeds were discovered in Cyprus, dating from the second half of the second millennium BCE. Citron seeds were also found in Ramat Rachel south of Jerusalem, in the remains of a palace garden dating from the fifth century BCE.

Branches of date palms: The date palm, *Phoenix dactylifera*, grows in the Arava Desert, in the Dead Sea Basin, and in the Lower Jordan Valley, near springs or places with high ground water. Cultivated for its edible, sweet fruit, this palm is a medium-sized tree, 10 to 20 m tall. The branches grow at the top of the tree; they spread out, reaching a length of up to 3 m. Green leaflets, sharp and narrow, grow on each side of the branches' spines. The Sages identified the branches referred to in this verse as the young branches of the date palm, the leaves of which have yet to separate and are still bound to the branch's spine (*Sukka* 31a).

A bough of a leafy tree: The Sages identify this leafy tree as the myrtle, *Myrtus communis*, an evergreen shrub whose small, hard leaves grow tightly together. Its height ranges from 0.5 to 2 m. It grows wild in the Golan, the Upper Galilee, and the Carmel and on the banks of streams in the north of Israel. It has a pleasant fragrance; an aromatic oil is extracted from it and used for medicinal purposes as well as in perfumes. In Isaiah's prophecies of comfort and redemption, this tree symbolizes a change for the good: "I will put cedar, acacia, myrtle, and pine tree in the wilderness" (Isaiah 41:19), and "Instead of the brier, will rise a myrtle" (Isaiah 55:13).

Willows of the brook: According to the characteristics by which the Sages identify this tree, the verse is referring to trees of the *Salix* and *Populus* genus, of the Salicaceae or willow family, which typically grow near ponds and streams. The willow family comprises roughly 170 species. Of these, two fit the Sages' definitions: The pointed willow, *Salix acmophylla Boiss*, and the white willow, *Salix alba*. It is difficult nowadays to identify the original willow, due to the hybridization of species.

The Arrangement of the Candelabrum and the Table in the Sanctuary
LEVITICUS 24:1–9

The following section completes the previous discussion of the offerings presented in the Temple at certain times during the year. It sets down the laws pertaining to two rites performed in the Temple throughout the year that do not involve offerings on the altar: the kindling of the lamps of the candelabrum, and the arrangement of the showbread on the table.

24 **1** **The Lord spoke to Moses, saying:**

Seventh aliya

2 **Command the children of Israel, and they shall take to you,** as the one in charge of this matter,[81] **pure olive oil,** which was not easily obtained in the wilderness, **beaten**[D] **for the lighting, to kindle a lamp continually.**[82]

3 On the candelabrum, **outside the curtain** which conceals the Ark **of the Testimony, in the Tent of Meeting,**[83] **Aaron shall arrange it,** the oil. He shall prepare the lamps, removing the residue from the previous night's kindling, cleaning the lamps, and placing new wicks in them,[84] so that they will be ready to be lit and to remain alight **from evening until morning**[D] **before the Lord continually.** Aaron must ensure that the candelabrum shines from evening till morning every day. This commandment does not pertain only to the Tabernacle in the wilderness, but is **an eternal statute for your generations.**

4 **On the pure candelabrum,** on the pure gold of the candelabrum, without any intervening matter, **he,** Aaron, **shall arrange the lamps.** The words "the pure candelabrum" may also refer to the clean candelabrum, after the removal of the previous night's remnants.[85] Furthermore, the candelabrum is designed for the single purpose of kindling. It is a vessel that symbolizes purity and radiance.[86] The lamps shall be arranged **before the Lord continuously.**

5 The arrangement of the showbread on the table is another rite performed weekly in the Temple: **You shall take high-quality flour and bake with it twelve loaves;**[D] **two-tenths of an ephah** of flour, which is a dry measure of volume corresponding to around 5 L, **shall be one loaf.** These are large loaves.

6 **You shall place them,** the twelve loaves, **in two arrangements, six** loaves **to the arrangement.** Four supporting panels rose up above the table for the showbread, between which were inserted rods, upon which the showbread was placed.[87] The loaves shall be placed **on the pure table,** on the pure gold covering the table without any intervening matter, **before the Lord.** The words "the pure table" may also refer to the fact that it is intended solely for the arrangement of the showbread and for no other purpose.

7 **You shall place pure frankincense on the arrangement,** either literally upon each of the two arrangements, or next to them.[88] **And it,** the frankincense, **shall be a memorial portion for the bread, a fire offering to the Lord.** The frankincense is burned upon the altar as a remembrance for the bread, which is not burned.[89]

Loaves

Table with the twelve loaves

8 **Each and every Sabbath day he shall arrange it,** the showbread, **before the Lord continuously.** Every Sabbath day, the priests bring twelve fresh loaves and arrange them on the table. At the same time, the old loaves are removed, and the frankincense that was placed with them is burned on the altar. Like the oil for the candelabrum, the showbread is a gift to the Temple **from the children of Israel,** from the entire nation, as **an eternal covenant.** The Jewish people are always obligated to present this gift to the Temple.

9 **It,** the showbread,[90] **shall be for Aaron and his sons, and they shall eat it in a holy place, for it is a sacred sacrament for him from the fire offerings of the Lord, an eternal statute.** The status of the showbread is comparable to that of the meal offerings, which are eaten by the priests in the Temple as gifts of the priesthood.

מד אֱלֹהֵיכֶם: וַיְדַבֵּר מֹשֶׁה אֶת־מֹעֲדֵי יהוה אֶל־בְּנֵי יִשְׂרָאֵל:

ב וַיְדַבֵּר יהוה אֶל־מֹשֶׁה לֵּאמֹר: צַו אֶת־בְּנֵי יִשְׂרָאֵל וְיִקְחוּ אֵלֶיךָ שֶׁמֶן זַיִת זָךְ כָּתִית שביעי

ג לַמָּאוֹר לְהַעֲלֹת נֵר תָּמִיד: מִחוּץ לְפָרֹכֶת הָעֵדֻת בְּאֹהֶל מוֹעֵד יַעֲרֹךְ אֹתוֹ אַהֲרֹן

ד מֵעֶרֶב עַד־בֹּקֶר לִפְנֵי יהוה תָּמִיד חֻקַּת עוֹלָם לְדֹרֹתֵיכֶם: עַל הַמְּנֹרָה הַטְּהֹרָה יַעֲרֹךְ אֶת־הַנֵּרוֹת לִפְנֵי יהוה תָּמִיד:

ה וְלָקַחְתָּ סֹלֶת וְאָפִיתָ אֹתָהּ שְׁתֵּים עֶשְׂרֵה חַלּוֹת שְׁנֵי עֶשְׂרֹנִים יִהְיֶה הַחַלָּה הָאֶחָת:

ו וְשַׂמְתָּ אוֹתָם שְׁתַּיִם מַעֲרָכוֹת שֵׁשׁ הַמַּעֲרָכֶת עַל הַשֻּׁלְחָן הַטָּהֹר לִפְנֵי יהוה: וְנָתַתָּ

ז עַל־הַמַּעֲרֶכֶת לְבֹנָה זַכָּה וְהָיְתָה לַלֶּחֶם לְאַזְכָּרָה אִשֶּׁה לַיהוה: בְּיוֹם הַשַּׁבָּת בְּיוֹם

ח הַשַּׁבָּת יַעַרְכֶנּוּ לִפְנֵי יהוה תָּמִיד מֵאֵת בְּנֵי־יִשְׂרָאֵל בְּרִית עוֹלָם: וְהָיְתָה לְאַהֲרֹן

רש"י

פרק כד

ב] צַו אֶת בְּנֵי יִשְׂרָאֵל. זוֹ פָּרָשַׁת מִצְוַת הַנֵּרוֹת. וּפָרָשַׁת 'וְאַתָּה תְּצַוֶּה' (שמות כז, כ) לֹא נֶאֶמְרָה אֶלָּא עַל סֵדֶר מְלֶאכֶת הַמִּשְׁכָּן לְפָרֵשׁ צֹרֶךְ הַמְּנוֹרָה, וְכֵן מַשְׁמָע: וְאַתָּה סוֹפְךָ לְצַוּוֹת אֶת בְּנֵי יִשְׂרָאֵל עַל כָּךְ: שֶׁמֶן זַיִת זָךְ. שְׁלֹשָׁה שְׁמָנִים יוֹצְאִים מִן הַזַּיִת, הָרִאשׁוֹן קָרוּי זָךְ, וְהֵן מְפֹרָשִׁין בִּמְנָחוֹת (דף פו ע"ח) וּבְתוֹרַת כֹּהֲנִים (פרשתא יג, א): תָּמִיד. מִלַּיְלָה לְלַיְלָה, כְּמוֹ: 'עֹלַת תָּמִיד' (במדבר כח, ו) שֶׁאֵינָה אֶלָּא מִיּוֹם לְיוֹם:

ג] לְפָרֹכֶת הָעֵדֻת. שֶׁלִּפְנֵי הָאָרוֹן שֶׁהוּא קָרוּי עֵדוּת. וְרַבּוֹתֵינוּ דָּרְשׁוּ עַל נֵר מַעֲרָבִי, שֶׁהוּא עֵדוּת לְכָל בָּאֵי עוֹלָם שֶׁהַשְּׁכִינָה שׁוֹרָה בְּיִשְׂרָאֵל, שֶׁנּוֹתֵן בָּהּ שֶׁמֶן כְּמִדַּת חַבְרוֹתֶיהָ, וּמִמֶּנָּה הָיָה מַתְחִיל וּבָהּ הָיָה מְסַיֵּם: יַעֲרֹךְ אֹתוֹ אַהֲרֹן מֵעֶרֶב עַד בֹּקֶר. יַעֲרֹךְ אוֹתוֹ עֲרִיכָה הָרְאוּיָה לְמִדַּת כָּל הַלַּיְלָה, וְשִׁעֲרוּ חֲכָמִים חֲצִי לֹג לְכָל נֵר וָנֵר, וְהֵן כְּדַאי אַף לְלֵילֵי תְקוּפַת טֵבֵת, וּמִדָּה זוֹ הֻקְבְּעָה לָהֶם:

ד] הַמְּנֹרָה הַטְּהֹרָה. שֶׁהִיא זָהָב טָהוֹר. דָּבָר אַחֵר, עַל טָהֳרָהּ שֶׁל מְנוֹרָה, שֶׁמְּטַהֲרָהּ וּמְדַשְּׁנָהּ תְּחִלָּה מִן הָאֵפֶר:

ו] שֵׁשׁ הַמַּעֲרֶכֶת. שֵׁשׁ חַלּוֹת הַמַּעֲרֶכֶת הָאֶחָת: הַשֻּׁלְחָן הַטָּהֹר. שֶׁל זָהָב טָהוֹר. דָּבָר אַחֵר, עַל טָהֳרוֹ שֶׁל שֻׁלְחָן, שֶׁלֹּא יִהְיוּ הַסְּנִיפִין מַגְבִּיהִין אֶת הַלֶּחֶם מֵעַל גַּבֵּי הַשֻּׁלְחָן:

ז] וְנָתַתָּ עַל הַמַּעֲרֶכֶת. עַל כָּל אַחַת מִשְּׁתֵּי הַמַּעֲרָכוֹת. הֲרֵי שְׁנֵי בְזִכֵי לְבוֹנָה, מְלֹא קֹמֶץ לְכָל אַחַת: וְהָיְתָה. הַלְּבוֹנָה הַזֹּאת: לַלֶּחֶם לְאַזְכָּרָה. שֶׁאֵין מִן הַלֶּחֶם לַגָּבוֹהַּ כְּלוּם, אֶלָּא הַלְּבוֹנָה נִקְטֶרֶת כְּשֶׁמְּסַלְּקִין אוֹתוֹ בְּכָל שַׁבָּת וְשַׁבָּת, וְהִיא לְזִכָּרוֹן לַלֶּחֶם, שֶׁעַל יָדָהּ הוּא נִזְכָּר לְמַעְלָה, כַּקֹּמֶץ שֶׁהוּא אַזְכָּרָה לַמִּנְחָה:

ט] וְהָיְתָה. הַמִּנְחָה הַזֹּאת, שֶׁכָּל דָּבָר הַבָּא מִן הַתְּבוּאָה בִּכְלַל מִנְחָה הוּא: וַאֲכָלֻהוּ. מוּסָב עַל הַלֶּחֶם שֶׁהוּא לְשׁוֹן זָכָר:

DISCUSSION

24:2 | Pure olive oil, beaten: The ripe olives are struck with a stone or similar object so that the oil flows out. Oil extracted in this manner contains fewer impurities than that produced by pressing the olives in an olive press after they have been beaten. When olives are beaten by hand, only the purest oil is extracted from the olives, while the rest of the oil remains in the olives (see Menaḥot 86a).

24:3 | From evening until morning: At times the lamps continued to burn for twenty-four hours and more (see Shabbat 22b; Yoma 39b; Temura 30b). However, the commandment primarily requires them to be kindled at night. Like the other vessels used in the Tabernacle, the candelabrum possesses symbolic meaning, and the kindling of its light throughout the darkness is an important aspect of that symbolism.

24:5 | Twelve loaves: According to the tradition of the Sages, the loaves of the showbread were molded in a complex form. Their unique design included a base with walls on two sides (see Menaḥot 94a–95a).

The Blasphemer and the Ensuing Commandments

LEVITICUS 24:10–23

The following section describes an appalling incident that occurred in the wilderness. It is unclear how this episode is connected to the matters discussed previously. Some commentaries note the sharp contrast between the respect and honor toward the divine service mandated by the many aforementioned commandments and the utter disrespect toward God displayed in the vile conduct of the blasphemer. The sin of blasphemy is so shocking that it is often referred to, both in the Bible and in the Talmud, by a euphemism, e.g., to bless God.[91]

10 **The son of an Israelite woman, and he** was not of solely Jewish descent, but **the son of an Egyptian man,**[D] **went out among the children of Israel.** This indicates that the son of a Jewish woman born from a gentile is considered a member of the Jewish people.[92] **And the son of the Israelite woman and the Israelite man,** one who was of solely Jewish descent and who remains anonymous, **fought in the camp.**

11 When the quarrel became heated, **the son of the Israelite woman blasphemed,**[93] explicitly mentioning **the Name** of God, **and he cursed,** speaking derogatively and mockingly.[94] This occurred in public, and **they,** the witnesses who heard him, **brought him to Moses. And the name of his mother was Shelomit, daughter of Divri, of the tribe of Dan.** The blasphemer's own name is not stated, while the mention of his mother's name in this context and in the context of her relationship with an Egyptian man is certainly not to her credit.

12 **They placed him in custody.**[D] It was clear that he had committed a transgression, but his precise punishment was unknown. They therefore waited for Moses **to clarify** his punishment **for them according to the Lord.** Unlike other prophets, Moses could address his questions directly to God and request His guidance.[95]

13 **The Lord spoke to Moses, saying:**

14 **Take the one who cursed outside the camp** for judgment; **and all** those **who heard** him, who witnessed his transgression, **shall lay their hands upon his head.** It is the witnesses' duty to designate him for punishment.[96] **And then the entire congregation shall stone him** to death. This directive was exceptional; generally one is not liable to receive the death penalty unless he

was aware of the potential punishment beforehand, whereas in this case the man knew that he was committing a transgression but he did not know what punishment was involved.[97]

15 The remainder of this passage contains commandments addressed to the entire people: **To the children of Israel you shall speak, saying: Each and every man who curses his God, then he shall bear his sin** and be punished.

16 **One who blasphemes the name of the Lord shall be put to death; the entire congregation shall stone him.** The same law applies to **the stranger,** that is, the convert, **and native alike, when he blasphemes the Name he shall be put to death.**

17 The passage now sets down several laws with regard to one who strikes another person or an animal. These laws are indirectly related to the aforementioned commandments: **If a man smites the life of a person,** killing him, **he shall be put to death** by the court.

18 **One who smites the life of an animal** that belongs to another **shall pay for it, a life for a life.** He must pay for the animal with either another animal or its equivalent value.[98]

19 **If a man** wounds and **inflicts a defect on his counterpart, as he did, so shall be done to him:**

20 **A break for a break, an eye for an eye, a tooth for a tooth; as he inflicted a defect on the person, so shall be inflicted on him.**[D] This is the punishment that he deserves.

21 **One who smites an animal shall pay for it. And one who** *Maftir* **smites a person,** even if he does not kill him but wounds him severely, **shall be put to death.**[D] Again, the verse indicates that he is deserving of death.

DISCUSSION

24:10 | **The son of an Israelite woman, and he was the son of an Egyptian man:** According to the Midrash, this was the only instance in the entire generation where a child was born to a Jewish woman and an Egyptian man (see Rashi; Ibn Ezra). The camp was organized on a tribal basis, with the division of tribes determined according to the patrilineal lineage. This meant that although the son of an Egyptian man was a member of the Jewish people he was not a member of any tribe. There was consequently no place for him in the camp. It is possible that this was the source of his quarrel with the

Israelite man, who did not want him as a neighbor (see Rashi; *Sifra, Emor* 14).

24:12 | **They placed him in custody:** Imprisonment is not a form of punishment included in Jewish penal law. People were generally placed in custody only to detain them until their punishment was determined (see also Jeremiah 32:2).

24:20 | **As he inflicted a defect on the person, so shall be inflicted on him:** According to Jewish law, this punishment is not actually carried out, nor was it ever the practice to inflict

bodily injury as punishment (see *Bava Kamma* 83b–84a; commentary on Exodus 21:25). The expressions in this verse can be interpreted as an indication that the person deserves to be punished with the injury that he inflicted. However, although he deserves to be punished in this manner, the Torah states elsewhere that there are only two cases where one cannot pay a ransom to avoid another punishment: One who unintentionally killed someone cannot avoid exile, and an intentional murderer is liable to receive the death penalty (see Numbers 35:31–32). The Sages derive from this that with regard to ◄◄

וּלְבָנָיו וַאֲכָלֻהוּ בְּמָקוֹם קָדֹשׁ כִּי קֹדֶשׁ קָדָשִׁים הוּא לוֹ מֵאִשֵּׁי יהוה חָק־עוֹלָם׃
י וַיֵּצֵא בֶּן־אִשָּׁה יִשְׂרְאֵלִית וְהוּא בֶּן־אִישׁ מִצְרִי בְּתוֹךְ בְּנֵי יִשְׂרָאֵל
יא וַיִּנָּצוּ בַּמַּחֲנֶה בֶּן הַיִּשְׂרְאֵלִית וְאִישׁ הַיִּשְׂרְאֵלִי׃ וַיִּקֹּב בֶּן־הָאִשָּׁה הַיִּשְׂרְאֵלִית
אֶת־הַשֵּׁם וַיְקַלֵּל וַיָּבִיאוּ אֹתוֹ אֶל־מֹשֶׁה וְשֵׁם אִמּוֹ שְׁלֹמִית בַּת־דִּבְרִי לְמַטֵּה־
יב דָן׃ וַיַּנִּיחֻהוּ בַּמִּשְׁמָר לִפְרֹשׁ לָהֶם עַל־פִּי יהוה׃
יג וַיְדַבֵּר יהוה אֶל־מֹשֶׁה לֵּאמֹר׃ הוֹצֵא אֶת־הַמְקַלֵּל אֶל־מִחוּץ לַמַּחֲנֶה וְסָמְכוּ
יד
טו כָל־הַשֹּׁמְעִים אֶת־יְדֵיהֶם עַל־רֹאשׁוֹ וְרָגְמוּ אֹתוֹ כָּל־הָעֵדָה׃ וְאֶל־בְּנֵי יִשְׂרָאֵל
טז תְּדַבֵּר לֵאמֹר אִישׁ אִישׁ כִּי־יְקַלֵּל אֱלֹהָיו וְנָשָׂא חֶטְאוֹ׃ וְנֹקֵב שֵׁם־יהוה מוֹת יוּמָת
יז רָגוֹם יִרְגְּמוּ־בוֹ כָּל־הָעֵדָה כַּגֵּר כָּאֶזְרָח בְּנָקְבוֹ־שֵׁם יוּמָת׃ וְאִישׁ כִּי יַכֶּה כָּל־נֶפֶשׁ
יח
יט אָדָם מוֹת יוּמָת׃ וּמַכֵּה נֶפֶשׁ־בְּהֵמָה יְשַׁלְּמֶנָּה נֶפֶשׁ תַּחַת נָפֶשׁ׃ וְאִישׁ כִּי־יִתֵּן מוּם
כ בַּעֲמִיתוֹ כַּאֲשֶׁר עָשָׂה כֵּן יֵעָשֶׂה לּוֹ׃ שֶׁבֶר תַּחַת שֶׁבֶר עַיִן תַּחַת עַיִן שֵׁן תַּחַת שֵׁן

רש"י

י | ויצא בן אשה ישראלית. מהיכן יצא? רבי לוי אומר: מעולמו יצא. רבי ברכיה אומר: מפרשה שלמעלה יצא, לגלג ואמר: "ביום השבת יערכנו" (לעיל פסוק ח), דרך המלך לאכול פת חמה בכל יום, שמא פת צוננת של תשעה ימים? בתמיהה. ומתניתא אמרה: מבית דינו של משה יצא מחויב. בא ליטע אהלו בתוך מחנה דן, אמרו לו, מה טיבך לכאן? אמר להם: מבני דן אני. אמרו לו: "איש על דגלו באתת לבית אבתם" כתיב (במדבר ב, ב), נכנס לבית דינו של משה ויצא מחויב, עמד וגדף: בן איש מצרי. הוא המצרי שהרג משה: בתוך בני ישראל. מלמד שנתגייר: וינצו במחנה. על עסקי המחנה: ואיש הישראלי. זה שכנגדו, שמיחה בו מטע אהלו:

יא | ויקב. כתרגומו: "ופרש", שנקב שם המיוחד וגדף, והוא שם המפורש ששמע מסיני: ושם אמו שלמית בת דברי. שבחן של ישראל שפרסמה הכתוב לזו, לומר שהיא לבדה היתה זונה: שלמית. דהות פטפטה, שלם עלך, שלם עלך, שלם עליכון, מפטפטת בדברים, שואלת בשלום הכל: בת דברי. דברנית היתה, מדברת עם כל אדם, לפיכך קלקלה: למטה דן. מגיד שהרשע גורם גנאי לו, גנאי לאביו, גנאי לשבטו. כיוצא בו: "אהליאב בן אחיסמך למטה דן" (שמות לא, ו), שבח לו, שבח לאביו, שבח לשבטו:

יב | ויניחהו. לבדו, ולא הניחו מקושש עמו, ששניהם היו בפרק אחד; ויודעים היו שהמקושש במיתה, אבל לא פורש להם באיזו מיתה, לכך נאמר: "כי לא פרש מה יעשה לו" (במדבר טו, לד), אבל במקלל הוא אומר "לפרש להם", שלא היו יודעים אם חייב מיתה אם לאו:

יד | השמעים. אלו העדים: כל. להביא את הדיינים: את ידיהם. אומרים לו, דמך בראשך, ואין אנו נענשים במיתתך שאתה גרמת לך: כל העדה. במעמד כל העדה, מכאן ששלוחו של אדם כמותו:

טו | ונשא חטאו. בכרת, כשאין התראה:

טז | ונקב שם. אינו חייב עד שיפרש את השם, ולא המקלל בכנוי: ונקב. לשון קללה, כמו: "מה אקב" (במדבר כג, ח):

יז | ואיש כי יכה. לפי שנאמר: "מכה איש" וגו' (שמות כא, יב), אין לי אלא שהרג את האיש, אשה וקטן מנין? תלמוד לומר: "כל נפש אדם":

כ | כן ינתן בו. פרשו רבותינו שאינו נתינת מום ממש, אלא תשלומי ממון – שמין אותו כעבד, לכך כתוב בו לשון נתינה, דבר הנתון מיד ליד:

DISCUSSION

→ all other punishments for interpersonal matters, e.g., inflicting an injury, even when the Torah states that the offender deserves bodily punishment, in practice he pays compensation instead (*Bava Kamma* 83b; Rambam, *Sefer Nezikin*, *Hilkhot Ḥovel UMazik* 1:3; *Rambam's Introduction to the Mishna*; see also Rambam, *Guide of the Perplexed* 3:41; commentary on Exodus 21:24).

24:21| **And one who smites a person shall be put to death:** In the case of murder, the verse above (24:17) stresses the punishment of death by combining the prescriptive verb with the infinitive, "*mot yumat,*" indicating that this punishment must be carried out by the court. In contrast, in the verse here, which refers to one who inflicts bodily harm upon another without killing him, the verse uses only the prescriptive verb "*yumat,*" which is less emphatic. This indicates that although the assailant is deserving of death, in practice this punishment is not carried out, but is transmuted to monetary recompense. This is stated explicitly elsewhere (see Exodus 21:18–19; see also *Bava Kamma* 83b; *Bekhor Shor*; Exodus 2:14). The term "*yumat*" appears elsewhere in contexts where the punishment of death is not carried out by the court (see, e.g., Exodus 21:19; Numbers 1:51, 3:10).

22 **There shall be one law for you,**[D] **the stranger and native alike,** whether the assailant is a born Jew and the victim a convert, or the reverse, **for I am the Lord your God.** You are all equal before Me, both with regard to your duties and with regard to your rights. Therefore, the same law applies to all.[99]

23 **Moses spoke to the children of Israel,** teaching them all of the aforementioned commandments, as God instructed him. Although some of these laws were mentioned previously,[100]

they are restated here in the context of the actions that are subsequently taken: **And they took the one who cursed outside the camp and stoned him with stones.**[D] **The children of Israel** accepted God's commandments, and from then on they **did as the Lord had commanded Moses,** with regard to the equality of all before the law, as well as the other laws stated here.

DISCUSSION

24:22 | **There shall be one law for you:** Although in theory most legal systems accept the concept of equality before the law, this principle was not fully implemented in the ancient world, and it is not always adhered to even nowadays. In various legal systems of the ancient world, the severity and extent of the punishment depended on the identity and status of the murdered victim. In contrast, by Torah law the same punishment is meted out

to whoever harms another, irrespective of the victim's identity.

24:23 | **And they took the one who cursed outside the camp and stoned him with stones:** The case of murder is somewhat related to the case of blasphemy. Just as the blasphemer intends to strike against God, so too the murderer indirectly strikes, as it were, against his Maker, as the verse states: "One who sheds the blood of man, by man shall his blood be shed,

as He made man in the image of God" (Genesis 9:6). Consequently, there is no atonement for a murderer other than his own death. This might explain why the Torah mentions the immediate execution of the blasphemer, despite the fact that the time and context of this episode are unknown.

This incident demonstrates vividly that God's commandments to the Jewish people are not merely theoretical ideas. They form a practical set of laws, which are to be implemented to the

↤

Parashat
Behar

The Sabbatical Year, Jubilee Year, and Related Laws

LEVITICUS 25:1–55

Although the *halakhot* discussed in this section concerning the Sabbatical Year and the Jubilee Year will be observed only after the Israelites reach their land, they are nevertheless delineated in the wilderness. With regard to the placement of these matters in the book of Leviticus, admittedly the main focus of this book is the sacrificial service, but it also includes many complex commandments pertaining to various areas of life. In broad terms, these commands relate to the total authority of God over His people, and the power of His rule. One central idea is that both the land and its inhabitants are considered the property of God, a principle that finds expression through the institution of the Sabbatical Year and the Jubilee Year. One year out of every seven is designated as the Sabbatical Year, during which the Land of Israel must be allowed to lie fallow and its produce made available to all. Likewise, every fiftieth year is set aside as the Jubilee, when all land sales that occurred during the previous fifty years are nullified and the land reverts to its original owners. This commandment demonstrates that real estate in the Land of Israel can never be fully sold, but merely leased for its produce. Slaves are also freed, as the general manumission of the Jubilee Year grants everyone the opportunity to start afresh and forge a new path in life, until the next Jubilee.

The Sabbatical Year and the Jubilee Year

LEVITICUS 25:1–24

25 1 **The Lord spoke to Moses at Mount Sinai** before the Israelites set out for the Land of Israel, despite the fact that the following *halakhot* would be practiced only when they reached their land, **saying:**

2 **Speak to the children of Israel, and say to them: When you come into the land that I am giving you, the land shall rest a Sabbath to the Lord.** Just as the weekly Sabbath, during which people must rest, expresses the sovereignty of God as

כא כַּאֲשֶׁר יִתֵּן מוּם בָּאָדָם כֵּן יִנָּתֶן בּוֹ: וּמַכֵּה בְהֵמָה יְשַׁלְּמֶנָּה וּמַכֵּה אָדָם יוּמָת: מפטיר
כב כג מִשְׁפַּט אֶחָד יִהְיֶה לָכֶם כַּגֵּר כָּאֶזְרָח יִהְיֶה כִּי אֲנִי יהוה אֱלֹהֵיכֶם: וַיְדַבֵּר מֹשֶׁה
אֶל־בְּנֵי יִשְׂרָאֵל וַיּוֹצִיאוּ אֶת־הַמְקַלֵּל אֶל־מִחוּץ לַמַּחֲנֶה וַיִּרְגְּמוּ אֹתוֹ אָבֶן וּבְנֵי־
יִשְׂרָאֵל עָשׂוּ כַּאֲשֶׁר צִוָּה יהוה אֶת־מֹשֶׁה:

רש״י

כא| וּמַכֵּה בְהֵמָה יְשַׁלְּמֶנָּה. לְמַעְלָה דִּבֵּר בְּהוֹרֵג בְּהֵמָה, וְכָאן דִּבֵּר בְּעוֹשֶׂה בָהּ חַבּוּרָה: וּמַכֵּה אָדָם יוּמָת. אֲפִלּוּ לֹא הֲרָגוֹ אֶלָּא עָשָׂה בוֹ חַבּוּרָה, שֶׁלֹּא נֶאֱמַר כָּאן ׳נֶפֶשׁ׳. וּבְמַכֶּה אָבִיו וְאִמּוֹ דִּבֵּר הַכָּתוּב, וּבָא לְהַקִּישׁוֹ לְמַכֵּה בְּהֵמָה, מָה מַכֵּה בְהֵמָה מֵחַיִּים, אַף מַכֵּה אָבִיו מֵחַיִּים, פְּרָט לְמַכֶּה לְאַחַר מִיתָה, לְפִי שֶׁמָּצִינוּ שֶׁהַמְקַלְּלוֹ לְאַחַר מִיתָה חַיָּב, הֻצְרַךְ לוֹמַר בְּמַכֶּה שֶׁפָּטוּר. וּמָה בִּבְהֵמָה בְּחַבָּלָה, שֶׁאִם אֵין חַבָּלָה אֵין תַּשְׁלוּמִין, אַף מַכֵּה אָבִיו אֵינוֹ חַיָּב עַד שֶׁיַּעֲשֶׂה בּוֹ חַבּוּרָה:

כב| אֲנִי ה׳ אֱלֹהֵיכֶם. אֱלֹהֵי כֻלְּכֶם, כְּשֵׁם שֶׁאֲנִי מְיַחֵד שְׁמִי עֲלֵיכֶם, כָּךְ אֲנִי מְיַחֲדוֹ עַל הַגֵּרִים:

כג| וּבְנֵי יִשְׂרָאֵל עָשׂוּ. כָּל הַמִּצְוָה הָאֲמוּרָה בִּסְקִילָה בְּמָקוֹם אַחֵר: דְּחִיָּה, רְגִימָה וּתְלִיָּה:

DISCUSSION

letter. In the case of the festivals, which were discussed previously, there is no need for the verse to state that they were celebrated in practice, as there is no reason to suppose otherwise. In contrast, when it comes to the implementation of a judicial system, which involves complex social changes, it is necessary to stress that God's commandments were indeed put into practice.

פרשת
בהר

א וַיְדַבֵּר יהוה אֶל־מֹשֶׁה בְּהַר סִינַי לֵאמֹר: דַּבֵּר אֶל־בְּנֵי יִשְׂרָאֵל וְאָמַרְתָּ אֲלֵהֶם
ב
ג כִּי תָבֹאוּ אֶל־הָאָרֶץ אֲשֶׁר אֲנִי נֹתֵן לָכֶם וְשָׁבְתָה הָאָרֶץ שַׁבָּת לַיהוה: שֵׁשׁ
ד שָׁנִים תִּזְרַע שָׂדֶךָ וְשֵׁשׁ שָׁנִים תִּזְמֹר כַּרְמֶךָ וְאָסַפְתָּ אֶת־תְּבוּאָתָהּ: וּבַשָּׁנָה

רש״י

א| בְּהַר סִינַי. מָה עִנְיַן שְׁמִטָּה אֵצֶל הַר סִינַי? וַהֲלֹא כָל הַמִּצְוֹת נֶאֶמְרוּ מִסִּינַי? אֶלָּא מַה שְּׁמִטָּה נֶאֶמְרוּ כְּלָלוֹתֶיהָ וּפְרָטוֹתֶיהָ וְדִקְדּוּקֶיהָ מִסִּינַי, אַף כֻּלָּן נֶאֶמְרוּ כְּלָלוֹתֵיהֶן וְדִקְדּוּקֵיהֶן מִסִּינַי. כָּךְ שְׁנוּיָה בְּתוֹרַת כֹּהֲנִים (פרשתא א, א). וְנִרְאֶה לִי שֶׁכָּךְ פֵּרוּשָׁהּ, לְפִי שֶׁלֹּא מָצִינוּ שְׁמִטַּת קַרְקָעוֹת שֶׁנִּשְׁנֵית בְּעַרְבוֹת מוֹאָב בְּמִשְׁנֵה תוֹרָה, לָמַדְנוּ שֶׁכְּלָלוֹתֶיהָ וּפְרָטוֹתֶיהָ כֻּלָּן נֶאֶמְרוּ מִסִּינַי, וּבָא הַכָּתוּב וְלִמֵּד כָּאן עַל כָּל דִּבּוּר שֶׁנִּדְבַּר לְמֹשֶׁה שֶׁמִּסִּינַי הָיוּ כֻּלָּם כְּלָלוֹתֵיהֶן וְדִקְדּוּקֵיהֶן, וְחָזְרוּ וְנִשְׁנוּ בְּעַרְבוֹת מוֹאָב:

ב| שַׁבָּת לַה׳. לְשֵׁם ה׳, כְּשֵׁם שֶׁנֶּאֱמַר בְּשַׁבַּת בְּרֵאשִׁית:

the Creator, so too this sabbatical year, which occurs once every seven years, represents God's lordship over the land.

3 **Six years you will sow your field, and six years you will prune your vineyard, and you will gather its produce.** You must harvest and collect everything you have planted before the beginning of the seventh year.

4 **In the seventh year, it shall be a sabbatical rest for the land,** just as the weekly Sabbath is a rest for people, **a Sabbath for the**

Lord; **your field you shall not sow, and your vineyard you shall not prune.**

5 **The aftergrowth of your reaping,** the produce that grows by itself from the remnants that fell to the ground during the previous harvest, without any plowing and sowing on your part, **you shall not reap** in the normal manner of an owner in his field, despite the fact that it is permitted to consume this produce. **And the uncultivated grapes of your vine,** the grapes of the seventh year, which are for the Lord,[1] or the grapes of highest quality,[2] **you shall not gather.** This year is not designated as a time of rest for humans; rather, **it shall be a sabbatical year for the land.**

6 **The Sabbath of the land,** the produce that grows during the seventh year, also called the *Shemitta* Year,[3] **shall be yours for eating, for you, and for your slave, and for your maidservant, and for your hired laborer, and for your resident alien who reside with you,** all the inhabitants of the Land of Israel.

7 **And for your animals,** your livestock, **and for the** wild **beasts,** including birds, **that are in your land, all of its,** the year's, **produce shall be to eat.**[D]

8 These Sabbatical Years are themselves part of a larger cycle: **You shall count for yourselves seven Sabbatical Years, seven years seven times, and they shall be to you the days of the seven Sabbatical Years, forty-nine years.**

9 After forty-nine years, **you shall sound an alarm blast of the shofar during the seventh month, on the tenth day; on the Day of Atonement you shall sound the shofar throughout your land,**[D] thereby proclaiming the start of a new year.

10 **You shall sanctify the fiftieth year,** in which there is an even more significant cessation of activities and transactions than in the Sabbatical Year, **and proclaim liberty in the land for all its inhabitants.** You must ensure that all slaves are freed from all bonds. **It shall be a Jubilee** Year, of blowing the shofar,[4] to

Shofar

you; **each man shall return to his ancestral portion,**[D] and **each man shall return to his family.** The fiftieth year is a year of manumission, at which point certain matters revert to their original state.

11 **It is a Jubilee, the fiftieth year shall be for you; you shall not sow, and you shall not reap its aftergrowth, and you shall not gather its uncultivated grapes.**

12 **Since it is a Jubilee, it shall be sacred for you;** you shall abstain from working the land and reaping its produce in the manner of an owner. **From the field you shall eat its produce,** which must be made available to all. As in the Sabbatical Year, the produce does not belong to you; rather, it is comparable to public property located in your custody.

13 **In this Jubilee Year you shall return each man to his ancestral portion.** If one sold his family's land during the previous forty-nine years, it will revert to his possession in the Jubilee Year.

14 The verse states a related *halakha*: **If you sell a sale item to your counterpart,** another citizen, **or acquire** an article **from the hand of your counterpart, you shall not exploit one another** by cheating. Of course, fraud is always prohibited, but it is mentioned in this context for a specific reason:

Second aliya

DISCUSSION

25:7 | And for your animals, and for the beasts that are in your land, all of its harvest shall be to eat: During this year, any produce belongs to everyone, man and animal alike, as the land reverts from its earthly owners to the exclusive possession of its divine Creator (see Jerusalem Talmud, *Pe'a* 6:1; *Tosafot, Rosh HaShana* 9b, and *Rashash* ad loc.; *Ḥazon Ish, Shevi'it* 14:4).

25:9 | On the Day of Atonement you shall sound the shofar throughout your land: The

year officially begins ten days earlier, on the first day of the seventh month, which is Rosh HaShana. With regard to this, Rabbi Yishmael, son of Rabbi Yoḥanan ben Beroka, says: From Rosh HaShana until Yom Kippur of the Jubilee Year Hebrew slaves were not released to their homes, but they were not enslaved to their masters either. Instead, they would eat, drink, and rejoice, and they would wear crowns on their heads. Once Yom Kippur arrived, the court would sound the shofar, slaves would

be released to their homes, and fields that had been sold would be returned to their original owners (*Rosh HaShana* 8b).

25:10 | Each man shall return to his ancestral portion: As explained below, in the Jubilee Year all sales of land that occurred during the previous forty-nine years are nullified, with the plots returning to their original owners. This is a cancellation of prior obligations and bonds.

הַשְּׁבִיעִת שַׁבַּת שַׁבָּתוֹן יִהְיֶה לָאָרֶץ שַׁבָּת לַיהוָה שָׂדְךָ לֹא תִזְרָע וְכַרְמְךָ לֹא
ה תִזְמֹר: אֵת סְפִיחַ קְצִירְךָ לֹא תִקְצוֹר וְאֶת־עִנְּבֵי נְזִירֶךָ לֹא תִבְצֹר שְׁנַת שַׁבָּתוֹן
ו יִהְיֶה לָאָרֶץ: וְהָיְתָה שַׁבַּת הָאָרֶץ לָכֶם לְאָכְלָה לְךָ וּלְעַבְדְּךָ וְלַאֲמָתֶךָ וְלִשְׂכִירְךָ
ז וּלְתוֹשָׁבְךָ הַגָּרִים עִמָּךְ: וְלִבְהֶמְתְּךָ וְלַחַיָּה אֲשֶׁר בְּאַרְצֶךָ תִּהְיֶה כָל־תְּבוּאָתָהּ
ח לֶאֱכֹל: וְסָפַרְתָּ לְךָ שֶׁבַע שַׁבְּתֹת שָׁנִים שֶׁבַע שָׁנִים שֶׁבַע פְּעָמִים
ט וְהָיוּ לְךָ יְמֵי שֶׁבַע שַׁבְּתֹת הַשָּׁנִים תֵּשַׁע וְאַרְבָּעִים שָׁנָה: וְהַעֲבַרְתָּ שׁוֹפַר תְּרוּעָה
בַּחֹדֶשׁ הַשְּׁבִעִי בֶּעָשׂוֹר לַחֹדֶשׁ בְּיוֹם הַכִּפֻּרִים תַּעֲבִירוּ שׁוֹפָר בְּכָל־אַרְצְכֶם:
י וְקִדַּשְׁתֶּם אֵת שְׁנַת הַחֲמִשִּׁים שָׁנָה וּקְרָאתֶם דְּרוֹר בָּאָרֶץ לְכָל־יֹשְׁבֶיהָ יוֹבֵל הִוא
יא תִּהְיֶה לָכֶם וְשַׁבְתֶּם אִישׁ אֶל־אֲחֻזָּתוֹ וְאִישׁ אֶל־מִשְׁפַּחְתּוֹ תָּשֻׁבוּ: יוֹבֵל הִוא שְׁנַת
הַחֲמִשִּׁים שָׁנָה תִּהְיֶה לָכֶם לֹא תִזְרָעוּ וְלֹא תִקְצְרוּ אֶת־סְפִיחֶיהָ וְלֹא תִבְצְרוּ
יב אֶת־נְזִרֶיהָ: כִּי יוֹבֵל הִוא קֹדֶשׁ תִּהְיֶה לָכֶם מִן־הַשָּׂדֶה תֹּאכְלוּ אֶת־תְּבוּאָתָהּ:
יג יד בִּשְׁנַת הַיּוֹבֵל הַזֹּאת תָּשֻׁבוּ אִישׁ אֶל־אֲחֻזָּתוֹ: וְכִי־תִמְכְּרוּ מִמְכָּר לַעֲמִיתֶךָ אוֹ כ שני

רש"י

ד| יִהְיֶה לָאָרֶץ. לַשָּׂדוֹת וְלַכְּרָמִים: לֹא תִזְמֹר. שֶׁקּוֹצְצִין זְמוֹרוֹתֶיהָ, וְתַרְגּוּמוֹ: "לָא תִכְסַח", וְדוֹמֶה לוֹ: "קוֹצִים כְּסוּחִים" (ישעיה לג, יב), "שְׂרֻפָה בָאֵשׁ כְּסוּחָה" (תהלים פ, יז):

ה| אֵת סְפִיחַ קְצִירְךָ. אֲפִלּוּ לֹא זְרַעְתָּהּ וְהִיא צָמְחָה מִן הַזֶּרַע שֶׁנָּפַל בָּהּ בְּעֵת הַקָּצִיר, הוּא קָרוּי 'סָפִיחַ': לֹא תִקְצוֹר. לִהְיוֹת מַחֲזִיק בּוֹ כִּשְׁאָר קָצִיר, אֶלָּא הֶפְקֵר יִהְיֶה לַכֹּל: נְזִירֶךָ. שֶׁהִנַּרְתָּ וְהִפְרַשְׁתָּ בְּנֵי אָדָם מֵהֶם וְלֹא הִפְקַרְתָּם: לֹא תִבְצֹר. אוֹתָם אֵינְךָ בּוֹצֵר, אֶלָּא מִן הַמֻּפְקָר:

ו| וְהָיְתָה שַׁבַּת הָאָרֶץ וְגוֹ'. אַף עַל פִּי שֶׁאֲסַרְתִּים עָלֶיךָ, לֹא בַאֲכִילָה וְלֹא בַהֲנָאָה אֲסַרְתִּים, אֶלָּא שֶׁלֹּא תִנְהַג בָּהֶם כְּבַעַל הַבַּיִת, אֶלָּא הַכֹּל יִהְיוּ שָׁוִים בָּהּ, אַתָּה וּשְׂכִירְךָ וְתוֹשָׁבְךָ: שַׁבַּת הָאָרֶץ לָכֶם לְאָכְלָה. מִן הַשָּׁבוּת אַתָּה אוֹכֵל, וְאִי אַתָּה אוֹכֵל מִן הַשָּׁמוּר: לְךָ וּלְעַבְדְּךָ וְלַאֲמָתֶךָ. לְפִי שֶׁנֶּאֱמַר: "וְאָכְלוּ אֶבְיֹנֵי עַמֶּךָ" (שמות כג, יא), יָכוֹל יִהְיוּ אֲסוּרִים בַּאֲכִילָה לָעֲשִׁירִים? תַּלְמוּד לוֹמַר: "לְךָ וּלְעַבְדְּךָ וְלַאֲמָתֶךָ", הֲרֵי בְּעָלִים וַעֲבָדִים וּשְׁפָחוֹת אֲמוּרִים כָּאן: וְלִשְׂכִירְךָ וּלְתוֹשָׁבְךָ. אַף הַגּוֹיִם:

ז| וְלִבְהֶמְתְּךָ וְלַחַיָּה. אִם חַיָּה אוֹכֶלֶת, בְּהֵמָה לֹא כָּל שֶׁכֵּן, שֶׁמְּזוֹנוֹתֶיהָ עָלֶיךָ, מַה תַּלְמוּד לוֹמַר: "וְלִבְהֶמְתְּךָ"? מַקִּישׁ בְּהֵמָה לְחַיָּה, כָּל זְמַן שֶׁחַיָּה אוֹכֶלֶת מִן הַשָּׂדֶה הַאֲכֵל לִבְהֶמְתְּךָ מִן הַבַּיִת, כָּלָה לַחַיָּה מִן הַשָּׂדֶה, כַּלֵּה לִבְהֶמְתְּךָ מִן הַבַּיִת:

ח| שַׁבְּתֹת שָׁנִים. שְׁמִטּוֹת שָׁנִים. יָכוֹל יַעֲשֶׂה שֶׁבַע שָׁנִים רְצוּפוֹת שְׁמִטָּה וְיַעֲשֶׂה יוֹבֵל אַחֲרֵיהֶם? תַּלְמוּד לוֹמַר: "שֶׁבַע שָׁנִים שֶׁבַע פְּעָמִים", הֱוֵי אוֹמֵר כָּל שְׁמִטָּה וּשְׁמִטָּה בִּזְמַנָּהּ: וְהָיוּ לְךָ יְמֵי שֶׁבַע וְגוֹ'. מַגִּיד לְךָ שֶׁאַף עַל פִּי שֶׁלֹּא עָשִׂיתָ שְׁמִטּוֹת, עֲשֵׂה יוֹבֵל לְסוֹף אַרְבָּעִים וָתֵשַׁע שָׁנִים. וּפְשׁוּטוֹ שֶׁל מִקְרָא: וְעָלוּ לְךָ חֶשְׁבּוֹן שְׁנוֹת הַשְּׁמִטּוֹת לְמִסְפַּר אַרְבָּעִים וָתֵשַׁע שָׁנִים:

ט| וְהַעֲבַרְתָּ. לְשׁוֹן "וַיַּעֲבִירוּ קוֹל בַּמַּחֲנֶה" (שמות לו, ו), לְשׁוֹן הַכְרָזָה: בְּיוֹם הַכִּפֻּרִים... בְּכָל אַרְצְכֶם. מִמַּשְׁמַע שֶׁנֶּאֱמַר "בְּיוֹם הַכִּפֻּרִים" אֵינִי יוֹדֵעַ שֶׁהוּא בֶּעָשׂוֹר לַחֹדֶשׁ? אִם כֵּן לָמָּה נֶאֱמַר "בֶּעָשׂוֹר לַחֹדֶשׁ"? אֶלָּא לוֹמַר לְךָ, תְּקִיעַת עָשׂוֹר לַחֹדֶשׁ דּוֹחָה שַׁבָּת בְּכָל אַרְצְכֶם, וְאֵין תְּקִיעַת רֹאשׁ הַשָּׁנָה דּוֹחָה שַׁבָּת בְּכָל אַרְצְכֶם, אֶלָּא בְּבֵית דִּין בִּלְבַד:

י| וְקִדַּשְׁתֶּם. בִּכְנִיסָתָהּ מְקַדְּשִׁין אוֹתָהּ בְּבֵית דִּין, וְאוֹמְרִים 'מְקֻדֶּשֶׁת הַשָּׁנָה': וּקְרָאתֶם דְּרוֹר. לַעֲבָדִים, בֵּין נִרְצָע בֵּין שֶׁלֹּא כָלוּ לוֹ שֵׁשׁ שָׁנִים מִשֶּׁנִּמְכַּר. אָמַר רַבִּי יְהוּדָה: מַהוּ לְשׁוֹן 'דְּרוֹר'? כִּמְדַיַּר בֵּי דַיְּרָא וְכוּ', שֶׁדָּר בְּכָל מָקוֹם שֶׁהוּא רוֹצֶה, וְאֵינוֹ בִּרְשׁוּת אֲחֵרִים: יוֹבֵל הִוא. שָׁנָה זֹאת מֻבְדֶּלֶת מִשְּׁאָר שָׁנִים בִּנְקִיבַת שֵׁם לָהּ לְבַדָּהּ, וּמַה שְּׁמָהּ? 'יוֹבֵל' שְׁמָהּ, עַל שֵׁם תְּקִיעַת שׁוֹפָר: וְשַׁבְתֶּם אִישׁ אֶל אֲחֻזָּתוֹ. שֶׁהַשָּׂדוֹת חוֹזְרוֹת לְבַעֲלֵיהֶן: וְאִישׁ אֶל מִשְׁפַּחְתּוֹ תָּשֻׁבוּ. לְרַבּוֹת אֶת הַנִּרְצָע:

יא| יוֹבֵל הִוא שְׁנַת הַחֲמִשִּׁים שָׁנָה. מַה תַּלְמוּד לוֹמַר? לְפִי שֶׁנֶּאֱמַר: "וְקִדַּשְׁתֶּם" וְגוֹ', כִּדְאִיתָא בְּרֹאשׁ הַשָּׁנָה (דף ח ע"ב) וּבְתוֹרַת כֹּהֲנִים (פרק ג, א): אֶת נְזִרֶיהָ. אֶת הָעֲנָבִים הַמְּשֻׁמָּרִים, אֲבָל בּוֹצֵר אַתָּה מִן הַמֻּפְקָרִים, כְּשֵׁם שֶׁנֶּאֱמַר בַּשְּׁבִיעִית כָּךְ נֶאֱמַר בַּיּוֹבֵל. נִמְצְאוּ שְׁתֵּי שָׁנִים קְדוֹשׁוֹת סְמוּכוֹת זוֹ לָזוֹ, שְׁנַת אַרְבָּעִים וָתֵשַׁע שְׁמִטָּה וּשְׁנַת הַחֲמִשִּׁים יוֹבֵל:

יב| קֹדֶשׁ תִּהְיֶה לָכֶם. תּוֹפֶסֶת דָּמֶיהָ כְּהֶקְדֵּשׁ. יָכוֹל תֵּצֵא הִיא לְחֻלִּין? תַּלְמוּד לוֹמַר: "תִּהְיֶה", בַּהֲוָיָתָהּ תְּהֵא: מִן הַשָּׂדֶה תֹּאכְלוּ. עַל יְדֵי הַשָּׂדֶה אַתָּה אוֹכֵל מִן הַבַּיִת, שֶׁאִם כָּלָה לַחַיָּה מִן הַשָּׂדֶה צָרִיךְ אַתָּה לְבַעֵר מִן הַבַּיִת, כְּשֵׁם שֶׁנֶּאֱמַר בַּשְּׁבִיעִית כָּךְ נֶאֱמַר בַּיּוֹבֵל:

יג| תָּשֻׁבוּ אִישׁ אֶל אֲחֻזָּתוֹ. וַהֲרֵי כְּבָר נֶאֱמַר: "וְשַׁבְתֶּם אִישׁ אֶל אֲחֻזָּתוֹ" (לעיל פסוק י)? אֶלָּא לְרַבּוֹת הַמּוֹכֵר שָׂדֵהוּ וְעָמַד בְּנוֹ וּגְאָלָהּ, שֶׁחוֹזֶרֶת לְאָבִיו בַּיּוֹבֵל:

יד| וְכִי תִמְכְּרוּ וְגוֹ'. לְפִי פְּשׁוּטוֹ, כְּמַשְׁמָעוֹ. וְעוֹד יֵשׁ דְּרָשָׁה: מִנַּיִן כְּשֶׁאַתָּה מוֹכֵר, מְכֹר לְיִשְׂרָאֵל חֲבֵרְךָ? תַּלְמוּד

15 The fact that land in the Land of Israel cannot be sold permanently, but merely leased until the Jubilee, affects the price of transactions. **On the basis of the number of years after the Jubilee you shall acquire from your counterpart.** The price of the land should be calculated based on the number of years that the sale will last. Here the word "after" should be understood to mean "until."[5] **On the basis of the number of crop years,** excluding the Sabbatical Years, which provide no profitable yield,[6] **he shall sell to you.**

16 **According to the abundance of the years,** if there are many years until the Jubilee, **you shall increase its price, and according to the paucity of the years you shall decrease its price, as it is the number of crops he is selling to you.** He is selling you only the right to the land's produce for a given number of years, not the land itself.

17 The Torah reiterates that **you shall not wrong one another, and you shall fear your God; for I am the Lord your God.** These *halakhot* are not easy to observe. Canceling all sales of land will likely lead to various complications and misunderstandings. Therefore, the Torah issues an extra warning.

18 **You shall perform My statutes,** including the Sabbatical Year and the Jubilee Year, **and My ordinances,** e.g., the *halakhot* regarding sale of land stated above,[7] **you shall observe, and perform them, and** then **you shall live on the land in security.**

Third aliya 19 **The land shall yield its produce,** as explained below, **and you shall eat your fill, and you shall live in security upon it.**

(Second aliya) 20 **If you shall say: What shall we eat during the seventh year? Behold,** due to these prohibitions, **we shall not sow, nor shall we gather our harvest.**

21 **I will command My blessing for you in the sixth year, and it shall generate the produce** so abundantly that it will provide food **for the three years:** the sixth year, the seventh year, and part of the eighth year.[8]

22 **You shall** be permitted to **sow** again in **the eighth year, and** meanwhile you will **eat of the old produce** from the sixth year, **until the ninth year, until the arrival of its produce** that you planted in the eighth year, **you shall eat the old.**

23 The Torah stresses once again: **The land,** the Land of Israel, **shall not be sold in perpetuity, as the land is Mine;**[D] **for you are strangers and resident aliens with Me,** as you live in My land under a special agreement, but it does not belong to you. The Sabbatical Year and the Jubilee Year are a reminder and our acknowledgment that the land is no one's personal property.

24 **In all the land of your ancestral portion,** the land of Canaan, which will become your ancestral property, **you shall provide redemption for the land** by returning all properties to their original owners.

The Sale of Real Estate in the Land of Israel

LEVITICUS 25:25–34

These statutes as well are included in the general law of the Jubilee outlined above.

Fourth aliya 25 The following *halakhot* also fall into the general framework of the Jubilee Year: **If your brother becomes poor and sells** a portion **from his ancestral portion** for his livelihood, **his redeemer,** a family member **who is close to him, shall come and redeem the sale of his brother.** This relative has the right to buy back the property.

DISCUSSION

25:23 | **As the land is mine:** The *halakhot* of the Sabbatical Year apply only in the Land of Israel. The phrase "the land" refers solely to this land, which is viewed as God's private royal territory.

טו קָנֹה מִיַּד עֲמִיתֶךָ אַל־תּוֹנוּ אִישׁ אֶת־אָחִיו: בְּמִסְפַּר שָׁנִים אַחַר הַיּוֹבֵל תִּקְנֶה
טז מֵאֵת עֲמִיתֶךָ בְּמִסְפַּר שְׁנֵי־תְבוּאֹת יִמְכָּר־לָךְ: לְפִי ׀ רֹב הַשָּׁנִים תַּרְבֶּה מִקְנָתוֹ
יז וּלְפִי מְעֹט הַשָּׁנִים תַּמְעִיט מִקְנָתוֹ כִּי מִסְפַּר תְּבוּאֹת הוּא מֹכֵר לָךְ: וְלֹא תוֹנוּ
יח אִישׁ אֶת־עֲמִיתוֹ וְיָרֵאתָ מֵאֱלֹהֶיךָ כִּי אֲנִי יְהוָה אֱלֹהֵיכֶם: וַעֲשִׂיתֶם אֶת־חֻקֹּתַי
יט וְאֶת־מִשְׁפָּטַי תִּשְׁמְרוּ וַעֲשִׂיתֶם אֹתָם וִישַׁבְתֶּם עַל־הָאָרֶץ לָבֶטַח: וְנָתְנָה הָאָרֶץ שלישי /שני/
כ פִּרְיָהּ וַאֲכַלְתֶּם לָשֹׂבַע וִישַׁבְתֶּם לָבֶטַח עָלֶיהָ: וְכִי תֹאמְרוּ מַה־נֹּאכַל בַּשָּׁנָה
כא הַשְּׁבִיעִת הֵן לֹא נִזְרָע וְלֹא נֶאֱסֹף אֶת־תְּבוּאָתֵנוּ: וְצִוִּיתִי אֶת־בִּרְכָתִי לָכֶם
כב בַּשָּׁנָה הַשִּׁשִּׁית וְעָשָׂת אֶת־הַתְּבוּאָה לִשְׁלֹשׁ הַשָּׁנִים: וּזְרַעְתֶּם אֵת הַשָּׁנָה
הַשְּׁמִינִת וַאֲכַלְתֶּם מִן־הַתְּבוּאָה יָשָׁן עַד ׀ הַשָּׁנָה הַתְּשִׁיעִת עַד־בּוֹא תְּבוּאָתָהּ
כג תֹּאכְלוּ יָשָׁן: וְהָאָרֶץ לֹא תִמָּכֵר לִצְמִתֻת כִּי־לִי הָאָרֶץ כִּי־גֵרִים וְתוֹשָׁבִים אַתֶּם
כד כה עִמָּדִי: וּבְכֹל אֶרֶץ אֲחֻזַּתְכֶם גְּאֻלָּה תִּתְּנוּ לָאָרֶץ: כִּי־יָמוּךְ רביעי
אָחִיךָ וּמָכַר מֵאֲחֻזָּתוֹ וּבָא גֹאֲלוֹ הַקָּרֹב אֵלָיו וְגָאַל אֵת מִמְכַּר אָחִיו:

רש"י

לוֹמַר: "וְכִי תִמְכְּרוּ מִמְכָּר – לַעֲמִיתֶךָ" מְכֹר. וּמִנַּיִן שֶׁאִם בָּאתָ לִקְנוֹת, קְנֵה מִיִּשְׂרָאֵל חֲבֵרְךָ? תַּלְמוּד לוֹמַר: "אוֹ קָנֹה – מִיַּד עֲמִיתֶךָ": אַל תּוֹנוּ. זוֹ אוֹנָאַת מָמוֹן:

טו | בְּמִסְפַּר שָׁנִים אַחַר הַיּוֹבֵל תִּקְנֶה. זֶהוּ פְּשׁוּטוֹ לְיַשֵּׁב הַמִּקְרָא עַל אָפְנָיו, עַל הָאוֹנָאָה בָּא לְהַזְהִיר: כְּשֶׁתִּמְכֹּר אוֹ תִּקְנֶה קַרְקַע דְּעוּ כַּמָּה שָׁנִים יֵשׁ עַד הַיּוֹבֵל, וּלְפִי הַשָּׁנִים וּתְבוּאוֹת הַשָּׂדֶה שֶׁהִיא רְאוּיָה לַעֲשׂוֹת יִמְכֹּר הַמּוֹכֵר וְיִקְנֶה הַקּוֹנֶה, שֶׁהֲרֵי סוֹפוֹ לְהַחֲזִירָהּ לוֹ בִּשְׁנַת הַיּוֹבֵל. וְאִם יֵשׁ שָׁנִים מוּעָטוֹת וְזֶה מוֹכְרָהּ בְּדָמִים יְקָרִים – הֲרֵי נִתְאַנָּה לוֹקֵחַ, וְאִם יֵשׁ שָׁנִים מְרֻבּוֹת וְאָכַל מִמֶּנָּה תְּבוּאוֹת הַרְבֵּה – הֲרֵי נִתְאַנָּה מוֹכֵר; לְפִיכָךְ צָרִיךְ לִקְנוֹתָהּ לְפִי הַזְּמַן. וְזֶהוּ שֶׁנֶּאֱמַר: "בְּמִסְפַּר שְׁנֵי תְבוּאֹת יִמְכָּר לָךְ" – לְפִי מִנְיַן שְׁנֵי הַתְּבוּאוֹת שֶׁתְּהֵא עוֹמֶדֶת בְּיַד הַלּוֹקֵחַ תִּמְכֹּר לוֹ. וְרַבּוֹתֵינוּ דָּרְשׁוּ מִכָּאן שֶׁהַמּוֹכֵר שָׂדֵהוּ אֵינוֹ רַשַּׁאי לִגְאֹל פָּחוֹת מִשְּׁתֵּי שָׁנִים, שֶׁתַּעֲמֹד שְׁתֵּי שָׁנִים בְּיַד הַלּוֹקֵחַ מִיּוֹם לְיוֹם, וַאֲפִלּוּ יֵשׁ שָׁלֹשׁ תְּבוּאוֹת בְּאוֹתָן שְׁתֵּי שָׁנִים, כְּגוֹן שֶׁמְּכָרָהּ לוֹ בְּקָמוֹתֶיהָ. וּ'שְׁנֵי' אֵינוֹ יוֹצֵא מִפְּשׁוּטוֹ, כְּלוֹמַר, מִסְפַּר שָׁנִים שֶׁל תְּבוּאוֹת וְלֹא שֶׁל שִׁדָּפוֹן, וּמִעוּט 'שָׁנִים' שְׁנַיִם:

טז | תַּרְבֶּה מִקְנָתוֹ. תִּמְכְּרֶנָּה בְּיֹקֶר: תַּמְעִיט מִקְנָתוֹ. תַּמְעִיט בְּדָמֶיהָ:

יז | וְלֹא תוֹנוּ אִישׁ אֶת עֲמִיתוֹ. כָּאן הִזְהִיר עַל אוֹנָאַת דְּבָרִים, שֶׁלֹּא יַקְנִיט אִישׁ אֶת חֲבֵרוֹ וְלֹא יַשִּׂיאֶנּוּ עֵצָה שֶׁאֵינָהּ הוֹגֶנֶת לוֹ לְפִי דַּרְכּוֹ וַהֲנָאָתוֹ שֶׁל יוֹעֵץ. וְאִם תֹּאמַר, מִי יוֹדֵעַ אִם נִתְכַּוַּנְתִּי לְרָעָה? לְכָךְ נֶאֱמַר: "וְיָרֵאתָ מֵאֱלֹהֶיךָ", הַיּוֹדֵעַ מַחֲשָׁבוֹת הוּא יוֹדֵעַ. כָּל דָּבָר הַמָּסוּר לַלֵּב, שֶׁאֵין מַכִּיר אֶלָּא מִי שֶׁהַמַּחֲשָׁבָה בְּלִבּוֹ, נֶאֱמַר בּוֹ "וְיָרֵאתָ מֵאֱלֹהֶיךָ":

יח | וִישַׁבְתֶּם עַל הָאָרֶץ לָבֶטַח. שֶׁבַּעֲוֹן שְׁמִטָּה יִשְׂרָאֵל גּוֹלִים, שֶׁנֶּאֱמַר: "אָז תִּרְצֶה הָאָרֶץ אֶת שַׁבְּתֹתֶיהָ... וְהִרְצָת אֶת שַׁבְּתֹתֶיהָ" (ויקרא כו, לד), וְשִׁבְעִים שָׁנָה שֶׁל גָּלוּת בָּבֶל כְּנֶגֶד שִׁבְעִים שְׁמִטּוֹת שֶׁבִּטְּלוּ הָיוּ (דברי הימים ב' לו, כא):

יט | וְנָתְנָה הָאָרֶץ וְגוֹ' וִישַׁבְתֶּם לָבֶטַח עָלֶיהָ. שֶׁלֹּא תִּדְאֲגוּ מִשְּׁנַת בַּצֹּרֶת: וַאֲכַלְתֶּם לָשֹׂבַע. אַף בְּתוֹךְ הַמֵּעַיִם תְּהֵא בּוֹ בְּרָכָה:

כ | וְלֹא נֶאֱסֹף. אֶל הַבַּיִת: אֶת תְּבוּאָתֵנוּ. כְּגוֹן יַיִן וּפֵרוֹת הָאִילָן וּסְפִיחִין הַבָּאִים מֵאֲלֵיהֶם:

כא | לִשְׁלֹשׁ הַשָּׁנִים. לִקְצָת הַשִּׁשִּׁית, מִנִּיסָן וְעַד רֹאשׁ הַשָּׁנָה, וְלַשְּׁבִיעִית וְלַשְּׁמִינִית, שֶׁיִּזְרְעוּ בַּשְּׁמִינִית בְּמַרְחֶשְׁוָן וְיִקְצְרוּ בְּנִיסָן:

כב | עַד הַשָּׁנָה הַתְּשִׁיעִת. עַד חַג הַסֻּכּוֹת שֶׁל תְּשִׁיעִית, שֶׁהוּא עֵת בּוֹא תְּבוּאָתָהּ שֶׁל שְׁמִינִית לְתוֹךְ הַבַּיִת, שֶׁכָּל יְמוֹת הַקַּיִץ הָיוּ בַּשָּׂדֶה בַּגְּרָנוֹת, וּבְתִשְׁרֵי הוּא עֵת הָאָסִיף לַבַּיִת. וּפְעָמִים שֶׁהָיְתָה צְרִיכָה לַעֲשׂוֹת לְאַרְבַּע שָׁנִים, בַּשִּׁשִּׁית שֶׁלִּפְנֵי הַשְּׁמִטָּה הַשְּׁבִיעִית, שֶׁהֵן בְּטֵלִין מֵעֲבוֹדַת קַרְקַע שְׁתֵּי שָׁנִים רְצוּפוֹת, הַשְּׁבִיעִית וְהַיּוֹבֵל, וּמִקְרָא זֶה נֶאֱמַר בִּשְׁאָר הַשְּׁמִטּוֹת כֻּלָּן:

כג | וְהָאָרֶץ לֹא תִמָּכֵר. לִתֵּן לָאו עַל חֲזָרַת שָׂדוֹת לִבְעָלִים בַּיּוֹבֵל, שֶׁלֹּא יְהֵא הַלּוֹקֵחַ כּוֹבְשָׁהּ: לִצְמִתֻת. לִפְסִיקָה, לִמְכִירָה פְּסוּקָה עוֹלָמִית: כִּי לִי הָאָרֶץ. אַל תֵּרַע עֵינְךָ בָּהּ, שֶׁאֵינָהּ שֶׁלְּךָ:

כד | וּבְכֹל אֶרֶץ אֲחֻזַּתְכֶם. לְרַבּוֹת בָּתִּים וְעֶבֶד עִבְרִי, וְדָבָר זֶה מְפֹרָשׁ בְּקִדּוּשִׁין בְּפֶרֶק רִאשׁוֹן (דף כא ע"א). וּלְפִי פְּשׁוּטוֹ סָמוּךְ לַפָּרָשָׁה שֶׁלְּאַחֲרָיו, שֶׁהַמּוֹכֵר אֲחֻזָּתוֹ רַשַּׁאי לְגָאֳלָהּ לְאַחַר שְׁתֵּי שָׁנִים, אוֹ הוּא אוֹ קְרוֹבוֹ, וְאֵין הַלּוֹקֵחַ יָכוֹל לְעַכֵּב:

כה | כִּי יָמוּךְ אָחִיךָ וּמָכַר. מְלַמֵּד שֶׁאֵין אָדָם רַשַּׁאי לִמְכֹּר שָׂדֵהוּ אֶלָּא מֵחֲמַת דֹּחַק עֹנִי: מֵאֲחֻזָּתוֹ. וְלֹא כֻּלָּהּ, לִמֵּד דֶּרֶךְ אֶרֶץ שֶׁיְּשַׁיֵּר שָׂדֶה לְעַצְמוֹ: וְגָאַל אֵת מִמְכַּר אָחִיו. וְאֵין הַלּוֹקֵחַ יָכוֹל לְעַכֵּב:

26 **If a man shall have no redeemer** who is able to exercise this
right, **and** after a period of time **he**, the original owner, **acquires**
the means and finds enough money **for its redemption,**
27 **he shall calculate the years of its sale,** the total number of
years that the land would have remained in the buyer's possession from the time of sale until the Jubilee Year, and subtract the number of years that it was actually under the buyer's control, **and return the balance,** the money for the remaining years, **to the man to whom he sold it,** as compensation to the buyer for the loss of the land's produce until the Jubilee Year. **And he shall return to his ancestral portion.**
28 **But if he does not acquire enough** money **for its return to**
him, then **his sale,** the property, **shall remain in the possession of the buyer until the Jubilee Year; and it shall go out** to the seller **in the Jubilee** without the need for redemption, **and he shall return to his ancestral portion.**[D]
Fifth aliya (Third aliya)
29 On the other hand, **if a man sells a house of residence in a**
walled city, its right of **redemption** by the seller **shall be until the conclusion of the year of its sale; its redemption shall be for** exactly **one year.**[9]
30 **If it,** the house, **shall not be redeemed until the comple-**
tion of one full year for it, as the seller was unable to find the means to redeem it during that period, **the house that is in the city that has a wall shall be established in perpetuity to the one who bought it for his generations; it shall not go out in the Jubilee.** The buyer will become the permanent owner of the house, which does not return to the original owner.
31 **But the houses in open cities that have no wall surrounding**
them shall be reckoned like the fields of the land;[D] **it,** such a house, **shall have redemption** like a field, **and in the Jubilee it shall go out.**
32 As for **the cities of the Levites,** with regard to **the houses of**
the cities of their ancestral portion, which are houses owned by Levites within their walled cities, **there shall be eternal redemption for the Levites.** Houses in the cities of Levites cannot be sold permanently, even if those cities are walled, as these houses are considered their primary property. For most Israelites, houses in cities were not usually sources of livelihood. For Levites, however, such houses were the only real estate they possessed, and therefore they had the same status as the agricultural land of other Israelites.[10]
33 Therefore **one who buys from the Levites, the sale of the**
house in the city, or of an entire city,[11] **of his ancestral property shall go out in the Jubilee; for the houses of the cities of the Levites are their ancestral portion in the midst of the children of Israel.** Consequently, even if the Levite seller is unable to redeem such property, it reverts to his possession in the Jubilee Year.
34 **But the fields of the open land of their cities,** surrounding
the Levites' cities,[12] which is the common property of all the residents of the city rather than of individual Levites,[13] **shall not be sold, as it is their eternal ancestral portion.**[D]

The Prohibition of Usury

LEVITICUS 25:35–38

Here, too, the Torah outlines *halakhot* that allow a poor person to recover economically and escape from poverty.

35 In a similar vein, the Torah suggests another method by which
a poor person's situation can be improved. **If your brother should become poor, and his means fail** while living **with you, you shall support him,** not only your brother but any

DISCUSSION

25:28 | **And it shall go out in the Jubilee, and he shall return to his ancestral portion:** In principle, land is a permanent inheritance that cannot be transferred between families. At most it can be leased until the Jubilee in order to provide a livelihood for the owner, who retains the right to redeem it even earlier than that. The goal of this system is that no one should become utterly impoverished, as one always retains the right to the portion of land he inherited (see Rambam, *Guide of the Perplexed* 3:39).

25:31 | **Shall be reckoned like the fields of the land:** Houses inside walled cities were often used as temporary places of residence or during times of danger, when the walls would provide protection (see, e.g., 26:25; Judges 5:7, 11; Jeremiah 4:5, 8:14). They would seldom serve as permanent dwellings. In contrast, houses outside cities, which stood on a family's agricultural land, were considered a permanent inheritance and a source of livelihood. Consequently, like fields, they could not be sold permanently (see *Bekhor Shor*).

25:34 | **As it is their eternal ancestral portion:** It is difficult to know the extent to which the *halakhot* of this chapter were observed in practice, and for how long. On one hand, one of the stated reasons given for the exile of the Israelites from the Land of Israel was their insufficient observance of these *halakhot* (see, e.g., 26:34–35; Jeremiah 25:8–14; II Chronicles 36:21). On the other hand, the redemption of land is described as having been performed in the time of Jeremiah and at other times (see Jeremiah 32:6–9; Ruth 4:3–5; Nehemiah 10:32).

In the ancient world, many civilizations recognized this principle and would return ancestral lands to their original owners. This would prevent a few rich and powerful individuals and families quickly amassing all the available real estate while reducing everyone else to a state of destitution. The Torah law that in the Jubilee Year all land returns to its original owners serves as a barrier against the permanent division of society into classes.

כו כז וְאִישׁ כִּי לֹא יִהְיֶה־לּוֹ גֹּאֵל וְהִשִּׂיגָה יָדוֹ וּמָצָא כְּדֵי גְאֻלָּתוֹ: וְחִשַּׁב אֶת־שְׁנֵי
כח מִמְכָּרוֹ וְהֵשִׁיב אֶת־הָעֹדֵף לָאִישׁ אֲשֶׁר מָכַר־לוֹ וְשָׁב לַאֲחֻזָּתוֹ: וְאִם לֹא־מָצְאָה
יָדוֹ דֵּי הָשִׁיב לוֹ וְהָיָה מִמְכָּרוֹ בְּיַד הַקֹּנֶה אֹתוֹ עַד שְׁנַת הַיּוֹבֵל וְיָצָא בַּיֹּבֵל וְשָׁב
כט לַאֲחֻזָּתוֹ: וְאִישׁ כִּי־יִמְכֹּר בֵּית־מוֹשַׁב עִיר חוֹמָה וְהָיְתָה חמישי /שלישי/
ל גְּאֻלָּתוֹ עַד־תֹּם שְׁנַת מִמְכָּרוֹ יָמִים תִּהְיֶה גְאֻלָּתוֹ: וְאִם לֹא־יִגָּאֵל עַד־מְלֹאת
לוֹ שָׁנָה תְמִימָה וְקָם הַבַּיִת אֲשֶׁר־בָּעִיר אֲשֶׁר־לא חֹמָה לַצְּמִיתֻת לַקֹּנֶה אֹתוֹ לוֹ
לא לְדֹרֹתָיו לֹא יֵצֵא בַּיֹּבֵל: וּבָתֵּי הַחֲצֵרִים אֲשֶׁר אֵין־לָהֶם חֹמָה סָבִיב עַל־שְׂדֵה
לב הָאָרֶץ יֵחָשֵׁב גְּאֻלָּה תִּהְיֶה־לּוֹ וּבַיֹּבֵל יֵצֵא: וְעָרֵי הַלְוִיִּם בָּתֵּי עָרֵי אֲחֻזָּתָם גְּאֻלַּת
לג עוֹלָם תִּהְיֶה לַלְוִיִּם: וַאֲשֶׁר יִגְאַל מִן־הַלְוִיִּם וְיָצָא מִמְכַּר־בַּיִת וְעִיר אֲחֻזָּתוֹ בַּיֹּבֵל
לד כִּי בָתֵּי עָרֵי הַלְוִיִּם הִוא אֲחֻזָּתָם בְּתוֹךְ בְּנֵי יִשְׂרָאֵל: וּשְׂדֵה מִגְרַשׁ עָרֵיהֶם לֹא
לה יִמָּכֵר כִּי־אֲחֻזַּת עוֹלָם הוּא לָהֶם: **כא** וְכִי־יָמוּךְ אָחִיךָ וּמָטָה יָדוֹ עִמָּךְ

רש"י

כו | **וְאִישׁ כִּי לֹא יִהְיֶה לוֹ גֹּאֵל.** וְכִי יֵשׁ לְךָ אָדָם בְּיִשְׂרָאֵל שֶׁאֵין לוֹ גּוֹאֲלִים? אֶלָּא גּוֹאֵל שֶׁיּוּכַל לִגְאֹל מִמְכָּרוֹ:

כז | **וְחִשַּׁב אֶת שְׁנֵי מִמְכָּרוֹ.** כַּמָּה שָׁנִים הָיוּ עַד הַיּוֹבֵל? כָּךְ וְכָךְ; וּבְכַמָּה מְכַרְתִּיהָ לְךָ? בְּכָךְ וְכָךְ; עָתִיד הָיִיתָ לְהַחֲזִירָהּ בַּיּוֹבֵל, נִמְצֵאתָ קוֹנֶה מִסְפַּר הַתְּבוּאוֹת כְּפִי חֶשְׁבּוֹן שֶׁל כָּל שָׁנָה, אָכַלְתָּ אוֹתָהּ שָׁלֹשׁ שָׁנִים אוֹ אַרְבַּע, הוֹצֵא אֶת דְּמֵיהֶן מִן הַחֶשְׁבּוֹן וְטֹל אֶת הַשְּׁאָר; וְזֶהוּ: "וְהֵשִׁיב אֶת הָעֹדֵף" בִּדְמֵי הַמִּקָּח עַל הָאֲכִילָה שֶׁאֲכָלָהּ, וְיִתְּנֵם לַלּוֹקֵחַ: **לָאִישׁ אֲשֶׁר מָכַר לוֹ.** הַמּוֹכֵר הַזֶּה שֶׁבָּא לְגָאֳלָהּ:

כח | **דֵּי הָשִׁיב לוֹ.** מִכָּאן שֶׁאֵינוֹ גּוֹאֵל לַחֲצָאִין: **עַד שְׁנַת הַיּוֹבֵל.** שֶׁלֹּא יִכָּנֵס לְתוֹךְ אוֹתָהּ שָׁנָה כְּלוּם, שֶׁהַיּוֹבֵל מְשַׁמֵּט בִּתְחִלָּתוֹ:

כט | **בֵּית מוֹשַׁב עִיר חוֹמָה.** בַּיִת בְּתוֹךְ עִיר הַמֻּקֶּפֶת חוֹמָה מִימוֹת יְהוֹשֻׁעַ בִּן נוּן: **וְהָיְתָה גְאֻלָּתוֹ.** לְפִי שֶׁנֶּאֱמַר בְּשָׂדֶה שֶׁיָּכוֹל לְגָאֳלָהּ מִשְּׁתֵּי שָׁנִים וְאֵילָךְ כָּל זְמַן שֶׁיִּרְצֶה, וּבְתוֹךְ שְׁתֵּי שָׁנִים הָרִאשׁוֹנוֹת אֵינוֹ יָכוֹל לְגָאֳלָהּ, הֻצְרַךְ לְפָרֵשׁ בָּזֶה שֶׁהוּא חִלּוּף, שֶׁאִם רָצָה לִגְאֹל בַּשָּׁנָה רִאשׁוֹנָה גּוֹאֲלָהּ, וּלְאַחַר מִכָּאן אֵינוֹ גּוֹאֲלָהּ: **וְהָיְתָה גְאֻלָּתוֹ.** שֶׁל בַּיִת: **יָמִים.** יְמֵי שָׁנָה שְׁלֵמָה קְרוּיִים 'יָמִים', וְכֵן: "תֵּשֵׁב הַנַּעֲרָ אִתָּנוּ יָמִים" (בראשית כד, נה):

ל | **וְקָם הַבַּיִת... לַצְּמִיתֻת.** יָצָא מִכֹּחוֹ שֶׁל מוֹכֵר וְעוֹמֵד בְּכֹחוֹ שֶׁל קוֹנֶה: **לֹא יֵצֵא בַּיֹּבֵל.** אָמַר רַב סַפְרָא: אִם פָּגַע בּוֹ יוֹבֵל בְּתוֹךְ שְׁנָתוֹ, לֹא יָצָא:

לא | **וּבָתֵּי הַחֲצֵרִים.** כְּתַרְגּוּמוֹ: "פַּצְחַיָּא", עֲיָרוֹת פְּתוּחוֹת מֵאֵין חוֹמָה, וְיֵשׁ הַרְבֵּה בְּסֵפֶר יְהוֹשֻׁעַ (פרקים יג-יט) "הֶעָרִים וְחַצְרֵיהֶם", "בְּחַצְרֵיהֶם וּבְטִירֹתָם" (בראשית כה, טז): **עַל שְׂדֵה הָאָרֶץ יֵחָשֵׁב.** הֲרֵי הֵן כְּשָׂדוֹת שֶׁנִּגְאָלִים עַד הַיּוֹבֵל, וְיוֹצְאִין בַּיּוֹבֵל לַבְּעָלִים אִם לֹא נִגְאֲלוּ: **גְּאֻלָּה תִּהְיֶה לּוֹ.** מִיָּד, אִם יִרְצֶה, וְזֶה יָפֶה כֹּחוֹ מִכֹּחַ שָׂדוֹת, שֶׁהַשָּׂדוֹת אֵין נִגְאָלוֹת עַד שְׁתֵּי שָׁנִים: **וּבַיֹּבֵל יֵצֵא.** בְּחִנָּם:

לב | **וְעָרֵי הַלְוִיִּם.** אַרְבָּעִים וּשְׁמוֹנֶה עִיר שֶׁנִּתְּנוּ לָהֶם: **גְּאֻלַּת עוֹלָם.** גּוֹאֵל מִיָּד אֲפִלּוּ לִפְנֵי שְׁתֵּי שָׁנִים, אִם מָכְרוּ שָׂדֶה מִשְּׂדוֹתֵיהֶם הַנְּתוּנוֹת לָהֶם בְּאַלְפַּיִם אַמָּה סְבִיבוֹת הֶעָרִים, אוֹ אִם מָכְרוּ בַּיִת בְּעִיר חוֹמָה, גּוֹאֲלִין לְעוֹלָם וְאֵינוֹ חָלוּט לְסוֹף שָׁנָה:

לג | **וַאֲשֶׁר יִגְאַל מִן הַלְוִיִּם.** וְאִם יִקְנֶה בַּיִת אוֹ עִיר מֵהֶם, וְיָצָא בַּיּוֹבֵל אוֹתוֹ מִמְכָּר שֶׁל בַּיִת אוֹ שֶׁל עִיר וְיָשׁוּב לַלֵּוִי שֶׁמְּכָרוֹ, וְלֹא יִהְיֶה חָלוּט כִּשְׁאָר בָּתֵּי עָרֵי חוֹמָה שֶׁל יִשְׂרָאֵל; וּ'גְאֻלָּה' זוֹ לְשׁוֹן מְכִירָה. דָּבָר אַחֵר, לְפִי שֶׁנֶּאֱמַר: "גְּאֻלַּת עוֹלָם תִּהְיֶה לַלְוִיִּם" (לעיל פסוק לב), יָכוֹל לֹא דִּבֶּר הַכָּתוּב אֶלָּא בְּלוֹקֵחַ יִשְׂרָאֵל שֶׁקָּנָה בַּיִת בְּעָרֵי הַלְוִיִּם, אֲבָל לֵוִי שֶׁקָּנָה מִלֵּוִי יִהְיֶה חָלוּט? תַּלְמוּד לוֹמַר: "וַאֲשֶׁר יִגְאַל מִן הַלְוִיִּם", אַף הַגּוֹאֵל מִיַּד לֵוִי גּוֹאֵל גְּאֻלַּת עוֹלָם. "וְיָצָא מִמְכַּר בַּיִת" – הֲרֵי זוֹ מִצְוָה אַחֶרֶת: וְאִם לֹא גְאָלָהּ יוֹצְאָה בַּיּוֹבֵל, וְאֵינוֹ נֶחְלָט לְסוֹף שָׁנָה כְּבַיִת שֶׁל יִשְׂרָאֵל: **כִּי בָתֵּי עָרֵי הַלְוִיִּם הִוא אֲחֻזָּתָם.** לֹא הָיוּ לָהֶם נַחֲלַת שָׂדוֹת וּכְרָמִים אֶלָּא עָרִים לָשֶׁבֶת וּמִגְרְשֵׁיהֶם, לְפִיכָךְ הֵם לָהֶם בִּמְקוֹם שָׂדוֹת וְיֵשׁ לָהֶם גְּאֻלָּה כְּשָׂדוֹת, כְּדֵי שֶׁלֹּא תִּפָּקַע נַחֲלָתָם מֵהֶם:

לד | **וּשְׂדֵה מִגְרַשׁ עָרֵיהֶם לֹא יִמָּכֵר.** מֶכֶר גִּזְבָּר, שֶׁאִם הִקְדִּישׁ בֶּן לֵוִי אֶת שָׂדֵהוּ וְלֹא גְאָלָהּ וּמְכָרָהּ גִּזְבָּר, אֵינָהּ יוֹצְאָה לַכֹּהֲנִים בַּיּוֹבֵל, כְּמוֹ שֶׁנֶּאֱמַר בְּיִשְׂרָאֵל: "וְאִם מָכַר אֶת הַשָּׂדֶה לְאִישׁ אַחֵר לֹא יִגָּאֵל עוֹד" (ויקרא כז, כ), אֲבָל בֶּן לֵוִי גּוֹאֵל לְעוֹלָם:

stranger or resident alien, and offer him the help he needs so that **he shall live with you.**

36 **Do not take interest,**[D] that is, do not lend money on the condition that the longer the borrower delays repayment the more he is forced to pay, **or increase,** demand a fixed fee that must be paid in addition to the loan, **from him; you shall fear your God,** who prohibits these practices, despite the fact that most people consider them normal. **And your brother shall live with you.** When one offers a loan to someone who needs money, it is only natural to seek to profit from such a transaction. The Torah warns against succumbing to such temptation.

37 **Your silver you shall not give him with interest, and with increase you shall not give him** even **your food.** The prohibition applies to loans of all items, not only money.

38 **I am the Lord your God, who brought you out of the land of Egypt to give you the land of Canaan, to be your God.** This statement serves to emphasize that God is the master of the Jewish people, as He provides them with everything they have. Therefore, one may use his property only in accordance with God's commandments.

The Hebrew Slave

LEVITICUS 25:39–55

Sixth aliya (Fourth aliya)

39 **If your brother shall become poor with you and is sold to you** as a slave due to his financial situation, **you shall not work him as a slave** by forcing him to perform menial tasks.

40 In general, a master does not hesitate to compel his slaves to perform those denigrating tasks that he would not assign to a hired hand, who possesses enough leverage to refuse to do such work.[14] Therefore, the Torah commands: **As a hired laborer, as a resident** of your area, **he,** the slave, **shall be with you.** Furthermore, **until the Jubilee Year he shall work with you.**

41 Then **he shall go out from you, he and his children with him.** Anyone who buys a slave also acquires his family by default, as they have no one else to support them. When the slave goes free, his family leaves with him.[15] **He shall return to his family, and to the ancestral portion of his fathers he shall return.**

42 The same principle that was stated above with regard to the land, "The land shall not be sold in perpetuity, as the land is Mine" (verse 23), is applied here to the children of Israel. They too may not be sold permanently, **for they are My servants, whom I brought out of the land of Egypt.** The servants of God possess a lofty status,[16] and therefore **they shall not be sold as slaves.** One may not treat them disrespectfully by putting them up for sale in a slave market.[17]

43 Furthermore, **you shall not oppress him with** uncommonly **hard labor; you shall fear your God.**[D]

44 **But your slaves and your maidservants whom you shall have from the nations that surround you: From them,** but not from your fellow Israelites, **you may buy a slave or a maidservant.** Gentile slaves, who are not your brothers and do not merit special treatment, may be purchased from the neighboring peoples.

45 **Also from the children of the resident aliens who reside with you,** gentiles who are resident aliens in the Land of Israel, who accept certain basic norms of the Israelites but have not become fully part of the nation, **from them you shall buy, and from their families that are with you, which they have begotten in your land; they shall be an ancestral portion for you.** These slaves may be bought, and you may use them throughout your lives.

46 Furthermore, **you shall bequeath them to your children after you, to inherit as an ancestral portion;** like all your other possessions, they are inherited by your children. **You shall enslave them forever;**[D] there is no set date when you must emancipate them. Indeed, this verse indicates that it is undesirable to free them at all. **But with regard to your brethren the children of Israel, one to another, you shall not oppress him with hard labor.** You must treat them gently and with respect.

47 **If a stranger who is a resident with you,** a gentile from a different nation who resides among you and who does not worship idolatry, **shall acquire means, and your brother**

Seventh aliya

DISCUSSION

25:36 | **Do not take interest:** Undoubtedly, an economic system in which interest is prohibited would be entirely different from those with which we are familiar. Much effort and creativity has been invested by rabbis in modern times to bring the *halakha* and economic reality into harmony with one another.

25:43 | **You shall fear your God:** There is a principle of the Sages that the phrase "you shall fear your God" typically appears in relation to actions whose motivations are difficult to discern to an outside observer (see *Bava Metzia* 58b). One of the definitions of hard labor is unnecessary work that is assigned merely to force the worker to toil (see Rashi; *Sifra*; Rambam, *Sefer Kinyan*, *Hilkhot Avadim* 1:6). Since it is difficult to prove whether or not a given task is required by the master, the prohibition is accompanied with a specific warning that he must fear God, who knows everyone's true intentions.

25:46 | **You shall enslave them forever:** The Sages interpret this as a prohibition against releasing Canaanite slaves. Nevertheless, it is

לו וְהֶחֱזַקְתָּ בּוֹ גֵּר וְתוֹשָׁב וָחַי עִמָּךְ: אַל־תִּקַּח מֵאִתּוֹ נֶשֶׁךְ וְתַרְבִּית וְיָרֵאתָ מֵאֱלֹהֶיךָ

לז וְחֵי אָחִיךָ עִמָּךְ: אֶת־כַּסְפְּךָ לֹא־תִתֵּן לוֹ בְּנֶשֶׁךְ וּבְמַרְבִּית לֹא־תִתֵּן אָכְלֶךָ: אֲנִי

לח יְהֹוָה אֱלֹהֵיכֶם אֲשֶׁר־הוֹצֵאתִי אֶתְכֶם מֵאֶרֶץ מִצְרָיִם לָתֵת לָכֶם אֶת־אֶרֶץ כְּנַעַן

לָהְיוֹת לָכֶם לֵאלֹהִים: ששי/רביעי

לט וְכִי־יָמוּךְ אָחִיךָ עִמָּךְ וְנִמְכַּר־לָךְ לֹא־תַעֲבֹד

מ בּוֹ עֲבֹדַת עָבֶד: כְּשָׂכִיר כְּתוֹשָׁב יִהְיֶה עִמָּךְ עַד־שְׁנַת הַיֹּבֵל יַעֲבֹד עִמָּךְ: וְיָצָא

מא מֵעִמָּךְ הוּא וּבָנָיו עִמּוֹ וְשָׁב אֶל־מִשְׁפַּחְתּוֹ וְאֶל־אֲחֻזַּת אֲבֹתָיו יָשׁוּב: כִּי־עֲבָדַי

מב הֵם אֲשֶׁר־הוֹצֵאתִי אֹתָם מֵאֶרֶץ מִצְרָיִם לֹא יִמָּכְרוּ מִמְכֶּרֶת עָבֶד: לֹא־תִרְדֶּה

מג בוֹ בְּפָרֶךְ וְיָרֵאתָ מֵאֱלֹהֶיךָ: וְעַבְדְּךָ וַאֲמָתְךָ אֲשֶׁר יִהְיוּ־לָךְ מֵאֵת הַגּוֹיִם אֲשֶׁר

מד סְבִיבֹתֵיכֶם מֵהֶם תִּקְנוּ עֶבֶד וְאָמָה: וְגַם מִבְּנֵי הַתּוֹשָׁבִים הַגָּרִים עִמָּכֶם מֵהֶם תִּקְנוּ

מה וּמִמִּשְׁפַּחְתָּם אֲשֶׁר עִמָּכֶם אֲשֶׁר הוֹלִידוּ בְּאַרְצְכֶם וְהָיוּ לָכֶם לַאֲחֻזָּה: וְהִתְנַחַלְתֶּם

אֹתָם לִבְנֵיכֶם אַחֲרֵיכֶם לָרֶשֶׁת אֲחֻזָּה לְעֹלָם בָּהֶם תַּעֲבֹדוּ וּבְאַחֵיכֶם בְּנֵי־יִשְׂרָאֵל

מו אִישׁ בְּאָחִיו לֹא־תִרְדֶּה בוֹ בְּפָרֶךְ:   וְכִי תַשִּׂיג יַד גֵּר וְתוֹשָׁב עִמָּךְ וּמָךְ   שביעי

רש"י

לה| וְהֶחֱזַקְתָּ בּוֹ. אַל תַּנִּיחֵהוּ שֶׁיֵּרֵד וְיִפּוֹל וְיִהְיֶה קָשֶׁה
לַהֲקִימוֹ, אֶלָּא חַזְּקֵהוּ מִשְּׁעַת מוֹטַת הַיָּד. לְמָה זֶה דּוֹמֶה?
לְמַשּׂאוֹי שֶׁעַל הַחֲמוֹר – עוֹדֵהוּ עַל הַחֲמוֹר, אֶחָד תּוֹפֵס
בּוֹ וּמַעֲמִידוֹ, נָפַל לָאָרֶץ, חֲמִשָּׁה אֵין מַעֲמִידִין אוֹתוֹ: גֵּר
וְתוֹשָׁב. אַף אִם הוּא גֵּר אוֹ תוֹשָׁב. וְאֵיזֶהוּ תוֹשָׁב? כָּל
שֶׁקִּבֵּל עָלָיו שֶׁלֹּא לַעֲבֹד עֲבוֹדָה זָרָה זֶה וְאוֹכֵל נְבֵלוֹת:
לו| נֶשֶׁךְ וְתַרְבִּית. חַד שַׁוְיוּהוּ רַבָּנַן, וְלַעֲבֹר עָלָיו בִּשְׁנֵי
לָאוִין: וְיָרֵאתָ מֵאֱלֹהֶיךָ. לְפִי שֶׁדַּעְתּוֹ שֶׁל אָדָם נִמְשֶׁכֶת
אַחַר הָרִבִּית וְקָשֶׁה לִפְרֹשׁ הֵימֶנּוּ, וּמוֹרֶה לְעַצְמוֹ הֶתֵּר
בִּשְׁבִיל מְעוֹתָיו שֶׁהָיוּ בְּטֵלוֹת אֶצְלוֹ, הֻצְרַךְ לוֹמַר "וְיָרֵאתָ
מֵאֱלֹהֶיךָ". אוֹ הַתּוֹלֶה מְעוֹתָיו בְּגוֹי כְּדֵי לְהַלְוֹתָם לְיִשְׂרָאֵל
בְּרִבִּית, הֲרֵי זֶה דָּבָר הַמָּסוּר לְלִבּוֹ שֶׁל אָדָם וּמַחְשַׁבְתּוֹ,
לְכָךְ הֻצְרַךְ לוֹמַר "וְיָרֵאתָ מֵאֱלֹהֶיךָ":

לח| אֲשֶׁר הוֹצֵאתִי וְגו'. וְהִבְחַנְתִּי בֵּין בְּכוֹר לְשֶׁאֵינוֹ בְּכוֹר,
אַף אֲנִי יוֹדֵעַ וְנִפְרָע מִן הַמַּלְוֶה מָעוֹת לְיִשְׂרָאֵל בְּרִבִּית
וְאוֹמֵר שֶׁל גוֹי הֵם. דָּבָר אַחֵר. "אֲשֶׁר הוֹצֵאתִי אֶתְכֶם מֵאֶרֶץ
מִצְרָיִם", עַל מְנָת שֶׁתְּקַבְּלוּ עֲלֵיכֶם מִצְוֹתַי וַאֲפִלּוּ הֵן
כְּבֵדוֹת עֲלֵיכֶם: לָתֵת לָכֶם אֶת אֶרֶץ כְּנַעַן. בִּשְׂכַר שֶׁתְּקַבְּלוּ
מִצְוֹתַי: לִהְיוֹת לָכֶם לֵאלֹהִים. שֶׁכָּל הַדָּר בְּאֶרֶץ יִשְׂרָאֵל
אֲנִי לוֹ לֵאלֹהִים, וְכָל הַיּוֹצֵא מִמֶּנָּה כְּעוֹבֵד עֲבוֹדָה זָרָה:

לט| עֲבֹדַת עָבֶד. עֲבוֹדָה שֶׁל גְּנַאי שֶׁיְּהֵא נִכָּר בָּהּ כְּעָבֶד,
שֶׁלֹּא יוֹלִיךְ כֵּלָיו אַחֲרָיו לְבֵית הַמֶּרְחָץ, וְלֹא יִנְעֹל לוֹ
מִנְעָלָיו:

מ| כְּשָׂכִיר כְּתוֹשָׁב. עֲבוֹדַת קַרְקַע וּמְלֶאכֶת אֻמָּנוּת, כְּשְׁאָר
שְׂכִירִים הִתְנַהֵג בּוֹ: עַד שְׁנַת הַיֹּבֵל. אִם פָּגַע בּוֹ יוֹבֵל לִפְנֵי
שֵׁשׁ שָׁנִים, הַיֹּבֵל מוֹצִיאוֹ:

מא| הוּא וּבָנָיו עִמּוֹ. אָמַר רַבִּי שִׁמְעוֹן. אִם הוּא נִמְכַּר
בָּנָיו מִי מְכָרָן? אֶלָּא מִכָּאן שֶׁרַבּוֹ חַיָּב בִּמְזוֹנוֹת בָּנָיו:
וְאֶל אֲחֻזַּת אֲבֹתָיו. אֶל כְּבוֹד אֲבוֹתָיו, וְאֵין לְזַלְזְלוֹ בְּכָךְ:
אֲחֻזַּת. חֲזָקַת:

מב| כִּי עֲבָדַי הֵם. שְׁטָרִי קוֹדֵם: לֹא יִמָּכְרוּ מִמְכֶּרֶת עָבֶד.
בְּהַכְרָזָה: "כָּאן יֵשׁ עֶבֶד לִמְכֹּר", וְלֹא יַעֲמִידֶנּוּ עַל אֶבֶן
הַלֶּקַח:

מג| לֹא תִרְדֶּה בוֹ בְּפָרֶךְ. מְלָאכָה שֶׁלֹּא לְצֹרֶךְ כְּדֵי לְעַנּוֹתוֹ,
אַל תֹּאמַר לוֹ: "הָחֵם לִי אֶת הַכּוֹס הַזֶּה" וְהוּא אֵינוֹ
צָרִיךְ, "עֲדֹר תַּחַת הַגֶּפֶן עַד שֶׁאָבוֹא". שֶׁמָּא תֹּאמַר: אֵין
מַכִּיר בַּדָּבָר אִם לְצֹרֶךְ אִם לָאו, וְאוֹמֵר אֲנִי לוֹ שֶׁהוּא
לְצֹרֶךְ – הֲרֵי הַדָּבָר הַזֶּה מָסוּר לַלֵּב, לְכָךְ נֶאֱמַר "וְיָרֵאתָ":

מד| וְעַבְדְּךָ וַאֲמָתְךָ אֲשֶׁר יִהְיוּ לָךְ. אִם תֹּאמַר, אִם כֵּן

בַּמֶּה אֶשְׁתַּמֵּשׁ? בַּעֲבָדַי אֵינִי מוֹשֵׁל, בְּאֻמּוֹת אֵינִי נוֹחֵל,
שֶׁהֲרֵי הִזְהַרְתַּנִי: "לֹא תְחַיֶּה כָּל נְשָׁמָה" (דברים כ, טז),
אֶלָּא מִי יְשַׁמְּשֵׁנִי? מֵאֵת הַגּוֹיִם. הֵם יִהְיוּ לְךָ לַעֲבָדִים:
אֲשֶׁר סְבִיבֹתֵיכֶם. וְלֹא שֶׁבְּתוֹךְ גְּבוּל אַרְצְכֶם, שֶׁהֲרֵי בָּהֶם
אָמַרְתִּי: "לֹא תְחַיֶּה כָּל נְשָׁמָה":

מה| וְגַם מִבְּנֵי הַתּוֹשָׁבִים. שֶׁבָּאוּ מִסְּבִיבוֹתֵיכֶם לִשָּׂא נָשִׁים
בְּאַרְצְכֶם וְיָלְדוּ לָהֶם, הַבֵּן הוֹלֵךְ אַחַר הָאָב וְאֵינוֹ בִּכְלַל
"לֹא תְחַיֶּה", אֶלָּא אַתָּה מֻתָּר לִקְנוֹתוֹ כְּעָבֶד: מֵהֶם תִּקְנוּ.
אוֹתָם תִּקְנוּ:

מו| וְהִתְנַחַלְתֶּם אֹתָם לִבְנֵיכֶם. הַחֲזִיקוּ בָּהֶם לְנַחֲלָה
לְצֹרֶךְ בְּנֵיכֶם אַחֲרֵיכֶם. וְלֹא יִתָּכֵן לְפָרֵשׁ הַנְחִילוּם
לִבְנֵיכֶם, שֶׁאִם כֵּן הָיָה לוֹ לִכְתֹּב "וְהִנְחַלְתֶּם אֹתָם
לִבְנֵיכֶם". "וְהִתְנַחַלְתֶּם" כְּמוֹ (במדבר לג, נד)
"וְהִתְנַחַלְתֶּם": אִישׁ בְּאָחִיו. לְהָבִיא נָשִׂיא בְּעַמָּיו וּמֶלֶךְ בְּמִשְׁרְתָיו שֶׁלֹּא
לִרְדּוֹת בְּפָרֶךְ:

מז| גֵּר וְתוֹשָׁב. גֵּר וְהוּא תוֹשָׁב, כְּתַרְגּוּמוֹ: "עָרֵל
וְתוֹתָב", וְסוֹפוֹ מוֹכִיחַ: "וְנִמְכַּר לְגֵר תּוֹשָׁב": וְכִי תַשִּׂיג יַד
גֵּר וְתוֹשָׁב עִמָּךְ. מִי גָּרַם לוֹ שֶׁיַּעֲשִׁיר? דִּבּוּקוֹ עִמָּךְ: וּמָךְ
אָחִיךָ עִמּוֹ. מִי גָּרַם לוֹ שֶׁיָּמוּךְ? דִּבּוּקוֹ עִמּוֹ, עַל יְדֵי שֶׁלָּמַד
מִמַּעֲשָׂיו: מִשְׁפַּחַת גֵּר. זֶה הַגּוֹי. כְּשֶׁהוּא אוֹמֵר "לְעֵקֶר",

becomes poor with, in comparison to, **him and he is sold to** that wealthy **stranger who is a resident with you, or to an off-shoot**^D **of a stranger's family** who does worship other gods,

48 in both such cases, the sale is valid. However, **after he,** the Israelite, **is sold** as a slave, **he shall have redemption; one of his brothers shall redeem him.** One of the slave's relatives is obligated to do his utmost to buy his freedom.[18]

49 **Or his uncle or his cousin shall redeem him, or** another relative **from his close kin from his family shall redeem him; or if he** himself **acquires** the **means, he shall be redeemed** with his own money.

50 **He shall calculate with his buyer from the year of his sale to him until the Jubilee Year, and his sale price shall be according to the number of years.** All Hebrew slaves go free at the advent of the Jubilee Year, even those owned by gentiles. Therefore, the price of the slave is calculated as a lease until the Jubilee: **As the time of a hired laborer, he,** the slave, **shall be with him.**

51 **If there are still many years** for the slave to work until the Jubilee, **in accordance with them he shall repay the cost of his redemption from the silver of his purchase.**

52 **If a few remain of the years until the Jubilee Year, he shall calculate for him; in accordance with his years he shall**

repay the cost of his redemption. This slave was initially bought at a certain price for a certain number of years' labor. When he or another comes to redeem him before the Jubilee, he must buy back the years of labor that are left, as dictated by the original price.

53 **As a yearly hired laborer he shall be with him.** Even gentiles residing in the Land of Israel are obligated to treat Israelite slaves with the respect accorded to hired workers. **He,** the gentile master, **shall not oppress him with hard labor before your eyes.** Since the master is not an Israelite, he might not observe the requirements of the Torah if he is not watched carefully.

54 **If he shall not be redeemed by** one of **these** relatives, his uncle, cousin, or any other relative, and he does not acquire the means to redeem himself, nevertheless **he shall go out in the Jubilee Year; he, and his children with him.**

55 The chapter summarizes the guiding principle of these *Maftir* *halakhot:* **For to Me the children of Israel are slaves; they are My slaves whom I took out of the land of Egypt. I am the Lord your God.** Since God is the Master of Israel, and the people are His exclusive property, they cannot be treated as chattel, and their servitude is regulated by the terms outlined here.

The Affirmation of the Covenant of Sinai

LEVITICUS 26:1–46

As stated earlier, in addition to its extensive focus on offerings, Leviticus deals with various *halakhot* pertaining to divine authority and God's rule over His people. These *halakhot* came to a conclusion with the commandments of the Sabbatical Year and the Jubilee Year, which appeared in the previous section. Toward the end of the book, the Torah reemphasizes the eternal nature of this covenant. The commitment of the people to God and the covenant between them cannot be broken. Therefore, any rebellion against God and disobedience of His commandments will lead to severe consequences. Another connection between these last subjects within Leviticus is the relationship between Israel and its land: If the people fail to observe the prohibitions of the land and do not allow it to rest of their own free will, the land will find its rest in their absence from it.

26 1 **You shall not make for you false gods, and you shall not establish for you an idol or a pillar,** whether in the likeness of other gods or in service of God. **And an ornamented**^D **stone you shall not place in your land, to prostrate yourself upon it,**^D as idol worshippers would often bow on a mosaic floor as an act of worship.[19] **For I am the Lord your God.**

2 This section concludes with a mention of principles that are relevant to most of the issues discussed in the book of Leviticus: **You shall observe My Sabbaths,** the Sabbath and the festivals, **and you shall revere My Sanctuary.** The obligation to revere the Temple includes the scrupulous observance of the sacrificial rituals and the preservation of the Temple's ritual purity (see 16:16, 19:30). **I am the Lord.**

DISCUSSION

permitted to free gentile slaves in order to fulfill a commandment or for ethical reasons (see *Gittin* 38b; Rabbi Samson Raphael Hirsch).

25:47 | Offshoot [*eker*]: The commentaries propose various interpretations of this unique word. Their suggestions include an uprooted and isolated person; one who remains established; a descendant; or even that it is a term for idolatry. All of these suggestions are related to meanings of similar roots in Hebrew.

26:1 | Ornamented [*maskit*]: The translation here follows the opinion that the root of this word is *sin-kaf-heh*, which denotes looking. An ornamented stone invites viewers to look at its decoration (see Rashbam; Ezekiel 8:12).

מח אָחִיךָ עִמּוֹ וְנִמְכַּר לְגֵר תּוֹשָׁב עִמָּךְ אוֹ לְעֵקֶר מִשְׁפַּחַת גֵּר: אַחֲרֵי נִמְכַּר גְּאֻלָּה
מט תִּהְיֶה־לּוֹ אֶחָד מֵאֶחָיו יִגְאָלֶנּוּ: אוֹ־דֹדוֹ אוֹ בֶן־דֹּדוֹ יִגְאָלֶנּוּ אוֹ־מִשְּׁאֵר בְּשָׂרוֹ
נ מִמִּשְׁפַּחְתּוֹ יִגְאָלֶנּוּ אוֹ־הִשִּׂיגָה יָדוֹ וְנִגְאָל: וְחִשַּׁב עִם־קֹנֵהוּ מִשְּׁנַת הִמָּכְרוֹ לוֹ
נא עַד שְׁנַת הַיֹּבֵל וְהָיָה כֶּסֶף מִמְכָּרוֹ בְּמִסְפַּר שָׁנִים כִּימֵי שָׂכִיר יִהְיֶה עִמּוֹ: אִם־
נב עוֹד רַבּוֹת בַּשָּׁנִים לְפִיהֶן יָשִׁיב גְּאֻלָּתוֹ מִכֶּסֶף מִקְנָתוֹ: וְאִם־מְעַט נִשְׁאַר בַּשָּׁנִים
נג עַד־שְׁנַת הַיֹּבֵל וְחִשַּׁב־לוֹ כְּפִי שָׁנָיו יָשִׁיב אֶת־גְּאֻלָּתוֹ: כִּשְׂכִיר שָׁנָה בְּשָׁנָה יִהְיֶה
נד עִמּוֹ לֹא־יִרְדֶּנּוּ בְּפֶרֶךְ לְעֵינֶיךָ: וְאִם־לֹא יִגָּאֵל בְּאֵלֶּה וְיָצָא בִּשְׁנַת הַיֹּבֵל הוּא
נה וּבָנָיו עִמּוֹ: כִּי־לִי בְנֵי־יִשְׂרָאֵל עֲבָדִים עֲבָדַי הֵם אֲשֶׁר־הוֹצֵאתִי אוֹתָם מֵאֶרֶץ מפטיר
א מִצְרָיִם אֲנִי יְהוָה אֱלֹהֵיכֶם: לֹא־תַעֲשׂוּ לָכֶם אֱלִילִם וּפֶסֶל וּמַצֵּבָה לֹא־תָקִימוּ
לָכֶם וְאֶבֶן מַשְׂכִּית לֹא תִתְּנוּ בְּאַרְצְכֶם לְהִשְׁתַּחֲוֺת עָלֶיהָ כִּי אֲנִי יְהוָה אֱלֹהֵיכֶם:
ב אֶת־שַׁבְּתֹתַי תִּשְׁמֹרוּ וּמִקְדָּשִׁי תִּירָאוּ אֲנִי יְהוָה:

רש"י

זה הנמכר לעבודה זרה עצמה להיות לה שמש, ולא לאלהות אלא לחטב עצים ולשאב מים:

מח | **גאלה תהיה לו.** מיד, אל תניחהו שיטמע:

נ | **עד שנת היבל.** שהרי כל עצמו לא קנאו אלא לעבדו עד היובל, שהרי ביובל יצא, כמו שנאמר למטה: "ויצא בשנת היבל" (להלן פסוק נד). ובגוי שתחת ידך הכתוב מדבר, ואף על פי כן לא תבא עליו בעקיפין, מפני חלול השם, אלא כשבא לגאל, ידקדק בחשבון, לפי המגיע בכל שנה ושנה ינכה לו הגוי מן דמיו – אם היו עשרים שנה משנמכר עד היובל וקנאו בעשרים מנה, נמצא שקנה הגוי עבודת שנה במנה, ואם שהה זה אצלו חמש שנים ובא לגאל ינכה לו חמשת מנים ויתן לו העבד חמשה עשר מנים, וזהו: "והיה כסף ממכרו במספר שנים": **כימי שכיר יהיה עמו.** חשבון המגיע לכל שנה ושנה יחשב כאלו נשכר עמו כל שנה במנה וינכה לו:

נא | **אם עוד רבות בשנים.** עד היובל: **לפיהן וגו'.** הכל כמו שפרשתי:

נג | **לא ירדנו בפרך לעיניך.** כלומר, ואתה רואה:

נד | **ואם לא יגאל באלה.** באלה הוא נגאל, ואינו נגאל בשש:

נה | **כי לי בני ישראל עבדים.** שטרי קודם: **אני ה' אלהיכם.** כל המשעבדן מלמטה כאלו משעבד מלמעלה:

פרק כו

א | **לא תעשו לכם אלילם.** כנגד זה הנמכר לגוי, שלא יאמר: הואיל ורבי מגלה עריות אף אני כמותו, הואיל ורבי עובד עבודה זרה אף אני כמותו, הואיל ורבי מחלל שבת אף אני כמותו, לכך נאמרו מקראות הללו. ואף הפרשיות הללו נאמרו על הסדר: בתחלה הזהיר על השביעית, ואם חמד ממון ונחשד על השביעית סופו למכר מטלטליו, לכך סמך לה: "וכי תמכרו ממכר" (לעיל כה, יד). לא חזר בו, סוף מוכר אחזתו. לא חזר בו, סוף מוכר את ביתו. לא חזר בו, סוף לוה ברבית. כל אלו האחרונות קשות מן הראשונות. לא חזר בו, סוף מוכר את עצמו. לא חזר בו, לא דיו לישראל אלא אפלו לגוי: **ואבן משכית.** לשון כסוי, כמו: "ושכתי כפי" (שמות לג, כב), שמכסין הקרקע ברצפת אבנים: **להשתחות עליה.** אפלו לשמים, לפי שהשתחויה בפשוט ידים ורגלים היא, ואסרה תורה לעשות כן חוץ מן המקדש:

ב | **אני ה'.** נאמן לשלם שכר:

DISCUSSION

An ornamented stone you shall not place in your land, to prostrate yourself upon it: The Sages explain that this prohibition includes prostration on any stone. Complete prostration, lying prone on the ground rather than simply bowing, is considered a quintessential act of worship, which may not be performed on any stone at all outside of the Temple in Jerusalem. This is the basis for the prevalent custom of spreading carpets or other coverings over the floor of the synagogue at those points of the Yom Kippur service when the congregation bows to the ground. In this manner they avoid bowing upon an exposed stone (see *Megilla* 22b; Rambam, *Sefer HaMadda*, *Hilkhot Avoda Zara* 6:6–7; Rema, *Shulḥan Arukh*, *Oraḥ Ḥayyim* 131:8).

Parashat
Behukotai

A Promise of Blessing and the Threat of Punishment

LEVITICUS 26:3–46

After the assurance of a blessing and a life of goodness if the Israelites fulfill the word of God, the Torah details the heavy punishments for the abandonment of the Torah and its commandments. Tragically, all of the retributions listed here have befallen the Jewish people over the course of its long history, in its far-flung communities.

26 3 God promises: **If you follow My statutes** that I have made known to you, **and observe My commandments,** which further establish what paths one may not follow,[1] **and perform them,**

4 **I will provide your rains in their season.** For workers of the land, not only is the overall yearly amount of rainfall important, but their precise distribution during the agricultural year is of no less significance. **And** when rain falls at the desired times, then **the land shall yield its produce, and the tree of the field shall yield its fruit.** If rain does not come at the right time, the fertility of the land is reduced, and even if the plants and trees grow, the course of their development will be adversely affected.

5 When the harvest is successful, **your threshing,**[B] which starts at the beginning of the summer months, when the barley ripens, followed by the wheat harvest, **shall reach until grape harvest.** The grapes start to ripen during the months of Tammuz to Av, July to August. In a year of blessing, each one of these stages shall lengthen, so that they follow in an uninterrupted

sequence. **And** therefore the **grape harvest shall reach until sowing,** the season for sowing the fields at the beginning of the next agricultural year, after the summer. The unbroken succession of these agricultural seasons is indicative of the earth's fertility. **You shall eat your food to repletion, and** although a rich, productive land generally tempts enemies to come and seek to conquer it, **you shall live in your land in security.**

6 In addition to the granting of rain and the resultant blessing of fertility, **I shall grant peace in the land, and you shall lie without threat** of an enemy attack; **and I will banish wild beasts from the land.** When the land is tilled and the villages are inhabited, wild animals keep away from the settled areas. Furthermore, not only will you be spared a direct attack, but **a sword shall not pass in your land.**[D] Foreign forces will not dare even to pass through your territory.[2]

Second aliya

7 Not only shall armies not pass through your land, but **you shall pursue your enemies, and they shall fall before you by the sword.**

8 Furthermore, **five of you shall pursue one hundred, and one hundred of you shall pursue ten thousand;**[D] **and your enemies shall fall before you by the sword.**

9 Not only will you not encounter difficulties, but **I will turn to you** with a special blessing **and make you fruitful, and multiply you; and I will fulfill My covenant with you,** with all the promises the covenant includes.

10 **You shall eat old produce.** This is a double blessing: First, there will be a surplus of food beyond present consumption which will be placed in storage; and second, the produce will improve with age.[3] **And** as the land will continue to be fertile, **you shall remove the old from before the new.** You will have to take out the excess old produce in order to make room for the new.

Third aliya (Fifth aliya)

11 On a broader scale, **I will place My dwelling in your midst, and My self shall not reject you;** I shall willingly rest My presence among you.

Threshing

DISCUSSION

26:6 | A sword shall not pass in your land: From ancient times, Israel served as a corridor between other lands. Various conquerors were tempted to wage war over it, as they moved through the land on their way to more distant destinations, and as a result it was often captured by great kingdoms from the south or north.

פרשת

בחקתי

ג ד אִם־בְּחֻקֹּתַי תֵּלֵכוּ וְאֶת־מִצְוֺתַי תִּשְׁמְרוּ וַעֲשִׂיתֶם אֹתָם: וְנָתַתִּי גִשְׁמֵיכֶם בְּעִתָּם כב
ה וְנָתְנָה הָאָרֶץ יְבוּלָהּ וְעֵץ הַשָּׂדֶה יִתֵּן פִּרְיוֹ: וְהִשִּׂיג לָכֶם דַּיִשׁ אֶת־בָּצִיר וּבָצִיר
ו יַשִּׂיג אֶת־זָרַע וַאֲכַלְתֶּם לַחְמְכֶם לָשֹׂבַע וִישַׁבְתֶּם לָבֶטַח בְּאַרְצְכֶם: וְנָתַתִּי שָׁלוֹם שני
בָּאָרֶץ וּשְׁכַבְתֶּם וְאֵין מַחֲרִיד וְהִשְׁבַּתִּי חַיָּה רָעָה מִן־הָאָרֶץ וְחֶרֶב לֹא־תַעֲבֹר
ז ח בְּאַרְצְכֶם: וּרְדַפְתֶּם אֶת־אֹיְבֵיכֶם וְנָפְלוּ לִפְנֵיכֶם לֶחָרֶב: וְרָדְפוּ מִכֶּם חֲמִשָּׁה מֵאָה
ט וּמֵאָה מִכֶּם רְבָבָה יִרְדֹּפוּ וְנָפְלוּ אֹיְבֵיכֶם לִפְנֵיכֶם לֶחָרֶב: וּפָנִיתִי אֲלֵיכֶם וְהִפְרֵיתִי
י אֶתְכֶם וְהִרְבֵּיתִי אֶתְכֶם וַהֲקִימֹתִי אֶת־בְּרִיתִי אִתְּכֶם: וַאֲכַלְתֶּם יָשָׁן נוֹשָׁן וְיָשָׁן שלישי
יא יב מִפְּנֵי חָדָשׁ תּוֹצִיאוּ: וְנָתַתִּי מִשְׁכָּנִי בְּתוֹכְכֶם וְלֹא־תִגְעַל נַפְשִׁי אֶתְכֶם: וְהִתְהַלַּכְתִּי /חמישי/

רש"י

ג | **אם בחקתי תלכו.** יכול זה קיום המצות? כשהוא אומר: "ואת מצותי תשמרו" הרי קיום המצות אמור, הא מה אני מקיים: "אם בחקתי תלכו"? שתהיו עמלים בתורה: **ואת מצותי תשמרו.** הוו עמלים בתורה על מנת לשמר ולקים, כמו שנאמר: "ולמדתם אתם ושמרתם לעשתם" (דברים ה, א):

ד | **בעתם.** בשעה שאין דרך בני אדם לצאת, כגון בלילי שבתות: **ועץ השדה.** הן אילני סרק, ועתידין לעשות פרות:

ה | **והשיג לכם דיש את בציר.** שיהא הדיש מרבה ואתם עסוקים בו עד הבציר, ובבציר תעסקו עד שעת הזרע: **ואכלתם לחמכם לשבע.** אוכל קמעא והוא מתברך במעיו:

ו | **ונתתי שלום.** שמא תאמרו: הרי מאכל והרי משתה, אם אין שלום אין כלום! תלמוד לומר אחר כל זאת: "ונתתי שלום בארץ", מכאן שהשלום שקול כנגד הכל, וכן הוא אומר: "עשה שלום ובורא את הכל" (על פי ישעיה מה, ז): **וחרב לא תעבר בארצכם.** אין צריך לומר שלא יבואו למלחמה, אלא אפילו לעבר דרך ארצכם ממדינה למדינה:

ז | **לפניכם לחרב.** איש בחרב רעהו:

ח | **ורדפו מכם.** מן החלשים שבכם ולא מן הגבורים שבכם: **חמשה מאה ומאה מכם רבבה.** וכי כך הוא החשבון? והלא לא היה צריך לומר אלא 'ומאה מכם שני אלפים ירדפו'! אלא אינו דומה מועטין העושין את התורה למרבין העושין את התורה: **ונפלו איביכם וגו'.** שיהיו נופלין לפניכם שלא כדרך הארץ:

ט | **ופניתי אליכם.** אפנה מכל עסקי לשלם שכרכם. משל למה הדבר דומה? למלך ששכר פועלים וכו' [הרבה, והיה שם פועל אחד ועשה עמו מלאכה ימים הרבה. נכנסו הפועלים ליטול שכרם ונכנס אותו הפועל עמהם. אמר לו המלך לאותו הפועל: בני, אפנה לך, הרובים הללו שעשו עמי מלאכה ממועטת ואני נותן להם שכר מועט, אבל את - חשבון רב אני עתיד לחשב עמך], כדאיתא בתורת כהנים (ת"כ פרק ב, ה): **והפריתי אתכם.** בפריה ורביה: **והרביתי אתכם.** בקומה זקופה: **והקימתי את בריתי אתכם.** ברית חדשה, לא כברית הראשונה שהפרתם אותה אלא ברית חדשה שלא תופר, שנאמר: "וכרתי את בית ישראל ואת בית יהודה ברית חדשה... לא כברית" וגו' (ירמיה לא, ל-לא):

י | **ואכלתם ישן נושן.** הפרות יהיו משתמרין וטובים להתישן, שיהא ישן הנושן של שלש שנים יפה לאכול משל אשתקד: **וישן מפני חדש תוציאו.** שיהיו הגרנות מלאות חדש והאוצרות מלאות ישן, וצריכים אתם לפנות האוצרות למקום אחר לתת החדש לתוכן:

יא | **ונתתי משכני.** זה בית המקדש: **ולא תגעל נפשי.** אין רוחי קצה בכם. כל 'געילה' לשון פליטת דבר הבלוע בדבר, כמו: "כי שם נגעל מגן גבורים" (שמואל ב' א, כא),

BACKGROUND

26:5 | **Threshing:** This is a reference to the separation of the grain from the chaff, performed at the conclusion of the harvest, toward the end of the month of Iyar. In order to ready the produce for threshing, it would be spread over a rocky surface or across the granary. Pressure would then be applied to the produce: Either it was trampled under the feet of animals, or a special threshing implement in the form of a wooden board was dragged over it.

DISCUSSION

26:8 | **Five of you shall pursue one hundred, and one hundred of you shall pursue ten thousand:** Such a situation, in which five warriors give chase to one hundred enemy fighters, and similar ratios, are familiar both from Jewish and general history. An army renowned for its strength can deter an enemy even when its forces are few in number. If a fighting unit believes all is lost, superiority in numbers will not help, and its soldiers might even flee the battlefield and scatter.

12 I shall walk in your midst, openly and with satisfaction.[4] **I shall be your God, and you shall be My people.** The mutual relationship between the nation and its God will be apparent. You will feel that you are My people,[5] not only when you submit to My will, but also when you take shelter in My shade.

13 I am the Lord your God, who took you out of the land of Egypt, from being slaves to them; I broke the beams of your yoke,[B] **and caused you to walk upright.** By breaking the beams of the yoke, which force the wearer's head downward, I enabled you to lift up your heads and walk erect.[6]

14 Here the chapter starts the list of curses: **And if you do not heed Me, and do not perform all these commandments,**

15 but if you also despise My statutes, and if your soul rejects My ordinances,[D] **failing to perform all My commandments, in your violating My covenant,**

16 so too will I act like you, as I will do this to you: I will appoint over you panic, existential anxiety that is not caused by any particular event. I will also bring upon you diseases: **consumption**[B] **and fever, causing the eyes to seek and the soul to despair** with continuous suffering. There are sicknesses that are far more severe than the ones listed here, but those for the most part are circumscribed in that they start and end at defined points. Consumption and malaria, which is a classic example of the fever mentioned here, generally cause chronic pain for an extended period of time. **And** in a different realm of activity, **you shall sow your seed in vain, and your enemies shall eat it.**[D]

17 I shall direct My attention against you, in contrast to the blessing of verse 9: "I will turn to you."[7] In the Bible, the act of turning toward is invariably a positive move, a sign of affection, whereas the directing of attention, which is likewise a mark of providence, means that God will attend in a negative form.[8] **And you shall be smitten** in combat **before your enemies; those who hate you shall subjugate you; and you shall flee with no one pursuing you.** This is the reverse of the

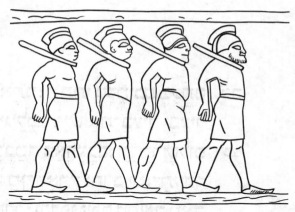

Captives in Assyria with a yoke around their necks. Relief from the Balawat Gates of Ashurnasirpal II, near Nineveh, ninth century BCE

description in verse 8. Panic, fear, and the loss of composure cause one to flee even when there is nobody chasing.

18 And if after these you do not heed Me, in your willful refusal to interpret your troubles as a punishment for your evil deeds, if you continue to live your lives in the same manner, without rectifying your behavior, **I will amplify chastising you,** I will continue to punish you **sevenfold for your sins.** Some commentaries, both here and with regard to similar expressions below, spell out precisely seven types of punishments, to which this alludes. Generally speaking, however, seven is a symbolic number, often used in an inexact manner, to denote a substantial amount.[9]

19 I will break the pride of your power, I will destroy the Temple.[10] This expression can also be interpreted as referring to the shattering of Israel's sense of power and strength. Such a feeling might be due to various causes, including years of famine and hunger, as indicated by the continuation: **And I**

————————— BACKGROUND —————————

26:13 | The beams of your yoke: This expression comes from the world of animal husbandry. Such yokes were also used for slaves and captives. A yoke was typically placed on the neck of a plowing ox, and beams were attached to the yoke in order to hold the animal's head and shoulders in place. The breaking of these beams would free the animal.

26:16 | Consumption [shaḥefet]: In modern Hebrew, shaḥefet refers to tuberculosis, an infectious disease which affects mainly the lungs. However, this is not necessarily the sickness referred to here. According to the Sages, shaḥefet is a gauntness accompanied by fever and depression (Sifra, Beḥukotai 2:2). Some commentaries maintain that this illness causes the skin to dry up and change in form (Rashi; Rambam). Others associate its root, shin-ḥet-peh, with the roots samekh-ḥet-bet and samekh-ḥet-peh, alluding to weakness and exhaustion. If so, it is similar to the ancient Arabic da'ifa.

————————— DISCUSSION —————————

26:15 | But if you despise My statutes, and if your soul rejects My ordinances: These expressions go beyond disobedience. They attest to an obtuseness of the soul, a lack of sensitivity toward Torah and commandments, and even a somewhat willful abandonment of the way of life expected from the people of Israel. A failure to fulfill the commandments out of contempt is a familiar phenomenon in the past and even the present.

26:16 | You shall sow your seed in vain, and your enemies shall eat it: The book of Judges describes the realization of this curse. The Israelites sowed their fields and began to harvest its produce, but the enemy came and took it for themselves (see Judges 6:3–4; see also commentary on Isaiah 62:8).

יג בְּתוֹכְכֶם וְהָיִיתִי לָכֶם לֵאלֹהִים וְאַתֶּם תִּהְיוּ־לִי לְעָם: אֲנִי יהוה אֱלֹהֵיכֶם אֲשֶׁר
הוֹצֵאתִי אֶתְכֶם מֵאֶרֶץ מִצְרַיִם מִהְיֹת לָהֶם עֲבָדִים וָאֶשְׁבֹּר מֹטֹת עֻלְּכֶם וָאוֹלֵךְ
אֶתְכֶם קוֹמְמִיּוּת:
יד טו וְאִם־לֹא תִשְׁמְעוּ לִי וְלֹא תַעֲשׂוּ אֵת כָּל־הַמִּצְוֹת הָאֵלֶּה: וְאִם־בְּחֻקֹּתַי תִּמְאָסוּ וְאִם
אֶת־מִשְׁפָּטַי תִּגְעַל נַפְשְׁכֶם לְבִלְתִּי עֲשׂוֹת אֶת־כָּל־מִצְוֹתַי לְהַפְרְכֶם אֶת־בְּרִיתִי:
טז אַף־אֲנִי אֶעֱשֶׂה־זֹּאת לָכֶם וְהִפְקַדְתִּי עֲלֵיכֶם בֶּהָלָה אֶת־הַשַּׁחֶפֶת וְאֶת־הַקַּדַּחַת
יז מְכַלּוֹת עֵינַיִם וּמְדִיבֹת נָפֶשׁ וּזְרַעְתֶּם לָרִיק זַרְעֲכֶם וַאֲכָלֻהוּ אֹיְבֵיכֶם: וְנָתַתִּי פָנַי
יח בָּכֶם וְנִגַּפְתֶּם לִפְנֵי אֹיְבֵיכֶם וְרָדוּ בָכֶם שֹׂנְאֵיכֶם וְנַסְתֶּם וְאֵין־רֹדֵף אֶתְכֶם: וְאִם־
יט עַד־אֵלֶּה לֹא תִשְׁמְעוּ לִי וְיָסַפְתִּי לְיַסְּרָה אֶתְכֶם שֶׁבַע עַל־חַטֹּאתֵיכֶם: וְשָׁבַרְתִּי

רש"י

לא יקבל המשיחה, שמושחין מגן של עור בחלב מבשל כדי להחליק מעליו מכת חץ או חנית, שלא יקב העור:

יב| **והתהלכתי בתוככם.** אטייל עמכם בגן עדן כאחד מכם ולא תהיו מזדעזעים ממני. יכול לא תיראו ממני? תלמוד לומר: "והייתי לכם לאלהים":

יג| **אני ה' אלהיכם.** כדאי אני שתאמינו בי שאני יכול לעשות כל אלה, שהרי "הוצאתי אתכם מארץ מצרים" ועשיתי לכם נסים גדולים: **מטת.** כמין יתד בשני ראשי העול המעכבים המוסרה שלא תצא מראש השור ויתיר הקשר, כמו: "עשה לך מוסרות ומטות" (ירמיה כז, ב), קביליי"א בלעז: **קוממיות.** בקומה זקופה:

יד| **ואם לא תשמעו לי.** להיות עמלים בתורה ולדעת מדרש חכמים. יכול לקיום המצות? כשהוא אומר: "ולא תעשו" וגו' הרי קיום מצות אמור, הא מה אני מקיים: "ואם לא תשמעו לי"? להיות עמלים בתורה. ומה תלמוד לומר: "לי"? אין "לי" אלא זה המכיר את רבונו ומתכוון למרד בו, וכן בנמרוד: "גבור ציד לפני ה'" (בראשית י, ט), שמכירו ומתכוון למרד בו, וכן באנשי סדום: "רעים וחטאים לה' מאד" (שם יג, יג), מכירים את רבונם ומתכוונים למרד בו: **ולא תעשו.** משלא תלמדו לא תעשו, הרי שתי עבירות:

טו| **ואם בחקתי תמאסו.** מואס באחרים העושים: **משפטי תגעל נפשכם.** שונא החכמים: **לבלתי עשות.** מונע את אחרים מעשות: **את כל מצותי.** כופר שלא צויתים, לכך נאמר: "את כל מצותי" ולא נאמר 'את כל המצות': **להפרכם את בריתי.** כופר בעיקר. הרי שבע עבירות, הראשונה גוררת השניה וכן עד השביעית, ואלו הן: לא למד, ולא עשה, מואס באחרים העושים, שונא את החכמים, מונע את האחרים מעשות, כופר במצות, כופר בעיקר:

טז| **והפקדתי עליכם.** וצויתי עליכם: **שחפת.** חולי שמשחף את הבשר, אנפולי"ש בלעז, דומה לנפוח שהוקלה נפיחתו, ומראית פניו זעופה: **קדחת.** חולי שמקדיח את הגוף ומחממו ומבעירו, כמו: "כי אש קדחה באפי" (דברים לב, כב): **מכלות עינים ומדיבת נפש.** העינים צופות וכלות לראות שיקל וירפא, וסוף שלא ירפא וידאבו הנפשות של משפחתו במותו. כל תאוה שאינה באה ותוחלת ממשכה קרויה 'כליון עינים': **וזרעתם לריק.** תזרעו ולא תצמח, ואם תצמח "ואכלהו איביכם":

יז| **ונתתי פני.** פנאי שלי, פונה אני מכל עסקי להרע לכם: **ורדו בכם שנאיכם.** כמשמעו, ישלטו בכם:

אגדת תורת כהנים מפרשה זו: **אף אני אעשה זאת.** איני מדבר אלא באף, וכן: "והלכתי אף אני עמכם בקרי" (להלן פסוק כד): **והפקדתי עליכם.** שיהיו המכות פוקדות אתכם מזו לזו, עד שהראשונה פקודה אצלכם תביא אחרת ואסמכנה לה: **בהלה.** מכה המבהלת את הבריות, ואי זו? זו מכת מותן: **את השחפת.** יש לך אדם שהוא חולה ומוטל במטה אבל בשרו שמור עליו, תלמוד לומר: "שחפת" שהוא נשחף. או עתים שהוא נשחף אבל נח ואינו מקדיח, תלמוד לומר: "ואת הקדחת", מלמד שהוא מקדיח. או עתים שהוא מקדיח וסבור הוא בעצמו שיחיה, תלמוד לומר: "מכלות עינים". או הוא אינו סבור בעצמו שיחיה אבל אחרים סבורים שיחיה, תלמוד לומר: "ומדיבת נפש" (לעיל פסוק טז): **וזרעתם לריק זרעכם.** זורעה ואינה מצמחת, ומעתה מה אויביכם באים ואוכלים, ומה תלמוד לומר "ואכלהו איביכם"? הא כיצד? זורעה שנה ראשונה ואינה מצמחת, שנה שניה מצמחת, ואויבים באים ומוצאים תבואה לימי המצור, ושבפנים מתים ברעב שלא לקטו תבואה אשתקד. דבר אחר: "וזרעתם לריק זרעכם", כנגד הבנים והבנות הכתוב מדבר, שאתה עמל בהם ומגדלן והחטא בא ומכלה אותם, שנאמר: "אשר טפחתי ורביתי איבי כלם" (איכה ב, כב): **ונתתי פני בכם.** כמו שנאמר בטובה: "ופניתי אליכם", כך נאמר ברעה: "ונתתי פני". משלו משל, למלך שאמר לעבדיו: פונה אני מכל עסקי ועוסק אני עמכם לרעה: **ונגפתם לפני איביכם.** שיהא המות הורג אתכם מבפנים ובעלי דבביכון מקיפין אתכם מבחוץ: **ורדו בכם שנאיכם.** שאיני מעמיד שונאים אלא מכם ובכם, שבשעה שאמות העולם עומדים על ישראל אינם מבקשים אלא מה שבגלוי, שנאמר: "והיה אם זרע ישראל ועלה מדין ועמלק ובני קדם וגו' ויחנו עליהם וישחיתו את יבול הארץ" (שופטים ו, ג-ד), אבל בשעה שאעמיד עליכם מכם ובכם, הם מחפשים אחר המטמוניות שלכם, וכן הוא אומר: "ואשר אכלו שאר עמי ועורם מעליהם הפשיטו" וגו' (מיכה ג, ג): **ונסתם.** מפני אימה: **ואין רדף אתכם.** מבלי כח:

יח| **ואם עד אלה.** ואם בעוד אלה לא תשמעו: **ויספתי.** עוד יסורין אחרים: **שבע על חטאתיכם.** שבע פרעניות על שבע עבירות האמורות למעלה:

יט| **ושברתי את גאון עזכם.** זה בית המקדש, וכן הוא אומר: "הנני מחלל את מקדשי גאון עזכם" (יחזקאל כד, כא): **ונתתי את שמיכם כברזל ואת ארצכם כנחשה.** זו קשה משל משה, ששם הוא אומר: "והיו שמיך אשר על ראשך נחשת" וגו' (דברים כח, כג), שיהיו השמים מזיעין כדרך שהנחשת מזיעה, והארץ אינה מזיעה כדרך שאין הברזל מזיע והיא משמרת פרותיה; אבל כאן השמים לא יהיו מזיעין כדרך שאין הברזל מזיע ויהא חורב בעולם, והארץ תהא מזיעה כדרך שהנחשת מזיעה והיא מאבדת פרותיה:

will render your sky like iron, which does not drip, **and your earth like bronze,** from which nothing grows.

20 **Your strength shall be** entirely **expended in vain.** During a drought, much time and effort is invested to work the land and draw water in various ways for irrigation, but all this shall be for naught: **And your land shall not yield its produce and the tree of the land shall not yield its fruit.**

21 **And if you walk recalcitrantly with Me,**[D] in rebellion, **and you do not** wish to **heed Me,** as you learn nothing from the punishments, then **I will amplify My blow upon you seven-fold in accordance with your sins.**

22 **I will send the beast of the field against you.**[D] In sharp contrast to the blessing: "I will banish wild beasts from the land" (verse 6), here wild beasts invade settled areas. **It will bereave you of your children,** the easiest prey, **and destroy your cattle, and diminish you; and your roads shall become desolate.** Due to their reduced number and out of fear, people will shut themselves up in their communities, and the roads will be deserted and laid waste.

23 **And if with these** too **you are not chastised to Me,** by accepting My reproof, **and you walk recalcitrantly with Me;**

24 **so I also will walk with you recalcitrantly,** in the same harsh and forceful manner, **and I too will smite you sevenfold for your sins.**

25 **I will bring upon you a sword** of war, **avenging the vengeance of the** broken **covenant; you shall be gathered into your cities,** to hide from the enemy. Also, **I will send forth pestilence among you.** When you are crowded within your cities, a plague will be all the more deadly. **And** eventually **you shall be delivered into the hand of an enemy,** as your cities will be unprotected.

26 **When I break for you the staff,** your support **of bread, ten women shall bake your bread in one oven.** This is an

exaggerated depiction of a lack of bread. Home ovens were like relatively small jugs, designed for baking the bread required by a single family. **And they shall return your bread by weight.** Since food will be so sparse, people will be unable to act in a broad-minded, generous manner, and swap portions freely; rather, they will weigh how much they put into the oven and how much they took out, to determine exactly what belongs to them and what belongs to their neighbor. **And** then **you shall eat, but you shall not be satisfied,** both due to the fact that there is not enough food and also because the feeling of scarcity itself will cause the meal to be unsatisfying.

Drawing of an oven from the Iron Age, Tel Qasile

27 **And if with** even **this,** actual hunger, when the hardships and disasters increase, **you do not heed Me, and you walk recalcitrantly with Me;**

28 **I will walk with you in recalcitrant fury.** After causing a food shortage and harming your welfare, I will bring further horrors upon you: **I, too, will chastise you sevenfold for your sins.**

29 **You shall eat the flesh of your sons,**[D] **and the flesh of your daughters you shall eat.** Due to the increasing hunger, you will eat the flesh of man, and not just any person; rather, you will cannibalize your very own children.

30 **I will destroy your high places,** the tall structures on which altars are built, **and destroy your sun idols,** images and monuments for the worship of the sun, **and I shall cast your carcasses on the carcasses of your idols.**[D] You will die, and your

---

DISCUSSION

26:21 | And if you walk recalcitrantly [*keri*] with Me: The word *keri* is from the root *kuf-reish-heh,* like *mikreh,* happenstance. Walking *keri* denotes a basic lack of reaction: An incident occurred but one thinks little about it. The diseases, famines, and wars described here are tragedies that bring about great suffering, and yet some continue to view them as coincidental and do not examine their moral states (see Rambam, *Sefer Zemanim, Hilkhot Ta'anit* 1:3; Rambam, *Guide of the Perplexed* 3:36). The troubles they encounter cause them to groan, but they carry on in the same manner regardless.

Many other commentaries interpret *keri* as hardness. According to this understanding, the verse refers to a stubborn stance in the face of retribution (see Onkelos; Rashi).

26:22 | I will send the beast of the field against you: In a time of famine and water shortage, it is natural for wild animals to infiltrate populated regions. Due to hunger, packs of animals overcome their fear of humans and enter villages and cities. The Sages call this phenomenon wolf attacks (*Bava Metzia* 93b).

26:29 | You shall eat the flesh of your sons: Terrible incidents of this type indeed occurred

among the people of Israel in times of siege and distress.

26:30 | And I shall cast your carcasses on the carcasses of your idols [*giluleikhem*]: *Gilulim* is one of several derogatory terms for idols. Presumably it is a variant form of *gelal,* animal dung (see *Sifra, Kedoshim;* Rashi, Deuteronomy 29:16). This extreme formulation describes the outcome of a war and conquest in which idolatrous temples are destroyed and the bodies of the pagan believers become intermingled with broken pieces of their idols. Not only in exile, but even when they were in their own land, which

כ את־גאון עזכם ונתתי את־שמיכם כברזל ואת־ארצכם כנחשה: ותם לריק
כא כחכם ולא־תתן ארצכם את־יבולה ועץ הארץ לא יתן פריו: ואם־תלכו עמי
כב קרי ולא תאבו לשמע לי ויספתי עליכם מכה שבע כחטאתיכם: והשלחתי
בכם את־חית השדה ושכלה אתכם והכריתה את־בהמתכם והמעיטה אתכם
כג כד ונשמו דרכיכם: ואם־באלה לא תוסרו לי והלכתם עמי קרי: והלכתי אף־אני
כה עמכם בקרי והכיתי אתכם גם־אני שבע על־חטאתיכם: והבאתי עליכם חרב
נקמת נקם־ברית ונאספתם אל־עריכם ושלחתי דבר בתוככם ונתתם ביד־
כו אויב: בשברי לכם מטה־לחם ואפו עשר נשים לחמכם בתנור אחד והשיבו
כז לחמכם במשקל ואכלתם ולא תשבעו: ואם־בזאת לא תשמעו
כח לי והלכתם עמי בקרי: והלכתי עמכם בחמת־קרי ויסרתי אתכם אף־אני שבע
כט ל על־חטאתיכם: ואכלתם בשר בניכם ובשר בנתיכם תאכלו: והשמדתי את־
במתיכם והכרתי את־חמניכם ונתתי את־פגריכם על־פגרי גלוליכם וגעלה

רש״י

כ| **ותם לריק כחכם.** הרי אדם שלא עמל, שלא חרש, שלא זרע, שלא נכש, שלא כסח, שלא עדר, ובשעת הקציר בא שדפון ומלקה אותו, אין בכך כלום. אבל אדם שעמל וחרש וזרע ונכש וכסח ועדר, ובא שדפון ומלקה אותו, הרי שניו של זה קהות: **ולא תתן ארצכם את יבולה.** אף מה שאתה מוביל לה בשעת הזרע: **ועץ הארץ.** אפילו מן הארץ יהא לקוי, שלא יחניט פרותיו בשעת החנטה: **לא יתן.** משמש למעלה ולמטה, אעץ ואפרי: **לא יתן פריו.** כשהוא מפרה, משיר פרותיו – הרי שתי קללות, ויש כאן שבע פרעניות:

כא| **ואם תלכו עמי קרי.** רבותינו אמרו: עראי, במקרה, שאינו אלא לפרקים, כן תלכו עראי במצות. ומנחם פרש: לשון מניעה, וכן "הקר רגלך" (משלי כה, יז), וכן "יקר רוח" (משלי יז, כז); וקרוב לשון זה לתרגומו של אונקלוס, לשון קשי, שמקשים לבם למנע מהתקרב אלי: **שבע כחטאתיכם.** שבע פרעניות אחרות במספר שבע, כחטאתיכם:

כב| **והשלחתי.** לשון גרוי: **ושכלה אתכם.** אין לי אלא חיה משכלת שדרכה בכך, בהמה שאין דרכה בכך מנין? תלמוד לומר: "ושן בהמות אשלח בם" (דברים לב, כד), הרי שתים. ומנין שתהא ממיתה בנשיכתה? תלמוד לומר: "עם חמת זחלי עפר" (שם), מה אלו נושכין וממיתין, אף אלו נושכין וממיתין, כבר היו שנים בארץ ישראל, חמור נושך וממית, ערוד נושך וממית: **ושכלה אתכם.** אלו הקטנים: **והכריתה את בהמתכם.** מבחוץ: **והמעיטה אתכם.** מבפנים: **ונשמו דרכיכם.** שבילים גדולים ושבילים קטנים. הרי שבע פרעניות: שן בהמה, ושן חיה, חמת זוחלי עפר, ושכלה, והכריתה, והמעיטה, ונשמו:

כג| **לא תוסרו לי.** לשוב אלי:

כה| **נקם ברית.** ויש נקם שאינו בברית כדרך שאר נקמות, וזהו סמוי עיניו של צדקיהו (מלכים ב׳ כה, ז). דבר אחר: "נקם ברית", נקמת בריתי אשר עברתם. כל הבאת חרב שבמקרא היא מלחמת חילות אויבים: **ונאספתם.** מן החוץ אל תוך הערים מפני המצור: **ושלחתי דבר בתוככם.** ועל ידי הדבר "ונתתם ביד" האויבים הצרים עליכם, לפי שאין מלינים את המת בירושלים, וכשהם מוציאים את המת לקברו נתנין ביד אויב:

כו| **מטה לחם.** לשון משען, כמו "מטה עז" (ירמיה מח, יז): **בשברי לכם מטה לחם.** אשבר לכם כל מסעד אכל, והם חלי רעב: **ואפו עשר נשים לחמכם בתנור אחד.** מחסר עצים: **והשיבו לחמכם במשקל.** שתהא התבואה נרקבת ונעשית פת נפולה ומתפרכת בתנור, והן יושבות ושוקלות את השברים לחלקם ביניהם: **ואכלתם ולא תשבעו.** זהו מארה בתוך המעים בלחם. הרי שבע פרעניות: חרב, מצור, דבר, שבר מטה לחם, חסר עצים, פת נפולה, מארה במעים. "ונתתם" אינה מן המנין, היא החרב:

ל| **במתיכם.** מגדלים ובירניות: **חמניכם.** מין עבודה זרה שמעמידין על הגגות, ועל שם שמעמידין בחמה קרויין 'חמנים': **ונתתי את פגריכם.** תפוחי רעב היו, ומוציאים יראתם מחיקם ומנשקים אותה, וכרסו נבקעת ונופל עליה: **וגעלה נפשי אתכם.** זה סלוק שכינה:

DISCUSSION

→ was subject to the influence of many foreign cultures, Jews adopted various alien religions. Nevertheless, for most of their history Jews did not abandon their faith entirely; rather, they practiced syncretism: People worshipped the God of Israel and practiced various forms of idolatry at the same time.

idols will likewise be smashed. **And My Soul shall reject you.** You will feel that you have no path to approach Me.[11]

31 **I will render your cities ruins, I will make your sanctuaries desolate, and I will not smell your pleasing aroma.** On the one hand, the idols upon which you relied shall be broken; on the other hand, I, God, will not answer you.

32 **I will make the land desolate, and** the result will be that **your enemies who live in it shall be desolate upon it.**[D] Even those who try to settle the land after you are gone will be unable to make it blossom.

33 The land will be desolate, and its settled areas, if there are any left at all, will be sparse and feeble. As for **you, I will scatter you among the nations, and I will draw [*harikoti*] the sword after you,** and it will consume you incessantly. *Harikoti* literally means, "I will empty." This is a graphic expression of a sheath left empty due to the frequent use of its sword. **Your land shall be desolate, and your cities shall be ruins.**

34 **Then the land shall be repaid for its sabbaths, all the days of its desolation, and you are in the land of your enemies; then the land shall rest and will repay its sabbaths.** Since you refused to observe the *halakhot* of the Sabbatical Year and let the land rest, as commanded in the previous section, the land shall find its own way to rest, when you have been exiled from it. It is as though the land itself will complete the missing years in which you did not keep the prohibitions of its rest. This is an ironic description of a measure-for-measure punishment.[12]

35 **All the days of its desolation it,** the land, **shall rest** from yielding produce; **that which it did not rest during your sabbaths, when you lived upon it.** This will be a cruel rest for the land. No labor will be performed in your cities on the Sabbath, as your cities will be deserted; the land will not be worked in the seventh year, because you will no longer live there.

36 **Of the survivors among you, I will bring cowardice,** weakness and spinelessness, **in their hearts in the lands of their enemies; the sound of a driven leaf,** or a falling or rustling leaf, **shall pursue them.** Due to their constant state of fear, as well as their sense of vulnerability and the knowledge that

they are surrounded by enemies on all sides, they will experience every slight noise as a sign that they are being chased. Consequently, **they shall flee, as one flees the sword, and they shall fall** while running **with no pursuer.** Their own panicked flight shall lead to their downfall, even though nobody is actually chasing after them.

37 **They shall stumble over one another** during their flight, **as before a sword,** like those who flee from war and hurt each other in their rush to escape, **with no pursuer. You shall have no recourse before your enemies.** You will be unable to rise up and face enemy attackers.

38 Moreover, **you shall perish among the nations, and the land of your enemies shall consume you.** There is no assurance that you will remain as you are, both on the personal and the national levels. The land of the gentiles shall destroy you and swallow you up. This is one of the harshest curses of all.[13]

39 **The survivors among you** after all these retributions **shall molder in,** due to, **their iniquity, in the lands of your enemies, and also in the iniquities of their fathers, with them they shall molder.**[D]

40 Ultimately, **they shall confess their iniquity and the iniquity of their fathers, in their trespass,** betrayal, **that they committed against Me, and also that they walked recalcitrantly with Me.** At some point they will acknowledge their betrayal and the rebellious nature of their acts. The time will come when they will recognize their impudence and their obtuse response to God's callings. The aim of the retributions, which appeared gradually, was not merely to punish them, but also to call upon them to change their perspectives, repent, and return to God.

41 This verse summarizes the above stages. **I too will walk recalcitrantly with them, and I will bring them into the land of their enemies,** the punishment of exile, which breaks all the frameworks of their lives; **or perhaps then,** when they have been exiled from their land, **their sealed** and dense **hearts will be humbled.** As described earlier, people will take no notice of the implications of the events that have befallen them, even when each tragedy is followed by a worse event. When the seal

---

DISCUSSION

26:32 | Your enemies who live in it shall be desolate upon it: These descriptions came to pass in full. At different periods the Land of Israel was desolate not only because the Israelites were exiled from it, but also because its conquerors found it uninhabitable. After the destruction of the Temple and the unremitting

ruin of the land, no nation was able to strike roots in it.

26:39 | In the iniquities of their fathers, with them they shall molder: Some people commit transgressions not out of any particular interest, but merely because they follow in their

fathers' footsteps. Having been born to parents who strayed from the proper path, the children continue their sins without noticing, lacking an informed will, and without having made an active decision to do evil. Nevertheless, they will be punished for these sins as well.

לא נַפְשִׁי אֶתְכֶם: וְנָתַתִּי אֶת־עָרֵיכֶם חׇרְבָּה וַהֲשִׁמּוֹתִי אֶת־מִקְדְּשֵׁיכֶם וְלֹא אָרִיחַ
לב בְּרֵיחַ נִיחֹחֲכֶם: וַהֲשִׁמֹּתִי אֲנִי אֶת־הָאָרֶץ וְשָׁמְמוּ עָלֶיהָ אֹיְבֵיכֶם הַיֹּשְׁבִים בָּהּ:
לג וְאֶתְכֶם אֱזָרֶה בַגּוֹיִם וַהֲרִיקֹתִי אַחֲרֵיכֶם חָרֶב וְהָיְתָה אַרְצְכֶם שְׁמָמָה וְעָרֵיכֶם
לד יִהְיוּ חׇרְבָּה: אָז תִּרְצֶה הָאָרֶץ אֶת־שַׁבְּתֹתֶיהָ כֹּל יְמֵי הֳשַׁמָּה וְאַתֶּם בְּאֶרֶץ
לה אֹיְבֵיכֶם אָז תִּשְׁבַּת הָאָרֶץ וְהִרְצָת אֶת־שַׁבְּתֹתֶיהָ: כׇּל־יְמֵי הׇשַּׁמָּה תִּשְׁבֹּת אֵת
לו אֲשֶׁר לֹא־שָׁבְתָה בְּשַׁבְּתֹתֵיכֶם בְּשִׁבְתְּכֶם עָלֶיהָ: וְהַנִּשְׁאָרִים בָּכֶם וְהֵבֵאתִי מֹרֶךְ
בִּלְבָבָם בְּאַרְצֹת אֹיְבֵיהֶם וְרָדַף אֹתָם קוֹל עָלֶה נִדָּף וְנָסוּ מְנֻסַת־חֶרֶב וְנָפְלוּ וְאֵין
לז רֹדֵף: וְכָשְׁלוּ אִישׁ־בְּאָחִיו כְּמִפְּנֵי־חֶרֶב וְרֹדֵף אָיִן וְלֹא־תִהְיֶה לָכֶם תְּקוּמָה לִפְנֵי
לח לט אֹיְבֵיכֶם: וַאֲבַדְתֶּם בַּגּוֹיִם וְאָכְלָה אֶתְכֶם אֶרֶץ אֹיְבֵיכֶם: וְהַנִּשְׁאָרִים בָּכֶם יִמַּקּוּ
מ בַּעֲוֺנָם בְּאַרְצֹת אֹיְבֵיכֶם וְאַף בַּעֲוֺנֹת אֲבֹתָם אִתָּם יִמָּקּוּ: וְהִתְוַדּוּ אֶת־עֲוֺנָם וְאֶת־
מא עֲוֺן אֲבֹתָם בְּמַעֲלָם אֲשֶׁר מָעֲלוּ־בִי וְאַף אֲשֶׁר־הָלְכוּ עִמִּי בְּקֶרִי: אַף־אֲנִי אֵלֵךְ

רש"י

לא| **וְנָתַתִּי אֶת עָרֵיכֶם חָרְבָּה.** יָכוֹל מֵאָדָם? כְּשֶׁהוּא אוֹמֵר: "וַהֲשִׁמֹּתִי אֲנִי אֶת הָאָרֶץ" (להלן פסוק לב) הֲרֵי אָדָם אָמוּר, הָא מָה אֲנִי מְקַיֵּם "חָרְבָּה"? מֵעוֹבֵר וָשָׁב: **וַהֲשִׁמּוֹתִי אֶת מִקְדְּשֵׁיכֶם.** יָכוֹל מִן הַקָּרְבָּנוֹת? כְּשֶׁהוּא אוֹמֵר: "וְלֹא אָרִיחַ" הֲרֵי קָרְבָּנוֹת אֲמוּרִים, הָא מָה אֲנִי מְקַיֵּם "וַהֲשִׁמּוֹתִי אֶת מִקְדְּשֵׁיכֶם"? מִן הַגְּדוּדִיּוֹת – שַׁיָּרוֹת שֶׁל יִשְׂרָאֵל שֶׁהָיוּ מִתְקַדְּשׁוֹת וְנוֹעָדוֹת לָבֹא שָׁם. הֲרֵי שֶׁבַע פֻּרְעָנֻיּוֹת: אֲכִילַת בְּשַׂר בָּנִים וּבָנוֹת וְהַשְׁמָדַת בָּמוֹת, הֲרֵי שְׁתַּיִם. כְּרִיתַת חַמָּנִים אֵין כָּאן פֻּרְעָנוּת, אֶלָּא עַל יְדֵי הַשְׁמָדַת הַבִּירָנִיּוֹת יִפְּלוּ הַחַמָּנִים שֶׁבְּרָאשֵׁי הַגַּגּוֹת וְיִכָּרְתוּ. "וְנָתַתִּי אֶת פִּגְרֵיכֶם" וְגוֹ', הֲרֵי שָׁלֹשׁ. סִלּוּק שְׁכִינָה, אַרְבַּע. חָרְבַּן עָרִים, שִׁמְמוֹן מִקְדָּשׁ מִן הַגְּדוּדִיּוֹת, "וְלֹא אָרִיחַ" קָרְבָּנוֹת, הֲרֵי שֶׁבַע:

לב| **וַהֲשִׁמֹּתִי אֲנִי אֶת הָאָרֶץ.** זוֹ מִדָּה טוֹבָה לְיִשְׂרָאֵל, שֶׁלֹּא יִמְצְאוּ הָאוֹיְבִים נַחַת רוּחַ בְּאַרְצָם, שֶׁתְּהֵא שׁוֹמֵמָה מִיּוֹשְׁבֶיהָ:

לג| **וְאֶתְכֶם אֱזָרֶה בַגּוֹיִם.** זוֹ מִדָּה קָשָׁה, שֶׁבְּשָׁעָה שֶׁבְּנֵי מְדִינָה גּוֹלִים לְמָקוֹם אֶחָד רוֹאִים זֶה אֶת זֶה וּמִתְנַחֲמִין, וְיִשְׂרָאֵל נִזְרוּ כְּבַמְּזָרֶה, כְּאָדָם הַזּוֹרֶה שְׂעוֹרִים בְּנָפָה וְאֵין אַחַת מֵהֶן דְּבוּקָה בַּחֲבֶרְתָּהּ: **וַהֲרִיקֹתִי.** כְּשֶׁשּׁוֹלֵף הַחֶרֶב מִתְרוֹקֵן הַנָּדָן. וּמִדְרָשׁוֹ: חֶרֶב הַנִּשְׁמֶטֶת אַחֲרֵיכֶם אֵינָהּ חוֹזֶרֶת מַהֵר, כְּאָדָם שֶׁמֵּרִיק אֶת הַמַּיִם וְאֵין סוֹפָן לַחֲזֹר: **וְהָיְתָה אַרְצְכֶם שְׁמָמָה.** שֶׁלֹּא תְּמַהֲרוּ לָשׁוּב לְתוֹכָהּ, וּמִתּוֹךְ כָּךְ "עָרֵיכֶם יִהְיוּ חָרְבָּה" – נִרְאוֹת לָכֶם חֲרֵבוֹת, שֶׁבְּשָׁעָה שֶׁאָדָם גּוֹלֶה מִבֵּיתוֹ וּמִכַּרְמוֹ וּמֵעִירוֹ וְסוֹפוֹ לַחֲזֹר, כְּאִלּוּ אֵין כַּרְמוֹ וּבֵיתוֹ חֲרֵבִים. כָּךְ שְׁנוּיָה בְּתוֹרַת כֹּהֲנִים (פרק ז, א):

לד| **אָז תִּרְצֶה.** תְּפַיֵּס אֶת כַּעַס הַמָּקוֹם שֶׁכָּעַס עַל שְׁמִטּוֹתֶיהָ: **וְהִרְצָת.** לַמֶּלֶךְ אֶת שַׁבְּתוֹתֶיהָ:

לה| **אֵת אֲשֶׁר לֹא שָׁבְתָה.** שִׁבְעִים שָׁנָה שֶׁל גָּלוּת בָּבֶל הֵן הָיוּ כְּנֶגֶד שִׁבְעִים שְׁנוֹת הַשְּׁמִטָּה וְיוֹבֵל שֶׁהָיוּ בַּשָּׁנִים שֶׁהִכְעִיסוּ יִשְׂרָאֵל בְּאַרְצָם לִפְנֵי הַמָּקוֹם, אַרְבַּע מֵאוֹת וּשְׁלֹשִׁים וָשֵׁשׁ שָׁנָה. שְׁלֹשׁ מֵאוֹת וְתִשְׁעִים הָיוּ שְׁנֵי עֲוֹנָם מִשֶּׁנִּכְנְסוּ לָאָרֶץ עַד שֶׁגָּלוּ עֲשֶׂרֶת הַשְּׁבָטִים, וּבְנֵי יְהוּדָה הִכְעִיסוּ לְפָנָיו אַרְבָּעִים שָׁנָה מִשֶּׁגָּלוּ עֲשֶׂרֶת הַשְּׁבָטִים עַד חָרְבוֹת יְרוּשָׁלַיִם. הוּא שֶׁנֶּאֱמַר בִּיחֶזְקֵאל: "וְאַתָּה שְׁכַב עַל צִדְּךָ הַשְּׂמָאלִי וְגוֹ' וְכִלִּיתָ אֶת אֵלֶּה וְשָׁכַבְתָּ עַל צִדְּךָ הַיְמָנִי שֵׁנִית, וְנָשָׂאתָ אֶת עֲוֹן בֵּית יְהוּדָה אַרְבָּעִים יוֹם" (יחזקאל ד, ד-ו), וּנְבוּאָה זוֹ נֶאֶמְרָה לִיחֶזְקֵאל בַּשָּׁנָה הַחֲמִישִׁית לְגָלוּת הַמֶּלֶךְ יְהוֹיָכִין (שם א, ב) וְעוֹד עָשׂוּ שֵׁשׁ שָׁנִים עַד גָּלוּת צִדְקִיָּהוּ, הֲרֵי אַרְבָּעִים וָשֵׁשׁ. וְאִם תֹּאמַר שְׁנוֹת מְנַשֶּׁה חֲמִשִּׁים וְחָמֵשׁ הָיוּ (מלכים ב' כא, א)! מְנַשֶּׁה עָשָׂה תְּשׁוּבָה שְׁלֹשִׁים וְשָׁלֹשׁ שָׁנָה, וְכָל שְׁנוֹת רִשְׁעוֹ עֶשְׂרִים וּשְׁתַּיִם, כְּמוֹ שֶׁאָמְרוּ בְּאַגָּדַת 'חֵלֶק' (סנהדרין קג ע"א), וְשֶׁל אָמוֹן שְׁתַּיִם (מלכים ב' כא, יט) וְאַחַת עֶשְׂרֵה לִיהוֹיָקִים (שם כג, לו) וּכְנֶגְדָּן לְצִדְקִיָּהוּ (שם כד, יח). צֵא וַחֲשֹׁב לְאַרְבַּע מֵאוֹת וּשְׁלֹשִׁים וָשֵׁשׁ שָׁנָה שְׁמִטִּין וְיוֹבְלוֹת שֶׁבָּהֶם, וְהֵם שֵׁשׁ עֶשְׂרֵה לְמֵאָה, אַרְבַּע עֶשְׂרֵה שְׁמִטִּין וּשְׁנֵי יוֹבְלוֹת, הֲרֵי לְאַרְבַּע מֵאוֹת שָׁנָה שִׁשִּׁים וְאַרְבַּע, לִשְׁלֹשִׁים וָשֵׁשׁ שָׁנָה חָמֵשׁ שְׁמִטּוֹת, הֲרֵי שִׁבְעִים חָסֵר אַחַת, וְעוֹד שָׁנָה יְתֵרָה שֶׁנִּכְנְסָה בַּשְּׁמִטָּה הַמַּשְׁלֶמֶת לְשִׁבְעִים, וַעֲלֵיהֶם נִגְזַר שִׁבְעִים שָׁנָה שְׁלֵמִים. וְכֵן הוּא אוֹמֵר: "עַד רָצְתָה הָאָרֶץ אֶת שַׁבְּתוֹתֶיהָ... לְמַלֹּאות שִׁבְעִים שָׁנָה" (דברי הימים ב' לו, כא):

לו| **וְהֵבֵאתִי מֹרֶךְ.** פַּחַד וְרֹךְ לֵבָב, מֵ"ם שֶׁל "מֹרֶךְ" יְסוֹד נוֹפֵל הוּא, כְּמוֹ מֵ"ם שֶׁל 'מוֹעֵד' וְשֶׁל 'מוֹקֵשׁ': **וְנָסוּ מְנֻסַת חֶרֶב.** כְּאִלּוּ רוֹדְפִים הוֹרְגִים אוֹתָם: **עָלֶה נִדָּף.** שֶׁהָרוּחַ דּוֹחֲפוֹ וּמַכֵּהוּ עַל עָלֶה אַחֵר וּמְקַשְׁקֵשׁ וּמוֹצִיא קוֹל, וְכֵן תַּרְגּוּמוֹ: "קָל טַרְפָא דְּשָׁקִיף", לְשׁוֹן חֲבָטָה, "שְׁדוּפֹת קָדִים" (בראשית מא, ו) 'שְׁקִיפָן קִדּוּם', וְהוּא לְשׁוֹן מַשְׁקוֹף (שמות יב, כב) מְקוֹם חֲבָטַת הַדֶּלֶת, וְכֵן תַּרְגּוּמוֹ שֶׁל "חַבּוּרָה" (שם כא, כה) 'מַשְׁקוֹפֵי':

לז| **וְכָשְׁלוּ אִישׁ בְּאָחִיו.** כְּשֶׁיִּרְצוּ לָנוּס יִכָּשְׁלוּ זֶה בָּזֶה, כִּי יִבָּהֲלוּ לָרוּץ: **כְּמִפְּנֵי חֶרֶב.** כְּאִלּוּ בּוֹרְחִים מִלִּפְנֵי הוֹרְגִים, שֶׁיְּהֵא בִלְבָבָם פַּחַד, וְכָל שָׁעָה סְבוּרִים שֶׁאָדָם רוֹדְפָם. וּמִדְרָשׁוֹ: "וְכָשְׁלוּ אִישׁ בְּאָחִיו", זֶה נִכְשָׁל בַּעֲוֹנוֹ שֶׁל זֶה, שֶׁכָּל יִשְׂרָאֵל עֲרֵבִין זֶה לָזֶה:

לח| **וַאֲבַדְתֶּם בַּגּוֹיִם.** כְּשֶׁתִּהְיוּ פְּזוּרִים תִּהְיוּ אֲבוּדִים זֶה מִזֶּה: **וְאָכְלָה אֶתְכֶם.** אֵלּוּ הַמֵּתִים בַּגּוֹלָה:

לט| **בַּעֲוֹנֹת אֲבֹתָם אִתָּם.** כְּשֶׁאוֹחֲזִים מַעֲשֵׂה אֲבוֹתֵיהֶם בִּידֵיהֶם: **יִמָּקּוּ.** לְשׁוֹן הֲמַסָּה, כְּמוֹ 'יִמַּסּוּ', וְכָמוֹהוּ "תִּמַּקְנָה בְחוֹרֵיהֶן" (זכריה יד, יב), "נָמַקּוּ חַבּוּרֹתָי" (תהלים לח, ו):

that blocks the heart is removed, they will become more sensitive to the meaning of these occurrences. **And they** will **then be repaid for their iniquity.** Their sins will be atoned for in exile, not only because punishment in general serves to atone for sins, but also because the shock of exile will cause them to return to God.

42 **I will remember My covenant** that I enacted **with Jacob, and also My covenant with Isaac, and also My covenant with Abraham I will remember; and the land** that I chose to give to you, which due to your sins became a remote, miserable province, **I will remember.**

43 Although I shall not forget it, **the land shall be forsaken of them,** during their exile, **and shall be repaid for her sabbaths** that they failed to observe, **in** the fact of **its desolation from them; and they shall repay their iniquity** through their punishment, as described above, **because they despised My ordinances, and their soul rejected** and abhorred **My statutes.** They did not merely neglect and abandon God's commandments, but they actively recoiled from them in revulsion and treated them with contempt.

44 Here comes a very important point: **Despite this,** after all the transgressions and punishments, and notwithstanding the people's indifference to the lessons of the past, even **when they are in the land of their enemies,** poor, downtrodden, lowly in spirit, and weak in body, **I will not have despised them and will not have rejected them** in order **to destroy them** entirely, and thereby **to violate My covenant with them, as I am the Lord their God.** Even when they transgress the commandments and rebel in every possible manner, My covenant will remain in force.

45 **I shall remember for them,** those who will live after many generations, **the covenant of their ancestors, that I took them out of the land of Egypt,**[D] not in the manner of individuals taking flight, but **before the eyes of the nations,** in public display, on a grand scale, **to be their God.** In conclusion, God states: **I am the Lord,** who is responsible for all these events.

46 In summary, **these are the statutes and ordinances and laws which the Lord gave between Him and the children of Israel at Mount Sinai,** before their many journeys in the wilderness, **at the hand of Moses.** At Mount Sinai, Israel received numerous commandments, instructions, and *halakhot*. In a certain sense, this chapter recapitulated all the central matters given at Sinai.

Laws of Consecration

LEVITICUS 27:1–34

In the section before the last, the Torah dealt with the sale of fields and houses, and their release in the Jubilee Year. After listing the blessings and curses, which are also connected to the Sabbatical Year and the land's rest (see 26:34–35, 43), this chapter serves as an addendum of sorts to the earlier issue. It addresses various forms of consecration, including a field or house one donates to the Sanctuary. As the state of mind of one who consecrates his property is likely to be similar to that of a person who brings an offering, the discussion of this topic is appropriate for Leviticus. Furthermore, this passage includes certain rights and duties of the priests, which is one of the main subjects discussed in Leviticus.

27 *Fourth aliya (Sixth aliya)*

Vows of Evaluation

LEVITICUS 27:1–8

1 **The Lord spoke to Moses, saying:**

2 **Speak to the children of Israel, and say to them: If a man articulates a vow**[D] **in accordance with the valuation of persons to the Lord,** when one obligates himself to give to God the value of a certain person. With regard to the term *erkekha*, "valuation," see commentary on 5:15.

3 **The valuation shall be:**[D] **For the male from twenty years old until sixty years old, the valuation** of such a man with regard to this form of dedication, **shall be fifty shekels of silver of the sacred shekel.**

4 **And if it is for a female,** in the same age range of twenty years old to sixty, **the valuation shall be thirty shekels.** Someone of this age is considered to be in his or her prime.

DISCUSSION

26:45 | **I shall remember for them the covenant of their ancestors, that I took them out of the land of Egypt:** A covenant remains intact even if one of the parties fails to fulfills its obligations. Consequently, the covenant between God and the Jewish people, which the prophet describes with the famous lines: "I remember for you the kindness of your youth, the love of your nuptials" (Jeremiah 2:2), is still valid. The people will attempt to break it, and God will punish them severely for their misdeeds, but the covenant itself, as well as the relationship and commitment first revealed at the exodus from Egypt with all its miracles and the wonder and uniqueness of the Israelite nation: all these shall last forever.

27:2 | **Articulates [*yafli*] a vow:** The word *pele* means a wonder, an event that is out of the ordinary, or an object outside the boundaries of the normal and the everyday (see Deuteronomy 30:11; Proverbs 30:18). One who articulates a vow

עמם בקרי והבאתי אתם בארץ איביהם או־אז יכנע לבבם הערל ואז ירצו
מב את־עונם: וזכרתי את־בריתי יעקוב ואף את־בריתי יצחק ואף את־בריתי
מג אברהם אזכר והארץ אזכר: והארץ תעזב מהם ותרץ את־שבתתיה בהשמה
מהם והם ירצו את־עונם יען וביען במשפטי מאסו ואת־חקתי געלה נפשם:
מד ואף גם־זאת בהיותם בארץ איביהם לא־מאסתים ולא־געלתים לכלתם להפר
מה בריתי אתם כי אני יהוה אלהיהם: וזכרתי להם ברית ראשנים אשר הוצאתי־
מו אתם מארץ מצרים לעיני הגוים להיות להם לאלהים אני יהוה: אלה החקים
והמשפטים והתורת אשר נתן יהוה בינו ובין בני ישראל בהר סיני ביד־משה:
כז א ב וידבר יהוה אל־משה לאמר: דבר אל־בני ישראל ואמרת אלהם איש כי יפלא רביעי / ששי
ג נדר בערכך נפשת ליהוה: והיה ערכך הזכר מבן עשרים שנה ועד בן־ששים
ד שנה והיה ערכך חמשים שקל כסף בשקל הקדש: ואם־נקבה הוא והיה ערכך

רש"י

מא| **והבאתי אתם.** אני בעצמי אביאם, זו מדה טובה לישראל, שלא יהיו אומרים, הואיל וגלינו בין האומות נעשה כמעשיהם, אני איני מניחם, אלא מעמיד אני את נביאי ומחזירן לתחת כנפי, שנאמר: "והעלה על רוחכם היו לא תהיה וגו', חי אני וגו' אם לא ביד חזקה" וגו' (יחזקאל כ, לב-לג): **או אז יכנע.** כמו "או נודע כי שור נגח הוא" (שמות כא, לו), אם אז יכנע. לשון אחר: אולי, שמא "אז יכנע לבבם" וגו': **ואז ירצו את עונם.** יכפרו על עונם ביסוריהם:

מב| **וזכרתי את בריתי יעקוב.** בחמשה מקומות נכתב מלא, ואליהו חסר בחמשה מקומות – יעקב נטל אות משמו של אליהו ערבון שיבוא ויבשר גאולת בניו: **וזכרתי את בריתי יעקוב.** למה נמנו אחורנית? כלומר כדאי הוא יעקב הקטן לכך, ואם אינו כדאי הרי יצחק עמו, ואם אינו כדאי הרי אברהם כדאי. ולמה לא נאמרה 'זכירה' ביצחק? אלא אפרו של יצחק נראה לפני צבור ומנח על המזבח:

מג| **יען וביען.** גמול ובגמול אשר במשפטי מאסו:

מד| **ואף גם זאת.** ואף אפלו אני עושה עמהם זאת הפרענות אשר אמרתי, בהיותם בארץ אויביהם לא אמאסם לכלתם ולהפר בריתי אשר אתם:

מה| **ברית ראשנים.** של שבטים:

מו| **והתורת.** אחת בכתב ואחת בעל פה, מגיד שכלם נתנו למשה בסיני:

פרק כז

ב| **כי יפלא.** יפריש בפיו: **בערכך נפשת.** לתן ערך נפשו, לומר ערך דבר שנפשו תלויה בו עלי:

ג| **והיה ערכך וגו'.** אין 'ערך' זה לשון דמים, אלא בין שהוא יקר בין שהוא זול, כפי שניו הוא הערך הקצוב עליו בפרשה זו: **ערכך.** כמו 'ערך', וכפל הכפי"ן לא ידעתי מאיזה לשון הוא:

DISCUSSION

expresses a clear, explicit promise that he is separating something from his control, his use, and the usage of others. Accordingly, a vow is an explicit declaration with regard to the demarcation of certain objects.

27:3| **The valuation shall be:** This valuation is not the value of the individual in question. If one wishes, he can vow to give someone's value to the Sanctuary, but in such a case the amount is determined by the value of his work; one estimates how much money the labor of that person would be worth (see *Arakhin* 13b). By contrast, the valuation discussed here is a fixed sum, determined by specific categories of sex and age alone; it has nothing whatsoever to do with the person's ability to work or function. In this regard there is no difference between the valuation of someone who is whole in body, strong, learned, and skilled in a craft, and an individual who is blemished, weak, and incapable of doing anything productive. According to some Sages, it also does not matter whether or not the person who is the subject of the valuation is Jewish (see *Arakhin* 5b; Rambam, *Sefer Hafla'a*, *Hilkhot Arakhin VaḤaramim* 1:6). With that said, there is a possible link between the fixed amounts listed here and the price of slaves in a public auction, although this connection is not explicit in the Torah, which simply presents a decree that only age and sex are to be taken into account for the purpose of valuations.

5 **And if from five years old until twenty years old, the valuation shall be: The male twenty shekels, and for the female ten shekels.**
6 **And if from one month old until five years old, the valuation shall be: The male five shekels of silver, and for the female, the valuation three shekels of silver.**
7 **And if from sixty years old and above: If a male, the valuation shall be fifteen shekels, and for the female ten shekels.**
8 **And if he,** the one who vowed, **is too poor** to pay **for the valuation, he shall be set before the priest, and the priest shall assess him; on the basis of what the one who vowed can afford, the priest shall assess him.**[D] The priest shall grant him a deduction.

Substitution

LEVITICUS 27:9–10

9 **And if it,** the subject of one's vow, **is a type of animal from which one would present an offering to the Lord,** an animal fit for the altar, **any that one gives of it to the Lord shall be sacred.** The sanctity of the vow applies to the body of the animal itself.
10 Consequently, the animal itself must be sacrificed upon the altar. **One shall not exchange it and not substitute it,** replacing a **good** animal **with** a **bad** one, **or** even a **bad** one **with** a **good** one; **if he substitutes an animal for an animal, it and its substitute shall be sacred.** [D] On the other hand, if one dedicates produce or other items, he is permitted to exchange them, to give the value of the object in its stead. Such an exchange is prohibited in the case of an animal that is fit for the altar, as the body of the animal itself is sanctified; it is not consecrated merely for its monetary value.[14] And yet **if he substitutes an animal for an animal, it and its substitute shall be sacred.**[D] Although it is prohibited to say that another animal should replace a consecrated animal, this declaration is not entirely without effect. This contrasts with most other situations, as the *halakha* generally does not recognize the validity of an action which constitutes a prohibition. In the formulation of the Talmud, if there is a matter about which God said: Do not do it, and one did it, his action is ineffective.[15] In this case, however, the animal which one sought to use as a substitute is indeed consecrated, although the original animal also retains its sanctity.

Consecration of Property Unfit for Sacrifice

LEVITICUS 27:11–15

11 **And if** a man consecrates an animal, and **it is any type of non-pure animal** or an animal **from which one does not present an offering to the Lord** for other reasons, e.g., if it is blemished,[16] **he shall set the animal before the priest.**
12 **The priest shall assess it, whether good or bad; as the priest's valuation, so shall it be.** The priest shall evaluate the worth of the animal standing before him, and his determination is final.
13 **And if,** after the owner consecrates the non-pure animal, **he redeems it,** seeks to reacquire it from Sanctuary property, **he shall add its one-fifth to the valuation** of its worth.
14 This verse presents a similar *halakha*: **And when a man consecrates his house sacred to the Lord, then the priest shall assess it, whether good or bad; as the priest assesses it, so shall it stand.**
15 **And if the one who consecrated it redeems his house** himself, **he shall add one-fifth the silver of the valuation to it,** and **then** the house **shall be his.**

DISCUSSION

27:8 | **On the basis of what the one who vowed can afford, the priest shall assess him:** In certain cases the Torah makes allowances for the indigent who are obligated to bring an offering. For example, instead of an animal offering they might bring a bird offering, and one who cannot afford even a bird offering may bring a meal offering of fine flour (see 5:6–11; 12:8; 14:21). In other instances there is no difference between rich and poor, and the obligation to bring the offering remains in force until one is able to do so. With regard to vows of valuation, the priest is authorized to determine the size of the deduction, which is not established by the Torah. The priest appraises the means of the one who vowed and decides how much he must pay. According to this explanation of the text, the person in this verse who is set before the priest and assessed is the one who undertook the vow. Some commentaries, however, maintain that the verse refers to the subject of the valuation, that is, the priest determines the valuation of the person whose value is being pledged by the one who vowed, in accordance with the means

ה שְׁלֹשִׁים שָׁקֶל: וְאִם מִבֶּן־חָמֵשׁ שָׁנִים וְעַד בֶּן־עֶשְׂרִים שָׁנָה וְהָיָה עֶרְכְּךָ הַזָּכָר
ו עֶשְׂרִים שְׁקָלִים וְלַנְּקֵבָה עֲשֶׂרֶת שְׁקָלִים: וְאִם מִבֶּן־חֹדֶשׁ וְעַד בֶּן־חָמֵשׁ שָׁנִים
וְהָיָה עֶרְכְּךָ הַזָּכָר חֲמִשָּׁה שְׁקָלִים כָּסֶף וְלַנְּקֵבָה עֶרְכְּךָ שְׁלֹשֶׁת שְׁקָלִים כָּסֶף:
ז וְאִם מִבֶּן־שִׁשִּׁים שָׁנָה וָמַעְלָה אִם־זָכָר וְהָיָה עֶרְכְּךָ חֲמִשָּׁה עָשָׂר שָׁקֶל וְלַנְּקֵבָה
ח עֲשָׂרָה שְׁקָלִים: וְאִם־מָךְ הוּא מֵעֶרְכֶּךָ וְהֶעֱמִידוֹ לִפְנֵי הַכֹּהֵן וְהֶעֱרִיךְ אֹתוֹ הַכֹּהֵן
ט עַל־פִּי אֲשֶׁר תַּשִּׂיג יַד הַנֹּדֵר יַעֲרִיכֶנּוּ הַכֹּהֵן: וְאִם־בְּהֵמָה אֲשֶׁר
י יַקְרִיבוּ מִמֶּנָּה קָרְבָּן לַיהוָה כֹּל אֲשֶׁר יִתֵּן מִמֶּנּוּ לַיהוָה יִהְיֶה־קֹּדֶשׁ: לֹא יַחֲלִיפֶנּוּ
וְלֹא־יָמִיר אֹתוֹ טוֹב בְּרָע אוֹ־רַע בְּטוֹב וְאִם־הָמֵר יָמִיר בְּהֵמָה בִּבְהֵמָה וְהָיָה־
יא הוּא וּתְמוּרָתוֹ יִהְיֶה־קֹּדֶשׁ: וְאִם כָּל־בְּהֵמָה טְמֵאָה אֲשֶׁר לֹא־יַקְרִיבוּ מִמֶּנָּה
יב קָרְבָּן לַיהוָה וְהֶעֱמִיד אֶת־הַבְּהֵמָה לִפְנֵי הַכֹּהֵן: וְהֶעֱרִיךְ הַכֹּהֵן אֹתָהּ בֵּין טוֹב
יג וּבֵין רָע כְּעֶרְכְּךָ הַכֹּהֵן כֵּן יִהְיֶה: וְאִם־גָּאֹל יִגְאָלֶנָּה וְיָסַף חֲמִישִׁתוֹ עַל־עֶרְכֶּךָ:
יד וְאִישׁ כִּי־יַקְדִּשׁ אֶת־בֵּיתוֹ קֹדֶשׁ לַיהוָה וְהֶעֱרִיכוֹ הַכֹּהֵן בֵּין טוֹב וּבֵין רָע כַּאֲשֶׁר
טו יַעֲרִיךְ אֹתוֹ הַכֹּהֵן כֵּן יָקוּם: וְאִם־הַמַּקְדִּישׁ יִגְאַל אֶת־בֵּיתוֹ וְיָסַף חֲמִישִׁית כֶּסֶף־

רש"י

ה| **וְאִם מִבֶּן חָמֵשׁ שָׁנִים.** לֹא שֶׁיְּהֵא הַנּוֹדֵר קָטָן, שֶׁאֵין בְּדִבְרֵי קָטָן כְּלוּם, אֶלָּא גָּדוֹל שֶׁאָמַר: 'עֵרֶךְ קָטָן זֶה שֶׁהוּא בֶּן חָמֵשׁ שָׁנִים, עָלַי':

ז| **וְאִם מִבֶּן שִׁשִּׁים שָׁנָה וְגוֹ'.** כְּשֶׁמַּגִּיעַ לִימֵי הַזִּקְנָה הָאִשָּׁה קְרוֹבָה לְהֵחָשֵׁב כְּאִישׁ, לְפִיכָךְ הָאִישׁ פּוֹחֵת כְּהִזְדַּקְּנוֹ יוֹתֵר מִשְּׁלִישׁ בְּעֶרְכּוֹ וְהָאִשָּׁה אֵינָהּ פּוֹחֶתֶת אֶלָּא שְׁלִישׁ בְּעֶרְכָּהּ, דְּאָמְרֵי אֱנָשֵׁי: סָבָא בְּבֵיתָא פַּחָא בְּבֵיתָא, סַבְתָּא בְּבֵיתָא סִימָא בְּבֵיתָא וְסִימָנָא טָבָא בְּבֵיתָא:

ח| **וְאִם מָךְ הוּא.** שֶׁאֵין יָדוֹ מַשֶּׂגֶת לִתֵּן הָעֵרֶךְ הַזֶּה: **עַל פִּי אֲשֶׁר תַּשִּׂיג.** לְפִי מַה שֶּׁיֵּשׁ לוֹ יְסַדְּרֶנּוּ, וְיַשְׁאִיר לוֹ כְּדֵי חַיָּיו, מִטָּה כַּר וָכֶסֶת וּכְלֵי אֻמָּנוּת, אִם הָיָה חַמָּר מַשְׁאִיר לוֹ חֲמוֹרוֹ:

ט| **כֹּל אֲשֶׁר יִתֵּן מִמֶּנּוּ.** אָמַר: 'רַגְלָהּ שֶׁל זוֹ עוֹלָה', דְּבָרָיו קַיָּמִין, וְתִמָּכֵר לְצָרְכֵי עוֹלָה, וְדָמֶיהָ חֻלִּין חוּץ מִדְּמֵי אוֹתוֹ הָאֵבֶר:

י| **טוֹב בְּרָע.** תָּם בְּבַעַל מוּם: **אוֹ רַע בְּטוֹב.** וְכָל שֶׁכֵּן טוֹב בְּטוֹב וְרַע בְּרָע:

יא| **וְאִם כָּל בְּהֵמָה טְמֵאָה.** בְּבַעֲלַת מוּם הַכָּתוּב מְדַבֵּר שֶׁהִיא טְמֵאָה לְהַקְרָבָה, וְלִמֶּדְךָ הַכָּתוּב שֶׁאֵין קָדָשִׁים תְּמִימִים יוֹצְאִין לְחֻלִּין בְּפִדְיוֹן, אֶלָּא אִם כֵּן הוּמְמוּ:

יב| **כְּעֶרְכְּךָ הַכֹּהֵן כֵּן יִהְיֶה.** לִשְׁאָר כָּל אָדָם הַבָּא לִקְנוֹתָהּ מִיַּד הֶקְדֵּשׁ:

יג| **וְאִם גָּאֹל יִגְאָלֶנָּה.** בַּבְּעָלִים הֶחְמִיר הַכָּתוּב לְהוֹסִיף חֹמֶשׁ, וְכֵן בְּמַקְדִּישׁ בַּיִת, וְכֵן בְּמַקְדִּישׁ אֶת הַשָּׂדֶה, וְכֵן בְּפִדְיוֹן מַעֲשֵׂר שֵׁנִי, הַבְּעָלִים מוֹסִיפִין חֹמֶשׁ וְלֹא שְׁאָר כָּל אָדָם:

DISCUSSION

→ of the one who vowed (see Rashi and *Ha'amek Davar*).

27:10| **It and its substitute shall be sacred:** This brief phrase is the focus of discussions and *halakhot* that span an entire tractate of the Talmud: Tractate *Temura*. *Temura* analyzes such issues as whether an animal consecrated as a substitute has the same level of sanctity as the original animal, whether one can consecrate a third animal by substituting it for a substitute, and whether a single substitution is effective only for one animal or for several animals (see *Temura* 9a, 12a).

Consecration of Fields
LEVITICUS 27:16–25

16 It was stated earlier (25:25–28) that one cannot transfer permanent ownership of an ancestral field, as it theoretically remains in the family's possession forever. Yet **if from the field of his ancestral portion a man consecrates to the Lord, the valuation,** the value of the field, **shall be according to its seed.** Since the field is not sold forever, this consecration is a gift for a limited number of years. Its value, for the purposes of redemption with money, is based on the following formula: **An area** that is required to be **sown with a ḥomer,**[B] a measure of volume **of barley, shall be redeemed for fifty shekels of silver.** The Sages refer to this area as a *beit kor*; in modern measurements it is roughly 18 dunams, about 4.5 acres.

Fifth aliya (Seventh aliya)

17 **If he consecrates his field from,** that is, immediately after, **the Jubilee Year,** when there is maximum time until the next Jubilee, **the valuation shall stand.** It shall be redeemed in accordance with the full sum.

18 **And if he consecrates his field after the Jubilee, the priest shall calculate for him the silver according to the remaining years until the Jubilee Year, and it shall be deducted from the valuation.** If fifty shekels of silver is the valuation of the field for forty-nine years, these must be divided into forty-nine parts, which means that slightly more than one shekel must be deducted from the total sum for each year that has passed.

19 **And if the one who consecrated it** himself **redeems the field, he shall add one-fifth of the silver of the valuation to it, and it shall be his.** This is a general principle with regard to the redemption of consecrated items: If a stranger, not the original owner, seeks to acquire it, he pays the amount determined by the priest, or its fixed valuation, whereas the original owner must add a fifth, a kind of compensation or surcharge to the Sanctuary.

20 **And if he does not redeem the field** from the Sanctuary property in all the years of the Jubilee cycle, **or if,** in the meantime, **he,** the Temple treasurer, **sold the field to another man, it shall no longer be redeemed** by the original owner, and his historical link to the field shall be severed.

21 **When the field goes out in the Jubilee, it shall be sacred to the Lord.** Just like all fields in Israel, this field shall leave the possession of the buyer at the Jubilee Year. However, as its owner consecrated it, the field now reverts to become Temple property. It is considered **like a proscribed field,** as explained below (verses 28–29); **his portion shall belong to the priest.**

22 **And if he consecrates to the Lord a field of his acquisition,** a field that he purchased from another, **that is not a field of his ancestral portion.** He does not have full ownership of this field, but merely the right of usage for fifty years at the most.

Sixth aliya

23 Consequently, **the priest shall calculate for him the sum of the valuation until the Jubilee Year,** the valuation in accordance with the number of years remaining until the Jubilee, and **he shall give the valuation as of that day** on which he comes to redeem it. The field shall thereby return to the possession of the redeemer, and **it,** the payment, **is sacred to the Lord.** No payment of an additional fifth is mentioned here, as the current owner is considered like a stranger with regard to this purchased field. The Sages disagree whether an acquired field is redeemed by its actual sale value, or in accordance with the fixed value established in verse 16 for an ancestral field.[17]

24 **In the Jubilee Year, the field shall return to the one from whom he acquired it,** the original seller, **to the one whose ancestral portion of the land it is.** The person who consecrated it did not have the right to permanently dedicate a field that did not belong to him. To summarize, in all cases the fields return to their original owners in the Jubilee Year, apart from an ancestral field that was consecrated and not redeemed.

25 **Every** payment of **valuation** discussed above **shall be in the sacred shekel; twenty gera**[B] **shall be** the value of **the shekel.** These *gera* are called *maot* in the terminology of the Sages.[18] Although there were smaller units of weight and coins, the *ma'a* was the basic silver coin, ten of which were worth a regular shekel, while twenty were worth the holy shekel, which was double in size.[19]

BACKGROUND

27:16 | Ḥomer: The *ḥomer,* which is the largest measure of volume for dry items, is equivalent to roughly 250 L. It is similar to the Akkadian *imeru,* which is also mentioned in documents from Ugarit. It is also called a *kor* (see, e.g., I Kings 5:2).

In ancient times an area was measured by the amount of seed sown there; for example, a *beit kor* (*Kilayim* 2:9), a *beit sa'atayim,* literally a house of two *se'a* (I Kings 18:32), and a *beit kav* (*Tosefta, Bava Kamma* 6:21).

27:25 | Gera: It is likely that the source for this name for a measurement of weight is the word *gar'in,* kernel or seed, similar to its use in the expression: "Brings up the cud [*gera*]" (11:3). The background for such a name is the ancient prac-

טז עֶרְכְּךָ עָלָיו וְהָיָה לוֹ: וְאִם ׀ מִשְּׂדֵה אֲחֻזָּתוֹ יַקְדִּישׁ אִישׁ לַיהוָה וְהָיָה עֶרְכְּךָ לְפִי חמישי /שביעי/
יז זַרְעוֹ זֶרַע חֹמֶר שְׂעֹרִים בַּחֲמִשִּׁים שֶׁקֶל כָּסֶף: אִם־מִשְּׁנַת הַיֹּבֵל יַקְדִּישׁ שָׂדֵהוּ
יח כְּעֶרְכְּךָ יָקוּם: וְאִם־אַחַר הַיֹּבֵל יַקְדִּישׁ שָׂדֵהוּ וְחִשַּׁב־לוֹ הַכֹּהֵן אֶת־הַכֶּסֶף עַל־
יט פִּי הַשָּׁנִים הַנּוֹתָרֹת עַד שְׁנַת הַיֹּבֵל וְנִגְרַע מֵעֶרְכֶּךָ: וְאִם־גָּאֹל יִגְאַל אֶת־הַשָּׂדֶה
כ הַמַּקְדִּישׁ אֹתוֹ וְיָסַף חֲמִשִׁית כֶּסֶף־עֶרְכְּךָ עָלָיו וְקָם לוֹ: וְאִם־לֹא יִגְאַל אֶת־הַשָּׂדֶה
כא וְאִם־מָכַר אֶת־הַשָּׂדֶה לְאִישׁ אַחֵר לֹא יִגָּאֵל עוֹד: וְהָיָה הַשָּׂדֶה בְּצֵאתוֹ בַיֹּבֵל
כב קֹדֶשׁ לַיהוָה כִּשְׂדֵה הַחֵרֶם לַכֹּהֵן תִּהְיֶה אֲחֻזָּתוֹ: וְאִם אֶת־שְׂדֵה מִקְנָתוֹ אֲשֶׁר ששי
כג לֹא מִשְּׂדֵה אֲחֻזָּתוֹ יַקְדִּישׁ לַיהוָה: וְחִשַּׁב־לוֹ הַכֹּהֵן אֵת מִכְסַת הָעֶרְכְּךָ עַד שְׁנַת
כד הַיֹּבֵל וְנָתַן אֶת־הָעֶרְכְּךָ בַּיּוֹם הַהוּא קֹדֶשׁ לַיהוָה: בִּשְׁנַת הַיּוֹבֵל יָשׁוּב הַשָּׂדֶה
כה לַאֲשֶׁר קָנָהוּ מֵאִתּוֹ לַאֲשֶׁר־לוֹ אֲחֻזַּת הָאָרֶץ: וְכָל־עֶרְכְּךָ יִהְיֶה בְּשֶׁקֶל הַקֹּדֶשׁ

רש״י

טז| **וְהָיָה עֶרְכְּךָ לְפִי זַרְעוֹ.** וְלֹא כְּפִי שָׁוְיָהּ; אַחַת שָׂדֶה טוֹבָה וְאַחַת שָׂדֶה רָעָה פִּדְיוֹן הֶקְדֵּשָׁן שָׁוֶה, בֵּית כּוֹר שְׂעוֹרִים בַּחֲמִשִּׁים שְׁקָלִים, כָּךְ גְּזֵרַת הַכָּתוּב. וְהוּא שֶׁבָּא לְגָאֳלָהּ בִּתְחִלַּת הַיּוֹבֵל. וְאִם בָּא לְגָאֳלָהּ בְּאֶמְצָעוֹ נוֹתֵן לְפִי הַחֶשְׁבּוֹן, סֶלַע וּפֻנְדְּיוֹן לְשָׁנָה, לְפִי שֶׁאֵינָהּ הֶקְדֵּשׁ אֶלָּא לְמִנְיַן שְׁנוֹת הַיּוֹבֵל, שֶׁאִם גְּאָלָהּ הֲרֵי טוֹב, וְאִם לָאו – הַגִּזְבָּר מוֹכְרָהּ בְּדָמִים הַלָּלוּ לְאַחֵר וְעוֹמֶדֶת בְּיַד הַלּוֹקֵחַ עַד הַיּוֹבֵל כִּשְׁאָר כָּל הַשָּׂדוֹת הַמְּכוּרוֹת, וּכְשֶׁהִיא יוֹצְאָה מִיָּדוֹ חוֹזֶרֶת לַכֹּהֲנִים שֶׁל אוֹתוֹ מִשְׁמָר שֶׁהַיּוֹבֵל פּוֹגֵעַ בּוֹ, וּמִתְחַלֶּקֶת בֵּינֵיהֶם. זֶהוּ הַמִּשְׁפָּט הָאָמוּר בְּמַקְדִּישׁ שָׂדֶה. וְעַכְשָׁיו אֲפָרְשֶׁנּוּ עַל סֵדֶר הַמִּקְרָאוֹת:

יז| **אִם מִשְּׁנַת הַיֹּבֵל יַקְדִּישׁ וְגוֹ׳.** אִם מִשֶּׁעָבְרָה שְׁנַת הַיּוֹבֵל מִיָּד הִקְדִּישָׁהּ, וּבָא זֶה לְגָאֳלָהּ מִיָּד: **כְּעֶרְכְּךָ יָקוּם.** כָּעֵרֶךְ הַזֶּה הָאָמוּר יִהְיֶה, חֲמִשִּׁים כֶּסֶף יִתֵּן:

יח| **וְאִם אַחַר הַיֹּבֵל יַקְדִּישׁ.** וְכֵן אִם הִקְדִּישָׁהּ מִשְּׁנַת הַיּוֹבֵל וְנִשְׁתַּהֵית בְּיַד גִּזְבָּר, וּבָא זֶה לְגָאֳלָהּ אַחַר הַיּוֹבֵל: **וְחִשַּׁב לוֹ הַכֹּהֵן אֶת הַכֶּסֶף עַל פִּי הַשָּׁנִים הַנּוֹתָרֹת.** כְּפִי חֶשְׁבּוֹן. כֵּיצַד? הֲרֵי קָצַב דָּמֶיהָ שֶׁל אַרְבָּעִים וְתֵשַׁע שָׁנָה חֲמִשִּׁים שֶׁקֶל, הֲרֵי שֶׁקֶל לְכָל שָׁנָה וְשֶׁקֶל יָתֵר עַל כֻּלָּן, וְהַשֶּׁקֶל – אַרְבָּעִים וּשְׁמוֹנָה פֻּנְדְּיוֹן, הֲרֵי סֶלַע וּפֻנְדְּיוֹן לְשָׁנָה, אֶלָּא שֶׁחָסֵר פֻּנְדְּיוֹן אֶחָד לְכֻלָּן, וְאָמְרוּ רַבּוֹתֵינוּ שֶׁאוֹתוֹ פֻּנְדְּיוֹן קָלְבּוֹן לִפְרוֹטְרוֹט, וְהַבָּא לִגְאֹל יִתֵּן סֶלַע וּפֻנְדְּיוֹן לְכָל שָׁנָה לַשָּׁנִים הַנּוֹתָרוֹת עַד שְׁנַת הַיּוֹבֵל: **וְנִגְרַע מֵעֶרְכֶּךָ.** מִנְיַן הַשָּׁנִים שֶׁמִּשְּׁנַת הַיּוֹבֵל עַד שְׁנַת הַפִּדְיוֹן:

יט| **וְאִם גָּאֹל יִגְאַל... הַמַּקְדִּישׁ אֹתוֹ.** יוֹסִיף חֹמֶשׁ עַל הַקִּצְבָה הַזֹּאת:

כ| **וְאִם לֹא יִגְאַל אֶת הַשָּׂדֶה.** הַמַּקְדִּישׁ: **וְאִם מָכַר.** הַגִּזְבָּר: **אֶת הַשָּׂדֶה לְאִישׁ אַחֵר לֹא יִגָּאֵל עוֹד.** לָשׁוּב לְיַד הַמַּקְדִּישׁ:

כא| **וְהָיָה הַשָּׂדֶה בְּצֵאתוֹ בַיֹּבֵל.** מִיַּד הַלּוֹקְחוֹ מִן הַגִּזְבָּר, כְּדֶרֶךְ שְׁאָר שָׂדוֹת הַיּוֹצְאוֹת מִיַּד לוֹקְחֵיהֶם בַּיּוֹבֵל: **קֹדֶשׁ לַה׳.** לֹא שֶׁיָּשׁוּב לְהֶקְדֵּשׁ בֶּדֶק הַבַּיִת לְיַד הַגִּזְבָּר, אֶלָּא "כִּשְׂדֵה הַחֵרֶם" הַנָּתוּן לַכֹּהֲנִים, שֶׁנֶּאֱמַר "כָּל חֵרֶם בְּיִשְׂרָאֵל לְךָ יִהְיֶה" (במדבר יח, יד), אַף זוֹ תִּתְחַלֵּק לַכֹּהֲנִים שֶׁל אוֹתוֹ מִשְׁמָר שֶׁיּוֹם הַכִּפּוּרִים שֶׁל יוֹבֵל פּוֹגֵעַ בּוֹ:

כב| **וְאִם אֶת שְׂדֵה מִקְנָתוֹ וְגוֹ׳.** חִלּוּק יֵשׁ בֵּין שְׂדֵה מִקְנָה לִשְׂדֵה אֲחֻזָּה, שֶׁשְּׂדֵה מִקְנָה לֹא תִּתְחַלֵּק לַכֹּהֲנִים בַּיּוֹבֵל, לְפִי שֶׁאֵינוֹ יָכוֹל לְהַקְדִּישָׁהּ אֶלָּא עַד הַיּוֹבֵל, שֶׁהֲרֵי בַּיּוֹבֵל הָיְתָה עֲתִידָה לָצֵאת מִיָּדוֹ וְלָשׁוּב לַבְּעָלִים. לְפִיכָךְ אִם בָּא לְגָאֳלָהּ, יִגְאַל בַּדָּמִים הַלָּלוּ הַקְּצוּבִים לִשְׂדֵה אֲחֻזָּה. וְאִם לֹא יִגְאַל וְיִמְכְּרֶנָּה הַגִּזְבָּר לְאַחֵר, אוֹ אִם יִגְאַל הוּא, "בִּשְׁנַת הַיּוֹבֵל יָשׁוּב הַשָּׂדֶה לַאֲשֶׁר קָנָהוּ מֵאִתּוֹ" (להלן פסוק כד), אוֹתוֹ שֶׁהִקְדִּישָׁהּ. וּפֶן תֹּאמַר: "לַאֲשֶׁר קָנָהוּ" הַלּוֹקֵחַ הַזֶּה הָאַחֲרוֹן "מֵאִתּוֹ", וְזֶהוּ הַגִּזְבָּר, לְכָךְ הֻצְרַךְ לוֹמַר: "לַאֲשֶׁר לוֹ אֲחֻזַּת הָאָרֶץ" (שם) מִירֻשַּׁת אָבוֹת, וְזֶהוּ בְּעָלִים הָרִאשׁוֹנִים שֶׁמְּכָרוּהָ לַמַּקְדִּישׁ:

כה| **וְכָל עֶרְכְּךָ יִהְיֶה בְּשֶׁקֶל הַקֹּדֶשׁ.** כָּל עֵרֶךְ שֶׁכָּתוּב בּוֹ 'שְׁקָלִים' יִהְיֶה בְּשֶׁקֶל הַקֹּדֶשׁ: **עֶשְׂרִים גֵּרָה.** עֶשְׂרִים מָעוֹת, כָּךְ הָיוּ מִתְּחִלָּה, וּלְאַחַר מִכָּאן הוֹסִיפוּ שְׁתוּת, וְאָמְרוּ רַבּוֹתֵינוּ: שֵׁשׁ מָעָה כֶּסֶף דִּינָר, עֶשְׂרִים וְאַרְבַּע מָעוֹת לַסֶּלַע:

BACKGROUND

→ tice of using the kernels of produce and fruit, such as barley (Ruth 3:15) and carobs, as small weights. Following the opinions of the Sages, the weight of a *gera* is 0.83 g, while researchers claim that it is roughly 0.5 g. Some contend that the name comes from *giru*, an Akkadian weight, 0.04 of an Akkadian shekel, meaning carob seed, and weighing about 0.2 g. The custom of using carob seeds or beans as units of weight led to the modern carat, which is still used as a unit of measurement for gold and precious stones.

The Firstborn Animal

LEVITICUS 27:26–27

26 Pursuant to the discussion of consecration and redemption, the Torah presents a related law: **However,** with regard to **a** male **firstborn that is born first to the Lord, from an animal, no man shall consecrate it,** since it is not anyone's property; **whether it is an ox or a sheep, it is the Lord's,** and must be brought as an offering.[20]
27 **And if it,** the firstborn animal, **is a non-pure beast,** which cannot be brought as an offering, **he,** the owner, **shall redeem it according to the valuation,** by paying the animal's worth, **and he shall add one additional fifth of it to it,** as one always must when redeeming consecrated items. **And if it is not redeemed** by the owner, **it shall be sold for the valuation.** Unlike pure animals, impure animals cannot be consecrated in and of themselves as offerings. Only their value is consecrated, and therefore the animal itself can be redeemed by paying its value to the Temple.[21] In practice, among all impure animals, only the firstborn of a donkey must be redeemed. As mentioned elsewhere in the Torah, it is redeemed in exchange for a sheep, or for silver or other objects equal in value to itself.[22]

Proscribed Items

LEVITICUS 27:28–29

28 **However,** in contrast to consecrated objects, which may be redeemed or sold, **anything proscribed that a man proscribes for the Lord**[D] **from all that is his, whether man,** e.g., one of his slaves, **or animal, or the field of his ancestral portion,** which is in the absolute possession of its owner, **shall not be sold and shall not be redeemed; anything proscribed is a sacred sacrament to the Lord.**

29 *Seventh aliya* **Anything proscribed with regard to people,** captives of war who have been proscribed, or one who has been sentenced to death for political or halakhic reasons[23] **shall not be redeemed; he shall be put to death.** This is referring to a human *ḥerem*, but there is also the *ḥerem* of an area or a city. In such cases all the objects go to Heaven, and they are prohibited for all benefit and earthly uses, and may not be redeemed or sold.[24]

The Tithe of Seed and Fruit, and the Animal Tithe

LEVITICUS 27:30–34

30 **All the tithe of the land,** a tenth separated **from the seed of the land,** such as wheat or barley, **or from the fruit of the tree,** wine, oil, and possibly other types of fruit as well,[25] **is the Lord's; it is sacred to the Lord.** It may not be treated like other fruit, but must be eaten near the Temple in a state of ritual purity.[26] The Sages call this the second tithe.
31 **And if a man shall redeem from his tithe,** if he wants to reacquire his tithe and be permitted to treat his produce like regular produce, **he shall add one-fifth of it to it,** like all who buy back their consecrated property from the Sanctuary.
32 In addition to the better-known tithe of produce, there is also
Maftir an animal tithe: **And all the tithe of cattle or the flock, any that passes under the rod,** the herdsman's staff, **the tenth shall be sacred to the Lord.** All herd and flock born during each year shall pass under the rod and be counted in that manner, and the herdsman shall mark every tenth animal.[27]
33 **He shall not distinguish between good and bad, nor shall he substitute it.** The counting of the animals serves to establish which is the tithe. The animal that is counted as tenth is consecrated and cannot be exchanged. it must be sacrificed to God, while its meat is eaten by the owner in compliance with the *halakhot* of offerings. **And if he substitutes it, it and its substitute shall be sacred,** in accordance with the *halakha* of substitution stated above (verse 10); **it shall not be redeemed.** The tithe remains consecrated to God; one may not redeem it.
34 This verse concludes the book of Leviticus: **These are the commandments that the Lord commanded Moses for the children of Israel on Mount Sinai.**

DISCUSSION

27:28 | **Anything proscribed that a man proscribes for the Lord:** This is apparently referring to a different type of vow. Proscribed items, *ḥerem*, are unique in that they may not be sold or redeemed. They become Sanctuary property, and are classified as consecrated for the Temple maintenance, or are given to a priest (see *Arakhin* 28b–29a; *Nedarim* 2a). Some explain that *ḥerem* means a curse or ruin, and therefore

כו עֶשְׂרִים גֵּרָה יִהְיֶה הַשָּׁקֶל: אַךְ־בְּכוֹר אֲשֶׁר יְבֻכַּר לַיהוָה בִּבְהֵמָה לֹא־יַקְדִּישׁ
כז אִישׁ אֹתוֹ אִם־שׁוֹר אִם־שֶׂה לַיהוָה הוּא: וְאִם בַּבְּהֵמָה הַטְּמֵאָה וּפָדָה בְעֶרְכְּךָ
כח וְיָסַף חֲמִשִׁתוֹ עָלָיו וְאִם־לֹא יִגָּאֵל וְנִמְכַּר בְּעֶרְכֶּךָ: אַךְ כָּל־חֵרֶם אֲשֶׁר יַחֲרִם אִישׁ
לַיהוָה מִכָּל־אֲשֶׁר־לוֹ מֵאָדָם וּבְהֵמָה וּמִשְּׂדֵה אֲחֻזָּתוֹ לֹא יִמָּכֵר וְלֹא יִגָּאֵל כָּל־
כט חֵרֶם קֹדֶשׁ־קָדָשִׁים הוּא לַיהוָה: כָּל־חֵרֶם אֲשֶׁר יָחֳרַם מִן־הָאָדָם לֹא יִפָּדֶה מוֹת שביעי
ל יוּמָת: וְכָל־מַעְשַׂר הָאָרֶץ מִזֶּרַע הָאָרֶץ מִפְּרִי הָעֵץ לַיהוָה הוּא קֹדֶשׁ לַיהוָה:
לא לב וְאִם־גָּאֹל יִגְאַל אִישׁ מִמַּעַשְׂרוֹ חֲמִשִׁיתוֹ יֹסֵף עָלָיו: וְכָל־מַעְשַׂר בָּקָר וָצֹאן כֹּל מפטיר
לג אֲשֶׁר־יַעֲבֹר תַּחַת הַשָּׁבֶט הָעֲשִׂירִי יִהְיֶה־קֹּדֶשׁ לַיהוָה: לֹא יְבַקֵּר בֵּין־טוֹב לָרַע
לד וְלֹא יְמִירֶנּוּ וְאִם־הָמֵר יְמִירֶנּוּ וְהָיָה־הוּא וּתְמוּרָתוֹ יִהְיֶה־קֹּדֶשׁ לֹא יִגָּאֵל: אֵלֶּה
הַמִּצְוֹת אֲשֶׁר צִוָּה יְהוָה אֶת־מֹשֶׁה אֶל־בְּנֵי יִשְׂרָאֵל בְּהַר סִינָי: חזק

רש״י

כו| **לֹא יַקְדִּישׁ אִישׁ אֹתוֹ.** לְשֵׁם קָרְבָּן אַחֵר, לְפִי שֶׁאֵינוֹ שֶׁלּוֹ:

כז| **וְאִם בַּבְּהֵמָה הַטְּמֵאָה וְגוֹ׳.** אֵין הַמִּקְרָא הַזֶּה מוּסָב עַל הַבְּכוֹר, שֶׁאֵין לוֹמַר בִּבְכוֹר בְּהֵמָה טְמֵאָה "וּפָדָה בְעֶרְכֶּךָ", וַחֲמוֹר אֵין זֶה, שֶׁהֲרֵי אֵין פִּדְיוֹן פֶּטֶר חֲמוֹר אֶלָּא טָלֶה, וְהוּא מַתָּנָה לַכֹּהֵן וְאֵינוֹ לַהֶקְדֵּשׁ; אֶלָּא הַכָּתוּב מוּסָב עַל הַהֶקְדֵּשׁ, שֶׁהַכָּתוּב שֶׁל מַעְלָה דִּבֶּר בְּפִדְיוֹן בְּהֵמָה טְהוֹרָה שֶׁהוּמְמָה, וְכָאן דִּבֶּר בְּמַקְדִּישׁ בְּהֵמָה טְמֵאָה לְבֶדֶק הַבַּיִת: **וּפָדָה בְעֶרְכֶּךָ.** כְּפִי מַה שֶּׁיַּעֲרִיכֶנָּה הַכֹּהֵן: **וְאִם לֹא יִגָּאֵל.** עַל יְדֵי בְּעָלִים: **וְנִמְכַּר בְּעֶרְכֶּךָ.** לַאֲחֵרִים:

כח| **אַךְ כָּל חֵרֶם וְגוֹ׳.** נֶחְלְקוּ רַבּוֹתֵינוּ בַּדָּבָר: יֵשׁ אוֹמְרִים סְתָם חֲרָמִים לַהֶקְדֵּשׁ, וּמָה אֲנִי מְקַיֵּם: "כָּל חֵרֶם בְּיִשְׂרָאֵל לְךָ יִהְיֶה" (במדבר יח, יד)? בְּחֶרְמֵי כֹהֲנִים, שֶׁפֵּרֵשׁ וְאָמַר: 'הֲרֵי זֶה חֵרֶם לַכֹּהֵן'; וְיֵשׁ שֶׁאָמְרוּ סְתָם חֲרָמִים לַכֹּהֲנִים: **לֹא יִמָּכֵר וְלֹא יִגָּאֵל.** אֶלָּא יִנָּתֵן לַכֹּהֵן. לְדִבְרֵי הָאוֹמֵר סְתָם חֲרָמִים לַכֹּהֲנִים, מְפָרֵשׁ מִקְרָא זֶה בִּסְתָם חֲרָמִים, וְהָאוֹמֵר סְתָם חֲרָמִים לְבֶדֶק הַבַּיִת, מְפָרֵשׁ מִקְרָא זֶה בְּחֶרְמֵי כֹהֲנִים, שֶׁהַכֹּל מוֹדִים שֶׁחֶרְמֵי כֹהֲנִים אֵין לָהֶם פִּדְיוֹן עַד שֶׁיָּבֹאוּ לְיַד כֹּהֵן, וְחֶרְמֵי גָבוֹהַּ נִפְדִּים: **כָּל חֵרֶם קֹדֶשׁ קָדָשִׁים הוּא.** הָאוֹמֵר סְתָם חֲרָמִים לְבֶדֶק הַבַּיִת מֵבִיא רְאָיָה מִכָּאן, וְהָאוֹמֵר סְתָם חֲרָמִים לַכֹּהֲנִים, מְפָרֵשׁ: "כָּל חֵרֶם קֹדֶשׁ קָדָשִׁים הוּא לַה׳" – לְלַמֵּד שֶׁחֶרְמֵי כֹהֲנִים חָלִים עַל קָדְשֵׁי קָדָשִׁים וְעַל קָדָשִׁים קַלִּים, וְנוֹתֵן לַכֹּהֵן, כְּמוֹ שֶׁשָּׁנִינוּ בְּמַסֶּכֶת עֲרָכִין (דף כח ע״ב): אִם נֶדֶר נוֹתֵן דְּמֵיהֶם, וְאִם נְדָבָה נוֹתֵן אֶת טוֹבָתָהּ: **מֵאָדָם.** כְּגוֹן שֶׁהֶחֱרִים עֲבָדָיו וְשִׁפְחוֹתָיו הַכְּנַעֲנִים:

כט| **כָּל חֵרֶם אֲשֶׁר יָחֳרַם וְגוֹ׳.** הַיּוֹצֵא לֵהָרֵג וְאָמַר אֶחָד: 'עֶרְכּוֹ עָלַי', לֹא אָמַר כְּלוּם: **מוֹת יוּמָת.** הֲרֵי הוֹלֵךְ לָמוּת, לְפִיכָךְ "לֹא יִפָּדֶה", אֵין לוֹ דָּמִים וְלֹא עֵרֶךְ:

ל| **וְכָל מַעְשַׂר הָאָרֶץ.** בְּמַעֲשֵׂר שֵׁנִי הַכָּתוּב מְדַבֵּר: **מִזֶּרַע הָאָרֶץ.** דָּגָן: **מִפְּרִי הָעֵץ.** תִּירוֹשׁ וְיִצְהָר: **לַה׳ הוּא.** קְנָאוֹ הַשֵּׁם, וּמִשֻּׁלְחָנוֹ צִוָּה לְךָ לַעֲלוֹת וְלֶאֱכֹל בִּירוּשָׁלַיִם, כְּמוֹ שֶׁנֶּאֱמַר: "וְאָכַלְתָּ לִפְנֵי ה׳ אֱלֹהֶיךָ... מַעְשַׂר דְּגָנְךָ תִּירֹשְׁךָ" וְגוֹ׳ (דברים יד, כג):

לא| **מִמַּעַשְׂרוֹ.** וְלֹא מִמַּעֲשַׂר חֲבֵרוֹ; הַפּוֹדֶה מַעֲשֵׂר שֶׁל חֲבֵרוֹ אֵין מוֹסִיף חֹמֶשׁ. וּמַה הִיא גְּאֻלָּתוֹ? כְּדֵי לְהַתִּירוֹ בַּאֲכִילָה בְּכָל מָקוֹם, וְהַמָּעוֹת יַעֲלֶה וְיֹאכַל בִּירוּשָׁלַיִם, כְּמוֹ שֶׁכָּתוּב: "וְנָתַתָּה בַּכָּסֶף" וְגוֹ׳ (שם פסוק כה):

לב| **תַּחַת הַשָּׁבֶט.** כְּשֶׁבָּא לְעַשְּׂרָן מוֹצִיאָן בַּפֶּתַח זֶה אַחַר זֶה, וְהָעֲשִׂירִי מַכֶּה בְּשֵׁבֶט צְבוּעָה בְּסִיקְרָא, לִהְיוֹת נִכָּר שֶׁהוּא מַעֲשֵׂר, כֵּן עוֹשֶׂה לִטְלָאִים וְלַעֲגָלִים שֶׁל כָּל שָׁנָה וְשָׁנָה: **יִהְיֶה קֹדֶשׁ.** לִקָּרֵב לַמִּזְבֵּחַ דָּמוֹ וְאֵמוּרָיו, וְהַבָּשָׂר נֶאֱכָל לַבְּעָלִים, שֶׁהֲרֵי לֹא נִמְנָה עִם שְׁאָר מַתְּנוֹת כְּהֻנָּה, וְלֹא מָצִינוּ שֶׁיְּהֵא נִתָּן לַכֹּהֲנִים:

לג| **לֹא יְבַקֵּר וְגוֹ׳.** לְפִי שֶׁנֶּאֱמַר: "וְכֹל מִבְחַר נִדְרֵיכֶם" (שם יב, יא), יָכוֹל יְהֵא בּוֹרֵר וּמוֹצִיא אֶת הַיָּפֶה? תַּלְמוּד לוֹמַר: "לֹא יְבַקֵּר בֵּין טוֹב לָרַע", בֵּין תָּם בֵּין בַּעַל מוּם חָלָה עָלָיו קְדֻשָּׁה. וְלֹא שֶׁיִּקְרַב בַּעַל מוּם, אֶלָּא יֵאָכֵל בְּתוֹרַת מַעֲשֵׂר, וְאָסוּר לִגָּזֵז וְלֵעָבֵד:

DISCUSSION

rendering an object *ḥerem* is to remove it from the world (see, e.g., Numbers 21:3). According to this interpretation, if someone declares that an item of his is *ḥerem*, it is a decree of the Torah that it shall be sacred to the Lord (see Ramban, verse 29, and in his book *Mishpat HaḤerem*; *Sefer HaḤinnukh* 357).

Book of
Numbers

NUMBERS

For my holy grandfather,
the *Bnei Yissaskhar,*
and for the entire congregation of Israel

May they fulfill the destiny of the *haftara* of Bemidbar:

"The number of the children of Israel will be like the sand of
the sea, which cannot be measured and cannot be counted."

Hoshea 2:1

לזכות הסבא הקדוש שלי

בעל הבני יששכר

ולזכות כלל ישראל שיקויים בהם היעוד

דהפטרת במדבר

והיה מספר בני ישראל כחול הים אשר לא ימד ולא יספר.

הושע ב:א

Bemidbar

INTRODUCTION TO NUMBERS

The book of Numbers describes the period of the Israelites' journeys in the wilderness, with all its hardships and upheavals. Although the book begins during the second year following the exodus from Egypt and concludes with the nation's fortieth year of wandering in the wilderness, it does not provide a continuous, chronological account. Nevertheless, when comparing the opening and conclusion of the book, the closing of a circle can be discerned: It opens with a counting of the people and the preparations of the camp for its travels in the wilderness of Sinai, and it ends with the confrontations faced as they approach settled areas on the eastern side of the Jordan River, and with their preparations to enter the Land of Israel.

In the Jewish national consciousness, the wandering in the wilderness is remembered as an idyllic period, when the Israelites were enwrapped by the clouds of glory and nourished with food bestowed upon them from heaven. In poetic language, the prophet Jeremiah famously depicts Israel's faithfulness to the One who leads them in the wilderness: "I have remembered for you the kindness of your youth, the love of your nuptials, your following Me in the wilderness, in a land not sown" (Jeremiah 2:2). However, the book of Numbers also describes the repeated disruptions of this harmony. The years of travel are depicted here and elsewhere as a period rife with errors and failures on the part of all or part of the nation, on account of which its entrance to the Promised Land is delayed for many years. In this context, it should be noted that all the events described in Numbers occur in the first and perhaps the second year of their wanderings, as well as in the final year or years.

The primary failure of the people was their lack of desire to enter the Land of Israel, and their rejection of God's land. Upon hearing the negative reports about the land from the spies, the entire nation weeps over their departure from Egypt to Canaan. Although as soon as they are criticized for this mistake they sincerely regret it, and are even ready to risk their lives in order to enter the Land of Israel, nevertheless this rejection is considered to be a terrible sin, and perhaps even worse than their worship of the Golden Calf. In addition to this failure, the Torah records the unceasing complaints and grumblings of the Israelites resulting from the harsh desert conditions, as well as the personal attacks on Moses. Those include that of Korah, who foments an ideological rebellion against Moses as leader, and the complaints of a very different, far less severe kind, of his sister Miriam and brother Aaron, with regard to Moses' personal conduct.

No other book in the Torah shows the personality of Moses depicted in as much complexity as in Numbers. His humble acceptance of matters is described alongside his decisive stance against those who seek to undermine the truth of his mission. His moments of weakness are recorded, such as his request to relinquish his position when he feels that he can no longer withstand the childish complaints of his people, and his tears when faced with the nation's collapse in Shitim. In addition, his serene generosity is evident within his comment that he would gladly share his prophecy with the entire people, as is his self-sacrifice for the Israelites in order to protect them from death and destruction. The book also portrays Moses' ultimate readiness to remove himself and his heirs from all positions of greatness in favor of one who is suitable and worthy to serve as his successor. In fact, God Himself describes Moses in the book as an individual exalted above the rest of humanity.

The book lists in detail the various censuses taken of the people as a whole and of parts of the nation: tribes, camps, patrilineal houses, princes, and warriors. For this reason, the Sages themselves called it the book of Counting or Numbers. It also includes poetic and prophetic chapters: The Song of the Well, in which praise is offered to God in the present, and the prophecy or blessing of Bilam, which in part looks toward the distant future. Numbers also contains several typically short sections of laws, most of which supplement certain commandments found in the book of Leviticus.

Alongside the stories of complaints and retributions, the book of Numbers also provides an account of the victories of Moses and the people over surrounding nations. These conquests allow for the continuation of the people's travels, as described in the book of Deuteronomy, until their entrance into the Promised Land, which occurs in the book of Joshua.

Parashat
Bemidbar

The Census

NUMBERS 1:1–54

At the start of the book, just over a year has passed from when the Israelites left Egypt. The construction of the Tabernacle has concluded, and the people are ready to continue their journey to the Land of Israel. The Israelites are currently traversing the open wilderness, and they anticipate that they will soon come to Canaan and inherit the land. Consequently, all their adult males are conscripted into a newly created army and are therefore called for a census to determine the precise number of available soldiers.

1 1 **The Lord spoke to Moses in the wilderness of Sinai, in the Tent of Meeting, on the first of the second month, in the second year of their exodus from the land of Egypt, saying:**

2 **Take a census of the entire congregation of the children of Israel, by their families, by their patrilineal house, according to the number of names.** This is not merely a technical count, as it will include both the names of those counted as well as the group to which they belong. Since this is a military census, it will not encompass the entire people, but only **every male, by their head count.** The census will be performed in their presence, so that their heads can be counted.[1]

3 **From twenty years old and above, all those fit for military service in Israel: You shall count them according to their hosts, you and Aaron.**

4 **With you shall be a man for each tribe.** One man shall be appointed over every tribe of Israel, and **each** man **is the head of his patrilineal house,** the leader of that tribe.

5 **These are the names of the men who shall stand with you** to administer the counting of their tribes. From the continuation below, it is evident that these men served as heads of their tribes with regard to other matters as well (7:10–84). **For Reuben, Elitzur son of Shede'ur.**[D]

6 **For Simeon, Shelumiel son of Tzurishadai.**

7 **For Judah, Nahshon son of Aminadav.**

8 **For Issachar, Netanel son of Tzuar.**

9 **For Zebulun, Eliav son of Helon.** The six sons of Leah, in order of birth, have now all been mentioned.

10 Following the sons of Leah, the sons of Rachel are listed. **For the sons of Joseph: for Ephraim, Elishama son of Amihud; for Manasseh, Gamliel son of Pedatzur.**

11 **For Benjamin, Avidan son of Gidoni.**

12 Next are the tribes of the sons of the maidservants. **For Dan,** the firstborn of these maidservants,[2] **Ahiezer son of Amishadai.**

13 **For Asher, Pagiel son of Okhran.**

14 **For Gad, Elyasaf son of De'uel.**

15 **For Naphtali, Ahira son of Einan.**

16 **These are the distinguished of the congregation, the princes of the tribes of their fathers; they are the heads of the thousands of Israel.**

17 **Moses and Aaron took these men,** listed above, **who were** also **designated by name** by God, and selected by Him for their important role.

18 **They assembled the entire congregation on the first of the second month, and they verified their lineages by their families, by their patrilineal house.** They all provided proof of their ancestry.[3] The tribes were not merely formal units; they were also comprised of groups and subgroups: families and houses of fathers. The lists included only the Israelites, and not members of other nations who left Egypt with them. These foreigners apparently lived in a different section of the camp. The Israelites were counted **according to the number of names, from twenty years old and above, by their head count.**

19 **As the Lord had commanded Moses, he counted them in the wilderness of Sinai.**

Second aliya 20 The Torah now lists the census of each tribe: **These were the**

DISCUSSION

1:5 | For Reuben, Elitzur son of Shede'ur: Although the Israelite names used here are seemingly random, one can discern an interesting phenomenon: There are twice as many theophoric names that incorporate the name of God among the children than their fathers. Perhaps the members of the previous generation, who were born in Egypt at the height of the servitude, eschewed such names. Alternatively,

perhaps there was a renewed commitment to the service of God in this generation, and there was a corresponding increase in names referring to God as well. A third possibility is that these were not the names given to them at birth but titles of sorts that they were granted due to their important status, as they probably served in that capacity even before they were officially appointed as princes (see commentary on

Genesis 11:29, 17:15). Another interesting point is that according to the division of camps detailed below (10:11–28), the names of the princes of the middle tribe in each camp, and only those names, contain the suffix *el*, which is generally considered one of the names of God: Shelumiel, Netanel, Gamliel, and Pagiel.

פרשת
במדבר

א

א וַיְדַבֵּר יְהוָה אֶל־מֹשֶׁה בְּמִדְבַּר סִינַי בְּאֹהֶל מוֹעֵד בְּאֶחָד לַחֹדֶשׁ הַשֵּׁנִי בַּשָּׁנָה א
ב הַשֵּׁנִית לְצֵאתָם מֵאֶרֶץ מִצְרַיִם לֵאמֹר: שְׂאוּ אֶת־רֹאשׁ כָּל־עֲדַת בְּנֵי־יִשְׂרָאֵל
ג לְמִשְׁפְּחֹתָם לְבֵית אֲבֹתָם בְּמִסְפַּר שֵׁמוֹת כָּל־זָכָר לְגֻלְגְּלֹתָם: מִבֶּן עֶשְׂרִים שָׁנָה
ד וָמַעְלָה כָּל־יֹצֵא צָבָא בְּיִשְׂרָאֵל תִּפְקְדוּ אֹתָם לְצִבְאֹתָם אַתָּה וְאַהֲרֹן: וְאִתְּכֶם
ה יִהְיוּ אִישׁ אִישׁ לַמַּטֶּה אִישׁ רֹאשׁ לְבֵית־אֲבֹתָיו הוּא: וְאֵלֶּה שְׁמוֹת הָאֲנָשִׁים אֲשֶׁר
ו יַעַמְדוּ אִתְּכֶם לִרְאוּבֵן אֱלִיצוּר בֶּן־שְׁדֵיאוּר: לְשִׁמְעוֹן שְׁלֻמִיאֵל בֶּן־צוּרִישַׁדָּי:
ז ח ט לִיהוּדָה נַחְשׁוֹן בֶּן־עַמִּינָדָב: לְיִשָּׂשכָר נְתַנְאֵל בֶּן־צוּעָר: לִזְבוּלֻן אֱלִיאָב בֶּן־
י חֵלֹן: לִבְנֵי יוֹסֵף לְאֶפְרַיִם אֱלִישָׁמָע בֶּן־עַמִּיהוּד לִמְנַשֶּׁה גַּמְלִיאֵל בֶּן־פְּדָהצוּר:
יא יב יג לְבִנְיָמִן אֲבִידָן בֶּן־גִּדְעֹנִי: לְדָן אֲחִיעֶזֶר בֶּן־עַמִּישַׁדָּי: לְאָשֵׁר פַּגְעִיאֵל בֶּן־עָכְרָן:
יד טו טז לְגָד אֶלְיָסָף בֶּן־דְּעוּאֵל: לְנַפְתָּלִי אֲחִירַע בֶּן־עֵינָן: אֵלֶּה קְרִיאֵי הָעֵדָה נְשִׂיאֵי קרואי
יז מַטּוֹת אֲבוֹתָם רָאשֵׁי אַלְפֵי יִשְׂרָאֵל הֵם: וַיִּקַּח מֹשֶׁה וְאַהֲרֹן אֵת הָאֲנָשִׁים הָאֵלֶּה
יח אֲשֶׁר נִקְּבוּ בְּשֵׁמוֹת: וְאֵת כָּל־הָעֵדָה הִקְהִילוּ בְּאֶחָד לַחֹדֶשׁ הַשֵּׁנִי וַיִּתְיַלְדוּ עַל־
מִשְׁפְּחֹתָם לְבֵית אֲבֹתָם בְּמִסְפַּר שֵׁמוֹת מִבֶּן עֶשְׂרִים שָׁנָה וָמַעְלָה לְגֻלְגְּלֹתָם:
יט כ כַּאֲשֶׁר צִוָּה יְהוָה אֶת־מֹשֶׁה וַיִּפְקְדֵם בְּמִדְבַּר סִינָי: וַיִּהְיוּ שני

רש"י

פרק א

א| בְּמִדְבַּר סִינַי בְּאֶחָד לַחֹדֶשׁ. מִתּוֹךְ חִבָּתָן לְפָנָיו מוֹנֶה אוֹתָם כָּל שָׁעָה. כְּשֶׁיָּצְאוּ מִמִּצְרַיִם מְנָאָן (שמות יב, לז), וּכְשֶׁנָּפְלוּ בָּעֵגֶל מְנָאָן לֵידַע מִנְיַן הַנּוֹתָרִים. וּכְשֶׁבָּא לְהַשְׁרוֹת שְׁכִינָתוֹ עֲלֵיהֶם מְנָאָם. בְּאֶחָד בְּנִיסָן הוּקַם הַמִּשְׁכָּן וּבְאֶחָד בְּאִיָּיר מְנָאָם:

ב| לְמִשְׁפְּחֹתָם. דַּע מִנְיַן כָּל שֵׁבֶט וָשֵׁבֶט: לְבֵית אֲבֹתָם. מִי שֶׁאָבִיו מִשֵּׁבֶט אֶחָד וְאִמּוֹ מִשֵּׁבֶט אַחֵר יָקוּם עַל שֵׁבֶט אָבִיו: לְגֻלְגְּלֹתָם. עַל יְדֵי שְׁקָלִים, בֶּקַע לַגֻּלְגֹּלֶת:

ג| כָּל יֹצֵא צָבָא. מַגִּיד שֶׁאֵין יוֹצֵא בַּצָּבָא פָּחוֹת מִבֶּן עֶשְׂרִים:

ד| וְאִתְּכֶם יִהְיוּ. כְּשֶׁתִּפְקְדוּ אוֹתָם יִהְיוּ עִמָּכֶם נְשִׂיא כָּל שֵׁבֶט וָשֵׁבֶט:

טז| אֵלֶּה קְרוּאֵי הָעֵדָה. הַנִּקְרָאִים לְכָל דְּבַר חֲשִׁיבוּת שֶׁבָּעֵדָה:

יז| אֵת הָאֲנָשִׁים הָאֵלֶּה. אֵת שְׁנֵים עָשָׂר נְשִׂיאִים הַלָּלוּ: אֲשֶׁר נִקְּבוּ. לוֹ כָּאן בְּשֵׁמוֹת:

יח| וַיִּתְיַלְדוּ עַל מִשְׁפְּחֹתָם. הֵבִיאוּ סִפְרֵי יִחוּסֵיהֶם וְעֵדֵי חֶזְקַת לֵדָתָם, כָּל אֶחָד וְאֶחָד לְהִתְיַחֵס עַל הַשֵּׁבֶט:

children of Reuben, Israel's firstborn, and their descendants. They were the individuals counted by their families, which were subgroups of and listed by their patrilineal house,ᴰ according to the number of names, by their head count, every male from twenty years old and above, all those fit for military service. This was a fixed formula, which was repeated for the census of each tribe.

21 Those counted, for the tribe of Reuben, were forty-six thousand five hundred.

22 For the children of Simeon, their descendants, by their families, by their patrilineal house, those counted, according to the number of names, by their head count, every male from twenty years old and above, all those fit for military service;

23 those counted, for the tribe of Simeon, were fifty-nine thousand three hundred.

24 For the children of Gad, their descendants, by their families, by their patrilineal house, according to the number of names, from twenty years old and above, all those fit for military service;

25 those counted, for the tribe of Gad, were forty-five thousand six hundred and fifty.ᴰ

26 For the children of Judah, their descendants, by their families, by their patrilineal house, according to the number of names, from twenty years old and above, all those fit for military service;

27 those counted, for the tribe of Judah, were seventy-four thousand six hundred. As befitting Judah's status as leader of the brothers, his tribe was exceptionally large.

28 For the children of Issachar, their descendants, by their families, by their patrilineal house, according to the number of names, from twenty years old and above, all those fit for military service;

29 those counted, for the tribe of Issachar, were fifty-four thousand four hundred.

30 For the children of Zebulun, their descendants, by their families, by their patrilineal house, according to the number of names, from twenty years old and above, all those fit for military service;

31 those counted, for the tribe of Zebulun, were fifty-seven thousand four hundred.

32 For the children of Joseph, for the children of Ephraim, their descendants, by their families, by their patrilineal house, according to the number of names, from twenty years old and above, all those fit for military service;

33 those counted, for the tribe of Ephraim, were forty thousand five hundred.

34 For the children of Manasseh, their descendants, by their families, by their patrilineal house, according to the number of names, from twenty years old and above, all those fit for military service;

35 those counted, for the tribe of Manasseh,ᴰ were thirty-two thousand two hundred.

36 For the children of Benjamin, their descendants, by their families, by their patrilineal house, according to the number of names, from twenty years old and above, all those fit for military service;

37 those counted, for the tribe of Benjamin, were thirty-five thousand four hundred.

DISCUSSION

1:20 | By their patrilineal house: This expression can bear a variety of meanings. Here it probably referred to the expanded family (see 3:30, 25:15). In contrast, in Joshua (7:17–18), it meant a unit smaller than a family, whereas in Exodus (12:3), it was likely a synonym for a family (see *Da'at Mikra*, 1:2).

1:25 | Forty-five thousand six hundred and fifty: It can be surmised that the numbers are rounded, as it is unlikely that each of the twelve tribes was comprised of an exact number of

hundreds, or of fifties as in the case of Gad. Furthermore, it is possible that the census was carried out based on military units, and therefore the totals were calculated on the basis of the leaders of hundreds and fifties, who were appointed over the people (see Exodus 18:25; see also Rav Yeshaya of Trani; *Meshekh Ḥokhma*; *Ha'amek Davar*). There is, however, an example of rounding off to tens in Judges (9:2, 5).

1:35 | For the tribe of Manasseh: Although Manasseh was the elder of the two, Ephraim is

listed here first, similar to the blessing of Jacob and Moses, which likewise places Ephraim first (Genesis 48:14–20; Deuteronomy 33:17). This is due to Ephraim's greater future importance and the greater number of his descendants. However, it should be noted that the other tribes are not listed here in accordance with their importance (see *Adderet Eliyahu*). In a different census in the book of Numbers, where the descendants of Manasseh are more numerous than the tribe of Ephraim, Manasseh appears first, by birth order by matriarch (see 26:28–37).

בְּנֵי־רְאוּבֵן בְּכֹר יִשְׂרָאֵל תּוֹלְדֹתָם לְמִשְׁפְּחֹתָם לְבֵית אֲבֹתָם בְּמִסְפַּר שֵׁמוֹת

כא לְגֻלְגְּלֹתָם כָּל־זָכָר מִבֶּן עֶשְׂרִים שָׁנָה וָמַעְלָה כֹּל יֹצֵא צָבָא: פְּקֻדֵיהֶם לְמַטֵּה
רְאוּבֵן שִׁשָּׁה וְאַרְבָּעִים אֶלֶף וַחֲמֵשׁ מֵאוֹת:

כב לִבְנֵי שִׁמְעוֹן תּוֹלְדֹתָם לְמִשְׁפְּחֹתָם לְבֵית אֲבֹתָם פְּקֻדָיו בְּמִסְפַּר שֵׁמוֹת לְגֻלְגְּלֹתָם

כג כָּל־זָכָר מִבֶּן עֶשְׂרִים שָׁנָה וָמַעְלָה כֹּל יֹצֵא צָבָא: פְּקֻדֵיהֶם לְמַטֵּה שִׁמְעוֹן תִּשְׁעָה
וַחֲמִשִּׁים אֶלֶף וּשְׁלֹשׁ מֵאוֹת:

כד לִבְנֵי גָד תּוֹלְדֹתָם לְמִשְׁפְּחֹתָם לְבֵית אֲבֹתָם בְּמִסְפַּר שֵׁמוֹת מִבֶּן עֶשְׂרִים שָׁנָה

כה וָמַעְלָה כֹּל יֹצֵא צָבָא: פְּקֻדֵיהֶם לְמַטֵּה גָד חֲמִשָּׁה וְאַרְבָּעִים אֶלֶף וְשֵׁשׁ מֵאוֹת
וַחֲמִשִּׁים:

כו לִבְנֵי יְהוּדָה תּוֹלְדֹתָם לְמִשְׁפְּחֹתָם לְבֵית אֲבֹתָם בְּמִסְפַּר שֵׁמֹת מִבֶּן עֶשְׂרִים שָׁנָה

כז וָמַעְלָה כֹּל יֹצֵא צָבָא: פְּקֻדֵיהֶם לְמַטֵּה יְהוּדָה אַרְבָּעָה וְשִׁבְעִים אֶלֶף וְשֵׁשׁ מֵאוֹת:

כח לִבְנֵי יִשָּׂשכָר תּוֹלְדֹתָם לְמִשְׁפְּחֹתָם לְבֵית אֲבֹתָם בְּמִסְפַּר שֵׁמֹת מִבֶּן עֶשְׂרִים

כט שָׁנָה וָמַעְלָה כֹּל יֹצֵא צָבָא: פְּקֻדֵיהֶם לְמַטֵּה יִשָּׂשכָר אַרְבָּעָה וַחֲמִשִּׁים אֶלֶף
וְאַרְבַּע מֵאוֹת:

ל לִבְנֵי זְבוּלֻן תּוֹלְדֹתָם לְמִשְׁפְּחֹתָם לְבֵית אֲבֹתָם בְּמִסְפַּר שֵׁמֹת מִבֶּן עֶשְׂרִים שָׁנָה

לא וָמַעְלָה כֹּל יֹצֵא צָבָא: פְּקֻדֵיהֶם לְמַטֵּה זְבוּלֻן שִׁבְעָה וַחֲמִשִּׁים אֶלֶף וְאַרְבַּע מֵאוֹת:

לב לִבְנֵי יוֹסֵף לִבְנֵי אֶפְרַיִם תּוֹלְדֹתָם לְמִשְׁפְּחֹתָם לְבֵית אֲבֹתָם בְּמִסְפַּר שֵׁמֹת מִבֶּן

לג עֶשְׂרִים שָׁנָה וָמַעְלָה כֹּל יֹצֵא צָבָא: פְּקֻדֵיהֶם לְמַטֵּה אֶפְרַיִם אַרְבָּעִים אֶלֶף
וַחֲמֵשׁ מֵאוֹת:

לד לִבְנֵי מְנַשֶּׁה תּוֹלְדֹתָם לְמִשְׁפְּחֹתָם לְבֵית אֲבֹתָם בְּמִסְפַּר שֵׁמוֹת מִבֶּן עֶשְׂרִים שָׁנָה

לה וָמַעְלָה כֹּל יֹצֵא צָבָא: פְּקֻדֵיהֶם לְמַטֵּה מְנַשֶּׁה שְׁנַיִם וּשְׁלֹשִׁים אֶלֶף וּמָאתָיִם:

לו לִבְנֵי בִנְיָמִן תּוֹלְדֹתָם לְמִשְׁפְּחֹתָם לְבֵית אֲבֹתָם בְּמִסְפַּר שֵׁמֹת מִבֶּן עֶשְׂרִים שָׁנָה

לז וָמַעְלָה כֹּל יֹצֵא צָבָא: פְּקֻדֵיהֶם לְמַטֵּה בִנְיָמִן חֲמִשָּׁה וּשְׁלֹשִׁים אֶלֶף וְאַרְבַּע
מֵאוֹת:

38 For the children of Dan, their descendants, by their families, by their patrilineal house, according to the number of names, from twenty years old and above, all those fit for military service;

39 those counted, for the tribe of Dan, were sixty-two thousand seven hundred.

40 For the children of Asher, their descendants, by their families, by their patrilineal house, according to the number of names, from twenty years old and above, all those fit for military service;

41 those counted, for the tribe of Asher, were forty-one thousand five hundred.

42 For the children of Naphtali, their descendants, by their families, by their patrilineal house, according to the number of names, from twenty years old and above, all those fit for military service;

43 those counted, for the tribe of Naphtali, were fifty-three thousand four hundred.

44 In summary, **these are the counted**[D] that Moses, Aaron, and the princes of Israel counted; they were twelve men, one each for his patrilineal house.

45 These were all the counted of the children of Israel by their patrilineal house, from twenty years old and above, all those fit for military service in Israel.

46 All the counted were six hundred thousand three thousand five hundred and fifty.

47 But the Levites by the tribe of their fathers were not counted among them, as they were not part of the army, as the Torah explains below.[4]

48 **The Lord spoke to Moses,** prior to the above census,[5] **saying:**

49 **However, the tribe of Levi you shall not count, and you shall not take a census of them among the children of Israel.**

The members of the tribe of Levi will not serve in the army, and they will not conquer nor inherit any portion of the land.

50 **You, appoint the Levites over the Tabernacle of the Testimony, over all its vessels, and over everything that is associated with it. They shall bear the Tabernacle and all its vessels, and they shall minister to it.** They shall function as a special unit for safeguarding the sacred items and serving in the Tabernacle. This role is already alluded to in Exodus 38:21, among other places. Likewise, the Levites' inheritance of designated cities in Israel is previously mentioned in Leviticus 25:32. **Around the Tabernacle they shall encamp.** They shall not reside together with the other tribes, but in the center of the camp, surrounding and keeping in close proximity to the Tabernacle of the Testimony.

51 **When the Tabernacle travels, the Levites shall dismantle it, and when the Tabernacle encamps, the Levites shall erect it; and the stranger,** a non-Levite, **who approaches** the Tabernacle and the sacred vessels to care for them, **shall be put to death,** as this service must be performed by the Levites alone.

52 **The children of Israel shall encamp, each man in his camp, and each man at his banner,**[D] **according to their hosts.** Every member of Israel shall encamp in his designated spot.

53 **The Levites shall encamp around the Tabernacle of the Testimony, and there shall not be** divine **rage against the congregation of the children of Israel, and the Levites shall protect the integrity of the Tabernacle of the Testimony,** to ensure that the Israelites do not touch the Tabernacle and perish.

54 **The children of Israel did according to everything that the Lord had commanded Moses, so they did,** with regard to the division into consolidated groups, the counting of the military census, and keeping their distance from the Tabernacle.

DISCUSSION

1:44 | **These are the counted:** On a basic level, the census was required for very specific purposes: To determine the number of military men from each tribe, and to create a list of those who will inherit the land that the nation expects to enter soon (see Ramban, verse 45). In this regard, the experiences of each tribe from one census to another were reflected in the changes in the sum totals reported. On a deeper level, by its very nature, a counting can blur the distinctive personalities of the individual members. Therefore, the Israelites were counted both as individuals by their personal names as well as numbers that are part of greater units. This serves to emphasize that each member of the Israelites was unique, and was not swallowed up by the whole.

1:52 | **Each at his banner:** This is possibly the first literary mention of the idea that a banner represents membership in a specific group.

לח לִבְנֵי דָן תּוֹלְדֹתָם לְמִשְׁפְּחֹתָם לְבֵית אֲבֹתָם בְּמִסְפַּר שֵׁמֹת מִבֶּן עֶשְׂרִים שָׁנָה
לט וָמַעְלָה כֹּל יֹצֵא צָבָא: פְּקֻדֵיהֶם לְמַטֵּה דָן שְׁנַיִם וְשִׁשִּׁים אֶלֶף וּשְׁבַע מֵאוֹת:
מ לִבְנֵי אָשֵׁר תּוֹלְדֹתָם לְמִשְׁפְּחֹתָם לְבֵית אֲבֹתָם בְּמִסְפַּר שֵׁמֹת מִבֶּן עֶשְׂרִים שָׁנָה
מא וָמַעְלָה כֹּל יֹצֵא צָבָא: פְּקֻדֵיהֶם לְמַטֵּה אָשֵׁר אֶחָד וְאַרְבָּעִים אֶלֶף וַחֲמֵשׁ מֵאוֹת:
מב בְּנֵי נַפְתָּלִי תּוֹלְדֹתָם לְמִשְׁפְּחֹתָם לְבֵית אֲבֹתָם בְּמִסְפַּר שֵׁמֹת מִבֶּן עֶשְׂרִים שָׁנָה
מג וָמַעְלָה כֹּל יֹצֵא צָבָא: פְּקֻדֵיהֶם לְמַטֵּה נַפְתָּלִי שְׁלֹשָׁה וַחֲמִשִּׁים אֶלֶף וְאַרְבַּע
מֵאוֹת:
מד אֵלֶּה הַפְּקֻדִים אֲשֶׁר פָּקַד מֹשֶׁה וְאַהֲרֹן וּנְשִׂיאֵי יִשְׂרָאֵל שְׁנֵים עָשָׂר אִישׁ אִישׁ־
מה אֶחָד לְבֵית־אֲבֹתָיו הָיוּ: וַיִּהְיוּ כָּל־פְּקוּדֵי בְנֵי־יִשְׂרָאֵל לְבֵית אֲבֹתָם מִבֶּן עֶשְׂרִים
מו שָׁנָה וָמַעְלָה כָּל־יֹצֵא צָבָא בְּיִשְׂרָאֵל: וַיִּהְיוּ כָּל־הַפְּקֻדִים שֵׁשׁ־מֵאוֹת אֶלֶף וּשְׁלֹשֶׁת
מז אֲלָפִים וַחֲמֵשׁ מֵאוֹת וַחֲמִשִּׁים: וְהַלְוִיִּם לְמַטֵּה אֲבֹתָם לֹא הָתְפָּקְדוּ בְּתוֹכָם:
מח מט וַיְדַבֵּר יְהוָה אֶל־מֹשֶׁה לֵּאמֹר: אַךְ אֶת־מַטֵּה לֵוִי לֹא תִפְקֹד וְאֶת־רֹאשָׁם לֹא
נ תִשָּׂא בְּתוֹךְ בְּנֵי יִשְׂרָאֵל: וְאַתָּה הַפְקֵד אֶת־הַלְוִיִּם עַל־מִשְׁכַּן הָעֵדֻת וְעַל כָּל־
כֵּלָיו וְעַל כָּל־אֲשֶׁר־לוֹ הֵמָּה יִשְׂאוּ אֶת־הַמִּשְׁכָּן וְאֶת־כָּל־כֵּלָיו וְהֵם יְשָׁרְתֻהוּ
נא וְסָבִיב לַמִּשְׁכָּן יַחֲנוּ: וּבִנְסֹעַ הַמִּשְׁכָּן יוֹרִידוּ אֹתוֹ הַלְוִיִּם וּבַחֲנֹת הַמִּשְׁכָּן יָקִימוּ
נב אֹתוֹ הַלְוִיִּם וְהַזָּר הַקָּרֵב יוּמָת: וְחָנוּ בְּנֵי יִשְׂרָאֵל אִישׁ עַל־מַחֲנֵהוּ וְאִישׁ עַל־
נג דִּגְלוֹ לְצִבְאֹתָם: וְהַלְוִיִּם יַחֲנוּ סָבִיב לְמִשְׁכַּן הָעֵדֻת וְלֹא־יִהְיֶה קֶצֶף עַל־עֲדַת
נד בְּנֵי יִשְׂרָאֵל וְשָׁמְרוּ הַלְוִיִּם אֶת־מִשְׁמֶרֶת מִשְׁכַּן הָעֵדוּת: וַיַּעֲשׂוּ בְּנֵי יִשְׂרָאֵל כְּכֹל
אֲשֶׁר צִוָּה יְהוָה אֶת־מֹשֶׁה כֵּן עָשׂוּ:

רש״י

מט] אַךְ אֶת מַטֵּה לֵוִי לֹא תִפְקֹד. כְּדַאי הוּא לִגְיוֹן שֶׁל מֶלֶךְ לִהְיוֹת נִמְנֶה לְבַדּוֹ. דָּבָר אַחֵר, צָפָה הַקָּדוֹשׁ בָּרוּךְ הוּא שֶׁעֲתִידָה לַעֲמֹד גְּזֵרָה עַל כָּל הַנִּמְנִין מִבֶּן עֶשְׂרִים שָׁנָה וָמַעְלָה שֶׁיָּמוּתוּ בַּמִּדְבָּר, אָמַר: אַל יִהְיוּ אֵלּוּ בִּכְלָל, לְפִי שֶׁהֵם שֶׁלִּי, שֶׁלֹּא טָעוּ בָּעֵגֶל.

נ] וְאַתָּה הַפְקֵד אֶת הַלְוִיִּם. כְּתַרְגּוּמוֹ "מַנִּי", לְשׁוֹן מִנּוּי שְׂרָרָה עַל דָּבָר שֶׁהוּא מְמֻנֶּה עָלָיו, כְּמוֹ "וְיַפְקֵד הַמֶּלֶךְ פְּקִידִים" (אסתר ב, ג).

נא] יוֹרִידוּ אֹתוֹ. כְּתַרְגּוּמוֹ: "יְפָרְקוּן", כְּשֶׁבָּאִין לִסַּע בַּמִּדְבָּר מִמַּסָּע לְמַסָּע הָיוּ מְפָרְקִין אוֹתוֹ מֵהֲקָמָתוֹ, וְנוֹשְׂאִין אוֹתוֹ עַד מְקוֹם אֲשֶׁר יִשְׁכֹּן שָׁם הֶעָנָן וְיַחֲנוּ שָׁם, וּמְקִימִין אוֹתוֹ: וְהַזָּר הַקָּרֵב. לַעֲבוֹדָתָם זוֹ: יוּמָת. בִּידֵי שָׁמַיִם:

נב] וְאִישׁ עַל דִּגְלוֹ. כְּמוֹ שֶׁהַדְּגָלִים סְדוּרִים בְּסֵפֶר זֶה, שְׁלֹשָׁה שְׁבָטִים לְכָל דֶּגֶל.

נג] וְלֹא יִהְיֶה קֶצֶף. אִם תַּעֲשׂוּ כְּמִצְוָתִי לֹא יִהְיֶה קֶצֶף, וְאִם לָאו, שֶׁיִּכָּנְסוּ זָרִים בַּעֲבוֹדָתָם זוֹ, יִהְיֶה קֶצֶף, כְּמוֹ שֶׁמָּצִינוּ בְּמַעֲשֵׂה קֹרַח: "כִּי יָצָא הַקֶּצֶף" וְגוֹ' (להלן יז, יא).

The Encampment of the Israelites

NUMBERS 2:1–34

Toward the end of the previous section, the Torah stated in general terms: "The children of Israel shall encamp, each in his camp, and each at his banner, according to their hosts" (1:52). The following chapter details their encampment based on the four directions of the compass, which signals a change in their style of encampment. Until this point, the camp had traveled in a haphazard fashion. It can be assumed that the members of each tribe stayed close to each other, and would travel and encamp together, though there may have been exceptions. However, once the Tabernacle, situated in the heart of the camp, is constructed, the arrangement of the encampments of all of the tribes in relation to each other becomes fixed.

2

Third aliya

1 **The Lord spoke to Moses and to Aaron, saying:**

2 **Each man at his banner, with the insignias of their patrilineal house, the children of Israel shall encamp.** Each tribe shall be represented by its own symbol. **At a distance, around the Tent of Meeting they shall encamp.**

3 **Those who encamp at the front, to the east** side of the camp, **were the banner of the camp of Judah, according to their hosts; and the prince of the children of Judah is Nahshon son of Aminadav.**

4 **Its host and those counted were seventy-four thousand six hundred.**

5 **Those who encamp with it**[6] **were the tribe of Issachar; and the prince of the children of Issachar was Netanel son of Tzuar.**

6 **Its host and its count was fifty-four thousand four hundred.**

7 **Alongside them shall encamp the tribe of Zebulun; and the prince of the children of Zebulun was Eliav son of Helon.**

8 **Its host and its count was fifty-seven thousand four hundred.**

9 **The sum total of all the counted for the camp of Judah,**[D] which includes the tribes of Issachar and Zebulun, were **one hundred thousand eighty thousand six thousand four hundred, according to their hosts; they shall travel first.** Although these tribes were encamped to the east, when traveling they would always lead, regardless of the direction of the journey.

10 **The banner of the camp of Reuben was to the south according to their hosts; and the prince of the children of Reuben was Elitzur son of Shede'ur.**

11 **Its host and its count was forty-six thousand five hundred.**

12 **Those who encamp with it were the tribe of Simeon; and the prince of the children of Simeon was Shelumiel son of Tzurishadai.**

13 **Its host and those counted were fifty-nine thousand three hundred.**

14 **The tribe of Gad;**[D] **and the prince of the children of Gad was Elyasaf son of Re'uel.**

15 **Its host and those counted were forty-five thousand six hundred and fifty.**

16 **All the counted for the camp of Reuben were one hundred thousand fifty-one thousand four hundred and fifty, according to their hosts; and they shall travel second** when departing the encampment, after the camp of the banner of Judah.

17 After the camp of Reuben has begun to travel, **the Tent of Meeting,** which constituted a distinct camp, called the camp of the Divine Presence by the Sages,[7] shall travel. And around it shall be **the Levite camp,** which **shall travel in the midst of the camps; as they encamp so shall they travel,** with **every man in his** designated **place, according to their banners.**

18 **The banner of the camp of Ephraim according to their hosts was to the west; and the prince of the children of Ephraim was Elishama son of Amihud.**

19 **Its host and those counted were forty thousand five hundred.**

20 **With it was the tribe of Manasseh; and the prince of the children of Manasseh was Gamliel son of Pedatzur.**

DISCUSSION

2:9 | For the camp of Judah: This division of tribes was based on their relative importance. The tribe of Judah was chosen as the head of the first camp not only because of its size and strength but also due to its status as the central tribe among the sons of Jacob. Its banner was shared by Issachar and Zebulun, who were also sons of Leah, and who, unlike Jacob's eldest two sons, Reuben and Simeon, did not have any major flaws (see Genesis 34:25–30, 35:22; see also Jacob's last speech, 49:3–7).

2:14 | Gad: Gad was the firstborn of Zilpa, Leah's maidservant, and therefore his descendants encamped alongside the tribes of Leah's sons. Since Leah had six sons, they could theoretically have formed two full banners of three tribes each. However, as the tribe of Levi, one of the sons of Leah, was not included in the camps surrounding the Tabernacle on the outside, her sons Reuben and Simeon were joined by the tribe of Gad, the firstborn of her maidservant.

א ב וַיְדַבֵּר יְהוָה אֶל־מֹשֶׁה וְאֶל־אַהֲרֹן לֵאמֹר: אִישׁ עַל־דִּגְלוֹ בְאֹתֹת לְבֵית אֲבֹתָם ב שלישי
ג יַחֲנוּ בְּנֵי יִשְׂרָאֵל מִנֶּגֶד סָבִיב לְאֹהֶל־מוֹעֵד יַחֲנוּ: וְהַחֹנִים קֵדְמָה מִזְרָחָה דֶּגֶל
ד מַחֲנֵה יְהוּדָה לְצִבְאֹתָם וְנָשִׂיא לִבְנֵי יְהוּדָה נַחְשׁוֹן בֶּן־עַמִּינָדָב: וּצְבָאוֹ וּפְקֻדֵיהֶם
ה אַרְבָּעָה וְשִׁבְעִים אֶלֶף וְשֵׁשׁ מֵאוֹת: וְהַחֹנִים עָלָיו מַטֵּה יִשָּׂשכָר וְנָשִׂיא לִבְנֵי
ו יִשָּׂשכָר נְתַנְאֵל בֶּן־צוּעָר: וּצְבָאוֹ וּפְקֻדָיו אַרְבָּעָה וַחֲמִשִּׁים אֶלֶף וְאַרְבַּע מֵאוֹת:
ז ח מַטֵּה זְבוּלֻן וְנָשִׂיא לִבְנֵי זְבוּלֻן אֱלִיאָב בֶּן־חֵלֹן: וּצְבָאוֹ וּפְקֻדָיו שִׁבְעָה וַחֲמִשִּׁים
ט אֶלֶף וְאַרְבַּע מֵאוֹת: כָּל־הַפְּקֻדִים לְמַחֲנֵה יְהוּדָה מְאַת אֶלֶף וּשְׁמֹנִים אֶלֶף
י וְשֵׁשֶׁת־אֲלָפִים וְאַרְבַּע־מֵאוֹת לְצִבְאֹתָם רִאשֹׁנָה יִסָּעוּ: דֶּגֶל
יא מַחֲנֵה רְאוּבֵן תֵּימָנָה לְצִבְאֹתָם וְנָשִׂיא לִבְנֵי רְאוּבֵן אֱלִיצוּר בֶּן־שְׁדֵיאוּר: וּצְבָאוֹ
יב וּפְקֻדָיו שִׁשָּׁה וְאַרְבָּעִים אֶלֶף וַחֲמֵשׁ מֵאוֹת: וְהַחוֹנִם עָלָיו מַטֵּה שִׁמְעוֹן וְנָשִׂיא
יג לִבְנֵי שִׁמְעוֹן שְׁלֻמִיאֵל בֶּן־צוּרִישַׁדָּי: וּצְבָאוֹ וּפְקֻדֵיהֶם תִּשְׁעָה וַחֲמִשִּׁים אֶלֶף
יד טו וּשְׁלֹשׁ מֵאוֹת: וּמַטֵּה גָּד וְנָשִׂיא לִבְנֵי גָד אֶלְיָסָף בֶּן־רְעוּאֵל: וּצְבָאוֹ וּפְקֻדֵיהֶם
טז חֲמִשָּׁה וְאַרְבָּעִים אֶלֶף וְשֵׁשׁ מֵאוֹת וַחֲמִשִּׁים: כָּל־הַפְּקֻדִים לְמַחֲנֵה רְאוּבֵן
מְאַת אֶלֶף וְאֶחָד וַחֲמִשִּׁים אֶלֶף וְאַרְבַּע־מֵאוֹת וַחֲמִשִּׁים לְצִבְאֹתָם וּשְׁנִיִּם
יז יִסָּעוּ: וְנָסַע אֹהֶל־מוֹעֵד מַחֲנֵה הַלְוִיִּם בְּתוֹךְ הַמַּחֲנֹת כַּאֲשֶׁר
יח יַחֲנוּ כֵּן יִסָּעוּ אִישׁ עַל־יָדוֹ לְדִגְלֵיהֶם: דֶּגֶל מַחֲנֵה אֶפְרַיִם
יט לְצִבְאֹתָם יָמָּה וְנָשִׂיא לִבְנֵי אֶפְרַיִם אֱלִישָׁמָע בֶּן־עַמִּיהוּד: וּצְבָאוֹ וּפְקֻדֵיהֶם אַרְבָּעִים
כ אֶלֶף וַחֲמֵשׁ מֵאוֹת: וְעָלָיו מַטֵּה מְנַשֶּׁה וְנָשִׂיא לִבְנֵי מְנַשֶּׁה גַּמְלִיאֵל בֶּן־פְּדָהצוּר:

רש"י

פרק ב

ב| **בְּאֹתֹת.** כָּל דֶּגֶל יִהְיֶה לוֹ אוֹת, מַפָּה צְבוּעָה תְּלוּיָה בּוֹ, צִבְעוֹ שֶׁל זֶה לֹא כְּצִבְעוֹ שֶׁל זֶה, צֶבַע כָּל אֶחָד כְּגוֹן אַבְנוֹ הַקְּבוּעָה בַּחֹשֶׁן, וּמִתּוֹךְ כָּךְ יַכִּיר כָּל אֶחָד אֶת דִּגְלוֹ. דָּבָר אַחֵר, "בְּאֹתֹת לְבֵית אֲבֹתָם", בָּאוֹת שֶׁמָּסַר לָהֶם יַעֲקֹב אֲבִיהֶם כְּשֶׁנְּשָׂאוּהוּ מִמִּצְרַיִם, שֶׁנֶּאֱמַר: "וַיַּעֲשׂוּ בָנָיו לוֹ כֵּן כַּאֲשֶׁר צִוָּם" (בראשית נ, יב) – יְהוּדָה וְיִשָּׂשכָר וּזְבוּלֻן יִשָּׂאוּהוּ מִן הַמִּזְרָח, וּרְאוּבֵן וְשִׁמְעוֹן וְגָד מִן הַדָּרוֹם וְכוּ׳, כִּדְאִיתָא בְּתַנְחוּמָא בְּפָרָשָׁה זוֹ (יב): **מִנֶּגֶד.** מֵרָחוֹק מִיל, כְּמוֹ שֶׁנֶּאֱמַר בִּיהוֹשֻׁעַ: "אַךְ רָחוֹק יִהְיֶה בֵּינֵיכֶם וּבֵינָו כְּאַלְפַּיִם אַמָּה" (יהושע ג, ד), שֶׁיּוּכְלוּ לָבֹא בְּשַׁבָּת. מֹשֶׁה וְאַהֲרֹן וּבָנָיו וְהַלְוִיִּם חוֹנִים בְּסָמוּךְ לוֹ:

ג| **קֵדְמָה.** לִפְנֵי הַקְּרוּיִים 'קֶדֶם', וְאֵיזוֹ? זוֹ רוּחַ מִזְרָחִית, וְהַמַּעֲרָב קָרוּי אָחוֹר:

ט| **רִאשֹׁנָה יִסָּעוּ.** כְּשֶׁרוֹאִין הֶעָנָן מִסְתַּלֵּק, תּוֹקְעִין הַכֹּהֲנִים בַּחֲצוֹצְרוֹת וְנוֹסֵעַ מַחֲנֵה יְהוּדָה תְּחִלָּה; וּכְשֶׁהוֹלְכִין – הוֹלְכִין כְּדֶרֶךְ חֲנִיָּתָן, הַלְוִיִּם וְהָעֲגָלוֹת בָּאֶמְצַע, דֶּגֶל יְהוּדָה בַּמִּזְרָח, וְשֶׁל רְאוּבֵן בַּדָּרוֹם, וְשֶׁל אֶפְרַיִם בַּמַּעֲרָב, וְשֶׁל דָּן בַּצָּפוֹן:

יז| **וְנָסַע אֹהֶל מוֹעֵד.** לְאַחַר שְׁנֵי דְּגָלִים הַלָּלוּ: **כַּאֲשֶׁר יַחֲנוּ כֵּן יִסָּעוּ.** כְּמוֹ שֶׁפֵּרַשְׁתִּי, הֲלִיכָתָן כַּחֲנִיָּתָן, כָּל דֶּגֶל מְהַלֵּךְ לָרוּחַ הַקָּבוּעַ לוֹ: **עַל יָדוֹ.** עַל מְקוֹמוֹ, וְאֵין לְשׁוֹן 'יָד' זָז מִמַּשְׁמָעוֹ, רוּחַ שֶׁל צִדּוֹ קָרוּי "עַל יָדוֹ", הַסְּמוּכָה לוֹ לְכָל הוֹשָׁטַת יָדוֹ, אינשו"ן איס"א בְּלַעַז:

כ| **וְעָלָיו.** כְּתַרְגּוּמוֹ: "וּדְסָמְכִין עֲלוֹהִי":

21 **Its host and those counted were thirty-two thousand two hundred.**
22 **The tribe of Benjamin; and the prince of the children of Benjamin was Avidan son of Gidoni.**
23 **Its host and those counted were thirty-five thousand four hundred.**
24 **All those counted for the camp of Ephraim**[D] **were one hundred thousand eight thousand one hundred, according to their hosts; and they shall travel third.** They journeyed either directly behind the Levites, or on their side, parallel to them.
25 **The banner of the camp of Dan**[D] **was to the north according to their hosts; and the prince of the children of Dan was Ahiezer son of Amishadai.**
26 **Its host and those counted were sixty-two thousand seven hundred.**
27 **Those who encamp with it were the tribe of Asher; and the prince of the children of Asher was Pagiel son of Okhran.**
28 **Its host and those counted were forty-one thousand five hundred.**
29 **The tribe of Naphtali; and the prince of the children of Naphtali was Ahira son of Einan.**
30 **Its host and those counted were fifty-three thousand four hundred.**
31 **All those counted for the camp of Dan were one hundred thousand fifty-seven thousand six hundred; they shall travel last by their banners.**
32 **These are those who were counted of the children of Israel by their patrilineal house; all those counted of the camps according to their hosts were six hundred thousand three thousand five hundred and fifty.**
33 **The Levites were not counted among the children of Israel, as the Lord had commanded Moses.** The unusual form for the words "were not counted" [*hotpakdu*] indicated that they did not count themselves, nor did others count them.[8]
34 **The children of Israel did according to everything that the Lord had commanded Moses, so they encamped according to their banners,**[D] **and so they traveled, each** man **according to his families, by his patrilineal house.**

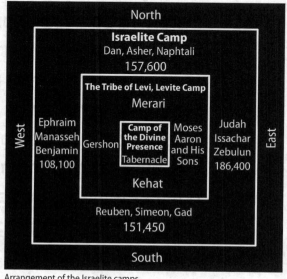

Arrangement of the Israelite camps

The Descendants of Levi

NUMBERS 3:1–51

As was mentioned above, the tribe of Levi is not counted together with the rest of the Israelites. This section focuses on various issues relevant specifically to the members of this tribe: the results of their census, their encampment adjacent to the Tabernacle, and the general function of each of the three central patrilineal houses. After the Levites have been counted, the Torah depicts how they assumed their responsibilities from the firstborn, who formerly performed the sacred service. The consecration of the Levites in place of the firstborn is another stage in the census of the people, as it almost entirely negates the previous unique status of the firstborn, who are now reincorporated into the general community of the rest of the people.

3 1 **These are the descendants of Aaron and Moses on the day that the Lord spoke with Moses on Mount Sinai.** Despite the mention of the descendants of Moses, only the descendants of Aaron are listed in the next verse. Moses' descendants are only indirectly mentioned in verse 27, via the wording "the family of the Amramites," as Amram had no sons other than Moses and Aaron, and this cannot be referring to Aaron's descendants, who are listed before that verse. Nevertheless, their names are not specified.[9] The reason for this is that the descendants of Aaron alone were granted a special role. Although Aaron himself was secondary to his younger brother Moses, his sons served as priests. In contrast, Moses' descendants were ordinary Levites like the rest of their tribe.

Fourth aliya

2 **These are the names of the sons of Aaron: the firstborn, Nadav, and Avihu, Elazar, and Itamar.**

כא כב וּצְבָאוֹ וּפְקֻדֵיהֶם שְׁנַיִם וּשְׁלֹשִׁים אֶלֶף וּמָאתָיִם: וּמַטֵּה בִּנְיָמִן וְנָשִׂיא לִבְנֵי בִנְיָמִן
כג כד אֲבִידָן בֶּן־גִּדְעֹנִי: וּצְבָאוֹ וּפְקֻדֵיהֶם חֲמִשָּׁה וּשְׁלֹשִׁים אֶלֶף וְאַרְבַּע מֵאוֹת: כָּל־
הַפְּקֻדִים לְמַחֲנֵה אֶפְרַיִם מְאַת אֶלֶף וּשְׁמֹנַת־אֲלָפִים וּמֵאָה לְצִבְאֹתָם וּשְׁלִשִׁים
כה יִסָּעוּ: דֶּגֶל מַחֲנֵה דָן צָפֹנָה לְצִבְאֹתָם וְנָשִׂיא לִבְנֵי דָן אֲחִיעֶזֶר בֶּן־
כו כז עַמִּישַׁדָּי: וּצְבָאוֹ וּפְקֻדֵיהֶם שְׁנַיִם וְשִׁשִּׁים אֶלֶף וּשְׁבַע מֵאוֹת: וְהַחֹנִים עָלָיו מַטֵּה
כח אָשֵׁר וְנָשִׂיא לִבְנֵי אָשֵׁר פַּגְעִיאֵל בֶּן־עָכְרָן: וּצְבָאוֹ וּפְקֻדֵיהֶם אֶחָד וְאַרְבָּעִים
כט ל אֶלֶף וַחֲמֵשׁ מֵאוֹת: וּמַטֵּה נַפְתָּלִי וְנָשִׂיא לִבְנֵי נַפְתָּלִי אֲחִירַע בֶּן־עֵינָן: וּצְבָאוֹ
לא וּפְקֻדֵיהֶם שְׁלֹשָׁה וַחֲמִשִּׁים אֶלֶף וְאַרְבַּע מֵאוֹת: כָּל־הַפְּקֻדִים לְמַחֲנֵה דָן מְאַת
אֶלֶף וְשִׁבְעָה וַחֲמִשִּׁים אֶלֶף וְשֵׁשׁ מֵאוֹת לָאַחֲרֹנָה יִסְעוּ לְדִגְלֵיהֶם:
לב אֵלֶּה פְּקוּדֵי בְנֵי־יִשְׂרָאֵל לְבֵית אֲבֹתָם כָּל־פְּקוּדֵי הַמַּחֲנֹת לְצִבְאֹתָם שֵׁשׁ־מֵאוֹת
לג אֶלֶף וּשְׁלֹשֶׁת אֲלָפִים וַחֲמֵשׁ מֵאוֹת וַחֲמִשִּׁים: וְהַלְוִיִּם לֹא הָתְפָּקְדוּ בְּתוֹךְ בְּנֵי
לד יִשְׂרָאֵל כַּאֲשֶׁר צִוָּה יְהוָה אֶת־מֹשֶׁה: וַיַּעֲשׂוּ בְּנֵי יִשְׂרָאֵל כְּכֹל אֲשֶׁר־צִוָּה יְהוָה
אֶת־מֹשֶׁה כֵּן־חָנוּ לְדִגְלֵיהֶם וְכֵן נָסָעוּ אִישׁ לְמִשְׁפְּחֹתָיו עַל־בֵּית אֲבֹתָיו:
ג א ב וְאֵלֶּה תּוֹלְדֹת אַהֲרֹן וּמֹשֶׁה בְּיוֹם דִּבֶּר יְהוָה אֶת־מֹשֶׁה בְּהַר סִינָי: וְאֵלֶּה שְׁמוֹת ג רביעי

רש"י

פרק ג

א| וְאֵלֶּה תּוֹלְדֹת אַהֲרֹן וּמֹשֶׁה. וְאֵינוֹ מַזְכִּיר אֶלָּא בְּנֵי אַהֲרֹן, וְנִקְרְאוּ תּוֹלְדוֹת מֹשֶׁה, לְפִי שֶׁלִּמְּדָן תּוֹרָה, מְלַמֵּד שֶׁכָּל הַמְלַמֵּד אֶת בֶּן חֲבֵרוֹ תּוֹרָה מַעֲלֶה עָלָיו הַכָּתוּב כְּאִלּוּ יְלָדוֹ: בְּיוֹם דִּבֶּר ה' אֶת מֹשֶׁה. נַעֲשׂוּ אֵלּוּ הַתּוֹלָדוֹת שֶׁלּוֹ, שֶׁלִּמְּדָן מַה שֶּׁלָּמַד מִפִּי הַגְּבוּרָה:

DISCUSSION

2:24 | **The camp of Ephraim:** This camp, which included Ephraim, Manasseh, and Benjamin, was the camp of the descendants of Rachel. It was possible that the location of this camp was related to the idea that the Divine Presence was located in the west (see *Zevaḥim* 54b; *Bava Batra* 25a; *Zohar* 3:119:2). The First and Second Temples were in fact built in the portions of Rachel's sons: The Tabernacle in Shilo was situated in Joseph's inherited land, while the Temple was situated in Benjamin's land (see *Bemidbar Rabba* 2:9; Abravanel).

2:25 | **The camp of Dan:** This camp consisted of the sons of the maidservants. It was headed by Dan, the firstborn of Bilha, Rachel's maidservant, who was accompanied by Naphtali, Bilha's other son, and Asher, son of Zilpa, Leah's maidservant.

As mentioned above, the largest camp was that of Judah, but the camp of Dan was second in size. It is likely no coincidence that the two camps of Judah and Dan, which were significantly larger than the rest, were instructed to lead the way and travel at the rear, respectively (see Ramban, verse 2). Moreover, the entire structure of the camp appeared to be similar to an organized battle formation, including banners and trumpets. Although the people did not actually engage in war on their journey until near the end of the forty years in the wilderness, they nevertheless traveled in a similar manner to a military camp. In addition to their visible shape, the arrangement of the camps also revealed an esoteric symbolic meaning (see *Bemidbar Rabba* 2:10).

2:34 | **So they encamped according to their banners:** According to tradition, each tribe's banner had its own color, identical to the color of the precious stone that represented it on the High Priest's breast piece (*Bemidbar Rabba* 2:7; Rashi, verse 2). In addition to the banners of the individual tribes, each group of tribes that encamped together had its own banner, which

3 **These are the names of the sons of Aaron, the anointed priests, whom he invested to serve as priests,** at the time of the inauguration of the Tabernacle.
4 However, soon after they were anointed, **Nadav and Avihu died before the Lord, when they presented strange fire before the Lord,** as a result of which they were burned and died[10] **in the wilderness of Sinai, and they had no children;**[D] **and Elazar and Itamar served as priests**[D] **in the presence of Aaron, their father.** In addition to Elazar and Itamar's role as Levites, they were also appointed to serve as priests.
5 **The Lord spoke to Moses, saying:**
6 **Bring the tribe of Levi near,**[D] **and stand it before Aaron the priest, and they shall serve him.** From this point onward, the Levites shall serve the priests and the Tabernacle.
7 **They shall keep his,** Aaron's, **commission, and the commission of the entire congregation before the Tent of Meeting, to perform the service of the Tabernacle.** The Levites will become the guard of the Tabernacle and will encamp around it in close proximity. This is not a military guard; rather, they are responsible to tend to the needs of the priests and the Tabernacle.
8 **They shall safeguard all the vessels of the Tent of Meeting, and the commission of the children of Israel, to perform the service of the Tabernacle.**
9 **You shall give the Levites to Aaron and to his sons** as appointed assistants to the priests. **They are** entirely **given to him from the children of Israel.** The Levites, a relatively small tribe, are considered here as a gift from the Israelites to the priests to aid in the Tabernacle service. As stated elsewhere, the Israelites must also designate cities for the Levites and give them a tithe from their produce.[11]
10 **You shall count Aaron and his sons, and they shall observe their priesthood,** to the exclusion of all others, who may not serve in their capacity; **and the stranger who approaches shall be put to death.**
11 **The Lord spoke to Moses, saying:**
12 **I have hereby taken the Levites from among the children of Israel in place of every firstborn, first issue of the womb from the children of Israel,** who previously performed the sacred service. The priests mentioned at Mount Sinai are in fact identified as the firstborns.[12] **And the Levites shall be Mine.**
13 **For every firstborn is Mine; on the day that I smote all the firstborn in the land of Egypt I sanctified to Me every firstborn in Israel, from man to animal; they shall be Mine; I am the Lord.** Upon the striking of all firstborns in Egypt, including both man and beast, both the firstborn Israelites and their animals became consecrated to God. Now the unique status of Jewish male firstborns, and their function and rights, passes to the Levites.[13]
Fifth aliya 14 **The Lord spoke to Moses in the wilderness of Sinai, saying:**
15 **Count the children of Levi by their patrilineal house, by their families; every male from one month old and above you shall count them.** Unlike the counting of the other tribes, which was similar to a military census, and therefore included only those aged twenty and upward, the counting of the Levites applied even to children as young as a month old, when their health is considered stable and they are classified as viable offspring.[14]

DISCUSSION

incorporated the colors of the three tribes collectively (see *Targum Yonatan*). It was also possible that each of the patrilineal houses had their own smaller banners or emblems.

3:4| **And they had no children:** There is an opinion in the Midrash that Nadav and Avihu did not marry (see *Vayikra Rabba* 20:9). It is also possible that they married late, and therefore had not fathered children, or that they had only daughters. If so, the word "children" should be translated as sons.

And Elazar and Itamar served as priests: In addition to the three priests listed here, Aaron and two of his sons, it is logical that there were others as well. For instance, Elazar's son Pinhas is mentioned as a hero toward the end of this book (25:11–13). Likewise, Elazar and Itamar may have had other sons, whose identity and function is not mentioned here, perhaps because they were young or unimportant. It is also quite possible that those descendants were not appointed to the priestly role together with Aaron and his sons (see Ibn Ezra, verse 10; commentary on 25:13).

3:6| **Bring the tribe of Levi near:** The tribe of Levi was counted independently, and the sum of its members was listed separately from those of the other tribes. This was consistent with the establishment of the Levites' unique status among the children of Israel. This tribe, which according to the Sages was not enslaved in Egypt, was to be distinguished from the rest of the people in their public, social, and cultural life. The tribe was dedicated to the sacred service, and its members did not participate in the worship of the Golden Calf with much of the rest of the nation. On the contrary, the Levites' loyalty to God and Moses enabled them to smite even their close relatives on that occasion (Exodus 32:26–29). Furthermore, the tribe of Levi did not join the misguided initiative to send spies to the land of Canaan.

The Levites, however, did not inherit a portion in the land, and did not work in fields or vineyards, but rather dwelled in cities that belonged to the other tribes. Their livelihoods were generally unsteady and irregular, and they had to rely on the gifts given to them by their brethren. Their growth rate was also far lower than that of the other tribes. As the King's legion, as it were, it is fitting for the tribe of Levi to be counted by itself (*Midrash Aggada*, cited by Rashi, 1:49).

ג בְּנֵי־אַהֲרֹן הַבְּכֹר ׀ נָדָב וַאֲבִיהוּא אֶלְעָזָר וְאִיתָמָר: אֵלֶּה שְׁמוֹת בְּנֵי אַהֲרֹן הַכֹּהֲנִים
ד הַמְּשֻׁחִים אֲשֶׁר־מִלֵּא יָדָם לְכַהֵן: וַיָּמָת נָדָב וַאֲבִיהוּא לִפְנֵי יְהוָה בְּהַקְרִבָם אֵשׁ
זָרָה לִפְנֵי יְהוָה בְּמִדְבַּר סִינַי וּבָנִים לֹא־הָיוּ לָהֶם וַיְכַהֵן אֶלְעָזָר וְאִיתָמָר עַל־פְּנֵי
אַהֲרֹן אֲבִיהֶם:
ה ו וַיְדַבֵּר יְהוָה אֶל־מֹשֶׁה לֵּאמֹר: הַקְרֵב אֶת־מַטֵּה לֵוִי וְהַעֲמַדְתָּ אֹתוֹ לִפְנֵי אַהֲרֹן
ז הַכֹּהֵן וְשֵׁרְתוּ אֹתוֹ: וְשָׁמְרוּ אֶת־מִשְׁמַרְתּוֹ וְאֶת־מִשְׁמֶרֶת כָּל־הָעֵדָה לִפְנֵי אֹהֶל
ח מוֹעֵד לַעֲבֹד אֶת־עֲבֹדַת הַמִּשְׁכָּן: וְשָׁמְרוּ אֶת־כָּל־כְּלֵי אֹהֶל מוֹעֵד וְאֶת־מִשְׁמֶרֶת
ט בְּנֵי יִשְׂרָאֵל לַעֲבֹד אֶת־עֲבֹדַת הַמִּשְׁכָּן: וְנָתַתָּה אֶת־הַלְוִיִּם לְאַהֲרֹן וּלְבָנָיו נְתוּנִם
י נְתוּנִם הֵמָּה לוֹ מֵאֵת בְּנֵי יִשְׂרָאֵל: וְאֶת־אַהֲרֹן וְאֶת־בָּנָיו תִּפְקֹד וְשָׁמְרוּ אֶת־
כְּהֻנָּתָם וְהַזָּר הַקָּרֵב יוּמָת:
יא יב וַיְדַבֵּר יְהוָה אֶל־מֹשֶׁה לֵּאמֹר: וַאֲנִי הִנֵּה לָקַחְתִּי אֶת־הַלְוִיִּם מִתּוֹךְ בְּנֵי יִשְׂרָאֵל
יג תַּחַת כָּל־בְּכוֹר פֶּטֶר רֶחֶם מִבְּנֵי יִשְׂרָאֵל וְהָיוּ לִי הַלְוִיִּם: כִּי לִי כָּל־בְּכוֹר בְּיוֹם
הַכֹּתִי כָל־בְּכוֹר בְּאֶרֶץ מִצְרַיִם הִקְדַּשְׁתִּי לִי כָל־בְּכוֹר בְּיִשְׂרָאֵל מֵאָדָם עַד־
בְּהֵמָה לִי יִהְיוּ אֲנִי יְהוָה:
יד טו וַיְדַבֵּר יְהוָה אֶל־מֹשֶׁה בְּמִדְבַּר סִינַי לֵאמֹר: פְּקֹד אֶת־בְּנֵי לֵוִי לְבֵית אֲבֹתָם חמישי
לְמִשְׁפְּחֹתָם כָּל־זָכָר מִבֶּן־חֹדֶשׁ וָמַעְלָה תִּפְקְדֵם:

רש״י

ד | **עַל פְּנֵי אַהֲרֹן.** בְּחַיָּיו:

ו | **וְשֵׁרְתוּ אֹתוֹ.** וּמַהוּ הַשֵּׁרוּת? "וְשָׁמְרוּ אֶת מִשְׁמַרְתּוֹ". לְפִי שֶׁשְּׁמִירַת הַמִּקְדָּשׁ עָלָיו שֶׁלֹּא יִקְרַב זָר, כְּמוֹ שֶׁנֶּאֱמַר: "אַתָּה וּבָנֶיךָ וּבֵית אָבִיךָ אִתָּךְ תִּשְׂאוּ אֶת עֲוֹן הַמִּקְדָּשׁ" (להלן יח, א), וְהַלְוִיִּם הַלָּלוּ מְסַיְּעִין אוֹתָם, זוֹ הִיא הַשֵּׁרוּת:

ז | **וְשָׁמְרוּ אֶת מִשְׁמַרְתּוֹ.** כָּל מִנּוּי שֶׁהָאָדָם מְמֻנֶּה עָלָיו וּמֻטָּל עָלָיו לַעֲשׂוֹתוֹ קָרוּי 'מִשְׁמֶרֶת' בְּכָל הַמִּקְרָא וּבִלְשׁוֹן מִשְׁנָה, כְּמוֹ שֶׁאָמְרוּ בְּבִגְתָן וָתֶרֶשׁ: "וַהֲלֹא אֵין מִשְׁמַרְתִּי וּמִשְׁמַרְתְּךָ שָׁוָה", וְכֵן מִשְׁמְרוֹת כְּהֻנָּה וּלְוִיָּה:

ח | **וְאֶת מִשְׁמֶרֶת בְּנֵי יִשְׂרָאֵל.** שֶׁכֻּלָּן הָיוּ זְקוּקִין לְצָרְכֵי הַמִּקְדָּשׁ, אֶלָּא שֶׁהַלְוִיִּם בָּאִים תַּחְתֵּיהֶם בִּשְׁלִיחוּתָם, לְפִיכָךְ לוֹקְחִים מֵהֶם הַמַּעַשְׂרוֹת בִּשְׂכָרָן, שֶׁנֶּאֱמַר: "כִּי שָׂכָר הוּא לָכֶם חֵלֶף עֲבֹדַתְכֶם" (להלן יח, לא):

ט | **נְתוּנִם הֵמָּה לוֹ.** לְעֶזְרָה: **מֵאֵת בְּנֵי יִשְׂרָאֵל.** כְּמוֹ 'מִתּוֹךְ בְּנֵי יִשְׂרָאֵל', כְּלוֹמַר מִשְּׁאָר כָּל הָעֵדָה נִבְדְּלוּ לְכָךְ בִּגְזֵרַת הַמָּקוֹם וְהוּא נְתָנָם לוֹ, שֶׁנֶּאֱמַר: "וָאֶתְּנָה אֶת הַלְוִיִּם נְתֻנִים" וְגוֹ' (להלן ח, יט):

י | **וְאֶת אַהֲרֹן וְאֶת בָּנָיו תִּפְקֹד.** לְשׁוֹן פְּקִידוּת, וְאֵינוֹ לְשׁוֹן מִנְיָן: **וְשָׁמְרוּ אֶת כְּהֻנָּתָם.** קַבָּלַת דָּמִים וּזְרִיקָה וְהַקְטָרָה וַעֲבוֹדוֹת הַמְּסוּרוֹת לַכֹּהֲנִים:

יב | **וַאֲנִי הִנֵּה לָקַחְתִּי.** וַאֲנִי מֵהֵיכָן זָכִיתִי בָּהֶן "מִתּוֹךְ בְּנֵי יִשְׂרָאֵל", שֶׁיִּהְיוּ יִשְׂרָאֵל שׂוֹכְרִין אוֹתָן לְשֵׁרוּת שֶׁלִּי? עַל יְדֵי הַבְּכוֹרוֹת זָכִיתִי בָּהֶם וּלְקַחְתִּים תְּמוּרָתָם. לְפִי שֶׁהָיְתָה הָעֲבוֹדָה בַּבְּכוֹרוֹת, וּכְשֶׁחָטְאוּ בָּעֵגֶל נִפְסְלוּ, וְהַלְוִיִּם שֶׁלֹּא עָבְדוּ עֲבוֹדָה זָרָה נִבְחֲרוּ תַּחְתֵּיהֶם:

טו | **מִבֶּן חֹדֶשׁ וָמַעְלָה.** מִשֶּׁיָּצָא מִכְּלַל נְפָלִים הוּא נִמְנֶה לִקָּרֵא שׁוֹמֵר מִשְׁמֶרֶת הַקֹּדֶשׁ. אָמַר רַבִּי יְהוּדָה בְּרַבִּי שָׁלוֹם: לָמוּד הוּא אוֹתוֹ הַשֵּׁבֶט לִהְיוֹת נִמְנֶה מִן הַבֶּטֶן, שֶׁנֶּאֱמַר: "אֲשֶׁר יָלְדָה אֹתָהּ לְלֵוִי בְּמִצְרָיִם" (להלן כו, נט), עִם כְּנִיסָתָהּ בְּפֶתַח מִצְרַיִם יְלָדָה אוֹתָהּ, וְנִמְנֵית בְּשִׁבְעִים נֶפֶשׁ, שֶׁכְּשֶׁאַתָּה מוֹנֶה חֶשְׁבּוֹנָם לֹא תִּמְצָאֵם אֶלָּא שִׁבְעִים חָסֵר אַחַת, וְהִיא הִשְׁלִימָה אֶת הַמִּנְיָן:

16 **Moses counted them according to the directive of the Lord, as he was commanded.** Since this census included children and newborns, it was harder to perform than that of the rest of the people, where all those counted were adults who could appear in person. Therefore, the verse stresses that God assisted Moses in the count.[15]

17 **These were the sons of Levi by their names: Gershon, Kehat, and Merari.**

18 **These were the names of the sons of Gershon by their families: Livni and Shimi.**

19 **The sons of Kehat by their families: Amram, Yitzhar, Hebron,**[D] **and Uziel.**

20 **The sons of Merari by their families: Mahli and Mushi. These are the families of the Levites by their patrilineal house.**

21 Following the listing of the names of the Levite families, the Torah details their numbers, the place of their encampment in relation to the Tabernacle, and their role in carrying the Tabernacle. **For Gershon, the family of the Livnites, and the family of the Shimiites; these are the families of the Gershonites.**

22 **Those counted,** of the descendants of Gershon, **according to the number of all males from one month old and above; those counted were seven thousand five hundred.**

23 **The families of the Gershonites shall encamp behind the Tabernacle to the west.**

24 **The prince of the patrilineal house of the Gershonites was Elyasaf son of Lael.**

25 **The commission of the sons of Gershon in the Tent of Meeting was** the responsibility for the curtains of dyed wool and linen, that was above **the Tabernacle, and the Tent,** the upper curtains of goats' hair, **its** outer **covering** of rams' skins and sealskins, **and the screen of the entrance of the Tent of Meeting,**

26 **and the hangings of the courtyard, and the screen of the entrance of the courtyard that is near the Tabernacle, and near** the altar surrounding, **and its cords,** which hold the screen of the courtyard as well. It is possible that stretched cords were also used to tie the coverings of the Tabernacle to the ground. Furthermore, the descendants of Gershon were responsible **for all its work,** which included handling all the textiles, skins, and ropes of the Tabernacle, in addition to their other tasks.[16]

27 **For Kehat, the family of the Amramites, the family of the Yitzharites, the family of the Hebronites, and the family of the Uzielites; these are the families of the Kehatites.**

28 **According to the number of all males, from one month old and above, eight thousand six hundred, keepers of the commission of the sacred.** They were entrusted with the special task of carrying the sacred vessels, as detailed below.

29 **The families of the sons of Kehat shall encamp on the side of the Tabernacle to the south.**

30 **The prince of the patrilineal house of the families of the Kehatites was Elitzafan son of Uziel.**[D]

31 **Their commission** that they must perform is to carry **the ark, the table, the candelabrum, the altars, and the sacred vessels with which they would serve, and the screen,** which divides the Holy of Holies from the Sanctuary,[17] **and all** the rest of **its work.** Alternatively, "the screen" refers to the screen of the courtyard, and "all its work" refers to its cords.[18]

32 Serving above the princes of the three patrilineal houses of the tribe of Levi was a prince of the whole tribe, from the Kehatites: **The prince of the princes of the Levites was Elazar son of Aaron the priest,** and he was given **the appointment over the keepers of the commission of the sacred.** Aaron himself had a special role in the Tabernacle. He was not the prince of the Levites; rather, that task was entrusted to his firstborn son.

33 **For Merari, the family of the Mahlites, and the family of the Mushites; these are the families of Merari.**

34 **Those counted, according to the number of all males, from one month old and above, were six thousand two hundred.**

35 **The prince of the patrilineal house of the families of Merari was Tzuriel son of Avihayil; they shall encamp on the side of the Tabernacle to the north.**

DISCUSSION

3:19| **Hebron:** This individual may have been named after the city of Hebron in the land of Canaan. Alternatively, this name is similar to that of Hever, which means friend or colleague. There are four people in the Bible with that name (see Genesis 46:17; Judges 4:17; I Chronicles 4:18, 8:17).

3:30| **Elitzafan son of Uziel:** Undoubtedly, Kehat was considered the senior patrilineal house, as Moses and Aaron, the leaders of the people, were the sons of Amram, the firstborn of Kehat. The fact that the prince of this patrilineal house was the son of the third son, Uziel, rather than the son of the older Yitzhar, is cited as one reason for Korah's bitterness toward Moses and Aaron that motivated his rebellion (see 16:1–3), as he had received no public appointment in the family of the Kehatites (*Bemidbar Rabba* 18:2).

טז וַיִּפְקֹד אֹתָם מֹשֶׁה עַל־פִּי יְהוָה כַּאֲשֶׁר צֻוָּה: וַיִּהְיוּ־אֵלֶּה בְנֵי־לֵוִי בִּשְׁמֹתָם גֵּרְשׁוֹן

יז וּקְהָת וּמְרָרִי: וְאֵלֶּה שְׁמוֹת בְּנֵי־גֵרְשׁוֹן לְמִשְׁפְּחֹתָם לִבְנִי וְשִׁמְעִי: וּבְנֵי קְהָת

כ לְמִשְׁפְּחֹתָם עַמְרָם וְיִצְהָר חֶבְרוֹן וְעֻזִּיאֵל: וּבְנֵי מְרָרִי לְמִשְׁפְּחֹתָם מַחְלִי וּמוּשִׁי

כא אֵלֶּה הֵם מִשְׁפְּחֹת הַלֵּוִי לְבֵית אֲבֹתָם: לְגֵרְשׁוֹן מִשְׁפַּחַת הַלִּבְנִי וּמִשְׁפַּחַת הַשִּׁמְעִי

כב אֵלֶּה הֵם מִשְׁפְּחֹת הַגֵּרְשֻׁנִּי: פְּקֻדֵיהֶם בְּמִסְפַּר כָּל־זָכָר מִבֶּן־חֹדֶשׁ וָמָעְלָה פְּקֻדֵיהֶם

כג שִׁבְעַת אֲלָפִים וַחֲמֵשׁ מֵאוֹת: מִשְׁפְּחֹת הַגֵּרְשֻׁנִּי אַחֲרֵי הַמִּשְׁכָּן יַחֲנוּ יָמָּה: וּנְשִׂיא

כה בֵית־אָב לַגֵּרְשֻׁנִּי אֶלְיָסָף בֶּן־לָאֵל: וּמִשְׁמֶרֶת בְּנֵי־גֵרְשׁוֹן בְּאֹהֶל מוֹעֵד הַמִּשְׁכָּן

כו וְהָאֹהֶל מִכְסֵהוּ וּמָסַךְ פֶּתַח אֹהֶל מוֹעֵד: וְקַלְעֵי הֶחָצֵר וְאֶת־מָסַךְ פֶּתַח הֶחָצֵר

כז אֲשֶׁר עַל־הַמִּשְׁכָּן וְעַל־הַמִּזְבֵּחַ סָבִיב וְאֵת מֵיתָרָיו לְכֹל עֲבֹדָתוֹ: וְלִקְהָת

מִשְׁפַּחַת הָעַמְרָמִי וּמִשְׁפַּחַת הַיִּצְהָרִי וּמִשְׁפַּחַת הַחֶבְרֹנִי וּמִשְׁפַּחַת הָעָזִּיאֵלִי

כח אֵלֶּה הֵם מִשְׁפְּחֹת הַקְּהָתִי: בְּמִסְפַּר כָּל־זָכָר מִבֶּן־חֹדֶשׁ וָמָעְלָה שְׁמֹנַת אֲלָפִים

כט וְשֵׁשׁ מֵאוֹת שֹׁמְרֵי מִשְׁמֶרֶת הַקֹּדֶשׁ: מִשְׁפְּחֹת בְּנֵי־קְהָת יַחֲנוּ עַל יֶרֶךְ הַמִּשְׁכָּן

ל תֵּימָנָה: וּנְשִׂיא בֵית־אָב לְמִשְׁפְּחֹת הַקְּהָתִי אֱלִיצָפָן בֶּן־עֻזִּיאֵל: וּמִשְׁמַרְתָּם

לא הָאָרֹן וְהַשֻּׁלְחָן וְהַמְּנֹרָה וְהַמִּזְבְּחֹת וּכְלֵי הַקֹּדֶשׁ אֲשֶׁר יְשָׁרְתוּ בָּהֶם וְהַמָּסָךְ וְכֹל

לב עֲבֹדָתוֹ: וּנְשִׂיא נְשִׂיאֵי הַלֵּוִי אֶלְעָזָר בֶּן־אַהֲרֹן הַכֹּהֵן פְּקֻדַּת שֹׁמְרֵי מִשְׁמֶרֶת

לג הַקֹּדֶשׁ: לִמְרָרִי מִשְׁפַּחַת הַמַּחְלִי וּמִשְׁפַּחַת הַמּוּשִׁי אֵלֶּה הֵם מִשְׁפְּחֹת מְרָרִי:

לד וּפְקֻדֵיהֶם בְּמִסְפַּר כָּל־זָכָר מִבֶּן־חֹדֶשׁ וָמָעְלָה שֵׁשֶׁת אֲלָפִים וּמָאתָיִם: וּנְשִׂיא

לה בֵית־אָב לְמִשְׁפְּחֹת מְרָרִי צוּרִיאֵל בֶּן־אֲבִיחָיִל עַל יֶרֶךְ הַמִּשְׁכָּן יַחֲנוּ צָפֹנָה:

רש"י

טז] עַל פִּי ה'. אָמַר מֹשֶׁה לִפְנֵי הַקָּדוֹשׁ בָּרוּךְ הוּא: הֵיאַךְ אֲנִי נִכְנָס לְתוֹךְ אָהֳלֵיהֶם לָדַעַת מִנְיַן יוֹנְקֵיהֶם? אָמַר לוֹ הַקָּדוֹשׁ בָּרוּךְ הוּא: עֲשֵׂה אַתָּה שֶׁלְּךָ וַאֲנִי אֶעֱשֶׂה שֶׁלִּי. הָלַךְ מֹשֶׁה וְעָמַד עַל פֶּתַח הָאֹהֶל, וְהַשְּׁכִינָה מַקְדֶּמֶת לְפָנָיו, וּבַת קוֹל יוֹצֵאת מִן הָאֹהֶל וְאוֹמֶרֶת: כָּךְ וְכָךְ תִּינוֹקוֹת יֵשׁ בְּאֹהֶל זֶה, לְכָךְ נֶאֱמַר: "עַל פִּי ה'":

כא] לְגֵרְשׁוֹן מִשְׁפַּחַת הַלִּבְנִי. כְּלוֹמַר, לְגֵרְשׁוֹן הָיוּ

הַפְּקוּדִים מִשְׁפַּחַת הַלִּבְנִי וּמִשְׁפַּחַת הַשִּׁמְעִי, פְּקוּדֵיהֶם כָּךְ וְכָךְ:

כה] הַמִּשְׁכָּן. יְרִיעוֹת הַתַּחְתּוֹנוֹת: וְהָאֹהֶל. יְרִיעוֹת עִזִּים הָעֲשׂוּיוֹת לְגַג: מִכְסֵהוּ. עוֹרוֹת אֵילִים וּתְחָשִׁים: וּמָסַךְ פֶּתַח. הוּא הַוִּילוֹן:

כו] וְאֵת מֵיתָרָיו. שֶׁל מִשְׁכָּן וְשֶׁל אֹהֶל, וְלֹא שֶׁל חָצֵר:

כט] מִשְׁפְּחֹת בְּנֵי קְהָת יַחֲנוּ... תֵּימָנָה. וְסָמוּךְ לָהֶם

דֶּגֶל רְאוּבֵן הַחוֹנִים תֵּימָנָה, אוֹי לָרָשָׁע וְאוֹי לִשְׁכֵנוֹ, לְכָךְ לָקוּ מֵהֶם דָּתָן וַאֲבִירָם וּמָאתַיִם וַחֲמִשִּׁים אִישׁ עִם קֹרַח וַעֲדָתוֹ, שֶׁנִּמְשְׁכוּ עִמָּהֶם בְּמַחְלָקְתָּם:

לא] וְהַמָּסָךְ. הוּא הַפָּרֹכֶת, שֶׁאַף הוּא קָרוּי "פָּרֹכֶת הַמָּסָךְ" (להלן ד, ה):

לב] וּנְשִׂיא נְשִׂיאֵי הַלֵּוִי. מְמֻנֶּה עַל כֻּלָּם, וְעַל מַה הָיָה נְשִׂיאוּתוֹ? "פְּקֻדַּת שֹׁמְרֵי מִשְׁמֶרֶת", עַל יָדוֹ הָיָה פְּקֻדַּת כֻּלָּם:

36 **The appointed commission of the sons of Merari** was the responsibility for **the beams of the Tabernacle, its bars, its pillars, its sockets, all its** accompanying **instruments, and all its work,**

37 **and the pillars of the courtyard all around, their sockets, their pegs, and their cords.**

38 The previous verses detailed the functions of the three patrilineal houses of the tribe of Levi: The descendants of Kehat, who were the most important, were in charge of the sacred vessels. The descendants of Gershon, the firstborn, dealt with the woven fabrics and the skins of the Tabernacle, while the descendants of Merari had the most physically taxing job, to carry all the heavy, solid components of the Tabernacle, including the beams, sockets, pegs, and the like. When the Israelites were encamped, these three patrilineal houses surrounded the Tabernacle on three sides, with Gershon to the west, Kehat to the south, and Merari to the north. On the remaining side, **those encamped in front of the Tabernacle,** where its entrance was located, **to the east, in front of the Tent of Meeting: Moses, and Aaron, and his sons, keeping the commission of the Sanctuary, for the commission of the children of Israel; and the stranger who approaches shall be put to death.** Although Moses was not a priest, due to his unique status he encamped alongside his brother.

39 **All those counted of the Levites, whom Moses and Aaron counted by the mandate of the Lord, by their families, all males from one month old and above, were twenty-two thousand.**

40 **The Lord said to Moses: Count all the firstborn males of the**
Sixth aliya **children of Israel from one month old and above, and take the number of their names.** Corresponding to the counting of the Levites, you must conduct another census, that of the Israelite firstborns. Since this counting is also unrelated to military roles, but is rather to determine the number of firstborns, it too includes newborns.

41 **You shall** then **take the Levites for Me, I am the Lord, in place of all the firstborn among the children of Israel.** The firstborns are thereby removed from the Tabernacle service and all ritual functions and are replaced by the Levites. The firstborns will retain only a minor element of sanctity, for which they require redemption, as will be explained below. **And** likewise, you shall take **the animals of the Levites in place of all the firstborn among the animals of the children of Israel,** which were consecrated to God.[19]

42 **Moses counted, as the Lord had commanded him, all firstborn among the children of Israel.**

43 **All the firstborn males according to the number of names, from one month old and above, by their count, were twenty-two thousand two hundred and seventy-three.**[D]

44 **The Lord spoke to Moses, saying:**

45 **Take the Levites in place of all the firstborn among the children of Israel, and the animals of the Levites instead of their animals,** those of the Israelites; **and the Levites shall be Mine,** as a special group dedicated to the Tabernacle, **I am the Lord.**

46 Each firstborn is removed from his function and replaced by one of the Levites. As the number of firstborns is not identical to the number of Levites, **for the redemptions of the two hundred and seventy-three of the firstborn of the children of Israel, who remain beyond the Levites,**

47 **you shall take five shekels each by head,** for every additional firstborn. **In the sacred shekel you shall take; twenty gera**[B] **is the shekel.**[20]

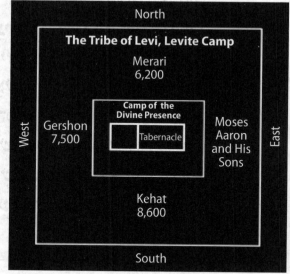

Levite families and those counted

DISCUSSION

3:43| **Twenty-two thousand two hundred and seventy-three:** A comparison of the number of firstborns to the total number of the children of Israel (603,550) indicates that there was an unusually high number of children in each household. One possible explanation for this is a high mortality rate, as in ancient times more than half of all children died before the age of five, and the firstborn often did not survive. Therefore, the total number of children could be significantly disproportionate to the number of firstborns. Another suggestion is that in the final years of slavery in Egypt, the severity of the servitude, which included the killing of children, brought about a decrease in the number of Israelites. Consequently, a relatively large number of children who were not firstborns survived.

לו וּפְקֻדַּת מִשְׁמֶרֶת בְּנֵי מְרָרִי קַרְשֵׁי הַמִּשְׁכָּן וּבְרִיחָיו וְעַמֻּדָיו וַאֲדָנָיו וְכָל־כֵּלָיו
לז לח וְכֹל עֲבֹדָתוֹ: וְעַמֻּדֵי הֶחָצֵר סָבִיב וְאַדְנֵיהֶם וִיתֵדֹתָם וּמֵיתְרֵיהֶם: וְהַחֹנִים לִפְנֵי
הַמִּשְׁכָּן קֵדְמָה לִפְנֵי אֹהֶל־מוֹעֵד ׀ מִזְרָחָה מֹשֶׁה ׀ וְאַהֲרֹן וּבָנָיו שֹׁמְרִים מִשְׁמֶרֶת
לט הַמִּקְדָּשׁ לְמִשְׁמֶרֶת בְּנֵי יִשְׂרָאֵל וְהַזָּר הַקָּרֵב יוּמָת: כָּל־פְּקוּדֵי הַלְוִיִּם אֲשֶׁר
פָּקַד מֹשֶׁה וְאַהֲרֹן עַל־פִּי יְהוָה לְמִשְׁפְּחֹתָם כָּל־זָכָר מִבֶּן־חֹדֶשׁ וָמַעְלָה שְׁנַיִם
מ וְעֶשְׂרִים אָלֶף: וַיֹּאמֶר יְהוָה אֶל־מֹשֶׁה פְּקֹד כָּל־בְּכֹר זָכָר לִבְנֵי ששי
מא יִשְׂרָאֵל מִבֶּן־חֹדֶשׁ וָמָעְלָה וְשָׂא אֵת מִסְפַּר שְׁמֹתָם: וְלָקַחְתָּ אֶת־הַלְוִיִּם לִי אֲנִי
יְהוָה תַּחַת כָּל־בְּכֹר בִּבְנֵי יִשְׂרָאֵל וְאֵת בֶּהֱמַת הַלְוִיִּם תַּחַת כָּל־בְּכוֹר בְּבֶהֱמַת
מב בְּנֵי יִשְׂרָאֵל: וַיִּפְקֹד מֹשֶׁה כַּאֲשֶׁר צִוָּה יְהוָה אֹתוֹ אֶת־כָּל־בְּכוֹר בִּבְנֵי יִשְׂרָאֵל:
מג וַיְהִי כָל־בְּכוֹר זָכָר בְּמִסְפַּר שֵׁמֹת מִבֶּן־חֹדֶשׁ וָמַעְלָה לִפְקֻדֵיהֶם שְׁנַיִם וְעֶשְׂרִים
אֶלֶף שְׁלֹשָׁה וְשִׁבְעִים וּמָאתָיִם:
מד מה וַיְדַבֵּר יְהוָה אֶל־מֹשֶׁה לֵּאמֹר: קַח אֶת־הַלְוִיִּם תַּחַת כָּל־בְּכוֹר בִּבְנֵי יִשְׂרָאֵל
מו וְאֶת־בֶּהֱמַת הַלְוִיִּם תַּחַת בְּהֶמְתָּם וְהָיוּ־לִי הַלְוִיִּם אֲנִי יְהוָה: וְאֵת פְּדוּיֵי
מז הַשְּׁלֹשָׁה וְהַשִּׁבְעִים וְהַמָּאתָיִם הָעֹדְפִים עַל־הַלְוִיִּם מִבְּכוֹר בְּנֵי יִשְׂרָאֵל: וְלָקַחְתָּ
חֲמֵשֶׁת חֲמֵשֶׁת שְׁקָלִים לַגֻּלְגֹּלֶת בְּשֶׁקֶל הַקֹּדֶשׁ תִּקָּח עֶשְׂרִים גֵּרָה הַשָּׁקֶל:

רש״י

לח | **מֹשֶׁה וְאַהֲרֹן וּבָנָיו.** וּסְמוּכִין לָהֶם דֶּגֶל מַחֲנֵה יְהוּדָה וְהַחוֹנִים עָלָיו יִשָּׂשכָר וּזְבוּלֻן, טוֹב לַצַּדִּיק טוֹב לִשְׁכֵנוֹ, לְפִי שֶׁהָיוּ שְׁכֵנָיו שֶׁל מֹשֶׁה שֶׁהָיָה עוֹסֵק בַּתּוֹרָה, נַעֲשׂוּ גְּדוֹלִים בַּתּוֹרָה, שֶׁנֶּאֱמַר: "יְהוּדָה מְחֹקְקִי" (תהלים ס, ט), "וּמִבְּנֵי יִשָּׂשכָר יוֹדְעֵי בִינָה" וְגוֹ׳ (דברי הימים א׳ יב, לג) מָאתַיִם רָאשֵׁי סַנְהֶדְרָאוֹת, "וּמִזְּבוּלֻן מֹשְׁכִים בְּשֵׁבֶט סֹפֵר" (שופטים ה, יד):

לט | **אֲשֶׁר פָּקַד מֹשֶׁה וְאַהֲרֹן.** נָקוּד עַל וְאַהֲרֹן, לוֹמַר שֶׁלֹּא הָיָה בְּמִנְיַן הַלְוִיִּם: **שְׁנַיִם וְעֶשְׂרִים אָלֶף.** וּבִפְרָטָן אַתָּה מוֹצֵא שְׁלֹשׁ מֵאוֹת יְתֵרִים: בְּנֵי גֵרְשׁוֹן שִׁבְעַת אֲלָפִים וַחֲמֵשׁ מֵאוֹת, בְּנֵי קְהָת שְׁמֹנַת אֲלָפִים וְשֵׁשׁ מֵאוֹת, בְּנֵי מְרָרִי שֵׁשֶׁת אֲלָפִים וּמָאתַיִם! וְלָמָּה לֹא כְּלָלָן עִם הַשְּׁאָר וְיִפְדּוּ אֶת הַבְּכוֹרוֹת, וְלֹא יִהְיוּ זְקוּקִים הַשְּׁלֹשָׁה וְשִׁבְעִים וּמָאתַיִם בְּכוֹרוֹת הָעוֹדְפִים עַל הַמִּנְיָן לְפִדְיוֹן? אָמְרוּ רַבּוֹתֵינוּ בְּמַסֶּכֶת בְּכוֹרוֹת (דף ה ע״א): אוֹתָן שְׁלֹשׁ מֵאוֹת לְוִיִּם בְּכוֹרוֹת הָיוּ, וְדַיָּם שֶׁיַּפְקִיעוּ עַצְמָם מִן הַפִּדְיוֹן:

מ | **פְּקֹד כָּל בְּכֹר זָכָר וְגוֹ׳ מִבֶּן חֹדֶשׁ וָמָעְלָה.** מִשֶּׁיָּצָא מִכְּלַל סְפֵק נְפָלִים:

מה | **וְאֶת בֶּהֱמַת הַלְוִיִּם וְגוֹ׳.** לֹא פָּדוּ בַּהֲמוֹת הַלְוִיִּם אֶת בְּכוֹרֵי בְּהֵמָה טְהוֹרָה שֶׁל יִשְׂרָאֵל, אֶלָּא אֶת פִּטְרֵי חֲמוֹרֵיהֶם, וְשֶׂה אֶחָד שֶׁל בֶּן לֵוִי פָּטַר כַּמָּה פִּטְרֵי חֲמוֹרִים שֶׁל יִשְׂרָאֵל. תֵּדַע, שֶׁהֲרֵי מָנָה הָעוֹדְפִים בָּאָדָם וְלֹא מָנָה הָעוֹדְפִים בַּבְּהֵמָה:

מו-מז | **וְאֵת פְּדוּיֵי הַשְּׁלֹשָׁה וְגוֹ׳.** וְאֶת הַבְּכוֹרוֹת הַצְּרִיכִין לְהִפָּדוֹת בָּהֶם, אֵלּוּ שְׁלֹשָׁה וְשִׁבְעִים וּמָאתַיִם הָעוֹדְפִים בָּהֶם יְתֵרִים עַל הַלְוִיִּם, מֵהֶם תִּקַּח חֲמֵשֶׁת שְׁקָלִים לַגֻּלְגֹּלֶת. כָּךְ הָיְתָה מְכִירָתוֹ שֶׁל יוֹסֵף, עֶשְׂרִים כֶּסֶף, שֶׁהָיָה בְּכוֹרָהּ שֶׁל רָחֵל:

BACKGROUND

3:47 | **Gera:** This is the smallest measurement of weight for silver, probably equivalent to 0.83 g, and is called a *ma'a* by the Sages. Ten of these gera is worth a regular shekel, while twenty is equal to the sacred shekel (see commentary on Leviticus 27:25).

48 **You shall give the silver to Aaron and to his sons; the redemptions of those among them who remain.** This money shall serve to redeem those firstborns for whom there is no Levite to replace them.

49 **Moses took the silver of the redemption from those who remain beyond the redemptions of the Levites.**[D]

50 **From the firstborn of the children of Israel he took the silver: One thousand three hundred and sixty-five shekels, in the sacred shekels.** Five shekels were paid for each of the 273 remaining firstborns.

51 **Moses gave the silver of the redemption to Aaron and to his sons, according to the directive of the Lord, as the Lord had commanded Moses.**[D]

The Service of the Levites and Their Census

NUMBERS 4:1–49

The division of labor for the Tabernacle between the three patrilineal families of the tribe of Levi (Kehat, Gershon, and Merari), mentioned briefly in the previous section, is spelled out in detail here. The Torah describes the function of each patrilineal family during this time that the Israelites embark on a journey, which involves the dismantling of the Tabernacle and the bearing of its various parts. In the previous chapter, the Levites were counted from the age of one month. This is a significant factor contributing to their identity as Levites, and to their replacing the firstborn in their duties. By contrast, the census conducted here is part of the practical preparations for the Levites to bear the Tabernacle and its vessels, and therefore only includes men between the ages of thirty and fifty. The assistance of the Levites in such matters is especially vital in the wilderness, as the number of priests at this time is negligible compared to the size of the people.

The Sages comment that the repetition and detail with regard to these matters indicates the Torah's great love for them.

4 1 **The Lord spoke to Moses and to Aaron, saying:**

Seventh aliya 2 **Take the census of the sons of Kehat,** and appoint them for their important task, **from among the sons of Levi, by their families, by their patrilineal house.**

3 **From thirty years old and above and until fifty years old,**[D] **all those enlisted for duty, to perform labor in the Tent of Meeting.**

4 **This is the work of the sons of Kehat in the Tent of Meeting: the sacred sacraments [*kodesh hakodashim*].** Here, this expression does not bear its usual meaning of the Holy of Holies, which is the location behind the curtain in the Sanctuary where the ark was located but rather means the sacred sacraments.

5 The priests must prepare the vessels before the Kehatites may carry them. **Aaron and his sons shall come when the camp travels, and they shall remove the curtain that screens,** divides between the Sanctuary and the Holy of Holies, **and with it they shall cover the Ark of the Testimony.** The curtain, which itself is part of the Sanctuary, shall serve as the first cover over the ark.

6 **They shall** then **place upon it,** the ark, above the curtain, **a covering of the hide of a taḥash,**[B] which is stronger and more impermeable than the curtain, **and they shall spread** a third layer, **a cloth entirely of sky-blue wool,** a valuable woven material, **over it, and they shall** straighten and **fasten its staves**[D] in preparation for its journey.

7 **On the table for the showbread they shall spread a cloth of**

Dugong, possibly the *taḥash*

DISCUSSION

3:49 | From those who remain beyond the redemptions of the Levites: The Sages explained that in order to determine which of the firstborn would be considered "those who remain," all of them participated in a lottery. On twenty-two thousand slips, the word "Levite" was written, and the firstborn who picked these slips were exempt from payment, as a Levite had been chosen to replace each firstborn. On the 273 remaining slips it was written that they had to pay the redemption (see *Tanḥuma, Bemidbar* 25; Rashi, verse 50).

3:51 | As the Lord had commanded Moses: This emphasis is important, as it might appear that Moses is granting favorable status to his family. One of the motivations for Korah's rebellion against him and his brother Aaron was in fact such suggestions of nepotism (chap. 16). Therefore, the verses stress on several occasions that everything was performed upon God's command (see *Or HaḤayyim*).

4:3 | From thirty years old and above and until fifty years old: In comparison to the Israelite males fit for conscription, who were counted from the age of twenty (1:3), the Levites were only fit for service to carry the sacred vessels at the age of thirty and were counted from that age. As such, their period of service in the Tabernacle was shorter perhaps due to the

מח וְנָתַתָּה הַכֶּסֶף לְאַהֲרֹן וּלְבָנָיו פְּדוּיֵי הָעֹדְפִים בָּהֶם׃ וַיִּקַּח מֹשֶׁה אֵת כֶּסֶף הַפִּדְיוֹם
מט
נ מֵאֵת הָעֹדְפִים עַל פְּדוּיֵי הַלְוִיִּם׃ מֵאֵת בְּכוֹר בְּנֵי יִשְׂרָאֵל לָקַח אֶת־הַכָּסֶף חֲמִשָּׁה
נא וְשִׁשִּׁים וּשְׁלֹשׁ מֵאוֹת וָאֶלֶף בְּשֶׁקֶל הַקֹּדֶשׁ׃ וַיִּתֵּן מֹשֶׁה אֶת־כֶּסֶף הַפְּדֻיִם לְאַהֲרֹן
וּלְבָנָיו עַל־פִּי יְהוָה כַּאֲשֶׁר צִוָּה יְהוָה אֶת־מֹשֶׁה׃
א וַיְדַבֵּר יְהוָה אֶל־מֹשֶׁה וְאֶל־אַהֲרֹן לֵאמֹר׃ נָשֹׂא אֶת־רֹאשׁ בְּנֵי קְהָת מִתּוֹךְ בְּנֵי שביעי
ב
ג לֵוִי לְמִשְׁפְּחֹתָם לְבֵית אֲבֹתָם׃ מִבֶּן שְׁלֹשִׁים שָׁנָה וָמַעְלָה וְעַד בֶּן־חֲמִשִּׁים
ד שָׁנָה כָּל־בָּא לַצָּבָא לַעֲשׂוֹת מְלָאכָה בְּאֹהֶל מוֹעֵד׃ זֹאת עֲבֹדַת בְּנֵי־קְהָת
ה בְּאֹהֶל מוֹעֵד קֹדֶשׁ הַקֳּדָשִׁים׃ וּבָא אַהֲרֹן וּבָנָיו בִּנְסֹעַ הַמַּחֲנֶה וְהוֹרִדוּ אֵת
ו פָּרֹכֶת הַמָּסָךְ וְכִסּוּ־בָהּ אֵת אֲרֹן הָעֵדֻת׃ וְנָתְנוּ עָלָיו כְּסוּי עוֹר תַּחַשׁ וּפָרְשׂוּ
ז בֶגֶד־כְּלִיל תְּכֵלֶת מִלְמָעְלָה וְשָׂמוּ בַּדָּיו׃ וְעַל | שֻׁלְחַן הַפָּנִים יִפְרְשׂוּ בֶּגֶד

רש״י

מט | **הָעֹדְפִים עַל פְּדוּיֵי הַלְוִיִּם.** עַל אוֹתָן שֶׁפָּדוּ הַלְוִיִּם בְּגוּפָן:

נ | **חֲמִשָּׁה וְשִׁשִּׁים וּשְׁלֹשׁ מֵאוֹת וָאֶלֶף.** כָּךְ סְכוּם הַחֶשְׁבּוֹן: חֲמֵשֶׁת שְׁקָלִים לַגֻּלְגֹּלֶת, לְמָאתַיִם בְּכוֹרוֹת – אֶלֶף שֶׁקֶל, לְשִׁבְעִים בְּכוֹרוֹת – שְׁלֹשׁ מֵאוֹת וַחֲמִשִּׁים שֶׁקֶל, לִשְׁלֹשָׁה בְּכוֹרוֹת – חֲמִשָּׁה עָשָׂר שֶׁקֶל. אָמַר: כֵּיצַד אֶעֱשֶׂה? בְּכוֹר שֶׁאֹמַר לוֹ: תֵּן חֲמֵשֶׁת שְׁקָלִים! יֹאמַר לִי: אֲנִי מִפְּדוּיֵי הַלְוִיִּם. מֶה עָשָׂה? הֵבִיא שְׁנַיִם וְעֶשְׂרִים אֶלֶף פִּתְקִין וְכָתַב עֲלֵיהֶם 'בֶּן לֵוִי', וּמָאתַיִם וְשִׁבְעִים וּשְׁלֹשָׁה פִּתְקִין כָּתַב עֲלֵיהֶן 'חֲמֵשֶׁת שְׁקָלִים'. בְּלָלָן וּנְתָנָן בְּקַלְפֵּי. אָמַר לָהֶם: בּוֹאוּ וּטְלוּ פִּתְקֵיכֶם לְפִי הַגּוֹרָל:

פרק ד

ב | **נָשֹׂא אֶת רֹאשׁ וְגוֹ'.** מְנֵה מֵהֶם אֶת הָרְאוּיִין לַעֲבוֹדַת מַשָּׂא, וְהֵם מִבֶּן שְׁלֹשִׁים וְעַד בֶּן חֲמִשִּׁים שָׁנָה, וְהַפָּחוֹת מִשְּׁלֹשִׁים לֹא נִתְמַלֵּא כֹּחוֹ, מִכָּאן אָמְרוּ: "בֶּן שְׁלֹשִׁים לַכֹּחַ" (אבות ה, כא), וְהַיּוֹתֵר עַל בֶּן חֲמִשִּׁים כֹּחוֹ מַכְחִישׁ מֵעַתָּה:

ד | **קֹדֶשׁ הַקֳּדָשִׁים.** הַמְקֻדָּשׁ שֶׁבְּכֻלָּן, הָאָרוֹן וְהַשֻּׁלְחָן וְהַמְּנוֹרָה וְהַמִּזְבְּחוֹת וְהַפָּרֹכֶת וּכְלֵי שָׁרֵת:

ה | **וּבָא אַהֲרֹן וּבָנָיו וְגוֹ'.** יַכְנִיסוּ כָּל כְּלִי וּכְלִי לְנַרְתִּיקוֹ הַמְפֹרָשׁ לוֹ בְּפָרָשָׁה זוֹ, וְלֹא יִצְטָרְכוּ הַלְוִיִּם בְּנֵי קְהָת אֶלָּא לָשֵׂאת: **בִּנְסֹעַ הַמַּחֲנֶה.** כְּשֶׁהֶעָנָן מִסְתַּלֵּק, הֵן יוֹדְעִין שֶׁיִּסְעוּ:

DISCUSSION

necessary training they received before beginning the service, which commenced prior to age thirty (see Rashi and Ramban, 8:24; *Ḥullin* 24a). Furthermore, beyond the physical effort which the Levites' work entailed, their proximity to the sacred vessels and the Tabernacle required a serious, composed state of mind, as well as an alertness and a respectful attitude more typical of mature adults.

4:6| **And they shall fasten its staves:** This does not mean that the staves were placed on the ark, as even when the ark was at rest the staves were never removed from its rings

BACKGROUND

4:6| **Taḥash:** The identity of the *taḥash* is uncertain. It is mentioned in the book of Ezekiel as an expensive material used for making shoes: "I clothed you in embroidery, and shod you with sealskin [*taḥash*], and I wrapped you with linen and covered you with silk" (Ezekiel 16:10). Some maintain that *taḥash* is the name of a color; purple according to Rabbi Yehuda in the Jerusalem Talmud (*Shabbat* 2:3). Alternatively, Onkelos and *Targum Yonatan* translate it simply as a colorful hide. Interestingly, researchers note the similarity between this name and *tah-si-a*, mentioned in the Nuzi Tablets, fourteenth century BCE, which means a yellow or pink hide.

Others hold that the *taḥash* is an animal, but there has never been any consensus as to which. The Talmud (*Shabbat* 28b) identifies the *taḥash* as an extinct unicorn. In light of the Arabic cognate, it may be the dugong, a porpoise that can be found in the Red Sea, and whose skin is sometimes used by the Bedouin in shoemaking. Some posit that the *taḥash* is a narwhal, a species of arctic whale. Narwhals travel in small groups and can grow to 6 m in length. The narwhal is mostly light yellow with dark spots,

sky-blue wool, and place upon it the bowls and the spoons, the supports, which were the pillars on the sides of the table, **and the covering tubes,** which were the thin tubes installed on the supports. In short, all the movable appurtenances of the table are placed upon the cloth. **And the perpetual bread shall remain upon it,** the table which is beneath the cloth of sky-blue wool. The bread may not be removed from the table during the journey.

8 **They shall spread upon them** another **cloth of scarlet wool, and they shall cover it** as well **with a covering of the hide of a taḥash, and shall place its staves,** with which the table for the showbread shall be carried.

9 **They shall take a cloth of sky-blue wool, and cover the candelabrum of the light, its lamps, its tongs, its fire-pans, and all its oil vessels with which they serve it.**

10 **They shall place it and all its vessels into a covering of the hide of a taḥash, and shall place it on a pole.** In contrast to the table for the showbread and the Ark of the Covenant, the candelabrum did not have staves inserted into rings. In order to carry it, the candelabrum must be placed inside a covering of a *taḥash* hide, into which a pole is inserted, and the pole is carried by two Levites.

11 **Upon the golden altar they shall spread a cloth of sky-blue wool, and cover it with a covering of the hide of a taḥash, and they shall place its staves.** They shall insert the staves with which the altar is carried into the rings of the altar.

12 **They shall take all the service vessels with which they serve in the Sanctuary, and they shall place them in a cloth of sky-blue wool, and cover them with a covering of the hide of a taḥash, and they shall place them** all on the pole.

13 The chapter now moves from discussing the vessels that were placed inside the Tent of Meeting to those vessels located outside the Tent. **They shall remove the ashes**[D] **from the altar, and spread a cloth of purple**[B] **wool over it.**

14 **They shall place upon it all its vessels with which they serve upon it: the fire-pans,** which are spoon-like utensils, **the forks,** for handling the flesh of offerings, **the shovels,** for sweeping the ashes, **and the basins,** for collecting and sprinkling the blood. This was done for **all the vessels of the altar; and they shall spread upon it a covering of the hide of a taḥash, and place its staves** for carrying the altar. Despite its size, the altar was not heavy, as it was hollow.

15 **Aaron and his sons shall conclude to cover the sacred, and all the sacred vessels, when the camp travels. And thereafter, the sons of Kehat shall come to bear.** Only after the priests have prepared and covered the vessels for the journey are the sons of Kehat permitted to carry them, so **that they shall not touch the sacred and die,** as direct contact with the sacred vessels is permitted to the priests alone. **These are the burden of the sons of Kehat in the Tent of Meeting.**

16 **The charge,** the area of responsibility,[21] **of Elazar son of Aaron the priest,** who, as the oldest of Aaron's remaining sons, has a special role, **is** the bearing of **the illuminating oil, the fragrant incense, the meal offering of the daily offering, and the anointing oil.** He did not necessarily bear these himself, but it was his job to ensure that they were carried.[22] As the prince of the princes of the Levites (3:32), he also had **the charge of the entire Tabernacle, and of all that is in it, in the sacred, and in its vessels.**

Maftir 17 **The Lord spoke to Moses and to Aaron, saying:**

18 **Do not excise,** or cause the death of **the tribe of the families**

BACKGROUND

and it is the only spotted cetacean. A twisted tooth, up to three meters long, grows out of one side of its mouth, and throughout history its horn has been mistaken for that of the unicorn. According to Rabbi Neḥemya (Jerusalem Talmud, *Shabbat* 2:3), the *taḥash* is the *galaktinin*, a small weasel-like creature (*Arukh*).

4:13 | Purple: This is a reddish-purple dye extracted from the spiny dye-murex, *Murex brandaris*, a type of sea snail. Early documents indicate that wool dyed with this substance was four times more expensive than other

dyed wool. In addition to its use together with the sky-blue dye in the construction of the Tabernacle, as mentioned frequently in the Bible, it also was used in knitting the covers of the Tabernacle's accoutrements and the vestments of the High Priest. The dye also appears in external sources dating from the fourteenth century BCE. In the Roman period, purple dye was used mainly by priests, kings, and ministers. Due to its importance and high price, its production was monitored, and free commerce with the dye was prohibited.

DISCUSSION

(Exodus 25:15). Perhaps the staves were generally left loose inside the rings, possibly so that they could be inserted into the sockets of the cover. Consequently, when the ark was carried, the staves had to be fixed firmly to the rings to prevent them from moving (see *Bekhor Shor*; Ramban; *Panim Yafot*; *Bekhor Shor*, Exodus 25:16; *Responsa of the Radbaz* 6:2190).

4:13 | They shall remove [*vedishnu*] the ashes: This verb is one of those that has conflicting meanings: It either means placing the ashes on the altar or removing the ashes (see Rashi and Ibn Ezra, Exodus 27:3).

תְּכֵלֶת וְנָתְנוּ עָלָיו אֶת־הַקְּעָרֹת וְאֶת־הַכַּפֹּת וְאֶת־הַמְּנַקִּיֹּת וְאֵת קְשׂוֹת הַנָּסֶךְ

ח וְלֶחֶם הַתָּמִיד עָלָיו יִהְיֶה: וּפָרְשׂוּ עֲלֵיהֶם בֶּגֶד תּוֹלַעַת שָׁנִי וְכִסּוּ אֹתוֹ בְּמִכְסֵה

ט עוֹר תַּחַשׁ וְשָׂמוּ אֶת־בַּדָּיו: וְלָקְחוּ ׀ בֶּגֶד תְּכֵלֶת וְכִסּוּ אֶת־מְנֹרַת הַמָּאוֹר וְאֶת־ נֵרֹתֶיהָ וְאֶת־מַלְקָחֶיהָ וְאֶת־מַחְתֹּתֶיהָ וְאֵת כָּל־כְּלֵי שַׁמְנָהּ אֲשֶׁר יְשָׁרְתוּ־לָהּ

יא בָּהֶם: וְנָתְנוּ אֹתָהּ וְאֶת־כָּל־כֵּלֶיהָ אֶל־מִכְסֵה עוֹר תַּחַשׁ וְנָתְנוּ עַל־הַמּוֹט: וְעַל ׀ מִזְבַּח הַזָּהָב יִפְרְשׂוּ בֶּגֶד תְּכֵלֶת וְכִסּוּ אֹתוֹ בְּמִכְסֵה עוֹר תַּחַשׁ וְשָׂמוּ אֶת־בַּדָּיו:

יב וְלָקְחוּ אֶת־כָּל־כְּלֵי הַשָּׁרֵת אֲשֶׁר יְשָׁרְתוּ־בָם בַּקֹּדֶשׁ וְנָתְנוּ אֶל־בֶּגֶד תְּכֵלֶת וְכִסּוּ אוֹתָם בְּמִכְסֵה עוֹר תַּחַשׁ וְנָתְנוּ עַל־הַמּוֹט:

יג וְדִשְּׁנוּ אֶת־הַמִּזְבֵּחַ וּפָרְשׂוּ עָלָיו

יד בֶּגֶד אַרְגָּמָן: וְנָתְנוּ עָלָיו אֶת־כָּל־כֵּלָיו אֲשֶׁר יְשָׁרְתוּ עָלָיו בָּהֶם אֶת־הַמַּחְתֹּת אֶת־הַמִּזְלָגֹת וְאֶת־הַיָּעִים וְאֶת־הַמִּזְרָקֹת כֹּל כְּלֵי הַמִּזְבֵּחַ וּפָרְשׂוּ עָלָיו כְּסוּי עוֹר

טו תַּחַשׁ וְשָׂמוּ בַדָּיו: וְכִלָּה אַהֲרֹן־וּבָנָיו לְכַסֹּת אֶת־הַקֹּדֶשׁ וְאֶת־כָּל־כְּלֵי הַקֹּדֶשׁ בִּנְסֹעַ הַמַּחֲנֶה וְאַחֲרֵי־כֵן יָבֹאוּ בְנֵי־קְהָת לָשֵׂאת וְלֹא־יִגְּעוּ אֶל־הַקֹּדֶשׁ וָמֵתוּ

טז אֵלֶּה מַשָּׂא בְנֵי־קְהָת בְּאֹהֶל מוֹעֵד: וּפְקֻדַּת אֶלְעָזָר ׀ בֶּן־אַהֲרֹן הַכֹּהֵן שֶׁמֶן הַמָּאוֹר וּקְטֹרֶת הַסַּמִּים וּמִנְחַת הַתָּמִיד וְשֶׁמֶן הַמִּשְׁחָה פְּקֻדַּת כָּל־הַמִּשְׁכָּן וְכָל־אֲשֶׁר־בּוֹ בְּקֹדֶשׁ וּבְכֵלָיו:

יז וַיְדַבֵּר יְהֹוָה אֶל־מֹשֶׁה וְאֶל־אַהֲרֹן לֵאמֹר: אַל־תַּכְרִיתוּ אֶת־שֵׁבֶט מִשְׁפְּחֹת ד מפטיר

רש"י

ז] **קְעָרֹת וְכַפֹּת וּקְשׂוֹת וּמְנַקִּיֹּת.** כְּבָר פֵּרַשְׁתִּים בִּמְלֶאכֶת הַמִּשְׁכָּן (שמות כה, כט): **הַנָּסֶךְ.** לְשׁוֹן מָסָךְ, כְּדִכְתִיב: "אֲשֶׁר יֻסַּךְ בָּהֵן" (שם):

טז] **מַלְקָחֶיהָ.** כְּמִין עֶצֶת שְׁמוֹשֵׁךְ בָּה אֶת הַפְּתִילָה לְכָל צַד שֶׁיִּרְצֶה: **מַחְתֹּתֶיהָ.** כְּמִין כַּף קְטַנָּה וְשׁוּלֶיהָ פְּשׁוּטִין וְלֹא סֻגַלְגַּלִּים וְאֵין לָהּ מְחִצָּה לְפָנֶיהָ מִצִּדֶּיהָ, וְחוֹתֶה בָּהּ אֶת דֶּשֶׁן הַנֵּרוֹת כְּשֶׁמְּטִיבָן: **נֵרֹתֶיהָ.** לוי"ש בְּלַעַז, שֶׁנּוֹתְנִים בָּהֶן הַשֶּׁמֶן וְהַפְּתִילוֹת:

י] **אֶל־מִכְסֵה עוֹר תָּחַשׁ.** כְּמִין מַרְטוּף:

יב] **אֶת־כָּל־כְּלֵי הַשָּׁרֵת אֲשֶׁר יְשָׁרְתוּ בָם בַּקֹּדֶשׁ.** בְּתוֹךְ

הַמִּשְׁכָּן שֶׁהוּא קֹדֶשׁ, וְהֵן כְּלֵי הַקְּטֹרֶת שֶׁמְּשָׁרְתִין בָּהֶם בַּמִּזְבֵּחַ הַפְּנִימִי:

יג] **וְדִשְּׁנוּ אֶת־הַמִּזְבֵּחַ.** מִזְבַּח הַנְּחֹשֶׁת: **וְדִשְּׁנוּ.** יִטְּלוּ אֶת הַדֶּשֶׁן מֵעָלָיו: **וּפָרְשׂוּ עָלָיו בֶּגֶד אַרְגָּמָן.** וְאֵשׁ שֶׁיָּרְדָה מִן הַשָּׁמַיִם רְבוּצָה תַּחַת הַבֶּגֶד כַּאֲרִי בִּשְׁעַת הַמַּסָּעוֹת, וְאֵינָהּ שׂוֹרַפְתּוֹ, שֶׁהָיוּ כּוֹפִין עָלֶיהָ פְּסַכְתֵּר שֶׁל נְחֹשֶׁת:

יד] **מַחְתֹּת.** שֶׁבָּהֶן חוֹתִים גֶּחָלִים לִתְרוּמַת הַדֶּשֶׁן. עֲשׂוּיָה כְּמִין מַחֲבַת שֶׁאֵין לָהּ אֶלָּא שֶׁלֹּשׁ מְחִצּוֹת, וּמִלְּפָנֶיהָ שׁוֹאֶבֶת אֶת הַגֶּחָלִים: **הַמִּזְלָגֹת.** מַזְלֵגוֹת. עֲגוֹרוֹת שֶׁל נְחֹשֶׁת שֶׁבָּהֶן מַכִּין בַּבְּשָׂרִים שֶׁעַל הַמִּזְבֵּחַ לְהָפְכָן כְּדֵי שֶׁיִּתְעַכְּלוּ יָפֶה וּמַהֵר: **יָעִים.** הֵם מַגְרֵפוֹת, וּבְלַעַז וודי"ל, וְהֵן שֶׁל נְחֹשֶׁת, וּבָהֶן מְכַבְּדִין אֶת הַדֶּשֶׁן מֵעַל הַמִּזְבֵּחַ:

טו] **לְכַסֹּת אֶת הַקֹּדֶשׁ.** הָאָרוֹן וְהַמִּזְבֵּחַ: **וְאֶת־כָּל־כְּלֵי הַקֹּדֶשׁ.** הַמְּנוֹרָה וּכְלֵי שָׁרֵת: **וָמֵתוּ.** שֶׁאִם יִגְּעוּ חַיָּבִין מִיתָה בִּידֵי שָׁמַיִם:

טז] **וּפְקֻדַּת אֶלְעָזָר.** שֶׁהוּא מְמֻנֶּה עֲלֵיהֶם לָשֵׂאת אוֹתָם, שֶׁמֶן וּקְטֹרֶת וְשֶׁמֶן הַמִּשְׁחָה וּמִנְחַת הַתָּמִיד, עָלָיו מֻטָּל לְצַוּוֹת וְלֵזָרֵז וּלְהַקְרִיב בְּעֵת חֲנִיָּתָם: **פְּקֻדַּת כָּל־הַמִּשְׁכָּן.** וְעוֹד הָיָה מְמֻנֶּה עַל מַשָּׂא בְּנֵי קְהָת, לְצַוּוֹת אִישׁ אִישׁ עַל עֲבֹדָתוֹ וְעַל מַשָּׂאוֹ, וְהוּא הַמִּשְׁכָּן וְכָל אֲשֶׁר בּוֹ, כָּל הַסְּדוּרִים לְמַעְלָה בַּפָּרָשָׁה זוֹ, אֲבָל מַשָּׂא בְּנֵי גֵרְשׁוֹן וּמְרָרִי, שֶׁאֵינָן מִקֹּדֶשׁ הַקֳּדָשִׁים, עַל פִּי אִיתָמָר הָיָה, כְּמוֹ שֶׁכָּתוּב בְּפָרָשַׁת "נָשֹׂא" (להלן ד, כח. לג):

יח] **אַל־תַּכְרִיתוּ.** אַל תְּגַרְמוּ לָהֶם שֶׁיָּמוּתוּ:

of the Kehatites from among the Levites, due to lack of appropriate caution.

19 **But this do for them, and they will live, and will not die, upon their approach to [*et*] the Holy of Holies.** Although "to" is usually signified by the Hebrew word *el*, a similar example where the word *et* means "to" can be found in I Samuel 9:18. **Aaron and his sons** alone **shall come, and assign them, the**

Levites, **each man to his work and to his burden.** The Levites shall do nothing of their own accord.[23] All the vessels shall be covered by the priests and be ready for the journey when the Kehatites enter the Holy of Holies.

20 **They shall not come to see while the sacred is covered,** when the priests cover the sacred vessels.[24] And the reason is **that** if they gaze upon the holy to satisfy their curiosity,[25] **they will die.**

Parashat
Naso

The Service of the Levites and Their Census

NUMBERS 4:21–49

This is the continuation of the section which presents the details of the division of labor in the carrying of the Tabernacle between the three patrilineal families of the tribe of Levi: Kehat, Gershon, and Merari. The previous passage dealt with the family of Kehat. The following passages deal with the families of Gershon and Merari and with the sums of their censuses.

21 **The Lord spoke to Moses saying:**
22 **Take the census of the sons of Gershon as well,** in addition to Kehat, **by their patrilineal house, by their families.**
23 **From thirty years old and above until fifty years old you shall count them,** and appoint them to their task: **Everyone enlisted to perform a duty, to perform work in the Tent of Meeting.**
24 **This is the work of the families of the Gershonites, to work** when the people encamp. The service which the Levites performed in the Tabernacle once it was erected is not detailed here, but they were probably responsible for ongoing maintenance jobs and to aid the priests in such tasks as the Levites later performed in the Temple, e.g., reciting the songs that accompanied the offerings, slaughtering, flaying, and cleaning the animals.[1] **And** they were also responsible **for bearing** the burdens, when the Tabernacle traveled with the people in the wilderness.
25 The Torah lists the items that the Gershonites were to carry: **They shall bear the sheet of the Tabernacle; and** also the curtains of **the Tent of Meeting,** made of goats' hair; and **its covering,** of rams' skins dyed red; **and the covering of the taḥash** that is upon it from above; **and the screen for the entrance of the Tent of Meeting;**

26 **and the hangings of the courtyard; and the screen for the entrance of the gate of the courtyard, that is near the Tabernacle, and near the altar, all around; and their cords,** for the hangings; **and all the instruments of their work; and everything that shall be fashioned for them, and they shall serve.**

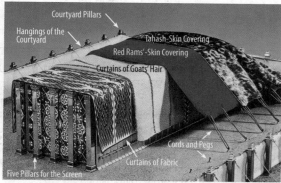

Tabernacle, its curtains, cords, and pegs, showing the different layers of the Tabernacle's coverings

יט הַקְּהָתִי מִתּוֹךְ הַלְוִיִּם: וְזֹאת עֲשׂוּ לָהֶם וְחָיוּ וְלֹא יָמֻתוּ בְּגִשְׁתָּם אֶת־קֹדֶשׁ
הַקֳּדָשִׁים אַהֲרֹן וּבָנָיו יָבֹאוּ וְשָׂמוּ אוֹתָם אִישׁ אִישׁ עַל־עֲבֹדָתוֹ וְאֶל־מַשָּׂאוֹ:
כ וְלֹא־יָבֹאוּ לִרְאוֹת כְּבַלַּע אֶת־הַקֹּדֶשׁ וָמֵתוּ:

רש"י

כ| וְלֹא יָבֹאוּ לִרְאוֹת כְּבַלַּע אֶת הַקֹּדֶשׁ. לְתוֹךְ נַרְתִּיק שֶׁלּוֹ, כְּמוֹ שֶׁפֵּרַשְׁתִּי לְמַעְלָה בַּפָּרָשָׁה זוֹ (פסוק ה), וּפָרְשׂוּ עָלָיו בֶּגֶד פְּלוֹנִי וְכִסּוּ אוֹתוֹ בְּמִכְסֵה פְּלוֹנִי, וּבִלּוּעַ שֶׁלּוֹ הוּא כִּסּוּיוֹ:

פרשת
נשא

כא
כב וַיְדַבֵּר יְהוָה אֶל־מֹשֶׁה לֵּאמֹר: נָשֹׂא אֶת־רֹאשׁ בְּנֵי גֵרְשׁוֹן גַּם־הֵם לְבֵית אֲבֹתָם
כג לְמִשְׁפְּחֹתָם: מִבֶּן שְׁלֹשִׁים שָׁנָה וָמַעְלָה עַד בֶּן־חֲמִשִּׁים שָׁנָה תִּפְקֹד אוֹתָם
כד כָּל־הַבָּא לִצְבֹא צָבָא לַעֲבֹד עֲבֹדָה בְּאֹהֶל מוֹעֵד: זֹאת עֲבֹדַת מִשְׁפְּחֹת
כה הַגֵּרְשֻׁנִּי לַעֲבֹד וּלְמַשָּׂא: וְנָשְׂאוּ אֶת־יְרִיעֹת הַמִּשְׁכָּן וְאֶת־אֹהֶל מוֹעֵד מִכְסֵהוּ
כו וּמִכְסֵה הַתַּחַשׁ אֲשֶׁר־עָלָיו מִלְמָעְלָה וְאֶת־מָסַךְ פֶּתַח אֹהֶל מוֹעֵד: וְאֵת קַלְעֵי
הֶחָצֵר וְאֶת־מָסַךְ ׀ פֶּתַח ׀ שַׁעַר הֶחָצֵר אֲשֶׁר עַל־הַמִּשְׁכָּן וְעַל־הַמִּזְבֵּחַ סָבִיב
וְאֵת מֵיתְרֵיהֶם וְאֶת־כָּל־כְּלֵי עֲבֹדָתָם וְאֵת כָּל־אֲשֶׁר יֵעָשֶׂה לָהֶם וְעָבָדוּ:

רש"י

כב| נָשֹׂא אֶת רֹאשׁ בְּנֵי גֵרְשׁוֹן גַּם הֵם. כְּמוֹ שֶׁצִּוִּיתִיךָ עַל בְּנֵי קְהָת, לִרְאוֹת כַּמָּה יֵשׁ שֶׁהִגִּיעוּ לִכְלַל עֲבוֹדָה:

כה| אֶת יְרִיעֹת הַמִּשְׁכָּן. עֶשֶׂר תַּחְתּוֹנוֹת: וְאֶת אֹהֶל מוֹעֵד. יְרִיעוֹת עִזִּים הָעֲשׂוּיוֹת לְאֹהֶל עָלָיו: מִכְסֵהוּ. עוֹרוֹת אֵילִים מְאָדָּמִים: מָסַךְ פֶּתַח. וִילוֹן הַמִּזְרָחִי:

כו| אֲשֶׁר עַל הַמִּשְׁכָּן. כְּלוֹמַר: הַקְּלָעִים וְהַמָּסָךְ שֶׁל חָצֵר, הַסּוֹכְכִים וּמְגִנִּים עַל הַמִּשְׁכָּן וְעַל מִזְבַּח הַנְּחֹשֶׁת סָבִיב: וְאֵת כָּל אֲשֶׁר יֵעָשֶׂה לָהֶם. כְּתַרְגּוּמוֹ: "וְיָת כָּל דְּיִתְמְסַר לְהוֹן", לִבְנֵי גֵּרְשׁוֹן:

27 **According to the directive of Aaron and his sons shall be all the work of the sons of the Gershonites, for all their burden, and for all their work; you shall assign them all of their burden as a commission,** in an organized fashion.[2]

28 **This is the work of the families of the sons of the Gershonites in the Tent of Meeting; and their commission shall be in the hand of Itamar son of Aaron the priest,** under his command. Itamar was the second surviving son of Aaron.

29 **The sons of Merari, by their families, by their patrilineal house, you shall count them.**[D]

30 **From thirty years old and above until fifty years old you shall count them, everyone that enlists for the duty, to perform the work of the Tent of Meeting.**

31 Whereas the Gershonites' burden consisted chiefly of those parts of the Tabernacle made of woven fabrics or skins, the sons of Merari must bear the heavier objects: **This is the commission of their burden for all their work in the Tent of Meeting: the beams of the Tabernacle, its bars, its pillars, and its sockets;**

32 **and the pillars of the courtyard all around, their sockets, their pegs, and their cords, with all their instruments, and for all their work. By names you shall appoint the instruments of the commission of their burden.** For reasons of efficiency, and so as not to delay the people's departure on a journey due to the work of dismantling the Tabernacle, each member of the family of Merari must be familiar with his specific responsibility.

33 **This is the work of the families of the sons of Merari, for all their work in the Tent of Meeting,** which is also a responsibility placed **in the hand of Itamar son of Aaron the priest.**

34 After stating God's command, the Torah relates its fulfillment in practice: **Moses, and Aaron, and the princes of the congregation counted the sons of the Kehatites by their families, and by their patrilineal house.**

35 The Kehatites were counted **from thirty years old and above until fifty years old, everyone who enlisted for duty, for work in the Tent of Meeting.**

36 **Those counted, by their families, were two thousand seven hundred and fifty.**

37 **These are the counted of the families of the Kehatites, all who worked in the Tent of Meeting, whom Moses and Aaron counted according to the directive of the Lord at the hand of Moses.**

Second aliya

38 **The counted of the sons of Gershon, by their families, and by their patrilineal house,**

39 **from thirty years old and above until fifty years old, everyone who enlisted for duty, for work in the Tent of Meeting.**

40 **Those counted, by their families, by their patrilineal house, were two thousand six hundred and thirty.**

41 **These are the counted of the families of the sons of Gershon, all who worked in the Tent of Meeting, whom Moses and Aaron counted according to the directive of the Lord.**

42 **The counted of the families of the sons of Merari, by their families, by their patrilineal house,**

43 **from thirty years old and above until fifty years old, everyone who enlisted for duty, for work in the Tent of Meeting,**

44 **those counted by their families were three thousand two hundred.** The number of adult males in the family of Merari was significantly larger than in the families of Kehat and Gershon. This might be the reason why they were chosen to carry the heavier burdens.[3]

45 **These are the counted of the families of the sons of Merari, whom Moses and Aaron counted according to the directive of the Lord at the hand of Moses.**

DISCUSSION

4:29 | **You shall count them:** With regard to the counting of the sons of Merari, the verse uses this simple expression rather than the term "take the census," which is used in the cases of Kehat and Gershon (verses 2, 22). This is probably because the duties of Merari were more straightforward, and it is perhaps for this reason that in contrast to the passages with regard to Kehat and Gershon, the passage with regard to the census of Merari is not introduced with a separate address of "The Lord spoke to Moses saying" (see Rabbi Ḥayyim Paltiel; *Or HaḤayyim*).

כז עַל־פִּי אַהֲרֹן וּבָנָיו תִּהְיֶה כָּל־עֲבֹדַת בְּנֵי הַגֵּרְשֻׁנִּי לְכָל־מַשָּׂאָם וּלְכֹל עֲבֹדָתָם
כח וּפְקַדְתֶּם עֲלֵהֶם בְּמִשְׁמֶרֶת אֵת כָּל־מַשָּׂאָם: זֹאת עֲבֹדַת מִשְׁפְּחֹת בְּנֵי הַגֵּרְשֻׁנִּי
כט בְּאֹהֶל מוֹעֵד וּמִשְׁמַרְתָּם בְּיַד אִיתָמָר בֶּן־אַהֲרֹן הַכֹּהֵן: בְּנֵי
ל מְרָרִי לְמִשְׁפְּחֹתָם לְבֵית־אֲבֹתָם תִּפְקֹד אֹתָם: מִבֶּן שְׁלֹשִׁים שָׁנָה וָמַעְלָה וְעַד
לא בֶּן־חֲמִשִּׁים שָׁנָה תִּפְקְדֵם כָּל־הַבָּא לַצָּבָא לַעֲבֹד אֶת־עֲבֹדַת אֹהֶל מוֹעֵד: וְזֹאת
מִשְׁמֶרֶת מַשָּׂאָם לְכָל־עֲבֹדָתָם בְּאֹהֶל מוֹעֵד קַרְשֵׁי הַמִּשְׁכָּן וּבְרִיחָיו וְעַמּוּדָיו
לב וַאֲדָנָיו: וְעַמּוּדֵי הֶחָצֵר סָבִיב וְאַדְנֵיהֶם וִיתֵדֹתָם וּמֵיתְרֵיהֶם לְכָל־כְּלֵיהֶם וּלְכֹל
לג עֲבֹדָתָם וּבְשֵׁמֹת תִּפְקְדוּ אֶת־כְּלֵי מִשְׁמֶרֶת מַשָּׂאָם: זֹאת עֲבֹדַת מִשְׁפְּחֹת
לד בְּנֵי מְרָרִי לְכָל־עֲבֹדָתָם בְּאֹהֶל מוֹעֵד בְּיַד אִיתָמָר בֶּן־אַהֲרֹן הַכֹּהֵן: וַיִּפְקֹד
לה מֹשֶׁה וְאַהֲרֹן וּנְשִׂיאֵי הָעֵדָה אֶת־בְּנֵי הַקְּהָתִי לְמִשְׁפְּחֹתָם וּלְבֵית אֲבֹתָם: מִבֶּן
שְׁלֹשִׁים שָׁנָה וָמַעְלָה וְעַד בֶּן־חֲמִשִּׁים שָׁנָה כָּל־הַבָּא לַצָּבָא לַעֲבֹדָה בְּאֹהֶל
לו
לז מוֹעֵד: וַיִּהְיוּ פְקֻדֵיהֶם לְמִשְׁפְּחֹתָם אַלְפַּיִם שְׁבַע מֵאוֹת וַחֲמִשִּׁים: אֵלֶּה פְקוּדֵי
מִשְׁפְּחֹת הַקְּהָתִי כָּל־הָעֹבֵד בְּאֹהֶל מוֹעֵד אֲשֶׁר פָּקַד מֹשֶׁה וְאַהֲרֹן עַל־פִּי
לח יְהוָה בְּיַד־מֹשֶׁה: וּפְקוּדֵי בְּנֵי גֵרְשׁוֹן לְמִשְׁפְּחוֹתָם וּלְבֵית שני
לט אֲבֹתָם: מִבֶּן שְׁלֹשִׁים שָׁנָה וָמַעְלָה וְעַד בֶּן־חֲמִשִּׁים שָׁנָה כָּל־הַבָּא לַצָּבָא
מ לַעֲבֹדָה בְּאֹהֶל מוֹעֵד: וַיִּהְיוּ פְּקֻדֵיהֶם לְמִשְׁפְּחֹתָם לְבֵית אֲבֹתָם אַלְפַּיִם וְשֵׁשׁ
מא מֵאוֹת וּשְׁלֹשִׁים: אֵלֶּה פְקוּדֵי מִשְׁפְּחֹת בְּנֵי גֵרְשׁוֹן כָּל־הָעֹבֵד בְּאֹהֶל מוֹעֵד
מב אֲשֶׁר פָּקַד מֹשֶׁה וְאַהֲרֹן עַל־פִּי יְהוָה: וּפְקוּדֵי מִשְׁפְּחֹת בְּנֵי מְרָרִי לְמִשְׁפְּחֹתָם
מג לְבֵית אֲבֹתָם: מִבֶּן שְׁלֹשִׁים שָׁנָה וָמַעְלָה וְעַד בֶּן־חֲמִשִּׁים שָׁנָה כָּל־הַבָּא לַצָּבָא
מד לַעֲבֹדָה בְּאֹהֶל מוֹעֵד: וַיִּהְיוּ פְקֻדֵיהֶם לְמִשְׁפְּחֹתָם שְׁלֹשֶׁת אֲלָפִים וּמָאתָיִם:
מה אֵלֶּה פְּקוּדֵי מִשְׁפְּחֹת בְּנֵי מְרָרִי אֲשֶׁר פָּקַד מֹשֶׁה וְאַהֲרֹן עַל־פִּי יְהוָה בְּיַד־מֹשֶׁה:

רש״י

כז] עַל פִּי אַהֲרֹן וּבָנָיו. וְאֵי זֶה מֵהַבָּנִים מְמֻנֶּה עֲלֵיהֶם? "בְּיַד אִיתָמָר בֶּן אַהֲרֹן הַכֹּהֵן" (לְהַלָּן פָּסוּק כח).

לב] וִיתֵדֹתָם וּמֵיתְרֵיהֶם. שֶׁל עַמּוּדִים, שֶׁהֲרֵי יְתֵדוֹת וּמֵיתָרִים שֶׁל קְלָעִים בְּמַשָּׂא בְּנֵי גֵרְשׁוֹן הָיוּ, יְתֵדוֹת וּמֵיתָרִים הָיוּ לַיְרִיעוֹת וְלַקְּלָעִים מִלְּמַטָּה שֶׁלֹּא תַּגְבִּיהֵם הָרוּחַ, וִיתֵדוֹת וּמֵיתָרִים הָיוּ לָעַמּוּדִים סָבִיב לִתְלוֹת בָּהֶם הַקְּלָעִים בִּשְׂפָתָם הָעֶלְיוֹנָה בִּכְלוֹנָסוֹת וְקוּנְטְיסִין, כְּמוֹ שֶׁשְּׁנוּיָה בִּמְלֶאכֶת הַמִּשְׁכָּן (ברייתא דמלאכת המשכן פרק ה).

46 The sum total of **all the counted, whom Moses and Aaron and the princes of Israel counted of the Levites, by their families, and by their patrilineal house,** was as follows:

47 They **were** counted **from thirty years old and above until fifty years old, everyone who came to perform the service of work and the service of bearing in the Tent of Meeting.**

48 **Those counted were eight thousand five hundred and eighty.**

49 **According to the directive of the Lord he counted them, at the hand of Moses,** under his supervision,[4] **each man to his work and to his burden. And** these were the results of **his count** that **was** performed **as the Lord commanded Moses.**

Sending the Ritually Impure Outside the Camp

NUMBERS 5:1–4

The previous sections dealt with the organization of the camp, the arrangement of the banners and the division of the tribes' encampments as military units. The Tabernacle was in the center, surrounded on three sides by the camp of the Levites and on the fourth side by Moses and Aaron, while the Israelite's camp formed the outer ring. The arrangement of the camp is followed by a commandment that pertains to the sanctity of the camps: In certain cases of ritual impurity, the impure individuals are prohibited from entering the camps which are arranged around God's Tabernacle.

5 1 **The Lord spoke to Moses, saying:**

Third aliya 2 **Command the children of Israel, and they shall send out from the camp every leper,** one afflicted with *tzara'at,* commonly translated as leprosy,[5] **and anyone with a discharge.** This includes a man who emits a gonorrhea-like discharge from the member, and a woman who emits a discharge of blood from the uterus.[6] **And** you shall also send from the camp **anyone**

impure by means of a corpse. The details of this type of impurity are discussed elsewhere (19:11–22).

3 **Male and female,** adults and minors **alike, you shall send out, outside the camp you shall send them;**[D] **and they shall not render impure their camp, in which I dwell in their midst.**

4 **The children of Israel did so, and sent them outside the camp; as the Lord spoke to Moses, so the children of Israel did.**

Payments and Gifts Due to the Priests

NUMBERS 5:5–10

The following brief passage completes the discussion of certain laws that were already mentioned in Leviticus. After detailing the order of the camp according to the tribal banners and the lineage of the Jewish people according to their families, this passage deals with those who joined the Jewish people but were not members of the twelve tribes, as stated in Exodus: "And a mixed multitude came up with them" (12:38). These converts often did not have any relatives in the camp. If someone unlawfully took money from a convert and he died leaving behind no heirs, the thief is unable to return the stolen property to its rightful owner. He must therefore give it to a priest, who is God's representative. Besides returning the principal, the thief must pay an additional fine and bring an atonement offering. Both this matter and the matter discussed in the subsequent section are somewhat related to the purity of the camp previously discussed. While the previous sections dealt with maintaining the ritual purity of the camp, these sections deal with the moral purity of the camp.

5 **The Lord spoke to Moses, saying:**

6 **Speak to the children of Israel: A man or woman, when they perform any sin of a person, committing a trespass,**[D] betraying the trust of another through theft, stealing, or cheating, he

thereby also sins **against the Lord.** Aside from the fact that the transgressor betrays a person's trust, he also does not take into consideration the fact that God is watching and is aware of his deed. **And** therefore, **that person is guilty.**

DISCUSSION

Families of the Levites, Their Numbers and Their Tasks

	Gershon	Kehat	Merari
Items under their responsibility	The curtains, screens, and hangings	The sacred vessels	The beams, pillars, and sockets
Families	Livni, Shimi	Amram, Yitzhar, Hevron, Uziel	Mahli, Mushi
Numbers, from one month old	7500	8600	6200
Numbers, between thirty and fifty years of age	2630 (roughly 35% of all the Levites)	2750 (less than one-third of all the Levites)	3200 (more than half of the Levites)
Place of encampment	West	South	North
Prince of their house	Elyasaf son of Lael	Elitzafan son of Uziel Elazar son of Aaron, the prince of the princes of the Levites	Tzuriel son of Avihayil

מו כָּל־הַפְּקֻדִ֡ים אֲשֶׁר֩ פָּקַ֨ד מֹשֶׁ֤ה וְאַהֲרֹן֙ וּנְשִׂיאֵ֣י יִשְׂרָאֵ֔ל אֶת־הַלְוִיִּ֖ם לְמִשְׁפְּחֹתָ֑ם

מז וּלְבֵ֖ית אֲבֹתָ֑ם מִבֶּן֩ שְׁלֹשִׁ֨ים שָׁנָ֤ה וָמַ֙עְלָה֙ וְעַ֛ד בֶּן־חֲמִשִּׁ֥ים שָׁנָ֖ה כָּל־הַבָּ֣א לַעֲבֹ֗ד

מח עֲבֹדַ֤ת עֲבֹדָה֙ וַעֲבֹדַ֣ת מַשָּׂ֔א בְּאֹ֖הֶל מוֹעֵֽד׃ וַיִּהְי֣וּ פְקֻדֵיהֶ֔ם שְׁמֹנַ֥ת אֲלָפִ֖ים וַחֲמֵ֥שׁ

מאוֹת וּשְׁמֹנִ֑ים׃ עַל־פִּ֨י יְהוָ֜ה פָּקַ֤ד אוֹתָם֙ בְּיַד־מֹשֶׁ֔ה אִ֥ישׁ אִ֖ישׁ עַל־עֲבֹדָת֣וֹ וְעַל־

מט מַשָּׂא֑וֹ וּפְקֻדָ֕יו אֲשֶׁר־צִוָּ֥ה יְהוָ֖ה אֶת־מֹשֶֽׁה׃

ב וַיְדַבֵּ֥ר יְהוָ֖ה אֶל־מֹשֶׁ֥ה לֵּאמֹֽר׃ צַ֞ו אֶת־בְּנֵ֣י יִשְׂרָאֵ֗ל וִֽישַׁלְּחוּ֙ מִן־הַֽמַּחֲנֶ֔ה כָּל־צָר֖וּעַ שלישי

ג וְכָל־זָ֑ב וְכֹ֖ל טָמֵ֣א לָנָ֑פֶשׁ׃ מִזָּכָ֤ר עַד־נְקֵבָה֙ תְּשַׁלֵּ֔חוּ אֶל־מִח֥וּץ לַֽמַּחֲנֶ֖ה תְּשַׁלְּח֑וּם

ד וְלֹ֤א יְטַמְּאוּ֙ אֶת־מַ֣חֲנֵיהֶ֔ם אֲשֶׁ֥ר אֲנִ֖י שֹׁכֵ֥ן בְּתוֹכָֽם׃ וַיַּֽעֲשׂוּ־כֵן֙ בְּנֵ֣י יִשְׂרָאֵ֔ל וַיְשַׁלְּח֣וּ

אוֹתָ֔ם אֶל־מִח֖וּץ לַֽמַּחֲנֶ֑ה כַּאֲשֶׁ֨ר דִּבֶּ֤ר יְהוָה֙ אֶל־מֹשֶׁ֔ה כֵּ֥ן עָשׂ֖וּ בְּנֵ֥י יִשְׂרָאֵֽל׃

ה וַיְדַבֵּ֥ר יְהוָ֖ה אֶל־מֹשֶׁ֥ה לֵּאמֹֽר׃ דַּבֵּר֙ אֶל־בְּנֵ֣י יִשְׂרָאֵ֔ל אִ֣ישׁ אֽוֹ־אִשָּׁ֗ה כִּ֤י יַעֲשׂוּ֙ מִכָּל־

ו חַטֹּ֣את הָֽאָדָ֔ם לִמְעֹ֥ל מַ֖עַל בַּיהוָ֑ה וְאָֽשְׁמָ֖ה הַנֶּ֥פֶשׁ הַהִֽוא׃ וְהִתְוַדּ֗וּ אֶת־חַטָּאתָם֮

ז אֲשֶׁ֣ר עָשׂוּ֒ וְהֵשִׁ֤יב אֶת־אֲשָׁמוֹ֙ בְּרֹאשׁ֔וֹ וַחֲמִישִׁת֖וֹ יֹסֵ֣ף עָלָ֑יו וְנָתַ֕ן לַאֲשֶׁ֖ר אָשַׁ֥ם לֽוֹ׃

רש"י

מו **עֲבֹדַת עֲבֹדָה.** הוּא הַשִּׁיר בִּמְצִלְתַּיִם וְכִנּוֹרוֹת, שֶׁהִיא עֲבוֹדָה לַעֲבוֹדָה אַחֶרֶת: **וַעֲבֹדַת מַשָּׂא.** כְּמַשְׁמָעוֹ:

מט **וּפְקֻדָיו אֲשֶׁר צִוָּה ה' אֶת מֹשֶׁה.** וְאוֹתָן הַפְּקוּדִים הָיוּ בְּמַעְלָה מִבֶּן שְׁלֹשִׁים שָׁנָה וְעַד בֶּן חֲמִשִּׁים:

פרק ה

ב **צַו אֶת בְּנֵי יִשְׂרָאֵל וְגו'.** פָּרָשָׁה זוֹ נֶאֶמְרָה בַּיּוֹם שֶׁהוּקַם

הַמִּשְׁכָּן, וּשְׁמוֹנֶה פָּרָשִׁיּוֹת נֶאֶמְרוּ בּוֹ בַּיּוֹם, כִּדְאִיתָא בְּמַסֶּכֶת גִּטִּין בְּפֶרֶק הַנִּזָּקִין (דף ס ע"א): **וִישַׁלְּחוּ מִן הַמַּחֲנֶה.** שָׁלֹשׁ מַחֲנוֹת הָיוּ שָׁם בִּשְׁעַת חֲנִיָּתָן: תּוֹךְ הַקְּלָעִים הִיא מַחֲנֵה שְׁכִינָה, חֲנִיַּת הַלְוִיִּם סָבִיב כְּמוֹ שֶׁמְּפֹרָשׁ בְּפָרָשַׁת בְּמִדְבַּר סִינַי (לעיל א, נ) הִיא מַחֲנֵה לְוִיָּה, וּמִשָּׁם וְעַד סוֹף מַחֲנֵה הַדְּגָלִים לְכָל אַרְבַּע הָרוּחוֹת הִיא מַחֲנֵה יִשְׂרָאֵל. הַצָּרוּעַ נִשְׁתַּלַּח חוּץ לְכֻלָּם, הַזָּב מֻתָּר בְּמַחֲנֵה יִשְׂרָאֵל וּמְשֻׁלָּח מִן הַשְּׁתַּיִם, וְטָמֵא לָנֶפֶשׁ מֻתָּר אַף בְּשֶׁל לֵוִיָּה וְאֵינוֹ

מִשְׁתַּלֵּחַ אֶלָּא מִשֶּׁל שְׁכִינָה. וְכָל זֶה דָּרְשׁוּ רַבּוֹתֵינוּ מִן הַמִּקְרָאוֹת בְּמַסֶּכֶת פְּסָחִים (דף סז ע"א): **טָמֵא לָנָפֶשׁ.** לְטַמֵּא נַפְשׁוֹ דְּאָדָם, כְּלוֹמַר אֲנִי שֶׁהוּא אָדָם בִּלְשׁוֹן חֲכָמִים, וְהַרְבֵּה יֵשׁ בִּבְרֵאשִׁית רַבָּה: "אַדְרִיָּנוּס שְׁחִיק טְמַיָּא", שְׁחִיק עֲצָמוֹת:

ז **לִמְעֹל מַעַל בָּהּ.** הֲרֵי חָזַר וְכָתַב כָּאן פָּרָשַׁת גֹּזֵל וְנִשְׁבָּע עַל שֶׁקֶר, הִיא הָאֲמוּרָה בְּפָרָשַׁת וַיִּקְרָא: "וּמָעֲלָה מַעַל

---

7 **They shall confess their sin that they had committed; and he shall** first **make restitution in its principal,** the sum stolen.[7] **And he shall add its one-fifth to it** in order to atone for his sin, **and he shall give it to the one to whom he is guilty,** the person from whom he took the money.

DISCUSSION

5:3 | Outside the camp you shall send them: The Sages derive from the complex wording here, and through a comparison with the Torah's statements elsewhere, that the impure individuals mentioned here were not all distanced from the camp to the same degree. Only the leper was required to remain outside the Israelite camp, the outermost camp where most of the people dwelt (see Leviticus 13:46). Those individuals who experienced a discharge could remain in the Israelite camp. However, they could not enter the camp of the Divine Presence, the innermost camp consisting of the Tabernacle and its courtyard, nor the Levites' camp, the camp of the Tabernacle's guards and ministers which surrounded the Tabernacle. Individuals who were impure with impurity imparted by a corpse were only required to remain outside the camp of the Divine Presence (see Rashi; Bekhor Shor; Pesahim 67a–68a).

5:6 | A trespass: The verse does not explain the form of trespass involved here. Nevertheless, it may be inferred from the phrase "any sin of a person" that the verse is not referring to making personal use of consecrated items, although this is referred to elsewhere as a trespass (see Leviticus 5:15). Rather, the verse is referring to the misappropriation of money or property belonging to another person (see Leviticus 5:21).

8 In a case where the transgressor seeks to make restitution only after the victim died, he must return the misappropriated property to the victim's heirs. **But if the man** from whom the property was stolen **has no redeeemer**[D] **to make restitution to him, the restitution is returned to the Lord,** and is given **to the priest** as one of the gifts of the priesthood in order to atone for the sinner's transgression. The restitution is given to the priests **besides the ram of atonement,** which is a guilt offering also consumed by the priests,[8] **with which he will further atone for it.**

9 **Every gift of all the sacred items of the children of Israel that they shall bring to the priest, shall be his,** the priest's.

This includes all of the portions separated for the priests from various types of produce, as well as all of the different gifts which are given to the priests, as detailed in various places in the Torah.[9]

10 The verse states another law concerning the consecrated items and the sacred portion separated from the produce and given to the priests: **A man's sacred items shall be his,** the priest's.[10] The sacred items become the priest's property, and the former owners retain no rights in them. Nevertheless, the owner has the right to determine beforehand which priest will receive the portion separated from the produce, or which of the priestly watches in the Temple will receive the consecrated items.[11] **Anything that a man gives the priest, shall be his,** the priest's.

The Woman Suspected of Unfaithfulness

NUMBERS 5:11–31

The following passage deals with the case of a married woman who knowingly secluded herself with a man other than her husband, and her husband suspects that she has been unfaithful to him. The Torah prescribes a detailed ritual, the purpose of which is to resolve the uncertainty by means of a miraculous intervention. This ritual is exceptional, as in the case of no other commandment is the outcome dependent upon divine intervention.

Fourth **11** **The Lord spoke to Moses, saying:**

aliya **12** **Speak to the children of Israel, and say to them: If any man's wife shall go astray and commit a trespass** of betrayal **against him,**[D] the following ritual must be performed.

13 **And** the betrayal committed is that **a man lay with her sexually. And it was hidden from the eyes of her husband, and she was secluded** with the man **and she was defiled** by engaging in intercourse with him. **And** yet **there is no witness** who can testify **against her, and she was not coerced.**

14 In the absence of both witnesses **and** evidence, there are two possibilities: Either **a spirit of jealousy overcame him,** the

husband, **and he was jealous with regard to his wife,**[D] and she was indeed **defiled,** and therefore he was rightfully jealous, **or a spirit of jealousy overcame him, and he was jealous with regard to his wife, and she was not defiled,** and his jealousy was unjustified. It is possible that the husband's suspicion merely stems from paranoia. Conversely, his allegation might be accurate.

15 **The man shall bring his wife to the priest. And he shall bring her offering for her, one-tenth of an ephah,** which is 2–4 L, **of barley flour.**[D] **He shall not pour oil upon it, and he shall not place frankincense upon it, for it is a meal offering**

DISCUSSION

5:8 | But if the man has no redeemer: Since the Jewish people are all descendants of the twelve tribes, every individual by definition has a redeemer, even if he is a very distant relative. Only a convert who dies childless has no redeemer whatsoever, and it is to this case that the verse refers here (Rashi; *Sifrei* 4).

The Sages explain that this passage is dealing with the same case as described in the parallel passage in Leviticus (5:20–26): The person who misappropriates the money denied doing so and swore falsely that he does not owe the money to the victim. When he confesses his sin, he must make restitution by repaying the principal together with an additional fine of one-fifth of the total. In addition to paying the fine as a form of punishment, he must bring a guilt offering to the priest to atone for his sin (see *Sifrei*; *Bava Kamma* 109a).

5:12 | And commit a trespass against him: A previous passage also made reference to a trespass that was committed (5:6). There, the trespass involved the misappropriation of property by force or by deceit. Similarly, the trespass referred to in this verse undermines the trust between people. Both trespasses are considered a sin against one's fellow man as well as a transgression against God.

5:14 | And a spirit of jealousy overcame him and he was jealous with regard to his wife: If a husband holds suspicions that his wife is unfaithful to him, his suspicions can be grounds for divorce. This passage deals with a specific case of uncertainty.

The term jealousy has two different connotations in Hebrew: In this first sense, one might be jealous of something which another person

possesses, e.g., wealth, wisdom, or greatness; but one might also be jealous for the sake of another. In this second sense, jealousy is a powerful expression of concern and love for another, demanding their whole, absolute, and exclusive commitment, and not tolerating the intrusion of anyone else. In a similar sense God is described as "a zealous God," as He demands exclusive commitment, leaving no place for other gods (e.g., Exodus 20:5; see also Song of Songs 8:6).

Since the husband is full of jealous love for his wife, he feels torn and is unwilling to resolve the situation by simply divorcing her. The complex and emotionally charged ordeal described below is intended not only to shed light on the woman's status, but also to resolve the husband's uncertainty and to determine the couple's future.

ח וְאִם־אֵין לָאִישׁ גֹּאֵל לְהָשִׁיב הָאָשָׁם אֵלָיו הָאָשָׁם הַמּוּשָׁב לַיהוה לַכֹּהֵן מִלְּבַד
ט אֵיל הַכִּפֻּרִים אֲשֶׁר יְכַפֶּר־בּוֹ עָלָיו׃ וְכָל־תְּרוּמָה לְכָל־קָדְשֵׁי בְנֵי־יִשְׂרָאֵל אֲשֶׁר־
י יַקְרִיבוּ לַכֹּהֵן לוֹ יִהְיֶה׃ וְאִישׁ אֶת־קֳדָשָׁיו לוֹ יִהְיוּ אִישׁ אֲשֶׁר־יִתֵּן לַכֹּהֵן לוֹ יִהְיֶה׃
יא יב וַיְדַבֵּר יהוה אֶל־מֹשֶׁה לֵּאמֹר׃ דַּבֵּר אֶל־בְּנֵי יִשְׂרָאֵל וְאָמַרְתָּ אֲלֵהֶם אִישׁ אִישׁ ה רביעי
יג כִּי־תִשְׂטֶה אִשְׁתּוֹ וּמָעֲלָה בוֹ מָעַל׃ וְשָׁכַב אִישׁ אֹתָהּ שִׁכְבַת־זֶרַע וְנֶעְלַם מֵעֵינֵי
יד אִישָׁהּ וְנִסְתְּרָה וְהִיא נִטְמָאָה וְעֵד אֵין בָּהּ וְהִוא לֹא נִתְפָּשָׂה׃ וְעָבַר עָלָיו רוּחַ־
קִנְאָה וְקִנֵּא אֶת־אִשְׁתּוֹ וְהִוא נִטְמָאָה אוֹ־עָבַר עָלָיו רוּחַ־קִנְאָה וְקִנֵּא אֶת־אִשְׁתּוֹ
טו וְהִיא לֹא נִטְמָאָה׃ וְהֵבִיא הָאִישׁ אֶת־אִשְׁתּוֹ אֶל־הַכֹּהֵן וְהֵבִיא אֶת־קָרְבָּנָהּ עָלֶיהָ
עֲשִׂירִת הָאֵיפָה קֶמַח שְׂעֹרִים לֹא־יִצֹק עָלָיו שֶׁמֶן וְלֹא־יִתֵּן עָלָיו לְבֹנָה כִּי־מִנְחַת

רש״י

בה׳ וכחש בעמיתו״ וגו׳ (ויקרא ה, כא); ונשנית כאן בשביל שני דברים שנתחדשו בה: האחד – שכתב ״והתודו״ (להלן פסוק ז), למד שאינו חייב חומש ואשם על פי עדים עד שיודה בדבר; והשני – שפרש על גזל הגר שהוא נתן לכהנים:

ז| את אשמו בראשו. הוא הקרן שנשבע עליו: לאשר אשם לו. למי שנתחייב לו:

ח| ואם אין לאיש גאל. שמת התובע שהשביעו ואין לו יורשים: להשיב האשם אליו. כשנמלך זה להתודות על עונו. ואמרו רבותינו: וכי יש לך אדם בישראל שאין לו גואלים, או בן או בת או אח או שאר בשר הקרוב ממשפחת אביו למעלה עד יעקב? אלא זה הגר שמת ואין לו יורשים: האשם המושב. זה הקרן והחומש: לה׳ לכהן. קנאו השם ונתנו לכהן שבאותו משמר: מלבד איל הכפרים. האמור בויקרא (ה, כה) שהוא צריך להביא:

ט| וכל תרומה וגו׳. אמר רבי ישמעאל, וכי תרומה מקריבין לכהן? והלא הוא המחזר אחריה לבית הגרנות, ומה תלמוד לומר: ״אשר יקריבו לכהן״? אלו הבכורים, שנאמר בהם: ״תביא בית ה׳ אלהיך״ (שמות כג, יט), ואיני יודע מה יעשה בהם, תלמוד לומר: ״לכהן לו יהיה״, בא הכתוב ולמד על הבכורים שיהיו נתנין לכהן:

י| ואיש את קדשיו לו יהיו. לפי שנאמרו מתנות כהנה ולויה, יכול יבואו ויטלום בזרוע? תלמוד לומר: ״ואיש את קדשיו לו יהיו״, מגיד שטובת הנאתן לבעלים. ועוד מדרשים הרבה דרשו בו בספרי (ו). ומדרש אגדה: ״ואיש את קדשיו לו יהיו״, מי שמעכב מעשרותיו ואינו נותנן, לו יהיו המעשרות, סוף שאין שדהו עושה אלא אחד מעשרה שהיתה למודה לעשות. ״איש אשר יתן לכהן״ מתנות הראויות לו, ״לו יהיה״ ממון הרבה:

יב| איש איש כי תשטה אשתו. מה כתוב למעלה מן הענין? ״ואיש את קדשיו לו יהיו״ (לעיל פסוק י), אם אתה מעכב מתנות הכהן, חייך שתצטרך לבא אצלו להביא לו את הסוטה: כי תשטה. תט מדרכי צניעות ותחשד בעיניו, כמו: ״שטה מעליו ועבר״ (משלי ד, טו), ״אל ישט אל דרכיה לבך״ (שם ז, כה): ומעלה בו מעל. ומהו המעל? ״ושכב איש אתה״:

יג| ונעלם מעיני אישה. הא אם היה רואה ומעמעם, אין המים בודקין אותה: ונסתרה. שעור שתהא לטמאת ביאה: ועד אין בה. הא אם יש בה אפילו עד אחד שאמר ׳נטמאת׳, לא היתה שותה: ועד אין בה. בטמאה, אבל יש עדים לסתירה: נתפשה. נאנסה, כמו: ״ותפשה ושכב עמה״ (דברים כב, כח):

יד| ועבר עליו. קדם לסתירה: רוח קנאה וקנא. פרשו רבותינו לשון התראה, שמתרה בה: ׳אל תסתרי עם איש פלוני׳: והוא נטמאה או עבר עליו וגו׳. כלומר, הוא התרה בה ועברה על התראתו, ואין ידוע אם נטמאה אם לאו:

טו| קמח. שלא יהא מסלת: שערים. ולא חטים, היא עשתה מעשה בהמה וקרבנה מאכל בהמה: לא יצק עליו שמן. שלא יהא קרבנה מהדר, שהשמן קרוי ׳אור׳ והיא עשתה בחשך: ולא יתן עליו לבנה. שהאמהות נקראות לבונה, שנאמר: ״אל גבעת הלבונה״ (שיר השירים ד, ו), והיא פרשה מדרכיהן: כי מנחת קנאת הוא. הקמח הזה, ׳קמח׳ לשון זכר: מנחת קנאת. מעוררת עליה שתי קנאות, קנאת המקום וקנאת הבעל:

DISCUSSION

The Mishna and Talmud devote the tractate of *Sota* to this matter. The Sages explain that a husband cannot initiate the ritual described below on the basis of mere suspicion. His suspicions must be supported to a certain extent by factual evidence. A woman is considered to be suspected of unfaithfulness only if the husband explicitly warned his wife not to seclude herself with a certain man, and she subsequently ignored his warning and secluded herself with that man (see *Sota* 2a).

5:15| **Barley flour:** This meal offering is brought only in order to resolve the crisis in the couple's relationship. It is not brought to atone, nor to serve as a pleasing aroma to God. It therefore reflects the circumstances of its owner, and it is inferior to other meal offerings (see *Sota* 14a; *Bekhor Shor*). Other meal offerings consist of fine wheat flour, and are presented with oil and fragrant frankincense. Conversely, not only is the meal offering of the woman suspected of unfaithfulness brought from barley flour, which is considered of lesser quality, but it is also brought from inferior flour, derived from the more finely crushed part of the grain, and not from high quality flour (see commentary on Leviticus 2:1).

of jealousy, a meal offering of remembrance, a recollection of iniquity. It is neither a gift offering, a thanks offering, nor a sin offering that is brought when one regrets his transgression, but an offering brought due to the suspicion of sin. It is therefore the lowliest type of meal offering.

16 **The priest shall bring her near, and cause her to stand before the Lord,** in the Temple.[12] Alternatively, the verse means that the priest shall set the meal offering before the Lord.[13]

17 **The priest shall take sacred water** from the basin **in an earthenware vessel.** Like other service vessels, the basin consecrates its contents. The priests regularly use the water in the basin to wash their hands and feet before performing the divine service.[14] **And the priest shall take** a small amount **from the dirt that is on the floor of the Tabernacle,**[D] **and he shall place it into the water.**

Ritual earthenware vessel from the Second Temple period

18 **The priest shall cause the woman to stand before the Lord,** opposite the Tabernacle's entrance,[15] **and he shall expose** the hair of **the woman's head,**[D] **and he shall place on her palms the meal offering of remembrance, it is the meal offering of jealousy; and in the hand of the priest shall** also **be the imprecatory water of bitterness.**[D] Once the dust from the floor of the Tabernacle is placed in the sacred water, it becomes bitter and the source of a curse.

19 **The priest shall administer an oath to her, and he shall say to the woman: If no man has lain with you, and if you have not gone astray** to engage **in** an act of **defilement while subject to your husband, be absolved of this imprecatory water of bitterness.**[D] The water itself is not poisonous, and if you have not sinned it will do you no harm. The priest first mentions the positive outcome in the case of her innocence. Since the woman's guilt has not yet been confirmed, it is improper to begin by stating the outcome of her possible guilt.[16]

20 **But you, if you have gone astray while subject to your husband,**[17] **and if you were defiled, and a man has lain sexually with you, other than your husband...** then the water of bitterness will cause your death, as detailed below. The verse leaves the consequences of the woman's possible unfaithfulness unsaid.

21 **The priest shall administer to the woman the oath of the curse,** spelling out the consequences of the curse, **and the priest shall say to the woman:** If you are guilty, **may the Lord render you as a curse and an oath among your people, when the Lord causes your thigh to** shrivel and **fall, and your belly to distend.** The woman will become a symbol and archetype of a curse.[18]

22 **May this imprecatory water enter your intestines to cause a belly to distend, and a thigh to fall. The woman shall say: Amen, amen.** The woman accepts the conditional curse with a double response, which serves to reinforce her acquiescence.

23 **The priest shall write these curses in the scroll, and he shall dissolve them into the water of bitterness.** The priest soaks the parchment on which the curses are written in the water, until the ink dissolves.

24 **He shall give the woman to drink the imprecatory water of bitterness and the imprecatory water shall enter her for bitterness.** Although there would appear to be insufficient bitterness in the water for its effect to be greatly felt, the indication that it causes a curse is the instant sensation of bitterness and the suffering involved in drinking it.

DISCUSSION

5:17 | From the dirt that is on the floor of the Tabernacle: In the Tabernacle, the floor was unpaved, so this did not present any difficulty. In the Temple, however, the floor was paved with stones, and it was therefore necessary to raise a certain flagstone by means of a ring that was fixed in it in order to take some of the dirt underneath (see *Sota* 15b).

5:18 | And he shall expose the woman's head: Revealing the woman's hair is part of a ritual that is intended to demean the woman.

The Sages derive from this that married women cover their heads (see *Ketubot* 72a).

At this stage, it is as yet unknown whether or not the woman was unfaithful. Nevertheless, the priest humiliates her by revealing her hair because she placed herself in an undesirable situation by secluding herself with a man other than her husband. Even if she did not commit a severe transgression, her behavior was inappropriate.

And in the hand of the priest shall be the imprecatory water of bitterness: According to one opinion among the Sages, a substance was added to the water to give it a bitter taste. According to this interpretation, "the water of bitterness" means the water with bitter medicaments (*Sota* 20a; see *Meiri* ad loc.).

5:19 | Be absolved of this imprecatory water of bitterness: The Sages liken the bitter water to a powerful dry poison which is placed on one's skin. If the skin is whole, the poison does not have any effect. If, however, the skin is wounded, the poison seeps through and causes harm (*Sota* 7b).

טז קַנָאֹת הוּא מִנְחַת זִכָּרוֹן מַזְכֶּרֶת עָוֹן: וְהִקְרִיב אֹתָהּ הַכֹּהֵן וְהֶעֱמִדָהּ לִפְנֵי יהוה:

יז וְלָקַח הַכֹּהֵן מַיִם קְדֹשִׁים בִּכְלִי־חָרֶשׂ וּמִן־הֶעָפָר אֲשֶׁר יִהְיֶה בְּקַרְקַע הַמִּשְׁכָּן יִקַּח הַכֹּהֵן וְנָתַן אֶל־הַמָּיִם:

יח וְהֶעֱמִיד הַכֹּהֵן אֶת־הָאִשָּׁה לִפְנֵי יהוה וּפָרַע אֶת־רֹאשׁ הָאִשָּׁה וְנָתַן עַל־כַּפֶּיהָ אֵת מִנְחַת הַזִּכָּרוֹן מִנְחַת קְנָאֹת הִוא וּבְיַד הַכֹּהֵן יִהְיוּ מֵי הַמָּרִים הַמְאָרְרִים:

יט וְהִשְׁבִּיעַ אֹתָהּ הַכֹּהֵן וְאָמַר אֶל־הָאִשָּׁה אִם־לֹא שָׁכַב אִישׁ אֹתָךְ וְאִם־לֹא שָׂטִית טֻמְאָה תַּחַת אִישֵׁךְ הִנָּקִי מִמֵּי הַמָּרִים הַמְאָרְרִים הָאֵלֶּה:

כ וְאַתְּ כִּי שָׂטִית תַּחַת אִישֵׁךְ וְכִי נִטְמֵאת וַיִּתֵּן אִישׁ בָּךְ אֶת־שְׁכָבְתּוֹ מִבַּלְעֲדֵי אִישֵׁךְ:

כא וְהִשְׁבִּיעַ הַכֹּהֵן אֶת־הָאִשָּׁה בִּשְׁבֻעַת הָאָלָה וְאָמַר הַכֹּהֵן לָאִשָּׁה יִתֵּן יהוה אוֹתָךְ לְאָלָה וְלִשְׁבֻעָה בְּתוֹךְ עַמֵּךְ בְּתֵת יהוה אֶת־יְרֵכֵךְ נֹפֶלֶת וְאֶת־בִּטְנֵךְ צָבָה:

כב וּבָאוּ הַמַּיִם הַמְאָרְרִים הָאֵלֶּה בְּמֵעַיִךְ לַצְבּוֹת בֶּטֶן וְלַנְפִּל יָרֵךְ וְאָמְרָה הָאִשָּׁה אָמֵן ׀ אָמֵן:

כג וְכָתַב אֶת־הָאָלֹת הָאֵלֶּה הַכֹּהֵן בַּסֵּפֶר וּמָחָה אֶל־מֵי הַמָּרִים: וְהִשְׁקָה אֶת־הָאִשָּׁה אֶת־מֵי הַמָּרִים הַמְאָרְרִים וּבָאוּ בָהּ הַמַּיִם הַמְאָרְרִים לְמָרִים:

<hr />

רש"י

יז מַיִם קְדֹשִׁים. שֶׁקִּדְּשׁוּ בַּכִּיּוֹר. לְפִי שֶׁנַּעֲשָׂה הַכִּיּוֹר מִנְּחֹשֶׁת מַרְאוֹת הַצּוֹבְאוֹת, וְזוֹ פֵּרְשָׁה מִדַּרְכֵּיהֶן, שֶׁהָיוּ נִבְעָלוֹת לְבַעֲלֵיהֶן בְּמִצְרַיִם תַּחַת הַתַּפּוּחַ, וְזוֹ קִלְקְלָה לְאַחֵר, תִּבָּדֵק בּוֹ: בִּכְלִי־חָרֶשׂ. הִיא הִשְׁקַתַּ אֶת הַנּוֹאֵף יַיִן מְשֻׁבָּח בְּכוֹסוֹת מְשֻׁבָּחִים, לְפִיכָךְ תִּשְׁתֶּה מַיִם הַמָּרִים בְּמִקְדָה בְּזוּיָה שֶׁל חָרֶשׂ:

יח וְהֶעֱמִיד הַכֹּהֵן וְגו'. וַהֲלֹא כְּבָר נֶאֱמַר (לְעֵיל פָּסוּק טז) וְהֶעֱמִדָהּ לִפְנֵי ה'? אֶלָּא מַסִּיעִין הָיוּ אוֹתָהּ מִמָּקוֹם לְמָקוֹם, כְּדֵי לְיַגְּעָהּ וְתִטָּרֵף דַּעְתָּהּ וְתוֹדֶה: וּפָרַע. סוֹתֵר אֶת קְלִיעַת שְׂעָרָהּ כְּדֵי לְבַזּוֹתָהּ, מִכַּאן לִבְנוֹת יִשְׂרָאֵל שֶׁגִּלּוּי הָרֹאשׁ גְּנַאי לָהֶן: לִפְנֵי ה'. בְּשַׁעַר נִיקָנוֹר, הוּא שַׁעַר הָעֲזָרָה הַמִּזְרָחִי, דֶּרֶךְ כָּל הַנִּכְנָסִים: וְנָתַן עַל כַּפֶּיהָ. לְיַגְּעָהּ, אוּלַי תִּטָּרֵף דַּעְתָּהּ וְתוֹדֶה, וְלֹא יִמָּחֶה שֵׁם הַמְפֹרָשׁ עַל הַמָּיִם: הַמָּרִים. עַל שֵׁם סוֹפָן, שֶׁהֵם מָרִים לָהּ: הַמְאָרְרִים. הַמְחַסְּרִים אוֹתָהּ מִן הָעוֹלָם, לְשׁוֹן "סִלּוֹן מַמְאִיר" (יְחֶזְקֵאל כח, כד). וְלֹא יִתָּכֵן לְפָרֵשׁ מַיִם אֲרוּרִים שֶׁהֲרֵי קְדוֹשִׁים הֵן, וְלֹא "אֲרוּרִים" כָּתַב הַכָּתוּב,

אֶלָּא "מְאָרְרִים" אֶת אֲחֵרִים. וְאַף אוֹנְקְלוֹס לֹא תִרְגֵּם "לִיטַיָּא" אֶלָּא "מְלַטְטַיָּא", שְׁמַרְאוֹת קְלָלָה בְּגוּפָהּ שֶׁל זוֹ:

יט וְהִשְׁבִּיעַ וְגו'. וּמַה הִיא הַשְּׁבוּעָה? "אִם לֹא שָׁכַב הִנָּקִי", "אִם שָׁכַב - חַנְּקִי", שֶׁמִּכְּלַל לָאו אַתָּה שׁוֹמֵעַ הֵן, אֶלָּא שֶׁמִּצְוָה לִפְתּוֹחַ בִּדְינֵי נְפָשׁוֹת תְּחִלָּה לִזְכוּת:

כ וְאַתְּ כִּי שָׂטִית. "כִּי" מְשַׁמֵּשׁ בִּלְשׁוֹן "אִם":

כא בִּשְׁבֻעַת הָאָלָה. שְׁבוּעָה שֶׁל קְלָלָה: יִתֵּן ה' אוֹתָךְ לְאָלָה וְגו'. שֶׁיִּהְיוּ הַכֹּל מְקַלְּלִין בִּיךְ: יִתֵּן ה' כָּךְ יְחַךְ כִּדְרֶךְ שֶׁבָּא לָךְ לְקַלְלוּת: וְלִשְׁבֻעָה. שֶׁיִּהְיוּ הַכֹּל נִשְׁבָּעִין בִּיךְ, אִם לֹא יֵדַע בְּ... כְּדֶרֶךְ שֶׁאֵרַע לִפְלוֹנִית, אִם לֹא יֵדַע בְּ... כִּדְרֶךְ שֶׁאֵרַע לִפְלוֹנִית, וְכֵן הוּא אוֹמֵר "וְהִנַּחְתֶּם שֶׁמְכֶם לִשְׁבוּעָה לִבְחִירַי" (יְשַׁעְיָהוּ סה, טו), שֶׁהַצַּדִּיקִים נִשְׁבָּעִים בְּפֻרְעֲנוּתָן שֶׁל רְשָׁעִים. וְכֵן לְעִנְיַן הַבְּרָכָה: "וְנִבְרְכוּ" וְגו' (בְּרֵאשִׁית יב, ג), "בְּךָ יְבָרֵךְ יִשְׂרָאֵל לֵאמֹר" (שָׁם מח, כ): אֶת יְרֵכֵךְ. בַּקְּלָלָה יֵרֵךְ לַבֶּטֶן, לְפִי שֶׁבָּהּ הִתְחִילָה בָּעֲבֵרָה תְּחִלָּה: צָבָה. כְּתַרְגּוּמוֹ: נְפִיחָה:

כב לַצְבּוֹת בֶּטֶן. כְּמוֹ לְהַצְבּוֹת בֶּטֶן, זֶהוּ שִׁמּוּשׁ פַּתָּח שֶׁהַלַּמֶ"ד נְקוּדָה בּוֹ. וְכֵן "לַנְחֹתָם הַדֶּרֶךְ" (שְׁמוֹת יג, כא), וְכֵן "לַרְאֹתְכֶם בַּדֶּרֶךְ אֲשֶׁר תֵּלְכוּ בָהּ" (דְּבָרִים א, לג), וְכֵן "לַנְפִּל יָרֵךְ", שֶׁהַמַּיִם מַצְבִּים אֶת הַבֶּטֶן וּמַפִּילִים הַיָּרֵךְ: לַצְבּוֹת בֶּטֶן וְלַנְפִּל יָרֵךְ. בִּטְנָהּ וִירֵכָהּ שֶׁל נוֹאֵף. אוֹ אֵינוֹ אֶלָּא שֶׁל נִבְעֶלֶת? כְּשֶׁהוּא אוֹמֵר: "אֶת יְרֵכֵךְ נֹפֶלֶת וְאֶת בִּטְנֵךְ צָבָה" (לְעֵיל פָּסוּק כא), הֲרֵי שֶׁל נִבְעֶלֶת אָמוּר: אָמֵן אָמֵן. קַבָּלַת שְׁבוּעָה, אָמֵן אִם מֵאִישׁ זֶה אָמֵן מֵאִישׁ אַחֵר, אָמֵן אִם הָאָלָה אָמֵן עַל הַשְּׁבוּעָה:

כג וְהִשְׁקָה אֶת הָאִשָּׁה. אֵין זֶה סֵדֶר הַמַּעֲשֶׂה, שֶׁהֲרֵי בַּתְּחִלָּה מַקְרִיב מִנְחָתָהּ, אֶלָּא הַכָּתוּב מְבַשֶּׂרְךָ שֶׁכְּשֶׁיַּשְׁקֶנָּה יָבוֹאוּ בָהּ לְמָרִים. לְפִי שֶׁנֶּאֱמַר בֶּטֶן וְיָרֵךְ, מִנַּיִן לִשְׁאָר כָּל הַגּוּף? תַּלְמוּד לוֹמַר: "וּבָאוּ בָהּ", בְּכֻלָּהּ, אִם כֵּן מַה תַּלְמוּד לוֹמַר בֶּטֶן וְיָרֵךְ? לְפִי שֶׁהֵן הִתְחִילוּ בָעֲבֵרָה תְּחִלָּה, לְפִיכָךְ הִתְחִיל מֵהֶם הַפֻּרְעָנוּת: לְמָרִים. לִהְיוֹת לָהּ רָעִים וּמָרִים:

25 **The priest shall take the meal offering of jealousy from the woman's hand, and he shall wave the meal offering before the Lord, and bring it near to the altar.**
26 **The priest shall take a handful from the meal offering,** the amount held between the three middle fingers when they are bent over the palm, which is **its memorial portion. And** the priest shall **burn it upon the altar, and then he shall give the woman to drink the water.**
27 **He shall give her to drink the water, and it shall be, if she was defiled, and committed a trespass against her husband, the imprecatory water shall enter her for** immediate **bitterness, and her belly shall distend, and her thigh shall fall; and the woman shall become a curse among her people,** possibly even dying as a result.[19]
28 **But if the woman was not defiled, and is untainted, she will be absolved** from any suspicion through drinking the water. **And** furthermore, she **will conceive offspring,**[D] as compensation for the frightening and demeaning process she endured.
29 **This is the law of jealousy, when a woman goes astray while subject to her husband and becomes defiled,**
30 **or when a man is overcome with the spirit of jealousy and is jealous with regard to his wife and causes the woman to stand before the Lord,** although she was not actually defiled.[20] In either case **the priest shall perform for her this entire ritual.** The husband must take this into account before he initiates the aforementioned process, considering all the possible ramifications of this course of action. Alternatively, the verse may be interpreted as follows: If a man will be overcome with the spirit of jealousy, and he will be jealous with regard to his wife, he shall cause her to stand before the Lord.[21]
31 If the woman was affected by the water, her belly distended and her thigh fell, **the man shall be clear from iniquity,**[D] **and that woman shall bear her iniquity.**[D]

The Nazirite

NUMBERS 6:1–21

The figure of the nazirite stands in complete contrast to the unfaithful woman, the laws of which were discussed in the previous passage. The unfaithful woman is an outcast from society because she chooses to veer from the path of morality. Conversely, while the nazirite also deviates from the social norms and separates himself from the surrounding society, he does so out of a desire to sanctify himself. The Sages suggest that one might take upon himself the nazirite vows as a response upon witnessing the failings of the unfaithful woman.[22]

In contrast to the ascetics of other religions, who detach themselves completely from society and strive to totally abstain from worldly activities, the Jewish nazirite does not remove himself from ordinary life. He continues to live a normal life, abstaining only from certain activities detailed below.

In general, the Torah's purpose is to cultivate an entire holy nation that adheres to the path of God. Nevertheless, in this case the Torah presents a unique path that is not required of all members of the people. It is a viable option for an individual who wishes, at a certain point in his life, to sanctify himself beyond the ability of the rest of the people and to attain greater closeness to God by adhering to certain restrictions.

Fresh grapes

6 1 **The Lord spoke to Moses, saying:**
2 **Speak to the children of Israel, and say to them: When a man or a woman articulates**[D] and declares his intent unambiguously **to vow a vow of a nazirite, to abstain** from certain matters and to separate himself from the surrounding society **for** the sake of drawing close to **the Lord,** he shall abstain from the following matters:
3 **He shall abstain from wine and intoxicating drink,**[D] a beverage of concentrated wine, produced from grapes. **Vinegar of wine and vinegar of intoxicating drink he shall not drink; he shall not drink anything in which grapes were soaked,** e.g., raisin wine; **and grapes** in any form, **fresh or dried, he shall not eat.**

Dried grapes

DISCUSSION

5:28 | **And will conceive offspring:** The Sages explain that even if she gave birth to children previously, she will still benefit from this blessing, as the ones she bears from then onward will be more beautiful and successful (see *Sota* 26a).

5:31 | **The man shall be clear from iniquity:** The evaluation of the woman by means of the water of bitterness is based on the expectation of a miracle. The woman's evident punishment is proof of her sin. Conversely, if she suffers no adverse effects from the water, she is absolved of any suspicion. Nevertheless, the Sages teach that the effectiveness of the water depends, among other factors, on the condition that the husband was loyal to his wife. If he is also tainted by a similar transgression, the water will have no effect upon his wife regardless of her actions, and it would be advisable for him to avoid causing his wife to undergo this evaluation (*Sota* 28a).

Similarly, the Mishna states that the priests ceased to administer the water of bitterness to women even before the destruction of the Second Temple. As long as the examination of a woman suspected of unfaithfulness was a rare occurrence, one could anticipate God's miraculous intervention. However, when more and more men entertained suspicions that their wives were unfaithful, as adultery became more widespread, there was no longer any point in

כה וְלָקַח הַכֹּהֵן מִיַּד הָאִשָּׁה אֵת מִנְחַת הַקְּנָאֹת וְהֵנִיף אֶת־הַמִּנְחָה לִפְנֵי יהוה

וְהִקְרִיב אֹתָהּ אֶל־הַמִּזְבֵּחַ: וְקָמַץ הַכֹּהֵן מִן־הַמִּנְחָה אֶת־אַזְכָּרָתָהּ וְהִקְטִיר כו

הַמִּזְבֵּחָה וְאַחַר יַשְׁקֶה אֶת־הָאִשָּׁה אֶת־הַמָּיִם: וְהִשְׁקָהּ אֶת־הַמַּיִם וְהָיְתָה כז

אִם־נִטְמְאָה וַתִּמְעֹל מַעַל בְּאִישָׁהּ וּבָאוּ בָהּ הַמַּיִם הַמְאָרֲרִים לְמָרִים וְצָבְתָה

בִטְנָהּ וְנָפְלָה יְרֵכָהּ וְהָיְתָה הָאִשָּׁה לְאָלָה בְּקֶרֶב עַמָּהּ: וְאִם־לֹא נִטְמְאָה הָאִשָּׁה כח

וּטְהֹרָה הִוא וְנִקְּתָה וְנִזְרְעָה זָרַע: זֹאת תּוֹרַת הַקְּנָאֹת אֲשֶׁר תִּשְׂטֶה אִשָּׁה תַּחַת כט

אִישָׁהּ וְנִטְמָאָה: אוֹ אִישׁ אֲשֶׁר תַּעֲבֹר עָלָיו רוּחַ קִנְאָה וְקִנֵּא אֶת־אִשְׁתּוֹ וְהֶעֱמִיד ל

אֶת־הָאִשָּׁה לִפְנֵי יהוה וְעָשָׂה לָהּ הַכֹּהֵן אֵת כָּל־הַתּוֹרָה הַזֹּאת: וְנִקָּה הָאִישׁ לא

מֵעָוֹן וְהָאִשָּׁה הַהִוא תִּשָּׂא אֶת־עֲוֺנָהּ:

ו א וַיְדַבֵּר יהוה אֶל־מֹשֶׁה לֵּאמֹר: דַּבֵּר אֶל־בְּנֵי יִשְׂרָאֵל וְאָמַרְתָּ אֲלֵהֶם אִישׁ אוֹ־ ב

אִשָּׁה כִּי יַפְלִא לִנְדֹּר נֶדֶר נָזִיר לְהַזִּיר לַיהוה: מִיַּיִן וְשֵׁכָר יַזִּיר חֹמֶץ יַיִן וְחֹמֶץ ג

שֵׁכָר לֹא יִשְׁתֶּה וְכָל־מִשְׁרַת עֲנָבִים לֹא יִשְׁתֶּה וַעֲנָבִים לַחִים וִיבֵשִׁים לֹא יֹאכֵל:

רש"י

כה | וְהֵנִיף. מוֹלִיךְ וּמֵבִיא מַעֲלֶה וּמוֹרִיד, וְאַף הִיא הָיְתָה מְנִיפָה עִמּוֹ, שֶׁיָּדָהּ לְמַעְלָה מִיָּדוֹ שֶׁל כֹּהֵן. וְהִקְרִיב אֹתָהּ. זוֹ הִיא הַגָּשָׁתָהּ בְּקֶרֶן דְּרוֹמִית מַעֲרָבִית שֶׁל מִזְבֵּחַ קֹדֶם קְמִיצָה, כִּשְׁאָר מְנָחוֹת:

כו | אַזְכָּרָתָהּ. הוּא הַקֹּמֶץ, שֶׁעַל יְדֵי הַקְטָרָתוֹ הַמִּנְחָה בָּאָה לְזִכָּרוֹן לַגָּבוֹהַּ:

כז | וְהִשְׁקָהּ אֶת הַמַּיִם. לְרַבּוֹת שְׁאָר חֲמוּרָה 'אֵינֵי שׂוֹתָה' לְאַחַר שֶׁנִּמְחֲקָה הַמְּגִלָּה, מְעַרְעֲרִין אוֹתָהּ וּמַשְׁקִין אוֹתָהּ בְּעַל כָּרְחָהּ, אֶלָּא אִם כֵּן אָמְרָה 'טְמֵאָה אֲנִי'. וְצָבְתָה בִטְנָהּ וְגוֹ'. אַף עַל פִּי שֶׁבַּקְּלָלָה הִזְכִּיר יָרֵךְ תְּחִלָּה, הַמַּיִם אֵינָם בּוֹדְקִין אֶלָּא כְּדֶרֶךְ כְּנִיסָתָן בָּהּ: וְהָיְתָה הָאִשָּׁה לְאָלָה.

כמו שֶׁפֵּרַשְׁתִּי, שֶׁיִּהְיוּ הַכֹּל אָלִין בָּהּ: בְּקֶרֶב עַמָּהּ. קְּפֶרֶשׁ יֵשׁ בֵּין אָדָם הַמִּתְנַוֵּל בִּמְקוֹם שֶׁנִּכָּר לְאָדָם הַמִּתְנַוֵּל בִּמְקוֹם שֶׁאֵינוֹ נִכָּר:

כח | וְאִם לֹא נִטְמְאָה הָאִשָּׁה. בִּסְתִירָה זוֹ: וּטְהֹרָה הִוא. מִמָּקוֹם אַחֵר: וְנִקְּתָה. מִמַּיִם הַמְאָרֲרִים, וְלֹא עוֹד אֶלָּא "וְנִזְרְעָה זָרַע", אִם הָיְתָה יוֹלֶדֶת בְּצַעַר תֵּלֵד בְּרֶוַח, אִם הָיְתָה יוֹלֶדֶת שְׁחוֹרִים יוֹלֶדֶת לְבָנִים:

ל | אוֹ אִישׁ. כְּמוֹ "אוֹ נוֹדַע" (שמות כא, לו), כְּלוֹמַר, אִם אִישׁ קַנַּאי הוּא, לְכָךְ "וְהֶעֱמִיד אֶת הָאִשָּׁה":

לא | וְנִקָּה הָאִישׁ מֵעָוֹן. אִם בְּדָקוּהָ הַמַּיִם, אַל יִדְאַג לוֹמַר 'חַבְתִּי בְּמִיתָתָהּ', נָקִי הוּא מִן הָעֹנֶשׁ. דָּבָר אַחֵר,

---

מִשֶּׁיַּשְׁקֶנָּה תְּהֵא אֶצְלוֹ בְּהֶיְתֵּר, וְנִקָּה מֵעָוֹן, שֶׁהַסּוֹטָה אֲסוּרָה לְבַעְלָהּ:

פרק ו

ב | יַפְלִא. "יַפְרִישׁ". לָמָּה נִסְמְכָה פָרָשַׁת נָזִיר לְפָרָשַׁת סוֹטָה? לוֹמַר לְךָ שֶׁכָּל הָרוֹאֶה סוֹטָה בְּקִלְקוּלָהּ יַזִּיר עַצְמוֹ מִן הַיַּיִן שֶׁהוּא מֵבִיא לִידֵי נִאוּף. נֶדֶר נָזִיר. אֵין נָזִיר בְּכָל מָקוֹם אֶלָּא פְרִישָׁה, אַף כָּאן שֶׁפֵּרַשׁ מִן הַיַּיִן: לְהַזִּיר לַה'. לְהַבְדִּיל עַצְמוֹ מִן הַיַּיִן לְשֵׁם שָׁמַיִם:

ג | מִיַּיִן וְשֵׁכָר. כְּתַרְגּוּמוֹ: "מֵחֲמַר חֲדַת וְעַתִּיק", שֶׁהַיַּיִן מְשַׁכֵּר כְּשֶׁהוּא יָשֵׁן: וְכָל מִשְׁרַת. לְשׁוֹן צְבִיעָה בַּמַּיִם אוֹ בְּכָל מַשְׁקֶה, וּבִלְשׁוֹן מִשְׁנָה יֵשׁ הַרְבֵּה: "אֵין שׁוֹרִין דְּיוֹ וְסַמְמָנִים" (שבת יז ע"א), "נָזִיר שֶׁשָּׁרָה פִתּוֹ בְּיַיִן" (נזיר לז ע"א):

DISCUSSION

→ conducting this evaluation (see *Sota* 47b; see also Hosea 4:14).

And that woman shall bear her iniquity: The husband does not wish to divorce his wife without further investigation. Since he has mixed feelings toward his wife, he comes to the Temple in order to dispel his doubts with regard to her fidelity. When the water evaluates her and her guilt is proven, the husband might blame

himself for her fate. The verse therefore emphasizes that he shall be clear from iniquity, as he took the proper course of action. The unfaithful woman alone bears the responsibility for her punishment (see Rashi; *Bemidbar Rabba* 9:23).

6:2 | When a man or a woman articulates: The term *yafli*, "to articulate," stems from the root peh-lamed-aleph, which also appears elsewhere (15:3) in the context of a vow offering. It

can mean to articulate a vow or to fulfill a vow. It also alludes to a noticeably unusual event (see Ibn Ezra; *Bekhor Shor*, Exodus 8:18).

6:3 | Intoxicating drink: In talmudic and modern Hebrew the term *shekhar*, "an intoxicating drink," includes alcoholic beverages that are not produced from grapes. Here, however, the term refers specifically to beverages produced from grapes (see *Targum Onkelos*; Rashi).

4 **All the days of his naziriteship, from anything that may be derived from the grapevine, from pits to skin,**[23] **he shall not eat.** The nazirite may neither eat nor drink anything derived from the vine.

5 **All the days of his vow of nazir-iteship,** as long as the vow is in effect, **a razor shall not pass on his head.** He may not shave his hair. **Until completion of the days that he shall abstain for the Lord, he shall be holy; the hair of his head shall be grown out.**[D]

6 **All the days of his abstinence to the Lord, he shall not approach a corpse.** He may not come into contact with a dead body under any circumstances.

Razor for shaving hair, from ancient Egypt

7 Even **to his father and to his mother, to his brother and to his sister, he shall not become impure for them upon their death.** Similarly, the priests are also prohibited to approach a corpse.[24] However, the common priests may become impure upon the death of a close relative, whereas a nazirite may not become impure even in the case of a close relative, **since the crown of his God is upon his head.**[D] The nazirite's long hair is a tangible symbol of his naziriteship and his unique closeness to God.

8 **All the days of his naziriteship he is holy to the Lord.** This is evident in the nazirite's deviation from social norms: in the restrictions upon his eating and drinking habits, in his long hair, and in his caution not to approach the dead.

9 Even if the nazirite tries to avoid all contact with the dead, an unforeseen event might occur. **If a corpse dies near him with unexpected suddenness,** while he is under the same roof, the corpse renders him impure, **and** thereby **renders the head of his naziriteship,** the crown of his long hair, **impure;** that is, his naziriteship is compromised.[25] The impurity imparted by a corpse lasts for seven days. Therefore, **he shall shave his head on the day of his purification; on the seventh day shall he shave it.**

10 **And on the eighth day he shall bring two turtledoves, or two young pigeons, to the priest, to the entrance of the Tent of Meeting.**

11 **The priest shall prepare one** of the birds **as a sin offering, and** the other **one as a burnt offering, and** the priest shall **atone for him, for that which he sinned with regard to the corpse.**[D] Even if the nazirite became impure due to circumstances beyond his control, his naziriteship is compromised and he requires atonement. **And he shall sanctify his head on that day,** the eighth day, when his hair shall again be consecrated with the sanctity of naziriteship.

12 **He shall dedicate to the Lord the days of his naziriteship,** commencing his period of naziriteship anew, **and** in addition he **shall bring a sheep in its first year as a guilt offering** to complete his atonement. **And the first days** of his naziriteship **shall be void.**[D] The days prior to his impurity do not count toward the fulfillment of his vow, **as his naziriteship is impure.**

13 The previous verses presented the laws that pertain to a nazirite who became impure due to circumstances beyond his control, and who was unable to complete his naziriteship: He is required to shave; to bring a sin offering, a burnt offering, and a guilt offering; and to observe his period of naziriteship anew. The following verses detail the laws that apply when the nazirite successfully completes his period of naziriteship without mishap: **And this is the law of the nazirite, on the day of the completion of the days of his naziriteship: He shall bring it,** the set of offerings listed below,[26] **to the entrance of the Tent of Meeting.** Alternatively, the verse means that he shall bring himself to the entrance of the Tent of Meeting.[27]

14 **He shall present his offering to the Lord: one unblemished lamb in its first year as a burnt offering, one unblemished ewe in its first year as a sin offering, and one unblemished ram as a peace offering,**

DISCUSSION

6:5 | The hair of his head shall be grown out: According to the Sages' tradition, the minimum period of naziriteship is thirty days. If one is a nazirite for merely thirty days, the growth of his hair will not necessarily be noticeable, but in the case of a lengthy period of naziriteship the hair might grow extremely long, as in the case of Samson, Avshalom, and perhaps also the prophet Samuel (see Judges 13:5; I Samuel 1:11; II Samuel 14:25–26; *Nazir* 66a).

6:7 | Since the crown of his God is upon his head: The term *nezer*, "a crown," is derived from the same root as the term *nezirut*, "naziriteship." In this verse, the two meanings of the root *nun-zayin-reish* merge together. The nazirite abstains from indulging in luxuries, sometimes turning his back on social life and worldly matters (see, e.g., Jeremiah 35:6–19; Lamentations 4:7). While he abstains from these matters, he is adorned with the crown of his God. The purpose of a crown is to emphasize the elevated status of the wearer. It would therefore appear that there is a linguistic connection between these two meanings.

6:11 | And atone for him for that which he sinned with regard to the corpse: Since the verse is referring to the unavoidable impurity of the nazirite in the case of a sudden death, it is difficult to understand why the nazirite requires atonement. Some of the Sages therefore explain that the sin which requires atonement is not the fact that he became impure, but his ◄

ד ה כֹּל יְמֵי נִזְרוֹ מִכֹּל אֲשֶׁר יֵעָשֶׂה מִגֶּפֶן הַיַּיִן מֵחַרְצַנִּים וְעַד־זָג לֹא יֹאכֵל: כָּל־יְמֵי
נֶדֶר נִזְרוֹ תַּעַר לֹא־יַעֲבֹר עַל־רֹאשׁוֹ עַד־מְלֹאת הַיָּמִם אֲשֶׁר־יַזִּיר לַיהוָה קָדֹשׁ
ו יִהְיֶה גַּדֵּל פֶּרַע שְׂעַר רֹאשׁוֹ: כָּל־יְמֵי הַזִּירוֹ לַיהוָה עַל־נֶפֶשׁ מֵת לֹא יָבֹא:
ז לְאָבִיו וּלְאִמּוֹ לְאָחִיו וּלְאַחֹתוֹ לֹא־יִטַּמָּא לָהֶם בְּמֹתָם כִּי נֵזֶר אֱלֹהָיו עַל־רֹאשׁוֹ:
ח ט כֹּל יְמֵי נִזְרוֹ קָדֹשׁ הוּא לַיהוָה: וְכִי־יָמוּת מֵת עָלָיו בְּפֶתַע פִּתְאֹם וְטִמֵּא רֹאשׁ
י נִזְרוֹ וְגִלַּח רֹאשׁוֹ בְּיוֹם טָהֳרָתוֹ בַּיּוֹם הַשְּׁבִיעִי יְגַלְּחֶנּוּ: וּבַיּוֹם הַשְּׁמִינִי יָבִא שְׁתֵּי
יא תֹרִים אוֹ שְׁנֵי בְּנֵי יוֹנָה אֶל־הַכֹּהֵן אֶל־פֶּתַח אֹהֶל מוֹעֵד: וְעָשָׂה הַכֹּהֵן אֶחָד
לְחַטָּאת וְאֶחָד לְעֹלָה וְכִפֶּר עָלָיו מֵאֲשֶׁר חָטָא עַל־הַנָּפֶשׁ וְקִדַּשׁ אֶת־רֹאשׁוֹ
יב בַּיּוֹם הַהוּא: וְהִזִּיר לַיהוָה אֶת־יְמֵי נִזְרוֹ וְהֵבִיא כֶּבֶשׂ בֶּן־שְׁנָתוֹ לְאָשָׁם וְהַיָּמִים
יג הָרִאשֹׁנִים יִפְּלוּ כִּי טָמֵא נִזְרוֹ: וְזֹאת תּוֹרַת הַנָּזִיר בְּיוֹם מְלֹאת יְמֵי נִזְרוֹ יָבִיא אֹתוֹ
יד אֶל־פֶּתַח אֹהֶל מוֹעֵד: וְהִקְרִיב אֶת־קָרְבָּנוֹ לַיהוָה כֶּבֶשׂ בֶּן־שְׁנָתוֹ תָמִים אֶחָד
לְעֹלָה וְכַבְשָׂה אַחַת בַּת־שְׁנָתָהּ תְּמִימָה לְחַטָּאת וְאַיִל־אֶחָד תָּמִים לִשְׁלָמִים:

רש״י

ד | **חַרְצַנִּים.** הֵם הַגַּרְעִינִין: **זָג.** הֵם קְלִפּוֹת שֶׁמִּבַּחוּץ, שֶׁהַחַרְצַנִּים בְּתוֹכָן כְּעִנְבָּל בַּזּוּג:

ה | **קָדֹשׁ יִהְיֶה.** הַשֵּׂעָר שֶׁלּוֹ, לְגַדֵּל הַפֶּרַע שֶׁל שְׂעַר רֹאשׁוֹ: **פֶּרַע שְׂעַר.** נָקוּד פַּתָּח לְפִי שֶׁהוּא דָּבוּק לְ״שְׂעַר רֹאשׁוֹ״, פֶּרַע שֶׁל שֵׂעָר. וּפֵרוּשׁוֹ שֶׁל ״פֶּרַע״ גִּדּוּל שֶׁל שֵׂעָר. וְכֵן ״אֶת רֹאשׁוֹ לֹא יִפְרָע״ (ויקרא כא, י), וְאֵין קָרוּי פֶּרַע פָּחוּת מִשְּׁלֹשִׁים יוֹם:

ח | **כֹּל יְמֵי נִזְרוֹ קָדֹשׁ הוּא.** זוֹ קְדֻשַּׁת הַגּוּף מִלְּטַמֵּא לְמֵתִים:

ט | **פֶּתַע.** זֶה אֹנֶס: **פִּתְאֹם.** זֶה שׁוֹגֵג. וְיֵשׁ אוֹמְרִים: ״פֶּתַע פִּתְאֹם״ דָּבָר אֶחָד הוּא, מִקְרֶה שֶׁל פִּתְאֹם: **וְכִי יָמוּת מֵת עָלָיו.** בָּאֹהֶל שֶׁהוּא בּוֹ: **בְּיוֹם טָהֳרָתוֹ.** בְּיוֹם הַזָּאָתוֹ. אוֹ אֵינוֹ אֶלָּא בַּשְּׁמִינִי שֶׁהוּא טָהוֹר לְגַמְרֵי? תַּלְמוּד לוֹמַר: ״בַּיּוֹם הַשְּׁבִיעִי״. אִי שְׁבִיעִי, יָכוֹל אֲפִלּוּ לֹא הִזָּה? תַּלְמוּד לוֹמַר: ״בְּיוֹם טָהֳרָתוֹ״:

י | **וּבַיּוֹם הַשְּׁמִינִי יָבִא שְׁתֵּי תֹרִים.** לְהוֹצִיא אֶת הַשְּׁבִיעִי. אוֹ אֵינוֹ אֶלָּא לְהוֹצִיא אֶת הַתְּשִׁיעִי? קָבַע זְמַן לַקָּרֵבִין וְקָבַע זְמַן לַמַּקְרִיבִין, מַה קָּרֵבִין הִכְשִׁיר שְׁמִינִי וּמִשְּׁמִינִי וָהָלְאָה, אַף מַקְרִיבִין שְׁמִינִי וּמִשְּׁמִינִי וָהָלְאָה:

יא | **מֵאֲשֶׁר חָטָא עַל הַנָּפֶשׁ.** שֶׁלֹּא נִזְהַר מִטֻּמְאַת הַמֵּת. רַבִּי אֶלְעָזָר הַקַּפָּר אוֹמֵר: שֶׁצִּעֵר עַצְמוֹ מִן הַיַּיִן: **וְקִדַּשׁ אֶת רֹאשׁוֹ.** לַחֲזֹר וּלְהַתְחִיל מִנְיַן נְזִירוּתוֹ:

יב | **וְהִזִּיר לַה׳ אֶת יְמֵי נִזְרוֹ.** יַחֲזֹר וְיִמְנֶה נְזִירוּתוֹ כְּבַתְּחִלָּה: **וְהַיָּמִים הָרִאשֹׁנִים יִפְּלוּ.** לֹא יַעֲלוּ מִן הַמִּנְיָן:

יג | **יָבִיא אֹתוֹ.** יָבִיא אֶת עַצְמוֹ, וְזֶה אֶחָד מִשְּׁלֹשָׁה אֶתִּים שֶׁהָיָה רַבִּי יִשְׁמָעֵאל דּוֹרֵשׁ כֵּן. כַּיּוֹצֵא בוֹ: ״וְהִשִּׂיאוּ אוֹתָם עֲוֹן אַשְׁמָה״ (ויקרא כב, טז), אֶת עַצְמָם; כַּיּוֹצֵא בוֹ: ״וַיִּקְבֹּר אֹתוֹ בַגַּי״ (דברים לד, ו), הוּא קָבַר אֶת עַצְמוֹ:

DISCUSSION

initial decision to become a nazirite. The nazirite undertook his naziriteship out of a desire to sanctify himself for a limited amount of time. Since he became impure, he must start anew, extending the period of his naziriteship. It is possible that at this stage he regrets his vow, and no longer retains his original intention of sanctification. His abstinence therefore no longer serves its intended purpose, and requires atonement. This concept is expressed in the words of Rabbi Elazar HaKappar: With what soul did the nazirite sin? Rather, he sinned by the distress he caused himself by abstaining from wine (*Ta'anit* 11a). According to this interpretation, the verse would be rendered: He shall atone for him, for that which he sinned with regard to his person.

6:12 | **And the first days shall be void:** The Talmud relates the story of Queen Helene, who vowed to be a nazirite for seven years. However, toward the conclusion of that period she became impure and had to start her naziriteship anew (*Nazir* 19b).

15 and he shall also bring **a basket of unleavened bread,** of two types: **Loaves of high quality flour mixed with oil, and thin wafers of unleavened bread spread with oil. And** with the animal offerings he shall bring **their meal offering, and their libations.** The meal offerings and libations that must be brought with a burnt offering or a peace offering are detailed elsewhere (15:1–16).

16 **The priest shall bring them before the Lord, and shall perform his sin offering, and his burnt offering.**

17 **The ram he shall make a peace offering to the Lord,** together **with the basket of unleavened bread; and the priest shall perform its meal offering and its libation.**

18 Once the rites of the offerings have been performed, **the nazirite shall shave the head of his naziriteship at the entrance of the Tent of Meeting.** In contrast to the case of a nazirite who shaves because he became impure, when a nazirite completes his period of naziriteship his shaving symbolizes the conclusion of his naziriteship and his return to ordinary social life. **And he shall take the hair of the head of his naziriteship,** after he has shaved it, **and he shall place it on the fire that is beneath the peace offering.** The same fire is used to cook the peace offering and to burn the shaved-off hairs. This may indicate that the hairs are sacred to a certain extent, and therefore they may not be used for any other purpose. The Mishna lists the hair of

the nazirite among those items from which deriving benefit is prohibited.[28]

19 **The priest shall take the cooked foreleg of the ram** peace offering, **and one loaf of unleavened bread from the basket, and one wafer of unleavened bread, and he shall place** all three of **them on the palms of the nazirite, after he** has **shaved** the head of **his naziriteship.** The palms of the nazirite are waved together with the offerings. This alludes to the fact that the status of the nazirite himself is similar to that of an offering.

20 **The priest shall wave them as a wave offering before the Lord. It,** the foreleg of the ram, **is sacred for the priest.** It is given to the priest as one of the gifts of the priesthood together **with the breast of waving and with the haunch of lifting,** which are given to the priests in the case of every peace offering. **And then the nazirite may drink wine,** as his naziriteship has concluded.

21 **This is the law of the nazirite who vows his offering to the Lord for his naziriteship.** The aforementioned offerings are required of every nazirite, **besides that for which his means suffice.** If the nazirite has the means to bring more offerings, and he vowed to do so, then **in accordance with his vow that he vows,**[D] **so shall he perform** together **with the** fixed **law of his naziriteship:** the lamb, the ewe, the ram, and the unleavened bread, which are incumbent upon every nazirite.

The Priestly Benediction

NUMBERS 6:22–27

The commandment to bless the people is part of the priests' duties. The following section, which discusses the priestly benediction, is therefore connected to the subsequent section which discusses the organization of the Tabernacle. However, the priests' sanctity and elevated spiritual status does not stem only from their service in the Temple. This is expressed in the priestly benediction which is performed in all places, even today when the Temple does not exist. One can also discern a connection between the priest and the nazirite, who was the subject of the previous section, as both the priest and the nazirite are on an elevated spiritual plane.

The priests do not bless the people as private individuals, or because of their personal virtues; rather, the blessing emanates from the unique spiritual ability with which God invested the descendants of Aaron.

22 **The Lord spoke to Moses, saying:**

23 **Speak to Aaron and to his sons, saying: So shall you bless the children of Israel, say to them**[D] the following:

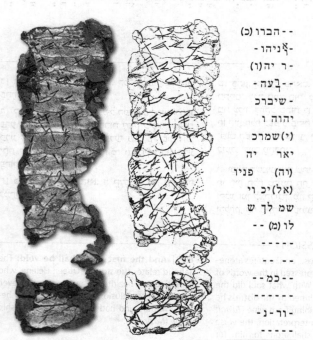

- - הברו (כ)
-אָ֗ניהו -
- ר יה (ו) -
- -בָּ֗עה -
- שיברך -
יהוה ו
(י)שמרכ
יאר   יה
(יה)   פניו
(אל)יכ וי
שמ לך ש
לו (מ) - -
- - - - -
- -- ---
- - כמ- -
- - - - -
-ור - נ - -
- - - - -

Priestly benediction on a silver plate from the First Temple period; Ketef Hinom, Jerusalem

טו וְסַל מַצּוֹת סֹלֶת חַלֹּת בְּלוּלֹת בַּשֶּׁמֶן וּרְקִיקֵי מַצּוֹת מְשֻׁחִים בַּשָּׁמֶן וּמִנְחָתָם

טז וְנִסְכֵּיהֶם: וְהִקְרִיב הַכֹּהֵן לִפְנֵי יהוה וְעָשָׂה אֶת־חַטָּאתוֹ וְאֶת־עֹלָתוֹ: וְאֶת־הָאַיִל

יז יַעֲשֶׂה זֶבַח שְׁלָמִים לַיהוה עַל סַל הַמַּצּוֹת וְעָשָׂה הַכֹּהֵן אֶת־מִנְחָתוֹ וְאֶת־נִסְכּוֹ:

יח וְגִלַּח הַנָּזִיר פֶּתַח אֹהֶל מוֹעֵד אֶת־רֹאשׁ נִזְרוֹ וְלָקַח אֶת־שְׂעַר רֹאשׁ נִזְרוֹ וְנָתַן

יט עַל־הָאֵשׁ אֲשֶׁר־תַּחַת זֶבַח הַשְּׁלָמִים: וְלָקַח הַכֹּהֵן אֶת־הַזְּרֹעַ בְּשֵׁלָה מִן־הָאַיִל

וְחַלַּת מַצָּה אַחַת מִן־הַסַּל וּרְקִיק מַצָּה אֶחָד וְנָתַן עַל־כַּפֵּי הַנָּזִיר אַחַר הִתְגַּלְּחוֹ

כ אֶת־נִזְרוֹ: וְהֵנִיף אוֹתָם הַכֹּהֵן ׀ תְּנוּפָה לִפְנֵי יהוה קֹדֶשׁ הוּא לַכֹּהֵן עַל חֲזֵה

הַתְּנוּפָה וְעַל שׁוֹק הַתְּרוּמָה וְאַחַר יִשְׁתֶּה הַנָּזִיר יָיִן: זֹאת תּוֹרַת הַנָּזִיר אֲשֶׁר

כא יִדֹּר קָרְבָּנוֹ לַיהוה עַל־נִזְרוֹ מִלְּבַד אֲשֶׁר־תַּשִּׂיג יָדוֹ כְּפִי נִדְרוֹ אֲשֶׁר יִדֹּר כֵּן יַעֲשֶׂה

עַל תּוֹרַת נִזְרוֹ:

כב וַיְדַבֵּר יהוה אֶל־מֹשֶׁה לֵּאמֹר: דַּבֵּר אֶל־אַהֲרֹן וְאֶל־בָּנָיו לֵאמֹר כֹּה תְבָרֲכוּ אֶת־בְּנֵי

כג

רש"י

טו | וּמִנְחָתָם וְנִסְכֵּיהֶם. שֶׁל עוֹלָה וּשְׁלָמִים, לְפִי שֶׁהָיוּ בִּכְלָל וְיָצְאוּ לָדוֹן בְּדָבָר חָדָשׁ שֶׁיִּטָּעֲנוּ לֶחֶם, הֶחֱזִירָן לִכְלָלָן שֶׁיִּטָּעֲנוּ נְסָכִים כְּדִין עוֹלָה וּשְׁלָמִים: חַלֹּת בְּלוּלֹת וּרְקִיקֵי מַצּוֹת. עֶשֶׂר מִכָּל מִין:

יז | זֶבַח שְׁלָמִים לַה׳. אֶת סַל הַמַּצּוֹת: יִשְׁחַט אֶת הַשְּׁלָמִים עַל מְנָת לְקַדֵּשׁ אֶת הַלֶּחֶם: אֶת מִנְחָתוֹ וְאֶת נִסְכּוֹ. שֶׁל אַיִל:

יח | וְגִלַּח הַנָּזִיר פֶּתַח אֹהֶל מוֹעֵד. יָכוֹל יְגַלַּח בָּעֲזָרָה? הֲרֵי

זֶה דֶּרֶךְ בִּזָּיוֹן! אֶלָּא "וְגִלַּח הַנָּזִיר" לְאַחַר שְׁחִיטַת הַשְּׁלָמִים שֶׁכָּתוּב בָּהֶן: "וּשְׁחָטוֹ פֶּתַח אֹהֶל מוֹעֵד" (ויקרא ג, ב): אֲשֶׁר תַּחַת זֶבַח הַשְּׁלָמִים. תַּחַת הַדּוּד שֶׁהוּא מְבַשְּׁלָן בּוֹ, לְפִי שֶׁשַּׁלְמֵי נָזִיר הָיוּ מִתְבַּשְּׁלִין בָּעֲזָרָה, שֶׁצָּרִיךְ לִטֹּל הַכֹּהֵן הַזְּרוֹעַ אַחַר שֶׁנִּתְבַּשְּׁלָה וּלְהָנִיף לִפְנֵי ה׳:

יט | הַזְּרֹעַ בְּשֵׁלָה. לְאַחַר שֶׁנִּתְבַּשְּׁלָה:

כ | קֹדֶשׁ הוּא לַכֹּהֵן. הַחַלָּה וְהָרָקִיק וְהַזְּרוֹעַ תְּרוּמָה הֵן לַכֹּהֵן: עַל חֲזֵה הַתְּנוּפָה. מִלְּבַד חֲזֵה וְשׁוֹק הָרְאוּיִים לוֹ

מִכָּל שְׁלָמִים, מוּסָף עַל שַׁלְמֵי נָזִיר עוֹד הַזְּרוֹעַ הַזֶּה. לְפִי שֶׁהָיוּ שַׁלְמֵי נָזִיר בִּכְלָל וְיָצְאוּ לָדוֹן בְּדָבָר חָדָשׁ לְהַפְרָשַׁת זְרוֹעַ, הֻצְרַךְ לְהַחֲזִירָן לִכְלָלָן לָדוֹן אַף בְּחָזֶה וָשׁוֹק:

כא | מִלְּבַד אֲשֶׁר תַּשִּׂיג יָדוֹ. שֶׁאִם אָמַר: הֲרֵינִי נָזִיר עַל מְנָת לְגַלֵּחַ עַל מֵאָה עוֹלוֹת וְעַל מֵאָה שְׁלָמִים: "כְּפִי נִדְרוֹ אֲשֶׁר יִדֹּר כֵּן יַעֲשֶׂה" מוּסָף "עַל תּוֹרַת נִזְרוֹ", עַל תּוֹרַת הַנָּזִיר מוֹסִיף וְלֹא יִחְסַר, שֶׁאִם אָמַר: הֲרֵינִי נָזִיר חָמֵשׁ נְזִירוֹת עַל מְנָת לְגַלֵּחַ עַל שָׁלֹשׁ בְּהֵמוֹת הַלָּלוּ, אֵין אֲנִי קוֹרֵא בוֹ "כַּאֲשֶׁר יִדֹּר כֵּן יַעֲשֶׂה":

DISCUSSION

6:21 | In accordance with his vow that he vows: One might vow out of a desire to sanctify oneself, as an act of gratitude toward God, or in a situation where one greatly wishes to obtain a certain outcome. In such cases the vow might be uttered conditionally, that if a certain event

comes to pass, the individual will fulfill the terms of the vow (see, e.g., 21:2; Genesis 28:20; Psalms 56:13–14; 66:13–14).

6:23 | Say to them: The Sages derive from the phrase, "say to them," that a representative of

the congregation first addresses the priests and calls upon them to bless the people. The congregation's representative reads out the benediction to the priests one word after another, and they recite the blessing after him (see Sota 38a; Targum Onkelos).

765

24 **The Lord shall bless you,**[D] **and keep you.** Even when one receives a gift directly, he might have the misfortune to lose it. The blessing that the Lord will keep you, may be interpreted as a blessing of protection. Not only will the Lord bless the people, but he will also protect them from such misfortune, preserving the goodness which He bestowed upon them.[29]

25 **The Lord shall shine His countenance to you.** He shall treat you with benevolence, **and** He shall **be gracious to you.** You will find favor in His eyes.

26 **The Lord shall lift His countenance to you,**[D] giving you preferential status, **and** He shall **grant you peace:**[D] wholeness, serenity, satisfaction, and completeness.

27 **They shall place My name upon the children of Israel.** The priests shall bless the people with these three verses, in each of which My name appears, and thereby they will place My name upon them. **And I shall bless them.** The priests serve merely as a conduit: By means of the priestly benediction, God's bountiful goodness is transmitted to the Jewish people. Alternatively, the verse means that when the priests bless the people, God in turn blesses the priests themselves.[30]

The Dedication of the Altar of Burnt Offerings

NUMBERS 7:1–89

Until this point, there has been little narrative development in the book of Numbers. The book thus far deals with commandments and instructions with regard to the organization of the Tabernacle and the surrounding camps, together with all their details; with the appointment of the Levites and the details of their service; with the requirement to ensure the purity of those dwelling in the camp; and finally with the priests' duty to bless the people. In the following section, the Torah continues to relate the events that take place on the day that Moses finishes erecting the Tabernacle, the eighth day of the inauguration. On that day fire emerges from before the Lord and consumes Aaron's offerings upon the altar in the presence of the people.[31]

7 1 It was on the day that Moses concluded to erect the Tabernacle, that he anointed it with the anointing oil and thereby sanctified it, all its vessels and the altar and all its vessels; he anointed them and sanctified them.

Fifth aliya

2 **The princes of Israel, the heads of their patrilineal houses, brought** the **offerings** stated below. **They were the princes of the tribes.** The Torah previously described the establishment of a hierarchy of judges and officers who were appointed over the people.[32] Nevertheless, the tribal division remained the most significant division of the people into separate groups, each of which was represented by a prince. **They were those who stood over those who were counted,** those who assisted Moses in the census (1:4–15).

3 **They brought their offering before the Lord, six covered wagons.** Alternatively, the verse may mean decorated wagons.[33] Covered wagons were probably unusual in that period.

Presumably, the princes built these wagons specifically for the Tabernacle, as it is unlikely that they brought them from Egypt. **And** the princes also brought **twelve cattle**[D] to pull the wagons. **A wagon** was brought **for each two princes.** Each pair of princes contributed one wagon. This indicates that the princes coordinated their gifts. **And an ox** was brought **for each one,** totaling twelve oxen. **And they brought them** near **before the Tabernacle.**

4 **The Lord spoke to Moses, saying:**

5 **Take** these gifts **from them,** despite the fact that they did not appear in the original list of required items,[34] **and they shall be to perform the service of the Tent of Meeting,** to transport the different parts of the Tabernacle. **And you shall give them,** the wagons and cattle, **to the Levites,** dividing them among the Levites, **each according to his work.**

DISCUSSION

6:24 | The Lord shall bless you: The three verses of the priestly benediction are considered three separate blessings (see *Sota* 38a). Outside the Temple, one responds "amen" after each of the three blessings. Nevertheless, according to the *Tosefta* (*Menaḥot* 6) each of the three blessings is indispensable, and if a priest recited only one or two verses he has not fulfilled his obligation. Furthermore, the verses clearly form a single structural unit, of three, five, and seven words respectively (see also *Minhagei Yisrael* 2:5, p. 184; with regard to such structural units, see *Sanhedrin* 10b; *Megilla* 23a).

6:26 | The Lord shall lift His countenance to you: The judges are prohibited from favoring people in judgment. Nevertheless, the priests request that God grant the Jewish people preferential status, as they seek to act in His name beyond the requirements of the letter of the law (see *Berakhot* 20b).

And grant you peace: In biblical Hebrew the term *shalom*, "peace," does not only denote the absence of war, but also includes many forms of goodness. It is therefore a fitting conclusion for both the priestly benediction and for other

benedictions of later origin. The term became a blessing by itself, used both when greeting people and when departing from their presence.

7:3 | Six covered wagons and twelve cattle: The vast majority of the donations for the erection of the Tabernacle came from the common people, who gave in accordance with their means and their generosity. Some people donated a few threads or fabrics, or the skin of a goat, while others donated copper, silver, or gold items. The princes and other wealthy individuals donated the precious stones, of which ◀▶

כד כה יִשְׂרָאֵל אָמוֹר לָהֶם: יְבָרֶכְךָ יְהוָה וְיִשְׁמְרֶךָ: יָאֵר יְהוָה | פָּנָיו
כו כז אֵלֶיךָ וִיחֻנֶּךָּ: יִשָּׂא יְהוָה | פָּנָיו אֵלֶיךָ וְיָשֵׂם לְךָ שָׁלוֹם: וְשָׂמוּ
א אֶת־שְׁמִי עַל־בְּנֵי יִשְׂרָאֵל וַאֲנִי אֲבָרְכֵם: וַיְהִי בְּיוֹם כַּלּוֹת מֹשֶׁה חמישי
לְהָקִים אֶת־הַמִּשְׁכָּן וַיִּמְשַׁח אֹתוֹ וַיְקַדֵּשׁ אֹתוֹ וְאֶת־כָּל־כֵּלָיו וְאֶת־הַמִּזְבֵּחַ
ב וְאֶת־כָּל־כֵּלָיו וַיִּמְשָׁחֵם וַיְקַדֵּשׁ אֹתָם: וַיַּקְרִיבוּ נְשִׂיאֵי יִשְׂרָאֵל רָאשֵׁי בֵּית
ג אֲבֹתָם הֵם נְשִׂיאֵי הַמַּטֹּת הֵם הָעֹמְדִים עַל־הַפְּקֻדִים: וַיָּבִיאוּ אֶת־קָרְבָּנָם לִפְנֵי
יְהוָה שֵׁשׁ־עֶגְלֹת צָב וּשְׁנֵי־עָשָׂר בָּקָר עֲגָלָה עַל־שְׁנֵי הַנְּשִׂאִים וְשׁוֹר לְאֶחָד
ד ה וַיַּקְרִיבוּ אוֹתָם לִפְנֵי הַמִּשְׁכָּן: וַיֹּאמֶר יְהוָה אֶל־מֹשֶׁה לֵּאמֹר: קַח מֵאִתָּם וְהָיוּ
לַעֲבֹד אֶת־עֲבֹדַת אֹהֶל מוֹעֵד וְנָתַתָּה אוֹתָם אֶל־הַלְוִיִּם אִישׁ כְּפִי עֲבֹדָתוֹ:

רש"י

כג | **אמור להם.** כמו 'זכור', 'שמור', בלעז דישנ"ט: **אמור להם.** שיהיו כלם שומעים: **אמור.** מלא, לא תברכם בחפזון ובהלות אלא בכונה ובלב שלם:

כד | **יברכך.** שיתברכו נכסיך: **וישמרך.** שלא יבואו עליך שודדים לטול ממונך, שהנותן מתנה לעבדו אינו יכול לשמרו מכל אדם, וכיון שבאים לסטים עליו ונוטלין אותה ממנו, מה הנאה יש לו במתנה זו; אבל הקדוש ברוך הוא, הוא הנותן הוא השומר. והרבה מדרשים דרשו בו בספרי (מ):

כה | **יאר ה' פניו אליך.** יראה לך פנים שוחקות, פנים צהובות: **ויחנך.** יתן לך חן:

כו | **ישא ה' פניו אליך.** יכבש כעסו:

כז | **ושמו את שמי.** יברכום בשם המפרש: **ואני אברכם.** לישראל, ואסכים עם הכהנים. דבר אחר, "ואני אברכם" לכהנים:

פרק ז

א | **ויהי ביום כלות משה.** 'כלת' כתיב, יום הקמת המשכן היו ישראל ככלה הנכנסת לחפה: **כלות משה.** בצלאל ואהליאב וכל חכם לב עשו את המשכן ותלאו הכתוב במשה, לפי שמסר נפשו עליו לראות תבנית כל דבר ודבר כמו שהראהו בהר, להורות לעושי המלאכה, ולא טעה בתבנית אחת. וכן מצינו בדוד, לפי שמסר נפשו על בנין בית המקדש, שנאמר: "זכור ה' לדוד את כל ענותו אשר נשבע לה'" וגו' (תהלים קלב, א-ב), לפיכך נקרא על שמו, שנאמר: "ראה ביתך דוד" (מלכים א' יב, טז): **ביום כלות משה להקים.** ולא נאמר: 'ביום הקים', מלמד שכל שבעת ימי המלואים היה משה מעמידו ומפרקו, ובאותו היום העמידו ולא פרקו, לכך נאמר: "ביום כלות משה להקים", אותו היום כלו הקמותיו, וראש חדש ניסן היה. בשני – נשרפה הפרה, בשלישי – הזו הזיה ראשונה, ובשביעי – גלחו:

ב | **הם נשיאי המטת.** שהיו שוטרים עליהם במצרים והיו מכים עליהם, שנאמר: "ויכו שטרי בני ישראל" וגו' (שמות ה, יד): **הם העמדים על הפקדים.** שעמדו עם משה ואהרן כשמנו את ישראל, שנאמר: "ואתכם יהיו" וגו' (לעיל א, ד):

ג | **שש עגלת צב.** אין "צב" אלא מחפים, וכן: "בצבים ובפרדים" (ישעיה סו, כ), עגלות מכסות קרויות 'צבים': **ויקריבו אותם לפני המשכן.** שלא קבל משה מידם עד שנאמר לו מפי המקום. אמר רבי נתן: מה ראו הנשיאים להתנדב כאן בתחלה ובמלאכת המשכן לא התנדבו תחלה? אלא כך אמרו הנשיאים: יתנדבו צבור מה שיתנדבו ומה שמחסרין אנו משלימין; כיון שראו שהשלימו צבור את הכל, שנאמר: "והמלאכה היתה דים" (שמות לו, ז), אמרו: מעתה מה לנו לעשות? הביאו אבני השהם ואבני המלואים לאפוד ולחשן (שם לה, כז), לכך התנדבו כאן תחלה:

DISCUSSION

only a few were required for the Tabernacle (see Exodus 35:27). Apparently, the princes subsequently agreed among themselves to bring a unique gift of their own. One might understand why the leaders would think of presenting this gift. The rest of the people donated the necessary materials for the actual construction of the Tabernacle. However, the princes had the foresight to take into consideration the logistics involved in transporting the Tabernacle. Since Moses did not arrange a special collection for the materials required in order to carry the Tabernacle, the princes donated the wagons and the cattle of their own accord.

The Sages make the following observation with regard to the princes' gifts: The princes should have been the main contributors for the construction of the Tabernacle, as they were the dignitaries of the people, and were presumably among their wealthier members. In practice, however, the erection of the Tabernacle was not based on the donations of the wealthy members of the people, but on the generosity of the nation as a whole. For example, a woman donated one of her bracelets; a man contributed a chain or a few copper nails. All participated in the construction of the Tabernacle. By the time the princes got around to bringing their donations, they were no longer needed. In order to express their regret for delaying to participate in the collection for the Tabernacle, the princes eagerly brought gifts for the dedication of the altar (*Bemidbar Rabba* 12:16).

6 **Moses took the wagons and the cattle, and gave them to the Levites.**

7 **Two of the wagons and four of the cattle, he gave to the sons of Gershon, according to their work.** The Gershonites primarily carried the coverings, fashioned from woven fabrics and animal skins. Although these items could be carried by hand, it was easier to transport the large number of items on wagons. The size of the wagons is not specified, but they were presumably quite large, as two were sufficient for the entire burden of the Gershonites.

8 **Four of the wagons and eight of the cattle he gave to the sons of Merari, according to their work, in the hand of Itamar son of Aaron the priest.** The sons of Merari bore the heavy beams and pillars of the Tabernacle, and therefore they required more wagons.

9 **But he did not give to the sons of Kehat** any wagons or cattle, **because the sacred service,** the burden of the sacred Tabernacle vessels, **is upon them.** The burden was borne by the Kehatites physically, and they were not permitted to place them upon animals or to use any other means of transportation. **They shall bear** the sacred vessels **on the shoulder.**^D

10 **The princes brought the dedication of the altar on the day that it was anointed; and the princes** themselves **brought their** unique **offering before the altar.**³⁵

11 **The Lord said to Moses: One prince on each day shall present their offering for the dedication of the altar.** God commanded that an identical ritual should be observed for the offerings of each of the princes. A separate day shall be devoted to the offerings of each of them, for the first twelve days following the inauguration of the altar, according each its appropriate place.

12 **The one who presented his offering on the first day was Nahshon son of Aminadav,**^D **of the tribe of Judah.**

13 **His offering** was comprised of the following: **one silver dish, its weight one hundred and thirty**^B silver shekels; **one silver basin,** thinner than the dish,³⁶ and **of** the weight of **seventy shekels, in the sacred shekel.** The basins were used in the Tabernacle to hold liquids; they were the receptacles in which the blood of the offerings was collected and from which the blood was sprinkled upon the altar. Here, however, they do not yet serve their intended purpose. Rather, **both of them,** the dish and the basin, **were full of high quality flour mixed with oil as a meal offering.**

14 In addition, Nahshon brought **one ladle of** the weight of **ten** shekels **of gold, full of incense.** Although the ladle was smaller

Ram

"Ladle," for the incense

Basin

than the dish and basin, it contained incense, which was more expensive than flour. The offering or gift included both the vessels and their contents.

15 The previous verses listed the gifts made from inanimate materials and from vegetable matter. The gift also included the following animal offerings: **one young bull, one ram, one lamb in its first year,**^D **as a burnt offering;**

ו ז וַיִּקַּח מֹשֶׁה אֶת־הָעֲגָלֹת וְאֶת־הַבָּקָר וַיִּתֵּן אוֹתָם אֶל־הַלְוִיִּם: אֵת ׀ שְׁתֵּי
ח הָעֲגָלוֹת וְאֵת אַרְבַּעַת הַבָּקָר נָתַן לִבְנֵי גֵרְשׁוֹן כְּפִי עֲבֹדָתָם: וְאֵת ׀ אַרְבַּע
הָעֲגָלֹת וְאֵת שְׁמֹנַת הַבָּקָר נָתַן לִבְנֵי מְרָרִי כְּפִי עֲבֹדָתָם בְּיַד אִיתָמָר בֶּן־
ט אַהֲרֹן הַכֹּהֵן: וְלִבְנֵי קְהָת לֹא נָתָן כִּי־עֲבֹדַת הַקֹּדֶשׁ עֲלֵהֶם בַּכָּתֵף יִשָּׂאוּ:
י וַיַּקְרִיבוּ הַנְּשִׂאִים אֵת חֲנֻכַּת הַמִּזְבֵּחַ בְּיוֹם הִמָּשַׁח אֹתוֹ וַיַּקְרִיבוּ הַנְּשִׂיאִם אֶת־
יא קָרְבָּנָם לִפְנֵי הַמִּזְבֵּחַ: וַיֹּאמֶר יְהוָה אֶל־מֹשֶׁה נָשִׂיא אֶחָד לַיּוֹם נָשִׂיא אֶחָד
יב לַיּוֹם יַקְרִיבוּ אֶת־קָרְבָּנָם לַחֲנֻכַּת הַמִּזְבֵּחַ: וַיְהִי הַמַּקְרִיב
יג בַּיּוֹם הָרִאשׁוֹן אֶת־קָרְבָּנוֹ נַחְשׁוֹן בֶּן־עַמִּינָדָב לְמַטֵּה יְהוּדָה: וְקָרְבָּנוֹ קַעֲרַת־
כֶּסֶף אַחַת שְׁלֹשִׁים וּמֵאָה מִשְׁקָלָהּ מִזְרָק אֶחָד כֶּסֶף שִׁבְעִים שֶׁקֶל בְּשֶׁקֶל
יד הַקֹּדֶשׁ שְׁנֵיהֶם ׀ מְלֵאִים סֹלֶת בְּלוּלָה בַשֶּׁמֶן לְמִנְחָה: כַּף אַחַת עֲשָׂרָה זָהָב
טו מְלֵאָה קְטֹרֶת: פַּר אֶחָד בֶּן־בָּקָר אַיִל אֶחָד כֶּבֶשׂ־אֶחָד בֶּן־שְׁנָתוֹ לְעֹלָה:

רש"י

ז| **כפי עבדתם.** שהיה משא בני גרשון קל משל מררי שהיו נושאים הקרשים והעמודים והאדנים:

ט| **כי עבדת הקדש עלהם.** משא דבר הקדושה, "הארון והשלחן" וגו' (לעיל ג, לא), לפיכך "בכתף ישאו":

י| **ויקריבו הנשאים את חנכת המזבח.** לאחר שהתנדבו העגלות והבקר לשאת המשכן, נשאם לבם להתנדב קרבנות המזבח לחנכו: **ויקריבו הנשיאם את קרבנם לפני המזבח.** כי לא קבל משה מידם עד שנאמר לו מפי הגבורה:

יא| **יקריבו את קרבנם לחנכת המזבח.** ועדין לא היה יודע משה היאך יקריבו, אם כסדר תולדותם אם כסדר המסעות, עד שנאמר לו מפי הקדוש ברוך הוא: יקריבו למסעות איש יומו:

יב| **ביום הראשון.** אותו היום נטל עשר עטרות, ראשון למעשה בראשית, ראשון לנשיאים וכו', כדאיתא בסדר עולם (פרק ז): **למטה יהודה.** יחסו הכתוב על שבטו, ולא שגבה משבטו והקריב. או אינו אומר "למטה יהודה" אלא שגבה משבטו והביא? תלמוד לומר: "זה קרבן נחשון" (להלן פסוק יז), משלו הביא:

יג| **שניהם מלאים סלת.** למנחת נדבה:

יד| **עשרה זהב.** כתרגומו, משקל עשר שקלי הקדש היה בה: **מלאה קטרת.** לא מצינו קטרת ליחיד ולא על מזבח החיצון אלא זו בלבד, והוראת שעה היתה:

טו| **פר אחד.** מיחד שבעדרו:

BACKGROUND

7:13| **Its weight one hundred and thirty:** According to the commonly accepted calculations, the shekel weighed 9.6 g. The average weight of shekels found in archaeological excavations is approximately 11.4 g. The silver dishes therefore weighed roughly 1300–1500 g. Depending on its shape and thickness, the dish might have had a diameter of up to 50 cm.

DISCUSSION

7:9| **They shall bear on the shoulder:** Many generations later, when King David sought to bring the Ark of the Covenant to Jerusalem, it was placed on wagons. Despite the stately appearance of this manner of transport, it was prohibited, as the sacred vessels must be carried only upon the shoulder, and the erroneous decision resulted in tragedy (see II Samuel 6:2–8; *Sota* 35a).

7:12| **Nahshon son of Aminadav:** Nahshon was the prince of the tribe of Judah (1:7, 2:3). He was the only prince whose name is mentioned here without the title "prince." This was probably due to his unique status. Nahshon was Aaron's brother-in-law (Exodus 6:23), and according to several *midrashim* he was the first to summon the courage to jump into the Red Sea before it was split by God (see *Sota* 37a; *Bemidbar Rabba* 13:7). Since he was well-known in his own right, it was unnecessary to mention his title (see Abravanel; *Or HaḤayyim*).

7:15| **One ram, one lamb in its first year:** Although the ram and the lamb offering are of the same species, the lamb must be in its first year, whereas the ram must be older.

16 one male **goat as a sin offering;**[D]

17 **and for the peace offering:** partaken of both by its owner and by the priests, **two cattle, five rams, five** male **goats, and five sheep in their first year. This was the offering of Nahshon son of Aminadav.**

Goat

18 **On the second day**[D] **presented** his offering **Netanel son of Tzuar, prince of Issachar.**[D] The prince of Issachar presented his offering immediately after the prince of Judah as Issachar is the second tribe in the camp of Judah (2:1–5).

19 **He presented his offering,** which was identical to that of Nahshon: **One silver dish, its weight one hundred and**

thirty; **one silver basin of seventy shekels, in the sacred shekel; both of them full of high quality flour mixed with oil as a meal offering;**

20 **one ladle of ten** shekels **of gold, full of incense;**

21 **one young bull, one ram, one lamb in its first year, as a burnt offering;**

22 **one goat as a sin offering;**

23 **and for the peace offering: two cattle, five rams, five goats, five sheep in their first year. This was the offering of Netanel son of Tzuar.**

24 The gifts of all the princes are listed, in accordance with the same standard formula as above: **On the third day, prince of the children of Zebulun, Eliav son of Helon.**

25 **His offering was one silver dish, its weight one hundred and thirty; one silver basin of seventy shekels, in the sacred shekel; both of them full of high quality flour mixed with oil as a meal offering;**

26 **one ladle of ten of gold, full of incense;**

27 **one young bull, one ram, one lamb in its first year, as a burnt offering;**

28 **one goat as a sin offering;**

29 **and for the peace offering: two cattle, five rams, five goats, five sheep in their first year. This was the offering of Eliav son of Helon.**

DISCUSSION

7:16 | **One goat as a sin offering:** All of the princes presented male goats as sin offerings, although the Talmud refers to them collectively as the goat of Nahshon, since he was the first to present his offering (*Zevaḥim* 48b). These offerings were exceptional, as the sin offering usually brought in the case of an unwitting transgression is a female sheep or goat (Leviticus 4:28, 4:32). Although the Torah states that a *nasi*, usually translated as "a prince," must bring a male goat as a sin offering (Leviticus 4:22–24), the verse there is referring to a supreme ruler (see commentary ad loc.), whereas here the verse refers to the princes of the tribes. The sin offerings presented by the princes were also exceptional in other ways: The offering was not brought due to a specific sin, but as part of the inauguration of the altar. Since each of the princes presented the same offering, it appears that the offerings were not brought due to any personal failing on the part of the princes, but for the atonement of the entire community, similar to the goats brought as sin offerings on the New Moon and festivals (see *Shevuot* 9a; *Sifrei*; *Zevaḥim* 48b). Furthermore, while sin offerings are usually consumed by the priests, the sin offerings of the

princes were burnt in their entirety on the altar, with no part of them consumed by the priests (see *Zevaḥim* 9b). Since these offerings were exceptional, they required divine sanction, as stated above (7:5; see *Bemidbar Rabba*; *Sifrei* 51; *Menaḥot* 50a).

7:18 | **On the second day:** Although some of the princes were heads of large tribes, whereas others represented small tribes, from a legal and governmental perspective they shared equal status. Consequently, their offerings were completely identical, as the princes presented them as leaders of their tribes and not as private individuals. This was presumably due to a prior arrangement between them. The fact that the princes' gifts were presented due to their status explains the order in which they were presented, which follows the order of their camps: first the camp of Judah, followed by the camp of Reuben, then the camp of Ephraim, and lastly the three tribes of the camp of Dan. The Israelite camp was organized in the manner of a military camp, and the princes, who had clearly defined roles, were like the officers of the different camps.

Presented Netanel son of Tzuar, prince of Issachar: In contrast to the princes listed after him, whose title precedes their name, Netanel's name precedes his title of prince. This is the only instance in which the verb *hikriv*, "presented," appears twice. The verb *hikriv* is usually used as an intransitive verb; however, its grammatical form could indicate the causative form. The repetition of the verb *hikriv* may therefore indicate the presence of both meanings: Netanel presented offerings, and he caused others to present offerings. This may be the source for the opinion of the Sages that the princes' decision to present their own offerings was the initiative of Netanel (see Rashi; *Bekhor Shor*; *Ketav Sofer*; *Bemidbar Rabba* 13; *Sifrei* 52).

The majority of the names of the princes incorporate the name of God, *El*. These so-called theophoric names are far more prevalent among the princes than among their fathers, whose names are also mentioned here. It is possible that the generation of the exodus, who received the Torah, expressed their spirit of faith by means of these names (see commentary on 1:5).

שְׂעִיר־עִזִּים אֶחָד לְחַטָּאת: וּלְזֶבַח הַשְּׁלָמִים בָּקָר שְׁנַיִם אֵילִם חֲמִשָּׁה עַתּוּדִים
חֲמִשָּׁה כְּבָשִׂים בְּנֵי־שָׁנָה חֲמִשָּׁה זֶה קָרְבַּן נַחְשׁוֹן בֶּן־עַמִּינָדָב:

בַּיּוֹם הַשֵּׁנִי הִקְרִיב נְתַנְאֵל בֶּן־צוּעָר נְשִׂיא יִשָּׂשכָר: הִקְרִב אֶת־קָרְבָּנוֹ קַעֲרַת־
כֶּסֶף אַחַת שְׁלֹשִׁים וּמֵאָה מִשְׁקָלָהּ מִזְרָק אֶחָד כֶּסֶף שִׁבְעִים שֶׁקֶל בְּשֶׁקֶל הַקֹּדֶשׁ
שְׁנֵיהֶם ׀ מְלֵאִים סֹלֶת בְּלוּלָה בַשֶּׁמֶן לְמִנְחָה: כַּף אַחַת עֲשָׂרָה זָהָב מְלֵאָה קְטֹרֶת:
פַּר אֶחָד בֶּן־בָּקָר אַיִל אֶחָד כֶּבֶשׂ־אֶחָד בֶּן־שְׁנָתוֹ לְעֹלָה: שְׂעִיר־עִזִּים אֶחָד
לְחַטָּאת: וּלְזֶבַח הַשְּׁלָמִים בָּקָר שְׁנַיִם אֵילִם חֲמִשָּׁה עַתֻּדִים חֲמִשָּׁה כְּבָשִׂים
בְּנֵי־שָׁנָה חֲמִשָּׁה זֶה קָרְבַּן נְתַנְאֵל בֶּן־צוּעָר:

בַּיּוֹם הַשְּׁלִישִׁי נָשִׂיא לִבְנֵי זְבוּלֻן אֱלִיאָב בֶּן־חֵלֹן: קָרְבָּנוֹ קַעֲרַת־כֶּסֶף אַחַת
שְׁלֹשִׁים וּמֵאָה מִשְׁקָלָהּ מִזְרָק אֶחָד כֶּסֶף שִׁבְעִים שֶׁקֶל בְּשֶׁקֶל הַקֹּדֶשׁ שְׁנֵיהֶם ׀
מְלֵאִים סֹלֶת בְּלוּלָה בַשֶּׁמֶן לְמִנְחָה: כַּף אַחַת עֲשָׂרָה זָהָב מְלֵאָה קְטֹרֶת:
פַּר אֶחָד בֶּן־בָּקָר אַיִל אֶחָד כֶּבֶשׂ־אֶחָד בֶּן־שְׁנָתוֹ לְעֹלָה: שְׂעִיר־עִזִּים אֶחָד
לְחַטָּאת: וּלְזֶבַח הַשְּׁלָמִים בָּקָר שְׁנַיִם אֵילִם חֲמִשָּׁה עַתֻּדִים חֲמִשָּׁה כְּבָשִׂים
בְּנֵי־שָׁנָה חֲמִשָּׁה זֶה קָרְבַּן אֱלִיאָב בֶּן־חֵלֹן:

רש"י

טז) שְׂעִיר עִזִּים אֶחָד לְחַטָּאת. לְכַפֵּר עַל קֶבֶר הַתְּהוֹם, טֻמְאַת סָפֵק:

יח-יט) הִקְרִב נְתַנְאֵל בֶּן צוּעָר, הִקְרֵב אֶת קָרְבָּנוֹ. מַה תַּלְמוּד לוֹמַר: "הִקְרִיב" בְּשִׁבְטוֹ שֶׁל יִשָּׂשכָר מַה שֶּׁלֹּא נֶאֱמַר בְּכָל הַשְּׁבָטִים? לְפִי שֶׁבָּא רְאוּבֵן וְעִרְעֵר וְאָמַר: דַּי שֶׁקְּדָמַנִי יְהוּדָה אָחִי, אַקְרִיב אֲנִי אַחֲרָיו. אָמַר לוֹ מֹשֶׁה: מִפִּי הַגְּבוּרָה נֶאֱמַר לִי שֶׁיַּקְרִיבוּ כְּסֵדֶר מַסָּעָן לְדִגְלֵיהֶם. לְכָךְ אָמַר: "הִקְרִב אֶת קָרְבָּנוֹ" וְהוּא חָסֵר יו"ד, שֶׁהוּא מַשְׁמַע "הִקְרַב" לְשׁוֹן צִוּוּי, שֶׁמִּפִּי הַגְּבוּרָה נִצְטַוָּה "הַקְרֵב". וּמַהוּ "הִקְרִיב הִקְרִב" שְׁנֵי פְּעָמִים? שֶׁבִּשְׁבִיל שְׁנֵי דְּבָרִים זָכָה לְהַקְרִיב הַקְרָבָנוֹ שְׁנֵי לַשְּׁבָטִים: אַחַת, שֶׁהָיוּ יוֹדְעִים בַּתּוֹרָה, שֶׁנֶּאֱמַר: "וּמִבְּנֵי יִשָּׂשכָר יוֹדְעֵי בִינָה לַעִתִּים" (דברי הימים א' יב, לג), וְאַחַת – שֶׁהֵם נָתְנוּ עֵצָה לַנְּשִׂיאִים לְהִתְנַדֵּב קָרְבָּנוֹת הַלָּלוּ.

וּבִיסוֹדוֹ שֶׁל רַבִּי מֹשֶׁה הַדַּרְשָׁן מָצָאתִי: אָמַר רַבִּי פִּנְחָס בֶּן יָאִיר: נְתַנְאֵל בֶּן צוּעָר הִשִּׂיאָן עֵצָה זוֹ: קַעֲרַת כָּסֶף.

מִנְיַן אוֹתִיּוֹתֶיהָ בְּגִימַטְרִיָּא תתק"ל, כְּנֶגֶד שְׁנוֹתָיו שֶׁל אָדָם הָרִאשׁוֹן: שְׁלֹשִׁים וּמֵאָה מִשְׁקָלָהּ. עַל שֵׁם שֶׁכְּשֶׁהֶעֱמִיד תּוֹלְדוֹת לְקִיּוּם הָעוֹלָם בֶּן מֵאָה וּשְׁלֹשִׁים שָׁנָה הָיָה, שֶׁנֶּאֱמַר: "וַיְחִי אָדָם שְׁלֹשִׁים וּמְאַת שָׁנָה וַיּוֹלֶד בִּדְמוּתוֹ" וְגוֹ' (בראשית ה, ג). מִזְרָק אֶחָד כָּסֶף. בְּגִימַטְרִיָּא תק"כ, עַל שֵׁם נֹחַ שֶׁהֶעֱמִיד תּוֹלְדוֹת בֶּן ת"ק שָׁנָה, וְעַל שֵׁם עֶשְׂרִים שָׁנָה שֶׁנִּגְזְרָה גְּזֵרַת הַמַּבּוּל קֹדֶם תּוֹלְדוֹתָיו, כְּמוֹ שֶׁפֵּרַשְׁתִּי אֵצֶל "וְהָיוּ יָמָיו מֵאָה וְעֶשְׂרִים שָׁנָה" (שם ו, ג). לְפִיכָךְ נֶאֱמַר: "מִזְרָק אֶחָד כָּסֶף" וְלֹא נֶאֱמַר "מִזְרַק כָּסֶף אֶחָד" כְּמוֹ שֶׁנֶּאֱמַר בַּקְּעָרָה, לוֹמַר שֶׁאַף אוֹתִיּוֹת שֶׁל 'אֶחָד' מִצְטָרְפוֹת לַמִּנְיָן: שִׁבְעִים שֶׁקֶל. כְּנֶגֶד שִׁבְעִים אֻמּוֹת שֶׁיָּצְאוּ מִבָּנָיו: כַּף אַחַת. כְּנֶגֶד הַתּוֹרָה שֶׁנִּתְּנָה מִיָּדוֹ שֶׁל הַקָּדוֹשׁ בָּרוּךְ הוּא: עֲשָׂרָה זָהָב. כְּנֶגֶד עֲשֶׂרֶת הַדִּבְּרוֹת: מְלֵאָה קְטֹרֶת. גִּימַטְרִיָּא שֶׁל קְטֹרֶת תרי"ג מִצְווֹת, וּבִלְבַד שֶׁתַּחֲלִיף קו"ף בְּדָלֶ"ת עַל יְדֵי א"ת ב"ש ג"ר ד"ק: פַּר אֶחָד. כְּנֶגֶד אַבְרָהָם, שֶׁנֶּאֱמַר: "וַיִּקַּח בֶּן בָּקָר" (שם יח, ז): אַיִל אֶחָד. כְּנֶגֶד יִצְחָק, שֶׁנֶּאֱמַר: "וַיִּקַּח אֶת

הָאַיִל" וְגוֹ' (שם כב, יג): כֶּבֶשׂ אֶחָד. כְּנֶגֶד יַעֲקֹב, שֶׁנֶּאֱמַר: "וְהַכְּשָׂבִים הִפְרִיד יַעֲקֹב" (שם ל, מ): שְׂעִיר עִזִּים. לְכַפֵּר עַל מְכִירַת יוֹסֵף, שֶׁנֶּאֱמַר בּוֹ: "וַיִּשְׁחֲטוּ שְׂעִיר עִזִּים" (שם לז, לא): וּלְזֶבַח הַשְּׁלָמִים בָּקָר שְׁנַיִם. כְּנֶגֶד מֹשֶׁה וְאַהֲרֹן שֶׁנָּתְנוּ שָׁלוֹם בֵּין יִשְׂרָאֵל לַאֲבִיהֶם שֶׁבַּשָּׁמַיִם: אֵילִם עַתּוּדִים כְּבָשִׂים. שְׁלֹשָׁה מִינִים, כְּנֶגֶד כֹּהֲנִים וּלְוִיִּם וְיִשְׂרָאֵלִים, וּכְנֶגֶד תּוֹרָה נְבִיאִים וּכְתוּבִים: שְׁלֹשָׁה חֲמִשִּׁיּוֹת, כְּנֶגֶד חֲמִשָּׁה חֻמָּשִׁין, וַחֲמֵשֶׁת הַדִּבְּרוֹת הַכְּתוּבִין עַל לוּחַ אֶחָד, וַחֲמֵשֶׁת הַכְּתוּבִין עַל הַשֵּׁנִי. עַד כָּאן מִיסוֹדוֹ שֶׁל רַבִּי מֹשֶׁה הַדַּרְשָׁן:

כד) בַּיּוֹם הַשְּׁלִישִׁי נָשִׂיא וְגוֹ'. בַּיּוֹם הַשְּׁלִישִׁי הָיָה הַנָּשִׂיא הַמַּקְרִיב לִבְנֵי זְבוּלֻן, וְכֵן כֻּלָּם. אֲבָל בִּנְתַנְאֵל שֶׁנֶּאֱמַר בּוֹ: "הִקְרִיב נְתַנְאֵל" (לעיל פסוק יח) נוֹפֵל אַחֲרָיו הַלָּשׁוֹן לוֹמַר: "נָשִׂיא יִשָּׂשכָר", לְפִי שֶׁכְּבָר הִזְכִּיר שְׁמוֹ וְהִקְרִיבַתְנִי, וּבִשְׁאָר כֻּלָּם נֶאֱמַר בָּהֶן "הִקְרִיב", נוֹפֵל עֲלֵיהֶן לָשׁוֹן זֶה: נָשִׂיא לִבְנֵי פְּלוֹנִי, אוֹתוֹ הַיּוֹם הָיָה הַנָּשִׂיא הַמַּקְרִיב לְשֵׁבֶט פְּלוֹנִי:

30 On the fourth day, prince of the children of Reuben, Elitzur son of Shede'ur.

31 His offering was one silver dish, its weight one hundred and thirty; one silver basin of seventy shekels, in the sacred shekel; both of them full of high quality flour mixed with oil as a meal offering;

32 one ladle of ten of gold, full of incense;

33 one young bull, one ram, one lamb in its first year, as a burnt offering;

34 one goat as a sin offering;

35 and for the peace offering: two cattle, five rams, five goats, five sheep in their first year. This was the offering of Elitzur son of Shede'ur.

36 On the fifth day, prince of the children of Simeon, Shelumiel son of Tzurishadai.

37 His offering was one silver dish, its weight one hundred and thirty; one silver basin of seventy shekels, in the sacred shekel; both of them full of high quality flour mixed with oil as a meal offering;

38 one ladle of ten of gold, full of incense;

39 one young bull, one ram, one lamb in its first year, as a burnt offering;

40 one goat as a sin offering;

41 and for the peace offering: two cattle, five rams, five goats, five sheep in their first year. This was the offering of Shelumiel son of Tzurishadai.

Sixth 42 On the sixth day, prince of the children of Gad, Elyasaf son
aliya   of De'uel.

43 His offering was one silver dish, its weight one hundred and thirty; one silver basin of seventy shekels, in the sacred shekel; both of them full of high quality flour mixed with oil as a meal offering;

44 one ladle of ten of gold, full of incense;

45 one young bull, one ram, one lamb in its first year, as a burnt offering;

46 one goat as a sin offering;

47 and for the peace offering: two cattle, five rams, five goats, five sheep in their first year. This was the offering of Elyasaf son of De'uel.

48 On the seventh day, prince of the children of Ephraim, Elishama son of Amihud.

49 His offering was one silver dish, its weight one hundred and thirty; one silver basin of seventy shekels, in the sacred shekel; both of them full of high quality flour mixed with oil as a meal offering;

50 one ladle of ten of gold, full of incense;

51 one young bull, one ram, one lamb in its first year, as a burnt offering;

52 one goat as a sin offering;

53 and for the peace offering: two cattle, five rams, five goats, five sheep in their first year. This was the offering of Elishama son of Amihud.

Ancient silver dish

DISCUSSION

The Transition from God's Miraculous Leadership to His Natural Leadership: Lists of the tribes of Israel appear in several places in the Torah (Genesis 46, 49; Exodus 1; Numbers 1, 2, 7, 10, 13, 26, 34; Deuteronomy 27, 33). The lists vary; in some the order is chronological, in others it is not. In some Levi and Joseph are listed, in others Joseph's sons are listed in their stead.

One of differences between the two censuses conducted by Moses in the book of Numbers, the first one in the second year (chap. 1) and second one in the fortieth year (chap. 26), is the order in which the tribes of Manasseh and Ephraim are listed. In the first census, Ephraim precedes Manasseh, the same order in which they appeared in the blessing that Jacob bestowed upon them before his death (Genesis 48). In the second census, Manasseh precedes Ephraim.

The Netziv from Volozhin in his introduction to his *Haamek Davar* on the book of Numbers explains that Numbers marks the transition between God's miraculous leadership of the children of Israel in the wilderness and God's natural leadership of the children of Israel as they prepared to enter the Land of Israel. That transition starts at the beginning of chapter 11 after the second inverted letter *nun*. After the immediate punishment that they incurred for the relatively minor infraction of the mourners, the children of Israel felt that they could no longer live with the intimate presence of God in their midst. It was that sentiment that ultimately led to the sin of the spies.

In the first census, which reflected the miraculous leadership of God, Ephraim was listed first because his superiority over his elder brother was in the spiritual realm. In the second census, which reflected the natural leadership of God, Manasseh the elder took precedence.

ל לא בַּיּוֹם הָרְבִיעִי נָשִׂיא לִבְנֵי רְאוּבֵן אֱלִיצוּר בֶּן־שְׁדֵיאוּר: קָרְבָּנוֹ קַעֲרַת־כֶּסֶף
אַחַת שְׁלֹשִׁים וּמֵאָה מִשְׁקָלָהּ מִזְרָק אֶחָד כֶּסֶף שִׁבְעִים שֶׁקֶל בְּשֶׁקֶל הַקֹּדֶשׁ
לב שְׁנֵיהֶם ׀ מְלֵאִים סֹלֶת בְּלוּלָה בַשֶּׁמֶן לְמִנְחָה: כַּף אַחַת עֲשָׂרָה זָהָב מְלֵאָה קְטֹרֶת:
לג לד פַּר אֶחָד בֶּן־בָּקָר אַיִל אֶחָד כֶּבֶשׂ־אֶחָד בֶּן־שְׁנָתוֹ לְעֹלָה: שְׂעִיר־עִזִּים אֶחָד
לה לְחַטָּאת: וּלְזֶבַח הַשְּׁלָמִים בָּקָר שְׁנַיִם אֵילִם חֲמִשָּׁה עַתֻּדִים חֲמִשָּׁה כְּבָשִׂים
בְּנֵי־שָׁנָה חֲמִשָּׁה זֶה קָרְבַּן אֱלִיצוּר בֶּן־שְׁדֵיאוּר:

לו לז בַּיּוֹם הַחֲמִישִׁי נָשִׂיא לִבְנֵי שִׁמְעוֹן שְׁלֻמִיאֵל בֶּן־צוּרִישַׁדָּי: קָרְבָּנוֹ קַעֲרַת־כֶּסֶף
אַחַת שְׁלֹשִׁים וּמֵאָה מִשְׁקָלָהּ מִזְרָק אֶחָד כֶּסֶף שִׁבְעִים שֶׁקֶל בְּשֶׁקֶל הַקֹּדֶשׁ
לח שְׁנֵיהֶם ׀ מְלֵאִים סֹלֶת בְּלוּלָה בַשֶּׁמֶן לְמִנְחָה: כַּף אַחַת עֲשָׂרָה זָהָב מְלֵאָה
לט מ קְטֹרֶת: פַּר אֶחָד בֶּן־בָּקָר אַיִל אֶחָד כֶּבֶשׂ־אֶחָד בֶּן־שְׁנָתוֹ לְעֹלָה: שְׂעִיר־עִזִּים
מא אֶחָד לְחַטָּאת: וּלְזֶבַח הַשְּׁלָמִים בָּקָר שְׁנַיִם אֵילִם חֲמִשָּׁה עַתֻּדִים חֲמִשָּׁה כְּבָשִׂים
בְּנֵי־שָׁנָה חֲמִשָּׁה זֶה קָרְבַּן שְׁלֻמִיאֵל בֶּן־צוּרִישַׁדָּי:

מב מג בַּיּוֹם הַשִּׁשִּׁי נָשִׂיא לִבְנֵי גָד אֶלְיָסָף בֶּן־דְּעוּאֵל: קָרְבָּנוֹ קַעֲרַת־כֶּסֶף אַחַת שְׁלֹשִׁים ששי
וּמֵאָה מִשְׁקָלָהּ מִזְרָק אֶחָד כֶּסֶף שִׁבְעִים שֶׁקֶל בְּשֶׁקֶל הַקֹּדֶשׁ שְׁנֵיהֶם ׀ מְלֵאִים
מד מה סֹלֶת בְּלוּלָה בַשֶּׁמֶן לְמִנְחָה: כַּף אַחַת עֲשָׂרָה זָהָב מְלֵאָה קְטֹרֶת: פַּר אֶחָד
מו בֶּן־בָּקָר אַיִל אֶחָד כֶּבֶשׂ־אֶחָד בֶּן־שְׁנָתוֹ לְעֹלָה: שְׂעִיר־עִזִּים אֶחָד לְחַטָּאת:
מז וּלְזֶבַח הַשְּׁלָמִים בָּקָר שְׁנַיִם אֵילִם חֲמִשָּׁה עַתֻּדִים חֲמִשָּׁה כְּבָשִׂים בְּנֵי־שָׁנָה
חֲמִשָּׁה זֶה קָרְבַּן אֶלְיָסָף בֶּן־דְּעוּאֵל:

מח מט בַּיּוֹם הַשְּׁבִיעִי נָשִׂיא לִבְנֵי אֶפְרָיִם אֱלִישָׁמָע בֶּן־עַמִּיהוּד: קָרְבָּנוֹ קַעֲרַת־כֶּסֶף ז
אַחַת שְׁלֹשִׁים וּמֵאָה מִשְׁקָלָהּ מִזְרָק אֶחָד כֶּסֶף שִׁבְעִים שֶׁקֶל בְּשֶׁקֶל הַקֹּדֶשׁ
נ שְׁנֵיהֶם ׀ מְלֵאִים סֹלֶת בְּלוּלָה בַשֶּׁמֶן לְמִנְחָה: כַּף אַחַת עֲשָׂרָה זָהָב מְלֵאָה
נא נב קְטֹרֶת: פַּר אֶחָד בֶּן־בָּקָר אַיִל אֶחָד כֶּבֶשׂ־אֶחָד בֶּן־שְׁנָתוֹ לְעֹלָה: שְׂעִיר־עִזִּים
נג אֶחָד לְחַטָּאת: וּלְזֶבַח הַשְּׁלָמִים בָּקָר שְׁנַיִם אֵילִם חֲמִשָּׁה עַתֻּדִים חֲמִשָּׁה כְּבָשִׂים
בְּנֵי־שָׁנָה חֲמִשָּׁה זֶה קָרְבַּן אֱלִישָׁמָע בֶּן־עַמִּיהוּד:

54 On the eighth day, prince of the children of Manasseh, Gamliel son of Pedatzur.
55 His offering was one silver dish, its weight one hundred and thirty; one silver basin of seventy shekels, in the sacred shekel; both of them full of high quality flour mixed with oil as a meal offering;
56 one ladle of ten of gold, full of incense;
57 one young bull, one ram, one lamb in its first year, as a burnt offering;
58 one goat as a sin offering;
59 and for the peace offering: two cattle, five rams, five goats, five sheep in their first year. This was the offering of Gamliel son of Pedatzur.
60 On the ninth day, prince of the children of Benjamin, Avidan son of Gidoni.
61 His offering was one silver dish, its weight one hundred and thirty; one silver basin of seventy shekels, in the sacred shekel; both of them full of high quality flour mixed with oil as a meal offering;
62 one ladle of ten of gold, full of incense;
63 one young bull, one ram, one lamb in its first year, as a burnt offering;
64 one goat as a sin offering;
65 and for the peace offering: two cattle, five rams, five goats, five sheep in their first year. This was the offering of Avidan son of Gidoni.
66 On the tenth day, prince of the children of Dan, Ahiezer son of Amishadai.
67 His offering was one silver dish, its weight one hundred and thirty; one silver basin of seventy shekels, in the sacred shekel; both of them full of high quality flour mixed with oil as a meal offering;
68 one ladle of ten of gold, full of incense;
69 one young bull, one ram, one lamb in its first year, as a burnt offering;
70 one goat as a sin offering;
71 and for the peace offering: two cattle, five rams, five goats, five sheep in their first year. This was the offering of Ahiezer son of Amishadai.
Seventh aliya
72 On the eleventh day, prince of the children of Asher, Pagiel son of Okhran.
73 His offering was one silver dish, its weight one hundred and thirty; one silver basin of seventy shekels, in the sacred shekel; both of them full of high quality flour mixed with oil as a meal offering;
74 one ladle of ten of gold, full of incense;
75 one young bull, one ram, one lamb in its first year, as a burnt offering;
76 one goat as a sin offering;
77 and for the peace offering: two cattle, five rams, five goats, five sheep in their first year. This was the offering of Pagiel son of Okhran.

DISCUSSION

First Day of the First Month: The Talmud, based on the opinion that the Torah was not given in its entirety at Sinai, but rather was given by God to Moses scroll by scroll (see *Gittin* 60a), states that Rabbi Levi says: Eight portions were stated on the day that the Tabernacle was established. They are: the portion of the priests (Leviticus 21:1–22:26); the portion of the Levites (Numbers 8:5–26); the portion of the impure (Leviticus 13:1–14:57); the portion of the sending away of the impure (Numbers 5:1–4); the portion beginning with the words "after the death" (Leviticus, chap. 16), in which the details of the Yom Kippur service, including the prohibition of entering the Holy of Holies on any day other than Yom Kippur, are articulated; the portion dealing with priests intoxicated with wine (Leviticus 10:8–11); the portion of the lamps (Numbers 8:1–7); and the section of the red heifer (Numbers, chap. 19), as all of these portions are directly related to the service in the Tabernacle.

In a note at the end of this chapter, a dispute whether the inauguration of the Tabernacle took place on the first day or on the eighth day of the first month is cited. The opinion that appears more often in rabbinic literature and in the commentaries is that the Tabernacle was established and inaugurated on the first day of the first month. According to that opinion, all the commandments in the above portions were commanded on the first day of the first month.

The Talmud arrives at the conclusion that the details of the Yom Kippur service were commanded on that day based on the introduction to that portion: "The Lord spoke to Moses after the death of the two sons of Aaron, when they approached before the Lord and they died" (Leviticus 16:1). Nadav and Avihu were killed during the inauguration of the Temple; therefore, the passage commanded after their deaths was apparently commanded on that day.

There is an additional portion, not listed in the passage cited above, that was stated on that day: The portion of the second *Pesaḥ* (Num. 9:1–14). The portion begins: "The Lord spoke to Moses in the wilderness of Sinai, during the second year since their exodus from the land of Egypt, in the first month, saying." Because no date is mentioned, presumably it was on the first of the month. It is not included in the passage cited above because although the paschal lamb, whether offered on the fourteenth day of the first month or on the fourteenth day of the second month, is offered in the Tabernacle, it is not a necessary prerequisite to the functioning of the Tabernacle.

נה בַּיּוֹם֙ הַשְּׁמִינִ֔י נָשִׂ֖יא לִבְנֵ֣י מְנַשֶּׁ֑ה גַּמְלִיאֵ֖ל בֶּן־פְּדָהצֽוּר: קׇרְבָּנ֞וֹ קַֽעֲרַת־כֶּ֣סֶף אַחַ֗ת

שְׁלֹשִׁ֣ים וּמֵאָה֮ מִשְׁקָלָהּ֒ מִזְרָ֤ק אֶחָד֙ כֶּ֔סֶף שִׁבְעִ֥ים שֶׁ֖קֶל בְּשֶׁ֣קֶל הַקֹּ֑דֶשׁ שְׁנֵיהֶ֣ם ׀

נו מְלֵאִ֗ים סֹ֛לֶת בְּלוּלָ֥ה בַשֶּׁ֖מֶן לְמִנְחָֽה: כַּ֥ף אַחַ֛ת עֲשָׂרָ֥ה זָהָ֖ב מְלֵאָ֥ה קְטֹֽרֶת:

נז נח פַּ֣ר אֶחָ֞ד בֶּן־בָּקָ֗ר אַ֧יִל אֶחָ֛ד כֶּֽבֶשׂ־אֶחָ֥ד בֶּן־שְׁנָת֖וֹ לְעֹלָֽה: שְׂעִיר־עִזִּ֥ים אֶחָ֖ד

נט לְחַטָּֽאת: וּלְזֶ֣בַח הַשְּׁלָמִים֮ בָּקָ֣ר שְׁנַ֒יִם֒ אֵילִ֤ם חֲמִשָּׁה֙ עַתֻּדִ֣ים חֲמִשָּׁ֔ה כְּבָשִׂ֥ים

בְּנֵֽי־שָׁנָ֖ה חֲמִשָּׁ֑ה זֶ֛ה קׇרְבַּ֥ן גַּמְלִיאֵ֖ל בֶּן־פְּדָהצֽוּר:

בַּיּוֹם֙ הַתְּשִׁיעִ֔י נָשִׂ֖יא לִבְנֵ֣י בִנְיָמִ֑ן אֲבִידָ֖ן בֶּן־גִּדְעֹנִֽי: קׇרְבָּנ֞וֹ קַֽעֲרַת־כֶּ֣סֶף אַחַ֗ת

סא שְׁלֹשִׁ֣ים וּמֵאָה֮ מִשְׁקָלָהּ֒ מִזְרָ֤ק אֶחָד֙ כֶּ֔סֶף שִׁבְעִ֥ים שֶׁ֖קֶל בְּשֶׁ֣קֶל הַקֹּ֑דֶשׁ שְׁנֵיהֶ֣ם ׀

סב מְלֵאִ֗ים סֹ֛לֶת בְּלוּלָ֥ה בַשֶּׁ֖מֶן לְמִנְחָֽה: כַּ֥ף אַחַ֛ת עֲשָׂרָ֥ה זָהָ֖ב מְלֵאָ֥ה קְטֹֽרֶת:

סג סד פַּ֣ר אֶחָ֞ד בֶּן־בָּקָ֗ר אַ֧יִל אֶחָ֛ד כֶּֽבֶשׂ־אֶחָ֥ד בֶּן־שְׁנָת֖וֹ לְעֹלָֽה: שְׂעִיר־עִזִּ֥ים אֶחָ֖ד

סה לְחַטָּֽאת: וּלְזֶ֣בַח הַשְּׁלָמִים֮ בָּקָ֣ר שְׁנַ֒יִם֒ אֵילִ֤ם חֲמִשָּׁה֙ עַתֻּדִ֣ים חֲמִשָּׁ֔ה כְּבָשִׂ֥ים

בְּנֵֽי־שָׁנָ֖ה חֲמִשָּׁ֑ה זֶ֛ה קׇרְבַּ֥ן אֲבִידָ֖ן בֶּן־גִּדְעֹנִֽי:

סו סז בַּיּוֹם֙ הָֽעֲשִׂירִ֔י נָשִׂ֖יא לִבְנֵ֣י דָ֑ן אֲחִיעֶ֖זֶר בֶּן־עַמִּֽישַׁדָּֽי: קׇרְבָּנ֞וֹ קַֽעֲרַת־כֶּ֣סֶף אַחַ֗ת

שְׁלֹשִׁ֣ים וּמֵאָה֮ מִשְׁקָלָהּ֒ מִזְרָ֤ק אֶחָד֙ כֶּ֔סֶף שִׁבְעִ֥ים שֶׁ֖קֶל בְּשֶׁ֣קֶל הַקֹּ֑דֶשׁ שְׁנֵיהֶ֣ם ׀

סח מְלֵאִ֗ים סֹ֛לֶת בְּלוּלָ֥ה בַשֶּׁ֖מֶן לְמִנְחָֽה: כַּ֥ף אַחַ֛ת עֲשָׂרָ֥ה זָהָ֖ב מְלֵאָ֥ה קְטֹֽרֶת:

סט ע פַּ֣ר אֶחָ֞ד בֶּן־בָּקָ֗ר אַ֧יִל אֶחָ֛ד כֶּֽבֶשׂ־אֶחָ֥ד בֶּן־שְׁנָת֖וֹ לְעֹלָֽה: שְׂעִיר־עִזִּ֥ים אֶחָ֖ד

עא לְחַטָּֽאת: וּלְזֶ֣בַח הַשְּׁלָמִים֮ בָּקָ֣ר שְׁנַ֒יִם֒ אֵילִ֤ם חֲמִשָּׁה֙ עַתֻּדִ֣ים חֲמִשָּׁ֔ה כְּבָשִׂ֥ים

בְּנֵֽי־שָׁנָ֖ה חֲמִשָּׁ֑ה זֶ֛ה קׇרְבַּ֥ן אֲחִיעֶ֖זֶר בֶּן־עַמִּֽישַׁדָּֽי:

עב עג בַּיּוֹם֙ עַשְׁתֵּ֣י עָשָׂ֣ר י֔וֹם נָשִׂ֖יא לִבְנֵ֣י אָשֵׁ֑ר פַּגְעִיאֵ֖ל בֶּן־עׇכְרָֽן: קׇרְבָּנ֞וֹ קַֽעֲרַת־כֶּ֣סֶף שביעי

אַחַ֗ת שְׁלֹשִׁ֣ים וּמֵאָה֮ מִשְׁקָלָהּ֒ מִזְרָ֤ק אֶחָד֙ כֶּ֔סֶף שִׁבְעִ֥ים שֶׁ֖קֶל בְּשֶׁ֣קֶל הַקֹּ֑דֶשׁ

עד שְׁנֵיהֶ֣ם ׀ מְלֵאִ֗ים סֹ֛לֶת בְּלוּלָ֥ה בַשֶּׁ֖מֶן לְמִנְחָֽה: כַּ֥ף אַחַ֛ת עֲשָׂרָ֥ה זָהָ֖ב מְלֵאָ֥ה

עה עו קְטֹֽרֶת: פַּ֣ר אֶחָ֞ד בֶּן־בָּקָ֗ר אַ֧יִל אֶחָ֛ד כֶּֽבֶשׂ־אֶחָ֥ד בֶּן־שְׁנָת֖וֹ לְעֹלָֽה: שְׂעִיר־עִזִּ֥ים

עז אֶחָ֖ד לְחַטָּֽאת: וּלְזֶ֣בַח הַשְּׁלָמִים֮ בָּקָ֣ר שְׁנַ֒יִם֒ אֵילִ֤ם חֲמִשָּׁה֙ עַתֻּדִ֣ים חֲמִשָּׁ֔ה כְּבָשִׂ֥ים

בְּנֵֽי־שָׁנָ֖ה חֲמִשָּׁ֑ה זֶ֛ה קׇרְבַּ֥ן פַּגְעִיאֵ֖ל בֶּן־עׇכְרָֽן:

78 **On the twelfth day, prince of the children of Naphtali, Ahira son of Einan.**
79 **His offering was one silver dish, its weight one hundred and thirty; one silver basin of seventy shekels, in the sacred shekel; both of them full of high quality flour mixed with oil as a meal offering;**
80 **one ladle of ten of gold, full of incense;**
81 **one young bull, one ram, one lamb in its first year, as a burnt offering;**
82 **one goat as a sin offering;**
83 **and for the peace offering: two cattle, five rams, five goats, five sheep in their first year. This was the offering of Ahira son of Einan.**[D]
84 The chapter sums up the total number of offerings presented: **This was the dedication of the altar, on the day when it was anointed,** the gift **from the princes of Israel: twelve silver dishes, twelve silver basins, twelve golden ladles.**
85 The Torah reiterates the particulars of these gifts: **One hundred and thirty** shekels **was** the weight of **each silver dish and seventy** shekels was the weight of **each basin. All the silver of the vessels** donated by the princes **was two thousand and four hundred, in the sacred shekel.**
86 The list continues: **Twelve golden ladles, full of incense, ten** shekels was the weight of **each ladle, in the sacred shekel; all the gold of the ladles was one hundred and twenty** shekels, not including the incense.
87 *Maftir* **All the cattle for the burnt offering** totaled **twelve bulls, twelve rams,** and **twelve sheep in their first year. And** these were accompanied by **their meal offering,** as all burnt offerings must be. **And twelve goats** were brought, each of them **as a sin offering.**
88 **All the cattle of the peace offerings were twenty-four bulls, sixty rams, sixty goats,** and **sixty sheep in their first year. This was the dedication of the altar, after it was anointed.** These celebratory offerings were brought as part of the dedication ceremony.
89 These gifts were presented after the Tabernacle was anointed and the Divine Presence was revealed there. Yet the Divine Presence did not reside in the Tabernacle merely temporarily. **When Moses went into the Tent of Meeting to speak with Him, he heard the voice speaking to him from above the ark cover that was upon the Ark of the Testimony, from between the two cherubs. And** in this manner **He,** God, **spoke to him.** This concluding verse serves as an explanation for all the aforementioned gifts and donations: The Tabernacle is no mere construction. It is the tent in which God meets with Moses. It is the place where God communicates with His world, through a direct encounter that occurs when Moses approaches the Ark of the Covenant.

DISCUSSION

Was the Inauguration of the Tabernacle on the First Day of the First Month?: The seven days of investiture [*miluim*] culminated with the inauguration of the Tabernacle on the eighth day, which is described in detail in Leviticus (chap. 9). There is a dispute between the Sages (see *Seder Olam* 7:1; *Sifrei Bemidbar* 9:6), and a dispute between the commentaries with regard to the date when the seven days of investiture commenced, and the date one week later when the Tabernacle was inaugurated.

Rashi explains that the investiture commenced on the twenty-third day of Adar, and the inauguration was on the New Moon of Nisan. This is based on the opinion cited by the Sages (*Sifra Tzav*) who explain that the sin offering about which Moses inquired on the day of the inauguration, and was angry when he discovered that it was burned, was the sin offering of the New Moon.

Ibn Ezra explains that the investiture commenced on the New Moon of Nisan and the inauguration was on the eighth day of Nisan. This is based on the opinion cited by the Sages (*Sifrei Bemidbar* 9:6) that the people who were impure by means of a corpse and expressed their desire to offer the paschal lamb were Mishael and Eltzafan, who carried their brethren, Nadav and Avihu, from inside the Sanctuary on the day of the inauguration of the Tabernacle. They were impurified on the eighth and could not complete the purification process before the fourteenth, the day on which the paschal lamb is offered.

7:83 | **This was the offering of Ahira son of Einan:** The verses which describe the offerings of the princes are repeated on each occasion word for word, letter by letter, with the same vowels, and the same cantillation notes. It can be suggested that this repetition is not merely due to the Torah's regard for the princes and their gifts (see Ramban); it also serves to emphasize the uniqueness of each of the princes. Despite the fact that they all agreed at the outset to bring the same gifts, each had his own intentions. Although they brought identical gifts that expressed their common public status, each prince was a unique individual, and therefore each offering had its distinct significance. For this reason, ancient midrashic sources found symbolic meanings in each of the gifts, which relate to the character of the prince who presented the gift, to the events of his life, and to his inheritance in the Land of Israel. This is in spite of the fact that the source material for these expositions: the gifts, their weights, and their numbers, are all identical. These expositions are based on the idea that the same act holds diverse meanings when performed by different individuals (*Bemidbar Rabba* 13:9–14:10).

עח
עט
בְּיוֹם שְׁנֵים עָשָׂר יוֹם נָשִׂיא לִבְנֵי נַפְתָּלִי אֲחִירַע בֶּן־עֵינָן: קָרְבָּנוֹ קַעֲרַת־כֶּסֶף אַחַת שְׁלֹשִׁים וּמֵאָה מִשְׁקָלָהּ מִזְרָק אֶחָד כֶּסֶף שִׁבְעִים שֶׁקֶל בְּשֶׁקֶל הַקֹּדֶשׁ

פ
שְׁנֵיהֶם ׀ מְלֵאִים סֹלֶת בְּלוּלָה בַשֶּׁמֶן לְמִנְחָה: כַּף אַחַת עֲשָׂרָה זָהָב מְלֵאָה

פא
פב
קְטֹרֶת: פַּר אֶחָד בֶּן־בָּקָר אַיִל אֶחָד כֶּבֶשׂ־אֶחָד בֶּן־שְׁנָתוֹ לְעֹלָה: שְׂעִיר־עִזִּים אֶחָד לְחַטָּאת: וּלְזֶבַח הַשְּׁלָמִים בָּקָר שְׁנַיִם אֵילִם חֲמִשָּׁה עַתֻּדִים חֲמִשָּׁה כְּבָשִׂים

פג
בְּנֵי־שָׁנָה חֲמִשָּׁה זֶה קָרְבַּן אֲחִירַע בֶּן־עֵינָן:

פד
זֹאת ׀ חֲנֻכַּת הַמִּזְבֵּחַ בְּיוֹם הִמָּשַׁח אֹתוֹ מֵאֵת נְשִׂיאֵי יִשְׂרָאֵל קַעֲרֹת כֶּסֶף שְׁתֵּים

פה
עֶשְׂרֵה מִזְרְקֵי־כֶסֶף שְׁנֵים עָשָׂר כַּפּוֹת זָהָב שְׁתֵּים עֶשְׂרֵה: שְׁלֹשִׁים וּמֵאָה הַקְּעָרָה הָאַחַת כֶּסֶף וְשִׁבְעִים הַמִּזְרָק הָאֶחָד כֹּל כֶּסֶף הַכֵּלִים אַלְפַּיִם וְאַרְבַּע־מֵאוֹת

פו
בְּשֶׁקֶל הַקֹּדֶשׁ: כַּפּוֹת זָהָב שְׁתֵּים־עֶשְׂרֵה מְלֵאֹת קְטֹרֶת עֲשָׂרָה עֲשָׂרָה הַכַּף

פז
מפטיר
בְּשֶׁקֶל הַקֹּדֶשׁ כָּל־זְהַב הַכַּפּוֹת עֶשְׂרִים וּמֵאָה: כָּל־הַבָּקָר לָעֹלָה שְׁנֵים עָשָׂר פָּרִים אֵילִם שְׁנֵים־עָשָׂר כְּבָשִׂים בְּנֵי־שָׁנָה שְׁנֵים עָשָׂר וּמִנְחָתָם וּשְׂעִירֵי עִזִּים

פח
שְׁנֵים עָשָׂר לְחַטָּאת: וְכֹל ׀ בְּקַר זֶבַח הַשְּׁלָמִים עֶשְׂרִים וְאַרְבָּעָה פָּרִים אֵילִם שִׁשִּׁים עַתֻּדִים שִׁשִּׁים כְּבָשִׂים בְּנֵי־שָׁנָה שִׁשִּׁים זֹאת חֲנֻכַּת הַמִּזְבֵּחַ אַחֲרֵי הִמָּשַׁח

פט
אֹתוֹ: וּבְבֹא מֹשֶׁה אֶל־אֹהֶל מוֹעֵד לְדַבֵּר אִתּוֹ וַיִּשְׁמַע אֶת־הַקּוֹל מִדַּבֵּר אֵלָיו מֵעַל הַכַּפֹּרֶת אֲשֶׁר עַל־אֲרֹן הָעֵדֻת מִבֵּין שְׁנֵי הַכְּרֻבִים וַיְדַבֵּר אֵלָיו:

פד | בְּיוֹם הִמָּשַׁח אֹתוֹ. בּוֹ בַּיּוֹם שֶׁנִּמְשַׁח הִקְרִיב, וּמָה אֲנִי מְקַיֵּם "אַחֲרֵי הִמָּשַׁח" (להלן פסוק פח)? שֶׁנִּמְשַׁח תְּחִלָּה וְאַחַר כָּךְ הִקְרִיב. אוֹ "אַחֲרֵי הִמָּשַׁח" לְאַחַר זְמַן, וְלֹא בָּא לְלַמֵּד "בְּיוֹם הִמָּשַׁח" אֶלָּא לוֹמַר שֶׁנִּמְשַׁח בַּיּוֹם? כְּשֶׁהוּא אוֹמֵר: "בְּיוֹם מָשְׁחוֹ אֹתָם" (ויקרא ז, לו), לָמַדְנוּ שֶׁנִּמְשַׁח בַּיּוֹם, וּמַה תַּלְמוּד לוֹמַר: "בְּיוֹם הִמָּשַׁח אֹתוֹ"? בַּיּוֹם שֶׁנִּמְשַׁח הִקְרִיב: קַעֲרֹת כֶּסֶף שְׁתֵּים עֶשְׂרֵה. הֵם הֵם שֶׁהִתְנַדְּבוּ, וְלֹא אֵרַע בָּהֶם פְּסוּל:

פה | שְׁלֹשִׁים וּמֵאָה הַקְּעָרָה הָאַחַת וְגו'. מַה תַּלְמוּד לוֹמַר? לְפִי שֶׁנֶּאֱמַר: "שְׁלֹשִׁים וּמֵאָה מִשְׁקָלָהּ" וְלֹא פֵּרַשׁ בְּאֵי זוֹ שֶׁקֶל, לְכָךְ חָזַר וּשְׁנָאָהּ כָּאן וְכָלַל בְּכֻלָּן: "כֹּל כֶּסֶף

הַכֵּלִים... בְּשֶׁקֶל הַקֹּדֶשׁ": כֹּל כֶּסֶף הַכֵּלִים וְגו'. לִמֶּדְךָ שֶׁהָיוּ כְּלֵי הַמִּקְדָּשׁ מְכֻוָּנִים בְּמִשְׁקָלָן, שׁוֹקְלָן אֶחָד אֶחָד וְשׁוֹקְלָן כֻּלָּן כְּאֶחָד, לֹא רִבָּה וְלֹא מִעֵט:

פו | כַּפּוֹת זָהָב שְׁתֵּים עֶשְׂרֵה. לָמָּה נֶאֱמַר? לְפִי שֶׁנֶּאֱמַר: "כַּף אַחַת עֲשָׂרָה זָהָב", הִיא שֶׁל זָהָב וּמִשְׁקָלָהּ עֲשָׂרָה שְׁקָלִים שֶׁל כֶּסֶף; אוֹ אֵינוֹ אֶלָּא כַּף אַחַת שֶׁל כֶּסֶף וּמִשְׁקָלָהּ עֲשָׂרָה שִׁקְלֵי זָהָב חִין מִשְׁקָלָם שָׁוֶה לַעֲשָׂרָה שֶׁל כֶּסֶף? תַּלְמוּד לוֹמַר: "כַּפּוֹת זָהָב", שֶׁל זָהָב הָיוּ:

פט | וּבְבֹא מֹשֶׁה. שְׁנֵי כְתוּבִים הַמַּכְחִישִׁים זֶה אֶת זֶה, בָּא שְׁלִישִׁי וְהִכְרִיעַ בֵּינֵיהֶם. כָּתוּב אֶחָד אוֹמֵר: "וַיְדַבֵּר ה' אֵלָיו

מֵאֹהֶל מוֹעֵד" (ויקרא א, א), וְהוּא חוּץ לַפָּרֹכֶת, וְכָתוּב אֶחָד אוֹמֵר: "וְדִבַּרְתִּי אִתְּךָ מֵעַל הַכַּפֹּרֶת" (שמות כה, כב), בָּא זֶה וְהִכְרִיעַ בֵּינֵיהֶם: מֹשֶׁה בָּא אֶל אֹהֶל מוֹעֵד, וְשָׁם שׁוֹמֵעַ אֶת הַקּוֹל הַבָּא מֵעַל הַכַּפֹּרֶת מִבֵּין שְׁנֵי הַכְּרֻבִים, הַקּוֹל יוֹצֵא מִן הַשָּׁמַיִם לְבֵין שְׁנֵי הַכְּרֻבִים, וּמִשָּׁם יוֹצֵא לְאֹהֶל מוֹעֵד: מִדַּבֵּר. כְּמוֹ 'מִתְדַּבֵּר', כְּבוֹדוֹ שֶׁל מַעְלָה לוֹמַר כֵּן, מִדַּבֵּר בֵּינוֹ לְבֵין עַצְמוֹ, וּמֹשֶׁה שׁוֹמֵעַ מֵאֵלָיו: וַיְדַבֵּר אֵלָיו. לְמַעֵט אֶת אַהֲרֹן מִן הַדִּבְּרוֹת: וַיִּשְׁמַע אֶת הַקּוֹל. יָכוֹל קוֹל נָמוּךְ? תַּלְמוּד לוֹמַר: "אֶת הַקּוֹל", הוּא הַקּוֹל שֶׁנִּדְבַּר עִמּוֹ בְּסִינַי, וּכְשֶׁמַּגִּיעַ לַפֶּתַח הָיָה נִפְסָק וְלֹא הָיָה יוֹצֵא חוּץ לָאֹהֶל:

777

Parashat
Behaalotekha

Kindling the Candelabrum
NUMBERS 8:1–4

Kindling the candelabrum has already been mentioned twice in the Torah.[1] However, this passage contains a practical command that was not previously stated, and which is relevant beginning from the very first day of service in the Tabernacle. Some explain that this passage appears here in order to complement the preceding description of the gifts of the tribal princes to the Tabernacle. Each tribe's prince gave a donation, with the exception of Aaron, prince of the tribe of Levi. Therefore, the verse mentions Aaron's role in kindling the candelabrum, which is parallel to the offerings brought by the other tribal princes in honor of the inauguration of the Tabernacle.[2]

8 1 **The Lord spoke to Moses, saying:**

2 **Speak to Aaron, and say to him: When you kindle the lamps, the seven lamps shall illuminate toward the front of the candelabrum,** the middle branch, which forms the body of the candelabrum. The branches of the candelabrum culminated with lamps, which were vessels that held the oil and wicks with a spout that could be turned in any direction. Aaron was commanded to ensure that these spouts would face the middle branch of the candelabrum.[3] Alternatively, some commentaries explain that this verse means that the spouts should face the area in front of the candelabrum,[4] either the curtain separating the Sanctuary from the Holy of Holies or the table for the showbread.[5]

3 **Aaron did so; toward the front of the candelabrum he kindled its lamps, as the Lord had commanded Moses.**

4 **This is the craftsmanship of the candelabrum: Hammered gold; from its base to its** decorative **flowers on its branches, it is hammered;** the entire candelabrum was sculpted from one piece of gold, without welding or otherwise attaching other pieces. **Like the vision that the Lord showed Moses, so he crafted the candelabrum.** From the descriptions in the Torah, it is difficult to fully understand what the candelabrum was supposed to look like, including the shape and number of its decorative knobs and flowers. Consequently, God showed Moses an image of the candelabrum on Mount Sinai, and then Moses was able to instruct the artisans as to its construction.

Kindling the lamps of the candelabrum

Taking the Levites
NUMBERS 8:5–26

The work of the Levites in the Tabernacle was described in the opening chapters of Numbers. However, their role requires more than just the performance of certain actions; it requires a high level of sanctity. Consequently, their induction includes a purification ritual. After describing the role of the priests in kindling the candelabrum, the Torah issues a command with regard to the manner in which the Levites, who are subordinate to the priests, are to be inducted into their role.

5 **The Lord spoke to Moses, saying:**

6 **Take the Levites from among the children of Israel, and purify them.**

7 **So shall you do to them, to purify them: Sprinkle upon them purification water** from a red heifer (see 19:1–13), **and they shall pass a razor over all their flesh,** shaving off all the

פרשת
בהעלתך

ח א וַיְדַבֵּר יְהוָֹה אֶל־מֹשֶׁה לֵּאמֹר: דַּבֵּר אֶל־אַהֲרֹן וְאָמַרְתָּ אֵלָיו בְּהַעֲלֹתְךָ אֶת־
ג הַנֵּרֹת אֶל־מוּל פְּנֵי הַמְּנוֹרָה יָאִירוּ שִׁבְעַת הַנֵּרוֹת: וַיַּעַשׂ כֵּן אַהֲרֹן אֶל־מוּל פְּנֵי
ד הַמְּנוֹרָה הֶעֱלָה נֵרֹתֶיהָ כַּאֲשֶׁר צִוָּה יְהוָֹה אֶת־מֹשֶׁה: וְזֶה מַעֲשֵׂה הַמְּנֹרָה מִקְשָׁה
זָהָב עַד־יְרֵכָהּ עַד־פִּרְחָהּ מִקְשָׁה הִוא כַּמַּרְאֶה אֲשֶׁר הֶרְאָה יְהוָֹה אֶת־מֹשֶׁה כֵּן
עָשָׂה אֶת־הַמְּנֹרָה:

ה וַיְדַבֵּר יְהוָֹה אֶל־מֹשֶׁה לֵּאמֹר: קַח אֶת־הַלְוִיִּם מִתּוֹךְ בְּנֵי יִשְׂרָאֵל וְטִהַרְתָּ אֹתָם:
ז וְכֹה־תַעֲשֶׂה לָהֶם לְטַהֲרָם הַזֵּה עֲלֵיהֶם מֵי חַטָּאת וְהֶעֱבִירוּ תַעַר עַל־כָּל־בְּשָׂרָם
ח וְכִבְּסוּ בִגְדֵיהֶם וְהִטֶּהָרוּ: וְלָקְחוּ פַּר בֶּן־בָּקָר וּמִנְחָתוֹ סֹלֶת בְּלוּלָה בַשָּׁמֶן וּפַר־
ט שֵׁנִי בֶן־בָּקָר תִּקַּח לְחַטָּאת: וְהִקְרַבְתָּ אֶת־הַלְוִיִּם לִפְנֵי אֹהֶל מוֹעֵד וְהִקְהַלְתָּ

רש"י

ב] בְּהַעֲלֹתְךָ. לָמָּה נִסְמְכָה פָּרָשַׁת הַמְּנוֹרָה לְפָרָשַׁת הַנְּשִׂיאִים? לְפִי שֶׁכְּשֶׁרָאָה אַהֲרֹן חֲנֻכַּת הַנְּשִׂיאִים חָלְשָׁה דַעְתּוֹ, שֶׁלֹּא הָיָה עִמָּהֶם בַּחֲנֻכָּה לֹא הוּא וְלֹא שִׁבְטוֹ, אָמַר לוֹ הַקָּדוֹשׁ בָּרוּךְ הוּא: חַיֶּיךָ, שֶׁלְּךָ גְּדוֹלָה מִשֶּׁלָּהֶם, שֶׁאַתָּה מַדְלִיק וּמֵיטִיב אֶת הַנֵּרוֹת: עַל שֵׁם שֶׁהַלֶּהַב עוֹלֶה כָּתוּב בְּהַדְלָקָתָן לְשׁוֹן עֲלִיָּה, שֶׁצָּרִיךְ לְהַדְלִיק עַד שֶׁתְּהֵא שַׁלְהֶבֶת עוֹלָה מֵאֵלֶיהָ. וְעוֹד דָּרְשׁוּ רַבּוֹתֵינוּ מִכַּאן שֶׁמַּעֲלָה הָיְתָה לִפְנֵי הַמְּנוֹרָה שֶׁעָלֶיהָ הַכֹּהֵן עוֹמֵד וּמֵיטִיב. אֶל מוּל נֵר הַמַּעֲרָבִי, שֶׁאֵינוֹ בָּקָנִים אֶלָּא בְּגוּף שֶׁל מְנוֹרָה. שֶׁבַּע שֶׁעַל שֵׁשֶׁת הַקָּנִים, שְׁלֹשָׁה הַמִּזְרָחִיִּים פּוֹנִים לְמוּל הָאֶמְצָעִי, הַפְּתִילוֹת שֶׁבָּהֶן, וְכֵן שְׁלֹשָׁה הַמַּעֲרָבִיִּים רָאשֵׁי הַפְּתִילוֹת לְמוּל הָאֶמְצָעִי. וְלָמָּה? כְּדֵי שֶׁלֹּא יֹאמְרוּ: לְאוֹרָה הוּא צָרִיךְ:

ג] וַיַּעַשׂ כֵּן אַהֲרֹן. לְהַגִּיד שִׁבְחוֹ שֶׁל אַהֲרֹן שֶׁלֹּא שִׁנָּה:

ד] וְזֶה מַעֲשֵׂה הַמְּנֹרָה. שֶׁהֶרְאָהוּ הַקָּדוֹשׁ בָּרוּךְ הוּא בְּאֶצְבַּע, לְפִי שֶׁנִּתְקַשָּׁה בָהּ, לְכָךְ נֶאֱמַר: "זֶה": מִקְשָׁה. בטדי"ץ בְּלַעַז, לְשׁוֹן: "דַּח לְדָח נָקְשָׁן" (דניאל ה, ו). עֲשַׁת שֶׁל כִּכַּר זָהָב הָיְתָה, וּמַקִּישׁ בְּקֻרְנָס וְחוֹתֵךְ בְּכַשְׁיִל לְפַשֵּׁט אֵיבָרֶיהָ כְּתִקּוּנָן, וְלֹא נַעֲשֵׂית אֵיבָרִים אֵיבָרִים עַל יְדֵי חִבּוּר: עַד יְרֵכָהּ עַד פִּרְחָהּ. יְרֵכָהּ הִיא הַשִּׁדָּה שֶׁעַל הָרַגְלַיִם, חָלוּל, כְּדֶרֶךְ מְנוֹרוֹת כֶּסֶף שֶׁלִּפְנֵי הַשָּׂרִים: עַד יְרֵכָהּ עַד פִּרְחָהּ. כְּלוֹמַר גּוּפָהּ שֶׁל מְנוֹרָה כֻּלָּהּ וְכָל הַתָּלוּי בָּהּ: עַד יְרֵכָהּ. שֶׁהוּא אֵיבָר גָּדוֹל עַד פִּרְחָהּ. שֶׁהוּא מַעֲשֵׂה דַּק שֶׁבָּהּ, הַכֹּל "מִקְשָׁה". וְדֶרֶךְ 'עַד' לְשַׁמֵּשׁ בְּלָשׁוֹן זֶה, כְּמוֹ: "מִגָּדִישׁ וְעַד קָמָה וְעַד כֶּרֶם זָיִת" (שופטים טו, ה): כַּמַּרְאֶה אֲשֶׁר הֶרְאָה וְגו'. כַּתַּבְנִית אֲשֶׁר הֶרְאָהוּ בָּהָר, כְּמוֹ שֶׁנֶּאֱמַר: "וּרְאֵה וַעֲשֵׂה בְּתַבְנִיתָם" וְגו' (שמות כה, מ): כֵּן עָשָׂה אֶת הַמְּנֹרָה. מִי שֶׁעֲשָׂאָהּ. וּמִדְרַשׁ אַגָּדָה: עַל יְדֵי הַקָּדוֹשׁ בָּרוּךְ הוּא נַעֲשֵׂית מֵאֵלֶיהָ:

ו] קַח אֶת הַלְוִיִּם. קָחֵם בִּדְבָרִים: 'אַשְׁרֵיכֶם שֶׁתִּזְכּוּ לִהְיוֹת שַׁמָּשִׁים לַמָּקוֹם':

ז] הַזֵּה עֲלֵיהֶם מֵי חַטָּאת. שֶׁל אֵפֶר הַפָּרָה, מִפְּנֵי טְמֵאֵי מֵתִים שֶׁבָּהֶם: וְהֶעֱבִירוּ תַעַר. מָצָאתִי בְּדִבְרֵי רַבִּי מֹשֶׁה הַדַּרְשָׁן, לְפִי שֶׁנִּתְּנוּ כַּפָּרָה עַל הַבְּכוֹרוֹת שֶׁעָבְדוּ עֲבוֹדָה זָרָה, וְהִיא קְרוּיָה "זִבְחֵי מֵתִים" (תהלים קו, כח), וְהַמְצֹרָע קָרוּי "מֵת" (להלן יב, יב), הִזְקִיקָם תִּגְלַחַת כַּמְצֹרָעִים:

ח] וְלָקְחוּ פַּר בֶּן בָּקָר. וְהוּא עוֹלָה, כְּמוֹ שֶׁנֶּאֱמַר: "וַעֲשֵׂה אֶת הָאֶחָד... עֹלָה" (להלן פסוק יב), וְהוּא קָרְבַּן צִבּוּר בַּעֲבוֹדָה זָרָה (להלן טו, כד): וּפַר שֵׁנִי. מַה תַּלְמוּד לוֹמַר "שֵׁנִי"? לוֹמַר לְךָ, מַה עוֹלָה לֹא נֶאֱכֶלֶת אַף חַטָּאת לֹא נֶאֱכֶלֶת, וּבְזוֹ יֵשׁ סֶמֶךְ לְדִבְרָיו בְּתוֹרַת כֹּהֲנִים (חובה פרק ג, ז). וַאֲנִי אוֹמֵר חַטַּאת שֶׁהוֹרָאַת שָׁעָה הָיְתָה, שֶׁצָּעִיר זֶה הָיָה לָהֶם לִהְיוֹת לְחַטָּאת שָׁעָה זֶה עִם פַּר הָעוֹלָה:

ט] וְהִקְהַלְתָּ אֶת כָּל עֵדַת. לְפִי שֶׁהַלְוִיִּם נְתוּנִים קָרְבָּן

---

hair on their heads, beards and bodies, **and they shall wash their clothes and become pure** by immersing in a ritual bath.
8 **They,** the Levites, **shall take a young bull** as a burnt offering, **and its meal offering,** made from **high-quality flour mixed**

with oil; and a second young bull you, Moses, shall take as a sin offering as part of their purification process.
9 **You shall bring the Levites before the Tent of Meeting and**

you shall assemble the entire congregation of the children of Israel, as this matter pertains to them as well.

10 **You shall bring the Levites before the Lord; and the** representatives of the **children of Israel shall lay their hands upon the Levites.** The representatives may have been the Sanhedrin or the firstborn, who were replaced by the Levites.[6] The laying of the hands in this ceremony was parallel to the rite of one who brings an offering, who must lay his hands upon the head of the offering he brings. By this act, the Levites were designated as a sort of offering, consecrated by the nation to work in the Tabernacle instead of the firstborn and to act as representatives of the entire nation.[7]

11 **Aaron shall wave the Levites as a wave offering before the Lord from the children of Israel, and they shall be** designated **to perform the service of the Lord.** Similar to an offering, the Levites were bestowed with a special status, for which they had to undergo preparatory rites parallel to those of an offering. Just as a priest waves parts of certain offerings, so Aaron was commanded to wave the Levites. This was a difficult procedure that required great physical strength.

12 The children of Israel shall lay their hands on the heads of the Levites, and **the Levites shall lay their hands upon the heads of the** two **bulls,** which are the offerings actually sacrificed on the altar; **and you shall perform the one as a sin offering, and the one as a burnt offering, to the Lord, to atone for the Levites.**

13 **You shall have the Levites stand before Aaron and before his sons, and** you, Moses, shall also **wave them as a wave offering to the Lord** as part of their rite of sanctification.

14 **You shall separate the Levites from the midst of the children of Israel, and the Levites shall be Mine** as My honor guard.

15 **Thereafter the Levites shall come to serve the Tent of Meeting; you shall purify them, and wave them as a wave offering** before they come to serve.

Second aliya

16 **For they are given to Me**[D] **from among the children of Israel. In place of the one that emerges first from each womb, the firstborn, of all the children of Israel, I have taken them for Myself.**

17 **For all the firstborn among the children of Israel are Mine, man and animal; on the day that I smote all the firstborn in the land of Egypt I sanctified them for Myself,** to serve Me.

18 **I have** then **taken the Levites in place of all the firstborn among the children of Israel.**

19 **I have given the Levites, given to Aaron and to his sons from among the children of Israel, to perform the service of the children of Israel in the Tent of Meeting, and to atone for the children of Israel, and** accordingly **there shall not be a stroke against the children of Israel, when the children of Israel approach the Sanctuary.** The regular watch of the Levites will ensure that the Israelites do not touch sanctified items improperly, and it will thereby protect the Israelites from harm. The Levites required training for their position to remain in the Tabernacle or Temple, to perform services there and to prevent those who were not fit from entering. It was difficult to demand this of the firstborn of every Israelite household, but possible to set aside one small tribe for this purpose.[8]

20 **Moses, Aaron, and the entire congregation of the children of Israel did to the Levites in accordance with everything that the Lord commanded Moses with regard to the Levites, so the children of Israel did to them.**

21 **The Levites purified themselves, and they washed their clothes, and Aaron waved them as a wave offering before the Lord. Aaron atoned for them to purify them** and thereby elevate them so that they would be worthy of their task.

22 **Thereafter the Levites came to perform their service in the Tent of Meeting before Aaron, and before his sons; as the Lord had commanded Moses with regard to the Levites, so they did to them.**

23 The Torah continues the previous topic and concludes the section: **The Lord spoke to Moses, saying:**

24 **This is with regard to the Levites: From twenty-five years**

DISCUSSION

8:16 | **For they are given [*netunim netunim*] to Me:** The word given [*netunim*] is repeated in this phrase in order to indicate that the Levites are entirely given to God, to the point that their status applies even to their children. Another interpretation is that they are given in two manners: Once by their own free will, and once in that they have been selected by God. Alternatively, they are given on their own merit and as replacements for the firstborn (see Sforno).

8:24 | **From twenty-five years old and above:** This instruction is different than what was stated above, with regard to the Levites from the family of Kehat: "From thirty years old and above and until fifty years old, all those enlisted for duty, to perform labor in the Tent of Meeting" (4:3). Apparently, the Levites began their service at the age of twenty-five, therefore for the first five years they trained and acted as replacements in the performance of the actual service. When they reached the age of thirty, they were considered mature and reliable enough to be appointed to their own positions of service (see *Bekhor Shor* here, and 4:3, 22).

אֶת־כׇּל־עֲדַת בְּנֵי יִשְׂרָאֵל: וְהִקְרַבְתָּ אֶת־הַלְוִיִּם לִפְנֵי יהוה וְסָמְכוּ בְנֵי־יִשְׂרָאֵל י
אֶת־יְדֵיהֶם עַל־הַלְוִיִּם: וְהֵנִיף אַהֲרֹן אֶת־הַלְוִיִּם תְּנוּפָה לִפְנֵי יהוה מֵאֵת בְּנֵי יא
יִשְׂרָאֵל וְהָיוּ לַעֲבֹד אֶת־עֲבֹדַת יהוה: וְהַלְוִיִּם יִסְמְכוּ אֶת־יְדֵיהֶם עַל רֹאשׁ יב
הַפָּרִים וַעֲשֵׂה אֶת־הָאֶחָד חַטָּאת וְאֶת־הָאֶחָד עֹלָה לַיהוה לְכַפֵּר עַל־הַלְוִיִּם:
וְהַעֲמַדְתָּ אֶת־הַלְוִיִּם לִפְנֵי אַהֲרֹן וְלִפְנֵי בָנָיו וְהֵנַפְתָּ אֹתָם תְּנוּפָה לַיהוה: וְהִבְדַּלְתָּ יג יד
אֶת־הַלְוִיִּם מִתּוֹךְ בְּנֵי יִשְׂרָאֵל וְהָיוּ לִי הַלְוִיִּם: וְאַחֲרֵי־כֵן יָבֹאוּ הַלְוִיִּם לַעֲבֹד שני טו
אֶת־אֹהֶל מוֹעֵד וְטִהַרְתָּ אֹתָם וְהֵנַפְתָּ אֹתָם תְּנוּפָה: כִּי נְתֻנִים נְתֻנִים הֵמָּה לִי טז
מִתּוֹךְ בְּנֵי יִשְׂרָאֵל תַּחַת פִּטְרַת כׇּל־רֶחֶם בְּכוֹר כֹּל מִבְּנֵי יִשְׂרָאֵל לָקַחְתִּי אֹתָם
לִי: כִּי לִי כׇל־בְּכוֹר בִּבְנֵי יִשְׂרָאֵל בָּאָדָם וּבַבְּהֵמָה בְּיוֹם הַכֹּתִי כׇל־בְּכוֹר בְּאֶרֶץ יז
מִצְרַיִם הִקְדַּשְׁתִּי אֹתָם לִי: וָאֶקַּח אֶת־הַלְוִיִּם תַּחַת כׇּל־בְּכוֹר בִּבְנֵי יִשְׂרָאֵל: יח
וָאֶתְּנָה אֶת־הַלְוִיִּם נְתֻנִים ׀ לְאַהֲרֹן וּלְבָנָיו מִתּוֹךְ בְּנֵי יִשְׂרָאֵל לַעֲבֹד אֶת־עֲבֹדַת יט
בְּנֵי־יִשְׂרָאֵל בְּאֹהֶל מוֹעֵד וּלְכַפֵּר עַל־בְּנֵי יִשְׂרָאֵל וְלֹא יִהְיֶה בִּבְנֵי יִשְׂרָאֵל נֶגֶף
בְּגֶשֶׁת בְּנֵי־יִשְׂרָאֵל אֶל־הַקֹּדֶשׁ: וַיַּעַשׂ מֹשֶׁה וְאַהֲרֹן וְכׇל־עֲדַת בְּנֵי־יִשְׂרָאֵל כ
לַלְוִיִּם כְּכֹל אֲשֶׁר־צִוָּה יהוה אֶת־מֹשֶׁה לַלְוִיִּם כֵּן־עָשׂוּ לָהֶם בְּנֵי יִשְׂרָאֵל: כא
וַיִּתְחַטְּאוּ הַלְוִיִּם וַיְכַבְּסוּ בִּגְדֵיהֶם וַיָּנֶף אַהֲרֹן אֹתָם תְּנוּפָה לִפְנֵי יהוה וַיְכַפֵּר
עֲלֵיהֶם אַהֲרֹן לְטַהֲרָם: וְאַחֲרֵי־כֵן בָּאוּ הַלְוִיִּם לַעֲבֹד אֶת־עֲבֹדָתָם בְּאֹהֶל כב
מוֹעֵד לִפְנֵי אַהֲרֹן וְלִפְנֵי בָנָיו כַּאֲשֶׁר צִוָּה יהוה אֶת־מֹשֶׁה עַל־הַלְוִיִּם כֵּן עָשׂוּ
לָהֶם: וַיְדַבֵּר יהוה אֶל־מֹשֶׁה לֵּאמֹר: זֹאת אֲשֶׁר לַלְוִיִּם מִבֶּן חָמֵשׁ וְעֶשְׂרִים כג כד

רש"י

כַּפָּרָה תַּחְתֵּיהֶם, יָבוֹאוּ וְיַעַמְדוּ עַל קׇרְבָּנָם וְיִסְמְכוּ אֶת יְדֵיהֶם עֲלֵיהֶם:

יא] וְהֵנִיף אַהֲרֹן אֶת הַלְוִיִּם תְּנוּפָה. כְּדֶרֶךְ שֶׁאָשָׁם מְצֹרָע טָעוּן תְּנוּפָה חַי (ויקרא יד, יב). שָׁלֹשׁ תְּנוּפוֹת נֶאֶמְרוּ בְּפָרָשָׁה זוֹ: הָרִאשׁוֹנָה לִבְנֵי קְהָת, לְכָךְ נֶאֱמַר בָּם: "וְהָיוּ לַעֲבֹד אֶת עֲבֹדַת ה'", לְפִי שֶׁעֲבוֹדַת קֹדֶשׁ הַקֳּדָשִׁים עֲלֵיהֶם, "הָאָרֹן וְהַשֻּׁלְחָן" וְגוֹ' (לעיל ג, לא). הַשְּׁנִיָּה לִבְנֵי גֵרְשׁוֹן, לְכָךְ נֶאֱמַר בָּם: "תְּנוּפָה לַה'" (להלן פסוק יג), שֶׁאַף עֲלֵיהֶם הָיְתָה עֲבוֹדַת הַקֹּדֶשׁ – יְרִיעוֹת וּקְרָסִים הַנִּרְאִים בְּבֵית קֹדֶשׁ הַקֳּדָשִׁים; וְהַשְּׁלִישִׁית לִבְנֵי מְרָרִי (להלן פסוק טו):

טז] נְתֻנִים נְתֻנִים. נְתוּנִים לְמַשָּׂא, נְתוּנִים לְשִׁיר. פִּטְרַת. פְּתִיחַת.

יז] כִּי לִי כׇל בְּכוֹר. שֶׁלִּי הָיוּ הַבְּכוֹרוֹת בְּקַו הַדִּין, שֶׁהִגַּנְתִּי עֲלֵיהֶם בֵּין בְּכוֹרֵי מִצְרַיִם וְלָקַחְתִּי אוֹתָם לִי, עַד שֶׁטָּעוּ בָּעֵגֶל, וְעַכְשָׁיו: "וָאֶקַּח אֶת הַלְוִיִּם" וְגוֹ' (להלן פסוק יח).

יט] וָאֶתְּנָה וְגוֹ'. חֲמִשָּׁה פְּעָמִים נֶאֱמַר 'בְּנֵי יִשְׂרָאֵל' בְּמִקְרָא זֶה, לְהוֹדִיעַ חִבָּתָן, שֶׁנִּכְפְּלוּ אַזְכָּרוֹתֵיהֶן בְּמִקְרָא אֶחָד כְּמִנְיַן חֲמִשָּׁה חֻמְשֵׁי תוֹרָה, כָּךְ רָאִיתִי בִּבְרֵאשִׁית רַבָּה (ג, ה). וְלֹא יִהְיֶה בִּבְנֵי יִשְׂרָאֵל נֶגֶף. שֶׁלֹּא יִצְטָרְכוּ לָגֶשֶׁת אֶל הַקֹּדֶשׁ, שֶׁאִם יִגְּשׁוּ יִהְיֶה נֶגֶף:

כ] וַיַּעַשׂ מֹשֶׁה וְאַהֲרֹן וְכׇל עֲדַת וְגוֹ'. מֹשֶׁה הֶעֱמִידָן, וְאַהֲרֹן הֵנִיף, וְיִשְׂרָאֵל סָמְכוּ אֶת יְדֵיהֶם:

כב] כַּאֲשֶׁר צִוָּה ה' וְגוֹ' כֵּן עָשׂוּ. לְהַגִּיד שִׁבְחָן שֶׁל הָעוֹשִׂין וְהַנַּעֲשָׂה בָהֶן, שֶׁאֶחָד מֵהֶם לֹא עִכֵּב:

old and above[D] **he shall enlist to perform duty in the work**
of the Tent of Meeting.
25 **From fifty years old, he shall return from the duty of the**
work, and he shall work no more in physically demanding
labor such as carrying the vessels.
26 **He shall serve with his brethren**[D] **in the Tent of Meeting,** as
an aid to the other Levites, **to stand a watch** over the Levites'
other tasks, **but** physical **work he shall not perform. So shall**
you do with the Levites with regard to their watches.[9]

Second Pesaḥ

NUMBERS 9:1–14

This passage, which precedes the opening section of the book of Numbers chronologically, begins with a reminder to the Israelites to sacrifice the paschal lamb in the year following the exodus from Egypt. Now that the Tabernacle has been constructed and the Divine Presence rests there, the nation is commanded to bring this offering, which in the previous year, in Egypt, had been mandated as a personal commandment to each individual. The nation as a whole observes this commandment, but there are individuals who are unable to do so due to being ritually impure. In response to their request, God introduces the laws of the second *Pesaḥ*. This is one of the few instances in the Torah where a commandment is introduced as a divine solution to a human request.

9 1 **The Lord spoke to Moses** in the Tent of Meeting **in the wil-**
Third aliya **derness of Sinai, during the second year,** one full year **since**
their exodus from the land of Egypt, in the first month,
Nisan, **saying:**
2 **The children of Israel shall offer the paschal lamb**[D] **at its ap-**
pointed time.
3 **On the fourteenth day of that month, in the afternoon,** from
when the sun begins its descent in the western portion of the
sky until it completely sets,[10] **you shall offer it at its appointed**
time; in accordance with all its statutes and in accordance
with all its ordinances, you shall offer it. There were commandments issued with regard to the paschal lamb offered in
Egypt that applied only that year, such as the requirement to
apply its blood to the lintel and side-posts instead of applying
the blood to the altar. However, other commandments that
were issued with regard to the paschal lamb in Egypt apply for
all time.[11]
4 **Moses spoke to the children of Israel, to offer the paschal**
lamb.
5 **They offered the paschal lamb during the first month, on**
the fourteenth day of the month, in the afternoon, in the
wilderness of Sinai; in accordance with everything that the
Lord commanded Moses, so the children of Israel did.
6 **There were men** in the camp **who were impure by means of**
a corpse,[D] **and they were unable to offer the paschal lamb**
on that day, as one who is ritually impure is prohibited from
entering the sacred areas or partaking of sacrificial food; **and**
they approached Moses and Aaron on that day.
7 **Those men said to him: We are impure by means of a corpse**
through no fault of our own; generally, one who becomes impure from a corpse has acted properly by attending to the burial
needs of his relative.[12] Consequently, **why shall we be deprived**

DISCUSSION

8:25–26 | **From fifty years old.... He shall serve with their brethren:** The Levites' term of service begins later and ends earlier than that of Israelites: Whereas Israelites would be counted as soldiers from the age of twenty until sixty, Levites served from age thirty to fifty. However, in practice the Levites would begin their training at age twenty-five, and even after they reached the age of fifty they would continue to serve as guards and perhaps to perform other tasks such as opening and closing the gates of the Temple, loading the wagons to transport the Tabernacle through the wilderness, and supervising the performance of other tasks (see Rashi; Ramban; *Ḥullin* 24a; *Sifrei*; Ramban, *Sefer HaMitzvot*, *Shoresh* 3).

9:2 | **The children of Israel shall offer the paschal lamb:** Although the Israelites had already been commanded to observe all of the festivals, it is possible that Passover was the only one that was actually observed in the wilderness with the consumption of offerings (see Ramban, 28:2 and Leviticus 23:2). Another explanation for the fact that a reminder is issued only with regard to Passover is that the initial commandment to sacrifice the paschal lamb was issued on the first day of the month of Nisan, before the exodus from Egypt (Exodus chap. 12), one year before the reminder mentioned in this passage. It would be possible to mistakenly think that the offering sacrificed in Egypt was a preparatory ritual for the exodus, whereas the permanent commandment to sacrifice the paschal lamb would apply only in the land of Israel, as the verse indicates: "It shall be when you come to the land… you shall observe this service" (Exodus 12:25; see

כה שָׁנָה וָמַעְלָה יָבוֹא לִצְבֹא צָבָא בַּעֲבֹדַת אֹהֶל מוֹעֵד: וּמִבֶּן חֲמִשִּׁים שָׁנָה יָשׁוּב

כו מִצְּבָא הָעֲבֹדָה וְלֹא יַעֲבֹד עוֹד: וְשֵׁרֵת אֶת־אֶחָיו בְּאֹהֶל מוֹעֵד לִשְׁמֹר מִשְׁמֶרֶת וַעֲבֹדָה לֹא יַעֲבֹד כָּכָה תַּעֲשֶׂה לַלְוִיִּם בְּמִשְׁמְרֹתָם:

שלישי

א וַיְדַבֵּר יְהוָה אֶל־מֹשֶׁה בְמִדְבַּר־סִינַי בַּשָּׁנָה הַשֵּׁנִית לְצֵאתָם מֵאֶרֶץ מִצְרַיִם בַּחֹדֶשׁ

ב הָרִאשׁוֹן לֵאמֹר: וְיַעֲשׂוּ בְנֵי־יִשְׂרָאֵל אֶת־הַפָּסַח בְּמוֹעֲדוֹ: בְּאַרְבָּעָה עָשָׂר־יוֹם

ג בַּחֹדֶשׁ הַזֶּה בֵּין הָעַרְבַּיִם תַּעֲשׂוּ אֹתוֹ בְּמֹעֲדוֹ כְּכָל־חֻקֹּתָיו וּכְכָל־מִשְׁפָּטָיו תַּעֲשׂוּ

ד אֹתוֹ: וַיְדַבֵּר מֹשֶׁה אֶל־בְּנֵי יִשְׂרָאֵל לַעֲשֹׂת הַפָּסַח: וַיַּעֲשׂוּ אֶת־הַפֶּסַח בָּרִאשׁוֹן

ה בְּאַרְבָּעָה עָשָׂר יוֹם לַחֹדֶשׁ בֵּין הָעַרְבַּיִם בְּמִדְבַּר סִינָי כְּכֹל אֲשֶׁר צִוָּה יְהוָה אֶת־

מֹשֶׁה כֵּן עָשׂוּ בְּנֵי יִשְׂרָאֵל: וַיְהִי אֲנָשִׁים אֲשֶׁר הָיוּ טְמֵאִים לְנֶפֶשׁ אָדָם וְלֹא־יָכְלוּ

ו לַעֲשֹׂת־הַפֶּסַח בַּיּוֹם הַהוּא וַיִּקְרְבוּ לִפְנֵי מֹשֶׁה וְלִפְנֵי אַהֲרֹן בַּיּוֹם הַהוּא: וַיֹּאמְרוּ

ז הָאֲנָשִׁים הָהֵמָּה אֵלָיו אֲנַחְנוּ טְמֵאִים לְנֶפֶשׁ אָדָם לָמָּה נִגָּרַע לְבִלְתִּי הַקְרִיב

רש"י

פרק ט

א בַּחֹדֶשׁ הָרִאשׁוֹן. פָּרָשָׁה שֶׁבְּרֹאשׁ הַסֵּפֶר לֹא נֶאֶמְרָה עַד אִיָּר, לָמַדְתָּ שֶׁאֵין סֵדֶר מֻקְדָּם וּמְאֻחָר בַּתּוֹרָה. וְלָמָּה לֹא פָתַח בְּזוֹ? מִפְּנֵי שֶׁהוּא גְּנוּתָן שֶׁל יִשְׂרָאֵל, שֶׁכָּל אַרְבָּעִים שָׁנָה שֶׁהָיוּ יִשְׂרָאֵל בַּמִּדְבָּר לֹא הִקְרִיבוּ אֶלָּא פֶּסַח זֶה בִּלְבַד:

ב בְּמֹעֲדוֹ. אַף בְּשַׁבָּת. אַף בְּטֻמְאָה:

ג כְּכָל חֻקֹּתָיו. אֵלּוּ מִצְוֹת שֶׁבְּגוּפוֹ: "שֶׂה תָמִים זָכָר בֶּן שָׁנָה" (שמות יב, ה). **וּכְכָל מִשְׁפָּטָיו.** אֵלּוּ מִצְוֹת שֶׁעַל גּוּפוֹ מִמָּקוֹם אַחֵר: לִשְׁבַּעַת יָמִים לַמַּצָּה וּלְבִעוּר חָמֵץ:

ד וַיְדַבֵּר מֹשֶׁה וְגו'. מַה תַּלְמוּד לוֹמַר? וַהֲלֹא כְּבָר נֶאֱמַר: "וַיְדַבֵּר מֹשֶׁה אֶת מֹעֲדֵי ה'" (ויקרא כג, מד)? אֶלָּא כְּשֶׁשָּׁמַע

כד זֹאת אֲשֶׁר לַלְוִיִּם. שָׁנִים פּוֹסְלִים בָּהֶם, וְאֵין הַמּוּמִין פּוֹסְלִים בָּהֶם: מִבֶּן חָמֵשׁ וְעֶשְׂרִים. וּבְמָקוֹם אַחֵר אוֹמֵר: "מִבֶּן שְׁלֹשִׁים שָׁנָה" (לעיל ד, ג). הָא כֵּיצַד? מִבֶּן עֶשְׂרִים וְחָמֵשׁ בָּא לִלְמֹד הִלְכוֹת עֲבוֹדָה וְלוֹמֵד חָמֵשׁ שָׁנִים, וּבֶן שְׁלֹשִׁים עוֹבֵד. מִכָּאן לְתַלְמִיד שֶׁלֹּא רָאָה סִימָן יָפֶה בְּמִשְׁנָתוֹ בְּחָמֵשׁ שָׁנִים, שׁוּב אֵינוֹ רוֹאֶה:

כה וְלֹא יַעֲבֹד עוֹד. עֲבוֹדַת מַשָּׂא בַּכָּתֵף, אֲבָל חוֹזֵר הוּא לִנְעִילַת שְׁעָרִים וְלָשִׁיר וְלִטְעֹן עֲגָלוֹת, וְזֶהוּ: "וְשֵׁרֵת אֶת אֶחָיו" (להלן פסוק כו), עִם אֶחָיו, כְּתַרְגּוּמוֹ:

כו לִשְׁמֹר מִשְׁמֶרֶת. לַחֲנוֹת סָבִיב לָאֹהֶל וּלְהָקִים וּלְהוֹרִיד בְּשָׁעַת הַמַּסָעוֹת:

פָּרָשַׁת מוֹעֲדִים מִסִּינַי אָמְרָה חָזַר וְהִזְהִירָם בִּשְׁעַת מַעֲשֵׂה:

ו לִפְנֵי מֹשֶׁה וְלִפְנֵי אַהֲרֹן. כְּשֶׁשְּׁנֵיהֶם יוֹשְׁבִין בְּבֵית הַמִּדְרָשׁ בָּאוּ וּשְׁאָלוּם. וְלֹא יִתָּכֵן לוֹמַר זֶה אַחַר זֶה, שֶׁאִם מֹשֶׁה לֹא הָיָה יוֹדֵעַ, אַהֲרֹן מִנַּיִן לוֹ:

ז לָמָּה נִגָּרַע. אָמַר לָהֶם: אֵין קָדָשִׁים קְרֵבִים בְּטֻמְאָה. אָמְרוּ לוֹ: יִזָּרֵק הַדָּם עָלֵינוּ בְּכֹהֲנִים טְהוֹרִים וְיֵאָכֵל הַבָּשָׂר לַטְּהוֹרִים, אָמַר לָהֶם: "עִמְדוּ וְאֶשְׁמְעָה" (להלן פסוק ח), כְּתַלְמִיד הַמֻּבְטָח לִשְׁמֹעַ מִפִּי רַבּוֹ. אַשְׁרֵי יְלוּד אִשָּׁה שֶׁכָּךְ מֻבְטָח, שֶׁכָּל זְמַן שֶׁהָיָה רוֹצֶה הָיָה מְדַבֵּר עִם הַשְּׁכִינָה. וּרְאוּיָה הָיְתָה פָרָשָׁה זוֹ לְהֵאָמֵר עַל יְדֵי מֹשֶׁה כְּשְׁאָר כָּל הַתּוֹרָה כֻּלָּהּ, אֶלָּא שֶׁזָּכוּ אֵלּוּ שֶׁתֵּאָמֵר עַל יְדֵיהֶן, שֶׁמְּגַלְגְּלִין זְכוּת עַל יְדֵי זַכַּאי:

DISCUSSION

➤ also Exodus 13:5–6). Consequently, it was necessary the following year to emphasize that this offering was to be brought each year (based upon the *Zohar*; *Sifrei* 67; Ibn Ezra; Ramban).

9:6 | There were men who were impure by means of a corpse: Naturally, in a camp the size of the Israelite camp there were people who died, and therefore there were individuals who became impure due to contact with a corpse. However, some identify these impure individuals as specifically those who carried the corpses of Nadav and Avihu, the sons of Aaron, from the Tabernacle following their death (see *Sukka* 25a–b).

and not present the offering of the Lord at its appointed time among the children of Israel?

8 **Moses said to them: Stand, and I will hear what the Lord will command you.** This is one of the cases where Moses tells individuals who have consulted with him to wait until God instructs him about how to act in their case. Moses speaks with God "face to face as a man speaks to his neighbor."[13] He can therefore initiate dialogue with God in order to request instruction.

9 **The Lord spoke to Moses, saying:**

10 **Speak to the children of Israel, saying: When any man shall be impure by means of a corpse, or on a distant journey,** far from the Tabernacle or Temple, **for you or for your** future **generations, he shall offer the paschal lamb to the Lord.**

11 **During the second month,** Iyar, **on the fourteenth day in the afternoon,** exactly one month after the first *Pesaḥ*, **they shall offer it; with unleavened bread and bitter herbs they shall eat it,** similar to the first *Pesaḥ*.

12 **They shall not leave from it until the morning, and they shall not break a bone in it; in accordance with the entire statute of the paschal lamb they shall do it.**

13 **But the man who is pure, and was not on a journey, and** who yet **refrains from offering the paschal lamb,**[D] **that person shall be excised from his people; because he did not present the offering of the Lord at its appointed time, that man shall bear his sin.**[D]

14 **If a stranger** from another nation **shall reside among you, and will offer the paschal lamb to the Lord: In accordance with the statute of the paschal lamb, and in accordance with its ordinance, so shall he do; there shall be one statute for you, for the stranger, and for the native of the land.** The paschal lamb and the festival of Passover commemorate and celebrate the national experience of the exodus from Egypt. Since the convert is not a descendant of those who left Egypt, one might think that he is not included in these commandments. This verse teaches that converts are included, because these commandments do not pertain to an individual or familial experience or memory but to the national experience, and therefore all those who join the nation are included.[14]

The Travels of the Israelites and the Role of the Cloud

NUMBERS 9:15–23

The cloud above the Tabernacle is a sign that the Divine Presence rests upon the Jewish people, as the Divine Presence is often accompanied by lack of clarity and impaired visibility.[15] The sign of the cloud is noticeable primarily during the day, and therefore at night it is replaced by the appearance of a fire. The movements of the cloud are like a form of sign language by which God directs the Israelites with regard to the pace of their travels through the wilderness, the direction in which they are to move, and the timing of their traveling and encampments.

15 **On the day that the Tabernacle was erected, the cloud covered the Tabernacle, to the Tent of the Testimony;** the cloud covered only the tent itself, which housed the Tablets of the Testimony, but did not cover the courtyard.[16] **And in the evening there would be upon the Tabernacle as the appearance of fire, until morning.**

Fourth aliya

16 **So it would be always: The cloud would cover it** by day, **and the appearance of fire at night.**

17 **In accordance with the** timing and direction of the **ascent of the cloud from upon the Tent,**[17] **thereafter the children of Israel would travel, and in the place where the cloud would stop, there the children of Israel would encamp.**

18 **According to the directive of the Lord the children of Israel would travel, and according to the directive of the Lord they encamped: As all the days that the cloud would rest upon the Tabernacle they would encamp.**

19 **When the cloud lingered upon the Tabernacle many days, the children of Israel kept the commission of the Lord, and did not travel.**

20 **At times, the cloud would be several days upon the**

DISCUSSION

9:13 | **And refrains from offering the paschal lamb:** This commandment and the commandment of circumcision, which represent one's inclusion in the Israelite nation, are the only two positive commandments which carry a punishment of excision for one who fails to fulfill them.

That man shall bear his sin: Each individual is obligated to sacrifice the paschal lamb at the appointed time. The option of sacrificing the offering a month later is available *ab initio* only to those who could not sacrifice the offering on the fourteenth of Nisan because they were ritually impure, on a distant journey, or due to some other unavoidable circumstance. Nevertheless, the liability to the punishment of excision mentioned in the verse here for intentionally refraining from offering the paschal lamb is limited by the Sages to where one did not offer the second *Pesaḥ* as well. One who did offer the second *Pesaḥ* is not liable to excision (see *Pesaḥim* 93a; Rambam, *Hilkhot Korban Pesaḥ* 5:2).

ח אֶת־קָרְבַּן יְהוָה בְּמֹעֲדוֹ בְּתוֹךְ בְּנֵי יִשְׂרָאֵל: וַיֹּאמֶר אֲלֵהֶם מֹשֶׁה עִמְדוּ וְאֶשְׁמְעָה
מַה־יְצַוֶּה יְהוָה לָכֶם:
ט י וַיְדַבֵּר יְהוָה אֶל־מֹשֶׁה לֵּאמֹר: דַּבֵּר אֶל־בְּנֵי יִשְׂרָאֵל לֵאמֹר אִישׁ אִישׁ כִּי־יִהְיֶה
יא טָמֵא לָנֶפֶשׁ אוֹ בְדֶרֶךְ רְחֹקָה לָכֶם אוֹ לְדֹרֹתֵיכֶם וְעָשָׂה פֶסַח לַיהוָה: בַּחֹדֶשׁ
הַשֵּׁנִי בְּאַרְבָּעָה עָשָׂר יוֹם בֵּין הָעַרְבַּיִם יַעֲשׂוּ אֹתוֹ עַל־מַצּוֹת וּמְרֹרִים יֹאכְלֻהוּ:
יב לֹא־יַשְׁאִירוּ מִמֶּנּוּ עַד־בֹּקֶר וְעֶצֶם לֹא יִשְׁבְּרוּ־בוֹ כְּכָל־חֻקַּת הַפֶּסַח יַעֲשׂוּ אֹתוֹ:
יג וְהָאִישׁ אֲשֶׁר־הוּא טָהוֹר וּבְדֶרֶךְ לֹא־הָיָה וְחָדַל לַעֲשׂוֹת הַפֶּסַח וְנִכְרְתָה הַנֶּפֶשׁ
הַהִוא מֵעַמֶּיהָ כִּי קָרְבַּן יְהוָה לֹא הִקְרִיב בְּמֹעֲדוֹ חֶטְאוֹ יִשָּׂא הָאִישׁ הַהוּא:
יד וְכִי־יָגוּר אִתְּכֶם גֵּר וְעָשָׂה פֶסַח לַיהוָה כְּחֻקַּת הַפֶּסַח וּכְמִשְׁפָּטוֹ כֵּן יַעֲשֶׂה חֻקָּה
טו אַחַת יִהְיֶה לָכֶם וְלַגֵּר וּלְאֶזְרַח הָאָרֶץ: וּבְיוֹם הָקִים אֶת־הַמִּשְׁכָּן רביעי
כִּסָּה הֶעָנָן אֶת־הַמִּשְׁכָּן לְאֹהֶל הָעֵדֻת וּבָעֶרֶב יִהְיֶה עַל־הַמִּשְׁכָּן כְּמַרְאֵה־אֵשׁ
טז יז עַד־בֹּקֶר: כֵּן יִהְיֶה תָמִיד הֶעָנָן יְכַסֶּנּוּ וּמַרְאֵה־אֵשׁ לָיְלָה: וּלְפִי הֵעָלֹת הֶעָנָן
מֵעַל הָאֹהֶל וְאַחֲרֵי כֵן יִסְעוּ בְּנֵי יִשְׂרָאֵל וּבִמְקוֹם אֲשֶׁר יִשְׁכָּן־שָׁם הֶעָנָן שָׁם
יח יַחֲנוּ בְּנֵי יִשְׂרָאֵל: עַל־פִּי יְהוָה יִסְעוּ בְּנֵי יִשְׂרָאֵל וְעַל־פִּי יְהוָה יַחֲנוּ כָּל־יְמֵי אֲשֶׁר
יט יִשְׁכֹּן הֶעָנָן עַל־הַמִּשְׁכָּן יַחֲנוּ: וּבְהַאֲרִיךְ הֶעָנָן עַל־הַמִּשְׁכָּן יָמִים רַבִּים וְשָׁמְרוּ
כ בְנֵי־יִשְׂרָאֵל אֶת־מִשְׁמֶרֶת יְהוָה וְלֹא יִסָּעוּ: וְיֵשׁ אֲשֶׁר יִהְיֶה הֶעָנָן יָמִים מִסְפָּר

רש"י

י | **אוֹ בְדֶרֶךְ רְחֹקָה.** נָקוּד עָלָיו, לוֹמַר לֹא שֶׁרְחוֹקָה וַדַּאי, אֶלָּא שֶׁהָיָה חוּץ לְאַסְקֻפַּת הָעֲזָרָה כָּל זְמַן שְׁחִיטָה. פֶּסַח שֵׁנִי – מַצָּה וְחָמֵץ עִמּוֹ בַּבַּיִת, וְאֵין שָׁם יוֹם טוֹב, וְאֵין אִסּוּר חָמֵץ אֶלָּא עִמּוֹ בַּאֲכִילָתוֹ:

יד | **וְכִי יָגוּר אִתְּכֶם גֵּר וְעָשָׂה פֶסַח.** יָכוֹל כָּל הַמִּתְגַּיֵּר יַעֲשֶׂה פֶּסַח מִיָּד? תַּלְמוּד לוֹמַר: "חֻקָּה אַחַת" וְגוֹ', אֶלָּא כָּךְ מַשְׁמָעוֹ: "וְכִי יָגוּר אִתְּכֶם גֵּר" וּבָא עֵת לַעֲשׂוֹת פֶּסַח עִם חֲבֵרָיו, כַּחֻקָּה וְכַמִּשְׁפָּט יַעֲשֶׂה:

טו | **הַמִּשְׁכָּן לְאֹהֶל הָעֵדֻת.** הַמִּשְׁכָּן הֶעָשׂוּי לִהְיוֹת אֹהֶל לַלּוּחוֹת הָעֵדוּת: **יִהְיֶה עַל הַמִּשְׁכָּן.** כְּמוֹ 'הֹוֶה עַל הַמִּשְׁכָּן', וְכֵן לְשׁוֹן כָּל הַפָּרָשָׁה:

יז | **הֵעָלֹת הֶעָנָן.** כְּתַרְגּוּמוֹ: "אִסְתַּלָּקוּת", וְכֵן: "וְנַעֲלָה הֶעָנָן" (להלן פסוק כא). וְלֹא יִתָּכֵן לִכְתֹּב: 'וּלְפִי עֲלוֹת הֶעָנָן וְעָלָה הֶעָנָן', שֶׁאֵין זֶה לְשׁוֹן סִלּוּק אֶלָּא גִּמּוּי וַעֲלִיָּה, כְּמוֹ: "הִנֵּה עָב קְטַנָּה כְּכַף אִישׁ עֹלָה מִיָּם" (מלכים א' יח, מד):

יח | **עַל פִּי ה' יִסְעוּ.** שָׁנִינוּ בִּמְלֶאכֶת הַמִּשְׁכָּן (בברייתא דמלאכת המשכן פי"ג): כֵּיוָן שֶׁהָיוּ יִשְׂרָאֵל נוֹסְעִים, הָיָה עַמּוּד הֶעָנָן מִתְקַפֵּל וְנִמְשָׁךְ עַל גַּבֵּי בְּנֵי יְהוּדָה כְּמִין קוֹרָה, תָּקְעוּ וְהֵרִיעוּ וְתָקְעוּ, וְלֹא הָיָה מְהַלֵּךְ עַד שֶׁמֹּשֶׁה אוֹמֵר: "קוּמָה ה'" (להלן י, לה), וְנָסַע דֶּגֶל מַחֲנֵה יְהוּדָה. זוֹ בְּסִפְרֵי (פד): **וְעַל פִּי ה' יַחֲנוּ.** כֵּיוָן שֶׁהָיוּ יִשְׂרָאֵל חוֹנִים, עַמּוּד הֶעָנָן מִתַּמֵּר וְעוֹלֶה וְנִמְשָׁךְ עַל גַּבֵּי בְּנֵי יְהוּדָה כְּמִין סֻכָּה, וְלֹא הָיָה נִפְרָשׂ עַד שֶׁמֹּשֶׁה אוֹמֵר: "שׁוּבָה ה' רִבְבוֹת אַלְפֵי יִשְׂרָאֵל" (להלן י, לו), הֱוֵי אוֹמֵר: עַל פִּי ה' וּבְיַד מֹשֶׁה (ראה להלן פסוק כג):

כ | **וְיֵשׁ.** כְּלוֹמַר, וּפְעָמִים: **יָמִים מִסְפָּר.** יָמִים מוּעָטִים:

Tabernacle; **according to the directive of the Lord they would encamp, and according to the directive of the Lord they would travel.** God's instructions, referred to as the word of the Lord, were relayed by means of the cloud's movements rather than by actual speech.

21 **At times the cloud would be** in place only **from evening until morning; the cloud would ascend in the morning, and they would travel; or** the cloud would remain in place for **a day and a night, and the cloud would ascend and they would travel.** It is possible that at times the Israelites traveled at night.[18]

22 **Or two days, or one month, or one year, when the cloud lingered upon the Tabernacle, to rest upon it, the children of Israel would encamp, and would not travel; with its ascent, they would travel.**

23 **At the directive of the Lord they would camp, and at the directive of the Lord they would travel;**[D] **the commission of the Lord they kept, according to the directive of the Lord** as expressed through the movements of the cloud, **at the hand of Moses,** who explained to them the significance of the cloud's movements and resting.

Israelite camp in the wilderness

The Trumpets

NUMBERS 10:1–10

The previous passage stated that the departure of the cloud from atop the Tabernacle indicated that it was time for the children of Israel to travel. The manner in which the camp would travel has also been described in Numbers chap. 2. However, in addition to the heavenly sign that it was time to travel, which may not have been seen or correctly interpreted by the nation, an official proclamation by the nation's leadership was necessary, indicating when it was time to travel or to stop. This is alluded to in the concluding verse of the previous passage, which stated that the people traveled "according to the directive of the Lord at the hand of Moses." For this purpose, Moses was commanded to fashion trumpets. The upcoming passage describes a system of communication based upon two basic sounds: A long, straight trumpet blast and a series of short trumpet blasts.

Having mentioned the role of the trumpets in the wilderness, the Torah then goes on to mention a range of uses for the trumpets for future generations. In these functions as well the type of sound produced is significant: The sound of a long, straight blast corresponds to a state of physical stability and mental focus. Conversely, the series of short trumpet blasts is appropriate for situations of physical movement, mental awakening, or for sounding an alarm.

10 1 **The Lord spoke to Moses, saying:**

2 **Craft for you two silver trumpets; hammered** from one piece of silver, **you shall craft them,** rather than attaching together separate pieces of silver; **they shall be for you for summoning the congregation, and for causing the camps to travel** by notifying them that it is time to begin traveling.

3 **They shall sound them, and the entire congregation shall assemble to you at the entrance of the Tent of Meeting.**

4 **If they shall sound one** trumpet, **the princes, the heads of the thousands of Israel, shall assemble to you.**

5 **You shall sound an alarm, and** this sound indicates that **the camps that encamp to the east,** the banner of the camp of Judah, **shall travel.**

6 **You shall sound an alarm again, and the camps that encamp to the south shall travel;** following that, the camps that encamp to the west shall travel; and finally, the camps that encamp to the north, which are the tribes of the banner of Dan, shall travel. **They shall sound an alarm**[D] **for their travels,** with each series of blasts signaling to one of the sets of camps that it is time to travel.[19] However, according to the Ibn Ezra only the two alarms mentioned explicitly in the verses were blown. These were sounded for the tribes encamped to the east and to the south because the Tabernacle and its vessels traveled with those tribes.

כא על־המשכן על־פי יהוה יחנו ועל־פי יהוה יסעו: ויש אשר יהיה הענן מערב
כב עד־בקר ונעלה הענן בבקר ונסעו או יומם ולילה ונעלה הענן ונסעו: או־ימים
או־חדש או־ימים בהאריך הענן על־המשכן לשכן עליו יחנו בני־ישראל ולא
כג יסעו ובהעלתו יסעו: על־פי יהוה יחנו ועל־פי יהוה יסעו את־משמרת יהוה
שמרו על־פי יהוה ביד־משה:

י א ב וידבר יהוה אל־משה לאמר: עשה לך שתי חצוצרת כסף מקשה תעשה ט
אתם והיו לך למקרא העדה ולמסע את־המחנות: ותקעו בהן ונועדו אליך
ג
ד כל־העדה אל־פתח אהל מועד: ואם־באחת יתקעו ונועדו אליך הנשיאים
ה ו ראשי אלפי ישראל: ותקעתם תרועה ונסעו המחנות החנים קדמה: ותקעתם
תרועה שנית ונסעו המחנות החנים תימנה תרועה יתקעו למסעיהם:

רש״י

כב | או ימים. שנה, כמו: ״ימים תהיה גאלתו״ (ויקרא כה, כט):

פרק י

ב | למקרא העדה. כשתרצה לדבר עם הסנהדרין ושאר העם ותקראם לאסף אליך, תקראם על ידי חצוצרות: ולמסע את המחנות. בשעת סלוק מסעות תתקעו בהם לסימן. נמצאת אתה אומר, על פי שלשה היו נוסעים: על פי הקדוש ברוך הוא ועל פי משה ועל פי חצוצרות: מקשה. מן העשת תעשה בהקשת הקורנס:

ג | ותקעו בהן. בשתיהן, והוא סימן למקרא העדה, שנאמר: ״ונועדו אליך כל העדה אל פתח אהל מועד״:

ד | ואם באחת יתקעו. הוא סימן למקרא הנשיאים, שנאמר: ״ונועדו אליך הנשיאים״, ואף הן יעידתן אל פתח אהל מועד, ומגזרה שוה הוא בא בספרי (עג):

ה | ותקעתם תרועה. סימן מסע המחנות: תקיעה תרועה ותקיעה, כך הוא נדרש בספרי מן המקראות היתרים (שם):

ז | ובהקהיל את הקהל וגו׳. לפי שהוא אומר: ״והיו לך למקרא העדה ולמסע את המחנות״ (לעיל פסוק ב), מה מקרא העדה תוקע בשני כהנים ובשתיהן, שנאמר: ״ותקעו בהן״ וגו׳ (לעיל פסוק ג), אף מסע המחנות בשתיהם. יכול מה מסע המחנות תוקע ומריע ותוקע, אף מקרא העדה תוקע ומריע ותוקע, ומעתה אין חלוק בין מקרא העדה למסע את המחנות? תלמוד לומר: ״ובהקהיל את הקהל״ וגו׳, לומר שאין תרועה למקרא העדה, והוא הדין לנשיאים. הרי סימן לשלשתם: מקרא העדה בשתים, ושל נשיאים באחת, וזו וזו אין בהם תרועה, ומסע המחנות בשתים על ידי תרועה ותקיעה:

ח | ובני אהרן יתקעו. במקראות ובמסעות הללו:

DISCUSSION

9:23 | **At the directive of the Lord they would travel:** The many repetitions of the fact that the Jewish people traveled according to the movements of the cloud are meant to express the absolute commitment that was required in order to travel in this manner. The people could never prepare for what was to come next, as they could never know in advance how long they would stay in place, when they would travel and how long they would travel for (see Ramban, 9:19; Sforno, 9:17, 33:2; Rabbi Samson Raphael Hirsch).

The Ramban adds though that it is possible that the actual journeys through the wilderness took place only in the methods described in this passage: The cloud stayed in one location either from night to the next morning, for a day and a night, for two days, for a month, for a year, or as in Kadesh Barnea, for many years (see Deuteronomy 1:46).

10:6 | **You shall sound an alarm [*tekatem terua*]…they shall sound an alarm [*terua yitke'u*]:** The verb used to indicate sounding the trumpets is a form of the word *tekia*, which can also be used to indicate a long, straight blast. The verse first employs this verb before the word *terua*, which indicates short broken sounds, and then reverses the order and mentions *terua* before the word *tekia*. The Talmud (*Rosh HaShana* 34a) derives from this that the short, broken sound [*terua*] is both preceded and followed by a long, straight blast [*tekia*], and that this is the procedure on Rosh HaShana as well. Perhaps this is hinted at in the next verse as well, which states that, as opposed to when traveling, "when assembling the assembly, you shall sound a blast, but you shall not sound an alarm," meaning that there are long blasts not separated by short blasts.

7 **When assembling the assembly, you shall sound a blast, but you shall not sound an alarm.**

8 **The sons of Aaron, the priests, shall sound the trumpets; they shall be for you as an eternal statute for your generations.** The trumpets referred to in verse 2 above were to be used exclusively by Moses and his generation, based on the repetitive use of the expression "for you" there.[20] In contrast, the trumpets referred to here were to be used by the priests in future generations as well. Clearly, these trumpets were not meant to signal that the camp was to start traveling, rather they served other functions, as described below.

9 **When you go to war in your land against the enemy who oppresses you, you shall sound an alarm with the trumpets;**[D]

and you shall be remembered before the Lord your God, and you shall be delivered from your enemies. These trumpets were not military trumpets, but the trumpets used in the Temple. Consequently, the blasts are not part of a military procedure, but rather serve as a call to spiritual awakening, similar to a prayer to God.

10 The role of the trumpets in the Tabernacle and Temple is not limited to sounding an alarm in case of emergency. **On the day of your rejoicing, at your appointed times, and on your New Moons, you shall sound the trumpets over your** communal **burnt offerings, and over your** communal **peace offerings; they shall be a remembrance for you before your God, I am the Lord your God.**

The Camp Departs on a Journey
NUMBERS 10:11–34

The Israelites construct the Tabernacle in the wilderness of Sinai after the giving of the Torah. The Tabernacle is inaugurated on the first day of the first month, Nisan, almost a full year after the exodus from Egypt, at which time the regular service in the Tabernacle commences. Those who are ritually impure due to contact with a corpse sacrifice the paschal lamb on the fourteenth day of the second month, Iyar, and a few days later the cloud ascends from above the Tabernacle, and the Israelites depart on their journey.

The manner in which the camp travels matches the description of the camp stated at the beginning of the book of Numbers (chap. 2). However, that passage prescribed the proper organization of the camp, whereas the upcoming passage describes how that organization is manifested during the first subsequent journey undertaken by the Israelites, as they depart from the wilderness of Sinai. Additionally, this passage describes the role of the Levites during the travels.

11 **It was during the second year, in the second month,** Iyar, **on the twentieth of the month, the cloud ascended from upon the Tabernacle of the Testimony.**

Fifth aliya

12 **The children of Israel traveled on their journeys from the wilderness of Sinai; the cloud rested in the wilderness of Paran.** Since the cloud moved forward, the Israelites followed it in the direction of the wilderness of Paran, in the Sinai Peninsula.

13 **They traveled from the beginning according to the directive of the Lord,** as expressed by the movement of the cloud, and **at the hand of Moses** via the blowing of the trumpets.

14 **The banner of the camp of the sons of Judah traveled first according to their hosts; and over its host was Nahshon son of Aminadav.**

15 **Over the host of the tribe of the children of Issachar was Netanel son of Tzuar.**

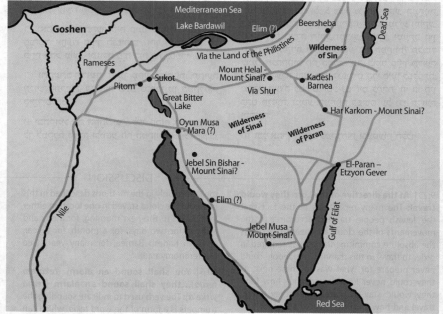

Main travel routes in the Sinai Peninsula

ז ח וּבְהַקְהִיל אֶת־הַקָּהָל תִּתְקְעוּ וְלֹא תָרִיעוּ: וּבְנֵי אַהֲרֹן הַכֹּהֲנִים יִתְקְעוּ בַּחֲצֹצְרוֹת
ט וְהָיוּ לָכֶם לְחֻקַּת עוֹלָם לְדֹרֹתֵיכֶם: וְכִי־תָבֹאוּ מִלְחָמָה בְּאַרְצְכֶם עַל־הַצַּר הַצֹּרֵר
אֶתְכֶם וַהֲרֵעֹתֶם בַּחֲצֹצְרוֹת וְנִזְכַּרְתֶּם לִפְנֵי יהוה אֱלֹהֵיכֶם וְנוֹשַׁעְתֶּם מֵאֹיְבֵיכֶם:
י וּבְיוֹם שִׂמְחַתְכֶם וּבְמוֹעֲדֵיכֶם וּבְרָאשֵׁי חָדְשֵׁיכֶם וּתְקַעְתֶּם בַּחֲצֹצְרֹת עַל עֹלֹתֵיכֶם
וְעַל זִבְחֵי שַׁלְמֵיכֶם וְהָיוּ לָכֶם לְזִכָּרוֹן לִפְנֵי אֱלֹהֵיכֶם אֲנִי יהוה אֱלֹהֵיכֶם:
יא וַיְהִי בַּשָּׁנָה הַשֵּׁנִית בַּחֹדֶשׁ הַשֵּׁנִי בְּעֶשְׂרִים בַּחֹדֶשׁ נַעֲלָה הֶעָנָן מֵעַל מִשְׁכַּן חמישי
יב הָעֵדֻת: וַיִּסְעוּ בְנֵי־יִשְׂרָאֵל לְמַסְעֵיהֶם מִמִּדְבַּר סִינָי וַיִּשְׁכֹּן הֶעָנָן בְּמִדְבַּר פָּארָן:
יג יד וַיִּסְעוּ בָּרִאשֹׁנָה עַל־פִּי יהוה בְּיַד־מֹשֶׁה: וַיִּסַּע דֶּגֶל מַחֲנֵה בְנֵי־יְהוּדָה בָּרִאשֹׁנָה
טו לְצִבְאֹתָם וְעַל־צְבָאוֹ נַחְשׁוֹן בֶּן־עַמִּינָדָב: וְעַל־צְבָא מַטֵּה בְּנֵי יִשָּׂשכָר נְתַנְאֵל
טז יז בֶּן־צוּעָר: וְעַל־צְבָא מַטֵּה בְּנֵי זְבוּלֻן אֱלִיאָב בֶּן־חֵלֹן: וְהוּרַד הַמִּשְׁכָּן וְנָסְעוּ
יח בְנֵי־גֵרְשׁוֹן וּבְנֵי מְרָרִי נֹשְׂאֵי הַמִּשְׁכָּן: וְנָסַע דֶּגֶל מַחֲנֵה רְאוּבֵן לְצִבְאֹתָם וְעַל־
יט צְבָאוֹ אֱלִיצוּר בֶּן־שְׁדֵיאוּר: וְעַל־צְבָא מַטֵּה בְּנֵי שִׁמְעוֹן שְׁלֻמִיאֵל בֶּן־צוּרִישַׁדָּי:

רש"י

י | עַל עֹלֹתֵיכֶם. בְּקָרְבַּן צִבּוּר הַכָּתוּב מְדַבֵּר: אֲנִי ה' אֱלֹהֵיכֶם. מִכָּאן לָמַדְנוּ מַלְכֻיּוֹת עִם זִכְרוֹנוֹת וְשׁוֹפָרוֹת, שֶׁנֶּאֱמַר: "וּתְקַעְתֶּם" – הֲרֵי שׁוֹפָרוֹת, "לְזִכָּרוֹן" – הֲרֵי זִכְרוֹנוֹת, "אֲנִי ה' אֱלֹהֵיכֶם" – זוֹ מַלְכֻיּוֹת וְכוּ':

יא | בַּחֹדֶשׁ הַשֵּׁנִי. נִמְצֵאתָ אַתָּה אוֹמֵר, שָׁנִים עָשָׂר חֹדֶשׁ חָסֵר עֲשָׂרָה יָמִים עָשׂוּ בְּחוֹרֵב, שֶׁהֲרֵי בְּרֹאשׁ חֹדֶשׁ סִיוָן חָנוּ שָׁם (שמות יט, א) וְלֹא נָסְעוּ עַד עֶשְׂרִים בְּאִיָּר לַשָּׁנָה הַבָּאָה:

יב | לְמַסְעֵיהֶם. כְּמִשְׁפַּט הַמְפֹרָשׁ לְמַסַּע דִּגְלֵיהֶם מִי רִאשׁוֹן וּמִי אַחֲרוֹן: בְּמִדְבַּר פָּארָן. קִבְרוֹת הַתַּאֲוָה בְּמִדְבַּר פָּארָן הָיָה, וְשָׁם חָנוּ מִמַּסַּע זֶה:

יז | וְהוּרַד הַמִּשְׁכָּן. כֵּיוָן שֶׁנּוֹסַע דֶּגֶל יְהוּדָה, נִכְנְסוּ אַהֲרֹן וּבָנָיו וּפֵרְקוּ אֶת הַפָּרֹכֶת וְכִסּוּ בָהּ אֶת הָאָרוֹן, שֶׁנֶּאֱמַר: "וּבָא אַהֲרֹן וּבָנָיו בִּנְסֹעַ הַמַּחֲנֶה" (לעיל ד, ה), וּבְנֵי גֵרְשׁוֹן וּבְנֵי מְרָרִי פּוֹרְקִין הַמִּשְׁכָּן וְטוֹעֲנִין אוֹתוֹ בָּעֲגָלוֹת, וְהָאָרוֹן וּכְלֵי הַקֹּדֶשׁ שֶׁל מַשָּׂא בְנֵי קְהָת עוֹמְדִים מְכֻסִּין וּנְתוּנִין עַל

16 **Over the host of the tribe of the children of Zebulun was Eliav son of Helon.** These three tribes, Judah, Issachar and Zebulun, comprised the banner of the camp of Judah.

17 When the banner of the camp of Judah began traveling, **the Tabernacle was dismantled, and the sons of Gershon and the sons of Merari, the bearers of the Tabernacle, traveled.** The sons of Gershon carried primarily the textile portions of the Tabernacle, and the sons of Merari carried the beams and the other components of the structure of the Tabernacle.

18 **The banner of the camp of Reuben traveled according to their hosts; and over its host was Elitzur son of Shede'ur.**

19 **Over the host of the tribe of the children of Simeon was Shelumiel son of Tzurishadai.**

DISCUSSION

10:9 | **The trumpets:** The function of the trumpets was not to provide musical accompaniment to the Temple service, which was accomplished by other musical instruments used in the Temple. Rather, the trumpet blasts served as calls for attention or to action on the part of the Jewish people or God, similar to the *shofar* blasts on Rosh HaShana or at the beginning of the Jubilee Year (see *Sefer HaḤinnukh* 384).

Both the trumpets and *shofar* were blown in the Temple, and the Sages addressed the differences between the manners of blowing each of these instruments (see *Rosh HaShana* 26b–27a). Clearly, the sound produced by the trumpets was different than that produced by the *shofar*, both because of the different materials from which these instruments were made and because of their different shapes, as the trumpets were straight and the *shofar* was curved, at least according to the opinion in the Talmud accepted in Jewish law.

20 **Over the host of the tribe of the children of Gad was Elyasaf son of De'uel.** These three tribes, Reuben, Simeon and Gad, comprised the banner of the camp of Reuben.

21 After the Tabernacle had been dismantled and the banner of Reuben traveled, **the Kehatites, bearers of the** sacred vessels of the **Sanctuary traveled; they,** the sons of Gershon and Merari,²¹ **erected the Tabernacle before their arrival.**

22 **The banner of the camp of the children of Ephraim traveled according to their hosts; and over its host was Elishama son of Amihud.**

23 **Over the host of the tribe of the children of Manasseh was Gamliel son of Pedatzur.**

24 **Over the host of the tribe of the children of Benjamin was Avidan son of Gidoni.** These three tribes, Ephraim, Manasseh and Benjamin comprised the banner of the camp of Ephraim.

25 **The banner of the camp of the children of Dan, the rear guard of all the camps, traveled** following the banner of the camp of Ephraim **according to their hosts; and over its host was Ahiezer son of Amishadai.**

26 **Over the host of the tribe of the children of Asher was Pagiel son of Okhran.**

27 **Over the host of the tribe of the children of Naphtali was Ahira son of Einan.**

28 **These are the travels of the children of Israel according to their hosts; and they traveled.**

29 **Moses said to Hovav son of Re'uel the Midyanite, father-in-law of Moses: We are traveling to the place that the Lord said: I will give it to you; you should also come with us, and we will be good to you**ᴰ by giving you a portion of the land;

as the Lord has spoken good about Israel. It is not clear whether Hovav or Re'uel is the second name of Yitro, Moses' father-in-law. Hovav may have been Tzipora's brother, who was the head of the family at that time; alternatively, it is possible that Hovav was Yitro and Re'uel was Tzipora's grandfather.²²

30 **He,** Hovav, **said to him: I will not go** with you; **rather, to my land, and to the land of my birth, I will go.** You have hosted me honorably in your camp, but I have my own home to which I will return.

31 **He,** Moses, **said: Please do not leave us; for since you know our encampment in the wilderness, you shall be for us as eyes.** I am not inviting you just for your benefit but for ours as well. Hovav was a Midyanite, and although the Midyanites had permanent settlements, according to one assessment they were essentially nomads. Consequently, Hovav could assist the Jewish people in their journey through the wilderness.²³

32 **It shall be, if you go with us, that good that the Lord shall grant us, we will be good to you.** The Torah does not relate the conclusion of this story. It is possible that some members of Hovav's family returned to their land, however, it is clear that some continued to journey with the Israelites.²⁴

33 **They,** the Israelites, **traveled from the mountain of the Lord a journey of three days and the Ark of the Covenant of the Lord was traveling before them a journey of three days, to scout for them a resting place.** Additionally, the Israelites did not need to determine which path would be the easiest to travel on foot as the ark traveled before them and led them on the best path.

DISCUSSION

10:29 | **Come with us, and we will be good to you:** In fact, at least a part of Yitro's family did travel with the Israelites to the Land of Israel.

These people were known as the Kenites and Rekhavites, and lived on their own parcels of land in Israel until the end of the First Temple era

(see Judges 1:16; Radak; Judges 4:11; Jeremiah 35:2; I Chronicles 2:55; *Sota* 11a; *Sanhedrin* 104a).

כ כא ועל־צבא מטה בני־גד אליסף בן־דעואל: ונסעו הקהתים נשאי המקדש
כב והקימו את־המשכן עד־באם: ונסע דגל מחנה בני־אפרים לצבאתם ועל־
כג צבאו אלישמע בן־עמיהוד: ועל־צבא מטה בני מנשה גמליאל בן־פדהצור:
כד כה ועל־צבא מטה בני בנימן אבידן בן־גדעוני: ונסע דגל מחנה בני־דן מאסף
כו לכל־המחנת לצבאתם ועל־צבאו אחיעזר בן־עמישדי: ועל־צבא מטה בני
כז כח אשר פגעיאל בן־עכרן: ועל־צבא מטה בני נפתלי אחירע בן־עינן: אלה
כט מסעי בני־ישראל לצבאתם ויסעו: ויאמר משה לחבב בן־
רעואל המדיני חתן משה נסעים | אנחנו אל־המקום אשר אמר יהוה אתו
ל אתן לכם לכה אתנו והטבנו לך כי־יהוה דבר־טוב על־ישראל: ויאמר אליו
לא לא אלך כי אם־אל־ארצי ואל־מולדתי אלך: ויאמר אל־נא תעזב אתנו כי
לב על־כן ידעת חנתנו במדבר והיית לנו לעינים: והיה כי־תלך עמנו והיה |
לג הטוב ההוא אשר ייטיב יהוה עמנו והטבנו לך: ויסעו מהר יהוה דרך שלשת
ימים וארון ברית־יהוה נסע לפניהם דרך שלשת ימים לתור להם מנוחה:

רש"י

המוטות, עד שנסע דגל מחנה ראובן, ואחר כך "ונסעו הקהתים" (להלן פסוק כא):

כא| **נשאי המקדש.** נושאי דברים המקודשים: **והקימו את המשכן.** בני גרשון ובני מררי, שהיו קודמים להם מסע שני דגלים, היו מקימין את המשכן כשהיה הענן שוכן, וסימן החניה נראה בדגל מחנה יהודה והם חונים, ועדיין בני קהת באים מאחריהם עם שני דגלים האחרונים, היו בני גרשון ובני מררי מקימין את המשכן, וכשבאים בני קהת מוצאים אותו על מכונו, ומכניסין בו הארון והשלחן והמנורה והמזבחות. וזהו משמעות המקרא: "והקימו" מקימי המשכן אותו, "עד" – טרם "באם" של בני קהת:

כה| **מאסף לכל המחנת.** תלמוד ירושלמי (עירובין ה, א), לפי שהיה שבטו של דן מרובה באוכלוסין היה נוסע באחרונה, וכל מי שהיה מאבד דבר היה מחזירו לו. אתיא כמאן דאמר כתבה היו מהלכין, ומפיק ליה מן "כאשר יחנו כן יסעו" (לעיל ב, יז), ואית דאמרי: כקורה היו מהלכין, ומפיק ליה מן "מאסף לכל המחנת":

כח| **אלה מסעי.** זה סדר מסעיהם: **ויסעו.** ביום ההוא נסעו:

כט| **חבב.** הוא יתרו, שנאמר: "מבני חבב חתן משה" (שופטים ד, יא), ומה תלמוד לומר: "ותבאנה אל רעואל אביהן" (שמות ב, יח)? מלמד שהתינוקות קורין לאבי אביהן 'אבא'. ושמות הרבה היו לו: יתרו – על שם שיתר פרשה אחת בתורה, חובב – על שחבב את התורה וכו': **נסעים אנחנו אל המקום.** מיד עד שלשה ימים אנו נכנסין לארץ, שבמסע זה הראשון נסעו על מנת ליכנס לארץ ישראל, אלא שחטאו במתאוננים. ומפני מה שתף משה עצמו עמהם? שעדין לא נגזרה גזרה עליו וכסבור שהוא נכנס:

ל| **אל ארצי ואל מולדתי.** אם בשביל נכסי אם בשביל משפחתי:

לא| **אל נא תעזב.** אין 'נא' אלא לשון בקשה, שלא יאמרו לא נתגייר יתרו מחבה, סבור היה שיש לגרים חלק בארץ, עכשיו שראה שאין להם חלק הניחם והלך לו: **כי על כן ידעת חנתנו במדבר.** כי נאה לך לעשות זאת, על אשר ידעת חנותנו במדבר וראית נסים וגבורות שנעשו לנו: **כי על כן ידעת.** כמו: 'על אשר ידעת', כמו: "כי על כן לא נתתיה לשלה בני" (בראשית לח, כו), "כי על כן באו" (שם יט, ח), "כי על כן ראיתי פניך" (שם לג, י): **והיית לנו לעינים.** לשון עבר, כתרגומו. דבר אחר לשון עתיד, כל דבר ודבר שיתעלם מעינינו תהיה מאיר עינינו. דבר אחר, שתהא חביב עלינו כגלגל עינינו, שנאמר: "ואהבתם את הגר" (דברים י, יט):

לב| **והיה הטוב ההוא וגו'.** מה טובה היטיבו לו? אמרו, כשהיו ישראל מחלקין את הארץ היה דשנה של יריחו חמש מאות אמה על חמש מאות אמה, והניחוהו מלחלק. אמרו, מי שיבנה בית המקדש בחלקו הוא יטלנו, ובין כך ובין כך נתנוהו לבני יתרו ליונדב בן רכב:

לג| **דרך שלשת ימים.** מהלך שלשת ימים הלכו ביום אחד, שהיה הקדוש ברוך הוא חפץ להכניסם לארץ מיד: **וארון ברית ה' נסע לפניהם דרך שלשת ימים.** זה הארון היוצא עמהם למלחמה ובו שברי לוחות מנחים, ומקדים לפניהם דרך שלשת ימים לתקן להם מקום חניה:

34 **The cloud of the Lord was upon them by day, when they traveled from the camp.** The cloud covered the Israelite camp and shielded them during the daytime hours in the desert, and when they traveled it would move with them.

Moses' Prayers upon the Movement and Resting of the Ark
NUMBERS 10:35–36

When the children of Israel depart on their journey and arrive at a resting place, they will blow Moses' trumpets. Moses recites prayers to accompany the departure of the ark from its place in the Holy of Holies and its return to the Holy of Holies.

According to tradition, these two verses are surrounded by unique symbols in the form of a backward *nun*, which serve like parentheses. Perhaps this is because the content of these two verses is not specific to the first journey but applies to all the journeys of the children of Israel through the wilderness, and therefore should have been mentioned earlier. Some saw these verses as a small book in their own right, which also divides the book of Numbers into two sections: The first part of Numbers deals primarily with the arrangement of the camp around the Tabernacle and the preparations for traveling through the wilderness, and the rest of Numbers describes the upcoming travels through the wilderness, with the good and bad times that accompanied them.

35 **It was when the ark traveled** at the beginning of a journey, **Moses said: Arise Lord, and may Your enemies,** the enemies of Israel, **be dispersed and may those who hate You flee from before You.** The Ark of the Covenant, which contained the tablets, represented God's Divine Presence in the world, and therefore its movement from its place of resting served as a threat to the enemies of the children of Israel.[25]

36 **When it rested, he said:**[D] **Repose O Lord,**[26] among **the myriad thousands of Israel.** Moses would pray that God would rest His Presence in the midst of the people.[27]

Sixth aliya

Tavera and Kivrot HaTaava
NUMBERS 11:1–35

This chapter begins to tell the story of the hardships encountered by the children of Israel in the wilderness. The longer their stay in the wilderness continues, the more difficult their lives become. The Israelites do not have any obvious activities with which to occupy themselves, and their futures are murky. In such a state, it is no surprise that various complaints continuously surface.

11 1 **The people were** expressing their distress, **as do mourners;** the verse does not specify what they were complaining about, but **it was evil in the ears of the Lord. The Lord heard it, His wrath was enflamed** over their complaints, **and the fire of the Lord burned in their midst, and consumed the edge of the camp.**

2 **The people cried out to Moses** about the supernatural fire consuming the camp; **Moses prayed to the Lord, and the fire subsided.**

3 **He called the name of that place** at the edge of the camp[28] **Tavera, because the fire of the Lord burned [ba'ara] in their midst.**

4 In continuation of the nation's complaining, the verse relates: **The mob that was in their midst expressed a craving;** this mob was comprised of slaves from other nations who were unhappy in Egypt and joined the exodus of the children of Israel, but never became an organic part of the nation.[29] Their talk of food aroused a desire and even a feeling of need.[30] **And the children of Israel,** who did not initiate this complaint, were nonetheless influenced by the mob, and they **responded and wept as well and said: Who will feed us meat?** The primary sustenance for the children of Israel in the wilderness was the manna. Although some had sheep, they refrained from slaughtering them for food due to the difficulty in raising sheep in the wilderness and replacing the ones that had been slaughtered.

5 The children of Israel did not suffice with desiring meat; they aroused nostalgic feelings about their lives in Egypt, ignoring the subjugation and suffering they experienced there. **We remember the fish that we would eat in Egypt for free;** presumably they did not receive fish from Pharaoh but caught them on their own in the Nile and its tributaries. We also remember fondly **the cucumbers,**[B] **the watermelons, the leeks,**[B] **the onions, and the garlic** that we ate in Egypt. All of these foods stimulate the appetite, and the manna did not have a taste similar to any of these.

6 **But now our soul is parched; there is nothing at all; nothing**

Adzhur melon

Leek

DISCUSSION

10:36 | **When it rested, he said:** Moses' prayers continue to be recited even nowadays in synagogues. The first verse is recited when the Torah scroll is removed from the ark and the second verse is recited when it is returned to the ark after it is has been read.

לד לה וַעֲנַן יְהוָה עֲלֵיהֶם יוֹמָם בְּנָסְעָם מִן־הַמַּחֲנֶה: ׆ וַיְהִי בִּנְסֹעַ הָאָרֹן ששי
לו וַיֹּאמֶר מֹשֶׁה קוּמָה ׀ יְהוָה וְיָפֻצוּ אֹיְבֶיךָ וְיָנֻסוּ מְשַׂנְאֶיךָ מִפָּנֶיךָ: וּבְנֻחֹה יֹאמַר
שׁוּבָה יְהוָה רִבְבוֹת אַלְפֵי יִשְׂרָאֵל: ׆
א וַיְהִי הָעָם כְּמִתְאֹנְנִים רַע בְּאָזְנֵי יְהוָה וַיִּשְׁמַע יְהוָה וַיִּחַר אַפּוֹ וַתִּבְעַר־בָּם אֵשׁ
ב יְהוָה וַתֹּאכַל בִּקְצֵה הַמַּחֲנֶה: וַיִּצְעַק הָעָם אֶל־מֹשֶׁה וַיִּתְפַּלֵּל מֹשֶׁה אֶל־יְהוָה
ג וַתִּשְׁקַע הָאֵשׁ: וַיִּקְרָא שֵׁם־הַמָּקוֹם הַהוּא תַּבְעֵרָה כִּי־בָעֲרָה בָם אֵשׁ יְהוָה:
ד וְהָאסַפְסֻף אֲשֶׁר בְּקִרְבּוֹ הִתְאַוּוּ תַּאֲוָה וַיָּשֻׁבוּ וַיִּבְכּוּ גַּם בְּנֵי יִשְׂרָאֵל וַיֹּאמְרוּ מִי
ה יַאֲכִלֵנוּ בָּשָׂר: זָכַרְנוּ אֶת־הַדָּגָה אֲשֶׁר־נֹאכַל בְּמִצְרַיִם חִנָּם אֵת הַקִּשֻּׁאִים וְאֵת
ו הָאֲבַטִּחִים וְאֶת־הֶחָצִיר וְאֶת־הַבְּצָלִים וְאֶת־הַשּׁוּמִים: וְעַתָּה נַפְשֵׁנוּ יְבֵשָׁה אֵין

רש״י

לד| וענן ה׳ עליהם יומם. שבעה עננים כתובים במסעיהם, ארבעה מארבע רוחות, ואחד למעלה ואחד למטה, ואחד לפניהם, מנמיך את הגבוה ומגביה את הנמוך והורג נחשים ועקרבים:

לה| ויהי בנסע הארן. עשה לו סימניות מלפניו ומלאחריו לומר שאין זה מקומו; ולמה נכתב כאן? כדי להפסיק בין פורענות לפורענות וכו׳, כדאיתא בכל כתבי הקדש׳ (שבת קטו ע״ב – קטז ע״א): קומה ה׳. לפי שהיה מקדים לפניהם מהלך שלשת ימים, היה משה אומר: עמד והמתן לנו ואל תתרחק יותר. במדרש תנחומא בויקהל (ז): ויפצו איביך. המכונסין: וינסו משנאיך. אלו הרודפים: משנאיך. אלו שונאי ישראל, שכל השונא את ישראל שונא את מי שאמר והיה העולם, שנאמר: ״ומשנאיך נשאו ראש״ (תהלים פג, ג), ומי הם? ״על עמך יערימו סוד״ (שם ד):

לו| שובה ה׳. מנחם תרגמו לשון מרגוע, וכן: ״בשובה ונחת תושעון״ (ישעיה ל, טו): רבבות אלפי ישראל. מגיד שאין השכינה שורה בישראל פחותים משני אלפים ושתי רבבות:

פרק יא

א| ויהי העם כמתאננים. אין ׳העם׳ אלא רשעים, וכן הוא אומר: ״מה אעשה לעם הזה״ (שמות יז, ד). ואומר: ״העם הזה הרע״ (ירמיה יג, י). וכשהם כשרים קרואים ׳עמי׳, שנאמר: ״שלח עמי״ (שמות ח, טז), ״עמי מה עשיתי לך״ (מיכה ו, ג): כמתאננים. אין ׳מתאוננים׳ אלא לשון עלילה, מבקשים עלילה היאך לפרוש מאחרי המקום, וכן הוא אומר בשמשון: ״כי תאנה הוא מבקש״ (שופטים יד, ד): רע באזני ה׳. תואנה שהיא רעה באזני ה׳, שמתכוונים שתבוא באזניו ויקניט. אמרו: אוי לנו, כמה לבטנו בדרך הזה, שלשה ימים שלא נחנו מעינוי הדרך: ויחר אפו. אני הייתי מתכוון לטובתכם שתכנסו לארץ מיד: בקצה המחנה. במקוין שבהם לשפלות, אלו ערב רב. רבי שמעון בן מנסיא אומר: בקצינים שבהם ובגדולים:

ב| ויצעק העם אל משה. משל למלך בשר ודם שכעס על בנו, והלך הבן אצל אוהבו של אביו ואמר לו: צא ובקש עלי מאבא: ותשקע האש. שקעה במקומה בארץ, שאלו חזרה לאחת הרוחות היתה מקפלת והולכת כל אותו הרוח:

ד| והאספסף. אלו ערב רב שנאספו עליהם בצאתם ממצרים: וישבו. גם בני ישראל ויבכו עמהם: מי יאכלנו בשר. וכי לא היה להם בשר? והלא כבר נאמר: ״וגם ערב רב עלה אתם וצאן ובקר״ וגו׳ (שמות יב, לח), ואם תאמר אכלום, והלא בכניסתם לארץ נאמר: ״ומקנה רב היה לבני ראובן״ וגו׳ (להלן לב, א), אלא שמבקשים עלילה:

ה| אשר נאכל במצרים חנם. אם תאמר שמצרים נותנים להם דגים חנם, והלא כבר נאמר: ״ותבן לא ינתן לכם״ (שמות ה, יח), אם תבן לא היו נותנים להם חנם, דגים היו נותנין להם חנם?! ומהו אומר: ״חנם״? חנם מן המצוות: את הקשאים. אמר רבי שמעון: מפני מה המן משתנה לכל דבר חוץ מאלו? מפני שהן קשים למיניקות; אומרים לאשה: אל תאכלי שום ובצל, מפני התינוק. משל למלך כו׳ [בשר ודם שמסר בנו לפידגוג, והיה יושב ומפקדו ואומר לו, הנראה שלא יאכל מאכל רע ולא ישתה משקה רע. ובכל כך היה הבן ההוא מתרעם על אביו לומר, לא מפני שאוהבני, אלא מפני שאי אפשר לו שאוכל], כדאיתא בספרי (פז): הקשאים. הם קוקומבר״ש בלעז: אבטחים. בודיק״ש: החציר. כרישין, פוריל״ש, ותרגומו: ״ית בוציניא״ וכו׳:

BACKGROUND

11:5| Cucumbers [*kishuim*]: The Aramaic translations identify this as the Adzhur melon, otherwise known as the Armenian cucumber (Scientific name: *Cucumis melo var. chate*), a type of melon from the gourd family, which is similar to a long, hairy cucumber. The Greek and Latin translations identify this as the cucumber (Scientific name: *Cucumis savitus*).

Leeks [*hatzir*]: This is not the same as the modern Hebrew term *ḥatzir*, which means hay. According to the commentaries, *ḥatzir* in this verse refers to the leek, *Allium porrum*, which is related to the onion.

but the manna before our eyes. The manna is our only source of sustenance. The children of Israel forgot about the decrees of Pharaoh, and their own subservience and suffering, while remembering only the aroma and taste of their old cuisine.

7 The Torah now provides background detail that is not part of the complaint of the children of Israel: **The manna that they complained about was like** a round **coriander seed**[B] in size and shape, **and its appearance was like the appearance of bdellium;** it was white, like bdellium, rather than brown like coriander.[31]

8 **The people roamed about, and gathered and ground it in a mill, or crushed it in a mortar, or boiled it in a pot,**[B] **and made it into cakes and its taste was like the taste of a cake moist with oil.** The manna was not dry; its taste was similar to that of a food saturated with oil.

9 **With the falling of the dew upon the camp at night, the manna fell upon it.**

10 **Moses heard the people weeping, according to their families, each** man **at the entrance of his tent.** This was not a mass demonstration; rather people saw each other weeping, which spread, along with the sense of lacking and longing, throughout the nation. **The wrath of the Lord was greatly enflamed and in the eyes of Moses it was bad** that the nation was weeping.

11 **Moses said to the Lord: Why have You mistreated Your servant and why have I not found favor in Your eyes, to place the burden of this entire people upon me?** Am I so unfavorable in Your eyes that you have given me such a difficult job?

12 **Did I conceive this entire people; did I give birth to it, that You should say to me: Carry it in your bosom, as a nurse carries the suckling babe to the land with regard to which You took an oath to its forefathers?** Moses compares the people to dependent children, and asks God why he has been tasked with the responsibility to care for them. He feels that this task is beyond his natural abilities.

Detail from a tablet found in Nineveh, depicting an Israelite woman carrying an infant, eighth century BCE

13 **From where do I have meat to give to this entire people that they cry to me, saying: Give us meat, and we shall eat.** Their request is unreasonable and I have no way to fulfill it.

14 **I cannot bear this entire people alone, because it is too heavy for me.**

15 **If this is what You do to me, please kill me,**[D] **if I have found favor in Your eyes and let me not see my wretchedness.** I would prefer that you kill me so that I will not have to remain in this wretched state.[32]

Coriander plant

Coriander seed

Pot

Mortar

Mill

BACKGROUND

11:7 | Coriander seed [*zera gad*]: This is identified by commentaries and scholars as coriander (Scientific name: *Coriandrum sativum*), an annual herb in the family Apiaceae. It grows to a height of 50 cm and has round seeds that have a diameter of 2–4 mm.

11:8 | Pot [*parur*]: The word *parur* refers to a pot used for cooking (see Judges 6:19). Based upon Ben Sira (13:2), it appears that it is an earthenware pot rather than an iron pot.

ז ח כֹּל בִּלְתִּי אֶל־הַמָּן עֵינֵינוּ: וְהַמָּן כִּזְרַע־גַּד הוּא וְעֵינוֹ כְּעֵין הַבְּדֹלַח: שָׁטוּ הָעָם
וְלָקְטוּ וְטָחֲנוּ בָרֵחַיִם אוֹ דָכוּ בַּמְּדֹכָה וּבִשְּׁלוּ בַּפָּרוּר וְעָשׂוּ אֹתוֹ עֻגוֹת וְהָיָה
ט טַעְמוֹ כְּטַעַם לְשַׁד הַשָּׁמֶן: וּבְרֶדֶת הַטַּל עַל־הַמַּחֲנֶה לָיְלָה יֵרֵד הַמָּן עָלָיו:
י וַיִּשְׁמַע מֹשֶׁה אֶת־הָעָם בֹּכֶה לְמִשְׁפְּחֹתָיו אִישׁ לְפֶתַח אָהֳלוֹ וַיִּחַר־אַף יהוה
יא מְאֹד וּבְעֵינֵי מֹשֶׁה רָע: וַיֹּאמֶר מֹשֶׁה אֶל־יהוה לָמָה הֲרֵעֹתָ לְעַבְדֶּךָ וְלָמָּה לֹא־
יב מָצָתִי חֵן בְּעֵינֶיךָ לָשׂוּם אֶת־מַשָּׂא כָּל־הָעָם הַזֶּה עָלָי: הֶאָנֹכִי הָרִיתִי אֵת כָּל־
הָעָם הַזֶּה אִם־אָנֹכִי יְלִדְתִּיהוּ כִּי־תֹאמַר אֵלַי שָׂאֵהוּ בְחֵיקֶךָ כַּאֲשֶׁר יִשָּׂא הָאֹמֵן
יג אֶת־הַיֹּנֵק עַל הָאֲדָמָה אֲשֶׁר נִשְׁבַּעְתָּ לַאֲבֹתָיו: מֵאַיִן לִי בָּשָׂר לָתֵת לְכָל־הָעָם
יד הַזֶּה כִּי־יִבְכּוּ עָלַי לֵאמֹר תְּנָה־לָּנוּ בָשָׂר וְנֹאכֵלָה: לֹא־אוּכַל אָנֹכִי לְבַדִּי לָשֵׂאת
טו אֶת־כָּל־הָעָם הַזֶּה כִּי כָבֵד מִמֶּנִּי: וְאִם־כָּכָה ׀ אַתְּ־עֹשֶׂה לִּי הָרְגֵנִי נָא הָרֹג אִם־
מָצָאתִי חֵן בְּעֵינֶיךָ וְאַל־אֶרְאֶה בְּרָעָתִי:

רש"י

ו| **אֶל הַמָּן עֵינֵינוּ.** מָן בַּשַּׁחַר, מָן בָּעֶרֶב:

ז| **וְהַמָּן כִּזְרַע גַּד.** מִי שֶׁאָמַר זֶה לֹא אָמַר זֶה. יִשְׂרָאֵל אוֹמְרִים: "בִּלְתִּי אֶל הַמָּן עֵינֵינוּ", וְהַקָּדוֹשׁ בָּרוּךְ הוּא הִכְתִּיב בַּתּוֹרָה: "וְהַמָּן כִּזְרַע גַּד" וְגוֹ', כְּלוֹמַר, רְאוּ בָּאֵי עוֹלָם עַל מַה מִּתְלוֹנְנִים בָּנַי, וְהַמָּן כָּךְ וְכָךְ הוּא חָשׁוּב: **כִּזְרַע גַּד.** עָגֹל כְּגִדָּא, זֶרַע קוליינדר"ו: **בְּדֹלַח.** שֵׁם אֶבֶן טוֹבָה, קריסט"ל:

ח| **שָׁטוּ.** אֵין 'שַׁיִט' אֶלָּא לְשׁוֹן טִיּוּל, אישבני"ר, בְּלֹא עָמָל: **וְטָחֲנוּ בָרֵחַיִם וְגוֹ'.** לֹא יָרַד בָּרֵיחַיִם וְלֹא בַּקְּדֵרָה וְלֹא בַּמְּדוֹכָה, אֶלָּא מִשְׁתַּנֶּה הָיָה טַעְמוֹ לְנִטְחָנִין וְלִנְדּוֹכִין וְלִמְבֻשָּׁלִין: **בַּפָּרוּר.** קְדֵרָה: **לְשַׁד הַשָּׁמֶן.** לִחְלוּחַ שֶׁל שֶׁמֶן, כָּךְ פֵּרְשׁוֹ דּוּנַשׁ. וְדוֹמֶה לוֹ: "נֶהְפַּךְ לְשַׁדִּי בְּחַרְבֹנֵי קַיִץ" (תהלים לב, ד), וְהַלָּמֶ"ד יְסוֹד, נֶהְפַּךְ לִחְלוּחִי בְּחַרְבוֹנֵי קַיִץ. וְרַבּוֹתֵינוּ פֵּרְשׁוּהוּ לְשׁוֹן שָׁדַיִם, אַךְ אֵין עִנְיַן שָׁדַיִם אֵצֶל שֶׁמֶן. וְאִי אֶפְשָׁר לוֹמַר "לְשַׁד הַשָּׁמֶן" לְשׁוֹן "וַיִּשְׁמַן יְשֻׁרוּן" (דברים לב, טו), שֶׁאִם כֵּן הָיָה הַמֵּ"ם נָקוּד קָמָץ קָטָן (צירי) וְטַעְמוֹ לְמַטָּה תַּחַת הַמֵּ"ם, עַכְשָׁיו שֶׁהַמֵּ"ם נָקוּד פַּתָּח קָטָן (סגול) וְהַטַּעַם תַּחַת הַשִּׁי"ן, לְשׁוֹן שֶׁמֶן הוּא, וְהַשִּׁי"ן הַנְּקוּדָה בְּקָמָץ גָּדוֹל וְאֵינָהּ נְקוּדָה בְּפַתָּח קָטָן מִפְּנֵי שֶׁהוּא סוֹף פָּסוּק. דָּבָר אַחֵר, "לְשַׁד" לְשׁוֹן נוֹטָרִיקוֹן לַיִשׁ שֶׁמֶן דְּבַשׁ, כְּעִסָּה הַנִּלּוֹשָׁה בְּשֶׁמֶן וּקְטוּפָה בִּדְבַשׁ. וְתַרְגּוּם שֶׁל אוּנְקְלוֹס דִּמְתַרְגֵּם: "דְּלִישׁ בִּמְשַׁח" נוֹטֶה לְפִתְרוֹנוֹ שֶׁל דּוּנַשׁ, שֶׁהָעִסָּה הַנִּלּוֹשָׁה בְּשֶׁמֶן לַחְלוּחִית שֶׁמֶן יֵשׁ בָּהּ:

י| **בֹּכֶה לְמִשְׁפְּחֹתָיו.** מִשְׁפָּחוֹת מִשְׁפָּחוֹת נֶאֱסָפִים וּבוֹכִים, לְפַרְסֵם תַּרְעֻמְתָּן בְּגָלוּי. וְרַבּוֹתֵינוּ אָמְרוּ: "לְמִשְׁפְּחֹתָיו", עַל עִסְקֵי מִשְׁפָּחוֹת, עַל עֲרָיוֹת הַנֶּאֱסָרוֹת לָהֶם:

יב| **כִּי תֹאמַר אֵלַי.** שֶׁאַתָּה אוֹמֵר אֵלַי: שָׂאֵהוּ בְּחֵיקֶךָ, וְהֵיכָן אָמַר לוֹ כֵּן? "לֵךְ נְחֵה אֶת הָעָם" (שמות לב, לד), וְאוֹמֵר: "וַיְצַוֵּם אֶל בְּנֵי יִשְׂרָאֵל" (שם ו, יג), עַל מְנָת שֶׁיִּהְיוּ סוֹקְלִים אֶתְכֶם וּמְחָרְפִין אֶתְכֶם: **עַל הָאֲדָמָה אֲשֶׁר נִשְׁבַּעְתָּ לַאֲבֹתָיו.** אַתָּה אוֹמֵר לִי לְשֵׂאתָם בְּחֵיקִי:

טו| **וְאִם כָּכָה אַתְּ עֹשֶׂה לִּי.** תָּשַׁשׁ כֹּחוֹ שֶׁל מֹשֶׁה כִּנְקֵבָה כְּשֶׁהֶרְאָהוּ הַקָּדוֹשׁ בָּרוּךְ הוּא הַפֻּרְעָנוּת שֶׁהוּא עָתִיד לְהָבִיא עֲלֵיהֶם עַל זֹאת, אָמַר לְפָנָיו: אִם כֵּן, הָרְגֵנִי תְּחִלָּה: **וְאַל אֶרְאֶה בְּרָעָתִי.** 'בְּרָעָתָם' הָיָה לוֹ לִכְתֹּב, אֶלָּא שֶׁכִּנָּה הַכָּתוּב, וְזֶה אֶחָד מִתִּקּוּנֵי סוֹפְרִים בַּתּוֹרָה לְכִנּוּי וּלְתִקּוּן לָשׁוֹן:

DISCUSSION

11:15| **If this is what You do to me, please kill me:** Moses responded harshly because he was unable to understand the people around him. He was already more than eighty years old and had lived in solitude, engaged in a spiritual search, even before receiving his divine charge. In fact, the *Zohar* (Balak, section 3, 187b–188a) compares Moses in a society of men to a fish out of water. Moreover, Moses was able to live for forty days and nights without food or drink (Exodus 34:28); he therefore had a difficult time comprehending people who were concerned that they did not have food for the next day, and whose whole complaint focused on nostalgia for the tastes of certain foods.

16 **The Lord said to Moses: Gather to Me seventy men of the elders of Israel, whom you know to be the elders of the people, and its officers; and you shall take them to the Tent of Meeting, and they will stand there with you.** Take the men who are most prominent and respected, and who function as the leaders of the people.

17 **I will descend and speak with you there, and I will draw from the spirit** of prophecy **that is upon you,** as well as a portion of your spiritual character, **and I will place it upon them; they shall bear with you**[D] **the burden of the people, and you shall not bear** it **alone.**

18 **To the people you shall say: Prepare yourselves for tomorrow, and you shall eat meat; for you have wept in the ears of the Lord, saying: Who will feed us meat, as it is better for us in Egypt; and the Lord will give you meat, and you shall eat.**

19 **You shall have so much meat that you shall eat not one day, nor two days, nor five days, nor ten days, nor twenty days.**

20 **Until a month of days, until it comes out of your nose** and you regurgitate it, **and it shall be loathsome for you;** the Lord is angry with you **because you despised the Lord who is in your midst, and you wept before Him, saying: Why is it that we left Egypt?**

21 **Moses said:** More than **six hundred thousand men on foot is the people that I am in their midst, and You said: I will give them meat, and they will eat for a month of days.**

22 **Will** it be possible to gather enough **flocks and cattle to be slain for them and it suffice for them?**[D] **If all the fish of the sea will be gathered for them, will it suffice for them?**

23 **The Lord said to Moses: Shall the hand of the Lord be inadequate? Now you will see whether My statement will transpire for you or not.**

24 **Moses emerged** from the Tent of Meeting[33] **and spoke the words of the Lord to the people,** informing them that they would receive meat the following day; **he gathered seventy men of the elders of the people, and he had them stand around the Tent.**

25 **The Lord descended in the cloud, and spoke to him, and** simultaneously **drew from the spirit that was upon him, and put it upon the seventy elders;**[D] it was, as the spirit rested **upon them, they prophesied, but did not continue.** These elders prophesied at that time but did not become regular prophets.

DISCUSSION

11:17 | They shall bear with you: The elders were more embedded in the nation than Moses was, and therefore they would be able to speak to the people and to calm them (see Ramban). Here they were to undergo a type of partial spiritual cloning process in which they would receive some of the inner character of Moses so that they would be able to comprehend the will of God. In this manner the elders would become like an extension of Moses; they would not merely receive instructions from him, but would identify with him.

The institution of the High Court of seventy-one Sages, or Sanhedrin, that would function during the Second Temple era, would be a continuation of this group of seventy elders that was presided over by Moses. It was they who would communicate the message of Moses to future generations (see Mishna *Sanhedrin* 1:6; see also Ezekiel 8:11).

11:22 | Will flocks and cattle be slain for them and it suffice for them: Despite the fact that God was providing manna for His people on a daily basis, Moses had difficulty believing that sufficient meat could be found for all. Unlike manna, which was food provided in a supernatural manner, the people wanted meat, which exists in the natural realm. Moses saw no way to procure meat in the wilderness in a natural fashion.

11:25 | And drew from the spirit that was upon him, and put it upon the seventy elders: The seventy elders were exposed to prophecy by being included in the prophecy that was experienced by Moses at that time. In this manner they came to understand the nature of Moses' experience and to appreciate his greatness. From then on, they would respect him and his decisions, they would be loyal to him, and would fight his battles (see Ramban, 11:17).

טז וַיֹּאמֶר יְהוָה אֶל־מֹשֶׁה אֶסְפָה־לִּי שִׁבְעִים אִישׁ מִזִּקְנֵי יִשְׂרָאֵל אֲשֶׁר יָדַעְתָּ י
כִּי־הֵם זִקְנֵי הָעָם וְשֹׁטְרָיו וְלָקַחְתָּ אֹתָם אֶל־אֹהֶל מוֹעֵד וְהִתְיַצְּבוּ שָׁם עִמָּךְ׃
יז וְיָרַדְתִּי וְדִבַּרְתִּי עִמְּךָ שָׁם וְאָצַלְתִּי מִן־הָרוּחַ אֲשֶׁר עָלֶיךָ וְשַׂמְתִּי עֲלֵיהֶם וְנָשְׂאוּ
יח אִתְּךָ בְּמַשָּׂא הָעָם וְלֹא־תִשָּׂא אַתָּה לְבַדֶּךָ׃ וְאֶל־הָעָם תֹּאמַר הִתְקַדְּשׁוּ לְמָחָר
וַאֲכַלְתֶּם בָּשָׂר כִּי בְּכִיתֶם בְּאָזְנֵי יְהוָה לֵאמֹר מִי יַאֲכִלֵנוּ בָּשָׂר כִּי־טוֹב לָנוּ בְּמִצְרָיִם
יט וְנָתַן יְהוָה לָכֶם בָּשָׂר וַאֲכַלְתֶּם׃ לֹא יוֹם אֶחָד תֹּאכְלוּן וְלֹא יוֹמָיִם וְלֹא ׀ חֲמִשָּׁה
כ יָמִים וְלֹא עֲשָׂרָה יָמִים וְלֹא עֶשְׂרִים יוֹם׃ עַד ׀ חֹדֶשׁ יָמִים עַד אֲשֶׁר־יֵצֵא מֵאַפְּכֶם
וְהָיָה לָכֶם לְזָרָא יַעַן כִּי־מְאַסְתֶּם אֶת־יְהוָה אֲשֶׁר בְּקִרְבְּכֶם וַתִּבְכּוּ לְפָנָיו לֵאמֹר
כא לָמָּה זֶּה יָצָאנוּ מִמִּצְרָיִם׃ וַיֹּאמֶר מֹשֶׁה שֵׁשׁ־מֵאוֹת אֶלֶף רַגְלִי הָעָם אֲשֶׁר אָנֹכִי
כב בְּקִרְבּוֹ וְאַתָּה אָמַרְתָּ בָּשָׂר אֶתֵּן לָהֶם וְאָכְלוּ חֹדֶשׁ יָמִים׃ הֲצֹאן וּבָקָר יִשָּׁחֵט
לָהֶם וּמָצָא לָהֶם אִם אֶת־כָּל־דְּגֵי הַיָּם יֵאָסֵף לָהֶם וּמָצָא לָהֶם׃
כג וַיֹּאמֶר יְהוָה אֶל־מֹשֶׁה הֲיַד יְהוָה תִּקְצָר עַתָּה תִרְאֶה הֲיִקְרְךָ דְבָרִי אִם־לֹא׃ יא
כד וַיֵּצֵא מֹשֶׁה וַיְדַבֵּר אֶל־הָעָם אֵת דִּבְרֵי יְהוָה וַיֶּאֱסֹף שִׁבְעִים אִישׁ מִזִּקְנֵי הָעָם
כה וַיַּעֲמֵד אֹתָם סְבִיבֹת הָאֹהֶל׃ וַיֵּרֶד יְהוָה ׀ בֶּעָנָן וַיְדַבֵּר אֵלָיו וַיָּאצֶל מִן־הָרוּחַ אֲשֶׁר
עָלָיו וַיִּתֵּן עַל־שִׁבְעִים אִישׁ הַזְּקֵנִים וַיְהִי כְּנוֹחַ עֲלֵיהֶם הָרוּחַ וַיִּתְנַבְּאוּ וְלֹא יָסָפוּ׃

רש״י

טז| **אספה לי.** הרי תשובה לתלונתך שאמרת: "לא אוכל אנכי לבדי" (לעיל פסוק יד). והזקנים הראשונים היכן היו? והלא אף במצרים ישבו עמהם, שנאמר: "לך ואספת את זקני ישראל" (שמות ג, טז), אלא באש תבערה מתו. וראויים היו לכך מסיני, דכתיב: "ויחזו את האלהים" (שמות כד, יא), שנהגו קלות ראש כנושך פתו ומדבר בפני המלך, וזהו: "ויאכלו וישתו" (שם), ולא רצה הקדוש ברוך הוא ליתן אבלות במתן תורה, ופרע להם כאן: **אשר ידעת כי הם וגו'.** אותן שאתה מכיר שנתמנו עליהם שוטרים במצרים בעבודת פרך, והיו מרחמים עליהם ומוכים על ידם, שנאמר: "ויכו שוטרי בני ישראל" (שמות ה, יד), עתה יתמנו בגדלתן, כדרך שנצטערו בצרתן: **ולקחת אתם.** קחם בדברים, אשריכם שנתמניתם פרנסים על בניו של מקום: **והתיצבו שם עמך.** כדי שיראו ישראל וינהגו בהם גדלה וכבוד, ויאמרו: חביבין אלו שנכנסו עם משה לשמוע דבור מפי הקדוש ברוך הוא:

יז| **וירדתי.** זו אחת מעשר ירידות הכתובות בתורה: **ודברתי עמך.** ולא עמהם: **ואצלתי.** כתרגומו: "וארבי", כמו: "ואל אצילי בני ישראל" (שמות כד, יא): **ושמתי עליהם.** למה משה דומה באותה שעה? לנר שמונח על גבי מנורה, והכל מדליקין הימנו ואין אורו חסר כלום: **ונשאו אתך.** התנה עמהם, על מנת שיקבלו עליהם טרח בני, שהם טרחנים וסרבנים: **ולא תשא אתה לבדך.** הרי תשובה למה שאמרת "לא אוכל אנכי לבדי" (לעיל פסוק יד):

יח| **התקדשו.** הזמינו עצמכם לפורענות, וכן הוא אומר: "והקדשם ליום הרגה" (ירמיה יב, ג):

כ| **עד חדש ימים.** זו בכשרים שמתמצין על מטותיהן ואחר כך נשמתן יוצאה; וברשעים הוא אומר "הבשר עודנו בין שניהם" (להלן פסוק לג), כך היא שנויה בספרי (עג). אבל במכילתא (ויסע פ"ד) שנויה חילוף: הרשעים אוכלין ומצטערין שלשים יום, והכשרים – "הבשר עודנו בין שניהם": **עד אשר יצא מאפכם.** כתרגומו: "דתקוצון ביה", יהא דומה לכם כאלו אכלתם ממנו יותר מדאי עד שיוצא ונגעל לחוץ דרך האף: **והיה לכם לזרא.** שתהיו מרחקין אותו יותר ממה שקרבתם. ובדברי רבי משה הדרשן ראיתי, שיש לשון שקורין לחרב 'זרא': **את ה' אשר בקרבכם.** אם לא שנטעתי שכינתי ביניכם, לא גבה לבבכם לכנס לכל הדברים הללו:

כא| **שש מאות אלף רגלי.** לא חש למנות את הפרט, שלשת אלפים היתרים (לעיל א, מו). ורבי משה הדרשן פרש, שלא בכו אלא אותן שיצאו ממצרים:

כב-כג| **הצאן ובקר ישחט.** זה אחד מארבעה דברים שהיה רבי עקיבא דורש ואין רבי שמעון דורש כמותו. רבי עקיבא אומר: "שש מאות אלף רגלי, ואתה אמרת בשר אתן להם ואכלו חדש ימים, הצאן ובקר" וגו', הכל כמשמעו, מי מספיק להם? כענין שנאמר: "ומצא

26 **Two men remained in the camp; the name of the one was Eldad, and the name of the second was Meidad.** According to the midrash, the elders of Israel were to be selected from a group of candidates comprised of six men from each tribe. Since there were a total of seventy-two candidates, two of them would not be selected. Eldad and Meidad decided not to go out to the Tent of Meeting so that the spirit of Moses would rest on the remaining seventy men.[34] Nonetheless, **the spirit rested upon them and they were among those written** on the list of potential candidates,[35] **but they did not go out to the Tent and they prophesied in the camp.**

27 **The young man ran and told Moses, and he said: Eldad and Meidad are prophesying in the camp;** they remained in the camp, and nonetheless they are prophesying.

28 **Joshua son of Nun, servant of Moses** who had been devoted to Moses **from his youth,**[36] **spoke up and said: My lord Moses, incarcerate them**[D] for prophesying without authorization. Alternatively, some commentaries interpret the first part of the verse as stating that Joshua was one of Moses' finest attendants.[37]

29 **Moses said to him: Are you zealous on my behalf?** Are you angry that prophecy has been granted to others? On the contrary, **would that all the people of the Lord be prophets,**[D] **that the Lord would place His spirit upon them.** Ideally, the whole nation should be close to God to the point that they experience prophecy.

Seventh aliya 30 **Moses returned** from the Tent of Meeting **to the camp, he and the elders of Israel.**

31 **A wind went from the Lord, and displaced** a group of **quails**[B] **from** their larger group that was flying over **the sea, and dispersed them over the camp.** This flock of birds was so enormous that it extended from the camp **approximately a day's journey here,** in one direction, **and approximately a day's journey there, around the camp, and** there were so many birds that they were piled to a height of **approximately two cubits above the face of the earth.**

Quail

32 **The people arose all that day, all the night, and all the next day, and they gathered the quail** with gluttonous appetite, having become disgusted with eating the same food every day; **he who did the least, gathered ten piles,** while those who were more gluttonous or more efficient undoubtedly gathered more; **and they spread them around the camp.** There were too many quails to store them in vessels, so they left them to dry around the camp.

33 **The meat was still between their teeth, it was not yet** entirely **finished, and the wrath of the Lord was enflamed against the people, and the Lord struck the people with a very great blow.**[D]

34 **He called the name of that place Kivrot Hataava, because there they buried [*kaveru*] the people that lusted [*hamitavim*].**

35 **From Kivrot Hataava the people traveled to Hatzerot,** where they presumably build enclosures [*ḥatzerot*] as temporary living quarters; **and they were in Hatzerot.**

DISCUSSION

11:28 | **Incarcerate them:** The Sages explained that Eldad and Meidad prophesied that Moses would die and Joshua would take his place. This explains the severe reaction of Joshua (see Rashi; *Sanhedrin* 17a).

11:29 | **Would that all the people of the Lord be prophets:** Moses expresses here a democratic view of the nature of prophecy: Prophecy is appropriate for anyone worthy of it, and not just the seventy elders who received their prophetic abilities from Moses and became almost like his clones. This perspective of Moses is expressed in other instances as well when Moses relates to other people vis-à-vis his own status (see 12:3; 16:5–7; Deuteronomy 10:12; see also the introduction to Numbers).

11:33 | **And the Lord struck the people with a very great blow:** God sent them meat so that there would be no room to doubt His omnipotence. Yet in His anger He struck those who had doubted His power, both due to their lack of faith, and due to the fact that they immediately rushed to gather quail rather than standing in amazement over God's greatness.

BACKGROUND

11:31 | **Quails:** The quail (Scientific name: *Coturnix coturnix*) is a small bird from the pheasant family Phasianidae. Its body is small and plump, reaching a length of about 18 cm and a weight of about 100 g. At the end of the summer it migrates east from Central Europe to the shores in Northern Sinai and Eastern Egypt, a distance of approximately 750 km in one night. Due to the long journey, the quail arrive exhausted and it is easy to collect them. When quail are found nowadays, they are spread on the ground over a large area but they are not found piled on top of one another.

כו וַיִּשָּׁאֲרוּ שְׁנֵי־אֲנָשִׁים ׀ בַּמַּחֲנֶה שֵׁם הָאֶחָד ׀ אֶלְדָּד וְשֵׁם הַשֵּׁנִי מֵידָד וַתָּנַח עֲלֵהֶם
כז הָרוּחַ וְהֵמָּה בַּכְּתֻבִים וְלֹא יָצְאוּ הָאֹהֱלָה וַיִּתְנַבְּאוּ בַּמַּחֲנֶה׃ וַיָּרָץ הַנַּעַר וַיַּגֵּד
כח לְמֹשֶׁה וַיֹּאמַר אֶלְדָּד וּמֵידָד מִתְנַבְּאִים בַּמַּחֲנֶה׃ וַיַּעַן יְהוֹשֻׁעַ בִּן־נוּן מְשָׁרֵת מֹשֶׁה
כט מִבְּחֻרָיו וַיֹּאמַר אֲדֹנִי מֹשֶׁה כְּלָאֵם׃ וַיֹּאמֶר לוֹ מֹשֶׁה הַמְקַנֵּא אַתָּה לִי וּמִי יִתֵּן
ל כָּל־עַם יהוה נְבִיאִים כִּי־יִתֵּן יהוה אֶת־רוּחוֹ עֲלֵיהֶם׃ וַיֵּאָסֵף מֹשֶׁה אֶל־הַמַּחֲנֶה
לא הוּא וְזִקְנֵי יִשְׂרָאֵל׃ וְרוּחַ נָסַע ׀ מֵאֵת יהוה וַיָּגָז שַׂלְוִים מִן־הַיָּם וַיִּטֹּשׁ עַל־הַמַּחֲנֶה
לב כְּדֶרֶךְ יוֹם כֹּה וּכְדֶרֶךְ יוֹם כֹּה סְבִיבוֹת הַמַּחֲנֶה וּכְאַמָּתַיִם עַל־פְּנֵי הָאָרֶץ׃ וַיָּקָם
הָעָם כָּל־הַיּוֹם הַהוּא וְכָל־הַלַּיְלָה וְכֹל ׀ יוֹם הַמָּחֳרָת וַיַּאַסְפוּ אֶת־הַשְּׂלָו הַמַּמְעִיט
לג אָסַף עֲשָׂרָה חֳמָרִים וַיִּשְׁטְחוּ לָהֶם שָׁטוֹחַ סְבִיבוֹת הַמַּחֲנֶה׃ הַבָּשָׂר עוֹדֶנּוּ בֵּין
לד שִׁנֵּיהֶם טֶרֶם יִכָּרֵת וְאַף יהוה חָרָה בָעָם וַיַּךְ יהוה בָּעָם מַכָּה רַבָּה מְאֹד׃ וַיִּקְרָא
אֶת־שֵׁם־הַמָּקוֹם הַהוּא קִבְרוֹת הַתַּאֲוָה כִּי־שָׁם קָבְרוּ אֶת־הָעָם הַמִּתְאַוִּים׃
לה מִקִּבְרוֹת הַתַּאֲוָה נָסְעוּ הָעָם חֲצֵרוֹת וַיִּהְיוּ בַּחֲצֵרוֹת׃

רש"י

כְּדֵי גְאֻלָּתוֹ" (ויקרא כה, כו). וְאֵיזוֹ קָשָׁה, זוֹ אוֹ "שִׁמְעוּ נָא הַמֹּרִים" (להלן כ, י)? אֶלָּא לְפִי שֶׁלֹּא אָמַר בָּרַבִּים, חִסֵּךְ לוֹ הַכָּתוּב וְלֹא נִפְרַע מִמֶּנּוּ, וְזוֹ שֶׁל מְרִיבָה הָיְתָה בַּגָּלוּי, לְפִיכָךְ לֹא חִסֵּךְ לוֹ הַכָּתוּב. רַבִּי שִׁמְעוֹן אוֹמֵר: חַס וְשָׁלוֹם, לֹא עָלְתָה עַל דַּעְתּוֹ שֶׁל אוֹתוֹ צַדִּיק כָּךְ! מִי שֶׁכָּתוּב בּוֹ: "בְּכָל בֵּיתִי נֶאֱמָן הוּא" (להלן יב, ז) יֹאמַר: 'אֵין הַמָּקוֹם מַסְפִּיק לָנוּ'?! אֶלָּא, כָּךְ אָמַר: "שֵׁשׁ מֵאוֹת אֶלֶף רַגְלִי וְגוֹ'", וְאַתָּה אָמַרְתָּ "בָּשָׂר אֶתֵּן" לְחֹדֶשׁ יָמִים, וְאַחַר כָּךְ תַּהֲרֹג אֻמָּה גְּדוֹלָה כָּזוֹ, "הֲצֹאן וּבָקָר יִשָּׁחֵט לָהֶם" כְּדֵי שֶׁיֵּהָרְגוּ וּתְהֵא אֲכִילָה זוֹ מְסַפַּקְתָּן עַד עוֹלָם? וְכִי שִׁבְחֲךָ הוּא זֶה? אוֹמְרִים לוֹ לַחֲמוֹר: טֹל כֹּר שְׂעוֹרִים וְנַחְתֹּךְ רֹאשְׁךָ? הֵשִׁיבוֹ הַקָּדוֹשׁ בָּרוּךְ הוּא: וְאִם לֹא אֶתֵּן, יֹאמְרוּ שֶׁקָּצְרָה יָדִי, הֲטוֹב בְּעֵינֶיךָ שֶׁיַּד ה' תִּקְצַר בְּעֵינֵיהֶם? יֹאבְדוּ הֵם וּמֵאָה כַּיּוֹצֵא בָּהֶם וְאַל תְּהִי יָדִי קְצָרָה לִפְנֵיהֶם אֲפִלּוּ שָׁעָה אַחַת, "עַתָּה תִרְאֶה הֲיִקְרְךָ דְבָרִי". רַבָּן גַּמְלִיאֵל בְּנוֹ שֶׁל רַבִּי יְהוּדָה הַנָּשִׂיא אוֹמֵר: אִי אֶפְשָׁר לַעֲמֹד עַל הַטָּפֵל, מֵאַחַר שֶׁאֵינָן מְבַקְשִׁים אֶלָּא עֲלִילָה לֹא תַסְפִּיק לָהֶם, סוֹפָן לָדוּן אַחֲרֶיךָ, אִם אַתָּה נוֹתֵן לָהֶם בְּשַׂר בְּהֵמָה גַּסָּה, יֹאמְרוּ: דַּקָּה בִּקַּשְׁנוּ, וְאִם אַתָּה נוֹתֵן לָהֶם דַּקָּה, יֹאמְרוּ: גַּסָּה בִּקַּשְׁנוּ, חַיָּה וָעוֹף בִּקַּשְׁנוּ, דָּגִים וַחֲגָבִים בִּקַּשְׁנוּ. אָמַר לוֹ: אִם כֵּן יֹאמְרוּ שֶׁקָּצְרָה יָדִי. אָמַר לְפָנָיו: הֲרֵינִי הוֹלֵךְ וּמְפַיְּסָן. אָמַר לוֹ: "עַתָּה תִרְאֶה הֲיִקְרְךָ דְבָרִי", שֶׁלֹּא יִשְׁמְעוּ לְךָ. הָלַךְ מֹשֶׁה לְפַיְּסָן, אָמַר לָהֶם: "הֲיַד ה' תִּקְצָר", "הֵן הִכָּה צוּר וַיָּזוּבוּ מַיִם וְגוֹ' הֲגַם לֶחֶם יוּכַל תֵּת" (תהלים עח, כ). אָמְרוּ: פְּשָׁרָה הִיא זוֹ, אֵין בּוֹ כֹּחַ לְמַלֹּאת שְׁאֵלָתֵנוּ, וְזֶהוּ שֶׁנֶּאֱמַר: "וַיֵּצֵא מֹשֶׁה וַיְדַבֵּר אֶל הָעָם" (להלן פסוק כד), כֵּיוָן שֶׁלֹּא שָׁמְעוּ לוֹ, "וַיֶּאֱסֹף שִׁבְעִים אִישׁ" וְגוֹ' (שם):

כה | **וְלֹא יָסָפוּ.** לֹא נִתְנַבְּאוּ אֶלָּא אוֹתוֹ הַיּוֹם לְבַדּוֹ, כָּךְ מְפֹרָשׁ בְּסִפְרֵי (צה), וְאוּנְקְלוֹס תִּרְגֵּם: "וְלָא פָסְקִין", שֶׁלֹּא פָּסְקָה נְבוּאָה מֵהֶם:

כו | **וַיִּשָּׁאֲרוּ שְׁנֵי אֲנָשִׁים.** מֵאוֹתָן שֶׁנִּבְחֲרוּ, אָמְרוּ: אֵין אָנוּ כְּדַאי לִגְדֻלָּה זוֹ: **וְהֵמָּה בַּכְּתֻבִים.** בַּמְבֹרָרִים שֶׁבָּהֶם לְסַנְהֶדְרִין. וְנִכְתְּבוּ כֻּלָּם נְקוּבִים בְּשֵׁמוֹת וְעַל יְדֵי גוֹרָל, לְפִי שֶׁהַחֶשְׁבּוֹן עוֹלֶה לִשְׁנֵים עָשָׂר שְׁבָטִים שִׁשָּׁה שִׁשָּׁה לְכָל שֵׁבֶט וָשֵׁבֶט, חוּץ מִשְּׁנֵי שְׁבָטִים שֶׁאֵין מַגִּיעַ אֲלֵיהֶם אֶלָּא חֲמִשָּׁה חֲמִשָּׁה. אָמַר מֹשֶׁה: אֵין שֵׁבֶט שׁוֹמֵעַ לִי לִפְחוֹת מִשִּׁבְטוֹ זָקֵן אֶחָד. מֶה עָשָׂה? נָטַל שִׁבְעִים וּשְׁנַיִם פְּתָקִין וְכָתַב עַל שִׁבְעִים 'זָקֵן' וְעַל שְׁנַיִם חָלָק, וּבֵרֵר מִכָּל שֵׁבֶט וָשֵׁבֶט שִׁשָּׁה, וְהָיוּ שִׁבְעִים וּשְׁנַיִם. אָמַר לָהֶם: טְלוּ פִּתְקֵיכֶם מִתּוֹךְ קַלְפִּי. מִי שֶׁעָלָה בְּיָדוֹ 'זָקֵן' נִתְקַדֵּשׁ; מִי שֶׁעָלָה בְּיָדוֹ חָלָק, אָמַר לוֹ: הַמָּקוֹם לֹא חֲפֵצְךָ:

כז | **וַיָּרָץ הַנַּעַר.** יֵשׁ אוֹמְרִים: גֵּרְשֹׁם בֶּן מֹשֶׁה הָיָה:

כח | **כְּלָאֵם.** הַטֵּל עֲלֵיהֶם צָרְכֵי צִבּוּר וְהֵם כָּלִים מֵאֲלֵיהֶם. דָּבָר אַחֵר, תְּנֵם אֶל בֵּית הַכֶּלֶא, לְפִי שֶׁהָיוּ מִתְנַבְּאִים: מֹשֶׁה מֵת וִיהוֹשֻׁעַ מַכְנִיס אֶת יִשְׂרָאֵל לָאָרֶץ:

כט | **הַמְקַנֵּא אַתָּה לִי.** "הַקִּנְאֲתִי אַתְּ מְקַנֵּא": לִי. כְּמוֹ בִּשְׁבִילִי. כָּל לְשׁוֹן קִנְאָה, אָדָם הַנּוֹתֵן לֵב עַל הַדָּבָר אוֹ לִנְקֹם אוֹ לַעֲזֹר, אנפרנמ"ט בְּלַעַז, אוֹחֵז בְּעָבְרֵי הַמַּשָּׂא:

ל | **וַיֵּאָסֵף מֹשֶׁה.** מִפֶּתַח אֹהֶל מוֹעֵד: **אֶל הַמַּחֲנֶה.** נִכְנְסוּ אִישׁ לְאָהֳלוֹ: **וַיֵּאָסֵף.** לְשׁוֹן כְּנִיסָה אֶל הַבַּיִת, כְּמוֹ: "וַאֲסַפְתּוֹ אֶל תּוֹךְ בֵּיתֶךָ" (דברים כב, ב), וְאָב לְכֻלָּם: "יִצְבֹּר וְלֹא יֵדַע מִי אֹסְפָם" (תהלים לט, ז). מְלַמֵּד שֶׁלֹּא הֵבִיא עֲלֵיהֶם פֻּרְעָנוּת עַד שֶׁנִּכְנְסוּ הַצַּדִּיקִים אִישׁ לְאָהֳלוֹ:

לא | **וַיָּגָז.** וַיַּפְרִיחַ, וְכֵן: "כִּי גָז חִישׁ" (תהלים צ, י), "וְכֵן נָגוֹזּוּ וְעָבָר" (נחום א, יב): **וַיִּטֹּשׁ.** וַיִּפְשֹׁט, כְּמוֹ "וְהִנֵּה נְטֻשִׁים עַל פְּנֵי כָל הָאָרֶץ" (שמואל א' ל, טז), "וּנְטַשְׁתִּיךָ הַמִּדְבָּרָה" (יחזקאל כט, ה): **וּכְאַמָּתַיִם.** פּוֹרְחוֹת בְּגֹבַהּ עַד שֶׁהֵן כְּנֶגֶד לִבּוֹ שֶׁל אָדָם, כְּדֵי שֶׁלֹּא יְהֵא טֹרַח בַּאֲסִיפָתָן לֹא לְהַגְבִּיהַּ וְלֹא לִשְׁחוֹת:

לב | **הַמַּמְעִיט.** מִי שֶׁאוֹסֵף פָּחוֹת מִכֻּלָּם, הָעַצְלִים וְהַחִגְּרִים, "אָסַף עֲשָׂרָה חֳמָרִים": **וַיִּשְׁטְחוּ.** עָשׂוּ אוֹתָן מַשְׁטִיחִין מַשְׁטִיחִין:

לג | **טֶרֶם יִכָּרֵת.** כְּתַרְגּוּמוֹ: "עַד לָא פְסַק". דָּבָר אַחֵר, אֵינוֹ מַסְפִּיק לְפָסְקוֹ בְּשִׁנָּיו עַד שֶׁנִּשְׁמָתוֹ יוֹצְאָה:

Moses and His Siblings' Criticism
NUMBERS 12:1–16

Moses does not have to deal only with the burden of leadership of the entire nation. In the upcoming passage, he is confronted by negative personal comments about him that are uttered by his older siblings, Miriam and Aaron. It is specifically in light of this criticism by his own family members that God expresses His most direct and exalted praise of Moses, and mentions his uniqueness among humankind. Due to his great humility, Moses is not sensitive to critique, but God zealously defends Moses' honor.

The Torah also relates the punishment meted out to Miriam, who began the slanderous discussion about Moses. Later, the nation would be commanded to remember this event for future generations in order to internalize how serious a sin slander is. Although slander is not punishable in court, its consequences can be extremely destructive.

12 **1** **Miriam and Aaron spoke against Moses,** at Miriam's initiative, **with regard to the Kushite woman whom he had married; for he had married a Kushite woman,**[D] Tzipora the Midyanite.[38] It is possible that the Midyanites, who were nomads, mixed with other peoples.[39] It is also possible that Tzipora was called Kushite because the Kushites were known for their black skin and Tzipora's skin was darker than usual among the Israelites, whose skin color was a light brown.[40] Although she was Moses' wife, Moses had separated from her and refrained from marital relations in order to commune with God in the Tabernacle.[41]

2 **They said: Was it only with Moses that the Lord spoke; didn't he speak with us as well?** Since we are also prophets, we do not see what right Moses has to act in this way with regard to his wife. Moses married Tzipora, her father later brought her to the Israelite camp from Midyan, and yet Moses is ignoring her. This was a private conversation between Miriam and Aaron, but **the Lord heard**.[42]

3 The fact that Miriam and Aaron spoke about Moses in third person indicates that they were not directly addressing Moses. However, it is possible that they would not have minded if he had heard about their conversation, and perhaps they even intended for him to hear about it, thereby sending him an indirect message. It is possible that Moses heard and did not respond.[43] However, the verse testifies that even if Moses had been present when this conversation was taking place he would not have responded or have been insulted due to his great humility: **And the man Moses was very humble,**[D] **more than any person on**

the face of the earth. Moses did not demand special status or extra rights; he saw himself simply as a servant and messenger of God who was transmitting His word and His Torah.[44]

4 **The Lord said suddenly to Moses, to Aaron, and to Miriam: Go out the three of you,** together, **to the Tent of Meeting. The three of them went out.**

5 **The Lord descended in a pillar of cloud, and stood at the entrance of the Tent. He called Aaron and Miriam and both of them came out** from the Tent and moved closer to the cloud.

6 **He said: Hear now My words:** Even **if your prophet is** truly a prophet **of the Lord,** as you are, **I will** nonetheless **reveal Myself to him** indirectly, **in a vision** that must be deciphered, or **in a dream I will speak to him.** Regular prophets do not hear My words while they are fully conscious, but rather while in a deep trance.

7 **Not so My servant Moses,**[D] who is different from you and from all other prophets; **in all My house he is** the most **trusted,** so much so that I speak with him on a regular basis.

8 **Mouth to mouth I will speak with him,** in a direct manner, unlike the visions of other prophets from which they deduce the presence of God; **and a** clear **vision that is not in riddles** that require interpretation; **and the image of the Lord he will behold.**[D] That being the case, **why did you not fear to speak against My servant, against Moses?** How do you dare to equate yourselves to Moses and to criticize his conduct?

9 **The wrath of the Lord was enflamed against them and He departed.**

DISCUSSION

12:1 | **He had married a Kushite woman:** Some have identified this woman as someone other than Tzipora. It is related in some *midrashim* that when Moses initially fled from Pharaoh, he spent time in Kush before arriving in Midyan, where he eventually married Tzipora. In Kush he had married a woman, perhaps the queen of Kush herself. According to these opinions, Miriam and Aaron spoke about the fact that this matter had not been closed (see *Targum Yerushalmi;* Ibn Ezra; Rashbam; *Yalkut Shimoni, Shemot* 168).

12:3 | **And the man Moses was very humble:** The fact that Moses was so humble does not mean that he did not value or appreciate his position, rather Moses felt that he was merely doing his job. Consequently, it would never have occurred to him that because of his status he was immune from critique or that he had extra rights. This is because humility consists of an awareness of one's status unaccompanied by feelings of superiority. The greater the individual is, the more he views himself as insignificant compared to that which is above him, rather than measuring himself by those beneath him.

12:7 | **My servant Moses:** There are several other instances when Moses is called the servant of the Lord, as in the next verse (see also Exodus 14:31; Joshua 11:15). This depiction expresses not only Moses' subservience to God, but also his closeness, much like the expression "the king's servant" (see II Samuel 18:29; II Kings 25:8; Jeremiah 38:7–12). Archeological excavations have uncovered beautiful signet rings containing the words "servant of the king," or "servant of King so-and-so," indicating a lofty social status. The term, "servant of the Lord" is ◄●

א וַתְּדַבֵּ֨ר מִרְיָ֤ם וְאַהֲרֹן֙ בְּמֹשֶׁ֔ה עַל־אֹד֛וֹת הָאִשָּׁ֥ה הַכֻּשִׁ֖ית אֲשֶׁ֣ר לָקָ֑ח כִּי־אִשָּׁ֥ה

ב כֻשִׁ֖ית לָקָֽח: וַיֹּאמְר֗וּ הֲרַ֤ק אַךְ־בְּמֹשֶׁה֙ דִּבֶּ֣ר יְהוָ֔ה הֲלֹ֖א גַּם־בָּ֣נוּ דִבֵּ֑ר וַיִּשְׁמַ֖ע יְהוָֽה:

ג וְהָאִ֥ישׁ מֹשֶׁ֖ה עָנָ֣ו מְאֹ֑ד מִכֹּל֙ הָֽאָדָ֔ם אֲשֶׁ֖ר עַל־פְּנֵ֥י הָֽאֲדָמָֽה: וַיֹּ֨אמֶר

ד יְהוָ֜ה פִּתְאֹ֗ם אֶל־מֹשֶׁ֤ה וְאֶֽל־אַהֲרֹן֙ וְאֶל־מִרְיָ֔ם צְא֥וּ שְׁלָשְׁתְּכֶ֖ם אֶל־אֹ֣הֶל

ה מוֹעֵ֑ד וַיֵּצְא֖וּ שְׁלָשְׁתָּֽם: וַיֵּ֤רֶד יְהוָה֙ בְּעַמּ֣וּד עָנָ֔ן וַיַּעֲמֹ֖ד פֶּ֣תַח הָאֹ֑הֶל וַיִּקְרָא֙

ו אַהֲרֹ֣ן וּמִרְיָ֔ם וַיֵּצְא֖וּ שְׁנֵיהֶֽם: וַיֹּ֖אמֶר שִׁמְעוּ־נָ֣א דְבָרָ֑י אִם־יִֽהְיֶה֙ נְבִ֣יאֲכֶ֔ם

ז יְהוָ֗ה בַּמַּרְאָה֙ אֵלָ֣יו אֶתְוַדָּ֔ע בַּחֲל֖וֹם אֲדַבֶּר־בּֽוֹ: לֹא־כֵ֖ן עַבְדִּ֣י מֹשֶׁ֑ה בְּכָל־

ח בֵּיתִ֖י נֶאֱמָ֥ן הֽוּא: פֶּ֣ה אֶל־פֶּ֞ה אֲדַבֶּר־בּ֗וֹ וּמַרְאֶה֙ וְלֹ֣א בְחִידֹ֔ת וּתְמֻנַ֥ת יְהוָ֖ה

ט יַבִּ֑יט וּמַדּ֙וּעַ֙ לֹ֣א יְרֵאתֶ֔ם לְדַבֵּ֖ר בְּעַבְדִּ֣י בְמֹשֶֽׁה: וַיִּֽחַר־אַ֧ף יְהוָ֛ה בָּ֖ם וַיֵּלַֽךְ:

רש"י

פרק יב

א וַתְּדַבֵּר. אֵין דִּבּוּר בְּכָל מָקוֹם אֶלָּא לְשׁוֹן קָשָׁה, וְכֵן הוּא אוֹמֵר: "דִּבֶּר הָאִישׁ אֲדֹנֵי הָאָרֶץ אִתָּנוּ קָשׁוֹת" (בראשית מב, ל), וְאֵין אֲמִירָה בְּכָל מָקוֹם אֶלָּא לְשׁוֹן תַּחֲנוּנִים, וְכֵן הוּא אוֹמֵר: "וַיֹּאמֶר אַל נָא אַחַי תָּרֵעוּ" (בראשית יט, ז), "וַיֹּאמֶר שִׁמְעוּ נָא דְבָרָי" (להלן פסוק ו), כָּל "נָא" לְשׁוֹן בַּקָּשָׁה: **וַתְּדַבֵּר מִרְיָם וְאַהֲרֹן.** הִיא פָתְחָה בַּדִּבּוּר תְּחִלָּה, לְפִיכָךְ הִקְדִּימָהּ הַכָּתוּב. וּמִנַּיִן הָיְתָה יוֹדַעַת מִרְיָם שֶׁפֵּרַשׁ מֹשֶׁה מִן הָאִשָּׁה? רַבִּי נָתָן אוֹמֵר: מִרְיָם הָיְתָה בְּצַד צִפּוֹרָה בְּשָׁעָה שֶׁנֶּאֱמַר לְמֹשֶׁה: "אֶלְדָּד וּמֵידָד מִתְנַבְּאִים בַּמַּחֲנֶה" (לעיל יא, כז), כֵּיוָן שֶׁשָּׁמְעָה צִפּוֹרָה אָמְרָה: אוֹי לְנְשׁוֹתֵיהֶן שֶׁל אֵלּוּ אִם הֵם נִזְקָקִים לִנְבוּאָה, שֶׁיִּהְיוּ פוֹרְשִׁין מִנְּשׁוֹתֵיהֶן כְּדֶרֶךְ שֶׁפֵּרַשׁ בַּעְלִי מִמֶּנִּי, וּמִשָּׁם יָדְעָה מִרְיָם וְהִגִּידָה לְאַהֲרֹן. וּמָה מִרְיָם שֶׁלֹּא נִתְכַּוְּנָה לִגְנוּתוֹ כָּךְ נֶעֶנְשָׁה, קַל וָחֹמֶר לְמְסַפֵּר בִּגְנוּתוֹ שֶׁל חֲבֵרוֹ: **הָאִשָּׁה הַכֻּשִׁית.** מַגִּיד שֶׁהַכֹּל מוֹדִים בְּיָפְיָהּ, כְּשֵׁם שֶׁהַכֹּל מוֹדִים בְּשַׁחֲרוּתוֹ שֶׁל כּוּשִׁי: **כֻּשִׁית.** בְּגִימַטְרִיָּא יְפַת מַרְאֶה: **עַל אֹדוֹת הָאִשָּׁה.** עַל אֹדוֹת גֵּרוּשֶׁיהָ: **כִּי אִשָּׁה**

כֻשִׁית לָקָח. מַה תַּלְמוּד לוֹמַר? אֶלָּא יֵשׁ לְךָ אִשָּׁה נָאָה בְּיָפְיָהּ וְאֵינָהּ נָאָה בְּמַעֲשֶׂיהָ, בְּמַעֲשֶׂיהָ וְלֹא בְיָפְיָהּ, אֲבָל זֹאת נָאָה בַכֹּל: **הָאִשָּׁה הַכֻּשִׁית.** עַל שֵׁם נוֹיָהּ נִקְרֵאת "כֻּשִׁית", כְּאָדָם הַקּוֹרֵא אֶת בְּנוֹ נָאֶה "כּוּשִׁי" כְּדֵי שֶׁלֹּא תִשְׁלֹט בּוֹ עַיִן רָעָה: **כִּי אִשָּׁה כֻשִׁית לָקָח.** וְעַתָּה גֵּרְשָׁהּ:

ב הֲרַק אַךְ בְּמֹשֶׁה. עִמּוֹ לְבַדּוֹ "דִּבֶּר ה'": **הֲלֹא גַם בָּנוּ** דִּבֵּר. וְלֹא פֵרַשְׁנוּ מִדֶּרֶךְ אֶרֶץ:

ג עָנָו. שָׁפָל וְסַבְלָן:

ד פִּתְאֹם. נִגְלָה עֲלֵיהֶם פִּתְאֹם וְהֵם טְמֵאִים בְּדֶרֶךְ אֶרֶץ וְהָיוּ צוֹעֲקִים: מַיִם מַיִם, לְהוֹדִיעָם שֶׁיָּפֶה עָשָׂה מֹשֶׁה שֶׁפֵּרַשׁ מִן הָאִשָּׁה, מֵאַחַר שֶׁנִּגְלֵית עָלָיו שְׁכִינָה תָּדִיר וְאֵין עֵת קְבוּעָה לַדִּבּוּר: **צְאוּ שְׁלָשְׁתְּכֶם.** מַגִּיד שֶׁשְּׁלָשְׁתָּן נִקְרְאוּ בְּדִבּוּר אֶחָד, מַה שֶּׁאִי אֶפְשָׁר לַפֶּה לוֹמַר וְלָאֹזֶן לִשְׁמֹעַ:

ה בְּעַמּוּד עָנָן. יָצָא יְחִידִי, שֶׁלֹּא כְמִדַּת בָּשָׂר וָדָם: מֶלֶךְ בָּשָׂר וָדָם כְּשֶׁיּוֹצֵא לַמִּלְחָמָה יוֹצֵא בְּאֻכְלוּסִין וּכְשֶׁיּוֹצֵא לְשָׁלוֹם יוֹצֵא בְּמֻעֲטִין, וּמִדַּת הַקָּדוֹשׁ בָּרוּךְ הוּא יוֹצֵא לַמִּלְחָמָה יְחִידִי, שֶׁנֶּאֱמַר: "ה' אִישׁ מִלְחָמָה" (שמות טו, ג), וְיוֹצֵא לְשָׁלוֹם בְּאֻכְלוּסִין, שֶׁנֶּאֱמַר: "רֶכֶב אֱלֹהִים רִבֹּתַיִם אַלְפֵי שִׁנְאָן" (תהלים סח, יח): **וַיִּקְרָא אַהֲרֹן וּמִרְיָם.** שֶׁיִּהְיוּ נִמְשָׁכִין וְיוֹצְאִין מִן הֶחָצֵר לִקְרַאת הַדִּבּוּר: **וַיֵּצְאוּ שְׁנֵיהֶם.** וּמִפְּנֵי מָה מָשְׁכָן וְהִפְרִידָן מִמֹּשֶׁה, לְפִי שֶׁאוֹמְרִים מִקְצָת שִׁבְחוֹ שֶׁל אָדָם בְּפָנָיו וְכֻלּוֹ שֶׁלֹּא בְּפָנָיו, וְכֵן מָצִינוּ בְּנֹחַ, שֶׁלֹּא בְּפָנָיו נֶאֱמַר: "אִישׁ צַדִּיק תָּמִים" (בראשית ו, ט), וּבְפָנָיו נֶאֱמַר: "כִּי אֹתְךָ רָאִיתִי צַדִּיק לְפָנַי" (שם ז, א): **דָּבָר אַחֵר.** שֶׁלֹּא יִשְׁמַע בִּנְזִיפָתוֹ שֶׁל אַהֲרֹן:

ו שִׁמְעוּ נָא דְבָרָי. אֵין נָא אֶלָּא לְשׁוֹן בַּקָּשָׁה: **אִם יִהְיֶה נְבִיאֲכֶם.** אִם יִהְיוּ לָכֶם נְבִיאִים: **ה' בַּמַּרְאָה אֵלָיו אֶתְוַדָּע.** שְׁכִינַת שְׁמִי אֵין נִגְלֵית עָלָיו בְּאַסְפַּקְלַרְיָא הַמְּאִירָה, אֶלָּא בַּחֲלוֹם וְחָזוֹן:

ח פֶּה אֶל פֶּה. אָמַרְתִּי לוֹ לִפְרֹשׁ מִן הָאִשָּׁה, וְהֵיכָן אָמַרְתִּי לוֹ? בְּסִינַי: "לֵךְ אֱמֹר לָהֶם שׁוּבוּ לָכֶם לְאָהֳלֵיכֶם וְאַתָּה פֹּה עֲמֹד עִמָּדִי" (דברים ה, כו-כח): **וּמַרְאֶה וְלֹא בְחִידֹת.** "וּמַרְאֶה" זֶה מַרְאֵה דִבּוּר, שֶׁאֲנִי מְפָרֵשׁ לוֹ דִּבּוּרִי בְּמַרְאִית פָּנִים שֶׁבּוֹ, וְאֵינִי סוֹתְמוֹ לוֹ בְּחִידוֹת, כָּעִנְיָן שֶׁנֶּאֱמַר לִיחֶזְקֵאל: "חוּד חִידָה" (יחזקאל יז, ב) וְגוֹ'. יָכוֹל מַרְאֵה שְׁכִינָה? תַּלְמוּד לוֹמַר: "לֹא תוּכַל לִרְאֹת אֶת פָּנָי" (שמות לג, כ): **וּתְמֻנַת ה' יַבִּיט.** זֶה מַרְאֵה אֲחוֹרַיִם, כָּעִנְיָן שֶׁנֶּאֱמַר: "וְרָאִיתָ אֶת אֲחֹרָי" (שמות לג, כג): **בְּעַבְדִּי בְמֹשֶׁה.** אֵינוֹ אוֹמֵר "בְּעַבְדִּי מֹשֶׁה", אֶלָּא "בְּעַבְדִּי בְמֹשֶׁה", בְּמֹשֶׁה אַף עַל פִּי שֶׁאֵינוֹ עַבְדִּי, בְּמֹשֶׁה שֶׁהוּא עַבְדִּי, כְּדַאי הֱיִיתֶם לִירֹא מִפָּנַי, וְכָל שֶׁכֵּן שֶׁהוּא עַבְדִּי, וְעֶבֶד מֶלֶךְ – מֶלֶךְ, וְהָיָה לָכֶם לוֹמַר: אֵין הַמֶּלֶךְ אוֹהֲבוֹ חִנָּם, וְאִם תֹּאמְרוּ אֵינִי מַכִּיר בְּמַעֲשָׂיו – זוֹ קָשָׁה מִן הָרִאשׁוֹנָה:

ט וַיִּחַר אַף ה' וַיֵּלַךְ. מֵאַחַר שֶׁהוֹדִיעָם סִרְחוֹנָם גָּזַר עֲלֵיהֶם נִדּוּי, קַל וָחֹמֶר לְבָשָׂר וָדָם, שֶׁלֹּא יִכְעֹס עַל חֲבֵרוֹ עַד שֶׁיּוֹדִיעֶנּוּ סִרְחוֹנוֹ:

DISCUSSION

→ an elevated title, and Moses is one of the only people in the Bible who was awarded this title.

12:8 | And the image of the Lord he will behold: Precisely because Moses saw the "image of the Lord," he knew better than anyone else that God does not have a body or any physical

form. The Rambam (Sefer HaMadda, Hilkhot Yesodei HaTorah 7:6; 9:1) speaks clearly and strongly about the uniqueness of the level and experience of Moses' prophecy, and about its centrality with regard to the sanctity of Torah. The Sages expressed this in the following way:

All the prophets observed their prophecies through an obscure looking glass; Moses observed his prophecies through a clear looking glass (Yevamot 49b). It is precisely because the other prophets observed their prophecies through an obscure looking glass that they saw

10 **The cloud,** representing God's revelation, **withdrew from upon the Tent, and behold, Miriam was leprous like snow,** which was an expression of God's anger. **Aaron turned to Miriam; and behold,** he discovered that **she was leprous.** Moses was also present, or at least in close proximity, to this incident, but he was, at this point, uninvolved. God addressed Aaron and Miriam, and it was they who were chastised and punished. The Sages said that Aaron was also struck with leprosy but the verse does not mention this point in order to protect Aaron's honor, as he was the High Priest and he was not the one who initiated the discussion about Moses.[45]

11 **Aaron said to Moses: Please my lord, do not place sin upon us, as we have been foolish, and we have sinned** by saying things that we should not have said. Aaron, Moses' older brother, had already been following Moses' directives before this incident, and had served as his assistant, but he had viewed himself as comparable to Moses. Now, after hearing God's rebuke, Aaron can only speak to Moses with absolute subservience. Their brotherly relationship and working relationship are no longer relevant, and Aaron turns to his brother with his supplication.

12 **Please, let her not be as a corpse, who when he emerges from his mother's womb, half his flesh was consumed.** Some interpret the verse as follows: Please, do not be as a corpse. According to this interpretation, Aaron is not requesting that Miriam should not be like a corpse, but is rather asking Moses not to be like a corpse. Since Miriam is his sister, and it is as though she is almost dead, it is as though part of Moses' flesh is consumed as well. A similar example can be found in Genesis 37:27, where Judah states about Joseph: "as he is our brother, our flesh." Consequently, Aaron says to Moses: Even if you do not want to act on our behalf, act for the benefit of your own flesh.[46]

13 **Moses cried out**[D] **to the Lord, saying: God, please, heal her now.**

14 **The Lord said to Moses: If her father spit in her face** and
Maftir thereby humiliated her, **wouldn't she be ashamed** to leave her house for **seven days** until the humiliation would subside? God afflicted Miriam with leprosy as a form of public disgrace, which is equivalent to spitting in her face. Consequently, **she shall be quarantined outside the camp seven days** as a leper, **and then she shall be readmitted** to the camp. Alternatively, the last phrase of this verse may be rendered: And then she shall be cured.[47]

15 **Miriam was quarantined outside the camp seven days,** in accordance with the law of a leper; **and the people did not travel until Miriam's readmission,** because despite her sin she was an eminent individual and deserved the honor of the nation waiting for her.

16 **Then,** when Miriam had recovered, **the people traveled from Hatzerot, and encamped** in a different location **in the wilderness of Paran.**[48]

DISCUSSION

extraneous images. This lack of clarity, though, was in the eyes of the beholder or the glass through which he was looking. One who clearly observes the prophetic vision as it is does not see extraneous images.

12:13 | **Moses cried out:** There were instances when Moses engaged in lengthy prayers, whether for himself or for the Israelites. Here, Moses prays succinctly and intensely for another individual standing nearby, with the brevity of the prayer expressing Moses' personal pain. This is not a prayer that was carefully formulated but rather a desperate plea for a cure for his sister (see *Sifrei*; *Berakhot* 34a).

י וְהֶעָנָן סָר מֵעַל הָאֹהֶל וְהִנֵּה מִרְיָם מְצֹרַעַת כַּשָּׁלֶג וַיִּפֶן אַהֲרֹן אֶל־מִרְיָם וְהִנֵּה
יא מְצֹרָעַת: וַיֹּאמֶר אַהֲרֹן אֶל־מֹשֶׁה בִּי אֲדֹנִי אַל־נָא תָשֵׁת עָלֵינוּ חַטָּאת אֲשֶׁר
יב נוֹאַלְנוּ וַאֲשֶׁר חָטָאנוּ: אַל־נָא תְהִי כַּמֵּת אֲשֶׁר בְּצֵאתוֹ מֵרֶחֶם אִמּוֹ וַיֵּאָכֵל חֲצִי
יג בְשָׂרוֹ: וַיִּצְעַק מֹשֶׁה אֶל־יהוה לֵאמֹר אֵל נָא רְפָא נָא לָהּ:
יד וַיֹּאמֶר יהוה אֶל־מֹשֶׁה וְאָבִיהָ יָרֹק יָרַק בְּפָנֶיהָ הֲלֹא תִכָּלֵם שִׁבְעַת יָמִים תִּסָּגֵר מפטיר
טו שִׁבְעַת יָמִים מִחוּץ לַמַּחֲנֶה וְאַחַר תֵּאָסֵף: וַתִּסָּגֵר מִרְיָם מִחוּץ לַמַּחֲנֶה שִׁבְעַת
טז יָמִים וְהָעָם לֹא נָסַע עַד־הֵאָסֵף מִרְיָם: וְאַחַר נָסְעוּ הָעָם מֵחֲצֵרוֹת וַיַּחֲנוּ בְּמִדְבַּר
פָּארָן:

רש״י

י | **וְהֶעָנָן סָר.** וְאַחַר כָּךְ "וְהִנֵּה מִרְיָם מְצֹרַעַת כַּשָּׁלֶג", מָשָׁל לְמֶלֶךְ שֶׁאָמַר לַפֵּדָגוֹג: רְדֵה אֶת בְּנִי, אֲבָל לֹא תִרְדֶּנּוּ עַד שֶׁאֵלֵךְ מֵאֶצְלְךָ, שֶׁרַחֲמַי עָלָיו:

יא | **נוֹאַלְנוּ.** כְּתַרְגּוּמוֹ, לְשׁוֹן אֱוִיל:

יב | **אַל נָא תְהִי.** אֲחוֹתֵנוּ זוֹ: **כַּמֵּת.** שֶׁהַמְּצֹרָע חָשׁוּב כַּמֵּת, מָה מֵת מְטַמֵּא בְּבִיאָה אַף מְצֹרָע מְטַמֵּא בְּבִיאָה: **אֲשֶׁר בְּצֵאתוֹ מֵרֶחֶם אִמּוֹ.** 'אִמֵּנוּ' הָיָה לוֹ לוֹמַר, אֶלָּא שֶׁכִּנָּה הַכָּתוּב. וְכֵן 'חֲצִי בְּשָׂרֵנוּ' הָיָה לוֹ לוֹמַר, אֶלָּא שֶׁכִּנָּה הַכָּתוּב. מֵאַחַר שֶׁיָּצָאת מֵרֶחֶם אִמֵּנוּ, הִיא לָנוּ כְּאִלּוּ נֶאֱכַל חֲצִי בְּשָׂרֵנוּ, כָּעִנְיָן שֶׁנֶּאֱמַר: "כִּי אָחִינוּ בְשָׂרֵנוּ הוּא" (בראשית לז, כז). וּלְפִי מַשְׁמָעוֹ, אַף הוּא נִרְאֶה כֵּן, אֵין רָאוּי לָאָח לְהַנִּיחַ אֶת אֲחוֹתוֹ לִהְיוֹת כַּמֵּת: **אֲשֶׁר בְּצֵאתוֹ.** מֵאַחַר שֶׁיָּצָא זֶה מֵרֶחֶם אִמּוֹ שֶׁל זֶה שֶׁיֵּשׁ כֹּחַ בְּיָדוֹ לַעֲזֹר וְאֵינוֹ עוֹזְרוֹ, הֲרֵי נֶאֱכַל חֲצִי בְּשָׂרוֹ, שֶׁאָחִיו בְּשָׂרוֹ הוּא. דָּבָר אַחֵר, "אַל נָא תְהִי כַּמֵּת" – אִם אֵינְךָ רוֹפְאָהּ בִּתְפִלָּה, מִי מַסְגִּירָהּ אוֹ מִי מְטַהֲרָהּ? אֲנִי אִי אֶפְשָׁר לִרְאוֹתָהּ, שֶׁאֲנִי קָרוֹב וְאֵין קָרוֹב רוֹאֶה אֶת הַנְּגָעִים, וְכֹהֵן אַחֵר אֵין בָּעוֹלָם. וְזֶהוּ "אֲשֶׁר בְּצֵאתוֹ מֵרֶחֶם אִמּוֹ":

יג | **אֵל נָא רְפָא נָא לָהּ.** בָּא הַכָּתוּב לְלַמֶּדְךָ דֶּרֶךְ אֶרֶץ, שֶׁהַשּׁוֹאֵל דָּבָר מֵחֲבֵרוֹ צָרִיךְ לוֹמַר שְׁנַיִם אוֹ שְׁלֹשָׁה דִּבְרֵי תַחֲנוּנִים, וְאַחַר כָּךְ יְבַקֵּשׁ שְׁאֵלוֹתָיו: **לֵאמֹר.** מַה תַּלְמוּד לוֹמַר? אָמַר לוֹ: הֲשִׁיבֵנִי אִם אַתָּה מְרַפֵּא אוֹתָהּ אִם לָאו, עַד שֶׁהֱשִׁיבוֹ: "וְאָבִיהָ יָרֹק יָרַק" וְגוֹ'. רַבִּי אֶלְעָזָר בֶּן עֲזַרְיָה אוֹמֵר: בְּאַרְבָּעָה מְקוֹמוֹת בִּקֵּשׁ מֹשֶׁה מִלִּפְנֵי הַקָּדוֹשׁ בָּרוּךְ הוּא לַהֲשִׁיבוֹ אִם יַעֲשֶׂה שְׁאֵלוֹתָיו אִם לָאו. כַּיּוֹצֵא בוֹ: "וַיְדַבֵּר מֹשֶׁה לִפְנֵי ה' לֵאמֹר" וְגוֹ' (שמות ו, יב), מַה תַּלְמוּד לוֹמַר: "לֵאמֹר"? הֲשִׁיבֵנִי אִם גּוֹאֲלָם אַתָּה אִם לָאו, עַד שֶׁהֱשִׁיבוֹ: "עַתָּה תִרְאֶה" וְגוֹ' (שם פסוק א). כַּיּוֹצֵא בוֹ: "וַיְדַבֵּר מֹשֶׁה אֶל ה' לֵאמֹר יִפְקֹד ה' אֱלֹהֵי הָרוּחֹת לְכָל בָּשָׂר" (להלן כז, טו-טז), הֱשִׁיבוֹ: "קַח לְךָ" (שם פסוק יח). כַּיּוֹצֵא בוֹ: "וָאֶתְחַנַּן אֶל ה' בָּעֵת הַהִוא לֵאמֹר" (דברים ג, כג), הֱשִׁיבוֹ: "רַב לָךְ" (שם פסוק כו): **רְפָא נָא לָהּ.** מִפְּנֵי מָה לֹא הֶאֱרִיךְ מֹשֶׁה בִּתְפִלָּה? שֶׁלֹּא יִהְיוּ יִשְׂרָאֵל אוֹמְרִים, אֲחוֹתוֹ עוֹמֶדֶת בְּצָרָה וְהוּא עוֹמֵד וּמַרְבֶּה בִּתְפִלָּה:

יד | **וְאָבִיהָ יָרֹק יָרַק בְּפָנֶיהָ.** וְאִם אָבִיהָ הֶרְאָה לָהּ פָּנִים זוֹעֲפוֹת "הֲלֹא תִכָּלֵם שִׁבְעַת יָמִים", קַל וָחֹמֶר לַשְּׁכִינָה אַרְבָּעָה עָשָׂר יוֹם, אֶלָּא דַּיּוֹ לַבָּא מִן הַדִּין לִהְיוֹת כַּנִּדּוֹן, לְפִיכָךְ אַף בִּנְזִיפָתִי "תִּסָּגֵר שִׁבְעַת יָמִים": **וְאַחַר תֵּאָסֵף.** אוֹמֵר אֲנִי, כָּל הָאֲסִיפוֹת הָאֲמוּרוֹת בַּמְּצֹרָעִים, עַל שֵׁם שֶׁהוּא מְשֻׁלָּח מִחוּץ לַמַּחֲנֶה וּכְשֶׁהוּא נִרְפָּא נֶאֱסָף אֶל הַמַּחֲנֶה, לְכָךְ כְּתוּב בּוֹ אֲסִיפָה, לְשׁוֹן הַכְנָסָה:

טו | **וְהָעָם לֹא נָסַע.** זֶה הַכָּבוֹד חָלַק לָהּ הַמָּקוֹם בִּשְׁבִיל שָׁעָה אַחַת שֶׁנִּתְעַכְּבָה לְמֹשֶׁה כְּשֶׁהֻשְׁלַךְ לַיְאוֹר, שֶׁנֶּאֱמַר: "וַתֵּתַצַּב אֲחֹתוֹ מֵרָחֹק" וְגוֹ' (שמות ב, ד):

Parashat
Shelah

The Scouts and Those Who Dared Ascend toward the Land
NUMBERS 13:1–14:45

The land of Canaan differs dramatically from Egypt. Canaan is a hilly, mountainous region that is dependent upon rainfall, whereas the terrain of Egypt is flat and is irrigated from the Nile. The cultures and systems of government in the two countries were also completely dissimilar at the time. Consequently, the children of Israel were troubled by the prospect of an unfamiliar way of life and by the dangerous challenges of the conquests ahead. Therefore, they wished to send scouts to Canaan.

The weakness and cowardice displayed by the people after they hear the report of the scouts leads to God's decree that this generation will not enter Canaan. Subsequently, a group rises up and insists that they want to ascend to the land, ignoring Moses' warnings to desist. But this brazen move is also doomed to failure, as it represents a rebellion against the divine decree that this generation will wander in the wilderness for forty years until they have all passed away.

13 1 **The Lord spoke to Moses, saying:**
2 **Send you men**[D] **that they may scout** out **the land of Canaan**[D] **that I am giving to the children of Israel** in order to become familiar with it; **you shall send one man** for every tribe, **each** as a representative **for the tribe of his fathers, every one a prince among them.** They must be leaders and men of stature, whose reports will be accepted and trusted by the members of their tribes. The men chosen were not the actual heads of the tribes, who are listed in the earlier census and at the festivities for the dedication of the altar (1:4–15, 7:12–78). It is possible that those tribal princes were too old for a mission of this nature. The men who were sent as scouts were prominent members of their tribes, but they were younger, probably at the peak of their strength.[1] One of the scouts, Caleb son of Yefuneh, will later state that he was forty years old at the time of this mission.[2]
3 **Moses sent them from the wilderness of Paran according to the directive of the Lord; all of them were personages; they were heads of the children of Israel.**

4 **These were their names:**[D] **For the tribe of Reuben,** they sent **Shamua son of Zakur.**
5 **For the tribe of Simeon, Shafat son of Hori.**
6 **For the tribe of Judah, Caleb son of Yefuneh.**
7 **For the tribe of Issachar, Yigal son of Joseph.**
8 **For the tribe of Ephraim, Hoshe'a son of Nun.**[D]
9 **For the tribe of Benjamin, Palti son of Rafu.**
10 **For the tribe of Zebulun, Gadiel son of Sodi.**
11 **For the tribe of Joseph: For the tribe of Manasseh,**[D] **Gadi son of Susi.**
12 **For the tribe of Dan, Amiel son of Gemali.**
13 **For the tribe of Asher, Setur son of Mikhael.**
14 **For the tribe of Naphtali, Nahbi son of Vofsi.**
15 **For the tribe of Gad, Geuel son of Makhi.**
16 **These are the names of the men whom Moses sent to scout the land. Moses called Hoshe'a son of Nun, Joshua.**[D] The name Hoshe'a means salvation. The addition of the letter *yod* is a reference to God. Hence, the name Joshua, like the related name Isaiah, means may God save.

DISCUSSION

13:2 | Send you men: This episode is also described in detail in the book of Deuteronomy in one of the lengthy speeches Moses gave prior to his death. According to that account, it was the children of Israel who initiated the plan to send scouts to Canaan, and Moses acceded to their request (Deuteronomy 1:22–23). However, the text here describes it as God's command.

It is likely that the people initiated the plan and Moses then relayed their request to God, who agreed. If so, the description here is truncated, with the first few stages omitted. Although the fateful idea was the people's initiative, their suggestion could have been rejected, and hence this verse emphasizes God's own

instruction that the plan should be followed and the scouts sent (see Rashi; *Sota* 34b, and Rashi ad loc.).

That they may scout the land of Canaan: This chapter does not use the word *meraglim*, "spies," but rather *tarim*, "scouts." To be sure, they were not merely tourists; the purpose of their trip was to gather information. With that said, though, they were not spies in the full sense of the term either, as their mission did not attempt to uncover secrets about the land or its inhabitants.

It would seem that from the outset Moses and the Israelites had different attitudes toward the scouts and their mission. Moses felt that their mission could be helpful in mapping out the

country and its entry routes, but the Israelites wanted a description of the current state of the country: Was it still a good land? Would it be feasible to conquer it at this point in time? The Israelites' knowledge of the land was limited to stories from the distant past and promises of a bright future; they wanted a current, accurate report of the state of affairs. It seems that the choice to send a representative from each of the tribes was due to these insecurities and worries. Had this mission been purely for the purpose of espionage, the individuals included would have been chosen for their professional qualifications rather than their social status or public reputations (see Ramban; *Bekhor Shor*).

פרשת
שלח

א ב וַיְדַבֵּר יְהוָה אֶל־מֹשֶׁה לֵּאמֹר: שְׁלַח־לְךָ אֲנָשִׁים וְיָתֻרוּ אֶת־אֶרֶץ כְּנַעַן אֲשֶׁר־אֲנִי יב
נֹתֵן לִבְנֵי יִשְׂרָאֵל אִישׁ אֶחָד אִישׁ אֶחָד לְמַטֵּה אֲבֹתָיו תִּשְׁלָחוּ כֹּל נָשִׂיא בָהֶם:
ג וַיִּשְׁלַח אֹתָם מֹשֶׁה מִמִּדְבַּר פָּארָן עַל־פִּי יְהוָה כֻּלָּם אֲנָשִׁים רָאשֵׁי בְנֵי־יִשְׂרָאֵל
ד ה הֵמָּה: וְאֵלֶּה שְׁמוֹתָם לְמַטֵּה רְאוּבֵן שַׁמּוּעַ בֶּן־זַכּוּר: לְמַטֵּה שִׁמְעוֹן שָׁפָט בֶּן־חוֹרִי:
ו ז ח לְמַטֵּה יְהוּדָה כָּלֵב בֶּן־יְפֻנֶּה: לְמַטֵּה יִשָּׂשכָר יִגְאָל בֶּן־יוֹסֵף: לְמַטֵּה אֶפְרָיִם הוֹשֵׁעַ
ט י בִּן־נוּן: לְמַטֵּה בִנְיָמִן פַּלְטִי בֶּן־רָפוּא: לְמַטֵּה זְבוּלֻן גַּדִּיאֵל בֶּן־סוֹדִי: לְמַטֵּה
יא יב יג יוֹסֵף לְמַטֵּה מְנַשֶּׁה גַּדִּי בֶּן־סוּסִי: לְמַטֵּה דָן עַמִּיאֵל בֶּן־גְּמַלִּי: לְמַטֵּה אָשֵׁר סְתוּר
יד טו טז בֶּן־מִיכָאֵל: לְמַטֵּה נַפְתָּלִי נַחְבִּי בֶּן־וָפְסִי: לְמַטֵּה גָד גְּאוּאֵל בֶּן־מָכִי: אֵלֶּה שְׁמוֹת
הָאֲנָשִׁים אֲשֶׁר־שָׁלַח מֹשֶׁה לָתוּר אֶת־הָאָרֶץ וַיִּקְרָא מֹשֶׁה לְהוֹשֵׁעַ בִּן־נוּן יְהוֹשֻׁעַ:

רש״י

פרק יג

ב] **שְׁלַח לְךָ אֲנָשִׁים.** לָמָּה נִסְמְכָה פָּרָשַׁת מְרַגְּלִים לְפָרָשַׁת מִרְיָם? לְפִי שֶׁלָּקְתָה עַל עִסְקֵי דִבָּה שֶׁדִּבְּרָה בְּאָחִיהָ, וּרְשָׁעִים הַלָּלוּ רָאוּ וְלֹא לָקְחוּ מוּסָר: שְׁלַח לְךָ. לְדַעְתְּךָ, אֲנִי אֵינִי מְצַוֶּה לְךָ, אִם תִּרְצֶה שְׁלַח. לְפִי שֶׁבָּאוּ יִשְׂרָאֵל וְאָמְרוּ: "נִשְׁלְחָה אֲנָשִׁים לְפָנֵינוּ" (דברים א, כב), כְּמָה שֶׁנֶּאֱמַר: "וַתִּקְרְבוּן אֵלַי כֻּלְּכֶם" וְגוֹ' (שם), וּמֹשֶׁה נִמְלַךְ בַּשְּׁכִינָה, אָמַר: אֲנִי אָמַרְתִּי לָהֶם שֶׁהִיא טוֹבָה, שֶׁנֶּאֱמַר: "אַעֲלֶה אֶתְכֶם מֵעֳנִי מִצְרַיִם" וְגוֹ' (שמות ג, יז), חַיֵּיהֶם שֶׁאֲנִי נוֹתֵן לָהֶם מָקוֹם לִטְעוֹת בְּדִבְרֵי הַמְרַגְּלִים, לְמַעַן לֹא יִירָשׁוּהָ:

ג] **עַל פִּי ה'.** בִּרְשׁוּתוֹ, שֶׁלֹּא עִכֵּב עַל יָדוֹ: **כֻּלָּם אֲנָשִׁים.** כָּל 'אֲנָשִׁים' שֶׁבַּמִּקְרָא לְשׁוֹן חֲשִׁיבוּת, וְאוֹתָהּ שָׁעָה כְּשֵׁרִים הָיוּ:

טז] **וַיִּקְרָא מֹשֶׁה לְהוֹשֵׁעַ וְגוֹ'.** נִתְפַּלֵּל עָלָיו: יָהּ יוֹשִׁיעֲךָ מֵעֲצַת מְרַגְּלִים:

DISCUSSION

13:4| **These were their names:** The order of the tribes listed here is not in accordance with their grouping under the banners, which was the military formation of the camp, nor does it follow their birth order. It is possible that they are listed in accordance with their social status, as these men were not sent as representatives of military units, but as agents of civil groups (see Ramban; *Ha'amek Davar*).

13:8| **Hoshe'a son of Nun:** Hoshe'a is Joshua son of Nun, Moses' attendant, who has already been mentioned (11:28; Exodus 33:11). In addition to Joshua's closeness to Moses, he was an important person in his own right. In the genealogical list in I Chronicles (7:26–27), Joshua appears as the grandson of the prince of the tribe of Ephraim. This is further proof of the high social status of the men selected for this mission, as well as the considerations of age that might have prevented the actual princes of the tribes undertaking the mission to Canaan.

13:11| **For the tribe of Joseph: for the tribe of Manasseh:** The description of Manasseh as the representative of Joseph is another indication that this list does not follow the military formation of the banners in the wilderness, as the banner of Joseph was headed by Ephraim. Rather, it follows the civilian structure of the tribes, and Manasseh was Joseph's firstborn.

13:16| **Moses called Hoshe'a son of Nun, Joshua:** Moses seemed to be uneasy about sending the delegation and perhaps he felt it was unnecessary, but nevertheless agreed to send scouts in order to placate the Israelites, following God's instruction. He therefore requested divine protection for his closest attendant, Hoshe'a (see Rashi; *Sota* 34b). This new name is significant not only for the current episode, but also for subsequent history. The change in name signifies Joshua's status as a future leader, similar to the new names given to kings and ministers upon their appointments (see Genesis 41:45; II Kings 23:34; see also *Bekhor Shor*; *Ḥizkuni*, Genesis 17:5).

17 Moses wanted to give the scouts a specifically defined mandate. The information they were asked to provide was strategic rather than tactical; for example, he did not ask them about particular fortifications or roads. Rather, **Moses sent them to scout the land of Canaan,** and **he said to them: Ascend,**[D] enter the land from **there in the South, and climb the highland.**

18 **You shall see the land, what it is** like in general. And **the people that lives in it, is it strong or is it weak? Are they few or many?** How densely populated is the land?

19 **What is the** type of **land in which it lives,** with regard to its climate and fauna? **Is it a good** land **or a bad** one? **What are the cities in which it lives? Is it in camps,** unwalled settlements, **or in** cities that have walls as **fortifications?**[D]

20 **What is the** nature of the **land? Is it fat or lean?** How fertile is its soil? Relatively speaking, which areas are more fertile and which ones less so? This information could also be relevant to understanding the locations of major population centers and the natures of the different possible travel routes. **Are there trees in it, or not?** Egypt does not have many natural trees, and some of those that have been growing there have been cut down. By contrast, at this time the entire central region of Canaan is thickly wooded.[3] In addition, Moses instructed them: **You shall strengthen yourselves, and you shall take** samples **from the fruit of the land** and bring them back to show your brethren. At this juncture, **the** verse notes parenthetically that these **days were the days of the first grapes,** which ripen in the late spring.

21 **They ascended and scouted** all **the land,** traversing the entire
Second aliya territory of Canaan **from the wilderness of Tzin**[B] **to Rehov,**[B] a place located **at Levo Hamat**[B] in northern Syria.

22 **They ascended in the South, and he came until Hebron.** The second clause is stated in the singular despite the fact that the first clause is in the plural. It is possible that the scouts did not advance as a single unit for the entire trip, and therefore only one of them reached Hebron. According to the Sages, this was Caleb.[4] It is likely that the people had preserved the memory of Hebron as the city of the forefathers. **And Ahiman, Sheshai, and Talmai, children of the giant, were there.** Parenthetically, the verse notes here that **Hebron was built seven years before Tzo'an,**[B] a very important city **of Egypt.** Tzo'an was a well-known ancient city, and unlike other Egyptian cities, the time period of its establishment was also known. The verse therefore underscores the importance of the ancient city of Hebron by stating that it was founded even earlier than Tzo'an.

23 Toward the end of their journey back,[5] **they came to the Eshkol Ravine, and cut from there a vine with one cluster**

Cluster of grapes

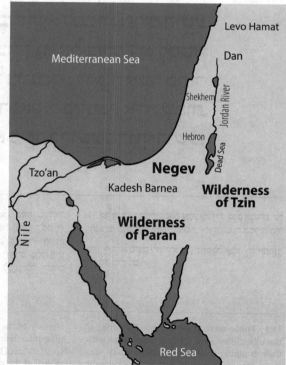

Places mentioned in the account of the scouts

DISCUSSION

13:17| **Ascend:** In the Bible, the verb "to ascend" can refer to a northward journey (see, e.g., Genesis 13:1; Exodus 13:18), but it can also refer to one entering the Land of Israel (e.g., II Samuel 5:17; II Kings 18:9; Isaiah 36:10; Zechariah 14:16–17; Ezra 2:1; see *Kiddushin* 69b).

13:19| **Is it in camps or in fortifications:** These details were indeed significant during the conquest of the land. The open cities were captured straightaway, whereas the fortified cities were able to resist and delay the progress of Joshua's army in the early stages of the campaign (see Joshua 6–8, 10:19–20; Rashbam).

וַיִּשְׁלַ֤ח אֹתָם֙ מֹשֶׁ֔ה לָת֖וּר אֶת־אֶ֣רֶץ כְּנָ֑עַן וַיֹּ֣אמֶר אֲלֵהֶ֗ם עֲל֥וּ זֶה֙ בַּנֶּ֔גֶב וַעֲלִיתֶ֖ם אֶת־ יז

הָהָֽר: וּרְאִיתֶ֥ם אֶת־הָאָ֖רֶץ מַה־הִ֑וא וְאֶת־הָעָם֙ הַיֹּשֵׁ֣ב עָלֶ֔יהָ הֶחָזָ֥ק הוּא֙ הֲרָפֶ֔ה יח

הַמְעַ֥ט ה֖וּא אִם־רָֽב: וּמָ֣ה הָאָ֗רֶץ אֲשֶׁר־הוּא֙ יֹשֵׁ֣ב בָּ֔הּ הֲטוֹבָ֥ה הִ֖וא אִם־רָעָ֑ה וּמָ֣ה יט

הֶֽעָרִ֗ים אֲשֶׁר־הוּא֙ יוֹשֵׁ֣ב בָּהֵ֔נָּה הַבְּמַֽחֲנִ֖ים אִ֥ם בְּמִבְצָרִֽים: וּמָ֣ה הָ֠אָ֠רֶץ הַשְּׁמֵנָ֨ה הִ֜וא כ

אִם־רָזָ֗ה הֲיֵֽשׁ־בָּ֥הּ עֵץ֙ אִם־אַ֔יִן וְהִ֨תְחַזַּקְתֶּ֔ם וּלְקַחְתֶּ֖ם מִפְּרִ֣י הָאָ֑רֶץ וְהַ֨יָּמִ֔ים יְמֵ֖י

בִּכּוּרֵ֥י עֲנָבִֽים: וַֽיַּעֲל֖וּ וַיָּתֻ֣רוּ אֶת־הָאָ֑רֶץ מִמִּדְבַּר־צִ֥ן עַד־רְחֹ֖ב לְבֹ֥א חֲמָֽת: וַיַּעֲל֣וּ כא שני

בַנֶּגֶב֮ וַיָּבֹ֣א עַד־חֶבְרוֹן֒ וְשָׁ֤ם אֲחִימַן֙ שֵׁשַׁ֣י וְתַלְמַ֔י יְלִידֵ֖י הָעֲנָ֑ק וְחֶבְר֗וֹן שֶׁ֤בַע שָׁנִים֙ כב

נִבְנְתָ֔ה לִפְנֵ֖י צֹ֥עַן מִצְרָֽיִם: וַיָּבֹ֜אוּ עַד־נַ֣חַל אֶשְׁכֹּ֗ל וַיִּכְרְת֨וּ מִשָּׁ֤ם זְמוֹרָה֙ וְאֶשְׁכּ֤וֹל כג

רש"י

יז| עֲלוּ זֶה בַּנֶּגֶב. הוּא הָיָה הַפְּסֹלֶת שֶׁל אֶרֶץ יִשְׂרָאֵל, שֶׁכֵּן דֶּרֶךְ הַתַּגָּרִים, מַרְאִים אֶת הַפְּסֹלֶת תְּחִלָּה וְאַחַר כָּךְ מַרְאִים אֶת הַשֶּׁבַח:

יח| אֶת הָאָרֶץ מַה הִוא. יֵשׁ אֶרֶץ מְגַדֶּלֶת גִּבּוֹרִים וְיֵשׁ אֶרֶץ מְגַדֶּלֶת חַלָּשִׁים, יֵשׁ מְגַדֶּלֶת אֻכְלוּסִין וְיֵשׁ מְמַעֶטֶת אֻכְלוּסִין: **הֶחָזָק הוּא הֲרָפֶה.** סִימָן מָסַר לָהֶם, אִם בִּכְרַכִּים יוֹשְׁבִין – חֲזָקִים הֵם, שֶׁסּוֹמְכִין עַל גְּבוּרָתָם, וְאִם בַּעֲרִים בְּטוּרוֹת הֵם יוֹשְׁבִין – חַלָּשִׁים הֵם:

יט| הַבְּמַחֲנִים. תַּרְגּוּמוֹ "הַבְּפַצְחִין", כְּרַכִּין פְּתִיחִין וּפְתִיחִין מֵאֵין חוֹמָה. **הֲטוֹבָה הִוא.** בְּמַעְיָנוֹת וּתְהוֹמוֹת טוֹבִים וּבְרִיאִים:

כ| הֲיֵשׁ בָּהּ עֵץ. אִם יֵשׁ בָּהֶם אָדָם כָּשֵׁר שֶׁיָּגֵן עֲלֵיהֶם בִּזְכוּתוֹ: **בִּכּוּרֵי עֲנָבִים.** יָמִים שֶׁהָעֲנָבִים מִתְבַּשְּׁלִין בְּכִבּוּר:

כא| מִמִּדְבַּר צִן עַד רְחֹב לְבֹא חֲמָת. הָלְכוּ בִּגְבוּלֶיהָ בְּאֹרֶךְ וּבְרֹחַב כְּמִין "גַּאם", הָלְכוּ רוּחַ גְּבוּל דְּרוֹמִית מִמִּקְצוֹעַ מִזְרָח עַד מִקְצוֹעַ מַעֲרָב, כְּמוֹ שֶׁצִּוָּה מֹשֶׁה, "עֲלוּ זֶה בַּנֶּגֶב" (לְעֵיל פָּסוּק יז) דֶּרֶךְ גְּבוּל דְּרוֹמִית מִזְרָחִית, עַד הַיָּם, שֶׁהַיָּם הוּא גְּבוּל מַעֲרָבִי, וּמִשָּׁם חָזְרוּ וְהָלְכוּ כָּל גְּבוּל מַעֲרָבִי עַל שְׂפַת הַיָּם עַד לְבֹא חֲמָת, שֶׁהוּא אֵצֶל הֹר הָהָר בְּמִקְצוֹעַ מַעֲרָבִית צְפוֹנִית, כְּמוֹ שֶׁמְּפֹרָשׁ בִּגְבוּלוֹת הָאָרֶץ בְּפָרָשַׁת אֵלֶּה מַסְעֵי (לְהַלָּן לד, ז):

כב| וַיָּבֹא עַד חֶבְרוֹן. כָּלֵב לְבַדּוֹ הָלַךְ שָׁם, וְנִשְׁתַּטֵּחַ עַל קִבְרֵי אָבוֹת שֶׁלֹּא יְהֵא נִסָּת לַחֲבֵרָיו לִהְיוֹת בַּעֲצָתָם, וְכֵן

הוּא אוֹמֵר: "וְלוֹ אֶתֵּן אֶת הָאָרֶץ אֲשֶׁר דָּרַךְ בָּהּ" (דְּבָרִים א, לו). וּכְתִיב: "וַיִּתְּנוּ לְכָלֵב אֶת חֶבְרוֹן" (שׁוֹפְטִים א, כ): **שֶׁבַע שָׁנִים נִבְנְתָה.** אֶפְשָׁר שֶׁבָּנָה חָם אֶת חֶבְרוֹן לְכְנַעַן בְּנוֹ הַקָּטָן קֹדֶם שֶׁיִּבְנֶה אֶת צֹעַן לְמִצְרַיִם בְּנוֹ הַגָּדוֹל? אֶלָּא שֶׁהָיְתָה מְבֻנָּה בְּכָל טוּב עַל אֶחָד מִשִּׁבְעָה בְּצֹעַן, וּבָא לְהוֹדִיעֲךָ שִׁבְחָהּ שֶׁל אֶרֶץ יִשְׂרָאֵל, שֶׁאֵין לְךָ טְרָשִׁין בְּאֶרֶץ יִשְׂרָאֵל יוֹתֵר מֵחֶבְרוֹן, לְפִיכָךְ הִקְצוּהָ לִקְבוּרַת מֵתִים, וְאֵין לְךָ מְעֻלָּה בְּכָל הָאֲרָצוֹת כְּמִצְרַיִם, שֶׁנֶּאֱמַר: "כְּגַן ה' כְּאֶרֶץ מִצְרַיִם" (בְּרֵאשִׁית יג, י), וְצֹעַן הִיא הַמְעֻלָּה שֶׁבְּאֶרֶץ מִצְרַיִם, שֶׁשָּׁם מוֹשַׁב הַמְּלָכִים, שֶׁנֶּאֱמַר: "כִּי הָיוּ בְצֹעַן שָׂרָיו" (יְשַׁעְיָה ל, ד), וְהָיְתָה חֶבְרוֹן טוֹבָה מִמֶּנָּה שִׁבְעָה חֲלָקִים:

כג| זְמוֹרָה. שׂוֹכַת גֶּפֶן, וְאֶשְׁכּוֹל שֶׁל עֲנָבִים תָּלוּי בָּהּ:

BACKGROUND

13:21| From the wilderness of Tzin: Some say that this wilderness is in the eastern side of the Sinai Peninsula, north of Kadesh Barnea (Ein el-Qudeirat), while others locate it between Eilat and Wadi Jira, southeast of central Sinai, in the same region. There are also other opinions that place it north of the Arava desert, or even further east in the territory of Edom (see Joshua 15:1).

The name Tzin, or Sin, refers to the prickly edges of plants. It perhaps alludes to desert regions that contain springs of water, such as were found at Eilim and Kadesh Barnea (20:1, 27:14). This environment is characterized by its prickly palm trees.

Rehov: There are several places in the Bible with this name: A city in the portion of the tribe of Asher, near Sidon in Lebanon (Joshua 21:31); another is Beit Rehov, in the Hula Valley (Judges 18:28); and a third city is Beit Rehov mentioned in II Samuel 10:6, one of the kingdoms of Aram in the north of the Beqaa Valley in Lebanon, which is probably the place referred to here. According to *Targum Yonatan*, this is the passageway to Levo Hamat.

At Levo Hamat: Some explain that *levo* refers to the route from the coast to Hamat. Others claim that it is the name of a place in Hamat, which they identify with the village of Laboue, north of Baalbek in the Beqaa Valley.

13:22| Tzo'an: A city in Lower Egypt. According to Onkelos and the Septuagint, it is the city of Tanis. Tanis was the capital of Egypt between the eleventh and seventh centuries BCE. From the sixth century onward it decreased in importance, due to the expansion of the Nile Delta, which caused Tanis to be farther from the Mediterranean.

Contemporary scholars identify ancient Tzo'an with a site near San al-Hagar, in the Delta northeast of Tanis, or with Avaris, the capital of Egypt during the seventeenth to fifteenth centuries BCE, located slightly further south.

of grapes, and two of them bore it upon a pole.[D] Due to its immense size, it could not be borne by a single person. **And they also brought back samples from the** local **pomegranates, and from the figs.**

24 The verse notes: **That place he,** or they, **called the Eshkol Ravine.** It can be assumed that this valley was close to the wilderness, and therefore the scouts did not have to carry the grapes throughout the entire length of Canaan. Some commentaries suggest that the Eshkol Ravine should be identified with one of the streambeds planted with many vineyards found to the north of Hebron. The valley became commonly known as the Eshkol Ravine **because of the cluster [***eshkol***]** of grapes **that the children of Israel cut from there.**

25 Since their mission was limited to gaining a general impression and their mandate did not include gathering detailed information, **they returned from scouting the land at the conclusion of forty days.**

26 **They went and came to** report back to **Moses, and to Aaron, and to the entire congregation of the children of Israel, to the wilderness of Paran,** more specifically **to** the place known as **Kadesh.**[B] And they **brought back word to them and to the entire congregation,** who gathered to hear their account. This phrase serves as an additional indication that the scouts viewed themselves not only as emissaries of the leadership, but as agents of the entire nation. **And** in addition to their verbal testimony, they also **showed them the fruit of the land.**

27 Addressing Moses directly in the presence of the assembled crowd, **they related** the details of their journey **to him, and** they **said: We came to the land to which you sent us, and indeed it is flowing with milk and honey.** It is a very fertile land, as God has told us,[6] **and this is** a sample of some of **its fruit.**

28 **Only,** you must know that **the people that lives in the land is mighty.** Its inhabitants are not meek or complacent, and therefore it will be difficult for us to subjugate them quickly. **And** furthermore **the cities** in which they live **are fortified and very great;**[D] **we also saw the children of the giant there.**

29 **Amalek lives in the southern region,** along our route. According to the original plan for entering Canaan, the Israelites would have traveled north, through the Negev, and would have encountered opposition from the Amalekites. **And in addition, the Hitites, the Yevusites, and the Emorites live in the highland, and the Canaanites live along the sea and alongside the Jordan.**

30 Although the scouts' report was formally addressed to Moses, it was meant for the nation's ears as well. Since the people trusted the scouts, they became fearful upon hearing their report, and they began to murmur among themselves and to voice their concerns. In response, **Caleb silenced the people** and directed their attention **toward Moses.** As the leader of the nation and the recipient of the scouts' report, the response to the report should have come from him rather than from the initial reaction of the masses. Furthermore, Caleb added encouraging words of his own, **and he said:** Do not fear or hesitate! **We shall** be able to **ascend and inherit it,** the land, **for we can prevail over it.**

31 **But the** other **men who ascended** to the land along **with him** and with Joshua, representatives of the other tribes, contradicted him and **said: We will not be able to ascend** to the land, **against the people, for it is stronger than we are.** We do not have the military strength to fight those mighty armies. The Israelites, who until recently had been slaves in Egypt, were afraid to engage in open warfare.

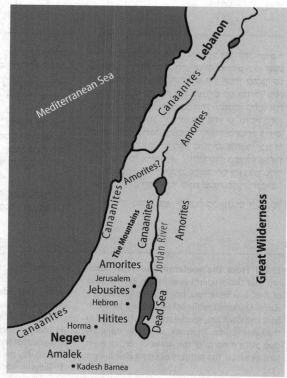

Canaanite nations

— DISCUSSION —

13:23 | **And two of them bore it upon a pole:** According to some midrashim, this cluster was even larger than might be inferred from a straightforward reading of the text (see *Sota* 34a). The Sages relate that in their time as well, there were reports of massive clusters of grapes that were as large as calves and goats (see *Ketubot* 112a).

כד ענבים אחד וישאהו במוט בשנים ומן־הרמנים ומן־התאנים: למקום ההוא
כה קרא נחל אשכול על אדות האשכול אשר־כרתו משם בני ישראל: וישבו
כו מתור הארץ מקץ ארבעים יום: וילכו ויבאו אל־משה ואל־אהרן ואל־כל־
עדת בני־ישראל אל־מדבר פארן קדשה וישיבו אתם דבר ואת־כל־העדה
כז ויראום את־פרי הארץ: ויספרו־לו ויאמרו באנו אל־הארץ אשר שלחתנו
כח וגם זבת חלב ודבש הוא וזה־פריה: אפס כי־עז העם הישב בארץ והערים
כט בצרות גדלת מאד וגם־ילדי הענק ראינו שם: עמלק יושב בארץ הנגב
ל והחתי והיבוסי והאמרי יושב בהר והכנעני יושב על־הים ועל יד הירדן: ויהס
כלב את־העם אל־משה ויאמר עלה נעלה וירשנו אתה כי־יכול נוכל לה:
לא והאנשים אשר־עלו עמו אמרו לא נוכל לעלות אל־העם כי־חזק הוא ממנו:

רש"י

כד| **וישאהו במוט בשנים.** ממשמע שנאמר: "וישאהו במוט", איני יודע שהוא בשנים? מה תלמוד לומר "בשנים"? בשני מוטות. הא כיצד? שמונה נטלו אשכול, אחד נטל תאנה ואחד רמון. יהושע וכלב לא נטלו כלום, לפי שכל עצמם להוציא דבה נתכונו: כשם שפריה משנה כך עמה משנה. ואם חפץ אתה לידע כמה משאוי אחד מהם, צא ולמד מאבנים שהקימו בגלגל, הרימו להם איש אבן אחת מן הירדן על שכמו והקימוה בגלגל, ושקלום רבותינו משקל כל אחת ארבעים סאה, וגמירי, טונא דמדלי אינש על כתפיה אינו אלא שליש משאוי כמשאוי שמסייעין אותו להרים:

כה| **וישבו מתור הארץ מקץ ארבעים יום.** והלא ארבע מאות פרסה על ארבע מאות פרסה היא, ומהלך אדם בינוני עשרה פרסאות ליום, הרי מהלך ארבעים יום מן המזרח למערב, והם הלכו ארכה ורחבה! אלא שגלוי לפני הקדוש ברוך הוא שיגזור עליהם יום לשנה, קצר לפניהם את הדרך:

כו| **וילכו ויבאו.** מהו "וילכו", להקיש הליכתן לביאתן, מה ביאתן בעצה רעה, אף הליכתן בעצה רעה: **וישיבו אתם דבר.** את משה ואת אהרן:

כז| **זבת חלב ודבש.** כל דבר שקר שאין אומרים בו קצת אמת בתחלתו, אין מתקיים בסופו:

כח| **בצרות.** לשון חוזק, ותרגומו: "כריכן", לשון בירניות עגלות, ובלשון ארמי 'כריך' – עגל:

כט| **עמלק יושב וגו'.** לפי שנכוו בעמלק כבר, הזכירוהו מרגלים כדי ליראם: **ועל יד הירדן.** 'יד' כמשמעו, אצל הירדן, ולא תוכלו לעבר:

ל| **ויהס כלב.** השתיק את כלם: **אל משה.** לשמע מה שידבר במשה, צוח ואמר: וכי זו בלבד עשה לנו בן עמרם? השומע היה סבור שבא לספר בגנותו, ומתוך שהיה בלבם על משה בשביל דברי המרגלים שתקו כלם לשמע גנותו. אמר: והלא קרע לנו את הים, והוריד לנו את המן, והגיז לנו את השלו: **עלה נעלה.** אפילו בשמים, והוא אומר: עשו סלמות ועלו שם! נצליח בכל דבריו: **ויהס.** לשון שתיקה, וכן: "הס כל בשר" (זכריה ב, יז), "הס כי לא להזכיר" (עמוס ו, י), כן דרך בני אדם, הרוצה לשתק אגדת אנשים אומר ס"ט:

לא| **חזק הוא ממנו.** כביכול כלפי מעלה אמרו:

BACKGROUND

13:26| **To the wilderness of Paran, to Kadesh:** The mention of Paran serves to differentiate this Kadesh from other places with the same name. Some identify the place mentioned in this verse with the Kadesh located in the wilderness of Tzin (27:14; Deuteronomy 1:2), which marked the southern border of the Land of Israel (Genesis 16:14, 20:1). It is generally accepted that this Kadesh is the same place known as Kadesh Barnea, and is identified with the desert oasis known today as Ein el-Qudeirat, an important junction approximately 25 km south of Nitzana, along the route from the Arabian Peninsula to Gaza. Indeed, one of the springs there is called Ein el-Qadeis.

However, some researchers hold that the Kadesh of Paran is different from the Kadesh in the wilderness of Tzin, as that Kadesh was on the border of Edom. In addition, there is also another city by the name of Kadesh in the portion of Naftali, in the Upper Galilee (Joshua 20:7).

DISCUSSION

13:28| **And the cities are fortified, very great:** The inhabitants of the city-states in Canaan belonged to a variety of nations, including Canaanites, Yevusites, Emorites, and other nations from among the descendants of Shem and Ham. As a result, there was often hostility between them (see, e.g., Judges 1:7). Therefore, although it is a small land, Canaan's cities were fortified and very large, due to the constant battles and general instability in the region.

32 At first, the scouts provided a relatively objective account of what they had seen, answering the questions that were posed to them. But now **they promulgated a slanderous report of the land that they scouted to the children of Israel.** Their portrayals may not have been entirely false, but they were slanted in a deliberate effort to create a negative impression,[7] **saying: The land, which we passed through to scout it, is a land that devours its inhabitants.** There are many diseases and untimely deaths there. **And** conversely, **all the people whom we saw in it were people of size,**[D] large individuals. Although the mortality rate is high, large people with strong bodies are able to live there.

33 **There we saw the Nefilim, sons of a giant, from** among the **Nefilim,**[D] an ancient race of giants.[8] **We were as grasshoppers in our eyes** when we stood opposite these enormous individuals, **and so we were in their eyes;** they also related to us as small, worthless creatures. The huge fruits the scouts brought back also served to vividly illustrate for their listeners the likely dimensions of the people who inhabited the land.

14 1 **The entire congregation** who were present at the time then **raised and sounded their voice; and the people wept that night.**

2 **All the children of Israel complained against Moses and against Aaron; and the entire congregation said to them: If only we had died in the land of Egypt, or in this wilderness; if only we had died** in peace and tranquility.

3 **Why does the Lord bring us to this land,** Canaan, **to fall by the sword?** Rather than living a full life and dying of natural causes, we will instead perish before our time in battle, and **our wives and our children will be** taken **for loot.** Faced with such a prospect, **isn't it better for us to return to Egypt?**

4 As a result of the crying and commotion, the people's bitterness and resentment progressively increased. Finally, **they said one to another:** It is not wise to continue in the direction of Canaan, so instead **let us appoint a leader**[9] **and return to Egypt.**

5 Upon hearing this, **Moses and Aaron fell upon their faces before the entire assembly of the congregation of the children of Israel.**

6 **Joshua son of Nun and Caleb son of Yefuneh,** who were **from those** men **who** had **scouted the land, rent their garments.**

7 **They said to the entire congregation of the children of Israel, saying: The land through which we passed to scout it, the land is exceedingly good.**

8 As for your concerns, **if the Lord is favorably disposed to us, He will bring us to this land and will give it to us, a land flowing with milk and honey.** The land is excellent, and our success depends only on God's will.

Third aliya

9 **However, do not rebel against the Lord** by refusing to enter the land. **And you,** who have received a direct promise from God, **do not fear the people of the land,** even if others might justifiably do so,[10] **as they are** like **our bread;** our triumph over them will be as simple as eating bread. **Their protection has withdrawn from them,** and they have nowhere to shelter and take refuge, **and** by contrast **the Lord is with us;** therefore, **do not fear them.**

10 **The entire congregation said to stone them,** referring to Joshua and Caleb and perhaps also to Moses and Aaron,[11] **with stones, and the glory of the Lord appeared in the Tent of Meeting to all the children of Israel.**

11 It appears that Moses went to the Tent of Meeting, and then **the Lord said to Moses: Until when will this people scorn** and profane **Me, and until when will they not believe in Me,**

"A land flowing with milk and honey"

DISCUSSION

13:32 | And all the people whom we saw in it were people of size: The Egyptians were an ethnocentric people who saw themselves at the center of global civilization. They viewed all lands to their north as primitive, disparaging their cultures and the strength of their inhabitants. The scouts sought to undermine that impression.

They warned them not to take the residents of Canaan lightly, and emphasized that it was not a relatively unsettled frontier area. Rather, it was a built-up and populated country with fortified cities and developed agriculture. The children of Israel, who were not trained fighters, should

therefore anticipate a difficult war that might well be beyond their abilities.

13:33 | Sons of a giant, from the Nefilim: Later, the Torah mentions Og, king of Bashan (21:33), who was himself one of the last of these giants who had lived in earlier generations (see Deuteronomy 2:11, 3:11).

לב וַיֹּצִיאוּ דִּבַּת הָאָרֶץ אֲשֶׁר תָּרוּ אֹתָהּ אֶל־בְּנֵי יִשְׂרָאֵל לֵאמֹר הָאָרֶץ אֲשֶׁר עָבַרְנוּ
בָהּ לָתוּר אֹתָהּ אֶרֶץ אֹכֶלֶת יוֹשְׁבֶיהָ הִוא וְכָל־הָעָם אֲשֶׁר־רָאִינוּ בְתוֹכָהּ אַנְשֵׁי
לג מִדּוֹת׃ וְשָׁם רָאִינוּ אֶת־הַנְּפִילִים בְּנֵי עֲנָק מִן־הַנְּפִלִים וַנְּהִי בְעֵינֵינוּ כַּחֲגָבִים וְכֵן
א הָיִינוּ בְּעֵינֵיהֶם׃ וַתִּשָּׂא כָּל־הָעֵדָה וַיִּתְּנוּ אֶת־קוֹלָם וַיִּבְכּוּ הָעָם בַּלַּיְלָה הַהוּא׃
ב וַיִּלֹּנוּ עַל־מֹשֶׁה וְעַל־אַהֲרֹן כֹּל בְּנֵי יִשְׂרָאֵל וַיֹּאמְרוּ אֲלֵהֶם כָּל־הָעֵדָה לוּ־מַתְנוּ
ג בְּאֶרֶץ מִצְרַיִם אוֹ בַּמִּדְבָּר הַזֶּה לוּ־מָתְנוּ׃ וְלָמָה יְהוָה מֵבִיא אֹתָנוּ אֶל־הָאָרֶץ
ד הַזֹּאת לִנְפֹּל בַּחֶרֶב נָשֵׁינוּ וְטַפֵּנוּ יִהְיוּ לָבַז הֲלוֹא טוֹב לָנוּ שׁוּב מִצְרָיְמָה׃ וַיֹּאמְרוּ
ה אִישׁ אֶל־אָחִיו נִתְּנָה רֹאשׁ וְנָשׁוּבָה מִצְרָיְמָה׃ וַיִּפֹּל מֹשֶׁה וְאַהֲרֹן עַל־פְּנֵיהֶם
ו לִפְנֵי כָּל־קְהַל עֲדַת בְּנֵי יִשְׂרָאֵל׃ וִיהוֹשֻׁעַ בִּן־נוּן וְכָלֵב בֶּן־יְפֻנֶּה מִן־הַתָּרִים אֶת־
ז הָאָרֶץ קָרְעוּ בִּגְדֵיהֶם׃ וַיֹּאמְרוּ אֶל־כָּל־עֲדַת בְּנֵי־יִשְׂרָאֵל לֵאמֹר הָאָרֶץ אֲשֶׁר
ח עָבַרְנוּ בָהּ לָתוּר אֹתָהּ טוֹבָה הָאָרֶץ מְאֹד מְאֹד׃ אִם־חָפֵץ בָּנוּ יְהוָה וְהֵבִיא שלישי
ט אֹתָנוּ אֶל־הָאָרֶץ הַזֹּאת וּנְתָנָהּ לָנוּ אֶרֶץ אֲשֶׁר־הִוא זָבַת חָלָב וּדְבָשׁ׃ אַךְ בַּיהוָה
אַל־תִּמְרֹדוּ וְאַתֶּם אַל־תִּירְאוּ אֶת־עַם הָאָרֶץ כִּי לַחְמֵנוּ הֵם סָר צִלָּם מֵעֲלֵיהֶם
י וַיהוָה אִתָּנוּ אַל־תִּירָאֻם׃ וַיֹּאמְרוּ כָּל־הָעֵדָה לִרְגּוֹם אֹתָם בָּאֲבָנִים וּכְבוֹד יְהוָה
נִרְאָה בְּאֹהֶל מוֹעֵד אֶל־כָּל־בְּנֵי יִשְׂרָאֵל׃
יא וַיֹּאמֶר יְהוָה אֶל־מֹשֶׁה עַד־אָנָה יְנַאֲצֻנִי הָעָם הַזֶּה וְעַד־אָנָה לֹא־יַאֲמִינוּ בִי יג

רש"י

לב] אֹכֶלֶת יוֹשְׁבֶיהָ. בְּכָל מָקוֹם שֶׁעָבַרְנוּ מְצָאנוּם קוֹבְרֵי מֵתִים, וְהַקָּדוֹשׁ בָּרוּךְ הוּא עָשָׂה לְטוֹבָה כְּדֵי לְטָרְדָם בְּאֶבְלָם וְלֹא יִתְּנוּ לֵב לָאֵלּוּ: אַנְשֵׁי מִדּוֹת. גְּדוֹלִים וּגְבוֹהִים, וְצָרִיךְ לִתֵּן לָהֶם מִדָּה, כְּגוֹן גָּלְיָת: "גָּבְהוֹ שֵׁשׁ אַמּוֹת וָזָרֶת" (שמואל א' יז, ד), וְכֵן: "אִישׁ מָדוֹן" (שמואל ב' כא, כ), "אִישׁ מִדָּה" (דברי הימים א' יא, כג).

לג] הַנְּפִילִים. עֲנָקִים, מִבְּנֵי שַׁמְחַזַאי וַעֲזָאֵל שֶׁנָּפְלוּ מִן הַשָּׁמַיִם בִּימֵי דּוֹר אֱנוֹשׁ: וְכֵן הָיִינוּ בְּעֵינֵיהֶם. שָׁמַעְנוּ אוֹמְרִים זֶה לָזֶה: נְמָלִים יֵשׁ בַּכְּרָמִים כַּאֲנָשִׁים: עֲנָק. שֶׁמַּעֲנִיקִים חַמָּה בְּקוֹמָתָן:

פרק יד

ב] לוּ מַתְנוּ. הַלְוַאי וּמַתְנוּ:

ד] נִתְּנָה רֹאשׁ. כְּתַרְגּוּמוֹ: "נְמַנֵּי רֵישָׁא", נָשִׂים עָלֵינוּ מֶלֶךְ. וְרַבּוֹתֵינוּ פֵּרְשׁוּ, לְשׁוֹן עֲבוֹדָה זָרָה.

ט] אַל תִּמְרֹדוּ. וְשׁוּב "וְאַתֶּם אַל תִּירְאוּ": כִּי לַחְמֵנוּ הֵם. נֹאכְלֵם כַּלֶּחֶם: סָר צִלָּם. מְגִנָּם וְחָזְקָם, כְּשֵׁרִים שֶׁבָּהֶם מֵתוּ, אִיּוֹב שֶׁהָיָה מֵגֵן עֲלֵיהֶם. דָּבָר אַחֵר, צִלּוֹ שֶׁל הַמָּקוֹם סָר מֵעֲלֵיהֶם.

י] לִרְגּוֹם אֹתָם. אֶת יְהוֹשֻׁעַ וְכָלֵב: וּכְבוֹד ה'. הֶעָנָן יָרַד שָׁם.

יא] עַד אָנָה. עַד הֵיכָן: יְנַאֲצֻנִי. יַרְגִּיזוּנִי:

with, and despite, **all the signs** and miracles **that I have performed in their midst?**

12 Because of their obstinacy, **I will smite them, with the pestilence, and I will destroy them, and will make you,** Moses, **into a nation greater and mightier than they.** God thereby indicated His intention to destroy the people, and to wait for a new nation to evolve from Moses' descendants. Although this nation would in some way be the continuation of the children of Israel, in a more direct sense it would be a new nation called the children of Moses.

13 **Moses said to the Lord: Egypt will hear** what has happened, **that You took up this people** of Israel **with Your might from its midst.**

14 **And** if You destroy them, **they will** then **say to,** meaning about, **the inhabitants of this land** of Canaan, to which the children of Israel were supposed to go; until now **they,** the Egyptians, had **heard that You, the Lord, are** to be found **in the midst of this people; that with their very eyes You, the Lord, were seen** by that people, **and Your cloud stands over them; and in a pillar of cloud You go before them by day, and in a pillar of fire by night.**

15 But **if You** now suddenly **kill this people as one man** in a plague, the Egyptians and **the nations that have heard of Your renown will** wonder why You have done that. They will conclude that You must have lacked the power to fulfill your promise to them, and **say** that You therefore killed them. They will thereby desecrate Your name, **saying:**

16 Although **the Lord** did manage to take them out of Egypt, at this time He **lacks ability to bring this people into the land with regard to which He took an oath to them.** He is obviously unable to defeat the nations of Canaan, **and** for that reason **He slaughtered them in the wilderness.**

17 **Now,** therefore, **please, let the might of my Lord be great.** Let Your power be revealed to Israel in a more exalted and loftier way, **as You spoke** and promised me, by teaching Me Your attributes of mercy after the sin of the Golden Calf,[12] **saying:**

18 **The Lord is** patient and **slow to anger and abounding in kindness, bearing iniquity and transgression. But** at the same time, though, **He will not** completely **exonerate** the iniquity. Although God awaits the sinner's repentance and the sin is then forgiven, it is not entirely cleansed.[13] Rather, He will continue **reckoning the iniquity of the fathers** and enacting restitution for it **upon the children, upon the third and upon the fourth generation.**[D] God is exceedingly merciful, and consequently does not punish one's descendants eternally for their forefathers' sins. But He also does not bring the complete punishment upon the sinner at one time, as this would lead to the sinner's total destruction. Instead, He extends the punishment over several generations and places some of the burden upon the sinner's descendants, but only until the fourth generation. Furthermore, if the children refrain from committing additional sins, and thereby refrain from evoking the memory of their ancestor's iniquity, the sin is erased completely and they are not punished at all.[14] These attributes of God are similar to the ones God Himself mentioned in Exodus 34, after the sin of the Golden Calf. However, there are some differences between them; see the chart below.[15]

19 **Please pardon the iniquity of this people in accordance with the greatness of Your kindness, and** reduce their severe punishment to a lighter penalty,[16] **as You have** patiently **borne** and forgiven the sin of **this people, from Egypt until now.**

20 **The Lord said: I have pardoned in accordance with your word,**[D] as you requested, since your reasoning is valid. Moses' prayer succeeded insofar as God annulled the original decree to destroy the entire people at once and replace them with a new nation descended from Moses.

21 **However, as I live,** I swear by My life, **the entire earth shall be filled with the glory of the Lord.** This was an additional expression of an oath:[17]

22 **For all the people who have seen My glory, and My signs, which I performed in Egypt and in the wilderness,** meaning

---

DISCUSSION

14:18 | God's Attributes of Mercy

The attributes after the sin of the scouts (14:18)	The attributes after God forgave the people for the sin of the Golden Calf (Exodus 34:6–7)
The Lord	The Lord, the Lord, merciful and gracious
Slow to anger and abounding in kindness	Slow to anger and abounding in kindness and truth
Bearing iniquity and transgression	He maintains kindness to the thousands, bearing iniquity and transgression and sin
But He will not exonerate	But He will not exonerate
Reckoning the iniquity of the fathers upon the children, upon the third and upon the fourth generation	Reckoning the iniquity of the fathers upon children, and upon the children's children, upon the third and upon the fourth generation

יב בְּכֹל הָאֹתוֹת אֲשֶׁר עָשִׂיתִי בְּקִרְבּוֹ: אַכֶּנּוּ בַדֶּבֶר וְאוֹרִשֶׁנּוּ וְאֶעֱשֶׂה אֹתְךָ לְגוֹי־
יג גָּדוֹל וְעָצוּם מִמֶּנּוּ: וַיֹּאמֶר מֹשֶׁה אֶל־יְהוָה וְשָׁמְעוּ מִצְרַיִם כִּי־הֶעֱלִיתָ בְכֹחֲךָ
יד אֶת־הָעָם הַזֶּה מִקִּרְבּוֹ: וְאָמְרוּ אֶל־יוֹשֵׁב הָאָרֶץ הַזֹּאת שָׁמְעוּ כִּי־אַתָּה יְהוָה
בְּקֶרֶב הָעָם הַזֶּה אֲשֶׁר־עַיִן בְּעַיִן נִרְאָה ׀ אַתָּה יְהוָה וַעֲנָנְךָ עֹמֵד עֲלֵהֶם וּבְעַמֻּד
טו עָנָן אַתָּה הֹלֵךְ לִפְנֵיהֶם יוֹמָם וּבְעַמּוּד אֵשׁ לָיְלָה: וְהֵמַתָּה אֶת־הָעָם הַזֶּה כְּאִישׁ
טז אֶחָד וְאָמְרוּ הַגּוֹיִם אֲשֶׁר־שָׁמְעוּ אֶת־שִׁמְעֲךָ לֵאמֹר: מִבִּלְתִּי יְכֹלֶת יְהוָה לְהָבִיא
יז אֶת־הָעָם הַזֶּה אֶל־הָאָרֶץ אֲשֶׁר־נִשְׁבַּע לָהֶם וַיִּשְׁחָטֵם בַּמִּדְבָּר: וְעַתָּה יִגְדַּל־
יח נָא כֹּחַ אֲדֹנָי כַּאֲשֶׁר דִּבַּרְתָּ לֵאמֹר: יְהוָה אֶרֶךְ אַפַּיִם וְרַב־חֶסֶד נֹשֵׂא עָוֺן וָפָשַׁע
יט וְנַקֵּה לֹא יְנַקֶּה פֹּקֵד עֲוֺן אָבוֹת עַל־בָּנִים עַל־שִׁלֵּשִׁים וְעַל־רִבֵּעִים: סְלַח־נָא
לַעֲוֺן הָעָם הַזֶּה כְּגֹדֶל חַסְדֶּךָ וְכַאֲשֶׁר נָשָׂאתָה לָעָם הַזֶּה מִמִּצְרַיִם וְעַד־הֵנָּה:
כ כא וַיֹּאמֶר יְהוָה סָלַחְתִּי כִּדְבָרֶךָ: וְאוּלָם חַי־אָנִי וְיִמָּלֵא כְבוֹד־יְהוָה אֶת־כָּל־הָאָרֶץ:

רש"י

בכל האותות. בשביל כל הנסים שעשיתי להם היה להם להאמין שהיכלת בידי לקים הבטחתי:

יב| ואורשנו. כתרגומו, תרוכין. ואם תאמר: מה אעשה לשבועת אבות? "ואעשה אתך לגוי גדול", שאתה מזרעם:

יג-יד| ושמעו מצרים. ושמעו את אשר תהרגם: כי העלית. 'כי' משמש בלשון 'אשר'. והם ראו את אשר העלית בכחך הגדול אותם מקרבם, וכשישמעו שאתה הורגם, לא יאמרו שחטאו לך, אלא יאמרו שכנגדם יכלת להלחם אבל כנגד יושבי הארץ לא יכלת להלחם, וזו היא: ואמרו אל יושב הארץ הזאת. כמו 'על יושב הארץ הזאת'. ומה יאמרו עליהם? מה שאמור בסוף הענין: "מבלתי יכלת ה'" (להלן פסוק טז), בשביל ש"שמעו כי אתה ה'" שוכן בקרבם ועין בעין אתה נראה להם, והכל בדרך חבה, ולא הכירו בך שנתקה אהבתך מהם עד הנה:

טו| והמתה את העם הזה כאיש אחד. פתאם, ומתוך כך: "ואמרו הגוים אשר שמעו את שמעך" וגו':

טז| מבלתי יכלת וגו'. לפי שיושבי הארץ חזקים וגבורים, ואינו דומה פרעה לשלשים ואחד מלכים, זאת יאמרו על יושבי הארץ הזאת: "מבלתי יכלת", מתוך שלא היה יכלת בידו להביאם, שחטם: יכלת. שם דבר הוא:

יז-יח| כאשר דברת לאמר. ומהו הדבור? ה' ארך אפים. לצדיקים ולרשעים. כשעלה משה למרום מצאו משה להקדוש ברוך הוא שהיה יושב וכותב: "ה' ארך אפים", אמר לו: לצדיקים? אמר לו הקדוש ברוך הוא: אף לרשעים. אמר לו: רשעים יאבדו. אמר לו הקדוש ברוך הוא: חייך שתצטרך לדבר. כשחטאו ישראל בעגל ובמרגלים התפלל משה לפניו ב'ארך אפים', אמר לו הקדוש ברוך הוא: והלא אמרת לי 'לצדיקים'! אמר לו: והלא אתה אמרת לי 'אף לרשעים': יגדל נא כח אדני. לעשות דבורך: ונקה. לשבים: לא ינקה. לשאינן שבים:

כ| כדברך. בשביל מה שאמרת, פן יאמרו: "מבלתי יכלת ה'" (לעיל פסוק טז):

כא-כג| ואולם. כמו 'אבל', זאת אעשה להם: חי אני. לשון שבועה, כשם שאני חי וכבודי ימלא את כל הארץ, כך אקים להם, "כי כל האנשים הראים וגו' אם יראו את הארץ"; הרי זה מקרא מסרס: חי אני כי כל האנשים אם יראו את הארץ, וכבודי ימלא את כל הארץ, שלא יתחלל שמי במגפה הזאת לאמר: 'מבלתי יכלת ה'' להביאם, שלא אמיתם פתאם כאיש אחד, אלא באחור ארבעים שנה מעט מעט:

DISCUSSION

14:20| **I have pardoned in accordance with your word:** God was certainly aware of Moses' claims beforehand, but He wanted to hear them from him. God grants people a certain amount of leeway to speak and act, and gives them the ability to change, as it were, God's own decrees. Herein lies the power of prayer.

the entire people of Israel, **and they have tested Me these ten times, and have not heeded My voice,**

23 I swear that **they shall not see the land with regard to which I took an oath to their fathers. And** certainly **all those who scorned Me,** whether they were among those who incited others to rebel, or were themselves incited by others; whether they were seized by terror as a result of the negative report they heard from the scouts, or they objected to Moses' leadership for personal reasons; they all **shall not see it.**

24 **But** in contrast to them, **My servant Caleb, because another spirit was with him,** and although he had been one of the scouts, he remained fully faithful to My wishes and commands **and he followed Me wholeheartedly, will I** therefore **bring him** at a future time **to the land into which he** already **came.** This time he will enter the land as a conqueror, **and his descendants shall take possession of it.**

25 If you insist on trying to enter the land despite My decree, you will not succeed, as **the Amalekites and the Canaanites dwell in the valley,** and they will prevent you from entering. Therefore, **tomorrow, turn** back **and travel you to the wilderness,** and travel back **by way of the Red Sea.**

Fourth 26 **The Lord spoke to Moses and to Aaron, saying:**
aliya 27 **Until when** shall I have tolerance **for this evil congregation that bring complaints against Me?** In this context, the term "congregation" refers mainly to the scouts themselves.[18] **I have heard the complaints of the children of Israel that they,** the scouts, **brought against Me.**

28 Therefore, **say to them:** I swear **as I live – the utterance of the Lord – surely as you** yourselves **spoke in My ears,** when you said that you will die without succeeding to conquer the land, **so I shall do to you.**

29 **Your carcasses shall fall in this wilderness, and** this fate will befall **all those of you who were counted in any of your censuses** taken for any reason,[19] meaning all those **from twenty years old and above, who brought complaints against Me.**

Your predictions will come true: You will all die. However, this will not happen as a result of war, but rather after years of wandering in the wilderness.

30 **You shall not come into the land, with regard to which I raised My hand** and took an oath **that I would settle you in it.** None of those who are adults today shall reach the Promised Land, **except for** two single individuals who will be exempt from this decree: **Caleb son of Yefuneh and Joshua son of Nun.**

31 Instead, I will fulfill My promise to **your children, about whom you said they would be** taken by the Canaanites **for loot. I will bring them** into the land, **and they shall know the land that you have despised.**

32 **But your carcasses, you, shall fall in this wilderness,** which you will not escape.

33 While this is happening, **your children shall be wandering about in the wilderness,** drifting from place to place[20] for **forty years. And they shall bear** the consequences of **your harlotry until the demise of your carcasses** falling **in the wilderness,** and all of you have passed away.

34 **In accordance with the number of the days that you scouted the land, forty days, each day for a year, you shall bear your iniquities,** adding up to a total of **forty years. And** as a result of this punishment, **you shall know** the extent of **My estrangement** from you, or how far you have strayed from following Me.[21] Alternatively, this means: You shall know the price of refusing to follow My commands.[22]

35 **I am the Lord; I have spoken; surely, I will do this to this entire evil congregation that congregated against Me; in this wilderness they shall expire, and there they shall die.** Only the next generation will conquer the land.

36 **The men whom Moses sent to scout the land and returned and brought the entire congregation to complain against him** continued **to promulgate a slanderous report of the land.**

רש"י

כב] וַיְנַסּוּ. כְּמַשְׁמָעוֹ: זֶה עֶשֶׂר פְּעָמִים. שְׁנַיִם בַּיָּם וּשְׁנַיִם בַּסְּלָו וְכוּ', כִּדְאִיתָא בְּמַסֶּכֶת עֲרָכִין (דף טז ע"א - טז ע"ב):

כג] אִם יִרְאוּ. לֹא יִרְאוּ:

כד] רוּחַ אַחֶרֶת. שְׁתֵּי רוּחוֹת, אַחַת בַּפֶּה וְאַחַת בַּלֵּב. לַמְרַגְּלִים אָמַר: חַי עִמָּכֶם בָּעֵצָה, וּבְלִבּוֹ הָיָה לוֹמַר הָאֱמֶת, וְעַל יְדֵי כֵן הָיָה בּוֹ כֹּחַ לְהַשְׁתִּיקָם, כְּמוֹ שֶׁנֶּאֱמַר: "וַיַּהַס כָּלֵב" (לעיל יג, ל), שֶׁהָיוּ סְבוּרִים שֶׁיֹּאמַר כְּמוֹתָם. זֶהוּ שֶׁנֶּאֱמַר בְּסֵפֶר יְהוֹשֻׁעַ: "וָאָשֵׁב אֹתוֹ דָּבָר כַּאֲשֶׁר עִם

לְבָבִי" (יהושע יד, ז), וְלֹא כַאֲשֶׁר עִם פִּי: וַיְמַלֵּא אַחֲרָי. וַיְמַלֵּא אֶת לִבּוֹ אַחֲרַי, זֶה מִקְרָא קָצֵר: אֲשֶׁר בָּא שָׁמָּה. חֶבְרוֹן תִּנָּתֵן לוֹ: יוֹרִשֶׁנָּה. כְּתַרְגּוּמוֹ: "יְתָרְכִנַּהּ", יוֹרִישׁוּ אֶת הָעֲנָקִים וְאֶת הָעָם אֲשֶׁר בָּהּ, וְאֵין לְתַרְגְּמוֹ 'יִרְתְּנַהּ' אֶלָּא בִּמְקוֹם 'יִירָשֶׁנָּה':

כה] וְהָעֲמָלֵקִי וְגו'. אִם תֵּלְכוּ שָׁם יַהַרְגוּ אֶתְכֶם, מֵאַחַר שֶׁאֵינִי עִמָּכֶם: מָחָר פְּנוּ. לַאֲחוֹרֵיכֶם, "וּסְעוּ לָכֶם" וְגו':

כז] לָעֵדָה הָרָעָה וְגו'. אֵלּוּ הַמְרַגְּלִים, מִכָּאן לְעֵדָה שֶׁהִיא עֲשָׂרָה: אֲשֶׁר הֵמָּה מַלִּינִים. אֶת יִשְׂרָאֵל "עָלָי":

אֶת תְּלֻנּוֹת בְּנֵי יִשְׂרָאֵל אֲשֶׁר הֵמָּה. הַמְרַגְּלִים, "מַלִּינִים" אוֹתָם "עָלַי", שָׁמַעְתִּי:

כח] חַי אָנִי. לְשׁוֹן שְׁבוּעָה, אִם לֹא כֵן אֶעֱשֶׂה – כִּבְיָכוֹל אֵינִי חַי: כַּאֲשֶׁר דִּבַּרְתֶּם. שֶׁבִּקַּשְׁתֶּם מִמֶּנִּי: "אוֹ בַּמִּדְבָּר הַזֶּה לוּ מָתְנוּ" (לעיל פסוק ב):

כט] וְכָל פְּקֻדֵיכֶם לְכָל מִסְפַּרְכֶם. כָּל הַנִּמְנֶה לְכָל מִסְפָּר שֶׁאַתֶּם נִמְנִים בּוֹ, כְּגוֹן לָצֵאת וְלָבוֹא לַצָּבָא וְלָתֵת שְׁקָלִים, כָּל הַמְּנוּיִים לְכָל אוֹתָן מִסְפָּרוֹת יָמוּתוּ, וְאֵלּוּ הֵן: "מִבֶּן

כב כִּי כָל־הָאֲנָשִׁים הָרֹאִים אֶת־כְּבֹדִי וְאֶת־אֹתֹתַי אֲשֶׁר־עָשִׂיתִי בְמִצְרַיִם וּבַמִּדְבָּר
כג וַיְנַסּוּ אֹתִי זֶה עֶשֶׂר פְּעָמִים וְלֹא שָׁמְעוּ בְּקוֹלִי: אִם־יִרְאוּ אֶת־הָאָרֶץ אֲשֶׁר נִשְׁבַּעְתִּי
כד לַאֲבֹתָם וְכָל־מְנַאֲצַי לֹא יִרְאוּהָ: וְעַבְדִּי כָלֵב עֵקֶב הָיְתָה רוּחַ אַחֶרֶת עִמּוֹ וַיְמַלֵּא
כה אַחֲרָי וַהֲבִיאֹתִיו אֶל־הָאָרֶץ אֲשֶׁר־בָּא שָׁמָּה וְזַרְעוֹ יוֹרִשֶׁנָּה: וְהָעֲמָלֵקִי וְהַכְּנַעֲנִי
יוֹשֵׁב בָּעֵמֶק מָחָר פְּנוּ וּסְעוּ לָכֶם הַמִּדְבָּר דֶּרֶךְ יַם־סוּף:
כו כז וַיְדַבֵּר יְהוָה אֶל־מֹשֶׁה וְאֶל־אַהֲרֹן לֵאמֹר: עַד־מָתַי לָעֵדָה הָרָעָה הַזֹּאת אֲשֶׁר רביעי
הֵמָּה מַלִּינִים עָלָי אֶת־תְּלֻנּוֹת בְּנֵי יִשְׂרָאֵל אֲשֶׁר הֵמָּה מַלִּינִים עָלַי שָׁמָעְתִּי:
כח אֱמֹר אֲלֵהֶם חַי־אָנִי נְאֻם־יְהוָה אִם־לֹא כַּאֲשֶׁר דִּבַּרְתֶּם בְּאָזְנָי כֵּן אֶעֱשֶׂה לָכֶם:
כט בַּמִּדְבָּר הַזֶּה יִפְּלוּ פִגְרֵיכֶם וְכָל־פְּקֻדֵיכֶם לְכָל־מִסְפַּרְכֶם מִבֶּן עֶשְׂרִים שָׁנָה
ל וָמָעְלָה אֲשֶׁר הֲלִינֹתֶם עָלָי: אִם־אַתֶּם תָּבֹאוּ אֶל־הָאָרֶץ אֲשֶׁר נָשָׂאתִי אֶת־יָדִי
לא לְשַׁכֵּן אֶתְכֶם בָּהּ כִּי אִם־כָּלֵב בֶּן־יְפֻנֶּה וִיהוֹשֻׁעַ בִּן־נוּן: וְטַפְּכֶם אֲשֶׁר אֲמַרְתֶּם
לב לָבַז יִהְיֶה וְהֵבֵיאתִי אֹתָם וְיָדְעוּ אֶת־הָאָרֶץ אֲשֶׁר מְאַסְתֶּם בָּהּ: וּפִגְרֵיכֶם אַתֶּם
לג יִפְּלוּ בַּמִּדְבָּר הַזֶּה: וּבְנֵיכֶם יִהְיוּ רֹעִים בַּמִּדְבָּר אַרְבָּעִים שָׁנָה וְנָשְׂאוּ אֶת־זְנוּתֵיכֶם
לד עַד־תֹּם פִּגְרֵיכֶם בַּמִּדְבָּר: בְּמִסְפַּר הַיָּמִים אֲשֶׁר־תַּרְתֶּם אֶת־הָאָרֶץ אַרְבָּעִים
יוֹם יוֹם לַשָּׁנָה יוֹם לַשָּׁנָה תִּשְׂאוּ אֶת־עֲוֺנֹתֵיכֶם אַרְבָּעִים שָׁנָה וִידַעְתֶּם אֶת־
לה תְּנוּאָתִי: אֲנִי יְהוָה דִּבַּרְתִּי אִם־לֹא | זֹאת אֶעֱשֶׂה לְכָל־הָעֵדָה הָרָעָה הַזֹּאת
לו הַנּוֹעָדִים עָלָי בַּמִּדְבָּר הַזֶּה יִתַּמּוּ וְשָׁם יָמֻתוּ: וְהָאֲנָשִׁים אֲשֶׁר־שָׁלַח מֹשֶׁה
לָתוּר אֶת־הָאָרֶץ וַיָּשֻׁבוּ וילונו עָלָיו אֶת־כָּל־הָעֵדָה לְהוֹצִיא דִבָּה עַל־הָאָרֶץ: וַיַּלִּינוּ

רש"י

עֶשְׂרִים שָׁנָה" וְגוֹ' – לְהוֹצִיא שִׁבְטוֹ שֶׁל לֵוִי שֶׁאֵין פְּקוּדֵיהֶם מִבֶּן עֶשְׂרִים:

לב | וּפִגְרֵיכֶם אַתֶּם. כְּתַרְגּוּמוֹ, לְפִי שֶׁדִּבֵּר עַל הַבָּנִים לְהַכְנִיסָם לָאָרֶץ וּבִקֵּשׁ לוֹמַר: 'וְאַתֶּם תָּמוּתוּ', נוֹפֵל לָשׁוֹן זֶה כָּאן לוֹמַר "אַתֶּם":

לג | אַרְבָּעִים שָׁנָה. לֹא מֵת אֶחָד מֵהֶם פָּחוֹת מִבֶּן שִׁשִּׁים, לְכָךְ נִגְזַר אַרְבָּעִים, כְּדֵי שֶׁיִּהְיוּ אוֹתָם שֶׁל בְּנֵי עֶשְׂרִים מַגִּיעִין לִכְלַל שִׁשִּׁים. וְשָׁנָה רִאשׁוֹנָה הָיְתָה בַּכְּלָל, וְאַף עַל פִּי שֶׁקָּדְמָה לְשִׁלּוּחַ הַמְרַגְּלִים, לְפִי שֶׁמִּשֶּׁעָשׂוּ אֶת הָעֵגֶל עָלְתָה גְּזֵרָה זוֹ בְּמַחֲשָׁבָה, אֶלָּא שֶׁהִמְתִּין לָהֶם עַד שֶׁתִּתְמַלֵּא סְאָתָם, וְזֶהוּ שֶׁנֶּאֱמַר: "וּבְיוֹם פָּקְדִי", בַּמְרַגְּלִים, "וּפָקַדְתִּי עֲלֵיהֶם חַטָּאתָם" (שמות לב, לד), וְאַף כָּאן נֶאֱמַר: "תִּשְׂאוּ אֶת עֲוֹנֹתֵיכֶם", שְׁתֵּי עֲוֹנוֹת, שֶׁל עֵגֶל וְשֶׁל תְּלוּנָה, וְחִשֵּׁב לָהֶם בְּמִנְיַן חַיֵּיהֶם מִקְצָת שָׁנָה כְּכֻלָּהּ, וּכְשֶׁנִּכְנְסוּ לִשְׁנַת שִׁשִּׁים מֵתוּ אוֹתָם שֶׁל בְּנֵי עֶשְׂרִים: וְנָשְׂאוּ אֶת זְנוּתֵיכֶם. כְּתַרְגּוּמוֹ, יְסַבְּלוּן יָת חוֹבֵיכוֹן:

לד | אֶת תְּנוּאָתִי. שֶׁהֲנִיאוֹתֶם אֶת לְבַבְכֶם מֵאַחֲרַי. 'תְּנוּאָה' לְשׁוֹן הֲסָרָה, כְּמוֹ: "כִּי הֵנִיא אָבִיהָ אֹתָהּ" (להלן ל, ו):

לו | וַיָּשֻׁבוּ וַיַּלִּינוּ עָלָיו. וּכְשֶׁשָּׁבוּ מִתּוּר הָאָרֶץ הִרְעִימוּ עָלָיו אֶת כָּל הָעֵדָה בְּהוֹצָאַת דִּבָּה, אוֹתָן הָאֲנָשִׁים "וַיָּמֻתוּ" (להלן פסוק לז). כָּל הוֹצָאַת דִּבָּה לְשׁוֹן חִנּוּךְ דְּבָרִים, שֶׁמַּלְקִיאִים לְשׁוֹנָם לְאָדָם לְדַבֵּר בּוֹ, כְּמוֹ: "דּוֹבֵב שִׂפְתֵי יְשֵׁנִים" (שיר השירים ז, י), וְיֶשְׁנָהּ לְטוֹבָה וְיֶשְׁנָהּ לְרָעָה, לְכָךְ נֶאֱמַר כָּאן: "מוֹצִאֵי דִבַּת הָאָרֶץ רָעָה" (להלן פסוק לז), שֶׁיֵּשׁ דִּבָּה שֶׁהִיא טוֹבָה: דִּבָּה. פרלדי"ץ בְּלַעַז:

37 The men, promulgators of the evil slanderous report of the land, died in the plague before the Lord. The scouts themselves were the first to die, and they died a difficult, unnatural death. The definite article in the term "the plague" indicates something well-known and terrible.[23]

38 But Joshua son of Nun, and Caleb son of Yefuneh, lived from among those men who went to scout the land. This was a clear indication that the scouts did not die as a result of some infectious disease they had contracted during their journey, but rather as a direct punishment that afflicted only those who were guilty of circulating slander about the land.

39 Moses spoke these words to all the children of Israel. He informed all the adults that as they had rejected the land, and there will be no returning to Egypt, it has been decreed that they will remain in the wilderness until their deaths. And upon hearing this, the people mourned greatly, since they believed in God and in Moses.

40 Because the children of Israel felt this remorse, they awoke early in the morning, and ascended to the top of the mountain, saying: Here we are, and we will ascend to the place that the Lord said, the land of Canaan. We wish to repair our earlier error, because we sinned by refusing to go to the land.

41 But Moses said to them: Why are you violating the directive of the Lord? God has already issued His decree and therefore it, this initiative of yours, shall not succeed.

42 Do not ascend to try to fight for the land, as the Lord is not in your midst. There is no chance that you will emerge victorious. Consequently, it would be wise to refrain from trying, so that you will not be struck down before your enemies.

43 For the Amalekites and the Canaanites are there before you on the path leading to the land, and if you attempt to enter, you shall fall by the sword; since you have withdrawn from following the Lord, and therefore the Lord will not be with you.

44 Nevertheless, they ventured[D] to go up to the top of the mountain range that stood before them on the way to Canaan; yet the Ark of the Covenant of the Lord, and Moses, did not move from the midst of the camp.

45 The Amalekites and the Canaanites, who lived on that mountain, came down and smote them and crushed them, chasing them until a place that later became known as Horma, because those people met their destruction [*horbanam*] there.[24] They were routed in battle and retreated in humiliation.

Various Commandments
NUMBERS 15:1–41

Although in the previous section it was decreed that the entire generation would die in the wilderness, nothing has changed with regard to the fundamental relationship between God and His people. The nation's arrival in the Promised Land will be delayed until the next generation, but nevertheless, it still awaits them.

This reassuring message can be inferred from several of the commandments that appear below, as they apply only in the Land of Israel, and are to be fulfilled by the descendants of the current generation. In the following cases the Torah emphasizes that the commands apply equally to the stranger living among the people in the land, as it does to the citizen. These details serve to strengthen the hope that the people will indeed arrive at the Promised Land, which the text describes with the words "that I am giving to you" (verse 2) and "that I am bringing you there" (verse 18).

This section contains a variety of commandments: the laws of meal offerings and libations; the portion of dough set aside for priests [*halla*]; the offerings that provide atonement for the unwitting sin of idolatry, after which appears, by way of contrast, the prohibition against disparaging the name of God by acting high-handedly and blaspheming; and finally the commandment of ritual fringes [*tzitzit*]. In connection with the prohibition of sinning high-handedly against God, the Torah relates a short narrative detailing an episode involving someone who publicly desecrates the Sabbath in the wilderness.

15 1 The Lord spoke to Moses, saying:

2 The following commandment is addressed not to the adult individuals then assembled in the wilderness, but rather to the children of Israel as a people, since only their descendants would enter the land. Speak to the children of Israel, and say to them: When you will come into the land of your dwellings that I am giving to you,

3 and you will perform of your own free will a fire offering to the Lord, either in the form of a burnt offering or a peace offering to fulfill a vow, or if you bring a particular animal as a pledge, a gift offering, or at your appointed times, to create a pleasing aroma to the Lord, from the cattle, or from the flock;

לח וַיָּמֻ֙תוּ֙ הָֽאֲנָשִׁ֔ים מֽוֹצִאֵ֥י דִבַּת־הָאָ֖רֶץ רָעָ֑ה בַּמַּגֵּפָ֖ה לִפְנֵ֥י יְהֹוָֽה: וִיהוֹשֻׁ֣עַ בִּן־נ֔וּן

לט וְכָלֵ֣ב בֶּן־יְפֻנֶּ֔ה חָיוּ֙ מִן־הָֽאֲנָשִׁ֣ים הָהֵ֔ם הַהֹֽלְכִ֖ים לָת֣וּר אֶת־הָאָ֑רֶץ: וַיְדַבֵּ֤ר מֹשֶׁה֙

מ אֶת־הַדְּבָרִ֣ים הָאֵ֔לֶּה אֶל־כָּל־בְּנֵ֖י יִשְׂרָאֵ֑ל וַיִּֽתְאַבְּל֥וּ הָעָ֖ם מְאֹֽד: וַיַּשְׁכִּ֣מוּ בַבֹּ֔קֶר

וַיַּֽעֲל֥וּ אֶל־רֹֽאשׁ־הָהָ֖ר לֵאמֹ֑ר הִנֶּ֗נּוּ וְעָלִ֛ינוּ אֶל־הַמָּק֛וֹם אֲשֶׁר־אָמַ֥ר יְהֹוָ֖ה כִּ֥י

מא חָטָ֑אנוּ: וַיֹּ֣אמֶר מֹשֶׁ֗ה לָ֤מָּה זֶּה֙ אַתֶּ֣ם עֹֽבְרִ֔ים אֶת־פִּ֖י יְהֹוָ֑ה וְהִ֖וא לֹ֥א תִצְלָֽח:

מב אַֽל־תַּֽעֲל֔וּ כִּ֛י אֵ֥ין יְהֹוָ֖ה בְּקִרְבְּכֶ֑ם וְלֹא֙ תִּנָּֽגְפ֔וּ לִפְנֵ֖י אֹֽיְבֵיכֶֽם: מג כִּי֩ הָֽעֲמָלֵקִ֨י וְהַֽכְּנַֽעֲנִ֜י

שָׁ֣ם לִפְנֵיכֶ֗ם וּנְפַלְתֶּ֖ם בֶּחָ֑רֶב כִּֽי־עַל־כֵּ֤ן שַׁבְתֶּם֙ מֵאַֽחֲרֵ֣י יְהֹוָ֔ה וְלֹֽא־יִֽהְיֶ֥ה יְהֹוָ֖ה

מד עִמָּכֶֽם: וַיַּעְפִּ֕לוּ לַֽעֲל֖וֹת אֶל־רֹ֣אשׁ הָהָ֑ר וַֽאֲר֤וֹן בְּרִית־יְהֹוָה֙ וּמֹשֶׁ֔ה לֹא־מָ֖שׁוּ מִקֶּ֥רֶב

מה הַֽמַּֽחֲנֶֽה: וַיֵּ֤רֶד הָֽעֲמָֽלֵקִי֙ וְהַֽכְּנַֽעֲנִ֔י הַיֹּשֵׁ֖ב בָּהָ֣ר הַה֑וּא וַיַּכּ֥וּם וַֽיַּכְּת֖וּם עַד־הַֽחָרְמָֽה:

יד א וַיְדַבֵּ֥ר יְהֹוָ֖ה אֶל־מֹשֶׁ֥ה לֵּאמֹֽר: ב דַּבֵּר֙ אֶל־בְּנֵ֣י יִשְׂרָאֵ֔ל וְאָֽמַרְתָּ֖ אֲלֵהֶ֑ם כִּ֣י תָבֹ֗אוּ אֶל־

אֶ֨רֶץ֙ מֽוֹשְׁבֹ֣תֵיכֶ֔ם אֲשֶׁ֥ר אֲנִ֖י נֹתֵ֥ן לָכֶֽם: ג וַֽעֲשִׂיתֶ֨ם אִשֶּׁ֤ה לַֽיהֹוָה֙ עֹלָ֣ה אֽוֹ־זֶ֔בַח לְפַלֵּא־

נֶ֨דֶר֙ א֣וֹ בִנְדָבָ֔ה א֖וֹ בְּמֹֽעֲדֵיכֶ֑ם לַֽעֲשׂ֞וֹת רֵ֤יחַ נִיחֹ֨חַ֙ לַֽיהֹוָ֔ה מִן־הַבָּקָ֖ר א֥וֹ מִן־הַצֹּֽאן:

לח | **בַּמַּגֵּפָ֖ה לִפְנֵ֖י ה'.** בְּאוֹתָהּ מִיתָה הַהֲגוּנָה לָהֶם, מִדָּה כְּנֶגֶד מִדָּה. הֵם חָטְאוּ בַּלָּשׁוֹן, וְנִשְׁתַּרְבַּב לְשׁוֹנָם עַד טַבּוּרָם, וְתוֹלָעִים יוֹצְאִים מִלְּשׁוֹנָם וּבָאִין לְתוֹךְ טַבּוּרָם, לְכָךְ נֶאֱמַר: "בַּמַּגֵּפָה", וְלֹא "בַּמַּגֵּפָה", זֶהוּ "לִפְנֵי ה'", בְּאוֹתָהּ הָרְאוּיָה לָהֶם עַל פִּי מִדּוֹתָיו שֶׁל הַקָּדוֹשׁ בָּרוּךְ הוּא שֶׁהוּא מוֹדֵד מִדָּה כְּנֶגֶד מִדָּה:

לח | **וִיהוֹשֻׁ֣עַ וְכָלֵ֣ב חָיוּ֙ וְגוֹ'.** מַה תַּלְמוּד לוֹמַר: "חָיוּ מִן הָֽאֲנָשִׁים הָהֵם"? אֶלָּא מְלַמֵּד שֶׁנָּטְלוּ חֶלְקָם שֶׁל מְרַגְּלִים בָּאָרֶץ וְקָמוּ תַּחְתֵּיהֶם לַחַיִּים:

מ | **אֶל־רֹ֣אשׁ הָהָ֑ר.** הִיא הַדֶּרֶךְ הָעוֹלֶה לְאֶרֶץ יִשְׂרָאֵל:

הִנֶּ֗נּוּ וְעָלִ֛ינוּ אֶל־הַמָּקוֹם. לְאֶרֶץ יִשְׂרָאֵל: **אֲשֶׁר אָמַר ה'.** לְתִתָּהּ לָנוּ, שָׁם נַעֲלֶה: **כִּי חָטָאנוּ.** עַל אֲשֶׁר אָמַרְנוּ: "הֲלוֹא טוֹב לָנוּ שׁוּב מִצְרָיְמָה" (לעיל פסוק ג):

מא | **וְהִ֖וא לֹ֥א תִצְלָֽח.** זוֹ שֶׁאַתֶּם עוֹשִׂים לֹא תִצְלָח:

מג | **כִּי־עַל־כֵּ֤ן שַׁבְתֶּ֑ם.** כְּלוֹמַר, כִּי זֹאת תָּבֹא לָכֶם עַל אֲשֶׁר שַׁבְתֶּם וְגוֹ':

מד | **וַיַּעְפִּ֕לוּ.** לְשׁוֹן חֹזֶק, וְכֵן: "הִנֵּה עֻפְּלָה" (חבקוק ב, ד), אײנגרי"ש בְּלַעַז, לְשׁוֹן עַזּוּת, וְכֵן: "עֹ֫פֶל בַּת צִיּוֹן" (מיכה ד, ח), "עֹפֶל וָבַחַן" (ישעיה לב, יד). וּמִדְרַשׁ תַּנְחוּמָא מְפָרְשׁוֹ לְשׁוֹן אֹפֶל, הָלְכוּ חֲשֵׁכִים שֶׁלֹּא בִרְשׁוּת:

מה | **וַֽיַּכְּת֖וּם.** כְּמוֹ: "וָֽאֶכֹּ֥ת אֹת֖וֹ טָח֑וֹן" (דברים ט, כא), מַכָּה אַחַר מַכָּה: **עַד הַֽחָרְמָֽה.** שֵׁם הַמָּקוֹם נִקְרָא עַל שֵׁם הַמְּאֹרָע:

פרק טו

ב | **כִּ֣י תָבֹ֗אוּ.** בִּשֵּׂר לָהֶם שֶׁיִּכָּנְסוּ לָאָרֶץ:

ג | **וַֽעֲשִׂיתֶ֨ם אִשֶּׁ֤ה.** אֵין זֶה צִוּוּי, אֶלָּא כְּשֶׁתָּבֹ֫אוּ שָׁם וְתַֽעֲלֶה עַל לִבְּכֶ֫ם לַֽעֲשׂוֹת אִשֶּׁה לַה': **רֵ֤יחַ נִיחֹ֨חַ.** לְפַלֵּא נֶדֶר אוֹ בִנְדָבָה. נַחַת רוּחַ לְפָנַי, אוֹ שֶׁתַּֽעֲשׂוּ הָחֵ֫שָׁה בִּשְׁבִיל חוֹבַת מוֹֽעֲדֵיכֶם, שֶׁחַיַּבְתִּי אֶתְכֶם לַֽעֲשׂוֹת בַּמּוֹעֵד:

14:44 | They ventured [vayapilu]: Rashi explains that this term indicates that they acted brazenly. Others suggest that it means they stubbornly strengthened themselves (see Sforno; Ha'amek Davar), or they rebelliously transgressed (see Onkelos; Rav Se'adya Gaon). Some maintain that the root of this word, ayin-peh-lamed, initially had the same meaning as the root gimmel-beit-heh, which indicates height (see Ibn Ezra; Radak, Habakkuk 2:4). This interpretation is accepted by most modern linguists. If so, the verse may be referring to the haughtiness of the people who chose to ignore Moses, or it may have a more neutral connotation, merely indicating their ascent to the mountain.

In the twentieth century, this word took on a slightly different, more positive meaning, as it was used to describe Jews who attempted to immigrate to Israel in defiance of the British blockade. However, most commentaries agree that it has a negative connotation in its original context.

4 **the one who presents his offering to the Lord shall present a meal offering.** He must bring a meal offering from the world of vegetation to accompany his animal offering, in accordance with these measurements: **One-tenth** of an ephah **of high-quality flour** made from ground wheat kernels, **mixed with one-fourth of a hin of oil.** In contemporary terms, one-tenth of an ephah is more than 2 L, and a hin is somewhat larger than 1 L.

5 **And** in addition, you shall also bring **wine** to be poured upon the altar **as the libation: One-fourth of a hin you shall make** these amounts of flour, oil, and wine **with the burnt offering or for the peace offering, for one sheep.** As explained in the coming verses, the amounts change in accordance with the type of animal brought as an offering.

6 **Or for** an offering consisting of **a ram,** which is an older animal from the same species as the sheep, in the second year of its life, **you shall perform a meal offering** consisting of **two-tenths** of an ephah **of high-quality flour mixed with one-third of a hin of oil.**

7 **And you shall present wine as the libation: One-third of a hin, a pleasing aroma to the Lord.**

Fifth aliya 8 **When you render a young bull a burnt offering, or a peace offering, to fulfill a vow or a peace offering to the Lord,**

9 one shall present with the young bull a meal offering: **Three-tenths** of an ephah **of high-quality flour,** which is three times as large as the meal offering for a sheep, **mixed with one-half a hin of oil,** twice the amount brought with a sheep.

10 **And you shall present wine as the libation: One-half a hin as a fire offering of a pleasing aroma to the Lord.**

11 In general, **so shall be done for one bull, or for one ram, or for a lamb, or for a kid.**

12 **According to the number** of offerings **that you shall do, so shall you do for each according to their number.** The meal offerings and libations that accompany these offerings shall correspond to the number and type of animals that are offered.

13 **Every native shall do these in this** precise **manner, to present a fire offering of a pleasing aroma to the Lord.** There are fixed amounts for the meal offerings and libations brought with the offerings.

14 **If a stranger will reside with you** as a full-fledged convert who has become a member of the nation[25] or one **who is** already[26] living **in your midst for your generations, and will perform a fire offering of a pleasing aroma to the Lord, as you do, so he shall do.** There is no difference between an Israelite from birth and a convert who has joined the nation.

15 The verse addresses **the assembly:** There shall be **one statute for you and for the stranger who resides, an eternal statute for your generations; like you, so the stranger shall be before the Lord.** With regard to obligations toward God, such as these rules regarding meal offerings and libations that accompany offerings, the law applies equally to Israelites from birth and to converts.

16 **One law and one ordinance shall be for you and for the stranger who resides with you.** This principle goes beyond the specific topic at hand, as it refers to all the statutes and ordinances given to the children of Israel. These laws apply to all members of the nation, whether they are Israelites from birth or converts who have joined the nation.[27]

Sixth aliya 17 The next commandment will also take effect only after the Israelites enter the land. **The Lord spoke to Moses, saying:**

18 **Speak to the children of Israel, and say to them: When you come to the land that I am bringing you there,**

19 **it shall be, when you eat from the bread of the land, you shall separate** from it **a gift for the Lord.**

20 From **the first of your kneading basket you shall separate a loaf [*ḥalla*] as a gift.** Due to this verse, the portion separated from the dough is known as *ḥalla.* **Like the gift from the threshing floor,** the portion known as *teruma* that is set aside from produce for the priests, **so shall you separate it,**[D] the *ḥalla* from the dough.

DISCUSSION

15:20 | Like the gift from the threshing floor, so shall you separate it: The *teruma* of the threshing floor mentioned here should have already been separated from the flour before making dough, which then incurs a separate obligation of *ḥalla.*

These two gifts, *ḥalla* and *teruma,* are similar in three ways: First, both must be given to the priests, and only priests may eat them in a state of ritual purity. Second, in both cases the Torah does not specify how much must be given; it was the Sages who established the required quantities (see Rashi; Mishna *Ḥalla* 2:7; Mishna *Terumot* 4:3). Finally, the prohibition against eating non-tithed food applies in both cases. In other words, just as it is forbidden to consume produce before *teruma* has been removed from it and set aside, so too a baked product is forbidden until its *ḥalla* has been removed, ideally while it is still dough, and if not, then after baking.

ד וְהִקְרִיב הַמַּקְרִיב קׇרְבָּנוֹ לַיהוָה מִנְחָה סֹלֶת עִשָּׂרוֹן בָּלוּל בִּרְבִעִית הַהִין שָׁמֶן׃
ה ו וְיַיִן לַנֶּסֶךְ רְבִיעִית הַהִין תַּעֲשֶׂה עַל־הָעֹלָה אוֹ לַזָּבַח לַכֶּבֶשׂ הָאֶחָד׃ אוֹ לָאַיִל
ז תַּעֲשֶׂה מִנְחָה סֹלֶת שְׁנֵי עֶשְׂרֹנִים בְּלוּלָה בַשֶּׁמֶן שְׁלִשִׁית הַהִין׃ וְיַיִן לַנֶּסֶךְ שְׁלִשִׁית
ח הַהִין תַּקְרִיב רֵיחַ־נִיחֹחַ לַיהוָה׃ וְכִי־תַעֲשֶׂה בֶן־בָּקָר עֹלָה אוֹ־זָבַח לְפַלֵּא־נֶדֶר חמישי
ט אוֹ־שְׁלָמִים לַיהוָה׃ וְהִקְרִיב עַל־בֶּן־הַבָּקָר מִנְחָה סֹלֶת שְׁלֹשָׁה עֶשְׂרֹנִים בָּלוּל
י יא בַּשֶּׁמֶן חֲצִי הַהִין׃ וְיַיִן תַּקְרִיב לַנֶּסֶךְ חֲצִי הַהִין אִשֵּׁה רֵיחַ־נִיחֹחַ לַיהוָה׃ כָּכָה
יב יֵעָשֶׂה לַשּׁוֹר הָאֶחָד אוֹ לָאַיִל הָאֶחָד אוֹ־לַשֶּׂה בַכְּבָשִׂים אוֹ בָעִזִּים׃ כַּמִּסְפָּר אֲשֶׁר
יג תַּעֲשׂוּ כָּכָה תַּעֲשׂוּ לָאֶחָד כְּמִסְפָּרָם׃ כׇּל־הָאֶזְרָח יַעֲשֶׂה־כָּכָה אֶת־אֵלֶּה לְהַקְרִיב
יד אִשֵּׁה רֵיחַ־נִיחֹחַ לַיהוָה׃ וְכִי־יָגוּר אִתְּכֶם גֵּר אוֹ אֲשֶׁר־בְּתוֹכְכֶם לְדֹרֹתֵיכֶם וְעָשָׂה
טו אִשֵּׁה רֵיחַ־נִיחֹחַ לַיהוָה כַּאֲשֶׁר תַּעֲשׂוּ כֵּן יַעֲשֶׂה׃ הַקָּהָל חֻקָּה אַחַת לָכֶם וְלַגֵּר
טז הַגָּר חֻקַּת עוֹלָם לְדֹרֹתֵיכֶם כָּכֶם כַּגֵּר יִהְיֶה לִפְנֵי יְהוָה׃ תּוֹרָה אַחַת וּמִשְׁפָּט אֶחָד
יִהְיֶה לָכֶם וְלַגֵּר הַגָּר אִתְּכֶם׃
יז יח וַיְדַבֵּר יְהוָה אֶל־מֹשֶׁה לֵּאמֹר׃ דַּבֵּר אֶל־בְּנֵי יִשְׂרָאֵל וְאָמַרְתָּ אֲלֵהֶם בְּבֹאֲכֶם אֶל־ ששי
יט הָאָרֶץ אֲשֶׁר אֲנִי מֵבִיא אֶתְכֶם שָׁמָּה׃ וְהָיָה בַּאֲכׇלְכֶם מִלֶּחֶם הָאָרֶץ תָּרִימוּ תְרוּמָה
כ לַיהוָה׃ רֵאשִׁית עֲרִסֹתֵכֶם חַלָּה תָּרִימוּ תְרוּמָה כִּתְרוּמַת גֹּרֶן כֵּן תָּרִימוּ אֹתָהּ׃

רש"י

ד| וְהִקְרִיב הַמַּקְרִיב. תַּקְרִיבוּ נְסָכִים וּמִנְחָה לְכָל בְּהֵמָה, הַמִּנְחָה כָּלִיל וְהַשֶּׁמֶן נִבְלָל בְּתוֹכָהּ, וְהַיַּיִן לַסְּפָלִים, כְּמוֹ שֶׁשָּׁנִינוּ בְּמַסֶּכֶת סֻכָּה (דף מח ע"ב):

ה| לַכֶּבֶשׂ הָאֶחָד. עַל כָּל הָאָמוּר לְמַעְלָה הוּא מוּסָב, עַל הַמִּנְחָה וְעַל הַשֶּׁמֶן וְעַל הַיַּיִן:

ו| אוֹ לָאַיִל. וְאִם אַיִל הוּא. וְרַבּוֹתֵינוּ דָּרְשׁוּ: "אוֹ" לְרַבּוֹת אֶת הַפַּלְגָּס לִנְסָכֵי אַיִל:

י| אִשֵּׁה רֵיחַ. אֵינוֹ מוּסָב אֶלָּא עַל הַמִּנְחָה וְהַשֶּׁמֶן, אֲבָל הַיַּיִן אֵינוֹ אִשֶּׁה, שֶׁאֵינוֹ נִתָּן עַל הָאֵשׁ:

יא| אוֹ לַשֶּׂה. בֵּין שֶׁהוּא בַּכְּבָשִׂים בֵּין שֶׁהוּא בָּעִזִּים. 'כֶּבֶשׂ' וָ'שֶׂה' קְרוּיִם בְּתוֹךְ שְׁנָתָם, 'אַיִל' בֶּן שְׁלֹשָׁה עָשָׂר חֹדֶשׁ וְיוֹם אֶחָד:

יב| כַּמִּסְפָּר אֲשֶׁר תַּעֲשׂוּ. כְּמִסְפַּר הַבְּהֵמוֹת אֲשֶׁר תַּקְרִיבוּ לְקָרְבָּן, כָּכָה תַּעֲשׂוּ נְסָכִים לְכָל אֶחָד מֵהֶם, כְּמִסְפָּרָם שֶׁל בְּהֵמוֹת מִסְפָּרָם שֶׁל נְסָכִים:

טו| כָּכֶם כַּגֵּר. כְּמוֹתְכֶם כֵּן גֵּר, וְכֵן דֶּרֶךְ לְשׁוֹן עִבְרִית: "כְּגַן ה' כְּאֶרֶץ מִצְרַיִם" (בראשית יג, י) כֵּן אֶרֶץ מִצְרַיִם, "כָּמוֹנִי כָמוֹךָ כְּעַמִּי כְעַמֶּךָ" (מלכים א' כב, ד):

יח| בְּבֹאֲכֶם אֶל הָאָרֶץ. מְשֻׁנָּה בִּיאָה זוֹ מִכׇּל בִּיאוֹת שֶׁבַּתּוֹרָה, שֶׁבְּכֻלָּן נֶאֱמַר: "כִּי תָבֹא" "כִּי תָבֹאוּ", לְפִיכָךְ כֻּלָּן לִמְּדוּת זוֹ מִזּוֹ, וְכֵיוָן שֶׁפֵּרַט לְךָ הַכָּתוּב בְּאַחַת מֵהֶן שֶׁאֵינָהּ אֶלָּא לְאַחַר יְרֻשָּׁה וִישִׁיבָה, אַף כֻּלָּן כֵּן. אֲבָל זוֹ נֶאֱמַר בָּהּ: "בְּבֹאֲכֶם", מִשֶּׁנִּכְנְסוּ בָּהּ וְאָכְלוּ מִלַּחְמָהּ נִתְחַיְּבוּ בַּחַלָּה:

כ| רֵאשִׁית עֲרִסֹתֵכֶם. כְּשֶׁתָּלוּשׁוּ כְּדֵי עֲרִיסוֹתֵיכֶם שֶׁאַתֶּם רְגִילִין לָלוּשׁ בַּמִּדְבָּר, וְכַמָּה הִיא? "וַיָּמֹדּוּ בָעֹמֶר" (שמות טז, יח), "עֹמֶר לַגֻּלְגֹּלֶת" (שם פסוק טז), תָּרִימוּ מֵרֵאשִׁיתָהּ, כְּלוֹמַר, קֹדֶם שֶׁתֹּאכְלוּ מִמֶּנָּה, רֵאשִׁית חֶלְקָהּ חַלָּה אַחַת מִמֶּנָּה "תָּרִימוּ תְרוּמָה" לְשֵׁם ה': חַלָּה. טורטי"ל בְּלַעַז: כִּתְרוּמַת גֹּרֶן. שֶׁלֹּא נֶאֱמַר בָּהּ שִׁעוּר, וְלֹא כִּתְרוּמַת מַעֲשֵׂר שֶׁנֶּאֱמַר בָּהּ שִׁעוּר. אֲבָל חֲכָמִים נָתְנוּ שִׁעוּר, לְבַעַל הַבַּיִת אֶחָד מֵעֶשְׂרִים וְאַרְבָּעָה, וְלַנַּחְתּוֹם אֶחָד מֵאַרְבָּעִים וּשְׁמוֹנָה:

21 **From the first of your kneading basket[D] you shall give to the Lord a gift for your generations.**
22 **If you act unwittingly[D] and do not observe all these commandments that the Lord spoke to Moses,**
23 **everything that the Lord commanded to you at the hand of Moses, from the day that the Lord commanded and onward for your generations.** According to the tradition of the Sages, the unwitting act described here, which leads to a neglect of all the commandments, refers to the specific, fundamental sin of idolatry.[28] This was the first prohibition Israel received in the Ten Precepts: "I am the Lord your God.... You shall have no other gods before Me."[29] These verses discuss a situation where one transgresses this prohibition unwittingly, as can happen in complicated cases or situations involving a lack of clarity in one's thoughts or action. However, in a case where one worshipped idols intentionally, atonement cannot be achieved by means of an offering.
24 **It shall be, if from the eyes of the congregation it was performed unwittingly,** as a result of an erroneous ruling by the court, then **the entire congregation,** meaning the court, which represents the entire congregation of Israel, **shall render one young bull as a burnt offering for a pleasing aroma to the Lord, and its meal offering and its libation according to the ordinance, and one goat as a sin offering.** This is different from a comparable case of a communal sin as a result of an erroneous ruling with regard to other sins, in which case the congregation brings a bull as a sin offering.
25 **The priest shall atone for the entire congregation of the children of Israel, and it will be forgiven for them, as it was an unwitting act, and** when they became aware of their error **they brought their offering, a fire offering to the Lord, and their sin offering before the Lord, for their unwitting act.**
26 **The entire congregation of the children of Israel shall be forgiven.** Even if the sin was not actually performed by every member of the congregation, an erroneous ruling on the part of the upper echelon of the nation's leadership, which is then acted upon by the general public, is considered a transgression of the entire congregation. Therefore, the offering brought by the court serves to atone for both its own sin and that of the entire nation, **and** also for **the stranger that resides in their midst,** since he too is part of the congregation, **as it was** an **unwitting** transgression **for the entire people.**

Seventh aliya

27 After discussing an unwitting sin of idolatry performed by the congregation as a result of a mistaken ruling by the court, the Torah continues with a case of the same sin committed unwittingly by an individual: **If one person will sin unwittingly, he shall present a female goat in its first year as a sin offering.** For an ordinary sin offering, one may bring either a female lamb or a female goat. However, for the specific transgression of idolatry one must bring a goat, as is the case for other offerings connected with this sin.
28 **The priest shall atone for the unwitting person, when he sins unwittingly, before the Lord, to atone for him; and it shall be forgiven for him.**
29 **The native of the children of Israel and for the stranger that resides in their midst: There shall be one law for you, for one who acts unwittingly.**
30 The aforementioned offerings atone for an individual or a community that committed the sin of idolatry due to an error of judgment or as a result of a habitual, unthinking action. In contrast, **the person that will act high-handedly,[D]** purposely and with malicious intent, **whether native or stranger, it is the Lord that he blasphemes,[30] and that person shall be excised from among his people,[D]** wherever he is. This punishment is inflicted by God and it is not within the jurisdiction of the court.

DISCUSSION

15:21| **From the first of your kneading basket:** In the past, *ḥalla* was actually given to a priest as mentioned above, but nowadays this is not done, since the laws of ritual purity are not observed and therefore the *ḥalla* may not be eaten. Instead, a small amount is separated from the dough, as it remains prohibited to consume the dough until the *ḥalla* has been set aside (see Rema, *Yoreh De'a* 322:8; *Birkei Yosef*).

In order to commemorate this commandment, the Sages enacted a requirement to separate *ḥalla* even outside the Land of Israel (see *Bekhorot* 27a).

15:22| **If you act unwittingly:** A detailed discussion of the offerings brought by unwitting sinners has already appeared in Leviticus (chaps. 4–5). To a certain extent, therefore, the book of Numbers completes the laws of offerings listed in the previous book.

Despite the similarities between this passage and the chapters in Leviticus, there are also differences between them: With regard to all other commandments, apart from the transgression mention here, in the event of a communal error, the court is obligated to bring a bull as a sin offering. However, in these verses it is commanded to bring a bull as a burnt offering and a goat as a sin offering. Furthermore, with regard to an individual who sinned unwittingly, in the case of other commandments he brings either a female lamb or female goat, whereas these verses specify only a female goat.

Some commentaries explain that according to the plain meaning of the text, this passage refers to an offering brought by one who unwittingly denied the Torah, for example, one who left his people and joined another nation. With regard to an entire community, this is possible, for example, if they think that the time of the Torah has already passed and that it is not eternal, or if they reason: Why did the Omnipresent speak? Was it not so that we should act and receive a reward? We will not act, and we will relinquish the reward (Ramban).

כא כב מֵרֵאשִׁית עֲרִסֹתֵיכֶם תִּתְּנוּ לַיהוָה תְּרוּמָה לְדֹרֹתֵיכֶם: וְכִי תִשְׁגּוּ
כג וְלֹא תַעֲשׂוּ אֵת כָּל־הַמִּצְוֹת הָאֵלֶּה אֲשֶׁר־דִּבֶּר יהוָה אֶל־מֹשֶׁה: אֵת כָּל־אֲשֶׁר
כד צִוָּה יהוָה אֲלֵיכֶם בְּיַד־מֹשֶׁה מִן־הַיּוֹם אֲשֶׁר צִוָּה יהוָה וָהָלְאָה לְדֹרֹתֵיכֶם: וְהָיָה
אִם מֵעֵינֵי הָעֵדָה נֶעֶשְׂתָה לִשְׁגָגָה וְעָשׂוּ כָל־הָעֵדָה פַּר בֶּן־בָּקָר אֶחָד לְעֹלָה
כה לְרֵיחַ נִיחֹחַ לַיהוָה וּמִנְחָתוֹ וְנִסְכּוֹ כַּמִּשְׁפָּט וּשְׂעִיר־עִזִּים אֶחָד לְחַטָּת: וְכִפֶּר הַכֹּהֵן
עַל־כָּל־עֲדַת בְּנֵי יִשְׂרָאֵל וְנִסְלַח לָהֶם כִּי־שְׁגָגָה הִוא וְהֵם הֵבִיאוּ אֶת־קָרְבָּנָם
כו אִשֶּׁה לַיהוָה וְחַטָּאתָם לִפְנֵי יהוָה עַל־שִׁגְגָתָם: וְנִסְלַח לְכָל־עֲדַת בְּנֵי יִשְׂרָאֵל
כז וְלַגֵּר הַגָּר בְּתוֹכָם כִּי לְכָל־הָעָם בִּשְׁגָגָה: וְאִם־נֶפֶשׁ אַחַת תֶּחֱטָא שביעי
כח בִשְׁגָגָה וְהִקְרִיבָה עֵז בַּת־שְׁנָתָהּ לְחַטָּאת: וְכִפֶּר הַכֹּהֵן עַל־הַנֶּפֶשׁ הַשֹּׁגֶגֶת
כט בְּחֶטְאָה בִשְׁגָגָה לִפְנֵי יהוָה לְכַפֵּר עָלָיו וְנִסְלַח לוֹ: הָאֶזְרָח בִּבְנֵי יִשְׂרָאֵל וְלַגֵּר הַגָּר
ל בְּתוֹכָם תּוֹרָה אַחַת יִהְיֶה לָכֶם לָעֹשֶׂה בִּשְׁגָגָה: וְהַנֶּפֶשׁ אֲשֶׁר־תַּעֲשֶׂה ׀ בְּיָד רָמָה
מִן־הָאֶזְרָח וּמִן־הַגֵּר אֶת־יהוָה הוּא מְגַדֵּף וְנִכְרְתָה הַנֶּפֶשׁ הַהִוא מִקֶּרֶב עַמָּהּ:

רש"י

כא| **מֵרֵאשִׁית עֲרִסֹתֵיכֶם.** לָמָּה נֶאֱמַר? לְפִי שֶׁנֶּאֱמַר: "רֵאשִׁית עֲרִסֹתֵכֶם" (לעיל פסוק כ), שׁוֹמֵעַ אֲנִי רִאשׁוֹנָה שֶׁבָּעִסּוֹת? תַּלְמוּד לוֹמַר: "מֵרֵאשִׁית", מִקְצָתָהּ וְלֹא כֻלָּהּ. תִּתְּנוּ לַה' תְּרוּמָה. לְפִי שֶׁלֹּא שָׁמַעְנוּ שִׁעוּר לַחַלָּה נֶאֱמַר: "תִּתְּנוּ", שֶׁיְּהֵא בָהּ כְּדֵי נְתִינָה:

כב| **וְכִי תִשְׁגּוּ וְלֹא תַעֲשׂוּ.** עֲבוֹדָה זָרָה הָיְתָה בִּכְלַל כָּל הַמִּצְוֹת שֶׁהַצִּבּוּר מְבִיאִין עָלֶיהָ פַּר, וַהֲרֵי הַכָּתוּב מוֹצִיאָהּ כָּאן מִכְּלָלָהּ לָדוּן בְּפַר לְעוֹלָה וְשָׂעִיר לְחַטָּאת: וְכִי תִשְׁגּוּ וְגוֹ'. בַּעֲבוֹדָה זָרָה הַכָּתוּב מְדַבֵּר, אוֹ אֵינוֹ אֶלָּא בְּאַחַת מִכָּל הַמִּצְוֹת? תַּלְמוּד לוֹמַר: "אֵת כָּל הַמִּצְוֹת הָאֵלֶּה", מִצְוָה אַחַת שֶׁהִיא כְּכָל הַמִּצְוֹת. מָה הָעוֹבֵר עַל כָּל הַמִּצְוֹת פּוֹרֵק עֹל וּמֵפֵר בְּרִית וּמְגַלֶּה פָּנִים, אַף מִצְוָה זוֹ פּוֹרֵק בָּהּ עֹל וּמֵפֵר בְּרִית וּמְגַלֶּה פָנִים, וְאֵיזוֹ זוֹ? זוֹ עֲבוֹדָה זָרָה: אֲשֶׁר דִּבֶּר ה' אֶל מֹשֶׁה. "אָנֹכִי" וְ"לֹא יִהְיֶה לְךָ" מִפִּי הַגְּבוּרָה שְׁמַעְנוּם. "אַחַת דִּבֶּר אֱלֹהִים שְׁתַּיִם זוּ שָׁמָעְתִּי" (תהלים סב, יב):

כג| **אֵת כָּל אֲשֶׁר צִוָּה וְגוֹ'.** מַגִּיד שֶׁכָּל הַמּוֹדֶה בַּעֲבוֹדָה זָרָה כְּכוֹפֵר בְּכָל הַתּוֹרָה כֻּלָּהּ וּבְכָל מַה שֶּׁנִּתְנַבְּאוּ הַנְּבִיאִים, שֶׁנֶּאֱמַר: "מִן הַיּוֹם אֲשֶׁר צִוָּה ה' וָהָלְאָה":

כד| **אִם מֵעֵינֵי הָעֵדָה נֶעֶשְׂתָה לִשְׁגָגָה.** אִם מֵעֵינֵי הָעֵדָה נֶעֶשְׂתָה עֲבֵרָה זוֹ עַל יְדֵי שׁוֹגֵג, כְּגוֹן שֶׁשָּׁגְגוּ וְהוֹרוּ עַל אַחַת מִן הָעֲבוֹדוֹת שֶׁהִיא מֻתֶּרֶת לַעֲבֹד עֲבוֹדָה זָרָה בְּכָךְ: לְחַטָּת. חָסֵר אָלֶ"ף, שֶׁאֵינוֹ כִּשְׁאָר חַטָּאוֹת, שֶׁכָּל חַטָּאוֹת שֶׁבַּתּוֹרָה הַבָּאוֹת עִם עוֹלָה, הַחַטָּאת קוֹדֶמֶת לָעוֹלָה, שֶׁנֶּאֱמַר: "וְאֶת הַשֵּׁנִי יַעֲשֶׂה עֹלָה" (ויקרא ה, י), וְזוֹ עוֹלָה קוֹדֶמֶת לְחַטָּאת:

כה| **הֵבִיאוּ אֶת קָרְבָּנָם אִשֶּׁה לַה'.** זֶה הָאָמוּר בַּפָּרָשָׁה, הוּא פַּר הָעוֹלָה, שֶׁנֶּאֱמַר: "אִשֶּׁה לַה'": וְחַטָּאתָם. זֶה הַשָּׂעִיר:

כז| **תֶּחֱטָא בִשְׁגָגָה.** בַּעֲבוֹדָה זָרָה: **עֵז בַּת שְׁנָתָהּ.** שְׁאָר עֲבֵרוֹת יָחִיד מֵבִיא כִּשְׂבָּה אוֹ שְׂעִירָה, וְכָאן קָבַע לָהּ שְׂעִירָה:

ל| **בְּיָד רָמָה.** בְּמֵזִיד: **מְגַדֵּף.** מְחָרֵף, כְּמוֹ: "וְהָיְתָה חֶרְפָּה וּגְדוּפָה" (יחזקאל ה, טו), "אֲשֶׁר גִּדְּפוּ נַעֲרֵי מֶלֶךְ אַשּׁוּר"

DISCUSSION

It is possible that this section is written specifically here as a reference to the sin of the congregation, who said: "Let us appoint a leader and return to Egypt" (14:4). They wished to go back to their previous state as they had existed in Egypt, without the Torah or its commandments (see Ramban; Abravanel).

15:30| **The person that will act high-handedly:** According to one opinion, this does not refer to blasphemy, but to intentional idol worship, in contrast to the unwitting sin of idolatry discussed in the previous verses (see *Karetot* 7b). Others maintain that this passage applies to any sin committed in a high-handed manner, as someone who purposely rebels against God is comparable to one who believes in idols and rejects the entire Torah (see Rambam, *Guide of the Perplexed* 3:41; *Ha'amek Davar*).

And that person shall be excised from among his people: The laws presented in this chapter follow a logical progression. After discussing unwitting sins, for which one can achieve atonement by means of an offering, the Torah turns to sins committed intentionally but not in the presence of witnesses. Consequently, they are punished by God with the sinner's excision from among his people. Following this, the Torah addresses severe transgressions performed intentionally, following a warning and in the presence of witnesses. The punishment

31 **Because he scorned the word of the Lord** by committing the transgression, **and he violated His commandment; as a result, that person shall be excised; his iniquity is upon him.**

32 In connection with the descriptions of high-handed sins like idolatry and blasphemy, the Torah relates an incident that illustrates how the children of Israel responded to a serious public violation of one of the commandments that occurred in their midst during their wanderings in the wilderness: **The children of Israel were in the wilderness and they found a man gathering wood**[D] **on the Sabbath day.**

33 **Those who found him gathering wood brought him to Moses and Aaron, and to the entire congregation,** and testified that he had desecrated Sabbath in a high-handed manner.

34 **They placed him in custody, because it had not been explicated what** precisely **should be done to him.** It was clear that he was liable to receive the death penalty, as the verse states explicitly: "You shall observe the Sabbath, as it is sacred for you; its desecrators shall be put to death."[31] However, it was necessary to determine the precise manner in which he was to be executed.

35 The Lord said to Moses: **The man shall be put to death** by stoning; **the entire congregation shall stone him with stones outside the camp.**

36 **The entire congregation took him outside the camp, and they stoned him with stones, and he died, as the Lord had commanded Moses.**

Maftir **37** **The Lord spoke to Moses, saying:**

38 **Speak to the children of Israel, and say to them: They shall make for themselves a fringe** consisting of a group of hanging threads[32] **on the corners of their garments**[D] **for their generations,** and in addition, **they shall put on the fringe of the corner a sky-blue thread.**[D]

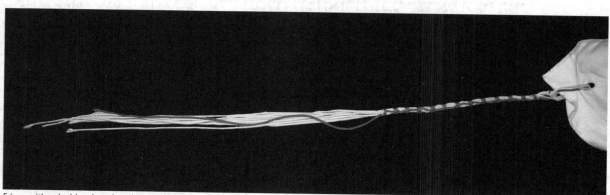
Fringe with a sky-blue thread on the corner of a garment

DISCUSSION

for this type of sin is the death penalty, administered by the court. This category is introduced by way of the narrative concerning the man who gathered wood.

Certain sins are performed not due to negative intention but as a result of negative, ingrained patterns of behavior. Therefore, this passage is followed by the commandment of ritual fringes, which are designed to awaken the wearer to a life of sanctity, by reminding him of God's commandments in spite of the distractions of daily life.

15:32 | Gathering wood: There are different opinions among the Sages with regard to the precise nature of this man's sin. One possibility is that the violation was caused by the act of gathering itself, as one of the prohibited labors on Sabbath is gathering sheaves or wood into a pile for any purpose, even if they are not actually used on Shabbat (see *Shabbat* 73b). Others maintain that the man cut branches that were still growing, or that he carried the wood in the public domain (*Shabbat* 96b).

15:38 | On the corners of their garments: The wording of the verse indicates that it is not discussing a type of special, sanctified garment, but rather the simple clothing worn by ordinary people. In the desert climates of the Middle East, which are characterized by sharp variations in temperature between day and night and ↤

לא כִּי דְבַר־יהוה בָּזָה וְאֶת־מִצְוָתוֹ הֵפַר הִכָּרֵת ׀ תִּכָּרֵת הַנֶּפֶשׁ הַהִוא עֲוֺנָה בָהּ׃
לב לג וַיִּהְיוּ בְנֵי־יִשְׂרָאֵל בַּמִּדְבָּר וַיִּמְצְאוּ אִישׁ מְקֹשֵׁשׁ עֵצִים בְּיוֹם הַשַּׁבָּת׃ וַיַּקְרִיבוּ
אֹתוֹ הַמֹּצְאִים אֹתוֹ מְקֹשֵׁשׁ עֵצִים אֶל־מֹשֶׁה וְאֶל־אַהֲרֹן וְאֶל כָּל־הָעֵדָה׃
לד לה וַיַּנִּיחוּ אֹתוֹ בַּמִּשְׁמָר כִּי לֹא פֹרַשׁ מַה־יֵּעָשֶׂה לוֹ׃ וַיֹּאמֶר יהוה
אֶל־מֹשֶׁה מוֹת יוּמַת הָאִישׁ רָגוֹם אֹתוֹ בָאֲבָנִים כָּל־הָעֵדָה מִחוּץ לַמַּחֲנֶה׃
לו וַיֹּצִיאוּ אֹתוֹ כָּל־הָעֵדָה אֶל־מִחוּץ לַמַּחֲנֶה וַיִּרְגְּמוּ אֹתוֹ בָּאֲבָנִים וַיָּמֹת כַּאֲשֶׁר
צִוָּה יהוה אֶת־מֹשֶׁה׃
לז לח וַיֹּאמֶר יהוה אֶל־מֹשֶׁה לֵּאמֹר׃ דַּבֵּר אֶל־בְּנֵי יִשְׂרָאֵל וְאָמַרְתָּ אֲלֵהֶם וְעָשׂוּ מפטיר
לָהֶם צִיצִת עַל־כַּנְפֵי בִגְדֵיהֶם לְדֹרֹתָם וְנָתְנוּ עַל־צִיצִת הַכָּנָף פְּתִיל תְּכֵלֶת׃

רש״י

(ישעיה לז, ו). וְעוֹד דָּרְשׁוּ רַבּוֹתֵינוּ, מִכָּאן לַמְבָרֵךְ אֶת הַשֵּׁם שֶׁהוּא בְּכָרֵת:

לא| דְּבַר ה׳. אַזְהָרַת עֲבוֹדָה זָרָה מִפִּי הַגְּבוּרָה, וְהַשְּׁאָר מִפִּי מֹשֶׁה: עֲוֺנָה בָהּ. בִּזְמַן שֶׁעֲוֺנָהּ בָּהּ, שֶׁלֹּא עָשָׂה תְשׁוּבָה:

לב| וַיִּהְיוּ בְנֵי יִשְׂרָאֵל בַּמִּדְבָּר וַיִּמְצְאוּ. בִּגְנוּתָן שֶׁל יִשְׂרָאֵל דִּבֵּר הַכָּתוּב, שֶׁלֹּא שָׁמְרוּ אֶלָּא שַׁבָּת רִאשׁוֹנָה, וּבַשְּׁנִיָּה בָּא זֶה וְחִלְּלָהּ:

לג| הַמֹּצְאִים אֹתוֹ מְקֹשֵׁשׁ. שֶׁהִתְרוּ בּוֹ, וְלֹא הִנִּיחַ מִלְּקוֹשֵׁשׁ אַף מִשֶּׁמְּצָאוּהוּ וְהִתְרוּ בּוֹ:

לד| כִּי לֹא פֹרַשׁ מַה יֵּעָשֶׂה לוֹ. לֹא הָיוּ יוֹדְעִים בְּאֵיזוֹ מִיתָה יָמוּת, אֲבָל יוֹדְעִים הָיוּ שֶׁהַמְחַלֵּל שַׁבָּת בְּמִיתָה:

לה| רָגוֹם. עָשֹׂה, פיישנ״ט בְּלַעַז, וְכֵן: ״הָלוֹךְ״ אלנ״ט, וְכֵן: ״זָכוֹר״ (שמות כ, ח) וְ״שָׁמוֹר״ (דברים ה, יב):

לו| וַיֹּצִיאוּ אֹתוֹ. מִכָּאן שֶׁבֵּית הַסְּקִילָה חוּץ וְרָחוֹק מִבֵּית דִּין:

לח| וְעָשׂוּ לָהֶם צִיצִת. עַל שֵׁם הַפְּתִילִים הַתְּלוּיִים בָּהּ, כְּמוֹ: ״וַיִּקָּחֵנִי בְּצִיצִת רֹאשִׁי״ (יחזקאל ח, ג). דָּבָר אַחֵר, ״צִיצִת״ עַל שֵׁם ״וּרְאִיתֶם אֹתוֹ״, כְּמוֹ ״מֵצִיץ מִן הַחֲרַכִּים״ (שיר השירים ב, ט): תְּכֵלֶת. צֶבַע יָרֹק שֶׁל חִלָּזוֹן:

DISCUSSION

between different seasons, it was common to wear a basic garment, which was nothing more than a rectangular piece of woolen or linen cloth. When the weather was hot, these garments could be folded over the wearer's shoulders, and when it got cold he could wrap himself in them (see Deuteronomy 22:12: "You shall make for you twisted threads on the four corners of your garment, with which you cover").

It can be inferred from the phrase "for their generations" that this command is to remain in effect at all times, even if clothing styles change in the future. Indeed, although practical considerations eventually caused people to stop wearing these four-cornered garments, Jews have continued to don four-cornered garments in order to fulfill the commandment.

A sky-blue [*tekhelet*] thread: Although the threads of the fringes themselves, which according to tradition are white (see *Menaḥot* 38a), can be made of wool or linen, the sky-blue thread must be made of wool. In the Torah, the word *tekhelet* invariably refers to wool dyed sky blue, as wool was the only material used for this purpose at the time (see *Menaḥot* 38a–39b). The detailed laws concerning the fringes, such as the number of threads and knots they are required to have and the manner in which they are to be attached to the garments, are based on rabbinic tradition, and some of them are derived from close readings of the verses.

39 It shall be for you a fringe,[D] and you shall see it and remember[D] all the commandments of the Lord, and perform them. The garments with fringes shall serve as a reminder of God's commandments **and you shall not rove after your heart and after your eyes,**[D] after which you stray. The combination of a lusting heart and seeing eye is a dangerous one, as it can lead one to violate the Torah's laws.

40 So that you shall remember and perform all My commandments throughout your daily lives and mundane pursuits, **and be holy to your God** in all your ways, thoughts, and actions.

41 I am the Lord your God, who took you out of the land of Egypt, to be your God: I am the Lord your God. By taking the children of Israel out of Egypt, God consecrated them as His servants. In order to ensure that they preserve this sanctity by observing the commandments, the Israelites are in need of these fixed signs on their garments.

DISCUSSION

15:39 | It shall be for you a fringe [*tzitzit*]: Some commentaries associate this term with peeking or glancing [*hatzatza*] (*Sifrei*; Rashbam), while others maintain that the word is derived from the word for flower, or bud [*tzitz*]. Indeed, the fringes are not a functional part of the garment, but a kind of decoration, like a flower (see *Menaḥot* 42a; Rabbi Samson Raphael Hirsch, 15:38).

These two interpretations are connected, just as the word for sprouting or germinating [*nevita*] is also related to the word for looking [*habata*]. When a plant first sprouts from the ground, it becomes visible to an observer for the first time, and can also be described as seeing the world itself for the first time.

The threads of the ritual fringes appear to shoot out of the garments like buds sprouting from the ground. It should be noted that the High Priest's similarly named frontplate [*tzitz*], which was his most prominent decorative item of clothing, was worn on the forehead and tied around his head with a thread of sky-blue wool (see Exodus 28:26–37).

And you shall see it and remember: Nowadays, the ritual *tallit* is donned during prayers on top of the worshipper's regular clothing, while a smaller four-cornered garment is worn underneath throughout the entire day, in order to remember all of God's commandments and keep them present in one's consciousness.

And you shall not rove after your heart and after your eyes: The verb for "rove" [*tur*] is the same as the one used with regard to the scouts (13:2), and it rarely appears in other contexts.

Perhaps the similarity of the terms, as well as the discussion of this commandment in the section immediately following the narrative of the scouts, alludes to the idea that the scouts followed their own hearts and eyes, and abandoned the path of God.

The verse mentions the heart before the eyes because it is not always one's sensory perceptions that cause the desires of the heart. Quite often the reverse is the case; the desires come first, and then when the desired item is seen, the lust in one's heart increases and pushes the person to act. Hence, one who tames the desires of his heart from the outset will be less likely to be drawn to forbidden actions by that which he sees with his eyes.

וְהָיָ֣ה לָכֶם֮ לְצִיצִת֒ וּרְאִיתֶ֣ם אֹת֗וֹ וּזְכַרְתֶּם֙ אֶת־כָּל־מִצְוֺ֣ת יְהֹוָ֔ה וַעֲשִׂיתֶ֖ם
אֹתָ֑ם וְלֹֽא־תָת֜וּרוּ אַחֲרֵ֤י לְבַבְכֶם֙ וְאַחֲרֵ֣י עֵֽינֵיכֶ֔ם אֲשֶׁר־אַתֶּ֥ם זֹנִ֖ים אַחֲרֵיהֶֽם׃

מא לְמַ֣עַן תִּזְכְּר֔וּ וַעֲשִׂיתֶ֖ם אֶת־כָּל־מִצְוֺתָ֑י וִהְיִיתֶ֥ם קְדֹשִׁ֖ים לֵאלֹֽהֵיכֶֽם׃ אֲנִ֞י יְהֹוָ֣ה
אֱלֹֽהֵיכֶ֗ם אֲשֶׁ֨ר הוֹצֵ֤אתִי אֶתְכֶם֙ מֵאֶ֣רֶץ מִצְרַ֔יִם לִהְי֥וֹת לָכֶ֖ם לֵאלֹהִ֑ים אֲנִ֖י יְהֹוָ֥ה
אֱלֹהֵיכֶֽם׃

רש״י

לט | וּזְכַרְתֶּם אֶת כָּל מִצְוֺת ה׳. שֶׁמִּנְיַן גִּימַטְרִיָּא שֶׁל צִיצִית שֵׁשׁ מֵאוֹת, וּשְׁמוֹנָה חוּטִים וַחֲמִשָּׁה קְשָׁרִים הֲרֵי תַּרְיַ״ג: **וְלֹא תָתוּרוּ אַחֲרֵי לְבַבְכֶם.** כְּמוֹ "מִתּוּר הָאָרֶץ" (לעיל יג, כה). הַלֵּב וְהָעֵינַיִם הֵם מְרַגְּלִים לַגּוּף, מְסַרְסְרִים לוֹ אֶת הָעֲבֵרוֹת, הָעַיִן רוֹאָה וְהַלֵּב חוֹמֵד וְהַגּוּף עוֹשֶׂה אֶת הָעֲבֵרוֹת:

מא | אֲנִי ה׳. נֶאֱמָן לְשַׁלֵּם שָׂכָר: **אֱלֹהֵיכֶם.** נֶאֱמָן לִפָּרַע: **אֲשֶׁר הוֹצֵאתִי אֶתְכֶם.** עַל מְנַת כֵּן פְּדִיתִי אֶתְכֶם שֶׁתְּקַבְּלוּ עֲלֵיכֶם גְּזֵרוֹתַי: **אֲנִי ה׳ אֱלֹהֵיכֶם.** עוֹד לָמָּה נֶאֱמַר? כְּדֵי שֶׁלֹּא יֹאמְרוּ יִשְׂרָאֵל: מִפְּנֵי מָה אָמַר הַמָּקוֹם, לֹא שֶׁנַּעֲשֶׂה וְנִטֹּל שָׂכָר? אָנוּ לֹא עוֹשִׂים וְלֹא נוֹטְלִים שָׂכָר! עַל כָּרְחֲכֶם

חֲנִי מַלְכְּכֶם. וְכֵן הוּא אוֹמֵר: "אִם לֹא בְּיָד חֲזָקָה... אֶמְלוֹךְ עֲלֵיכֶם" (יחזקאל כ, לג). דָּבָר אַחֵר, לָמָּה נֶאֱמַר יְצִיאַת מִצְרַיִם? אֲנִי הוּא שֶׁהִבְחַנְתִּי בְּמִצְרַיִם בֵּין טִפָּה שֶׁל בְּכוֹר לְשֶׁאֵינָהּ שֶׁל בְּכוֹר, אֲנִי הוּא עָתִיד לְהַבְחִין וּלְהִפָּרַע מִן הַתּוֹלֶה קָלָא אִילָן בְּבִגְדּוֹ וְאוֹמֵר: תְּכֵלֶת הִיא:

וּמִיסוֹדוֹ שֶׁל רַבִּי מֹשֶׁה הַדַּרְשָׁן הֶעְתַּקְתִּי: לָמָּה נִסְמְכָה פָּרָשַׁת מְקוֹשֵׁשׁ לְפָרָשַׁת עֲבוֹדָה זָרָה? לוֹמַר שֶׁהַמְחַלֵּל אֶת הַשַּׁבָּת כְּעוֹבֵד עֲבוֹדָה זָרָה, שֶׁאַף הִיא שְׁקוּלָה כְּכָל הַמִּצְוֺת, וְכֵן הוּא אוֹמֵר בְּעֶזְרָא: "וְעַל הַר סִינַי יָרַדְתָּ..." וַתִּתֵּן לְעַמְּךָ תּוֹרָה וּמִצְוֺת "וְאֶת שַׁבַּת קָדְשְׁךָ הוֹדַעְתָּ לָהֶם"

(נחמיה ט, יג-יד). וְאַף פָּרָשַׁת צִיצִית נִסְמְכָה לְכָךְ נִסְמְכָה לְחַלָּל, לְפִי שֶׁאַף הִיא שְׁקוּלָה כְּנֶגֶד כָּל הַמִּצְוֺת, שֶׁנֶּאֱמַר: "וַעֲשִׂיתֶם אֶת כָּל מִצְוֺתָי" (לעיל פסוק מ): **עַל כַּנְפֵי בִגְדֵיהֶם.** כְּנֶגֶד "וָאֶשָּׂא אֶתְכֶם עַל כַּנְפֵי נְשָׁרִים" (שמות יט, ד). **עַל אַרְבַּע כַּנְפוֹת,** וְלֹא בַּעֲלַת שָׁלֹשׁ וְלֹא בַּעֲלַת חָמֵשׁ, כְּנֶגֶד אַרְבַּע לְשׁוֹנוֹת שֶׁל גְּאֻלָּה שֶׁנֶּאֶמְרוּ בְּמִצְרַיִם: "וְהוֹצֵאתִי", "וְהִצַּלְתִּי", "וְגָאַלְתִּי", "וְלָקַחְתִּי" (שמות ו, ו-ז): **פְּתִיל תְּכֵלֶת.** עַל שֵׁם שִׁכּוּל בְּכוֹרוֹת, תַּרְגּוּמוֹ שֶׁל שִׁכּוּל: "תְּכֵלָא". וּמַכָּתָם הָיְתָה בַּלַּיְלָה, וְכֵן צֶבַע הַתְּכֵלֶת דּוֹמֶה לָרָקִיעַ הַמַּשְׁחִיר לְעֵת עֶרֶב. וּשְׁמוֹנָה חוּטִים שֶׁבָּהּ, כְּנֶגֶד שְׁמוֹנָה יָמִים שֶׁשָּׁהוּ יִשְׂרָאֵל מִשֶּׁיָּצְאוּ מִמִּצְרַיִם עַד שֶׁאָמְרוּ שִׁירָה עַל הַיָּם:

Parashat
Korah

Korah and His Congregation

NUMBERS 16:1–17:15

In this section, Korah leads an internal rebellion against the leadership that was chosen by God, rejecting the authority of Moses and the priesthood of Aaron and his sons. The Torah does not state when exactly this episode occurs. Aaron and his sons are already serving in the Tabernacle, but it is possible that they have only recently been appointed to their posts. Korah and his congregation then audaciously suggest that Moses invented this new status of the priesthood.

The immediate and miraculous response to this revolt is essential. Korah, Datan and Aviram, and the two hundred and fifty people who offer the incense do not merely besmirch the reputation of Moses, they seek to undermine his prophecy and the truth of his words, which are the basis for one's entire belief in the Torah.

16 1 **Korah son of Yitzhar,** Amram's brother, **son of Kehat, son of Levi,**[D] **and Datan and Aviram sons of Eliav, and On son of Pelet,** all three of whom were **sons of Reuben,**[D] **took** men.

2 **They,** Korah and his accomplices, **arose before Moses, and** with them were **two hundred and fifty people from the children of Israel, princes of the congregation, the distinguished of the convocation,** men who would be called for important gatherings, to hear judgments, and to the Tent of Meeting.[1] Alternatively, this phrase means that they had the authority to gather the assembly together. In addition, they were **people of renown,** making this a rebellion of the elite.

3 They **assembled against Moses and against Aaron, and said to them: It is too much for you.**[D] You have taken for yourselves too many positions of authority.[2] **As the entire congregation** of Israel, **all of them are holy, and the Lord is** found **among them; why do you elevate yourselves over the assembly of the Lord** by giving yourself these positions?

4 **Moses heard and he fell upon his face** in shock, as this was not the cry of a mob (see 11:4), but an attack from men with whom he was intimately familiar, and who were respected by the people.

5 After falling on his face Moses received a prophecy. **He** then **spoke to Korah and to his entire congregation** in the name of God, **saying:** Tomorrow, **in the morning the Lord will disclose who is His, and who is holy, and will bring him near to Him; whom He shall choose** as the one to perform His sacred service for future generations, and that person alone[3] **He will bring near to Him.** You will then realize that it is not I who decided the various appointments.

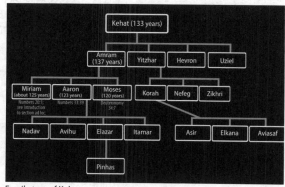

Family tree of Kehat

DISCUSSION

16:1 | Korah son of Yitzhar, son of Kehat, son of Levi: Korah was Moses' cousin, as Aaron and Moses were the sons of Kehat's firstborn, Amram. Elitzafan son of Kehat's third son was chosen as prince of the Kehatites (3:30). One can therefore understand Korah's frustration at this apparent unfairness, that the family of his father Yitzhar, Kehat's second son, did not receive any public appointment (*Bemidbar Rabba* 18:2).

Sons of Reuben: The fact that these three individuals were from the tribe of Reuben is significant. Their bitterness most probably stemmed from the fact that Jacob had taken the birthright from Reuben, his first son, and given it to Joseph, and transferred the kingship to Judah (see I Chronicles 5:1–2; *Bereshit Rabba* 49:8). At a later stage the sacred service, which was also initially a function of the firstborn, was granted to Levi (3:44–51; Mishna *Zevaḥim* 14:4). These men attributed their failure to land any position of importance to the lust for power of the current leaders.

The Sages further note that due to the arrangements of the encampment of the tribes, Korah and his family were adjacent to the tribe of Reuben. Consequently, it is possible that their neighborly relations were also a contributing

פרשת
קרח

טז א וַיִּקַּח קֹרַח בֶּן־יִצְהָר בֶּן־קְהָת בֶּן־לֵוִי וְדָתָן וַאֲבִירָם בְּנֵי אֱלִיאָב וְאוֹן בֶּן־פֶּלֶת טו
ב בְּנֵי רְאוּבֵן: וַיָּקֻמוּ לִפְנֵי מֹשֶׁה וַאֲנָשִׁים מִבְּנֵי־יִשְׂרָאֵל חֲמִשִּׁים וּמָאתָיִם נְשִׂיאֵי
ג עֵדָה קְרִאֵי מוֹעֵד אַנְשֵׁי־שֵׁם: וַיִּקָּהֲלוּ עַל־מֹשֶׁה וְעַל־אַהֲרֹן וַיֹּאמְרוּ אֲלֵהֶם רַב־
לָכֶם כִּי כָל־הָעֵדָה כֻּלָּם קְדֹשִׁים וּבְתוֹכָם יְהוָה וּמַדּוּעַ תִּתְנַשְּׂאוּ עַל־קְהַל יְהוָה:
ד ה וַיִּשְׁמַע מֹשֶׁה וַיִּפֹּל עַל־פָּנָיו: וַיְדַבֵּר אֶל־קֹרַח וְאֶל־כָּל־עֲדָתוֹ לֵאמֹר בֹּקֶר וְיֹדַע
יְהוָה אֶת־אֲשֶׁר־לוֹ וְאֶת־הַקָּדוֹשׁ וְהִקְרִיב אֵלָיו וְאֵת אֲשֶׁר יִבְחַר־בּוֹ יַקְרִיב אֵלָיו:

רש"י

פרק טז

א| **ויקח קרח.** פרשה זו יפה נדרשת במדרש רבי תנחומא: **ויקח קרח.** לקח את עצמו לצד אחד להיות נחלק מתוך העדה לעורר על הכהנה, וזהו שתרגם אונקלוס: "ואתפליג", נחלק משאר העדה להחזיק במחלקת. וכן: "מה יקחך לבך" (איוב טו, יב), לוקח אותך להפליגך משאר בני אדם. דבר אחר, "ויקח קרח", משך ראשי סנהדראות שבהם בדברים, כמו שנאמר: "קח את אהרן" (ויקרא ח, ב), "קחו עמכם דברים" (הושע יד, ג): **בן יצהר בן קהת בן לוי.** ולא הזכיר 'בן יעקב', שבקש רחמים על עצמו שלא יזכר שמו על מחלקתם, שנאמר: "בקהלם אל תחד כבדי" (בראשית מט, ו). והיכן נזכר שמו על קרח? בהתיחסם על הדוכן בדברי הימים, שנאמר: "בן אביסף בן קרח בן יצהר בן קהת בן לוי בן ישראל" (דברי הימים א' ו, כב-כג): **ודתן ואבירם.** בשביל שהיה שבט ראובן שרוי בחנייתם תימנה, שכן לקהת ובניו החונים תימנה, נשתתפו עם קרח במחלקתו, אוי לרשע אוי לשכנו. ומה ראה קרח לחלק עם משה? נתקנא על נשיאותו של אליצפן בן עזיאל, שמנהו משה נשיא על בני קהת על פי הדבור. אמר קרח: אחי אבא ארבעה היו, שנאמר: "ובני קהת" וגו' (שמות ו, יח), עמרם הבכור נטלו שני בניו גדלה, אחד מלך ואחד כהן גדול, מי ראוי לטול את השניה? לא אני, שאני בן יצהר שהוא שני לעמרם? והוא מנה נשיא את בן אחיו הקטן מכלם! הריני חולק עליו ומבטל את דבריו. מה עשה? עמד וכנס מאתים וחמשים ראשי סנהדראות, רבן משבט ראובן שכניו, והם אליצור בן שדיאור וחבריו וכיוצא בו, שנאמר: "נשיאי עדה קראי מועד" (להלן פסוק ב), ולהלן הוא אומר: "אלה קרואי העדה" (לעיל א, טז), והלבישן טליתות שכלן תכלת, באו ועמדו לפני משה, אמרו לו: טלית שכלה של תכלת חיבת בציצית או פטורה? אמר להם: חיבת. התחילו לשחק עליו: אפשר טלית של מין אחר, חוט אחד של תכלת פוטרה, זו שכלה תכלת לא תפטור את עצמה?!: **בני ראובן.** דתן ואבירם ואון בן פלת:

ג| **רב לכם.** הרבה יותר מדאי לקחתם לעצמכם גדלה: **כלם קדשים.** כלם שמעו דברים בסיני מפי הגבורה: **ומדוע תתנשאו.** אם לקחת אתה מלכות, לא היה לך לברר לאחיך כהנה. לא אתם לבדכם שמעתם בסיני: "אנכי ה' אלהיך", כל העדה שמעו:

ד| **ויפל על פניו.** מפני המחלקת, שכבר זה בידם סרחון רביעי. [חטאו בעגל, "ויחל משה" (שמות לב, יא); במתאוננים, "ויתפלל משה" (לעיל יא, ב); במרגלים, "ויאמר משה אל ה' ושמעו מצרים" (לעיל יד, יג). במחלקתו של קרח נתרשלו ידיו]. משל לבן מלך שסרח על אביו, ופיס עליו אוהבו פעם ושתים ושלש, כשסרח רביעית נתרשלו ידי האוהב ההוא, אמר: עד מתי אטריח על המלך? שמא לא יקבל עוד ממני:

ה| **בקר וידע וגו'.** עתה עת שכרות הוא לנו ולא נכון להראות לפניו. והוא היה מתכון לדחותם, שמא יחזרו בהם: **בקר וידע ה' את אשר לו.** לעבודת לויה: **ואת הקדוש.** לכהנה: **והקריב.** אותם "אליו":

DISCUSSION

factor in this collaboration (see Rashi; *Bemidbar Rabba* 18:5).

16:3| **It is too much for you:** Korah and his group leveled a double accusation at Moses and Aaron. From a theological perspective, they rejected the very requirement for a priestly caste. If the entire congregation is holy, there is no need for priests. On the political level, they argued that even if priests are necessary, Moses and Aaron should not have taken the positions of authority for themselves.

The first claim, that "the entire congregation, all of them are holy, and the Lord is among them," expresses the idea that all the people have the potential to reach the highest level. This is in fact similar to a statement of Moses himself to Joshua: "Would that all the people of the Lord would be prophets" (11:29). This can be understood as a call for democratization and the annulment of social classes (see *Tzidkat HaTzaddik* 65, 231).

6 In order to remove any doubt, **this you shall do:**[D] **Take for you fire-pans** for the incense, **Korah, and all his congregation.**
7 **Place fire in them, and place incense upon them before the Lord tomorrow,** if you wish to burn incense yourselves. Yet **it shall be the man whom the Lord will choose, he** alone **is the holy one.** Up to this point, Moses has spoken to the entire congregation of Korah. Now he turns his focus specifically to the Levites among them: **It is too much for you, sons of Levi.** You should be satisfied with the honorable role you have been given.
8 **Moses said to Korah: Hear now, sons of Levi:**
9 **Is it not enough for you that the God of Israel has distinguished you from the congregation of Israel, to bring you near to Him, to perform the service of the Tabernacle of the Lord, and to stand before the congregation to serve them?**
10 **He brought you,** Korah, **near, and all your brethren the sons of Levi with you, and will you seek the priesthood as well?** Why isn't your unique status as Levites in the Temple sufficient for you? Furthermore, your request that the entire people should have equal status is inconsistent with the fact that you as a tribe have been singled out and granted a special role. Evidently, you are hiding your personal ambitions for the priesthood.
11 **Therefore, you and all your congregation** are people **who are** in effect **congregated against the Lord;**[D] **and Aaron, what is he that you bring complaints against him?** Aaron did not choose his position as High Priest.
12 **Moses sent to summon Datan and Aviram, sons of Eliav,** in order to talk to them personally; **and they said: We will not go up,** as we reject your authority.
13 **Is it not enough that you brought us up from a land flowing with milk and honey?** Datan and Aviram appropriate Moses' own description of the land of Canaan,[4] and use it to refer to Egypt, which they claim was a place of bountiful goodness and comfort. Their echoing of Moses is designed to harangue him.[5] Is it not enough that you took us up **to kill us in the wilderness? Will you also reign over us?** You took us from our land to a vast wilderness from which you are unable to extract us, and in addition you seek to lord over us.
14 **Yet you did not take us to a land flowing with milk and honey, and** you did not **give us an inheritance of field and vineyard,** as you promised. **Will you gouge out the eyes of these men,** meaning our eyes; do you think we cannot see what is happening?[6] We see no evidence of the blessings of milk and honey you mentioned, but only the thorns of desert shrubbery. **We will not go up,** as we place no trust in your statements.

Second aliya

15 **Moses was very incensed, and said to the Lord: Do not turn to their offering** or any of their prayers,[7] as **not one donkey did I take from them** as a tax, **nor did I wrong one of them.** There is no justification for their behavior.
16 **Moses said to Korah: You and all your congregation, be before the Lord: You, and they, and Aaron, tomorrow.**

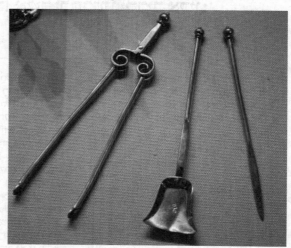

Fire-pan

DISCUSSION

16:6 | **This you shall do:** Moses suggests here that they act in accordance with their convictions. If, as they maintain, the leadership was not chosen by God but was the result of political and social motivations, then anyone can function as a priest. He therefore invites them to attempt to burn incense. However, he assumes that they certainly recall the tragic deaths of Aaron's sons, who burnt incense when they were not commanded to do so and subsequently died (see Leviticus 10:1–2). Moses assumes that this traumatic memory will deter the rebels from approaching the sacred area, as one who sacrifices incense without a command from God is clearly placing his life in danger.

16:11 | **Therefore, you and all your congregation who are congregated against the Lord:** When Moses saw that Korah and his congregation were casting doubt on the reliability of his claims that he and his brother were chosen by God, he feared for the status of the entire Torah. Consequently, he abandoned his usual quiet, humble stance.

ו ז זֹאת עֲשׂוּ קְחוּ־לָכֶם מַחְתּוֹת קֹרַח וְכָל־עֲדָתוֹ: וּתְנוּ־בָהֵן ׀ אֵשׁ וְשִׂימוּ עֲלֵיהֶן ׀
קְטֹרֶת לִפְנֵי יהוה מָחָר וְהָיָה הָאִישׁ אֲשֶׁר־יִבְחַר יהוה הוּא הַקָּדוֹשׁ רַב־לָכֶם
ח ט בְּנֵי לֵוִי: וַיֹּאמֶר מֹשֶׁה אֶל־קֹרַח שִׁמְעוּ־נָא בְּנֵי לֵוִי: הַמְעַט מִכֶּם כִּי־הִבְדִּיל
אֱלֹהֵי יִשְׂרָאֵל אֶתְכֶם מֵעֲדַת יִשְׂרָאֵל לְהַקְרִיב אֶתְכֶם אֵלָיו לַעֲבֹד אֶת־עֲבֹדַת
י מִשְׁכַּן יהוה וְלַעֲמֹד לִפְנֵי הָעֵדָה לְשָׁרְתָם: וַיַּקְרֵב אֹתְךָ וְאֶת־כָּל־אַחֶיךָ בְנֵי־לֵוִי
יא אִתָּךְ וּבִקַּשְׁתֶּם גַּם־כְּהֻנָּה: לָכֵן אַתָּה וְכָל־עֲדָתְךָ הַנֹּעָדִים עַל־יהוה וְאַהֲרֹן מַה־
יב הוּא כִּי תלונו עָלָיו: וַיִּשְׁלַח מֹשֶׁה לִקְרֹא לְדָתָן וְלַאֲבִירָם בְּנֵי אֱלִיאָב וַיֹּאמְרוּ תַלִּינוּ
יג לֹא נַעֲלֶה: הַמְעַט כִּי הֶעֱלִיתָנוּ מֵאֶרֶץ זָבַת חָלָב וּדְבַשׁ לַהֲמִיתֵנוּ בַּמִּדְבָּר
יד כִּי־תִשְׂתָּרֵר עָלֵינוּ גַּם־הִשְׂתָּרֵר: אַף לֹא אֶל־אֶרֶץ זָבַת חָלָב וּדְבַשׁ הֲבִיאֹתָנוּ שני
טו וַתִּתֶּן־לָנוּ נַחֲלַת שָׂדֶה וָכָרֶם הַעֵינֵי הָאֲנָשִׁים הָהֵם תְּנַקֵּר לֹא נַעֲלֶה: וַיִּחַר לְמֹשֶׁה
מְאֹד וַיֹּאמֶר אֶל־יהוה אַל־תֵּפֶן אֶל־מִנְחָתָם לֹא חֲמוֹר אֶחָד מֵהֶם נָשָׂאתִי וְלֹא
טז הֲרֵעֹתִי אֶת־אַחַד מֵהֶם: וַיֹּאמֶר מֹשֶׁה אֶל־קֹרַח אַתָּה וְכָל־עֲדָתְךָ הֱיוּ לִפְנֵי יהוה

רש"י

ו-ז | [תוספת מאיגרת רבינו שמעיה: **זאת עשו קחו לכם מחתות.** מה ראה לומר להם כך? אמר להם: בדרכי הגוים יש נימוסים הרבה וכמרים הרבה, ואין כלם מתקבצים בבית אחד. אנו אין לנו אלא ה' אחד, ארון אחד ותורה אחת ומזבח אחד וכהן גדול אחד, ואתם חמשים ומאתים איש מבקשים כהנה גדולה? אף אני רוצה בכך. הא לכם תשמיש חביב מכל, היא הקטרת החביבה מכל הקרבנות, וסם המות נתון בתוכו שבו נשרפו נדב ואביהוא, לפיכך התרה בהם: "והיה האיש אשר יבחר ה' הוא הקדוש" (להלן פסוק ז), כבר הוא בקדשתו, וכי אין אנו יודעים שמי שיבחר הוא הקדוש? אלא אמר להם משה: הריני אומר לכם, שלא תתחיבו: מי שיבחר בו יצא חי וכלכם אובדים: **רב לכם בני לוי.** דבר גדול אמרתי לכם. ולא טפשים היו שככך התרה בהם וקבלו עליהם לקרב, אלא הם חטאו על נפשותם, שנאמר: "את מחתות החטאים האלה בנפשתם" (להלן יז, ג). וקרח שפקח היה, מה ראה לשטות זו? עינו הטעתו, ראה שלשלת גדולה יוצאה ממנו – שמואל ששקול כנגד משה ואהרן, אמר: בשבילו אני נמלט; ועשרים וארבע משמרות עומדות לבני בניו כלם מתנבאים ברוח הקדש, שנאמר: "כל אלה בנים להימן" (דברי הימים א' כה, ה), אמר: אפשר כל הגדלה הזאת עתידה לעמד ממנו ואני אדם? לכך נשתתף לבא לאותה חזקה, ששמע מפי משה שכלם אובדים ואחד נמלט – "אשר יבחר ה' הוא הקדוש", טעה ותלה בעצמו. ולא ראה יפה, לפי שבניו עשו תשובה, ומשה היה רואה. תנחומא (ה)] **מחתות.** כלים שאוחזין בהם גחלים ויש להם בית יד: **רב לכם.** דבר גדול נטלתם בעצמכם, לחלק על הקדוש ברוך הוא:

ח | **ויאמר משה אל קרח שמעו נא בני לוי.** התחיל לדבר עמו דברים רכים, כיון שראהו קשה ערף, אמר: עד שלא ישתתפו שאר השבטים ויאבדו עמו אדבר גם אל כלם. התחיל לזרז בהם: "שמעו נא בני לוי":

ט | **ולעמד לפני העדה.** לשיר על הדוכן:

י | **ויקרב אתך.** לאותו שרות שהרחיק ממנו שאר עדת ישראל:

יא | **לכן.** בשביל כך, "אתה וכל עדתך הנעדים" אתך "על ה'", כי בשליחותו עשיתי לתת כהנה לאהרן, ולא לנו הוא המחלקת הזה:

יב | **וישלח משה וגו'.** מכאן שאין מחזיקין במחלקת, שהיה משה מחזר אחריהם להשלימם בדברי שלום: **לא נעלה.** פיהם הכשילם, שאין להם אלא ירידה:

יד | **ותתן לנו.** הדבר מוסב על 'לא' האמור למעלה, כלומר: לא הביאתנו ולא נתת לנו נחלת שדה וכרם. אמרת לנו: "אעלה אתכם מעני מצרים אל ארץ טובה וגו'" (שמות ג, ח; יז), משם הוצאתנו, ולא אל ארץ זבת חלב ודבש הביאתנו, אלא גזרת עלינו להמיתנו במדבר, שאמרת לנו: "במדבר הזה יפלו פגריכם" (לעיל יד, כט): **העיני האנשים ההם תנקר וגו'.** אפלו אתה שולח לנקר את עינינו אם לא נעלה אליך, לא נעלה: **האנשים ההם.** כאדם התולה קללתו בחברו:

טו | **אל תפן אל מנחתם.** לפי פשוטו, הקטרת שהם מקריבין לפניך מחר אל תפן אליהם. והמדרש אומר: יודע אני שיש להם חלק בתמידי צבור, אף חלקם לא יקבל לפניך לרצון, תניחנו האש ולא תאכלנו: **לא חמור אחד מהם נשאתי.** לא חמורו של אחד מהם נטלתי. אפלו כשהלכתי ממדין למצרים והרכבתי את אשתי ואת בני על החמור, והיה לי לטל אותו החמור משלהם, לא נטלתי אלא משלי. "שחרית", לשון ארמי, כך נקראת אנגריא של מלך 'שחור':

טז | **והם.** עדתך:

17 **Each of you shall take his fire-pan and you shall place incense upon** each of **them, and each of you shall bring his fire-pan before the Lord, two hundred and fifty fire-pans; and you, and Aaron, each his fire-pan.** Since you claim that Aaron received his position by my choice alone, and not by God's command due to his individual persona, you shall stand next to him for a test tomorrow.

18 **Each man** from that group **took up his fire-pan; they put fire on them and placed incense on them, and stood at the entrance of the Tent of Meeting with Moses and Aaron.**

19 **Korah assembled the entire congregation against them to the entrance of the Tent of Meeting,** as he was convinced of the justness of his cause; **and the glory of the Lord appeared to the entire congregation.**

Third aliya

20 **The Lord spoke to Moses and to Aaron, saying:**

21 **Separate yourselves from the midst of this congregation, and I will destroy them in a moment.** The congregation refers to the entire congregation of Israel, which was gathered by Korah, as is evident from the next verse where Moses and Aaron pray on behalf of all Israel.[8]

22 **They,** Moses and Aaron, **fell upon their faces** in prayer,[9] **and said: God, God of the spirits of all flesh,** You know each man's spirit. **Shall one man sin, and You will rage against the entire congregation?** This is a transgression of isolated individuals, not a rebellion of the entire congregation of Israel against You or us.

23 **The Lord spoke to Moses, saying:**

24 **Speak to the congregation, saying: Depart from around the dwelling of Korah, Datan, and Aviram.**

25 **Moses arose and went to Datan and Aviram; and the elders of Israel followed him.**

26 **He spoke to the congregation** that had gathered there, **saying: Depart now from near the tents of these wicked men, and do not touch anything that is theirs.** It is recommended that you stay away from their location and their possessions, **lest you be destroyed for all their sins.** When divine retribution arrives, it can sometimes strike others in the vicinity of the sinners.

27 **They departed from around the dwelling of Korah, Datan, and Aviram.** Meanwhile **Datan and Aviram emerged and stood at the entrance of their tents with their wives, their sons, and their children.** The entire family came out in a brazen display of self-confidence and rebellion against Moses' authority. They did so in the presence of the congregation, which had distanced themselves, but continued to watch the unfolding events.

28 **Moses said: With this you will know that the Lord has sent me to perform all these actions,** the appointments about which you accuse me of favoritism, **as it is not from my heart.** I did not initiate them, but received them as commands from God.

29 **If these** men **die like the death of all people, and the destiny of all people,** the punishment of all mankind, which is the death of the spirit while the body returns to dust,[10] **is visited upon them,** you will know that **the Lord has not sent me.** If they die in a normal manner, my prophecy will have been shown to be false.

30 **But if the Lord creates a creation** here, **and the ground opens its mouth and swallows them and everything that is theirs, and they descend** while still **alive into the abyss, you shall know that these people have scorned the Lord,** and this is their punishment.

31 **It was as he concluded to speak all these words; the ground that was beneath them split.** At first, cracks appeared in the earth.

32 Then **the earth opened its mouth** wide **and swallowed them, their households, all the people who were with Korah,** his family, **and all the property.**

רש״י

יז | **וְהִקְרַבְתֶּם... אִישׁ מַחְתָּתוֹ.** הַחֲמִשִּׁים וּמָאתַיִם אִישׁ שֶׁבָּכֶם:

יט | **וַיַּקְהֵל עֲלֵיהֶם קֹרַח.** בְּדִבְרֵי לֵיצָנוּת. כָּל הַלַּיְלָה הַהוּא הָלַךְ אֵצֶל הַשְּׁבָטִים וּפִתָּה אוֹתָם: כִּסְבוּרִין אַתֶּם שֶׁעָלַי לְבַדִּי אֲנִי מַקְפִּיד? אֵינִי מַקְפִּיד אֶלָּא בִּשְׁבִיל כֻּלְּכֶם, אֵלּוּ בָּאִין וְנוֹטְלִין כָּל הַגְּדֻלּוֹת, לוֹ הַמַּלְכוּת וּלְאָחִיו הַכְּהֻנָּה! עַד שֶׁנִּתְפַּתּוּ כֻּלָּם: **וַיֵּרָא כְבוֹד ה׳.** בָּא בְּעַמּוּד עָנָן:

כב | **אֵל אֱלֹהֵי הָרוּחֹת.** יוֹדֵעַ מַחֲשָׁבוֹת. אֵין מִדָּתְךָ כְּמִדַּת בָּשָׂר וָדָם, מֶלֶךְ בָּשָׂר וָדָם שֶׁסָּרְחָה עָלָיו מִקְצָת מְדִינָה אֵינוֹ יוֹדֵעַ מִי הַחוֹטֵא, לְפִיכָךְ כְּשֶׁהוּא כּוֹעֵס נִפְרָע מִכֻּלָּם. אֲבָל אַתָּה, לְפָנֶיךָ גְּלוּיוֹת כָּל הַמַּחֲשָׁבוֹת וְיוֹדֵעַ אַתָּה מִי הַחוֹטֵא: **הָאִישׁ אֶחָד.** הוּא הַחוֹטֵא וְאַתָּה ״עַל כָּל הָעֵדָה תִּקְצֹף״? אָמַר הַקָּדוֹשׁ בָּרוּךְ הוּא: יָפֶה אֲמַרְתֶּם, אֲנִי יוֹדֵעַ וּמוֹדִיעַ מִי חָטָא וּמִי לֹא חָטָא:

כד | **הֵעָלוּ וְגוֹ׳.** כְּתַרְגּוּמוֹ, ״אִסְתַּלָּקוּ״ מִסְּבִיבוֹת מִשְׁכַּן קֹרַח:

כה | **וַיָּקָם מֹשֶׁה.** כְּסָבוּר שֶׁיִּשְׂאוּ לוֹ פָּנִים וְלֹא עָשׂוּ:

יז אַתָּה וָהֵם וְאַהֲרֹן מָחָר: וּקְחוּ ׀ אִישׁ מַחְתָּתוֹ וּנְתַתֶּם עֲלֵיהֶם קְטֹרֶת וְהִקְרַבְתֶּם
לִפְנֵי יהוה אִישׁ מַחְתָּתוֹ חֲמִשִּׁים וּמָאתַיִם מַחְתֹּת וְאַתָּה וְאַהֲרֹן אִישׁ מַחְתָּתוֹ:
יח וַיִּקְחוּ אִישׁ מַחְתָּתוֹ וַיִּתְּנוּ עֲלֵיהֶם אֵשׁ וַיָּשִׂימוּ עֲלֵיהֶם קְטֹרֶת וַיַּעַמְדוּ פֶּתַח
יט אֹהֶל מוֹעֵד וּמֹשֶׁה וְאַהֲרֹן: וַיַּקְהֵל עֲלֵיהֶם קֹרַח אֶת־כָּל־הָעֵדָה אֶל־פֶּתַח אֹהֶל
כ מוֹעֵד וַיֵּרָא כְבוֹד־יהוה אֶל־כָּל־הָעֵדָה: וַיְדַבֵּר יהוה אֶל־מֹשֶׁה שלישי
כא כב וְאֶל־אַהֲרֹן לֵאמֹר: הִבָּדְלוּ מִתּוֹךְ הָעֵדָה הַזֹּאת וַאֲכַלֶּה אֹתָם כְּרָגַע: וַיִּפְּלוּ
עַל־פְּנֵיהֶם וַיֹּאמְרוּ אֵל אֱלֹהֵי הָרוּחֹת לְכָל־בָּשָׂר הָאִישׁ אֶחָד יֶחֱטָא וְעַל כָּל־
כג כד הָעֵדָה תִּקְצֹף: וַיְדַבֵּר יהוה אֶל־מֹשֶׁה לֵּאמֹר: דַּבֵּר אֶל־הָעֵדָה
כה לֵאמֹר הֵעָלוּ מִסָּבִיב לְמִשְׁכַּן־קֹרַח דָּתָן וַאֲבִירָם: וַיָּקָם מֹשֶׁה וַיֵּלֶךְ אֶל־דָּתָן
כו וַאֲבִירָם וַיֵּלְכוּ אַחֲרָיו זִקְנֵי יִשְׂרָאֵל: וַיְדַבֵּר אֶל־הָעֵדָה לֵאמֹר סוּרוּ נָא מֵעַל אָהֳלֵי
הָאֲנָשִׁים הָרְשָׁעִים הָאֵלֶּה וְאַל־תִּגְּעוּ בְּכָל־אֲשֶׁר לָהֶם פֶּן־תִּסָּפוּ בְּכָל־חַטֹּאתָם:
כז וַיֵּעָלוּ מֵעַל מִשְׁכַּן־קֹרַח דָּתָן וַאֲבִירָם מִסָּבִיב וְדָתָן וַאֲבִירָם יָצְאוּ נִצָּבִים פֶּתַח
כח אָהֳלֵיהֶם וּנְשֵׁיהֶם וּבְנֵיהֶם וְטַפָּם: וַיֹּאמֶר מֹשֶׁה בְּזֹאת תֵּדְעוּן כִּי־יהוה שְׁלָחַנִי
כט לַעֲשׂוֹת אֵת כָּל־הַמַּעֲשִׂים הָאֵלֶּה כִּי־לֹא מִלִּבִּי: אִם־כְּמוֹת כָּל־הָאָדָם יְמֻתוּן
ל אֵלֶּה וּפְקֻדַּת כָּל־הָאָדָם יִפָּקֵד עֲלֵיהֶם לֹא יהוה שְׁלָחָנִי: וְאִם־בְּרִיאָה יִבְרָא
יהוה וּפָצְתָה הָאֲדָמָה אֶת־פִּיהָ וּבָלְעָה אֹתָם וְאֶת־כָּל־אֲשֶׁר לָהֶם וְיָרְדוּ חַיִּים
לא שְׁאֹלָה וִידַעְתֶּם כִּי נִאֲצוּ הָאֲנָשִׁים הָאֵלֶּה אֶת־יהוה: וַיְהִי כְּכַלֹּתוֹ לְדַבֵּר אֵת
לב כָּל־הַדְּבָרִים הָאֵלֶּה וַתִּבָּקַע הָאֲדָמָה אֲשֶׁר תַּחְתֵּיהֶם: וַתִּפְתַּח הָאָרֶץ אֶת־
פִּיהָ וַתִּבְלַע אֹתָם וְאֶת־בָּתֵּיהֶם וְאֵת כָּל־הָאָדָם אֲשֶׁר לְקֹרַח וְאֵת כָּל־הָרְכוּשׁ:

רש״י

כז| **יָצְאוּ נִצָּבִים.** בְּקוֹמָה זְקוּפָה לְחָרֵף וּלְגַדֵּף, כְּמוֹ: "וַיִּתְיַצֵּב אַרְבָּעִים יוֹם" דִּגְלְיַת (שמואל א׳ יז, טז): **וּנְשֵׁיהֶם וּבְנֵיהֶם וְטַפָּם.** בֹּא וּרְאֵה כַּמָּה קָשָׁה הַמַּחְלֹקֶת, שֶׁהֲרֵי בֵּית דִּין שֶׁל מַטָּה אֵין עוֹנְשִׁין אֶלָּא עַד שֶׁיָּבִיא שְׁתֵּי שְׂעָרוֹת, וּבֵית דִּין שֶׁל מַעְלָה עַד עֶשְׂרִים שָׁנָה, וְכָאן אָבְדוּ אַף יוֹנְקֵי שָׁדַיִם:

כח| **לַעֲשׂוֹת אֵת כָּל הַמַּעֲשִׂים הָאֵלֶּה.** שֶׁעָשִׂיתִי עַל פִּי הַדִּבּוּר, לָתֵת לְאַהֲרֹן כְּהֻנָּה גְּדוֹלָה, וּבָנָיו סְגָנֵי כְּהֻנָּה, וֶאֱלִיצָפָן נְשִׂיא הַקְּהָתִי:

כט| **לֹא ה׳ שְׁלָחָנִי.** אֶלָּא אֲנִי עָשִׂיתִי הַכֹּל מִדַּעְתִּי, וּבְדִין הוּא חוֹלֵק עָלַי:

ל| **וְאִם בְּרִיאָה.** חֲדָשָׁה: **יִבְרָא ה׳.** לְהָמִית אוֹתָם בְּמִיתָה שֶׁלֹּא מֵת בָּהּ אָדָם עַד הֵנָּה, וּמָה הִיא הַבְּרִיאָה? "וּפָצְתָה הָאֲדָמָה אֶת פִּיהָ" וְתִבְלָעֵם, אָז "וִידַעְתֶּם כִּי נִאֲצוּ" הֵם, וַאֲנִי מִפִּי הַגְּבוּרָה אָמַרְתִּי. וְרַבּוֹתֵינוּ פֵּרְשׁוּ: "אִם בְּרִיאָה" – פֶּה לָאָרֶץ מִשֵּׁשֶׁת יְמֵי בְרֵאשִׁית, מוּטָב, וְאִם לָאו – "יִבְרָא ה'":

33 **They, and everything that was theirs descended alive into
the abyss. The earth covered them and they were lost from
the midst of the assembly** in body and soul.
34 **All Israel that were** standing **around them fled due to their
sound, as they said: Lest the earth swallow us.**[D]
35 **Fire emerged from the Lord, and consumed the two hundred and fifty men,**[D] **the presenters of the incense.** Since
they had encroached upon the sacred by acting in a capacity
that was not assigned to them, they were punished in the manner of Nadav and Avihu, who offered strange fire.[11]

17 1 **The Lord spoke to Moses, saying:**
2 **Say to Elazar son of Aaron the priest that he shall lift up the
fire-pans,** in which the incense was sacrificed, **from the midst
of the fire** that consumed the men who brought it, **and the fire**
of the incense, which was still burning in the coals, he should
cast onwards to a distant location; **for they,** these fire-pans,
became holy to God by being designated for sacrifice, despite
the fact that the incense was brought unlawfully.[12]
3 **The fire-pans of these sinners** who sinned **with their lives,
they shall render them,** the fire-pans, **beaten sheet metal,**
flattened until they can be used as **a covering for the altar; for
they brought them before the Lord, and they became holy.**
Consequently, they must remain near the altar and **they shall
be as a sign to the children of Israel** that they must not rebel
against the sanctity of the priesthood again.
4 **Elazar the priest took the bronze fire-pans that those who
were burned** had **brought** near with the incense, **and they
beat them as a covering for the altar.**
5 This covering served as **a remembrance to the children of
Israel, so that a non-priestly man who is not from the descendants of Aaron shall not draw near to burn incense
before the Lord, and he will not be like Korah and like his
congregation as the Lord spoke** with regard **to him at the
hand of Moses.**
6 All of these events, the opening of the ground and the descent
of the heavenly fire, occurred on a single day. However, despite
these miraculous punishments, the arguments that Korah and
his congregation voiced had left an impression upon the people. Consequently, **the entire congregation of the children
of Israel complained against Moses and against Aaron the
next day, saying: You have killed**[D] **the people of the Lord.**
Although you turned to God in order to protect yourselves, you
should not have decreed death upon the rebels.
7 **It was when the congregation was assembled** and complaining **against Moses and against Aaron, they turned toward
the Tent of Meeting and behold, the cloud covered it, and
the glory of the Lord appeared** within the cloud.
8 **Moses and Aaron came before the Tent of Meeting** to hear
the word of God.
Fourth aliya 9 **The Lord spoke to Moses, saying:**
10 **Remove yourselves**[D] **from among this congregation, and
I will destroy them,** the entire congregation, **in a moment.
They,** Moses and Aaron, **fell upon their faces,** beseeching God
not to do so. However, a plague had already begun to spread
among the people, and some had already died.
11 **Moses said to Aaron: Take the fire-pan, put fire on it from
upon the altar and place incense, and go quickly** with the
fire-pan and the incense **to the congregation and atone for
them;**[D] **for the rage has emerged from before the Lord: The
plague has begun.**
12 **Aaron took** a fire-pan **as Moses had spoken, and ran to the
midst of the assembly** with it; **and behold, the plague had
begun among the people; he placed the incense, and atoned
for the people** by means of the incense.

DISCUSSION

16:34 | **Lest the earth swallow us:** Although the nation had previously witnessed miracles, some of which had entailed people's deaths, the sight of the ground opening up and literally swallowing people alive terrified them. They were stunned by the way the earth consumed some people and not others. Furthermore, Datan and Aviram did not live in precisely the same place as Korah, and yet all the sinners were swallowed in their respective locations.

16:35 | **And consumed the two hundred and fifty men:** The men who sacrificed the incense were well-known, respected individuals. They joined the rebellion in the belief that the priesthood should be available to all who wish to approach the Sanctuary, as was common in other cultures. It is possible that some of them chose to burn the incense out of a sincere belief that they would thereby achieve closeness to God, but this act was in opposition to God's explicit will as transmitted through His prophet, Moses.

17:6 | **You have killed:** The people could not deny that Korah and his assembly received a divine punishment. The dramatic events which unfolded before their own eyes attested to the greatness and power of Moses and Aaron. However, the very fact that Moses' request was answered in such wondrous fashion led the people to hold him and Aaron responsible for the harsh retribution (see *Tzidkat HaTzaddik* 64). These complaints indicated that they did not fully understand the nature of the relationship between God and His messengers Moses and Aaron.

17:10 | **Remove yourselves [*heromu*]:** Although the word *harama* generally refers to lifting, it can also refer to an act of separation, as with regard to the separation of the priestly gift [*haramat teruma*] (e.g., 15:19–20; see also Onkelos; *Targum Yonatan*).

17:11 | **And atone for them:** It can be assumed that it was not Moses' own idea that atonement could be attained for the people by means of incense held by Aaron, but rather a suggestion he received from God. There are passages in the Torah where it explicitly states that Moses spoke in the name of God, but on occasion he also received divine instructions which are not related in the Torah, through a form of direct, personal conversation with God, "face-to-face as a man speaks to his neighbor" (Exodus 33:11).

לג וַיֵּרְדוּ הֵם וְכָל־אֲשֶׁר לָהֶם חַיִּים שְׁאֹלָה וַתְּכַס עֲלֵיהֶם הָאָרֶץ וַיֹּאבְדוּ מִתּוֹךְ
לד הַקָּהָל: וְכָל־יִשְׂרָאֵל אֲשֶׁר סְבִיבֹתֵיהֶם נָסוּ לְקֹלָם כִּי אָמְרוּ פֶּן־תִּבְלָעֵנוּ
לה הָאָרֶץ: וְאֵשׁ יָצְאָה מֵאֵת יְהוָה וַתֹּאכַל אֵת הַחֲמִשִּׁים וּמָאתַיִם אִישׁ מַקְרִיבֵי
א ב הַקְּטֹרֶת: וַיְדַבֵּר יְהוָה אֶל־מֹשֶׁה לֵּאמֹר: אֱמֹר אֶל־אֶלְעָזָר בֶּן־
אַהֲרֹן הַכֹּהֵן וְיָרֵם אֶת־הַמַּחְתֹּת מִבֵּין הַשְּׂרֵפָה וְאֶת־הָאֵשׁ זְרֵה־הָלְאָה כִּי קָדֵשׁוּ:
ג אֵת מַחְתּוֹת הַחַטָּאִים הָאֵלֶּה בְּנַפְשֹׁתָם וְעָשׂוּ אֹתָם רִקֻּעֵי פַחִים צִפּוּי לַמִּזְבֵּחַ
ד כִּי־הִקְרִיבֻם לִפְנֵי־יְהוָה וַיִּקְדָּשׁוּ וְיִהְיוּ לְאוֹת לִבְנֵי יִשְׂרָאֵל: וַיִּקַּח אֶלְעָזָר הַכֹּהֵן
ה אֵת מַחְתּוֹת הַנְּחֹשֶׁת אֲשֶׁר הִקְרִיבוּ הַשְּׂרֻפִים וַיְרַקְּעוּם צִפּוּי לַמִּזְבֵּחַ: זִכָּרוֹן לִבְנֵי
יִשְׂרָאֵל לְמַעַן אֲשֶׁר לֹא־יִקְרַב אִישׁ זָר אֲשֶׁר לֹא מִזֶּרַע אַהֲרֹן הוּא לְהַקְטִיר
קְטֹרֶת לִפְנֵי יְהוָה וְלֹא־יִהְיֶה כְקֹרַח וְכַעֲדָתוֹ כַּאֲשֶׁר דִּבֶּר יְהוָה בְּיַד־מֹשֶׁה לוֹ:
ו וַיִּלֹּנוּ כָּל־עֲדַת בְּנֵי־יִשְׂרָאֵל מִמָּחֳרָת עַל־מֹשֶׁה וְעַל־אַהֲרֹן לֵאמֹר אַתֶּם הֲמִתֶּם
ז אֶת־עַם יְהוָה: וַיְהִי בְּהִקָּהֵל הָעֵדָה עַל־מֹשֶׁה וְעַל־אַהֲרֹן וַיִּפְנוּ אֶל־אֹהֶל
ח מוֹעֵד וְהִנֵּה כִסָּהוּ הֶעָנָן וַיֵּרָא כְּבוֹד יְהוָה: וַיָּבֹא מֹשֶׁה וְאַהֲרֹן אֶל־פְּנֵי אֹהֶל
ט י מוֹעֵד: וַיְדַבֵּר יְהוָה אֶל־מֹשֶׁה לֵּאמֹר: הֵרֹמּוּ מִתּוֹךְ הָעֵדָה הַזֹּאת רביעי
יא וַאֲכַלֶּה אֹתָם כְּרָגַע וַיִּפְּלוּ עַל־פְּנֵיהֶם: וַיֹּאמֶר מֹשֶׁה אֶל־אַהֲרֹן קַח אֶת־הַמַּחְתָּה
וְתֶן־עָלֶיהָ אֵשׁ מֵעַל הַמִּזְבֵּחַ וְשִׂים קְטֹרֶת וְהוֹלֵךְ מְהֵרָה אֶל־הָעֵדָה וְכַפֵּר
יב עֲלֵיהֶם כִּי־יָצָא הַקֶּצֶף מִלִּפְנֵי יְהוָה הֵחֵל הַנָּגֶף: וַיִּקַּח אַהֲרֹן כַּאֲשֶׁר ׀ דִּבֶּר מֹשֶׁה
וַיָּרָץ אֶל־תּוֹךְ הַקָּהָל וְהִנֵּה הֵחֵל הַנֶּגֶף בָּעָם וַיִּתֵּן אֶת־הַקְּטֹרֶת וַיְכַפֵּר עַל־הָעָם:

רש"י

לד | נָסוּ לְקֹלָם. בִּשְׁבִיל הַקּוֹל הַיּוֹצֵא עַל בְּלִיעָתָן:

פרק יז

ב | וְאֶת הָאֵשׁ. שֶׁבְּתוֹךְ הַמַּחְתּוֹת: זְרֵה הָלְאָה. לָאָרֶץ מֵעַל הַמַּחְתּוֹת: כִּי קָדֵשׁוּ. הַמַּחְתּוֹת, וַאֲסוּרִין בַּהֲנָאָה, שֶׁהֲרֵי עֲשָׂאוּם כְּלֵי שָׁרֵת:

ג | הַחַטָּאִים הָאֵלֶּה בְּנַפְשֹׁתָם. שֶׁנַּעֲשׂוּ פּוֹשְׁעִים בְּנַפְשׁוֹתָם, שֶׁנֶּחְלְקוּ עַל הַקָּדוֹשׁ בָּרוּךְ הוּא: רִקֻּעֵי. רְדוּדִין: פַּחִים. טַסִּים מְרֻדָּדִין, טינבי"ש בְּלַעַז: צִפּוּי לַמִּזְבֵּחַ. לְמִזְבַּח הַנְּחֹשֶׁת: וְיִהְיוּ לְאוֹת. לְזִכָּרוֹן, שֶׁיֹּאמְרוּ: אֵלּוּ הָיוּ מֵאוֹתָן שֶׁנֶּחְלְקוּ עַל הַכְּהֻנָּה וְנִשְׂרְפוּ:

ד | וַיְרַקְּעוּם. אינטינבירינ"ט בְּלַעַז:

ה | וְלֹא יִהְיֶה כְקֹרַח. כְּדֵי שֶׁלֹּא יִהְיֶה כְּקֹרַח: כַּאֲשֶׁר דִּבֶּר ה' בְּיַד מֹשֶׁה לוֹ. כְּמוֹ 'עָלָיו', עַל אַהֲרֹן דִּבֶּר אֶל מֹשֶׁה שֶׁיִּהְיֶה הוּא וּבָנָיו כֹּהֲנִים, לְפִיכָךְ "לֹא יִקְרַב אִישׁ זָר אֲשֶׁר לֹא מִזֶּרַע אַהֲרֹן" וְגוֹ'. וְכֵן כָּל 'לִי' וְ'לוֹ' וְ'לָהֶם' הַסְּמוּכִים אֵצֶל דִּבּוּר, פִּתְרוֹנָם כְּמוֹ 'עַל'. וּמִדְרָשׁוֹ, עַל קֹרַח. וּמַהוּ "בְּיַד מֹשֶׁה" וְלֹא כָּתַב 'אֶל מֹשֶׁה'? רֶמֶז לַחוֹלְקִים עַל הַכְּהֻנָּה שֶׁלּוֹקִין בְּצָרַעַת כְּמוֹ שֶׁלָּקָה מֹשֶׁה בְּיָדוֹ, שֶׁנֶּאֱמַר: "וַיּוֹצִאָהּ וְהִנֵּה יָדוֹ מְצֹרַעַת כַּשָּׁלֶג" (שמות ד, ו), וְעַל כֵּן לָקָה עֻזִּיָּהוּ בְּצָרַעַת (דברי הימים ב' כו, טז-כ):

יא | וְכַפֵּר עֲלֵיהֶם. רָז זֶה מָסַר לוֹ מַלְאַךְ הַמָּוֶת כְּשֶׁעָלָה לָרָקִיעַ, שֶׁהַקְּטֹרֶת עוֹצֶרֶת הַמַּגֵּפָה, כִּדְאִיתָא בְּמַסֶּכֶת שַׁבָּת (דף פט ע"א):

13 **He stood between the dead** from the plague **and the living; and the plague was stopped.**
14 **The dead in the plague were fourteen thousand seven hundred; besides the** previous **dead over the matter of Korah.**
15 **Aaron returned to Moses to the entrance of the Tent of Meeting, and the plague was stopped.**

A Reaffirmation of the Status of the Priests and the Levites

NUMBERS 17:16–18:32

The objections of the rebels against the idea of a priesthood rooted in one man or a single family could have been supported by the fact that Aaron was consecrated for his role in a ritual that involved no clear divine affirmation of his selection. The miracles that took place as the rebellion was crushed served to reinforce the status of Moses and Aaron through the negative means of the death of their opponents. Now, God provides a positive sign, involving flowering and fertility, to indicate the divine choice of the tribe of Levi and of Aaron.

In the continuation of the section, the people express their fears of the grave power of the sanctity that resides in the camp. In response, God emphasizes the responsibility of the priests and the Levites to guard the Sanctuary. Furthermore, the elevated status of the priests is stressed once again, as the verses list the gifts to which they are entitled, as well as the functions of the Levites.

Fifth aliya 16 **The Lord spoke to Moses, saying:**
17 **Speak to the children of Israel, and take from them one staff for each patrilineal house, from each of their princes according to their patrilineal house, twelve staffs;**[D] **each man's name you shall write upon his staff.**
18 **You shall write Aaron's name upon the staff of Levi, for there shall be one staff for the head of their patrilineal house.** In addition to Aaron's other roles, he is also the prince and representative of his tribe. This division of the tribes is not based on military camps, as it is for the encampments and the travels of the Israelites. Rather, it follows the original tribes of Israel. Consequently, it includes the tribe of Levi, and it is likely that Joseph was not split into two tribes.[13]
19 **You shall place them,** the staffs, **in the Tent of Meeting before the testimony,** the covenant that was inside the Ark, **where I will meet with you,** in the Holy of Holies.
20 **It shall be** that **the man whom I shall choose, his staff will blossom and I will quell from upon Me the complaints of the children of Israel that they bring against you.**
21 **Moses spoke** these matters **to the children of Israel, and all their princes gave him one staff for each prince according to their patrilineal house, twelve staffs** in total; **and the staff of Aaron was among their staffs.** Moses did not place Aaron's staff at any particular spot, but simply as one staff among the others, so that no one could argue that it blossomed due to its position.[14]
22 **Moses placed the staffs before the Lord in the Tent of the Testimony.**
23 **It was on the next day, and Moses came into the Tent of the Testimony and behold, the staff of Aaron of the house of Levi had blossomed; it had produced a blossom, and had sprouted a bud,** the first part of the fruit that develops from a blossom after the petals have fallen off, **and had brought forth almonds.**[D] Unlike the natural gradual process, where the almonds ripen only six months after blossoming, here the blossom, bud, and almonds all miraculously appeared together.
24 **Moses took out all the staffs from before the Lord to all the children of Israel and they saw, and each took his staff.** In this manner, all the princes saw proof that they had not been chosen to serve as priests in the Sanctuary.

Almond bud and fruit

Almond blossom

DISCUSSION

Unlike other prophets, Moses could communicate with God whenever he wished. Ordinary prophets experienced their prophecy as traumatic events, which often entailed a breakdown in their daily routine and even their personalities. By contrast, Moses' prophecy was part of his regular life (see Rambam, *Sefer HaMadda, Hilkhot Yesodei HaTorah* 7:6; Rambam, *Guide of the Perplexed* 2:39, 44, 45).

Only the day before the people had witnessed the inherent danger of burning incense. Yet, Moses knew that Aaron alone could help them escape death here. On Moses' command, Aaron used the incense in the opposite manner, as a life-saving substance (see Rashi, verse 13; *Bemidbar Rabba* 4:20).

17:17 | **Twelve staffs [*mattot*]:** The word "staff" [*matteh*], like *shevet*, has a double meaning.

יד וַיַּעֲמֹד בֵּין־הַמֵּתִים וּבֵין הַחַיִּים וַתֵּעָצַר הַמַּגֵּפָה: וַיִּהְיוּ הַמֵּתִים בַּמַּגֵּפָה אַרְבָּעָה

טו עָשָׂר אֶלֶף וּשְׁבַע מֵאוֹת מִלְּבַד הַמֵּתִים עַל־דְּבַר־קֹרַח: וַיָּשָׁב אַהֲרֹן אֶל־מֹשֶׁה אֶל־פֶּתַח אֹהֶל מוֹעֵד וְהַמַּגֵּפָה נֶעֱצָרָה:

טז חמישי וַיְדַבֵּר יְהֹוָה אֶל־מֹשֶׁה לֵּאמֹר: דַּבֵּר ׀ אֶל־בְּנֵי יִשְׂרָאֵל וְקַח מֵאִתָּם מַטֶּה מַטֶּה

יז לְבֵית אָב מֵאֵת כָּל־נְשִׂיאֵהֶם לְבֵית אֲבֹתָם שְׁנֵים עָשָׂר מַטּוֹת אִישׁ אֶת־שְׁמוֹ

יח תִּכְתֹּב עַל־מַטֵּהוּ: וְאֵת שֵׁם אַהֲרֹן תִּכְתֹּב עַל־מַטֵּה לֵוִי כִּי מַטֶּה אֶחָד לְרֹאשׁ

יט בֵּית אֲבוֹתָם: וְהִנַּחְתָּם בְּאֹהֶל מוֹעֵד לִפְנֵי הָעֵדוּת אֲשֶׁר אִוָּעֵד לָכֶם שָׁמָּה: וְהָיָה

כ הָאִישׁ אֲשֶׁר אֶבְחַר־בּוֹ מַטֵּהוּ יִפְרָח וַהֲשִׁכֹּתִי מֵעָלַי אֶת־תְּלֻנּוֹת בְּנֵי יִשְׂרָאֵל אֲשֶׁר

כא הֵם מַלִּינִם עֲלֵיכֶם: וַיְדַבֵּר מֹשֶׁה אֶל־בְּנֵי יִשְׂרָאֵל וַיִּתְּנוּ אֵלָיו ׀ כָּל־נְשִׂיאֵיהֶם מַטֶּה לְנָשִׂיא אֶחָד מַטֶּה לְנָשִׂיא אֶחָד לְבֵית אֲבֹתָם שְׁנֵים עָשָׂר מַטּוֹת וּמַטֵּה אַהֲרֹן

כב בְּתוֹךְ מַטּוֹתָם: וַיַּנַּח מֹשֶׁה אֶת־הַמַּטֹּת לִפְנֵי יְהֹוָה בְּאֹהֶל הָעֵדֻת: וַיְהִי מִמָּחֳרָת

כג וַיָּבֹא מֹשֶׁה אֶל־אֹהֶל הָעֵדוּת וְהִנֵּה פָּרַח מַטֵּה־אַהֲרֹן לְבֵית לֵוִי וַיֹּצֵא פֶרַח וַיָּצֵץ

כד צִיץ וַיִּגְמֹל שְׁקֵדִים: וַיֹּצֵא מֹשֶׁה אֶת־כָּל־הַמַּטֹּת מִלִּפְנֵי יְהֹוָה אֶל־כָּל־בְּנֵי יִשְׂרָאֵל וַיִּרְאוּ וַיִּקְחוּ אִישׁ מַטֵּהוּ:

רש״י

יג) וַיַּעֲמֹד בֵּין־הַמֵּתִים וגו׳. אָחַז אֶת הַמַּלְאָךְ וְהֶעֱמִידוֹ עַל כָּרְחוֹ. אָמַר לוֹ הַמַּלְאָךְ: הַנַּח לִי לַעֲשׂוֹת שְׁלִיחוּתִי. אָמַר לוֹ: מֹשֶׁה צִוַּנִי לַעֲכֵב עַל יָדֶךָ. אָמַר לוֹ: אֲנִי שְׁלוּחוֹ שֶׁל מָקוֹם וְאַתָּה שְׁלוּחוֹ שֶׁל מֹשֶׁה. אָמַר לוֹ: אֵין מֹשֶׁה אוֹמֵר כְּלוּם מִלִּבּוֹ אֶלָּא מִפִּי הַגְּבוּרָה, אִם אֵין אַתָּה מַאֲמִין, הֲרֵי הַקָּדוֹשׁ בָּרוּךְ הוּא וּמֹשֶׁה אֶל פֶּתַח אֹהֶל מוֹעֵד, בֹּא עִמִּי וּשְׁאַל. וְזֶהוּ שֶׁנֶּאֱמַר: "וַיָּשָׁב אַהֲרֹן אֶל מֹשֶׁה" (לְהַלָּן פָּסוּק טו). דָּבָר אַחֵר, לָמָּה בַּקְּטֹרֶת? לְפִי שֶׁהָיוּ יִשְׂרָאֵל מְלִיזִים וּמְרַנְּנִים אַחַר הַקְּטֹרֶת לוֹמַר: סַם הַמָּוֶת הוּא, עַל יָדוֹ מֵתוּ נָדָב וַאֲבִיהוּא, עַל יָדוֹ נִשְׂרְפוּ חֲמִשִּׁים וּמָאתַיִם

אִישׁ. אָמַר הַקָּדוֹשׁ בָּרוּךְ הוּא: תִּרְאוּ שֶׁעוֹצֵר מַגֵּפָה הוּא, וְהַחֵטְא הוּא הַמֵּמִית:

יח) כִּי מַטֶּה אֶחָד. אַף עַל פִּי שֶׁחֲלַקְתִּים לִשְׁתֵּי מִשְׁפָּחוֹת, מִשְׁפַּחַת כְּהֻנָּה לְבַד וּלְוִיָּה לְבַד, מִכָּל מָקוֹם שֵׁבֶט אֶחָד הוּא:

כ) וַהֲשִׁכֹּתִי. כְּמוֹ: "וַיָּשֹׁכּוּ הַמָּיִם" (בְּרֵאשִׁית ח, א), "וַחֲמַת הַמֶּלֶךְ שָׁכָכָה" (אֶסְתֵּר ז, י):

כא) בְּתוֹךְ מַטּוֹתָם. הִנִּיחוֹ בָּאֶמְצַע, שֶׁלֹּא יֹאמְרוּ: מִפְּנֵי שֶׁהִנִּיחוֹ בְּצַד שְׁכִינָה פָּרַח:

כג) וַיֹּצֵא פֶרַח. כְּמַשְׁמָעוֹ. **צִיץ.** הוּא חֲנָטַת הַפְּרִי כְּשֶׁהַפֶּרַח נוֹבֵל. **וַיִּגְמֹל שְׁקֵדִים.** כְּשֶׁהֻכַּר הַפְּרִי הֻכַּר שֶׁהֵן שְׁקֵדִים, לָשׁוֹן: "וַיִּגְדַּל הַיֶּלֶד וַיִּגָּמַל" (בְּרֵאשִׁית כא, ח), וְלָשׁוֹן זֶה מָצוּי בִּפְרִי הָאִילָן, כְּמוֹ: "וּבֹסֶר גֹּמֵל יִהְיֶה נִצָּה" (יְשַׁעְיָה יח, ה). וְלָמָּה שְׁקֵדִים? הוּא הַפְּרִי הַמְמַהֵר לְהַפְרִיחַ מִכָּל הַפֵּרוֹת, אַף הַמְעוֹרֵר עַל הַכְּהֻנָּה פֻּרְעָנוּתוֹ מְמַהֶרֶת לָבֹא, כְּמוֹ שֶׁמָּצִינוּ בְּעֻזִּיָּהוּ: "וְהַצָּרַעַת זָרְחָה בְמִצְחוֹ" (דִּבְרֵי הַיָּמִים ב' כו, יט). וְתַרְגּוּמוֹ: "וְכַפֵּית שִׁגְדִּין", כְּמִין אֶשְׁכּוֹל שְׁקֵדִים יַחַד כְּפוּתִים זֶה עַל זֶה:

כה) וּתְכַל תְּלֻנּוֹתָם. כְּמוֹ "וּתְכַלֶּה תְלוּנֹתָם", לְשׁוֹן שֵׁם

DISCUSSION

➤ Principally, both terms refer to a staff, stick, or branch held by a leader as a symbol of his authority. Indeed, a judge or leader himself can also be called a *shevet* (see II Samuel 7:7; Radak). By extension, these words can also refer to a group of individuals who are a branch of an

entire people. It is possible that here the Torah uses both meanings of the term in the same verse, as a play on words: Take one stick from each of the twelve tribes.

17:23 | **It had produced a blossom, and had sprouted a bud, and had brought forth**

almonds: It would seem that this blossom did not wither even after the fruit appeared. Consequently, Aaron's staff remained adorned with a blossom, bud, and almonds forever (see *Da'at Zekenim*; *Yoma* 52b, and *Tosafot Yeshanim* ad loc.).

25 **The Lord said to Moses: Return the staff of Aaron before**
Sixth aliya **the testimony.** After such a unique miracle has occurred with it, it may no longer be used for non-sacred purposes. Instead, it must be returned to the Sanctuary **for safekeeping, as a sign for the defiant ones,** for anyone who might consider rebelling in the future. **And their complaints will** thereby **cease from Me, and they will not die,** as the plague came due to their complaints.
26 **Moses did as the Lord had commanded him; so he did.** From that point onward Aaron's staff was kept at the side of the Ark of the Covenant.
27 Although the Tabernacle was at the heart of the Israelites' national life, the people saw that it was not merely a source of security and shelter. On the contrary, the swallowing of Korah and his congregation by the ground, the burning of those who brought the incense, the plague that afflicted the people, and the earlier deaths of Nadav and Avihu,[15] all combined with the repeated warnings against the approach of non-priests to the Sanctuary (1:51, 3:10, 38, 8:19) to produce a feeling of terror. **The children of Israel spoke to Moses, saying: Behold, we perish, we are lost, all of us are lost.**
28 **Anyone who approaches the Tabernacle of the Lord will die. Have we ceased to perish,** or will the tremendous power of the Tabernacle of God continue to claim victims?

18 1 **The Lord said to Aaron: You and your sons** the priests, **and your patrilineal house,** the Kehatites, **with you shall bear the iniquity of the Sanctuary,** as you will be held accountable for any breach of the sacred. **And** in addition, **you and your sons with you shall bear the iniquity of your priesthood:** The responsibility for the lack of fulfillment of the duties of the priesthood shall fall upon you.
2 **Also your brethren, the tribe of Levi,**[D] **the tribe of your father, bring near with you, and they shall accompany you, and serve you. And** only **you and your sons with you** will serve **before the Tent of the Testimony,** not the Levites, whose function is outside this area.[16]
3 **They shall keep your commission, and the commission of all the** surrounding **Tent; however, they shall not come close to the sacred vessels and to the altar, and neither they nor you will die.** Although the Levites must carry and guard the Tabernacle, they are prohibited from touching its vessels.
4 **They,** the Levites, **shall accompany you** and your family, the priests, **and** they shall **keep the commission of the Tent of Meeting, for all the service of the Tent; a non-priest shall not approach you.**
5 **You shall keep the commission of the sacred and the commission of the altar,** by ensuring that non-priests shall not approach the Sanctuary and the altar,[17] **and there will be no more rage against the children of Israel,** due to any breach of the sanctity of the altar.
6 **And I, behold, I have taken your brethren the Levites from among the children of Israel; to you they are given as a gift for the Lord, to perform the service of the Tent of Meeting.**
7 **You and your sons with you shall keep your priesthood with regard to any matter of the altar, and with regard to that which is within the curtain, and you shall serve.** You are responsible for ensuring that the entire service, both inside and outside the Sanctuary, is performed in the proper manner. **As a service of gift I give** you **your priesthood.** Your service as a priest is not a form of subjugation but rather a privilege bestowed solely upon you, whereas **the non-priest who approaches shall be put to death.**
8 **The Lord spoke to Aaron: Behold, I have given you the commission of My gifts; with regard to all the consecrated**

DISCUSSION

18:2| **Also your brethren, the tribe of Levi:** The task of assisting the priests was already previously assigned to the Levites (1:48–54, 3:6–10, 8:18). Here, after the uprising against the priesthood, Aaron was given the additional command that the priests and Levites have the permanent job of safeguarding the sacred vessels and tending to the upkeep of the Sanctuary. Such maintenance tasks were far more important in the Temple in Jerusalem than in the Tabernacle, which was a smaller structure with fewer priests serving.

כה וַיֹּאמֶר יְהוָה אֶל־מֹשֶׁה הָשֵׁב אֶת־מַטֵּה אַהֲרֹן לִפְנֵי הָעֵדוּת לְמִשְׁמֶרֶת לְאוֹת ששי
כו לִבְנֵי־מֶרִי וּתְכַל תְּלוּנֹּתָם מֵעָלַי וְלֹא יָמֻתוּ: וַיַּעַשׂ מֹשֶׁה כַּאֲשֶׁר צִוָּה יְהוָה אֹתוֹ
כֵּן עָשָׂה:
כז כח וַיֹּאמְרוּ בְּנֵי יִשְׂרָאֵל אֶל־מֹשֶׁה לֵאמֹר הֵן גָּוַעְנוּ אָבַדְנוּ כֻּלָּנוּ אָבָדְנוּ: כֹּל הַקָּרֵב ׀
א הַקָּרֵב אֶל־מִשְׁכַּן יְהוָה יָמוּת הַאִם תַּמְנוּ לִגְוֹעַ: וַיֹּאמֶר יְהוָה אֶל־אַהֲרֹן
אַתָּה וּבָנֶיךָ וּבֵית־אָבִיךָ אִתָּךְ תִּשְׂאוּ אֶת־עֲוֺן הַמִּקְדָּשׁ וְאַתָּה וּבָנֶיךָ אִתָּךְ תִּשְׂאוּ
ב אֶת־עֲוֺן כְּהֻנַּתְכֶם: וְגַם אֶת־אַחֶיךָ מַטֵּה לֵוִי שֵׁבֶט אָבִיךָ הַקְרֵב אִתָּךְ וְיִלָּווּ עָלֶיךָ
ג וִישָׁרְתוּךָ וְאַתָּה וּבָנֶיךָ אִתָּךְ לִפְנֵי אֹהֶל הָעֵדֻת: וְשָׁמְרוּ מִשְׁמַרְתְּךָ וּמִשְׁמֶרֶת כָּל־
הָאֹהֶל אַךְ אֶל־כְּלֵי הַקֹּדֶשׁ וְאֶל־הַמִּזְבֵּחַ לֹא יִקְרָבוּ וְלֹא־יָמֻתוּ גַם־הֵם גַּם־אַתֶּם:
ד וְנִלְווּ עָלֶיךָ וְשָׁמְרוּ אֶת־מִשְׁמֶרֶת אֹהֶל מוֹעֵד לְכֹל עֲבֹדַת הָאֹהֶל וְזָר לֹא־יִקְרַב
ה אֲלֵיכֶם: וּשְׁמַרְתֶּם אֵת מִשְׁמֶרֶת הַקֹּדֶשׁ וְאֵת מִשְׁמֶרֶת הַמִּזְבֵּחַ וְלֹא־יִהְיֶה עוֹד
ו קֶצֶף עַל־בְּנֵי יִשְׂרָאֵל: וַאֲנִי הִנֵּה לָקַחְתִּי אֶת־אֲחֵיכֶם הַלְוִיִּם מִתּוֹךְ בְּנֵי יִשְׂרָאֵל
ז לָכֶם מַתָּנָה נְתֻנִים לַיהוָה לַעֲבֹד אֶת־עֲבֹדַת אֹהֶל מוֹעֵד: וְאַתָּה וּבָנֶיךָ אִתְּךָ
תִּשְׁמְרוּ אֶת־כְּהֻנַּתְכֶם לְכָל־דְּבַר הַמִּזְבֵּחַ וּלְמִבֵּית לַפָּרֹכֶת וַעֲבַדְתֶּם עֲבֹדַת
מַתָּנָה אֶתֵּן אֶת־כְּהֻנַּתְכֶם וְהַזָּר הַקָּרֵב יוּמָת:
ח וַיְדַבֵּר יְהוָה אֶל־אַהֲרֹן וַאֲנִי הִנֵּה נָתַתִּי לְךָ אֶת־מִשְׁמֶרֶת תְּרוּמֹתָי לְכָל־קָדְשֵׁי

רש"י

מִפְעָל יָחִיד לִנְקֵבָה כְּמוֹ מורמורדי"ן בְּלַעַז: לְמִשְׁמֶרֶת לְאוֹת. לְזִכָּרוֹן שֶׁבָּחַרְתִּי בְּאַהֲרֹן לְכֹהֵן, וְלֹא יַלִּינוּ עוֹד עַל הַכְּהֻנָּה:

כח| כֹּל הַקָּרֵב הַקָּרֵב וגו'. אֵין אָנוּ יְכוֹלִין לִהְיוֹת זְהִירִין בְּכָךְ, כֻּלָּנוּ רַשָּׁאִין לְהִכָּנֵס לַחֲצַר אֹהֶל מוֹעֵד, וְאֶחָד שֶׁיַּקְרִיב עַצְמוֹ יוֹתֵר מֵחֲבֵרָיו וְיִכָּנֵס לְתוֹךְ אֹהֶל מוֹעֵד יָמוּת: הַאִם תַּמְנוּ לִגְוֹעַ. שֶׁמָּא הֻפְקַרְנוּ לְמִיתָה?!:

פרק יח

א| וַיֹּאמֶר ה' אֶל אַהֲרֹן. לְמֹשֶׁה אָמַר שֶׁיֹּאמַר לְאַהֲרֹן, לְהַזְהִירוֹ עַל תַּקָּנַת יִשְׂרָאֵל שֶׁלֹּא יִכָּנְסוּ לַמִּקְדָּשׁ: אַתָּה וּבָנֶיךָ וּבֵית אָבִיךָ. הֵם בְּנֵי קְהָת אֲבִי עַמְרָם: תִּשְׂאוּ אֶת עֲוֹן הַמִּקְדָּשׁ. עֲלֵיכֶם אֲנִי מַטִּיל עֹנֶשׁ הַזָּרִים שֶׁיֶּחֶטְאוּ בְּעִסְקֵי הַדְּבָרִים הַמְקֻדָּשִׁים הַמְּסוּרִים לָכֶם, הוּא הָאֹהֶל וְהָאָרוֹן וְהַשֻּׁלְחָן וּכְלֵי הַקֹּדֶשׁ, אַתֶּם תֵּשְׁבוּ וְתַזְהִירוּ עַל כָּל זָר הַבָּא לִגַּע: וְאַתָּה וּבָנֶיךָ. הַכֹּהֲנִים: תִּשְׂאוּ אֶת עֲוֹן כְּהֻנַּתְכֶם. שֶׁאֵינָהּ מְסוּרָה לַלְוִיִּם, וְתַזְהִירוּ הַלְוִיִּם הַשּׁוֹגְגִים שֶׁלֹּא יִגְּעוּ אֲלֵיכֶם בַּעֲבוֹדַתְכֶם:

ב| וְגַם אֶת אַחֶיךָ. בְּנֵי גֵרְשׁוֹן וּבְנֵי מְרָרִי: וְיִלָּווּ. וְיִתְחַבְּרוּ אֲלֵיכֶם, לְהַזְהִיר גַּם אֶת הַזָּרִים מִלִּקְרַב אֲלֵיהֶם: וִישָׁרְתוּךָ. בִּשְׁמִירַת הַשְּׁעָרִים וּלְמַנּוֹת מֵהֶם גִּזְבָּרִין וַאֲמַרְכָּלִין:

ד| וְזָר לֹא יִקְרַב אֲלֵיכֶם. אֶתְכֶם אֲנִי מַזְהִיר עַל כָּךְ:

ה| וְלֹא יִהְיֶה עוֹד קֶצֶף. כְּמוֹ שֶׁהָיָה כְּבָר, שֶׁנֶּאֱמַר: "כִּי יָצָא הַקֶּצֶף" (לעיל יז, יא):

ו| לָכֶם מַתָּנָה נְתֻנִים. יָכוֹל לַעֲבוֹדַתְכֶם שֶׁל הֶדְיוֹט? תַּלְמוּד לוֹמַר: "לַה'", כְּמוֹ שֶׁמְּפֹרָשׁ לְמַעְלָה, לִשְׁמֹר מִשְׁמֶרֶת גִּזְבָּרִין וַאֲמַרְכָּלִין:

ז| עֲבֹדַת מַתָּנָה. בְּמַתָּנָה נְתַתִּיהָ לָכֶם:

ח| וַאֲנִי הִנֵּה נָתַתִּי לְךָ. בְּשִׂמְחָה. לְשׁוֹן שִׂמְחָה הוּא זֶה, כְּמוֹ: "הִנֵּה הוּא יֹצֵא לִקְרָאתֶךָ וְרָאֲךָ וְשָׂמַח בְּלִבּוֹ" (שמות ד, יד). מָשָׁל לְמֶלֶךְ שֶׁנָּתַן שָׂדֶה לְאוֹהֲבוֹ וְלֹא כָתַב וְלֹא חָתַם וְלֹא הֶעֱלָה בָּעֲרְכָּאִין. בָּא אֶחָד וְעִרְעֵר עַל הַשָּׂדֶה, אָמַר לוֹ הַמֶּלֶךְ: כָּל מִי שֶׁיִּרְצֶה יָבֹא וִיעַרְעֵר לְנֶגְדְּךָ, הֲרֵינִי כוֹתֵב וְחוֹתֵם לְךָ וּמַעֲלֶה בָּעֲרְכָּאִין. אַף כָּאן, לְפִי שֶׁבָּא קֹרַח וְעִרְעֵר כְּנֶגֶד אַהֲרֹן עַל הַכְּהֻנָּה, בָּא הַכָּתוּב וְנָתַן לוֹ עֶשְׂרִים וְאַרְבַּע מַתְּנוֹת כְּהֻנָּה בִּבְרִית מֶלַח עוֹלָם, וּלְכָךְ נִסְמְכָה פָּרָשָׁה זוֹ לְכָאן: מִשְׁמֶרֶת תְּרוּמֹתָי. שֶׁאַתָּה צָרִיךְ לְשָׁמְרָן בְּטָהֳרָה:

items of the children of Israel I have given them to you for prominence, as a mark of greatness,[18] and to your sons, as an eternal allotment.

9 The Torah provides a list of the gifts of the priesthood: **This shall be for you from the sacred sacraments, from the fire, the offerings of the most sacred order that are burnt upon the altar: Every offering of theirs, every meal offering of theirs, every sin offering of theirs, and every guilt offering of theirs that they shall return to Me; it is a sacred sacrament for you and for your sons.** Only the priests are entitled to these gifts.

10 **In the sacred sanctum shall you eat it,**[D] in the courtyard, which is the designated place for the consumption of offerings of the most sacred order: meal offerings, sin offerings, and guilt offerings.[19] **Every male may eat it;**[D] **it shall be sacred to you.**

11 **This is yours: The separation of their gift, for all the wave offerings of the children of Israel,** the specific portions of peace offerings that are set aside and waved,[20] **I have given them to you, and to your sons and to your daughters with you, as an eternal allotment; all pure in your household may eat it,** in accordance with the law of offerings of lesser sanctity, which may be eaten by all ritually pure members of a priest's household.

12 **All the best of the oil, and all the best of the wine and of the grain, the first of them that they will give to the Lord,** which is the portion that the children of Israel separate for God,[21] in practice **to you,** the priests and their families, **have I given them.**[D]

13 **The first fruits of all that is in their land that they bring to the Lord,** to the Temple, **shall be yours; all pure in your household may eat it.** This includes slaves, who are referred to as an "acquisition of his silver," who are permitted to partake of the meat of offerings permitted to the priests, the portion of produce allotted to the priest, or *teruma*, and first fruits, if the slaves are ritually pure.[22] In certain cases, when *teruma* is unfit for human consumption, it may even be given to animals.[23]

14 **Everything proscribed in Israel,** movable property and real estate that were consecrated, but not for the Temple maintenance, **shall be yours.**

15 **Every first issue of the womb of all flesh, which they offer to the Lord, of man and of animal, shall be yours; however, the firstborn of man you shall redeem,** by means of money that is given to you, **and the firstborn of the impure animal you shall redeem.** Since you may not eat this animal, you shall receive its value instead. It is clarified elsewhere that the impure animal mentioned here is a donkey, which is redeemed with a lamb given to a priest.[24]

16 **Its redeemed, of a woman's firstborn son, from one month old shall you redeem,**[D] **with a value of five shekels of silver in the sacred shekel; it is twenty gera.** The *gera* is the smallest unit of weight for silver, which is referred to as a *ma'a* by the Sages. The sacred shekel is twice the value of a regular shekel, which is worth ten *gera*.[25]

17 **However, the firstborn of an ox, or the firstborn of a sheep, or the firstborn of a goat, you shall not redeem, they** themselves **are sacred. You shall sprinkle their blood on the altar, and you shall burn their fat as a fire offering for a pleasing aroma to the Lord,** as these portions are not eaten.

18 In contrast to the blood and fat, **their meat,** of the firstborn kosher animals, **shall be for you, like the breast of the waving and like the right haunch** of peace offerings, which are eaten by priests and the members of their household in a state of ritual purity. The same applies to the meat of firstborn animals; **it shall be yours.**

19 The Torah once again summarizes: **All the gifts of the consecrated items that the children of Israel separate for the Lord,** those stated explicitly here, as well as other gifts alluded to in these verses, and those mentioned elsewhere, **I have given you, and your sons and your daughters with you,**

DISCUSSION

18:10 | In the sacred sanctum shall you eat it: Some suggest that this phrase is not referring to the location where these offerings are to be consumed, but rather to the state of being in which the priests are to consume them. Accordingly, the verse states: In accordance with the guidelines of the most sacred order of offerings shall you eat it (see Ramban; Rabbi Samson Raphael Hirsch).

Every male may eat it: The Sages derive from here that even male priests who are not permitted to perform the sacred service in practice, such as those who are blemished, are nevertheless entitled to partake of consecrated foods (see *Zevaḥim* 102a).

18:12 | To you have I given them: A minimum amount of the portion of produce allotted to

the priest, known as *teruma*, and dough allotted to the priest, known as *ḥalla* (see 15:20) are set aside even nowadays. However, they are not given to the priests but are burnt. This is because priests too are prohibited to eat these portions, as they do not currently observe the laws of ritual purity.

ט בְּנֵי־יִשְׂרָאֵל לְךָ נְתַתִּים לְמָשְׁחָה וּלְבָנֶיךָ לְחָק־עוֹלָם: זֶה יִהְיֶה לְךָ מִקֹּדֶשׁ
הַקֳּדָשִׁים מִן־הָאֵשׁ כָּל־קָרְבָּנָם לְכָל־מִנְחָתָם וּלְכָל־חַטָּאתָם וּלְכָל־אֲשָׁמָם
י אֲשֶׁר יָשִׁיבוּ לִי קֹדֶשׁ קָדָשִׁים לְךָ הוּא וּלְבָנֶיךָ: בְּקֹדֶשׁ הַקֳּדָשִׁים תֹּאכְלֶנּוּ כָּל־
יא זָכָר יֹאכַל אֹתוֹ קֹדֶשׁ יִהְיֶה־לָּךְ: וְזֶה־לְּךָ תְּרוּמַת מַתָּנָם לְכָל־תְּנוּפֹת בְּנֵי יִשְׂרָאֵל
לְךָ נְתַתִּים וּלְבָנֶיךָ וְלִבְנֹתֶיךָ אִתְּךָ לְחָק־עוֹלָם כָּל־טָהוֹר בְּבֵיתְךָ יֹאכַל אֹתוֹ:
יב כֹּל חֵלֶב יִצְהָר וְכָל־חֵלֶב תִּירוֹשׁ וְדָגָן רֵאשִׁיתָם אֲשֶׁר־יִתְּנוּ לַיהוָה לְךָ נְתַתִּים:
יג בִּכּוּרֵי כָּל־אֲשֶׁר בְּאַרְצָם אֲשֶׁר־יָבִיאוּ לַיהוָה לְךָ יִהְיֶה כָּל־טָהוֹר בְּבֵיתְךָ יֹאכְלֶנּוּ:
יד טו כָּל־חֵרֶם בְּיִשְׂרָאֵל לְךָ יִהְיֶה: כָּל־פֶּטֶר רֶחֶם לְכָל־בָּשָׂר אֲשֶׁר־יַקְרִיבוּ לַיהוָה
בָּאָדָם וּבַבְּהֵמָה יִהְיֶה־לָּךְ אַךְ ׀ פָּדֹה תִפְדֶּה אֵת בְּכוֹר הָאָדָם וְאֵת בְּכוֹר־הַבְּהֵמָה
טז הַטְּמֵאָה תִּפְדֶּה: וּפְדוּיָו מִבֶּן־חֹדֶשׁ תִּפְדֶּה בְּעֶרְכְּךָ כֶּסֶף חֲמֵשֶׁת שְׁקָלִים בְּשֶׁקֶל
יז הַקֹּדֶשׁ עֶשְׂרִים גֵּרָה הוּא: אַךְ בְּכוֹר־שׁוֹר אוֹ־בְכוֹר כֶּשֶׂב אוֹ־בְכוֹר עֵז לֹא תִפְדֶּה
קֹדֶשׁ הֵם אֶת־דָּמָם תִּזְרֹק עַל־הַמִּזְבֵּחַ וְאֶת־חֶלְבָּם תַּקְטִיר אִשֶּׁה לְרֵיחַ נִיחֹחַ
יח יט לַיהוָה: וּבְשָׂרָם יִהְיֶה־לָּךְ כַּחֲזֵה הַתְּנוּפָה וּכְשׁוֹק הַיָּמִין לְךָ יִהְיֶה: כֹּל ׀ תְּרוּמֹת
הַקֳּדָשִׁים אֲשֶׁר יָרִימוּ בְנֵי־יִשְׂרָאֵל לַיהוָה נָתַתִּי לְךָ וּלְבָנֶיךָ וְלִבְנֹתֶיךָ אִתְּךָ

רש״י

לְמָשְׁחָה. לִגְדֻלָּה:

ט | מִן הָאֵשׁ. לְאַחַר הַקְטָרַת הָאִשִּׁים: כָּל קָרְבָּנָם. כְּגוֹן זִבְחֵי שַׁלְמֵי צִבּוּר: מִנְחָתָם חַטָּאתָם וַאֲשָׁמָם. כְּמַשְׁמָעוֹ: אֲשֶׁר יָשִׁיבוּ לִי. זֶה גֶּזֶל הַגֵּר:

י | בְּקֹדֶשׁ הַקֳּדָשִׁים תֹּאכְלֶנּוּ וְגוֹ׳. לִמֵּד עַל קָדְשֵׁי קָדָשִׁים שֶׁאֵין נֶאֱכָלִין אֶלָּא בָּעֲזָרָה וּלְזִכְרֵי כְהֻנָּה:

יא | תְּרוּמַת מַתָּנָם. הַמּוּרָם מִן הַתּוֹדָה וּמֵהַשְּׁלָמִים וּמֵאֵיל נָזִיר: לְכָל תְּנוּפֹת. שֶׁהֲרֵי אֵלּוּ טְעוּנִין תְּנוּפָה: כָּל טָהוֹר. וְלֹא טְמֵאִים. דָּבָר אַחֵר, "כָּל טָהוֹר" לְרַבּוֹת אִשְׁתּוֹ:

יב | רֵאשִׁיתָם. הִיא תְּרוּמָה גְּדוֹלָה:

יח | כַּחֲזֵה הַתְּנוּפָה וּכְשׁוֹק הַיָּמִין. שֶׁל שְׁלָמִים, שֶׁנֶּאֱכָלִים לַכֹּהֲנִים וְלִנְשֵׁיהֶם לִבְנֵיהֶם וּלְעַבְדֵיהֶם לִשְׁנֵי יָמִים וְלַיְלָה אֶחָד, אַף הַבְּכוֹר נֶאֱכָל לִשְׁנֵי יָמִים וְלַיְלָה אֶחָד: לְךָ יִהְיֶה. בָּא רַבִּי עֲקִיבָא וְלִמֵּד: הוֹסִיף לְךָ הַכָּתוּב הֲוָיָה אַחֶרֶת, שֶׁלֹּא תֹּאמַר, כֶּחָזֶה וָשׁוֹק שֶׁל תּוֹדָה שֶׁאֵינוֹ נֶאֱכָל אֶלָּא לְיוֹם וָלַיְלָה:

יט | כֹּל תְּרוּמֹת הַקֳּדָשִׁים. מֵחִבָּתָהּ שֶׁל פָּרָשָׁה זוֹ, כְּלָלָהּ בַּתְּחִלָּה וּכְלָלָהּ בַּסּוֹף וּפֵרַט בָּאֶמְצַע:

DISCUSSION

18:16| **Shall you redeem:** The redemption of the firstborn son with the equivalent of five sacred shekel, and the redemption of a firstborn donkey by means of a lamb given to a priest, are practiced to this day, since Jews remain obligated to redeem their firstborns. However, as priests have no definitive proof of their priestly lineage, this commandment cannot be fulfilled in the ideal manner.

With regard to the firstborn of a kosher animal, it automatically has the sanctity of an offering but it cannot be sacrificed nowadays. Therefore, the common practice is to prevent the animal from becoming holy in the first place, by selling part of the mother's body to a gentile, as in such a situation the animal does not become consecrated. This aids in avoiding a situation where an animal is sacred but cannot be brought to the Temple, and may not be put to work or eaten either (see *Bekhorot* 13a).

as an eternal allotment; it is an everlasting covenant[26] **of salt**[D] **before the Lord to you and to your descendants with you.** The Sages list twenty-four gifts of the priesthood.[27]

20 **The Lord said to Aaron:** On the one hand, you and your descendants will receive gifts from the rest of the children of Israel; on the other hand, **you shall not inherit in their land, and you shall not have a portion** of land **in their midst; I am your portion and your inheritance among the children of Israel.**

21 **To the children of Levi,** who also serve in the Temple, **behold,**
Seventh aliya **I have given all the tithe,**[D] a tenth of all produce, **in Israel as an inheritance, in exchange for their service that they perform, the service of the Tent of Meeting.**

22 **The children of Israel shall not approach the Tent of Meeting anymore, to bear sin, to die.** The Levites will care for the Temple maintenance, through their singing and the assistance they provide to the priests, and they must also prevent the Israelites from performing these functions and from approaching the Sanctuary.

23 **The Levite himself shall perform the service of the Tent of Meeting, and they,** the Levites, **shall bear their iniquity;** they are responsible for the sins that might result from their service. **It shall be an eternal statute for your generations, and among the children of Israel, they,** the entire tribe of Levi, **shall not inherit an inheritance** in the land of Israel.

24 **For the tithe of the children of Israel that they will separate to the Lord as a gift, I have given to the Levites as an inheritance; therefore, I said to them: In the midst of the children of Israel they shall not inherit an inheritance.**

25 **The Lord spoke to Moses, saying:**

26 **To the Levites you shall speak, and say to them: When you take from the children of Israel the tithe that I have given you from them for your inheritance, you shall separate from it a gift to the Lord.** From the tithe that you receive from the Israelites, you must set aside **a tithe from the tithe.**

27 After you have separated a tithe from the tithe that you received from an Israelite, then **your gift** to the priest **shall be considered for you like the grain from the threshing floor, and like the fill**[28] **of the winepress,** like the produce that grows in one's property, from which *teruma*, the portion of produce allotted to the priest, is set aside and given to the priest.[29]

Threshing floor

Winepress

DISCUSSION

18:19| **An everlasting covenant of salt:** Salt is a symbol of eternity because it withstands changing conditions. Furthermore, one of the rites of enacting a covenant was to divide bread and salt between the parties (see commentary on Leviticus 2:13).

The Gifts of the Priesthood That Are Explicitly Stated in the Torah

Consecrated food that must be eaten in the Temple courtyard (offerings of the most sacred order)	The meat of sin offerings, guilt offerings, and communal peace offerings; the surplus of the *omer*; the remainders of meal offerings of Israelites; the two loaves; the showbread; the leper's *log* of oil
Gifts from the Temple that are not eaten	Hides of consecrated animals
Consecrated food that must be eaten in Jerusalem (offerings of lesser sanctity)	The breast and thigh of peace offerings brought by an individual; the portions separated from the loaves of the thanks offering and the Nazirite's ram; the firstborn of a kosher animal; first fruits
Gifts in the Land of Israel that have sanctity	*Teruma*; tithe of the tithe; *ḥalla*, the portion of the dough given to the priests
Gifts in the Land of Israel that do not have sanctity	The first shearing of wool; an ancestral field
Gifts that apply in all places	The right foreleg, the cheeks, and the maw of non-sacred meat; the redemption of the firstborn son and the redemption of the firstborn donkey; payment for that which was stolen from a convert who died without heirs; a dedicated field

כ לְחָק־עוֹלָם בְּרִית מֶלַח עוֹלָם הִוא לִפְנֵי יְהוָה לְךָ וּלְזַרְעֲךָ אִתָּךְ: וַיֹּאמֶר יְהוָה אֶל־
אַהֲרֹן בְּאַרְצָם לֹא תִנְחָל וְחֵלֶק לֹא־יִהְיֶה לְךָ בְּתוֹכָם אֲנִי חֶלְקְךָ וְנַחֲלָתְךָ בְּתוֹךְ
כא בְּנֵי יִשְׂרָאֵל: וְלִבְנֵי לֵוִי הִנֵּה נָתַתִּי כָּל־מַעֲשֵׂר בְּיִשְׂרָאֵל לְנַחֲלָה חֵלֶף שביעי
כב עֲבֹדָתָם אֲשֶׁר־הֵם עֹבְדִים אֶת־עֲבֹדַת אֹהֶל מוֹעֵד: וְלֹא־יִקְרְבוּ עוֹד בְּנֵי יִשְׂרָאֵל
כג אֶל־אֹהֶל מוֹעֵד לָשֵׂאת חֵטְא לָמוּת: וְעָבַד הַלֵּוִי הוּא אֶת־עֲבֹדַת אֹהֶל מוֹעֵד
כד וְהֵם יִשְׂאוּ עֲוֺנָם חֻקַּת עוֹלָם לְדֹרֹתֵיכֶם וּבְתוֹךְ בְּנֵי יִשְׂרָאֵל לֹא יִנְחֲלוּ נַחֲלָה: כִּי
אֶת־מַעְשַׂר בְּנֵי־יִשְׂרָאֵל אֲשֶׁר יָרִימוּ לַיהוָה תְּרוּמָה נָתַתִּי לַלְוִיִּם לְנַחֲלָה עַל־כֵּן
אָמַרְתִּי לָהֶם בְּתוֹךְ בְּנֵי יִשְׂרָאֵל לֹא יִנְחֲלוּ נַחֲלָה:
כה וַיְדַבֵּר יְהוָה אֶל־מֹשֶׁה לֵּאמֹר: וְאֶל־הַלְוִיִּם תְּדַבֵּר וְאָמַרְתָּ אֲלֵהֶם כִּי־תִקְחוּ יז
כו מֵאֵת בְּנֵי־יִשְׂרָאֵל אֶת־הַמַּעֲשֵׂר אֲשֶׁר נָתַתִּי לָכֶם מֵאִתָּם בְּנַחֲלַתְכֶם וַהֲרֵמֹתֶם
כז מִמֶּנּוּ תְּרוּמַת יְהוָה מַעֲשֵׂר מִן־הַמַּעֲשֵׂר: וְנֶחְשַׁב לָכֶם תְּרוּמַתְכֶם כַּדָּגָן מִן־הַגֹּרֶן

רש״י

בְּרִית מֶלַח עוֹלָם. כָּרַת בְּרִית עִם אַהֲרֹן בְּדָבָר הַבָּרִיא וּמִתְקַיֵּם וּמַבְרִיא אֶת אֲחֵרִים: בְּרִית מֶלַח. כִּבְרִית הַכְּרוּתָה לַמֶּלַח, שֶׁאֵינוֹ מַסְרִיחַ לְעוֹלָם:

כ | וְחֵלֶק לֹא יִהְיֶה לְךָ בְּתוֹכָם. אַף בַּבִּזָּה:

כג | וְהֵם. הַלְוִיִּם, ״יִשְׂאוּ עֲוֹנָם״ שֶׁל יִשְׂרָאֵל, שֶׁעֲלֵיהֶם לְהַזְהִיר הַזָּרִים מִגֶּשֶׁת אֲלֵיהֶם:

כד | אֲשֶׁר יָרִימוּ לַה׳ תְּרוּמָה. הַכָּתוּב קְרָאוֹ ׳תְּרוּמָה׳ עַד שֶׁיַּפְרִישׁ מִמֶּנּוּ תְּרוּמַת מַעֲשֵׂר:

כז | וְנֶחְשַׁב לָכֶם תְּרוּמַתְכֶם כַּדָּגָן מִן הַגֹּרֶן. תְּרוּמַת מַעֲשֵׂר שֶׁלָּכֶם אֲסוּרָה לְזָרִים וְלִטְמֵאִים, וְחַיָּבִין עָלֶיהָ מִיתָה וְחֹמֶשׁ, כִּתְרוּמָה גְּדוֹלָה שֶׁנִּקְרֵאת רֵאשִׁית דָּגָן מִן הַגֹּרֶן:

DISCUSSION

18:21 | To the children of Levi, behold, I have given all the tithe: This tithe, which becomes the property of the Levite to whom it is given, has no inherent sanctity, and there are no special preconditions for its consumption (see verse 31). Since nowadays the Levites cannot prove their lineage, Israelites are not obligated by the letter of the law to give them their tithes. Nevertheless, there are some that still give the tithe today to those who have the presumptive status of Levites. Either way, the tithe must be separated and designated as such, by saying, with regard to a tenth of one's produce: This is the tithe. The separation of the tithe and its delivery to a Levite are two independent stages; even when one does not fulfill the commandment to give the tithe to a Levite, the commandment to set it aside must be performed.

28 **So you too shall separate the gift of the Lord from all your tithes**[D] **that you receive from the children of Israel; you shall give from it the gift of the Lord to Aaron the priest,** meaning to one of the priests. The tithe that the Levites receive from the Israelites is their sustenance. Just as the children of Israel give *teruma* to a priest from their produce, so too the Levites must give *teruma* to a priest from the portion they receive.

29 **From all your gifts** that you receive from the children of Israel **you shall separate all the gifts of the Lord,**[D] **of all its finest** portions, you must give to the priest **its sacred part from it.**

30 **You shall say to them: When you separate its finest,** the tithe
Maftir of the tithe for the priests, **from it,** the other nine-tenths of the tithe, **it shall be considered for the Levites like the produce of the threshing floor, and like the produce of the winepress.** The remainder of the tithe has the status of nonsacred produce.

31 **You may eat it,** the tithe, **in any place, you and your households, for it is your wage in exchange for your service in the Tent of Meeting.**

32 **You shall not bear sin on its account when you separate its finest from it.** You must give the choicest part of the produce received from an Israelite to the priest. It is derived from here that one may not set aside poor-quality produce for the priest. **The sacred items of the children of Israel you shall not profane,**[D] **and you will not die.** By separating the tithe of the tithe for the priest, the Levite prevents the profanation of the sacred gifts of the Israelites that were given to him.[30]

DISCUSSION

18:28 | **So you too shall separate the gift of the Lord from all your tithes:** This obligation of the tithe of the tithe, which is one-hundredth of the entire crop, given by the Levites to the priests, remains in effect nowadays. Although this commandment was given to the Levites, it has ramifications for all, as the tithe of the tithe possesses sanctity and may be eaten only in a state of ritual purity. Since today the Levites are not entitled to their tithe by law, Israelites are obligated to separate a tithe of the tithe in their stead, which they must treat in the manner of the regular *teruma*.

18:29 | **From all your gifts you shall separate all the gifts of the Lord:** The Sages derive the following law from the expansive phrase, "you shall separate all the gifts of the Lord": If a Levite received a tithe from produce which had already been subject to the obligation of *teruma*, but for whatever reason its Israelite owner had neglected to separate and give it to a priest, the Levite is obligated to set aside *teruma* that had not been separated, in addition to the tithe of the tithe (see *Beitza* 13b).

18:32 | **The sacred items of the children of Israel you shall not profane:** The Sages derive another prohibition from here, that the various tithes must be given in accordance with the wishes of the owner of the produce. If a particular priest or Levite offers any sort of incentive or payment to an Israelite in order to be the recipient of his gifts, the priest or Levite has thereby profaned the sacred items of the children of Israel, and they receive a severe punishment (see *Bekhorot* 26b).

כח וְכַמְלֵאָה מִן־הַיָּקֶב׃ כֵּן תָּרִימוּ גַם־אַתֶּם תְּרוּמַת יְהוָה מִכֹּל מַעְשְׂרֹתֵיכֶם אֲשֶׁר
כט תִּקְחוּ מֵאֵת בְּנֵי יִשְׂרָאֵל וּנְתַתֶּם מִמֶּנּוּ אֶת־תְּרוּמַת יְהוָה לְאַהֲרֹן הַכֹּהֵן׃ מִכֹּל
ל מַתְּנֹתֵיכֶם תָּרִימוּ אֵת כָּל־תְּרוּמַת יְהוָה מִכָּל־חֶלְבּוֹ אֶת־מִקְדְּשׁוֹ מִמֶּנּוּ׃ וְאָמַרְתָּ מפטיר
אֲלֵהֶם בַּהֲרִימְכֶם אֶת־חֶלְבּוֹ מִמֶּנּוּ וְנֶחְשַׁב לַלְוִיִּם כִּתְבוּאַת גֹּרֶן וְכִתְבוּאַת יָקֶב׃
לא וַאֲכַלְתֶּם אֹתוֹ בְּכָל־מָקוֹם אַתֶּם וּבֵיתְכֶם כִּי־שָׂכָר הוּא לָכֶם חֵלֶף עֲבֹדַתְכֶם
לב בְּאֹהֶל מוֹעֵד׃ וְלֹא־תִשְׂאוּ עָלָיו חֵטְא בַּהֲרִימְכֶם אֶת־חֶלְבּוֹ מִמֶּנּוּ וְאֶת־קָדְשֵׁי
בְנֵי־יִשְׂרָאֵל לֹא תְחַלְּלוּ וְלֹא תָמוּתוּ׃

רש״י

וְכַמְלֵאָה מִן הַיָּקֶב. כִּתְרוּמַת תִּירוֹשׁ וְיִצְהָר הַנִּטֶּלֶת מִן הַיְקָבִים: מְלֵאָה. לְשׁוֹן בִּשּׁוּל תְּבוּאָה שֶׁנִּתְמַלֵּאת: יָקֶב. הוּא הַבּוֹר שֶׁלִּפְנֵי הַגַּת שֶׁהַיַּיִן יוֹרֵד לְתוֹכוֹ. וְכָל לְשׁוֹן ׳יֶקֶב׳ חֲפִירַת קַרְקַע הוּא, וְכֵן: ״יִקְבֵי הַמֶּלֶךְ״ (זכריה יד, י), הוּא יָם אוֹקְיָנוֹס, חֲפִירָה שֶׁחָפַר מַלְכּוֹ שֶׁל עוֹלָם:

כח| כֵּן תָּרִימוּ גַם אַתֶּם. כְּמוֹ שֶׁיִּשְׂרָאֵל מְרִימִים מִגָּרְנָם וּמִיִּקְבֵיהֶם תָּרִימוּ אַתֶּם מִמַּעֲשֵׂר שֶׁלָּכֶם, כִּי הוּא נַחֲלַתְכֶם:

כט| מִכֹּל מַתְּנֹתֵיכֶם תָּרִימוּ אֵת כָּל תְּרוּמַת ה׳. בִּתְרוּמָה גְּדוֹלָה הַכָּתוּב מְדַבֵּר, שֶׁאִם הִקְדִּים לֵוִי אֶת הַכֹּהֵן בַּכְּרִי וְקִבֵּל מַעַשְׂרוֹתָיו קֹדֶם שֶׁיִּטֹּל כֹּהֵן תְּרוּמָה גְּדוֹלָה מִן הַכְּרִי, צָרִיךְ לְהַפְרִישׁ הַלֵּוִי מִן הַמַּעֲשֵׂר תְּחִלָּה אֶחָד מֵחֲמִשִּׁים לִתְרוּמָה גְּדוֹלָה, וְיַחֲזֹר וְיַפְרִישׁ תְּרוּמַת מַעֲשֵׂר:

ל| בַּהֲרִימְכֶם אֶת חֶלְבּוֹ מִמֶּנּוּ. לְאַחַר שֶׁתָּרִימוּ תְּרוּמַת מַעֲשֵׂר מִמֶּנּוּ, ״וְנֶחְשַׁב״ הַמּוֹתָר ״לַלְוִיִּם״ חֻלִּין גְּמוּרִין, ״כִּתְבוּאַת גֹּרֶן״ לְיִשְׂרָאֵל. שֶׁלֹּא תֹּאמַר: הוֹאִיל וּקְרָאוֹ הַכָּתוּב ׳תְּרוּמָה׳, שֶׁנֶּאֱמַר: ״כִּי אֶת מַעְשַׂר בְּנֵי יִשְׂרָאֵל אֲשֶׁר יָרִימוּ לַה׳ תְּרוּמָה״ (לעיל פסוק כד), יָכוֹל יְהֵא כֻּלּוֹ אָסוּר? תַּלְמוּד לוֹמַר: ״וְנֶחְשַׁב לַלְוִיִּם כִּתְבוּאַת גֹּרֶן״, מַה שֶּׁל יִשְׂרָאֵל חֻלִּין, אַף שֶׁל לֵוִי חֻלִּין:

לא| בְּכָל מָקוֹם. אֲפִלּוּ בְּבֵית הַקְּבָרוֹת:

לב| וְלֹא תִשְׂאוּ עָלָיו חֵטְא וְגוֹ׳. הָא אִם לֹא תָרִימוּ, תִּשְׂאוּ חֵטְא: וְלֹא תָמוּתוּ. הָא אִם תְּחַלְּלוּ, תָּמוּתוּ:

Parashat
Hukat

The Red Heifer
NUMBERS 19:1–22

The laws of ritual impurity and purity are difficult to comprehend in general, but the statute of the red heifer is the most mysterious of them all. The red heifer is burned in an elaborate ritual, and its ashes are used to purify an individual who becomes impure through contact with a corpse, which is one of the most severe forms of impurity.

Besides the enigma of the very use of these ashes in the purification process, the process itself contains a paradox: The ritually impure individual is rendered pure through these ashes, while ritually pure individuals who participated in the purification process are rendered impure through it.

The statute of the red heifer belongs to the murky region between death and life, impurity and purity. The springwater in which the ashes of the red heifer are mingled act as a type of healing potion for the impurity associated with death, yet it impairs the status of the person who had no contact with death.

19 1 **The Lord spoke to Moses and to Aaron, saying:**
2 **This is the statute of the law**[D] **that the Lord had commanded, saying: Speak to the children of Israel, and they shall take to you an unflawed**[D] **red heifer,**[D] a heifer whose color is distinctly red and **in which there is no blemish, and upon which a yoke was not placed**[D] for any sort of work.
3 **You shall give it to Elazar the priest,**[D] **and he shall take it out of the camp,**[D] **and one shall slaughter** it **before him.** Since the heifer is not an offering, its rites are performed outside the Temple.
4 **Elazar the priest shall take from its blood with his finger, and sprinkle from its blood toward the front of the Tent of Meeting seven times.**

5 **One shall burn the heifer before his eyes: Its skin, its flesh, and its blood, with its dung, he shall burn.** The heifer must be burned in its entirety.
6 **The priest shall take cedarwood,**[B] **hyssop,**[B] **and a scarlet thread,**[B] as in the purification rite of a leper, **and** he shall **cast** these items **into the burning of the heifer.** Consequently, the ashes will be comprised of a combination of the heifer, the wood of the pyre, and these three items.
7 The individuals involved in this ritual are rendered impure: **The priest shall wash his garments, and he shall bathe,** immerse, **his flesh**[D] **in water, and then he may come to the camp. The priest shall be impure until the evening.**
8 **He who burns it shall** also **wash his garments in water, and**

DISCUSSION

19:2 | This is the statute of the law: A statute is a decree or command whose rationale cannot be explained. There have been numerous attempts throughout the generations to solve the mystery of the red heifer, but none have achieved complete success. In the words of the Sages: The Holy One, blessed be He, said: I legislated a statute, I enacted a decree, and you may not transgress it (*Bemidbar Rabba* 19:1).

Unflawed: The plain meaning of the verse is that the term "unflawed" is elaborated upon by the phrase "in which there is no blemish." However, this would appear to be a redundancy. The Sages therefore understand that the term "unflawed" is a description of the heifer's color: The heifer must be completely red (*Sifrei*; Rashi; see Ibn Ezra; Abravanel).

Red heifer: It is difficult to know what exactly the Torah considers red. Strains of cows that are brown tending toward red, while rare, can be found in various locations around the world.

The ritual described in this passage was performed until near the end of the Second Temple period. However, valid red heifers were exceedingly scarce; as such, they were extremely valuable (see *Kiddushin* 31a). Likewise, the rite of slaughtering and burning a red heifer was an incredibly rare occurrence (see Mishna *Para* 3:5). The ashes of the red heifer would be preserved and used for many years, and was apparently in use until the early generations of the Sages of the Talmud. An entire tractate of the Mishna and the *Tosefta*, tractate *Para*, is devoted to the details of the laws of the red heifer.

Upon which a yoke was not placed: The verse refers to a heifer and not a calf, meaning that the

animal is at least one or two years old. Therefore, it would have been necessary to ensure that the animal was not used for plowing. Accordingly, if an animal was considered potentially suitable for this special rite, they would guard it and ensure that no yoke was ever placed upon it.

19:3 | You shall give it to Elazar the priest: Although this red heifer was given specifically to Elazar, who was the deputy High Priest, this is not a general requirement (see *Yoma* 42b). In fact, apart from this instance and perhaps on a few other occasions, the rites of the red heifer were performed by the High Priest himself. Tractate *Para* provides a list of High Priests in whose days the rites of the red heifer were performed (Mishna *Para* 3:5).

Out of the camp: When the rite of the red heifer was performed in Jerusalem, the animal was ◄◄

פרשת
חקת

אב וַיְדַבֵּר יְהוָֹה אֶל־מֹשֶׁה וְאֶל־אַהֲרֹן לֵאמֹר: זֹאת חֻקַּת הַתּוֹרָה אֲשֶׁר־צִוָּה יְהוָֹה לֵאמֹר דַּבֵּר ׀ אֶל־בְּנֵי יִשְׂרָאֵל וְיִקְחוּ אֵלֶיךָ פָרָה אֲדֻמָּה תְּמִימָה אֲשֶׁר אֵין־בָּהּ

ג מוּם אֲשֶׁר לֹא־עָלָה עָלֶיהָ עֹל: וּנְתַתֶּם אֹתָהּ אֶל־אֶלְעָזָר הַכֹּהֵן וְהוֹצִיא אֹתָהּ

ד אֶל־מִחוּץ לַמַּחֲנֶה וְשָׁחַט אֹתָהּ לְפָנָיו: וְלָקַח אֶלְעָזָר הַכֹּהֵן מִדָּמָהּ בְּאֶצְבָּעוֹ וְהִזָּה

ה אֶל־נֹכַח פְּנֵי אֹהֶל־מוֹעֵד מִדָּמָהּ שֶׁבַע פְּעָמִים: וְשָׂרַף אֶת־הַפָּרָה לְעֵינָיו אֶת־

ו עֹרָהּ וְאֶת־בְּשָׂרָהּ וְאֶת־דָּמָהּ עַל־פִּרְשָׁהּ יִשְׂרֹף: וְלָקַח הַכֹּהֵן עֵץ אֶרֶז וְאֵזוֹב וּשְׁנִי

ז תוֹלָעַת וְהִשְׁלִיךְ אֶל־תּוֹךְ שְׂרֵפַת הַפָּרָה: וְכִבֶּס בְּגָדָיו הַכֹּהֵן וְרָחַץ בְּשָׂרוֹ בַּמַּיִם

ח וְאַחַר יָבֹא אֶל־הַמַּחֲנֶה וְטָמֵא הַכֹּהֵן עַד־הָעָרֶב: וְהַשֹּׂרֵף אֹתָהּ יְכַבֵּס בְּגָדָיו בַּמַּיִם

פרק יט

ב | **זֹאת חֻקַּת הַתּוֹרָה.** לְפִי שֶׁהַשָּׂטָן וְאֻמּוֹת הָעוֹלָם מוֹנִין אֶת יִשְׂרָאֵל, לוֹמַר: מָה הַמִּצְוָה הַזֹּאת וּמַה טַעַם יֵשׁ בָּהּ? לְפִיכָךְ כָּתַב בָּהּ 'חֻקָּה' – גְּזֵרָה הִיא מִלְּפָנַי, אֵין לְךָ רְשׁוּת לְהַרְהֵר אַחֲרֶיהָ: וְיִקְחוּ אֵלֶיךָ. לְעוֹלָם הִיא נִקְרֵאת עַל שִׁמְךָ, פָּרָה שֶׁעָשָׂה מֹשֶׁה בַּמִּדְבָּר: אֲדֻמָּה תְּמִימָה.

שֶׁתְּהֵא תְמִימָה בְּאַדְמִימוּת, שֶׁאִם הָיוּ בָהּ שְׁתֵּי שְׂעָרוֹת שְׁחוֹרוֹת פְּסוּלָה:

ג | **אֶלְעָזָר.** מִצְוָתָהּ בַּסְּגָן: אֶל מִחוּץ לַמַּחֲנֶה. חוּץ לְשָׁלֹשׁ מַחֲנוֹת: וְשָׁחַט אֹתָהּ לְפָנָיו. זָר שׁוֹחֵט וְאֶלְעָזָר רוֹאֶה:

ד | **אֶל נֹכַח פְּנֵי אֹהֶל מוֹעֵד.** עוֹמֵד בְּמִזְרָחוֹ שֶׁל יְרוּשָׁלַיִם וּמִתְכַּוֵּן וְרוֹאֶה פִתְחוֹ שֶׁל הֵיכָל בִּשְׁעַת הַזָּאַת הַדָּם:

ז | **אֶל הַמַּחֲנֶה.** לְמַחֲנֵה שְׁכִינָה, שֶׁאֵין טָמֵא מְשֻׁלָּח חוּץ לִשְׁתֵּי מַחֲנוֹת אֶלָּא זָב וּבַעַל קֶרִי וּמְצֹרָע: וְטָמֵא הַכֹּהֵן עַד הָעָרֶב. סָרְסֵהוּ וְדָרְשֵׁהוּ: וְטָמֵא עַד הָעֶרֶב וְאַחַר יָבֹא אֶל הַמַּחֲנֶה:

BACKGROUND

19:6 | Cedarwood: The Lebanon cedar, *Cedrus libani*, from the family Pinaceae, is a coniferous tree that is impressive in both height and beauty. It can grow to a height of almost 50 m, while its trunk can reach 2–3 m in diameter. It is found in cold, elevated locations, mainly in Lebanon. Due to its strength, and its straight, tall branches, cedarwood has been used throughout history for building, especially for public structures and palaces. It also serves as a symbol of strength and fortitude.

Hyssop [ezov]: The *ezov* is generally identified with the common hyssop plant, *Majorana syriaca*. The hyssop is a flowering plant from the mint family, Lamiaceae, that can grow up to a height of 1 m. It grows in rocky terrain throughout the Middle East and is considered to have healing properties. The hyssop is also a central ingredient of za'atar, a

Mediterranean condiment. The *ezov* is used in the purification rites of lepers, and is also regarded as a symbol of lowliness (I Kings 5:13).

Scarlet thread: Scarlet dye was extracted from scale insects by drying, grinding, and then cooking them. It was commonly used to dye wool and expensive fabrics, and scarlet threads were also used in the purification of lepers (Leviticus 14:4–6). In a description of the Temple appearing in II Chronicles (2:6–13), scarlet is referred to as *karmil*, which is the name of the insect from which the dye was extracted (see Rav Se'adya Gaon; Rashi; Radak). Researchers today identify this as the *Kermes echinatus*, an insect that feeds on the sap of evergreen trees. This identification fits with a description found in the Midrash (*Pesikta Rabbati* 20).

DISCUSSION

burned on the Mount of Olives, referred to in the Mishna as the Mount of Anointing (Mishna *Para* 3:6). From there, one could look to the west and peer directly through the entrance of the Temple (see Mishna *Middot* 2:4; *Mikdash David* 12:8), as described in the next verse.

19:7 | The priest shall wash his garments, and he shall bathe his flesh: The priest who burns the red heifer is situated at the mysterious juncture between life and death. The priest comes from the Temple, which is the locus of life and holiness, and deals with the red heifer, which symbolizes fertility and the power of life. He then proceeds to burn it to ash. This experience requires that he be purified at its conclusion.

bathe his flesh in water, and he shall be impure until the evening.
9 **A pure man shall gather the ashes of the heifer, and place them outside the camp in a pure place, and it,** this collection of ashes, **shall be for the congregation of the children of Israel a keepsake, as a water of sprinkling [*nidda*]; it,** the heifer, **is** a means of **purification.**[D] In this context, *nidda*, which usually denotes a menstruating woman, means throwing.[1]
10 **He who gathers the ashes of the heifer shall** also **wash his garments, and he shall be impure until the evening; it shall be for the children of Israel, and to the stranger who resides among them for an eternal statute.**
11 Until now, the Torah described the rite of the heifer and the preparation of its ashes. Now, it will describe the use of these ashes: **One who touches the corpse of any person shall be impure seven days.**
12 **He shall purify himself with it,** the mixture of water and ashes, **on the third day and on the seventh day** of his impurity, and then **he shall be pure; however, if he does not purify himself on the third day and on the seventh day, he shall not be pure** even after seven days have elapsed.
13 The potential consequences of not purifying oneself with the ashes of the heifer are severe: **Anyone who touches a corpse of a person who has died and does not purify himself** and enters the Tabernacle **has defiled the Tabernacle of the Lord; that person shall be excised from Israel because the water of sprinkling was not sprinkled upon him; he shall be impure; his impurity is still upon him.**
14 Contrary to what might have been expected, this passage began with a description of the process by which one purifies oneself with the red heifer. The Torah describes at this point how one enters into a state of ritual impurity in the first place: **This is the law: When a man dies in a tent,** or in any roofed structure, **anyone who comes into the tent** while the corpse is there, **and anything that is in the tent** while the corpse is there, **shall be impure seven days.** This is known as impurity imparted by a tent, meaning that the impurity due to the corpse spreads throughout the entire space under the roof covering the corpse.

Stopper for sealing an earthenware jug

Therefore, one may be rendered impure even without touching or carrying the corpse.
15 **Any open vessel** in the tent **that does not have a tight-fitting lid upon it is impure.**
16 **Anyone who will touch in the open field,**[D] in an unroofed area, **one slain with a sword, or one who died**[D] through other means, **or a bone of a man, or a grave** of a person, **shall be impure seven days.** In cases where the source of impurity is not situated under a roof, impurity is imparted through physical contact.
17 **They shall take for the impure from the ashes of the burning of the purification,** the ashes of the heifer, **and he shall place springwater upon it in a vessel.**
18 **A pure person shall take hyssop, and dip it in the water, and**
Second aliya **sprinkle it on the tent,** which is made of leather or flax,[2] **and on all the vessels, and on the people who were there, and on one who touched the bone, or the slain, or the dead, or the grave.**
19 **The pure shall sprinkle upon the impure on the third day and on the seventh day and he shall purify him on the seventh day; he,** the one undergoing purification, **shall** then **wash his garments, and bathe in water, and be pure in the evening.**

DISCUSSION

19:9 | **It is purification [*ḥatat*]:** This expression indicates that the heifer cleanses one of impurity, as a verse in Psalms states: "Purify me [*teḥate'eini*] with hyssop, and I will be clean" (51:9, based on Rambam, *Guide of the Perplexed* 3:47). Furthermore, due to this expression, although the heifer is not itself an offering, it is in many ways equated to a *ḥatat*, sin offering (see, e.g., *Hullin* 11a).

19:16 | **Who will touch in the open field:** The Sages derive from this phrase that one who overlies a corpse or a grave is considered to have touched it. The same is true if a corpse overlies a person or a vessel (see, e.g., *Nazir* 53b; Mishna *Oholot* 3:1).

One slain with a sword, or one who died: With regard to ritual impurity, there is no difference between one who was murdered and one who died through other means. The Sages therefore derive from the phrase "one slain with a sword" that the sword used to murder a person is rendered impure to the same degree as the one slain with it (see *Pesaḥim* 79a).

ט וְרָחַ֥ץ בְּשָׂר֖וֹ בַּמָּ֑יִם וְטָמֵ֖א עַד־הָעָֽרֶב׃ וְאָסַ֣ף ׀ אִ֣ישׁ טָה֗וֹר אֵ֚ת אֵ֣פֶר הַפָּרָ֔ה וְהִנִּ֛יחַ
מִח֥וּץ לַֽמַּחֲנֶ֖ה בְּמָק֣וֹם טָה֑וֹר וְ֠הָיְתָה לַעֲדַ֨ת בְּנֵֽי־יִשְׂרָאֵ֧ל לְמִשְׁמֶ֛רֶת לְמֵ֥י נִדָּ֖ה
י חַטָּ֥את הִֽוא׃ וְ֠כִבֶּס הָאֹסֵ֨ף אֶת־אֵ֤פֶר הַפָּרָה֙ אֶת־בְּגָדָ֔יו וְטָמֵ֖א עַד־הָעָ֑רֶב וְהָֽיְתָ֞ה
יא לִבְנֵ֤י יִשְׂרָאֵל֙ וְלַגֵּ֣ר הַגָּ֣ר בְּתוֹכָ֔ם לְחֻקַּ֖ת עוֹלָֽם׃ הַנֹּגֵ֥עַ בְּמֵ֖ת לְכָל־נֶ֣פֶשׁ אָדָ֑ם וְטָמֵ֖א
יב שִׁבְעַ֥ת יָמִֽים׃ ה֣וּא יִתְחַטָּא־ב֞וֹ בַּיּ֧וֹם הַשְּׁלִישִׁ֛י וּבַיּ֥וֹם הַשְּׁבִיעִ֖י יִטְהָ֑ר וְאִם־לֹ֨א
יג יִתְחַטָּ֜א בַּיּ֧וֹם הַשְּׁלִישִׁ֛י וּבַיּ֥וֹם הַשְּׁבִיעִ֖י לֹ֥א יִטְהָֽר׃ כָּל־הַנֹּגֵ֡עַ בְּמֵ֣ת בְּנֶפֶשׁ֩ הָֽאָדָ֨ם
אֲשֶׁר־יָמ֜וּת וְלֹ֣א יִתְחַטָּ֗א אֶת־מִשְׁכַּ֤ן יְהוָה֙ טִמֵּ֔א וְנִכְרְתָ֛ה הַנֶּ֥פֶשׁ הַהִ֖וא מִיִּשְׂרָאֵ֑ל
יד כִּ֣י מֵ֣י נִדָּ֞ה לֹא־זֹרַ֤ק עָלָיו֙ טָמֵ֣א יִהְיֶ֔ה ע֖וֹד טֻמְאָת֥וֹ בֽוֹ׃ זֹ֚את הַתּוֹרָ֔ה אָדָ֖ם כִּֽי־יָמ֣וּת
טו בְּאֹ֑הֶל כָּל־הַבָּ֤א אֶל־הָאֹ֙הֶל֙ וְכָל־אֲשֶׁ֣ר בָּאֹ֔הֶל יִטְמָ֖א שִׁבְעַ֥ת יָמִֽים׃ וְכֹל֙ כְּלִ֣י פָת֔וּחַ
טז אֲשֶׁ֛ר אֵין־צָמִ֥יד פָּתִ֖יל עָלָ֑יו טָמֵ֖א הֽוּא׃ וְכֹ֨ל אֲשֶׁר־יִגַּ֜ע עַל־פְּנֵ֣י הַשָּׂדֶ֗ה בַּֽחֲלַל־חֶ֙רֶב֙
יז א֣וֹ בְמֵ֔ת אוֹ־בְעֶ֥צֶם אָדָ֖ם א֣וֹ בְקָ֑בֶר יִטְמָ֖א שִׁבְעַ֥ת יָמִֽים׃ וְלָֽקְחוּ֙ לַטָּמֵ֔א מֵעֲפַ֖ר
יח שְׂרֵפַ֣ת הַֽחַטָּ֑את וְנָתַ֥ן עָלָ֛יו מַ֥יִם חַיִּ֖ים אֶל־כֶּֽלִי׃ וְלָקַ֨ח אֵז֜וֹב וְטָבַ֣ל בַּמַּ֘יִם֮ אִ֣ישׁ שני
טָהוֹר֒ וְהִזָּ֣ה עַל־הָאֹ֔הֶל וְעַל־כָּל־הַכֵּלִ֔ים וְעַל־הַנְּפָשׁ֖וֹת אֲשֶׁ֣ר הָֽיוּ־שָׁ֑ם וְעַֽל־הַנֹּגֵ֗עַ
יט בַּעֶ֙צֶם֙ א֣וֹ בֶֽחָלָ֔ל א֥וֹ בַמֵּ֖ת א֥וֹ בַקָּֽבֶר׃ וְהִזָּ֣ה הַטָּהֹר֙ עַל־הַטָּמֵ֔א בַּיּ֥וֹם הַשְּׁלִישִׁ֖י
וּבַיּ֣וֹם הַשְּׁבִיעִ֑י וְחִטְּאוֹ֙ בַּיּ֣וֹם הַשְּׁבִיעִ֔י וְכִבֶּ֧ס בְּגָדָ֛יו וְרָחַ֥ץ בַּמַּ֖יִם וְטָהֵ֥ר בָּעָֽרֶב׃

רש"י

ט | **וְהִנִּיחַ מִחוּץ לַמַּחֲנֶה.** לִשְׁלֹשָׁה חֲלָקִים מְחַלְּקָהּ: אֶחָד נָתַן בְּהַר הַמִּשְׁחָה, וְאֶחָד מִתְחַלֵּק לְכָל הַמִּשְׁמָרוֹת, וְאֶחָד נָתַן בַּחֵיל. זֶה שֶׁל מִשְׁמָרוֹת הָיָה חוּץ לָעֲזָרָה, לִטֹּל מִמֶּנּוּ בְּנֵי הָעֲיָרוֹת וְכָל הַצְּרִיכִין לְהִטַּהֵר. וְזֶה שֶׁבְּהַר הַמִּשְׁחָה כֹּהֲנִים גְּדוֹלִים לְפָרוֹת אֲחֵרוֹת מְקַדְּשִׁין הֵימֶנָּה. וְזֶה שֶׁבַּחֵיל נָתוּן לְמִשְׁמֶרֶת מִגְּזֵרַת הַכָּתוּב, שֶׁנֶּאֱמַר: "וְהָיְתָה לַעֲדַת בְּנֵי יִשְׂרָאֵל לְמִשְׁמֶרֶת": **לְמֵי נִדָּה.** לְמֵי הַזָּיָה, כְּמוֹ: "וַיַּדּוּ אֶבֶן בִּי" (איכה ג, נג), "לְיַדּוֹת אֶת קַרְנוֹת הַגּוֹיִם" (זכריה ב, ד), לְשׁוֹן זְרִיקָה: **חַטָּאת הִוא.** לְשׁוֹן חִטּוּי כִּפְשׁוּטוֹ. וּלְפִי הִלְכוֹתָיו קְרָאָהּ הַכָּתוּב 'חַטָּאת', לוֹמַר שֶׁהִיא כְּקָדָשִׁים לֶאֱסֹר בַּהֲנָאָה:

יב | **הוּא יִתְחַטָּא בוֹ.** בְּאֵפֶר הַפָּרָה:

יג | **בְּמֵת בְּנֶפֶשׁ.** וְאֵיזֶה מֵת? שֶׁל "נֶפֶשׁ הָאָדָם", לְהוֹצִיא נֶפֶשׁ בְּהֵמָה שֶׁאֵין טֻמְאָתָהּ צְרִיכָה הַזָּאָה. דָּבָר אַחֵר, "בְּנֶפֶשׁ" זוֹ רְבִיעִית דָּם: **אֶת מִשְׁכַּן ה' טִמֵּא.** אִם נִכְנַס לָעֲזָרָה, אֲפִלּוּ בִּטְבִילָה, בְּלֹא הַזָּאַת שְׁלִישִׁי וּשְׁבִיעִי: **עוֹד טֻמְאָתוֹ בוֹ.** אַף עַל פִּי שֶׁטָּבַל:

יד | **כָּל הַבָּא אֶל הָאֹהֶל.** בְּעוֹד שֶׁהַמֵּת בְּתוֹכוֹ:

טו | **וְכֹל כְּלִי פָתוּחַ.** בִּכְלִי חֶרֶס הַכָּתוּב מְדַבֵּר, שֶׁאֵין מְקַבֵּל טֻמְאָה מִגַּבּוֹ אֶלָּא מִתּוֹכוֹ, לְפִיכָךְ אִם אֵין מְגוּפַת צְמִידָתוֹ פְּתוּלָה עָלָיו יָפֶה בְּחִבּוּר "טָמֵא הוּא", הָא אִם יֵשׁ צָמִיד פָּתִיל עָלָיו – טָהוֹר. "פָּתִיל" לְשׁוֹן מְחֻבָּר בִּלְשׁוֹן עֲרָבִי, וְכֵן: "נַפְתּוּלֵי אֱלֹהִים נִפְתַּלְתִּי" (בראשית ל, ח), נִתְחַבַּרְתִּי עִם אֲחוֹתִי:

טז | **עַל פְּנֵי הַשָּׂדֶה.** רַבּוֹתֵינוּ דָּרְשׁוּ לְרַבּוֹת גּוֹלֵל וְדוֹפֵק. וּפְשׁוּטוֹ: "עַל פְּנֵי הַשָּׂדֶה", שֶׁאֵין שָׁם אֹהֶל, מְטַמֵּא הַמֵּת שָׁם בִּנְגִיעָה:

יט | **וְחִטְּאוֹ בַּיּוֹם הַשְּׁבִיעִי.** הוּא גְּמַר טָהֳרָתוֹ:

20 **A man who is impure, and does not purify himself,** and nevertheless enters the Temple or eats from sacrificial items, **that person shall be excised from the midst of the assembly, because he has rendered the Sanctuary of the Lord impure; the water of sprinkling has not been sprinkled on him; he is impure.** Although it is not a sin to be impure, an impure individual is prohibited from entering the Temple or consuming sacrificial food.

21 **It shall be an eternal statute for them; he who sprinkles the water**[D] **of sprinkling shall wash his garments,** as he is rendered impure, **and he who touches the water of sprinkling**

shall also **be impure until the evening.** This water has great powers of purification; nevertheless, if a person who does not require purification through this water comes into contact with it, that person is rendered impure by the water. However, the degree of impurity is not as severe as the impurity imparted by a corpse. One does not require sprinkling on the third and seventh days, but merely immersion in a ritual bath and the arrival of nightfall.

22 **Anything that the impure person shall touch shall be impure; and the person who touches** the impure individual **shall** himself **be impure until the evening.**

The Death of Miriam and the Water of Dispute

NUMBERS 20:1–13

This passage opens with a reference to the month in which the following events begin to take place; the precise year, however, is not revealed by the Torah. According to the Sages, the events of this passage, which tells of the death of Miriam, occurs in the fortieth year of the Israelites' wanderings in the wilderness, long after the events recorded in the preceding passages. The events that follow Miriam's death ultimately lead to the deaths of her two brothers, Moses and Aaron, leaders of Israel before the Israelites would enter the land of Canaan. Consequently, a tragic outcome unfolds: These three siblings, the faithful shepherds of Israel who led the people out of Egypt and through all the suffering, hardship, and dangers of their wanderings, will not enter the Promised Land.

The passage concludes with the phrase "and He was sanctified [*vayikadesh*] through them" (20:13). God was sanctified through the execution of judgment upon those close to Him. Therefore, there is an additional significance to Kadesh, the name of the place in which these events occurred.

20 1 **The children of Israel, the entire congregation, came to the wilderness of Tzin during the first month and the people lived in Kadesh,** in the wilderness of Tzin. Later, Kadesh will be referred to as a city situated on the edge of the border of Edom (20:16). **Miriam died there, and she was buried there.**

2 **There was no water for the congregation;**[D] **and they assembled against Moses and against Aaron.**

3 **The people quarreled with Moses, and they said, saying: If only we had perished in the perishing of our brethren before the Lord.** At least our brethren, who died due to the sin of the spies and other transgressions, died a quick death.[3]

4 **Why did you bring the assembly of the Lord to this wilderness, that we and our animals should die there?**

5 **Why did you bring us up from Egypt, to bring us to this wretched place? It is not a place of seed, or figs, or vines, or pomegranates,** fruits for which the Promised Land is praised.[4] Now, we are neither in Egypt nor in Canaan, **and there is no water to drink.**

6 **Moses and Aaron came from before the assembly,** and were forced by the angry crowd **to the entrance of the Tent of Meeting, and they fell upon their faces** in prayer, **and the glory of the Lord appeared to them.**

Figs, vines, and pomegranates

DISCUSSION

19:21| **He who sprinkles the water:** According to tradition, this verse does not mean that one who sprinkles the water on an impure individual is rendered impure. Rather, the verse is referring to one who carried the water for purposes other than the sprinkling of purification. The verse refers to "he who sprinkles the water" to indicate

that one is rendered impure through carrying the water only if he carried a sufficient quantity of water to carry out the sprinkling (see *Yoma* 14a).

20:2| **There was no water for the congregation:** According to the Sages, there is a

connection between Miriam's death and the absence of water: In Miriam's merit, the children of Israel were provided with a miraculous well that moved with the people as they wandered through the wilderness (*Tosefta, Sota* 11). Upon Miriam's passing, this miraculous well disappeared.

כ וְאִישׁ אֲשֶׁר־יִטְמָא וְלֹא יִתְחַטָּא וְנִכְרְתָה הַנֶּפֶשׁ הַהִוא מִתּוֹךְ הַקָּהָל כִּי אֶת־
כא מִקְדַּשׁ יהוה טִמֵּא מֵי נִדָּה לֹא־זֹרַק עָלָיו טָמֵא הוּא: וְהָיְתָה לָהֶם לְחֻקַּת עוֹלָם
כב וּמַזֵּה מֵי־הַנִּדָּה יְכַבֵּס בְּגָדָיו וְהַנֹּגֵעַ בְּמֵי הַנִּדָּה יִטְמָא עַד־הָעָרֶב: וְכֹל אֲשֶׁר־יִגַּע־
בּוֹ הַטָּמֵא יִטְמָא וְהַנֶּפֶשׁ הַנֹּגַעַת תִּטְמָא עַד־הָעָרֶב:
א וַיָּבֹאוּ בְנֵי־יִשְׂרָאֵל כָּל־הָעֵדָה מִדְבַּר־צִן בַּחֹדֶשׁ הָרִאשׁוֹן וַיֵּשֶׁב הָעָם בְּקָדֵשׁ
ב וַתָּמָת שָׁם מִרְיָם וַתִּקָּבֵר שָׁם: וְלֹא־הָיָה מַיִם לָעֵדָה וַיִּקָּהֲלוּ עַל־מֹשֶׁה וְעַל־
ג אַהֲרֹן: וַיָּרֶב הָעָם עִם־מֹשֶׁה וַיֹּאמְרוּ לֵאמֹר וְלוּ גָוַעְנוּ בִּגְוַע אַחֵינוּ לִפְנֵי יהוה:
ד וְלָמָה הֲבֵאתֶם אֶת־קְהַל יהוה אֶל־הַמִּדְבָּר הַזֶּה לָמוּת שָׁם אֲנַחְנוּ וּבְעִירֵנוּ:
ה וְלָמָה הֶעֱלִיתֻנוּ מִמִּצְרַיִם לְהָבִיא אֹתָנוּ אֶל־הַמָּקוֹם הָרָע הַזֶּה לֹא מְקוֹם זֶרַע
ו וּתְאֵנָה וְגֶפֶן וְרִמּוֹן וּמַיִם אַיִן לִשְׁתּוֹת: וַיָּבֹא מֹשֶׁה וְאַהֲרֹן מִפְּנֵי הַקָּהָל אֶל־פֶּתַח
אֹהֶל מוֹעֵד וַיִּפְּלוּ עַל־פְּנֵיהֶם וַיֵּרָא כְבוֹד־יהוה אֲלֵיהֶם:

רש"י

כ| וְאִישׁ אֲשֶׁר יִטְמָא וְגוֹ'. אִם נֶאֱמַר 'מִקְדָּשׁ' לָמָּה נֶאֱמַר 'מִשְׁכָּן' (לעיל פסוק יג)? כו' כִּדְאִיתָא בִּשְׁבוּעוֹת (דף טז ע"ב):

כא| וּמַזֵּה מֵי הַנִּדָּה. רַבּוֹתֵינוּ אָמְרוּ שֶׁהַמַּזֶּה טָהוֹר, וְזֶה בָּא לְלַמֵּד שֶׁהַנּוֹשֵׂא מֵי חַטָּאת טָמֵא טֻמְאָה חֲמוּרָה לְטַמֵּא בְּגָדִים שֶׁעָלָיו, מַה שֶּׁאֵין כֵּן בַּנּוֹגֵעַ. וְזֶה שֶׁהוֹצִיא בִּלְשׁוֹן 'מַזֶּה', לוֹמַר לְךָ שֶׁאֵינָן מְטַמְּאִין עַד שֶׁיְּהֵא בָהֶן שִׁעוּר הַזָּאָה: וְהַנֹּגֵעַ... יִטְמָא. וְאֵין טָעוּן כִּבּוּס בְּגָדִים:

כב| וְכֹל אֲשֶׁר יִגַּע בּוֹ הַטָּמֵא. הַזֶּה שֶׁנִּטְמָא בְּמֵת, "יִטְמָא": וְהַנֶּפֶשׁ הַנֹּגַעַת. בּוֹ בִּטְמֵא מֵת: תִּטְמָא עַד הָעָרֶב. כָּאן לָמַדְנוּ שֶׁהַמֵּת אֲבִי אֲבוֹת הַטֻּמְאָה, וְהַנּוֹגֵעַ בּוֹ אַב הַטֻּמְאָה וּמְטַמֵּא אָדָם. זֶהוּ פֵּרוּשָׁהּ לְפִי מַשְׁמָעָהּ וְהִלְכוֹתֶיהָ:

וּמִדְרַשׁ אַגָּדָה הֶעְתַּקְתִּי מִיסוֹדוֹ שֶׁל רַבִּי מֹשֶׁה הַדַּרְשָׁן. וְזֶהוּ:

ב| וְיִקְחוּ אֵלֶיךָ. מִשֶּׁלָּהֶם. כְּשֵׁם שֶׁהֵם פֵּרְקוּ נִזְמֵי הַזָּהָב לָעֵגֶל מִשֶּׁלָּהֶם, כָּךְ יָבִיאוּ זוֹ לְכַפָּרָה מִשֶּׁלָּהֶם: פָּרָה אֲדֻמָּה. מָשָׁל לְבֶן שִׁפְחָה שֶׁטִּנֵּף פַּלְטֵין שֶׁל מֶלֶךְ, אָמְרוּ: תָּבֹא אִמּוֹ וּתְקַנֵּחַ הַצּוֹאָה; כָּךְ תָּבֹא פָּרָה וּתְכַפֵּר עַל הָעֵגֶל: אֲדֻמָּה. עַל שֵׁם: "אִם יַאְדִּימוּ כַתּוֹלָע" (ישעיה א, יח), שֶׁהַחֵטְא קָרוּי אָדֹם: תְּמִימָה. עַל שֵׁם יִשְׂרָאֵל שֶׁהָיוּ תְּמִימִים וְנַעֲשׂוּ בוֹ בַּעֲלֵי מוּמִין, תָּבֹא זוֹ וּתְכַפֵּר עֲלֵיהֶם וְיַחְזְרוּ לְתַמּוּתָם: לֹא עָלָה עָלֶיהָ עֹל. כְּשֵׁם שֶׁפָּרְקוּ מֵעֲלֵיהֶם עֹל שָׁמַיִם:

ג| אֶל אֶלְעָזָר הַכֹּהֵן. כְּשֵׁם שֶׁנִּקְהֲלוּ עַל אַהֲרֹן, שֶׁהוּא כֹּהֵן, לַעֲשׂוֹת הָעֵגֶל. וּלְפִי שֶׁאַהֲרֹן עָשָׂה אֶת הָעֵגֶל לֹא נַעֲשֵׂית עֲבוֹדָה זוֹ עַל יָדוֹ, שֶׁאֵין קַטֵּגוֹר נַעֲשֶׂה סַנֵּגוֹר:

ד| וְשָׂרַף אֶת הַפָּרָה. כְּשֵׁם שֶׁנִּשְׂרַף הָעֵגֶל:

ו| עֵץ אֶרֶז וְאֵזוֹב וּשְׁנִי תוֹלָעַת. שְׁלֹשָׁה מִינִין הַלָּלוּ כְּנֶגֶד שְׁלֹשֶׁת אֲלָפִים אִישׁ שֶׁנָּפְלוּ בָעֵגֶל. וְאֶרֶז הוּא הַגָּבוֹהַּ מִכָּל הָאִילָנוֹת, וְאֵזוֹב נָמוּךְ מִכֻּלָּם, סִימָן שֶׁהַגָּבוֹהַּ שֶׁנִּתְגָּאָה וְחָטָא יַשְׁפִּיל אֶת עַצְמוֹ כְּאֵזוֹב וְתוֹלַעַת וְיִתְכַּפֵּר לוֹ:

ט| לְמִשְׁמֶרֶת. כְּמוֹ שֶׁפֶּשַׁע הָעֵגֶל שָׁמוּר לְדוֹרוֹת לְפֻרְעָנוּת, וְאֵין לְךָ פְּקֻדָּה שֶׁאֵין בָּהּ מִפְּקֻדַּת הָעֵגֶל, שֶׁנֶּאֱמַר: "וּבְיוֹם פָּקְדִי וּפָקַדְתִּי" וְגוֹ' (שמות לב, לד). וּכְשֵׁם שֶׁהָעֵגֶל מְטַמֵּא כָּל הָעוֹסְקִין בּוֹ, כָּךְ פָּרָה מְטַמְּאָה כָּל הָעוֹסְקִין בָּהּ, וּכְשֵׁם שֶׁנִּטַּהֲרוּ בְאֶפְרוֹ, שֶׁנֶּאֱמַר: "וַיִּזֶר עַל פְּנֵי הַמַּיִם" וְגוֹ' (שמות לב, כ), כָּךְ: "וְלָקְחוּ לַטָּמֵא מֵעֲפַר שְׂרֵפַת הַחַטָּאת" וְגוֹ' (להלן פסוק יז):

פרק כ

א| כָּל הָעֵדָה. עֵדָה הַשְּׁלֵמָה, שֶׁכְּבָר מֵתוּ מֵתֵי מִדְבָּר וְאֵלּוּ פֵּרְשׁוּ לַחַיִּים: וַתָּמָת שָׁם מִרְיָם. לָמָּה נִסְמְכָה מִיתַת מִרְיָם לְפָרָשַׁת פָּרָה אֲדֻמָּה? לוֹמַר לְךָ, מַה קָּרְבָּנוֹת מְכַפְּרִין, אַף מִיתַת צַדִּיקִים מְכַפֶּרֶת: וַתָּמָת שָׁם מִרְיָם. אַף הִיא בִּנְשִׁיקָה מֵתָה, וּמִפְּנֵי מָה לֹא נֶאֱמַר בָּהּ: 'עַל פִּי ה''? שֶׁאֵינוֹ דֶּרֶךְ כָּבוֹד שֶׁל מַעְלָה. וּבְאַהֲרֹן נֶאֱמַר: "עַל פִּי ה'" בְּאֵלֶּה מַסְעֵי (להלן לג, לח):

ב| וְלֹא הָיָה מַיִם לָעֵדָה. מִכָּאן שֶׁכָּל אַרְבָּעִים שָׁנָה הָיָה לָהֶם הַבְּאֵר בִּזְכוּת מִרְיָם:

ג| וְלוּ גָוַעְנוּ. הַלְוַאי שֶׁגָּוַעְנוּ: בִּגְוַע אַחֵינוּ. בְּמִיתַת אַחֵינוּ בַּדֶּבֶר, לִמֵּד שֶׁמִּיתַת צָמָא מְגֻנָּה מִמֶּנָּה: בִּגְוַע. שֵׁם דָּבָר הוּא, כְּמוֹ: 'בְּמִיתַת אַחֵינוּ'. וְלֹא יִתָּכֵן לְפָרְשׁוֹ כְּשֶׁמֵּתוּ אַחֵינוּ, שֶׁאִם כֵּן הָיָה לוֹ לְהִנָּקֵד 'בִּגְוֹעַ':

Third aliya (Second aliya)
7 **The Lord spoke to Moses, saying:**
8 **Take the staff** with which you performed all the miracles and wonders,[5] **and assemble the congregation, you, and Aaron your brother, and speak to the rock before their eyes, and it,** the rock, **will provide its water.** You will thereby **extract water for them from the rock and you shall give drink to the congregation and their animals.**
9 **Moses took the staff from before the Lord, as He had commanded him.** It is possible that this was the staff placed before God "for safekeeping, as a sign for the rebellious ones."[6]
10 **Moses and Aaron assembled the assembly before the rock, and said to them: Hear now, defiant ones:**[7] **From this rock will we bring out water for you?** Why do you quarrel with us? Do you think we have the power to bring out water from this rock? You should have turned and prayed to God.[8] Alternatively, Moses asked them: Defiant ones, do you doubt God's ability to bring water from this rock?[9]
11 **Moses raised his hand, and he struck the rock with his staff twice; a great deal of water came out, and the congregation and their animals drank.**
12 Although the rock miraculously provided water, **the Lord said to Moses and Aaron: Because you did not** cause the people to **have faith in Me,**[10] **to sanctify Me before the eyes of the children of Israel; therefore, you shall not bring this assembly into the land that I have given them.**
13 **These are the waters of dispute,**[D] **where the children of Israel quarreled with the Lord, and He was sanctified through them.** God was sanctified through the execution of judgment upon those close to Him. A similar expression appears with regard to the deaths of Aaron's sons: "Through those who are near to Me I will be sanctified."[11]

Israel Approaches Edom

NUMBERS 20:14–21

As the children of Israel draw near to settled areas, they must begin dealing with external forces. Their first challenge will not be a collection of nomadic tribes such as Amalek, whom they fought in the first year of their exodus from Egypt, but the established and fortified nation of Edom. Since the kingdom of Edom is located to the southeast of Canaan, the children of Israel do not seek to conquer Edom but merely to pass through it.

14 **Moses sent messengers from Kadesh,** south of Edom, **to the king of Edom: So said your brother Israel,** as Jacob was the brother of Esau, the father of the nation of Edom:[12] **You know all the travail that we have encountered.**
Fourth aliya
15 **Our ancestors descended to Egypt, and we lived in Egypt many years; the Egyptians mistreated us and our ancestors.**
16 **We cried to the Lord and He heard our voice,** and **sent an angel.** The verse may be referring to Moses, the messenger of God,[13] or to an actual angel of God.[14] **And He took us out of Egypt; behold, we are** now **in Kadesh, a city at the edge of your border.**
17 Therefore, we ask: **Please, let us pass through your land;** we promise that **we will not pass in a field or in a vineyard,** in your settled areas, **and we will not drink well water; we will go on the king's way,** the public thoroughfares that pass through the cities.[15] Alternatively, this refers to whatever road the king of Edom would instruct them to use.[16] **We will not turn right or left until we will pass your border;** we will pass through your land quietly, without causing any damage.

DISCUSSION

20:13 | **The waters of dispute:** This episode is mentioned in several places in the Bible (see Deuteronomy 32:51; Ezekiel 47:19, 48:28; Psalms 81:8, 95:8, 106:32). Various explanations have been offered regarding the nature of the sin that warranted such a severe response from God. One of the most accepted opinions is that Moses and Aaron sinned by not speaking to the rock, as God had commanded, and instead Moses struck the rock (see Rashi, verse 11). Although producing water from a rock by striking it is also miraculous, Moses and Aaron squandered the opportunity to perform the even greater miracle of producing water from the rock by speaking to it. According to other commentaries, Moses sinned by becoming angry with the people and calling them "defiant ones" (20:10; see *Devarim Rabba* 1:8; *Derashot HaRan* 8). Once Moses expressed his personal frustrations, he lost his direct connection to God. Additionally, the fact that Moses hit the rock twice perhaps indicates that he acted out of anger (see Ibn Ezra, verse 8; Ramban, verse 1).

Over the generations, many scholars have offered alternative explanations of this episode, perhaps bothered by the question of how it could be that Moses, the faithful shepherd of the Israelites, was barred from entering the Land of Israel. One of the great sages of recent generations summed up this matter beautifully: Any sin whose severity can be grasped by an ordinary person is unsuitable for the towering figure of Moses. Presumably, the actions of Moses pertained to some sublime realities beyond our perception. Whatever Moses did would not have been considered a severe transgression by us. Moses, however, was judged according to his lofty level.

ז ח וַיְדַבֵּר יְהוָה אֶל־מֹשֶׁה לֵּאמֹר: קַח אֶת־הַמַּטֶּה וְהַקְהֵל אֶת־הָעֵדָה אַתָּה וְאַהֲרֹן שלישי /שני/
אָחִיךָ וְדִבַּרְתֶּם אֶל־הַסֶּלַע לְעֵינֵיהֶם וְנָתַן מֵימָיו וְהוֹצֵאתָ לָהֶם מַיִם מִן־הַסֶּלַע
ט וְהִשְׁקִיתָ אֶת־הָעֵדָה וְאֶת־בְּעִירָם: וַיִּקַּח מֹשֶׁה אֶת־הַמַּטֶּה מִלִּפְנֵי יְהוָה כַּאֲשֶׁר
י צִוָּהוּ: וַיַּקְהִלוּ מֹשֶׁה וְאַהֲרֹן אֶת־הַקָּהָל אֶל־פְּנֵי הַסָּלַע וַיֹּאמֶר לָהֶם שִׁמְעוּ־נָא
יא הַמֹּרִים הֲמִן־הַסֶּלַע הַזֶּה נוֹצִיא לָכֶם מָיִם: וַיָּרֶם מֹשֶׁה אֶת־יָדוֹ וַיַּךְ אֶת־הַסֶּלַע
יב בְּמַטֵּהוּ פַּעֲמָיִם וַיֵּצְאוּ מַיִם רַבִּים וַתֵּשְׁתְּ הָעֵדָה וּבְעִירָם: וַיֹּאמֶר
יְהוָה אֶל־מֹשֶׁה וְאֶל־אַהֲרֹן יַעַן לֹא־הֶאֱמַנְתֶּם בִּי לְהַקְדִּישֵׁנִי לְעֵינֵי בְּנֵי יִשְׂרָאֵל לָכֵן
יג לֹא תָבִיאוּ אֶת־הַקָּהָל הַזֶּה אֶל־הָאָרֶץ אֲשֶׁר־נָתַתִּי לָהֶם: הֵמָּה מֵי מְרִיבָה אֲשֶׁר־
יד רָבוּ בְנֵי־יִשְׂרָאֵל אֶת־יְהוָה וַיִּקָּדֵשׁ בָּם: וַיִּשְׁלַח מֹשֶׁה מַלְאָכִים יח רביעי
מִקָּדֵשׁ אֶל־מֶלֶךְ אֱדוֹם כֹּה אָמַר אָחִיךָ יִשְׂרָאֵל אַתָּה יָדַעְתָּ אֵת כָּל־הַתְּלָאָה אֲשֶׁר
טו מְצָאָתְנוּ: וַיֵּרְדוּ אֲבֹתֵינוּ מִצְרַיְמָה וַנֵּשֶׁב בְּמִצְרַיִם יָמִים רַבִּים וַיָּרֵעוּ לָנוּ מִצְרַיִם
טז וְלַאֲבֹתֵינוּ: וַנִּצְעַק אֶל־יְהוָה וַיִּשְׁמַע קֹלֵנוּ וַיִּשְׁלַח מַלְאָךְ וַיֹּצִאֵנוּ מִמִּצְרָיִם וְהִנֵּה
יז אֲנַחְנוּ בְקָדֵשׁ עִיר קְצֵה גְבוּלֶךָ: נַעְבְּרָה־נָּא בְאַרְצֶךָ לֹא נַעֲבֹר בְּשָׂדֶה וּבְכֶרֶם וְלֹא
נִשְׁתֶּה מֵי בְאֵר דֶּרֶךְ הַמֶּלֶךְ נֵלֵךְ לֹא נִטֶּה יָמִין וּשְׂמֹאול עַד אֲשֶׁר־נַעֲבֹר גְּבֻלֶךָ:

רש"י

ח| **וְאֶת בְּעִירָם.** מִכָּאן שֶׁחָס הַקָּדוֹשׁ בָּרוּךְ הוּא עַל מָמוֹנָם שֶׁל יִשְׂרָאֵל:

י| **וַיַּקְהִלוּ וְגוֹ׳.** זֶה אֶחָד מִן הַמְּקוֹמוֹת שֶׁהֶחֱזִיק מֻעָט אֶת הַמְּרֻבֶּה: **הֲמִן הַסֶּלַע הַזֶּה נוֹצִיא.** לְפִי שֶׁלֹּא הָיוּ מַכִּירִין אוֹתוֹ, לְפִי שֶׁהָלַךְ הַסֶּלַע וְיָשַׁב לוֹ בֵּין הַסְּלָעִים כְּשֶׁנִּסְתַּלֵּק הַבְּאֵר, וְהָיוּ יִשְׂרָאֵל אוֹמְרִים לָהֶם: מַה לָּכֶם, מֵאֵיזֶה סֶלַע תּוֹצִיאוּ לָנוּ מַיִם? לְכָךְ אָמַר לָהֶם: ׳הַמֹּרִים׳, סַרְבָנִים, לְשׁוֹן יְוָנִי שׁוֹטִים, מוֹרִים אֶת מוֹרֵיהֶם, "הֲמִן הַסֶּלַע הַזֶּה" שֶׁלֹּא נִצְטַוִּינוּ עָלָיו, "נוֹצִיא לָכֶם מָיִם"?:

יא| **פַּעֲמָיִם.** לְפִי שֶׁבָּרִאשׁוֹנָה לֹא הוֹצִיא אֶלָּא טִפִּין, לְפִי שֶׁלֹּא צִוָּה הַמָּקוֹם לְהַכּוֹתוֹ, אֶלָּא "וְדִבַּרְתֶּם אֶל הַסֶּלַע", וְהֵמָּה דִּבְּרוּ אֶל סֶלַע אַחֵר וְלֹא הוֹצִיא, אָמְרוּ: שֶׁמָּא צָרִיךְ לְהַכּוֹתוֹ כְּבָרִאשׁוֹנָה, שֶׁנֶּאֱמַר: "וְהִכִּיתָ בַצּוּר" (שמות יז, ו), וְנִזְדַּמֵּן לָהֶם אוֹתוֹ סֶלַע וְהִכָּהוּ:

יב| **לְהַקְדִּישֵׁנִי.** שֶׁאִלּוּ דִּבַּרְתֶּם אֶל הַסֶּלַע וְהוֹצִיא, הָיִיתִי מְקֻדָּשׁ לְעֵינֵי הָעֵדָה, וְאוֹמְרִים: מַה סֶּלַע זֶה, שֶׁאֵינוֹ מְדַבֵּר וְאֵינוֹ שׁוֹמֵעַ וְאֵינוֹ צָרִיךְ לְפַרְנָסָה, מְקַיֵּם דִּבּוּרוֹ שֶׁל מָקוֹם, קַל וָחֹמֶר אָנוּ: **לָכֵן לֹא תָבִיאוּ.** בִּשְׁבוּעָה, נִשְׁבַּע בִּקְפִיצָה, שֶׁלֹּא יַרְבּוּ בִתְפִלָּה עַל כָּךְ: **יַעַן לֹא הֶאֱמַנְתֶּם בִּי.** גִּלָּה הַכָּתוּב שֶׁאִלּוּלֵי חֵטְא זֶה בִּלְבַד הָיוּ נִכְנָסִין לָאָרֶץ, כְּדֵי שֶׁלֹּא יֹאמְרוּ עֲלֵיהֶם: כַּעֲוֹן שְׁאָר דּוֹר הַמִּדְבָּר שֶׁנִּגְזַר עֲלֵיהֶם שֶׁלֹּא יִכָּנְסוּ לָאָרֶץ, כָּךְ הָיָה עֲוֹן מֹשֶׁה וְאַהֲרֹן. וַהֲלֹא "הֲצֹאן וּבָקָר יִשָּׁחֵט" קָשֶׁה מִזּוֹ? אֶלָּא לְפִי שֶׁבַּסֵּתֶר חָסַךְ עָלָיו הַכָּתוּב, וְכָאן שֶׁבְּמַעֲמַד כָּל יִשְׂרָאֵל לֹא חָסַךְ עָלָיו הַכָּתוּב, מִפְּנֵי קִדּוּשׁ הַשֵּׁם:

יג| **הֵמָּה מֵי מְרִיבָה.** הֵם הַנִּזְכָּרִים בְּמָקוֹם אַחֵר, אֶת אֵלּוּ רָאוּ אִצְטַגְנִינֵי פַרְעֹה שֶׁמּוֹשִׁיעָן שֶׁל יִשְׂרָאֵל לוֹקֶה בַּמַּיִם, לְכָךְ גָּזְרוּ: "כָּל הַבֵּן הַיִּלּוֹד הַיְאֹרָה תַּשְׁלִיכֻהוּ" (שמות א, כב): **וַיִּקָּדֵשׁ בָּם.** שֶׁמֵּתוּ מֹשֶׁה וְאַהֲרֹן עַל יָדָם, שֶׁכְּשֶׁהַקָּדוֹשׁ בָּרוּךְ הוּא עוֹשֶׂה דִּין בִּמְקֻדָּשָׁיו הוּא יָרֵאוּי וּמִתְקַדֵּשׁ עַל הַבְּרִיּוֹת, וְכֵן הוּא אוֹמֵר: "נוֹרָא אֱלֹהִים מִמִּקְדָּשֶׁיךָ" (תהלים סח, לו), וְכֵן הוּא אוֹמֵר: "בִּקְרֹבַי אֶקָּדֵשׁ" (ויקרא י, ג):

יד| **אָחִיךָ יִשְׂרָאֵל.** מָה רָאָה לְהַזְכִּיר כָּאן אַחְוָה? אֶלָּא אָמַר לוֹ: אַחִים אֲנַחְנוּ בְּנֵי אַבְרָהָם, שֶׁנֶּאֱמַר לוֹ: "כִּי גֵר יִהְיֶה זַרְעֲךָ" (בראשית טו, יג) וְעַל שְׁנֵינוּ הָיָה אוֹתוֹ הַחוֹב לְפָרְעוֹ: **אַתָּה יָדַעְתָּ אֵת כָּל הַתְּלָאָה.** לְפִיכָךְ פֵּרַשׁ אֲבִיכֶם מֵעַל אָבִינוּ, שֶׁנֶּאֱמַר: "וַיֵּלֶךְ אֶל אֶרֶץ מִפְּנֵי יַעֲקֹב אָחִיו" (שם לו, ו), מִפְּנֵי הַשְּׁטָר חוֹב הַמֻּטָּל עֲלֵיהֶם, וְהִטִּילוּ עַל יַעֲקֹב:

טו| **וַיָּרֵעוּ לָנוּ.** סָבַלְנוּ צָרוֹת רַבּוֹת: **וְלַאֲבֹתֵינוּ.** מִכָּאן שֶׁהָאָבוֹת מִצְטַעֲרִים בַּקֶּבֶר כְּשֶׁפֻּרְעָנוּת בָּאָה עַל יִשְׂרָאֵל:

טז| **וַיִּשְׁמַע קֹלֵנוּ.** בַּבְּרָכָה שֶׁבֵּרְכָנוּ אָבִינוּ: "הַקֹּל קוֹל יַעֲקֹב" (בראשית כז, כב), שֶׁאָנוּ צוֹעֲקִים וְנַעֲנִים: **מַלְאָךְ.** זֶה מֹשֶׁה, מִכָּאן שֶׁהַנְּבִיאִים קְרוּיִין מַלְאָכִים, וְאוֹמֵר: "וַיִּהְיוּ מַלְעִבִים בְּמַלְאֲכֵי הָאֱלֹהִים" (דברי הימים ב׳ לו, טז):

יז| **נַעְבְּרָה נָּא בְאַרְצֶךָ.** אֵין לְךָ לְעוֹרֵר עַל הַיְרֻשָּׁה שֶׁל אֶרֶץ יִשְׂרָאֵל, כְּשֵׁם שֶׁלֹּא פָּרַעְתָּ הַחוֹב, עֲשֵׂה לָנוּ עֵזֶר מְעַט לַעֲבֹר דֶּרֶךְ אַרְצְךָ: **וְלֹא נִשְׁתֶּה מֵי בְאֵר.** ׳מֵי בוֹרוֹת׳ הָיָה צָרִיךְ לוֹמַר, אֶלָּא כָּךְ אָמַר מֹשֶׁה: אַף עַל פִּי שֶׁיֵּשׁ בְּיָדֵינוּ מָן לֶאֱכֹל וּבְאֵר לִשְׁתּוֹת, לֹא נִשְׁתֶּה מִמֶּנּוּ, אֶלָּא נִקְנֶה מִכֶּם אֹכֶל וּמַיִם לַהֲנָאַתְכֶם. מִכָּאן לְאַכְסְנַאי שֶׁאַף עַל פִּי שֶׁיֵּשׁ בְּיָדוֹ לֶאֱכֹל יִקְנֶה מִן הַחֶנְוָנִי, כְּדֵי לְהַנּוֹת אֶת אֻשְׁפִּיזוֹ: **דֶּרֶךְ הַמֶּלֶךְ נֵלֵךְ וְגוֹ׳.** אָנוּ אוֹסְמִים אֶת בְּהֶמְתֵּנוּ וְלֹא יִטּוּ לְכָאן וּלְכָאן לֶאֱכֹל:

18 The king of **Edom said to him,** Moses, or Israel: **You shall not pass through me, lest I come out toward you with the sword.** If you attempt to pass through, I will wage war against you.

19 Despite the threats of Edom, **the children of Israel said to him:** If you do not permit us to use the king's road, which is in the valley and surrounded by fields and vineyards, **we will go up on the** mountain **highway,**[17] even though it is a less

comfortable road. **And if we drink your water, I or my cattle, I will give its price; only it is no matter,** no harm will be caused, **let me pass on foot.** We will not travel in military chariots.

20 He, Edom, said: You shall not pass. Edom came out toward him with a great multitude, and with a powerful hand.

21 **Edom refused to allow Israel to pass in his border and Israel turned from him.**[D] They turned eastward in order to bypass the land of Edom.

The Death of Aaron
NUMBERS 20:22–29

In this passage, the death of Aaron is described in detail. Toward the conclusion of the book of Numbers, the Torah states that Aaron died at the age of 123 on the first day of the fifth month, in the fortieth year following the exodus of Israel from Egypt,[18] mere months before the Israelites entered the land of Canaan.

Fifth aliya (Third aliya)

22 **They traveled from Kadesh; and the children of Israel, the entire congregation, came to Hor Mountain.** It was known by the name Hor, which itself means mountain, due to its regional prominence.

23 **The Lord spoke to Moses and Aaron at Hor Mountain, on the border of the land of Edom, saying:**

24 **Aaron shall be gathered to his people,**[D] the time has come for him to die; his soul shall be returned to its source. **For he shall not come into the land that I gave to the children of Israel because you defied My directive at the** incident of the **waters of dispute** (20:7–13).

25 **Take Aaron and Elazar his son, and take them up Hor Mountain.**

26 **Undress Aaron of his** priestly **vestments, and dress Elazar his son in them.** In this way, Aaron will merit to see his son assume the position of High Priest in his place.[19] **Aaron will be gathered** to his people, **and he will die there,** in perfect serenity, in the presence of only his brother and one of his sons.

27 **Moses did as the Lord had commanded and they went up to Hor Mountain before the eyes of the entire congregation,** in a ceremonial and public fashion. It is evident from the verse that Aaron did not die from old age or frailty, as he was capable of ascending the mountain alongside his brother and son.

28 **Moses undressed Aaron of his vestments, and dressed Elazar his son in them; and Aaron died there**[D] **at the top of the mountain; and Moses and Elazar descended from the mountain.**

29 **The entire congregation saw that Aaron had perished.** Although the people knew that Moses, Aaron, and Elazar ascended the mountain, they were unaware of the purpose of this ascent. Now they saw that Moses and Elazar returned without Aaron.[20] **And they wept for Aaron thirty days, the**

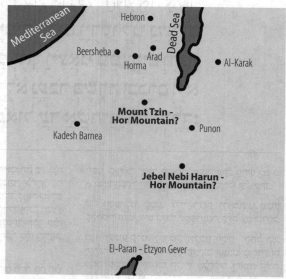

Hor Mountain

DISCUSSION

20:21 | And Israel turned from him: It can be concluded from elsewhere that Edom did not pose a substantial threat to Israel. The fact that the Edomite king is not even mentioned by name, unlike the Emorite kings (see 21:21, 33), is a further indication that Edom was not particularly strong (see Ramban). The Israelites were

not afraid of entering Edom; they refrained from passing through only because of Esau's relation to Jacob (see Deuteronomy 2:4–5, 23:8). A similar reason will be indicated with regard to Amon and Moav (see Deuteronomy 2:9, 19). Out of a sense of obligation between brothers or relatives, Moses saw fit to avoid waging war against

Edom despite their refusal to allow the Israelites to pass through their land.

20:24 | Aaron shall be gathered to his people: This expression appears in the Torah only in reference to the death of a righteous individual (see, e.g., Genesis 25:8).

יח יט וַיֹּאמֶר אֵלָיו אֱדוֹם לֹא תַעֲבֹר בִּי פֶּן־בַּחֶרֶב אֵצֵא לִקְרָאתֶךָ׃ וַיֹּאמְרוּ אֵלָיו בְּנֵי־
יִשְׂרָאֵל בַּמְסִלָּה נַעֲלֶה וְאִם־מֵימֶיךָ נִשְׁתֶּה אֲנִי וּמִקְנַי וְנָתַתִּי מִכְרָם רַק אֵין־דָּבָר
כ בְּרַגְלַי אֶעֱבֹרָה׃ וַיֹּאמֶר לֹא תַעֲבֹר וַיֵּצֵא אֱדוֹם לִקְרָאתוֹ בְּעַם כָּבֵד וּבְיָד חֲזָקָה׃
כא וַיְמָאֵן אֱדוֹם נְתֹן אֶת־יִשְׂרָאֵל עֲבֹר בִּגְבֻלוֹ וַיֵּט יִשְׂרָאֵל מֵעָלָיו׃
כב כג וַיִּסְעוּ מִקָּדֵשׁ וַיָּבֹאוּ בְנֵי־יִשְׂרָאֵל כָּל־הָעֵדָה הֹר הָהָר׃ וַיֹּאמֶר יְהוָה אֶל־מֹשֶׁה חמישי /שלישי/
כד וְאֶל־אַהֲרֹן בְּהֹר הָהָר עַל־גְּבוּל אֶרֶץ־אֱדוֹם לֵאמֹר׃ יֵאָסֵף אַהֲרֹן אֶל־עַמָּיו כִּי
לֹא יָבֹא אֶל־הָאָרֶץ אֲשֶׁר נָתַתִּי לִבְנֵי יִשְׂרָאֵל עַל אֲשֶׁר־מְרִיתֶם אֶת־פִּי לְמֵי
כה כו מְרִיבָה׃ קַח אֶת־אַהֲרֹן וְאֶת־אֶלְעָזָר בְּנוֹ וְהַעַל אֹתָם הֹר הָהָר׃ וְהַפְשֵׁט אֶת־
כז אַהֲרֹן אֶת־בְּגָדָיו וְהִלְבַּשְׁתָּם אֶת־אֶלְעָזָר בְּנוֹ וְאַהֲרֹן יֵאָסֵף וּמֵת שָׁם׃ וַיַּעַשׂ מֹשֶׁה
כח כַּאֲשֶׁר צִוָּה יְהוָה וַיַּעֲלוּ אֶל־הֹר הָהָר לְעֵינֵי כָּל־הָעֵדָה׃ וַיַּפְשֵׁט מֹשֶׁה אֶת־אַהֲרֹן
אֶת־בְּגָדָיו וַיַּלְבֵּשׁ אֹתָם אֶת־אֶלְעָזָר בְּנוֹ וַיָּמָת אַהֲרֹן שָׁם בְּרֹאשׁ הָהָר וַיֵּרֶד מֹשֶׁה
כט וְאֶלְעָזָר מִן־הָהָר׃ וַיִּרְאוּ כָּל־הָעֵדָה כִּי גָוַע אַהֲרֹן וַיִּבְכּוּ אֶת־אַהֲרֹן שְׁלֹשִׁים יוֹם

רש"י

יח| **פֶּן בַּחֶרֶב אֵצֵא לִקְרָאתֶךָ.** אַתֶּם מִתְגָּאִים בַּקּוֹל שֶׁהוֹרִישְׁכֶם אֲבִיכֶם, וְאוֹמְרִים: "וַנִּצְעַק אֶל ה' וַיִּשְׁמַע קֹלֵנוּ" (לעיל פסוק טז), וַאֲנִי אֵצֵא עֲלֵיכֶם בְּמַה שֶּׁהוֹרִישַׁנִי אָבִי: "וְעַל חַרְבְּךָ תִחְיֶה" (בראשית כז, מ):

יט| **רַק אֵין דָּבָר.** אֵין שׁוּם דָּבָר מַזִּיקְךָ:

כ| **וּבְיָד חֲזָקָה.** בְּהַבְטָחַת זְקֵנוֹ: "וְהַיָּדַיִם יְדֵי עֵשָׂו" (בראשית כז, כב):

כב| **כָּל הָעֵדָה.** כֻּלָּם שְׁלֵמִים וְעוֹמְדִים לִיכָּנֵס לָאָרֶץ, שֶׁלֹּא הָיָה בָּהֶן אֶחָד מֵאוֹתָם שֶׁנִּגְזְרָה גְּזֵרָה עֲלֵיהֶם, שֶׁכְּבָר כָּלוּ מֵתֵי מִדְבָּר, וְאֵלּוּ מֵאוֹתָן שֶׁכָּתוּב בָּהֶן: "חַיִּים כֻּלְּכֶם הַיּוֹם" (דברים ד, ד). **הֹר הָהָר.** הַר עַל גַּבֵּי הַר, כְּתַפּוּחַ קָטָן עַל גַּבֵּי תַפּוּחַ גָּדוֹל. וְאַף עַל פִּי שֶׁהֶעָנָן הוֹלֵךְ לִפְנֵיהֶם וּמַשְׁוֶה אֶת הֶהָרִים, שְׁלֹשָׁה נִשְׁאֲרוּ בָהֶן: הַר סִינַי לַתּוֹרָה, הֹר הָהָר לִקְבוּרַת אַהֲרֹן, וְהַר נְבוֹ לִקְבוּרַת מֹשֶׁה:

כג| **עַל גְּבוּל אֶרֶץ אֱדוֹם.** מַגִּיד שֶׁמִּפְּנֵי שֶׁנִּתְחַבְּרוּ כָּאן לְהִתְקָרֵב לְעֵשָׂו הָרָשָׁע נִפְרְצוּ מַעֲשֵׂיהֶם וְחָסְרוּ הַצַּדִּיק הַזֶּה:

כה| **קַח אֶת אַהֲרֹן.** בִּדְבָרִים שֶׁל נִחוּמִים, אֱמֹר לוֹ: אַשְׁרֶיךָ שֶׁתִּרְאֶה כִּתְרְךָ נָתוּן לִבְנְךָ, מַה שֶּׁאֵין אֲנִי זַכַּאי לְכָךְ:

כו| **אֶת בְּגָדָיו.** בִּגְדֵי כְהֻנָּה גְדוֹלָה הִלְבִּישׁוֹ וְהִפְשִׁיטָם מֵעָלָיו לְתִתָּם עַל בְּנוֹ בְּפָנָיו. אָמַר לוֹ: הִכָּנֵס לַמְּעָרָה, וְנִכְנַס. רָאָה מִטָּה מֻצַּעַת וְנֵר דָּלוּק. אָמַר לוֹ: עֲלֵה לַמִּטָּה, וְעָלָה. פְּשֹׁט יָדֶיךָ, וּפָשַׁט. קְמֹץ פִּיךָ, וְקָמַץ. עֲצֹם עֵינֶיךָ, וְעָצַם. מִיָּד חָמַד מֹשֶׁה לְאוֹתָהּ מִיתָה. וְזֶהוּ שֶׁנֶּאֱמַר לוֹ: "כַּאֲשֶׁר מֵת אַהֲרֹן אָחִיךָ" (דברים לב, נ), מִיתָה שֶׁנִּתְאַוִּיתָ לָהּ:

כז| **וַיַּעַשׂ מֹשֶׁה.** אַף עַל פִּי שֶׁהַדָּבָר קָשֶׁה לוֹ, לֹא עִכֵּב:

כט| **וַיִּרְאוּ כָּל הָעֵדָה וְגוֹ'.** כְּשֶׁרָאוּ מֹשֶׁה וְאֶלְעָזָר יוֹרְדִים וְאַהֲרֹן לֹא יָרַד, אָמְרוּ: הֵיכָן הוּא אַהֲרֹן? אָמַר לָהֶם: מֵת. אָמְרוּ: אֶפְשָׁר מִי שֶׁעָמַד כְּנֶגֶד הַמַּלְאָךְ וְעָצַר אֶת הַמַּגֵּפָה (במדבר יז, יג) יִשְׁלֹט בּוֹ מַלְאַךְ הַמָּוֶת?! מִיָּד בִּקֵּשׁ מֹשֶׁה רַחֲמִים וְהֶרְאוּהוּ מַלְאֲכֵי הַשָּׁרֵת לָהֶם מֻטָּל בַּמִּטָּה, רָאוּ וְהֶאֱמִינוּ: **כֹּל בֵּית יִשְׂרָאֵל.** הָאֲנָשִׁים וְהַנָּשִׁים, לְפִי שֶׁהָיָה אַהֲרֹן רוֹדֵף שָׁלוֹם וּמֵטִיל אַהֲבָה בֵּין בַּעֲלֵי מְרִיבָה וּבֵין

DISCUSSION

20:28| **And Aaron died there:** Aaron did not experience any shock in the moments of his death. He calmly removed his clothes and perhaps dressed himself in shrouds, and then passed away in a state of rest, without any of the mental anguish that normally accompanies death. Aaron was told that it was his time to leave this world, and that his son would inherit his position, and Aaron departed to God in a state of tranquility.

entire house of Israel. Aaron was a prophet of the nation of Israel even before the arrival of Moses, and he was also the High Priest. The spontaneous weeping of the entire house of Israel testifies to the love that the entire nation felt for Aaron.

The War with the King of Arad

NUMBERS 21:1–3

Although the general direction of Israel's travels is northeast, they follow a circuitous path. This passage describes the challenge they face from the king of Arad. Although his land does not lie on their route, he is fearful of a possible invasion and attacks them.

21 1 **The Canaanite, king of Arad,**[B] **who lives in the South,** to the west of Israel's route, **heard that Israel came via Atarim,**[B] a place that perhaps served as one of the entrances to Canaan. According to the Sages, the king of Arad ruled over a mixed population of Amalekites and Canaanites.[21] **And he fought against Israel, and** although this was not a particularly large-scale war, the people were dispirited by Aaron's recent death,[22] and the king **took a captive from them.**

2 **Israel took a vow to the Lord, and said: If You will deliver this people into my hand, I will destroy their cities.** None of us will take from the spoils.

3 **The Lord heeded the voice of Israel, and delivered the Canaanites** into their hands; **it destroyed** [*vayaḥarem*] **them and their cities; and** from then onward, **it,** the people, **called the name of the place Ḥorma,** after the destruction [*ḥerem*]. Some commentaries say that it was called by that name because after its destruction, no permanent settlement was ever erected there.[23]

The Bronze Serpent

NUMBERS 21:4–9

As a punishment for their complaints, God strikes Israel with a plague of serpents. Anyone struck by this plague will be healed by gazing at the form of a serpent that Moses is commanded to fashion and place before them. The fact that one is healed by looking at an image of the very creature that caused his life-threatening wound serves to emphasize that it is the hand of God that both gives life and takes it.

4 **They,** the children of Israel, **traveled from Hor Mountain via the Red Sea.** They turned southward, toward the modern-day Gulf of Aqaba, in order **to circumvent the land of Edom. The soul of the people grew restive on the way,** as they appeared to be heading away from Canaan.[24]

5 **The people spoke** harshly **against God and against Moses: Why did you bring us up from Egypt to die in the wilderness, for there is no real bread and there is no** natural **water, and our soul loathes this insubstantial bread,**[D] the manna.

6 **The Lord sent the fiery serpents** whose poison burns human

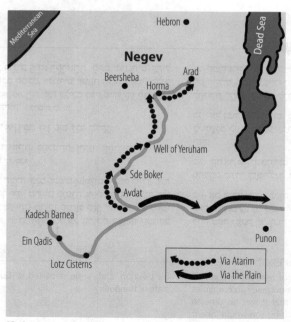

Via Atarim

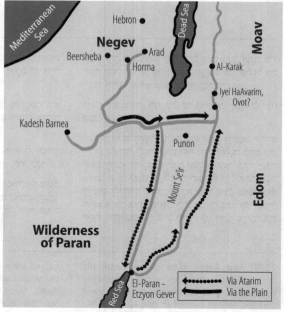

Circumvention of the land of Edom

854

כָּל בֵּית יִשְׂרָאֵל: וַיִּשְׁמַע הַכְּנַעֲנִי מֶלֶךְ־עֲרָד יֹשֵׁב הַנֶּגֶב כִּי

א

בָּא יִשְׂרָאֵל דֶּרֶךְ הָאֲתָרִים וַיִּלָּחֶם בְּיִשְׂרָאֵל וַיִּשְׁבְּ | מִמֶּנּוּ שֶׁבִי: וַיִּדַּר יִשְׂרָאֵל

ב

נֶדֶר לַיהוָה וַיֹּאמַר אִם־נָתֹן תִּתֵּן אֶת־הָעָם הַזֶּה בְּיָדִי וְהַחֲרַמְתִּי אֶת־עָרֵיהֶם:

וַיִּשְׁמַע יְהוָה בְּקוֹל יִשְׂרָאֵל וַיִּתֵּן אֶת־הַכְּנַעֲנִי וַיַּחֲרֵם אֶתְהֶם וְאֶת־עָרֵיהֶם וַיִּקְרָא

ג

שֵׁם־הַמָּקוֹם חָרְמָה:

וַיִּסְעוּ מֵהֹר הָהָר דֶּרֶךְ יַם־סוּף לִסְבֹב אֶת־אֶרֶץ אֱדוֹם וַתִּקְצַר נֶפֶשׁ־הָעָם בַּדָּרֶךְ:

ד

וַיְדַבֵּר הָעָם בֵּאלֹהִים וּבְמֹשֶׁה לָמָה הֶעֱלִיתֻנוּ מִמִּצְרַיִם לָמוּת בַּמִּדְבָּר כִּי אֵין לֶחֶם

ה

וְאֵין מַיִם וְנַפְשֵׁנוּ קָצָה בַּלֶּחֶם הַקְּלֹקֵל: וַיְשַׁלַּח יְהוָה בָּעָם אֵת הַנְּחָשִׁים הַשְּׂרָפִים

ו

רש"י

איש לאשתו: כי גוע. אומר אני שהמתרגם: 'דהא מית' טועה הוא, אלא אם כן מתרגם: 'ויראו' – 'ואתחזיאו', שלא אמרו רבותינו זכרונם לברכה 'כי' זה משמש בלשון 'דהא', אלא על מדרש שנסתלקו ענני כבוד, וכדאמר רבי אבהו: אל תקרי 'ויראו' אלא 'וייראו', ועל לשון זה נופל לשון 'דהא', לפי שהיא נתינת טעם למה שלמעלה הימנו: למה וייראו? לפי שהרי מת אהרן. אבל על תרגום: "וחזו כל כנשתא" אין לשון 'דהא' נופל, אלא לשון 'אשר', שהוא מגזרת שמוש 'אי', שמשמש 'אם' משמש בלשון 'אשר', כמו: "ואם מדוע לא תקצר רוחי" (איוב כא, ד), והרבה מפרשים מזה הלשון: "אם חרוצים ימיו" (שם יד, ה):

פרק כא

א| וישמע הכנעני. שמע שמת אהרן ונסתלקו ענני כבוד כו', כדאיתא בראש השנה (דף ג ע"א). ועמלק מעולם רצועת מרדות לישראל, מזמן בכל עת לפרענות: ישב הנגב. זה עמלק, שנאמר: "עמלק יושב בארץ הנגב" (לעיל יג, כט), ושנה את לשונו לדבר בלשון כנען, כדי שיהיו ישראל מתפללים להקדוש ברוך הוא לתת כנענים בידם, והם אינן כנענים. ראו ישראל לבושיהם כלבושי עמלקים ולשונם לשון כנען, אמרו: נתפלל סתם, שנאמר: "אם נתן תתן את העם הזה בידי" (להלן פסוק ב): דרך האתרים. דרך הנגב שהלכו בה מרגלים, שנאמר: "ויעלו בנגב" (לעיל יג, כב). דבר אחר, "דרך האתרים", דרך התייר הגדול הנוסע לפניהם, שנאמר: "דרך שלשת ימים לתור להם מנוחה" (לעיל י, לג): וישב ממנו שבי. אינה אלא שפחה אחת:

ב| והחרמתי. אקדיש שללם לגבוה:

ג| ויחרם אתהם. בהריגה: ואת עריהם. חרמי גבוה:

ד| דרך ים סוף. כיון שמת אהרן ובאת עליהם מלחמה זו, חזרו לאחוריהם דרך ים סוף, הוא הדרך שחזרו להם כשנגזרה עליהם גזרת מרגלים, שנאמר: "וסעו המדברה דרך ים סוף" (דברים א, מ). וכאן חזרו לאחוריהם שבע מסעות, שנאמר: "ובני ישראל נסעו מבארת בני יעקן מוסרה שם מת אהרן" (שם י, ו), וכי במוסרה מת? והלא בהר ההר מת! אלא שם חזרו והתאבלו עליו והספידוהו כאלו הוא בפניהם. וצא ובדוק במסעות ותמצאם שבע מסעות מן מוסרה עד הר ההר: לסבב את ארץ אדום. שלא נתנם לעבר בארצו: ותקצר נפש העם בדרך. בטורח הדרך שהקשה להם, אמרו: עכשיו היינו קרובים לכנס לארץ ואנו חוזרים לאחורינו, כך חזרו אבותינו ונשתהו שלשים ושמונה שנה עד היום, לפיכך קצרה נפשם בענוי הדרך. ובלשון לעז אנקרוטלו"ר. ולא יתכן לומר "ותקצר נפש העם בדרך" בהיותם בדרך ולא פרש בו במה קצרה, שכל מקום שתמצא קצור נפש במקרא מפרש שם במה קצרה, כגון: "ותקצר נפשי בהם" (זכריה יא, ח), וכגון: "ותקצר נפשו בעמל ישראל" (שופטים י, טז), וכל דבר הקשה על אדם נופל בו לשון קצור נפש, כאדם שהטורח בא עליו ואין דעתו רחבה לקבל אותו הדבר, ואין לו מקום בתוך לבו לגור שם אותו הצער, ובדבר המטריח נופל לשון גדל, שגדול הוא וכבד על האדם, כגון: "וגם נפשם בחלה בי" (זכריה שם), גדלה עלי, "ותגאה כשחל תצודני" (איוב י, טז). כללו של פרוש: כל לשון קצור נפש בדבר, לשון 'שאין יכול לסבלו' הוא, שאין הדעת סובלתו:

ה| באלהים ובמשה. השוו עבד לקונו: למה העליתנו. שניהם שוים: ונפשנו קצה. אף זה לשון קצור נפש ומאוס: בלחם הקלקל. לפי שהמן נבלע באיברים קראוהו 'קלקל', אמרו: עתיד המן הזה שיתפח במעינו, כלום יש ילוד אשה שמכניס ואינו מוציא?:

BACKGROUND

21:1 | **Arad:** Tel Arad is located on the northern slopes of the Valley of Arad, on the crossroads between the Judean hills and the Negev, and on the route ascending from Edom and the Arava to the coastal plain.

Via Atarim: Some commentaries explain that this refers to the route followed by the *tarim*, spies, when they ascended from Kadesh Barnea to Arad. This is one of the central routes in the Negev; its terrain is easily traversed and it is rich in water wells.

DISCUSSION

21:5 | **And our soul loathes this insubstantial bread:** Although the manna nourished the children of Israel, its consumption may be likened to the nourishment one receives intravenously. While the people were provided the necessary nutrients, they did not receive the satisfaction that comes with eating and enjoying a hearty meal. Although the people's complaints addressed specific issues, they were merely an expression of their mounting frustration at their life of wandering.

flesh, **against the people, and they bit the people, and a large multitude of Israel died** from the plague of serpents.

7 **The people came to Moses, and they said: We sinned, for we spoke against the Lord, and against you; pray to the Lord, and He will remove the serpents from us.** Unlike on earlier occasions when the people complained about their situation in a rebellious spirit, this time the people accepted responsibility for their current state. **Moses prayed on behalf of the people.**

8 **The Lord said to Moses: Craft for yourself a fiery,** poisonous **serpent, and place it upon a standard,** or a tall pillar; **it shall be that anyone who was bitten** by a serpent **will see it and live.**

9 **Moses crafted a bronze serpent.**[D] Although God did not tell Moses with which material to fashion the serpent, Moses chose to use bronze [*neḥoshet*] due to its similarity to the word *naḥash*, serpent, as if God's instructions alluded to the metal he should use.[25] Alternatively, he did not want to use a precious metal, as that might have led the people to deify the serpent. **And Moses placed it on the standard and it was that if a serpent bit a man, he would look at the bronze serpent and live.**

The Travels along the Border of Moav

NUMBERS 21:10–15

This passage, like the short passages that follow it, features prosaic descriptions of the journeys of the children of Israel, alongside obscure and poetic references to miracles that are performed for Israel. The details of these miracles have been lost; all that remains are distant echoes of these miraculous events.

Sixth 10 **The children of Israel traveled and encamped in Ovot.**
aliya 11 **They traveled from Ovot, and encamped at Iyei HaAvarim,** the ruins of the passageways [*ma'abarim*] between Moav and the Emorites,[26] **in the wilderness that is before Moav, to the east** of Moav **toward the sun.**

12 **From there they traveled** north, **and encamped in the Zered Ravine,**[B] which descends from the mountains of modern-day Jordan.

13 **From there they traveled and encamped across the Arnon,**[B] **which is in the wilderness, that emerges from the border of the Emorites, for Arnon is the border of Moav,**[D] **between Moav and the Emorites.**

14 **Therefore, it is said in the book of the Wars of the Lord:**[D] **Vahev,** the name of a place,[27] the children of Israel conquered **by storm, and also the tributaries of the Arnon;**

15 **the outpouring of the streams that tended toward the settled area of Ar,**[B] an important Moavite city, **and** this estuary **abuts the border of Moav.**

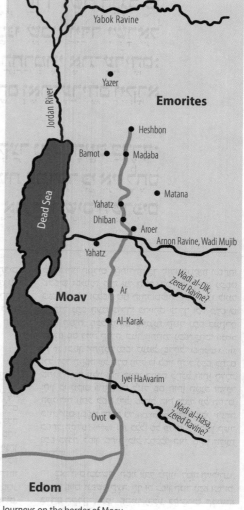

Journeys on the border of Moav

DISCUSSION

21:9 | A bronze serpent: This serpent was preserved by Israel for many generations. Not only was it brought into the Land of Israel, but it was kept in the various Tabernacles until the period of the kings. Eventually, King Hizkiya destroyed it because it had become an attraction for idol worshippers due to its antiquity, its sanctity, and its history (see II Kings 18:4).

21:13 | Arnon is the border of Moav: The fact that the Arnon Ravine was one of the borders

of Moav would have significance for many generations. The plains north of the ravine were the focus of numerous disputes between the nations of Israel and Amon and Moav, both in the period of the judges (Judges 11) and, according to the Mesha Stele, in the period of the kings. It is therefore important for the verse to establish that the Arnon is the border of Moav.

21:14 | In the book of the Wars of the Lord: Alongside the mysterious book of the Wars of the

Lord, the Bible makes reference to other books, including the book of the Upright (e.g., Joshua 10:13; II Samuel 1:18; I Kings 11:41). It may be assumed that some of these books were collections of ancient poetry that were not preserved because they were not considered sacred. Consequently, only allusions to these books remain (Rav Se'adya Gaon; Ibn Ezra). Some commentaries claim that the book of the Wars of the Lord, as well as similar names, refer to the Torah itself, or to parts of it (see *Targum Yonatan*; *Rokeaḥ*; Rav Yehuda HaḤasid).

ז וַיְנַשְּׁכוּ אֶת־הָעָם וַיָּמָת עַם־רָב מִיִּשְׂרָאֵל׃ וַיָּבֹא הָעָם אֶל־מֹשֶׁה וַיֹּאמְרוּ חָטָאנוּ
כִּי־דִבַּרְנוּ בַיהוה וָבָךְ הִתְפַּלֵּל אֶל־יהוה וְיָסֵר מֵעָלֵינוּ אֶת־הַנָּחָשׁ וַיִּתְפַּלֵּל
ח מֹשֶׁה בְּעַד הָעָם׃ וַיֹּאמֶר יהוה אֶל־מֹשֶׁה עֲשֵׂה לְךָ שָׂרָף וְשִׂים אֹתוֹ עַל־נֵס
ט וְהָיָה כָּל־הַנָּשׁוּךְ וְרָאָה אֹתוֹ וָחָי׃ וַיַּעַשׂ מֹשֶׁה נְחַשׁ נְחֹשֶׁת וַיְשִׂמֵהוּ עַל־הַנֵּס
י וְהָיָה אִם־נָשַׁךְ הַנָּחָשׁ אֶת־אִישׁ וְהִבִּיט אֶל־נְחַשׁ הַנְּחֹשֶׁת וָחָי׃ וַיִּסְעוּ בְּנֵי ששי
יא יִשְׂרָאֵל וַיַּחֲנוּ בְּאֹבֹת׃ וַיִּסְעוּ מֵאֹבֹת וַיַּחֲנוּ בְּעִיֵּי הָעֲבָרִים בַּמִּדְבָּר אֲשֶׁר עַל־
יב יג פְּנֵי מוֹאָב מִמִּזְרַח הַשָּׁמֶשׁ׃ מִשָּׁם נָסָעוּ וַיַּחֲנוּ בְּנַחַל זָרֶד׃ מִשָּׁם נָסָעוּ וַיַּחֲנוּ
מֵעֵבֶר אַרְנוֹן אֲשֶׁר בַּמִּדְבָּר הַיֹּצֵא מִגְּבֻל הָאֱמֹרִי כִּי אַרְנוֹן גְּבוּל מוֹאָב בֵּין
יד מוֹאָב וּבֵין הָאֱמֹרִי׃ עַל־כֵּן יֵאָמַר בְּסֵפֶר מִלְחֲמֹת יהוה אֶת־וָהֵב בְּסוּפָה וְאֶת־
טו הַנְּחָלִים אַרְנוֹן׃ וְאֶשֶׁד הַנְּחָלִים אֲשֶׁר נָטָה לְשֶׁבֶת עָר וְנִשְׁעַן לִגְבוּל מוֹאָב׃

רש"י

ו| **את הנחשים השרפים.** ששורפים את האדם בארס שיניהם: **וינשכו את העם.** יבא נחש שלקה על הוצאת דבה ויפרע ממוציאי דבה, יבא נחש שכל המינין נטעמין לו טעם אחד ויפרע מכפויי טובה שדבר אחד משתנה להם לכמה טעמים:

ז| **ויתפלל משה.** מכאן למי שמבקשים ממנו מחילה שלא יהא אכזרי מלמחול:

ח| **על נס.** על כלונס שקורין פירק"א בלעז, וכן: "וכנס על הגבעה" (ישעיה ל, יז), "ארים נסי" (שם מט, כב), "שאו נס" (שם יג, ב), ולפי שהוא גבוה לאות ולראיה קוראו 'נס': **כל הנשוך.** אפילו כלב או חמור נושכו היה נזוק ומתנונה והולך, אלא שנשיכת הנחש ממהרת להמית, לכך נאמר כאן: "וראה אתו" ראיה בעלמא, ובנשיכת הנחש נאמר: "והביט", "והיה אם נשך הנחש את איש והביט" וגו' (להלן פסוק ט), שלא היה ממהר נשוך הנחש להתרפאות אלא אם כן מביט בו בכונה. ואמרו רבותינו: וכי נחש ממית או מחיה? אלא בזמן שהיו ישראל מסתכלין כלפי מעלה ומשעבדין את לבם לאביהם שבשמים היו מתרפאים, ואם לאו היו נמוקים:

ט| **נחש נחשת.** לא נאמר לו לעשותו של נחשת, אלא אמר משה: הקדוש ברוך הוא קוראו נחש ואני אעשנו של נחשת, לשון נופל על לשון:

יא| **בעיי העברים.** לא ידעתי למה נקרא שמם עיים, ו'עי' לשון חרבה הוא, דבר הטאטא במטאטא, והעי"ן בו יסוד לבדה, והוא מלשון "יעים" (לעיל ד, יד), "ויעה ברד" (ישעיה כח, יז): **העברים.** דרך מעבר העוברים שם את הר נבו אל ארץ כנען, שהוא מפסיק בין ארץ מואב לארץ אמורי: **על פני מואב ממזרח השמש.** במזרחה של ארץ מואב:

יג| **מגבל האמרי.** תחום סוף מצר שלהם, וכן "גבול מואב", לשון קצה וסוף: **מעבר ארנון.** הקיפו ארץ מואב כל דרומה ומזרחה, עד שבאו מעבר השני לארנון בתוך ארץ האמורי, בצפונה של ארץ מואב: **היצא מגבל האמרי.** רצועה יוצאה מגבול האמורי והיא של אמוריים, ונכנסת לגבול מואב עד ארנון שהוא גבול מואב, ושם חנו ישראל ולא באו לגבול מואב, "כי ארנון גבול מואב", והם לא נתנו להם רשות לעבר בארצם. ואף על פי שלא פרשה משה, פרשה יפתח, כמו שאמר יפתח: "וגם אל מלך מואב שלח ולא אבה" (שופטים יא, יז), ומשה רמזה: "כאשר עשו לי בני עשו הישבים בשעיר והמואבים הישבים בער" (דברים ב, כט), מה אלו לא נתנום לעבר בתוך ארצם אלא הקיפום סביב, אף מואב כן:

יד-טו| **על כן.** על חניה זו ונסים שנעשו בה "יאמר בספר מלחמת ה'", כשמספרים נסים שנעשו לאבותינו, יספרו: "את והב" וגו': **את והב.** כמו 'את יהב', כמו שיאמר מן 'יעד' 'ועד', כן יאמר מן יהב 'והב', והוי"ו יסוד הוא, כלומר את אשר יהב להם והרבה נסים בים סוף: **ואת הנחלים ארנון.** כשם שמספרים בנסי ים סוף, כך יש לספר בנסי נחלי ארנון, שאף כאן נעשו נסים גדולים, ומה הם הנסים?: **ואשד הנחלים.** תרגום של שפך - 'אשד', שפך הנחלים, שנשפך שם דם אמוריים

BACKGROUND

21:12| **In the Zered Ravine:** Many researchers identify this valley with Wadi al-Hasa, whose stream empties into the southern part of the Dead Sea, and which forms the border between the mountains of Moav and the mountains of Edom. Others claim that it is one of the valleys in northeast Moav, which connect to the Arnon Ravine, specifically Wadi al-Dik, or another valley whose stream flows near Aroer (Elitzur).

21:13| **Arnon:** This refers to Wadi Mujib, which empties into the Dead Sea. It contains the largest river in Israel after the Jordan and served as a natural border due to its size and depth (see Joshua 12–13). Consequently, its crossings were of great strategic value.

21:15| **Ar:** This refers either to a southern province of Moav or to the ancient city of Areopolis, the Greek name for Rabat Moav, modern-day Rabba, located south of Wadi Mujib, and northeast of Al-Karak.

More Travels and the Song of the Well

NUMBERS 21:16–20

Just a few days after the children of Israel left Egypt, the Red Sea split before their eyes. There, the verse states: "Then Moses and the children of Israel sang this song to the Lord."[28] Now, as they approach Canaan, they sing another song involving water, this time for the opening of a source of fresh water. The fact that this song is introduced in a similar fashion, "Then Israel sang this song" (verse 17), serves to highlight the great difference between them: Only after Moses has led the children of Israel for many years have the people arrived at a point where they can initiate a song of gratitude to God even without the guidance of Moses.

16 **From there** Israel traveled **to the well; that is the well where the Lord said to Moses: Assemble the people, and I will give them water.** It is possible that this is the well that opened for them at the incident of the water of dispute (20:11–13).

17 **Then Israel sang this song:**[D] **Rise, well; give voice for it,** in honor of the well.

18 **A well that princes dug, the nobles of the people excavated, with a ruler's staff,**[B] meaning with the staffs in their hands, which symbolized their leadership, and **with their canes.** This was not a typical well dug by common laborers. The verse now proceeds with a list of places through which Israel passed: **And from the wilderness** they journeyed **to** a place called **Matana,**[B] perhaps because of the abundance that was found there.[29]

19 **And from Matana** they came **to** a place called **Nahaliel,** after its streams [*nehalim*]; **and from Nahaliel to Bamot,**[B] which was probably an elevated area, like a *bima*, platform;

20 **and from Bamot** they traveled **to the canyon that is in the field of Moav,** and **at the top of the peak** above, one could see Moav on one side, **and** the other side **overlooks the surface of the desert,** east of Moav.

Wars with Sihon and Og

The Wars with Sihon and Og

NUMBERS 21:21–22:1

At this point in the narrative, the Israelites have arrived at the northern border of Moav. Further north are two great kings who reign over the Emorites: Sihon in Heshbon and Og in Bashan. Perhaps as with Edom, Israel wanted no more than to pass through their lands or perhaps they sought to conquer this territory. In any event, the Israelites initiate their confrontation with the Emorites with polite negotiation. In this passage, the verse emphasizes that although the cities that are captured by Israel belonged to Moav in the distant past, Israel does not take these cities from their cousins, the Moavites, but from the Emorite kings who had previously captured them from Moav.

Seventh *aliya* (Fourth *aliya*)

21 **Israel sent messengers to Sihon, king of the Emorites, saying:**

22 **Let me pass in your land; we will not turn to a field or to a vineyard; we will not drink well water** from your wells; **we will go on the king's way,** the public thoroughfares that pass through the cities.[30] Alternatively, we will go on whatever road you instruct us to use,[31] **until we will pass your border** on the way to Canaan.

23 **Sihon did not allow Israel to pass in his border.**[D] Perhaps he was emboldened to refuse Israel safe passage because they

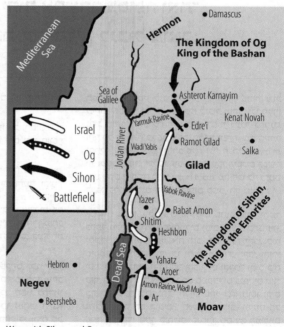

DISCUSSION

21:17 | **Then Israel sang this song:** It is possible that this ancient song also appeared in the book of the Wars of the Lord mentioned in the earlier passage (verse 14), or that it was included in the songs of the allegorists, which will be mentioned in the upcoming passage (verse 27). Like the book of the Wars of the Lord, the songs of the allegorists describe ancient events in a cryptic manner.

21:23 | **Sihon did not allow Israel to pass in his border:** Perhaps Sihon and Og (see verse 33), were border barons, powerful rulers charged with defending the borders of Canaan against invading marauders arriving from the wilderness. Indeed, such a threat would on occasion materialize (see Judges 6:1–6). It is even possible that the nations on the western side of the Jordan River paid these kings to protect their borders. Consequently, had Sihon and Og accepted Israel's request, they would have betrayed their function and the trust placed in them (see Rashi; *Bemidbar Rabba* 19:29; *Tanhuma, Hukat* 23).

טז וּמִשָּׁם בְּאֵרָה הִוא הַבְּאֵר אֲשֶׁר אָמַר יְהוָה לְמֹשֶׁה אֱסֹף אֶת־הָעָם וְאֶתְּנָה לָהֶם
יז מָיִם: אָז יָשִׁיר יִשְׂרָאֵל אֶת־הַשִּׁירָה הַזֹּאת עֲלִי בְאֵר עֱנוּ־לָהּ: בְּאֵר
יח
יט חֲפָרוּהָ שָׂרִים כָּרוּהָ נְדִיבֵי הָעָם בִּמְחֹקֵק בְּמִשְׁעֲנֹתָם וּמִמִּדְבָּר מַתָּנָה: וּמִמַּתָּנָה
כ נַחֲלִיאֵל וּמִנַּחֲלִיאֵל בָּמוֹת: וּמִבָּמוֹת הַגַּיְא אֲשֶׁר בִּשְׂדֵה מוֹאָב רֹאשׁ הַפִּסְגָּה
וְנִשְׁקָפָה עַל־פְּנֵי הַיְשִׁימֹן:
כא וַיִּשְׁלַח יִשְׂרָאֵל מַלְאָכִים אֶל־סִיחֹן מֶלֶךְ־הָאֱמֹרִי לֵאמֹר: אֶעְבְּרָה בְאַרְצֶךָ שביעי
כב לֹא נִטֶּה בְּשָׂדֶה וּבְכֶרֶם לֹא נִשְׁתֶּה מֵי בְאֵר בְּדֶרֶךְ הַמֶּלֶךְ נֵלֵךְ עַד אֲשֶׁר־נַעֲבֹר /רביעי/
כג גְּבֻלֶךָ: וְלֹא־נָתַן סִיחֹן אֶת־יִשְׂרָאֵל עֲבֹר בִּגְבֻלוֹ וַיֶּאֱסֹף סִיחֹן אֶת־כָּל־עַמּוֹ

רש"י

שהיו נחבאים שם; לפי שהיו ההרים גבוהים והנחל עמוק וקצר וההרים סמוכים זה לזה, אדם עומד על ההר מזה ומדבר עם חבירו בהר מזה, והדרך עובר בתוך הנחל, אמרו אמוריים: כשיכנסו ישראל לתוך הנחל לעבור, נצא מן המערות שבהרים שלמעלה מהם ונהרגם בחצים ואבני בליסטראות, והיו אותן הנקעים בהר של צד מואב, ובהר של צד אמוריים היו כנגד אותן נקעים כמין קרנות ושדים בולטין לחוץ, כיון שבאו ישראל לעבור, נזדעזע ההר של ארץ ישראל כשפחה היוצאת להקביל פני גבירתה, ונתקרב לצד הר של מואב, ונכנסו אותן השדים לתוך אותן נקעים והרגום, וזהו: "אשר נטה לשבת ער", שההר נטה ממקומו ונתקרב לצד מואב ונדבק בו, וזהו: "ונשען לגבול מואב":

טז | **ומשם בארה.** משם בא האשד אל הבאר. כיצד? אמר הקדוש ברוך הוא, מי מודיע לבני הנסים הללו? המשל אומר: נתת פת לתינוק, הודע לאמו. לאחר שעברו חזרו ההרים למקומם, והבאר ירדה לתוך הנחל והעלתה משם דם ההרוגים וזרועות ואיברים ומוליכתן סביב המחנה, וישראל ראו ואמרו שירה:

יז | **עלי באר.** מתוך הנחל והעלי מה שאת מעלה. ומנין שהבאר הודיעה להם? שנאמר: "ומשם בארה", וכי משם היתה? והלא מתחלת ארבעים שנה היתה עמהם! אלא שירדה לפרסם את הנסים. וכן "אז ישיר", השירה הזאת נאמרה בסוף ארבעים, והבאר נתנה להם מתחלת ארבעים, מה ראה לכתב כאן? אלא הענין הזה נדרש למעלה הימנו:

יח-כ | **באר חפרוה.** זאת היא הבאר אשר "חפרוה שרים", משה ואהרן: **במשענתם.** במטה: **וממדבר.** נתנה להם: **וממתנה נחליאל.** כתרגומו: **ומבמות הגיא אשר בשדה מואב.** כי שם מת משה ושם בטלה הבאר. דבר אחר, **כרוה נדיבי העם.** כל נשיא ונשיא כשהיו חונים נוטל מקלו ומושך אצל דגלו ומחנהו, ומי הבאר נמשכין דרך אותו סימן ובאין לפני חנית כל שבט ושבט: **במחקק.** על פי משה שנקרא מחוקק, שנאמר: "כי שם חלקת מחקק ספון" (דברים לג, כא). ולמה לא נזכר משה בשירה זו? לפי שלקה על ידי הבאר. וכיון שלא נזכר שמו של משה לא נזכר שמו של הקדוש ברוך הוא. משל למלך שהיו מזמנין אותו לסעודה, אמר: אם אוהבי שם אני שם, ואם לאו איני הולך: **ראש הפסגה.** כתרגומו: "ריש רמתא": **פסגה.** לשון גבה, וכן "פסגו ארמנותיה" (תהלים מח, יד), הגביהו ארמנותיה: **ונשקפה.** אותה הפסגה, על פני המקום ששמו "ישימן", והוא לשון מדבר שהוא שמם. דבר אחר, "ונשקפה" הבאר "על פני הישימן", שנגנזה בימה של טבריא, והעומד על הישימון מביט ורואה כמין כברה בים והיא הבאר. כך דרש רבי תנחומא (כא):

כא | **וישלח ישראל מלאכים.** ובמקום אחר תולה השליחות במשה, שנאמר: "ואשלח מלאכים ממדבר קדמות" (דברים ב, כו), וכן: "וישלח משה מלאכים מקדש אל מלך אדום" (לעיל כ, יד), וביפתח הוא אומר: "וישלח ישראל מלאכים אל מלך אדום" וגו' (שופטים יא, יז); הכתובים הללו צריכים זה לזה, זה נועל וזה פותח, שמשה הוא ישראל וישראל הם משה, לומר לך שנשיא הדור הוא ככל הדור, כי הנשיא הוא הכל:

כב | **אעברה בארצך.** אף על פי שלא נצטוו לפתח להם בשלום בקשו מהם שלום:

כג | **ולא נתן סיחן וגו'.** לפי שכל מלכי כנען היו מעלין לו מס, שהיה שומרם שלא יעברו עליהם גייסות, כיון שאמרו לו ישראל: "אעברה בארצך", אמר להם: כל

BACKGROUND

21:18| **With a ruler's staff** [*meḥokek*]: It is possible that the leaders would literally engrave statutes [*meḥokek ḥukkim*] into stone with the sharp ends of these staffs, hence the term *meḥokek* (see Rabbi Samson Raphael Hirsch, Genesis 49:10).

Matana: Some commentaries identify Matana with Khirbet al-Mudayna, located in Wadi ath-Thamad in northeastern Moav, which connects to the Zarqa Ravine. According to Nelson Glueck in 1942, the underground water in this area is relatively close to the surface and can be reached after a little digging, "with a ruler's staff, with their canes."

21:19| **Bamot:** This is an elevated area south of the Arnon Ravine, on the edge of the border of Moav, and possibly synonymous with the "heights of Baal" mentioned in connection to Bilam (22:41). However, most researchers believe the heights of Baal to be on one of the mountains north of the Arnon, e.g., Mount Attarus. According to the Jerusalem Talmud (*Shevi'it* 9:2), the heights of Baal was actually a plain or a hilly region.

approached him in a polite manner. **Sihon gathered his entire people, and came out toward Israel to the wilderness; he came to** the city of **Yahatz;**[B] **and he fought against Israel.**

24 **Israel smote him by sword, and took possession of his land from** the **Arnon** Ravine, on the border of Moav, **until** the **Yabok** Ravine,[32] **until the children of Amon; for the border of the children of Amon was strongly defended**[D] and closed to them.

25 **Israel took all these cities** in Sihon's land, **and Israel dwelt in all the cities of the Emorites, in** the city of **Heshbon,**[B] **and in all its environs.**

26 **For Heshbon was the city of Sihon, king of the Emorites; he,** Sihon, **fought against the first king of Moav, and took all his land from his possession, until Arnon,** including the city of Heshbon, which changed hands several times.

27 **Therefore, the allegorists will say.**[D] These allegorists were ancient poets who spoke in metaphor and parable,[33] and sang songs of the heroism displayed by the Emorites during their victorious wars against Moav. They will say: **Come,** let us go **to** conquer **Heshbon. The city of Sihon will be built and established** in this place, on the spot of the Moavite Heshbon.

28 **For a fire emerged from Heshbon, a flame from the city of Sihon.** After Heshbon was captured by the Emorites, it became known as the city of Sihon. The allegorists called for the heat of battle to continue from Heshbon to the other Moavite cities: **It consumed Ar,** a city **of Moav,** and **the shrines of the high places of Arnon.** The ancient song reiterated the small territory held by Moav at that time: Arnon was its northern border, as Heshbon, further north and formerly a Moavite city, had already been conquered by the Emorites.

29 **Woe to you, Moav, you are lost, people of Kemosh,** god of Moav. **He,** Kemosh, **has rendered his sons refugees, and his daughters are in captivity, to the Emorite king, Sihon.**

30 **Their fields were lost from Heshbon until Divon,**[B] another Moavite city.[34] Alternatively, the verse means: Their authority was lost from Heshbon and removed from Divon.[35] Or the verse means: We cast them from Heshbon until Divon.[36] **And we laid waste till Nofah that reaches to Medva.**[B] The poets depict Sihon's great victory over Moav, in which the border of Moav was pushed southward, and the entire region between the Arnon and Yabok Ravines became Emorite territory. When the Israelites conquered Sihon, they settled in this area.

31 **Israel dwelt in the land of the Emorites,** which was not densely populated, but was mainly pasture and farmland.

———— DISCUSSION ————

21:24 | For the border of the children of Amon was strongly defended: Not only did Sihon refuse to grant passage to the Israelites, he even came out to fight them. As there was nothing preventing the Israelites from engaging Sihon in battle, they fought Sihon and conquered his land. By contrast, the Israelites could not wage war against the children of Amon, even though they were not as strong as Sihon, because God prohibited the Israelites from doing so (Deuteronomy 2:19). Consequently, the Israelites considered the border of Amon impassable, not due to the military might of the Amonites, but because of the command of God (see Rashi).

21:27 | Therefore, the allegorists will say: In this passage, and in the preceding passages, the Torah cites fragments of ancient songs and allegories whose language is archaic. The homilies of the prophet Bilam (chaps. 23–24) are similar in this regard, as he, too, was an allegorist; the only remnants of his writings are those recorded in the Torah. These citations appear only toward the end of the Israelites' wanderings in the wilderness; before then, the Israelites were not exposed to other civilized nations. Only when they reached the edge of inhabited lands were they exposed to history, literature, and poetry, and only then could they cite the ancient songs of these lands.

———— BACKGROUND ————

21:23 | Yahatz: This city, which is mentioned in the ancient Mesha Stele, later became a Levite city in the territory of Reuben (see Joshua 13:18; I Chronicles 6:63). The verse seems to indicate that it was in the wilderness. Some identify Yahatz with one of two Iron Age fortresses situated on the ancient King's Highway, roughly 6 km north of Dhiban and overlooking Wadi Hidan. Others identify Yahatz with Tel Alian, roughly 12 km northeast of Dhiban.

21:25 | Heshbon: Heshbon was an important city located on the borders of the portions of Gad and Reuben (Joshua 13:17). It is generally identified with Tel Hesban, which sits on the ancient King's Highway, on the mountain range above the Madaba Plains, about 20 km southwest of Rabat Amon. According to Josephus Flavius, control of Heshbon passed through several hands during various

wars, and was even under Israelite control during the Hasmonean period. It can be inferred from Song of Songs (7:5) that the Israelites were familiar with this city (see Ramban, 32:38).

21:30 | Divon: Divon is generally identified with modern-day Dhiban, a major city on the ancient King's Highway, 4 km north of the Arnon Ravine. This city lies in the territory of the tribe of Reuben (Joshua 13:17), and was the capital of Moav in the ninth century BCE. Excavations of this site have yielded important archaeological discoveries, among them the Mesha Stele, named after Mesha, king of Moav. This inscription describes Mesha's war against Israel and various construction projects initiated by him throughout Moav and specifically in Divon. Some claim that in southern Moav, near the valley of Zered, there is another Divon, known as Divon Gad (see 32:34).

↢

כד ויצא לקראת ישראל המדברה ויבא יהצה וילחם בישראל: ויכהו ישראל
לפי־חרב ויירש את־ארצו מארנן עד־יבק עד־בני עמון כי עז גבול בני
כה עמון: ויקח ישראל את כל־הערים האלה וישב ישראל בכל־ערי האמרי
כו בחשבון ובכל־בנתיה: כי חשבון עיר סיחן מלך האמרי הוא והוא נלחם
כז במלך מואב הראשון ויקח את־כל־ארצו מידו עד־ארנן: על־כן יאמרו
כח המשלים באו חשבון תבנה ותכונן עיר סיחון: כי־אש יצאה מחשבון להבה
כט מקרית סיחן אכלה ער מואב בעלי במות ארנן: אוי־לך מואב אבדת עם־
ל כמוש נתן בניו פליטם ובנתיו בשבית למלך אמרי סיחון: ונירם אבד חשבון
לא עד־דיבן ונשים עד־נפח אשר עד־מידבא: וישב ישראל בארץ האמרי:

רש"י

עַצְמִי אֵינִי יוֹשֵׁב כָּאן אֶלָּא לְשָׁמְרָם מִפְּנֵיכֶם, וְאַתֶּם אוֹמְרִים כָּךְ?!: **וַיֵּצֵא לִקְרַאת יִשְׂרָאֵל.** אִלּוּ הָיְתָה חֶשְׁבּוֹן מְלֵאָה יַתּוּשִׁין אֵין כָּל בְּרִיָּה יְכוֹלָה לְכָבְשָׁהּ, וְאִם הָיָה סִיחוֹן בִּכְפָר חַלָּשׁ אֵין כָּל אָדָם יָכוֹל לְכָבְשׁוֹ, וְכָל שֶׁכֵּן שֶׁהָיָה בְּחֶשְׁבּוֹן. אָמַר הַקָּדוֹשׁ בָּרוּךְ הוּא: מָה אֲנִי מַטְרִיחַ עַל בָּנַי כָּל זֹאת לָצוּר עַל כָּל עִיר וָעִיר, נָתַן בְּלֵב כָּל אַנְשֵׁי הַמִּלְחָמָה לָצֵאת מִן הֶעָיָרוֹת, וְנִתְקַבְּצוּ כֻּלָּם לְמָקוֹם אֶחָד, וְשָׁם נָפְלוּ, וּמִשָּׁם הָלְכוּ יִשְׂרָאֵל אֶל הֶעָרִים וְאֵין עוֹמֵד לְנֶגְדָּם, כִּי אֵין שָׁם אִישׁ אֶלָּא נָשִׁים וָטָף:

כד| **כִּי עַז.** וּמַהוּ חָזְקוֹ? הַתְרָאָתוֹ שֶׁל הַקָּדוֹשׁ בָּרוּךְ הוּא שֶׁאָמַר לָהֶם: "אַל תְּגָרֶם" וְגוֹ' (דברים ב, יט):

כה| **בְּנֹתֶיהָ.** כְּפָרִים הַסְּמוּכִים לָהּ:

כו| **וְהוּא נִלְחַם וְגוֹ'.** לָמָּה הֻצְרַךְ לִכָּתֵב? לְפִי שֶׁנֶּאֱמַר: "אַל תָּצַר אֶת מוֹאָב" (דברים ב, ט), וְחֶשְׁבּוֹן מִשֶּׁל מוֹאָב הָיְתָה, כָּתַב לָנוּ שֶׁסִּיחוֹן לְקָחָהּ מֵהֶם וְעַל יָדוֹ טָהֲרָה לְיִשְׂרָאֵל: **מִיָּדוֹ.** מֵרְשׁוּתוֹ:

כז| **עַל כֵּן.** עַל אוֹתָהּ מִלְחָמָה שֶׁנִּלְחַם סִיחוֹן בְּמוֹאָב: **יֹאמְרוּ הַמֹּשְׁלִים.** בִּלְעָם, שֶׁנֶּאֱמַר בּוֹ: "וַיִּשָּׂא מְשָׁלוֹ" (להלן כג, ז): **הַמֹּשְׁלִים.** בִּלְעָם וּבְעוֹר, וְהֵם אָמְרוּ: "בֹּאוּ חֶשְׁבּוֹן", שֶׁלֹּא הָיָה סִיחוֹן יָכוֹל לְכָבְשָׁהּ וְהָלַךְ וְשָׂכַר אֶת בִּלְעָם לְקַלְּלוֹ, וְזֶהוּ שֶׁאָמַר לוֹ בָּלָק: "כִּי יָדַעְתִּי אֵת אֲשֶׁר תְּבָרֵךְ מְבֹרָךְ" וְגוֹ' (להלן כב, ו): **תִּבָּנֶה וְתִכּוֹנֵן.** חֶשְׁבּוֹן בְּשֵׁם סִיחוֹן לִהְיוֹת עִירוֹ:

כח| **כִּי אֵשׁ יָצְאָה מֵחֶשְׁבּוֹן.** מִשֶּׁכְּבָשָׁהּ סִיחוֹן: **אָכְלָה עָר מוֹאָב.** שֵׁם אוֹתָהּ הַמְּדִינָה קָרוּי 'עָר' בִּלְשׁוֹן עִבְרִי וּ'לְחָיַת' בִּלְשׁוֹן אֲרַמִּי: **עָר מוֹאָב.** עָר שֶׁל מוֹאָב:

כט| **אוֹי לְךָ מוֹאָב.** שֶׁקִּלְּלוּ אֶת מוֹאָב שֶׁיִּמָּסְרוּ בְּיָדוֹ: **כְּמוֹשׁ.** שֵׁם אֱלֹהֵי מוֹאָב (שופטים יא, כד): **נָתַן.** הַנּוֹתֵן אֶת בָּנָיו שֶׁל מוֹאָב: **פְּלֵיטִם.** נָסִים וּפְלֵטִים מֵחֶרֶב, וְאֶת בְּנֹתָיו בַּשְּׁבִית וְגוֹ':

ל| **וַנִּירָם אָבַד.** מַלְכוּת שֶׁלָּהֶם: **אָבַד חֶשְׁבּוֹן עַד דִּיבֹן.** מַלְכוּת וְעֹל שֶׁהָיָה לְמוֹאָב בְּחֶשְׁבּוֹן אָבַד מִשָּׁם, וְכֵן "עַד דִּיבֹן", תַּרְגּוּם שֶׁל 'סָר' – 'עַד', כְּלוֹמַר סָר נִיר מִדִּיבֹן. 'נִיר' לְשׁוֹן מַלְכוּת וְעֹל מֶמְשֶׁלֶת אִישׁ, כְּמוֹ: "לְמַעַן הֱיוֹת נִיר לְדָוִיד עַבְדִּי" (מלכים א' יא, לו): **וַנַּשִּׁים.** שִׁי"ן דְּגוּשָׁה, לְשׁוֹן שְׁמָמָה. כָּךְ יֹאמְרוּ הַמּוֹשְׁלִים: "וַנַּשִּׁים" אוֹתָם "עַד נֹפַח", הַשְּׁמָמוֹן עַד נֹפַח:

BACKGROUND

Medva: Medva, or Madaba, is a known city which has retained its name until today. It is located approximately 10 km south of Heshbon, in the portion of the tribe of Reuben. The city is built on a hill in the middle of a mountain range that ascends from the Jordan Valley. Its reconquest from Israel is mentioned in the Mesha Stele. Today, Madaba is known primarily for a mosaic that was uncovered there, the Madaba Map, which contains a cartographic depiction of Israel during the Byzantine period.

32 **Moses sent to spy out Yazer,**[B] which was also in the land of
Sihon. **They** first **captured its environs,** the small settlements
surrounding the city, after which they captured Yazer itself, **and
dispossessed the Emorites who were there.**

33 Once the children of Israel had conquered the land of Sihon,
they continued to move northward. Later, they would travel
back south, cross the Jordan River, and enter the land of
Canaan near Jericho **They turned and ascended via the
Bashan,** the broad and fertile region which includes the modern-day Golan Heights. The Bashan extends from the Yarmuk
River in the south to Mount Hermon, with the Jordan Valley
and the Sea of Galilee on the west and Jabal al-Druze on the
east. **And Og, king of Bashan,** also an Emorite king,[37] **came
out against them, he and his entire people, to the battle**

against Israel **at the city of Edre'i.**[B]

34 **The Lord said to Moses: Do not fear him.** Og, and perhaps
Maftir those in the surrounding areas, were "from the rest of the
Refaim,"[38] a race of giants. Some members of this race lived on
the western side of the Jordan, and it is they who caused the
spies of Israel to be afraid (13:33). God therefore tells Moses not
to fear. **For I have delivered him into your hand, him and his
entire people, and his land; you shall do to him as you did
to Sihon, king of the Emorites, who lives in Heshbon.**

35 **They smote him,**[D] **and his sons, and his entire people, until
they left no remnant of him; and they took possession of his
land.**

22 1 **The children of Israel traveled** southward, **and encamped on
the plains of Moav across the Jordan** River **from Jericho.**

BACKGROUND

21:32 | **Yazer:** Yazer was a central settlement that
served as a demarcation point for the southern border of Gilad and Amon (see Joshua 13:25). It is also
mentioned as one of the cities of the Levite family of
Merari (I Chronicles 6:66). Several possible locations
of ancient Yazer have been proposed: Khirbet Sar,
west of Rabat Amon; Tel Arima; and Khirbet Jazar,
south of Al-Salt. Some place it northeast of the Dead
Sea, in the region of Machaerus.

DISCUSSION

21:35 | **They smote him:** The reason for these
conquests is explained later, in the book of
Deuteronomy: "Rise, and travel, and cross
Arnon Ravine; see, I have placed Sihon, king
of Heshbon, the Emorite, and his land in your
hand; begin taking possession, and provoke
war with him. This day I will begin to place
terror of you and fear of you upon the peoples

under all the heavens, who will hear your reputation and will tremble, and be in trepidation
because of you" (2:24–25). The same may be
inferred from comments made by Rahav (see
Joshua 2:10), namely that the conquest of the
two Emorite kings deterred the inhabitants of
Canaan, and caused them to fear Israel.

לב וַיִּשְׁלַח מֹשֶׁה לְרַגֵּל אֶת־יַעְזֵר וַיִּלְכְּדוּ בְּנֹתֶיהָ וַיִּירֶשׁ אֶת־הָאֱמֹרִי אֲשֶׁר־שָׁם׃ וַיּוֹרֶשׁ
לג וַיִּפְנוּ וַיַּעֲלוּ דֶּרֶךְ הַבָּשָׁן וַיֵּצֵא עוֹג מֶלֶךְ־הַבָּשָׁן לִקְרָאתָם הוּא וְכָל־עַמּוֹ לַמִּלְחָמָה
לד אֶדְרֶעִי׃ וַיֹּאמֶר יהוה אֶל־מֹשֶׁה אַל־תִּירָא אֹתוֹ כִּי בְיָדְךָ נָתַתִּי אֹתוֹ וְאֶת־כָּל־עַמּוֹ מפטיר
וְאֶת־אַרְצוֹ וְעָשִׂיתָ לּוֹ כַּאֲשֶׁר עָשִׂיתָ לְסִיחֹן מֶלֶךְ הָאֱמֹרִי אֲשֶׁר יוֹשֵׁב בְּחֶשְׁבּוֹן׃
לה וַיַּכּוּ אֹתוֹ וְאֶת־בָּנָיו וְאֶת־כָּל־עַמּוֹ עַד־בִּלְתִּי הִשְׁאִיר־לוֹ שָׂרִיד וַיִּירְשׁוּ אֶת־אַרְצוֹ׃
כב א וַיִּסְעוּ בְּנֵי יִשְׂרָאֵל וַיַּחֲנוּ בְּעַרְבוֹת מוֹאָב מֵעֵבֶר לְיַרְדֵּן יְרֵחוֹ׃

רש״י

לב] **וישלח משה לרגל את יעזר וגו׳.** הַמְרַגְּלִים לְכָדוּהָ, אָמְרוּ: לֹא נַעֲשֶׂה כָּרִאשׁוֹנִים, בְּטוּחִים אָנוּ בְּכֹחַ תְּפִלָּתוֹ שֶׁל מֹשֶׁה לְהִלָּחֵם:

לד] **אל תירא אתו.** שֶׁהָיָה מֹשֶׁה יָרֵא לְהִלָּחֵם, שֶׁמָּא תַּעֲמֹד לוֹ זְכוּתוֹ שֶׁל אַבְרָהָם, שֶׁנֶּאֱמַר: ״וַיָּבֹא הַפָּלִיט״ (בראשית יד, יג), הוּא עוֹג שֶׁפָּלַט מִן הָרְפָאִים שֶׁהִכּוּ כְּדָרְלָעֹמֶר וַחֲבֵרָיו בְּעַשְׁתְּרֹת קַרְנַיִם, שֶׁנֶּאֱמַר: ״רַק עוֹג מֶלֶךְ הַבָּשָׁן נִשְׁאַר מִיֶּתֶר הָרְפָאִים״ (דברים ג, יא):

לה] **ויכו אתו.** מֹשֶׁה הֲרָגוֹ, כִּדְאִיתָא בִּבְרָכוֹת בְּ״הָרוֹאֶה״ (דף נד ע״ב): עֲקַר טוּרָא בַּר תְּלָתָא פַּרְסֵי וְכוּ׳:

BACKGROUND

21:33| **Edre'i:** This refers to Daraa, a provincial city and an important crossroads in the south of the Bashan, located in southern Syria. Archaeologists have found artifacts in Edre'i dating back to the third millennium BCE, and it is mentioned in ancient Egyptian records. Edre'i was included in the portion of half the tribe of Manasseh. Historical records testify to an Israelite presence in Edre'i from the Second Temple period until the Middle Ages.

Parashat
Balak

Balak and Bilam
NUMBERS 22:2–24:25

The previous section related that Sihon king of the Emorites triumphed over the Moavites during their first king's reign. When Balak, the reigning king of Moav, sees that the kingdom that defeated his land suffers a dramatic defeat at the hands of Israel, he considers the presence of the children of Israel in the region as a threat. He therefore decides to deploy a weapon that has yet to be tried against them, namely, the supernatural power of the sorcerer Bilam, who would curse the people. The episode of Balak and Bilam is important for two main reasons: First, the entire story demonstrates God's providence and care for Israel, as He protects the Israelites from any curse. Second, Bilam's poetic verses are significant in their own right; his speeches are to a certain extent unrelated to his motivations and his personality, as they are placed in his mouth against his will, in the form of a lofty prophecy that incorporates basic truths about the nation of Israel and its future.

2 **Balak son of Tzipor,** king of Moav, **saw all that Israel had done to the Emorites.**

3 **Moav was very alarmed by the people because they were numerous; and** furthermore, **Moav was disgusted by the children of Israel.** Although the Israelites were commanded not to harass the Moavites,[1] and they had not done anything to provoke them, nevertheless, the Israelites' very presence near their land agitated the Moavites.

4 **Moav said to the elders,** the leaders **of Midyan,** which was a group of nomadic tribes dwelling close to Moav: **Now this** large **assembly** of Israel **will lick clean,** consume, **all our surroundings, as the ox licks clean the grass of the field.** Even if they refrain from attacking us, in order to survive here they will inevitably consume everything in their surroundings. The verse notes: **Balak son of Tzipor was king of Moav at that time.** It is possible that he was recently crowned as king. Certain sources indicate that Balak was considered a powerful, successful king.[2]

"Ox licks clean the grass of the field"

5 **Therefore, he,** Balak, **sent messengers to Bilam son of Beor,**ᴰ **to** a place called **Petor that is by the** Euphrates **River,** far north

of Moav, **in the land of the members of his,** Balak's, **people,**[3] or Bilam's people.[4] He sent those messengers **to summon him, saying: Behold, a people emerged from Egypt; behold, it has covered the face of the earth.** This is a metaphor of the earth covered by so many people that it is as though it can no longer be seen.[5] **And it,** this nation, **dwells across from me.**

6 **Now, please come curse this people for me, as they are too mighty for me; perhaps I will be able to smite** [*nakeh*] **them,** or to reduce it [*lenakot*] from its greatness. Some commentaries explain that this is a plural form, as Balak is saying that he and Bilam, or he and Midyan, will be able to smite Israel.[6] **And I will drive them from the land, for I know that he whom you bless is blessed, and he whom you curse is cursed.** As a great sorcerer and prophet, your blessings and curses come to pass.

7 **The elders of Moav and the elders of Midyan went with the tools of sorcery in their hand.** These tools helped them navigate their way, and they also took them to present to Bilam, in case he would claim that his tools of divination were unavailable.[7] **And they came to Bilam,** after a very lengthy journey, **and spoke to him the words of Balak.**

8 **He,** Bilam, **said to them,** the elders of Moav and Midyan: **Spend the night here, and I will reply to you as the Lord will speak to me.** I expect that God will reveal Himself to me in a nightly vision. **The princes of Moav stayed** overnight **with Bilam,** hoping he would have a revelation in a dream.

DISCUSSION

22:5 | **Bilam son of Beor:** Bilam's name is preserved in archaeological findings as well. An extant inscription, which includes one of his prophecies or curses, indicates that Bilam was well known throughout the entire region. These statements of Bilam survived on a wall for thousands of years, but they remain obscure.

In addition to Bilam's dalliance in magic, as a sorcerer and a soothsayer, he was also a prophet of God. Perhaps he was among the group of people who believed in God and observed an ancient form of worship of "God, the Most High," a group which included Malkitzedek king of Shalem (Genesis 14:18). Balak saw that the

gods of the Egyptians and the Emorites, and all other idols, had failed to withstand Israel, and he reasoned that if anyone could defeat them, it must be someone who can utilize the source of their own power. In short, he wanted to find a way for the God who supports Israel to be used against them.

פרשת

בלק

כב ב ג וַיַּרְא בָּלָק בֶּן־צִפּוֹר אֵת כָּל־אֲשֶׁר־עָשָׂה יִשְׂרָאֵל לָאֱמֹרִי׃ וַיָּגָר מוֹאָב מִפְּנֵי הָעָם יט
ד מְאֹד כִּי רַב־הוּא וַיָּקָץ מוֹאָב מִפְּנֵי בְּנֵי יִשְׂרָאֵל׃ וַיֹּאמֶר מוֹאָב אֶל־זִקְנֵי מִדְיָן
עַתָּה יְלַחֲכוּ הַקָּהָל אֶת־כָּל־סְבִיבֹתֵינוּ כִּלְחֹךְ הַשּׁוֹר אֵת יֶרֶק הַשָּׂדֶה וּבָלָק בֶּן־
ה צִפּוֹר מֶלֶךְ לְמוֹאָב בָּעֵת הַהִוא׃ וַיִּשְׁלַח מַלְאָכִים אֶל־בִּלְעָם בֶּן־בְּעֹר פְּתוֹרָה
אֲשֶׁר עַל־הַנָּהָר אֶרֶץ בְּנֵי־עַמּוֹ לִקְרֹא־לוֹ לֵאמֹר הִנֵּה עַם יָצָא מִמִּצְרַיִם הִנֵּה
ו כִסָּה אֶת־עֵין הָאָרֶץ וְהוּא יֹשֵׁב מִמֻּלִי׃ וְעַתָּה לְכָה־נָּא אָרָה־לִּי אֶת־הָעָם הַזֶּה
כִּי־עָצוּם הוּא מִמֶּנִּי אוּלַי אוּכַל נַכֶּה־בּוֹ וַאֲגָרְשֶׁנּוּ מִן־הָאָרֶץ כִּי יָדַעְתִּי אֵת
ז אֲשֶׁר־תְּבָרֵךְ מְבֹרָךְ וַאֲשֶׁר תָּאֹר יוּאָר׃ וַיֵּלְכוּ זִקְנֵי מוֹאָב וְזִקְנֵי מִדְיָן וּקְסָמִים
ח בְּיָדָם וַיָּבֹאוּ אֶל־בִּלְעָם וַיְדַבְּרוּ אֵלָיו דִּבְרֵי בָלָק׃ וַיֹּאמֶר אֲלֵיהֶם לִינוּ פֹה הַלַּיְלָה
וַהֲשִׁבֹתִי אֶתְכֶם דָּבָר כַּאֲשֶׁר יְדַבֵּר יְהוָה אֵלָי וַיֵּשְׁבוּ שָׂרֵי־מוֹאָב עִם־בִּלְעָם׃

רש״י

פרק כב

ב | **וַיַּרְא בָּלָק בֶּן צִפּוֹר אֵת כָּל אֲשֶׁר עָשָׂה יִשְׂרָאֵל לָאֱמֹרִי.** אָמַר: אֵלּוּ שְׁנֵי מְלָכִים שֶׁהָיִינוּ בְּטוּחִים עֲלֵיהֶם לֹא עָמְדוּ בִּפְנֵיהֶם, אָנוּ עַל אַחַת כַּמָּה וְכַמָּה, לְפִיכָךְ: "וַיָּגָר מוֹאָב":

ג | **וַיָּגָר.** לְשׁוֹן מוֹרָא, כְּמוֹ: "גּוּרוּ לָכֶם" (איוב יט, כט): **וַיָּקָץ מוֹאָב.** קָצוּ בְּחַיֵּיהֶם:

ד | **אֶל זִקְנֵי מִדְיָן.** וַהֲלֹא מֵעוֹלָם הָיוּ שׂוֹנְאִים זֶה אֶת זֶה, שֶׁנֶּאֱמַר: "הַמַּכֶּה אֶת מִדְיָן בִּשְׂדֵה מוֹאָב" (בראשית לו, לה), שֶׁבָּאוּ מִדְיָן עַל מוֹאָב לַמִּלְחָמָה! אֶלָּא מִיִּרְאָתָן שֶׁל יִשְׂרָאֵל עָשׂוּ שָׁלוֹם בֵּינֵיהֶם. וּמָה רָאָה מוֹאָב לִטֹּל עֵצָה מִמִּדְיָן? כֵּיוָן שֶׁרָאוּ אֶת יִשְׂרָאֵל נוֹצְחִים שֶׁלֹּא כְּמִנְהַג הָעוֹלָם, אָמְרוּ: מַנְהִיגָם שֶׁל אֵלּוּ בְּמִדְיָן נִתְגַּדֵּל, נִשְׁאַל מֵהֶם מַה מִּדָּתוֹ. אָמְרוּ לָהֶם: אֵין כֹּחוֹ אֶלָּא בְּפִיו. אָמְרוּ: אַף אָנוּ נָבוֹא עֲלֵיהֶם בְּאָדָם שֶׁכֹּחוֹ בְּפִיו: **כִּלְחֹךְ הַשּׁוֹר.** כָּל מַה שֶּׁהַשּׁוֹר מְלַחֵךְ אֵין בּוֹ בְּרָכָה: **בָּעֵת הַהִוא.** לֹא הָיָה רָאוּי לְמַלְכוּת, מִנְּסִיכֵי מִדְיָן הָיָה, וְכֵיוָן שֶׁמֵּת סִיחוֹן מִנּוּהוּ עֲלֵיהֶם לְצֹרֶךְ שָׁעָה:

ה | **פְּתוֹרָה.** כַּשֻּׁלְחָנִי הַזֶּה שֶׁהַכֹּל מְרִיצִין לוֹ מָעוֹת, כָּךְ כָּל הַמְּלָכִים מְרִיצִין לוֹ אִגְּרוֹתֵיהֶם. וּלְפִי פְּשׁוּטוֹ שֶׁל מִקְרָא כָּךְ שֵׁם הַמָּקוֹם: **אֶרֶץ בְּנֵי עַמּוֹ.** שֶׁל בָּלָק, מִשָּׁם הָיָה, וְזֶה הָיָה מִתְנַבֵּא וְאוֹמֵר לוֹ: עָתִיד אַתָּה לִמְלֹךְ. וְאִם תֹּאמַר: מִפְּנֵי מָה הִשְׁרָה הַקָּדוֹשׁ בָּרוּךְ הוּא שְׁכִינָתוֹ עַל גּוֹי רָשָׁע? כְּדֵי שֶׁלֹּא יִהְיֶה פִּתְחוֹן פֶּה לָאֻמּוֹת לוֹמַר: אִלּוּ הָיוּ לָנוּ נְבִיאִים חָזַרְנוּ לְמוּטָב. הֶעֱמִיד לָהֶם נְבִיאִים, וְהֵם פָּרְצוּ גֶּדֶר הָעוֹלָם, שֶׁבַּתְּחִלָּה הָיוּ גְּדוּרִים בַּעֲרָיוֹת, וְזֶה נָתַן לָהֶם עֵצָה לְהַפְקִיר עַצְמָן לִזְנוּת: **לִקְרֹא לוֹ.** הַקְּרִיאָה הָיְתָה שֶׁלּוֹ וּלַהֲנָאָתוֹ, שֶׁהָיָה פּוֹסֵק לוֹ מָמוֹן הַרְבֵּה: **עַם יָצָא מִמִּצְרַיִם.** וְאִם תֹּאמַר: מַה מַּזִּיקְךָ? **הִנֵּה כִסָּה אֶת עֵין הָאָרֶץ.** סִיחוֹן וְעוֹג שֶׁהָיוּ שׁוֹמְרִים אוֹתָנוּ, עָמְדוּ עֲלֵיהֶם וַהֲרָגוּם: **וְהוּא יֹשֵׁב מִמֻּלִי.** חָסֵר כְּתִיב, קְרוֹבִים הֵם לְהַכְרִיתֵנִי, כְּמוֹ: "כִּי אֲמִילַם" (תהלים קיח, י):

ו | **נַכֶּה בּוֹ.** אֲנִי וְעַמִּי נַכֶּה בָּהֶם. דָּבָר אַחֵר, לְשׁוֹן מִשְׁנָה הוּא: "מְנַכֶּה לוֹ מִן הַדָּמִים" (חולין קלב ע"א), לְחַסֵּר מֵהֶם מְעַט: **כִּי יָדַעְתִּי וְגוֹ׳.** עַל יְדֵי מִלְחֶמֶת סִיחוֹן שֶׁעֲזַרְתּוֹ לְהַכּוֹת אֶת מוֹאָב:

ז | **וּקְסָמִים בְּיָדָם.** כָּל מִינֵי קְסָמִים, שֶׁלֹּא יֹאמַר: אֵין כְּלֵי תַּשְׁמִישִׁי עִמִּי. דָּבָר אַחֵר, קֶסֶם זֶה נָטְלוּ בְּיָדָם זִקְנֵי מִדְיָן, אָמְרוּ: אִם יָבֹא עִמָּנוּ בַּפַּעַם הַזֹּאת יֵשׁ בּוֹ מַמָּשׁ, וְאִם יִדְחֵנוּ אֵין בּוֹ תּוֹעֶלֶת. לְפִיכָךְ כְּשֶׁאָמַר לָהֶם: "לִינוּ פֹה הַלַּיְלָה" (להלן פסוק ח) אָמְרוּ: אֵין בּוֹ תִּקְוָה, הִנִּיחוּהוּ וְהָלְכוּ לָהֶם, שֶׁנֶּאֱמַר: "וַיֵּשְׁבוּ שָׂרֵי מוֹאָב עִם בִּלְעָם" (שם), אֲבָל זִקְנֵי מִדְיָן הָלְכוּ לָהֶם:

ח | **לִינוּ פֹה הַלַּיְלָה.** אֵין רוּחַ הַקֹּדֶשׁ שׁוֹרָה עָלָיו אֶלָּא בַּלַּיְלָה, וְכֵן לְכָל נְבִיאֵי אֻמּוֹת הָעוֹלָם, וְכֵן לָבָן בַּחֲלוֹם הַלַּיְלָה, שֶׁנֶּאֱמַר: "וַיָּבֹא אֱלֹהִים אֶל לָבָן הָאֲרַמִּי בַּחֲלֹם הַלָּיְלָה" (בראשית לא, כד), כְּאָדָם הַהוֹלֵךְ אֵצֶל פִּילַגְשׁוֹ בְּהֶחְבֵּא: **כַּאֲשֶׁר יְדַבֵּר ה׳ אֵלָי.** אִם יַמְלִיכֵנִי לָלֶכֶת עִם בְּנֵי אָדָם כְּמוֹתְכֶם אֵלֵךְ עִמָּכֶם, שֶׁמָּא אֵין כְּבוֹדוֹ לְתִתִּי לַהֲלֹךְ אֶלָּא עִם שָׂרִים גְּדוֹלִים: **וַיֵּשְׁבוּ.** לְשׁוֹן עַכָּבָה:

9 Indeed, **God came to Bilam, and said,** in order to initiate conversation with him: **Who are these men with you?**[D]

10 **Bilam said to God: Balak son of Tzipor, king of Moav, sent to me:**

11 **Behold, the people that has come out of Egypt and it has covered the face of the earth; now, come curse them for me; perhaps** they will be weakened by your curse, and then **I will be able to make war against them, and I will drive them away.**

12 **God said to Bilam: You shall not go with them; you shall not** succeed in your wish to **curse the people, as it is blessed.**

13 **Bilam arose in the morning, and said to the princes of**
Second aliya (Fifth aliya)
Balak: Go to your land, as the Lord refused to allow me to go with you. I have no choice, as I received an unambiguous message from God, whose commands I must obey. Bilam considered himself a servant of God, not an idolater.

14 **The princes of Moav rose, and they came to Balak, and they said: Bilam refused to go with us.** This suggests that Bilam did not cite God's exact statement, but spoke to them in such a manner that they understood there was something holding him back. The continuation of the story indicates that the princes did not take his response as an absolute refusal.

15 Assuming that the first delegation failed in its mission because it was insufficiently impressive, **Balak continued sending additional princes, more numerous and more prestigious than those** he had sent before.

16 **They came to Bilam and said to him: So said Balak son of Tzipor;** he instructed us to say to you: **Please, do not refrain from going to me.**

17 **For I will honor you greatly, and anything that you say to me I will do;** just **please go curse this people for me.**

18 **Bilam answered and said to the servants of Balak:** Even if **Balak were to give me his house full of silver and gold,**[D] **I would be unable to violate the directive of the Lord my God, to perform a small or a great matter.** I must reiterate that I cannot do as I please. I am but a messenger, an instrument of God, and I can act only in accordance with His instructions.

19 **Now, please, you too, remain here also this night,** as it is possible that I will receive a prophetic vision tonight as well. I will

Donkey

pass on your suggestion to God, **and I will know more what the Lord will speak to me,** which I will relay to you.

20 **God came to Bilam at night, and He said** a different message **to him: If the people came to summon you,** then **rise, go with them;** you may accompany them as they have requested. **However, only the matter that I will speak to you shall you do.** You are permitted to go to Moav, but you must remember that you are still obligated to fulfill My bidding, and you cannot know what you will be required to do there.

21 **Bilam arose in the morning, saddled his donkey, and went**
Third aliya
with the princes of Moav. He agreed to accompany them on the lengthy journey.

22 **God's wrath was enflamed because he was going.** The initial instruction Bilam received from God was clear: Do not go and do not curse the Israelites. Bilam continued to beseech God for permission to accompany Balak's men and was therefore granted God's reluctant consent. However, God allowed him only to go with the princes of Moav. It was clear from the way Bilam accompanied the princes that he desired the same result as them, but as God's servant he had to placate Him first. Consequently, God was angry with him.[8] **And the angel of the Lord stood on the way as an impediment to him. He,** Bilam,

---

DISCUSSION

22:9 | Who are these men with you: In several places in the Bible, God begins His address to a person with questions of this type, about his place and deeds. This is not in order to clarify a matter of which God is unaware, but to help His listeners ease into the conversation, so that they

should not be too frightened to answer (see Rashi, Genesis 3:9).

22:18 | If Balak were to give me his house full of silver and gold: Although Bilam speaks as a servant of God, the Sages infer from his

language that he had several bad qualities: an evil eye, a haughty spirit, and a desirous soul (*Avot* 5:19). Although no clear offer has been made to Bilam at this stage, he imagines that he will receive enormous treasures, such as the king's own house filled with silver and gold.

ט וַיָּבֹא אֱלֹהִים אֶל־בִּלְעָם וַיֹּאמֶר מִי הָאֲנָשִׁים הָאֵלֶּה עִמָּךְ׃ וַיֹּאמֶר בִּלְעָם אֶל־
יא הָאֱלֹהִים בָּלָק בֶּן־צִפֹּר מֶלֶךְ מוֹאָב שָׁלַח אֵלָי׃ הִנֵּה הָעָם הַיֹּצֵא מִמִּצְרַיִם וַיְכַס
יב אֶת־עֵין הָאָרֶץ עַתָּה לְכָה קָבָה־לִּי אֹתוֹ אוּלַי אוּכַל לְהִלָּחֶם בּוֹ וְגֵרַשְׁתִּיו׃ וַיֹּאמֶר
יג אֱלֹהִים אֶל־בִּלְעָם לֹא תֵלֵךְ עִמָּהֶם לֹא תָאֹר אֶת־הָעָם כִּי בָרוּךְ הוּא׃ וַיָּקָם שני
בִּלְעָם בַּבֹּקֶר וַיֹּאמֶר אֶל־שָׂרֵי בָלָק לְכוּ אֶל־אַרְצְכֶם כִּי מֵאֵן יְהוָה לְתִתִּי לַהֲלֹךְ /חמישי/
יד טו עִמָּכֶם׃ וַיָּקוּמוּ שָׂרֵי מוֹאָב וַיָּבֹאוּ אֶל־בָּלָק וַיֹּאמְרוּ מֵאֵן בִּלְעָם הֲלֹךְ עִמָּנוּ׃ וַיֹּסֶף
טז עוֹד בָּלָק שְׁלֹחַ שָׂרִים רַבִּים וְנִכְבָּדִים מֵאֵלֶּה׃ וַיָּבֹאוּ אֶל־בִּלְעָם וַיֹּאמְרוּ לוֹ כֹּה
יז אָמַר בָּלָק בֶּן־צִפּוֹר אַל־נָא תִמָּנַע מֵהֲלֹךְ אֵלָי׃ כִּי־כַבֵּד אֲכַבֶּדְךָ מְאֹד וְכֹל
יח אֲשֶׁר־תֹּאמַר אֵלַי אֶעֱשֶׂה וּלְכָה־נָּא קָבָה־לִּי אֵת הָעָם הַזֶּה׃ וַיַּעַן בִּלְעָם וַיֹּאמֶר
אֶל־עַבְדֵי בָלָק אִם־יִתֶּן־לִי בָלָק מְלֹא בֵיתוֹ כֶּסֶף וְזָהָב לֹא אוּכַל לַעֲבֹר אֶת־פִּי
יט יְהוָה אֱלֹהָי לַעֲשׂוֹת קְטַנָּה אוֹ גְדוֹלָה׃ וְעַתָּה שְׁבוּ נָא בָזֶה גַּם־אַתֶּם הַלָּיְלָה
כ וְאֵדְעָה מַה־יֹּסֵף יְהוָה דַּבֵּר עִמִּי׃ וַיָּבֹא אֱלֹהִים ׀ אֶל־בִּלְעָם לַיְלָה וַיֹּאמֶר לוֹ
אִם־לִקְרֹא לְךָ בָּאוּ הָאֲנָשִׁים קוּם לֵךְ אִתָּם וְאַךְ אֶת־הַדָּבָר אֲשֶׁר־אֲדַבֵּר אֵלֶיךָ
כא אֹתוֹ תַעֲשֶׂה׃ וַיָּקָם בִּלְעָם בַּבֹּקֶר וַיַּחֲבֹשׁ אֶת־אֲתֹנוֹ וַיֵּלֶךְ עִם־שָׂרֵי מוֹאָב׃ שלישי
כב וַיִּחַר־אַף אֱלֹהִים כִּי־הוֹלֵךְ הוּא וַיִּתְיַצֵּב מַלְאַךְ יְהוָה בַּדֶּרֶךְ לְשָׂטָן לוֹ וְהוּא

רש״י

ט | **מִי הָאֲנָשִׁים הָאֵלֶּה עִמָּךְ.** לְהַטְעוֹתוֹ בָּא, אָמַר: פְּעָמִים שֶׁאֵין הַכֹּל גָּלוּי לְפָנָיו, אֵין דַּעְתּוֹ שָׁוָה עָלָיו, אַף אֲנִי אֶרְאֶה עֵת שֶׁאוּכַל לְקַלֵּל וְלֹא יָבִין:

י | **בָּלָק בֶּן צִפֹּר מֶלֶךְ מוֹאָב.** אַף עַל פִּי שֶׁאֵינִי חָשׁוּב בְּעֵינֶיךָ, חָשׁוּב אֲנִי בְּעֵינֵי הַמְּלָכִים:

יא | **קָבָה לִּי.** זוֹ קָשָׁה מֵ״אָרָה לִּי״, שֶׁהוּא נוֹקֵב וּמְפָרֵשׁ: **וְגֵרַשְׁתִּיו.** מִן הָעוֹלָם, וּבָלָק לֹא אָמַר אֶלָּא ״וַאֲגָרְשֶׁנּוּ מִן הָאָרֶץ״ (לעיל פסוק ו), אֵינִי מְבַקֵּשׁ אֶלָּא לְהַסִּיעָם מֵעָלַי, וּבִלְעָם הָיָה שׂוֹנְאָם יוֹתֵר מִבָּלָק:

יב | **לֹא תֵלֵךְ עִמָּהֶם.** אָמַר לוֹ: אִם כֵּן אֲקַלְּלֵם בִּמְקוֹמִי. אָמַר לוֹ: ״לֹא תָאֹר אֶת הָעָם״. אָמַר לוֹ: אִם כֵּן אֲבָרְכֵם. אָמַר לוֹ: אֵינָם צְרִיכִים לְבִרְכָתְךָ ״כִּי בָרוּךְ הוּא״. מָשָׁל, אוֹמְרִים לַצִּרְעָה: לֹא מִדֻּבְשֵׁךְ וְלֹא מֵעֻקְצֵךְ:

יג | **לַהֲלֹךְ עִמָּכֶם.** אֶלָּא עִם שָׂרִים גְּדוֹלִים מִכֶּם. לָמַדְנוּ שֶׁרוּחוֹ גְּבוֹהָה, וְלֹא רָצָה לְגַלּוֹת שֶׁהוּא בִּרְשׁוּתוֹ שֶׁל מָקוֹם אֶלָּא בִּלְשׁוֹן גַּסּוּת, לְפִיכָךְ ״וַיֹּסֶף עוֹד בָּלָק״ (להלן פסוק טו):

יז | **כִּי כַבֵּד אֲכַבֶּדְךָ מְאֹד.** יוֹתֵר מִמַּה שֶּׁהָיִיתָ נוֹטֵל לְשֶׁעָבַר אֲנִי נוֹתֵן לְךָ:

יח | **מְלֹא בֵיתוֹ כֶּסֶף וְזָהָב.** לָמַדְנוּ שֶׁנַּפְשׁוֹ רְחָבָה וּמְחַמֵּד מָמוֹן אֲחֵרִים. אָמַר: רָאוּי לוֹ לִתֵּן לִי כָּל כֶּסֶף וְזָהָב שֶׁלּוֹ, שֶׁהֲרֵי צָרִיךְ לִשְׂכֹּר חֲיָלוֹת רַבּוֹת, סָפֵק נוֹצֵחַ סָפֵק אֵינוֹ נוֹצֵחַ, וַאֲנִי וַדַּאי נוֹצֵחַ: **לֹא אוּכַל לַעֲבֹר.** עַל כָּרְחוֹ גִּלָּה שֶׁהוּא בִּרְשׁוּת אֲחֵרִים, וְנִתְנַבֵּא כָּאן שֶׁאֵינוֹ יָכוֹל לְבַטֵּל הַבְּרָכוֹת שֶׁנִּתְבָּרְכוּ הָאָבוֹת מִפִּי הַשְּׁכִינָה:

יט | **גַּם אַתֶּם.** פִּיו הִכְשִׁילוֹ, ״גַּם אַתֶּם״ סוֹפְכֶם לֵילֵךְ בְּפַחֵי נֶפֶשׁ כָּרִאשׁוֹנִים: **מַה יֹּסֵף.** לֹא יְשַׁנֶּה דְּבָרָיו מִבְּרָכָה לִקְלָלָה, הַלְוַאי שֶׁלֹּא יוֹסִיף לְבָרֵךְ. כָּאן נִתְנַבֵּא שֶׁעָתִיד לְהוֹסִיף לָהֶם בְּרָכוֹת עַל יָדוֹ:

כ | **אִם לִקְרֹא לְךָ.** אִם הַקְּרִיאָה שֶׁלְּךָ וְסָבוּר אַתָּה לִטֹּל עָלֶיהָ שָׂכָר, ״קוּם לֵךְ אִתָּם״: **וְאַךְ.** עַל כָּרְחֲךָ ״אֶת הַדָּבָר אֲשֶׁר אֲדַבֵּר אֵלֶיךָ אֹתוֹ תַעֲשֶׂה״, וְאַף עַל פִּי כֵן: ״וַיֵּלֶךְ בִּלְעָם״, אָמַר: שֶׁמָּא אֲפַתֶּנּוּ וְיִתְרַצֶּה:

כא | **וַיַּחֲבֹשׁ אֶת אֲתֹנוֹ.** מִכָּאן שֶׁהַשִּׂנְאָה מְקַלְקֶלֶת אֶת הַשּׁוּרָה, שֶׁחָבַשׁ הוּא בְּעַצְמוֹ. אָמַר הַקָּדוֹשׁ בָּרוּךְ הוּא: רָשָׁע, כְּבָר קְדָמְךָ אַבְרָהָם אֲבִיהֶם, שֶׁנֶּאֱמַר: ״וַיַּשְׁכֵּם אַבְרָהָם בַּבֹּקֶר וַיַּחֲבֹשׁ אֶת חֲמֹרוֹ״ (בראשית כב, ג): **עִם שָׂרֵי מוֹאָב.** לִבּוֹ כְּלִבָּם שָׁוֶה:

כב | **כִּי הוֹלֵךְ הוּא.** רָאָה שֶׁהַדָּבָר רַע בְּעֵינֵי הַמָּקוֹם וְנִתְאַוָּה לֵילֵךְ: **לְשָׂטָן לוֹ.** מַלְאָךְ שֶׁל רַחֲמִים הָיָה, וְהָיָה רוֹצֶה לְמָנְעוֹ מִלַּחֲטֹא שֶׁלֹּא יֶחֱטָא וְיֹאבַד: **וּשְׁנֵי נְעָרָיו עִמּוֹ.** מִכָּאן לְאָדָם חָשׁוּב הַיּוֹצֵא לַדֶּרֶךְ יוֹלִיךְ עִמּוֹ שְׁנֵי אֲנָשִׁים לְשַׁמְּשׁוֹ, וְחוֹזְרִים וּמְשַׁמְּשִׁים זֶה אֶת זֶה:

as a distinguished individual, **was riding on his donkey, and his two servants were with him.**

23 **The donkey saw the angel of the Lord standing on the way, and his sword was drawn in his hand.** It is unclear what exactly the donkey saw or understood, but it certainly felt threatened. **And the donkey turned from the way, and went into the field. Bilam struck the donkey, to turn it** back **to the way.**

24 After the donkey turned from the road into a field, **the angel of the Lord stood in the path of the vineyards, a** vineyard **fence on this side** of the path, **and a** vineyard **fence on that side** of the path, with the angel in between.

25 **The donkey saw the angel of the Lord, and it**, the donkey, **was pressed to the wall,** to bypass the angel, who did not fill the entire width of the path. On the one hand, the donkey was being struck in order that it should continue forward; on the other hand, a terrifying being stood opposite it. It therefore turned aside, **and it pressed Bilam's foot,** which extended beyond the donkey's body, **against the wall; and he carried on striking it,** due to its puzzling behavior.

26 **The angel of the Lord continued passing, and stood in a narrow place, where there is no way to turn right or left.** The entire passageway was blocked.

27 **The donkey saw the angel of the Lord, and it lay down underneath Bilam. Bilam's wrath was enflamed, and he struck the donkey,** perhaps this time delivering harsher blows, **with the staff.**

28 At this point a miracle occurred: **The Lord opened the mouth of the donkey,**[D] **and it said to Bilam: What did I do to you that you struck me these three times?**

29 Anyone else would have perhaps fainted at hearing a donkey speak, but Bilam, a sorcerer who was accustomed to supernatural occurrences, simply gave it a straightforward answer. **Bilam said to the donkey: Because you abused me; if only there were a sword in my hand, I would have killed you now.**

30 **The donkey said to Bilam: Am I not your donkey that you have ridden upon me from your start until this day? Have I made it a habit to do so,** to act in this manner **to you? He said: No,** you have never done this to me. Indeed, I don't understand what has happened to you.

31 **The Lord uncovered the eyes of Bilam, and he saw the angel of the Lord standing on the way, and his sword was drawn in his hand; he,** Bilam, **bowed his head, and he prostrated himself to him,** the angel.

32 **The angel of the Lord said to him: For what** reason **did you smite your donkey these three times? Behold, I came out to be an obstacle;** I blocked your path, **because the path was altered** for the donkey, and the donkey strayed from the road,[9] as it was **against me,** opposite me, leaving the donkey no choice.[10]

33 **The donkey saw me, and turned from before me these three times; had it not turned from before me,** but had continued to advance, **then now I would have indeed slain you and spared it.**[D] Nothing would have happened to the donkey, whose actions saved you.

DISCUSSION

22:28 | The Lord opened the mouth of the donkey: This story, of a donkey seeing an angel that Bilam was unable to discern, serves to mock and satirize him. The great prophet, who had the power to bless and curse, and who was able to see the entire world and the future, as he will boast about himself below, perceived less than his own donkey.

The miracle of the speaking donkey can be understood only as a tool for conveying the message of the entire story. The satirical motif continues: The prophet does not see, and yet the donkey sees; the prophet does not know what to say, whereas the donkey speaks.

22:33 | Then now I would have indeed slain you and spared it: It is unclear from the verse whether the donkey remained alive after it had spoken. Most likely it died, and Bilam was left alone and embarrassed (see Rashi; *Bemidbar Rabba* 20:15).

כג רֹכֵב עַל־אֲתֹנוֹ וּשְׁנֵי נְעָרָיו עִמּוֹ: וַתֵּרֶא הָאָתוֹן אֶת־מַלְאַךְ יְהוָה נִצָּב בַּדֶּרֶךְ
וְחַרְבּוֹ שְׁלוּפָה בְּיָדוֹ וַתֵּט הָאָתוֹן מִן־הַדֶּרֶךְ וַתֵּלֶךְ בַּשָּׂדֶה וַיַּךְ בִּלְעָם אֶת־
כד הָאָתוֹן לְהַטֹּתָהּ הַדָּרֶךְ: וַיַּעֲמֹד מַלְאַךְ יְהוָה בְּמִשְׁעוֹל הַכְּרָמִים גָּדֵר מִזֶּה וְגָדֵר
כה מִזֶּה: וַתֵּרֶא הָאָתוֹן אֶת־מַלְאַךְ יְהוָה וַתִּלָּחֵץ אֶל־הַקִּיר וַתִּלְחַץ אֶת־רֶגֶל בִּלְעָם
כו אֶל־הַקִּיר וַיֹּסֶף לְהַכֹּתָהּ: וַיּוֹסֶף מַלְאַךְ־יְהוָה עֲבוֹר וַיַּעֲמֹד בְּמָקוֹם צָר אֲשֶׁר
כז אֵין־דֶּרֶךְ לִנְטוֹת יָמִין וּשְׂמֹאול: וַתֵּרֶא הָאָתוֹן אֶת־מַלְאַךְ יְהוָה וַתִּרְבַּץ
כח תַּחַת בִּלְעָם וַיִּחַר־אַף בִּלְעָם וַיַּךְ אֶת־הָאָתוֹן בַּמַּקֵּל: וַיִּפְתַּח יְהוָה אֶת־פִּי
כט הָאָתוֹן וַתֹּאמֶר לְבִלְעָם מֶה־עָשִׂיתִי לְךָ כִּי הִכִּיתַנִי זֶה שָׁלֹשׁ רְגָלִים: וַיֹּאמֶר
ל בִּלְעָם לָאָתוֹן כִּי הִתְעַלַּלְתְּ בִּי לוּ יֶשׁ־חֶרֶב בְּיָדִי כִּי עַתָּה הֲרַגְתִּיךְ: וַתֹּאמֶר
הָאָתוֹן אֶל־בִּלְעָם הֲלוֹא אָנֹכִי אֲתֹנְךָ אֲשֶׁר־רָכַבְתָּ עָלַי מֵעוֹדְךָ עַד־הַיּוֹם הַזֶּה
לא הַהַסְכֵּן הִסְכַּנְתִּי לַעֲשׂוֹת לְךָ כֹּה וַיֹּאמֶר לֹא: וַיְגַל יְהוָה אֶת־עֵינֵי בִלְעָם וַיַּרְא
אֶת־מַלְאַךְ יְהוָה נִצָּב בַּדֶּרֶךְ וְחַרְבּוֹ שְׁלֻפָה בְּיָדוֹ וַיִּקֹּד וַיִּשְׁתַּחוּ לְאַפָּיו:
לב וַיֹּאמֶר אֵלָיו מַלְאַךְ יְהוָה עַל־מָה הִכִּיתָ אֶת־אֲתֹנְךָ זֶה שָׁלוֹשׁ רְגָלִים הִנֵּה אָנֹכִי
לג יָצָאתִי לְשָׂטָן כִּי־יָרַט הַדֶּרֶךְ לְנֶגְדִּי: וַתִּרְאַנִי הָאָתוֹן וַתֵּט לְפָנַי זֶה שָׁלֹשׁ
רְגָלִים אוּלַי נָטְתָה מִפָּנַי כִּי עַתָּה גַּם־אֹתְכָה הָרַגְתִּי וְאוֹתָהּ הֶחֱיֵיתִי:

רש"י

כג| **וַתֵּרֶא הָאָתוֹן.** וְהוּא לֹא רָאָה, שֶׁנָּתַן הַקָּדוֹשׁ בָּרוּךְ הוּא רְשׁוּת לַבְּהֵמָה לִרְאוֹת יוֹתֵר מִן הָאָדָם, שֶׁמִּתּוֹךְ שֶׁיֵּשׁ בּוֹ דַּעַת תִּטָּרֵף דַּעְתּוֹ כְּשֶׁיִּרְאֶה מַזִּיקִין: **וְחַרְבּוֹ שְׁלוּפָה בְּיָדוֹ.** אָמַר: רָשָׁע זֶה הִנִּיחַ כְּלֵי אֻמָּנוּתוֹ, שֶׁכְּלֵי זַיִן שֶׁל אֻמּוֹת הָעוֹלָם בַּחֶרֶב, וְהוּא בָּא עֲלֵיהֶם בְּפִיו שֶׁהוּא אֻמָּנוּת שֶׁלָּהֶם, אַף אֲנִי אֶתְפֹּשׂ אֶת שֶׁלּוֹ וְאָבֹא עָלָיו בְּאֻמָּנוּתוֹ, וְכֵן הָיָה סוֹפוֹ: "וְאֵת בִּלְעָם בֶּן בְּעוֹר הָרְגוּ בֶּחָרֶב" (להלן לא, ח):

כד| **בְּמִשְׁעוֹל.** כְּתַרְגּוּמוֹ: "בִּשְׁבִיל", וְכֵן: "אִם יִשְׂפֹּק עֲפַר שֹׁמְרוֹן לִשְׁעָלִים" (מלכים א' כ, י), עָפָר הַנִּדְבָּק בְּכַפּוֹת הָרַגְלַיִם בְּהִלּוּכָן. וְכֵן: "מִי מָדַד בְּשָׁעֳלוֹ מַיִם" (ישעיה מ, יב), בְּרַגְלָיו וּבְהִלּוּכוֹ: **גָּדֵר מִזֶּה וְגָדֵר מִזֶּה.** סְתָם 'גָּדֵר' שֶׁל אֲבָנִים הוּא:

כה| **וַתִּלָּחֵץ.** הִיא עַצְמָהּ: **וַתִּלְחַץ.** אֶת אֲחֵרִים, אֶת רֶגֶל בִּלְעָם:

כו| **וַיּוֹסֶף מַלְאַךְ ה' עֲבוֹר.** לַעֲבֹר עוֹד לְפָנָיו לַהֲלֹךְ לִהְיוֹת לְפָנָיו בְּמָקוֹם אַחֵר, כְּמוֹ: "וְהוּא עָבַר לִפְנֵיהֶם" (בראשית לג, ג). וּמִדְרַשׁ אַגָּדָה יֵשׁ בְּתַנְחוּמָא, מָה רָאָה לַעֲמֹד בִּשְׁלֹשָׁה מְקוֹמוֹת? סִימָנֵי אָבוֹת הֶרְאָהוּ:

כח| **זֶה שָׁלֹשׁ רְגָלִים.** רָמְזָה לוֹ, אַתָּה מְבַקֵּשׁ לַעֲקֹר אֻמָּה הַחוֹגֶגֶת שָׁלֹשׁ רְגָלִים בַּשָּׁנָה:

כט| **הִתְעַלַּלְתְּ.** כְּתַרְגּוּמוֹ, לְשׁוֹן גְּנַאי וּבִזָּיוֹן: **לוּ יֶשׁ חֶרֶב בְּיָדִי.** גְּנוּת גְּדוֹלָה הָיָה לוֹ דָּבָר זֶה בְּעֵינֵי הַשָּׂרִים, זֶה הוֹלֵךְ לַהֲרֹג אֻמָּה שְׁלֵמָה בְּפִיו, וְלָאָתוֹן זוֹ צָרִיךְ לִכְלֵי זַיִן:

ל| **הַהַסְכֵּן הִסְכַּנְתִּי.** כְּתַרְגּוּמוֹ, וְכֵן: "הַלְאֵל יִסְכָּן גָּבֶר" (איוב כב, ב). וְרַבּוֹתֵינוּ דָּרְשׁוּ מִקְרָא זֶה בַּתַּלְמוּד: אָמְרוּ לֵיהּ: מַאי טַעְמָא לָא רָכְבַתְּ אַסּוּסְיָא? אֲמַר לְהוֹן: בִּרְטִיבָא שְׁדָאִי לֵיהּ כו', כִּדְאִיתָא בְּמַסֶּכֶת עֲבוֹדָה זָרָה (דף ד ע"ב):

לב| **כִּי יָרַט הַדֶּרֶךְ לְנֶגְדִּי.** רַבּוֹתֵינוּ חַכְמֵי הַמִּשְׁנָה דְּרָשׁוּהוּ נוֹטָרִיקוֹן: יָרְאָה, רָאֲתָה, נָטְתָה, בִּשְׁבִיל שֶׁהַדֶּרֶךְ לְנֶגְדִּי, כְּלוֹמַר לְקִנְאָתִי וּלְהַקְנִיטֵנִי. וּלְפִי מַשְׁמָעוֹ, כִּי חָרַד הַדֶּרֶךְ לְנֶגְדִּי, לְשׁוֹן רֶטֶט, כִּי רָאִיתִי בַּעַל הַדֶּרֶךְ שֶׁחָרַד וּמִהֵר הַדֶּרֶךְ שֶׁהוּא לְכַעְסִי וּלְהַמְרוֹתִי, וּמִקְרָא קָצָר הוּא, כְּמוֹ: "וַתְּכַל דָּוִד" (שמואל ב' יג, לט) שֶׁרוֹצֶה לוֹמַר: וַתְּכַל נֶפֶשׁ דָּוִד. לָשׁוֹן אַחֵר, 'יָרַט' לְשׁוֹן רָצוֹן, וְכֵן: "וְעַל יְדֵי רְשָׁעִים יִרְטֵנִי" (איוב טז, יא), מְפַיֵּס וּמְנַחֵם אוֹתִי עַל יְדֵי רְשָׁעִים, שֶׁאֵינָן אֶלָּא מַקְנִיטִים:

לג| **אוּלַי נָטְתָה.** כְּמוֹ לוּלֵא, פְּעָמִים שֶׁ'אוּלַי' מְשַׁמֵּשׁ בִּלְשׁוֹן לוּלֵא: **גַּם אֹתְכָה הָרַגְתִּי.** הֲרֵי זֶה מִקְרָא מְסֹרָס, וְהוּא כְּמוֹ: 'גַּם הָרַגְתִּי אוֹתְךָ'. כְּלוֹמַר, לֹא הָעַכָּבָה בִּלְבַד קָרָאתְךָ עַל יָדִי, כִּי גַּם הַהֲרִיגָה: **וְאוֹתָהּ הֶחֱיֵיתִי.** וְעַתָּה מִפְּנֵי שֶׁדִּבְּרָה וְהוֹכִיחַתְךָ, וְלֹא יָכֹלְתָּ לַעֲמֹד בְּתוֹכַחְתָּהּ, כְּמוֹ שֶׁכָּתוּב: "וַיֹּאמֶר לֹא" (לעיל פסוק ל) – הֲרַגְתִּיהָ, שֶׁלֹּא יֹאמְרוּ: זוֹ הִיא שֶׁסִּלְּקָה אֶת בִּלְעָם בְּתוֹכַחְתָּהּ וְלֹא יָכֹל לְהָשִׁיב, שֶׁחָס הַמָּקוֹם עַל כְּבוֹד הַבְּרִיּוֹת. וְכֵן: "וְאֶת הַבְּהֵמָה תַּהֲרֹגוּ" (ויקרא כ, טו), וְכֵן: "וְהָרַגְתָּ אֶת הָאִשָּׁה וְאֶת הַבְּהֵמָה" (שם פסוק טז):

34 **Bilam said to the angel of the Lord: I have sinned, for I did not know that you were standing opposite me on the way; now, if it,** my journey, **is wrong in your eyes, I will return.**

35 **The angel of the Lord said to Bilam: Go with the men,** as God said to you in the nighttime vision; **but only the matter that I will speak to you shall you speak.** You have no right to say anything else as a prophecy. **Bilam went** on **with the princes of Balak.** It is likely that the princes of Balak had observed nothing out of the ordinary, other than the irregular behavior of the donkey, and Bilam seemingly talking to no one. However, they were aware that Bilam was a sorcerer who could perceive beings that they were unable to see.

36 **Balak heard** from messengers **that Bilam had come, and came out to meet him, to the city of Moav,** the city **which is on the border of** the **Arnon** Ravine, **which is on the edge of the border.**

37 **Balak said to Bilam: Did I not send to you to summon you** once before? **Why didn't you come to me** on the first occasion? **Is it true that** you thought **I cannot honor you** and bestow upon you the proper reward? That is not so, as I am a king.

38 **Bilam said to Balak:** Although I initially refused, **behold, I have come to you; now,** what do you think? **Will I be able to speak anything** that I choose? **The matter that God places in my mouth, that** alone **I will** be able to **speak.**D I declare from the outset that that I am merely God's mouthpiece. Now perhaps you will understand why I did not come straight away.

Fourth aliya 39 **Bilam went with Balak, and they came to Kiryat Hutzot,** the name of a central, public place of many streets [*huzot*].

(Sixth aliya) 40 **Balak slaughtered cattle and sheep, and sent to Bilam and to the princes who were with him.** Bilam and those who accompanied him received large portions of food and stayed overnight in Kiryat Hutzot.

41 **It was in the morning, and Balak took Bilam, and brought him up to the heights of Baal,** at the top of a mountain, **and he saw from there the edge of** the camp of **the people.** The Israelite camp was extremely large; according to tradition, it spread over an area of roughly 12 km.[11] It is difficult to see such a large area unless one is standing on a tall spot. After leading Bilam to a place from where he could see some of the people, Balak invited him to use his powers.

23 1 **Bilam said to Balak: Build me,** right **here** and now, **seven altars, and prepare me here seven bulls and seven rams** as offerings.

2 **Balak did as Bilam had spoken; Balak and Bilam** together **offered up a bull and a ram on each altar.** The joint offering of Balak and Bilam on the same altar strengthened the bond between them, enabling Bilam to represent Balak in his actions.

3 **Bilam said to Balak: Stand with your burnt offering, and I will go** from here; **perhaps the Lord will happen upon me and He will show me some matter and I will tell you.** I cannot induce a vision or demand one. I have done what I can by sacrificing the offerings; if I go off by myself there is a chance that God will reveal Himself to me. **He went alone** [*shefi*], quietly, without disturbances,[12] or bent over [*shafuf*],[13] while Balak remained near the altar.

4 Indeed, **God happened upon Bilam, and he,** Bilam, **said to Him: The seven altars I have prepared, and I offered up a bull and a ram on each altar.**

5 **The Lord placed speech in Bilam's mouth, and He said: Return to Balak, and so you shall speak.** The verse indicates that Bilam received a general message that he had to formulate for Balak, rather than exact words to be recited.

DISCUSSION

22:38 | The matter that God places in my mouth, that I will speak: It is hard to get a firm grasp on Bilam's personality from the narrative up to this point. Undoubtedly, he was a unique individual, as God spoke through him. Bilam was blessed with supernatural powers and with the ability to perceive lofty matters. However, the Torah certainly does not depict him as a righteous man, and in fact he seems to be a somewhat demonic figure. Although Bilam was

a prophet of God, he saw no reason to love all God's servants and His people. He did not reject Balak's idea himself, and was more than willing to curse Israel, had God not prevented him from doing so. The Sages depict him as an animal trying to open its mouth despite the muzzle that has been placed over it.

Among the Israelites, prophecy was granted only to individuals on a high moral plane, who were also gifted with the ability to receive divine statements. By contrast, Bilam, the gentile prophet, had the capacity to be inspired and hear the word of God regardless of his character and moral worth. Bilam's prophecy was found fit for inclusion in the Torah, not because of any merit of his, but due to the essential truth of its message.

לד ויאמר בלעם אל-מלאך יהוה חטאתי כי לא ידעתי כי אתה נצב לקראתי
לה בדרך ועתה אם-רע בעיניך אשובה לי: ויאמר מלאך יהוה אל-בלעם לך
עם-האנשים ואפס את-הדבר אשר-אדבר אליך אתו תדבר וילך בלעם עם-
לו שרי בלק: וישמע בלק כי-בא בלעם ויצא לקראתו אל-עיר מואב אשר
לז על-גבול ארנן אשר בקצה הגבול: ויאמר בלק אל-בלעם הלא שלח שלחתי
לח אליך לקרא-לך למה לא-הלכת אלי האמנם לא אוכל כבדך: ויאמר בלעם
אל-בלק הנה-באתי אליך עתה היכל אוכל דבר מאומה הדבר אשר ישים
לט מ אלהים בפי אתו אדבר: וילך בלעם עם-בלק ויבאו קרית חצות: ויזבח בלק רביעי /ששי/
מא בקר וצאן וישלח לבלעם ולשרים אשר אתו: ויהי בבקר ויקח בלק את-בלעם
ויעלהו במות בעל וירא משם קצה העם: א ויאמר בלעם אל-בלק בנה-לי בזה
ב שבעה מזבחת והכן לי בזה שבעה פרים ושבעה אילים: ויעש בלק כאשר
ג דבר בלעם ויעל בלק ובלעם פר ואיל במזבח: ויאמר בלעם לבלק התיצב
על-עלתך ואלכה אולי יקרה יהוה לקראתי ודבר מה-יראני והגדתי לך וילך
ד שפי: ויקר אלהים אל-בלעם ויאמר אליו את-שבעת המזבחת ערכתי ואעל
ה פר ואיל במזבח: וישם יהוה דבר בפי בלעם ויאמר שוב אל-בלק וכה תדבר:

רש"י

לד] כי לא ידעתי. גם זה גנותו, ועל כרחו הודה, שהוא היה משתבח שיודע דעת עליון, ופיו העיד: "לא ידעתי". אם רע בעיניך אשובה לי. להתריס נגד המקום היא תשובה זו. אמר לו: הוא בעצמו צוני ללכת ואתה מלאך מבטל את דבריו, למוד הוא בכך שאומר דבר ומלאך מחזירו, אמר לאברהם: "קח נא את בנך" וגו' (בראשית כב, ב) ועל ידי מלאך בטל את דברו, אף אני אם רע בעיניך צריך אני לשוב.

לה] לך עם האנשים. בדרך שאדם רוצה לילך בה מוליכין אותו: לך עם האנשים. כי חלקך עמהם וסופך לאבד מן העולם. ואפס. על כרחך, "את הדבר אשר אדבר" וגו'. עם שרי בלק. שמח לקללם כמותם.

לו] וישמע בלק. שלח שלוחים לבשרו. אל עיר מואב. אל מטרופולין שלו, עיר החשובה שלו, לומר: ראה מה אלו מבקשים לעקור:

לז] האמנם לא אוכל כבדך. נתנבא שסופו לצאת מעמו בקלון:

לט] קרית חצות. עיר מלאה שווקים אנשים נשים וטף בחוצותיה, לומר: ראה והס שלא יעקרו אלו:

מ] בקר וצאן. דבר מועט, בקר אחד וצאן אחד בלבד:

מא] במות בעל. כתרגומו: "לרמת דחלתיה", שם עבודה זרה:

פרק כג

ג] אולי יקרה ה' לקראתי. אינו רגיל לדבר עמי ביום: וילך שפי. כתרגומו: "יחידי", לשון שפי ושקט, שאין עמו אלא שתיקה:

ד] ויקר. לשון עראי, לשון גנאי, לשון טומאת קרי, כלומר בקשי ובבזיון, ולא היה נגלה עליו ביום אלא בשביל להראות חבתן של ישראל: את שבעת המזבחת. "שבעה מזבחת ערכתי" אין כתיב כאן אלא "את שבעת המזבחת", אמר לפניו: אבותיהם של אלו בנו לפניך שבעה מזבחות, ואני ערכתי כנגד כלן. אברהם בנה ארבעה: "ויבן שם מזבח לה' הנראה אליו" (בראשית יב, ז), "ויעתק משם ההרה" וגו' (שם פסוק ח), "ויאהל אברם" וגו' (שם יג, יח), ואחד בהר המוריה (שם כב, ט); ויצחק בנה אחד, "ויבן שם מזבח וגו' ויכרו שם עבדי יצחק באר" (שם כו, כה); ויעקב בנה שנים: אחד בשכם (שם לג, כ) ואחד בבית אל (שם לה, ז). ואעל פר ואיל במזבח. ואברהם לא העלה אלא איל אחד:

6 **He returned to him, and behold, he,** Balak, **was standing with his burnt offering, he, and all the princes of Moav.**
7 **He launched his oration,** or his poetic allegory,[14] **and said: From Aram,** as Bilam lived on the Euphrates River in Aram (see 22:5), **Balak leads me,** and calls me; **the king of Moav from the highlands of the east,** saying: **Go, curse Jacob for me, and go, censure [*zo'ama*] Israel.** Cause rage [*za'am*] to descend upon them, or issue pronouncements of rage against the nation of Israel.
8 **How will I curse,** when **God has not cursed? How will I censure,** when **the Lord has not censured?** I am unable to fulfill Balak's request to curse and censure if God does not allow me to do so. God does not want this people to be cursed, as they are special. Bilam proceeds to depict the people's unique qualities.
9 **For from the top of precipices I will see it,** the nation of Israel, **and from hills I behold it.** Since I am standing in a physically high location, on the heights of Baal, and I also have a metahistorical perspective, I can observe Israel from "above": **Behold, it is a people that shall dwell alone, and shall not be reckoned among the nations.** This people is not part of the family of nations.
10 **Who has counted the dust of Jacob?** Who can count the dust trodden under the feet of Jacob? Alternatively, this means: Who can count the descendants of Jacob, as they are as numerous as the dust.[15] **Or** who has **tallied**[16] even **one quarter [*rova*] of Israel?** *Rova* is referring to one of the four smaller camps that comprise the entire Israelite camp.[17] **Let me die the death of the upright, and let my end be like his,** like one of the children of Israel.
11 **Balak said to Bilam,** in shock: **What have you done to me? To curse my enemies I took you, and behold, you have blessed them.**
12 **He,** Bilam, **answered and said: Is it not that which the Lord will place in my mouth, that I will take care to speak?** I cannot speak according to your will.
13 **Balak said to him: Please, go with me to another place that you may see them,** the Israelites, **from there; you will see only their edge, but you will not see all of them; curse them for me from there.** If you gaze upon the Israelites from a different angle, perhaps you will be able to curse them.

Fifth aliya

14 **He took him to the field of Tzofim,**[B] again **to the top of the peak, and he built seven altars, and offered up a bull and a ram on each altar,** in accordance with Bilam's instructions.
15 **He said to Balak: Stand here** as you are, **with your burnt offering, and I will be happened upon there.** I will walk until I receive a prophecy.
16 **The Lord happened upon Bilam,**[D] **and** again **placed speech in his mouth, and said: Return to Balak, and so you shall speak.** Bilam was now instilled with the word of God, although it is possible that he did not yet know what he was about to say.
17 **He came to him,** Balak, **and behold, he was standing with his burnt offering,** as Bilam had commanded, **and the princes of Moav** were there **with him. Balak,** who could tell that Bilam had received a prophecy, **said to him: What did the Lord speak?** Balak mocked Bilam with this question: Since you have repeatedly stated that it is not you who speaks but God, what, then, did God say?[18]
18 **He launched his oration, and said: Rise, Balak, and hear; listen to me, son of Tzipor:** Perhaps he addressed him in this manner in response to the disparaging tone he detected in Balak's comment.

BACKGROUND

23:14 | **The field of Tzofim:** According to Onkelos and the Septuagint, this is a description of a place, the field of lookouts [*tzofim*]. Conversely, some researchers maintain that Tzofim was the name of the place. For reasons of similarity it has been identified with Tal'at-es-Safa, a group of mountains on the northwestern edge of the range that descends steeply to the Dead Sea.

DISCUSSION

23:16 | **The Lord happened upon Bilam:** This verb, "happened upon," which is repeated on several occasions in this chapter, is indicative of the nature of Bilam's prophecy. Although Bilam made efforts to achieve prophecy, he experienced it as a chance event. Other prophets could not actively initiate prophecy but considered it a gift of God, bestowed upon them by divine will. Bilam, by contrast, perceived his inspiration as happenstance, not an intentional act of God.

ו ז וַיָּשָׁב אֵלָיו וְהִנֵּה נִצָּב עַל־עֹלָתוֹ הוּא וְכָל־שָׂרֵי מוֹאָב׃ וַיִּשָּׂא מְשָׁלוֹ וַיֹּאמַר מִן־
אֲרָם יַנְחֵנִי בָלָק מֶלֶךְ־מוֹאָב מֵהַרְרֵי־קֶדֶם לְכָה אָרָה־לִּי יַעֲקֹב וּלְכָה זֹעֲמָה
ח ט יִשְׂרָאֵל׃ מָה אֶקֹּב לֹא קַבֹּה אֵל וּמָה אֶזְעֹם לֹא זָעַם יהוה׃ כִּי־מֵרֹאשׁ צֻרִים
י אֶרְאֶנּוּ וּמִגְּבָעוֹת אֲשׁוּרֶנּוּ הֶן־עָם לְבָדָד יִשְׁכֹּן וּבַגּוֹיִם לֹא יִתְחַשָּׁב׃ מִי מָנָה עֲפַר כ
יַעֲקֹב וּמִסְפָּר אֶת־רֹבַע יִשְׂרָאֵל תָּמֹת נַפְשִׁי מוֹת יְשָׁרִים וּתְהִי אַחֲרִיתִי כָּמֹהוּ׃
יא וַיֹּאמֶר בָּלָק אֶל־בִּלְעָם מֶה עָשִׂיתָ לִי לָקֹב אֹיְבַי לְקַחְתִּיךָ וְהִנֵּה בֵּרַכְתָּ בָרֵךְ׃
יב יג וַיַּעַן וַיֹּאמַר הֲלֹא אֵת אֲשֶׁר יָשִׂים יהוה בְּפִי אֹתוֹ אֶשְׁמֹר לְדַבֵּר׃ וַיֹּאמֶר אֵלָיו חמישי
בָּלָק לְךָ־נָּא אִתִּי אֶל־מָקוֹם אַחֵר אֲשֶׁר תִּרְאֶנּוּ מִשָּׁם אֶפֶס קָצֵהוּ תִרְאֶה וְכֻלּוֹ
יד לֹא תִרְאֶה וְקָבְנוֹ־לִי מִשָּׁם׃ וַיִּקָּחֵהוּ שְׂדֵה צֹפִים אֶל־רֹאשׁ הַפִּסְגָּה וַיִּבֶן שִׁבְעָה
טו מִזְבְּחֹת וַיַּעַל פָּר וָאַיִל בַּמִּזְבֵּחַ׃ וַיֹּאמֶר אֶל־בָּלָק הִתְיַצֵּב כֹּה עַל־עֹלָתֶךָ וְאָנֹכִי
טז אִקָּרֶה כֹּה׃ וַיִּקָּר יהוה אֶל־בִּלְעָם וַיָּשֶׂם דָּבָר בְּפִיו וַיֹּאמֶר שׁוּב אֶל־בָּלָק וְכֹה
יז תְדַבֵּר׃ וַיָּבֹא אֵלָיו וְהִנּוֹ נִצָּב עַל־עֹלָתוֹ וְשָׂרֵי מוֹאָב אִתּוֹ וַיֹּאמֶר לוֹ בָּלָק מַה־
יח דִּבֶּר יהוה׃ וַיִּשָּׂא מְשָׁלוֹ וַיֹּאמַר קוּם בָּלָק וּשְׁמָע הַאֲזִינָה עָדַי בְּנוֹ צִפֹּר׃

רש"י

ז | **אָרָה לִּי יַעֲקֹב וּלְכָה זֹעֲמָה יִשְׂרָאֵל.** בִּשְׁנֵי שְׁמוֹתֵיהֶם אָמַר לוֹ לְקַלְּלָם, שֶׁמָּא אֶחָד מֵהֶם אֵינוֹ מֻבְהָק:

ח | **מָה אֶקֹּב לֹא קַבֹּה אֵל.** כְּשֶׁהָיוּ רְאוּיִים לְהִתְקַלֵּל לֹא נִתְקַלְּלוּ, כְּשֶׁהִזְכִּיר אֲבִיהֶם אֶת עֲוֹנָם: "כִּי בְאַפָּם הָרְגוּ אִישׁ" (בראשית מט, ו), לֹא קִלֵּל אֶלָּא אַפָּם, שֶׁנֶּאֱמַר: "אָרוּר אַפָּם" (שם פסוק ז), כְּשֶׁנִּכְנַס אֲבִיהֶם בְּמִרְמָה אֵצֶל אָבִיו הָיָה רָאוּי לְהִתְקַלֵּל; מַה נֶּאֱמַר שָׁם – "גַּם בָּרוּךְ יִהְיֶה" (שם כז, לג). בַּמְבָרְכִים נֶאֱמַר: "אֵלֶּה יַעַמְדוּ לְבָרֵךְ אֶת הָעָם" (דברים כז, יב), בַּמְקַלְּלִים לֹא נֶאֱמַר: 'וְאֵלֶּה יַעַמְדוּ לְקַלֵּל אֶת הָעָם', אֶלָּא "וְאֵלֶּה יַעַמְדוּ עַל הַקְּלָלָה" (שם פסוק יג), לֹא רָצָה לְהַזְכִּיר עֲלֵיהֶם שֵׁם קְלָלָה: **לֹא זָעַם ה'.** אֲנִי אֵין כֹּחִי אֶלָּא שֶׁאֲנִי יוֹדֵעַ לְכַוֵּן הַשָּׁעָה שֶׁהַקָּדוֹשׁ בָּרוּךְ הוּא כּוֹעֵס בָּהּ, וְהוּא לֹא כָעַס כָּל הַיָּמִים הַלָּלוּ שֶׁבָּאתִי אֵלֶיךָ, וְזֶהוּ שֶׁנֶּאֱמַר: "עַמִּי זְכָר נָא מַה יָּעַץ וְגוֹ' וּמֶה עָנָה אֹתוֹ בִּלְעָם וְגוֹ' לְמַעַן דַּעַת צִדְקוֹת ה'" (מיכה ו, ה):

ט | **כִּי מֵרֹאשׁ צֻרִים אֶרְאֶנּוּ.** אֲנִי מִסְתַּכֵּל בְּרֵאשִׁיתָם וּבִתְחִלַּת שָׁרְשֵׁיהֶם, וַאֲנִי רוֹאֶה אוֹתָם מְיֻסָּדִים וַחֲזָקִים כְּצוּרִים וּגְבָעוֹת הַלָּלוּ, עַל יְדֵי אָבוֹת וְאִמָּהוֹת: **הֶן עָם לְבָדָד יִשְׁכֹּן.** הוּא אֲשֶׁר זָכוּ לוֹ אֲבוֹתָיו לִשְׁכֹּן בָּדָד, כְּתַרְגּוּמוֹ: **וּבַגּוֹיִם לֹא יִתְחַשָּׁב.** כְּתַרְגּוּמוֹ, לֹא יִהְיוּ נַעֲשִׂין כָּלָה עִם שְׁאָר הָאֻמּוֹת, שֶׁנֶּאֱמַר: "כִּי אֶעֱשֶׂה כָלָה בְּכָל הַגּוֹיִם" וְגוֹ' (ירמיה ל, יא), אֵינָן נִמְנִין עִם הַשְּׁאָר. דָּבָר אַחֵר, כְּשֶׁהֵן שְׂמֵחִין אֵין אֻמָּה שְׂמֵחָה עִמָּהֶם, שֶׁנֶּאֱמַר: "ה' בָּדָד יַנְחֶנּוּ" (דברים לב, יב). וּכְשֶׁהָאֻמּוֹת בְּטוֹבָה הֵם אוֹכְלִין עִם כָּל אֶחָד וְאֶחָד וְאֵין עוֹלֶה לָהֶם מִן הַחֶשְׁבּוֹן, וְזֶהוּ: "וּבַגּוֹיִם לֹא יִתְחַשָּׁב":

י | **מִי מָנָה עֲפַר יַעֲקֹב וְגוֹ'.** כְּתַרְגּוּמוֹ: "דַּעְדְּקַיָּא דְּבֵית יַעֲקֹב כּוּ' מֵאַרְבַּע מַשְׁרְיָתָא" מֵאַרְבָּעָה דְּגָלִים. דָּבָר אַחֵר, "עֲפַר יַעֲקֹב", אֵין חֶשְׁבּוֹן בַּמִּצְוֹת שֶׁהֵם מְקַיְּמִין בֶּעָפָר: "לֹא תַחֲרֹשׁ בְּשׁוֹר וּבַחֲמֹר" (דברים כב, י), "לֹא תִזְרַע כִּלְאָיִם" (ויקרא יט, יט), אֵפֶר פָּרָה (לעיל יט, ט) וַעֲפַר סוֹטָה (לעיל ה, יז) וְכַיּוֹצֵא בָּהֶם: **וּמִסְפָּר אֶת רֹבַע יִשְׂרָאֵל.** רְבִיעוֹתֵיהֶן, זֶרַע הַיּוֹצֵא מִן הַתַּשְׁמִישׁ שֶׁלָּהֶם: **תָּמֹת נַפְשִׁי מוֹת יְשָׁרִים.** שֶׁבָּהֶם:

יג | **וְקָבְנוֹ לִי.** לְשׁוֹן צִוּוּי, קַלְּלֵהוּ לִי:

יד | **שְׂדֵה צֹפִים.** מָקוֹם גָּבוֹהַּ הָיָה, שֶׁשָּׁם הַצּוֹפֶה עוֹמֵד לִשְׁמֹר אִם יָבֹא חַיִל עַל הָעִיר: **רֹאשׁ הַפִּסְגָּה.** בִּלְעָם לֹא הָיָה קוֹסֵם כְּבָלָק, רָאָה בָּלָק שֶׁעֲתִידָה פִּרְצָה לְהִפָּרֵץ בְּיִשְׂרָאֵל מִשָּׁם, שֶׁשָּׁם מֵת מֹשֶׁה, כִּסְבוּר שֶׁשָּׁם תָּחוּל עֲלֵיהֶם הַקְּלָלָה וְזוֹ הִיא הַפִּרְצָה שֶׁאֲנִי רוֹאֶה:

טו | **אִקָּרֶה כֹּה.** מֵאֵת הַקָּדוֹשׁ בָּרוּךְ הוּא. 'אִקָּרֶה' לְשׁוֹן אֶתְפַּעֵל:

טז | **וַיָּשֶׂם דָּבָר בְּפִיו.** וּמָה הִיא הַשִּׂימָה הַזֹּאת, וּמֶה חָסֵר הַמִּקְרָא בְּאָמְרוֹ: "שׁוּב אֶל בָּלָק וְכֹה תְדַבֵּר"? אֶלָּא כְּשֶׁהָיָה שׁוֹמֵעַ שֶׁאֵינוֹ נִרְשֶׁה לְקַלֵּל, אָמַר: מָה אֲנִי חוֹזֵר אֵצֶל בָּלָק לְצַעֲרוֹ, וְנָתַן לוֹ הַקָּדוֹשׁ בָּרוּךְ הוּא רֶסֶן וְחַכָּה בְּפִיו כְּאָדָם הַפּוֹקֵס בְּהֵמָה בְּחַכָּה לְהוֹלִיכָהּ אֶל אֲשֶׁר יִרְצֶה, אָמַר לוֹ: עַל כָּרְחֲךָ תָּשׁוּב אֶל בָּלָק:

יז | **וְשָׂרֵי מוֹאָב אִתּוֹ.** וּלְמַעְלָה הוּא אוֹמֵר: "וְכָל שָׂרֵי מוֹאָב" (לעיל פסוק ו), כֵּיוָן שֶׁרָאוּ שֶׁאֵין בּוֹ תִּקְוָה הָלְכוּ לָהֶם מִקְצָתָם, וְלֹא נִשְׁאֲרוּ אֶלָּא מִקְצָתָם: **מַה דִּבֶּר ה'.** לְשׁוֹן צְחוֹק הוּא זֶה, כְּלוֹמַר אֵינְךָ בִּרְשׁוּתְךָ:

יח | **קוּם בָּלָק.** כֵּיוָן שֶׁרָאָהוּ מְצַחֵק בּוֹ, נִתְכַּוֵּן לְצַעֲרוֹ: עֲמֹד עַל רַגְלֶיךָ, אֵינְךָ רַשַּׁאי לֵישֵׁב וַאֲנִי שָׁלוּחַ אֵלֶיךָ בִּשְׁלִיחוּתוֹ שֶׁל מָקוֹם: **בְּנוֹ צִפֹּר.** לְשׁוֹן מִקְרָא הוּא כֵּן, כְּמוֹ: "חַיְתוֹ יָעַר" (תהלים נ, י), "וְחַיְתוֹ אֶרֶץ" (בראשית א, כד), "לְמַעְיְנוֹ מָיִם" (תהלים קיד, ח):

19 **God is not a man that He will lie** and not fulfill His promises, **or the son of man** who changes his mind, **that He will reconsider; will He say and not perform, or** would He **speak and not fulfill** His word?[19]

20 This is God's statement: **Behold, for blessing I have taken him,** Bilam, **and he will bless, and I will not retract it.** The blessing will not be retracted, as God loves this nation.

21 **One has not beheld evil in Jacob, and not seen sin in Israel.**[D] When God looks upon His people, He sees nothing reprehensible in them. **The Lord his God is with him, and the blast [*teru'at*] of the King is in its midst.** The people sound the blast of the shofar, or of some other instrument, or they cheer in the King's honor. Alternatively, this means that the people are befriended by [*mitro'ea*] their King and are near to Him, and the King wants this close relationship.[20]

22 **God who took them out of Egypt** is exalted, elevated **like the great, impressive horns of the wild ox [*re'em*]**[B] **for it.**

23 **For there is no divination** that can have an effect **in Jacob, and no sorcery in Israel.** No sorcery, divination, or magic that I might perform will have any effect upon Israel. God sees no flaw in them, and He elevates them so that I cannot harm them. **Now, what God has wrought is what shall be said of Jacob and of Israel.** Their fortunes are decided directly by God and cannot be influenced by witchcraft.

24 **Behold, a people will rise like a great cat,**[B] **and like a lion will raise itself.** One who sees a lion rising from a crouching position may observe the strength and sheer power of that movement alone. Furthermore, he knows that the lion will succeed in its quest; **it will not lie** down again **until it will devour prey,** and until **the blood of the slain it will drink.**

25 **Balak said to Bilam: Do not curse them; also do not bless them.** If you refuse to curse them, at least do not bless them.

26 **Bilam answered and said to Balak: Did I not speak to you** and warn you, **saying: Everything that the Lord speaks, that I will do?** I do not speak of my own volition.

27 **Balak said to Bilam: Come please, I will take you to another place; perhaps it will be proper in the eyes of God and you will curse it for me from there.** Maybe there our plan will find favor in God's eyes, and He will allow you to curse Israel.

Sixth aliya (Seventh aliya)

28 **Balak took Bilam**[D] **to the top of Peor,**[B] once again to a mountain peak, this time to one **that overlooks upon the wilderness,** at the edge of the border of Canaan.

29 Yet again, **Bilam said to Balak: Build me here seven altars, and prepare me here seven bulls and seven rams.**

30 **Balak did as Bilam said, and offered up a bull and a ram on each altar.**

24 1 **Bilam saw that it was good in the eyes of the Lord to bless Israel,** and that there was no point in trying to seek a way to curse them. **And** therefore **he did not go as each other**

Aurochs   Lion

BACKGROUND

23:22 | *Re'em*: This is a type of ox, mentioned on several occasions in the Bible (see Deuteronomy 33:17; Psalms 22:22, 29:6). Researchers identify it with the aurochs, an extinct species of large wild cattle, whose scientific name is *Bos primigenius*, *rimu* in Akkadian. Aurochs, common in the Land of Israel in biblical times, were far larger than modern cattle, as they reached a length of roughly 3 m, while the height of their shoulders was about 2 m, and they weighed up to a ton. This is not the *re'em* of modern Hebrew, which is the oryx, called *dishon* in the Bible.

23:24 | A great cat [*lavi*]: There are six names for lions in the Bible: *ari, kefir, lavi, layish, shaḥal,* and *shaḥatz* (see *Avot deRabbi Natan*, version A, 39). Some claim that these differences in name reflect various stages in the animal's development and appearance. Others contend that the many names are due to different strains of the beast, from diverse countries of origin, and which differ in size and bodily shape. It should be noted that current zoological literature differentiates between about ten types of lion.

23:28 | The top of Peor: Identified with Râs es-Siyagha, on the slopes of Mount Nevo.

DISCUSSION

23:21 | One has not beheld evil [*aven*] in Jacob, and not seen sin [*amal*] in Israel: *Aven* and *amal* are synonyms for sin. These terms emphasize the contempt of the act rather than its evil nature, the vanity and lack of purpose and value in an unworthy deed (see Isaiah 1:13, 41:29, 59:4, and commentary ad loc.; Psalms 90:10). God does not see even such shortcomings in His people.

23:28 | Balak took Bilam: The Sages note that although he was not a prophet on Bilam's level, Balak himself had spiritual insight. He was therefore able to take Bilam to those locations where he sensed that misfortune would occur to Israel, such as the top of Peor, a place where the people would soon suffer a moral downfall (25:3; see Rashi).

יט לֹא אִישׁ אֵל וִיכַזֵּב וּבֶן־אָדָם וְיִתְנֶחָם הַהוּא אָמַר וְלֹא יַעֲשֶׂה וְדִבֶּר וְלֹא יְקִימֶנָּה:
כ כא הִנֵּה בָרֵךְ לָקָחְתִּי וּבֵרֵךְ וְלֹא אֲשִׁיבֶנָּה: לֹא־הִבִּיט אָוֶן בְּיַעֲקֹב וְלֹא־רָאָה עָמָל
כב בְּיִשְׂרָאֵל יְהוָה אֱלֹהָיו עִמּוֹ וּתְרוּעַת מֶלֶךְ בּוֹ: אֵל מוֹצִיאָם מִמִּצְרָיִם כְּתוֹעֲפֹת
כג רְאֵם לוֹ: כִּי לֹא־נַחַשׁ בְּיַעֲקֹב וְלֹא־קֶסֶם בְּיִשְׂרָאֵל כָּעֵת יֵאָמֵר לְיַעֲקֹב וּלְיִשְׂרָאֵל
כד מַה־פָּעַל אֵל: הֶן־עָם כְּלָבִיא יָקוּם וְכַאֲרִי יִתְנַשָּׂא לֹא יִשְׁכַּב עַד־יֹאכַל טֶרֶף
כה וְדַם־חֲלָלִים יִשְׁתֶּה: וַיֹּאמֶר בָּלָק אֶל־בִּלְעָם גַּם־קֹב לֹא תִקֳּבֶנּוּ גַּם־בָּרֵךְ לֹא
כו תְבָרְכֶנּוּ: וַיַּעַן בִּלְעָם וַיֹּאמֶר אֶל־בָּלָק הֲלֹא דִּבַּרְתִּי אֵלֶיךָ לֵאמֹר כֹּל אֲשֶׁר־יְדַבֵּר
כז יְהוָה אֹתוֹ אֶעֱשֶׂה: וַיֹּאמֶר בָּלָק אֶל־בִּלְעָם לְכָה־נָּא אֶקָּחֲךָ אֶל־מָקוֹם אַחֵר אוּלַי ששי / שביעי
כח יִישַׁר בְּעֵינֵי הָאֱלֹהִים וְקַבֹּתוֹ לִי מִשָּׁם: וַיִּקַּח בָּלָק אֶת־בִּלְעָם רֹאשׁ הַפְּעוֹר
כט הַנִּשְׁקָף עַל־פְּנֵי הַיְשִׁימֹן: וַיֹּאמֶר בִּלְעָם אֶל־בָּלָק בְּנֵה־לִי בָזֶה שִׁבְעָה מִזְבְּחֹת
ל וְהָכֵן לִי בָּזֶה שִׁבְעָה פָרִים וְשִׁבְעָה אֵילִים: וַיַּעַשׂ בָּלָק כַּאֲשֶׁר אָמַר בִּלְעָם וַיַּעַל
א פַּר וָאַיִל בַּמִּזְבֵּחַ: וַיַּרְא בִּלְעָם כִּי טוֹב בְּעֵינֵי יְהוָה לְבָרֵךְ אֶת־יִשְׂרָאֵל וְלֹא־הָלַךְ

רש"י

יט | **לא איש אל וגו'.** כבר נשבע להם להביאם ולהורישם ארץ שבעה עממים, ואתה סבור להמיתם במדבר?: **ההוא אמר וגו'.** בלשון תמה, ותרגומו: "תיבין ומתמלכין", חוזרים ונמלכין לחזור בהם:

כ | **הנה ברך לקחתי.** אתה שואלני: "מה דבר ה'" (לעיל פסוק יז), קבלתי ממנו לברך אותם: **וברך ולא אשיבנה.** הוא ברך אותם, ואני לא אשיב את ברכתו: **וברך.** כמו 'ובירך', וכן הוא גזרת רי"ש, כמו: "אויב חרף" (תהלים עד, יח) כמו 'חירף', וכן: "ובוצע ברך" (שם י, ג), המהלל ומברך את הגוזל ואומר לו: אל תירא כי לא תענש, שלום יהיה לך, מרגיז הוא להקדוש ברוך הוא. ואין לומר 'ברך' שם דבר, שאם כן היה נקוד בפתח קטן (סגול) וטעמו למעלה, אבל לפי שהוא לשון פעל, הוא נקוד קמץ קטן (צירי) וטעמו למטה:

כא | **לא הביט און וגו'.** כתרגומו. דבר אחר, אחרי פשוטו הוא נדרש מדרש נאה: "לא הביט" הקדוש ברוך הוא און שביעקב, שכשהן עוברין על דבריו, אינו מדקדק אחריהם להתבונן באוניות שלהם ובעמלן שהן עוברין על דתו: **עמל.** לשון עבירה, כמו: "הרה עמל" (איוב טו, לה), "כי אתה עמל וכעס תביט" (תהלים י, יד), לפי שהעבירה היא עמל לפני המקום: **ה' אלהיו עמו.** אפילו מכעיסין וממרים לפניו אינו זז מתוכן: **ותרועת מלך בו.** לשון חבה ורעות, כמו: "רעה דוד" (שמואל ב' טו, לז), אוהב דוד, "ויתנה למרעהו" (שופטים טו, ו). וכן תרגם אונקלוס: "ושכינת מלכהון בינהון":

כב | **אל מוציאם ממצרים.** אתה אמרת: "הנה עם יצא ממצרים" (לעיל כב, ה), לא יצא מעצמו אלא האלהים הוציאם: **כתועפת ראם לו.** כתקף רום וגבה שלו, וכן: "וכסף תועפות" (איוב כב, כה), לשון מעוז הוא. ואומר אני שהוא לשון: "ועוף יעופף" (בראשית א, כ), המעופף ברום וגבה, ותקף רב הוא זה, "ותועפת ראם" עפיפת גבה. דבר אחר, "תועפת ראם", תקף ראמים, ואמרו רבותינו: אלו השדים:

כג | **כי לא נחש ביעקב.** כי ראוים הם לברכה, שאין בהם מנחשים וקוסמים: **כעת יאמר ליעקב וגו'.** עוד עתיד להיות עת כעת הזאת אשר תגלה חבתן לעין כל, שהן יושבין לפניו ולומדים תורה מפיו ומחצתן לפנים ממלאכי השרת, והם ישאלו להם: "מה פעל אל", וזהו שנאמר: "והיו עיניך ראות את מוריך" (ישעיה ל, כ). דבר אחר, "יאמר ליעקב" אינו לשון עתיד אלא לשון הוה, אינן צריכים למנחש וקוסם, כי בכל עת שצריך להאמר ליעקב ולישראל מה פעל הקדוש ברוך הוא ומה גזרותיו במרום, אינן מנחשים וקוסמים, אלא נאמר להם על פי נביאיהם מה היא גזרת המקום, או אורים ותמים מגידים להם. ואונקלוס לא תרגם כן:

כד | **הן עם כלביא יקום וגו'.** כשהן עומדין משנתם שחרית הן מתגברים כלביא וכארי לחטוף את המצות, ללבש טלית, לקרא את שמע ולהניח תפלין: **לא ישכב.** בלילה על מטתו עד שהוא אוכל ומחבל כל מזיק הבא לטרפו. כיצד? קורא את שמע על מטתו ומפקיד רוחו ביד המקום. בא מחנה וגיס להזיקם, הקדוש ברוך הוא שומרם ונלחם מלחמותיהם ומפילם חללים. דבר אחר, "הן עם כלביא יקום" וגו', כתרגומו: **ודם חללים ישתה.** נתנבא שאין משה מת עד שיפיל מלכי מדין חללים ויהרג הוא עמהם, שנאמר: "ואת בלעם בן בעור הקוסם הרגו בני ישראל בחרב אל חלליהם" (יהושע יג, כב):

כה | **גם קב לא תקבנו.** "גם" ראשון מוסף על "גם" השני ו"גם" שני על "גם" ראשון, וכן: "גם לי גם לך לא יהיה" (מלכים א' ג, כו), וכן: "גם בחור גם בתולה" (דברים לב, כה):

כז | **וקבתו לי.** אין זה לשון צווי כמו "וקבנו" (לעיל פסוק יג), אלא לשון עתיד, אולי יישר בעיניו ותקבנו לי משם. מלדיר"ש לו"י בלעז:

כח | **ראש הפעור.** קוסם גדול היה בלק, וראה שהן עתידין ללקות על ידי פעור, ולא היה יודע במה. אמר: שמא הקללה תחול עליהם משם. וכן כל החוזים בכוכבים רואים ואין יודעין מה רואים:

פרק כד

א | **וירא בלעם כי טוב וגו'.** אמר: איני צריך לבדק

time toward divinations, which had been proven ineffective, **but he set his face to the wilderness,** to the east of Moav, and did not attempt to do anything.

2 **Bilam raised his eyes, and he saw Israel dwelling** quietly **according to its tribes and** then **the spirit of God was upon him.**

3 **He launched his oration, and said: The utterance of Bilam son of Beor, and the utterance of the open-eyed [*shetum ha'ayin*] man.** The word *shetum* denotes perforation, and accordingly, *shetum ha'ayin* means one who sees, who has an open eye.[21]

4 **The utterance of one who hears the sayings of God, the vision of the Almighty he will see; he falls** when he receives a vision, in the usual manner of prophets, who would be unable to stand due to the overwhelming force of the prophecy.[22] When he falls, it seems like he has lost all consciousness; however, he receives the revelation **with uncovered eyes,** as the message is revealed to him:

5 After the introductory self-description of the previous verses, Bilam opens this prophecy with a simple blessing: **How goodly are your tents, Jacob,**[D] **your dwellings, Israel.**

6 **Like streams they,** the tents of Israel, **diverged,** spreading out from one area to another, **like gardens** that sprout and thrive **beside a river; like marigolds**[B] **planted by the Lord, like cedars beside the water.** Cedars are generally planted on mountains rather than near a water source. This metaphor therefore emphasizes the Israelites' greatness and might: The cedar is large and, as mighty as it is, how much more so would it be if it were planted near water.

Marigolds

7 More and more **water**[D] **will flow from its drawings,** from Israel's buckets that draw water, **and its seed** shall sprout and further spread **in many waters; its king shall rise above Agag,**[D] king of the Amalekites, **and its,** Israel's, **kingdom shall be exalted.**

8 **God, who took it out of Egypt,** is **like the lofty,** powerful, and prominent **horns of the wild ox for it.** God, whose visible power is compared here to the horns of the aurochs, a herbivore, is immediately depicted as a carnivorous lion: **He will consume nations of its adversaries; He will crush [*yigarem*] their bones, and break its arrows.** Alternatively, *yigarem* means scrape, as their flesh will be scraped off their bones.[23]

9 Whereas the previous verse was apparently referring to the power of God, fighting on behalf of His people, the allegory now passes seamlessly to the might of Israel itself, received from God: **It crouched, it lay like a lion.** When the people are resting in their place like a lion and are not waging war, they have the magnificence and power of a crouching lion. **And like a great cat, who shall rouse it?** Nobody would dare provoke them, as **those who bless you are blessed, and those who curse you are cursed.**

10 **Balak's wrath was enflamed against Bilam,** as this last prophecy was all about Israel's success in the present and the future. **And he clapped his hands** in anger; and **Balak said to Bilam: I called you to curse my enemies and behold, you have blessed them these three times.**

11 **Now flee to your place.** Go home, for **I said** that if you succeeded **I would honor you, and behold, the Lord,** who speaks through your mouth, **has precluded you from honor.**

12 **Bilam said to Balak:** You have no cause to be angry with me, for **did I not also speak to your messengers that you**

BACKGROUND

24:6 | **Marigolds [*ahalim*]:** Identified with the Egyptian fig-marigold, *Mesembryanthemum nodiflorum*, a fleshy desert plant that trails low on the ground. This plant grows rapidly, has bright green leaves and colorful flowers, and contains a scented resin. In the Bible, it features as a fragrant plant (Psalms 45:9; Proverbs 7:17; Song of Songs 4:14), while the Sages state that *ahal* was used in the laundering process (*Zevaḥim* 88a), although that might be referring to the ice plant, *Mesembryanthemum crystallinum L.*

DISCUSSION

24:5 | **How goodly are your tents, Jacob:** In addition to the aesthetic beauty of the Israelite camp, the Sages explain that Bilam discerned a moral beauty in their arrangement, with each family granted privacy, and the camp residing in harmony (see Rashi, 24:2; *Bava Batra* 60a).

24:7 | **Water:** Although Bilam was gazing at the parched wilderness, water is featured prominently in his blessing. This contrast perhaps further highlights the fact that whereas Bilam and Balak sought to find a negative aspect of the Israelites so that he could curse them, he found himself blessing them against his will.

Its king shall rise above Agag: This prophecy indeed came to pass centuries later, as Israel's first king, Saul, triumphed over Agag, the sworn enemy of Israel (see Rashi; I Samuel 15). Some commentaries claim that Agag is the generic name of Amalekite kings over the generations, like Pharaoh, rather than the personal name of a specific king (see *Bekhor Shor*; Ramban).

ב כְּפַעַם־בְּפַעַם לִקְרַאת נְחָשִׁים וַיָּשֶׁת אֶל־הַמִּדְבָּר פָּנָיו: וַיִּשָּׂא בִלְעָם אֶת־עֵינָיו

ג וַיַּרְא אֶת־יִשְׂרָאֵל שֹׁכֵן לִשְׁבָטָיו וַתְּהִי עָלָיו רוּחַ אֱלֹהִים: וַיִּשָּׂא מְשָׁלוֹ וַיֹּאמַר

ד נְאֻם בִּלְעָם בְּנוֹ בְעֹר וּנְאֻם הַגֶּבֶר שְׁתֻם הָעָיִן: נְאֻם שֹׁמֵעַ אִמְרֵי־אֵל אֲשֶׁר מַחֲזֵה

ה שַׁדַּי יֶחֱזֶה נֹפֵל וּגְלוּי עֵינָיִם: מַה־טֹּבוּ אֹהָלֶיךָ יַעֲקֹב מִשְׁכְּנֹתֶיךָ יִשְׂרָאֵל: כִּנְחָלִים

ו נִטָּיוּ כְּגַנֹּת עֲלֵי נָהָר כַּאֲהָלִים נָטַע יְהוָה כַּאֲרָזִים עֲלֵי־מָיִם: יִזַּל־מַיִם מִדָּלְיָו

ז וְזַרְעוֹ בְּמַיִם רַבִּים וְיָרֹם מֵאֲגַג מַלְכּוֹ וְתִנַּשֵּׂא מַלְכֻתוֹ: אֵל מוֹצִיאוֹ מִמִּצְרַיִם

ח כְּתוֹעֲפֹת רְאֵם לוֹ יֹאכַל גּוֹיִם צָרָיו וְעַצְמֹתֵיהֶם יְגָרֵם וְחִצָּיו יִמְחָץ: כָּרַע שָׁכַב

ט כַּאֲרִי וּכְלָבִיא מִי יְקִימֶנּוּ מְבָרֲכֶיךָ בָרוּךְ וְאֹרֲרֶיךָ אָרוּר: וַיִּחַר־אַף בָּלָק אֶל־בִּלְעָם

י וַיִּסְפֹּק אֶת־כַּפָּיו וַיֹּאמֶר בָּלָק אֶל־בִּלְעָם לָקֹב אֹיְבַי קְרָאתִיךָ וְהִנֵּה בֵּרַכְתָּ בָרֵךְ

יא זֶה שָׁלֹשׁ פְּעָמִים: וְעַתָּה בְּרַח־לְךָ אֶל־מְקוֹמֶךָ אָמַרְתִּי כַּבֵּד אֲכַבֶּדְךָ וְהִנֵּה

יב מְנָעֲךָ יְהוָה מִכָּבוֹד: וַיֹּאמֶר בִּלְעָם אֶל־בָּלָק הֲלֹא גַּם אֶל־מַלְאָכֶיךָ אֲשֶׁר

רש"י

עוֹד כְּהַקָּדוֹשׁ בָּרוּךְ הוּא, כִּי לֹא יַחְפֹּץ לְקַלְּלָם: וְלֹא הָלַךְ כְּפַעַם בְּפַעַם. כַּאֲשֶׁר עָשָׂה שְׁתֵּי פְעָמִים: לִקְרַאת נְחָשִׁים. לְנַחֵשׁ אוּלַי יִקָּרֶה ה' לִקְרָאתוֹ כִּרְצוֹנוֹ. אָמַר: רוֹצֶה וְלֹא רוֹצֶה לְקַלְלָם, מַזְכִּיר עֲוֹנוֹתֵיהֶם, וְהַקְּלָלָה עַל הַזְכָּרַת עֲוֹנֹתֵיהֶם תָּחוּל: וַיָּשֶׁת אֶל־הַמִּדְבָּר פָּנָיו. כְּתַרְגּוּמוֹ:

ב וַיִּשָּׂא בִלְעָם אֶת־עֵינָיו. בִּקֵּשׁ לְהַכְנִיס בָּהֶם עַיִן רָעָה. וַהֲרֵי יֵשׁ לְךָ שָׁלֹשׁ מִדּוֹתָיו: עַיִן רָעָה, וְרוּחַ גְּבֹהָה וְנֶפֶשׁ רְחָבָה הַאֲמוּרִים לְמַעְלָה: שֹׁכֵן לִשְׁבָטָיו. רָאָה כָּל שֵׁבֶט וְשֵׁבֶט שׁוֹכֵן לְעַצְמוֹ וְאֵינָן מְעֹרָבִין, רָאָה שֶׁאֵין פִּתְחֵיהֶם מְכֻוָּנִין זֶה כְּנֶגֶד זֶה, שֶׁלֹּא יָצִיץ לְתוֹךְ אֹהֶל חֲבֵרוֹ: וַתְּהִי עָלָיו רוּחַ אֱלֹהִים. עָלָה בְלִבּוֹ שֶׁלֹּא יְקַלְּלֵם:

ג בְּנוֹ בְעֹר. כְּמוֹ: "לְמַעְיְנוֹ מָיִם" (תהלים קיד, ח), וּמִדְרַשׁ אַגָּדָה, שְׁנֵיהֶם הָיוּ גְדוֹלִים מֵאֲבוֹתֵיהֶם: בָּלָק "בְּנוֹ צִפֹּר" (לעיל כב, יח), אָבִיו בְּנוֹ הוּא בְּמַלְכוּת, וּבִלְעָם גָּדוֹל מֵאָבִיו בִּנְבִיאוּת, מְנָה בֶּן פְּרֹר הָיָה: שְׁתֻם הָעָיִן. עֵינוֹ נְקוּרָה וּמוֹצֵאת לַחוּץ וְחוֹר שֶׁלָּהּ נִרְאֶה פָתוּחַ. וּלְשׁוֹן מִשְׁנָה הוּא: "כְּדֵי שֶׁיִּשְׁתֹּם וְיִסְתֹּם וְיִגֹּב" (עבודה זרה סט ע"ב). וְרַבּוֹתֵינוּ אָמְרוּ: לְפִי שֶׁאָמַר: "וּמִסְפָּר אֶת רֹבַע יִשְׂרָאֵל" (לעיל כב, י), שֶׁהַקָּדוֹשׁ בָּרוּךְ הוּא יוֹשֵׁב וּמוֹנֶה רְבִיעִיּוֹתֵיהֶן שֶׁל יִשְׂרָאֵל מָתַי תָּבוֹא טִפָּה שֶׁלָּהּ הַצַּדִּיק מִמֶּנָּה, אָמַר בְּלִבּוֹ, מִי שֶׁהוּא קָדוֹשׁ וּמְשָׁרְתָיו קְדוֹשִׁים יִסְתַּכֵּל בַּדְּבָרִים הַלָּלוּ, וְעַל דָּבָר זֶה נִסְמֵית עֵינוֹ שֶׁל בִּלְעָם. וְיֵשׁ מְפָרְשִׁים שְׁתֻם הָעָיִן, כְּמוֹ שָׁתוּם תִּרְגֵּם אֻנְקְלוֹס, וְעַל שֶׁאָמַר

שְׁתֻם הָעָיִן. וְלֹא אָמַר "שְׁתֻם הָעֵינַיִם" לְמַדְנוּ שֶׁסּוּמָא בְּאַחַת מֵעֵינָיו הָיָה:

ד נֹפֵל וּגְלוּי עֵינָיִם. פְּשׁוּטוֹ כְּתַרְגּוּמוֹ, שֶׁאֵין נִרְאֶה עָלָיו אֶלָּא בַּלַּיְלָה כְּשֶׁהוּא שׁוֹכֵב. וּמִדְרָשׁוֹ: כְּשֶׁהָיָה נִגְלֶה עָלָיו לֹא הָיָה בּוֹ כֹּחַ לַעֲמֹד עַל רַגְלָיו וְנוֹפֵל עַל פָּנָיו, לְפִי שֶׁהָיָה עָרֵל, וּמָאוּס לִהְיוֹת נִגְלֶה עָלָיו בְּקוֹמָה זְקוּפָה לְפָנָיו:

ה מַה־טֹּבוּ אֹהָלֶיךָ. עַל שֶׁרָאָה פִתְחֵיהֶם שֶׁאֵינָן מְכֻוָּנִין זֶה מוּל זֶה: מִשְׁכְּנֹתֶיךָ. חֲנִיּוֹתֶיךָ, כְּתַרְגּוּמוֹ. דָּבָר אַחֵר, "מַה טֹּבוּ אֹהָלֶיךָ", מַה טֹּבוּ אֹהֶל שִׁילֹה וּבֵית עוֹלָמִים בְּיִשּׁוּבָן, שֶׁמַּקְרִיבִין בָּהֶן קָרְבָּנוֹת לְכַפֵּר עֲלֵיכֶם: מִשְׁכְּנֹתֶיךָ. אַף כְּשֶׁהֵן חֲרֵבִין, לְפִי שֶׁהֵן מַשְׁכּוֹן עֲלֵיכֶם וְחֻרְבָּנָן כַּפָּרָה עַל הַנְּפָשׁוֹת, שֶׁנֶּאֱמַר: "כִּלָּה ה' אֶת חֲמָתוֹ" (איכה ד, יא), וּבַמֶּה כִלָּה? "וַיַּצֶּת אֵשׁ בְּצִיּוֹן" (שם):

ו כִּנְחָלִים נִטָּיוּ. שֶׁנִּמְשָׁכִין וְנִמְתָּחִין לָנֶטוֹת לְמֵרָחוֹק. אָמְרוּ רַבּוֹתֵינוּ: מִבִּרְכוֹתָיו שֶׁל אוֹתוֹ רָשָׁע אָנוּ לְמֵדִים מַה הָיָה בְלִבּוֹ לְקַלְלָם כְּשֶׁאָמַר לְהָשִׁית אֶל הַמִּדְבָּר פָּנָיו, וּכְשֶׁהָפַךְ הַמָּקוֹם אֶת פִּיו בֵּרְכָם מֵעֵין אוֹתָם קְלָלוֹת שֶׁבִּקֵּשׁ לוֹמַר כו', כִּדְאִיתָא בְּ'חֵלֶק' (סנהדרין קה ע"ב): כַּאֲהָלִים. כְּתַרְגּוּמוֹ, לְשׁוֹן "מֹר וַאֲהָלוֹת" (תהלים מה, ט). בְּגַן עֵדֶן. דָּבָר אַחֵר, "כַּאֲהָלִים נָטַע ה'", כַּשָּׁמַיִם הַמְּתוּחִין כְּאֹהֶל, שֶׁנֶּאֱמַר: "וַיִּמְתָּחֵם כָּאֹהֶל לָשָׁבֶת" (ישעיה מ, כב): נָטַע ה'. לְשׁוֹן נְטִיעָה מָצִינוּ בְּאֹהָלִים, שֶׁנֶּאֱמַר: "וְיִטַּע אָהֳלֵי אַפַּדְנוֹ" (דניאל יא, מה):

ז מִדָּלְיָו. מִבְּאֵרוֹתָיו, וּפֵרוּשׁוֹ כְּתַרְגּוּמוֹ: וְזַרְעוֹ בְּמַיִם רַבִּים. לְשׁוֹן הַצְלָחָה הוּא זֶה, כְּזֶרַע הַזָּרוּעַ עַל פְּנֵי הַמָּיִם: וְיָרֹם מֵאֲגַג מַלְכּוֹ. מֶלֶךְ רִאשׁוֹן שֶׁלָּהֶם יִכְבֹּשׁ אֶת אֲגַג מֶלֶךְ עֲמָלֵק: וְתִנַּשֵּׂא מַלְכֻתוֹ. שֶׁל יַעֲקֹב יוֹתֵר וְיוֹתֵר, שֶׁיָּבֹא אַחֲרָיו דָּוִד וּשְׁלֹמֹה:

ח אֵל מוֹצִיאוֹ מִמִּצְרַיִם. מִי גּוֹרֵם לָהֶם הַגְּדֻלָּה הַזֹּאת? אֵל הַמּוֹצִיאָם מִמִּצְרַיִם, בְּתֹקֶף וְרוּם שֶׁלּוֹ "יֹאכַל אֶת הַגּוֹיִם" שֶׁהֵם "צָרָיו": וְעַצְמֹתֵיהֶם. שֶׁל צָרִים: יְגָרֵם. מְנַחֵם פָּתַר בּוֹ לְשׁוֹן שְׁבִירָה, וְכֵן: "לֹא גָרְמוּ לַבֹּקֶר" (צפניה ג, ג), וְכֵן: "וְאֶת חֲרָשֶׂיהָ תְּגָרֵמִי" (יחזקאל כג, לד). וַאֲנִי אוֹמֵר, לְשׁוֹן עֶצֶם הוּא, שֶׁמְּגָרֵר הַבָּשָׂר בְּשִׁנָּיו מִסָּבִיב וְהַמֹּחַ שֶׁבִּפְנִים, וּמַעֲמִיד הָעֶצֶם עַל עַרְמִימוּתוֹ: וְחִצָּיו יִמְחָץ. אֻנְקְלוֹס תִּרְגֵּם "חִצָּיו" שֶׁל צָרִים, חֲלָקָם שֶׁלָּהֶם, כְּמוֹ: "בַּעֲלֵי חִצִּים" (בראשית מט, כג), מָרֵי פַלְגּוּתָא - לְשׁוֹן חֲלָקָה וַחֲצָיִין. וְכֵן "יִמְחָץ" לְשׁוֹן "וּמָחֲצָה וְחָלְפָה רַקָּתוֹ" (שופטים ה, כו), שֶׁיַּשְׁמִיט אֶת חַרְצַם. וְיֵשׁ לִפְתֹּר לְשׁוֹן חִצִּים מַמָּשׁ, שֶׁל צָרִים, יְקַבֵּל וְיִטְבַּע בְּדָמָם, כְּמוֹ: "לְמַעַן תִּמְחַץ רַגְלְךָ בְּדָם" (תהלים סח, כד), וְאֵינוֹ זָז מִלְּשׁוֹן מַכָּה, כְּמוֹ: "מָחַצְתִּי" (דברים לב, לט), שֶׁהַטָּבַע בְּדָם נִרְאֶה כְּאִלּוּ מָחוּץ וְנָגוּעַ:

ט כָּרַע שָׁכַב כַּאֲרִי. כְּתַרְגּוּמוֹ, יִתְיַשְּׁבוּ כְתַרְגָּם בְּכֹחַ וּבִגְבוּרָה:

י וַיִּסְפֹּק. הִכָּה זוֹ עַל זוֹ:

sent to me, saying:

13 **If Balak gives me his house full of silver and gold, I will be unable to violate the directive of the Lord, to perform good or bad on my own; that which the Lord will speak, I will speak?** I understand that you will not pay me, as I did not do as you requested. I also accept that you will not honor me, as I failed to fulfill your aspirations. However, your disappointment in me is unwarranted; I did not mislead you, as I informed you upfront that my powers are limited.

14 **Now, behold, I am going to my people.** However, **come, I will advise you.** I will tell you something else in the form of prophetic knowledge,[24] with regard to **what this people will do to your people at the end of days.** In contrast to the previous speeches, which referred mainly to the present, the next allegory is a prophecy that will come to pass in the future, although it is difficult to know the exact period to which it refers.

Seventh aliya

15 **He launched his oration, and said: The utterance of Bilam son of Beor, and the utterance of the open-eyed man.** This is the same preamble that appeared in his previous speech; it includes Bilam's self-presentation and boast that he is an all-knowing prophet (24:3).

16 **The utterance of one who hears the sayings of God, and knows the knowledge of the Most High, he shall see the vision of the Almighty; he falls with uncovered eyes** during his revelations.

17 **I see him** in a vision of future events, **but not now. I behold him, but** he will **not** rise in the **near** future; I do not know when my prophecy will happen, but I can see that it will occur only in the distant future. **A star,** a sparkling leader, **shall rise [*darakh*] from Jacob,** shooting out like an arrow from an outstretched [*darukh*] bow.[25] Some commentaries explain that *darakh* means embark on its route. **And a** ruling **scepter shall rise from Israel, and shall crush the outskirts of Moav, and destroy all the descendants of Seth,** all of mankind. As stated in Genesis 5, all of surviving humanity is the offspring of Seth son of Adam, as Abel was killed, and the descendants of Cain did not survive the deluge.

18 **Edom shall be a possession** for Israel; Israel will occupy and possess Edom. **And a possession shall be Se'ir,** Edom, for Israel, as they are **its enemies,** since the Edomites did not let Israel pass through their land. **Israel will achieve success.**

19 **One shall rule from Jacob, and will rid a remnant from the city,**[D] from all the cities of Edom,[26] or from every city in the world.[27]

20 **He saw Amalek,** either with his eyes, residing close to Israel, or in a vision,[28] **and he launched his oration, and said: Amalek was the first of the nations** to fight Israel;[29] **and its end will be oblivion.**

21 **He saw the Kenites,** Yitro's children and family, who were nomads that maintained ties with Amalek,[30] **and launched his oration, and said: Firm is your dwelling. Place your nest in the rock,** from where it cannot be removed, as you are a friend of Israel.

22 **Nevertheless,** when **Kayin shall** eventually **be expelled, until when will Assyria take you captive?** You will be captured by Assyria only temporarily.[31]

23 **He launched his oration, and said: Alas, who shall live after God's implementation** of His plan? In those future days, distant nations will come to conquer the region:

24 **Seafarers** will emerge **from Kitim,** Rome[32] or Greece,[33] and they **will afflict Assyria, and afflict the riverbank,** the residents of the western side of the Euphrates River, not only the children of Israel, **and it too,** this nation that metes out affliction, **will end in oblivion.** Bilam describes distant events with a broad brush: Great nations will break the nations that preceded them, before eventually being destroyed in turn. Only Israel and those close with them, such as the Kenite, will survive. This prophecy is also relevant for Moav, as it teaches that even if the Moavites hold firm for the moment, they will eventually be destroyed as well.

25 **Bilam rose, and went, and returned to his place** without receiving any reward. It seems that he was granted no more great prophecies after his return. It can be inferred from below that after Bilam went home he offered evil council against Israel, not as a prophet but as a private individual, and perhaps as a sorcerer as well (see 31:16). **And Balak too went on his way,** dissatisfied and frustrated, after hearing about his people's ultimate end, whereas Israel would continue to exist.

DISCUSSION

24:19 | And will rid a remnant from the city: Some commentaries explain that this prophecy is referring to the destruction of Rome in the distant future (see *Targum Yonatan*; Rashi), as Christianity is identified with the kingdom of Edom (see commentary on Isaiah 21:11).

יג שְׁלַחְתָּ אֵלַי דִּבַּרְתִּי לֵאמֹר: אִם־יִתֶּן־לִי בָלָק מְלֹא בֵיתוֹ כֶּסֶף וְזָהָב לֹא אוּכַל
לַעֲבֹר אֶת־פִּי יהוה לַעֲשׂוֹת טוֹבָה אוֹ רָעָה מִלִּבִּי אֲשֶׁר־יְדַבֵּר יהוה אֹתוֹ אֲדַבֵּר:
יד וְעַתָּה הִנְנִי הוֹלֵךְ לְעַמִּי לְכָה אִיעָצְךָ אֲשֶׁר יַעֲשֶׂה הָעָם הַזֶּה לְעַמְּךָ בְּאַחֲרִית שביעי
טו טז הַיָּמִים: וַיִּשָּׂא מְשָׁלוֹ וַיֹּאמַר נְאֻם בִּלְעָם בְּנוֹ בְעֹר וּנְאֻם הַגֶּבֶר שְׁתֻם הָעָיִן: נְאֻם
יז שֹׁמֵעַ אִמְרֵי־אֵל וְיֹדֵעַ דַּעַת עֶלְיוֹן מַחֲזֵה שַׁדַּי יֶחֱזֶה נֹפֵל וּגְלוּי עֵינָיִם: אֶרְאֶנּוּ וְלֹא
עַתָּה אֲשׁוּרֶנּוּ וְלֹא קָרוֹב דָּרַךְ כּוֹכָב מִיַּעֲקֹב וְקָם שֵׁבֶט מִיִּשְׂרָאֵל וּמָחַץ פַּאֲתֵי
יח מוֹאָב וְקַרְקַר כָּל־בְּנֵי־שֵׁת: וְהָיָה אֱדוֹם יְרֵשָׁה וְהָיָה יְרֵשָׁה שֵׂעִיר אֹיְבָיו וְיִשְׂרָאֵל
יט כ עֹשֶׂה חָיִל: וְיֵרְדְּ מִיַּעֲקֹב וְהֶאֱבִיד שָׂרִיד מֵעִיר: וַיַּרְא אֶת־עֲמָלֵק וַיִּשָּׂא מְשָׁלוֹ
כא וַיֹּאמַר רֵאשִׁית גּוֹיִם עֲמָלֵק וְאַחֲרִיתוֹ עֲדֵי אֹבֵד: וַיַּרְא אֶת־הַקֵּינִי וַיִּשָּׂא מְשָׁלוֹ
כב וַיֹּאמַר אֵיתָן מוֹשָׁבֶךָ וְשִׂים בַּסֶּלַע קִנֶּךָ: כִּי אִם־יִהְיֶה לְבָעֵר קָיִן עַד־מָה אַשּׁוּר
כג כד תִּשְׁבֶּךָּ: וַיִּשָּׂא מְשָׁלוֹ וַיֹּאמַר אוֹי מִי יִחְיֶה מִשֻּׂמוֹ אֵל: וְצִים מִיַּד כִּתִּים וְעִנּוּ אַשּׁוּר
כה וְעִנּוּ־עֵבֶר וְגַם־הוּא עֲדֵי אֹבֵד: וַיָּקָם בִּלְעָם וַיֵּלֶךְ וַיָּשָׁב לִמְקֹמוֹ וְגַם־בָּלָק
הָלַךְ לְדַרְכּוֹ:

רש״י

יג| **לַעֲבֹר אֶת פִּי ה'.** כָּאן לֹא נֶאֱמַר 'אֱלֹהַי', כְּמוֹ שֶׁאָמַר בָּרִאשׁוֹנָה, לְפִי שֶׁיָּדַע שֶׁנִּגְנַס בְּהַקָּדוֹשׁ בָּרוּךְ הוּא וְנִטְרַד:

יד| **הוֹלֵךְ לְעַמִּי.** מֵעַתָּה הֲרֵינִי כְּאֶחָד עַמִּי, שֶׁנִּסְתַּלֵּק הַקָּדוֹשׁ בָּרוּךְ הוּא מֵעָלָיו: **לְכָה אִיעָצְךָ.** מַה לְּךָ לַעֲשׂוֹת, וּמַה הִיא הָעֵצָה? אֱלֹהֵיהֶם שֶׁל אֵלּוּ שׂוֹנֵא זִמָּה הוּא כוּ', כִּדְאִיתָא בְּ'חֵלֶק' (סנהדרין קו ע״א). תֵּדַע שֶׁבִּלְעָם הַשִּׂיא עֵצָה זוֹ לְהַכְשִׁילָם בְּזִמָּה, שֶׁהֲרֵי נֶאֱמַר: "הֵן הֵנָּה הָיוּ לִבְנֵי יִשְׂרָאֵל בִּדְבַר בִּלְעָם" (להלן לא, טז): **אֲשֶׁר יַעֲשֶׂה הָעָם הַזֶּה לְעַמְּךָ.** מִקְרָא קָצָר הוּא זֶה, אִיעָצְךָ לְהַכְשִׁילָם, וְאֹמַר לְךָ מַה שֶּׁהֵן עֲתִידִין לְהָרַע לְמוֹאָב בְּאַחֲרִית הַיָּמִים: "וּמָחַץ פַּאֲתֵי מוֹאָב" (להלן פסוק יז). הַתַּרְגּוּם מְפָרֵשׁ קֹצֶר הָעִבְרִי:

טז| **וְיֹדֵעַ דַּעַת עֶלְיוֹן.** לְכַוֵּן הַשָּׁעָה שֶׁכּוֹעֵס בָּהּ:

יז| **אֶרְאֶנּוּ.** רוֹאֶה אֲנִי שִׁבְחוֹ שֶׁל יַעֲקֹב וּגְדֻלָּתוֹ, אַךְ לֹא עַתָּה הוּא אֶלָּא לְאַחַר זְמַן: **דָּרַךְ כּוֹכָב מִיַּעֲקֹב.** כְּתַרְגּוּמוֹ, לְשׁוֹן: "דָּרַךְ קַשְׁתּוֹ" (איכה ב, ד), שֶׁהַכּוֹכָב עוֹבֵר כְּחֵץ, וּבְלַעַז דישטינ״ט, כְּלוֹמַר יָקוּם מַזָּל: **וְקָם שֵׁבֶט.** מֶלֶךְ רוֹדֶה וּמוֹשֵׁל: **וּמָחַץ פַּאֲתֵי מוֹאָב.** זֶה דָּוִד, שֶׁנֶּאֱמַר בּוֹ: "הַשְׁכֵּב אוֹתָם אַרְצָה וַיְמַדֵּד שְׁנֵי חֲבָלִים לְהָמִית" וְגוֹ' (שמואל ב' ח, ב): **וְקַרְקַר.** לְשׁוֹן קוֹרֶה, כְּמוֹ: "אֲנִי קַרְתִּי" (מלכים ב' יט, כד), "מַקֶּבֶת בּוֹר נֻקַּרְתֶּם" (ישעיה נא, א), "יִקְּרוּהָ עֹרְבֵי נַחַל" (משלי ל, יז), פוריי״ר בְּלַעַז: **כָּל בְּנֵי שֵׁת.** כָּל הָאֻמּוֹת, שֶׁכֻּלָּם יָצְאוּ מִן שֵׁת בְּנוֹ שֶׁל אָדָם הָרִאשׁוֹן:

יח| **וְהָיָה יְרֵשָׁה שֵׂעִיר אֹיְבָיו.** לְאוֹיְבָיו יִשְׂרָאֵל:

יט| **וְיֵרְדְּ מִיַּעֲקֹב.** וְעוֹד יִהְיֶה מוֹשֵׁל אַחֵר מִיַּעֲקֹב: **וְהֶאֱבִיד שָׂרִיד מֵעִיר.** הַחֲשׁוּבָה שֶׁל אֱדוֹם, הִיא רוֹמִי. וְעַל מֶלֶךְ הַמָּשִׁיחַ אוֹמֵר כֵּן, שֶׁנֶּאֱמַר בּוֹ: "וְיֵרְדְּ מִיָּם עַד יָם" (תהלים עב, ח), "וְלֹא יִהְיֶה שָׂרִיד לְבֵית עֵשָׂו" (עובדיה א, יח):

כ| **וַיַּרְא אֶת עֲמָלֵק.** נִסְתַּכֵּל בְּפֻרְעָנוּתוֹ שֶׁל עֲמָלֵק: **רֵאשִׁית גּוֹיִם עֲמָלֵק.** הוּא קָדַם אֶת כֻּלָּם לְהִלָּחֵם בְּיִשְׂרָאֵל, וְכָךְ תִּרְגֵּם אוּנְקְלוֹס, "וְאַחֲרִיתוֹ" לֵאָבֵד בְּיָדָם, שֶׁנֶּאֱמַר: "תִּמְחֶה אֶת זֵכֶר עֲמָלֵק" (דברים כה, יט):

כא| **וַיַּרְא אֶת הַקֵּינִי.** לְפִי שֶׁהָיָה קֵינִי תָּקוּעַ אֵצֶל עֲמָלֵק, כָּעִנְיָן שֶׁנֶּאֱמַר: "וַיֹּאמֶר שָׁאוּל אֶל הַקֵּינִי" וְגוֹ' (שמואל א' טו, ו), הִזְכִּירוֹ אַחַר עֲמָלֵק. נִסְתַּכֵּל בִּגְדֻלָּתָם שֶׁל בְּנֵי יִתְרוֹ שֶׁנֶּאֱמַר בָּהֶם: "תִּרְעָתִים שִׁמְעָתִים שׂוּכָתִים" (דברי הימים א' ב, נה): **אֵיתָן מוֹשָׁבֶךָ.** תָּמֵהַּ אֲנִי מֵהֵיכָן זָכִיתָ לְכָךְ, הֲלֹא אַתָּה עִמִּי הָיִיתָ בַּעֲצַת "הָבָה נִתְחַכְּמָה לוֹ" (שמות א, י), וְעַתָּה נִתְיַשַּׁבְתָּ בְּאֵיתָן וּמָעוֹז שֶׁל יִשְׂרָאֵל:

כב| **כִּי אִם יִהְיֶה לְבָעֵר קָיִן וְגוֹ'.** אַשְׁרֶיךָ שֶׁנִּתְקַעְתָּ לְתֹקֶף זֶה, שֶׁאֵינְךָ נִטְרָד עוֹד מִן הָעוֹלָם, כִּי אַף אִם אַתָּה עָתִיד לִגְלוֹת עִם עֲשֶׂרֶת הַשְּׁבָטִים וְתִהְיֶה לְבָעֵר מִמָּקוֹם שֶׁנִּתְיַשַּׁבְתָּ שָׁם, מַה בְּכָךְ?: **עַד מָה אַשּׁוּר תִּשְׁבֶּךָּ.** עַד הֵיכָן הוּא מַגְלֶה אוֹתְךָ, שֶׁמָּא לַחְלַח וְחָבוֹר, אֵין זֶה טֵרוּד מִן הָעוֹלָם, אֶלָּא טִלְטוּל מִמָּקוֹם לְמָקוֹם, וְתָשׁוּב עִם שְׁאָר הַגָּלֻיּוֹת:

כג-כד| **וַיִּשָּׂא מְשָׁלוֹ וְגוֹ'.** כֵּיוָן שֶׁהִזְכִּיר אֶת שְׁבִיַּת אַשּׁוּר, אָמַר: **אוֹי מִי יִחְיֶה מִשֻּׂמוֹ אֵל.** מִי יָכוֹל לְהַחֲיוֹת אֶת עַצְמוֹ מִשּׂוּמוֹ אֶת אֵלֶּה, שֶׁלֹּא יָשִׂים עָלָיו הַגּוֹזֵר אֶת אֵלֶּה, שֶׁיַּעֲמֹד סַנְחֵרִיב וִיבַלְבֵּל אֶת כָּל הָאֻמּוֹת, וְעוֹד יָבוֹאוּ "צִים מִיַּד כִּתִּים" וְיַעַבְרוּ כִּתִּיִּים שֶׁהֵן רוֹמִיִּים בְּבִירָנִיּוֹת גְּדוֹלוֹת עַל אַשּׁוּר: **וְעִנּוּ עֵבֶר.** וְעִנּוּ אוֹתָם שֶׁבְּעֵבֶר הַנָּהָר: **וְגַם הוּא עֲדֵי אֹבֵד.** וְכֵן פֵּרֵשׁ דָּנִיֵּאל: "עַד דִּי קְטִילַת חֵיוְתָא וְהוּבַד גִּשְׁמַהּ" (דניאל ז, יא): **וְצִים.** סְפִינוֹת גְּדוֹלוֹת, כִּדְכְתִיב: "וְצִי אַדִּיר" (ישעיה לג, כא), תַּרְגּוּמוֹ "וּבוּרְנִי רַבְּתָא":

Israel's Sins in Shitim

NUMBERS 25:1–18

In the previous section, Balak sought to fight Israel through heavenly forces alone. He suffered a crushing defeat in this supernatural battle, as Bilam's mouth, which was supposed to serve as the Moavites' weapon against Israel, was the very means through which God displayed His love for His people, the Israelites. In Bilam's prophecies and blessings, Balak heard that even if Moav were to rise above Israel at certain points in history, ultimately Moav and all of the Israel's enemies would be destroyed, whereas the Israelites would survive. In the meantime, the Moavites turn to other means to oppose Israel: They try and cause the people to sin, in an effort to turn their hearts away from God. Straight after the wonderful descriptions of Israel's noble qualities, the people fall into the depths of sin, succumbing to licentiousness and idolatry.

25 1 **Israel was living in Shitim,**[B] a place near Moav, where acacia plants [*shittim*] likely grew, **and the people began to engage in licentiousness with the daughters of Moav.**[D]
2 As a result, **they invited the people to the offerings of their gods; the people ate and prostrated themselves to their gods.** The Israelites did not immediately succumb to the sin of idolatry, but as they were interested in the daughters of the land, they participated in the rites of their cults.
3 Ultimately, **Israel adhered to Baal Peor,**[BD] the Moavite god who was presumed to control that area; **and the wrath of the Lord was enflamed against Israel,** for their licentiousness and idol worship.
4 **The Lord said to Moses: Take all the leaders of the people,** the judges appointed to execute sinners, **and** since nobody has yet objected to their actions, **hang them,** those who participated in the sin, **for the Lord opposite the sun.** This should be done in a public, decisive manner, in order to express the severity of the act, **and** then **the enflamed wrath of the Lord will be withdrawn from Israel.**
5 **Moses said to the judges,** the leaders **of Israel: Each of you, kill his men,** the men under his charge[34] **who are adhering to Baal Peor.**
6 **Behold,** an important **man**[D] **from the children of Israel**[35] **came and brought near to his brethren the Midyanite woman**[D] he had found, and brought her to the tent, **before the eyes of Moses, and before the eyes of the entire congregation of the children of Israel.** He did this in public in order to demonstrate that in his opinion there was nothing wrong in the act. **And they,** the Israelites, **were weeping at the entrance of the Tent of Meeting,** as they sensed that the act was very repulsive, but they felt helpless, as they did not know what they were supposed to do.
7 **Pinhas, son of Elazar, son of Aaron the** High **Priest,** who was
Maftir present at the time alongside Moses and the other leaders of the people, **saw** this act, **and he rose from among the congregation, and he took a spear in his hand.**
8 **He went after the man of Israel** who had brought the Midyanite woman **into the tent, and stabbed both of them** as they were engaged in the act, **the man of Israel, and the woman through her abdomen,** her sexual organ.[36] **The plague was stopped**[D] **from the children of Israel,** because of this stabbing.
9 **Those who died in the plague were twenty-four thousand.**[D]

DISCUSSION

25:1| **And the people began to engage in licentiousness with the daughters of Moav:** Since the Moavites decided to refrain from waging war with the Israelites, who were dwelling in their vicinity, some Israelites living on the edge of the camp became friendly with Moavite men and women. After long years of wandering, during which the Israelites lived under a rigid system, they arrived at settled areas, whose residents lived more comfortably. The inhabitants of these places were their distant relatives and even spoke a related language, as it is evident from the Mesha Stele that the Moavite tongue was very similar to Hebrew. Naturally, some of the people developed friendly relations with their new neighbors. It is clear from below that the leaders of Moav, who did not want the Israelites to harass or attack them, encouraged these ties. At first, the meetings with the daughters of Moav were not for the sake of licentiousness, but were social encounters between the nomads and the Moavite and Midyanite inhabitants of the land. However, forbidden relationships eventually developed between them (see *Bemidbar Rabba* 20:23; see also commentary on Deuteronomy 2:19).

25:3| **Israel adhered to Baal Peor:** The people who sinned with the daughters of Moav, and subsequently worshipped Baal Peor, were born during the wanderings in the wilderness. They were not directly influenced by Egyptian culture, but had been raised to observe God's commandments, given by Moses. After many years living in a society with a framework of defined laws, the Israelites presumably sensed that their current relationships were inappropriate. However, when faced with the temptations from the ties that had developed between them and the local women, the ideals that they had absorbed from many years living near the Tabernacle faded away. The reason they succumbed might have been because there was not yet an extended tradition among the people of Torah observance, or perhaps it was due to the fact that until that point sexual relations with women from other nations had not been specifically prohibited to the Israelites. It is even possible that they saw nothing wrong with their behavior, according to the standards of basic human morality, as the women were not forced but participated willingly, out of mutual affection.

25:6| **Man [*ish*]:** The use of the term *ish* in reference to a notably powerful individual is found in other places as well (see, e.g., I Samuel 26:15; I Kings 2:2; Rashi, 13:3 and I Samuel 1:11; Ibn Ezra, 13:2).

The Midyanite woman: As stated earlier, the elders of Midyan joined the elders of Moav in their approach to Bilam (22:7). In this seduction of the Israelites, the Midyanites were apparently even more active than the Moavites, as indicated below (25:17–18).

א וַיֵּשֶׁב יִשְׂרָאֵל בַּשִּׁטִּים וַיָּחֶל הָעָם לִזְנוֹת אֶל־בְּנוֹת מוֹאָב: וַתִּקְרֶאןָ לָעָם לְזִבְחֵי כא
ב אֱלֹהֵיהֶן וַיֹּאכַל הָעָם וַיִּשְׁתַּחֲוֻ לֵאלֹהֵיהֶן: וַיִּצָּמֶד יִשְׂרָאֵל לְבַעַל פְּעוֹר וַיִּחַר־אַף
ג יְהוָה בְּיִשְׂרָאֵל: וַיֹּאמֶר יְהוָה אֶל־מֹשֶׁה קַח אֶת־כָּל־רָאשֵׁי הָעָם וְהוֹקַע אוֹתָם
ד לַיהוָה נֶגֶד הַשָּׁמֶשׁ וְיָשֹׁב חֲרוֹן אַף־יְהוָה מִיִּשְׂרָאֵל: וַיֹּאמֶר מֹשֶׁה אֶל־שֹׁפְטֵי
ה יִשְׂרָאֵל הִרְגוּ אִישׁ אֲנָשָׁיו הַנִּצְמָדִים לְבַעַל פְּעוֹר: וְהִנֵּה אִישׁ מִבְּנֵי יִשְׂרָאֵל בָּא
ו וַיַּקְרֵב אֶל־אֶחָיו אֶת־הַמִּדְיָנִית לְעֵינֵי מֹשֶׁה וּלְעֵינֵי כָּל־עֲדַת בְּנֵי־יִשְׂרָאֵל וְהֵמָּה
בֹכִים פֶּתַח אֹהֶל מוֹעֵד: וַיַּרְא פִּינְחָס בֶּן־אֶלְעָזָר בֶּן־אַהֲרֹן הַכֹּהֵן וַיָּקָם מִתּוֹךְ מפטיר
ז הָעֵדָה וַיִּקַּח רֹמַח בְּיָדוֹ: וַיָּבֹא אַחַר אִישׁ־יִשְׂרָאֵל אֶל־הַקֻּבָּה וַיִּדְקֹר אֶת־שְׁנֵיהֶם
ח אֵת אִישׁ יִשְׂרָאֵל וְאֶת־הָאִשָּׁה אֶל־קֳבָתָהּ וַתֵּעָצַר הַמַּגֵּפָה מֵעַל בְּנֵי יִשְׂרָאֵל:
ט וַיִּהְיוּ הַמֵּתִים בַּמַּגֵּפָה אַרְבָּעָה וְעֶשְׂרִים אָלֶף:

רש״י

פרק כה

א) **בַּשִּׁטִּים.** כָּךְ שְׁמָהּ: **לִזְנוֹת אֶל בְּנוֹת מוֹאָב.** עַל יְדֵי עֲצַת בִּלְעָם, כִּדְאִיתָא בְּחֵלֶק (סנהדרין קו ע״א):

ב) **וַיִּשְׁתַּחֲוֻ לֵאלֹהֵיהֶן.** כְּשֶׁתְּקָפוֹ יִצְרוֹ עָלָיו וְאוֹמֵר לָהּ הִשְּׁמְעִי לִי, וְהִיא מוֹצִיאָה לוֹ דְּמוּת פְּעוֹר מֵחֵיקָהּ וְאוֹמֶרֶת לוֹ הִשְׁתַּחֲוֵה לָזֶה:

ג) **פְּעוֹר.** עַל שֵׁם שֶׁפּוֹעֲרִין לְפָנָיו פִּי הַטַּבַּעַת וּמוֹצִיאִין רֶעִי, וְזוֹ הִיא עֲבוֹדָתוֹ: **וַיִּחַר אַף ה' בְּיִשְׂרָאֵל.** שָׁלַח בָּם מַגֵּפָה:

ד) **קַח אֶת כָּל רָאשֵׁי הָעָם.** לִשְׁפֹּט אֶת הָעוֹבְדִים לִפְעוֹר: **וְהוֹקַע אוֹתָם.** אֶת הָעוֹבְדִים: **וְהוֹקַע.** הִיא תְּלִיָּה, כְּמוֹ שֶׁמָּצִינוּ בִּבְנֵי שָׁאוּל: ״וְהוֹקַעֲנוּם לַה'״ (שמואל ב' כא, ו), וְשָׁם

תְּלִיָּה מְפֹרֶשֶׁת, עֲבוֹדָה זָרָה בִּסְקִילָה, וְכָל הַנִּסְקָלִין נִתְלִין: **נֶגֶד הַשָּׁמֶשׁ.** לְעֵין כֹּל. וּמִדְרַשׁ אַגָּדָה: הַשֶּׁמֶשׁ מוֹדִיעַ אֶת הַחוֹטְאִים, הֶעָנָן נִקְפָּל מִכְּנֶגְדּוֹ וְהַחַמָּה זוֹרַחַת עָלָיו:

ה) **הִרְגוּ אִישׁ אֲנָשָׁיו.** כָּל אֶחָד וְאֶחָד מִדַּיָּנֵי יִשְׂרָאֵל הָיָה הוֹרֵג שְׁנַיִם, וְדַיָּנֵי יִשְׂרָאֵל שִׁבְעָה רִבּוֹא וּשְׁמוֹנַת אֲלָפִים, כִּדְאִיתָא בְּסַנְהֶדְרִין (דף יח ע״א):

ו) **וְהִנֵּה אִישׁ וְגוֹ'.** נִתְקַבְּצוּ שִׁבְטוֹ שֶׁל שִׁמְעוֹן אֵצֶל זִמְרִי שֶׁהָיָה נָשִׂיא שֶׁלָּהֶם, אָמְרוּ לוֹ: אָנוּ נִדּוֹנִין בְּמִיתָה וְאַתָּה יוֹשֵׁב? וְכוּ', כִּדְאִיתָא בְּאֵלּוּ הֵן הַנִּשְׂרָפִין (סנהדרין פב ע״א): **אֶת הַמִּדְיָנִית.** כָּזְבִּי בַּת צוּר: **לְעֵינֵי מֹשֶׁה.** אָמְרוּ לוֹ: מֹשֶׁה, זוֹ אֲסוּרָה אוֹ מֻתֶּרֶת? אִם תֹּאמַר אֲסוּרָה, בַּת יִתְרוֹ מִי הִתִּירָהּ לְךָ? וְכוּ', כִּדְאִיתָא הָתָם: **וְהֵמָּה בֹכִים.** נִתְעַלְּמָה מִמֶּנּוּ הֲלָכָה, גָּעוּ כֻּלָּם בִּבְכִיָּה. בָּעֵגֶל עָמַד

מֹשֶׁה כְּנֶגֶד שִׁשִּׁים רִבּוֹא, שֶׁנֶּאֱמַר: ״וַיִּטְחַן עַד אֲשֶׁר דָּק״ וְגוֹ' (שמות לב, כ), וְכָאן רָפוּ יָדָיו? אֶלָּא כְּדֵי שֶׁיָּבֹא פִּינְחָס וְיִטֹּל אֶת הָרָאוּי לוֹ:

ז) **וַיַּרְא פִּינְחָס.** רָאָה מַעֲשֶׂה וְנִזְכַּר הֲלָכָה. אָמַר לוֹ לְמֹשֶׁה: מְקֻבְּלַנִי מִמְּךָ, הַבּוֹעֵל אֲרַמִּית קַנָּאִין פּוֹגְעִין בּוֹ. אָמַר לוֹ: קַרְיָנָא דְּאִגַּרְתָּא אִיהוּ לֶהֱוֵי פַּרְוַנְקָא. מִיָּד – ״וַיִּקַּח רֹמַח בְּיָדוֹ״ וְגוֹ':

ח) **אֶל הַקֻּבָּה.** אֶל הָאֹהֶל: **אֶל קֳבָתָהּ.** כְּמוֹ ״וְהַלְּחָיַיִם וְהַקֵּבָה״ (דברים יח, ג), כִּוֵּן בְּתוֹךְ זַכְרוּת שֶׁל זִמְרִי וְנַקְבוּת שֶׁלָּהּ, וְרָאוּ כֻּלָּם שֶׁלֹּא לְחִנָּם הֲרָגָם, וְהַרְבֵּה נִסִּים נַעֲשׂוּ לוֹ וְכוּ', כִּדְאִיתָא הָתָם (סנהדרין פב ע״ב):

BACKGROUND

25:1 | Shitim: Many researchers identify this with Khirbet el-Kefrain, north of Wadi el-Kefrain, on the eastern side of the Jordan River. Others claim that it is Tel el-Hammam, east of Khirbet el-Kefrain.

25:3 | Baal Peor: This was a god of the Baal type, which belonged specifically to the locale of Peor. Some associate this cult with offerings sacrificed to the dead (see Psalms 106:28). According to the Talmud, the ritual of Baal Peor was particularly repulsive, as it involved *peira*, the exposure of one's body for the purpose of defecation.

DISCUSSION

25:8 | The plague was stopped: Just as that man acted flagrantly in public, to show that he was doing nothing wrong, so too Pinhas opposed him in an open, unambiguous manner. Pinhas' decisive act not only halted the plague itself, in that people stopped dying, but it also responded to the cause of the plague, as the entire congregation saw from his dramatic deed that such behavior was

unacceptable, and that one who continued to act in such a manner would meet his end.

25:9 | Those who died in the plague were twenty-four thousand: In light of the censuses of the tribes below, it seems likely that all the dead were from the tribe of Simeon (based on Jerusalem Talmud, *Sota* 7:4; see commentary on Numbers 26:14).

Parashat **Pinhas**

Pinhas and the Eternal Priesthood

NUMBERS 25:10–18

The narrative continues with Pinhas' reward for placating God's wrath in the matter of bringing the forbidden Midyanite woman into the Israelite camp. As a result, Pinhas merits the covenant of eternal priesthood.

10 **The Lord spoke to Moses, saying:**
11 **Pinhas, son of Elazar, son of Aaron the priest, has caused My wrath to be withdrawn from the children of Israel, in that he was zealous on my behalf among them;** Pinhas felt that it was his responsibility to zealously guard My presence in the midst of the children of Israel, and therefore took extreme action that he had not been commanded to take. It was only because of that action **that I did not destroy the children of Israel in My zealotry;** had he not taken action, the plague would have spread and consumed the entire nation.
12 **Therefore, say: Behold, I am giving him My covenant of peace.** This special covenant of peace was given to Pinhas not because he was a man of peace but rather because he brought about peace between the children of Israel and their Father in Heaven. Through his action, Pinhas proclaimed that the Israelites belong exclusively to God. This zealous position did not allow for any foreign entity to interfere with the intimate relationship between God and Israel.
13 **It shall be for him, and for his descendants after him, a covenant of an eternal priesthood;**[D] Pinhas receives this gift **because he was zealous for his God, and he atoned for the children of Israel.**
14 The Torah provides details to round out the story: **The name of the man of Israel who was slain, who was slain with the Midyanite woman** while performing a sinful act, **was Zimri son of Salu, prince of a patrilineal house of the Simeonites.**[D]
15 **The name of the Midyanite woman who was slain was Kozbi daughter of Tzur; he was head of the nations of a patrilineal house in Midyan.**[D] The Midyanites were comprised of distinct tribes that were affiliated with one another. Tzur was the leader of the largest or most important clan in Midyan.
16 **The Lord spoke to Moses, saying:**
17 **Bear enmity to the Midyanites, and smite them.** God spared the Moavites, but commanded the children of Israel to battle the Midyanites.
18 This is **because they are enemies to you, with their deceits that they deceived you in the matter of Peor, and in the matter of Kozbi, daughter of the prince of Midyan, their**

DISCUSSION

25:13| **It shall be for him, and for his descendants after him, a covenant of an eternal priesthood:** It would seem that Pinhas, a son of Elazar the priest, was already a priest and therefore would not need a new covenant of eternal priesthood. However, when the priests were originally sanctified and appointed, only Aaron and his sons were sanctified. It was then stated that their future descendants would also have the status of priests. However, the sons who were already born, such as Pinhas, were not necessarily sanctified as priests. Therefore Pinhas' status as a priest was unclear until he was granted this covenant of eternal priesthood for him and his descendants. Just as the tribe of Levi attained its elevated status due to the fact that it fought for God in the aftermath of the sin of the Golden Calf, so too Pinhas was granted priestly status because he fought on behalf of God and thereby atoned for the children of Israel (Rashi; *Zevaḥim* 101b).

The covenant of eternal priesthood that was promised to Pinhas was fulfilled in a manner superseding the simple appointment of Pinhas as a priest: For the majority of the duration of the kingdom of Israel, the High Priests were descendants of Tzadok, who himself was a descendant of Pinhas (see I Kings 2:27, 4:2; I Chronicles 5:27–34; Ibn Ezra here and Numbers 25:12; see also commentary on I Samuel 2:30 and Ezekiel 44:15).

25:14| **Prince of a patrilineal house of the Simeonites:** It would seem that Zimri was not the prince of the tribe of Simeon but rather the head of one of the families that comprised the tribe of Simeon. Consequently, he was at the

פרשת פינחס

י יא וַיְדַבֵּר יְהוָה אֶל־מֹשֶׁה לֵּאמֹר: פִּינְחָס בֶּן־אֶלְעָזָר בֶּן־אַהֲרֹן הַכֹּהֵן הֵשִׁיב אֶת־ כב
חֲמָתִי מֵעַל בְּנֵי־יִשְׂרָאֵל בְּקַנְאוֹ אֶת־קִנְאָתִי בְּתוֹכָם וְלֹא־כִלִּיתִי אֶת־בְּנֵי־
יב יג יִשְׂרָאֵל בְּקִנְאָתִי: לָכֵן אֱמֹר הִנְנִי נֹתֵן לוֹ אֶת־בְּרִיתִי שָׁלוֹם: וְהָיְתָה לּוֹ וּלְזַרְעוֹ
אַחֲרָיו בְּרִית כְּהֻנַּת עוֹלָם תַּחַת אֲשֶׁר קִנֵּא לֵאלֹהָיו וַיְכַפֵּר עַל־בְּנֵי יִשְׂרָאֵל:
יד וְשֵׁם אִישׁ יִשְׂרָאֵל הַמֻּכֶּה אֲשֶׁר הֻכָּה אֶת־הַמִּדְיָנִית זִמְרִי בֶּן־סָלוּא נְשִׂיא בֵית־
טו אָב לַשִּׁמְעֹנִי: וְשֵׁם הָאִשָּׁה הַמֻּכָּה הַמִּדְיָנִית כָּזְבִּי בַת־צוּר רֹאשׁ אֻמּוֹת בֵּית־אָב
בְּמִדְיָן הוּא:
טז יז יח וַיְדַבֵּר יְהוָה אֶל־מֹשֶׁה לֵּאמֹר: צָרוֹר אֶת־הַמִּדְיָנִים וְהִכִּיתֶם אוֹתָם: כִּי־צֹרְרִים הֵם
לָכֶם בְּנִכְלֵיהֶם אֲשֶׁר־נִכְּלוּ לָכֶם עַל־דְּבַר פְּעוֹר וְעַל־דְּבַר כָּזְבִּי בַת־נְשִׂיא מִדְיָן

רש״י

יא| **פִּינְחָס בֶּן אֶלְעָזָר בֶּן אַהֲרֹן הַכֹּהֵן.** לְפִי שֶׁהָיוּ הַשְּׁבָטִים מְבַזִּים אוֹתוֹ, הַרְאִיתֶם בֶּן פּוּטִי זֶה שֶׁפִּטֵּם אֲבִי אִמּוֹ עֲגָלִים לַעֲבוֹדָה זָרָה וְהָרַג נְשִׂיא שֵׁבֶט מִיִּשְׂרָאֵל, לְפִיכָךְ בָּא הַכָּתוּב וְיִחֲסוֹ אַחַר אַהֲרֹן: **בְּקַנְאוֹ אֶת קִנְאָתִי.** בְּנָקְמוֹ אֶת נִקְמָתִי, בְּקָצְפּוֹ אֶת הַקֶּצֶף שֶׁהָיָה לִי לִקְצֹף. כָּל לְשׁוֹן ׳קִנְאָה׳ הוּא הַמִּתְחָרֶה לִנְקֹם נִקְמַת דָּבָר, אנפרנמנ״ט בְּלַעַז:

יב| **אֶת בְּרִיתִי שָׁלוֹם.** שֶׁתְּהֵא לוֹ לִבְרִית שָׁלוֹם, כְּאָדָם הַמַּחֲזִיק טוֹבָה וְחַנּוּת לְמִי שֶׁעוֹשֶׂה עִמּוֹ טוֹבָה, אַף כָּאן פֵּרֵשׁ לוֹ הַקָּדוֹשׁ בָּרוּךְ הוּא שְׁלוֹמוֹתָיו:

יג| **וְהָיְתָה לּוֹ.** בְּרִיתִי זֹאת: **בְּרִית כְּהֻנַּת עוֹלָם.** שֶׁאַף עַל פִּי שֶׁכְּבָר נִתְּנָה כְּהֻנָּה לְזַרְעוֹ שֶׁל אַהֲרֹן, לֹא נִתְּנָה אֶלָּא לְאַהֲרֹן וּלְבָנָיו שֶׁנִּמְשְׁחוּ עִמּוֹ וּלְתוֹלְדוֹתֵיהֶם שֶׁיּוֹלִידוּ אַחַר הַמְשָׁחָתָן, אֲבָל פִּינְחָס שֶׁנּוֹלַד קֹדֶם לָכֵן וְלֹא נִמְשַׁח, לֹא בָּא לִכְלַל כְּהֻנָּה עַד כָּאן. וְכֵן שָׁנִינוּ בִּזְבָחִים: לֹא נִתְכַּהֵן פִּינְחָס עַד שֶׁהֲרָגוֹ לְזִמְרִי (זבחים קא ע״ב): **לֵאלֹהָיו.** בִּשְׁבִיל אֱלֹהָיו, כְּמוֹ: ״הַמְקַנֵּא אַתָּה לִי״ (לעיל יא, כט), ״קִנֵּאתִי לְצִיּוֹן״ (זכריה ח, ב), בִּשְׁבִיל צִיּוֹן:

יד| **וְשֵׁם אִישׁ יִשְׂרָאֵל וְגוֹ׳.** בִּמְקוֹם שֶׁיִּחֵס אֶת הַצַּדִּיק לְשֶׁבַח, יִחֵס אֶת הָרָשָׁע לִגְנַאי: **נְשִׂיא בֵית אָב לַשִּׁמְעֹנִי.** לְאֶחָד מֵחֲמֵשֶׁת בָּתֵּי אָבוֹת שֶׁהָיוּ לְשֵׁבֶט שִׁמְעוֹן. דָּבָר אַחֵר, לְהוֹדִיעַ שִׁבְחוֹ שֶׁל פִּינְחָס, שֶׁאַף עַל פִּי שֶׁזֶּה הָיָה נָשִׂיא, לֹא מָנַע אֶת עַצְמוֹ מִלְּקַנֵּא לְחִלּוּל הַשֵּׁם, לְכָךְ הוֹדִיעֲךָ הַכָּתוּב מִי הוּא הַמֻּכֶּה:

טו| **וְשֵׁם הָאִשָּׁה הַמֻּכָּה וְגוֹ׳.** לְהוֹדִיעֲךָ שִׂנְאָתָן שֶׁל מִדְיָנִים, שֶׁהִפְקִירוּ בַּת מֶלֶךְ לִזְנוּת כְּדֵי לְהַחֲטִיא אֶת יִשְׂרָאֵל: **רֹאשׁ אֻמּוֹת.** אֶחָד מֵחֲמֵשֶׁת מַלְכֵי מִדְיָן: ״אֶת אֱוִי וְאֶת רֶקֶם וְאֶת צוּר״ וְגוֹ׳ (להלן לא, ח), וְהוּא הָיָה חָשׁוּב מִכֻּלָּם, שֶׁנֶּאֱמַר: ״רֹאשׁ אֻמּוֹת״, וּלְפִי שֶׁנָּהַג בִּזָּיוֹן בְּעַצְמוֹ לְהַפְקִיר בִּתּוֹ מְנָאוֹ שְׁלִישִׁי: **בֵּית אָב.** חֲמִשָּׁה בָּתֵּי אָבוֹת הָיוּ לְמִדְיָן: ״עֵיפָה וָעֵפֶר וַחֲנֹךְ וַאֲבִידָע וְאֶלְדָּעָה״ (בראשית כה, ד), וְזֶה הָיָה מֶלֶךְ לְאֶחָד מֵהֶם:

יז| **צָרוֹר.** כְּמוֹ: ׳זָכוֹר׳, ׳שָׁמוֹר׳, לְשׁוֹן הֹוֶה, עֲלֵיכֶם לְאַיֵּב אוֹתָם:

יח| **כִּי צֹרְרִים הֵם לָכֶם וְגוֹ׳ עַל דְּבַר פְּעוֹר.** שֶׁהִפְקִירוּ בְּנוֹתֵיהֶם לִזְנוּת כְּדֵי לְהַטְעוֹתְכֶם אַחַר פְּעוֹר. וְאֶת מוֹאָב לֹא צִוָּה לְהַשְׁמִיד, מִפְּנֵי רוּת שֶׁהָיְתָה עֲתִידָה לָצֵאת מֵהֶם, כִּדְאָמְרִינַן בְּבָבָא קַמָּא (דף לח ע״ב):

DISCUSSION

third level of leadership of Israel (see Rashi). However, a midrash states that Zimri was the prince of the entire tribe, and the verse refers to him a leader of lesser standing in order to protect the honor of the tribe (*Bemidbar Rabba* 21:3).

25:15| **Kozbi daughter of Tzur; he was head of the nations of a patrilineal house in Midyan:** Kozbi's lineage explains why the Israelite prince paraded her in front of the entire nation. He took pride in her because she was a Midyanite princess, and he was also demonstrating solidarity and peace between the two nations. Pinhas put an end to this cosmopolitan flashiness.

sister, who was slain on the day of the plague in the matter of Peor. The Midyanites were connected to Moav, as the elders of Midyan traveled with the elders of Moav to convince Bilam to curse Israel. However, it seems that Midyan hated Israel even more than Moav did. It is clear from the verses later on (31:7–16) that the idea to seduce the Israelite men via Moavite and Midyanite women was a conscious strategy that was planned

by Bilam and the Midyanites, based on their understanding that the existence of the Israelite nation was dependent on their distinctiveness and sanctity. Consequently, they were willing to send their daughters, including even the daughter of their prince, to cause the Israelite men to sin and thereby to lead to their downfall.

The Census and Division of the Land
NUMBERS 26:1–65

The children of Israel were counted shortly after their exodus from Egypt. Now, in their final year of wandering through the wilderness, Moses and Aaron's son, Elazar, are commanded to conduct another census. This census has military significance, among other purposes,[1] as the nation will shortly enter the land of Canaan, where they will engage in military combat. It is possible, as hinted in the opening phrase of this chapter, that a census is conducted now in order to determine how many people are left after the plague that struck the Israelites in the previous incident.

26 1 **It was after the plague; and the Lord said to Moses and to Elazar son of Aaron the priest, saying:**

2 **Take a census of the entire congregation of the children of Israel, from twenty years old and above, by their patrilineal house, all those fit for military service in Israel.**

3 **Moses and Elazar the priest spoke with them on the plains of Moav along the Jordan opposite Jericho, saying:**

4 **From twenty years old and above,** in the same manner **as the Lord had commanded Moses and the children of Israel** to count them **when coming out from the land of Egypt,** so that the results of the two censuses may be compared.

5 **Reuben, the firstborn of Israel, the sons of Reuben:** Second aliya **Hanokh,** whose descendants comprised **the family of the Hanokhites; for Palu,** another son of Reuben, **the family of the Paluites;**

6 **for Hetzron, the family of the Hetzronites; for Karmi, the family of the Karmites.**

7 **These are the families of the Reubenites; those counted were forty-three thousand seven hundred and thirty.**

8 **And the sons of Palu,** his only son: **Eliav.**

9 **And the sons of Eliav: Nemuel, Datan, and Aviram. This is Datan and Aviram, the distinguished of the congregation, who incited against Moses and against Aaron in the**

congregation of Korah, when they incited against the Lord. Although the report of the census generally includes only the names of the families within each tribe and not the names of the individuals in each family, the Torah gives details about the Paluite family in order to mention Palu's grandsons, Datan and Aviram, who were leaders in the rebellion of Korah and his congregation.

10 **The earth opened its mouth, and swallowed them and Korah, with the death of the congregation, when the fire devoured two hundred and fifty men, and they became a sign.**

11 The Torah notes that **the sons of Korah did not die,** despite the fact that they were involved, to a certain degree, in the rebellion.[2]

12 **The sons of Simeon by their families: for Nemuel, the family of the Nemuelites; for Yamin, the family of the Yaminites; for Yakhin, the family of the Yakhinites;**

13 **for Zerah, the family of the Zerahites; for Shaul, the family of the Shaulites.**

14 **These are the families of the Simeonites, twenty-two thousand two hundred.**[D]

15 **The sons of Gad by their families: for Tzefon, the family**

DISCUSSION

26:14 | **The families of the Simeonites, twenty-two thousand two hundred:** This number indicates a decline of over 37,000 men since the time of the first census taken in the wilderness (see 1:23). It is possible that this precipitous decline is due in part to the plague that struck the nation in the previous incident. This plague may have primarily targeted the tribe of Simeon, either because they were encamped closest to the Moavites, because they had particular affection for them, or because their leader, Zimri, encouraged them to engage with the foreign women and even publicly and brazenly brought a Midyanite woman into the Israelite camp in order to sin (Rashi; see Jerusalem Talmud, *Sota* 4:7).

א אֲחֹתָם הַמֻּכָּה בְיוֹם־הַמַּגֵּפָה עַל־דְּבַר פְּעוֹר: וַיְהִי אַחֲרֵי הַמַּגֵּפָה
ב וַיֹּאמֶר יְהוָה אֶל־מֹשֶׁה וְאֶל אֶלְעָזָר בֶּן־אַהֲרֹן הַכֹּהֵן לֵאמֹר: שְׂאוּ אֶת־רֹאשׁ
כָּל־עֲדַת בְּנֵי־יִשְׂרָאֵל מִבֶּן עֶשְׂרִים שָׁנָה וָמַעְלָה לְבֵית אֲבֹתָם כָּל־יֹצֵא צָבָא
ג בְּיִשְׂרָאֵל: וַיְדַבֵּר מֹשֶׁה וְאֶלְעָזָר הַכֹּהֵן אֹתָם בְּעַרְבֹת מוֹאָב עַל־יַרְדֵּן יְרֵחוֹ
ד לֵאמֹר: מִבֶּן עֶשְׂרִים שָׁנָה וָמָעְלָה כַּאֲשֶׁר צִוָּה יְהוָה אֶת־מֹשֶׁה וּבְנֵי יִשְׂרָאֵל
ה הַיֹּצְאִים מֵאֶרֶץ מִצְרָיִם: רְאוּבֵן בְּכוֹר יִשְׂרָאֵל בְּנֵי רְאוּבֵן חֲנוֹךְ מִשְׁפַּחַת הַחֲנֹכִי
ו לְפַלּוּא מִשְׁפַּחַת הַפַּלֻּאִי: לְחֶצְרֹן מִשְׁפַּחַת הַחֶצְרוֹנִי לְכַרְמִי מִשְׁפַּחַת הַכַּרְמִי:
ז אֵלֶּה מִשְׁפְּחֹת הָראוּבֵנִי וַיִּהְיוּ פְקֻדֵיהֶם שְׁלֹשָׁה וְאַרְבָּעִים אֶלֶף וּשְׁבַע מֵאוֹת
ח ט וּשְׁלֹשִׁים: וּבְנֵי פַלּוּא אֱלִיאָב: וּבְנֵי אֱלִיאָב נְמוּאֵל וְדָתָן וַאֲבִירָם הוּא־דָתָן וַאֲבִירָם
קְרוּאֵי הָעֵדָה אֲשֶׁר הִצּוּ עַל־מֹשֶׁה וְעַל־אַהֲרֹן בַּעֲדַת־קֹרַח בְּהַצֹּתָם עַל־יְהוָה:
י וַתִּפְתַּח הָאָרֶץ אֶת־פִּיהָ וַתִּבְלַע אֹתָם וְאֶת־קֹרַח בְּמוֹת הָעֵדָה בַּאֲכֹל הָאֵשׁ אֵת
יא יב חֲמִשִּׁים וּמָאתַיִם אִישׁ וַיִּהְיוּ לְנֵס: וּבְנֵי־קֹרַח לֹא־מֵתוּ: בְּנֵי שִׁמְעוֹן
לְמִשְׁפְּחֹתָם לִנְמוּאֵל מִשְׁפַּחַת הַנְּמוּאֵלִי לְיָמִין מִשְׁפַּחַת הַיָּמִינִי לְיָכִין מִשְׁפַּחַת
יג יד הַיָּכִינִי: לְזֶרַח מִשְׁפַּחַת הַזַּרְחִי לְשָׁאוּל מִשְׁפַּחַת הַשָּׁאוּלִי: אֵלֶּה מִשְׁפְּחֹת הַשִּׁמְעֹנִי
טו שְׁנַיִם וְעֶשְׂרִים אֶלֶף וּמָאתָיִם: בְּנֵי גָד לְמִשְׁפְּחֹתָם לִצְפוֹן מִשְׁפַּחַת

רש"י

פרק כו

א| ויהי אחרי המגפה וגו'. משל לרועה שנכנסו זאבים לתוך עדרו והרגו בהן, והוא מונה אותן לידע מנין הנותרות. דבר אחר, כשיצאו ממצרים ונמסרו למשה, נמסרו לו במנין, עכשיו שקרב למות ולהחזיר צאנו, מחזירם במנין:

ב| לבית אבתם. על שבט האב יתיחסו ולא אחר האם:

ג| וידבר משה ואלעזר הכהן אתם. דברו עמם על זאת, שצוה המקום למנותם: לאמר. אמרו להם צריכים אתם להמנות:

ד| מבן עשרים שנה ומעלה כאשר צוה וגו'. שיהא מנינם מבן עשרים שנה ומעלה, שנאמר: "כל העבר על הפקדים" וגו' (שמות ל, יג):

ה| משפחת החנכי. לפי שהיו האמות מבזין אותם ואומרים, מה אלו מתיחסין על שבטיהם? סבורין הם שלא שלטו המצרים באמותיהם? אם בגופם היו מושלים קל וחומר בנשותיהם! לפיכך הטיל הקדוש ברוך הוא שמו עליהם, ה"א מצד זה ויו"ד מצד זה, לומר, מעיד אני עליהם שהם בני אבותיהם. וזה הוא שמפורש על ידי דוד: "שבטי יה עדות לישראל" (תהלים קכב, ד), השם הזה מעיד עליהם לשבטיהם. לפיכך בכלם כתיב: "החנכי", "הפלאי", אבל ב"ימנה" (להלן פסוק מד) לא הוצרך לומר 'משפחת הימני', לפי שהשם קבוע בו, יו"ד בראש וה"א בסוף:

ט| אשר הצו. את ישראל "על משה": בהצתם. את העם "על ה'": הצו. השיאו את ישראל לריב "על משה", לשון הפעילו:

י| ויהיו לנס. לאות ולזכרון, למען אשר לא יקרב איש זר לחלק עוד על הכהנה:

יא| ובני קרח לא מתו. הם היו בעצה תחלה, ובשעת המחלקת הרהרו תשובה בלבם, לפיכך נתבצר להם מקום גבוה בגיהנם וישבו שם:

יג| לזרח. הוא צחר (שמות ו, טו), לשון צהר, אבל משפחת אהד בטלה. וכן חמש משבט בנימין, שהרי בעשרה בנים ירד למצרים (בראשית מו, כא) וכאן לא מנה אלא חמשה, וכן אצבון לגד, הרי שבע משפחות. ומצאתי בתלמוד ירושלמי (סוטה א, י) שכשמת אהרן נסתלקו ענני כבוד ובאו הכנענים להלחם בישראל, ונתנו לב לחזור למצרים, וחזרו לאחוריהם שמונה מסעות מהר ההר למוסרה, שנאמר: "ובני ישראל נסעו מבארת בני יעקן מוסרה, שם מת אהרן" (דברים י, ו), והלא בהר ההר מת, וממוסרה עד הר ההר שמונה מסעות יש למפרע? אלא שחזרו לאחוריהם, ורדפו בני לוי אחריהם להחזירם, והרגו מהם שבע משפחות, ומבני לוי נפלו ארבע משפחות: משפחת שמעי, ועזיאלי,

of the Tzefonites; for Hagi, the family of the Hagites; for Shuni, the family of the Shunites;

16 **for Ozni,** referred to elsewhere as Etzbon,[3] **the family of the Oznites; for Eri, the family of the Erites;**

17 **for Arod, the family of the Arodites; for Areli, the family of the Arelites.**

18 **These are the families of the sons of Gad by their count, forty thousand five hundred.**

19 **The sons of Judah: Er and Onan. Er and Onan died in the land of Canaan.** Although Er and Onan died childless and were therefore insignificant with regard to the census, there are several places in the Bible where they are memorialized by being mentioned among the offspring of the tribe of Judah.[4]

20 **The sons of Judah by their families were: for Shela, the family of the Shelanites; for Peretz, the family of the Peretzites; for Zerah, the family of the Zerahites.**

21 **The sons of Peretz were** further subdivided: **for Hetzron, the family of the Hetzronites; for Hamul, the family of the Hamulites.**

22 **These are the families of Judah by their count, seventy-six thousand five hundred.**

23 **The sons of Issachar by their families: for Tola, the family of the Tola'ites; for Puva, the family of the Punites;**

24 **for Yashuv, the family of the Yashuvites; for Shimron, the family of the Shimronites.**

25 **These are the families of Issachar by their count, sixty-four thousand three hundred.**

26 **The sons of Zebulun by their families: for Sered, the family of the Seredites; for Elon, the family of the Elonites; for**

Yahle'el, the family of the Yahle'elites.

27 **These are the families of the Zebulunites by their count, sixty thousand five hundred.**

28 **The sons of Joseph by their families: Manasseh and Ephraim.** In the first census, Ephraim is mentioned before Manasseh whereas here the order is reversed (see 1:32–35). Perhaps the reason for this is that in the first census Ephraim was larger than Manasseh. Over the years Manasseh grew larger and Ephraim became smaller, and now, when Manasseh was much larger than Ephraim, it was mentioned first.

29 **The sons of Manasseh: for Makhir, the family of the Makhirites, and Makhir begot Gilad; for Gilad, the family of the Giladites,** which became known as a distinct and prominent family in its own right, with a strip of land known as the land of Gilad.

30 **These are the sons of Gilad: for Iezer, the family of the Iezerites; for Helek, the family of the Helekites;**

31 **Asriel, the family of the Asrielites; Shekhem, the family of the Shekhemites;**

32 **Shemida, the family of the Shemida'ites; Hefer, the family of the Heferites.** The Torah again mentions names of people within a family because they are relevant with regard to a particular incident, as will be related in the upcoming section (27:1–11).

33 **Tzelofhad son of Hefer did not have sons, but daughters. The names of the daughters of Tzelofhad were Mahla, Noa, Hogla, Milka, and Tirtza.**

טז הַצְּפוֹנִ֔י לְחַגִּ֕י מִשְׁפַּ֖חַת הַֽחַגִּ֑י לְשׁוּנִ֕י מִשְׁפַּ֖חַת הַשּׁוּנִֽי׃ לְאׇזְנִ֕י מִשְׁפַּ֖חַת הָאׇזְנִ֑י
יז לְעֵרִ֕י מִשְׁפַּ֖חַת הָעֵרִֽי׃ לַאֲר֕וֹד מִשְׁפַּ֖חַת הָאֲרוֹדִ֑י לְאַ֨רְאֵלִ֔י מִשְׁפַּ֖חַת הָאַרְאֵלִֽי׃
יח יט אֵ֛לֶּה מִשְׁפְּחֹ֥ת בְּנֵי־גָ֖ד לִפְקֻדֵיהֶ֑ם אַרְבָּעִ֥ים אֶ֖לֶף וַחֲמֵ֥שׁ מֵאֽוֹת׃ בְּנֵ֥י
כ יְהוּדָ֖ה עֵ֣ר וְאוֹנָ֑ן וַיָּ֥מׇת עֵ֛ר וְאוֹנָ֖ן בְּאֶ֥רֶץ כְּנָֽעַן׃ וַיִּהְי֣וּ בְנֵי־יְהוּדָה֮ לְמִשְׁפְּחֹתָם֒
כא לְשֵׁלָ֗ה מִשְׁפַּ֙חַת֙ הַשֵּׁ֣לָנִ֔י לְפֶ֕רֶץ מִשְׁפַּ֖חַת הַפַּרְצִ֑י לְזֶ֕רַח מִשְׁפַּ֖חַת הַזַּרְחִֽי׃ וַיִּהְי֣וּ
כב בְנֵי־פֶ֔רֶץ לְחֶצְרֹ֕ן מִשְׁפַּ֖חַת הַֽחֶצְרֹנִ֑י לְחָמ֕וּל מִשְׁפַּ֖חַת הֶחָמוּלִֽי׃ אֵ֛לֶּה מִשְׁפְּחֹ֥ת
כג יְהוּדָ֖ה לִפְקֻדֵיהֶ֑ם שִׁשָּׁ֧ה וְשִׁבְעִ֛ים אֶ֖לֶף וַחֲמֵ֥שׁ מֵאֽוֹת׃ בְּנֵ֤י יִשָּׂשכָר֙
כד לְמִשְׁפְּחֹתָ֔ם תּוֹלָ֕ע מִשְׁפַּ֖חַת הַתּוֹלָעִ֑י לְפֻוָ֕ה מִשְׁפַּ֖חַת הַפּוּנִֽי׃ לְיָשׁ֕וּב מִשְׁפַּ֖חַת
כה הַיָּשֻׁבִ֑י לְשִׁמְרֹ֕ן מִשְׁפַּ֖חַת הַשִּׁמְרֹנִֽי׃ אֵ֛לֶּה מִשְׁפְּחֹ֥ת יִשָּׂשכָ֖ר לִפְקֻדֵיהֶ֑ם אַרְבָּעָ֧ה
כו וְשִׁשִּׁ֛ים אֶ֖לֶף וּשְׁלֹ֥שׁ מֵאֽוֹת׃ בְּנֵ֣י זְבוּלֻן֮ לְמִשְׁפְּחֹתָם֒ לְסֶ֗רֶד מִשְׁפַּ֙חַת֙
כז הַסַּרְדִּ֔י לְאֵל֕וֹן מִשְׁפַּ֖חַת הָאֵלֹנִ֑י לְיַ֨חְלְאֵ֔ל מִשְׁפַּ֖חַת הַיַּחְלְאֵלִֽי׃ אֵ֛לֶּה מִשְׁפְּחֹ֥ת
כח הַזְּבוּלֹנִ֖י לִפְקֻדֵיהֶ֑ם שִׁשִּׁ֥ים אֶ֖לֶף וַחֲמֵ֥שׁ מֵאֽוֹת׃ בְּנֵ֥י יוֹסֵ֖ף לְמִשְׁפְּחֹתָ֑ם
כט מְנַשֶּׁ֖ה וְאֶפְרָֽיִם׃ בְּנֵ֣י מְנַשֶּׁ֗ה לְמָכִיר֙ מִשְׁפַּ֣חַת הַמָּכִירִ֔י וּמָכִ֖יר הוֹלִ֣יד אֶת־גִּלְעָ֑ד
ל לְגִלְעָ֕ד מִשְׁפַּ֖חַת הַגִּלְעָדִֽי׃ אֵ֚לֶּה בְּנֵ֣י גִלְעָ֔ד אִיעֶ֕זֶר מִשְׁפַּ֖חַת הָאִיעֶזְרִ֑י לְחֵ֕לֶק
לא מִשְׁפַּ֖חַת הַֽחֶלְקִֽי׃ וְאַשְׂרִיאֵ֕ל מִשְׁפַּ֖חַת הָֽאַשְׂרִֽאֵלִ֑י וְשֶׁ֕כֶם מִשְׁפַּ֖חַת הַשִּׁכְמִֽי׃
לב לג וּשְׁמִידָ֕ע מִשְׁפַּ֖חַת הַשְּׁמִידָעִ֑י וְחֵ֕פֶר מִשְׁפַּ֖חַת הַֽחֶפְרִֽי׃ וּצְלׇפְחָ֣ד בֶּן־חֵ֗פֶר לֹא־הָ֥יוּ
ל֛וֹ בָּנִ֖ים כִּ֣י אִם־בָּנ֑וֹת וְשֵׁם֙ בְּנ֣וֹת צְלׇפְחָ֔ד מַחְלָ֣ה וְנֹעָ֔ה חׇגְלָ֥ה מִלְכָּ֖ה וְתִרְצָֽה׃

רש״י

וּמִבְּנֵי יִצְהָר לֹא נִמְנוּ כָּאן אֶלָּא מִשְׁפַּחַת הַקׇּרְחִי, וְהָרְבִיעִית לֹא יָדַעְתִּי מַה הִיא. וְרַבִּי תַּנְחוּמָא דָּרַשׁ שֶׁמֵּתוּ בַּמַּגֵּפָה בִּדְבַר בִּלְעָם (מדרש תנחומא ה), אֲבָל לְפִי הַחֶסְרוֹן שֶׁחָסֵר מִשֵּׁבֶט שִׁמְעוֹן בְּמִנְיָן זֶה מִמִּנְיָן הָרִאשׁוֹן שֶׁבְּמִדְבַּר סִינַי, נִרְאֶה שֶׁכׇּל עֶשְׂרִים וְאַרְבָּעָה אֶלֶף נָפְלוּ מִשִּׁבְטוֹ שֶׁל שִׁמְעוֹן:

טז| לְאׇזְנִי. אוֹמֵר אֲנִי שֶׁזּוֹ מִשְׁפַּחַת אֶצְבּוֹן, וְאֵינִי יוֹדֵעַ לָמָּה לֹא נִקְרֵאת מִשְׁפַּחְתּוֹ עַל שְׁמוֹ:

כד| לְיָשׁוּב. הוּא יוֹב הָאָמוּר בְּיוֹרְדֵי מִצְרַיִם, כִּי כׇּל הַמִּשְׁפָּחוֹת נִקְרְאוּ עַל שֵׁם יוֹרְדֵי מִצְרַיִם, וְהַנּוֹלָדִין מִשָּׁם וָהָלְאָה לֹא נִקְרְאוּ הַמִּשְׁפָּחוֹת עַל שְׁמָם, חוּץ מִמִּשְׁפְּחוֹת אֶפְרַיִם וּמְנַשֶּׁה שֶׁנּוֹלְדוּ כֻּלָּם בְּמִצְרַיִם, וְאַרְדְּ וְנַעֲמָן בְּנֵי בֶלַע בֶּן בִּנְיָמִין. וּמָצָאתִי בִּיסוֹדוֹ שֶׁל רַבִּי מֹשֶׁה הַדַּרְשָׁן, שֶׁיָּרְדָה אִמָּן לְמִצְרַיִם כְּשֶׁהָיְתָה מְעֻבֶּרֶת מֵהֶם, לְכָךְ נֶחְלְקוּ לְמִשְׁפָּחוֹת, כְּחֶצְרוֹן וְחָמוּל שֶׁהָיוּ בְּנֵי בָנִים לִיהוּדָה, וְחֶבֶר וּמַלְכִּיאֵל שֶׁהָיוּ בְּנֵי בָנִים שֶׁל אָשֵׁר. וְאִם אַגָּדָה הִיא הֲרֵי טוֹב, וְאִם לָאו אוֹמֵר אֲנִי שֶׁהָיוּ לְבֶלַע בְּנֵי בָנִים הַרְבֵּה, וּמִשְּׁנַיִם הַלָּלוּ אַרְדְּ וְנַעֲמָן יָצְאָה מִכׇּל אֶחָד מִשְׁפָּחָה רַבָּה, וְנִקְרְאוּ תּוֹלְדוֹת שְׁאָר הַבָּנִים עַל שֵׁם בֶּלַע, וְתוֹלְדוֹת הַשְּׁנַיִם הַלָּלוּ נִקְרְאוּ עַל שְׁמָם. וְכֵן אֲנִי אוֹמֵר בִּבְנֵי מָכִיר שֶׁנֶּחְלְקוּ לִשְׁתֵּי מִשְׁפָּחוֹת, אַחַת נִקְרֵאת עַל שְׁמוֹ וְאַחַת נִקְרֵאת עַל שֵׁם גִּלְעָד בְּנוֹ. חָמֵשׁ מִשְׁפָּחוֹת חָסְרוּ מִבָּנָיו שֶׁל בִּנְיָמִין, כָּאן נִתְקַיְּמָה מִקְצָת נְבוּאַת אִמּוֹ שֶׁקְּרָאַתּוּ "בֶּן אוֹנִי" (בראשית לה, יח), בֶּן אֲנִינוּתִי, וּבְפִילֶגֶשׁ בְּגִבְעָה נִתְקַיְּמָה כֻּלָּהּ. זוֹ מָצָאתִי בִּיסוֹדוֹ שֶׁל רַבִּי מֹשֶׁה הַדַּרְשָׁן:

34 These are the families of Manasseh; those counted were fifty-two thousand seven hundred.

35 These are the sons of Ephraim by their families: for Shutelah, the family of the Shutelahites; for Bekher, the family of the Bekherites; for Tahan, the family of the Tahanites.

36 These are the sons of Shutelah: for Eran, the family of the Eranites.

37 These are the families of the sons of Ephraim by their count, thirty-two thousand five hundred. These are the sons of Joseph by their families.

38 The sons of Benjamin by their families: for Bela, the family of the Bela'ites; for Ashbel, the family of the Ashbelites; for Ahiram, the family of the Ahiramites;

39 for Shefufam, the family of the Shufamites; for Hufam, the family of the Hufamites. Hufam was referred to as Hupim when the sons of Jacob descended to Egypt; Shefufam was referred to as Mupim.[5]

40 The sons of Bela were Ard and Naaman; the family of the Ardites; for Naaman, the family of the Naamites.

41 These are the sons of Benjamin by their families; and their counted were forty-five thousand six hundred.

42 These are the sons of Dan by their families: for Shuham, the family of the Shuhamites. These are the families of Dan by their families. Dan apparently had only one son, Shuham, who is referred to as Hushim in Genesis (46:23). Nonetheless his offspring were known as the tribe of Dan as well as the family of Shuham.

43 All the families of the Shuhamites, by their count, were sixty-four thousand four hundred.

44 The sons of Asher by their families: for Yimna, the family of the Yimnites; for Yishvi, the family of the Yishvites; for Beria, the family of the Beriites.

45 For the sons of Beria: for Hever, the family of the Heverites; for Malkiel, the family of the Malkielites.

46 The name of the daughter of Asher: Serah.[D]

47 These are the families of the sons of Asher by their count, fifty-three thousand four hundred.

48 The sons of Naphtali by their families: for Yahtze'el, the family of the Yahtze'elites; for Guni, the family of the Gunites;

49 for Yetzer, the family of the Yetzerites; for Shilem, the family of the Shilemites.

50 These are the families of Naphtali by their families; their counted were forty-five thousand four hundred.

51 These are the counted of the children of Israel, six hundred thousand one thousand seven hundred and thirty.[D]

Third aliya 52 The Lord spoke to Moses, saying:

53 To these families listed above the land shall be divided as an inheritance, according to the number of names. The census was not meant merely to serve a military function, but also to delineate those to whom the land will be divided.

DISCUSSION

26:46 | **Daughter of Asher: Serah:** Serah stands out in this list of names, which generally includes only male heads of families. Some commentaries say that Serah was still alive at that time, making her the oldest woman in the entire nation, as she was also alive when Jacob and his family first immigrated to Egypt (Genesis 46:17). Consequently, she carried memories of the entire history of the nation (see *Sota* 13a). According to a different midrash, she was

blessed by Jacob that she would never die (*Batei Midrashot* 2, *Midrash Eshet Ḥayyil*). One version of Onkelos asserts that Serah was not actually Asher's daughter but rather his stepdaughter (see Ramban). Nevertheless, since she grew up in Asher's house she was included in his family and is mentioned with the tribe of Asher.

26:51 | **Six hundred thousand one thousand seven hundred and thirty:** This is close to the number of the children of Israel at the time

of the exodus from Egypt (see Exodus 38:26). Although the numbers of each tribe changed over the forty years in the wilderness, the total number of the people stayed approximately the same. Consequently, the number six hundred thousand has been seen as a significant number, representing the nature and essence of the Jewish people (see *Pirkei deRabbi Eliezer* 39; Rabbeinu Baḥya, Genesis 46:27; this is a common theme in the writings of the Maharal).

לד אֵלֶּה מִשְׁפְּחֹת מְנַשֶּׁה וּפְקֻדֵיהֶם שְׁנַיִם וַחֲמִשִּׁים אֶלֶף וּשְׁבַע מֵאוֹת: אֵלֶּה
לה בְנֵי־אֶפְרַיִם לְמִשְׁפְּחֹתָם לְשׁוּתֶלַח מִשְׁפַּחַת הַשֻּׁתַלְחִי לְבֶכֶר מִשְׁפַּחַת הַבַּכְרִי
לְתַחַן מִשְׁפַּחַת הַתַּחֲנִי: וְאֵלֶּה בְּנֵי שׁוּתָלַח לְעֵרָן מִשְׁפַּחַת הָעֵרָנִי: אֵלֶּה
לו
לז מִשְׁפְּחֹת בְּנֵי־אֶפְרַיִם לִפְקֻדֵיהֶם שְׁנַיִם וּשְׁלֹשִׁים אֶלֶף וַחֲמֵשׁ מֵאוֹת אֵלֶּה בְנֵי־
יוֹסֵף לְמִשְׁפְּחֹתָם: בְּנֵי בִנְיָמִן לְמִשְׁפְּחֹתָם לְבֶלַע מִשְׁפַּחַת הַבַּלְעִי
לח
לט לְאַשְׁבֵּל מִשְׁפַּחַת הָאַשְׁבֵּלִי לַאֲחִירָם מִשְׁפַּחַת הָאֲחִירָמִי: לִשְׁפוּפָם מִשְׁפַּחַת
הַשּׁוּפָמִי לְחוּפָם מִשְׁפַּחַת הַחוּפָמִי: וַיִּהְיוּ בְנֵי־בֶלַע אַרְדְּ וְנַעֲמָן מִשְׁפַּחַת הָאַרְדִּי
מ לְנַעֲמָן מִשְׁפַּחַת הַנַּעֲמִי: אֵלֶּה בְנֵי־בִנְיָמִן לְמִשְׁפְּחֹתָם וּפְקֻדֵיהֶם חֲמִשָּׁה וְאַרְבָּעִים
מא אֶלֶף וְשֵׁשׁ מֵאוֹת: אֵלֶּה בְנֵי־דָן לְמִשְׁפְּחֹתָם לְשׁוּחָם מִשְׁפַּחַת
מב הַשּׁוּחָמִי אֵלֶּה מִשְׁפְּחֹת דָּן לְמִשְׁפְּחֹתָם: כָּל־מִשְׁפְּחֹת הַשּׁוּחָמִי לִפְקֻדֵיהֶם
מג אַרְבָּעָה וְשִׁשִּׁים אֶלֶף וְאַרְבַּע מֵאוֹת: בְּנֵי אָשֵׁר לְמִשְׁפְּחֹתָם
מד לְיִמְנָה מִשְׁפַּחַת הַיִּמְנָה לְיִשְׁוִי מִשְׁפַּחַת הַיִּשְׁוִי לִבְרִיעָה מִשְׁפַּחַת הַבְּרִיעִי:
לִבְנֵי בְרִיעָה לְחֶבֶר מִשְׁפַּחַת הַחֶבְרִי לְמַלְכִּיאֵל מִשְׁפַּחַת הַמַּלְכִּיאֵלִי: וְשֵׁם בַּת־
מה
מו אָשֵׁר שָׂרַח: אֵלֶּה מִשְׁפְּחֹת בְּנֵי־אָשֵׁר לִפְקֻדֵיהֶם שְׁלֹשָׁה וַחֲמִשִּׁים אֶלֶף וְאַרְבַּע
מז מֵאוֹת: בְּנֵי נַפְתָּלִי לְמִשְׁפְּחֹתָם לְיַחְצְאֵל מִשְׁפַּחַת הַיַּחְצְאֵלִי לְגוּנִי
מח מִשְׁפַּחַת הַגּוּנִי: לְיֵצֶר מִשְׁפַּחַת הַיִּצְרִי לְשִׁלֵּם מִשְׁפַּחַת הַשִּׁלֵּמִי: אֵלֶּה מִשְׁפְּחֹת
מט
נ נַפְתָּלִי לְמִשְׁפְּחֹתָם וּפְקֻדֵיהֶם חֲמִשָּׁה וְאַרְבָּעִים אֶלֶף וְאַרְבַּע מֵאוֹת: אֵלֶּה פְּקוּדֵי
נא בְּנֵי יִשְׂרָאֵל שֵׁשׁ־מֵאוֹת אֶלֶף וָאָלֶף שְׁבַע מֵאוֹת וּשְׁלֹשִׁים:
נב וַיְדַבֵּר יְהוָה אֶל־מֹשֶׁה לֵּאמֹר: לָאֵלֶּה תֵּחָלֵק הָאָרֶץ בְּנַחֲלָה בְּמִסְפַּר שֵׁמוֹת: כג שלישי
נג

רש״י

לו) וְאֵלֶּה בְּנֵי שׁוּתָלַח וְגו׳. שָׁאָר בְּנֵי שׁוּתֶלַח נִקְרְאוּ
תוֹלְדוֹתֵיהֶם עַל שֵׁם שׁוּתֶלַח, וּמֵעֵרָן יָצְאָה מִשְׁפָּחָה רַבָּה
וְנִקְרֵאת עַל שְׁמוֹ, וְנֶחְשְׁבוּ בְּנֵי שׁוּתֶלַח לִשְׁתֵּי מִשְׁפָּחוֹת.
צֵא וַחֲשֹׁב, וְתִמְצָא בְּפָרָשָׁה זוּ חֲמִשִּׁים וּשְׁמֹנֶה מִשְׁפָּחוֹת
וּמִבְּנֵי לֵוִי שְׁמוֹנֶה, הֲרֵי שִׁשִּׁים וָחָמֵשׁ, וְזֶהוּ שֶׁנֶּאֱמַר: "כִּי
אַתֶּם הַמְעַט״ וְגו׳ (דברים ז, ז), ה״א מְעַט, חָמֵשׁ חָסֵר אַתֶּם
חֲסֵרִים מִמִּשְׁפְּחוֹת כָּל הָעַמִּים שֶׁהֵן שִׁבְעִים. אַף זֶה
הַבַּנְתִּי מִיסוֹדוֹ שֶׁל רַבִּי מֹשֶׁה הַדַּרְשָׁן, אַךְ הֻצְרַכְתִּי לִמְחוֹק
וּלְהוֹסִיף בִּדְבָרָיו:

לח) לַאֲחִירָם. הוּא אֲחִי שֶׁיָּרַד לְמִצְרַיִם (בראשית מו,
כא), וּלְפִי שֶׁנִּקְרָא עַל שֵׁם יוֹסֵף שֶׁהָיָה אֲחִיו וְרָם מִמֶּנּוּ
נִקְרָא אֲחִירָם:

לט) לִשְׁפוּפָם. הוּא מֻפִּים (בראשית שם), עַל שֵׁם שֶׁהָיָה
יוֹסֵף שָׁפוּף בֵּין הָאֻמּוֹת:

מב) לְשׁוּחָם. הוּא חֻשִׁים (שם כג):

מו) וְשֵׁם בַּת אָשֵׁר שָׂרַח. לְפִי שֶׁהָיְתָה קַיֶּמֶת בַּחַיִּים
מְנָאָהּ כָּאן:

נג) לָאֵלֶּה תֵּחָלֵק הָאָרֶץ. וְלֹא לִפְחוּתִים מִבֶּן עֶשְׂרִים, אַף
עַל פִּי שֶׁבָּאוּ לִכְלַל עֶשְׂרִים בְּטֶרֶם חִלּוּק הָאָרֶץ, שֶׁהֲרֵי
שֶׁבַע שָׁנִים כָּבְשׁוּ וְשֶׁבַע חִלְּקוּ, לֹא נָטְלוּ חֵלֶק בָּאָרֶץ אֶלָּא
אֵלּוּ שֵׁשׁ מֵאוֹת אֶלֶף וָאֶלֶף, וְאִם הָיוּ לְאֶחָד מֵהֶם שִׁשָּׁה
בָנִים, לֹא נָטְלוּ אֶלָּא חֵלֶק אֲבִיהֶם לְבַדּוֹ:

54 On the one hand, **to the** family that is **greater** in number **you shall increase its inheritance, and to the** family that is **lesser** in number **you shall decrease its inheritance; each** family, **according to its counted, its inheritance shall be given.**

55 **However,** on the other hand, **by lot the land shall be divided; according to the names of the tribes of their fathers they shall inherit.**

56 **Their inheritance shall be divided by lot whether the many or the few.**[D]

57 **These are the counted of the Levites,** who will not inherit portions of the land but are nevertheless counted along with the rest of the nation, **according to their families: for Gershon, the family of the Gershonites; for Kehat, the family of the Kehatites; for Merari, the family of the Merarites.**

58 **These are the families of Levi** divided into more specific family groups: **the family of the Livnites, the family of the Hebronites, the family of the Mahlites, the family of the Mushites, the family of the Korahites. Kehat begot Amram.**

59 **The name of Amram's wife was Yokheved daughter of Levi, who was born to Levi in Egypt.** This is one of the verses from which the Sages derive that Yokheved was born as the family of Jacob entered Egypt. The verse is understood to mean although Yokheved was born in Egypt, she was not conceived there.[6] **She bore to Amram: Aaron, Moses, and Miriam their sister.**

60 **To Aaron were born: Nadav, Avihu, Elazar, and Itamar.**

61 **Nadav and Avihu died when they offered strange fire before the Lord.** It would appear that Nadav and Avihu did not have sons, although it is possible that they had daughters. Similar to Judah's sons, Er and Onan, although Nadav and Avihu died at a young age without sons, they are memorialized through the mention of their names in the genealogy of their father's family.

62 **Those counted were twenty-three thousand, each male from one month old and above; for they were not counted among the children of Israel, because no inheritance was given to them among the children of Israel.**

63 **These are the counted of Moses and Elazar the priest, who counted the children of Israel on the plains of Moav by the Jordan opposite Jericho.**

64 **Among these** people, who were counted in preparation for entering the land of Canaan, **there was not a man from the counted of Moses and Aaron the priest, who counted the children of Israel in the wilderness of Sinai.**

65 **As the Lord said of them,** in response to the sin of the spies (14:23–24): **They will die in the wilderness. No man was left of them, except Caleb son of Yefuneh, and Joshua son of Nun.**

The Inheritance of the Daughters of Tzelofhad

NUMBERS 27:1–11

In the previous chapter, the families counted in the plains of Moav were determined as the basic units to which the land was to be divided. The Torah provides greater detail as to why the daughters of Tzelofhad were also mentioned in the counting and about the significance of their story.

27 1 **The daughters of Tzelofhad, son of Hefer, son of Gilad, son of Makhir, son of Manasseh, from the families of Manasseh** son of Joseph, approached; these are the names of his daughters: Mahla, Noa, Hogla, Milka, and Tirtza.

DISCUSSION

26:56| **Their inheritance shall be divided by lot whether the many or the few:** These two descriptions of the method of dividing the land would seem to be inconsistent: Was the land divided according to a lottery or based upon the size of the family? Some commentaries explain that the size of each tribe or family's inheritance was determined by the census, but the location of that territory was determined by lottery (see 33:54; Rashi; Ramban).

נד לָרַב תַּרְבֶּה נַחֲלָתוֹ וְלַמְעַט תַּמְעִיט נַחֲלָתוֹ אִישׁ לְפִי פְקֻדָיו יֻתַּן נַחֲלָתוֹ: אַךְ־

נה בְּגוֹרָל יֵחָלֵק אֶת־הָאָרֶץ לִשְׁמוֹת מַטּוֹת־אֲבֹתָם יִנְחָלוּ: עַל־פִּי הַגּוֹרָל תֵּחָלֵק

נו נַחֲלָתוֹ בֵּין רַב לִמְעָט:

נז וְאֵלֶּה פְקוּדֵי הַלֵּוִי לְמִשְׁפְּחֹתָם לְגֵרְשׁוֹן מִשְׁפַּחַת

הַגֵּרְשֻׁנִּי לִקְהָת מִשְׁפַּחַת הַקְּהָתִי לִמְרָרִי מִשְׁפַּחַת הַמְּרָרִי: אֵלֶּה ׀ מִשְׁפְּחֹת לֵוִי

מִשְׁפַּחַת הַלִּבְנִי מִשְׁפַּחַת הַחֶבְרֹנִי מִשְׁפַּחַת הַמַּחְלִי מִשְׁפַּחַת הַמּוּשִׁי מִשְׁפַּחַת

הַקָּרְחִי וּקְהָת הוֹלִד אֶת־עַמְרָם: וְשֵׁם ׀ אֵשֶׁת עַמְרָם יוֹכֶבֶד בַּת־לֵוִי אֲשֶׁר יָלְדָה

נט אֹתָהּ לְלֵוִי בְּמִצְרָיִם וַתֵּלֶד לְעַמְרָם אֶת־אַהֲרֹן וְאֶת־מֹשֶׁה וְאֵת מִרְיָם אֲחֹתָם:

סא וַיִּוָּלֵד לְאַהֲרֹן אֶת־נָדָב וְאֶת־אֲבִיהוּא אֶת־אֶלְעָזָר וְאֶת־אִיתָמָר: וַיָּמָת נָדָב

סב וַאֲבִיהוּא בְּהַקְרִיבָם אֵשׁ־זָרָה לִפְנֵי יְהֹוָה: וַיִּהְיוּ פְקֻדֵיהֶם שְׁלֹשָׁה וְעֶשְׂרִים אֶלֶף

כָּל־זָכָר מִבֶּן־חֹדֶשׁ וָמָעְלָה כִּי ׀ לֹא הָתְפָּקְדוּ בְּתוֹךְ בְּנֵי יִשְׂרָאֵל כִּי לֹא־נִתַּן

סג לָהֶם נַחֲלָה בְּתוֹךְ בְּנֵי יִשְׂרָאֵל: אֵלֶּה פְּקוּדֵי מֹשֶׁה וְאֶלְעָזָר הַכֹּהֵן אֲשֶׁר פָּקְדוּ

סד אֶת־בְּנֵי יִשְׂרָאֵל בְּעַרְבֹת מוֹאָב עַל יַרְדֵּן יְרֵחוֹ: וּבְאֵלֶּה לֹא־הָיָה אִישׁ מִפְּקוּדֵי

סה מֹשֶׁה וְאַהֲרֹן הַכֹּהֵן אֲשֶׁר פָּקְדוּ אֶת־בְּנֵי יִשְׂרָאֵל בְּמִדְבַּר סִינָי: כִּי־אָמַר יְהֹוָה

לָהֶם מוֹת יָמֻתוּ בַּמִּדְבָּר וְלֹא־נוֹתַר מֵהֶם אִישׁ כִּי אִם־כָּלֵב בֶּן־יְפֻנֶּה וִיהוֹשֻׁעַ

בִּן־נוּן: וַתִּקְרַבְנָה בְּנוֹת צְלָפְחָד בֶּן־חֵפֶר בֶּן־גִּלְעָד בֶּן־מָכִיר בֶּן־מְנַשֶּׁה

א לְמִשְׁפְּחֹת מְנַשֶּׁה בֶן־יוֹסֵף וְאֵלֶּה שְׁמוֹת בְּנֹתָיו מַחְלָה נֹעָה וְחׇגְלָה וּמִלְכָּה וְתִרְצָה:

רש"י

נד) לָרַב תַּרְבֶּה נַחֲלָתוֹ. לְשֵׁבֶט שֶׁהָיָה מְרֻבֶּה בְּאֻכְלוּסִין נָתְנוּ חֵלֶק רַב. וְאַף עַל פִּי שֶׁלֹּא הָיוּ הַחֲלָקִים שָׁוִים, שֶׁהֲרֵי הַכֹּל לְפִי רִבּוּי הַשֵּׁבֶט חִלְּקוּ הַחֲלָקִים, לֹא עָשׂוּ אֶלָּא עַל יְדֵי גוֹרָל, וְהַגּוֹרָל הָיָה עַל פִּי רוּחַ הַקֹּדֶשׁ, כְּמוֹ שֶׁמְּפֹרָשׁ בְּבָבָא בַתְרָא (דף קכב ע"א). אֶלְעָזָר הַכֹּהֵן הָיָה מְלֻבָּשׁ בְּאוּרִים וְתֻמִּים וְאוֹמֵר בְּרוּחַ הַקֹּדֶשׁ: אִם שֵׁבֶט פְּלוֹנִי עוֹלֶה, תְּחוּם פְּלוֹנִי עוֹלֶה עִמּוֹ. וְהַשְּׁבָטִים הָיוּ כְתוּבִים בְּשָׁנֵים עָשָׂר פְּתָקִין וּשְׁנֵים עָשָׂר גְּבוּלִין בִּשְׁנֵים עָשָׂר פְּתָקִין, וּבְלָלוּם בְּקַלְפֵּי, וְהִשִּׁיא יָדוֹ לְתוֹכָהּ וְנָטַל שְׁנֵי פְתָקִין. עוֹלֶה בְּיָדוֹ פְּתָק שֶׁל שֵׁם שִׁבְטוֹ וּפְתָק שֶׁל גְּבוּל הַמְעֹרָב לוֹ, וְהַגּוֹרָל עַצְמוֹ הָיָה צוֹוֵחַ וְאוֹמֵר: אֲנִי הַגּוֹרָל עָלִיתִי לִגְבוּל פְּלוֹנִי לְשֵׁבֶט פְּלוֹנִי, שֶׁנֶּאֱמַר: "עַל פִּי הַגּוֹרָל". וְלֹא נִתְחַלְּקָה הָאָרֶץ בְּמִדָּה, לְפִי שֶׁיֵּשׁ גְּבוּל מְשֻׁבָּח מֵחֲבֵרוֹ, אֶלָּא בְּשׁוּמָא: בֵּית כּוֹר רַע כְּנֶגֶד בֵּית סְאָה טוֹב, הַכֹּל לְפִי הַדָּמִים.

נה) לִשְׁמוֹת מַטּוֹת אֲבֹתָם. אֵלּוּ יוֹצְאֵי מִצְרָיִם. שִׁנָּה הַכָּתוּב נַחֲלָה זוֹ מִכָּל הַנְּחָלוֹת שֶׁבַּתּוֹרָה, שֶׁכָּל הַנְּחָלוֹת הַחַיִּים יוֹרְשִׁים אֶת הַמֵּתִים, וְכָאן מֵתִים יוֹרְשִׁים אֶת הַחַיִּים. כֵּיצַד? שְׁנֵי אַחִים מִיּוֹצְאֵי מִצְרַיִם שֶׁהָיוּ לָהֶם בָּנִים בְּבָאֵי הָאָרֶץ, לָזֶה אֶחָד וְלָזֶה שְׁלֹשָׁה, הָאֶחָד נָטַל חֵלֶק אֶחָד, וְהַשְּׁלֹשָׁה נָטְלוּ שְׁלֹשָׁה, שֶׁנֶּאֱמַר: "לָאֵלֶּה תֵּחָלֵק הָאָרֶץ", חָזְרָה נַחֲלָתָן אֵצֶל אֲבִי אֲבִיהֶן וְחִלְּקוּ הַכֹּל בְּשָׁוֶה, וְזֶהוּ שֶׁנֶּאֱמַר: "לִשְׁמוֹת מַטּוֹת אֲבֹתָם יִנְחָלוּ", שֶׁאַחַר שֶׁנָּטְלוּ הַבָּנִים חִלְּקוּם לְפִי הָאָבוֹת שֶׁיָּצְאוּ מִמִּצְרָיִם. וְאִלּוּ מִתְּחִלָּה חִלְּקוּ לְמִנְיַן יוֹצְאֵי מִצְרַיִם לֹא הָיוּ נוֹטְלִין אֵלּוּ הָאַרְבָּעָה אֶלָּא שְׁנֵי חֲלָקִים, עַכְשָׁיו נָטְלוּ אַרְבָּעָה חֲלָקִים.

נו) עַל פִּי הַגּוֹרָל. הַגּוֹרָל הָיָה מְדַבֵּר כְּמוֹ שֶׁפֵּרַשְׁתִּי לְמַעְלָה, מַגִּיד שֶׁנִּתְחַלְּקָה בְּרוּחַ הַקֹּדֶשׁ, וְכֵן הוּא אוֹמֵר: "יִתְּנוּ לְכָלֵב אֶת חֶבְרוֹן (על פי ה')" [כַּאֲשֶׁר דִּבֶּר מֹשֶׁה)] עַל פִּי ה': וְאוֹמֵר: "עַל פִּי ה' נָתְנוּ לוֹ אֶת הָעִיר אֲשֶׁר שָׁאָל" (יהושע יט, כ): מַטּוֹת אֲבֹתָם. יָצְאוּ גֵּרִים וַעֲבָדִים.

נח) אֵלֶּה מִשְׁפְּחֹת לֵוִי. חָסֵר כָּאן מִשְׁפְּחוֹת הַשִּׁמְעִי וְהָעָזִיאֵלִי וּקְצָת מִן הַיִּצְהָרִי:

נט) אֲשֶׁר יָלְדָה אֹתָהּ לְלֵוִי בְּמִצְרָיִם. אִשְׁתּוֹ יְלָדַתָּה בְּמִצְרַיִם, וְאֵין הוֹרָתָהּ בְּמִצְרַיִם, כְּשֶׁנִּכְנְסוּ לְתוֹךְ הַחוֹמָה יְלָדַתָּה, וְהִיא הִשְׁלִימָה מִנְיַן שִׁבְעִים, שֶׁהֲרֵי בִּפְרָטָן אִי אַתָּה מוֹצֵא אֶלָּא שִׁשִּׁים וָתֵשַׁע:

סב) כִּי לֹא הָתְפָּקְדוּ בְּתוֹךְ בְּנֵי יִשְׂרָאֵל. לִהְיוֹת נִמְנִין בְּנֵי עֶשְׂרִים שָׁנָה, מַה טַּעַם? "כִּי לֹא נִתַּן לָהֶם נַחֲלָה", וְהַנִּמְנִין מִבֶּן עֶשְׂרִים שָׁנָה הָיוּ בְּנֵי נַחֲלָה, שֶׁנֶּאֱמַר: "אִישׁ לְפִי פְקֻדָיו יֻתַּן נַחֲלָתוֹ" (לעיל פסוק נד):

סד) וּבְאֵלֶּה לֹא הָיָה אִישׁ וְגוֹ'. אֲבָל עַל הַנָּשִׁים לֹא נִגְזְרָה גְּזֵרַת הַמְרַגְּלִים, לְפִי שֶׁהֵן הָיוּ מְחַבְּבוֹת אֶת הָאָרֶץ, הָאֲנָשִׁים אוֹמְרִים: "נִתְּנָה רֹאשׁ וְנָשׁוּבָה מִצְרָיְמָה" (לעיל יד, ד), וְהַנָּשִׁים אוֹמְרוֹת: "תְּנָה לָּנוּ אֲחֻזָּה" (להלן כז, ד), לְכָךְ נִסְמְכָה פָּרָשַׁת בְּנוֹת צְלָפְחָד לְכָאן:

פרק כז

א) לְמִשְׁפְּחֹת מְנַשֶּׁה בֶן יוֹסֵף. לָמָּה נֶאֱמַר? וַהֲלֹא כְּבָר נֶאֱמַר: "בֶּן מְנַשֶּׁה", אֶלָּא לוֹמַר לְךָ, יוֹסֵף חִבֵּב אֶת

2 **They stood before Moses, before Elazar the priest, before the princes and the entire congregation, at the entrance of the Tent of Meeting, saying:**

3 **Our father died in the wilderness, and he was not among the congregation of those who congregated against the Lord in the congregation of Korah,** and therefore he did not die in a miraculous and dramatic fashion, **as he died for his own sin,**D like any regular person,7 **and he had no sons.**

4 **Why should the name of our father be subtracted from among his family because he had no son?** Since we are his daughters, **give us a portion among the brothers of our father,** as his heirs.

5 **Moses brought their case before the Lord,** as he did not have clear instructions pertaining to this type of case.

Fourth
aliya
6 **The Lord spoke to Moses, saying:**

7 **The daughters of Tzelofhad speak justly:** Consequently, **you shall give them a portion for inheritance among their father's brothers and you shall convey the inheritance of their father to them.**D

8 The specific instruction given in response to the request of the daughters of Tzelofhad is now formulated as a general principle: **To the children of Israel, you shall speak, saying: If a man will die, and he has no son, you shall convey his inheritance to his daughter.**

9 **If he has no daughter** either, **you shall give his inheritance to his brothers.**

10 **If he has no brothers, you shall give his inheritance to his father's brothers.**

11 **If his father has no brothers, you shall give his inheritance to his next of kin from his family, and he shall take possession of it. It shall be for the children of Israel a statute of justice, as the Lord had commanded Moses.** The basic principle of the law of inheritance, as explained by the Oral Law, is that the estate of the deceased is transferred according to a downward-upward-downward scheme. When an individual dies, his property is inherited by his offspring; if he has sons they inherit the property, and if not, his daughters inherit the property. If the deceased has no living descendants, the property goes up a generation to the father of the deceased. If he is not alive, it goes down to his children, meaning the siblings of the deceased. If the father of the deceased has no living descendants, it goes up another generation to the paternal grandfather of the deceased and to his offspring, and so on, as far as necessary until an heir is located.8

Preparation for the Demise of Moses

NUMBERS 27:12–23

Moses was not granted permission to enter the land of Canaan. The task of conquering and dividing the land will therefore have to be accomplished by his replacement. Before Aaron's death God commanded him to pass on his position to his son, Elazar. Now, in light of Moses' impending death and with a sense of responsibility toward the nation that he led for so many years, he requests that God appoint a fitting replacement who will become the nation's leader after his demise.

Although this passage addresses the impending death of Moses, it does not actually relate the historical event of his death. This is because the remainder of the book discusses other tasks that Moses had to complete before his death. Only at the end of Deuteronomy, after Moses' long farewell address to the nation, does Moses obey the command that appears in this passage to ascend the highlands of Avarim, where he would depart from the world.

12 **The Lord said to Moses: Ascend to this highlands of Avarim,**B **and see the land that I have given to the children of Israel.** Some commentaries explain that Moses was to ascend a mountain peak that could be seen from each direction [*ever*] and which overlooked the entire area.

13 **You will see it, and you also will be gathered to your people,**

— BACKGROUND —

27:12 | This highlands of Avarim: It appears that Avarim is a general name for the mountain range of northwest Moav, one of whose peaks was Mount Nevo (see 33:47; Deuteronomy 32:49).

— DISCUSSION —

27:3 | As he died for his own sin: In the Talmud (*Shabbat* 96b) it is explained that this expression refers to a specific sin: Tzelofhad was the individual caught gathering wood on the Sabbath (15:32). This is quoted by most of the commentaries on this verse. According to this explanation, the contrast between Tzelofhad and the congregation of Korah is meant to indicate that Tzelofhad died for his personal sin and did not cause an entire congregation to sin or others to die. Consequently, his death should suffice as punishment for his sin, and his descendants should inherit his rightful portion of the Land of Israel.

27:7 | And you shall convey the inheritance of their father to them: Tzelofhad was no longer alive, yet his rights to a portion of the Land of Israel were honored due to the fact that he was among those who left Egypt. This proves that the Land of Israel was apportioned to those who left Egypt. Their descendants, who were the ones who actually entered the Land of Israel, inherited the rights of those who had left Egypt (see *Bava Batra* 116b–117b).

ב ותעמדנה לפני משה ולפני אלעזר הכהן ולפני הנשיאם וכל־העדה פתח
ג אהל־מועד לאמר: אבינו מת במדבר והוא לא־היה בתוך העדה הנועדים
ד על־יהוה בעדת־קרח כי־בחטאו מת ובנים לא־היו לו: למה יגרע שם־אבינו
ה מתוך משפחתו כי אין לו בן תנה־לנו אחזה בתוך אחי אבינו: ויקרב משה
את־משפטן לפני יהוה:
ו ז ויאמר יהוה אל־משה לאמר: כן בנות צלפחד דברת נתן תתן להם אחזת רביעי
ח נחלה בתוך אחי אביהם והעברת את־נחלת אביהן להן: ואל־בני ישראל
ט תדבר לאמר איש כי־ימות ובן אין לו והעברתם את־נחלתו לבתו: ואם־
י אין לו בת ונתתם את־נחלתו לאחיו: ואם־אין לו אחים ונתתם את־נחלתו
יא לאחי אביו: ואם־אין אחים לאביו ונתתם את־נחלתו לשארו הקרב אליו
ממשפחתו וירש אתה והיתה לבני ישראל לחקת משפט כאשר צוה יהוה
את־משה:
יב ויאמר יהוה אל־משה עלה אל־הר העברים הזה וראה את־הארץ אשר
יג נתתי לבני ישראל: וראיתה אתה ונאספת אל־עמיך גם־אתה כאשר

רש"י

הארץ, שנאמר: "והעלתם את עצמתי" וגו' (בראשית נ, כה), ובנותיו חבבו את הארץ, שנאמר: "תנה לנו אחזה" (להלן פסוק ד). וללמדך שהיו כלם צדיקים, שכל מי שמעשיו ומעשה אבותיו סתומים ופרט לך הכתוב באחד מהם ליחסו לשבח, הרי זה צדיק בן צדיק, ואם יחסו לגנאי, כגון: "בא ישמעאל בן נתניה בן אלישמע" (מלכים ב' כה, כה), בידוע שכל הנזכרים עמו רשעים היו: מחלה נעה וגו'. ולהלן (לו, יא) הוא אומר: "ותהיינה מחלה תרצה", מגיד שכלן שקולות זו כזו, לפיכך שנה את סדרן:

ב| **לפני משה ולפני אלעזר.** מגיד שלא עמדו לפניהם אלא בשנת הארבעים אחר שמת אהרן: **לפני משה.** ואחר כך "לפני אלעזר", אפשר אם משה לא ידע אלעזר יודע? אלא סרס המקרא ודרשהו, דברי רבי יאשיה. אבא חנן משום רבי אליעזר אומר: בבית המדרש היו יושבים, ועמדו לפני כלם:

ג| **והוא לא היה וגו'.** לפי שהיו באות לומר "בחטאו מת", נזקקו לומר: לא בחטא מתלוננים ולא בעדת קרח שהצו על הקדוש ברוך הוא, אלא בחטאו לבדו מת ולא החטיא את אחרים עמו. רבי עקיבא אומר: מקושש עצים היה; ורבי שמעון אומר: מן המעפילים היה:

ד| **למה יגרע שם אבינו.** אנו במקום בן עומדות, ואם אין הנקבות חשובות זרע תתיבם אמנו ליבם: **כי אין לו בן.** הא אם היה לו בן לא היו תובעות כלום, מגיד שחכמניות היו:

ה| **ויקרב משה את משפטן.** נתעלמה הלכה ממנו. וכאן נפרע על שנטל עטרה לומר: "והדבר אשר יקשה מכם תקרבון אלי" (דברים א, יז). דבר אחר, ראויה היתה פרשה זו להכתב על ידי משה, אלא שזכו בנות צלפחד ונכתבה על ידן:

ז| **כן בנות צלפחד דברת.** כתרגומו: "יאות". כך כתובה פרשה זו לפני במרום, מגיד שראתה עינן מה שלא ראתה עינו של משה: **כן בנות צלפחד דברת.** יפה תבעו, אשרי אדם שהקדוש ברוך הוא מודה לדבריו: **נתן תתן.** שני חלקים, חלק אביהן שהיה מיוצאי מצרים, וחלקו עם אחיו בנכסי חפר: **והעברת.** לשון עברה הוא, במי שאינו מניח בן ליורשו. דבר אחר, על שם שהבת מעברת נחלה משבט לשבט, שבנה ובעלה יורשין אותה, ש"לא תסב נחלה" (להלן לו, ז) לא נצטוה אלא לאותו הדור בלבד, וכן: "והעברתם את נחלתו לבתו" (להלן פסוק ח), בכלן הוא אומר: "ונתתם" (להלן פסוקים ט-יא) ובבת הוא אומר: "והעברתם":

יא| **לשארו הקרב אליו ממשפחתו.** ואין משפחה קרויה אלא משפחת האב:

יב| **עלה אל הר העברים.** למה נסמכה לכאן? כיון שאמר הקדוש ברוך הוא: "נתן תתן להם" (לעיל פסוק ז), אמר: אותי צוה המקום להנחיל, שמא הותרה הגזרה ואכנס לארץ, אמר לו הקדוש ברוך הוא: גזרתי במקומה עומדת. דבר אחר, כיון שנכנס משה לנחלת בני גד ובני ראובן, שמח ואמר: כמדמה שהתר לי נדרי. משל למלך שגזר על בנו שלא יכנס לפתח פלטין שלו, נכנס לשער והוא אחריו, לחצר והוא אחריו, לטרקלין והוא אחריו, כיון שבא להכנס לקיטון אמר לו: בני, מכאן ואילך אתה אסור לכנס:

יג| **כאשר נאסף אהרן אחיך.** מכאן שנתאוה משה למיתתו של אהרן. דבר אחר, אין אתה טוב ממנו. "על אשר לא קדשתם" (דברים לב, נא), הא אם קדשתם אותי עדין לא הגיע זמנכם להפטר מן העולם. בכל מקום

you will die, **as Aaron your brother was gathered;** just as Aaron died without suffering, your soul will depart in absolute tranquility and will be attached to its Creator.[9]

14 You will not enter the land **because you defied My directive in the wilderness of Tzin, in the dispute of the congregation,**[10] **to sanctify Me with the water before their eyes. It is the water of dispute in Kadesh in the wilderness of Tzin.** Consequently, I decreed that you and Aaron would die in the wilderness.

15 Moses did not ascend the mountain immediately because he had important matters that he needed to attend to first. The first issue was his future replacement. **Moses spoke to the Lord, saying:**

16 **May the Lord, God of the spirits of all flesh,**[D] **appoint a man over the congregation,**

17 **who will go out before them** when they go out to war, **who will come before them** for other matters,[11] **who will take them out, and who will bring them in,** ensuring the unity of the nation, so **that the congregation of the Lord will not be like a flock that has no shepherd.**

18 **The Lord said to Moses:** Since you are searching for a man of this type, **take you Joshua son of Nun, a man in whom there is,** already now, a lofty **spirit, and lay your hand upon him** in order to transfer to him your unique abilities and authority.

19 **Stand him before Elazar the priest, and before the entire congregation, and command him before their eyes.** You shall instruct him about his position of leadership in the presence of the congregation so that they will respect his authority and obey his instructions.

20 **You shall confer from your** unique **grandeur upon him,**[D] **so that the entire congregation of the children of Israel will heed.**

21 However, unlike you, Moses, who receives instructions directly from Me, Joshua will need an intermediary to receive My instructions: **Before Elazar the priest he shall stand, and he will inquire for him regarding the judgment of the Urim before the Lord,** by way of the lights that will brighten in the stones of the breast piece and thereby communicate God's will to the priest;[12] **at his,** Elazar's, **directive**[13] **they shall go out, and at his directive they shall come, he and all the children of Israel with him, and the entire congregation.**

22 **Moses did as the Lord had commanded him; he took Joshua, and stood him before Elazar the priest, and before the entire congregation.**

23 **He laid his hands upon him, and commanded him, as the Lord spoke at the hand of Moses.**

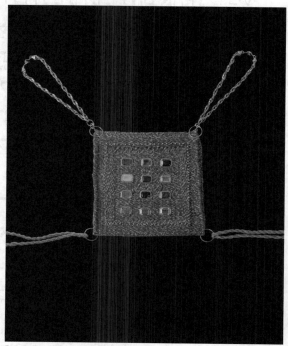

Breast piece of the High Priest

DISCUSSION

27:16| **The Lord, God of the spirits of all flesh:** Moses chose to address God in this unique manner due to the nature of his request. Moses requested that God, who understands the nature and character of each person, appoint a replacement for him who would know how to relate to each member of the nation (see Rashi).

27:20| **You shall confer from your grandeur upon him:** It is possible that this grandeur is Moses' honor (Ibn Ezra; Sforno), his wisdom, or his other character traits. However, it is also possible that this is referring to the radiance of Moses' face, as the verses in Exodus state that "the skin of his face was radiant" (34:29–30). The Sages say that people would compare the faces of the two leaders, saying that Moses' face was like the sun and Joshua's face was like the moon, meaning that Joshua's face also shone, but it was less bright than Moses' face (*Bava Batra* 75a).

יד נאסף אהרן אחיך: כאשר מריתם פי במדבר־צן במריבת העדה להקדישני
טו במים לעיניהם הם מי־מריבת קדש מדבר־צן: וידבר משה אל־ כד
טז יז יהוה לאמר: יפקד יהוה אלהי הרוחת לכל־בשר איש על־העדה: אשר־יצא
לפניהם ואשר יבא לפניהם ואשר יוציאם ואשר יביאם ולא תהיה עדת יהוה
יח כצאן אשר אין־להם רעה: ויאמר יהוה אל־משה קח־לך את־יהושע בן־נון
יט איש אשר־רוח בו וסמכת את־ידך עליו: והעמדת אתו לפני אלעזר הכהן
כ ולפני כל־העדה וצויתה אתו לעיניהם: ונתתה מהודך עליו למען ישמעו כל־
כא עדת בני ישראל: ולפני אלעזר הכהן יעמד ושאל לו במשפט האורים לפני
כב יהוה על־פיו יצאו ועל־פיו יבאו הוא וכל־בני־ישראל אתו וכל־העדה: ויעש
משה כאשר צוה יהוה אתו ויקח את־יהושע ויעמדהו לפני אלעזר הכהן
כג ולפני כל־העדה: ויסמך את־ידיו עליו ויצוהו כאשר דבר יהוה ביד־משה:

רש"י

שכתב מיתתם כתב סרחנם, לפי שנגזרה גזרה על דור המדבר למות במדבר בעון שלא האמינו, לכך בקש משה שיכתב סרחנו, שלא יאמרו: אף הוא מן הממרים היה. משל לשתי נשים שלוקות בבית דין, אחת קלקלה ואחת אכלה פגי שביעית וכו' [אמרה להן אותה שאכלה פגי שביעית: בבקשה מכם, הודיעו על מה היא לוקה, שלא יאמרו על מה שזו לוקה זו לוקה. הביאו פגי שביעית ותלו בצווארה, והיו מכריזין לפניה ואומרין: על עסקי שביעית היא לוקה] (יומא פו ע"ב), אף כאן בכל מקום שהזכיר מיתתן הזכיר סרחנן, להודיע שלא היתה בהם אלא זו בלבד:

יד | הם מי מריבת קדש. הם לבדם, אין בהם עון אחר. דבר אחר, הם שהמרו במרה, הם היו שהמרו בים סוף, הם עצמם שהמרו במדבר צן:

טו | וידבר משה אל ה' וגו'. להודיע שבחן של צדיקים, שכשנפטרים מן העולם מניחין צרכן ועוסקין בצרכי צבור: לאמר. אמר לו: השיבני אם אתה ממנה להם פרנס אם לאו:

טז | יפקד ה'. כיון ששמע משה שאמר לו המקום: תן נחלת צלפחד לבנותיו, אמר: הגיע שעה שאתבע צרכי שירשו בני את גדלתי. אמר לו הקדוש ברוך הוא: לא כך עלתה במחשבה לפני, כדאי הוא יהושע ליטול שכר שמושו, שלא מש מתוך האהל. וזהו שאמר שלמה: "נצר תאנה יאכל פריה" (משלי כז, יח): אלהי הרוחת. למה נאמר? אמר לפניו: רבונו של עולם, גלוי לפניך דעתו של כל אחד ואחד ואינן דומין זה לזה, מנה עליהם מנהיג שיהא סובל כל אחד ואחד לפי דעתו:

יז | אשר יצא לפניהם. לא כדרך מלכי האמות שיושבים בבתיהם ומשלחין את חיילותיהם למלחמה, אלא כמו שעשיתי אני, שנלחמתי בסיחון ועוג, שנאמר: "אל תירא אתו" (במדבר כא, לד), וכדרך שעשה יהושע, שנאמר: "וילך יהושע אליו ויאמר לו הלנו אתה" וגו' (יהושע ה, יג), וכן בדוד הוא אומר: "כי הוא יוצא ובא לפניהם" (שמואל א' יח, טז), יוצא בראש ונכנס בראש: ואשר יוציאם. בזכיותיו: ואשר יביאם. בזכיותיו. דבר אחר, "ואשר יביאם", שלא תעשה לו כדרך שאתה עושה לי, שאיני מכניסן לארץ:

יח | קח לך. קחנו בדברים, אשריך שזכית להנהיג בניו של מקום: לך. את שבדוק לך, את זה אתה מכיר: אשר רוח בו. כאשר שאלת, שיוכל להלך כנגד רוחו של כל אחד ואחד: וסמכת את ידך עליו. תן לו מתרגמן שידרש בחייך, שלא יאמרו עליו: לא היה לו להרים ראש בימי משה:

יט | וצויתה אתו. על ישראל: דע שטרחנין הם, סרבנים הם, על מנת שתקבל עליך:

כ | ונתתה מהודך עליו. זה קרון עור פנים: מהודך. ולא כל הודך, נמצינו למדין, פני משה כחמה, פני יהושע כלבנה: למען ישמעו כל עדת בני ישראל. שיהיו נוהגין בו כבוד ויראה כדרך שנוהגין בך:

כא | ולפני אלעזר הכהן יעמד. הרי שאלתך שאלת, שאין הכבוד הזה זז מבית אביך, שאף יהושע יהא צריך לאלעזר: ושאל לו. כשיצטרך לצאת למלחמה: על פיו. של אלעזר: וכל העדה. סנהדרין:

כב | ויקח את יהושע. לקחו בדברים, והודיעו מתן שכר פרנסי ישראל לעולם הבא:

כג | ויסמך את ידיו. בעין יפה, יותר ויותר ממה שנצטוה, שהקדוש ברוך הוא אמר לו: "וסמכת את ידך" (לעיל פסוק יח) והוא עשה בשתי ידיו, ועשאו ככלי מלא וגדוש ומלאו חכמתו בעין יפה: כאשר דבר ה'. אף לענין ההוד, נתן מהודו עליו:

The Continual and Additional Offerings

NUMBERS 28:1–30:1

The upcoming passage discusses the communal offerings that must be brought at specific times: The continual offering, as well as the additional offerings that are brought on the Sabbath, New Moons, and festivals. Most of these offerings were not offered in the wilderness at all. Consequently, they are first mentioned here, shortly before the entry of Israel into the land. The festivals are mentioned here only as they pertain to the laws of the communal offerings that are brought at those times. Other rites and laws of the festivals are not mentioned, other than a reminder that these are sacred times and that one may not perform forbidden labors on the festivals.

28 1 **The Lord spoke to Moses, saying:**

Fifth aliya 2 **Command the children of Israel, and say to them: My offering,** which is **My food, for My fires, My pleasing aroma, you shall take care to present to Me at its appointed time.** One should not delay bringing any offering, but one must be particularly careful about the offerings that have a set time, which may be brought only at that appointed time.

3 **You shall say to them: This is the fire offering that you shall bring to the Lord** and burn on the altar: **Unblemished lambs in the first year, two each day, a continual burnt offering.**

4 **The one lamb you shall offer in the morning, and the second lamb you shall offer in the afternoon.**

5 This offering is accompanied by **one-tenth of an ephah**[B] of **high-quality flour as a meal offering, mixed with one-fourth of a hin**[B] **of virgin oil,** fine oil produced by beating on olives that are specially chosen as they ripened.

6 **It is a continual burnt offering that was** already **done at Mount Sinai,** as stated in Exodus 24:5, **as a pleasing aroma, a fire offering to the Lord.**

7 **And its libation is one-fourth of a hin for the one lamb; in the holy place, pour a libation of** an **intoxicating drink [*shekhar*], wine, to the Lord.** This is the law of the wine libation which is poured onto the altar from a vessel. Although the term *shekhar* in the Bible is often understood to mean beer, it is in fact not the name of a particular beverage, but a term that refers to any intoxicating drink.

8 This is the law of the morning lamb. **The other lamb you shall offer in the afternoon; like the meal offering of the morning, and like its libation, you shall offer a fire offering of a pleasing aroma to the Lord.**

9 **On the Sabbath day, two unblemished lambs in the first year, two-tenths** of an ephah **of high-quality flour as a meal offering, mixed with oil, and its libation.** It is unclear what the pronoun "its" at the end of this sentence is referring to; it may be the meal offering, such that the verse is referring to the libation that accompanies the meal offering. Alternatively, it could be a reference to the Sabbath.[14]

10 **This is the burnt offering of each Sabbath on its Sabbath, with the continual burnt offering and its libation.** These two lambs are sacrificed as burnt offerings every Sabbath, and are known as the additional offering of Sabbath. They are brought in addition to the two lambs sacrificed as a continual offering.

11 **On your New Moons you shall present a burnt offering to the Lord: Two young bulls, and one ram, seven lambs in the first year, unblemished.**

12 **Three-tenths** of an ephah **of high-quality flour as a meal offering, mixed with oil,** accompanying the offering **for each bull and two-tenths of high-quality flour as a meal offering, mixed with oil, for the one ram.**

13 **One-tenth** of an ephah **of high-quality flour mixed with oil as a meal offering for each lamb;** all of these are **a burnt offering of a pleasing aroma, a fire offering to the Lord.**

14 **Their libations,** the libations that are brought with these offerings, **shall be one-half hin of wine for a bull, and one-third of a hin for the ram, and one-fourth of a hin for a lamb.**

BACKGROUND

28:5 | **One-tenth of an ephah:** An ancient measurement of volume that corresponds to approximately 2.4 L, or, according to some, to about 4 L. It is probable that the term "ephah" is derived from the Egyptian term *ephat*, which means counting.

Hin: A measurement of liquid that is more than 4 L. The source of this term is Egyptian and it originally referred to a receptacle.

א ב וַיְדַבֵּר יְהוָה אֶל־מֹשֶׁה לֵּאמֹר: צַו אֶת־בְּנֵי יִשְׂרָאֵל וְאָמַרְתָּ אֲלֵהֶם אֶת־קָרְבָּנִי חמישי
ג לַחְמִי לְאִשַּׁי רֵיחַ נִיחֹחִי תִּשְׁמְרוּ לְהַקְרִיב לִי בְּמוֹעֲדוֹ: וְאָמַרְתָּ לָהֶם זֶה הָאִשֶּׁה
ד אֲשֶׁר תַּקְרִיבוּ לַיהוָה כְּבָשִׂים בְּנֵי־שָׁנָה תְמִימִם שְׁנַיִם לַיּוֹם עֹלָה תָמִיד: אֶת־
ה הַכֶּבֶשׂ אֶחָד תַּעֲשֶׂה בַבֹּקֶר וְאֵת הַכֶּבֶשׂ הַשֵּׁנִי תַּעֲשֶׂה בֵּין הָעַרְבָּיִם: וַעֲשִׂירִית
ו הָאֵיפָה סֹלֶת לְמִנְחָה בְּלוּלָה בְּשֶׁמֶן כָּתִית רְבִיעִת הַהִין: עֹלַת תָּמִיד הָעֲשֻׂיָה
ז בְּהַר סִינַי לְרֵיחַ נִיחֹחַ אִשֶּׁה לַיהוָה: וְנִסְכּוֹ רְבִיעִת הַהִין לַכֶּבֶשׂ הָאֶחָד בַּקֹּדֶשׁ
ח הַסֵּךְ נֶסֶךְ שֵׁכָר לַיהוָה: וְאֵת הַכֶּבֶשׂ הַשֵּׁנִי תַּעֲשֶׂה בֵּין הָעַרְבָּיִם כְּמִנְחַת הַבֹּקֶר
וּכְנִסְכּוֹ תַּעֲשֶׂה אִשֵּׁה רֵיחַ נִיחֹחַ לַיהוָה:
ט וּבְיוֹם הַשַּׁבָּת שְׁנֵי־כְבָשִׂים בְּנֵי־שָׁנָה תְּמִימִם וּשְׁנֵי עֶשְׂרֹנִים סֹלֶת מִנְחָה בְּלוּלָה
י בַשֶּׁמֶן וְנִסְכּוֹ: עֹלַת שַׁבַּת בְּשַׁבַּתּוֹ עַל־עֹלַת הַתָּמִיד וְנִסְכָּהּ:
יא וּבְרָאשֵׁי חָדְשֵׁיכֶם תַּקְרִיבוּ עֹלָה לַיהוָה פָּרִים בְּנֵי־בָקָר שְׁנַיִם וְאַיִל אֶחָד
יב כְּבָשִׂים בְּנֵי־שָׁנָה שִׁבְעָה תְּמִימִם: וּשְׁלֹשָׁה עֶשְׂרֹנִים סֹלֶת מִנְחָה בְּלוּלָה בַשֶּׁמֶן
יג לַפָּר הָאֶחָד וּשְׁנֵי עֶשְׂרֹנִים סֹלֶת מִנְחָה בְּלוּלָה בַשֶּׁמֶן לָאַיִל הָאֶחָד: וְעִשָּׂרֹן
עִשָּׂרוֹן סֹלֶת מִנְחָה בְּלוּלָה בַשֶּׁמֶן לַכֶּבֶשׂ הָאֶחָד עֹלָה רֵיחַ נִיחֹחַ אִשֶּׁה לַיהוָה:
יד וְנִסְכֵּיהֶם חֲצִי הַהִין יִהְיֶה לַפָּר וּשְׁלִישִׁת הַהִין לָאַיִל וּרְבִיעִת הַהִין לַכֶּבֶשׂ יָיִן

רש״י

פרק כח

ב| צַו אֶת בְּנֵי יִשְׂרָאֵל. מָה אָמוּר לְמַעְלָה? "יִפְקֹד ה'" (לעיל כז, טז), אָמַר לוֹ הַקָּדוֹשׁ בָּרוּךְ הוּא: עַד שֶׁאַתָּה מְצַוֵּנִי עַל בָּנַי, צַוֵּה אֶת בָּנַי עָלַי. מָשָׁל לְבַת מֶלֶךְ שֶׁהָיְתָה נִפְטֶרֶת מִן הָעוֹלָם וְהָיְתָה מְפַקֶּדֶת לְבַעְלָהּ עַל בָּנֶיהָ וְכוּ' [אמרה לו: בבקשה ממך הזהר לי בבניי. אמר לה: עד שאת מפקדתני על בניי פקדי את בניי עלי, שלא ימרדו בי ושלא ינהגו בי מנהג ביזיון], כִּדְאִיתָא בְּסִפְרֵי (קמב): קָרְבָּנִי. זֶה הַדָּם: לַחְמִי. אֵלּוּ אֵמוּרִין, וְכֵן הוּא אוֹמֵר: "וְהִקְטִירָם הַכֹּהֵן הַמִּזְבֵּחָה לֶחֶם אִשֶּׁה" (ויקרא ג, טו): לְאִשַּׁי. הַנִּתָּנִין לְאִשֵּׁי מִזְבְּחִי: תִּשְׁמְרוּ. שֶׁיִּהְיוּ כֹּהֲנִים וּלְוִיִּם וְיִשְׂרְאֵלִים עוֹמְדִין עַל גַּבָּיו, מִכָּאן לָמְדוּ וְתִקְּנוּ מַעֲמָדוֹת: בְּמוֹעֲדוֹ. בְּכָל יוֹם הוּא מוֹעֵד הַתְּמִידִים:

ג| וְאָמַרְתָּ לָהֶם. אַזְהָרָה לְבֵית דִּין: שְׁנַיִם לַיּוֹם. כִּפְשׁוּטוֹ. וְעִקָּרוֹ בָּא לְלַמֵּד שֶׁיִּהְיוּ נִשְׁחָטִין כְּנֶגֶד הַיּוֹם, תָּמִיד שֶׁל שַׁחַר בַּמַּעֲרָב וְשֶׁל בֵּין הָעַרְבַּיִם בַּמִּזְרָח שֶׁל טַבָּעוֹת:

ד| אֶת הַכֶּבֶשׂ אֶחָד. אַף עַל פִּי שֶׁכְּבָר נֶאֱמַר בְּפָרָשַׁת וְאַתָּה תְּצַוֶּה: "וְזֶה אֲשֶׁר תַּעֲשֶׂה" וְגוֹ' (שמות כט, לח-לט), הִיא הָיְתָה אַזְהָרָה לִימֵי הַמִּלּוּאִים, וְכָאן צִוָּה לְדוֹרוֹת:

ה| סֹלֶת לְמִנְחָה. מִנְחַת נְסָכִים:

ו| הָעֲשֻׂיָה בְּהַר סִינַי. כְּאוֹתָן שֶׁנַּעֲשׂוּ בִּימֵי הַמִּלּוּאִים. דָּבָר אַחֵר, "הָעֲשֻׂיָה בְּהַר סִינַי", מַקִּישׁ עוֹלַת תָּמִיד לְעוֹלַת הַר סִינַי, אוֹתָהּ שֶׁקָּרְבָה לִפְנֵי מַתַּן תּוֹרָה שֶׁכָּתוּב בָּהּ: "וַיָּשֶׂם בָּאַגָּנֹת" (שמות כד, ו), מְלַמֵּד שֶׁטְּעוּנָה כְּלִי:

ז| וְנִסְכּוֹ. יַיִן: בַּקֹּדֶשׁ הַסֵּךְ. עַל הַמִּזְבֵּחַ יִתְנַסְּכוּ: נֶסֶךְ שֵׁכָר. יַיִן הַמְשַׁכֵּר, פְּרָט לְיַיִן מִגִּתּוֹ:

ח| רֵיחַ נִיחֹחַ. נַחַת רוּחַ לְפָנַי שֶׁאָמַרְתִּי וְנַעֲשָׂה רְצוֹנִי:

י| עֹלַת שַׁבַּת בְּשַׁבַּתּוֹ. וְלֹא עוֹלַת שַׁבָּת בְּשַׁבָּת אַחֶרֶת, הֲרֵי שֶׁלֹּא הִקְרִיב בְּשַׁבָּת זוֹ, שׁוֹמֵעַ אֲנִי יַקְרִיב שְׁתַּיִם לַשַּׁבָּת הַבָּאָה? תַּלְמוּד לוֹמַר: "בְּשַׁבַּתּוֹ", מַגִּיד שֶׁאִם עָבַר יוֹמוֹ בָּטֵל קָרְבָּנוֹ: עַל עֹלַת הַתָּמִיד. אֵלּוּ מוּסָפִין, לְבַד אוֹתָן שְׁנֵי כְּבָשִׂים שֶׁל עוֹלַת הַתָּמִיד. וּמַגִּיד שֶׁאֵין קְרֵבִין אֶלָּא בֵּין שְׁנֵי הַתְּמִידִין, וְכֵן בְּכָל הַמּוּסָפִין נֶאֱמַר: "עַל עוֹלַת הַתָּמִיד" לְתַלְמוּד זֶה:

יב| וּשְׁלֹשָׁה עֶשְׂרֹנִים. כְּמִשְׁפַּט נִסְכֵּי פָּר, שֶׁכֵּן הֵן קְצוּבִין בְּפָרָשַׁת נְסָכִים (לעיל טו, ח-י):

יד| זֹאת עֹלַת חֹדֶשׁ בְּחָדְשׁוֹ. שֶׁאִם עָבַר יוֹמוֹ בָּטֵל קָרְבָּנוֹ וְשׁוּב אֵין לוֹ תַּשְׁלוּמִין:

This is the burnt offering of the New Moon, brought **for each New Moon for** all **the months of the year.**

15 Additionally, **one goat** is brought on the New Moon **as a sin offering to the Lord;**[D] **with the continual burnt offering and its libation it shall be offered.**

16 Having discussed the offerings of the New Moon, the Torah
Sixth aliya now discusses the offerings of the festivals in the order that they occur during the year. **In the first month,** Nisan, **on the fourteenth day of the month, is the paschal lamb** to be offered **to the Lord.**

17 **On the fifteenth day of that month shall be a festival;**[D] **seven days unleavened bread shall be eaten.**

18 **On the first day** of Passover you shall have **a holy convocation,** a gathering to which the entire nation is invited for sacred purposes.[15] **You shall not perform any toilsome labor;** this includes forms of labor that one generally performs for the sake of his livelihood or to enhance his property, as opposed to food preparation, such as cooking, which is permitted on a festival.[16] Conversely, with regard to the Sabbath, the verse states that one may not perform "any labor,"[17] implying that even food preparation is prohibited.[18]

19 **You shall present a fire offering, a burnt offering to the Lord: Two young bulls, and one ram, and seven lambs in the first year; they shall be unblemished for you;**

20 **and their meal offering: High-quality flour mixed with oil;** you shall give **three-tenths for a bull, and two-tenths for the ram;**

21 **one-tenth shall you offer for each lamb for the seven lambs.**

22 **And one goat as a sin offering, to atone for you** in case you unintentionally transmitted ritual impurity to the Temple over the course of the year.[19]

23 **Besides the burnt offering of the morning that is for the continual burnt offering, you shall offer these.** These additional offerings are sacrificed after the continual morning offering, which is the first offering of the day.

24 **Like these you shall offer for each day, for seven days: It is the food of the fire offering, a pleasing aroma to the Lord; with the continual burnt offering, and its libation, it shall be offered.**

25 **On the seventh day** of Passover **it shall be a holy convocation for you; you shall not perform any toilsome labor,** just as on the first day.

26 **On the day of the first fruits, when you present a new meal offering to the Lord,** the offering of the two loaves, which is the first offering of the year that is brought from the new crop of grain,[20] **on your Festival of Weeks** [***Shavuot***], as this festival occurs seven weeks after the sheaf [*omer*] offering is brought on the second day of Passover,[21] **it shall be a holy convocation for you; you shall not perform any toilsome labor.**

27 **You shall present a burnt offering for a pleasing aroma to the Lord: Two young bulls, one ram, seven lambs in the first year;**

28 **and their meal offering: High-quality flour mixed with oil, three-tenths for each bull, two-tenths for the one ram,**

29 **one-tenth for each lamb for the seven lambs;**

30 **one goat, to atone for you.**

31 **Besides the continual burnt offering, and its meal offering, you shall offer** these; **they shall be unblemished for you, and their libations.** The prohibition of labor, as well as the additional animal offerings, and the meal offerings and libations that accompany them, are identical on Passover and on Shavuot.

DISCUSSION

28:15 | **As a sin offering to the Lord:** Previously (verse 11), the burnt offering brought on the New Moon was referred to as a "burnt offering to the Lord." This is understandable, as the purpose of a burnt offering is to honor the altar and to express Israel's goodwill toward God. However, it is difficult to understand why this verse refers to the sin offering brought on the New Moon as "a sin offering to the Lord," as a sin offering is brought to atone for sins rather than to express devotion to God.

The Sages interpret this phrase homiletically, explaining that God requests that on every New Moon a sin offering be brought on His behalf, as it were, for reducing the size of the moon (*Ḥullin* 60b). Additionally, all sin offerings [*ḥatat*] that are not brought to atone for a specific sin, but are rather brought on fixed dates, serve to cleanse [*leḥatei*], to atone for instances of ritual impurity in the Temple. The sin offering brought on the New Moon belongs to this category, and atones for all such sins that were committed due to unknown ritual impurity. It is called "a sin offering to the Lord" because it atones for sins known only to God (*Shevuot* 9a).

28:16–17 | **On the fourteenth day of the month is the paschal lamb [*Pesaḥ*] to the Lord.... On the fifteenth day of that month shall be a festival:** It is common in modern times to refer to the entire seven-day holiday as the festival of Passover [*Pesaḥ*]. However, the Torah distinguishes between the fourteenth of Nisan, when the paschal lamb [*Pesaḥ*] is brought, and the seven-day festival that begins the following day, which it calls the Festival of Unleavened Bread. This festival also commemorates the exodus from Egypt, but it is not directly related to the paschal lamb.

On the other hand, it is noteworthy that the connection between the day of the paschal lamb and the subsequent seven-day festival is emphasized elsewhere in the Bible. In Deuteronomy (16:2–3) it is stated: "You shall slaughter the paschal offering to the Lord your God.... Seven days you shall eat with it unleavened bread, the bread of affliction, as in haste you came out from the land of Egypt." Similarly, another verse states: "In the first month, on the fourteenth day of the month, there shall be the paschal lamb for you, a festival of seven days; unleavened bread shall be eaten" (Ezekiel 45:21).

טו זֹאת עֹלַת חֹדֶשׁ בְּחָדְשׁוֹ לְחָדְשֵׁי הַשָּׁנָה: וּשְׂעִיר עִזִּים אֶחָד לְחַטָּאת לַיהוָה
טז עַל־עֹלַת הַתָּמִיד יֵעָשֶׂה וְנִסְכּוֹ: וּבַחֹדֶשׁ הָרִאשׁוֹן בְּאַרְבָּעָה ששי
יז עָשָׂר יוֹם לַחֹדֶשׁ פֶּסַח לַיהוָה: וּבַחֲמִשָּׁה עָשָׂר יוֹם לַחֹדֶשׁ הַזֶּה חָג שִׁבְעַת
יח יָמִים מַצּוֹת יֵאָכֵל: בַּיּוֹם הָרִאשׁוֹן מִקְרָא־קֹדֶשׁ כָּל־מְלֶאכֶת עֲבֹדָה לֹא תַעֲשׂוּ:
יט וְהִקְרַבְתֶּם אִשֶּׁה עֹלָה לַיהוָה פָּרִים בְּנֵי־בָקָר שְׁנַיִם וְאַיִל אֶחָד וְשִׁבְעָה כְבָשִׂים
כ בְּנֵי שָׁנָה תְּמִימִם יִהְיוּ לָכֶם: וּמִנְחָתָם סֹלֶת בְּלוּלָה בַשָּׁמֶן שְׁלֹשָׁה עֶשְׂרֹנִים
כא לַפָּר וּשְׁנֵי עֶשְׂרֹנִים לָאַיִל תַּעֲשׂוּ: עִשָּׂרוֹן עִשָּׂרוֹן תַּעֲשֶׂה לַכֶּבֶשׂ הָאֶחָד לְשִׁבְעַת
כב כג הַכְּבָשִׂים: וּשְׂעִיר חַטָּאת אֶחָד לְכַפֵּר עֲלֵיכֶם: מִלְּבַד עֹלַת הַבֹּקֶר אֲשֶׁר לְעֹלַת
כד הַתָּמִיד תַּעֲשׂוּ אֶת־אֵלֶּה: כָּאֵלֶּה תַּעֲשׂוּ לַיּוֹם שִׁבְעַת יָמִים לֶחֶם אִשֵּׁה רֵיחַ־נִיחֹחַ
כה לַיהוָה עַל־עוֹלַת הַתָּמִיד יֵעָשֶׂה וְנִסְכּוֹ: וּבַיּוֹם הַשְּׁבִיעִי מִקְרָא־קֹדֶשׁ יִהְיֶה לָכֶם
כו כָּל־מְלֶאכֶת עֲבֹדָה לֹא תַעֲשׂוּ: וּבְיוֹם הַבִּכּוּרִים בְּהַקְרִיבְכֶם כה
מִנְחָה חֲדָשָׁה לַיהוָה בְּשָׁבֻעֹתֵיכֶם מִקְרָא־קֹדֶשׁ יִהְיֶה לָכֶם כָּל־מְלֶאכֶת עֲבֹדָה
כז לֹא תַעֲשׂוּ: וְהִקְרַבְתֶּם עוֹלָה לְרֵיחַ נִיחֹחַ לַיהוָה פָּרִים בְּנֵי־בָקָר שְׁנַיִם אַיִל
כח אֶחָד שִׁבְעָה כְבָשִׂים בְּנֵי שָׁנָה: וּמִנְחָתָם סֹלֶת בְּלוּלָה בַשָּׁמֶן שְׁלֹשָׁה עֶשְׂרֹנִים
כט לַפָּר הָאֶחָד שְׁנֵי עֶשְׂרֹנִים לָאַיִל הָאֶחָד: עִשָּׂרוֹן עִשָּׂרוֹן לַכֶּבֶשׂ הָאֶחָד לְשִׁבְעַת
ל לא הַכְּבָשִׂים: שְׂעִיר עִזִּים אֶחָד לְכַפֵּר עֲלֵיכֶם: מִלְּבַד עֹלַת הַתָּמִיד וּמִנְחָתוֹ תַּעֲשׂוּ
תְּמִימִם יִהְיוּ־לָכֶם וְנִסְכֵּיהֶם:

רש״י

טו| **וּשְׂעִיר עִזִּים וְגוֹ׳.** כָּל שְׂעִירֵי הַמּוּסָפִין בָּאִין לְכַפֵּר עַל טֻמְאַת מִקְדָּשׁ וְקָדָשָׁיו, הַכֹּל כְּמוֹ שֶׁמְּפֹרָשׁ בְּמַסֶּכֶת שְׁבוּעוֹת (דף ב ע״א-ע״ב). וְנִשְׁתַּנָּה שְׂעִיר רֹאשׁ חֹדֶשׁ שֶׁנֶּאֱמַר בּוֹ: ״לַה׳״, לְלַמֶּדְךָ שֶׁמְּכַפֵּר עַל שֶׁאֵין בּוֹ יְדִיעָה לֹא בַּתְּחִלָּה וְלֹא בַּסּוֹף, שֶׁאֵין מַכִּיר בַּחֵטְא אֶלָּא הַקָּדוֹשׁ בָּרוּךְ הוּא בִּלְבַד, וּשְׁאָר הַשְּׂעִירִין לְמֵדִין מִמֶּנּוּ. וּמִדְרָשׁוֹ בָּאַגָּדָה: אָמַר הַקָּדוֹשׁ בָּרוּךְ הוּא: הָבִיאוּ כַּפָּרָה עָלַי עַל שֶׁמִּעַטְתִּי אֶת הַיָּרֵחַ: **עַל עֹלַת הַתָּמִיד יֵעָשֶׂה.** כָּל הַקָּרְבָּן הַזֶּה: **וְנִסְכּוֹ.** אֵין ׳וְנִסְכּוֹ׳ מוּסָב עַל הַשָּׂעִיר, שֶׁאֵין נְסָכִים לְחַטָּאת:

יח| **כָּל מְלֶאכֶת עֲבֹדָה.** אֲפִלּוּ מְלָאכָה הַצְּרִיכָה לָכֶם, כְּגוֹן דָּבָר הָאָבֵד הַמֻּתָּר בְּחֻלּוֹ שֶׁל מוֹעֵד, אֲסוּרָה בְּיוֹם טוֹב:

יט| **פָּרִים.** כְּנֶגֶד אַבְרָהָם, שֶׁנֶּאֱמַר: ״וְאֶל הַבָּקָר רָץ אַבְרָהָם״ (בראשית יח, ז): **אֵילִים.** כְּנֶגֶד אֵילוֹ שֶׁל יִצְחָק (שם כב, יג): **כְּבָשִׂים.** כְּנֶגֶד יַעֲקֹב, שֶׁנֶּאֱמַר: ״וְהַכְּשָׂבִים הִפְרִיד יַעֲקֹב״ (שם ל, מ). בִּיסוֹדוֹ שֶׁל רַבִּי מֹשֶׁה הַדַּרְשָׁן רָאִיתִי זֹאת:

כד| **כָּאֵלֶּה תַּעֲשׂוּ לַיּוֹם.** שֶׁלֹּא יִהְיוּ פּוֹחֲתִין וְהוֹלְכִין כְּפָרֵי הֶחָג:

כו| **וּבְיוֹם הַבִּכּוּרִים.** חַג הַשָּׁבוּעוֹת קָרוּי: ״בִּכּוּרֵי קְצִיר חִטִּים״ (שמות לד, כב), עַל שֵׁם שְׁתֵּי הַלֶּחֶם שֶׁהֵם רִאשׁוֹנִים לְמִנְחַת חִטִּים הַבָּאָה מִן הֶחָדָשׁ:

לא| **תְּמִימִם יִהְיוּ לָכֶם וְנִסְכֵּיהֶם.** אַף הַנְּסָכִים יִהְיוּ תְּמִימִים, לָמְדוּ רַבּוֹתֵינוּ מִכָּאן שֶׁהַיַּיִן שֶׁהֶעֱלָה קְמָחִין פָּסוּל לִנְסָכִים:

29 1 **In the seventh month,** Tishrei, **on the first of the month,**[D] Rosh HaShana, **it shall be a holy convocation for you; you shall not perform any toilsome labor; a day of sounding the alarm** of the shofar **it shall be for you.**
2 **You shall perform a burnt offering for a pleasing aroma to the Lord: One young bull, one ram, seven lambs in the first year, unblemished;**
3 **and their meal offering: High-quality flour mixed with oil, three-tenths for the bull, two-tenths for the ram,**
4 **and one-tenth for each lamb for the seven lambs.**
5 **And one goat as a sin offering, to atone for you.**
6 These offerings are **besides the burnt offering of the New Moon and its meal offering,** as this festival occurs on the New Moon, **and the continual burnt offering and its meal offering,**[D] **and their libations, in accordance with their ordinance,** as discussed above (28:5–7, 12–14) **for a pleasing aroma, a fire offering to the Lord.**
7 **On the tenth of this seventh month,** Yom Kippur, **it shall be a holy convocation for you;** but on this day **you shall afflict your souls** by fasting. Furthermore, **you shall not perform any labor,** including labor undertaken for food preparation, just like on the Sabbath.
8 **You shall present a burnt offering to the Lord, a pleasing aroma: One young bull, one ram, seven lambs in the first year, unblemished.** This is identical to the additional offering of Rosh HaShana.
9 **And their meal offering: High-quality flour mixed with oil, three-tenths for the bull, two-tenths for the one ram,**
10 **one-tenth for each lamb for the seven lambs.**
11 **One goat as a sin offering; besides the** bull and goat brought on Yom Kippur as a special **sin offering of atonement, and the continual burnt offering, and its meal offering, and their libations.** The special sin offerings of a bull and goat are not specifically mentioned here because they do not belong to the general category of additional offerings on the festivals, as they serve a different purpose.[22]
12 **On the fifteenth day of the seventh month it shall be a holy**
Seventh aliya **convocation,** Sukkot, **for you; you shall not perform any toilsome labor, and you shall celebrate a festival to the Lord seven days.**[B]
13 **You shall present a burnt offering, a fire offering, a pleasing aroma to the Lord: Thirteen young bulls, two rams, fourteen lambs of the first year, they shall be unblemished;**
14 **and their meal offering: High-quality flour mixed with oil, three-tenths for each bull for the thirteen bulls, two-tenths for each ram for the two rams,**
15 **and one-tenth for each lamb for the fourteen lambs.**
16 **And one goat as a sin offering; besides the continual burnt offering, its meal offering, and its libation.**
17 On Passover, the additional offering is the same for each of the seven days of the festival. In contrast, on Sukkot, each day is

BACKGROUND

29:12 | **Seven days:** Other than the number of bulls brought as burnt offerings each day, the verses pertaining to the different days of this festival are practically identical. Nevertheless, there are small differences with regard to the conclusions of the verses. The verses about each day conclude with the expression "and its libation," except for the second day, where the verse states "and their libations" (29:19) and the sixth day, where the verse states "and its libations" (29:31). Furthermore, the verses employ the expression "in accordance with its ordinance" with regard to all of the days except the seventh day, where the verse states "in accordance with their ordinance" (29:33).

These small differences do not affect the plain meaning of the verses, but the Sages find hidden meaning in these nuances. In Hebrew, the differences in expression are created by the simple addition of a total of three letters to the regular expressions. These letters, *mem*, *yod*, and *mem*, spell the word *mayim*, water, and the Sages interpret this as an allusion to the water libation, an offering brought on Sukkot that is not mentioned explicitly in the verses (*Ta'anit* 2b).

The number of bulls brought as burnt offerings changes each day: On the first day thirteen bulls are brought, and the number decreases by one on each subsequent day. The total number of bulls sacrificed as burnt offerings over the festival is seventy. This number is identical to the number of nations in the world, as per the list of the descendants of Noah (Genesis 10). The seventy bulls brought as burnt offerings therefore symbolize the onset of peace among all the nations of the world (*Sukka* 55b). The universal nature of Sukkot is also expressed by the prophecy of Zechariah (see Zechariah 14:16).

DISCUSSION

29:1 | **In the seventh month, on the first of the month:** The Torah does not refer to this day as Rosh HaShana, meaning the New Year, but rather as "a day of sounding the alarm" or "a remembrance by means of an alarm blast" (Leviticus 23:24). The term *rosh hashana* is mentioned in Ezekiel (40:1), but there it refers to a season rather than to a specific day (see also Exodus 34:22). The Torah also does not explain the significance of the day or the meaning of the alarm blasts. It is unclear from the Torah if the blast marks the beginning of a new year, as the month of Nisan has already been identified as the first month of the year (Exodus 12:2). It is possible that the shofar blast marks the beginning of the many festivals that occur in the month of Tishrei. According to the tradition of the Oral Torah, the first of Tishrei is indeed the New Year, and the shofar blast serves to declare God the King of the world, and to announce His judgment of the world on this day. This is alluded to in Psalms (81:4–5; see *Rosh HaShana* 8a, 16a; commentary on Leviticus 23:25).

29:6 | **Besides the burnt offering of the New Moon and its meal offering, and the continual burnt offering and its meal offering:** The order in which the offerings are sacrificed depends upon their frequency. The continual offering is always sacrificed first. If it is also the Sabbath and New Moon, the additional offering of the Sabbath follows the continual offering, and the additional offering of the New Moon follows after that.

א וּבַחֹ֣דֶשׁ הַשְּׁבִיעִ֣י בְּאֶחָ֣ד לַחֹ֗דֶשׁ מִֽקְרָא־קֹ֨דֶשׁ֙ יִהְיֶ֣ה לָכֶ֔ם כָּל־מְלֶ֥אכֶת עֲבֹדָ֖ה לֹ֣א

ב תַעֲשׂ֑וּ י֥וֹם תְּרוּעָ֖ה יִהְיֶ֥ה לָכֶֽם׃ וַעֲשִׂיתֶ֨ם עֹלָ֜ה לְרֵ֤יחַ נִיחֹ֨חַ֙ לַֽיהוָ֔ה פַּ֧ר בֶּן־בָּקָ֛ר אֶחָ֖ד

ג אַ֣יִל אֶחָ֑ד כְּבָשִׂ֧ים בְּנֵֽי־שָׁנָ֛ה שִׁבְעָ֖ה תְּמִימִֽם׃ וּמִ֨נְחָתָ֔ם סֹ֖לֶת בְּלוּלָ֣ה בַשָּׁ֑מֶן שְׁלֹשָׁ֣ה

ד עֶשְׂרֹנִ֗ים לַפָּ֔ר שְׁנֵ֥י עֶשְׂרֹנִ֖ים לָאָ֑יִל׃ וְעִשָּׂר֣וֹן אֶחָ֗ד לַכֶּ֨בֶשׂ֙ הָֽאֶחָ֔ד לְשִׁבְעַ֖ת הַכְּבָשִֽׂים׃

ה וּשְׂעִיר־עִזִּ֥ים אֶחָ֖ד חַטָּ֑את לְכַפֵּ֖ר עֲלֵיכֶֽם׃ מִלְּבַד֙ עֹלַ֣ת הַחֹ֔דֶשׁ וּמִ֨נְחָתָ֔הּ וְעֹלַ֥ת

ו הַתָּמִ֖יד וּמִנְחָתָ֑הּ וְנִסְכֵּיהֶ֖ם כְּמִשְׁפָּטָ֑ם לְרֵ֣יחַ נִיחֹ֔חַ אִשֶּׁ֖ה לַֽיהוָֽה׃ וּבֶעָשׂ֣וֹר

ז לַחֹ֩דֶשׁ֩ הַשְּׁבִיעִ֨י הַזֶּ֜ה מִֽקְרָא־קֹ֨דֶשׁ֙ יִהְיֶ֣ה לָכֶ֔ם וְעִנִּיתֶ֖ם אֶת־נַפְשֹֽׁתֵיכֶ֑ם כָּל־מְלָאכָ֖ה

ח לֹ֥א תַעֲשֽׂוּ׃ וְהִקְרַבְתֶּ֨ם עֹלָ֤ה לַֽיהוָה֙ רֵ֣יחַ נִיחֹ֔חַ פַּ֧ר בֶּן־בָּקָ֛ר אֶחָ֖ד אַ֥יִל אֶחָ֖ד כְּבָשִׂ֞ים

ט בְּנֵֽי־שָׁנָ֛ה שִׁבְעָ֖ה תְּמִימִ֣ם יִהְי֣וּ לָכֶֽם׃ וּמִ֨נְחָתָ֔ם סֹ֖לֶת בְּלוּלָ֣ה בַשָּׁ֑מֶן שְׁלֹשָׁ֣ה עֶשְׂרֹנִ֗ים

י לַפָּ֔ר שְׁנֵ֥י עֶשְׂרֹנִ֖ים לָאַ֥יִל הָֽאֶחָֽד׃ עִשָּׂרוֹן֙ עִשָּׂר֔וֹן לַכֶּ֨בֶשׂ֙ הָֽאֶחָ֔ד לְשִׁבְעַ֖ת הַכְּבָשִֽׂים׃

יא שְׂעִיר־עִזִּ֥ים אֶחָ֖ד חַטָּ֑את מִלְּבַ֞ד חַטַּ֤את הַכִּפֻּרִים֙ וְעֹלַ֣ת הַתָּמִ֔יד וּמִנְחָתָ֖הּ

יב וְנִסְכֵּיהֶֽם׃ וּבַחֲמִשָּׁה֩ עָשָׂ֨ר י֜וֹם לַחֹ֣דֶשׁ הַשְּׁבִיעִ֗י מִֽקְרָא־קֹ֨דֶשׁ֙

יִהְיֶ֣ה לָכֶ֔ם כָּל־מְלֶ֥אכֶת עֲבֹדָ֖ה לֹ֣א תַעֲשׂ֑וּ וְחַגֹּתֶ֥ם חַ֛ג לַֽיהוָ֖ה שִׁבְעַ֥ת יָמִֽים׃

יג וְהִקְרַבְתֶּ֨ם עֹלָ֜ה אִשֵּׁ֨ה רֵ֤יחַ נִיחֹ֨חַ֙ לַֽיהוָ֔ה פָּרִ֧ים בְּנֵֽי־בָקָ֛ר שְׁלֹשָׁ֥ה עָשָׂ֖ר אֵילִ֣ם

יד שְׁנָ֑יִם כְּבָשִׂ֧ים בְּנֵֽי־שָׁנָ֛ה אַרְבָּעָ֥ה עָשָׂ֖ר תְּמִימִ֣ם יִהְיֽוּ׃ וּמִנְחָתָ֔ם סֹ֖לֶת בְּלוּלָ֣ה

בַשָּׁ֑מֶן שְׁלֹשָׁ֣ה עֶשְׂרֹנִ֗ים לַפָּ֤ר הָֽאֶחָד֙ לִשְׁלֹשָׁ֤ה עָשָׂר֙ פָּרִ֔ים שְׁנֵ֣י עֶשְׂרֹנִ֔ים לָאַ֧יִל

טו הָֽאֶחָ֛ד לִשְׁנֵ֥י הָֽאֵילִֽם׃ וְעִשָּׂר֤וֹן עִשָּׂרוֹן֙ לַכֶּ֣בֶשׂ הָֽאֶחָ֔ד לְאַרְבָּעָ֥ה עָשָׂ֖ר כְּבָשִֽׂים׃

טז וּשְׂעִיר־עִזִּ֥ים אֶחָ֖ד חַטָּ֑את מִלְּבַד֙ עֹלַ֣ת הַתָּמִ֔יד מִנְחָתָ֖הּ וְנִסְכָּֽהּ׃ וּבַיּוֹם֙

פרק כט

ו| מִלְּבַד עֹלַת הַחֹדֶשׁ. מוּסְפֵי לֶחֶם חֹדֶשׁ שֶׁהוּא בְּיוֹם לֶחֶם הַשֶּׁנָה:

יא| מִלְּבַד חַטַּאת הַכִּפֻּרִים. שָׂעִיר הַנַּעֲשֶׂה בִּפְנִים

הָאָמוּר בְּאַחֲרֵי מוֹת (ויקרא טז, ט, טו), שֶׁגַּם הוּא חַטָּאת: וְעֹלַת הַתָּמִיד. וּמִלְּבַד עֹלַת הַתָּמִיד תַּעֲשׂוּ "תַּעֲשׂוּ", וְהוּא לְשׁוֹן צִוּוּי, מִלְּבַד עֹלַת הַתָּמִיד וּמִנְחָתָהּ תַּעֲשׂוּ אֶת אֵלֶּה וְנִסְכֵּיהֶם. וְכֵן כָּל "וְנִסְכֵּיהֶם" הָאֲמוּרִים

כָּל הַמּוֹעֲדוֹת, חוּץ מִשֶּׁל קָרְבְּנוֹת הַחַג, שֶׁכָּל "וְנִסְכָּה", "וְנִסְכֵּיהֶם", "וּנְסָכֶיהָ" שֶׁבָּהֶם מוּסָּבִים עַל הַתָּמִיד וְאֵינָן לְשׁוֹן צִוּוּי, שֶׁהֲרֵי נִסְכֵּיהֶם שֶׁל מוּסָפִין כְּתוּבִין לְעַצְמָן בְּכָל יוֹם וָיוֹם:

unique; despite the same basic composition of the additional offering, there is a change from one day to the next. **On the second day, twelve young bulls,** one less than the previous day, **as well as two rams, fourteen lambs in the first year, unblemished;**

18 **and their meal offering and their libations for the bulls, for the rams, and for the lambs, according to their number, in accordance with the ordinance.** There shall be accompanying meal offerings and libations for each of the animals sacrificed, as per the guidelines set forth above (verses 14–15).

19 **And one goat as a sin offering; besides the continual burnt offering, and its meal offering, and their libations.**

20 **On the third day, eleven bulls, two rams, fourteen lambs in the first year, unblemished;**

21 **and their meal offering and their libations for the bulls, for the rams, and for the lambs, according to their number, in accordance with the ordinance.**

22 **And one goat as a sin offering; besides the continual burnt offering, and its meal offering, and its libation.**

23 **On the fourth day, ten bulls, two rams, fourteen lambs in the first year, unblemished;**

24 **their meal offering and their libations for the bulls, for the rams, and for the lambs, according to their number, in accordance with the ordinance.**

25 **And one goat as a sin offering; besides the continual burnt offering, its meal offering, and its libation.**

26 **On the fifth day, nine bulls, two rams, fourteen lambs in the first year, unblemished;**

27 **and their meal offering and their libations for the bulls, for the rams, and for the lambs, according to their number, in accordance with the ordinance.**

28 **And one goat as a sin offering; besides the continual burnt offering, and its meal offering, and its libation.**

29 **On the sixth day, eight bulls, two rams, fourteen lambs in the first year, unblemished;**

30 **and their meal offering and their libations for the bulls, for the rams, and for the lambs, according to their number, in accordance with the ordinance.**

31 **And one goat as a sin offering; besides the continual burnt offering, and its meal offering, and its libations.**

32 **On the seventh day,** the final day of Sukkot, which the Sages refer to as the Day of the Willow and which is currently known as Hoshana Rabba, **seven bulls, two rams, fourteen lambs in the first year, unblemished;**

33 **and their meal offering and their libations for the bulls, for the rams, and for the lambs, according to their number, in accordance with their ordinance.**

34 **And one goat for a sin offering; besides the regular burnt offering, its meal offering, and its libation.**

35 **On the eighth** [*shemini*] **day it shall be an assembly**[B] [*atzeret*] *Maftir* **for you,** an additional festival day that serves as the summation of all the preceding days; **you shall not perform any toilsome labor.** This day is referred to by the Sages as Shemini Atzeret. The seventh day of Passover is also referred to as an assembly.[23] However, when the Sages use the term *atzeret*, they are referring to Shavuot, which stops [*otzer*] and concludes the spiritual growth that has developed since the beginning of Passover.[24]

36 **You shall present a burnt offering, a fire offering, a pleasing**

—— BACKGROUND ——

29:35 | Assembly: This day concludes the celebration of the thrice-yearly pilgrimage festivals. Passover, which is celebrated in Nisan, the first month, is the first pilgrimage festival of the yearly cycle, and this cycle concludes with a great assembly, Shemini Atzeret, at the end of the seventh month, Tishrei. Since Hanukkah and Purim are not Torah festivals, as they were instituted later, Shemini Atzeret marks the beginning of the ordinary days, when there are no festivals.

—— DISCUSSION ——

29:38 | The offerings of the eighth day of Sukkot: The additional offerings of the eighth day, which are one bull, one ram, seven lambs, and one goat, are identical to the additional offerings of the first and tenth days of the month, Rosh HaShana and Yom Kippur. They are different from the offerings of the pilgrimage festivals, when at least two bulls are offered.

This implies that although Shemini Atzeret concludes the cycle of the pilgrimage festivals, it is somewhat more similar to Rosh HaShana and Yom Kippur. While the other pilgrimage festivals are mentioned in the Torah as joyful times associated with the agricultural cycle (see Exodus 23:15–16), Shemini Atzeret has no such description.

הַשֵּׁנִי פָּרִים בְּנֵי־בָקָר שְׁנֵים עָשָׂר אֵילִם שְׁנָיִם כְּבָשִׂים בְּנֵי־שָׁנָה אַרְבָּעָה עָשָׂר
יח יט תְּמִימִם׃ וּמִנְחָתָם וְנִסְכֵּיהֶם לַפָּרִים לָאֵילִם וְלַכְּבָשִׂים בְּמִסְפָּרָם כַּמִּשְׁפָּט׃ וּשְׂעִיר־
כ עִזִּים אֶחָד חַטָּאת מִלְּבַד עֹלַת הַתָּמִיד וּמִנְחָתָהּ וְנִסְכֵּיהֶם׃ וּבַיּוֹם
הַשְּׁלִישִׁי פָּרִים עַשְׁתֵּי־עָשָׂר אֵילִם שְׁנָיִם כְּבָשִׂים בְּנֵי־שָׁנָה אַרְבָּעָה עָשָׂר תְּמִימִם׃
כא כב וּמִנְחָתָם וְנִסְכֵּיהֶם לַפָּרִים לָאֵילִם וְלַכְּבָשִׂים בְּמִסְפָּרָם כַּמִּשְׁפָּט׃ וּשְׂעִיר חַטָּאת
כג אֶחָד מִלְּבַד עֹלַת הַתָּמִיד וּמִנְחָתָהּ וְנִסְכָּהּ׃ וּבַיּוֹם הָרְבִיעִי פָּרִים עֲשָׂרָה
כד אֵילִם שְׁנָיִם כְּבָשִׂים בְּנֵי־שָׁנָה אַרְבָּעָה עָשָׂר תְּמִימִם׃ מִנְחָתָם וְנִסְכֵּיהֶם לַפָּרִים
כה לָאֵילִם וְלַכְּבָשִׂים בְּמִסְפָּרָם כַּמִּשְׁפָּט׃ וּשְׂעִיר־עִזִּים אֶחָד חַטָּאת מִלְּבַד עֹלַת
כו הַתָּמִיד מִנְחָתָהּ וְנִסְכָּהּ׃ וּבַיּוֹם הַחֲמִישִׁי פָּרִים תִּשְׁעָה אֵילִם שְׁנָיִם
כז כְּבָשִׂים בְּנֵי־שָׁנָה אַרְבָּעָה עָשָׂר תְּמִימִם׃ וּמִנְחָתָם וְנִסְכֵּיהֶם לַפָּרִים לָאֵילִם
כח וְלַכְּבָשִׂים בְּמִסְפָּרָם כַּמִּשְׁפָּט׃ וּשְׂעִיר חַטָּאת אֶחָד מִלְּבַד עֹלַת הַתָּמִיד וּמִנְחָתָהּ
כט וְנִסְכָּהּ׃ וּבַיּוֹם הַשִּׁשִּׁי פָּרִים שְׁמֹנָה אֵילִם שְׁנָיִם כְּבָשִׂים בְּנֵי־שָׁנָה אַרְבָּעָה
ל עָשָׂר תְּמִימִם׃ וּמִנְחָתָם וְנִסְכֵּהֶם לַפָּרִים לָאֵילִם וְלַכְּבָשִׂים בְּמִסְפָּרָם כַּמִּשְׁפָּט׃
לא לב וּשְׂעִיר חַטָּאת אֶחָד מִלְּבַד עֹלַת הַתָּמִיד מִנְחָתָהּ וּנְסָכֶיהָ׃ וּבַיּוֹם
הַשְּׁבִיעִי פָּרִים שִׁבְעָה אֵילִם שְׁנָיִם כְּבָשִׂים בְּנֵי־שָׁנָה אַרְבָּעָה עָשָׂר תְּמִימִם׃
לג לד וּמִנְחָתָם וְנִסְכֵּהֶם לַפָּרִים לָאֵילִם וְלַכְּבָשִׂים בְּמִסְפָּרָם כְּמִשְׁפָּטָם׃ וּשְׂעִיר
לה חַטָּאת אֶחָד מִלְּבַד עֹלַת הַתָּמִיד מִנְחָתָהּ וְנִסְכָּהּ׃ בַּיּוֹם הַשְּׁמִינִי מפטיר
לו עֲצֶרֶת תִּהְיֶה לָכֶם כָּל־מְלֶאכֶת עֲבֹדָה לֹא תַעֲשׂוּ׃ וְהִקְרַבְתֶּם עֹלָה אִשֵּׁה רֵיחַ

רש״י

יח | וּמִנְחָתָם וְנִסְכֵּיהֶם לַפָּרִים. פָּרֵי הֶחָג שִׁבְעִים הֵם, כְּנֶגֶד שִׁבְעִים אֻמּוֹת, שֶׁמִּתְמַעֲטִים וְהוֹלְכִים, סִימַן כְּלָיָה הוּא לָהֶם, וּבִימֵי הַמִּקְדָּשׁ הָיוּ מְגִנִּים עֲלֵיהֶם מִן הַיִּסּוּרִין, וְהַכְּבָשִׂים כְּנֶגֶד יִשְׂרָאֵל שֶׁנִּקְרְאוּ: "שֶׂה פְזוּרָה" (ירמיה נ, יז), וְהֵם קְבוּעִים, וּמִנְיָנָם תִּשְׁעִים וּשְׁמוֹנָה, לְכַלּוֹת מֵהֶם תִּשְׁעִים וּשְׁמוֹנֶה קְלָלוֹת שֶׁבְּמִשְׁנֵה תוֹרָה. בַּשֵּׁנִי נֶאֱמַר: "וְנִסְכֵּיהֶם" (להלן פסוק יט) עַל שְׁנֵי תְמִידֵי הַיּוֹם, וְלֹא שִׁנָּה הַלָּשׁוֹן אֶלָּא לִדְרֹשׁ, כְּמוֹ שֶׁאָמְרוּ רַבּוֹתֵינוּ זִכְרוֹנָם לִבְרָכָה: בַּשֵּׁנִי "וְנִסְכֵּיהֶם", בַּשִּׁשִּׁי "וּנְסָכֶיהָ" (להלן פסוק לא), בַּשְּׁבִיעִי "כְּמִשְׁפָּטָם" (להלן פסוק לג), מֵ"ם יוּ"ד מֵ"ם, הֲרֵי כָּאן 'מַיִם', רֶמֶז לְנִסּוּךְ הַמַּיִם מִן הַתּוֹרָה בֶּחָג:

לה | עֲצֶרֶת תִּהְיֶה לָכֶם. עֲצוּרִים בַּעֲשִׂיַּת מְלָאכָה. דָּבָר אַחֵר, "עֲצֶרֶת", עִצְרוּ מִלָּצֵאת, מְלַמֵּד שֶׁטָּעוּן לִינָה. וּמִדְרָשׁוֹ בָּאַגָּדָה: לְפִי שֶׁכָּל יְמוֹת הָרֶגֶל הִקְרִיבוּ כְּנֶגֶד שִׁבְעִים אֻמּוֹת, וּכְשֶׁבָּאִין לְלֶכֶת, אָמַר לָהֶם הַמָּקוֹם: בְּבַקָּשָׁה מִכֶּם עֲשׂוּ לִי סְעוּדָה קְטַנָּה, כְּדֵי שֶׁאֵהָנֶה מִכֶּם:

aroma to the Lord: One bull, one ram, seven lambs in the first year, unblemished;

37 their meal offering and their libations for the bull, for the ram, and for the lambs, according to their number, in accordance with the ordinance.

38 And one goat as a sin offering; besides the continual burnt offering, and its meal offering, and its libation.[D]

39 In conclusion, **these** communal offerings **you shall offer to the Lord in your appointed times, besides your vows, and your**

pledges, for your burnt offerings, and for your meal offerings, and for your libations, and for your peace offerings. These are the personal offerings brought to the Temple during the festival or on other days.

30 1 Moses said to the children of Israel in accordance with everything that the Lord commanded Moses with regard to the appointed times of the year.[D]

DISCUSSION

30:1 | Chart of the Fixed Communal Offerings

Time of year	Burnt offerings	Sin offerings	Other offerings
Every day	2 lambs		
Sabbath	2 lambs		
New Moon	2 bulls 1 ram 7 lambs	1 goat	
Passover	2 bulls 1 ram 7 lambs	1 goat	
Shavuot	2 bulls 1 ram 7 lambs	1 goat	2 lambs as peace offerings
Rosh HaShana	1 bull 1 ram 7 lambs	1 goat	Additional offerings for the New Moon
Yom Kippur	1 bull 1 ram 7 lambs	1 goat	Offerings of the service of Yom Kippur
Sukkot (day 1)	13 bulls 2 rams 7 lambs	1 goat	

לז נִיחֹחַ לַיהוָה פַּר אֶחָד אַיִל אֶחָד כְּבָשִׂים בְּנֵי־שָׁנָה שִׁבְעָה תְּמִימִם: מִנְחָתָם
לח וְנִסְכֵּיהֶם לַפָּר לָאַיִל וְלַכְּבָשִׂים בְּמִסְפָּרָם כַּמִּשְׁפָּט: וּשְׂעִיר חַטָּאת אֶחָד מִלְּבַד
לט עֹלַת הַתָּמִיד וּמִנְחָתָהּ וְנִסְכָּהּ: אֵלֶּה תַּעֲשׂוּ לַיהוָה בְּמוֹעֲדֵיכֶם לְבַד מִנִּדְרֵיכֶם
א וְנִדְבֹתֵיכֶם לְעֹלֹתֵיכֶם וּלְמִנְחֹתֵיכֶם וּלְנִסְכֵּיכֶם וּלְשַׁלְמֵיכֶם: וַיֹּאמֶר מֹשֶׁה אֶל־בְּנֵי
יִשְׂרָאֵל כְּכֹל אֲשֶׁר־צִוָּה יְהוָה אֶת־מֹשֶׁה:

רש״י

לז) פַּר אֶחָד אַיִל אֶחָד. אֵלּוּ כְּנֶגֶד יִשְׂרָאֵל, הִתְעַכְּבוּ לִי מְעַט עוֹד, וּלְשׁוֹן חִבָּה הוּא זֶה, כְּבָנִים הַנִּפְטָרִים מֵאֲבִיהֶם וְהוּא אוֹמֵר לָהֶם: קָשָׁה עָלַי פְּרֵדַתְכֶם, עַכְּבוּ עוֹד יוֹם אֶחָד. מָשָׁל לְמֶלֶךְ שֶׁעָשָׂה סְעוּדָה וְכוּ׳, כִּדְאִיתָא בְּמַסֶּכֶת סֻכָּה (דף נה ע״ב) [מָשָׁל לְמֶלֶךְ בָּשָׂר וָדָם שֶׁאָמַר לַעֲבָדָיו: עֲשׂוּ לִי סְעוּדָה גְּדוֹלָה. לְיוֹם אַחֲרוֹן אָמַר לְאוֹהֲבוֹ: עֲשֵׂה לִי סְעוּדָה קְטַנָּה, כְּדֵי שֶׁאֵהָנֶה מִמְּךָ]. וּבְמִדְרַשׁ רַבִּי תַּנְחוּמָא (יז) לִמְּדָה תּוֹרָה דֶּרֶךְ אֶרֶץ, שֶׁמִּי שֶׁיֵּשׁ לוֹ אַכְסְנַאי, יוֹם רִאשׁוֹן יַאֲכִילֶנּוּ פְּטוּמוֹת, לְמָחָר יַאֲכִילֶנּוּ דָּגִים, לְמָחָר יַאֲכִילֶנּוּ בְּשַׂר בְּהֵמָה, לְמָחָר מַאֲכִילוֹ קִטְנִיּוֹת, לְמָחָר מַאֲכִילוֹ יָרָק, פּוֹחֵת וְהוֹלֵךְ כְּפָרֵי הֶחָג:

לט) אֵלֶּה תַּעֲשׂוּ לַה׳ בְּמוֹעֲדֵיכֶם. דָּבָר הַקָּצוּב לְחוֹבָה: לְבַד מִנִּדְרֵיכֶם. אִם בָּאתֶם לִדֹּר קָרְבָּנוֹת בָּרֶגֶל, מִצְוָה הִיא בְּיֶדְכֶם, אוֹ נְדָרִים אוֹ נְדָבוֹת שֶׁנְּדַרְתֶּם כָּל הַשָּׁנָה הַקְרִיבוּם בָּרֶגֶל, שֶׁמָּא יִקְשֶׁה לוֹ לַחֲזֹר וְלַעֲלוֹת לִירוּשָׁלַיִם וּלְהַקְרִיב נְדָרָיו, וְנִמְצָא עוֹבֵר בְּבַל תְּאַחֵר:

פרק ל

א) וַיֹּאמֶר מֹשֶׁה אֶל בְּנֵי יִשְׂרָאֵל. לְהַפְסִיק הָעִנְיָן, דִּבְרֵי רַבִּי יִשְׁמָעֵאל. לְפִי שֶׁעַד כָּאן דְּבָרָיו שֶׁל מָקוֹם וּפָרָשַׁת נְדָרִים מַתְחֶלֶת בְּדִבּוּרוֹ שֶׁל מֹשֶׁה, הֻצְרַךְ לְהַפְסִיק תְּחִלָּה וְלוֹמַר שֶׁחָזַר מֹשֶׁה וְאָמַר פָּרָשָׁה זוֹ לְיִשְׂרָאֵל, שֶׁאִם לֹא כֵן יֵשׁ בְּמַשְׁמָע שֶׁלֹּא אָמַר לָהֶם זוֹ, אֶלָּא בְּפָרָשַׁת נְדָרִים הִתְחִיל דְּבָרָיו:

DISCUSSION

Time of year	Burnt offerings	Sin offerings	Other offerings
Sukkot (day 2)	12 bulls 2 rams 7 lambs	1 goat	
Sukkot (day 3)	11 bulls 2 rams 7 lambs	1 goat	
Sukkot (day 4)	10 bulls 2 rams 7 lambs	1 goat	
Sukkot (day 5)	9 bulls 2 rams 7 lambs	1 goat	
Sukkot (day 6)	8 bulls 2 rams 7 lambs	1 goat	
Sukkot (day 7)	7 bulls 2 rams 7 lambs	1 goat	
Shemini Atzeret	1 bull 1 ram 7 lambs	1 goat	

Parashat
Matot

Vows and Oaths of Prohibitions

NUMBERS 30:2–17

Vows in the Torah are often commitments to dedicate something to God, as an offering or a gift to the priesthood. This obligation to keep one's word applies to any individual who takes a vow. Nevertheless, the commandments with regard to vows are addressed specifically to the heads of the tribes, as these statutes have social and familial ramifications beyond their personal significance.

2 **Moses spoke to the heads of the tribes**[D] **of the children of Israel,** who served as a kind of supreme council of the people, **saying: This is the matter that the Lord commanded.**

3 Moses begins with a general, fundamental law: **If a man takes a vow to the Lord, or** if he **takes an oath**[D] **to impose a prohibition upon himself,** by declaring that he will refrain from particular actions or from deriving benefit from certain people or items, **he shall not profane his word** by disregarding his commitment; **he shall act in accordance with everything that emerges from his mouth.**

4 The Torah turns to the social aspects of vows. **If a woman takes a vow to the Lord and imposes a prohibition** when she is unmarried **in her father's house, in her youth,**

5 **and her father hears her vow and her prohibition that she imposed upon herself, and** when he hears about her vow **her father keeps silent toward her,** and does not interfere or object, **all her vows shall be upheld, and every prohibition that she imposed upon herself shall be upheld,** and she is obligated to fulfill them.

6 **But if her father prevented her,** by annulling her vows **on the day of his hearing** the vow, **all her vows and her prohibitions that she imposed upon herself,** both positive and negative

vows, **shall not be upheld,** they do not take effect; **and the Lord will forgive her** for failing to conform to the vow she uttered, **because her father prevented her,** and she did not violate her word of her own accord.

7 **If** a young woman vows when she is single, and **she is** betrothed **to a husband, and her vows are upon her, or the expression of her lips with which she prohibited herself,**

8 **and her husband hears** that she has vowed before their betrothal, **and keeps silent toward her on the day of his hearing** and does not object, **her vows shall be upheld, and her prohibitions that she imposed upon herself shall be upheld.**

9 **But if on the day of her husband's hearing, he prevents her**[D] by expressing his objection, **and nullifies her vow that is upon her or the expression of her lips that she imposed upon herself,** then **the Lord will forgive her,** despite the fact that she did not uphold her vow, as she must act in accordance with her husband's wishes.

10 **But the vow of a widow, or a divorcée,** who is not under anyone's authority, as she left her father's domain when she married, and her husband's authority lapsed upon his death or with the divorce, **anything that she imposed upon herself shall be upheld for her.**

DISCUSSION

30:2 | Moses spoke to the heads of the tribes: The Sages derive from the fact that these laws are addressed to the leaders of the tribes that judges and sages have a special right to intervene in the cases dealt with here (see *Nedarim* 78a).

30:3 | Takes a vow to the Lord, or takes an oath: The term "vow" can refer to a commitment to bring an offering, which is known as a vow of consecration, or to the imposition of a prohibition upon a specific article, which is known as a vow of prohibition. Upon taking a vow of

prohibition, the object becomes fully or partially prohibited, and one no longer has full control over it. An example would be if a person says: This food is forbidden to me like consecrated property. Conversely, an oath is focused on the one who articulates it rather than the object, e.g., if a person says: I am taking an oath that I will, or I will not, eat this food. In the wording of the Sages, a vow is a prohibition that applies to the object, whereas an oath is a prohibition that applies to the person (see *Nedarim* 2b).

30:9 | But if on the day of her husband's hearing, he prevents her: A plain reading of the verses indicates that a man may nullify those vows of his wife that she uttered while she was still single. However, the Sages derived that these verses apply only during the stage of betrothal to vows that she took that day (see *Nedarim* 72a; Rashbam; Ibn Ezra; *Bekhor Shor*). Nevertheless, there may be a difference of opinion in this regard (see *Sifra*).

פרשת
מטות

ב וַיְדַבֵּ֤ר מֹשֶׁה֙ אֶל־רָאשֵׁ֣י הַמַּטּ֔וֹת לִבְנֵ֥י יִשְׂרָאֵ֖ל לֵאמֹ֑ר זֶ֣ה הַדָּבָ֔ר אֲשֶׁ֖ר צִוָּ֥ה יְהוָֽה׃
ג אִישׁ֩ כִּֽי־יִדֹּ֨ר נֶ֜דֶר לַֽיהוָ֗ה אֽוֹ־הִשָּׁ֤בַע שְׁבֻעָה֙ לֶאְסֹ֤ר אִסָּר֙ עַל־נַפְשׁ֔וֹ לֹ֥א יַחֵ֖ל דְּבָר֑וֹ
ד כְּכָל־הַיֹּצֵ֥א מִפִּ֖יו יַעֲשֶֽׂה׃ וְאִשָּׁ֕ה כִּֽי־תִדֹּ֥ר נֶ֖דֶר לַֽיהוָ֑ה וְאָסְרָ֥ה אִסָּ֛ר בְּבֵ֥ית אָבִ֖יהָ
ה בִּנְעֻרֶֽיהָ׃ וְשָׁמַ֨ע אָבִ֜יהָ אֶת־נִדְרָ֗הּ וֶֽאֱסָרָהּ֙ אֲשֶׁ֣ר אָסְרָ֣ה עַל־נַפְשָׁ֔הּ וְהֶחֱרִ֥ישׁ לָ֖הּ
ו אָבִ֑יהָ וְקָ֙מוּ֙ כָּל־נְדָרֶ֔יהָ וְכָל־אִסָּ֛ר אֲשֶׁר־אָסְרָ֥ה עַל־נַפְשָׁ֖הּ יָקֽוּם׃ וְאִם־הֵנִ֨יא
אָבִ֣יהָ אֹתָהּ֮ בְּי֣וֹם שָׁמְעוֹ֒ כָּל־נְדָרֶ֗יהָ וֶֽאֱסָרֶ֛יהָ אֲשֶׁר־אָסְרָ֥ה עַל־נַפְשָׁ֖הּ לֹ֣א יָק֑וּם
ז וַֽיהוָה֙ יִסְלַח־לָ֔הּ כִּֽי־הֵנִ֥יא אָבִ֖יהָ אֹתָֽהּ׃ וְאִם־הָי֤וֹ תִֽהְיֶה֙ לְאִ֔ישׁ וּנְדָרֶ֖יהָ עָלֶ֑יהָ א֚וֹ
ח מִבְטָ֣א שְׂפָתֶ֔יהָ אֲשֶׁ֥ר אָסְרָ֖ה עַל־נַפְשָֽׁהּ׃ וְשָׁמַ֥ע אִישָׁ֛הּ בְּי֥וֹם שָׁמְע֖וֹ וְהֶחֱרִ֣ישׁ לָ֑הּ
ט וְקָ֣מוּ נְדָרֶ֗יהָ וֶֽאֱסָרָ֛הּ אֲשֶׁר־אָסְרָ֥ה עַל־נַפְשָׁ֖הּ יָקֻֽמוּ׃ וְאִ֠ם בְּי֨וֹם שְׁמֹ֣עַ אִישָׁהּ֮ יָנִ֣יא
אוֹתָהּ֒ וְהֵפֵ֗ר אֶת־נִדְרָהּ֙ אֲשֶׁ֣ר עָלֶ֔יהָ וְאֵת֙ מִבְטָ֣א שְׂפָתֶ֔יהָ אֲשֶׁ֥ר אָסְרָ֖ה עַל־נַפְשָׁ֑הּ
י וַֽיהוָ֖ה יִֽסְלַֽח־לָֽהּ׃ וְנֵ֥דֶר אַלְמָנָ֖ה וּגְרוּשָׁ֑ה כֹּ֛ל אֲשֶׁר־אָסְרָ֥ה עַל־נַפְשָׁ֖הּ יָק֥וּם עָלֶֽיהָ׃

רש"י

ב| **ראשי המטות.** חלק כבוד לנשיאים ללמדם תחלה, ואחר כך לכל בני ישראל. ומנין שאף שאר הדברות כן? תלמוד לומר: "וישבו אליו אהרן וכל הנשאים בעדה וידבר משה אליהם, ואחרי כן נגשו כל בני ישראל" (שמות לד, לא-לב). ומה ראה לאמרה כאן? למד שהפרת נדרים ביחיד מומחה, ואם אין יחיד מומחה מפר בשלשה הדיוטות. או יכול שלא אמר משה פרשה זו אלא לנשיאים בלבד? נאמר כאן: "זה הדבר", ונאמר בשחוטי חוץ: "זה הדבר" (ויקרא יז, ב), מה להלן נאמרה לאהרן ולבניו ולכל בני ישראל, שנאמר: "דבר אל אהרן" וגו' (שם), אף זו נאמרה לכלן: **זה הדבר.** משה נתנבא ב"כה אמר ה' כחצת הלילה" (שמות יא, ד) והנביאים נתנבאו ב"כה אמר ה'", מוסף עליהם משה, שנתנבא בלשון "זה הדבר". דבר אחר, "זה הדבר" מעוט הוא, לומר שהחכם בלשון התרה ובעל בלשון הפרה, כלשון הכתוב כאן, ואם אלפו אין מתר ואין מופר:

ג| **נדר.** האומר: הרי עלי קונם שלא אכל או שלא אעשה דבר פלוני. יכול אפלו נשבע שיאכל נבלות אני קורא עליו: "ככל היצא מפיו יעשה"? תלמוד לומר: "לאסר אסר", לאסר את המתר ולא להתיר את האסור: **לא יחל דברו.** כמו: לא יחלל דברו, לא יעשה דבריו חלין:

ד| **בבית אביה.** ברשות אביה, ואפלו אינה בביתו: **בנעריה.** ולא קטנה ולא בוגרת, שהקטנה אין נדרה נדר, והבוגרת אינה ברשותו של אביה להפר נדריה. ואי זו היא קטנה? אמרו רבותינו: בת אחת עשרה שנה ויום אחד נדריה נבדקין, אם ידעה לשם מי נדרה ולשם מי הקדישה, נדרה נדר. בת שתים עשרה שנה ויום אחד אינה צריכה לבדק:

ו| **ואם הניא אביה אתה.** אם מנע אותה מן הנדר, כלומר שהפר לה. הנאה זו איני יודע מה היא, כשהוא אומר: "ואם ביום שמע אישה יניא אותה והפר" (להלן פסוק ט), הוי אומר הנאה זו הפרה. ופשוטו, לשון מניעה והסרה, וכן: "ולמה תניאון" (להלן לב, ז), וכן: "שמן ראש אל יני ראשי" (תהלים קמא, ה), וכן: "וידעתם את תנואתי" (לעיל יד, לד), את אשר סרתם מעלי: **וה' יסלח לה.** במה הכתוב מדבר? באשה שנדרה בנזיר ושמע בעלה והפר לה והיא לא ידעה, ועוברת על נדרה ושותה יין ומטמאה למתים, זו היא שצריכה סליחה ואף על פי שהוא מופר. ואם המופרין צריכין סליחה, קל וחמר לשאינן מופרין:

ז| **ואם היו תהיה לאיש.** זו ארוסה; או אינו אלא נשואה? כשהוא אומר: "ואם בית אישה נדרה" (להלן פסוק יא), הרי נשואה אמור, וכאן בארוסה, ובא לחלק בה, שאביה ובעלה מפירין נדריה. הפר האב ולא הפר הבעל, או הפר הבעל ולא הפר האב, הרי זה אינו מופר, ואין צריך לומר אם קים אחד מהם: **ונדריה עליה.** שנדרה בבית אביה ולא שמע בהן אביה, ולא הופרו ולא הוקמו:

ח| **ושמע אישה וגו'.** הרי לך שאם קים הבעל שהוא קים:

ט| **והפר את נדרה אשר עליה.** יכול אפלו לא הפר האב? תלמוד לומר: "בנעריה בית אביה" (להלן פסוק יז), כל שבנעוריה ברשות אביה היא:

י| **אשר אסרה על נפשה יקום עליה.** לפי שאינה לא ברשות אב ולא ברשות בעל, ובאלמנה מן הנשואין הכתוב מדבר, אבל אלמנה מן הארוסין, מת הבעל, נתרוקנה וחזרה לרשות אב:

11 **If she vowed in her husband's house,** when she was married, **or imposed a prohibition upon herself with an oath,**

12 **and her husband heard and kept silent toward her, he did not prevent her, then all her vows shall be upheld, and every prohibition that she imposed upon herself shall be upheld.**

13 **But if her husband nullifies them on the day of his hearing,** anything that emerges from her lips for her vows or for the prohibitions of herself shall not be upheld: **Her husband has nullified them and the Lord will forgive her.**

14 **Every vow and every oath of prohibition to afflict the soul, her husband shall uphold it, and her husband shall nullify it.** The husband's right to nullify his wife's vows does not apply to all vows, but only to so-called vows of affliction, those vows that cause the woman to suffer or that affect the couple's relationship.[1]

15 **But if her husband keeps silent toward her from day to day, and he** thereby **upholds all her vows, or all her prohibitions that are upon her, he has upheld them,** and the vows can no longer be nullified, **because he kept silent toward her on the day that he heard them.**

16 **But if he nullifies them after his hearing**[D] them, and did not react on the day he heard, **he shall bear her iniquity.** He, not she, is guilty of the sin of her violating the vow if she does so, as she mistakenly thought that he still had the authority to nullify them.[2]

17 In summary, **these are the statutes that the Lord commanded Moses, between a man and his wife, between a father and his daughter, in her youth, in her father's house.**

The War with Midyan

NUMBERS 31:1–54

With the assistance of the Moavites, the Midyanites had caused the children of Israel to sin and thereby brought a terrible plague upon them. The vengeance against Midyan, which God commanded Moses to carry out immediately after those events, is one of his last missions. Earlier in his life, Moses handed down the Torah of God to Israel, the foundation of which is loyalty to God and His commandments. Now, just before he dies, Moses rescues his people from the ploys of the Midyanites and protects them from licentiousness and idolatry.

31 1 **The Lord spoke to Moses, saying:**

Second aliya 2 **Avenge the vengeance of the children of Israel on the Midyanites; and then you shall be gathered to your people** and die.

3 **Moses spoke to the people, saying: Select from among you men for the army, and they shall be against Midyan, to execute the vengeance of the Lord against Midyan.** Since Midyan was not a large nation and consisted mainly of tent-dwellers, Moses asked for only a few fighters from each of the tribes of Israel as volunteers to execute a campaign of retribution against them.

4 **One thousand from each tribe, from all the tribes of Israel, you shall send to the army.**

5 **One thousand per tribe from the thousands of Israel were provided,**[D] **twelve thousand mobilized soldiers.**

6 **Moses sent them, one thousand per tribe, to the army, them**

Silver trumpets

DISCUSSION

30:16 | But if he nullifies them after his hearing: Since a family home cannot be established without coordination and agreement, in certain cases the Torah permits one of the partners to prevent fulfillment of the other's vow. These laws explicitly grant an asymmetrical right to a father over his daughter, and not his son, and to a husband over his wife, and not vice versa. A wife might prevent her husband from fulfilling

his vows, but that is a practical matter, not a legal one.

According to some opinions, the limitation on vows that can be nullified to vows of affliction applies specifically to a husband. In contrast, a father has the right to nullify all vows of his daughter while she is a young woman. Others contend that like a husband, a father may also nullify only those vows that relate to him or

that cause his daughter suffering (see Rambam, *Sefer Hafla'a, Hilkhot Nedarim* 12:1; Ran and Rosh, *Nedarim* 79b; *Bekhor Shor*, verse 6).

Some of the repetitions in the passage are explained by the Sages as referring to a betrothed woman. During this period she is under the authority of her father and the man who is betrothed to her; therefore she requires them both to nullify her vow (*Nedarim* 66b–67a).

יא-יב וְאִם־בֵּית אִישָׁהּ נָדָרָה אוֹ־אָסְרָה אִסָּר עַל־נַפְשָׁהּ בִּשְׁבֻעָה: וְשָׁמַע אִישָׁהּ
וְהֶחֱרִשׁ לָהּ לֹא הֵנִיא אֹתָהּ וְקָמוּ כָּל־נְדָרֶיהָ וְכָל־אִסָּר אֲשֶׁר־אָסְרָה עַל־נַפְשָׁהּ
יג יָקוּם: וְאִם־הָפֵר יָפֵר אֹתָם ׀ אִישָׁהּ בְּיוֹם שָׁמְעוֹ כָּל־מוֹצָא שְׂפָתֶיהָ לִנְדָרֶיהָ
יד וּלְאִסַּר נַפְשָׁהּ לֹא יָקוּם אִישָׁהּ הֲפֵרָם וַיהוָה יִסְלַח־לָהּ: כָּל־נֵדֶר וְכָל־שְׁבֻעַת
טו אִסָּר לְעַנֹּת נָפֶשׁ אִישָׁהּ יְקִימֶנּוּ וְאִישָׁהּ יְפֵרֶנּוּ: וְאִם־הַחֲרֵשׁ יַחֲרִישׁ לָהּ אִישָׁהּ
מִיּוֹם אֶל־יוֹם וְהֵקִים אֶת־כָּל־נְדָרֶיהָ אוֹ אֶת־כָּל־אֱסָרֶיהָ אֲשֶׁר עָלֶיהָ הֵקִים אֹתָם
טז כִּי־הֶחֱרִשׁ לָהּ בְּיוֹם שָׁמְעוֹ: וְאִם־הָפֵר יָפֵר אֹתָם אַחֲרֵי שָׁמְעוֹ וְנָשָׂא אֶת־עֲוֺנָהּ:
יז אֵלֶּה הַחֻקִּים אֲשֶׁר צִוָּה יְהוָה אֶת־מֹשֶׁה בֵּין אִישׁ לְאִשְׁתּוֹ בֵּין־אָב לְבִתּוֹ בִּנְעֻרֶיהָ
בֵּית אָבִיהָ:

א-ב וַיְדַבֵּר יְהוָה אֶל־מֹשֶׁה לֵּאמֹר: נְקֹם נִקְמַת בְּנֵי יִשְׂרָאֵל מֵאֵת הַמִּדְיָנִים אַחַר כז שני
ג תֵּאָסֵף אֶל־עַמֶּיךָ: וַיְדַבֵּר מֹשֶׁה אֶל־הָעָם לֵאמֹר הֵחָלְצוּ מֵאִתְּכֶם אֲנָשִׁים
ד לַצָּבָא וְיִהְיוּ עַל־מִדְיָן לָתֵת נִקְמַת־יְהוָה בְּמִדְיָן: אֶלֶף לַמַּטֶּה אֶלֶף לַמַּטֶּה
ה לְכֹל מַטּוֹת יִשְׂרָאֵל תִּשְׁלְחוּ לַצָּבָא: וַיִּמָּסְרוּ מֵאַלְפֵי יִשְׂרָאֵל אֶלֶף לַמַּטֶּה
ו שְׁנֵים־עָשָׂר אֶלֶף חֲלוּצֵי צָבָא: וַיִּשְׁלַח אֹתָם מֹשֶׁה אֶלֶף לַמַּטֶּה לַצָּבָא אֹתָם

רש״י

יא| וְאִם בֵּית אִישָׁהּ נָדָרָה. בִּנְשׂוּאָה הַכָּתוּב מְדַבֵּר:

יד| כָּל נֵדֶר וְכָל שְׁבֻעַת אִסָּר וְגוֹ׳. לְפִי שֶׁאָמַר שֶׁהַבַּעַל מֵפֵר, יָכוֹל כָּל נְדָרִים בַּמַּשְׁמָע? תַּלְמוּד לוֹמַר: "לְעַנֹּת נָפֶשׁ", אֵינוֹ מֵפֵר אֶלָּא נִדְרֵי עִנּוּי נֶפֶשׁ בִּלְבַד, וְהֵם מְפֹרָשִׁים בְּמַסֶּכֶת נְדָרִים (דף עט ע״א ואילך):

טו| מִיּוֹם אֶל יוֹם. שֶׁלֹּא תֹּאמַר מֵעֵת לְעֵת, לְכָךְ נֶאֱמַר: "מִיּוֹם אֶל יוֹם", לְלַמֶּדְךָ שֶׁאֵין מֵפֵר אֶלָּא עַד שֶׁתֶּחְשַׁךְ:

טז| אַחֲרֵי שָׁמְעוֹ. אַחֲרֵי שֶׁשָּׁמַע וְקִיֵּם, שֶׁאָמַר: אֶפְשִׁי בּוֹ, וְחָזַר וְהֵפֵר לָהּ, אֲפִלּוּ בּוֹ בַּיּוֹם: וְנָשָׂא אֶת עֲוֺנָהּ. הוּא נִכְנָס תַּחְתֶּיהָ. לָמַדְנוּ מִכָּאן שֶׁהַגּוֹרֵם תַּקָּלָה לַחֲבֵרוֹ הוּא נִכְנָס תַּחְתָּיו לְכָל עָנְשִׁין:

פרק לא

ב| מֵאֵת הַמִּדְיָנִים. וְלֹא מֵאֵת הַמּוֹאָבִים, שֶׁהַמּוֹאָבִים נִכְנְסוּ לַדָּבָר מֵחֲמַת יִרְאָה, שֶׁהָיוּ יְרֵאִים מֵהֶם שֶׁיִּהְיוּ שׁוֹלְלִים אוֹתָם, שֶׁלֹּא נֶאֱמַר אֶלָּא "אַל תִּתְגָּר בָּם מִלְחָמָה" (דברים ב, ט), אֲבָל מִדְיָנִים נִתְעַבְּרוּ עַל רִיב לֹא לָהֶם. דָּבָר אַחֵר, מִפְּנֵי שְׁתֵּי פְּרֵידוֹת טוֹבוֹת שֶׁיֵּשׁ לִי לְהוֹצִיא מֵהֶם, רוּת הַמּוֹאֲבִיָּה וְנַעֲמָה הָעַמּוֹנִית:

ג| וַיְדַבֵּר מֹשֶׁה וְגוֹ׳. אַף עַל פִּי שֶׁשָּׁמַע שֶׁמִּיתָתוֹ תְּלוּיָה בַּדָּבָר, עָשָׂה בְּשִׂמְחָה וְלֹא אֵחַר: הֵחָלְצוּ. כְּתַרְגּוּמוֹ, לְשׁוֹן חֲלוּצֵי צָבָא, מְזֻיָּנִים: אֲנָשִׁים. צַדִּיקִים, וְכֵן: "בְּחַר לָנוּ אֲנָשִׁים" (שמות יז, ט), וְכֵן: "אֲנָשִׁים חֲכָמִים וּנְבֹנִים" (דברים א, יג): נִקְמַת ה׳. שֶׁהָעוֹמֵד כְּנֶגֶד יִשְׂרָאֵל כְּאִלּוּ עוֹמֵד כְּנֶגֶד הַקָּדוֹשׁ בָּרוּךְ הוּא:

ד| לְכֹל מַטּוֹת יִשְׂרָאֵל. לְרַבּוֹת שֵׁבֶט לֵוִי:

ה| וַיִּמָּסְרוּ. לְהוֹדִיעֲךָ שִׁבְחָן שֶׁל רוֹעֵי יִשְׂרָאֵל, כַּמָּה הֵם חֲבִיבִים עַל יִשְׂרָאֵל. עַד שֶׁלֹּא שָׁמְעוּ בְּמִיתָתוֹ, מַה הוּא אוֹמֵר? "עוֹד מְעַט וּסְקָלֻנִי" (שמות יז, ד), וּמִשֶּׁשָּׁמְעוּ שֶׁמִּיתַת מֹשֶׁה תְּלוּיָה בְּנִקְמַת מִדְיָן, לֹא רָצוּ לָלֶכֶת עַד שֶׁנִּמְסְרוּ עַל כָּרְחָן:

ו| אֹתָם וְאֶת פִּינְחָס. מַגִּיד שֶׁהָיָה פִּינְחָס שָׁקוּל כְּנֶגֶד כֻּלָּם. וּמִפְּנֵי מָה הָלַךְ פִּינְחָס וְלֹא הָלַךְ אֶלְעָזָר? אָמַר הַקָּדוֹשׁ בָּרוּךְ הוּא: מִי שֶׁהִתְחִיל בַּמִּצְוָה, שֶׁהָרַג כָּזְבִּי בַּת צוּר, יִגְמֹר. דָּבָר אַחֵר, שֶׁהָלַךְ לִנְקֹם נִקְמַת יוֹסֵף אֲבִי אִמּוֹ, שֶׁנֶּאֱמַר: "וְהַמְּדָנִים מָכְרוּ אֹתוֹ" (בראשית לז, לו). וּמִנַּיִן שֶׁהָיְתָה אִמּוֹ שֶׁל פִּינְחָס מִשֶּׁל יוֹסֵף? שֶׁנֶּאֱמַר: "מִבְּנוֹת פּוּטִיאֵל" (שמות ו, כה), מִזֶּרַע יִתְרוֹ שֶׁפִּטֵּם עֲגָלִים לַעֲבוֹדָה זָרָה, וּמִזֶּרַע

DISCUSSION

31:5| **Were provided:** According to the Midrash, the passive form of this verb is indicative of an unwillingness on the part of the warriors. This was because the children of Israel knew that Moses' death would not occur until this mission had been completed; therefore they sought to delay fighting so that their leader would live longer (see Rashi; *Bemidbar Rabba* 22:2).

and Pinhas son of Elazar the priest, to the army, with the holy vessels and the trumpets of alarm in his hand. Pinhas was not a man of war, but the presence of a priest was important for all military campaigns.[3]

7 **They campaigned against Midyan** by surrounding the Midyanite camp, **as the Lord had commanded Moses; and they killed every male.**

8 **They killed the** following **kings of Midyan among those they slayed: Evi, Rekem, Tzur** the father of Kozbi (see 25:15), **Hur, and Reva, the five kings of Midyan; and Bilam son of Beor, they killed with the sword.** They executed Bilam because he advised them to tempt the children of Israel to sin with the daughters of Moav and Midyan (see verse 16).

9 **The children of Israel took the women of Midyan and their** young **children captive; all their animals, all their livestock, and all their wealth, they looted.**

10 **All their cities in their dwellings and all their fortresses they burned with fire.**

11 **They took all the spoils and all the plunder of man and of animal.**

12 **They brought** all these **to Moses and to Elazar the priest and to the congregation of the children of Israel, the** human **captives, the plunder,** animals, **and the** other items taken as **spoils, to the camp, to the plains of Moav, which are along the Jordan at Jericho.**

Third aliya (Second aliya)

13 **Moses, Elazar the priest, and all the princes of the congregation came out toward them, to outside the camp,** to greet the victorious army.

14 **Moses became angry at the commanders of the army,** the highest command, **the officers of the thousands and the officers of the hundreds, who came from the army of the battle.**

15 **Moses said to them: Did you keep all the females alive?**

16 **Behold, they were for the children of Israel, by the word of Bilam,** a stumbling block, that led them **to commit trespass against the Lord in the matter of Peor.** They caused both the licentiousness and the idolatry, **and** due to these women **the plague was among the congregation of the Lord.** Now you are bringing those same women back with you to the camp?

17 **Now, kill every male among the children, and kill every woman who has known a man by lying with a male.** Every adult woman who can be presumed to have had sexual relations with any man, you shall kill.

18 **However, all the** young female **children among the women, who have not known lying with a male, keep alive for yourselves** as captives.

DISCUSSION

Daughters of Midyan or Daughters of Moav?

After discovering that "the children of Israel took the women of Midyan…captive (31:9), Moses was angry at "the commanders of the army, the officers of the thousands and the officers of the hundreds" (31:14), who had just returned from the battle with Midyan. Moses said to them: "Did you keep all the females alive? Behold, they were for the children of Israel, by the word of Bilam, to commit trespass against the Lord in the matter of Peor, and the plague was among the congregation of the Lord" (31:15–16).

Based on previous verses, Moses' reaction is a bit surprising. Above, the Torah relates: "Israel was living in Shitim, and the people began to engage in licentiousness with the daughters of Moav. They invited the people to the offerings of their gods; the people ate and prostrated themselves to their gods. Israel adhered to Baal Peor, and the wrath of the Lord was enflamed against Israel" (25:1–3).

It is clear from these verses that it was the women of Moav who seduced the children of Israel to worship Baal Peor, not the women of Midyan. Why then did Moses command regarding the Midyanite women: "Kill every woman who has known a man by lying with a male" (31:17)?

The Abravanel (25:1) asserts that it was in fact Midyanite women disguised as Moavite women who seduced the children of Israel. That is the reason that Moses was angry, and that is the reason that he commanded: "Kill every woman who has known a man by lying with a male." He cites several proofs supporting this understanding.

First, in explaining the prohibition "An Amonite or a Moavite shall not enter into the assembly of the Lord" (Deuteronomy 23:4), the Torah states: "Because they did not greet you with bread and with water on the way upon your exodus from Egypt, and because he hired against you Bilam son of Beor, from Petor, Aram Naharayim, to curse you" (Deuteronomy 23:5). It does not mention anywhere in the verses that the Moavites seduced the children of Israel to worship Baal Peor, a transgression no less egregious.

Second, consider to whom the prohibition applies: An Amonite but not an Amonitess, a Moavite but not a Moavitess (*Yevamot* 69a). Had it been the daughters of Moav who performed this transgression, marrying the women would have been prohibited more than marrying the men.

Third, it was the Midyanites whom God commanded that the Israelites put to death for their participation in this episode: "Bear enmity to the Midyanites, and smite them, because they are enemies to you, with their deceits that they deceived you in the matter of Peor" (25:17–18). In addition, it was specifically with regard to the daughters of Midyan that Moses stated: "They were for the children of Israel, by the word of Bilam, to commit trespass against the Lord in the matter of Peor" (31:16).

ואת־פינחס בן־אלעזר הכהן לצבא וכלי הקדש וחצצרות התרועה בידו:
ז ח ויצבאו על־מדין כאשר צוה יהוה את־משה ויהרגו כל־זכר: ואת־מלכי
מדין הרגו על־חלליהם את־אוי ואת־רקם ואת־צור ואת־חור ואת־רבע
ט חמשת מלכי מדין ואת בלעם בן־בעור הרגו בחרב: וישבו בני־ישראל את־
נשי מדין ואת־טפם ואת כל־בהמתם ואת־כל־מקנהם ואת־כל־חילם בזזו:
י יא ואת כל־עריהם במושבתם ואת כל־טירתם שרפו באש: ויקחו את־כל־השלל
יב ואת כל־המלקוח באדם ובבהמה: ויבאו אל־משה ואל־אלעזר הכהן ואל־
עדת בני־ישראל את־השבי ואת־המלקוח ואת־השלל אל־המחנה אל־ערבת
יג מואב אשר על־ירדן ירחו: ויצאו משה ואלעזר הכהן וכל־ שלישי /שני/
יד נשיאי העדה לקראתם אל־מחוץ למחנה: ויקצף משה על פקודי החיל שרי
טו האלפים ושרי המאות הבאים מצבא המלחמה: ויאמר אליהם משה החייתם
טז כל־נקבה: הן הנה היו לבני ישראל בדבר בלעם למסר־מעל ביהוה על־דבר
יז פעור ותהי המגפה בעדת יהוה: ועתה הרגו כל־זכר בטף וכל־אשה ידעת
יח איש למשכב זכר הרגו: וכל הטף בנשים אשר לא־ידעו משכב זכר החיו לכם:

רש"י

יוסף שפטפט בידו. דבר אחר, שהיה משוח מלחמה: וכלי הקדש. זה הארון והציץ, שהיה בלעם עמהם ומפריח מלכי מדין בכשפים, והוא עצמו פורח עמהם; הראה להם את הציץ שהשם חקוק בו, והם נופלים, לכך נאמר: "על חלליהם" (להלן פסוק ח) במלכי מדין, שנופלים על החללים מן האויר. וכן בבלעם כתיב: "אל חלליהם" בספר יהושע (יג, כב): בידו. ברשותו, וכן: "ויקח את כל ארצו מידו" (במדבר כא, כו):

ח| חמשת מלכי מדין. וכי איני רואה שחמשה מנה הכתוב? למה הזקק לומר 'חמשת'? אלא ללמדך ששוו כלם בעצה והשוו כלם בפרענות. בלעם הלך שם לטול שכר עשרים וארבעה אלף שהפיל מישראל בעצתו, ויצא ממדין לקראת ישראל ומשיאן עצה רעה, אמר להם: אם כשהייתם ששים רבוא לא יכלתם להם, עתה בשנים עשר אלף אתם באים להלחם? נתנו לו שכרו משלם ולא קפחוהו: בחרב. הוא בא על ישראל והחליף אמנותו באמנותם, שאין נושעים אלא בפיהם על ידי תפלה ובקשה, ובא הוא ותפש אמנותם לקללם בפיו, אף הם באו עליו והחליפו אמנותם באמנות האמות שבאין בחרב, שנאמר: "ועל חרבך תחיה" (בראשית כז, מ):

י| טירתם. מקום פלטרין שלהם, שהוא לשון מושב כמרים יודעי חקיהם. דבר אחר, לשון מושב שריהם, כמו שמתרגם "סרני פלשתים" (יהושע יג, ג) – "טורני פלשתאי":

יא| ויקחו את כל השלל וגו'. מגיד שהיו כשרים וצדיקים, ולא נחשדו על הגזל לשלח יד בבזה שלא ברשות, שנאמר: "את כל השלל" וגו', ועליהם מפרש בקבלה: "שניך כעדר הרחלים" וגו' (שיר השירים ו, ו), אף אנשי המלחמה שבך כלם צדיקים: שלל. הן מטלטלין של מלבוש ותכשיטין: "בז" הוא בזת מטלטלין שאינם תכשיטין: מלקוח. אדם ובהמה. ובמקום שכתוב 'שבי' אצל 'מלקוח', 'שבי' באדם ו'מלקוח' בבהמה:

יג| ויצאו משה ואלעזר הכהן. לפי שראו את נערי ישראל יוצאים לחטף מן הבזה:

יד| ויקצף משה על פקודי החיל. ממנים על החיל, ללמדך שכל סרחון הדור תלוי בגדולים, שיש כח בידם למחות:

טז| הן הנה. מגיד שהיו מכירים אותן, זו היא שנכשל פלוני בה: בדבר בלעם. אמר להם: אפלו אתם מכניסים כל המונות שבעולם אין אתם יכולים להם, שמא מרבים אתם מן המצרים שהיו שש מאות רכב בחור (שמות יד, ז)? בואו ואשיאכם עצה: אלהיהם של אלו שונא זמה הוא וכו', כדאיתא ב'חלק' (סנהדרין קו ע"א) ובספרי (קנז):

יז| וכל אשה ידעת איש. ראויה להבעל, אף על פי שלא נבעלה, ולפני הציץ העבירום, והראויה להבעל פניה מוריקות: הרגו. למה חזר ואמר? להפסיק הענין, דברי רבי ישמעאל, שאם אני קורא: "הרגו כל זכר בטף וכל אשה ידעת איש... וכל הטף בנשים" וגו', איני יודע אם להרג עם הזכרים או להחיות עם הטף, לכך נאמר: "הרגו":

19 And you, encamp outside the camp seven days; anyone of you who went to war and **who killed a person and anyone of** you **who touched a dead body,** you shall purify yourselves from the ritual impurity of the dead, with the waters of purification of the red heifer, **on the third day and on the seventh day, you and your** human **captives** who have joined the nation of Israel.[4]

20 **Every garment, every vessel of hide, anything fabricated from goats, and every wooden vessel** that came into contact with the dead, **you shall purify** them as well.

21 **Elazar the priest said to the men of the army**[D] who came to, returned from, **the battle:**[5] **This is the statute of the law that the Lord has commanded Moses:**

22 **Even the gold** items, **the silver** ones, **the bronze, the iron, the tin, and the lead** ones,

23 **everything** from among these metals **that may come through the fire** during its normal usage, **you shall pass through the fire, and it shall** thereby **be purified** and permitted for use by the children of Israel. Vessels for food require this procedure because they were previously used by gentiles. **However,** in addition, **it shall be purified** from any possible contact with the dead[6] **with the water of sprinkling,** the waters containing the ashes of the red heifer (see 19:9); **and everything that may not come through the fire,** those vessels which are not used with fire, such as wooden or leather utensils, **you shall pass through the water.**

24 **You shall wash your garments on the seventh day, and you** too **shall be purified,** since you killed people, **and** only **then you shall come to the camp.**

Fourth aliya 25 The Lord spoke to Moses, saying:

26 Take a census of the plunder of the captives, of human and of animal, you, Elazar the priest, and the heads of the fathers of the congregation.

27 **You shall divide the plunder in half, between those who took part in the war, who went out with the army, and the entire congregation.** The plunder is not the private property of the soldiers. Half of the spoils of the battle should be transferred to the rest of the congregation, whom the fighters represented, while the other half shall be given as a special reward to the warriors.

28 Furthermore, **you shall separate a levy to the Lord from the men of war that go out with the army,** by the ratio of **one being from five hundred, from the persons, from the cattle, from the donkeys, and from the flocks.**

29 **From their half,** the half received by the soldiers, **you shall take** one from five hundred **and give it to Elazar the priest** as **a gift for the Lord.**

30 **From the half of the children of Israel, you shall take one** part **drawn from fifty,** two percent, **from the persons, from the cattle, from the donkeys, from the flocks, from all the animals, and you shall give them to the Levites, keepers of the commission of the Tabernacle of the Lord.** The soldiers shall give to Elazar the priest one part of five hundred, whereas the civilians shall give ten times as much to the Levites, two percent of their portion.

DISCUSSION

31:21 | Elazar the priest said to the men of the army: Although God gave this commandment to Moses, it was Elazar the priest who conveyed the instruction to the children of Israel. It is possible that Moses did not want to talk to the Israelites due to his anger at them. He therefore asked Elazar to inform the warriors of the commands in his name in a calm and organized manner (see Rashi; *Vayikra Rabba* 13:1).

912

יט וְאַתֶּם חֲנוּ מִחוּץ לַמַּחֲנֶה שִׁבְעַת יָמִים כֹּל הֹרֵג נֶפֶשׁ וְכֹל ׀ נֹגֵעַ בֶּחָלָל תִּתְחַטְּאוּ

כ בַּיּוֹם הַשְּׁלִישִׁי וּבַיּוֹם הַשְּׁבִיעִי אַתֶּם וּשְׁבִיכֶם וְכָל־בֶּגֶד וְכָל־כְּלִי־עוֹר וְכָל־

כא מַעֲשֵׂה עִזִּים וְכָל־כְּלִי־עֵץ תִּתְחַטָּאוּ: וַיֹּאמֶר אֶלְעָזָר הַכֹּהֵן אֶל־

אַנְשֵׁי הַצָּבָא הַבָּאִים לַמִּלְחָמָה זֹאת חֻקַּת הַתּוֹרָה אֲשֶׁר־צִוָּה יהוה אֶת־

כב מֹשֶׁה: אַךְ אֶת־הַזָּהָב וְאֶת־הַכָּסֶף אֶת־הַנְּחֹשֶׁת אֶת־הַבַּרְזֶל אֶת־הַבְּדִיל וְאֶת־

כג הָעֹפָרֶת: כָּל־דָּבָר אֲשֶׁר־יָבֹא בָאֵשׁ תַּעֲבִירוּ בָאֵשׁ וְטָהֵר אַךְ בְּמֵי נִדָּה יִתְחַטָּא

כד וְכֹל אֲשֶׁר לֹא־יָבֹא בָּאֵשׁ תַּעֲבִירוּ בַמָּיִם: וְכִבַּסְתֶּם בִּגְדֵיכֶם בַּיּוֹם הַשְּׁבִיעִי

כה וּטְהַרְתֶּם וְאַחַר תָּבֹאוּ אֶל־הַמַּחֲנֶה: וַיֹּאמֶר יהוה אֶל־מֹשֶׁה כח רביעי

כו לֵּאמֹר: שָׂא אֵת רֹאשׁ מַלְקוֹחַ הַשְּׁבִי בָּאָדָם וּבַבְּהֵמָה אַתָּה וְאֶלְעָזָר הַכֹּהֵן

כז וְרָאשֵׁי אֲבוֹת הָעֵדָה: וְחָצִיתָ אֶת־הַמַּלְקוֹחַ בֵּין תֹּפְשֵׂי הַמִּלְחָמָה הַיֹּצְאִים

כח לַצָּבָא וּבֵין כָּל־הָעֵדָה: וַהֲרֵמֹתָ מֶכֶס לַיהוה מֵאֵת אַנְשֵׁי הַמִּלְחָמָה הַיֹּצְאִים

לַצָּבָא אֶחָד נֶפֶשׁ מֵחֲמֵשׁ הַמֵּאוֹת מִן־הָאָדָם וּמִן־הַבָּקָר וּמִן־הַחֲמֹרִים וּמִן־

כט הַצֹּאן: מִמַּחֲצִיתָם תִּקָּחוּ וְנָתַתָּה לְאֶלְעָזָר הַכֹּהֵן תְּרוּמַת יהוה: וּמִמַּחֲצִת

ל בְּנֵי־יִשְׂרָאֵל תִּקַּח ׀ אֶחָד ׀ אָחֻז מִן־הַחֲמִשִּׁים מִן־הָאָדָם מִן־הַבָּקָר מִן־הַחֲמֹרִים

וּמִן־הַצֹּאן מִכָּל־הַבְּהֵמָה וְנָתַתָּה אֹתָם לַלְוִיִּם שֹׁמְרֵי מִשְׁמֶרֶת מִשְׁכַּן יהוה:

רש"י

יט מחוץ למחנה. שֶׁלֹּא יִכָּנְסוּ לָעֲזָרָה. **כֹל הֹרֵג נֶפֶשׁ.** רַבִּי מֵאִיר אוֹמֵר: בְּהוֹרֵג בְּדָבָר הַמְקַבֵּל טֻמְאָה הַכָּתוּב מְדַבֵּר, וּלְמֶדְךָ הַכָּתוּב, שֶׁהַכְּלִי מְטַמֵּא אָדָם בְּחִבּוּרֵי הַמֵּת, כְּאִלּוּ נוֹגֵעַ בַּמֵּת עַצְמוֹ. אוֹ אֵינוֹ זָכִךְ בּוֹ חֵן וַהֲרָגוֹ? תַּלְמוּד לוֹמַר: "וְכֹל נֹגֵעַ בֶּחָלָל", הִקִּישׁ הוֹרֵג לְנוֹגֵעַ, מַה נּוֹגֵעַ עַל יְדֵי חִבּוּרוֹ, אַף הוֹרֵג עַל יְדֵי חִבּוּרוֹ. **תִּתְחַטָּאוּ.** בְּמֵי נִדָּה, כְּדִין שְׁאָר טְמֵאֵי מֵתִים, שֶׁאַף לְדִבְרֵי הָאוֹמֵר קִבְרֵי גוֹיִם אֵינָם מְטַמְּאִין בְּאֹהֶל, שֶׁנֶּאֱמַר: "וְאַתֵּן צֹאנִי צֹאן מַרְעִיתִי אָדָם אַתֶּם" (יחזקאל לד, לא), מוֹדֶה הוּא שֶׁהַגּוֹיִם מְטַמְּאִין בְּמַגָּע וּבְמַשָּׂא, שֶׁלֹּא נֶאֱמַר 'אָדָם' אֶלָּא אֵצֶל טֻמְאַת אֹהָלוֹת, שֶׁנֶּאֱמַר: "אָדָם כִּי יָמוּת בְּאֹהֶל" (לעיל יט, יד). **אַתֶּם וּשְׁבִיכֶם.** לֹא שֶׁהַגּוֹיִם מְקַבְּלִין טֻמְאָה וּצְרִיכִין הַזָּאָה, אֶלָּא מַה אַתֶּם בְּנֵי בְרִית, אַף שְׁבִיכֶם כְּשֶׁיָּבוֹאוּ לַבְּרִית וְיִטַּמְּאוּ צְרִיכִין הַזָּאָה:

כו וְכָל מַעֲשֵׂה עִזִּים. לְהָבִיא כְּלֵי הַקַּרְנַיִם וְהַטְּלָפַיִם וְהָעֲצָמוֹת:

כא וַיֹּאמֶר אֶלְעָזָר הַכֹּהֵן וְגו'. לְפִי שֶׁבָּא מֹשֶׁה לִכְלַל כַּעַס בָּא לִכְלַל טָעוּת, שֶׁנִּתְעַלְּמוּ מִמֶּנּוּ הִלְכוֹת גְּעוּלֵי גוֹיִם. וְכֵן אַתָּה מוֹצֵא בַּשְּׁמִינִי לַמִּלּוּאִים, שֶׁנֶּאֱמַר: "וַיִּקְצֹף עַל אֶלְעָזָר וְעַל אִיתָמָר" (ויקרא י, טז), בָּא לִכְלַל כַּעַס, בָּא לִכְלַל טָעוּת. וְכֵן בְּ"שִׁמְעוּ נָא הַמֹּרִים" - "וַיַּךְ אֶת הַסֶּלַע" (לעיל כ, יא), עַל יְדֵי הַכַּעַס טָעָה. **אֲשֶׁר צִוָּה ה' וְגו'.** תָּלָה הַהוֹרָאָה בְּרַבּוֹ:

כב אַךְ אֶת הַזָּהָב וְגו'. אַף עַל פִּי שֶׁלֹּא הִזְהִיר לָכֶם מֹשֶׁה אֶלָּא עַל הִלְכוֹת טֻמְאָה, עוֹד יֵשׁ לְהַזְהִיר לָכֶם עַל הִלְכוֹת גְּעוּל. וְאַ"ךְ לְשׁוֹן מִעוּט, כְּלוֹמַר מִמְעֲטִין אַתֶּם מִלְּהִשְׁתַּמֵּשׁ בַּכֵּלִים, אֲפִלּוּ לְאַחַר טָהֳרָתָן מִטֻּמְאַת הַמֵּת, עַד שֶׁיְּטַהֲרוּ מִבְּלִיעַת אִסּוּר נְבֵלוֹת. וְרַבּוֹתֵינוּ אָמְרוּ: "אַךְ אֶת הַזָּהָב", לוֹמַר, שֶׁצָּרִיךְ לְהַעֲבִיר חֲלֻדָּה שֶׁלּוֹ קֹדֶם שֶׁיַּגְעִילֶנּוּ, וְזֶהוּ לְשׁוֹן 'אַךְ', שֶׁלֹּא יְהֵא שָׁם חֲלֻדָּה, אַךְ הַמַּתֶּכֶת יִהְיֶה כְּמוֹת שֶׁהוּא:

כג כָּל דָּבָר אֲשֶׁר יָבֹא בָאֵשׁ. לְבַשֵּׁל בּוֹ כְּלוּם: **תַּעֲבִירוּ בָאֵשׁ.** כְּדֶרֶךְ תַּשְׁמִישׁוֹ הַגְעָלָתוֹ, מַה שֶּׁתַּשְׁמִישׁוֹ עַל יְדֵי חַמִּין יַגְעִילֶנּוּ בְּחַמִּין, וּמַה שֶּׁתַּשְׁמִישׁוֹ עַל יְדֵי צְלִי, כְּגוֹן הַשַּׁפּוּד וְהָאַסְכְּלָה, יְלַבְּנֶנּוּ בָּאוּר: **אַךְ בְּמֵי נִדָּה יִתְחַטָּא.** לְפִי פְשׁוּטוֹ, חִטּוּי זֶה לְטַהֲרוֹ מִטֻּמְאַת מֵת, אָמַר לָהֶם: צְרִיכִין הַכֵּלִים גְּעוּל לְטַהֲרָם מִן הָאִסּוּר וְחִטּוּי לְטַהֲרָן מִן הַטֻּמְאָה. וְרַבּוֹתֵינוּ דָּרְשׁוּ מִכָּאן שֶׁאַף לְהַכְשִׁירָן מִן הָאִסּוּר הִטְעִין טְבִילָה לִכְלֵי מַתָּכוֹת, וּ"מֵי נִדָּה" הַכְּתוּבִין כָּאן דָּרְשׁוּ: מַיִם הָרְאוּיִין לִטְבֹּל בָּהֶם נִדָּה, וְכַמָּה הֵם? אַרְבָּעִים סְאָה:

כד אֶל הַמַּחֲנֶה. לְמַחֲנֵה שְׁכִינָה, שֶׁאֵין טְמֵא מֵת טָעוּן שִׁלּוּחַ מִמַּחֲנֵה לֵוִיָּה וּמִמַּחֲנֵה יִשְׂרָאֵל:

כו שָׂא אֵת רֹאשׁ. קַח אֶת חֶשְׁבּוֹן:

כז וְחָצִיתָ אֶת הַמַּלְקוֹחַ בֵּין תֹּפְשֵׂי הַמִּלְחָמָה וְגו'. חֶצְיוֹ לָאֵלּוּ וְחֶצְיוֹ לָאֵלּוּ:

31 Moses and Elazar the priest did as the Lord had commanded Moses.

32 **The plunder, the rest of the loot,** the objects that were neither people nor animals, **that the men of the army looted** for themselves, as those were not brought before Moses for the separation of the tax, **was flocks, six hundred and seventy-five thousand,** as many Midyanites were shepherds;

33 and cattle, seventy-two thousand;

34 and donkeys, sixty-one thousand;

35 and human beings, from the women who had not known lying with a male, thirty-two thousand.

36 The half, the portion of those who went out in the army, the number of the flock was three hundred thirty-seven thousand five hundred.

37 The levy to the Lord from the sheep was six hundred and seventy-five.

38 And the cattle, thirty-six thousand, and their levy to the Lord, seventy-two.

39 And the donkeys, thirty thousand five hundred, and their levy to the Lord, sixty-one.

40 And human beings, sixteen thousand, and their levy to the Lord, thirty-two people.

41 Moses gave the levy, the gift to the Lord, to Elazar the priest, as the Lord had commanded Moses.

42 **And from the half of** the plunder distributed to **the children**
Fifth **of Israel,** that Moses had **divided,** taken, **from the men who**
aliya **campaigned,** and gave to the Israelites,

43 the half of the congregation, which was transferred to them, from the flock was three hundred thirty-seven thousand five hundred;

44 and cattle, thirty-six thousand;

45 and donkeys, thirty thousand five hundred;

46 and human beings, sixteen thousand.

47 Moses took from the half of the children of Israel the one drawn from fifty, from the humans and from the animals, and he gave them to the Levites, keepers of the commission of the Tabernacle of the Lord, as the Lord had commanded Moses.

48 Those appointed over the thousands of the army,[7] the officers of thousands and the officers of hundreds, the higher echelon of command, approached Moses, by themselves.

Bangle

Egyptian women with bangles on their arms. Fresco, Thebes, Egypt, fourteenth century BCE

49 **They said to Moses: Your servants took a census of the men of war in our charge,** and it was discovered that **not one man is missing from us,** and no one was killed. This is a very rare occurrence, even when the enemy is caught unawares, and even for armies far better trained and organized than the Israelites.

50 Therefore, **we have brought the offering of the Lord: Any man** among us **who found a gold ornament** in the Midyanite camp, **a bangle**[B] **or a bracelet, a ring, an earring, or a girdle,**[B] **to atone for our souls before the Lord.** As a thanks offering to God for the miraculous deliverance of all the soldiers, we have brought an atonement for our souls.[8]

BACKGROUND

31:50 | **Bangle [etzada]:** According to the description in II Samuel 1:10, this ornament was placed on the arm, and may have been a symbol of royalty. It has similar letters to the word *adi*, an ornament, although some maintain that the root *tzadi-ayin-dalet* indicates that it was placed on the leg, as *tza'ad* means a step.

Girdle [kumaz]: The Sages state that this was a mold in the shape of the womb (*Shabbat* 64a), which was used to cover the genitals. There is evidence of an ornament of this kind from Ugarit, Syria, from the fourteenth century BCE. Some maintain that this was a string of tiny balls, as *kumzat* in Arabic means a small ball.

לא וַיַּעַשׂ מֹשֶׁה וְאֶלְעָזָר הַכֹּהֵן כַּאֲשֶׁר צִוָּה יְהוָה אֶת־מֹשֶׁה: וַיְהִי הַמַּלְקוֹחַ יֶתֶר הַבָּז
לב אֲשֶׁר בָּזְזוּ עַם הַצָּבָא צֹאן שֵׁשׁ־מֵאוֹת אֶלֶף וְשִׁבְעִים אֶלֶף וַחֲמֵשֶׁת אֲלָפִים: וּבָקָר
לג שְׁנַיִם וְשִׁבְעִים אָלֶף: וַחֲמֹרִים אֶחָד וְשִׁשִּׁים אָלֶף: וְנֶפֶשׁ אָדָם מִן־הַנָּשִׁים אֲשֶׁר
לד לֹא־יָדְעוּ מִשְׁכַּב זָכָר כָּל־נֶפֶשׁ שְׁנַיִם וּשְׁלֹשִׁים אָלֶף: וַתְּהִי הַמֶּחֱצָה חֵלֶק הַיֹּצְאִים
לה בַּצָּבָא מִסְפַּר הַצֹּאן שְׁלֹשׁ־מֵאוֹת אֶלֶף וּשְׁלֹשִׁים אֶלֶף וְשִׁבְעַת אֲלָפִים וַחֲמֵשׁ
לו מֵאוֹת: וַיְהִי הַמֶּכֶס לַיהוָה מִן־הַצֹּאן שֵׁשׁ מֵאוֹת חָמֵשׁ וְשִׁבְעִים: וְהַבָּקָר שִׁשָּׁה
לז וּשְׁלֹשִׁים אָלֶף וּמִכְסָם לַיהוָה שְׁנַיִם וְשִׁבְעִים: וַחֲמֹרִים שְׁלֹשִׁים אֶלֶף וַחֲמֵשׁ מֵאוֹת
לח וּמִכְסָם לַיהוָה אֶחָד וְשִׁשִּׁים: וְנֶפֶשׁ אָדָם שִׁשָּׁה עָשָׂר אָלֶף וּמִכְסָם לַיהוָה שְׁנַיִם
לט וּשְׁלֹשִׁים נָפֶשׁ: וַיִּתֵּן מֹשֶׁה אֶת־מֶכֶס תְּרוּמַת יְהוָה לְאֶלְעָזָר הַכֹּהֵן כַּאֲשֶׁר צִוָּה
מ יְהוָה אֶת־מֹשֶׁה: וּמִמַּחֲצִית בְּנֵי יִשְׂרָאֵל אֲשֶׁר חָצָה מֹשֶׁה מִן־הָאֲנָשִׁים הַצֹּבְאִים:
מא חֲמִישִׁי
מב וַתְּהִי מֶחֱצַת הָעֵדָה מִן־הַצֹּאן שְׁלֹשׁ־מֵאוֹת אֶלֶף וּשְׁלֹשִׁים אֶלֶף שִׁבְעַת אֲלָפִים
מג וַחֲמֵשׁ מֵאוֹת: וּבָקָר שִׁשָּׁה וּשְׁלֹשִׁים אָלֶף: וַחֲמֹרִים שְׁלֹשִׁים אֶלֶף וַחֲמֵשׁ מֵאוֹת:
מד וְנֶפֶשׁ אָדָם שִׁשָּׁה עָשָׂר אָלֶף: וַיִּקַּח מֹשֶׁה מִמַּחֲצִת בְּנֵי־יִשְׂרָאֵל אֶת־הָאָחֻז אֶחָד
מה מִן־הַחֲמִשִּׁים מִן־הָאָדָם וּמִן־הַבְּהֵמָה וַיִּתֵּן אֹתָם לַלְוִיִּם שֹׁמְרֵי מִשְׁמֶרֶת מִשְׁכַּן
מו יְהוָה כַּאֲשֶׁר צִוָּה יְהוָה אֶת־מֹשֶׁה: וַיִּקְרְבוּ אֶל־מֹשֶׁה הַפְּקֻדִים אֲשֶׁר לְאַלְפֵי הַצָּבָא
מז שָׂרֵי הָאֲלָפִים וְשָׂרֵי הַמֵּאוֹת: וַיֹּאמְרוּ אֶל־מֹשֶׁה עֲבָדֶיךָ נָשְׂאוּ אֶת־רֹאשׁ אַנְשֵׁי
מח הַמִּלְחָמָה אֲשֶׁר בְּיָדֵנוּ וְלֹא־נִפְקַד מִמֶּנּוּ אִישׁ: וַנַּקְרֵב אֶת־קָרְבַּן יְהוָה אִישׁ אֲשֶׁר
נ מָצָא כְלִי־זָהָב אֶצְעָדָה וְצָמִיד טַבַּעַת עָגִיל וְכוּמָז לְכַפֵּר עַל־נַפְשֹׁתֵינוּ לִפְנֵי יְהוָה:

רש״י

לב) וַיְהִי הַמַּלְקוֹחַ יֶתֶר הַבָּז. לְפִי שֶׁלֹּא נִצְטַוּוּ לְהַפְרִישׁ
מֶכֶס מִן הַמִּטַּלְטְלִין אֶלָּא מִן הַמַּלְקוֹחַ, כְּתַב אֵת הַלָּשׁוֹן
הַזֶּה: "וַיְהִי הַמַּלְקוֹחַ" שֶׁבָּא לִכְלַל חֲלֻקָּה וּלְכְלַל מֶכֶס,
שֶׁהָיָה עוֹדֵף עַל בַּז הַמִּטַּלְטְלִין "אֲשֶׁר בָּזְזוּ עַם הַצָּבָא"
חוּץ לוֹ וְלֹא בָא לִכְלַל חֲלֻקָּה, מִסְפַּר הַצֹּאן וְגוֹ':

מב) וּמִמַּחֲצִית בְּנֵי יִשְׂרָאֵל אֲשֶׁר חָצָה מֹשֶׁה. לָעֵדָה,
וְהוֹצִיאָהּ לָהֶם "מִן הָאֲנָשִׁים הַצֹּבְאִים":

מג-מו) וַתְּהִי מֶחֱצַת הָעֵדָה. כָּךְ וְכָךְ, "וַיִּקַּח מֹשֶׁה"
וְגוֹ':

מח) הַפְּקֻדִים. הַמְמֻנִּים:

מט) וְלֹא נִפְקָד. לֹא נֶחְסַר. וְתַרְגּוּמוֹ: "וְלָא שְׁגָא", אַף הוּא
בִּלְשׁוֹן חִסָּרוֹן חֲסֵרוֹן, כְּמוֹ: "אֲנֹכִי אֲחַטֶּנָּה" (בראשית לא, לט),
תַּרְגּוּמוֹ: "דַּהֲוַת שַׁגְיָא מִמִּנְיָנָא", וְכֵן: "כִּי יִפָּקֵד מוֹשָׁבֶךָ"
(שמואל א' כ, יח), יֶחְסַר מְקוֹם מוֹשָׁבֶךָ, אִישׁ הָרָגִיל לֵישֵׁב
שָׁם. וְכֵן: "וַיִּפָּקֵד מְקוֹם דָּוִד" (שם פסוק כה), נֶחְסַר מְקוֹמוֹ
וְאֵין אִישׁ יוֹשֵׁב שָׁם:

נ) אֶצְעָדָה. אֵלּוּ צְמִידִים שֶׁל רֶגֶל. וְצָמִיד. שֶׁל יָד
עָגִיל. נִזְמֵי אֹזֶן. וְכוּמָז. דְּפוּס שֶׁל בֵּית הָרֶחֶם, לְכַפֵּר עַל
הִרְהוּר הַלֵּב שֶׁל בְּנוֹת מִדְיָן:

915

51 **Moses and Elazar the priest took the gold from them, all wrought vessels.**

52 **All the gold of the gift that they donated to the Lord was sixteen thousand seven hundred and fifty shekels, from the officers of the thousands, and from the officers of the hundreds.**

53 However, **each of** the rest of **the men of the army looted for himself.** Every soldier took what he wanted, without providing an account of those items.

54 **Moses and Elazar the priest took the gold of the officers of the thousands and of the hundreds and brought it to the Tent of Meeting, a remembrance for the children of Israel before the Lord.** Presumably, the gold was later used when needed.

The Inheritance of the Two and a Half Tribes

NUMBERS 32:1–42

Like the previous section, this passage also deals with some final practical matters handled by Moses before his death. Two tribes come before him requesting that they receive their inheritance on the eastern side of the Jordan River for economic reasons. Moses sharply rebukes them for their desire to remain outside the borders of Canaan and not to assist in its conquest. After agreeing to aid their brothers in conquering the land, promising that they would return to their preferred inheritance only after the cessation of war, Moses accepts their request. However, he warns them in the presence of Elazar the priest, Joshua son of Nun, and the heads of the tribes, that they must fight on the front lines with their brethren until the end of the conquest. Moses formulates this agreement by issuing a so-called compound condition, in which both the positive and negative outcomes are spelled out. He also includes half of the tribe of Manasseh within their group, as that was also a populous tribe whose members were powerful warriors.

32 1 **The children of Reuben and the children of Gad had much livestock** from what they had brought from Egypt, as well as the plunder of Midyan; **it was very considerable.** Since they wanted to work as shepherds, it is also possible that they exchanged goods with the other tribes for their animals, which further augmented their flocks. **They saw the land of Yazer and the land of Gilad** on the eastern side of the Jordan River, **and behold, the place was a place for livestock.** It contained large tracts that were unsuitable for agriculture, but were perfect for raising flocks.

Sixth aliya (Third aliya)

2 **The children of Gad and the children of Reuben came and said to Moses, to Elazar the priest, and to the princes of the congregation, saying:**

3 The cities of **Atarot, Divon, Yazer, Nimra, Heshbon, Elaleh, Sevam, Nevo, and Beon,**

4 **all the land that the Lord smote before the congregation of Israel** on the eastern side of the Jordan River, **it is a land of livestock, and we, your servants, have livestock.**

5 **They said: If we have found favor in your eyes, may this land,** which is suited for our occupation, **be given to your servants as an ancestral portion; do not take us across the Jordan.** We prefer to stay here.

6 **Moses said to the children of Gad and to the children of Reuben: Will your brethren go to the war, and you will sit here,** quietly tending to your flocks?

7 **And why will you dishearten the children of Israel from crossing into the land that the Lord has given them?** God has promised the land of Canaan to you, on the western side of the Jordan. By staying here, you are liable to weaken your brothers' resolve and perhaps they too will be reluctant to cross the Jordan.

8 **So did your fathers,** the spies, **when I sent them from Kadesh Barnea to see the land,** during the second year in the wilderness (chap. 13).

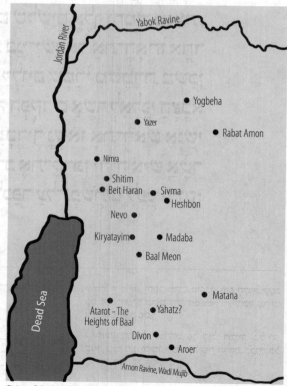

Cities of Gad and Reuben

נב וַיִּקַּ֨ח מֹשֶׁ֜ה וְאֶלְעָזָ֤ר הַכֹּהֵן֙ אֶת־הַזָּהָ֔ב מֵֽאִתָּ֑ם כֹּ֖ל כְּלִ֣י מַעֲשֶֽׂה: וַיְהִ֣י ׀ כָּל־זְהַ֣ב
הַתְּרוּמָ֗ה אֲשֶׁ֤ר הֵרִ֙ימוּ֙ לַֽיהֹוָ֔ה שִׁשָּׁ֨ה עָשָׂ֥ר אֶ֛לֶף שְׁבַע־מֵא֥וֹת וַחֲמִשִּׁ֖ים שָֽׁקֶל

נג מֵאֵת֙ שָׂרֵ֣י הָאֲלָפִ֔ים וּמֵאֵ֖ת שָׂרֵ֣י הַמֵּא֑וֹת: אַנְשֵׁי֙ הַצָּבָ֔א בָּזְז֖וּ אִ֥ישׁ לֽוֹ: וַיִּקַּ֨ח מֹשֶׁ֜ה
נד וְאֶלְעָזָ֤ר הַכֹּהֵן֙ אֶת־הַזָּהָ֔ב מֵאֵ֛ת שָׂרֵ֥י הָאֲלָפִ֖ים וְהַמֵּא֑וֹת וַיָּבִ֤אוּ אֹתוֹ֙ אֶל־אֹ֣הֶל
מוֹעֵ֔ד זִכָּר֥וֹן לִבְנֵֽי־יִשְׂרָאֵ֖ל לִפְנֵ֥י יְהֹוָֽה:

א וּמִקְנֶ֣ה ׀ רַ֗ב הָיָ֞ה לִבְנֵ֧י רְאוּבֵ֛ן וְלִבְנֵי־גָ֖ד עָצ֣וּם מְאֹ֑ד וַיִּרְא֞וּ אֶת־אֶ֤רֶץ יַעְזֵר֙ וְאֶת־
ב אֶ֣רֶץ גִּלְעָ֔ד וְהִנֵּ֥ה הַמָּק֖וֹם מְק֥וֹם מִקְנֶֽה: וַיָּבֹ֥אוּ בְנֵי־גָ֖ד וּבְנֵ֣י רְאוּבֵ֑ן וַיֹּאמְר֤וּ
ג אֶל־מֹשֶׁה֙ וְאֶל־אֶלְעָזָ֣ר הַכֹּהֵ֔ן וְאֶל־נְשִׂיאֵ֖י הָעֵדָ֥ה לֵאמֹֽר: עֲטָר֤וֹת וְדִיבֹן֙ וְיַעְזֵ֣ר
ד וְנִמְרָ֔ה וְחֶשְׁבּ֖וֹן וְאֶלְעָלֵ֑ה וּשְׂבָ֥ם וּנְב֖וֹ וּבְעֹֽן: הָאָ֗רֶץ אֲשֶׁ֨ר הִכָּ֤ה יְהֹוָה֙ לִפְנֵי֙ עֲדַ֣ת
ה יִשְׂרָאֵ֔ל אֶ֥רֶץ מִקְנֶ֖ה הִ֑וא וְלַעֲבָדֶ֖יךָ מִקְנֶֽה: וַיֹּאמְר֗וּ אִם־מָצָ֤אנוּ
חֵן֙ בְּעֵינֶ֔יךָ יֻתַּ֞ן אֶת־הָאָ֧רֶץ הַזֹּ֛את לַעֲבָדֶ֖יךָ לַאֲחֻזָּ֑ה אַל־תַּעֲבִרֵ֖נוּ אֶת־הַיַּרְדֵּֽן:
ו וַיֹּ֣אמֶר מֹשֶׁ֔ה לִבְנֵי־גָ֖ד וְלִבְנֵ֣י רְאוּבֵ֑ן הַאַֽחֵיכֶ֗ם יָבֹ֙אוּ֙ לַמִּלְחָמָ֔ה וְאַתֶּ֖ם תֵּ֥שְׁבוּ פֹֽה:
ז וְלָ֣מָּה תְנִיא֔וּן אֶת־לֵ֖ב בְּנֵ֣י יִשְׂרָאֵ֑ל מֵֽעֲבֹר֙ אֶל־הָאָ֔רֶץ אֲשֶׁר־נָתַ֥ן לָהֶ֖ם יְהֹוָֽה: כֹּ֤ה
ח עָשׂוּ֙ אֲבֹ֣תֵיכֶ֔ם בְּשָׁלְחִ֥י אֹתָ֛ם מִקָּדֵ֥שׁ בַּרְנֵ֖עַ לִרְא֣וֹת אֶת־הָאָֽרֶץ: וַֽיַּעֲל֞וּ עַד־נַ֣חַל
ט אֶשְׁכּ֗וֹל וַיִּרְאוּ֙ אֶת־הָאָ֔רֶץ וַיָּנִ֕יאוּ אֶת־לֵ֖ב בְּנֵ֣י יִשְׂרָאֵ֑ל לְבִלְתִּי־בֹא֙ אֶל־הָאָ֔רֶץ
אֲשֶׁר־נָתַ֥ן לָהֶ֖ם יְהֹוָֽה: וַיִּֽחַר־אַ֥ף יְהֹוָ֖ה בַּיּ֣וֹם הַה֑וּא וַיִּשָּׁבַ֖ע לֵאמֹֽר: אִם־יִרְאוּ֩
יא הָאֲנָשִׁ֨ים הָעֹלִ֜ים מִמִּצְרַ֗יִם מִבֶּ֨ן עֶשְׂרִ֤ים שָׁנָה֙ וָמַ֔עְלָה אֵ֚ת הָאֲדָמָ֔ה אֲשֶׁ֥ר נִשְׁבַּ֖עְתִּי

כט ששי
/שלישי/

תְנִיאוּן

ז| וְלָמָּה תְנִיאוּן. תָּסִירוּ וְתַמְנִיעוּ לְבָם "מֵעֲבֹר", שֶׁיִּהְיוּ
סְבוּרִים שֶׁאַתֶּם יְרֵאִים לַעֲבֹר מִפְּנֵי הַמִּלְחָמָה וְחֹזֶק
הֶעָרִים וְהָעָם:

ח| מִקָּדֵשׁ בַּרְנֵעַ. כָּךְ שְׁמָהּ, וּשְׁתֵּי קַדֵשׁ הָיוּ:

פרק לב

ג| עֲטָרוֹת וְדִיבֹן וְגו'. מֵאֶרֶץ סִיחוֹן וְעוֹג הָיוּ:

ו| הַאַחֵיכֶם. לְשׁוֹן תְּמִיהָה הוּא:

---

9 They went up until the Eshkol Ravine, and they saw the land, and when they said that it was unsatisfactory for them, they disheartened the children of Israel, so as not to desire to come to the land that the Lord had given them.

10 The Lord's anger was enflamed on that day, and He took an oath, saying:

11 The men who came up from Egypt, from twenty years old and above, shall not see the land about which I took an oath

to Abraham, to Isaac, and to Jacob, because they did not wholeheartedly follow Me and My instructions,

12 **except** for **Caleb son of Yefuneh the Kenizite, and Joshua son of Nun; because they wholeheartedly followed the Lord.**

13 **The Lord's anger was enflamed against Israel, and He caused them to wander in the wilderness forty years, until the end of the entire generation that did evil in the eyes of the Lord.** As a result of God's anger, the people wandered in the wilderness for forty years, waiting for that entire sinful generation to die out.

14 **And behold, you,** the children of Gad and the children of Reuben, **have risen in place of your fathers, a breed of sinful men,**[9] **to further exacerbate the enflamed wrath of the Lord against Israel.**

15 **If you will turn from following Him** and His path, **He will continue to leave them,** the people, **in the wilderness** for longer;[10] **and so you will bring harm to this entire people.**

16 **They,** the children of Gad and the children of Reuben, **approached him, and said:** Let us present our request in a more appropriate manner: **We will build sheep enclosures for our livestock here, and cities,** settled areas, **for our** young **children** and wives.[11]

17 **And we,** the men, **will swiftly set out as a vanguard** for war **before the children of Israel, until we have taken them to their place,** on the western side of the Jordan, and in the meantime **our children shall live in the fortified cities, due to the inhabitants of the land** who might attack those left here.

18 **We will not return to our homes until each of the children of Israel has inherited his inheritance** in the land of Canaan,

19 **as we will not inherit with them across the Jordan and beyond, as our inheritance has come to us on the east side of the Jordan.** We had no intention of shirking our duty and will fight with the rest of our brethren. However, we relinquish our portion on the western side of the Jordan from the outset.

Seventh aliya (Fourth aliya)

20 **Moses said to them: If you will do this matter: If you will** indeed **be a vanguard before the Lord to the war,**

21 **all of the vanguard from you will cross the Jordan** and fight as the vanguard of the army on the western side of the Jordan, **before the Lord, until** the enemies are weakened, and until **His dispossession of His enemies from before Him,** so that your brothers may inherit the land.

22 **The land will be conquered before the Lord, and** only **then you will return**[D] here, when the wars, which will certainly last years, are concluded; **and you shall be absolved before the Lord and before Israel, and this land shall be for you as an ancestral portion before the Lord.**

23 **But if you will not do so,** but remain here on the eastern side of the Jordan River, **behold, you have sinned to the Lord; and know your sin that will find you.** You will not escape punishment for your transgression.

24 Therefore, **build cities for your children and enclosures for your flocks, and that which comes out of your mouth,** that which you promised, **you shall do.**

25 **The children of Gad and the children of Reuben said to Moses, saying:** We, **your servants, will do as** you, **my lord, commands.**

26 **Our children, our wives, our livestock, and all our animals, will be there in the cities of Gilad.**

27 **And your servants will cross, all the vanguard soldiers, before the Lord to war, as my lord speaks.**

DISCUSSION

32:22 | **And then you will return:** The children of Gad and Reuben might make better soldiers than the other tribes as they will not be troubled by worries over their wives and children. Since they will leave their families safely behind on the eastern side of the Jordan River, they can set out to battle with greater peace of mind.

יב לאברהם ליצחק וליעקב כי לא־מלאו אחרי: בלתי כלב בן־יפנה הקנזי ויהושע
יג בן־נון כי מלאו אחרי יהוה: ויחר־אף יהוה בישראל וינעם במדבר ארבעים
יד שנה עד־תם כל־הדור העשה הרע בעיני יהוה: והנה קמתם תחת אבתיכם
טו תרבות אנשים חטאים לספות עוד על חרון אף־יהוה אל־ישראל: כי תשובן
טז מאחריו ויסף עוד להניחו במדבר ושחתם לכל־העם הזה: ויגשו
יז אליו ויאמרו גדרת צאן נבנה למקננו פה וערים לטפנו: ואנחנו נחלץ חשים
לפני בני ישראל עד אשר אם־הביאנם אל־מקומם וישב טפנו בערי המבצר
יח מפני ישבי הארץ: לא נשוב אל־בתינו עד התנחל בני ישראל איש נחלתו:
יט כי לא ננחל אתם מעבר לירדן והלאה כי באה נחלתנו אלינו מעבר הירדן
מזרחה:
כ ויאמר אליהם משה אם־תעשון את־הדבר הזה אם־תחלצו לפני יהוה שביעי /רביעי/
כא למלחמה: ועבר לכם כל־חלוץ את־הירדן לפני יהוה עד הורישו את־איביו
כב מפניו: ונכבשה הארץ לפני יהוה ואחר תשבו והייתם נקים מיהוה ומישראל
כג והיתה הארץ הזאת לכם לאחזה לפני יהוה: ואם־לא תעשון כן הנה חטאתם
כד ליהוה ודעו חטאתכם אשר תמצא אתכם: בנו־לכם ערים לטפכם וגדרת
כה לצנאכם והיצא מפיכם תעשו: ויאמר בני־גד ובני ראובן אל־משה לאמר
כו עבדיך יעשו כאשר אדני מצוה: טפנו נשינו מקננו וכל־בהמתנו יהיו־שם בערי
כז הגלעד: ועבדיך יעברו כל־חלוץ צבא לפני יהוה למלחמה כאשר אדני דבר:

רש"י

יב | **הקנזי.** חורגו של קנז היה, וילדה לו אמו של כלב את עתניאל:

יג | **וינעם.** ויטלטלם, מן "נע ונד" (בראשית ד, יב):

יד | **לספות.** כמו: "ספו שנה על שנה" (ישעיה כט, א), "עלותיכם ספו" וגו' (ירמיה ז, כא), לשון תוספת:

טז | **נבנה למקננו פה.** חסים היו על ממונם יותר מבניהם ובנותיהם, שהקדימו מקניהם לטפם. אמר להם משה: לא כן, עשו העקר עקר והטפל טפל, בנו לכם תחלה ערים לטפכם ואחר כך גדרות לצאנכם (להלן פסוק כד):

יז | **ואנחנו נחלץ חשים.** נזדין מהירים, כמו: "מהר שלל חש בז" (ישעיה ח, ג), "ימהר יחישה" (שם ה, יט): [**לפני בני ישראל.** בראשי גיסות, מתוך שגבורים היו, שכן נאמר בגד: "וטרף זרוע אף קדקד" (דברים לג, כ). ואף משה חזר ופרש להם באלה הדברים: "ואצו אתכם בעת ההוא וגו' חלוצים תעברו לפני אחיכם בני ישראל כל בני חיל" (דברים ג, יח), וביריחו כתיב: "והחלוץ הלך לפניהם" (יהושע ו, יג), זה ראובן וגד שקימו תנאם: – תוספת מרבינו שמעיה שהעיד: "זוני רבי להגיה"] **וישב טפנו.** בעודנו אצל אחינו: **בערי המבצר.** שנבנה עכשיו:

יט | **מעבר לירדן וגו'.** בעבר המערבי: **כי באה נחלתנו.** כבר קבלנוה בעבר המזרחי:

כד | **לצנאכם.** תבה זו מגזרת "צנה ואלפים כלם" (תהלים ח, ח), שאין בו אל"ף מפסיק בין נו"ן לצד"י, ואל"ף שבה כאן אחר הנו"ן, במקום ה"א של "צנה" הוא. מיסודו של רבי משה למדתי: **והיצא מפיכם תעשו.** לגבוה, שקבלתם עליכם לעבר למלחמה עד כבוש וחלוק, שמשה לא בקש מהם אלא "ונכבשה... ואחר תשבו" (לעיל פסוק כב), והם קבלו עליהם "עד התנחל" (לעיל פסוק יח), הרי הוסיפו להתעכב שבע שחלקו, וכן עשו:

כה | **ויאמר בני גד.** כלם כאיש אחד:

28 **Moses commanded Elazar the priest, and Joshua son of Nun, and the heads of the fathers,** the leaders, **of the tribes of the children of Israel in their regard.** Since this agreement will be fulfilled only after Moses' death, he entrusts it to the future leaders of the people.

29 **Moses said to them: If the children of Gad and the children of Reuben will cross the Jordan with you, all the vanguard to war before the Lord, and the land will be conquered before you, you shall give them the land of Gilad as a portion.**

30 **But if they will not cross as a vanguard with you, they will receive their portion in your midst, in the land of Canaan.**

31 **The children of Gad and the children of Reuben answered, saying: That which the Lord has spoken to your servants, so we will do.**

32 **We will cross as a vanguard before the Lord into the land of Canaan, and for us** the rights **to the portion of our inheritance will be across the Jordan.** It will be kept in trust for us until we have fulfilled all our obligations.

33 **Moses gave to them, to the children of Gad, to the children of Reuben, and to half the tribe of Manasseh son of Joseph,** which also possessed flocks and wished to accept the conditions of the children of Gad and Reuben,[12] **the kingdom of Sihon, king of the Emorites, and the kingdom of Og, king of Bashan, the land with its cities, within the borders** set aside for each tribe and comprised **of the cities of the land all around.** Moses permitted the shepherds who preferred an inheritance on the eastern side of the Jordan River to join the agreement of the tribes of Gad and Reuben. The other half of the tribe of Manasseh crossed the Jordan and settled on its western side.[13]

34 **The children of Gad built Divon, Atarot, Aroer,**

35 **Atrot Shofan, Yazer, Yogbeha,**[B]

36 **Beit Nimra, and Beit Haran,** which were **fortified cities and enclosures for sheep.** Some of these places were already cities before the tribes arrived, and the children of Gad reconstructed them to serve as dwelling places for their families. They presumably left a small guard of men there as well.

37 **The children of Reuben** likewise **built Heshbon, Elaleh, and Kiryatayim;**[B]

38 **and Nevo and Baal Meon, with changed names.** They gave these cities different names, as some of them were named after idols, such as Nevo and Baal Meon;[14] **and Sivma, and they designated names for the cities that they built.** Some of these were their old names, while others were given new names.

39 **The children of Makhir son of Manasseh went to Gilad and conquered it, and dispossessed the Emorites who were in it.**

40 **Moses gave the Gilad to Makhir son of Manasseh, and he**
Maftir **dwelt in it.**

41 **Ya'ir son of Manasseh**[D] **went and captured their ranches [*ḥavvot*],** which they used for a temporary residence and for raising flocks and herds, **and he called them Havot Ya'ir,** after his own name.

42 **And Novah,** an unknown individual, probably an adventurer who preferred to remain a shepherd in the wild east rather than live as a farmer in Canaan, joined half the tribe of Manasseh and **went and captured** the city of **Kenat,**[B] **and its** surrounding **environs, and he called it Novah, after his name.**

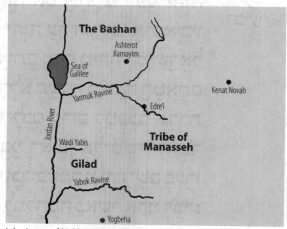

Inheritance of Makhir son of Manasseh

BACKGROUND

32:35 | Yogbeha: Following the order of the cities as they are presented in these verses, this is the northernmost city in the territory of the tribe of Gad. Yogbeha is mentioned as an eastern city in Gideon's wars with the Midyanites (Judges 8:11). It is identified with Ajebeihat, which is located north of Rabat Amon.

32:37 | Kiryatayim: This place is mentioned in Genesis (14:5) and is also referred to in the book of Joshua (13:19) as located within the inheritance of Reuben. The name also appears in external sources, such as the Mesha Stele, ninth century BCE. The geographical descriptions refer to a prominent mountain on a plain. Researchers have suggested various identifications: Khirbet el-Qereiyâ, west of Madaba; Khirbet el-Qereiyât, southwest of Madaba; or Jalul, to the east.

32:42 | Kenat: Generally identified with Canatha, in the east of the Bashan, a provincial city on the slopes of Jabal al-Druze, the Mountain of the Druze, in Havran. Kenat is mentioned in early Egyptian documents dating back to the first half of the second millennium BCE. It was a city of the Decapolis in the Hellenistic period, a group of ten cities that possessed a measure of autonomy. In the period of the Mishna, Kenat marked the border of the Land of Israel for the separation of tithes (*Tosefta, Shevi'it* 4:11).

כה וַיְצַו לָהֶם מֹשֶׁה אֵת אֶלְעָזָר הַכֹּהֵן וְאֵת יְהוֹשֻׁעַ בִּן-נוּן וְאֶת-רָאשֵׁי אֲבוֹת הַמַּטּוֹת

לִבְנֵי יִשְׂרָאֵל: כט וַיֹּאמֶר מֹשֶׁה אֲלֵהֶם אִם-יַעַבְרוּ בְנֵי-גָד וּבְנֵי-רְאוּבֵן ׀ אִתְּכֶם אֶת-

הַיַּרְדֵּן כָּל-חָלוּץ לַמִּלְחָמָה לִפְנֵי יְהוָה וְנִכְבְּשָׁה הָאָרֶץ לִפְנֵיכֶם וּנְתַתֶּם לָהֶם

אֶת-אֶרֶץ הַגִּלְעָד לַאֲחֻזָּה: ל וְאִם-לֹא יַעַבְרוּ חֲלוּצִים אִתְּכֶם וְנֹאחֲזוּ בְתֹכְכֶם

בְּאֶרֶץ כְּנָעַן: לא וַיַּעֲנוּ בְנֵי-גָד וּבְנֵי רְאוּבֵן לֵאמֹר אֵת אֲשֶׁר דִּבֶּר יְהוָה אֶל-עֲבָדֶיךָ

כֵּן נַעֲשֶׂה: לב נַחְנוּ נַעֲבֹר חֲלוּצִים לִפְנֵי יְהוָה אֶרֶץ כְּנָעַן וְאִתָּנוּ אֲחֻזַּת נַחֲלָתֵנוּ

מֵעֵבֶר לַיַּרְדֵּן: לג וַיִּתֵּן לָהֶם ׀ מֹשֶׁה לִבְנֵי-גָד וְלִבְנֵי רְאוּבֵן וְלַחֲצִי ׀ שֵׁבֶט ׀ מְנַשֶּׁה

בֶן-יוֹסֵף אֶת-מַמְלֶכֶת סִיחֹן מֶלֶךְ הָאֱמֹרִי וְאֶת-מַמְלֶכֶת עוֹג מֶלֶךְ הַבָּשָׁן הָאָרֶץ

לְעָרֶיהָ בִּגְבֻלֹת עָרֵי הָאָרֶץ סָבִיב: לד וַיִּבְנוּ בְנֵי-גָד אֶת-דִּיבֹן וְאֶת-עֲטָרֹת וְאֵת

עֲרֹעֵר: לה וְאֶת-עַטְרֹת שׁוֹפָן וְאֶת-יַעְזֵר וְיָגְבְּהָה: לו וְאֶת-בֵּית נִמְרָה וְאֶת-בֵּית

הָרָן עָרֵי מִבְצָר וְגִדְרֹת צֹאן: לז וּבְנֵי רְאוּבֵן בָּנוּ אֶת-חֶשְׁבּוֹן וְאֶת-אֶלְעָלֵא וְאֵת

קִרְיָתָיִם: לח וְאֶת-נְבוֹ וְאֶת-בַּעַל מְעוֹן מוּסַבֹּת שֵׁם וְאֶת-שִׂבְמָה וַיִּקְרְאוּ בְשֵׁמֹת

אֶת-שְׁמוֹת הֶעָרִים אֲשֶׁר בָּנוּ: לט וַיֵּלְכוּ בְּנֵי מָכִיר בֶּן-מְנַשֶּׁה גִּלְעָדָה וַיִּלְכְּדֻהָ וַיּוֹרֶשׁ

אֶת-הָאֱמֹרִי אֲשֶׁר-בָּהּ: מ וַיִּתֵּן מֹשֶׁה אֶת-הַגִּלְעָד לְמָכִיר בֶּן-מְנַשֶּׁה וַיֵּשֶׁב בָּהּ: מפטיר

מא וְיָאִיר בֶּן-מְנַשֶּׁה הָלַךְ וַיִּלְכֹּד אֶת-חַוֺּתֵיהֶם וַיִּקְרָא אֶתְהֶן חַוֺּת יָאִיר:

מב וְנֹבַח הָלַךְ וַיִּלְכֹּד אֶת-קְנָת וְאֶת-בְּנֹתֶיהָ וַיִּקְרָא לָה נֹבַח בִּשְׁמוֹ:

רש"י

כה] וַיְצַו לָהֶם. כְּמוֹ "עֲלֵיהֶם", וְעַל תְּנָאָם מִנָּה אֶלְעָזָר וִיהוֹשֻׁעַ, כְּמוֹ: "ה' יִלָּחֵם לָכֶם" (שמות יד, יד).

לב] וְאִתָּנוּ אֲחֻזַּת נַחֲלָתֵנוּ. כְּלוֹמַר, בְּיָדֵנוּ וּבִרְשׁוּתֵנוּ תְּהִי חֲזָקַת נַחֲלָתֵנוּ מֵעֵבֶר הַזֶּה:

לו] עָרֵי מִבְצָר וְגִדְרֹת צֹאן. זֶה סוֹף פָּסוּק מוּסָב עַל תְּחִלַּת הָעִנְיָן, "וַיִּבְנוּ בְנֵי גָד" אֶת הֶעָרִים הַלָּלוּ לִהְיוֹת "עָרֵי מִבְצָר וְגִדְרֹת צֹאן":

לח] וְאֶת נְבוֹ וְאֶת בַּעַל מְעוֹן מוּסַבֹּת שֵׁם. נְבוֹ וּבַעַל מְעוֹן שְׁמוֹת עֲבוֹדָה זָרָה הֵם, וְהָיוּ הָאֱמוֹרִיִּים קוֹרִים עָרֵיהֶם עַל שֵׁם עֲבוֹדָה זָרָה שֶׁלָּהֶם, וּבְנֵי רְאוּבֵן הֵסֵבּוּ אֶת שְׁמָם לִשְׁמוֹת אֲחֵרִים, וְזֶהוּ: "מוּסַבֹּת שֵׁם": וְאֶת שִׂבְמָה. בָּנוּ שִׂבְמָה, וְהִיא שְׂבָם הָאֲמוּרָה לְמַעְלָה (פסוק ג):

לט] וַיּוֹרֶשׁ. כְּתַרְגּוּמוֹ: "וְתָרֵיךְ", שֶׁתִּרֵּשׁ 'רֵישׁ' מְשַׁמֶּשֶׁת שְׁתֵּי מַחֲלָקוֹת: לְשׁוֹן יְרֻשָּׁה וּלְשׁוֹן הוֹרָשָׁה, שֶׁהוּא טֵרוּד וְתָרֵיךְ:

מא] חַוֺּתֵיהֶם. "כַּפְרָנֵיהוֹן", "וַיִּקְרָא אֶתְהֶן חַוֺּת יָאִיר". לְפִי שֶׁלֹּא הָיוּ לוֹ בָּנִים קְרָאָם בִּשְׁמוֹ לְזִכָּרוֹן:

מב] וַיִּקְרָא לָה נֹבַח. "לָה" אֵינוֹ מַפִּיק ה"א, וְרָאִיתִי בִּיסוֹדוֹ שֶׁל רַבִּי מֹשֶׁה הַדַּרְשָׁן, לְפִי שֶׁלֹּא נִתְקַיֵּם לָהּ שֵׁם זֶה לְפִיכָךְ הוּא רָפֶה, שֶׁמַּשְׁמָעוֹ מִדְרָשׁוֹ כְּמוֹ לֹא: וּתְמַהֲנִי מַה יְּדֹרֵשׁ בִּשְׁתֵּי תֵבוֹת הַדּוֹמִין לָהּ, "וַיֹּאמֶר לָה בֹעַז" (רות ב, יד), "לִבְנוֹת לָה בָיִת" (זכריה ה, יא):

DISCUSSION

32:41 | **Ya'ir son of Manasseh:** This was not Manasseh's own son but a descendant of the tribe of Judah who married the daughter of Makhir son of Manasseh and resided in the portion of Makhir's family on the eastern side of the Jordan River (see I Chronicles 2:21–23).

Parashat
Masei

Summary of the Journeys in the Wilderness

NUMBERS 33:1–49

The Israelites have approached the edge of the land of Canaan, and are preparing to enter the land, and the narrative turns to summarizing their travels. It would appear that God led them in a zigzag, in fulfillment of His decree that they would wander in the wilderness until the entire generation that left Egypt had passed away. This section mainly lists the stops on the journey; therefore, not all the important events are mentioned. Apart from the date of the exodus from Egypt and Aaron's passing, there are also no references to time. Furthermore, there were places where the Israelites stayed for a few brief days, while they remained in other locations for several years. In fact, the Sages derive from the verse, "You lived in Kadesh many days, like the days that you lived there,"[1] that roughly half of the Israelites' years in the wilderness were spent in the region of Kadesh.

It is hard to identify accurately all the places listed here, as, with few exceptions, the names of these locations have not been preserved through history. If there was no prior settlement in a location, it is difficult to imagine that a camp established thousands of years ago in the desert would have left any archaeological evidence.

The commentaries interpret some of the names homiletically as esoteric allusions to lengthier journeys in the history of the Jewish people, humanity as a whole, and even the personal biographies of each individual.

33 1 **These are the journeys of the children of Israel, who came out from the land of Egypt according to their hosts, at the hand of Moses and Aaron.**

2 **Moses wrote their points of origin,** their starting points for each of **their journeys according to the directive of the Lord; these are their journeys from their points of origin.** Each journey ended at a place of encampment from which the next journey commenced.

3 **They traveled from Rameses**[B] **in the first month, on the fifteenth day of the first month;** on the day after the initial celebration of **Passover, the children of Israel exited with a high hand,** in a display of power and strength, **before the eyes of all Egypt,** not as runaways.

4 **The Egyptians were burying those whom the Lord had smitten among them, all their firstborn.** The Egyptians could do nothing about the departure of the children of Israel from Egypt, as they were busy mourning and burying their dead. **And** furthermore, **on their gods, the Lord administered punishments,** acts of vengeance as the children of Israel left Egypt.[2]

5 **The children of Israel traveled from Rameses, and encamped in Sukot.**[B]

6 **They traveled from Sukot, and encamped in Etam,**[B] **which is at the edge of the wilderness.** From here onward they left the land of Egypt and the region of the Nile, several of the river branches stretched further eastward in those times than they do today.

7 **They traveled from Etam, and** the people **went back to** near **Pi HaHirot,**[B] **which is before Baal Tzefon.**[B] They did not advance in one single direction, but turned around and retraced their steps.[3] Baal Tzefon was an Egyptian or Egyptian-Canaanite god that embodied the forces of evil. The Egyptians interpreted the Israelites' delay alongside this god as a sign that it had ensnared them with its powers, and they were thereby motivated to chase after Israel. **And they,** the Israelites, **encamped before Migdol.**[B]

8 **They traveled from Penei HaHirot, and they crossed in the midst of the** Red **Sea to the wilderness and they took a three-day journey in the wilderness of Etam, and they encamped in Mara,** where the bitter [*marim*] waters were sweetened for them.[4]

9 **They traveled from Mara,**[B] **and came to Eilim;**[B] **and in Eilim** there **were twelve springs of water,** corresponding to the

---

BACKGROUND

33:3 | Rameses: This is the land of Goshen, northeast of the Nile Delta, where the children of Israel resided (Genesis 47:11). It is also the name of a storehouse city built by the Hebrews (Exodus 1:11). Some commentaries say it is Pelusium, a city on the eastern edge of the Nile

Delta, which was destroyed in the Middle Ages. Nowadays the accepted identification is Tel-el-Dab'a, Avaris, an important city back in the sixteenth century BCE.

33:5 | Sukot: Some commentaries identify this with Tel el-Maskhuta, on the eastern edge of

Wadi Tumilat, which is Pitom. Others claim that Sukot is not referring to a specific place, but it is the name given to an area in which people lived in booths, *sukkot*.

33:6 | Etam: Some commentaries claim that this is a corrupted form of the Egyptian *ḥetam,* ↩

פרשת
מַסְעֵי

לֹ א אֵלֶּה מַסְעֵי בְנֵי־יִשְׂרָאֵל אֲשֶׁר יָצְאוּ מֵאֶרֶץ מִצְרַיִם לְצִבְאֹתָם בְּיַד־מֹשֶׁה וְאַהֲרֹן:

ב וַיִּכְתֹּב מֹשֶׁה אֶת־מוֹצָאֵיהֶם לְמַסְעֵיהֶם עַל־פִּי יְהוָֹה וְאֵלֶּה מַסְעֵיהֶם לְמוֹצָאֵיהֶם:

ג וַיִּסְעוּ מֵרַעְמְסֵס בַּחֹדֶשׁ הָרִאשׁוֹן בַּחֲמִשָּׁה עָשָׂר יוֹם לַחֹדֶשׁ הָרִאשׁוֹן מִמָּחֳרַת הַפֶּסַח יָצְאוּ בְנֵי־יִשְׂרָאֵל בְּיָד רָמָה לְעֵינֵי כָּל־מִצְרָיִם: ד וּמִצְרַיִם מְקַבְּרִים אֵת אֲשֶׁר הִכָּה יְהוָֹה בָּהֶם כָּל־בְּכוֹר וּבֵאלֹהֵיהֶם עָשָׂה יְהוָֹה שְׁפָטִים: ה וַיִּסְעוּ בְנֵי־יִשְׂרָאֵל מֵרַעְמְסֵס וַיַּחֲנוּ בְּסֻכֹּת: ו וַיִּסְעוּ מִסֻּכֹּת וַיַּחֲנוּ בְאֵתָם אֲשֶׁר בִּקְצֵה הַמִּדְבָּר: ז וַיִּסְעוּ מֵאֵתָם וַיָּשָׁב עַל־פִּי הַחִירֹת אֲשֶׁר עַל־פְּנֵי בַּעַל צְפוֹן וַיַּחֲנוּ לִפְנֵי מִגְדֹּל: ח וַיִּסְעוּ מִפְּנֵי הַחִירֹת וַיַּעַבְרוּ בְתוֹךְ־הַיָּם הַמִּדְבָּרָה וַיֵּלְכוּ דֶּרֶךְ שְׁלֹשֶׁת יָמִים בְּמִדְבַּר אֵתָם וַיַּחֲנוּ בְּמָרָה: ט וַיִּסְעוּ מִמָּרָה וַיָּבֹאוּ אֵילִמָה וּבְאֵילִם שְׁתֵּים עֶשְׂרֵה עֵינֹת מַיִם

רש״י

פרק לג

א אֵלֶּה מַסְעֵי. לָמָּה נִכְתְּבוּ הַמַּסָּעוֹת הַלָּלוּ? לְהוֹדִיעַ חֲסָדָיו שֶׁל מָקוֹם, שֶׁאַף עַל פִּי שֶׁגָּזַר עֲלֵיהֶם לְטַלְטְלָם וּלְהַנִיעָם בַּמִּדְבָּר, לֹא תֹאמַר שֶׁהָיוּ נָעִים וּמְטֻלְטָלִים מִמַּסָּע לְמַסָּע כָּל אַרְבָּעִים שָׁנָה וְלֹא הָיְתָה לָהֶם מְנוּחָה, שֶׁהֲרֵי אֵין כָּאן אֶלָּא אַרְבָּעִים וּשְׁתַּיִם מַסָּעוֹת. צֵא מֵהֶם אַרְבַּע עֶשְׂרֵה שֶׁכֻּלָּם הָיוּ בַּשָּׁנָה רִאשׁוֹנָה קֹדֶם גְּזֵרָה,

מִשֶּׁנָּסְעוּ מֵרַעְמְסֵס עַד שֶׁבָּאוּ לְרִתְמָה, שֶׁמִּשָּׁם נִשְׁתַּלְּחוּ הַמְרַגְּלִים, שֶׁנֶּאֱמַר: ״וְאַחַר נָסְעוּ הָעָם מֵחֲצֵרוֹת״ וְגוֹ׳ (לעיל יב, טז), ״שְׁלַח לְךָ אֲנָשִׁים״ וְגוֹ׳ (שם יג, ב), וְכָאן הוּא אוֹמֵר: ״וַיִּסְעוּ מֵחֲצֵרֹת וַיַּחֲנוּ בְּרִתְמָה״ (להלן פסוק יח), לָמַדְתָּ שֶׁהִיא בְּמִדְבַּר פָּארָן. וְעוֹד הוֹצֵא מִשָּׁם שְׁמוֹנֶה מַסָּעוֹת שֶׁהָיוּ לְאַחַר מִיתַת אַהֲרֹן, מֵהֹר הָהָר עַד עַרְבוֹת מוֹאָב

בִּשְׁנַת הָאַרְבָּעִים, נִמְצָא שֶׁכָּל שְׁמוֹנֶה וּשְׁלֹשִׁים שָׁנָה לֹא נָסְעוּ אֶלָּא עֶשְׂרִים מַסָּעוֹת. זֶה מִיסוֹדוֹ שֶׁל רַבִּי מֹשֶׁה. וְרַבִּי תַּנְחוּמָא דָּרַשׁ בּוֹ דְּרָשָׁה אַחֶרֶת: מָשָׁל לְמֶלֶךְ שֶׁהָיָה בְּנוֹ חוֹלֶה וְהוֹלִיכוֹ לְמָקוֹם רָחוֹק לְרַפְּאֹתוֹ. כֵּיוָן שֶׁהָיוּ חוֹזְרִין, הִתְחִיל אָבִיו מוֹנֶה כָּל הַמַּסָּעוֹת. אָמַר לוֹ: כָּאן יָשַׁנּוּ, כָּאן הוּקַרְנוּ, כָּאן חָשַׁשְׁתָּ אֶת רֹאשֶׁךָ וְכוּ׳ (תנחומא ג):

BACKGROUND

which means a fortress. Accordingly, they identify Etam with Tel Abu Sefa, east of El-Qantarah.

33:7 | Pi HaHirot: Two areas fit this geographical description. One is in the south, near the city of Suez (Mount Ataka), where there is the opening [*pi*] of a wadi near the Red Sea. The other is to the north, near the outlet of one of the Nile channels; this is possibly the eastern branch (Pelusiac) of the Nile, called Shihor, after the Egyptian god Horus (Isaiah 23:3; see also Exodus 14:2).

Baal Tzefon: This is the name of a Canaanite god, mentioned in an Egyptian letter from the sixth century BCE alongside the gods of Tahpanhes. It is also the name of the ancient temple of this god in Jebel Aqra, near Ugarit. Some

contend that this is the large mound known as Mons Casios (Mount Casius), located in the center of the cape of Lake Bardawil, but there is no archaeological basis for this theory. With that said, it should be noted that the same name was sometimes given to different places, as the names of locations near the Egyptian border recur in towns in the Land of Israel and further north, such as Sukot and Goshen.

Migdol: This was a consecrated or elevated place where there was presumably a fortress that controlled the route from Egypt to Canaan. It also appears in ancient Egyptians documents (Papyrus Anastasi, thirteenth century BCE). Some identify Migdol with the city of El-Qanta-

rah, while others claim that it is Tel el-Hesi, north of that city (see, e.g., Genesis 35:21; Joshua 15:37, 19:35; Judges 8:17, 9:51; II Kings 18:8).

33:9 | Mara: There are two proposed identifications of sulfurous springs for Mara: Bir el-Murrah, approximately 14 km southeast of the town of Suez; and Ein Hawara, south of Wadi Amarah, roughly 70 km southeast of Suez and about 8 km north of Ein Gharandal.

Eilim: The main identifications of this place are: Ein Musa, a large oasis 8 km south of Suez; Ein Gharandal, the largest oasis in Sinai, roughly 110 km south of Suez; or the more northern locations of the city Al-Arish or Abu-Ageila.

twelve tribes of Israel, **and seventy palm trees,** corresponding to the number of those who descended to Egypt;[5] **and they encamped there.** This place is memorable due to the symbolic importance of its springs and palm trees.
10 **They traveled from Eilim, and encamped near the Red Sea.**
Second aliya 11 **They traveled from the Red Sea, and encamped in the wilderness of Sin.**[6]
12 **They traveled from the wilderness of Sin, and encamped in Dofka.**
13 **They traveled from Dofka, and encamped in Alush.**
14 **They traveled from Alush, and encamped in Refidim;**[B] **there was no water for the people to drink there.** This was also the location of the war with Amalek.[7]
15 **They traveled from Refidim, and encamped in the wilderness of Sinai,** where the Torah was given and the Tabernacle was built. The people stayed there for a lengthy period of time; all the commandments and events described in Exodus 19:1–Numbers 10:12 occurred there.
16 **They traveled from the wilderness of Sinai, and encamped in Kivrot HaTaava.**
17 **They traveled from Kivrot HaTaava, and encamped in Hatzerot,**[B] where Miriam contracted leprosy (12:15–16).
18 **They traveled from Hatzerot, and encamped in Ritma.**[B]
19 **They traveled from Ritma, and encamped in Rimon Peretz,** possibly named after a breach [*pirtza*] or downfall that befell the people there.
20 **They traveled from Rimon Peretz, and encamped in Livna.**
21 **They traveled from Livna, and encamped in Risa.**
22 **They traveled from Risa, and encamped in Kehelata.** These last places have not been identified. It is possible that Korah assembled [*hikhil*] the congregation of Israel against Moses and Aaron in Kehelata.[8]
23 **They traveled from Kehelata, and encamped at Mount Shefer.**
24 **They traveled from Mount Shefer, and encamped in Harada.**[D]
25 **They traveled from Harada, and encamped in Mak'helot.**
26 **They traveled from Mak'helot, and encamped in Tahat,** which was possibly a low area, as *tahat* means underneath.
27 **They traveled from Tahat, and encamped in Terah.**
28 **They traveled from Terah, and encamped in Mitka.**
29 **They traveled from Mitka, and encamped in Hashmona.**
30 **They traveled from Hashmona, and encamped in Moserot.**
31 **They traveled from Moserot, and encamped in Benei Yaakan.**[B]
32 **They traveled from Benei Yaakan, and encamped at Hor HaGidgad,** which perhaps contained rocky crevices, as *ḥor* means a hole.[9]
33 **They traveled from Hor HaGidgad, and encamped in Yotvata.**[B]
34 **They traveled from Yotvata, and encamped in Avrona.**[B]
35 **They traveled from Avrona, and encamped in Etzyon Gever,** which is near Eilat,[10] although the location of the city of Eilat at the time is uncertain.
36 **They traveled from Etzyon Gever, and encamped in the wilderness of Tzin, that is, Kadesh.**
37 **They traveled from Kadesh, and encamped at Hor Mountain,**[B] **at the edge of the land of Edom.** They turned northeast, in order to bypass the land of Edom.
38 **Aaron the priest ascended Hor Mountain at the directive of the Lord, and he died there.** Aaron did not die a regular death; rather, he died in peace by God's word, **in the fortieth year of the exodus of the children of Israel from the land of Egypt, in the fifth month, on the first of the month.**

BACKGROUND

33:14 | **Refidim:** It can be inferred from Exodus 19:2 that Refidim was near Mount Sinai. In accordance with the various identifications of Mount Sinai, four locations have been suggested for Refidim: the opening of Wadi Sudr, to the east of Ein Musa in western Sinai; Wadi Feiran, in southwest Sinai; Be'er Karkom, about 7 km north of Mount Karkom in central Sinai; and Wadi Rufaid, southeast of Al-Arish in northern Sinai.

33:17 | **Hatzerot:** Due to the similarity of the names, some suggest that this is Ein-Khudra, on the route from Jebel Musa to Etzyon Gever. Others claim it is the town of Hazira, on the southern edge of Mount Helal, in central Sinai.

33:18 | **Ritma:** In Wadi Sudr, about 20 km east of Jebel Sen Bashar, there is an oasis called Ein Ritma, however it is uncertain that this is the Ritma referred to here.

33:31 | **Benei Yaakan:** According to the verses here, Benei Yaakan was between Moserot and Hor HaGidgad, whereas in Deuteronomy it states: "And the children of Israel journeyed from Be'erot Benei Yaakan to Mosera; there Aaron died, and he was buried; and Elazar his son served as priest in his place. From there they traveled to Gudgod" (Deuteronomy

DISCUSSION

33:24 | **They traveled from Mount Shefer, and encamped in Harada:** No explanation is given for the names of most of these places. It is possible that some of them were unknown locations prior to the arrival of the Israelites, and their names were given in light of the Israelites' stay there. Perhaps Mount Shefer, which means beauty, was named for its pleasant surroundings or the Israelites' comfortable stay there (see *Targum Yonatan*). In an esoteric vein, the travel from Mount Shefer to Harada symbolizes a stage in the journey of life, from a location of beauty and comfort to a place where fear and anxiety [*ḥarada*] reign (see *Mei HaShiloaḥ* vol. 1). It is further expounded in *Mei HaShiloaḥ* with regard to the next destination of Mak'helot, which means assemblies, that when God wishes to gather the Jewish people, He will instill bravery in their hearts so that they will not be afraid. The author of *Mei HaShiloaḥ* concludes: "May that come to pass, speedily in our days."

י יא ושבעים תמרים ויחנו־שם: ויסעו מאילם ויחנו על־ים־סוף: ויסעו מים־
יב יג סוף ויחנו במדבר־סין: ויסעו ממדבר־סין ויחנו בדפקה: ויסעו מדפקה
יד ויחנו באלוש: ויסעו מאלוש ויחנו ברפידם ולא־היה שם מים לעם לשתות:
טו טז ויסעו מרפידם ויחנו במדבר סיני: ויסעו ממדבר סיני ויחנו בקברת התאוה:
יז יח יט ויסעו מקברת התאוה ויחנו בחצרת: ויסעו מחצרת ויחנו ברתמה: ויסעו
כ כא מרתמה ויחנו ברמן פרץ: ויסעו מרמן פרץ ויחנו בלבנה: ויסעו מלבנה ויחנו
כב כג כד ברסה: ויסעו מרסה ויחנו בקהלתה: ויסעו מקהלתה ויחנו בהר־שפר: ויסעו
כה כו מהר־שפר ויחנו בחרדה: ויסעו מחרדה ויחנו במקהלת: ויסעו ממקהלת
כז כח כט ויחנו בתחת: ויסעו מתחת ויחנו בתרח: ויסעו מתרח ויחנו במתקה: ויסעו
ל לא ממתקה ויחנו בחשמנה: ויסעו מחשמנה ויחנו במסרות: ויסעו ממסרות
לב לג ויחנו בבני יעקן: ויסעו מבני יעקן ויחנו בחר הגדגד: ויסעו מחר הגדגד ויחנו
לד לה ביטבתה: ויסעו מיטבתה ויחנו בעברנה: ויסעו מעברנה ויחנו בעצין גבר:
לו לז ויסעו מעצין גבר ויחנו במדבר־צן הוא קדש: ויסעו מקדש ויחנו בהר ההר
לח בקצה ארץ אדום: ויעל אהרן הכהן אל־הר ההר על־פי יהוה וימת שם בשנת
הארבעים לצאת בני־ישראל מארץ מצרים בחדש החמישי באחד לחדש:

רש״י

יח ויחנו ברתמה. על שם לשון הרע של מרגלים, שנאמר: ״מה יתן לך ומה יסיף לך לשון רמיה, חצי גבור שנונים עם גחלי רתמים״ (תהלים קכ, ג-ד).

לח על פי ה׳. מלמד שמת בנשיקה:

BACKGROUND

10:6–7). Some commentaries claim that Moserot and Mosera are the same location, as are Hor HaGidgad and Gudgod. They identify Be'erot Benei Yaakan with the water wells [*be'erot*] in Biriin, near the settlement of Ezuz.

33:33 | **Yotvata:** Depicted in Deuteronomy 10:7 as "a land of streams of water," its name also alludes to its good [*tov*] qualities. The conjectures with regard to its identity include Ein Radian, roughly 40 km north of Eilat, which is near modern-day Kibbutz Yotvata; Sabkhat et-Taba, at the foot of the Mountains of Edom, east of Kibbutz Yahel; or, due to the similarities in name, Bir et-Taba in Wadi Taba, 10 km south of Eilat.

33:34 | **Avrona:** Avrona is identified as Ein Defiyeh, nowadays called Ein Avrona, about 13 km north of Eilat; or Tel el-Kheleifah, between Aqaba and Eilat.

33:37 | **Hor Mountain:** There are two mountains of this name in the Torah. The one mentioned here is on the edge of the land of Edom, while the other is on the northern border of Israel (34:7). Some identify the southern Hor Mountain with Mount Tzin, Jebel Madera, southwest of Maaleh Akrabim; while others say it is Jebel Nebi Harun, in the mountains of Edom, about 4 km west of Petra. Both have the unusual structure of a mountain that is flat on top, and which has a large protrusion halfway up. It is possible that Hor Mountain [*Hor HaHar*] is not the name of a specific mountain, but a reference to the structure of one mountain [*har*] on top of another (see Rashi, 20:22; *Bemidbar Rabba* 19:16).

39 **Aaron was one hundred twenty and three years old when he died on Hor Mountain.**
40 **The Canaanite king of Arad, who lived in the south in the land of Canaan, heard of the arrival of the children of Israel** to his region (see 21:1). This led to a war, in which the Israelites defeated the king of Arad. However, the victorious Israelites did not enter Canaan from the south, but continued to encircle Edom and turned toward the lands adjacent to the eastern bank of the Jordan River.
41 **They traveled from Hor Mountain, and encamped in Tzalmona.**[B]
42 **They traveled from Tzalmona, and encamped in Punon.**[B]
43 **They traveled from Punon, and encamped in Ovot.**
44 **They traveled from Ovot, and encamped in Iyei Avarim,** the ruins of the passageways [*ma'abarim*],[11] **at the border of Moav.**
45 **They traveled from Iyim, and encamped in Divon Gad.**
46 **They traveled from Divon Gad, and encamped in Almon Divlataim.**[B]
47 **They traveled from Almon Divlataim, and encamped in the highlands of Avarim, before Nevo.**
48 **They traveled from the highlands of Avarim, and encamped on the plains of Moav along the Jordan at,** opposite, **Jericho.**
49 **They encamped along the Jordan, from Beit Yeshimot**[B] **until Avel Shitim.**[B] The camp was not concentrated in one spot, but was spread out over several kilometers along the Jordan, **on the plains of Moav.** Nevertheless, the Moavites did not dare to provoke Israel.

Instructions and Commandments in Preparation for the Entry to the Land

NUMBERS 33:50–35:34

From here until the end of the book of Numbers, the Torah cites various commandments God gives the Israelites through Moses, before he hands over the leadership to Joshua and before their entrance into Canaan. As part of the orderly transfer of leadership, Moses has to prepare the Israelites for entrance into the land, instructing them with regard to the nations that were living there, the manner of its division among the tribes, the demarcation of its borders, the names of those charged with the division of the land, and the arrangement of the Levite cities and the cities of refuge.

Moses had not received divine communication for the majority of the duration of the Israelites' wandering in the wilderness, however, for the purpose of the commandments here, God addresses Moses. According to tradition, God did not speak to Moses in his usual special manner until the entire generation that left Egypt had passed away, since like the rest of the people Moses was sad, lonely, and disappointed during those years.[12]

Third aliya (Fifth aliya)

50 **The Lord spoke to Moses on the plains of Moav along the Jordan at Jericho, saying:**
51 **Speak to the children of Israel, and say to them: When you cross the Jordan** on your way **to** entering **the land of Canaan,**
52 **you shall dispossess**[13] **all the inhabitants of the land from before you, and you shall destroy all their ornamented stones,** the decorations they made for their idolatrous rites, **and all their cast images,** their idols, **you shall destroy, and all their high places,** their altars, **you shall demolish.**
53 **You shall take possession of the land** from the nations that are currently residing there, **and you shall settle in it, as to you I have given the land to take possession of it.**
54 **You shall allocate the land by lot according to** the size of **your families: To the greater you shall increase his allocation, and to the lesser you shall decrease his allocation; wherever the lot shall fall for him, it shall be his; according to the tribes of your fathers you shall allocate.** The land shall be divided according to lot, first to tribes and then to families. The size of each family's portion shall depend on the number of the heads of that family. Its members shall subsequently distribute the plots of land internally between them.[14]

BACKGROUND

33:41 | **Tzalmona:** Identified with the Roman fortress Celamona in the Arava, north of Punon.

33:42 | **Punon:** Also known as Feinan, the great center of copper mines located near the mouth of Wadi Dana on the slopes of the mountains of Edom, approximately 35 km southeast of the Dead Sea.

33:46 | **Almon Divlataim:** This was a Moavite city located on the road to Divlataim. The mention of Divlataim serves to differentiate this Almon from the city of the same name in the tribal territory of Benjamin (Joshua 21:18). The Divlataim in Moav is mentioned in Jeremiah (48:22) and in the Mesha Stele as a city north of Arnon, near Nevo and Baal Meon.

33:49 | **Beit Yeshimot:** This city demarcates the southern border of the kingdom of Sihon and the portion of the tribe of Reuben (see Joshua 12:3, 13:20). It is identified with Sweimeh, about 2 km northeast of the Dead Sea. Some claim that it is Tel el-'Azeimeh, 5 km east of Khirbet es-Suweimeh.

Avel Shitim: Most experts identify this with Khirbet el-Kefrein, or with the nearby fertile wadi, roughly 20 km east of Jericho. The name Avel was added to several locations, such as Avel Beit Maakha (I Kings 15:20), Avel Mehola (e.g., Judges 7:22), Avel Mitzrayim (Genesis 50:11), and Avel Keramim (Judges 11:33), among others. It is possible that Avel is derived from *yuval*, a tributary, and it indicates that the town was near water.

לט וְאַהֲרֹן בֶּן־שָׁלֹשׁ וְעֶשְׂרִים וּמְאַת שָׁנָה בְּמֹתוֹ בְּהֹר הָהָר׃ וַיִּשְׁמַע
מ
מא הַכְּנַעֲנִי מֶלֶךְ עֲרָד וְהוּא־יֹשֵׁב בַּנֶּגֶב בְּאֶרֶץ כְּנָעַן בְּבֹא בְּנֵי יִשְׂרָאֵל׃ וַיִּסְעוּ
מב מג מֵהֹר הָהָר וַיַּחֲנוּ בְּצַלְמֹנָה׃ וַיִּסְעוּ מִצַּלְמֹנָה וַיַּחֲנוּ בְּפוּנֹן׃ וַיִּסְעוּ מִפּוּנֹן וַיַּחֲנוּ
מד מה בְּאֹבֹת׃ וַיִּסְעוּ מֵאֹבֹת וַיַּחֲנוּ בְּעִיֵּי הָעֲבָרִים בִּגְבוּל מוֹאָב׃ וַיִּסְעוּ מֵעִיִּים וַיַּחֲנוּ
מו מז בְּדִיבֹן גָּד׃ וַיִּסְעוּ מִדִּיבֹן גָּד וַיַּחֲנוּ בְּעַלְמֹן דִּבְלָתָיְמָה׃ וַיִּסְעוּ מֵעַלְמֹן דִּבְלָתָיְמָה
מח וַיַּחֲנוּ בְּהָרֵי הָעֲבָרִים לִפְנֵי נְבוֹ׃ וַיִּסְעוּ מֵהָרֵי הָעֲבָרִים וַיַּחֲנוּ בְּעַרְבֹת מוֹאָב
מט עַל יַרְדֵּן יְרֵחוֹ׃ וַיַּחֲנוּ עַל־הַיַּרְדֵּן מִבֵּית הַיְשִׁמֹת עַד אָבֵל הַשִּׁטִּים בְּעַרְבֹת
נ מוֹאָב׃ וַיְדַבֵּר יְהוָה אֶל־מֹשֶׁה בְּעַרְבֹת מוֹאָב עַל־יַרְדֵּן יְרֵחוֹ לֵאמֹר׃ שלישי
/חמישי/
נא דַּבֵּר אֶל־בְּנֵי יִשְׂרָאֵל וְאָמַרְתָּ אֲלֵהֶם כִּי אַתֶּם עֹבְרִים אֶת־הַיַּרְדֵּן אֶל־אֶרֶץ
נב כְּנָעַן׃ וְהוֹרַשְׁתֶּם אֶת־כָּל־יֹשְׁבֵי הָאָרֶץ מִפְּנֵיכֶם וְאִבַּדְתֶּם אֵת כָּל־מַשְׂכִּיֹּתָם
נג וְאֵת כָּל־צַלְמֵי מַסֵּכֹתָם תְּאַבֵּדוּ וְאֵת כָּל־בָּמוֹתָם תַּשְׁמִידוּ׃ וְהוֹרַשְׁתֶּם אֶת־
נד הָאָרֶץ וִישַׁבְתֶּם־בָּהּ כִּי לָכֶם נָתַתִּי אֶת־הָאָרֶץ לָרֶשֶׁת אֹתָהּ׃ וְהִתְנַחַלְתֶּם
אֶת־הָאָרֶץ בְּגוֹרָל לְמִשְׁפְּחֹתֵיכֶם לָרַב תַּרְבּוּ אֶת־נַחֲלָתוֹ וְלַמְעַט תַּמְעִיט אֶת־
נַחֲלָתוֹ אֶל אֲשֶׁר־יֵצֵא לוֹ שָׁמָּה הַגּוֹרָל לוֹ יִהְיֶה לְמַטּוֹת אֲבֹתֵיכֶם תִּתְנֶחָלוּ׃

רש״י

מ| **וַיִּשְׁמַע הַכְּנַעֲנִי.** לְלַמֶּדְךָ שֶׁמִּיתַת אַהֲרֹן הִיא הַשְּׁמוּעָה, שֶׁנִּסְתַּלְּקוּ עַנְנֵי כָבוֹד, וְכָסְבוּר שֶׁנִּתְּנָה רְשׁוּת לְהִלָּחֵם בְּיִשְׂרָאֵל, לְפִיכָךְ חָזַר וְכָתְבָהּ:

מד| **בְּעִיֵּי הָעֲבָרִים.** לְשׁוֹן חֳרָבוֹת וְגַלִּים, כְּמוֹ: "לְעִי הַשָּׂדֶה" (מיכה א, ו), "שָׂמוּ אֶת יְרוּשָׁלַםִ לְעִיִּים" (תהלים עט, א):

מט| **מִבֵּית הַיְשִׁמֹת עַד אָבֵל הַשִּׁטִּים.** כָּאן לִמֶּדְךָ שִׁעוּר מַחֲנֵה יִשְׂרָאֵל שְׁנֵים עָשָׂר מִיל, דְּאָמַר רַבָּה בַּר בַּר חָנָה: לְדִידִי חֲזֵי לִי הַהוּא אַתְרָא וְכוּ': **אָבֵל הַשִּׁטִּים.** מִישׁוֹר שֶׁל שִׁטִּים 'אָבֵל' שְׁמוֹ:

נא-נב| **כִּי אַתֶּם עֹבְרִים אֶת הַיַּרְדֵּן וגו' וְהוֹרַשְׁתֶּם וגו'.** וַהֲלֹא כַּמָּה פְעָמִים הֻזְהֲרוּ עַל כָּךְ! אֶלָּא כָּךְ אָמַר לָהֶם מֹשֶׁה: כְּשֶׁאַתֶּם עוֹבְרִים בַּיַּרְדֵּן בַּיַּבָּשָׁה, עַל מְנָת כֵּן תַּעַבְרוּ, וְאִם לָאו, בָּאִים מַיִם וְשׁוֹטְפִין אֶתְכֶם. וְכֵן מָצִינוּ שֶׁאָמַר לָהֶם יְהוֹשֻׁעַ עוֹדָם בַּיַּרְדֵּן (יהושע ד, י). בְּמַסֶּכֶת סוֹטָה (לד ע"א) וּבְתוֹסֶפְתָּא דְסוֹטָה (ח, ה):

נב| **וְהוֹרַשְׁתֶּם.** וְגֵרַשְׁתֶּם: **מַשְׂכִּיֹּתָם.** כְּתַרְגּוּמוֹ: "בֵּית סִגְדַּתְהוֹן", עַל שֵׁם שֶׁהָיוּ מְסַכְּכִין אֶת הַקַּרְקַע בְּרִצְפַּת אֲבָנִים שַׁיִשׁ לְהִשְׁתַּחֲווֹת עָלֶיהָ בְּפִשּׁוּט יָדַיִם וְרַגְלַיִם, כִּדְכְתִיב: "וְאֶבֶן מַשְׂכִּית... לְהִשְׁתַּחֲוֹת עָלֶיהָ" (ויקרא כו, א): **מַסֵּכֹתָם.** כְּתַרְגּוּמוֹ: "מַתְּכָתְהוֹן":

נג| **וְהוֹרַשְׁתֶּם אֶת הָאָרֶץ.** וְהוֹרַשְׁתֶּם אוֹתָהּ מִיּוֹשְׁבֶיהָ, וְאָז "וִישַׁבְתֶּם בָּהּ" – תּוּכְלוּ לְהִתְקַיֵּם בָּהּ, וְאִם לָאו – לֹא תוּכְלוּ לְהִתְקַיֵּם בָּהּ:

נד| **אֶל אֲשֶׁר יֵצֵא לוֹ שָׁמָּה.** מִקְרָא קָצָר הוּא זֶה, אֶל מָקוֹם אֲשֶׁר יֵצֵא לוֹ שָׁמָּה הַגּוֹרָל לוֹ יִהְיֶה: **לְמַטּוֹת אֲבֹתֵיכֶם.** לְפִי חֶשְׁבּוֹן יוֹצְאֵי מִצְרַיִם. דָּבָר אַחֵר, בִּשְׁנֵים עָשָׂר גְּבוּלִין כְּמִנְיַן הַשְּׁבָטִים:

55 **But if you will not dispossess the inhabitants of the land from before you, it shall be that those who you will leave from them,** who remain in the land, **will be as thorns in your eyes, and as sharp stones in your sides, and they will bear enmity to you in the land in which you dwell.** It is prohibited to attempt to exist alongside them in peace, as you will be unable to live together. Even if you make the effort to do so temporarily, they will eventually cause you to stumble into sin.

56 **It shall be that as I imagined to do to them,** to drive them from the land, **I will do to you.**^D

34 1 **The Lord spoke to Moses, saying:**

2 **Command the children of Israel, and say to them: When you come to the land of Canaan,**^D **this shall be the land that shall fall to you as an inheritance, the land of Canaan according to its borders.**

3 **The southern side shall be for you from the wilderness of Tzin alongside Edom,** on the southeastern edge of the border, **and your southern border shall begin at the** southern **edge of the Dead Sea eastward.** This shall be the easternmost point of the southern border of the land.

4 **Your border shall turn,** from the Dead Sea, **south of Maaleh Akrabim,**^B **and pass toward Tzin, and its terminus shall be,** the border shall pass **south of Kadesh Barnea, and it shall emerge to Hatzar Adar,**^B **and pass toward Atzmon.**^B

5 **The border shall turn from Atzmon toward the Ravine of Egypt,** which is Wadi El-Arish, according to the standard tradition¹⁵ **and its terminus shall be at the** Mediterranean **Sea.**

6 **The western border shall be for you the Great Sea,** the Mediterranean Sea, **and its coast,** which includes everything near the shore, such as reefs and small islands;¹⁶ **this shall be the western border for you.**

7 **This shall be the northern border for you; from the Great Sea** in the west, **you shall veer**¹⁷ **toward Hor Mountain.** Alternatively, this means, that you shall mark a route for yourselves that turns toward Hor Mountain.¹⁸

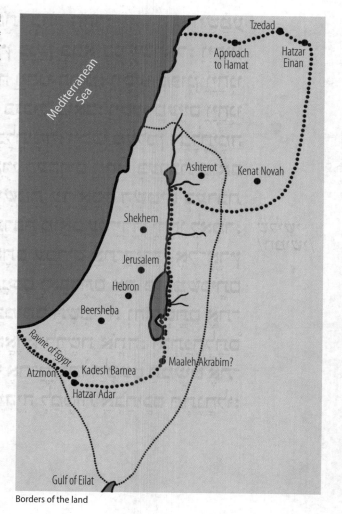

Borders of the land

——— BACKGROUND ———

34:4 | **Maaleh Akrabim:** Generally identified with Naqb es-Safa, about 20 km southeast of Dimona.

Hatzar Adar: Possibly Hetzron, on the border of the inheritance of the tribe of Judah (see Joshua 15:3). Alternatively, it is Ein el-Qedeis, near Kadesh Barnea.

Atzmon: The accepted identification is Ein el-Qaseimeh, 30 km west of Nitzana.

——— DISCUSSION ———

33:56 | **It shall be that as I imagined to do to them, I will do to you:** Clearing the Land of Israel in its entirety was a duty as well as a right. God warned the children of Israel that if they did not fulfill this command they would be banished from the land. Indeed, the failure of the Israelites to rid the land of its local inhabitants brought upon them many troubles that continued throughout the entire period of the judges (see Judges 2:1–3, 6:7–10).

34:2 | **Canaan:** Although the land of Canaan was considered one country, it had never belonged to a single tribe or nation. Rather, many nations and tribes, who came from various other places, lived alongside one another in Canaan. Consequently, the borders of Canaan were not properly defined, and it was necessary for the Torah to delineate them.

נה וְאִם־לֹא תוֹרִישׁוּ אֶת־יֹשְׁבֵי הָאָרֶץ מִפְּנֵיכֶם וְהָיָה אֲשֶׁר תּוֹתִירוּ מֵהֶם לְשִׂכִּים
בְּעֵינֵיכֶם וְלִצְנִינִם בְּצִדֵּיכֶם וְצָרְרוּ אֶתְכֶם עַל־הָאָרֶץ אֲשֶׁר אַתֶּם יֹשְׁבִים בָּהּ׃
נו וְהָיָה כַּאֲשֶׁר דִּמִּיתִי לַעֲשׂוֹת לָהֶם אֶעֱשֶׂה לָכֶם׃
א ב וַיְדַבֵּר יְהוָה אֶל־מֹשֶׁה לֵּאמֹר׃ צַו אֶת־בְּנֵי יִשְׂרָאֵל וְאָמַרְתָּ אֲלֵהֶם כִּי־אַתֶּם בָּאִים לא
ג אֶל־הָאָרֶץ כְּנָעַן זֹאת הָאָרֶץ אֲשֶׁר תִּפֹּל לָכֶם בְּנַחֲלָה אֶרֶץ כְּנַעַן לִגְבֻלֹתֶיהָ׃ וְהָיָה
לָכֶם פְּאַת־נֶגֶב מִמִּדְבַּר־צִן עַל־יְדֵי אֱדוֹם וְהָיָה לָכֶם גְּבוּל נֶגֶב מִקְצֵה יָם־הַמֶּלַח
ד קֵדְמָה׃ וְנָסַב לָכֶם הַגְּבוּל מִנֶּגֶב לְמַעֲלֵה עַקְרַבִּים וְעָבַר צִנָה וְהָיָה תּוֹצְאֹתָיו וְהָיוּ
ה מִנֶּגֶב לְקָדֵשׁ בַּרְנֵעַ וְיָצָא חֲצַר־אַדָּר וְעָבַר עַצְמֹנָה׃ וְנָסַב הַגְּבוּל מֵעַצְמוֹן נַחְלָה
ו מִצְרָיִם וְהָיוּ תוֹצְאֹתָיו הַיָּמָּה׃ וּגְבוּל יָם וְהָיָה לָכֶם הַיָּם הַגָּדוֹל וּגְבוּל זֶה־יִהְיֶה
ז לָכֶם גְּבוּל יָם׃ וְזֶה־יִהְיֶה לָכֶם גְּבוּל צָפוֹן מִן־הַיָּם הַגָּדֹל תְּתָאוּ לָכֶם הֹר הָהָר׃

רש״י

נה | **והיה אשר תותירו מהם.** יהיו לכם לרעה: **לשכים בעיניכם.** ליתדות המנקרות עיניכם. תרגום של יתדות: "סכיא": **ולצנינם.** פותרים בו הפותרים לשון משוכת קוצים הסוככת אתכם, לסגר ולכלא אתכם מאין יוצא ובא: **וצררו אתכם.** כתרגומו:

פרק לד

ב | **זאת הארץ אשר תפל לכם וגו׳.** לפי שהרבה מצות נוהגות בארץ ואין נוהגות בחוצה לארץ, הצרך לכתב מצרני גבולי רוחותיה סביב, לומר לך, מן הגבולים הללו ולפנים המצות נוהגות: **תפל לכם.** על שם שנחלקה בגורל נקראת חלוקה לשון נפילה. ומדרש אגדה אומר: על ידי שהפיל הקדוש ברוך הוא שריהם של שבעה אמות מן השמים וכפתן לפני משה, אמר לו: ראה אין בהם עוד כח:

ג | **והיה לכם פאת נגב.** רוח דרומית אשר מן המזרח למערב: **ממדבר צן.** אשר אצל אדום, מתחיל מקצוע דרומית מזרחית של ארץ תשעת המטות. כיצד? שלש ארצות יושבות בדרומה של ארץ ישראל זו אצל זו: קצת ארץ מצרים, וארץ אדום כלה, וארץ מואב כלה. ארץ מצרים במקצוע דרומית מערבית, שנאמר בפרשה זו: "מעצמון נחלה מצרים והיו תוצאתיו הימה" (להלן פסוק ה), ונחל מצרים היה מהלך על פני כל ארץ מצרים, שנאמר: "מן השיחור אשר על פני מצרים" (יהושע יג, ג), ומפסיק בין ארץ מצרים לארץ ישראל. וארץ אדום אצלה לצד המזרח, וארץ מואב אצל ארץ אדום, בסוף הדרום למזרח. וכשיצאו ישראל ממצרים, אם רצה המקום לקרב את כניסתם לארץ, היה מעבירם את הפלשת לצד צפון ובאין לארץ ישראל, ולא עשה כן, וזהו שנאמר: "ולא נחם אלהים דרך ארץ פלשתים" (שמות יג, יז) שהם יושבים על הים במערבה של ארץ כנען, כענין שנאמר בפלשתים: "ישבי חבל הים גוי כרתים" (צפניה ב, ה), ולא נחם אותו הדרך, אלא הסבן והוציאם דרך דרומה אל המדבר, והוא שקראו יחזקאל: "מדבר העמים" (יחזקאל כ, לה) לפי שהיו כמה אמות יושבים בצדו. והולכין אצל דרומה מן המערב כלפי מזרח תמיד, עד שבאו לדרומה של ארץ אדום, ובקשו ממלך אדום שיניחם לעבר דרך ארצו ולהכנס לארץ דרך רחבה, ולא רצה, והצרכו לסבב את כל דרומה של אדום עד בואם לדרומה של ארץ מואב, שנאמר: "וגם אל מלך מואב שלח ולא אבה" (שופטים יא, יז), והלכו כל דרומה של מואב עד סופה, ומשם הפכו פניהם לצפון עד שסבבו כל מצר מזרחי שלה לרחבה, וכשכלו את מזרחה מצאו את ארץ סיחון ועוג שהיו יושבין במזרחה של ארץ כנען, והירדן מפסיק ביניהם, וזהו שנאמר ביפתח: "וילך במדבר ויסב את ארץ אדום ואת ארץ מואב ויבא ממזרח שמש לארץ מואב" (שם פסוק יח), וכבשו את ארץ סיחון ועוג שהיתה בצפונה של ארץ מואב, וקרבו עד הירדן, והוא כנגד מקצוע צפונית מערבית של ארץ מואב. נמצא שארץ כנען שבעבר הירדן למערב, היה מקצוע דרומית מזרחית שלה אצל אדום:

ד | **ונסב לכם הגבול מנגב למעלה עקרבים.** כל מקום שנאמר: ׳ונסב׳ או ׳ויצא׳, מלמד שלא היה המצר שוה, אלא הולך ויוצא לחוץ. יוצא המצר ועוקם לצד צפונו של עולם באלכסון למערב, ועובר המצר בדרומה של מעלה עקרבים, נמצא מעלה עקרבים לפנים מן המצר: **ועבר צנה.** אל צן, כמו: ׳מצרימה׳: **והיו תוצאתיו.** קצותיו, בדרומה של קדש ברנע: **ויצא חצר אדר.** מתפשט המצר ומרחיב לצד צפון, ונמשך עוד באלכסון למערב, ובא לו לחצר אדר ומשם לעצמון ומשם לנחל מצרים. ולשון ׳ונסב׳ האמור כאן, לפי שכתב: "ויצא חצר אדר", שהתחיל להרחיב משעבר את קדש ברנע, ורחב אותה רצועה שבלטה לצד צפון היתה מקדש עד עצמון, ומשם והלאה נתקצר המצר ונסב לצד הדרום ובא לו לנחל מצרים, ומשם לצד המערב אל הים הגדול, שהוא מצר מערבה של כל ארץ ישראל, נמצא שנחל מצרים במקצוע מערבית דרומית:

ה | **והיו תוצאתיו הימה.** אל מצר המערב, שאין עוד גבול נגב מאריך לצד המערב משם והלאה:

ו | **וגבול ים.** ומצר מערבי מהו?: **והיה לכם הים הגדול.** למצר: **וגבול.** הנסין שבתוך הים אף הם מן הגבול, והם איים שקורין איסל״ש:

ז | **וגבול צפון.** מצר צפון: **מן הים הגדל תתאו לכם הר ההר.** שהוא במקצוע צפונית מערבית, וראשו משפיע ונכנס לתוך הים, ויש מרחב הים לפנים הימנו וחוצה הימנו: **תתאו.** תשפעו לכם לנטות ממערב לצפון אל הר ההר: **תתאו.** לשון סבה, כמו: "אל תא הרצים" (דברי הימים ב׳ יב, יא), "ותאי השער" (יחזקאל מ, י), היציע שקורין אפנדי״ץ, שהוא מוסב ומשפע:

8 **From Hor Mountain you shall veer toward the approach to** [*levo*] **Hamat.** Some explain that Levo Hamat[19] is the name of a place in the land of Hamat.[20] **And the terminus of the border shall be toward Tzedad.**[B]

9 **The border shall go out toward Zifrona, and its terminus shall be Hatzar Einan;**[B] **this shall be your northern border.** Although the identity of all these locations is uncertain, they are known to be in the region of the northern border of modern Syria. In *Targum Yonatan* (verse 7), Hor Mountain is identified as the Amanus range of the Taurus Mountains, which separates Syria and Turkey. The northern border of the land extends very far, as it incorporates even the city of Aleppo in northern Syria. *Fourth aliya (Sixth aliya)*

10 **You shall veer,** or mark a route **toward the east border, from Hatzar Einan to Shefam.**

11 **The border shall descend from Shefam to Rivla,**[B] **east of the spring,** possibly referring to Lake Hula, **and the border shall descend** in an almost straight line, **and shall converge** and touch **upon the bank of the Sea of Galilee eastward,** on the eastern shore of the Sea of Galilee.

12 **The border shall descend to the Jordan** River, **and its terminus shall be at the Dead Sea; this shall be your land according to its borders all around.**[D]

13 **Moses commanded the children of Israel, saying: This is the land that you shall allocate by lot, that the Lord commanded to give to the nine tribes, and to half the tribe;**

14 **for the tribe of the children of Reuben, according to their patrilineal houses, and the tribe of the children of Gad, according to their patrilineal houses, have taken** a portion, **and half the tribe of Manasseh has taken their inheritance** on the eastern side of the Jordan River.

15 **The two tribes and the half tribe have taken their inheritance across the Jordan from Jericho to the east.** The practical division of the tribal portions on the western side of the Jordan is delineated in greater detail in the book of Joshua, chapters 14–17.

16 **The Lord spoke to Moses, saying:**

17 **These are the names of the men who shall allocate the land on your behalf: Elazar the** High **Priest, and Joshua son of Nun.**

18 **You shall take one prince from each tribe,** as their representatives, **to allocate the land.**

19 **These are the names of the men: From the tribe of Judah, Caleb son of Yefuneh,** one of the few surviving elderly members of the generation that left Egypt.

20 **From the tribe of the children of Simeon, Shmuel son of Amihud.**

21 **From the tribe of Benjamin, Elidad son of Kislon.**

22 **From the tribe of the children of Dan,** the representative was a prince,[D] **Buki son of Yogli.**

23 **From the children of Joseph: From the tribe of the children of Manasseh a prince, Haniel son of Efod;**

24 **From the tribe of the children of Ephraim a prince, Kemuel son of Shiftan.**

25 **From the tribe of the children of Zebulun a prince, Elitzafan son of Parnakh.**

26 **From the tribe of the children of Issachar a prince, Paltiel the son of Azan.**

27 **From the tribe of the children of Asher a prince, Ahihud son of Shelomi.**

BACKGROUND

34:8 | **Tzedad:** Generally identified with the village of Sadad, roughly 100 km northeast of Damascus, near the road between Damascus and Homs.

34:9 | **Zifrona; Hatzar Einan:** Some identify these locations with two oases, Huwwarin and El Qaryatein, east of Tzedad.

34:11 | **Rivla:** This is the capital city of the land of Hamat, to which the kings of Judah were exiled (II Kings 23:33; Jeremiah 39:6, 52:27). It is identified as Ribleh, on the bank of the Orontes, about 30 km south of Homs. Some claim that the descriptions, "east of the spring, and the border shall descend," do not fit Ribleh, but are referring to a different place, southeast of that town, near the Sea of Galilee. Yet others say it is the springs at Lyon, north of the Yarmuk, roughly 5 km east of the Sea of Galilee.

DISCUSSION

34:12 | **This shall be your land according to its borders all around:** These borders are known as borders of those who ascended from Egypt (*Ḥagiga* 3b). In practice, Israel was never in control of this entire area. There were always enclaves inhabited by foreign nations, some of which the Israelites did not even attempt to conquer. For example, no attempt was even made to capture the areas of Tyre and Sidon, occupied by the Phoenicians, the Sidonians, and the Tyrians. Additionally, the Philistines dwelled in the coastal strip of the southern plains, and despite efforts to conquer this region in the days of David, Solomon, and probably the Hasmoneans as well, the task was never completed.

Nonetheless, in the era of David and Solomon, the border of Israel reached the northernmost edge mentioned here, and extended even further. In fact, it is stated that Solomon built the city of Palmyra, an oasis in the Syrian desert, far to the east of the border (II Chronicles 8:1–6). However, a full conquest of all the territory included in the borders of the land was never carried out. The expanse of Israel as depicted here includes the entire modern-day State of Israel, as well as most of modern-day Syria. Conversely, according to certain opinions, the borders delineated in this chapter do not include the southern Negev, which is part of the State of Israel.

34:22 | **From the tribe of the children of Dan a prince:** It seems that the representatives of the previous tribes were not princes but dignified members of that tribe. In verse 18 they are all called princes, but that appointment applied only for the purpose of dividing the land, not for other matters. Consequently, in the list they are mentioned by name alone, without the title of prince (see *Ha'amek Davar*).

ח ט מֵהֹר הָהָר תְּתָאוּ לְבֹא חֲמָת וְהָיוּ תּוֹצְאֹת הַגְּבֻל צְדָדָה: וְיָצָא הַגְּבֻל זִפְרֹנָה וְהָיוּ
י תוֹצְאֹתָיו חֲצַר עֵינָן זֶה־יִהְיֶה לָכֶם גְּבוּל צָפוֹן: וְהִתְאַוִּיתֶם לָכֶם לִגְבוּל קֵדְמָה
יא מֵחֲצַר עֵינָן שְׁפָמָה: וְיָרַד הַגְּבֻל מִשְּׁפָם הָרִבְלָה מִקֶּדֶם לָעָיִן וְיָרַד הַגְּבֻל וּמָחָה
יב עַל־כֶּתֶף יָם־כִּנֶּרֶת קֵדְמָה: וְיָרַד הַגְּבוּל הַיַּרְדֵּנָה וְהָיוּ תוֹצְאֹתָיו יָם הַמֶּלַח זֹאת
יג תִּהְיֶה לָכֶם הָאָרֶץ לִגְבֻלֹתֶיהָ סָבִיב: וַיְצַו מֹשֶׁה אֶת־בְּנֵי יִשְׂרָאֵל לֵאמֹר זֹאת
הָאָרֶץ אֲשֶׁר תִּתְנַחֲלוּ אֹתָהּ בְּגוֹרָל אֲשֶׁר צִוָּה יְהוָה לָתֵת לְתִשְׁעַת הַמַּטּוֹת
יד וַחֲצִי הַמַּטֶּה: כִּי לָקְחוּ מַטֵּה בְנֵי הָרְאוּבֵנִי לְבֵית אֲבֹתָם וּמַטֵּה בְנֵי־הַגָּדִי לְבֵית
טו אֲבֹתָם וַחֲצִי מַטֵּה מְנַשֶּׁה לָקְחוּ נַחֲלָתָם: שְׁנֵי הַמַּטּוֹת וַחֲצִי הַמַּטֶּה לָקְחוּ נַחֲלָתָם
מֵעֵבֶר לְיַרְדֵּן יְרֵחוֹ קֵדְמָה מִזְרָחָה:

טז יז וַיְדַבֵּר יְהוָה אֶל־מֹשֶׁה לֵּאמֹר: אֵלֶּה שְׁמוֹת הָאֲנָשִׁים אֲשֶׁר־יִנְחֲלוּ לָכֶם אֶת־הָאָרֶץ רביעי /ששי/
יח אֶלְעָזָר הַכֹּהֵן וִיהוֹשֻׁעַ בִּן־נוּן: וְנָשִׂיא אֶחָד נָשִׂיא אֶחָד מִמַּטֶּה תִּקְחוּ לִנְחֹל אֶת־
יט כ הָאָרֶץ: וְאֵלֶּה שְׁמוֹת הָאֲנָשִׁים לְמַטֵּה יְהוּדָה כָּלֵב בֶּן־יְפֻנֶּה: וּלְמַטֵּה בְּנֵי שִׁמְעוֹן
כא כב שְׁמוּאֵל בֶּן־עַמִּיהוּד: לְמַטֵּה בִנְיָמִן אֱלִידָד בֶּן־כִּסְלוֹן: וּלְמַטֵּה בְנֵי־דָן נָשִׂיא בֻּקִּי
כג כד בֶּן־יָגְלִי: לִבְנֵי יוֹסֵף לְמַטֵּה בְנֵי־מְנַשֶּׁה נָשִׂיא חַנִּיאֵל בֶּן־אֵפֹד: וּלְמַטֵּה בְנֵי־אֶפְרַיִם
כה כו נָשִׂיא קְמוּאֵל בֶּן־שִׁפְטָן: וּלְמַטֵּה בְנֵי־זְבוּלֻן נָשִׂיא אֱלִיצָפָן בֶּן־פַּרְנָךְ: וּלְמַטֵּה
כז בְנֵי־יִשָּׂשכָר נָשִׂיא פַּלְטִיאֵל בֶּן־עַזָּן: וּלְמַטֵּה בְנֵי־אָשֵׁר נָשִׂיא אֲחִיהוּד בֶּן־שְׁלֹמִי:

רש"י

ח | **מהר ההר.** תסבו ותלכו אל מצר הצפון לצד המזרח, ותפגעו ב"לבא חמת", זו אנטוכיא: **תוצאת הגבל.** סופי הגבול. כל מקום שנאמר: 'תוצאות הגבול', או המצר כלה שם לגמרי ואינו עובר להלן כלל, או משם מתפשט ומרחיב ויוצא לאחוריו להמשך להלן באלכסון יותר מן הרחב הראשון, ולענין רחב המדה הראשון קרוי 'תוצאות', שמשם כלתה אותה מדה:

ט-יב | **והיו תוצאתיו חצר עינן.** הוא היה סוף המצר הצפוני, ונמצא חצר עינן במקצוע צפונית מזרחית, ומשם "והתאויתם לכם" אל מצר המזרחי: **והתאויתם.** לשון הסבה ונטיה, כמו: "תתאו": **שפמה.** במצר המזרחי, ומשם הרבלה: **מקדם לעין.** שם מקום, והמצר הולך במזרחו, ונמצא העין לפנים מן המצר, ומארץ ישראל הוא: **וירד הגבל.** כל שהגבול הולך מצפון לדרום, הוא יורד והולך: **ומחה על כתף ים כנרת קדמה.** שיהא ים כנרת תוך לגבול במערב, והגבול במזרח ים כנרת, ומשם ירד אל הירדן, והירדן מושך ובא מן הצפון לדרום באלכסון, נוטה לצד מזרח, ומתקרב לצד ארץ כנען כנגד ים כנרת, ומושך לצד מזרחה של ארץ ישראל כנגד ים כנרת, עד שנופל בים המלח, ומשם כלה הגבול בתוצאותיו אל ים המלח, שממנו התחלת מצר מקצוע דרומית מזרחית, הרי סבבת אותה לארבע רוחותיה:

טו | **קדמה מזרחה.** אל פני העולם שהם במזרח, שרוח מזרחית קרויה פנים ומערבית קרויה אחור, לפיכך דרום לימין וצפון לשמאל:

יז | **אשר ינחלו לכם.** בשבילכם, כל נשיא ונשיא אפוטרופוס לשבטו, ומחלק נחלת השבט למשפחות ולגברים, ובורר לכל אחד ואחד חלק הגון, ומה שהם עושים יהיה עשוי כאלו עשאום שלוחים. ולא יתכן לפרש 'לכם' זה ככל 'לכם' שבמקרא, שאם כן היה לו לכתב: 'ינחילו לכם', "ינחלו" משמע שהם נוחלים לכם בשבילכם ובמקומכם, כמו: "ה' ילחם לכם" (שמות יד, יד):

יח | **לנחל את הארץ.** שיהא נוחל וחולק אותה במקומכם:

28 **From the tribe of the children of Naphtali a prince, Pedahel son of Amihud.**

29 **These are those** men **whom the Lord commanded to allocate the inheritance to the children of Israel,** to ensure that all inherit their rightful portion, **in the land of Canaan.**

35 1 Each of the nine and a half tribes was to receive a fair portion on the western side of the Jordan. Reuben, Gad, and half the tribe of Manasseh had already been promised their portion on the eastern side of the Jordan River. Now God commanded that each of the tribes had to set aside from their territory residential areas for the Levites. **The Lord spoke to Moses on the plains of Moav along the Jordan at Jericho, saying:**

Fifth aliya

2 **Command the children of Israel, and they shall give to the Levites from the allocation of their ancestral portion cities in which to live, and** an open **for the cities around them, you shall give to the Levites.**

3 **The cities shall be for them to live, and their tracts** surrounding their cities **shall be for their animals, and for their property, and for all their provisions.**[21]

4 **The** surrounding **tracts of the cities that you shall give to the Levites, from the wall of the city and outward, one thousand cubits all around.**

5 In all, **you shall measure outside the city:** on **the eastern side two thousand cubits,**[D] **and the southern side two thousand cubits, and the western side two thousand cubits, and the northern side two thousand cubits, and the city in the middle. This shall be for them the** surrounding **tracts of the cities.**

6 Included in **the cities that you shall give to the Levites,** there shall be **the six cities of refuge that you shall give for the murderer to flee there.** Six of the Levite cities shall be cities of refuge, **and with them you shall give forty-two** additional **cities.**[D]

7 **All the cities that you shall give to the Levites are forty-eight cities, them,** the cities themselves, **and their surrounding tracts.** Since the portions of each tribe had yet to be delineated, the chapter does not list these cities.

8 **The cities which you shall give from the portion of the children of Israel, from the greater** tribes **you shall increase,** by giving the Levites more cities, **and from the lesser,** the smaller tribes, **you shall decrease;**[22] **each tribe according to its inheritance that it will inherit shall give from its cities to the Levites.** The Levites shall receive small tracts of land scattered among the portions of the tribes.[23]

9 Apropos the mention of the Levite cities, the Torah reiterates the laws of the unwitting murderer, who must flee to one of those cities. **The Lord spoke to Moses, saying:**

Sixth aliya (Seventh aliya)

10 **Speak to the children of Israel, and say to them: When you cross the Jordan to the land of Canaan,**

11 **you shall designate cities, cities of refuge they shall be for you; and the murderer who smites a person unwittingly shall flee there.**

12 **The cities shall be for you for refuge from the** blood **redeemer, that the murderer shall not die, until he stands before the congregation for judgment.** These cities will initially absorb all murderers until they stand trial, protecting them from the relatives of the deceased. The murderer who arrives there is under the protection of God's statutes until the court decides whether he indeed murdered unwittingly and must remain in exile in a city of refuge; whether he is an intentional murderer, and is therefore liable to receive the death penalty; or whether he is entirely exempt.[24]

13 **The cities that you shall give, six cities of refuge you shall have.**

14 **Three cities you shall place across the Jordan,**[D] **and three cities you shall give in the land of Canaan; they shall be cities of refuge.**

15 The chapter explains the details of this law: **For the children of Israel, and for the stranger and for the resident alien among**

DISCUSSION

35:5 | **You shall measure outside the city: the eastern side two thousand cubits:** An area extending 2000 cubits in each direction was allotted to each city (see Ramban; *Ha'amek Davar*). One thousand cubits of this extension was the surrounding tract mentioned in verses 2–4. The purpose of the further thousand cubits is not stated here; it probably served as forest land and for various requirements of the city, such as fields and vineyards (see Rashi on verse 4; *Sota* 26b; *Eruvim* 56b). The whole area, 2000 cubits, in all directions is also referred to as the surrounding tract of the city (See Leviticus 25:34; Joshua 21).

35:6 | **For the murderer to flee there, and with them you shall give forty-two cities:** According to the tradition of the Sages, murderers could be absorbed by any of the Levite cities, at least temporarily, with the agreement of the residents of that city. The difference was that six of the cities were specifically designated for this purpose, and the signposts on roads leading to them stated that they were cities of refuge (see *Makkot* 10a, 13a; *Likkutei Sefat Emet; Or HaḤayyim*).

35:14 | **Three cities you shall place across the Jordan:** Although the land of Canaan was to be more densely populated than on the eastern side of the Jordan River, it is for this very reason that there was a need for an equal number of three cities on the eastern side of the river, one in each region, due to the great distance between settlements. Furthermore, the Sages explain that murderers were more commonly found in the Gilad region than on the western side of the Jordan River (*Makkot* 9b).

כח כט וּלְמַטֵּה בְנֵי־נַפְתָּלִי נָשִׂיא פְּדַהְאֵל בֶּן־עַמִּיהוּד: אֵלֶּה אֲשֶׁר צִוָּה יְהוָה לְנַחֵל
אֶת־בְּנֵי־יִשְׂרָאֵל בְּאֶרֶץ כְּנָעַן:
א ב וַיְדַבֵּר יְהוָה אֶל־מֹשֶׁה בְּעַרְבֹת מוֹאָב עַל־יַרְדֵּן יְרֵחוֹ לֵאמֹר: צַו אֶת־בְּנֵי יִשְׂרָאֵל חמישי
וְנָתְנוּ לַלְוִיִּם מִנַּחֲלַת אֲחֻזָּתָם עָרִים לָשָׁבֶת וּמִגְרָשׁ לֶעָרִים סְבִיבֹתֵיהֶם תִּתְּנוּ
ג לַלְוִיִּם: וְהָיוּ הֶעָרִים לָהֶם לָשָׁבֶת וּמִגְרְשֵׁיהֶם יִהְיוּ לִבְהֶמְתָּם וְלִרְכֻשָׁם וּלְכֹל חַיָּתָם:
ד ה וּמִגְרְשֵׁי הֶעָרִים אֲשֶׁר תִּתְּנוּ לַלְוִיִּם מִקִּיר הָעִיר וָחוּצָה אֶלֶף אַמָּה סָבִיב: וּמַדֹּתֶם
מִחוּץ לָעִיר אֶת־פְּאַת־קֵדְמָה אַלְפַּיִם בָּאַמָּה וְאֶת־פְּאַת־נֶגֶב אַלְפַּיִם בָּאַמָּה וְאֶת־
פְּאַת־יָם אַלְפַּיִם בָּאַמָּה וְאֵת פְּאַת צָפוֹן אַלְפַּיִם בָּאַמָּה וְהָעִיר בַּתָּוֶךְ זֶה יִהְיֶה
ו לָהֶם מִגְרְשֵׁי הֶעָרִים: וְאֵת הֶעָרִים אֲשֶׁר תִּתְּנוּ לַלְוִיִּם אֵת שֵׁשׁ־עָרֵי הַמִּקְלָט
ז אֲשֶׁר תִּתְּנוּ לָנֻס שָׁמָּה הָרֹצֵחַ וַעֲלֵיהֶם תִּתְּנוּ אַרְבָּעִים וּשְׁתַּיִם עִיר: כָּל־הֶעָרִים
ח אֲשֶׁר תִּתְּנוּ לַלְוִיִּם אַרְבָּעִים וּשְׁמֹנֶה עִיר אֶתְהֶן וְאֶת־מִגְרְשֵׁיהֶן: וְהֶעָרִים אֲשֶׁר
תִּתְּנוּ מֵאֲחֻזַּת בְּנֵי־יִשְׂרָאֵל מֵאֵת הָרַב תַּרְבּוּ וּמֵאֵת הַמְעַט תַּמְעִיטוּ אִישׁ כְּפִי
נַחֲלָתוֹ אֲשֶׁר יִנְחָלוּ יִתֵּן מֵעָרָיו לַלְוִיִּם:
ט וַיְדַבֵּר יְהוָה אֶל־מֹשֶׁה לֵּאמֹר: דַּבֵּר אֶל־בְּנֵי יִשְׂרָאֵל וְאָמַרְתָּ אֲלֵהֶם כִּי אַתֶּם לב ששי /שביעי/
יא עֹבְרִים אֶת־הַיַּרְדֵּן אַרְצָה כְּנָעַן: וְהִקְרִיתֶם לָכֶם עָרִים עָרֵי מִקְלָט תִּהְיֶינָה
יב לָכֶם וְנָס שָׁמָּה רֹצֵחַ מַכֵּה־נֶפֶשׁ בִּשְׁגָגָה: וְהָיוּ לָכֶם הֶעָרִים לְמִקְלָט מִגֹּאֵל
יג וְלֹא יָמוּת הָרֹצֵחַ עַד־עָמְדוֹ לִפְנֵי הָעֵדָה לַמִּשְׁפָּט: וְהֶעָרִים אֲשֶׁר תִּתֵּנוּ שֵׁשׁ־
יד עָרֵי מִקְלָט תִּהְיֶינָה לָכֶם: אֵת ׀ שְׁלֹשׁ הֶעָרִים תִּתְּנוּ מֵעֵבֶר לַיַּרְדֵּן וְאֵת שְׁלֹשׁ
טו הֶעָרִים תִּתְּנוּ בְּאֶרֶץ כְּנָעַן עָרֵי מִקְלָט תִּהְיֶינָה: לִבְנֵי יִשְׂרָאֵל וְלַגֵּר וְלַתּוֹשָׁב

כט] לְנַחֵל אֶת בְּנֵי יִשְׂרָאֵל. שֶׁהֵם יַנְחִילוּ אוֹתָהּ לָהֶם לְמַחְלְקוֹתֶיהָ:

פרק לה

ב] וּמִגְרָשׁ. רֶוַח מָקוֹם חָלָק חוּץ לָעִיר סָבִיב לִהְיוֹת לְנוֹי לָעִיר, וְאֵין רַשָּׁאִין לִבְנוֹת שָׁם בַּיִת וְלֹא לִנְטֹעַ כֶּרֶם וְלֹא לִזְרֹעַ זְרִיעָה:

ג] וּלְכֹל חַיָּתָם. לְכָל צָרְכֵיהֶם.

ד] אֶלֶף אַמָּה סָבִיב. וְאַחֲרָיו הוּא אוֹמֵר: "אַלְפַּיִם בָּאַמָּה" (פסוק ה), הָא כֵּיצַד? אַלְפַּיִם הוּא נוֹתֵן לָהֶם סָבִיב, וּמֵהֶם הָאֶלֶף הַפְּנִימִיִּים לְמִגְרָשׁ וְהַחִיצוֹנִים לְשָׂדוֹת וּכְרָמִים:

יא] וְהִקְרִיתֶם. אֵין הַקְרָיָה אֶלָּא לְשׁוֹן הַזְמָנָה, וְכֵן הוּא אוֹמֵר: "כִּי הִקְרָה ה' אֱלֹהֶיךָ לְפָנָי" (בראשית כז, כ).

יב] מִגֹּאֵל. מִפְּנֵי גּוֹאֵל הַדָּם שֶׁהוּא קָרוֹב לַנִּרְצָח:

יג] שֵׁשׁ עָרֵי מִקְלָט. מַגִּיד שֶׁאַף עַל פִּי שֶׁהִבְדִּיל מֹשֶׁה בְּחַיָּיו שָׁלֹשׁ עָרִים בְּעֵבֶר הַיַּרְדֵּן, לֹא הָיוּ קוֹלְטוֹת עַד שֶׁנִּבְחֲרוּ שָׁלֹשׁ שֶׁנָּתַן יְהוֹשֻׁעַ בְּאֶרֶץ כְּנָעַן:

יד] אֵת שְׁלֹשׁ הֶעָרִים וְגוֹ'. אַף עַל פִּי שֶׁבְּאֶרֶץ כְּנַעַן תִּשְׁעָה שְׁבָטִים וְכָאן אֵינָן אֶלָּא שְׁנַיִם, הִשְׁוָה מִנְיַן עָרֵי מִקְלָט שֶׁלָּהֶם, מִשּׁוּם דִּבְגִלְעָד נְפִישֵׁי רוֹצְחִים, דִּכְתִיב: "גִּלְעָד קִרְיַת פֹּעֲלֵי אָוֶן עֲקֻבָּה מִדָּם" (הושע ו, ח).

them, these six cities shall be for refuge to flee there, anyone who kills a person unwittingly.

16 But if he smote him with an instrument of iron, or some other destructive implement, and he died, he is a murderer; the murderer shall be put to death. Since he struck the person with a utensil that could cause death, it is assumed that he meant to kill him and he is sentenced as a murderer, unless his innocence is proven.

17 Similarly, if he smote him with a hand-sized stone,[25] or a sizable stone that is used as a tool for handiwork,[26] by means of which one may likely die, and he died, he is a murderer; the murderer shall be put to death.

18 Or if he smote him with a hand-sized weapon of wood, by means of which one may likely die, and he died, he is a murderer. When one fatally strikes a person with an implement that is likely to kill, he is presumed to have committed the act on purpose, and therefore the murderer shall be put to death.

19 The blood redeemer, a relative of the deceased; if he had no relative, the court appoints a blood redeemer for him;[27] he shall put the murderer to death;[D] when he encounters him, he shall put him to death. He has permission to kill the murderer.

20 If he shoved him with enmity, without using an implement, but he pushed him violently in a manner designed to cause harm, or cast upon him some object intentionally, with malice forethought, and he died;

21 or he smote him with his hand with animosity, and he died; in all such cases the assailant shall be put to death; he is a murderer; the blood redeemer shall put the murderer to death when he encounters him.

22 But if there is no apparent reason to suspect that he meant to kill him, e.g., he shoved him suddenly, unintentionally,[28]

and without animosity, or he cast upon him any vessel without intention.

23 or with any stone, by means of which one may die, without seeing him, as he was unaware of the presence of the victim, and he dropped it upon him, and he died, and he did not bear enmity to him nor did he seek his harm,

24 the congregation of Israel, represented by the court, shall judge between the assailant and the blood redeemer[D] according to these ordinances.

25 The congregation shall deliver the murderer from the hand of the blood redeemer, if it is established that he committed the act unwittingly and he is worthy of being saved, and the congregation shall restore him to the city of his refuge, where he fled, as he was taken from the city of refuge to stand trial in the region where the crime was committed. And he shall live in it, the city of refuge, until the death of the High Priest,[D] who was anointed[29] with the sacred oil. The murderer must remain in exile in the city of refuge for an unknown period of time, as it depends on the age and health of the High Priest, and other factors over which the accidental murderer has no control. Consequently, he might be tempted to leave his city of refuge.

26 But if the murderer emerges, for whatever reason, from the border of the city of his refuge to which he flees,

27 and the blood redeemer finds him outside the border of the city of his refuge, and the blood redeemer murders the murderer;[D] he has no bloodguilt meaning that the blood redeemer is free of guilt.

28 Because he shall live within the city of his refuge until the death of the High Priest; and after the death of the High

---

DISCUSSION

35:19 | **The blood redeemer, he shall put the murderer to death:** According to some commentaries, this is referring to an unwitting murderer who has left his city of refuge (Rashi, *Sanhedrin* 45b). Some say that this verse applies only in the case of an intentional murderer, if the court is unable to execute him for some reason (see Ramban, *Sefer HaMitzvot*, omitted positive commandment 13; see also Rabbi Samson Raphael Hirsch; *Ha'amek Davar*).

35:24 | **The congregation shall judge between the assailant and the blood redeemer:** The blood redeemer is not depicted here as hotheaded, consumed by feelings of hatred toward the murderer and eager to avenge the blood of his relative. Rather, he serves as a prosecutor at the murder trial. For this reason, the Sages state that if the victim of a murder has no relative who can serve as his blood redeemer, the

court must appoint one on his behalf, to find the guilty party and stand against him in court (see *Sanhedrin* 45b; Ralbag, II Samuel 14:7).

35:25 | **Until the death of the High Priest:** The High Priest is the holiest individual in Israel, and therefore his death atones for the entire nation. Someone who killed a person unwittingly and has been exiled to a city of refuge is in a sense under the patronage of the High Priest. He goes free when the High Priest dies because he no longer requires his protection. Furthermore, the accidental killing of someone contradicts the basic mission of the priests, represented by the High Priest. The function of the priest is atonement, instruction, and the correction of people's ways. When someone performs the terrible transgression of killing a person through lack of foresight, it serves as a warning to the priests and their most senior member. Therefore, the

death of the High Priest concludes the atonement process for the tragic incident (see Rabbi Samson Raphael Hirsch). Some suggest a different explanation: The death of a great personality, admired by all, serves to calm the spirit of the blood redeemer. He is comforted from his personal tragedy by his participation in the national tragedy (Rambam, *Guide of the Perplexed* 3:40).

35:27 | **And the blood redeemer murders the murderer:** In effect, the blood redeemer is not only the prosecutor at the trial, but also the one responsible for executing the punishment determined by the court. If the unwitting murderer leaves the vicinity of his city of refuge, the blood redeemer has the right to carry out his punishment without the need for further intervention on the part of the court.

בְּתוֹכְכֶם תִּהְיֶינָה שֵׁשׁ־הֶעָרִים הָאֵלֶּה לְמִקְלָט לָנֻס שָׁמָּה כָּל־מַכֵּה־נֶפֶשׁ בִּשְׁגָגָה:

טז וְאִם־בִּכְלִי בַרְזֶל | הִכָּהוּ וַיָּמֹת רֹצֵחַ הוּא מוֹת יוּמַת הָרֹצֵחַ: וְאִם בְּאֶבֶן יָד אֲשֶׁר־

יז יָמוּת בָּהּ הִכָּהוּ וַיָּמֹת רֹצֵחַ הוּא מוֹת יוּמַת הָרֹצֵחַ: אוֹ בִּכְלִי עֵץ־יָד אֲשֶׁר יָמוּת

יח בּוֹ הִכָּהוּ וַיָּמֹת רֹצֵחַ הוּא מוֹת יוּמַת הָרֹצֵחַ: גֹּאֵל הַדָּם הוּא יָמִית אֶת־הָרֹצֵחַ

יט בְּפִגְעוֹ־בוֹ הוּא יְמִתֶנּוּ: וְאִם־בְּשִׂנְאָה יֶהְדָּפֶנּוּ אוֹ־הִשְׁלִיךְ עָלָיו בִּצְדִיָּה וַיָּמֹת:

כ אוֹ בְאֵיבָה הִכָּהוּ בְיָדוֹ וַיָּמֹת מוֹת־יוּמַת הַמַּכֶּה רֹצֵחַ הוּא גֹּאֵל הַדָּם יָמִית אֶת־

כא הָרֹצֵחַ בְּפִגְעוֹ־בוֹ: וְאִם־בְּפֶתַע בְּלֹא־אֵיבָה הֲדָפוֹ אוֹ־הִשְׁלִיךְ עָלָיו כָּל־כְּלִי בְּלֹא

כב צְדִיָּה: אוֹ בְכָל־אֶבֶן אֲשֶׁר־יָמוּת בָּהּ בְּלֹא רְאוֹת וַיַּפֵּל עָלָיו וַיָּמֹת וְהוּא לֹא־אוֹיֵב

כג לוֹ וְלֹא מְבַקֵּשׁ רָעָתוֹ: וְשָׁפְטוּ הָעֵדָה בֵּין הַמַּכֶּה וּבֵין גֹּאֵל הַדָּם עַל הַמִּשְׁפָּטִים

כד הָאֵלֶּה: וְהִצִּילוּ הָעֵדָה אֶת־הָרֹצֵחַ מִיַּד גֹּאֵל הַדָּם וְהֵשִׁיבוּ אֹתוֹ הָעֵדָה אֶל־עִיר

כה מִקְלָטוֹ אֲשֶׁר־נָס שָׁמָּה וְיָשַׁב בָּהּ עַד־מוֹת הַכֹּהֵן הַגָּדֹל אֲשֶׁר־מָשַׁח אֹתוֹ בְּשֶׁמֶן

כו הַקֹּדֶשׁ: וְאִם־יָצֹא יֵצֵא הָרֹצֵחַ אֶת־גְּבוּל עִיר מִקְלָטוֹ אֲשֶׁר יָנוּס שָׁמָּה: וּמָצָא

אֹתוֹ גֹּאֵל הַדָּם מִחוּץ לִגְבוּל עִיר מִקְלָטוֹ וְרָצַח גֹּאֵל הַדָּם אֶת־הָרֹצֵחַ אֵין לוֹ דָּם:

טז וְאִם־בִּכְלִי בַרְזֶל הִכָּהוּ. אֵין זֶה מְדַבֵּר בְּהוֹרֵג בְּשׁוֹגֵג אֶלָּא בְּהוֹרֵג בְּמֵזִיד, וּבָא לְלַמֵּד שֶׁהַהוֹרֵג בְּכָל דָּבָר צָרִיךְ שֶׁיְּהֵא בּוֹ שִׁעוּר כְּדֵי לְהָמִית, שֶׁנֶּאֱמַר בְּכֻלָּם: "אֲשֶׁר יָמוּת בּוֹ", כְּדִמְתַרְגְּמִינָן: "דְּהָיֵא כְמִסַּת דִּימוּת בָּהּ", חוּץ מִן הַבַּרְזֶל, שֶׁגָּלוּי וְיָדוּעַ לִפְנֵי הַקָּדוֹשׁ בָּרוּךְ הוּא שֶׁהַבַּרְזֶל מֵמִית בְּכָל שֶׁהוּא, אֲפִלּוּ מַחַט, לְפִיכָךְ לֹא נָתְנָה בוֹ תוֹרָה שִׁעוּר לִכְתֹּב בּוֹ: "אֲשֶׁר יָמוּת בּוֹ". וְאִם תֹּאמַר בְּהוֹרֵג בְּשׁוֹגֵג הַכָּתוּב מְדַבֵּר, הֲרֵי הוּא אוֹמֵר לְמַטָּה: "אוֹ בְכָל אֶבֶן אֲשֶׁר יָמוּת בָּהּ בְּלֹא רְאוֹת" וְגו' (להלן פסוק כג), לְמַד עַל הָאֲמוּרִים לְמַעְלָה שֶׁבְּהוֹרֵג בְּמֵזִיד הַכָּתוּב מְדַבֵּר:

יז בְּאֶבֶן יָד. שֶׁיֵּשׁ בָּהּ מְלֹא יָד: **אֲשֶׁר יָמוּת בָּהּ.** שֶׁיֵּשׁ בָּהּ שִׁעוּר לְהָמִית, כְּתַרְגּוּמוֹ. לְפִי שֶׁנֶּאֱמַר: "וְהִכָּה אִישׁ אֶת רֵעֵהוּ בְּאֶבֶן" (שמות כא, יח) וְלֹא נָתַן בָּהּ שִׁעוּר, יָכוֹל כָּל שֶׁהוּא? לְכָךְ נֶאֱמַר: "אֲשֶׁר יָמוּת בָּהּ":

יח אוֹ בִכְלִי עֵץ יָד. לְפִי שֶׁנֶּאֱמַר: "וְכִי יַכֶּה אִישׁ אֶת עַבְדּוֹ אוֹ אֶת אֲמָתוֹ בַּשֵּׁבֶט" (שם פסוק כ), יָכוֹל כָּל שֶׁהוּא? לְכָךְ נֶאֱמַר בְּעֵץ: "אֲשֶׁר יָמוּת בּוֹ", שֶׁיֵּהֵא בּוֹ כְּדֵי לְהָמִית:

יט בְּפִגְעוֹ בוֹ. אֲפִלּוּ בְּתוֹךְ עָרֵי מִקְלָט:

כא בִּצְדִיָּה. כְּתַרְגּוּמוֹ: "בְּכַמְנָא", בְּמַאֲרָב:

כב בְּפֶתַע. בְּאֹנֶס, וְתַרְגּוּמוֹ: "בִּתְכֵף", שֶׁהָיָה סָמוּךְ לוֹ, וְלֹא הָיָה לוֹ שְׁהוּת לְהִזָּהֵר עָלָיו:

כג אוֹ בְכָל אֶבֶן אֲשֶׁר יָמוּת בָּהּ. הִכָּהוּ: **בְּלֹא רְאוֹת.** שֶׁלֹּא רָאָהוּ: **וַיַּפֵּל עָלָיו.** מִכָּאן אָמְרוּ, הַהוֹרֵג דֶּרֶךְ יְרִידָה – גּוֹלֶה, דֶּרֶךְ עֲלִיָּה – אֵינוֹ גוֹלֶה:

כה עַד מוֹת הַכֹּהֵן הַגָּדֹל. שֶׁהוּא בָּא לְהַשְׁרוֹת שְׁכִינָה בְּיִשְׂרָאֵל וּלְהַאֲרִיךְ יְמֵיהֶם, וְהָרוֹצֵחַ בָּא לְסַלֵּק אֶת הַשְּׁכִינָה

מִיִּשְׂרָאֵל וּמְקַצֵּר אֶת יְמֵי הַחַיִּים, אֵינוֹ כְדַאי לִהְיוֹת לִפְנֵי כֹהֵן גָּדוֹל. דָּבָר אַחֵר, לְפִי שֶׁהָיָה לוֹ לְכֹהֵן גָּדוֹל לְהִתְפַּלֵּל שֶׁלֹּא תֶאֱרַע תַּקָּלָה זוֹ לְיִשְׂרָאֵל בְּחַיָּיו: **אֲשֶׁר מָשַׁח אֹתוֹ בְּשֶׁמֶן הַקֹּדֶשׁ.** לְפִי פְשׁוּטוֹ, מִן הַמִּקְרָאוֹת הַקְּצָרִים הוּא שֶׁלֹּא פֵּרַשׁ מִי מְשָׁחוֹ, אֶלָּא כְּמוֹ: אֲשֶׁר מָשַׁח הַמּוֹשֵׁחַ אוֹתוֹ בְּשֶׁמֶן הַקֹּדֶשׁ. וְרַבּוֹתֵינוּ דְּרָשׁוּהוּ בְּמַסֶּכֶת מַכּוֹת (דף יא ע"ב) לְהַרְבּוֹת דָּבָר, לְלַמֵּד שֶׁאִם עַד שֶׁלֹּא נִגְמַר דִּינוֹ מֵת הַכֹּהֵן הַגָּדוֹל וּמִנּוּ אַחֵר תַּחְתָּיו, וּלְאַחַר מִכָּאן נִגְמַר דִּינוֹ, חוֹזֵר בְּמִיתָתוֹ שֶׁל שֵׁנִי, שֶׁנֶּאֱמַר: "אֲשֶׁר מָשַׁח אֹתוֹ", וְכִי הוּא מְשָׁחוֹ לַכֹּהֵן, אוֹ הַכֹּהֵן מָשַׁח אוֹתוֹ? אֶלָּא לְהָבִיא אֶת הַנִּמְשָׁח בְּיָמָיו שֶׁמַּחֲזִירוֹ בְּמִיתָתוֹ:

כו אֵין לוֹ דָּם. הֲרֵי הוּא כְהוֹרֵג אֶת הַמֵּת, שֶׁאֵין לוֹ דָּם:

Priest the murderer shall return to the land of his ancestral portion.

29 Although the laws of the cities of refuge are connected to the approaching historical event dealt with in this section, the settlement of the land, nevertheless, **these** laws, of unwitting and intentional murderers, **shall be for you as a statute of justice**[D] **for your generations in all your dwellings.**

30 This verse mentions two additional laws that are also related to murder. **Anyone who kills a person, on the basis of witnesses one shall murder the murderer.** The court may execute a murderer based only on eyewitness testimony and not based on mere circumstantial evidence. **But one witness shall not testify against a person to die.** One witness is not sufficient evidence for a death sentence, despite the fact that such testimony creates grave suspicions of his guilt.

31 **You shall not take ransom for the life of a murderer, who is condemned to die;**[D] as instead **he shall be put to death.**

32 **You shall not take** payment of **ransom from one who** unwittingly killed a person, and **fled to the city of his refuge,** in order **to return and to live in the land, until the death of the** High **Priest.** Some commentaries explain this to mean that a ransom is not taken from an intentional murderer who wishes to change his punishment from the death sentence and instead to flee to a city of refuge until the death of the High Priest.[30]

33 **You shall not** thereby **tarnish**[31] **the land in which you are, as the blood,** if judgment is not executed upon the one who shed it, **will tarnish the land; and the land will not be atoned for the blood that is shed in it, except through the blood of its shedder.**[D] The only atonement for the blood of someone who was intentionally killed is the death of his murderer.

34 **You shall not defile the land in which you live, in the midst of which I rest; for I am the Lord, who rests in the midst of the children of Israel.**

Marriage for Women Who Inherit

NUMBERS 36:1–13

This last section of the book of Numbers also deals with a commandment involving settlement of the land. However, this topic differs from the previous instructions in that it does not begin with a commandment of God but with the children of Gilad approaching Moses. They were concerned that part of their portion of the land might be transferred to another tribe if the daughters of Tzelofhad, who had been promised their father's inheritance, would marry men from outside their tribe. There is a clear parallel between the earlier appeal of the daughters of Tzelofhad and this address by the children of Gilad. Likewise, God's answer was similar in both cases: He affirmed the rightness of the women's claim, and He accepted the concerns of the children of Gilad.

36 1 **The heads of the fathers of the family of the children of Gilad, son of Makhir, son of Manasseh, from the families of the sons of Joseph, approached, and they spoke before Moses, and before the princes, the heads of the fathers of the children of Israel.**

Seventh aliya

2 **They said:** On the one hand, **the Lord commanded my lord,** Moses, **to give the land as inheritance by lot to the children of Israel,** the men, **and** on the other hand **my lord was commanded by the Lord to give the inheritance of Tzelofhad our brother to his daughters.** These two commands lead to a contradiction of sorts:

3 If **they,** the daughters of Tzelofhad, **shall be to the sons of the tribes of the children of Israel for wives,** then they will join a different tribe, **and their inheritance will be deducted from the inheritance of our fathers, and it will be added to the inheritance of the tribe to which they will be** joined through marriage. In this manner a portion of our tribe's inheritance will be transferred to another tribe, **and** ultimately **from the lot of our inheritance it shall be deducted.**

4 **When the Jubilee will be for the children of Israel,** when the members of every tribe return to their original inheritance,[32]

DISCUSSION

35:29 | **These shall be for you as a statute of justice:** The fact that these laws are called a statute of justice serves to teach that although the outcome of the trial is subject to debate and the judge's discretion, which is free and autonomous, the judge must nevertheless apply the punishment that is fixed by statute. He does not have the authority to decide that in a particular case a criminal should not receive the punishment he deserves, whether it is death or exile.

35:31 | **You shall not take ransom for the life of a murderer, who is condemned to die:** This contrasts with other punishments, which are substituted for monetary payment. The Sages explain that the expressions "an eye for an eye" and "a foot for a foot" (Exodus 21:24) are referring to payment of ransom as a punishment for the physical harm the offender inflicted (*Bava Kamma* 83b; see Exodus 21:29–30).

35:33 | **The blood will tarnish the land; and the land will not be atoned for the blood that is shed in it, except through the blood of its shedder:** A society that does not demand retribution for spilt human blood has broken the basic condition under which the land was given to people. The blood of a living person carries his soul and it is through the blood that man's physical body merges with a divine soul. When it is spilled, the blood tarnishes and contaminates the land, which holds back the blessing stored inside it, and the expectations that people have from the land will not be realized. The continued life of an intentional murderer serves as an affront to the lofty status of man, and this breaches the contract for mankind's sustained existence on earth (Rabbi Samson Raphael Hirsch).

כח כי בעיר מקלטו ישב עד־מות הכהן הגדל ואחרי־מות הכהן הגדל ישוב הרצח
כט אל־ארץ אחזתו: והיו אלה לכם לחקת משפט לדרתיכם בכל מושבתיכם:
ל כל־מכה־נפש לפי עדים ירצח את־הרצח ועד אחד לא־יענה בנפש למות:
לא לב ולא־תקחו כפר לנפש רצח אשר־הוא רשע למות כי־מות יומת: ולא־תקחו
לג כפר לנוס אל־עיר מקלטו לשוב לשבת בארץ עד־מות הכהן: ולא־תחניפו
את־הארץ אשר אתם בה כי הדם הוא יחניף את־הארץ ולארץ לא־יכפר
לד לדם אשר שפך־בה כי־אם בדם שפכו: ולא תטמא את־הארץ אשר אתם
ישבים בה אשר אני שכן בתוכה כי אני יהוה שכן בתוך בני ישראל:
א ויקרבו ראשי האבות למשפחת בני־גלעד בן־מכיר בן־מנשה ממשפחת
בני יוסף וידברו לפני משה ולפני הנשאים ראשי אבות לבני ישראל:
ב ויאמרו את־אדני צוה יהוה לתת את־הארץ בנחלה בגורל לבני ישראל
ג ואדני צוה ביהוה לתת את־נחלת צלפחד אחינו לבנתיו: והיו לאחד מבני
שבטי בני־ישראל לנשים ונגרעה נחלתן מנחלת אבתינו ונוסף על נחלת
ד המטה אשר תהיינה להם ומגרל נחלתנו יגרע: ואם־יהיה היבל לבני ישראל

רש"י

כט| בכל מושבתיכם. למד שתהא סנהדרין נוהגת בחוצה לארץ כל זמן שנוהגת בארץ ישראל:

ל| כל מכה נפש וגו׳. הבא להרגו על שהכה את הנפש: לפי עדים ירצח. שיעידו שבמזיד ובהתראה הרגו:

לא| ולא תקחו כפר. לא יפטר בממון:

לב| ולא תקחו כפר לנוס אל עיר מקלטו. למי שנס אל עיר מקלט, שהרג בשוגג, אינו נפטר מגלות בממון לתן כפר "לשוב לשבת בארץ" בטרם ימות הכהן: לנוס. כמו 'לנס', כמו: "שובי מלחמה" (מיכה ב, ח), ששבו מן המלחמה, "נוגי ממועד" (צפניה ג, יח), "כי מלים היו" (יהושע ה, ה), כאשר תאמר 'שוב' על מי ששב כבר, ו'מול' על שמל כבר, כן תאמר 'לנוס' על מי שנס כבר, וקורהו 'נוס' – מברח. ואם תאמר 'לנוס' – לברח, ותפרשהו: לא תקחו כפר למי שיש לו לברח לפטרו מן הגלות, לא ידעתי היאך יאמר: "לשוב לשבת בארץ", הרי עדין לא נס, ומהיכן ישוב?

לג| ולא תחניפו. ולא תרשיעו, כתרגומו: "ולא תחיבון":

לד| אשר אני שכן בתוכה. שלא תשכינו אותי בטמאתה:

כי אני ה׳ שכן בתוך בני ישראל. אף בזמן שהם טמאים, שכינה ביניהם:

פרק לו

ג| ונוסף על נחלת המטה. שהרי בנה יורשה, והבן מתיחס על שבט אביו:

ד| ואם יהיה היבל. מכאן היה רבי יהודה אומר: עתיד היובל שיפסק: ואם יהיה היבל. כלומר, אין זו מכירה שחוזרת ביובל, שהירשה אינה חוזרת, ואפלו אם יהיה היובל לא תחזור הנחלה לשבטו, ונמצא שנוספה "על נחלת המטה אשר תהיינה להם":

their inheritance will be added to the inheritance of the tribe to which they will be, and from the inheritance of the tribe of our fathers, their inheritance will be deducted. Their father's inheritance will be transferred to their husbands not only temporarily, but it will remain in the possession of that tribe forever. Consequently, the commandment that women are also entitled to inherit their father's portion will cause their tribe's land to diminish.

5 Moses commanded the children of Israel according to the directive of the Lord, saying: The tribe of the sons of Joseph speaks justly. Their claim was correct. Moses did not have a ready answer for them himself; therefore, he had to hear a response from God.

6 This is the matter that the Lord commanded with regard to the daughters of Tzelofhad,[D] saying: To whomever is good in their eyes they shall be wives; however, there is one condition, that they shall be wives to the family of the tribe of their father. They can marry any man of their choice, provided that he is a member of their tribe.

7 No inheritance of the children of Israel shall pass from tribe to tribe, as each of the children of Israel shall cleave to the inheritance of the tribe of his fathers. This command is

not referring to the daughters of Tzelofhad alone; rather, it is a general instruction:

8 Every daughter who inherits an inheritance from the tribes of the children of Israel, shall be a wife to one from the families of the tribe of her father, so that each of the children of Israel will inherit the inheritance of his fathers.

9 No inheritance shall pass from tribe to tribe, as each of the children of Israel shall cleave to his inheritance.

10 As the Lord commanded Moses, so the daughters of Tzelofhad did.

11 Mahla, Tirtza, Hogla, Milka, and Noa, daughters of
Maftir Tzelofhad, were married to the sons of their uncles.

12 From the families of the sons of Manasseh son of Joseph, they were wives and their inheritance was with the tribe of the family of their father. Their inheritance thereby remained within their tribe.

13 These are the last commandments and the ordinances which the Lord commanded at the hand of Moses to the children of Israel on the plains of Moav along the Jordan at Jericho. This concludes the series of statutes related to the nation's entrance into the land of Canaan.

DISCUSSION

36:6 | **This is the matter that the Lord commanded with regard to the daughters of Tzelofhad:** This law, with regard to which the Torah does not state that it is for your generations, or an everlasting statute, or some similar phrase of that kind, seemed to be implemented only during the initial period during and after the division of the land; it was subsequently annulled, and women who inherited were technically permitted to marry men from other tribes, although this was perhaps not the accepted custom in practice. According to one opinion, the festivities of matchmaking and marriage held on the fifteenth of Av marked the day on which the tribes were formally permitted to marry among each other, even in the case of women inheriting their fathers' land (see *Ta'anit* 30b; Radak, Judges 11:1; *Responsa of the Rashbatz* 3:322).

וְנוֹסְפָה נַחֲלָתָן עַל נַחֲלַת הַמַּטֶּה אֲשֶׁר תִּהְיֶינָה לָהֶם וּמִנַּחֲלַת מַטֵּה אֲבֹתֵינוּ
ה יִגָּרַע נַחֲלָתָן: וַיְצַו מֹשֶׁה אֶת־בְּנֵי יִשְׂרָאֵל עַל־פִּי יְהוָה לֵאמֹר כֵּן מַטֵּה בְנֵי־יוֹסֵף
ו דֹּבְרִים: זֶה הַדָּבָר אֲשֶׁר־צִוָּה יְהוָה לִבְנוֹת צְלָפְחָד לֵאמֹר לַטּוֹב בְּעֵינֵיהֶם תִּהְיֶינָה
ז לְנָשִׁים אַךְ לְמִשְׁפַּחַת מַטֵּה אֲבִיהֶם תִּהְיֶינָה לְנָשִׁים: וְלֹא־תִסֹּב נַחֲלָה לִבְנֵי
יִשְׂרָאֵל מִמַּטֶּה אֶל־מַטֶּה כִּי אִישׁ בְּנַחֲלַת מַטֵּה אֲבֹתָיו יִדְבְּקוּ בְּנֵי יִשְׂרָאֵל:
ח וְכָל־בַּת יֹרֶשֶׁת נַחֲלָה מִמַּטּוֹת בְּנֵי יִשְׂרָאֵל לְאֶחָד מִמִּשְׁפַּחַת מַטֵּה אָבִיהָ תִּהְיֶה
ט לְאִשָּׁה לְמַעַן יִירְשׁוּ בְּנֵי יִשְׂרָאֵל אִישׁ נַחֲלַת אֲבֹתָיו: וְלֹא־תִסֹּב נַחֲלָה מִמַּטֶּה
י לְמַטֶּה אַחֵר כִּי־אִישׁ בְּנַחֲלָתוֹ יִדְבְּקוּ מַטּוֹת בְּנֵי יִשְׂרָאֵל: כַּאֲשֶׁר צִוָּה יְהוָה אֶת־
יא מֹשֶׁה כֵּן עָשׂוּ בְּנוֹת צְלָפְחָד: וַתִּהְיֶינָה מַחְלָה תִרְצָה וְחָגְלָה וּמִלְכָּה וְנֹעָה בְּנוֹת מפטיר
יב צְלָפְחָד לִבְנֵי דֹדֵיהֶן לְנָשִׁים: מִמִּשְׁפְּחֹת בְּנֵי־מְנַשֶּׁה בֶן־יוֹסֵף הָיוּ לְנָשִׁים וַתְּהִי
יג נַחֲלָתָן עַל־מַטֵּה מִשְׁפַּחַת אֲבִיהֶן: אֵלֶּה הַמִּצְוֹת וְהַמִּשְׁפָּטִים אֲשֶׁר צִוָּה יְהוָה
בְּיַד־מֹשֶׁה אֶל־בְּנֵי יִשְׂרָאֵל בְּעַרְבֹת מוֹאָב עַל יַרְדֵּן יְרֵחוֹ: חזק

רש"י

ח| וְכָל בַּת יֹרֶשֶׁת נַחֲלָה. שֶׁלֹּא הָיָה בֵּן לְאָבִיהָ: יא| מַחְלָה תִרְצָה וְגוֹ׳. כָּאן מְנָאָן לְפִי גְּדֻלָּתָן זוֹ מִזּוֹ בְּשָׁנִים, וְנִשְּׂאוּ כְּסֵדֶר תּוֹלְדוֹתָן, וּבְכָל הַמִּקְרָא מְנָאָן לְפִי חָכְמָתָן, וּמַגִּיד שֶׁשְּׁקוּלוֹת זוֹ כְּזוֹ:

Book of

Deuteronomy

DEUTERONOMY

And you shall love the Lord your God with all your heart, with all your soul, and with all your might. Take to heart these instructions with which I charge you this day. Impress them upon your children. Recite them when you stay at home and when you are away, when you lie down and when you get up. Bind them as a sign on your hand and let them serve as a frontlet between your eyes.

Deuteronomy 6:5–8

This book is dedicated by

Barbara K. and Ira A. Lipman

Devarim

INTRODUCTION TO DEUTERONOMY

This book is called by the Sages the "Repetition of the Law" [*Mishneh Torah*], and its name in many European languages, Deuteronomy, has the same meaning. It bears this name for a good reason, as the book mainly reviews commandments of the Torah that appear in the earlier books. The time frame of Deuteronomy is extremely short, a mere few weeks at the end of Moses' life, and the vast majority of the book is a farewell speech that Moses our teacher delivered in the presence of all Israel. A sermon of this magnitude, which incorporates summaries, reviews, and even certain novel teachings on central themes of the Torah, certainly could not have been delivered in a single day, or even several days.

Deuteronomy is unique in the manner of its composition. The other books of the Torah are related from the point of view of an anonymous, omniscient narrator, as both the words of God and statements of various characters, including Moses, are delivered in the third person. Not only are the commandments and obligations presented in this detached fashion, as it were, but also the deeds and speeches of God and man. By contrast, the narrator in the book of Deuteronomy is Moses himself, and he speaks in the first person. Therefore, the common introductory verse of the previous books, "And God spoke to Moses, saying," does not appear in the book of Deuteronomy at all.

The book of Deuteronomy contains three main speeches. In his first discourse (1:1–4:49), Moses reproves the people while reviewing various events in the history of the nation, from their departure from Egypt to the present day. The second speech (5:1–27:8) presents various commandments. Both of these orations conclude with an addendum. The third and final speech (27:9–31:13) deals with the covenant between God and Israel. The end of this section depicts Moses taking leave of his people, and it includes two poetic addenda: the Song of Haazinu, which is written in the style of a poetic prophecy; and Moses' blessings to Israel.[1] The book concludes with a description, once again in the third person, of the death and burial of Moses, and a brief summary of his great deeds.

In his recounting of various events, Moses revisits incidents that were related in earlier books. Some of his audience would have been old enough to remember the momentous exodus from Egypt, although there were probably only a few such individuals. These would have been extremely elderly people who were not subject to the sentence of death in the wilderness pronounced on the generation of the exodus due to the sin of the spies. They included the entire tribe of Levi, which did not participate in that sin; and women, as the decree applied only to those who go to war, namely males. Most of those who heard Moses' speech had not personally witnessed the giving of the Torah and all the other events that occurred in the first year after the exodus, and if they had been present, they would have been too young to remember much. Many, no doubt, had heard about these important events from their parents, but others perhaps heard about them now for the first time.

In any case, Moses does not simply reiterate the facts and report his conversations with God. He inserts into his narrative the moral messages one should learn from them, and even adds a personal dimension; he records his thoughts and feelings at the time of the events and his reactions and responses to the various incidents, while reproving the people for their misdeeds. Despite the relatively small number of people in his audience who witnessed those early events, Moses stresses their presence among his listeners, as such witnesses could corroborate the truth of the history he described (see, e.g., 11:2–7).

The Sages compare Moses' recollections in this book to parallel accounts of the same events in other places in the Torah, and note differences in both style and content. There is no section of the book of Deuteronomy that does not contain some novelty, large or small, when compared to the corresponding passage in a previous book. With regard to the entire book of Deuteronomy, it is stated that "the Divine Presence spoke through Moses' throat,"[2] and this applies not merely when Moses directly relays

the word of God but also when he speaks about himself. Consequently, this book of the "Repetition of the Law" has the same sanctity and authority as the rest of the books of the Torah. Indeed, on occasion (e.g., 11:13–15), Moses initially speaks in his own voice, as Moses the man, before seamlessly changing to the word of God in the first person.

In general terms, the book of Deuteronomy deals with all the different types of commandments of the Torah, although there is less focus on the offerings and the laws of ritual purity and impurity than in other books. According to the Talmud, one can derive teachings from juxtapositions in the book of Deuteronomy;[3] that is, lessons can be learned from the fact that certain commandments appear alongside one another. Sometimes such links even have ramifications for practical *halakha*. Nevertheless, commentaries on the Torah have not managed to clarify fully the reasons for the order of all the commandments in the book, and this matter requires further analysis and study.

The manner in which many of the commandments are presented in this book is unique from another perspective: Moses is preparing Israel for the future. Consequently, he instructs them on how they must live once they have crossed into the Land of Israel. Moses situates the commandments, both those that have already appeared in the Torah as well as new commandments, in the context of a nation living in its land which must establish its public and political institutions.

Moses bids farewell to his people through the songs and blessings that appear at the end of the book of Deuteronomy. He does not leave his flock only with commandments, but also offers abstract ideas and moral messages that have become part of the collective memory over the generations. These include his blessings, which differ from those of Jacob at the conclusion of the book of Genesis in their details and emphases, but resemble Jacob's blessings in the sense that they too are a kind of benediction from a father to his children.

The book of Deuteronomy concludes with the death of Moses our teacher, the most important figure in Jewish history, just before the beginning of a new era for the nation. The children of Israel are about to enter their land, accompanied by the Torah of Moses and fortified with the blessings and mission bestowed upon them by their great leader.

Since the book of Deuteronomy is Moses' parting speech to the people, through which he seeks to implant in their hearts many values, commandments, warnings, and instructions, it repeats itself often. Due to Moses' rhetorical style, it is not easy to divide the book's major parts into clearly defined sections. The divisions that appear in this volume, and the headings given to them, should be taken as no more than suggestions of the book's structure, as an aid to the reader.

Parashat
Devarim

Moses' Speech Begins

DEUTERONOMY 1:1–2:1

Deuteronomy starts by noting the location where Moses delivered his great closing address to the children of Israel, and by mentioning certain places where and about which he spoke. It then begins to cite the contents of his address. Moses explains that the people's journey to the Land of Israel should have taken a mere few days, but it was extended due to their fear of entering the land. Eventually, God decreed that they must wander in the wilderness until the generation that left Egypt had died out. Those who attempted to enter the land before receiving permission to do so were killed in battle. In this survey, Moses incidentally mentions his delegation of judicial responsibility to judges and officers, a process accompanied by his admonition to the judges to rule justly.

1 **1** **These are the words that Moses spoke to all Israel beyond the Jordan, in the wilderness** that stretches along the eastern side of the Jordan, **in the Arava** which extends from the Dead Sea to the Gulf of Eilat, **opposite the Red Sea, between Paran**[B] **and Tofel, and Lavan,**[B] **and Hatzerot,**[B] **and Di Zahav.**[B] These places serve to pinpoint the precise locations where Moses spoke.[4] Alternatively, Moses repeated here various commandments that he had imparted to the people when they were in these places.[5] Additionally, these names allude to certain events to which Moses refers in his address.[6]

2 **Eleven days from Horev,**[B] Mount Sinai, **via Mount Se'ir**[B] **until Kadesh Barnea.** The journey from Mount Sinai to Kadesh Barnea, on the southern border of the Land of Israel,[7] took eleven days. However, it was only many years after the people arrived in Kadesh Barnea that they were able to enter Israel.

3 **It was in the fortieth year, in the eleventh month,** which would later be called Shevat, **on the first of the month,**[D] that **Moses spoke to the children of Israel, in accordance with everything that the Lord had commanded him to them.**

4 **After his smiting of Sihon, king of the Emorites, who lived in Heshbon,**[B] **and Og, king of Bashan, who lived in**

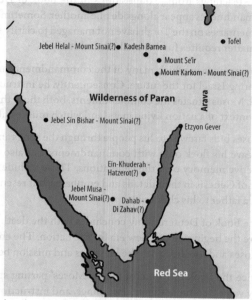

Locations mentioned by Moses

DISCUSSION

1:3 | **In the eleventh month, on the first of the month:** According to tradition, Moses died on the seventh of Adar, the twelfth month (see *Kiddushin* 38a). Since he began his farewell speech on the first of Shevat, the entire book of Deuteronomy, virtually all of which is Moses' last address to his people, encompasses a period of just over one month.

BACKGROUND

1:1 | **Paran:** A general name for the Sinai Peninsula, which includes several deserts: Tzin, Sinai, Eitam, and Shur. Additionally, Paran is the name of a specific location (Genesis; I Kings 11:18), possibly a mountain range west of the Arava, opposite Mount Se'ir (see 33:2), or in southern Sinai. It should be noted that southwest of the Sinai Peninsula there is a prominent wadi with a similar name, Wadi Feiran.

Tofel and Lavan: These locations have not been positively identified. Some claim that Tofel is the

village Tafila in Jordan, based on the similarity of the names. This village is located 25 km southeast of the Dead Sea.

Hatzerot: The identification of this location depends upon a dispute with regard to Mount Sinai. Those who identify Mount Sinai with Yaval Musa in the southern part of the Sinai Peninsula would claim that Hatzerot is Ein Khuderah, on the route from Yaval Musa to Eilat, Etzyon Gever. Others claim that ←

פרשת
דברים

א

א אֵלֶּה הַדְּבָרִים אֲשֶׁר דִּבֶּר מֹשֶׁה אֶל־כָּל־יִשְׂרָאֵל בְּעֵבֶר הַיַּרְדֵּן בַּמִּדְבָּר בָּעֲרָבָה א
ב מוֹל סוּף בֵּין־פָּארָן וּבֵין־תֹּפֶל וְלָבָן וַחֲצֵרֹת וְדִי זָהָב: אַחַד עָשָׂר יוֹם מֵחֹרֵב דֶּרֶךְ
ג הַר־שֵׂעִיר עַד קָדֵשׁ בַּרְנֵעַ: וַיְהִי בְּאַרְבָּעִים שָׁנָה בְּעַשְׁתֵּי־עָשָׂר חֹדֶשׁ בְּאֶחָד
ד לַחֹדֶשׁ דִּבֶּר מֹשֶׁה אֶל־בְּנֵי יִשְׂרָאֵל כְּכֹל אֲשֶׁר צִוָּה יְהוָה אֹתוֹ אֲלֵהֶם: אַחֲרֵי
הַכֹּתוֹ אֵת סִיחֹן מֶלֶךְ הָאֱמֹרִי אֲשֶׁר יוֹשֵׁב בְּחֶשְׁבּוֹן וְאֵת עוֹג מֶלֶךְ הַבָּשָׁן אֲשֶׁר־

רש"י

פרק א

א| **אלה הדברים.** לפי שהן דברי תוכחות, ומנה כאן כל המקומות שהכעיסו לפני המקום בהן, לפיכך סתם את הדברים והזכירם ברמז, מפני כבודן של ישראל: **אל כל ישראל.** אלו הוכיח מקצתן, היו אלו שבשוק אומרים: אתם הייתם שומעים מבן עמרם ולא השיבותם דבר, מכך וכך, אלו היינו שם היינו משיבין אותו; לכך כנסם כלם ואמר להם: הרי כלכם כאן, כל מי שיש לו תשובה ישיב: **במדבר.** לא במדבר היו אלא בערבות מואב, ומהו "במדבר"? אלא בשביל מה שהכעיסוהו במדבר, שאמרו: "מי יתן מותנו" וגו' (שמות טז, ג): **בערבה.** בשביל הערבה, שחטאו בבעל פעור בשטים בערבות מואב: **מול סוף.** על מה שהמרו בים סוף, בבואם לים סוף, שאמרו: "המבלי אין קברים במצרים" (שמות יד, יא), וכן בנסעם מתוך הים, שנאמר: "וימרו על ים בים סוף" (תהלים קו, ז), כדאיתא בערכין (דף טו ע"א): **בין פארן ובין תפל ולבן.** אמר רבי יוחנן: חזרנו על כל המקרא ולא מצינו מקום ששמו תפל ולבן, אלא הוכיחן על הדברים שתפלו על המן שהוא לבן, שאמרו: "ונפשנו קצה בלחם הקלקל" (במדבר כא, ה), ועל מה שעשו במדבר פארן על ידי המרגלים: **וחצרת.** במחלקתו של קרח. דבר אחר, אמר להם: היה לכם ללמד ממה שעשיתי למרים בחצרות בשביל לשון הרע, ואתם נדברתם במקום: **ודי זהב.** הוכיחן על העגל שעשו בשביל רב זהב שהיה להם, שנאמר: "וכסף הרביתי לה וזהב עשו לבעל" (הושע ב, י):

ב| **אחד עשר יום מחרב.** אמר להם משה: ראו מה שגרמתם, אין לכם דרך קצרה מחורב לקדש ברנע כדרך הר שעיר, ואף היא מהלך אחד עשר יום ואתם הלכתם אותה בשלשה ימים, שהרי בעשרים באייר נסעו מחורב, שנאמר: "ויהי בשנה השנית בחדש השני בעשרים בחדש" וגו' (במדבר י, יא), ובעשרים ותשעה בסיון שלחו את המרגלים מקדש ברנע, צא מהם שלשים יום שעשו בקברות התאוה שאכלו הבשר חדש ימים, ושבעה ימים שעשו בחצרות להסגר של מרים, נמצא בשלשה ימים הלכו כל אותו הדרך, וכל כך היתה השכינה מתלבטת בשבילכם למהר ביאתכם לארץ דרך הר שעיר, ובשביל שקלקלתם הסב אתכם סביבות הר שעיר ארבעים שנה:

ג| **ויהי בארבעים שנה בעשתי עשר חדש באחד לחדש.** מלמד שלא הוכיחן אלא סמוך למיתה. ממי למד? מיעקב, שלא הוכיח את בניו אלא סמוך למיתה. אמר: ראובן בני, אני אומר לך מפני מה לא הוכחתיך כל השנים הללו, כדי שלא תניחני ותלך ותדבק בעשו אחי. ומפני ארבעה דברים אין מוכיחין את האדם אלא סמוך למיתה: כדי שלא יהא מוכיחו וחוזר ומוכיחו, ושלא יהא חברו רואהו ומתבייש ממנו וכו', כדאיתא בספרי (ב). וכן יהושע לא הוכיח את ישראל אלא סמוך למיתה. וכן שמואל, שנאמר: "הנני ענו בי" (שמואל א' יב, ג). וכן דוד את שלמה בנו:

ד| **אחרי הכתו.** אמר משה: אם אני מוכיחם קודם שיכנסו לקצת הארץ, יאמרו: מה לזה עלינו, מה היטיב לנו, אינו בא אלא לקנתר ולמצא עלה, שאין בו כח להכניסנו לארץ. לפיכך המתין עד שהפיל סיחון ועוג לפניהם והורישם את ארצם, ואחר כך הוכיחן: **סיחן... אשר יושב בחשבון.** אלו לא היה סיחון קשה והיה שרוי בחשבון, היה קשה, שהמדינה קשה. ואלו היתה עיר אחרת וסיחון שרוי בתוכה, היה קשה, שהמלך

BACKGROUND

→ it is the settlement Hazira, on the southern edge of Mount Helal, in the north of central Sinai.

Di Zahav: Some identify this as Dahab, a port on the southeastern coast of the Sinai Peninsula.

1:2| **Eleven days from Horev:** Travelers in caravans of camels testified that they traversed the area from Yaval Musa, which some identify as Mount Sinai, to Kadesh Barnea, in ten or eleven days (*Biblical Researches in Palestine and Adjacent Countries*, 561–62 (three volumes, Boston and London, 1841; German edition, Halle, 1841; second edition, enlarged, 1856 [English and German]; Robinson, 1934). Those who identify Mount Sinai with Har Karkom note that there are ten wells between there and Kadesh Barnea, each separated by roughly 10–15 km, which is the maximum distance that a large group can travel in one day.

Via Mount Se'ir: Some claim that Mount Se'ir is Yaval Seira or Mount Harif, which are near the road leading from northern Sinai toward Etzyon Gever.

1:4| **Heshbon:** An important city located on the borders of the portions of the tribes of Gad and Reuben (Joshua 13:17). It is generally identified with Tel Hesban, located on the King's Highway, on the range above the Madaba Plains, about 20 km southwest of Rabat Amon. According to Josephus Flavius, Heshbon passed through several hands after various wars, and was even under Israelite control in the Hasmonean period. It can be inferred from Song of Songs 7:5 that this city was familiar to the Israelites (see also Ramban, Numbers 32:28).

Ashtarot,[B] in battle[8] **at Edre'i.**[B] Alternatively, the conclusion of the verse may be rendered: Who dwelled in Ashtarot and Edre'i, as both were cities in Og's kingdom.[9] Yet another possibility is that Ashtarot is not a place-name, but it means strength and sharp cliffs, and it describes the tall, harsh mountains of Edre'i.[10] Although Moses did not bring the people into the Land of Israel, he prepared the way by defeating two powerful kings. He mentions these victories in order to solidify the nation's confidence toward their next step of entering the land;

5 **beyond the Jordan, in the land of Moav, Moses began [*ho'il*]**[11] **expounding this Torah, saying.** Others explain that *ho'il* means wanted, that Moses sought to expound the law of the Torah:[12]

6 **The Lord our God spoke to us** when we were **at Horev, saying: Enough of your living at this mountain,** where you received the Torah;

7 **turn** from Horev, **and set you out, and come to the highlands of the Emorites and all their neighbors, in the Arava, on the highlands, and on the plain, and in the south, and on the seashore; the land of the Canaanites, and the Lebanon, until the great river, the Euphrates River.**

8 **See, I have placed the land before you. Come and take possession of the land about which the Lord took an oath to your fathers, to Abraham, to Isaac, and to Jacob, to give** it **to them and to their descendants after them.** God commands the people to depart upon a journey that will eventually lead to their entry into the Land of Israel.

9 **I spoke to you**[D] **at that time, saying: I am unable to bear you alone.**

10 The burden was too heavy for me because **the Lord your God has multiplied you, and behold, you are today as the stars of the heavens in abundance.**

11 After mentioning the great size of the people, Moses stresses
Second that he is not complaining about the growth of the nation; on
aliya the contrary, he says: It is my wish that **the Lord, God of your fathers, shall add to you one thousand times** as many people **as you are** now, **and** that **He will bless you,** and fulfill His promises, **as He spoke to,** about, **you.**

"Stars of the heavens in abundance"

12 Nevertheless, as you are so numerous, **how shall I bear alone your troubles** that require resolutions, **your** personal **burdens** with which each of you troubles me, **and your** internal **quarrels?**

13 **Get for you,** choose, **men, wise, and understanding, and** who are not strangers or loners but who are well **known to your tribes** and have good reputations, **and I will place them at your head.** I presented you with a suggestion that was basically the one initially proposed by Yitro.

BACKGROUND

1:4| **Ashtarot:** Also known as Ashterot Karnayim, this was a city in the inheritance of Manasseh in Bashan, which was given to the Levites. It is also called Be'eshtera, which is perhaps a shortened form of Beit Ashterot, the House of Ashterot (Joshua 21:27). This city controlled the main road of Bashan. It was the capital city of the province of Karnayim, and as this verse mentions, it was the home of Og, king of Bashan. It is identified with Al-Shaykh Saad, in Syria.

Edre'i: Daraa, a provincial city and an important crossroads in the south of the Bashan in southern Syria. Archaeological finds have been unearthed there dating back to the third century BCE, and it is mentioned in ancient Egyptian hieroglyphic tablets. Edre'i was included in the inheritance of half the tribe of Manasseh. According to historical testimonies, Jews lived there in the Second Temple period, in the periods of the Mishna and the Talmud, and in the Middle Ages.

DISCUSSION

1:9| **I spoke to you:** The Torah stated earlier that the appointment of judges was a result of Yitro's suggestion (Exodus 18:13–26), but that episode is not mentioned here. Moses certainly understood how hard it was to function as the sole judge of such a large community, and he was familiar with organized governmental systems. Consequently, Yitro's advice should not be seen as the sole catalyst for change, but rather as encouragement to Moses to act quickly. When Moses mentions this event in his speech, in which he generally presents his own perspective, he emphasizes the difficulties he experienced, as well as the selection of the judges and their appointment, but he does not find it necessary to mention the private advice he had previously received from his father-in-law.

ה יֹשֵׁב בְּעַשְׁתָּרֹת בְּאֶדְרֶעִי: בְּעֵבֶר הַיַּרְדֵּן בְּאֶרֶץ מוֹאָב הוֹאִיל מֹשֶׁה בֵּאֵר אֶת־
ו הַתּוֹרָה הַזֹּאת לֵאמֹר: יהוה אֱלֹהֵינוּ דִּבֶּר אֵלֵינוּ בְּחֹרֵב לֵאמֹר רַב־לָכֶם שֶׁבֶת
ז בָּהָר הַזֶּה: פְּנוּ וּסְעוּ לָכֶם וּבֹאוּ הַר הָאֱמֹרִי וְאֶל־כָּל־שְׁכֵנָיו בָּעֲרָבָה בָהָר
וּבַשְּׁפֵלָה וּבַנֶּגֶב וּבְחוֹף הַיָּם אֶרֶץ הַכְּנַעֲנִי וְהַלְּבָנוֹן עַד־הַנָּהָר הַגָּדֹל נְהַר־פְּרָת:
ח רְאֵה נָתַתִּי לִפְנֵיכֶם אֶת־הָאָרֶץ בֹּאוּ וּרְשׁוּ אֶת־הָאָרֶץ אֲשֶׁר נִשְׁבַּע יהוה לַאֲבֹתֵיכֶם
ט לְאַבְרָהָם לְיִצְחָק וּלְיַעֲקֹב לָתֵת לָהֶם וּלְזַרְעָם אַחֲרֵיהֶם: וָאֹמַר אֲלֵכֶם בָּעֵת
י הַהִוא לֵאמֹר לֹא־אוּכַל לְבַדִּי שְׂאֵת אֶתְכֶם: יהוה אֱלֹהֵיכֶם הִרְבָּה אֶתְכֶם וְהִנְּכֶם
יא הַיּוֹם כְּכוֹכְבֵי הַשָּׁמַיִם לָרֹב: יהוה אֱלֹהֵי אֲבוֹתֵכֶם יֹסֵף עֲלֵיכֶם כָּכֶם אֶלֶף פְּעָמִים
יב וִיבָרֵךְ אֶתְכֶם כַּאֲשֶׁר דִּבֶּר לָכֶם: אֵיכָה אֶשָּׂא לְבַדִּי טָרְחֲכֶם וּמַשַּׂאֲכֶם וְרִיבְכֶם:
יג הָבוּ לָכֶם אֲנָשִׁים חֲכָמִים וּנְבֹנִים וִידֻעִים לְשִׁבְטֵיכֶם וַאֲשִׂימֵם בְּרָאשֵׁיכֶם:

רש״י

קשה. על אחת כמה וכמה שהמלך קשה והמדינה קשה: **אשר יושב בעשתרת.** המלך קשה והמדינה קשה: **עשתרת.** הוא לשון צוקין וקושי, כמו: "עשתרות קרנים" (בראשית יד, ה), ו'עשתרות' זה הוא עשתרות קרנים שהיו שם רפאים שהכה אמרפל, שנאמר: "ויכו את רפאים בעשתרת קרנים" (שם), ועוג נמלט מהם, והוא שנאמר: "ויבא הפליט" (שם פסוק יג), ואומר: "כי רק עוג מלך הבשן נשאר מיתר הרפאים" (להלן ג, יא): **באדרעי.** שם המלכות.

ה] **הואיל.** התחיל, כמו: "הנה נא הואלתי" (בראשית יח, כז): **באר את התורה.** בשבעים לשון פירשה להם.

ו] **רב לכם שבת.** כפשוטו, ויש מדרש אגדה: הרבה גדלה לכם ושכר על ישיבתכם בהר הזה, עשיתם משכן מנורה וכלים, קבלתם תורה, מניתם לכם סנהדרין שרי אלפים ושרי מאות.

ז] **פנו וסעו לכם.** זו דרך ערד וחרמה: **ובאו הר האמרי.** כמשמעו: **ואל כל שכניו.** עמון ומואב והר שעיר: **בערבה.** זה מישור של יער: **בהר.** זה הר המלך: **ובשפלה.** זו שפלת דרום: **ובנגב ובחוף הים.** אשקלון ועזה וקסרי וכו', כדאיתא בספרי (ו): **עד הנהר הגדל.** מפני שנזכר עם ארץ ישראל קורהו גדול, משל הדיוט אומר: עבד מלך מלך, הדבק לשחור וישתחוו לך, קרב לגבי דהינא ואידהן.

ח] **ראה נתתי.** בעיניכם אתם רואים, איני אומר לכם מאומד ומשמועה: **באו ורשו.** אין מערער בדבר ואינכם צריכים למלחמה, אלו לא שלחו מרגלים לא היו צריכים לכלי זין: **לאבתיכם.** למה הזכיר שוב "לאברהם ליצחק וליעקב"? אלא אברהם כדאי לעצמו, יצחק כדאי לעצמו, יעקב כדאי לעצמו.

ט] **ואמר אלכם בעת ההוא לאמר.** מהו 'לאמר'? אמר להם משה: לא מעצמי אני אומר לכם אלא מפי הקדוש ברוך הוא: **לא אוכל לבדי וגו'.** אפשר שלא היה משה יכול לדון את ישראל? אדם שהוציאם ממצרים, וקרע להם את הים, והוריד את המן, והגיז את השלו, לא היה יכול לדונם? אלא כך אמר להם: "ה' אלהיכם הרבה אתכם" (להלן פסוק י) – הגדיל והרים אתכם על דייניכם, נטל את העונש מכם ונתנו על הדיינים. וכן אמר שלמה: "כי מי יוכל לשפט את עמך הכבד הזה" (מלכים א' ג, ט), אפשר מי שכתוב בו: "ויחכם מכל האדם" (שם ה, יא) אומר: "מי יוכל לשפט"? אלא כך אמר שלמה: אין דייני אמה זו כדייני שאר האמות, שאם דן והורג ומכה וחונק ומטה את דינו וגוזל אין בכך כלום, אני אם חייבתי ממון שלא כדין, נפשות אני נתבע, שנאמר: "וקבע את קבעיהם נפש" (משלי כב, כג).

י] **והנכם היום ככוכבי השמים.** וכי ככוכבי השמים היו באותו היום? והלא לא היו אלא ששים רבוא, מהו "והנכם היום"? הנכם משולים כיום, קיימים לעולם כחמה ולבנה וכוכבים.

יא] **יסף עליכם ככם אלף פעמים.** מהו שוב "ויברך אתכם כאשר דבר לכם"? אלא אמרו לו: משה, אתה נותן קצבה לברכותינו, כבר הבטיח הקדוש ברוך הוא את אברהם: "אשר אם יוכל איש למנות" וגו' (בראשית יג, טז). אמר להם: זו משלי היא, אבל הוא "יברך אתכם כאשר דבר לכם".

יב] **איכה אשא לבדי.** אם אומר לקבל שכר, לא אוכל, זו היא שאמרתי לכם: לא מעצמי אני אומר לכם אלא מפי הקדוש ברוך הוא: **טרחכם.** מלמד שהיו ישראל טרחנין, היה אחד מהם רואה את בעל דינו נוצח בדין, אומר: יש לי עדים להביא, יש לי ראיות להביא, מוסיף אני עליכם דיינין: **ומשאכם.** מלמד שהיו אפיקורסין, הקדים משה לצאת, אמרו: מה ראה בן עמרם לצאת? שמא אינו שפוי בתוך ביתו. איחר לצאת, אמרו: מה ראה בן עמרם שלא לצאת? מה אתם סבורים, יושב ויועץ עליכם עצות רעות וחושב עליכם מחשבות: **וריבכם.** מלמד שהיו רוגנים.

יג] **הבו לכם.** הזמינו עצמכם לדבר: **אנשים.** וכי תעלה על דעתך נשים? מה תלמוד לומר: אנשים? צדיקים: **חכמים.** כסופים: **ונבנים.** מבינים דבר מתוך דבר, זהו ששאל אריוס את רבי יוסי: מה בין חכמים לנבונים? חכם דומה לשלחני עשיר, כשמביאין לו דינרין לראות רואה, וכשאין מביאין לו יושב ותוהה. נבון דומה לשלחני תגר, כשמביאין לו מעות לראות רואה, וכשאין מביאין לו הוא מחזר ומביא משלו: **וידעים לשבטיכם.** שהם נכרים לכם, שאם בא לפני מעוטף בטליתו איני יודע מי הוא ומאיזה שבט הוא ואם הגון הוא, אבל אתם מכירין בו, שאתם גדלתם אותו, לכך נאמר: "וידעים לשבטיכם": **בראשיכם.** ראשים ומכובדים עליכם, שתהיו נוהגין בהם כבוד ויראה: **ואשמם.** חסר יו"ד, למד שאשמותיהם של ישראל תלויות בראשי דייניהם, שהיה להם למחות ולכוון אותם לדרך הישרה.

14 **You answered me and said: The matter is good that you have spoken to do.**

15 With your consent, and based on your personal testimony, **I took the heads of your tribes, men wise and known, and I placed them** as **heads over you.** These men were appointed **leaders of thousands, and leaders of hundreds, and leaders of fifties, and leaders of tens, and officers for your tribes.**

16 **I commanded your judges at that time, saying: Hear** the arguments **between your brethren** and attempt to understand the wishes of each side, **and judge righteousness between man and his brother, and a stranger to him,** including those who have no family relatives.

17 **You shall not give preference** to either side **in judgment; small and great alike you shall hear** equally, to safeguard justice and honesty. **You shall not fear** speaking your mind or remaining silent **due to any man, as judgment is God's.** No personal considerations may enter the judge's decision making, as his task is to relay God's judgment to the litigants. Consequently, any perversion of justice is a sin against God and

a betrayal of His agency.[13] **And the matter that is too difficult for you, you shall bring near to me, and I will hear it,** and attempt to find a solution.

18 **I commanded you at that time all the matters that you shall do.**

19 **We traveled from Horev, and we went through the entire great and awesome wilderness that you saw, via the Emorite highlands, as the Lord our God had commanded us, and we came to Kadesh Barnea.**

20 **I said to you: You have come to the Emorite highlands, which the Lord our God is giving us.**

21 You can **see,** from your experiences to this point,[14] that **the Lord your God has placed the land before you; ascend, take possession, as the Lord, God of your fathers, spoke to you; do not fear, and do not be frightened** and lose the will to fight. Go forth to battle, as you will be victorious.

22 When I informed you that you would soon be entering the

Third aliya land, **you all approached me and said: Let us send men[D] before us, and they will spy the land for us, and they will**

DISCUSSION

1:22 | Let us send men: This verse apparently contradicts the account in Numbers, where it is stated that God commanded Moses to send spies (Numbers 13:1–2). It is best to consider these versions as two complementary accounts. One explanation is that the nation initially approached Moses and requested to send spies. Moses accepted their proposal and added that there should be one representative for each tribe, to render it an official delegation of sorts. Finally, God instructed them on how to carry out the mission properly (Ramban, Numbers 13:2).

Appointment of Judges and Leaders: In recounting the commandment to appoint leaders of thousands, hundreds, fifties, and tens along with the commandments directed toward the judges, Moses encapsulates several earlier episodes into one seamless narrative. First he describes the impetus for the appointment of the various echelons of leadership: "I spoke to you at that time, saying: I am unable to bear you alone" (1:9) and "How shall I bear alone your troubles, your burdens, and your quarrels" (1:12)? In response, God commands: "Get for you men, wise, and understanding, and known to your tribes, and I will place them at your head" (1:13). Moses

then attests: "I took the heads of your tribes, men wise and known, and I placed them heads over you, leaders of thousands, and leaders of hundreds, and leaders of fifties, and leaders of tens, and officers for your tribes" (1:15).

Indeed we find, in the book of Numbers, in response to the breakdown of the children of Israel that began with their talk that was "evil in the ears of the Lord" (11:1), followed by the mob that "expressed a craving" (11:4) and complained about the manna (11:6), culminating in Moses hearing the "people weeping…each man at the entrance of his tent" (11:10)," Moses said: "Why have You mistreated Your servant and why have I not found favor in Your eyes, to place the burden of this entire people upon Me?" (11:11).

God answered Moses: "Gather to Me seventy men of the elders of Israel, whom you know to be elders of the people, and its officers…. They shall bear with you the burden of the people, and you shall not bear alone" (11:16–17). This is the Torah source for the Great Sanhedrin, the court of seventy-one judges, the highest tribunal in Judaism.

In the book of Exodus, the impetus for the appointment of the leadership configuration is

different. Moses' father-in-law, Yitro, visits, and he sees Moses sitting and judging the people and observes: "The people stood over Moses from the morning until the evening" (18:13). He comments: "It is not a good thing that you are doing" (18:17). Yitro counsels Moses: "You shall identify from all the people capable men, fearers of God, men of truth, haters of ill-gotten gain; set over them leaders of thousands, leaders of hundreds, leaders of fifties, and leaders of tens" (18:21). The Torah relates: "Moses heeded the voice of his father-in-law and did everything that he said" (18:24).

Here, in the book of Deuteronomy, Moses omits any mention of Yitro. He reprises the despair that he expressed in the book of Numbers and the solution that he adopted in Exodus. He continues with an allusion to the solution that God provided in Deuteronomy, instructions to judges: "Hear between your brethren and judge righteousness between man and his brother, and a stranger to him. You shall not give preference in judgment; small and great alike you shall hear. You shall not fear due to any man, as judgment is God's" (1:16–17).

יד וַתַּעֲנוּ אֹתִי וַתֹּאמְרוּ טוֹב־הַדָּבָר אֲשֶׁר־דִּבַּרְתָּ לַעֲשׂוֹת: וָאֶקַּח אֶת־רָאשֵׁי
שִׁבְטֵיכֶם אֲנָשִׁים חֲכָמִים וִידֻעִים וָאֶתֵּן אוֹתָם רָאשִׁים עֲלֵיכֶם שָׂרֵי אֲלָפִים וְשָׂרֵי
טו מֵאוֹת וְשָׂרֵי חֲמִשִּׁים וְשָׂרֵי עֲשָׂרֹת וְשֹׁטְרִים לְשִׁבְטֵיכֶם: וָאֲצַוֶּה אֶת־שֹׁפְטֵיכֶם
בָּעֵת הַהִוא לֵאמֹר שָׁמֹעַ בֵּין־אֲחֵיכֶם וּשְׁפַטְתֶּם צֶדֶק בֵּין־אִישׁ וּבֵין־אָחִיו וּבֵין
יז גֵּרוֹ: לֹא־תַכִּירוּ פָנִים בַּמִּשְׁפָּט כַּקָּטֹן כַּגָּדֹל תִּשְׁמָעוּן לֹא תָגוּרוּ מִפְּנֵי־אִישׁ כִּי
הַמִּשְׁפָּט לֵאלֹהִים הוּא וְהַדָּבָר אֲשֶׁר יִקְשֶׁה מִכֶּם תַּקְרִבוּן אֵלַי וּשְׁמַעְתִּיו: וָאֲצַוֶּה
יח אֶתְכֶם בָּעֵת הַהִוא אֵת כָּל־הַדְּבָרִים אֲשֶׁר תַּעֲשׂוּן: וַנִּסַּע מֵחֹרֵב וַנֵּלֶךְ אֵת כָּל־
יט הַמִּדְבָּר הַגָּדוֹל וְהַנּוֹרָא הַהוּא אֲשֶׁר רְאִיתֶם דֶּרֶךְ הַר הָאֱמֹרִי כַּאֲשֶׁר
צִוָּה יְהוָה אֱלֹהֵינוּ אֹתָנוּ וַנָּבֹא עַד קָדֵשׁ בַּרְנֵעַ: וָאֹמַר אֲלֵכֶם בָּאתֶם עַד־הַר
כ הָאֱמֹרִי אֲשֶׁר־יְהוָה אֱלֹהֵינוּ נֹתֵן לָנוּ: רְאֵה נָתַן יְהוָה אֱלֹהֶיךָ לְפָנֶיךָ אֶת־הָאָרֶץ
כא עֲלֵה רֵשׁ כַּאֲשֶׁר דִּבֶּר יְהוָה אֱלֹהֵי אֲבֹתֶיךָ לָךְ אַל־תִּירָא וְאַל־תֵּחָת: וַתִּקְרְבוּן שְׁלִישִׁי
כב אֵלַי כֻּלְּכֶם וַתֹּאמְרוּ נִשְׁלְחָה אֲנָשִׁים לְפָנֵינוּ וְיַחְפְּרוּ־לָנוּ אֶת־הָאָרֶץ

רש"י

יד וַתַּעֲנוּ אֹתִי וְגו'. חֲלַטְתֶּם אֶת הַדָּבָר לַהֲנָאַתְכֶם, הָיָה
לָכֶם לְהָשִׁיב: רַבֵּנוּ מֹשֶׁה, מִמִּי נָאֶה לִלְמֹד, מִמְּךָ אוֹ
מִתַּלְמִידְךָ? לֹא מִמְּךָ שֶׁנִּצְטַעַרְתָּ עָלֶיהָ? אֶלָּא יָדַעְתִּי
מַחְשְׁבוֹתֵיכֶם, הֱיִיתֶם אוֹמְרִים: עַכְשָׁיו יִתְמַנּוּ עָלֵינוּ דַּיָּנִין
הַרְבֵּה, אִם אֵין מַכִּירֵנוּ, אָנוּ מְבִיאִין לוֹ דּוֹרוֹן וְהוּא נוֹשֵׂא
לָנוּ פָנִים. לַעֲשׂוֹת. אִם הָיִיתִי מִתְעַצֵּל, אַתֶּם אוֹמְרִים
עֲשֵׂה מְהֵרָה:

טו וָאֶקַּח אֶת רָאשֵׁי שִׁבְטֵיכֶם. מְשֻׁכְתִּים בִּדְבָרִים.
אַשְׁרֵיכֶם, עַל מִי בָּאתֶם לְהִתְמַנּוֹת, עַל בְּנֵי אַבְרָהָם
יִצְחָק וְיַעֲקֹב, עַל בְּנֵי שֶׁנִּקְרְאוּ אַחִים וְרֵעִים, חֵלֶק
וְנַחֲלָה, וְכָל לְשׁוֹן חִבָּה: אֲנָשִׁים חֲכָמִים וִידֻעִים. אֲבָל
נְבוֹנִים לֹא מָצָאתִי. זוֹ אַחַת מִשֶּׁבַע מִדּוֹת שֶׁאָמַר יִתְרוֹ
לְמֹשֶׁה, וְלֹא מָצָא אֶלָּא שָׁלֹשׁ: אֲנָשִׁים צַדִּיקִים, חֲכָמִים
וִידֻעִים: רָאשִׁים עֲלֵיכֶם. שֶׁתִּנְהֲגוּ בָהֶם כָּבוֹד, רָאשִׁים
בְּמִקָּח, רָאשִׁים בְּמִמְכָּר, רָאשִׁים בְּמַשָּׂא וּמַתָּן, נִכְנָס אַחֲרוֹן
וְיוֹצֵא רִאשׁוֹן: שָׂרֵי אֲלָפִים. אֶחָד מְמֻנֶּה עַל אֶלֶף: שָׂרֵי
מֵאוֹת. אֶחָד מְמֻנֶּה עַל מֵאָה: וְשֹׁטְרִים. אֵלּוּ הַכּוֹפְתִין
"לְשִׁבְטֵיכֶם", אֵלּוּ הַכּוֹפְתִין וְהַמַּכִּין בִּרְצוּעָה עַל פִּי הַדַּיָּנִין:

טז וָאֲצַוֶּה אֶת שֹׁפְטֵיכֶם. אָמַרְתִּי לָהֶם: הֱווּ מְתוּנִים בַּדִּין,
אִם בָּא דִּין לְפָנֶיךָ פַּעַם אַחַת שְׁתַּיִם וְשָׁלֹשׁ, אַל תֹּאמַר:
כְּבָר בָּא דִין זֶה לְפָנַי פְּעָמִים הַרְבֵּה, אֶלָּא הֱיוּ נוֹשְׂאִים

וְנוֹתְנִים בּוֹ: בָּעֵת הַהִוא. מִשֶּׁמִּנִּיתִים אָמַרְתִּי לָהֶם: אֵין
עַכְשָׁיו כִּלְשֶׁעָבַר, לְשֶׁעָבַר הֱיִיתֶם בִּרְשׁוּת עַצְמְכֶם, עַכְשָׁיו
הֲרֵי אַתֶּם מְשֻׁעְבָּדִים לַצִּבּוּר: שָׁמֹעַ. לְשׁוֹן הוֶֹה, אודנ"ט
בְּלַעַז, כְּמוֹ זָכוֹר וְשָׁמוֹר: וּבֵין גֵּרוֹ. זֶה בַּעַל דִּינוֹ שֶׁאוֹגֵר
עָלָיו דְּבָרִים. דָּבָר אַחֵר, "וּבֵין גֵּרוֹ", אַף עַל עִסְקֵי דִירָה,
בֵּין חֲלֻקַּת אַחִים, אֲפִלּוּ בֵּין תַּנּוּר לְכִירַיִם:

יז לֹא תַכִּירוּ פָנִים בַּמִּשְׁפָּט. זֶה הַמְמֻנֶּה לְהוֹשִׁיב הַדַּיָּנִים,
שֶׁלֹּא יֹאמַר: אִישׁ פְּלוֹנִי נָאֶה אוֹ גִּבּוֹר, אוֹשִׁיבֶנּוּ דַּיָּן, אִישׁ
פְּלוֹנִי קְרוֹבִי, אוֹשִׁיבֶנּוּ דַּיָּן בָּעִיר, וְהוּא אֵינוֹ בָּקִי בְּדִינִין,
נִמְצָא מְחַיֵּב אֶת הַזַּכַּאי וּמְזַכֶּה אֶת הַחַיָּב, מַעֲלֶה אֲנִי עַל
מִי שֶׁמִּנָּהוּ כְּאִלּוּ הִכִּיר פָּנִים בַּדִּין: כַּקָּטֹן כַּגָּדֹל תִּשְׁמָעוּן.
שֶׁיְּהֵא חָבִיב עָלֶיךָ דִּין שֶׁל פְּרוּטָה כְּדִין שֶׁל מֵאָה מָנֶה,
שֶׁאִם קָדַם וּבָא לְפָנֶיךָ לֹא תְסַלְּקֶנּוּ לָאַחֲרוֹנָה. דָּבָר אַחֵר,
"כַּקָּטֹן כַּגָּדֹל תִּשְׁמָעוּן", כְּתַרְגּוּמוֹ, שֶׁלֹּא תֹאמַר: זֶה עָנִי
הוּא וַחֲבֵרוֹ עָשִׁיר וּמְצֻוֶּה לְפַרְנְסוֹ, אֲזַכֶּה אֶת הֶעָנִי וְנִמְצָא
מִתְפַּרְנֵס בְּנִקִיּוּת. דָּבָר אַחֵר, שֶׁלֹּא תֹאמַר: הֵיאַךְ אֲנִי
פּוֹגֵם בִּכְבוֹדוֹ שֶׁל עָשִׁיר זֶה בִּשְׁבִיל דִּינָר, אֲחַיְּבֶנּוּ עַכְשָׁיו,
וּכְשֶׁיֵּצֵא לַחוּץ, אֹמַר לוֹ: תֵּן לוֹ, שֶׁאַתָּה חַיָּב לוֹ: לֹא תָגוּרוּ
מִפְּנֵי אִישׁ. לֹא תִירְאוּ. דָּבָר אַחֵר, "לֹא תָגוּרוּ", לֹא תַכְנִיס
דְּבָרֶיךָ מִפְּנֵי אִישׁ, לְשׁוֹן: "אֹגֵר בַּקַּיִץ" (משלי י, ה): כִּי
הַמִּשְׁפָּט לֵאלֹהִים הוּא. מַה שֶּׁאַתָּה נוֹטֵל מִזֶּה שֶׁלֹּא כַדִּין

חַתָּה מַזְקִיקֵנִי לְהַחֲזִיר לוֹ, נִמְצָא שֶׁהִטֵּיתָ עָלַי הַמִּשְׁפָּט:
תַּקְרִבוּן אֵלַי. עַל דָּבָר זֶה נִסְתַּלֵּק מִמֶּנּוּ מִשְׁפַּט בְּנוֹת
צְלָפְחָד. וְכֵן שְׁמוּאֵל אָמַר לְשָׁאוּל: "אָנֹכִי הָרֹאֶה" (שמואל־א
ט, יט), אָמַר לוֹ הַקָּדוֹשׁ בָּרוּךְ הוּא: חַיֶּיךָ שֶׁאֵין אַתָּה מוֹדִיעַ
שֶׁאֵין אַתָּה רוֹאֶה. וְאֵימָתַי הוֹדִיעוֹ? כְּשֶׁבָּא לִמְשֹׁחַ אֶת
דָּוִד, "וַיַּרְא אֶת אֱלִיאָב וַיֹּאמֶר אַךְ נֶגֶד ה' מְשִׁיחוֹ" (שמואל־א
טז, ו), אָמַר לוֹ הַקָּדוֹשׁ בָּרוּךְ הוּא: וְלֹא אָמַרְתָּ "אָנֹכִי
הָרֹאֶה"? "אַל תַּבֵּט אֶל מַרְאֵהוּ" (שם פסוק ז):

יח אֵת כָּל הַדְּבָרִים אֲשֶׁר תַּעֲשׂוּן. אֵלּוּ עֲשֶׂרֶת הַדְּבָרִים
שֶׁבֵּין דִּינֵי מָמוֹנוֹת לְדִינֵי נְפָשׁוֹת:

יט הַמִּדְבָּר הַגָּדוֹל וְהַנּוֹרָא. שֶׁהָיוּ בוֹ נְחָשִׁים כְּקוֹרוֹת
וְעַקְרַבִּים כִּקְשָׁתוֹת:

כב וַתִּקְרְבוּן אֵלַי כֻּלְּכֶם. בְּעִרְבּוּבְיָא, וּלְהַלָּן הוּא אוֹמֵר:
"וַתִּקְרְבוּן אֵלַי כָּל רָאשֵׁי שִׁבְטֵיכֶם וְזִקְנֵיכֶם, וַתֹּאמְרוּ
הֵן הֶרְאָנוּ" וְגו' (להלן ה, כ-כא), אוֹתָהּ קְרִיבָה הָיְתָה
הוֹגֶנֶת, יְלָדִים מְכַבְּדִים אֶת הַזְּקֵנִים וּשְׁלָחוּם לִפְנֵיהֶם,
וּזְקֵנִים מְכַבְּדִים אֶת הָרָאשִׁים לָלֶכֶת לִפְנֵיהֶם, אֲבָל כָּאן,
"וַתִּקְרְבוּן אֵלַי כֻּלְּכֶם", בְּעִרְבּוּבְיָא, יְלָדִים דּוֹחֲפִין אֶת
הַזְּקֵנִים וּזְקֵנִים דּוֹחֲפִין אֶת הָרָאשִׁים: וְיַשֻׁבוּ אֹתָנוּ דָבָר.
בְּאֵיזֶה לָשׁוֹן הֵם מְדַבְּרִים: אֶת הַדֶּרֶךְ אֲשֶׁר נַעֲלֶה בָּהּ:

return word to us: The way that we will ascend, and the cities at which we will arrive.

23 **The matter was good in my eyes; and I took from you twelve men, one man for each tribe.**

24 **They,** the men, **turned and they ascended to the highlands, and they came until the Eshkol Ravine, and spied it,** the land.

25 **They took in their hand from the fruit of the land and brought it down to us; they brought back word to us, and said: The land that the Lord our God is giving to us is good.** According to the parallel account in Numbers, after the spies admitted that the land was good, they added other comments which ruined what would otherwise have been a positive report.[15] However, in this speech, Moses is generally not interested in emphasizing private sins. He therefore highlights the positive aspect of the spies' report.

26 **But** despite the positive report, **you were not willing to ascend, and you defied the directive of the Lord your God.**

27 **You murmured** your complaints **in your tents, and you said: In the Lord's hatred of us, He took us out of the land of Egypt, to deliver us into the hand of the Emorites, to destroy us.** God is sending us to Canaan only because He wants to destroy us.

28 **Where are we ascending? Our brethren,** the spies, **have melted our heart, saying: A people greater and taller than** we; **cities great and fortified to the heavens; and we have also seen the sons of the giants there.** We cannot possibly conquer the inhabitants of Canaan.

29 **I said to you: Do not be intimidated and do not fear them.**

30 **The Lord your God who goes before you, He will make war for you, like everything that He did for you in Egypt before your eyes.** You saw in Egypt how God fought for you without any effort on your part. He will continue to battle on your behalf in the future as well.

31 In addition to the miracles you witnessed in Egypt, you experienced many wonders **in the wilderness, where you saw that the Lord your God bore you as a man would bear his son,** with strength, love, and gentleness, **in the entire path that you went, until you came to this place.**

32 **But in this matter** of conquering the land, which is far less complicated, **you do not have faith in the Lord your God,**

33 **who goes before you on the way, to scout for you a place for your encampment with fire** that descends **by night, to show you the path on which you shall go, and in the cloud by day.**

34 However, the nation did not listen to Moses, and objected to entering the land. And **the Lord heard the sound of your words, and He was enraged and took an oath, saying:**

35 **If any man among these men, this wicked generation, will see the good land about which I took an oath to give** it **to**

DISCUSSION

Caleb, Joshua, and Moses: The Torah account of the sin of the spies ends with a list of its repercussions. The list begins with the punishment of the children of Israel: "The Lord…was enraged and took an oath, saying: If any man among these men, this wicked generation, will see the good land about which I took an oath to give to your fathers" (1:34–35). It continues with Caleb's reward: "Except Caleb son of Yefuneh, he shall see it and to him I will give the land in which he trod, and to his children, because he followed the Lord wholeheartedly" (1:36). It concludes with Joshua's reward: "Joshua son of Nun, who stands before you, he shall come there; strengthen him, for he shall bequeath it to Israel" (1:38).

The verse that appears in the text between the reward for Caleb and the reward for Joshua presents a difficulty not due to its content but due to its placement. The verse says: "Also the Lord was incensed with me because of you, saying: You too shall not come there" (1:37). Though the fact that Moses was not going to enter the Land of Israel was already known, its mention in the context of the sin of the spies is surprising. Wasn't the punishment that he would not enter the land administered due to the sin of the waters of dispute? Does it not say: "Because you did not have faith in Me, to sanctify Me before the eyes of the children of Israel; therefore, you shall not bring this assembly into the land that I have given them" (Numbers 20:12)?

The Abravanel explains that despite the plain understanding of this verse, the sin of the waters of dispute was not the reason that Moses was punished; rather, he was punished for his role in the sin of the spies. God commanded Moses to send men to scout the land of Canaan (Numbers 13:2), a command to get a general sense of the land. The people requested: "Let us send men before us, and they will spy the land for us, and they will return word to us: The way that we will ascend, and the cities at which we will arrive" (Deuteronomy 1:22). The request was limited to ascertaining the ideal path to take to the first city they would conquer. Moses, with the best of intentions, as he was confident in God's promise, added to the mission of the spies and thereby compromised that mission: "You shall see the land, what it is. The people that lives in it, is it strong or is it weak? Are they few or many? What is the land in which it lives? Is it good or bad? What are the cities in which it lives? Is it in camps or in fortifications?" (Numbers 13:18–19). Those questions directed the focus of the spies to the might of the people, the strength of the cities, and the fact that the land devoured its inhabitants. Therefore, it is only natural that Moses' punishment was mentioned in this context.

The Ramban explains that Moses' punishment is totally unrelated to the sin of the spies. Rather, his punishment is mentioned in order to make sense of the verse about Joshua that follows. In order to understand why Joshua would be leading the people into the land of Canaan, it was first necessary to explain that Moses would not be entering the land.

וַיֵּשְׁבוּ אֹתָנוּ דָּבָר אֶת־הַדֶּרֶךְ אֲשֶׁר נַעֲלֶה־בָּהּ וְאֵת הֶעָרִים אֲשֶׁר נָבֹא אֲלֵיהֶן:

כג וַיִּיטַב בְּעֵינַי הַדָּבָר וָאֶקַּח מִכֶּם שְׁנֵים עָשָׂר אֲנָשִׁים אִישׁ אֶחָד לַשָּׁבֶט: וַיִּפְנוּ

כה וַיַּעֲלוּ הָהָרָה וַיָּבֹאוּ עַד־נַחַל אֶשְׁכֹּל וַיְרַגְּלוּ אֹתָהּ: וַיִּקְחוּ בְיָדָם מִפְּרִי הָאָרֶץ

וַיּוֹרִדוּ אֵלֵינוּ וַיָּשִׁבוּ אֹתָנוּ דָבָר וַיֹּאמְרוּ טוֹבָה הָאָרֶץ אֲשֶׁר־יְהֹוָה אֱלֹהֵינוּ נֹתֵן

כו לָנוּ: וְלֹא אֲבִיתֶם לַעֲלֹת וַתַּמְרוּ אֶת־פִּי יְהֹוָה אֱלֹהֵיכֶם: וַתֵּרָגְנוּ בְאָהֳלֵיכֶם

וַתֹּאמְרוּ בְּשִׂנְאַת יְהֹוָה אֹתָנוּ הוֹצִיאָנוּ מֵאֶרֶץ מִצְרָיִם לָתֵת אֹתָנוּ בְּיַד הָאֱמֹרִי

כח לְהַשְׁמִידֵנוּ: אָנָה ׀ אֲנַחְנוּ עֹלִים אַחֵינוּ הֵמַסּוּ אֶת־לְבָבֵנוּ לֵאמֹר עַם גָּדוֹל וָרָם

כט מִמֶּנּוּ עָרִים גְּדֹלֹת וּבְצוּרֹת בַּשָּׁמָיִם וְגַם־בְּנֵי עֲנָקִים רָאִינוּ שָׁם: וָאֹמַר אֲלֵכֶם

ל לֹא־תַעַרְצוּן וְלֹא־תִירְאוּן מֵהֶם: יְהֹוָה אֱלֹהֵיכֶם הַהֹלֵךְ לִפְנֵיכֶם הוּא יִלָּחֵם לָכֶם

לא כְּכֹל אֲשֶׁר עָשָׂה אִתְּכֶם בְּמִצְרַיִם לְעֵינֵיכֶם: וּבַמִּדְבָּר אֲשֶׁר רָאִיתָ אֲשֶׁר נְשָׂאֲךָ

יְהֹוָה אֱלֹהֶיךָ כַּאֲשֶׁר יִשָּׂא־אִישׁ אֶת־בְּנוֹ בְּכָל־הַדֶּרֶךְ אֲשֶׁר הֲלַכְתֶּם עַד־בֹּאֲכֶם

לב עַד־הַמָּקוֹם הַזֶּה: וּבַדָּבָר הַזֶּה אֵינְכֶם מַאֲמִינִם בַּיהֹוָה אֱלֹהֵיכֶם: הַהֹלֵךְ לִפְנֵיכֶם

לג בַּדֶּרֶךְ לָתוּר לָכֶם מָקוֹם לַחֲנֹתְכֶם בָּאֵשׁ ׀ לַיְלָה לַרְאֹתְכֶם בַּדֶּרֶךְ אֲשֶׁר תֵּלְכוּ־בָהּ

לד וּבֶעָנָן יוֹמָם: וַיִּשְׁמַע יְהֹוָה אֶת־קוֹל דִּבְרֵיכֶם וַיִּקְצֹף וַיִּשָּׁבַע לֵאמֹר: אִם־יִרְאֶה

לה אִישׁ בָּאֲנָשִׁים הָאֵלֶּה הַדּוֹר הָרָע הַזֶּה אֵת הָאָרֶץ הַטּוֹבָה אֲשֶׁר נִשְׁבַּעְתִּי לָתֵת

רש״י

אֵין דֶּרֶךְ שֶׁאֵין בָּהּ עֲקַמִּימוּת. וְאֵת הֶעָרִים אֲשֶׁר נָבֹא אֲלֵיהֶן. תְּחִלָּה לְכָבְּשָׁם:

כג וַיִּיטַב בְּעֵינַי הַדָּבָר. בְּעֵינַי וְלֹא בְּעֵינֵי הַמָּקוֹם. וְאִם בְּעֵינֵי מֹשֶׁה הָיָה טוֹב, לָמָּה אֲמָרָהּ בַּתּוֹכָחוֹת? מָשָׁל לְאָדָם שֶׁאוֹמֵר לַחֲבֵרוֹ: מְכֹר לִי חֲמוֹרְךָ זֶה, אָמַר לוֹ: הֵן. נוֹתְנוֹ לְךָ לְנִסָּיוֹן? אָמַר לוֹ: הֵן. בֶּהָרִים וּבַגְּאָיוֹת? אָמַר לוֹ: הֵן. כֵּיוָן שֶׁרָאָה שֶׁאֵין מְעַכְּבוֹ כְלוּם, אָמַר הַלּוֹקֵחַ בְּלִבּוֹ: בָּטוּחַ הוּא זֶה שֶׁלֹּא אֶמְצָא בּוֹ מוּם. מִיָּד אָמַר לוֹ: טֹל מְעוֹתֶיךָ וַאֲנִי אֵינִי מְנַסֵּהוּ מֵעַתָּה. אַף אֲנִי הוֹדֵיתִי לְדִבְרֵיכֶם, שֶׁמָּא תַחְזְרוּ בָכֶם כְּשֶׁתִּרְאוּ שֶׁאֵינִי מְעַכֵּב, וְאַתֶּם לֹא חֲזַרְתֶּם בָּכֶם: וָאֶקַּח מִכֶּם. מִן הַבְּרוּרִים שֶׁבָּכֶם, מִן הַמֻּבְחָרִים שֶׁבָּכֶם: שְׁנֵים עָשָׂר אֲנָשִׁים אִישׁ אֶחָד לַשָּׁבֶט. מַגִּיד שֶׁלֹּא הָיָה שֵׁבֶט לֵוִי עִמָּהֶם:

כד עַד נַחַל אֶשְׁכֹּל. מַגִּיד שֶׁנִּקְרָא עַל שֵׁם סוֹפוֹ: וַיְרַגְּלוּ אֹתָהּ. מְלַמֵּד שֶׁהִלְּכוּ בָהּ אַרְבָּעָה אֻמָּנִין שְׁתִי וָעֵרֶב:

כה וַיּוֹרִדוּ אֵלֵינוּ. מַגִּיד שֶׁאֶרֶץ יִשְׂרָאֵל גְּבוֹהָה מִכָּל הָאֲרָצוֹת: וַיֹּאמְרוּ טוֹבָה הָאָרֶץ. מִי הֵם שֶׁאָמְרוּ טוֹבָתָהּ? יְהוֹשֻׁעַ וְכָלֵב:

כו וַתַּמְרוּ. לְשׁוֹן הַתְרָסָה, הִתְרַסְתֶּם כְּנֶגֶד מַאֲמָרוֹ:

כז וַתֵּרָגְנוּ. לְשׁוֹן הָרָע, וְכֵן: ״דִּבְרֵי נִרְגָּן״ (משלי יח, ח), אָדָם הַמּוֹצִיא דִּבָּה. בְּשִׂנְאַת ה' אֹתָנוּ. וְהוּא הָיָה אוֹהֵב אֶתְכֶם, אֲבָל אַתֶּם שׂוֹנְאִים אוֹתוֹ. מָשָׁל הֶדְיוֹט אוֹמֵר: מַה דְּבִלִבָּךְ עַל רְחִימָךְ, מַה דְּבִלִבֵּיהּ עֲלָךְ: בְּשִׂנְאַת ה' הוֹצִיאָנוּ מֵאֶרֶץ מִצְרָיִם. הוֹצָאָתוֹ לְשִׂנְאָה הָיְתָה. מָשָׁל לְמֶלֶךְ בָּשָׂר וָדָם שֶׁהָיוּ לוֹ שְׁנֵי בָנִים וְיֵשׁ לוֹ שְׁתֵּי שָׂדוֹת, אַחַת שֶׁל שַׁלְחִין וְאַחַת שֶׁל בַּעַל, לְמִי שֶׁהוּא אוֹהֵב נוֹתֵן שֶׁל שַׁלְחִין וּלְמִי שֶׁהוּא שׂוֹנֵא נוֹתֵן לוֹ שֶׁל בַּעַל. אֶרֶץ מִצְרַיִם שֶׁל שַׁלְחִין הִיא, שֶׁנִּילוּס עוֹלֶה וּמַשְׁקֶה אוֹתָהּ, וְאֶרֶץ כְּנַעַן שֶׁל בַּעַל. וְהוֹצִיאָנוּ מִמִּצְרַיִם לָתֵת לָנוּ אֶת אֶרֶץ כְּנַעַן:

כח עָרִים גְּדֹלֹת וּבְצוּרֹת בַּשָּׁמָיִם. דִּבְּרוּ הַכְּתוּבִים לְשׁוֹן הֲבַאי:

כט לֹא תַעַרְצוּן. לְשׁוֹן שְׁבִירָה כְּתַרְגּוּמוֹ, וְדוֹמֶה לוֹ: ״בַּעֲרוֹץ נְחָלִים״ (איוב ל, ו), לִשְׁבֹּר הַנְּחָלִים:

לֹא יִלָּחֵם לָכֶם. בִּשְׁבִילְכֶם:

לא וּבַמִּדְבָּר אֲשֶׁר רָאִיתָ. מוּסָב עַל מִקְרָא שֶׁלְּמַעְלָה הֵימֶנּוּ: ״כְּכֹל אֲשֶׁר עָשָׂה אִתְּכֶם בְּמִצְרַיִם״ וְעָשָׂה אַף בַּמִּדְבָּר, ״אֲשֶׁר רָאִיתָ אֲשֶׁר נְשָׂאֲךָ״ וְגו': כַּאֲשֶׁר יִשָּׂא־אִישׁ אֶת־בְּנוֹ. כְּמוֹ שֶׁפֵּרַשְׁתִּי אֵצֶל ״וַיִּסַּע מַלְאַךְ הָאֱלֹהִים הַהֹלֵךְ״ וְגו' (שמות יד, יט-כ), מָשָׁל לִמְהַלֵּךְ בַּדֶּרֶךְ וּבְנוֹ לְפָנָיו, בָּאוּ לִסְטִים לִשְׁבּוֹתוֹ וְכו', [נְטָלוֹ מִלְּפָנָיו נְתָנוֹ לְאַחֲרָיו, בָּא זְאֵב מֵאַחֲרָיו, נְתָנוֹ לְפָנָיו, וְחִזְקָם מֵאַחֲרָיו, נְתָנוֹ עַל זְרוֹעוֹתָיו]. כָּךְ: ״וְאָנֹכִי תִרְגַּלְתִּי לְאֶפְרַיִם קָחָם עַל זְרוֹעוֹתָיו״ (הושע יא, ג):

לב וּבַדָּבָר הַזֶּה. שֶׁהוּא מַבְטִיחֲכֶם לַהֲבִיאֲכֶם אֶל הָאָרֶץ, ״אֵינְכֶם מַאֲמִינִם״ בּוֹ:

לג לַרְאֹתְכֶם. כְּמוֹ ״לְהַרְאֹתְכֶם״, וְכֵן: ״לַנְחֹתָם הַדֶּרֶךְ״ (שמות יג, כא), וְכֵן: ״לַשְׁמִיעַ בְּקוֹל תּוֹדָה״ (תהלים כו, ז), וְכֵן: ״לָלֶכֶת לַגִּיד בְּיִזְרְעֶאל״ (מלכים ב' ט, טו ועיין רש״י שם):

your fathers. I will not allow any of these men to see the land,

36 **except** for **Caleb son of Yefuneh, he shall see it,** the land; **and to him I will give the land in which he trod, and to his children, because he followed the** instruction of the **Lord wholeheartedly,** and provided an accurate description of the land, while assuring the people that they could conquer it.

37 **Also the Lord was incensed with me because of you, saying:** Due to your sin, **you too shall not come there.** Although Moses sinned on a different occasion,[16] he already received a hint in the aftermath of the sin of the spies that he too would not enter the land.[17]

38 **Joshua son of Nun, who stands before you,** to serve you, **he shall come there; strengthen him, for he shall bequeath it to Israel.**

39 God addresses the people: **And** ironically, **your children, whom you said would be** taken by your enemies as **captives** and killed, **and your** young **sons, who today do not know** how to distinguish between **good and evil, they will come there,** to the land of Canaan, **and to them I will give it, and they will take possession of it.**

Fourth
aliya

40 Meanwhile **you, turn** back **and travel into the wilderness via** the route leading to **the Red Sea,** as you will wander in the wilderness until you die.

41 **You answered and you said to me: We sinned against the Lord, we will go up and make war, in accordance with everything that the Lord our God had commanded; and you girded each man his weapons of war, and decided to ascend to the mountain.** Alternatively, this means: And you dared to ascend to the mountain, or: And you readied yourselves to ascend to the mountain.[18]

42 **The Lord said to me: Say to them: Do not go up and do not make war, as I am not in your midst, and** if you obey Me, **you will not be routed before your enemies.**

43 **I spoke to you** and told you not to set out to war, reminding you that all your previous victories were achieved only through divine assistance, not your own military power; **but you did not heed, and you defied the directive of the Lord, and you intentionally ascended to the mountain.**

44 **The Emorites, who live on that mountain, came out toward you, and pursued you, as bees would do, and** they **beat** and broke[19] **you in Se'ir until Horma.** The Emorites surrounded you like a swarm of bees, leaving no avenue of escape. This place was later called Horma, in commemoration of the destruction [*ḥurban*] that occurred there.

Swarm of bees

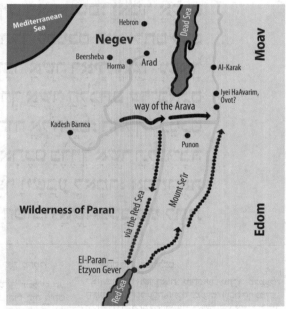

Circling of Mount Se'ir

45 **You returned and wept before the Lord,** in regret for your sins, begging for forgiveness and mercy; **but the Lord did not heed your voice, and He did not listen to you.**

46 **You lived in Kadesh many days, like the days that you lived there.**

2 1 **We turned and we traveled** back **into the wilderness via the Red Sea, as the Lord spoke to me; and we circled Mount Se'ir**

לו לַאֲבֹתֵיכֶם: זוּלָתִי כָּלֵב בֶּן־יְפֻנֶּה הוּא יִרְאֶנָּה וְלוֹ־אֶתֵּן אֶת־הָאָרֶץ אֲשֶׁר דָּרַךְ־בָּהּ
לז וּלְבָנָיו יַעַן אֲשֶׁר מִלֵּא אַחֲרֵי יְהוָה: גַּם־בִּי הִתְאַנַּף יְהוָה בִּגְלַלְכֶם לֵאמֹר גַּם־אַתָּה
לח לֹא־תָבֹא שָׁם: יְהוֹשֻׁעַ בִּן־נוּן הָעֹמֵד לְפָנֶיךָ הוּא יָבֹא שָׁמָּה אֹתוֹ חַזֵּק כִּי־הוּא
לט יַנְחִלֶנָּה אֶת־יִשְׂרָאֵל: וְטַפְּכֶם אֲשֶׁר אֲמַרְתֶּם לָבַז יִהְיֶה וּבְנֵיכֶם אֲשֶׁר לֹא־יָדְעוּ רביעי
מ הַיּוֹם טוֹב וָרָע הֵמָּה יָבֹאוּ שָׁמָּה וְלָהֶם אֶתְּנֶנָּה וְהֵם יִירָשׁוּהָ: וְאַתֶּם פְּנוּ לָכֶם
מא וּסְעוּ הַמִּדְבָּרָה דֶּרֶךְ יַם־סוּף: וַתַּעֲנוּ ׀ וַתֹּאמְרוּ אֵלַי חָטָאנוּ לַיהוָה אֲנַחְנוּ
נַעֲלֶה וְנִלְחַמְנוּ כְּכֹל אֲשֶׁר־צִוָּנוּ יְהוָה אֱלֹהֵינוּ וַתַּחְגְּרוּ אִישׁ אֶת־כְּלֵי מִלְחַמְתּוֹ
מב וַתָּהִינוּ לַעֲלֹת הָהָרָה: וַיֹּאמֶר יְהוָה אֵלַי אֱמֹר לָהֶם לֹא תַעֲלוּ וְלֹא
מג תִלָּחֲמוּ כִּי אֵינֶנִּי בְּקִרְבְּכֶם וְלֹא תִּנָּגְפוּ לִפְנֵי אֹיְבֵיכֶם: וָאֲדַבֵּר אֲלֵיכֶם
מד וְלֹא שְׁמַעְתֶּם וַתַּמְרוּ אֶת־פִּי יְהוָה וַתָּזִדוּ וַתַּעֲלוּ הָהָרָה: וַיֵּצֵא הָאֱמֹרִי הַיֹּשֵׁב
בָּהָר הַהוּא לִקְרַאתְכֶם וַיִּרְדְּפוּ אֶתְכֶם כַּאֲשֶׁר תַּעֲשֶׂינָה הַדְּבֹרִים וַיַּכְּתוּ אֶתְכֶם
מה בְּשֵׂעִיר עַד־חָרְמָה: וַתָּשֻׁבוּ וַתִּבְכּוּ לִפְנֵי יְהוָה וְלֹא־שָׁמַע יְהוָה בְּקֹלְכֶם וְלֹא
מו א הֶאֱזִין אֲלֵיכֶם: וַתֵּשְׁבוּ בְקָדֵשׁ יָמִים רַבִּים כַּיָּמִים אֲשֶׁר יְשַׁבְתֶּם: וַנֵּפֶן
וַנִּסַּע הַמִּדְבָּרָה דֶּרֶךְ יַם־סוּף כַּאֲשֶׁר דִּבֶּר יְהוָה אֵלָי וַנָּסָב אֶת־הַר־שֵׂעִיר

רש"י

לו| **אֲשֶׁר דָּרַךְ בָּהּ.** חֶבְרוֹן, שֶׁנֶּאֱמַר: "וַיָּבֹא עַד חֶבְרוֹן" (במדבר יג, כב):

לז| **הִתְאַנַּף.** נִתְמַלֵּא רֹגֶז:

מ| **פְּנוּ לָכֶם.** אָמַרְתִּי לְהַעֲבִיר אֶתְכֶם דֶּרֶךְ רֹחַב אֶרֶץ אֱדוֹם לְצַד צָפוֹן לִכָּנֵס לָאָרֶץ, קִלְקַלְתֶּם וּגְרַמְתֶּם לָכֶם עִכּוּב: **פְּנוּ לָכֶם.** לַאֲחוֹרֵיכֶם, וְתֵלְכוּ בַּמִּדְבָּר לְצַד יַם סוּף, שֶׁהַמִּדְבָּר שֶׁהָיוּ הוֹלְכִים בּוֹ לִדְרוֹמָהּ שֶׁל הַר שֵׂעִיר הָיָה, מַפְסִיק בֵּין יַם סוּף לְהַר שֵׂעִיר, עַתָּה הִמָּשְׁכוּ לְצַד הַיָּם וְתִסַּבְּבוּ אֶת הַר שֵׂעִיר כָּל דְּרוֹמוֹ מִן הַמַּעֲרָב לַמִּזְרָח:

מא| **וַתָּהִינוּ.** לְשׁוֹן: "הִנֶּנּוּ וְעָלִינוּ אֶל הַמָּקוֹם" (במדבר יד, מ), זֶה הַלָּשׁוֹן שֶׁאֲמַרְתֶּם, לְשׁוֹן הֵן, כְּלוֹמַר נִזְדַּמַּנְתֶּם:

מב| **לֹא תַעֲלוּ.** לֹא עֲלִיָּה תְּהֵא לָכֶם אֶלָּא יְרִידָה:

מד| **כַּאֲשֶׁר תַּעֲשֶׂינָה הַדְּבֹרִים.** מַה הַדְּבוֹרָה הַזֹּאת כְּשֶׁהִיא מַכָּה אֶת הָאָדָם מִיָּד מֵתָה, אַף הֵם כְּשֶׁהָיוּ נוֹגְעִים בָּכֶם מִיָּד מֵתִים:

מה| **וְלֹא שָׁמַע ה' בְּקֹלְכֶם.** כִּבְיָכוֹל עֲשִׂיתֶם מִדַּת רַחֲמָיו כְּאִלּוּ אַכְזָרִי:

מו| **וַתֵּשְׁבוּ בְקָדֵשׁ יָמִים רַבִּים.** תְּשַׁע עֶשְׂרֵה שָׁנָה, שֶׁנֶּאֱמַר: "כַּיָּמִים אֲשֶׁר יְשַׁבְתֶּם" בִּשְׁאָר הַמַּסָּעוֹת, וְהֵם הָיוּ שְׁלֹשִׁים וּשְׁמֹנֶה שָׁנָה, תְּשַׁע עֶשְׂרֵה מֵהֶם עָשׂוּ בְּקָדֵשׁ וּתְשַׁע עֶשְׂרֵה שָׁנָה הוֹלְכִים וּמְטֹרָפִים וְחָזְרוּ לְקָדֵשׁ, כְּמוֹ שֶׁנֶּאֱמַר: "וַיְנִעֵם בַּמִּדְבָּר" (במדבר לב, יג). כָּךְ מָצָאתִי בְּסֵדֶר עוֹלָם (פרק ח):

פרק ב

א| **וַנִּסַּע הַמִּדְבָּרָה.** אִלּוּ לֹא חָטְאוּ הָיוּ עוֹבְרִים דֶּרֶךְ הַר שֵׂעִיר לִכָּנֵס לָאָרֶץ מִדְּרוֹמוֹ לִצְפוֹנוֹ, וּבִשְׁבִיל שֶׁקִּלְקְלוּ הִפְנָן לְצַד הַמִּדְבָּר שֶׁהוּא בֵּין יַם סוּף לִדְרוֹמוֹ שֶׁל הַר שֵׂעִיר, וְהָלְכוּ אֵצֶל דְּרוֹמוֹ מִן הַמַּעֲרָב לַמִּזְרָח דֶּרֶךְ יְצִיאָתָן מִמִּצְרַיִם שֶׁהוּא בְּמִקְצוֹעַ דְּרוֹמִית מַעֲרָבִית, מִשָּׁם הָיוּ

many days. For years, we stayed in the region of Mount Se'ir, and we did not travel in the direction of Canaan until the generation that left Egypt had died out.

Moses' Speech Continues: Confrontations Lands on the Eastern Side of the Jordan River

DEUTERONOMY 2:2–3:22

Moses continues to summarize the past, turning next to recent events that most of his audience would remember: The abstention from war against nations that are considered family relations of the children of Israel, namely Edom, Amon, and Moav, as well as the military victories over the two Emorite kings. Toward the end of the section, Moses describes how he apportioned the land on the eastern side of the Jordan River to certain tribes and families, after which he blesses Joshua and encourages him for the upcoming conquest of the territory on the western side of the Jordan.

This is a new context for such words of encouragement. Although Moses took the nation out of Egypt and led them through the wilderness for many years, his comments gain extra credibility from his recent conquest of two powerful kings and his division of land to a portion of the nation. Even if the full vision for the future has yet to be realized, Moses has fulfilled part of it. Consequently, he emphasizes the details of his military victories as well as the conquest of the region and its settlement as a model for the nation's wars after it crosses the Jordan.

Fifth
aliya

2 After a long time had passed, **the Lord said to me, saying:**

3 **Enough for you circling this mountain,** Mount Se'ir, and staying in the same region all the time. After all this aimless wandering, **turn you** to a specific direction, **to the north.**

4 **Command the people, saying: You are passing through the border of your brethren the children of Esau, who live in Se'ir; they will be afraid of you,** because you are a great nation, **and even so, you shall be very careful.**

5 **Do not provoke them, for I will not give you even the tread of the sole of a foot from their land, because I have given Mount Se'ir to be an inheritance to Esau.** Esau was granted Mount Se'ir as his portion of God's promise to Abraham and his family.[20] In the future, this territory will revert to its true permanent owner, the nation of Israel. However, for the moment it will remain in the possession of the descendants of Esau, and Israel was prohibited from taking any part of it.[21]

6 Consequently, in order to eat, **you shall purchase**[22] **from them food with silver, and eat; and also water you shall purchase**[23] **from them with silver, and drink.**

7 **For the Lord your God blessed you in all your handiwork; He has known** what you required[24] in **your walking through this great wilderness, these forty years the Lord your God has been with you; you have not lacked anything.** Since you were isolated from civilization and commerce in the wilderness, and your needs were provided for by God, you did not require money. Now you can spend the money that you possess.[25]

8 **We passed from our brethren the children of Esau, who live in Se'ir, from the way of the Arava, from Eilat and from Etzyon Gever,** which is next to Eilat, **and we turned** northward **and passed via the wilderness of Moav.** In the Bible, of all the nations, only the children of Esau are called the brethren of Israel,[26] as they are the Israelites' closest family; no other nation is referred to by this term. Here this family relationship is mentioned in support of the admonition against threatening the territory of Esau.

9 **The Lord said to me: Do not besiege Moav, and do not provoke war with them, as I will not give you from his land a possession; because to the children of Lot I have given** the region of **Ar,** in Moav, **as a possession.**

10 Here, the chapter records some pertinent details from the distant past: **The Emim,** a nation or tribe, perhaps so named because it engendered fear [*eima*] in others, **dwelt there previously,** in the land currently inhabited by Moav; **a people great, numerous, and tall, like giants.**

11 **Refaim,**[B] another ancient people, **would also be regarded as giants; but the Moavites,** whose language was similar to Hebrew, **would call them Emim,** because they aroused fear [*eima*].

12 The chapter similarly notes: **In Se'ir the Horites lived previously, and the children of Esau took possession from them and they destroyed them from before them, and dwelled in their place, as Israel did to the land of its possession,** the land of Sihon and Og, **which the Lord gave to them.** The

---

BACKGROUND

2:11| Refaim: Only fragments of information remain about this ancient people. The Torah's historical descriptions of this and other nations, and its mention of how they were known to the other nations in the region, serve to clarify that these were not mere figments of the imagination or mythical characters, but real peoples who played a role in the history of the region. Furthermore, the depiction of these nations is designed to prevent future generations of Israel from considering their own possession of the land as unquestionable, as it is stated: "I destroyed the Emorites from before them, whose height was like the height of cedars and who were strong as the oaks; I destroyed his fruit from above and his roots from below" (Amos 2:9).

ב ג ימים רבים: ויאמר יהוה אלי לאמר: רב־לכם סב את־ההר הזה ב חמישי
ד פנו לכם צפנה: ואת־העם צו לאמר אתם עברים בגבול אחיכם בני־עשו
ה הישבים בשעיר וייראו מכם ונשמרתם מאד: אל־תתגרו בם כי לא־אתן לכם
ו מארצם עד מדרך כף־רגל כי־ירשה לעשו נתתי את־הר שעיר: אכל תשברו
ז מאתם בכסף ואכלתם וגם־מים תכרו מאתם בכסף ושתיתם: כי יהוה אלהיך
ברכך בכל מעשה ידך ידע לכתך את־המדבר הגדל הזה זה | ארבעים שנה
ח יהוה אלהיך עמך לא חסרת דבר: ונעבר מאת אחינו בני־עשו הישבים
בשעיר מדרך הערבה מאילת ומעצין גבר ונפן ונעבר דרך מדבר
ט מואב: ויאמר יהוה אלי אל־תצר את־מואב ואל־תתגר בם מלחמה כי לא־
י אתן לך מארצו ירשה כי לבני־לוט נתתי את־ער ירשה: האמים לפנים ישבו
יא בה עם גדול ורב ורם כענקים: רפאים יחשבו אף־הם כענקים והמאבים יקראו
יב להם אמים: ובשעיר ישבו החרים לפנים ובני עשו יירשום וישמידום מפניהם
וישבו תחתם כאשר עשה ישראל לארץ ירשתו אשר־נתן יהוה להם:

רש"י

הולכים לצד המזרח: ונסב את הר שעיר. כל דרומו עד ארץ מואב:

ג| פנו לכם צפנה. סבו לכם לרוח מזרחית מן הדרום לצפון פניכם לצפון, נמצאו הולכים את רוח מזרחית, וזהו שנאמר: "ויבא ממזרח שמש לארץ מואב" (שופטים יא, יח):

ד| ונשמרתם מאד. ומהו השמירה? "אל תתגרו בם" (להלן פסוק ה):

ה| עד מדרך כף רגל. (אפילו כדי מדרך כף רגל), [כלומר אפילו דריסת הרגל איני מרשה לכם לעבור בארצם שלא ברשות – רבינו שמעיה העיד: "רבי נוה להגיה"]. ומדרש אגדה, עד שיבוא יום דריסת כף רגל על הר הזיתים, שנאמר: "ועמדו רגליו" וגו' (זכריה יד, ד): ירשה לעשו. מאברהם. עשרה עממים נתתי לו, שבעה לכם, וקיני וקנזי וקדמוני הן עמון ומואב ושעיר, אחת מהם לעשו, והשנים לבני לוט בשכר שהלך אתו למצרים ושתק על מה שהיה אומר על אשתו 'אחותי היא', לפיכך עשאו כבנו:

ו| תכרו. לשון מקח, וכן: "אשר כריתי לי" (בראשית נ, ה), שכן בכרכי הים קורין למכירה כירה:

ז| כי ה' אלהיך ברכך. לפיכך לא תכפו את טובתו להראות כאלו אתם עניים, אלא הראו עצמכם עשירים:

ח| ונפן ונעבר. לצד צפון, הפכנו פנים להלך רוח מזרחית:

ט| ואל תתגר בם. לא אסר להם על מואב אלא מלחמה, אבל מיראים היו אותם ונראים להם כשהם מזוינים, לפיכך כתיב: "ויגר מואב מפני העם" (במדבר כב, ג), שהיו שוללים ובוזזים אותם, אבל בבני עמון נאמר: "ואל תתגר בם" (להלן פסוק יט), שום גרוי, בשכר צניעות אמם שלא פרסמה על אביה כמו שעשתה הבכירה שקראתה שם בנה מואב: ער. שם המדינה:

י| האמים לפנים וגו'. אתה סבור שזו ארץ רפאים שנתתי לו לאברהם (בראשית טו, כ), לפי שהאמים שהם רפאים ישבו בה לפנים, אבל לא זו היא, כי אותן רפאים הורשתי מפני בני לוט והושבתים תחתם:

יא-יב| רפאים יחשבו וגו'. רפאים היו נחשבין אותם אמים, כענקים הנקראים רפאים, על שם שכל הרואה אותם ידיו מתרפות: אמים. על שם שאימתם מטלת על הבריות. וכן: "ובשעיר ישבו החרים" ונתתים לבני עשו: יירשום. לשון הווה, כלומר נתתי בהם כח שהיו מורישים אותם והולכים:

children of Esau did not entirely destroy the Horites, as they intermingled with them.[27] The children of Esau were the de facto rulers of Se'ir, while the Horites cooperated and maintained cordial relations with them.

13 **Now** that you have approached the Land of Israel, **rise, and cross the Zered Ravine.**[B] This ravine was perhaps named for its trees or shrubbery [*zeradim*].[28] **And we crossed the Zered Ravine.** This was the point of transition from the Israelites' wandering in the wilderness to their arrival at the border of the Promised Land.

14 **The days that we went from Kadesh Barnea, until we crossed the Zered Ravine, were thirty-eight years,** as we waited **until the demise of the entire generation,** all those who had been counted in the first census as **the men of war,** males who were between ages twenty and sixty at the time. Eventually, all those men passed away **from the midst of the camp, as the Lord swore to them.**

15 **The hand of the Lord,** divine intervention, **was also among them, to destroy them from the midst of the camp, until their demise.** Thirty-eight years would not have been enough for them all to die of natural means, and therefore God accelerated the process.

16 **It was when all the men of war concluded to die from among the people,** that the great journey to enter the land began, as

17 **the Lord spoke to me, saying:**

18 **You are passing today the border of Moav, Ar;**

19 **you will approach opposite the children of Amon; do not besiege them and do not provoke them** to battle,[29] **as I will not give you from the land of the children of Amon as a possession; because to the children of Lot I have given it as a possession,** in Abraham's merit.

20 **It, too,** the land of the descendants of Amon, **is considered a land of Refaim,** as **Refaim lived in it previously, and the Amonites call them,** those people, **Zamzumim.**

21 The lands on the eastern side of the Jordan River were once populated by the Refaim, who were **a people great, and numerous, and tall as the giants;** but **the Lord destroyed them,**[D] the Refaim, **from before them,** the Amonites, the descendants of Lot, **and they took possession from them, and settled in their place,**

22 **as He did for the children of Esau, who live in Se'ir, that He destroyed the Horites from before them and they took possession from them, and settled in their place until this day.** Since Canaan serves as a crossing point for other regions, there have always been nations that spoke different languages, living in close proximity to this land. Like the Refaim, the Horites, who were apparently originally from Asia Minor, lived on the eastern side of the Jordan River until the arrival of the descendants of Esau.

23 Similar to the previous verse, this verse is not directly related to the narrative at hand, as it describes ancient demographic and historical shifts. As for **the Avim, who lived in unwalled cities until Gaza,** a coastal region in the southern part of the land, **Kaftorim, who emerged from Kaftor,**[B] the island of Crete, **destroyed them, and settled in their place.**[D] The Philistines, who settled this coastal area, were descendants of the Kaftorim.[30]

24 After this historical and geographical description, God commands: **Rise, and travel, and cross the Arnon Ravine; see, I have placed Sihon, king of Heshbon, the Emorite, and his land in your hand; begin taking possession, and provoke war with him.** The Edomites, descendants of Esau, and the Moavites and Amonites, descendants of Lot, came from the same family as the patriarchs of Israel. Due to the oath to Abraham and his family, these nations also inherited portions on the eastern side of the Jordan River. Consequently, the children of Israel were warned not to attack them. However, this warning does not apply to Israel attacking other nations, and therefore the children of Israel were permitted and commanded to begin inheriting the land of Sihon.

DISCUSSION

2:21 | The Lord destroyed them: Even many years after these large men had ceased to exist, their very mention was enough to instill fear in people. It is unclear how numerous the Refaim were, and it is possible that in actual fact they were not exceptionally powerful. After all, they were destroyed by people who were physically far smaller than they were. However, perhaps they were destroyed because they were scattered over a large area (see verse 11; Numbers 13:33, 21:34).

2:23 | Destroyed them, and settled in their place: In contrast to the conventional wisdom of ancient times, that all peoples are set in their places, the Torah emphasizes that God moves nations and kingdoms. Not only does Israel, with its unique mission, undergo travels, but also other nations are transported from place to place. Their ability to remain settled in one region depends upon the grace of God (see Amos 9:7–9).

יג יד עַתָּה קֻמוּ וְעִבְרוּ לָכֶם אֶת־נַחַל זֶרֶד וַנַּעֲבֹר אֶת־נַחַל זֶרֶד: וְהַיָּמִים אֲשֶׁר־הָלַכְנוּ ׀
מִקָּדֵשׁ בַּרְנֵעַ עַד אֲשֶׁר־עָבַרְנוּ אֶת־נַחַל זֶרֶד שְׁלֹשִׁים וּשְׁמֹנֶה שָׁנָה עַד־תֹּם כָּל־
טו הַדּוֹר אַנְשֵׁי הַמִּלְחָמָה מִקֶּרֶב הַמַּחֲנֶה כַּאֲשֶׁר נִשְׁבַּע יְהוָה לָהֶם: וְגַם יַד־יְהוָה
טז הָיְתָה בָּם לְהֻמָּם מִקֶּרֶב הַמַּחֲנֶה עַד תֻּמָּם: וַיְהִי כַאֲשֶׁר־תַּמּוּ כָּל־אַנְשֵׁי הַמִּלְחָמָה
יז יח לָמוּת מִקֶּרֶב הָעָם: וַיְדַבֵּר יְהוָה אֵלַי לֵאמֹר: אַתָּה עֹבֵר הַיּוֹם
יט אֶת־גְּבוּל מוֹאָב אֶת־עָר: וְקָרַבְתָּ מוּל בְּנֵי עַמּוֹן אַל־תְּצֻרֵם וְאַל־תִּתְגָּר בָּם כִּי
כ לֹא־אֶתֵּן מֵאֶרֶץ בְּנֵי־עַמּוֹן לְךָ יְרֻשָּׁה כִּי לִבְנֵי־לוֹט נְתַתִּיהָ יְרֻשָּׁה: אֶרֶץ־רְפָאִים
כא תֵּחָשֵׁב אַף־הִוא רְפָאִים יָשְׁבוּ־בָהּ לְפָנִים וְהָעַמֹּנִים יִקְרְאוּ לָהֶם זַמְזֻמִּים: עַם
כב גָּדוֹל וְרַב וָרָם כָּעֲנָקִים וַיַּשְׁמִידֵם יְהוָה מִפְּנֵיהֶם וַיִּירָשֻׁם וַיֵּשְׁבוּ תַחְתָּם: כַּאֲשֶׁר
עָשָׂה לִבְנֵי עֵשָׂו הַיֹּשְׁבִים בְּשֵׂעִיר אֲשֶׁר הִשְׁמִיד אֶת־הַחֹרִי מִפְּנֵיהֶם וַיִּירָשֻׁם וַיֵּשְׁבוּ
כג תַחְתָּם עַד הַיּוֹם הַזֶּה: וְהָעַוִּים הַיֹּשְׁבִים בַּחֲצֵרִים עַד־עַזָּה כַּפְתֹּרִים הַיֹּצְאִים
כד מִכַּפְתֹּר הִשְׁמִידֻם וַיֵּשְׁבוּ תַחְתָּם: קוּמוּ סְּעוּ וְעִבְרוּ אֶת־נַחַל אַרְנֹן רְאֵה נָתַתִּי
בְיָדְךָ אֶת־סִיחֹן מֶלֶךְ־חֶשְׁבּוֹן הָאֱמֹרִי וְאֶת־אַרְצוֹ הָחֵל רָשׁ וְהִתְגָּר בּוֹ מִלְחָמָה:

רש"י

טו| **היתה בם.** למהר ולהמם בתוך ארבעים שנה, שלא יגרמו לבניהם עוד להתעכב במדבר:

טז-יז| **ויהי כאשר תמו וגו' וידבר ה' אלי וגו'.** אבל משלוח המרגלים עד כאן לא נאמר 'וידבר' בפרשה זו אלא 'ויאמר', ללמדך שכל שלשים ושמונה שנה שהיו ישראל נזופים, לא נתיחד עמו הדבור בלשון חבה פנים אל פנים וישוב, ללמדך שאין השכינה שורה על הנביאים אלא בשביל ישראל: אנשי המלחמה. מבן עשרים שנה היוצאים בצבא:

יח-יט| **אתה עבר היום את גבול מואב.** אל 'מול בני עמון', מכאן שארץ עמון לצד צפון:

כ| **ארץ רפאים תחשב.** ארץ רפאים נחשבת אף היא לפי שהרפאים ישבו בה לפנים, אבל לא זו היא שנתתי לאברהם:

כג| **והעוים הישבים בחצרים וגו'.** עוים מפלשתים הם, שעמהם הם נחשבים בספר יהושע, שנאמר: "חמשת סרני פלשתים העזתי והאשדודי האשקלוני הגתי והעקרוני והעוים" (יהושע יג, ג), ומפני השבועה שנשבע אברהם לאבימלך לא יכלו ישראל להוציא ארצם מידם, והבאתי עליהם כפתורים והשמידום וישבו תחתם, ועכשיו אתם מתרים לקחתה מידם:

BACKGROUND

2:13| **Zered Ravine:** Many researchers identify this with Wadi al-Hisa, which flows to the south end of the Dead Sea, and forms the border between the mountains of Moav and the mountains of Edom. Others claim that it is one of the wadis in northeast Moav, which lead to the Arnon Ravine, Wadi Mujib, either Wadi al-Dik or another wadi that flows near Aroer (Elitzur).

2:23| **Kaftor:** This is the name for Crete in early documents (see also Amos 9:7; Jeremiah 47:4). Some maintain that this is the place called Keftiu in Egyptian sources dating from the second millennium BCE, perhaps because Egyptians did not pronounce the sound "r." The residents of this island were called Philistines (Ezekiel 25:16; Zephaniah 2:5). Historical sources indicate that some of the nations whom the Egyptians called Sea Peoples were foreign invaders, descendants of the Cretans who came to the land of Canaan.

25 From **this day** onward **I will begin to place terror of you and fear of you upon the peoples under all the heavens, who will hear your reputation and will tremble, and be in trepidation because of you.** Until now, the children of Israel were considered by other peoples as an almost mythical nation of nomads, about whom they related miraculous stories from forty years earlier. Now this nation would become a real threat.

26 **I sent messengers from the wilderness of Kedemot,** in the east [*kedem*], **to Sihon, king of Heshbon, with words of peace, saying:** Although God had told Moses that the children of Israel would have to wage war against Sihon, Moses nevertheless sent a message of peace. This gesture highlights the value of attempting dialogue before waging war.[31] Similarly, the Rambam writes that one does not wage war, whether an optional or a compulsory war, without first extending an offer of peace.[32]

27 **Let me pass through your land,** and I promise that **I will go only on the** main **path, I will not diverge** to the sides, **right or left.**

28 As in the case of the children of Esau (2:6), Israel proposes: **You will sell me food for silver, and I will eat, and you will give me water for silver, and I will drink; only let me pass on my feet.** All we ask is for permission to pass through your territory; we guarantee not to cause any damage to the surroundings, the people, or the animals. Furthermore, you will profit from the arrangement, as we will pay for anything we eat,

29 **like the children of Esau, who live in Se'ir, and the Moavites, who live in Ar, did for me.** The children of Israel did not pass through Se'ir or Moav. Rather, this is apparently a reference to the commercial ties that they maintained with these nations. With regard to Moav, see Numbers 25:1–3; it is possible that there was a similar arrangement with Edom.[33] Israel adds: I request this assistance only **until I will cross the Jordan into the land that the Lord our God is giving us.**

30 **But Sihon, king of Heshbon, was unwilling**[D] **to let us pass through it,** his land, **for the Lord your God hardened his spirit, and made his heart obstinate, in order to deliver him into your hand, like this day.**

31 **The Lord said to me: See, I have begun delivering before you Sihon and his land; begin taking possession of his land** without delay.

Sixth aliya

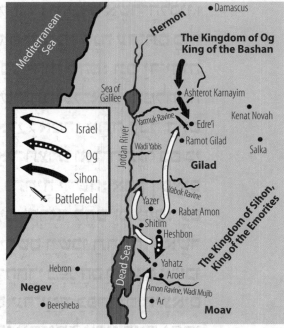

Wars against Sihon and Og

32 **Sihon came out to war toward us, he and his entire people, to Yahatz.**[B]

33 **The Lord our God delivered him before us and we smote him, and his sons,** who were also prominent individuals or warriors, **and his entire people.**

34 **We captured all his cities at that time, and we destroyed** the men of **every inhabited city, and** also **the women, and the children.** We took everything, and **we left no remnant** from its inhabitants.

35 **Only the animals we looted for ourselves, and the spoils of the cities that we captured.**

36 We conquered all the cities **from Aroer, which is on the** northern **edge of the Arnon Ravine, and the city that is in the ravine**[B] **until the Gilad,** far to the north of Aroer. **There was no city that was too high for us,** or too strong for us to conquer; **everything, the Lord our God delivered before us.**

DISCUSSION

2:30 | **But Sihon, king of Heshbon, was unwilling:** It is possible that Sihon was a border ruler, a leader charged with defending the boundaries of the land of Canaan against infiltrators from the wilderness, as would occasionally happen (see Judges 6:1–6). Although Sihon is presented as a great ruler, his land was not well populated like Canaan; rather, his importance lay in his protection of the residents of Canaan from invaders from the east (see *Bemidbar Rabba* 19:29; *Tanḥuma, Hukat* 52; Rashi, Numbers 21:23). Furthermore, it is possible that Sihon's refusal stemmed from an assumption that the children of Israel would respond as they did to earlier refusals from other nations. When the Edomites, for example, refused to allow passage through their land, the children of Israel circumvented Edom, and the same happened with Moav and Amon. Sihon might have thought that if he responded in the negative to Israel's request and gathered his army as a deterrent, he would be treated likewise. However, in this case God did not grant him immunity from attack.

כה הַיּוֹם הַזֶּה אָחֵל תֵּת פַּחְדְּךָ וְיִרְאָתְךָ עַל־פְּנֵי הָעַמִּים תַּחַת כָּל־הַשָּׁמָיִם אֲשֶׁר
כו יִשְׁמְעוּן שִׁמְעֲךָ וְרָגְזוּ וְחָלוּ מִפָּנֶיךָ: וָאֶשְׁלַח מַלְאָכִים מִמִּדְבַּר קְדֵמוֹת אֶל־סִיחוֹן
כז מֶלֶךְ חֶשְׁבּוֹן דִּבְרֵי שָׁלוֹם לֵאמֹר: אֶעְבְּרָה בְאַרְצֶךָ בַּדֶּרֶךְ בַּדֶּרֶךְ אֵלֵךְ לֹא אָסוּר
כח יָמִין וּשְׂמֹאול: אֹכֶל בַּכֶּסֶף תַּשְׁבִּרֵנִי וְאָכַלְתִּי וּמַיִם בַּכֶּסֶף תִּתֶּן־לִי וְשָׁתִיתִי רַק
כט אֶעְבְּרָה בְרַגְלָי: כַּאֲשֶׁר עָשׂוּ־לִי בְּנֵי עֵשָׂו הַיֹּשְׁבִים בְּשֵׂעִיר וְהַמּוֹאָבִים הַיֹּשְׁבִים
בְּעָר עַד אֲשֶׁר־אֶעֱבֹר אֶת־הַיַּרְדֵּן אֶל־הָאָרֶץ אֲשֶׁר־יְהוָה אֱלֹהֵינוּ נֹתֵן לָנוּ:
ל וְלֹא אָבָה סִיחֹן מֶלֶךְ חֶשְׁבּוֹן הַעֲבִרֵנוּ בּוֹ כִּי־הִקְשָׁה יְהוָה אֱלֹהֶיךָ אֶת־רוּחוֹ וְאִמֵּץ
לא אֶת־לְבָבוֹ לְמַעַן תִּתּוֹ בְיָדְךָ כַּיּוֹם הַזֶּה: ג ששי וַיֹּאמֶר יְהוָה אֵלַי רְאֵה
לב הַחִלֹּתִי תֵּת לְפָנֶיךָ אֶת־סִיחֹן וְאֶת־אַרְצוֹ הָחֵל רָשׁ לָרֶשֶׁת אֶת־אַרְצוֹ: וַיֵּצֵא סִיחֹן
לג לִקְרָאתֵנוּ הוּא וְכָל־עַמּוֹ לַמִּלְחָמָה יָהְצָה: וַיִּתְּנֵהוּ יְהוָה אֱלֹהֵינוּ לְפָנֵינוּ וַנַּךְ אֹתוֹ
לד וְאֶת־בָּנָו וְאֶת־כָּל־עַמּוֹ: וַנִּלְכֹּד אֶת־כָּל־עָרָיו בָּעֵת הַהִוא וַנַּחֲרֵם אֶת־כָּל־עִיר
לה מְתִם וְהַנָּשִׁים וְהַטָּף לֹא הִשְׁאַרְנוּ שָׂרִיד: רַק הַבְּהֵמָה בָּזַזְנוּ לָנוּ וּשְׁלַל הֶעָרִים
לו אֲשֶׁר לָכָדְנוּ: מֵעֲרֹעֵר אֲשֶׁר עַל־שְׂפַת־נַחַל אַרְנֹן וְהָעִיר אֲשֶׁר בַּנַּחַל וְעַד־הַגִּלְעָד
לֹא הָיְתָה קִרְיָה אֲשֶׁר שָׂגְבָה מִמֶּנּוּ אֶת־הַכֹּל נָתַן יְהוָה אֱלֹהֵינוּ לְפָנֵינוּ:

רש״י

כה| תַּחַת כָּל הַשָּׁמָיִם. לִמֵּד שֶׁעָמְדָה חַמָּה לְמֹשֶׁה בְּיוֹם מִלְחֶמֶת עוֹג, וְנוֹדַע הַדָּבָר תַּחַת כָּל הַשָּׁמָיִם:

כו| מִמִּדְבַּר קְדֵמוֹת. אַף עַל פִּי שֶׁלֹּא צִוַּנִי הַמָּקוֹם לִקְרֹא לְסִיחוֹן לְשָׁלוֹם, לָמַדְתִּי מִמִּדְבַּר סִינַי, מִן הַתּוֹרָה שֶׁקָּדְמָה לָעוֹלָם, כְּשֶׁבָּא הַקָּדוֹשׁ בָּרוּךְ הוּא לִתְּנָהּ לְיִשְׂרָאֵל חִזֵּר אוֹתָהּ עַל עֵשָׂו וְיִשְׁמָעֵאל, וְגָלוּי לְפָנָיו שֶׁלֹּא יְקַבְּלוּהָ, וְאַף עַל פִּי כֵן פָּתַח לָהֶם בְּשָׁלוֹם, אַף אֲנִי קִדַּמְתִּי אֶת סִיחוֹן בְּדִבְרֵי שָׁלוֹם.

כט| כַּאֲשֶׁר עָשׂוּ לִי בְּנֵי עֵשָׂו. לֹא לְעִנְיַן לַעֲבֹר בְּאַרְצָם, אֶלָּא לְעִנְיַן מֶכֶר אֹכֶל וּמַיִם:

לב| וַיֵּצֵא סִיחֹן. לֹא שָׁלַח בִּשְׁבִיל עוֹג לַעֲזֹר לוֹ, לְלַמֶּדְךָ שֶׁלֹּא הָיוּ צְרִיכִים זֶה לָזֶה:

לג| וְאֶת בָּנָו. ׳בְּנוֹ׳ כְּתִיב, שֶׁהָיָה לוֹ בֵּן גִּבּוֹר כָּמוֹתוֹ:

לד| מְתִם. אֲנָשִׁים. בְּבִזַּת סִיחוֹן נֶאֱמַר: "בָּזַזְנוּ לָנוּ" (להלן פסוק לה), לְשׁוֹן בִּזָּה, שֶׁהָיְתָה חֲבִיבָה עֲלֵיהֶם וּבוֹזְזִים אִישׁ לוֹ, וּכְשֶׁבָּאוּ לְבִזַּת עוֹג כְּבָר הָיוּ שְׂבֵעִים וּמְלֵאִים, וְהָיְתָה בְּזוּיָה בְּעֵינֵיהֶם וּמְקַרְעִין וּמַשְׁלִיכִין בְּהֵמָה וּבְגָדִים, כִּי אִם כֶּסֶף וְזָהָב, לְכָךְ נֶאֱמַר: "בַּזּוֹנוּ לָנוּ" (להלן ג, ז), לְשׁוֹן בִּזָּיוֹן. כָּךְ נִדְרָשׁ בְּסִפְרֵי בְּפָרָשַׁת ׳וַיֵּשֶׁב יִשְׂרָאֵל בַּשִּׁטִּים׳ (ספרי במדבר קלא).

BACKGROUND

2:32| **Yahatz:** This later became a Levite city, of the family of Merari, in the portion of Reuben (see Joshua 13:18; I Chronicles 6:63). It is also mentioned in the Mesha Inscription, ninth century BCE. The identity of Yahatz is uncertain.

2:36| **The city that is in the ravine:** A similar expression appears elsewhere in the Bible. In Joshua 13:9, "the city that is within the ravine" is mentioned as a point along the border between the tribal territories of Gad and Reuben. However, it is unclear whether this was an independent settlement whose precise location is currently unknown, whether it was part of Aroer, or if it was an isolated fortress.

37 Only to the land of the children of Amon you did not approach, all the area adjacent to the Yabok Ravine, and the cities of the highlands, and everywhere that the Lord our God had commanded us. The children of Israel fought Sihon, whose kingdom encompassed a large territory which reached until the border of Amon, but they were careful not to encroach upon the territory of Amon.

3 1 We turned, and went up northward via the Bashan, to the northeast of the Sea of Galilee; and Og, king of the Bashan, came out toward us, he and his entire people, to war at the city of Edre'i. It is possible that any turn to the north is called an ascent in the Bible.[34]

2 The Lord said to me: Do not fear him as I have delivered him and his entire people and his land into your hand; you shall do to him as you did to Sihon, king of the Emorites, who lives in Heshbon.

3 The Lord our God also delivered into our hand Og, king of Bashan, and all his people; and we smote him until we left him no remnant.

4 We took all his cities at that time; there was no city in that entire region that we did not take from them, including[35] the sixty cities comprising the entire region of Argov, the kingdom of Og in the Bashan. The precise location of the region of Argov is unknown. Its name possibly derives from the term for a clod [*regev*] of dirt, or a den [*gov*] of a lion [*arye*].[36]

5 All these were strong, fortified cities, surrounded by a high wall, with gates and a bar, besides the very many smaller, unwalled cities that we conquered.

6 We destroyed them, as we did to Sihon, king of Heshbon, destroying every inhabited city, the women, and the children.

7 But all the animals, and the spoils of the cities, we looted for ourselves.

8 We took, at that time, the land from the hand of the two kings of the Emorites, Sihon and Og, that were beyond the Jordan, from the Arnon Ravine until Mount Hermon.

9 The chapter adds a comment on Hermon, the most prominent mountain range south of Lebanon: Sidonians, who lived on the other side of the mountain, would call Hermon Siryon, and the Emorites would call it Senir.[D]

10 All the cities of the plain, and all the Gilad, and all the Bashan, until Salka[B] and Edre'i, cities of the kingdom of Og in the Bashan.

11 As only Og, king of the Bashan, remained from the rest of the Refaim who once dwelled on the eastern side of the Jordan River, most of whom had died (see 2:20). Behold, his bed[D] was a bed of iron, which was unusual at that time. It was made of iron because Og was exceptionally large and heavy.[37] This bed survived and was transferred over time; isn't it in Raba of the children of Amon? Nine cubits is its length, and four cubits its width, by the cubit of a man. Since the height of an average individual is three to four cubits,[38] one whose bed measures nine cubits in length is indeed a giant.

Mount Hermon

DISCUSSION

3:9| Sidonians would call Hermon Siryon, and the Emorites would call it Senir: The verse provides references to Hermon in various languages, similar to the manner in which it cites different names for the Refaim (see 2:11 and the commentary ad loc.). The people of that generation were already aware of these details, but they are mentioned due to their importance for later generations. The fact that different nations dwelled in or near the Hermon and had their own names for it is indicative of the mountain's regional significance. Mount Hermon serves as a point of reference at the edge of the area conquered by the children of Israel, but it was not actually part of their inheritance.

3:11| His bed: Some explain that this is a reference to Og's cradle as a baby, which means that he was far larger when fully grown (see Rashbam).

BACKGROUND

3:10| Salka: A city in the territory of the half of the tribe of Manasseh that settled on the eastern side of the Jordan River. According to I Chronicles 5:11, in practice Salka was inhabited by members of the tribe of Gad. Salka is identified with the modern town called Salkhad, which lies near the southern foot of Yaval al-Druze in southern Syria.

962

לז רַק אֶל־אֶרֶץ בְּנֵי־עַמּוֹן לֹא קָרָבְתָּ כָּל־יַד נַחַל יַבֹּק וְעָרֵי הָהָר וְכֹל אֲשֶׁר־צִוָּה
א יְהוָה אֱלֹהֵינוּ: וַנֵּפֶן וַנַּעַל דֶּרֶךְ הַבָּשָׁן וַיֵּצֵא עוֹג מֶלֶךְ־הַבָּשָׁן לִקְרָאתֵנוּ הוּא וְכָל־
ב עַמּוֹ לַמִּלְחָמָה אֶדְרֶעִי: וַיֹּאמֶר יְהוָה אֵלַי אַל־תִּירָא אֹתוֹ כִּי בְיָדְךָ נָתַתִּי אֹתוֹ
וְאֶת־כָּל־עַמּוֹ וְאֶת־אַרְצוֹ וְעָשִׂיתָ לּוֹ כַּאֲשֶׁר עָשִׂיתָ לְסִיחֹן מֶלֶךְ הָאֱמֹרִי אֲשֶׁר
ג יוֹשֵׁב בְּחֶשְׁבּוֹן: וַיִּתֵּן יְהוָה אֱלֹהֵינוּ בְּיָדֵנוּ גַּם אֶת־עוֹג מֶלֶךְ־הַבָּשָׁן וְאֶת־כָּל־עַמּוֹ
ד וַנַּכֵּהוּ עַד־בִּלְתִּי הִשְׁאִיר־לוֹ שָׂרִיד: וַנִּלְכֹּד אֶת־כָּל־עָרָיו בָּעֵת הַהִוא לֹא הָיְתָה
קִרְיָה אֲשֶׁר לֹא־לָקַחְנוּ מֵאִתָּם שִׁשִּׁים עִיר כָּל־חֶבֶל אַרְגֹּב מַמְלֶכֶת עוֹג
ה בַּבָּשָׁן: כָּל־אֵלֶּה עָרִים בְּצֻרֹת חוֹמָה גְבֹהָה דְּלָתַיִם וּבְרִיחַ לְבַד מֵעָרֵי הַפְּרָזִי
ו הַרְבֵּה מְאֹד: וַנַּחֲרֵם אוֹתָם כַּאֲשֶׁר עָשִׂינוּ לְסִיחֹן מֶלֶךְ חֶשְׁבּוֹן הַחֲרֵם כָּל־עִיר
ז ח מְתִם הַנָּשִׁים וְהַטָּף: וְכָל־הַבְּהֵמָה וּשְׁלַל הֶעָרִים בַּזּוֹנוּ לָנוּ: וַנִּקַּח בָּעֵת הַהִוא
אֶת־הָאָרֶץ מִיַּד שְׁנֵי מַלְכֵי הָאֱמֹרִי אֲשֶׁר בְּעֵבֶר הַיַּרְדֵּן מִנַּחַל אַרְנֹן עַד־הַר
ט י חֶרְמוֹן: צִידֹנִים יִקְרְאוּ לְחֶרְמוֹן שִׂרְיֹן וְהָאֱמֹרִי יִקְרְאוּ־לוֹ שְׂנִיר: כֹּל | עָרֵי
הַמִּישֹׁר וְכָל־הַגִּלְעָד וְכָל־הַבָּשָׁן עַד־סַלְכָה וְאֶדְרֶעִי עָרֵי מַמְלֶכֶת עוֹג בַּבָּשָׁן:
יא כִּי רַק־עוֹג מֶלֶךְ הַבָּשָׁן נִשְׁאַר מִיֶּתֶר הָרְפָאִים הִנֵּה עַרְשׂוֹ עֶרֶשׂ בַּרְזֶל הֲלֹה הִוא
בְּרַבַּת בְּנֵי עַמּוֹן תֵּשַׁע אַמּוֹת אָרְכָּהּ וְאַרְבַּע אַמּוֹת רָחְבָּהּ בְּאַמַּת־אִישׁ:

רש״י

לז| **כָּל יַד נַחַל יַבֹּק.** כָּל אֵצֶל נַחַל יַבֹּק: **וְכֹל אֲשֶׁר צִוָּה ה׳ אֱלֹהֵינוּ.** שֶׁלֹּא לִכְבֹּשׁ, הִנַּחְנוּ:

פרק ג

א| **וַנֵּפֶן וַנַּעַל.** כָּל לְצַד צָפוֹן עֲלִיָּה הִיא:

ב| **אַל תִּירָא אֹתוֹ.** וּבְסִיחוֹן לֹא הֻצְרַךְ לוֹמַר ״אַל תִּירָא אֹתוֹ״, אֶלָּא מִתְיָרֵא הָיָה מֹשֶׁה שֶׁלֹּא תַעֲמֹד לוֹ זְכוּת שֶׁשִּׁמֵּשׁ לְאַבְרָהָם, שֶׁנֶּאֱמַר: ״וַיָּבֹא הַפָּלִיט״ (בראשית יד, יג) וְהוּא עוֹג:

ד| **חֶבֶל אַרְגֹּב.** מְתַרְגְּמִינַן: ״בֵּית פֶּלֶךְ טְרָכוֹנָא״. וְרָאִיתִי תַּרְגּוּם יְרוּשַׁלְמִי בִּמְגִלַּת אֶסְתֵּר (א, ג) קוֹרֵא פָּלָטִין – טְרָכוֹנִין, לָמַדְתִּי ״חֶבֶל אַרְגֹּב״ – הַפַּרְכְיָא שֶׁל הֵיכַל הַמֶּלֶךְ, כְּלוֹמַר שֶׁהַמַּלְכוּת נִקְרָא עַל שְׁמָהּ וְכֵן: ״אֶת אַרְגֹּב״ דִּמְלָכִים (ב׳ טו, כה), אֵצֶל הֵיכַל הַמֶּלֶךְ הֲרָגוֹ פֶּקַח לִ[פְקַחְיָה בֶּן] מְנַחֵם:

ה| **מֵעָרֵי הַפְּרָזִי.** פְּרוּזוֹת וּפְתוּחוֹת בְּלֹא חוֹמָה, וְכֵן: ״פְּרָזוֹת תֵּשֵׁב יְרוּשָׁלַםִ״ (זכריה ב, ח):

ו| **הַחֲרֵם.** לְשׁוֹן הֹוֶה, הָלוֹךְ וְכַלּוֹת:

ח| **מִיַּד.** מֵרְשׁוּת:

ט| **צִידֹנִים יִקְרְאוּ לְחֶרְמוֹן וְגוֹ׳.** וּבְמָקוֹם אַחֵר הוּא אוֹמֵר: ״וְעַד הַר שִׂיאֹן הוּא חֶרְמוֹן״ (להלן ד, מח), הֲרֵי לוֹ אַרְבָּעָה שֵׁמוֹת. לָמָּה הֻצְרְכוּ לִכָּתֵב? לְהַגִּיד שֶׁבַח אֶרֶץ יִשְׂרָאֵל, שֶׁהָיוּ אַרְבַּע מַלְכֻיּוֹת מִתְפָּאֲרוֹת בְּכָךְ, זוֹ אוֹמֶרֶת עַל שְׁמִי יִקָּרֵא, וְזוֹ אוֹמֶרֶת עַל שְׁמִי יִקָּרֵא: **שְׂנִיר.** הוּא שֶׁלֶג בִּלְשׁוֹן אַשְׁכְּנַז וּבִלְשׁוֹן כְּנַעַן:

יא| **מִיֶּתֶר הָרְפָאִים.** שֶׁהָרְגוּ אַמְרָפֶל וַחֲבֵרָיו בְּעַשְׁתְּרוֹת קַרְנַיִם, וְהוּא פָּלַט מִן הַמִּלְחָמָה, שֶׁנֶּאֱמַר: ״וַיָּבֹא הַפָּלִיט״ (בראשית יד, יג), זֶהוּ עוֹג: **בְּאַמַּת אִישׁ.** בְּאַמַּת עוֹג:

12 **This land we took possession of at that time, from Aroer,**
which is near the Arnon Ravine, in the south, near Moav, **and**
half of Mount Gilad, and its cities, I gave to the Reubenite
and to the Gadite tribes.
13 **The rest of Gilad, and all the Bashan,** which is **the kingdom**
of Og, I gave to half the tribe of Manasseh; the entire re-
gion of Argov for the entire Bashan, that would be called
the land of Refaim, especially the area of Bashan.
14 **Ya'ir son of Manasseh,** among others, **took the entire re-**
gion of Argov until the border of the Geshurite and the
Maakhatite,[B] two small kingdoms north of Israel, **and he**
called them after his name, the Bashan he called **Havvoth**
Ya'ir, to this day.
Seventh aliya 15 **To Makhir,** a family from the tribe of Manasseh, **I gave Gilad**
as an inheritance.
16 **To the Reubenite and to the Gadite I gave from the Gilad**
until the Arnon Ravine, which included the area **within the**
ravine and around **its border, until the Yabok Ravine, the**
border of the children of Amon. The Arnon Ravine is the
border of Moav, while the Yabok Ravine is the border of Amon.
The entire adjacent region was given to the tribes of Reuben
and Gad.
17 This territory included **the Arava, and the Jordan, and its**
border, its bank. The Jordan was included in their land and
comprised the western border of the portion of these tribes.
From the Sea of Galilee until the sea of the Arava, the Dead
Sea, under the waterfalls of the peak to the east, near the
Jordan. Alternatively, this last phrase means: The streams that
flow to the Jordan from the east.
18 **I commanded you at that time, saying:**[D] **The Lord, your**
God, gave you, the tribes of Reuben and Gad and half the
tribe of Manasseh, **this land to take possession of it; all those**
mobilized shall pass before your brethren the children of
Israel, all those **capable men,** who are fit to wage war.
19 **Only your wives, and your children, and your livestock,** I
know that you have much livestock, they shall live in your
cities that I gave you on the eastern side of the Jordan River.

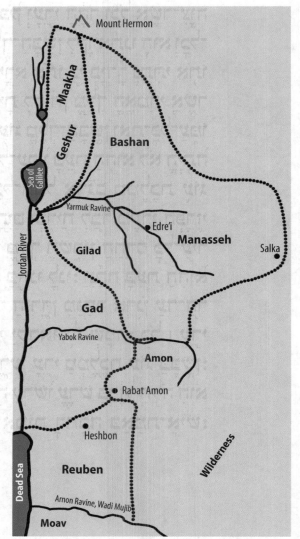

Inheritance of the tribes that settled on the eastern side of the Jordan River

DISCUSSION

3:18 | **I commanded you at that time, saying:** The incident in which the tribes of Reuben and Gad received their inheritances is yet another example of a story that is retold differently from the way it was previously related (Numbers 32). It is not mentioned here that these tribes requested to receive their portions on the eastern side of the Jordan, that Moses scolded them, or that they suggested going to battle alongside the rest of the nation as a condition for their settlement on the eastern side of the Jordan River. These differences are due to the context. In Moses' last speech he mentions only the public aspects of the debate: His stipulation in the presence of the entire nation, in which he formally authorized these tribes to settle east of the Jordan, and the fact that this permission is contingent upon their participation in the upcoming military encounters west of the Jordan.

יב וְאֶת־הָאָרֶץ הַזֹּאת יָרַשְׁנוּ בָּעֵת הַהִוא מֵעֲרֹעֵר אֲשֶׁר־עַל־נַחַל אַרְנֹן וַחֲצִי הַר־
יג הַגִּלְעָד וְעָרָיו נָתַתִּי לָרֽאוּבֵנִי וְלַגָּדִי׃ וְיֶתֶר הַגִּלְעָד וְכָל־הַבָּשָׁן מַמְלֶכֶת עוֹג
נָתַתִּי לַחֲצִי שֵׁבֶט הַמְנַשֶּׁה כֹּל חֶבֶל הָאַרְגֹּב לְכָל־הַבָּשָׁן הַהוּא יִקָּרֵא
יד אֶרֶץ רְפָאִים׃ יָאִיר בֶּן־מְנַשֶּׁה לָקַח אֶת־כָּל־חֶבֶל אַרְגֹּב עַד־גְּבוּל הַגְּשׁוּרִי
וְהַמַּעֲכָתִי וַיִּקְרָא אֹתָם עַל־שְׁמוֹ אֶת־הַבָּשָׁן חַוֹּת יָאִיר עַד הַיּוֹם הַזֶּה׃
טו טז וּלְמָכִיר נָתַתִּי אֶת־הַגִּלְעָד׃ וְלָרֽאוּבֵנִי וְלַגָּדִי נָתַתִּי מִן־הַגִּלְעָד וְעַד־נַחַל אַרְנֹן שביעי
יז תּוֹךְ הַנַּחַל וּגְבֻל וְעַד יַבֹּק הַנַּחַל גְּבוּל בְּנֵי עַמּוֹן׃ וְהָעֲרָבָה וְהַיַּרְדֵּן וּגְבֻל מִכִּנֶּרֶת
יח וְעַד יָם הָעֲרָבָה יָם הַמֶּלַח תַּחַת אַשְׁדֹּת הַפִּסְגָּה מִזְרָחָה׃ וָאֲצַו אֶתְכֶם בָּעֵת
הַהִוא לֵאמֹר יְהוָה אֱלֹהֵיכֶם נָתַן לָכֶם אֶת־הָאָרֶץ הַזֹּאת לְרִשְׁתָּהּ
יט חֲלוּצִים תַּעַבְרוּ לִפְנֵי אֲחֵיכֶם בְּנֵי־יִשְׂרָאֵל כָּל־בְּנֵי־חָיִל׃ רַק נְשֵׁיכֶם וְטַפְּכֶם
וּמִקְנֵכֶם יָדַעְתִּי כִּי־מִקְנֶה רַב לָכֶם יֵשְׁבוּ בְּעָרֵיכֶם אֲשֶׁר נָתַתִּי לָכֶם׃

רש״י

יב] **וְאֶת הָאָרֶץ הַזֹּאת.** הָאֲמוּרָה לְמַעְלָה מִנַּחַל אַרְנֹן וְעַד הַר חֶרְמוֹן (לעיל פסוק ח), "יָרַשְׁנוּ בָּעֵת הַהִוא": מֵעֲרֹעֵר אֲשֶׁר עַל נַחַל אַרְנֹן. אֵינוֹ מְחֻבָּר לְרֹאשׁוֹ שֶׁל מִקְרָא אֶלָּא לְסוֹפוֹ, עַל "נָתַתִּי לָרְאוּבֵנִי וְלַגָּדִי", אֲבָל לְעִנְיַן יְרֻשָּׁה עַד הַר חֶרְמוֹן הָיָה:

יג] **הַהוּא יִקָּרֵא אֶרֶץ רְפָאִים.** הִיא אוֹתָהּ שֶׁנָּתַתִּי לְאַבְרָהָם:

טז] **תּוֹךְ הַנַּחַל וּגְבֻל.** כָּל הַנַּחַל וְעַד מֵעֵבֶר לִשְׂפָתוֹ, כְּלוֹמַר, עַד וְעַד בִּכְלָל, וְיוֹתֵר מִכָּאן:

יז] **כִּנֶּרֶת.** מֵעֵבֶר הַיַּרְדֵּן הַמַּעֲרָבִי הָיָה, וְנַחֲלַת בְּנֵי גָד מֵעֵבֶר הַיַּרְדֵּן הַמִּזְרָחִי, וְנָפַל בְּגוֹרָלָם רֹחַב הַיַּרְדֵּן כְּנֶגְדָּם וְעוֹד מֵעֵבֶר לִשְׂפָתוֹ עַד כִּנֶּרֶת, וְזֶהוּ שֶׁנֶּאֱמַר: "וְהַיַּרְדֵּן וּגְבֻל", הַיַּרְדֵּן וּמֵעֵבֶר לוֹ:

יח] **וָאֲצַו אֶתְכֶם.** לִבְנֵי רְאוּבֵן וְגָד הָיָה מְדַבֵּר: **לִפְנֵי אֲחֵיכֶם.** הֵם הָיוּ הוֹלְכִים לִפְנֵי יִשְׂרָאֵל לַמִּלְחָמָה, לְפִי שֶׁהָיוּ גִּבּוֹרִים וְאוֹיְבִים נוֹפְלִים לִפְנֵיהֶם, שֶׁנֶּאֱמַר: "וְטָרַף זְרוֹעַ אַף קָדְקֹד" (דברים לג, כ):

BACKGROUND

3:14| The Geshurite and the Maakhatite: These were Aramean kingdoms in the Golan: Geshur to the south and Maakha to the north. These kingdoms were not conquered by Joshua (Joshua 13:13). The friendly relations between the Israelite kingdom and the Geshurite kingdom found expression in the marriage of David to Maakha, daughter of the king of Geshur. She bore him his son Avshalom (II Samuel 3:3), who lived for a period of time with his grandfather in Geshur (II Samuel 13:37). The kingdoms of Geshur and Maakha are also mentioned in Egyptian inscriptions, in the Amarna letters, fourteenth century BCE.

20 However, you must remember that those fit for war are obli-
Maftir gated to go forth in battle at the vanguard of the army, **until the Lord will give rest to your brethren,** the other tribes, **like you, and they too will take possession of the land that the Lord your God is giving them beyond the Jordan**, to the west. Only then, when the wars are concluded, **each man shall return to his possession that I gave** and divided among **you,** and which awaits you on this side of the Jordan.

21 Although Joshua served as one of Moses' generals,[39] Moses personally commanded the battles against Sihon and Og. Now Moses refers directly to Joshua. **I commanded Joshua at that time, saying: It is your eyes that have seen everything that the Lord your God has done to these two kings,** as they were utterly defeated; **so shall the Lord do to all the kingdoms that you are crossing there.**

22 There are many more kingdoms on the western side of the Jordan, and the settled areas there are both larger and more crowded. Nevertheless, **you shall not fear them, as it is the Lord your God who makes war for you.**

Parashat
Va'ethanan

Moses and the Land

DEUTERONOMY 3:23–29

The previous *parasha* concluded with words of encouragement that Moses gave Joshua as the nation prepared to enter the Land of Israel. Moses continues his address by pleading to God to cancel the decree barring him from entering the land.

Despite the personal perspective used by Moses to deliver his speech in the book of Deuteronomy, nearly all of the stories related are not personal in nature, but apply to the entire nation. The following passage, though, is the exception, in which Moses pleads to God to allow him to enter the Land of Israel. Perhaps Moses' goal in relating this information is to tell the people: I was your leader, I helped to bear your burdens, and even in my old age I fought on your behalf. Nevertheless, I am not permitted to enter the land, but only to view it from afar. You, in contrast, will cross over the Jordan River and enter the land, and you should appreciate the significance of this great privilege.

23 **I pleaded with the Lord at that time,** when God instructed me to speak to Joshua and prepare the nation to enter the Land of Israel, **saying:**

24 **My Lord God, You began to show Your servant Your greatness and Your mighty hand,** through the great miracles performed in Egypt, at the Red Sea, and during the recent conquests; **that who is a god in the heavens or on the earth, who can perform like Your actions, and like Your mighty deeds?** I now turn to you with a small request.

25 I accept the fact that I have completed my job, but I request of You to **please, let me cross** the Jordan River, **and I will see the good land that is beyond the Jordan, that good mountain, and** until **the Lebanon.** Please show me the mountainous region of the Promised Land with its borders.[1]

26 **The Lord was irate with me because of you,**[D] or: For your benefit and honor,[2] **and did not heed me, and the Lord said to me: Enough for you, do not continue speaking** and praying **to Me anymore about this matter.**

27 **Ascend to the top of the peak, and lift your eyes to the**

DISCUSSION

3:26| **Because of you:** Moses is not saying here that God prevented him from entering the land due to the incident of the waters of dispute (Numbers 20:9–13), as that could be construed as an affront to the dignity of the nation, which was listening to his speech. Rather, Moses is explaining that he was prohibited from crossing the Jordan River because the people he took out of Egypt remained on the other side. Since his flock all perished in the wilderness, he must remain with them. While God's denial of Moses and Aaron's entry into the land could have been linked to a specific transgression, the primary reason presented here for God's decree is that leaders must remain with their people (see

כ עַד אֲשֶׁר־יָנִיחַ יְהוָה לַאֲחֵיכֶם כָּכֶם וְיָרְשׁוּ גַם־הֵם אֶת־הָאָרֶץ אֲשֶׁר יְהוָה אֱלֹהֵיכֶם מפטיר
נֹתֵן לָהֶם בְּעֵבֶר הַיַּרְדֵּן וְשַׁבְתֶּם אִישׁ לִירֻשָּׁתוֹ אֲשֶׁר נָתַתִּי לָכֶם׃ וְאֶת־יְהוֹשׁוּעַ
כא צִוֵּיתִי בָּעֵת הַהִוא לֵאמֹר עֵינֶיךָ הָרֹאֹת אֵת כָּל־אֲשֶׁר עָשָׂה יְהוָה אֱלֹהֵיכֶם לִשְׁנֵי
כב הַמְּלָכִים הָאֵלֶּה כֵּן־יַעֲשֶׂה יְהוָה לְכָל־הַמַּמְלָכוֹת אֲשֶׁר אַתָּה עֹבֵר שָׁמָּה׃ לֹא
תִּירָאוּם כִּי יְהוָה אֱלֹהֵיכֶם הוּא הַנִּלְחָם לָכֶם׃

פרשת ואתחנן

כג כד וָאֶתְחַנַּן אֶל־יְהוָה בָּעֵת הַהִוא לֵאמֹר׃ אֲדֹנָי יֱהוִה אַתָּה הַחִלּוֹתָ לְהַרְאוֹת אֶת־ ד
עַבְדְּךָ אֶת־גָּדְלְךָ וְאֶת־יָדְךָ הַחֲזָקָה אֲשֶׁר מִי־אֵל בַּשָּׁמַיִם וּבָאָרֶץ אֲשֶׁר־יַעֲשֶׂה
כה כְמַעֲשֶׂיךָ וְכִגְבוּרֹתֶךָ׃ אֶעְבְּרָה־נָּא וְאֶרְאֶה אֶת־הָאָרֶץ הַטּוֹבָה אֲשֶׁר בְּעֵבֶר הַיַּרְדֵּן
כו הָהָר הַטּוֹב הַזֶּה וְהַלְּבָנֹן׃ וַיִּתְעַבֵּר יְהוָה בִּי לְמַעַנְכֶם וְלֹא שָׁמַע אֵלָי וַיֹּאמֶר יְהוָה
כז אֵלַי רַב־לָךְ אַל־תּוֹסֶף דַּבֵּר אֵלַי עוֹד בַּדָּבָר הַזֶּה׃ עֲלֵה ׀ רֹאשׁ הַפִּסְגָּה וְשָׂא עֵינֶיךָ

רש"י

כג| **וָאֶתְחַנַּן.** אֵין חִנּוּן בְּכָל מָקוֹם אֶלָּא לְשׁוֹן מַתְּנַת חִנָּם. אַף עַל פִּי שֶׁיֵּשׁ לָהֶם לַצַּדִּיקִים לִתְלוֹת בְּמַעֲשֵׂיהֶם הַטּוֹבִים, אֵין מְבַקְשִׁים מֵאֵת הַמָּקוֹם אֶלָּא מַתְּנַת חִנָּם. דָּבָר אַחֵר, זֶה אֶחָד מֵעֲשָׂרָה לְשׁוֹנוֹת שֶׁנִּקְרֵאת תְּפִלָּה, כִּדְאִיתָא בְּסִפְרֵי (כו): **בָּעֵת הַהִוא.** לְאַחַר שֶׁכָּבַשְׁתִּי אֶרֶץ סִיחוֹן וְעוֹג, דִּמִּיתִי שֶׁמָּא הֻתַּר הַנֶּדֶר: **לֵאמֹר.** זֶה אֶחָד מִשְּׁלֹשָׁה מְקוֹמוֹת שֶׁאָמַר מֹשֶׁה לִפְנֵי הַמָּקוֹם: אֵינִי מַנִּיחֲךָ עַד שֶׁתּוֹדִיעֵנִי אִם תַּעֲשֶׂה שְׁאֵלָתִי אִם לָאו:

כד| **ה' אֱלֹהִים.** רַחוּם בַּדִּין: **אַתָּה הַחִלּוֹתָ לְהַרְאוֹת אֶת עַבְדְּךָ.** פֶּתַח לִהְיוֹת עוֹמֵד וּמִתְפַּלֵּל אַף עַל פִּי שֶׁנִּגְזְרָה גְּזֵרָה. אָמַר לוֹ: מִמְּךָ לָמַדְתִּי, שֶׁאָמַרְתָּ לִי: "וְעַתָּה הַנִּיחָה לִּי" (שמות לב, י), וְכִי תּוֹפֵס הָיִיתִי בְּךָ? אֶלָּא לִפְתֹּחַ פֶּתַח, שֶׁבִּי הָיָה תָּלוּי לְהִתְפַּלֵּל עֲלֵיהֶם: **אֶת גָּדְלְךָ.** זוֹ מִדַּת טוּבְךָ, וְכֵן הוּא אוֹמֵר: "וְעַתָּה יִגְדַּל נָא כֹּחַ אֲדֹנָי" (במדבר יד, יז): **וְאֶת יָדְךָ.** זוֹ יְמִינְךָ שֶׁהִיא פְּשׁוּטָה לְכָל בָּאֵי עוֹלָם: **הַחֲזָקָה.** שֶׁאַתָּה כּוֹבֵשׁ בְּרַחֲמִים אֶת מִדַּת הַדִּין בַּחֲזָקָה: **אֲשֶׁר מִי אֵל וְגוֹ'.** אֵינְךָ דּוֹמֶה לְמֶלֶךְ בָּשָׂר וָדָם, שֶׁיֵּשׁ לוֹ יוֹעֲצִין וְסַנְקָתֶדְרִין הַמְמַחִין בְּיָדוֹ כְּשֶׁרוֹצֶה לַעֲשׂוֹת חֶסֶד וְלַעֲבֹר עַל מִדּוֹתָיו, אַתָּה אֵין מִי יִמְחֶה בְּיָדְךָ אִם תִּמְחֹל לִי וּתְבַטֵּל גְּזֵרָתְךָ:

כה| **אֶעְבְּרָה נָּא.** אֵין 'נָא' אֶלָּא לְשׁוֹן בַּקָּשָׁה: **הָהָר הַטּוֹב הַזֶּה.** זוֹ יְרוּשָׁלַיִם: **וְהַלְּבָנֹן.** זֶה בֵּית הַמִּקְדָּשׁ:

כו| **וַיִּתְעַבֵּר ה'.** נִתְמַלֵּא חֵמָה: **לְמַעַנְכֶם.** אַתֶּם גְּרַמְתֶּם לִי, וְכֵן הוּא אוֹמֵר: "וַיַּקְצִיפוּ עַל מֵי מְרִיבָה וַיֵּרַע לְמֹשֶׁה בַּעֲבוּרָם" (תהלים קו, לב): **רַב לָךְ.** שֶׁלֹּא יֹאמְרוּ, הָרַב כַּמָּה קָשֶׁה וְהַתַּלְמִיד כַּמָּה סַרְבָן וּמַפְצִיר. דָּבָר אַחֵר, "רַב לָךְ", הַרְבֵּה מִזֶּה שָׁמוּר לְךָ רַב טוּב הַצָּפוּן לְךָ:

west, to the north, to the south, and to the east, and see the land **with your eyes** as far as you can, **as you will not cross this Jordan.**

28 **Command Joshua, and strengthen him and encourage him, as he will cross before this people, and he will allocate to them the land that you will see.** You are permitted only to see it, but not to enter.

29 **We dwelled in the canyon opposite Beit Peor.** Moses alludes here to the tragic occurrences that took place there.[3] At this point, the nation of Israel remains in place for some time. The book of Deuteronomy will conclude with the death of Moses at the end of the winter. Joshua will enter the land during the month of Nisan, at the beginning of the warm season, which is the time of year best suited for wars in the Middle East. Until that time arrives, the people remain in the valley, opposite Beit Peor, and listen to Moses' speech.

General Warnings

DEUTERONOMY 4:1–40

Following the brief historical summary presented in the previous passages, Moses now emphasizes to those waiting to enter and live in the Land of Israel the importance of fulfilling the laws of the Torah. In the continuation of his speech, Moses blends rebuke and encouragement with a few specific laws. Highlighted in particular is the prohibition of idolatry under the influence of those currently dwelling in the land. Moses' speech reflects the great responsibility shouldered by the one who brought down the Torah from Mount Sinai to the people and who is about to take his leave from them. Before they enter a land full of idolatry, Moses seeks to etch in their memory the giving of the Torah at Mount Sinai, where they experienced divine revelation but where God did not appear in physical form.

At the conclusion of this passage, Moses stresses to the nation that their continued existence in the land should not be taken for granted, but is dependent on their deeds. If they are not faithful to their covenant with God, and do not retain the historical perspective that Moses seeks to impart, then they will be liable to be exiled.

Over the course of his speech, Moses moves from addressing the people as a single unit to addressing them in the plural. In addition, there is some ambiguity as to whether certain statements are warnings of what will happen if they fail to heed the word of God or prophecies describing events that will transpire in any case.

4 1 **Now, Israel, heed the statutes and the ordinances that I am teaching you to perform, so that you will live, and you will come and take possession of the land that the Lord, God of your fathers, is giving you.**

2 **You shall not add**[D] **to the matter that I am commanding you, and you shall not subtract from it, to observe the commandments of the Lord your God that I am commanding you.** These commandments are not rooted in mutual consent, either individual or national; they do not change depending on the times or changes in accepted beliefs. This is the Torah, and one may not add to it or subtract from it.

3 Moses now delineates a warning: **It is your eyes that have seen that which the Lord** recently **did concerning Baal Peor, as every man who followed Baal Peor, the Lord your God destroyed him from your midst** by means of a plague, as you all remember.[4]

4 **But you, who cleave to the Lord your God, all of you live today.**

5 **See, I have taught you statutes and ordinances, as the Lord my God had commanded me to do so,** to comply with these statutes and ordinances, **in the midst of the land that you are coming there to take possession of it.** Not all of the laws given by Moses were designed to be fulfilled in the wilderness; the complete fulfillment of the Torah will be possible only in the Land of Israel.

Second aliya

6 **You shall observe and you shall perform, as this,** the fulfillment of the Torah, **is your wisdom and your understanding in the eyes of the peoples; when they hear all these statutes, they will say: It is a particularly wise and understanding people, this great nation.**[D] If you continue to fulfill the Torah, you will be honored because of it.

DISCUSSION

Ḥizkuni). The new generation will be led into the new land by other leaders, and Moses was not even granted the privilege of entering the land.

4:2| **You shall not add:** Due to the critical importance of this commandment, Moses places it prior to presenting the laws to the people. This prohibition against adding or subtracting from the commandments is enumerated as one of the 613 commandments of the Torah (see Rambam, *Sefer HaMitzvot*, negative commandments 313–314).

4:6| **Great nation:** The Torah states below that the nation of Israel is "the fewest of all the peoples" (7:7). Here and in the following verses,

כח ימה וצפנה ותימנה ומזרחה וראה בעיניך כי־לא תעבר את־הירדן הזה: וצו
את־יהושע וחזקהו ואמצהו כי־הוא יעבר לפני העם הזה והוא ינחיל אותם
כט את־הארץ אשר תראה: ונשב בגיא מול בית פעור:
א ועתה ישראל שמע אל־החקים ואל־המשפטים אשר אנכי מלמד אתכם
לעשות למען תחיו ובאתם וירשתם את־הארץ אשר יהוה אלהי אבתיכם נתן
ב לכם: לא תספו על־הדבר אשר אנכי מצוה אתכם ולא תגרעו ממנו לשמר את־
ג מצות יהוה אלהיכם אשר אנכי מצוה אתכם: עיניכם הראות את אשר־עשה
יהוה בבעל פעור כי כל־האיש אשר הלך אחרי בעל־פעור השמידו יהוה אלהיך
ד ה מקרבך: ואתם הדבקים ביהוה אלהיכם חיים כלכם היום: ראה | למדתי אתכם שני
חקים ומשפטים כאשר צוני יהוה אלהי לעשות כן בקרב הארץ אשר אתם
ו באים שמה לרשתה: ושמרתם ועשיתם כי הוא חכמתכם ובינתכם לעיני העמים
אשר ישמעון את כל־החקים האלה ואמרו רק עם־חכם ונבון הגוי הגדול הזה:

רש"י

כז| **וראה בעיניך.** בקשת ממני: "ואראה את הארץ הטובה" (לעיל פסוק כה), אני מראה לך את כלה, שנאמר: "ויראהו ה' את כל הארץ" (להלן לד, א):

כח| **וצו את יהושע.** על הטרחות ועל המשאות ועל המריבות: **וחזקהו ואמצהו.** בדבריך, שלא ירך לבו לומר: כשם שנענש רבי עליהם כך סופי לענש עליהם, מבטיחו אני כי "הוא יעבר והוא ינחיל": **כי הוא יעבר.** אם יעבר לפניהם – ינחלו, ואם לאו – לא ינחלו. וכן אתה מוצא כששלח מן העם אל העי והוא ישב: "ויכו מהם אנשי העי" וגו' (יהושע ז, ה), וכיון שנפל על פניו, אמר לו: "קם לך" (שם פסוק י), 'קם לך' כתיב, אתה הוא העומד במקומך ומשלח את בני למלחמה, "למה זה אתה נפל על פניך", לא כך אמרתי למשה רבך: אם הוא עובר עוברין ואם לאו אין עוברין?

כט| **ונשב בגיא וגו'.** ונצמדתם לעבודה זרה, ואף על פי כן: "ועתה ישראל שמע אל החקים" (להלן ד, א), והכל מחול לך, ואני לא זכיתי למחל לי:

פרק ד

ב| **לא תספו.** כגון חמש פרשיות בתפלין, חמשת מינין בלולב וחמש ציציות, וכן "לא תגרעו":

ו| **ושמרתם.** זו משנה: **ועשיתם.** כמשמעו: **כי הוא חכמתכם ובינתכם וגו'.** בזאת תחשבו חכמים ונבונים "לעיני העמים":

DISCUSSION

in contrast, it is referred to three times as a great nation. Evidently, this means a complete nation, rather than large in quantity. Perhaps the threefold repetition of this expression is necessary because these traits are generally found only among elite members of society. However, the Torah stresses that the people of Israel are unique in that the entire nation exemplifies faith, closeness to God, and fulfillment of the wise and divine laws.

7 You are not just a wise nation, but also an important one; **for who is a great nation that has God near it, as the Lord our God,** who is close to us **in all of our calling to Him?**

8 **Who is a great nation that has righteous statutes and ordinances like this entire Torah that I place before you today?**

9 Moses now details specific commandments: **Only beware, and protect yourself greatly, lest you forget the matters that your eyes saw, and lest they move from your heart all the days of your life.** Aside from statutes and ordinances, the nation of Israel must retain certain memories in its consciousness. At its core stands its collective memory, which is supposed to be retained not by experts or academics alone; rather: **And you shall impart them to your children and to your children's children.**

10 One of the occurrences that you must remember is **the day that you stood before the Lord**[D] **your God at Horev,** at Mount Sinai, to receive the Torah, **when the Lord said to me: Assemble the people for Me, and I will have them hear My words,** so that they will learn to fear Me all the days that they live on the earth, and so that **they will** also **teach their children.**

11 **You approached and stood at the foot of the mountain [*taḥat hahar*].** This phrase has also been understood in a literal sense, meaning that the mountain was suspended over their heads so that they stood beneath the mountain.[5] **And the mountain was burning with fire to the heart of the heavens, darkness, cloud, and fog** surrounding it.

12 **The Lord spoke to you from the midst of the fire; the sound of words** alone **you were hearing, but an image you were not seeing, only a sound.** Had there been any physical image, you would have seen it. The fact that there was none is the basis for the prohibition of sculpting an idol or an image mentioned in the following verses. In addition, realize that the miracles and wonders were not the primary focus of the event at Mount Sinai. Rather, you must remember the content of the revelation, which is the basis for the entire Torah.

13 **He told you His covenant that He commanded you to perform, the Ten Precepts,**[D] **and He inscribed them on two tablets of stone.**

14 **To me, the Lord commanded at that time to teach you statutes and ordinances, to have you perform them in the land that you are crossing there to take possession of it.** Due to its unusual Hebrew syntax, the phrase "to have you perform them" is interpreted homiletically to mean that while you fulfill the statutes, the statutes will also mold you as individuals.[6]

15 **You shall greatly beware for your lives, as you did not see any image on the day that the Lord your God spoke to you at Horev from the midst of the fire,**

16 **lest you act corruptly and make for yourselves an idol, the image of any shape.**[7] Even though the people did not see any images at Mount Sinai, they may be tempted to create their own images and worship them, due to the surrounding pagan influence. Therefore, the Torah reemphasizes the prohibition, and even details various kinds of images, the primary one being **the form of a male or a female** human;

17 or **the form of any beast that is on the earth,** such as the Golden Calf, **the form of any winged bird that flies in the heavens,**

18 **the form of any being that creeps on the ground,** such as the bronze serpent, which also became an object of worship over time,[8] or **the form of any fish that is in the water under the earth,** such as the primordial leviathan. These images symbolized various forces in other cultures.

19 **And** likewise, you must also be careful **lest you lift your eyes to the heavens, and see the sun and the moon and the stars, all the host of the heavens, and you are led astray and prostrate yourselves to them, and serve them,** the host of the heavens, **which the Lord your God distributed to all the peoples under all the heavens,** as luminaries and to help determine time,[9] but not to worship. Alternatively, in contrast to the nation of Israel, which was explicitly warned against worshipping natural forces, the other nations of the world were not explicitly forbidden to include natural forces in their worship.[10]

Sun

Moon and stars

DISCUSSION

4:10 | **The day that you stood before the Lord:** Moses again describes to the people the event that occurred on Mount Sinai, referred to by the Ramban as the Great Event, and seen by many Jewish philosophers as the most critical event in the history of the Jewish people (see Ramban, verse 9).

4:13 | **Ten Precepts:** The familiar term Ten Commandments is translated here as Ten Precepts. In three places the Torah recounts the writing of the ten *devarim* on the Tablets of the Covenant (Exodus 34:28; Deuteronomy 4:13, 10:4). *Devarim* is best translated as statements or precepts, not commandments. Furthermore, the passages in which these are stated (Exodus 20:2–14; Deuteronomy 5:6–18, with minor variations) can readily be divided up into ten precepts, while it is difficult to divide them into ten commandments.

ז כִּי מִי־גוֹי גָּדוֹל אֲשֶׁר־לוֹ אֱלֹהִים קְרֹבִים אֵלָיו כַּיהוָה אֱלֹהֵינוּ בְּכָל־קָרְאֵנוּ אֵלָיו׃
ח וּמִי גּוֹי גָּדוֹל אֲשֶׁר־לוֹ חֻקִּים וּמִשְׁפָּטִים צַדִּיקִם כְּכֹל הַתּוֹרָה הַזֹּאת אֲשֶׁר אָנֹכִי
ט נֹתֵן לִפְנֵיכֶם הַיּוֹם׃ רַק הִשָּׁמֶר לְךָ וּשְׁמֹר נַפְשְׁךָ מְאֹד פֶּן־תִּשְׁכַּח אֶת־הַדְּבָרִים
אֲשֶׁר־רָאוּ עֵינֶיךָ וּפֶן־יָסוּרוּ מִלְּבָבְךָ כֹּל יְמֵי חַיֶּיךָ וְהוֹדַעְתָּם לְבָנֶיךָ וְלִבְנֵי בָנֶיךָ׃
י יוֹם אֲשֶׁר עָמַדְתָּ לִפְנֵי יהוה אֱלֹהֶיךָ בְּחֹרֵב בֶּאֱמֹר יהוה אֵלַי הַקְהֶל־לִי אֶת־
הָעָם וְאַשְׁמִעֵם אֶת־דְּבָרָי אֲשֶׁר יִלְמְדוּן לְיִרְאָה אֹתִי כָּל־הַיָּמִים אֲשֶׁר הֵם חַיִּים
יא עַל־הָאֲדָמָה וְאֶת־בְּנֵיהֶם יְלַמֵּדוּן׃ וַתִּקְרְבוּן וַתַּעַמְדוּן תַּחַת הָהָר וְהָהָר בֹּעֵר
יב בָּאֵשׁ עַד־לֵב הַשָּׁמַיִם חֹשֶׁךְ עָנָן וַעֲרָפֶל׃ וַיְדַבֵּר יהוה אֲלֵיכֶם מִתּוֹךְ הָאֵשׁ קוֹל
יג דְּבָרִים אַתֶּם שֹׁמְעִים וּתְמוּנָה אֵינְכֶם רֹאִים זוּלָתִי קוֹל׃ וַיַּגֵּד לָכֶם אֶת־בְּרִיתוֹ
יד אֲשֶׁר צִוָּה אֶתְכֶם לַעֲשׂוֹת עֲשֶׂרֶת הַדְּבָרִים וַיִּכְתְּבֵם עַל־שְׁנֵי לֻחוֹת אֲבָנִים׃ וְאֹתִי
צִוָּה יהוה בָּעֵת הַהִוא לְלַמֵּד אֶתְכֶם חֻקִּים וּמִשְׁפָּטִים לַעֲשֹׂתְכֶם אֹתָם בָּאָרֶץ
טו אֲשֶׁר אַתֶּם עֹבְרִים שָׁמָּה לְרִשְׁתָּהּ׃ וְנִשְׁמַרְתֶּם מְאֹד לְנַפְשֹׁתֵיכֶם כִּי לֹא רְאִיתֶם
טז כָּל־תְּמוּנָה בְּיוֹם דִּבֶּר יהוה אֲלֵיכֶם בְּחֹרֵב מִתּוֹךְ הָאֵשׁ׃ פֶּן־תַּשְׁחִתוּן וַעֲשִׂיתֶם
יז לָכֶם פֶּסֶל תְּמוּנַת כָּל־סָמֶל תַּבְנִית זָכָר אוֹ נְקֵבָה׃ תַּבְנִית כָּל־בְּהֵמָה אֲשֶׁר
יח בָּאָרֶץ תַּבְנִית כָּל־צִפּוֹר כָּנָף אֲשֶׁר תָּעוּף בַּשָּׁמָיִם׃ תַּבְנִית כָּל־רֹמֵשׂ בָּאֲדָמָה
יט תַּבְנִית כָּל־דָּגָה אֲשֶׁר־בַּמַּיִם מִתַּחַת לָאָרֶץ׃ וּפֶן־תִּשָּׂא עֵינֶיךָ הַשָּׁמַיְמָה וְרָאִיתָ
אֶת־הַשֶּׁמֶשׁ וְאֶת־הַיָּרֵחַ וְאֶת־הַכּוֹכָבִים כֹּל צְבָא הַשָּׁמַיִם וְנִדַּחְתָּ וְהִשְׁתַּחֲוִיתָ
לָהֶם וַעֲבַדְתָּם אֲשֶׁר חָלַק יהוה אֱלֹהֶיךָ אֹתָם לְכֹל הָעַמִּים תַּחַת כָּל־הַשָּׁמָיִם׃

רש"י

ח | **חקים ומשפטים צדיקם.** הגונים ומקבלים:

ט | **רק השמר לך וגו' פן תשכח את הדברים.** אז כשלא תשכחו אותם ותעשום על אמתתם, תחשבו חכמים ונבונים, ואם תעותו אותם מתוך שכחה, תחשבו שוטים:

י | **יום אשר עמדת.** מוסב על מקרא שלמעלה ממנו: אשר ראו עיניך יום אשר עמדת בחרב, אשר ראית את הקולות ואת הלפידים: **ילמדון.** לעצמם:

יד | **ואתי צוה ה' בעת ההוא ללמד אתכם.** תורה שבעל פה:

טז | **סמל.** צורה:

יט | **ופן תשא עיניך.** להסתכל בדבר ולתת לב לטעות אחריהם: **אשר חלק ה'.** להאיר להם. דבר אחר, לאלהות, לא מנען מלטעות אחריהם, אלא החליקם בדברי הבליהם לטרדם, וכן הוא אומר: "כי החליק אליו בעיניו למצא עונו לשנא" (תהלים לו, ג):

20 As for **you, the Lord has taken** you for Himself, **and He took you out from the iron crucible, from Egypt, to be for Him a people of inheritance, as this day.** Your exodus from Egypt manifests your unique status and your separation from the other nations.[11]

21 **The Lord was incensed with me because of your deeds** at the waters of dispute, as I sinned by becoming angry due to your conduct,[12] **and He took an oath that I not cross the Jordan, and not come to the good land which the Lord your God is giving you as an inheritance.**

22 **For I will die in this land; I am not crossing the Jordan, and you are crossing** without me, **and you will take possession of that good land.**

23 Therefore, I must strongly warn you that with the pagan presence in the new land, and without me, everything is liable to unravel. Moreover, it is possible that just as you made a calf when I was on Mount Sinai, in the future, in my absence from your lives, you may decide again to create a symbolic image to represent God. Therefore, **beware, lest you forget the covenant of the Lord your God, which He made with you, and you make for yourselves an idol, the image of anything that the Lord your God has commanded you** not to make.

24 **For the Lord your God is** like **a consuming fire,**[13] whose judgment is harsh.[14] Alternatively, this statement means that God is like a consuming fire in that He is constantly active rather than a distant and neutral entity. He is **a zealous God** and demands exclusive, uncompromising commitment to the relationship.[15]

25 It is reasonable to assume that the first generation that conquers the land will sense that God accompanies them throughout their battles. However, **when you will beget children, and children's children, and** eventually **you will have been long in the land,** future generations may take their existence there for granted, **and** consequently **you** will **act corruptly and make an idol, the image of anything,** due to your integration into the cultural surroundings and your loss of your uniqueness. **And** when this occurs, **you will perform evil in the eyes of the Lord your God,** which will serve **to anger Him,** as He is a zealous God, as mentioned above.

26 **I call today to the heavens and earth,** which are eternal witnesses,[16] **to bear witness against you, that** if you do so, **you will be quickly eradicated from upon the land that you are crossing the Jordan there to take possession of it; you will not extend your days upon it, as you will be destroyed.** Although your entry into the land and conquest of it are promised, the continuation of your dwelling there is contingent upon your actions.

27 **The Lord will disperse you among the peoples, and you will remain few in number among the nations where the Lord will lead you.**

28 **You will serve gods there, the handiwork of man,**[D] **wood and stone, which neither see, nor hear, nor eat, nor smell.** If you are expelled from the land, you will find yourselves in locations where the inhabitants worship idolatry much more blatantly than you do (see 28:36).

29 **You will seek from there the Lord your God, and you will find Him, when you search for Him with all your heart and with all your soul.**

30 **When you are in distress** in exile, **and all these matters befall you, by the end of days,** i.e., in the near or distant future, **you will return to the Lord your God, and you will heed His voice.**

31 **As the Lord your God is a merciful God,** not just a zealous God, it is possible to return to Him. At that time, **He will neither forsake you, nor destroy you, nor forget the covenant of your fathers with regard to which He took an oath to them.**

32 **For** with regard to the oath and the covenant with God, **ask**

DISCUSSION

4:28| **The handiwork of man:** The images mentioned above (verse 25) refer to images designed to represent God, such as the Golden Calf in the wilderness, and the golden calves that would ultimately be crafted in Beit El and Dan (I Kings 12:28–29). Moses warned them that if they are exiled from the land, they will find worship of inanimate objects, such as wood or stone, as gods, in their new destinations.

כ וְאֶתְכֶם לָקַח יְהוָֹה וַיּוֹצִא אֶתְכֶם מִכּוּר הַבַּרְזֶל מִמִּצְרָיִם לִהְיוֹת לוֹ לְעַם נַחֲלָה

כא כַּיּוֹם הַזֶּה: וַיהוָֹה הִתְאַנַּף־בִּי עַל־דִּבְרֵיכֶם וַיִּשָּׁבַע לְבִלְתִּי עָבְרִי אֶת־הַיַּרְדֵּן

כב וּלְבִלְתִּי־בֹא אֶל־הָאָרֶץ הַטּוֹבָה אֲשֶׁר יְהוָֹה אֱלֹהֶיךָ נֹתֵן לְךָ נַחֲלָה: כִּי אָנֹכִי מֵת בָּאָרֶץ הַזֹּאת אֵינֶנִּי עֹבֵר אֶת־הַיַּרְדֵּן וְאַתֶּם עֹבְרִים וִירִשְׁתֶּם אֶת־הָאָרֶץ הַטּוֹבָה

כג הַזֹּאת: הִשָּׁמְרוּ לָכֶם פֶּן־תִּשְׁכְּחוּ אֶת־בְּרִית יְהוָֹה אֱלֹהֵיכֶם אֲשֶׁר כָּרַת עִמָּכֶם

כד וַעֲשִׂיתֶם לָכֶם פֶּסֶל תְּמוּנַת כֹּל אֲשֶׁר צִוְּךָ יְהוָֹה אֱלֹהֶיךָ: כִּי יְהוָֹה אֱלֹהֶיךָ אֵשׁ אֹכְלָה הוּא אֵל קַנָּא:

כה כִּי־תוֹלִיד בָּנִים וּבְנֵי בָנִים וְנוֹשַׁנְתֶּם בָּאָרֶץ וְהִשְׁחַתֶּם וַעֲשִׂיתֶם פֶּסֶל תְּמוּנַת

כו כֹּל וַעֲשִׂיתֶם הָרַע בְּעֵינֵי־יְהוָֹה־אֱלֹהֶיךָ לְהַכְעִיסוֹ: הַעִידֹתִי בָכֶם הַיּוֹם אֶת־ הַשָּׁמַיִם וְאֶת־הָאָרֶץ כִּי־אָבֹד תֹּאבֵדוּן מַהֵר מֵעַל הָאָרֶץ אֲשֶׁר אַתֶּם עֹבְרִים

כז אֶת־הַיַּרְדֵּן שָׁמָּה לְרִשְׁתָּהּ לֹא־תַאֲרִיכֻן יָמִים עָלֶיהָ כִּי הִשָּׁמֵד תִּשָּׁמֵדוּן: וְהֵפִיץ יְהוָֹה אֶתְכֶם בָּעַמִּים וְנִשְׁאַרְתֶּם מְתֵי מִסְפָּר בַּגּוֹיִם אֲשֶׁר יְנַהֵג יְהוָֹה אֶתְכֶם שָׁמָּה:

כח וַעֲבַדְתֶּם־שָׁם אֱלֹהִים מַעֲשֵׂה יְדֵי אָדָם עֵץ וָאֶבֶן אֲשֶׁר לֹא־יִרְאוּן וְלֹא יִשְׁמְעוּן

כט וְלֹא יֹאכְלוּן וְלֹא יְרִיחֻן: וּבִקַּשְׁתֶּם מִשָּׁם אֶת־יְהוָֹה אֱלֹהֶיךָ וּמָצָאתָ כִּי תִדְרְשֶׁנּוּ

ל בְּכָל־לְבָבְךָ וּבְכָל־נַפְשֶׁךָ: בַּצַּר לְךָ וּמְצָאוּךָ כֹּל הַדְּבָרִים הָאֵלֶּה בְּאַחֲרִית הַיָּמִים

לא וְשַׁבְתָּ עַד־יְהוָֹה אֱלֹהֶיךָ וְשָׁמַעְתָּ בְּקֹלוֹ: כִּי אֵל רַחוּם יְהוָֹה אֱלֹהֶיךָ לֹא יַרְפְּךָ

לב וְלֹא יַשְׁחִיתֶךָ וְלֹא יִשְׁכַּח אֶת־בְּרִית אֲבֹתֶיךָ אֲשֶׁר נִשְׁבַּע לָהֶם: כִּי שְׁאַל־נָא

רש"י

כו | הַעִידֹתִי בָכֶם. הִנְנִי מַזְמִינָם לִהְיוֹת עֵדִים שֶׁהִתְרֵיתִי בָכֶם.

כח | וַעֲבַדְתֶּם שָׁם אֱלֹהִים. כְּתַרְגּוּמוֹ, מִשֶּׁאַתֶּם עוֹבְדִים לְעוֹבְדֵיהֶם כְּאִלּוּ אַתֶּם עוֹבְדִים לָהֶם:

לא | לֹא יַרְפְּךָ. מִלְּהַחֲזִיק בְּךָ בְּיָדָיו, וּלְשׁוֹן "לֹא יַרְפְּךָ" לְשׁוֹן הִפְעִיל הוּא, לֹא יִתֵּן לְךָ רִפְיוֹן, לֹא יַפְרִישׁ אוֹתְךָ מֵאֶצְלוֹ, וְכֵן: "אֲחַזְתִּיו וְלֹא אַרְפֶּנּוּ" (שיר השירים ג, ד), שֶׁלֹּא נֶּקֶד "אַרְפֶּנּוּ". כָּל לְשׁוֹן רִפְיוֹן מוּסָב עַל לְשׁוֹן מַפְעִיל

כד | אֵל קַנָּא. מְקַנֵּא לִנְקֹם, אנפרנמנ"ט בְּלַעַ"ז, מִתְחָרֶה עַל רָגְזוֹ לְהִפָּרַע מֵעוֹבְדֵי עֲבוֹדָה זָרָה:

כה | וְנוֹשַׁנְתֶּם. רָמַז לָהֶם שֶׁיִּגְלוּ מִמֶּנָּה לְסוֹף שְׁמוֹנֶה מֵאוֹת וַחֲמִשִּׁים וּשְׁתַּיִם שָׁנָה כְּמִנְיַן "וְנוֹשַׁנְתֶּם", וְהוּא הִקְדִּים וְהִגְלָם לְסוֹף שְׁמוֹנֶה מֵאוֹת וַחֲמִשִּׁים, וְהִקְדִּים שְׁתֵּי שָׁנִים לְ"וְנוֹשַׁנְתֶּם", כְּדֵי שֶׁלֹּא יִתְקַיֵּם בָּהֶם: "כִּי אָבֹד תֹּאבֵדוּן" (להלן פסוק כו), וְזֶהוּ שֶׁנֶּאֱמַר: "וַיִּשְׁקֹד ה' עַל הָרָעָה וַיְבִיאֶהָ עָלֵינוּ כִּי צַדִּיק ה' אֱלֹהֵינוּ" (דניאל ט, יד), צְדָקָה עָשָׂה עִמָּנוּ שְׁמִהֵר לַהֲבִיאָהּ שְׁתֵּי שָׁנִים לִפְנֵי זְמַנָּהּ:

כו | מִכּוּר. כּוּר הוּא כְּלִי שֶׁמְּזַקְּקִים בּוֹ אֶת הַזָּהָב:

כא | הִתְאַנַּף. נִתְמַלֵּא רֹגֶז: עַל דִּבְרֵיכֶם. עַל אֹדוֹתֵיכֶם, עַל עִסְקֵיכֶם:

כב | כִּי אָנֹכִי מֵת וְגו' אֵינֶנִּי עֹבֵר. מֵאַחַר שֶׁמֵּת מֵהֵיכָן יַעֲבֹר?! אֶלָּא אַף עַצְמוֹתַי אֵינָם עוֹבְרִים:

כג | תְּמוּנַת כֹּל. תְּמוּנַת כָּל דָּבָר: אֲשֶׁר צִוְּךָ ה'. אֲשֶׁר צִוְּךָ שֶׁלֹּא לַעֲשׂוֹת:

now of the early days that were before you, from the day that God created man upon the earth, and from the end of the heavens to the end of the heavens. Examine the history of the entire world; **has there been anything like this great thing, or has anything been heard like it?**

33 **Has a people heard the voice of God speaking from the midst of the fire, as you heard, and lived?** One who is exposed to a revelation of that magnitude typically dies immediately,[17] but you heard God speaking and remained alive.

34 **Or has a god sought to come and take for himself a nation from the midst of a nation, with** wondrous **tribulations,** such as the ten plagues with which God struck Egypt, **with signs, and with wonders** that served as ominous warnings, such as the plagues of blood and darkness, **and with war, and with a mighty hand, and with an outstretched arm, and with fearsome deeds, like everything that the Lord your God did for you in Egypt before your eyes?** Have there ever been occurrences such as those that you saw with your own eyes?

35 **You have been shown** these events **in order to know that the Lord, He is the God; there is no other besides Him.** No one can prevent Him from executing His will.

36 **From the heavens He had you hear His voice, to chastise you; and upon earth He showed you His great fire** on the mountain **and you heard His words from the midst of the fire.**

37 This is **because He loved your forefathers,**[18] **and He chose their descendants after them.**[19] Alternatively, the reference is specifically to Jacob's descendants, as this Hebrew phrase is actually formulated in the singular.[20] **And He took you out before Him,** due to His will,[21] and with miraculous divine events,[22] **with His great power, from Egypt,**

38 **to dispossess nations greater and mightier than you from before you, to bring you, to give you their land as an inheritance, as it is this day.**

39 **You shall know this day, and** moreover, **restore to your heart that the Lord, He is the God in the heavens above and upon the earth below; there is no other.** Do not suffice with the memory of that which you hear from me; you must internalize it in your soul.

40 If you internalize this message, **you shall** consequently **observe His statutes and His commandments, which I am commanding you this day,** and on account of **that, He will do good to you, and to your children after you, and so that you may extend your days upon the land that the Lord your God is giving you, for all the days.**

Designating the Cities of Refuge

DEUTERONOMY 4:41–43

In the book of Numbers, the nation of Israel was instructed to prepare cities of refuge, to provide asylum for one who unwittingly kills another, thereby avoiding the vengeance of the victim's blood avenger. Here, as an addendum to Moses' speech of reproach, where he raised awareness of the challenges inherent in the entry to the Land of Israel, he designates three cities on the eastern side of the Jordan River, which has already would be conquered, for this purpose.

According to tradition, at this stage these cities did not yet provide asylum for murderers. Rather, they would fulfill their function only after an additional three cities were designated west of the Jordan River. Nevertheless, by designating these cities at this point, Moses establishes that this region was not merely conquered land, but rather it possesses a certain degree of the sanctity of the Land of Israel.

Third aliya 41 **Then Moses designated three cities beyond the Jordan,** in the east, **toward the eastern sunrise;**

42 these cities were designated **for the murderer to flee there,** one **who will kill his neighbor unwittingly and he does not hate him previously,** as was described earlier in the Torah;[23]

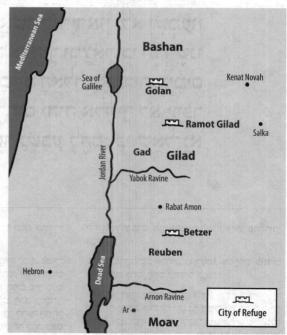

Cities of refuge on the eastern side of the Jordan River

לְיָמִים רִאשֹׁנִים אֲשֶׁר־הָיוּ לְפָנֶיךָ לְמִן־הַיּוֹם אֲשֶׁר בָּרָא אֱלֹהִים ׀ אָדָם עַל־הָאָרֶץ
וּלְמִקְצֵה הַשָּׁמַיִם וְעַד־קְצֵה הַשָּׁמָיִם הֲנִהְיָה כַּדָּבָר הַגָּדוֹל הַזֶּה אוֹ הֲנִשְׁמַע
לג כָּמֹהוּ: הֲשָׁמַע עָם קוֹל אֱלֹהִים מְדַבֵּר מִתּוֹךְ־הָאֵשׁ כַּאֲשֶׁר־שָׁמַעְתָּ אַתָּה וַיֶּחִי:
לד אוֹ ׀ הֲנִסָּה אֱלֹהִים לָבוֹא לָקַחַת לוֹ גוֹי מִקֶּרֶב גּוֹי בְּמַסֹּת בְּאֹתֹת וּבְמוֹפְתִים
וּבְמִלְחָמָה וּבְיָד חֲזָקָה וּבִזְרוֹעַ נְטוּיָה וּבְמוֹרָאִים גְּדֹלִים כְּכֹל אֲשֶׁר־עָשָׂה לָכֶם
לה יְהוָה אֱלֹהֵיכֶם בְּמִצְרַיִם לְעֵינֶיךָ: אַתָּה הׇרְאֵתָ לָדַעַת כִּי יְהוָה הוּא הָאֱלֹהִים אֵין
לו עוֹד מִלְבַדּוֹ: מִן־הַשָּׁמַיִם הִשְׁמִיעֲךָ אֶת־קֹלוֹ לְיַסְּרֶךָּ וְעַל־הָאָרֶץ הֶרְאֲךָ אֶת־אִשּׁוֹ
לז הַגְּדוֹלָה וּדְבָרָיו שָׁמַעְתָּ מִתּוֹךְ הָאֵשׁ: וְתַחַת כִּי אָהַב אֶת־אֲבֹתֶיךָ וַיִּבְחַר בְּזַרְעוֹ
לח אַחֲרָיו וַיּוֹצִאֲךָ בְּפָנָיו בְּכֹחוֹ הַגָּדֹל מִמִּצְרָיִם: לְהוֹרִישׁ גּוֹיִם גְּדֹלִים וַעֲצֻמִים מִמְּךָ
לט מִפָּנֶיךָ לַהֲבִיאֲךָ לָתֶת־לְךָ אֶת־אַרְצָם נַחֲלָה כַּיּוֹם הַזֶּה: וְיָדַעְתָּ הַיּוֹם וַהֲשֵׁבֹתָ
אֶל־לְבָבֶךָ כִּי יְהוָה הוּא הָאֱלֹהִים בַּשָּׁמַיִם מִמַּעַל וְעַל־הָאָרֶץ מִתָּחַת אֵין עוֹד:
מ וְשָׁמַרְתָּ אֶת־חֻקָּיו וְאֶת־מִצְוֺתָיו אֲשֶׁר אָנֹכִי מְצַוְּךָ הַיּוֹם אֲשֶׁר יִיטַב לְךָ וּלְבָנֶיךָ
אַחֲרֶיךָ וּלְמַעַן תַּאֲרִיךְ יָמִים עַל־הָאֲדָמָה אֲשֶׁר יְהוָה אֱלֹהֶיךָ נֹתֵן לְךָ כׇּל־הַיָּמִים:
מא מב אָז יַבְדִּיל מֹשֶׁה שָׁלֹשׁ עָרִים בְּעֵבֶר הַיַּרְדֵּן מִזְרְחָה שָׁמֶשׁ: לָנֻס שָׁמָּה רוֹצֵחַ ה שלישי
אֲשֶׁר יִרְצַח אֶת־רֵעֵהוּ בִּבְלִי־דַעַת וְהוּא לֹא־שֹׂנֵא לוֹ מִתְּמֹל שִׁלְשֹׁם

רש״י

וּמִתְפַּעֵל, כְּמוֹ "הַרְפֵּה לָהּ" (מלכים ב׳ ד, כז), תֵּן לָהּ רִפְיוֹן, "הֶרֶף מִמֶּנִּי" (להלן ט, יד), הִתְרַפֵּה מִמֶּנִּי:

לב| **לְיָמִים רִאשֹׁנִים.** עַל יָמִים רִאשׁוֹנִים: **וּלְמִקְצֵה הַשָּׁמַיִם.** וְגַם שְׁאַל לְכָל הַבְּרוּאִים אֲשֶׁר מִקָּצֶה אֶל קָצֶה, זֶהוּ פְּשׁוּטוֹ. וּמִדְרָשׁוֹ, מְלַמֵּד עַל קוֹמָתוֹ שֶׁל אָדָם שֶׁהָיְתָה מִן הָאָרֶץ עַד הַשָּׁמַיִם, וְהוּא הַשִּׁעוּר עַצְמוֹ אֲשֶׁר מִקָּצֶה אֶל קָצֶה: **הֲנִהְיָה כַּדָּבָר הַגָּדוֹל הַזֶּה.** מַהוּ הַדָּבָר הַגָּדוֹל? "הֲשָׁמַע עָם" וְגוֹ׳ (להלן פסוק לג):

לד| **אוֹ הֲנִסָּה אֱלֹהִים.** הֲכִי עָשָׂה נִסִּים שׁוּם אֱלוֹהַּ "לָבוֹא לָקַחַת לוֹ גוֹי" וְגוֹ׳, כָּל הֵהִי"ן הַלָּלוּ תְּמִיהוֹת הֵן, לְכָךְ נְקוּדוֹת הֵן בַּחֲטַף פַּתָּח: הֲנִהְיָה, הֲנִשְׁמַע, הֲשָׁמַע, הֲנִסָּה: **בְּמַסֹּת.** עַל יְדֵי נִסְיוֹנוֹת הוֹדִיעָם גְּבוּרוֹתָיו, כְּגוֹן: "הִתְפָּאֵר עָלַי" (שמות ח, ה) אִם אוּכַל לַעֲשׂוֹת כֵּן, הֲרֵי זֶה נִסָּיוֹן: **בְּאֹתֹת.** בְּסִימָנִים לְהַאֲמִין שֶׁהוּא שְׁלוּחוֹ שֶׁל מָקוֹם, כְּגוֹן: "מַה זֶּה בְיָדֶךָ" (שם ד, ב): **וּבְמוֹפְתִים.** הֵם נִפְלָאוֹת, שֶׁהֵבִיא עֲלֵיהֶם מַכּוֹת מֻפְלָאוֹת: **וּבְמִלְחָמָה.** בַּיָּם, שֶׁנֶּאֱמַר: "כִּי ה׳ נִלְחָם לָהֶם" (שם יד, כה):

לה| **הָרְאֵתָ.** כְּתַרְגּוּמוֹ: "אִתַּחְזֵיתָא", כְּשֶׁנָּתַן הַקָּדוֹשׁ בָּרוּךְ הוּא אֶת הַתּוֹרָה פָּתַח לָהֶם שִׁבְעָה רְקִיעִים וּכְשֵׁם שֶׁקָּרַע אֶת הָעֶלְיוֹנִים כָּךְ קָרַע אֶת הַתַּחְתּוֹנִים וְרָאוּ שֶׁהוּא יְחִידִי, לְכָךְ נֶאֱמַר: "אַתָּה הָרְאֵתָ לָדַעַת":

לז| **וְתַחַת כִּי אָהַב.** וְכָל זֶה תַּחַת אֲשֶׁר אָהַב: **וַיּוֹצִאֲךָ בְּפָנָיו.** כְּאָדָם הַמַּנְהִיג בְּנוֹ לְפָנָיו, שֶׁנֶּאֱמַר: "וַיִּסַּע מַלְאַךְ הָאֱלֹהִים הַהֹלֵךְ וְגוֹ׳ וַיֵּלֶךְ מֵאַחֲרֵיהֶם" (שמות יד, יט). דָּבָר אַחֵר, "וַיּוֹצִאֲךָ בְּפָנָיו", בִּפְנֵי אֲבוֹתָיו, כְּמָה שֶׁנֶּאֱמַר: "נֶגֶד אֲבוֹתָם עָשָׂה פֶלֶא" (תהלים עח, יב). וְאַל תִּתְמַהּ עַל שֶׁהִזְכִּירָם בִּלְשׁוֹן יָחִיד, שֶׁהֲרֵי כְּתָבָם בִּלְשׁוֹן יָחִיד, "וַיִּבְחַר בְּזַרְעוֹ אַחֲרָיו":

לח| **מִמְּךָ מִפָּנֶיךָ.** סָרְסֵהוּ וְדָרְשֵׁהוּ: לְהוֹרִישׁ מִפָּנֶיךָ גּוֹיִם גְּדֹלִים וַעֲצֻמִים מִמְּךָ: **כַּיּוֹם הַזֶּה.** כַּאֲשֶׁר אַתָּה רוֹאֶה הַיּוֹם:

מא| **אָז יַבְדִּיל.** נָתַן לֵב לִהְיוֹת חָרֵד לַדָּבָר שֶׁיַּבְדִּילֵם, וְאַף עַל פִּי שֶׁאֵינָן קוֹלְטוֹת עַד שֶׁיִּבָּדְלוּ אוֹתָן שֶׁבְּאֶרֶץ כְּנַעַן, אָמַר מֹשֶׁה: מִצְוָה שֶׁאֶפְשָׁר לְקַיְּמָהּ אֲקַיְּמֶנָּה: **בְּעֵבֶר הַיַּרְדֵּן מִזְרְחָה שָׁמֶשׁ.** בְּאוֹתוֹ עֵבֶר שֶׁבְּמִזְרָחוֹ שֶׁל יַרְדֵּן: **מִזְרְחָה שָׁמֶשׁ.** לְפִי שֶׁהוּא דָּבוּק נְקוּדָה רֵי"שׁ בַּחֲטָף, מִזְרַח שֶׁל שֶׁמֶשׁ, מְקוֹם זְרִיחַת הַשֶּׁמֶשׁ:

he shall flee to one of these cities and live.

43 Moses designated the city of **Betzer in the wilderness, in the land of the plain for the Reubenites** in their tribal region; **and Ramot in Gilad for the Gadites; and Golan in the Bashan for the Manassites.**

Mount Bental in the Golan Heights

Introduction to the Detailing of the Commandments

DEUTERONOMY 4:44–49

According to the division suggested in the introduction to the book of Deuteronomy, these verses introduce the second section of the book.[24] However, some view them as a summary of the previous speech.[25]

44 **This,** the content recorded below,[26] **is the Torah that Moses placed before the children of Israel.**

45 **These are the testimonies, and the statutes, and the ordinances, which Moses spoke to the children of Israel, when they emerged from Egypt,**

46 **beyond the Jordan, in the canyon opposite Beit Peor, in the land of Sihon king of the Emorites, who lived in Heshbon, whom Moses and the children of Israel smote, upon their emergence from Egypt.**

47 **They took possession of his land, and the land of Og king of the Bashan, the two kings of the Emorites, which are beyond the Jordan toward the eastern sunrise.**

48 The areas which Israel conquered on the eastern side of the Jordan River were **from Aroer, which is on the bank of the Arnon Ravine, until Mount Sion, which is Hermon,**

49 **and all the Arava beyond the Jordan to the east, until the sea of the plain,** the Dead Sea, **under the waterfall of the peak.**

Recounting the Giving of the Torah on Mount Sinai

DEUTERONOMY 5:1–28

In this passage, Moses recounts the event of the giving of the Torah at Mount Sinai, both as a reminder to the older people who had witnessed it and to describe the event to the younger generation. He repeats the Ten Precepts and describes the entire experience of the event. He recalls the fear of those who were present and their request that Moses serve as an intermediary between them and God.

The formulation of the Ten Precepts used by Moses here is not identical to that found in the book of Exodus. It is possible that the text there is the formulation of the precepts that appeared on the first tablets, which Moses broke, while the formulation here was engraved upon the second tablets. Alternatively, this may have been an explication of additional themes that are embedded in the original words. In any case, the precepts here and in Exodus are nearly identical, and presumably, the differences between them teach additional details that are not explicitly mentioned.

This section concludes with Moses relating that God called the entire nation to resume their daily lives following the revelation, and He requested that Moses remain with Him. God then assigned Moses the responsibility of transmitting the Torah to the people.

5 1 **Moses called all Israel, and said to them: Hear, Israel, the statutes and the ordinances that I am speaking in your ears today, and you shall learn them, and** then **you shall take care to perform them.**

Fourth aliya

2 **The Lord our God established a covenant with us at Horev,** Sinai.

3 **Not with our forefathers** alone **did the Lord establish this covenant, but with us, we, who are here, all of us alive today.** The covenant included the younger generation that was born following the revelation as well.[27]

4 Moses begins to relate the details of the revelation: **Face-to-face the Lord spoke with you at the mountain from the midst of the fire.** Some of those listening to Moses were present themselves at the giving of the Torah when they were younger. Consequently, this could not have been viewed as an ancient event that occurred in earlier generations.

5 **I was standing** as an intermediary **between the Lord and you at that time, to tell you the word of the Lord, because you were afraid due to the fire, and you did not ascend the mountain.** God too did not permit the people to approach the mountain to hear His words directly,[28] **saying:**

6 **I am the Lord your God,**[D] **who took you out of the land of Egypt, from the house of bondage.** According to some commentaries, this is not a separate precept, but the Speaker introducing Himself, without which there is no significance to the precepts that follow.[29] Others maintain that this is the first precept: Belief in God and knowledge of Him.[30]

מג וְנָ֗ס אֶל־אַחַ֛ת מִן־הֶעָרִ֥ים הָאֵ֖ל וָחָֽי׃ אֶת־בֶּ֧צֶר בַּמִּדְבָּ֛ר בְּאֶ֥רֶץ הַמִּישֹׁ֖ר לָראוּבֵנִ֑י
מד וְאֶת־רָאמֹ֤ת בַּגִּלְעָד֙ לַגָּדִ֔י וְאֶת־גּוֹלָ֥ן בַּבָּשָׁ֖ן לַֽמְנַשִּֽׁי׃ וְזֹ֖את הַתּוֹרָ֑ה אֲשֶׁר־שָׂ֣ם
מה מֹשֶׁ֔ה לִפְנֵ֖י בְּנֵ֥י יִשְׂרָאֵֽל׃ אֵ֚לֶּה הָעֵדֹ֔ת וְהַחֻקִּ֖ים וְהַמִּשְׁפָּטִ֑ים אֲשֶׁ֨ר דִּבֶּ֤ר מֹשֶׁה֙
מו אֶל־בְּנֵ֣י יִשְׂרָאֵ֔ל בְּצֵאתָ֖ם מִמִּצְרָֽיִם׃ בְּעֵ֣בֶר הַיַּרְדֵּ֗ן בַּגַּ֨יְא מ֜וּל בֵּ֣ית פְּע֔וֹר בְּאֶ֗רֶץ
סִיחֹן֙ מֶ֣לֶךְ הָֽאֱמֹרִ֔י אֲשֶׁ֥ר יוֹשֵׁ֖ב בְּחֶשְׁבּ֑וֹן אֲשֶׁ֨ר הִכָּ֤ה מֹשֶׁה֙ וּבְנֵ֣י יִשְׂרָאֵ֔ל בְּצֵאתָ֖ם
מז מִמִּצְרָֽיִם׃ וַיִּֽירְשׁ֨וּ אֶת־אַרְצ֜וֹ וְאֶת־אֶ֣רֶץ ׀ ע֣וֹג מֶֽלֶךְ־הַבָּשָׁ֗ן שְׁנֵי֙ מַלְכֵ֣י הָֽאֱמֹרִ֔י
מח אֲשֶׁ֖ר בְּעֵ֣בֶר הַיַּרְדֵּ֑ן מִזְרַ֖ח שָֽׁמֶשׁ׃ מֵעֲרֹעֵ֞ר אֲשֶׁ֨ר עַל־שְׂפַת־נַ֧חַל אַרְנֹ֛ן וְעַד־הַ֥ר
מט שִׂיאֹ֖ן ה֥וּא חֶרְמֽוֹן׃ וְכָל־הָ֨עֲרָבָ֜ה עֵ֤בֶר הַיַּרְדֵּן֙ מִזְרָ֔חָה וְעַ֖ד יָ֣ם הָעֲרָבָ֑ה תַּ֖חַת
אַשְׁדֹּ֥ת הַפִּסְגָּֽה׃

ה א וַיִּקְרָ֣א מֹשֶׁה֮ אֶל־כָּל־יִשְׂרָאֵל֒ וַיֹּ֣אמֶר אֲלֵהֶ֗ם שְׁמַ֤ע יִשְׂרָאֵל֙ אֶת־הַֽחֻקִּ֣ים וְאֶת־ רביעי
הַמִּשְׁפָּטִ֔ים אֲשֶׁ֧ר אָנֹכִ֛י דֹּבֵ֥ר בְּאָזְנֵיכֶ֖ם הַיּ֑וֹם וּלְמַדְתֶּ֣ם אֹתָ֔ם וּשְׁמַרְתֶּ֖ם לַעֲשֹׂתָֽם׃
ב ג יְהוָ֣ה אֱלֹהֵ֗ינוּ כָּרַ֥ת עִמָּ֛נוּ בְּרִ֖ית בְּחֹרֵֽב׃ לֹ֣א אֶת־אֲבֹתֵ֔ינוּ כָּרַ֥ת יְהוָ֖ה אֶת־
ד הַבְּרִ֣ית הַזֹּ֑את כִּ֣י אִתָּ֔נוּ אֲנַ֨חְנוּ אֵ֥לֶּה פֹ֛ה הַיּ֖וֹם כֻּלָּ֥נוּ חַיִּֽים׃ פָּנִ֣ים ׀ בְּפָנִ֗ים
ה דִּבֶּ֨ר יְהוָ֧ה עִמָּכֶ֛ם בָּהָ֖ר מִתּ֥וֹךְ הָאֵֽשׁ׃ אָנֹכִ֞י עֹמֵ֤ד בֵּין־יְהוָה֙ וּבֵ֣ינֵיכֶ֔ם בָּעֵ֣ת
הַהִ֔וא לְהַגִּ֥יד לָכֶ֖ם אֶת־דְּבַ֣ר יְהוָ֑ה כִּ֤י יְרֵאתֶם֙ מִפְּנֵ֣י הָאֵ֔שׁ וְלֹֽא־עֲלִיתֶ֥ם בָּהָ֖ר
ו לֵאמֹֽר׃ אָנֹכִי֙ יְהוָ֣ה אֱלֹהֶ֔יךָ אֲשֶׁ֧ר הוֹצֵאתִ֛יךָ מֵאֶ֥רֶץ מִצְרַ֖יִם מִבֵּ֣ית עֲבָדִ֑ים

רש״י

מד | וְזֹאת הַתּוֹרָה. זוֹ שֶׁהוּא עָתִיד לְסַדֵּר אַחַר פָּרָשָׁה זוֹ:

מה-מו | אֵלֶּה הָעֵדֹת וְגוֹ׳ אֲשֶׁר דִּבֶּר. הֵם הֵם אֲשֶׁר דִּבֶּר בְּצֵאתָם מִמִּצְרַיִם דִּבֶּר לָהֶם בְּעַרְבוֹת מוֹאָב אֲשֶׁר בְּעֵבֶר הַיַּרְדֵּן שֶׁהוּא בַּמִּזְרָח, שֶׁהָעֵבֶר הַשֵּׁנִי הָיָה בַּמַּעֲרָב: בְּעֵבֶר הַיַּרְדֵּן. חָזַר וְשָׁנָה לָהֶם:

פרק ה

ג | לֹא אֶת אֲבֹתֵינוּ. בִּלְבַד ״כָּרַת ה׳״ וְגוֹ׳:

ד | פָּנִים בְּפָנִים. אָמַר רַבִּי בֶּרֶכְיָה: כָּךְ אָמַר מֹשֶׁה: אַל תֹּאמְרוּ אֲנִי מַטְעֶה אֶתְכֶם עַל לֹא דָבָר כְּדֶרֶךְ שֶׁהַסַּרְסוּר עוֹשֶׂה בֵּין הַמּוֹכֵר לַלּוֹקֵחַ, הֲרֵי (הַלּוֹקֵחַ) [הַמּוֹכֵר] עַצְמוֹ מְדַבֵּר עִמָּכֶם:

ד-ה | לֵאמֹר. מוּסָב עַל ״דִּבֶּר ה׳ עִמָּכֶם בָּהָר מִתּוֹךְ הָאֵשׁ״ לֵאמֹר, וְ״אָנֹכִי עֹמֵד בֵּין ה׳ וּבֵינֵיכֶם״:

ז | עַל פָּנָי. בְּכָל מָקוֹם אֲשֶׁר אֲנִי שָׁם, וְזֶהוּ כָּל הָעוֹלָם. דָּבָר אַחֵר, כָּל זְמַן שֶׁאֲנִי קַיָּם:

עֲשֶׂרֶת הַדִּבְּרוֹת כְּבָר פֵּרַשְׁתִּים.

DISCUSSION

5:6| I am the Lord your God: The first topic of the Ten Precepts, which appears in both a positive and a negative formulation, is the existence of God. This matter must necessarily precede all the others, as the practical precepts that follow are based on the existence of a Commander. Although some of the precepts also have social value, their importance is not merely due to their practicality. Rather, the precepts given on this lofty occasion mainly serve to establish values of good and evil. Furthermore, the opening declaration: "I am the Lord your God," identifies the Giver of the Torah as the One who saved Israel from Egypt, and it provides the moral justification for the ensuing commands. These are not statutes that must be fulfilled due to fear of judgment or enforcement; rather, it is due to their independent, absolute value.

7 The previous declaration leads to the demand for exclusivity: **You shall have no other gods before Me,** in addition to Me. There is no god but Me.

8 In addition to belief in God, **you shall not make for you an idol** to worship, nor **any image of that which is in the heavens above or that which is** anywhere **on the earth below or that which is in the water beneath the earth.** Any image created for the sake of worship is forbidden here, whether it corresponds to a physical creature in the heaven or earth or whether it represents any other force.

9 **You shall not prostrate yourself to them and you shall not worship them, because I am the Lord your God, a zealous [*kanna*] God,**[D] I demand exclusivity and cannot allow any god to be worshipped with Me, **who reckons the iniquity of the fathers against the children, and against the third generation,** the grandchildren, **and against the fourth generation, to My enemies.** I remember transgressions for generationsand punish one's descendants until the fourth generation, if they continue on their forefathers' evil path.[31] Some maintain that this principle applies only to the severe transgression of idolatry, whose worshippers are called "My enemies."[32]

10 Yet I am also a God **who engages in kindness for the thousands** of generations, **for those who love Me and observe My commandments.** The demand for exclusivity and God's zealotry entail both the negation of all competitors as well as a great love for the faithful.

11 The previous precept of not worshipping other gods leads to the requirement to honor and fear God: **You shall not take the name of the Lord your God in vain,**[D] **as the Lord will not absolve one who takes His name in vain.** The primary purpose of this prohibition is not to prohibit taking a false oath or deceiving another, but to prohibit utilizing His name for no purpose. The severity of the prohibition is much greater than other transgressions, and one who violates it cannot atone for his sin.[33]

12 The next precept is the one that creates the basic framework for the life of Israelites: **Observe the Sabbath day;** pay attention to it, take care not to desecrate it, and wait for it, **to keep it holy,** as a sacred day, **as the Lord your God commanded you** in Mara[34] and in the wilderness of Sin.[35]

13 **Six days you shall work and perform all your labor.** The six weekdays are meant for working and accomplishing all of one's necessary tasks.

14 **The seventh day is a Sabbath to the Lord your God.** On this day God rested, as related at the beginning of the Torah.[36] **You,** people, as well, **shall not perform any labor** on this day. The same restrictions apply to the members of your extended household: **You, and your son, and your daughter, and your slave, and your maidservant, and your ox, and your donkey, and all your animals, and your stranger who is within your gates, so that your slave and your maidservant may rest like you.**

15 **You shall remember that you were a slave in the land of Egypt, and the Lord your God took you out from there with a mighty hand and with an outstretched arm; therefore, the Lord your God commanded you to observe the Sabbath**[D] **day.** The social aspect of the Sabbath is especially significant for Israel and those associated with it. By being slaves in Egypt, the Israelites learned that slaves also require free time, one day of rest from their other activities, in order to pursue more lofty spiritual matters.

16 **Honor your father and your mother,**[D] **as the Lord your God commanded you** in Mara,[37] **so that your days will be extended.** In a society in which the elder generation is respected, people will live long lives, as aging parents can be confident that they can rely on the younger generation to care for them, and they will feel valued as important members of the family and of society at large.[38] **And** you shall also do this so **that it will be good**

DISCUSSION

5:9 | A zealous [*kanna*] God: Although the root *kuf-nun-alef* usually refers to jealousy, here the meaning is closer to zealotry. To the degree that jealousy is relevant in describing God's attitude toward sinners, it is not a jealousy of desire, but of love, as in the verse: "As love is as intense as death, jealousy is as cruel as the grave" (Song of Songs 8:6). It is characterized by the demand for complete, exclusive ownership. Both here and in its human, social manifestation, jealousy is expressed not merely through a lack of tolerance toward the intimacy of the beloved with another, but also through a desire for vengeance and a combative spirit (see *Bekhor Shor*, Exodus 20:4). Indeed, the expressions of jealousy attributed to God in the Bible appear invariably in the context of idolatry, which is essentially the betrayal of God (based on Ramban).

5:11 | You shall not take the name of the Lord your God in vain: This verse teaches that the very name of God must be treated with reverence. In addition, it is derived from here that there are limitations on mentioning the ineffable name of God for no purpose or in a negative context. God's name is usually replaced by terms such as Hashem, which literally means The Name, in order to prevent people from using the actual name of God in a disrespectful manner.

This precept is also interpreted as a general reference to the desecration of the honor of God in other ways. Since, over the course of history, the nation of Israel became identified as the people of God, any clearly negative behavior on their part in the presence of others is

ז ח לֹא־יִהְיֶה לְךָ אֱלֹהִים אֲחֵרִים עַל־פָּנָי: לֹא־תַעֲשֶׂה לְךָ פֶסֶל כָּל־תְּמוּנָה אֲשֶׁר
ט בַּשָּׁמַיִם מִמַּעַל וַאֲשֶׁר בָּאָרֶץ מִתָּחַת וַאֲשֶׁר בַּמַּיִם מִתַּחַת לָאָרֶץ: לֹא־תִשְׁתַּחֲוֶה
לָהֶם וְלֹא תָעָבְדֵם כִּי אָנֹכִי יהוה אֱלֹהֶיךָ אֵל קַנָּא פֹּקֵד עֲוֺן אָבוֹת עַל־בָּנִים
י וְעַל־שִׁלֵּשִׁים וְעַל־רִבֵּעִים לְשֹׂנְאָי: וְעֹשֶׂה חֶסֶד לַאֲלָפִים לְאֹהֲבַי וּלְשֹׁמְרֵי
יא מצותו: לֹא תִשָּׂא אֶת־שֵׁם־יהוה אֱלֹהֶיךָ לַשָּׁוְא כִּי לֹא יְנַקֶּה יהוה אֵת מִצְוֺתָי
יב אֲשֶׁר־יִשָּׂא אֶת־שְׁמוֹ לַשָּׁוְא: שָׁמוֹר אֶת־יוֹם הַשַּׁבָּת לְקַדְּשׁוֹ כַּאֲשֶׁר
יג יד צִוְּךָ יהוה אֱלֹהֶיךָ: שֵׁשֶׁת יָמִים תַּעֲבֹד וְעָשִׂיתָ כָּל־מְלַאכְתֶּךָ: וְיוֹם הַשְּׁבִיעִי שַׁבָּת
לַיהוה אֱלֹהֶיךָ לֹא־תַעֲשֶׂה כָל־מְלָאכָה אַתָּה ׀ וּבִנְךָ־וּבִתֶּךָ וְעַבְדְּךָ־וַאֲמָתֶךָ
וְשׁוֹרְךָ וַחֲמֹרְךָ וְכָל־בְּהֶמְתֶּךָ וְגֵרְךָ אֲשֶׁר בִּשְׁעָרֶיךָ לְמַעַן יָנוּחַ עַבְדְּךָ וַאֲמָתְךָ
טו כָּמוֹךָ: וְזָכַרְתָּ כִּי עֶבֶד הָיִיתָ בְּאֶרֶץ מִצְרַיִם וַיֹּצִאֲךָ יהוה אֱלֹהֶיךָ מִשָּׁם בְּיָד חֲזָקָה
טז וּבִזְרֹעַ נְטוּיָה עַל־כֵּן צִוְּךָ יהוה אֱלֹהֶיךָ לַעֲשׂוֹת אֶת־יוֹם הַשַּׁבָּת: כַּבֵּד
אֶת־אָבִיךָ וְאֶת־אִמֶּךָ כַּאֲשֶׁר צִוְּךָ יהוה אֱלֹהֶיךָ לְמַעַן ׀ יַאֲרִיכֻן יָמֶיךָ וּלְמַעַן יִיטַב

רש״י

יב | שָׁמוֹר. וּבָרִאשׁוֹנוֹת הוּא אוֹמֵר: "זָכוֹר" (שמות כ, ח), שְׁנֵיהֶם בְּדִבּוּר אֶחָד וּבְתֵבָה אַחַת נֶאֶמְרוּ וּבִשְׁמִיעָה אַחַת נִשְׁמְעוּ: כַּאֲשֶׁר צִוְּךָ. קֹדֶם מַתַּן תּוֹרָה, בְּמָרָה:

טו | וְזָכַרְתָּ כִּי עֶבֶד הָיִיתָ וְגוֹ'. עַל מְנָת כֵּן פְּדָאֲךָ, שֶׁתִּהְיֶה לוֹ עֶבֶד וְתִשְׁמֹר מִצְוֺתָיו:

טז | כַּאֲשֶׁר צִוְּךָ. אַף עַל כִּבּוּד אָב וָאֵם נִצְטַוּוּ בְּמָרָה, שֶׁנֶּאֱמַר: "שָׁם שָׂם לוֹ חֹק וּמִשְׁפָּט" (שמות טו, כה):

DISCUSSION

a desecration of the name of God. When they act in that manner, their actions do not merely damage their own good names and the honor of their families and their nation, but even the name of God Himself (see the midrash cited here in *Torah Shelema*; *Sha'arei Teshuva* 2:45; *Yoma* 86a).

5:15| **Sabbath:** The formulation of this precept in the book of Deuteronomy is different from the one in the book of Exodus. There, the Sabbath is mentioned as God's day of rest from creating the world, while here a more humanistic and current explanation is given; the need for a weekly day of rest is based on the memory of our enslavement in Egypt.

At Mount Sinai, the specific prohibitions of the Sabbath were not given. Certainly resting on the Sabbath does not require one to sit motionless for the entire day. The prohibition applies to the performance of labor, which is a defined act not necessarily synonymous with hard work. Work refers to a physical action, whereas labor in this context is a deliberate creative act.

5:16| **Honor your father and your mother:** Although this precept was not explicitly mentioned in the Torah before the Ten Precepts, it was already a basic value one thousand years beforehand, as is evident from the story of Noah's sons (see Genesis 9:20–23).

Honoring one's parents is now presented as a fundamental principle of the Torah. It is not presented as part of the obligation to respect one's elders, alongside the precept: "You shall rise before the graybeard, and show deference before the elderly" (Leviticus 19:32). Instead, it appears as one of the Ten Precepts, which detail the basic principles of worshipping God, as one's attitude toward his parents should parallel his attitude toward God. The first precept ties the people of Israel to God by virtue of the fact that He fashioned them as a nation: "Who took you out of the land of Egypt, from the house of bondage" (verse 6). The precept to observe the Sabbath that appears just before this one is associated with God's creation of the entire world (in Exodus), as well as to His redemption of the people of Israel from Egypt (in Deuteronomy). The duty to honor one's parents extends this theme in that it is not dependent upon the individual personalities of the parents, but rather on the fact that they, like God, are the source of a person's existence (see Ramban, Exodus 20:11; *Kiddushin* 30b).

for you, on the land which the Lord your God gives you. Despite the difficulties inherent in properly honoring one's parents, this precept applies to everyone. The precept is not simply for the parents' benefit; it is also an integral part of a fulfilling lifestyle that the Torah teaches, and as a result, one is rewarded with prosperity and longevity.

17 **You shall not murder.**^D **And you shall not commit adultery.**^D This prohibition of sexual misconduct is defined by Jewish law and in the traditional commentaries as pertaining to the relationship of a married woman with a man other than her husband.³⁹ **And you shall not steal.** Following the severe prohibitions that define the basis of a person's behavior toward his fellow man, such as murder, adultery, and stealing, the Torah presents a precept that is seemingly less severe than the previous ones, but which relates to a common social situation: **And you shall not bear false witness against your neighbor.**^D According to the Sages, the definition of this prohibition is the submission of false testimony in court, which could, at times, lead even to the death of the accused. Such testimony undermines the trust between people.

18 **You shall not covet**^D **your neighbor's wife; and you shall not desire your neighbor's house, his field, or his slave, or his maidservant, his ox, or his donkey, or anything that is your neighbor's.**

19 **These ten words the Lord spoke to your entire assembly at** *Fifth* **the mountain from the midst of the fire, the cloud, and the** *aliya* **fog, a great voice that did not cease.** Although God did not continue to speak, the noise continued.⁴⁰ **And He inscribed them on two stone tablets, and He gave them to me.**

Diagram of the stone tablets

20 **It was when you heard the voice from the midst of the darkness, and the mountain was burning with fire, that you approached me, all the heads of your tribes, and your elders.**

21 **You said** in fear: **Behold, the Lord our God has shown us His glory and His greatness, and His voice we heard from the midst of the fire; this day we have seen that God will speak with man, and he may live.**

22 **And now, why should we die, when this great,** unusual **fire will consume us? If we continue to hear the voice of the Lord our God, we shall die.** This voice, which emanates from above and beyond this world, is making contact with us in some manner, but we are concerned that we cannot survive if we continue to hear it.

23 **For who of all flesh that heard the voice of the living God speaking from the midst of the fire like us, has lived?**

24 **You,** Moses, **approach and hear everything that the Lord our God will say; and you will speak to us**^D **everything that the Lord our God will speak to you, and we will hear it and we will perform it.**

DISCUSSION

5:17 | You shall not murder [*lo tirtzaḥ*]: The foundation of social coexistence is the basic sense of security felt by each individual, which is contingent upon his confidence that others will not attempt to kill him. In a society in which murder is permitted, humanity in general and each individual in particular is in a constant state of peril. Even in the animal kingdom, among many species, animals in a pack do not attack one another. However, in the Ten Precepts, this fundamental prohibition is imbued with meaning that goes beyond its social utility, as indicated by the formulation *lo tirtzaḥ*, which repudiates murder entirely, rather than *al tirtzaḥ*, which is merely a prohibition. In effect, the Torah is saying: There

shall be no murder, as acts of this kind simply are not part of your world. A similar formulation is employed in the subsequent precepts as well.

And you shall not commit adultery: Other sexual prohibitions, such as incest and prohibitions that stem from the elevated status of the nation of Israel or of certain individuals, are not included in this precept. This is true despite the fact that they are no less severe than adultery, and the punishment for some of them is in fact more severe. The reason adultery appears here is because it undermines the most basic social unit, the family. In addition, it violates a concept that goes back to creation: "Therefore, a man shall leave his father and his mother, and he

shall cleave to his wife, and they shall become one flesh" (Genesis 2:24). Likewise, the prohibition against murder too, relates to a verse in Genesis (9:6): "One who sheds the blood of man, by man shall his blood be shed, as He made man in the image of God."

And you shall not bear false witness against your neighbor: This precept may be interpreted as including a broad range of situations in which one speaks falsely about another (see *Bekhor Shor*, Exodus 23:1). If people would refrain from speaking falsehoods entirely, each man could rely on another, with full confidence that other people's statements are spoken in good faith.

יז לָךְ עַל הָאֲדָמָה אֲשֶׁר־יהוה אֱלֹהֶיךָ נֹתֵן לָךְ: לֹא תִּרְצָח וְלֹא

יח תִּנְאָף וְלֹא תִּגְנֹב וְלֹא־תַעֲנֶה בְרֵעֲךָ עֵד שָׁוְא: וְלֹא תַחְמֹד

אֵשֶׁת רֵעֶךָ וְלֹא תִתְאַוֶּה בֵּית רֵעֶךָ שָׂדֵהוּ וְעַבְדּוֹ וַאֲמָתוֹ שׁוֹרוֹ וַחֲמֹרוֹ

יט וְכֹל אֲשֶׁר לְרֵעֶךָ: אֶת־הַדְּבָרִים הָאֵלֶּה דִּבֶּר יהוה אֶל־כָּל־קְהַלְכֶם בָּהָר חמישי

מִתּוֹךְ הָאֵשׁ הֶעָנָן וְהָעֲרָפֶל קוֹל גָּדוֹל וְלֹא יָסָף וַיִּכְתְּבֵם עַל־שְׁנֵי לֻחֹת אֲבָנִים וַיִּתְּנֵם

כ אֵלָי: וַיְהִי כְּשָׁמְעֲכֶם אֶת־הַקּוֹל מִתּוֹךְ הַחֹשֶׁךְ וְהָהָר בֹּעֵר בָּאֵשׁ וַתִּקְרְבוּן אֵלַי כָּל־

כא רָאשֵׁי שִׁבְטֵיכֶם וְזִקְנֵיכֶם: וַתֹּאמְרוּ הֵן הֶרְאָנוּ יהוה אֱלֹהֵינוּ אֶת־כְּבֹדוֹ וְאֶת־גָּדְלוֹ

וְאֶת־קֹלוֹ שָׁמַעְנוּ מִתּוֹךְ הָאֵשׁ הַיּוֹם הַזֶּה רָאִינוּ כִּי־יְדַבֵּר אֱלֹהִים אֶת־הָאָדָם וָחָי:

כב וְעַתָּה לָמָּה נָמוּת כִּי תֹאכְלֵנוּ הָאֵשׁ הַגְּדֹלָה הַזֹּאת אִם־יֹסְפִים אֲנַחְנוּ לִשְׁמֹעַ אֶת־

כג קוֹל יהוה אֱלֹהֵינוּ עוֹד וָמָתְנוּ: כִּי מִי כָל־בָּשָׂר אֲשֶׁר שָׁמַע קוֹל אֱלֹהִים חַיִּים מְדַבֵּר

כד מִתּוֹךְ־הָאֵשׁ כָּמֹנוּ וַיֶּחִי: קְרַב אַתָּה וּשֲׁמָע אֵת כָּל־אֲשֶׁר יֹאמַר יהוה אֱלֹהֵינוּ

וְאַתְּ ׀ תְּדַבֵּר אֵלֵינוּ אֵת כָּל־אֲשֶׁר יְדַבֵּר יהוה אֱלֹהֵינוּ אֵלֶיךָ וְשָׁמַעְנוּ וְעָשִׂינוּ:

רש"י

יז] וְלֹא תִּנְאָף. אֵין לְשׁוֹן נִאוּף אֶלָּא בְּאֵשֶׁת אִישׁ:

יח] לֹא תִתְאַוֶּה. אַף הוּא לְשׁוֹן חֶמְדָּה, כְּמוֹ "נֶחְמָד לְמַרְאֶה" (בראשית ב, ט) דִּמְתַרְגְּמִינָן: "דִּמְרַגֵּג לְמֶחֱזֵי:

יט] וְלֹא יָסָף. מְתַרְגְּמִינָן "וְלָא פָסָק", כִּי קוֹלוֹ חָזָק וְקַיָּם לְעוֹלָם. דָּבָר אַחֵר, "וְלֹא יָסָף", לֹא הוֹסִיף לְהֵרָאוֹת בְּאוֹתוֹ פֻּמְבֵּי:

כד] וְאַתְּ תְּדַבֵּר אֵלֵינוּ. הִתַּשְׁתֶּם אֶת כֹּחִי כִּנְקֵבָה,

שֶׁנִּצְטַעַרְתִּי עֲלֵיכֶם וְרִפִּיתֶם אֶת יָדִי, כִּי רָאִיתִי שֶׁאֵינְכֶם חֲרֵדִים לְהִתְקָרֵב אֵלָיו מֵאַהֲבָה. וְכִי לֹא הָיָה יָפֶה לָכֶם לִלְמֹד מִפִּי הַגְּבוּרָה וְלֹא לִלְמֹד מִמֶּנִּי?:

DISCUSSION

5:18 | You shall not covet: Ostensibly, a prohibition of this kind has no place in a legal system, as legal codes refer to actions rather than people's thoughts and desires. Only God can command people not to desire something, and only God can place limits on the intrigues and desires hidden in the heart of man. Nonetheless, due to the unique nature of this prohibition among the other precepts, most of which apply to actions and words, the Sages interpreted this prohibition in a more limited manner, as prohibiting taking action to dispossess another of an item that belongs to him (see Rambam, *Sefer*

HaMitzvot, negative commandment 265). This applies not only to methods that are otherwise prohibited, but also to otherwise permitted means of persuasion, pressure, or manipulation that a person might employ to compel another to transfer ownership of his belongings to him, or to cause another person's wife to become his. Coveting in this sense is somewhat akin to the villainy identified as the sin of the generation of the flood (Genesis 6:11–13), as it too was a moral, rather than a legal transgression. Accordingly, this final precept serves to prohibit practical planning and scheming for the purpose of

appropriating that which belongs to someone else.

5:24 | You will speak to us: A mere several months earlier, the children of Israel were still slaves. Therefore, it was difficult for them to conceive that it would be possible to forge a direct connection with God. They felt that they were incapable of surviving the direct encounter in which they experienced the voice of God speaking to them from nothingness; therefore, they requested that Moses intermediate between them.

25 **The Lord heard the sound of your words upon your speaking to me; and the Lord said to me: I heard the sound of the
words of this people that they spoke to you; they did well in
everything that they spoke.**
26 **Would that this heart shall be for them to fear Me and to
observe all My commandments for all days, so that it will
be good for them and for their children forever.** Within the
conditions allowing the world to exist, there are numerous situations in which God conceals His presence, and only with great
difficulty can a person recognize and fulfill his responsibilities.
It is even more rare that a person's descendants will succeed in
achieving this goal.[41]
27 **Go say to them: Return to your tents,** to the regular responsibilities and lifestyle of married people.
28 **But you,** Moses, **stand here with Me,** and do not return to
regular daily life like the rest of the people. You must abstain
from normal worldly activities, including relations with your
wife. **And I will speak to you all the commandment, and the
statutes, and the ordinances that you will teach them, and
they will perform them in the land that I am giving them to
take possession of it.**

General Commands and Objectives

DEUTERONOMY 5:29–6:3

In the following verses, Moses is no longer recounting the past, but is addressing his audience with regard to the present.

29 **You shall take care to act as the Lord your God commanded
you; you shall not deviate right or left.** You shall fulfill the
commandments with the same awe and fear as you would have
had you heard all of them directly from the voice of God.
30 **In the entire path that the Lord your God commanded you,
you shall walk.** You received the gift of the Torah, and you
must now uphold its sanctity, as well as that of your new elevated status, **so that you will live, and that it will be good for
you, and you will extend your days in the land of which you
will take possession.**
6 1 **And this is the commandment, the statutes, and the ordinances that the Lord your God commanded to teach you,
to perform them in the land into which you are crossing to
take possession of it**
2 **so that you will fear the Lord your God, to observe all His
statutes and His commandments that I am commanding
you: You, your son, and your son's son, all the days of your
life; and so that your days will be extended,** and there will be
continuity of the nation of Israel.
3 **You shall hear, Israel, and you shall take care to perform,
so that it will be good for you, and so that you will increase
greatly, as the Lord, the God of your forefathers, spoke to
you,** and you will experience this goodness in **a land flowing
with milk and honey.** You are about to enter the good land and
live a normal life there. If you fulfill your responsibilities, I will
ensure that you have plentiful food and other necessities.

Shema

DEUTERONOMY 6:4–9

The introductory verse of this section consists of one of the few abstract declarations found in the Torah. It expresses the belief in the oneness of God, and it is the most significant verse in the Torah in many respects. This section was ultimately called *Shema*. It is recited twice daily, and throughout the generations, many Jews have recited it prior to their death. In addition to declaring God's unity, one is also required to love Him, and this is in fact the first time in the Torah where a person is commanded to love God. Belief in the oneness of God requires actions involving both speech and writing that serve to internalize this faith in God. In this manner, a Jew's faith is present throughout his daily routine.

4 **Hear, Israel:** With these words, Moses was not merely address-
Sixth aliya ing Israel, but also declaring the essence and faith of the people.
He made two declarations:[42] **The Lord is our God,** and **the
Lord is one.**
5 Based on the fundamental declaration, the following commands are derived: **You shall love the Lord your God with all**
the desire of **your heart,** and your heart shall not disagree with
this,[43] **and with all your soul,** to the point of giving up your life
for His sake,[44] **and with all your might.** You are commanded to
love God at all times and in all places, and you shall increase the
extent of this love as much as possible.[45]
6 **These matters that I command you today shall be upon your
heart** by remembering them constantly.
7 **You shall inculcate them in your children, and you shall
speak of them** and review them **while you are sitting in your
house, and while you are walking on the way,** in every place
that you may be, **and while you are lying down, and while
you are rising,** so that you will remember them.

כה וַיִּשְׁמַע יְהוָה אֶת־קוֹל דִּבְרֵיכֶם בְּדַבֶּרְכֶם אֵלָי וַיֹּאמֶר יְהוָה אֵלַי שָׁמַעְתִּי אֶת־קוֹל

כו דִּבְרֵי הָעָם הַזֶּה אֲשֶׁר דִּבְּרוּ אֵלֶיךָ הֵיטִיבוּ כָּל־אֲשֶׁר דִּבֵּרוּ: מִי־יִתֵּן וְהָיָה לְבָבָם זֶה לָהֶם לְיִרְאָה אֹתִי וְלִשְׁמֹר אֶת־כָּל־מִצְוֹתַי כָּל־הַיָּמִים לְמַעַן יִיטַב לָהֶם וְלִבְנֵיהֶם

כז לְעֹלָם: לֵךְ אֱמֹר לָהֶם שׁוּבוּ לָכֶם לְאָהֳלֵיכֶם: וְאַתָּה פֹּה עֲמֹד עִמָּדִי וַאֲדַבְּרָה

כח אֵלֶיךָ אֵת כָּל־הַמִּצְוָה וְהַחֻקִּים וְהַמִּשְׁפָּטִים אֲשֶׁר תְּלַמְּדֵם וְעָשׂוּ בָאָרֶץ אֲשֶׁר אָנֹכִי נֹתֵן לָהֶם לְרִשְׁתָּהּ: וּשְׁמַרְתֶּם לַעֲשׂוֹת כַּאֲשֶׁר צִוָּה יְהוָה אֱלֹהֵיכֶם אֶתְכֶם

כט לֹא תָסֻרוּ יָמִין וּשְׂמֹאל: בְּכָל־הַדֶּרֶךְ אֲשֶׁר צִוָּה יְהוָה אֱלֹהֵיכֶם אֶתְכֶם תֵּלֵכוּ לְמַעַן

ל תִּחְיוּן וְטוֹב לָכֶם וְהַאֲרַכְתֶּם יָמִים בָּאָרֶץ אֲשֶׁר תִּירָשׁוּן: וְזֹאת הַמִּצְוָה הַחֻקִּים

א וְהַמִּשְׁפָּטִים אֲשֶׁר צִוָּה יְהוָה אֱלֹהֵיכֶם לְלַמֵּד אֶתְכֶם לַעֲשׂוֹת בָּאָרֶץ אֲשֶׁר אַתֶּם

ב עֹבְרִים שָׁמָּה לְרִשְׁתָּהּ: לְמַעַן תִּירָא אֶת־יְהוָה אֱלֹהֶיךָ לִשְׁמֹר אֶת־כָּל־חֻקֹּתָיו וּמִצְוֹתָיו אֲשֶׁר אָנֹכִי מְצַוֶּךָ אַתָּה וּבִנְךָ וּבֶן־בִּנְךָ כֹּל יְמֵי חַיֶּיךָ וּלְמַעַן יַאֲרִכֻן יָמֶיךָ:

ג וְשָׁמַעְתָּ יִשְׂרָאֵל וְשָׁמַרְתָּ לַעֲשׂוֹת אֲשֶׁר יִיטַב לְךָ וַאֲשֶׁר תִּרְבּוּן מְאֹד כַּאֲשֶׁר דִּבֶּר יְהוָה אֱלֹהֵי אֲבֹתֶיךָ לָךְ אֶרֶץ זָבַת חָלָב וּדְבָשׁ:

ד שְׁמַע יִשְׂרָאֵל יְהוָה אֱלֹהֵינוּ יְהוָה ׀ אֶחָד: וְאָהַבְתָּ אֵת יְהוָה אֱלֹהֶיךָ בְּכָל־לְבָבְךָ וּ   ששי

ו וּבְכָל־נַפְשְׁךָ וּבְכָל־מְאֹדֶךָ: וְהָיוּ הַדְּבָרִים הָאֵלֶּה אֲשֶׁר אָנֹכִי מְצַוְּךָ הַיּוֹם עַל־לְבָבֶךָ:

ז וְשִׁנַּנְתָּם לְבָנֶיךָ וְדִבַּרְתָּ בָּם בְּשִׁבְתְּךָ בְּבֵיתֶךָ וּבְלֶכְתְּךָ בַדֶּרֶךְ וּבְשָׁכְבְּךָ וּבְקוּמֶךָ:

רש"י

פרק ו

ד ה' אֱלֹהֵינוּ ה' אֶחָד. ה' שֶׁהוּא "אֱלֹהֵינוּ" עַתָּה וְלֹא אֱלֹהֵי הָאֻמּוֹת, הוּא עָתִיד לִהְיוֹת "ה' אֶחָד", שֶׁנֶּאֱמַר: "כִּי אָז אֶהְפֹּךְ אֶל עַמִּים שָׂפָה בְרוּרָה לִקְרֹא כֻלָּם בְּשֵׁם ה'" (צפניה ג, ט), וְנֶאֱמַר: "בַּיּוֹם הַהוּא יִהְיֶה ה' אֶחָד וּשְׁמוֹ אֶחָד" (זכריה יד, ט):

ה וְאָהַבְתָּ. עֲשֵׂה דְבָרָיו מֵאַהֲבָה. אֵינוֹ דוֹמֶה עוֹשֶׂה מֵאַהֲבָה לְעוֹשֶׂה מִיִּרְאָה. הָעוֹשֶׂה אֵצֶל רַבּוֹ מִיִּרְאָה, כְּשֶׁהוּא מַטְרִיחַ עָלָיו מַנִּיחוֹ וְהוֹלֵךְ לוֹ: בְּכָל־לְבָבְךָ. בִּשְׁנֵי יְצָרֶיךָ. דָּבָר אַחֵר, "בְּכָל לְבָבְךָ", שֶׁלֹּא יִהְיֶה לִבְּךָ חָלוּק עַל הַמָּקוֹם: וּבְכָל־נַפְשְׁךָ. אֲפִלּוּ הוּא נוֹטֵל אֶת נַפְשֶׁךָ: וּבְכָל־מְאֹדֶךָ. בְּכָל מָמוֹנְךָ, יֵשׁ לְךָ אָדָם שֶׁמָּמוֹנוֹ חָבִיב

עָלָיו מִגּוּפוֹ, לְכָךְ נֶאֱמַר: "בְּכָל מְאֹדֶךָ". דָּבָר אַחֵר, "וּבְכָל מְאֹדֶךָ", בְּכָל מִדָּה וּמִדָּה שֶׁמּוֹדֵד לְךָ, בֵּין בְּמִדָּה טוֹבָה בֵּין בְּמִדַּת פֻּרְעָנוּת, וְכֵן דָּוִד הוּא אוֹמֵר: "כּוֹס יְשׁוּעוֹת אֶשָּׂא" וּבִשְׁמַע ה' אֶקְרָא" (תהלים קטז, יג), "צָרָה וְיָגוֹן אֶמְצָא וּבְשֵׁם ה' אֶקְרָא" (שם פסוקים ג-ד):

ו וְהָיוּ הַדְּבָרִים. מַהוּ הָאַהֲבָה? "וְהָיוּ הַדְּבָרִים הָאֵלֶּה", שֶׁמִּתּוֹךְ כָּךְ אַתָּה מַכִּיר בְּהַקָּדוֹשׁ בָּרוּךְ הוּא וּמִדַּבֵּק בִּדְרָכָיו: אֲשֶׁר אָנֹכִי מְצַוְּךָ הַיּוֹם. לֹא יִהְיוּ בְּעֵינֶיךָ כִּדְיוֹטַגְמָא יְשָׁנָה שֶׁאֵין אָדָם סוֹפְנָהּ, אֶלָּא כַּחֲדָשָׁה שֶׁהַכֹּל רָצִין לִקְרֹאתָהּ. דְּיוֹטַגְמָא – מְצַת הַמֶּלֶךְ הַבָּאָה בְּמִכְתָּב:

ז וְשִׁנַּנְתָּם. לְשׁוֹן חִדּוּד הוּא, שֶׁיִּהְיוּ מְחֻדָּדִים בְּפִיךָ, שֶׁאִם יִשְׁאָלְךָ אָדָם דָּבָר לֹא תְהֵא צָרִיךְ לְגַמְגֵּם בּוֹ, אֶלָּא

אֱמֹר לוֹ מִיָּד: לְבָנֶיךָ. אֵלּוּ הַתַּלְמִידִים. מָצִינוּ בְּכָל מָקוֹם שֶׁהַתַּלְמִידִים קְרוּיִים בָּנִים, שֶׁנֶּאֱמַר: "בָּנִים אַתֶּם לַה' אֱלֹהֵיכֶם" (להלן יד, א), וְאוֹמֵר: "בְּנֵי הַנְּבִיאִים אֲשֶׁר בֵּית אֵל" (מלכים ב ב, ג), וְכֵן בְּחִזְקִיָּהוּ שֶׁלִּמֵּד תּוֹרָה לְכָל יִשְׂרָאֵל וּקְרָאָם בָּנִים, שֶׁנֶּאֱמַר: "בָּנַי עַתָּה אַל תִּשָּׁלוּ" (דברי הימים ב כט, יא). וּכְשֵׁם שֶׁהַתַּלְמִידִים קְרוּיִים בָּנִים, כָּךְ הָרַב קָרוּי אָב, שֶׁנֶּאֱמַר: "אָבִי אָבִי רֶכֶב יִשְׂרָאֵל וְגוֹ'" (מלכים ב ב, יב): וְדִבַּרְתָּ בָּם. שֶׁלֹּא יְהֵא עִקַּר דִּבּוּרְךָ אֶלָּא בָּם, עֲשֵׂם עִקָּר וְאַל תַּעֲשֵׂם טָפֵל: וּבְשָׁכְבְּךָ. יָכוֹל אֲפִלּוּ שָׁכַב בַּחֲצִי הַיּוֹם? תַּלְמוּד לוֹמַר: "וּבְלֶכְתְּךָ בַדֶּרֶךְ", דֶּרֶךְ אֶרֶץ דִּבְּרָה תוֹרָה, זְמַן שְׁכִיבָה וּזְמַן קִימָה:

8 **You shall bind them as a sign on your arm** by making square black boxes, inside which these words shall be written. This refers to the phylacteries bound on the arm, the binding of which symbolizes one's connection to God. **And they shall be for ornaments,** which function as an emblem or a symbol,[46] **between your eyes,** centered in between the eyes above the forehead.[47] This refers to the phylacteries bound on the head.
9 **You shall write them on the doorposts of your** private **house, and on your gates** of the cities.

Phylacteries

שמע ישראל יהוה אלהינו יהוה אחד ואהבת את
יהוה אלהיך בכל לבבך ובכל נפשך ובכל מאדך והיו
הדברים האלה אשר אנכי מצוך היום על לבבך ושננתם
לבניך ודברת בם בשבתך בביתך ובלכתך בדרך
ובשכבך ובקומך וקשרתם לאות על ידך והיו לטטפת
בין עיניך וכתבתם על מזזות ביתך ובשעריך
והיה אם שמע תשמעו אל מצותי אשר אנכי
מצוה אתכם היום לאהבה את יהוה אלהיכם ולעבדו
בכל לבבכם ובכל נפשכם ונתתי מטר ארצכם בעתו
יורה ומלקוש ואספת דגנך ותירשך ויצהרך ונתתי
עשב בשדך לבהמתך ואכלת ושבעת השמרו לכם
פן יפתה לבבכם וסרתם ועבדתם אלהים אחרים
והשתחויתם להם וחרה אף יהוה בכם ועצר את
השמים ולא יהיה מטר והאדמה לא תתן את יבולה
ואבדתם מהרה מעל הארץ הטבה אשר יהוה נתן לכם
ושמתם את דברי אלה על לבבכם ועל נפשכם וקשרתם
אתם לאות על ידכם והיו לטוטפת בין עיניכם ולמדתם
אתם את בניכם לדבר בם בשבתך בביתך ובלכתך
בדרך ובשכבך ובקומך וכתבתם על מזוזות ביתך
ובשעריך למען ירבו ימיכם וימי בניכם על האדמה
אשר נשבע יהוה לאבתיכם לתת להם כימי השמים
על הארץ

Parchment containing the passages of the mezuzah, which one must affix on one's doorpost

Remembering the Kindness of God and Being Faithful to Him

DEUTERONOMY 6:10–9:7

The following section contains several themes related to remembering and forgetting in the Land of Israel. The opening verses address the concern that the memory of the divine kindness and the resulting commitment to God will be erased when the children of Israel become accustomed to the great plenty available there. Moses bases his instructions to Israel to follow God without question on memories of the recent past, among them the trials that the children of Israel tried God in the wilderness that ended with disastrous consequences. He also mentions the exodus from Egypt, which many knew about only from their parents, in order to strengthen their commitment to observing the Torah and its commandments.

Not only was there concern that the comfortable economic conditions in the Land of Israel would likely erode the loyalty of the people to God and the Torah, there was also concern that the inhabitants might entice them to adopt their idol worship and their beliefs. Therefore, in the continuation of the section, Moses warns the people against the negative influence of those inhabitants and instructs them to destroy them along with all vestiges of their idols.

As part of the struggle against complacency that was likely to develop as Israel would live securely in its land, Moses attempts to instill in the national consciousness the memory of their dependence upon God in the wilderness, as well as the kindnesses He performed for them. Although their remaining in the land in future generations would depend on their actions, their entry was entirely dependent upon the merit of their ancestors, and the wickedness of the previous inhabitants. All of the miracles that God will perform will be due to His kindness, and not due to the righteousness of Israel.

10 **It shall be when the Lord your God will take you into the land with regard to which He took an oath to your forefathers, to Abraham, to Isaac, and to Jacob, to give to you, great and good cities that you did not build,** but will already be present,
11 **and houses full of everything good,** such as food and other stored items, **that you did not fill** or gather, **and hewn cisterns** for water **that you did not hew,** and likewise, **vineyards and olive trees that you did not plant, and you shall eat** all of these **and you shall be satisfied.**
12 **Beware, lest you forget the Lord, who took you out of the land of Egypt, from the house of bondage.**
13 **You shall fear the Lord your God,** by treating Him with reverence, **and Him you shall serve, and** only afterward,[48] if you must take an oath,[49] **by His name you shall swear,** and thereby connect yourself to Him.

ח ט וקשרתם לאות על־ידך והיו לטטפת בין עיניך: וכתבתם על־מזזות ביתך
י ובשעריך: והיה כי־יביאך | יהוה אלהיך אל־הארץ אשר נשבע
לאבתיך לאברהם ליצחק וליעקב לתת לך ערים גדלת וטבת אשר לא־
יא בנית: ובתים מלאים כל־טוב אשר לא־מלאת וברת חצובים אשר לא־חצבת
יב כרמים וזיתים אשר לא־נטעת ואכלת ושבעת: השמר לך פן־תשכח את־
יג יהוה אשר הוציאך מארץ מצרים מבית עבדים: את־יהוה אלהיך תירא ואתו
יד תעבד ובשמו תשבע: לא תלכון אחרי אלהים אחרים מאלהי העמים אשר
טו סביבותיכם: כי אל קנא יהוה אלהיך בקרבך פן־יחרה אף־יהוה אלהיך בך

רש"י

ח | וקשרתם לאות על ידך. אלו תפלין שבזרוע: והיו לטטפת בין עיניך. אלו תפלין שבראש. ועל שם מנין פרשיותיהם נקראו טוטפת, 'טט' בכתפי שתים, 'פת' באפריקי שתים:

ט | מזוזת ביתך. 'מזוזת' כתיב, שאין צריך אלא אחת: ובשעריך. לרבות שערי חצרות ושערי מדינות ושערי עירות:

יא | חצובים. לפי שהיו מקום טרשין וסלעים נופל בו לשון חציבה:

יב | מבית עבדים. כתרגומו: "מבית עבדותא", ממקום שהייתם שם עבדים:

יג | ובשמו תשבע. אם יש בך כל המדות הללו, שאתה ירא את שמו ועובד אותו, אז "בשמו תשבע", שמתוך שאתה ירא את שמו תהא זהיר בשבועתך, ואם לאו לא תשבע:

יד | מאלהי העמים אשר סביבותיכם. הוא הדין לרחוקים, אלא לפי שאתה רואה את סביבותיך תועים אחריהם הצרך להזהיר עליהם ביותר:

14 **You shall not follow other gods** to worship them or to take an oath by them,[50] **from the gods of the peoples that are around you.**

15 **For the Lord your God is a zealous God in your midst.** God's love for you requires you to worship Him exclusively. He will not allow you to worship the gods of other nations; **lest the wrath of the Lord your God will be enflamed against you,**

Pit dug for water storage from the Nabatean period next to Khirbet Uza in the Judean Desert, aerial view

Vineyard in the Golan Heights

Grove of olive trees

and He will destroy you from upon the face of the earth.

16 When you encounter a challenge, and you require His assistance, **you shall not test the Lord your God.** Do not request your needs from Him as a test or an attempt for proof that God is present, **as you tested Him in Masa,** as your attempt there ended badly, resulting in Amalek's attack.[51]

17 **You shall observe the commandments of the Lord your God, and His testimonies, and His statutes that He commanded you.**

18 The Torah contains numerous commandments that address every aspect of life. Here, however, the Torah refers to a demand more general than merely fulfilling specific commandments. **You shall do the right and the good in the eyes of the Lord,** even if it is not stated explicitly in the Torah; **so that it will be good for you, and you will come and you will take possession of the good land with regard to which the Lord took an oath to your forefathers,**

19 **to cast all your enemies from before you, as the Lord spoke.** If the children of Israel conduct themselves as described in the previous verse, God will be good to them and protect them from their enemies.

20 **When your son asks you tomorrow,** when you are already settled in the Land of Israel, **saying: What are the testimonies,** the commandments that serve as symbols for other commandments and call attention to particular messages of the Torah, or those that serve to commemorate past events; **and the statutes,** laws whose reasons are unknown or unclear; **and the ordinances,** commandments with clear and understandable reasons,[52] **that the Lord our God commanded you?** What are the reasons for the numerous commandments in the Torah, and why is their fulfillment required specifically of us?

21 **You shall say to your son: We were slaves to Pharaoh in Egypt, and the Lord took us out of Egypt with a mighty hand.**

22 **The Lord provided signs and wonders, great and awful, against Egypt, against Pharaoh, and against his entire household, before our eyes.** We saw God strike the Egyptians and their king with our own eyes.

23 **He took us out of there,** not due to our righteousness, but rather **so that He would bring us, to give us the land with** regard to which He took an oath to our forefathers. His purpose was to fulfill His covenant that He had made with our forefathers.

24 **The Lord commanded us to perform all these statutes, to fear the Lord our God, for our good all the days,** in order **to keep us alive** continuously, just **as** we are alive on **this day.**

25 **Justice,** a just action,[53] or a reward,[54] or a privilege,[55] **will be had for us, if we take care to perform all of this commandment,** to be remembered **before the Lord our God, as He commanded us.**

7 1 When the Lord your God will bring you to the land into
Seventh which you are coming to take possession of it, and He
aliya will banish many nations from before you, specifically the following: **the Hitites, the Girgashites, the Emorites, the Canaanites, the Perizites, the Hivites, and the Yevusites, seven nations** that are all **greater and mightier than you.**

2 But nevertheless, **the Lord your God will deliver them before you, and you will smite them; you shall destroy them** entirely; **you shall not establish a covenant with them, and you shall not show them favor** by having mercy upon them.[56]

3 **You shall not marry them,**[57] in either of the following forms: **Your daughter you shall not give to his son, and his daughter you shall not take for your son;**

4 either form is forbidden **because he will divert your son from following Me, and they will serve other gods.** If someone from a foreign nation marries into the family, his beliefs and actions will certainly influence future generations. **And the wrath of the Lord will be enflamed against you, and He will destroy you quickly.**

5 Do not make a covenant with the inhabitants of the land, and do not establish ties of marriage with them. **Rather, so you shall do to them: Their altars you shall smash, and their monuments,** which are built out of one stone, **you shall shatter, and their sacred trees** that they worship **you shall cut down, and their idols you shall burn in fire.** You shall destroy all idols and everything connected to idol worship.

6 **For you are a holy people to the Lord your God; the Lord your God has chosen you to be His people of distinction,**

טז וְהִשְׁמִידְךָ מֵעַל פְּנֵי הָאֲדָמָה׃ לֹא תְנַסּוּ אֶת־יְהוָה אֱלֹהֵיכֶם כַּאֲשֶׁר
יז נִסִּיתֶם בַּמַּסָּה׃ שָׁמוֹר תִּשְׁמְרוּן אֶת־מִצְוֹת יְהוָה אֱלֹהֵיכֶם וְעֵדֹתָיו וְחֻקָּיו אֲשֶׁר
יח צִוָּךְ׃ וְעָשִׂיתָ הַיָּשָׁר וְהַטּוֹב בְּעֵינֵי יְהוָה לְמַעַן יִיטַב לָךְ וּבָאתָ וְיָרַשְׁתָּ אֶת־הָאָרֶץ
יט הַטֹּבָה אֲשֶׁר־נִשְׁבַּע יְהוָה לַאֲבֹתֶיךָ׃ לַהֲדֹף אֶת־כָּל־אֹיְבֶיךָ מִפָּנֶיךָ כַּאֲשֶׁר דִּבֶּר
כ יְהוָה׃ כִּי־יִשְׁאָלְךָ בִנְךָ מָחָר לֵאמֹר מָה הָעֵדֹת וְהַחֻקִּים וְהַמִּשְׁפָּטִים
כא אֲשֶׁר צִוָּה יְהוָה אֱלֹהֵינוּ אֶתְכֶם׃ וְאָמַרְתָּ לְבִנְךָ עֲבָדִים הָיִינוּ לְפַרְעֹה בְּמִצְרָיִם
כב וַיֹּצִיאֵנוּ יְהוָה מִמִּצְרַיִם בְּיָד חֲזָקָה׃ וַיִּתֵּן יְהוָה אוֹתֹת וּמֹפְתִים גְּדֹלִים וְרָעִים ׀
כג בְּמִצְרַיִם בְּפַרְעֹה וּבְכָל־בֵּיתוֹ לְעֵינֵינוּ׃ וְאוֹתָנוּ הוֹצִיא מִשָּׁם לְמַעַן הָבִיא אֹתָנוּ
כד לָתֶת לָנוּ אֶת־הָאָרֶץ אֲשֶׁר נִשְׁבַּע לַאֲבֹתֵינוּ׃ וַיְצַוֵּנוּ יְהוָה לַעֲשׂוֹת אֶת־כָּל־הַחֻקִּים
הָאֵלֶּה לְיִרְאָה אֶת־יְהוָה אֱלֹהֵינוּ לְטוֹב לָנוּ כָּל־הַיָּמִים לְחַיֹּתֵנוּ כְּהַיּוֹם הַזֶּה׃
כה וּצְדָקָה תִּהְיֶה־לָּנוּ כִּי־נִשְׁמֹר לַעֲשׂוֹת אֶת־כָּל־הַמִּצְוָה הַזֹּאת לִפְנֵי יְהוָה אֱלֹהֵינוּ
א כַּאֲשֶׁר צִוָּנוּ׃ כִּי יְבִיאֲךָ יְהוָה אֱלֹהֶיךָ אֶל־הָאָרֶץ אֲשֶׁר־אַתָּה בָא־שָׁמָּה שביעי
לְרִשְׁתָּהּ וְנָשַׁל גּוֹיִם־רַבִּים ׀ מִפָּנֶיךָ הַחִתִּי וְהַגִּרְגָּשִׁי וְהָאֱמֹרִי וְהַכְּנַעֲנִי וְהַפְּרִזִּי
ב וְהַחִוִּי וְהַיְבוּסִי שִׁבְעָה גוֹיִם רַבִּים וַעֲצוּמִים מִמֶּךָּ׃ וּנְתָנָם יְהוָה אֱלֹהֶיךָ לְפָנֶיךָ
ג וְהִכִּיתָם הַחֲרֵם תַּחֲרִים אֹתָם לֹא־תִכְרֹת לָהֶם בְּרִית וְלֹא תְחָנֵּם׃ וְלֹא תִתְחַתֵּן
ד בָּם בִּתְּךָ לֹא־תִתֵּן לִבְנוֹ וּבִתּוֹ לֹא־תִקַּח לִבְנֶךָ׃ כִּי־יָסִיר אֶת־בִּנְךָ מֵאַחֲרַי וְעָבְדוּ
ה אֱלֹהִים אֲחֵרִים וְחָרָה אַף־יְהוָה בָּכֶם וְהִשְׁמִידְךָ מַהֵר׃ כִּי־אִם־כֹּה תַעֲשׂוּ לָהֶם
מִזְבְּחֹתֵיהֶם תִּתֹּצוּ וּמַצֵּבֹתָם תְּשַׁבֵּרוּ וַאֲשֵׁירֵהֶם תְּגַדֵּעוּן וּפְסִילֵיהֶם תִּשְׂרְפוּן בָּאֵשׁ׃
ו כִּי עַם קָדוֹשׁ אַתָּה לַיהוָה אֱלֹהֶיךָ בְּךָ בָּחַר ׀ יְהוָה אֱלֹהֶיךָ לִהְיוֹת לוֹ לְעַם סְגֻלָּה

רש״י

טז| **במסה.** כשיצאו ממצרים שנסוהו במים, שנאמר: "היש ה' בקרבנו" (שמות יז, ז):

יח| **הישר והטוב.** זו פשרה לפנים משורת הדין:

יט| **כאשר דבר.** והיכן דבר? "והמתי את כל העם" וגו' (שמות כג, כז):

כ| **כי ישאלך בנך מחר.** יש מחר שהוא אחר זמן:

פרק ז

א| **ונשל.** לשון השלכה והתזה, וכן: "ונשל הברזל" (להלן יט, ה):

ב| **ולא תחנם.** לא תתן להם חן, אסור לו לאדם לומר: כמה נאה גוי זה. דבר אחר, לא תתן להם חניה בארץ:

ד| **כי יסיר את בנך מאחרי.** בנו של גוי כשישא את בתך, יסיר את בנך אשר תלד לו בתך מאחרי. למדנו שבן בתך הבא מן הגוי קרוי בנך, אבל בנך הבא מן הגויה אינו קרוי בנך, שהרי לא נאמר על בתו: לא תקח, כי תסיר את בנך מאחרי:

ה| **מזבחותיהם.** של בנין: **ומצבתם.** אבן אחת: **ואשירהם.** אילנות שעובדין אותן: **ופסיליהם.** צלמים:

ז| **לא מרבכם.** כפשוטו. ומדרשו, לפי שאין אתם

from all the peoples that are on the face of the earth. Therefore, you must separate yourselves entirely from the impurity of the gentile nations and their practices.
7 **It is not for your multitude,** because you are the biggest nation, **that the Lord desired you and chose you, as you are the fewest of all the peoples.**
8 **Rather, it is from the Lord's love of you, and from His observance of the oath that He took to your forefathers that the Lord took you out with a mighty hand, and He redeemed you from the house of bondage, from the hand of Pharaoh king of Egypt.**

9 **You shall know,** contemplate, and internalize, **that the Lord**
Maftir **your God, He is the God, the faithful God, who maintains the covenant and the kindness to those who love Him and those who observe His commandments, for** up to **one thousand generations.**
10 **And** on the other hand, **He repays His enemies to his face,** in their lifetime, **to destroy them.** With regard to His enemies, God punishes far more quickly. **He will not delay for His enemy, to his face He will repay him** his punishment.
11 **You shall observe the commandment, and the statutes, and the ordinances that I command you today, to perform them.**

Parashat
Ekev

Remembering God and His Commandments

DEUTERONOMY 7:12–9:7

This passage exhorts the nation of Israel not to forget God upon entering the Land of Israel. The danger exists that people will become discouraged when they see the powerful inhabitants of the land. Additionally, they might be negatively influenced by those nations, or they may forget their dependence upon God and their commitment to Him when they experience security and prosperity. Moses therefore warns the people not to forget what God performed for them in the wilderness, and he cites certain commandments that will assist them in remembering God and remaining loyal to Him.

12 **It shall be, because you heed these ordinances, and observe and perform them, the Lord your God will maintain for you the covenant and the kindness with regard to which He took an oath to your forefathers.**

ז מִכׇּל־הָעַמִּים אֲשֶׁר עַל־פְּנֵי הָאֲדָמָה: לֹא מֵרֻבְּכֶם מִכׇּל־הָעַמִּים חָשַׁק יְהֹוָה בָּכֶם
ח וַיִּבְחַר בָּכֶם כִּי־אַתֶּם הַמְעַט מִכׇּל־הָעַמִּים: כִּי מֵאַהֲבַת יְהֹוָה אֶתְכֶם וּמִשׇּׁמְרוֹ
אֶת־הַשְּׁבֻעָה אֲשֶׁר נִשְׁבַּע לַאֲבֹתֵיכֶם הוֹצִיא יְהֹוָה אֶתְכֶם בְּיָד חֲזָקָה וַיִּפְדְּךָ
ט מִבֵּית עֲבָדִים מִיַּד פַּרְעֹה מֶלֶךְ־מִצְרָיִם: וְיָדַעְתָּ כִּי־יְהֹוָה אֱלֹהֶיךָ הוּא הָאֱלֹהִים מפטיר
י הָאֵל הַנֶּאֱמָן שֹׁמֵר הַבְּרִית וְהַחֶסֶד לְאֹהֲבָיו וּלְשֹׁמְרֵי מִצְוֺתָו לְאֶלֶף דּוֹר: וּמְשַׁלֵּם
יא לְשֹׂנְאָיו אֶל־פָּנָיו לְהַאֲבִידוֹ לֹא יְאַחֵר לְשֹׂנְאוֹ אֶל־פָּנָיו יְשַׁלֶּם־לוֹ: וְשָׁמַרְתָּ אֶת־
הַמִּצְוָה וְאֶת־הַחֻקִּים וְאֶת־הַמִּשְׁפָּטִים אֲשֶׁר אָנֹכִי מְצַוְּךָ הַיּוֹם לַעֲשׂוֹתָם:

רש"י

מַגְדִּילִים עַצְמְכֶם כְּשֶׁאֲנִי מַשְׁפִּיעַ לָכֶם טוֹבָה, לְפִיכָךְ חָשַׁק בָּכֶם: כִּי אַתֶּם הַמְעַט. הַמְמַעֲטִים עַצְמְכֶם, כְּמוֹ: "וְאָנֹכִי עָפָר וָאֵפֶר" (בראשית יח, כז), "וְנַחְנוּ מָה" (שמות טז, ז); לֹא כִּנְבוּכַדְנֶצַּר שֶׁאָמַר: "אֲדַמֶּה לְעֶלְיוֹן" (ישעיה יד, יד), וְסַנְחֵרִיב שֶׁאָמַר: "מִי בְּכָל אֱלֹהֵי הָאֲרָצוֹת" (שם לו, כ), וְחִירָם שֶׁאָמַר: "אֵל אָנִי מוֹשַׁב אֱלֹהִים יָשַׁבְתִּי" (יחזקאל כח, ב): כִּי אַתֶּם הַמְעַט. הֲרֵי "כִּי" מְשַׁמֵּשׁ בִּלְשׁוֹן "דְּהָא":

ח| כִּי מֵאַהֲבַת ה'. הֲרֵי 'כִּי' מְשַׁמֵּשׁ בִּלְשׁוֹן 'אֶלָּא', לֹא מֵרֻבְּכֶם חָשַׁק ה' בָּכֶם אֶלָּא מֵאַהֲבַת ה' אֶתְכֶם: וּמִשׇּׁמְרוֹ אֶת הַשְּׁבֻעָה. מֵחֲמַת שֶׁשָּׁמְרוֹ אֶת הַשְּׁבוּעָה:

ט| לְאֶלֶף דּוֹר. וּלְהַלָּן הוּא אוֹמֵר: "לַאֲלָפִים" (לעיל ה, י), כָּאן שֶׁהוּא סָמוּךְ אֵצֶל "לְשֹׁמְרֵי מִצְוֺתָיו" הוּא אוֹמֵר "לְאֶלֶף", וּלְהַלָּן שֶׁהוּא סָמוּךְ אֵצֶל "לְאֹהֲבַי" הוּא אוֹמֵר "לַאֲלָפִים": לְאֹהֲבָיו. אֵלּוּ הָעוֹשִׂין מֵאַהֲבָה: וּלְשֹׁמְרֵי מִצְוֺתָיו. אֵלּוּ הָעוֹשִׂין מִיִּרְאָה:

י| וּמְשַׁלֵּם לְשֹׂנְאָיו אֶל פָּנָיו. בְּחַיָּיו מְשַׁלֵּם לוֹ גְּמוּלוֹ הַטּוֹב, כְּדֵי לְהַאֲבִידוֹ מִן הָעוֹלָם הַבָּא:

יא| הַיּוֹם לַעֲשׂוֹתָם. וּלְמָחָר, לָעוֹלָם הַבָּא, לִטֹּל שְׂכָרָם:

פרשת

עקב

יב וְהָיָה עֵקֶב תִּשְׁמְעוּן אֵת הַמִּשְׁפָּטִים הָאֵלֶּה וּשְׁמַרְתֶּם וַעֲשִׂיתֶם אֹתָם ז
וְשָׁמַר יְהֹוָה אֱלֹהֶיךָ לְךָ אֶת־הַבְּרִית וְאֶת־הַחֶסֶד אֲשֶׁר נִשְׁבַּע לַאֲבֹתֶיךָ:

רש"י

יב| וְהָיָה עֵקֶב תִּשְׁמְעוּן. אִם הַמִּצְוֹת הַקַּלּוֹת שֶׁאָדָם דָּשׁ בַּעֲקֵבָיו תִּשְׁמְעוּן: וְשָׁמַר ה' וְגוֹ'. יִשְׁמֹר לְךָ הַבְטָחָתוֹ:

13 **He will love you, bless you, and multiply you; He will bless the fruit of your womb and the fruit of your land, your grain, your wine, and your oil, the calves of your herds and the lambs of your flock,**[D] **in the land with regard to which He took an oath to your forefathers to give to you.**

14 **You shall be blessed more than all peoples:** First and foremost, **there shall not be an infertile male or a barren female among you, or among your animals.**

15 **The Lord will remove from you all illness and all of the evil maladies of Egypt that you knew,** which you saw in Egypt, **he will not place them among you; rather, he will give them to your enemies.**

16 **You shall consume all the peoples that the Lord your God shall deliver to you; your eye shall not pity them; and,** Moses emphasizes once again, **you shall not serve their gods, for it is a snare for you.**

17 **If you shall say in your heart: These nations are more numerous than I; how can I dispossess** all of **them?**

18 **You shall not fear them; remember that which the Lord your God did to Pharaoh, and to all of Egypt.**

19 **The great tests,**[1] or miracles,[2] or events **that your eyes saw, and the signs, and the wonders, and the mighty hand, and the outstretched arm, with which the Lord your God took you out; so will the Lord your God do,** employing signs and wonders and delivering retribution **to all the peoples from whom you fear.**

20 In addition to your victories in war, God will assist you in other ways as well: **The hornets [*tzira*]**[B] **too, the Lord your God will dispatch among them** to chase them out of their hiding places.[3] Alternatively, *tzira* is a type of illness, similar to the term for leprosy [*tzara'at*], which your enemies will contract,[4] **until the annihilation of those remaining and those hiding from before you.**

21 **Do not be broken before them**[5] or fear them; **as the Lord your God is in your midst, the great and awesome God.** It is appropriate to fear only God, not your enemies.

22 **The Lord your God will banish those nations from before you little by little, you will be unable to eliminate them quickly,** as that outcome would not benefit you,[6] **lest the beasts of the field increase against you.** If these nations were destroyed all at once, the emptied expanses of the land would become inhabited by wild beasts.

"Calves of your herds"

"Lambs of your flock"

Oriental hornet, *Vespa orientalis*

DISCUSSION

7:13 | **And the lambs of your flock:** It is possible that the term employed here for lambs, *ashterot*, is related to wealth [*osher*], as in the growth of one's flock is an indication of material success (see Rashi; *Ḥullin* 84b).

יג וְאֲהֵבְךָ וּבֵרַכְךָ וְהִרְבֶּךָ וּבֵרַךְ פְּרִי־בִטְנְךָ וּפְרִי־אַדְמָתֶךָ דְּגָנְךָ וְתִירֹשְׁךָ וְיִצְהָרֶךָ
יד שְׁגַר־אֲלָפֶיךָ וְעַשְׁתְּרֹת צֹאנֶךָ עַל הָאֲדָמָה אֲשֶׁר־נִשְׁבַּע לַאֲבֹתֶיךָ לָתֶת לָךְ׃ בָּרוּךְ
תִּהְיֶה מִכָּל־הָעַמִּים לֹא־יִהְיֶה בְךָ עָקָר וַעֲקָרָה וּבִבְהֶמְתֶּךָ׃ וְהֵסִיר יְהוָה מִמְּךָ כָּל־ טו
חֹלִי וְכָל־מַדְוֵי מִצְרַיִם הָרָעִים אֲשֶׁר יָדַעְתָּ לֹא יְשִׂימָם בָּךְ וּנְתָנָם בְּכָל־שֹׂנְאֶיךָ׃
טז וְאָכַלְתָּ אֶת־כָּל־הָעַמִּים אֲשֶׁר יְהוָה אֱלֹהֶיךָ נֹתֵן לָךְ לֹא־תָחוֹס עֵינְךָ עֲלֵיהֶם
יז וְלֹא תַעֲבֹד אֶת־אֱלֹהֵיהֶם כִּי־מוֹקֵשׁ הוּא לָךְ׃ כִּי תֹאמַר בִּלְבָבְךָ
יח רַבִּים הַגּוֹיִם הָאֵלֶּה מִמֶּנִּי אֵיכָה אוּכַל לְהוֹרִישָׁם׃ לֹא תִירָא מֵהֶם זָכֹר תִּזְכֹּר אֵת
יט אֲשֶׁר־עָשָׂה יְהוָה אֱלֹהֶיךָ לְפַרְעֹה וּלְכָל־מִצְרָיִם׃ הַמַּסֹּת הַגְּדֹלֹת אֲשֶׁר־רָאוּ עֵינֶיךָ
וְהָאֹתֹת וְהַמֹּפְתִים וְהַיָּד הַחֲזָקָה וְהַזְּרֹעַ הַנְּטוּיָה אֲשֶׁר הוֹצִאֲךָ יְהוָה אֱלֹהֶיךָ כֵּן
כ יַעֲשֶׂה יְהוָה אֱלֹהֶיךָ לְכָל־הָעַמִּים אֲשֶׁר־אַתָּה יָרֵא מִפְּנֵיהֶם׃ וְגַם אֶת־הַצִּרְעָה
כא יְשַׁלַּח יְהוָה אֱלֹהֶיךָ בָּם עַד־אֲבֹד הַנִּשְׁאָרִים וְהַנִּסְתָּרִים מִפָּנֶיךָ׃ לֹא תַעֲרֹץ
כב מִפְּנֵיהֶם כִּי־יְהוָה אֱלֹהֶיךָ בְּקִרְבֶּךָ אֵל גָּדוֹל וְנוֹרָא׃ וְנָשַׁל יְהוָה אֱלֹהֶיךָ אֶת־הַגּוֹיִם
הָאֵל מִפָּנֶיךָ מְעַט מְעָט לֹא תוּכַל כַּלֹּתָם מַהֵר פֶּן־תִּרְבֶּה עָלֶיךָ חַיַּת הַשָּׂדֶה׃

רש״י

יג| שְׁגַר אֲלָפֶיךָ. וַלְדֵי בְקָרְךָ שֶׁהַנְּקֵבָה מְשַׁגֶּרֶת מִמֵּעֶיהָ: וְעַשְׁתְּרֹת צֹאנֶךָ. מְנַחֵם פֵּרַשׁ: ״אַבִּירֵי בָשָׁן״ (תהלים כב, יג) מִבְחַר הַצֹּאן, כְּמוֹ: ׳עַשְׁתְּרֹת קַרְנַיִם׳, לְשׁוֹן חֹזֶק, וְאוּנְקְלוֹס תִּרְגֵּם: ״וְעֶדְרֵי עָנָךְ״, וְרַבּוֹתֵינוּ אָמְרוּ: לָמָּה נִקְרָא שְׁמָם ׳עַשְׁתָּרוֹת׳? שֶׁמְּעַשְּׁרוֹת אֶת בַּעֲלֵיהֶן:

יד| עָקָר. שֶׁאֵינוֹ מוֹלִיד:

יז-יח| כִּי תֹאמַר בִּלְבָבְךָ. עַל כָּרְחֲךָ לְשׁוֹן ׳דִּלְמָא׳ הוּא, שֶׁמָּא תֹּאמַר בִּלְבָבְךָ מִפְּנֵי שֶׁהֵם רַבִּים לֹא אוּכַל לְהוֹרִישָׁם, אַל תֹּאמַר כֵּן, ״לֹא תִירָא מֵהֶם״! וְלֹא יִתָּכֵן לְפָרְשׁוֹ בְּאֶחָד מֵאַרְבַּע לְשׁוֹנוֹת שֶׁל ׳כִּי׳ שֶׁיִּפֹּל עָלָיו סוֹף ״לֹא תִירָא מֵהֶם״:

יט| הַמַּסֹּת. נִסְיוֹנוֹת: וְהָאֹתֹת. כְּגוֹן: ״וַיְהִי לְנָחָשׁ״ (שמות ד, ג), ״וְהָיוּ לְדָם בַּיַּבָּשֶׁת״ (שם ט): וְהַמֹּפְתִים. הַמַּכּוֹת הַמֻּפְלָאוֹת: וְהַיָּד הַחֲזָקָה. זֶה הַדֶּבֶר: וְהַזְּרֹעַ הַנְּטוּיָה. זוֹ הַחֶרֶב שֶׁל מַכַּת בְּכוֹרוֹת:

כ| הַצִּרְעָה. מִין שֶׁרֶץ הָעוֹף, שֶׁהָיְתָה זוֹרֶקֶת בָּהֶם מָרָה וּמְסָרַסְתָּן וּמְסַמְּאָה אֶת עֵינֵיהֶם בְּכָל מָקוֹם שֶׁהָיוּ נִסְתָּרִים שָׁם:

כב| פֶּן תִּרְבֶּה עָלֶיךָ חַיַּת הַשָּׂדֶה. וַהֲלֹא אִם עוֹשִׂין רְצוֹנוֹ שֶׁל מָקוֹם אֵין מִתְיָרְאִין מִן הַחַיָּה, שֶׁנֶּאֱמַר: ״וְחַיַּת הַשָּׂדֶה הָשְׁלְמָה לָךְ״ (איוב ה, כג)? אֶלָּא גָּלוּי הָיָה לְפָנָיו שֶׁעֲתִידִין לַחֲטֹא:

BACKGROUND

7:20| **The hornets** [*tzira*]: The oriental hornet, *Vespa orientalis*, is an insect 20–22 mm in length, with a painful sting.

23 **The Lord your God will deliver them before you, and He will confound them a great confusion, until their destruction.**

24 **He shall deliver their kings into your hand, and** for your part, **you will eradicate their name from under the heavens.** You must not allow the names of idol worshippers to be memorialized, all the more so the names of their idols. **No man will stand before you, until you have destroyed them.**

25 **The idols of their gods you shall burn in fire; you shall not covet** even the **silver or gold that is on them and take it for you,** despite the temptation to keep those valuable items for oneself, **lest you be ensnared by it,** and it will cause you to sin, **as it is an abomination to the Lord your God.**

26 **You shall not bring an abomination** or items related to it **into your house, or** else **you will be proscribed** and abominated like it; rather, **you shall detest it, and you shall abhor it, as it is proscribed,** and you may have no contact with it.

8 1 **All the commandment that I command you this day,** both the commandments already mentioned and those to be stated below, **you shall take care to perform, so that you will live,** as you have already seen that those who abandoned their connection with God were destroyed (4:3). **And** beyond your survival, a life of commandments will bring you: You will **multiply and come and take possession of the land with regard to which the Lord took an oath to your forefathers.**

2 Apart from the practical obedience to God's commandments, it is important for Israel to maintain its collective national memory, which encompasses the period of the wanderings in the wilderness that it is about to conclude. **You shall remember the entire way that the Lord your God led you these forty years in the wilderness,** and He did so **to afflict you,** so that you would become accustomed to nomadic conditions and exile,[7] and also in order **to test you,**[D] **to know** and reveal[8] **what is in your heart: Will you keep His commandments or not.**

3 **He afflicted you, and starved you, and** then He **fed you the manna,** which is a food **that you did not know, and your fathers did not know; in order to impart to you that man does not live by bread alone; rather, it is by everything that emanates from the mouth of the Lord**[D] **that man lives.**

4 **Your garment did not grow worn from upon you, and your foot did not swell, these forty years.** Despite the extensive travels and walking, all your needs were provided for by God.

5 When you consider the matter, **you shall know in your heart that** just **as a man chastises his son** due to his concern and love, **so the Lord your God chastises you.** The child understands that his father punishes him because he cares about him and is acting in his best interests. Furthermore, he realizes that even if his father chastens him, he will not stop providing for his needs. Similarly, you saw that even when you were being punished, the manna did not cease for even a single day.

6 **You shall observe the commandments of the Lord your God, to walk in His ways, and to fear Him.** Your relationship with God is not based on love and acceptance alone; it includes a commitment to law and justice, based on the fear of God.

7 **For the Lord your God is bringing you to a good land, a land of streams of water, of springs and depths, coming out in the valley and on the highlands.** These plentiful sources

Natural spring in Wadi Sa'ar, Golan Heights

DISCUSSION

8:2 | **To afflict you, to test you:** During their forty years in the wilderness, Israel established itself as a people that observes God's commandments. The nation's suffering did not end when it left the iron crucible of Egyptian slavery (4:20). The long journeys in the desert were also full of ordeals, and their time there also served as a crucible that forged the people's character. Their experiences in the wilderness were designed to test whether the people would remain faithful to God and His commandments even when they had no material concerns, as He tended to all their needs in the wilderness.

8:3 | **It is by everything that emanates from the mouth of the Lord:** Your experiences in the wilderness have taught you that it is possible to survive without consuming bread that emerged from the ground. One who reflects further on the matter will realize that even supposedly natural bread, prepared from grain, exists only through the creative statements of God.

כג כד ונתנם יהוה אלהיך לפניך והמם מהומה גדלה עד השמדם: ונתן מלכיהם
בידך והאבדת את־שמם מתחת השמים לא־יתיצב איש בפניך עד השמדך
כה אתם: פסילי אלהיהם תשרפון באש לא־תחמד כסף וזהב עליהם ולקחת לך
כו פן תוקש בו כי תועבת יהוה אלהיך הוא: ולא־תביא תועבה אל־ביתך והיית
חרם כמהו שקץ | תשקצנו ותעב | תתעבנו כי־חרם הוא:
ח א כל־המצוה אשר אנכי מצוך היום תשמרון לעשות למען תחיון ורביתם
ב ובאתם וירשתם את־הארץ אשר־נשבע יהוה לאבתיכם: וזכרת את־כל־
הדרך אשר הוליכך יהוה אלהיך זה ארבעים שנה במדבר למען ענתך
ג לנסתך לדעת את־אשר בלבבך התשמר מצותו אם־לא: ויענך וירעבך
ויאכלך את־המן אשר לא־ידעת ולא ידעון אבתיך למען הודיעך כי לא
על־הלחם לבדו יחיה האדם כי על־כל־מוצא פי־יהוה יחיה האדם:
ד ה שמלתך לא בלתה מעליך ורגלך לא בצקה זה ארבעים שנה: וידעת
ו עם־לבבך כי כאשר ייסר איש את־בנו יהוה אלהיך מיסרך: ושמרת את־
ז מצות יהוה אלהיך ללכת בדרכיו וליראה אתו: כי יהוה אלהיך מביאך
אל־ארץ טובה ארץ נחלי מים עינת ותהמת יצאים בבקעה ובהר:

רש"י

כג] והמם. נקוד קמץ כלו, לפי שאין מ"ם אחרונה מן היסוד, והרי הוא כמו: והם אותם, אבל "והמם גלגל עגלתו" (ישעיה כח, כח) כלו יסוד, לפיכך חציו קמץ וחציו פתח, כשאר פעל של שלש אותיות:

פרק ח

א] כל המצוה. כפשוטו. ומדרש אגדה, אם התחלת במצוה, גמור אותה, שאינה נקראת אלא על שם הגומרה, שנאמר: "ואת עצמות יוסף אשר העלו בני ישראל ממצרים קברו בשכם" (יהושע כד, לב), והלא משה לבדו נתעסק בהם להעלותם (שמות יג, יט)? אלא לפי שלא הספיק לגמרה וגמרוה ישראל, נקראת על שמם:

ב] התשמר מצותו. שלא תנסהו ולא תהרהר אחריו:

ד] שמלתך לא בלתה. ענני כבוד היו שפים בכסותם ומגהצים אותם כמין כלים מגהצים, ואף קטניהם כמו שהיו גדלים, היה גדל לבושן עמהם, כלבוש הזה של חמט שגדל עמו: לא בצקה. לא נפחה כבצק, כדרך הולכי יחף שרגליהם נפוחות:

of water in the Promised Land contrast starkly not only with the parched desert but also with the land of Egypt. Although water is plentiful in Egypt, virtually all of it comes from a single source, the Nile, whereas in the land of Canaan there are streams and small rivers, as well as a great number of springs.

8 **A land** praised for the types of food that grow there. It is a land **of wheat and barley, grapevines, figs, pomegranates; a land of oil olives,** olives from which oil is produced, **and** date **honey;**⁹

9 **a land in which you shall eat bread without poverty,** as it gives forth bountiful produce. **You shall not lack anything in it; a land whose stones are iron, and from whose hills you will excavate copper.** The land also contains deposits of various types of metals.

10 **You will eat and be satisfied, and you shall bless**ᴰ **the Lord your God for the good land that He gave you.**

Second aliya

11 **Beware, lest you forget the Lord your God, to not observe His commandments, and His ordinances, and His statutes that I am commanding you today.**

12 **Lest you eat and be satisfied** with the economic success that you have been promised, **and you will build good houses, and settle** in them. You are currently nomads who live in huts, at best, but you will soon be able to build houses and your lives will become increasingly comfortable.

13 **And your cattle and your flocks increase; and silver and gold increase for you; and everything that is yours increases,** following your settlement of the land;

14 **and your heart will grow haughty, and you will forget the Lord your God, who took you out of the land of Egypt, from the house of bondage.** It is natural that once you become accustomed to the easy life in Canaan, you will come to take it for granted, and you will forget that it is incumbent upon you to be grateful to God.

15 **Who guides you in the great and awesome wilderness,** a place inhabited by the **snake** known as the **fiery serpent,** whose venom burns like fire, **and scorpion, and thirst where there is no water; who took water for you** even **from the rock of flint,** which is a hard rock.¹⁰ You must constantly

Seven species:

Wheat

Barley

Grapes

Figs

Pomegranate

Olives

Dates, a source of honey

Scorpion

Fiery serpent, Ein Gedi

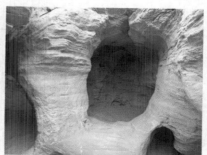
Copper mine, Timna

אֶרֶץ חִטָּה וּשְׂעֹרָה וְגֶפֶן וּתְאֵנָה וְרִמּוֹן אֶרֶץ־זֵית שֶׁמֶן וּדְבָשׁ: אֶרֶץ אֲשֶׁר לֹא

בְמִסְכֵּנֻת תֹּאכַל־בָּהּ לֶחֶם לֹא־תֶחְסַר כֹּל בָּהּ אֶרֶץ אֲשֶׁר אֲבָנֶיהָ בַרְזֶל וּמֵהֲרָרֶיהָ

תַּחְצֹב נְחֹשֶׁת: וְאָכַלְתָּ וְשָׂבָעְתָּ וּבֵרַכְתָּ אֶת־יְהֹוָה אֱלֹהֶיךָ עַל־הָאָרֶץ הַטֹּבָה

אֲשֶׁר נָתַן־לָךְ: הִשָּׁמֶר לְךָ פֶּן־תִּשְׁכַּח אֶת־יְהֹוָה אֱלֹהֶיךָ לְבִלְתִּי שְׁמֹר מִצְוֺתָיו

וּמִשְׁפָּטָיו וְחֻקֹּתָיו אֲשֶׁר אָנֹכִי מְצַוְּךָ הַיּוֹם: פֶּן־תֹּאכַל וְשָׂבָעְתָּ וּבָתִּים טֹבִים

תִּבְנֶה וְיָשָׁבְתָּ: וּבְקָרְךָ וְצֹאנְךָ יִרְבְּיֻן וְכֶסֶף וְזָהָב יִרְבֶּה־לָּךְ וְכֹל אֲשֶׁר־לְךָ יִרְבֶּה:

וְרָם לְבָבֶךָ וְשָׁכַחְתָּ אֶת־יְהֹוָה אֱלֹהֶיךָ הַמּוֹצִיאֲךָ מֵאֶרֶץ מִצְרַיִם מִבֵּית עֲבָדִים:

הַמּוֹלִיכֲךָ בַּמִּדְבָּר הַגָּדֹל וְהַנּוֹרָא נָחָשׁ שָׂרָף וְעַקְרָב וְצִמָּאוֹן אֲשֶׁר אֵין־מָיִם

הַמּוֹצִיא לְךָ מַיִם מִצּוּר הַחַלָּמִישׁ: הַמַּאֲכִלְךָ מָן בַּמִּדְבָּר אֲשֶׁר לֹא־יָדְעוּן אֲבֹתֶיךָ

לְמַעַן עַנֹּתְךָ וּלְמַעַן נַסֹּתֶךָ לְהֵיטִבְךָ בְּאַחֲרִיתֶךָ: וְאָמַרְתָּ בִּלְבָבֶךָ כֹּחִי וְעֹצֶם יָדִי

עָשָׂה לִי אֶת־הַחַיִל הַזֶּה: וְזָכַרְתָּ אֶת־יְהֹוָה אֱלֹהֶיךָ כִּי הוּא הַנֹּתֵן לְךָ כֹּחַ לַעֲשׂוֹת

חָיִל לְמַעַן הָקִים אֶת־בְּרִיתוֹ אֲשֶׁר־נִשְׁבַּע לַאֲבֹתֶיךָ כַּיּוֹם הַזֶּה:

רַשִׁ״י

ח | זֵית שֶׁמֶן. זֵיתִים הָעוֹשִׂים שֶׁמֶן:

---

remind yourselves and your children of the goodness that God bestowed upon you;

16 **who feeds you manna in the wilderness, which your fathers did not know, in order to afflict you, and in order to test you, to do good for you in your future,** so that you will learn through this dependency about the true source of all blessings. The affliction mentioned here was caused by the unusual nature of the manna. Although it provided sustenance, it was always food of the same type and it could not be preserved for the next day to enable a sense of security. Furthermore, consumption of the manna did not create a true sense of satiation.[11]

17 **And you will say in your heart: My power and the might of my hand made me these riches.**[12]

18 **You shall remember the Lord your God, as it is He who gives you power to generate riches, in order to fulfill His covenant with regard to which He took an oath to your fore-fathers, as** you can remember **this day.**[13]

DISCUSSION

8:10 | You will eat and be satisfied, and you shall bless: This verse is the source for the obligation to recite Grace after Meals, a blessing attributed to the earliest generations of the nation of Israel, if not literally in its current formulation, then at least in its basic structure (see *Berakhot* 21a, 48b). Grace after Meals includes general thanks for the food one has eaten, as well as special gratitude for the land, whose formula includes the citation of this verse.

19 **It shall be if you shall forget the Lord**[D] **your God, and you shall follow other gods, and serve them, and prostrate yourself before them, I am warning you today that you shall be annihilated** from the land.

20 **Like the nations that the Lord annihilates from before you, so you will be annihilated, because you would not heed the voice of the Lord your God.**

9 1 Although the question of whether Israel will remain in their land or suffer exile is contingent on their actions; here Moses underscores that their entrance into Canaan is not due to the merit of their deeds or their righteousness. **Hear, Israel: You are crossing the Jordan today,** in the near future, **to come to take possession from nations greater and mightier than you, cities great and** very strong, **fortified to the heavens;** this description is hyperbole.[14]

2 In these cities dwells **a people great and tall, sons of giants,** about **whom you knew and you heard** from afar: **Who can stand before the sons of giants?** Who can defeat them?

3 Nevertheless, **you shall know today that the Lord your God is He who passes before you, a devouring fire; He will destroy them, and He will subdue them before you, and you will dispossess them and eradicate them quickly, as the Lord spoke to you.** Despite the difficult challenges ahead, you will emerge victorious, with God's help.

4 However, I am warning you: **Do not say in your heart, upon the Lord your God casting them from before you, saying: Due to my righteousness, the Lord has brought me to take possession of this land; and** in fact it is **due to the wickedness of these nations** that **the Lord dispossesses them from before you.** The cause of the banishment of those nations is due more to their culpability than to your own good deeds.[15]

Third aliya

5 **It is not due to your righteousness, or due to the uprightness of your heart, that you are coming to take possession of their land; rather, it is due to the wickedness of these nations that the Lord your God dispossesses them from before you.** These nations will be driven from the land because of their wickedness, **and** additionally, this will be performed **in order to keep the word with regard to which the Lord took an oath to your forefathers, to Abraham, to Isaac, and to Jacob.**

6 **You should know that it is not due to your righteousness that the Lord your God is giving you this good land to take possession of it, as you are a stiff-necked,** stubborn **people.**

7 Moses reiterates: **Remember; do not forget that you infuriated the Lord your God in the wilderness. From the day that you emerged from the land of Egypt until your arrival at this place, you have been defiant against the Lord.**

The Breaking of the First Tablets of the Covenant and Its Aftermath

DEUTERONOMY 9:8–10:11

As an example of Israel's defiance against God, mentioned at the conclusion of the previous section, Moses reminds the Israelites of their sin of the Golden Calf. In addition, Moses recounts God's mercy, manifest in His acceptance of Moses' prayers and His giving of the second tablets. Apropos this episode, Moses also mentions the change in the status of the Levites following the sin of the Golden Calf, a change that will have further ramifications when the nation enters the land.

Moses relates the story of the Golden Calf intermittently. In the context of his memories and impressions of the sin and God's reaction to it, Moses relates in passing other transgressions that the Israelites committed in the wilderness. Two verses deal with Aaron's recent death, in the fortieth year since the Israelites' exodus from Egypt, and the journeys that preceded and followed that event.

8 **At Horev,** Mount Sinai, **you provoked the Lord, and the Lord was incensed with you to destroy you**

9 **when I had ascended to the mountaintop to take the tablets of stone, the Tablets of the Covenant that the Lord made with you; I remained on the mountain forty days and forty nights;** and throughout that entire period, **bread I did not eat and water I did not drink,** as I was in a different state of existence.

10 **The Lord gave me the two tablets of stone** that were **inscribed with the finger of God and on them corresponding to all the words that the Lord spoke with you on the mountain from the midst of the fire on the day of the assembly,** when the Torah was given. That day is referred to as the day of the assembly in other places as well (see 10:4; 18:16). In later generations this was called the day of the great event.[16]

DISCUSSION

8:19| **If you shall forget the Lord:** Unlike other nations, who are not required to remember God and think of Him continuously, Israel is obligated not only to observe God's commandments but also to have Him in mind at all times.

יט וְהָיָ֣ה אִם־שָׁכֹ֤חַ תִּשְׁכַּח֙ אֶת־יְהוָ֣ה אֱלֹהֶ֔יךָ וְהָֽלַכְתָּ֗ אַחֲרֵי֙ אֱלֹהִ֣ים אֲחֵרִ֔ים וַעֲבַדְתָּ֖ם

כ וְהִֽשְׁתַּחֲוִ֣יתָ לָהֶ֑ם הַעִדֹ֨תִי בָכֶ֤ם הַיּוֹם֙ כִּ֣י אָבֹ֣ד תֹּאבֵד֔וּן כַּגּוֹיִ֗ם אֲשֶׁ֤ר יְהוָה֙ מַאֲבִ֣יד מִפְּנֵיכֶ֔ם כֵּ֣ן תֹּאבֵד֑וּן עֵ֕קֶב לֹ֣א תִשְׁמְע֔וּן בְּק֖וֹל יְהוָ֥ה אֱלֹהֵיכֶֽם:

ח א שְׁמַ֣ע יִשְׂרָאֵ֗ל אַתָּ֨ה עֹבֵ֤ר הַיּוֹם֙ אֶת־הַיַּרְדֵּ֔ן לָבֹא֙ לָרֶ֣שֶׁת גּוֹיִ֔ם גְּדֹלִ֥ים וַעֲצֻמִ֖ים

ב מִמֶּ֑ךָּ עָרִ֛ים גְּדֹלֹ֥ת וּבְצֻרֹ֖ת בַּשָּׁמָֽיִם: עַם־גָּד֥וֹל וָרָ֖ם בְּנֵ֣י עֲנָקִ֑ים אֲשֶׁ֨ר אַתָּ֤ה יָדַ֙עְתָּ֙

ג וְאַתָּ֣ה שָׁמַ֔עְתָּ מִ֣י יִתְיַצֵּ֔ב לִפְנֵ֖י בְּנֵ֣י עֲנָֽק: וְיָדַעְתָּ֣ הַיּ֗וֹם כִּ֣י יְהוָ֣ה אֱלֹהֶ֗יךָ הֽוּא־הָעֹבֵ֤ר לְפָנֶ֙יךָ֙ אֵ֣שׁ אֹֽכְלָ֔ה ה֧וּא יַשְׁמִידֵ֛ם וְה֥וּא יַכְנִיעֵ֖ם לְפָנֶ֑יךָ וְהֽוֹרַשְׁתָּ֤ם וְהַֽאֲבַדְתָּ֣ם

שלישי ד מַהֵ֔ר כַּאֲשֶׁ֛ר דִּבֶּ֥ר יְהוָ֖ה לָֽךְ: אַל־תֹּאמַ֣ר בִּלְבָבְךָ֗ בַּהֲדֹ֣ף יְהוָ֣ה אֱלֹהֶ֩יךָ֩ אֹתָ֨ם מִלְּפָנֶ֜יךָ לֵאמֹ֗ר בְּצִדְקָתִי֙ הֱבִיאַ֣נִי יְהוָ֔ה לָרֶ֖שֶׁת אֶת־הָאָ֣רֶץ הַזֹּ֑את וּבְרִשְׁעַת֙ הַגּוֹיִ֣ם

ה הָאֵ֔לֶּה יְהוָ֖ה מוֹרִישָׁ֥ם מִפָּנֶֽיךָ: לֹ֣א בְצִדְקָתְךָ֗ וּבְיֹ֙שֶׁר֙ לְבָ֣בְךָ֔ אַתָּ֥ה בָ֖א לָרֶ֣שֶׁת אֶת־אַרְצָ֑ם כִּ֣י בְּרִשְׁעַ֣ת ׀ הַגּוֹיִ֣ם הָאֵ֗לֶּה יְהוָ֤ה אֱלֹהֶ֙יךָ֙ מוֹרִישָׁ֣ם מִפָּנֶ֔יךָ וּלְמַ֜עַן הָקִ֣ים אֶת־הַדָּבָ֗ר אֲשֶׁ֨ר נִשְׁבַּ֤ע יְהוָה֙ לַאֲבֹתֶ֔יךָ לְאַבְרָהָ֥ם לְיִצְחָ֖ק וּֽלְיַעֲקֹֽב: וְיָדַעְתָּ֗

ו כִּ֣י לֹ֣א בְצִדְקָתְךָ֗ יְהוָ֤ה אֱלֹהֶ֙יךָ֙ נֹתֵ֣ן לְךָ֔ אֶת־הָאָ֧רֶץ הַטּוֹבָ֛ה הַזֹּ֖את לְרִשְׁתָּ֑הּ כִּ֥י

ז עַם־קְשֵׁה־עֹ֖רֶף אָֽתָּה: זְכֹר֙ אַל־תִּשְׁכַּ֔ח אֵ֧ת אֲשֶׁר־הִקְצַ֛פְתָּ אֶת־יְהוָ֥ה אֱלֹהֶ֖יךָ בַּמִּדְבָּ֑ר לְמִן־הַיּ֨וֹם אֲשֶׁר־יָצָ֣אתָ ׀ מֵאֶ֣רֶץ מִצְרַ֗יִם עַד־בֹּֽאֲכֶם֙ עַד־הַמָּק֣וֹם הַזֶּ֔ה

ח מַמְרִ֥ים הֱיִיתֶ֖ם עִם־יְהוָֽה: וּבְחֹרֵ֥ב הִקְצַפְתֶּ֖ם אֶת־יְהוָ֑ה וַיִּתְאַנַּ֧ף יְהוָ֛ה בָּכֶ֖ם

ט לְהַשְׁמִ֥יד אֶתְכֶֽם: בַּעֲלֹתִ֣י הָהָ֗רָה לָקַ֜חַת לוּחֹ֤ת הָֽאֲבָנִים֙ לוּחֹ֣ת הַבְּרִ֔ית אֲשֶׁר־כָּרַ֥ת יְהוָ֖ה עִמָּכֶ֑ם וָאֵשֵׁ֣ב בָּהָ֗ר אַרְבָּעִ֥ים יוֹם֙ וְאַרְבָּעִ֣ים לַ֔יְלָה לֶ֚חֶם לֹ֣א אָכַ֔לְתִּי וּמַ֖יִם

י לֹ֥א שָׁתִֽיתִי: וַיִּתֵּ֨ן יְהוָ֜ה אֵלַ֗י אֶת־שְׁנֵי֙ לוּחֹ֣ת הָֽאֲבָנִ֔ים כְּתֻבִ֖ים בְּאֶצְבַּ֣ע אֱלֹהִ֑ים וַעֲלֵיהֶ֗ם כְּֽכָל־הַדְּבָרִ֡ים אֲשֶׁ֣ר דִּבֶּר֩ יְהוָ֨ה עִמָּכֶ֥ם בָּהָ֛ר מִתּ֥וֹךְ הָאֵ֖שׁ בְּי֥וֹם הַקָּהָֽל:

רש״י

פרק ט
א] גְּדֹלִים וַעֲצֻמִים מִמֶּךָ. אַתָּה עָצוּם וְהֵם עֲצוּמִים מִמְּךָ:

ד] אַל תֹּאמַר בִּלְבָבְךָ. צִדְקָתִי וְרִשְׁעַת הַגּוֹיִם גָּרְמוּ:

ה] לֹא בְצִדְקָתְךָ וְגו' אַתָּה בָא לָרֶשֶׁת וְגו' כִּי בְּרִשְׁעַת הַגּוֹיִם. הֲרֵי 'כִּי' מְשַׁמֵּשׁ בִּלְשׁוֹן 'אֶלָּא':

ט] וָאֵשֵׁב בָּהָר. אֵין יְשִׁיבָה אֶלָּא לְשׁוֹן עַכָּבָה:

י] לוּחֹת. 'לֻחֹת' כְּתִיב, שֶׁשְּׁתֵּיהֶן שָׁווֹת:

11 It was at the end of forty days and forty nights, that the Lord gave me the two tablets of stone, the Tablets of the Covenant.

12 The Lord said to me: Rise, descend quickly from here, as your people that you took out of Egypt acted corruptly; they deviated quickly from the path that I had commanded them, they made for them a cast figure.

13 The Lord said to me, saying: I have seen this people, and behold, it is a stiff-necked, stubborn people that does not accept authority.

14 Let Me, and I will destroy them and I will erase their name from under the heavens and I will make you a nation mightier and more numerous than they. Here Moses does not mention his response to this offer.[17]

15 I turned and descended the mountain, and the mountain was still burning in fire, and the two Tablets of the Covenant were in my two hands.

16 I saw, and, behold, you had sinned against the Lord your God, you made yourselves a cast figure of a calf, you quickly deviated from the path that the Lord had commanded you. You had heard the prohibition against worshipping idols, and yet you had committed this transgression. Furthermore, you sinned at Mount Sinai itself, while the fire was still burning upon the mountain.

17 I grasped the two tablets, inscribed by the finger of God, I cast them from my two hands, and I shattered them before your eyes, in order to exemplify the abrogation of the covenant, as the people were no longer worthy of receiving these tablets.

18 I subsequently fell before the Lord, as at the first occasion, for forty days and forty nights, I did not eat bread and I did not drink water, for all of your sin that you sinned, to perform evil in the eyes of the Lord, to anger Him.

19 For I was daunted due to the wrath and the fury that the Lord raged against you to destroy you and the Lord heeded me that time as well.

20 And the Lord was incensed with Aaron to destroy him, as he was the one who had actually fashioned the calf; and I prayed for Aaron too, at that time, so God would have mercy upon him.

21 I took your sin that you made, the calf, and I burned it in fire; I pulverized it until it was well ground into dust and I cast its dust into the ravine that descends from the mountain, so that it would be carried away by the water, and no trace of it would remain.

22 The Golden Calf was your worst and most conspicuous, but not your only, sin. In Tavera,[18] and in Masa,[19] and in Kivrot HaTaava,[20] you also enraged the Lord.

23 Moses mentions another severe transgression of Israel, the sin of the spies: Upon the Lord's sending you from Kadesh Barnea, saying: Go up and take possession of the land that I have given you, you could have entered the land, but you defied the directive of the Lord your God, you did not trust Him, and you did not heed His voice, to enter the land.

24 In general, you have been defiant of the Lord from the day that I first knew you.

25 Moses returns to the main event that he mentioned, the sin of the Golden Calf, but turns his focus to God's mercy: I fell before the Lord the forty days and forty nights that I fell, as mentioned above in verse 18,[21] because the Lord had said to destroy you.

יא וַיְהִי מִקֵּץ אַרְבָּעִים יוֹם וְאַרְבָּעִים לָיְלָה נָתַן יְהוָה אֵלַי אֶת־שְׁנֵי לֻחֹת הָאֲבָנִים
יב לֻחוֹת הַבְּרִית׃ וַיֹּאמֶר יְהוָה אֵלַי קוּם רֵד מַהֵר מִזֶּה כִּי שִׁחֵת עַמְּךָ אֲשֶׁר
יג הוֹצֵאתָ מִמִּצְרָיִם סָרוּ מַהֵר מִן־הַדֶּרֶךְ אֲשֶׁר צִוִּיתִם עָשׂוּ לָהֶם מַסֵּכָה׃ וַיֹּאמֶר
יד יְהוָה אֵלַי לֵאמֹר רָאִיתִי אֶת־הָעָם הַזֶּה וְהִנֵּה עַם־קְשֵׁה־עֹרֶף הוּא׃ הֶרֶף מִמֶּנִּי
וְאַשְׁמִידֵם וְאֶמְחֶה אֶת־שְׁמָם מִתַּחַת הַשָּׁמָיִם וְאֶעֱשֶׂה אוֹתְךָ לְגוֹי־עָצוּם
טו וָרָב מִמֶּנּוּ׃ וָאֵפֶן וָאֵרֵד מִן־הָהָר וְהָהָר בֹּעֵר בָּאֵשׁ וּשְׁנֵי לוּחֹת הַבְּרִית עַל
טז שְׁתֵּי יָדָי׃ וָאֵרֶא וְהִנֵּה חֲטָאתֶם לַיהוָה אֱלֹהֵיכֶם עֲשִׂיתֶם לָכֶם עֵגֶל מַסֵּכָה
יז סַרְתֶּם מַהֵר מִן־הַדֶּרֶךְ אֲשֶׁר־צִוָּה יְהוָה אֶתְכֶם׃ וָאֶתְפֹּשׂ בִּשְׁנֵי הַלֻּחֹת וָאַשְׁלִכֵם
יח מֵעַל שְׁתֵּי יָדָי וָאֲשַׁבְּרֵם לְעֵינֵיכֶם׃ וָאֶתְנַפַּל לִפְנֵי יְהוָה כָּרִאשֹׁנָה אַרְבָּעִים יוֹם
וְאַרְבָּעִים לַיְלָה לֶחֶם לֹא אָכַלְתִּי וּמַיִם לֹא שָׁתִיתִי עַל כָּל־חַטַּאתְכֶם אֲשֶׁר
יט חֲטָאתֶם לַעֲשׂוֹת הָרַע בְּעֵינֵי יְהוָה לְהַכְעִיסוֹ׃ כִּי יָגֹרְתִּי מִפְּנֵי הָאַף וְהַחֵמָה
אֲשֶׁר קָצַף יְהוָה עֲלֵיכֶם לְהַשְׁמִיד אֶתְכֶם וַיִּשְׁמַע יְהוָה אֵלַי גַּם בַּפַּעַם הַהִוא׃
כ וּבְאַהֲרֹן הִתְאַנַּף יְהוָה מְאֹד לְהַשְׁמִידוֹ וָאֶתְפַּלֵּל גַּם־בְּעַד אַהֲרֹן בָּעֵת הַהִוא׃
כא וְאֶת־חַטַּאתְכֶם אֲשֶׁר־עֲשִׂיתֶם אֶת־הָעֵגֶל לָקַחְתִּי וָאֶשְׂרֹף אֹתוֹ ׀ בָּאֵשׁ וָאֶכֹּת אֹתוֹ
טָחוֹן הֵיטֵב עַד אֲשֶׁר־דַּק לְעָפָר וָאַשְׁלִךְ אֶת־עֲפָרוֹ אֶל־הַנַּחַל הַיֹּרֵד מִן־הָהָר׃
כב כג וּבְתַבְעֵרָה וּבְמַסָּה וּבְקִבְרֹת הַתַּאֲוָה מַקְצִפִים הֱיִיתֶם אֶת־יְהוָה׃ וּבִשְׁלֹחַ יְהוָה
אֶתְכֶם מִקָּדֵשׁ בַּרְנֵעַ לֵאמֹר עֲלוּ וּרְשׁוּ אֶת־הָאָרֶץ אֲשֶׁר נָתַתִּי לָכֶם וַתַּמְרוּ אֶת־פִּי
כד יְהוָה אֱלֹהֵיכֶם וְלֹא הֶאֱמַנְתֶּם לוֹ וְלֹא שְׁמַעְתֶּם בְּקֹלוֹ׃ מַמְרִים הֱיִיתֶם עִם־יְהוָה
כה מִיּוֹם דַּעְתִּי אֶתְכֶם׃ וָאֶתְנַפַּל לִפְנֵי יְהוָה אֵת אַרְבָּעִים הַיּוֹם וְאֶת־אַרְבָּעִים הַלַּיְלָה

רש״י

יח | **וָאֶתְנַפַּל לִפְנֵי ה׳ כָּרִאשֹׁנָה אַרְבָּעִים יוֹם.** שֶׁנֶּאֱמַר: "וְעַתָּה אֶעֱלֶה אֶל ה׳ אוּלַי אֲכַפְּרָה" (שמות לב, ל), בְּאוֹתָהּ עֲלִיָּה נִתְעַכַּבְתִּי אַרְבָּעִים יוֹם, נִמְצְאוּ כָּלִים בְּעֶשְׂרִים וְתִשְׁעָה בְּאָב, שֶׁהוּא עָלָה בִּשְׁמוֹנָה עָשָׂר בְּתַמּוּז. בּוֹ בַּיּוֹם נִתְרַצָּה הַקָּדוֹשׁ בָּרוּךְ הוּא לְיִשְׂרָאֵל וְאָמַר לְמֹשֶׁה: "פְּסָל לְךָ שְׁנֵי לֻחֹת" (שם לד, א), עָשָׂה עוֹד אַרְבָּעִים יוֹם, נִמְצְאוּ כָּלִים בְּיוֹם הַכִּפּוּרִים. בּוֹ בַּיּוֹם נִתְרַצָּה הַקָּדוֹשׁ בָּרוּךְ הוּא לְיִשְׂרָאֵל בְּשִׂמְחָה, וְאָמַר לוֹ לְמֹשֶׁה: "סָלַחְתִּי כִּדְבָרֶךָ" (במדבר יד, כ), לְכָךְ הֻקְבַּע לִמְחִילָה וְלִסְלִיחָה. וּמִנַּיִן שֶׁנִּתְרַצָּה בְּרָצוֹן שָׁלֵם? שֶׁנֶּאֱמַר בָּאַרְבָּעִים שֶׁל לוּחוֹת אַחֲרוֹנוֹת: "וְאָנֹכִי עָמַדְתִּי בָהָר כַּיָּמִים הָרִאשֹׁנִים" (להלן י, י), מָה הָרִאשׁוֹנִים בְּרָצוֹן אַף אַחֲרוֹנִים בְּרָצוֹן, אֱמֹר מֵעַתָּה אֶמְצָעִיִּים הָיוּ בְּכַעַס:

כ | **וּבְאַהֲרֹן הִתְאַנַּף ה׳.** לְפִי שֶׁשָּׁמַע לָכֶם: **לְהַשְׁמִידוֹ.** זֶה כִּלּוּי בָּנִים, וְכֵן הוּא אוֹמֵר: "וָאַשְׁמִיד פִּרְיוֹ מִמַּעַל" (עמוס ב, ט): **וָאֶתְפַּלֵּל גַּם בְּעַד אַהֲרֹן.** וְהוֹעִילָה תְּפִלָּתִי לְכַפֵּר מֶחֱצָה, וּמֵתוּ שְׁנַיִם וְנִשְׁאֲרוּ הַשְּׁנַיִם:

כא | **טָחוֹן.** לְשׁוֹן הֹוֶה, כְּמוֹ "הָלוֹךְ וְגָדוֹל" (שמואל ב׳ ה, י; דברי הימים א׳ יא, ט). מולא"נט בְּלַעַז:

כה | **וָאֶתְנַפַּל וְגוֹ׳.** אֵלּוּ הֵן עַצְמָן הָאֲמוּרִים לְמַעְלָה, וּכְפָלָן כָּאן לְפִי שֶׁכָּתוּב כָּאן סֵדֶר תְּפִלָּתוֹ, שֶׁנֶּאֱמַר: "ה׳ אֱלֹהִים אַל תַּשְׁחֵת עַמְּךָ" וְגוֹ׳ (להלן פסוק כו):

26 **I prayed to the Lord, and said: My Lord God, do not destroy Your people and Your inheritance, Your chosen portion, that You have redeemed in Your greatness, that You took out of Egypt with a mighty hand.**

27 **Remember Your servants, Abraham, Isaac, and Jacob; do not turn to the stubbornness of this people, or to its wickedness, or to its sin.**

28 Moses states another reason why God should spare the people: **Lest the inhabitants of the land that You took us out from there say: Due to the lack of the ability of the Lord to bring them to the land with regard to which He spoke to them, and due to His hatred of them, He took them out to kill them in the wilderness.** They might think that God is incapable of helping the Israelites conquer the land; therefore, He sought a pretext to rid Himself of them in the wilderness.

29 **They are Your people and Your inheritance, that You took out with Your great power and with Your outstretched arm.** Therefore, please have mercy upon them.

10 1 **At that time the Lord said to me: Carve for yourself**[D] **two**
Fourth **tablets of stone like the first** tablets, **and ascend to Me to the**
aliya **mountain; and make for yourself a wooden ark,** in which to place the tablets.

2 **I will inscribe on the tablets the statements that were on the first tablets that you shattered, and you shall place them in the ark.** Both the first tablets and the writing upon them were the work of God, whereas the second tablets were crafted by man, and then God wrote upon them the same content that were written on the first tablets.

3 **I made an ark of acacia wood, I carved two tablets of stone like the first, and I** again **ascended to the mountaintop,** Mount Sinai, **and the two tablets were in my hand.**

4 **He,** God, **inscribed on the tablets like the first inscription, the Ten Precepts that the Lord spoke to you on the mountain from the midst of the fire on the day of the assembly,** on the day of the revelation at Mount Sinai; **and the Lord gave them to me.**

5 **I turned and I descended from the mount, and I placed the tablets in the ark**[D] **that I had made and they were there, as the Lord had commanded me.**

6 Here, Moses skips in time from the events at Sinai to the fortieth year in the wilderness: **The children of Israel traveled from Be'erot Benei Yaakan**[B] **to Mosera; there Aaron died,**[D] **and he was buried there, and Elazar his son served as priest in his place.**

Acacia tree

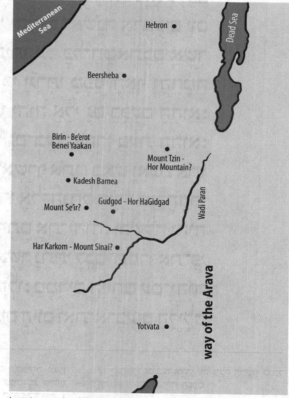

Locations on the children of Israel's travels

BACKGROUND

10:6 | **From Be'erot Benei Yaakan:** Generally identified with the water wells [be'erot], in Biriin, near the settlement of Ezuz.

כו אֲשֶׁר הִתְנַפַּלְתִּי כִּי־אָמַר יְהוָה לְהַשְׁמִיד אֶתְכֶם׃ וָאֶתְפַּלֵּל אֶל־יְהוָה וָאֹמַר אֲדֹנָי
יְהוִה אַל־תַּשְׁחֵת עַמְּךָ וְנַחֲלָתְךָ אֲשֶׁר פָּדִיתָ בְּגָדְלֶךָ אֲשֶׁר־הוֹצֵאתָ מִמִּצְרַיִם בְּיָד
כז חֲזָקָה׃ זְכֹר לַעֲבָדֶיךָ לְאַבְרָהָם לְיִצְחָק וּלְיַעֲקֹב אַל־תֵּפֶן אֶל־קְשִׁי הָעָם הַזֶּה
כח וְאֶל־רִשְׁעוֹ וְאֶל־חַטָּאתוֹ׃ פֶּן־יֹאמְרוּ הָאָרֶץ אֲשֶׁר הוֹצֵאתָנוּ מִשָּׁם מִבְּלִי יְכֹלֶת
יְהוָה לַהֲבִיאָם אֶל־הָאָרֶץ אֲשֶׁר־דִּבֶּר לָהֶם וּמִשִּׂנְאָתוֹ אוֹתָם הוֹצִיאָם לַהֲמִתָם
כט בַּמִּדְבָּר׃ וְהֵם עַמְּךָ וְנַחֲלָתֶךָ אֲשֶׁר הוֹצֵאתָ בְּכֹחֲךָ הַגָּדֹל וּבִזְרֹעֲךָ הַנְּטוּיָה׃
א בָּעֵת הַהִוא אָמַר יְהוָה אֵלַי פְּסָל־לְךָ שְׁנֵי־לוּחֹת אֲבָנִים כָּרִאשֹׁנִים וַעֲלֵה ט רביעי
ב אֵלַי הָהָרָה וְעָשִׂיתָ לְּךָ אֲרוֹן עֵץ׃ וְאֶכְתֹּב עַל־הַלֻּחֹת אֶת־הַדְּבָרִים אֲשֶׁר
ג הָיוּ עַל־הַלֻּחֹת הָרִאשֹׁנִים אֲשֶׁר שִׁבַּרְתָּ וְשַׂמְתָּם בָּאָרוֹן׃ וָאַעַשׂ אֲרוֹן עֲצֵי
שִׁטִּים וָאֶפְסֹל שְׁנֵי־לֻחֹת אֲבָנִים כָּרִאשֹׁנִים וָאַעַל הָהָרָה וּשְׁנֵי הַלֻּחֹת בְּיָדִי׃
ד וַיִּכְתֹּב עַל־הַלֻּחֹת כַּמִּכְתָּב הָרִאשׁוֹן אֵת עֲשֶׂרֶת הַדְּבָרִים אֲשֶׁר דִּבֶּר יְהוָה אֲלֵיכֶם
ה בָּהָר מִתּוֹךְ הָאֵשׁ בְּיוֹם הַקָּהָל וַיִּתְּנֵם יְהוָה אֵלָי׃ וָאֵפֶן וָאֵרֵד מִן־הָהָר וָאָשִׂם
ו אֶת־הַלֻּחֹת בָּאָרוֹן אֲשֶׁר עָשִׂיתִי וַיִּהְיוּ שָׁם כַּאֲשֶׁר צִוַּנִי יְהוָה׃ וּבְנֵי יִשְׂרָאֵל נָסְעוּ
מִבְּאֵרֹת בְּנֵי־יַעֲקָן מוֹסֵרָה שָׁם מֵת אַהֲרֹן וַיִּקָּבֵר שָׁם וַיְכַהֵן אֶלְעָזָר בְּנוֹ תַּחְתָּיו׃

רש"י

פרק י

א) **בעת ההוא.** לסוף ארבעים יום נתרצה לי ואמר לי: "פסל לך" ואחר כך: "ועשית לך ארון", ואני עשיתי ארון תחלה, שכשאבוא והלוחות בידי היכן אתנם. ולא זה הוא הארון שעשה בצלאל, שהרי משכן לא נתעסקו בו עד לאחר יום הכפורים, כי בירידתו מן ההר צוה להם על מלאכת המשכן, ובצלאל עשה משכן תחלה ואחר כך ארון וכלים, נמצא זה ארון אחר היה, וזהו שהיה יוצא עמהם למלחמה, ואותו שעשה בצלאל לא יצא למלחמה אלא בימי עלי, ונענשו עליו ונשבה:

ו-ז) **ובני ישראל נסעו מבארת בני יעקן מוסרה.** מה ענין זה לכאן? ועוד, וכי מבארות בני יעקן נסעו למוסרה?

DISCUSSION

10:1 | **Carve for yourself:** The first tablets were not the handiwork of man, but were crafted by God and given to Moses. Since Moses had seen their form, he could reproduce them from material of his own. The Sages state that the second tablets were fashioned from precious stones (see Jerusalem Talmud, *Shekalim* 5:2), but the material from which the first tablets were made is unknown. It is likely that they were a singular creation, as reflected in the Mishna (*Avot* 5:6), that the writing, the inscription, and the tablets were among the items created before the beginning of the history of the world.

10:5 | **In the ark:** The Torah does not state how long the tablets remained in this particular ark. In any case, when the Tabernacle and its vessels were built, the Ark of the Covenant was also constructed, and the tablets were placed in that ark (Exodus 25:16). That was not the wooden ark constructed by Moses, but a specially designed wooden ark plated with gold (Exodus 25:9–15). The ark that Moses crafted was temporary, whereas the ark fashioned by the craftsman of the Tabernacle, Betzalel the son of Uri, served as the permanent place for the Tablets of the Covenant (see *Bava Batra* 14a–b).

10:6 | **There Aaron died:** Some explain that Moses mentions this incident in his retelling of the sin of the Golden Calf in response to a challenge posed to him: If, as you claim, you prayed on Aaron's behalf with regard to this sin, why did he die? Perhaps your prayer was ineffective. Moses therefore stresses that Aaron did not die because of his part in the sin of the Golden Calf, as he died elsewhere many years later. He was even privileged to transfer his title of High Priest to his son in a dignified manner (Rashbam).

7 **From there they traveled to Gudgod,**[B] **and from Gudgod to Yotvata, a land of streams of water.** Perhaps it was named Yotvata due to its plentiful sources of water and its overall goodness [*tuva*].

8 Moses returns to the repercussions of the sin of the Golden Calf. **At that time,** after the giving of the second tablets, **the Lord designated the tribe of Levi to carry the Ark of the Covenant of the Lord, to stand before the Lord to serve Him, and to bless in His name to this day.**

9 **Therefore Levi did not have a portion or an inheritance with his brethren, the Lord is his inheritance, as the Lord your God spoke to him.** The Levites, who are designated for the service of God, will be considered an independent social unit because they did not participate in the sin of the Golden Calf.[22]

10 Having concluded his account of the second tablets, Moses fills in some previously omitted details of earlier events. **I stayed on the mountain** in prayer so that God would forgive the sins of Israel, **like** I remained there **the first time,** when I received the Torah,[23] **forty days and forty nights, and the Lord heeded me that time as well, the Lord was unwilling to destroy you** and had mercy upon you.

Yotvata against the backdrop of the mountains of Edom

11 **The Lord said to me: Rise, go on a journey before the people, and they will come and take possession of the land, with regard to which I took an oath to their forefathers to give to them.**

The Commandments and Love of God

DEUTERONOMY 10:12–11:25

In this section, Moses reiterates several times the demand that Israel worship and love God. This demand is repeatedly predicated on the relationship between God and Israel, past and future; as well as God's greatness and His attributes of kindness, righteousness, and justice.

To emphasize Israel's obligation to God, Moses mentions past events such as the miracles of the exodus from Egypt, the splitting of the sea, and the earth opening to swallow Datan and Aviram. He also promises future success, in the form of the inheritance of the land and the possibility of a good life there, if the people will follow the path of God. This section includes a passage (11:13–21) that deals with the reward and punishment for Israel's behavior in its land, which will come in the form of rain or drought. Due to its great importance, as it speaks of the acceptance of the commandments, this passage is recited twice daily as the second portion of *Shema*. It is also one of the Torah passages written in a mezuza and placed on one's doorposts and written in phylacteries.

12 Having summarized many of the events of the past years, Moses
Fifth aliya continues: **Now, Israel, what does the Lord your God ask of you? Only**[D] **to fear the Lord your God, to walk in all His ways, and to love Him, and to serve the Lord your God with all your heart and with all your soul,**

13 **to observe the commandments of the Lord, and His statutes that I command you today,** not for God's sake but **for your** own **good.**

14 **Behold, to the Lord your God are the heavens,** which are not the edge of reality, as even the heavens have heavens; **and the heavens of heavens, the earth and everything that is in it.** Since the entire universe belongs to Him, He does not need your observance of the commandments; rather, their fulfillment is for your own good alone.

DISCUSSION

10:12 | What does the Lord your God ask of you? Only…: Moses appears to present God's demands from Israel, which include fear, following God's ways, loving Him, worshipping Him, and performing His commandments, as minor expectations (see *Berakhot* 33b). Indeed, this rhetorical question serves to emphasize that the nation of Israel is not asked to perform actions that require a change of human nature. The Israelites must cleave to God, but this does not mean that they must be superhuman. The Torah and the commandments must be observed in the manner that people do.

ז ח מִשָּׁם נָסְעוּ הַגֻּדְגֹּדָה וּמִן־הַגֻּדְגֹּדָה יָטְבָתָה אֶרֶץ נַחֲלֵי־מָיִם: בָּעֵת הַהִוא הִבְדִּיל
יְהוָה אֶת־שֵׁבֶט הַלֵּוִי לָשֵׂאת אֶת־אֲרוֹן בְּרִית־יְהוָה לַעֲמֹד לִפְנֵי יְהוָה לְשָׁרְתוֹ
ט וּלְבָרֵךְ בִּשְׁמוֹ עַד הַיּוֹם הַזֶּה: עַל־כֵּן לֹא־הָיָה לְלֵוִי חֵלֶק וְנַחֲלָה עִם־אֶחָיו יְהוָה
י הוּא נַחֲלָתוֹ כַּאֲשֶׁר דִּבֶּר יְהוָה אֱלֹהֶיךָ לוֹ: וְאָנֹכִי עָמַדְתִּי בָהָר כַּיָּמִים הָרִאשֹׁנִים
אַרְבָּעִים יוֹם וְאַרְבָּעִים לָיְלָה וַיִּשְׁמַע יְהוָה אֵלַי גַּם בַּפַּעַם הַהִוא לֹא־אָבָה יְהוָה
יא הַשְׁחִיתֶךָ: וַיֹּאמֶר יְהוָה אֵלַי קוּם לֵךְ לְמַסַּע לִפְנֵי הָעָם וְיָבֹאוּ וְיִירְשׁוּ אֶת־הָאָרֶץ
אֲשֶׁר־נִשְׁבַּעְתִּי לַאֲבֹתָם לָתֵת לָהֶם:
יב וְעַתָּה יִשְׂרָאֵל מָה יְהוָה אֱלֹהֶיךָ שֹׁאֵל מֵעִמָּךְ כִּי אִם־לְיִרְאָה אֶת־יְהוָה אֱלֹהֶיךָ חמישי
לָלֶכֶת בְּכָל־דְּרָכָיו וּלְאַהֲבָה אֹתוֹ וְלַעֲבֹד אֶת־יְהוָה אֱלֹהֶיךָ בְּכָל־לְבָבְךָ
יג וּבְכָל־נַפְשֶׁךָ: לִשְׁמֹר אֶת־מִצְוֹת יְהוָה וְאֶת־חֻקֹּתָיו אֲשֶׁר אָנֹכִי מְצַוְּךָ הַיּוֹם
יד לְטוֹב לָךְ: הֵן לַיהוָה אֱלֹהֶיךָ הַשָּׁמַיִם וּשְׁמֵי הַשָּׁמָיִם הָאָרֶץ וְכָל־אֲשֶׁר־בָּהּ:

רש״י

וַהֲלֹא מִמּוֹסֵרָה בָּאוּ לִבְנֵי יַעֲקָן, שֶׁנֶּאֱמַר: ״וַיִּסְעוּ מִמֹּסֵרוֹת״ וְגוֹ׳ (במדבר לג, לא)! וְעוֹד, ״שָׁם מֵת אַהֲרֹן״ – וַהֲלֹא בְּהֹר הָהָר מֵת! צֵא וַחֲשֹׁב וְתִמְצָא שְׁמוֹנָה מַסָּעוֹת מִמּוֹסֵרוֹת לְהֹר הָהָר! אֶלָּא אַף זוֹ מִן הַתּוֹכָחָה: וְעוֹד עֲשִׂיתֶם זֹאת, כְּשֶׁמֵּת אַהֲרֹן בְּהֹר הָהָר לְסוֹף אַרְבָּעִים שָׁנָה וְנִסְתַּלְּקוּ עַנְנֵי כָבוֹד, יְרֵאתֶם לָכֶם מִמִּלְחֶמֶת מֶלֶךְ עֲרָד וּנְתַתֶּם רֹאשׁ לַחֲזֹר לְמִצְרַיִם, וַחֲזַרְתֶּם לַאֲחוֹרֵיכֶם שְׁמוֹנָה מַסָּעוֹת עַד בְּנֵי יַעֲקָן וּמִשָּׁם לְמוֹסֵרָה, שָׁם נִלְחֲמוּ בָּכֶם בְּנֵי לֵוִי וְהָרְגוּ מִכֶּם וְאַתֶּם מֵהֶם, עַד שֶׁהֶחֱזִירוּ אֶתְכֶם בְּדֶרֶךְ חֲזָרַתְכֶם, וּמִשָּׁם חֲזַרְתֶּם ״הַגֻּדְגֹּדָה״ הוּא חֹר הַגִּדְגָּד, ״וּמִן הַגֻּדְגֹּדָה יָטְבָתָה״. וּבְמוֹסֵרָה עֲשִׂיתֶם אֵבֶל כָּבֵד עַל מִיתָתוֹ שֶׁל אַהֲרֹן שֶׁגָּרְמָה לָכֶם זֹאת, וְנִדְמָה לָכֶם כְּאִלּוּ מֵת שָׁם. וְסָמַךְ מֹשֶׁה תּוֹכָחָה זוֹ לִשְׁבִירַת הַלּוּחוֹת, לוֹמַר שֶׁקָּשָׁה מִיתָתָן שֶׁל צַדִּיקִים לִפְנֵי הַקָּדוֹשׁ בָּרוּךְ הוּא כַּיּוֹם שֶׁנִּשְׁתַּבְּרוּ בּוֹ הַלּוּחוֹת, וּלְהוֹדִיעֲךָ שֶׁהִקְשָׁה לוֹ מַה שֶּׁנָּתְנוּ רֹאשׁ לִפְרֹשׁ מִמֶּנּוּ, כְּיוֹם שֶׁעָשׂוּ בּוֹ אֶת הָעֵגֶל:

ח| **בָּעֵת הַהִוא הִבְדִּיל ה׳** וְגוֹ׳. מוּסָב לָעִנְיָן הָרִאשׁוֹן, ״בָּעֵת הַהִוא״ בַּשָּׁנָה הָרִאשׁוֹנָה לְצֵאתְכֶם מִמִּצְרַיִם וּטְעִיתֶם בָּעֵגֶל וּבְנֵי לֵוִי לֹא טָעוּ, הִבְדִּילָם הַמָּקוֹם מִכֶּם. וְסָמַךְ מִקְרָא זֶה לַחֲזָרַת בְּנֵי יַעֲקָן, לוֹמַר שֶׁאַף בְּזוֹ לֹא טָעוּ בָּהּ בְּנֵי לֵוִי אֶלָּא עָמְדוּ בֶּאֱמוּנָתָם: **לָשֵׂאת אֶת אֲרוֹן.** הַלְוִיִּם: **לַעֲמֹד... לְשָׁרְתוֹ וּלְבָרֵךְ בִּשְׁמוֹ.** הַכֹּהֲנִים, וְהוּא נְשִׂיאוּת כַּפַּיִם:

ט| **עַל כֵּן לֹא הָיָה לְלֵוִי חֵלֶק.** לְפִי שֶׁהֻבְדְּלוּ לַעֲבוֹדַת מִזְבֵּחַ וְאֵינָן פְּנוּיִין לַחֲרֹשׁ וְלִזְרֹעַ: **ה׳ הוּא נַחֲלָתוֹ.** נוֹטֵל פְּרָס מְזֻמָּן מִבֵּית הַמֶּלֶךְ:

י| **וְאָנֹכִי עָמַדְתִּי בָהָר.** לְקַבֵּל לוּחוֹת הָאַחֲרוֹנוֹת, וּלְפִי שֶׁלֹּא פֵּרַשׁ לְמַעְלָה כַּמָּה עָמַד בָּהָר בַּעֲלִיָּה אַחֲרוֹנָה זוֹ, חָזַר וְהִתְחִיל בָּהּ: **כַּיָּמִים הָרִאשֹׁנִים.** שֶׁל לוּחוֹת הָרִאשׁוֹנוֹת, מָה הֵם בְּרָצוֹן, אַף אֵלּוּ בְּרָצוֹן, אֲבָל הָאֶמְצָעִיִּים שֶׁעָמַדְתִּי שָׁם לְהִתְפַּלֵּל עֲלֵיכֶם הָיוּ בְּכַעַס:

יא| **וַיֹּאמֶר ה׳ אֵלַי** וְגוֹ׳. אַף עַל פִּי שֶׁסַּרְתֶּם מֵאַחֲרָיו וּטְעִיתֶם בָּעֵגֶל, אָמַר לִי: ״לֵךְ נְחֵה אֶת הָעָם״ (שמות לב, לד):

יב| **וְעַתָּה יִשְׂרָאֵל.** אַף עַל פִּי שֶׁעֲשִׂיתֶם כָּל זֹאת, עוֹדֶנּוּ רַחֲמָיו וְחִבָּתוֹ עֲלֵיכֶם, וּמִכָּל מַה שֶּׁחֲטָאתֶם לְפָנָיו אֵינוֹ שׁוֹאֵל מִכֶּם ״כִּי אִם לְיִרְאָה״ וְגוֹ׳. וְרַבּוֹתֵינוּ דָּרְשׁוּ מִכָּאן: הַכֹּל בִּידֵי שָׁמַיִם חוּץ מִיִּרְאַת שָׁמַיִם:

יג| **לִשְׁמֹר אֶת מִצְוֹת ה׳.** וְאַף הִיא לֹא לְחִנָּם, אֶלָּא ״לְטוֹב לָךְ״, שֶׁתְּקַבְּלוּ שָׂכָר:

יד-טו| **הֵן לַה׳ אֱלֹהֶיךָ.** הַכֹּל, וְאַף עַל פִּי כֵן, ״רַק

BACKGROUND

10:7| **Gudgod:** In Numbers (33:32) it is related that the children of Israel traveled from Benei Yaakan and encamped in Hor HaGidgad. Due to the similarity of the names, this place is identified with Be'erot Oded in Wadi Oded, roughly 15 km southeast of Mitzpe Ramon, or with Wadi Hadhad, which enters Wadi Paran from the south, north of Kontila.

15 **Yet the Lord desired your forefathers, to love them, and He chose their descendants after them, you, from all the peoples, as this day,** and therefore He charged you with the fulfillment of His commandments.

16 Therefore, **remove the** metaphorical **obstruction of your heart;** restore your sensitivity so that you will stand before God wholeheartedly.[24] **And do not stiffen your neck anymore;** cease acting stubbornly.

17 **For the Lord your God, He is the God of gods, and the Lord of lords, the great, the valorous, and the awesome God, who will not show favor** to people because of their status or achievements, **and will not take a bribe.** People might delude themselves that they can bribe God by performing good deeds or by mentioning His name, but He does not require anyone's actions or praise.[25]

18 God does not favor the nobility, as **He executes justice for the orphan and the widow, and loves the stranger, to give him food and garment.** He cares for the lowly and the downtrodden.[26] It is specifically due to God's greatness that He supports those at the lowest strata of society. Consequently, you will not become more acceptable to God by building lavish temples, or by decorating them with expensive ornamentations.

19 In passing, Moses adds: You should learn from God's attributes and **you** too **shall love the stranger,** just as God does; and furthermore, **as you were strangers in the land of Egypt,** you should remember the misery of the foreign, subjugated exile, and you should act with compassion toward strangers in your land.

20 In summation, **the Lord your God you shall fear, Him you shall serve, and to Him you shall cleave,**[D] **and in His name you shall take an oath.** If you must take an oath, you are obligated to do so in His name.

21 **He is your glory, and He is your God,** and there is nothing besides Him; it is He **who performed for you these great and awesome deeds that your eyes saw.**

22 **With seventy people your ancestors descended to Egypt, and now the Lord your God has rendered you as the stars of the heavens in abundance.** Your immense increase in numbers is an indication of God's special providence over you and His love for you.

11 1 You shall love the Lord your God, and observe His charge. You must be faithful to Him, and stand ready to fulfill His instructions, **and** also to observe **His statutes, and His ordinances, and His commandments, all the days.**

2 **You shall know today that it is not with your children** that I am speaking, **who did not know, and who have not seen the chastising of the Lord your God, His greatness, His mighty hand, and His outstretched arm,**

3 **and His signs, and His actions that He performed in the midst of Egypt to Pharaoh king of Egypt, and to his entire land,**

4 **and what He did to the army of Egypt, to its horses, and to its chariots; that He inundated the water of the Red Sea upon them in their pursuit of you, and the Lord annihilated them to this day;**

5 **and what He did for you in the wilderness, until you arrived at this place;**

6 **and what He did to Datan and Aviram,**[D] **sons of Eliav son of Reuben; that the earth opened its mouth, swallowed them, their households, their tents, and all the property that was at their feet,** the possessions through which they established their social status,[27] **in the midst of all Israel.**

7 **Rather, it is your** own **eyes that see**[D] **all the great work of the Lord that He performed.**

DISCUSSION

10:20 | And to Him you shall cleave: Unlike other religions, in which people's lives are for the most part independent of their religious worship, Judaism is theocentric. The God of Israel demands full commitment from His people: They must fear Him, worship Him, cleave to Him, and take oaths exclusively in His name. God is the center of their lives, and they have no existence without Him.

11:6 | And what He did to Datan and Aviram: It is interesting that the instigator of that rebellion, Korah, is not mentioned here. Perhaps this is because Korah's argument with Moses and Aaron was an internal family dispute, which Moses chooses to omit from an address before the entire nation.

11:7 | Your eyes that see: Although a large proportion of Moses' listeners were born in the wilderness and did not actually witness the early events cited here, some had indeed seen them with their own eyes, and Moses addresses his comments to those individuals. His audience includes all those survivors who were not of military age at the time of the sin of the spies, either because they were too young or too old, as well as women and the tribe of Levi, upon whom God did not impose the decree to die in the wilderness due to the sin of the spies.

טו רַק בַּאֲבֹתֶיךָ חָשַׁק יְהוָה לְאַהֲבָה אוֹתָם וַיִּבְחַר בְּזַרְעָם אַחֲרֵיהֶם בָּכֶם מִכׇּל־
טז יז הָעַמִּים כַּיּוֹם הַזֶּה׃ וּמַלְתֶּם אֵת עׇרְלַת לְבַבְכֶם וְעׇרְפְּכֶם לֹא תַקְשׁוּ עוֹד׃ כִּי יְהוָה
אֱלֹהֵיכֶם הוּא אֱלֹהֵי הָאֱלֹהִים וַאֲדֹנֵי הָאֲדֹנִים הָאֵל הַגָּדֹל הַגִּבֹּר וְהַנּוֹרָא אֲשֶׁר
יח לֹא־יִשָּׂא פָנִים וְלֹא יִקַּח שֹׁחַד׃ עֹשֶׂה מִשְׁפַּט יָתוֹם וְאַלְמָנָה וְאֹהֵב גֵּר לָתֶת לוֹ לֶחֶם
יט כ וְשִׂמְלָה׃ וַאֲהַבְתֶּם אֶת־הַגֵּר כִּי־גֵרִים הֱיִיתֶם בְּאֶרֶץ מִצְרָיִם׃ אֶת־יְהוָה אֱלֹהֶיךָ
כא תִּירָא אֹתוֹ תַעֲבֹד וּבוֹ תִדְבָּק וּבִשְׁמוֹ תִּשָּׁבֵעַ׃ הוּא תְהִלָּתְךָ וְהוּא אֱלֹהֶיךָ אֲשֶׁר־
כב עָשָׂה אִתְּךָ אֶת־הַגְּדֹלֹת וְאֶת־הַנּוֹרָאֹת הָאֵלֶּה אֲשֶׁר רָאוּ עֵינֶיךָ׃ בְּשִׁבְעִים נֶפֶשׁ
א יָרְדוּ אֲבֹתֶיךָ מִצְרָיְמָה וְעַתָּה שָׂמְךָ יְהוָה אֱלֹהֶיךָ כְּכוֹכְבֵי הַשָּׁמַיִם לָרֹב׃ וְאָהַבְתָּ
אֵת יְהוָה אֱלֹהֶיךָ וְשָׁמַרְתָּ מִשְׁמַרְתּוֹ וְחֻקֹּתָיו וּמִשְׁפָּטָיו וּמִצְוֺתָיו כׇּל־הַיָּמִים׃
ב וִידַעְתֶּם הַיּוֹם כִּי לֹא אֶת־בְּנֵיכֶם אֲשֶׁר לֹא־יָדְעוּ וַאֲשֶׁר לֹא־רָאוּ אֶת־מוּסַר יְהוָה
ג אֱלֹהֵיכֶם אֶת־גׇּדְלוֹ אֶת־יָדוֹ הַחֲזָקָה וּזְרֹעוֹ הַנְּטוּיָה׃ וְאֶת־אֹתֹתָיו וְאֶת־מַעֲשָׂיו
ד אֲשֶׁר עָשָׂה בְּתוֹךְ מִצְרָיִם לְפַרְעֹה מֶלֶךְ־מִצְרַיִם וּלְכׇל־אַרְצוֹ׃ וַאֲשֶׁר עָשָׂה לְחֵיל
מִצְרַיִם לְסוּסָיו וּלְרִכְבּוֹ אֲשֶׁר הֵצִיף אֶת־מֵי יַם־סוּף עַל־פְּנֵיהֶם בְּרׇדְפָם אַחֲרֵיכֶם
ה וַיְאַבְּדֵם יְהוָה עַד הַיּוֹם הַזֶּה׃ וַאֲשֶׁר עָשָׂה לָכֶם בַּמִּדְבָּר עַד־בֹּאֲכֶם עַד־הַמָּקוֹם
ו הַזֶּה׃ וַאֲשֶׁר עָשָׂה לְדָתָן וְלַאֲבִירָם בְּנֵי אֱלִיאָב בֶּן־רְאוּבֵן אֲשֶׁר פָּצְתָה הָאָרֶץ
אֶת־פִּיהָ וַתִּבְלָעֵם וְאֶת־בָּתֵּיהֶם וְאֶת־אׇהֳלֵיהֶם וְאֵת כׇּל־הַיְקוּם אֲשֶׁר בְּרַגְלֵיהֶם
ז בְּקֶרֶב כׇּל־יִשְׂרָאֵל׃ כִּי עֵינֵיכֶם הָרֹאֹת אֶת כׇּל־מַעֲשֵׂה יְהוָה הַגָּדֹל אֲשֶׁר עָשָׂה׃

רש״י

טו) בַּאֲבֹתֶיךָ חָשַׁק ה׳ מִן הַכֹּל: בָּכֶם. כְּמוֹ שֶׁאַתֶּם רוֹאִים אֶתְכֶם חֲשׁוּקִים מִכׇּל הָעַמִּים הַיּוֹם הַזֶּה:

טז) עׇרְלַת לְבַבְכֶם. אֹטֶם לְבַבְכֶם וְכִסּוּיוֹ:

יז) וַאֲדֹנֵי הָאֲדֹנִים. לֹא יוּכַל שׁוּם אָדוֹן לְהַצִּיל אֶתְכֶם מִיָּדוֹ: לֹא יִשָּׂא פָנִים. אִם תִּפְרְקוּ עֻלּוֹ: וְלֹא יִקַּח שֹׁחַד. לְפַיְּסוֹ בְּמָמוֹן:

יח) עֹשֶׂה מִשְׁפַּט יָתוֹם וְאַלְמָנָה. הֲרֵי גְבוּרָה, וְאֵצֶל גְּבוּרָתוֹ אַתָּה מוֹצֵא עַנְוְתָנוּתוֹ: וְאֹהֵב גֵּר לָתֶת לוֹ לֶחֶם וְשִׂמְלָה. וְדָבָר חָשׁוּב הוּא זֶה, שֶׁכָּל עַצְמוֹ שֶׁל יַעֲקֹב אָבִינוּ עַל זֶה נִתְפַּלֵּל: "וְנָתַן לִי לֶחֶם לֶאֱכֹל וּבֶגֶד לִלְבֹּשׁ" (בראשית כח, כ):

יט) כִּי גֵרִים הֱיִיתֶם. מוּם שֶׁבְּךָ אַל תֹּאמַר לַחֲבֵרְךָ:

כ) אֶת ה׳ אֱלֹהֶיךָ תִּירָא. וְתַעַבְדוֹ וְתִדְבַּק בּוֹ, וּלְאַחַר שֶׁיִּהְיוּ בְךָ כׇּל הַמִּדּוֹת הַלָּלוּ, אָז "בִּשְׁמוֹ תִּשָּׁבֵעַ":

פרק יא

ב) וִידַעְתֶּם הַיּוֹם. תְּנוּ לֵב לָדַעַת וּלְהָבִין וּלְקַבֵּל תּוֹכַחְתִּי: כִּי לֹא אֶת בְּנֵיכֶם. אֲנִי מְדַבֵּר עַכְשָׁיו, שֶׁיּוּכְלוּ לוֹמַר: אֲנוּ לֹא יָדַעְנוּ וְלֹא רָאִינוּ בְּכׇל זֶה:

ו) בְּקֶרֶב כׇּל יִשְׂרָאֵל. כׇּל מָקוֹם שֶׁהָיָה אֶחָד מֵהֶם בּוֹרֵחַ, הָאָרֶץ נִבְקַעַת מִתַּחְתָּיו וּבוֹלַעְתּוֹ, אֵלּוּ דִּבְרֵי רַבִּי יְהוּדָה. אָמַר לוֹ רַבִּי נְחֶמְיָה: וַהֲלֹא כְּבָר נֶאֱמַר: "וַתִּפְתַּח הָאָרֶץ אֶת פִּיהָ" (במדבר טז, לב) וְלֹא 'פִּיּוֹתֶיהָ'? אָמַר לוֹ: וּמָה אֲנִי מְקַיֵּם "בְּקֶרֶב כׇּל יִשְׂרָאֵל"? אָמַר לוֹ: שֶׁנַּעֲשֵׂית הָאָרֶץ מִדְרוֹן כְּמַשְׁפֵּךְ, וְכׇל מָקוֹם שֶׁהָיָה אֶחָד מֵהֶם, הָיָה מִתְגַּלְגֵּל וּבָא עַד מְקוֹם הַבְּקִיעָה: וְאֵת כׇּל הַיְקוּם אֲשֶׁר בְּרַגְלֵיהֶם. זֶה מָמוֹנוֹ שֶׁל אָדָם שֶׁמַּעֲמִידוֹ עַל רַגְלָיו:

ז) כִּי עֵינֵיכֶם הָרֹאֹת. מוּסָב עַל הַמִּקְרָא הָאָמוּר לְמַעְלָה (לעיל פסוק ב): "כִּי לֹא אֶת בְּנֵיכֶם אֲשֶׁר לֹא יָדְעוּ" וְגוֹ׳, כִּי אִם עִמָּכֶם, אֲשֶׁר "עֵינֵיכֶם הָרֹאֹת" וְגוֹ׳:

8 Therefore, **you shall observe the entire commandment that I command you this day, so that you will be strong, and come and take possession of the land, that you are crossing there to take possession of it;**

9 **and** in addition, you should observe the commandments **so that you may extend your days upon the land, with regard to which the Lord took an oath to your forefathers to give to them and to their descendants,** and which is **a land flowing with milk and honey.**

10 One special feature of the Promised Land is that it is clear that one's sustenance there depends upon God: **For the land that you are coming there to take possession of it is not like the land of Egypt, from which you emerged, where you would sow your seed, and water it on foot, like a vegetable garden.** Thanks to the Nile, water is constantly available in Egypt. It is

Sixth aliya

transferred through canals, from which it is carried in buckets to fields and gardens.

11 **Rather the land that you are crossing there to take possession of it is a land of mountains and valleys; according to the rain of the heavens it drinks water.**

12 **A land that the Lord your God seeks** and oversees; **always the eyes of the Lord your God are upon it, from the beginning of the year until year end.** Unlike the land of Egypt, where the supply of water is naturally steady, in Canaan there is no certainty that one will receive sufficient water for his needs. In the land of Canaan, one is made aware that he is under God's constant supervision.

13 **It shall be if you will heed My commandments that I command you today, to love the Lord your God, and to serve Him with all your heart and with all your soul,**

Agriculture along the Nile

Cultivated terraces in the hills of Gush Etzion

ח וּשְׁמַרְתֶּם֙ אֶת־כׇּל־הַמִּצְוָ֔ה אֲשֶׁ֛ר אָנֹכִ֥י מְצַוְּךָ֖ הַיּ֑וֹם לְמַ֣עַן תֶּחֶזְק֗וּ וּבָאתֶם֙ וִֽירִשְׁתֶּ֣ם
ט אֶת־הָאָ֔רֶץ אֲשֶׁ֛ר אַתֶּ֥ם עֹבְרִ֖ים שָׁ֑מָּה לְרִשְׁתָּֽהּ׃ וּלְמַ֙עַן֙ תַּאֲרִ֤יכוּ יָמִים֙ עַל־הָ֣אֲדָמָ֔ה
י אֲשֶׁ֣ר נִשְׁבַּ֧ע יהוה לַאֲבֹתֵיכֶ֛ם לָתֵ֥ת לָהֶ֖ם וּלְזַרְעָ֑ם אֶ֛רֶץ זָבַ֥ת חָלָ֖ב וּדְבָֽשׁ׃ כִּ֣י י ששי
הָאָ֗רֶץ אֲשֶׁ֨ר אַתָּ֤ה בָא־שָׁ֙מָּה֙ לְרִשְׁתָּ֔הּ לֹ֤א כְאֶ֙רֶץ֙ מִצְרַ֣יִם הִ֔וא אֲשֶׁ֥ר יְצָאתֶ֖ם
יא מִשָּׁ֑ם אֲשֶׁ֤ר תִּזְרַע֙ אֶֽת־זַרְעֲךָ֔ וְהִשְׁקִ֥יתָ בְרַגְלְךָ֖ כְּגַ֥ן הַיָּרָֽק׃ וְהָאָ֗רֶץ אֲשֶׁ֨ר אַתֶּ֜ם
יב עֹבְרִ֥ים שָׁ֙מָּה֙ לְרִשְׁתָּ֔הּ אֶ֥רֶץ הָרִ֖ים וּבְקָעֹ֑ת לִמְטַ֥ר הַשָּׁמַ֖יִם תִּשְׁתֶּה־מָּֽיִם׃ אֶ֕רֶץ
אֲשֶׁר־יהוה אֱלֹהֶ֖יךָ דֹּרֵ֣שׁ אֹתָ֑הּ תָּמִ֗יד עֵינֵ֨י יהוה אֱלֹהֶ֙יךָ֙ בָּ֔הּ מֵֽרֵשִׁית֙ הַשָּׁנָ֔ה וְעַ֖ד
יג אַחֲרִ֥ית שָׁנָֽה׃ וְהָיָ֗ה אִם־שָׁמֹ֤עַ תִּשְׁמְעוּ֙ אֶל־מִצְוֺתַ֔י אֲשֶׁ֧ר אָנֹכִ֛י מְצַוֶּ֥ה
אֶתְכֶ֖ם הַיּ֑וֹם לְאַהֲבָ֞ה אֶת־יהוה אֱלֹֽהֵיכֶם֙ וּלְעׇבְד֔וֹ בְּכׇל־לְבַבְכֶ֖ם וּבְכׇל־נַפְשְׁכֶֽם׃

רש"י

י | **לֹא כְאֶרֶץ מִצְרַיִם הִוא.** אֶלָּא טוֹבָה הֵימֶנָּה. וְנֶאֶמְרָה הַבְטָחָה זוֹ לְיִשְׂרָאֵל בִּיצִיאָתָם מִמִּצְרַיִם, שֶׁהָיוּ אוֹמְרִים, שֶׁמָּא לֹא נָבוֹא אֶל אֶרֶץ טוֹבָה וְיָפָה כָּזוֹ. יָכוֹל בִּגְנוּתָהּ הַכָּתוּב מְדַבֵּר, וְכָךְ אָמַר לָהֶם: לֹא כְּאֶרֶץ מִצְרַיִם הִיא אֶלָּא רָעָה הֵימֶנָּה? תַּלְמוּד לוֹמַר: "וְחֶבְרוֹן שֶׁבַע שָׁנִים נִבְנְתָה לִפְנֵי צֹעַן מִצְרָיִם" (במדבר יג, כב), אָדָם אֶחָד בְּנָאָן, אִם בָּנָה צֹעַן לְמִצְרַיִם בְּנוֹ וְחֶבְרוֹן לִכְנַעַן; דֶּרֶךְ אֶרֶץ אָדָם בּוֹנֶה אֶת הַנָּאֶה וְאַחַר כָּךְ בּוֹנֶה אֶת הַכָּעוּר, שֶׁפְּסׇלְתּוֹ שֶׁל רִאשׁוֹן הוּא נוֹתֵן בַּשֵּׁנִי, וּבְכׇל מָקוֹם הֶחָבִיב קוֹדֵם, הָא לָמַדְתָּ שֶׁחֶבְרוֹן יָפָה מִצֹּעַן. וּמִצְרַיִם מְשֻׁבַּחַת מִכׇּל הָאֲרָצוֹת, שֶׁנֶּאֱמַר: "כְּגַן ה' כְּאֶרֶץ מִצְרַיִם" (בראשית יג, י), וְצֹעַן שְׁבַח מִצְרַיִם הִיא, שֶׁהָיְתָה מְקוֹם מַלְכוּת, שֶׁכֵּן הוּא אוֹמֵר: "כִּי הָיוּ בְצֹעַן שָׂרָיו" (ישעיה ל, ד), וְחֶבְרוֹן פְּסׇלְתָּהּ שֶׁל אֶרֶץ יִשְׂרָאֵל, לְכָךְ הִקְצוּהָ לִקְבוּרַת מֵתִים, וְאַף עַל פִּי כֵן הִיא יָפָה מִצֹּעַן. וּבִכְתֻבּוֹת (דף קיב ע"א) דָּרְשׁוּ בְּעִנְיָן אַחֵר: אֶפְשָׁר אָדָם בּוֹנֶה בַּיִת לִבְנוֹ הַקָּטָן וְאַחַר כָּךְ לִבְנוֹ הַגָּדוֹל? אֶלָּא שֶׁמְּבֻנָּה עַל אֶחָד מִשִּׁבְעָה בְּצֹעַן: **אֲשֶׁר יְצָאתֶם מִשָּׁם.** אֲפִלּוּ אֶרֶץ רַעְמְסֵס אֲשֶׁר יְשַׁבְתֶּם בָּהּ וְהִיא בְּמֵיטַב אֶרֶץ מִצְרַיִם, שֶׁנֶּאֱמַר: "בְּמֵיטַב הָאָרֶץ" וְגוֹ' (בראשית מז, יא), אַף הִיא אֵינָהּ כְּאֶרֶץ יִשְׂרָאֵל: **וְהִשְׁקִיתָ בְרַגְלְךָ.** אֶרֶץ מִצְרַיִם – הָיִיתָ צָרִיךְ לְהָבִיא מַיִם מִנִּילוּס בְּרַגְלְךָ וּלְהַשְׁקוֹתָהּ, וְצָרִיךְ אַתָּה לִנְדֹּד אֶת שְׁנָתְךָ וְלַעֲמֹל, וְהַנָּמוּךְ שׁוֹתֶה וְלֹא הַגָּבוֹהַּ, וְאַתָּה מַעֲלֶה הַמַּיִם מִן הַנָּמוּךְ לַגָּבוֹהַּ. אֲבָל זוֹ – "לִמְטַר הַשָּׁמַיִם תִּשְׁתֶּה מָּיִם" (להלן פסוק יא), אַתָּה יָשֵׁן עַל מִטָּתְךָ וְהַקָּדוֹשׁ בָּרוּךְ הוּא מַשְׁקֶה נָמוּךְ וְגָבוֹהַּ, גָּלוּי וְשֶׁאֵינוֹ גָּלוּי כְּאַחַת: **כְּגַן הַיָּרָק.** שֶׁאֵין דַּי לוֹ בִּגְשָׁמִים וּמַשְׁקִים אוֹתוֹ בָּרֶגֶל וּבַכָּתֵף:

יא | **אֶרֶץ הָרִים וּבְקָעֹת.** מְשֻׁבָּח הָהָר מִן הַמִּישׁוֹר, שֶׁהַמִּישׁוֹר בְּבֵית כּוֹר אַתָּה זוֹרֵעַ כּוֹר, אֲבָל הָהָר בֵּית כּוֹר מִמֶּנּוּ חֲמֵשֶׁת כּוֹרִין, אַרְבָּעָה מֵאַרְבָּעָה שִׁפּוּעָיו וְאֶחָד בְּרֹאשׁוֹ: **וּבְקָעֹת.** הֵן מִישׁוֹר:

יב | **אֲשֶׁר ה' אֱלֹהֶיךָ דֹּרֵשׁ אֹתָהּ.** וַהֲלֹא כׇּל הָאֲרָצוֹת הוּא דּוֹרֵשׁ, שֶׁנֶּאֱמַר: "לְהַמְטִיר עַל אֶרֶץ לֹא אִישׁ" (איוב לח, כו)! אֶלָּא כִּבְיָכוֹל אֵינוֹ דּוֹרֵשׁ אֶלָּא אוֹתָהּ, וְעַל יְדֵי אוֹתָהּ דְּרִישָׁה שֶׁדּוֹרְשָׁהּ דּוֹרֵשׁ אֶת כׇּל הָאֲרָצוֹת עִמָּהּ: **תָּמִיד עֵינֵי ה' אֱלֹהֶיךָ בָּהּ.** לִרְאוֹת מַה הִיא צְרִיכָה וּלְחַדֵּשׁ בָּהּ גְּזֵרוֹת, עִתִּים לְטוֹבָה וְעִתִּים לְרָעָה וְכוּ', כִּדְאִיתָא בְּרֹאשׁ הַשָּׁנָה (דף יז ע"ב): **מֵרֵשִׁית הַשָּׁנָה.** מֵרֹאשׁ הַשָּׁנָה נִדּוֹן מַה יְּהֵא בְּסוֹפָהּ:

יג | **וְהָיָה אִם שָׁמֹעַ תִּשְׁמְעוּ.** אִם תִּשְׁמַע בַּיָּשָׁן, תִּשְׁמַע בֶּחָדָשׁ, וְכֵן: "וְהָיָה אִם שָׁכֹחַ תִּשְׁכַּח" (לעיל ח, יט), אִם הִתְחַלְתָּ לִשְׁכֹּחַ סוֹפְךָ שֶׁתִּשְׁכַּח כֻּלָּהּ, כְּתִיב בִּמְגִלָּה: אִם תַּעַזְבֵנִי יוֹם, יוֹמַיִם אֶעֶזְבֶךָּ (ראה ספרי מח): **מְצַוֶּה אֶתְכֶם הַיּוֹם.** שֶׁיִּהְיוּ עֲלֵיכֶם חֲדָשִׁים כְּאִלּוּ שְׁמַעְתֶּם בּוֹ בַּיּוֹם: **לְאַהֲבָה אֶת ה'.** שֶׁלֹּא תֹּאמַר: הֲרֵי אֲנִי לָמֵד בִּשְׁבִיל שֶׁאֶהְיֶה עָשִׁיר, בִּשְׁבִיל שֶׁאֶקָּרֵא רַב, בִּשְׁבִיל שֶׁאֲקַבֵּל שָׂכָר, אֶלָּא כׇּל מַה שֶּׁתַּעֲשׂוּ עֲשׂוּ מֵאַהֲבָה, וְסוֹף הַכָּבוֹד לָבֹא: **וּלְעׇבְדוֹ בְּכׇל לְבַבְכֶם.** עֲבוֹדָה שֶׁהִיא בַּלֵּב, וְזוֹ הִיא תְּפִלָּה, שֶׁהַתְּפִלָּה קְרוּיָה עֲבוֹדָה, שֶׁנֶּאֱמַר: "אֱלָהָךְ דִּי אַנְתְּ פָּלַח לֵהּ בִּתְדִירָא" (דניאל ו, יז), וְכִי יֵשׁ פׇּלְחָן בְּבָבֶל? אֶלָּא עַל שֶׁהָיָה מִתְפַּלֵּל, שֶׁנֶּאֱמַר: "וְכַוִּין פְּתִיחָן לֵהּ" וְגוֹ' (שם יא), וְכֵן בְּדָוִד הוּא אוֹמֵר: "תִּכּוֹן תְּפִלָּתִי קְטֹרֶת לְפָנֶיךָ" (תהלים קמא, ב): **בְּכׇל לְבַבְכֶם וּבְכׇל נַפְשְׁכֶם.** וַהֲלֹא כְּבָר הִזְהִיר: "בְּכׇל לְבָבְךָ וּבְכׇל נַפְשְׁךָ" (דברים ו, ה)? אֶלָּא, אַזְהָרָה לַיָּחִיד, אַזְהָרָה לַצִּבּוּר:

14 **I will provide the rain of your land at its appointed time,**[D] **the early rain and the late rain, and you will gather your grain, and your wine, and your oil,** all the major crops.

15 **I will provide grass in your field for your animals,** as the rain will irrigate your fields of crops as well as areas designated for pasture, **and you will eat and you will be satisfied.**

16 **Beware, lest your heart be seduced, and you stray and serve other gods, and prostrate yourself before them.**

17 **The wrath of the Lord will be enflamed against you, and He will curb the heavens and there will be no rain, and** since the land in which you will be living depends on regular rainfall, **the ground will not yield its produce; and** due to the ensuing famine **you will be quickly eradicated from upon the good land that the Lord is giving you.**

18 Due to the importance of these matters, the people are commanded to keep them in mind at all times. In this regard, Moses issues statements that can be interpreted as general, metaphorical expressions of internalization and remembrance, but which also require practical implementation: **You shall place these words of Mine upon your heart and upon your soul,** as you must pay attention to them; **and you shall bind them as a sign** of remembrance **upon your arm,** in that you must remember and observe them, and in addition you must bind them in

written form upon your arm. **And they shall be as ornaments between** and above **your eyes,** an ornament of sorts placed above the forehead.[28] This sign, the phylacteries, identifies each male as a member of the people of Israel.

19 **You shall teach them to your children to speak of them** wherever you are, and whatever your situation; **while you are sitting in your house, while you are walking on the way,**

Gathering grain

Phylacteries of the head

Gathering olives

Gathering grapes

יד וְנָתַתִּי מְטַר־אַרְצְכֶם בְּעִתּוֹ יוֹרֶה וּמַלְקוֹשׁ וְאָסַפְתָּ דְגָנֶךָ וְתִירֹשְׁךָ וְיִצְהָרֶךָ:
טו טז וְנָתַתִּי עֵשֶׂב בְּשָׂדְךָ לִבְהֶמְתֶּךָ וְאָכַלְתָּ וְשָׂבָעְתָּ: הִשָּׁמְרוּ לָכֶם פֶּן־יִפְתֶּה לְבַבְכֶם
יז וְסַרְתֶּם וַעֲבַדְתֶּם אֱלֹהִים אֲחֵרִים וְהִשְׁתַּחֲוִיתֶם לָהֶם: וְחָרָה אַף־יְהוָה בָּכֶם
וְעָצַר אֶת־הַשָּׁמַיִם וְלֹא־יִהְיֶה מָטָר וְהָאֲדָמָה לֹא תִתֵּן אֶת־יְבוּלָהּ וַאֲבַדְתֶּם
יח מְהֵרָה מֵעַל הָאָרֶץ הַטֹּבָה אֲשֶׁר יְהוָה נֹתֵן לָכֶם: וְשַׂמְתֶּם אֶת־דְּבָרַי אֵלֶּה
עַל־לְבַבְכֶם וְעַל־נַפְשְׁכֶם וּקְשַׁרְתֶּם אֹתָם לְאוֹת עַל־יֶדְכֶם וְהָיוּ לְטוֹטָפֹת בֵּין
יט עֵינֵיכֶם: וְלִמַּדְתֶּם אֹתָם אֶת־בְּנֵיכֶם לְדַבֵּר בָּם בְּשִׁבְתְּךָ בְּבֵיתֶךָ וּבְלֶכְתְּךָ בַדֶּרֶךְ

רש"י

יד | **וְנָתַתִּי מְטַר אַרְצְכֶם.** עֲשִׂיתֶם מַה שֶּׁעֲלֵיכֶם, אַף אֲנִי אֶעֱשֶׂה מַה שֶּׁעָלַי: **בְּעִתּוֹ.** בַּלֵּילוֹת, שֶׁלֹּא יַטְרִיחוּ אֶתְכֶם. דָּבָר אַחֵר, "בְּעִתּוֹ", בְּלֵילֵי שַׁבָּתוֹת, שֶׁהַכֹּל מְצוּיִין בְּבָתֵּיהֶם: **יוֹרֶה.** הִיא רְבִיעָה הַנּוֹפֶלֶת לְאַחַר הַזְּרִיעָה, שֶׁמַּרְוָה אֶת הָאָרֶץ וְאֶת הַזְּרָעִים: **וּמַלְקוֹשׁ.** רְבִיעָה הַיּוֹרֶדֶת סָמוּךְ לַקָּצִיר לְמַלֹּאת הַתְּבוּאָה בְּקַשֶּׁיהָ. וּלְשׁוֹן "מַלְקוֹשׁ" דָּבָר הַמְאֻחָר, כִּדְמִתַּרְגְּמִינַן: "וְהָיָה הָעֲטֻפִים לְלָבָן" – "לַקִּישַׁיָּא" (בראשית ל, מב). דָּבָר אַחֵר, לְכָךְ נִקְרֵאת "מַלְקוֹשׁ", שֶׁיּוֹרֶדֶת עַל הַמְּלִילוֹת וְעַל הַקַּשִּׁין: **וְאָסַפְתָּ דְגָנֶךָ.** אַתָּה תַּאַסְפֶנּוּ אֶל הַבַּיִת וְלֹא אוֹיְבֶיךָ, כְּעִנְיָן שֶׁנֶּאֱמַר: "אִם אֶתֵּן אֶת דְּגָנֵךְ עוֹד מַאֲכָל לְאֹיְבַיִךְ וְגוֹ' כִּי מְאַסְפָיו יֹאכְלֻהוּ" (ישעיה סב, ח-ט), וְלֹא כְּעִנְיָן שֶׁנֶּאֱמַר: "וְהָיָה אִם זָרַע יִשְׂרָאֵל וְעָלָה מִדְיָן וַעֲמָלֵק וּבְנֵי קֶדֶם" וְגוֹ' (שופטים ו, ג):

טו | **וְנָתַתִּי עֵשֶׂב בְּשָׂדְךָ.** שֶׁלֹּא תִצְטָרֵךְ לְהוֹלִיכָהּ לַמִּדְבָּרוֹת. דָּבָר אַחֵר, שֶׁתִּהְיֶה גּוֹזֵז תְּבוּאָתְךָ כָּל יְמוֹת הַגְּשָׁמִים וּמַשְׁלִיךְ לִפְנֵי בְהֶמְתְּךָ, וְאַתָּה מוֹנֵעַ יָדְךָ מִמֶּנָּה שְׁלֹשִׁים יוֹם קֹדֶם לַקָּצִיר וְאֵינָהּ פּוֹחֶתֶת מִדְּגָנָהּ: **וְאָכַלְתָּ וְשָׂבָעְתָּ.** הֲרֵי זוֹ בְּרָכָה אַחֶרֶת, שֶׁתְּהֵא בְּרָכָה מְצוּיָה בַּפַּת בְּתוֹךְ הַמֵּעַיִם:

טו-טז | **וְאָכַלְתָּ וְשָׂבָעְתָּ, הִשָּׁמְרוּ לָכֶם.** כֵּיוָן שֶׁתִּהְיוּ אוֹכְלִים וּשְׂבֵעִים, הִשָּׁמְרוּ לָכֶם שֶׁלֹּא תִבְעָטוּ, שֶׁאֵין אָדָם מוֹרֵד בְּהַקָּדוֹשׁ בָּרוּךְ הוּא אֶלָּא מִתּוֹךְ שְׂבִיעָה, שֶׁנֶּאֱמַר: "פֶּן תֹּאכַל וְשָׂבָעְתָּ... וּבְקָרְךָ וְצֹאנְךָ יִרְבְּיֻן" (לעיל ח, יב-יג), מַה הוּא אוֹמֵר אַחֲרָיו? "וְרָם לְבָבֶךָ וְשָׁכַחְתָּ" (שם יד): **וְסַרְתֶּם.** לִפְרֹשׁ מִן הַתּוֹרָה, וּמִתּוֹךְ כָּךְ: "וַעֲבַדְתֶּם אֱלֹהִים אֲחֵרִים", שֶׁכֵּיוָן שֶׁאָדָם פּוֹרֵשׁ מִן הַתּוֹרָה, הוֹלֵךְ וּמִדַּבֵּק בַּעֲבוֹדָה זָרָה. וְכֵן דָּוִד אוֹמֵר: "כִּי גֵרְשׁוּנִי הַיּוֹם מֵהִסְתַּפֵּחַ בְּנַחֲלַת ה' לֵאמֹר לֵךְ עֲבֹד אֱלֹהִים אֲחֵרִים" (שמואל א' כו, יט), וּמִי אָמַר לוֹ כֵּן? אֶלָּא כֵּיוָן שֶׁאֲנִי מְגֹרָשׁ מִלַּעֲסֹק בַּתּוֹרָה, הֲרֵינִי קָרוֹב לַעֲבֹד אֱלֹהִים אֲחֵרִים: **אֱלֹהִים אֲחֵרִים.** שֶׁהֵם אֲחֵרִים לְעוֹבְדֵיהֶם, צוֹעֵק אֵלָיו וְאֵינוֹ עוֹנֵהוּ, נִמְצָא עָשׂוּי לוֹ כְּנָכְרִי:

יז | **אֶת יְבוּלָהּ.** אַף מַה שֶּׁאַתָּה מוֹבִיל לָהּ, כְּעִנְיָן שֶׁנֶּאֱמַר: "זְרַעְתֶּם הַרְבֵּה וְהָבֵא מְעָט" (חגי א, ו): **וַאֲבַדְתֶּם מְהֵרָה.** עַל כָּל שְׁאָר הַיִּסּוּרִין, אַגְלֶה אֶתְכֶם מִן הָאֲדָמָה שֶׁגָּרְמָה לָכֶם לַחֲטֹא. מָשָׁל לְמֶלֶךְ שֶׁשָּׁלַח בְּנוֹ לְבֵית הַמִּשְׁתֶּה וְהָיָה יוֹשֵׁב וּמְפַקְּדוֹ: אַל תֹּאכַל יוֹתֵר מִצָּרְכְּךָ שֶׁתָּבוֹא נָקִי לְבֵיתְךָ, וְלֹא הִשְׁגִּיחַ הַבֵּן הַהוּא, אָכַל וְשָׁתָה יוֹתֵר מִצָּרְכּוֹ וְהֵקִיא וְטִנֵּף אֶת כָּל בְּנֵי הַמְּסִבָּה, נְטָלוּהוּ בְּיָדָיו וּבְרַגְלָיו וּזְרָקוּהוּ אֲחוֹרֵי פַלְטֵרִין: **מְהֵרָה.** אֵינִי נוֹתֵן לָכֶם אַרְכָּא. וְאִם תֹּאמְרוּ, וַהֲלֹא נִתְּנָה אַרְכָּא לְדוֹר הַמַּבּוּל, שֶׁנֶּאֱמַר: "וְהָיוּ יָמָיו מֵאָה וְעֶשְׂרִים שָׁנָה" (בראשית ו, ג)? דּוֹר הַמַּבּוּל לֹא הָיָה לָהֶם מִמִּי לִלְמֹד, וְאַתֶּם יֵשׁ לָכֶם מִמִּי לִלְמֹד:

יח | **וְשַׂמְתֶּם אֶת דְּבָרַי.** אַף לְאַחַר שֶׁתִּגְלוּ הֱיוּ מְצֻיָּנִים בַּמִּצְוֹת, הַנִּיחוּ תְּפִלִּין עֲשׂוּ מְזוּזוֹת, כְּדֵי שֶׁלֹּא יִהְיוּ לָכֶם חֲדָשִׁים כְּשֶׁתַּחְזְרוּ, וְכֵן הוּא אוֹמֵר: "הַצִּיבִי לָךְ צִיֻּנִים" (ירמיה לא, כ):

יט-כא | **לְדַבֵּר בָּם.** מִשָּׁעָה שֶׁהַבֵּן יוֹדֵעַ לְדַבֵּר, לַמְּדֵהוּ "תּוֹרָה צִוָּה לָנוּ מֹשֶׁה" (להלן לג, ד), שֶׁיְּהֵא זֶה לִמּוּד דִּבּוּרוֹ. מִכָּאן אָמְרוּ: כְּשֶׁהַתִּינוֹק מַתְחִיל לְדַבֵּר, אָבִיו מֵשִׂיחַ עִמּוֹ בִּלְשׁוֹן הַקֹּדֶשׁ וּמְלַמְּדוֹ תּוֹרָה, וְאִם לֹא עָשָׂה כֵן הֲרֵי הוּא כְּאִלּוּ קוֹבְרוֹ, שֶׁנֶּאֱמַר: "וְלִמַּדְתֶּם אֹתָם אֶת בְּנֵיכֶם לְדַבֵּר בָּם וְגוֹ' לְמַעַן יִרְבּוּ יְמֵיכֶם וִימֵי בְנֵיכֶם" – אִם עֲשִׂיתֶם

DISCUSSION

11:14 | I will provide the rain of your land at its appointed time: In general, the book of Deuteronomy is addressed to the entire congregation of Israel, not to individuals. The rainfall and the lack thereof, are also tied to the conduct of the community as a whole, not to the deeds of any particular individual. According to one opinion, the fulfillment of these promises is a miraculous event, and miracles of this kind transpire only to the entire nation of Israel, when it is complete, but not to private individuals (Ramban, Genesis 17:1, Leviticus 26:10). Consequently, any change in the conduct of the community, for good or bad, is immediately noticeable.

while you are lying, and while you are arising, so that your children will continue in the path of the Torah.
20 Additionally, **you shall write them on the doorposts**[D] **of your house, and on your gates;**
21 **so that your days will be increased, and the days of your children, on the land with regard to which the Lord took an oath to your forefathers to give them,** and the length of those days is **like the days of the heavens above the earth,** as long as the world exists.
Seventh aliya Maftir 22 **For if you shall observe this entire commandment that I command you to perform it, to love the Lord your God, to walk in all His ways, and to cleave to Him,**
23 **the Lord will dispossess all these nations from before you, and you will take possession from nations greater and mightier than you.**
24 **Every place on which the sole of your foot shall tread will be yours, from the wilderness and the Lebanon, from the river, the Euphrates River, until the ultimate sea will be your border.** Not only will you receive the land that was promised to you in advance, but you will also succeed in conquering other places.
25 **No man will stand before you,** since **the Lord your God will place terror of you and fear of you upon the entire land on which you will tread, as He spoke to you.**

Mezuza on a gate

DISCUSSION

11:20 | **The doorposts:** According to tradition, these words are not actually written on the doorposts, but on parchment, which is then appended to the doorpost. These are called mezuzot, literally, doorposts (see *Menaḥot* 34a).

כ כא וּבְשָׁכְבְּךָ וּבְקוּמֶךָ׃ וּכְתַבְתָּם עַל־מְזוּזוֹת בֵּיתֶךָ וּבִשְׁעָרֶיךָ׃ לְמַעַן יִרְבּוּ יְמֵיכֶם וִימֵי
בְנֵיכֶם עַל הָאֲדָמָה אֲשֶׁר נִשְׁבַּע יְהוָה לַאֲבֹתֵיכֶם לָתֵת לָהֶם כִּימֵי הַשָּׁמַיִם עַל־
כב הָאָרֶץ׃ כִּי אִם־שָׁמֹר תִּשְׁמְרוּן אֶת־כָּל־הַמִּצְוָה הַזֹּאת אֲשֶׁר אָנֹכִי שביעי ומפטיר
מְצַוֶּה אֶתְכֶם לַעֲשֹׂתָהּ לְאַהֲבָה אֶת־יְהוָה אֱלֹהֵיכֶם לָלֶכֶת בְּכָל־דְּרָכָיו וּלְדָבְקָה־
כג בוֹ׃ וְהוֹרִישׁ יְהוָה אֶת־כָּל־הַגּוֹיִם הָאֵלֶּה מִלִּפְנֵיכֶם וִירִשְׁתֶּם גּוֹיִם גְּדֹלִים וַעֲצֻמִים
כד מִכֶּם׃ כָּל־הַמָּקוֹם אֲשֶׁר תִּדְרֹךְ כַּף־רַגְלְכֶם בּוֹ לָכֶם יִהְיֶה מִן־הַמִּדְבָּר וְהַלְּבָנוֹן
כה מִן־הַנָּהָר נְהַר־פְּרָת וְעַד הַיָּם הָאַחֲרוֹן יִהְיֶה גְּבֻלְכֶם׃ לֹא־יִתְיַצֵּב אִישׁ בִּפְנֵיכֶם
פַּחְדְּכֶם וּמוֹרַאֲכֶם יִתֵּן ׀ יְהוָה אֱלֹהֵיכֶם עַל־פְּנֵי כָל־הָאָרֶץ אֲשֶׁר תִּדְרְכוּ־בָהּ
כַּאֲשֶׁר דִּבֶּר לָכֶם׃

רש״י

כֵּן יִרְבּוּ, וְאִם לָאו לֹא יִרְבּוּ, שֶׁדִּבְרֵי תוֹרָה נִדְרָשִׁין מִכְּלַל לָאו הֵן וּמִכְּלַל הֵן לָאו: **לָתֵת לָהֶם.** 'לָתֵת לָכֶם' אֵין כְּתִיב כָּאן, אֶלָּא "לָתֵת לָהֶם", מִכָּאן מָצִינוּ לְמֵדִים תְּחִיַּת הַמֵּתִים מִן הַתּוֹרָה:

כב | **שָׁמֹר תִּשְׁמְרוּן.** אַזְהָרַת שְׁמִירוֹת הַרְבֵּה, לְהִזָּהֵר בְּתַלְמוּדוֹ שֶׁלֹּא יִשְׁתַּכַּח: **לָלֶכֶת בְּכָל דְּרָכָיו.** הוּא רַחוּם וְאַתָּה תְּהֵא רַחוּם, הוּא גּוֹמֵל חֲסָדִים וְאַתָּה גּוֹמֵל חֲסָדִים: **וּלְדָבְקָה בוֹ.** אֶפְשָׁר לוֹמַר כֵּן, וַהֲלֹא "אֵשׁ אֹכְלָה הוּא" (לעיל ד, כד)? אֶלָּא הִדָּבֵק בַּתַּלְמִידִים וּבַחֲכָמִים, וּמַעֲלֶה אֲנִי עָלֶיךָ כְּאִלּוּ נִדְבַּקְתָּ בוֹ:

כג | **וְהוֹרִישׁ ה'.** עֲשִׂיתֶם מַה שֶּׁעֲלֵיכֶם, אַף אֲנִי אֶעֱשֶׂה מַה שֶּׁעָלַי: **וַעֲצֻמִים מִכֶּם.** אַתֶּם גִּבּוֹרִים וְהֵם גִּבּוֹרִים מִכֶּם, שֶׁאִם לֹא שֶׁיִּשְׂרָאֵל גִּבּוֹרִים, מַה הַשֶּׁבַח הַהוּא שֶׁמְּשַׁבֵּחַ אֶת הָאֱמוֹרִיִּים לוֹמַר: "וַעֲצֻמִים מִכֶּם"? אֶלָּא אַתֶּם גִּבּוֹרִים מִשְּׁאָר הָאֻמּוֹת, וְהֵם גִּבּוֹרִים מִכֶּם:

כה | **לֹא יִתְיַצֵּב אִישׁ וְגוֹ'.** אֵין לִי אֶלָּא אִישׁ, אֻמָּה וּמִשְׁפָּחָה וְאִשָּׁה בִּכְשָׁפֶיהָ מִנַּיִן? תַּלְמוּד לוֹמַר: "לֹא יִתְיַצֵּב", מִכָּל מָקוֹם. אִם כֵּן, מַה תַּלְמוּד לוֹמַר: "אִישׁ"? אֲפִלּוּ כְּעוֹג מֶלֶךְ הַבָּשָׁן: **פַּחְדְּכֶם וּמוֹרַאֲכֶם.** וַהֲלֹא פַּחַד הוּא מוֹרָא? אֶלָּא "פַּחְדְּכֶם" עַל הַקְּרוֹבִים "וּמוֹרַאֲכֶם" עַל הָרְחוֹקִים. 'פַּחַד' לְשׁוֹן בְּעִיתַת פִּתְאֹם, 'מוֹרָא' לְשׁוֹן דְּאָגָה מִיָּמִים רַבִּים: **כַּאֲשֶׁר דִּבֶּר לָכֶם.** וְהֵיכָן דִּבֶּר? "אֶת אֵימָתִי אֲשַׁלַּח לְפָנֶיךָ" וְגוֹ' (שמות כג, כז):

Parashat
Re'eh

The Blessing and the Curse
DEUTERONOMY 11:26–32

Moses' declaration regarding the blessing to be bestowed upon the people in the Land of Israel if they fulfill God's commandments, and the curse that will befall them if they fail to do so, is a transition and introduction to the detailed discussion of the commandments that follows.

26 **See, I put before you this day a blessing and a curse.**

27 **The blessing, if you heed the commandments of the Lord your God, that I am commanding you today,**

28 **and the curse, if you will not heed the commandments of the Lord your God, and you stray from the path that I am commanding you today, to follow other gods that you did not know.** The blessing and the curse relate to the observance of all of the Torah's commandments, but their primary focus is upon the prohibition of idolatry.

29 The blessing and the curse will also have a ceremonial manifestation: **It shall be when the Lord your God brings you into the land that you are coming there to take possession of it, you shall present the blessing on Mount Gerizim,**[B] **and the curse on Mount Eival.**[B] Blessings will be proclaimed facing Mount Gerizim, while curses will be pronounced facing Mount Eival.[1]

30 The verse clarifies the location of these two mountains: **Aren't they beyond the Jordan, beyond the path of the setting of the sun,** heading westward, **in the land of the Canaanite that lives in the plain, opposite the Gilgal, beside the plains of Moreh?**[2]

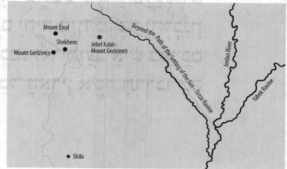

Locations of Mount Gerizim and Mount Eival

31 **For you are crossing the Jordan to come to take possession of the land that the Lord your God is giving you, and you shall take possession of it, and you shall reside in it.**

32 **You shall take care to perform all the statutes and the ordinances that I put before you today.**

Mount Gerizim and Mount Eival

פרשת
ראה

כו כז רְאֵה אָנֹכִי נֹתֵן לִפְנֵיכֶם הַיּוֹם בְּרָכָה וּקְלָלָה: אֶת־הַבְּרָכָה אֲשֶׁר תִּשְׁמְעוּ אֶל־מִצְוֺת
כח יהוה אֱלֹהֵיכֶם אֲשֶׁר אָנֹכִי מְצַוֶּה אֶתְכֶם הַיּוֹם: וְהַקְּלָלָה אִם־לֹא תִשְׁמְעוּ אֶל־מִצְוֺת
יהוה אֱלֹהֵיכֶם וְסַרְתֶּם מִן־הַדֶּרֶךְ אֲשֶׁר אָנֹכִי מְצַוֶּה אֶתְכֶם הַיּוֹם לָלֶכֶת אַחֲרֵי
כט אֱלֹהִים אֲחֵרִים אֲשֶׁר לֹא־יְדַעְתֶּם: וְהָיָה כִּי יְבִיאֲךָ יהוה אֱלֹהֶיךָ אֶל־
הָאָרֶץ אֲשֶׁר־אַתָּה בָא־שָׁמָּה לְרִשְׁתָּהּ וְנָתַתָּה אֶת־הַבְּרָכָה עַל־הַר גְּרִזִים וְאֶת־
ל הַקְּלָלָה עַל־הַר עֵיבָל: הֲלֹא־הֵמָּה בְּעֵבֶר הַיַּרְדֵּן אַחֲרֵי דֶּרֶךְ מְבוֹא הַשֶּׁמֶשׁ בְּאֶרֶץ
לא הַכְּנַעֲנִי הַיֹּשֵׁב בָּעֲרָבָה מוּל הַגִּלְגָּל אֵצֶל אֵלוֹנֵי מֹרֶה: כִּי אַתֶּם עֹבְרִים אֶת־הַיַּרְדֵּן
לָבֹא לָרֶשֶׁת אֶת־הָאָרֶץ אֲשֶׁר־יהוה אֱלֹהֵיכֶם נֹתֵן לָכֶם וִירִשְׁתֶּם אֹתָהּ וִישַׁבְתֶּם־בָּהּ:
לב וּשְׁמַרְתֶּם לַעֲשׂוֹת אֵת כָּל־הַחֻקִּים וְאֶת־הַמִּשְׁפָּטִים אֲשֶׁר אָנֹכִי נֹתֵן לִפְנֵיכֶם הַיּוֹם:

רש״י

כו | **רְאֵה אָנֹכִי. בְּרָכָה וּקְלָלָה.** הָאֲמוּרוֹת בְּהַר גְּרִזִּים וּבְהַר עֵיבָל (להלן כז, טו-כו):

כז | **אֶת הַבְּרָכָה.** עַל מְנָת ״אֲשֶׁר תִּשְׁמְעוּ״:

כח | **מִן הַדֶּרֶךְ אֲשֶׁר אָנֹכִי מְצַוֶּה אֶתְכֶם הַיּוֹם לָלֶכֶת וְגוֹ׳.** הָא לָמַדְתָּ שֶׁכָּל הָעוֹבֵד עֲבוֹדָה זָרָה הֲרֵי הוּא סָר מִכָּל הַדֶּרֶךְ שֶׁנִּצְטַוּוּ יִשְׂרָאֵל. מִכָּאן אָמְרוּ: כָּל הַמּוֹדֶה בַּעֲבוֹדָה זָרָה כְּכוֹפֵר בְּכָל הַתּוֹרָה כֻּלָּהּ:

כט | **וְנָתַתָּה אֶת הַבְּרָכָה.** כְּתַרְגּוּמוֹ: ״יָת מְבָרְכַיָּא״, אֶת הַמְבָרְכִים: **עַל הַר גְּרִזִּים.** כְּלַפֵּי הַר גְּרִזִּים הוֹפְכִים פְּנֵיהֶם וּפָתְחוּ בִּבְרָכָה: ׳בָּרוּךְ הָאִישׁ אֲשֶׁר לֹא יַעֲשֶׂה פֶסֶל וּמַסֵּכָה׳ וְגוֹ׳, כָּל הָאֲרוּרִים שֶׁבַּפָּרָשָׁה אָמְרוּ תְּחִלָּה בִּלְשׁוֹן ׳בָּרוּךְ׳, וְאַחַר כָּךְ הָפְכוּ פְּנֵיהֶם כְּלַפֵּי הַר עֵיבָל וּפָתְחוּ בִּקְלָלָה:

ל | **הֲלֹא הֵמָּה.** נָתַן לָהֶם סִימָן: **אַחֲרֵי.** אַחַר הַעֲבָרַת הַיַּרְדֵּן הַרְבֵּה וְהָלְאָה לְמֵרָחוֹק, וְזֶהוּ לְשׁוֹן ׳אַחֲרֵי׳. כָּל מָקוֹם שֶׁנֶּאֱמַר ׳אַחֲרֵי׳ מֻפְלָג הוּא: **דֶּרֶךְ מְבוֹא הַשֶּׁמֶשׁ.** לְהַלָּן מִן הַיַּרְדֵּן לְצַד מַעֲרָב. וְטַעַם הַמִּקְרָא מוֹכִיחַ שֶׁהֵם שְׁנֵי דְּבָרִים, שֶׁנֶּנְקְדוּ בִּשְׁנֵי טְעָמִים, ׳אַחֲרֵי׳ נָקוּד בְּפַשְׁטָא, וְ׳דֶרֶךְ׳ נָקוּד בְּמַשְׁפֵּל וְהוּא דָּגוּשׁ, וְאִם הָיָה ׳אַחֲרֵי דֶּרֶךְ׳ דִּבּוּר אֶחָד, הָיָה נָקוּד ׳אַחֲרֵי׳ בִּמְשָׁרֵת, בְּשׁוֹפָר הָפוּךְ, וְ׳דֶרֶךְ׳ בְּפַשְׁטָא וְרָפֶה: **מוּל הַגִּלְגָּל.** רָחוֹק מִן הַגִּלְגָּל: **אֵלוֹנֵי מֹרֶה.** שְׁכֶם הוּא, שֶׁנֶּאֱמַר: ״עַד מְקוֹם שְׁכֶם עַד אֵלוֹן מוֹרֶה״ (בראשית יב, ו):

לא | **כִּי אַתֶּם עֹבְרִים אֶת הַיַּרְדֵּן וְגוֹ׳.** נִסִּים שֶׁל יַרְדֵּן יִהְיוּ סִימָן בְּיֶדְכֶם שֶׁתָּבֹאוּ וְתִירְשׁוּ אֶת הָאָרֶץ:

BACKGROUND

11:29 | **Mount Gerizim:** The mountain currently known as Mount Gerizim is located south of Nablus and rises to an elevation of 881 m above sea level. It is considered sacred by the Samaritans. Some identify Mount Gerizim with Jebel Kabir, which is east of Mount Eival.

Mount Eival: The mountain currently known as Mount Eival is located north of Nablus. It rises to an elevation of 940 m above sea level, making it the highest peak in central and northern Samaria. The Samaritans call it *Har Askar*, after the village located at the foot of the mountain in the valley of Ein Sukar. The remnants of an altar were excavated on the northeastern side of Mount Eival, and were identified as the remains of the altar constructed by Joshua (see 27:1–11; Joshua 8:30–33).

Commandments Connected to the Temple and to Idolatry in the Land of Israel

DEUTERONOMY 12:1–31

Moses' long presentation of the commandments (spanning from 12:1 to 26:19) includes some new commandments as well as others that appeared in earlier books of the Torah. However, in those earlier books of the Torah, fulfillment of the commandments is generally not restricted to a specific location, whereas in Deuteronomy a close connection between fulfillment of commandments and entry into the Land of Israel is introduced. In this regard, this section includes commandments related to the nation dwelling in its land, those pertaining to the establishment of a state with its own spiritual leadership and judiciary, commandments relating to the Temple, and commandments that apply to other parts of the land, some of which stem from the agricultural lifestyle the nation will adopt in its land. Among the most prominent prohibitions are those related to idolatry.

In this first section, which pertains mainly to the role of the Temple, the relationship between one commandment and the next is not always readily apparent. Some of the juxtapositions have been explained through homiletic interpretation.

12 **1** **These are the statutes and the ordinances that you shall take care to perform in the land that the Lord, God of your fathers, has given you to take possession of it, all the days that you live on the earth,** forever.

2 Upon entering the land, **you shall eradicate** the idols in **all the places**[3] **where the nations from whom you are taking possession served their gods.** To this end you must seek and destroy idols everywhere: **on the high mountains, and on the hills, and under every flourishing tree.** The reference here is not to trees that were worshipped, but to trees that were chosen to serve as cultic sites. Since trees of that kind were typically not hewed or trimmed, their form was conspicuous.

3 **You shall smash their altars, and you shall shatter their monuments, and their sacred trees you shall burn in fire, and the idols of their gods you shall cut down** and destroy; **and** in addition **you shall eradicate their name from that place.** You must change or corrupt the names of places named for the pagan rites practiced there,[4] or refrain from referring to such places by name.

4 **You shall not do so to the Lord your God;** you shall not destroy or smash an altar or holy place built for Him. Alternatively, you shall not sacrifice offerings to Him in all places.[5]

5 **Rather, to the** presently undisclosed **place that the Lord your God will choose** one day **from all your tribes to place His name there, you shall seek for His resting place, and you shall come there,** and there you shall conduct public ceremonies of religious worship.

6 **You shall bring there,** to the Temple that will be built on that site, **your burnt offerings,** which are burnt on the altar in their entirety, **and your peace offerings,** parts of which are eaten, **and your** animal **tithes** from your herds and flocks, **and the gift of your hand, and your vows** that you undertook to consecrate to the Temple, **and your pledges** that you designated for the Temple, **and the firstborn of your cattle and of your flocks.**

7 **You shall eat** the offerings **there before the Lord your God, and you shall rejoice in all** you have acquired through **your endeavors, you and your households, with which the Lord your God has blessed you.**

8 **You shall not do** in the land **like all that we are doing here today, each man anything that is right in his eyes.** Many laws, and in particular the laws related to bringing offerings to the Temple and eating them there, did not take effect in the wilderness, and would become relevant only after the people entered the land. In the wilderness, a person who did not sin was not obligated to bring any offerings, and even one who brought an offering of his own free will could eat it wherever he wanted. Once God chooses a location in which to rest His Presence, it will be prohibited to eat consecrated meat anywhere else, and private offerings, e.g., animal tithes, firstborns, and festival offerings, will become obligatory.[6]

9 **For you have not yet come to the haven and to the inheritance that the Lord your God is giving you,** and there is still no place that has been chosen as the exclusive location where one may bring offerings, as the Tabernacle is itinerant.

10 **You shall cross the Jordan, and you will live in the land that the Lord your God is bequeathing to you, and He will give you respite from all your enemies around, and you will live securely,** following the war of conquest.

א אֵלֶּה הַחֻקִּים וְהַמִּשְׁפָּטִים אֲשֶׁר תִּשְׁמְרוּן לַעֲשׂוֹת בָּאָרֶץ אֲשֶׁר נָתַן יְהוָה אֱלֹהֵי
אֲבֹתֶיךָ לְךָ לְרִשְׁתָּהּ כָּל־הַיָּמִים אֲשֶׁר־אַתֶּם חַיִּים עַל־הָאֲדָמָה: ב אַבֵּד תְּאַבְּדוּן
אֶת־כָּל־הַמְּקֹמוֹת אֲשֶׁר עָבְדוּ־שָׁם הַגּוֹיִם אֲשֶׁר אַתֶּם יֹרְשִׁים אֹתָם אֶת־אֱלֹהֵיהֶם
עַל־הֶהָרִים הָרָמִים וְעַל־הַגְּבָעוֹת וְתַחַת כָּל־עֵץ רַעֲנָן: ג וְנִתַּצְתֶּם אֶת־מִזְבְּחֹתָם
וְשִׁבַּרְתֶּם אֶת־מַצֵּבֹתָם וַאֲשֵׁרֵיהֶם תִּשְׂרְפוּן בָּאֵשׁ וּפְסִילֵי אֱלֹהֵיהֶם תְּגַדֵּעוּן
וְאִבַּדְתֶּם אֶת־שְׁמָם מִן־הַמָּקוֹם הַהוּא: ד לֹא־תַעֲשׂוּן כֵּן לַיהוָה אֱלֹהֵיכֶם: ה כִּי
אִם־אֶל־הַמָּקוֹם אֲשֶׁר־יִבְחַר יְהוָה אֱלֹהֵיכֶם מִכָּל־שִׁבְטֵיכֶם לָשׂוּם אֶת־שְׁמוֹ
שָׁם לְשִׁכְנוֹ תִדְרְשׁוּ וּבָאתָ שָּׁמָּה: ו וַהֲבֵאתֶם שָׁמָּה עֹלֹתֵיכֶם וְזִבְחֵיכֶם וְאֵת
מַעְשְׂרֹתֵיכֶם וְאֵת תְּרוּמַת יֶדְכֶם וְנִדְרֵיכֶם וְנִדְבֹתֵיכֶם וּבְכֹרֹת בְּקַרְכֶם וְצֹאנְכֶם:
ז וַאֲכַלְתֶּם־שָׁם לִפְנֵי יְהוָה אֱלֹהֵיכֶם וּשְׂמַחְתֶּם בְּכֹל מִשְׁלַח יֶדְכֶם אַתֶּם וּבָתֵּיכֶם
אֲשֶׁר בֵּרַכְךָ יְהוָה אֱלֹהֶיךָ: ח לֹא תַעֲשׂוּן כְּכֹל אֲשֶׁר אֲנַחְנוּ עֹשִׂים פֹּה הַיּוֹם
אִישׁ כָּל־הַיָּשָׁר בְּעֵינָיו: ט כִּי לֹא־בָאתֶם עַד־עָתָּה אֶל־הַמְּנוּחָה וְאֶל־הַנַּחֲלָה
אֲשֶׁר־יְהוָה אֱלֹהֶיךָ נֹתֵן לָךְ: י וַעֲבַרְתֶּם אֶת־הַיַּרְדֵּן וִישַׁבְתֶּם בָּאָרֶץ אֲשֶׁר־יְהוָה
אֱלֹהֵיכֶם מַנְחִיל אֶתְכֶם וְהֵנִיחַ לָכֶם מִכָּל־אֹיְבֵיכֶם מִסָּבִיב וִישַׁבְתֶּם־בֶּטַח:

רש"י

פרק יב
ב אַבֵּד תְּאַבְּדוּן. "אַבֵּד" וְאַחַר כָּךְ "תְּאַבְּדוּן", מִכָּאן
לְעוֹקֵר עֲבוֹדָה זָרָה שֶׁצָּרִיךְ לְשָׁרֵשׁ אַחֲרֶיהָ: אֶת כָּל
הַמְּקֹמוֹת אֲשֶׁר עָבְדוּ שָׁם וְגוֹ'. וּמַה תְּאַבְּדוּן מֵהֶם? "אֶת
אֱלֹהֵיהֶם" אֲשֶׁר "עַל הֶהָרִים":

ג מִזְבֵּחַ. שֶׁל אֲבָנִים הַרְבֵּה: מַצֵּבָה. שֶׁל אֶבֶן אַחַת, וְהִיא
'בִּימוֹס' שֶׁשָּׁנִינוּ בַּמִּשְׁנָה: "אֶבֶן שֶׁחֲצָבָהּ מִתְּחִלָּתָהּ לַבִּימוֹס"
(עבודה זרה מז ע"ב): אֲשֵׁרָה. אִילָן הַנֶּעֱבָד: וְאִבַּדְתֶּם אֶת
שְׁמָם. לְכַנּוֹת לָהֶם שֵׁם לִגְנַאי, בֵּית גַּלְיָא קוֹרִין לָהּ בֵּית
כַּרְיָא, עֵין כֹּל עֵין קוֹץ:

ד לֹא תַעֲשׂוּן כֵּן. לְהַקְטִיר לַשָּׁמַיִם בְּכָל מָקוֹם, כִּי אִם
בַּמָּקוֹם אֲשֶׁר יִבְחַר (להלן פסוק יא). דָּבָר אַחֵר, וְנִתַּצְתֶּם אֶת
מִזְבְּחֹתָם... וְאִבַּדְתֶּם אֶת שְׁמָם - לֹא תַעֲשׂוּן כֵּן, אַזְהָרָה
לַמּוֹחֵק אֶת הַשֵּׁם וְלַנּוֹתֵץ אֶבֶן אַחַת מִן הַמִּזְבֵּחַ אוֹ מִן הָעֲזָרָה.
אָמַר רַבִּי יִשְׁמָעֵאל: וְכִי תַעֲלֶה עַל דַּעְתְּךָ שֶׁיִּשְׂרָאֵל נוֹתְצִין

אֶת הַמִּזְבְּחוֹת? אֶלָּא שֶׁלֹּא תַעֲשׂוּ כְּמַעֲשֵׂיהֶם, וְיִגְרְמוּ
עֲוֹנוֹתֵיכֶם לְמִקְדַּשׁ אֲבוֹתֵיכֶם שֶׁיֵּחָרֵב:

ה לְשִׁכְנוֹ תִדְרְשׁוּ. זֶה מִשְׁכַּן שִׁילֹה:

ו וְזִבְחֵיכֶם. שַׁלְמֵי חוֹבָה: מַעְשְׂרֹתֵיכֶם. מַעֲשַׂר
בְּהֵמָה וּמַעֲשֵׂר שֵׁנִי, לֶאֱכֹל לִפְנִים מִן הַחוֹמָה: תְּרוּמַת
יֶדְכֶם. אֵלּוּ הַבִּכּוּרִים, שֶׁנֶּאֱמַר בָּהֶם: "וְלָקַח הַכֹּהֵן הַטֶּנֶא
מִיָּדֶךָ" (להלן כו, ד): וּבְכֹרֹת בְּקַרְכֶם. לְתִתָּם לַכֹּהֵן וְיַקְרִיבֵם
שָׁם:

ז אֲשֶׁר בֵּרַכְךָ ה'. לְפִי הַבְּרָכָה הָבֵא:

ח לֹא תַעֲשׂוּן כְּכֹל אֲשֶׁר אֲנַחְנוּ עֹשִׂים וְגוֹ'. מוּסָב
לְמַעְלָה, עַל "כִּי אַתֶּם עֹבְרִים אֶת הַיַּרְדֵּן וְגוֹ'" (לעיל יא,
לא), כְּשֶׁתַּעַבְרוּ אֶת הַיַּרְדֵּן מִיָּד מֻתָּרִים אַתֶּם לְהַקְרִיב
בַּבָּמָה כָּל אַרְבַּע עֶשְׂרֵה שָׁנָה שֶׁל כִּבּוּשׁ וְחִלּוּק, וּבַבָּמָה
לֹא תַקְרִיבוּ כָּל מַה שֶּׁאַתֶּם מַקְרִיבִים פֹּה הַיּוֹם בַּמִּשְׁכָּן

שֶׁהוּא עִמָּכֶם וְנִמְשַׁח, וְהוּא כָּשֵׁר לְהַקְרִיב בּוֹ חַטָּאוֹת
וַאֲשָׁמוֹת נְדָרִים וּנְדָבוֹת, אֲבָל בַּבָּמָה אֵין קָרֵב אֶלָּא הַנִּדָּר
וְהַנִּדָּב, וְזֶהוּ "אִישׁ כָּל הַיָּשָׁר בְּעֵינָיו", נְדָרִים וּנְדָבוֹת שֶׁאַתֶּם
מִתְנַדְּבִים עַל יְדֵי שֶׁיָּשָׁר בְּעֵינֵיכֶם לַהֲבִיאָם וְלֹא עַל יְדֵי
חוֹבָה, אוֹתָם תַּקְרִיבוּ בַּבָּמָה:

ט כִּי לֹא בָאתֶם. כָּל אוֹתָן אַרְבַּע עֶשְׂרֵה שָׁנָה: עַד עָתָּה.
כְּמוֹ עֲדַיִן: אֶל הַמְּנוּחָה. זוֹ שִׁילֹה: הַנַּחֲלָה. זוֹ יְרוּשָׁלַיִם:

י-יא וַעֲבַרְתֶּם אֶת הַיַּרְדֵּן וִישַׁבְתֶּם בָּאָרֶץ. שֶׁתִּתְחַלֵּק
וְיִהְיֶה כָּל אֶחָד מַכִּיר אֶת חֶלְקוֹ וְאֶת שִׁבְטוֹ: וְהֵנִיחַ לָכֶם.
לְאַחַר כִּבּוּשׁ וְחִלּוּק, וּמְנוּחָה מִן "הַגּוֹיִם אֲשֶׁר ה'
לְנַסּוֹת בָּם אֶת יִשְׂרָאֵל" (שופטים ג, א), וְאֵין זֶה אֶלָּא בִּימֵי
דָוִד, אָז "וְהָיָה הַמָּקוֹם וְגוֹ'" - בְּנוּ לָכֶם בֵּית הַמִּקְדָּשׁ
בִּירוּשָׁלַיִם. וְכֵן הוּא אוֹמֵר בְּדָוִד: "וַיְהִי כִּי יָשַׁב הַמֶּלֶךְ
בְּבֵיתוֹ וַה' הֵנִיחַ לוֹ מִסָּבִיב מִכָּל אֹיְבָיו, וַיֹּאמֶר הַמֶּלֶךְ
אֶל נָתָן הַנָּבִיא, רְאֵה נָא אָנֹכִי יוֹשֵׁב בְּבֵית אֲרָזִים וְחָרֹן

11 **It shall be the** particular **place that the Lord your God will**
Second **choose to rest His name there; there you shall bring every-**
aliya **thing that I command you: Your burnt offerings, and your**
peace offerings, your tithes, and the gifts of your hand, and
all your choice vows that you vow to the Lord. Moses does
not know which place will be chosen, but he does know that at
some future time a particular site will be selected.
12 **You shall rejoice before the Lord your God, you, and your**
sons, and your daughters, and your slaves, and your maid-
servants, and the Levite who is within your gates, as he has
no share and inheritance with you. Since the Levite has no
land of his own, he will be sustained by tithes. For this reason
the Levites are counted among the impoverished of the community (see 14:29).
13 **Beware, lest you offer up your burnt offerings in any place**
that you see. Once a specific location is selected as the site of
the permanent Temple, it will no longer be permitted to sacrifice offerings anywhere else.[7]
14 **Rather, in the place that the Lord will choose in one of your**
tribes, there you shall offer up your burnt offerings, and
there you shall do everything that I command you.
15 In the wilderness, the people of Israel were not permitted to
eat meat from an animal that had not been brought as an offering in the Tabernacle.[8] Once they settle the land and the
tribes are dispersed, this policy would change. **Only, with all of**
your heart's desire, you may
slaughter and eat meat in ac-
cordance with the blessing
of the Lord your God[D] **that**
He gave you within all your
gates, in all the places where
you live. This meat is non-
consecrated food and wholly
void of sanctity. Therefore, **the**
pure and the impure may eat
it together, **like the gazelle**[B]
and like the deer,[B] common game animals whose consumption is permitted but they may not be offered on the altar, and
are therefore cited as representatives of non-consecrated food.
16 **Only the blood you shall not eat;**[D] apart from the reason for
this prohibition mentioned elsewhere,[9] blood is used in sacrificial rituals, and it is therefore connected to idolatry. This explains the importance of the repeated prohibition to never eat
blood, neither that of sacrificial offerings nor that of unconsecrated animals.[10] Rather, **you shall pour it on the ground like**
water.
17 **You may not eat** anywhere **within your gates the tithe of**
your grain and your wine and your oil, or the firstborn of
your cattle and of your flocks, or any of your vows that you
will vow, or your pledges, or the gift of your hand. Just as offerings may be sacrificed only in a particular place, so too, tithes
and the meat of offerings may only be eaten in a specific place.
18 **Rather, before the Lord your God you shall eat them in the**
place that the Lord your God will choose; and when you
bring them to the Temple, you should not come alone; rather,
it shall be **you, and your son, and your daughter, and your**
slave, and your maidservant, and the Levite who is within
your gates and appended to your family; **and you shall rejoice**
before the Lord your God in all your endeavors. A discussion of this tithe, called second tithe, can be found below; see
14:22–26).

Gazelle

Roe Deer

DISCUSSION

12:15 | **You may slaughter and eat meat in accordance with the blessing of the Lord your God:** The Sages interpreted this verse, which is reiterated below (see verses 20–24), as referring to animals that had initially been fit for the altar, but later became disqualified for sacrifice, e.g., they became blemished. Those animals were treated like non-consecrated animals and even in the wilderness it was permitted to slaughter them anywhere (see *Sifrei*; Rashi; 15:21–23).

12:16 | **Only the blood you shall not eat:** When offerings were slaughtered in the Temple, the blood that would spurt from the animal was collected by the priests for use in the sacred service. In contrast, when animals were slaughtered in private circumstances, greater caution was required. Therefore, the prohibition of blood is mentioned in connection with non-consecrated meat.

יא וְהָיָה הַמָּקוֹם אֲשֶׁר־יִבְחַר יְהֹוָה אֱלֹהֵיכֶם בּוֹ לְשַׁכֵּן שְׁמוֹ שָׁם שָׁמָּה תָבִיאוּ אֵת שני
כָּל־אֲשֶׁר אָנֹכִי מְצַוֶּה אֶתְכֶם עוֹלֹתֵיכֶם וְזִבְחֵיכֶם מַעְשְׂרֹתֵיכֶם וּתְרֻמַת יֶדְכֶם וְכֹל
מִבְחַר נִדְרֵיכֶם אֲשֶׁר תִּדְּרוּ לַיהֹוָה: יב וּשְׂמַחְתֶּם לִפְנֵי יְהֹוָה אֱלֹהֵיכֶם אַתֶּם וּבְנֵיכֶם
וּבְנֹתֵיכֶם וְעַבְדֵיכֶם וְאַמְהֹתֵיכֶם וְהַלֵּוִי אֲשֶׁר בְּשַׁעֲרֵיכֶם כִּי אֵין לוֹ חֵלֶק וְנַחֲלָה
אִתְּכֶם: יג הִשָּׁמֶר לְךָ פֶּן־תַּעֲלֶה עֹלֹתֶיךָ בְּכָל־מָקוֹם אֲשֶׁר תִּרְאֶה: יד כִּי אִם־בַּמָּקוֹם
אֲשֶׁר־יִבְחַר יְהֹוָה בְּאַחַד שְׁבָטֶיךָ שָׁם תַּעֲלֶה עֹלֹתֶיךָ וְשָׁם תַּעֲשֶׂה כֹּל אֲשֶׁר אָנֹכִי
מְצַוֶּךָּ: טו רַק בְּכָל־אַוַּת נַפְשְׁךָ תִּזְבַּח וְאָכַלְתָּ בָשָׂר כְּבִרְכַּת יְהֹוָה אֱלֹהֶיךָ אֲשֶׁר נָתַן
לְךָ בְּכָל־שְׁעָרֶיךָ הַטָּמֵא וְהַטָּהוֹר יֹאכְלֶנּוּ כַּצְּבִי וְכָאַיָּל: רַק הַדָּם לֹא תֹאכֵלוּ עַל־
הָאָרֶץ תִּשְׁפְּכֶנּוּ כַּמָּיִם: יז לֹא־תוּכַל לֶאֱכֹל בִּשְׁעָרֶיךָ מַעְשַׂר דְּגָנְךָ וְתִירֹשְׁךָ וְיִצְהָרֶךָ
וּבְכֹרֹת בְּקָרְךָ וְצֹאנֶךָ וְכָל־נְדָרֶיךָ אֲשֶׁר תִּדֹּר וְנִדְבֹתֶיךָ וּתְרוּמַת יָדֶךָ: יח כִּי אִם־לִפְנֵי
יְהֹוָה אֱלֹהֶיךָ תֹּאכְלֶנּוּ בַּמָּקוֹם אֲשֶׁר יִבְחַר יְהֹוָה אֱלֹהֶיךָ בּוֹ אַתָּה וּבִנְךָ וּבִתֶּךָ
וְעַבְדְּךָ וַאֲמָתֶךָ וְהַלֵּוִי אֲשֶׁר בִּשְׁעָרֶיךָ וְשָׂמַחְתָּ לִפְנֵי יְהֹוָה אֱלֹהֶיךָ בְּכֹל מִשְׁלַח יָדֶךָ:

רש"י

הָאֱלֹהִים יֹשֵׁב בְּתוֹךְ הַיְרִיעָה" (שמואל ב' ז, ב-כב): שָׁמָּה תָבִיאוּ וְגו'. לְמַעְלָה אָמוּר לְעִנְיַן שִׁילֹה, וְכָאן אָמוּר לְעִנְיַן יְרוּשָׁלַיִם, וּלְכָךְ חִלְּקָם הַכָּתוּב, לִתֵּן הֶתֵּר בֵּין זוֹ לָזוֹ, מִשֶּׁחָרְבָה שִׁילֹה וּבָאוּ לְנוֹב וְחָרְבָה נוֹב וּבָאוּ לְגִבְעוֹן, הָיוּ הַבָּמוֹת מֻתָּרוֹת, עַד שֶׁבָּאוּ לִירוּשָׁלַיִם: מִבְחַר נִדְרֵיכֶם. מְלַמֵּד שֶׁיָּבִיא מִן הַמֻּבְחָר:

יג| הִשָּׁמֶר לְךָ. לִתֵּן לֹא תַעֲשֶׂה עַל הַדָּבָר: אֲשֶׁר תִּרְאֶה. אֲשֶׁר יַעֲלֶה בְּלִבְּךָ, אֲבָל אַתָּה מַקְרִיב עַל פִּי נָבִיא, כְּגוֹן אֵלִיָּהוּ בְּהַר הַכַּרְמֶל:

יד| בְּאַחַד שְׁבָטֶיךָ. בְּחֶלְקוֹ שֶׁל בִּנְיָמִין, וּלְמַעְלָה (לעיל פסוק ה) הוּא אוֹמֵר: "מִכָּל שִׁבְטֵיכֶם", הָא כֵּיצַד? כְּשֶׁקָּנָה דָּוִד אֶת הַגֹּרֶן מֵאֲרַוְנָה הַיְבוּסִי גָּבָה הַזָּהָב מִכָּל הַשְּׁבָטִים, וּמִכָּל מָקוֹם הַגֹּרֶן בְּחֶלְקוֹ שֶׁל בִּנְיָמִין הָיָה:

טו| רַק בְּכָל אַוַּת נַפְשְׁךָ. בַּמֶּה הַכָּתוּב מְדַבֵּר? אִם בִּבְשַׂר

תַּאֲוָה לְהַתִּירָהּ לָהֶם בְּלֹא הַקְרָבַת אֵמוּרִים, הֲרֵי אָמוּר בְּמָקוֹם אַחֵר: "כִּי יַרְחִיב ה'... אֶת גְּבֻלְךָ וְגו' וְאָמַרְתָּ אֹכְלָה בָשָׂר" וְגו' (להלן פסוק כ), בַּמֶּה זֶה מְדַבֵּר? בִּקְדָשִׁים שֶׁנָּפַל בָּהֶם מוּם שֶׁיִּפָּדוּ וְיֵאָכְלוּ בְּכָל מָקוֹם. יָכוֹל יִפָּדוּ עַל מוּם עוֹבֵר? תַּלְמוּד לוֹמַר: "רַק". תִּזְבַּח וְאָכַלְתָּ. אֵין לְךָ בָּהֶם הֶתֵּר גִּזָּה וְחָלָב, אֶלָּא אֲכִילָה עַל יְדֵי זְבִיחָה: הַטָּמֵא וְהַטָּהוֹר. לְפִי שֶׁבָּאוּ מִכֹּחַ קָדָשִׁים שֶׁנֶּאֱמַר בָּהֶם "וְהַבָּשָׂר אֲשֶׁר יִגַּע בְּכָל טָמֵא לֹא יֵאָכֵל" (ויקרא ז, יט), הֻצְרַךְ לְהַתִּיר בּוֹ שֶׁטָּמֵא וְטָהוֹר אוֹכְלִים בִּקְעָרָה אַחַת: כַּצְּבִי וְכָאַיָּל. שֶׁאֵין קָרְבָּן בָּא מֵהֶם: כַּצְּבִי וְכָאַיָּל. לְפָטְרָן מִן הַזְּרוֹעַ וְהַלְּחָיַיִם וְהַקֵּבָה:

טז| רַק הַדָּם לֹא תֹאכֵלוּ. אַף עַל פִּי שֶׁאָמַרְתִּי שֶׁאֵין לְךָ בּוֹ זְרִיקַת דָּם בַּמִּזְבֵּחַ, לֹא תֹאכְלֶנּוּ: תִּשְׁפְּכֶנּוּ כַּמָּיִם. לוֹמַר לְךָ שֶׁאֵין צָרִיךְ כִּסּוּי. דָּבָר אַחֵר, הֲרֵי הוּא כַּמַּיִם לְהַכְשִׁיר אֶת הַזְּרָעִים:

יז| לֹא תוּכַל. בָּא הַכָּתוּב לִתֵּן לֹא תַעֲשֶׂה עַל הַדָּבָר: לֹא תוּכַל. רַבִּי יְהוֹשֻׁעַ בֶּן קָרְחָה אוֹמֵר: יָכוֹל אַתָּה אֲבָל אֵינְךָ רַשַּׁאי. כַּיּוֹצֵא בּוֹ: "וְאֶת הַיְבוּסִי יוֹשְׁבֵי יְרוּשָׁלַיִם לֹא יָכְלוּ בְנֵי יְהוּדָה לְהוֹרִישָׁם" (יהושע טו, סג), יְכוֹלִים הָיוּ אֶלָּא שֶׁאֵינָן רַשָּׁאִין, לְפִי שֶׁכָּרַת לָהֶם אַבְרָהָם בְּרִית כְּשֶׁלָּקַח מֵהֶם מְעָרַת הַמַּכְפֵּלָה, וְלֹא יְבוּסִים הָיוּ אֶלָּא חִתִּיִּים הָיוּ, חֶלֶק אֶחָד שָׁם הָעִיר שֶׁשְּׁמָהּ "יְבוּס". כָּךְ מְפֹרָשׁ בְּפִרְקֵי דְּרַבִּי אֱלִיעֶזֶר (פ' לו). וְהוּא שֶׁנֶּאֱמַר: "כִּי אִם הֱסִירְךָ הָעִוְרִים וְהַפִּסְחִים" (שמואל ב' ה, ו), צְלָמִים שֶׁכָּתְבוּ עֲלֵיהֶם אֶת הַשְּׁבוּעָה: וּבְכֹרֹת בְּקָרְךָ. אַזְהָרָה לַכֹּהֲנִים: וּתְרוּמַת יָדֶךָ. אֵלּוּ הַבִּכּוּרִים:

יח| לִפְנֵי ה'. לִפְנִים מִן הַחוֹמָה: וְהַלֵּוִי אֲשֶׁר בִּשְׁעָרֶיךָ. אִם אֵין לְךָ לָתֵת לוֹ מֵחֶלְקוֹ כְּגוֹן מַעֲשֵׂר רִאשׁוֹן, תֵּן לוֹ מַעֲשַׂר עָנִי, אֵין לְךָ מַעֲשַׂר עָנִי, הַזְמִינֵהוּ עַל שְׁלָמֶיךָ:

BACKGROUND

12:15 | Gazelle: A mammal from the Bovidae family, the gazelle, scientific name: *Gazella*, chews its cud and has split hooves. It has horns rather than antlers. It grows to a height of about 75 cm and weighs, on average, 18–25 kg. The gazelle is common in Israel.

Deer: Customarily identified as the roe deer, *Capreolus capreolus*, this mammal from the deer family chews its cud and has split hooves. The roe deer became extinct in Israel in the early twentieth century, but in recent years there has been an attempt to reintroduce it to the wild in the area of Mount Carmel. It grows to a length of 95–135 cm, a height of about 75 cm, and an average weight of 15–30 kg. The deer is different from the gazelle in its horns, which are branched antlers that are shed and regrow every year.

19 **Beware, lest you forsake the Levite all your days upon your land.** Since Levites are denied the opportunity to live ordinary lives, they are dependent upon you. Therefore a severe warning is issued here to tend to the Levites, God's servants.

20 Here the Torah elaborates on what was written earlier:[11] **When the Lord your God will expand your border** and you become wealthy,[12] **as He spoke to you, and you will say: I will eat meat, because your heart will desire to eat meat; with all your heart's desire you may eat meat.**

21 **If the place that the Lord your God will choose to place His name there will be far from you;** in the wilderness the distance between the encampments of the children of Israel and the Tabernacle was not great. Those who wished to eat meat would sacrifice peace offerings and eat most of the meat themselves, leaving a small portion for the priests. But following their settlement in the Land of Israel, the distance would be too great and a different arrangement would become necessary. Consequently, **you shall slaughter from your herd and from your flock that the Lord gave you, as I commanded you, and you shall eat within your gates,** in all your cities, **with all your heart's desire.**

22 **However, just as the gazelle or the deer is eaten,** freely, in the manner that game animals are eaten, **so you shall eat it; the pure and the impure may eat it together,** without the restrictions of ritual purity that are in effect with regard to consecrated animals.

23 Once again the Torah emphasizes: **Only be strong to not eat the blood, as the blood is the life, and you shall not eat the life with the meat;** even though the blood comes together with the meat, it may not be eaten.

24 **You shall not eat it; you shall pour it on the earth like water.**

25 **You shall not eat it,**[D] **so that it will be good for you and for your children after you, when you will do that which is right in the eyes of the Lord.**

26 **Only your sacraments that you will have,** your obligatory offerings, **and your vows,** the offerings that you freely commit yourself to bring, **you shall carry, and come to the place that the Lord will choose.**

27 **You shall perform your burnt offerings** in the Temple that will stand there, **the meat and the blood, on the altar of the Lord your God; and the blood of your offerings** that are to be eaten **shall be poured on the altar of the Lord your God, and only the meat you shall eat.** Even the blood of offerings most of whose meat is eaten may not be consumed or used in any way by human beings.

28 The Torah reiterates a general command: **Observe and heed all these matters that I command you, so that it will be good for you and for your children after you forever, when you perform the good and the right in the eyes of the Lord your God.**

29 **When the Lord your God will excise the nations that you**
Third aliya **are coming there to take possession from them from before you and you will take possession from them and live in their land.** In light of Israel's conquest of the land in the name of God, one would have thought that the gods of the nations, who brought no benefit to those who worshipped them, would immediately lose all their allure, and the children of Israel would have an attitude of absolute contempt toward them. Nevertheless, owing to the overwhelming influence of societal pressure, the Torah repeats its admonition:

30 **Beware lest you be ensnared after them, after they are destroyed from before you and lest you seek their gods,**

DISCUSSION

12:25 | **You shall not eat it:** Here the prohibition against eating blood joins other commandments relating to ritual slaughter. The repeated warning against eating blood indicates that this practice was an accepted norm among the Jewish people (see Rashi; *Sifrei, Devarim* 78). Eating blood was apparently associated with various cultic rituals, as in most cultures blood is not eaten on its own. In ancient times, various nations would offer blood to their gods and eat part of it. The promise in the verse might be an allusion to the view prevalent among the surrounding nations that eating blood had advantageous effects (see also commentary on Leviticus 17:13; I Samuel 14:32–35).

יט כ הִשָּׁמֶר לְךָ פֶּן־תַּעֲזֹב אֶת־הַלֵּוִי כָּל־יָמֶיךָ עַל־אַדְמָתֶךָ׃ כִּי־יַרְחִיב
יְהוָה אֱלֹהֶיךָ אֶת־גְּבֻלְךָ כַּאֲשֶׁר דִּבֶּר־לָךְ וְאָמַרְתָּ אֹכְלָה בָשָׂר כִּי־תְאַוֶּה נַפְשְׁךָ
כא לֶאֱכֹל בָּשָׂר בְּכָל־אַוַּת נַפְשְׁךָ תֹּאכַל בָּשָׂר׃ כִּי־יִרְחַק מִמְּךָ הַמָּקוֹם אֲשֶׁר יִבְחַר
יְהוָה אֱלֹהֶיךָ לָשׂוּם שְׁמוֹ שָׁם וְזָבַחְתָּ מִבְּקָרְךָ וּמִצֹּאנְךָ אֲשֶׁר נָתַן יְהוָה לְךָ כַּאֲשֶׁר
כב צִוִּיתִךָ וְאָכַלְתָּ בִּשְׁעָרֶיךָ בְּכֹל אַוַּת נַפְשֶׁךָ׃ אַךְ כַּאֲשֶׁר יֵאָכֵל אֶת־הַצְּבִי וְאֶת־
כג הָאַיָּל כֵּן תֹּאכְלֶנּוּ הַטָּמֵא וְהַטָּהוֹר יַחְדָּו יֹאכְלֶנּוּ׃ רַק חֲזַק לְבִלְתִּי אֲכֹל הַדָּם
כד כִּי הַדָּם הוּא הַנָּפֶשׁ וְלֹא־תֹאכַל הַנֶּפֶשׁ עִם־הַבָּשָׂר׃ לֹא תֹּאכְלֶנּוּ עַל־הָאָרֶץ
כה תִּשְׁפְּכֶנּוּ כַּמָּיִם׃ לֹא תֹּאכְלֶנּוּ לְמַעַן יִיטַב לְךָ וּלְבָנֶיךָ אַחֲרֶיךָ כִּי־תַעֲשֶׂה הַיָּשָׁר
כו בְּעֵינֵי יְהוָה׃ רַק קֳדָשֶׁיךָ אֲשֶׁר־יִהְיוּ לְךָ וּנְדָרֶיךָ תִּשָּׂא וּבָאתָ אֶל־הַמָּקוֹם אֲשֶׁר־
כז יִבְחַר יְהוָה׃ וְעָשִׂיתָ עֹלֹתֶיךָ הַבָּשָׂר וְהַדָּם עַל־מִזְבַּח יְהוָה אֱלֹהֶיךָ וְדַם־זְבָחֶיךָ
כח יִשָּׁפֵךְ עַל־מִזְבַּח יְהוָה אֱלֹהֶיךָ וְהַבָּשָׂר תֹּאכֵל׃ שְׁמֹר וְשָׁמַעְתָּ אֵת כָּל־הַדְּבָרִים
הָאֵלֶּה אֲשֶׁר אָנֹכִי מְצַוֶּךָּ לְמַעַן יִיטַב לְךָ וּלְבָנֶיךָ אַחֲרֶיךָ עַד־עוֹלָם כִּי תַעֲשֶׂה
כט הַטּוֹב וְהַיָּשָׁר בְּעֵינֵי יְהוָה אֱלֹהֶיךָ׃ כִּי־יַכְרִית יְהוָה אֱלֹהֶיךָ אֶת־ שלישי
הַגּוֹיִם אֲשֶׁר אַתָּה בָא־שָׁמָּה לָרֶשֶׁת אוֹתָם מִפָּנֶיךָ וְיָרַשְׁתָּ אֹתָם וְיָשַׁבְתָּ בְּאַרְצָם׃
ל הִשָּׁמֶר לְךָ פֶּן־תִּנָּקֵשׁ אַחֲרֵיהֶם אַחֲרֵי הִשָּׁמְדָם מִפָּנֶיךָ וּפֶן־תִּדְרֹשׁ לֵאלֹהֵיהֶם

רש"י

יט| **הִשָּׁמֶר לְךָ.** לִתֵּן לֹא תַעֲשֶׂה עַל הַדָּבָר: **עַל אַדְמָתֶךָ.** אֲבָל בַּגּוֹלָה אֵינְךָ מֻזְהָר עָלָיו יוֹתֵר מֵעֲנִיֵּי יִשְׂרָאֵל:

כ| **כִּי יַרְחִיב וְגוֹ׳.** לִמְּדָה תוֹרָה דֶּרֶךְ אֶרֶץ, שֶׁלֹּא יִתְאַוֶּה אָדָם לֶאֱכֹל בָּשָׂר אֶלָּא מִתּוֹךְ רַחֲבַת יָדַיִם וָעֹשֶׁר: **בְּכָל אַוַּת נַפְשְׁךָ וְגוֹ׳.** אֲבָל בַּמִּדְבָּר נֶאֱסַר לָהֶם בְּשַׂר חֻלִּין, אֶלָּא אִם כֵּן מַקְדִּישָׁהּ וּמַקְרִיבָהּ שְׁלָמִים:

כא| **כִּי יִרְחַק מִמְּךָ הַמָּקוֹם.** וְלֹא תּוּכַל לָבוֹא וְלַעֲשׂוֹת שְׁלָמִים בְּכָל יוֹם, כְּמוֹ עַכְשָׁיו שֶׁהַמִּשְׁכָּן הוֹלֵךְ עִמָּכֶם: **וְזָבַחְתָּ... כַּאֲשֶׁר צִוִּיתִךָ.** לָמַדְנוּ שֶׁיֵּשׁ צִוּוּי בִּזְבִיחָה הֵיאַךְ יִשְׁחֹט, וְהֵן הִלְכוֹת שְׁחִיטָה שֶׁנֶּאֶמְרוּ לְמֹשֶׁה בְּסִינַי:

כב| **אַךְ כַּאֲשֶׁר יֵאָכֵל אֶת הַצְּבִי וְגוֹ׳.** אֵינְךָ מֻזְהָר לְאָכְלָן בְּטָהֳרָה. אִי מַה צְּבִי וְאַיִל חֶלְבָּן מֻתָּר אַף חֻלִּין חֶלְבָּן מֻתָּר? תַּלְמוּד לוֹמַר: "אַךְ":

כג| **רַק חֲזַק לְבִלְתִּי אֲכֹל הַדָּם.** מִמַּה שֶּׁנֶּאֱמַר "חֲזַק" אַתָּה לָמֵד שֶׁהָיוּ שְׁטוּפִים בַּדָּם לְאָכְלוֹ, לְפִיכָךְ הֻצְרַךְ לוֹמַר "חֲזַק", דִּבְרֵי רַבִּי יְהוּדָה. רַבִּי שִׁמְעוֹן בֶּן עַזַּאי אוֹמֵר: לֹא בָּא הַכָּתוּב אֶלָּא לְהַזְהִירְךָ וּלְלַמֶּדְךָ עַד כַּמָּה אַתָּה צָרִיךְ לְהִתְחַזֵּק בְּמִצְוֹת, אִם הַדָּם שֶׁהוּא קַל לְהִשָּׁמֵר מִמֶּנּוּ, שֶׁאֵין אָדָם מִתְאַוֶּה לוֹ, הֻצְרַךְ לְחַזֶּקְךָ בְּאַזְהָרָתוֹ, קַל וָחֹמֶר לִשְׁאָר מִצְוֹת: **וְלֹא תֹאכַל הַנֶּפֶשׁ עִם הַבָּשָׂר.** אַזְהָרָה לְאֵבֶר מִן הַחַי:

כד| **לֹא תֹּאכְלֶנּוּ.** אַזְהָרָה לְדַם הַתַּמְצִית:

כה| **לֹא תֹּאכְלֶנּוּ.** אַזְהָרָה לְדַם הָאֵבָרִים: **לְמַעַן יִיטַב לְךָ וְגוֹ׳.** צֵא וּלְמַד מַתַּן שְׂכָרָן שֶׁל מִצְוֹת, אִם הַדָּם שֶׁנַּפְשׁוֹ שֶׁל אָדָם קָצָה מִמֶּנּוּ, הַפּוֹרֵשׁ מִמֶּנּוּ זוֹכֶה לוֹ וּלְבָנָיו אַחֲרָיו, קַל וָחֹמֶר לְגָזֵל וַעֲרָיוֹת שֶׁנַּפְשׁוֹ שֶׁל אָדָם מִתְאַוָּה לָהֶם:

כו| **רַק קָדָשֶׁיךָ.** אַף עַל פִּי שֶׁאַתָּה מֻתָּר לִשְׁחֹט חֻלִּין, לֹא הִתַּרְתִּי לְךָ לִשְׁחֹט אֶת הַקֳּדָשִׁים וּלְאָכְלָן בִּשְׁעָרֶיךָ בְּלֹא הַקְרָבָה, אֶלָּא הֲבִיאֵם לְבֵית הַבְּחִירָה:

כז| **וְעָשִׂיתָ עֹלֹתֶיךָ.** אִם עוֹלוֹת הֵן, תֵּן "הַבָּשָׂר וְהַדָּם" עַל גַּבֵּי הַמִּזְבֵּחַ, וְאִם זִבְחֵי שְׁלָמִים הֵם, "דַּם זְבָחֶיךָ יִשָּׁפֵךְ" עַל הַמִּזְבֵּחַ תְּחִלָּה, וְאַחַר כָּךְ "וְהַבָּשָׂר תֹּאכֵל". וְעוֹד דָּרְשׁוּ רַבּוֹתֵינוּ, "רַק קָדָשֶׁיךָ", שֶׁבָּא לְלַמֵּד עַל הַקֳּדָשִׁים שֶׁבְּחוּצָה לָאָרֶץ, וּלְלַמֵּד עַל הַתְּמוּרוֹת וְעַל וַלְדוֹת קָדָשִׁים שֶׁיַּקְרִיבוּ:

כח| **שְׁמֹר.** זוֹ מִשְׁנָה, שֶׁאַתָּה צָרִיךְ לְשָׁמְרָהּ בְּבִטְנְךָ שֶׁלֹּא תִשְׁכַּח, כְּעִנְיָן שֶׁנֶּאֱמַר: "כִּי נָעִים כִּי תִשְׁמְרֵם בְּבִטְנֶךָ" (משלי כב, יח), וְאִם שָׁנִיתָ, אֶפְשָׁר שֶׁתִּשְׁמַע וּתְקַיֵּם. הָא כָּל שֶׁאֵינוֹ בִּכְלַל מִשְׁנָה אֵינוֹ בִּכְלַל מַעֲשֶׂה: **אֵת כָּל הַדְּבָרִים.** שֶׁתְּהֵא חֲבִיבָה עָלֶיךָ מִצְוָה קַלָּה כְּמִצְוָה חֲמוּרָה: **הַטּוֹב.** בְּעֵינֵי הַשָּׁמַיִם: **וְהַיָּשָׁר.** בְּעֵינֵי אָדָם:

ל| **פֶּן תִּנָּקֵשׁ.** אוּנְקְלוֹס תִּרְגֵּם לְשׁוֹן מוֹקֵשׁ. וַאֲנִי אוֹמֵר שֶׁלֹּא חָשׁ לְדַקְדֵּק בַּלָּשׁוֹן, שֶׁלֹּא מָצִינוּ נוּ"ן בִּלְשׁוֹן יוֹקֵשׁ, וַאֲפִלּוּ לִיסוֹד הַנּוֹפֵל מִמֶּנּוּ. אֲבָל בִּלְשׁוֹן טֵרוּף וְהַקְּשָׁה מָצִינוּ נוּ"ן: "וְאַרְכֻבָּתֵהּ דָּא לְדָא נָקְשָׁן" (דניאל ה, ו). וְאַף זֶה אֲנִי אוֹמֵר, "פֶּן תִּנָּקֵשׁ אַחֲרֵיהֶם", פֶּן תִּטָּרֵף אַחֲרֵיהֶם לִהְיוֹת כָּרוּךְ אַחַר מַעֲשֵׂיהֶם. וְכֵן: "יְנַקֵּשׁ נוֹשֶׁה לְכָל אֲשֶׁר לוֹ" (תהלים קט, יא), מְקַלֵּל אֶת הָרָשָׁע לִהְיוֹת עָלָיו נוֹשִׁים רַבִּים, וִיהְיוּ מַחֲזִירִין וּמִתְנַקְּשִׁין אַחַר מָמוֹנוֹ: **אַחֲרֵי הִשָּׁמְדָם מִפָּנֶיךָ.** אַחַר שֶׁתִּרְאֶה שֶׁאֲשְׁמִידֵם מִפָּנֶיךָ, יֵשׁ לְךָ לָתֵת לֵב מִפְּנֵי מָה נִשְׁמְדוּ אֵלּוּ? מִפְּנֵי מַעֲשִׂים מְקֻלְקָלִים שֶׁבִּידֵיהֶם. אַף אַתָּה לֹא תַעֲשֶׂה כָּךְ, שֶׁלֹּא יָבוֹאוּ אֲחֵרִים וְיַשְׁמִידוּךָ:

showing a practical interest in them and **saying: How do these nations serve their gods? I will do so as well.**[D] The Torah prohibits here not only actual idolatry, but even imitating idolatrous modes of worship.

31 **You shall not do so to the Lord your God, as every abomination of the Lord that He hates, they have done to their gods, as,** for example, **they also burn their sons and their daughters in the fire to their gods,** and they lack the natural revulsion to that evil act.

Those Who Entice Others to Idolatry

DEUTERONOMY 13:1–19

This section opens with a declaration concerning the absolute nature of the Torah. Unlike governments in which the king or the parliament is the source of the law, the Torah is rigid and stable. It does not automatically change according to historical circumstances or preferences of the people, even though it too has mechanisms through which it can deal with changes that transpire in the world. Against the backdrop of this declaration, the Torah presents three different scenarios of people who incite against the laws of the Torah, and in particular to violate the prohibition of idolatry: One who falsely presents himself as a prophet, one who does not claim to be a prophet but entices the members of his family to engage in idolatry, and an entire society of idol worshippers. Their support for idolatry and their attempts to attract followers seal their fate, and they are subject to the death penalty.

13 1 **All this matter that I command you, you shall take care to perform; you shall not add to it and you shall not subtract from it;** the system of Torah law is immutable.

2 **If a prophet,** who expresses himself in an articulate manner, **rises in your midst, or a dreamer of a** prophetic **dream, and he provides you with a sign or a wonder,** a marvel that transcends the natural order, in order to validate his words,

3 **and the sign or the wonder that he spoke to you comes to pass,** ostensibly indicating that he is a true prophet, who is prophesying on behalf of a different religion or seeking to institute changes to the Jewish religion, **saying: Let us follow other gods that you did not know and serve them.** The problem in this case is not due to his cooperation with the enemies surrounding Israel, as the verse speaks of the gods of distant nations, who are not known to the people.

4 In that case, **you shall not heed the words of that prophet, or that dreamer of a dream,** even if he provided a sign or a wonder to validate his words. This is puzzling: How did he receive divine assistance if his message is antithetical to the word of God? The verse explains: **As the Lord your God is testing you, to know whether you love the Lord your God with all your heart and with all your soul.**

5 Ultimately, **you shall follow the Lord your God, and Him you shall fear, and His commandments you shall observe, and His voice you shall heed, and Him you shall serve, and to Him you shall cleave.** You must do whatever you can do to cleave to God to the extent that no factor in the world will be able to separate you.

6 **That prophet, or that dreamer of a dream, shall be put to death,** whether he actually dreamed false dreams or he concocted them, **because he spoke fabrication about the Lord your God, who took you out of the land of Egypt and redeemed you from the house of bondage, to lead you astray from the path on which the Lord your God commanded you to walk; and you shall eliminate the evil from your midst.** Since God would not have instructed you to serve gods other than Himself, anyone who asserts otherwise is a charlatan, even if his claims are supported by a sign or a wonder. He does not have the authority to change the laws of the Torah, and certainly not to incite people to worship other gods.

7 **If** a relative or someone close to you, e.g., **your brother, son of your mother,** who for various reasons might be particularly close to you, as maternal brothers from different fathers do not quarrel even over matters of inheritance, as each brother inherits his own father,[13] **or your son, or your daughter, or the wife of your bosom, or your** close **friend, who is like your own soul,** and with whom you identify very closely, **entices you secretly, saying: Let us go and serve other gods that you did not know, you and your fathers,**

8 whether the inciter is an agent of that idolatrous cult, or if he is an enthusiastic acolyte and wishes to share his new insights with a family member or close friend, and he urges you to worship a deity **from the gods of the peoples that are around you, that are near to you, or that are far from you, from one end of the earth to the other,**

DISCUSSION

12:30 | **How do these nations serve their gods, I will do so as well:** The children of Israel knew how they were supposed to act; however they were liable to be swayed and negatively influenced by their neighbors. At a different time and in a different manner something similar happened to the Samaritans, who were exiled from their native lands to Samaria. They wanted to observe the religious rituals that they brought with them, but they also wished to maintain good relations with "the God of the land," seeking to appease Him when things did not go as they desired (see II Kings 17:26–34).

לֵאמֹר אֵיכָה יַעַבְדוּ הַגּוֹיִם הָאֵלֶּה אֶת־אֱלֹהֵיהֶם וְאֶעֱשֶׂה־כֵּן גַּם־אָנִי: לֹא־תַעֲשֶׂה

כֵן לַיהוָה אֱלֹהֶיךָ כִּי כָל־תּוֹעֲבַת יְהוָה אֲשֶׁר שָׂנֵא עָשׂוּ לֵאלֹהֵיהֶם כִּי גַם אֶת־

יג בְּנֵיהֶם וְאֶת־בְּנֹתֵיהֶם יִשְׂרְפוּ בָאֵשׁ לֵאלֹהֵיהֶם: אֵת כָּל־הַדָּבָר אֲשֶׁר אָנֹכִי מְצַוֶּה

אֶתְכֶם אֹתוֹ תִשְׁמְרוּ לַעֲשׂוֹת לֹא־תֹסֵף עָלָיו וְלֹא תִגְרַע מִמֶּנּוּ:

ב-ג כִּי־יָקוּם בְּקִרְבְּךָ נָבִיא אוֹ חֹלֵם חֲלוֹם וְנָתַן אֵלֶיךָ אוֹת אוֹ מוֹפֵת: וּבָא הָאוֹת

וְהַמּוֹפֵת אֲשֶׁר־דִּבֶּר אֵלֶיךָ לֵאמֹר נֵלְכָה אַחֲרֵי אֱלֹהִים אֲחֵרִים אֲשֶׁר לֹא־יְדַעְתָּם

ד וְנָעָבְדֵם: לֹא תִשְׁמַע אֶל־דִּבְרֵי הַנָּבִיא הַהוּא אוֹ אֶל־חוֹלֵם הַחֲלוֹם הַהוּא

כִּי מְנַסֶּה יְהוָה אֱלֹהֵיכֶם אֶתְכֶם לָדַעַת הֲיִשְׁכֶם אֹהֲבִים אֶת־יְהוָה אֱלֹהֵיכֶם

ה בְּכָל־לְבַבְכֶם וּבְכָל־נַפְשְׁכֶם: אַחֲרֵי יְהוָה אֱלֹהֵיכֶם תֵּלֵכוּ וְאֹתוֹ תִירָאוּ וְאֶת־

ו מִצְוֹתָיו תִּשְׁמֹרוּ וּבְקֹלוֹ תִשְׁמָעוּ וְאֹתוֹ תַעֲבֹדוּ וּבוֹ תִדְבָּקוּן: וְהַנָּבִיא הַהוּא אוֹ

חֹלֵם הַחֲלוֹם הַהוּא יוּמָת כִּי דִבֶּר־סָרָה עַל־יְהוָה אֱלֹהֵיכֶם הַמּוֹצִיא אֶתְכֶם

מֵאֶרֶץ מִצְרַיִם וְהַפֹּדְךָ מִבֵּית עֲבָדִים לְהַדִּיחֲךָ מִן־הַדֶּרֶךְ אֲשֶׁר צִוְּךָ יְהוָה אֱלֹהֶיךָ

ז לָלֶכֶת בָּהּ וּבִעַרְתָּ הָרָע מִקִּרְבֶּךָ: כִּי יְסִיתְךָ אָחִיךָ בֶן־אִמֶּךָ אוֹ־

בִנְךָ אוֹ־בִתְּךָ אוֹ אֵשֶׁת חֵיקֶךָ אוֹ רֵעֲךָ אֲשֶׁר כְּנַפְשְׁךָ בַּסֵּתֶר לֵאמֹר נֵלְכָה

ח וְנַעַבְדָה אֱלֹהִים אֲחֵרִים אֲשֶׁר לֹא יָדַעְתָּ אַתָּה וַאֲבֹתֶיךָ: מֵאֱלֹהֵי הָעַמִּים אֲשֶׁר

סְבִיבֹתֵיכֶם הַקְּרֹבִים אֵלֶיךָ אוֹ הָרְחֹקִים מִמֶּךָּ מִקְצֵה הָאָרֶץ וְעַד־קְצֵה הָאָרֶץ:

רש"י

אֵיכָה יַעַבְדוּ. לְפִי שֶׁלֹּא עָנַשׁ עַל עֲבוֹדָה זָרָה זֹה אֶלָּא עַל זֶבַח וְקִטּוּר וְנִסּוּךְ וְהִשְׁתַּחֲוָאָה, כְּמוֹ שֶׁכָּתוּב: "בִּלְתִּי לַה' לְבַדּוֹ" (שמות כב, יט) – דְּבָרִים הַנַּעֲשִׂים לַגָּבוֹהַּ, בָּא וְלִמֶּדְךָ כָּאן שֶׁאִם דַּרְכָּהּ שֶׁל עֲבוֹדָה זָרָה לַעֲבָדָהּ בְּדָבָר אַחֵר, כְּגוֹן פּוֹעֵר לְפַעוֹר וְזוֹרֵק אֶבֶן לְמַרְקוּלִיס, זוֹ הִיא עֲבוֹדָתוֹ וְחַיָּב, חֲבָל זֶבַח וְקִטּוּר וְנִסּוּךְ וְהִשְׁתַּחֲוָאָה אֲפִלּוּ שֶׁלֹּא כְדַרְכָּהּ חַיָּב:

לא כִּי גַם אֶת בְּנֵיהֶם. "גַּם" לְרַבּוֹת אֶת אֲבוֹתֵיהֶם וְחַמֹּתֵיהֶם. אָמַר רַבִּי עֲקִיבָא: אֲנִי רָאִיתִי גּוֹי שֶׁכְּפָתוֹ לְאָבִיו לִפְנֵי כַלְבּוֹ וַאֲכָלוֹ:

פרק יג

א אֵת כָּל הַדָּבָר. קַלָּה כַחֲמוּרָה. **תִּשְׁמְרוּ לַעֲשׂוֹת.** לִתֵּן לֹא תַעֲשֶׂה עַל עֲשֵׂה הָאֲמוּרִים בְּפָרָשָׁה, שֶׁכָּל "הִשָּׁמֶר" בִּלְשׁוֹן לֹא תַעֲשֶׂה הוּא, אֶלָּא שֶׁאֵין לוֹקִין עַל "הִשָּׁמֶר" שֶׁל עֲשֵׂה. **לֹא תֹסֵף עָלָיו.** חֲמִשָּׁה טוֹטָפוֹת, חֲמִשָּׁה מִינִין בַּלּוּלָב, אַרְבַּע בְּרָכוֹת בְּבִרְכַּת כֹּהֲנִים:

ב וְנָתַן אֵלֶיךָ אוֹת. בַּשָּׁמַיִם, כְּעִנְיָן שֶׁנֶּאֱמַר בְּגִדְעוֹן: "וַעֲשִׂיתָ לִּי אוֹת" (שופטים ו, יז), וְאוֹמֵר: "יְהִי נָא חֹרֶב אֶל הַגִּזָּה" וְגוֹ' (שם פסוק לז): **אוֹ מוֹפֵת.** בָּאָרֶץ אַף עַל פִּי כֵן לֹא תִשְׁמַע לוֹ. וְאִם תֹּאמַר: מִפְּנֵי מָה נוֹתֵן לוֹ הַקָּדוֹשׁ בָּרוּךְ הוּא מֶמְשָׁלָה לַעֲשׂוֹת אוֹת? "כִּי מְנַסֶּה ה' אֱלֹהֵיכֶם אֶתְכֶם" (להלן פסוק ד):

ה וְאֶת מִצְוֹתָיו תִּשְׁמֹרוּ. תּוֹרַת מֹשֶׁה. **וּבְקֹלוֹ תִשְׁמָעוּ.** בְּקוֹל הַנְּבִיאִים: **וְאֹתוֹ תַעֲבֹדוּ.** בְּמִקְדָּשׁוֹ. **וּבוֹ תִדְבָּקוּן.** הַדְּבֵק בִּדְרָכָיו: גְּמֹל חֲסָדִים, קְבֹר מֵתִים, בַּקֵּר חוֹלִים, כְּמוֹ שֶׁעָשָׂה הַקָּדוֹשׁ בָּרוּךְ הוּא:

ו סָרָה. דָּבָר הַמּוּסָר מִן הָעוֹלָם, שֶׁלֹּא הָיָה וְלֹא נִבְרָא וְלֹא צִוִּיתִי לְדַבֵּר כֵּן, דֶּשְׂטוֹלְוִד"א בְּלַעַז. **וְהַפֹּדְךָ מִבֵּית עֲבָדִים.** אֲפִלּוּ אֵין לוֹ עָלֶיךָ אֶלָּא שֶׁפְּדָאֲךָ, דַּיּוֹ:

ז כִּי יְסִיתְךָ. אֵין הַסָּתָה אֶלָּא גֵרוּי, שֶׁנֶּאֱמַר: "אִם ה' הֱסִיתְךָ בִּי" (שמואל א' כו, יט), אמיטיר"א בְּלַעַז, שֶׁמַּשִּׂיאוֹ לַעֲשׂוֹת כֵּן:

אָחִיךָ. מֵאָב, אוֹ "בֶן אִמֶּךָ", מֵאֵם. **חֵיקֶךָ.** הַשּׁוֹכֶבֶת בְּחֵיקֶךָ וּמְחֻקָּה בְּךָ, אֲפִיקִיד"א בְּלַעַז, וְכֵן: "מֵחֵיק הָאָרֶץ" (יחזקאל מג, יד), מִיסוֹד הַתִּקּוּעַ בָּאָרֶץ. **אֲשֶׁר כְּנַפְשְׁךָ.** זֶה אָבִיךָ. פֵּרֵשׁ לְךָ הַכָּתוּב אֶת הַחֲבִיבִין לְךָ, קַל וָחֹמֶר לַאֲחֵרִים. **בַּסֵּתֶר.** דִּבֶּר הַכָּתוּב בַּהֹוֶה, שֶׁאֵין דִּבְרֵי מֵסִית אֶלָּא בַּסֵּתֶר, וְכֵן שְׁלֹמֹה הוּא אוֹמֵר: "בְּנֶשֶׁף בְּעֶרֶב יוֹם בְּאִישׁוֹן לַיְלָה וַאֲפֵלָה" (משלי ז, ט): **אֲשֶׁר לֹא יָדַעְתָּ אַתָּה וַאֲבֹתֶיךָ.** דָּבָר זֶה גְּנַאי גָּדוֹל הוּא לְךָ, שֶׁאַף הָאֻמּוֹת אֵין מַנִּיחִין מַה שֶּׁמָּסְרוּ לָהֶם אֲבוֹתֵיהֶם, וְזֶה אוֹמֵר לְךָ: עֲזֹב מַה שֶּׁמָּסְרוּ לְךָ אֲבוֹתֶיךָ:

ח הַקְּרֹבִים אֵלֶיךָ אוֹ הָרְחֹקִים. לָמָּה פֵּרֵט קְרוֹבִים וּרְחוֹקִים? אֶלָּא כָּךְ אָמַר הַכָּתוּב: מִטִּיבָן שֶׁל קְרוֹבִים אַתָּה לָמֵד טִיבָן שֶׁל רְחוֹקִים, כְּשֵׁם שֶׁאֵין מַמָּשׁ בַּקְּרוֹבִים כָּךְ אֵין מַמָּשׁ בָּרְחוֹקִים: **מִקְצֵה הָאָרֶץ.** זוֹ חַמָּה וּלְבָנָה וּצְבָא הַשָּׁמַיִם, שֶׁהֵן מְהַלְּכִין מִסּוֹף הָעוֹלָם וְעַד סוֹפוֹ:

9 **you shall not accede to him, and you shall not heed him, and your eye shall not pity him, and you shall not be compassionate, and you shall not cover up for him** to spare him from punishment. Even though he is very close to you, it is your duty to expose him.
10 **Rather, you shall kill him** in the following manner: **Your hand shall be against him first to put him to death, and the hand of all the people last.** In the case of one executed for idolatry, the witnesses are the first to carry out the execution (17:7). Here, in the case of one executed for attempting to entice others to commit idolatry, the individual that he tried to entice is the first to do so.
11 **You shall stone him with stones and he shall die because he sought to lead you astray from the Lord your God, who took you out of the land of Egypt, from the house of bondage.**
12 **All Israel shall hear and shall fear, and they will not continue to perform like this evil matter in your midst.** This case may recur; you must nip this evil in the bud, even if there was no actual commission of a transgression, but only verbal incitement to sin.[14]
13 **If you shall hear in** regard to **one of your cities that the Lord your God is giving you to live there, saying:**
14 Incorrigible **wicked people have emerged from your midst, and have led the inhabitants of their city astray, saying: Let us go and serve other gods that you did not know.** Here it is not a single individual who clandestinely incites his relative or friend to sin, but rather a well-organized public propaganda campaign in the streets of the city that incites the residents to engage in idolatry. In that case, responsibility to take action falls upon the court, Israel's judicial authority, and it is its members that the Torah addresses.
15 **You shall inquire, and interrogate, and ask diligently,** investigate meticulously, **and behold,** if **it is** found to be **true, the matter is correct,** and not mere rumor, **this abomination was** indeed **performed in your midst,** the entire city was incited to idolatry.
16 **You shall smite the inhabitants of that city by sword; destroy it, and all that is in it, and its animals by sword;** you shall destroy all those found in the city, including the animals.
17 **You shall gather all its spoils into the midst of its square, and you shall burn in fire the city, and all its spoils, completely, to the Lord your God;** the entire city shall go up in flames to God like an offering; **and** after the city is destroyed, **it shall be an eternal mound,** serving as a severe and tangible warning to others; **it shall not be rebuilt.**
18 **There shall not cleave anything of the proscribed property to your hand, so that the Lord will abandon His enflamed wrath, and He will give you mercy, and He will be merciful to you,[D] and He will multiply you, as He took an oath to your fathers,**
19 **when you will heed the voice of the Lord your God, to observe all His commandments that I am commanding you today, to perform the right in the eyes of the Lord your God.**

Prohibitions Relating to the Sanctity of Israel

DEUTERONOMY 14:1–21

The sanctity of the Jewish people is expressed, among other ways, in their attitude toward their bodies. Here the Torah prohibits them from mutilating their bodies when they are in mourning. It also provides a list of foods that they may not ingest because they are considered an abomination.

14 1 **You are children to the Lord your God,** and this lofty sta-
Fourth aliya tus obligates you to abstain from practices that are common among the nations that surround you. **You shall not** stab or **cut yourselves** with knives as a sign of mourning, **and you shall not** pluck the hair from the center of your head and thereby **place a bald spot between your eyes for the dead.**

DISCUSSION

13:18 | **And He will give you mercy, and He will be merciful to you:** In order for God to have mercy on Israel and for His wrath to be removed from them, they must, somewhat paradoxically, do something harsh and seemingly cruel. In truth, however, there is no contradiction: Even a good doctor, whose compassion is not merely superficial and sentimental, will perform surgery on his patient when necessary. The doctor may express his mercy by removing a diseased organ or amputating a limb in order to save the patient, despite the fact that this causes pain to the patient. Similarly, the eradication of idolatry in a swift and powerful manner preserves the very existence of the nation.

ט לֹא־תֹאבֶה לוֹ וְלֹא תִשְׁמַע אֵלָיו וְלֹא־תָחוֹס עֵינְךָ עָלָיו וְלֹא־תַחְמֹל וְלֹא־תְכַסֶּה
י עָלָיו׃ כִּי הָרֹג תַּהַרְגֶנּוּ יָדְךָ תִּהְיֶה־בּוֹ בָרִאשׁוֹנָה לַהֲמִיתוֹ וְיַד כָּל־הָעָם בָּאַחֲרֹנָה׃
יא וּסְקַלְתּוֹ בָאֲבָנִים וָמֵת כִּי בִקֵּשׁ לְהַדִּיחֲךָ מֵעַל יהוה אֱלֹהֶיךָ הַמּוֹצִיאֲךָ מֵאֶרֶץ
יב מִצְרַיִם מִבֵּית עֲבָדִים׃ וְכָל־יִשְׂרָאֵל יִשְׁמְעוּ וְיִרָאוּן וְלֹא־יוֹסִפוּ לַעֲשׂוֹת כַּדָּבָר
יג הָרָע הַזֶּה בְּקִרְבֶּךָ׃ כִּי־תִשְׁמַע בְּאַחַת עָרֶיךָ אֲשֶׁר יהוה אֱלֹהֶיךָ נֹתֵן
יד לְךָ לָשֶׁבֶת שָׁם לֵאמֹר׃ יָצְאוּ אֲנָשִׁים בְּנֵי־בְלִיַּעַל מִקִּרְבֶּךָ וַיַּדִּיחוּ אֶת־יֹשְׁבֵי עִירָם
טו לֵאמֹר נֵלְכָה וְנַעַבְדָה אֱלֹהִים אֲחֵרִים אֲשֶׁר לֹא־יְדַעְתֶּם׃ וְדָרַשְׁתָּ וְחָקַרְתָּ וְשָׁאַלְתָּ
טז הֵיטֵב וְהִנֵּה אֱמֶת נָכוֹן הַדָּבָר נֶעֶשְׂתָה הַתּוֹעֵבָה הַזֹּאת בְּקִרְבֶּךָ׃ הַכֵּה תַכֶּה
אֶת־יֹשְׁבֵי הָעִיר הַהִוא לְפִי־חָרֶב הַחֲרֵם אֹתָהּ וְאֶת־כָּל־אֲשֶׁר־בָּהּ וְאֶת־בְּהֶמְתָּהּ
יז לְפִי־חָרֶב׃ וְאֶת־כָּל־שְׁלָלָהּ תִּקְבֹּץ אֶל־תּוֹךְ רְחֹבָהּ וְשָׂרַפְתָּ בָאֵשׁ אֶת־הָעִיר וְאֶת־
יח כָּל־שְׁלָלָהּ כָּלִיל לַיהוה אֱלֹהֶיךָ וְהָיְתָה תֵּל עוֹלָם לֹא תִבָּנֶה עוֹד׃ וְלֹא־יִדְבַּק בְּיָדְךָ
מְאוּמָה מִן־הַחֵרֶם לְמַעַן יָשׁוּב יהוה מֵחֲרוֹן אַפּוֹ וְנָתַן־לְךָ רַחֲמִים וְרִחַמְךָ וְהִרְבֶּךָ
יט כַּאֲשֶׁר נִשְׁבַּע לַאֲבֹתֶיךָ׃ כִּי תִשְׁמַע בְּקוֹל יהוה אֱלֹהֶיךָ לִשְׁמֹר אֶת־כָּל־מִצְוֹתָיו
א אֲשֶׁר אָנֹכִי מְצַוְּךָ הַיּוֹם לַעֲשׂוֹת הַיָּשָׁר בְּעֵינֵי יהוה אֱלֹהֶיךָ׃ בָּנִים יב רביעי
אַתֶּם לַיהוה אֱלֹהֵיכֶם לֹא תִתְגֹּדְדוּ וְלֹא־תָשִׂימוּ קָרְחָה בֵּין עֵינֵיכֶם לָמֵת׃

רש"י

ט | **לא תאבה לו.** לא תהא תאב לו, לא תאהבנו, לפי שנאמר: "ואהבת לרעך כמוך" (ויקרא יט, יח), את זה לא תאהב: **ולא תשמע אליו.** בהתחננו על נפשו למחול לו, לפי שנאמר: "עזב תעזב עמו" (שמות כג, ה), לזה לא תעזב: **ולא תחוס עינך עליו.** לפי שנאמר: "לא תעמד על דם רעך" (ויקרא יט, טז), על זה לא תחוס: **ולא תחמל.** לא תהפך בזכותו: **ולא תכסה עליו.** אם אתה יודע לו חובה, אינך רשאי לשתק:

י | **כי הרג תהרגנו.** אם יצא מבית דין זכאי החזירהו לחובה, יצא מבית דין חיב אל תחזירהו לזכות: **ידך תהיה בו בראשונה.** מצוה ביד הנסת להמיתו. לא מת בידו – ימות ביד אחרים, שנאמר: "ויד כל העם" וגו':

יג-יד | **לשבת שם.** פרט לירושלים שלא נתנה לדירה: **בני בליעל.** בלי על, שפרקו עלו של מקום: **אנשים.** ולא נשים: **ישבי עירם.** ולא יושבי עיר אחרת, מכאן אמרו: אין נעשית עיר הנדחת עד שידיחוה אנשים, ועד שיהיו מדיחיה מתוכה:

טו | **ודרשת וחקרת ושאלת היטב.** מכאן למדו שבע חקירות מרבוי המקרא. כאן יש שלש: דרישה וחקירה ו"היטב". "ושאלת" אינו מן המנין, וממנו למדו בדיקות. ובמקום אחר הוא אומר: "ודרשו השפטים היטב" (להלן יט, יח), ובמקום אחר הוא אומר: "ודרשת היטב" (להלן יז, ד), ולמדו "היטב" "היטב" לגזרה שוה, לתן האמור של זה בזה:

טז | **הכה תכה.** אם אינך יכול להמיתם במיתה הכתובה בהם, המיתם באחרת:

יז | **לה' אלהיך.** לשמו ובשבילו:

יח | **למען ישוב ה' מחרון אפו.** שכל זמן שעבודה זרה בעולם, חרון אף בעולם:

פרק יד

א | **לא תתגדדו.** לא תתנו גדידה ושרט בבשרכם על מת כדרך שהאמוריים עושין, לפי שאתם בניו של מקום, ואתם ראויין להיות נאים ולא גדודים ומקרחים: **בין עיניכם.** אצל הפדחת, ובמקום אחר הוא אומר: "לא יקרחו קרחה בראשם" (ויקרא כא, ה), לעשות כל הראש כבין העינים:

2 God does not want His children to mutilate their bodies and render themselves unsightly,[15] **for you are a holy people ded‐ icated to the Lord your God, and you the Lord chose to be His people of distinction from all the peoples that are on the face of the earth.**

3 **You shall not eat any** item considered an **abomination.** According to some, this includes items that are despicable in the eyes of the surrounding nations as well.[16]

4 **These are the animals that you may eat: an ox, a sheep, and a goat;**

5 in addition to the aforementioned domestic animals, you may also eat **a deer, a gazelle, a fallow deer,**[B] **a wild goat,**[B] **an oryx,**[B] **an aurochs,**[B] **and a mouflon sheep.**[BD]

6 **Any animal that has hooves, and** unlike the horse and don‐ key, which have only one hoof on each foot, **the** animal has **two hooves** on each foot and they **are** entirely **split,** and it also **brings up the cud among the animals, that you may eat.**

7 **However, these you shall not eat from those that bring up the cud, or from those with a split hoof,** creatures that have only one of the characteristics of kosher animals but not both: **The camel,**[B] **and the hare, and the hyrax**[B] because they bring

Fallow deer

Nubian ibex

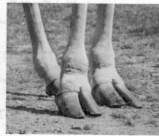
Arabian oryx

Split hooves

Aurochs

Mouflon ram

Giraffe

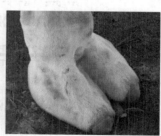
Top of a camel's foot

Hare

Hyrax

Bottom of a camel's foot

DISCUSSION

14:5 | Deer...a mouflon sheep: The identifica‐ tion of the animals listed here is not certain, but this has little significance regarding the fact that it is permitted to eat them, as the Torah spells

out the physical characteristics on the basis of which it may be determined whether an animal is permitted to be eaten or not (see *Ḥullin* 71a). The customary practice, however, is to eat only

those animals about which there is a tradition that they are permitted, e.g., the deer and the gazelle (see *Ḥokhmat Adam* 36:1; *Zivḥei Tzedek* 80:2).

ב כִּי עַם קָדוֹשׁ אַתָּה לַיהוָה אֱלֹהֶיךָ וּבְךָ בָּחַר יְהוָה לִהְיוֹת לוֹ לְעַם סְגֻלָּה מִכֹּל
ג ד הָעַמִּים אֲשֶׁר עַל־פְּנֵי הָאֲדָמָה: לֹא תֹאכַל כָּל־תּוֹעֵבָה: זֹאת
ה הַבְּהֵמָה אֲשֶׁר תֹּאכֵלוּ שׁוֹר שֵׂה כְשָׂבִים וְשֵׂה עִזִּים: אַיָּל וּצְבִי וְיַחְמוּר וְאַקּוֹ
ו וְדִישֹׁן וּתְאוֹ וָזָמֶר: וְכָל־בְּהֵמָה מַפְרֶסֶת פַּרְסָה וְשֹׁסַעַת שֶׁסַע שְׁתֵּי פְרָסוֹת
ז מַעֲלַת גֵּרָה בַּבְּהֵמָה אֹתָהּ תֹּאכֵלוּ: אַךְ אֶת־זֶה לֹא תֹאכְלוּ מִמַּעֲלֵי הַגֵּרָה
וּמִמַּפְרִיסֵי הַפַּרְסָה הַשְּׁסוּעָה אֶת־הַגָּמָל וְאֶת־הָאַרְנֶבֶת וְאֶת־הַשָּׁפָן כִּי־

רש״י

ב| **כִּי עַם קָדוֹשׁ אַתָּה.** קְדֻשַּׁת עַצְמְךָ מֵאֲבוֹתֶיךָ, וְעוֹד: "וּבְךָ בָּחַר ה'":

ג| **כָּל תּוֹעֵבָה.** כָּל שֶׁתִּעַבְתִּי לְךָ, כְּגוֹן צָרַם אֹזֶן בְּכוֹר כְּדֵי לְשָׁחֲטוֹ בַּמְּדִינָה, הֲרֵי דָּבָר שֶׁתִּעַבְתִּי לְךָ: "כָּל מוּם לֹא יִהְיֶה בּוֹ" (ויקרא כב, כא), כָּאן לִמֵּד כָּאן שֶׁלֹּא יִשְׁחַט וְיֹאכַל עַל אוֹתוֹ הַמּוּם. בִּשֵּׁל בָּשָׂר בְּחָלָב, הֲרֵי דָּבָר שֶׁתִּעַבְתִּי לְךָ, הִזְהִיר כָּאן עַל אֲכִילָתוֹ:

ד-ה| **זֹאת הַבְּהֵמָה... אַיָּל וּצְבִי וְיַחְמוּר.** לִמְּדָנוּ שֶׁהַחַיָּה בִּכְלַל בְּהֵמָה, וְלִמְּדָנוּ שֶׁהַבְּהֵמָה וְחַיָּה טְמֵאָה מְרֻבָּה מִן הַטְּהוֹרָה, שֶׁבְּכָל מָקוֹם פּוֹרֵט הֶחָת הַמּוּעָט: **וְאַקּוֹ.** מְתֻרְגָּם: "יַעְלָא", "יַעֲלֵי סָלַע" הוּא אשטנבו"ק: **וּתְאוֹ.** "תּוֹרְבָּלָא", שׁוֹר הַיַּעַר, 'בָּלָא' – יַעַר בִּלְשׁוֹן אֲרַמִּי:

ו| **מַפְרֶסֶת.** סְדוּקָה, כְּתַרְגּוּמוֹ: **פַּרְסָה.** פלנט"א: **וְשֹׁסַעַת.** חֲלוּקָה בִּשְׁתֵּי צִפָּרְנַיִם, שֶׁיֵּשׁ סְדוּקָה וְאֵינָהּ חֲלוּקָה בְּצִפָּרְנַיִם וְהִיא טְמֵאָה: **בַּבְּהֵמָה.** מַשְׁמַע מָה שֶׁנִּמְצָא בַּבְּהֵמָה אֱכֹל, מִכָּאן אָמְרוּ שֶׁהַשְּׁלִיל מֻתָּר בִּשְׁחִיטַת אִמּוֹ:

ז| **הַשְּׁסוּעָה.** בְּרִיָּה הִיא שֶׁיֵּשׁ לָהּ שְׁנֵי גַבִּין וּשְׁתֵּי שִׁדְרָאוֹת. אָמְרוּ רַבּוֹתֵינוּ: לָמָּה נִשְׁנוּ? בַּבְּהֵמָה מִפְּנֵי הַשְּׁסוּעָה וּבָעוֹפוֹת מִפְּנֵי הָרָאָה (להלן פסוק יג), שֶׁלֹּא נֶאֶמְרוּ בְּתוֹרַת כֹּהֲנִים:

BACKGROUND

14:5| **Fallow deer [*yaḥmur*]:** A type of deer; it chews its cud and has split hooves. The *yaḥmur* is commonly identified as the Persian fallow deer, *Dama dama mesopotamica.* The length of its body reaches 2 m. The average weight of a male is about 80 kg and that of a female is about 50 kg. Its antlers are spread less widely than those of other deer. The biblical name *yaḥmur* has been preserved in Aramaic and Arabic. It is possible that the name is attributed to the reddish-brown color of the animal, similar to *ḥamar*, which is wine (see, e.g., Isaiah 27:5). All the Aramaic translations use the name *yaḥmur*, as does the Arabic translation of Rav Se'adya Gaon. The Persian fallow deer is known as the *yaḥmur* in northwestern Iran, which hosts the last remaining natural population of Persian fallow deer in the world. However, some have identified the *yaḥmur* as the hartebeest (*Alcelaphus buselaphus*), an antelope that has curved horns similar to those of cattle.

Wild goat [*ako*]: Identified by most of the Aramaic translations as the goat-antelope, *Caprinae*, a wild goat from the Bovidae family. These goats live in open areas and on rocky, mountainous terrain (see Psalms 104:18). In Israel, the only commonly found wild goat is the Nubian ibex (*Capra ibex nubiana*). Wild goats grow to a body length of 100–120 cm and a weight of 45–80 kg. The horns of the male reach a length of 130 cm, while those of the female reach a length of 40 cm.

Oryx [*dishon*]: According to the Aramaic translations, this is the oryx, and it is customarily identified as the Arabian oryx, *Oryx leucoryx*, which in the past was commonly found in desert plains in Israel, but became extinct from those areas in the early twentieth century due to hunting. It grows to a body length of 2 m, a height of 70 cm, and a weight of 70 kg. Its horns are straight and sharp.

Aurochs [*te'o*]: According to the Aramaic translations, this is a wild ox identified as the aurochs, *Bos primigenius*, which was common to Israel in biblical times but is currently extinct. It was much larger than modern-day cattle. It reached a length of about 3 m, a shoulder height of about 2 m, and a weight of over 1,000 kg. Its horns reached a length of 80 cm. Some have identified the *te'o* with the water buffalo, *Bubalus bubalis*. However, no water buffalo remains have been uncovered in archaeological excavations from the biblical era. Apparently, the water buffalo reached Israel only in post-biblical times.

Mouflon sheep [*zamer*]: Rav Se'adya Gaon identified the *zamer* as the giraffe, *giraffa*, which has all the characteristics of a kosher animal. The giraffe lived in Egypt in biblical times, but archaeologists have yet to uncover any giraffe remains in Israel from that time period. Others have identified the *zamer* as a type of mouflon sheep, *Ovis orientalis*, or the barbary sheep, *Ammotragus lervia*, or the wild goat, *Capra aegagrus*, but there is no hard evidence for any of these claims.

14:7| **The camel:** The upper, visible part of the camel's foot appears to be split, but its underside appears to be one unit. In any event, the camel walks on several fairly soft toes.

The hare and the hyrax: The hare and hyrax do not actually return food from their stomachs to their mouths to be chewed for a second time, but to the external observer they chew their

up the cud but do not have hooves; they are impure for you and you
may not eat them;
8 **and the pig**[B] too you shall not eat, **because it has hooves,** and its
hooves are split, **but** it **does not bring up the cud, it is impure for
you; from their meat** of all these impure animals **you shall not eat,
and their carcasses you shall not touch.**[D]
9 **This you may eat from all that is in the water: Anything that has
fins,**[B] the limb by means of which it swims through the water, **and
scales**[B] that cover its body, **you may eat;**
10 **and anything that does not have fins and scales you may not eat; it
is impure for you.** This prohibition is not limited to fish, but includes
all aquatic creatures lacking fins and scales.
11 **All pure birds you may eat.**
12 **This is that which you may not eat from them: The griffon vulture,**[B]
the bearded vulture,[B] **and
the lappet-faced vulture;**[B]
13 **the glede, the buzzard,**[B]
and the kite,[B] various birds
of prey, **after its kinds;**
14 **every raven after its kinds;**

Characteristics of a kosher fish

Griffon vulture

Bearded vulture

Lappet-faced vulture

European honey buzzard

Common buzzard

Black kite

Raven

DISCUSSION

14:8 | **And their carcasses you shall not touch:** The Sages derived from other verses that contact with the carcass of a non-kosher animal is not prohibited; it is prohibited only for a person who came into contact with it to approach the Temple and consecrated objects, e.g., during the pilgrimage festivals (see *Rosh HaShana* 16b; see also commentary on Leviticus 15:31; 17:16; and Leviticus 11:8). Some explain this part of the verse as reinforcing the prohibition against eating a carcass: You shall not touch their carcasses in order to eat them (see *Bekhor Shor*).

BACKGROUND

food in a manner similar to that of ruminants who chew their cud.

14:8 | **Pig:** This refers to the wild boar, *Sus scrofa*, a large animal from the pig family. It grows to a length of up to a 1.5 m, and a height of up to 1 m. Its body is hairy and is covered with strong bristles. The wild boar will eat almost anything, including vegetation, birds' eggs, chicks, small rodents, and even carcasses. Unlike ruminants, which have four stomachs, this animal has a single stomach. The wild boar is common in northern and central Israel in marshes, thickets, and agricultural areas. Remainders of pig bones have been uncovered in almost all non-Israelite settlements in Israel.

14:9 | **Fins:** A bony protrusion on the side of a fish's stomach, which it uses to glide through the water. On the back and tail of a fish there are also fins that do not move.

Scales: Flat protrusions on the skin of a fish, which overlap like tiles, with their edges angled toward the tail. There are fish whose scales deteriorate, their connection to the body loosens, and they are shed with age.

ח מַעֲלֵה גֵרָה הֵמָּה וּפַרְסָה לֹא הִפְרִיסוּ טְמֵאִים הֵם לָכֶם׃ וְאֶת־הַחֲזִיר כִּי־
מַפְרִיס פַּרְסָה הוּא וְלֹא גֵרָה טָמֵא הוּא לָכֶם מִבְּשָׂרָם לֹא תֹאכֵלוּ וּבְנִבְלָתָם
ט לֹא תִגָּעוּ׃ אֶת־זֶה תֹּאכְלוּ מִכֹּל אֲשֶׁר בַּמָּיִם כֹּל אֲשֶׁר־לוֹ סְנַפִּיר
י וְקַשְׂקֶשֶׂת תֹּאכֵלוּ׃ וְכֹל אֲשֶׁר אֵין־לוֹ סְנַפִּיר וְקַשְׂקֶשֶׂת לֹא תֹאכֵלוּ טָמֵא הוּא
יא יב לָכֶם׃ כָּל־צִפּוֹר טְהֹרָה תֹּאכֵלוּ׃ וְזֶה אֲשֶׁר לֹא־תֹאכְלוּ מֵהֶם הַנֶּשֶׁר
יג יד וְהַפֶּרֶס וְהָעָזְנִיָּה׃ וְהָרָאָה וְאֶת־הָאַיָּה וְהַדַּיָּה לְמִינָהּ׃ וְאֵת כָּל־עֹרֵב לְמִינוֹ׃

רש"י

ח| וּבְנִבְלָתָם לֹא תִגָּעוּ. רַבּוֹתֵינוּ פֵּרְשׁוּ: בָּרֶגֶל, שֶׁאָדָם חַיָּב לְטַהֵר אֶת עַצְמוֹ בָּרֶגֶל. יָכוֹל יְהוּ מֻזְהָרִים בְּכָל הַשָּׁנָה? תַּלְמוּד לוֹמַר: "אֱמֹר אֶל הַכֹּהֲנִים" וְגוֹ' (ויקרא כא, א), וּמָה טֻמְאַת הַמֵּת חֲמוּרָה, כֹּהֲנִים מֻזְהָרִים וְאֵין יִשְׂרָאֵל מֻזְהָרִים, טֻמְאַת נְבֵלָה קַלָּה לֹא כָּל שֶׁכֵּן?:

יא| כָּל צִפּוֹר טְהֹרָה תֹּאכֵלוּ. לְהַתִּיר מְשֻׁלַּחַת שֶׁבַּמְּצֹרָע:

יב| וְזֶה אֲשֶׁר לֹא תֹאכְלוּ. לֶאֱסֹר אֶת הַשְּׁחוּטָה:

יג| וְהָרָאָה וְאֶת הָאַיָּה וְגוֹ'. הִיא רָאָה, הִיא אַיָּה, הִיא דַּיָּה, וְלָמָּה נִקְרָא שְׁמָהּ 'רָאָה'? שֶׁרוֹאָה בְּיוֹתֵר. וְלָמָּה הִזְהִירְךָ בְּכָל שְׁמוֹתֶיהָ? שֶׁלֹּא לִתֵּן פִּתְחוֹן פֶּה לְבַעַל דִּין לַחֲלֹק, שֶׁלֹּא יְהֵא הָאוֹסְרָהּ קוֹרֵא אוֹתָהּ 'רָאָה' וְהַבָּא לְהַתִּיר אוֹמֵר זוֹ 'דַּיָּה' שְׁמָהּ אוֹ 'אַיָּה' שְׁמָהּ, וְזוֹ לֹא אָסַר הַכָּתוּב. וּבָעוֹפוֹת פֵּרַט לְךָ הַטְּמֵאִים, לְלַמֶּדְךָ שֶׁעוֹפוֹת טְהוֹרִים מְרֻבִּים עַל הַטְּמֵאִים, לְפִיכָךְ פֵּרַט אֶת הַמּוּעָט:

BACKGROUND

14:12| **Griffon vulture [*nesher*]:** The griffon vulture, *Gyps fulvus*, is a large bird that is characterized by its nesting and soaring at high altitudes, allowing it to swiftly glide toward its food (see Jeremiah 48:40; Obadia 1:4; Micah 1:16; Habakkuk 1:8; Job 39:27–28). This bird was a royal symbol in Egypt and Assyria. Its wingspan stretches to 2.5 m, and it weighs roughly 10 kg. Its head and neck are bare, as though its feathers shed [*nashar*]; perhaps for this reason the vulture is known as the *nesher*. Some opinions identify the *nesher* with the eagle, *Aquila chrysaetos*, which was a very important Roman symbol, while others maintain that *nesher* is a general term that refers to several different birds of prey.

Bearded vulture [*peres*]: It is commonly accepted to identify the *peres* with the bearded vulture, *Gypaetus barbatus*, which is known to drop its prey from high altitudes in order to shatter [*pores*] its bones. In Arabic it is known as *mukhlafa*, *kasar al-atam*, which means bone-breaker. In the nineteenth century this vulture nested in all the rocky, mountainous areas in Israel. The bearded vulture has a body length of approximately 100–115 cm, a wingspan of 265–280 cm, and weighs 4.5–8 kg. It has sharp-edged wings, and a diamond-shaped tail.

Lappet-faced vulture [*ozniyya*]: From the root *ayin-zayin-zayin*, meaning strong or powerful (Radak). The Mishna refers to it as the *oz* (*Keilim* 17:14). According to the Sages, the *ozniyya* is solitary and does not live near settled areas (*Ḥullin* 62a). The Septuagint translates *ozniyya* as the white-tailed eagle, *Haliaeetus albicilla*, which is rarely seen in Israel. As such, it is commonly accepted to identify the *ozniyya* with the lappet-faced vulture, *Torgos tracheliotus*, from the family Accipitriformes. The lappet-faced vulture's neck and head are bald and pink, it has a wingspan of 3 m, and it can weigh as much as 14 kg. It has a large, powerful beak that can tear through the skin of animals and break bones. Some opinions maintain that the *ozniyya* is the cinereous vulture, *Aegypius monachus*, which passes through Israel but is rarely sighted there nowadays (see *Encyclopaedia Biblica*).

14:13| **Buzzard [*ayya*]:** The *ayya* is described in Job (28:7) as a bird that can see across great distances. It is identified as the common buzzard, *Buteo buteo*, a nomadic bird of prey from the family Accipitridae whose wingspan is about 120 cm, and can weigh up to 900 gm. Alternatively, it is identified as the European honey buzzard, *Pernis apivorus*, also a nomadic bird of prey from the family Accipitridae, which may be found in Israel. It is of medium size, with a body length of 53–58 cm, a wingspan of 145 cm, and it weighs 460–800 gm. In any event, the prohibition stated in this verse relates not to a particular bird, but to a group of closely related birds. The Talmud states: In the east there are one hundred non-kosher birds, all of the species of *ayya* (Ḥullin 63b).

Kite [*dayya*]: The Sages consider *da'a* and *ayya* general terms for various birds with similar characteristics (*Ḥullin* 63b). The *dayya* is also known as the *da'a* (see Leviticus 11:14, and Onkelos ad loc.). It is depicted as a desert bird that gathers in packs to sleep and eat (see Isaiah 34:15), and is commonly identified as the black kite, *Milvus migrans*, a scavenger bird from the family Accipitridae, which can be found in Israel. The black kite weighs 600–1000 gm, is 55–60 cm in length, and has a wingspan of 135–150 cm. It hunts mice, medium-sized birds, and chicks, but it feeds on carrion and trash, and will occasionally snatch food that has been abandoned or left in the open. It nests in trees or on rocks.

15 the ostrich,[B] the swift,[B] the seagull,[B] and the sparrow hawk[B] after its kinds;

16 the little owl,[B] the short-eared owl,[B] and the barn owl,[B] all nocturnal birds of prey;

17 the eagle owl,[B] the roller,[B] and the fish owl;[B]

18 the stork,[B] the heron[B]

Ostrich

Swift

Common kestrel

Seagull

Eurasian sparrow hawk

Little owl

Short-eared owl

Barn owl

Eagle owl

Houbara bustard

Roller

Egyptian vulture

Osprey

Brown fish owl

Stork

BACKGROUND

14:15 | Ostrich [*bat haya'ana*]: This bird is mentioned elsewhere in the Bible among desert animals and birds (Isaiah 34:13; Jeremiah 50:9; Micah 1:8). Its name probably stems from the root *vav-ayin-nun* or *yod-ayin-nun*, which means greedy in Syriac. Alternatively, it comes from the root *ayin-nun-yod* or *ayin-nun-heh*, which refers to the screeching sound [*anot*] it makes. Some opinions, based on Onkelos and *Targum Yonatan*, identify the *bat hayaana* as the ostrich, *Struthio camelus* (Rav Se'adya Gaon; Malbim). The ostrich once populated the deserts of Syria, Iraq, the Arabian Peninsula, and the Negev. Ostriches reach a height of approximately 2.5 m, and can weigh as much as 150 kg. Others, however, note that the *bat haya'ana* is listed in the verse together with nocturnal birds of prey from the owl family, and therefore identify it as the pharaoh eagle-owl, *Bubo ascalaphus*, which

grows to a size of approximately 40 cm, a weight of about 2 kg, and emits a howling sound.

Swift [*taḥmas*]: Based on the root of its name, *ḥet-mem-samekh*, which denotes robbery, commentaries and researchers alike maintain that the *taḥmas* is a bird that is characterized by snatching or theft. Indeed, *Targum Yonatan* translates *taḥmas* as *ḥatfita*, which may be translated as snatcher, while Onkelos translates it as *tzitza*, a swift, *Apus apus*, which is noted for the manner in which it snatches flying insects during its flight. Some identify the *taḥmas* with nightjars, *Caprimulgus*, small nocturnal birds of prey, which are also known by this name in modern Hebrew. The nightjar weighs roughly 80 g, and is also known for preying on flying insects. Others suggest that the *taḥmas* is the common kestrel [*baz*], *Falco tinnunculus*, whose

name also refers to looting [*biza*] or stealing. The common kestrel is a brown, speedy bird of prey that can be found throughout Israel. It is the size of a large pigeon, with a wingspan of 70–80 cm, and a weight of roughly 150 gm; it feeds on birds, rodents, and insects.

Seagull [*shaḥaf*]: Following the Septuagint, which translates *shaḥaf* as *laron*, some identify it with the gull, *Larus*, often referred to as seagull, called *shaḥaf* in modern Hebrew. Several species of gull may be found near water sources in Israel. Its size ranges from 25–70 centimeters; its wings are long and sharp, and it has three webbed toes. It feeds on fish, carrion, and trash.

Sparrow hawk [*netz*]: Based on the translation appearing in the Septuagint, the *netz* has been identified as the Eurasian sparrow hawk, *Accipiter nisus*, one of the most common and notice-

טו טז וְאֵת בַּת הַיַּעֲנָה וְאֶת־הַתַּחְמָס וְאֶת־הַשָּׁחַף וְאֶת־הַנֵּץ לְמִינֵהוּ: אֶת־הַכּוֹס
יז יח וְאֶת־הַיַּנְשׁוּף וְהַתִּנְשָׁמֶת: וְהַקָּאָת וְאֶת־הָרָחָמָה וְאֶת־הַשָּׁלָךְ: וְהַחֲסִידָה

רש״י

טז | הַתִּנְשָׁמֶת. קלב״ח סורי״ן: יז | שָׁלָךְ. הַשּׁוֹלֶה דָּגִים מִן הַיָּם:

BACKGROUND

able birds of prey in Israel (see also Rashi here and *Ḥullin* 63a). The Eurasian sparrow hawk is 30 to 40 cm in length, while its wingspan reaches up to 65 cm. Its back is brownish-gray, and it has a striped tail. It would seem that the phrase: "The sparrow hawk [*netz*] after its kinds," includes other types of birds of prey of similar size that are found in Israel, such as the peregrine falcon, *Falco peregrinus*, the Eurasian hobby, *Falco subbuteo*, the lanner falcon, *Falco biarmicus*, and the saker falcon, *Falco cherrug*. The Midrash refers to the fact that the *netz* hunts other birds, as it states: To what was Israel comparable at that hour? To a dove fleeing from a *netz* (*Mekhilta Beshalah, Masekhta DeVayehi* 2).

14:16| **Little owl [*kos*]:** The *kos* is depicted in Psalms (102:7) as a solitary desert bird that inhabits wastelands and ruins. Aramaic translations, the Septuagint, and the majority of commentaries and researchers identify the *kos* as the little owl, *Athene noctua saharae*, a small, nocturnal bird of prey from the owl family. The little owl measures up to 21 cm, with a wingspan of approximately 60 cm, while the weight of an adult can reach up to 150 g. The little owl is commonly found in open areas, and dwells among ruins and in rocky terrain. Some claim that the *kos* is a water bird, similar to the pelican, due to the fact that it is listed alongside the *shalakh* in Leviticus (11:17).

The short-eared owl [*yanshuf*]: According to Isaiah (34:10–11), the *yanshuf* is a bird that lives in ruins and wastelands. The commentaries maintain that it is a nocturnal bird whose name is derived from the noun *neshef*, meaning night (Ibn Ezra; Radak), or from the sounds it emits when exhaling [*neshifa*]. Onkelos and the Talmud (*Nidda* 23a) identify it by the Aramaic term *kifofa*, a bird that is similar in appearance to a monkey [*kof*], in that its eyes are situated at the front of its head. This description fits the nocturnal birds of prey from the owl family. Nowadays, this is indeed the accepted identification of the *yanshuf*. Two species of owl are found in Israel: The long-eared owl, *Asio otus*, and the short-eared owl, *Asio flammeus*. Their length can reach up to 40 cm, their wingspans are about 1 m, and they weigh up to 300 g.

Barn owl [*tinshamet*]: The barn owl, *Tyto alba*, is a common nocturnal bird from the owl family. Onkelos calls it *bavta*, while the Talmud refers to it as *ba'ut* (*Ḥullin* 63a). Its length is 34 cm, and it is recognizable by the heart-shaped feathers around its eyes. The barn owl lives in pits, ruins, and caves, and hunts field mice and small birds.

14:17| **Eagle owl [*kaat*]:** The *kaat* lives in wastelands and desolated areas (Isaiah 34:11; Zephaniah 2:14; Psalms 102:7). Its name alludes to its habit of vomiting [*hakaa*] undigested food pellets, something done primarily by nocturnal birds of prey. Some identify the *kaat* with the eagle owl, which is a desert owl, since the *kaat* is mentioned in this verse immediately following other nocturnal birds of prey. Others suggest that it is the houbara bustard, *Chlamydotis undulata*, a large, land bird with long legs and an elongated neck. Its length extends up to 65 cm and it has a wingspan of 150 cm.

Roller [*raḥama*]: The translation of *raḥama* as the roller follows the Talmud (*Ḥullin* 63a) and *Targum Yonatan*, who identify it as the *sherakrak*. As recent authorities such as R. Yaakov Tzvi Mecklenburg and R. Joseph Schwartz note, this is the Arabic term for a roller. The European roller, *Coracias garrulus*, is around the size of a jackdaw, with a slightly hooked beak, and it preys on small mammals, reptiles, and insects. Some have understood the Talmud as referring to the bird making a whistling sound, and identify it instead as a bee-eater (which used to be sometimes confused with a roller), but the bee-eater is not at all predatory and would be out of place in this list. Rav Se'adya Gaon identifies the *raḥam* as the Egyptian vulture, *Neophron percnopterus*, based on the fact that this is its name in Arabic. The Egyptian vulture is approximately 60 cm in length, with a wingspan of 150 to 170 cm, and it weighs up to about 2 kg. Some commentaries contend that the *raḥam* is a nocturnal bird of prey, since it is mentioned alongside the *kaat* and the *tinshemet*.

Fish owl [*shalakh*]: According to the Septuagint and the Sages, the *shalakh* snatches fish from the sea (*Ḥullin* 63a). Some claim that it is the osprey, *Pandion haliaetus*, which feeds almost entirely off fish. The Septuagint translates *shalakh* as the cormorant, which dives into the sea to catch fish and is found near large bodies of water in Israel. Researchers suggest other possibilities: the pelican; the white-throated kingfisher, *Halcyon smyrnensis*; or the pied kingfisher, *Ceryle rudis*. Some have suggested that it is the brown fish owl, *Ketupa zeylonensis*, a small, nocturnal bird of prey from the owl family, which also hunts fish.

14:18| **The stork [*ḥasida*]:** The *ḥasida* is mentioned in the Bible as a nomadic, gliding bird that nests in cypress trees (Jeremiah 8:7; Zechariah 5:9; Psalms 104:17; Job 39:13). The Sages describe it as a bird that performs acts of kindness [*hessed*] with its young and others of its type (*Ḥullin* 63a; *Midrash Tehillim* 22:14). According to the commentaries, the name *ḥasida* denotes a characteristic, and is not necessarily the proper name of any particular bird. Consequently, different birds have been suggested as the *ḥasida* according to the context in which the term appears in the Bible. The Aramaic translations, the Talmud (*Ḥullin* 63a), and Rav Se'adya Gaon identify it as either the white *dayya* or a hawk. The Septuagint, the Vulgate, and Rashi claim that it is a bird from the family Ciconiiformes. These birds, which generally live near swamps or on river banks, include the pelican, the heron, and the stork. Ancient cultures viewed the stork as a symbol of dedication to family and respect for one's parents. This identification of the *ḥasida* as the stork has long been accepted and is accepted today by the majority of researchers. However, there were times when Jews in certain communities ate stork, apparently considering it to be a kosher bird (see *Responsa of the Rosh*, 20:20).

The heron [*anafa*]: According to the Talmud (*Ḥullin* 63a), the *anafa* is similar to the *ḥasida* in appearance and in its flight. It is accepted to identify the *anafa* with the heron, a carnivorous

after its kinds, the hoopoe,[B] and the bat.[B]

19 **Every flying swarming creature,** small, winged creatures that creep on the ground and also fly, **is impure for you; they shall not be eaten.**

20 **All pure flying creatures,** including any flying creature that does not appear on the list provided here, **you may eat.**[D] Some commentaries explain this verse as adding to what is stated above (verse 11) by indicating that grasshoppers may also be eaten.[17]

21 **You shall not eat any unslaughtered carcass,** an animal that died in any manner other than proper ritual slaughter; **to the stranger who is within your gates,** a resident alien, who lives in the land but is not integrated into national life because he has not accepted upon himself all the commandments,[18] **you may give it and he will eat it; or you may sell it to a foreigner, as you are a holy people for the Lord your God. You shall not cook a kid in its mother's milk;**[D] cooking a kid in the milk from which it was to receive its nurture is seen as cruel.[19]

Heron

Hoopoe

Kid nursing from its mother

Bat

"Flying swarming creature"

Tithes

DEUTERONOMY 14:22–29

This passage opens with the tithe referred to by the Sages as second tithe, which is not given to others but rather is eaten by its owner in Jerusalem. This tithe was briefly mentioned earlier (12:17–18) along with other matters related to the place that God will choose. It is also mentioned in Leviticus (27:30) in the context of the laws of consecrated property. Here, additional details are provided with regard to this tithe. The discussion continues with the laws pertaining to the tithes that are given to the Levite and to the poor.

22 **You shall tithe the entire crop of your sowing,** your produce **that comes out in the field year by year.** The tithes are determined according to the year of the Sabbatical cycle, as will be explained below. The Sages learned from this verse that the produce of one year cannot be set aside as tithe for the produce of a different year.[20]

Fifth aliya

23 **You shall eat before the Lord your God, in the place which He will choose to rest His name there,** in close proximity to the Temple, **the tithe of your grain, your wine, and your oil, and the firstborn of your cattle and your flocks, so that you will learn to fear the Lord your God all the days.** The dispersal of the nation across the country, with no regular communication, may cause the people to lose sight of their unique essence. Therefore every farmer must come at least once a year to the Temple. Staying in the holy city together with his family,

as they consume a tenth of their annual yield, will strengthen his and his family's identification as members of the Jewish people, and will revitalize them as they return to their homes and regular lives.[21]

24 **If the way is too great for you, as you are unable to carry it,** your tithe, from your home to Jerusalem, **because the place that the Lord your God will choose to place His name there is too far from you, when the Lord your God blesses you,** and the population will not be concentrated in one area; rather, it will be dispersed over a spacious country, and you will have abundant crops;

25 **you shall** be permitted to **exchange it for silver,** by selling the tithe to someone else or by redeeming it on your own, **and you shall bind the silver in your hand, and you shall go to the**

יט וְהָאֲנָפָה לְמִינָהּ וְהַדּוּכִיפַת וְהָעֲטַלֵּף: וְכֹל שֶׁרֶץ הָעוֹף טָמֵא הוּא לָכֶם לֹא יֵאָכֵלוּ:
כ כא כָּל־עוֹף טָהוֹר תֹּאכֵלוּ: לֹא־תֹאכְלוּ כָל־נְבֵלָה לַגֵּר אֲשֶׁר־בִּשְׁעָרֶיךָ תִּתְּנֶנָּה וַאֲכָלָהּ
אוֹ מָכֹר לְנָכְרִי כִּי עַם קָדוֹשׁ אַתָּה לַיהוָה אֱלֹהֶיךָ לֹא־תְבַשֵּׁל גְּדִי בַּחֲלֵב אִמּוֹ:
כב כג עַשֵּׂר תְּעַשֵּׂר אֵת כָּל־תְּבוּאַת זַרְעֶךָ הַיֹּצֵא הַשָּׂדֶה שָׁנָה שָׁנָה: וְאָכַלְתָּ לִפְנֵי ׀ יְהוָה חמישי
אֱלֹהֶיךָ בַּמָּקוֹם אֲשֶׁר־יִבְחַר לְשַׁכֵּן שְׁמוֹ שָׁם מַעְשַׂר דְּגָנְךָ תִּירֹשְׁךָ וְיִצְהָרֶךָ וּבְכֹרֹת
כד בְּקָרְךָ וְצֹאנֶךָ לְמַעַן תִּלְמַד לְיִרְאָה אֶת־יְהוָה אֱלֹהֶיךָ כָּל־הַיָּמִים: וְכִי־יִרְבֶּה מִמְּךָ
הַדֶּרֶךְ כִּי לֹא תוּכַל שְׂאֵתוֹ כִּי־יִרְחַק מִמְּךָ הַמָּקוֹם אֲשֶׁר יִבְחַר יְהוָה אֱלֹהֶיךָ
כה לָשׂוּם שְׁמוֹ שָׁם כִּי יְבָרֶכְךָ יְהוָה אֱלֹהֶיךָ: וְנָתַתָּה בַּכָּסֶף וְצַרְתָּ הַכֶּסֶף בְּיָדְךָ וְהָלַכְתָּ

רש״י

יח| **דוּכִיפַת.** הוּא תַּרְנְגוֹל הַבָּר, וּבְלַעַז הרופ״א וְכַרְבָּלְתּוֹ כְּפוּלָה:

יט| **שֶׁרֶץ הָעוֹף.** הֵם הַנְּמוּכִים הָרוֹחֲשִׁים עַל הָאָרֶץ, כְּגוֹן זְבוּבִים וּצְרָעִים וַחֲגָבִים טְמֵאִים, הֵם קְרוּיִים ׳שֶׁרֶץ׳:

כ| **כָּל עוֹף טָהוֹר תֹּאכֵלוּ.** וְלֹא אֶת הַטָּמֵא, בָּא לִתֵּן עֲשֵׂה עַל לֹא תַעֲשֶׂה; וְכֵן בַּבְּהֵמָה: ״אֹתָהּ תֹּאכֵלוּ״ (לעיל פסוק ו) וְלֹא בְּהֵמָה טְמֵאָה; לָאו הַבָּא מִכְּלַל עֲשֵׂה עֲשֵׂה, לַעֲבֹר עֲלֵיהֶם בַּעֲשֵׂה וְלֹא תַעֲשֶׂה:

כא| **לַגֵּר אֲשֶׁר בִּשְׁעָרֶיךָ.** גֵּר תּוֹשָׁב שֶׁקִּבֵּל עָלָיו שֶׁלֹּא לַעֲבֹד עֲבוֹדָה זָרָה וְאוֹכֵל נְבֵלוֹת: **כִּי עַם קָדוֹשׁ אַתָּה לַה׳.** קַדֵּשׁ אֶת עַצְמְךָ בַּמֻּתָּר לְךָ, דְּבָרִים הַמֻּתָּרִים וַאֲחֵרִים נוֹהֲגִים בָּהֶם אִסּוּר אַל תַּתִּירֵם בִּפְנֵיהֶם: **לֹא תְבַשֵּׁל גְּדִי.** שָׁלֹשׁ פְּעָמִים (שמות כג, יט; שם לד, כו), פְּרָט לְחַיָּה וּלְעוֹפוֹת וְלִבְהֵמָה טְמֵאָה:

כא-כב| **לֹא תְבַשֵּׁל גְּדִי. עַשֵּׂר תְּעַשֵּׂר.** מָה עִנְיַן זֶה אֵצֶל זֶה? אָמַר לָהֶם הַקָּדוֹשׁ בָּרוּךְ הוּא לְיִשְׂרָאֵל: אַל תִּגְרְמוּ לִי לְבַשֵּׁל גְּדָיִים שֶׁל תְּבוּאָה עַד שֶׁהֵן בִּמְעֵי אִמּוֹתֵיהֶן, שֶׁאִם אֵין אַתֶּם מְעַשְּׂרִים מַעַשְׂרוֹת כָּרָאוּי, כְּשֶׁהוּא סָמוּךְ לְהִתְבַּשֵּׁל אֲנִי מוֹצִיא רוּחַ קָדִים וְהִיא מְשַׁדַּפְתָּן, שֶׁנֶּאֱמַר: ״וּשְׁדֵפָה לִפְנֵי קָמָה״ (מלכים ב׳ יט, כו), וְכֵן לְעִנְיַן בִּכּוּרִים: **שָׁנָה שָׁנָה.** מִכָּאן שֶׁאֵין מְעַשְּׂרִין מִן הֶחָדָשׁ עַל הַיָּשָׁן:

כג| **וְאָכַלְתָּ וְגוֹ׳.** זֶה מַעֲשֵׂר שֵׁנִי, שֶׁכְּבָר לָמַדְנוּ לִתֵּן מַעֲשֵׂר אֶחָד לַלְוִיִּם, שֶׁנֶּאֱמַר: ״כִּי תִקְחוּ מֵאֵת בְּנֵי יִשְׂרָאֵל״ וְגוֹ׳ (במדבר יח, כו), וְנָתַן לָהֶם רְשׁוּת לְאָכְלוֹ בְּכָל מָקוֹם, שֶׁנֶּאֱמַר: ״וַאֲכַלְתֶּם אֹתוֹ בְּכָל מָקוֹם״ (שם פסוק לא), עַל כָּרְחֲךָ זֶה מַעֲשֵׂר אַחֵר הוּא:

כד| **כִּי יְבָרֶכְךָ.** שֶׁתְּהֵא הַתְּבוּאָה מְרֻבָּה לָשֵׂאת:

BACKGROUND

bird from the family Ardeidae, which resembles the stork (see Rashi). Several species of heron are found in Israel. While these species differ in size, herons all possess long legs, a long neck, and a long beak. Herons live in and around water.

The hoopoe [*dukhifat*]: According to the Talmud (*Ḥullin* 63a), this is referring to a bird whose comb appears bent [*hodo kafut*]. The Aramaic translations refer to it as *naggar tura*, which the Talmud (*Gittin* 68a) identifies as a wild rooster. According to the Septuagint, as well as the Latin translations, the *dukhifat* is identified as the hoopoe, *Upupa epops*, a bird with a distinctive colorful comb on its head consisting of feathers that appear either folded over or spread out. Its length is roughly 28 cm, with a wingspan of about 44 cm, and its weight ranges from 46–70 g.

The bat [*atalef*]: From the order Chiroptera, the bat is a flying mammal that lives in trees and caves. It is a nocturnal creature, which sustains itself on insects and fruit. There are dozens of species of bats in Israel. Although the bat is not classified nowadays as a bird from a zoological perspective, it is nevertheless a flying creature and is included in the list presented in this passage along with other flying creatures.

DISCUSSION

14:20| **All pure flying creatures you may eat:** Apparently, the Torah deems kosher any bird not included in the list of twenty-four species of forbidden birds. The Torah employs a concise manner of expression; therefore, it lists the kosher animals, because most animals are non-kosher, and it lists the non-kosher birds, because most birds are kosher (see *Ḥullin* 63b). In practice, however, Jewish tradition did not accept this leniency. Due to the concern for a lack of proficiency in identifying all of the non-kosher species listed, halakhic authorities banned many species of birds, and therefore Jews eat only those species of birds for which there is a clear tradition that they are kosher.

14:21| **You shall not cook a kid in its mother's milk:** The plain meaning of the verse is clear, but the verse is also understood as a directive that all kinds of meat must not be cooked or eaten with milk products, as one of the restrictions on eating relating to the sanctity of the people of Israel (see Ḥullin 113–114a; Rambam, *Sefer HaMitzvot*, negative precepts 183–184). Perhaps this is based on the fact that a person often cannot know for certain whether the milk that he buys came from the animal from which the meat that he bought originated (see Ibn Ezra, Exodus 23:19). In any

place that the Lord your God will choose.
26 **You shall spend the silver for whatever your heart desires, for cattle, or for sheep, or for wine, or for** other **intoxicating drink, or for whatever** food **your heart shall wish** to purchase, **and you shall eat** it **there**[D] **before the Lord your God,**[D] **and you shall rejoice, you and your household.**
27 **The Levite who is within your gates,** your cities, **you shall not forsake him, as he has no portion or inheritance with you,** and as a result he typically has no produce of his own.
28 Therefore, **at the end of** every **three years,** when you separate the various tithes, **you shall take out all the tithe of your crop in that year, and,** as opposed to the tithes of the two previous years, which were brought by the owner of the produce to Jerusalem, this year **you shall deposit it** for the needy **within your gates.**[22] The Sages also derived from here the obligation, once in three years, to remove from one's house all the tithes of the previous three years which for one reason or another did not reach their intended recipient. This commandment is discussed later at greater length (26:12).
29 **The Levite, because he has no portion or inheritance with you, and the stranger, and the orphan, and the widow, who are within your gates,** all of whom have no property or independent source of income, and are therefore in need of the tithe, they **shall come, and they shall eat and be satisfied, so that,** as a result, **the Lord your God will bless you in all your endeavors that you do.**

Remittal of Loans

DEUTERONOMY 15:1–11

The people of Israel were already commanded to have their agricultural lands lie fallow once every seven years, in the Sabbatical Year, ceasing all agricultural labor and declaring the produce ownerless. The Torah now adds that in that same year each person must relinquish his right to collect loans that he lent to others.

15 1 **At the end of seven years you shall perform a remittal.**
Sixth aliya 2 **This is the matter of the remittal: Every creditor that has extended credit to his neighbor shall remit,** abrogate his right to demand repayment. When the appointed time arrives, **he shall not demand it,** repayment of loans that he has given them, **from his neighbor or his brother, because remittal has been proclaimed for the Lord,**[23] or alternatively, because the fixed time for abrogation for the Lord already passed,[24] and all debts were abrogated.
3 **From the foreigner you may demand it;**[D] **but that which you will have with your brother, you shall remit your claim.**
4 The social background of this commandment is the presumed existence of impoverished people who are forced to borrow money from the wealthy, and yet are unable to repay their debts. In light of this presumptive situation, a note of hope and blessing is introduced here:[25] **It is only** our true hope **that there will be no indigent among you, as the Lord will bless you in the land that the Lord your God is giving you as an inheritance to take possession of it,**
5 **if you only heed the voice of the Lord your God, to take care to perform this entire commandment that I command you today,** both the commandments mentioned earlier and those that appear below.
6 **For the Lord your God has blessed you, as He spoke to you, and you will lend to many nations but you will not borrow,**

DISCUSSION

event, according to the *halakha*, even when it is known that the milk is not from the kid's mother, the milk and meat may not be eaten together. It has been suggested that this prohibition is related to the customary practice of idolaters to eat meat and milk together (see commentary on Shemot 23:19).

14:26| **And you shall eat there:** One-tenth of the annual harvest, or its monetary equivalent, is liable to be a rather significant amount. This sum cannot be used for anything but the purchase of food that must then be eaten in Jerusalem, which for most people is not where they live. Consequently, people would share their tithes with their friends in Jerusalem and with the city's poor, or they would bring needy people with them to Jerusalem. Additionally, there were financial repercussions for priests, pilgrims, and everyone in Jerusalem due to the fact that Jerusalem would be inundated with produce; the increased supply meant that Jerusalem's markets would be filled with inexpensive produce (see Rambam, *Guide of the Perplexed* 3:39, 46).

And you shall eat there before the Lord your God: According to what is stated in Numbers (18:21), a tenth of the crop is given each year to the Levites. This is what the Sages refer to as first tithe. In the first and second years of the Sabbatical cycle, an additional tenth of the produce, known as second tithe, is separated to be eaten in a state of ritual purity in Jerusalem by the owner of the produce and the members of his household. In the third year of the cycle, instead of second tithe, one separates one tenth of his produce to give to the poor; this is known as the poor man's tithe. The first tithe and the poor man's tithe are non-sacred; as such, anyone may eat them, anywhere, and even by one who is ritually impure.

After the third year this sequence is repeated: In the fourth and fifth years of the cycle one separates second tithe, and in the sixth year one separates the poor man's tithe. The seventh year in the cycle is the Sabbatical Year, during which no tithes whatsoever are separated, because all of the year's produce is ownerless.

The laws of tithes are in effect even today. However, since second tithe may be eaten only in a state of ritual purity and in proximity to the Temple, it may not be eaten today. Therefore, second tithe is redeemed by transferring its sanctity onto a coin. This may be done even with a coin that does not match the value of the produce. It is then prohibited to use the coin. The first tithe and the poor man's tithe may be eaten today. Therefore, when it is known with

כו אֶל־הַמָּקוֹם אֲשֶׁר יִבְחַר יְהוָה אֱלֹהֶיךָ בּוֹ: וְנָתַתָּה הַכֶּסֶף בְּכֹל אֲשֶׁר־תְּאַוֶּה
נַפְשְׁךָ בַּבָּקָר וּבַצֹּאן וּבַיַּיִן וּבַשֵּׁכָר וּבְכֹל אֲשֶׁר תִּשְׁאָלְךָ נַפְשֶׁךָ וְאָכַלְתָּ שָּׁם לִפְנֵי
כז יְהוָה אֱלֹהֶיךָ וְשָׂמַחְתָּ אַתָּה וּבֵיתֶךָ: וְהַלֵּוִי אֲשֶׁר־בִּשְׁעָרֶיךָ לֹא תַעַזְבֶנּוּ כִּי אֵין
כח לוֹ חֵלֶק וְנַחֲלָה עִמָּךְ: מִקְצֵה שָׁלֹשׁ שָׁנִים תּוֹצִיא אֶת־כָּל־מַעְשַׂר
כט תְּבוּאָתְךָ בַּשָּׁנָה הַהִוא וְהִנַּחְתָּ בִּשְׁעָרֶיךָ: וּבָא הַלֵּוִי כִּי אֵין־לוֹ חֵלֶק וְנַחֲלָה
עִמָּךְ וְהַגֵּר וְהַיָּתוֹם וְהָאַלְמָנָה אֲשֶׁר בִּשְׁעָרֶיךָ וְאָכְלוּ וְשָׂבֵעוּ לְמַעַן יְבָרֶכְךָ יְהוָה
א אֱלֹהֶיךָ בְּכָל־מַעֲשֵׂה יָדְךָ אֲשֶׁר תַּעֲשֶׂה: מִקֵּץ שֶׁבַע־שָׁנִים תַּעֲשֶׂה ששי
ב שְׁמִטָּה: וְזֶה דְּבַר הַשְּׁמִטָּה שָׁמוֹט כָּל־בַּעַל מַשֵּׁה יָדוֹ אֲשֶׁר יַשֶּׁה בְּרֵעֵהוּ לֹא־
ג יִגֹּשׂ אֶת־רֵעֵהוּ וְאֶת־אָחִיו כִּי־קָרָא שְׁמִטָּה לַיהוָה: אֶת־הַנָּכְרִי תִּגֹּשׂ וַאֲשֶׁר יִהְיֶה
ד לְךָ אֶת־אָחִיךָ תַּשְׁמֵט יָדֶךָ: אֶפֶס כִּי לֹא יִהְיֶה־בְּךָ אֶבְיוֹן כִּי־בָרֵךְ יְבָרֶכְךָ יְהוָה
ה בָּאָרֶץ אֲשֶׁר יְהוָה אֱלֹהֶיךָ נֹתֵן־לְךָ נַחֲלָה לְרִשְׁתָּהּ: רַק אִם־שָׁמוֹעַ תִּשְׁמַע בְּקוֹל
יְהוָה אֱלֹהֶיךָ לִשְׁמֹר לַעֲשׂוֹת אֶת־כָּל־הַמִּצְוָה הַזֹּאת אֲשֶׁר אָנֹכִי מְצַוְּךָ הַיּוֹם:
ו כִּי־יְהוָה אֱלֹהֶיךָ בֵּרַכְךָ כַּאֲשֶׁר דִּבֶּר־לָךְ וְהַעֲבַטְתָּ גּוֹיִם רַבִּים וְאַתָּה לֹא תַעֲבֹט

רש"י

כו | בְּכֹל אֲשֶׁר תְּאַוֶּה נַפְשְׁךָ. כְּלָל: בַּבָּקָר וּבַצֹּאן וּבַיַּיִן וּבַשֵּׁכָר. פְּרָט: וּבְכֹל אֲשֶׁר תִּשְׁאָלְךָ נַפְשֶׁךָ. חָזַר וְכָלַל, מַה הַפְּרָט מְפֹרָשׁ וְלַד וְלָדוֹת הָאָרֶץ וְרָאוּי לְמַאֲכַל אָדָם וְכוּ':

כז | וְהַלֵּוִי... לֹא תַעַזְבֶנּוּ. מִלִּתֵּן לוֹ מַעֲשֵׂר רִאשׁוֹן: כִּי אֵין לוֹ חֵלֶק וְנַחֲלָה עִמָּךְ. יָצְאוּ לֶקֶט שִׁכְחָה וּפֵאָה וְהֶפְקֵר, שֶׁאַף הוּא יֵשׁ לוֹ חֵלֶק עִמְּךָ בָּהֶן כָּמוֹךָ, וְאֵינָן חַיָּבִין בְּמַעֲשֵׂר:

כח | מִקְצֵה שָׁלֹשׁ שָׁנִים. בָּא וְלִמֵּד שֶׁאִם הִשְׁהָה מַעַשְׂרוֹתָיו שֶׁל שָׁנָה רִאשׁוֹנָה וּשְׁנִיָּה לַשְּׁמִטָּה, שֶׁיְּבַעֲרֵם מִן הַבַּיִת בַּשְּׁלִישִׁית:

כט | וּבָא הַלֵּוִי. וְיִטֹּל מַעֲשֵׂר רִאשׁוֹן: וְהַגֵּר וְהַיָּתוֹם. וְיִטְּלוּ מַעֲשֵׂר שֵׁנִי, שֶׁהוּא שֶׁל עָנִי שֶׁל שָׁנָה זוֹ, וְלֹא תֹּאכְלֶנּוּ אַתָּה בִּירוּשָׁלַיִם כְּדֶרֶךְ שֶׁנִּזְקַקְתָּ לֶאֱכֹל מַעֲשֵׂר שֵׁנִי שֶׁל שְׁתֵּי שָׁנִים: וְאָכְלוּ וְשָׂבֵעוּ. תֵּן לָהֶם כְּדֵי שָׂבְעָן, מִכָּאן אָמְרוּ: "אֵין פּוֹחֲתִין לֶעָנִי בַּגֹּרֶן" וְכוּ' (ספרי קי). וְאַתָּה הוֹלֵךְ לִירוּשָׁלַיִם בְּמַעֲשַׂר שֶׁל שָׁנָה רִאשׁוֹנָה וּשְׁנִיָּה שֶׁהִשְׁהֵיתָ, וּמִתְוַדֶּה: "בִּעַרְתִּי הַקֹּדֶשׁ מִן הַבַּיִת" (להלן כו, יג) כְּמוֹ שֶׁמְּפֹרָשׁ 'כִּי תְכַלֶּה לַעְשֵׂר' (שם פסוק יב):

פרק טו

א | מִקֵּץ שֶׁבַע שָׁנִים. יָכוֹל שֶׁבַע שָׁנִים לְכָל מִלְוָה וּמִלְוָה? תַּלְמוּד לוֹמַר: "קָרְבָה שְׁנַת הַשֶּׁבַע" (להלן פסוק ט), וְאִם אַתָּה אוֹמֵר שֶׁבַע שָׁנִים לְכָל מִלְוָה וּמִלְוָה, לְהַלְוָאַת כָּל אֶחָד וְאֶחָד, הֵיאַךְ הִיא קְרֵבָה? הָא לָמַדְתָּ שֶׁבַע שָׁנִים לְמִנְיַן הַשְּׁמִטִּים:

ב | שָׁמוֹט כָּל בַּעַל מַשֵּׁה יָדוֹ. שָׁמוֹט אֶת יָדוֹ שֶׁל כָּל בַּעַל מַשֶּׁה:

ד | אֶפֶס כִּי לֹא יִהְיֶה בְּךָ אֶבְיוֹן. וּלְהַלָּן הוּא אוֹמֵר: "כִּי לֹא יֶחְדַּל אֶבְיוֹן" (להלן פסוק יא)! אֶלָּא בִּזְמַן שֶׁאַתֶּם עוֹשִׂים רְצוֹנוֹ שֶׁל מָקוֹם, אֶבְיוֹנִים בַּאֲחֵרִים וְלֹא בָּכֶם, וּכְשֶׁאֵין אַתֶּם עוֹשִׂים רְצוֹנוֹ שֶׁל מָקוֹם אֶבְיוֹנִים בָּכֶם: אֶבְיוֹן. דַּל מֵעָנִי, וּלְשׁוֹן 'אֶבְיוֹן' שֶׁהוּא תָּאֵב לְכָל דָּבָר:

ה | רַק אִם שָׁמוֹעַ תִּשְׁמַע. אָז לֹא יִהְיֶה בְּךָ אֶבְיוֹן: שָׁמוֹעַ תִּשְׁמַע. שָׁמַע קִמְעָא, מַשְׁמִיעִין אוֹתוֹ הַרְבֵּה:

ו | כַּאֲשֶׁר דִּבֶּר לָךְ. וְהֵיכָן דִּבֵּר? "בָּרוּךְ אַתָּה בָּעִיר" (להלן כח, ג): וְהַעֲבַטְתָּ גּוֹיִם. יָכוֹל שֶׁתְּהֵא לֹוֶה מִזֶּה וּמַלְוֶה

DISCUSSION

certainty that particular produce is subject to first tithe or the poor man's tithe, the produce itself is given to a Levite or a poor person, or else the monetary value of the produce is given to them in accordance with an agreement made with them in advance.

15:3 | **From the foreigner you may demand it:** The seventh year does not eliminate all private property, nor does it cancel all monetary obligations. The laws of abrogation apply only between Jews, but not to the dealings between them and members of other nations. Accordingly, it is permitted to demand payment of a debt from a gentile.

and you will rule many nations but they will not rule you. This being the case, there will be no need for the abrogation of debts in the seventh year.

7 This desired situation is not realized in actuality. Therefore, **if there is among you an indigent** person **from your brethren, within your gates,** in one of the places where you live, **in your land that the Lord your God is giving you, you shall not harden your heart** and ignore his request, **and you shall not close your hand from your indigent brother** by denying him even a small gift.[26]

8 **Rather, you shall open your hand to him, and you shall lend him** money with collateral, **enough for his need,** to provide all that will be lacking for him.

9 **Beware, lest there be a wicked thought in your heart, saying: The seventh year, the year of remittal, is** quickly approaching, and **your eye will be miserly toward your indigent brother, and you will not give him** a significant loan, which is liable to cause you to incur a heavy loss. **And he,** your needy brother, **will cry to the Lord against you, and it will be a sin for you.** Although the Torah does not require a person to lend money to the poor when that loan will definitely cause the lender a loss, beyond the general obligation to do good and act in an equitable manner; nevertheless, if a person refuses to lend money to the poor before the Sabbatical Year because of a Torah commandment designed to help the poor, he is a sinner.

10 **You shall give him** the loan, even though you know that it might not be repaid after the seventh year, **and your heart shall not be miserly when you give to him.** Giving charity and providing assistance to others are not merely external actions. The donor's state of mind is also significant, and one should not give unwillingly or with a sense of bitterness.[27] **Because due to this matter,** your generous giving in a spirit of amity, **the Lord your God will bless you in all your actions, and in all your endeavors.**

11 **For the indigent will never cease from the land;**[D] in practice there will always be people in need, notwithstanding the wish expressed above that this not be the case in an ideal world. **Therefore, I command you, saying: You shall open your hand to your brother, to your poor, and to your indigent, in your land.**

The Release of Slaves
DEUTERONOMY 15:12–18

Although the laws of a Hebrew slave and a Hebrew maidservant are not land-based commandments, as they apply even outside the land provided that most of the Jewish people dwell in Israel, these laws appear immediately after the laws of the abrogation of debts due to several similarities between them: Debts are abrogated in the collective seventh year, and the Hebrew slave is released in the seventh year of his enslavement. In both cases, a time comes when a person must relinquish something that until then was considered his. The Torah demands generosity both from one who lends money adjacent to the seventh year and from one who liberates his slave or maidservant; and it promises that in both cases the generous person will be blessed. The upcoming section also includes a discussion regarding a Hebrew slave who does not want to go free.

12 **If your brother, a Hebrew man, or a Hebrew woman,** who fell into debt for one reason or another, **is sold to you, he shall serve you six years,** as this fixed period of slavery is his last resort for repayment;[28] **and in the seventh year you shall set him free from you.**

13 **When you set him free from you, you shall not release him empty-handed.**

14 **You shall grant him from your flock, and from your threshing floor, and from your winepress;** from **that** with which the Lord your God has blessed you, you shall give him a substantial gift when he is released.

15 By right this should not be necessary, as he already received compensation for his service; nevertheless, you are demanded to grant your fellow Jew a gift at this time, as you yourself come from slaves. **You shall remember that you were a slave in the land of Egypt, and the Lord your God redeemed you; therefore I command you this matter today.**

Threshing floor

Winepress

ז וּמָשַׁלְתָּ בְּגוֹיִם רַבִּים וּבְךָ לֹא יִמְשֹׁלוּ: כִּי־יִהְיֶה בְךָ אֶבְיוֹן מֵאַחַד יג
אַחֶיךָ בְּאַחַד שְׁעָרֶיךָ בְּאַרְצְךָ אֲשֶׁר־יְהוָה אֱלֹהֶיךָ נֹתֵן לָךְ לֹא תְאַמֵּץ אֶת־
ח לְבָבְךָ וְלֹא תִקְפֹּץ אֶת־יָדְךָ מֵאָחִיךָ הָאֶבְיוֹן: כִּי־פָתֹחַ תִּפְתַּח אֶת־יָדְךָ לוֹ
ט וְהַעֲבֵט תַּעֲבִיטֶנּוּ דֵּי מַחְסֹרוֹ אֲשֶׁר יֶחְסַר לוֹ: הִשָּׁמֶר לְךָ פֶּן־יִהְיֶה דָבָר עִם־
לְבָבְךָ בְלִיַּעַל לֵאמֹר קָרְבָה שְׁנַת־הַשֶּׁבַע שְׁנַת הַשְּׁמִטָּה וְרָעָה עֵינְךָ בְּאָחִיךָ
י הָאֶבְיוֹן וְלֹא תִתֵּן לוֹ וְקָרָא עָלֶיךָ אֶל־יְהוָה וְהָיָה בְךָ חֵטְא: נָתוֹן תִּתֵּן לוֹ וְלֹא־
יֵרַע לְבָבְךָ בְּתִתְּךָ לוֹ כִּי בִּגְלַל ׀ הַדָּבָר הַזֶּה יְבָרֶכְךָ יְהוָה אֱלֹהֶיךָ בְּכָל־מַעֲשֶׂךָ
יא וּבְכֹל מִשְׁלַח יָדֶךָ: כִּי לֹא־יֶחְדַּל אֶבְיוֹן מִקֶּרֶב הָאָרֶץ עַל־כֵּן אָנֹכִי מְצַוְּךָ לֵאמֹר
יב פָּתֹחַ תִּפְתַּח אֶת־יָדְךָ לְאָחִיךָ לַעֲנִיֶּךָ וּלְאֶבְיֹנְךָ בְּאַרְצֶךָ: כִּי־יִמָּכֵר
לְךָ אָחִיךָ הָעִבְרִי אוֹ הָעִבְרִיָּה וַעֲבָדְךָ שֵׁשׁ שָׁנִים וּבַשָּׁנָה הַשְּׁבִיעִת תְּשַׁלְּחֶנּוּ
יג יד חָפְשִׁי מֵעִמָּךְ: וְכִי־תְשַׁלְּחֶנּוּ חָפְשִׁי מֵעִמָּךְ לֹא תְשַׁלְּחֶנּוּ רֵיקָם: הַעֲנֵיק תַּעֲנִיק
טו לוֹ מִצֹּאנְךָ וּמִגָּרְנְךָ וּמִיִּקְבֶךָ אֲשֶׁר בֵּרַכְךָ יְהוָה אֱלֹהֶיךָ תִּתֶּן־לוֹ: וְזָכַרְתָּ כִּי עֶבֶד
הָיִיתָ בְּאֶרֶץ מִצְרַיִם וַיִּפְדְּךָ יְהוָה אֱלֹהֶיךָ עַל־כֵּן אָנֹכִי מְצַוְּךָ אֶת־הַדָּבָר הַזֶּה הַיּוֹם:

רש"י

לזה? תלמוד לומר: "ואתה לא תעבט". ומשלת בגוים רבים. יכול גוים אחרים מושלים עליך? תלמוד לומר: "ובך לא ימשלו":

ז| כי יהיה בך אביון. התאב תאב קודם: מאחד אחיך. אחיך מאביך קודם לאחיך מאמך: שעריך. עניי עירך קודמים: לא תאמץ. יש לך אדם שמצטער אם יתן אם לא יתן, לכך נאמר: "לא תאמץ". יש לך אדם שפושט את ידו וקופצה, לכך נאמר: "ולא תקפץ": מאחיך האביון. אם לא תתן לו, סופך להיות אחיו של אביון:

ח| פתח תפתח. אפילו כמה פעמים: כי פתח תפתח. הרי 'כי' משמש בלשון 'אלא': והעבט תעביטנו. אם לא רצה במתנה, תן לו בהלואה: די מחסרו. ואי אתה מצוה לעשרו: אשר יחסר לו. אפילו סוס לרכב עליו ועבד לרוץ לפניו: לו. זו אשה, וכן הוא אומר: "אעשה לו עזר כנגדו" (בראשית ב, יח):

ט| וקרא עליך. יכול מצוה? תלמוד לומר: "ולא יקרא" (להלן כד, טו): והיה בך חטא. מכל מקום, אפילו לא יקרא. אם כן למה נאמר: "וקרא עליך"? ממהר אני לפרע על ידי הקורא יותר ממי שאינו קורא:

י| נתון תתן לו. אפילו מאה פעמים: לו. בינו ובינך: כי בגלל הדבר. אפילו אמרת לתן, אתה נוטל שכר האמירה עם שכר המעשה:

יא| על כן. מפני כן: לאמר. עצה לטובתך אני משיאך: לאחיך לעניך. לאי זה אח? לעני: לעניך. ביו"ד אחד – לשון עני אחד הוא, אבל 'ענייך' בשני יודי"ן – שני עניים:

יב| כי ימכר לך. על ידי אחרים, במכרוהו בית דין בגנבתו הכתוב מדבר. והרי כבר נאמר: "כי תקנה עבד עברי" (שמות כא, ב), ובמכרוהו בית דין הכתוב מדבר? אלא מפני שני דברים שנתחדשו כאן: אחת, שכתוב "או העבריה" – אף היא תצא בשש, ולא שמכרוה בית דין, שאין האשה נמכרת בגנבתה, שנאמר "בגנבתו" (שם כב, ב) ולא 'בגנבתה', אלא בקטנה שמכרה אביה, ולמד כאן שאם יצאו שש שנים קדם שתביא סימנין – תצא. ועוד חדש כאן: "הענק תעניק":

יד| הענק תעניק. לשון עדי, בגבה ובמראית העין, דבר שיהא נכר שהטיבות לו. ויש מפרשים לשון הטענה על צוארו: מצאנך ומגרנך ומיקבך. יכול אין לי אלא אלו בלבד? תלמוד לומר: "אשר ברכך", מכל מה שברכך בוראך. ולמה נאמרו אלו? מה אלו מיחדים שהם בכלל ברכה, אף כל שהוא בכלל ברכה, יצאו פרדות. ולמדו רבותינו במסכת קדושין (דף יז ע"א) בגזרה שוה, כמה נותן לו מכל מין ומין:

טו| וזכרת כי עבד היית. והענקתי ושניתי לך מביזת מצרים וביזת הים, אף אתה הענק ושנה לו:

DISCUSSION

15:11| **For the indigent will never cease from the land:** These words may also contain a veiled threat: I command you to give to others because, although you are not poor, you are liable to become poor. From here the command ensues: Open your hand and give, so that you will not become one of the needy (see *Sifrei*; *Tanḥuma Mishpatim* 8).

16 Ordinarily a Hebrew slave goes free after six years of servitude, but there is an alternative: **It shall be that if he says to you: I will not leave you** in the seventh year, **because he loves you and** the members of **your household, because it is good for him with you;** perhaps he is afraid to assume the responsibilities and obligations incumbent upon a free man.

17 **You shall take the awl,** a cobbler's piercing tool, consisting of a pointed metal blade inserted into a wood or bone handle; **and you shall place it through his ear and the door.** You shall set the slave's ear against the door, and pierce it with the awl, creating a hole through to the door; **and** by doing so **he shall be an** **eternal slave**[D] **to you,** and not go free in the seventh year; **and so to your maidservant you shall do likewise.**[D]

18 **It shall not be difficult in your eyes in your setting him free from you,** unlike non-Hebrew slaves, who remain in your possession forever; **as twice the wage of a hired man he has served you six years.** The standard contract of a hired hand extended for three years,[29] and thus he will have worked for you twice as long as a hired hand, and apparently at a lower cost. In any case, he is your brother, a member of the people of Israel, and you must consider his needs and provide him with a comfortable basis for starting out on his new path, **and the Lord your God will bless you in all that you will do.**

A Firstborn Animal
DEUTERONOMY 15:19–23

The Torah now commands to sanctify to God the firstborns of one's herd and flock. As mentioned earlier, these animals were given to a priest, who would bring them as an offering and eat most of its meat in a family celebration. The passage here adds several details to that which was stated previously.

19 **Any firstborn that shall be born of your cattle and of your** *Seventh* **flocks you shall sanctify the males to the Lord your God;** *aliya* **you shall not work with the firstborn of your ox, and you shall not shear** the wool of **the firstborn of your flock.**[D]

20 **You shall eat it before the Lord your God year by year,** each year, **in the place that the Lord shall choose, you and your household.**

21 **And if there is a blemish on it,** the firstborn, for example: **Lameness, or blindness,** or **any** other **severe blemish, you shall not slaughter it to the Lord your God.**

22 **You shall eat it,** the meat of a blemished firstborn, anywhere **within your gates,** wherever you live; **the impure and the pure alike, like the gazelle** is eaten, **and like the deer** is eaten; these two animals are unfit to be brought as offerings; therefore, they do not have any special laws governing their sanctity.

Shearing a sheep

23 **Only its blood you shall not eat; you shall pour it on the ground like water.**

The Three Pilgrimage Festivals
DEUTERONOMY 16:1–17

The commandments that follow relate to the yearly cycle. Not all of them apply exclusively in the Land of Israel, but this passage emphasizes the unique connection between the festivals and the place that God will choose.

16 1 **Observe the month of ripening,**[D] **and you shall perform the paschal offering to the Lord your God;** make sure that the first month of the year, which is when the paschal lamb is sacrificed, always coincides with the time of year when the new grain ripens; **for in the month of ripening, the Lord your God took you out of Egypt at night.**

2 **You shall slaughter** in that month **the paschal offering to the Lord your God, sheep** for the paschal offering itself, **and cattle**[D] for the festive meal and other offerings that accompany the

---

DISCUSSION

15:17| An eternal slave: Rabbinic tradition interprets this phrase in a more restrictive fashion: The Hebrew slave does not serve forever; rather, he serves until the Jubilee Year (see *Kiddushin* 21b; Rashi). In general, the term "eternal" is used in the Bible in the sense of a very long time rather than actual eternity.

And so to your maidservant you shall do likewise: According to rabbinic tradition, this verse likens the law of a Hebrew maidservant to the law of a Hebrew slave so that the maidservant too is set free after six years and is entitled to gifts upon her release (*Kiddushin* 17b). However, unlike a Hebrew slave, a Hebrew maidservant cannot have her ear pierced and thereby extend the period of her slavery as she is subject to special laws. In effect, she is acquired by her master only until she reaches puberty and majority. Her master is granted the right to designate her as a bride for himself or for his son, even though the money that he paid to purchase her as a

↤

טז וְהָיָה כִּי־יֹאמַר אֵלֶיךָ לֹא אֵצֵא מֵעִמָּךְ כִּי אֲהֵבְךָ וְאֶת־בֵּיתֶךָ כִּי־טוֹב לוֹ עִמָּךְ:
יז וְלָקַחְתָּ אֶת־הַמַּרְצֵעַ וְנָתַתָּה בְאָזְנוֹ וּבַדֶּלֶת וְהָיָה לְךָ עֶבֶד עוֹלָם וְאַף לַאֲמָתְךָ
יח תַּעֲשֶׂה־כֵּן: לֹא־יִקְשֶׁה בְעֵינֶךָ בְּשַׁלֵּחֲךָ אֹתוֹ חָפְשִׁי מֵעִמָּךְ כִּי מִשְׁנֶה שְׂכַר שָׂכִיר
עֲבָדְךָ שֵׁשׁ שָׁנִים וּבֵרַכְךָ יְהוָה אֱלֹהֶיךָ בְּכֹל אֲשֶׁר תַּעֲשֶׂה:
יט כָּל־הַבְּכוֹר אֲשֶׁר יִוָּלֵד בִּבְקָרְךָ וּבְצֹאנְךָ הַזָּכָר תַּקְדִּישׁ לַיהוָה אֱלֹהֶיךָ לֹא תַעֲבֹד שביעי
כ בִּבְכֹר שׁוֹרֶךָ וְלֹא תָגֹז בְּכוֹר צֹאנֶךָ: לִפְנֵי יְהוָה אֱלֹהֶיךָ תֹאכְלֶנּוּ שָׁנָה בְשָׁנָה
כא בַּמָּקוֹם אֲשֶׁר־יִבְחַר יְהוָה אַתָּה וּבֵיתֶךָ: וְכִי־יִהְיֶה בוֹ מוּם פִּסֵּחַ אוֹ עִוֵּר כֹּל מוּם
כב רָע לֹא תִזְבָּחֶנּוּ לַיהוָה אֱלֹהֶיךָ: בִּשְׁעָרֶיךָ תֹּאכְלֶנּוּ הַטָּמֵא וְהַטָּהוֹר יַחְדָּו כַּצְּבִי
כג וְכָאַיָּל: רַק אֶת־דָּמוֹ לֹא תֹאכֵל עַל־הָאָרֶץ תִּשְׁפְּכֶנּוּ כַּמָּיִם:
א שָׁמוֹר אֶת־חֹדֶשׁ הָאָבִיב וְעָשִׂיתָ פֶּסַח לַיהוָה אֱלֹהֶיךָ כִּי בְּחֹדֶשׁ הָאָבִיב הוֹצִיאֲךָ
ב יְהוָה אֱלֹהֶיךָ מִמִּצְרַיִם לָיְלָה: וְזָבַחְתָּ פֶּסַח לַיהוָה אֱלֹהֶיךָ צֹאן וּבָקָר בַּמָּקוֹם

רש"י

יז| **עבד עולם.** יכול כמשמעו? תלמוד לומר: "ושבתם איש אל אחזתו ואיש אל משפחתו תשבו" (ויקרא כה, י), הא למדת שאין זה אלא עולמו של יובל: **ואף לאמתך תעשה כן.** הענק לה. יכול אף לרציעה השוה הכתוב אותה? תלמוד לומר: "ואם אמר יאמר העבד" (שמות כא, ה), עבד נרצע ואין אמה נרצעת:

יח| **כי משנה שכר שכיר.** מכאן אמרו: עבד עברי עובד בין ביום ובין בלילה, וזהו כפלים שבעבודת שכירי יום. ומהו עבודתו בלילה? רבו מוסר לו שפחה כנענית והולדות לאדון:

יט| **כל הבכור... תקדיש.** ובמקום אחר הוא אומר: "לא יקדיש איש אתו" (ויקרא כז, כו)! אינו מקדישו לקרבן אחר, וכאן למד שמצוה לומר: 'הרי אתה קדוש לבכורה'. דבר אחר, אי אפשר לומר "תקדיש" שכבר נאמר "לא יקדיש", ואי אפשר לומר "לא יקדיש" שהרי כבר נאמר "תקדיש", הא כיצד? מקדישו אתה הקדש עלוי ונותן להקדש כפי טובת הנאה שבו: **לא תעבד בבכר שורך ולא תגז וגו'.** אף החלוף למדו רבותינו שאסור, אלא שדבר הכתוב בהוה:

כ| **לפני ה' אלהיך תאכלנו.** לכהן הוא אומר, שכבר מצינו שהוא ממתנות כהנה, אחד תם ואחד בעל מום, שנאמר: "ובשרם יהיה לך" וגו' (במדבר יח, יח): **שנה בשנה.** מכאן שאין מאחרין אותו יותר על שנתו. יכול יהא פסול משעברה שנתו? כבר הקיש למעשר, שנאמר: "ואכלת לפני ה' אלהיך... מעשר דגנך תירשך ויצהרך ובכרת בקרך וצאנך" (לעיל יד, כג), מה מעשר שני אינו נפסל משנה לחברתה, אף בכור אינו נפסל, אלא שמצוה בתוך שנתו: **שנה בשנה.** אם שחטו בסוף שנתו, אוכלו אותו היום ויום אחד משנה אחרת, למד שנאכל לשני ימים ולילה אחד:

כא| **מום.** כלל: **פסח או עור.** פרט: **כל מום רע.** חזר וכלל, מה הפרט מפרש מום הגלוי ואינו חוזר, אף כל מום שבגלוי ואינו חוזר:

כג| **רק את דמו לא תאכל.** שלא תאמר: הואיל וכלו היתר הבא מכלל אסור הוא, שהרי קדוש ונשחט בחוץ בלא פדיון ונאכל, יכול יהא אף הדם מתר? תלמוד לומר: "רק את דמו לא תאכל":

פרק טז

א| **שמור את חדש האביב.** מקדם בואו שמר שיהא ראוי לאביב, להקריב בו את מנחת העמר, ואם לאו – עבר את השנה: **ממצרים לילה.** והלא ביום יצאו, שנאמר: "ממחרת הפסח יצאו בני ישראל" וגו' (במדבר לג, ג)? אלא לפי שבלילה נתן להם פרעה רשות לצאת, שנאמר: "ויקרא למשה ולאהרן לילה" וגו' (שמות יב, לא):

ב| **וזבחת פסח לה' אלהיך צאן.** שנאמר: "מן הכבשים

DISCUSSION

maidservant was not actually given for the purpose of betrothal (see Exodus 21:7–11).

15:19| **You shall not work with the firstborn of your ox, and you shall not shear the firstborn of your flock:** The verse expresses the prohibition in common cases, but it would certainly apply equally to less common cases of working a firstborn sheep or goat and shearing a firstborn ox (see Rashi; *Ḥullin* 137a).

16:1| **Observe the month of ripening:** Since the months of the Jewish calendar are determined by the moon, and the lunar year is eleven days shorter than the solar year, each holiday could theoretically occur in any season, as is the case with the Muslim calendar. To avoid that situation, the Torah commands that care must be taken that Nisan, the month of redemption, will coincide with the month of ripening, the beginning of spring, as it did at the time of the actual redemption. To this end, the mechanism of intercalation was introduced into the Jewish calendar (*Rosh HaShana* 7a; *Sanhedrin* 11b).

16:2| **And cattle:** Pilgrims coming to sacrifice the paschal lamb would remain in Jerusalem for the week and celebrate the festival. Consequently, they would bring additional animals with them to present as offerings, and

paschal lamb,[30] **in the place that the Lord shall choose to rest His name there.**

3 **You shall not eat with it,** the paschal lamb, **leavened bread; seven days you shall eat with it unleavened bread,**[D] bread whose dough was not allowed to rise, which is **the bread of affliction,** the bread of the poor, **as in haste you came out from the land of Egypt;** eating unleavened bread serves as a reminder both of the haste imposed upon Israel in Egypt, not allowing them to tarry there until their dough could rise, and of the affliction and exile that preceded the exodus,[31] **so that you will remember the day of your exodus from the land of Egypt all the days of your life.**

4 **No leaven [*se'or*]**[B] **shall be seen by you within all your borders seven days. And** another prohibition: **The meat** of the paschal lamb **that you slaughter in the evening on the first day,** preceding the seven days of the festival, **shall not remain overnight until morning.** You must eat all of it during the night. Elsewhere, it is stated that the meat that remains overnight must be burned.[32]

Dough that has has risen due to leavening

Leaven

5 The laws about the paschal lamb that have been stated until now have been taught previously; the upcoming law is introduced here for the first time. **You may not slaughter the paschal lamb within any of your gates that the Lord your God is giving you.** Although the paschal lamb is not eaten by the priests, but by each Jew together with his family, it may not be offered just anywhere;

6 **except at the place that the Lord your God shall choose to rest His name,** in the Temple, **there you shall slaughter the paschal lamb in the evening, as the sun sets,** on the fourteenth of Nisan, **the appointed time of your exodus from Egypt;** in actuality, the exodus took place only on the morning of the fifteenth, but the children of Israel were ready to leave the previous evening.

7 **You shall** not prepare the meat of the paschal lamb in water, but rather **cook**[D] it over a fire **and eat** it **in the place that the Lord your God shall choose, and you shall turn in the morning,** and not before, **and go** home **to your tents.** The Sages understood this as a general law applying to anyone who offers a sacrifice in the Temple, that he must not return to his city immediately after offering his sacrifice, but rather he must spend the night in Jerusalem and only the next morning go on his way.[33]

8 **Six days you shall eat unleavened bread; and on the seventh day,** on which you shall continue to eat unleavened bread, there **shall** also **be a** day of **solemn assembly to the Lord your God,** on which **you shall perform no labor.** Even if you do not remain in the Temple all seven days, you must still celebrate the seventh day as a festival day.[34]

9 **You shall count seven weeks for you; from the start of the**

DISCUSSION

to eat over the course of the week. People of means would bring cattle for their offerings. Support for this interpretation may be adduced from the description of the Passover celebration during the reigns of the last kings of Judah (see II Chronicles 35:7–13; Ramban).

16:3 | **Seven days you shall eat with it unleavened bread:** These are two separate festivals (see Numbers 28:16–17). Passover, when the paschal lamb is offered, is on the fourteenth of Nisan in the afternoon, on the eve of the exodus from Egypt. The Festival of Unleavened Bread begins on the fifteenth of Nisan, and is observed for seven days. Only in rabbinic Hebrew is the Festival of Unleavened Bread referred to as Passover. These two festivals are observed in succession, and they are related, as is evident here; there is no separation between the prohibition against eating leavened bread with the paschal lamb and the obligation to eat unleavened bread during the seven days of the ensuing festival.

16:7 | **You shall cook [*uvishalta*]:** The root *bet-shin-lamed* is often understood as connoting cooking in liquid. However, in the book of Exodus (12:9) it is stated explicitly that the paschal lamb must be roasted directly over a fire, not cooked in liquid. From the fact that the verse here and in II Chronicles (35:13) employ the term *bishul* with regard to the paschal lamb, it appears that the broader meaning of this term in the Bible is preparing food through heat, and not necessarily in water or some other liquid (see *Nedarim* 49a). Perhaps the Torah uses the more general term *bishul* here in order to include the other offerings that accompany the paschal lamb and that may be cooked in liquid.

ג אֲשֶׁר יִבְחַר יְהוָה לְשַׁכֵּן שְׁמוֹ שָׁם: לֹא־תֹאכַל עָלָיו חָמֵץ שִׁבְעַת יָמִים תֹּאכַל־
עָלָיו מַצּוֹת לֶחֶם עֹנִי כִּי בְחִפָּזוֹן יָצָאתָ מֵאֶרֶץ מִצְרַיִם לְמַעַן תִּזְכֹּר אֶת־יוֹם צֵאתְךָ
ד מֵאֶרֶץ מִצְרַיִם כֹּל יְמֵי חַיֶּיךָ: וְלֹא־יֵרָאֶה לְךָ שְׂאֹר בְּכָל־גְּבֻלְךָ שִׁבְעַת יָמִים
ה וְלֹא־יָלִין מִן־הַבָּשָׂר אֲשֶׁר תִּזְבַּח בָּעֶרֶב בַּיּוֹם הָרִאשׁוֹן לַבֹּקֶר: לֹא תוּכַל לִזְבֹּחַ
ו אֶת־הַפָּסַח בְּאַחַד שְׁעָרֶיךָ אֲשֶׁר־יְהוָה אֱלֹהֶיךָ נֹתֵן לָךְ: כִּי אִם־אֶל־הַמָּקוֹם
אֲשֶׁר־יִבְחַר יְהוָה אֱלֹהֶיךָ לְשַׁכֵּן שְׁמוֹ שָׁם תִּזְבַּח אֶת־הַפֶּסַח בָּעָרֶב כְּבוֹא הַשֶּׁמֶשׁ
ז מוֹעֵד צֵאתְךָ מִמִּצְרָיִם: וּבִשַּׁלְתָּ וְאָכַלְתָּ בַּמָּקוֹם אֲשֶׁר יִבְחַר יְהוָה אֱלֹהֶיךָ בּוֹ
ח וּפָנִיתָ בַבֹּקֶר וְהָלַכְתָּ לְאֹהָלֶיךָ: שֵׁשֶׁת יָמִים תֹּאכַל מַצּוֹת וּבַיּוֹם הַשְּׁבִיעִי עֲצֶרֶת
ט לַיהוָה אֱלֹהֶיךָ לֹא תַעֲשֶׂה מְלָאכָה: שִׁבְעָה שָׁבֻעֹת תִּסְפָּר־לָךְ מֵהָחֵל

רש"י

"וּמִן הָעִזִּים תִּקָּחוּ" (שמות יב, ה): **וּבָקָר.** תִּזְבַּח לַחֲגִיגָה, שֶׁאִם נִמְנוּ עַל הַפֶּסַח חֲבוּרָה מְרֻבָּה, מְבִיאִים עִמּוֹ חֲגִיגָה כְּדֵי שֶׁיְּהֵא נֶאֱכָל עַל הַשֹּׂבַע. וְעוֹד לָמְדוּ רַבּוֹתֵינוּ דְּבָרִים הַרְבֵּה מִפָּסוּק זֶה:

ג | **לֶחֶם עֹנִי.** לֶחֶם שֶׁמַּזְכִּיר אֶת הָעֹנִי שֶׁנִּתְעַנּוּ בְּמִצְרַיִם: **כִּי בְחִפָּזוֹן יָצָאתָ.** וְלֹא הִסְפִּיק בָּצֵק לְהַחֲמִיץ, וְזֶה יִהְיֶה לְךָ לְזִכָּרוֹן. וְחִפָּזוֹן לֹא שֶׁלְּךָ הָיָה אֶלָּא שֶׁל מִצְרַיִם, שֶׁכֵּן הוּא אוֹמֵר: "וַתֶּחֱזַק מִצְרַיִם עַל הָעָם" וְגוֹ' (שמות יב, לג): **לְמַעַן תִּזְכֹּר.** עַל יְדֵי אֲכִילַת הַפֶּסַח וְהַמַּצָּה "אֶת יוֹם צֵאתְךָ":

ד | **וְלֹא יָלִין מִן הַבָּשָׂר אֲשֶׁר תִּזְבַּח בָּעֶרֶב בַּיּוֹם הָרִאשׁוֹן לַבֹּקֶר.** אַזְהָרָה לַמּוֹתִיר בְּפֶסַח דּוֹרוֹת, לְפִי שֶׁלֹּא נֶאֱמַר אֶלָּא בְּפֶסַח מִצְרַיִם, וְיוֹם רִאשׁוֹן הָאָמוּר כָּאן הוּא אַרְבָּעָה עָשָׂר בְּנִיסָן, כְּמָה דְאַתְּ אָמַר: "אַךְ בַּיּוֹם הָרִאשׁוֹן תַּשְׁבִּיתוּ שְׂאֹר מִבָּתֵּיכֶם" (שמות יב, טו). וּלְפִי שֶׁנִּסְתַּלֵּק הַכָּתוּב מֵעִנְיָנוֹ שֶׁל פֶּסַח וְהִתְחִיל לְדַבֵּר בַּחֲקוֹת שִׁבְעַת יָמִים, כְּגוֹן: "שִׁבְעַת יָמִים תֹּאכַל עָלָיו מַצּוֹת", "וְלֹא יֵרָאֶה לְךָ שְׂאֹר בְּכָל גְּבֻלְךָ", הֻצְרַךְ לְפָרֵשׁ בְּאֵיזוֹ זְבִיחָה הוּא מַזְהִיר, שֶׁאִם כָּתַב: 'וְלֹא יָלִין מִן הַבָּשָׂר אֲשֶׁר תִּזְבַּח בָּעֶרֶב לַבֹּקֶר', הָיִיתִי אוֹמֵר, שְׁלָמִים הַנִּשְׁחָטִים כָּל שִׁבְעָה כֻּלָּן בְּבַל תּוֹתִירוּ וְאֵינָן נֶאֱכָלִין אֶלָּא לְיוֹם וָלַיְלָה, לְכָךְ כָּתַב: "בָּעֶרֶב בַּיּוֹם הָרִאשׁוֹן". דָּבָר אַחֵר, בַּחֲגִיגַת אַרְבָּעָה עָשָׂר הַכָּתוּב מְדַבֵּר, וְלִמֵּד עָלֶיהָ שֶׁנֶּאֱכֶלֶת לִשְׁנֵי יָמִים, וְ"הָרִאשׁוֹן" הָאָמוּר כָּאן – בְּיוֹם טוֹב הָרִאשׁוֹן הַכָּתוּב מְדַבֵּר, וְכֵן מַשְׁמָעוּת הַמִּקְרָא: בְּשַׂר חֲגִיגָה אֲשֶׁר תִּזְבַּח בָּעֶרֶב לֹא יָלִין בְּיוֹם טוֹב הָרִאשׁוֹן עַד בָּקְרוֹ שֶׁל שֵׁנִי, אֲבָל נֶאֱכֶלֶת הִיא בְּאַרְבָּעָה עָשָׂר וּבַחֲמִשָּׁה עָשָׂר. וְכָךְ הִיא שְׁנוּיָה בְּמַסֶּכֶת פְּסָחִים (דף עא ע"א – עא ע"ב):

ו | **בָּעֶרֶב כְּבוֹא הַשֶּׁמֶשׁ מוֹעֵד צֵאתְךָ מִמִּצְרָיִם.** הֲרֵי שְׁלֹשָׁה זְמַנִּים חֲלוּקִים: 'בָּעֶרֶב' מִשֵּׁשׁ שָׁעוֹת וּלְמַעְלָה זָבְחֵהוּ, וּ'כְבוֹא הַשֶּׁמֶשׁ' תֹּאכְלֵהוּ, וּ'מוֹעֵד צֵאתְךָ' אַתָּה שׂוֹרְפֵהוּ, כְּלוֹמַר נַעֲשָׂה נוֹתָר וְיֵצֵא לְבֵית הַשְּׂרֵפָה:

ז | **וּבִשַּׁלְתָּ.** זֶהוּ צְלִי אֵשׁ, שֶׁאַף הוּא קָרוּי בִּשּׁוּל: **וּפָנִיתָ בַבֹּקֶר.** לְבָקְרוֹ שֶׁל שֵׁנִי, מְלַמֵּד שֶׁטָּעוּן לִינָה לֵיל שֶׁל מוֹצָאֵי יוֹם טוֹב:

ח | **שֵׁשֶׁת יָמִים תֹּאכַל מַצּוֹת.** וּבְמָקוֹם אַחֵר הוּא אוֹמֵר: "שִׁבְעַת יָמִים" (שמות יב, טו)! שִׁבְעָה מִן הַיָּשָׁן וְשִׁשָּׁה מִן הֶחָדָשׁ. דָּבָר אַחֵר, לִמֵּד עַל אֲכִילַת מַצָּה בַּשְּׁבִיעִי שֶׁאֵינָהּ חוֹבָה, וּמִכָּאן אַתָּה לָמֵד לְשֵׁשֶׁת יָמִים, שֶׁהֲרֵי שְׁבִיעִי בִּכְלָל הָיָה וְיָצָא מִן הַכְּלָל לְלַמֵּד שֶׁאֵין אֲכִילַת מַצָּה בּוֹ חוֹבָה אֶלָּא רְשׁוּת, וְלֹא לְלַמֵּד עַל עַצְמוֹ יָצָא אֶלָּא לְלַמֵּד עַל הַכְּלָל כֻּלּוֹ יָצָא, מַה שְּׁבִיעִי רְשׁוּת אַף כֻּלָּם רְשׁוּת, חוּץ מִלַּיְלָה הָרִאשׁוֹן שֶׁהַכָּתוּב קְבָעוֹ חוֹבָה, שֶׁנֶּאֱמַר: "בָּעֶרֶב תֹּאכְלוּ מַצֹּת" (שמות יב, יח): **עֲצֶרֶת לַה' אֱלֹהֶיךָ.** עֲצֹר עַצְמְךָ מִן הַמְּלָאכָה. דָּבָר אַחֵר, כְּנוּפְיָא שֶׁל מַאֲכָל וּמִשְׁתֶּה, לְשׁוֹן: "נַעַצְרָה נָּא אוֹתָךְ" (שופטים יג, טו):

BACKGROUND

16:4 | **Leaven [*se'or*]:** Sourdough, fermented dough that is used to facilitate the leavening of other dough.

harvest, when the **sickle** is used **in the standing grain,**^{D} you shall start to count seven weeks.

Harvesting with a sickle, wall fresco in a tomb in Thebes, Egypt

10 **You shall hold the Festival of Weeks to the Lord your God;** nothing yet has been said about the nature of this festival, only that its name is derived from the fact that it occurs after a count of seven weeks. **The measure of the pledge of your hand which you shall give will be as the Lord your God will bless you.** This festival takes place at the beginning of the summer, when the year's crops begin to ripen and are harvested. At this time each person can see how God has blessed him that year, and in accordance with the quantity and quality of his produce, he must bring a gift to God.

11 **You shall rejoice before the Lord your God, you,** and your entire family, including **your son, your daughter, your slave, your maidservant, and the Levite who is within your gates,** as the Levite, who had no property of his own, was provided for by the landowners; **and the stranger, the orphan, and the**

widow, who are in your midst; all this transpires **in the place that the Lord your God shall rest His name there.**

12 **You shall remember that you were a slave in Egypt;** even though you are celebrating the festival in freedom and with plenty, you must remember that this was not always the situation, nor is it to be taken for granted, and you shall be grateful to God for all the good that He has done for you, **and you shall observe and you shall perform these statutes.**

13 **You shall hold the Festival of Tabernacles seven days, upon**
Maftir **your gathering** the produce **from your threshing floor and from your winepress** at the end of the agricultural season. This is a festival of thanksgiving to God for all the kindness that He has bestowed upon His people in the wilderness and in the Land of Israel.

14 **You shall rejoice on your festival, you, your son, your daughter, your slave, your maidservant, and the Levite; the stranger, the orphan, and the widow who are within your gates;** all those who eat at your table.

15 **Seven days you shall celebrate to the Lord your God in the place that the Lord shall choose, as the Lord your God will bless you in your entire crop, and in all your endeavors, and you shall be completely joyous,** free of all worry and concern.

16 In summation, **three times in the year all your males shall appear**^{D} **before the Lord your God** in His chosen Sanctuary **in the place that He shall choose: On the Festival of Unleavened Bread, and on the Festival of Weeks, and on the Festival of Tabernacles, and they shall not appear before the Lord empty-handed;** when they appear before God, they must bring a gift.

17 **Each man** shall bring **according to the gift of his hand, in accordance with the blessing of the Lord your God that He gave you;** the gift is not defined, and each person may bring as he sees fit.

DISCUSSION

16:9| From the start of the sickle in the standing grain: The count begins from the time of a special ceremony of cutting the grain for the *omer* offering, which took place on the night of the sixteenth of Nisan and marked the beginning of the grain harvest. A verse in Leviticus (23:11) states that this ceremony takes place "on the day after the sabbath." This vague expression was the basis of a dispute that began

during the Second Temple era, and continued into later periods. The *halakha* has determined that the term sabbath in this context does not refer to the seventh day of the week; rather it refers to the first day of Passover. On the following day the *omer* offering is brought and the count of seven weeks begins (see *Menaḥot* 65b).

16:16| Shall appear: The people of Israel do not make pilgrimages in order to see God and experience a revelation. Rather, they appear before God and remain in the place of His choosing in order to demonstrate that they are still committed to the covenant and to maintaining their relationship with Him. This also explains the importance of remembering Israel's bondage in Egypt.

י חֶרְמֵשׁ בַּקָּמָה תָּחֵל לִסְפֹּר שִׁבְעָה שָׁבֻעוֹת: וְעָשִׂיתָ חַג שָׁבֻעוֹת לַיהוָה אֱלֹהֶיךָ
יא מִסַּת נִדְבַת יָדְךָ אֲשֶׁר תִּתֵּן כַּאֲשֶׁר יְבָרֶכְךָ יְהוָה אֱלֹהֶיךָ: וְשָׂמַחְתָּ לִפְנֵי ׀ יְהוָה
אֱלֹהֶיךָ אַתָּה וּבִנְךָ וּבִתֶּךָ וְעַבְדְּךָ וַאֲמָתֶךָ וְהַלֵּוִי אֲשֶׁר בִּשְׁעָרֶיךָ וְהַגֵּר וְהַיָּתוֹם
וְהָאַלְמָנָה אֲשֶׁר בְּקִרְבֶּךָ בַּמָּקוֹם אֲשֶׁר יִבְחַר יְהוָה אֱלֹהֶיךָ לְשַׁכֵּן שְׁמוֹ שָׁם:
יב וְזָכַרְתָּ כִּי־עֶבֶד הָיִיתָ בְּמִצְרָיִם וְשָׁמַרְתָּ וְעָשִׂיתָ אֶת־הַחֻקִּים הָאֵלֶּה:
יג יד חַג הַסֻּכֹּת תַּעֲשֶׂה לְךָ שִׁבְעַת יָמִים בְּאָסְפְּךָ מִגָּרְנְךָ וּמִיִּקְבֶךָ: וְשָׂמַחְתָּ בְּחַגֶּךָ מפטיר
אַתָּה וּבִנְךָ וּבִתֶּךָ וְעַבְדְּךָ וַאֲמָתֶךָ וְהַלֵּוִי וְהַגֵּר וְהַיָּתוֹם וְהָאַלְמָנָה אֲשֶׁר בִּשְׁעָרֶיךָ:
טו שִׁבְעַת יָמִים תָּחֹג לַיהוָה אֱלֹהֶיךָ בַּמָּקוֹם אֲשֶׁר־יִבְחַר יְהוָה כִּי יְבָרֶכְךָ יְהוָה
טז אֱלֹהֶיךָ בְּכֹל תְּבוּאָתְךָ וּבְכֹל מַעֲשֵׂה יָדֶיךָ וְהָיִיתָ אַךְ שָׂמֵחַ: שָׁלוֹשׁ פְּעָמִים ׀
בַּשָּׁנָה יֵרָאֶה כָל־זְכוּרְךָ אֶת־פְּנֵי ׀ יְהוָה אֱלֹהֶיךָ בַּמָּקוֹם אֲשֶׁר יִבְחָר בְּחַג הַמַּצּוֹת
יז וּבְחַג הַשָּׁבֻעוֹת וּבְחַג הַסֻּכּוֹת וְלֹא יֵרָאֶה אֶת־פְּנֵי יְהוָה רֵיקָם: אִישׁ כְּמַתְּנַת יָדוֹ
כְּבִרְכַּת יְהוָה אֱלֹהֶיךָ אֲשֶׁר נָתַן־לָךְ:

רש"י

ט | **מֵהָחֵל חֶרְמֵשׁ בַּקָּמָה.** מִשֶּׁנִּקְצַר הָעֹמֶר שֶׁהוּא רֵאשִׁית הַקָּצִיר:

י | **מִסַּת נִדְבַת יָדְךָ.** דֵּי נִדְבַת יָדְךָ, הַכֹּל לְפִי הַבְּרָכָה הָבֵא שַׁלְמֵי שִׂמְחָה וְקַדֵּשׁ קְרוּאִים לֶאֱכֹל:

יא | **וְהַלֵּוִי וְהַגֵּר וְהַיָּתוֹם וְהָאַלְמָנָה.** אַרְבָּעָה שֶׁלִּי כְּנֶגֶד אַרְבָּעָה שֶׁלְּךָ: "בִּנְךָ וּבִתֶּךָ וְעַבְדְּךָ וַאֲמָתֶךָ", אִם אַתָּה מְשַׂמֵּחַ אֶת שֶׁלִּי אֲנִי מְשַׂמֵּחַ אֶת שֶׁלְּךָ:

יב | **וְזָכַרְתָּ כִּי עֶבֶד הָיִיתָ וְגוֹ'.** עַל מְנָת כֵּן פְּדִיתִיךָ, שֶׁתִּשְׁמֹר וְתַעֲשֶׂה אֶת הַחֻקִּים הָאֵלֶּה:

יג | **בְּאָסְפְּךָ.** בִּזְמַן הָאָסִיף, שֶׁאַתָּה מַכְנִיס לַבַּיִת פֵּרוֹת הַקַּיִץ. דָּבָר אַחֵר, "בְּאָסְפְּךָ מִגָּרְנְךָ וּמִיִּקְבֶךָ", לָמַד שֶׁמְּסַכְּכִין אֶת הַסֻּכָּה בִּפְסֹלֶת גֹּרֶן וָיֶקֶב:

טו | **וְהָיִיתָ אַךְ שָׂמֵחַ.** לְפִי פְשׁוּטוֹ אֵין זֶה לְשׁוֹן צִוּוּי אֶלָּא לְשׁוֹן הַבְטָחָה. וּלְפִי תַלְמוּדוֹ לָמְדוּ מִכָּאן לְרַבּוֹת לֵילֵי יוֹם טוֹב הָאַחֲרוֹן לְשִׂמְחָה:

טז | **וְלֹא יֵרָאֶה אֶת פְּנֵי ה' רֵיקָם.** אֶלָּא הָבֵא עוֹלוֹת רְאִיָּה וְשַׁלְמֵי חֲגִיגָה:

יז | **אִישׁ כְּמַתְּנַת יָדוֹ.** מִי שֶׁיֵּשׁ לוֹ אוֹכְלִין הַרְבֵּה וּנְכָסִים מְרֻבִּים יָבִיא עוֹלוֹת מְרֻבּוֹת וּשְׁלָמִים מְרֻבִּים:

Parashat
Shofetim

Appointing Judges and Pursuing Justice
DEUTERONOMY 16:18–20

In order to create a just, law-abiding society, a community must establish a system of law enforcement and a judiciary. The appointed officials must be careful to avoid any distortion of justice.

18 **Judges and officers you shall place for you within all your gates that the Lord your God is giving you for your tribes.** Israel is obligated to appoint judges and officers in all their dwelling places. **And they shall judge the people a fair judgment,** which is a necessary precondition for the existence of a nation.

19 This verse addresses the judges: **You shall not distort judgment, you shall not give preference** to a litigant who is your acquaintance; **and you shall not take a bribe, as the bribe will blind** even **the eyes of the wise,** who thereby lose their impartiality, **and corrupt the words of the righteous.** The latter phrase may also be understood to mean that a bribe will

cause words that are correct to appear corrupt. The reference here is not only a benefit offered for the express purpose of rendering a particular verdict. The very acceptance of a favor from someone, even with no stipulation of a quid pro quo, is enough to cause a judge to view matters differently, which will prevent him from reaching a just decision.

20 It is not enough merely for the law to be just; rather, **justice, justice you shall pursue,** take the initiative to impose justice, **so that you will live, and take possession of the land that the Lord your God is giving you,** by establishing a civilized state, where integrity and justice reign.

Prohibitions against Planting a Sacred Tree or Establishing a Monument
DEUTERONOMY 16:21–22

The Torah bans syncretism, the integration of foreign rites into the service of God. Here The Torah prohibits using sacred trees or monuments even in the service of the God of Israel.

21 **You shall not plant for you any kind of sacred tree next to the altar of the Lord your God that you shall make for you.** Do not seek to honor God in the same manner that idols are worshipped.

22 Similarly, **you shall not establish for you a monument,**[D] a stone or tall construction used as a focal point for worship,[1] **which the Lord your God hates.**

Prohibition of Blemished Offerings
DEUTERONOMY 17:1

The verse mentions another prohibition involving the worship of God and the altar.

17 1 **You shall not slaughter to the Lord your God an ox, or a lamb,** an animal from the herd or flock, **in which there is a blemish,** as defined in the Torah,[2] or a cow or sheep that has **any bad thing,** other flaws that are not classified as blemishes but which disfigure the animal or render it unacceptable as an

offering, e.g., conspicuous signs of old age,[3] **as that is an abomination of the Lord your God.** The blemish itself is not an abomination; it is the act of offering the blemished animal to God that is an abomination. One's gift to God must be as respectable as possible.

Law of an Idol Worshipper
DEUTERONOMY 17:2–7

Idolatry is a severe transgression against God. In order to eradicate this phenomenon, the court is empowered to punish anyone who betrays the covenant with God in this manner.

2 **If there will be found in your midst, within any of your gates,** your places of settlement, **that the Lord your God is giving you, a man or a woman who will perform evil in the eyes of the Lord your God, to violate His covenant;**
3 **he went and served other gods, and prostrated himself before them.** Idolatry is not merely a violation of one Torah

prohibition among others; rather, it is a breach of the fundamental covenant with God. Perhaps this is the reason for the phrase "he went," as that person distances himself from the Jewish religion. Indeed, the Torah frequently uses forms of the verb "to go" to describe Jews who worship idols, as they thereby depart from God.[4] It makes no difference whether one bowed

פרשת
שופטים

יח שֹׁפְטִים וְשֹׁטְרִים תִּתֶּן־לְךָ בְּכָל־שְׁעָרֶיךָ אֲשֶׁר יְהוָה אֱלֹהֶיךָ נֹתֵן לְךָ לִשְׁבָטֶיךָ
יט וְשָׁפְטוּ אֶת־הָעָם מִשְׁפַּט־צֶדֶק: לֹא־תַטֶּה מִשְׁפָּט לֹא תַכִּיר פָּנִים וְלֹא־תִקַּח
כ שֹׁחַד כִּי הַשֹּׁחַד יְעַוֵּר עֵינֵי חֲכָמִים וִיסַלֵּף דִּבְרֵי צַדִּיקִם: צֶדֶק צֶדֶק תִּרְדֹּף לְמַעַן
כא תִּחְיֶה וְיָרַשְׁתָּ אֶת־הָאָרֶץ אֲשֶׁר־יְהוָה אֱלֹהֶיךָ נֹתֵן לָךְ: לֹא־תִטַּע
כב לְךָ אֲשֵׁרָה כָּל־עֵץ אֵצֶל מִזְבַּח יְהוָה אֱלֹהֶיךָ אֲשֶׁר תַּעֲשֶׂה־לָּךְ: וְלֹא־תָקִים לְךָ
א מַצֵּבָה אֲשֶׁר שָׂנֵא יְהוָה אֱלֹהֶיךָ: לֹא־תִזְבַּח לַיהוָה אֱלֹהֶיךָ שׁוֹר וָשֶׂה
ב אֲשֶׁר יִהְיֶה בוֹ מוּם כֹּל דָּבָר רָע כִּי תוֹעֲבַת יְהוָה אֱלֹהֶיךָ הוּא: כִּי־יִמָּצֵא
בְקִרְבְּךָ בְּאַחַד שְׁעָרֶיךָ אֲשֶׁר־יְהוָה אֱלֹהֶיךָ נֹתֵן לָךְ אִישׁ אוֹ־אִשָּׁה אֲשֶׁר יַעֲשֶׂה
ג אֶת־הָרַע בְּעֵינֵי יְהוָה־אֱלֹהֶיךָ לַעֲבֹר בְּרִיתוֹ: וַיֵּלֶךְ וַיַּעֲבֹד אֱלֹהִים אֲחֵרִים
וַיִּשְׁתַּחוּ לָהֶם וְלַשֶּׁמֶשׁ ׀ אוֹ לַיָּרֵחַ אוֹ לְכָל־צְבָא הַשָּׁמַיִם אֲשֶׁר לֹא־צִוִּיתִי:

רש״י

יח | **שֹׁפְטִים וְשֹׁטְרִים.** "שֹׁפְטִים" דַּיָּנִים הַפּוֹסְקִים אֶת הַדִּין, "וְשֹׁטְרִים" הָרוֹדִין אֶת הָעָם אַחַר מִצְוָתָם, שֶׁמַּכִּין וְכוֹפְתִין בְּמַקֵּל וּבִרְצוּעָה עַד שֶׁיְּקַבֵּל עָלָיו אֶת דִּין הַשּׁוֹפֵט: **בְּכָל שְׁעָרֶיךָ.** בְּכָל עִיר וָעִיר: **לִשְׁבָטֶיךָ.** מוּסָב עַל "תִּתֶּן לְךָ": שֹׁפְטִים וְשֹׁטְרִים תִּתֶּן לְךָ לִשְׁבָטֶיךָ בְּכָל שְׁעָרֶיךָ אֲשֶׁר ה׳ אֱלֹהֶיךָ נֹתֵן לְךָ: **לִשְׁבָטֶיךָ.** מְלַמֵּד שֶׁמּוֹשִׁיבִין דַּיָּנִין לְכָל שֵׁבֶט וָשֵׁבֶט וּבְכָל עִיר וָעִיר: **וְשָׁפְטוּ אֶת הָעָם וְגוֹ׳.** מַנֵּה דַּיָּנִין מֻמְחִים וְצַדִּיקִים לִשְׁפֹּט צֶדֶק:

יט | **לֹא תַטֶּה מִשְׁפָּט.** כְּמַשְׁמָעוֹ: **לֹא תַכִּיר פָּנִים.** אַף בִּשְׁעַת הַטְּעָנוֹת, שֶׁלֹּא יְהֵא רַךְ לָזֶה וְקָשֶׁה לָזֶה, אֶחָד עוֹמֵד וְאֶחָד יוֹשֵׁב, לְפִי שֶׁכְּשֶׁרוֹאֶה זֶה שֶׁהַדַּיָּן מְכַבֵּד אֶת חֲבֵרוֹ מִסְתַּתְּמִין טַעֲנוֹתָיו: **וְלֹא תִקַּח שֹׁחַד.** אֲפִלּוּ לִשְׁפֹּט צֶדֶק: **כִּי הַשֹּׁחַד יְעַוֵּר.** מִשֶּׁקִּבֵּל שֹׁחַד מִמֶּנּוּ, אִי אֶפְשָׁר שֶׁלֹּא יַטֶּה אֶת לִבּוֹ אֶצְלוֹ לַהֲפֹךְ בִּזְכוּתוֹ: **דִּבְרֵי צַדִּיקִם.** דְּבָרִים הַמְצֻדָּקִים, מִשְׁפְּטֵי אֱמֶת:

כ | **צֶדֶק צֶדֶק תִּרְדֹּף.** הֵלֵךְ אַחַר בֵּית דִּין יָפֶה: **לְמַעַן תִּחְיֶה וְיָרַשְׁתָּ.** כְּדַאי הוּא מִנּוּי הַדַּיָּנִין הַכְּשֵׁרִים לְהַחֲיוֹת אֶת יִשְׂרָאֵל וּלְהוֹשִׁיבָן עַל אַדְמָתָן:

כא | **לֹא תִטַּע לְךָ אֲשֵׁרָה.** לְחַיְּבוֹ עָלֶיהָ מִשְּׁעַת נְטִיעָתָהּ, וַאֲפִלּוּ לֹא עֲבָדָהּ עוֹבֵר בְּלֹא תַעֲשֶׂה עַל נְטִיעָתָהּ. וְ"לֹא תִטַּע לְךָ... כָּל עֵץ אֵצֶל מִזְבַּח" – אַזְהָרָה לְנוֹטֵעַ אִילָן וּלְבוֹנֶה בַיִת בְּהַר הַבַּיִת:

כב | **וְלֹא תָקִים לְךָ מַצֵּבָה.** מַצֵּבָה, אֶבֶן אַחַת לְהַקְרִיב עָלֶיהָ, אֲפִלּוּ לַשָּׁמַיִם: **אֲשֶׁר שָׂנֵא.** מִזְבַּח אֲבָנִים וּמִזְבַּח אֲדָמָה צִוָּה לַעֲשׂוֹת, וְאֶת זוֹ שָׂנֵא, כִּי חֹק הָיְתָה לַכְּנַעֲנִים. וְאַף עַל פִּי שֶׁהָיְתָה אֲהוּבָה לוֹ בִּימֵי הָאָבוֹת, עַכְשָׁיו שְׂנֵאָהּ, מֵאַחַר שֶׁעֲשָׂאוּהָ אֵלּוּ חֹק לַעֲבוֹדָה זָרָה:

פרק יז

א | **לֹא תִזְבַּח וְגוֹ׳ כָּל דָּבָר רָע.** אַזְהָרָה לִמְפַגֵּל בְּקָדָשִׁים עַל יְדֵי דִּבּוּר רָע. וְעוֹד נִדְרְשׁוּ בוֹ שְׁאָר דְּרָשׁוֹת בִּשְׁחִיטַת קָדָשִׁים:

ב | **לַעֲבֹר בְּרִיתוֹ.** אֲשֶׁר כָּרַת ה׳ אִתְּכֶם שֶׁלֹּא לַעֲבֹד עֲבוֹדָה זָרָה:

ג | **אֲשֶׁר לֹא צִוִּיתִי.** לַעֲבֹד:

DISCUSSION

16:22 | **You shall not establish for you a monument:** The construction of pillars and the planting of trees as memorials are not despicable rituals in and of themselves. Abraham planted a tree as a memorial in Beersheba (Genesis 21:33), while Jacob built a pillar for God (Genesis 28:18, 35:14). However, over time actions of that kind became identified with idolatry; therefore God despises them and one may not perform them for ritualistic purposes or near the altar (see Rashi; *Sifrei*, *Devarim*, 146).

to an idol, **or to the sun, or to the moon, or to any of the host of the heavens that I did not command,** which I commanded you not to worship or honor. Alternatively, this means that God did not grant the host of the heavens dominion or influence over the world, as their worshippers suppose.[5]

4 It, this occurrence, **will be told to you, and you will hear, and you shall inquire** and clarify **diligently.** Like all cases that come to the court, the judge may not rule based on rumors alone; he must examine all the details of the case in order to establish the truth. **And behold,** it turns out that **it is true, the matter is correct, this abomination was performed in Israel.**

5 **You shall take out that man or that woman who has performed this evil thing to your gates, the man or the woman**[D] who committed idolatry; **you shall stone them with stones, and they will die.**[6]

6 Here the Torah provides a general principle that goes beyond the parameters of this particular case. **At the word of two**

witnesses, or three witnesses, a person shall be put to death. In capital cases it is vital that testimony be received from at least two witnesses. **He shall not be put to death at the word of one witness.**[D]

7 In addition to the court's examination, there is another role assigned to the witnesses that indirectly serves as a moral deterrent to them. **The hand of the witnesses shall be first upon him to put him to death, and the hand of all the people last, and you shall eliminate the evil from your midst.** Although the witnesses do not carry out the death penalty in its entirety, they start implementing the verdict.[7] Consequently, if witnesses falsely accuse someone, they might be frightened into reconsidering their action and retract their testimony at the last minute when they realize that they will have to participate in implementing the ruling of capital punishment that was reached due to their testimony.

The Central Court
DEUTERONOMY 17:8–13

After describing a severe transgression whose matter was resolved and the sinner punished, the Torah addresses a situation that a local court is unable to resolve.

This section also serves as the basis for the authority of the Sages of Israel to decide all legal questions that arise over the course of the generations, and the duty of the people to obey them. In essence, this is the foundation of the Oral Law.

8 The Torah addresses a local judge and instructs him with regard to a doubt that might arise in a case that comes before him. For example: **If a matter of judgment will be obscure to you,** and you do not know how to distinguish **between** the **blood** of one who is not guilty of a capital offense **and** the **blood** of one who is guilty,[8] or alternatively, between blood that is ritually pure and blood that is ritually impure;[9] or you do not know how to decide **between** one monetary **case and** another similar **case** in order to determine which of them can serve as a legal precedent for the case that is currently being adjudicated; **or between** one type of leprous **mark and** a different type of leprous **mark;** the difference of opinion between two or more judges is liable to lead to **matters of dispute within your gates,** the place of the local court.[10] Therefore, **you shall arise, and you shall go up to the place that the Lord your God shall choose,** which is the seat of the greatest experts in Torah law.

9 **You shall come to the priests,** who are all **Levites,** who study the Torah regularly and teach it, **and to the** highest **judge,** the head of the Great Sanhedrin, **who shall be in those days, and you shall inquire, and they shall tell you the statement of**

judgment. Not only are these judges likely to know the correct ruling of the Torah, but they are granted the ultimate authority to decide these cases.

10 **You shall do according to the statement that they will tell you from that place that the Lord shall choose, and you shall take care to perform in accordance with everything that they,** the judges of the highest court, **will instruct you.**

11 **On the basis of the law that they,** those judges, **will instruct you, and the judgment that they will say to you, you shall act; you shall not deviate from the matter that they will tell you, right or left.**[D]

12 Since these matters are subject to dispute and argumentation, the verse stresses that one who ignores the ruling of the court has committed a very serious transgression. **The man**[D] who **shall perform with intent, to not heed the priest who stands to serve the Lord your God there,** the High Priest,[11] **or the judge** who heads the court, **that man shall die, and you shall eliminate the evil,** of undermining the authority of the central judiciary body, **from Israel.**

DISCUSSION

17:5 | **The man or the woman:** The repeated mention of "the man and the woman" distinguishes this transgression from the worship of idols by an entire community. A different punishment is imposed in that case (13:13–17; see *Sanhedrin* 16b).

17:6 | **He shall not be put to death at the word of one witness:** Although one witness can provide support, his account alone does ←↩

ד וְהֻגַּד־לְךָ וְשָׁמָעְתָּ וְדָרַשְׁתָּ הֵיטֵב וְהִנֵּה אֱמֶת נָכוֹן הַדָּבָר נֶעֶשְׂתָה הַתּוֹעֵבָה
ה הַזֹּאת בְּיִשְׂרָאֵל: וְהוֹצֵאתָ אֶת־הָאִישׁ הַהוּא אוֹ אֶת־הָאִשָּׁה הַהִוא אֲשֶׁר עָשׂוּ
אֶת־הַדָּבָר הָרָע הַזֶּה אֶל־שְׁעָרֶיךָ אֶת־הָאִישׁ אוֹ אֶת־הָאִשָּׁה וּסְקַלְתָּם בָּאֲבָנִים
ו וָמֵתוּ: עַל־פִּי ׀ שְׁנַיִם עֵדִים אוֹ שְׁלֹשָׁה עֵדִים יוּמַת הַמֵּת לֹא יוּמַת עַל־פִּי עֵד
ז אֶחָד: יַד הָעֵדִים תִּהְיֶה־בּוֹ בָרִאשֹׁנָה לַהֲמִיתוֹ וְיַד כָּל־הָעָם בָּאַחֲרֹנָה וּבִעַרְתָּ
הָרָע מִקִּרְבֶּךָ:
ח כִּי יִפָּלֵא מִמְּךָ דָבָר לַמִּשְׁפָּט בֵּין־דָּם ׀ לְדָם בֵּין־דִּין לְדִין וּבֵין נֶגַע לָנֶגַע דִּבְרֵי
ט רִיבֹת בִּשְׁעָרֶיךָ וְקַמְתָּ וְעָלִיתָ אֶל־הַמָּקוֹם אֲשֶׁר יִבְחַר יהוה אֱלֹהֶיךָ בּוֹ: וּבָאתָ
אֶל־הַכֹּהֲנִים הַלְוִיִּם וְאֶל־הַשֹּׁפֵט אֲשֶׁר יִהְיֶה בַּיָּמִים הָהֵם וְדָרַשְׁתָּ וְהִגִּידוּ לְךָ אֵת
י דְּבַר הַמִּשְׁפָּט: וְעָשִׂיתָ עַל־פִּי הַדָּבָר אֲשֶׁר יַגִּידוּ לְךָ מִן־הַמָּקוֹם הַהוּא אֲשֶׁר יִבְחַר
יא יהוה וְשָׁמַרְתָּ לַעֲשׂוֹת כְּכֹל אֲשֶׁר יוֹרוּךָ: עַל־פִּי הַתּוֹרָה אֲשֶׁר יוֹרוּךָ וְעַל־הַמִּשְׁפָּט
אֲשֶׁר־יֹאמְרוּ לְךָ תַּעֲשֶׂה לֹא תָסוּר מִן־הַדָּבָר אֲשֶׁר־יַגִּידוּ לְךָ יָמִין וּשְׂמֹאל:
יב וְהָאִישׁ אֲשֶׁר־יַעֲשֶׂה בְזָדוֹן לְבִלְתִּי שְׁמֹעַ אֶל־הַכֹּהֵן הָעֹמֵד לְשָׁרֶת שָׁם אֶת־
יהוה אֱלֹהֶיךָ אוֹ אֶל־הַשֹּׁפֵט וּמֵת הָאִישׁ הַהוּא וּבִעַרְתָּ הָרָע מִיִּשְׂרָאֵל:

רש״י

ד | **נָכוֹן.** מְכֻוָּן הָעֵדוּת:

ה | **וְהוֹצֵאתָ אֶת הָאִישׁ הַהוּא וְגוֹ׳ אֶל שְׁעָרֶיךָ.** הַמְתַרְגֵּם "אֶל שְׁעָרֶיךָ" – 'לִתְרַע בֵּית דִּינָךְ' טוֹעֶה, שֶׁכֵּן שָׁנִינוּ: "אֶל שְׁעָרֶיךָ" זֶה שַׁעַר שֶׁעָבַד בּוֹ, אוֹ אֵינוֹ אֶלָּא שַׁעַר שֶׁנִּדּוֹן בּוֹ? נֶאֱמַר "שְׁעָרֶיךָ" לְמַטָּה וְנֶאֱמַר "שְׁעָרֶיךָ" לְמַעְלָה (לעיל פסוק ב), מָה "שְׁעָרֶיךָ" הָאָמוּר לְמַעְלָה שַׁעַר שֶׁעָבַד בּוֹ, אַף "שְׁעָרֶיךָ" הָאָמוּר לְמַטָּה שַׁעַר שֶׁעָבַד בּוֹ. וְתַרְגּוּמוֹ: "לְקִרְוָךְ":

ו | **שְׁנַיִם עֵדִים אוֹ שְׁלֹשָׁה.** אִם מִתְקַיֶּמֶת עֵדוּת בִּשְׁנַיִם, לָמָּה פֵּרַט לְךָ שְׁלֹשָׁה? לְהַקִּישׁ שְׁלֹשָׁה לִשְׁנַיִם, מַה שְּׁנַיִם עֵדוּת אַחַת, אַף שְׁלֹשָׁה עֵדוּת אַחַת, וְאֵין נַעֲשִׂין זוֹמְמִין עַד שֶׁיִּזּוֹמּוּ כֻּלָּם:

ח | **כִּי יִפָּלֵא.** כָּל הַפְלָאָה לְשׁוֹן הַבְדָּלָה וּפְרִישָׁה, שֶׁהַדָּבָר נִבְדָּל וּמְכֻסֶּה מִמְּךָ: **בֵּין דָּם לְדָם.** בֵּין דָּם טָמֵא לְדָם טָהוֹר: **בֵּין דִּין לְדִין.** בֵּין דִּין זַכַּאי לְדִין חַיָּב: **וּבֵין נֶגַע לָנֶגַע.** בֵּין נֶגַע טָמֵא לְנֶגַע טָהוֹר: **דִּבְרֵי רִיבֹת.** שֶׁיִּהְיוּ חַכְמֵי הָעִיר חוֹלְקִים בַּדָּבָר, זֶה מְטַמֵּא וְזֶה מְטַהֵר, זֶה מְחַיֵּב וְזֶה מְזַכֶּה: **וְקַמְתָּ וְעָלִיתָ.** מְלַמֵּד שֶׁבֵּית הַמִּקְדָּשׁ גָּבוֹהַּ מִכָּל הַמְּקוֹמוֹת:

ט | **הַכֹּהֲנִים הַלְוִיִּם.** הַכֹּהֲנִים שֶׁיָּצְאוּ מִשֵּׁבֶט לֵוִי: **וְאֶל הַשֹּׁפֵט אֲשֶׁר יִהְיֶה בַּיָּמִים הָהֵם.** וַאֲפִלּוּ אֵינוֹ כִּשְׁאָר שׁוֹפְטִים שֶׁהָיוּ לְפָנָיו, אַתָּה צָרִיךְ לִשְׁמֹעַ לוֹ, אֵין לְךָ אֶלָּא שׁוֹפֵט שֶׁבְּיָמֶיךָ:

יא | **יָמִין וּשְׂמֹאל.** אֲפִלּוּ אוֹמֵר לְךָ עַל יָמִין שֶׁהוּא שְׂמֹאל וְעַל שְׂמֹאל שֶׁהוּא יָמִין, וְכָל שֶׁכֵּן שֶׁאוֹמֵר לְךָ עַל יָמִין יָמִין וְעַל שְׂמֹאל שְׂמֹאל:

DISCUSSION

not suffice to put an accused party to death. Two witnesses are considered more objective and reliable than one, as each must leave his private sphere of knowledge, emotion, and experience, and enter the shared domain of two people. Naturally, each of these witnesses is cross-examined separately, and the statement of each is verified against that of his colleague (see *Sanhedrin* 29a).

17:11| **Right or left:** This expression is interpreted in two different ways: First, one must obey the judges even if they are wrong, e.g., if they tell you that right is left and left is right, as the authority to decide is theirs (Rashi; *Sifrei, Devarim* 154). Others explain that one is obligated to obey them only if they say that right is right and left is left (Jerusalem Talmud, *Horayot* 1:1). It is possible that these interpretations reflect conflicting opinions with regard to the court (see also *Horayot* 2b; *Tosafot*).

17:12| **The man:** In the Bible, man [*ish*] refers to someone of distinguished status (see Exodus 11:3; Numbers 13:3; II Samuel 17:25). The punishment stated here is not meted out to anyone who fails to abide by a ruling of the High Court. Rather, the verse is speaking specifically

13 **All the people shall hear** that this person was executed for de-
fying the central court, **and they shall fear,**[D] **and they will not
act with** evil **intent anymore.**

The Monarchy

DEUTERONOMY 17:14–20

A straightforward reading of this section indicates that although the Torah does not mandate a specific form of government, if Israel chooses a centralized regime, the establishment of a monarchy is subject to the conditions presented here.

14 **When you will come to the land that the Lord your God is**
Second aliya **giving you, and you shall take possession of it, and you shall
live in it, and you shall say: I will place a king over me, like
all the nations that are around me;**
15 **you shall place a king over you, whom the Lord your God
shall choose,** through a prophet. Perhaps this is an indication
that the king is not selected by his people. **From among your
brethren you shall place a king over you; you may not place
over you a foreign man, who is not your brother.**[D]
16 **Only he shall not amass horses for himself.** This prohibition serves to curb the natural desire of a king to establish
for himself a large cavalry for his army. In earlier generations,
horses were used primarily for war, while other animals were
used for work.[12] The Torah does not permit a king to increase
his stable when the horses are not necessary but are collected
merely to showcase his power. **And he,** the king, **shall not return the people to Egypt, in order to amass horses, as the
Lord** has **said to you: You shall not return again**[D] **on that
way anymore.** Before the establishment of the Hitite kingdom,
war horses were bred primarily in Egypt. A king who sought to
amass horses would be forced to maintain close relations with
Egypt, which is undesirable.
17 **He shall not amass wives.**[D] The Torah seeks to restrain the
well-known tendency of kings to marry many women, for van-
ity, among other reasons. **And his heart will not stray** due to
his interactions with his many wives. **And silver and gold he
shall not amass greatly.**[D] Although every king requires money
to run his kingdom, and he is entitled to collect taxes for this
purpose, he must not become overly involved in financial
matters.
18 In addition to the special prohibitions that apply to a king, there
is also a positive commandment that he is obligated to perform:
**It shall be upon his sitting on the throne of his kingdom, he
shall write for himself,** either by his own hand or through the
agency of a scribe specially appointed to write on behalf of the
king,[13] **a copy**[14] **of this Torah in a scroll, from that which is
before the priests, the Levites,** who are in possession of the
original text of the Torah.
19 **It,** the Torah scroll, **shall be with him,**[D] **and he shall read
from it all the days of his life, so that he will learn**[D] **to fear
the Lord his God, to observe all the words of this Torah and
these statutes, in order to perform them.**

Horses

DISCUSSION

of a significant personage, a judge who issues a practical ruling to others contrary to the ruling of the Sanhedrin. The Sages call this individual a "rebellious elder according to the court" (Mishna *Sanhedrin* 11:1).

17:13 | **And all the people shall hear, and they shall fear:** So that all the people will be aware of the matter, and so that the punishment that the rebellious elder receives will not remain a mere rumor, he is not sentenced immediately. Rather, his public execution is delayed until all Israel ascend to the Temple on the pilgrimage festival (Mishna *Sanhedrin* 11:4).

17:15 | **You may not place over you a foreign man, who is not your brother:** Both in ancient times and in the modern world, there have been cases where kings were brought from distant lands. Indeed, there is a certain advantage to a king who did not grow up among the people. Nevertheless, the Torah requires that the king

יג יד וְכָל־הָעָם יִשְׁמְעוּ וְיִרָאוּ וְלֹא יְזִידוּן עוֹד׃ ס שני כִּי־תָבֹא אֶל־הָאָרֶץ אֲשֶׁר
יְהוָה אֱלֹהֶיךָ נֹתֵן לָךְ וִירִשְׁתָּהּ וְיָשַׁבְתָּה בָּהּ וְאָמַרְתָּ אָשִׂימָה עָלַי מֶלֶךְ כְּכָל־
טו הַגּוֹיִם אֲשֶׁר סְבִיבֹתָי׃ שׂוֹם תָּשִׂים עָלֶיךָ מֶלֶךְ אֲשֶׁר יִבְחַר יְהוָה אֱלֹהֶיךָ בּוֹ
מִקֶּרֶב אַחֶיךָ תָּשִׂים עָלֶיךָ מֶלֶךְ לֹא תוּכַל לָתֵת עָלֶיךָ אִישׁ נָכְרִי אֲשֶׁר לֹא־
טז אָחִיךָ הוּא׃ רַק לֹא־יַרְבֶּה־לּוֹ סוּסִים וְלֹא־יָשִׁיב אֶת־הָעָם מִצְרַיְמָה לְמַעַן
יז הַרְבּוֹת סוּס וַיהוָה אָמַר לָכֶם לֹא תֹסִפוּן לָשׁוּב בַּדֶּרֶךְ הַזֶּה עוֹד׃ וְלֹא יַרְבֶּה־
יח לּוֹ נָשִׁים וְלֹא יָסוּר לְבָבוֹ וְכֶסֶף וְזָהָב לֹא יַרְבֶּה־לּוֹ מְאֹד׃ וְהָיָה כְשִׁבְתּוֹ עַל
כִּסֵּא מַמְלַכְתּוֹ וְכָתַב לוֹ אֶת־מִשְׁנֵה הַתּוֹרָה הַזֹּאת עַל־סֵפֶר מִלִּפְנֵי הַכֹּהֲנִים
יט הַלְוִיִּם׃ וְהָיְתָה עִמּוֹ וְקָרָא בוֹ כָּל־יְמֵי חַיָּיו לְמַעַן יִלְמַד לְיִרְאָה אֶת־יְהוָה
אֱלֹהָיו לִשְׁמֹר אֶת־כָּל־דִּבְרֵי הַתּוֹרָה הַזֹּאת וְאֶת־הַחֻקִּים הָאֵלֶּה לַעֲשֹׂתָם׃

רש״י

יג | וְכָל הָעָם יִשְׁמְעוּ. מִכָּאן שֶׁמַּמְתִּינִין לוֹ עַד הָרֶגֶל וּמְמִיתִין אוֹתוֹ בָּרֶגֶל:

טז | לֹא יַרְבֶּה לוֹ סוּסִים. אֶלָּא כְּדֵי מֶרְכַּבְתּוֹ, שֶׁלֹּא יָשִׁיב אֶת הָעָם מִצְרַיְמָה, שֶׁהַסּוּסִים בָּאִים מִשָּׁם, כְּמָה שֶׁנֶּאֱמַר בִּשְׁלֹמֹה: "וַתַּעֲלֶה וַתֵּצֵא מֶרְכָּבָה מִמִּצְרַיִם בְּשֵׁשׁ מֵאוֹת כֶּסֶף וְסוּס בַּחֲמִשִּׁים וּמֵאָה" (מלכים א' י, כט):

יז | וְלֹא יַרְבֶּה לוֹ נָשִׁים. אֶלָּא שְׁמוֹנֶה עֶשְׂרֵה, שֶׁמָּצִינוּ שֶׁהָיוּ לוֹ לְדָוִד שֵׁשׁ נָשִׁים (שמואל ב' ג, ב-ה) וְנֶאֱמַר לוֹ: "וְאִם מְעָט וְאֹסִפָה לְּךָ כָּהֵנָּה וְכָהֵנָּה" (שם יב, ח): וְכֶסֶף וְזָהָב לֹא יַרְבֶּה לוֹ מְאֹד. אֶלָּא כְּדֵי לִתֵּן לְאַכְסַנְיָא:

יח | וְהָיָה כְשִׁבְתּוֹ. אִם עָשָׂה כֵן, כְּדַאי הוּא שֶׁתִּתְקַיֵּם מַלְכוּתוֹ: אֶת מִשְׁנֵה הַתּוֹרָה. שְׁתֵּי סִפְרֵי תוֹרוֹת, אַחַת שֶׁהִיא מֻנַּחַת בְּבֵית גְּנָזָיו וְאַחַת שֶׁנִּכְנֶסֶת וְיוֹצְאָה עִמּוֹ:

DISCUSSION

must come from the people of Israel, to prevent the adoption of foreign cultural mores.

17:16| **You shall not return again:** The command not to return to Egypt does not mean that it is prohibited to stay in that land on a temporary basis; rather, it is living there permanently and maintaining close ties with Egypt that is prohibited (see Jerusalem Talmud *Sanhedrin* 10:8; Rambam, *Sefer HaMitzvot*, negative commandment 46; *Sefer HaḤinnukh* 500).

17:17| **He shall not amass wives:** In various cultures, beyond their marital ties, the king's wives served as his companions and close friends. However, there were kingdoms in which the people were effectively ruled by a harem. In those cases, the many wives became a dominant force in the kingdom, and the king was constantly distracted from his official tasks in order to deal with his wives.

And silver and gold he shall not amass greatly: One possible reason for this prohibition is that hoarding a large treasury of silver and gold can ruin the country's economy, as it is liable to undermine the productivity of its citizens. This could endanger the stability of the entire country, beyond the deleterious moral effect of that sort of greed upon the king himself, his heirs, and his close advisors (see I Kings 10:21).

17:19| **It shall be with him:** The Torah scroll is not merely another item in the king's possession or available for him to peruse if he so chooses. Rather, it is a kind of symbol of his reign. Some claim that the king had a small Torah scroll tied to his arm (see *Sanhedrin* 21b). Unlike other kings, who hold a scepter in their hand and wear a crown on their heads, the king of Israel's appearance as the representative of the people includes a Torah scroll, whether it is in his hand, near his body, or carried before him by others (see Mishna *Sanhedrin* 2:4).

So that he will learn: The king is not part of the legal system discussed in the previous section; for example, he does not deal with the laws of leprosy. Rather, he is considered the highest authority only in the area of civil law and politics. There are many cases in the Bible of petitions to the king relating to matters of that kind (see I Kings 3:16–23, 20:39–40; II Kings 6:26–29; see also commentary on II Samuel 14:4).

20 The king must observe the aforementioned laws so **that his heart will not be elevated above his brethren,** as he must not forget his roots and become haughty, **and** so that he **not deviate from the commandment right or left.**[D] The king who acts in this manner will be rewarded, **so that he may extend his days over his kingdom, he and his sons in the midst of Israel.** A righteous king will merit to bequeath his throne to his descendants.

Priests and Levites

DEUTERONOMY 18:1–8

After dealing with the laws of civil leadership, the Torah focuses on the nation's spiritual mentors.

18 **1** **There shall not be for the priests,** who are all **Levites,** and for **the entire tribe of Levi, a portion and an inheritance with Israel.** Their unique status is tied to the tasks that are imposed upon them and is a great honor; however, it does not provide them with economic security. **The fire offerings of the Lord and His inheritance they shall eat.** They eat from the altar, described as the table of God,[15] as they are entitled to parts of certain offerings for their sustenance.

Third aliya

2 **He shall not have an inheritance** of land **among his brethren; the Lord is their inheritance.** The priests and Levites receive their livelihood from their service of God. Although it is permitted for them to engage in any occupation, they have no rights to ancestral lands, and each is supposed to focus on Godly matters, **as He had spoken to him.**

3 **This shall be the allocation of the priests,** their legal rights, **from the people.** First, they receive a portion **from those who perform slaughter** of a non-consecrated animal, **if it is an ox or if it is a lamb: He shall give the priest** part of **the** right **foreleg** of the animal, **and the** lower **jaw** and the tongue,[16] **and the stomach.** These gifts of the priesthood need not be eaten in a state of ritual purity, as they are non-sacred.

4 The chapter lists additional gifts that must be given to the priests: **You shall give him the first fruits of your grain, of your wine, and of your oil** as *teruma,* **and** likewise you shall give him **the first of the fleece of your flock,** in the form of a non-sacred gift.[17]

5 **For the Lord your God has chosen him from all your tribes,** and therefore his job is **to stand** and **to serve in the name of the Lord, he and his sons all the days.**

Parts of an animal given to priests

6 **And if a Levite shall come from one of your gates**[D] **from all of Israel where he resides, and he comes with all the desire of his heart,**[D] when he wishes to do so, **to the place that the Lord will choose, he** is permitted to volunteer to perform the Temple service, even at times beyond his appointed Levite watch;

Fourth aliya

7 **he shall serve in the name of the Lord his God, like all his brethren the Levites, who stand there before the Lord,** on their assigned watch.

Grain

Grapes for wine

Olives for oil

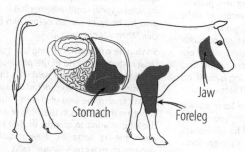

כ לְבִלְתִּי רוּם־לְבָבוֹ מֵאֶחָיו וּלְבִלְתִּי סוּר מִן־הַמִּצְוָה יָמִין וּשְׂמֹאול לְמַעַן יַאֲרִיךְ
יח א יָמִים עַל־מַמְלַכְתּוֹ הוּא וּבָנָיו בְּקֶרֶב יִשְׂרָאֵל׃ לֹא־יִהְיֶה לַכֹּהֲנִים שלישי
ב הַלְוִיִּם כָּל־שֵׁבֶט לֵוִי חֵלֶק וְנַחֲלָה עִם־יִשְׂרָאֵל אִשֵּׁי יְהוָה וְנַחֲלָתוֹ יֹאכֵלוּן׃ וְנַחֲלָה
ג לֹא־יִהְיֶה־לּוֹ בְּקֶרֶב אֶחָיו יְהוָה הוּא נַחֲלָתוֹ כַּאֲשֶׁר דִּבֶּר־לוֹ׃ וְזֶה
יִהְיֶה מִשְׁפַּט הַכֹּהֲנִים מֵאֵת הָעָם מֵאֵת זֹבְחֵי הַזֶּבַח אִם־שׁוֹר אִם־שֶׂה וְנָתַן
ד לַכֹּהֵן הַזְּרֹעַ וְהַלְּחָיַיִם וְהַקֵּבָה׃ רֵאשִׁית דְּגָנְךָ תִּירֹשְׁךָ וְיִצְהָרֶךָ וְרֵאשִׁית גֵּז
ה צֹאנְךָ תִּתֶּן־לוֹ׃ כִּי בוֹ בָּחַר יְהוָה אֱלֹהֶיךָ מִכָּל־שְׁבָטֶיךָ לַעֲמֹד לְשָׁרֵת בְּשֵׁם־
ו יְהוָה הוּא וּבָנָיו כָּל־הַיָּמִים׃ וְכִי־יָבֹא הַלֵּוִי מֵאַחַד שְׁעָרֶיךָ רביעי
מִכָּל־יִשְׂרָאֵל אֲשֶׁר־הוּא גָּר שָׁם וּבָא בְּכָל־אַוַּת נַפְשׁוֹ אֶל־הַמָּקוֹם אֲשֶׁר־יִבְחַר
ז יְהוָה׃ וְשֵׁרֵת בְּשֵׁם יְהוָה אֱלֹהָיו כְּכָל־אֶחָיו הַלְוִיִּם הָעֹמְדִים שָׁם לִפְנֵי יְהוָה׃

רש"י

כ | וּלְבִלְתִּי סוּר מִן הַמִּצְוָה. אֲפִלּוּ מִצְוָה קַלָּה שֶׁל נָבִיא: לְמַעַן יַאֲרִיךְ יָמִים. מִכְּלַל הֵן אַתָּה שׁוֹמֵעַ לָאו, וְכֵן מָצִינוּ בְּשָׁאוּל שֶׁאָמַר לוֹ שְׁמוּאֵל: "שִׁבְעַת יָמִים תּוֹחֵל עַד בּוֹאִי אֵלֶיךָ" לְהַעֲלוֹת הָעֹלָה (שמואל א׳ י, ח), וּכְתִיב: "וַיּוֹחֶל שִׁבְעַת יָמִים" (שם יג, ח), וְלֹא שָׁמַר הַבְטָחָתוֹ לִשְׁמֹר כָּל הַיּוֹם, וְלֹא הִסְפִּיק לְהַעֲלוֹת הָעוֹלָה עַד שֶׁבָּא שְׁמוּאֵל וְאָמַר לוֹ: "נִסְכָּלְתָּ לֹא שָׁמַרְתָּ וְגוֹ׳ וְעַתָּה מַמְלַכְתְּךָ לֹא תָקוּם" (שם פסוקים יג-יד), הָא לָמַדְתָּ שֶׁבִּשְׁבִיל מִצְוָה קַלָּה שֶׁל נָבִיא נֶעֱנַשׁ: הוּא וּבָנָיו. מַגִּיד שֶׁאִם בְּנוֹ הָגוּן לְמַלְכוּת הוּא קוֹדֵם לְכָל אָדָם:

פרק יח

א-ב | כָּל שֵׁבֶט לֵוִי. בֵּין תְּמִימִין בֵּין בַּעֲלֵי מוּמִין: חֵלֶק. בַּבִּזָּה: וְנַחֲלָה. בָּאָרֶץ: אִשֵּׁי ה׳. קָדְשֵׁי הַמִּקְדָּשׁ: וְנַחֲלָתוֹ. אֵלּוּ קָדְשֵׁי הַגְּבוּל, תְּרוּמוֹת וּמַעַשְׂרוֹת, אֲבָל "נַחֲלָה" גְּמוּרָה "לֹא יִהְיֶה לּוֹ בְּקֶרֶב אֶחָיו". וּבְסִפְרֵי דָּרְשׁוּ: "וְנַחֲלָה לֹא יִהְיֶה לּוֹ, זוֹ נַחֲלַת אַחֵר. בְּקֶרֶב אֶחָיו, זוֹ נַחֲלַת חֲמִשָּׁה". וְאֵינִי יוֹדֵעַ מַה הִיא. וְנִרְאֶה לִי שֶׁאֶרֶץ כְּנַעַן שֶׁמֵּעֵבֶר הַיַּרְדֵּן וְאֵילָךְ נִקְרֵאת אֶרֶץ חֲמִשָּׁה עֲמָמִים, וְשֶׁל סִיחוֹן וְעוֹג שְׁנֵי עֲמָמִים, אֱמוֹרִי וּכְנַעֲנִי, וְנַחֲלַת אַחֵר לְרַבּוֹת קֵינִי וּקְנִזִּי וְקַדְמוֹנִי. וְכֵן דּוֹרֵשׁ בְּפָרָשַׁת מַתָּנוֹת שֶׁנֶּאֶמְרוּ לְאַהֲרֹן: "עַל כֵּן לֹא הָיָה לְלֵוִי" וְגוֹ׳ (לעיל י, ט), לְהַזְהִיר עַל קֵינִי וּקְנִזִּי וְקַדְמוֹנִי: כַּאֲשֶׁר דִּבֶּר לוֹ. "בְּאַרְצָם לֹא תִנְחָל וְגוֹ׳ אֲנִי חֶלְקְךָ" (במדבר יח, כ):

ג | מֵאֵת הָעָם. וְלֹא מֵאֵת הַכֹּהֲנִים: אִם שׁוֹר אִם שֶׂה. פְּרָט לְחַיָּה: הַזְּרֹעַ. מִן הַפֶּרֶק שֶׁל אַרְכֻּבָּה עַד כַּף שֶׁל יָד שֶׁקּוֹרִין אשפלדו"ן: וְהַלְּחָיַיִם. עִם הַלָּשׁוֹן. דּוֹרְשֵׁי רְשׁוּמוֹת הָיוּ אוֹמְרִים: 'זְרוֹעַ' תַּחַת יָד, שֶׁנֶּאֱמַר: "וַיִּקַּח רֹמַח בְּיָדוֹ" (במדבר כה, ז). 'לְחָיַיִם' תַּחַת תְּפִלָּה, שֶׁנֶּאֱמַר: "וַיַּעֲמֹד פִּינְחָס וַיְפַלֵּל" (תהלים קו, ל). 'וְהַקֵּבָה' תַּחַת "הָאִשָּׁה אֶל קֳבָתָהּ" (במדבר כה, ח):

ד | רֵאשִׁית דְּגָנְךָ. זוֹ תְּרוּמָה, וְלֹא פֵּרַשׁ בָּהּ שִׁעוּר, אֲבָל רַבּוֹתֵינוּ נָתְנוּ בָּהּ שִׁעוּר: עַיִן יָפָה אֶחָד מֵאַרְבָּעִים, עַיִן רָעָה אֶחָד מִשִּׁשִּׁים, בֵּינוֹנִית אֶחָד מֵחֲמִשִּׁים. וְסָמְכוּ עַל הַמִּקְרָא שֶׁלֹּא לִפְחוֹת מֵאֶחָד מִשִּׁשִּׁים, שֶׁנֶּאֱמַר: "וְשִׁשִּׁיתֶם הָאֵיפָה מֵחֹמֶר הַשְּׂעֹרִים" (יחזקאל מה, יג), שִׁשִּׁית הָאֵיפָה חֲצִי סְאָה, כְּשֶׁאַתָּה נוֹתֵן חֲצִי סְאָה לְכוֹר, הֲרֵי אֶחָד מִשִּׁשִּׁים, שֶׁהַכּוֹר שְׁלֹשִׁים סְאִין: וְרֵאשִׁית גֵּז צֹאנְךָ. כְּשֶׁאַתָּה גוֹזֵז צֹאנְךָ בְּכָל שָׁנָה תֵּן מִמֶּנָּה רֵאשִׁית לַכֹּהֵן, וְלֹא פֵּרַשׁ בָּהּ שִׁעוּר. וְרַבּוֹתֵינוּ נָתְנוּ בָּהּ שִׁעוּר – אֶחָד מִשִּׁשִּׁים. וְכַמָּה צֹאן חַיָּבוֹת בְּרֵאשִׁית הַגֵּז? חָמֵשׁ רְחֵלוֹת, שֶׁנֶּאֱמַר: "וְחָמֵשׁ צֹאן עֲשׂוּיוֹת" (שמואל א׳ כה, יח):

ה | לַעֲמֹד לְשָׁרֵת. מִכָּאן שֶׁאֵין שֵׁרוּת אֶלָּא מְעוּמָּד:

ו-ז | וְכִי יָבֹא הַלֵּוִי. יָכוֹל בְּבֶן לֵוִי וַדַּאי הַכָּתוּב מְדַבֵּר? תַּלְמוּד לוֹמַר: "וְשֵׁרֵת", יָצְאוּ לְוִיִּם שֶׁאֵין רְאוּיִין לְשֵׁרוּת: וּבָא בְּכָל אַוַּת נַפְשׁוֹ... וְשֵׁרֵת. לִמֵּד עַל הַכֹּהֵן שֶׁבָּא וּמַקְרִיב

DISCUSSION

17:20 | And not deviate from the commandment right or left: The restrictions and the positive obligations incumbent upon a king are designed to eliminate factors liable to cause him to deviate from the path of the Torah, and to direct him to the will of God. A king requires chariots of war, gold and silver to fund the kingdom, and wives, but he must accumulate them in moderation. The Torah scroll that must be with him at all times serves as a continuous reminder that his authority stems from the Torah, and that he remains subordinate to its laws.

18:6 | And if a Levite shall come from one of your gates: Like the priests, the Levites also served in the Temple, e.g., they stood guard and they sang during the sacrifice of offerings. However, there were too many Levites for them to remain in the Temple precincts on a permanent basis. Instead, they would live in designated cities scattered throughout the country, where they would receive the gifts from their brethren on which their livelihood depended (Numbers 35:1–8).

With all the desire of his heart: The Levites and priests were divided into watches from early times, perhaps already from the days of Moses, and certainly by the era of King David, based on Samuel's prophecy (see *Ta'anit* 27a). Nevertheless, a Levite was permitted to volunteer to serve even at times not designated for his watch turn.

8 When the Levite arrives there, **portion by portion they shall eat.** He is entitled to a portion together with those serving on the official watch, **except for that which was sold by the ancestors.** This is referring to agreements, similar to sales contracts, between the ancestors of the Levite families, by which the share of each watch was determined. A Levite will not receive a portion that has been guaranteed to members of a different watch.[18]

The Prohibition of Sorcery and the Status of the Prophet

DEUTERONOMY 18:9–22

In its discussion of the institutions of the spiritual leadership of the people, the Torah redirects its focus from those who serve God in the Temple, and their rights, to the status of the prophet, who acts as a channel of communication between God and man. First, the Torah rejects the methods by which gentiles sought to know and control the future.

9 **When you come into the land that the Lord your God is giving you, you shall not learn to act in accordance with the abominations of those nations.** The reference here does not necessarily involve the worship of foreign gods or sexual licentiousness. Rather, they are rites that contain an element of magic designed to enable their performers to control the future.[19]

10 **There shall not be found among you any one who passes his son or his daughter through the fire,** a Canaanite ritual that was designed to consecrate the child or to ensure future success;[20] **a sorcerer; a soothsayer** [*me'onen*], one who foresees which seasons [*onot*] are favorable for certain activities,[21] or one who tells the future based on the appearance of clouds, [*ananim*];[22] or **a diviner,** who tries to discern future events by means of signs, similar to the modern practice of reading tea leaves; **or a warlock,** someone who seeks esoteric knowledge through unholy means;

11 **or an enchanter,** who engages in sorcery by gathering animals together; **or a medium,**[D] who seeks to communicate with the dead; **or an oracle,** one who tells the future by means of the bones of the dead.[23] All these are professional sorcerers who seek to contact hidden worlds. The verse adds: **Or a necromancer,** an individual who prays to the dead for their assistance.

12 **For anyone who performs these is an abomination to the Lord, and due to these abominations the Lord your God dispossesses them,** the Canaanites, **from before you.**[D] These are considered abominations not because they are superstitions, but because those who perform them are devoted to forces of evil, destruction, and death.

13 **You,** by contrast, **shall be wholehearted**[24] **with the Lord your God.** Even if you are beset by troubles which lead you to seek reassurances and answers to your questions, do not look for a response by embracing foreign beliefs and strange forms of worship. Rather, you must wholeheartedly follow God alone.

14 **For these nations from whom you are taking possession**
Fifth aliya **heed soothsayers and sorcerers; but you, not so did the Lord your God give to you, and it is** prohibited for you to engage in those practices.

15 Even one who seeks to follow God wholeheartedly, and who does not attempt to ascertain the future through sorcery, will often wonder how to act when confronted with ever-changing circumstances. It is only natural that he will want to amend his way of life when the normative conduct of his life proves unsatisfactory. The Torah provides an answer for this need:[25] **A prophet from your midst, from your brethren,** who will be **like me,** both in that he will be a great man and that his identity and lineage are as widely known as mine,[26] **the Lord your God will establish for you; him you shall heed;**

16 **in accordance with everything that you asked of the Lord your God at Horev on the day of the assembly,** at the revelation on Mount Sinai, **saying: I will not continue to hear the voice of the Lord my God, and I will not see this great fire anymore so that I will not die.** Fearing the direct encounter with God, you petitioned me to mediate between Him and you.[27]

17 **The Lord said to me** in response to your request: **They did well in that which they spoke.**

18 **I will establish a prophet for them from among their brethren, like you, and I will place My words in his mouth, and he will speak to them everything that I will command him.** He will relay the word of God, but he will not function as a constant channel of communication between the people and God, and he will not be a member of your ruling class. Rather, God will endow this individual with prophetic abilities, through which he will convey His instructions when God deems this necessary.

19 God, who chooses and establishes the prophet, continues: **It shall be that the man who will not heed My words that he will speak in My name, I will demand it from him.** I will punish him for his refusal to obey.

חֵלֶק כְּחֵלֶק יֹאכֵלוּ לְבַד מִמְכָּרָיו עַל־הָאָבוֹת: כִּי אַתָּה בָּא אֶל־
הָאָרֶץ אֲשֶׁר־יְהוָה אֱלֹהֶיךָ נֹתֵן לָךְ לֹא־תִלְמַד לַעֲשׂוֹת כְּתוֹעֲבֹת הַגּוֹיִם הָהֵם:
לֹא־יִמָּצֵא בְךָ מַעֲבִיר בְּנוֹ־וּבִתּוֹ בָּאֵשׁ קֹסֵם קְסָמִים מְעוֹנֵן וּמְנַחֵשׁ וּמְכַשֵּׁף: וְחֹבֵר
חָבֶר וְשֹׁאֵל אוֹב וְיִדְּעֹנִי וְדֹרֵשׁ אֶל־הַמֵּתִים: כִּי־תוֹעֲבַת יְהוָה כָּל־עֹשֵׂה אֵלֶּה
וּבִגְלַל הַתּוֹעֵבֹת הָאֵלֶּה יְהוָה אֱלֹהֶיךָ מוֹרִישׁ אוֹתָם מִפָּנֶיךָ: תָּמִים תִּהְיֶה עִם
יְהוָה אֱלֹהֶיךָ: כִּי הַגּוֹיִם הָאֵלֶּה אֲשֶׁר אַתָּה יוֹרֵשׁ אוֹתָם אֶל־מְעֹנְנִים וְאֶל־קֹסְמִים
יִשְׁמָעוּ וְאַתָּה לֹא כֵן נָתַן לְךָ יְהוָה אֱלֹהֶיךָ: נָבִיא מִקִּרְבְּךָ מֵאַחֶיךָ כָּמֹנִי יָקִים לְךָ
יְהוָה אֱלֹהֶיךָ אֵלָיו תִּשְׁמָעוּן: כְּכֹל אֲשֶׁר־שָׁאַלְתָּ מֵעִם יְהוָה אֱלֹהֶיךָ בְּחֹרֵב בְּיוֹם
הַקָּהָל לֵאמֹר לֹא אֹסֵף לִשְׁמֹעַ אֶת־קוֹל יְהוָה אֱלֹהָי וְאֶת־הָאֵשׁ הַגְּדֹלָה הַזֹּאת
לֹא־אֶרְאֶה עוֹד וְלֹא אָמוּת: וַיֹּאמֶר יְהוָה אֵלָי הֵיטִיבוּ אֲשֶׁר דִּבֵּרוּ: נָבִיא אָקִים
לָהֶם מִקֶּרֶב אֲחֵיהֶם כָּמוֹךָ וְנָתַתִּי דְבָרַי בְּפִיו וְדִבֶּר אֲלֵיהֶם אֵת כָּל־אֲשֶׁר אֲצַוֶּנּוּ:
וְהָיָה הָאִישׁ אֲשֶׁר לֹא־יִשְׁמַע אֶל־דְּבָרַי אֲשֶׁר יְדַבֵּר בִּשְׁמִי אָנֹכִי אֶדְרֹשׁ מֵעִמּוֹ:

חמישי

רש"י

קָרְבָּנוֹת נְדָבָתָן אוֹ חוֹבָתָן, וְאָכְלוּ בְּמִשְׁמָר שֶׁאֵינוֹ שֶׁלּוֹ. דָּבָר
אַחֵר, עוֹד לִמֵּד עַל הַכֹּהֲנִים הַבָּאִים לָרֶגֶל שֶׁמַּקְרִיבִין
בַּמִּשְׁמָר וְעוֹבְדִין בַּקָּרְבָּנוֹת הַבָּאוֹת מֵחֲמַת הָרֶגֶל, כְּגוֹן
מוּסְפֵי הָרֶגֶל, וְאַף עַל פִּי שֶׁאֵין הַמִּשְׁמָר שֶׁלָּהֶם:

ח חֵלֶק כְּחֵלֶק יֹאכֵלוּ. מְלַמֵּד שֶׁחוֹלְקִין בָּעוֹרוֹת וּבִבְשַׂר
שְׂעִירֵי חַטָּאוֹת. יָכוֹל אַף בִּדְבָרִים הַבָּאִים שֶׁלֹּא מֵחֲמַת
הָרֶגֶל, כְּגוֹן תְּמִידִין וּמוּסְפֵי שַׁבָּת וּנְדָרִים וּנְדָבוֹת? תַּלְמוּד
לוֹמַר: "לְבַד מִמְכָּרָיו עַל הָאָבוֹת", חוּץ מִמַּה שֶּׁמָּכְרוּ
הָאָבוֹת, בִּימֵי דָּוִד וּשְׁמוּאֵל שֶׁנִּקְבְּעוּ הַמִּשְׁמָרוֹת וּמָכְרוּ
זֶה לָזֶה, טֹל אַתָּה שַׁבַּתְּךָ וַאֲנִי אֶטֹּל שַׁבַּתִּי:

ט לֹא תִלְמַד לַעֲשׂוֹת. אֲבָל אַתָּה לָמֵד לְהָבִין וּלְהוֹרוֹת,
כְּלוֹמַר לְהָבִין מַעֲשֵׂיהֶם כַּמָּה הֵם מְקֻלְקָלִין וּלְהוֹרוֹת
לְבָנֶיךָ לֹא תַעֲשֶׂה כָּךְ וְכָךְ, שֶׁזֶּה הוּא חֹק הַגּוֹיִם:

י מַעֲבִיר בְּנוֹ וּבִתּוֹ בָּאֵשׁ. הִיא עֲבוֹדַת הַמֹּלֶךְ, עוֹשֶׂה
מְדוּרוֹת אֵשׁ מִכָּאן וּמִכָּאן וּמַעֲבִירוֹ בֵּין שְׁתֵּיהֶם: קֹסֵם
קְסָמִים. אֵיזֶהוּ קוֹסֵם? הָאוֹחֵז אֶת מַקְלוֹ וְאוֹמֵר: אִם אֵלֵךְ
אִם לֹא אֵלֵךְ. וְכֵן הוּא אוֹמֵר: "עַמִּי בְּעֵצוֹ יִשְׁאָל וּמַקְלוֹ
יַגִּיד לוֹ" (הושע ד, יב): מְעוֹנֵן. רַבִּי עֲקִיבָא אוֹמֵר: אֵלּוּ נוֹתְנֵי
עוֹנוֹת שֶׁאוֹמְרִים: עוֹנָה פְּלוֹנִית יָפָה לְהַתְחִיל. וַחֲכָמִים
אוֹמְרִים: אֵלּוּ אוֹחֲזֵי הָעֵינַיִם: מְנַחֵשׁ. פִּתּוֹ נָפְלָה מִפִּיו,
צְבִי הִפְסִיקוֹ בַּדֶּרֶךְ, מַקְלוֹ נָפַל מִיָּדוֹ:

יא וְחֹבֵר חָבֶר. שֶׁמְּצָרֵף נָחָשׁ וְעַקְרַבִּים אוֹ שְׁאָר חַיַּת
לְמָקוֹם אֶחָד: וְשֹׁאֵל אוֹב. זֶה מְכַשְּׁפוּת שֶׁשְּׁמוֹ פִּיתוֹם
וּמְדַבֵּר מִשֶּׁחְיוֹ וּמַעֲלֶה אֶת הַמֵּת בְּבֵית הַשֶּׁחִי שֶׁלּוֹ: וְיִדְּעֹנִי.
מַכְנִיס עֶצֶם חַיָּה שֶׁשְּׁמָהּ יַדּוּעַ לְתוֹךְ פִּיו, וּמְדַבֵּר הָעֶצֶם:

עַל יְדֵי מְכַשְּׁפוּת: וְדֹרֵשׁ אֶל הַמֵּתִים. כְּגוֹן הַמַּעֲלֶה בִזְכוּרוֹ
וְהַנִּשְׁאָל בְּגֻלְגֹּלֶת:

יב כָּל עֹשֵׂה אֵלֶּה. "עוֹשֵׂה כָּל אֵלֶּה" לֹא נֶאֱמַר, אֶלָּא "כָּל
עֹשֵׂה אֵלֶּה", אֲפִלּוּ אַחַת מֵהֶן:

יג תָּמִים תִּהְיֶה עִם ה' אֱלֹהֶיךָ. הִתְהַלֵּךְ עִמּוֹ בִּתְמִימוּת
וּתְצַפֶּה לוֹ וְלֹא תַחְקֹר אַחַר הָעֲתִידוֹת, אֶלָּא כָּל מַה שֶּׁיָּבוֹא
עָלֶיךָ קַבֵּל בִּתְמִימוּת, וְאָז תִּהְיֶה עִמּוֹ וּלְחֶלְקוֹ:

יד לֹא כֵן נָתַן לְךָ ה' אֱלֹהֶיךָ. לִשְׁמֹעַ אֶל מְעוֹנְנִים וְאֶל
קוֹסְמִים, שֶׁהֲרֵי הִשְׁרָה שְׁכִינָה עַל הַנְּבִיאִים וְאוּרִים וְתֻמִּים:

טו מִקִּרְבְּךָ מֵאַחֶיךָ כָּמֹנִי. כְּמוֹ שֶׁאֲנִי מִקִּרְבְּךָ מֵאַחֶיךָ
יָקִים לְךָ תַּחְתַּי, וְכֵן מִנָּבִיא לְנָבִיא:

DISCUSSION

18:11 | **Or a medium:** A biblical example of a desperate attempt to turn to these forces is the sad story of King Saul's demise. In his distress, he sought out a woman who was an oracle (I Samuel 28:3–25). He sinned in this manner due to his great anxiety regarding his own future, the future of his family, and that of the nation as a whole. Ultimately, however, he met his demise (see I Chronicles 10:13).

18:12 | **And due to these abominations the Lord your God dispossesses them from before you:** These practices share the common feature of an inquiry into hidden worlds, which was more typical of Canaanites than of Egyptians. The religion of Egypt was organized and institutionalized, whereas the Canaanites were a collection of nations with diverse origins, cultures, languages, beliefs, and modes of worship. Despite the relatively small size of the land of Canaan, there was a greater variety of idol worship there than in the expansive territory of Egypt, whose religion was more systematized and structured.

20 Since a prophet has great influence, the parameters of his prophecy must be defined. **However, the prophet who will speak with intent a matter in My name that I did not command him to speak,**D or even worse, one **who will speak in the name of other gods,** even if he does not preach the worship of idols, but he claims that he was sent by other forces, **that prophet shall die.**

21 **If you say in your heart,**D when a prophet arrives and speaks in the name of God: **How shall we know the matter that the Lord did not speak?** Unlike Levites and priests, whose status is determined by their lineage, one can easily err in the identification of a true prophet. He is not recognizable by any outward characteristics or from his origins, as he is simply one of the people who purports to speak in God's name.

22 **That which a prophet will speak in the name of the Lord, and the matter will not be and will not come to pass, that is the matter that the Lord did not speak.**D The true word of God is clear and perfect; therefore, if a prophet says something that does not occur, you will know that **the prophet spoke with** evil **intent,** and from a desire to sin. **You shall not be daunted by him,** a prophet of that kind.

Cities of Refuge
DEUTERONOMY 19:1–13

Moses already designated three cities on the eastern side of the Jordan River to serve as asylum for unwitting murderers (4:41–43). Those cities are not yet operational. Now he commands those entering Canaan to designate additional cities of refuge west of the Jordan. These laws exemplify the fact that it is the Torah that determines and reshapes ancient societal customs.

19 1 **When the Lord your God shall excise the nations that the Lord your God is giving you their land, and you take possession from them and live in their cities and in their houses,** after the conquest of the land, when you are living there in peace;

2 **you shall separate three cities for you in the midst of your land that the Lord your God is giving you to take possession of it.**

3 Furthermore, **you shall prepare the path for you.** The roads to these cities must be well paved and there must be signs directing toward them;[28] **and you shall divide** the area within **the boundaries of your land that the Lord your God will bequeath to you into three** equal **parts,** so that there will be a comparable distance from the borders to the cities and from one city to the next, **and it shall be for every murderer to flee there.**

4 The punishment for murder is limited, but not negated, by the existence of cities of refuge. **This is the matter of the murderer, who shall flee there and live. He,** the murderer who is protected by a city of refuge, is one **who will kill his neighbor without knowledge,** premeditated intent, **and he does not hate him previously.** Rather, the unfortunate incident was a complete accident. In many cases where someone kills his enemy, even if there is no evidence that he did do so intentionally, presumably, it was not completely unwitting. There is no asylum for a murderer under those circumstances.[29]

DISCUSSION

18:20| **Speak with intent a matter in My name that I did not command him to speak:** A prophet who receives the word of God is liable to be tempted to issue statements in His name that God did not command him to say. Although he is certainly a special individual, as evidenced by the fact that God chose him for this lofty task (see *Nedarim* 38a), this does not give him the right to ascribe to God his own comments or explanations beyond the prophecy that he received. Like his listeners, he may analyze his prophecy in an attempt to understand its meaning, but he may not state in the name of God anything that God did not authorize him to say in His name.

18:21| **And if you say in your heart:** There are only a few instances in which the Torah presents a hypothetical question that one might raise (see, e.g., 7:17; Leviticus 25:20). Here the question is a necessary one: How can a true prophecy be distinguished from a false one?

18:22| **That is the matter that the Lord did not speak:** Part of the difficulty in identifying a true prophet is that God sends him not only to predict the future but also to rebuke the people for their sins. Accordingly, his reproofs are frequently accompanied by threats, but those threats will not necessarily come to pass. If the people obey the word of God that he conveyed, the disasters he prophesied will not occur.

The story of the prophet Jonah exemplifies these ideas. Jonah actually wanted his prophecy to be realized and for the retribution that he predicted to be visited upon the inhabitants of Nineveh. However, the residents of ◄◄

כ אַךְ הַנָּבִיא אֲשֶׁר יָזִיד לְדַבֵּר דָּבָר בִּשְׁמִי אֵת אֲשֶׁר לֹא־צִוִּיתִיו לְדַבֵּר וַאֲשֶׁר יְדַבֵּר
כא בְּשֵׁם אֱלֹהִים אֲחֵרִים וּמֵת הַנָּבִיא הַהוּא׃ וְכִי תֹאמַר בִּלְבָבֶךָ אֵיכָה נֵדַע אֶת־הַדָּבָר
כב אֲשֶׁר לֹא־דִבְּרוֹ יהוה׃ אֲשֶׁר יְדַבֵּר הַנָּבִיא בְּשֵׁם יהוה וְלֹא־יִהְיֶה הַדָּבָר וְלֹא יָבֹא
א הוּא הַדָּבָר אֲשֶׁר לֹא־דִבְּרוֹ יהוה בְּזָדוֹן דִּבְּרוֹ הַנָּבִיא לֹא תָגוּר מִמֶּנּוּ׃ כִּי־
יַכְרִית יהוה אֱלֹהֶיךָ אֶת־הַגּוֹיִם אֲשֶׁר יהוה אֱלֹהֶיךָ נֹתֵן לְךָ אֶת־אַרְצָם וִירִשְׁתָּם
ב וְיָשַׁבְתָּ בְעָרֵיהֶם וּבְבָתֵּיהֶם׃ שָׁלוֹשׁ עָרִים תַּבְדִּיל לָךְ בְּתוֹךְ אַרְצְךָ אֲשֶׁר יהוה
ג אֱלֹהֶיךָ נֹתֵן לְךָ לְרִשְׁתָּהּ׃ תָּכִין לְךָ הַדֶּרֶךְ וְשִׁלַּשְׁתָּ אֶת־גְּבוּל אַרְצְךָ אֲשֶׁר
ד יַנְחִילְךָ יהוה אֱלֹהֶיךָ וְהָיָה לָנוּס שָׁמָּה כָּל־רֹצֵחַ׃ וְזֶה דְּבַר הָרֹצֵחַ אֲשֶׁר־יָנוּס
שָׁמָּה וָחָי אֲשֶׁר יַכֶּה אֶת־רֵעֵהוּ בִּבְלִי־דַעַת וְהוּא לֹא־שֹׂנֵא לוֹ מִתְּמֹל שִׁלְשֹׁם׃

רש״י

כ| **אֲשֶׁר לֹא צִוִּיתִיו לְדַבֵּר.** אֲבָל צִוִּיתִי לַחֲבֵרוֹ: **וַאֲשֶׁר יְדַבֵּר בְּשֵׁם אֱלֹהִים אֲחֵרִים.** אֲפִלּוּ כִּוֵּן אֶת הַהֲלָכָה לֶאֱסֹר אֶת הָאָסוּר וּלְהַתִּיר אֶת הַמֻּתָּר: **וּמֵת.** בְּחֶנֶק. שְׁלֹשָׁה מִיתָתָן בִּידֵי אָדָם: הַמִּתְנַבֵּא מַה שֶּׁלֹּא שָׁמַע, וּמַה שֶּׁלֹּא נֶאֱמַר לוֹ וְנֶאֱמַר לַחֲבֵרוֹ, וְהַמִּתְנַבֵּא בְּשֵׁם עֲבוֹדָה זָרָה. אֲבָל הַכּוֹבֵשׁ אֶת נְבוּאָתוֹ וְהָעוֹבֵר עַל דִּבְרֵי נָבִיא וְהָעוֹבֵר עַל דִּבְרֵי עַצְמוֹ, מִיתָתָן בִּידֵי שָׁמַיִם, שֶׁנֶּאֱמַר: "אָנֹכִי אֶדְרֹשׁ מֵעִמּוֹ" (לעיל פסוק יט):

כא| **וְכִי תֹאמַר בִּלְבָבְךָ.** עֲתִידִין אַתֶּם לוֹמַר, כְּשֶׁיָּבֹא חֲנַנְיָה בֶּן עַזּוּר וּמִתְנַבֵּא: "הִנֵּה כְלֵי בֵית ה' מוּשָׁבִים מִבָּבֶלָה עַתָּה מְהֵרָה" (ירמיה כז, טז), וְיִרְמְיָהוּ עוֹמֵד וְצוֹוֵחַ עַל הָעַמּוּדִים וְעַל הַיָּם וְעַל יֶתֶר הַכֵּלִים שֶׁלֹּא גָלוּ עִם יְכָנְיָה: "בָּבֶלָה יוּבָאוּ" (שם פסוק כב) עִם גָּלוּת צִדְקִיָּהוּ:

כב| **אֲשֶׁר יְדַבֵּר הַנָּבִיא.** וְיֹאמַר: דָּבָר זֶה עָתִיד לָבוֹא עֲלֵיכֶם, וְתִרְאוּ שֶׁלֹּא יָבוֹא, "הוּא הַדָּבָר אֲשֶׁר לֹא דִבְּרוֹ ה'" וַהֲרֹג אוֹתוֹ. וְאִם תֹּאמַר: זוֹ בְּמִתְנַבֵּא עַל הָעֲתִידוֹת, הֲרֵי שֶׁבָּא וְאָמַר עֲשׂוּ כָּךְ וְכָךְ וּמִפִּי הַקָּדוֹשׁ בָּרוּךְ הוּא אֲנִי אוֹמֵר - כְּבָר נִצְטַוּוּ שֶׁאִם בָּא לְהַדִּיחֲךָ מֵאַחַת מִכָּל הַמִּצְוֹת לֹא תִשְׁמַע לוֹ (דברים יג, ד), אֶלָּא אִם כֵּן מֻמְחֶה הוּא לְךָ שֶׁהוּא צַדִּיק גָּמוּר, כְּגוֹן אֵלִיָּהוּ בְּהַר הַכַּרְמֶל שֶׁהִקְרִיב בַּבָּמָה בִּשְׁעַת אִסּוּר הַבָּמוֹת כְּדֵי לִגְדֹּר אֶת יִשְׂרָאֵל, הַכֹּל לְפִי צֹרֶךְ שָׁעָה וּסְיָג הַפִּרְצָה, לְכָךְ נֶאֱמַר: "אֵלָיו תִּשְׁמָעוּן" (לעיל פסוק טו): **לֹא תָגוּר מִמֶּנּוּ.** לֹא תִמְנַע עַצְמְךָ מִלְּלַמֵּד עָלָיו חוֹבָה, וְלֹא תִירָא לֵעָנֵשׁ עָלָיו:

פרק יט

ג| **תָּכִין לְךָ הַדָּרֶךְ.** 'מִקְלָט' 'מִקְלָט' הָיָה כָּתוּב עַל פָּרָשַׁת דְּרָכִים: **וְשִׁלַּשְׁתָּ אֶת גְּבוּל אַרְצְךָ.** שֶׁיְּהֵא מִתְּחִלַּת הַגְּבוּל עַד הָעִיר הָרִאשׁוֹנָה שֶׁל עִיר מִקְלָט כְּשִׁעוּר מַהֲלָךְ שֶׁיֵּשׁ מִמֶּנָּה עַד הַשְּׁנִיָּה, וְכֵן מִשְּׁנִיָּה לַשְּׁלִישִׁית, וְכֵן מִן הַשְּׁלִישִׁית עַד הַגְּבוּל הַשֵּׁנִי שֶׁל אֶרֶץ יִשְׂרָאֵל:

DISCUSSION

Nineveh believed in his prophecy and repented, and therefore his prophecy was not realized (Jonah 3:1–4:3). The Sages explain that Jonah fled from before God for this very reason; he feared his prophecy would be taken seriously, which would render his words an empty threat (Jerusalem Talmud, *Sanhedrin* 11:5). By contrast, a different prophecy of his, in which he predicted a positive outcome, was realized in its entirety (II Kings 14:25).

It can be inferred from here that the truth of a prophecy can be established only in the case of a positive prophecy stated to the public, as then it will be clearly seen whether the prophet overstepped his authority. Furthermore, fundamentally, even a prophet who in other contexts was as a true, outstanding prophet, might betray his loyalty to his mission and his Sender (*Sanhedrin* 89a). Consequently, a prophet can earn the full trust of the people only over a period of time during which all of his good prophecies come to pass, as it is stated with regard to Samuel: And all Israel from Dan to Beersheba knew that Samuel was established to be a prophet of the Lord (I Samuel 3:20; Rambam, *Sefer HaMadda*, *Hilkhot Yesodei HaTorah* 10:2; Rambam's introduction to his Commentary on the Mishna; *Or Hashem*; Abravanel; see also commentary on Jeremiah 23:27, 28:9).

The Bible focuses mainly on the statements of true, righteous prophets, not on false prophets. Nevertheless, it does mention people who sinned by stating prophecies that they were not commanded to say (see I Kings 22; Jeremiah 22:14–18). No written work of false prophets remains (see also commentary on Jeremiah 23:27).

5 The verse provides an example of unwitting murder: **One who will come with his neighbor in the forest to hew trees,**[D] **and his hand will slip from the axe while** he is **chopping the tree, and the blade comes off the wood** handle, or a sliver will be displaced from the tree that is being chopped down due to the force of the axe,[30] **and finds his neighbor, and he dies,** then **he,** the one who caused his death, **shall flee to one of these cities and he shall live.**

Chopping wood

6 **Lest the blood redeemer,**[D] who is typically a relative of the deceased, **pursue the murderer, because his heart is incensed,**[B] in his passion for revenge, **and he will overtake him, because the way** to the city of refuge **is** too **great, and he will smite him mortally. And for him,** the unwitting murderer, **there is no sentence of death,** and he does not deserve this fate, **as he does not hate him,** his victim, **previously,** before the tragic mishap occurred.

7 **Therefore,** in order to prevent the death of an unwitting murderer, **I command you, saying: You shall separate three cities for you,**[D] appropriately distributed across the land and with directions plainly marked on the roads leading to those cities.

8 **When**[31] **the Lord your God will expand**[D] **your border,** beyond the land of Canaan as delineated in Numbers 34:1–12, when it was an Egyptian province, **as He has taken an oath to your forefathers, and He will give you the entire land that He spoke to give to your forefathers.** This is a far more expansive territory, stretching from the river or brook of Egypt, which is the Nile or one of its tributaries, to the Euphrates River, which includes a large portion of the Fertile Crescent;[32]

9 because you will observe this entire commandment to perform it, that I am commanding you today, to love the Lord your God, and to walk in His ways always, then your land shall increase, and there will be a need to add cities for unwitting murders. Therefore, **you shall add for you three more cities,** in the new areas, together **with these three** west of the Jordan River, which are in addition to the three east of the Jordan.

10 In this manner, **innocent blood will be not spilled in the midst of your land that the Lord your God is giving you as an inheritance, and** if it is spilled, then **the blood will be upon you,** the people as a whole. The spilling of blood defiles the land, and therefore action must be taken to forestall potential murders as well as vengeance for those acts by the victims' blood redeemers.

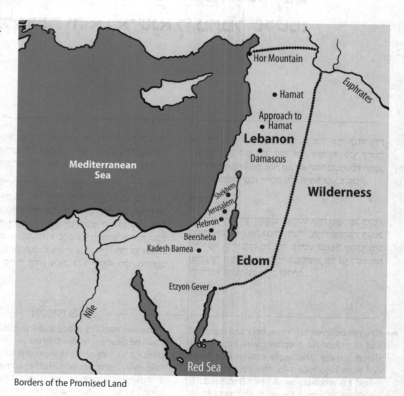

Borders of the Promised Land

BACKGROUND

19:6 | **Because his heart is incensed:** This applies only if the blood redeemer is actually incensed, but not if he has a different motive for killing the murderer (see Radak, II Samuel 14:7).

DISCUSSION

19:5 | **One who will come with his neighbor in the forest to hew trees:** From this example one can infer a general definition of the type of unwitting murderer who is absorbed in a city of refuge. Not everyone who unintentionally causes another's death is included in this category, e.g., it does not apply to one who killed due to circumstances beyond his control.

ה וַאֲשֶׁר יָבֹא אֶת־רֵעֵהוּ בַיַּעַר לַחְטֹב עֵצִים וְנִדְּחָה יָדוֹ בַגַּרְזֶן לִכְרֹת הָעֵץ וְנָשַׁל
הַבַּרְזֶל מִן־הָעֵץ וּמָצָא אֶת־רֵעֵהוּ וָמֵת הוּא יָנוּס אֶל־אַחַת הֶעָרִים־הָאֵלֶּה וָחָי׃
ו פֶּן־יִרְדֹּף גֹּאֵל הַדָּם אַחֲרֵי הָרֹצֵחַ כִּי יֵחַם לְבָבוֹ וְהִשִּׂיגוֹ כִּי־יִרְבֶּה הַדֶּרֶךְ וְהִכָּהוּ
ז נָפֶשׁ וְלוֹ אֵין מִשְׁפַּט־מָוֶת כִּי לֹא־שֹׂנֵא הוּא לוֹ מִתְּמוֹל שִׁלְשׁוֹם׃ עַל־כֵּן אָנֹכִי
ח מְצַוְּךָ לֵאמֹר שָׁלֹשׁ עָרִים תַּבְדִּיל לָךְ׃ וְאִם־יַרְחִיב יהוה אֱלֹהֶיךָ אֶת־גְּבֻלְךָ כַּאֲשֶׁר
ט נִשְׁבַּע לַאֲבֹתֶיךָ וְנָתַן לְךָ אֶת־כָּל־הָאָרֶץ אֲשֶׁר דִּבֶּר לָתֵת לַאֲבֹתֶיךָ׃ כִּי־תִשְׁמֹר
אֶת־כָּל־הַמִּצְוָה הַזֹּאת לַעֲשֹׂתָהּ אֲשֶׁר אָנֹכִי מְצַוְּךָ הַיּוֹם לְאַהֲבָה אֶת־יהוה אֱלֹהֶיךָ
י וְלָלֶכֶת בִּדְרָכָיו כָּל־הַיָּמִים וְיָסַפְתָּ לְךָ עוֹד שָׁלֹשׁ עָרִים עַל הַשָּׁלֹשׁ הָאֵלֶּה׃ וְלֹא
יִשָּׁפֵךְ דָּם נָקִי בְּקֶרֶב אַרְצְךָ אֲשֶׁר יהוה אֱלֹהֶיךָ נֹתֵן לְךָ נַחֲלָה וְהָיָה עָלֶיךָ דָּמִים׃

רש״י

ה | וְנִדְּחָה יָדוֹ. כְּשֶׁבָּא לְהַפִּיל הַגַּרְזֶן עַל הָעֵץ, וְתַרְגּוּמוֹ: "וְתִתְמְרֵיג יְדֵיהּ", לְשׁוֹן וְנִשְׁמְטָה יָדוֹ לְהַפִּיל מַכַּת הַגַּרְזֶן עַל הָעֵץ. "כִּי שָׁמְטוּ הַבָּקָר" (שמואל ב׳ ו, ו) תַּרְגֵּם יוֹנָתָן: "אֲרֵי מַרְגוּהִי תּוֹרַיָּא": וְנָשַׁל הַבַּרְזֶל מִן הָעֵץ. יֵשׁ מֵרַבּוֹתֵינוּ אוֹמְרִים: נִשְׁמַט הַבַּרְזֶל מִקַּתּוֹ, וְיֵשׁ מֵהֶם אוֹמְרִים: שֶׁיָּשַׁל הַבַּרְזֶל לַחֲתִיכָה מִן הָעֵץ הַמִּתְבַּקֵּעַ וְהִיא נִתְּזָה וְהָרְגָה:

ו | פֶּן יִרְדֹּף גֹּאֵל הַדָּם. לְכָךְ אֲנִי אוֹמֵר לְהָכִין לְךָ דֶּרֶךְ וְעָרֵי מִקְלָט רַבִּים:

ח | וְאִם יַרְחִיב. כַּאֲשֶׁר נִשְׁבַּע לָתֵת לְךָ אֶרֶץ קֵינִי וּקְנִזִּי וְקַדְמֹנִי (בראשית טו, יט):

ט | וְיָסַפְתָּ לְךָ עוֹד שָׁלֹשׁ. הֲרֵי תֵּשַׁע: שָׁלֹשׁ שֶׁבְּעֵבֶר הַיַּרְדֵּן וְשָׁלֹשׁ שֶׁבְּאֶרֶץ כְּנַעַן וְשָׁלֹשׁ לֶעָתִיד לָבוֹא:

DISCUSSION

The verse is referring specifically to cases where one's actions verge on criminal negligence. Athough that person is not an intentional murderer, his behavior warrants punishment (see *Makkot* 7a). Therefore, he must flee to a city of refuge and remain confined there for a period of time that might be quite lengthy.

19:6 | **The blood redeemer:** The commandment to designate cities to absorb unwitting murderers already appeared in Numbers (35:9–29), as well as earlier in Deuteronomy (4:41–43), where it is stated that Moses began the task of designating the cities of refuge east of the Jordan River. The numerous repetitions of this matter (see also Joshua 20–21) are not indicative that killing was frequent among the people. Rather, they express the general principle of the Torah's authority over all aspects of life. The Torah does not adopt in full the institution of the blood redeemer, which was common among the surrounding nations. In certain cultures, the blood redeemer was considered above the law. The custom that the blood redeemer is allowed the freedom to act on his own burning sense of vengeance is based on the notion that certain actions lie outside the framework of the law. By contrast, the Torah counters the passion of the blood redeemer by repeatedly insisting on the need to preserve law and order. It does not tolerate modes of behavior outside its jurisdiction. It is for this reason that Josephus calls the Jewish state a divine nomocracy, a government based on the rule of divine law.

19:7 | **You shall separate three cities for you:** Unwitting murderers as well as blood redeemers must be aware of the existence of these cities. The blood redeemer must know that as long as the murderer is in a city of refuge he may not harm him. The murderer must know the cities that will protect him from the blood redeemer. Yet he does not release himself from his responsibility for his deed By fleeing to a city of refuge, he does not absolve himself of responsibility for his action; rather, he enters a legal and judicial framework and he is sentenced to a punishment of partial confinement.

19:8 | **When the Lord your God will expand:** There were indeed periods in the history of the nation when Israel's control extended far beyond its usual borders, e.g., in the days of David and Solomon (II Samuel 8:3; I Kings 5:4), Yorovam II (II Kings 14:25), and even during the reign of Alexander Jannaeus, the Hasmonean king.

11 **But if there will be a man who hates his neighbor, and he ambushed him and rose against him, and smote him mortally and he died and he,** this intentional murderer, **flees to one of these cities** of refuge, where he is legally entitled to temporary asylum until he stands trial;[33]
12 **the elders of his city shall send and take him from there** to face justice, **and will place him into the hand of the blood redeemer** to stand trial as demanded by the victim's relative, who seeks justice on his behalf, **and he,** the murderer, **will die,** once his death sentence has been pronounced.
13 **Your eye shall not pity him,** the murderer;[34] **you shall eliminate the blood of the innocent from Israel, and it will be good for you.**

Prohibition against Moving a Boundary

DEUTERONOMY 19:14

It has been suggested that the reason the prohibition against moving a boundary is juxtaposed with the law of cities of refuge is that the earlier section mentioned the borders of the land. Some commentaries note a causal link between the intentional murderer and this prohibition: Respect for borders between neighbors prevents squabbles that are liable to deteriorate into disputes that can eventually lead to murder.

14 **You shall not move your neighbor's boundary that the pre-**
Sixth aliya **decessors demarcated, in your inheritance that you will inherit, in the land that the Lord your God is giving you to take possession of it.** Do not adjust the established border between your property and that of your neighbor in order to encroach upon his territory and increase your own property.

Commandments Relating to Witnesses

DEUTERONOMY 19:15–21

After explaining in previous sections that the judiciary is the sole authority with the right to impose punishments, to determine the prohibited and the permitted, and to establish people's obligations and rights, the Torah clarifies the laws of the primary evidentiary source upon which the court relies in arriving at its decision, i.e., eyewitness testimony.

15 **One witness shall not stand against a man for any iniquity, or for any sin, in any sin that he may sin,** as it is always possible that the testimony of an individual is distorted by his subjective viewpoint. Instead, **according to two witnesses, or according to three witnesses, a matter shall be established.** Admittedly, the testimony of two or more witnesses does not prove a claim absolutely, and it too must be scrutinized carefully, but the presence of two people serves to move their account from a private experience to the objective realm, where their respective versions can be compared and analyzed.
16 Although the testimony of two witnesses is generally considered reliable, it is no guarantee against deception. **If a corrupt,** lying **witness shall stand** with another witness **against a man to testify a fabrication against him,** to accuse him falsely,
17 **both the men, between whom there is a dispute,** the two litigants, or the two witnesses,[35] **shall stand before the Lord, before the priests and the judges who will be in those days.**
18 **The judges shall inquire** and examine the witnesses **diligently,** to uncover any errors, lies, or conspiracies. **And behold,** as a result of their investigation they discover that **the witness is a false witness; he testified falsehood against his brother.** This is no innocuous lie, as had their incriminating testimony been accepted, an innocent man would have been punished, as he would be required to pay, receive corporal punishment, or even forfeit his life.
19 Consequently, **you shall do to him as he had conspired to do to his brother, and you shall eliminate the evil from your midst.** In this case, the witness is guilty of attempting to harm another person. This is an anomalous case in Torah law, which generally deals with actual damages, not with unsuccessful attempts to cause damage.
20 **The survivors shall hear, and fear, and shall not continue to do like this evil matter in your midst anymore.** The knowledge that a false witness was severely punished for his attempt to harm another will send shockwaves through the populace. They will realize that the submission of testimony is a serious matter which must be undertaken with care, precision, and seriousness.
21 With regard to the punishment of a conspiring witness, although he did not inflict any damage in practice, nevertheless **your eye shall not pity** him, as he intended to cause severe harm. If his testimony was designed to take **a life,** then he shall pay **for** it with **a life,** as he himself shall be killed. If he testified that someone blinded **an eye** of another, he must pay **for** the

יא וְכִי־יִהְיֶה אִישׁ שֹׂנֵא לְרֵעֵהוּ וְאָרַב לוֹ וְקָם עָלָיו וְהִכָּהוּ נֶפֶשׁ וָמֵת וְנָס אֶל־אַחַת

יב הֶעָרִים הָאֵל: וְשָׁלְחוּ זִקְנֵי עִירוֹ וְלָקְחוּ אֹתוֹ מִשָּׁם וְנָתְנוּ אֹתוֹ בְּיַד גֹּאֵל הַדָּם

יג וָמֵת: לֹא־תָחוֹס עֵינְךָ עָלָיו וּבִעַרְתָּ דַם־הַנָּקִי מִיִּשְׂרָאֵל וְטוֹב לָךְ:

לֹא ששי

יד תַשִּׂיג גְּבוּל רֵעֲךָ אֲשֶׁר גָּבְלוּ רִאשֹׁנִים בְּנַחֲלָתְךָ אֲשֶׁר תִּנְחַל בָּאָרֶץ אֲשֶׁר יְהֹוָה אֱלֹהֶיךָ נֹתֵן לְךָ לְרִשְׁתָּהּ:

טו לֹא־יָקוּם עֵד אֶחָד בְּאִישׁ לְכָל־עָו‍ֹן וּלְכָל־חַטָּאת בְּכָל־חֵטְא אֲשֶׁר יֶחֱטָא עַל־פִּי | שְׁנֵי עֵדִים אוֹ עַל־פִּי שְׁלֹשָׁה־

טז עֵדִים יָקוּם דָּבָר: כִּי־יָקוּם עֵד־חָמָס בְּאִישׁ לַעֲנוֹת בּוֹ סָרָה: וְעָמְדוּ שְׁנֵי־הָאֲנָשִׁים אֲשֶׁר־לָהֶם הָרִיב לִפְנֵי יְהֹוָה לִפְנֵי הַכֹּהֲנִים וְהַשֹּׁפְטִים אֲשֶׁר יִהְיוּ בַּיָּמִים הָהֵם:

יח וְדָרְשׁוּ הַשֹּׁפְטִים הֵיטֵב וְהִנֵּה עֵד־שֶׁקֶר הָעֵד שֶׁקֶר עָנָה בְאָחִיו: וַעֲשִׂיתֶם לוֹ

יט כַּאֲשֶׁר זָמַם לַעֲשׂוֹת לְאָחִיו וּבִעַרְתָּ הָרָע מִקִּרְבֶּךָ: וְהַנִּשְׁאָרִים יִשְׁמְעוּ וְיִרָאוּ

כא וְלֹא־יֹסִפוּ לַעֲשׂוֹת עוֹד כַּדָּבָר הָרָע הַזֶּה בְּקִרְבֶּךָ: וְלֹא תָחוֹס עֵינֶךָ נֶפֶשׁ בְּנֶפֶשׁ עַיִן

יא וְכִי־יִהְיֶה אִישׁ שֹׂנֵא לְרֵעֵהוּ. עַל יְדֵי שִׂנְאָתוֹ הוּא בָּא לִידֵי "וְאָרַב לוֹ", מִכָּאן אָמְרוּ: עָבַר אָדָם עַל מִצְוָה קַלָּה סוֹפוֹ לַעֲבֹר עַל מִצְוָה חֲמוּרָה, לְפִי שֶׁעָבַר עַל "לֹא תִשְׂנָא" (ויקרא יט, יז) סוֹפוֹ לָבֹא לִידֵי שְׁפִיכוּת דָּמִים, לְכָךְ נֶאֱמַר: "כִּי יִהְיֶה אִישׁ שֹׂנֵא לְרֵעֵהוּ" וְגוֹ', שֶׁהָיָה לוֹ לִכְתֹּב: "וְכִי יָקוּם אִישׁ וְאָרַב לְרֵעֵהוּ וְהִכָּהוּ נָפֶשׁ":

יג לֹא תָחוֹס עֵינְךָ. שֶׁלֹּא תֹאמַר: הָרִאשׁוֹן כְּבָר נֶהֱרַג, מַה אָנוּ הוֹרְגִים אֶת זֶה, וְנִמְצְאוּ שְׁנֵי יִשְׂרְאֵלִים הֲרוּגִים?

יד לֹא תַסִּיג גְּבוּל. לְשׁוֹן: "נָסֹגוּ אָחוֹר" (ישעיה מב, יז; ירמיה לח, כב), שֶׁמַּחֲזִיר סִימָן חֲלֻקַּת הַקַּרְקַע לְאָחוֹר לְתוֹךְ שְׂדֵה חֲבֵרוֹ לְמַעַן הַרְחִיב אֶת שֶׁלּוֹ. וַהֲלֹא כְבָר נֶאֱמַר: "לֹא תִגְזֹל" (ויקרא יט, יג), מַה תַּלְמוּד לוֹמַר: "לֹא תַסִּיג"? לְמֵד עַל הָעוֹקֵר תְּחוּם חֲבֵרוֹ שֶׁעוֹבֵר בִּשְׁנֵי לָאוִין. יָכוֹל אַף בְּחוּצָה לָאָרֶץ? תַּלְמוּד לוֹמַר: "בְּנַחֲלָתְךָ אֲשֶׁר תִּנְחַל" וְגוֹ', בְּאֶרֶץ יִשְׂרָאֵל עוֹבֵר בִּשְׁנֵי לָאוִין, בְּחוּצָה לָאָרֶץ אֵינוֹ עוֹבֵר אֶלָּא מִשּׁוּם "לֹא תִגְזֹל":

טו עֵד אֶחָד. זֶה בָּנָה אָב, כָּל "עֵד" שֶׁבַּתּוֹרָה שְׁנַיִם, חֶלָּא אִם כֵּן פָּרַט לְךָ בּוֹ "אֶחָד": **לְכָל עָו‍ֹן וּלְכָל חַטָּאת.** לִהְיוֹת חֲבֵרוֹ נֶעֱנָשׁ עַל עֵדוּתוֹ, לֹא עֹנֶשׁ מָמוֹן, חֶלָּא קָם הוּא לִשְׁבוּעָה. אָמַר לַחֲבֵרוֹ: תֵּן לִי מָנֶה שֶׁהִלְוִיתִיךְ, אָמַר לוֹ: אֵין לְךָ בְּיָדִי כְּלוּם, וְעַד אֶחָד מְעִידוֹ שֶׁיֵּשׁ לוֹ, חַיָּב לִשָּׁבַע לוֹ: **עַל פִּי שְׁנֵי עֵדִים.** וְלֹא שֶׁיִּכְתְּבוּ עֵדוּתָם בְּאִגֶּרֶת וְיִשְׁלְחוּ לְבֵית דִּין, וְלֹא שֶׁיַּעֲמֹד תֻּרְגְּמָן בֵּין הָעֵדִים וּבֵין הַדַּיָּנִים:

טז לַעֲנוֹת בּוֹ סָרָה. דָּבָר שֶׁאֵינוֹ, שֶׁהוּסַר הָעֵד הַזֶּה מִכָּל הָעֵדוּת הַזֹּאת. כֵּיצַד? שֶׁאָמְרוּ לָהֶם: וַהֲלֹא עִמָּנוּ הֱיִיתֶם בְּאוֹתוֹ הַיּוֹם בְּמָקוֹם פְּלוֹנִי: **וְעָמְדוּ שְׁנֵי הָאֲנָשִׁים.** בָּעֵדִים הַכָּתוּב מְדַבֵּר, וְלָמַד שֶׁאֵין עֵדוּת בְּנָשִׁים, וְלָמַד שֶׁצְּרִיכִין לְהָעִיד לָעֵדִים עֵדוּתָן מְעֻמָּד: **אֲשֶׁר לָהֶם הָרִיב.** אֵלּוּ בַּעֲלֵי הַדִּין: **לִפְנֵי ה'.** יִהְיֶה דוֹמֶה לָהֶם כְּאִלּוּ עוֹמְדִין לִפְנֵי הַמָּקוֹם, שֶׁנֶּאֱמַר: "בְּקֶרֶב אֱלֹהִים יִשְׁפֹּט" (תהלים פב, א): **אֲשֶׁר יִהְיוּ בַּיָּמִים הָהֵם.** יִפְתָּח בְּדוֹרוֹ כִּשְׁמוּאֵל בְּדוֹרוֹ, צָרִיךְ אַתָּה לִנְהֹג בּוֹ כָּבוֹד:

יח וְהִנֵּה עֵד שֶׁקֶר. כָּל מָקוֹם שֶׁנֶּאֱמַר "עֵד" בִּשְׁנַיִם הַכָּתוּב מְדַבֵּר: **וְדָרְשׁוּ הַשֹּׁפְטִים הֵיטֵב.** עַל פִּי הַמְזִמִּים אוֹתָם, וּבוֹדְקִים וְחוֹקְרִים אֶת הַבָּאִים לַהֲזִמָּם בִּדְרִישָׁה וּבַחֲקִירָה:

יט כַּאֲשֶׁר זָמַם. וְלֹא כַּאֲשֶׁר עָשָׂה, מִכָּאן אָמְרוּ: הָרְגוּ – אֵין נֶהֱרָגִין. מַה כָּאן לוֹמַר: "לְאָחִיו"? לְמֵד עַל זוֹמְמֵי בַת כֹּהֵן נְשׂוּאָה שֶׁאֵינָן בִּשְׂרֵפָה חֶלָּא כְמִיתַת הַבּוֹעֵל שֶׁהוּא בְחֶנֶק, שֶׁנֶּאֱמַר: "בָּאֵשׁ תִּשָּׂרֵף" (ויקרא כא, ט), הִיא וְלֹא בּוֹעֲלָהּ, לְכָךְ נֶאֱמַר כָּאן: "לַאֲחִיו", כַּאֲשֶׁר זָמַם לַעֲשׂוֹת לְאָחִיו וְלֹא כַאֲשֶׁר זָמַם לַעֲשׂוֹת לַאֲחוֹתוֹ. חֶבָל בְּכָל שְׁאָר מִיתוֹת הִשְׁוָה הַכָּתוּב אִשָּׁה לְאִישׁ, וְזוֹמְמֵי אִשָּׁה נֶהֱרָגִין כְּזוֹמְמֵי אִישׁ, כְּגוֹן שֶׁהֵעִידוּהָ שֶׁהָרְגָה אֶת הַנֶּפֶשׁ, שֶׁחִלְּלָה אֶת הַשַּׁבָּת – נֶהֱרָגִין בְּמִיתָתָהּ, שֶׁלֹּא מִעֵט כָּאן אֲחוֹתוֹ חֶלָּא בְּמָקוֹם שֶׁיֵּשׁ לְקַיֵּם בָּהֶן הֲזָמָה בְּמִיתַת הַבּוֹעֵל:

כ יִשְׁמְעוּ וְיִרָאוּ. מִכָּאן שֶׁצְּרִיכִין הַכְרָזָה: אִישׁ פְּלוֹנִי וּפְלוֹנִי נֶהֱרָגִין עַל שֶׁהוּזַמּוּ בְּבֵית דִּין:

כא עַיִן בְּעַיִן. מָמוֹן. וְכֵן: "שֵׁן בְּשֵׁן" וְגוֹ':

---

damages of **an eye,** which he sought to impose upon the accused. Likewise, **a tooth for a tooth, a hand for a hand, a foot for a foot;**[D] the penalty for all those schemes to force someone to pay for damages is the payment of a like sum. Just as the world stands on peace, so too it stands on law,[36] and elimination of evil from the world will enable the world to continue to exist for many years.

Laws Relating to War

DEUTERONOMY 20:1–20

This section, which deals with the laws of war, begins with Israel's pre-battle preparations and lists the categories of men who are exempt from military duty. It continues with a discussion relating to the conduct of war itself, before closing with a command involving the proper treatment of trees during a siege.

20 1 **When you go out to war against your enemies,**[D] **and you shall see horses and chariots,** in an organized camp belonging to **a people more numerous than you, you shall not fear them, as the Lord your God is with you, who took you up from the land of Egypt.** Since God has already performed many signs and miracles and routed your enemies, trust that He will continue to help you.

"Horses and chariots." Detail from the palace of Shalmaneser III

2 **It will be when ou advance to the war,** the battlefield, **the priest,** an especially dignified member of the priesthood appointed specifically for the war preparations, **shall approach and speak to the people.** The Sages call this man the priest anointed for war.[37]

3 **He shall say to them: Hear, Israel.** Listen! **You are advancing today to war against your enemies; let your heart not be faint, do not fear, do not panic, and do not be broken before them,**

4 **for it is the Lord your God who goes with you to wage war for you against your enemies to save you.**

5 After declaring that God is with the soldiers, the military officers shall seek to raise the quality of the military force by calling upon those liable to weaken it to return home. **The officers**[D] **shall speak to the people, saying: Who is the man who built a new house, and did not dedicate it** by dwelling there? **Let him go and return to his house, lest he die in the war and another man dedicate it.** A soldier who is preoccupied by the thought that he might never be privileged to live in his new home will not perform well in the battlefield.

6 **And who is the man who planted a vineyard and did not celebrate it?**[38] During the first three years after the planting of a vineyard, its fruit is forbidden. Only in the fourth year are the grapes consecrated to God, and they may be redeemed and enjoyed by its owner. The officers shall announce that one who did not yet have the opportunity to eat the fruit of his vineyard, **let him go and return to his house, lest he die in the war, and another man will celebrate it.** This is an important celebration.[39] If a man has planted a vineyard and has not yet been able to enjoy it, he might not be focused on the task at hand to fight properly.

7 **And** similarly, **who is the man who betrothed a woman,**[D] **and has not married her? Let him go and return to his house, lest he die in the war, and another man will marry her.**

DISCUSSION

19:21 | **A tooth for a tooth, a hand for a hand, a foot for a foot:** In practice, when witnesses testify falsely that someone inflicted bodily harm upon another, they are not conspiring to have him suffer a similar fate; rather, they seek to have him pay a sum of money (see commentary on Exodus 21:25). Therefore, the punishment of these witnesses is likewise monetary (see *Targum Yonatan*; Rashi; *Bava Kamma* 84a).

20:1 | **When you go out to war against your enemies:** This is apparently not referring to a war of survival or a defensive war; rather, it is referring to what the Sages call an optional war, initiated by Israel for purposes of conquest for economic or political benefit (see *Sota* 44b). Some of the campaigns of David and Saul were of this variety. If so, it is puzzling that Judah the Maccabee permitted his soldiers to choose whether or not to join the battle, in accordance with the ritual described below, as his was certainly not an optional war (Maccabees 1:3). It is possible that Judah's procedure was based on an interpretation that maintains that these verses are referring even to mandatory wars, but it is more likely that he acted beyond the letter of the law.

א בְּעַיִן שֵׁן בְּשֵׁן יָד בְּיָד רֶגֶל בְּרֶגֶל: כִּי־תֵצֵא לַמִּלְחָמָה עַל־אֹיְבֶךָ וְרָאִיתָ סוּס וָרֶכֶב עַם רַב מִמְּךָ לֹא תִירָא מֵהֶם כִּי־יהוה אֱלֹהֶיךָ עִמָּךְ הַמַּעַלְךָ

ב מֵאֶרֶץ מִצְרָיִם: וְהָיָה כְּקָרָבְכֶם אֶל־הַמִּלְחָמָה וְנִגַּשׁ הַכֹּהֵן וְדִבֶּר אֶל־הָעָם:

ג וְאָמַר אֲלֵהֶם שְׁמַע יִשְׂרָאֵל אַתֶּם קְרֵבִים הַיּוֹם לַמִּלְחָמָה עַל־אֹיְבֵיכֶם אַל־

ד יֵרַךְ לְבַבְכֶם אַל־תִּירְאוּ וְאַל־תַּחְפְּזוּ וְאַל־תַּעַרְצוּ מִפְּנֵיהֶם: כִּי יהוה אֱלֹהֵיכֶם

ה הַהֹלֵךְ עִמָּכֶם לְהִלָּחֵם לָכֶם עִם־אֹיְבֵיכֶם לְהוֹשִׁיעַ אֶתְכֶם: וְדִבְּרוּ הַשֹּׁטְרִים אֶל־הָעָם לֵאמֹר מִי־הָאִישׁ אֲשֶׁר בָּנָה בַיִת־חָדָשׁ וְלֹא חֲנָכוֹ יֵלֵךְ וְיָשֹׁב לְבֵיתוֹ

ו פֶּן־יָמוּת בַּמִּלְחָמָה וְאִישׁ אַחֵר יַחְנְכֶנּוּ: וּמִי־הָאִישׁ אֲשֶׁר נָטַע כֶּרֶם וְלֹא חִלְּלוֹ

ז יֵלֵךְ וְיָשֹׁב לְבֵיתוֹ פֶּן־יָמוּת בַּמִּלְחָמָה וְאִישׁ אַחֵר יְחַלְּלֶנּוּ: וּמִי־הָאִישׁ אֲשֶׁר אֵרַשׂ אִשָּׁה וְלֹא לְקָחָהּ יֵלֵךְ וְיָשֹׁב לְבֵיתוֹ פֶּן־יָמוּת בַּמִּלְחָמָה וְאִישׁ אַחֵר יִקָּחֶנָּה:

רש"י

פרק כ

א **כִּי תֵצֵא לַמִּלְחָמָה.** סָמַךְ הַכָּתוּב יְצִיאַת מִלְחָמָה לְכָאן, לוֹמַר לְךָ שֶׁאֵין מְחֻסַּר אֵבֶר יוֹצֵא לַמִּלְחָמָה. דָּבָר אַחֵר, לוֹמַר לְךָ, אִם עָשִׂיתָ מִשְׁפָּט צֶדֶק אַתָּה מֻבְטָח שֶׁאִם תֵּצֵא לַמִּלְחָמָה אַתָּה נוֹצֵחַ, וְכֵן דָּוִד הוּא אוֹמֵר: "עָשִׂיתִי מִשְׁפָּט וָצֶדֶק בַּל תַּנִּיחֵנִי לְעוֹשְׁקָי" (תהלים קיט, קכא): **עַל אֹיְבֶךָ.** יִהְיוּ בְּעֵינֶיךָ כְּאוֹיְבִים, אַל תְּרַחֵם עֲלֵיהֶם כִּי לֹא יְרַחֲמוּ עָלֶיךָ: **סוּס וָרֶכֶב.** בְּעֵינַי כֻּלָּם כְּסוּס אֶחָד, וְכֵן הוּא אוֹמֵר: "וְהִכִּיתָ אֶת מִדְיָן כְּאִישׁ אֶחָד" (שופטים ו, טז), וְכֵן הוּא אוֹמֵר: "כִּי בָא סוּס פַּרְעֹה" (שמות טו, יט): **עַם רַב מִמְּךָ.** בְּעֵינֶיךָ הוּא רַב, אֲבָל בְּעֵינַי אֵינוֹ רַב:

ב **כְּקָרָבְכֶם אֶל הַמִּלְחָמָה.** סָמוּךְ לַצֵּאתְכֶם מִן הַסְּפָר, מִגְּבוּל אַרְצְכֶם: **וְנִגַּשׁ הַכֹּהֵן.** הַמָּשׁוּחַ לְכָךְ, וְהוּא הַנִּקְרָא מְשׁוּחַ מִלְחָמָה: **וְדִבֶּר אֶל הָעָם.** בִּלְשׁוֹן הַקֹּדֶשׁ:

ג **שְׁמַע יִשְׂרָאֵל.** אֲפִלּוּ אֵין בָּכֶם זְכוּת אֶלָּא קְרִיאַת שְׁמַע בִּלְבַד, כְּדַאי אַתֶּם שֶׁיּוֹשִׁיעַ אֶתְכֶם: **עַל אֹיְבֵיכֶם.** אֵין אֵלּוּ חֲלוּ אֲחֵיכֶם, שֶׁאִם תִּפְּלוּ בְּיָדָם אֵינָם מְרַחֲמִים עֲלֵיכֶם, אֵין זוֹ כְּמִלְחֶמֶת יְהוּדָה עִם יִשְׂרָאֵל, שֶׁנֶּאֱמַר: "וַיָּקֻמוּ הָאֲנָשִׁים אֲשֶׁר נִקְּבוּ בְשֵׁמוֹת וַיַּחֲזִיקוּ בַשִּׁבְיָה וְכָל מַעֲרֻמֵּיהֶם הִלְבִּישׁוּ מִן הַשָּׁלָל וַיַּלְבִּשׁוּם וַיַּנְעִלוּם וַיַּאֲכִלוּם וַיַּשְׁקוּם וַיְסֻכוּם וַיְנַהֲלוּם בַּחֲמֹרִים לְכָל כּוֹשֵׁל וַיְבִיאוּם יְרֵחוֹ עִיר הַתְּמָרִים אֵצֶל אֲחֵיהֶם וַיָּשׁוּבוּ שֹׁמְרוֹן" (דברי הימים ב' כח, טו), עַל אֹיְבֵיכֶם אַתֶּם הוֹלְכִים, לְפִיכָךְ הִתְחַזְּקוּ לַמִּלְחָמָה:

ד **אַל יֵרַךְ לְבַבְכֶם אַל תִּירְאוּ וְאַל תַּחְפְּזוּ וְאַל תַּעַרְצוּ.** אַרְבַּע אַזְהָרוֹת, כְּנֶגֶד אַרְבָּעָה דְּבָרִים שֶׁמַּלְכֵי הָאֻמּוֹת עוֹשִׂין: מְגִיפִין בְּתָרֵיסֵיהֶם כְּדֵי לְהַקִּישָׁם זֶה לָזֶה כְּדֵי לְהַשְׁמִיעַ קוֹל שֶׁיַּחְפְּזוּ אֵלּוּ שֶׁכְּנֶגְדָּם וְיָנֻסוּ, וְרוֹמְסִים בְּסוּסֵיהֶם וּמַצְהִילִין אוֹתָם לְהַשְׁמִיעַ קוֹל שַׁעֲטַת פַּרְסוֹת סוּסֵיהֶם, וְצוֹוְחִין בְּקוֹלָם, וְתוֹקְעִין בַּשּׁוֹפָרוֹת וּמִינֵי מַשְׁמִיעֵי קוֹל. "אַל יֵרַךְ לְבַבְכֶם", מִצָּהֳלַת סוּסִים. "אַל תִּירְאוּ", מֵהֲגָפַת הַתְּרִיסִין. "וְאַל תַּחְפְּזוּ", מִקּוֹל הַקְּרָנוֹת. "וְאַל תַּעַרְצוּ", מִקּוֹל הַצְּוָחָה:

ד **כִּי ה' אֱלֹהֵיכֶם וְגוֹ'.** הֵם בָּאִים בְּנִצְחוֹנוֹ שֶׁל בָּשָׂר וָדָם, וְאַתֶּם בָּאִים בְּנִצְחוֹנוֹ שֶׁל מָקוֹם. פְּלִשְׁתִּים בָּאוּ בְּנִצְחוֹנוֹ שֶׁל גָּלְיָת, מֶה הָיָה סוֹפוֹ? נָפַל וְנָפְלוּ עִמּוֹ: **הַהֹלֵךְ עִמָּכֶם.** זֶה מַחֲנֵה הָאָרוֹן:

ה **וְלֹא חֲנָכוֹ.** וְלֹא דָּר בּוֹ. "חֲנֻכָּה" לְשׁוֹן הַתְחָלָה: **וְאִישׁ אַחֵר יַחְנְכֶנּוּ.** וְדָבָר שֶׁל עָגְמַת נֶפֶשׁ הוּא זֶה:

ו **וְלֹא חִלְּלוֹ.** לֹא פְּדָאוֹ בַּשָּׁנָה הָרְבִיעִית, שֶׁהַפֵּרוֹת טְעוּנִים לְהֵאָכֵל בִּירוּשָׁלַיִם, אוֹ לְחַלְּלָם בְּדָמִים וְלֶאֱכֹל הַדָּמִים בִּירוּשָׁלַיִם:

ז-ח **וְיָסְפוּ הַשֹּׁטְרִים.** לָמָּה נֶאֱמַר כָּאן "וְיָסְפוּ"? מוֹסִיפִין זֶה עַל דִּבְרֵי הַכֹּהֵן, כֵּהֵן מְדַבֵּר וּמַשְׁמִיעַ מִן "שְׁמַע יִשְׂרָאֵל" עַד "לְהוֹשִׁיעַ אֶתְכֶם", וּמִי הָאִישׁ", וְשׁוֹטֵר מַשְׁמִיעַ וְשׁוֹטֵר מְדַבֵּר

DISCUSSION

20:5 | The officers [shoterim]: It is likely that the officers mentioned here were high-ranking officials who were not personally involved in maintaining public order, like modern-day police officers, who are also called *shoterim*. This is similar to the role of the constable in several countries, which was originally a title given to a high-ranking minister of the king, appointed as the director of law enforcement. A similar conclusion can be inferred from the only verse in the Bible that mentions a *shoter* by name (II Chronicles 26:11).

20:7 | Who betrothed a woman: This verse is referring only to a betrothed man. Later, the Torah will state explicitly that one who actually married a woman is completely exempt from military duty during the first year of marriage. He does not go out to battle at all; rather, "he shall be free for his house one year, and shall cause his wife, whom he took, to rejoice" (24:5).

8 **The officers shall continue to speak**[D] **to the people, and they shall say: Who is the man who is fearful and fainthearted,** and not brave enough to face war? **Let him go and return to his house, that he shall not melt his brethren's heart like his heart.** Soldiers who do not wish to fight are usually the first to flee or shirk difficult challenges, and they are liable to dishearten others.

9 **It shall be when the officers conclude to speak to the people,** and a select group of highly motivated fighters remain, **and they appoint the captains of the guard at the head of the people.** The army of Israel comprised mainly reservists, and even the upper echelon of command was appointed during the preparations for war.[40]

10 **When you approach a city to wage war against it,**[D] first of all
Seventh aliya **you shall call to it for peace.** You shall offer a peace treaty to its residents.

11 **It shall be, if it responds peace to you,** by accepting your offer, **and it opens** its gates **for you,** you shall agree to terms with it. However, this is not a peace between equals, as **the entire people that is found in it shall be for tribute for you, and they shall serve you.** The city will become a conquered territory subject to the authority of Israelite rule.

12 **If it will not make peace with you, but will wage war against you and you besiege it,**

13 **the Lord your God will deliver it into your hand, and you shall smite all its males by sword.** You are permitted to kill all its male inhabitants, as they are the enemy.

14 **Only the women, and the** young **children, and the animals, and everything that is in the city, all its spoils, you shall loot for you.** Since the women and children are considered plunder, not the enemy, you may take them captive rather than killing them. **And you shall consume the spoils of your enemies that the Lord your God has given you.**

15 **So you shall do to all the cities that are very far from you, that are not from the cities of these nations** in the boundaries of the land that you are about to enter;

16 **however, from the cities of these peoples that the Lord your God is giving you as inheritance, you shall not keep any person alive.** The law with regard to cities in Canaan is more severe than that of distant cities. If a city that is far from your land makes peace with you, accepting your terms, it will remain intact. Even if it refuses to accept your stipulations and attacks you, only its males are killed.

17 **Rather, you shall destroy them,** those cities in Canaan, and kill all their inhabitants: **The Hitites, and the Emorites, the Canaanites, and the Perizites, the Hivites, and the Yevusites, as the Lord your God has commanded you.** The reason for the annihilation of the inhabitants of those cities is neither racial nor nationalistic. Elsewhere the Torah cites security justifications, the concern that the foreigners who remain in Canaan might pose a threat to the lives of Israelites.[41] Here the Torah states a different reason:

18 **So that they will not teach you to do like all their abominations that they performed with their gods, and you will sin against the Lord your God.** You might be adversely influenced by their culture and religion.

19 **When you will besiege**[D] **a city many days to wage war against it to seize it,** you might think of chopping down the trees near the city to take the wood as plunder, or in order to construct a wall or fortification, or alternatively, to prevent the inhabitants of the city from enjoying the fruit, or to prevent them from using the trees as cover to escape the city to rearm. Nevertheless, **you shall not destroy its** fruit **trees to wield an axe against them, as from them,** the trees in your vicinity, **you will eat, and** therefore **you shall not cut them down.**

DISCUSSION

20:8 | **The officers shall continue to speak:** Although it might appear that the release of the fainthearted from battle is a separate stage in the officers' speech, the Sages have a tradition that all these announcements were issued together. Not many cowards have the courage, when standing in formation with the entire army, to step back from their line and effectively declare that they are returning home motivated by fear. It would be easier for them to avoid that shame by leaving together with the group of men who built a house, planted a vineyard, or betrothed a woman (*Sota* 44a).

20:10 | **When you approach a city to make war against it:** It is clear from verse 15 that the reference is to an attack against a city beyond the borders of the land, in the course of an optional war (see *Sifrei, Devarim* 199; Rashi). However, there is an opinion that maintains that even during a mandatory war for the conquest of the land of Canaan one must first offer peace, and war is waged only if that proposal is rejected (see Jerusalem Talmud, *Shevi'it* 6:1; Rambam, *Sefer Shofetim, Hilkhot Melakhim* 6:4–5, and Ra'avad ad loc.; Ramban; see also the sources cited in the commentary on Joshua 9:5).

20:19 | **When you will besiege:** This law teaches that even during the chaos of war, not everything is permitted. The prohibition against destroying fruit trees during a siege serves as a reminder that despite the violence and chaos of wartime, one must take care to avoid gratuitous waste and destruction.

ח וְיָסְפוּ הַשֹּׁטְרִים לְדַבֵּר אֶל־הָעָם וְאָמְרוּ מִי־הָאִישׁ הַיָּרֵא וְרַךְ הַלֵּבָב יֵלֵךְ וְיָשֹׁב

ט לְבֵיתוֹ וְלֹא יִמַּס אֶת־לְבַב אֶחָיו כִּלְבָבוֹ: וְהָיָה כְּכַלֹּת הַשֹּׁטְרִים לְדַבֵּר אֶל־

י הָעָם וּפָקְדוּ שָׂרֵי צְבָאוֹת בְּרֹאשׁ הָעָם: כִּי־תִקְרַב אֶל־עִיר   טז שביעי

יא לְהִלָּחֵם עָלֶיהָ וְקָרָאתָ אֵלֶיהָ לְשָׁלוֹם: וְהָיָה אִם־שָׁלוֹם תַּעַנְךָ וּפָתְחָה לָךְ וְהָיָה

יב כָּל־הָעָם הַנִּמְצָא־בָהּ יִהְיוּ לְךָ לָמַס וַעֲבָדוּךָ: וְאִם־לֹא תַשְׁלִים עִמָּךְ וְעָשְׂתָה

יג עִמְּךָ מִלְחָמָה וְצַרְתָּ עָלֶיהָ: וּנְתָנָהּ יְהוָה אֱלֹהֶיךָ בְּיָדֶךָ וְהִכִּיתָ אֶת־כָּל־זְכוּרָהּ

יד לְפִי־חָרֶב: רַק הַנָּשִׁים וְהַטַּף וְהַבְּהֵמָה וְכֹל אֲשֶׁר יִהְיֶה בָעִיר כָּל־שְׁלָלָהּ תָּבֹז

טו לָךְ וְאָכַלְתָּ אֶת־שְׁלַל אֹיְבֶיךָ אֲשֶׁר נָתַן יְהוָה אֱלֹהֶיךָ לָךְ: כֵּן תַּעֲשֶׂה לְכָל־

טז הֶעָרִים הָרְחֹקֹת מִמְּךָ מְאֹד אֲשֶׁר לֹא־מֵעָרֵי הַגּוֹיִם־הָאֵלֶּה הֵנָּה: רַק מֵעָרֵי

יז הָעַמִּים הָאֵלֶּה אֲשֶׁר יְהוָה אֱלֹהֶיךָ נֹתֵן לְךָ נַחֲלָה לֹא תְחַיֶּה כָּל־נְשָׁמָה: כִּי־

הַחֲרֵם תַּחֲרִימֵם הַחִתִּי וְהָאֱמֹרִי הַכְּנַעֲנִי וְהַפְּרִזִּי הַחִוִּי וְהַיְבוּסִי כַּאֲשֶׁר צִוְּךָ

יח יְהוָה אֱלֹהֶיךָ: לְמַעַן אֲשֶׁר לֹא־יְלַמְּדוּ אֶתְכֶם לַעֲשׂוֹת כְּכֹל תּוֹעֲבֹתָם אֲשֶׁר

יט עָשׂוּ לֵאלֹהֵיהֶם וַחֲטָאתֶם לַיהוָה אֱלֹהֵיכֶם: כִּי־תָצוּר אֶל־עִיר

יָמִים רַבִּים לְהִלָּחֵם עָלֶיהָ לְתָפְשָׂהּ לֹא־תַשְׁחִית אֶת־עֵצָהּ לִנְדֹּחַ עָלָיו גַּרְזֶן

<hr/>

רש״י

וְשׁוֹטֵר מַשְׁמִיעַ, וְזֶה שׁוֹטֵר מְדַבֵּר וְשׁוֹטֵר מַשְׁמִיעַ: **הַיָּרֵא וְרַךְ הַלֵּבָב.** רַבִּי עֲקִיבָא אוֹמֵר: כְּמַשְׁמָעוֹ, שֶׁאֵינוֹ יָכוֹל לַעֲמֹד בְּקִשְׁרֵי הַמִּלְחָמָה וְלִרְאוֹת חֶרֶב שְׁלוּפָה. רַבִּי יוֹסֵי הַגְּלִילִי אוֹמֵר: הַיָּרֵא מֵעֲבֵרוֹת שֶׁבְּיָדוֹ, וּלְכָךְ תָּלְתָה לוֹ תּוֹרָה לַחֲזֹר עַל בַּיִת וְכֶרֶם וְאִשָּׁה, לְכַסּוֹת עַל הַחוֹזְרִים בִּשְׁבִיל עֲבֵרוֹת שֶׁבְּיָדָם, שֶׁלֹּא יָבִינוּ שֶׁהֵם בַּעֲלֵי עֲבֵרָה, וְהָרוֹאֵהוּ חוֹזֵר אוֹמֵר: שֶׁמָּא בָּנָה בַּיִת אוֹ נָטַע כֶּרֶם אוֹ אֵרַשׂ אִשָּׁה: **פֶּן יָמוּת בַּמִּלְחָמָה.** יָשׁוּב פֶּן יָמוּת, שֶׁאִם לֹא יִשְׁמַע לְדִבְרֵי הַכֹּהֵן כְּדַאי הוּא שֶׁיָּמוּת:

ט | **שָׂרֵי צְבָאוֹת.** שֶׁמַּעֲמִידִין זַקָּפִין מִלִּפְנֵיהֶם וּמֵאַחֲרֵיהֶם וְכַשִּׁילִין שֶׁל בַּרְזֶל בִּידֵיהֶם, וְכָל מִי שֶׁרוֹצֶה לַחֲזֹר הָרְשׁוּת בְּיָדוֹ לְקַפֵּחַ אֶת שׁוֹקָיו. זַקָּפִין - בְּנֵי אָדָם עוֹמְדִין בִּקְצֵה הַמַּעֲרָכָה לִזְקֹף אֶת הַנּוֹפְלִים וּלְחַזְּקָם

בִּדְבָרִים, שׁוּבוּ אֶל הַמִּלְחָמָה וְלֹא תָנוּסוּ, שֶׁתְּחִלַּת נְפִילָה נִיסָה:

י | **כִּי תִקְרַב אֶל עִיר.** בְּמִלְחֶמֶת הָרְשׁוּת הַכָּתוּב מְדַבֵּר, כְּמוֹ שֶׁמְּפֹרָשׁ בָּעִנְיָן: "כֵּן תַּעֲשֶׂה לְכָל הֶעָרִים הָרְחֹקֹת" וְגוֹ' (לְהַלָּן פָּסוּק טו):

יא | **כָּל הָעָם הַנִּמְצָא בָהּ.** אֲפִלּוּ אַתָּה מוֹצֵא בָהּ מִשִּׁבְעָה עֲמָמִין שֶׁנִּצְטַוֵּיתָ לְהַחֲרִימָם, אַתָּה רַשַּׁאי לְקַיְּמָם: **לָמַס וַעֲבָדוּךָ.** עַד שֶׁיְּקַבְּלוּ עֲלֵיהֶם מִסִּים וְשִׁעְבּוּד:

יב | **וְאִם לֹא תַשְׁלִים עִמְּךָ וְעָשְׂתָה עִמְּךָ מִלְחָמָה.** הַכָּתוּב מְבַשֶּׂרְךָ שֶׁאִם לֹא תַשְׁלִים עִמְּךָ, סוֹפָהּ לְהִלָּחֵם בְּךָ אִם תַּנִּיחֶנָּה וְתֵלֵךְ. **וְצַרְתָּ עָלֶיהָ.** אַף לְהַרְעִיבָהּ וּלְהַצְמִיאָהּ וְלַהֲמִיתָהּ מִיתַת תַּחֲלוּאִים:

יג | **וּנְתָנָהּ ה' אֱלֹהֶיךָ בְּיָדֶךָ.** אִם עָשִׂיתָ כָּל הָאָמוּר בָּעִנְיָן, סוֹף שֶׁה' נוֹתְנָהּ בְּיָדֶךָ:

יד | **וְהַטַּף.** אַף טַף שֶׁל זְכָרִים. וּמָה אֲנִי מְקַיֵּם: "וְהִכִּיתָ אֶת כָּל זְכוּרָהּ"? בַּגְּדוֹלִים:

יז | **כַּאֲשֶׁר צִוְּךָ.** לְרַבּוֹת אֶת הַגִּרְגָּשִׁי:

יח | **לְמַעַן אֲשֶׁר לֹא יְלַמְּדוּ.** הָא אִם עָשׂוּ תְּשׁוּבָה וּמִתְגַּיְּרִין, אַתָּה רַשַּׁאי לְקַבְּלָם:

יט | **יָמִים.** שְׁנַיִם. **רַבִּים.** שְׁלֹשָׁה. מִכָּאן אָמְרוּ: אֵין צָרִין עַל עֲיָרוֹת שֶׁל גּוֹי פָּחוֹת מִשְּׁלֹשָׁה יָמִים קֹדֶם לַשַּׁבָּת. וְלִמֵּד שֶׁפּוֹתֵחַ בְּשָׁלוֹם שְׁנַיִם אוֹ שְׁלֹשָׁה יָמִים, וְכֵן הוּא אוֹמֵר: "וַיֵּשֶׁב דָּוִד בְּצִקְלַג יָמִים שְׁנָיִם" (שְׁמוּאֵל ב' א, א). וּבְמִלְחֶמֶת

1061

For is the tree of the field a man, to retreat from you during the siege?[D] Is the tree a person, that you are waging war against it?[42] Your war should be directed against people, not nature.

20 **Only a tree that you will know that it is not a food tree, it you may destroy and cut down.** It is sometimes difficult to distinguish between a fruit-bearing tree whose fruit has fallen off or has yet to sprout, and a tree that does not bear fruit. Consequently, the Torah stresses that one may destroy only those trees that he knows for certain are not fruit trees. **And you will build** from the wood of those trees **a siege against the city that makes war with you, until its fall,** meaning until the city's defeat[43] or until its walls fall.[44]

Wood cut from trees

The Beheaded Calf

DEUTERONOMY 21:1–9

After dealing with war waged by the nation, this section addresses the murder of a private individual under unknown circumstances. The Torah teaches that a community may not divest itself of responsibility for one whose life was taken by another, even if it knows nothing of the details of the tragic event.

21 1 **If a dead body will be found in the land that the Lord your God is giving you to take possession of it, fallen in the field, and it is not known who smote him.** It is evident that the man was murdered but no one knows what exactly happened or the identity of the killer.

2 The very fact that a body was discovered in the Land of Israel is a shameful scandal, a sin and a stain upon the people. Consequently, **your elders and your judges,** the foremost leaders of the people, the members of the Great Sanhedrin,[45] **shall go out, and they shall measure** the distance from the body **to the cities that are surrounding the body.**[D]

3 **It shall be** assumed **that the city that is nearest to the body** is the most likely to be the home of the killer, despite the fact that there is no proof to this effect. Therefore, **the elders of that particular city shall take a calf of the herd,** in its first year, or according to a dissenting opinion, in the second year of its life,[46] **with which work was not performed, and which has not drawn a yoke** for plowing or any other labor. This would be a young, small calf, as a yoke would generally be placed on larger calves, if only to accustom them to the burden.[47]

4 **The elders of that city shall take the calf down to a harsh ravine,** hard and stony,[48] or according to some commentaries, a ravine with a strong, constant stream of water,[49] **in which work will not be done and it will not be sown,** because it is too steep and rocky, or because of the water. Although it is near a settled area, the spot itself is desolate. **And they shall behead the calf there in the ravine,**[D] from the nape, unlike the ritual slaughter of an animal, which is performed from the neck.

5 **The priests, sons of Levi, shall approach, as the Lord your God chose them to serve Him and to bless in the name of the Lord, and** in many cases, **by their word shall be every dispute and every affliction.**[D] They too shall participate in the ritual, together with the elders of the city.

6 **And all the elders of that city, who,** after the measurement, **are** found to be **nearest to the body shall wash their hands over the calf that was beheaded in the ravine.**

7 **They shall proclaim and say: Our hands did not shed this**
Maftir **blood, and our eyes did not see.** In action, washing their hands, and in statement, they are declaring, as representatives of their city, that they are in no way responsible for this murder, not even through inaction.[50] They are also saying that they do not know the identity of the guilty party. It is derived from here that if there is a suspect for the murder, then the rituals of the measurement and the beheading of the calf are not performed; rather, the accused is brought to trial.

8 **Atone for Your people Israel, whom You have redeemed, Lord, and do not let there be innocent blood, in the midst**

DISCUSSION

For is the tree of the field a man, to retreat from you during the siege: It is derived from here that there is a general obligation to preserve nature, and not to destroy items unnecessarily (see *Bava Kamma* 91b).

21:2 | And they shall measure to the cities that are surrounding the body: The aim of this ritual of measuring the distance is to send shockwaves throughout all the neighboring cities. According to the tradition of the Sages, the measuring must be performed even when it is obvious which city is the closest (*Sota* 45a).

This shows that the measuring is not designed merely to establish which city is nearest to the corpse. Rather, its ritualistic performance serves to express the idea that all the inhabitants of that region are implicated in the terrible event, and to highlight the great value of every individual, even an unidentified nomad.

כִּי מִמֶּ֣נּוּ תֹאכֵ֔ל וְאֹת֖וֹ לֹ֣א תִכְרֹ֑ת כִּ֤י הָֽאָדָם֙ עֵ֣ץ הַשָּׂדֶ֔ה לָבֹ֥א מִפָּנֶ֖יךָ בַּמָּצֽוֹר:

כ רַ֣ק עֵ֞ץ אֲשֶׁר־תֵּדַ֗ע כִּֽי־לֹא־עֵ֤ץ מַֽאֲכָל֙ ה֔וּא אֹת֥וֹ תַשְׁחִ֖ית וְכָרָ֑תָּ וּבָנִ֣יתָ מָצ֗וֹר עַל־הָעִיר֙ אֲשֶׁר־הִ֨וא עֹשָׂ֧ה עִמְּךָ֛ מִלְחָמָ֖ה עַ֥ד רִדְתָּֽהּ:

א כִּֽי־יִמָּצֵ֣א חָלָ֗ל בָּֽאֲדָמָה֙ אֲשֶׁר֩ יְהֹוָ֨ה אֱלֹהֶ֜יךָ נֹתֵ֤ן לְךָ֙ לְרִשְׁתָּ֔הּ נֹפֵ֖ל בַּשָּׂדֶ֑ה לֹ֥א

ב נוֹדַ֖ע מִ֥י הִכָּֽהוּ: וְיָֽצְא֥וּ זְקֵנֶ֖יךָ וְשֹֽׁפְטֶ֑יךָ וּמָֽדְד֗וּ אֶל־הֶ֣עָרִ֔ים אֲשֶׁ֖ר סְבִיבֹ֥ת הֶֽחָלָֽל:

ג וְהָיָ֣ה הָעִ֔יר הַקְּרֹבָ֖ה אֶל־הֶֽחָלָ֑ל וְלָֽקְח֡וּ זִקְנֵי֩ הָעִ֨יר הַהִ֜וא עֶגְלַ֣ת בָּקָ֗ר אֲשֶׁ֤ר לֹֽא־

ד עֻבַּד֙ בָּ֔הּ אֲשֶׁ֥ר לֹֽא־מָשְׁכָ֖ה בְּעֹֽל: וְהוֹרִ֡דוּ זִקְנֵי֩ הָעִ֨יר הַהִ֤וא אֶת־הָֽעֶגְלָה֙ אֶל־

ה נַ֣חַל אֵיתָ֔ן אֲשֶׁ֛ר לֹֽא־יֵֽעָבֵ֥ד בּ֖וֹ וְלֹ֣א יִזָּרֵ֑עַ וְעָֽרְפוּ־שָׁ֥ם אֶת־הָֽעֶגְלָ֖ה בַּנָּֽחַל: וְנִגְּשׁ֣וּ הַכֹּֽהֲנִים֮ בְּנֵ֣י לֵוִי֒ כִּ֣י בָ֗ם בָּחַ֞ר יְהֹוָ֤ה אֱלֹהֶ֨יךָ֙ לְשָׁ֣רְת֔וֹ וּלְבָרֵ֖ךְ בְּשֵׁ֣ם יְהֹוָ֑ה וְעַל־פִּיהֶ֥ם

ו יִֽהְיֶ֖ה כׇּל־רִ֥יב וְכׇל־נָֽגַע: וְכֹ֗ל זִקְנֵי֙ הָעִ֣יר הַהִ֔וא הַקְּרֹבִ֖ים אֶל־הֶֽחָלָ֑ל יִרְחֲצוּ֙ אֶת־

ז יְדֵיהֶ֔ם עַל־הָֽעֶגְלָ֖ה הָֽעֲרוּפָ֥ה בַנָּֽחַל: וְעָנ֖וּ וְאָֽמְר֑וּ יָדֵ֗ינוּ לֹ֤א שָֽׁפְכוּ֙ אֶת־הַדָּ֣ם הַזֶּ֔ה

ח וְעֵינֵ֖ינוּ לֹ֥א רָאֽוּ: כַּפֵּר֩ לְעַמְּךָ֙ יִשְׂרָאֵ֤ל אֲשֶׁר־פָּדִ֨יתָ֙ יְהֹוָ֔ה וְאַל־תִּתֵּן֙ דָּ֣ם נָקִ֔י בְּקֶ֖רֶב

מפטיר
שָׁפְכוּ

הָֽרְשׁוּת הַכָּתוּב מְדַבֵּר: **כִּי הָֽאָדָם עֵץ הַשָּׂדֶה.** הֲרֵי "כִּי" מְשַׁמֵּשׁ בִּלְשׁוֹן "דִּלְמָא", שֶׁמָּא הָֽאָדָם עֵץ הַשָּׂדֶה לְהִכָּנֵס בְּתוֹךְ הַמָּצוֹר מִפָּנֶיךָ לְהִתְיַסֵּר בְּיִסּוּרֵי רָעָב וְצָמָא כְּאַנְשֵׁי הָעִיר? לָמָּה תַשְׁחִיתֶנּוּ?

כ עַד רִדְתָּהּ. לְשׁוֹן רִדּוּי, שֶׁתְּהֵא כְּפוּפָה לָֽךְ:

פרק כא
ב וְיָֽצְאוּ זְקֵנֶיךָ. מְיֻחָדֶיךָ, סַנְהֶדְרֵי גְדוֹלָה: **וּמָֽדְדוּ.** מִמָּקוֹם שֶׁהֶֽחָלָל שׁוֹכֵב: **אֶל הֶעָרִים אֲשֶׁר סְבִיבֹת הֶֽחָלָל.** לְכָל צַד, לֵידַע אֵיזוֹ קְרוֹבָה:

ד אֶל נַחַל אֵיתָן. קָשֶׁה, שֶׁלֹּֽא נֶעֱבַד: **וְעָֽרְפוּ.** קוֹצֵץ עׇרְפָּהּ בְּקוֹפִיץ. אָמַר הַקָּדוֹשׁ בָּרוּךְ הוּא, תָּבֹא עֶגְלָה בַּת שְׁנָתָהּ

שֶׁלֹּֽא עָשְׂתָה פֵרוֹת, וְתֵעָרֵף בְּמָקוֹם שֶׁאֵינוֹ עוֹשֶׂה פֵרוֹת, לְכַפֵּר עַל הֲרִיגָתוֹ שֶׁל זֶה שֶׁלֹּֽא הִנִּיחוּהוּ לַֽעֲשׂוֹת פֵּרוֹת:

ז יָדֵינוּ לֹא שָׁפְכוּ. וְכִי עׇלְתָה עַל לֵב שֶׁזִּקְנֵי בֵית דִּין שׁוֹפְכֵי דָמִים הֵם? אֶלָּֽא לֹֽא רְאִינוּהוּ וּפְטַרְנוּהוּ בְּלֹֽא מְזוֹנוֹת וּבְלֹֽא לְוָיָה:

ח הַכֹּֽהֲנִים אוֹמְרִים: כַּפֵּר לְעַמְּךָ יִשְׂרָאֵל. וְנִכַּפֵּר לָהֶם הַדָּם. הַכָּתוּב מְבַשְּׂרָם, שֶׁמִּשֶּׁעָשׂוּ כֵּן יְכֻפַּר לָהֶם הֶעָוֹן:

DISCUSSION

21:4 | And they shall behead the calf there in the ravine: The details of this ritual are symbolic of the deceased: The earth from which nothing will grow; the young calf never produced off-spring and never performed labor; and its be-heading from the nape, which, as opposed to ritual slaughter from the neck, does not enable

the animal to be eaten. All these are examples of potential that was not realized, just like the murder victim whose life was cut short (see *Sota* 46a).

21:5 | By their word shall be every dispute and every affliction: From the earliest days of

the Israelite nation, before Torah study was officially organized, the priests had a tradition of scholarship, which continued throughout the generations (see also 17:9, 17:18, 19:17, 31:9, 33:10; Jeremiah 18:18; Ezekiel 7:26, 22:26; Malachi 2:7).

of your people Israel, and the blood will be atoned for them. Elsewhere it is stated: "And the land will not be atoned for the blood that is shed in it, except for through the blood of its shedder."[51] The elders pray to God that since they do not know who the guilty party is, He should atone for the bloodshed despite the fact that they cannot punish the murderer.

9 **You shall eliminate the innocent blood from your midst,**[D] **when you shall do the right in the eyes of the Lord.**

DISCUSSION

21:9 | You shall eliminate the innocent blood from your midst: As stated above, this ritual serves to atone only when nothing is known about the murder and the murderer. However, it does not provide absolution for the murder, nor does it absolve society of the obligation to investigate the matter. On the contrary, society remains responsible even for the unsolved cases, and the ritual is in part a request for forgiveness until the matter is fully clarified. Furthermore, the elaborate rites of the measuring and the beheading of the calf by the elders would certainly generate publicity and general awareness of the incident. This might help shed light on the details of the crime. In any case, where society is able to clarify the truth and punish the criminal, it is obligated to do so (see Rashi; *Sota* 47a).

Parashat
Ki Tetze

A Beautiful Captive Woman
DEUTERONOMY 21:10–14

This section discusses a specific case in the context of war. The Torah's ruling allowing a man to marry a captive woman recognizes the tendency of carnal desires to be unleashed during wartime, a time of chaos and an outbreak of violence, but requires that this tendency be restrained.

10 **When you go out to war,** referring not to the war of conquering the land of Canaan, about which Israel was commanded: "You shall not keep any person alive" (20:16), but to an optional war,[1] **against your enemies, and the Lord your God delivers them into your hand, and you capture its captives.** During biblical times, enemies were taken captive in war, and most of them were sold into slavery.

11 **And you see among the captives a beautiful woman, and you desire her, and you** may **take her for you as a wife.** However, in order to do so, a special procedure must be followed. This is not a standard marriage, as the captive woman cannot refuse. Nevertheless, the required procedure is considerate of the woman.

12 **You shall bring her into your house, and she shall shave her head, and she shall do her nails.** Some Sages understand this to mean that she should grow her nails long, and others explain that she should clip them. According to both opinions, this action symbolizes unsightliness and mourning.[2] Perhaps it depends on the standard in the woman's locale: If they grow long fingernails for beauty, she must clip them, and if they typically keep their fingernails short, she must grow them long.

13 **She shall remove the garment of her captivity,** which might be elegant, as she was taken from her home, **from her, and she shall remain in your house, and she shall lament her father and her mother a month of days.** She should mourn them, as presumably she was taken from a house whose other residents were killed by the soldiers. She may have been married, but her marriage is now void, and she therefore grieves her past.[3] **And** only **thereafter you may consort with her, and engage in intercourse with her,** but not during her period of mourning, as that would be inconsiderate and inappropriate.[4] After this entire process of shaving her head, doing her nails, removing her garment, and continued grieving, perhaps you will no longer be attracted to her. If you still wish to marry her, you may do so, **and she shall be a wife to you.**

14 **It shall be** that **if you do not desire her,** due to her new appearance or for any other reason, **you shall release her on her own,**

ט עַמְּךָ יִשְׂרָאֵל וְנִכַּפֵּר לָהֶם הַדָּם: וְאַתָּה תְּבַעֵר הַדָּם הַנָּקִי מִקִּרְבֶּךָ כִּי־תַעֲשֶׂה
הַיָּשָׁר בְּעֵינֵי יְהוָה:

רש״י

ט| וְאַתָּה תְּבַעֵר. מַגִּיד שֶׁאִם נִמְצָא הַהוֹרֵג אַחַר שֶׁנִּתְעָרְפָה הָעֶגְלָה, הֲרֵי זֶה יֵהָרֵג, וְהוּא ״הַיָּשָׁר בְּעֵינֵי ה׳״:

פרשת

כי תצא

י יא כִּי־תֵצֵא לַמִּלְחָמָה עַל־אֹיְבֶיךָ וּנְתָנוֹ יְהוָה אֱלֹהֶיךָ בְּיָדֶךָ וְשָׁבִיתָ שִׁבְיוֹ: וְרָאִיתָ
יב בַּשִּׁבְיָה אֵשֶׁת יְפַת־תֹּאַר וְחָשַׁקְתָּ בָהּ וְלָקַחְתָּ לְךָ לְאִשָּׁה: וַהֲבֵאתָהּ אֶל־תּוֹךְ
יג בֵּיתֶךָ וְגִלְּחָה אֶת־רֹאשָׁהּ וְעָשְׂתָה אֶת־צִפָּרְנֶיהָ: וְהֵסִירָה אֶת־שִׂמְלַת שִׁבְיָהּ
מֵעָלֶיהָ וְיָשְׁבָה בְּבֵיתֶךָ וּבָכְתָה אֶת־אָבִיהָ וְאֶת־אִמָּהּ יֶרַח יָמִים וְאַחַר כֵּן תָּבוֹא
יד אֵלֶיהָ וּבְעַלְתָּהּ וְהָיְתָה לְךָ לְאִשָּׁה: וְהָיָה אִם־לֹא חָפַצְתָּ בָּהּ וְשִׁלַּחְתָּהּ לְנַפְשָׁהּ

רש״י

י| כִּי תֵצֵא לַמִּלְחָמָה. בְּמִלְחֶמֶת הָרְשׁוּת הַכָּתוּב מְדַבֵּר, שֶׁבְּמִלְחֶמֶת אֶרֶץ יִשְׂרָאֵל אֵין לוֹמַר ״וְשָׁבִיתָ שִׁבְיוֹ״, שֶׁהֲרֵי כְּבָר נֶאֱמַר: ״לֹא תְחַיֶּה כָּל נְשָׁמָה״ (לעיל כ, טז): וְשָׁבִיתָ שִׁבְיוֹ. לְרַבּוֹת כְּנַעֲנִים שֶׁבְּתוֹכָהּ, וְאַף עַל פִּי שֶׁהֵן מִשִּׁבְעָה אֻמּוֹת:

יא| וְלָקַחְתָּ לְךָ לְאִשָּׁה. לֹא דִּבְּרָה תוֹרָה אֶלָּא כְּנֶגֶד יֵצֶר הָרָע, שֶׁאִם אֵין הַקָּדוֹשׁ בָּרוּךְ הוּא מַתִּירָהּ יִשָּׂאֶנָּה בְּאִסּוּר, אֲבָל אִם נְשָׂאָהּ סוֹפוֹ לִהְיוֹת שׂוֹנְאָהּ, שֶׁנֶּאֱמַר אַחֲרָיו: ״כִּי תִהְיֶיןָ לְאִישׁ״ וְגוֹ׳ (להלן פסוק טו), וְסוֹפוֹ לְהוֹלִיד מִמֶּנָּה בֵּן סוֹרֵר וּמוֹרֶה (להלן פסוק יח), לְכָךְ נִסְמְכוּ פָּרָשִׁיּוֹת הַלָּלוּ: אֵשֶׁת. אֲפִלּוּ אֵשֶׁת אִישׁ:

יב| וְעָשְׂתָה אֶת צִפָּרְנֶיהָ. תְּגַדֵּל כְּדֵי שֶׁתִּתְנַוֵּל:

יג| וְהֵסִירָה אֶת שִׂמְלַת שִׁבְיָהּ. לְפִי שֶׁהֵם נָאִים, שֶׁהַגּוֹיִם הָאֲרוּרִים בְּנוֹתֵיהֶם מִתְקַשְּׁטוֹת בַּמִּלְחָמָה בִּשְׁבִיל לְהַזְנוֹת אֲחֵרִים עִמָּהֶם: וְיָשְׁבָה בְּבֵיתֶךָ. בַּבַּיִת שֶׁמִּשְׁתַּמֵּשׁ בּוֹ. נִכְנָס וְנִתְקָל בָּהּ, יוֹצֵא וְנִתְקָל בָּהּ, רוֹאֶה בְּבִכְיָתָהּ רוֹאֶה בְּנִוּוּלָהּ, כְּדֵי שֶׁתִּתְגַּנֶּה עָלָיו: וּבָכְתָה אֶת אָבִיהָ. כָּל כָּךְ לָמָּה? כְּדֵי שֶׁתְּהֵא בַּת יִשְׂרָאֵל שְׂמֵחָה וְזוֹ עֲצֵבָה, בַּת יִשְׂרָאֵל מִתְקַשֶּׁטֶת וְזוֹ מִתְנַוֶּלֶת:

יד| וְהָיָה אִם לֹא חָפַצְתָּ בָּהּ. הַכָּתוּב מְבַשֶּׂרְךָ שֶׁסּוֹפְךָ

and **you shall not sell her for silver,** even though she is a prisoner and her legal status is that of a maidservant. **You shall not enslave her,** or abuse her,[5] **because you afflicted her.** By designating her for marriage, you have effectively offered her a future better than that of a maidservant. Since she has already become accustomed to this elevated status, you lack the moral right to afflict her with more suffering; therefore, you must release her.

The Beloved Son and the Hated Son

DEUTERONOMY 21:15–17

After delineating the laws of a captive woman, the Torah states the laws of inheritance in a case where a man has sons from two wives. The Sages explain homiletically that there is a connection between these two matters, based on circumstantial cause and effect: When a married soldier brings a captive woman into his home as a new wife, a stressful relationship between the two wives is likely to develop, and he may prefer one of his wives over the other.

15 **If a man has two wives, the one beloved, and the** other **one hated.** Clearly, he does not actually hate her, as in that case he would divorce her; rather, it means that she is not as beloved as the other wife is. **And they bear him children, the beloved and the hated, and the firstborn son is of the hated,**

16 **it shall be on the day that he,** the father, **bequeaths to his sons that** property **which he has, he may not prefer the son of the beloved,** who is not the firstborn, **over the son of the hated, the firstborn.**

17 **Rather, he shall acknowledge the firstborn, son of the hated,**[6] **to give him double**[D] **from everything that is found with him.** According to Torah law, when an inheritance is divided among a person's sons, the firstborn receives a double portion. **As he is the first of his potency,**[D] his first child, therefore **his is the right of the firstborn.**

A Defiant and Rebellious Son

DEUTERONOMY 21:18–21

The homiletic interpretation explaining the connection between the issue of a captive woman and the law of a firstborn son from a hated wife, mentioned above, extends to the law of a defiant and rebellious son as well: A family in which the man displays favoritism and hatred toward his wives is liable to produce this type of child. The Torah describes an extreme situation in which parents decide to bring their son to the city elders in order to initiate a process that culminates in the death penalty.

18 **If a man has a defiant and rebellious son,**[D] **who does not heed the voice of his father, or the voice of his mother, and they,** his parents, **chastise [*yisseru*] him, and** nevertheless **he does not heed them.** The Sages interpret the word *yisseru* as referring to the penalty of lashes.[7] Accordingly, the verse means that the son commits many transgressioad loc.ntil eventually he is liable to be flogged, and his parents bring him to court to receive this punishment. Nevertheless, he does not heed them.

19 **His father and his mother shall seize him, and they shall take him out to the elders,** the judges, **of his city, to the gate,** the court, **of his place.**

20 **They shall say to the elders of his city: This son of ours is defiant and rebellious; he does not heed our voice.** Moreover, he is also **a glutton and a drunkard;**[D] his behavior is disgraceful.

21 **All the men of his city shall stone him with stones, and he shall die, and you shall eliminate the evil from your midst.** Once it is clear that he is completely corrupt and incorrigible, he is sentenced to death. **And all Israel shall hear and fear.** The purpose of this law is to send a clear message that crime among youth will not be tolerated and that obedience is essential. Therefore the son receives the death penalty even though his actions in and of themselves do not warrant a punishment so severe.[8]

The Hanging of an Executed Criminal

DEUTERONOMY 21:22–23

The Sages explain the position of this section too, based on circumstantial cause and effect: If a defiant and rebellious son is not punished while he is still young, he is liable to commit more severe crimes as an adult, which will lead to his being executed and hanged.

22 **If there is in a man a sin with a death sentence, and he is put**
Second aliya **to death, you shall hang him on a tree**[D] after his execution.
Hanging is not a method of execution in Torah law.

DISCUSSION

21:17 | **To give him double:** It is unclear whether legal systems prior to the giving of the Torah considered the firstborn as the primary heir, but it was common in legal systems after this period (see commentary on Genesis 25:34).

As he is the first of his potency: The inheritance rights of the firstborn are not dependent on the will of the father. The father may advise his sons with regard to the estate, but it is not in his power to decide what will be done with it. A child's right of inheritance derives from the fact that the estate is the inheritance of

טו וּמָכֹר לֹא־תִמְכְּרֶנָּה בַּכָּסֶף לֹא־תִתְעַמֵּר בָּהּ תַּחַת אֲשֶׁר עִנִּיתָהּ: כִּי־
תִהְיֶיןָ לְאִישׁ שְׁתֵּי נָשִׁים הָאַחַת אֲהוּבָה וְהָאַחַת שְׂנוּאָה וְיָלְדוּ־לוֹ בָנִים

טז הָאֲהוּבָה וְהַשְּׂנוּאָה וְהָיָה הַבֵּן הַבְּכֹר לַשְּׂנִיאָה: וְהָיָה בְּיוֹם הַנְחִילוֹ אֶת־בָּנָיו
אֵת אֲשֶׁר־יִהְיֶה לוֹ לֹא יוּכַל לְבַכֵּר אֶת־בֶּן־הָאֲהוּבָה עַל־פְּנֵי בֶן־הַשְּׂנוּאָה

יז הַבְּכֹר: כִּי אֶת־הַבְּכֹר בֶּן־הַשְּׂנוּאָה יַכִּיר לָתֶת לוֹ פִּי שְׁנַיִם בְּכֹל אֲשֶׁר־יִמָּצֵא
לוֹ כִּי־הוּא רֵאשִׁית אֹנוֹ לוֹ מִשְׁפַּט הַבְּכֹרָה: כִּי־יִהְיֶה לְאִישׁ בֵּן סוֹרֵר

יח וּמוֹרֶה אֵינֶנּוּ שֹׁמֵעַ בְּקוֹל אָבִיו וּבְקוֹל אִמּוֹ וְיִסְּרוּ אֹתוֹ וְלֹא יִשְׁמַע אֲלֵיהֶם:

יט וְתָפְשׂוּ בוֹ אָבִיו וְאִמּוֹ וְהוֹצִיאוּ אֹתוֹ אֶל־זִקְנֵי עִירוֹ וְאֶל־שַׁעַר מְקֹמוֹ: וְאָמְרוּ
אֶל־זִקְנֵי עִירוֹ בְּנֵנוּ זֶה סוֹרֵר וּמֹרֶה אֵינֶנּוּ שֹׁמֵעַ בְּקֹלֵנוּ זוֹלֵל וְסֹבֵא: וּרְגָמֻהוּ

כא כָּל־אַנְשֵׁי עִירוֹ בָאֲבָנִים וָמֵת וּבִעַרְתָּ הָרָע מִקִּרְבֶּךָ וְכָל־יִשְׂרָאֵל יִשְׁמְעוּ

כב וְיִרָאוּ: וְכִי־יִהְיֶה בְאִישׁ חֵטְא מִשְׁפַּט־מָוֶת וְהוּמָת וְתָלִיתָ אֹתוֹ עַל־עֵץ: שני

רש״י

לַשְּׂנִיאָה. לֹא תִתְעַמֵּר בָּהּ. לֹא תִשְׁתַּמֵּשׁ בָּהּ, בִּלְשׁוֹן פַּרְסִי קוֹרִין לַעַבְדוּת וְשִׁמּוּשׁ עִימְרָאָה. מִיסוֹדוֹ שֶׁל רַבִּי מֹשֶׁה הַדַּרְשָׁן לָמַדְתִּי כֵּן.

יז פִּי שְׁנַיִם. כְּנֶגֶד שְׁנֵי אַחִים. מִכָּאן שֶׁאֵין הַבְּכוֹר נוֹטֵל פִּי שְׁנַיִם בָּרָאוּי לָבֹא לַחֵלֶק לְאַחַר מִיתַת הָאָב כְּבַמּוּחְזָק.

יח סוֹרֵר. סָר מִן הַדֶּרֶךְ. וּמוֹרֶה. מְסָרֵב בְּדִבְרֵי אָבִיו, לְשׁוֹן "מַמְרִים" (לעיל ט, ז). וְיִסְּרוּ אֹתוֹ. מַתְרִין בּוֹ בִּפְנֵי שְׁלֹשָׁה וּמַלְקִין אוֹתוֹ. בֵּן סוֹרֵר וּמוֹרֶה אֵינוֹ חַיָּב עַד שֶׁיִּגְנֹב וְיֹאכַל תַּרְטֵימַר בָּשָׂר וְיִשְׁתֶּה חֲצִי לֹג יַיִן, שֶׁנֶּאֱמַר: "זוֹלֵל וְסֹבֵא" (להלן פסוק כ), וְנֶאֱמַר: "אַל תְּהִי בְסֹבְאֵי יָיִן בְּזֹלֲלֵי בָשָׂר לָמוֹ" (משלי כג, כ), וּבֵן סוֹרֵר וּמוֹרֶה נֶהֱרָג עַל שֵׁם סוֹפוֹ, הִגִּיעָה תוֹרָה לְסוֹף דַּעְתּוֹ, סוֹף שֶׁמְּכַלֶּה מָמוֹן אָבִיו וּמְבַקֵּשׁ לִמּוּדוֹ וְאֵינוֹ מוֹצֵא, וְעוֹמֵד בְּפָרָשַׁת דְּרָכִים וּמְלַסְטֵם אֶת הַבְּרִיּוֹת, אָמְרָה תּוֹרָה יָמוּת זַכַּאי וְאַל יָמוּת חַיָּב:

כא וְכָל יִשְׂרָאֵל יִשְׁמְעוּ וְיִרָאוּ. מִכָּאן שֶׁצָּרִיךְ הַכְרָזָה בְּבֵית דִּין: פְּלוֹנִי נִסְקָל עַל שֶׁהָיָה בֶן סוֹרֵר וּמוֹרֶה:

כב וְכִי יִהְיֶה בְאִישׁ חֵטְא מִשְׁפַּט מָוֶת. סְמִיכוּת הַפָּרָשִׁיּוֹת מַגִּיד שֶׁאִם חָסִים עָלָיו אָבִיו וְאִמּוֹ, סוֹף שֶׁיֵּצֵא לְתַרְבּוּת רָעָה וְיַעֲבֹר עֲבֵרוֹת וְיִתְחַיֵּב מִיתָה בְּבֵית דִּין: וְתָלִיתָ אֹתוֹ עַל עֵץ. רַבּוֹתֵינוּ אָמְרוּ: כָּל הַנִּסְקָלִין נִתְלִין, שֶׁנֶּאֱמַר: "כִּי קִלְלַת אֱלֹהִים תָּלוּי", וְהַמְבָרֵךְ ה' בִּסְקִילָה:

DISCUSSION

his forefathers. It is possible for a father to circumvent this law by giving his estate away as a gift, rather than leaving it as an inheritance, but within the framework of inheritance law, he cannot prevent his firstborn son from receiving a double share (see *Bava Batra* 126b).

21:18 | **A defiant and rebellious son:** The Sages interpret several details of this law literally, creating conditions that render implementation impossible. Consequently, some of the Sages claim that there never was nor will there ever be a case that met the conditions (*Sanhedrin* 71a). For example, the Sages derive from the repetitive mention of both the father and mother that if the son rebelled against only one of his parents, or if only one of his parents brought him to court for the legal procedure to be initiated,

the capital punishment is not administered. The Sages also derive from the phrase "he does not heed our voice" that the parents must have the same voice. The age of the son to whom this law applies is also defined very narrowly by the Sages, approximately between the ages of thirteen and thirteen and a half. This is an age when the parents still have the authority to take their son to the elders, but he is already legally accountable for his actions and considered independent in that regard (*Sanhedrin* 68b). Some Sages consider the law of the defiant and rebellious son to be a hypothetical passage that is to be studied but not practiced.

21:20 | **A glutton and a drunkard:** According to the definitions of the Sages, in order for the boy to be deemed a defiant and rebellious son,

the son must steal money from his parents and use it for gluttony and drunkenness. The Sages precisely define the required gluttony and drunkenness (see *Sanhedrin* 71a).

21:22 | **A sin with a death sentence, and he is put to death, you shall hang him on a tree:** Not all those who are executed are then hanged on a tree. According to one opinion, only those executed by stoning, the most severe form of execution, are included. Others maintain that it applies only to transgressions punishable by stoning that are particularly appalling. The Sages determined that this commandment is performed by hanging the body on a tree just before sunset, and immediately removing the body and burying it (see *Sanhedrin* 45b–46a).

23 **His carcass shall not remain overnight upon the tree; rather you shall bury him on that day** on which he was executed, **as one hanged is a curse,** a disgrace, **of God.**[D] Since man was created in the image of God, the existence of a hanging human body is a disgrace to its Creator.[9] Consequently, this law applies not only to an executed Israelite, but also to a gentile who was executed and then hanged.[10] **And you shall not defile your land that the Lord your God is giving you as an inheritance** by leaving a dead body hanging on a tree.

Returning a Lost Item

DEUTERONOMY 22:1–3

The commandment to return another person's lost item, whether one is acquainted with him or not, is an act of uprightness and righteousness that causes one to develop sensitivity toward others and their property, and encourages mutual responsibility and friendship.

22 **1** **You shall not see your brother's ox,** the ox of your fellow Israelite, **or his sheep wandering** alone outside of its proper area, **and disregard them.** Do not say to yourself that since the animals do not belong to you, they need not concern you; rather, **you shall return them to your brother.**
2 In many cases, identifying the owner of the lost animal is quite simple, as he might be an acquaintance, e.g., a neighbor or a worker in a nearby field, and perhaps the finder even recognizes the animal. Furthermore, animals are sometimes marked for identification. However, **if your brother is not near to you, and you do not know him;** the animal is clearly lost but you do not know who the owner is, **you shall gather it into your house, and it shall be with you until your brother seeks it,**[D] until the owner searches for his lost property and reaches you, **and** then **you shall return it to him.**
3 This law applies not only to kosher animals, such as an ox or a sheep. **So you shall do with his donkey,** which is also liable to get lost on its way, **and so you shall do** even **with his** lost **garment,** an inanimate object, **and so you shall do with every lost item of your brother that shall be lost from him, and you found it, you shall not disregard.** You are obligated to take it with you in order to return it to its owner.

Helping Another's Animal

DEUTERONOMY 22:4

This commandment, like the previous one, requires one not to neglect the needs of another person.

4 **You shall not see your brother's donkey or his ox fallen on the road,**[D] buckling under its load, **and disregard them;** rather, **you shall raise it with him.** You must help the owner stand his animal on its feet.

Differentiating between Men's Clothing and Women's Clothing

DEUTERONOMY 22:5

In addition to commandments that emphasize one's involvement in the life of others, there are commandments that stress the distinction between different segments of society. Cross-dressing is prohibited, as it may lead to non-standard relations between the sexes. Moreover, blurring the distinction between male and female is undesirable.

5 **A man's garment,** ornament, or accessory **shall not be on a woman and a man shall not wear a woman's garment,**[D] **as it is an abomination to the Lord your God anyone who does these.** These deviations from the accepted standards of dress contain sexual overtones of licentiousness and a breach of convention.

DISCUSSION

21:23| **As one hanged is a curse of God:** While the commandment of the beheaded calf at the end of the previous parasha is meant to inspire sensitivity to the lives of innocent victims of murder, this commandment emphasizes the dignity of even the criminal who has been sentenced to death. Even he must be treated with dignity as a person who was created in the image of God. This law is one of the group of commandments that express both compassion and unforgiving demands.

22:2| **Until your brother seeks it:** In small villages, news of a found animal would spread quickly, but in larger towns it was the norm throughout history to announce publicly that so-and-so found an ox, a sheep, or any other lost item. However, the found item is not given automatically to any stranger who claims it. In order to prevent error or deception, one who claims that the object belongs to him must prove his claim by citing distinguishing marks on the object. If he is correct, he receives the lost item. Consequently, the commandment to return lost items is limited to cases in which the item has a distinguishing mark that can be cited as proof of ownersHe profferses not have a mark, the finder may keep it, as the owner presumably despairs of recovering it, recognizing that the owner has no way to prove that it is his (see *Bava Metzia*, chap. 2).

22:4| **Fallen on the road:** This can happen due to the weight of the load or the weakness of the animal. Presumably, the owner is also present,

כג לא־תלין נבלתו על־העץ כי־קבור תקברנו ביום ההוא כי־קללת אלהים תלוי
כב א ולא תטמא את־אדמתך אשר יהוה אלהיך נתן לך נחלה: לא־תראה
ב את־שור אחיך או את־שיו נדחים והתעלמת מהם השב תשיבם לאחיך: ואם־
לא קרוב אחיך אליך ולא ידעתו ואספתו אל־תוך ביתך והיה עמך עד דרש
ג אחיך אתו והשבתו לו: וכן תעשה לחמרו וכן תעשה לשמלתו וכן תעשה לכל־
ד אבדת אחיך אשר־תאבד ממנו ומצאתה לא תוכל להתעלם: לא־
תראה את־חמור אחיך או שורו נפלים בדרך והתעלמת מהם הקם תקים
ה עמו: לא־יהיה כלי־גבר על־אשה ולא־ילבש גבר שמלת אשה כי
תועבת יהוה אלהיך כל־עשה אלה:

רש"י

כג| כי קללת אלהים תלוי. זלזולו של מלך הוא, שאדם עשוי בדמות דיוקנו וישראל הם בניו. משל לשני אחים תאומים שהיו דומים זה לזה, אחד נעשה מלך ואחד נתפס לליסטיות ונתלה, כל הרואה אותו אומר: המלך תלוי. כל 'קללה' שבמקרא לשון הקל וזלזול, כמו: "והוא קללני קללה נמרצת" (מלכים א' ב, ח):

פרק כב

א| והתעלמת. כובש עין כאלו אינו רואהו: לא תראה...

והתעלמת. לא תראה אותו שתתעלם ממנו, זהו פשוטו. ורבותינו דרשו: פעמים שאתה מתעלם וכו':

ב| עד דרש אחיך. וכי תעלה על דעתך שיתנהו לו קודם שידרשהו? אלא דרשהו שלא יהא רמאי: והשבתו לו. שתהא בו השבה, שלא יאכל בביתך כדי דמיו ותתבעם ממנו. מכאן אמרו: כל דבר שעושה ואוכל יעשה ויאכל, ושאינו עושה ואוכל ימכר:

ג| לא תוכל להתעלם. לכבוש עינך כאלו אינך רואה אותו:

ד| הקם תקים. זו טעינה, להטעין משאוי שנפל מעליו: עמו. עם בעליו, אבל אם הלך וישב לו ואמר לו: הואיל ועליך מצוה, אם רצית לטעון טעון, פטור:

ה| לא יהיה כלי גבר על אשה. שתהא דומה לאיש כדי שתלך בין האנשים, שאין זו אלא לשם ניאוף: ולא ילבש גבר שמלת אשה. לילך לישב בין הנשים. דבר אחר, שלא יסיר שער הערוה ושער של בית השחי: כי תועבת. לא אסרה תורה אלא לבוש המביא לידי תועבה:

DISCUSSION

→ but it is difficult for him to stand a burdened animal on its feet without assistance. Even if the animal was not injured by its fall, and even if it does not have trouble walking, it may be difficult for it to rise after falling, and it might insist on remaining on the ground even after its load is removed. Therefore, the assistance of another is important.

22:5| **A man's garment shall not be on a woman and a man shall not wear a woman's garment:** According to the Rambam, cross-dressing was an idolatrous ritual (*Sefer HaMitzvot*, negative commandment 39). It undoubtedly had sexual overtones as well. The prohibition refers not only to dress but also to jewelry, and perhaps to hairstyles and conduct as well (Onkelos; *Targum Yonatan*; see *Makkot* 20b). The simple meaning of the verse does not refer to garments worn by both men and women. In addition, there is nothing wrong with a man using an item that belongs to a woman, or vice versa, unless it is an accessory used exclusively by the other gender (see *Nazir* 59a). It should be noted that the verse speaks in general categories; the specific definitions of a man's garment and a woman's garment change from era to era and from society to society. Items that were once worn only by women or only by men can become common to both genders, or vice versa.

Releasing the Mother Bird from the Nest
DEUTERONOMY 22:6–7

This commandment, which begins on a new line in a Torah scroll, an open portion [*parasha petuḥa*], is the first of a series of commandments primarily tied to the establishment of a home, some of which pertain to the preservation of the natural order. In the commandment to release the mother bird from the nest, one is required to respect the motherhood inherent in nature.

6 **If a bird's nest will happen before you on the way, on any tree or on the ground, with fledglings or eggs** in the nest, **and the mother is crouching**^D **on the fledglings or on the eggs,** if you are interested in taking them, **you shall not take the mother** while it is **with the offspring.** The bird's maternal instinct can cause it to remain close to the nest even while it sees danger approaching. It endangers itself in order to protect its fledglings, which facilitates its capture.

7 If you want the fledglings or eggs, **you shall send forth the mother, and the offspring** you may then **take for yourself, so**

that it will be good for you, and you will extend your days. By refraining from exploiting the mother's care for its fledglings, one shows respect for life and motherhood. Therefore, God will repay this act with long life and prosperity.

Bird's nest with eggs inside

Building a Parapet
DEUTERONOMY 22:8

Following a commandment pertaining to the way (verse 6), the Torah proceeds to detail commandments regarding one's home. Like the injunction to release the mother bird, the law of erecting a parapet around one's roof stresses that building and settling the world will not be accompanied by damage and destruction.

8 **If you build a new house, you shall make a parapet for your**
Third **roof,**^D **and you shall not place blood,** cause blood to be spilled,
aliya **in your house, if someone falls from it.** In ancient times, roofs were flat and were utilized as living space.¹¹ Therefore a parapet was necessary to prevent one from falling off the roof.

Diverse Kinds
DEUTERONOMY 22:9–11

The next three laws mandate separating different plant species in the vineyard, among work animals, and in garments. The theme of this prohibition is similar to that of cross-dressing, cited earlier (verse 5).

9 **You shall not sow your vineyard with diverse kinds.** It is prohibited to sow grain seeds in a vineyard, **lest the growth be forbidden** [*tikdash*] literally, become consecrated,¹² **the seed that you will sow and the produce of the vineyard.** Alternatively, the word *tikdash* may be a euphemism for "be impure,"¹³ or it may mean "become mixed."¹⁴ Not only is sowing grain seeds in a vineyard prohibited, but if those seeds are sown, it is prohibited to eat the produce that grows as well as the grapes of the vine. Deriving benefit from them is forbidden as well.¹⁵

10 The Torah states another prohibition similar to that of diverse kinds: **You shall not plow with an ox and a donkey together.** Although plowing with each species individually is permitted, allowing both animals to pull a plow, a carriage, or the like, is prohibited. Since they do not have equal strength, their combination increases the workload of both, causing them unnecessary suffering.¹⁶

Vineyard sown with diverse kinds

Plowing with an ox and a donkey together

וּ כִּי יִקָּרֵא קַן־צִפּוֹר ׀ לְפָנֶיךָ בַּדֶּרֶךְ בְּכָל־עֵץ ׀ אוֹ עַל־הָאָרֶץ אֶפְרֹחִים אוֹ בֵיצִים יז
וְהָאֵם רֹבֶצֶת עַל־הָאֶפְרֹחִים אוֹ עַל־הַבֵּיצִים לֹא־תִקַּח הָאֵם עַל־הַבָּנִים:
ז שַׁלֵּחַ תְּשַׁלַּח אֶת־הָאֵם וְאֶת־הַבָּנִים תִּקַּח־לָךְ לְמַעַן יִיטַב לָךְ וְהַאֲרַכְתָּ
יָמִים: ח כִּי תִבְנֶה בַּיִת חָדָשׁ וְעָשִׂיתָ מַעֲקֶה לְגַגֶּךָ וְלֹא־תָשִׂים דָּמִים שלישי
בְּבֵיתֶךָ כִּי־יִפֹּל הַנֹּפֵל מִמֶּנּוּ: ט לֹא־תִזְרַע כַּרְמְךָ כִּלְאָיִם פֶּן־תִּקְדַּשׁ הַמְלֵאָה הַזֶּרַע
אֲשֶׁר תִּזְרָע וּתְבוּאַת הַכָּרֶם: י לֹא־תַחֲרֹשׁ בְּשׁוֹר־וּבַחֲמֹר יַחְדָּו:

רש"י

ו וְכִי יִקָּרֵא. פְּרָט לִמְזֻמָּן: לֹא תִקַּח הָאֵם. בְּעוֹדָהּ עַל בָּנֶיהָ:

ז לְמַעַן יִיטַב לָךְ וְגוֹ'. אִם מִצְוָה קַלָּה שֶׁאֵין בָּהּ חֶסְרוֹן כִּיס אָמְרָה תּוֹרָה: "לְמַעַן יִיטַב לָךְ וְהַאֲרַכְתָּ יָמִים", קַל וָחֹמֶר לְמַתַּן שְׂכָרָן שֶׁל מִצְווֹת חֲמוּרוֹת:

ח כִּי תִבְנֶה בַּיִת חָדָשׁ. אִם קִיַּמְתָּ מִצְוַת שִׁלּוּחַ הַקֵּן, סוֹפְךָ

לִבְנוֹת בַּיִת חָדָשׁ וּתְקַיֵּם מִצְוַת מַעֲקֶה, שֶׁמִּצְוָה גּוֹרֶרֶת מִצְוָה (אבות ד, ב), וְתַגִּיעַ לְכֶרֶם וְשָׂדֶה וְלִבְגָדִים נָאִים, לְכָךְ נִסְמְכוּ פָּרָשִׁיּוֹת הַלָּלוּ: מַעֲקֶה. גֶּדֶר סָבִיב. וְאוֹנְקְלוֹס תִּרְגֵּם: "תְּיָקָא", כְּגוֹן תִּיק שֶׁמְשַׁמֵּר מַה שֶּׁבְּתוֹכוֹ: כִּי יִפֹּל הַנֹּפֵל. רָאוּי זֶה לִפֹּל, וְאַף עַל פִּי כֵן לֹא תִתְגַּלְגֵּל מִיתָתוֹ עַל יָדְךָ, שֶׁמְּגַלְגְּלִין חוֹבָה עַל יְדֵי חַיָּב:

ט כִּלְאָיִם. חִטָּה וּשְׂעוֹרָה וְחַרְצָן בְּמַפֹּלֶת יָד: פֶּן תִּקְדָּשׁ.

כְּתַרְגּוּמוֹ: "תִּסְתָּאַב", כָּל דָּבָר הַנִּתְעָב עַל הָאָדָם, בֵּין לְשֶׁבַח כְּגוֹן הֶקְדֵּשׁ, בֵּין לִגְנַאי כְּגוֹן אִסּוּר, נוֹפֵל בּוֹ לְשׁוֹן קֹדֶשׁ, כְּמוֹ: "אַל תִּגַּשׁ בִּי כִּי קְדַשְׁתִּיךָ" (ישעיה סה, ה):

י לֹא תַחֲרֹשׁ בְּשׁוֹר וּבַחֲמֹר. הוּא הַדִּין לְכָל שְׁנֵי מִינִים שֶׁבָּעוֹלָם, וְהוּא הַדִּין לְהַנְהִיגָם יַחַד קְשׁוּרִים זוּגִים בְּהוֹלָכַת שׁוּם מַשָּׂא:

DISCUSSION

22:6 | And the mother is crouching: The Torah refers specifically to the mother here, as it is usually the female that hatches the eggs. The Talmud discusses whether this law applies in a case in which a male bird is the one sitting on

the eggs as well, as there are species of birds among which both sexes hatch (*Ḥullin* 140b).

22:8 | A parapet for your roof: The Sages say that the requirement to build a parapet applies even to the flat roof of the Temple (*Sifrei,*

Devarim 229). They also expand the prohibition of "you shall not place blood in your house" to include any action that might endanger others, e.g., keeping a rickety ladder in one's home, or owning a belligerent dog (see *Bava Kamma* 15b).

11 **You shall not wear** fabric that contains **a mixture of fibers** [*sha'atnez*],^D **wool and linen**, woven **together.**

Ritual Fringes
DEUTERONOMY 22:12

The Sages explain the juxtaposition of the commandment of ritual fringes with the prohibition of diverse fibers as indicating that this prohibition applies to all garments other than a garment with ritual fringes on the four corners of the garment.

12 **You shall make for yourself twisted threads on the four corners of your garment, with which you cover** yourself.^D

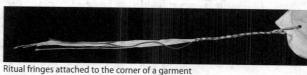

Ritual fringes attached to the corner of a garment

Laws Pertaining to Marriage
DEUTERONOMY 22:13–23:9

This section contains a collection of laws that mainly concern a woman's personal status and her legal relationship with the men in her life: her father, her husband, her fiancé, and a man who engages in sexual intercourse with her.

13 **If a man takes,** marries, **a wife, and consorts with her, and** discovers that **he hates her** for whatever reason.

14 If he wants to harass or perhaps to free himself of his monetary obligation toward her in the case of divorce, **and** therefore, **he proffers a libelous matter against her,**^D and thereby has **disseminated an evil name about her and said: I took this woman, and I approached her, and** although she was supposed to be a virgin, **I did not find signs of her virginity,** claiming thereby that she had engaged in intercourse with another man before the marriage.

15 The husband's claim is challenged in court. Although it cannot be refuted definitively, circumstantial evidence can be brought to indicate that it was false. **The father of the young woman and her mother take and bring the signs of the virginity of the young woman,** the bedsheet upon which the initial act of intercourse between the husband and wife took place, **out to the elders of the city to the** city **gate,** the courthouse. If there are bloodstains on the sheet, this proves that the wife was a virgin.¹⁷ There were eras when newlyweds would use a special bedsheet that could serve as proof of the wife's virginity. In this case, it indeed serves as legal evidence.

16 **The father of the young woman shall say to the elders: I gave my daughter to this man for a wife, and he hated her.**

17 **Behold, he proffered libelous words, saying: I did not find signs of virginity for your daughter, but these are the signs of virginity of my daughter. They shall spread the garment before the elders of the city.**

18 **The elders of that city shall take the man and they shall chastise [*veyisseru*] him.** The Sages interpret the word *yisseru* as referring to administering lashes.¹⁸

19 In addition, **they shall punish him** by imposing a payment of **one hundred shekels of silver,** double the amount that was normally given as a bride price,¹⁹ **and they shall give it to the** **father of the young woman** as compensation, **because he disseminated an evil name about a virgin of Israel. And** furthermore, **she shall be a wife to him; he may not release her all his days.** After a despicable attempt to rid himself of her by endangering her, he may never divorce her at his initiative. If she chooses, she may exercise her right to remain married to him for the rest of their lives, or alternatively, she can demand that he divorce her.²⁰

20 The case discussed until now was one of a slanderous lie, **but** there is another possible outcome: **If this matter was true, and the signs of virginity were not found for the daughter,** and it was proven in court that the bride betrayed her husband and committed adultery during the period between betrothal and marriage,²¹

21 **they shall take the young woman out to the entrance of her father's house, and the people of her city shall stone her with stones and she shall die.** She must be stoned outside the entrance to her father's house **because she performed a despicable act in Israel, to engage in licentiousness in her father's house.** Engaging in sexual relations with another man after her betrothal, even though she was not married yet and still lived in her parents' home, is a serious act of betrayal toward her husband, and it disgraces her family as well. **And you shall eliminate the evil from your midst** in a public ceremony, deterring any future transgressors. Although most of those condemned to death by stoning receive their punishment at a designated location outside the city,²² this woman is stoned outside her parents' home, so that the family will be shamed by this act for generations to come.²³

22 A man who commits adultery likewise receives capital punishment. **If a man shall be found lying with a woman** who is **married to a husband, the two of them shall die, the man who lay with the woman, and the woman.** Since both of them

יא יב לֹא תִלְבַּשׁ שַׁעַטְנֵז צֶמֶר וּפִשְׁתִּים יַחְדָּו: גְּדִלִים תַּעֲשֶׂה־לָּךְ עַל־אַרְבַּע
יג כַּנְפוֹת כְּסוּתְךָ אֲשֶׁר תְּכַסֶּה־בָּהּ: כִּי־יִקַּח אִישׁ אִשָּׁה וּבָא אֵלֶיהָ
יד וּשְׂנֵאָהּ: וְשָׂם לָהּ עֲלִילֹת דְּבָרִים וְהוֹצִא עָלֶיהָ שֵׁם רָע וְאָמַר אֶת־הָאִשָּׁה הַזֹּאת
טו לָקַחְתִּי וָאֶקְרַב אֵלֶיהָ וְלֹא־מָצָאתִי לָהּ בְּתוּלִים: וְלָקַח אֲבִי הַנַּעֲרָ וְאִמָּהּ וְהוֹצִיאוּ
טז אֶת־בְּתוּלֵי הַנַּעֲרָ אֶל־זִקְנֵי הָעִיר הַשָּׁעְרָה: וְאָמַר אֲבִי הַנַּעֲרָ אֶל־
יז הַזְּקֵנִים אֶת־בִּתִּי נָתַתִּי לָאִישׁ הַזֶּה לְאִשָּׁה וַיִּשְׂנָאֶהָ: וְהִנֵּה־הוּא שָׂם עֲלִילֹת
דְּבָרִים לֵאמֹר לֹא־מָצָאתִי לְבִתְּךָ בְּתוּלִים וְאֵלֶּה בְּתוּלֵי בִתִּי וּפָרְשׂוּ הַשִּׂמְלָה
יח יט לִפְנֵי זִקְנֵי הָעִיר: וְלָקְחוּ זִקְנֵי הָעִיר־הַהִוא אֶת־הָאִישׁ וְיִסְּרוּ אֹתוֹ: וְעָנְשׁוּ
אֹתוֹ מֵאָה כֶסֶף וְנָתְנוּ לַאֲבִי הַנַּעֲרָה כִּי הוֹצִיא שֵׁם רָע עַל בְּתוּלַת יִשְׂרָאֵל
כ וְלוֹ־תִהְיֶה לְאִשָּׁה לֹא־יוּכַל לְשַׁלְּחָהּ כָּל־יָמָיו: וְאִם־אֱמֶת
כא הָיָה הַדָּבָר הַזֶּה לֹא־נִמְצְאוּ בְתוּלִים לַנַּעֲרָ: וְהוֹצִיאוּ אֶת־הַנַּעֲרָ אֶל־פֶּתַח בֵּית־
אָבִיהָ וּסְקָלוּהָ אַנְשֵׁי עִירָהּ בָּאֲבָנִים וָמֵתָה כִּי־עָשְׂתָה נְבָלָה בְּיִשְׂרָאֵל לִזְנוֹת
כב בֵּית אָבִיהָ וּבִעַרְתָּ הָרָע מִקִּרְבֶּךָ: כִּי־יִמָּצֵא אִישׁ שֹׁכֵב | עִם־
אִשָּׁה בְעֻלַת־בַּעַל וּמֵתוּ גַּם־שְׁנֵיהֶם הָאִישׁ הַשֹּׁכֵב עִם־הָאִשָּׁה וְהָאִשָּׁה

רש״י

יא | **שַׁעַטְנֵז.** לְשׁוֹן עִרּוּב, וְרַבּוֹתֵינוּ דָּרְשׁוּ: שׁוּעַ טָווּי וְנוּז:

יב | **גְּדִלִים תַּעֲשֶׂה לָּךְ.** אַף מִן הַכִּלְאַיִם, לְכָךְ סְמָכָן הַכָּתוּב:

יג-יד | **וּבָא אֵלֶיהָ וּשְׂנֵאָהּ.** סוֹפוֹ: "וְשָׂם לָהּ עֲלִילֹת דְּבָרִים", עֲבֵרָה גוֹרֶרֶת עֲבֵרָה (אבות ד, ב), עָבַר עַל "לֹא תִשְׂנָא" (ויקרא יט, יז), סוֹפוֹ לָבֹא לִידֵי לְשׁוֹן הָרָע: **אֶת הָאִשָּׁה הַזֹּאת.** מִכָּאן שֶׁאֵין אוֹמֵר דָּבָר אֶלָּא בִּפְנֵי בַּעַל דִּין:

טו | **אֲבִי הַנַּעֲרָה וְאִמָּהּ.** מִי שֶׁגִּדְּלוּ גִּדּוּלִים הָרָעִים יִתְבַּזּוּ עָלֶיהָ:

טז | **וְאָמַר אֲבִי הַנַּעֲרָה.** מְלַמֵּד שֶׁאֵין רְשׁוּת לָאִשָּׁה לְדַבֵּר בִּפְנֵי הָאִישׁ:

יז | **וּפָרְשׂוּ הַשִּׂמְלָה.** הֲרֵי זֶה מָשָׁל, מְחַוְּרִין הַדְּבָרִים כְּשִׂמְלָה:

יח | **וְיִסְּרוּ אֹתוֹ.** מַלְקוּת:

כ | **וְאִם אֱמֶת הָיָה הַדָּבָר.** בְּעֵדִים וְהַתְרָאָה שֶׁזִּנְּתָה לְאַחַר אֵרוּסִין:

כא | **אֶל פֶּתַח בֵּית אָבִיהָ.** רְאוּ גִּדּוּלִים שֶׁגִּדַּלְתֶּם לִזְנוּת בֵּית אָבִיהָ. כְּמוֹ בְּבֵית אָבִיהָ: **אַנְשֵׁי עִירָהּ.** בְּמַעֲמַד כָּל אַנְשֵׁי עִירָהּ:

כב | **וּמֵתוּ גַּם שְׁנֵיהֶם.** לְהוֹצִיא מַעֲשֵׂה חִדּוּדִים שֶׁאֵין הָאִשָּׁה נֶהֱנֵית מֵהֶם: **גַּם.** לְרַבּוֹת הַבָּאִים מֵאַחֲרֵיהֶם. דָּבָר אַחֵר, "גַּם שְׁנֵיהֶם", לְרַבּוֹת אֶת הַוָּלָד, שֶׁאִם הָיְתָה מְעֻבֶּרֶת אֵין מַמְתִּינִין לָהּ עַד שֶׁתֵּלֵד:

DISCUSSION

22:11| **A mixture of fibers [*sha'atnez*]:** This enigmatic term is interpreted by the Sages as a kind of acronym (Jerusalem Talmud, *Kilayim* 9:5). However, it would seem that it is foreign in origin, and means mixture. There is no sufficient explanation for the prohibition to mix wool and linen specifically; it is one of the decrees of the Torah.

22:12| **Threads on the four corners of your garment:** In biblical times, many people wore a four cornered shawl as a garment. The Torah commands that one tie strings twisted together at each of the four corners. One of the strings on each corner must be made of wool dyed sky-blue (see Numbers 15:38). Since the garment and other strings could be made of linen, one might think that the prohibition of mixing wool and linen mentioned in the previous verse would apply. The Sages understood that the juxtaposition of these commandments teaches that it does not, and the obligation to put ritual fringes on a garment, including the woolen string, applies even to linen. (*Targum Yonatan*; Rashi; *Nazir* 58a).

22:14| **He proffers a libelous matter against her:** In principle, if a man marries a woman

participated in the act willingly, both are put to death, **and you shall eliminate the evil from Israel.**

23 This is true also in the case of a betrothed woman. **If there is a young virgin betrothed [*me'orasa*]**[D] **to a man,** but not yet married to him, **and** another **man finds her in the city, and lies with her,** and the act is discovered,

24 **you shall take the two of them out to** be judged at **the gate,** the court, **of that city, and you shall stone them with stones and they shall die.** Although **the young woman** will presumably claim that she was raped, her claim is not accepted, as it is assumed that she was complicit **because she did not cry out in the city.**[D] Had she cried out, the people of the city would have heard her and come to help. The fact that she did not cry for help in a location where it would have been effective proves that she was complicit. **And the man** is punished **because he afflicted [*inna*]** the betrothed **wife of his neighbor,** despite the fact that she consented.[24] According to another interpretation, *inna* means damaged; the man damaged her marital status, causing it to become prohibited for her to remain with her husband.[25] This is so because a betrothed woman is considered a wife even before marriage. For example, Jacob said to Laban with regard to Rachel, to whom he was not yet married: "Give me my wife."[26] **And you shall eliminate the evil from your midst.**

25 **But if the man shall find the betrothed young woman in the field,** away from a residential area, in a place where she has no way of defending herself, **and the man seized her, and lay with her, the man who lay with her shall die alone;** he is guilty of adultery and is therefore punishable by death.

26 **But to the young woman you shall do nothing,** as **the young woman has no sin worthy of death.** She is not guilty of adultery since she was raped. **As just like a man rises against his neighbor and murders him,**[D] **so is this matter.** The woman is comparable to a victim of murder in that she was incapable of preventing the act. Therefore she cannot be judged as a participant in the transgression.

27 **For he,** the rapist, **found her in the field; the betrothed young woman** presumably **cried out, and there is no rescuer for her.**

28 All of the previous cases pertained to a married or betrothed woman, and the described act of sexual intercourse was a violation of the severe prohibition of "You shall not commit adultery,"[27] which is punishable by death. The law is different in the case presented here: **If a man finds a young virgin who is not betrothed, and he seizes her** forcibly, **and lies with her,** rapes her (in rabbinic literature, a victim of rape is sometimes referred to as a seized woman),[28] **and they are found,**

29 since the young woman is unmarried, **the man who lay with her** is not subject to the death penalty; rather, he **shall give to the young woman's father fifty silver shekels,** which was the set bride price in biblical times. Since he behaved as though she were his wife, he must pay the accepted amount, **and** besides the monetary fine **she shall be a wife to him, because he afflicted,** raped **her; he may not release her,**[D] divorce her against her will, **all his days.**[29]

23 1 The Torah now presents a series of laws that deal with restrictions on marriage. **A man shall not take his father's wife,**[D] even after his father dies or gets divorced, **and he shall not uncover the edge of his father's garment,** his father's nakedness.

2 **One with crushed testicles and one with a severed** or severely damaged **penis**[D] **shall not enter into the assembly of the Lord** by marrying a daughter of Israel.[30]

DISCUSSION

under the assumption that she is a virgin, and discovers upon marrying her that she is not, he may divorce her. In the case here, the man apparently does not wish to get divorced, but due to his animosity prefers to slander her and damage her reputation. According to the tradition of the Sages, the husband's claim is understood to be supported by testimony of adultery after betrothal, which is punishable by death, as stated in the verses below. In fact, the objective of the husband may be to cause his wife to receive the death penalty. According to halakhic tradition, the cloth mentioned below is not sufficient proof of the woman's virginity; her parents must provide testimony to counter the testimony of the husband's witnesses. In this manner, the passage takes on a defined legal character (see Rashi, verses 17, 20; Ketubot 46a).

22:23 | **Betrothed [*me'orasa*]:** In modern Hebrew, the word *me'oreset* means engaged;

however, in biblical and rabbinic Hebrew, *me'orasa* or *me'oreset* refers to a woman who is betrothed to a man but does not yet live with him. In previous generations, there was a lengthy gap between the betrothal and the wedding. In the interim, although her legal status for all intents and purposes would be that of a wife, the woman would reside with her parents, and would effectively be between two authorities, her father and her husband. In that condition, she might tend to do as she pleases. Therefore, adultery with a betrothed young woman carries an even more severe penalty (stoning) than adultery with a married woman (strangulation).

22:24 | **Because she did not cry out in the city:** Of course, it is possible that she was raped in the city but was incapable of crying out, or that she was raped in a basement or an isolated courtyard where no one could have heard her

scream. The verses indicate that in a case where the act was seen by witnesses, but they do not know whether or not the woman consented, the *halakha* is determined based on the location of the act: If it happened in a place where people could have easily heard her shout and come to her rescue, but she did not shout, it can be assumed that she cooperated with the attacker. Even if she did not initiate the act, she did not resist with all her might and did not cry for help. However, if it was a place where there were no passersby who could have heard her shout, even if she did not cry for help, it is presumed she was raped, until it can be proven otherwise (see Ramban; Ḥizkuni).

22:26 | **Just like a man rises against his neighbor and murders him:** The law exempting a victim of rape from punishment as an adulteress is the source for the general halakhic principle that states that one who transgresses

כג ובערת הרע מישראל: כי יהיה נער בתולה מארשה לאיש ומצאה
כד איש בעיר ושכב עמה: והוצאתם את־שניהם אל־שער | העיר ההוא וסקלתם
אתם באבנים ומתו את־הנער על־דבר אשר לא־צעקה בעיר ואת־האיש על־
כה דבר אשר־ענה את־אשת רעהו ובערת הרע מקרבך: ואם־
בשדה ימצא האיש את־הנער המארשה והחזיק־בה האיש ושכב עמה ומת
כו האיש אשר־שכב עמה לבדו: ולנער לא־תעשה דבר אין לנער חטא מות כי
כז כאשר יקום איש על־רעהו ורצחו נפש כן הדבר הזה: כי בשדה מצאה צעקה
כח הנער המארשה ואין מושיע לה: כי־ימצא איש נער
כט בתולה אשר לא־ארשה ותפשה ושכב עמה ונמצאו: ונתן האיש השכב עמה
לאבי הנער חמשים כסף ולו־תהיה לאשה תחת אשר ענה לא־יוכל
א שלחה כל־ימיו: לא־יקח איש את־אשת אביו ולא יגלה
ב כנף אביו: לא־יבא פצוע־דכא וכרות שפכה בקהל

רש"י

כג | ומצאה איש בעיר. לפיכך "שכב עמה", פרצה קוראה לגנב, הא אלו ישבה בביתה לא ארע לה:

כו | כי כאשר יקום וגו'. לפי פשוטו זהו משמעו: כי אנוסה היא ובחזקה עמד עליה, כאדם העומד על חברו להרגו. ורבותינו דרשו בו (פסחים כה ע"ב ועוד): הרי זה בא ללמד ונמצא למד וכו':

פרק כג

א | לא יקח. אין לו בה לקוחין, ואין קדושין תופסין בה: ולא יגלה כנף אביו. שומרת יבם של אביו הראויה לאביו. והרי כבר הזהר עליה משום "ערות אחי אביך" (ויקרא יח, יד)? אלא לעבר על זו בשני לאוין, ולסמך לה: "לא יבא ממזר" (להלן פסוק ג), ללמד שאין ממזר אלא מחיבי כריתות, וקל וחמר מחיבי מיתות בית דין, שאין בעריות מיתת בית דין שאין בה כרת:

ב | פצוע דכה. שנפצעו או שנדכאו ביצים שלו: וכרות שפכה. שנכרת הגיד ושוב אינו יורה קלוח זרע, אלא שופך ושותת ואינו מוליד:

DISCUSSION

a prohibition due to circumstances beyond his control is not liable for his action (*Bava Kamma* 28b). Th is because it is not considered that he performed the transgression; rather, those who compelled him performed the transgression through him.

22:29| **He may not release her:** Just as in a case of a husband who proffered a libelous matter against his wife, the young woman (or her father, in this case) can decline marriage to the bridegroom. In that case, he is obligated only to pay the fine (see *Ketubot* 39b). The prohibition to divorce her is meant to deter men from engaging in intercourse with young women and then ignoring the effect it will have on their lives. This law is especially significant in the case of a rapist from a strong, wealthy, or influential family, who is liable to choose to rape a poor young woman who does not have the support of a prominent family. That woman is entitled to remain with him as long as she chooses.

23:1| **His father's wife:** Some of the Sages of the Mishna interpret this law as prohibiting marriage with any woman who engaged in intercourse with his father, whether or not they were married, and whether or not she consented. However, the *halakha* rules in accordance with the opinion that this prohibition applies only to a woman who was married to his father, even if it was only for a short period of time (see *Yevamot* 97a). Otherwise, if the son marries her it is not considered incest, but it is considered to be a display of contempt for his father.

23:2| **One with crushed testicles and one with a severed penis:** This prohibition does not judge the character of one with these deformities. Although he may not marry a woman included in the category of "the assembly of the Lord," he may marry other women, e.g., a convert (*Yevamot* 76a). The Oral Law discusses which men are included in this classification, and the halakhic conclusion is that the prohibition applies only to a man who was injured due to external circumstances, e.g., mutilation by man or animal, sitting on a thorn, or another accident, as opposed to one whose condition resulted from a birth defect or from an illness (see *Yevamot* 79b).

3 **A child born from incest or adultery [***mamzer***]**D **shall not enter into the assembly of the Lord;** he may not marry an Israelite woman of unflawed lineage. This prohibition applies to his descendants as well; **even the tenth generation** and beyond, that is, forever,[31] **he shall not enter into the assembly of the Lord.** There is no remedy for this person or his descendants. On the other hand, he remains a member of the people of Israel with regard to every other matter, and it is permitted for him to marry women of similarly flawed lineage, e.g., a *mamzeret*.[32]

4 The following restrictions on marriage stem from the collective memory of the nation of Israel. **An Amonite or a Moavite**D convert **shall not enter into the assembly of the Lord; even the tenth generation** and beyond **shall not enter into the assembly of the Lord forever.** In contrast to the previous verse, here the Torah explicitly states that the prohibition is in effect forever.

5 This is **because** the Amonites and Moavites did not cooperate with Israel; **they did not** even **greet you with bread and with water,** basic humanitarian aid, **on the way, upon your exodus from Egypt,** but rather avoided all contact with you (see 2:1–19). **And it is also because he,** the king of Moav, **hired against you Bilam son of Beor, from Petor, Aram Naharayim, to curse you.** This was the most powerful weapon that they could have used against you.

6 **But the Lord your God was unwilling to heed** the curses **of Bilam, and the Lord your God transformed for you the curse into a blessing.** Although Bilam desired and attempted to curse you, he ended up showering Israel with beautiful blessings, **because the Lord your God loved you.**[33] However, this does not diminish the guilt of the Amonites and the Moavites.

7 Because Moav and Amon refused to aid Israel, and because of their attempt to harm you with their contemptible conspiracy, **you shall not seek their peace or their welfare all your days, forever.** Their sin is unforgivable, and it is therefore inappropriate to assist them.

8 On the other hand, **you shall not** completely **despise an Edomite,**D **as he is your brother.** Edom is the nation that has the closest genealogical relation to Israel,[34] while Amon and Moav are more distantly related. Whereas Lot, the father of Amon and Moav, was Abraham's nephew, Edom, a name for Esau, was Jacob's brother and the son of Isaac and Rebecca. In addition, **you shall not despise an Egyptian,** but for another reason: **As you were a stranger in his land.** Although the Egyptians enslaved Israel for many years, they initially hosted the nation in their land and treated them well,[35] and gratitude must be expressed to them. Just as you must remember the negative behavior of Amon and Moav, so too you must remember the Egyptians' ambivalent treatment of you.

Fourth aliya

9 Therefore, **children that will be born to them,** Egyptian and Edomite converts, **in the third generation, shall enter into the assembly of the Lord.** By Torah law, only the grandchildren of those converts may enter into the nation of Israel through marriage.

Laws regarding the Sanctity of the Camp
DEUTERONOMY 23:10–15

The limitations on marriage stated above are part of the group of commandments meant to maintain the sanctity of the nation. The two subsequent laws preserve the sanctity in another respect: The first deals with ritual impurity, and the second underscores the importance of maintaining cleanliness and dignity in a military encampment. Both derive from the sanctity inherent in the Israelite military camp due to God's presence there.

10 **When you go out in a camp against your enemies, you shall be vigilant from every evil thing.** In the military and in wartime people tend toward a spiritual and moral decline, leading to a breach of the standards of conduct. Therefore, observance of purity and holiness is critical.

11 **If,** for example, **there is among you,** in the camp, **a man who will not be pure due to a nocturnal incident,** an unintended seminal emission, which is liable to occur at night especially to young men, **he shall go outside the camp** when he awakens and realizes what happened. **He shall not come into the midst of the camp.**

DISCUSSION

23:3 | **A child born from incest or adultery [***mamzer***]:** This word appears in only one other place in the Bible (Zechariah 9:6), and there too its meaning is not clear. It is apparently derived from the word *zar*, meaning strange or stranger, indicating that such a person was conceived under strange circumstances, or that his parents are "strangers" to each other; that they are not fit to marry each other (see Ibn Ezra; *Yevamot* 76b). The halakhic definition of a *mamzer* is one who was born from forbidden sexual relations punishable by excision from the World to Come [*karet*]. An exception to this definition is the case of a menstruating woman who engaged in intercourse; although this transgression is punishable by *karet*, the offspring is not a *mamzer*, as the prohibition involves the timing of the relations and not the identity of the parents (see *Yevamot* 44a–45a, 49).

A *mamzer* is not to blame for his status; he may be an exemplary individual. Rather, the restrictions on his marriage are only due to his parents. Despite the problematic circumstances of his conception, he is legally the son of his ←●

1076

ג יְהוָה: לֹא־יָבֹא מַמְזֵר בִּקְהַל יְהוָה גַּם דּוֹר עֲשִׂירִי לֹא־יָבֹא

ד לוֹ בִּקְהַל יְהוָה: לֹא־יָבֹא עַמּוֹנִי וּמוֹאָבִי בִּקְהַל יְהוָה

ה גַּם דּוֹר עֲשִׂירִי לֹא־יָבֹא לָהֶם בִּקְהַל יְהוָה עַד־עוֹלָם: עַל־דְּבַר אֲשֶׁר לֹא־קִדְּמוּ אֶתְכֶם בַּלֶּחֶם וּבַמַּיִם בַּדֶּרֶךְ בְּצֵאתְכֶם מִמִּצְרָיִם וַאֲשֶׁר שָׂכַר עָלֶיךָ

ו אֶת־בִּלְעָם בֶּן־בְּעוֹר מִפְּתוֹר אֲרַם נַהֲרַיִם לְקַלְלֶךָּ: וְלֹא־אָבָה יְהוָה אֱלֹהֶיךָ לִשְׁמֹעַ אֶל־בִּלְעָם וַיַּהֲפֹךְ יְהוָה אֱלֹהֶיךָ לְּךָ אֶת־הַקְּלָלָה לִבְרָכָה כִּי אֲהֵבְךָ יְהוָה אֱלֹהֶיךָ:

ז לֹא־תִדְרֹשׁ שְׁלֹמָם וְטֹבָתָם כָּל־יָמֶיךָ לְעוֹלָם: רביעי לֹא־תְתַעֵב

ח אֲדֹמִי כִּי אָחִיךָ הוּא לֹא־תְתַעֵב מִצְרִי כִּי־גֵר הָיִיתָ בְאַרְצוֹ: בָּנִים אֲשֶׁר־יִוָּלְדוּ

ט לָהֶם דּוֹר שְׁלִישִׁי יָבֹא לָהֶם בִּקְהַל יְהוָה: כִּי־תֵצֵא מַחֲנֶה יח

י עַל־אֹיְבֶיךָ וְנִשְׁמַרְתָּ מִכֹּל דָּבָר רָע: כִּי־יִהְיֶה בְךָ אִישׁ אֲשֶׁר לֹא־יִהְיֶה

יא טָהוֹר מִקְּרֵה־לָיְלָה וְיָצָא אֶל־מִחוּץ לַמַּחֲנֶה לֹא יָבֹא אֶל־תּוֹךְ הַמַּחֲנֶה:

ג| לֹא יָבֹא מַמְזֵר בִּקְהַל ה'. לֹא יִשָּׂא יִשְׂרְאֵלִית:

ד| לֹא יָבֹא עַמּוֹנִי. לֹא יִשָּׂא יִשְׂרְאֵלִית:

ה| עַל דְּבַר. עַל הָעֵצָה שֶׁיָּעֲצוּ אֶתְכֶם לְהַחֲטִיאֲכֶם כְּדִכְתִיב "בִּדְבַר בִּלְעָם" (במדבר לא, טז). בַּדֶּרֶךְ. כְּשֶׁהֱיִיתֶם בְּטֵרוּף:

ז| לֹא תִדְרֹשׁ שְׁלֹמָם. מִכְּלָל שֶׁנֶּאֱמַר: "עִמְּךָ יֵשֵׁב בְּקִרְבְּךָ" (להלן פסוק יז), יָכוֹל אַף זֶה כֵּן? תַּלְמוּד לוֹמַר: "לֹא תִדְרֹשׁ שְׁלֹמָם":

ח-ט| לֹא תְתַעֵב אֲדֹמִי. לְגַמְרֵי, וְאַף עַל פִּי שֶׁרָאוּי לְךָ לְתַעֲבוֹ, שֶׁיָּצָא בַּחֶרֶב לִקְרָאתֶךָ: לֹא תְתַעֵב מִצְרִי. מִכֹּל וָכֹל, אַף עַל פִּי שֶׁזָּרְקוּ זְכוּרֵיכֶם לַיְאוֹר, מַה טַּעַם? שֶׁהָיוּ לָכֶם אַכְסַנְיָה בִּשְׁעַת הַדְּחָק, לְפִיכָךְ: בָּנִים אֲשֶׁר יִוָּלְדוּ לָהֶם דּוֹר שְׁלִישִׁי וְגו'. וּשְׁאָר אֻמּוֹת מֻתָּרִין מִיָּד. הָא לָמַדְתָּ שֶׁהַמַּחֲטִיא לְאָדָם קָשֶׁה לוֹ מִן הַהוֹרְגוֹ, שֶׁהַהוֹרְגוֹ הוֹרְגוֹ בָּעוֹלָם הַזֶּה, וְהַמַּחֲטִיאוֹ מוֹצִיאוֹ מִן הָעוֹלָם הַזֶּה וּמִן הָעוֹלָם הַבָּא. לְפִיכָךְ אֱדוֹם שֶׁקִּדְּמָם

בַּחֶרֶב לֹא נִתְעַב, וְכֵן מִצְרַיִם שֶׁטִּבְּעוּם, וְאֵלּוּ שֶׁהֶחֱטִיאוּם נִתְעֲבוּ:

י| כִּי תֵצֵא מַחֲנֶה וְגו' וְנִשְׁמַרְתָּ. שֶׁהַשָּׂטָן מְקַטְרֵג בִּשְׁעַת הַסַּכָּנָה:

יא| מִקְּרֵה לָיְלָה. דִּבֶּר הַכָּתוּב בַּהֹוֶה: וְיָצָא אֶל מִחוּץ לַמַּחֲנֶה. זוֹ מִצְוַת עֲשֵׂה: לֹא יָבֹא אֶל תּוֹךְ הַמַּחֲנֶה. זוֹ מִצְוַת לֹא תַעֲשֶׂה. וְאָסוּר לִכָּנֵס לְמַחֲנֶה לְוִיָּה וְכָל שֶׁכֵּן לְמַחֲנֶה שְׁכִינָה:

DISCUSSION

father, if his father's identity is known, and he inherits his property. The Sages established that although a High Priest has the loftiest lineage among the people of Israel, while a *mamzer* has the basest, the deference due a *mamzer* who is a Torah scholar is greater than that due a High Priest who is ignorant (see *Yevamot 22; Horayot 13a*).

23:4 | An Amonite or a Moavite: According to the tradition of the Sages, this prohibition applies only to male Moavites and Amonites; female converts from Moav and Amon are permitted to marry Israelite men of unflawed lineage. This is also derived from the wording of the verse,

which employs the terms Amonite and Moavite, to the exclusion of an Amonitess or Moavitess. In the book of Ruth it is related that King David was a descendant of a Moavite convert (Ruth 4:17). In addition, his grandson Rehavam was born to Naama the Amonitess (I Kings 14:21). The fact that the great Davidic dynasty, whose future return was promised to the prophets, were descendants of a Moavitess and an Amonitess, illustrates the fact that this prohibition does not apply to women.

With regard to Egyptians and Edomites, mentioned below, there is a dispute between the Sages whether the prohibition applies to

women. The majority opinion is that it applies even to women (*Yevamot* 76b).

23:8 | You shall not despise an Edomite: There were instances of Edomite conversion to Judaism, e.g., the mass conversion initiated by John Hyrcanus in the second century BCE. Although that conversion was coerced, many of the converts remained part of the Jewish nation and identified with it completely, despite of the fact that they were still called Edomites due to their origin. During the Great Revolt against Rome, Edomite converts fought fearlessly to preserve the Temple (see *Antiquities of the Jews* XIII:257–58; *Wars of the Jews* V:6).

12 It shall be that **toward evening** of that day **he shall bathe in water,** immerse himself in a ritual bath, **and with the setting of the sun, he shall come into the camp.** A man who experiences a seminal emission is ritually impure for one day; once he immerses in a ritual bath, he is pure at nightfall. The Sages explain that the reason a man who experienced a seminal emission must leave the camp is that the Ark of the Covenant would accompany the military encampment of Israel, causing it to have sanctified status. A man who has had a seminal emission is prohibited from entering the Temple proper, known as the camp of the Divine Presence, and the entire Temple complex surrounding it, known as the camp of the Levites. [36]

13 An additional law with regard to the cleanliness and sanctity of the military camp is presented: **A** designated **place**[37] **shall** be for you outside the camp, and you shall go out there. A special place for relieving oneself must be designated outside the camp.

14 Furthermore, **a spade shall be for you with your weapons,** e.g., your sword or spear,[38] **and it shall be, upon your sitting outside** to relieve yourself, **you shall dig with it,** with the spade, a small hole in the ground, **and** once you finish **you shall return and cover your excrement.**

15 The reason for all these laws is: **As the Lord your God walks in the midst of your camp to save you, and to deliver your enemies** defeated **before you.** The Israelite military fights in the name of God, and therefore **your camp shall be holy, and** this is so that **He shall not see a shameful matter among you, and** consequently **turn from behind you,** leave you.[39]

The Prohibition against Turning In a Slave
DEUTERONOMY 23:16–17

In this section, the Torah stresses that the Land of Israel must absorb runaway slaves and grant them refuge. Although it is not stated explicitly, it seems that this commandment is rooted in the fact that the children of Israel were themselves slaves.

16 **You shall not hand over to his master** [D] a runaway Canaanite **slave,** whether his master is Israelite or gentile,[40] **who has been liberated to you,** who flees to your land, **from his master,** even if his master claims him from you.

17 **With you he shall reside in your midst,** among the people of Israel, **in the place that he will choose within one of your gates in which it is good for him; you shall not mistreat him.**

Prohibitions regarding Prostitution
DEUTERONOMY 23:18–19

The following two prohibitions relate to various aspects of prostitution. Some say that the background for the first prohibition is the licentiousness that was part of the worship in many pagan temples in Canaan. The second prohibition addresses the bringing of gifts that include an element of contempt to the Temple of God.

18 **There shall not be a prostitute** [*kedesha*], especially one who engages in ritual prostitution,[41] **from the daughters of Israel, and there shall not be a** male **prostitute** [*kadesh*],[D] whether for heterosexual or homosexual relations, **from the sons of Israel.**

19 **You shall not bring** a gift that was given as **the fee of a harlot,** or that you received as **the price of a dog, to the House of the Lord your God for any vow,** as fulfillment of a vow to the House of God, **for the two of them,** the fee of a harlot and the price of a dog, **are an abomination to the Lord your God.** Therefore it is inappropriate to bring them to His Temple.[42]

The Prohibition of Interest
DEUTERONOMY 23:20–21

Taking interest is prohibited only between members of the people of Israel. This indicates that taking interest is not considered to be an immoral act in and of itself.

20 **You shall not lend**[43] **with interest**[D] **to your brother,** your fellow Jew, **interest** [*neshekh*][D] **of silver** that was lent, **interest of food,** or **interest of any item that is lent with interest.**

Interest is called *neshekh*, bite, because with it the lender "bites" that which is not his.

יב יג וְהָיָה לִפְנוֹת־עֶרֶב יִרְחַץ בַּמָּיִם וּכְבֹא הַשֶּׁמֶשׁ יָבֹא אֶל־תּוֹךְ הַמַּחֲנֶה: וְיָד תִּהְיֶה
יד לְךָ מִחוּץ לַמַּחֲנֶה וְיָצָאתָ שָּׁמָּה חוּץ: וְיָתֵד תִּהְיֶה לְךָ עַל־אֲזֵנֶךָ וְהָיָה בְּשִׁבְתְּךָ
טו חוּץ וְחָפַרְתָּה בָהּ וְשַׁבְתָּ וְכִסִּיתָ אֶת־צֵאָתֶךָ: כִּי יְהוָה אֱלֹהֶיךָ מִתְהַלֵּךְ | בְּקֶרֶב
מַחֲנֶךָ לְהַצִּילְךָ וְלָתֵת אֹיְבֶיךָ לְפָנֶיךָ וְהָיָה מַחֲנֶיךָ קָדוֹשׁ וְלֹא־יִרְאֶה בְךָ עֶרְוַת
טז דָּבָר וְשָׁב מֵאַחֲרֶיךָ: לֹא־תַסְגִּיר עֶבֶד אֶל־אֲדֹנָיו אֲשֶׁר־יִנָּצֵל
יז אֵלֶיךָ מֵעִם אֲדֹנָיו: עִמְּךָ יֵשֵׁב בְּקִרְבְּךָ בַּמָּקוֹם אֲשֶׁר־יִבְחַר בְּאַחַד שְׁעָרֶיךָ בַּטּוֹב
יח לוֹ לֹא תּוֹנֶנּוּ: לֹא־תִהְיֶה קְדֵשָׁה מִבְּנוֹת יִשְׂרָאֵל וְלֹא־יִהְיֶה קָדֵשׁ
יט מִבְּנֵי יִשְׂרָאֵל: לֹא־תָבִיא אֶתְנַן זוֹנָה וּמְחִיר כֶּלֶב בֵּית יְהוָה אֱלֹהֶיךָ לְכָל־נֶדֶר כִּי
כ תוֹעֲבַת יְהוָה אֱלֹהֶיךָ גַּם־שְׁנֵיהֶם: לֹא־תַשִּׁיךְ לְאָחִיךָ נֶשֶׁךְ כֶּסֶף נֶשֶׁךְ

רש"י

יב| **והיה לפנות ערב.** סמוך להערב שמשו יטבל, שאינו טהור בלא הערב השמש:

יג| **ויד תהיה לך.** כתרגומו, כמו: "איש על ידו" (במדבר ב, יז): **מחוץ למחנה.** חוץ לענן:

יד| **על אזנך.** לבד משאר כלי תשמישך: **אזנך.** כמו כלי זין: **ולא יראה בך.** הקדוש ברוך הוא, "ערות דבר":

טז| **לא תסגיר עבד.** כתרגומו. דבר אחר, אפילו עבד כנעני של ישראל שברח מחוצה לארץ לארץ ישראל:

יח| **לא תהיה קדשה.** מפקרת, מקדשת ומזמנת לזנות: **ולא יהיה קדש.** מזמן למשכב זכור. ואונקלוס תרגם: "לא תהי איתתא מבנת ישראל לגבר עבד", שאף זו מפקרת לבעילת זנות היא, מאחר שאין קדושין תופסין לו בה, שהרי הקשו לחמור, שנאמר: "שבו לכם פה עם החמור" (בראשית כב, ה), עם הדומה לחמור, "ולא יסב גברא מבני ישראל אתתא אמא", שאף הוא נעשה קדש על ידה, שכל בעילותיו בעילות זנות שאין קדושין תופסין לו בה:

יט| **אתנן זונה.** נתן לה טלה באתננה, פסול להקרבה: **ומחיר כלב.** החליף שה בכלב: **גם שניהם.** לרבות שנוייהם, כגון חטים ועשאן סלת:

DISCUSSION

23:16| **You shall not hand over to his master:** Torah law requires that the authorities enforce the manumission of a slave who fled from his master to the Land of Israel, and compel the master to release him formally by writing him a deed of manumission. Concurrently, the slave is obligated to write his master a promissory note for his value (see Rambam, *Sefer Kinyan*, *Hilkhot Avadim* 8:10; *Shulḥan Arukh*, *Yoreh De'a* 267:85).

23:18| **Prostitute [*kedesha, kadesh*]:** Some commentaries explain that these terms are referring to professional prostitution, as opposed to the words *sota* and *zona*, which typically refer to casual licentiousness (see Rashi; *Bekhor Shor*). However, the fact that these words derive from the root *kuf-dalet-shin* implies that there is a ritual aspect as well (see commentary on Genesis 28:31). The nature of this ritual practice is unclear, as it no longer exists nowadays. The linguistic distinction between these words and *kedusha* and *kadosh*, which mean holy, emphasizes the disgracefulness of this occupation, as it is the antithesis of holiness. Likewise, the Torah intentionally distorts the names of idols (see Numbers 32:38, and Rashi ad loc.; *Avoda Zara* 46a).

23:20| **You shall not lend with interest:** In the *Sifrei* and the Talmud it is derived from these verses that it is also prohibited to borrow with interest and to repay interest.

Interest [*neshekh*]: The synonyms *neshekh* and *tarbit* appear together in Leviticus (25:36–37), Ezekiel (18:8–17, 22:12), and Proverbs (28:8). *Halakha* does not distinguish between *neshekh* and *tarbit* (*Bava Metzia* 60b–61a), but some explain that *neshekh* is a loan for which the interest rises as time passes, whereas *tarbit* refers to a fixed amount that the borrower is obligated to pay beyond the sum of the loan (see Ramban, Leviticus 25:36).

21 To the foreigner, a gentile, **you shall lend with interest,** it is permitted to borrow or lend with interest, **but to your brother, a fellow Jew, you shall not lend with interest,**[D] so that the Lord your God will bless you in all your endeavors, on the land that you are coming there to take possession of it.

Vows
DEUTERONOMY 23:22–24

22 **When you shall take a vow to** bring a donation to the Temple of **the Lord your God, you shall not delay to pay it;** you must pay it by the deadline. The Sages discuss the definition of this deadline and conclude that it is three pilgrimage festivals after having taken the vow. Nevertheless, one is commanded to fulfill his vow already at the first pilgrimage festival *ab initio*.[44] If you delay payment beyond the deadline, **the Lord your God will** ultimately **seek it from you, and there will be a sin,** a deficiency, **in you.**

23 **If you shall refrain from vowing, there will be no sin in you.** One is not obligated to vow, as no sin is performed by refraining from donating money to the Temple. The sin is when you violate your word and delay your commitment.

24 Therefore **that which emerges from your lips you shall observe and you shall perform as you vowed a pledge to the Lord your God,** of your volition, **that you spoke with your mouth.**

Eating from the Vineyard and from the Field
DEUTERONOMY 23:25–26

Just as it is prohibited for the owner of a field to muzzle an ox while threshing, rather, he must allow the animal to eat from the produce of the field in which it is working, so too one may not prevent a laborer from enjoying the produce of a vineyard or field in which he is working. However, the laborer must remember that he is not the owner, and his benefit from the produce is limited.

25 **When you come into your neighbor's vineyard** as a laborer,
Fifth **you may eat grapes as you desire to your contentment, but**
aliya **into your vessel you shall not place them.**

26 Likewise, **when you come into your neighbor's standing grain** to work, **you may pick** ripe **stalks with your hand, but you shall not wield a sickle on your neighbor's standing grain.** You may not use a tool to harvest stalks of grain for yourself. Although one of the Sages in the Mishna interprets this verse literally, as referring to anyone who enters another's vineyard or field, the other Sages disagree, maintaining that it refers only to a laborer. These are benefits to which a laborer is entitled for his work, and are limited to what can be gathered in the field without collecting a large amount to take home.[45]

Harvesting grapes from a vineyard, tomb of Nakht, Egypt, fifteenth century BCE | Stalks

The Remarriage of a Divorcée to Her First Husband after Marriage to Another Man
DEUTERONOMY 24:1–4

It is prohibited for a man to remarry his divorcée after her marriage to another man in the interim. They may remarry only if she did not marry in the interim. This is one of the few places in the Torah where divorce is mentioned. The Torah indicates here that marriage is not eternal; it may be terminated with a bill of divorce, a *get* in rabbinic terminology.

24 **1** **When a man takes,** betroths, **a wife and engages in intercourse with her, it shall be that if she does not find favor in his eyes, because he found in her an indecent matter,**[D] either a trait that he deems deficient, or immoral sexual behavior, albeit that which is insufficiently corrupt for him to be obligated to divorce her, but he decided to do so anyway, **and he wrote**

כא אֹכֵל נֶשֶׁךְ כָּל־דָּבָר אֲשֶׁר יִשָּׁךְ: לַנָּכְרִי תַשִּׁיךְ וּלְאָחִיךָ לֹא תַשִּׁיךְ לְמַעַן יְבָרֶכְךָ יְהוָה אֱלֹהֶיךָ בְּכֹל מִשְׁלַח יָדֶךָ עַל־הָאָרֶץ אֲשֶׁר־אַתָּה בָא־שָׁמָּה לְרִשְׁתָּהּ:

כב כִּי־תִדֹּר נֶדֶר לַיהוָה אֱלֹהֶיךָ לֹא תְאַחֵר לְשַׁלְּמוֹ כִּי־ יט דָרֹשׁ יִדְרְשֶׁנּוּ יְהוָה אֱלֹהֶיךָ מֵעִמָּךְ וְהָיָה בְךָ חֵטְא: וְכִי תֶחְדַּל לִנְדֹּר לֹא־יִהְיֶה בְךָ חֵטְא: מוֹצָא שְׂפָתֶיךָ תִּשְׁמֹר וְעָשִׂיתָ כַּאֲשֶׁר נָדַרְתָּ לַיהוָה אֱלֹהֶיךָ נְדָבָה אֲשֶׁר דִּבַּרְתָּ בְּפִיךָ: כה כִּי תָבֹא בְּכֶרֶם רֵעֶךָ וְאָכַלְתָּ עֲנָבִים כְּנַפְשְׁךָ חמישי שָׂבְעֶךָ וְאֶל־כֶּלְיְךָ לֹא תִתֵּן: כו כִּי תָבֹא בְּקָמַת רֵעֶךָ וְקָטַפְתָּ מְלִילֹת בְּיָדֶךָ וְחֶרְמֵשׁ לֹא תָנִיף עַל קָמַת רֵעֶךָ: כד א כִּי־יִקַּח אִישׁ אִשָּׁה וּבְעָלָהּ וְהָיָה אִם־לֹא תִמְצָא־חֵן בְּעֵינָיו כִּי־מָצָא בָהּ עֶרְוַת דָּבָר וְכָתַב

רש"י

כו לֹא תַשִּׁיךְ. אַזְהָרָה לַלֹּוֶה שֶׁלֹּא יִתֵּן רִבִּית לַמַּלְוֶה. וְאַחַר כָּךְ אַזְהָרָה לַמַּלְוֶה – "אֶת כַּסְפְּךָ לֹא תִתֵּן לוֹ בְּנֶשֶׁךְ" (ויקרא כה, לז):

כא לַנָּכְרִי תַשִּׁיךְ. וְלֹא לְאָחִיךָ, לָאו הַבָּא מִכְּלַל עֲשֵׂה – עֲשֵׂה, לַעֲבֹר עָלָיו בִּשְׁנֵי לָאוִין וַעֲשֵׂה:

כב לֹא תְאַחֵר לְשַׁלְּמוֹ. שְׁלֹשָׁה רְגָלִים, וּלְמָדוּהוּ רַבּוֹתֵינוּ מִן הַמִּקְרָא:

כד מוֹצָא שְׂפָתֶיךָ תִּשְׁמֹר. לִתֵּן עֲשֵׂה עַל לֹא תַעֲשֶׂה:

כה כִּי תָבֹא בְּכֶרֶם רֵעֶךָ. בְּפוֹעֵל הַכָּתוּב מְדַבֵּר:

וְאֶל־ כֶּלְיְךָ לֹא תִתֵּן. מִכָּאן שֶׁלֹּא דִבְּרָה תוֹרָה אֶלָּא בִּשְׁעַת הַבָּצִיר, בִּזְמַן שֶׁאַתָּה נוֹתֵן לְכֶלְיוֹ שֶׁל בַּעַל הַבַּיִת, אֲבָל חָס

בָּהּ לְעָבֵד וּלְקֻשְׁקָשׁ אֵינוֹ אוֹכֵל: כְּנַפְשְׁךָ. כַּמָּה שֶׁתִּרְצֶה: שָׂבְעֶךָ. וְלֹא אֲכִילָה גַסָּה:

כו כִּי תָבֹא בְּקָמַת רֵעֶךָ. אַף זוֹ בְּפוֹעֵל הַכָּתוּב מְדַבֵּר:

פרק כד

א כִּי מָצָא בָהּ עֶרְוַת דָּבָר. מִצְוָה עָלָיו לְגָרְשָׁהּ שֶׁלֹּא תִמְצָא חֵן בְּעֵינָיו:

DISCUSSION

23:21 | To the foreigner you shall lend with interest, but to your brother you shall not lend with interest: The fact that it is permitted to lend to a non-Jew with interest indicates that the Torah does not consider this an immoral act, as the loan can be seen as tantamount to rental of money for a profit, or as an investment in the borrower's business. Accordingly, when a person invests money in another person's business, he should get a share of the revenue. Rather, the prohibition against lending with interest to the children of Israel is based on the concept that the Israelite nation is one family, and within the family behavior of this kind is inappropriate;

parents do not keep a record of the food they give their children for the purpose of collecting payment in the future with interest.

According to several commentaries, the term *tashikh*, which is translated here as "lend with interest," actually means borrow with interest. According to this opinion, one may not pay interest to an Israelite, as it is prohibited for the lender to take interest; but it is permitted for one who borrowed from a gentile with interest, and therefore he is obligated to pay the interest to which he agreed (see *Targum Yonatan*; Rashi; Sforno).

24:1 | Because he found in hy Torah law, divorce can be initiated only by the husband. The Sages debate what constitutes a valid reason for divorce. According to one opinion, he may divorce her only when he finds in her an "indecent matter," licentious behavior with another man. According to another, he may divorce her simply for not performing her responsibilities as a wife. The example given is that she burns his food. A third opinion is that there need be greater grounds for divorce than the fact that "she does not find favor in his eyes" (*Gittin* 90a).

her a bill of divorce,^D and he placed it in her hand, and he sent her from his house,

2 and she departed from his house, and she went and was married **to another man,**

3 and the latter man also **hated her, and he wrote her a bill of divorce and placed it in her hand, and sent her from his house, or** alternatively, **if the latter man, who took her as his wife, died,**

4 her former husband, who sent her, **may not take her again to be a wife for him,** even though she is permitted to marry

anyone else, besides a priest,⁴⁶ **after she was defiled,**^D forbidden to other men upon marriage to her second husband.⁴⁷ Although the divorce from, or death of, her second husband renders her permitted again to marry other men, she remains forbidden to her first husband forever, **as it,** remarrying her first husband, **is an abomination before the Lord,** as it may facilitate sexual licentiousness and exchange of wives under the ruse of legal marriage.⁴⁸ **And you shall not bring sin to the land that the Lord your God is giving you as an inheritance.**

Prohibition of Going to War during the First Year of Marriage

DEUTERONOMY 24:5

The following prohibition relates to marriage as well, and underscores the importance of maintaining a proper and loving relationship between husband and wife. The obligation of creating a happy marriage is incumbent upon the husband, and during the first year of marriage, he must dedicate himself to cultivating it even at the price of refraining from other obligations to society.

5 **When a man takes a new wife,** a woman for whom it is her first
Sixth marriage,⁴⁹ or alternatively, a woman whom he is marrying for
aliya the first time,⁵⁰ **he shall not go out** to serve **in the army.**^D **And** not only may he not participate in a life-threatening activity, but **for no matter shall he be obligated** at all. He may not join

the army even in a supporting position, engaging in the duties performed by soldiers who are not fit for combat or who are exempt for reasons stated above.⁵¹ **He shall be free for his house,** his wife, for **one year,** exempt from all responsibilities toward the state, **and shall cause his wife, whom he took, to rejoice.**

Forbidden Collateral

DEUTERONOMY 24:6

This commandment, too, stresses the importance of protecting the well-being of a household. One may not take another's means for preparing food as collateral, even when doing so is legally justified.

6 **One,** a creditor, **shall not take the lower millstone [*reḥayim*] or the upper millstone [*rekhev*] as collateral.** A flour mill consists of two stones. The lower one [*reḥayim*] is the primary part of the mill, and therefore, the mill as a whole is also referred to by the same term. Some interpret the word *reḥayim* as referring to both stones, and explain that one may not take both stones as collateral, or even the upper stone [*rekhev*] alone,

which is mobile and can be taken easily, **as** by taking the means of preparing bread, **he takes a life as collateral.**

Upper Millstone

Lower Millstone

Flour mill

Abduction

DEUTERONOMY 24:7

The previous commandment states that one who takes a tool used in the preparation of food as collateral is likened to one who takes a person's life. While that analogy is an exaggeration, here the Torah relates to one who directly robs another of his freedom and his dignity.

7 **If a man is found abducting**^D **any of his brethren of the children of Israel, and he enslaved [*hitamer*] or abused him**⁵²

and then **sold him to another, that thief shall die,** you shall execute him, **and you shall eliminate the evil from your midst.**

Leprosy

DEUTERONOMY 24:8–9

As explained in Leviticus (chap. 13), the leprosy mentioned in the Torah is a divine sign of misconduct. Therefore, it is treated not by a doctor but by priests, the spiritual leaders. The commandment that appears here, against physically removing leprosy from the body, confirms this statement. According to the verses in Leviticus, the punishment of a leper is social isolation. He must remain outside the camp until the leprosy is cured. A leper would naturally be inclined to remove his mark of leprosy in order to return to his home and regain his freedom; therefore the Torah explicitly prohibits this action. The connection between this law and the previous verse can be understood as follows: Just as it is severely prohibited to deprive another person of his freedom, so too it is prohibited for one to take his freedom of movement into his own hands when Torah law requires his isolation.

8 **Be careful with the mark of leprosy, to greatly take care** of all of its laws **and to act in accordance with everything that the priests, the Levites, will instruct you; as I had commanded**

them in detail,⁵³ **you shall take care to perform.** The priests were commanded with regard to the details, and you must obey their instructions.

ב לָהּ סֵפֶר כְּרִיתֻת וְנָתַן בְּיָדָהּ וְשִׁלְּחָהּ מִבֵּיתוֹ: וְיָצְאָה מִבֵּיתוֹ וְהָלְכָה וְהָיְתָה
ג לְאִישׁ־אַחֵר: וּשְׂנֵאָהּ הָאִישׁ הָאַחֲרוֹן וְכָתַב לָהּ סֵפֶר כְּרִיתֻת וְנָתַן בְּיָדָהּ וְשִׁלְּחָהּ
ד מִבֵּיתוֹ אוֹ כִי יָמוּת הָאִישׁ הָאַחֲרוֹן אֲשֶׁר־לְקָחָהּ לוֹ לְאִשָּׁה: לֹא־יוּכַל בַּעְלָהּ
הָרִאשׁוֹן אֲשֶׁר־שִׁלְּחָהּ לָשׁוּב לְקַחְתָּהּ לִהְיוֹת לוֹ לְאִשָּׁה אַחֲרֵי אֲשֶׁר הֻטַּמָּאָה
כִּי־תוֹעֵבָה הִוא לִפְנֵי יְהוָה וְלֹא תַחֲטִיא אֶת־הָאָרֶץ אֲשֶׁר יְהוָה אֱלֹהֶיךָ נֹתֵן לְךָ
ה נַחֲלָה: כִּי־יִקַּח אִישׁ אִשָּׁה חֲדָשָׁה לֹא יֵצֵא בַּצָּבָא וְלֹא־יַעֲבֹר ששי
עָלָיו לְכָל־דָּבָר נָקִי יִהְיֶה לְבֵיתוֹ שָׁנָה אֶחָת וְשִׂמַּח אֶת־אִשְׁתּוֹ אֲשֶׁר־לָקָח:
ו ז לֹא־יַחֲבֹל רֵחַיִם וָרָכֶב כִּי־נֶפֶשׁ הוּא חֹבֵל: כִּי־יִמָּצֵא אִישׁ גֹּנֵב
נֶפֶשׁ מֵאֶחָיו מִבְּנֵי יִשְׂרָאֵל וְהִתְעַמֶּר־בּוֹ וּמְכָרוֹ וּמֵת הַגַּנָּב הַהוּא וּבִעַרְתָּ
ח הָרָע מִקִּרְבֶּךָ: הִשָּׁמֶר בְּנֶגַע־הַצָּרַעַת לִשְׁמֹר מְאֹד וְלַעֲשׂוֹת
כְּכֹל אֲשֶׁר־יוֹרוּ אֶתְכֶם הַכֹּהֲנִים הַלְוִיִּם כַּאֲשֶׁר צִוִּיתִם תִּשְׁמְרוּ לַעֲשׂוֹת:

רש"י

ב| לְאִישׁ אַחֵר. אֵין זֶה בֶּן זוּגוֹ שֶׁל רִאשׁוֹן, הוּא הוֹצִיא רְשָׁעָה מִתּוֹךְ בֵּיתוֹ וְזֶה הִכְנִיסָהּ:

ג| וּשְׂנֵאָהּ הָאִישׁ הָאַחֲרוֹן. הַכָּתוּב מְבַשְּׂרוֹ שֶׁסּוֹפוֹ לִשְׂנֹאתָהּ, וְאִם לָאו – קוֹבַרְתּוֹ, שֶׁנֶּאֱמַר: "אוֹ כִי יָמוּת":

ד| אַחֲרֵי אֲשֶׁר הֻטַּמָּאָה. לְרַבּוֹת סוֹטָה שֶׁנִּסְתְּרָה:

ה| אִשָּׁה חֲדָשָׁה. שֶׁהִיא חֲדָשָׁה לוֹ, וַאֲפִלּוּ אַלְמָנָה, פְּרָט לְמַחֲזִיר גְּרוּשָׁתוֹ: וְלֹא יַעֲבֹר עָלָיו. דְּבַר הַצָּבָא: לְכָל דָּבָר. שֶׁהוּא צֹרֶךְ הַצָּבָא, לֹא לְסַפֵּק מַיִם וּמָזוֹן וְלֹא לְתַקֵּן דְּרָכִים. אֲבָל הַחוֹזְרִים מֵעוֹרְכֵי הַמִּלְחָמָה עַל פִּי כֹהֵן, כְּגוֹן בָּנָה בַיִת וְלֹא חֲנָכוֹ אוֹ אֵרַשׂ אִשָּׁה וְלֹא לְקָחָהּ, מַסְפִּיקִין מַיִם וּמָזוֹן וּמְתַקְּנִין אֶת הַדְּרָכִים: יִהְיֶה לְבֵיתוֹ. אַף בִּשְׁבִיל בֵּיתוֹ, אִם בָּנָה בַיִת וַחֲנָכוֹ וְאִם נָטַע כֶּרֶם וְחִלְּלוֹ, אֵינוֹ זָז מִבֵּיתוֹ בִּשְׁבִיל צָרְכֵי הַמִּלְחָמָה: לְבֵיתוֹ. זֶה בֵּיתוֹ: יִהְיֶה. לְרַבּוֹת אֶת כַּרְמוֹ: וְשִׂמַּח. יְשַׂמַּח אֶת אִשְׁתּוֹ, וְתַרְגּוּמוֹ: "וְיַחְדֵּי יָת אִתְּתֵיהּ", וְהַמְתַרְגֵּם: 'וְיֶחֱדֵי עִם אִתְּתֵיהּ' טוֹעֶה הוּא, שֶׁאֵין זֶה תַּרְגּוּם שֶׁל 'וְשִׂמַּח' אֶלָּא שֶׁל 'וְשָׂמַח':

ו| רֵחַיִם. הִיא הַתַּחְתּוֹנָה: וָרֶכֶב. הִיא הָעֶלְיוֹנָה: לֹא יַחֲבֹל. אִם בָּא לְמַשְׁכְּנוֹ עַל חוֹבוֹ בְּבֵית דִּין, לֹא יְמַשְׁכְּנֶנּוּ בִּדְבָרִים שֶׁעוֹשִׂים בָּהֶן אֹכֶל נֶפֶשׁ:

ז| כִּי יִמָּצֵא. בְּעֵדִים וְהַתְרָאָה, וְכֵן כָּל 'יִמָּצֵא' שֶׁבַּתּוֹרָה: וְהִתְעַמֶּר בּוֹ. אֵינוֹ חַיָּב עַד שֶׁיִּשְׁתַּמֵּשׁ בּוֹ:

ח| הִשָּׁמֶר בְּנֶגַע הַצָּרַעַת. שֶׁלֹּא תִּתְלֹשׁ סִימָנֵי טֻמְאָה וְלֹא תָּקֹץ אֶת הַבַּהֶרֶת: כְּכֹל אֲשֶׁר יוֹרוּ אֶתְכֶם. אִם לְהַסְגִּיר, אִם לְהַחְלִיט, אִם לְטַהֵר:

ט| זָכוֹר אֵת אֲשֶׁר עָשָׂה ה' אֱלֹהֶיךָ לְמִרְיָם. אִם בָּאתָ

DISCUSSION

A bill of divorce: This is the only place in the Torah where a bill of divorce is mentioned, and no details of its content are given. It seems that the Torah assumes the existence of a normative procedure of divorce and therefore does not see a need to describe it. Details of this procedure are described only in post-biblical halakhic sources.

24:4| **After she was defiled:** This description does not refer to actual impurity, as there is clearly nothing impure or immoral about the woman's second marriage, which was completely legal. Furthermore, the Talmud states that if the divorcée did not marry another man, but engaged in non-marital sexual intercourse, it is permitted for her to remarry her first husband (*Yevamot* 56b). Evidently, it is the legal relationship with another man that prevents her from remarrying her first husband.

24:5| **He shall not go out in the army:** This commandment applies to an optional war initiated by the Israelite leadership, not to an obligatory war, such as a war of defense or security emergency (see Mishna *Sota* 8:7).

24:7| **A man is found abducting:** According to tradition, the prohibition "You shall not steal" in the Ten Precepts (Exodus 20:13) refers to abduction (*Sanhedrin* 86a). Although the verse here clearly expresses the severity of this action, nevertheless there is a halakhic principle that maintains that a punishment may be administered only if there is an explicit Torah prohibition. The prohibition in the Ten Precepts therefore serves as the requisite prohibition for the death penalty stated here.

9 An addition to this warning is now presented: **Remember that which the Lord your God did to Miriam**[D] the prophetess, Moses' sister, **on the way upon your exodus from Egypt.** Miriam was afflicted with leprosy and spent seven days in isolation.[54] Although the people honored her by remaining in place until she healed, her status did not save her from leprosy and isolation.

Commandments regarding Collateral

DEUTERONOMY 24:10–13

The commandment of the Torah to take the borrower's condition into account turns the act of taking collateral, in many cases, from an act of coercion to an almost symbolic act.

10 **When you lend your neighbor a loan of any amount,** and he is required to repay it, and you wish to collect the debt, **you shall not go into his house to take his collateral.**
11 **Outside you shall stand, and the man to whom you lend shall bring the collateral to you outside.** You are allowed to demand collateral worth the money you are owed, but you must be sensitive to the dignity of the borrower. You may not invade his house and choose one of his belongings as collateral, as that would humiliate him.
12 **If he,** the borrower, **is a poor man,** who can give you only a garment, which he presumably uses as a bed sheet or blanket, **you shall not sleep with his collateral.** You are allowed to use it, but you may not sleep at night with the collateral in your possession.[55]
13 Instead, you shall **return him the collateral with the setting of the sun and he will sleep in his garment, and he will bless you** for giving it back to him, as he now has a garment in which to sleep. **And** besides the blessing of the poor person, **for you it will be** considered **righteousness before the Lord your God.**

The Wage of a Poor Person

DEUTERONOMY 24:14–15

This commandment, too, deals with treatment of the poor.

14 **You shall not exploit a poor or indigent hired laborer from**
Seventh aliya **your brethren,** your people. It is prohibited to exploit any hired laborer, but the Torah refers to a reality in which most hired laborers were poor. The average person would work the land he inherited from his father, and the hired laborers were those who did not have land, or who did not have the means to work their field. **Or** a hired laborer **from your stranger who is in your land within your gates,** as he too does not have land of his own. A hired laborer is dependent on his employer. The Torah therefore attempts to prevent employers from exploiting their laborers.
15 Furthermore, **on his day,** until the end of his workday, **you shall give his wage, and the sun shall not set upon it.** He must receive his wage before sunset, **as he is poor, and he anticipates it;** if his daily wage is his only money, he will need it to buy food. **Lest he cry out against you to the Lord** if you do not pay him on that same day. Even if you intend to pay him another time, and even if your failure to pay him is unintentional, he is liable to pray against you for causing him misery, **and it will be a sin in you.**

Individual Punishment

DEUTERONOMY 24:16

This commandment is directed at the judicial and governmental authorities. Similar to the previous commandments, it deals with disadvantaged people. Here the verse relates to the children of criminals.

16 **Fathers shall not be put to death for** the sins of **sons,**[D] **and sons shall not be put to death for** the sins of **fathers.** People should not be punished for the sins of their family members;[56] **each** man **shall be put to death** only **for his** own **sin.**

Commandments Relating to the Helpless

DEUTERONOMY 24:17–22

The memory that the nation of Israel was enslaved in Egypt should accompany every Jew at all times and affect his behavior toward the helpless everywhere.

17 **You shall not distort the judgment of a stranger or an orphan,** who are defenseless and vulnerable. Besides the general obligation of justice, the Torah demands of a judge special care in deciding the case of a weak litigant. **And** likewise, **you shall not take a widow's garment as collateral,**[D] as opposed to other people, from whom it is stated above (verses 12–13) that taking collateral is permitted.
18 **You shall remember that you were a slave in Egypt, and**

ט זָכוֹר אֵת אֲשֶׁר־עָשָׂה יהוה אֱלֹהֶיךָ לְמִרְיָם בַּדֶּרֶךְ בְּצֵאתְכֶם
מִמִּצְרָיִם: י כִּי־תַשֶּׁה בְרֵעֲךָ מַשַּׁאת מְאוּמָה לֹא־תָבֹא אֶל־בֵּיתוֹ לַעֲבֹט
עֲבֹטוֹ: יא בַּחוּץ תַּעֲמֹד וְהָאִישׁ אֲשֶׁר אַתָּה נֹשֶׁה בוֹ יוֹצִיא אֵלֶיךָ אֶת־הָעֲבוֹט
הַחוּצָה: יב וְאִם־אִישׁ עָנִי הוּא לֹא תִשְׁכַּב בַּעֲבֹטוֹ: יג הָשֵׁב תָּשִׁיב לוֹ אֶת־הָעֲבוֹט
כְּבוֹא הַשֶּׁמֶשׁ וְשָׁכַב בְּשַׂלְמָתוֹ וּבֵרְכֶךָּ וּלְךָ תִּהְיֶה צְדָקָה לִפְנֵי יהוה
אֱלֹהֶיךָ: יד לֹא־תַעֲשֹׁק שָׂכִיר עָנִי וְאֶבְיוֹן מֵאַחֶיךָ אוֹ מִגֵּרְךָ אֲשֶׁר בְּאַרְצְךָ שביעי
בִּשְׁעָרֶיךָ: טו בְּיוֹמוֹ תִתֵּן שְׂכָרוֹ וְלֹא־תָבוֹא עָלָיו הַשֶּׁמֶשׁ כִּי עָנִי הוּא וְאֵלָיו הוּא
נֹשֵׂא אֶת־נַפְשׁוֹ וְלֹא־יִקְרָא עָלֶיךָ אֶל־יהוה וְהָיָה בְךָ חֵטְא: טז לֹא־יוּמְתוּ
אָבוֹת עַל־בָּנִים וּבָנִים לֹא־יוּמְתוּ עַל־אָבוֹת אִישׁ בְּחֶטְאוֹ יוּמָתוּ: יז לֹא
תַטֶּה מִשְׁפַּט גֵּר יָתוֹם וְלֹא תַחֲבֹל בֶּגֶד אַלְמָנָה: יח וְזָכַרְתָּ כִּי עֶבֶד הָיִיתָ בְּמִצְרַיִם

רש"י

לְהִזָּהֵר שֶׁלֹּא תִלְקֶה בְּצָרַעַת, אַל תְּסַפֵּר לָשׁוֹן הָרָע. זְכוֹר הֶעָשׂוּי לְמִרְיָם שֶׁדִּבְּרָה בְּאָחִיהָ וְלָקְתָה בִּנְגָעִים:

יא כִּי תַשֶּׁה בְרֵעֲךָ. תָּחוּב בַּחֲבֵרְךָ: מַשַּׁאת מְאוּמָה. חוֹב שֶׁל כְּלוּם:

יב לֹא תִשְׁכַּב בַּעֲבֹטוֹ. לֹא תִשְׁכַּב וַעֲבֹטוֹ אֶצְלֶךָ:

יג כְּבוֹא הַשֶּׁמֶשׁ. אִם כְּסוּת לַיְלָה הוּא, וְאִם כְּסוּת יוֹם הַחֲזִירֵהוּ בַּבֹּקֶר, וּכְבָר כָּתוּב בִּ"וְאֵלֶּה הַמִּשְׁפָּטִים": "עַד בֹּא הַשֶּׁמֶשׁ תְּשִׁיבֶנּוּ" (שמות כב, כה), כָּל הַיּוֹם תְּשִׁיבֶנּוּ לוֹ וּכְבֹא הַשֶּׁמֶשׁ תִּקָּחֶנּוּ: וּבֵרְכֶךָּ. וְאִם אֵינוֹ מְבָרֶכְךָ, מִכָּל מָקוֹם "וּלְךָ תִּהְיֶה צְדָקָה":

בַּעֲוֹן בָּנִים. כְּבָר אָמוּר: "אִישׁ בְּחֶטְאוֹ יוּמָתוּ", אֲבָל מִי שֶׁאֵינוֹ אִישׁ מֵת בַּעֲוֹן אָבִיו, וְהַקְּטַנִּים מֵתִים בַּעֲוֹן אֲבוֹתָם בִּידֵי שָׁמַיִם:

יז לֹא תַטֶּה מִשְׁפַּט גֵּר יָתוֹם. וְעַל הֶעָשִׁיר כְּבָר הִזְהִיר: "לֹא תַטֶּה מִשְׁפָּט" (לעיל טז, יט), וְשָׁנָה בֶּעָנִי לַעֲבֹר עָלָיו בִּשְׁנֵי לָאוִין, לְפִי שֶׁנָּקֵל לְהַטּוֹת מִשְׁפַּט עָנִי יוֹתֵר מִשֶּׁל עָשִׁיר, לְכָךְ הִזְהִיר וְשָׁנָה עָלָיו: וְלֹא תַחֲבֹל. שֶׁלֹּא בִּשְׁעַת הַהַלְוָאָה:

יח וְזָכַרְתָּ. עַל מְנָת כֵּן פְּדִיתִיךָ, לִשְׁמֹר חֻקּוֹתַי אֲפִלּוּ יֵשׁ חֶסְרוֹן כִּיס בַּדָּבָר:

יד לֹא תַעֲשֹׁק שָׂכִיר. וַהֲלֹא כְּבָר כָּתוּב? אֶלָּא לַעֲבֹר עַל הָאֶבְיוֹן בִּשְׁנֵי לָאוִין: "לֹא תַעֲשֹׁק שְׂכַר שָׂכִיר שֶׁהוּא עָנִי וְאֶבְיוֹן", וְעַל הֶעָשִׁיר כְּבָר הַזְהִיר: "לֹא תַעֲשֹׁק אֶת רֵעֲךָ" (ויקרא יט, יג): אֶבְיוֹן. הַתָּאֵב לְכָל דָּבָר: מִגֵּרְךָ. זֶה גֵּר צֶדֶק: בִּשְׁעָרֶיךָ. זֶה גֵּר תּוֹשָׁב הָאוֹכֵל נְבֵלוֹת: אֲשֶׁר בְּאַרְצְךָ. לְרַבּוֹת שְׂכַר בְּהֵמָה וְכֵלִים:

טו וְאֵלָיו הוּא נֹשֵׂא אֶת נַפְשׁוֹ. אֶל הַשָּׂכָר הַזֶּה הוּא נֹשֵׂא אֶת נַפְשׁוֹ לָמוּת, עָלָה בַּכֶּבֶשׁ וְנִתְלָה בָּאִילָן: וְהָיָה בְךָ חֵטְא. מִכָּל מָקוֹם, אֶלָּא שֶׁמְּמַהֲרִין לְפָרַע עַל יְדֵי הַקּוֹרֵא: טז לֹא יוּמְתוּ אָבוֹת עַל בָּנִים. בְּעֵדוּת בָּנִים. וְאִם תֹּאמַר

DISCUSSION

24:9 | Remember that which the Lord your God did to Miriam: This warning is interpreted homiletically as follows: The mark of leprosy is a punishment for inappropriate behavior, and even Miriam was punished with leprosy for speaking disparagingly of Moses. Therefore, one must beware of the mark of leprosy and of behavior that causes it, as it is liable to appear even among the distinguished (see *Targum Yonatan*; Rashi). Some maintain that this miracle afflicted mainly people of stature, as a sign of misconduct, as in the case of Miriam (see commentary, introduction to Leviticus 13). It is also possible that this verse is a warning to treat all people equally with regard to the laws of leprosy, and

to place even the most prominent individuals in isolation if that is what the law requires (see *Bekhor Shor*).

24:16 | Fathers shall not be put to death for sons: In II Kings (14:5–6) this verse is understood as a prohibition against punishing the sons of a sinner. It is related there that Amatzya, king of Judah, executed the servants who killed his father, "but the children of those who smote he did not put to death in accordance with that which is written in the book of the Torah of Moses, that the Lord commanded, saying: Fathers will not be put to death for the sons, and sons will not be put to death for fathers; each will be put to death for his sin." In the Talmud

another interpretation of the verse is offered: Fathers may not be sentenced to death, or to any other punishment, based on the testimony of their sons, and likewise, the testimony of fathers is not accepted in the trial of their sons. In general, this means that one is disqualified from testifying for or against a relative. In contrast to other legal systems, where the testimony of relatives is taken into consideration but accorded less authority, here that type of testimony is completely excluded (*Targum Yonatan*; Rashi; *Sanhedrin* 27b, *Ḥiddushei HaRan, Sanhedrin* 27b).

24:17 | You shall not take a widow's garment as collateral: A widow is perceived here as a poor and needy woman. According to one

the Lord your God redeemed you from there; therefore I command you to do this thing. As people who were abused yourselves, you must see to the rights of others who suffer.

19 The next three laws apply outside one's home, in the field, the orchard, and the vineyard, and also require that one refrain from exercising his full legal and property rights when dealing with the poor. When you reap your harvest in your field, and you forget a sheaf in the field, you shall not return to take it; for the stranger, the orphan, and the widow it shall be. Harvesters would tie together sheaves and leave them in the field for collection at the end of the day. If a sheaf was forgotten, you may not return later to take it. Once it is forgotten, leave it for the needy, so that the Lord your God will bless you in all your endeavors. This commandment is performed unintentionally, as you did not intend to leave the sheaf in the field, and your forgetfulness may have been caused by Heaven. However, if you are not eager to retrieve that which you lost, but instead leave your forgotten sheaf for the disadvantaged, you will be blessed, as a blessing is found only in an object that is hidden from the eye.[57] If you are not particular about what you deserve, Heaven will treat you generously as well.

Beating olives

20 A similar law is presented: When you beat your olive tree to knock down the olives, you shall not search the boughs again to find any remaining olives that did not fall but are caught in the leaves or branches, or that are not yet ripe; for the stranger, the orphan, and the widow it shall be. Here, too, you are required to relinquish the small remnants of which you have legal ownership to the needy.

21 Likewise, when you harvest your vineyard, you shall not glean the small, individual grapes that did not form into clusters behind you after harvesting the complete clusters; rather, for the stranger, the orphan, and the widow it shall be.

Sheaves of wheat in a field

Grapes in a vineyard

22 The Torah once again stresses: You shall remember that you were a slave in Egypt. You understand the desperation of one who is impoverished, and how finding objects of this kind can bring him joy. Therefore I command you to perform this matter. After everything you experienced, you are better able to understand and fulfill this commandment.

וּפְדְךָ יְהוָה אֱלֹהֶיךָ מִשָּׁם עַל־כֵּן אָנֹכִי מְצַוְּךָ לַעֲשׂוֹת אֶת־הַדָּבָר
יט הַזֶּה׃ כִּי תִקְצֹר קְצִירְךָ בְשָׂדֶךָ וְשָׁכַחְתָּ עֹמֶר בַּשָּׂדֶה לֹא תָשׁוּב
לְקַחְתּוֹ לַגֵּר לַיָּתוֹם וְלָאַלְמָנָה יִהְיֶה לְמַעַן יְבָרֶכְךָ יְהוָה אֱלֹהֶיךָ בְּכֹל מַעֲשֵׂה
כ יָדֶיךָ׃ כִּי תַחְבֹּט זֵיתְךָ לֹא תְפַאֵר אַחֲרֶיךָ לַגֵּר לַיָּתוֹם וְלָאַלְמָנָה
כא כב יִהְיֶה׃ כִּי תִבְצֹר כַּרְמְךָ לֹא תְעוֹלֵל אַחֲרֶיךָ לַגֵּר לַיָּתוֹם וְלָאַלְמָנָה יִהְיֶה׃ וְזָכַרְתָּ
כִּי־עֶבֶד הָיִיתָ בְּאֶרֶץ מִצְרָיִם עַל־כֵּן אָנֹכִי מְצַוְּךָ לַעֲשׂוֹת אֶת־הַדָּבָר
א הַזֶּה׃ כִּי־יִהְיֶה רִיב בֵּין אֲנָשִׁים וְנִגְּשׁוּ אֶל־הַמִּשְׁפָּט וּשְׁפָטוּם
ב וְהִצְדִּיקוּ אֶת־הַצַּדִּיק וְהִרְשִׁיעוּ אֶת־הָרָשָׁע׃ וְהָיָה אִם־בִּן הַכּוֹת הָרָשָׁע

רש״י

יט| **ושכחת עמר.** ולא גדיש, מכאן אמרו: עמר שיש בו סאתים ושכחו אינו שכחה (פאה ו, ו): **בשדה.** לרבות שכחת קמה ששכח מקצתה מלקצר: **לא תשוב לקחתו.** מכאן אמרו: שלאחריו שכחה, שלפניו אינו שכחה, שאינו בבל תשוב (פאה ו, ד): **למען יברכך.** ואף על פי שבאת לידו שלא במתכוון, קל וחומר לעושה במתכוון. אמור מעתה, נפלה סלע מידו ומצאה עני ונתפרנס בה, הרי הוא מתברך עליה:

כ| **לא תפאר.** לא תטול תפארתו ממנו, מכאן שמניחין פאה לאילן: **אחריך.** זו שכחה:

כא| **לא תעולל.** מצאת בה עוללת, לא תקחנה. ואיזו היא עוללת? כל שאין לה לא כתף ולא נטף. יש לה אחד מהם, הרי היא לבעל הבית. וראיתי בתלמוד ירושלמי (פאה ז, ד): אי זו היא כתף? פסיגין זה על גב זה. נטף – אלו התלויות בשדרה ויורדות:

פרק כה

א| **כי יהיה ריב.** סופם להיות נגשים אל המשפט. אמור מעתה, אין שלום יוצא מתוך מריבה; מי גרם ללוט לפרוש מן הצדיק? הוי אומר זו מריבה: **והרשיעו את הרשע.** יכול כל המתחייבין בדין לוקין? תלמוד לומר: "והיה אם בן הכות הרשע" (להלן פסוק ב), פעמים לוקה ופעמים אינו לוקה. ומי הוא הלוקה? למד מן הענין: "לא תחסם שור בדישו" (להלן פסוק ד), לאו שלא נתק לעשה:

Lashes

DEUTERONOMY 25:1–3

Following several commandments that deal with the well-being of people who are helpless due to their socio-economic circumstances, the next commandment encourages people to be considerate of a transgressor flogged in court, and to treat him with dignity.

25 1 **When there is a quarrel between men, and they approach** the court **to** receive **judgment, and they judge them,** in cases of both civil and criminal law, **and they,** the judges, **exonerate the righteous,** the one who is deemed righteous and wins the case, **and they convict the** one who is deemed **wicked** in this case,

2 **if the wicked man will be liable for flogging,** as not only did he cause harm to his counterpart but he also transgressed a law

DISCUSSION

opinion, the prohibition against taking a widow's garment as collateral is due to the above obligation (verses 12–13) to return a poor person's garment taken as collateral every day. If the widow's creditor acts with her in this manner, coming to her house every evening and morning, it might lead people to cast aspersions on her. Therefore, one of the *tanna'im* maintains that taking a wealthy widow's garment as collateral is permitted, as she does not need it returned daily (see *Targum Yonatan*; *Bava Metzia* 115a).

for which one is liable to receive lashes, **the judge shall cast him down [*vehippilo*],** he shall bend him over. Although the root *nun-peh-lamed* is understood to mean falling on the ground, in the Bible it can refer to any bending of the body.[58] According to the Talmud, before getting flogged a person would be stood and leaned a bit on an angle.[59] **And he,** the judge, **shall flog him before him,**[D] **in accordance with his wickedness, by number.** The number of lashes is not fixed; rather the number he is capable of enduring is deemed sufficient for his wickedness.[60]

Also, one who is convicted of several transgressions is flogged for each one, increasing the number accordingly.[61]

3 **Forty he shall flog him; he shall not continue.**[D] A convict is not flogged more than forty lashes for one transgression, **lest he continue to flog him beyond these a great blow, and your brother will be degraded before your eyes.** Any blow beyond what he deserves disgraces him unnecessarily. Another explanation: If his pain causes him to lose control of his orifices in front of all those present, he will be degraded, and his sentence is lashes, not degradation.[62]

The Prohibition of Muzzling an Ox While It Works
DEUTERONOMY 25:4

The Sages interpret the juxtaposition of this commandment with the matter of lashes as indicating that one is liable to receive lashes only for prohibitions that are similar to the prohibition of muzzling an ox. Therefore, prohibitions transgressed through passivity and not through action are excluded. Also excluded are prohibitions that are transgressed through speech; transgressions that can be remedied, e.g., returning a stolen object; and general prohibitions. All of these prohibitions are distinct from, and more lenient than, the prohibition of muzzling an ox during its threshing.

4 **You shall not muzzle an ox,** preventing it from eating grain, **in its threshing.** Naturally, an ox performing this labor wants to eat from the grain before it. Besides the fact that causing suffering to living creatures is prohibited, the owner of the animal is legally entitled for his animal to enjoy the grain of the field. Therefore, one who prevents the animal from doing so must pay the owner the value of the food he must now give it.[63]

Oxen during threshing

The Law of Levirate Marriage
DEUTERONOMY 25:5–10

Levirate marriage was practiced in Israel even before the Torah was given, and was practiced in many other cultures as well. The form of levirate marriage described in the Torah is meant to restrict this custom and define it. Whereas among other nations, or before the giving of the Torah, the obligation of levirate marriage applied to all relatives of the deceased, the Torah limits the commandment to his brothers alone. Likewise, the purpose of the commandment is to bring children into the world to sustain the name of the deceased; consequently, if the man or woman is infertile, the obligation does not apply.

5 **If brothers** who are sons of the same father[64] **will live together, and one of them dies, and he has no child** at the time of his death, **the wife of the dead shall not be married outside** of the family **to a strange man,** one who is not related. The Sages derive from the phrase "will live together" that the brothers must be alive at the same time; if one is born after his brother dies, there is no obligation of levirate marriage. Rather, **her husband's brother shall consort with her, and** thereby **take her as a wife, and perform levirate marriage with her.**

6 **It shall be that the firstborn that she will bear will perpetuate the name of his dead brother.** Although this literally means that the child should receive the name of the brother who died, the Sages interpret it figuratively, meaning that the firstborn is treated as the child of the brother who died, and not as the child of his biological father.[65] **And** the purpose of this is that **his name will not be expunged from Israel.** When a person dies without children, it is as though his name has

been erased, as he has no future. Therefore, his brother is commanded to marry his widow, and attempt to have a child with her.

7 **If the man does not wish to take his brother's widow, his brother's widow shall go up to the gate,** the location of the court, **to the elders,** the judges, **and say** to them: **My husband's brother refused to perpetuate a name for his brother in Israel; he is unwilling to perform levirate marriage with me.**

8 **The elders of his city shall call him and speak to him,** they shall advise him based on the circumstances. Sometimes they will try to convince him to perform levirate marriage, but other times the potential marriage may be imprudent, e.g., if there is a large age gap between them. In that case, the elders will advise him not to marry her.[66] **And he shall stand, and he shall say: I do not wish to take her.**

ג וְהִפִּילוֹ הַשֹּׁפֵט וְהִכָּהוּ לְפָנָיו כְּדֵי רִשְׁעָתוֹ בְּמִסְפָּר׃ אַרְבָּעִים יַכֶּנּוּ לֹא יֹסִיף פֶּן־
ד יֹסִיף לְהַכֹּתוֹ עַל־אֵלֶּה מַכָּה רַבָּה וְנִקְלָה אָחִיךָ לְעֵינֶיךָ׃ לֹא־תַחְסֹם שׁוֹר
ה בְּדִישׁוֹ׃ כִּי־יֵשְׁבוּ אַחִים יַחְדָּו וּמֵת אַחַד מֵהֶם וּבֵן אֵין־לוֹ
לֹא־תִהְיֶה אֵשֶׁת־הַמֵּת הַחוּצָה לְאִישׁ זָר יְבָמָהּ יָבֹא עָלֶיהָ וּלְקָחָהּ לוֹ לְאִשָּׁה
ו וְיִבְּמָהּ׃ וְהָיָה הַבְּכוֹר אֲשֶׁר תֵּלֵד יָקוּם עַל־שֵׁם אָחִיו הַמֵּת וְלֹא־יִמָּחֶה שְׁמוֹ
ז מִיִּשְׂרָאֵל׃ וְאִם־לֹא יַחְפֹּץ הָאִישׁ לָקַחַת אֶת־יְבִמְתּוֹ וְעָלְתָה יְבִמְתּוֹ הַשַּׁעְרָה
אֶל־הַזְּקֵנִים וְאָמְרָה מֵאֵן יְבָמִי לְהָקִים לְאָחִיו שֵׁם בְּיִשְׂרָאֵל לֹא אָבָה יַבְּמִי׃
ח וְקָרְאוּ־לוֹ זִקְנֵי־עִירוֹ וְדִבְּרוּ אֵלָיו וְעָמַד וְאָמַר לֹא חָפַצְתִּי לְקַחְתָּהּ׃

רש״י

ב | **וְהִפִּילוֹ הַשֹּׁפֵט.** מְלַמֵּד שֶׁאֵין מַלְקִין אוֹתוֹ לֹא עוֹמֵד וְלֹא יוֹשֵׁב אֶלָּא מֻטֶּה: **לְפָנָיו כְּדֵי רִשְׁעָתוֹ.** וּלְאַחֲרָיו כְּדֵי שְׁתַּיִם, מִכָּאן אָמְרוּ: מַלְקִין אוֹתוֹ שְׁתֵּי יָדוֹת מִלְּאַחֲרָיו וּשְׁלִישׁ מִלְּפָנָיו: **בְּמִסְפָּר.** וְאֵינוֹ נָקוּד 'בַּמִּסְפָּר', לִמֵּד שֶׁהוּא דָּבוּק, לוֹמַר בְּמִסְפַּר אַרְבָּעִים וְלֹא אַרְבָּעִים שְׁלֵמִים, אֶלָּא מִנְיָן שֶׁהוּא סוֹכֵם וּמַשְׁלִים לְאַרְבָּעִים, וְהֵן אַרְבָּעִים חָסֵר אַחַת:

ג | **לֹא יֹסִיף.** מִכָּאן אַזְהָרָה לַמַּכֶּה אֶת חֲבֵרוֹ: **וְנִקְלָה אָחִיךָ.** כָּל הַיּוֹם קוֹרְאֵהוּ 'רָשָׁע', וּמִשֶּׁלָּקָה קוֹרְאֵהוּ 'אָחִיךָ':

ד | **לֹא תַחְסֹם שׁוֹר.** דִּבֶּר הַכָּתוּב בַּהוֶֹה, וְהוּא הַדִּין לְכָל בְּהֵמָה חַיָּה וָעוֹף וּלְכָל מְלָאכָה שֶׁהִיא כְּדְבַר מַאֲכָל. אִם כֵּן לָמָּה נֶאֱמַר "שׁוֹר"? לְהוֹצִיא אֶת הָאָדָם: **בְּדִישׁוֹ.** יָכוֹל יַחְסְמֶנּוּ מִבַּחוּץ? תַּלְמוּד לוֹמַר: "לֹא תַחְסֹם שׁוֹר", מִכָּל מָקוֹם. וְלָמָּה נֶאֱמַר 'דַּיִשׁ'? לוֹמַר לְךָ מַה 'דַּיִשׁ' מְיֻחָד, דָּבָר שֶׁלֹּא נִגְמְרָה מְלַאכְתּוֹ וְגִדּוּלוֹ מִן הָאָרֶץ, אַף כָּל כַּיּוֹצֵא בוֹ, יָצָא הַחוֹלֵב וְהַמְגַבֵּן וְהַמְחַבֵּץ שֶׁאֵין גִּדּוּלוֹ מִן הָאָרֶץ, יָצָא הַלָּשׁ וְהַמְקַטֵּף שֶׁנִּגְמְרָה מְלַאכְתּוֹ לְחַלָּה, יָצָא הַבּוֹדֵל בִּתְמָרִים וּבִגְרוֹגָרוֹת שֶׁנִּגְמְרָה מְלַאכְתָּן לְמַעֲשֵׂר:

ה | **כִּי יֵשְׁבוּ אַחִים יַחְדָּו.** שֶׁהָיְתָה לָהֶם יְשִׁיבָה אַחַת בָּעוֹלָם, פְּרָט לְאֵשֶׁת אָחִיו שֶׁלֹּא הָיָה בְּעוֹלָמוֹ: **יַחְדָּו.** הַמְיֻחָדִים בְּנַחֲלָה, פְּרָט לְאָחִיו מִן הָאֵם: **וּבֵן אֵין לוֹ.** עַיֵּן עָלָיו, בֵּן אוֹ בַּת אוֹ בֶּן הַבֵּן אוֹ בֶּן הַבַּת אוֹ בַּת הַבֵּן אוֹ בַּת הַבַּת:

ו | **וְהָיָה הַבְּכוֹר.** גְּדוֹל הָאַחִים הוּא מְיַבֵּם אוֹתָהּ: **אֲשֶׁר תֵּלֵד.** פְּרָט לְאַיְלוֹנִית שֶׁאֵינָהּ יוֹלֶדֶת: **יָקוּם עַל שֵׁם אָחִיו.** זֶה שֶׁיְּיַבֵּם אֶת אִשְׁתּוֹ יִטֹּל נַחֲלַת הַמֵּת בְּנִכְסֵי אָבִיו: **וְלֹא יִמָּחֶה שְׁמוֹ.** פְּרָט לְאֵשֶׁת סָרִיס שֶׁשְּׁמוֹ מָחוּי:

ז | **הַשַּׁעְרָה.** כְּתַרְגּוּמוֹ: "לִתְרַע בֵּית דִּינָא":

ח | **וְעָמַד.** בַּעֲמִידָה: **וְאָמַר.** בִּלְשׁוֹן הַקֹּדֶשׁ, וְאַף הִיא דְּבָרֶיהָ בִּלְשׁוֹן הַקֹּדֶשׁ:

DISCUSSION

25:2 | **The judge shall cast him down and he shall flog him before him:** This expression indicates that the judges decide the number of lashes on a per-case basis (see Ibn Ezra). According to Jewish tradition, there is a fixed number for a convicted transgressor, thirty-nine lashes. However, since the purpose of the flogging is not to kill the convict but to significantly afflict him, an expert determines ahead of time how many of the thirty-nine lashes he is capable of withstanding (see *Or HaḤayyim*; *Makkot* 22).

25:3 | **Forty he shall flog him:** The Sages combine these verses to read: By number forty. They interpreted this phrase as referring to the number before forty, thirty-nine lashes (see Rashi, verse 2; *Makkot* 22). Since the number forty is mentioned in the verse as a maximum number, and if one exceeds it he is guilty, the Sages lowered the limit by one in order to prevent that from happening. According to tradition, one-third of the lashes are administered on the front of the body, and two-thirds are administered on the back (see *Makkot* 22a–23a; *Sefer HaḤinnukh* 595).

He shall not continue: By *a fortiori* inference from this verse, the Sages derive a general prohibition against striking another Jew. If a court-appointed attendant, who is subordinate to the judge, is prohibited from striking the convict beyond the exact number of lashes dictated to him by the judge, then an ordinary person, who is not authorized to administer punishment for a transgression, is certainly prohibited from striking another (see Rashi; *Ketubot* 33a).

9 **His brother's widow shall approach him before the eyes of the elders, and she shall remove his shoe from his foot, and spit** on the ground[67] **before him, and she shall proclaim and say: So,** in this disgraceful manner, **shall be done to the man who will not build the house of his brother.**[D]

10 **His name,** the name of his family, **shall be called in Israel: The house of one whose shoe was removed.** The purpose of this

act is to condemn one who refuses to perform an act of kindness for his dead brother. However, it can also be understood as an act of expiation, which allows the man to avoid fulfillment of this commandment in cases where the court advises against doing so.[68]

A Woman Who Grabs a Man's Genitals
DEUTERONOMY 25:11–12

The Torah details elsewhere the various categories of restitution one must pay for injuring another: damage, loss of livelihood, medical costs, and pain.[69] Here the Torah adds another right of the injured party.

11 **If men fight together one with another,** grabbing each other in a way that they cannot be separated, **and the wife of the one,** afraid that her husband will be overwhelmed by his adversary, **approaches to rescue her husband from the hand of the one who is striking him,** willing to do whatever she can to save him, **and she extends her hand, and grabs his genitals,** the genitals of the other man, in order to cause him pain, causing him to release his hold on her husband,

12 due to the danger and humiliation involved, **you shall sever her hand** with which she grabbed him in this manner; **your eye shall not pity** her. This verse is interpreted by the Sages in two

manners. The first interpretation is literal: The verse addresses any bystanders that might be present, and requires them to save the life of the man who was attacked by the woman and her husband, even if it involves physically mutilating the woman in order to release her hold on him.[70] The second interpretation is symbolic: The woman is required to pay restitution after the incident. This is similar to the rabbinic interpretation of the phrase "a hand for a hand."[71] Accordingly, this commandment addresses the judges, and introduces the concept of restitution for shame, whereby one who shames another by striking him or by any other physical act is required to pay.[72]

Weights and Justice
DEUTERONOMY 25:13–16

The purpose of the next commandment is to prevent deceit in the use of weights and other measurements.

13 **You shall not have in your pouch different weights,** a **great** one to use when buying, **and** a **small** one to use when selling, in order to profit from the difference between the weight you use and the actual weight of the item.

14 Likewise, **you shall not have in your house different measures** for measuring volume, a **great** measure for buying **and** a **small** one for selling. Even if it is not your intention to use them for deceit, do not own two different-sized measures for any purpose,[73] as merely keeping them in your possession might tempt you to use them deceitfully.

15 Rather, **you shall have a whole and just weight; you shall have a whole and just measure, so that your days will be extended on the land that the Lord your God is giving you.**

16 **As** injustice is not merely a social matter, but rather **it is an abomination to the Lord your God, all who do these, all who do injustice.**

Weights

ט וְנִגְּשָׁ֨ה יְבִמְתּ֣וֹ אֵלָיו֮ לְעֵינֵ֣י הַזְּקֵנִים֒ וְחָלְצָ֤ה נַעֲלוֹ֙ מֵעַ֣ל רַגְל֔וֹ וְיָרְקָ֖ה בְּפָנָ֑יו וְעָֽנְתָה֙
י וְאָ֣מְרָ֔ה כָּ֚כָה יֵעָשֶׂ֣ה לָאִ֔ישׁ אֲשֶׁ֥ר לֹא־יִבְנֶ֖ה אֶת־בֵּ֥ית אָחִֽיו׃ וְנִקְרָ֥א שְׁמ֖וֹ בְּיִשְׂרָאֵ֑ל
יא בֵּ֖ית חֲל֥וּץ הַנָּֽעַל׃ כִּֽי־יִנָּצ֨וּ אֲנָשִׁ֜ים יַחְדָּו֙ אִ֣ישׁ וְאָחִ֔יו וְקָֽרְבָה֙
אֵ֣שֶׁת הָֽאֶחָ֔ד לְהַצִּ֥יל אֶת־אִישָׁ֖הּ מִיַּ֣ד מַכֵּ֑הוּ וְשָׁלְחָ֣ה יָדָ֔הּ וְהֶחֱזִ֖יקָה בִּמְבֻשָֽׁיו׃
יב יג וְקַצֹּתָ֖ה אֶת־כַּפָּ֑הּ לֹ֥א תָח֖וֹס עֵינֶֽךָ׃ לֹא־יִהְיֶ֥ה לְךָ֛ בְּכִֽיסְךָ֖ אֶ֣בֶן וָאָ֑בֶן
יד טו גְּדוֹלָ֖ה וּקְטַנָּֽה׃ לֹא־יִהְיֶ֥ה לְךָ֛ בְּבֵיתְךָ֖ אֵיפָ֣ה וְאֵיפָ֑ה גְּדוֹלָ֖ה וּקְטַנָּֽה׃ אֶ֣בֶן שְׁלֵמָ֤ה
וָצֶ֙דֶק֙ יִֽהְיֶה־לָּ֔ךְ אֵיפָ֧ה שְׁלֵמָ֛ה וָצֶ֖דֶק יִֽהְיֶה־לָּ֑ךְ לְמַ֙עַן֙ יַאֲרִ֣יכוּ יָמֶ֔יךָ עַ֚ל הָֽאֲדָמָ֔ה
טז אֲשֶׁר־יְהוָ֥ה אֱלֹהֶ֖יךָ נֹתֵ֥ן לָֽךְ׃ כִּ֧י תוֹעֲבַ֛ת יְהוָ֥ה אֱלֹהֶ֖יךָ כָּל־עֹ֣שֵׂה אֵ֑לֶּה כֹּ֖ל
עֹ֥שֵׂה עָֽוֶל׃

רש״י

ט| וְיָרְקָה בְּפָנָיו. עַל גַּבֵּי קַרְקַע: אֲשֶׁר לֹא יִבְנֶה. מִכָּאן לְמִי שֶׁחָלַץ שֶׁלֹּא יַחְזֹר וְיִיַבֵּם, דְּלָא כְּתִיב ׳אֲשֶׁר לֹא בָנָה׳ אֶלָּא ״אֲשֶׁר לֹא יִבְנֶה״, כֵּיוָן שֶׁלֹּא בָנָה שׁוּב לֹא יִבְנֶה:

י| וְנִקְרָא שְׁמוֹ וְגוֹ׳. מִצְוָה עַל כָּל הָעוֹמְדִים שָׁם לוֹמַר: ״חֲלוּץ הַנַּעַל״:

יא| כִּי יִנָּצוּ אֲנָשִׁים. סוֹפָן לָבֹא לִידֵי מַכּוֹת, כְּמוֹ שֶׁנֶּאֱמַר: ״מִיַּד מַכֵּהוּ״, אֵין שָׁלוֹם יוֹצֵא מִתַּחַת יְדֵי מַצּוּת:

יב| וְקַצֹּתָה אֶת כַּפָּהּ. מָמוֹן דְּמֵי בָשְׁתּוֹ, הַכֹּל לְפִי הַמְבַיֵּשׁ וְהַמִּתְבַּיֵּשׁ. אוֹ אֵינוֹ אֶלָּא יָדָהּ מַמָּשׁ? נֶאֱמַר כָּאן ״לֹא תָחוֹס״, וְנֶאֱמַר לְהַלָּן בְּעֵדִים זוֹמְמִין ״לֹא תָחוֹס״ (לעיל יט, כא), מַה לְּהַלָּן מָמוֹן, אַף כָּאן מָמוֹן:

יג| גְּדוֹלָה וּקְטַנָּה. גְּדוֹלָה שֶׁמַּכְחֶשֶׁת אֶת הַקְּטַנָּה, שֶׁלֹּא יְהֵא נוֹטֵל בַּגְּדוֹלָה וּמַחֲזִיר בַּקְּטַנָּה: לֹא יִהְיֶה לְךָ. אִם עָשִׂיתָ כֵּן, לֹא יִהְיֶה לְךָ כְּלוּם: אֶבֶן וָאָבֶן. מִשְׁקָלוֹת:

טו| אֶבֶן שְׁלֵמָה וָצֶדֶק יִהְיֶה לָּךְ. אִם עָשִׂיתָ כֵּן, יִהְיֶה לְךָ הַרְבֵּה:

DISCUSSION

25:9| **And she shall proclaim and say: So shall be done to the man who will not build the house of his brother:** According to tradition, she must recite this statement exactly, word for word, in Hebrew (see *Sota* 32a).

Remembering Amalek and Expunging It

DEUTERONOMY 25:17–19

Amalek was the grandson of Esau. It is prohibited for Israel to harass the descendants of Esau; Amalek is an exception. Because of the Amalekites' irrational hatred of the children of Israel, not only is it permitted to wage war against them, Israel is also commanded to kill them, and to eternally remember the obligation to eradicate their memory from the world.

17 **Remember that which Amalek did to you on the way, upon**
Maftir **your exodus from Egypt.**

18 Amalek was a small nation, and did not engage in all-out war against Israel.[74] Rather, what occurred was **that he encountered you on the way, and he attacked from behind you**[D] **all the stragglers behind you,** the weak who walked slowly and with difficulty, **when you,** the children of Israel, **were faint and weary** from the years of slavery in Egypt and from traveling in the wilderness, **and he did not fear God.**[75] Alternatively, and you were not God-fearing, and therefore the weak of the nation were killed in the battle.[76]

19 Since Amalek initiated this attack motivated by pure wickedness, without any provocation on the part of Israel and with no rational reason, **it shall be when the Lord your God gives you rest from all your surrounding enemies, in the land that the Lord your God gives you as an inheritance to take possession of it, you shall expunge the memory of Amalek from under the heavens,** wherever it exists. **You shall not forget,** so that Amalek will not threaten you again, and also in order to exact revenge against them, as they were the first enemy of Israel whose hatred was ideological.

DISCUSSION

25:18 | That he encountered you on the way, and he attacked from behind you: Amalek's attack on Israel served no apparent interest. While Egypt's harassment of Israel stemmed from fear of their conquering the country, and other nations likewise worried that Israel might attack them, Amalek did not reside in Israel's path of travel, nor did they live in the land that Israel was to settle. While Amalek's attack may have simply been an attempted plunder by a nomadic tribe, this explanation is also suspect, ◄●

יז זָכ֕וֹר אֵ֛ת אֲשֶׁר־עָשָׂ֥ה לְךָ֖ עֲמָלֵ֑ק בַּדֶּ֖רֶךְ בְּצֵאתְכֶ֥ם מִמִּצְרָֽיִם: אֲשֶׁ֨ר קָֽרְךָ֜ בַּדֶּ֗רֶךְ מפטיר
יח
יט וַיְזַנֵּ֤ב בְּךָ֙ כָּל־הַנֶּחֱשָׁלִ֣ים אַחֲרֶ֔יךָ וְאַתָּ֖ה עָיֵ֣ף וְיָגֵ֑עַ וְלֹ֥א יָרֵ֖א אֱלֹהִֽים: וְהָיָ֡ה בְּהָנִ֣יחַ
יְהוָ֣ה אֱלֹהֶ֣יךָ ׀ לְ֠ךָ֠ מִכָּל־אֹ֨יְבֶ֜יךָ מִסָּבִ֗יב בָּאָ֙רֶץ֙ אֲשֶׁ֣ר־יְהוָֽה־אֱ֠לֹהֶ֠יךָ נֹתֵ֨ן לְךָ֤ נַחֲלָה֙
לְרִשְׁתָּ֔הּ תִּמְחֶה֙ אֶת־זֵ֣כֶר עֲמָלֵ֔ק מִתַּ֖חַת הַשָּׁמָ֑יִם לֹ֖א תִּשְׁכָּֽח:

רש״י

יז | זָכוֹר אֵת אֲשֶׁר עָשָׂה לְךָ. אִם שִׁקַּרְתָּ בְּמִדּוֹת וּבְמִשְׁקָלוֹת, הֱוֵי דּוֹאֵג מִגֵּרוּי הָאוֹיֵב, שֶׁנֶּאֱמַר: "מֹאזְנֵי מִרְמָה תּוֹעֲבַת ה'" וּכְתִיב בַּתְרֵיהּ: "בָּא זָדוֹן וַיָּבֹא קָלוֹן" (משלי יא, א-ב):

יח | אֲשֶׁר קָרְךָ בַּדֶּרֶךְ. לְשׁוֹן מִקְרֶה. דָּבָר אַחֵר, לְשׁוֹן קֶרִי וְטֻמְאָה, שֶׁהָיָה מְטַמְּאָן בְּמִשְׁכַּב זָכוּר. דָּבָר אַחֵר, לְשׁוֹן קֹר וָחֹם, צִנֶּנְךָ וְהִפְשִׁירְךָ מֵרְתִיחָתְךָ, שֶׁהָיוּ הָאֻמּוֹת יְרֵאִים לְהִלָּחֵם בָּכֶם, וּבָא זֶה וְהִתְחִיל וְהֶרְאָה מָקוֹם לַאֲחֵרִים. מָשָׁל לְאַמְבָּטִי רוֹתַחַת שֶׁאֵין כָּל בְּרִיָּה יְכוֹלָה לֵירֵד בְּתוֹכָהּ, בָּא בֶּן בְּלִיַּעַל אֶחָד קָפַץ וְיָרַד לְתוֹכָהּ, אַף עַל פִּי שֶׁנִּכְוָה, הֵקֵרָה אוֹתָהּ בִּפְנֵי אֲחֵרִים: וַיְזַנֵּב בְּךָ. מַכַּת זָנָב, חוֹתֵךְ מִילוֹת וְזוֹרֵק כְּלַפֵּי מַעְלָה: כָּל הַנֶּחֱשָׁלִים אַחֲרֶיךָ. חַסְרֵי כֹּחַ מֵחֲמַת חֶטְאָם, שֶׁהָיָה הֶעָנָן פּוֹלְטָן: וְאַתָּה עָיֵף וְיָגֵעַ. 'עָיֵף' בַּצָּמָא, דִּכְתִיב: "וַיִּצְמָא שָׁם הָעָם לַמַּיִם" (שמות יז, ג), וּכְתִיב אַחֲרָיו: "וַיָּבֹא עֲמָלֵק" (שם פסוק ח): וְיָגֵעַ. בַּדֶּרֶךְ: וְלֹא יָרֵא. עֲמָלֵק, "אֱלֹהִים" מִלְּהָרַע לְךָ:

יט | תִּמְחֶה אֶת זֵכֶר עֲמָלֵק. "מֵאִישׁ עַד אִשָּׁה מֵעוֹלֵל וְעַד יוֹנֵק מִשּׁוֹר וְעַד שֶׂה" (שמואל א' טו, ג), שֶׁלֹּא יְהֵא שֵׁם עֲמָלֵק נִזְכָּר אֲפִלּוּ עַל הַבְּהֵמָה, לוֹמַר, בְּהֵמָה זוֹ מִשֶּׁל עֲמָלֵק הָיְתָה:

DISCUSSION

→ as presumably they did not know what property Israel had in its possession.

In addition, Amalek did not seek to annihilate Israel, as the people of Israel were too numerous; rather, they sought to deter them or harm them. Given these factors, it appears that they were motivated by pure hatred. Consequently, the memory of Amalek in the national consciousness of Israel reflects opposition and hostility toward Israel no matter what the circumstances; it is the archetype of anti-Semitism throughout history. Although this hatred can occasionally be rationalized by various pretexts, it is primarily pure hatred of the essence of Israel.

Parashat
Ki Tavo

Gifts from the Crops That Require Declarations

DEUTERONOMY 26:1–19

The following section presents two commandments that will apply only when the nation reaches the land of Canaan. The first is the commandment to bring one's first fruits to the Temple each year. By means of this act, one demonstrates his recognition of the goodness of the land and its agricultural produce. The person who brings the first fruits expresses his gratitude with a speech in which he declares the goodness that God bestowed upon His people, and which enabled him to attain his current status. The second commandment is called the confession of tithes, a declaration made in the Temple to the effect that one has fulfilled his obligations with regard to tithes. Following these festive declarations, the section ends with a brief passage which concludes the portion of Moses' speech that deals with commandments.

26 1 **It shall be when you will come into the land that the Lord your God is giving you as an inheritance, and you take possession of it, and live in it.** The following commandment applies only after the conquest and settlement of the land, which takes fourteen years.[1]

2 **You shall take from the first of all the fruit of the ground**[D] **that you will bring from your land that the Lord your God is giving you.** These first fruits are separated before any of the other gifts that are given to the priests and Levites. **And you shall place it,** the first fruit, **in a wide,** flat **basket, and you shall go to the place that the Lord your God will choose to rest His name there,**[D] the Temple in Jerusalem.

3 **You shall come to the priest who will be in those days,**[D] **and you shall say to him,** in the manner of a ceremonial declaration: **I am telling today to the Lord your God that I have come to the land with regard to which the Lord took an oath to our fathers to give to us,** and this is its fruit.

4 **The priest shall take the basket from your hand, and he shall place it before the altar of the Lord your God.** The first fruits are not an offering that is burned on the altar. They are placed next to the altar, where the ritual waving of the basket is performed.[2]

5 **You shall proclaim and you shall say**[D] the following standard formula **before the Lord your God: A wandering Aramean was my father,** my forefather Jacob. Jacob married the daughters of the Aramean Laban and dwelled far from his homeland as part of an Aramean family.[3] Alternatively, some render the verse: An Aramean, close to annihilation, was my father. Others explain that the term "Aramean" refers to Laban, who sought to annihilate my father Jacob.[4] **And he,** Jacob, **descended to Egypt, and resided there, few in number,** arriving in Egypt with a family of merely seventy members. **And** during the years that his descendants dwelled in Egypt, **he became there a nation, great, mighty, and numerous.**

First fruits

DISCUSSION

26:2| **From the first of all the fruit of the ground:** The verse does not specify which types of fruit should be brought to the Temple. According to rabbinic tradition, the commandment to bring the first fruit to the Temple applies only to the seven species with which the Land of Israel is blessed (see 8:8). One may supplement them with other types of fruit, but one does not thereby fulfill the commandment (see Mishna *Bikkurim* 1:3, 3:9). Likewise, the amount that one must bring is not stated in the Torah. The Sages teach that each person may bring as much as he desires (Mishna *Pe'a* 1:1). The time for bringing the first fruit commences with the Festival of Weeks, Shavuot, which is also called the Day of the First Fruits (Numbers 28:26), the day on which two wheat loaves made from the first of the new wheat crop are presented in the Temple. The first fruits should be brought until the end of the Festival of Tabernacles. However, if one did not bring them until then, they may be brought until Hanukkah (Mishna *Bikkurim* 1:3, 1:6).

פרשת

כי תבוא

א והיה כי־תבוא אל־הארץ אשר יהוה אלהיך נתן לך נחלה וירשתה וישבת בה: כא
ב ולקחת מראשית ׀ כל־פרי האדמה אשר תביא מארצך אשר יהוה אלהיך נתן
לך ושמת בטנא והלכת אל־המקום אשר יבחר יהוה אלהיך לשכן שמו שם:
ג ובאת אל־הכהן אשר יהיה בימים ההם ואמרת אליו הגדתי היום ליהוה אלהיך
ד כי־באתי אל־הארץ אשר נשבע יהוה לאבתינו לתת לנו: ולקח הכהן הטנא
ה מידך והניחו לפני מזבח יהוה אלהיך: וענית ואמרת לפני ׀ יהוה אלהיך ארמי
אבד אבי וירד מצרימה ויגר שם במתי מעט ויהי־שם לגוי גדול עצום ורב:

רש״י

פרק כו

א| והיה כי תבוא. וירשתה וישבת בה. מגיד שלא נתחיבו בבכורים עד שכבשו את הארץ וחלקוה:

ב| מראשית. ולא כל ראשית, שאין כל הפרות חיבין בבכורים אלא שבעת המינין בלבד, נאמר כאן "ארץ" ונאמר להלן "ארץ חטה ושערה" וגו׳ (לעיל ח, ח), מה להלן משבעת המינים שנשתבחה בהן ארץ ישראל, אף כאן שבח ארץ ישראל. "זית שמן", זית אגורי ששמנו אגור בתוכו. "ודבש", הוא דבש תמרים: מראשית. אדם יורד לתוך שדהו ורואה תאנה שבכרה, כורך עליה גמי לסימן, ואומר: ׳הרי זו בכורים׳:

ג| אשר יהיה בימים ההם. אין לך אלא כהן שבימיך, כמו שהוא: ואמרת אליו. שאינך כפוי טובה: הגדתי היום. פעם אחת בשנה ולא שתי פעמים:

ד| ולקח הכהן הטנא מידך. להניף אותו, כהן מניח ידו תחת יד הבעלים ומניף:

ה| וענית. לשון הרמת קול: ארמי אבד אבי. מזכיר חסדי המקום: "ארמי אבד אבי", לבן בקש לעקר את הכל כשרדף אחר יעקב, ובשביל שחשב לעשות, חשב לו המקום כאלו עשה, שאמות העולם חושב להם הקדוש ברוך הוא מחשבה כמעשה: וירד מצרימה. ועוד אחרים באו לכלותנו, שאחרי זאת ירד יעקב למצרים: במתי מעט. בשבעים נפש:

DISCUSSION

Although one may perform this commandment individually, the Mishna describes the public manner in which the first fruits were brought during the Second Temple period: The residents of each town or province would ascend to Jerusalem together in a dramatic ceremonial procession that included decorations and much music (Mishna *Bikkurim* 3:2–4).

To the place that the Lord your God will choose to rest His name there: Before the Temple was built in Jerusalem, the first fruits were brought to the Tabernacle (see *Tosafot*, *Pesaḥim* 36b and *Zevaḥim* 119a). Some maintain that the first fruits were brought only to the Temple in Jerusalem, as the Torah states that they must be brought to "the house of the Lord" (Exodus 23:19), whereas the Tabernacle is not defined as a house. Furthermore, the Sages state that compulsory offerings for which there is no set time are presented only in the Temple, and there is no specific date for the bringing of the first fruits (see *Tosafot*, *Pesaḥim* 38b; Ramban).

26:3| **To the priest who will be in those days:** The first fruits may be brought to whichever priest is serving in the Temple. Although some explain that the verse refers specifically to the High Priest (*Targum Yonatan*; see Joshua 20:6), that is not the accepted opinion.

26:5| **You shall proclaim and you shall say:** This declaration, which one recites upon bringing the first fruits to the Temple, includes a brief description of the Israelites' descent to Egypt and their exodus, concluding with their arrival in the Land of Israel. It is referred to in the Mishna as the recitation of the first fruits (*Sota* 7:2). Like other ceremonial recitations, it must be recited in a precise manner. An official was therefore appointed who was responsible for reading the passage, and the one bringing the first fruits would repeat it after him. The recitation would be done in this manner even if the one bringing the fruit did not require assistance, so as not to shame those unable to read (see Mishna *Bikkurim* 3:7).

6 **The Egyptians mistreated us, and afflicted us, and imposed upon us hard labor.**

7 **We cried out to the Lord, God of our fathers, and the Lord heard our voice, and He saw** the extent of **our affliction**[5] **and our toil,** the tasks imposed upon us for the sole purpose of causing us suffering, **and our oppression.**

8 **The Lord took us out of Egypt with a mighty hand, and with an outstretched arm, and with** deeds that inspired **great awe** in those that witnessed them, **and with signs, and with wonders.**

9 **He brought us to this place,** the Land of Israel, **and He gave us this land, a land flowing with milk and honey.**

10 **Now,** since You performed this great kindness with our ancestors, I have come to thank You: **Behold, I have brought the first of the fruit of the land that You have given me, Lord. You shall place it before the Lord your God,** before the altar, **and you shall prostrate yourself before the Lord your God.**

11 **You shall rejoice in all the good that the Lord your God has given to you and to your household: you, and the Levite, and the stranger who is in your midst.** Having brought the first fruits to the Temple, you should take advantage of the opportunity to remain in the vicinity of the Temple and rejoice before God together with all your dependents.

12 **When you shall conclude to tithe all the tithes of your produce in the third year** of the Sabbatical cycle,[6] the third and sixth years after each Sabbatical Year, each of which is **the year of the** poor man's **tithe,**[D] **as you gave it to the Levite, to the stranger, to the orphan, and to the widow.** These include those individuals who do not possess an inheritance in the land, as well as the lower classes of society. **And they ate within your gates,** wherever they wished, not necessarily in the vicinity of the Temple, **and were satisfied.**

Second aliya

13 The harvest of the crop of the third and sixth years is completed toward the festival of Passover of the fourth and seventh years respectively, when the fruits of the trees that began to develop in the third and sixth years have all fully ripened. When you have performed all your obligations with regard to these crops, toward the end of the festival of Passover, you shall make the following declaration, stating that you have fulfilled the commandments of all the tithes of the last three years in accordance with the law: **You shall say before the Lord your God,** in the Temple: **I have disposed of the** portion of the produce that was **consecrated** to give to others, removing it **from my house, and also I gave them to the Levite, and to the stranger, to the orphan, and to the widow, in accordance with all Your commandment that You commanded me.** I gave each portion of the produce to those entitled to it. **I did not violate any of Your commandments, and I did not forget** to give each of the gifts in the correct manner and in their proper order.[7]

14 The following part of the declaration refers specifically to the second tithe, which must be eaten in Jerusalem by the owner and those who accompany him, in a state of ritual purity:[8] **I did not eat from it during my** acute **mourning, and I did not dispose of it in** a manner that would cause it to attain **a state of impurity, and I did not give from it,** its monetary exchange, toward the purchase of a shroud or coffin **for the dead.** In general, **I heeded the voice of the Lord my God, I have acted in accordance with everything that You commanded me.** Obviously, if someone is unable to honestly make this declaration, for example, if he ate of the second tithe during his acute mourning, he does not recite the passage.

15 The declaration is followed by a prayer: **Look** upon the land **from Your holy abode, from the heavens, and bless Your**

DISCUSSION

26:12 | In the third year, the year of the tithe: The year after the Sabbatical Year is the first year in the Sabbatical cycle. Each year other than the Sabbatical Year, first tithe is given to the Levites (Numbers 18:21–24). In addition, in the first and second years after the Sabbatical Year, second tithe is separated from the produce, which is not given to another but is brought to Jerusalem and consumed there with joy, in a state of ritual purity. In the third year, instead of second tithe, poor man's tithe is separated from the produce and given to the poor. This cycle is then repeated: In the fourth and fifth years second tithe is separated, while in the sixth year poor man's tithe is separated instead (see 14:22–29; Rashi here, and *Rosh HaShana* 12b; commentary on Deuteronomy 14:29).

ז וַיָּרֵעוּ אֹתָנוּ הַמִּצְרִים וַיְעַנּוּנוּ וַיִּתְּנוּ עָלֵינוּ עֲבֹדָה קָשָׁה: וַנִּצְעַק אֶל־יְהֹוָה אֱלֹהֵי אֲבֹתֵינוּ וַיִּשְׁמַע יְהֹוָה אֶת־קֹלֵנוּ וַיַּרְא אֶת־עָנְיֵנוּ וְאֶת־עֲמָלֵנוּ וְאֶת־לַחֲצֵנוּ:

ח וַיּוֹצִאֵנוּ יְהֹוָה מִמִּצְרַיִם בְּיָד חֲזָקָה וּבִזְרֹעַ נְטוּיָה וּבְמֹרָא גָּדֹל וּבְאֹתוֹת וּבְמֹפְתִים:

ט וַיְבִאֵנוּ אֶל־הַמָּקוֹם הַזֶּה וַיִּתֶּן־לָנוּ אֶת־הָאָרֶץ הַזֹּאת אֶרֶץ זָבַת חָלָב וּדְבָשׁ:

י וְעַתָּה הִנֵּה הֵבֵאתִי אֶת־רֵאשִׁית פְּרִי הָאֲדָמָה אֲשֶׁר־נָתַתָּה לִּי יְהֹוָה וְהִנַּחְתּוֹ לִפְנֵי יְהֹוָה אֱלֹהֶיךָ וְהִשְׁתַּחֲוִיתָ לִפְנֵי יְהֹוָה אֱלֹהֶיךָ:

יא וְשָׂמַחְתָּ בְכָל־הַטּוֹב אֲשֶׁר נָתַן־לְךָ יְהֹוָה אֱלֹהֶיךָ וּלְבֵיתֶךָ אַתָּה וְהַלֵּוִי וְהַגֵּר אֲשֶׁר בְּקִרְבֶּךָ:

שני

יב כִּי תְכַלֶּה לַעְשֵׂר אֶת־כָּל־מַעְשַׂר תְּבוּאָתְךָ בַּשָּׁנָה הַשְּׁלִישִׁת שְׁנַת הַמַּעֲשֵׂר וְנָתַתָּה לַלֵּוִי לַגֵּר לַיָּתוֹם וְלָאַלְמָנָה וְאָכְלוּ בִשְׁעָרֶיךָ וְשָׂבֵעוּ:

יג וְאָמַרְתָּ לִפְנֵי יְהֹוָה אֱלֹהֶיךָ בִּעַרְתִּי הַקֹּדֶשׁ מִן־הַבַּיִת וְגַם נְתַתִּיו לַלֵּוִי וְלַגֵּר לַיָּתוֹם וְלָאַלְמָנָה כְּכָל־מִצְוָתְךָ אֲשֶׁר צִוִּיתָנִי לֹא־עָבַרְתִּי מִמִּצְוֹתֶיךָ וְלֹא שָׁכָחְתִּי:

יד לֹא־אָכַלְתִּי בְאֹנִי מִמֶּנּוּ וְלֹא־בִעַרְתִּי מִמֶּנּוּ בְּטָמֵא וְלֹא־נָתַתִּי מִמֶּנּוּ לְמֵת שָׁמַעְתִּי בְּקוֹל יְהֹוָה אֱלֹהָי עָשִׂיתִי כְּכֹל אֲשֶׁר צִוִּיתָנִי:

טו הַשְׁקִיפָה מִמְּעוֹן קָדְשְׁךָ מִן־הַשָּׁמַיִם וּבָרֵךְ אֶת־עַמְּךָ אֶת־

ט אֶל הַמָּקוֹם הַזֶּה. זֶה בֵּית הַמִּקְדָּשׁ: וַיִּתֶּן לָנוּ אֶת הָאָרֶץ. כְּמַשְׁמָעוֹ:

י וְהִנַּחְתּוֹ. מַגִּיד שֶׁנּוֹטְלוֹ אַחַר הֲנָחַת הַכֹּהֵן, וְאוֹחֲזוֹ בְּיָדוֹ כְּשֶׁהוּא קוֹרֵא, וְחוֹזֵר וּמֵנִיף:

יא וְשָׂמַחְתָּ בְכָל הַטּוֹב. מִכָּאן אָמְרוּ: אֵין קוֹרִין מִקְרָא בִּכּוּרִים אֶלָּא בִּזְמַן שִׂמְחָה, מֵעֲצֶרֶת וְעַד הֶחָג, שֶׁאָדָם מְלַקֵּט תְּבוּאָתוֹ וּפֵרוֹתָיו וְיֵינוֹ וְשַׁמְנוֹ, אֲבָל מִן הֶחָג וְאֵילָךְ מֵבִיא וְאֵינוֹ קוֹרֵא: אַתָּה וְהַלֵּוִי. אַף הַלֵּוִי חַיָּב בַּבִּכּוּרִים אִם נָטְעוּ בְּתוֹךְ עָרֵיהֶם: וְהַגֵּר אֲשֶׁר בְּקִרְבֶּךָ. מֵבִיא וְאֵינוֹ קוֹרֵא, שֶׁאֵינוֹ יָכוֹל לוֹמַר לַאֲבֹתֵינוּ:

יב כִּי תְכַלֶּה לַעְשֵׂר אֶת כָּל מַעְשַׂר תְּבוּאָתְךָ בַּשָּׁנָה הַשְּׁלִישִׁת. כְּשֶׁתִּגְמֹר לְהַפְרִישׁ מַעַשְׂרוֹת שֶׁל שָׁנָה הַשְּׁלִישִׁית, קָבַע זְמַן הַבִּעוּר וְהַוִּדּוּי בְּעֶרֶב הַפֶּסַח הַסָּמוּךְ שֶׁל שָׁנָה הָרְבִיעִית, שֶׁנֶּאֱמַר: "מִקְצֵה שָׁלֹשׁ שָׁנִים תּוֹצִיא" וְגוֹ' (לעיל יד, כח), נֶאֱמַר כָּאן: "מִקְצֵה", וְנֶאֱמַר לְהַבָּל: "מִקֵּץ שֶׁבַע שָׁנִים" (להלן לא, י) לְעִנְיַן הַקְהֵל, מַה לְהַלָּן רֶגֶל, אַף כָּאן רֶגֶל, אִי מַה לְהַלָּן חַג הַסֻּכּוֹת אַף כָּאן חַג הַסֻּכּוֹת, תַּלְמוּד לוֹמַר: "כִּי תְכַלֶּה לַעְשֵׂר" מַעַשְׂרוֹת שֶׁל שָׁנָה הַשְּׁלִישִׁית, רֶגֶל שֶׁהַמַּעַשְׂרוֹת כָּלִין בּוֹ וְזֶהוּ פֶּסַח, שֶׁהַרְבֵּה אִילָנוֹת יֵשׁ שֶׁנִּלְקָטִים אַחַר הַסֻּכּוֹת,

נִמְצְאוּ מַעַשְׂרוֹת שֶׁל שְׁלִישִׁית כָּלִין בַּפֶּסַח שֶׁל רְבִיעִית, וְכָל מִי שֶׁשָּׁהָה מַעַשְׂרוֹתָיו הֵרִיכוֹ לְבַעֲרוֹ מִן הַבַּיִת: שְׁנַת הַמַּעֲשֵׂר. שָׁנָה שֶׁאֵין נוֹהֵג בָּהּ אֶלָּא מַעֲשֵׂר אֶחָד מִשְּׁנֵי מַעַשְׂרוֹת שֶׁנָּהֲגוּ בִּשְׁתֵּי שָׁנִים שֶׁלְּפָנֶיהָ, שָׁנָה רִאשׁוֹנָה שֶׁל שְׁמִטָּה נוֹהֵג בָּהּ מַעֲשֵׂר רִאשׁוֹן, כְּמוֹ שֶׁנֶּאֱמַר: "כִּי תִקְחוּ מֵאֵת בְּנֵי יִשְׂרָאֵל אֶת הַמַּעֲשֵׂר" (במדבר יח, כו), וּמַעֲשֵׂר שֵׁנִי, שֶׁנֶּאֱמַר: "וְאָכַלְתָּ לִפְנֵי ה' אֱלֹהֶיךָ... מַעְשַׂר דְּגָנְךָ תִּירֹשְׁךָ וְיִצְהָרֶךָ" (לעיל יד, כג), הֲרֵי שְׁתֵּי מַעַשְׂרוֹת, וּבָא וְלִמֶּדְךָ כָּאן בַּשָּׁנָה הַשְּׁלִישִׁית, שֶׁאֵין נוֹהֵג מֵאוֹתָן שְׁתֵּי מַעַשְׂרוֹת אֶלָּא הָאֶחָד, וְאֵי זֶה? זֶה מַעֲשֵׂר רִאשׁוֹן, וְתַחַת מַעֲשֵׂר שֵׁנִי יִתֵּן מַעֲשַׂר עָנִי, שֶׁנֶּאֱמַר כָּאן: "וְנָתַתָּה לַלֵּוִי" אֶת אֲשֶׁר לוֹ, זֶה מַעֲשֵׂר רִאשׁוֹן: "לַגֵּר לַיָּתוֹם וְלָאַלְמָנָה" זֶה מַעֲשֵׂר עָנִי: וְאָכְלוּ בִשְׁעָרֶיךָ וְשָׂבֵעוּ. תֵּן לָהֶם כְּדֵי שָׂבְעָן, מִכָּאן אָמְרוּ: אֵין פּוֹחֲתִין לֶעָנִי בַּגֹּרֶן מֵחֲצִי קַב חִטִּים וְכוּ':

יג וְאָמַרְתָּ לִפְנֵי ה' אֱלֹהֶיךָ. הִתְוַדֵּה שֶׁנָּתַתָּ מַעַשְׂרוֹתֶיךָ: בִּעַרְתִּי הַקֹּדֶשׁ מִן הַבַּיִת. זֶה מַעֲשֵׂר שֵׁנִי וְנֶטַע רְבָעִי, וְלִמֶּדְךָ שֶׁאִם שָׁהָה מַעַשְׂרוֹתָיו שֶׁל שְׁתֵּי שָׁנִים וְלֹא הֶעֱלָם לִירוּשָׁלַיִם, שֶׁצָּרִיךְ לְהַעֲלוֹתָם עַכְשָׁיו: וְגַם נְתַתִּיו לַלֵּוִי. זֶה מַעֲשֵׂר רִאשׁוֹן. וְגַם. לְרַבּוֹת תְּרוּמוֹת וּבִכּוּרִים: וְלַגֵּר לַיָּתוֹם

וְלָאַלְמָנָה. זֶה מַעֲשַׂר עָנִי: כְּכָל מִצְוָתְךָ. נְתַתִּים כְּסִדְרָן, לֹא הִקְדַּמְתִּי תְרוּמָה לַבִּכּוּרִים וְלֹא מַעֲשֵׂר לַתְּרוּמָה וְלֹא שֵׁנִי לָרִאשׁוֹן, שֶׁהַתְּרוּמָה קְרוּיָה "רֵאשִׁית" (לעיל יח, ד), שֶׁהִיא רִאשׁוֹנָה מִשֶּׁנַּעֲשָׂה דָגָן, וּכְתִיב: "מְלֵאָתְךָ וְדִמְעֲךָ לֹא תְאַחֵר" (שמות כב, כח), לֹא תְשַׁנֶּה אֶת הַסֵּדֶר: לֹא עָבַרְתִּי מִמִּצְוֹתֶיךָ. לֹא הִפְרַשְׁתִּי מִמִּין עַל שֶׁאֵינוֹ מִינוֹ, וּמִן הֶחָדָשׁ עַל הַיָּשָׁן: וְלֹא שָׁכָחְתִּי. מִלְּבָרֶכְךָ עַל הַפְרָשַׁת מַעַשְׂרוֹת:

יד לֹא אָכַלְתִּי בְאֹנִי מִמֶּנּוּ. מִכָּאן שֶׁאָסוּר לְאוֹנֵן: וְלֹא בִעַרְתִּי מִמֶּנּוּ בְּטָמֵא. בֵּין שֶׁאֲנִי טָמֵא וְהוּא טָהוֹר, בֵּין שֶׁאֲנִי טָהוֹר וְהוּא טָמֵא, וְהֵיכָן הֻזְהַר עַל כָּךְ: "לֹא תוּכַל לֶאֱכֹל בִּשְׁעָרֶיךָ" וְגוֹ' (לעיל יב, יז) — זוֹ אֲכִילַת טֻמְאָה, כְּמוֹ שֶׁנֶּאֱמַר בְּפָסוּלֵי הַמֻּקְדָּשִׁין: "בִּשְׁעָרֶיךָ תֹּאכְלֶנּוּ הַטָּמֵא וְהַטָּהוֹר" וְגוֹ' (לעיל טו, כב), אֲבָל זֶה לֹא תוּכַל לֶאֱכֹל דֶּרֶךְ אֲכִילַת שְׁעָרֶיךָ הָאָמוּר בְּמָקוֹם אַחֵר: וְלֹא נָתַתִּי מִמֶּנּוּ לְמֵת. לַעֲשׂוֹת לוֹ אָרוֹן וְתַכְרִיכִין: שָׁמַעְתִּי בְּקוֹל ה' אֱלֹהָי. הֲבִיאוֹתִיו לְבֵית הַבְּחִירָה: עָשִׂיתִי כְּכֹל אֲשֶׁר צִוִּיתָנִי. שָׂמַחְתִּי וְשִׂמַּחְתִּי בּוֹ:

טו הַשְׁקִיפָה מִמְּעוֹן קָדְשְׁךָ. עָשִׂינוּ מַה שֶּׁגָּזַרְתָּ עָלֵינוּ, עֲשֵׂה אַתָּה מַה שֶּׁעָלֶיךָ לַעֲשׂוֹת, שֶׁאָמַרְתָּ: "אִם בְּחֻקֹּתַי

people Israel, who fulfill Your will, **and the land that You gave us, as You took an oath to our fathers, a land flowing with milk and honey.**

16 Although the aforementioned gifts are given to people, the
Third first fruits to the priests and the tithes to the needy, they are
aliya primarily a fulfillment of God's commandments. Like those that preceded them, their primary importance is as part of the divine service. **This day, the Lord your God is commanding you to perform these statutes,** the commandments that you cannot comprehend, **and the ordinances,** which can be comprehended logically, **and you shall observe and you shall perform them with all your heart, and with all your soul.** Ensure that you perform each commandment at the proper time, in the appropriate place, according to the required measure, and with total dedication.

17 Even commandments that have social value should not be performed merely from the goodness of one's heart. You should perform them because **you have elevated** God's status in the world, and honored **the Lord today** by choosing Him **to be your God.**[9] Alternatively, the verse means that you have crowned Him today to be your King and your God.[10] **And this obligates you to walk in His ways, and to observe His statutes, and His commandments, and His ordinances, and to heed His voice.**

18 **And** likewise, **the Lord has elevated you today.** This relationship is mutual: You worship God alone and proclaim His unity, and similarly, He has chosen you alone, **to be a people of distinction for Him,** a unique nation, **as He spoke to you** before giving you the Torah: "You shall be distinguished for Me from among all the peoples."[11] **And** God also elevated you by choosing you **to observe all His commandments.**[D]

19 **To place you uppermost over all the nations that He made, for** your **praise, and for** your **renown, and for** your **splendor, and for you to be a holy people to the Lord your God, as He spoke,** on the same occasion, before giving you the Torah: "You shall be for Me a kingdom of priests, and a holy nation."[12]

The Public Recitation of the Blessings and Curses
DEUTERONOMY 27:1–26

In a one-time ceremony that will take place upon the arrival of the nation in the Land of Israel, the covenant with God is reaffirmed. As part of the ceremony, offerings are brought and a feast is held, as all the people confirm their commitment to the observance of God's commandments. In this unique ritual, all the tribes of Israel denounce those who clandestinely act improperly and praise those who behave morally even in private. In practice, this ceremony was held after the conquest of Jericho.[13]

27 1 **Moses and the elders of Israel commanded the people.** The
Fourth overall responsibility for the ceremony will be passed to Joshua,
aliya the next leader of the people. Nevertheless, due to the organizational aspects of the ceremony, the elders of Israel are also involved, and were presumably placed in charge of their tribes' part in the ceremony. They commanded the people, **saying: Observe the entire commandment,** all the details of the subsequent commandments, **that I am commanding you today.**

2 **It shall be on the day that you will cross the Jordan to the land that the Lord your God is giving you, you shall erect for you great stones, and plaster them with lime,** so that they will be smooth and form a suitable writing surface.

3 **You shall write on them all the words of this Torah, upon your crossing** the Jordan River, **so that you will come to the land that the Lord your God is giving you, a land flowing with milk and honey, as the Lord, God of your fathers, spoke to you.**

4 **It shall be upon your crossing of the Jordan, you shall erect these stones that I am commanding you today on Mount Eival, and you shall plaster them with lime.**[D]

5 **You shall build there an altar to the Lord your God, an altar**

Remnants of an altar on Mount Eival from the thirteenth century BCE, possibly the altar built by Joshua

ישראל ואת האדמה אשר נתתה לנו כאשר נשבעת לאבתינו ארץ זבת
טז חלב ודבש: היום הזה יהוה אלהיך מצוך לעשות את־החקים שלישי
יז האלה ואת־המשפטים ושמרת ועשית אותם בכל־לבבך ובכל־נפשך: את־
יהוה האמרת היום להיות לך לאלהים וללכת בדרכיו ולשמר חקיו ומצותיו
יח ומשפטיו ולשמע בקלו: ויהוה האמירך היום להיות לו לעם סגלה כאשר
יט דבר־לך ולשמר כל־מצותיו: ולתתך עליון על כל־הגוים אשר עשה לתהלה
ולשם ולתפארת ולהיתך עם־קדש ליהוה אלהיך כאשר דבר:
כז א ויצו משה וזקני ישראל את־העם לאמר שמר את־כל־המצוה אשר אנכי רביעי
ב מצוה אתכם היום: והיה ביום אשר תעברו את־הירדן אל־הארץ אשר־יהוה
ג אלהיך נתן לך והקמת לך אבנים גדלות ושדת אתם בשיד: וכתבת עליהן
את־כל־דברי התורה הזאת בעברך למען אשר תבא אל־הארץ אשר־יהוה
אלהיך נתן לך ארץ זבת חלב ודבש כאשר דבר יהוה אלהי־אבתיך לך:
ד והיה בעברכם את־הירדן תקימו את־האבנים האלה אשר אנכי מצוה אתכם
ה היום בהר עיבל ושדת אותם בשיד: ובנית שם מזבח ליהוה אלהיך מזבח

רש"י

תלכו... ונתתי גשמיכם בעתם" (ויקרא כו, ג-ד): אשר נתתה לנו כאשר נשבעת לאבתינו. לתת לנו, וקימת, "ארץ זבת חלב ודבש":

טז| היום הזה ה' אלהיך מצוך. בכל יום יהיו בעיניך חדשים כאלו בו ביום נצטוית עליהם: ושמרת ועשית אותם. בת קול מברכתו: הבאת בכורים היום, תשנה לשנה הבאה:

יז-יח| האמרת, האמירך. אין להם עד במקרא, ולי נראה שהם לשון הפרשה והבדלה, הבדלתו מאלהי הנכר "להיות לך לאלהים", והוא הפרישך אליו מעמי הארץ "להיות לו לעם סגלה") לשון תפארת, כמו: "יתאמרו כל פעלי און" (תהלים צד, ד):

יח| כאשר דבר לך. "והייתם לי סגלה" (שמות יט, ה):

יט| ולהיתך עם קדש וגו' כאשר דבר. "והייתם לי קדשים" (ויקרא כ, כו):

פרק כז

א| שמר את כל המצוה. לשון הוה, גרדנ"ט בלעז:

ב| והקמת לך. בירדן, ואחר כך תוציאו משם אחרות ותבנו מהן מזבח בהר עיבל. נמצאת אתה אומר, שלשה מיני אבנים היו: שתים עשרה בירדן, וכנגדן בגלגל, וכנגדן בהר עיבל, כדאיתא במסכת סוטה (דף לה ע"ב):

DISCUSSION

26:18| And the Lord has elevated you… to observe all His commandments: By addressing His commandments to you alone, God bestows a gift upon you and elevates your status. This concept is echoed in the formula of blessings recited over the performance of commandments: "Who sanctified us through His commandments," as well as in the Kiddush for the three pilgrimage festivals: "Who chose us from all peoples…and sanctified us through His commandments." Similarly, upon the fulfillment of every commandment that is performed periodically, one recites the blessing "Who has given us life, and sustained us, and brought us to this time," just as one gives thanks upon acquiring a new garment.

27:4| And you shall plaster them with lime: According to the plain meaning of the verses, the stones were covered with lime in order to form a smooth surface on which to write. However, some derive from the repetition of this instruction that the lime was placed on top of the writing in order to preserve it. According to this opinion, one would peel off the outer layer of lime in order to read the text (*Sota* 35b; see *Responsa of the Rashbatz* 53).

of stones; you shall not wield iron upon them.

6 Of **whole stones you shall build the altar of the Lord your God,** as it is prohibited to chisel stones with iron implements for use in the construction of an altar.[14] **And you shall offer up on it burnt offerings to the Lord your God.**

7 In addition, **you shall slaughter peace offerings, and you shall eat** them **there, and you shall rejoice before the Lord your God** through this public feast.

8 **You shall write on the stones all the words of this Torah,** which until now were written only on the Tablets of the Covenant and in the Torah scroll. You shall ensure that the writing is **very clearly**[D] readable by all and properly elucidated.

9 **Moses and the priests,** who are from the tribe of **the Levites, spoke to all Israel, saying: Listen and heed, Israel, this day you have become a people for the Lord your God.**

10 Therefore, the following is required of you: **You shall heed the voice of the Lord your God, and you shall perform His commandments and His statutes that I am commanding you today.** This covenant is enacted with the entire people now, before they enter the land of Canaan. The same covenant will be reaffirmed by the people after they enter the land.

Fifth aliya

11 **Moses commanded the people on that day, saying:**

12 **These** tribes **shall stand to bless the people**[D] **upon Mount Gerizim upon your crossing of the Jordan: Simeon, and Levi, and Judah, and Issachar, and Joseph, and Benjamin.** It is possible that these tribes were selected because they were considered the more distinguished tribes, as they are the sons of Leah and Rachel.[15]

13 **And these shall stand for the curse upon Mount Eival:**[16] **Reuben, Gad, and Asher, and Zebulun, Dan, and Naphtali.**

14 **The Levites,** who shall stand between the two mountains, **shall proclaim** the following curses and their parallel blessings, **and say** them **to every man of Israel in a loud voice.** When the Levites recited the blessings, they turned toward Mount Gerizim and faced the tribes that stood there, and when they recited the curses they turned toward Mount Eival and faced the tribes that stood on that mountain.[17] According to a different opinion, the Levites also stood on the mountains, and if that is the case, the blessings and curses were recited by people who stood on the mountains themselves:[18]

15 The following eleven curses do not pertain to those prohibitions which are of the greatest severity; neither do they include fundamental precepts such as those which appear in the Ten Precepts. Rather, the curses pertain to those transgressions that are performed in secret. Since the transgressors assume that their deeds will not be discovered, the people must publicly take an oath not to perform these actions.[19] For example, the focus of the first curse is not the prohibition against crafting a molten image in itself, but the secretive worship of idolatry. If any Jew openly worships idols, the court is obligated to eliminate him from among the people. However, if one conceals his idolatrous worship, no one is aware of his deeds, and therefore, the public oath is necessary. The Levites shall proclaim: **Cursed is the man who makes an idol or a cast figure, an abomination of the Lord,** an idol which is **the handiwork of a craftsman, and places it in secret. And** upon hearing this curse, **the entire people,** both the tribes standing on Mount Eival for the curse and those standing on Mount Gerizim for the blessing, **shall answer and say: Amen,** thereby taking an oath not to perform this transgression.

16 Once the people accept the first curse and its parallel blessing, the Levites recite the second curse: **Cursed is one who demeans his father or his mother, and the entire people shall say: Amen.** One who acts in this manner does not publicize his behavior, and his parents are likely to be reluctant to discuss it as well, particularly if they need him or are dependent upon him. The matter therefore remains a family secret. This curse also pertains to cases in which even one's parents are unaware of their son's behavior, e.g., when a son avoids his filial duty to honor his parents by means of deceit and false pretenses.[20]

17 **Cursed is one who moves his neighbor's boundary** into his neighbor's domain, thereby extending his own domain. This is obviously done in secret, based on the assumption that one's neighbor will not notice the change. The Sages include in this prohibition any incursion into another's domain or encroachment on an area under another's authority that is performed in a covert or deceitful manner.[21] **And the entire people shall say: Amen.**

18 **Cursed is one who misleads the blind on the way, and the entire people shall say: Amen.** This curse evokes the prohibition, "You shall not place an obstruction before the blind."[22] It applies to anyone who misleads others by giving them bad advice, even if they are not blind but merely lack necessary information and may make an erroneous decision on the basis of the advice that they were given.[23] In this case, the victim is unaware that he is being misled, and the responsibility is entirely upon the one who gave the advice. Therefore, a public oath is required.

19 **Cursed is one who distorts the judgment of a stranger, an orphan, or a widow, and the entire people shall say: Amen.** These individuals are not always aware of the fact that their judgment has been distorted. The stranger might be unfamiliar with local laws and customs, the orphan is young and inexperienced, and the widow, accustomed to being under the aegis of her husband, would not typically be familiar with legal and procedural matters. Therefore, it is often a simple matter for the judges to distort their judgment without the matter coming to light.[24]

ו אֲבָנִים לֹא־תָנִיף עֲלֵיהֶם בַּרְזֶל: אֲבָנִים שְׁלֵמוֹת תִּבְנֶה אֶת־מִזְבַּח יהוה אֱלֹהֶיךָ

ז וְהַעֲלִיתָ עָלָיו עוֹלֹת לַיהוה אֱלֹהֶיךָ: וְזָבַחְתָּ שְׁלָמִים וְאָכַלְתָּ שָּׁם וְשָׂמַחְתָּ

ח לִפְנֵי יהוה אֱלֹהֶיךָ: וְכָתַבְתָּ עַל־הָאֲבָנִים אֶת־כָּל־דִּבְרֵי הַתּוֹרָה הַזֹּאת בַּאֵר

ט הֵיטֵב: וַיְדַבֵּר מֹשֶׁה וְהַכֹּהֲנִים הַלְוִיִּם אֶל כָּל־יִשְׂרָאֵל לֵאמֹר הַסְכֵּת וּ

י שְׁמַע יִשְׂרָאֵל הַיּוֹם הַזֶּה נִהְיֵיתָ לְעָם לַיהוה אֱלֹהֶיךָ: וְשָׁמַעְתָּ בְּקוֹל יהוה אֱלֹהֶיךָ

יא וְעָשִׂיתָ אֶת־מִצְוֹתָו וְאֶת־חֻקָּיו אֲשֶׁר אָנֹכִי מְצַוְּךָ הַיּוֹם: וַיְצַו מֹשֶׁה אֶת־ **חמישי**

יב הָעָם בַּיּוֹם הַהוּא לֵאמֹר: אֵלֶּה יַעַמְדוּ לְבָרֵךְ אֶת־הָעָם עַל־הַר גְּרִזִים בְּעָבְרְכֶם

יג אֶת־הַיַּרְדֵּן שִׁמְעוֹן וְלֵוִי וִיהוּדָה וְיִשָּׂשׂכָר וְיוֹסֵף וּבִנְיָמִן: וְאֵלֶּה יַעַמְדוּ עַל־הַקְּלָלָה

יד בְּהַר עֵיבָל רְאוּבֵן גָּד וְאָשֵׁר וּזְבוּלֻן דָּן וְנַפְתָּלִי: וְעָנוּ הַלְוִיִּם וְאָמְרוּ אֶל־כָּל־אִישׁ

טו יִשְׂרָאֵל קוֹל רָם: אָרוּר הָאִישׁ אֲשֶׁר יַעֲשֶׂה פֶסֶל וּמַסֵּכָה תּוֹעֲבַת

טז יהוה מַעֲשֵׂה יְדֵי חָרָשׁ וְשָׂם בַּסָּתֶר וְעָנוּ כָל־הָעָם וְאָמְרוּ אָמֵן: אָרוּר

יז מַקְלֶה אָבִיו וְאִמּוֹ וְאָמַר כָּל־הָעָם אָמֵן: אָרוּר מַסִּיג גְּבוּל רֵעֵהוּ

יח וְאָמַר כָּל־הָעָם אָמֵן: אָרוּר מַשְׁגֶּה עִוֵּר בַּדָּרֶךְ וְאָמַר כָּל־הָעָם

יט אָמֵן: אָרוּר מַטֶּה מִשְׁפַּט גֵּר־יָתוֹם וְאַלְמָנָה וְאָמַר כָּל־הָעָם אָמֵן:

רש״י

ח] **בַּאֵר הֵיטֵב.** בְּשִׁבְעִים לָשׁוֹן:

ט] **הַסְכֵּת.** כְּתַרְגּוּמוֹ: הַיּוֹם הַזֶּה נִהְיֵיתָ לְעָם. בְּכָל יוֹם יִהְיֶה בְּעֵינֶיךָ כְּאִלּוּ הַיּוֹם בָּאתָ עִמּוֹ בַּבְּרִית:

יב] **לְבָרֵךְ אֶת־הָעָם.** כְּדְאִיתָא בְּמַסֶּכֶת סוֹטָה (לב ע״ב): שִׁשָּׁה שְׁבָטִים עָלוּ לְרֹאשׁ הַר גְּרִזִים וְשִׁשָּׁה לְרֹאשׁ הַר

עֵיבָל, וְהַכֹּהֲנִים וְהַלְוִיִּם וְהָאָרוֹן לְמַטָּה בָּאֶמְצַע. הָפְכוּ לְוִיִּם פְּנֵיהֶם כְּלַפֵּי הַר גְּרִזִים וּפָתְחוּ בַּבְּרָכָה: ״בָּרוּךְ הָאִישׁ אֲשֶׁר לֹא יַעֲשֶׂה פֶסֶל וּמַסֵּכָה״ וְגוֹ׳, וְאֵלּוּ וָאֵלּוּ עוֹנִין אָמֵן. חָזְרוּ וְהָפְכוּ פְּנֵיהֶם כְּלַפֵּי הַר עֵיבָל וּפָתְחוּ בַּקְּלָלָה, וְאוֹמְרִים: ״אָרוּר הָאִישׁ אֲשֶׁר יַעֲשֶׂה פֶסֶל״ וְגוֹ׳, וְכֵן כֻּלָּם עַד ״אָרוּר אֲשֶׁר לֹא יָקִים״:

טז] **מַקְלֶה אָבִיו.** מְזַלְזֵל, לְשׁוֹן: ״וְנִקְלָה אָחִיךָ״ (לעיל כה, ג):

יז] **מַסִּיג גְּבוּל.** מַחֲזִירוֹ לַאֲחוֹרָיו וְגוֹנֵב אֶת הַקַּרְקַע, לְשׁוֹן: ״הַסֵּג אָחוֹר״ (ישעיה נט, יד):

יח] **מַשְׁגֶּה עִוֵּר.** הַסּוּמָא בַּדָּבָר וּמַשִּׂיאוֹ עֵצָה רָעָה:

DISCUSSION

27:8 | Very clearly: Some maintain that the Torah was written on these stones together with its elucidation. According to one interpretation, it was written in seventy languages, that is, in all known languages (see *Targum Yonatan*; Rashi; *Sota* 32a). However, it is unlikely that these interpretations are to be understood literally, since one would need extremely large stones in order to write the words of the Torah alone. If the stones were to include the Torah's elucidation as well, enormous boulders would be required (see

Ramban, 27:3). Indeed, others contend that it was not the entire Torah, from beginning to end, that was written on the stones, but only a list of the commandments, accessible to all (Ibn Ezra, 27:1, citing Rav Se'adya Gaon).

27:12 | To bless the people: Although the proclamation of the Levites contains only curses, apparently each of the curses was formulated as a blessing as well. After the recitation of each curse, which opened with the formula "Cursed is the man who will…," the Levites turned to the mountain of blessing, Mount Gerizim, and recited a parallel blessing, beginning with "Blessed is the man who will not…" (*Sota* 32a). The fact that the Torah mentions the curses alone, while omitting the corresponding blessings, is unusual, and is likely due to considerations of brevity. Almost all of the curses pertain to prohibitions, and therefore their formulation as a blessing is more complex. For example, in the case of the curse, "Cursed is one who moves

20 The forbidden sexual relations mentioned below are also those that are likely to be committed in private, concealed from public view, due to the structure of society. **Cursed is one who lies with the wife of his father,** even after his father's death.[25] The widow might live alone in her deceased husband's house, while his adult son abuses her and she has no means of objecting, or they might both consent to the act. He is cursed **as he** thereby **exposed the edge of his father's garment,** shaming his father's nakedness, **and the entire people shall say: Amen.**

21 **Cursed is one who lies with any beast, and the entire people shall say: Amen.** This transgression would probably remain unknown as well, as the man himself would not report it, and the animal is of course unable to object.[26]

22 **Cursed is one who lies with his sister, the daughter of his father, or the daughter of his mother, and the entire people shall say: Amen.** An adult brother might use his authority and power to abuse his minor sister and prevent her from objecting and publicizing the matter. For this reason, the transgression can remain unknown to others, sometimes for many years.[27]

23 **Cursed is one who lies with his mother-in-law,** whether or not she is married. This severe transgression also shames the family. In this case the extent of their kinship might not be sufficient to deter them from the act, but they are close enough to develop an intimate relationship, and the affair would not be publicized. **And the entire people shall say: Amen.**

24 **Cursed is one who smites his neighbor in secret,** by attacking him in the dark, or by covering the eyes of the victim so that he cannot identify his assailant. The Sages interpret this verse as referring to verbal blows as well, e.g., the defamation of another when he is not present.[28] **And the entire people shall say: Amen.**

25 **Cursed is one who takes a bribe to slay a person of innocent blood, and the entire people shall say: Amen.** Neither the party who gives the bribe nor the one who accepts it is likely to publicize his actions. A judge who begins by accepting a bribe in relatively minor monetary cases is liable to deviate from the path of justice in cases involving large inheritances as well. Eventually, he is liable to be swayed through bribery to even cause a person's death.

26 The list concludes with a general curse: **Cursed is one who will not uphold the matters of this Torah to perform them.** Cursed is one who fails to do all that is in his power to ensure that the matters of this Torah, written before you on the stones (27:8), will be upheld. **And the entire people shall say: Amen.** The entire people of Israel thereby publicly committed to uphold the Torah: Each person must do his part in order to ensure that the Torah's commandments are fulfilled. The Sages therefore state that even if one studied the Torah and taught it to others, observed the Torah and performed its commandments, if he was able to support and bolster the Torah and he did not do so, he is included in this curse.[29]

The Blessings and Curses Stated in the Plains of Moav

DEUTERONOMY 28:1–69

The people are encamped in the plains of Moav, soon to enter the land of Canaan. Moses informs them of the blessings they will merit if they observe the commandments of God, and of the curses that will befall those who defy the word of God. The Torah first states the blessings, followed by a far longer and more detailed list of curses. There are fewer blessings than curses because the fundamental blessing is that one should be safe and healthy and lack no basic needs. By contrast, the illnesses and troubles that are liable to upset one's tranquility and well-being are many and diverse.

28 1 **It shall be if you shall heed the voice of the Lord your God to take care to perform all His commandments that I am commanding you today,** all forms of goodness will come to you. **The Lord your God will place you uppermost over all the nations of the earth.** Your status among the nations will be great.

2 **All these blessings will come upon you, and reach you.** They will pursue you, even if you do not endeavor to achieve them,[30] **if you shall heed the voice of the Lord your God.**

3 **Blessed are you in the city,** in the settled areas, **and blessed are you in the field,** in your workplaces.

4 **Blessed is the fruit of your womb,** your children, **and the fruit of your land, and the fruit of your animals: the calving of your cattle,**[31] **and the lambing of your flock.**

5 **Blessed is your basket,** in which you place the produce of your fields, **and your kneading bowl.**[D] You will find the contents of your vessels blessed.

6 **Blessed are you upon your arrival, and blessed are you upon your departure.**

Basket

Earthenware kneading bowl, Galilee, second millennium BCE

כ כא אָרוּר שֹׁכֵב עִם־אֵשֶׁת אָבִיו כִּי גִלָּה כְּנַף אָבִיו וְאָמַר כָּל־הָעָם אָמֵן: אָרוּר
כב שֹׁכֵב עִם־כָּל־בְּהֵמָה וְאָמַר כָּל־הָעָם אָמֵן: אָרוּר שֹׁכֵב עִם־אֲחֹתוֹ בַּת־
כג אָבִיו אוֹ בַת־אִמּוֹ וְאָמַר כָּל־הָעָם אָמֵן: אָרוּר שֹׁכֵב עִם־חֹתַנְתּוֹ וְאָמַר כָּל־
כד כה הָעָם אָמֵן: אָרוּר מַכֵּה רֵעֵהוּ בַּסָּתֶר וְאָמַר כָּל־הָעָם אָמֵן: אָרוּר
כו לֹקֵחַ שֹׁחַד לְהַכּוֹת נֶפֶשׁ דַּם נָקִי וְאָמַר כָּל־הָעָם אָמֵן: אָרוּר אֲשֶׁר לֹא־
יָקִים אֶת־דִּבְרֵי הַתּוֹרָה־הַזֹּאת לַעֲשׂוֹת אוֹתָם וְאָמַר כָּל־הָעָם אָמֵן:
כח א וְהָיָה אִם־שָׁמוֹעַ תִּשְׁמַע בְּקוֹל יְהוָה אֱלֹהֶיךָ לִשְׁמֹר לַעֲשׂוֹת אֶת־כָּל־מִצְוֺתָיו
ב אֲשֶׁר אָנֹכִי מְצַוְּךָ הַיּוֹם וּנְתָנְךָ יְהוָה אֱלֹהֶיךָ עֶלְיוֹן עַל כָּל־גּוֹיֵי הָאָרֶץ: וּבָאוּ
ג עָלֶיךָ כָּל־הַבְּרָכוֹת הָאֵלֶּה וְהִשִּׂיגֻךָ כִּי תִשְׁמַע בְּקוֹל יְהוָה אֱלֹהֶיךָ: בָּרוּךְ אַתָּה
ד בָּעִיר וּבָרוּךְ אַתָּה בַּשָּׂדֶה: בָּרוּךְ פְּרִי־בִטְנְךָ וּפְרִי אַדְמָתְךָ וּפְרִי בְהֶמְתֶּךָ
ה ו שְׁגַר אֲלָפֶיךָ וְעַשְׁתְּרוֹת צֹאנֶךָ: בָּרוּךְ טַנְאֲךָ וּמִשְׁאַרְתֶּךָ: בָּרוּךְ אַתָּה בְּבֹאֶךָ
ז וּבָרוּךְ אַתָּה בְּצֵאתֶךָ: יִתֵּן יְהוָה אֶת־אֹיְבֶיךָ הַקָּמִים עָלֶיךָ נִגָּפִים לְפָנֶיךָ ששי
ח בְּדֶרֶךְ אֶחָד יֵצְאוּ אֵלֶיךָ וּבְשִׁבְעָה דְרָכִים יָנוּסוּ לְפָנֶיךָ: יְצַו יְהוָה אִתְּךָ אֶת־
הַבְּרָכָה בַּאֲסָמֶיךָ וּבְכֹל מִשְׁלַח יָדֶךָ וּבֵרַכְךָ בָּאָרֶץ אֲשֶׁר־יְהוָה אֱלֹהֶיךָ נֹתֵן לָךְ:

רש״י

כד | **מַכֵּה רֵעֵהוּ בַּסָּתֶר.** עַל לָשׁוֹן הָרָע הוּא אוֹמֵר. רָאִיתִי יְסוֹדוֹ שֶׁל רַבִּי מֹשֶׁה הַדַּרְשָׁן: אַחַד עָשָׂר אֲרוּרִים יֵשׁ כָּאן, כְּנֶגֶד אַחַד עָשָׂר שְׁבָטִים, וּכְנֶגֶד שִׁמְעוֹן לֹא כָתַב אָרוּר, לְפִי שֶׁלֹּא הָיָה בְּלִבּוֹ לְבָרְכוֹ לִפְנֵי מוֹתוֹ כְּשֶׁבֵּרַךְ שְׁאָר הַשְּׁבָטִים, לְכָךְ לֹא רָצָה לְקַלְּלוֹ:

כו | **אֲשֶׁר לֹא יָקִים.** כָּאן כָּלַל אֶת כָּל הַתּוֹרָה כֻּלָּהּ, וְקִבְּלוּהָ עֲלֵיהֶם בְּאָלָה וּבִשְׁבוּעָה:

פרק כח

ד | **שְׁגַר אֲלָפֶיךָ.** וַלְדוֹת בְּקָרְךָ שֶׁהַבְּהֵמָה מְשַׁגֶּרֶת מִמֵּעֶיהָ: **וְעַשְׁתְּרוֹת צֹאנֶךָ.** כְּתַרְגּוּמוֹ. וְרַבּוֹתֵינוּ אָמְרוּ: לָמָּה נִקְרָא שְׁמָן ׳עַשְׁתָּרוֹת׳? שֶׁמַּעֲשִׁירוֹת אֶת בַּעְלֵיהֶן וּמַחֲזִיקוֹת אוֹתָן, כְּעַשְׁתָּרוֹת הַלָּלוּ שֶׁהֵן סְלָעִים חֲזָקִים:

ה | **בָּרוּךְ טַנְאֲךָ.** פֵּרוֹתֶיךָ. דָּבָר אַחֵר, ״טַנְאֲךָ״, דָּבָר לַח שֶׁאַתָּה מְסַנֵּן בִּסְלִים: **וּמִשְׁאַרְתֶּךָ.** דָּבָר יָבֵשׁ שֶׁנִּשְׁאָר בַּכְּלִי וְאֵינוֹ זָב:

ו | **בָּרוּךְ אַתָּה בְּבֹאֶךָ וּבָרוּךְ אַתָּה בְּצֵאתֶךָ.** שֶׁתְּהֵא יְצִיאָתְךָ מִן הָעוֹלָם בְּלֹא חֵטְא כְּבִיאָתְךָ לָעוֹלָם:

ז | **וּבְשִׁבְעָה דְרָכִים יָנוּסוּ לְפָנֶיךָ.** כֵּן דֶּרֶךְ הַנִּבְהָלִים לִבְרֹחַ לִהְיוֹת מִתְפַּזְּרִין לְכָל צַד:

7 **The Lord will render your enemies who rise against you** defeated and **routed before you. On one path they will emerge toward you,** in the manner of warriors setting out to war, **and on seven paths they will flee before you.** When an army loses a battle, its soldiers flee in different directions.

Sixth aliya

8 **The Lord will command for you the blessing in your silos, and in all your** various **endeavors, and He will bless you in the land that the Lord your God is giving you.**

DISCUSSION

his neighbor's boundary," the parallel blessing is "Blessed is one who will not move his neighbor's boundary," which is a more cumbersome sentence. The Torah therefore presents only the more succinct formulation of the curses.

28:5 | **And your kneading bowl:** The term *mishartekha*, "your kneading bowl," may be related to *se'or*, leaven, the dough left in the bowl until it becomes leaven and subsequently used as a leavening agent for the rest of the dough.

9 Furthermore, **the Lord will establish you as a holy people to Him, as He took an oath to you.** This shall be **if you shall observe the commandments of the Lord your God, and walk in His ways.**

10 Then, **all the peoples of the earth will see that the name of the Lord is invoked upon you,** as you constantly mention His name and honor Him, **and they shall fear you.** They will not provoke you in any manner.

11 **The Lord will increase you for good.** He will give you abundant blessing, even more than you expect or request, **in the fruit of your womb, and in the fruit of your animals, and in the fruit of your land.** He will bless you with all this, **on the land with regard to which the Lord took an oath to your fathers to give you.**

12 **The Lord will open for you His good storehouse, the heavens, to provide** you with **the rain of your land at its time, and to bless all your handiwork.** And due to this plenty, **you shall lend to many nations,** as they will need your help, **but you shall not borrow,** as you will not require the assistance of others.

13 **The Lord will set you as a head, and not as a tail.** In all matters you will take the lead, and you will not follow others. **And you will be only above, and you will not be below.** All this shall come to pass, **if you shall heed the commandments of the Lord your God that I am commanding you today, to observe and to perform** them.

14 **You shall not stray from any of the matters that I am commanding you today right or left,** the fundamental commandment being not **to follow other gods to serve them.** This concludes the blessings.

15 It shall be, **if you do not heed the voice of the Lord your God, to take care to perform all His commandments and His statutes that I am commanding you today, all these curses will come upon you and find you.**

16 Some of the curses parallel the aforementioned blessings: **Cursed are you in the city, and cursed are you in the field.**

17 **Cursed is your basket and your kneading bowl.**

18 **Cursed is the fruit of your womb, and the fruit of your land, the calving of your cattle, and the lambing of your flock.**

19 **Cursed are you upon your arrival, and cursed are you upon your departure.**

20 **The Lord will release among you the curse, the confusion,** panic and disorder, **and the** process of **diminution.**[D] These will befall you **in all your endeavors that you will perform, until your destruction, and until your swift annihilation, because of the wickedness of your deeds, that** you performed when **you forsook Me.**

21 **The Lord will attach the pestilence,** an infectious plague, **to you, until it eradicates you from upon the land that you are coming there to take possession of it.**

22 **The Lord will smite you with consumption,**[B] **and with fever, and with inflammation,**[B] **and with desiccation,** a disease of dryness, **and with the enemy's sword,**[32] **and with blight,** the loss of bulk and weight of crops or a living body, **and with mildew,**[B] a disease that ruins the crops.[33] Alternatively, the verse may be referring to the human disease of jaundice. **And they,** all these plagues, **shall pursue you until your annihilation.**

23 **Your heavens that are over your head will be** as impenetrable as **bronze,** and will not produce rain, **and the earth that is**

DISCUSSION

28:20 | And the diminution: Alternatively, the term *hamigeret* means that everyone will berate you (*Bekhor Shor*), or that you will suffer pangs of guilt (Rabbi Samson Raphael Hirsch).

BACKGROUND

28:22 | With consumption: In modern Hebrew the term *shaḥefet* refers to tuberculosis. However, the biblical *shaḥefet* is not the same disorder. The Sages state that one afflicted with *shaḥefet* wastes away; he becomes thin, and suffers from fever and depression (*Sifra, Behukotai* 2:2). Some explain that this disease causes the skin to swell and dry (Rashi; Rambam). Others suggest that the term indicates weakness and fatigue (Rabbi Samson Raphael Hirsch). If so, it is similar to an ancient Arabic word with that meaning.

And with inflammation: Alternatively, the term *daleket* may refer to a local infection that causes a fever.

And with desiccation and with the sword: The term *ḥarḥur* may be derived from the root *ḥet-reish-reish,* in which case it would indicate dryness and heat (Radak,

Sefer HaShorashim; Ibn Ezra). Others maintain that it is an onomatopoeic term, reflecting a raspy breathing sound. If so, the term indicates a disease of the respiratory organs, e.g., pneumonia or asthma. With regard to the term *ḥerev,* while this term usually means sword, some interpret the term as being related to *ḥorev,* parched dryness, as indicated by the context here (*Bekhor Shor*; Rabbi Samson Raphael Hirsch).

And with mildew: The term *yerakon* is derived from *yarok,* which means green in modern Hebrew. However, in biblical Hebrew, in talmudic terminology, as well as in Akkadian, the term can refer to the color yellow (see *Shabbat* 134a; *Ḥullin* 47b; *Yalkut Shimoni, Esther* 1053). Accordingly, *yerakon* is either a disease of the crops, which causes them to yellow, or the human disease of jaundice, which causes one's skin to acquire a yellowish tinge.

ט יְקִימְךָ יְהוָה לוֹ לְעַם קָדוֹשׁ כַּאֲשֶׁר נִשְׁבַּע־לָךְ כִּי תִשְׁמֹר אֶת־מִצְוֺת יְהוָה אֱלֹהֶיךָ
י וְהָלַכְתָּ בִּדְרָכָיו׃ וְרָאוּ כָּל־עַמֵּי הָאָרֶץ כִּי שֵׁם יְהוָה נִקְרָא עָלֶיךָ וְיָרְאוּ מִמֶּךָּ׃
יא וְהוֹתִרְךָ יְהוָה לְטוֹבָה בִּפְרִי בִטְנְךָ וּבִפְרִי בְהֶמְתְּךָ וּבִפְרִי אַדְמָתֶךָ עַל הָאֲדָמָה
יב אֲשֶׁר נִשְׁבַּע יְהוָה לַאֲבֹתֶיךָ לָתֶת לָךְ׃ יִפְתַּח יְהוָה ׀ לְךָ אֶת־אוֹצָרוֹ הַטּוֹב אֶת־
הַשָּׁמַיִם לָתֵת מְטַר־אַרְצְךָ בְּעִתּוֹ וּלְבָרֵךְ אֵת כָּל־מַעֲשֵׂה יָדֶךָ וְהִלְוִיתָ גּוֹיִם רַבִּים
יג וְאַתָּה לֹא תִלְוֶה׃ וּנְתָנְךָ יְהוָה לְרֹאשׁ וְלֹא לְזָנָב וְהָיִיתָ רַק לְמַעְלָה וְלֹא תִהְיֶה
לְמָטָּה כִּי־תִשְׁמַע אֶל־מִצְוֺת ׀ יְהוָה אֱלֹהֶיךָ אֲשֶׁר אָנֹכִי מְצַוְּךָ הַיּוֹם לִשְׁמֹר
יד וְלַעֲשׂוֹת׃ וְלֹא תָסוּר מִכָּל־הַדְּבָרִים אֲשֶׁר אָנֹכִי מְצַוֶּה אֶתְכֶם הַיּוֹם יָמִין וּשְׂמֹאול
לָלֶכֶת אַחֲרֵי אֱלֹהִים אֲחֵרִים לְעָבְדָם׃
טו וְהָיָה אִם־לֹא תִשְׁמַע בְּקוֹל יְהוָה אֱלֹהֶיךָ לִשְׁמֹר לַעֲשׂוֹת אֶת־כָּל־מִצְוֺתָיו וְחֻקֹּתָיו
טז אֲשֶׁר אָנֹכִי מְצַוְּךָ הַיּוֹם וּבָאוּ עָלֶיךָ כָּל־הַקְּלָלוֹת הָאֵלֶּה וְהִשִּׂיגוּךָ׃ אָרוּר אַתָּה
יז יח בָּעִיר וְאָרוּר אַתָּה בַּשָּׂדֶה׃ אָרוּר טַנְאֲךָ וּמִשְׁאַרְתֶּךָ׃ אָרוּר פְּרִי־בִטְנְךָ וּפְרִי
יט אַדְמָתֶךָ שְׁגַר אֲלָפֶיךָ וְעַשְׁתְּרֹת צֹאנֶךָ׃ אָרוּר אַתָּה בְּבֹאֶךָ וְאָרוּר אַתָּה בְּצֵאתֶךָ׃
כ יְשַׁלַּח יְהוָה ׀ בְּךָ אֶת־הַמְּאֵרָה אֶת־הַמְּהוּמָה וְאֶת־הַמִּגְעֶרֶת בְּכָל־מִשְׁלַח
יָדְךָ אֲשֶׁר תַּעֲשֶׂה עַד הִשָּׁמֶדְךָ וְעַד־אֲבָדְךָ מַהֵר מִפְּנֵי רֹעַ מַעֲלָלֶיךָ אֲשֶׁר עֲזַבְתָּנִי׃
כא יַדְבֵּק יְהוָה בְּךָ אֶת־הַדָּבֶר עַד כַּלֹּתוֹ אֹתְךָ מֵעַל הָאֲדָמָה אֲשֶׁר־אַתָּה בָא־שָׁמָּה
כב לְרִשְׁתָּהּ׃ יַכְּכָה יְהוָה בַּשַּׁחֶפֶת וּבַקַּדַּחַת וּבַדַּלֶּקֶת וּבַחַרְחֻר וּבַחֶרֶב וּבַשִּׁדָּפוֹן
כג וּבַיֵּרָקוֹן וּרְדָפוּךָ עַד אָבְדֶךָ׃ וְהָיוּ שָׁמֶיךָ אֲשֶׁר עַל־רֹאשְׁךָ נְחֹשֶׁת וְהָאָרֶץ אֲשֶׁר־

רש״י

כ| **המארה.** חסרון, כמו "צרעת ממארת" (ויקרא יג, נא): **המהומה.** שגוש, קול בהלות:

כב| **בשחפת.** שבשרו נשחף ונפוח: **ובקדחת.** לשון: "כי אש קדחה באפי" (להלן לב, כב), והוא אש של חולים, מלוו"י בלעז, שהיא חמה מאד: **ובדלקת.** חמה יותר מקדחת, ומיני חלאים הם: **ובחרחר.** חולי המחממו תוך הגוף ועמא תמיד למים, ובלעז אישטרדימנ"ט, לשון: "ועצמי חרה מני חרב" (איוב ל, ל), "נחר מפח מאש" (ירמיה ו, כט): **ובחרב.** יביא עליך גיסות: **ובשדפון ובירקון.** מכת תבואה שבשדות: **שדפון.** רוח קדים, השלי"ד בלעז: **ירקון.** יבש, ופני התבואה מכסיפין ונהפכין לירקון, קרו"א בלעז: **עד אבדך.** תרגום: "עד דתיבד", כלומר עד אבד אותך, שתכלה מאליך:

כג| **והיו שמיך אשר על ראשך נחשת.** קללות הללו משה מפי עצמו אמרן, ושבתורת כהנים מפי הקדוש ברוך הוא אמרן כמשמען: "ואם לא תשמעו לי" (ויקרא כו, יד), "ואם תלכו עמי קרי" (שם פסוק כא), וכאן הוא אומר: "בקול ה' אלהיך" (לעיל פסוק טו), "ידבק ה' בך" (לעיל פסוק כא), "יככה ה'" (לעיל פסוק כב). והקל משה בקללותיו לאמרן בלשון יחיד, וגם כן בקללה זו הקל, שבראשונות הוא אומר: "את שמיכם כברזל ואת ארצכם כנחשה" (ויקרא כו, יט), שלא יהיו השמים מזיעין כדרך שאין הברזל מזיע, ומתוך כך יהא חורב בעולם, והארץ תהא מזיעה כדרך שהנחשת מזיע, והיא מרקבת פירותיה. וכאן הוא אומר: שמיך נחשת וארצך ברזל, שיהיו שמים מזיעין, אף על פי שלא יריקו מטר, מכל מקום לא יהיה חורב של אבדון בעולם, והארץ לא תהיה מזיעה כדרך שאין הברזל

beneath you will be as dry and unfruitful as **iron.**

24 **The Lord will render the rain of your land dust and dirt; from the heavens it will descend upon you, until your destruction.** Rather than rain falling and facilitating growth, the wind will blow and bring dust and dirt.

25 **The Lord will render you routed before your enemies; on one path you will go out toward him, and on seven paths you will flee before him.** This is the exact opposite of the blessing stated earlier (28:7). **You will be a horror,** a paradigm of a nightmare scenario, **to all the kingdoms of the earth.**

26 **Your carcass will be for food for every bird of the heavens, and for the animals of the earth, and there is none to frighten them.** No one will prevent the birds and animals from feasting upon your corpses.

27 **The Lord will smite you with the rash**[D] **of Egypt,** a skin disease that causes swelling and irritation, with which the Egyptians were stricken.[34] **And** He will also strike you **with hemorrhoids,**[D] sores and diseases in the area of the anus, **with skin eruptions, and with dry boils,**[D] skin diseases that cause lesions and great embarrassment, **from which you will be unable to be healed.**

28 **The Lord will smite you with madness, and with blindness, and with confusion of the heart,** the disorientation of one's thoughts and will.

29 As a result, **you shall grope at noon as the blind gropes in the dark.** You will not know the path to follow and you will lose your orientation. **And you will not succeed on your way, and you will only be exploited and robbed all the days, and there is no savior.** You will be unable to put up any resistance, you will fail in all your endeavors, and you will lose everything.

30 **You will betroth a woman and another man will lie with her; you will build a house and** yet **you will not live in it; you will plant a vineyard, and you will not celebrate it.**

31 Having intended to slaughter and consume your ox, you will find that **your ox is slaughtered before your eyes, and you will not eat from it. Your donkey is robbed from before you and will not return to you,** as the robber will never release it; **your flock is given to your enemies, and there is no savior for you.**

32 **Your sons and your daughters are given to another people,** they are taken captive and enslaved, **and** even if they work as hired hands in distant, foreign lands, **your eyes see** them as they depart, **and long for them all the day, and you are powerless** to do anything about it.

33 **A nation that you did not know will eat the fruit of your land and all your toil.** A foreign nation will raid your land and take all of your produce, leaving you with nothing. **You will be only exploited and broken all the days,** both by external enemies that plunder your possessions, and by internal troubles.

34 Everything will go against you. In every direction in which you look you will see only troubles and distress. When you perceive this, **you will be mad from the sight of your eyes that you will see.**

35 **The Lord will smite you with a terrible rash on the knees and on the shins from which you will be unable to be healed, from the sole of your foot to the top of your head.**

36 **The Lord will lead you and your king whom you will establish over you to a nation that you did not know, you or your ancestors, and you will serve there other gods, of wood and stone.** In exile you will be subjugated to your oppressors in every manner. Pagan influences will dominate your lives.[35]

DISCUSSION

28:27 | With the rash: The term *sheḥin*, boils, is derived from the root *shin-ḥet-nun*, which is related to heat in most Semitic languages. Researchers associate *sheḥin* with several skin conditions that cause a sensation of heat and severe irritation, such as urticaria, commonly known as hives, which appears in the form of a rash.

With hemorrhoids: In the written text of the Torah, the word is *afolim*; however, it is read as *teḥorim*. This phenomenon, in which there is a difference between the way a word is written and how it is pronounced, is found in several other places in the Torah, and even more often in the Prophets and Writings. It seems that the reason here for this difference is that the word

as written is considered overly coarse. Since it is improper to utter this word, it is substituted with a more refined term (see II Kings 6:25, 18:27; *Megilla* 25b; Rambam, *Guide of the Perplexed* 3:8). The term *ofel* indicates something that is raised or protruding. It is possible that this is a euphemism for a disease of the lower part of the body. Similarly, the Sages refer to this disease as *taḥtoniyot* (see, e.g., *Berakhot* 55a), which means of the lower parts. Alternatively, the term *ofel* may be derived from the protruding, swollen blood vessels (see Radak and Abravanel, I Samuel 5:6).

With skin eruptions, and with dry boils: According to Leviticus 21:20, *garav*, skin eruptions, is one of the blemishes that disqualifies

a priest from serving in the Temple. The Sages explain that it is an affliction similar to *ḥares*, the dry boils that are mentioned immediately afterward. Based on the etymology of the term in Semitic languages, it has been suggested that *garav* is scabies, also called the seven-year itch, or pellagra, a vitamin deficiency disease. According to Rashi, *ḥares* is a type of inflammation. The term *ḥares* literally means earthenware and may indicate that the skin of the afflicted person becomes cracked like an earthenware vessel, and blood and other secretions flow through the cracks. Alternatively, it may allude to the fact that the afflicted person typically scratches himself with a piece of earthenware

כד תַּחְתֶּיךָ בַּרְזֶל: יִתֵּן יהוה אֶת־מְטַר אַרְצְךָ אָבָק וְעָפָר מִן־הַשָּׁמַיִם יֵרֵד עָלֶיךָ עַד
כה הִשָּׁמְדָךְ: יִתֶּנְךָ יהוה נִגָּף לִפְנֵי אֹיְבֶיךָ בְּדֶרֶךְ אֶחָד תֵּצֵא אֵלָיו וּבְשִׁבְעָה דְרָכִים
כו תָּנוּס לְפָנָיו וְהָיִיתָ לְזַעֲוָה לְכֹל מַמְלְכוֹת הָאָרֶץ: וְהָיְתָה נִבְלָתְךָ לְמַאֲכָל לְכָל־
כז עוֹף הַשָּׁמַיִם וּלְבֶהֱמַת הָאָרֶץ וְאֵין מַחֲרִיד: יַכְּכָה יהוה בִּשְׁחִין מִצְרַיִם ובעפלים וּבַטְּחֹרִים
כח וּבַגָּרָב וּבֶחָרֶס אֲשֶׁר לֹא־תוּכַל לְהֵרָפֵא: יַכְּכָה יהוה בְּשִׁגָּעוֹן וּבְעִוָּרוֹן וּבְתִמְהוֹן
כט לֵבָב: וְהָיִיתָ מְמַשֵּׁשׁ בַּצָּהֳרַיִם כַּאֲשֶׁר יְמַשֵּׁשׁ הָעִוֵּר בָּאֲפֵלָה וְלֹא תַצְלִיחַ אֶת־
ל דְּרָכֶיךָ וְהָיִיתָ אַךְ עָשׁוּק וְגָזוּל כָּל־הַיָּמִים וְאֵין מוֹשִׁיעַ: אִשָּׁה תְאָרֵשׂ וְאִישׁ
לא אַחֵר ישגלנה בַּיִת תִּבְנֶה וְלֹא־תֵשֵׁב בּוֹ כֶּרֶם תִּטַּע וְלֹא תְחַלְּלֶנּוּ: שׁוֹרְךָ טָבוּחַ יִשְׁכָּבֶנָּה
לְעֵינֶיךָ וְלֹא תֹאכַל מִמֶּנּוּ חֲמֹרְךָ גָּזוּל מִלְּפָנֶיךָ וְלֹא יָשׁוּב לָךְ צֹאנְךָ נְתֻנוֹת
לב לְאֹיְבֶיךָ וְאֵין לְךָ מוֹשִׁיעַ: בָּנֶיךָ וּבְנֹתֶיךָ נְתֻנִים לְעַם אַחֵר וְעֵינֶיךָ רֹאוֹת וְכָלוֹת
לג אֲלֵיהֶם כָּל־הַיּוֹם וְאֵין לְאֵל יָדֶךָ: פְּרִי אַדְמָתְךָ וְכָל־יְגִיעֲךָ יֹאכַל עַם אֲשֶׁר לֹא־
לד יָדָעְתָּ וְהָיִיתָ רַק עָשׁוּק וְרָצוּץ כָּל־הַיָּמִים: וְהָיִיתָ מְשֻׁגָּע מִמַּרְאֵה עֵינֶיךָ אֲשֶׁר
לה תִּרְאֶה: יַכְּכָה יהוה בִּשְׁחִין רָע עַל־הַבִּרְכַּיִם וְעַל־הַשֹּׁקַיִם אֲשֶׁר לֹא־תוּכַל
לו לְהֵרָפֵא מִכַּף רַגְלְךָ וְעַד קָדְקֳדֶךָ: יוֹלֵךְ יהוה אֹתְךָ וְאֶת־מַלְכְּךָ אֲשֶׁר תָּקִים עָלֶיךָ
אֶל־גּוֹי אֲשֶׁר לֹא־יָדַעְתָּ אַתָּה וַאֲבֹתֶיךָ וְעָבַדְתָּ שָּׁם אֱלֹהִים אֲחֵרִים עֵץ וָאָבֶן:

רש״י

מֵזִיעַ, וְאֵין הַפֵּרוֹת מַרְקִיבִין. וּמִכָּל מָקוֹם קְלָלָה הִיא, בֵּין שֶׁהִיא כִּנְחֹשֶׁת בֵּין שֶׁהִיא כְּבַרְזֶל לֹא תוֹצִיא פֵּרוֹת, וְכֵן הַשָּׁמַיִם לֹא יָרִיקוּ מָטָר:

כד| **מְטַר אַרְצְךָ אָבָק וְעָפָר.** זִיקָא דְּבָתַר מִטְרָא, מָטָר יוֹרֵד וְלֹא כָּל צָרְכּוֹ וְאֵין בּוֹ כְּדֵי לְהַרְבִּיץ אֶת הֶעָפָר, וְהָרוּחַ בָּאָה וּמַעֲלָה אֶת הָאָבָק וּמְכַסֶּה אֶת עֵשֶׂב הַזְּרָעִים שֶׁהֵן לַחִים מִן הַמַּיִם וְנִדְבָּק בָּהֶם, וְנַעֲשֶׂה טִיט וּמִתְיַבֵּשׁ וּמַרְקִיבָן:

כה| **לְזַעֲוָה.** לְאֵימָה וּלְזִיעַ, שֶׁיָּזוּעוּ כָּל שׁוֹמְעֵי מַכּוֹתֶיךָ מִמְּךָ, וְיֹאמְרוּ: אוֹי לָנוּ שֶׁלֹּא יָבֹא עָלֵינוּ כְּדֶרֶךְ שֶׁבָּא עַל אֵלּוּ:

כז| **בִּשְׁחִין מִצְרַיִם.** רַע הָיָה מְאֹד, לַח מִבִּפְנִים וְיָבֵשׁ מִבַּחוּץ, כִּדְאִיתָא בִּבְכוֹרוֹת (דף מא ע״א): **גָּרָב.** שְׁחִין לַח: **חָרֶס.** שְׁחִין יָבֵשׁ כְּחֶרֶס:

כח| **וּבְתִמְהוֹן לֵבָב.** אֹטֶם הַלֵּב, אשטורדישו״ן בְּלַעַז:

כט| **עָשׁוּק.** בְּכָל מַעֲשֶׂיךָ יְהִי עִרְעֵר:

ל| **יִשְׁגָּלֶנָּה.** לְשׁוֹן שֵׁגַל, פִּילֶגֶשׁ, וְהַכָּתוּב כִּנָּהוּ לְשֶׁבַח "יִשְׁכָּבֶנָּה", וְתִקּוּן סוֹפְרִים הוּא זֶה: **תְּחַלְּלֶנּוּ.** בַּשָּׁנָה הָרְבִיעִית לֶאֱכֹל פִּרְיוֹ:

לב| **וְכָלוֹת אֲלֵיהֶם.** מְצַפּוֹת אֲלֵיהֶם שֶׁיָּשׁוּבוּ וְאֵינָם שָׁבִים. כָּל תּוֹחֶלֶת שֶׁאֵינָהּ בָּאָה קְרוּיָה כִּלְיוֹן עֵינַיִם:

37 **You will become an astonishment, a proverb, and an adage among all the peoples that the Lord will lead you there.** Your very name will become an insult. When one wishes to speak of failures and miserable situations, he will compare them to your case as the classic example.

38 **Much seed you will take out to the field** to sow, **and little will you gather** from the field, **as the locust will consume it.**

39 **Vineyards you will plant and till, and** yet **you will not drink wine and you will not store it, as the worm will eat them,** the grapes.

Locust attacking wheat

40 **Olive trees you will have within all your borders, and** yet **you will not anoint** yourself with their **oil, as your olives will fall** to the ground before they ripen, and you will extract nothing from them.

41 **Sons and daughters will you beget and they will not be for you, as they will go into captivity.**

42 **All your trees and the fruit of your land, the worm**[D] **will deplete.**[36]

43 **The stranger who is** living **in your midst will ascend over you higher and higher, and you will descend lower and lower.**

44 **He,** the stranger, **will lend to you and you will not lend to him; he will be as a head, and you will be as a tail.**

45 **All these curses will come upon you, and will pursue you, and will find you until your destruction, because you did not heed the voice of the Lord your God, to observe His commandments and His statutes that He commanded you.**

46 **They,** all these troubles and plagues, **will be in you as a sign and as a wonder,** an indicator of your evil deeds, or as a paradigm of curses,[37] **and in your descendants forever;**

47 you will suffer these curses **because you did not serve the Lord your God** when you had the opportunity **with joy and with gladness of heart,**[D] **due to abundance of everything.**

48 Therefore, **you will serve your enemies whom the Lord will dispatch against you** in the reverse situation: **in** a state of **hunger, and in thirst, and in nakedness, and in the lack of everything; and he,** the enemy, **will place an iron yoke on your neck,** subjugating you **until he destroys you.**

49 **The Lord will bring a nation against you from afar, from the end of the earth.** It will appear suddenly, **as the eagle will swoop** down from a great height and from a vast distance, so that its approach is undetected. Since the enemies will come from afar, they will be **a nation whose language you will not understand,** and you will be unable to communicate with them.

Swooping eagle

50 It will be **a brazen nation that will not show favor to the elderly, and will not have mercy on the young.** It will not pity anyone.

51 **It will eat the fruit of your animals and the fruit of your land, until your destruction, which will not leave you grain, wine, or oil, the calving of your cattle, or the lambing of your flock, until it annihilates you.** Even if it does not act in a deliberately destructive manner, since it does not intend to settle in the conquered land it will exploit it without considering its long-term viability, leaving nothing intact.

52 **It will besiege you,** or torment you,[38] **at all your gates, until**

לז וְהָיִיתָ לְשַׁמָּה לְמָשָׁל וְלִשְׁנִינָה בְּכֹל הָעַמִּים אֲשֶׁר־יְנַהֶגְךָ יהוה שָׁמָּה: זֶרַע רַב

לח תּוֹצִיא הַשָּׂדֶה וּמְעַט תֶּאֱסֹף כִּי יַחְסְלֶנּוּ הָאַרְבֶּה: כְּרָמִים תִּטַּע וְעָבָדְתָּ וְיַיִן לֹא־

לט תִשְׁתֶּה וְלֹא תֶאֱגֹר כִּי תֹאכְלֶנּוּ הַתֹּלָעַת: זֵיתִים יִהְיוּ לְךָ בְּכָל־גְּבוּלֶךָ וְשֶׁמֶן לֹא

מ תָסוּךְ כִּי יִשַּׁל זֵיתֶךָ: בָּנִים וּבָנוֹת תּוֹלִיד וְלֹא־יִהְיוּ לָךְ כִּי יֵלְכוּ בַּשֶּׁבִי: כָּל־עֵצְךָ

מא מב וּפְרִי אַדְמָתֶךָ יְיָרֵשׁ הַצְּלָצַל: הַגֵּר אֲשֶׁר בְּקִרְבְּךָ יַעֲלֶה עָלֶיךָ מַעְלָה מָּעְלָה

מג וְאַתָּה תֵרֵד מַטָּה מָּטָּה: הוּא יַלְוְךָ וְאַתָּה לֹא תַלְוֶנּוּ הוּא יִהְיֶה לְרֹאשׁ וְאַתָּה

מד תִהְיֶה לְזָנָב: וּבָאוּ עָלֶיךָ כָּל־הַקְּלָלוֹת הָאֵלֶּה וּרְדָפוּךָ וְהִשִּׂיגוּךָ עַד הִשָּׁמְדָךְ

מה כִּי־לֹא שָׁמַעְתָּ בְּקוֹל יהוה אֱלֹהֶיךָ לִשְׁמֹר מִצְוֹתָיו וְחֻקֹּתָיו אֲשֶׁר צִוָּךְ: וְהָיוּ בְךָ

מו לְאוֹת וּלְמוֹפֵת וּבְזַרְעֲךָ עַד־עוֹלָם: תַּחַת אֲשֶׁר לֹא־עָבַדְתָּ אֶת־יהוה אֱלֹהֶיךָ

מז בְּשִׂמְחָה וּבְטוּב לֵבָב מֵרֹב כֹּל: וְעָבַדְתָּ אֶת־אֹיְבֶיךָ אֲשֶׁר יְשַׁלְּחֶנּוּ יהוה בָּךְ בְּרָעָב

מח וּבְצָמָא וּבְעֵירֹם וּבְחֹסֶר כֹּל וְנָתַן עֹל בַּרְזֶל עַל־צַוָּארֶךָ עַד הִשְׁמִידוֹ אֹתָךְ:

מט יִשָּׂא יהוה עָלֶיךָ גּוֹי מֵרָחֹק מִקְצֵה הָאָרֶץ כַּאֲשֶׁר יִדְאֶה הַנָּשֶׁר גּוֹי אֲשֶׁר לֹא־

נ תִשְׁמַע לְשֹׁנוֹ: גּוֹי עַז פָּנִים אֲשֶׁר לֹא־יִשָּׂא פָנִים לְזָקֵן וְנַעַר לֹא יָחֹן: וְאָכַל

נא פְּרִי בְהֶמְתְּךָ וּפְרִי־אַדְמָתְךָ עַד הִשָּׁמְדָךְ אֲשֶׁר לֹא־יַשְׁאִיר לְךָ דָּגָן תִּירוֹשׁ וְיִצְהָר

נב שְׁגַר אֲלָפֶיךָ וְעַשְׁתְּרֹת צֹאנֶךָ עַד הַאֲבִידוֹ אֹתָךְ: וְהֵצַר לְךָ בְּכָל־שְׁעָרֶיךָ עַד

רש"י

לז לְשַׁמָּה. אשטורדישו"ן, כָּל הָרוֹאֶה אוֹתְךָ יִשֹׁם עָלֶיךָ: לְמָשָׁל. כְּשֶׁתָּבֹא מַכָּה רָעָה עַל אָדָם יֹאמְרוּ: זוֹ דוֹמָה לְמַכַּת פְּלוֹנִי: וְלִשְׁנִינָה. לְשׁוֹן "וְשִׁנַּנְתָּם" (לעיל ו, ז), יְדַבְּרוּ בְךָ, וְכֵן תַּרְגּוּמוֹ: "וּלְשׁוֹעֵי", לְשׁוֹן סִפּוּר, וְאִשְׁתָּעֵי:

לח יַחְסְלֶנּוּ. יְכַלֶּנּוּ, וְעַל שֵׁם כָּךְ נִקְרָא 'חָסִיל', שֶׁמְּכַלֶּה אֶת הַכֹּל:

מו כִּי יִשַּׁל. יַשִּׁיר פֵּרוֹתָיו, לְשׁוֹן: "וְנָשַׁל הַבַּרְזֶל" (לעיל יט, ה):

מב יְיָרֵשׁ הַצְּלָצַל. יַעֲשֶׂנּוּ הֶחָרְבֶּה רָשׁ מִן הַפְּרִי: יְיָרֵשׁ. יַעֲנֵי: הַצְּלָצַל. מִין אַרְבֶּה. וְאִי אֶפְשָׁר לְפָרֵשׁ "יְיָרֵשׁ" לְשׁוֹן יְרֻשָּׁה, שֶׁאִם כֵּן הָיָה לוֹ לִכְתֹּב "יִירַשׁ", וְלֹא לְשׁוֹן הוֹרָשָׁה וְגֵרוּשִׁין, שֶׁאִם כֵּן הָיָה לוֹ לִכְתֹּב "יוֹרִישׁ":

מז מֵרֹב כֹּל. בְּעוֹד שֶׁהָיָה לְךָ כָּל טוּב:

מט כַּאֲשֶׁר יִדְאֶה הַנָּשֶׁר. פִּתְאֹם, וְדֶרֶךְ מִצְלַחַת וְיָקֵלּוּ סוּסָיו: לֹא תִשְׁמַע לְשֹׁנוֹ. שֶׁלֹּא תַכִּיר לְשׁוֹנוֹ, וְכֵן "תִּשְׁמַע חֲלוֹם לִפְתֹּר אֹתוֹ" (בראשית מא, טו), וְכֵן "כִּי שֹׁמֵעַ יוֹסֵף" (שם מב, כג), אינטינדר"א בְּלַעַ"ז:

DISCUSSION

for relief (see *Sifra* and Rashi, Leviticus 21:20; *Bekhorot* 41a; Job 2:8).

28:42 | The worm: Alternatively, the verse means that the trees and fruit will be depleted by the enemies (Ramban). According to this interpretation, the term *tzelatzal* is derived from

metzaltzel, ringing, and it is referring to the loud ringing sounds made by the enemy camp upon its arrival.

28:47 | You did not serve the Lord your God with joy and with gladness of heart: According to its straightforward meaning, this

verse is referring to a general, objective state of well-being, not an emotion. Nevertheless, some commentaries explain that part of the punishment is due to the fact that even when the people did serve God, they did not do so joyously (*Sha'arei Kedusha* 2:4, citing the Ari).

the downfall of your high and fortified walls upon which you rely throughout your land. The enemy will breach and break your walls, and you will realize that your supposedly strong cities do not guarantee your safety. And it will besiege you at all your gates throughout your land that the Lord your God gave you.

53 You shall eat the fruit of your womb, the flesh of your sons and your daughters that the Lord your God gave you, in siege and in the distress that your enemy will distress you. The famine in the besieged city will be so severe that you will be reduced to eating the flesh of your children.

54 These verses illustrate the horrors of the extreme famine: The man among you who is tender and very delicate will be selfish toward his brother, and even toward the wife of his bosom, and toward the remaining children that he will leave;

55 he will consume his children's flesh by himself, rather than give to one of them from the flesh of his children that he will eat. Not only will he eat the flesh of his own children, he will refuse to give any of it to his closest relatives, including his surviving children. He will do so because everything he had will be lost, not leaving anything for him. The hunger will be so intense that it will overcome love and the most intimate family ties. Any vestige of one's humanity will be wiped out, in the siege and in the distress that your enemy will distress you within all your gates.

56 The same will happen to the tender and delicate woman among you, who did not venture setting the sole of her foot on the ground due to her great delicacy and due to her tenderness. The most delicate of women will be selfish toward the husband of her bosom, and toward her son, and toward her daughter,

57 and toward her afterbirth that emerges from between her legs, her young babies,[39] and toward the rest of her children whom she will bear. She will be selfish as she will eat them in the lack of everything in secret. She will snatch her children to eat by herself in hiding, in the siege and in the distress that

your enemy will distress you at your gates. The siege will be so appalling that the people will be reduced to cannibalizing their own children, an act which shatters the moral boundaries of any human society.

58 All this will come to pass, if you will not take care to perform all the words of this Torah that are written in this book, to fear this revered and awesome name, the Lord your God;

59 then the Lord will intensify your blows, and the blows of your descendants, and they will increase in size and severity, great and profound blows, and dire and profound illnesses. Alternatively, the phrase means lengthy and persistent blows and illnesses.

60 He will return to you all the afflictions of Egypt of which you were terrified, when you saw the manner in which they were visited upon the Egyptians, and they will come and cleave to you.

61 Also, every illness and every blow that is not written in the book of this Torah, the Lord will pile them upon you, until your destruction. The list of afflictions will grow longer, and include other diseases not written here, as well as other afflictions that will demean and humiliate you.[40]

62 You shall remain few in number, instead of your having been like the stars of the heavens in plenitude. During your long history you were a great people, and through natural population increase you should have become an exceedingly great multitude. That is not the case, however, because you did not heed the voice of the Lord your God.

63 It shall be that as the Lord exulted over you to do you good, and to multiply you, when you followed His path and performed His will, so the Lord will cause others to exult over you to annihilate you and to destroy you, and you will be expelled from upon the land that you are coming there to take possession of it.

64 The Lord will disperse you among all the peoples from the end of the earth to the end of the earth. You will not all be exiled to one place; rather you will be scattered throughout the

רְדֶת חֹמֹתֶיךָ הַגְּבֹהֹת וְהַבְּצֻרוֹת אֲשֶׁר אַתָּה בֹּטֵחַ בָּהֵן בְּכָל־אַרְצֶךָ וְהֵצַר לְךָ
נג בְּכָל־שְׁעָרֶיךָ בְּכָל־אַרְצְךָ אֲשֶׁר נָתַן יְהוָה אֱלֹהֶיךָ לָךְ׃ וְאָכַלְתָּ פְרִי־בִטְנְךָ בְּשַׂר
בָּנֶיךָ וּבְנֹתֶיךָ אֲשֶׁר נָתַן־לְךָ יְהוָה אֱלֹהֶיךָ בְּמָצוֹר וּבְמָצוֹק אֲשֶׁר־יָצִיק לְךָ
נד אֹיְבֶךָ׃ הָאִישׁ הָרַךְ בְּךָ וְהֶעָנֹג מְאֹד תֵּרַע עֵינוֹ בְאָחִיו וּבְאֵשֶׁת חֵיקוֹ וּבְיֶתֶר בָּנָיו
נה אֲשֶׁר יוֹתִיר׃ מִתֵּת ׀ לְאַחַד מֵהֶם מִבְּשַׂר בָּנָיו אֲשֶׁר יֹאכֵל מִבְּלִי הִשְׁאִיר־לוֹ כֹּל
נו בְּמָצוֹר וּבְמָצוֹק אֲשֶׁר יָצִיק לְךָ אֹיִבְךָ בְּכָל־שְׁעָרֶיךָ׃ הָרַכָּה בְךָ וְהָעֲנֻגָּה אֲשֶׁר
לֹא־נִסְּתָה כַף־רַגְלָהּ הַצֵּג עַל־הָאָרֶץ מֵהִתְעַנֵּג וּמֵרֹךְ תֵּרַע עֵינָהּ בְּאִישׁ חֵיקָהּ
נז וּבִבְנָהּ וּבְבִתָּהּ׃ וּבְשִׁלְיָתָהּ הַיּוֹצֵת ׀ מִבֵּין רַגְלֶיהָ וּבְבָנֶיהָ אֲשֶׁר תֵּלֵד כִּי־תֹאכְלֵם
נח בְחֹסֶר־כֹּל בַּסָּתֶר בְּמָצוֹר וּבְמָצוֹק אֲשֶׁר יָצִיק לְךָ אֹיִבְךָ בִּשְׁעָרֶיךָ׃ אִם־לֹא תִשְׁמֹר
לַעֲשׂוֹת אֶת־כָּל־דִּבְרֵי הַתּוֹרָה הַזֹּאת הַכְּתֻבִים בַּסֵּפֶר הַזֶּה לְיִרְאָה אֶת־הַשֵּׁם
נט הַנִּכְבָּד וְהַנּוֹרָא הַזֶּה אֵת יְהוָה אֱלֹהֶיךָ׃ וְהִפְלָא יְהוָה אֶת־מַכֹּתְךָ וְאֵת מַכּוֹת
ס זַרְעֶךָ מַכּוֹת גְּדֹלֹת וְנֶאֱמָנוֹת וָחֳלָיִם רָעִים וְנֶאֱמָנִים׃ וְהֵשִׁיב בְּךָ אֵת כָּל־מַדְוֵה
סא מִצְרַיִם אֲשֶׁר יָגֹרְתָּ מִפְּנֵיהֶם וְדָבְקוּ בָּךְ׃ גַּם כָּל־חֳלִי וְכָל־מַכָּה אֲשֶׁר לֹא כָתוּב
סב בְּסֵפֶר הַתּוֹרָה הַזֹּאת יַעְלֵם יְהוָה עָלֶיךָ עַד הִשָּׁמְדָךְ׃ וְנִשְׁאַרְתֶּם בִּמְתֵי מְעָט
תַּחַת אֲשֶׁר הֱיִיתֶם כְּכוֹכְבֵי הַשָּׁמַיִם לָרֹב כִּי־לֹא שָׁמַעְתָּ בְּקוֹל יְהוָה אֱלֹהֶיךָ׃
סג וְהָיָה כַּאֲשֶׁר־שָׂשׂ יְהוָה עֲלֵיכֶם לְהֵיטִיב אֶתְכֶם וּלְהַרְבּוֹת אֶתְכֶם כֵּן יָשִׂישׂ יְהוָה
עֲלֵיכֶם לְהַאֲבִיד אֶתְכֶם וּלְהַשְׁמִיד אֶתְכֶם וְנִסַּחְתֶּם מֵעַל הָאֲדָמָה אֲשֶׁר־אַתָּה
סד בָא־שָׁמָּה לְרִשְׁתָּהּ׃ וֶהֱפִיצְךָ יְהוָה בְּכָל־הָעַמִּים מִקְצֵה הָאָרֶץ וְעַד־קְצֵה הָאָרֶץ

רש״י

נב | עד רדת חומתיך. לשון רדוי וכבוש:

נג | ואכלת... בשר בניך... במצור. מחמת שיהיו צרים על העיר ויהיה שם "מצוק", עקת רעבון:

נד | הרך בך. הרחמני ורך הלבב על בניו, תרע עינו בהם להעלים עינו מהם, מתת לאחד מהם מבשר בניו אשר יאכל. וביתר בניו אשר יותיר. מן השחוטין שישחט למאכלו, תהא עינו רעה ורעה בהם מלתת להם מבשר השחוטין:

נו | תרע עינה באיש חיקה ובבנה ובבתה. הגדולים:

נז | ובשליתה. בנים הקטנים, בכלן תהא עינה רעה כשתאכל את האחד מלתת לאשר אצלה מן הבשר: ובבניה אשר תלד. תרע עינה לשחטם ולאכלם בחוסר כל בסתר:

נט | והפלא ה׳ את מכתך. מפלאות ומבדלות משאר מכות. ונאמנות. לשרך לקיים שליחותן:

ס | אשר יגרת מפניהם. מפני המכות, כשהיו ישראל רואים מכות משנות הבאות על מצרים, היו יראים מהם שלא יבואו גם עליהם. תדע, שכן כתוב: "אם שמוע תשמע וגו׳ כל המחלה אשר שמתי במצרים לא אשים עליך" (שמות טו, כו), אין מיראין את האדם אלא בדבר שהוא יגור ממנו:

סא | יעלם. לשון עליה:

סב | ונשארתם במתי מעט תחת וגו׳. מועטין חלוף מרובין:

סג | כן ישיש ה׳. את אויביכם "עליכם, להאביד" וגו׳; ונסחתם. לשון עקירה, וכן: "בית גאים יסח ה׳" (משלי טו, כה):

סד | ועבדת שם אלהים אחרים. כתרגומו, לא עבודת

world. **And** when you are in exile **you shall** serve people who **serve there other gods that you did not know** (see verse 36), **you or your ancestors,** of **wood and stone.** The idol worship of your subjugators will be unfamiliar to you, and you will be unable to even imitate their actions.[41]

65 **Among these nations you will not be calm.** You will be in exile, scattered throughout the world, and unable to relax there. **And there will be no rest for the sole of your foot. The Lord will** also **give you there a trembling heart, and yearning eyes,** as you will long for an improvement in your situation, **and desolation of the soul.**

66 **Your life will be dangling before you.** You will feel completely insecure, as though your lives hang on a thread that might snap at any moment. **And you will fear night and day, and you will not believe in your life.**

67 **In the morning you will say: Would that it were** already **evening,** as the day is too grim. **And in the evening you will say: Would that it were morning.** These exclamations will come **from the fear of your heart that you will fear, and from the sight of your eyes that you will see.**

68 **The Lord will return you to Egypt in ships, on the way with regard to which I said to you: You will not see it ever again** (see 17:16). **And you will** even attempt to **sell yourselves there to your enemies as slaves and as maidservants,** merely in order to remain alive, **and** yet **there is no buyer.** No one will be willing to purchase you, as you will be considered worthless. This might be the most terrible curse of all.

69 **These are the words of the covenant that the Lord commanded Moses to make with the children of Israel in the land of Moav, besides the covenant that He made with them at Horev.**

The Enactment of the Covenant in the Plains of Moav

DEUTERONOMY 29:1–28

The previous section, which presented the blessings promised to those who observe the covenant, and the curses that will befall those who do not observe it, is entirely focused on the future. In the following section, Moses turns the attention of his listeners to the present, and to their memories of everything that occurred from the time they left Egypt.

The section concludes with Moses' declaration that those entering into the covenant are also responsible for the actions openly performed by other members of the children of Israel. However, they are not responsible for the covert actions of others. This declaration echoes the commandment to curse those who perform transgressions clandestinely at the public ceremony to be held on Mount Gerizim and Mount Eival, as stated above (27:11–26).

29 1 **Moses summoned all of Israel and he said to them: You have seen everything that the Lord performed before your eyes in the land of Egypt, to Pharaoh, and to all his servants, and to his entire land.** There are still those among you who witnessed and can remember the exodus from Egypt and the accompanying wondrous events;[42]

Seventh aliya

2 you witnessed **the great trials,** or great miracles,[43] **that your eyes saw, the signs and those great wonders.**

3 Although you witnessed all those miraculous events, **the Lord has not given you a heart to know, and eyes to see, and ears to hear, until this day.** Until now, you have not internalized these facts. I will therefore attempt to remind you of the events that occurred, so that you will contemplate the kindnesses of God:

4 **I have led you forty years in the wilderness.** Miraculously, **your garments did not wear out from upon you, and your shoe did not wear out from upon your foot.**

5 **Bread you did not eat and wine and intoxicating drink you did not drink.** All this was **so that you will know that I am the Lord your God,** who can sustain you on the miraculous manna alone, without these basic necessities.

6 **You came to this place, and Sihon king of Heshbon and Og king of Bashan emerged against us to war, and we** miraculously **smote them** with God's aid, despite the fact that you were unprepared for war.

Maftir

7 **We took their land and we gave it as an inheritance to the Reubenite, and to the Gadite, and to half the tribe of the Manassite.** God performed this kindness for us only recently, and you saw them with your own eyes. Therefore, you cannot disregard God's might.

8 **You shall observe the words of this covenant and you shall perform them, so that you will succeed in everything that you do.**

רש"י

אֱלֹהוּת מַמָּשׁ, אֶלָּא מַעֲלִים מַס וְגֻלְגָּלִיּוֹת לִכְמָרֵי עֲבוֹדָה זָרָה:

סה | **לֹא תַרְגִּיעַ.** לֹא תָנוּחַ, כְּמוֹ: "וְזֹאת הַמַּרְגֵּעָה" (ישעיה כח, יב): **לֵב רַגָּז.** לֵב חָרֵד, כְּתַרְגּוּמוֹ: "דָּחֵיל", כְּמוֹ: "שְׁאוֹל מִתַּחַת רָגְזָה לְךָ" (שם יד, ט), "שָׁמְעוּ עַמִּים יִרְגָּזוּן" (שמות טו, יד), "מוֹסְדוֹת הַשָּׁמַיִם יִרְגָּזוּ" (שמואל ב' כב, ח): **וְכִלְיוֹן עֵינַיִם.** מְצַפֶּה לִישׁוּעָה וְלֹא תָבֹא:

סו | **חַיֶּיךָ תְּלֻאִים לְךָ.** עַל הַסָּפֵק. כָּל סָפֵק קָרוּי 'תָּלוּי', שֶׁמָּא אָמוּת הַיּוֹם בַּחֶרֶב הַבָּאָה עָלֵינוּ. וְרַבּוֹתֵינוּ דָּרְשׁוּ: זֶה הַלּוֹקֵחַ תְּבוּאָה מִן הַשּׁוּק: **וְלֹא תַאֲמִין בְּחַיֶּיךָ.** זֶה הַסּוֹמֵךְ עַל הַפַּלְטֵר:

סז | **בַּבֹּקֶר תֹּאמַר מִי יִתֵּן.** וְהָיָה עֶרֶב שֶׁל אֶמֶשׁ: **וּבָעֶרֶב**

סה וְעָבַדְתָּ שָּׁם אֱלֹהִים אֲחֵרִים אֲשֶׁר לֹא־יָדַעְתָּ אַתָּה וַאֲבֹתֶיךָ עֵץ וָאָבֶן: וּבַגּוֹיִם
הָהֵם לֹא תַרְגִּיעַ וְלֹא־יִהְיֶה מָנוֹחַ לְכַף־רַגְלֶךָ וְנָתַן יְהוָה לְךָ שָׁם לֵב רַגָּז וְכִלְיוֹן
סו עֵינַיִם וְדַאֲבוֹן נָפֶשׁ: וְהָיוּ חַיֶּיךָ תְּלֻאִים לְךָ מִנֶּגֶד וּפָחַדְתָּ לַיְלָה וְיוֹמָם וְלֹא תַאֲמִין
סז בְּחַיֶּיךָ: בַּבֹּקֶר תֹּאמַר מִי־יִתֵּן עֶרֶב וּבָעֶרֶב תֹּאמַר מִי־יִתֵּן בֹּקֶר מִפַּחַד לְבָבְךָ
סח אֲשֶׁר תִּפְחָד וּמִמַּרְאֵה עֵינֶיךָ אֲשֶׁר תִּרְאֶה: וֶהֱשִׁיבְךָ יְהוָה | מִצְרַיִם בָּאֳנִיּוֹת בַּדֶּרֶךְ
אֲשֶׁר אָמַרְתִּי לְךָ לֹא־תֹסִיף עוֹד לִרְאֹתָהּ וְהִתְמַכַּרְתֶּם שָׁם לְאֹיְבֶיךָ לַעֲבָדִים
סט וְלִשְׁפָחוֹת וְאֵין קֹנֶה: אֵלֶּה דִבְרֵי הַבְּרִית אֲשֶׁר־צִוָּה יְהוָה אֶת־מֹשֶׁה
לִכְרֹת אֶת־בְּנֵי יִשְׂרָאֵל בְּאֶרֶץ מוֹאָב מִלְּבַד הַבְּרִית אֲשֶׁר־כָּרַת אִתָּם בְּחֹרֵב:

א וַיִּקְרָא מֹשֶׁה אֶל־כָּל־יִשְׂרָאֵל וַיֹּאמֶר אֲלֵהֶם אַתֶּם רְאִיתֶם אֵת כָּל־אֲשֶׁר עָשָׂה שביעי
ב יְהוָה לְעֵינֵיכֶם בְּאֶרֶץ מִצְרַיִם לְפַרְעֹה וּלְכָל־עֲבָדָיו וּלְכָל־אַרְצוֹ: הַמַּסּוֹת הַגְּדֹלֹת
ג אֲשֶׁר רָאוּ עֵינֶיךָ הָאֹתֹת וְהַמֹּפְתִים הַגְּדֹלִים הָהֵם: וְלֹא־נָתַן יְהוָה לָכֶם לֵב לָדַעַת
ד וְעֵינַיִם לִרְאוֹת וְאָזְנַיִם לִשְׁמֹעַ עַד הַיּוֹם הַזֶּה: וָאוֹלֵךְ אֶתְכֶם אַרְבָּעִים שָׁנָה בַּמִּדְבָּר
ה לֹא־בָלוּ שַׂלְמֹתֵיכֶם מֵעֲלֵיכֶם וְנַעַלְךָ לֹא־בָלְתָה מֵעַל רַגְלֶךָ: לֶחֶם לֹא אֲכַלְתֶּם
ו וְיַיִן וְשֵׁכָר לֹא שְׁתִיתֶם לְמַעַן תֵּדְעוּ כִּי אֲנִי יְהוָה אֱלֹהֵיכֶם: וַתָּבֹאוּ אֶל־הַמָּקוֹם מפטיר
ז הַזֶּה וַיֵּצֵא סִיחֹן מֶלֶךְ־חֶשְׁבּוֹן וְעוֹג מֶלֶךְ־הַבָּשָׁן לִקְרָאתֵנוּ לַמִּלְחָמָה וַנַּכֵּם: וַנִּקַּח
ח אֶת־אַרְצָם וַנִּתְּנָהּ לְנַחֲלָה לָראוּבֵנִי וְלַגָּדִי וְלַחֲצִי שֵׁבֶט הַמְנַשִּׁי: וּשְׁמַרְתֶּם אֶת־
דִּבְרֵי הַבְּרִית הַזֹּאת וַעֲשִׂיתֶם אֹתָם לְמַעַן תַּשְׂכִּילוּ אֵת כָּל־אֲשֶׁר תַּעֲשׂוּן:

רש"י

פרק כט

תֹּאמַר מִי־יִתֵּן בֹּקֶר. שֶׁל שַׁחֲרִית, שֶׁהַצָּרוֹת מִתְחַזְּקוֹת תָּמִיד,
וְכָל שָׁעָה מְרֻבָּה קִלְלָתָהּ מִשֶּׁלְּפָנֶיהָ:

סח בָּאֳנִיּוֹת. בִּסְפִינוֹת, בַּשִּׁבְיָה. וְהִתְמַכַּרְתֶּם שָׁם לְאֹיְבֶיךָ. אַתֶּם
מְבַקְשִׁים לִהְיוֹת נִמְכָּרִים לָהֶם "לַעֲבָדִים". וְאֵין
קֹנֶה. כִּי יִגְזְרוּ עָלֶיךָ הֶרֶג וְכִלָּיוֹן. בִּלְשׁוֹן
אִיטַרְוונְדֵרי"ן בּוּ"ש. וְלֹא יִתְכֵּן לְפָרֵשׁ "וְהִתְמַכַּרְתֶּם"
בִּלְשׁוֹן וְנִמְכַּרְתֶּם עַל יְדֵי מוֹכְרִים אֲחֵרִים:

סט לִכְרֹת אֶת בְּנֵי יִשְׂרָאֵל. שֶׁיְּקַבְּלוּ עֲלֵיהֶם הַתּוֹרָה
בְּאָלָה וּבִשְׁבוּעָה: מִלְּבַד הַבְּרִית. קְלָלוֹת שֶׁבְּתוֹרַת כֹּהֲנִים
שֶׁנֶּאֶמְרוּ בְּסִינַי:

ג-ח | וְלֹא נָתַן ה' לָכֶם לֵב לָדַעַת. לְהַכִּיר אֶת חַסְדֵי
הַקָּדוֹשׁ בָּרוּךְ הוּא וְלִדְבַּק בּוֹ: עַד הַיּוֹם הַזֶּה. שָׁמַעְתִּי
שֶׁאוֹתוֹ הַיּוֹם שֶׁנָּתַן מֹשֶׁה סֵפֶר הַתּוֹרָה לִבְנֵי לֵוִי, כְּמוֹ
שֶׁכָּתוּב: "וַיִּתְּנָהּ אֶל הַכֹּהֲנִים בְּנֵי לֵוִי" (להלן לא, ט), בָּאוּ
כָּל יִשְׂרָאֵל לִפְנֵי מֹשֶׁה וְאָמְרוּ לוֹ: מֹשֶׁה רַבֵּנוּ, אַף חָנוּ
עָמַדְנוּ בְּסִינַי וְקִבַּלְנוּ אֶת הַתּוֹרָה וְנִתְּנָה לָנוּ, וּמָה אַתָּה מַשְׁלִיט אֶת בְּנֵי
שִׁבְטְךָ עָלֶיהָ, וְיֹאמְרוּ לָנוּ יוֹם מָחָר, לֹא לָכֶם נִתְּנָה!
וְשָׂמַח מֹשֶׁה עַל הַדָּבָר, וְעַל זֹאת אָמַר לָהֶם: "הַיּוֹם הַזֶּה
נִהְיֵיתָ לְעָם" (לעיל כז, ט) וְגוֹ' (לעיל כז, ט). הַיּוֹם הַזֶּה הֵבַנְתִּי שֶׁאַתֶּם

דְּבֵקִים וַחֲפֵצִים בַּמָּקוֹם: וַתָּבֹאוּ אֶל הַמָּקוֹם הַזֶּה. עַתָּה
אַתֶּם רוֹאִים עַצְמְכֶם בִּגְדֻלָּה וְכָבוֹד, אַל תִּבְעֲטוּ בַּמָּקוֹם
וְאַל יָרוּם לְבַבְכֶם, "וּשְׁמַרְתֶּם אֶת דִּבְרֵי הַבְּרִית הַזֹּאת" וְגוֹ'
(להלן פסוק ח). דָּבָר אַחֵר, "וְלֹא נָתַן ה' לָכֶם לֵב לָדַעַת",
שֶׁאֵין אָדָם עוֹמֵד עַל סוֹף דַּעְתּוֹ שֶׁל רַבּוֹ וְחָכְמַת מִשְׁנָתוֹ
עַד אַרְבָּעִים שָׁנָה, וּלְפִיכָךְ לֹא הִקְפִּיד עֲלֵיכֶם הַמָּקוֹם
"עַד הַיּוֹם הַזֶּה", אֲבָל מִכָּאן וָאֵילָךְ יַקְפִּיד, וּלְפִיכָךְ
"וּשְׁמַרְתֶּם אֶת דִּבְרֵי הַבְּרִית הַזֹּאת" וְגוֹ':

Parashat
Nitzavim

The Covenant at the Plains of Moav
DEUTERONOMY 29:9–28

Moses continues the oration he began in the previous *parasha*, declaring that all those entering into the covenant are responsible for the actions openly performed by their counterparts in the children of Israel. However, they are not responsible for the covert actions of others.

9 **You are standing today, all of you, before the Lord your God.** Due to the importance of the following speech, the entire people is present: **Your heads,** leaders; the members of **your tribes;[1] your elders,** appointed over you; **and your officers;** and **every man of Israel,**

10 **your children, your wives, and your stranger who is in the midst of your camp,**D **from the hewer of your wood to the drawer of your water,**

Water bearer, eighth century BCE, Egypt

11 you are present in order **to pass you into the covenant of the Lord your God and into His oath that the Lord your God is making with you today.** The acceptance of an oath not only obligates one to fulfill an undertaking, but also entails a punishment should he fail to do so.[2]

12 God is enacting this covenant with you **in order to establish you today for Him as a people, and He will be your God.**
Second aliya There are two parties to the covenant, which entails an exclusive, mutual relationship between the children of Israel and God, **as He spoke to you, and as He took an oath to your forefathers, to Abraham, to Isaac, and to Jacob.** God's oath to the patriarchs continues with His oath to their descendants.

13 **But not with you by yourselves do I make this covenant and this oath;**

14 rather, I am establishing the covenant and the oath **with him who is here with us standing today before the Lord our God,** the entire assembly who are present, **and** also **with him**

who is not here with us today. This is referring either to people who were unable to participate in the assembly, or to future generations and converts who will later join the people.[3]

Third 15 **For you know how we lived in the land of Egypt, and how**
aliya **we passed in the midst of the nations that you passed.**

16 In all the places where you passed, you observed their behavior. **You saw their detestable things,** their gods,[4] **and their idols** of **wood and stone, silver and gold, that were with them.**

17 **Lest there is among you a man, or a woman, or a family, or a tribe,** who was impressed by the idols of the nations and **whose heart turns today from the Lord our God, to go to serve the gods of those nations,** I am therefore issuing this warning to them. At that time idolatry was not openly practiced among the Jewish people, but it is nevertheless possible that some people might have been influenced by the idolatrous nations. Although they would not yet publicly admit their beliefs, they are liable to do so at a later stage. Moses expresses this concern by means of a metaphor: **Lest there is among you a root producing gall and wormwood,**B bitter and possibly poisonous plants that are hard to discern when they are intermingled with a large quantity of produce;

Gall (hemlock)

Wormwood (*Artemisia absinthium*)

DISCUSSION

29:10 | **Your stranger who is in the midst of your camp:** These strangers may have been people who fled from Canaan and joined the children of Israel. They became part of the nation and dwelled in the Israelite camp, but they were not accorded the same legal status as full-fledged Israelites (see Rashi; *Yevamot* 79a).

BACKGROUND

29:17 | **Gall [*rosh*] and wormwood [*la'ana*]:** These are bitter and perhaps poisonous plants, which are often used as a metaphor for evil (Jeremiah 9:14, 23:15; Amos 5:7, 6:5; Lamentations 3:15). *Rosh* is commonly identified as hemlock, *Conium maculatum*, an extremely poisonous plant that was used for the execution of criminals in ancient Greece.

A herbaceous plant of the Apiaceae family that reaches a height of 1.5 m, hemlock grows by the roadside. Its flowers are white and its stalk is speckled with black spots. Others identify it with the poppy, *Papaver somniferum*. The fruit of the poppy resembles a head [*rosh*], and it is used to produce opium. Alternatively, *rosh* might be golden

פרשת
נצבים

ט אַתֶּם נִצָּבִים הַיּוֹם כֻּלְּכֶם לִפְנֵי יהוה אֱלֹהֵיכֶם רָאשֵׁיכֶם שִׁבְטֵיכֶם זִקְנֵיכֶם וְשֹׁטְרֵיכֶם כג
י כֹּל אִישׁ יִשְׂרָאֵל: טַפְּכֶם נְשֵׁיכֶם וְגֵרְךָ אֲשֶׁר בְּקֶרֶב מַחֲנֶיךָ מֵחֹטֵב עֵצֶיךָ עַד שֹׁאֵב
יא מֵימֶיךָ: לְעָבְרְךָ בִּבְרִית יהוה אֱלֹהֶיךָ וּבְאָלָתוֹ אֲשֶׁר יהוה אֱלֹהֶיךָ כֹּרֵת עִמְּךָ
יב הַיּוֹם: לְמַעַן הָקִים־אֹתְךָ הַיּוֹם | לוֹ לְעָם וְהוּא יִהְיֶה־לְּךָ לֵאלֹהִים כַּאֲשֶׁר דִּבֶּר־לָךְ שני
יג וְכַאֲשֶׁר נִשְׁבַּע לַאֲבֹתֶיךָ לְאַבְרָהָם לְיִצְחָק וּלְיַעֲקֹב: וְלֹא אִתְּכֶם לְבַדְּכֶם אָנֹכִי
יד כֹּרֵת אֶת־הַבְּרִית הַזֹּאת וְאֶת־הָאָלָה הַזֹּאת: כִּי אֶת־אֲשֶׁר יֶשְׁנוֹ פֹּה עִמָּנוּ עֹמֵד
טו הַיּוֹם לִפְנֵי יהוה אֱלֹהֵינוּ וְאֵת אֲשֶׁר אֵינֶנּוּ פֹּה עִמָּנוּ הַיּוֹם: כִּי־אַתֶּם יְדַעְתֶּם אֵת שלישי
אֲשֶׁר־יָשַׁבְנוּ בְּאֶרֶץ מִצְרָיִם וְאֵת אֲשֶׁר־עָבַרְנוּ בְּקֶרֶב הַגּוֹיִם אֲשֶׁר עֲבַרְתֶּם:
טז
יז וַתִּרְאוּ אֶת־שִׁקּוּצֵיהֶם וְאֵת גִּלֻּלֵיהֶם עֵץ וָאֶבֶן כֶּסֶף וְזָהָב אֲשֶׁר עִמָּהֶם: פֶּן־יֵשׁ
בָּכֶם אִישׁ אוֹ־אִשָּׁה אוֹ מִשְׁפָּחָה אוֹ־שֵׁבֶט אֲשֶׁר לְבָבוֹ פֹנֶה הַיּוֹם מֵעִם יהוה
אֱלֹהֵינוּ לָלֶכֶת לַעֲבֹד אֶת־אֱלֹהֵי הַגּוֹיִם הָהֵם פֶּן־יֵשׁ בָּכֶם שֹׁרֶשׁ פֹּרֶה רֹאשׁ וְלַעֲנָה:

רש״י

ט | אַתֶּם נִצָּבִים הַיּוֹם. מְלַמֵּד שֶׁכִּנְּסָם מֹשֶׁה לִפְנֵי הַקָּדוֹשׁ בָּרוּךְ הוּא בְּיוֹם מוֹתוֹ לְהַכְנִיסָם בַּבְּרִית: רָאשֵׁיכֶם שִׁבְטֵיכֶם. רָאשֵׁיכֶם לְשִׁבְטֵיכֶם: זִקְנֵיכֶם וְשֹׁטְרֵיכֶם. הֶחָשׁוּב חָשׁוּב קוֹדֵם, וְאַחַר כָּךְ "כֹּל אִישׁ יִשְׂרָאֵל":

י | מֵחֹטֵב עֵצֶיךָ. מְלַמֵּד שֶׁבָּאוּ כְּנַעֲנִיִּים לְהִתְגַּיֵּר בִּימֵי מֹשֶׁה כְּדֶרֶךְ שֶׁבָּאוּ גִּבְעוֹנִים בִּימֵי יְהוֹשֻׁעַ, וְזֶהוּ הָאָמוּר בַּגִּבְעוֹנִים: "וַיַּעֲשׂוּ גַם הֵמָּה בְּעָרְמָה" (יהושע ט, ד), וּנְתָנָם מֹשֶׁה חוֹטְבֵי עֵצִים וְשׁוֹאֲבֵי מַיִם:

יא | לְעָבְרְךָ בִּבְרִית. דֶּרֶךְ הַעֲבָרָה; כָּךְ הָיוּ כּוֹרְתִים בְּרִית: עוֹשִׂין מְחִצָּה מִכָּאן וּמְחִצָּה מִכָּאן וְעוֹבְרִים בֵּינְתַיִם, כְּמוֹ שֶׁנֶּאֱמַר: "הָעֵגֶל אֲשֶׁר כָּרְתוּ לִשְׁנַיִם וַיַּעַבְרוּ בֵּין בְּתָרָיו" (ירמיה לד, יח): לְעָבְרְךָ. לִהְיוֹתְךָ עוֹבֵר בַּבְּרִית, וְלֹא יִתָּכֵן לְפָרְשׁוֹ 'לְהַעֲבִירְךָ', אֶלָּא כְּמוֹ: "לַעֲשֹׂתְכֶם אֹתָם" (לעיל ד, יד):

יב | לְמַעַן הָקִים אֹתְךָ הַיּוֹם לוֹ לְעָם. כָּל כָּךְ הוּא נִכְנָס לִטֹרַח לְמַעַן קַיֵּם אוֹתְךָ לְפָנָיו לְעָם: וְהוּא יִהְיֶה לְּךָ לֵאלֹהִים. לְפִי שֶׁ"דִּבֶּר לָךְ וְנִשְׁבַּע לַאֲבֹתֶיךָ" שֶׁלֹּא לְהַחֲלִיף אֶת זַרְעָם בְּאֻמָּה אַחֶרֶת, לְכָךְ הוּא אוֹסֵר אֶתְכֶם בִּשְׁבוּעוֹת הַלָּלוּ שֶׁלֹּא תַּקְנִיטוּהוּ, אַחַר שֶׁהוּא אֵינוֹ יָכוֹל לְהִבָּדֵל מִכֶּם. עַד כָּאן פֵּרַשְׁתִּי לְפִי פְּשׁוּטָהּ שֶׁל פָּרָשָׁה.

וּמִדְרַשׁ אַגָּדָה: לָמָּה נִסְמְכָה פָּרָשַׁת "אַתֶּם נִצָּבִים" לַקְּלָלוֹת? לְפִי שֶׁשָּׁמְעוּ יִשְׂרָאֵל מֵאָה קְלָלוֹת חָסֵר שְׁתַּיִם, חוּץ מֵאַרְבָּעִים וְתֵשַׁע שֶׁבְּתוֹרַת כֹּהֲנִים, הוֹרִיקוּ פְּנֵיהֶם וְאָמְרוּ: מִי יוּכַל לַעֲמֹד בְּאֵלּוּ? הִתְחִיל מֹשֶׁה לְפַיְּסָם: "אַתֶּם נִצָּבִים הַיּוֹם", הַרְבֵּה הִכְעַסְתֶּם לַמָּקוֹם וְלֹא עָשָׂה אֶתְכֶם כְּלָיָה, וַהֲרֵי אַתֶּם קַיָּמִים לְפָנָיו "הַיּוֹם", כַּיּוֹם הַזֶּה שֶׁהוּא קַיָּם וְהוּא מַאֲפִיל וּמֵאִיר, כָּךְ הֵאִיר לָכֶם וְכָךְ עָתִיד לְהָאִיר לָכֶם, וְהַקְּלָלוֹת וְהַיִּסּוּרִין מְקַיְּמִין אֶתְכֶם וּמַצִּיבִין אֶתְכֶם לְפָנָיו. וְאַף הַפָּרָשָׁה שֶׁלְּמַעְלָה מִזּוֹ פִּיּוּסִין הֵם: "אַתֶּם רְאִיתֶם אֵת כָּל אֲשֶׁר עָשָׂה" וְגוֹ' (לעיל פסוק א). דָּבָר אַחֵר, "אַתֶּם נִצָּבִים", לְפִי שֶׁהָיוּ יִשְׂרָאֵל יוֹצְאִין מִפַּרְנָס לְפַרְנָס, מִמֹּשֶׁה לִיהוֹשֻׁעַ, לְפִיכָךְ עָשָׂה אוֹתָם מַצָּבָה לְזָרְזָם, וְכֵן עָשָׂה יְהוֹשֻׁעַ (יהושע כד, א), וְכֵן שְׁמוּאֵל: "הִתְיַצְּבוּ וְאִשָּׁפְטָה אִתְּכֶם" (שמואל א' יב, ז), כְּשֶׁיָּצְאוּ מִיָּדוֹ וְנִכְנְסוּ לְיָדוֹ שֶׁל שָׁאוּל:

יד | וְאֵת אֲשֶׁר אֵינֶנּוּ פֹּה. וְאַף עִם דּוֹרוֹת הָעֲתִידִים לִהְיוֹת:

טו-יז | כִּי אַתֶּם יְדַעְתֶּם וְגוֹ' וַתִּרְאוּ אֶת שִׁקּוּצֵיהֶם. לְפִי שֶׁרְאִיתֶם הָאֻמּוֹת עוֹבְדֵי עֲבוֹדָה זָרָה, וְשֶׁמָּא הִשִּׂיא לֵב אֶחָד מִכֶּם אוֹתוֹ לָלֶכֶת אַחֲרֵיהֶם: פֶּן יֵשׁ בָּכֶם וְגוֹ'. לְפִיכָךְ אֲנִי צָרִיךְ לְהַשְׁבִּיעֲכֶם:

BACKGROUND

henbane, *Hyoscyamus aureus*, which contains a strong poison.

La'ana is commonly identified with wormwood, *Artemisia absinthium*, which is common in Israel. The plant's flowers are yellow, and it reaches a height and width of 1.5 m.

It is also possible that *rosh* and *la'ana* are generic terms for various bitter or poisonous plants.

18 and it will be that upon his hearing the words of this curse that I am about to utter, **he,** who entertains idolatrous thoughts, **will bless himself in his heart, saying: Peace will be with me.** The curse will not affect me, but rather I will live happily and peacefully, **as I will follow the desire of my heart,** doing as I please, **so that the watered will be added to the dry.** Since the members of far-off nations did not witness God's greatness, their souls are called dry. They lack the divine experience that is the foundation of faith. By contrast, the souls of the Jewish people, whom God has accompanied and guided for many years, are considered properly watered. Therefore, the Israelites should not have learned from the way of life of those whose souls are dry merely because they passed through those heathen nations. If they do so, it is as though the watered has been added and adjoined to the dry.[5]

19 **The Lord will be unwilling to forgive him, as then the wrath of the Lord and His zealotry will smoke against that man.** God will be especially angry because that individual was present when the assembly accepted His oath, and yet he attempted to deceive Him, as it were. **And the entire curse that is written in this book shall rest upon him, and the Lord will expunge his name from under the heavens** until no memory of him remains.

20 If those with idolatrous thoughts are not merely individuals, but an entire family or an even larger group, they will be punished accordingly. **The Lord will separate him,** the family or group, **for evil, from all the tribes of Israel, in accordance with all the curses of the covenant that is written in this book of the Torah.**

21 Since you accept the covenant upon yourselves, if you break it and are punished, then **the latter generation, your children who will arise after you, and the foreigner who will come** to Israel **from a distant land, they will see the afflictions of that land, and the illnesses with which the Lord has blighted it, and they will say:**

22 The earth will be covered with **sulfur and salt, its entire land a fire. It will not be sown and will not produce, and no vegetation will grow in it,** as the soil will be blighted and acrid. It will look **like the aftermath of the upheaval of Sodom and Gomorrah, Adma and Tzevoyim,** the cities of the plain of the Jordan, **which the Lord overturned** because of their wickedness, **in His wrath and in His fury.**[6]

23 **All the** surrounding **nations will say: For what** reason **did the Lord do so to this land? What is** the cause of **this great enflamed wrath?**

24 **They will say** to themselves in response, or others will answer them: **It,** this occurrence, **is because they forsook the covenant of the Lord, God of their fathers, which He made with them when He took them out of the land of Egypt.**

25 **They went and served other gods and prostrated themselves before them, gods that they did not know them,** as the Canaanite gods were new to the Israelites. **And** these were gods that **He did not allot to them.** It might be the lot of gentile nations to engage in idolatry, but it is not the lot of the children of Israel.[7]

26 **The wrath of the Lord was enflamed against that land, to bring upon it the entire curse that is written in this book.**

Salt stalactites at the Dead Sea, near Mount Sodom

1116

יח וְהָיָ֡ה בְּשָׁמְעוֹ֩ אֶת־דִּבְרֵ֨י הָאָלָ֜ה הַזֹּ֗את וְהִתְבָּרֵ֤ךְ בִּלְבָבוֹ֙ לֵאמֹ֔ר שָׁל֖וֹם יִֽהְיֶה־לִּ֑י כִּ֚י

יט בִּשְׁרִר֣וּת לִבִּ֣י אֵלֵ֔ךְ לְמַ֛עַן סְפ֥וֹת הָרָוָ֖ה אֶת־הַצְּמֵאָֽה: לֹא־יֹאבֶ֣ה יְהוָה֮ סְלֹ֣חַֽ לוֹ֒ כִּ֣י

כ אָ֣ז יֶעְשַׁ֤ן אַף־יְהוָה֙ וְקִנְאָתוֹ֙ בָּאִ֣ישׁ הַה֔וּא וְרָ֤בְצָה בּוֹ֙ כָּל־הָֽאָלָ֔ה הַכְּתוּבָ֖ה בַּסֵּ֣פֶר

הַזֶּ֑ה וּמָחָ֤ה יְהוָה֙ אֶת־שְׁמ֔וֹ מִתַּ֖חַת הַשָּׁמָֽיִם: וְהִבְדִּיל֤וֹ יְהוָה֙ לְרָעָ֔ה מִכֹּ֖ל שִׁבְטֵ֣י

כא יִשְׂרָאֵ֑ל כְּכֹל֙ אָל֣וֹת הַבְּרִ֔ית הַכְּתוּבָ֕ה בְּסֵ֥פֶר הַתּוֹרָ֖ה הַזֶּֽה: וְאָמַ֞ר הַדּ֣וֹר הָאַחֲר֗וֹן

בְּנֵיכֶם֙ אֲשֶׁ֣ר יָק֣וּמוּ מֵאַחֲרֵיכֶ֔ם וְהַ֨נָּכְרִ֔י אֲשֶׁ֥ר יָבֹ֖א מֵאֶ֣רֶץ רְחוֹקָ֑ה וְ֠רָאוּ אֶת־מַכּ֞וֹת

כב הָאָ֤רֶץ הַהִוא֙ וְאֶת־תַּ֣חֲלֻאֶ֔יהָ אֲשֶׁר־חִלָּ֥ה יְהוָ֖ה בָּֽהּ: גָּפְרִ֣ית וָמֶלַח֮ שְׂרֵפָ֣ה כָל־

אַרְצָהּ֒ לֹ֤א תִזָּרַע֙ וְלֹ֣א תַצְמִ֔חַ וְלֹֽא־יַעֲלֶ֥ה בָ֖הּ כָּל־עֵ֑שֶׂב כְּֽמַהְפֵּכַ֞ת סְדֹ֤ם וַעֲמֹרָה֙

וּצְבוֹיִם֒ כג אַדְמָ֣ה וּצְבוֹיִ֔ם אֲשֶׁר֙ הָפַ֣ךְ יְהוָ֔ה בְּאַפּ֖וֹ וּבַחֲמָת֑וֹ: וְאָֽמְרוּ֙ כָּל־הַגּוֹיִ֔ם עַל־מֶ֥ה עָשָׂ֛ה

כד יְהוָ֖ה כָּ֣כָה לָאָ֣רֶץ הַזֹּ֑את מֶ֥ה חֳרִ֛י הָאַ֥ף הַגָּד֖וֹל הַזֶּֽה: וְאָ֣מְר֔וּ עַ֚ל אֲשֶׁ֣ר עָֽזְב֔וּ אֶת־

כה בְּרִ֥ית יְהוָ֖ה אֱלֹהֵ֣י אֲבֹתָ֑ם אֲשֶׁר֙ כָּרַ֣ת עִמָּ֔ם בְּהוֹצִיא֥וֹ אֹתָ֖ם מֵאֶ֣רֶץ מִצְרָֽיִם: וַיֵּלְכ֗וּ

וַיַּֽעַבְדוּ֙ אֱלֹהִ֣ים אֲחֵרִ֔ים וַיִּֽשְׁתַּחֲו֖וּ לָהֶ֑ם אֱלֹהִים֙ אֲשֶׁ֣ר לֹֽא־יְדָע֔וּם וְלֹ֥א חָלַ֖ק לָהֶֽם:

כו וַיִּֽחַר־אַ֥ף יְהוָ֖ה בָּאָ֣רֶץ הַהִ֑וא לְהָבִ֤יא עָלֶ֨יהָ֙ אֶת־כָּל־הַקְּלָלָ֔ה הַכְּתוּבָ֖ה בַּסֵּ֥פֶר הַזֶּֽה:

רש"י

טז| וַתִּרְאוּ אֶת שִׁקּוּצֵיהֶם. עַל שֵׁם שֶׁהֵם מְאוּסִים כַּשְּׁקָצִים: גִּלֻּלֵיהֶם. מְסֻרְחִים וּמְאוּסִין כַּגָּלָל: עֵץ וָאֶבֶן. אוֹתָן שֶׁל עֵץ וְשֶׁל אֶבֶן חֲמָנָם רְאִיתֶם בַּגָּלוּי, לְפִי שֶׁאֵין הַגּוֹי יָרֵא שֶׁמָּא יִגָּנֵב, אֲבָל שֶׁל כֶּסֶף וְזָהָב, "עִמָּהֶם" בְּחַדְרֵי מַשְׂכִּיתָם הֵם, לְפִי שֶׁהֵם יְרֵאִים שֶׁמָּא יִגָּנֵב:

יז| פֶּן יֵשׁ בָּכֶם. שֶׁמָּא יֵשׁ בָּכֶם: אֲשֶׁר לְבָבוֹ פֹנֶה הַיּוֹם. מִלְּקַבֵּל עָלָיו הַבְּרִית: שֹׁרֶשׁ פֹּרֶה רֹאשׁ וְלַעֲנָה. שֹׁרֶשׁ מְגַדֵּל עֵשֶׂב מַר, כְּגוֹן שֶׁהֵם מָרִים כַּלַּעֲנָה, כְּלוֹמַר, מַפְרֶה וּמַרְבֶּה רֶשַׁע בְּקִרְבְּכֶם:

יח| וְהִתְבָּרֵךְ בִּלְבָבוֹ. לְשׁוֹן בְּרָכָה, יַחֲשֹׁב בְּלִבּוֹ בִּרְכַּת שָׁלוֹם לְעַצְמוֹ לֵאמֹר, לֹא יְבוֹאוּנִי קְלָלוֹת הַלָּלוּ, אַךְ "שָׁלוֹם יִהְיֶה לִּי". בנ"דיר"א שנ"י בלע"ג, כְּמוֹ: "וְהִתְגַּלָּח" (ויקרא יג, לג), "וְהִתְפַּלֵּל" (מלכים א' ח, מב): בִּשְׁרִרוּת לִבִּי

אֵלֵךְ. בְּמַרְאִית לִבִּי, כְּמוֹ "אֲשׁוּרֵנּוּ וְלֹא קָרוֹב" (במדבר כד,): יט| כְּלוֹמַר, מַה שֶּׁלִּבִּי רוֹאֶה לַעֲשׂוֹת: לְמַעַן סְפוֹת הָרָוָה. לְפִי שֶׁאוֹסִיף לוֹ פֻּרְעָנִית עַל מַה שֶּׁעָשָׂה עַד הֵנָּה בְּשׁוֹגֵג וְהָיִיתִי מַעֲבִיר עֲלֵיהֶם, וְגוֹרֵם עַתָּה שֶׁאֲצָרְפֵם עִם הַמֵּזִיד וְאֶפָּרַע מִמֶּנוּ הַכֹּל. וְכֵן תִּרְגֵּם אוּנְקְלוֹס: "בְּדִיל לְאוֹסָפָא לֵיהּ חֲטָאֵי שָׁלוּתָא עַל זְדוֹנֵתָא", שֶׁאוֹסִיף אֲנִי לוֹ הַשְּׁגָגוֹת עַל הַזְּדוֹנוֹת: הָרָוָה. שׁוֹגֵג, שֶׁהוּא עוֹשֶׂה כְּאָדָם שִׁכּוֹר שֶׁלֹּא מִדַּעַת: הַצְּמֵאָה. שֶׁהוּא עוֹשֶׂה מִדַּעַת וּבְתַאֲוָה:

יט| יֶעְשַׁן אַף ה'. עַל יְדֵי כַּעַס, הַגּוּף מִתְחַמֵּם וְהֶעָשָׁן יוֹצֵא מִן הָאַף, וְכֵן: "עָלָה עָשָׁן בְּאַפּוֹ" (שמואל ב' כב, ט), וְאַף עַל פִּי שֶׁאֵין זוֹ לִפְנֵי הַמָּקוֹם, הַכָּתוּב מַשְׁמִיעַ אֶת הָאֹזֶן כְּדֶרֶךְ שֶׁהִיא רְגִילָה וִיכוֹלָה לִשְׁמוֹעַ, כְּפִי דֶּרֶךְ הָאָרֶץ: וְקִנְאָתוֹ. לְשׁוֹן חֵמָה, אַנְפַרְטְמנ"ט, אֲחִיזַת לְבִישַׁת נְקָמָה וְאֵינוֹ מַעֲבִיר עַל הַמִּדָּה:

כו| הַכְּתוּבָה בְּסֵפֶר הַתּוֹרָה הַזֶּה. וּלְמַעְלָה הוּא אוֹמֵר בְּסֵפֶר הַתּוֹרָה הַזֹּאת, גַּם כָּל חֳלִי וְכָל מַכָּה וְגוֹ' (לעיל כח, סא). "הַזֹּאת" לְשׁוֹן נְקֵבָה, מוּסָב עַל הַתּוֹרָה, "הַזֶּה" לְשׁוֹן זָכָר, מוּסָב עַל הַסֵּפֶר, וְעַל יְדֵי פִּסּוּק הַטְּעָמִים הֵן נֶחְלָקִין לִשְׁתֵּי לְשׁוֹנוֹת. בְּפָרָשַׁת קְלָלוֹת הַטַּעַם מַפְסִיק נְתוּנָה תַּחַת "בְּסֵפֶר", וְהַתּוֹרָה "הַזֹּאת" דְּבוּקִים זֶה לָזֶה, לְכָךְ אָמַר "הַזֹּאת", וְכָאן הַטַּעַם נָתוּן תַּחַת "הַתּוֹרָה" תֵּבַת "סֵפֶר הַתּוֹרָה" דְּבוּקִים זֶה לָזֶה, לְפִיכָךְ לְשׁוֹן זָכָר נוֹפֵל אַחֲרָיו, שֶׁהַלָּשׁוֹן נוֹפֵל עַל הַסֵּפֶר:

כה| לֹא יְדָעוּם. לֹא יָדְעוּ בָהֶם גְּבוּרַת אֱלֹהוּת: וְלֹא חָלַק לָהֶם. לֹא נְתָנָם לְחֶלְקָם, וְאוּנְקְלוֹס תִּרְגֵּם: "וְלָא אוֹטִיבָא לְהוֹן", לֹא הֵיטִיבוּ לָהֶם שׁוּם טוֹבָה, וְלֹא "חָלַק", אוֹתוֹ אֱלוֹהַּ שֶׁבָּחֲרוּ לָהֶם לֹא חָלַק לָהֶם שׁוּם נַחֲלָה וְשׁוּם חֵלֶק:

27 **The Lord uprooted them,** exiled them, **from upon their land with wrath, and with fury, and with great rage, and He cast them to another land, as** they are **this day.**

28 Moses concludes this section of his speech with a comment on the mutual responsibility of the people to uphold the covenant. **The concealed** deeds that you might commit **are** known only

for the Lord our God. God punishes those who engage in idol worship in secret, as He alone is aware of their behavior, and therefore the communal covenant does not apply to those transgressions. **But the revealed** sins, those performed openly, **are** a responsibility assigned **for us and for our children forever.** It is our duty to eliminate them,[8] as we have all undertaken **to perform all the matters of this Torah.**

The Concept of Repentance
DEUTERONOMY 30:1–10

In the previous sections, Moses portrayed an extremely rigid covenant: If one observes God's commandments, he receives the divine blessing; if he refuses to heed the word of God, he is cursed and many evils and troubles will befall him. In the following section, Moses' tone softens, as he introduces the possibility of repentance and change. Even if individuals or the community sinned, they can repent. Those who were exiled and distanced from the Divine Presence can eventually return.

This is a mutual process of repentance and return: The Jewish people will return to God, and God will likewise return the people to their land and restore their former status. These ideas are expressed by the many instances in this passage of the root *shin-vav-beit*, which means to return. The root appears in different forms and with different nuances throughout the section.

This is the first explicit mention in the Torah of the fundamental concept of repentance. The great power of repentance is the antidote to fatalistic beliefs and despair.

30 *Fourth aliya (Second aliya)* **1** **It shall be when all these matters will come upon you, the blessing and the curse that I have placed before you** (chap. 28), **that you shall restore to your heart;**[D] you will take your situation to heart and reflect upon your deeds and their consequences, while you are dwelling **among all the nations that the Lord your God has banished you there.**

2 **You shall** thereby **return to the Lord your God, and heed His voice, in accordance with everything that I command you today, you and your children, with all your heart, and with all your soul.**

3 As a result, **the Lord your God will restore your returnees** to their former status, to themselves. Alternatively, the verse means that He will return you from captivity.[9] **And He will be merciful to you, and,** just as He previously took you out of Egypt, **He will** once again **return and gather you from all the peoples, that the Lord your God dispersed you there.** In the Egyptian exile, the Israelites all dwelled in a single area. At the time of the future redemption, the Jewish people will be gathered from the many distant countries where they were scattered. *Fifth aliya (Third aliya)*

4 Although the people will be scattered, Moses reassures them: Even **if your banished** brethren **will be at the ends of the heavens, from there the Lord your God will gather you, and from there He will take you.** God will tend to each and every Jew.

5 **The Lord your God will** again **bring you to the land of which your fathers took possession, and you shall take possession of it and He will do good to you, and increase you beyond**

your fathers. Your situation will be better than that of your ancestors, and you will be greater in number than they were.

6 **The Lord your God will remove the obstruction from your heart and the heart of your descendants.** He will remove the layers of insensitivity that obstruct your heart (see 10:16). God will influence your newly revealed heart **to love the Lord your God with all your heart, and with all your soul, for the sake of your life.** You will no longer consider your service of God as a mere obligation; rather, it will be the very meaning of your life.

7 **The Lord your God will place all these curses,** about which I warned you, up**on your enemies, and upon those who hate you, who pursued you** when you were in exile and in distress.

8 **You shall return** to God, **and you shall heed the voice of the Lord.** Alternatively, this means that you shall once again heed the voice of the Lord. **And you shall perform all His commandments that I command you today.**

9 **The Lord your God will increase you in all your endeavors: In the fruit of your womb,** your children; **and in the fruit of your animals,** their brood; **and in the fruit of your land, for good, as the Lord will return to rejoice over you for good.** When God bestows good upon you He will again rejoice, **as He rejoiced over your fathers,** when they conducted themselves properly. This promise is the converse of the curse mentioned earlier (28:63), which will befall the nation if they do not observe the commandments: It shall be that as the Lord rejoiced over you to do you good and to multiply you, so the Lord will cause others to rejoice over you to annihilate you and to destroy you.

כז וַיִּתְּשֵׁם יְהוָה מֵעַל אַדְמָתָם בְּאַף וּבְחֵמָה וּבְקֶצֶף גָּדוֹל וַיַּשְׁלִכֵם אֶל־אֶרֶץ אַחֶרֶת
כח כַּיּוֹם הַזֶּה: הַנִּסְתָּרֹת לַיהוָה אֱלֹהֵינוּ וְהַנִּגְלֹת לָנוּ וּלְבָנֵינוּ עַד־עוֹלָם לַעֲשׂוֹת
ל א אֶת־כָּל־דִּבְרֵי הַתּוֹרָה הַזֹּאת: וְהָיָה כִי־יָבֹאוּ עָלֶיךָ כָּל־הַדְּבָרִים רביעי /שני/
הָאֵלֶּה הַבְּרָכָה וְהַקְּלָלָה אֲשֶׁר נָתַתִּי לְפָנֶיךָ וַהֲשֵׁבֹתָ אֶל־לְבָבֶךָ בְּכָל־הַגּוֹיִם
ב אֲשֶׁר הִדִּיחֲךָ יְהוָה אֱלֹהֶיךָ שָׁמָּה: וְשַׁבְתָּ עַד־יְהוָה אֱלֹהֶיךָ וְשָׁמַעְתָּ בְקֹלוֹ
ג כְּכֹל אֲשֶׁר־אָנֹכִי מְצַוְּךָ הַיּוֹם אַתָּה וּבָנֶיךָ בְּכָל־לְבָבְךָ וּבְכָל־נַפְשֶׁךָ: וְשָׁב יְהוָה
אֱלֹהֶיךָ אֶת־שְׁבוּתְךָ וְרִחֲמֶךָ וְשָׁב וְקִבֶּצְךָ מִכָּל־הָעַמִּים אֲשֶׁר הֱפִיצְךָ יְהוָה
ד אֱלֹהֶיךָ שָׁמָּה: אִם־יִהְיֶה נִדַּחֲךָ בִּקְצֵה הַשָּׁמָיִם מִשָּׁם יְקַבֶּצְךָ יְהוָה אֱלֹהֶיךָ
ה וּמִשָּׁם יִקָּחֶךָ: וֶהֱבִיאֲךָ יְהוָה אֱלֹהֶיךָ אֶל־הָאָרֶץ אֲשֶׁר־יָרְשׁוּ אֲבֹתֶיךָ וִירִשְׁתָּהּ
ו וְהֵיטִבְךָ וְהִרְבְּךָ מֵאֲבֹתֶיךָ: וּמָל יְהוָה אֱלֹהֶיךָ אֶת־לְבָבְךָ וְאֶת־לְבַב זַרְעֶךָ
ז לְאַהֲבָה אֶת־יְהוָה אֱלֹהֶיךָ בְּכָל־לְבָבְךָ וּבְכָל־נַפְשְׁךָ לְמַעַן חַיֶּיךָ: וְנָתַן יְהוָה חמישי /שלישי/
ח אֱלֹהֶיךָ אֵת כָּל־הָאָלוֹת הָאֵלֶּה עַל־אֹיְבֶיךָ וְעַל־שֹׂנְאֶיךָ אֲשֶׁר רְדָפוּךָ: וְאַתָּה
תָשׁוּב וְשָׁמַעְתָּ בְּקוֹל יְהוָה וְעָשִׂיתָ אֶת־כָּל־מִצְוֺתָיו אֲשֶׁר אָנֹכִי מְצַוְּךָ הַיּוֹם:
ט וְהוֹתִירְךָ יְהוָה אֱלֹהֶיךָ בְּכֹל מַעֲשֵׂה יָדֶךָ בִּפְרִי בִטְנְךָ וּבִפְרִי בְהֶמְתְּךָ וּבִפְרִי
אַדְמָתְךָ לְטֹבָה כִּי יָשׁוּב יְהוָה לָשׂוּשׂ עָלֶיךָ לְטוֹב כַּאֲשֶׁר־שָׂשׂ עַל־אֲבֹתֶיךָ:

רש״י

כז | **וַיִּתְּשֵׁם ה׳.** כְּתַרְגּוּמוֹ ״וְטַלְטֵלִנּוּן״, וְכֵן: ״הִנְנִי נֹתְשָׁם מֵעַל אַדְמָתָם״ (ירמיה יב, יד):

כח | **הַנִּסְתָּרֹת לַה׳ אֱלֹהֵינוּ.** וְאִם תֹּאמְרוּ, מַה בְּיָדֵנוּ לַעֲשׂוֹת? אַתָּה מַעֲנִישׁ אֶת הָרַבִּים עַל הִרְהוּרֵי הַיָּחִיד, שֶׁנֶּאֱמַר: ״פֶּן יֵשׁ בָּכֶם אִישׁ״ וְגוֹ׳ (לעיל פסוק יז) וְאַחַר כָּךְ: ״וְרָאוּ אֶת מַכּוֹת הָאָרֶץ הַהִוא״ (לעיל פסוק כא), וַהֲלֹא אֵין אָדָם יוֹדֵעַ טְמוּנוֹתָיו שֶׁל חֲבֵרוֹ? אֵין אֲנִי מַעֲנִישׁ אֶתְכֶם עַל ״הַנִּסְתָּרֹת״, שֶׁהֵן ״לַה׳ אֱלֹהֵינוּ״ וְהוּא יִפָּרַע מֵאוֹתוֹ יָחִיד, אֲבָל ״הַנִּגְלֹת לָנוּ וּלְבָנֵינוּ״ לְבַעֵר הָרָע מִקִּרְבֵּנוּ, וְאִם לֹא נַעֲשֶׂה דִין בָּהֶם יֵעָנְשׁוּ הָרַבִּים. נָקוּד עַל ״לָנוּ״ וְעַל ״לְבָנֵינוּ״ וְעַל ע׳ שֶׁבְּ״עַד״, לִדְרשׁ שֶׁאַף עַל הַנִּגְלוֹת לֹא עָנַשׁ אֶת הָרַבִּים עַד שֶׁעָבְרוּ אֶת הַיַּרְדֵּן, מִשֶּׁקִּבְּלוּ עֲלֵיהֶם אֶת הַשְּׁבוּעָה בְּהַר גְּרִזִּים וּבְהַר עֵיבָל וְנַעֲשׂוּ עֲרֵבִים זֶה לָזֶה:

פרק ל

ג | **וְשָׁב ה׳ אֱלֹהֶיךָ אֶת שְׁבוּתְךָ.** הָיָה לוֹ לִכְתֹּב: ׳וְהֵשִׁיב אֶת שְׁבוּתְךָ׳, רַבּוֹתֵינוּ לָמְדוּ מִכָּאן כִּבְיָכוֹל שֶׁהַשְּׁכִינָה שְׁרוּיָה עִם יִשְׂרָאֵל בְּצָרַת גָּלוּתָם, וּכְשֶׁנִּגְאָלִין הִכְתִּיב גְּאֻלָּה לְעַצְמוֹ שֶׁהוּא יָשׁוּב עִמָּהֶם. וְעוֹד יֵשׁ לוֹמַר שֶׁגָּדוֹל יוֹם קִבּוּץ גָּלֻיּוֹת וּבְקֹשִׁי, כְּאִלּוּ הוּא עַצְמוֹ צָרִיךְ לִהְיוֹת אוֹחֵז בְּיָדָיו מַמָּשׁ אִישׁ אִישׁ מִמְּקוֹמוֹ, כְּעִנְיָן שֶׁנֶּאֱמַר: ״וְאַתֶּם תְּלֻקְּטוּ לְאַחַד אֶחָד בְּנֵי יִשְׂרָאֵל״ (ישעיה כז, יב), וְאַף בְּגָלֻיּוֹת שְׁאָר הָאֻמּוֹת מָצִינוּ כֵּן: ״וְשַׁבְתִּי אֶת שְׁבוּת מִצְרַיִם״ (יחזקאל כט, יד):

DISCUSSION

30:1 | You shall restore to your heart: Some explain this phrase as: You shall answer yourself in your heart. As you contemplate the long and difficult period of exile, you will reconsider the values of your life. You will distinguish between those matters that are of utmost significance and those that are merely of secondary importance. You will find new answers to the fundamental questions of life, and you will consequently return to God.

10 You will receive these blessings **if you will heed the voice of the Lord your God, to observe His commandments and His statutes that are written in this book of the Torah, when you** **will return to the Lord your God with all your heart, and with all your soul.**

Choosing to Observe the Commandments
DEUTERONOMY 30:11–20

The following section contains general comments with regard to the covenant. The concept of repentance presented in the previous section provides hope for both the individual and the nation: Those who have distanced themselves from God can return to Him. In this section, the Torah stresses that God's commandments are readily accessible to everyone. Consequently, it is the responsibility of each person to choose life and good.

11 **For this commandment,** all the commandments of the Torah,

Sixth aliya **that I command you today, it is not obscured from you,** it is not strange or impossible to perform, **and it is not distant.** Some explain that this is referring specifically to the commandment of repentance.[10]

12 **It is not in the heavens,** which might lead the people **to say: Who will ascend for us to the heavens and take it for us, and communicate it to us, that we will perform it?** Although we desire to observe the Torah, it is too lofty and abstract for us. If someone would bring it down to us, we would observe it. To counter that claim, Moses explains that he has already brought the Torah down from the heavens, and it is now within their reach.

13 **It is not** distant, **across the sea,** which might lead them **to say: Who will cross for us to the other side of the sea and take it for us and communicate it to us, that we will perform it?** If it were a little nearer, we would observe it.

14 The suggestions that the Torah is too lofty or distant are incorrect. **Rather, the matter** of the Torah and its commandments **is very near to you.** The words of the Torah are **in your mouth** to speak them, **and in your heart** to understand them. Consequently you are able **to perform it,** the commandments of the Torah.

15 **See, I have placed before you today,** on the one hand, **life and**

Seventh aliya and Maftir (Fourth aliya) **good,** through your observance of the Torah and the covenant; **and** on the other hand, **death and evil,** if you do not obey. Life is naturally related to the good, whereas death is invariably associated with evil.

16 See **that I command you today to love the Lord your God, to walk in His ways and to observe His commandments, His statutes, and His ordinances.** When you choose to follow this path, **you will live and you will multiply, and the Lord your God will bless you in the land that you are coming there to take possession of it.** You will thereby choose life and the good.

17 **But if your heart will turn away, and you will not heed** these matters, **and you go astray** and veer from the path of the good, **and** you **prostrate yourself before other gods and serve them,**

18 **I am telling you today that you will be annihilated** from the world. Your lives are not mere random occurrences, as you are not alive merely to exist and multiply. Rather, your lives have a purpose. If you turn your backs on your destiny, **you will not extend your days upon the land that you are crossing the Jordan to go there to take possession of it,** but you will be exiled.

19 Moses reiterates the previous point, but this time he asks the people to choose correctly. **I call today to the heavens and the earth**[D] **to bear witness to you; I have placed life and death before you, the blessing and the curse.** I ask that **you shall choose life, so that you and your descendants will live.** Life, goodness, and a blessing are all one option, in contrast to death, evil, and a curse. I present you with both paths, but I want you to choose the positive option.[11]

20 Your choice should be **to love the Lord your God, to heed His voice, and to cleave to Him, for He is your life and the length of your days, so that you may live in the land with regard to which the Lord took an oath to your forefathers, to Abraham, to Isaac, and to Jacob, to give to them.** Your deeds and your attitude toward God will decide whether you will live a long, meaningful life in your land.

DISCUSSION

30:19 | The heavens and the earth: When Moses, who is about to depart from this world, administers the oath to the children of Israel, he chooses the heavens and the earth as eternal witnesses to ensure the fulfillment of the oath. Moses again calls upon the heavens and the earth to stand as witnesses at the beginning of the song of *Haazinu* (32:1; see also 31:28), and the prophet Isaiah does the same (Isaiah 1:2).

י כִּ֣י תִשְׁמַ֗ע בְּקוֹל֙ יְהוָ֣ה אֱלֹהֶ֔יךָ לִשְׁמֹ֤ר מִצְוֺתָיו֙ וְחֻקֹּתָ֔יו הַכְּתוּבָ֕ה בְּסֵ֥פֶר הַתּוֹרָ֖ה הַזֶּ֑ה
יא כִּ֤י תָשׁוּב֙ אֶל־יְהוָ֣ה אֱלֹהֶ֔יךָ בְּכָל־לְבָבְךָ֖ וּבְכָל־נַפְשֶֽׁךָ׃ כִּ֚י הַמִּצְוָ֣ה הַזֹּ֔את כד ששי
יב אֲשֶׁ֛ר אָנֹכִ֥י מְצַוְּךָ֖ הַיּ֑וֹם לֹֽא־נִפְלֵ֥את הִוא֙ מִמְּךָ֔ וְלֹ֥א רְחֹקָ֖ה הִֽוא׃ לֹ֥א בַשָּׁמַ֖יִם
יג הִ֑וא לֵאמֹ֗ר מִ֣י יַעֲלֶה־לָּ֤נוּ הַשָּׁמַ֙יְמָה֙ וְיִקָּחֶ֣הָ לָּ֔נוּ וְיַשְׁמִעֵ֥נוּ אֹתָ֖הּ וְנַעֲשֶֽׂנָּה׃ וְלֹֽא־
מֵעֵ֥בֶר לַיָּ֖ם הִ֑וא לֵאמֹ֗ר מִ֤י יַעֲבָר־לָ֙נוּ֙ אֶל־עֵ֣בֶר הַיָּ֔ם וְיִקָּחֶ֣הָ לָּ֔נוּ וְיַשְׁמִעֵ֥נוּ אֹתָ֖הּ
יד טו וְנַעֲשֶֽׂנָּה׃ כִּֽי־קָר֥וֹב אֵלֶ֛יךָ הַדָּבָ֖ר מְאֹ֑ד בְּפִ֥יךָ וּבִֽלְבָבְךָ֖ לַעֲשֹׂתֽוֹ׃ רְאֵ֨ה שביעי ומפטיר /רביעי/
טז נָתַ֤תִּי לְפָנֶ֙יךָ֙ הַיּ֔וֹם אֶת־הַֽחַיִּ֖ים וְאֶת־הַטּ֑וֹב וְאֶת־הַמָּ֖וֶת וְאֶת־הָרָֽע׃ אֲשֶׁ֨ר אָנֹכִ֣י
מְצַוְּךָ֮ הַיּוֹם֒ לְאַהֲבָ֞ה אֶת־יְהוָ֤ה אֱלֹהֶ֙יךָ֙ לָלֶ֣כֶת בִּדְרָכָ֔יו וְלִשְׁמֹ֛ר מִצְוֺתָ֥יו וְחֻקֹּתָ֖יו
וּמִשְׁפָּטָ֑יו וְחָיִ֣יתָ וְרָבִ֔יתָ וּבֵֽרַכְךָ֙ יְהוָ֣ה אֱלֹהֶ֔יךָ בָּאָ֕רֶץ אֲשֶׁר־אַתָּ֥ה בָא־שָׁ֖מָּה
יז לְרִשְׁתָּֽהּ׃ וְאִם־יִפְנֶ֥ה לְבָבְךָ֖ וְלֹ֣א תִשְׁמָ֑ע וְנִדַּחְתָּ֗ וְהִֽשְׁתַּחֲוִ֛יתָ לֵאלֹהִ֥ים אֲחֵרִ֖ים
יח וַעֲבַדְתָּֽם׃ הִגַּ֤דְתִּי לָכֶם֙ הַיּ֔וֹם כִּ֥י אָבֹ֖ד תֹּאבֵד֑וּן לֹא־תַאֲרִיכֻ֤ן יָמִים֙ עַל־הָ֣אֲדָמָ֔ה
יט אֲשֶׁ֨ר אַתָּ֤ה עֹבֵר֙ אֶת־הַיַּרְדֵּ֔ן לָב֥וֹא שָׁ֖מָּה לְרִשְׁתָּֽהּ׃ הַעִידֹ֨תִי בָכֶ֣ם הַיּוֹם֮ אֶת־הַשָּׁמַ֣יִם
וְאֶת־הָאָרֶץ֒ הַחַיִּ֤ים וְהַמָּ֙וֶת֙ נָתַ֣תִּי לְפָנֶ֔יךָ הַבְּרָכָ֖ה וְהַקְּלָלָ֑ה וּבָֽחַרְתָּ֙ בַּחַיִּ֔ים לְמַ֥עַן
כ תִּחְיֶ֖ה אַתָּ֥ה וְזַרְעֶֽךָ׃ לְאַהֲבָה֙ אֶת־יְהוָ֣ה אֱלֹהֶ֔יךָ לִשְׁמֹ֥עַ בְּקֹל֖וֹ וּלְדָבְקָה־ב֑וֹ כִּ֣י
ה֤וּא חַיֶּ֙יךָ֙ וְאֹ֣רֶךְ יָמֶ֔יךָ לָשֶׁ֣בֶת עַל־הָאֲדָמָ֗ה אֲשֶׁר֩ נִשְׁבַּ֨ע יְהוָ֧ה לַאֲבֹתֶ֛יךָ לְאַבְרָהָ֛ם
לְיִצְחָ֥ק וּֽלְיַעֲקֹ֖ב לָתֵ֥ת לָהֶֽם׃

רש"י

יא| **לֹא נִפְלֵאת הִוא מִמְּךָ.** לֹא מְכֻסָּה הִיא מִמְּךָ, כְּמוֹ שֶׁנֶּאֱמַר: "כִּי יִפָּלֵא" (לעיל יז, ח) – "אֲחַרֵי יִתְכַּסֵּי", "וַתֵּרֶד פְּלָאִים" (איכה א, ט) וַתֵּרֶד בְּמַטְמוֹנִיּוֹת, מְכֻסָּה חֲבוּשָׁה בְּטָמוּן:

יב| **לֹא בַשָּׁמַיִם הִוא.** שֶׁאִלּוּ הָיְתָה בַּשָּׁמַיִם, הָיִיתָ צָרִיךְ לַעֲלוֹת אַחֲרֶיהָ וְלִלְמְדָהּ:

יד| **כִּי קָרוֹב אֵלֶיךָ.** הַתּוֹרָה נִתְּנָה לָכֶם בִּכְתָב וּבְעַל פֶּה:

טו| **אֶת הַחַיִּים וְאֶת הַטּוֹב.** זֶה תָּלוּי בָּזֶה, אִם תַּעֲשֶׂה טוֹב הֲרֵי לְךָ חַיִּים, וְאִם תַּעֲשֶׂה רָע הֲרֵי לְךָ הַמָּוֶת, וְהַכָּתוּב מְפָרֵשׁ וְהוֹלֵךְ הֵיאַךְ:

טז| **אֲשֶׁר אָנֹכִי מְצַוְּךָ הַיּוֹם לְאַהֲבָה.** הֲרֵי הַטּוֹב, וּבוֹ תָּלוּי "וְחָיִיתָ וְרָבִיתָ", הֲרֵי הַחַיִּים:

יז| **וְאִם יִפְנֶה לְבָבְךָ.** הֲרֵי הָרָע:

יח| **כִּי אָבֹד תֹּאבֵדוּן.** הֲרֵי הַמָּוֶת:

יט| **הַעִדֹתִי בָכֶם הַיּוֹם אֶת הַשָּׁמַיִם וְאֶת הָאָרֶץ.** שֶׁהֵם קַיָּמִים לְעוֹלָם, וְכַאֲשֶׁר תִּקְרֶה אֶתְכֶם הָרָעָה יִהְיוּ עֵדִים שֶׁאֲנִי הִתְרֵיתִי בָּכֶם בְּכָל זֹאת. דָּבָר אַחֵר, "הַעִדֹתִי בָכֶם הַיּוֹם אֶת הַשָּׁמַיִם" וְגוֹ', אָמַר לָהֶם הַקָּדוֹשׁ בָּרוּךְ הוּא לְיִשְׂרָאֵל: הִסְתַּכְּלוּ בַּשָּׁמַיִם שֶׁבָּרָאתִי לְשַׁמֵּשׁ אֶתְכֶם, שֶׁמָּא שִׁנּוּ אֶת מִדָּתָם? שֶׁמָּא לֹא עָלָה גַּלְגַּל חַמָּה מִן הַמִּזְרָח וְהֵאִיר לְכָל הָעוֹלָם, כְּעִנְיָן שֶׁנֶּאֱמַר: "וְזָרַח הַשֶּׁמֶשׁ וּבָא הַשָּׁמֶשׁ" (קהלת א, ה)? הִסְתַּכְּלוּ בָּאָרֶץ שֶׁבָּרָאתִי לְשַׁמֵּשׁ אֶתְכֶם, שֶׁמָּא שִׁנְּתָה מִדָּתָהּ? שֶׁמָּא זְרַעְתֶּם אוֹתָהּ וְלֹא צָמְחָה, אוֹ שֶׁמָּא זְרַעְתֶּם חִטִּים וְהֶעֶלְתָה שְׂעוֹרִים? וּמָה אֵלּוּ שֶׁנַּעֲשׂוּ לֹא לְשָׂכָר וְלֹא לְהֶפְסֵד, אִם זוֹכִין אֵין מְקַבְּלִין שָׂכָר וְאִם חוֹטְאִין אֵין מְקַבְּלִין פֻּרְעָנוּת – לֹא שִׁנּוּ אֶת מִדָּתָם, אַתֶּם שֶׁאִם זְכִיתֶם תְּקַבְּלוּ שָׂכָר וְאִם חֲטָאתֶם תְּקַבְּלוּ פֻּרְעָנוּת, עַל אַחַת כַּמָּה וְכַמָּה: **וּבָחַרְתָּ בַּחַיִּים.** אֲנִי מוֹרֶה לָכֶם שֶׁתִּבְחֲרוּ בְּחֵלֶק הַחַיִּים, כְּאָדָם הָאוֹמֵר לִבְנוֹ, בְּרֹר לְךָ חֵלֶק יָפֶה בְּנַחֲלָתִי, וּמַעֲמִידוֹ עַל חֵלֶק הַיָּפֶה וְאוֹמֵר לוֹ: אֶת זֶה בְּרֹר לְךָ. וְעַל זֶה נֶאֱמַר: "ה' מְנָת חֶלְקִי וְכוֹסִי אַתָּה תּוֹמִיךְ גּוֹרָלִי" (תהלים טז, ה), הִנַּחְתָּ יָדִי עַל גּוֹרָל הַטּוֹב, לוֹמַר, אֶת זֶה קַח לְךָ:

Parashat
Vayelekh

Last Instructions before Moses' Departure

DEUTERONOMY 31:1–30

Moses is concluding his mission in this world. In this section, on the day of his death, he delivers his parting words to the children of Israel, in order to raise their spirits. Since he was everything to them, his loss will leave a massive void in the hearts of the people.

Not only with regard to his personality was there no one like Moses, with regard to the variety of leadership roles he filled there was also no one like him. He was a man of God, religious leader, transmitter of the Torah, in charge of the Tabernacle and the priests, judge, civil leader, and military commander. Moses therefore does everything he can to ensure that the chasm left by his death will not lead the people to despair. He comforts them and vigorously seeks to bolster them in preparation for future events.

From the beginning of the book of Deuteronomy until now, Moses has been instructing the people, but he knows that his commands will not be fully obeyed. He prophetically envisions that the people will ultimately abandon God and breach His covenant, and this outcome is beyond his control. In clear terms, he informs the people of future events both in prose and in poetry. The poetry appears in the *parasha* following this one, in the form of a song in which Moses briefly describes the highs and lows, the punishments and the ultimate redemption of Israel. Moses wants the nation to become familiar with this song, so that it will accompany them on their long, challenging path ahead, and help them preserve their collective memory and their faith.

31 1 **Moses went and spoke these** aforementioned **words,** from
the beginning of Deuteronomy,[1] **to all Israel.**
2 **He said to them: I am one hundred and twenty years old today.** It is possible that Moses turned one hundred and twenty on the very day that he passed away.[2] **I will no longer be able to go and come,** to lead the people, go before them to war, and deal with all their needs in an organized manner.[3] **And** yet the reason for this is not weakness, fatigue, or old age,[4] but because **the Lord said to me: You shall not cross this Jordan.** You, the children of Israel, are getting ready to cross the Jordan River, whereas I am prohibited from entering the Land of Israel.[5]
3 Moses seeks to reassure the people: Although I will not be with you, **the Lord your God, He is crossing before you,** just as He did in my day. **He will destroy these nations** west of the Jordan, **from before you, and you will take possession from them.** In addition to the unseen leadership from above, you will also have a capable flesh and blood leader: **Joshua, he is crossing before you, as the Lord spoke.** He is the leader chosen by God.
4 **The Lord will do to them,** those nations, **as He did to Sihon**
Second aliya **and to Og,**[D] the mighty **kings of the Emorites, and to their land, that He destroyed them,** as you will recall from the events of the last few months.
5 **The Lord will deliver them,** the inhabitants of Canaan, **before you, and you shall do to them in accordance with the entire commandment that I commanded you,** to eradicate them from the land.
6 **Be strong and courageous; do not fear or be intimidated before them,**[6] **as the Lord your God, it is He who goes with you,** and **He will not fail you,** or remove His grasp from you, **and He will not forsake you.**
7 **Moses summoned Joshua.** Since Joshua was always at Moses'
Third aliya (Fifth aliya) side, he was certainly present when Moses was speaking. However, Moses now summons him to come forward and stand before him in a ceremonial manner. **And** Moses **said to him before the eyes of all Israel: Be strong and courageous, as you will come with this people into the land with regard to which the Lord took an oath to their forefathers to give them, and you will bequeath it to them.**
8 **The Lord, it is He who goes before you; He will be with you, He will not fail you, and He will not forsake you;** and therefore **do not fear and do not be frightened.** By reiterating this message in public numerous times, Moses provides Joshua not only with the formal authority to rule over the people, but also with the might to perform this vital task.
9 **Moses wrote this Torah,** the Torah we have today, **and he gave it to the priests,**[D] **sons of Levi, who carry the Ark of the Covenant of the Lord; and** he gave it **to all the elders of**

פרשת
וילך

א ב וַיֵּלֶךְ מֹשֶׁה וַיְדַבֵּר אֶת־הַדְּבָרִים הָאֵלֶּה אֶל־כָּל־יִשְׂרָאֵל: וַיֹּאמֶר אֲלֵהֶם בֶּן־מֵאָה
וְעֶשְׂרִים שָׁנָה אָנֹכִי הַיּוֹם לֹא־אוּכַל עוֹד לָצֵאת וְלָבוֹא וַיהוה אָמַר אֵלַי לֹא
ג תַעֲבֹר אֶת־הַיַּרְדֵּן הַזֶּה: יהוה אֱלֹהֶיךָ הוּא ׀ עֹבֵר לְפָנֶיךָ הוּא־יַשְׁמִיד אֶת־הַגּוֹיִם
ד הָאֵלֶּה מִלְּפָנֶיךָ וִירִשְׁתָּם יְהוֹשֻׁעַ הוּא עֹבֵר לְפָנֶיךָ כַּאֲשֶׁר דִּבֶּר יהוה: וְעָשָׂה יהוה שני
לָהֶם כַּאֲשֶׁר עָשָׂה לְסִיחוֹן וּלְעוֹג מַלְכֵי הָאֱמֹרִי וּלְאַרְצָם אֲשֶׁר הִשְׁמִיד אֹתָם:
ה ו וּנְתָנָם יהוה לִפְנֵיכֶם וַעֲשִׂיתֶם לָהֶם כְּכָל־הַמִּצְוָה אֲשֶׁר צִוִּיתִי אֶתְכֶם: חִזְקוּ
וְאִמְצוּ אַל־תִּירְאוּ וְאַל־תַּעַרְצוּ מִפְּנֵיהֶם כִּי ׀ יהוה אֱלֹהֶיךָ הוּא הַהֹלֵךְ עִמָּךְ לֹא
ז יַרְפְּךָ וְלֹא יַעַזְבֶךָּ: וַיִּקְרָא מֹשֶׁה לִיהוֹשֻׁעַ וַיֹּאמֶר אֵלָיו לְעֵינֵי שלישי /חמישי/
כָל־יִשְׂרָאֵל חֲזַק וֶאֱמָץ כִּי אַתָּה תָּבוֹא אֶת־הָעָם הַזֶּה אֶל־הָאָרֶץ אֲשֶׁר נִשְׁבַּע
ח יהוה לַאֲבֹתָם לָתֵת לָהֶם וְאַתָּה תַּנְחִילֶנָּה אוֹתָם: וַיהוה הוּא ׀ הַהֹלֵךְ לְפָנֶיךָ הוּא
ט יִהְיֶה עִמָּךְ לֹא יַרְפְּךָ וְלֹא יַעַזְבֶךָּ לֹא תִירָא וְלֹא תֵחָת: וַיִּכְתֹּב מֹשֶׁה אֶת־הַתּוֹרָה
הַזֹּאת וַיִּתְּנָהּ אֶל־הַכֹּהֲנִים בְּנֵי לֵוִי הַנֹּשְׂאִים אֶת־אֲרוֹן בְּרִית יהוה וְאֶל־כָּל־זִקְנֵי

רש"י

פרק לא

ב| **לֹא אוּכַל עוֹד לָצֵאת וְלָבוֹא.** יָכוֹל שֶׁתָּשַׁשׁ כֹּחוֹ? תַּלְמוּד לוֹמַר: "לֹא כָהֲתָה עֵינוֹ וְלֹא נָס לֵחֹה" (להלן לד, ז), אֶלָּא מַהוּ "לֹא אוּכַל"? אֵינִי רַשַּׁאי, שֶׁנִּטְּלָה מִמֶּנִּי הָרְשׁוּת וְנִתְּנָה לִיהוֹשֻׁעַ: וַה' אָמַר אֵלַי. זֶהוּ פֵּרוּשׁ "לֹא אוּכַל עוֹד לָצֵאת וְלָבוֹא", לְפִי שֶׁה' אָמַר אֵלַי: **אָנֹכִי הַיּוֹם.** הַיּוֹם מָלְאוּ יָמַי וּשְׁנוֹתַי, בְּיוֹם זֶה נוֹלַדְתִּי וּבְיוֹם זֶה אָמוּת. דָּבָר אַחֵר, "לָצֵאת וְלָבוֹא" בְּדִבְרֵי תוֹרָה, מְלַמֵּד שֶׁנִּסְתְּמוּ מִמֶּנּוּ מְסוֹרוֹת וּמַעְיְנוֹת הַחָכְמָה:

ו| **לֹא יַרְפְּךָ.** לֹא יִתֵּן לְךָ רִפְיוֹן לִהְיוֹת נֶעֱזָב מִמֶּנּוּ:

ז| **כִּי אַתָּה תָּבוֹא אֶת הָעָם הַזֶּה.** כְּתַרְגּוּמוֹ: "אֲרֵי אַתְּ תֵּיעוֹל עִם עַמָּא הָדֵין". מֹשֶׁה אָמַר לוֹ לִיהוֹשֻׁעַ: זְקֵנִים שֶׁבַּדּוֹר יִהְיוּ עִמָּהֶם, הַכֹּל לְפִי דַּעְתָּן וַעֲצָתָן. אֲבָל הַקָּדוֹשׁ בָּרוּךְ הוּא אָמַר לִיהוֹשֻׁעַ: "כִּי אַתָּה תָּבִיא אֶת בְּנֵי יִשְׂרָאֵל אֶל הָאָרֶץ אֲשֶׁר נִשְׁבַּעְתִּי לָהֶם" (להלן פסוק כג), "תָּבִיא" עַל כָּרְחָם, הַכֹּל תָּלוּי בְּךָ, טֹל מַקֵּל וְהַךְ עַל קָדְקֳדָן, דַּבָּר אֶחָד לַדּוֹר וְלֹא שְׁנֵי דַּבָּרִים לַדּוֹר:

DISCUSSION

31:4| **The Lord will do to them as He did to Sihon and to Og:** Unlike the nations east of the Jordan River, some of the Canaanites on the western side of the Jordan maintained areas and settlements that had never been conquered and evacuated. Some of their inhabitants remained in place for many generations and intermingled with the Israelites. Indeed, Israel was warned and reproved on numerous occasions for not completing their conquest of the land (see Joshua 23:13; Judges 2–3).

31:9| **Moses wrote this Torah, and he gave it to the priests:** It is well known that one Torah was placed alongside the Ark of the Covenant at all times. This Torah scroll, also called the Book of the Courtyard, in reference to the Temple's courtyard, was the original version from which all other scrolls were copied. It is possible that this was the first copy of the Torah written, and it was written by Moses (see *Midrash Tanna'im*, *Devarim* 17:18; *Bava Batra* 14b).

Israel. They would later copy from this Torah, while the original would remain alongside the Tablets of the Covenant.

10 At this point, the last communal commandment in the Torah is

Fourth aliya stated: **Moses commanded them,** the sons of Levi and all the elders of Israel, **saying:** The following ceremony will take place **at the end of seven years in the appointed time of the year of remittal, during the Festival of the Tabernacles.** The ceremony will take place during the Sukkot immediately after the conclusion of the Sabbatical Year. Since Sukkot is the festival marking the conclusion of the harvest, it is associated with the previous year.

11 **Upon the arrival of all of Israel to appear before the Lord your God in the place that He will choose, you,** Joshua,[8] **shall read this Torah before all Israel in their ears,** in a clear, understandable manner.[9]

12 Aside from organizing the reading alone, you must also **assemble the people,**[D] **the men and the women and the children, and your stranger who is within your gates, so that they will hear, and so that they will learn, and they will fear the Lord your God, and they will take care to perform all the matters of this Torah.** Some of the people will only hear, while others will also learn.

13 The ultimate goal of this public recitation is that the Torah should be preserved and transmitted from one generation to another: **Their children, who do not know** anything, **they will hear, and they will learn to fear the Lord your God, all the days that you live on the land that you are crossing the Jordan to there, to take possession of it.**

14 **The Lord said to Moses: Behold, your days are drawing**

Fifth aliya (Sixth aliya) **near for you to die. Summon Joshua, and** both of you **stand in the Tent of Meeting,** the Tabernacle, **and** there **I will command him,** appoint him to his new task. **Moses and Joshua went and stood in the Tent of Meeting.** Moses could speak with God face-to-face, as it were, in the Tent of Meeting. On this occasion, he took Joshua with him as well. Their entrance together into the Tent of Meeting was a public, ceremonial act, and presumably, even those not invited to witness this event came to see what was happening.

15 **The Lord appeared in the tent in a pillar of cloud, and the pillar of cloud stood over the entrance of the tent.**

16 **The Lord said to Moses: Behold, you will lie with your fathers,** as you are about to die. You should know what will happen after your death: **This people will rise, and it will stray after the foreign gods of the land,**[D] or alternatively, the gods of the foreign people of the land,[10] **that it is coming there into their midst** of those nations.[11] **And it will forsake Me, and it will breach My covenant that I made with it.**

17 **My wrath will be enflamed against it on that day, and I will forsake them, and I will hide My face from them, and it,** this people, **will be for consumption.** All the foreign peoples will rule over the nation, oppressing it and destroying it. **Many evils and troubles**[D] **will find it, and it,** the nation of Israel, **will say on that day: Is it not because my God is not in my midst that these evils found me?** These evils are not random occurrences, but are a punishment for abandoning God.

18 **I will conceal My face**[D] **on that day,** in an undefined, future period, **because of all the evil that it,** Israel, **performed as it turned to other gods.**

19 **Now,** in light of the events to come, **write this song for you,** the song that appears later on (32:1–43), which is called the song of *Haazinu*, after its opening word, **and teach it to the children of Israel, place it in their mouths.** They shall write down this song and familiarize themselves with it until they can recite it, **so that this song will be a witness for Me for the children of Israel.** The song describes poetically, in highly condensed form, the rise of Israel, their sins, punishments, and redemption. Its poetic style is designed to facilitate remembering its contents throughout the generations.

DISCUSSION

31:12| **Assemble the people:** This commandment of assembling the people in the manner described was observed until the end of the Second Temple period. According to tradition, the king of Israel, or its most senior leader, would read the Torah before all of Israel in an area prepared especially for this purpose. He is not chosen because he is the greatest of Sages; rather, it is as part of his role as king (or leader) and the most distinguished member of the people. It should be noted as well that there is a distinction between the general commandment of ascending to Jerusalem for the pilgrimage festivals, and this commandment of assembling the people. Only adult males were obligated to ascend to Jerusalem for the pilgrimage festivals, although many came with their entire families. Here, however, the command is explicitly directed to all strata of the people, including foreigners living in the land. This ceremony in which the Torah is read publicly before so many people serves to express the entire nation's acceptance of the yoke of the Torah (see *Sota* 41a).

31:16| **And this people will rise, and it will stray after the foreign gods of the land:** Although each individual has free choice, the people as a whole will not maintain its observance of the Torah and its commandments for long (see Rambam, *Sefer HaMadda*, *Hilkhot Teshuva* 6:8). In fact, the process of internalizing the Torah among the people of Israel took hundreds of years. On many occasions the Israelites declared their acceptance of the Torah and its commandments, but they repeatedly strayed after the gods of the nations due to the influence

י יִשְׂרָאֵל: וַיְצַו מֹשֶׁה אוֹתָם לֵאמֹר מִקֵּץ ׀ שֶׁבַע שָׁנִים בְּמֹעֵד שְׁנַת הַשְּׁמִטָּה בְּחַג רביעי
יא הַסֻּכּוֹת: בְּבוֹא כָל־יִשְׂרָאֵל לֵרָאוֹת אֶת־פְּנֵי יהוה אֱלֹהֶיךָ בַּמָּקוֹם אֲשֶׁר יִבְחָר
יב תִּקְרָא אֶת־הַתּוֹרָה הַזֹּאת נֶגֶד כָּל־יִשְׂרָאֵל בְּאָזְנֵיהֶם: הַקְהֵל אֶת־הָעָם הָאֲנָשִׁים
וְהַנָּשִׁים וְהַטַּף וְגֵרְךָ אֲשֶׁר בִּשְׁעָרֶיךָ לְמַעַן יִשְׁמְעוּ וּלְמַעַן יִלְמְדוּ וְיָרְאוּ אֶת־יהוה
יג אֱלֹהֵיכֶם וְשָׁמְרוּ לַעֲשׂוֹת אֶת־כָּל־דִּבְרֵי הַתּוֹרָה הַזֹּאת: וּבְנֵיהֶם אֲשֶׁר לֹא־יָדְעוּ
יִשְׁמְעוּ וְלָמְדוּ לְיִרְאָה אֶת־יהוה אֱלֹהֵיכֶם כָּל־הַיָּמִים אֲשֶׁר אַתֶּם חַיִּים עַל־
הָאֲדָמָה אֲשֶׁר אַתֶּם עֹבְרִים אֶת־הַיַּרְדֵּן שָׁמָּה לְרִשְׁתָּהּ:
יד וַיֹּאמֶר יהוה אֶל־מֹשֶׁה הֵן קָרְבוּ יָמֶיךָ לָמוּת קְרָא אֶת־יְהוֹשֻׁעַ וְהִתְיַצְּבוּ בְּאֹהֶל כה חמישי /ששי/
טו מוֹעֵד וַאֲצַוֶּנּוּ וַיֵּלֶךְ מֹשֶׁה וִיהוֹשֻׁעַ וַיִּתְיַצְּבוּ בְּאֹהֶל מוֹעֵד: וַיֵּרָא יהוה בָּאֹהֶל בְּעַמּוּד
טז עָנָן וַיַּעֲמֹד עַמּוּד הֶעָנָן עַל־פֶּתַח הָאֹהֶל: וַיֹּאמֶר יהוה אֶל־מֹשֶׁה הִנְּךָ שֹׁכֵב עִם־
אֲבֹתֶיךָ וְקָם הָעָם הַזֶּה וְזָנָה ׀ אַחֲרֵי ׀ אֱלֹהֵי נֵכַר־הָאָרֶץ אֲשֶׁר הוּא בָא־שָׁמָּה
יז בְּקִרְבּוֹ וַעֲזָבַנִי וְהֵפֵר אֶת־בְּרִיתִי אֲשֶׁר כָּרַתִּי אִתּוֹ: וְחָרָה אַפִּי בוֹ בַיּוֹם־הַהוּא
וַעֲזַבְתִּים וְהִסְתַּרְתִּי פָנַי מֵהֶם וְהָיָה לֶאֱכֹל וּמְצָאֻהוּ רָעוֹת רַבּוֹת וְצָרוֹת וְאָמַר
יח בַּיּוֹם הַהוּא הֲלֹא עַל כִּי־אֵין אֱלֹהַי בְּקִרְבִּי מְצָאוּנִי הָרָעוֹת הָאֵלֶּה: וְאָנֹכִי הַסְתֵּר
אַסְתִּיר פָּנַי בַּיּוֹם הַהוּא עַל כָּל־הָרָעָה אֲשֶׁר עָשָׂה כִּי פָנָה אֶל־אֱלֹהִים אֲחֵרִים:
יט וְעַתָּה כִּתְבוּ לָכֶם אֶת־הַשִּׁירָה הַזֹּאת וְלַמְּדָהּ אֶת־בְּנֵי־יִשְׂרָאֵל שִׂימָהּ בְּפִיהֶם

רש״י

י | מִקֵּץ שֶׁבַע שָׁנִים. בְּשָׁנָה רִאשׁוֹנָה שֶׁל שְׁמִטָּה, הַשְּׁמִינִית. וְלָמָּה קוֹרֵא אוֹתָהּ "שְׁנַת הַשְּׁמִטָּה"? שֶׁעֲדַיִן שְׁבִיעִית נוֹהֶגֶת בָּהּ, בְּקָצִיר שֶׁל שְׁבִיעִית הַיּוֹצֵא לְמוֹצָאֵי שְׁבִיעִית:

יא | תִּקְרָא אֶת הַתּוֹרָה הַזֹּאת. הַמֶּלֶךְ הָיָה קוֹרֵא מִתְּחִלַּת 'אֵלֶּה הַדְּבָרִים', כִּדְאִיתָא בְּמַסֶּכֶת סוֹטָה (דף מא ע״א), עַל בִּימָה שֶׁל עֵץ שֶׁהָיוּ עוֹשִׂין בָּעֲזָרָה:

יב | הָאֲנָשִׁים. לִלְמֹד: וְהַנָּשִׁים. לִשְׁמֹעַ: וְהַטַּף. לָמָּה בָאִים? לִתֵּן שָׂכָר לִמְבִיאֵיהֶם:

יד | וַאֲצַוֶּנּוּ. וַאֲזָרְזֶנּוּ:

טז | נֵכַר הָאָרֶץ. גּוֹיֵי הָאָרֶץ:

יז | וְהִסְתַּרְתִּי פָנַי. כְּמוֹ שֶׁאֵינִי רוֹאֶה בְּצָרָתָם:

יט | אֶת הַשִּׁירָה הַזֹּאת. "הַאֲזִינוּ הַשָּׁמַיִם" עַד "וְכִפֶּר אַדְמָתוֹ עַמּוֹ" (להלן לב, א-מג):

DISCUSSION

of their rituals and beliefs. God informs Moses that the people will breach the covenant, as they will not only cease to observe God's commandments, they will even abandon their belief in His unity (4:35).

31:17| **And many evils and troubles [*tzarot*]:** The Sages interpreted this verse as a reference to the other meaning of *tzarot*, two rival women married to a single man (see *Bemidbar Rabba* 10:2; *Ḥagiga* 5a). Many troubles can stem from a single cause, but sometimes mutually exclusive challenges can befall a person which he cannot meet simultaneously. A situation of that kind causes confusion, despair, and a feeling that there is no way out.

31:18| **I will conceal My face:** God is not saying that He will abandon His people, but that it will appear to them as though He no longer cares for them. In that situation, the children of Israel will be in a state of terror due to their inability to sense God's presence. However, in truth God will be watching them, like a parent observing his young children from afar.

20 **For I will bring them to the land with regard to which I took**
Sixth **an oath to their forefathers,** which is a land **flowing with**
aliya **milk and honey, and** there **they will eat, and will be satisfied,**
(Seventh **and they will grow fat,** as the nation will be prosperous, **and**
aliya) **they will turn to other gods,**D **and will serve them, and scorn**
Me, and will breach My covenant.

21 **It will be when many evils and troubles find them, this song**
will testify before them as a witness, as it will not be forgot-
ten from the mouths of their descendants, as I know their
inclination from **what they do today, before I will bring**
them to the land with regard to which I took an oath. In
the meantime, you must memorize this song. Perhaps you will
not yet understand its contents, but as time passes it will speak
more to your heart. If you memorize the song, it will guide you
when you need it most.

22 **Moses wrote this song on that day, and he taught it to the**
children of Israel. The song was both written down and taught
orally, perhaps with a special tune that has been lost.

23 **He,** God, once again **commanded Joshua**D **son of Nun, and**
he said: Be strong and courageous, an expression repeated
on several occasions after Moses' death, both in God's statements to Joshua and the people's comments to him.[12] **As you**
shall bring the children of Israel into the land with regard
to which I took an oath to them; and I will be with you, and
with My assistance you will be able to conquer it.

24 **It was, as Moses finished writing the words of this Torah in**
a book, until their conclusionD in full,

Seventh 25 **Moses commanded the Levites, bearers of the Ark of the**
aliya **Covenant of the Lord, saying:**

26 **Take this book of the Torah, and place it at the side of the**
Ark of the Covenant of the Lord your God, near the Tablets
of the Covenant,[13] **and it,** the book, **will be there as a witness**
for you.

27 Moses addresses the people: **For I know your defiance, and**
your stiff neck; behold, although all of you know and fear me,
nevertheless, **while I am still alive with you today, you have**
been defiant with the Lord, as you are not fully obedient to
the word of God, **and so too,** all the more so **after my death.**
You already show a tendency to defy the will of God. Certainly
in more comfortable times you will be unable to resist the
greatest temptation that the people of Israel will face throughout its generations, of the quest for normalcy, which in effect
results in the abandonment of God. It is therefore best for you
to prepare yourselves beforehand for different times.

28 **Assemble to me all the elders of your tribes, and your of-**
Maftir **ficers, and I will speak these words in their ears, and I will**
call the heavens and the earth to testify for them. They must
hear the matters that will be spoken before the heavens and the
earth, which are the everlasting witnesses.

29 **For I know** that **after my death you will act corruptly, and**
you will deviate from the path that I commanded you and
evil will befall you at the end of days,D in a later period, **be-**
cause you will do that which is evil in the eyes of the Lord,
to anger Him with your handiwork.

30 **Moses spoke in the ears of the entire assembly of Israel the**
words of this song, until their conclusion.

DISCUSSION

31:20 | And they will eat, and will be sat-
isfied, and they will grow fat and they will
turn to other gods: The demand to maintain a
constant relationship with God is not easy, as He
is not a visible, material being. All forms of idolatry, whether the ancient gods of the Assyrians
and the Babylonians, or those of the sixteenth,
eighteenth, or twenty-first centuries CE, are
much more tangible. It is therefore not surprising that the children of Israel would abandon
God and breach their covenant with Him.

31:23 | He commanded Joshua: The Sages
comment that Moses did not hear this statement

of God to Joshua. Perhaps he sensed that the
time for the new leader had already arrived (see
Devarim Rabba 9:9)

31:24 | As Moses finished writing the words
of this Torah in a book, until their conclu-
sion: The Sages dispute how much of the Torah
was actually written by Moses, as it is unclear
whether he ceased writing after the phrase "until their conclusion," or whether he also wrote
the song below. In addition, the identity of the
author of the last verses of the Torah, which recount the death of Moses as well as the events
after his death, is also unclear. The majority of

the Sages maintain that the entire Torah was
given in its complete form, but the final verses
were not written in a sufficiently clear manner,
and they were clarified only later (see Ramban,
verse 24; Rashi, 34:5; *Bava Batra* 15a).

31:29 | At the end of days: In the Bible, the
expression "the end of days" does not necessarily refer to the end of history, as it does in the
language of the Sages and in common parlance.
Rather, it means a relative end of days, long after the present time. Similarly, the term "last" in
the Bible means "latter," not always last (see, e.g.,
Genesis 33:2).

כ לְמַעַן תִּהְיֶה־לִּי הַשִּׁירָה הַזֹּאת לְעֵד בִּבְנֵי יִשְׂרָאֵל: כִּי־אֲבִיאֶנּוּ אֶל־הָאֲדָמָה ׀ ששי
אֲשֶׁר־נִשְׁבַּעְתִּי לַאֲבֹתָיו זָבַת חָלָב וּדְבַשׁ וְאָכַל וְשָׂבַע וְדָשֵׁן וּפָנָה אֶל־אֱלֹהִים /שביעי/
כא אֲחֵרִים וַעֲבָדוּם וְנִאֲצוּנִי וְהֵפֵר אֶת־בְּרִיתִי: וְהָיָה כִּי־תִמְצֶאןָ אֹתוֹ רָעוֹת רַבּוֹת
וְצָרוֹת וְעָנְתָה הַשִּׁירָה הַזֹּאת לְפָנָיו לְעֵד כִּי לֹא תִשָּׁכַח מִפִּי זַרְעוֹ כִּי יָדַעְתִּי
אֶת־יִצְרוֹ אֲשֶׁר הוּא עֹשֶׂה הַיּוֹם בְּטֶרֶם אֲבִיאֶנּוּ אֶל־הָאָרֶץ אֲשֶׁר נִשְׁבָּעְתִּי:
כב כג וַיִּכְתֹּב מֹשֶׁה אֶת־הַשִּׁירָה הַזֹּאת בַּיּוֹם הַהוּא וַיְלַמְּדָהּ אֶת־בְּנֵי יִשְׂרָאֵל: וַיְצַו
אֶת־יְהוֹשֻׁעַ בִּן־נוּן וַיֹּאמֶר חֲזַק וֶאֱמָץ כִּי אַתָּה תָּבִיא אֶת־בְּנֵי יִשְׂרָאֵל אֶל־הָאָרֶץ
כד אֲשֶׁר־נִשְׁבַּעְתִּי לָהֶם וְאָנֹכִי אֶהְיֶה עִמָּךְ: וַיְהִי ׀ כְּכַלּוֹת מֹשֶׁה לִכְתֹּב אֶת־דִּבְרֵי
כה הַתּוֹרָה־הַזֹּאת עַל־סֵפֶר עַד תֻּמָּם: וַיְצַו מֹשֶׁה אֶת־הַלְוִיִּם נֹשְׂאֵי אֲרוֹן בְּרִית־ שביעי
כו יהוה לֵאמֹר: לָקֹחַ אֵת סֵפֶר הַתּוֹרָה הַזֶּה וְשַׂמְתֶּם אֹתוֹ מִצַּד אֲרוֹן בְּרִית־יהוה
כז אֱלֹהֵיכֶם וְהָיָה־שָׁם בְּךָ לְעֵד: כִּי אָנֹכִי יָדַעְתִּי אֶת־מֶרְיְךָ וְאֶת־עָרְפְּךָ הַקָּשֶׁה הֵן
כח בְּעוֹדֶנִּי חַי עִמָּכֶם הַיּוֹם מַמְרִים הֱיִתֶם עִם־יהוה וְאַף כִּי־אַחֲרֵי מוֹתִי: הַקְהִילוּ מפטיר
אֵלַי אֶת־כָּל־זִקְנֵי שִׁבְטֵיכֶם וְשֹׁטְרֵיכֶם וַאֲדַבְּרָה בְאָזְנֵיהֶם אֵת הַדְּבָרִים הָאֵלֶּה
כט וְאָעִידָה בָּם אֶת־הַשָּׁמַיִם וְאֶת־הָאָרֶץ: כִּי יָדַעְתִּי אַחֲרֵי מוֹתִי כִּי־הַשְׁחֵת תַּשְׁחִתוּן
וְסַרְתֶּם מִן־הַדֶּרֶךְ אֲשֶׁר צִוִּיתִי אֶתְכֶם וְקָרָאת אֶתְכֶם הָרָעָה בְּאַחֲרִית הַיָּמִים
ל כִּי־תַעֲשׂוּ אֶת־הָרַע בְּעֵינֵי יהוה לְהַכְעִיסוֹ בְּמַעֲשֵׂה יְדֵיכֶם: וַיְדַבֵּר מֹשֶׁה בְּאָזְנֵי
כָּל־קְהַל יִשְׂרָאֵל אֶת־דִּבְרֵי הַשִּׁירָה הַזֹּאת עַד תֻּמָּם:

רש"י

כ| וְנִאֲצוּנִי. וְהִכְעִיסוּנִי, וְכֵן כָּל 'נִאוּץ' לְשׁוֹן כַּעַס:

כא| וְעָנְתָה הַשִּׁירָה הַזֹּאת לְפָנָיו לְעֵד. שֶׁהִתְרֵיתִי בּוֹ בְּתוֹכָהּ עַל כָּל הַמּוֹצְאוֹת אוֹתוֹ: כִּי לֹא תִשָּׁכַח מִפִּי זַרְעוֹ. הֲרֵי זוֹ הַבְטָחָה לְיִשְׂרָאֵל שֶׁאֵין תּוֹרָה מִשְׁתַּכַּחַת מִזַּרְעָם לְגַמְרֵי:

כג| וַיְצַו אֶת יְהוֹשֻׁעַ בִּן נוּן. מוּסָב לְמַעְלָה כְּלַפֵּי שְׁכִינָה, כְּמוֹ שֶׁמְּפָרֵשׁ: "אֶל הָאָרֶץ אֲשֶׁר נִשְׁבַּעְתִּי לָהֶם":

כו| לָקֹחַ. כְּמוֹ: זָכוֹר, שָׁמוֹר, הָלוֹךְ: מִצַּד אֲרוֹן בְּרִית ה'. נֶחְלְקוּ בּוֹ חַכְמֵי יִשְׂרָאֵל בְּבָבָא בַּתְרָא (דף יד ע"ב), יֵשׁ מֵהֶם אוֹמְרִים: דַּף הָיָה בּוֹלֵט מִן הָאָרוֹן מִבַּחוּץ וְשָׁם הָיָה מֻנָּח, וְיֵשׁ אוֹמְרִים: מִצַּד הַלּוּחוֹת הָיָה מֻנָּח בְּתוֹךְ הָאָרוֹן:

כח| הַקְהִילוּ אֵלַי. וְלֹא תָקְעוּ אוֹתוֹ הַיּוֹם בַּחֲצוֹצְרוֹת לְהַקְהִיל אֶת הַקָּהָל, לְפִי שֶׁנֶּאֱמַר: "עֲשֵׂה לְךָ" (במדבר י, ב), וְלֹא הִשְׁלִיט יְהוֹשֻׁעַ עֲלֵיהֶם. וַאֲפִלּוּ בְּחַיָּיו נִגְנְזוּ קֹדֶם יוֹם מוֹתוֹ, לְקַיֵּם מַה שֶּׁנֶּאֱמַר: "וְאֵין שִׁלְטוֹן בְּיוֹם הַמָּוֶת" (קהלת ח, ח): וְאָעִידָה בָּם אֶת הַשָּׁמַיִם וְאֶת הָאָרֶץ. וְאִם תֹּאמַר, הֲרֵי כְּבָר הֵעִיד לְמַעְלָה: "הַעִידֹתִי בָכֶם הַיּוֹם" וְגוֹ' (לעיל ל, יט)? לְיִשְׂרָאֵל אָמַר אֲבָל לַשָּׁמַיִם וְלָאָרֶץ לֹא אָמַר, וְעַכְשָׁיו בָּא לוֹמַר: "הַאֲזִינוּ הַשָּׁמַיִם" וְגוֹ' (להלן לב, א):

כט| אַחֲרֵי מוֹתִי כִּי הַשְׁחֵת תַּשְׁחִתוּן. וַהֲרֵי כָּל יְמוֹת יְהוֹשֻׁעַ לֹא הִשְׁחִיתוּ, שֶׁנֶּאֱמַר: "וַיַּעַבְדוּ הָעָם אֶת ה' כֹּל יְמֵי יְהוֹשֻׁעַ" (שופטים ב, ז)? מִכָּאן שֶׁתַּלְמִידוֹ שֶׁל אָדָם חָבִיב עָלָיו כְּגוּפוֹ, כָּל זְמַן שֶׁיְּהוֹשֻׁעַ חַי הָיָה נִרְאֶה לְמֹשֶׁה כְּאִלּוּ הוּא חַי:

Parashat **Haazinu**

The Song of Haazinu and Closing Remarks

DEUTERONOMY 32:1–47

The song of *Haazinu*, which God commanded Moses to teach the people of Israel, was recited to them by Moses and Joshua. The song possesses a particular rhythm and contains many verses composed of two parallel halves. Although its elegant, poetic language is difficult to understand, at its core the message is that even though the children of Israel will act foolishly and abandon God, He will never abandon them. Any enemy of Israel is an enemy of God, and therefore, God will exact vengeance upon Israel's oppressors. The song also contains the message that ultimately, all the nations of the world will gather to sing songs of praise to the redeemed nation of Israel.

Following the conclusion of this song, Moses offers brief concluding remarks pertaining to the song itself and to the Torah in general.

32 1 The song begins with an introduction: **Listen, the heavens, and I will speak, and the earth will hear the sayings of my mouth.** Moses asks the heavens and the earth to bear witness to his speech. This is not the first time that he does so, as the heavens and the earth are ever present and may bear eternal witness (see 4:26). Moses' lofty status affords him the authority to command the heavens and the earth to listen to him.

2 **My lesson will fall as the rain,** and in parallel, **my saying will flow like dew, like rainstorms on grass, and like raindrops**[D] **on vegetation.** The lesson refers to harsh words containing elements of rebuke, which will bombard the people like torrential rain, while the mild sayings will fall upon them gently, like dew.

3 I am going to call the name of God and speak of Him. **When I proclaim the name of the Lord,** you must **acclaim greatness to our God.** My proclamation of His name obligates you, who will hear it, to ascribe honor and praise to God.

4 Moses begins to speak of God: **The Rock,** a metaphor for God that symbolizes His strength, or perhaps the fact that He is the source of existence, **His actions are perfect, as all His ways are justice:** He is **a faithful God, and there is no injustice** with Him; **righteous and upright is He.** Aside from God's strength, glory, and perfection, all of His actions are founded on the principles of loyalty and justice, even if it may sometimes seem otherwise to mankind.

5 It is **they** who **corrupted,** for corruption is **not from Him; His children, it is their blemish.**[1] Atrocities occur in this world not because God performs evil, but because His children are **a crooked and twisted generation.** They distort reality to justify their crookedness.[2]

6 **Will you repay the Lord** with **this,** your evil deeds, **crude and unwise people?**[3] You are causing harm only to yourselves. The corruption in the world is merely a response to man's evil ways. **Is He not your Father** and **your Redeemer,** who redeemed you from Egypt?[4] **He made you, and He established you.**

Dewdrops

DISCUSSION

32:2 | **Rainstorms [*se'irim*] and raindrops [*revivim*]:** It is possible that *se'irim* and *revivim* refer to two types of clouds: *Se'irim* could be dark clouds, whose color is reminiscent of goats [*se'irei izim*], whereas *revivim* could be white clouds, like the color of sheep's wool (see Psalms 144:13). The contrast between the different types of clouds parallels the contrast at the beginning of the verse between harsh rain, representing words of rebuke, and dew, representing light, pleasant words.

פרשת
האזינו

לב א הַאֲזִינוּ הַשָּׁמַיִם וַאֲדַבֵּרָה   וְתִשְׁמַע הָאָרֶץ אִמְרֵי־פִי׃
ב יַעֲרֹף כַּמָּטָר לִקְחִי   תִּזַּל כַּטַּל אִמְרָתִי
כִּשְׂעִירִם עֲלֵי־דֶשֶׁא   וְכִרְבִיבִים עֲלֵי־עֵשֶׂב׃
ג כִּי שֵׁם יְהוָה אֶקְרָא   הָבוּ גֹדֶל לֵאלֹהֵינוּ׃
ד הַצּוּר תָּמִים פָּעֳלוֹ   כִּי כָל־דְּרָכָיו מִשְׁפָּט
אֵל אֱמוּנָה וְאֵין עָוֶל   צַדִּיק וְיָשָׁר הוּא׃
ה שִׁחֵת לוֹ לֹא בָּנָיו מוּמָם   דּוֹר עִקֵּשׁ וּפְתַלְתֹּל׃
ו הַלְיהוָה תִּגְמְלוּ־זֹאת   עַם נָבָל וְלֹא חָכָם
הֲלוֹא־הוּא אָבִיךָ קָּנֶךָ   הוּא עָשְׂךָ וַיְכֹנְנֶךָ׃

רש"י

פרק לב

א| **האזינו השמים.** שאני מתרה בהם בישראל, ותהיו עדים בדבר, שכך אמרתי להם שאתם תהיו עדים, וכן "ותשמע הארץ". ולמה העיד בהם שמים וארץ? אמר משה: אני בשר ודם, למחר אני מת, אם יאמרו ישראל לא קבלנו עלינו הברית, מי בא ומכחישם? לפיכך העיד בהם שמים וארץ, עדים שהם קיימים לעולם. ועוד, שאם יזכו יבואו העדים ויתנו שכרם, "הגפן תתן פריה והארץ תתן את יבולה והשמים יתנו טלם" (זכריה ח, יב), ואם יתחיבו תהיה בהם יד העדים תחלה, "ועצר את השמים ולא יהיה מטר והאדמה לא תתן את יבולה", ואחר כך: "ואבדתם מהרה" (לעיל יא, יז) על ידי האמות:

ב| **יערף כמטר לקחי.** זו היא העדות שתעידו, שאני אומר בפניכם: תורה שנתתי לישראל שהיא חיים לעולם, כמטר הזה שהוא חיים לעולם, כאשר יערפו השמים טל ומטר: **יערף.** לשון יטיף, וכן: "יערפו טל" (להלן לג, כח), "ירעפון דשן" (תהלים סה, יב): **תזל כטל.** שהכל שמחים בו, לפי שהמטר יש בו עצבים, כגון הולכי דרכים ומי שהיה בורו מלא יין: **כשעירם.** לשון "רוח סערה", כתרגומו: "כרוחי מטרא", מה הרוחות הללו מחזקין את העשבים ומגדלין אותם, אף דברי תורה מחזקין את לומדיהן ומגדלין אותן: **וכרביבים.** טפי מטר, ונראה לי, על שם שיורה כחץ נקרא 'רביב', כמא דאת אמר: "רבה קשת" (בראשית כא, כ): **דשא.** ארברי"ן, עטיפת הארץ מכסה בירק: **עשב.** קלא אחד קרוי 'עשב', וכל מין ומין לעצמו קרוי 'עשב':

ג| **כי שם ה' אקרא.** הרי 'כי' משמש בלשון 'כאשר', כמו: "כי תבאו אל הארץ", כשאקרא ואזכיר שם ה', אתם "הבו גדל לאלהינו" וברכו שמו. מכאן שעונין: "ברוך שם כבוד מלכותו" אחר ברכה שבמקדש:

ד| **הצור תמים פעלו.** אף על פי שהוא חזק, כשמביא פרענות על עוברי רצונו, לא בשטף הוא מביא כי אם בדין, כי "תמים פעלו": **אל אמונה.** לשלם לצדיקים צדקתם לעולם הבא, ואף על פי שמאחר את תגמולם, סופו לאמן את דבריו: **ואין עול.** אף לרשעים משלם שכר צדקתם בעולם הזה: **צדיק וישר הוא.** הכל מצדיקים עליהם את דינו, וכך ראוי וישר להם. "צדיק" מפי הבריות "וישר הוא", וראוי להצדיקו:

ה| **שחת לו וגו'.** כתרגומו: "חבילו להון לא ליה": **בניו מומם.** בניו היו, והשחתה שהשחיתו היא מומם: **בניו מומם.** מומם של בניו היה ולא מומו: **דור עקש.** עקום ומעקל, כמו: "ואת כל הישרה יעקשו" (מיכה ג, ט), ובלשון משנה: "חלדה ששפיה עקומות ועקושות" (ראה חולין נו ע"א): **ופתלתל.** אנטורטליי"ן, כפתיל הזה שגודלין אותו ומקיפין אותו סביבות הגדיל: **פתלתל.** מן התיבות הכפולות כמו 'ירקרק' (ויקרא יג, מט), 'אדמדם' (שם), 'סחרחר' (תהלים לח, יא), 'סגלגל' (תרגום, מלכים א' ז, כג):

ו| **הלה' תגמלו זאת.** לשון תמה, וכי לפניו אתם מעיבין, שיש בידו לפרע מכם ושהיטיב לכם בכל הטובות?: **עם נבל.** ששכחו את העשוי להם: **ולא חכם.** להבין את הנולדות שיש בידו להיטיב ולהרע: **הלוא הוא אביך קנך.** שקנאך, שקננך בקן הסלעים ובארץ חזקה, שתקנך בכל מיני תקנה: **הוא עשך.** אמה באמות: **ויכננך.** אחרי כן בכל מיני בסיס וכן, מכם כהנים מכם נביאים ומכם מלכים, כרך שהכל תלוי בו:

7 Moses reminds Israel of God's kindness: **Remember the days** *Second aliya* **of yore; examine** the events of **the years of each generation,** the earlier generations in particular. **Ask your father, and he will tell you, your elders, and they will say to you.** Moses is about to recount events that are well-known to his audience. This song, however, is not addressed only to the people standing before Moses, but to all generations. Moses therefore stresses: In the distant future, when some of these matters will have been forgotten, ask your parents and your elders to recount them for you.

8 **When the Most High bequeathed** the various lands and characteristics **to the nations, when He separated the children of man** into tribes and nations, **He set the borders of the peoples according to the number of the children of Israel.** God divided mankind into seventy nations;[5] seventy is also the number of individuals who descended with Jacob to Egypt.[6] Other commentaries explain that Canaan and his sons, who inhabited the land of Canaan, numbered twelve, corresponding to the sons of Jacob.[7]

9 **For the portion of the Lord is His people; Jacob** is **the allotment of His inheritance.**

10 **He would find him,** Jacob, **in a wilderness land, and in emptiness, a howling wasteland.** Although it was God who led the people to the wilderness, it was there that He adopted them as His portion and inheritance.[8] **He would encircle him** protectively, **He would grant him understanding, He preserved him like the pupil of His eye,** as it were. God's protection of Israel is compared to the most important, most constant, and most natural form of protection.

11 **Like an eagle that would rouse its nest, over its fledglings it would hover.** Due to its size, the eagle does not rest upon its fledglings; rather, it circles them from above. When it finally approaches the nest, it situates itself adjacent to and above the nest, and thereby avoids landing inside the nest. **It would spread its wings and take it,** meaning the fledglings, and **it would carry it on its pinions.** God carried Israel through the wilderness in this manner.[9]

12 **The Lord alone would lead him.**[10] Alternatively, God led Israel when Israel was alone; the people relied on God and did not need assistance from others.[11] **And there was no foreign god with Him.**

13 **He would mount him on the elevations of the earth, and** *Third aliya* **he,** Israel, **ate the yield of the field,** meaning the manna, water, and quail provided for them in the wilderness. **He suckled him honey from a stone, and oil from a flinty rock.**

14 The people also received **butter of cattle, and milk of sheep, with fat of** large **lambs, and rams of the Bashan,** a fertile region in which exceptional crops and animals grow,[12] **and goats, with wheat fat as kidneys.** The wheat kernels evoke kidneys, perhaps because of the groove running through them. **And the**

Wheat

Goat

רש״י

ז| **זְכֹר יְמוֹת עוֹלָם.** מֶה עָשָׂה בָּרִאשׁוֹנִים שֶׁהִכְעִיסוּ לְפָנָיו: **בִּינוּ שְׁנוֹת דֹּר וָדֹר.** דּוֹר אֱנוֹשׁ שֶׁהֵצִיף עֲלֵיהֶם מֵי אוֹקְיָנוֹס, וְדוֹר הַמַּבּוּל שֶׁשְּׁטָפָם. דָּבָר אַחֵר, לֹא נְתַתֶּם לְבַבְכֶם עַל שֶׁעָבַר, ״בִּינוּ שְׁנוֹת דֹּר וָדֹר״ לְהַכִּיר לְהַבָּא, שֶׁיֵּשׁ בְּיָדוֹ לְהֵיטִיב לָכֶם וּלְהַנְחִיל לָכֶם יְמוֹת הַמָּשִׁיחַ וְהָעוֹלָם הַבָּא: **שְׁאַל אָבִיךָ.** אֵלּוּ הַנְּבִיאִים שֶׁנִּקְרְאוּ אָבוֹת, כְּמוֹ שֶׁנֶּאֱמַר בֶּאֱלִיָּהוּ: ״אָבִי אָבִי רֶכֶב יִשְׂרָאֵל״ (מלכים ב׳ ב, יב): **זְקֵנֶיךָ.** אֵלּוּ הַחֲכָמִים: **וְיֹאמְרוּ לָךְ.** הָרִאשׁוֹנוֹת:

ח| **בְּהַנְחֵל עֶלְיוֹן גּוֹיִם.** כְּשֶׁהִנְחִיל הַקָּדוֹשׁ בָּרוּךְ הוּא לְמַכְעִיסָיו אֶת חֶלְקָן נַחֲלָתָן, הֱצִיפָם וּשְׁטָפָם: **בְּהַפְרִידוֹ בְּנֵי אָדָם.** כְּשֶׁהֵפִיץ דּוֹר הַפַּלָּגָה הָיָה בְּיָדוֹ לְהַעֲבִירָם מִן הָעוֹלָם, וְלֹא עָשָׂה כֵן, אֶלָּא ״יַצֵּב גְּבֻלֹת עַמִּים״, קִיְּמָם וְלֹא אִבְּדָם: **לְמִסְפַּר בְּנֵי יִשְׂרָאֵל.** בִּשְׁבִיל מִסְפַּר בְּנֵי יִשְׂרָאֵל שֶׁעֲתִידִין לָצֵאת מִבְּנֵי שֵׁם, וּלְמִסְפַּר שִׁבְעִים נֶפֶשׁ שֶׁל בְּנֵי יִשְׂרָאֵל שֶׁיָּרְדוּ לְמִצְרַיִם הִצִּיב ״גְּבֻלֹת עַמִּים״ שִׁבְעִים לָשׁוֹן:

ט| **כִּי חֵלֶק ה׳ עַמּוֹ.** לָמָּה כָּל זֹאת? לְפִי שֶׁהָיָה חֶלְקוֹ כָּבוּשׁ בֵּינֵיהֶם וְעָתִיד לָצֵאת. וּמִי הוּא חֶלְקוֹ? ״עַמּוֹ״. וּמִי הוּא עַמּוֹ? ״יַעֲקֹב חֶבֶל נַחֲלָתוֹ״, וְהוּא הַשְּׁלִישִׁי בָּאָבוֹת, הַמְשֻׁלָּשׁ בְּשָׁלֹשׁ זְכֻיּוֹת, זְכוּת אֲבִי אָבִיו וּזְכוּת אָבִיו וּזְכוּתוֹ, הֲרֵי שָׁלֹשׁ, כַּחֶבֶל הַזֶּה שֶׁהוּא עָשׂוּי בִּשְׁלֹשָׁה גְּדִילִים; וְהוּא וּבָנָיו הָיוּ לוֹ לְנַחֲלָה, וְלֹא יִשְׁמָעֵאל בֶּן אַבְרָהָם וְלֹא עֵשָׂו בְּנוֹ שֶׁל יִצְחָק:

י| **יִמְצָאֵהוּ בְּאֶרֶץ מִדְבָּר.** אוֹתָם מָצָא לוֹ נֶאֱמָנִים בְּאֶרֶץ הַמִּדְבָּר, שֶׁקִּבְּלוּ תּוֹרָתוֹ וּמַלְכוּתוֹ וְעֻלּוֹ, מַה שֶּׁלֹּא עָשׂוּ יִשְׁמָעֵאל וְעֵשָׂו, שֶׁנֶּאֱמַר: ״וְזָרַח מִשֵּׂעִיר לָמוֹ הוֹפִיעַ מֵהַר פָּארָן״ (להלן לג, ב): **וּבְתֹהוּ יְלֵל יְשִׁמֹן.** אֶרֶץ צִיָּה וּשְׁמָמָה, מְקוֹם יִלְלַת תַּנִּים וּבְנוֹת יַעֲנָה, אַף שָׁם נִמְשְׁכוּ אַחַר

ז זְכֹר יְמוֹת עוֹלָם   בִּינוּ שְׁנוֹת דֹּר־וָדֹר   שני
שְׁאַל אָבִיךָ וְיַגֵּדְךָ   זְקֵנֶיךָ וְיֹאמְרוּ לָךְ:
ח בְּהַנְחֵל עֶלְיוֹן גּוֹיִם   בְּהַפְרִידוֹ בְּנֵי אָדָם
יַצֵּב גְּבֻלֹת עַמִּים   לְמִסְפַּר בְּנֵי יִשְׂרָאֵל:
ט כִּי חֵלֶק יְהוָה עַמּוֹ   יַעֲקֹב חֶבֶל נַחֲלָתוֹ:
י יִמְצָאֵהוּ בְּאֶרֶץ מִדְבָּר   וּבְתֹהוּ יְלֵל יְשִׁמֹן
יְסֹבְבֶנְהוּ יְבוֹנְנֵהוּ   יִצְּרֶנְהוּ כְּאִישׁוֹן עֵינוֹ:
יא כְּנֶשֶׁר יָעִיר קִנּוֹ   עַל־גּוֹזָלָיו יְרַחֵף
יִפְרֹשׂ כְּנָפָיו יִקָּחֵהוּ   יִשָּׂאֵהוּ עַל־אֶבְרָתוֹ:
יב יְהוָה בָּדָד יַנְחֶנּוּ   וְאֵין עִמּוֹ אֵל נֵכָר:
יג יַרְכִּבֵהוּ עַל־בָּמֳתֵי אָרֶץ   וַיֹּאכַל תְּנוּבֹת שָׂדָי   שלישי
במתי
וַיֵּנִקֵהוּ דְבַשׁ מִסֶּלַע   וְשֶׁמֶן מֵחַלְמִישׁ צוּר:
יד חֶמְאַת בָּקָר וַחֲלֵב צֹאן   עִם־חֵלֶב כָּרִים
וְאֵילִים בְּנֵי־בָשָׁן וְעַתּוּדִים   עִם־חֵלֶב כִּלְיוֹת חִטָּה

רש״י

הָאֱמוּנָה, וְלֹא אָמְרוּ לְמֹשֶׁה הֵיאַךְ נֵצֵא לַמִּדְבָּרוֹת מְקוֹם צִיָּה וְשִׁמָּמוֹן, כְּעִנְיָן שֶׁנֶּאֱמַר: "לֶכְתֵּךְ אַחֲרַי בַּמִּדְבָּר" (ירמיה ב, ב): **יְסֹבְבֶנְהוּ.** שָׁם סִבְּבָם וְהִקִּיפָם בַּעֲנָנִים, וְסִבְּבָם בִּדְגָלִים לְאַרְבַּע רוּחוֹת, וְסִבְּבָן בְּתַחְתִּית הָהָר שֶׁכְּפָאוֹ עֲלֵיהֶם כְּגִיגִית: **יְבוֹנְנֵהוּ.** שָׁם בְּתוֹרָה וּבִינָה: **יִצְּרֶנְהוּ.** מִנָּחָשׁ שָׂרָף וְעַקְרָב וּמִן הָאֻמּוֹת: **כְּאִישׁוֹן עֵינוֹ.** הוּא הַשָּׁחוֹר שֶׁבָּעַיִן שֶׁהַמָּאוֹר יוֹצֵא הֵימֶנּוּ. וְאוּנְקְלוֹס תִּרְגֵּם: "יִמְצָאֵהוּ" – יִסְפִּיקֵהוּ כָּל צָרְכּוֹ בַּמִּדְבָּר, כְּמוֹ: "וּמָצָא לָהֶם" (במדבר יא, כב), "לֹא יִמָּצֵא לָנוּ הָהָר" (יהושע יז, טז). "יְסֹבְבֶנְהוּ" – "אַשְׁרִינוּן סְחוֹר סְחוֹר לִשְׁכִינְתֵּיהּ", אֹהֶל מוֹעֵד בָּאֶמְצַע וְאַרְבָּעָה דְּגָלִים לְאַרְבַּע רוּחוֹת:

יא| **כְּנֶשֶׁר יָעִיר קִנּוֹ.** נִהֲגָם בְּרַחֲמִים וּבְחֶמְלָה כַּנֶּשֶׁר הַזֶּה רַחֲמָנִי עַל בָּנָיו, וְאֵינוֹ נִכְנָס לְקִנּוֹ פִּתְאוֹם עַד שֶׁהוּא מְקַשְׁקֵשׁ וּמְטָרֵף עַל בָּנָיו בִּכְנָפָיו בֵּין אִילָן לְאִילָן בֵּין שׂוֹכָה לַחֲבֶרְתָּהּ, כְּדֵי שֶׁיֵּעוֹרוּ בָּנָיו וִיהֵא בָּהֶן כֹּחַ לְקַבְּלוֹ: **יָעִיר קִנּוֹ.** יְעוֹרֵר בָּנָיו: **עַל גּוֹזָלָיו יְרַחֵף.** אֵינוֹ מַכְבִּיד עַצְמוֹ עֲלֵיהֶם אֶלָּא מְחוֹפֵף, נוֹגֵעַ וְאֵינוֹ נוֹגֵעַ, אַף הַקָּדוֹשׁ בָּרוּךְ הוּא "שַׁדַּי לֹא מְצָאנֻהוּ שַׂגִּיא כֹחַ" (איוב לז, כג), כְּשֶׁבָּא לִתֵּן תּוֹרָה לֹא נִגְלָה עֲלֵיהֶם מֵרוּחַ אַחַת אֶלָּא מֵאַרְבַּע רוּחוֹת, שֶׁנֶּאֱמַר: "ה' מִסִּינַי בָּא וְזָרַח מִשֵּׂעִיר לָמוֹ, הוֹפִיעַ מֵהַר פָּארָן" (להלן לג, ב), "אֱלוֹהַּ מִתֵּימָן יָבוֹא" (חבקוק ג, ג) זוֹ רוּחַ רְבִיעִית: **יִפְרֹשׂ כְּנָפָיו יִקָּחֵהוּ.** כְּשֶׁבָּא לְטָלְטְלָן מִמָּקוֹם לְמָקוֹם אֵינוֹ נוֹטְלָן בְּרַגְלָיו כִּשְׁאָר עוֹפוֹת, לְפִי שֶׁשְּׁאָר עוֹפוֹת יְרֵאִים מִן הַנֶּשֶׁר שֶׁהוּא מַגְבִּיהַּ לָעוּף וּפוֹרֵחַ עֲלֵיהֶם, לְפִיכָךְ נוֹשְׂאָן בְּרַגְלָיו מִפְּנֵי הַנֶּשֶׁר, אֲבָל הַנֶּשֶׁר אֵינוֹ יָרֵא אֶלָּא מִן הָאָדָם, לְפִיכָךְ נוֹשְׂאָן עַל כְּנָפָיו, אוֹמֵר: מוּטָב שֶׁיִּכָּנֵס הַחֵץ בִּי וְלֹא יִכָּנֵס בְּבָנַי. אַף הַקָּדוֹשׁ בָּרוּךְ הוּא, "וָאֶשָּׂא אֶתְכֶם עַל כַּנְפֵי נְשָׁרִים" (שמות יט, ד), כְּשֶׁנָּסְעוּ מִצְרַיִם אַחֲרֵיהֶם וְהִשִּׂיגוּם עַל הַיָּם הָיוּ זוֹרְקִים בָּהֶם חִצִּים וְאַבְנֵי בַּלִּיסְטְרָאוֹת, מִיָּד – "וַיִּסַּע מַלְאַךְ הָאֱלֹהִים וְגוֹ' וַיָּבֹא בֵּין מַחֲנֵה מִצְרַיִם" וְגוֹ' (שם יד, יט-כ):

יב| **ה' בָּדָד יַנְחֶנּוּ.** ה' בָּדָד וָבֶטַח נִהֲגָם בַּמִּדְבָּר: **וְאֵין עִמּוֹ אֵל נֵכָר.** לֹא הָיָה כֹּחַ בְּאֶחָד מִכָּל אֱלֹהֵי הַגּוֹיִם לְהַרְאוֹת כֹּחוֹ וּלְהִלָּחֵם עִמָּהֶם. וְרַבּוֹתֵינוּ דְּרָשׁוּהוּ עַל הֶעָתִיד, וְכֵן תִּרְגֵּם אוּנְקְלוֹס. וַאֲנִי אוֹמֵר, דִּבְרֵי תּוֹכָחָה הֵם לְהָעִיד הַשָּׁמַיִם וְהָאָרֶץ שֶׁתְּהֵא הַשִּׁירָה לְעֵד שֶׁסּוֹפָן לִבְגֹּד, וְלֹא יִזְכְּרוּ הָרִאשׁוֹנוֹת שֶׁעָשָׂה לָהֶם וְלֹא הַנּוֹלָדוֹת שֶׁהוּא עָתִיד לַעֲשׂוֹת לָהֶם. לְפִיכָךְ צָרִיךְ לְיַשֵּׁב הַדָּבָר לְכָאן וּלְכָאן, וְכָל הָעִנְיָן מוּסָב עַל "זְכֹר יְמוֹת עוֹלָם בִּינוּ שְׁנוֹת דֹּר וָדֹר" (לעיל פסוק ז), כֵּן עָשָׂה לָהֶם וְכֵן עָתִיד לַעֲשׂוֹת, כָּל זֶה הָיָה לָהֶם לִזְכֹּר:

יג-יד| **יַרְכִּבֵהוּ עַל בָּמֳתֵי אָרֶץ.** כָּל הַמִּקְרָא כְּתַרְגּוּמוֹ: **יַרְכִּבֵהוּ.** עַל שֵׁם שֶׁאֶרֶץ יִשְׂרָאֵל גְּבוֹהָה מִכָּל הָאֲרָצוֹת: **וַיֹּאכַל תְּנוּבֹת שָׂדָי.** אֵלּוּ פֵּרוֹת אֶרֶץ יִשְׂרָאֵל שֶׁקַּלִּים לָנוּב וּלְהִתְבַּשֵּׁל מִכָּל פֵּרוֹת הָאֲרָצוֹת: **וַיֵּנִקֵהוּ דְבַשׁ מִסֶּלַע.** מַעֲשֶׂה בְּאֶחָד שֶׁאָמַר לִבְנוֹ בְּסִיכְנִי: הָבֵא לִי קְצִיעוֹת מִן הֶחָבִית, הָלַךְ וּמָצָא הַדְּבַשׁ צָף עַל פִּיהָ, אָמַר לוֹ: זוֹ שֶׁל דְּבַשׁ הִיא, אָמַר לוֹ: הַשְׁקַע יָדְךָ לְתוֹכָהּ וְאַתָּה מַעֲלֶה קְצִיעוֹת מִתּוֹכָהּ: **וְשֶׁמֶן מֵחַלְמִישׁ צוּר.** אֵלּוּ זֵיתִים שֶׁל גּוּשׁ חָלָב: **חֶמְאַת בָּקָר וַחֲלֵב צֹאן.** זֶה הָיָה בִּימֵי שְׁלֹמֹה, שֶׁנֶּאֱמַר: "עֲשָׂרָה בָקָר בְּרִאִים וְעֶשְׂרִים בָּקָר רְעִי וּמֵאָה צֹאן" (מלכים א' ה, ג): **עִם חֵלֶב כָּרִים.** זֶה הָיָה בִּימֵי עֲשֶׂרֶת הַשְּׁבָטִים, שֶׁנֶּאֱמַר: "וְאֹכְלִים כָּרִים מִצֹּאן" (עמוס ו, ד): **עִם חֵלֶב כִּלְיוֹת חִטָּה.** זֶה הָיָה בִּימֵי שְׁלֹמֹה, שֶׁנֶּאֱמַר: "וַיְהִי לֶחֶם שְׁלֹמֹה" וְגוֹ' (מלכים א' ה, ב): **וְדַם**

blood of grapes, which begins as grape juice, **you would drink** as **wine.**

15 However, precisely because of this tremendous wealth and luxury, **Yeshurun grew fat and kicked;** Yeshurun rejected and disregarded its God. The name Yeshurun, which refers to the children of Israel, will appear again later.[13] **You became fat, you thickened, you grew obese; he,** Yeshurun, **forsook God his Maker,** viewing God as no longer relevant, **and reviled the Rock of his salvation.**

16 **They,** the children of Israel, **would** anger God and **infuriate Him with** their worship of **strangers,** other gods;[14] **with abominations they anger Him.**

17 Those who practiced idolatry did not worship only strange gods; **they would** even **slaughter to demons,** which they knew were **a non-god.** Nevertheless, they sacrificed to demons in order to find favor in their eyes. Due to the influence of the surrounding nations, they would worship **gods that they did not know, new ones that came recently; your fathers did not consider them.**[15] Alternatively, your fathers did not fear them,[16] or your fathers had no dealings with them.[17]

18 In contrast, **the Rock that gave birth to you, you forsook, and you forgot God, your Originator.**

Fourth aliya 19 **The Lord saw and scorned, due to the anger** caused by the idolatrous ways **of His sons and His daughters.**

20 **He,** God, **said: I will conceal My face from them.** I will not reveal Myself to them, and I will remove My providence from them. **I will see what their end is.** As God is aware of everything that will befall them, this is clearly a rhetorical statement, meaning: Without My guidance and intervention they will not survive. **As they are a generation of fickleness, children in whom there is no faithfulness.**

21 **They have infuriated Me with** their allegiance to **a non-god,** which has no significance or power whatsoever. **They** have **angered Me with their futilities,** as idolatry involves a primitive belief in charms and fortunes. **And** therefore, in a similar manner, **I will infuriate them with a non-people,** an enemy that is not a genuine nation. **With a crude nation,** a mixture of ignoble peoples, **I will anger them.**

22 **For** I was enraged; **a fire blazed in My nostrils, and it burned to the lowest depths, and it consumed the earth and its produce, and set ablaze the foundations of mountains.** The fire of My anger will shock the entire world.

23 **I will add evils upon them** aside from those already mentioned; **I will exhaust** all **My arrows,** instruments of My punishment, **on them.** Arrows will rain down upon them until none remain.

24 **They,** His sons and daughters, **will be wasted from hunger, and consumed by demons and evil spirits.**[18] Alternatively, they will be consumed by a terrible plague.[19] **And the teeth of animals I will** also **dispatch at them, with the venom of crawlers in the dust.** Not only venomous snakes, but even domesticated animals, will bite them.[20] Although this may seem like a milder punishment than the others mentioned here, those attacks will cause them to despair, as they will feel that they are under attack from all directions.

25 **Outside** their homes, **the sword will bereave** families, **and**

רש״י

עֵנָב תִּשְׁתֶּה חָמֶר. בִּימֵי עֲשֶׂרֶת הַשְּׁבָטִים, "הַשֹּׁתִים בְּמִזְרְקֵי יַיִן" (עמוס ו, ו): **בָּמֳתֵי אָרֶץ.** לְשׁוֹן גֹּבַהּ: **שָׂדָי.** לְשׁוֹן שָׂדֶה: **חַלְמִישׁ צוּר.** תָּקְפּוֹ וְחָזְקוֹ שֶׁל סֶלַע. כְּשֶׁאֵינוֹ דָּבוּק לַתֵּבָה שֶׁלְּאַחֲרָיו נָקוּד 'חַלָּמִישׁ' (לעיל ח, טו) וּכְשֶׁהוּא דָּבוּק נָקוּד 'חַלְמִישׁ': **חֶמְאַת בָּקָר.** הוּא שֻׁמָּן הַנִּלְקָט עַל גַּבֵּי חָלָב: **וַחֲלֵב צֹאן.** חָלָב שֶׁל צֹאן, וּכְשֶׁהוּא דָּבוּק נָקוּד 'חֲלֵב', כְּמוֹ: "כַּחֲלֵב חִמּוֹ" (לעיל יד, כא): **כָּרִים.** כְּבָשִׂים: **וְאֵילִים.** כְּמַשְׁמָעוֹ: **בְּנֵי בָשָׁן.** שְׁמֵנִים הָיוּ: **כִּלְיוֹת חִטָּה.** חִטִּים שְׁמֵנִים כְּחֵלֶב כְּלָיוֹת וְגַסִּין כִּכְלָיוֹת: **וְדַם עֵנָב.** הָיִיתָ שׁוֹתֶה טוֹב וְטוֹעֵם יַיִן חָשׁוּב: **חָמֶר.** יַיִן בִּלְשׁוֹן אֲרַמִּי: חֲמַר. אֵין זֶה שֵׁם דָּבָר אֶלָּא לְשׁוֹן מַשְׁקֶה בְּטַעַם, ווינו״ש בְּלַעַז. וְעוֹד יֵשׁ לְפָרֵשׁ שְׁנֵי מִקְרָאוֹת הַלָּלוּ אַחַר תַּרְגּוּם שֶׁל אוּנְקְלוֹס: "אַשְׁרִינוּן עַל תֻּקְפֵי אַרְעָא" וְגוֹ':

טו | **עָבִיתָ.** לְשׁוֹן עֹבִי: **כָּשִׂיתָ.** כְּמוֹ 'כָּסִיתָ', לְשׁוֹן: "כִּי כִסָּה פָנָיו בְּחֶלְבּוֹ" (איוב טו, כז), כְּאָדָם שֶׁשֻּׁמָּן מִבִּפְנִים וּכְסָלָיו נִכְפָּלִים מִבַּחוּץ, וְכֵן הוּא אוֹמֵר: "וַיַּעַשׂ פִּימָה עֲלֵי כָסֶל" (שם): **כָּשִׂיתָ.** יֵשׁ לְשׁוֹן קַל בִּלְשׁוֹן כִּסּוּי, כְּמוֹ: "וְכֹסֶה קָלוֹן עָרוּם" (משלי יב, טז), וְאִם כָּתַב 'כִּשִּׂיתָ' דָּגוּשׁ, הָיָה נִשְׁמַע כִּסִּיתָ אֶת אֲחֵרִים: **וַיְנַבֵּל צוּר יְשֻׁעָתוֹ.** גִּנָּהוּ וּבִזָּהוּ, כְּמוֹ שֶׁנֶּאֱמַר: "אֲחֹרֵיהֶם אֶל הֵיכַל ה'" וְגוֹ' (יחזקאל ח, טז), אֵין לְךָ נִבּוּל גָּדוֹל מִזֶּה:

טז | **יַקְנִאֻהוּ.** הִבְעִירוּ חֲמָתוֹ וְקִנְאָתוֹ: **בְּתוֹעֵבֹת.** בְּמַעֲשִׂים מְתֹעָבִים, כְּגוֹן מִשְׁכַּב זָכוּר וּכְשָׁפִים שֶׁנֶּאֱמַר בָּהֶם 'תּוֹעֵבָה':

יז | **לֹא אֱלֹהַּ.** כְּתַרְגּוּמוֹ: "דְּלֵית בְּהוֹן צְרוֹךְ", אִלּוּ הָיָה בָּהֶם צֹרֶךְ לֹא הָיְתָה קִנְאָה כְּפוּלָה כְּמוֹ עַכְשָׁיו: **חֲדָשִׁים מִקָּרֹב בָּאוּ.** אֲפִלּוּ הָאֻמּוֹת לֹא הָיוּ רְגִילִים בָּהֶם, גּוֹי שֶׁהָיָה רוֹאֶה אוֹתָם הָיָה אוֹמֵר: זֶה צֶלֶם יְהוּדִי: **לֹא שְׂעָרוּם אֲבֹתֵיכֶם.** לֹא יָרְאוּ מֵהֶם, לֹא עָמְדָה שַׂעֲרָתָם מִפְּנֵיהֶם, דֶּרֶךְ שַׂעֲרוֹת הָאָדָם לַעֲמֹד מֵחֲמַת יִרְאָה. כָּךְ נִדְרָשׁ בְּסִפְרֵי. וְיֵשׁ לְפָרֵשׁ עוֹד, "שְׂעָרוּם" לְשׁוֹן: "וּשְׂעִירִים יְרַקְּדוּ שָׁם" (ישעיה יג, כא), שְׂעִירִים הֵם שֵׁדִים, לֹא עָשׂוּ אֲבוֹתֵיכֶם שְׂעִירִים הַלָּלוּ:

יח | **תֶּשִׁי.** תִּשְׁכַּח. וְרַבּוֹתֵינוּ אָמְרוּ, כְּשֶׁבָּא לְהֵיטִיב לָכֶם אַתֶּם מַכְעִיסִין לְפָנָיו וּמַתִּישִׁים כֹּחוֹ מִלְּהֵיטִיב לָכֶם: **אֵל מְחֹלְלֶךָ.** מוֹצִיאֲךָ מֵרֶחֶם, לְשׁוֹן: "חֹלֵל אַיָּלוֹת" (איוב לט, א), "חִיל כַּיּוֹלֵדָה" (ירמיה ו, כד):

טו וְדַם־עֵנָב תִּשְׁתֶּה־חָמֶר׃ וַיִּשְׁמַן יְשֻׁרוּן וַיִּבְעָט

שָׁמַנְתָּ עָבִיתָ כָּשִׂיתָ וַיִּטֹּשׁ אֱלוֹהַ עָשָׂהוּ

טז וַיְנַבֵּל צוּר יְשֻׁעָתוֹ׃ יַקְנִאֻהוּ בְּזָרִים

יז בְּתוֹעֵבֹת יַכְעִיסֻהוּ׃ יִזְבְּחוּ לַשֵּׁדִים לֹא אֱלֹהַ

אֱלֹהִים לֹא יְדָעוּם חֲדָשִׁים מִקָּרֹב בָּאוּ

יח לֹא שְׂעָרוּם אֲבֹתֵיכֶם׃ צוּר יְלָדְךָ תֶּשִׁי

יט וַתִּשְׁכַּח אֵל מְחֹלְלֶךָ׃ וַיַּרְא יְהוָה וַיִּנְאָץ

כ מִכַּעַס בָּנָיו וּבְנֹתָיו׃ וַיֹּאמֶר אַסְתִּירָה פָנַי מֵהֶם

אֶרְאֶה מָה אַחֲרִיתָם כִּי דוֹר תַּהְפֻּכֹת הֵמָּה

כא בָּנִים לֹא־אֵמֻן בָּם׃ הֵם קִנְאוּנִי בְלֹא־אֵל

כִּעֲסוּנִי בְּהַבְלֵיהֶם וַאֲנִי אַקְנִיאֵם בְּלֹא־עָם

כב בְּגוֹי נָבָל אַכְעִיסֵם׃ כִּי־אֵשׁ קָדְחָה בְאַפִּי

וַתִּיקַד עַד־שְׁאוֹל תַּחְתִּית וַתֹּאכַל אֶרֶץ וִיבֻלָהּ

כג וַתְּלַהֵט מוֹסְדֵי הָרִים׃ אַסְפֶּה עָלֵימוֹ רָעוֹת

כד חִצַּי אֲכַלֶּה־בָּם׃ מְזֵי רָעָב וּלְחֻמֵי רֶשֶׁף

וְקֶטֶב מְרִירִי וְשֶׁן־בְּהֵמֹת אֲשַׁלַּח־בָּם

כה עִם־חֲמַת זֹחֲלֵי עָפָר׃ מִחוּץ תְּשַׁכֶּל־חֶרֶב

רש"י

כ| **מה אחריתם.** מה תעלה בהם בסופם: **כי דור תהפכת המה.** מהפכין רצוני לכעס: **לא אמן בם.** אין גדולי ניכרים בהם, כי הוריתים דרך טובה וסרו ממנה: **אמן.** לשון: "ויהי אומן" (אסתר ב, ז), נודריטור"א בלעז. דבר אחר, "אמן", לשון אמונה, כתרגומו, אמרו בסיני: "נעשה ונשמע" (שמות כד, ז), ולשעה קלה בטלו הבטחתם ועשו העגל:

כא| **קנאוני.** הבעירו חמתי: **בלא אל.** בדבר שאינו אלוה: **בלא עם.** באומה שאין לה שם, שנאמר: "הן ארץ כשדים זה העם לא היה" (ישעיה כג, יג); בעשו הוא אומר: "בזוי אתה מאד" (עובדיה א, ב): **בגוי נבל אכעיסם.** אלו המינין, וכן הוא אומר: "אמר נבל בלבו אין אלהים" (תהלים יד, א):

כב| **קדחה.** בערה: **ותיקד.** בכם עד היסוד: **ותאכל.** ארצכם ויבולה: **ותלהט.** את ירושלים המיוסדת על ההרים, שנאמר: "ירושלם הרים סביב לה" (תהלים קכה, ב):

כג| **אספה עלימו רעות.** אחביר רעה על רעה, לשון: "ספו שנה על שנה" (ישעיה כט, א), "ספות הרוה" (לעיל כט, יח), "עלותיכם ספו על זבחיכם" (ירמיה ז, כא). דבר אחר, "אספה", אכלה, כמו: "פן תספה" (בראשית יט, טו): **חצי אכלה בם.** כל חצי אשלים בהם, וקללה זו לפי הפרענות לברכה היא, חצי כלים והם אינם כלים:

כד| **מזי רעב.** אונקלוס תרגם: "נפיחי כפן" ואין לי עד מוכיח עליו. ומשמו של רבי יהודה הדרשן מטולוזא שמעתי, שעירי רעב, אדם כחוש מגדל שער על בשרו. 'מזי' לשון ארמי שער, מזיא, "דהוה מהפך במזייה" (מגילה דף יח ע"א): **ולחמי רשף.** השדים נלחמו בהם, שנאמר: "ובני רשף יגביהו עוף" (איוב ה, ז), והם שדים: **וקטב מרירי.** וכריתות שד ששמו מרירי: **קטב.** כריתה, כמו: "אהי קטבך שאול" (הושע יג, יד): **ושן בהמות.** מעשה היה והיו הרחלות נושכות וממיתות: **חמת זחלי עפר.** ארס נחשים המהלכים בגחונם על העפר כמים הזוחלים על הארץ. 'זחילה' לשון מרוצת המים על העפר, וכן כל מרוצת דבר המשפשף על העפר והולך:

כה| **מחוץ תשכל חרב.** מחוץ לעיר תשכלם חרב גייסות: **ומחדרים אימה.** כשבורח ונמלט מן החרב חדרי לבו

terror will do so **within, in** their hiding places. **Both a youth and a maiden, a suckling with a gray-haired man,** everyone will be punished and all will suffer.

26 **I said I would scatter them** [*af'eihem*] across the corners of the earth. The similar word *pe'a* meaning corners refers to the produce in the corner of the field left for the poor.[21] Alternatively, the verse means: I said I would stab them. **I would terminate their memory from man.**

27 Indeed, because of their insolence, ingratitude, and infidelity, I would destroy Israel, **were it not that I dread** [*agur*] **the enemy's anger.**[22] Alternatively, *agur* means gathered, i.e., were it not that the enemy's anger was pent up.[23] Yet another interpretation: Were it not that the enemy of Israel was angry.[24] However, under the circumstances, I am concerned **lest their adversaries misapprehend, lest they say: Our hand is mighty;** with our strength we subdued Israel, **and it is not the Lord who did all this.**

28 **For they,** Israel's enemies, **are a nation void of counsel, and there is no understanding in them.** Therefore, they will fail to recognize that their ascent to greatness was not through their own merit but because Israel was involved in those events.

29 **If they,** those enemies, **were wise,** if they contemplated their situation from the outset, **they would comprehend this, they would understand their end.** They would understand that their victories are the result of Israel's behavior. Alternatively, they would understand their own end, that their victories are supernatural, and ultimately, they will be held accountable for their sins just as Israel has been held accountable for its sins.[25]

Fifth aliya

30 The enemy would say: **How does one** of us **pursue one thousand** of Israel, **and two cause ten thousand to flee?** How is it that Israel falls so helplessly when facing our small forces, **if not that their Rock,** God, **sold them and the Lord delivered them** into our hands? Our victory is not due to our strength, but because God is punishing His people.

31 **For our Rock is not like their rock,** the rock of our enemies is not as strong as our Rock, **and** nevertheless, **our enemies are** our **judges**[D] and administer punishment to us.[26]

Hairy nightshade

32 **For their,** our enemy's, **vine is from the vine of Sodom, and from the fields of Gomorrah.** The source of their philosophy, their spirituality, and their codes of conduct is the evil and corrupt cities of Sodom and Gomorrah. **Their grapes are grapes of poison,**[B] **noxious clusters for them.**

33 **The venom of serpents is their wine, and the cruel poison of vipers.** Alternatively, the latter phrase may be rendered: And the head, or skull, of cruel vipers. The intense cruelty and venomous hatred to which the people of Israel will be exposed over the course of their exile cannot be accurately expressed even through the harsh words of this song.

Black viper

34 The nature of this hatred will defy explanation: **Is this not concealed with Me,**[D] **sealed in My treasuries?** The nations that will treat Israel with cruelty will not understand it; even besieged Israel will be incapable of grasping it. The matter will remain secret.

35 **Vengeance and recompense are Mine.** I will seek vengeance

BACKGROUND

32:32 | **Grapes of poison:** Some identify this as the hairy nightshade, *Solanum villosum*, a poisonous annual weed that has yellow or red berries. It reaches a height of 60 cm and grows in locations high in nitrogen: garbage dumps, gardens, the sides of roads, and irrigated fields.

DISCUSSION

32:31 | **And our enemies are judges:** The Israelites will be unable to prove their virtue in the courts of the other nations because they will not be treated as equals under the law. This problem is almost as ancient as the nation of Israel itself. Throughout various periods of history, Jews were required to debate and justify their position, despite the fact that the opposing side served as the judge. An arrangement of that kind left little chance for the possibility that the Jew would emerge victorious.

32:34 | **Is this not concealed with Me:** Futile are the many attempts to explain the fate of Israel through various economic, philosophical, or other explanations. The true foundations of anti-Semitism are unknown to man; they remain a divine secret.

וּמֵחֲדָרִים אֵימָה גַּם־בָּחוּר גַּם־בְּתוּלָה

כו יוֹנֵק עִם־אִישׁ שֵׂיבָה׃ אָמַרְתִּי אַפְאֵיהֶם

כז אַשְׁבִּיתָה מֵאֱנוֹשׁ זִכְרָם׃ לוּלֵי כַּעַס אוֹיֵב אָגוּר

פֶּן־יְנַכְּרוּ צָרֵימוֹ פֶּן־יֹאמְרוּ יָדֵנוּ רָמָה

כח וְלֹא יְהוָה פָּעַל כׇּל־זֹאת׃ כִּי־גוֹי אֹבַד עֵצוֹת הֵמָּה

כט וְאֵין בָּהֶם תְּבוּנָה׃ לוּ חָכְמוּ יַשְׂכִּילוּ זֹאת חמישי

ל יָבִינוּ לְאַחֲרִיתָם׃ אֵיכָה יִרְדֹּף אֶחָד אֶלֶף

וּשְׁנַיִם יָנִיסוּ רְבָבָה אִם־לֹא כִּי־צוּרָם מְכָרָם

לא וַיהוָה הִסְגִּירָם׃ כִּי לֹא כְצוּרֵנוּ צוּרָם

לב וְאֹיְבֵינוּ פְּלִילִים׃ כִּי־מִגֶּפֶן סְדֹם גַּפְנָם

וּמִשַּׁדְמֹת עֲמֹרָה עֲנָבֵמוֹ עִנְּבֵי־רוֹשׁ

לג אַשְׁכְּלֹת מְרֹרֹת לָמוֹ׃ חֲמַת תַּנִּינִם יֵינָם

לד וְרֹאשׁ פְּתָנִים אַכְזָר׃ הֲלֹא־הוּא כָּמֻס עִמָּדִי

לה חָתוּם בְּאוֹצְרֹתָי׃ לִי נָקָם וְשִׁלֵּם

רש"י

נקופים עליו מחמת אימה והוא מת והולך בה. דבר אחר, "ומחדרים אימה", בבית תהיה אימת דבר, כמה שנאמר: "כי עלה מות בחלונינו" (ירמיה ט, כ), וכן תרגם אונקלוס. דבר אחר, "מחוץ תשכל חרב" על מה שעשו בחוצות, שנאמר: "ומספר חצות ירושלם שמתם מזבחות לבשת" (שם יא, יג). "ומחדרים אימה" על מה שעשו בחדרי חדרים, שנאמר: "אשר זקני בית ישראל עשים בחשך איש בחדרי משכיתו" (יחזקאל ח, יב):

כו| **אמרתי אפאיהם.** אמרתי בלבי אפאה אותם. ויש לפרש "אפאיהם" אשיתם פאה, להשליכם מעלי הפקר, ודוגמתו מצינו בעזרא: "ותתן להם ממלכות ועממים ותחלקם לפאה" (נחמיה ט, כב), להפקר, וכן חברו מנחם. ויש פותרים אותו כתרגומו: "יחול רגזי עליהון", ולא יתכן, שאם כן היה לו לכתב 'אאפיהם', אלף לשמוש ואלף ליסוד, כמו: "אאזרך" (ישעיה מה, ה) "אאמצכם במו פי" (איוב טז, ה), והאל"ף התיכונה אינה ראויה בו כלל. ואונקלוס תרגם אחר לשון הברייתא השנויה בספרי (שכב) החולקת תבה זו לשלש תבות: 'אמרתי אף אי הם', אמרתי באפי אתנם כאלו אינם, שיאמרו רואיהם עליהם איה הם:

כז-כט| **לולי כעס אויב אגור.** אם לא שכעס האויב כנוס עליהם להשחית, ואם יוכל להם והשחיתם יתלה הגדלה בו ובאלהיו ולא יתלה הגדלה בי, וזהו שנאמר: "פן ינכרו צרימו", ינכרו הדבר לתלות גבורתי בנכרי שאין הגדלה שלו, "פן יאמרו ידנו רמה" וגו'. כי אותו גוי "אבד עצות המה ואין בהם תבונה", שאלו היו חכמים "ישכילו זאת... איכה ירדף" וגו': **יבינו לאחריתם.** יתנו לב להתבונן לסוף פרענותם של ישראל:

ל| **איכה ירדף אחד.** ממנו, אלף מישראל: **אם לא כי צורם מכרם וה' הסגירם.** מכרם ומסרם בידנו, דליבר"ר בלעז:

לא| **כי לא כצורנו צורם.** כל זה היה להם לאויבים להבין שהשם הסגירם ולא להם ולאלהיהם הנצחון, שהרי עד הנה לא יוכלו כלום אלהיהם כנגד צורנו, כי לא כסלענו סלעם. כל 'צור' שבמקרא לשון סלע: **ואיבינו פלילים.** ועכשיו אויבינו שופטים אותנו, הרי שצורנו מכרנו להם:

לב| **כי מגפן סדם גפנם.** מוסב למעלה, אמרתי בלבי אפאיהם ואשבית זכרם, לפי שמעשיהם מעשה סדום ועמורה: **שדמת.** שדה תבואה, כמו: "ושדמות לא עשה אכל" (חבקוק ג, יז), "בשדמות קדרון" (מלכים ב' כג, ד): **ענבי רוש.** עשב מר: **אשכלת מררת למו.** משקה מר ראוי להם, לפי מעשיהם פרענותם. וכן תרגם אונקלוס: "ותושלמת עובדיהון כמרדותהון":

לג| **חמת תנינם יינם.** כתרגומו: "הא כמרת תניניא כס פורענותהון", הנה כמרירת נחשים כוס משתה פרענותם: **וראש פתנים אכזר.** כוסם, שהוא אכזר לנשך – אויב אכזרי יבא ויפרע מהם:

לד| **הלא הוא כמס עמדי.** כתרגומו, כסבורים הם ששכחתי מעשיהם, כלם גנוזים ושמורים לפני: **הלא הוא.** פרי גפנם ותבואת שדמותם "כמס עמדי":

לה| **לי נקם ושלם.** עמי נכון ומזמן פרענות נקם, וישלם

at the time that their foot will collapse, when their evil will ruin them; **for** then, **the day of their calamity is near, and the future is rushing toward them.**

36 **When the Lord judges His people** after concealing His face from them, **and He regrets,** as it were, **with regard to** that which was done to **His servants,** as the suffering they will have endured due to their abandonment of God will have reached its full measure, **when He sees that their power is gone, and there is none protected** by the government, **or fortified,**[27]

37 **He,** God,[28] **will say: Where are their gods** in whom they placed their faith, **the rock in whom they sought refuge?** Alternatively, when the people of Israel are redeemed, they will say to the nations: Where are their gods, the rock in which they sought refuge?[29]

38 Where are those gods, **the fat of whose offerings they would eat, the wine of whose libations they would drink? They will** now **arise and help you; it,** those gods, **will be shelter over you.**

39 **See now,** at the time of the Redemption, when it will become clear to all that there is no substance to those gods whose shelter was sought, **that I, I am He, and there is no god with Me. I will kill and I will give life, I crushed and I will heal, and there is no rescuer from My hand;** everything is under My control.

40 **When I will raise My hand to heaven** to take an oath,[30] **and**
Sixth aliya **I will say: As I live forever.** Just as a person taking an oath states: As the Lord lives,[31] so too, when taking an oath, God invokes Himself, as it were.

41 **If,** or when, **I hone**[32] **My flashing sword** when it is removed from its sheath, **and My hand will grasp judgment,** then **I will return vengeance to My enemies, and to those who hate Me I will recompense.** Vengeance and recompense will be visited upon the enemies of Israel, as they are My enemies and they hate Me.[33] Although Israel is punished for its sins through its enemies, the latter do not seek to oppress Israel because of those sins. On the contrary, it is the bond between God and Israel and Israel's desire to call in the name of God and represent Him in this world that drive Israel's enemies to conspire against it. Therefore, Israel's enemies attack Israel due to a hatred of God.

42 Perhaps then **I will intoxicate My arrows with blood,** which is likened to wine,[34] **and** then **My sword will devour flesh,** and My arrows will be intoxicated **from the blood of the slain and the captive, from the heads of the enemy raiders.**

43 **Nations,** when God ultimately redeems Israel, **acclaim His people,** as it will then become clear that even when Israel suffered terribly, God never completely abandoned them; rather, He concealed His face from them so that it appeared that He was not with them. **As** when God will be revealed, **He will avenge the blood of His servants, and He will return vengeance to His adversaries, and He will atone for His land** and **His people.** When God avenges the blood of His servants, His land and His people will be purified.[35] Alternatively, His land will atone for His people when it absorbs the blood of His adversaries, or His people will purify His land through the killing of His murderous adversaries.[36]

רש"י

להם כמעשיהם, הנקם ישלם להם גמולם. ויש מפרשים "ושלם" שם דבר, כמו 'ושלום', והוא מגזרת: "והדבר אין בהם" (ירמיה ה, יג), כמו 'והדבור'. ואימתי אשלם להם? "לעת תמוט רגלם", כשיתמו זכות אבותם שהם סמוכים עליו: **כי קרוב יום אידם.** משארצה להביא עליהם יום אידם, קרוב ומזמן לפני להביא על ידי שלוחים הרבה: **וחש עתדת למו.** ומהר יבאו העתידות להם: **וחש.** כמו "ימהר יחישה" (ישעיה ה, יט).

עד כאן העיד עליהם משה דברי תוכחה להיות השירה הזאת לעד, כשתבוא עליהם הפרענות ידעו שאני הודעתים מראש. מכאן ואילך העיד עליהם דברי תנחומין שיבאו עליהם ככלות הפרענות, ככל אשר אמר למעלה: "והיה כי יבאו עליך... הברכה והקללה וגו' ושב ה' אלהיך את שבותך" וגו' (לעיל ל, א-ג):

לו | **כי ידין ה' עמו.** כשישפט אותם ביסורין הללו האמורים עליהם, כמו: "כי בם ידין עמים" (איוב לו, לא), ייסר עמים. 'כי' זה אינו משמש בלשון 'דהא' לתת טעם לדברים של מעלה, אלא לשון תחלת דבור, כמו: "כי תבאו אל הארץ" (ויקרא כה, ב), כשיבאו עליהם משפטים הללו ויתנחם הקדוש ברוך הוא על עבדיו לשוב ולרחם עליהם: **יתנחם.** לשון הפך מחשבה, להיטיב או להרע. כשתראה כי אזלת יד האויב הולכת וחזקה עליהם, ו"אפס" בהם "עצור ועזוב": **עצור.** נושע על ידי עוצר ומושל שיעצר בהם: **עזוב.** על ידי עוזב. 'עוצר' הוא המושל העוצר בעם שלא ילכו מפזרים בצאתם לצבא על האויב: **עצור.** הוא הנושע במעצור המושל: **עזוב.** מחזק, כמו: "ויעזבו ירושלם עד החומה" (נחמיה ג, ח), "איך לא עזבה עיר תהלת" (ירמיה מט, כה): **עצור.** מייטני"ר: **עזוב.** איפורצא"ר בלעז:

לז | **ואמר.** הקדוש ברוך הוא עליהם: "אי אלהימו" עבודה זרה שעבדו: **צור חסיו בו.** הסלע שהיו מתכסין בו מפני החמה והצנה, כלומר שהיו בטוחין בו להגן עליהם מן הרעה:

לח | **אשר חלב זבחימו.** היו אותן אלהות אוכלים, שהיו מקריבים לפניהם, ושותין "יין נסיכם": **יהי עליכם סתרה.** אותו הצור יהיה לכם מחסה ומסתור:

לט | **ראו עתה.** הבינו מן הפרענות שהבאתי עליכם ואין לכם מושיע, ומן התשועה שאושיעכם ואין מוחה בידי: **אני אני הוא.** אני להשפיל ואני להרים: **ואין אלהים**

לְעֵת תָּמוּט רַגְלָם | כִּי קָרוֹב יוֹם אֵידָם

לו וְחָשׁ עֲתִדֹת לָמוֹ: | כִּי־יָדִין יהוה עַמּוֹ

וְעַל־עֲבָדָיו יִתְנֶחָם | כִּי יִרְאֶה כִּי־אָזְלַת יָד

לז וְאֶפֶס עָצוּר וְעָזוּב: | וְאָמַר אֵי אֱלֹהֵימוֹ

לח צוּר חָסָיוּ בוֹ: | אֲשֶׁר חֵלֶב זְבָחֵימוֹ יֹאכֵלוּ

יִשְׁתּוּ יֵין נְסִיכָם | יָקוּמוּ וְיַעְזְרֻכֶם

לט יְהִי עֲלֵיכֶם סִתְרָה: | רְאוּ ׀ עַתָּה כִּי אֲנִי אֲנִי הוּא

וְאֵין אֱלֹהִים עִמָּדִי | אֲנִי אָמִית וַאֲחַיֶּה

מָחַצְתִּי וַאֲנִי אֶרְפָּא | וְאֵין מִיָּדִי מַצִּיל:

מ כִּי־אֶשָּׂא אֶל־שָׁמַיִם יָדִי | וְאָמַרְתִּי חַי אָנֹכִי לְעֹלָם: ששי

מא אִם־שַׁנּוֹתִי בְּרַק חַרְבִּי | וְתֹאחֵז בְּמִשְׁפָּט יָדִי

אָשִׁיב נָקָם לְצָרָי | וְלִמְשַׂנְאַי אֲשַׁלֵּם:

מב אַשְׁכִּיר חִצַּי מִדָּם | וְחַרְבִּי תֹּאכַל בָּשָׂר

מִדַּם חָלָל וְשִׁבְיָה | מֵרֹאשׁ פַּרְעוֹת אוֹיֵב:

מג הַרְנִינוּ גוֹיִם עַמּוֹ | כִּי דַם־עֲבָדָיו יִקּוֹם

וְנָקָם יָשִׁיב לְצָרָיו | וְכִפֶּר אַדְמָתוֹ עַמּוֹ:

רש"י

עמדי. עומד כנגדי למחות: **עמדי.** דגמתי וכמוני: **ואין מידי מציל.** הפושעים בי:

מ| **כי אשא אל שמים ידי.** כי בחרון אפי אשא ידי אל עצמי בשבועה: **ואמרתי חי אנכי.** לשון שבועה הוא, אני נשבע 'חי אני':

מא| **אם שנותי ברק חרבי.** אם אשנן את להב חרבי, כמו: "למען היות לה ברק", פלאנדו"ר: **ותאחז במשפט ידי.** להניח מדת רחמים באויבי שהרעו לכם, "אשר אני קצפתי מעט והמה עזרו לרעה" (זכריה א, טו), ותאחז ידי את מדת המשפט להחזיק בה ולנקם נקם: **אשיב נקם וגו'.** למדו רבותינו באגדה מתוך לשון המקרא שאמר: "ותאחז במשפט ידי" – לא כמדת בשר ודם מדת הקדוש ברוך הוא, מדת בשר ודם זורק חץ ואינו יכול להשיבו, והקדוש ברוך הוא זורק חציו ויש בידו להשיבם כאלו אוחזן בידו, שהרי ברק הוא חצו, שנאמר כאן: "ברק חרבי ותאחז במשפט ידי", והמשפט הזה לשון פרענות הוא, בלעז יושטיצי"א:

מב| **אשכיר חצי מדם.** האויב: **וחרבי תאכל.** בשרם: **מדם חלל ושביה.** זאת תהיה להם מעון דם חללי ישראל ושביה ששבו מהם: **מראש פרעות אויב.** מפסע תחלת פרעות האויב, כי כשהקדוש ברוך הוא נפרע מן האומות פוקד עליהם עונם ועונות אבותיהם מראשית פרצה שפרצו בישראל:

מג| **הרנינו גוים עמו.** לאותו הזמן ישבחו האומות את ישראל, ראו מה שבחה של אומה זו שדבקו בהקדוש ברוך הוא בכל התלאות שעברו עליהם ולא עזבוהו, יודעים היו בטובו ובשבחו: **כי דם עבדיו יקום.** שפיכות דמיהם, כמשמעו: **ונקם ישיב לצריו.** על הגזל ועל החמס, כענין שנאמר: "מצרים לשממה תהיה ואדום למדבר שממה תהיה, מחמס בני יהודה" (יואל ד, יט), ואומר: "מחמס אחיך יעקב" וגו' (עובדיה א, י): **וכפר אדמתו עמו.** ויפיס אדמתו ועמו על הצרות שעברו עליהם ושעשה להם האויב: **וכפר.** לשון רצוי ופיוס, כמו: "אכפרה פניו" – "אניחניה לרגזיה" (בראשית לב, כ; אונקלוס שם): **וכפר אדמתו.** ומה היא אדמתו? – "עמו", כשעמו מתנחמים ארצו מתנחמת, וכן הוא אומר: "רצית ה' ארצך" (תהלים פה, ב), במה רצית ארצך? "שבת שבות יעקב" (שם).

בפנים אחרים היא נדרשת בספרי ונחלקו בה רבי יהודה ורבי נחמיה. רבי יהודה דורש כלה כנגד ישראל, ורבי נחמיה דורש את כלה כנגד האומות. רבי יהודה דורשה

44 Moses came and he spoke all the words of this song in the
Seventh ears of the people, he, and Hoshe'a son of Nun. Joshua's orig-
aliya inal name was Hoshe'a, but Moses changed it to Joshua.[37] Moses
and Joshua presented this song to the nation together, primarily to honor Joshua. In this way, Moses publicly completed the
process of transferring his authority to Joshua. Hoshe'a, who
had been one of the people, assumes his status as Joshua, the
next great leader.

45 Moses finished speaking all these matters to all Israel.

46 He, Moses, again said to them: Set your heart to all the matters[D] that I attest to you today. Diligently observe these matters, and ensure that you will command them to your children, to take care to perform all the words of this Torah in

the future. The list of commandments, prohibitions, blessings,
curses, and punishments have already been stated in detail. The
song of *Haazinu* does not discuss the details of Israel's obligations to God; the entire book of Deuteronomy is devoted to
those obligations. Rather, the song relates to the general principles of loyalty to God and the observance of His laws.

47 For it is not an empty thing for you, as it is your life. Your life
depends on observing the Torah, as a man suspended above a
deep chasm depends on the rope that supports him, or as one
who sojourns through the desert depends on his last ration of
water. And through this matter you will extend your days on
the land[D] that you are crossing the Jordan to take possession of it.

Moses Receives His Final Commandment
DEUTERONOMY 32:48–52

The song of Moses has reached its conclusion, and with it, the song of his life is about to conclude.
Moses is now commanded to actualize the divine command he received previously.[38] The death of
Moses servant of God is described in this passage as a Master's commandment to His servant, with
a positive commandment and a prohibition: "Die on the mountain…but there you will not come"
(32:50–52).

48 The Lord spoke to Moses on that very day, the same day that
Maftir Moses recited the song of *Haazinu*,[39] and the last day of Moses'
life, saying:

49 Ascend to this highland of Avarim, a tall mountain visible
from all its sides [*avarav*], Mount Nevo, which is in the land
of Moav, which is opposite Jericho. The precise location of
this mountain is unknown nowadays. And from the mountain you shall see the land of Canaan that I am giving to the

children of Israel as a portion. I will thereby fulfill My promise that you will see the land.[40]

50 Your ascent upon the mountain is not only to see the land.
You are commanded to die on the mountain that you are
ascending there, and be gathered to your people, your soul
will return to its source. This latter expression is used only in
reference to the passing of a righteous individual. And you shall

---

DISCUSSION

32:45–46 | Moses finished speaking all these matters.... He said to them: Set your heart to all the matters: It is possible that these were not literally the last words of Moses (see Ibn Ezra, 31:1); rather, they were closing remarks that Moses would repeat again and again. Perhaps those who listened to Moses consid-ered his words to be the brilliant theories of a great sage and man of vision, words that were

not very relevant for the reality of the mundane lives they lived. Moses therefore reiterates to the people that the words of the Torah comprise the true reality.

32:47 | You will extend days on the land: After you conquer the land, establish a strong military, and become a powerful regional pres-ence, the Torah may come to be seen as a book

of merely historical or cultural interest, a collec-tion of traditions once observed by your ances-tors. Remember that even then, when you are a free people in your own land, the Torah is your life, and that without it your days in this land will be numbered, and sooner or later you will become yet another nation that was displaced from the land.

מד וַיָּבֹא מֹשֶׁה וַיְדַבֵּר אֶת־כׇּל־דִּבְרֵי הַשִּׁירָה־הַזֹּאת בְּאׇזְנֵי הָעָם הוּא וְהוֹשֵׁעַ בִּן־ שביעי
מה מו נוּן׃ וַיְכַל מֹשֶׁה לְדַבֵּר אֶת־כׇּל־הַדְּבָרִים הָאֵלֶּה אֶל־כׇּל־יִשְׂרָאֵל׃ וַיֹּאמֶר אֲלֵהֶם
שִׂימוּ לְבַבְכֶם לְכׇל־הַדְּבָרִים אֲשֶׁר אָנֹכִי מֵעִיד בָּכֶם הַיּוֹם אֲשֶׁר תְּצַוֻּם אֶת־בְּנֵיכֶם
מז לִשְׁמֹר לַעֲשׂוֹת אֶת־כׇּל־דִּבְרֵי הַתּוֹרָה הַזֹּאת׃ כִּי לֹא־דָבָר רֵק הוּא מִכֶּם כִּי־הוּא
חַיֵּיכֶם וּבַדָּבָר הַזֶּה תַּאֲרִיכוּ יָמִים עַל־הָאֲדָמָה אֲשֶׁר אַתֶּם עֹבְרִים אֶת־הַיַּרְדֵּן
שָׁמָּה לְרִשְׁתָּהּ׃
מח מט וַיְדַבֵּר יְהוָה אֶל־מֹשֶׁה בְּעֶצֶם הַיּוֹם הַזֶּה לֵאמֹר׃ עֲלֵה אֶל־הַר הָעֲבָרִים הַזֶּה מפטיר
הַר־נְבוֹ אֲשֶׁר בְּאֶרֶץ מוֹאָב אֲשֶׁר עַל־פְּנֵי יְרֵחוֹ וּרְאֵה אֶת־אֶרֶץ כְּנַעַן אֲשֶׁר אֲנִי
נ נֹתֵן לִבְנֵי יִשְׂרָאֵל לַאֲחֻזָּה׃ וּמֻת בָּהָר אֲשֶׁר אַתָּה עֹלֶה שָׁמָּה וְהֵאָסֵף אֶל־עַמֶּיךָ

רש״י

כְּלַפֵּי יִשְׂרָאֵל: **אָמַרְתִּי אַפְאֵיהֶם.** (לעיל פסוק כו) כְּמוֹ שֶׁפֵּרַשְׁתִּי, עַד "וְלֹא ה׳ פָּעַל כׇּל זֹאת" (לעיל פסוק כז): **כִּי גוֹי אֹבַד עֵצוֹת הֵמָּה.** (לעיל פסוק כח) אִבְּדוּ תּוֹרָתִי שֶׁהִיא לָהֶם עֵצָה נְכוֹנָה: **וְאֵין בָּהֶם תְּבוּנָה.** לְהִתְבּוֹנֵן "אֵיכָה יִרְדֹּף אֶחָד" מִן הָאֻמּוֹת "אֶלֶף" מֵהֶם, "אִם לֹא כִּי צוּרָם מְכָרָם" (לעיל פסוק ל). "כִּי לֹא כְצוּרֵנוּ צוּרָם" (לעיל פסוק לא), הַכֹּל כְּמוֹ שֶׁפֵּרַשְׁתִּי עַד תַּכְלִית.

וְרַבִּי נְחֶמְיָה דּוֹרְשָׁהּ כְּלַפֵּי הָאֻמּוֹת: **כִּי גוֹי אֹבַד עֵצוֹת הֵמָּה.** כְּמוֹ שֶׁפֵּרַשְׁתִּי תְּחִלָּה, עַד "וְאֹיְבֵינוּ פְּלִילִים" (לעיל פסוק לא):

לב| **כִּי מִגֶּפֶן סְדֹם גַּפְנָם.** שֶׁל אֻמּוֹת: **וּמִשַּׁדְמֹת עֲמֹרָה וְגוֹ׳.** וְלֹא יָשִׂימוּ לִבָּם לִתְלוֹת הַגְּדֻלָּה בִּי: **עֲנָבֵמוֹ עִנְּבֵי רוֹשׁ.** הוּא שֶׁאָמַר: "לוּלֵי כַּעַס אוֹיֵב אָגוּר" (לעיל פסוק כז) עַל יִשְׂרָאֵל לְהַרְעִילָם וּלְהַמְרִידָם, לְפִיכָךְ: "אַשְׁכְּלֹת מְרֹרֹת לָמוֹ" לְהַלְעִיט אוֹתָם עַל מַה שֶּׁעָשׂוּ לְבָנַי:

לג| **חֲמַת תַּנִּינִם יֵינָם.** מוּכָן לְהַשְׁקוֹתָם עַל מַה שֶּׁעוֹשִׂין לָהֶם:

לד| **כָּמֻס עִמָּדִי.** אוֹתוֹ הַכּוֹס, שֶׁנֶּאֱמַר: "כִּי כוֹס בְּיַד ה׳" וְגוֹ׳ (תהלים עה, ט):

לה| **לְעֵת תָּמוּט רַגְלָם.** כְּעִנְיָן שֶׁנֶּאֱמַר "תִּרְמְסֶנָּה רָגֶל" (ישעיה כו, ו):

לו| **כִּי יָדִין ה׳ עַמּוֹ.** כְּלָשׁוֹן זֶה מְשַׁמֵּשׁ "כִּי יָדִין" בִּלְשׁוֹן 'דְּהָא', וְאֵין "יָדִין" לְשׁוֹן יִסּוּרִין, אֶלָּא כְּמוֹ כִּי יָרִיב אֶת רִיבָם מִיַּד עוֹשְׁקֵיהֶם, "כִּי יִרְאֶה כִּי אָזְלַת יָד" וְגוֹ׳:

לז| **וְאָמַר אֵי אֱלֹהֵימוֹ.** וְהָאוֹיֵב יֹאמַר: "אֵי אֱלֹהֵימוֹ" שֶׁל יִשְׂרָאֵל, כְּמוֹ שֶׁאָמַר טִיטוּס הָרָשָׁע כְּשֶׁגִּדֵּר אֶת הַפָּרֹכֶת, כְּעִנְיָן שֶׁנֶּאֱמַר: "וְתֵרֶא אֹיַבְתִּי וּתְכַסֶּהָ בוּשָׁה הָאֹמְרָה אֵלַי אַיּוֹ ה׳ אֱלֹהָיִךְ" (מיכה ז, י):

לט| **רְאוּ עַתָּה כִּי אֲנִי וְגוֹ׳.** אָז יְגַלֶּה הַקָּדוֹשׁ בָּרוּךְ הוּא יְשׁוּעָתוֹ, וְיֹאמַר: "רְאוּ עַתָּה כִּי אֲנִי אֲנִי הוּא", מֵאִתִּי בָּאת עֲלֵיהֶם הָרָעָה, וּמֵאִתִּי תָּבֹא עֲלֵיהֶם הַטּוֹבָה: **וְאֵין מִיָּדִי מַצִּיל.** מִי שֶׁיַּצִּיל אֶתְכֶם מִן הָרָעָה אֲשֶׁר אָבִיא עֲלֵיכֶם:

מ| **כִּי אֶשָּׂא אֶל שָׁמַיִם יָדִי.** כְּמוֹ 'כִּי נָשָׂאתִי', תָּמִיד אֲנִי מַשְׁרֶה מְקוֹם שְׁכִינָתִי בַּשָּׁמַיִם, כְּתַרְגּוּמוֹ. אֲפִלּוּ אַלָּשׁ לְמַעְלָה וְגִבּוֹר לְמַטָּה, אֵימַת עֶלְיוֹן עַל הַתַּחְתּוֹן, וְכָל שֶׁכֵּן שֶׁגִּבּוֹר לְמַעְלָה וְחַלָּשׁ מִלְּמַטָּה: **יָדִי.** מְקוֹם שְׁכִינָתִי, כְּמוֹ: "אִישׁ עַל יָדוֹ" (במדבר ב, יז), וְהָיָה בְּיָדִי לְהִפָּרַע מִכֶּם, אֲבָל אָמַרְתִּי שֶׁ"חַי אָנֹכִי לְעֹלָם", אֵינִי מְמַהֵר לִפָּרַע לְפִי שֶׁיֵּשׁ שָׁהוּת בַּדָּבָר, אֲנִי חַי לְעוֹלָם וּבְדוֹרוֹת אַחֲרוֹנִים אֲנִי נִפְרָע מֵהֶם, וְהַיְּכֹלֶת בְּיָדִי לִפָּרַע מִן הַמֵּתִים וּמִן הַחַיִּים. מֶלֶךְ בָּשָׂר וָדָם שֶׁהוּא הוֹלֵךְ לָמוּת, מְמַהֵר נְקָמָתוֹ לִפָּרַע בְּחַיָּיו, כִּי שֶׁמָּא יָמוּת הוּא אוֹ אוֹיְבוֹ וְנִמְצָא שֶׁלֹּא רָאָה נְקָמָתוֹ מִמֶּנּוּ, אֲבָל אֲנִי חַי לְעוֹלָם, וְאִם יָמוּתוּ הֵם וְאֵינִי נִפְרָע בְּחַיֵּיהֶם, אֶפָּרַע בְּמוֹתָם:

מא| **אִם שַׁנּוֹתִי בְּרַק חַרְבִּי.** הַרְבֵּה 'אִם' יֵשׁ שֶׁאֵינָם תְּלוּיִין, כְּשֶׁאֶשְׁנֵן "בְּרַק חַרְבִּי וְתֹאחֵז בְּמִשְׁפָּט יָדִי", כֻּלּוֹ כְּמוֹ שֶׁפֵּרַשְׁתִּי לְמַעְלָה:

מד| **הוּא וְהוֹשֵׁעַ בִּן נוּן.** שַׁבָּת שֶׁל דְּיוֹזְגֵי הָיְתָה, נִטְּלָה רְשׁוּת מִזֶּה וְנִתְּנָה לָזֶה, הֶעֱמִיד לוֹ מֹשֶׁה מְתֻרְגְּמָן לִיהוֹשֻׁעַ שֶׁיְּהֵא דּוֹרֵשׁ בְּחַיָּיו, כְּדֵי שֶׁלֹּא יֹאמְרוּ יִשְׂרָאֵל: בְּחַיֵּי רַבְּךָ לֹא הָיָה לְךָ לְהָרִים רֹאשׁ. וְלָמָּה קוֹרֵהוּ כָּאן 'הוֹשֵׁעַ'? לוֹמַר שֶׁלֹּא זָחָה דַּעְתּוֹ עָלָיו, שֶׁאַף עַל פִּי שֶׁנִּתְּנָה לוֹ גְּדֻלָּה, הִשְׁפִּיל עַצְמוֹ כַּאֲשֶׁר מִתְּחִלָּתוֹ:

מו| **שִׂימוּ לְבַבְכֶם.** צָרִיךְ אָדָם שֶׁיִּהְיוּ עֵינָיו וְלִבּוֹ וְאׇזְנָיו מְכֻוָּנִים לְדִבְרֵי תוֹרָה, וְכֵן הוּא אוֹמֵר: "בֶּן אָדָם רְאֵה בְעֵינֶיךָ וּבְאׇזְנֶיךָ שְּׁמָע וְשִׂים לִבְּךָ" וְגוֹ׳ (יחזקאל מ, ד), וַהֲרֵי דְּבָרִים קַל וָחֹמֶר: וּמַה תַּבְנִית הַבַּיִת שֶׁהוּא נִרְאֶה לָעֵינַיִם וְנִמְדָּד בַּקָּנֶה, צָרִיךְ אָדָם שֶׁיִּהְיוּ עֵינָיו וְאׇזְנָיו וְלִבּוֹ מְכֻוָּנִים לְהָבִין, דִּבְרֵי תוֹרָה שֶׁהֵן כַּהֲרָרִין תְּלוּיִין בְּשַׂעֲרָה, עַל אַחַת כַּמָּה וְכַמָּה:

מז| **כִּי לֹא דָבָר רֵק הוּא מִכֶּם.** לֹא לְחִנָּם אַתֶּם יְגֵעִים בָּהּ, כִּי הַרְבֵּה שָׂכָר תָּלוּי בָּהּ, "כִּי הוּא חַיֵּיכֶם". דָּבָר אַחֵר, אֵין לְךָ דָּבָר רֵיקָן בַּתּוֹרָה שֶׁאִם תִּדְרְשֶׁנּוּ שֶׁאֵין בּוֹ מַתַּן שָׂכָר. תֵּדַע לְךָ, שֶׁכֵּן אָמְרוּ חֲכָמִים: "וַאֲחוֹת לוֹטָן תִּמְנָע" (בראשית לו, כב), "וְתִמְנַע הָיְתָה פִילֶגֶשׁ" וְגוֹ׳ (שם פסוק יב), לְפִי שֶׁאָמְרָה: אֵינִי כְּדַאי לִהְיוֹת לוֹ אִשָּׁה, הַלְוַאי וְאֶהְיֶה פִּילַגְשׁוֹ, וְכָל כָּךְ לָמָּה? לְהוֹדִיעַ שִׁבְחוֹ שֶׁל אַבְרָהָם, שֶׁהָיוּ שִׁלְטוֹנִים וּמְלָכִים מִתְאַוִּים לִדָּבֵק בְּזַרְעוֹ:

מח| **וַיְדַבֵּר ה׳ אֶל מֹשֶׁה בְּעֶצֶם הַיּוֹם הַזֶּה.** בִּשְׁלֹשָׁה מְקוֹמוֹת נֶאֱמַר "בְּעֶצֶם הַיּוֹם הַזֶּה": נֶאֱמַר בְּנֹחַ: "בְּעֶצֶם הַיּוֹם הַזֶּה בָּא נֹחַ" וְגוֹ׳ (בראשית ז, יג), בְּמַרְאִית אוֹרוֹ שֶׁל יוֹם; לְפִי שֶׁהָיוּ בְּנֵי דוֹרוֹ אוֹמְרִים, מִכָּךְ וְכָךְ, אִם אָנוּ מַרְגִּישִׁין בּוֹ אֵין אָנוּ מַנִּיחִין אוֹתוֹ לִכָּנֵס בַּתֵּבָה, וְלֹא עוֹד אֶלָּא אָנוּ נוֹטְלִין כַּשִּׁילִין וְקַרְדֻּמּוֹת וּמְבַקְּעִין אֶת הַתֵּבָה. אָמַר הַקָּדוֹשׁ בָּרוּךְ הוּא: הֲרֵינִי מַכְנִיסוֹ בַּחֲצִי הַיּוֹם, וְכָל מִי שֶׁיֵּשׁ בְּיָדוֹ כֹּחַ לִמְחוֹת יָבֹא וְיִמְחֶה. בְּמִצְרַיִם נֶאֱמַר: "בְּעֶצֶם הַיּוֹם הַזֶּה הוֹצִיא ה׳" (שמות יב, נא), לְפִי שֶׁהָיוּ מִצְרִיִּים אוֹמְרִים, מִכָּךְ וְכָךְ, אִם אָנוּ מַרְגִּישִׁין בָּהֶם אֵין אָנוּ מַנִּיחִין אוֹתָם לָצֵאת, וְלֹא עוֹד אֶלָּא אָנוּ נוֹטְלִין סַיָּפוֹת וּכְלֵי זַיִן וְהוֹרְגִין בָּהֶם. אָמַר הַקָּדוֹשׁ בָּרוּךְ הוּא: הֲרֵינִי מוֹצִיאָן בַּחֲצִי הַיּוֹם, וְכָל מִי שֶׁיֵּשׁ בּוֹ כֹּחַ לִמְחוֹת יָבֹא וְיִמְחֶה. אַף כָּאן בְּמִיתָתוֹ שֶׁל מֹשֶׁה נֶאֱמַר: "בְּעֶצֶם הַיּוֹם הַזֶּה", לְפִי שֶׁהָיוּ יִשְׂרָאֵל אוֹמְרִים, מִכָּךְ וְכָךְ, אִם אָנוּ מַרְגִּישִׁין בּוֹ אֵין אָנוּ מַנִּיחִין אוֹתוֹ, אָדָם שֶׁהוֹצִיאָנוּ מִמִּצְרַיִם, וְקָרַע לָנוּ אֶת הַיָּם, וְהוֹרִיד לָנוּ אֶת הַמָּן, וְהֵגִיז לָנוּ אֶת הַשְּׂלָו, וְהֶעֱלָה לָנוּ אֶת הַבְּאֵר, וְנָתַן לָנוּ אֶת הַתּוֹרָה, אֵין אָנוּ מַנִּיחִין אוֹתוֹ. אָמַר הַקָּדוֹשׁ בָּרוּךְ הוּא: הֲרֵינִי מַכְנִיסוֹ בַּחֲצִי הַיּוֹם וְכוּ׳:

die **as Aaron your brother died**[D] **on Hor Mountain, and he was gathered to his people.**

51 This is **because you trespassed against Me in the midst of the children of Israel at the waters of dispute of Kadesh, in the wilderness of Tzin; because you did not sanctify Me in the midst of the children of Israel.** You should have sanctified Me, but you failed to do so.[41] The punishment for this sin is not your death, which will come about because you have

completed your task in this world. The punishment is that after your extraordinary efforts to lead the children of Israel out of Egypt and through the struggles in the wilderness, you will not be privileged to enjoy the inheritance of the land.

52 **For from a distance you will see the land, but there you will not come, to the land that I am giving to the children of Israel.**

DISCUSSION

32:50 | As Aaron your brother died: By drawing a parallel to the death of Aaron, the verse indicates that Moses' death is a thematic continuation of the death of Aaron. This parallel also hints to a similarity in the manner of their deaths (see Numbers 20:23–29).

Even without the description of Aaron's death as portrayed by rabbinic tradition, it is clear that

his death was not due to natural causes, nor was it the typical experience of one who suffers before expiring. Aaron lay down to rest, ascended to God, and merged with the Divine. The Sages derive from the phrase "at the directive of the Lord [*al pi Hashem*]" (Numbers 33:38), which is mentioned with regard to Aaron's death, that he died from the kiss of death (see *Bava Batra* 17a),

whereby his soul united itself with its Maker. God informs Moses that he too will die in the same manner in which he witnessed Aaron die. His soul will cleave to its source, God, departing from his body without struggle, agitation, or crisis (see Rashi).

Parashat
Vezot HaBerakha

Moses Blesses the Tribes of Israel before His Death
DEUTERONOMY 33:1–29

Like Jacob's blessing to his sons, and to a certain extent the blessings of Abraham and Isaac to their sons, Moses' blessing to the people contains a combination of good wishes, blessings, and prophecies, both specific and general, which were to be fulfilled in the near or distant future. Because these blessings are prophetic, their significance goes beyond that of a standard blessing or spiritual testament that an individual gives before his death. Moreover, Moses is referred to in these blessings in the third person, which indicates that he was not expressing his personal thoughts but was transmitting the word of God.

Although the blessings focus primarily on each tribe individually, they are preceded and followed by statements addressed to the entire nation.

33 1 **This is the blessing that Moses, the man of God, blessed the children of Israel** with **before his death.**

2 Before addressing each tribe individually, Moses speaks to the entire nation and describes before them the most significant event in the Bible, and perhaps in history. **He said: The Lord came from Sinai, and shone from Se'ir for them,** Israel. The revelation at Sinai is described as an appearance of light emanating from several directions. **He appeared from Mount Paran, and He came from the holy myriads,** the angels.[1] The

verse may also mean that God appeared to them with a proliferation of holiness, or that He who is exalted above all holiness appeared from Mount Paran. **From His right** He brought **a fiery law to them.** This refers to the Torah, which was given in a fiery display and whose statements are like fire.[2]

3 **Indeed, He loves** all **the peoples** of the world.[3] Alternatively, He loves all the tribes of Israel.[4] Nevertheless, **all His holy ones,** the holy myriads above and the righteous individuals below, are kept **in Your hand; and they,** these holy ones, **fell at Your feet**

נא כַּאֲשֶׁר־מֵת אַהֲרֹן אָחִיךָ בְּהֹר הָהָר וַיֵּאָסֶף אֶל־עַמָּיו עַל אֲשֶׁר מְעַלְתֶּם בִּי בְּתוֹךְ בְּנֵי יִשְׂרָאֵל בְּמֵי־מְרִיבַת קָדֵשׁ מִדְבַּר־צִן עַל אֲשֶׁר לֹא־קִדַּשְׁתֶּם אוֹתִי בְּתוֹךְ בְּנֵי יִשְׂרָאֵל: **נב** כִּי מִנֶּגֶד תִּרְאֶה אֶת־הָאָרֶץ וְשָׁמָּה לֹא תָבוֹא אֶל־הָאָרֶץ אֲשֶׁר־אֲנִי נֹתֵן לִבְנֵי יִשְׂרָאֵל:

רש"י

נ] **כַּאֲשֶׁר מֵת אַהֲרֹן אָחִיךָ.** בְּאוֹתָהּ מִיתָה שֶׁרָאִיתָ וְחָמַדְתָּ אוֹתָהּ, שֶׁהִפְשִׁיט מֹשֶׁה אֶת אַהֲרֹן בֶּגֶד רִאשׁוֹן וְהִלְבִּישׁוֹ לְאֶלְעָזָר, וְכֵן שֵׁנִי, וְכֵן שְׁלִישִׁי, וְרָאָה בְּנוֹ בִּכְבוֹדוֹ. אָמַר לוֹ מֹשֶׁה: אַהֲרֹן אָחִי, עֲלֵה לַמִּטָּה, וְעָלָה. פְּשֹׁט יָדֶיךָ, וּפָשַׁט. פְּשֹׁט רַגְלֶיךָ, וּפָשַׁט. עֲצֹם עֵינֶיךָ, וְעָצַם. קְמֹץ פִּיךָ, וְקָמַץ. וְהָלַךְ לוֹ. אָמַר מֹשֶׁה: אַשְׁרֵי מִי שֶׁמֵּת בְּמִיתָה זוֹ:

נא] **עַל אֲשֶׁר מְרִיתֶם פִּי** (עַל פִּי בְּמִדְבַּר כ, כד; שָׁם כו). גְּרַמְתֶּם לַמְרוֹת פִּי: **עַל אֲשֶׁר לֹא קִדַּשְׁתֶּם אוֹתִי.** גְּרַמְתֶּם לִי שֶׁלֹּא אֶתְקַדֵּשׁ. אָמַרְתִּי לָכֶם: "וְדִבַּרְתֶּם אֶל הַסֶּלַע" (בְּמִדְבַּר כ, ח) וְהֵם הִכּוּהוּ, וְהֻצְרְכוּ לְהַכּוֹתוֹ פַּעֲמַיִם, וְאִלּוּ דִּבְּרוּ עִמּוֹ וְנָתַן מֵימָיו בְּלֹא הַכָּאָה, הָיָה מִתְקַדֵּשׁ שֵׁם שָׁמַיִם, שֶׁהָיוּ יִשְׂרָאֵל אוֹמְרִים: וּמַה הַסֶּלַע הַזֶּה שֶׁאֵינוֹ לְשָׂכָר וְלֹא לְפֻרְעָנוּת, אִם זָכָה אֵין לוֹ מַתַּן שָׂכָר וְאִם חָטָא אֵינוֹ לוֹקֶה, כָּךְ מְקַיֵּם מִצְוַת בּוֹרְאוֹ, אָנוּ לֹא כָל שֶׁכֵּן?:

נב] **כִּי מִנֶּגֶד.** מֵרָחוֹק: **תִּרְאֶה וְגוֹ'.** כִּי אִם לֹא תִרְאֶה עַכְשָׁיו, לֹא תִרְאֶנָּה עוֹד בְּחַיֶּיךָ: **וְשָׁמָּה לֹא תָבוֹא.** וְיָדַעְתִּי כִּי חֲבִיבָה הִיא לְךָ, עַל כֵּן אֲנִי אוֹמֵר לְךָ: "עֲלֵה... וּרְאֵה" (לְעֵיל פָּסוּק מט):

פרשת

וזאת הברכה

א וְזֹאת הַבְּרָכָה אֲשֶׁר בֵּרַךְ מֹשֶׁה אִישׁ הָאֱלֹהִים אֶת־בְּנֵי יִשְׂרָאֵל לִפְנֵי מוֹתוֹ: כז **ב** וַיֹּאמַר יְהוָה מִסִּינַי בָּא וְזָרַח מִשֵּׂעִיר לָמוֹ הוֹפִיעַ מֵהַר פָּארָן וְאָתָה מֵרִבְבֹת קֹדֶשׁ מִימִינוֹ אֵשׁ דָּת לָמוֹ: אַף חֹבֵב עַמִּים כָּל־קְדֹשָׁיו בְּיָדֶךָ וְהֵם תֻּכּוּ לְרַגְלֶךָ אֵשׁ דָּת

רש"י

פרק לג

א] **וְזֹאת הַבְּרָכָה. לִפְנֵי מוֹתוֹ.** סָמוּךְ לְמִיתָתוֹ, שֶׁאִם לֹא עַכְשָׁיו אֵימָתַי:

ב] **וַיֹּאמַר ה' מִסִּינַי בָּא.** פָּתַח תְּחִלָּה בְּשִׁבְחוֹ שֶׁל מָקוֹם וְאַחַר כָּךְ פָּתַח בְּצָרְכֵיהֶם שֶׁל יִשְׂרָאֵל, וּבַשֶּׁבַח שֶׁפָּתַח בּוֹ יֵשׁ בּוֹ הַזְכָּרַת זְכוּת לְיִשְׂרָאֵל, וְכָל זֶה דֶּרֶךְ רִצּוּי הוּא, כְּלוֹמַר כְּדַאי הֵם אֵלּוּ שֶׁתָּחוּל עֲלֵיהֶם בְּרָכָה: **מִסִּינַי בָּא.** יָצָא לִקְרָאתָם כְּשֶׁבָּאוּ לְהִתְיַצֵּב בְּתַחְתִּית הָהָר כְּחָתָן הַיּוֹצֵא לְהַקְבִּיל פְּנֵי כַלָּה, שֶׁנֶּאֱמַר: "לִקְרַאת הָאֱלֹהִים" (שְׁמוֹת יט, יז), לָמַדְנוּ שֶׁיָּצָא כְּנֶגְדָּם: **וְזָרַח מִשֵּׂעִיר לָמוֹ.** שֶׁפָּתַח לִבְנֵי עֵשָׂו שֶׁיְּקַבְּלוּ אֶת הַתּוֹרָה וְלֹא רָצוּ: **הוֹפִיעַ.** לָהֶם: **מֵהַר פָּארָן.** שֶׁהָלַךְ שָׁם וּפָתַח לִבְנֵי יִשְׁמָעֵאל שֶׁיְּקַבְּלוּהָ וְלֹא רָצוּ: **וְאָתָה.** לְיִשְׂרָאֵל: **מֵרִבְבֹת קֹדֶשׁ.** מִקְצָת רִבְבוֹת מַלְאֲכֵי קֹדֶשׁ, וְלֹא כֻלָּם וְלֹא רֻבָּם, וְלֹא כְּדֶרֶךְ בָּשָׂר וָדָם שֶׁמַּרְאֶה כָל כְּבוֹד עָשְׁרוֹ וְתִפְאַרְתּוֹ בְּיוֹם חֻפָּתוֹ: **אֵשׁ דָּת.** שֶׁהָיְתָה כְּתוּבָה מֵאָז לְפָנָיו בְּאֵשׁ שְׁחוֹרָה עַל גַּבֵּי אֵשׁ לְבָנָה, נָתַן לָהֶם בַּלּוּחוֹת כְּתָב יַד יְמִינוֹ. דָּבָר אַחֵר, "אֵשׁ דָּת", כְּתַרְגּוּמוֹ, שֶׁנִּתְּנָה לָהֶם מִתּוֹךְ הָאֵשׁ:

ג-ד] **אַף חֹבֵב עַמִּים.** גַּם חִבָּה יְתֵרָה חִבֵּב אֶת הַשְּׁבָטִים, כָּל אֶחָד וְאֶחָד קָרוּי "עַם", שֶׁהֲרֵי בִנְיָמִין לְבַדּוֹ הָיָה עָתִיד לְהִוָּלֵד כְּשֶׁאָמַר הַקָּדוֹשׁ בָּרוּךְ הוּא לְיַעֲקֹב: "גּוֹי וּקְהַל גּוֹיִם יִהְיֶה מִמֶּךָּ" (בְּרֵאשִׁית לה, יא): נַפְשׁוֹת הַצַּדִּיקִים גְּנוּזוֹת תַּחַת כִּסֵּא הַכָּבוֹד, כְּעִנְיָן שֶׁנֶּאֱמַר: "וְהָיְתָה נֶפֶשׁ אֲדֹנִי צְרוּרָה בִּצְרוֹר הַחַיִּים אֵת ה' אֱלֹהֶיךָ" (שְׁמוּאֵל א כה, כט): **וְהֵם תֻּכּוּ לְרַגְלֶךָ.** וְהֵם רְאוּיִים לְכָךְ, שֶׁהֲרֵי

in submission, **and** then **they received,** or accepted,[5] **Your sayings.**

4 The **Torah** that **Moses commanded us** is **a heritage of the assembly of Jacob.**[D] As these are words of prophecy, Moses speaks of himself in the third person.[6]

5 **He,** God, **became King in Yeshurun,** Israel, when He revealed Himself to them at Mount Sinai, **when the heads of the people were assembled,** and **the tribes of Israel** were assembled **together** with them. All of Israel was united and assembled in one spot.[7] Alternatively, some explain that the verse refers to ,Moses, the subject of the previous verse. Not only was Moses the teacher of Israel and its greatest prophet, he was also their leader and could therefore be described as their king. Moses was the only leader of Israel who ruled while all the tribes lived together, during the period of the wilderness.[8]

6 Moses proceeds to bless each tribe: **May** the tribe of **Reuben live and not die.** Although Reuben was the firstborn of Jacob, the tribe of Reuben was marginalized due to the sin of their progenitor,[9] and perhaps because no outstanding leaders emerged from the tribe. Moses therefore blessed this tribe with survival. This blessing may also be an allusion to the active participation of Reubenites in Korah's rebellion in the wilderness. In that affair, the descendants of Reuben demanded recognition of their firstborn status, and in its aftermath many of the tribe perished. Perhaps this blessing of life comes to replenish their ranks.[10] **And may his people be numerous.**[11]

7 **And this** is the blessing **for Judah, and he,** Moses, **said: Hear, Lord, the voice of Judah, and to his people bring him;**[D] **his hands are mighty for him, and You will be a helper against his adversaries.** Judah was a tribe of warriors and the vanguard of Israel.[12] Moses blessed them that they should return from battle unharmed.

8 **And of Levi**[D] he said: **Your Tumim and Your Urim,** the sys-

Second tem of holy namoteric matters in the breast piece of judgment,
aliya through which God communicated with His nation, are **for**

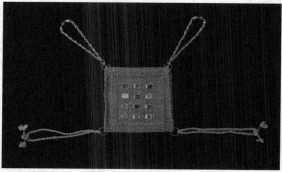

The breast piece

Your virtuous one, the High Priest. The first High Priest was Aaron, **whom You tested at Masa; You challenged him at the waters of Meriva.** Moses and Aaron were tested, and ultimately reproached and punished, at Masa and Meriva,[13] but this verse emphasizes that even after the reproach and punishment, Aaron remained God's pious one; he remained loyal to God and did not waver.

9 Whether following the incident of the Golden Calf or during other periods, the tribe of Levi served as a sort of royal guard for God.[14] The Levites fought zealously for the sake of Heaven, without regard for familial relationships: **Who said of his father, and of his mother: I did not see him; and his brothers he did not recognize, and his children he did not know.** Although none of the tribe of Levi participated in the sin, if a father or mother were among the sinners, they would not have afforded them special treatment, **because they observed Your saying, and Your covenant they upheld.**

10 In reward for their righteousness, **they,** the Levites, and in particular the priests, **shall teach Your ordinances to Jacob**[D] **and Your law to Israel.** For many generations, one of the responsibilities of the priests was to teach the Torah to Israel.[15]

DISCUSSION

33:4 | Torah Moses commanded us, a heritage of the congregation of Jacob: This well-known verse defines the relationship of Israel to the Torah. On the one hand, the Torah is the Torah of Moses, as it was transmitted to Israel through him. On the other hand, it is the inheritance of the entire congregation of Jacob. The

Sages teach that this should be the first verse that a father teaches his child when he begins to speak, thereby beginning to fulfill the commandment: "You shall inculcate them in your children" (6:7; see *Sukka* 42a).

33:7 | Hear, Lord, the voice of Judah, and to his people bring him: Judah's isolation from

the other tribes began long before the kingdom of Israel was divided; it originated when the Land of Israel was first partitioned among the tribes (see Judges 1; I Samuel 11:8). The tribe of Judah was therefore blessed that it should remain unified with the rest of the nation (see Ezekiel 23:2–4, 37:15–25).

ד ה יִשָּׂא מִדַּבְּרֹתֶיךָ: תּוֹרָה צִוָּה־לָנוּ מֹשֶׁה מוֹרָשָׁה קְהִלַּת יַעֲקֹב: וַיְהִי בִישֻׁרוּן
ו מֶלֶךְ בְּהִתְאַסֵּף רָאשֵׁי עָם יַחַד שִׁבְטֵי יִשְׂרָאֵל: יְחִי רְאוּבֵן וְאַל־יָמֹת וִיהִי מְתָיו
ז מִסְפָּר: וְזֹאת לִיהוּדָה וַיֹּאמַר שְׁמַע יהוה קוֹל יְהוּדָה וְאֶל־עַמּוֹ
תְּבִיאֶנּוּ יָדָיו רָב לוֹ וְעֵזֶר מִצָּרָיו תִּהְיֶה:
ח וּלְלֵוִי אָמַר תֻּמֶּיךָ וְאוּרֶיךָ לְאִישׁ חֲסִידֶךָ אֲשֶׁר נִסִּיתוֹ בְּמַסָּה תְּרִיבֵהוּ עַל־מֵי שני
ט מְרִיבָה: הָאֹמֵר לְאָבִיו וּלְאִמּוֹ לֹא רְאִיתִיו וְאֶת־אֶחָיו לֹא הִכִּיר וְאֶת־בָּנָו לֹא יָדָע
י כִּי שָׁמְרוּ אִמְרָתֶךָ וּבְרִיתְךָ יִנְצֹרוּ: יוֹרוּ מִשְׁפָּטֶיךָ לְיַעֲקֹב וְתוֹרָתְךָ לְיִשְׂרָאֵל יָשִׂימוּ

רש״י

תּוֹכוּ עַצְמָם לְתוֹךְ תַּחְתִּית הָהָר לְרַגְלֶיךָ בְּסִינַי. ״תֻּכּוּ״ לְשׁוֹן פֻּעֲלוּ, הִתְוַכּוּ לְתוֹךְ מַרְגְּלוֹתֶיךָ: **יִשָּׂא מִדַּבְּרֹתֶיךָ.** נָשְׂאוּ עֲלֵיהֶם עֹל תּוֹרָתֶךָ: **מִדַּבְּרֹתֶיךָ.** הַמֵּ״ם בּוֹ קָרוֹב לַיְסוֹד, כְּמוֹ: ״וַיִּשְׁמַע אֶת הַקּוֹל מִדַּבֵּר אֵלָיו״ (במדבר ז, פט), ״וָאֶשְׁמַע אֶת מִדַּבֵּר אֵלָי״ (יחזקאל ב, ב), כְּמוֹ: מִתְדַּבֵּר אֵלַי, אַף זֶה ״מִדַּבְּרֹתֶיךָ״, מַה שֶּׁהָיִיתָ מְדַבֵּר לְהַשְׁמִיעֵנִי לֵאמֹר לָהֶם, טי״ש פורפלידור״ש בְּלַעַז. וְאוּנְקְלוֹס תִּרְגֵּם, שֶׁהָיוּ נוֹסְעִים עַל פִּי דְּבָרֶיךָ, וְהַמֵּ״ם בּוֹ שִׁמּוּשׁ, מְשַׁמֶּשֶׁת לְשׁוֹן ׳מִן׳. דָּבָר אַחֵר, ״אַף חֹבֵב עַמִּים״, אַף בִּשְׁעַת חִבָּתָן שֶׁל אֻמּוֹת הָעוֹלָם, שֶׁהֶרְאֵיתָ לָאֻמּוֹת פָּנִים שׂוֹחֲקוֹת וּמָסַרְתָּ אֶת יִשְׂרָאֵל בְּיָדָם, ״כָּל קְדֹשָׁיו בְּיָדֶךָ״, כָּל צַדִּיקֵיהֶם וְטוֹבֵיהֶם דָּבְקוּ בְךָ וְלֹא מָשׁוּ מֵאַחֲרֶיךָ וְאַתָּה שׁוֹמְרָם: **וְהֵם תֻּכּוּ לְרַגְלֶךָ.** מִתְמַצְּעִים וּמִתְכַּנְּסִים לְתַחַת צִלְּךָ: **יִשָּׂא מִדַּבְּרֹתֶיךָ.** מְקַבְּלִין גְּזֵרוֹתֶיךָ וְדָתוֹתֶיךָ בְּשִׂמְחָה, וְאֵלֶּה דִּבְרֵיהֶם: **תּוֹרָה.** אֲשֶׁר ״צִוָּה לָנוּ מֹשֶׁה, מוֹרָשָׁה״ הִיא לִקְהִלַּת יַעֲקֹב, אֲחַזְנוּהָ וְלֹא נַעַזְבֶנָּה:

ה| **וַיְהִי.** הַקָּדוֹשׁ בָּרוּךְ הוּא: **בִישֻׁרוּן מֶלֶךְ.** תָּמִיד עֹל מַלְכוּתוֹ עֲלֵיהֶם, בְּכָל הִתְאַסֵּף רָאשֵׁי חֶשְׁבּוֹן אֲסִיפָתָם: **רָאשֵׁי.** כְּמוֹ: ״כִּי תִשָּׂא אֶת רֹאשׁ״ (שמות ל, יב), רְאוּיִין אֵלּוּ שֶׁאֲבָרְכֵם. דָּבָר אַחֵר, ״בְּהִתְאַסֵּף״, בְּהִתְאַסְּפָם יַחַד בַּאֲגֻדָּה אַחַת וְשָׁלוֹם בֵּינֵיהֶם – הוּא מַלְכָּם, וְלֹא כְּשֶׁיֵּשׁ מַחְלֹקֶת בֵּינֵיהֶם:

ו| **יְחִי רְאוּבֵן.** בָּעוֹלָם הַזֶּה: **וְאַל יָמֹת.** לָעוֹלָם הַבָּא, שֶׁלֹּא יִזָּכֵר לוֹ מַעֲשֵׂה בִלְהָה: **וִיהִי מְתָיו מִסְפָּר.** נִמְנִין בְּמִנְיַן שְׁאָר אֶחָיו, דֻּגְמָא הִיא זוֹ, כְּעִנְיָן שֶׁנֶּאֱמַר: ״וַיִּשְׁכַּב אֶת בִּלְהָה... וַיִּהְיוּ בְנֵי יַעֲקֹב שְׁנֵים עָשָׂר״ (בראשית לה, כב), שֶׁלֹּא יָצָא מִן הַמִּנְיָן:

ז| **וְזֹאת לִיהוּדָה.** סָמַךְ יְהוּדָה לִרְאוּבֵן מִפְּנֵי שֶׁשְּׁנֵיהֶם הוֹדוּ עַל קִלְקוּל שֶׁבְּיָדָם, שֶׁנֶּאֱמַר: ״אֲשֶׁר חֲכָמִים יַגִּידוּ וְגוֹ׳ לָהֶם לְבַדָּם נִתְּנָה הָאָרֶץ וְלֹא עָבַר זָר בְּתוֹכָם״ (איוב טו, יח-יט). וְעוֹד פֵּרְשׁוּ רַבּוֹתֵינוּ: כָּל אַרְבָּעִים שָׁנָה שֶׁהָיוּ יִשְׂרָאֵל בַּמִּדְבָּר, הָיוּ עַצְמוֹת יְהוּדָה מִתְגַּלְגְּלִין בָּאָרוֹן מִפְּנֵי נִדּוּי שֶׁקִּבֵּל עָלָיו, שֶׁנֶּאֱמַר: ״וְחָטָאתִי לְאָבִי כָּל הַיָּמִים״ (בראשית מד, לב), אָמַר מֹשֶׁה: מִי גָּרַם לִרְאוּבֵן שֶׁיּוֹדֶה? יְהוּדָה וְכוּ׳: **שְׁמַע ה׳ קוֹל יְהוּדָה.** תְּפִלַּת דָּוִד וּשְׁלֹמֹה, וְאָסָא מִפְּנֵי הַכּוּשִׁים, וִיהוֹשָׁפָט מִפְּנֵי הָעַמּוֹנִים, וְחִזְקִיָּה מִפְּנֵי סַנְחֵרִיב: **וְאֶל עַמּוֹ תְּבִיאֶנּוּ.** לְשָׁלוֹם מִפְּנֵי הַמִּלְחָמָה: **יָדָיו רָב לוֹ.** יָרִיבוּ רִיבוֹ וְיִנְקְמוּ נִקְמָתוֹ: **וְעֵזֶר מִצָּרָיו תִּהְיֶה.** עַל יְהוֹשָׁפָט נִתְפַּלֵּל, עַל מִלְחֶמֶת רָמוֹת גִּלְעָד, ״וַיִּזְעַק יְהוֹשָׁפָט וַה׳ עֲזָרוֹ״ (דברי הימים ב׳ יח, לא). דָּבָר אַחֵר, ״שְׁמַע ה׳ קוֹל יְהוּדָה״, כָּאן רָמַז בְּרָכָה לְשִׁמְעוֹן מִתּוֹךְ בִּרְכוֹתָיו שֶׁל יְהוּדָה, וְאַף כְּשֶׁחָלְקוּ אֶרֶץ יִשְׂרָאֵל נָטַל שִׁמְעוֹן מִתּוֹךְ גּוֹרָלוֹ שֶׁל יְהוּדָה, שֶׁנֶּאֱמַר: ״מֵחֶבֶל בְּנֵי יְהוּדָה נַחֲלַת בְּנֵי שִׁמְעוֹן״ (יהושע יט, ט):

ח| **וּלְלֵוִי אָמַר.** וְעַל לֵוִי אָמַר: **תֻּמֶּיךָ וְאוּרֶיךָ.** כְּלַפֵּי שְׁכִינָה הוּא מְדַבֵּר: **אֲשֶׁר נִסִּיתוֹ בְּמַסָּה.** שֶׁלֹּא נִתְלוֹנְנוּ עִם שְׁאָר הַמִּתְלוֹנְנִים: **תְּרִיבֵהוּ וְגוֹ׳.** כְּתַרְגּוּמוֹ. ״תְּרִיבֵהוּ עַל מֵי מְרִיבָה״, נִסְתַּקַּפְתָּ לוֹ לָבֹא בַּעֲלִילָה, אִם מֹשֶׁה אָמַר: ״שִׁמְעוּ נָא הַמֹּרִים״ (במדבר כ, י), אַהֲרֹן וּמִרְיָם מֶה עָשׂוּ?:

ט| **הָאֹמֵר לְאָבִיו וּלְאִמּוֹ לֹא רְאִיתִיו.** כְּשֶׁחָטְאוּ בָּעֵגֶל וְאָמַרְתִּי: ״מִי לַה׳ אֵלָי״ (שמות לב, כו) נֶאֶסְפוּ אֵלַי כָּל בְּנֵי לֵוִי, וְצִוִּיתִים לַהֲרֹג אֶת אֲבִי אִמּוֹ וְהוּא מִיִּשְׂרָאֵל אוֹ אֶת אָחִיו מֵאִמּוֹ אוֹ בֶּן בִּתּוֹ, וְכֵן עָשׂוּ. וְאִי אֶפְשָׁר לְפָרֵשׁ אָבִיו מַמָּשׁ, וְאָחִיו מֵאָבִיו, וְכֵן בָּנָיו מַמָּשׁ, שֶׁהֲרֵי לְוִיִּם הֵם, וּמִשֵּׁבֶט לֵוִי לֹא חָטָא אֶחָד מֵהֶם, שֶׁנֶּאֱמַר: ״כָּל בְּנֵי לֵוִי״ (שם): **כִּי שָׁמְרוּ אִמְרָתֶךָ.** ״לֹא יִהְיֶה לְךָ אֱלֹהִים אֲחֵרִים״ (שמות כ, ג): **וּבְרִיתְךָ יִנְצֹרוּ.** בְּרִית מִילָה, שֶׁאוֹתָם שֶׁנּוֹלְדוּ בַּמִּדְבָּר, שֶׁל יִשְׂרָאֵל לֹא מָלוּ אֶת בְּנֵיהֶם, וְהֵם הָיוּ מוֹלִין וּמָלִין אֶת בְּנֵיהֶם:

י| **יוֹרוּ מִשְׁפָּטֶיךָ.** רְאוּיִין אֵלּוּ לְכָךְ: **וְכָלִיל.** עוֹלָה:

DISCUSSION

33:8| **Simeon and Levi:** Moses' blessing served as a type of rectification for Jacob's rebuke of Simeon and Levi (Genesis 49:5–7). The tribe of Simeon is not mentioned explicitly in the verse, as it remained a small tribe following its involvement in the sin with the Midyanite women at Shitim and its resultant punishment (Numbers 25:1–15; see Jerusalem Talmud, *Sota* 7:4; Radak, Ezekiel 20:26). Nevertheless, some consider the phrase "Hear [*shema*], Lord, the voice of Judah" (33:7) as an allusion to Simeon, whose portion in Israel was absorbed into the portion of Judah (see *Midrash Tanna'im*; Rashi, verse 7). Levi, on the other hand, merited a long blessing, as it was rehabilitated and became an important tribe, devoted to the service of God.

33:10| **They shall teach Your ordinances to Jacob:** Some claim that throughout the generations, there has always been a disproportionate number of priests among the great Torah scholars. The Talmud states that a Sage who rules on

In addition to their lay duty as teachers, **they shall place incense before You, and** sacrifice **entire offerings,** burnt offerings, **on Your altar.**

11 **Bless, Lord, his might, and the work of his hands** in the Temple service **accept. Crush the loins of those who rise against him,**[D] **and his enemies,** prevent them **from rising.**[16]

12 **Of Benjamin he said:**[D] Benjamin is **the beloved, the Lord will dwell in safety with him,** as he is loyal to God. **He,** God, rests His presence over Benjamin and **hovers over him all the day, and He rests between his shoulders.**[D] This is a prophetic allusion to the time when the Temple would be built in Benjamin's portion of the land, as Jerusalem was in the portion of Benjamin more so than any other tribe. Additionally, the Temple Mount is not the highest mountain in its area, as the Mount of Olives, Mount Scopus, and Mount Zion are all higher; it is therefore referred to as between the shoulders.[17]

13 **And of Joseph he said:**[D] **Blessed of the Lord is his land;** it is

Third aliya

blessed from above, **from the sweetness of heaven, from dew, and** from below, **from** the groundwater of **the depths lying below;** Joseph's land will abound with water from above and from below;

14 **and from the sweetness of the crops of the sun,** that ripen in the sun, **and from the sweetness of the yield of the moons,** the new fruit that grow every month, by the moon so to speak, each species in its season;[18]

15 **and** the blessing will come **from the tops of the ancient mountains, and from the sweetness of the eternal hills.** Not only will the blessing come from heaven and the depths, from the sun and the moon, but it will also come from the fertile land in Joseph's portion, which included mountains and hills. According to *Sifrei,* the mountains and hills are an allusion to the patriarchs and matriarchs, who are also a source of Joseph's blessing.

The incense altar

16 **And from the sweetness of the earth and its fullness, and the will** and love **of He who rested in the bush** [*seneh*]. Moses refers to God in this manner because God first revealed Himself to Moses at the burning bush.[19] Ibn Ezra interprets the word *seneh* as a reference to heaven. **It,** this blessing, **shall come upon the head of Joseph, and upon the top of the head of the crowned of his brothers.**

17 **A firstborn bull is his majesty.** Joseph is likened to a majestic firstborn bull, as Joseph was his mother's firstborn son and because Reuben's rights of primogeniture were transferred to him. The bull, which became the symbol of the tribe of Joseph for better and for worse, represents the power of the tribe of Joseph.[20] **And his horns are the horns of** the aurochs [*re'em*], an extinct species of wild ox, or a large, ancient, mythical creature.[21] This animal symbolizes Joseph's splendor.[22] **With them,** these horns, figuratively speaking, **he will gore the peoples together,** even nations that live **at the ends of the earth. And** among the tribe of Joseph, **they are the myriads of Ephraim, and they are the thousands of Manasseh.** Two tribes emerged from Joseph, Manasseh, and Ephraim. Although there were periods when Manasseh was a larger tribe than Ephraim, Ephraim was considered the senior tribe. Therefore, myriads are attributed to Ephraim, whereas thousands are attributed to Manasseh.[23] The verse reflects the internal division of these tribes: The children of Manasseh were divided into units of thousands, while Ephraim was divided into tens of thousands.

Aurochs

18 **And of Zebulun he said: Rejoice, Zebulun, in your departure** for maritime commerce.[24] Moses prophesied that

Fourth aliya

Zebulun's portion of the land would be on the coast, as did Jacob in his blessing: "Zebulun shall dwell at the shore of seas, and he shall be a harbor for ships, and his border will be upon Sidon."[25] **And** rejoice, **Issachar, in your tents.**[D] The tribe of Issachar did not travel much; they remained on their land and engaged in farming.[26] The tents of Issachar also allude to the many prominent scholars that emerged from the tribe.[27]

DISCUSSION

Jewish law for the masses is presumed to be affiliated in some way with the tribe of Levi (see *Yoma* 26a).

33:11 | Crush the loins of those who rise against him: Some see this blessing as an

allusion to the period of the Hasmoneans, when the priests also filled a military role (see Rashi).

33:12 | Of Benjamin he said: The blessing of Benjamin is unique in that it is the only one that begins without the letter *vav,* which generally

indicates that it is a continuation of the preceding verse. Therefore, it is as though Benjamin's blessing is the first one (see Rabbeinu Baḥya).

And He rests between his shoulders [*keteifav*]: In general, many sections of Benjamin's

↩

יא קְטוֹרָה בְּאַפֶּךָ וְכָלִיל עַל־מִזְבְּחֶךָ: בָּרֵךְ יְהוָה חֵילוֹ וּפֹעַל יָדָיו תִּרְצֶה מְחַץ מָתְנַיִם
יב קָמָיו וּמְשַׂנְאָיו מִן־יְקוּמוּן: לְבִנְיָמִן אָמַר יְדִיד יְהוָה יִשְׁכֹּן לָבֶטַח
יג עָלָיו חֹפֵף עָלָיו כָּל־הַיּוֹם וּבֵין כְּתֵפָיו שָׁכֵן: וּלְיוֹסֵף אָמַר מְבֹרֶכֶת יְהוָה שלישי
יד אַרְצוֹ מִמֶּגֶד שָׁמַיִם מִטָּל וּמִתְּהוֹם רֹבֶצֶת תָּחַת: וּמִמֶּגֶד תְּבוּאֹת שָׁמֶשׁ וּמִמֶּגֶד
טו טז גֶּרֶשׁ יְרָחִים: וּמֵרֹאשׁ הַרְרֵי־קֶדֶם וּמִמֶּגֶד גִּבְעוֹת עוֹלָם: וּמִמֶּגֶד אֶרֶץ וּמְלֹאָהּ
יז וּרְצוֹן שֹׁכְנִי סְנֶה תָּבוֹאתָה לְרֹאשׁ יוֹסֵף וּלְקָדְקֹד נְזִיר אֶחָיו: בְּכוֹר שׁוֹרוֹ הָדָר לוֹ
וְקַרְנֵי רְאֵם קַרְנָיו בָּהֶם עַמִּים יְנַגַּח יַחְדָּו אַפְסֵי־אָרֶץ וְהֵם רִבְבוֹת אֶפְרַיִם וְהֵם
יח אַלְפֵי מְנַשֶּׁה: וְלִזְבוּלֻן אָמַר שְׂמַח זְבוּלֻן בְּצֵאתֶךָ וְיִשָּׂשכָר בְּאֹהָלֶיךָ: רביעי

רש"י

יא | **מחץ מתנים קמיו.** מחץ קמיו מכת מתנים, כענין שנאמר: "ומתניהם תמיד המעד" (תהלים סט, כד), ועל המעוררין על הכהנה אמר כן. דבר אחר, ראה שעתידין חשמונאי ובניו להלחם עם היונים, ונתפלל עליהם לפי שהיו מועטים, שנים עשר בני חשמונאי ואלעזר כנגד כמה רבבות, לכך נאמר: "ברך ה' חילו ופעל ידיו תרצה": **ומשנאיו מן יקומון.** מחץ קמיו ומשנאיו מהיות להם תקומה:

יב | **לבנימן אמר.** לפי שברכת לוי בעבודת הקרבנות ושל בנימין בבנין בית המקדש בחלקו, סמכן זה לזה, וסמך יוסף אחריו, שאף הוא משכן שילה היה בנוי בחלקו, שנאמר: "וימאס באהל יוסף" וגו' (תהלים עח, סז). ולפי שבית עולמים חביב משילה, לכך הקדים בנימין ליוסף: **חפף עליו.** מכסה אותו ומגן עליו: **כל היום.** לעולם, משנבחרה ירושלים לא שרתה שכינה במקום אחר: **ובין כתפיו שכן.** בגבה ארצו היה בית המקדש בנוי, אלא שנמוך עשרים ושלש אמה מעין עיטם, ושם היה דעתו של דוד לבנותו, כדאיתא בשחיטת קדשים (זבחים נד ע"ב): אמרי נחתי ביה פורתא משום דכתיב: "ובין כתפיו שכן", אין לך נאה בשור יותר מכתפיו:

יג | **מברכת ה' ארצו.** שלא היתה בנחלת השבטים ארץ מלאה כל טוב כארצו של יוסף: **ממגד.** לשון עדנים ומתק: **ומתהום.** שהתהום עולה ומלחלח אותה מלמטה. אתה מוצא בכל השבטים ברכתו של משה מעין ברכתו של יעקב:

יד | **וממגד תבואת שמש.** שהיתה ארצו פתוחה לחמה וממתקת הפרות: **גרש ירחים.** יש פרות שהלבנה מבשלתן, ואלו הן קשואין ודלועין. דבר אחר, "גרש ירחים", שהארץ מגרשת ומוציאה מחדש לחדש:

טו | **ומראש הררי קדם.** ומברכת מראשית בשול הפרות, שהרריה מקדימין לבכר בשול פרותיהם. דבר אחר, מגיד שקדמה בריאתן לשאר הרים: **גבעות עולם.** גבעות העושות פרות לעולם ואינן פוסקות מעצר הגשמים:

טז | **ורצון שכני סנה.** כמו: 'שוכן סנה', ותהא ארצו מברכת מרצונו ונחת רוחו של הקדוש ברוך הוא הנגלה עלי תחלה בסנה: **רצון.** נחת רוח ופיוס, וכן כל 'רצון' שבמקרא: **תבואתה.** ברכה זו "לראש יוסף": **נזיר אחיו.** שהפרש מאחיו במכירתו:

יז | **בכור שורו.** יש בכור שהוא לשון גדלה ומלכות, שנאמר: "אף אני בכור אתנהו" (תהלים פט, כח), וכן: "בני בכרי ישראל" (שמות ד, כב): **בכור.** מלך היוצא ממנו, והוא יהושע: **שורו.** שכחו קשה כשור לכבש כמה מלכים: **הדר לו.** נתון לו, שנאמר: "ונתתה מהודך עליו" (במדבר כז, כ): **וקרני ראם קרניו.** שור – כחו קשה ואין קרניו נאות, ראם – קרניו נאות ואין כחו קשה, נתן ליהושע כחו של שור ויפי קרני ראם: **אפסי ארץ.** שלשים ואחד מלכים, אפשר שכלם מארץ ישראל היו? אלא אין לך כל מלך ושלטון שלא קנה לו פלטרין ואחזה בארץ ישראל, שחשובה לכלם היא, שנאמר: "נחלת צבי צבאות גוים" (ירמיה ג, יט): **והם רבבות אפרים.** אותם המנגחים הם הרבבות שהרג יהושע שבא מאפרים: **והם אלפי מנשה.** הם האלפים שהרג גדעון במדין, שנאמר: "וזבח וצלמנע בקרקר" וגו' (שופטים ח, י):

יח-יט | **ולזבולן אמר.** אלו חמשה שבטים שברך באחרונה: זבולן גד דן ונפתלי ואשר, כפל שמותיהם לחזקם ולהגבירם, לפי שהיו חלשים שבכל השבטים, הם הם שהוליך יוסף לפני פרעה, שנאמר: "ומקצה אחיו לקח חמשה אנשים" (בראשית מז, ב), לפי שנראים חלשים ולא ישים אותם לו שרי מלחמתו: **שמח זבולן בצאתך ויששכר באהליך.** זבולון ויששכר עשו שתפות, זבולון יושב לחוף ימים ויוצא לפרקמטיא בספינות ומשתכר, ונותן לתוך פיו של יששכר, והם יושבים ועוסקים בתורה. לפיכך הקדים זבולון ליששכר, שתורתו של יששכר על

DISCUSSION

→ portion were considered to be between shoulders, that is, bordered by conspicuous hills, each referred to as *ketef* (see Joshua 15:10, 18:11–19).

33:13| **Of Joseph he said:** For various reasons, Joseph, Rachel's firstborn son, became one of the most prominent tribes. Therefore, the tribe received an especially long blessing. Over the years, the tribe of Joseph had a very large population, and most of the rulers of the Kingdom of Israel were descendants of Joseph. In the Bible, Israel as a whole was called after the tribe of Joseph, e.g., the house of Joseph, the remnant of Joseph (see II Samuel 19:21, and Ralbag ad loc.; Amos 5:15).

33:18| **Rejoice Zebulun in your departure and Issachar in your tents:** The Midrash describes an arrangement between Zebulun and Issachar whereby the tribe of Zebulun would travel for commerce and provide financial support to the tribe of Issachar, who would sit and engage in Torah study (see *Targum Yonatan*; Rashi; *Bereshit Rabba* 72:5).

19 Over the course of their travels and interactions with other nations, **they, the children of Zebulun, will call** other **peoples** to come **to the mountain** of God; **there shall they,** the other nations, **slaughter offerings of righteousness.** Contact with the tribe of Zebulun will cause the other nations to admire the God of Israel and His worship.²⁸ Indeed, the Bible records examples of peoples that believed in the God of Israel, some as a result of influence by Israelites.²⁹ **Because they,** the children of Zebulun, **will be nourished by the bounty of** fish and commerce by way of **the seas, and** they will also uncover **the hidden treasures of the sand,** pearls and jewels.³⁰

20 **And of Gad he said: Blessed is He who expands** the land of **Gad** east of the Jordan River. **Like a lion he rests,** confident in his power, **and mauls the arm, even the top of the head.** Like a lion that breaks the leg and head of its prey in one fell swoop, Gad will be a celebrated tribe of warriors capable of striking the enemy's arm and head with one swipe of the sword.³¹

21 **He saw the first** region that Israel conquered, east of the Jordan River, and chose it **for himself, as there the** burial **plot of the lawgiver,** Moses, **is hidden.**³² This too is a prophetic statement. Although the precise location of Moses' resting place is unknown, it is certain that he was buried in the portion of Gad east of the Jordan River (34:6). **He brings the heads of the people** of Israel to the land of Canaan, as he will serve as the vanguard in Israel's conquest of the land.³³ **He** thereby **performed the righteousness of the Lord and His ordinances with Israel.**³⁴

22 **And of Dan he said: Dan is a lion cub that leaps from the Bashan.** The Bashan was not originally included in Dan's portion of the land. Only after Dan felt congested in its original portion west of Judah on the coast of the Mediterranean Sea, it found an alternative tribal land near the Bashan.³⁵

Fifth aliya

Lion cub

23 **And of Naphtali he said: Naphtali, his desire is satisfied,** because his land is fertile **and full with the blessing of the Lord; he will take possession of the sea and south.** Naphtali's portion would border the Sea of Galilee, and its southern edge would include the Valley of Beit She'an.³⁶

24 **And of Asher he said: Blessed of** many **sons is Asher.**³⁷ **He will be the beloved of his brothers, and he dips his foot in oil.** The largest olive orchards in the Land of Israel are in the portion of Asher in the Galilee.³⁸

25 After blessing each tribe with the exception of the tribe of Simeon, Moses addresses the entire nation of Israel.³⁹ Alternatively, this verse is addressed specifically to the tribe of Asher: **Iron and copper** will be **your padlocks** [*minalekha*]. Your land will be safe, as if protected by barriers of iron and copper. Another interpretation: You will be able to rely on the mines containing these metals and on the tools fashioned from them, as one relies on sturdy shoes [*na'alayyim*] that enable one to walk safely.⁴⁰ **And like your days shall be your flow.** All your days an abundance of prosperity will flow to you.⁴¹

יט עמים הר־יקראו שם יזבחו זבחי־צדק כי שפע ימים יינקו ושפני טמוני
כ חול: ולגד אמר ברוך מרחיב גד כלביא שכן וטרף זרוע
כא אף־קדקד: וירא ראשית לו כי־שם חלקת מחקק ספון ויתא ראשי עם
כב צדקת יהוה עשה ומשפטיו עם־ישראל: ולדן אמר דן חמישי
כג גור אריה יזנק מן־הבשן: ולנפתלי אמר נפתלי שבע רצון ומלא ברכת
כד יהוה ים ודרום ירשה: ולאשר אמר ברוך מבנים אשר
כה יהי רצוי אחיו וטבל בשמן רגלו: ברזל ונחשת מנעלך וכימיך דבאך:

רש״י

ידי זבולון היתה: **שמח זבולן בצאתך.** הצלח בצאתך לסחורה: **ויששכר.** הצלח בישיבת אהליך לתורה, לישב ולעבר שנים ולקבע חדשים, כמו שנאמר: "ומבני יששכר יודעי בינה לעתים... ראשיהם מאתים" (דברי הימים א' יב, לג), ראשי סנהדרין היו עוסקים בכך. ועל פי קביעת עתיהם ועבוריהם, "עמים" של שבטי ישראל "הר יקראו" – להר המוריה יאספו. כל אספה על ידי קריאה היא, "ושם יזבחו" ברגלים "זבחי צדק": **כי שפע ימים יינקו.** יששכר וזבולון, ויהא להם פנאי לעסק בתורה: **ושפני טמוני חול.** כסויי טמוני חול, טרית וחלזון וזכוכית לבנה היוצאים מן הים ומן החול, ובחלקו של זבולון היה, כמו שאמור במסכת מגלה (דף ו ע"א): "זבלון עם חרף נפשו למות" (שופטים ה, יח) משום ד"נפתלי על מרומי שדה" (שם), היה מתרעם זבולון על חלקו, לאחי נתת שדות וכרמים וכו': **ושפני.** לשון כסוי, כמו שנאמר: "ויספן את הבית" (מלכים א' ו, ט), "וספון בארז" (ירמיה כב, יד), ותרגומו: "ומטלל בכיורי ארזיא". דבר אחר, "עמים הר יקראו", על ידי פרקמטיא של זבולון, תגרי אמות העולם באים אל ארצו, והיא עומדת על הספר, והם אומרים: הואיל ונצטערנו עד כאן נלך עד ירושלים ונראה מה יראתה של אמה זו ומה מעשיה, והם רואים כל ישראל עובדים לאלוה אחד ואוכלים מאכל אחד, לפי שהגוים אלהו של זה לא כאלהו של זה ומאכלו של זה לא כמאכלו של זה, והם אומרים: אין אמה כשרה כזו, ומתגיירין שם, שנאמר: "שם יזבחו זבחי צדק": **כי שפע ימים יינקו.** זבולון ויששכר, הים נותן להם ממון בשפע:

כ| **ברוך מרחיב גד.** מלמד שהיה תחומו של גד מרחיב והולך כלפי מזרח: **כלביא שכן.** לפי שהיה סמוך לספר לפיכך נמשל כאריות, שכל סמוכי ספר צריכים להיות גבורים: **וטרף זרוע אף קדקד.** הרוגיהם היו נכרים, חותכים הראש עם הזרוע במכה אחת:

כא| **וירא ראשית לו.** ראה לטל לו חלק בארץ סיחון ועוג שהיא ראשית כבוש הארץ: **כי שם חלקת.** כי ידע אשר שם בנחלתו חלקת שדה קבורת מחוקק, והוא משה: **ספון.** אותה חלקה ספונה וטמונה מכל בריה, שנאמר: "ולא ידע איש את קברתו" (להלן לד, ו): **ויתא.** גד: **ראשי עם.** הם היו הולכים לפני החלוץ בכבוש הארץ לפי שהיו גבורים, וכן הוא אומר: "חלוצים תעברו לפני אחיכם" וגו' (לעיל ג, יח): **צדקת ה' עשה.** שהאמינו דבריהם ושמרו הבטחתם לעבר את הירדן עד שכבשו וחלקו. דבר אחר, "ויתא" משה "ראשי עם". "צדקת ה' עשה" על משה אמור:

כב| **דן גור אריה.** אף הוא היה סמוך לספר, לפיכך מושלו באריות: **יזנק מן הבשן.** כתרגומו, שהיה הירדן יוצא מחלקו ממערת פמיאס, והיא לשם שהיא בחלקו של דן, שנאמר: "ויקראו ללשם דן" (יהושע יט, מז), וזנוקו וקלוחו מן הבשן. דבר אחר, מה זנוק זה יוצא ממקום אחד ונחלק לשני מקומות, כך שבטו של דן נטלו חלק בשני מקומות. תחלה נטלו בצפונית מערבית, עקרון וסביבותיה, ולא ספקו להם, ובאו ונלחמו עם לשם שהיא פמיאס, והיא בצפונית מזרחית, שהרי הירדן יוצא ממערת פמיאס והוא במזרחה של ארץ ישראל, ובא מהצפון לדרום, וכלה בקצה ים המלח שהוא במזרח יהודה שנטל בדרומה של ארץ ישראל, כמו שמפרש בספר יהושע, והוא שנאמר: "ויצא גבול בני דן מהם ויעלו בני דן וילחמו עם לשם" וגו' (יהושע שם), יצא גבולם מכל אותה הרוח שהתחילו לנחל בה:

כג| **שבע רצון.** שהיתה ארצו שבעה כל רצון יושביה: **ים ודרום ירשה.** ים כנרת נפל בחלקו, ונטל מלא חבל חרם בדרומה לפרש חרמים ומכמרות:

כד| **ברוך מבנים אשר.** ראיתי בספרי (שנה) אין לך בכל השבטים שנתברך בבנים כאשר. ואיני יודע כיצד: **יהי רצוי אחיו.** שהיה מתרצה לאחיו בשמן אנפיקינון. דבר אחר, "יהי רצוי אחיו", שהיו בנותיו נאות, והוא שנאמר בדברי הימים (א' ז, לא): "הוא אבי ברזית", שהיו בנותיו נשואות לכהנים גדולים ולמלכים הנמשחים בשמן זית: **וטבל בשמן רגלו.** שהיתה ארצו מושכת שמן כמעין. ומעשה שנצטרכו אנשי לודקיא לשמן, מנו להם פולמוסטוס אחד כו' [אמרו לו: לך והבא לנו שמן במאה ריבוא. הלך לירושלים, אמרו לו: לך לצור. הלך לצור, אמרו לו: לך לגוש חלב. הלך לגוש חלב, אמרו לו: לך אצל פלוני לשדה הלז, ומצאו שהיה עוזק תחת זיתיו. אמר לו: יש לך שמן במאה ריבוא שאני צריך? אמר לו: המתן לי עד שאסיים מלאכתי. המתין עד שסיים מלאכתו. לאחר שסיים מלאכתו, הפשיל כליו לאחוריו והיה מסקל ובא בדרך. אמר לו: יש לך שמן במאה ריבוא? כמדומה אני שצחוק שחקו בי היהודים. כיון שהגיע לעירו, הוציאה לו שפחתו קומקמוס של חמין ורחץ בו ידיו ורגליו, הוציאה לו ספל של זהב מלאה שמן וטבל בו ידיו ורגליו, לקיים מה שנאמר: "וטבל בשמן רגלו". לאחר שאכלו ושתו, מדד לו שמן במאה ריבוא. אמר לו: כלום אתה צריך ליותר? אמר לו: הן, אלא שאין לי דמים. אמר לו: אם אתה רוצה ליקח קח, ואני אלך עמך ואטול דמיו, מדד לו שמן בשמונה עשר ריבוא. אמרו: לא הניח אותו האיש לא סוס ולא פרד ולא גמל ולא חמור בארץ ישראל שלא שכרו. כיון שהגיע לעירו יצאו אנשי עירו לקלסו, אמר להם: לא לי קלסוני אלא לזה שבא עמי, שמדד לי שמן במאה ריבוא והרי נושה בי בשמונה עשרה ריבוא], כדאיתא במנחות (דף פה ע"ב):

כה| **ברזל ונחשת מנעלך.** עכשיו הוא מדבר כנגד כל ישראל, שהיו גבוריהם יושבים בערי הספר ונועלים אותה שלא יוכלו האויבים לכנס בה, כאלו היא סגורה במנעולים ובריחים של ברזל ונחשת. דבר אחר, "ברזל ונחשת מנעלך", ארצכם נעולה בהרים שחוצבין מהם ברזל ונחשת, וארצו של אשר היתה מנעולה של ארץ ישראל: **וכימיך דבאך.** וכימים שהם טובים לך, שהן ימי תחלתך, ימי נעוריך, כן יהיו ימי זקנותך שהם דואבים זבים ומתמוטטים. דבר אחר, "וכימיך דבאך", כמנין ימיך, כל הימים אשר אתם עושים רצונו של מקום, יהיו "דבאך", שכל הארצות יהיו דואבות כסף לארץ ישראל, שהיא מברכת בפרות וכל הארצות מתפרנסות הימנה, וממשיכות לה כספם וזהבם, אשקורנ"ט, הכסף כלה מהם שהן מזיבות אותו לארצכם:

26 **Yeshurun,** Israel, **there is none like God,**[42] or there is none like the God of Yeshurun,[43] **who rides the heavens** and is **in your assistance,** Israel; **and in His majesty,** He rules **the sky.**

27 **An abode is the God of eternity.**[44] A similar idea is expressed in Psalms (90:1): "Lord, You have been a dwelling place for us from generation to generation." **And below** the heavens, God carries all with **the eternal arms.**[45] **He banished the enemy from before you, and He said: Destroy** him.

Ḥatan Torah

28 A prophetic vision:[46] **Israel dwelled securely. Alone,** without needing others or being troubled by them, **is the spring of Jacob,** the descendants of Jacob,[47] when it comes **to a land of grain and wine. His heavens drip dew.**

29 **Happy are you, Israel, who is like you?** You are **a people saved by the Lord,** who is **the shield of your assistance, and Who is the sword of your honor. And your enemies will** therefore seek to **deceive you,** they will employ artifice in order to appease you. One of the signs of victory is that the defeated party seeks to appease the victor, and sometimes resorts to deceit to that end.[48] **And you will tread on their high places** and trample them.

The Death of Moses

DEUTERONOMY 34:1–12

The Torah of Moses ends with the death of its transmitter, the father of prophets, and with the transfer of leadership to his attendant, Joshua.

34 1 **Moses ascended from the plains of Moav to Mount Nevo, the top of the peak, that is opposite Jericho, and the Lord showed him**[D] **the entire land.** From the desolate area of Moav there was indeed a good view, but even if Mount Nevo was very high, it would be impossible for Moses to see the entire land from one end to the other end of Canaan with standard eyesight. Clearly, God granted Moses supernatural eyesight for this purpose.[49] God showed him **the Gilad** east of the Jordan River **until** the portion of the land's northern border that would later be known as **Dan.**[50]

2 **And** God also showed him **all of Naphtali,** which is also in the north, **and the land of Ephraim and Manasseh,** in Samaria and Carmel, **and the entire land of Judah until the last** [***aḥaron***] **sea,** the western sea, the Mediterranean Sea.[51] In the Bible, west is referred to as back [*aḥor*], while east is referred to as forward. As above, each region mentioned by the verse is identified according to the tribe that eventually settled there.

3 **And the South, and the Plain, the Valley of Jericho, city of the date palms, until Tzo'ar** on the bank of the Dead Sea. Moses' view of the land began at its most distant edge and continued to the area closest to him.

4 **The Lord said to him: This is the land with regard to which I took an oath to Abraham, to Isaac, and to Jacob, saying: To your descendants I will give it; I have shown it to you with your eyes, but there you will not cross.** So have I decreed.

5 **Moses servant of the Lord died there in the land of Moav, at the directive of the Lord,**[D] by God's command.

Jericho and the Plains of Moav as seen from the summit of Mount Nevo

Date-palm orchard in Jericho

DISCUSSION

34:1 | **And the Lord showed him:** According to the homiletic interpretation of the Sages, Moses' eyes were able to see not only these vast spaces but also future events that would take place in the land (see *Targum Yonatan*; Rashi, 34:1–3; *Sifrei, Vezot HaBerakha* 357).

34:5 | **At the directive of the Lord:** Translated literally, the verse means that Moses died by the mouth of God. According to the Midrash, this alludes to a type of death known as the kiss of death (see Rashi, Numbers 20:26; *Berakhot* 8a). Just as during Moses' lifetime, God spoke with him "mouth to mouth" (Numbers 12:8), so too,

כז אֵין כָּאֵל יְשֻׁרוּן רֹכֵב שָׁמַיִם בְּעֶזְרֶךָ וּבְגַאֲוָתוֹ שְׁחָקִים: מְעֹנָה אֱלֹהֵי קֶדֶם וּמִתַּחַת

כח זְרֹעֹת עוֹלָם וַיְגָרֶשׁ מִפָּנֶיךָ אוֹיֵב וַיֹּאמֶר הַשְׁמֵד: וַיִּשְׁכֹּן יִשְׂרָאֵל בֶּטַח בָּדָד עֵין

כט יַעֲקֹב אֶל־אֶרֶץ דָּגָן וְתִירוֹשׁ אַף־שָׁמָיו יַעַרְפוּ־טָל: אַשְׁרֶיךָ יִשְׂרָאֵל מִי כָמוֹךָ עַם נוֹשַׁע בַּיהוָה מָגֵן עֶזְרֶךָ וַאֲשֶׁר־חֶרֶב גַּאֲוָתֶךָ וְיִכָּחֲשׁוּ אֹיְבֶיךָ לָךְ וְאַתָּה עַל־

א בָּמוֹתֵימוֹ תִדְרֹךְ: וַיַּעַל מֹשֶׁה מֵעַרְבֹת מוֹאָב אֶל־הַר נְבוֹ רֹאשׁ הַפִּסְגָּה

ב אֲשֶׁר עַל־פְּנֵי יְרֵחוֹ וַיַּרְאֵהוּ יְהוָה אֶת־כָּל־הָאָרֶץ אֶת־הַגִּלְעָד עַד־דָּן: וְאֵת כָּל־

ג נַפְתָּלִי וְאֶת־אֶרֶץ אֶפְרַיִם וּמְנַשֶּׁה וְאֵת כָּל־אֶרֶץ יְהוּדָה עַד הַיָּם הָאַחֲרוֹן: וְאֶת־

ד הַנֶּגֶב וְאֶת־הַכִּכָּר בִּקְעַת יְרֵחוֹ עִיר הַתְּמָרִים עַד־צֹעַר: וַיֹּאמֶר יְהוָה אֵלָיו זֹאת הָאָרֶץ אֲשֶׁר נִשְׁבַּעְתִּי לְאַבְרָהָם לְיִצְחָק וּלְיַעֲקֹב לֵאמֹר לְזַרְעֲךָ אֶתְּנֶנָּה הֶרְאִיתִיךָ

ה בְעֵינֶיךָ וְשָׁמָּה לֹא תַעֲבֹר: וַיָּמָת שָׁם מֹשֶׁה עֶבֶד־יְהוָה בְּאֶרֶץ מוֹאָב עַל־פִּי יְהוָה:

רש"י

כו-כז] אֵין כָּאֵל יְשֻׁרוּן. דַּע לְךָ יְשֻׁרוּן, שֶׁאֵין כָּאֵל בְּכָל אֱלֹהֵי הָעַמִּים, וְלֹא כְּצוּרְךָ צוּרָם. **רֹכֵב שָׁמַיִם.** הוּא אוֹתוֹ אֱלוֹהַ שֶׁבְּעֶזְרֶךָ, **וּבְגַאֲוָתוֹ.** הוּא רוֹכֵב שְׁחָקִים: **מְעֹנָה אֱלֹהֵי קֶדֶם.** לְמָעוֹן הֵם הַשְּׁחָקִים לֵאלֹהֵי קֶדֶם, שֶׁקָּדַם לְכָל אֱלֹהִים, וּבֵרַר לוֹ שְׁחָקִים לְשִׁבְתּוֹ וּמְעוֹנָתוֹ, וּמִתַּחַת מְעוֹנָתוֹ כָּל בַּעֲלֵי זְרוֹעַ שׁוֹכְנִים: **זְרֹעֹת עוֹלָם.** סִיחוֹן וְעוֹג וּמַלְכֵי כְנַעַן תֹּקֶף וּגְבוּרָתָן שֶׁל עוֹלָם, לְפִיכָךְ עַל כָּרְחָם יֶחֶרְדוּ וְיָזוּעוּ וְכֹחָם חָלָשׁ מִפְּנֶיךָ, כִּי לְעוֹלָם חִימַת הַגָּבֹהַּ עַל הַנָּמוּךְ. וְהוּא, שֶׁהַכֹּחַ וְהַגְּבוּרָה שֶׁלּוֹ בְּעֶזְרֶךָ, **וַיְגָרֶשׁ מִפָּנֶיךָ אוֹיֵב.** וַיֹּאמֶר לְךָ, **הַשְׁמֵד.** אוֹתָם: **מְעֹנָה.** כָּל תֵּבָה שֶׁצְּרִיכָה לָמֶ"ד בִּתְחִלָּתָהּ הֵטִיל לָהּ הֵ"א בְּסוֹפָהּ:

כח] בֶּטַח בָּדָד. כָּל יָחִיד וְיָחִיד אִישׁ תַּחַת גַּפְנוֹ, מְפֻזָּרִים, וְאֵין צְרִיכִין לְהִתְאַסֵּף וְלֵשֵׁב יַחַד מִפְּנֵי הָאוֹיֵב: **עֵין יַעֲקֹב.** כְּמוֹ "וְעֵינוֹ כְּעֵין הַבְּדֹלַח" (במדבר יא, ז). כְּעֵין הַבְּרָכָה שֶׁבֵּרְכָם יַעֲקֹב. לֹא כְּבָדָד שֶׁל יִרְמְיָה: "כִּי הָיָה שָׁבַעְתִּי" (ירמיה טו, יז), אֶלָּא כְּעֵין הַבְטָחָה שֶׁהִבְטִיחָם יַעֲקֹב: "וְהָיָה אֱלֹהִים עִמָּכֶם וְהֵשִׁיב אֶתְכֶם אֶל אֶרֶץ אֲבֹתֵיכֶם" (בראשית מח, כא): **יַעַרְפוּ.** יִטְּפוּ: **אַף שָׁמָיו יַעַרְפוּ טָל.** אַף בִּרְכָתוֹ שֶׁל יִצְחָק נוֹסֶפֶת עַל שֶׁל יַעֲקֹב: "וְיִתֶּן לְךָ הָאֱלֹהִים מִטַּל הַשָּׁמַיִם" וְגוֹ' (בראשית כז, כח):

כט] אַשְׁרֶיךָ יִשְׂרָאֵל. לְאַחַר שֶׁפֵּרֵט לָהֶם בְּרָכוֹת, אָמַר לָהֶם: מַה לִּי לִפְרֹט לָכֶם? כְּלָל דָּבָר, הַכֹּל שֶׁלָּכֶם: **אַשְׁרֶיךָ יִשְׂרָאֵל מִי כָמוֹךָ.** תְּשׁוּעָתְךָ בַּה' אֲשֶׁר הוּא "מָגֵן עֶזְרֶךָ" "וְחֶרֶב גַּאֲוָתֶךָ". **וְיִכָּחֲשׁוּ אֹיְבֶיךָ לָךְ.** כְּגוֹן הַגִּבְעוֹנִים, שֶׁאָמְרוּ: "מֵאֶרֶץ רְחוֹקָה... בָּאוּ עֲבָדֶיךָ" וְגוֹ' (יהושע ט, ט): **וְאַתָּה עַל בָּמוֹתֵימוֹ תִדְרֹךְ.** כָּעִנְיָן שֶׁנֶּאֱמַר: "שִׂימוּ אֶת רַגְלֵיכֶם עַל צַוְּארֵי הַמְּלָכִים הָאֵלֶּה" (יהושע י, כד):

פרק לד

א] מֵעַרְבֹת מוֹאָב אֶל הַר נְבוֹ. כַּמָּה מַעֲלוֹת הָיוּ, וּפְסָעָן מֹשֶׁה בִּפְסִיעָה אַחַת: **אֶת כָּל הָאָרֶץ.** הֶרְאָהוּ אֶת כָּל אֶרֶץ יִשְׂרָאֵל בְּשַׁלְוָתָהּ, וְהַמְּצִיקִין הָעֲתִידִין לִהְיוֹת מְצִיקִין לָהּ: **עַד דָּן.** הֶרְאָהוּ בְּנֵי דָן עוֹבְדֵי עֲבוֹדָה זָרָה, שֶׁנֶּאֱמַר: "וַיָּקִימוּ לָהֶם בְּנֵי דָן אֶת הַפָּסֶל" (שופטים יח, ל), וְהֶרְאָהוּ שִׁמְשׁוֹן שֶׁעָתִיד לָצֵאת מִמֶּנּוּ לְמוֹשִׁיעַ:

ב] וְאֵת כָּל נַפְתָּלִי. הֶרְאָהוּ אַרְצוֹ בְּשַׁלְוָתָהּ וְחֻרְבָּנָהּ, וְהֶרְאָהוּ דְּבוֹרָה וּבָרָק מִקֶּדֶשׁ נַפְתָּלִי נִלְחָמִים עִם סִיסְרָא וַחֲיָלוֹתָיו: **וְאֵת אֶרֶץ אֶפְרַיִם וּמְנַשֶּׁה.** הֶרְאָהוּ אַרְצָם בְּשַׁלְוָתָהּ וּבְחֻרְבָּנָהּ, וְהֶרְאָהוּ יְהוֹשֻׁעַ נִלְחָם עִם מַלְכֵי כְנַעַן, שֶׁבָּא מֵאֶפְרַיִם, וְגִדְעוֹן שֶׁבָּא מִמְּנַשֶּׁה נִלְחָם עִם מִדְיָן וַעֲמָלֵק: **וְאֵת כָּל אֶרֶץ יְהוּדָה.** בְּשַׁלְוָתָהּ וּבְחֻרְבָּנָהּ,

וְהֶרְאָהוּ מַלְכוּת בֵּית דָּוִד וְנִצְחוֹנָם: **עַד הַיָּם הָאַחֲרוֹן.** אֶרֶץ הַמַּעֲרָב בְּשַׁלְוָתָהּ וּבְחֻרְבָּנָהּ. דָּבָר אַחֵר, אַל תִּקְרֵי "הַיָּם הָאַחֲרוֹן" אֶלָּא "הַיּוֹם הָאַחֲרוֹן" – כָּל הַמְּאֹרָעוֹת שֶׁעֲתִידִין לִישְׂרָאֵל עַד שֶׁיִּחְיוּ הַמֵּתִים:

ג] וְאֵת הַנֶּגֶב. אֶרֶץ הַדָּרוֹם. דָּבָר אַחֵר, מְעָרַת הַמַּכְפֵּלָה, שֶׁנֶּאֱמַר: "וַיַּעֲלוּ בַנֶּגֶב וַיָּבֹא עַד חֶבְרוֹן" (במדבר יג, כב): **וְאֵת הַכִּכָּר.** הֶרְאָהוּ שְׁלֹמֹה יוֹצֵק כְּלֵי בֵית הַמִּקְדָּשׁ בְּכִכַּר הַיַּרְדֵּן בְּמַעֲבֵה הָאֲדָמָה:

ד] לֵאמֹר לְזַרְעֲךָ אֶתְּנֶנָּה הֶרְאִיתִיךָ. כְּדֵי שֶׁתֵּלֵךְ וְתֹאמַר לְאַבְרָהָם לְיִצְחָק וּלְיַעֲקֹב, שְׁבוּעָה שֶׁנִּשְׁבַּע לָכֶם הַקָּדוֹשׁ בָּרוּךְ הוּא – קִיַּמְתִּיהָ, וְזֶהוּ "לֵאמֹר", לְכָךְ הֶרְאִיתִיהָ לָךְ, אֲבָל גְּזֵרָה הִיא מִלְּפָנַי שֶׁשָּׁמָּה לֹא תַעֲבֹר, שֶׁאִלּוּלֵי כָךְ הָיִיתִי מְקַיֶּמְךָ עַד שֶׁתִּרְאֶה אוֹתָם נְטוּעִים וּקְבוּעִים בָּהּ וְתֵלֵךְ וְתַגֵּד לָהֶם:

ה] וַיָּמָת שָׁם. אֶפְשָׁר מֹשֶׁה מֵת וְכָתַב: "וַיָּמָת שָׁם"? אֶלָּא עַד כָּאן כָּתַב מֹשֶׁה, מִכָּאן וְאֵילָךְ כָּתַב יְהוֹשֻׁעַ. רַבִּי מֵאִיר אוֹמֵר: אֶפְשָׁר סֵפֶר הַתּוֹרָה חָסֵר כְּלוּם, וְהוּא אוֹמֵר: "לָקֹחַ אֵת סֵפֶר הַתּוֹרָה הַזֶּה" (לעיל לא, כו)? אֶלָּא הַקָּדוֹשׁ בָּרוּךְ הוּא אוֹמֵר וּמֹשֶׁה כוֹתֵב בְּדֶמַע. **עַל פִּי ה'.** בִּנְשִׁיקָה:

DISCUSSION

➡ God ended Moses' life with a kiss on the mouth, as it were. In this manner, Moses' soul left his body by cleaving to God. Rambam writes that Moses did not die the way other people die; rather, his soul ascended to its Creator (Introduction to Commentary on the Mishna).

6 **He buried him,** Moses buried himself, by entering the place where he would die,[52] or God buried Moses,[53] **in the canyon in the land of Moav opposite Beit Peor. And** despite the detailed description of the region and terrain in which Moses was buried, **no man knows** the precise location of **his grave**[D] **to this day.**

7 **Moses was one hundred and twenty years old upon his death.** His death was not due to infirmity or old age, as his health did not deteriorate as he aged. Unlike other elderly individuals, **his eye had not dimmed, and his** skin **vitality had not departed.** Moses was as physically healthy in his advanced age as he was in his younger years; he did not display any physical manifestations of aging.

8 **The children of Israel wept for Moses in the plains of Moav thirty days,** the customary period for mourning,[54] **and** thereafter, **the days of weeping of the mourning of Moses concluded.**

9 **Joshua son of Nun was** then **full of the spirit of wisdom.**[55] Alternatively, Joshua was already full of the spirit of wisdom, **as**

Moses had placed his hands upon him;[D] **and the children of Israel heeded him, and acted as the Lord had commanded Moses,** by accepting Joshua as their leader.

10 The Torah concludes with closing remarks about Moses, the central figure in the Torah: **There has not risen another prophet in Israel like Moses, whom the Lord knew face-to-face.** Unlike the other prophets, who received prophecy in obscurity and through symbols and forms, Moses was privileged to receive direct and open revelation.

11 Moses stood apart from all the other leaders and prophets of Israel in other aspects as well: **With all the signs and the wonders that the Lord sent him to perform in the land of Egypt, to Pharaoh, and to all his servants, and to all his land.** No one ever performed a series of miracles comparable to what Moses performed in Egypt.

12 **And with all the mighty hand,** both in times of war and in times of peace, **and with all the great awe,** the awe of God upon Moses and the awe of Moses upon Israel. These were all the phenomena **that Moses performed before the eyes of all Israel.**

DISCUSSION

34:6 | And no man knows his grave: The Sages teach that the burial place of Moses was a special creation created by God specifically to bury Moses (see *Avot* 5:6). His grave remains a mystery; no one can even visit it (see *Sota* 13b–14a).

34:9 | Moses had placed his hands upon him: Moses merited that his attendant, Joshua, whom he ordained, would continue his path. Although Moses did not complete the mission of bringing the children of Israel to their land, his work was completed by his loyal disciple.

א וַיִּקָּבֵ֨ר אֹת֤וֹ בַגַּי֙ בְּאֶ֣רֶץ מוֹאָ֔ב מ֖וּל בֵּ֣ית פְּע֑וֹר וְלֹֽא־יָדַ֥ע אִישׁ֙ אֶת־קְבֻ֣רָת֔וֹ עַ֖ד הַיּ֥וֹם
ה הַזֶּֽה: וּמֹשֶׁ֗ה בֶּן־מֵאָ֧ה וְעֶשְׂרִ֛ים שָׁנָ֖ה בְּמֹת֑וֹ לֹא־כָהֲתָ֥ה עֵינ֖וֹ וְלֹא־נָ֥ס לֵחֹֽה: וַיִּבְכּ֨וּ
בְנֵ֤י יִשְׂרָאֵל֙ אֶת־מֹשֶׁ֔ה בְּעַֽרְבֹ֥ת מוֹאָ֖ב שְׁלֹשִׁ֣ים י֑וֹם וַיִּתְּמ֔וּ יְמֵ֥י בְכִ֖י אֵ֥בֶל מֹשֶֽׁה:
ט וִיהוֹשֻׁ֣עַ בִּן־נ֗וּן מָלֵא֙ ר֣וּחַ חָכְמָ֔ה כִּֽי־סָמַ֥ךְ מֹשֶׁ֛ה אֶת־יָדָ֖יו עָלָ֑יו וַיִּשְׁמְע֨וּ אֵלָ֤יו
י בְנֵֽי־יִשְׂרָאֵל֙ וַֽיַּעֲשׂ֔וּ כַּאֲשֶׁ֛ר צִוָּ֥ה יְהוָ֖ה אֶת־מֹשֶֽׁה: וְלֹֽא־קָ֨ם נָבִ֥יא ע֛וֹד בְּיִשְׂרָאֵ֖ל
יא כְּמֹשֶׁ֑ה אֲשֶׁר֙ יְדָע֣וֹ יְהוָ֔ה פָּנִ֖ים אֶל־פָּנִֽים: לְכָל־הָ֨אֹתֹ֜ת וְהַמּוֹפְתִ֗ים אֲשֶׁ֤ר שְׁלָחוֹ֙
יב יְהוָ֔ה לַעֲשׂ֖וֹת בְּאֶ֣רֶץ מִצְרָ֑יִם לְפַרְעֹ֥ה וּלְכָל־עֲבָדָ֖יו וּלְכָל־אַרְצֽוֹ: וּלְכֹל֙ הַיָּ֣ד הַחֲזָקָ֔ה
וּלְכֹ֖ל הַמּוֹרָ֣א הַגָּד֑וֹל אֲשֶׁר֙ עָשָׂ֣ה מֹשֶׁ֔ה לְעֵינֵ֖י כָּל־יִשְׂרָאֵֽל: חזק

ו | וַיִּקְבֹּר אֹתוֹ. הַקָּדוֹשׁ בָּרוּךְ הוּא בִּכְבוֹדוֹ. רַבִּי יִשְׁמָעֵאל
אוֹמֵר: הוּא קָבַר אֶת עַצְמוֹ, וְזֶה הוּא אֶחָד מִשְּׁלֹשָׁה אֵתִים
שֶׁהָיָה רַבִּי יִשְׁמָעֵאל דּוֹרֵשׁ כֵּן. כַּיּוֹצֵא בּוֹ: "בְּיוֹם מְלֹאת יְמֵי
נִזְרוֹ יָבִיא אֹתוֹ" (במדבר ו, יג), הוּא מֵבִיא אֶת עַצְמוֹ. כַּיּוֹצֵא
בּוֹ: "וְהִשִּׂיאוּ אוֹתָם עֲוֺן אַשְׁמָה" (ויקרא כב, טז), וְכִי אֲחֵרִים
מַשִּׂיאִים אוֹתָם? אֶלָּא הֵם מַשִּׂיאִים אֶת עַצְמָם: מוּל בֵּית
פְּעוֹר. קִבְרוֹ מוּכָן שָׁם מִשֵּׁשֶׁת יְמֵי בְרֵאשִׁית לְכַפֵּר עַל
מַעֲשֵׂה פְּעוֹר, וְזֶה אֶחָד מִן הַדְּבָרִים שֶׁנִּבְרְאוּ בְּעֶרֶב שַׁבָּת
בֵּין הַשְּׁמָשׁוֹת (אבות ה, ו):

ז | לֹא כָהֲתָה עֵינוֹ. אַף מִשֶּׁמֵּת: וְלֹא נָס לֵחֹה. לַחְלוּחִית
שֶׁבּוֹ. לֹא שָׁלַט בּוֹ רִקָּבוֹן וְלֹא נֶהְפַּךְ תֹּאַר פָּנָיו:

ח | בְּנֵי יִשְׂרָאֵל. הַזְּכָרִים, אֲבָל בְּאַהֲרֹן מִתּוֹךְ שֶׁהָיָה רוֹדֵף
שָׁלוֹם וְנוֹתֵן שָׁלוֹם בֵּין אִישׁ לְרֵעֵהוּ וּבֵין אִשָּׁה לְבַעֲלָהּ,
נֶאֱמַר: "כֹּל בֵּית יִשְׂרָאֵל" (במדבר כ, כט), זְכָרִים וּנְקֵבוֹת:

י | אֲשֶׁר יְדָעוֹ ה' פָּנִים אֶל פָּנִים. שֶׁהָיָה לִבּוֹ גַּס בּוֹ וּמְדַבֵּר
אֵלָיו בְּכָל עֵת שֶׁרוֹצֶה, כָּעִנְיָן שֶׁנֶּאֱמַר: "וְעַתָּה אֶעֱלֶה אֶל
ה'" (שמות לב, ל), "עִמְדוּ וְאֶשְׁמְעָה מַה יְצַוֶּה ה' לָכֶם"
(במדבר ט, ח):

יב | וּלְכֹל הַיָּד הַחֲזָקָה. שֶׁקִּבֵּל אֶת הַתּוֹרָה בַּלּוּחוֹת
בְּיָדָיו: וּלְכֹל הַמּוֹרָא הַגָּדוֹל. נִסִּים וּגְבוּרוֹת שֶׁבַּמִּדְבָּר
הַגָּדוֹל וְהַנּוֹרָא: לְעֵינֵי כָּל יִשְׂרָאֵל. שֶׁנְּשָׂאוֹ לִבּוֹ לִשְׁבֹּר
הַלּוּחוֹת לְעֵינֵיהֶם, שֶׁנֶּאֱמַר: "וָאֲשַׁבְּרֵם לְעֵינֵיכֶם" (לעיל ט,
יז), וְהִסְכִּימָה דַּעַת הַקָּדוֹשׁ בָּרוּךְ הוּא לְדַעְתּוֹ, שֶׁנֶּאֱמַר:
"אֲשֶׁר שִׁבַּרְתָּ" (שמות לד, א) – יִישַׁר כֹּחֲךָ שֶׁשִּׁבַּרְתָּ:

Haftarot

Haftara for **Bereshit**

Creation's Testimony about Its Creator

ISAIAH 42:5–43:10

This *haftara* describes God's servant and his mission. In the narrow sense of the term, the title "servant of God" refers to an individual chosen by God to redeem His people and enlighten His world. In a broader sense, this title refers to the entire nation of Israel. Throughout the exile, the servant of God feels that his Master has abandoned and rejected him. He is oppressed and his senses have been dulled. God comforts His servant by informing him that He will uphold the covenant between them, He will fight his battles, and He will convey him from darkness to light. Through this wondrous redemption, the servant will come to know his Master and bear witness to Him.

This passage was probably chosen as the *haftara* for *Parashat Bereshit* because a number of verses mention the creation of heaven and earth (Genesis 42:5, 43:7). However, there is another connection between the *haftara* and the *parasha*: Whereas *Bereshit* deals with the fall of man at the beginning of history, the *haftara* presents the servant of God, the final redeemer, whose destiny is to justify the existence of mankind.

42 5 So said the God, the Lord, Creator of the heavens and who
unfurled them, who spread out the earth and its progeny, who
gives breath to the people upon it and spirit to those who walk
6 in it: I, the Lord, have called you with justice; I have supported
your hand and have protected you, and I have set you for a cov-
7 enant to the people, as a light of nations, to open blind eyes,
to release a prisoner from confinement and dwellers in dark-
8 ness from prison. I am the Lord, that is My name, and I will not
9 give My glory to another, nor My praise to idols. Behold, the
first ones have come to pass and the new ones I relate; before
10 they burgeon I will pronounce them to you. Sing to the Lord
a new song, His praise from the ends of the earth, those who
11 go to sea and all that fill it, islands and their inhabitants. Let
the wilderness and its cities raise their voice, with courtyards
inhabited by Kedar; rock dwellers will sing; from mountain
12 peaks will they shout. They will grant glory to the Lord and will
13 relate His praise in the islands. The Lord will emerge like the
valiant one, He will arouse zealotry as a man of war; He will
14 roar, even scream; He will overwhelm His enemies. I have been
silent forever, I have been still and have restrained Myself; I will
cry out like a woman in childbirth, I will gasp and pant together.
15 I will destroy mountains and hills and all their vegetation will
I wither; I will transform rivers into islands and I will dry out
16 marshes. I will lead the blind on a way that they did not know,
on paths that they did not know will I guide them; I will render darkness before them into light and tortuous paths into a
plain. These are the things that I have done and I did not aban-
17 don them. They will draw back, will be deeply ashamed, those
who trust in idols, who say to cast images: You are our gods.
18 19 Hear, the deaf, and look to see, the blind. Who is blind but
My servant? Or deaf, like My messenger whom I send? Who
is blind like the perfect one and blind like the servant of the
20 Lord? Seeing much, but you do not observe; opening ears,
Seph. 21 but he does not hear. The Lord is desirous of him because of
end his righteousness; he will make the Torah great and glorious.
22 But it is a people looted and despoiled; the young men, all of
them, are blown away and have been trapped in prisons; they
were taken as loot with no savior, spoils with no one saying:
23 Return it. Who among you will listen to this, will pay atten-
24 tion and hear the ending? Who subjected Jacob to despoil-
ing and Israel to the looters? Wasn't it the Lord, He against
whom we sinned and were unwilling to walk in His ways and
25 did not heed His Torah? He poured upon it the fury of His
wrath and the might of war, scorched it from all around but it
43 1 did not know, burned in it but would not take it to heart. And
now, so said the Lord, your Creator, Jacob, and your Fashioner,
Israel: Do not fear, as I have redeemed you; I have called your
2 name, you are Mine. When you pass through the water, I am
with you, and through the rivers, they will not inundate you;
when you walk into fire, you will not be burned and a flame
3 will not ignite upon you. For I am the Lord your God, Holy
One of Israel, your Savior; I gave Egypt as your ransom, Kush
4 and Seva in your stead. Since you were precious in My eyes, you
were honored and I loved you; I will give men in your stead and
5 peoples instead of your life. Fear not, as I am with you; I will
bring your descendants from the East and from the West will I
6 gather you. I will say to the North: Give, and to the South: Do
not withhold; bring My sons from afar and My daughters from
7 the ends of the earth. Everything that is called by My name and
8 for My glory, I created it, I fashioned it, truly I made it, to free
a people that is blind though it has eyes, and deaf though they
9 have ears. All the nations gathered together and the peoples assembled; who among them will tell this and announce to us the
first things? Let them provide their witnesses and they will be
10 justified; and let them hear and they will say: Truth. You are My
witnesses – the utterance of the Lord – and My servant whom I
have chosen, so that you will know and trust in Me and understand that I am He; before Me no god was formed, and after Me
there will not be.

הפטרת

בראשית

ישעיה

מב ה כְּה־אָמַר הָאֵל ׀ יְהוָה בּוֹרֵא הַשָּׁמַיִם וְנוֹטֵיהֶם רֹקַע הָאָרֶץ וְצֶאֱצָאֶיהָ נֹתֵן נְשָׁמָה לָעָם עָלֶיהָ

ו וְרוּחַ לַהֹלְכִים בָּהּ: אֲנִי יְהוָה קְרָאתִיךָ בְצֶדֶק וְאַחְזֵק בְּיָדֶךָ וְאֶצָּרְךָ וְאֶתֶּנְךָ לִבְרִית עָם לְאוֹר

ז גּוֹיִם: לִפְקֹחַ עֵינַיִם עִוְרוֹת לְהוֹצִיא מִמַּסְגֵּר אַסִּיר מִבֵּית כֶּלֶא יֹשְׁבֵי חֹשֶׁךְ: אֲנִי יְהוָה הוּא שְׁמִי

ח וּכְבוֹדִי לְאַחֵר לֹא־אֶתֵּן וּתְהִלָּתִי לַפְּסִילִים: הָרִאשֹׁנוֹת הִנֵּה־בָאוּ וַחֲדָשׁוֹת אֲנִי מַגִּיד בְּטֶרֶם

ט תִּצְמַחְנָה אַשְׁמִיעַ אֶתְכֶם: שִׁירוּ לַיהוָה שִׁיר חָדָשׁ תְּהִלָּתוֹ מִקְצֵה הָאָרֶץ יוֹרְדֵי

יא הַיָּם וּמְלֹאוֹ אִיִּים וְיֹשְׁבֵיהֶם: יִשְׂאוּ מִדְבָּר וְעָרָיו חֲצֵרִים תֵּשֵׁב קֵדָר יָרֹנּוּ יֹשְׁבֵי סֶלַע מֵרֹאשׁ

יב הָרִים יִצְוָחוּ: יָשִׂימוּ לַיהוָה כָּבוֹד וּתְהִלָּתוֹ בָּאִיִּים יַגִּידוּ: יְהוָה כַּגִּבּוֹר יֵצֵא כְּאִישׁ מִלְחָמוֹת

יד יָעִיר קִנְאָה יָרִיעַ אַף־יַצְרִיחַ עַל־אֹיְבָיו יִתְגַּבָּר: הֶחֱשֵׁיתִי מֵעוֹלָם אַחֲרִישׁ אֶתְאַפָּק

טו כַּיּוֹלֵדָה אֶפְעֶה אֶשֹּׁם וְאֶשְׁאַף יָחַד: אַחֲרִיב הָרִים וּגְבָעוֹת וְכָל־עֶשְׂבָּם אוֹבִישׁ וְשַׂמְתִּי נְהָרוֹת

טז לָאִיִּים וַאֲגַמִּים אוֹבִישׁ: וְהוֹלַכְתִּי עִוְרִים בְּדֶרֶךְ לֹא יָדָעוּ בִּנְתִיבוֹת לֹא־יָדְעוּ אַדְרִיכֵם אָשִׂים

יז מַחְשָׁךְ לִפְנֵיהֶם לָאוֹר וּמַעֲקַשִּׁים לְמִישׁוֹר אֵלֶּה הַדְּבָרִים עֲשִׂיתִם וְלֹא עֲזַבְתִּים: נָסֹגוּ אָחוֹר

יח יֵבֹשׁוּ בֹשֶׁת הַבֹּטְחִים בַּפָּסֶל הָאֹמְרִים לְמַסֵּכָה אַתֶּם אֱלֹהֵינוּ: הַחֵרְשִׁים שְׁמָעוּ

יט וְהַעִוְרִים הַבִּיטוּ לִרְאוֹת: מִי עִוֵּר כִּי אִם־עַבְדִּי וְחֵרֵשׁ כְּמַלְאָכִי אֶשְׁלָח מִי עִוֵּר כִּמְשֻׁלָּם וְעִוֵּר

כא כְּעֶבֶד יְהוָה: רָאִיתָ רַבּוֹת וְלֹא תִשְׁמֹר פָּקוֹחַ אָזְנַיִם וְלֹא יִשְׁמָע: יְהוָה חָפֵץ לְמַעַן צִדְקוֹ יַגְדִּיל

רָאוֹת
הספרדים
מסיימים כאן
למפטיר

כב תּוֹרָה וְיַאְדִּיר: וְהוּא עַם־בָּזוּז וְשָׁסוּי הָפֵחַ בַּחוּרִים כֻּלָּם וּבְבָתֵּי כְלָאִים הָחְבָּאוּ הָיוּ לָבַז וְאֵין

כג מַצִּיל מְשִׁסָּה וְאֵין־אֹמֵר הָשַׁב: מִי בָכֶם יַאֲזִין זֹאת יַקְשֵׁב וְיִשְׁמַע לְאָחוֹר: מִי־נָתַן לִמְשׁוֹסָה

כד יַעֲקֹב וְיִשְׂרָאֵל לְבֹזְזִים הֲלוֹא יְהוָה זוּ חָטָאנוּ לוֹ וְלֹא־אָבוּ בִדְרָכָיו הָלוֹךְ וְלֹא שָׁמְעוּ בְּתוֹרָתוֹ:

כה וַיִּשְׁפֹּךְ עָלָיו חֵמָה אַפּוֹ וֶעֱזוּז מִלְחָמָה וַתְּלַהֲטֵהוּ מִסָּבִיב וְלֹא יָדָע וַתִּבְעַר־בּוֹ וְלֹא־יָשִׂים

מג א עַל־לֵב: וְעַתָּה כְּה־אָמַר יְהוָה בֹּרַאֲךָ יַעֲקֹב וְיֹצֶרְךָ יִשְׂרָאֵל אַל־תִּירָא כִּי גְאַלְתִּיךָ

ב קָרָאתִי בְשִׁמְךָ לִי־אָתָּה: כִּי־תַעֲבֹר בַּמַּיִם אִתְּךָ־אָנִי וּבַנְּהָרוֹת לֹא יִשְׁטְפוּךָ כִּי־תֵלֵךְ בְּמוֹ־אֵשׁ

ג לֹא תִכָּוֶה וְלֶהָבָה לֹא תִבְעַר־בָּךְ: כִּי אֲנִי יְהוָה אֱלֹהֶיךָ קְדוֹשׁ יִשְׂרָאֵל מוֹשִׁיעֶךָ נָתַתִּי כָפְרְךָ

ד מִצְרַיִם כּוּשׁ וּסְבָא תַּחְתֶּיךָ: מֵאֲשֶׁר יָקַרְתָּ בְעֵינַי נִכְבַּדְתָּ וַאֲנִי אֲהַבְתִּיךָ וְאֶתֵּן אָדָם תַּחְתֶּיךָ

ה וּלְאֻמִּים תַּחַת נַפְשֶׁךָ: אַל־תִּירָא כִּי אִתְּךָ־אָנִי מִמִּזְרָח אָבִיא זַרְעֶךָ וּמִמַּעֲרָב אֲקַבְּצֶךָ: אֹמַר

ו לַצָּפוֹן תֵּנִי וּלְתֵימָן אַל־תִּכְלָאִי הָבִיאִי בָנַי מֵרָחוֹק וּבְנוֹתַי מִקְצֵה הָאָרֶץ: כֹּל הַנִּקְרָא בִשְׁמִי

ז וְלִכְבוֹדִי בְּרָאתִיו יְצַרְתִּיו אַף־עֲשִׂיתִיו: הוֹצִיא עַם־עִוֵּר וְעֵינַיִם יֵשׁ וְחֵרְשִׁים וְאָזְנַיִם לָמוֹ: כָּל־

ח הַגּוֹיִם נִקְבְּצוּ יַחְדָּו וְיֵאָסְפוּ לְאֻמִּים מִי בָהֶם יַגִּיד זֹאת וְרִאשֹׁנוֹת יַשְׁמִיעֻנוּ יִתְּנוּ עֵדֵיהֶם וְיִצְדָּקוּ

ט וְיִשְׁמְעוּ וְיֹאמְרוּ אֱמֶת: אַתֶּם עֵדַי נְאֻם־יְהוָה וְעַבְדִּי אֲשֶׁר בָּחָרְתִּי לְמַעַן תֵּדְעוּ וְתַאֲמִינוּ לִי

י וְתָבִינוּ כִּי־אֲנִי הוּא לְפָנַי לֹא־נוֹצַר אֵל וְאַחֲרַי לֹא יִהְיֶה:

Haftara for
Noah

The Consolation of Construction
after Destruction
ISAIAH 54:1–55:5

This *haftara* contains an explicit reference to the main topic of the *parasha*, namely the flood (54:9). There is, however, another connection between the *haftara* and the *parasha*: In *Parashat Noah*, the Torah relates that the world was destroyed by a flood because it became filled with violence. In the *haftara*, the prophet describes the merciful redemption and consolation of the world following the destruction that occurs "in an outburst of rage" (54:8). In the future, the world will be reestablished through righteousness, when the people distance themselves from exploitation.

54 1 Sing, barren one, who did not give birth; burst into song and rejoice, one who did not go into labor, for the children of the desolate are more than the children of the married woman, said 2 the Lord. Expand the place of your tent and spread the curtains of your dwellings, do not spare; extend your cords and rein- 3 force your stakes. For you will spread out to the right and the left; and your descendants will inherit nations and they will set- 4 tle desolate cities. Do not fear, for you will not be shamed; do not feel humiliated, for you will not be disgraced, for you will forget the shame of your youth and you will not remember the 5 disgrace of your widowhood any longer. For your Husband is your Maker, the Lord of hosts is His name; and your Redeemer is the Holy One of Israel, the God of the entire world He will 6 be called. For as a wife forsaken and aggrieved of spirit the Lord called you, and as the wife of one's youth she will be de- 7 spised, said your God. For a brief moment I forsook you, and 8 with great mercy I will gather you. In an outburst of rage, I con- cealed My face from you for a moment, but with eternal grace 9 I will have mercy on you, said your Redeemer, the Lord. For this is for Me like the waters of Noah; as I took an oath that the waters of Noah would no longer pass over the earth, so I took an oath that I would not be furious with you, nor would I

Seph. 10 rebuke you. For the mountains will move and the hills will col-
end lapse, but My grace will not move from you and the covenant of My peace will not collapse, said the One who has mercy 11 on you, the Lord. Afflicted, storm-tossed one, she has not

been comforted; behold, I will set your flagstones with carbun- 12 cle and lay your foundation with sapphires. I will make your windows of chalcedony, your gates of ruby, and your entire 13 border of precious stones. All your children will be disciples 14 of the Lord and the peace of your children will be abundant. With righteousness, you will be established; distance your- self from exploitation, for you need not fear, and from ruin, 15 as it will not come near you. Behold, one who is not with Me will be afraid; whoever resides with you will fall in with 16 you. Behold, I created the smith who fans the fire of coal and produces a tool with his labor, and I created the destroyer to 17 cause harm. Any weapon crafted against you will not succeed and any tongue that will rise against you in judgment will be condemned. This is the heritage of the servants of the Lord and their just deserts from Me – the utterance of the Lord.

55 1 Ho, everyone thirsty, go to water, and one who has no silver, go purchase and eat; go purchase wine and milk without silver and 2 without cost. Why do you weigh our silver for no bread and your exertion for no satisfaction? Heed Me and eat well and your soul 3 will delight in fatness. Incline your ear and go to Me; take heed and your soul will live and I will establish with you an eternal 4 covenant, the enduring grace of David. Behold, I have set him a 5 witness for the peoples, a prince and commander to the peoples. Behold, you will call a nation that you do not know, and a nation that has not known you will run to you, for the sake of the Lord your God and for the Holy One of Israel, as He glorified you.

נח

רָנִּי עֲקָרָה לֹא יָלָדָה פִּצְחִי רִנָּה וְצַהֲלִי לֹא־חָלָה כִּי־רַבִּים בְּנֵי־שׁוֹמֵמָה מִבְּנֵי בְעוּלָה אָמַר יְהוָה: **ישעיה** נד א

הַרְחִיבִי ׀ מְקוֹם אָהֳלֵךְ וִירִיעוֹת מִשְׁכְּנוֹתַיִךְ יַטּוּ אַל־תַּחְשֹׂכִי הַאֲרִיכִי מֵיתָרַיִךְ וִיתֵדֹתַיִךְ חַזֵּקִי: ב

כִּי־יָמִין וּשְׂמֹאול תִּפְרֹצִי וְזַרְעֵךְ גּוֹיִם יִירָשׁ וְעָרִים נְשַׁמּוֹת יוֹשִׁיבוּ: אַל־תִּירְאִי כִּי־לֹא תֵבוֹשִׁי ג

וְאַל־תִּכָּלְמִי כִּי לֹא תַחְפִּירִי כִּי בֹשֶׁת עֲלוּמַיִךְ תִּשְׁכָּחִי וְחֶרְפַּת אַלְמְנוּתַיִךְ לֹא תִזְכְּרִי־עוֹד: כִּי ד

בֹעֲלַיִךְ עֹשַׂיִךְ יְהוָה צְבָאוֹת שְׁמוֹ וְגֹאֲלֵךְ קְדוֹשׁ יִשְׂרָאֵל אֱלֹהֵי כָל־הָאָרֶץ יִקָּרֵא: כִּי־כְאִשָּׁה ה

עֲזוּבָה וַעֲצוּבַת רוּחַ קְרָאָךְ יְהוָה וְאֵשֶׁת נְעוּרִים כִּי תִמָּאֵס אָמַר אֱלֹהָיִךְ: בְּרֶגַע קָטֹן עֲזַבְתִּיךְ ו

וּבְרַחֲמִים גְּדֹלִים אֲקַבְּצֵךְ: בְּשֶׁצֶף קֶצֶף הִסְתַּרְתִּי פָנַי רֶגַע מִמֵּךְ וּבְחֶסֶד עוֹלָם רִחַמְתִּיךְ אָמַר ז

גֹּאֲלֵךְ יְהוָה: כִּי־מֵי נֹחַ זֹאת לִי אֲשֶׁר נִשְׁבַּעְתִּי מֵעֲבֹר מֵי־נֹחַ עוֹד עַל־הָאָרֶץ כֵּן ח

נִשְׁבַּעְתִּי מִקְּצֹף עָלַיִךְ וּמִגְּעָר־בָּךְ: כִּי הֶהָרִים יָמוּשׁוּ וְהַגְּבָעוֹת תְּמוּטֶינָה וְחַסְדִּי מֵאִתֵּךְ ט

לֹא־יָמוּשׁ וּבְרִית שְׁלוֹמִי לֹא תָמוּט אָמַר מְרַחֲמֵךְ יְהוָה: עֲנִיָּה סֹעֲרָה לֹא נֻחָמָה **הספרדים מסיימים כאן** י

הִנֵּה אָנֹכִי מַרְבִּיץ בַּפּוּךְ אֲבָנַיִךְ וִיסַדְתִּיךְ בַּסַּפִּירִים: וְשַׂמְתִּי כַּדְכֹד שִׁמְשֹׁתַיִךְ וּשְׁעָרַיִךְ לְאַבְנֵי יא

אֶקְדָּח וְכָל־גְּבוּלֵךְ לְאַבְנֵי־חֵפֶץ: וְכָל־בָּנַיִךְ לִמּוּדֵי יְהוָה וְרַב שְׁלוֹם בָּנָיִךְ: בִּצְדָקָה תִּכּוֹנָנִי יב

רַחֲקִי מֵעֹשֶׁק כִּי־לֹא תִירָאִי וּמִמְּחִתָּה כִּי לֹא־תִקְרַב אֵלָיִךְ: הֵן גּוֹר יָגוּר אֶפֶס מֵאוֹתִי מִי־גָר יג

אִתָּךְ עָלַיִךְ יִפּוֹל: הֵן אָנֹכִי בָּרָאתִי חָרָשׁ נֹפֵחַ בְּאֵשׁ פֶּחָם וּמוֹצִיא כְלִי לְמַעֲשֵׂהוּ וְאָנֹכִי בָּרָאתִי **הִנֵּה** טו

מַשְׁחִית לְחַבֵּל: כָּל־כְּלִי יוּצַר עָלַיִךְ לֹא יִצְלָח וְכָל־לָשׁוֹן תָּקוּם־אִתָּךְ לַמִּשְׁפָּט תַּרְשִׁיעִי זֹאת טז

נַחֲלַת עַבְדֵי יְהוָה וְצִדְקָתָם מֵאִתִּי נְאֻם־יְהוָה: הוֹי כָּל־צָמֵא לְכוּ לַמַּיִם וַאֲשֶׁר אֵין נה א

לוֹ כָּסֶף לְכוּ שִׁבְרוּ וֶאֱכֹלוּ וּלְכוּ שִׁבְרוּ בְּלוֹא־כֶסֶף וּבְלוֹא מְחִיר יַיִן וְחָלָב: לָמָּה תִשְׁקְלוּ־כֶסֶף ב

בְּלוֹא־לֶחֶם וִיגִיעֲכֶם בְּלוֹא לְשָׂבְעָה שִׁמְעוּ שָׁמוֹעַ אֵלַי וְאִכְלוּ־טוֹב וְתִתְעַנַּג בַּדֶּשֶׁן נַפְשְׁכֶם:

הַטּוּ אָזְנְכֶם וּלְכוּ אֵלַי שִׁמְעוּ וּתְחִי נַפְשְׁכֶם וְאֶכְרְתָה לָכֶם בְּרִית עוֹלָם חַסְדֵי דָוִד הַנֶּאֱמָנִים: ג

הֵן עֵד לְאוּמִּים נְתַתִּיו נָגִיד וּמְצַוֵּה לְאֻמִּים: הֵן גּוֹי לֹא־תֵדַע תִּקְרָא וְגוֹי לֹא־יְדָעוּךָ אֵלֶיךָ ה

יָרוּצוּ לְמַעַן יְהוָה אֱלֹהֶיךָ וְלִקְדוֹשׁ יִשְׂרָאֵל כִּי פֵאֲרָךְ:

Haftara for
Lekh Lekha

God's Salvation and Judgment
ISAIAH 40:27–41:16

This *haftara* consists of a prophecy of consolation, in which the prophet seeks to strengthen and invigorate those who are weary and despairing. The prophet emphasizes the greatness of God, which is beyond any human classification or evaluation and calls upon the people to place their hopes in God alone. Among these messages of comfort and encouragement are statements of reproof and condemnation of the gentile nations. In this *haftara*, the prophet highlights the sharp contrast between the fear of idol worshippers on the one hand, and, on the other, the protection of the descendants of Abraham, who embodies this contrast as a destroyer of idols and a proponent of righteousness.

The prophecy in this *haftara* also depicts a great victor who brings redemption to the world, which the Sages consider an allusion to Abraham's wanderings through the Land of Israel. This link sheds fresh light on the figure of Abraham, who was not merely a nomad in a foreign land, but a great conqueror who wrought far-reaching change in the world.

40 27 Why do you say, Jacob, and speak, Israel: My way is hidden
from the Lord, and from my God my just deserts will have
28 passed? Didn't you know, didn't you hear, the Lord is the eternal God, Creator of the ends of the earth? He neither tires nor
29 wearies; there is no scrutinizing His understanding. He gives
30 strength to the tired, and to the powerless, He increases might.
The youths will be tired and weary and the young men will fal-
31 ter. But those who long for the Lord will renew their strength;
they will grow wings like eagles; they will run and will not
41 1 weary, they will walk and will not tire. Be silent for me, lands of
the sea, and let nations renew their strength; let them approach
and then they shall speak; together, let us approach for judg-
2 ment. Who awakens from the East, righteousness attends his
footstep? He will subdue nations before him and will subjugate
kings; He shall render his sword like dust, his bow like wind-
3 blown straw. He will pursue them and pass peacefully; he will
4 not come on a trail on his feet. Who acted and accomplished it?
He who proclaimed the generations from the beginning. I, the
5 Lord, am first and with the last I am He. The lands of the sea saw
and feared; the ends of the earth trembled, they approached
6 and came. Each would help his neighbor and would say to his
7 brother: Be strong. The carpenter encouraged the smith, the
one who smooths with a hammer, the one who strikes at the
start, saying of the join: It is good; he strengthened it with nails,
8 it would not fall apart. But it is you, Israel, My servant, Jacob,
whom I have chosen, descendants of Abraham who loved Me,
9 whom I have taken from the ends of the earth and from its noblemen, I called you; I said to you: You are My servant, I chose
10 you and did not despise you. Do not fear, as I am with you; do
not waver, as I am your God; I have made you firm; indeed, I
have helped you, even supported you with My righteous right
11 hand. Behold, all who provoke you will be ashamed and humiliated; all who provoke you will be like nothing and the people
12 who quarrel with you will perish. You will seek them, the people who contend with you, but you will not find them; the peo-
13 ple who make war on you will be like nothing and naught. For
I am the Lord your God, supporting your right hand, who says
14 to you: Do not fear, I help you. Do not fear, worm of Jacob, people of Israel; I am your help – the utterance of the Lord – and
15 your Redeemer, the Holy One of Israel. Behold, I will turn you
into a sharp new threshing board with teeth; you will thresh
16 mountains and pulverize them and make hills like chaff. You
will winnow them and the wind will carry them and the storm
will scatter them; but you will rejoice in the Lord, you will be
glorified in the Holy One of Israel.

ישעיה

כח לָמָּה תֹאמַר יַעֲקֹב וּתְדַבֵּר יִשְׂרָאֵל נִסְתְּרָה דַרְכִּי מֵיהוָה וּמֵאֱלֹהַי מִשְׁפָּטִי יַעֲבוֹר: הֲלוֹא יָדַעְתָּ אִם־לֹא שָׁמַעְתָּ אֱלֹהֵי עוֹלָם ׀ יהוה בּוֹרֵא קְצוֹת הָאָרֶץ לֹא יִיעַף וְלֹא יִיגָע אֵין חֵקֶר לִתְבוּנָתוֹ:

כט נֹתֵן לַיָּעֵף כֹּחַ וּלְאֵין אוֹנִים עָצְמָה יַרְבֶּה: וְיִעֲפוּ נְעָרִים וְיִגָעוּ וּבַחוּרִים כָּשׁוֹל יִכָּשֵׁלוּ: וְקֹוֵי יהוה

מא א יַחֲלִיפוּ כֹחַ יַעֲלוּ אֵבֶר כַּנְּשָׁרִים יָרוּצוּ וְלֹא יִיגָעוּ יֵלְכוּ וְלֹא יִיעָפוּ: הַחֲרִישׁוּ אֵלַי אִיִּים

ב וּלְאֻמִּים יַחֲלִיפוּ כֹחַ יִגְּשׁוּ אָז יְדַבֵּרוּ יַחְדָּו לַמִּשְׁפָּט נִקְרָבָה: מִי הֵעִיר מִמִּזְרָח צֶדֶק יִקְרָאֵהוּ

ג לְרַגְלוֹ יִתֵּן לְפָנָיו גּוֹיִם וּמְלָכִים יַרְדְּ יִתֵּן כֶּעָפָר חַרְבּוֹ כְּקַשׁ נִדָּף קַשְׁתּוֹ: יִרְדְּפֵם יַעֲבוֹר שָׁלוֹם אֹרַח

ד בְּרַגְלָיו לֹא יָבוֹא: מִי־פָעַל וְעָשָׂה קֹרֵא הַדֹּרוֹת מֵרֹאשׁ אֲנִי יהוה רִאשׁוֹן וְאֶת־אַחֲרֹנִים אֲנִי־הוּא:

ה רָאוּ אִיִּים וְיִירָאוּ קְצוֹת הָאָרֶץ יֶחֱרָדוּ קָרְבוּ וַיֶּאֱתָיוּן: אִישׁ אֶת־רֵעֵהוּ יַעְזֹרוּ וּלְאָחִיו יֹאמַר חֲזָק:

ז וַיְחַזֵּק חָרָשׁ אֶת־צֹרֵף מַחֲלִיק פַּטִּישׁ אֶת־הוֹלֶם פָּעַם אֹמֵר לַדֶּבֶק טוֹב הוּא וַיְחַזְּקֵהוּ בְמַסְמְרִים לֹא יִמּוֹט:

ח וְאַתָּה יִשְׂרָאֵל עַבְדִּי יַעֲקֹב אֲשֶׁר בְּחַרְתִּיךָ זֶרַע אַבְרָהָם אֹהֲבִי: אֲשֶׁר הֶחֱזַקְתִּיךָ מִקְצוֹת הָאָרֶץ וּמֵאֲצִילֶיהָ קְרָאתִיךָ וָאֹמַר לְךָ עַבְדִּי־אַתָּה בְּחַרְתִּיךָ וְלֹא מְאַסְתִּיךָ:

י אַל־תִּירָא כִּי עִמְּךָ־אָנִי אַל־תִּשְׁתָּע כִּי־אֲנִי אֱלֹהֶיךָ אִמַּצְתִּיךָ אַף־עֲזַרְתִּיךָ אַף־תְּמַכְתִּיךָ בִּימִין צִדְקִי: הֵן יֵבֹשׁוּ וְיִכָּלְמוּ כֹּל הַנֶּחֱרִים בָּךְ יִהְיוּ כְאַיִן וְיֹאבְדוּ אַנְשֵׁי רִיבֶךָ: תְּבַקְשֵׁם וְלֹא תִמְצָאֵם

יא אַנְשֵׁי מַצֻּתֶךָ יִהְיוּ כְאַיִן וּכְאֶפֶס אַנְשֵׁי מִלְחַמְתֶּךָ: כִּי אֲנִי יהוה אֱלֹהֶיךָ מַחֲזִיק יְמִינֶךָ הָאֹמֵר

יד לְךָ אַל־תִּירָא אֲנִי עֲזַרְתִּיךָ: אַל־תִּירְאִי תּוֹלַעַת יַעֲקֹב מְתֵי יִשְׂרָאֵל אֲנִי עֲזַרְתִּיךְ נְאֻם־יהוה וְגֹאֲלֵךְ קְדוֹשׁ יִשְׂרָאֵל: הִנֵּה שַׂמְתִּיךְ לְמוֹרַג חָרוּץ חָדָשׁ בַּעַל פִּיפִיּוֹת תָּדוּשׁ הָרִים

טז וְתָדֹק וּגְבָעוֹת כַּמֹּץ תָּשִׂים: תִּזְרֵם וְרוּחַ תִּשָּׂאֵם וּסְעָרָה תָּפִיץ אֹתָם וְאַתָּה תָּגִיל בַּיהוה בִּקְדוֹשׁ יִשְׂרָאֵל תִּתְהַלָּל:

Haftara for
Vayera

Elisha's Miracles on Behalf of Two Women and Their Children

II KINGS 4:1–37

This passage was probably selected as the *haftara* for this *parasha* because it relates the story of the miraculous birth of a child by virtue of a special prophetic blessing. It is interesting to note that the phrase *ka'et ḥaya*, "at this time next year," appears in both texts (Genesis 18:14; II Kings 4:16). Furthermore, in both the *parasha* and the *haftara*, the miraculous birth of the child follows a hospitable act.

4 1 A certain woman of the wives of the sons of the prophets cried out to Elisha, saying: Your servant, my husband, is dead, and you know that your servant feared the Lord, and the creditor is
2 coming to take my two children for himself as slaves. Elisha said to her: What shall I do for you? Tell me, what do you have in the house? She said: Your maidservant does not have anything in
3 the house, except for a flask of oil. He said: Go, borrow vessels for you from the outside, from all your neighbors, empty ves-
4 sels; do not skimp. You shall enter and shut the door on you and on your sons, and pour into all those vessels, and that which is
5 full, move aside. She went from him and shut the door on herself
6 and on her sons; they would hand to her, and she would pour. It was when the vessels were full that she said to her son: Hand me another vessel. He said to her: There is no other vessel, and
7 the oil stopped. She came and she told the man of God, and he said: Go, sell the oil and pay your debt, and you and your sons
8 shall live on the remainder. The day was that Elisha traveled to Shunem, and there was a great woman there and she implored him to eat bread, and so it was that whenever he passed, he
9 would turn there to eat bread. She said to her husband: Behold, now I know that he is a holy man of God, who visits us regularly.
10 Please, let us prepare a small loft, and place there a bed, a table, a chair, and a lamp for him; it shall be whenever he comes to us,
11 he will turn there. The day was that he came there, and he turned
12 to the loft and he lay down there. He said to Gehazi his lad: Summon that Shunamite woman. He summoned her, and she
13 stood before him. He said to him: Please say to her: Behold, you have exerted all this exertion for us. What to do for you? Should

one speak on your behalf to the king or to the commander of
14 the army? She said: I dwell among my people. He said: What can one do for her? Gehazi said: But she does not have a son,
15 and her husband is old. He said: Summon her. He summoned
16 her, and she stood in the entrance. He said: At this time next year, in this very time, you will embrace a son. She said: No, my
17 lord, man of God, do not deceive your maidservant. The woman conceived and bore a son at that time of year, at that very time,
18 as Elisha had spoken to her. The child grew, and the day was that
19 he went out to his father to the reapers. He said to his father: My head, my head. He said to his lad: Carry him to his mother.
20 He carried him, and he brought him to his mother; he sat on
21 her knees until noon and died. She went up and laid him on the bed of the man of God and shut the door on him and went out.
22 She called her husband and said: Please send me one of the lads and one of the donkeys, and I will run to the man of God and
23 return. He said: Why are you going to him today? It is not a New
Seph. 24 Moon and it is not Sabbath. She said: It is well. She saddled the
end donkey and she said to her lad: Lead and go; do not impede me
25 from riding, unless I say to you. She went and she came to the man of God, to Mount Carmel. It was when the man of God saw her from afar, he said to Gehazi his lad: Behold, it is that Shunamite
26 woman. Please, run now to meet her, and say to her: Is it well with you? Is it well with your husband? Is it well with the child?
27 She said: It is well. She came to the man of God, to the mountain, and she grasped his legs. Gehazi approached to push her away, but the man of God said: Leave her, as her soul is bitter within her, and the Lord has concealed it from me and did not tell me.

מלכים ב׳

ד א וְאִשָּׁה אַחַת מִנְּשֵׁי בְנֵי־הַנְּבִיאִים צָעֲקָה אֶל־אֱלִישָׁע לֵאמֹר עַבְדְּךָ אִישִׁי מֵת וְאַתָּה יָדַעְתָּ כִּי

ב עַבְדְּךָ הָיָה יָרֵא אֶת־יְהוָה וְהַנֹּשֶׁה בָּא לָקַחַת אֶת־שְׁנֵי יְלָדַי לוֹ לַעֲבָדִים: וַיֹּאמֶר אֵלֶיהָ אֱלִישָׁע
מָה אֶעֱשֶׂה־לָּךְ הַגִּידִי לִי מַה־יֶּשׁ־לָכִי בַּבָּיִת וַתֹּאמֶר אֵין לְשִׁפְחָתְךָ כֹל בַּבַּיִת כִּי אִם־אָסוּךְ

ג שָׁמֶן: וַיֹּאמֶר לְכִי שַׁאֲלִי־לָךְ כֵּלִים מִן־הַחוּץ מֵאֵת כָּל־שְׁכֵנָיִךְ כֵּלִים רֵקִים אַל־תַּמְעִיטִי:

ד וּבָאת וְסָגַרְתְּ הַדֶּלֶת בַּעֲדֵךְ וּבְעַד־בָּנַיִךְ וְיָצַקְתְּ עַל כָּל־הַכֵּלִים הָאֵלֶּה וְהַמָּלֵא תַּסִּיעִי: וַתֵּלֶךְ

ה מֵאִתּוֹ וַתִּסְגֹּר הַדֶּלֶת בַּעֲדָהּ וּבְעַד בָּנֶיהָ הֵם מַגִּשִׁים אֵלֶיהָ וְהִיא מיצקת: וַיְהִי כִּמְלֹאת

ו הַכֵּלִים וַתֹּאמֶר אֶל־בְּנָהּ הַגִּישָׁה אֵלַי עוֹד כֶּלִי וַיֹּאמֶר אֵלֶיהָ אֵין עוֹד כֶּלִי וַיַּעֲמֹד הַשָּׁמֶן:

ז וַתָּבֹא וַתַּגֵּד לְאִישׁ הָאֱלֹהִים וַיֹּאמֶר לְכִי מִכְרִי אֶת־הַשֶּׁמֶן וְשַׁלְּמִי אֶת־נשיכי וְאַתְּ בניכי

ח תִּחְיִי בַּנּוֹתָר: וַיְהִי הַיּוֹם וַיַּעֲבֹר אֱלִישָׁע אֶל־שׁוּנֵם וְשָׁם אִשָּׁה גְדוֹלָה וַתַּחֲזֶק־בּוֹ

ט לֶאֱכָל־לָחֶם וַיְהִי מִדֵּי עָבְרוֹ יָסֻר שָׁמָּה לֶאֱכָל־לָחֶם: וַתֹּאמֶר אֶל־אִישָׁהּ הִנֵּה־נָא יָדַעְתִּי כִּי

י אִישׁ אֱלֹהִים קָדוֹשׁ הוּא עֹבֵר עָלֵינוּ תָּמִיד: נַעֲשֶׂה־נָּא עֲלִיַּת־קִיר קְטַנָּה וְנָשִׂים לוֹ שָׁם מִטָּה

יא וְשֻׁלְחָן וְכִסֵּא וּמְנוֹרָה וְהָיָה בְּבֹאוֹ אֵלֵינוּ יָסוּר שָׁמָּה: וַיְהִי הַיּוֹם וַיָּבֹא שָׁמָּה וַיָּסַר אֶל־הָעֲלִיָּה

יב וַיִּשְׁכַּב־שָׁמָּה: וַיֹּאמֶר אֶל־גֵּיחֲזִי נַעֲרוֹ קְרָא לַשּׁוּנַמִּית הַזֹּאת וַיִּקְרָא־לָהּ וַתַּעֲמֹד לְפָנָיו: וַיֹּאמֶר

יג לוֹ אֱמָר־נָא אֵלֶיהָ הִנֵּה חָרַדְתְּ ׀ אֵלֵינוּ אֶת־כָּל־הַחֲרָדָה הַזֹּאת מֶה לַעֲשׂוֹת לָךְ הֲיֵשׁ לְדַבֶּר־

יד לָךְ אֶל־הַמֶּלֶךְ אוֹ אֶל־שַׂר הַצָּבָא וַתֹּאמֶר בְּתוֹךְ עַמִּי אָנֹכִי יֹשָׁבֶת: וַיֹּאמֶר וּמֶה לַעֲשׂוֹת

טו לָהּ וַיֹּאמֶר גֵּיחֲזִי אֲבָל בֵּן אֵין־לָהּ וְאִישָׁהּ זָקֵן: וַיֹּאמֶר קְרָא־לָהּ וַיִּקְרָא־לָהּ וַתַּעֲמֹד בַּפָּתַח:

טז וַיֹּאמֶר לַמּוֹעֵד הַזֶּה כָּעֵת חַיָּה אתי חֹבֶקֶת בֵּן וַתֹּאמֶר אַל־אֲדֹנִי אִישׁ הָאֱלֹהִים אַל־תְּכַזֵּב

יז בְּשִׁפְחָתֶךָ: וַתַּהַר הָאִשָּׁה וַתֵּלֶד בֵּן לַמּוֹעֵד הַזֶּה כָּעֵת חַיָּה אֲשֶׁר־דִּבֶּר אֵלֶיהָ אֱלִישָׁע: וַיִּגְדַּל

יח הַיָּלֶד וַיְהִי הַיּוֹם וַיֵּצֵא אֶל־אָבִיו אֶל־הַקֹּצְרִים: וַיֹּאמֶר אֶל־אָבִיו רֹאשִׁי ׀ רֹאשִׁי וַיֹּאמֶר אֶל־

יט הַנַּעַר שָׂאֵהוּ אֶל־אִמּוֹ: וַיִּשָּׂאֵהוּ וַיְבִיאֵהוּ אֶל־אִמּוֹ וַיֵּשֶׁב עַל־בִּרְכֶּיהָ עַד־

כ הַצָּהֳרַיִם וַיָּמֹת: וַתַּעַל וַתַּשְׁכִּבֵהוּ עַל־מִטַּת אִישׁ הָאֱלֹהִים וַתִּסְגֹּר בַּעֲדוֹ וַתֵּצֵא: וַתִּקְרָא אֶל־

כא אִישָׁהּ וַתֹּאמֶר שִׁלְחָה נָא לִי אֶחָד מִן־הַנְּעָרִים וְאַחַת הָאֲתֹנוֹת וְאָרוּצָה עַד־אִישׁ הָאֱלֹהִים

כב וְאָשׁוּבָה: וַיֹּאמֶר מַדּוּעַ אתי הֹלֶכֶת אֵלָיו הַיּוֹם לֹא־חֹדֶשׁ וְלֹא שַׁבָּת וַתֹּאמֶר שָׁלוֹם: וַתַּחֲבֹשׁ

כג הָאָתוֹן וַתֹּאמֶר אֶל־נַעֲרָהּ נְהַג וָלֵךְ אַל־תַּעֲצָר־לִי לִרְכֹּב כִּי אִם־אָמַרְתִּי לָךְ: וַתֵּלֶךְ וַתָּבֹא

כד אֶל־אִישׁ הָאֱלֹהִים אֶל־הַר הַכַּרְמֶל וַיְהִי כִּרְאוֹת אִישׁ־הָאֱלֹהִים אֹתָהּ מִנֶּגֶד וַיֹּאמֶר אֶל־גֵּיחֲזִי

כה נַעֲרוֹ הִנֵּה הַשּׁוּנַמִּית הַלָּז: עַתָּה רוּץ־נָא לִקְרָאתָהּ וֶאֱמָר־לָהּ הֲשָׁלוֹם לָךְ הֲשָׁלוֹם לְאִישֵׁךְ

כו הֲשָׁלוֹם לַיָּלֶד וַתֹּאמֶר שָׁלוֹם: וַתָּבֹא אֶל־אִישׁ הָאֱלֹהִים אֶל־הָהָר וַתַּחֲזֵק בְּרַגְלָיו וַיִּגַּשׁ גֵּיחֲזִי

לְהָדְפָהּ וַיֹּאמֶר אִישׁ הָאֱלֹהִים הַרְפֵּה־לָהּ כִּי־נַפְשָׁהּ מָרָה־לָהּ וַיהוָה הֶעְלִים מִמֶּנִּי וְלֹא הִגִּיד

Marginal qere notes (right-hand column):
לָךְ
שְׁכֵנָיִךְ
מוֹצֶקֶת
נָשַׁיִךְ וּבָנַיִךְ
אֶת

אֶת הלכת הספרדים מסיימים כאן

28 She said: Did I request a son from my lord? Didn't I say: Do
29 not mislead me? He said to Gehazi: Gird your loins and take my staff in your hand and go; if you encounter any man, do not greet him, and if any man greets you, do not answer him.
30 Place my staff on the lad's face. The mother of the lad said: As the Lord lives, and as you live, I will not leave you. He rose and
31 he followed her. Gehazi passed before them and placed the staff on the lad's face but there was no voice and no one listening. He returned to meet him, and he told him, saying: The lad has
32 not awakened. Elisha came to the house and behold, the lad was
33 dead, laid on his bed. He entered and shut the door on the two

34 of them, and he prayed to the Lord. He went up and lay upon the child; he placed his mouth on his mouth and his eyes on his eyes and his palms on his palms. He stretched himself over
35 him and the flesh of the child grew warm. He went back down, and walked in the house once to, and once fro, and went up and stretched himself over him; the lad sneezed seven times, and the
36 lad opened his eyes. He called Gehazi, and he said: Summon this Shunamite woman. He summoned her, and she came to
37 him, and he said: Take up your son. She entered, fell at his feet, and prostrated herself to the ground, and she took up her son and departed.

Haftara for
Hayei Sarah

King David's Old Age and the Right of Succession to His Throne
I KINGS 1:1–31

In King David's old age, his son Adoniya takes advantage of David's weakness and behaves as if he has been crowned king. David takes an oath before Batsheva that her son Solomon will inherit his throne, and not Solomon's elder half-brother Adoniya. David thereby seeks to mold the structure of the kingdom for generations. Similarly, in the *parasha*, Abraham in his old age administers an oath to his servant concerning the choice of a wife for Isaac. In this manner, Abraham effectively determines the future of the nation that will descend from him.

1
1 King David was old, advanced in years. They covered him in
2 garments, but he would not be warmed. His servants said to him: Have them seek for my lord the king a young virgin; she will stand before the king, and she will be an attendant for him, and she will lie in your bosom, and it will be warm for my lord
3 the king. They sought a beautiful young woman within the entire border of Israel, and they found Avishag the Shunamite and
4 brought her to the king. The young woman was exceedingly beautiful, and she became an attendant for the king and she
5 served him, but the king was not intimate with her. Adoniya son of Hagit exalted himself, saying: I will become king. He provided for himself chariots and horsemen, and fifty men ran
6 before him. His father never distressed him, saying: Why did you do so? Moreover, he was of very good form, and she bore

7 him after Avshalom. He consulted with Yoav son of Tzeruya, and with Evyatar the priest, and they supported Adoniyahu.
8 But Tzadok the priest, and Benayahu son of Yehoyada, and Natan the prophet, and Shimi, and Re'i, and the mighty men
9 who were with David were not with Adoniyahu. Adoniyahu slaughtered sheep, and oxen, and fatlings at the Tzohelet stone, which is near Ein Rogel, and he called all his brothers, the king's
10 sons, and all the men of Judah, the king's servants. But he did not call Natan the prophet, and Benayahu, and the mighty men,
11 and Solomon his brother. Natan spoke to Batsheva, mother of Solomon, saying: Haven't you heard that Adoniyahu son of Hagit, has become king, and David, our lord, does not know?
12 Now go, let me please counsel you, and save your life and the
13 life of your son Solomon. Go and come before King David,

כח כט לִי: וַתֹּאמֶר הֲשָׁאַלְתִּי בֵן מֵאֵת אֲדֹנִי הֲלֹא אָמַרְתִּי לֹא תַשְׁלֶה אֹתִי: וַיֹּאמֶר לְגֵיחֲזִי חֲגֹר
מָתְנֶיךָ וְקַח מִשְׁעַנְתִּי בְיָדְךָ וָלֵךְ כִּי־תִמְצָא אִישׁ לֹא תְבָרְכֶנּוּ וְכִי־יְבָרֶכְךָ אִישׁ לֹא תַעֲנֶנּוּ
ל וְשַׂמְתָּ מִשְׁעַנְתִּי עַל־פְּנֵי הַנָּעַר: וַתֹּאמֶר אֵם הַנַּעַר חַי־יהוה וְחֵי־נַפְשְׁךָ אִם־אֶעֶזְבֶךָּ וַיָּקָם וַיֵּלֶךְ
לא אַחֲרֶיהָ: וְגֵחֲזִי עָבַר לִפְנֵיהֶם וַיָּשֶׂם אֶת־הַמִּשְׁעֶנֶת עַל־פְּנֵי הַנַּעַר וְאֵין קוֹל וְאֵין קָשֶׁב וַיָּשָׁב
לב לִקְרָאתוֹ וַיַּגֶּד־לוֹ לֵאמֹר לֹא הֵקִיץ הַנָּעַר: וַיָּבֹא אֱלִישָׁע הַבָּיְתָה וְהִנֵּה הַנַּעַר מֵת מֻשְׁכָּב עַל־
לג לד מִטָּתוֹ: וַיָּבֹא וַיִּסְגֹּר הַדֶּלֶת בְּעַד שְׁנֵיהֶם וַיִּתְפַּלֵּל אֶל־יהוה: וַיַּעַל וַיִּשְׁכַּב עַל־הַיֶּלֶד וַיָּשֶׂם פִּיו
לה עַל־פִּיו וְעֵינָיו עַל־עֵינָיו וְכַפָּיו עַל־כַּפָּו וַיִּגְהַר עָלָיו וַיָּחָם בְּשַׂר הַיָּלֶד: וַיָּשָׁב וַיֵּלֶךְ בַּבַּיִת אַחַת
הֵנָּה וְאַחַת הֵנָּה וַיַּעַל וַיִּגְהַר עָלָיו וַיְזוֹרֵר הַנַּעַר עַד־שֶׁבַע פְּעָמִים וַיִּפְקַח הַנַּעַר אֶת־עֵינָיו:
לו וַיִּקְרָא אֶל־גֵּיחֲזִי וַיֹּאמֶר קְרָא אֶל־הַשֻּׁנַמִּית הַזֹּאת וַיִּקְרָאֶהָ וַתָּבוֹא אֵלָיו וַיֹּאמֶר שְׂאִי בְנֵךְ:
לז וַתָּבֹא וַתִּפֹּל עַל־רַגְלָיו וַתִּשְׁתַּחוּ אָרְצָה וַתִּשָּׂא אֶת־בְּנָהּ וַתֵּצֵא:

הפטרת

חיי שרה

מלכים א׳

א א ב וְהַמֶּלֶךְ דָּוִד זָקֵן בָּא בַּיָּמִים וַיְכַסֻּהוּ בַּבְּגָדִים וְלֹא יִחַם לוֹ: וַיֹּאמְרוּ לוֹ עֲבָדָיו יְבַקְשׁוּ לַאדֹנִי הַמֶּלֶךְ
ג נַעֲרָה בְתוּלָה וְעָמְדָה לִפְנֵי הַמֶּלֶךְ וּתְהִי־לוֹ סֹכֶנֶת וְשָׁכְבָה בְחֵיקֶךָ וְחַם לַאדֹנִי הַמֶּלֶךְ: וַיְבַקְשׁוּ
ד נַעֲרָה יָפָה בְּכֹל גְּבוּל יִשְׂרָאֵל וַיִּמְצְאוּ אֶת־אֲבִישַׁג הַשּׁוּנַמִּית וַיָּבִאוּ אֹתָהּ לַמֶּלֶךְ: וְהַנַּעֲרָה יָפָה
ה עַד־מְאֹד וַתְּהִי לַמֶּלֶךְ סֹכֶנֶת וַתְּשָׁרְתֵהוּ וְהַמֶּלֶךְ לֹא יְדָעָהּ: וַאֲדֹנִיָּה בֶן־חַגִּית מִתְנַשֵּׂא לֵאמֹר
ו אֲנִי אֶמְלֹךְ וַיַּעַשׂ לוֹ רֶכֶב וּפָרָשִׁים וַחֲמִשִּׁים אִישׁ רָצִים לְפָנָיו: וְלֹא־עֲצָבוֹ אָבִיו מִיָּמָיו לֵאמֹר
ז מַדּוּעַ כָּכָה עָשִׂיתָ וְגַם־הוּא טוֹב־תֹּאַר מְאֹד וְאֹתוֹ יָלְדָה אַחֲרֵי אַבְשָׁלוֹם: וַיִּהְיוּ דְבָרָיו עִם יוֹאָב
ח בֶּן־צְרוּיָה וְעִם אֶבְיָתָר הַכֹּהֵן וַיַּעְזְרוּ אַחֲרֵי אֲדֹנִיָּה: וְצָדוֹק הַכֹּהֵן וּבְנָיָהוּ בֶן־יְהוֹיָדָע וְנָתָן הַנָּבִיא
ט וְשִׁמְעִי וְרֵעִי וְהַגִּבּוֹרִים אֲשֶׁר לְדָוִד לֹא הָיוּ עִם־אֲדֹנִיָּהוּ: וַיִּזְבַּח אֲדֹנִיָּהוּ צֹאן וּבָקָר וּמְרִיא עִם
אֶבֶן הַזֹּחֶלֶת אֲשֶׁר־אֵצֶל עֵין רֹגֵל וַיִּקְרָא אֶת־כָּל־אֶחָיו בְּנֵי הַמֶּלֶךְ וּלְכָל־אַנְשֵׁי יְהוּדָה עַבְדֵי
י יא הַמֶּלֶךְ: וְאֶת־נָתָן הַנָּבִיא וּבְנָיָהוּ וְאֶת־הַגִּבּוֹרִים וְאֶת־שְׁלֹמֹה אָחִיו לֹא קָרָא: וַיֹּאמֶר נָתָן אֶל־
בַּת־שֶׁבַע אֵם־שְׁלֹמֹה לֵאמֹר הֲלוֹא שָׁמַעַתְּ כִּי מָלַךְ אֲדֹנִיָּהוּ בֶן־חַגִּית וַאֲדֹנֵינוּ דָוִד לֹא יָדָע:
יב יג וְעַתָּה לְכִי אִיעָצֵךְ נָא עֵצָה וּמַלְּטִי אֶת־נַפְשֵׁךְ וְאֶת־נֶפֶשׁ בְּנֵךְ שְׁלֹמֹה: לְכִי וּבֹאִי ׀ אֶל־הַמֶּלֶךְ דָּוִד

and say to him: Didn't you, my lord, the king, take an oath to your maidservant, saying that Solomon your son will become king after me, and he will sit upon my throne? Why has 14 Adoniyahu become king? Behold, while you are still speaking there with the king, I will come after you, and I will complete 15 your words. Batsheva came to the king, into the chamber; the king was very old, and Avishag the Shunamite was serving the 16 king. Batsheva bowed, and prostrated herself before the king, 17 and the king said: What happened to you? She said to him: My lord, you took an oath by the Lord your God to your maidservant that Solomon your son will become king after me, and he 18 will sit upon my throne. Now, behold, Adoniya has become 19 king; and now, my lord the king, you did not know. He slaughtered bulls, and fatlings, and sheep in abundance, and summoned all the sons of the king, and Evyatar the priest, and Yoav, commander of the army, but Solomon, your servant, he did not 20 summon. And you, my lord the king, the eyes of all Israel are upon you, to tell them who will sit upon the throne of my lord 21 the king after him. It will be that when my lord the king will lie 22 with his fathers, I and my son Solomon will be harmed. Behold, while she was still talking with the king, Natan the prophet 23 came. They told the king, saying: Here is Natan the prophet.

He came before the king and prostrated himself to the king on 24 his face to the ground. Natan said: My lord, the king, did you say: Adoniyahu will become king after me, and he will sit upon 25 my throne? For he went down today, and he slaughtered bulls, and fatlings and sheep in abundance, and he summoned all the king's sons, and the commanders of the army, and Evyatar the priest; here they are, eating and drinking before him, and they 26 are saying: Long live King Adoniyahu. But me, your servant, and Tzadok the priest, and Benayahu, son of Yehoyada, and 27 your servant Solomon, he did not summon. Is it from my lord the king that this matter came to be, and you did not inform your servant who will sit on the throne of my lord the king after 28 him? King David answered and said: Summon Batsheva to me. 29 She came before the king and stood before the king. The king took an oath and said: As the Lord lives, who has redeemed my 30 soul from every trouble, for as I took an oath to you by the Lord, God of Israel, saying that Solomon your son will become king after me, and he will sit upon my throne in my stead, so I will 31 do this day. Batsheva bowed with her face to the earth, and she prostrated herself to the king, and she said: May my lord, the King David, live forever.

וְאָמַרְתְּ אֵלָיו הֲלֹא־אַתָּה אֲדֹנִי הַמֶּלֶךְ נִשְׁבַּעְתָּ לַאֲמָתְךָ לֵאמֹר כִּי־שְׁלֹמֹה בְנֵךְ יִמְלֹךְ אַחֲרַי
יד וְהוּא יֵשֵׁב עַל־כִּסְאִי וּמַדּוּעַ מָלַךְ אֲדֹנִיָהוּ: הִנֵּה עוֹדָךְ מְדַבֶּרֶת שָׁם עִם־הַמֶּלֶךְ וַאֲנִי אָבוֹא
טו אַחֲרַיִךְ וּמִלֵּאתִי אֶת־דְּבָרָיִךְ: וַתָּבֹא בַת־שֶׁבַע אֶל־הַמֶּלֶךְ הַחַדְרָה וְהַמֶּלֶךְ זָקֵן מְאֹד וַאֲבִישַׁג
טז הַשּׁוּנַמִּית מְשָׁרַת אֶת־הַמֶּלֶךְ: וַתִּקֹּד בַּת־שֶׁבַע וַתִּשְׁתַּחוּ לַמֶּלֶךְ וַיֹּאמֶר הַמֶּלֶךְ מַה־לָּךְ:
יז וַתֹּאמֶר לוֹ אֲדֹנִי אַתָּה נִשְׁבַּעְתָּ בַּיהוָה אֱלֹהֶיךָ לַאֲמָתֶךָ כִּי־שְׁלֹמֹה בְנֵךְ יִמְלֹךְ אַחֲרָי וְהוּא
יח יט יֵשֵׁב עַל־כִּסְאִי: וְעַתָּה הִנֵּה אֲדֹנִיָּה מָלָךְ וְעַתָּה אֲדֹנִי הַמֶּלֶךְ לֹא יָדָעְתָּ: וַיִּזְבַּח שׁוֹר וּמְרִיא־
וְצֹאן לָרֹב וַיִּקְרָא לְכָל־בְּנֵי הַמֶּלֶךְ וּלְאֶבְיָתָר הַכֹּהֵן וּלְיֹאָב שַׂר הַצָּבָא וְלִשְׁלֹמֹה עַבְדְּךָ
כ לֹא קָרָא: וְאַתָּה אֲדֹנִי הַמֶּלֶךְ עֵינֵי כָל־יִשְׂרָאֵל עָלֶיךָ לְהַגִּיד לָהֶם מִי יֵשֵׁב עַל־כִּסֵּא אֲדֹנִי־
כא הַמֶּלֶךְ אַחֲרָיו: וְהָיָה כִּשְׁכַב אֲדֹנִי־הַמֶּלֶךְ עִם־אֲבֹתָיו וְהָיִיתִי אֲנִי וּבְנִי שְׁלֹמֹה חַטָּאִים:
כב כג וְהִנֵּה עוֹדֶנָּה מְדַבֶּרֶת עִם־הַמֶּלֶךְ וְנָתָן הַנָּבִיא בָּא: וַיַּגִּידוּ לַמֶּלֶךְ לֵאמֹר הִנֵּה נָתָן הַנָּבִיא
כד וַיָּבֹא לִפְנֵי הַמֶּלֶךְ וַיִּשְׁתַּחוּ לַמֶּלֶךְ עַל־אַפָּיו אָרְצָה: וַיֹּאמֶר נָתָן אֲדֹנִי הַמֶּלֶךְ אַתָּה אָמַרְתָּ
כה אֲדֹנִיָּהוּ יִמְלֹךְ אַחֲרָי וְהוּא יֵשֵׁב עַל־כִּסְאִי: כִּי ׀ יָרַד הַיּוֹם וַיִּזְבַּח שׁוֹר וּמְרִיא־וְצֹאן לָרֹב
וַיִּקְרָא לְכָל־בְּנֵי הַמֶּלֶךְ וּלְשָׂרֵי הַצָּבָא וּלְאֶבְיָתָר הַכֹּהֵן וְהִנָּם אֹכְלִים וְשֹׁתִים לְפָנָיו וַיֹּאמְרוּ
כו יְחִי הַמֶּלֶךְ אֲדֹנִיָּהוּ: וְלִי אֲנִי־עַבְדֶּךָ וּלְצָדֹק הַכֹּהֵן וְלִבְנָיָהוּ בֶן־יְהוֹיָדָע וְלִשְׁלֹמֹה עַבְדְּךָ לֹא
כז קָרָא: אִם מֵאֵת אֲדֹנִי הַמֶּלֶךְ נִהְיָה הַדָּבָר הַזֶּה וְלֹא הוֹדַעְתָּ אֶת־עַבְדֶּיךָ מִי יֵשֵׁב עַל־כִּסֵּא
כח אֲדֹנִי־הַמֶּלֶךְ אַחֲרָיו: וַיַּעַן הַמֶּלֶךְ דָּוִד וַיֹּאמֶר קִרְאוּ־לִי לְבַת־שָׁבַע וַתָּבֹא לִפְנֵי הַמֶּלֶךְ וַתַּעֲמֹד
כט ל לִפְנֵי הַמֶּלֶךְ: וַיִּשָּׁבַע הַמֶּלֶךְ וַיֹּאמַר חַי־יְהוָה אֲשֶׁר־פָּדָה אֶת־נַפְשִׁי מִכָּל־צָרָה: כִּי כַּאֲשֶׁר
נִשְׁבַּעְתִּי לָךְ בַּיהוָה אֱלֹהֵי יִשְׂרָאֵל לֵאמֹר כִּי־שְׁלֹמֹה בְנֵךְ יִמְלֹךְ אַחֲרַי וְהוּא יֵשֵׁב עַל־כִּסְאִי
לא תַּחְתָּי כִּי כֵּן אֶעֱשֶׂה הַיּוֹם הַזֶּה: וַתִּקֹּד בַּת־שֶׁבַע אַפַּיִם אֶרֶץ וַתִּשְׁתַּחוּ לַמֶּלֶךְ וַתֹּאמֶר יְחִי
אֲדֹנִי הַמֶּלֶךְ דָּוִד לְעֹלָם:

Haftara for **Toledot**

God's Selection of the House of Jacob and His Demand to Honor His Covenant

MALACHI 1:1–2:7

The first part of the *haftara* emphasizes one of the main themes of the *parasha*: Although Esau appeared to be the senior, more successful, and perhaps more upstanding brother, God chose the persecuted Jacob and rejected Esau, whose heart was full of hatred. Nevertheless, alongside the prophecy of God's hidden love for the house of Jacob, the prophet openly castigates the people for their lack of reverence in the performance of the Temple service. Israel's merit of the heavenly blessings placed upon the house of Jacob in this *parasha* depends on their respect for their loving Father, and on their observance of the covenant that God formed with those who love and serve Him.

1 2 The prophecy of the word of the Lord to Israel through Malachi.
I loved you, said the Lord, but you say: How have You loved us?
Wasn't Esau a brother to Jacob? – the utterance of the Lord –
3 and I loved Jacob. But I hated Esau and I rendered his mountains a desolation and his inheritance for the jackals of the wil-
4 derness. If Edom will say: We are ruined, but we will return and
build the ruins, so said the Lord of hosts: They will build, and
I will destroy; they will be called the boundary of wickedness,
5 and the people that the Lord rages against forever. Your eyes
will see, and you will say: May the Lord be glorified beyond the
6 boundary of Israel. A son will honor his father and a servant his
master. If I am a father, where is My honor? If I am a master,
where is My fear? The Lord of hosts says to you, the priests,
scorners of My name. And you say: How have we scorned Your
7 name? You present tainted bread on My altar and you say: How
have we tainted You? In your saying: The table of the Lord is
8 contemptible. When you present a blind animal for sacrifice, is
nothing wrong? When you present the lame and ill, is nothing
wrong? Present it now to your governor; will he be pleased with
9 you, or will he show you favor? said the Lord of hosts. Now,
please implore God, that He be gracious to us. This was from
your hand; will He show any of you favor? said the Lord of
10 hosts. If only there was even one among you who would shut the
doors, so you would not kindle My altar in vain. I have no desire
for you, said the Lord of hosts, and I will not accept an offering
11 from your hand. For from the rising of the sun to its setting,
My name is great among the nations and in every place burnt
offerings and pure meal offerings are presented to My name, for
12 My name is great among the nations, said the Lord of hosts. But
you profane it, in your saying: The table of the Lord is tainted,
13 and its fruit is contemptible as is its food. You say: Behold, this is
bothersome, and you disappointed Him, said the Lord of hosts,
and you brought the stolen, and the lame, and the ill, and you
brought the offering; should I accept it from your hand? said the
14 Lord. Cursed is the scoundrel, who has a ram in his flock, and
vows, and slaughters the blemished to the Lord, as I am a great
King, said the Lord of hosts, and My name is awesome among
2 1 the nations. And now, this commandment is to you, the priests.
2 If you will not heed, and if you will not take it to heart, to give
glory to My name, said the Lord of hosts, I will send among
you the curse, and I will curse your blessings; I also cursed it,
3 because you do not take it to heart. Behold, I berate the seed for
you, and I will scatter dung on your faces, the dung of your festi-
4 vals, and you will be carried to it. You shall know that I sent this
commandment to you, for My covenant to be with Levi, said
5 the Lord of hosts. My covenant was with him, life and peace,
and I gave it to him in fear, and they feared Me, and due to My
6 name he was intimidated. The Torah of truth was in his mouth,
and injustice was not found on his lips; he walked with Me in
7 peace and honesty and he returned many from iniquity. For the
lips of the priest will safeguard knowledge and they will seek
Torah from his mouth, as he is a messenger of the Lord of hosts.

הפטרת

תולדת

א א ב מַשָּׂא דְבַר־יְהוָה אֶל־יִשְׂרָאֵל בְּיַד מַלְאָכִי׃ אָהַבְתִּי אֶתְכֶם אָמַר יְהוָה וַאֲמַרְתֶּם בַּמָּה אֲהַבְתָּנוּ מלאכי
ג הֲלוֹא־אָח עֵשָׂו לְיַעֲקֹב נְאֻם־יְהוָה וָאֹהַב אֶת־יַעֲקֹב׃ וְאֶת־עֵשָׂו שָׂנֵאתִי וָאָשִׂים אֶת־הָרָיו
ד שְׁמָמָה וְאֶת־נַחֲלָתוֹ לְתַנּוֹת מִדְבָּר׃ כִּי־תֹאמַר אֱדוֹם רֻשַּׁשְׁנוּ וְנָשׁוּב וְנִבְנֶה חֳרָבוֹת כֹּה אָמַר
יְהוָה צְבָאוֹת הֵמָּה יִבְנוּ וַאֲנִי אֶהֱרוֹס וְקָרְאוּ לָהֶם גְּבוּל רִשְׁעָה וְהָעָם אֲשֶׁר־זָעַם יְהוָה עַד־עוֹלָם׃
ה ו וְעֵינֵיכֶם תִּרְאֶינָה וְאַתֶּם תֹּאמְרוּ יִגְדַּל יְהוָה מֵעַל לִגְבוּל יִשְׂרָאֵל׃ בֵּן יְכַבֵּד אָב וְעֶבֶד אֲדֹנָיו
וְאִם־אָב אָנִי אַיֵּה כְבוֹדִי וְאִם־אֲדוֹנִים אָנִי אַיֵּה מוֹרָאִי אָמַר ׀ יְהוָה צְבָאוֹת לָכֶם הַכֹּהֲנִים בּוֹזֵי
ז שְׁמִי וַאֲמַרְתֶּם בַּמֶּה בָזִינוּ אֶת־שְׁמֶךָ׃ מַגִּישִׁים עַל־מִזְבְּחִי לֶחֶם מְגֹאָל וַאֲמַרְתֶּם בַּמֶּה גֵאַלְנוּךָ
ח בֶּאֱמָרְכֶם שֻׁלְחַן יְהוָה נִבְזֶה הוּא׃ וְכִי־תַגִּשׁוּן עִוֵּר לִזְבֹּחַ אֵין רָע וְכִי תַגִּישׁוּ פִּסֵּחַ וְחֹלֶה אֵין רָע
ט הַקְרִיבֵהוּ נָא לְפֶחָתֶךָ הֲיִרְצְךָ אוֹ הֲיִשָּׂא פָנֶיךָ אָמַר יְהוָה צְבָאוֹת׃ וְעַתָּה חַלּוּ־נָא פְנֵי־אֵל וִיחָנֵנוּ
י מִיֶּדְכֶם הָיְתָה זֹּאת הֲיִשָּׂא מִכֶּם פָּנִים אָמַר יְהוָה צְבָאוֹת׃ מִי גַם־בָּכֶם וְיִסְגֹּר דְּלָתַיִם וְלֹא־תָאִירוּ
יא מִזְבְּחִי חִנָּם אֵין־לִי חֵפֶץ בָּכֶם אָמַר יְהוָה צְבָאוֹת וּמִנְחָה לֹא־אֶרְצֶה מִיֶּדְכֶם׃ כִּי מִמִּזְרַח־שֶׁמֶשׁ
וְעַד־מְבוֹאוֹ גָּדוֹל שְׁמִי בַּגּוֹיִם וּבְכָל־מָקוֹם מֻקְטָר מֻגָּשׁ לִשְׁמִי וּמִנְחָה טְהוֹרָה כִּי־גָדוֹל שְׁמִי
יב בַּגּוֹיִם אָמַר יְהוָה צְבָאוֹת׃ וְאַתֶּם מְחַלְּלִים אוֹתוֹ בֶּאֱמָרְכֶם שֻׁלְחַן אֲדֹנָי מְגֹאָל הוּא וְנִיבוֹ נִבְזֶה
יג אָכְלוֹ׃ וַאֲמַרְתֶּם הִנֵּה מַתְּלָאָה וְהִפַּחְתֶּם אוֹתוֹ אָמַר יְהוָה צְבָאוֹת וַהֲבֵאתֶם גָּזוּל וְאֶת־הַפִּסֵּחַ
יד וְאֶת־הַחוֹלֶה וַהֲבֵאתֶם אֶת־הַמִּנְחָה הַאֶרְצֶה אוֹתָהּ מִיֶּדְכֶם אָמַר יְהוָה׃ וְאָרוּר נוֹכֵל וְיֵשׁ
בְּעֶדְרוֹ זָכָר וְנֹדֵר וְזֹבֵחַ מָשְׁחָת לַאדֹנָי כִּי מֶלֶךְ גָּדוֹל אָנִי אָמַר יְהוָה צְבָאוֹת וּשְׁמִי נוֹרָא בַגּוֹיִם׃
ב א ב וְעַתָּה אֲלֵיכֶם הַמִּצְוָה הַזֹּאת הַכֹּהֲנִים׃ אִם־לֹא תִשְׁמְעוּ וְאִם־לֹא תָשִׂימוּ עַל־לֵב לָתֵת כָּבוֹד
לִשְׁמִי אָמַר יְהוָה צְבָאוֹת וְשִׁלַּחְתִּי בָכֶם אֶת־הַמְּאֵרָה וְאָרוֹתִי אֶת־בִּרְכוֹתֵיכֶם וְגַם אָרוֹתִיהָ
ג כִּי אֵינְכֶם שָׂמִים עַל־לֵב׃ הִנְנִי גֹעֵר לָכֶם אֶת־הַזֶּרַע וְזֵרִיתִי פֶרֶשׁ עַל־פְּנֵיכֶם פֶּרֶשׁ חַגֵּיכֶם וְנָשָׂא
ד אֶתְכֶם אֵלָיו׃ וִידַעְתֶּם כִּי שִׁלַּחְתִּי אֲלֵיכֶם אֵת הַמִּצְוָה הַזֹּאת לִהְיוֹת בְּרִיתִי אֶת־לֵוִי אָמַר
ה יְהוָה צְבָאוֹת׃ בְּרִיתִי ׀ הָיְתָה אִתּוֹ הַחַיִּים וְהַשָּׁלוֹם וָאֶתְּנֵם־לוֹ מוֹרָא וַיִּירָאֵנִי וּמִפְּנֵי שְׁמִי נִחַת
ו הוּא׃ תּוֹרַת אֱמֶת הָיְתָה בְּפִיהוּ וְעַוְלָה לֹא־נִמְצָא בִשְׂפָתָיו בְּשָׁלוֹם וּבְמִישׁוֹר הָלַךְ אִתִּי וְרַבִּים
ז הֵשִׁיב מֵעָוֹן׃ כִּי־שִׂפְתֵי כֹהֵן יִשְׁמְרוּ־דַעַת וְתוֹרָה יְבַקְשׁוּ מִפִּיהוּ כִּי מַלְאַךְ יְהוָה־צְבָאוֹת הוּא׃

Haftara for **Vayetze**

Israel's Rebelliousness, Suffering, and Repentance

HOSEA 11:7–14:10; JOEL 2:26–27

This *haftara* begins with words of consolation before moving on to a rebuke of the people for their deceitful and exploitative acts, idol worship, and the alliance that Israel wishes to forge with Assyria. After the prophet Hosea foresees a harsh retribution for the sinful nation, he calls upon the people to return to their God, as salvation shall sprout from Him alone.

The figure of Jacob recurs in this prophecy in various contexts. Hosea recounts to his audience, the citizens of the Kingdom of Israel, several events from Jacob's life that are recorded in *Parashat Vayetze* and the adjoining *parashot*. Jacob's suffering in exile, his trying conflicts, his perseverance, and the promise he received from God when he went into exile, namely that God will protect him and restore him to his rightful place, are signals to his descendants that despite their distance from God and the painful blows they have suffered, they will be healed from all their ailments and they will be restored to their former greatness.

11 7 My people waver about My return, and though they are called
Seph. begin 8 upward, they will not be uplifted together. How can I give you
up, Ephraim, turn you over, Israel? How can I render you like
Adma, set you like Tzevoyim? My heart is overturned in Me; all
9 My compassion was aroused. I will not act upon My enflamed
wrath; I will not return to destroy Ephraim. For I am God, and
not man; I am sacred in your midst, and I will not go to a city.
10 They will follow the Lord; He will roar like a lion, for He will
11 roar and the children of the west will come trembling. They
will come trembling like a bird from Egypt, and like a dove
from the land of Assyria, and I will settle them in their houses
12 1 – the utterance of the Lord. Ephraim surrounded Me with
falsehood, and the house of Israel with deceit; but Judah still
2 ruled with God, and he is faithful with the holy ones. Ephraim
herds wind and pursues the east wind; all day he proliferates
lies and robbery; they will establish a covenant with Assyria
3 and oil will be brought to Egypt. The Lord has a quarrel with
Judah, and will reckon with Jacob according to his ways; ac-
4 cording to his exploits He will recompense him. In the womb,
he was at his brother's heels, and with his strength he strove
5 with God. He strove with an angel and prevailed; he wept
and he pleaded with him; in Beit El he found him, and there
6 he will speak with us. And the Lord is the God of hosts; the
7 Lord is His appellation. And you, return to your God, attend
8 to kindness and justice, and long for your God constantly.
9 A trader, scales of deceit are in his hand; he loves to exploit.
Ephraim said: Indeed, I became rich, I found power for myself; in all my exertion they will not find in me iniquity that is
10 a sin. I am the Lord your God since the land of Egypt; I will
11 yet settle you in tents, as in the appointed days. I spoke to the
prophets, I proliferated visions, and I granted imagery to the
12 prophets. If Gilad is iniquitous, they were but futility; in Gilgal
Seph. end they slaughtered bulls; their altars too will be as heaps on the
Ashk. begin 13 furrows of the field.Jacob fled to the field of Aram, and Israel
14 worked for a wife, and for a wife he guarded. With a prophet,
the Lord took Israel up from Egypt, and with a prophet it
15 was guarded. Ephraim has angered bitterly and his blood will
rest upon him; his master will repay him with his disgrace.
13 1 When Ephraim spoke there was quaking; he exalted himself
2 in Israel but he became guilty through the Baal and died. Now
they continue to sin and they made themselves a cast image
from their silver, idols according to their form, in its entirety
the work of craftsmen; to them they say: Those who slaughter
3 men will be those who kiss the calves. Therefore, they will be
like the morning cloud, and like the early dew that passes, like
chaff blown from the threshing floor, and like smoke from a
4 roof vent. I am the Lord your God since the land of Egypt; you
shall not know a god other than Me, and there is no savior but
Some end 5 6 Me. I knew you in the wilderness, in a parched land. When they
were at their grazing, they were satiated; they were satiated and
7 their heart grew high; therefore, they forgot Me. I will be like a
8 lion for them, like a leopard I will lurk on the way. I will meet
them like a bereaved bear, and I will rend the encasement of
their heart; I will devour them there like a lion; the beast of the
9 field will rupture them. Your destruction, Israel, is because you
10 were against Me, your helper. Where, then, is your king, that he
may rescue you in all your cities, and your judges, of whom you
11 said: Give me a king and princes? I will give you a king in My
12 wrath, and I will take him in My ire. The iniquity of Ephraim is
13 bound; his sin is stored away. The throes of a woman in childbirth will come to him; he is an unwise son, because at the
14 time, he will not stay on the birthstool for children. From the
netherworld I have redeemed them, from death I have delivered them. I will be your death decree; I will be your excision to
15 the netherworld; regret will be hidden from My eyes. Though
he had been fruitful among the fields, an east wind, the wind
of the Lord, will come; it ascends from the wilderness, and it
will dry out his source and his spring will become parched;

הפטרת
ויצא

הושע

יא ז ח וְעַמִּי תְלוּאִים לִמְשׁוּבָתִי וְאֶל־עַל יִקְרָאֻהוּ יַחַד לֹא יְרוֹמֵם׃ אֵיךְ אֶתֶּנְךָ אֶפְרַיִם אֲמַגֶּנְךָ יִשְׂרָאֵל
ט אֵיךְ אֶתֶּנְךָ כְאַדְמָה אֲשִׂימְךָ כִּצְבֹאיִם נֶהְפַּךְ עָלַי לִבִּי יַחַד נִכְמְרוּ נִחוּמָי׃ לֹא אֶעֱשֶׂה חֲרוֹן אַפִּי
י לֹא אָשׁוּב לְשַׁחֵת אֶפְרָיִם כִּי אֵל אָנֹכִי וְלֹא־אִישׁ בְּקִרְבְּךָ קָדוֹשׁ וְלֹא אָבוֹא בְּעִיר׃ אַחֲרֵי יהוה
יא יֵלְכוּ כְּאַרְיֵה יִשְׁאָג כִּי־הוּא יִשְׁאַג וְיֶחֶרְדוּ בָנִים מִיָּם׃ יֶחֶרְדוּ כְצִפּוֹר מִמִּצְרַיִם וּכְיוֹנָה מֵאֶרֶץ
יב א אַשּׁוּר וְהוֹשַׁבְתִּים עַל־בָּתֵּיהֶם נְאֻם־יהוה׃ סְבָבֻנִי בְכַחַשׁ אֶפְרַיִם וּבְמִרְמָה בֵּית
ב יִשְׂרָאֵל וִיהוּדָה עֹד רָד עִם־אֵל וְעִם־קְדוֹשִׁים נֶאֱמָן׃ אֶפְרַיִם רֹעֶה רוּחַ וְרֹדֵף קָדִים כָּל־הַיּוֹם
ג כָּזָב וָשֹׁד יַרְבֶּה וּבְרִית עִם־אַשּׁוּר יִכְרֹתוּ וְשֶׁמֶן לְמִצְרַיִם יוּבָל׃ וְרִיב לַיהוה עִם־יְהוּדָה וְלִפְקֹד
ד ה עַל־יַעֲקֹב כִּדְרָכָיו כְּמַעֲלָלָיו יָשִׁיב לוֹ׃ בַּבֶּטֶן עָקַב אֶת־אָחִיו וּבְאוֹנוֹ שָׂרָה אֶת־אֱלֹהִים׃ וַיָּשַׂר
ו אֶל־מַלְאָךְ וַיֻּכָל בָּכָה וַיִּתְחַנֶּן־לוֹ בֵּית־אֵל יִמְצָאֶנּוּ וְשָׁם יְדַבֵּר עִמָּנוּ׃ וַיהוה אֱלֹהֵי הַצְּבָאוֹת
ז ח יהוה זִכְרוֹ׃ וְאַתָּה בֵּאלֹהֶיךָ תָשׁוּב חֶסֶד וּמִשְׁפָּט שְׁמֹר וְקַוֵּה אֶל־אֱלֹהֶיךָ תָּמִיד׃ כְּנַעַן בְּיָדוֹ
ט מֹאזְנֵי מִרְמָה לַעֲשֹׁק אָהֵב׃ וַיֹּאמֶר אֶפְרַיִם אַךְ עָשַׁרְתִּי מָצָאתִי אוֹן לִי כָּל־יְגִיעַי לֹא יִמְצְאוּ־
י לִי עָוֹן אֲשֶׁר־חֵטְא׃ וְאָנֹכִי יהוה אֱלֹהֶיךָ מֵאֶרֶץ מִצְרָיִם עֹד אוֹשִׁיבְךָ בָאֳהָלִים כִּימֵי מוֹעֵד׃
יא יב וְדִבַּרְתִּי עַל־הַנְּבִיאִים וְאָנֹכִי חָזוֹן הִרְבֵּיתִי וּבְיַד הַנְּבִיאִים אֲדַמֶּה׃ אִם־גִּלְעָד אָוֶן אַךְ־שָׁוְא
יג הָיוּ בַּגִּלְגָּל שְׁוָרִים זִבֵּחוּ גַּם מִזְבְּחוֹתָם כְּגַלִּים עַל תַּלְמֵי שָׂדָי׃ וַיִּבְרַח יַעֲקֹב שְׂדֵה אֲרָם וַיַּעֲבֹד
יד יִשְׂרָאֵל בְּאִשָּׁה וּבְאִשָּׁה שָׁמָר׃ וּבְנָבִיא הֶעֱלָה יהוה אֶת־יִשְׂרָאֵל מִמִּצְרָיִם וּבְנָבִיא נִשְׁמָר׃
יג טו א הִכְעִיס אֶפְרַיִם תַּמְרוּרִים וְדָמָיו עָלָיו יִטּוֹשׁ וְחֶרְפָּתוֹ יָשִׁיב לוֹ אֲדֹנָיו׃ כְּדַבֵּר אֶפְרַיִם רְתֵת
ב נָשָׂא הוּא בְּיִשְׂרָאֵל וַיֶּאְשַׁם בַּבַּעַל וַיָּמֹת׃ וְעַתָּה ׀ יוֹסִפוּ לַחֲטֹא וַיַּעֲשׂוּ לָהֶם מַסֵּכָה מִכַּסְפָּם
ג כִּתְבוּנָם עֲצַבִּים מַעֲשֵׂה חָרָשִׁים כֻּלֹּה לָהֶם הֵם אֹמְרִים זֹבְחֵי אָדָם עֲגָלִים יִשָּׁקוּן׃ לָכֵן יִהְיוּ
ד כַּעֲנַן־בֹּקֶר וְכַטַּל מַשְׁכִּים הֹלֵךְ כְּמֹץ יְסֹעֵר מִגֹּרֶן וּכְעָשָׁן מֵאֲרֻבָּה׃ וְאָנֹכִי יהוה אֱלֹהֶיךָ מֵאֶרֶץ
ה מִצְרָיִם וֵאלֹהִים זוּלָתִי לֹא תֵדָע וּמוֹשִׁיעַ אַיִן בִּלְתִּי׃ אֲנִי יְדַעְתִּיךָ בַּמִּדְבָּר בְּאֶרֶץ תַּלְאֻבוֹת׃
ו ז כְּמַרְעִיתָם וַיִּשְׂבָּעוּ שָׂבְעוּ וַיָּרָם לִבָּם עַל־כֵּן שְׁכֵחוּנִי׃ וָאֱהִי לָהֶם כְּמוֹ־שָׁחַל כְּנָמֵר עַל־דֶּרֶךְ
ח אָשׁוּר׃ אֶפְגְּשֵׁם כְּדֹב שַׁכּוּל וְאֶקְרַע סְגוֹר לִבָּם וְאֹכְלֵם שָׁם כְּלָבִיא חַיַּת הַשָּׂדֶה תְּבַקְּעֵם׃
ט י שִׁחֶתְךָ יִשְׂרָאֵל כִּי־בִי בְעֶזְרֶךָ׃ אֱהִי מַלְכְּךָ אֵפוֹא וְיוֹשִׁיעֲךָ בְּכָל־עָרֶיךָ וְשֹׁפְטֶיךָ אֲשֶׁר אָמַרְתָּ
יא יב תְּנָה־לִּי מֶלֶךְ וְשָׂרִים׃ אֶתֶּן־לְךָ מֶלֶךְ בְּאַפִּי וְאֶקַּח בְּעֶבְרָתִי׃ צָרוּר עֲוֹן אֶפְרָיִם
יג צְפוּנָה חַטָּאתוֹ׃ חֶבְלֵי יוֹלֵדָה יָבֹאוּ לוֹ הוּא־בֵן לֹא חָכָם כִּי־עֵת לֹא־יַעֲמֹד בְּמִשְׁבַּר בָּנִים׃
יד טו מִיַּד שְׁאוֹל אֶפְדֵּם מִמָּוֶת אֶגְאָלֵם אֱהִי דְבָרֶיךָ מָוֶת אֱהִי קָטָבְךָ שְׁאוֹל נֹחַם יִסָּתֵר מֵעֵינָי׃ כִּי
הוּא בֵּין אַחִים יַפְרִיא יָבוֹא קָדִים רוּחַ יהוה מִמִּדְבָּר עֹלֶה וְיֵבוֹשׁ מְקוֹרוֹ וְיֶחֱרַב מַעְיָנוֹ הוּא

הספרדים מתחילים כאן

הספרדים מסיימים כאן והאשכנזים מתחילים כאן

יש מסיימים כאן

14 1 it will plunder the treasury of all the precious vessels. Samaria
will be guilty, as it defied its God; they will fall by the sword;
their infants will be mangled and their pregnant women will
2 be ruptured. Return, Israel, to the Lord your God, for you
3 have stumbled in your iniquity. Take words with yourselves
and return to the Lord. Say to Him: Forgive all iniquity, and
4 accept good, and we will pay bulls with our lips. Assyria will
not save us; we will not ride on a horse and we will no longer say to our handiwork: Our gods, for it is in You that an
5 orphan will find mercy. I will heal their mischief; I will love
6 them gratuitously, for My wrath has turned from them. I will
be like the dew to Israel; it will blossom like the lily and it
7 will strike its roots like the Lebanon. Its branches will spread,
and its beauty will be like the olive tree, its fragrance like the
8 Lebanon. Those who dwell in its shade will return; they will
give life to grain and they will blossom like the vine; its repute
9 will be like the wine of Lebanon. Ephraim: What have I to do
with idols anymore? I have responded and I will gaze upon
10 them; I am like a lush juniper; from Me, your fruit is found.
Who is wise and will understand these, understanding and will
know them? For the ways of the Lord are straight; the righteous
will walk in them, and transgressors will stumble on them.

JOEL

2 26 You will eat, eating to satisfaction, and you will praise the name
Some of the Lord your God, who has acted with you wondrously, and
add 27 My people will not be ashamed forever. You will know that I am
in the midst of Israel, and I am the Lord your God and there is
no other, and My people will not be ashamed forever.

Haftara for **Vayishlah**

The End of Edom
OBADIAH 1:1–21

This *parasha*, beginning with the complex relationship between Jacob and Esau and concluding with a list of the kings of Edom, is accompanied by a *haftara* that deals with the ultimate fate of the Edomite kingdom, Esau's descendants, while also providing a general vision of the future. Obadiah considers Edom the nation that was historically closest to Israel, and yet it treated Israel with hostility. Although Edom was not always an independent nation, when it had power it oppressed Israel greatly. Edom cooperated with all of Israel's enemies and even sought to conquer the land of Judah. The dormant brotherly hatred in Esau's heart periodically breaks out through his descendants' lethal acts of violence toward Israel. Eventually, it will be the very sword of Edom that he raises over his brother that will bring about his own destruction.

1 1 The vision of Obadiah: So said the Lord God concerning
Edom: We have heard tidings from the Lord, and an envoy was
sent among the nations: Arise, and let us rise against it in war.
2 Behold, I rendered you small among the nations; you are greatly
3 despised. The malice of your heart has misled you who dwells
in the clefts of the rock; his dwelling place is lofty. He says in his
4 heart: Who will take me down to earth? If you raise yourself
like the eagle, or place your nest among the stars, from there I
5 will bring you down – the utterance of the Lord. If thieves came
for you, if plunderers of the night, how would you be totally
destroyed? Do they not steal just enough for them? If grape
harvesters came for you, would they not leave grape gleanings?
6 7 How was Esau searched, his hoards revealed? All the men of
your covenant escorted you to the border; your allies misled
you and overcame you; they who eat your bread will set a snare
8 in your place; there is no understanding in him. Will it not be
on that day – the utterance of the Lord – that I will eliminate
the wise from Edom and understanding from the highlands of
9 Esau? Your mighty, Teman, will be dismayed so that each man
10 from the highlands of Esau will be eliminated by slaughter. For

יד א יְשַׁסֶּה אוֹצַר כָּל־כְּלִי חֶמְדָּה: תֶּאְשַׁם שֹׁמְרוֹן כִּי מָרְתָה בֵּאלֹהֶיהָ בַּחֶרֶב יִפֹּלוּ עֹלְלֵיהֶם יְרֻטָּשׁוּ
ב וְהָרִיּוֹתָיו יְבֻקָּעוּ: שׁוּבָה יִשְׂרָאֵל עַד יְהוָה אֱלֹהֶיךָ כִּי כָשַׁלְתָּ בַּעֲוֹנֶךָ: קְחוּ עִמָּכֶם
ד דְּבָרִים וְשׁוּבוּ אֶל־יְהוָה אִמְרוּ אֵלָיו כָּל־תִּשָּׂא עָוֹן וְקַח־טוֹב וּנְשַׁלְמָה פָרִים שְׂפָתֵינוּ: אַשּׁוּר ׀
לֹא יוֹשִׁיעֵנוּ עַל־סוּס לֹא נִרְכָּב וְלֹא־נֹאמַר עוֹד אֱלֹהֵינוּ לְמַעֲשֵׂה יָדֵינוּ אֲשֶׁר־בְּךָ יְרֻחַם יָתוֹם:
ה אֶרְפָּא מְשׁוּבָתָם אֹהֲבֵם נְדָבָה כִּי שָׁב אַפִּי מִמֶּנּוּ: אֶהְיֶה כַטַּל לְיִשְׂרָאֵל יִפְרַח כַּשּׁוֹשַׁנָּה וְיַךְ
שָׁרָשָׁיו כַּלְּבָנוֹן: יֵלְכוּ יֹנְקוֹתָיו וִיהִי כַזַּיִת הוֹדוֹ וְרֵיחַ לוֹ כַּלְּבָנוֹן: יָשֻׁבוּ יֹשְׁבֵי בְצִלּוֹ יְחַיּוּ דָגָן
ז וְיִפְרְחוּ כַגֶּפֶן זִכְרוֹ כְּיֵין לְבָנוֹן: אֶפְרַיִם מַה־לִּי עוֹד לָעֲצַבִּים אֲנִי עָנִיתִי וַאֲשׁוּרֶנּוּ אֲנִי כִּבְרוֹשׁ
רַעֲנָן מִמֶּנִּי פֶּרְיְךָ נִמְצָא: מִי חָכָם וְיָבֵן אֵלֶּה נָבוֹן וְיֵדָעֵם כִּי־יְשָׁרִים דַּרְכֵי יְהוָה וְצַדִּקִים יֵלְכוּ
בָם וּפֹשְׁעִים יִכָּשְׁלוּ בָם:

ב כה וַאֲכַלְתֶּם אָכוֹל וְשָׂבוֹעַ וְהִלַּלְתֶּם אֶת־שֵׁם יְהוָה אֱלֹהֵיכֶם אֲשֶׁר־עָשָׂה עִמָּכֶם לְהַפְלִיא וְלֹא־   יואל
יש מוסיפים
כו יֵבֹשׁוּ עַמִּי לְעוֹלָם: וִידַעְתֶּם כִּי בְקֶרֶב יִשְׂרָאֵל אָנִי וַאֲנִי יְהוָה אֱלֹהֵיכֶם וְאֵין עוֹד וְלֹא־יֵבֹשׁוּ
עַמִּי לְעוֹלָם:

הפטרת
וישלח

א א חֲזוֹן עֹבַדְיָה כֹּה־אָמַר אֲדֹנָי יְהוִה לֶאֱדוֹם שְׁמוּעָה שָׁמַעְנוּ מֵאֵת יְהוָה וְצִיר בַּגּוֹיִם שֻׁלָּח   עובדיה
קוּמוּ וְנָקוּמָה עָלֶיהָ לַמִּלְחָמָה: הִנֵּה קָטֹן נְתַתִּיךָ בַּגּוֹיִם בָּזוּי אַתָּה מְאֹד: זְדוֹן לִבְּךָ הִשִּׁיאֶךָ
ד שֹׁכְנִי בְחַגְוֵי־סֶלַע מְרוֹם שִׁבְתּוֹ אֹמֵר בְּלִבּוֹ מִי יוֹרִדֵנִי אָרֶץ: אִם־תַּגְבִּיהַּ כַּנֶּשֶׁר וְאִם־
ה בֵּין כּוֹכָבִים שִׂים קִנֶּךָ מִשָּׁם אוֹרִידְךָ נְאֻם־יְהוָה: אִם־גַּנָּבִים בָּאוּ־לְךָ אִם־שׁוֹדְדֵי לַיְלָה
אֵיךְ נִדְמֵיתָה הֲלוֹא יִגְנְבוּ דַּיָּם אִם־בֹּצְרִים בָּאוּ לָךְ הֲלוֹא יַשְׁאִירוּ עֹלֵלוֹת: אֵיךְ נֶחְפְּשׂוּ
ז עֵשָׂו נִבְעוּ מַצְפֻּנָיו: עַד־הַגְּבוּל שִׁלְּחוּךָ כֹּל אַנְשֵׁי בְרִיתֶךָ הִשִּׁיאוּךָ יָכְלוּ לְךָ אַנְשֵׁי שְׁלֹמֶךָ
לַחְמְךָ יָשִׂימוּ מָזוֹר תַּחְתֶּיךָ אֵין תְּבוּנָה בּוֹ: הֲלוֹא בַּיּוֹם הַהוּא נְאֻם־יְהוָה וְהַאֲבַדְתִּי חֲכָמִים
ט מֵאֱדוֹם וּתְבוּנָה מֵהַר עֵשָׂו: וְחַתּוּ גִבּוֹרֶיךָ תֵּימָן לְמַעַן יִכָּרֶת־אִישׁ מֵהַר עֵשָׂו מִקָּטֶל:

the villainy to your brother Jacob, shame will cover you and you
11 will be eliminated forever. On the day that you stood opposite,
on the day that strangers captured his riches and foreigners entered his gates and cast lots on Jerusalem, you too were like one
12 of them. Do not gaze on the day of your brother, on the day of
his calamity; do not rejoice over the children of Judah on the
day of their destruction; do not open wide your mouth on the
13 day of distress. Do not enter the gate of My people on the day
of their destruction; you, do not also gaze on his misfortune
on the day of his ruin and do not reach for his riches on the
14 day of his ruin. Do not stand at the crossroads to eliminate his
survivors, and do not turn over his refugees on the day of dis-
15 tress. For the day of the Lord is near upon all the nations; what
you did will be done to you; your retribution will return upon
16 your head. For as you drank on My holy mountain, so will all
the nations drink always; they will drink and they will swallow,
17 and they will be as if they had not been. But on Mount Zion
there will be a remnant, and it will be holy, and the house of
18 Jacob will take possession from their dispossessors. The house
of Jacob will be fire, and the house of Joseph a flame, and the
house of Esau straw, and they will ignite them, and consume
them; there will not be any survivor of the house of Esau, as
19 the Lord has spoken. The South will take possession of the
highlands of Esau and the plain, the Philistines; they will take
possession of the field of Ephraim and the field of Samaria, and
20 Benjamin, the Gilad. The exile of this host of the children of
Israel, who are among the Canaanites, up to Tzarefat and the
exile of Jerusalem that is in Sefarad will take possession of the
21 cities of the South. Saviors will ascend Mount Zion to judge the
highlands of Esau, and the kingdom will be to the Lord.

Haftara for **Vayeshev**

On Hanukkah, the haftara on page 1280 is read.

Reproof and Retribution for the Unjust and Blasphemous

AMOS 2:6–3:8

Amos's description of Israel's first transgression, "For their sale of the righteous for silver" (Amos 2:6), has been explained by sages of later generations as a reference to the sale of Joseph, as related in *Parashat Vayeshev* (see *Tanḥuma*, Noah 5). In addition, Joseph's dreams and his ability to interpret the dreams of others are connected to Amos's statements concerning the talent for prophecy, which God grants certain individuals so that they will lead people on the upright path and which allows them a glimpse of future events.

2 6 So said the Lord: For three transgressions of Israel, but for
the fourth, I will not relent: For their sale of the righteous
for silver and the indigent for a pair of shoes. They tread on
the dust of the earth, on the head of the impoverished, and
divert the way of the humble; a man and his father go to the
8 same young woman in order to profane My holy name. They
recline on pawned garments beside every altar, and the wine
9 of the penalized they drink in the house of their God. I destroyed the Emorites from before them, whose height was like
the height of cedars and who were strong as the oaks; I de-
10 stroyed his fruit from above and his roots from below. I took
you up from the land of Egypt and led you in the wilderness
forty years, to take possession of the land of the Emorites.

יא מֵחֲמַס אָחִיךָ יַעֲקֹב תְּכַסְּךָ בוּשָׁה וְנִכְרַתָּ לְעוֹלָם׃ בְּיוֹם עֲמׇדְךָ מִנֶּגֶד בְּיוֹם שְׁבוֹת זָרִים חֵילוֹ
יב וְנׇכְרִים בָּאוּ שְׁעָרָו וְעַל־יְרוּשָׁלִַם יַדּוּ גוֹרָל גַּם־אַתָּה כְּאַחַד מֵהֶם׃ וְאַל־תֵּרֶא בְיוֹם־אָחִיךָ
יג בְּיוֹם נׇכְרוֹ וְאַל־תִּשְׂמַח לִבְנֵי־יְהוּדָה בְּיוֹם אׇבְדָם וְאַל־תַּגְדֵּל פִּיךָ בְּיוֹם צָרָה׃ אַל־תָּבוֹא
בְשַׁעַר־עַמִּי בְּיוֹם אֵידָם אַל־תֵּרֶא גַם־אַתָּה בְּרָעָתוֹ בְּיוֹם אֵידוֹ וְאַל־תִּשְׁלַחְנָה בְחֵילוֹ בְּיוֹם
יד טו אֵידוֹ׃ וְאַל־תַּעֲמֹד עַל־הַפֶּרֶק לְהַכְרִית אֶת־פְּלִיטָיו וְאַל־תַּסְגֵּר שְׂרִידָיו בְּיוֹם צָרָה׃ כִּי־
טז קָרוֹב יוֹם־יְהֹוָה עַל־כׇּל־הַגּוֹיִם כַּאֲשֶׁר עָשִׂיתָ יֵעָשֶׂה לָּךְ גְּמֻלְךָ יָשׁוּב בְּרֹאשֶׁךָ׃ כִּי כַּאֲשֶׁר
יז שְׁתִיתֶם עַל־הַר קׇדְשִׁי יִשְׁתּוּ כׇל־הַגּוֹיִם תָּמִיד וְשָׁתוּ וְלָעוּ וְהָיוּ כְּלוֹא הָיוּ׃ וּבְהַר צִיּוֹן תִּהְיֶה
יח פְלֵיטָה וְהָיָה קֹדֶשׁ וְיָרְשׁוּ בֵּית יַעֲקֹב אֵת מוֹרָשֵׁיהֶם׃ וְהָיָה בֵית־יַעֲקֹב אֵשׁ וּבֵית יוֹסֵף לֶהָבָה
יט וּבֵית עֵשָׂו לְקַשׁ וְדָלְקוּ בָהֶם וַאֲכָלוּם וְלֹא־יִהְיֶה שָׂרִיד לְבֵית עֵשָׂו כִּי יְהֹוָה דִּבֵּר׃ וְיָרְשׁוּ
הַנֶּגֶב אֶת־הַר עֵשָׂו וְהַשְּׁפֵלָה אֶת־פְּלִשְׁתִּים וְיָרְשׁוּ אֶת־שְׂדֵה אֶפְרַיִם וְאֵת שְׂדֵה שֹׁמְרוֹן
כ וּבִנְיָמִן אֶת־הַגִּלְעָד׃ וְגָלֻת הַחֵל־הַזֶּה לִבְנֵי יִשְׂרָאֵל אֲשֶׁר־כְּנַעֲנִים עַד־צָרְפַת וְגָלֻת יְרוּשָׁלִַם
כא אֲשֶׁר בִּסְפָרַד יִרְשׁוּ אֵת עָרֵי הַנֶּגֶב׃ וְעָלוּ מוֹשִׁעִים בְּהַר צִיּוֹן לִשְׁפֹּט אֶת־הַר עֵשָׂו וְהָיְתָה
לַיהֹוָה הַמְּלוּכָה׃

הפטרת
וישב

בחנוכה קוראים את ההפטרה בעמוד 1281.

עמוס

ב ו כֹּה אָמַר יְהֹוָה עַל־שְׁלֹשָׁה פִּשְׁעֵי יִשְׂרָאֵל וְעַל־אַרְבָּעָה לֹא אֲשִׁיבֶנּוּ עַל־מִכְרָם בַּכֶּסֶף
ז צַדִּיק וְאֶבְיוֹן בַּעֲבוּר נַעֲלָיִם׃ הַשֹּׁאֲפִים עַל־עֲפַר־אֶרֶץ בְּרֹאשׁ דַּלִּים וְדֶרֶךְ עֲנָוִים יַטּוּ וְאִישׁ
ח וְאָבִיו יֵלְכוּ אֶל־הַנַּעֲרָה לְמַעַן חַלֵּל אֶת־שֵׁם קׇדְשִׁי׃ וְעַל־בְּגָדִים חֲבֻלִים יַטּוּ אֵצֶל כׇּל־
ט מִזְבֵּחַ וְיֵין עֲנוּשִׁים יִשְׁתּוּ בֵּית אֱלֹהֵיהֶם׃ וְאָנֹכִי הִשְׁמַדְתִּי אֶת־הָאֱמֹרִי מִפְּנֵיהֶם אֲשֶׁר כְּגֹבַהּ
י אֲרָזִים גׇּבְהוֹ וְחָסֹן הוּא כָּאַלּוֹנִים וָאַשְׁמִיד פִּרְיוֹ מִמַּעַל וְשׇׁרָשָׁיו מִתָּחַת׃ וְאָנֹכִי הֶעֱלֵיתִי
אֶתְכֶם מֵאֶרֶץ מִצְרָיִם וָאוֹלֵךְ אֶתְכֶם בַּמִּדְבָּר אַרְבָּעִים שָׁנָה לָרֶשֶׁת אֶת־אֶרֶץ הָאֱמֹרִי׃

11 I raised up prophets from your sons, and Nazirites from your young men. Is this not so, children of Israel? – the utterance

12 of the Lord. You gave the Nazirites wine to drink, and com-

13 manded the prophets, saying: Do not prophesy. Behold, I will overburden you in your place, like a cart that is full of sheaves

14 is overburdened. Flight will elude the swift; the strong will not

15 exert his strength and the valiant will not save himself. The archer will not stand, and the swift of foot will not escape, and the

16 rider of the horse will not save himself. The courageous of heart among the valiant will flee naked on that day – the utterance

3 1 of the Lord. Hear this word that the Lord has spoken concerning you, children of Israel, concerning the entire family that I

2 took up from the land of Egypt, saying: Only you have I known from all the families of the earth; therefore, I will reckon upon

3 you all your iniquities. Will two walk together, unless they were

4 destined? Will a lion roar in the forest, if it has no prey? Will a young lion project its voice from its lair, unless it has captured?

5 Will a bird fall into a trap on the ground, and there is no snare

6 for it? Will a trap arise from the ground, and not capture? Will the shofar be sounded in a city, and the people not tremble? Will there be misfortune in a city, and the Lord did not do it?

7 For the Lord God will not do anything unless He revealed His

8 secret to His servants, the prophets. A lion roared, who will not fear? The Lord God spoke, who will not prophesy?

Haftara for
Miketz

On Hanukkah, the haftara on page 1280 is read. On the second Shabbat of Hanukkah, the haftara on page 1282 is read.

The Judgment of Solomon
I KINGS 3:15–4:1

In his prophetic dream, Solomon petitioned God for "an attentive heart" (I Kings 3:9), with which he could judge and lead the people, and God granted him his request. Likewise, in the *parasha*, Joseph displays through his wisdom and insight the spirit of God that is within him. In addition, the phrase "and he awoke…and behold, a dream," which appears near the beginning of the *parasha* (Genesis 41:7), is also the opening formula of the *haftara*.

3 15 Solomon awoke, and behold, a dream. He came to Jerusalem and stood before the Ark of the Covenant of the Lord, and he offered up burnt offerings, and he prepared peace offerings

16 and made a feast for all his servants. Then two women prosti-

17 tutes came to the king and stood before him. The one woman said: Please, my lord, I and this woman live in one house, and

18 I gave birth with her in the house. It was on the third day after my giving birth that this woman too gave birth, and we were together; there was no stranger with us in the house, other

19 than the two of us in the house. The son of this woman died

20 at night, because she lay upon him. She arose during the night, and she took my son from beside me, while your maidservant was asleep, and she laid him in her bosom, and she laid her

21 dead child in my bosom. I arose in the morning to nurse my son, and behold, he was dead; but when I examined him in the morning, behold, it was not my son to whom I gave birth.

22 The other woman said: No, for my son is the living and your son is the dead. But this one said: No, rather, your son is the dead and my son is the living, and they spoke before the king.

יא יב וָאָקִים מִבְּנֵיכֶם לִנְבִיאִים וּמִבַּחוּרֵיכֶם לִנְזִרִים הַאַף אֵין־זֹאת בְּנֵי יִשְׂרָאֵל נְאֻם־יהוה: וַתַּשְׁקוּ
יג אֶת־הַנְּזִרִים יָיִן וְעַל־הַנְּבִיאִים צִוִּיתֶם לֵאמֹר לֹא תִּנָּבְאוּ: הִנֵּה אָנֹכִי מֵעִיק תַּחְתֵּיכֶם כַּאֲשֶׁר
יד תָּעִיק הָעֲגָלָה הַמְלֵאָה לָהּ עָמִיר: וְאָבַד מָנוֹס מִקָּל וְחָזָק לֹא־יְאַמֵּץ כֹּחוֹ וְגִבּוֹר לֹא־יְמַלֵּט
טו טז נַפְשׁוֹ: וְתֹפֵשׂ הַקֶּשֶׁת לֹא יַעֲמֹד וְקַל בְּרַגְלָיו לֹא יְמַלֵּט וְרֹכֵב הַסּוּס לֹא יְמַלֵּט נַפְשׁוֹ: וְאַמִּיץ
ג א לִבּוֹ בַּגִּבּוֹרִים עָרוֹם יָנוּס בַּיּוֹם־הַהוּא נְאֻם־יהוה: שִׁמְעוּ אֶת־הַדָּבָר הַזֶּה אֲשֶׁר דִּבֶּר
ב יהוה עֲלֵיכֶם בְּנֵי יִשְׂרָאֵל עַל כָּל־הַמִּשְׁפָּחָה אֲשֶׁר הֶעֱלֵיתִי מֵאֶרֶץ מִצְרַיִם לֵאמֹר: רַק אֶתְכֶם
ג יָדַעְתִּי מִכֹּל מִשְׁפְּחוֹת הָאֲדָמָה עַל־כֵּן אֶפְקֹד עֲלֵיכֶם אֵת כָּל־עֲוֺנֹתֵיכֶם: הֲיֵלְכוּ שְׁנַיִם יַחְדָּו בִּלְתִּי
ד ה אִם־נוֹעָדוּ: הֲיִשְׁאַג אַרְיֵה בַּיַּעַר וְטֶרֶף אֵין לוֹ הֲיִתֵּן כְּפִיר קוֹלוֹ מִמְּעֹנָתוֹ בִּלְתִּי אִם־לָכָד: הֲתִפֹּל
ו צִפּוֹר עַל־פַּח הָאָרֶץ וּמוֹקֵשׁ אֵין לָהּ הֲיַעֲלֶה־פַּח מִן־הָאֲדָמָה וְלָכוֹד לֹא יִלְכּוֹד: אִם־יִתָּקַע שׁוֹפָר
ז בְּעִיר וְעָם לֹא יֶחֱרָדוּ אִם־תִּהְיֶה רָעָה בְּעִיר וַיהוה לֹא עָשָׂה: כִּי לֹא יַעֲשֶׂה אֲדֹנָי יהוה דָּבָר כִּי
ח אִם־גָּלָה סוֹדוֹ אֶל־עֲבָדָיו הַנְּבִיאִים: אַרְיֵה שָׁאָג מִי לֹא יִירָא אֲדֹנָי יהוה דִּבֶּר מִי לֹא יִנָּבֵא:

הפטרת

מקץ

בחנוכה קוראים את ההפטרה בעמ׳ 1281. בשבת השנייה של חנוכה קוראים את ההפטרה בעמ׳ 1283.

ג טו וַיִּקַץ שְׁלֹמֹה וְהִנֵּה חֲלוֹם וַיָּבוֹא יְרוּשָׁלַםִ וַיַּעֲמֹד ׀ לִפְנֵי ׀ אֲרוֹן בְּרִית־אֲדֹנָי וַיַּעַל עֹלוֹת מלכים א׳
טז וַיַּעַשׂ שְׁלָמִים וַיַּעַשׂ מִשְׁתֶּה לְכָל־עֲבָדָיו: אָז תָּבֹאנָה שְׁתַּיִם נָשִׁים זֹנוֹת
יז אֶל־הַמֶּלֶךְ וַתַּעֲמֹדְנָה לְפָנָיו: וַתֹּאמֶר הָאִשָּׁה הָאַחַת בִּי אֲדֹנִי אֲנִי וְהָאִשָּׁה הַזֹּאת יֹשְׁבֹת
יח בְּבַיִת אֶחָד וָאֵלֵד עִמָּהּ בַּבָּיִת: וַיְהִי בַּיּוֹם הַשְּׁלִישִׁי לְלִדְתִּי וַתֵּלֶד גַּם־הָאִשָּׁה הַזֹּאת
יט וַאֲנַחְנוּ יַחְדָּו אֵין־זָר אִתָּנוּ בַּבַּיִת זוּלָתִי שְׁתַּיִם־אֲנַחְנוּ בַּבָּיִת: וַיָּמָת בֶּן־הָאִשָּׁה הַזֹּאת
כ לָיְלָה אֲשֶׁר שָׁכְבָה עָלָיו: וַתָּקָם בְּתוֹךְ הַלַּיְלָה וַתִּקַּח אֶת־בְּנִי מֵאֶצְלִי וַאֲמָתְךָ יְשֵׁנָה
כא וַתַּשְׁכִּיבֵהוּ בְּחֵיקָהּ וְאֶת־בְּנָהּ הַמֵּת הִשְׁכִּיבָה בְחֵיקִי: וָאָקֻם בַּבֹּקֶר לְהֵינִיק אֶת־בְּנִי וְהִנֵּה־
כב מֵת וָאֶתְבּוֹנֵן אֵלָיו בַּבֹּקֶר וְהִנֵּה לֹא־הָיָה בְנִי אֲשֶׁר יָלָדְתִּי: וַתֹּאמֶר הָאִשָּׁה הָאַחֶרֶת לֹא
כִי בְּנִי הַחַי וּבְנֵךְ הַמֵּת וְזֹאת אֹמֶרֶת לֹא כִי בְּנֵךְ הַמֵּת וּבְנִי הֶחָי וַתְּדַבֵּרְנָה לִפְנֵי הַמֶּלֶךְ:

23 The king said: This one says: This is my living son, and your son is the dead; and that one says: No, rather, your son is the

24 dead, and my son is the living. The king said: Bring me a sword.

25 They brought a sword before the king. The king said: Cut the

26 living child in two, and give half to one and half to one. The woman whose son was the living child said to the king, because her mercy was aroused toward her son, and she said: Please,

my lord, give her the living baby, and do not put him to death. But that one was saying: It will not be mine and not yours; cut.

27 The king responded and said: Give her the living baby, and do

28 not put him to death; she is his mother. All Israel heard the judgment that the king adjudicated, and they feared the king, as they saw that the wisdom of God was in him, to perform justice.

4 1 King Solomon was king over all Israel.

Haftara for
Vayigash

The Gathering and Unification of Israel

EZEKIEL 37:15–28

The pattern of confrontation and subsequent reconciliation between Joseph and his brothers, led by Judah, recurred in different forms over the centuries. In this prophecy of comfort, issued after the destruction of the Temple, the prophet Ezekiel predicts the ultimate unification of the house of Israel under a single king from the tribe of Judah. Unlike most other prophecies, there is no demand here for the people's repentance or remorse as preconditions for redemption. Rather, God will act on His terms, and Israel is required only to be open to the possibility of redemption, which will bring about the Kingdom of Heaven on earth.

37 $^{15}_{16}$ The word of the Lord was with me, saying: You, Son of man, take for you one piece of wood and write on it: For Judah and for the children of Israel, his companions; and take another piece of wood and write on it: For Joseph, the wood of Ephraim, and

17 all the house of Israel, his companions. Draw them near one to another as one piece of wood for you, and they will be as one

18 in your hand. When the children of your people will speak to

19 you, saying: Will you not tell us what these are to you? Speak to them: So said the Lord God: Behold, I am taking the wood of Joseph that is in the hand of Ephraim and the tribes of Israel, his companions, and I will place them with him, with the wood of Judah, and I will make them as one piece of wood, and they

20 will be one in My hand. The pieces of wood upon which you

21 will write will be in your hand, before their eyes. Speak to them: So said the Lord God: Behold, I am taking the children of Israel from among the nations to which they went, and I will gather

22 them from all around, and I will bring them to their land. I will make them into one nation, in the land, on the mountains of Israel, and one king will be king for all of them, and they will no longer be two nations, and they will not be divided any

23 more into two kingdoms, ever. They will no longer be defiled with their idols and with their detestable things and with all their transgressions, and I will save them from all their dwellings in which they sinned, and I will purify them. They will be

24 My people, and I will be their God. My servant David will be king over them, and there will be one shepherd for all of them, and they will follow My ordinances and observe My statutes

25 and perform them. They will dwell in the land that I gave to My servant, to Jacob, in which your fathers dwelled. They will dwell in it, they and their children and their children's children, forever. And David My servant will be their prince forever.

כג וַיֹּאמֶר הַמֶּלֶךְ זֹאת אֹמֶרֶת זֶה־בְּנִי הַחַי וּבְנֵךְ הַמֵּת וְזֹאת אֹמֶרֶת לֹא כִי בְּנֵךְ הַמֵּת וּבְנִי
הֶחָי: כד וַיֹּאמֶר הַמֶּלֶךְ קְחוּ לִי־חָרֶב וַיָּבִאוּ הַחֶרֶב לִפְנֵי הַמֶּלֶךְ: כה וַיֹּאמֶר הַמֶּלֶךְ גִּזְרוּ
כו אֶת־הַיֶּלֶד הַחַי לִשְׁנָיִם וּתְנוּ אֶת־הַחֲצִי לְאַחַת וְאֶת־הַחֲצִי לְאֶחָת: וַתֹּאמֶר הָאִשָּׁה אֲשֶׁר־
בְּנָהּ הַחַי אֶל־הַמֶּלֶךְ כִּי־נִכְמְרוּ רַחֲמֶיהָ עַל־בְּנָהּ וַתֹּאמֶר ׀ בִּי אֲדֹנִי תְּנוּ־לָהּ אֶת־הַיָּלוּד הַחַי
כז וְהָמֵת אַל־תְּמִיתֻהוּ וְזֹאת אֹמֶרֶת גַּם־לִי גַם־לָךְ לֹא יִהְיֶה גְּזֹרוּ: וַיַּעַן הַמֶּלֶךְ וַיֹּאמֶר תְּנוּ־לָהּ
כח אֶת־הַיָּלוּד הַחַי וְהָמֵת לֹא תְמִיתֻהוּ הִיא אִמּוֹ: וַיִּשְׁמְעוּ כָל־יִשְׂרָאֵל אֶת־הַמִּשְׁפָּט אֲשֶׁר שָׁפַט
ד א הַמֶּלֶךְ וַיִּרְאוּ מִפְּנֵי הַמֶּלֶךְ כִּי רָאוּ כִּי־חָכְמַת אֱלֹהִים בְּקִרְבּוֹ לַעֲשׂוֹת מִשְׁפָּט: וַיְהִי הַמֶּלֶךְ
שְׁלֹמֹה מֶלֶךְ עַל־כָּל־יִשְׂרָאֵל:

הפטרת
ויגש

יחזקאל

לז וַיְהִי דְבַר־יְהוָה אֵלַי לֵאמֹר: וְאַתָּה בֶן־אָדָם קַח־לְךָ עֵץ אֶחָד וּכְתֹב עָלָיו לִיהוּדָה וְלִבְנֵי
ישראל חֲבֵרָו וּלְקַח עֵץ אֶחָד וּכְתוֹב עָלָיו לְיוֹסֵף עֵץ אֶפְרַיִם וְכָל־בֵּית יִשְׂרָאֵל חֲבֵרָו:
יח וְקָרַב אֹתָם אֶחָד אֶל־אֶחָד לְךָ לְעֵץ אֶחָד וְהָיוּ לַאֲחָדִים בְּיָדֶךָ: וְכַאֲשֶׁר יֹאמְרוּ אֵלֶיךָ
בְּנֵי עַמְּךָ לֵאמֹר הֲלוֹא־תַגִּיד לָנוּ מָה־אֵלֶּה לָּךְ: דַּבֵּר אֲלֵהֶם כֹּה־אָמַר אֲדֹנָי יְהוִה הִנֵּה
אֲנִי לֹקֵחַ אֶת־עֵץ יוֹסֵף אֲשֶׁר בְּיַד־אֶפְרַיִם וְשִׁבְטֵי יִשְׂרָאֵל חֲבֵרָו וְנָתַתִּי אוֹתָם עָלָיו אֶת־
כ עֵץ יְהוּדָה וַעֲשִׂיתִם לְעֵץ אֶחָד וְהָיוּ אֶחָד בְּיָדִי: וְהָיוּ הָעֵצִים אֲשֶׁר־תִּכְתֹּב עֲלֵיהֶם בְּיָדְךָ
כא לְעֵינֵיהֶם: וְדַבֵּר אֲלֵיהֶם כֹּה־אָמַר אֲדֹנָי יְהוִה הִנֵּה אֲנִי לֹקֵחַ אֶת־בְּנֵי יִשְׂרָאֵל מִבֵּין הַגּוֹיִם
כב אֲשֶׁר הָלְכוּ־שָׁם וְקִבַּצְתִּי אֹתָם מִסָּבִיב וְהֵבֵאתִי אוֹתָם אֶל־אַדְמָתָם: וְעָשִׂיתִי אֹתָם לְגוֹי
אֶחָד בָּאָרֶץ בְּהָרֵי יִשְׂרָאֵל וּמֶלֶךְ אֶחָד יִהְיֶה לְכֻלָּם לְמֶלֶךְ וְלֹא יִהְיֶה־עוֹד לִשְׁנֵי גוֹיִם וְלֹא יהיו
כג יֵחָצוּ עוֹד לִשְׁתֵּי מַמְלָכוֹת עוֹד: וְלֹא יִטַמְּאוּ עוֹד בְּגִלּוּלֵיהֶם וּבְשִׁקּוּצֵיהֶם וּבְכֹל פִּשְׁעֵיהֶם
וְהוֹשַׁעְתִּי אֹתָם מִכֹּל מוֹשְׁבֹתֵיהֶם אֲשֶׁר חָטְאוּ בָהֶם וְטִהַרְתִּי אוֹתָם וְהָיוּ־לִי לְעָם וַאֲנִי
כד אֶהְיֶה לָהֶם לֵאלֹהִים: וְעַבְדִּי דָוִד מֶלֶךְ עֲלֵיהֶם וְרוֹעֶה אֶחָד יִהְיֶה לְכֻלָּם וּבְמִשְׁפָּטַי יֵלֵכוּ
כה וְחֻקֹּתַי יִשְׁמְרוּ וְעָשׂוּ אוֹתָם: וְיָשְׁבוּ עַל־הָאָרֶץ אֲשֶׁר נָתַתִּי לְעַבְדִּי לְיַעֲקֹב אֲשֶׁר יָשְׁבוּ־בָהּ
אֲבוֹתֵיכֶם וְיָשְׁבוּ עָלֶיהָ הֵמָּה וּבְנֵיהֶם וּבְנֵי בְנֵיהֶם עַד־עוֹלָם וְדָוִד עַבְדִּי נָשִׂיא לָהֶם לְעוֹלָם:

26 I will establish a covenant of peace with them; it will be an eternal covenant with them. I will place them, and I will multiply

27 them, and I will place My Sanctuary in their midst forever. My dwelling place will be among them; I will be their God, and

28 they will be My people. And the nations will know that I am the Lord who sanctifies Israel when My Sanctuary is in their midst forever.

Haftara for
Vayhi

David's Last Will and His Death
I KINGS 2:1–12

Before King David departs from the world, he provides words of encouragement to his son Solomon and instructs him to follow the path of God and obey His laws. David also imposes upon the young king specific tasks, most of which are unpleasant, as he expects him to deal with some unfinished matters that he was unable to take care of himself. The opening phrase of the *haftara*, "The time for David to die approached" (I Kings 2:1), is clearly reminiscent of the beginning of the *parasha*: "The time for Israel to die approached" (Genesis 47:29). In the *parasha* as well, Jacob issues words of support to his sons and offers them guidance for the future.

2 1 The time for David to die approached, and he commanded

2 Solomon his son, saying: I am going the way of all the earth;

3 be strong, and become a man. You shall keep the commission of the Lord your God, to walk in His ways, to keep His statutes, His commandments, His ordinances, and His testimonies, as written in the Torah of Moses, so that you will succeed in every-

4 thing that you do, and wherever you turn; so that the Lord will fulfill His word that He spoke concerning me, saying: If your children keep their way, to walk before Me truly with all their heart and with all their soul, saying: A man of yours will never

5 be eliminated from upon the throne of Israel. Furthermore, you know that which Yoav son of Tzeruya did to me, what he did to the two captains of the hosts of Israel, to Avner son of Ner, and to Amasa son of Yeter. He killed them and shed the blood of war in peacetime, and he placed the blood of war on his belt that was on his waist, and on his shoes that were on his

6 feet. Act in accordance with your wisdom, and do not let his

7 white hair descend in peace to the grave. Act with kindness to the sons of Barzilai the Giladite, and they shall be among those who eat at your table, as they befriended me when I fled from

8 Avshalom your brother. Here with you is Shimi son of Gera, the Benjamite, of Bahurim; he cursed me with a substantial curse on the day that I went to Mahanayim. He came down to meet me at the Jordan, and I took an oath to him by the Lord, saying:

9 I will not put you to death by the sword. Now, do not absolve him, as you are a wise man; you will know what you should do to him, and you will cause his white hair to descend to the

10 grave in blood. David lay with his fathers, and he was buried in

11 the city of David. The days that David reigned over Israel were forty years: In Hebron he reigned seven years, and in Jerusalem

12 he reigned thirty-three years. Solomon sat upon the throne of David his father; and his kingdom was firmly established.

כו וְכָרַתִּי לָהֶם בְּרִית שָׁלוֹם בְּרִית עוֹלָם יִהְיֶה אוֹתָם וּנְתַתִּים וְהִרְבֵּיתִי אוֹתָם וְנָתַתִּי אֶת־מִקְדָּשִׁי
כז כח בְּתוֹכָם לְעוֹלָם׃ וְהָיָה מִשְׁכָּנִי עֲלֵיהֶם וְהָיִיתִי לָהֶם לֵאלֹהִים וְהֵמָּה יִהְיוּ־לִי לְעָם׃ וְיָדְעוּ הַגּוֹיִם
כִּי אֲנִי יְהוָה מְקַדֵּשׁ אֶת־יִשְׂרָאֵל בִּהְיוֹת מִקְדָּשִׁי בְּתוֹכָם לְעוֹלָם׃

הפטרת

ויחי

מלכים א׳

ב א ב וַיִּקְרְבוּ יְמֵי־דָוִד לָמוּת וַיְצַו אֶת־שְׁלֹמֹה בְנוֹ לֵאמֹר׃ אָנֹכִי הֹלֵךְ בְּדֶרֶךְ כָּל־הָאָרֶץ וְחָזַקְתָּ
ג וְהָיִיתָ לְאִישׁ׃ וְשָׁמַרְתָּ אֶת־מִשְׁמֶרֶת ׀ יְהוָה אֱלֹהֶיךָ לָלֶכֶת בִּדְרָכָיו לִשְׁמֹר חֻקֹּתָיו מִצְוֺתָיו
וּמִשְׁפָּטָיו וְעֵדְוֺתָיו כַּכָּתוּב בְּתוֹרַת מֹשֶׁה לְמַעַן תַּשְׂכִּיל אֵת כָּל־אֲשֶׁר תַּעֲשֶׂה וְאֵת כָּל־
ד אֲשֶׁר תִּפְנֶה שָׁם׃ לְמַעַן יָקִים יְהוָה אֶת־דְּבָרוֹ אֲשֶׁר דִּבֶּר עָלַי לֵאמֹר אִם־יִשְׁמְרוּ בָנֶיךָ
אֶת־דַּרְכָּם לָלֶכֶת לְפָנַי בֶּאֱמֶת בְּכָל־לְבָבָם וּבְכָל־נַפְשָׁם לֵאמֹר לֹא־יִכָּרֵת לְךָ אִישׁ מֵעַל
ה כִּסֵּא יִשְׂרָאֵל׃ וְגַם אַתָּה יָדַעְתָּ אֵת אֲשֶׁר־עָשָׂה לִי יוֹאָב בֶּן־צְרוּיָה אֲשֶׁר עָשָׂה לִשְׁנֵי־
שָׂרֵי צִבְאוֹת יִשְׂרָאֵל לְאַבְנֵר בֶּן־נֵר וְלַעֲמָשָׂא בֶן־יֶתֶר וַיַּהַרְגֵם וַיָּשֶׂם דְּמֵי־מִלְחָמָה בְּשָׁלֹם
ו וַיִּתֵּן דְּמֵי מִלְחָמָה בַּחֲגֹרָתוֹ אֲשֶׁר בְּמָתְנָיו וּבְנַעֲלוֹ אֲשֶׁר בְּרַגְלָיו׃ וְעָשִׂיתָ כְּחָכְמָתֶךָ וְלֹא־
ז תוֹרֵד שֵׂיבָתוֹ בְּשָׁלֹם שְׁאֹל׃ וְלִבְנֵי בַרְזִלַּי הַגִּלְעָדִי תַּעֲשֶׂה־חֶסֶד וְהָיוּ בְּאֹכְלֵי
ח שֻׁלְחָנֶךָ כִּי־כֵן קָרְבוּ אֵלַי בְּבָרְחִי מִפְּנֵי אַבְשָׁלוֹם אָחִיךָ׃ וְהִנֵּה עִמְּךָ שִׁמְעִי בֶן־גֵּרָא בֶן־
הַיְמִינִי מִבַּחֻרִים וְהוּא קִלְלַנִי קְלָלָה נִמְרֶצֶת בְּיוֹם לֶכְתִּי מַחֲנָיִם וְהוּא־יָרַד לִקְרָאתִי הַיַּרְדֵּן
ט וָאֶשָּׁבַע לוֹ בַיהוָה לֵאמֹר אִם־אֲמִיתְךָ בֶּחָרֶב׃ וְעַתָּה אַל־תְּנַקֵּהוּ כִּי אִישׁ חָכָם אָתָּה וְיָדַעְתָּ
י אֵת אֲשֶׁר תַּעֲשֶׂה־לּוֹ וְהוֹרַדְתָּ אֶת־שֵׂיבָתוֹ בְּדָם שְׁאוֹל׃ וַיִּשְׁכַּב דָּוִד עִם־אֲבֹתָיו וַיִּקָּבֵר
יא בְּעִיר דָּוִד׃ וְהַיָּמִים אֲשֶׁר מָלַךְ דָּוִד עַל־יִשְׂרָאֵל אַרְבָּעִים שָׁנָה בְּחֶבְרוֹן מָלַךְ
יב שֶׁבַע שָׁנִים וּבִירוּשָׁלַם מָלַךְ שְׁלֹשִׁים וְשָׁלֹשׁ שָׁנִים׃ וּשְׁלֹמֹה יָשַׁב עַל־כִּסֵּא דָּוִד אָבִיו וַתִּכֹּן
מַלְכֻתוֹ מְאֹד׃

Haftara for
Shemot

The Sufferings and Salvation of the House of Jacob

ISAIAH 27:6–28:13, 29:22–23

At the beginning of the *parasha*, the first exile of Jacob's descendants is recounted; in the *haftara*, Isaiah prophesies that the nation of Israel will ultimately return from exile and thrive in Jerusalem. Between the *haftara's* initial verses predicting salvation and its encouraging concluding words, the prophet depicts a corrupt and haughty nation that rebuffs, with indifference, any attempt to offer it reproof or teach its people Torah, and which claims that these matters are childish or simply irrelevant to contemporary discourse. The prophecy ends with a vision of a future transformation, when the house of Jacob will recognize and appreciate the Holy One, the God of Israel.

27 *Ashk. begin*

6 It is coming that Jacob will take root, Israel will bud and blos-
7 som, and the face of the earth will be filled with fruit. Did He strike it like the strike of its strikers? Was it killed like the kill-
8 ing of its killers? In measure, in sending it away, You contend with it; it roared its harsh wind on the day of the east wind.
9 Therefore, with this will the iniquity of Jacob be atoned, and this is the consequence of the removal of his sin: In rendering all the altar stones to be like shattered limestone; the sacred
10 trees and the sunstones will not stand. For the fortified city is alone, a habitation abandoned and forsaken like the wilder-ness; there the calf will graze, and there it will lie and consume
11 its branches. When its boughs wither, they will break; women will come and kindle it, for it is not a people of understanding; therefore, its Maker will not be merciful to it, and its Fashioner
12 will not show it grace. It will be on that day that the Lord will thrash from the current of the river until the ravine of Egypt,
13 and you will be gathered one by one, children of Israel. It will be on that day that a great shofar will be sounded, and the lost in the land of Assyria and the outcasts in the land of Egypt will come, and they will prostrate themselves to the Lord on the

28 1 holy mountain in Jerusalem. Woe, the crown of pride of the drunkards of Ephraim and the wilting diadem of his magnifi-cent splendor, which is on a head that is a valley of oils, stunned
2 with wine. Behold, strong and mighty for our Master, like a torrent of hail, a storm of destruction, as a torrent of mighty
3 flowing waters, He places it on the earth with His hand. With feet will the crown of pride of the drunkards of Ephraim be

4 trampled. The wilting diadem, his magnificent splendor that is on a head that is a valley of oils, will be like a ripened fig before the summer; when the observer sees it, while it is still in his
5 hand he will swallow it. On that day, the Lord of hosts will be a crown of glory and a diadem of beauty for the remnant of His
6 people and a spirit of judgment for one who sits in judgment
7 and valor for those who return war to the gate. These, too, erred with wine and strayed with intoxicating drink; the priest and the prophet erred with intoxicating drink, they were befuddled from wine; they strayed due to intoxicating drink, they erred
8 in sight, they distorted justice. For all tables are full of vomit,
9 excrement, with no room. To whom will one teach knowledge, and who will understand a message? Those weaned from the
10 milk, detached from breasts? For it is command by command, command by command, line by line, line by line, a bit here, a
11 bit there. For with garbled language and with a different tongue
12 one will speak to this people, saying to them: This is the rest, give rest to the weary and this is the respite, but they were un-
13 willing to hear. The word of the Lord will be for them command by command, command by command, line by line, line by line, a bit here, a bit there, so that they will go and falter backward

29 22 and be broken; they will be tripped and captured. Therefore, so says the Lord who redeemed Abraham to the house of Jacob: Not now will Jacob be ashamed, not now will his face pale,
23 for upon his seeing his children, My handiwork, in his midst, they will sanctify My name; they will sanctify the Holy One of Jacob, and they will venerate the God of Israel.

Ashk. end

ישעיה
לאשכנזים

כז הַבָּאִים יַשְׁרֵשׁ יַעֲקֹב יָצִיץ וּפָרַח יִשְׂרָאֵל וּמָלְאוּ פְנֵי־תֵבֵל תְּנוּבָה: הַכְּמַכַּת מַכֵּהוּ
ח הִכָּהוּ אִם־כְּהֶרֶג הֲרֻגָיו הֹרָג: בְּסַאסְּאָה בְּשַׁלְחָהּ תְּרִיבֶנָּה הָגָה בְּרוּחוֹ הַקָּשָׁה בְּיוֹם קָדִים: לָכֵן
ט בְּזֹאת יְכֻפַּר עֲוֺן־יַעֲקֹב וְזֶה כָּל־פְּרִי הָסִר חַטָּאתוֹ בְּשׂוּמוֹ ׀ כָּל־אַבְנֵי מִזְבֵּחַ כְּאַבְנֵי־גִר מְנֻפָּצוֹת
לֹא־יָקֻמוּ אֲשֵׁרִים וְחַמָּנִים: כִּי עִיר בְּצוּרָה בָּדָד נָוֶה מְשֻׁלָּח וְנֶעֱזָב כַּמִּדְבָּר שָׁם יִרְעֶה עֵגֶל וְשָׁם
יא יִרְבָּץ וְכִלָּה סְעִפֶיהָ: בִּיבֹשׁ קְצִירָהּ תִּשָּׁבַרְנָה נָשִׁים בָּאוֹת מְאִירוֹת אוֹתָהּ כִּי לֹא עַם־בִּינוֹת הוּא
יב עַל־כֵּן לֹא־יְרַחֲמֶנּוּ עֹשֵׂהוּ וְיֹצְרוֹ לֹא יְחֻנֶּנּוּ: וְהָיָה בַּיּוֹם הַהוּא יַחְבֹּט יְהוָה מִשִּׁבֹּלֶת
יג הַנָּהָר עַד־נַחַל מִצְרָיִם וְאַתֶּם תְּלֻקְּטוּ לְאַחַד אֶחָד בְּנֵי יִשְׂרָאֵל: וְהָיָה ׀ בַּיּוֹם הַהוּא
יִתָּקַע בְּשׁוֹפָר גָּדוֹל וּבָאוּ הָאֹבְדִים בְּאֶרֶץ אַשּׁוּר וְהַנִּדָּחִים בְּאֶרֶץ מִצְרָיִם וְהִשְׁתַּחֲווּ לַיהוָה
כח א בְּהַר הַקֹּדֶשׁ בִּירוּשָׁלָ͏ִם: הוֹי עֲטֶרֶת גֵּאוּת שִׁכֹּרֵי אֶפְרַיִם וְצִיץ נֹבֵל צְבִי תִפְאַרְתּוֹ
ב אֲשֶׁר עַל־רֹאשׁ גֵּיא־שְׁמָנִים הֲלוּמֵי יָיִן: הִנֵּה חָזָק וְאַמִּץ לַאדֹנָי כְּזֶרֶם בָּרָד שַׂעַר קָטֶב כְּזֶרֶם
ג מַיִם כַּבִּירִים שֹׁטְפִים הִנִּיחַ לָאָרֶץ בְּיָד: בְּרַגְלַיִם תֵּרָמַסְנָה עֲטֶרֶת גֵּאוּת שִׁכֹּרֵי אֶפְרָיִם: וְהָיְתָה
ד צִיצַת נֹבֵל צְבִי תִפְאַרְתּוֹ אֲשֶׁר עַל־רֹאשׁ גֵּיא שְׁמָנִים כְּבִכּוּרָהּ בְּטֶרֶם קַיִץ אֲשֶׁר יִרְאֶה הָרֹאֶה
ה אוֹתָהּ בְּעוֹדָהּ בְּכַפּוֹ יִבְלָעֶנָּה: בַּיּוֹם הַהוּא יִהְיֶה יְהוָה צְבָאוֹת לַעֲטֶרֶת צְבִי וְלִצְפִירַת
ו תִּפְאָרָה לִשְׁאָר עַמּוֹ: וּלְרוּחַ מִשְׁפָּט לַיּוֹשֵׁב עַל־הַמִּשְׁפָּט וְלִגְבוּרָה מְשִׁיבֵי מִלְחָמָה שָׁעְרָה:
ז וְגַם־אֵלֶּה בַּיַּיִן שָׁגוּ וּבַשֵּׁכָר תָּעוּ כֹּהֵן וְנָבִיא שָׁגוּ בַשֵּׁכָר נִבְלְעוּ מִן־הַיַּיִן תָּעוּ מִן־הַשֵּׁכָר שָׁגוּ
ח בָּרֹאֶה פָּקוּ פְּלִילִיָּה: כִּי כָּל־שֻׁלְחָנוֹת מָלְאוּ קִיא צֹאָה בְּלִי מָקוֹם: אֶת־מִי יוֹרֶה
ט דֵעָה וְאֶת־מִי יָבִין שְׁמוּעָה גְּמוּלֵי מֵחָלָב עַתִּיקֵי מִשָּׁדָיִם: כִּי צַו לָצָו צַו לָצָו קַו לָקָו קַו לָקָו
י זְעֵיר שָׁם זְעֵיר שָׁם: כִּי בְּלַעֲגֵי שָׂפָה וּבְלָשׁוֹן אַחֶרֶת יְדַבֵּר אֶל־הָעָם הַזֶּה: אֲשֶׁר ׀ אָמַר אֲלֵיהֶם
יא זֹאת הַמְּנוּחָה הָנִיחוּ לֶעָיֵף וְזֹאת הַמַּרְגֵּעָה וְלֹא אָבוּא שְׁמוֹעַ: וְהָיָה לָהֶם דְּבַר־יְהוָה צַו לָצָו
יב צַו לָצָו קַו לָקָו קַו לָקָו זְעֵיר שָׁם זְעֵיר שָׁם לְמַעַן יֵלְכוּ וְכָשְׁלוּ אָחוֹר וְנִשְׁבָּרוּ וְנוֹקְשׁוּ וְנִלְכָּדוּ:
כב לָכֵן כֹּה־אָמַר יְהוָה אֶל־בֵּית יַעֲקֹב אֲשֶׁר פָּדָה אֶת־אַבְרָהָם לֹא־עַתָּה יֵבוֹשׁ יַעֲקֹב וְלֹא עַתָּה
כג פָּנָיו יֶחֱוָרוּ: כִּי בִרְאֹתוֹ יְלָדָיו מַעֲשֵׂה יָדַי בְּקִרְבּוֹ יַקְדִּישׁוּ שְׁמִי וְהִקְדִּישׁוּ אֶת־קְדוֹשׁ יַעֲקֹב
וְאֶת־אֱלֹהֵי יִשְׂרָאֵל יַעֲרִיצוּ: יַעֲרִיצוּ

The Appointment of Jeremiah as a Prophet and His First Prophecy

JEREMIAH 1:1–2:3

This section of the *haftara* describes Jeremiah's initiation as a prophet, telling where, when, and how Jeremiah received his first prophecy and specifying to whom his prophecies would be addressed. Jeremiah is also offered words of encouragement as he takes the first steps on what will turn out to be a lonely path.

Like Moses, Jeremiah was reluctant to accept his mission as a prophet. The Midrash notes other commonalities between the two prophets: Both Moses and Jeremiah issued prophecies of reproof to Israel; both faced opponents from among the people of Israel who challenged them; both were put into dangerous places (a river and a pit, respectively); and finally, both prophesied for forty years (see *Pesikta DeRav Kahana* 13).

Although the book of Jeremiah is replete with reprimands of the nation, some of which are very harsh, Jeremiah's first prophecy is one of reconciliation, comfort, and love for Israel (see Malbim, Jeremiah 2:1). The words "Israel is sacred to the Lord, the first fruits of His crop" (Jeremiah 2:3), which appear at the end of the *haftara*, recall the words "My son, My firstborn, Israel" (Exodus 4:22) found in the *parasha*. According to both verses, one who harms Israel will be considered guilty of wronging a people whose Father in Heaven holds it sacred and dear.

1 1 The words of Jeremiah son of Hilkiyahu, of the priests who
Seph. begin 2 were in Anatot in the land of Benjamin, to whom the word of
the Lord was in the days of Yoshiyahu, son of Amon, king of
3 Judah, in the thirteenth year of his reign: It was in the days of
Yehoyakim, son of Yoshiyahu, king of Judah, until the conclusion of the eleventh year of Tzidkiyahu, son of Yoshiyahu, king
4 of Judah, until the exile of Jerusalem in the fifth month. The
5 word of the Lord was with me, saying: Before I formed you in
the belly I knew you, and before you emerged from the womb
6 I sanctified you; a prophet to the nations I set you. I said: Alas,
My Lord God, behold, I do not know to speak, for I am a lad.
7 The Lord said to me: Do not say: I am a lad, for to wherever I
will send you, you shall go, and whatever I will command you,
8 you shall speak. Do not fear them, as I am with you to save you
9 – the utterance of the Lord. The Lord sent His hand forth and
touched my mouth, and the Lord said to me: Behold, I have set
10 My words in your mouth. See, I appointed you this day over the
nations and over the kingdoms, to uproot and to smash and to
11 eradicate and to destroy, to build and to plant. The word of the
Lord was with me, saying: What do you see, Jeremiah? I said: I
12 see a branch of an almond tree [*shaked*]. The Lord said to me:
You have seen well, for I hasten [*shoked*] My word to perform
13 it. The word of the Lord was with me a second time, saying:
What do you see? I said: A boiling pot I see, and its opening is
14 facing toward the north. The Lord said to me: From the north
the evil shall be unleashed upon all the inhabitants of the land.
15 For behold, I am calling all the families of the kingdoms of the
north – the utterance of the Lord – and they will come, and
each man will place his throne at the entrance of the gates of
Jerusalem, and against all its walls around, and against all the
16 cities of Judah. I will speak My judgments against them for all
their evildoing, that they forsook Me, and burned to other gods,
17 and they prostrated themselves to their handiwork. You shall
gird your loins, and you shall arise, and you shall speak to them
everything that I will command you; do not be dismayed be-
18 cause of them, lest I devastate you before them. Behold, I have
rendered you today as a fortified city, and an iron pillar, and as
bronze walls, against the entire land, to the kings of Judah, to its
19 princes, to its priests, and to the people of the land. They will
battle against you, but they will not prevail against you, as I am
2 1 with you – the utterance of the Lord – to deliver you. The word
2 of the Lord was with me, saying: Go, and proclaim in the ears of
Jerusalem, saying: So said the Lord: I have remembered for you
the kindness of your youth, the love of your nuptials, your fol-
3 lowing Me in the wilderness, in a land not sown. Israel is sacred
to the Lord, the first of His crop, all those who devour it will be
guilty, evil will come upon them – the utterance of the Lord.

א א דִּבְרֵי יִרְמְיָהוּ בֶּן־חִלְקִיָּהוּ מִן־הַכֹּהֲנִים אֲשֶׁר בַּעֲנָתוֹת בְּאֶרֶץ בִּנְיָמִן: אֲשֶׁר הָיָה דְבַר־יְהוָה

ב אֵלָיו בִּימֵי יֹאשִׁיָּהוּ בֶן־אָמוֹן מֶלֶךְ יְהוּדָה בִּשְׁלֹשׁ־עֶשְׂרֵה שָׁנָה לְמָלְכוֹ: וַיְהִי בִּימֵי יְהוֹיָקִים בֶּן־

יֹאשִׁיָּהוּ מֶלֶךְ יְהוּדָה עַד־תֹּם עַשְׁתֵּי עֶשְׂרֵה שָׁנָה לְצִדְקִיָּהוּ בֶן־יֹאשִׁיָּהוּ מֶלֶךְ יְהוּדָה עַד־גְּלוֹת

ד יְרוּשָׁלִָם בַּחֹדֶשׁ הַחֲמִישִׁי: וַיְהִי דְבַר־יְהוָה אֵלַי לֵאמֹר: בְּטֶרֶם אצורך אֶצּוֹרְךָ בַבֶּטֶן יְדַעְתִּיךָ

ה וּבְטֶרֶם תֵּצֵא מֵרֶחֶם הִקְדַּשְׁתִּיךָ נָבִיא לַגּוֹיִם נְתַתִּיךָ: וָאֹמַר אֲהָהּ אֲדֹנָי יְהוִה הִנֵּה לֹא־יָדַעְתִּי

ו דַּבֵּר כִּי־נַעַר אָנֹכִי: וַיֹּאמֶר יְהוָה אֵלַי אַל־תֹּאמַר נַעַר אָנֹכִי כִּי עַל־כָּל־אֲשֶׁר אֶשְׁלָחֲךָ תֵּלֵךְ

ז וְאֵת כָּל־אֲשֶׁר אֲצַוְּךָ תְּדַבֵּר: אַל־תִּירָא מִפְּנֵיהֶם כִּי־אִתְּךָ אֲנִי לְהַצִּלֶךָ נְאֻם־יְהוָה: וַיִּשְׁלַח יְהוָה

ח אֶת־יָדוֹ וַיַּגַּע עַל־פִּי וַיֹּאמֶר יְהוָה אֵלַי הִנֵּה נָתַתִּי דְבָרַי בְּפִיךָ: רְאֵה הִפְקַדְתִּיךָ ׀ הַיּוֹם הַזֶּה

ט עַל־הַגּוֹיִם וְעַל־הַמַּמְלָכוֹת לִנְתוֹשׁ וְלִנְתוֹץ וּלְהַאֲבִיד וְלַהֲרוֹס לִבְנוֹת וְלִנְטוֹעַ: וַיְהִי

י דְבַר־יְהוָה אֵלַי לֵאמֹר מָה־אַתָּה רֹאֶה יִרְמְיָהוּ וָאֹמַר מַקֵּל שָׁקֵד אֲנִי רֹאֶה: וַיֹּאמֶר יְהוָה

יא אֵלַי הֵיטַבְתָּ לִרְאוֹת כִּי־שֹׁקֵד אֲנִי עַל־דְּבָרִי לַעֲשֹׂתוֹ: וַיְהִי דְבַר־יְהוָה ׀ אֵלַי

יב שֵׁנִית לֵאמֹר מָה אַתָּה רֹאֶה וָאֹמַר סִיר נָפוּחַ אֲנִי רֹאֶה וּפָנָיו מִפְּנֵי צָפוֹנָה: וַיֹּאמֶר יְהוָה אֵלַי

יג מִצָּפוֹן תִּפָּתַח הָרָעָה עַל כָּל־יֹשְׁבֵי הָאָרֶץ: כִּי ׀ הִנְנִי קֹרֵא לְכָל־מִשְׁפְּחוֹת מַמְלְכוֹת צָפוֹנָה

נְאֻם־יְהוָה וּבָאוּ וְנָתְנוּ אִישׁ כִּסְאוֹ פֶּתַח ׀ שַׁעֲרֵי יְרוּשָׁלִַם וְעַל כָּל־חוֹמֹתֶיהָ סָבִיב וְעַל כָּל־

יד עָרֵי יְהוּדָה: וְדִבַּרְתִּי מִשְׁפָּטַי אוֹתָם עַל כָּל־רָעָתָם אֲשֶׁר עֲזָבוּנִי וַיְקַטְּרוּ לֵאלֹהִים אֲחֵרִים

טו וַיִּשְׁתַּחֲווּ לְמַעֲשֵׂי יְדֵיהֶם: וְאַתָּה תֶּאְזֹר מָתְנֶיךָ וְקַמְתָּ וְדִבַּרְתָּ אֲלֵיהֶם אֵת כָּל־אֲשֶׁר אָנֹכִי

טז אֲצַוֶּךָּ אַל־תֵּחַת מִפְּנֵיהֶם פֶּן־אֲחִתְּךָ לִפְנֵיהֶם: וַאֲנִי הִנֵּה נְתַתִּיךָ הַיּוֹם לְעִיר מִבְצָר וּלְעַמּוּד

יז בַּרְזֶל וּלְחֹמוֹת נְחֹשֶׁת עַל־כָּל־הָאָרֶץ לְמַלְכֵי יְהוּדָה לְשָׂרֶיהָ לְכֹהֲנֶיהָ וּלְעַם הָאָרֶץ: וְנִלְחֲמוּ

יח אֵלֶיךָ וְלֹא־יוּכְלוּ לָךְ כִּי־אִתְּךָ אֲנִי נְאֻם־יְהוָה לְהַצִּילֶךָ: וַיְהִי דְבַר־יְהוָה אֵלַי לֵאמֹר:

ב א הָלֹךְ וְקָרָאתָ בְאָזְנֵי יְרוּשָׁלִַם לֵאמֹר כֹּה אָמַר יְהוָה זָכַרְתִּי לָךְ חֶסֶד נְעוּרַיִךְ אַהֲבַת כְּלוּלֹתָיִךְ

ב לֶכְתֵּךְ אַחֲרַי בַּמִּדְבָּר בְּאֶרֶץ לֹא זְרוּעָה: קֹדֶשׁ יִשְׂרָאֵל לַיהוָה רֵאשִׁית תְּבוּאָתֹה כָּל־אֹכְלָיו

ג יֶאְשָׁמוּ רָעָה תָּבֹא אֲלֵיהֶם נְאֻם־יְהוָה:

Haftara for **Va'era**

The Kingdom of Pharaoh Will Be Humiliated

EZEKIEL 28:25–29:21

As stated in the *parasha*, the plagues were not merely a punishment for Egypt's evil deeds, but were inflicted upon them "in order to promulgate My name in the entire earth" (Exodus 9:16). The humiliation of Egypt, and of Pharaoh, who was considered to be an omnipotent god by his people and himself, was intended to pave the way for a general recognition of the sovereignty of the true God. This is the main topic of the *haftara*, in which the expression "and they will know that I am the Lord," which appears in the *parasha* with regard to Egypt, occurs no less than six times.

28 25 So said the Lord God: When I gather the house of Israel from
the peoples among whom they were dispersed, I will be sanctified through them before the eyes of the nations, and they
will dwell in their land, which I gave to My servant, to Jacob.
26 They will dwell in it in security; they will build houses and plant
vineyards, and they will dwell in security when I administer
punishments upon all those around them who despise them,
29 1 and they will know that I am the Lord their God. In the tenth
year, in the tenth month, on the twelfth of the month, the word
2 of the Lord was with me, saying: Son of man, direct your attention to Pharaoh, king of Egypt, and prophesy concerning
3 him and concerning all Egypt. Speak and say: So said the Lord
God: Behold, I am against you, Pharaoh, king of Egypt, the
great crocodile that lies in the midst of his rivers, who has said:
4 My river is mine, and I made myself. I will put hooks into your
cheeks, and I will stick the fish of your rivers to your scales, and
I will take you up out of the midst of your rivers, and all the fish
5 of your rivers will stick to your scales. I will cast you into the
wilderness, you and all the fish of your rivers, upon the open
field you will fall; you will not be gathered, and you will not be
collected; I have given you to the beasts of the earth and to the
6 birds of the heavens to devour. All the inhabitants of Egypt will
know that I am the Lord, because they were a reed crutch for
7 the house of Israel. When they grasp you in the palm, you splin-
ter, and you wound their every shoulder, and when they lean
upon you, you snap, and you cause all their waists to collapse.
8 Therefore, so said the Lord God: Behold, I am bringing a sword
9 against you, and I will eliminate from you men and animals. The
land of Egypt will become desolation and ruins, and they will
know that I am the Lord, because he said: The Nile is mine, and
10 I made. Therefore, behold, I am against you and against your
rivers, and I will render the land of Egypt ruins, desolate ruins,
11 from Migdol to Sevene until the border of Kush. The foot of
man will not pass through it, and the foot of animals will not
12 pass through it, and it will not be inhabited for forty years. I will
render the land of Egypt a desolation among desolate lands, and
its cities will be desolation among ruined cities for forty years,
and I will disperse the Egyptians among the nations and scat-
13 ter them through the lands. For so said the Lord God: At the
end of forty years I will gather the Egyptians from the peoples
14 where they were dispersed. I will restore the returnees of Egypt,
and I will return them to the land of Patros, to the land of their
15 origins, and there they will be a lowly kingdom. It will be the
lowest of the kingdoms, and it will no longer exalt itself over the
nations, and I will diminish them so that they will not rule over
16 the nations. It will no longer be a support for the house of Israel,
evoking iniquity when they turn after them, and they will know
17 that I am the Lord God. It was in the twenty-seventh year, in the
first month, on the first of the month, the word of the Lord was
18 with me, saying: Son of man, Nebuchadrezzar, king of Babylon,
commissioned his army for a great undertaking against Tyre;
every head had been made bald and every shoulder peeled, but
he and his army had no reward from Tyre for the undertaking
19 that he performed against it. Therefore, so said the Lord God:
Behold, I am giving the land of Egypt to Nebuchadrezzar, king
of Babylon, and he will carry its multitude, take its spoils and
20 loot its loot, and it will be reward for his army. For the action
that he performed against it, I have given him the land of Egypt,
for that which they did for Me – the utterance of the Lord God.
21 On that day I will cause glory to flourish for the house of Israel,
and I will enable you to open your mouth in their midst, and
they will know that I am the Lord.

הפטרת

וארא

כח כה כֹּה־אָמַר אֲדֹנָי יֱהֹוִה בְּקַבְּצִי ׀ אֶת־בֵּית יִשְׂרָאֵל מִן־הָעַמִּים אֲשֶׁר נָפֹצוּ בָם וְנִקְדַּשְׁתִּי בָם יחזקאל
כו לְעֵינֵי הַגּוֹיִם וְיָשְׁבוּ עַל־אַדְמָתָם אֲשֶׁר נָתַתִּי לְעַבְדִּי לְיַעֲקֹב׃ וְיָשְׁבוּ עָלֶיהָ לָבֶטַח וּבָנוּ בָתִּים
וְנָטְעוּ כְרָמִים וְיָשְׁבוּ לָבֶטַח בַּעֲשׂוֹתִי שְׁפָטִים בְּכֹל הַשָּׁאטִים אֹתָם מִסְּבִיבוֹתָם וְיָדְעוּ כִּי אֲנִי
כט א יְהוָה אֱלֹהֵיהֶם׃ בַּשָּׁנָה הָעֲשִׂרִית בָּעֲשִׂרִי בִּשְׁנֵים עָשָׂר לַחֹדֶשׁ הָיָה דְבַר־יְהוָה
ב ג אֵלַי לֵאמֹר׃ בֶּן־אָדָם שִׂים פָּנֶיךָ עַל־פַּרְעֹה מֶלֶךְ מִצְרָיִם וְהִנָּבֵא עָלָיו וְעַל־מִצְרַיִם כֻּלָּהּ׃ דַּבֵּר
וְאָמַרְתָּ כֹּה־אָמַר ׀ אֲדֹנָי יֱהֹוִה הִנְנִי עָלֶיךָ פַּרְעֹה מֶלֶךְ־מִצְרַיִם הַתַּנִּים הַגָּדוֹל הָרֹבֵץ בְּתוֹךְ יְאֹרָיו
ד אֲשֶׁר אָמַר לִי יְאֹרִי וַאֲנִי עֲשִׂיתִנִי׃ וְנָתַתִּי חחיים בִּלְחָיֶיךָ וְהִדְבַּקְתִּי דְגַת־יְאֹרֶיךָ בְּקַשְׂקְשֹׂתֶיךָ חחים
ה וְהַעֲלִיתִיךָ מִתּוֹךְ יְאֹרֶיךָ וְאֵת כָּל־דְּגַת יְאֹרֶיךָ בְּקַשְׂקְשֹׂתֶיךָ תִּדְבָּק׃ וּנְטַשְׁתִּיךָ הַמִּדְבָּרָה
אוֹתְךָ וְאֵת כָּל־דְּגַת יְאֹרֶיךָ עַל־פְּנֵי הַשָּׂדֶה תִּפּוֹל לֹא תֵאָסֵף וְלֹא תִקָּבֵץ לְחַיַּת הָאָרֶץ וּלְעוֹף
ו הַשָּׁמַיִם נְתַתִּיךָ לְאָכְלָה׃ וְיָדְעוּ כָּל־יֹשְׁבֵי מִצְרַיִם כִּי אֲנִי יְהוָה יַעַן הֱיוֹתָם מִשְׁעֶנֶת קָנֶה לְבֵית
ז יִשְׂרָאֵל׃ בְּתָפְשָׂם בְּךָ בכפך תֵּרוֹץ וּבָקַעְתָּ לָהֶם כָּל־כָּתֵף וּבְהִשָּׁעֲנָם עָלֶיךָ תִּשָּׁבֵר וְהַעֲמַדְתָּ בַכַּף
ח לָהֶם כָּל־מָתְנָיִם׃ לָכֵן כֹּה אָמַר אֲדֹנָי יֱהֹוִה הִנְנִי מֵבִיא עָלַיִךְ חָרֶב וְהִכְרַתִּי מִמֵּךְ
ט אָדָם וּבְהֵמָה׃ וְהָיְתָה אֶרֶץ־מִצְרַיִם לִשְׁמָמָה וְחָרְבָּה וְיָדְעוּ כִּי־אֲנִי יְהוָה יַעַן אָמַר יְאֹר לִי וַאֲנִי
י עָשִׂיתִי׃ לָכֵן הִנְנִי אֵלֶיךָ וְאֶל־יְאֹרֶיךָ וְנָתַתִּי אֶת־אֶרֶץ מִצְרַיִם לְחָרְבוֹת חֹרֶב שְׁמָמָה מִמִּגְדֹּל
יא סְוֵנֵה וְעַד־גְּבוּל כּוּשׁ׃ לֹא תַעֲבָר־בָּהּ רֶגֶל אָדָם וְרֶגֶל בְּהֵמָה לֹא תַעֲבָר־בָּהּ וְלֹא תֵשֵׁב אַרְבָּעִים
יב שָׁנָה׃ וְנָתַתִּי אֶת־אֶרֶץ מִצְרַיִם שְׁמָמָה בְּתוֹךְ ׀ אֲרָצוֹת נְשַׁמּוֹת וְעָרֶיהָ בְּתוֹךְ עָרִים מָחֳרָבוֹת
יג תִּהְיֶיןָ שְׁמָמָה אַרְבָּעִים שָׁנָה וַהֲפִצֹתִי אֶת־מִצְרַיִם בַּגּוֹיִם וְזֵרִיתִים בָּאֲרָצוֹת׃ כִּי
כֹה אָמַר אֲדֹנָי יֱהֹוִה מִקֵּץ אַרְבָּעִים שָׁנָה אֲקַבֵּץ אֶת־מִצְרַיִם מִן־הָעַמִּים אֲשֶׁר־נָפֹצוּ שָׁמָּה׃
יד וְשַׁבְתִּי אֶת־שְׁבוּת מִצְרַיִם וַהֲשִׁבֹתִי אֹתָם אֶרֶץ פַּתְרוֹס עַל־אֶרֶץ מְכוּרָתָם וְהָיוּ שָׁם מַמְלָכָה
טו שְׁפָלָה׃ מִן־הַמַּמְלָכוֹת תִּהְיֶה שְׁפָלָה וְלֹא־תִתְנַשֵּׂא עוֹד עַל־הַגּוֹיִם וְהִמְעַטְתִּים לְבִלְתִּי רְדוֹת
טז בַּגּוֹיִם׃ וְלֹא יִהְיֶה־עוֹד לְבֵית יִשְׂרָאֵל לְמִבְטָח מַזְכִּיר עָוֺן בִּפְנוֹתָם אַחֲרֵיהֶם וְיָדְעוּ כִּי אֲנִי
יז אֲדֹנָי יֱהֹוִה׃ וַיְהִי בְּעֶשְׂרִים וָשֶׁבַע שָׁנָה בָּרִאשׁוֹן בְּאֶחָד לַחֹדֶשׁ הָיָה דְבַר־יְהוָה אֵלַי
יח לֵאמֹר׃ בֶּן־אָדָם נְבוּכַדְרֶאצַּר מֶלֶךְ־בָּבֶל הֶעֱבִיד אֶת־חֵילוֹ עֲבֹדָה גְדֹלָה אֶל־צֹר כָּל־רֹאשׁ
מֻקְרָח וְכָל־כָּתֵף מְרוּטָה וְשָׂכָר לֹא־הָיָה לוֹ וּלְחֵילוֹ מִצֹּר עַל־הָעֲבֹדָה אֲשֶׁר־עָבַד עָלֶיהָ׃
יט לָכֵן כֹּה אָמַר אֲדֹנָי יֱהֹוִה הִנְנִי נֹתֵן לִנְבוּכַדְרֶאצַּר מֶלֶךְ־בָּבֶל אֶת־אֶרֶץ מִצְרָיִם וְנָשָׂא הֲמֹנָהּ
כ וְשָׁלַל שְׁלָלָהּ וּבָזַז בִּזָּהּ וְהָיְתָה שָׂכָר לְחֵילוֹ׃ פְּעֻלָּתוֹ אֲשֶׁר־עָבַד בָּהּ נָתַתִּי לוֹ אֶת־אֶרֶץ מִצְרָיִם
כא אֲשֶׁר עָשׂוּ לִי נְאֻם אֲדֹנָי יֱהֹוִה׃ בַּיּוֹם הַהוּא אַצְמִיחַ קֶרֶן לְבֵית יִשְׂרָאֵל וּלְךָ אֶתֵּן פִּתְחוֹן־פֶּה
בְּתוֹכָם וְיָדְעוּ כִּי־אֲנִי יְהוָה׃

Haftara for
Bo

The Babylonian Defeat of Egypt
JEREMIAH 46:13–28

The plagues that were inflicted upon Egypt, its king, and its gods are a common theme in the last few *parashot* and in this *haftara*, in which Jeremiah prophesies a devastating and shocking defeat that God will bring upon Egypt through the agency of the Chaldeans. At the end of his prophecy, Jeremiah addresses the inhabitants of Judah with comforting words, assuring them that although they will be judged for their misdeeds, God will be with them forever, and they will ultimately be saved.

46 13 The matter that the Lord spoke to Jeremiah the prophet, concerning the coming of Nebuchadrezzar, king of Babylonia, to 14 smite the land of Egypt. Tell it in Egypt and proclaim in Migdol, and proclaim in Nof and in Tahpanhes; say: Stand and prepare 15 yourself, for the sword has consumed those around you. Why were your stallions swept away? It did not stand, because the 16 Lord cast it down. He increased stumbling; moreover, each man fell upon his neighbor, and they said: Arise, and let us return to our people and to the land of our birth from before 17 the sword of the oppressor. They called there: Pharaoh, king 18 of Egypt, is bluster; he passed by the appointed time. As I live – the utterance of the King, the Lord of hosts is His name – for it is like Tavor among the mountains, and like Carmel that 19 reaches to the sea. Tools of exile prepare for you, inhabitant of the daughter of Egypt, as Nof will become desolation and 20 will be destroyed, without inhabitants. Egypt is a very fair calf; 21 a slaughterer from the north is coming. Its mercenaries in its midst too are like fattened calves, for they too turned, fled together, they did not stand, for the day of their calamity came 22 upon them, the time of their reckoning. Its sound will go forth like a serpent, for they will go forth in force, and with axes they 23 came to it, like hewers of wood. They cut down its forest – the utterance of the Lord – for it cannot be estimated, as they out- 24 number locusts and they are innumerable. The daughter of Egypt is shamed; she is delivered into the hand of the people of 25 the north. The Lord of hosts, God of Israel, said: Behold, I am reckoning with Amon of No, and with Pharaoh and with Egypt, and with its gods and with its kings, and with Pharaoh and with 26 those who trust in him. I will deliver them into the hand of the seekers of their lives and into the hand of Nebuchadrezzar, king of Babylonia, and into the hand of his servants, but thereafter 27 it will dwell as in days of old – the utterance of the Lord. But you, do not fear, My servant Jacob, and do not be dismayed, Israel, for behold, I am saving you from afar and your descendants from the land of their captivity, and Jacob will return and 28 be calm and tranquil, and none will make him tremble. You, do not fear, My servant Jacob – the utterance of the Lord – for I am with you; for I will engender annihilation of all the nations where I banished you, but I will not engender annihilation of you; I will chastise you with justice, but I will not eradicate you.

יו יג הַדָּבָר֙ אֲשֶׁ֣ר דִּבֶּ֣ר יְהֹוָ֔ה אֶֽל־יִרְמְיָ֖הוּ הַנָּבִ֑יא לָב֗וֹא נְבֽוּכַדְרֶאצַּר֙ מֶ֣לֶךְ בָּבֶ֔ל לְהַכּ֖וֹת אֶת־אֶ֥רֶץ   יִרמיה

יד מִצְרָֽיִם: הַגִּ֤ידוּ בְמִצְרַ֙יִם֙ וְהַשְׁמִ֣יעוּ בְמִגְדּ֔וֹל וְהַשְׁמִ֥יעוּ בְנֹ֖ף וּבְתַחְפַּנְחֵ֑ס אִמְר֕וּ הִתְיַצֵּב֙ וְהָכֵ֣ן

טו לָ֔ךְ כִּֽי־אָכְלָ֥ה חֶ֖רֶב סְבִיבֶֽיךָ: מַדּ֖וּעַ נִסְחַ֣ף אַבִּירֶ֑יךָ לֹ֣א עָמַ֔ד כִּ֥י יְהֹוָ֖ה הֲדָפֽוֹ: הִרְבָּ֤ה כּוֹשֵׁל֙ גַּם־

טז נָפַ֗ל אִ֤ישׁ אֶל־רֵעֵ֙הוּ֙ וַיֹּ֣אמְר֔וּ ק֣וּמָה ׀ וְנָשֻׁ֣בָה אֶל־עַמֵּ֗נוּ וְאֶל־אֶ֙רֶץ֙ מֽוֹלַדְתֵּ֔נוּ מִפְּנֵ֖י חֶ֥רֶב הַיּוֹנָֽה:

יז קָרְא֣וּ שָׁ֔ם פַּרְעֹ֥ה מֶֽלֶךְ־מִצְרַ֖יִם שָׁא֑וֹן הֶעֱבִ֖יר הַמּוֹעֵֽד: חַי־אָ֙נִי֙ נְאֻם־הַמֶּ֔לֶךְ יְהֹוָ֥ה צְבָא֖וֹת

יח שְׁמ֑וֹ כִּ֚י כְּתָב֣וֹר בֶּֽהָרִ֔ים וּכְכַרְמֶ֖ל בַּיָּ֥ם יָבֽוֹא: כְּלֵ֤י גוֹלָה֙ עֲשִׂ֣י לָ֔ךְ יוֹשֶׁ֖בֶת בַּת־מִצְרָ֑יִם כִּֽי־נֹף֙

כ לְשַׁמָּ֣ה תִֽהְיֶ֔ה וְנִצְּתָ֖ה מֵאֵ֥ין יוֹשֵֽׁב: עֶגְלָ֥ה יְפֵֽה־פִיָּ֖ה מִצְרָ֑יִם קֶ֥רֶץ מִצָּפ֖וֹן בָּ֥א בָֽא:

כא גַּם־שְׂכִרֶ֤יהָ בְקִרְבָּהּ֙ כְּעֶגְלֵ֣י מַרְבֵּ֔ק כִּֽי־גַם־הֵ֧מָּה הִפְנ֛וּ נָ֥סוּ יַחְדָּ֖יו לֹ֣א עָמָ֑דוּ כִּ֣י י֥וֹם אֵידָ֛ם בָּ֥א

כב עֲלֵיהֶ֖ם עֵ֥ת פְּקֻדָּתָֽם: קוֹלָ֖הּ כַּנָּחָ֣שׁ יֵלֵ֑ךְ כִּֽי־בְחַ֣יִל יֵלֵ֔כוּ וּבְקַרְדֻּמּוֹת֙ בָּ֣אוּ לָ֔הּ כְּחֹטְבֵ֖י עֵצִֽים:

כג כָּרְת֤וּ יַעְרָהּ֙ נְאֻם־יְהֹוָ֔ה כִּ֖י לֹ֣א יֵֽחָקֵ֑ר כִּ֤י רַבּוּ֙ מֵֽאַרְבֶּ֔ה וְאֵ֥ין לָהֶ֖ם מִסְפָּֽר: הֹבִ֖ישָׁה בַּת־מִצְרָ֑יִם

כה נִתְּנָ֖ה בְּיַ֥ד עַם־צָפֽוֹן: אָמַר֩ יְהֹוָ֨ה צְבָא֜וֹת אֱלֹהֵ֣י יִשְׂרָאֵ֗ל הִנְנִ֤י פוֹקֵד֙ אֶל־אָמ֣וֹן מִנֹּ֔א וְעַל־פַּרְעֹה֙

כו וְעַל־מִצְרַ֔יִם וְעַל־אֱלֹהֶ֖יהָ וְעַל־מְלָכֶ֑יהָ וְעַל־פַּרְעֹ֕ה וְעַ֥ל הַבֹּטְחִ֖ים בּֽוֹ: וּנְתַתִּ֗ים בְּיַד֙ מְבַקְשֵׁ֣י

נַפְשָׁ֔ם וּבְיַ֛ד נְבֽוּכַדְרֶאצַּ֥ר מֶֽלֶךְ־בָּבֶ֖ל וּבְיַד־עֲבָדָ֑יו וְאַחֲרֵי־כֵ֛ן תִּשְׁכֹּ֥ן כִּֽימֵי־קֶ֖דֶם נְאֻם־יְהֹוָֽה:

כז וְ֠אַתָּ֠ה אַל־תִּירָ֞א עַבְדִּ֤י יַֽעֲקֹב֙ וְאַל־תֵּחַ֣ת יִשְׂרָאֵ֔ל כִּ֠י הִנְנִ֤י מֽוֹשִֽׁיעֲךָ֙ מֵֽרָח֔וֹק וְאֶֽת־זַרְעֲךָ֖ מֵאֶ֣רֶץ

כח שִׁבְיָ֑ם וְשָׁ֧ב יַעֲק֛וֹב וְשָׁקַ֥ט וְשַׁאֲנַ֖ן וְאֵ֥ין מַחֲרִֽיד: אַ֠תָּ֠ה אַל־תִּירָ֞א עַבְדִּ֤י יַֽעֲקֹב֙ נְאֻם־יְהֹוָ֔ה כִּ֥י

אִתְּךָ֖ אָ֑נִי כִּי֩ אֶעֱשֶׂ֨ה כָלָ֜ה בְּכׇל־הַגּוֹיִ֣ם ׀ אֲשֶׁ֧ר הִדַּחְתִּ֣יךָ שָּׁ֗מָּה וְאֹֽתְךָ֙ לֹֽא־אֶעֱשֶׂ֣ה כָלָ֔ה וְיִסַּרְתִּ֙יךָ֙

לַמִּשְׁפָּ֔ט וְנַקֵּ֖ה לֹ֥א אֲנַקֶּֽךָּ:

Haftara for **Beshalah**

The Song of Deborah

JUDGES 4:4–5:31

The Song of Deborah, which is one of the longest in the Bible, is similar to the Song at the Sea in its rhythm and content, and in some of its expressions. Both songs were recited to God in gratitude for His salvation of the people from a threatening army that was equipped with many hundreds of chariots and horses. In both cases, forces of nature aided the Israelites – in the form of the Red Sea and a strong east wind (Song at the Sea), and the Kishon Stream and the heavenly constellations (Song of Deborah). Likewise, in both instances the confusion that prevailed in the enemy's camp is expressed with the same term: "And He confounded..." (Exodus 14:24; Judges 4:15), and with regard to the enemy's destruction it is stated that "not even one remained" (Exodus 14:28; Judges 4:16).

Nevertheless, a comparison between the two songs also serves to highlight a major difference between them. The Song at the Sea is written in general terms; it records virtually no individual names, not even that of Moses himself, who composed the song. In contrast, the Song of Deborah is far more personal, singling out some people for praise while condemning others, and Deborah herself is mentioned on more than one occasion.

4 4 Deborah was a prophetess, the wife of Lappidot; she was judg-
Ashk. 5 ing Israel at that time. She was sitting beneath the date palm
begin of Deborah, between Rama and Beit El in the highlands of
Ephraim; and the children of Israel went up to her for judgment.
6 She sent and called Barak son of Avinoam, from Kedesh Naftali,
and said to him: Has not the Lord, God of Israel, commanded,
saying: Go and draw toward Mount Tavor, and take with you
ten thousand men from the children of Naphtali and from the
7 children of Zebulun? I will draw toward you, to the Kishon
Stream, Sisera, commander of Yavin's army, his chariots, and his
8 horde, and I will deliver him into your hand. Barak said to her:
If you will go with me, I will go, but if you will not go with me,
9 I will not go. She said: I will go with you. However, your glory
will not be on the path that you are walking, for the Lord will
dispatch Sisera by the hand of a woman. Deborah arose, and
10 she went with Barak to Kedesh. Barak mustered Zebulun and
Naphtali at Kedesh; he brought up with him ten thousand men,
11 and Deborah went up with him. Hever the Kenite had separated
from the Kenites, from the children of Hovav, father-in-law of
Moses, and he pitched his tent at Elon BeTzaanannim, which is
12 near Kedesh. They told Sisera that Barak son of Avinoam had
13 gone up Mount Tavor. Sisera mobilized all his chariots, nine
hundred chariots of iron, and all the people who were with him
14 from Haroshet Goyim to the Kishon Stream. Deborah said to
Barak: Rise, as this is the day on which the Lord has delivered
Sisera into your hand. Hasn't the Lord gone out before you?
Barak descended from Mount Tavor with ten thousand men
15 after him. The Lord confounded Sisera, all his chariots, and his
entire camp by the sword before Barak; Sisera got down from
16 his chariot and fled on foot. Barak pursued the chariots and the
camp to Haroshet Goyim, and the entire camp of Sisera fell by
17 the sword; not even one remained. Sisera fled on foot to the
tent of Yael, wife of Hever the Kenite, as there was peace between Yavin, king of Hatzor, and the house of Hever the Kenite.
18 Yael emerged to meet Sisera, and she said to him: Turn aside,
my lord, turn to me; do not fear. He turned aside to her, to the
19 tent, and she covered him with a blanket. He said to her: Please
give me a little water to drink, for I am thirsty. She opened the
skin of milk, and she gave him to drink, and she covered him.
20 He said to her: Stand at the entrance of the tent, and if it shall
be that a man should come and ask you, and say: Is there a man
21 here? You shall say: No. Yael, Hever's wife, took a tent peg, and
grasped a hammer in her hand, and came to him silently; she
drove the peg into his temple, and it sank into the ground; he
22 had fallen asleep, and was exhausted, and died. Behold, Barak
was pursuing Sisera, and Yael emerged to meet him, and said to
him: Come, and I will show you the man whom you seek. He
came in to her and, behold, Sisera was fallen, dead, and the peg
23 was in his temple. God subjugated Yavin, king of Canaan, on
24 that day before the children of Israel. The hand of the children
of Israel became gradually firmer over Yavin, king of Canaan,
until they eliminated Yavin, king of Canaan.

5 1
2 Deborah and Barak son of Avinoam, sang on that day, saying: When
Seph. rampage was rampant in Israel, when the people volunteered,
begin 3 bless the Lord. Hear, kings, listen, princes; to the Lord, will I
4 sing; I will make a song to the Lord, God of Israel. Lord, upon
Your emergence from Se'ir, upon Your marching from the field

הפטרת
בשלח

שופטים
האשכנזים מתחילים כאן

ד ד ה וּדְבוֹרָה אִשָּׁה נְבִיאָה אֵשֶׁת לַפִּידוֹת הִיא שֹׁפְטָה אֶת־יִשְׂרָאֵל בָּעֵת הַהִיא: וְהִיא יוֹשֶׁבֶת
תַּחַת־תֹּמֶר דְּבוֹרָה בֵּין הָרָמָה וּבֵין בֵּית־אֵל בְּהַר אֶפְרָיִם וַיַּעֲלוּ אֵלֶיהָ בְּנֵי יִשְׂרָאֵל לַמִּשְׁפָּט:
ו וַתִּשְׁלַח וַתִּקְרָא לְבָרָק בֶּן־אֲבִינֹעַם מִקֶּדֶשׁ נַפְתָּלִי וַתֹּאמֶר אֵלָיו הֲלֹא־צִוָּה ׀ יְהוָה אֱלֹהֵי־
יִשְׂרָאֵל לֵךְ וּמָשַׁכְתָּ בְּהַר תָּבוֹר וְלָקַחְתָּ עִמְּךָ עֲשֶׂרֶת אֲלָפִים אִישׁ מִבְּנֵי נַפְתָּלִי וּמִבְּנֵי זְבֻלוּן:
ז וּמָשַׁכְתִּי אֵלֶיךָ אֶל־נַחַל קִישׁוֹן אֶת־סִיסְרָא שַׂר־צְבָא יָבִין וְאֶת־רִכְבּוֹ וְאֶת־הֲמוֹנוֹ וּנְתַתִּיהוּ
ח ט בְּיָדֶךָ: וַיֹּאמֶר אֵלֶיהָ בָּרָק אִם־תֵּלְכִי עִמִּי וְהָלָכְתִּי וְאִם־לֹא תֵלְכִי עִמִּי לֹא אֵלֵךְ: וַתֹּאמֶר הָלֹךְ
אֵלֵךְ עִמָּךְ אֶפֶס כִּי לֹא תִהְיֶה תִּפְאַרְתְּךָ עַל־הַדֶּרֶךְ אֲשֶׁר אַתָּה הוֹלֵךְ כִּי בְיַד־אִשָּׁה יִמְכֹּר יְהוָה
י אֶת־סִיסְרָא וַתָּקָם דְּבוֹרָה וַתֵּלֶךְ עִם־בָּרָק קֶדְשָׁה: וַיַּזְעֵק בָּרָק אֶת־זְבוּלֻן וְאֶת־נַפְתָּלִי קֶדְשָׁה
יא וַיַּעַל בְּרַגְלָיו עֲשֶׂרֶת אַלְפֵי אִישׁ וַתַּעַל עִמּוֹ דְּבוֹרָה: וְחֶבֶר הַקֵּינִי נִפְרָד מִקַּיִן מִבְּנֵי חֹבָב חֹתֵן
יב מֹשֶׁה וַיֵּט אָהֳלוֹ עַד־אֵלוֹן בצענים אֲשֶׁר אֶת־קֶדֶשׁ: וַיַּגִּדוּ לְסִיסְרָא כִּי עָלָה בָּרָק בֶּן־אֲבִינֹעַם בצעננים
יג הַר־תָּבוֹר: וַיַּזְעֵק סִיסְרָא אֶת־כָּל־רִכְבּוֹ תְּשַׁע מֵאוֹת רֶכֶב בַּרְזֶל וְאֶת־כָּל־הָעָם אֲשֶׁר אִתּוֹ
יד מֵחֲרֹשֶׁת הַגּוֹיִם אֶל־נַחַל קִישׁוֹן: וַתֹּאמֶר דְּבֹרָה אֶל־בָּרָק קוּם כִּי זֶה הַיּוֹם אֲשֶׁר נָתַן יְהוָה
אֶת־סִיסְרָא בְּיָדֶךָ הֲלֹא יְהוָה יָצָא לְפָנֶיךָ וַיֵּרֶד בָּרָק מֵהַר תָּבוֹר וַעֲשֶׂרֶת אֲלָפִים אִישׁ אַחֲרָיו:
טו וַיָּהָם יְהוָה אֶת־סִיסְרָא וְאֶת־כָּל־הָרֶכֶב וְאֶת־כָּל־הַמַּחֲנֶה לְפִי־חֶרֶב לִפְנֵי בָרָק וַיֵּרֶד סִיסְרָא
טז מֵעַל הַמֶּרְכָּבָה וַיָּנָס בְּרַגְלָיו: וּבָרָק רָדַף אַחֲרֵי הָרֶכֶב וְאַחֲרֵי הַמַּחֲנֶה עַד חֲרֹשֶׁת הַגּוֹיִם וַיִּפֹּל
יז כָּל־מַחֲנֵה סִיסְרָא לְפִי־חֶרֶב לֹא נִשְׁאַר עַד־אֶחָד: וְסִיסְרָא נָס בְּרַגְלָיו אֶל־אֹהֶל יָעֵל אֵשֶׁת
יח חֶבֶר הַקֵּינִי כִּי שָׁלוֹם בֵּין יָבִין מֶלֶךְ־חָצוֹר וּבֵין בֵּית חֶבֶר הַקֵּינִי: וַתֵּצֵא יָעֵל לִקְרַאת סִיסְרָא
יט וַתֹּאמֶר אֵלָיו סוּרָה אֲדֹנִי סוּרָה אֵלַי אַל־תִּירָא וַיָּסַר אֵלֶיהָ הָאֹהֱלָה וַתְּכַסֵּהוּ בַּשְּׂמִיכָה: וַיֹּאמֶר
כ אֵלֶיהָ הַשְׁקִינִי־נָא מְעַט־מַיִם כִּי צָמֵאתִי וַתִּפְתַּח אֶת־נֹאוד הֶחָלָב וַתַּשְׁקֵהוּ וַתְּכַסֵּהוּ: וַיֹּאמֶר
כא אֵלֶיהָ עֲמֹד פֶּתַח הָאֹהֶל וְהָיָה אִם־אִישׁ יָבֹא וּשְׁאֵלֵךְ וְאָמַר הֲיֵשׁ־פֹּה אִישׁ וְאָמַרְתְּ אָיִן: וַתִּקַּח
יָעֵל אֵשֶׁת־חֶבֶר אֶת־יְתַד הָאֹהֶל וַתָּשֶׂם אֶת־הַמַּקֶּבֶת בְּיָדָהּ וַתָּבוֹא אֵלָיו בַּלָּאט וַתִּתְקַע אֶת־
כב הַיָּתֵד בְּרַקָּתוֹ וַתִּצְנַח בָּאָרֶץ וְהוּא־נִרְדָּם וַיָּעַף וַיָּמֹת: וְהִנֵּה בָרָק רֹדֵף אֶת־סִיסְרָא וַתֵּצֵא יָעֵל
לִקְרָאתוֹ וַתֹּאמֶר לוֹ לֵךְ וְאַרְאֶךָּ אֶת־הָאִישׁ אֲשֶׁר־אַתָּה מְבַקֵּשׁ וַיָּבֹא אֵלֶיהָ וְהִנֵּה סִיסְרָא
כג נֹפֵל מֵת וְהַיָּתֵד בְּרַקָּתוֹ: וַיַּכְנַע אֱלֹהִים בַּיּוֹם הַהוּא אֵת יָבִין מֶלֶךְ־כְּנָעַן לִפְנֵי בְּנֵי יִשְׂרָאֵל:
כד וַתֵּלֶךְ יַד בְּנֵי־יִשְׂרָאֵל הָלוֹךְ וְקָשָׁה עַל יָבִין מֶלֶךְ־כְּנָעַן עַד אֲשֶׁר הִכְרִיתוּ אֵת יָבִין מֶלֶךְ־כְּנָעַן:

ה א וַתָּשַׁר דְּבוֹרָה וּבָרָק בֶּן־אֲבִינֹעַם בַּיּוֹם הַהוּא
ב לֵאמֹר: בִּפְרֹעַ פְּרָעוֹת בְּיִשְׂרָאֵל בְּהִתְנַדֵּב
ג עָם בָּרְכוּ יְהוָה: שִׁמְעוּ מְלָכִים הַאֲזִינוּ

הספרדים מתחילים כאן

רֹזְנִים אָנֹכִי לַיהוָה אָנֹכִי אָשִׁירָה אֲזַמֵּר
ד לַיהוָה אֱלֹהֵי יִשְׂרָאֵל: יְהוָה בְּצֵאתְךָ
מִשֵּׂעִיר בְּצַעְדְּךָ מִשְּׂדֵה אֱדוֹם אֶרֶץ

of Edom, the earth quaked, indeed, the heavens dripped; in-
5 deed, the clouds dripped water. The mountains flowed before
6 the Lord; that is Sinai, before the Lord, God of Israel. In the
days of Shamgar son of Anat, in the days of Yael, caravans
ceased, and travelers on paths would go on tortuous routes.
7 Unwalled cities ceased in Israel, they ceased. Until I, Deborah,
8 arose; I arose a mother in Israel. He chose new gods, then there
was war at the gates; was a shield or a spear seen among forty
9 thousand in Israel? My heart is with the legislators of Israel,
10 the volunteers on behalf of the people. Bless the Lord. Riders
of white donkeys, sitters in judgment, and walkers on the way,
11 discuss! At the sounds flowing through the gravel, among the
drawers of water, there they will relate the righteous acts of the
Lord, the righteous acts of liberation in Israel. Then the people
12 of the Lord descended to the gates. Awaken, awaken, Deborah;
awaken, awaken, utter a song. Arise, Barak, and take your pris-
13 oners, son of Avinoam. Then the remnant of the mighty of
the people went down; the Lord came down for me with the
14 valiant. Out of Ephraim came they who uprooted Amalek; after you, Benjamin, came with your clans; out of Makhir came
down legislators, and from Zebulun, those who ply the scribe's
15 quill. Princes of Issachar were with Deborah, and Issachar,
like Barak, was sent forth into the valley on foot. Among the
16 divisions of Reuben are great deliberations of the heart. Why
did you sit between the sheepfolds, hearing the bleating of the
flocks? Among the divisions of Reuben are great consultations
17 of the heart. Gilad dwells beyond the Jordan, and Dan, why
does he reside in ships? Asher lived at the seashore and dwells

18 in its bays. Zebulun is a people that jeopardized its life to die,
19 as did Naphtali, on the heights of the field. Kings came, they
made war, then the kings of Canaan made war in Taanakh near
20 the waters of Megiddo; they took no monetary gain. From the
heavens, they made war; the stars from their courses made war
21 with Sisera. The Kishon Stream swept them away, the Kishon
Stream is an ancient Stream. Let my soul tread courageously.
22 Then the horsehoofs pounded, from the galloping, the gal-
23 loping of its warriors. Curse Meroz, said the messenger of the
Lord, curse its inhabitants thoroughly, because they did not
come to the aid of the Lord, to the aid of the Lord against the
24 valiant. Blessed above women is Yael, wife of Hever the Kenite;
25 among women in the tent, she shall be blessed. Water he requested, milk she gave; in a great bowl, she presented butter.
26 Her hand, to the peg she extended, and her right to the laborer's
hammer; she struck Sisera, crushed his head; and it smashed
27 and passed through his temple. At her feet he knelt, he fell,
he lay; at her feet he knelt, he fell; where he knelt, there he
28 fell dead. Through the window she gazed, and the mother of
Sisera sobbed through the lattice: Why does his chariot tarry
29 to arrive? Why are the hoofbeats of his chariot late? The wis-
est of her noblewomen answer her; she too, will respond with
30 her statements to herself: Aren't they finding, dividing spoils?
A beauty, two beauties, for each man; spoils of dyed garments
for Sisera, spoils of dyed embroidery, two dyed embroider-
31 ies for the necks of the plunderers? So may all Your enemies
perish, Lord, and may all those who love Him be like the sun
coming out in its might. The land was tranquil for forty years.

רָעָ֑שָׁה גַּם־שָׁמַ֣יִם נָטָ֑פוּ גַּם־עָבִ֖ים נָ֥טְפוּ
ה מָֽיִם׃ הָרִ֥ים נָזְל֖וּ מִפְּנֵ֣י יְהוָ֑ה זֶ֣ה
ו סִינַ֔י מִפְּנֵ֕י יְהוָ֖ה אֱלֹהֵ֥י יִשְׂרָאֵֽל׃ בִּימֵ֞י שַׁמְגַּ֤ר בֶּן־
עֲנָת֙ בִּימֵ֣י יָעֵ֔ל חָדְל֖וּ אֳרָח֑וֹת וְהֹלְכֵ֣י
ז נְתִיב֔וֹת יֵלְכ֕וּ אֳרָח֖וֹת עֲקַלְקַלּֽוֹת׃ חָדְל֧וּ פְרָז֛וֹן בְּיִשְׂרָאֵ֖ל
חָדֵ֑לּוּ עַ֤ד שַׁקַּ֙מְתִּי֙ דְּבוֹרָ֔ה שַׁקַּ֥מְתִּי
ח אֵ֖ם בְּיִשְׂרָאֵֽל׃ יִבְחַר֙ אֱלֹהִ֣ים
חֲדָשִׁ֔ים אָ֖ז לָחֶ֣ם שְׁעָרִ֑ים מָגֵ֤ן
אִם־יֵרָאֶה֙ וָרֹ֔מַח בְּאַרְבָּעִ֥ים אֶ֖לֶף
ט בְּיִשְׂרָאֵֽל׃ לִבִּי֙ לְחֽוֹקְקֵ֣י יִשְׂרָאֵ֔ל הַמִּֽתְנַדְּבִ֖ים
י בָּעָ֑ם בָּרְכ֖וּ יְהוָֽה׃ רֹכְבֵ֞י אֲתֹנ֣וֹת
צְחֹר֗וֹת יֹשְׁבֵ֛י עַל־מִדִּ֖ין וְהֹלְכֵ֥י
יא עַל־דֶּ֖רֶךְ שִֽׂיחוּ׃ מִקּ֣וֹל מְחַֽצְצִ֗ים בֵּ֚ין
מַשְׁאַבִּ֔ים שָׁ֤ם יְתַנּוּ֙ צִדְק֣וֹת יְהוָ֔ה צִדְקֹ֥ת
פִּרְזוֹנ֖וֹ בְּיִשְׂרָאֵ֑ל אָ֛ז יָרְד֥וּ לַשְּׁעָרִ֖ים עַם־
יב יְהוָֽה׃ ע֤וּרִי ע֙וּרִי֙ דְּבוֹרָ֔ה ע֥וּרִי
ע֖וּרִי דַּבְּרִי־שִׁ֑יר ק֤וּם בָּרָק֙ וּֽשֲׁבֵ֥ה שֶֽׁבְיְךָ֖ בֶּן־
יג אֲבִינֹֽעַם׃ אָ֚ז יְרַ֣ד שָׂרִ֔יד לְאַדִּירִ֖ים עָ֑ם יְהוָ֕ה
יד יְרַד־לִ֖י בַּגִּבּוֹרִֽים׃ מִנִּ֣י אֶפְרַ֗יִם שָׁרְשָׁם֙
בַּעֲמָלֵ֔ק אַחֲרֶ֥יךָ בִנְיָמִ֖ין בַּעֲמָמֶ֑יךָ מִנִּ֣י
מָכִ֗יר יָֽרְדוּ֙ מְחֹ֣קְקִ֔ים וּמִזְּבוּלֻ֔ן מֹשְׁכִ֖ים בְּשֵׁ֥בֶט
טו סֹפֵֽר׃ וְשָׂרַ֤י בְּיִשָּׂשכָר֙ עִם־דְּבֹרָ֔ה וְיִשָּׂשכָר֙
כֵּ֣ן בָּרָ֔ק בָּעֵ֖מֶק שֻׁלַּ֣ח
בְּרַגְלָ֑יו בִּפְלַגּ֣וֹת רְאוּבֵ֔ן גְּדֹלִ֖ים
טז חִקְקֵי־לֵֽב׃ לָ֣מָּה יָשַׁ֗בְתָּ בֵּ֚ין
הַֽמִּשְׁפְּתַ֔יִם לִשְׁמֹ֖עַ שְׁרִק֣וֹת עֲדָרִ֑ים לִפְלַגּ֣וֹת
יז רְאוּבֵ֔ן גְּדוֹלִ֖ים חִקְרֵי־לֵֽב׃ גִּלְעָ֗ד בְּעֵ֤בֶר הַיַּרְדֵּן֙
שָׁכֵ֔ן וְדָ֕ן לָ֥מָּה יָג֖וּר אֳנִיּ֑וֹת אָשֵׁ֗ר
יָשַׁב֙ לְח֣וֹף יַמִּ֔ים וְעַ֥ל מִפְרָצָ֖יו
יח יִשְׁכּֽוֹן׃ זְבֻל֗וּן עַ֣ם חֵרֵ֥ף נַפְשׁ֛וֹ לָמ֖וּת וְנַפְתָּלִ֑י
יט עַ֖ל מְר֥וֹמֵי שָׂדֶֽה׃ בָּ֤אוּ מְלָכִים֙
נִלְחָ֔מוּ אָ֤ז נִלְחֲמוּ֙ מַלְכֵ֣י כְנַ֔עַן בְּתַעְנַ֖ךְ
עַל־מֵ֣י מְגִדּ֑וֹ בֶּ֥צַע כֶּ֖סֶף לֹ֥א
כ לָקָֽחוּ׃ מִן־שָׁמַ֖יִם נִלְחָ֑מוּ הַכּֽוֹכָבִים֙
כא מִֽמְּסִלּוֹתָ֔ם נִלְחֲמ֖וּ עִם־סִֽיסְרָא׃ נַ֤חַל קִישׁוֹן֙
גְּרָפָ֔ם נַ֥חַל קְדוּמִ֖ים נַ֣חַל קִישׁ֑וֹן תִּדְרְכִ֥י
כב נַפְשִׁ֖י עֹֽז׃ אָ֥ז הָלְמ֖וּ עִקְּבֵי־
כג ס֑וּס מִֽדַּהֲר֖וֹת דַּהֲר֥וֹת אַבִּירָֽיו׃ א֣וֹרוּ
מֵר֗וֹז אָמַר֙ מַלְאַ֣ךְ יְהוָ֔ה אֹ֥רוּ אָר֖וֹר
יֹשְׁבֶ֑יהָ כִּ֤י לֹא־בָ֙אוּ֙ לְעֶזְרַ֣ת יְהוָ֔ה לְעֶזְרַ֥ת
כד יְהוָ֖ה בַּגִּבּוֹרִֽים׃ תְּבֹרַךְ֙ מִנָּשִׁ֔ים
יָעֵ֕ל אֵ֖שֶׁת חֶ֣בֶר הַקֵּינִ֑י מִנָּשִׁ֥ים
כה בָּאֹ֖הֶל תְּבֹרָֽךְ׃ מַ֥יִם שָׁאַ֖ל חָלָ֣ב
כו נָתָ֑נָה בְּסֵ֥פֶל אַדִּירִ֖ים הִקְרִ֥יבָה חֶמְאָֽה׃ יָדָהּ֙
לַיָּתֵ֣ד תִּשְׁלַ֔חְנָה וִֽימִינָ֖הּ לְהַלְמ֣וּת
עֲמֵלִ֑ים וְהָלְמָ֤ה סִֽיסְרָא֙ מָחֲקָ֣ה רֹאשׁ֔וֹ וּמָחֲצָ֥ה
כז וְחָלְפָ֖ה רַקָּתֽוֹ׃ בֵּ֣ין רַגְלֶ֗יהָ כָּרַ֛ע נָפַ֖ל
שָׁכָ֑ב בֵּ֤ין רַגְלֶ֙יהָ֙ כָּרַ֣ע נָפָ֔ל בַּאֲשֶׁ֣ר
כח כָּרַ֔ע שָׁ֖ם נָפַ֥ל שָׁדֽוּד׃ בְּעַ֨ד הַחַלּ֜וֹן נִשְׁקְפָ֧ה
וַתְּיַבֵּ֛ב אֵ֥ם סִֽיסְרָ֖א בְּעַ֣ד הָֽאֶשְׁנָ֑ב מַדּ֗וּעַ
בֹּשֵׁ֤שׁ רִכְבּוֹ֙ לָב֔וֹא מַדּ֣וּעַ אֶֽחֱר֔וּ פַּעֲמֵ֖י
כט מַרְכְּבוֹתָֽיו׃ חַכְמ֥וֹת שָׂרוֹתֶ֖יהָ תַּעֲנֶ֑ינָּה אַף־
ל הִ֕יא תָּשִׁ֥יב אֲמָרֶ֖יהָ לָֽהּ׃ הֲלֹ֨א יִמְצְא֜וּ יְחַלְּק֣וּ
שָׁלָ֗ל רַ֤חַם רַחֲמָתַ֙יִם֙ לְרֹ֣אשׁ גֶּ֔בֶר שְׁלַ֥ל
צְבָעִים֙ לְסִ֣יסְרָ֔א שְׁלַ֥ל צְבָעִ֖ים
רִקְמָ֑ה צֶ֥בַע רִקְמָתַ֛יִם לְצַוְּארֵ֥י שָׁלָֽל׃ כֵּ֠ן
לא יֹאבְד֤וּ כָל־אֽוֹיְבֶ֙יךָ֙ יְהוָ֔ה וְאֹ֣הֲבָ֔יו כְּצֵ֥את הַשֶּׁ֖מֶשׁ
בִּגְבֻרָת֑וֹ וַתִּשְׁקֹ֥ט הָאָ֖רֶץ אַרְבָּעִ֥ים שָׁנָֽה׃

Haftara for
Yitro

God's Revelation to Isaiah

ISAIAH 6:1–7:6, 9:5–6

The appearance of God to Israel on the day when we were established as "a kingdom of priests and a holy nation" (Exodus 19:6) was accompanied by fire, thick smoke, and sounds that made the mountain quake, all of which caused the people to tremble in deathly fear. The prophet Isaiah's description of his initiation into prophecy is analogous: There are noises that cause the doorposts to move, smoke fills the house (Isaiah 6:4), the prophet is afraid that the sight will silence or destroy him (Isaiah 6:5), and a fiery coal is touched to his lips (Isaiah 6:6–7). The concluding words of this vision, "the holy descendants will be its trunk" (Isaiah 6:13), express the eternity of the holy nation, which will survive the sternest of tests.

Some communities conclude the reading with a few more verses from the prophecies of Isaiah, which deal with the everlasting kingdom of Judah, heralding its peace, justice, and righteousness.

6 1 In the year of the death of King Uziya, I saw the Lord sitting on
a throne, high and exalted, and His hem filled the Sanctuary.
2 Seraphim were standing above Him, six wings to each one; with
two it would cover its face, with two it would cover its legs, and
3 with two it would fly. And this one called to that one and said:
Holy, holy, holy, is the Lord of hosts, the whole earth is full of
4 His glory. The doorposts moved at the voice of the caller and
5 the house filled with smoke: and I said: Woe is me, for I am
silenced, as I am a man of impure lips and I live in the midst of a
people of impure lips, for my eyes have seen the King, the Lord
6 of hosts. One of the seraphim flew to me, and in his hand was
7 a coal; he took it from upon the altar with tongs. He touched it
on my mouth and said: Behold, this touched your lips, and your
8 iniquity is removed and your sin atoned. I heard the voice of the
Lord, saying: whom will I send and who will go for us? I said:
9 Here I am, send me. He said: Go, tell this people: Hear, but do
10 not understand; see, but do not know. Bloat the heart of this
people, harden its hearing, and stop up its eyes, lest it see with
its eyes and hear with its ears, and its heart will understand and
11 it will repent and be healed. I said: Until when, my Lord? He
answered: Until cities will be devastated without inhabitant,
and houses without a person, and the land will be devastated
12 to desolation: and the Lord will banish man and the forsaken
13 will be many in the midst of the land. And there will still be a
Seph. tenth in it and it shall continue to be subject to elimination, and
end like the terebinth and like the oak when their leaves fall, their
7 1 trunk remains, the holy descendants will be its trunk. It was in
the days of Ahaz, son of Yotam, son of Uziyahu, king of Judah,
that Retzin, king of Aram, and Peka, son of Remalyahu, king of
Israel, went up to Jerusalem in a war against it, but could not
2 make war against it. It was told to the house of David, saying:
Aram has allied with Ephraim. His heart and the hearts of his
people trembled, like the trembling of the trees of the forest
3 from the wind. The Lord said to Isaiah: go out now to Ahaz,
you and She'ar Yashuv your son, to the end of the channel of
4 the upper pool, on the path of the launderers' field. Say to him:
Be secure and be calm, do not fear and let your heart not be
faint from these two smoldering butts of firebrands, from the
enflamed wrath of Retzin and Aram and the son of Remalya.
5 Because Aram plotted evil against you, with Ephraim and the
6 son of Remalya, saying: Let us go up against Judah, sunder it,
and breach it to us, and we will crown a king in its midst, the son
9 5 of Tavel. For a child is born to us, a son is given to us, and the
authority will be on his shoulders; he will be named Wondrous
6 Advisor, Mighty One, Everlasting Father, Prince of Peace. To
make potent the authority and for unending peace on the
throne of David and on his kingdom, to establish it and to support it with justice and with righteousness from now, forever;
the zealotry of the Lord of hosts will accomplish this.

הפטרת

יתרו

ו א בִּשְׁנַת־מוֹת הַמֶּלֶךְ עֻזִּיָּהוּ וָאֶרְאֶה אֶת־אֲדֹנָי יֹשֵׁב עַל־כִּסֵּא רָם וְנִשָּׂא וְשׁוּלָיו מְלֵאִים אֶת־ ישעיה
ב הַהֵיכָל: שְׂרָפִים עֹמְדִים ׀ מִמַּעַל לוֹ שֵׁשׁ כְּנָפַיִם שֵׁשׁ כְּנָפַיִם לְאֶחָד בִּשְׁתַּיִם ׀ יְכַסֶּה פָנָיו וּבִשְׁתַּיִם
ג יְכַסֶּה רַגְלָיו וּבִשְׁתַּיִם יְעוֹפֵף: וְקָרָא זֶה אֶל־זֶה וְאָמַר קָדוֹשׁ ׀ קָדוֹשׁ קָדוֹשׁ יהוה צְבָאוֹת מְלֹא
ד ה כָל־הָאָרֶץ כְּבוֹדוֹ: וַיָּנֻעוּ אַמּוֹת הַסִּפִּים מִקּוֹל הַקּוֹרֵא וְהַבַּיִת יִמָּלֵא עָשָׁן: וָאֹמַר אוֹי־לִי כִי־
נִדְמֵיתִי כִּי אִישׁ טְמֵא־שְׂפָתַיִם אָנֹכִי וּבְתוֹךְ עַם־טְמֵא שְׂפָתַיִם אָנֹכִי יֹשֵׁב כִּי אֶת־הַמֶּלֶךְ יהוה
ו ז צְבָאוֹת רָאוּ עֵינָי: וַיָּעָף אֵלַי אֶחָד מִן־הַשְּׂרָפִים וּבְיָדוֹ רִצְפָּה בְּמֶלְקַחַיִם לָקַח מֵעַל הַמִּזְבֵּחַ: וַיַּגַּע
ח עַל־פִּי וַיֹּאמֶר הִנֵּה נָגַע זֶה עַל־שְׂפָתֶיךָ וְסָר עֲוֹנֶךָ וְחַטָּאתְךָ תְּכֻפָּר: וָאֶשְׁמַע אֶת־קוֹל אֲדֹנָי אֹמֵר
ט אֶת־מִי אֶשְׁלַח וּמִי יֵלֶךְ־לָנוּ וָאֹמַר הִנְנִי שְׁלָחֵנִי: וַיֹּאמֶר לֵךְ וְאָמַרְתָּ לָעָם הַזֶּה שִׁמְעוּ שָׁמוֹעַ
י וְאַל־תָּבִינוּ וּרְאוּ רָאוֹ וְאַל־תֵּדָעוּ: הַשְׁמֵן לֵב־הָעָם הַזֶּה וְאָזְנָיו הַכְבֵּד וְעֵינָיו הָשַׁע פֶּן־יִרְאֶה
יא בְעֵינָיו וּבְאָזְנָיו יִשְׁמָע וּלְבָבוֹ יָבִין וָשָׁב וְרָפָא לוֹ: וָאֹמַר עַד־מָתַי אֲדֹנָי וַיֹּאמֶר עַד אֲשֶׁר אִם־
יב שָׁאוּ עָרִים מֵאֵין יוֹשֵׁב וּבָתִּים מֵאֵין אָדָם וְהָאֲדָמָה תִּשָּׁאֶה שְׁמָמָה: וְרִחַק יהוה אֶת־הָאָדָם
יג וְרַבָּה הָעֲזוּבָה בְּקֶרֶב הָאָרֶץ: וְעוֹד בָּהּ עֲשִׂרִיָּה וְשָׁבָה וְהָיְתָה לְבָעֵר כָּאֵלָה וְכָאַלּוֹן אֲשֶׁר
הספרדים מסיימים כאן
ז א בְּשַׁלֶּכֶת מַצֶּבֶת בָּם זֶרַע קֹדֶשׁ מַצַּבְתָּהּ: וַיְהִי בִּימֵי אָחָז בֶּן־יוֹתָם בֶּן־עֻזִּיָּהוּ מֶלֶךְ
יְהוּדָה עָלָה רְצִין מֶלֶךְ־אֲרָם וּפֶקַח בֶּן־רְמַלְיָהוּ מֶלֶךְ־יִשְׂרָאֵל יְרוּשָׁלַםִ לַמִּלְחָמָה עָלֶיהָ וְלֹא
ב יָכֹל לְהִלָּחֵם עָלֶיהָ: וַיֻּגַּד לְבֵית דָּוִד לֵאמֹר נָחָה אֲרָם עַל־אֶפְרָיִם וַיָּנַע לְבָבוֹ וּלְבַב עַמּוֹ כְּנוֹעַ
ג עֲצֵי־יַעַר מִפְּנֵי־רוּחַ: וַיֹּאמֶר יהוה אֶל־יְשַׁעְיָהוּ צֵא־נָא לִקְרַאת אָחָז אַתָּה וּשְׁאָר
ד יָשׁוּב בְּנֶךָ אֶל־קְצֵה תְּעָלַת הַבְּרֵכָה הָעֶלְיוֹנָה אֶל־מְסִלַּת שְׂדֵה כוֹבֵס: וְאָמַרְתָּ אֵלָיו הִשָּׁמֵר
וְהַשְׁקֵט אַל־תִּירָא וּלְבָבְךָ אַל־יֵרַךְ מִשְּׁנֵי זַנְבוֹת הָאוּדִים הָעֲשֵׁנִים הָאֵלֶּה בָּחֳרִי־אַף רְצִין
ה וַאֲרָם וּבֶן־רְמַלְיָהוּ: יַעַן כִּי־יָעַץ עָלֶיךָ אֲרָם רָעָה אֶפְרַיִם וּבֶן־רְמַלְיָהוּ לֵאמֹר: נַעֲלֶה בִיהוּדָה
ו וּנְקִיצֶנָּה וְנַבְקִעֶנָּה אֵלֵינוּ וְנַמְלִיךְ מֶלֶךְ בְּתוֹכָהּ אֵת בֶּן־טָבְאַל:
ט ה כִּי־יֶלֶד יֻלַּד־לָנוּ בֵּן נִתַּן־לָנוּ וַתְּהִי הַמִּשְׂרָה עַל־שִׁכְמוֹ וַיִּקְרָא שְׁמוֹ פֶּלֶא יוֹעֵץ אֵל גִּבּוֹר אֲבִי־
ו עַד שַׂר־שָׁלוֹם: לְםַרְבֵּה הַמִּשְׂרָה וּלְשָׁלוֹם אֵין־קֵץ עַל־כִּסֵּא דָוִד וְעַל־מַמְלַכְתּוֹ לְהָכִין אֹתָהּ לְמַרְבֵּה
וּלְסַעֲדָהּ בְּמִשְׁפָּט וּבִצְדָקָה מֵעַתָּה וְעַד־עוֹלָם קִנְאַת יהוה צְבָאוֹת תַּעֲשֶׂה־זֹּאת:

Haftara for
Mishpatim

On Shabbat Shekalim, the haftara on page 1282 is read.

The Fulfillment of the Covenant
JEREMIAH 34:8–22, 33:25–26

This *haftara* deals with the nation's breach of the covenant described at the end of the *parasha*. The prophet Jeremiah reproves the people for betraying the covenant at Sinai, which had been renewed in his days. He also rebukes them for unlawfully enslaving servants and maidservants. This issue, of a man having control over his brother, depriving him of his freedom, is also the first topic discussed in the *parasha*. Jeremiah declares that those who abandon the covenant will themselves be abandoned, warning that they will be delivered into the hands of their enemies and will suffer from hunger and disease.

In order not to end the *haftara* on a negative note, a section is added to the reading. It is the custom to read two verses from a different prophecy of Jeremiah, in which God promises that His covenant with the children of Israel and the house of David will be everlasting. Some communities continue with the adjoining chapter in the book of Jeremiah, which also discusses the reward for intergenerational loyalty to the observance of God's commandments.

34 8 This is the matter that was to Jeremiah from the Lord, after King Tzidkiya established a covenant with the entire people that was 9 in Jerusalem, to proclaim liberty for them, for each man to set his slave free, and each man his maidservant, the Hebrew man or the Hebrew woman, so that no man would enslave a Jew, his 10 brother. All the princes and all the people who entered into the covenant heeded, to set free each man his slave and each man his maidservant, so as not to enslave them any longer, and they 11 heeded, and they sent them forth. Thereafter, they reneged and brought back the slaves and the maidservants whom they had set free, and they subjugated them as slaves and as maidser- 12 vants. The word of the Lord was with Jeremiah from the Lord, 13 saying: So said the Lord, God of Israel: I established a covenant with your fathers on the day that I took them out of the land of 14 Egypt, from the house of bondage, saying: At the end of seven years you shall send forth, each man, his Hebrew brother who will be sold to you and shall serve you six years, after which you shall set him free from you: but your fathers did not heed Me, 15 and they did not incline their ear. You repented today, and you performed that which is upright in My eyes, to proclaim liberty each man for his neighbor, and you established a covenant be- 16 fore Me in the House upon which My name is called. But you reneged and profaned My name, and you brought back each man his slave and each man his maidservant, whom you had set free to themselves, and you subjugated them to be slaves and 17 maidservants for you. Therefore, so said the Lord: You did not

heed Me to proclaim liberty, each man for his brother and each man for his neighbor; behold, I am proclaiming for you liberty – the utterance of the Lord – for the sword, for pestilence and for famine, and I will render you a horror for all the kingdoms of 18 the earth. I will deliver the people who violated My covenant, who did not fulfill the matters of the covenant that they made before Me, the calf which they cut in two and passed between 19 its pieces: the princes of Judah and the princes of Jerusalem, the officers and the priests, and all the people of the land who 20 passed between the pieces of the calf. I will deliver them into the hand of their enemies and into the hand of the seekers of their life, and their corpses will be food for the birds of the heavens 21 and for the animals of the earth. And Tzidkiyahu king of Judah, and his princes, I will deliver into the hand of their enemies and into the hand of the seekers of their life, and into the hand of the army of the king of Babylonia, who have withdrawn from you. 22 Behold, I am commanding – the utterance of the Lord – and I will return them to this city, and they will make war against it, and they will capture it, and they will burn it in fire, and the cities of Judah I will render a wasteland, without inhabitants. **33** 25 So said the Lord: If My covenant of day and night were not, had 26 I not set the statutes of heaven and earth, I would also despise the descendants of Jacob and of David My servant, to cease to take from his descendants rulers over the descendants of Abraham, Isaac, and Jacob, for I will restore their returnees, and I will have compassion on them.

משפטים

בשבת פרשת שקלים קוראים את ההפטרה בעמ' 1283.

ירמיה	הַדָּבָר אֲשֶׁר־הָיָה אֶל־יִרְמְיָהוּ מֵאֵת יְהוָה אַחֲרֵי כְּרֹת הַמֶּלֶךְ צִדְקִיָּהוּ בְּרִית אֶת־כָּל־הָעָם	לד ח

אֲשֶׁר בִּירוּשָׁלִַם לִקְרֹא לָהֶם דְּרוֹר: לְשַׁלַּח אִישׁ אֶת־עַבְדּוֹ וְאִישׁ אֶת־שִׁפְחָתוֹ הָעִבְרִי וְהָעִבְרִיָּה

חָפְשִׁים לְבִלְתִּי עֲבָד־בָּם בִּיהוּדִי אָחִיהוּ אִישׁ: וַיִּשְׁמְעוּ כָל־הַשָּׂרִים וְכָל־הָעָם אֲשֶׁר־בָּאוּ בַבְּרִית

לְשַׁלַּח אִישׁ אֶת־עַבְדּוֹ וְאִישׁ אֶת־שִׁפְחָתוֹ חָפְשִׁים לְבִלְתִּי עֲבָד־בָּם עוֹד וַיִּשְׁמְעוּ וַיְשַׁלֵּחוּ:

וַיִּכְבְּשׁוּם	וַיָּשׁוּבוּ אַחֲרֵי־כֵן וַיָּשִׁבוּ אֶת־הָעֲבָדִים וְאֶת־הַשְּׁפָחוֹת אֲשֶׁר שִׁלְּחוּ חָפְשִׁים וַיִּכְבִּשׁוּם לַעֲבָדִים

וְלִשְׁפָחוֹת: וַיְהִי דְבַר־יְהוָה אֶל־יִרְמְיָהוּ מֵאֵת יְהוָה לֵאמֹר: כֹּה־אָמַר יְהוָה אֱלֹהֵי

יִשְׂרָאֵל אָנֹכִי כָּרַתִּי בְרִית אֶת־אֲבוֹתֵיכֶם בְּיוֹם הוֹצִאִי אוֹתָם מֵאֶרֶץ מִצְרַיִם מִבֵּית עֲבָדִים

לֵאמֹר: מִקֵּץ שֶׁבַע שָׁנִים תְּשַׁלְּחוּ אִישׁ אֶת־אָחִיו הָעִבְרִי אֲשֶׁר־יִמָּכֵר לְךָ וַעֲבָדְךָ שֵׁשׁ שָׁנִים

וְשִׁלַּחְתּוֹ חָפְשִׁי מֵעִמָּךְ וְלֹא־שָׁמְעוּ אֲבוֹתֵיכֶם אֵלַי וְלֹא הִטּוּ אֶת־אָזְנָם: וַתָּשֻׁבוּ אַתֶּם הַיּוֹם

וַתַּעֲשׂוּ אֶת־הַיָּשָׁר בְּעֵינַי לִקְרֹא דְרוֹר אִישׁ לְרֵעֵהוּ וַתִּכְרְתוּ בְרִית לְפָנַי בַּבַּיִת אֲשֶׁר־נִקְרָא

שְׁמִי עָלָיו: וַתָּשֻׁבוּ וַתְּחַלְּלוּ אֶת־שְׁמִי וַתָּשִׁבוּ אִישׁ אֶת־עַבְדּוֹ וְאִישׁ אֶת־שִׁפְחָתוֹ אֲשֶׁר־

שִׁלַּחְתֶּם חָפְשִׁים לְנַפְשָׁם וַתִּכְבְּשׁוּ אֹתָם לִהְיוֹת לָכֶם לַעֲבָדִים וְלִשְׁפָחוֹת: לָכֵן

לְזַעֲוָה	כֹּה־אָמַר יְהוָה אַתֶּם לֹא־שְׁמַעְתֶּם אֵלַי לִקְרֹא דְרוֹר אִישׁ לְאָחִיו וְאִישׁ לְרֵעֵהוּ הִנְנִי קֹרֵא לָכֶם דְּרוֹר נְאֻם־יְהוָה אֶל־הַחֶרֶב אֶל־הַדֶּבֶר וְאֶל־הָרָעָב וְנָתַתִּי אֶתְכֶם לְזַעֲוָה לְכֹל מַמְלְכוֹת

הָאָרֶץ: וְנָתַתִּי אֶת־הָאֲנָשִׁים הָעֹבְרִים אֶת־בְּרִתִי אֲשֶׁר לֹא־הֵקִימוּ אֶת־דִּבְרֵי הַבְּרִית אֲשֶׁר

כָּרְתוּ לְפָנַי הָעֵגֶל אֲשֶׁר כָּרְתוּ לִשְׁנַיִם וַיַּעַבְרוּ בֵּין בְּתָרָיו: שָׂרֵי יְהוּדָה וְשָׂרֵי יְרוּשָׁלִַם הַסָּרִסִים

וְהַכֹּהֲנִים וְכֹל עַם הָאָרֶץ הָעֹבְרִים בֵּין בִּתְרֵי הָעֵגֶל: וְנָתַתִּי אוֹתָם בְּיַד אֹיְבֵיהֶם וּבְיַד מְבַקְשֵׁי

נַפְשָׁם וְהָיְתָה נִבְלָתָם לְמַאֲכָל לְעוֹף הַשָּׁמַיִם וּלְבֶהֱמַת הָאָרֶץ: וְאֶת־צִדְקִיָּהוּ מֶלֶךְ־יְהוּדָה

וְאֶת־שָׂרָיו אֶתֵּן בְּיַד אֹיְבֵיהֶם וּבְיַד מְבַקְשֵׁי נַפְשָׁם וּבְיַד חֵיל מֶלֶךְ בָּבֶל הָעֹלִים מֵעֲלֵיכֶם: הִנְנִי

מְצַוֶּה נְאֻם־יְהוָה וַהֲשִׁבֹתִים אֶל־הָעִיר הַזֹּאת וְנִלְחֲמוּ עָלֶיהָ וּלְכָדוּהָ וּשְׂרָפֻהָ בָאֵשׁ וְאֶת־עָרֵי

יְהוּדָה אֶתֵּן שְׁמָמָה מֵאֵין יֹשֵׁב:

לג כה	כֹּה אָמַר יְהוָה אִם־לֹא בְרִיתִי יוֹמָם וָלָיְלָה חֻקּוֹת שָׁמַיִם וָאָרֶץ לֹא־שָׂמְתִּי: גַּם־זֶרַע יַעֲקוֹב

אָשִׁיב	וְדָוִד עַבְדִּי אֶמְאַס מִקַּחַת מִזַּרְעוֹ מֹשְׁלִים אֶל־זֶרַע אַבְרָהָם יִשְׂחָק וְיַעֲקֹב כִּי־אָשׁוּב אֶת־	

שְׁבוּתָם וְרִחַמְתִּים:

Haftara for
Teruma

On Shabbat Shekalim, the haftara on page 1282 is read. On Shabbat Zakhor, the haftara on page 1284 is read.

The Construction of the Temple
I KINGS 5:26–6:13

In contrast to the Tabernacle of Moses, which was expressly built through the generous donations of the people, Solomon's Temple was constructed with materials from the royal treasury and by means of a service tax that the king imposed on Israel.

God promised Solomon that His presence would always rest in this House, as long as the king would listen to His commandments and follow in His ways. God's statement ended with the assurance: "I will dwell among the children of Israel, and I will not forsake My people Israel" (I Kings 6:13). This is reminiscent of the conclusion of the commandment to build the Tabernacle in the parasha: "They shall make for Me a sanctuary, and I will dwell among them" (Exodus 25:8). The Tabernacle and the Temple caused the Divine Presence to dwell among His people, provided that the people were worthy of this great merit.

5 26 The Lord gave wisdom to Solomon, as He had said to him. There was peace between Hiram and Solomon, and the two 27 of them made a covenant. King Solomon imposed a levy from 28 all Israel; the levy was thirty thousand men. He sent them to Lebanon, ten thousand a month, in shifts: One month they would be in Lebanon, and two months he would be at his 29 home; and Adoniram was in charge of the levy. Solomon had seventy thousand carriers of burdens and eighty thousand hew- 30 ers in the mountains, besides Solomon's chief officers who were in charge of the labor, three thousand three hundred, who were 31 taskmasters over the people who performed the labor. The king commanded, and they quarried great stones, heavy stones, to 32 lay the foundation of the House with hewn stones. Solomon's builders, Hiram's builders, and the Gevalites shaped them, and **6** 1 they prepared the wood and the stones to build the House. It was in the four hundred and eightieth year after the exodus of the children of Israel from the land of Egypt, in the fourth year of Solomon's reign over Israel, in the month of Ziv, which is the second month, that he began to build the House for the Lord. 2 The House that King Solomon built for the Lord: Its length was 3 sixty cubits, its width twenty, and its height thirty cubits. The Hall before the Sanctuary of the House: Its length was twenty cubits along the width of the House; its width was ten cubits

4 before the House. He made for the House broad, narrowing 5 windows. Against the wall of the House he built an annex all around; it was against the walls of the House all around the Sanctuary and the Inner Sanctum, and he made side-chambers 6 all around. The lowest annex was five cubits wide, the middle was six cubits wide, and the third was seven cubits wide, since he made recesses in the wall of the House all around on the out- 7 side so as not to penetrate the walls of the House. The House, in its construction, was built of whole stones that were trans- ported, and hammers, the axe, or any iron tools were not heard 8 in the House in its construction. The entrance of the middle side-chambers was on the right side of the House, and they would ascend by a winding staircase to the middle, and from 9 the middle to the third. He built the House, and he completed it, and he installed a ceiling in the House with hollows and rows 10 of cedar beams. He built the annex along the entire House; its height was five cubits, and he paneled the House with cedar 11 12 wood. The word of the Lord was with Solomon, saying: This House that you are building: If you will follow My statutes, perform My ordinances, and observe all My commandments to follow them, I will fulfill My word with you that I spoke to 13 David your father. I will dwell among the children of Israel, and I will not forsake My people Israel.

תרומה

בשבת פרשת שקלים קוראים את ההפטרה בעמ׳ 1283. בשבת פרשת זכור קוראים את ההפטרה בעמ׳ 1285.

מלכים א׳ | ה כו וַיהוָה נָתַן חָכְמָה לִשְׁלֹמֹה כַּאֲשֶׁר דִּבֶּר־לֹו וַיְהִי שָׁלֹם בֵּין חִירָם וּבֵין שְׁלֹמֹה וַיִּכְרְתוּ בְרִית שְׁנֵיהֶם: כז וַיַּעַל הַמֶּלֶךְ שְׁלֹמֹה מַס מִכָּל־יִשְׂרָאֵל וַיְהִי הַמַּס שְׁלֹשִׁים אֶלֶף אִישׁ: וַיִּשְׁלָחֵם לְבָנֹונָה עֲשֶׂרֶת אֲלָפִים בַּחֹדֶשׁ חֲלִיפֹות חֹדֶשׁ יִהְיוּ בַלְּבָנֹון שְׁנַיִם חֳדָשִׁים בְּבֵיתֹו וַאֲדֹנִירָם עַל־ הַמַּס: כט וַיְהִי לִשְׁלֹמֹה שִׁבְעִים אֶלֶף נֹשֵׂא סַבָּל וּשְׁמֹנִים אֶלֶף חֹצֵב בָּהָר: לְבַד מִשָּׂרֵי הַנִּצָּבִים לִשְׁלֹמֹה אֲשֶׁר עַל־הַמְּלָאכָה שְׁלֹשֶׁת אֲלָפִים וּשְׁלֹשׁ מֵאֹות הָרֹדִים בָּעָם הָעֹשִׂים בַּמְּלָאכָה: לא וַיְצַו הַמֶּלֶךְ וַיַּסִּעוּ אֲבָנִים גְּדֹלֹות אֲבָנִים יְקָרֹות לְיַסֵּד הַבָּיִת אַבְנֵי גָזִית: לב וַיִּפְסְלוּ בֹּנֵי שְׁלֹמֹה וּבֹנֵי חִירֹום וְהַגִּבְלִים וַיָּכִינוּ הָעֵצִים וְהָאֲבָנִים לִבְנֹות הַבָּיִת: ו וַיְהִי בִשְׁמֹונִים שָׁנָה וְאַרְבַּע מֵאֹות שָׁנָה לְצֵאת בְּנֵי־יִשְׂרָאֵל מֵאֶרֶץ־מִצְרַיִם בַּשָּׁנָה הָרְבִיעִית בְּחֹדֶשׁ זִו הוּא הַחֹדֶשׁ הַשֵּׁנִי לִמְלֹךְ שְׁלֹמֹה עַל־יִשְׂרָאֵל וַיִּבֶן הַבַּיִת לַיהוָה: ב וְהַבַּיִת אֲשֶׁר בָּנָה הַמֶּלֶךְ שְׁלֹמֹה לַיהוָה שִׁשִּׁים־אַמָּה אָרְכֹּו וְעֶשְׂרִים רָחְבֹּו וּשְׁלֹשִׁים אַמָּה קֹומָתֹו: ג וְהָאוּלָם עַל־פְּנֵי הֵיכַל הַבַּיִת עֶשְׂרִים אַמָּה אָרְכֹּו עַל־פְּנֵי רֹחַב הַבָּיִת עֶשֶׂר בָּאַמָּה רָחְבֹּו עַל־פְּנֵי הַבָּיִת: ד וַיַּעַשׂ לַבָּיִת חַלֹּונֵי שְׁקֻפִים אֲטֻמִים: ה וַיִּבֶן עַל־קִיר הַבַּיִת יָצוּעַ סָבִיב אֶת־קִירֹות הַבַּיִת סָבִיב לַהֵיכָל וְלַדְּבִיר וַיַּעַשׂ יָצִיעַ צְלָעֹות סָבִיב: ו הַיָּצוּעַ הַתַּחְתֹּנָה חָמֵשׁ בָּאַמָּה רָחְבָּהּ וְהַתִּיכֹנָה שֵׁשׁ בָּאַמָּה רָחְבָּהּ וְהַשְּׁלִישִׁית הַיָּצִיעַ שֶׁבַע בָּאַמָּה רָחְבָּהּ כִּי מִגְרָעֹות נָתַן לַבַּיִת סָבִיב חוּצָה לְבִלְתִּי אֲחֹז בְּקִירֹות־הַבָּיִת: ז וְהַבַּיִת בְּהִבָּנֹתֹו אֶבֶן־שְׁלֵמָה מַסָּע נִבְנָה וּמַקָּבֹות וְהַגַּרְזֶן כָּל־כְּלִי בַרְזֶל לֹא־נִשְׁמַע בַּבַּיִת בְּהִבָּנֹתֹו: ח פֶּתַח הַצֵּלָע הַתִּיכֹנָה אֶל־כֶּתֶף הַבַּיִת הַיְמָנִית וּבְלוּלִּים יַעֲלוּ עַל־הַתִּיכֹנָה וּמִן־הַתִּיכֹנָה אֶל־הַשְּׁלִשִׁים: ט וַיִּבֶן אֶת־הַבַּיִת וַיְכַלֵּהוּ וַיִּסְפֹּן אֶת־הַבַּיִת גֵּבִים וּשְׂדֵרֹת בָּאֲרָזִים: ו וַיִּבֶן אֶת־ הַיָּצִיעַ עַל־כָּל־הַבַּיִת חָמֵשׁ אַמֹּות קֹומָתֹו וַיֶּאֱחֹז אֶת־הַבַּיִת בַּעֲצֵי אֲרָזִים: יא וַיְהִי דְּבַר־יְהוָה אֶל־שְׁלֹמֹה לֵאמֹר: יב הַבַּיִת הַזֶּה אֲשֶׁר־אַתָּה בֹּנֶה אִם־תֵּלֵךְ בְּחֻקֹּתַי וְאֶת־מִשְׁפָּטַי תַּעֲשֶׂה וְשָׁמַרְתָּ אֶת־כָּל־מִצְוֹתַי לָלֶכֶת בָּהֶם וַהֲקִמֹתִי אֶת־דְּבָרִי אִתָּךְ אֲשֶׁר דִּבַּרְתִּי אֶל־דָּוִד אָבִיךָ: יג וְשָׁכַנְתִּי בְּתֹוךְ בְּנֵי יִשְׂרָאֵל וְלֹא אֶעֱזֹב אֶת־עַמִּי יִשְׂרָאֵל:

Haftara for
Tetzaveh

On Shabbat Zakhor, the haftara on page 1284 is read.

The Inauguration of the Altar in the Prophecy of Ezekiel
EZEKIEL 43:10–27

The structure of the altar and the details of its inauguration process, as taught by the prophet Ezekiel to the exiles in Babylonia, bear some similarity to the structure of the altar fashioned by Moses and the details of the inauguration of the Tabernacle, which are discussed in the *parasha*. However, there are differences in the details of the two accounts. Moreover, the Second Temple, constructed in the days of Ezra the Scribe, was not built in accordance with the blueprint of the future Temple that Ezekiel had previously laid out, perhaps because his written descriptions were insufficiently clear (see Radak; Abravanel; *Menaḥot* 45a; Rambam, *Sefer Avoda, Hilkhot Beit HaBeḥira* 1:4).

43 10 You, Son of man, relate to the house of Israel about the House, and they will be humiliated by their iniquities, and they shall 11 measure the design. If they are humiliated by everything that they have done, inform them of the form of the House and its design, its exits, its entrances, and all its forms, and all its statutes, all its forms, and all its laws, and write it before their eyes, and they will keep its entire form and all its statutes, and per- 12 form them. This is the law of the House: Atop the mountain, its entire border all around is a sacred sanctum. Behold, this is the 13 law of the House. These are the measurements of the altar in cubits: each cubit is one cubit and a handbreadth; the founda- tion is one cubit and the width one cubit, and its border near its 14 edge all around, one span. This is the height of the altar. From the foundation on the ground until the lowest stratum is two cubits, and the width is one cubit, and from the low stratum to 15 the high stratum is four cubits, and the width is one cubit. The topmost stratum is four cubits, and above the topmost stratum 16 are the four horns. The topmost stratum is twelve in length by 17 twelve in width, square, to its four sides. The stratum is fourteen in length by fourteen in width to its four sides, and the border all around it is one-half of a cubit, its foundation is a cubit all 18 around, and its ramp faces east. He said to me: Son of man, so said the Lord God: These are the statutes of the altar on the day

of its making, to offer burnt offerings upon it and to sprinkle 19 blood upon it. You shall give a young bull as a sin offering to the priests, the Levites, who are from the descendants of Tzadok, who are near to Me – the utterance of the Lord God – to serve 20 me. You shall take from its blood, and you shall place it on its four horns, on the four corners of the stratum, and on the bor- 21 der all around, and you shall cleanse it and atone for it. You shall take the bull of the sin offering, and he shall burn it in the desig- 22 nated place of the House, outside the Sanctuary. On the second day you shall present an unblemished goat as a sin offering, and 23 they shall cleanse the altar as they cleansed with the bull. When you finish cleansing, you shall present an unblemished young 24 bull and an unblemished ram from the flock. You shall present them before the Lord, and the priests shall cast salt upon them 25 and offer them up as a burnt offering to the Lord. For seven days you shall offer a goat as a daily sin offering, and they shall 26 offer an unblemished young bull and ram from the flock. Seven days they shall atone for the altar and cleanse it, and they shall 27 inaugurate it. When they conclude the days, it shall be from the eighth day onward that the priests shall offer upon the altar your burnt offerings and your peace offerings, and I will grant you propitiation – the utterance of the Lord God.

הפטרת

תצוה

בשבת פרשת זכור קוראים את ההפטרה בעמ' 1285.

מג י אַתָּה בֶן־אָדָם הַגֵּד אֶת־בֵּית־יִשְׂרָאֵל אֶת־הַבַּיִת וְיִכָּלְמוּ מֵעֲוֺנוֹתֵיהֶם וּמָדְדוּ אֶת־תָּכְנִית: וְאִם־ יחזקאל
נִכְלְמוּ מִכֹּל אֲשֶׁר־עָשׂוּ צוּרַת הַבַּיִת וּתְכוּנָתוֹ וּמוֹצָאָיו וּמוֹבָאָיו וְכָל־צוּרֹתָו וְאֵת כָּל־חֻקֹּתָיו
וְכָל־צוּרֹתָו וְכָל־תּוֹרֹתָו הוֹדַע אוֹתָם וּכְתֹב לְעֵינֵיהֶם וְיִשְׁמְרוּ אֶת־כָּל־צוּרָתוֹ וְאֶת־כָּל־חֻקֹּתָיו
יב וְעָשׂוּ אוֹתָם: זֹאת תּוֹרַת הַבָּיִת עַל־רֹאשׁ הָהָר כָּל־גְּבֻלוֹ סָבִיב ׀ סָבִיב קֹדֶשׁ קָדָשִׁים הִנֵּה־
יג זֹאת תּוֹרַת הַבָּיִת: וְאֵלֶּה מִדּוֹת הַמִּזְבֵּחַ בָּאַמּוֹת אַמָּה אַמָּה וָטֹפַח וְחֵיק הָאַמָּה וְאַמָּה־רֹחַב
יד וּגְבוּלָהּ אֶל־שְׂפָתָהּ סָבִיב זֶרֶת הָאֶחָד וְזֶה גַּב הַמִּזְבֵּחַ: וּמֵחֵיק הָאָרֶץ עַד־הָעֲזָרָה הַתַּחְתּוֹנָה
שְׁתַּיִם אַמּוֹת וְרֹחַב אַמָּה אֶחָת וּמֵהָעֲזָרָה הַקְּטַנָּה עַד־הָעֲזָרָה הַגְּדוֹלָה אַרְבַּע אַמּוֹת וְרֹחַב
טו טז הָאַמָּה: וְהַהַרְאֵל אַרְבַּע אַמּוֹת וּמֵהָאֲרִאֵיל וּלְמַעְלָה הַקְּרָנוֹת אַרְבַּע: וְהָאֲרִאֵיל שְׁתֵּים עֶשְׂרֵה
יז אֹרֶךְ בִּשְׁתֵּים עֶשְׂרֵה רֹחַב רָבוּעַ אֶל אַרְבַּעַת רְבָעָיו: וְהָעֲזָרָה אַרְבַּע עֶשְׂרֵה אֹרֶךְ בְּאַרְבַּע
עֶשְׂרֵה רֹחַב אֶל אַרְבַּעַת רְבָעֶיהָ וְהַגְּבוּל סָבִיב אוֹתָהּ חֲצִי הָאַמָּה וְהַחֵיק־לָהּ אַמָּה סָבִיב
יח וּמַעֲלֹתֵהוּ פְּנוֹת קָדִים: וַיֹּאמֶר אֵלַי בֶּן־אָדָם כֹּה אָמַר אֲדֹנָי יֱהֹוִה אֵלֶּה חֻקּוֹת הַמִּזְבֵּחַ בְּיוֹם
יט הֵעָשׂוֹתוֹ לְהַעֲלוֹת עָלָיו עוֹלָה וְלִזְרֹק עָלָיו דָּם: וְנָתַתָּה אֶל־הַכֹּהֲנִים הַלְוִיִּם אֲשֶׁר הֵם מִזֶּרַע
כ צָדוֹק הַקְּרֹבִים אֵלַי נְאֻם אֲדֹנָי יֱהֹוִה לְשָׁרְתֵנִי פַּר בֶּן־בָּקָר לְחַטָּאת: וְלָקַחְתָּ מִדָּמוֹ וְנָתַתָּה עַל־
כא אַרְבַּע קַרְנֹתָיו וְאֶל־אַרְבַּע פִּנּוֹת הָעֲזָרָה וְאֶל־הַגְּבוּל סָבִיב וְחִטֵּאתָ אוֹתוֹ וְכִפַּרְתָּהוּ: וְלָקַחְתָּ
כב אֵת הַפָּר הַחַטָּאת וּשְׂרָפוֹ בְּמִפְקַד הַבַּיִת מִחוּץ לַמִּקְדָּשׁ: וּבַיּוֹם הַשֵּׁנִי תַּקְרִיב שְׂעִיר־עִזִּים
כג תָּמִים לְחַטָּאת וְחִטְּאוּ אֶת־הַמִּזְבֵּחַ כַּאֲשֶׁר חִטְּאוּ בַּפָּר: בְּכַלּוֹתְךָ מֵחַטֵּא תַּקְרִיב פַּר בֶּן־בָּקָר
כד תָּמִים וְאַיִל מִן־הַצֹּאן תָּמִים: וְהִקְרַבְתָּם לִפְנֵי יְהוָה וְהִשְׁלִיכוּ הַכֹּהֲנִים עֲלֵיהֶם מֶלַח וְהֶעֱלוּ
כה אוֹתָם עֹלָה לַיהוָה: שִׁבְעַת יָמִים תַּעֲשֶׂה שְׂעִיר־חַטָּאת לַיּוֹם וּפַר בֶּן־בָּקָר וְאַיִל מִן־הַצֹּאן
כו כז תְּמִימִים יַעֲשׂוּ: שִׁבְעַת יָמִים יְכַפְּרוּ אֶת־הַמִּזְבֵּחַ וְטִהֲרוּ אֹתוֹ וּמִלְאוּ יָדָו: וִיכַלּוּ אֶת־הַיָּמִים
וְהָיָה בַיּוֹם הַשְּׁמִינִי וָהָלְאָה יַעֲשׂוּ הַכֹּהֲנִים עַל־הַמִּזְבֵּחַ אֶת־עוֹלוֹתֵיכֶם וְאֶת־שַׁלְמֵיכֶם וְרָצָאתִי
אֶתְכֶם נְאֻם אֲדֹנָי יֱהֹוִה:

Haftara for
Ki Tisa

On Shabbat Para, the haftara on page 1288 is read.

Elijah and the Prophets of the Baal
I KINGS 18:1–39

Israel's main spiritual problem, from when it was first formed as a nation, was always its tendency to be influenced by the cultures and beliefs of the surrounding nations. Moses and all the subsequent prophets repeatedly warned each generation about this. The widespread desire in the pagan world to worship tangible gods that had tangible characteristics led to the sin of the Golden Calf and the ensuing punishment, as described in the *parasha*. In this regard, the reign of Ahav and his Zidonian wife Izevel is considered a particularly low point in the history of Israel. Ahav and Izevel centered their kingdom on the deliberate, calculated worship of a foreign god. This *haftara* recounts the efforts of the prophet Elijah to restore the people's faith in God.

18 1 Many days passed and the word of the Lord was with Elijah,
Ashk. in the third year, saying: Go, appear to Ahav, and I will send
begin 2 rain upon the land. Elijah went to appear to Ahav, and the fam-
3 ine was severe in Samaria. Ahav summoned Obadiah, who was
in charge of the household; Obadiah feared the Lord greatly.
4 It was when Izevel eliminated the prophets of the Lord that
Obadiah took one hundred prophets and concealed them, fifty
5 men to a cave, and provided them with bread and water. Ahav
said to Obadiah: Go through the land to all the springs of water
and to all the brooks; perhaps we will find forage and may sustain the horses and mules, that we will not be deprived of ani-
6 mals. They divided the land between them to pass through it.
Ahav went one way by himself, and Obadiah went one way by
7 himself. Obadiah was on the way, and behold, there was Elijah
to meet him. He recognized him, fell on his face, and said: Is
8 that you, my lord Elijah? He said to him: It is I. Go, say to your
9 lord: Here is Elijah. He said: How have I sinned, that you de-
10 liver your servant into the hand of Ahav, to put me to death? As
the Lord your God lives, there is no nation or kingdom that my
lord did not send to seek you; and they said: He is not here. He
administered an oath to the kingdom and the nation that they
11 could not find you. Now you say: Go, say to your lord: Here
12 is Elijah. It will be that I will leave you, and the spirit of the
Lord will carry you to where I will not know, and I will come
and tell Ahav, and he will not find you and he will kill me; but
13 your servant has feared the Lord from my youth. Was it not told
to my lord that which I did when Izevel killed the prophets of
the Lord? I concealed one hundred men of the prophets of the
Lord, fifty men to a cave, and I provided them with bread and
14 water. Now you say: Go, tell your lord: Here is Elijah; he will kill
15 me. Elijah said: As the Lord of hosts, before whom I have stood,
16 lives, I will appear to him today. Obadiah went to meet Ahav
17 and told him, and Ahav went to meet Elijah. It was when Ahav
18 saw Elijah, Ahav said to him: Is that you, troubler of Israel? He
said: I did not trouble Israel; rather, it was you and your father's
house, with your forsaking of the commandments of the Lord,
19 and you followed the Be'alim. Now send, assemble to me all of
Israel to Mount Carmel, and the prophets of the Baal, four hundred and fifty, and the prophets of the Ashera, four hundred,
Seph. 20 who eat at Izevel's table. Ahav sent among all the children of
begin 21 Israel, and he assembled the prophets to Mount Carmel. Elijah
approached all the people and he said: How long are you skipping between two branches? If the Lord is God, follow Him,
and if Baal, follow him. The people did not answer him a word.
22 Elijah said to the people: I alone remain a prophet of the Lord,
and the prophets of the Baal are four hundred and fifty men.
23 Let them give us two bulls, and let them choose one bull for
themselves, cut it in pieces, and place it on the wood, but let
them not place fire, and I will prepare one bull and place it on
24 the wood, and I will not place fire. You will call in the name
of your god, and I will call on the name of the Lord, and the
god who responds with fire, He is God. All the people answered
25 and said: The proposal is good. Elijah said to the prophets of

הפטרת

כי תשא

בשבת פרשת פרה קוראים את ההפטרה בעמ׳ 1289.

מלכים א׳ — האשכנזים מתחילים כאן

ח א ויהי ימים רבים ודבר־יהוה היה אל־אליהו בשנה השלישית לאמר לך הראה אל־אחאב
ב ג ואתנה מטר על־פני האדמה: וילך אליהו להראות אל־אחאב והרעב חזק בשמרון: ויקרא
ד אחאב אל־עבדיהו אשר על־הבית ועבדיהו היה ירא את־יהוה מאד: ויהי בהכרית איזבל
את נביאי יהוה ויקח עבדיהו מאה נביאים ויחביאם חמשים איש במערה וכלכלם לחם
ה ומים: ויאמר אחאב אל־עבדיהו לך בארץ אל־כל־מעיני המים ואל כל־הנחלים אולי ׀
ו נמצא חציר ונחיה סוס ופרד ולוא נכרית מהבהמה: ויחלקו להם את־הארץ לעבר־בה
ז אחאב הלך בדרך אחד לבדו ועבדיהו הלך בדרך־אחד לבדו: ויהי עבדיהו בדרך והנה
ח אליהו לקראתו ויכרהו ויפל על־פניו ויאמר האתה זה אדני אליהו: ויאמר לו אני לך אמר
ט לאדניך הנה אליהו: ויאמר מה חטאתי כי־אתה נתן את־עבדך ביד־אחאב להמיתני: חי ׀
יהוה אלהיך אם־יש־גוי וממלכה אשר לא־שלח אדני שם לבקשך ואמרו אין והשביע
יא את־הממלכה ואת־הגוי כי לא ימצאכה: ועתה אתה אמר לך אמר לאדניך הנה אליהו:
יב והיה אני ׀ אלך מאתך ורוח יהוה ׀ ישאך על אשר לא־אדע ובאתי להגיד לאחאב ולא
יג ימצאך והרגני ועבדך ירא את־יהוה מנערי: הלא־הגד לאדני את אשר־עשיתי בהרג איזבל
את נביאי יהוה ואחבא מנביאי יהוה מאה איש חמשים חמשים איש במערה ואכלכלם
יד טו לחם ומים: ועתה אתה אמר לך אמר לאדניך הנה אליהו והרגני: ויאמר אליהו חי יהוה
טז צבאות אשר עמדתי לפניו כי היום אראה אליו: וילך עבדיהו לקראת אחאב ויגד־לו וילך
יז אחאב לקראת אליהו: ויהי כראות אחאב את־אליהו ויאמר אחאב אליו האתה זה עכר
יח ישראל: ויאמר לא עכרתי את־ישראל כי אם־אתה ובית אביך בעזבכם את־מצות יהוה
יט ותלך אחרי הבעלים: ועתה שלח קבץ אלי את־כל־ישראל אל־הר הכרמל ואת־נביאי

הספרדים מתחילים כאן

כ הבעל ארבע מאות וחמשים ונביאי האשרה ארבע מאות אכלי שלחן איזבל: וישלח
כא אחאב בכל־בני ישראל ויקבץ את־הנביאים אל־הר הכרמל: ויגש אליהו אל־כל־העם
ויאמר עד־מתי אתם פסחים על־שתי הסעפים אם־יהוה האלהים לכו אחריו ואם־הבעל
כב לכו אחריו ולא־ענו העם אתו דבר: ויאמר אליהו אל־העם אני נותרתי נביא ליהוה
כג לבדי ונביאי הבעל ארבע־מאות וחמשים איש: ויתנו־לנו שנים פרים ויבחרו להם הפר
האחד וינתחהו וישימו על־העצים ואש לא ישימו ואני אעשה ׀ את־הפר האחד ונתתי
כד על־העצים ואש לא אשים: וקראתם בשם אלהיכם ואני אקרא בשם־יהוה והיה האלהים
כה אשר־יענה באש הוא האלהים ויען כל־העם ויאמרו טוב הדבר: ויאמר אליהו לנביאי

Baal: Choose one bull for yourselves and prepare it first, as you
are many, and call in the name of your god, but do not place fire.
26 They took the bull that he gave them, and they prepared. They
called in the name of the Baal from the morning until noon,
saying: The Baal, answer us. But there was no voice and no re-
27 spondent. They skipped about the altar that they prepared. It
was at noon and Elijah mocked them and said: Call in a loud
voice, as he is a god; perhaps he is in conversation, or he is
musing, or he is on the way; perhaps he is sleeping, and he will
28 awaken. They called in a loud voice and cut themselves in their
customary manner, with swords and spears, until blood spilled
29 on them. It was when noon passed; they prophesied until the
time of offering up the afternoon offering, but there was no
30 voice, nor respondent, nor listener. Elijah said to all the people:
Approach me. And all the people approached him. He repaired
31 the destroyed altar of the Lord. Elijah took twelve stones, according to the number of the tribes of the sons of Jacob, to
whom was the word of the Lord, saying: Israel shall be your
32 name. He built the stones into an altar in the name of the Lord;
and he made a trench around the altar as large as a field required
33 for sowing two se'a of seed. He arranged the wood, cut the bull
34 in pieces, and placed it on the wood. He said: Fill four jugs
with water and pour on the burnt offering and on the wood.
He said: Do it a second time. And they did it a second time.
35 He said: Do it a third time. And they did it a third time. The
water went around the altar; and he also filled the trench with
36 water. It was at the time of the presentation of the afternoon
offering that Elijah the prophet approached and said: Lord,
God of Abraham, Isaac, and Israel, let it be known today that
You are God in Israel and I am Your servant, and at Your word I
37 performed all these matters. Answer me, Lord, answer me, and
this people will know that You, Lord, are God, and it is You who
38 turned their heart back. Fire of the Lord fell and consumed the
burnt offering, the wood, the stones, and the dirt, and it vapor-
39 ized the water that was in the trench. All the people saw, fell on
their faces, and said: The Lord is the God; the Lord is the God.

Haftara for **Vayak'hel**

On Shabbat Shekalim, the haftara on page 1282 is read. On Shabbat Zakhor, the haftara on page 1284 is read. On Shabbat HaHodesh, the haftara on page 1290 is read.

The Temple Pillars and Vessels

I KINGS 7:13–26, 40–50

Both the Torah's account of the construction of the Tabernacle and its vessels and the description of the Temple of Solomon in the book of Kings are highly detailed and repetitious. This may be due to the importance attached to sacred objects and to fashioning them precisely according to God's instructions.

7 13
Seph. begin
14 King Solomon sent and took Hiram from Tyre. He was the
son of a widow from the tribe of Naphtali, and his father was
a Tyrian bronzesmith; he was filled with wisdom, understanding, and knowledge to perform all craftsmanship with bronze.
He came to King Solomon and he performed all his labor.
15 He fashioned the two bronze pillars; eighteen cubits was the
height of the one pillar, and a twelve-cubit string would cir-
16 cle the second pillar. He made: two capitals of cast bronze

הַבַּעַל בַּחֲרוּ לָכֶם הַפָּר הָאֶחָד וַעֲשׂוּ רִאשֹׁנָה כִּי אַתֶּם הָרַבִּים וְקִרְאוּ בְּשֵׁם אֱלֹהֵיכֶם וְאֵשׁ לֹא
כו תָשִׂימוּ: וַיִּקְחוּ אֶת־הַפָּר אֲשֶׁר־נָתַן לָהֶם וַיַּעֲשׂוּ וַיִּקְרְאוּ בְשֵׁם־הַבַּעַל מֵהַבֹּקֶר וְעַד־הַצָּהֳרַיִם
כז לֵאמֹר הַבַּעַל עֲנֵנוּ וְאֵין קוֹל וְאֵין עֹנֶה וַיְפַסְּחוּ עַל־הַמִּזְבֵּחַ אֲשֶׁר עָשָׂה: וַיְהִי בַצָּהֳרַיִם וַיְהַתֵּל
בָּהֶם אֵלִיָּהוּ וַיֹּאמֶר קִרְאוּ בְקוֹל־גָּדוֹל כִּי־אֱלֹהִים הוּא כִּי־שִׂיחַ וְכִי־שִׂיג לוֹ וְכִי־דֶרֶךְ לוֹ אוּלַי
כח יָשֵׁן הוּא וְיִקָץ: וַיִּקְרְאוּ בְּקוֹל גָּדוֹל וַיִּתְגֹּדְדוּ כְּמִשְׁפָּטָם בַּחֲרָבוֹת וּבָרְמָחִים עַד־שְׁפָךְ־דָּם
כט עֲלֵיהֶם: וַיְהִי כַּעֲבֹר הַצָּהֳרַיִם וַיִּתְנַבְּאוּ עַד לַעֲלוֹת הַמִּנְחָה וְאֵין־קוֹל וְאֵין־עֹנֶה וְאֵין קָשֶׁב:
ל וַיֹּאמֶר אֵלִיָּהוּ לְכָל־הָעָם גְּשׁוּ אֵלַי וַיִּגְּשׁוּ כָל־הָעָם אֵלָיו וַיְרַפֵּא אֶת־מִזְבַּח יְהוָה הֶהָרוּס: וַיִּקַּח
לא אֵלִיָּהוּ שְׁתֵּים עֶשְׂרֵה אֲבָנִים כְּמִסְפַּר שִׁבְטֵי בְנֵי־יַעֲקֹב אֲשֶׁר הָיָה דְבַר־יְהוָה אֵלָיו לֵאמֹר
לב יִשְׂרָאֵל יִהְיֶה שְׁמֶךָ: וַיִּבְנֶה אֶת־הָאֲבָנִים מִזְבֵּחַ בְּשֵׁם יְהוָה וַיַּעַשׂ תְּעָלָה כְּבֵית סָאתַיִם זֶרַע
לג סָבִיב לַמִּזְבֵּחַ: וַיַּעֲרֹךְ אֶת־הָעֵצִים וַיְנַתַּח אֶת־הַפָּר וַיָּשֶׂם עַל־הָעֵצִים: וַיֹּאמֶר מִלְאוּ אַרְבָּעָה
לה כַדִּים מַיִם וְיִצְקוּ עַל־הָעֹלָה וְעַל־הָעֵצִים וַיֹּאמֶר שְׁנוּ וַיִּשְׁנוּ וַיֹּאמֶר שַׁלֵּשׁוּ וַיְשַׁלֵּשׁוּ: וַיֵּלְכוּ
הַמַּיִם סָבִיב לַמִּזְבֵּחַ וְגַם אֶת־הַתְּעָלָה מִלֵּא־מָיִם: וַיְהִי ׀ בַּעֲלוֹת הַמִּנְחָה וַיִּגַּשׁ אֵלִיָּהוּ הַנָּבִיא
לו וַיֹּאמַר יְהוָה אֱלֹהֵי אַבְרָהָם יִצְחָק וְיִשְׂרָאֵל הַיּוֹם יִוָּדַע כִּי־אַתָּה אֱלֹהִים בְּיִשְׂרָאֵל וַאֲנִי עַבְדֶּךָ
לז וּבִדְבָרְךָ עָשִׂיתִי אֵת כָּל־הַדְּבָרִים הָאֵלֶּה: עֲנֵנִי יְהוָה עֲנֵנִי וְיֵדְעוּ הָעָם הַזֶּה כִּי־אַתָּה יְהוָה
לח הָאֱלֹהִים וְאַתָּה הֲסִבֹּתָ אֶת־לִבָּם אֲחֹרַנִּית: וַתִּפֹּל אֵשׁ־יְהוָה וַתֹּאכַל אֶת־הָעֹלָה וְאֶת־הָעֵצִים
לט וְאֶת־הָאֲבָנִים וְאֶת־הֶעָפָר וְאֶת־הַמַּיִם אֲשֶׁר־בַּתְּעָלָה לִחֵכָה: וַיַּרְא כָּל־הָעָם וַיִּפְּלוּ עַל־פְּנֵיהֶם
וַיֹּאמְרוּ יְהוָה הוּא הָאֱלֹהִים יְהוָה הוּא הָאֱלֹהִים:

ויקהל

בשבת פרשת שקלים קוראים את ההפטרה בעמ' 1283. בשבת פרשת זכור קוראים את ההפטרה בעמ' 1285. בשבת פרשת
החודש קוראים את ההפטרה בעמ' 1291.

מלכים א'
לספרדים

יג וַיִּשְׁלַח הַמֶּלֶךְ שְׁלֹמֹה וַיִּקַּח אֶת־חִירָם מִצֹּר: בֶּן־אִשָּׁה אַלְמָנָה הוּא מִמַּטֵּה נַפְתָּלִי וְאָבִיו
אִישׁ־צֹרִי חֹרֵשׁ נְחֹשֶׁת וַיִּמָּלֵא אֶת־הַחָכְמָה וְאֶת־הַתְּבוּנָה וְאֶת־הַדַּעַת לַעֲשׂוֹת כָּל־מְלָאכָה
בַּנְּחֹשֶׁת וַיָּבוֹא אֶל־הַמֶּלֶךְ שְׁלֹמֹה וַיַּעַשׂ אֶת־כָּל־מְלַאכְתּוֹ: וַיָּצַר אֶת־שְׁנֵי הָעַמּוּדִים נְחֹשֶׁת
טו שְׁמֹנֶה עֶשְׂרֵה אַמָּה קוֹמַת הָעַמּוּד הָאֶחָד וְחוּט שְׁתֵּים־עֶשְׂרֵה אַמָּה יָסֹב אֶת־הָעַמּוּד

to place on the tops of the pillars; five cubits was the height of
the one capital, and five cubits was the height of the second
17 capital; screens of meshwork and threads of chainwork for the
capitals that were on the tops of the pillars; there were seven for
18 the one capital, and seven for the second capital. He crafted the
pillars, and there were two rows all around on the one screen
to cover the capitals that were at the top with the pomegran-
19 ates; and likewise he did to the other capital. The capitals that
were atop the pillars to the Hall were of lily work, four cubits.
20 The capitals on the two pillars were also covered from the top,
from opposite the protrusion that was at the edge of the screen
and two hundred pomegranates were in rows around the sec-
21 ond capital. He erected the pillars for the Hall of the Sanctuary;
he erected the right pillar and called its name Yakhin, and he
22 erected the left pillar and called its name Boaz. Atop the pillars
23 was lily work; and the work of the pillars was completed. He
made the sea by casting. It was ten cubits from brim to brim,
circular all around, its height was five cubits, and a thirty-cu-
24 bit line would circle it all around. Bulbs were under its brim,
ten cubits all around circling it, surrounding the sea all around;
25 the bulbs were in two rows, cast with its casting. It stood upon
twelve oxen, three facing north, three facing west, three facing
south, and three facing east, and the sea was upon them from
26 above, and all their hind parts were inward. Its thickness was
a handbreadth, and its brim was like the craftsmanship of the
brim of a lily blossom cup; it would hold two thousand bat.

Seph. end

Ashk. begin

7 40 Hiram made the basins, the shovels, and the bowls, and Hiram
completed all the labor that he performed for King Solomon in
41 the House of the Lord: Two pillars; the two orbs of the capitals
that were atop the pillars; the two screens to cover the two orbs
42 of the capitals that were atop the pillars; the pomegranates, four
hundred for the two screens, two rows of pomegranates for
each screen, to cover the two orbs of the capitals that were atop
43 44 the pillars; the ten bases and the ten lavers on the bases; the
45 one sea and the twelve oxen beneath the sea; the pots, the shovels, the bowls, and all these vessels that Hiram crafted for King
Solomon in the House of the Lord were of burnished bronze.
46 The king cast them on the Jordan plain, in an excavation in the
47 ground between Sukot and Tzaretan. Solomon refrained with
regard to all the vessels, due to the exceedingly great quantity;
48 the weight of the bronze was not quantified. Solomon crafted
all the vessels that were in the House of the Lord: The golden
altar; the golden table upon which is the showbread, of gold;
49 the candelabra, five on the right and five on the left before the
Inner Sanctum, of pure gold; the flowers, the lamps, and the
50 tongs of gold; the jugs, the musical instruments, the bowls,
the ladles, and the pans of pure gold; the hinge sockets for the
doors of the inner house, the Holy of Holies, and for the doors
of the House, the Sanctuary, of gold.

טז הַשֵּׁנִי: וּשְׁתֵּי כֹתָרֹת עָשָׂה לָתֵת עַל־רָאשֵׁי הָעַמּוּדִים מֻצַק נְחֹשֶׁת חָמֵשׁ אַמּוֹת קוֹמַת
יז הַכֹּתֶרֶת הָאֶחָת וְחָמֵשׁ אַמּוֹת קוֹמַת הַכֹּתֶרֶת הַשֵּׁנִית: שְׂבָכִים מַעֲשֵׂה שְׂבָכָה גְּדִלִים
מַעֲשֵׂה שַׁרְשְׁרוֹת לַכֹּתָרֹת אֲשֶׁר עַל־רֹאשׁ הָעַמּוּדִים שִׁבְעָה לַכֹּתֶרֶת הָאֶחָת וְשִׁבְעָה
יח לַכֹּתֶרֶת הַשֵּׁנִית: וַיַּעַשׂ אֶת־הָעַמּוּדִים וּשְׁנֵי טוּרִים סָבִיב עַל־הַשְּׂבָכָה הָאֶחָת לְכַסּוֹת
יט אֶת־הַכֹּתָרֹת אֲשֶׁר עַל־רֹאשׁ הָרִמֹּנִים וְכֵן עָשָׂה לַכֹּתֶרֶת הַשֵּׁנִית: וְכֹתָרֹת אֲשֶׁר עַל־רֹאשׁ
כ הָעַמּוּדִים מַעֲשֵׂה שׁוּשַׁן בָּאוּלָם אַרְבַּע אַמּוֹת: וְכֹתָרֹת עַל־שְׁנֵי הָעַמּוּדִים גַּם־מִמַּעַל
מִלְּעֻמַּת הַבֶּטֶן אֲשֶׁר לְעֵבֶר שבכה וְהָרִמּוֹנִים מָאתַיִם טֻרִים סָבִיב עַל הַכֹּתֶרֶת הַשֵּׁנִית: הַשְּׂבָכָה
כא וַיָּקֶם אֶת־הָעַמֻּדִים לְאֻלָם הַהֵיכָל וַיָּקֶם אֶת־הָעַמּוּד הַיְמָנִי וַיִּקְרָא אֶת־שְׁמוֹ יָכִין וַיָּקֶם אֶת־
כב הָעַמּוּד הַשְּׂמָאלִי וַיִּקְרָא אֶת־שְׁמוֹ בֹּעַז: וְעַל רֹאשׁ הָעַמּוּדִים מַעֲשֵׂה שׁוֹשָׁן וַתִּתֹּם מְלֶאכֶת
כג הָעַמּוּדִים: וַיַּעַשׂ אֶת־הַיָּם מוּצָק עֶשֶׂר בָּאַמָּה מִשְּׂפָתוֹ עַד־שְׂפָתוֹ עָגֹל ׀ סָבִיב
כד וְחָמֵשׁ בָּאַמָּה קוֹמָתוֹ וקוה שְׁלֹשִׁים בָּאַמָּה יָסֹב אֹתוֹ סָבִיב: וּפְקָעִים מִתַּחַת לִשְׂפָתוֹ ׀ סָבִיב וְקָו
כה סֹבְבִים אֹתוֹ עֶשֶׂר בָּאַמָּה מַקִּפִים אֶת־הַיָּם סָבִיב שְׁנֵי טוּרִים הַפְּקָעִים יְצֻקִים בִּיצֻקָתוֹ: עֹמֵד
עַל־שְׁנֵי עָשָׂר בָּקָר שְׁלֹשָׁה פֹנִים ׀ צָפוֹנָה וּשְׁלֹשָׁה פֹנִים ׀ יָמָּה וּשְׁלֹשָׁה ׀ פֹּנִים נֶגְבָּה וּשְׁלֹשָׁה
כו פֹּנִים מִזְרָחָה וְהַיָּם עֲלֵיהֶם מִלְמָעְלָה וְכָל־אֲחֹרֵיהֶם בָּיְתָה: וְעָבְיוֹ טֶפַח וּשְׂפָתוֹ כְּמַעֲשֵׂה הספרדים
שְׂפַת־כּוֹס פֶּרַח שׁוֹשָׁן אַלְפַּיִם בַּת יָכִיל: מסיימים כאן

ז מ וַיַּעַשׂ חִירוֹם אֶת־הַכִּיֹּרוֹת וְאֶת־הַיָּעִים וְאֶת־הַמִּזְרָקוֹת וַיְכַל חִירָם לַעֲשׂוֹת אֶת־כָּל־הַמְּלָאכָה מלכים א׳ לאשכנזים
מא אֲשֶׁר עָשָׂה לַמֶּלֶךְ שְׁלֹמֹה בֵּית יְהוָה: עַמֻּדִים שְׁנַיִם וְגֻלֹּת הַכֹּתָרֹת אֲשֶׁר־עַל־רֹאשׁ הָעַמֻּ
דִים שְׁתָּיִם וְהַשְּׂבָכוֹת שְׁתַּיִם לְכַסּוֹת אֶת־שְׁתֵּי גֻּלּוֹת הַכֹּתָרֹת אֲשֶׁר עַל־רֹאשׁ הָעַמּוּדִים:
מב וְאֶת־הָרִמֹּנִים אַרְבַּע מֵאוֹת לִשְׁתֵּי הַשְּׂבָכוֹת שְׁנֵי־טוּרִים רִמֹּנִים לַשְּׂבָכָה הָאֶחָת לְכַסּוֹת
מג אֶת־שְׁתֵּי גֻּלֹּת הַכֹּתָרֹת אֲשֶׁר עַל־פְּנֵי הָעַמּוּדִים: וְאֶת־הַמְּכֹנוֹת עֶשֶׂר וְאֶת־הַכִּיֹּרֹת עֲשָׂרָה
מד מה עַל־הַמְּכֹנוֹת: וְאֶת־הַיָּם הָאֶחָד וְאֶת־הַבָּקָר שְׁנֵים־עָשָׂר תַּחַת הַיָּם: וְאֶת־הַסִּירוֹת וְאֶת־הַיָּעִים
וְאֶת־הַמִּזְרָקוֹת וְאֵת כָּל־הַכֵּלִים האהל אֲשֶׁר עָשָׂה חִירָם לַמֶּלֶךְ שְׁלֹמֹה בֵּית יְהוָה נְחֹשֶׁת הָאֵלֶּה
מו מז מְמֹרָט: בְּכִכַּר הַיַּרְדֵּן יְצָקָם הַמֶּלֶךְ בְּמַעֲבֵה הָאֲדָמָה בֵּין סֻכּוֹת וּבֵין צָרְתָן: וַיַּנַּח שְׁלֹמֹה אֶת־
מח כָּל־הַכֵּלִים מֵרֹב מְאֹד מְאֹד לֹא נֶחְקַר מִשְׁקַל הַנְּחֹשֶׁת: וַיַּעַשׂ שְׁלֹמֹה אֵת כָּל־הַכֵּלִים אֲשֶׁר
מט בֵּית יְהוָה אֵת מִזְבַּח הַזָּהָב וְאֶת־הַשֻּׁלְחָן אֲשֶׁר עָלָיו לֶחֶם הַפָּנִים זָהָב: וְאֶת־הַמְּנֹרוֹת חָמֵשׁ
נ מִיָּמִין וְחָמֵשׁ מִשְּׂמֹאול לִפְנֵי הַדְּבִיר זָהָב סָגוּר וְהַפֶּרַח וְהַנֵּרֹת וְהַמֶּלְקַחַיִם זָהָב: וְהַסִּפּוֹת
וְהַמְזַמְּרוֹת וְהַמִּזְרָקוֹת וְהַכַּפּוֹת וְהַמַּחְתּוֹת זָהָב סָגוּר וְהַפֹּתוֹת לְדַלְתוֹת הַבַּיִת הַפְּנִימִי לְקֹדֶשׁ
הַקֳּדָשִׁים לְדַלְתֵי הַבַּיִת לַהֵיכָל זָהָב:

Haftara for
Pekudei

On Shabbat Shekalim, the haftara on page 1282 is read. On Shabbat Para, the haftara on page 1288 is read. On Shabbat HaHodesh, the haftara on page 1290 is read.

The Inauguration of the Temple and Solomon's Blessings

I KINGS 7:40–8:21

The *haftara* of *Parashat Pekudei* is the continuation of the *haftara* of *Parashat Vayak'hel*. The Temple became the House of God when the Ark of the Covenant was brought inside. The ark was transported to Mount Moriah in a celebratory procession, and when it was placed was the Holy of Holies. God showed His affirmation with a cloud of smoke, which is similar to the description of the Tabernacle that appears at the end of the *parasha*. At this climactic moment, when the glory of God descended to rest in its permanent dwelling place in Jerusalem, Solomon spoke both to God and to the masses of people who had gathered for the event. His speech included words of gratitude and praise for the fulfillment of God's promise to his father David, as well as remarks on the magnitude of this occasion, when a permanent sanctuary was established for God, almost five hundred years after Israel first became a nation and was redeemed from Egypt.

7 40 Hiram made the basins, the shovels, and the bowls, and Hiram
Seph. completed all the labor that he performed for King Solomon in
begin 41 the House of the Lord: Two pillars; the two orbs of the capitals
that were atop the pillars; the two screens to cover the two orbs
42 of the capitals that were atop the pillars; the pomegranates, four
hundred for the two screens, two rows of pomegranates for
each screen, to cover the two orbs of the capitals that were atop
43
44 the pillars; the ten bases and the ten lavers on the bases; the
45 one sea and the twelve oxen beneath the sea; the pots, the shovels, the bowls, and all these vessels that Hiram crafted for King
Solomon in the House of the Lord were of burnished bronze.
46 The king cast them on the Jordan plain, in an excavation in the
47 ground between Sukot and Tzaretan. Solomon refrained with
regard to all the vessels, due to the exceedingly great quantity;
48 the weight of the bronze was not quantified. Solomon crafted
all the vessels that were in the House of the Lord: The golden
49 altar; the gold table upon which is the showbread; the candelabra, five on the right and five on the left before the Inner
Sanctum, of pure gold; the flowers, the lamps, and the tongs of
50 gold; the jugs, the musical instruments, the bowls, the ladles,
and the pans of pure gold; the hinge sockets for the doors of
the inner house, the Holy of Holies, and for the doors of the
Seph. 51 House, the Sanctuary, of gold. All the labor that King Solomon
end performed in the House of the Lord was completed. Solomon
Ashk. brought all the sacred items of David his father, the silver, the
begin gold, and the vessels, and he placed them in the treasuries of

8 1 the House of the Lord. Then Solomon assembled the elders of
Israel, all the heads of the tribes, the princes of the fathers of
the children of Israel, to King Solomon in Jerusalem, to bring
the Ark of the Covenant of the Lord up from the city of David,
2 which is Zion. All the men of Israel were assembled to King
Solomon on the festival, in the month of Etanim, which is the
3 seventh month. All the elders of Israel came, and the priests
4 carried the ark. They brought up the Ark of the Lord, the Tent
of Meeting, and all the sacred vessels that were in the Tent; the
5 priests and the Levites brought them up. King Solomon and the
entire congregation of Israel, who had congregated with him
before the ark, were offering sheep and cattle that could not be
6 numbered and could not be counted due to the quantity. The
priests brought the Ark of the Covenant of the Lord to its place,
to the Sanctuary of the House, to the Holy of Holies, to beneath
7 the wings of the cherubim. For the cherubim spread wings over
the area of the ark; the cherubim covered the ark and its staves
8 from above. They extended the staves, and the ends of the
staves were visible from the Inner Sanctum, in the front of the
Sanctuary, but they were not seen from the outside, and they
9 are there to this day. There is nothing in the ark but the two
tablets of stone that Moses placed there at Horev, with which
the Lord made a covenant with the children of Israel when they
10 came out of the land of Egypt. It was when the priests emerged
from the Sanctuary that the cloud filled the House of the Lord.
11 The priests were unable to stand and serve due to the cloud,

הפטרת

פקודי

בשבת פרשת שקלים קוראים את ההפטרה בעמ׳ 1283. בשבת פרשת פרה קוראים את ההפטרה בעמ׳ 1289. בשבת פרשת החודש קוראים את ההפטרה בעמ׳ 1291.

מלכים א׳
הספרדים
מתחילים כאן

מ וַיַּעַשׂ חִירוֹם אֶת־הַכִּיֹּרוֹת וְאֶת־הַיָּעִים וְאֶת־הַמִּזְרָקוֹת וַיְכַל חִירָם לַעֲשׂוֹת אֶת־כָּל־הַמְּלָאכָה

מא אֲשֶׁר עָשָׂה לַמֶּלֶךְ שְׁלֹמֹה בֵּית יְהוָה: עַמֻּדִים שְׁנַיִם וְגֻלֹּת הַכֹּתֶרֶת אֲשֶׁר־עַל־רֹאשׁ הָעַמּוּדִים

מב שְׁתָּיִם וְהַשְּׂבָכוֹת שְׁתַּיִם לְכַסּוֹת אֶת־שְׁתֵּי גֻּלֹּת הַכֹּתָרֹת אֲשֶׁר עַל־רֹאשׁ הָעַמּוּדִים: וְאֶת־הָרִמֹּנִים אַרְבַּע מֵאוֹת לִשְׁתֵּי הַשְּׂבָכוֹת שְׁנֵי־טוּרִים רִמֹּנִים לַשְּׂבָכָה הָאֶחָת לְכַסּוֹת אֶת־

מג שְׁתֵּי גֻּלֹּת הַכֹּתָרֹת אֲשֶׁר עַל־פְּנֵי הָעַמּוּדִים: וְאֶת־הַמְּכֹנוֹת עָשֶׂר וְאֶת־הַכִּיֹּרֹת עֲשָׂרָה עַל־

מד הַמְּכֹנוֹת: וְאֶת־הַיָּם הָאֶחָד וְאֶת־הַבָּקָר שְׁנֵים־עָשָׂר תַּחַת הַיָּם: וְאֶת־הַסִּירוֹת וְאֶת־הַיָּעִים

מה וְאֶת־הַמִּזְרָקוֹת וְאֵת כָּל־הַכֵּלִים הָאֹהֶל אֲשֶׁר עָשָׂה חִירָם לַמֶּלֶךְ שְׁלֹמֹה בֵּית יְהוָה נְחֹשֶׁת

הָאֵלֶּה

מו מְמֹרָט: בְּכִכַּר הַיַּרְדֵּן יְצָקָם הַמֶּלֶךְ בְּמַעֲבֵה הָאֲדָמָה בֵּין סֻכּוֹת וּבֵין צָרְתָן: וַיַּנַּח שְׁלֹמֹה אֶת־

מח כָּל־הַכֵּלִים מֵרֹב מְאֹד מְאֹד לֹא נֶחְקַר מִשְׁקַל הַנְּחֹשֶׁת: וַיַּעַשׂ שְׁלֹמֹה אֵת כָּל־הַכֵּלִים אֲשֶׁר

מט בֵּית יְהוָה אֵת מִזְבַּח הַזָּהָב וְאֶת־הַשֻּׁלְחָן אֲשֶׁר עָלָיו לֶחֶם הַפָּנִים זָהָב: וְאֶת־הַמְּנֹרוֹת חָמֵשׁ

נ מִיָּמִין וְחָמֵשׁ מִשְּׂמֹאול לִפְנֵי הַדְּבִיר זָהָב סָגוּר וְהַפֶּרַח וְהַנֵּרֹת וְהַמֶּלְקַחַיִם זָהָב: וְהַסִּפּוֹת וְהַמְזַמְּרוֹת וְהַמִּזְרָקוֹת וְהַכַּפּוֹת וְהַמַּחְתּוֹת זָהָב סָגוּר וְהַפֹּתוֹת לְדַלְתוֹת הַבַּיִת הַפְּנִימִי לְקֹדֶשׁ

הספרדים
מסיימים כאן
האשכנזים
מתחילים כאן

נא הַקֳּדָשִׁים לְדַלְתֵי הַבַּיִת לַהֵיכָל זָהָב: וַתִּשְׁלַם כָּל־הַמְּלָאכָה אֲשֶׁר עָשָׂה הַמֶּלֶךְ שְׁלֹמֹה בֵּית יְהוָה וַיָּבֵא שְׁלֹמֹה אֶת־קָדְשֵׁי | דָּוִד אָבִיו אֶת־הַכֶּסֶף וְאֶת־הַזָּהָב וְאֶת־הַכֵּלִים נָתַן בְּאֹצְרוֹת בֵּית יְהוָה:

ח א אָז יַקְהֵל שְׁלֹמֹה אֶת־זִקְנֵי יִשְׂרָאֵל אֶת־כָּל־רָאשֵׁי הַמַּטּוֹת נְשִׂיאֵי הָאָבוֹת לִבְנֵי יִשְׂרָאֵל אֶל־הַמֶּלֶךְ שְׁלֹמֹה יְרוּשָׁלִָם לְהַעֲלוֹת אֶת־אֲרוֹן בְּרִית־יְהוָה מֵעִיר

ב דָּוִד הִיא צִיּוֹן: וַיִּקָּהֲלוּ אֶל־הַמֶּלֶךְ שְׁלֹמֹה כָּל־אִישׁ יִשְׂרָאֵל בְּיֶרַח הָאֵתָנִים בֶּחָג הוּא הַחֹדֶשׁ

ג הַשְּׁבִיעִי: וַיָּבֹאוּ כֹּל זִקְנֵי יִשְׂרָאֵל וַיִּשְׂאוּ הַכֹּהֲנִים אֶת־הָאָרוֹן: וַיַּעֲלוּ אֶת־אֲרוֹן יְהוָה וְאֶת־אֹהֶל

ה מוֹעֵד וְאֶת־כָּל־כְּלֵי הַקֹּדֶשׁ אֲשֶׁר בָּאֹהֶל וַיַּעֲלוּ אֹתָם הַכֹּהֲנִים וְהַלְוִיִּם: וְהַמֶּלֶךְ שְׁלֹמֹה וְכָל־עֲדַת יִשְׂרָאֵל הַנּוֹעָדִים עָלָיו אִתּוֹ לִפְנֵי הָאָרוֹן מְזַבְּחִים צֹאן וּבָקָר אֲשֶׁר לֹא־יִסָּפְרוּ וְלֹא יִמָּנוּ

ו מֵרֹב: וַיָּבִאוּ הַכֹּהֲנִים אֶת־אֲרוֹן בְּרִית־יְהוָה אֶל־מְקוֹמוֹ אֶל־דְּבִיר הַבַּיִת אֶל־קֹדֶשׁ הַקֳּדָשִׁים

ז אֶל־תַּחַת כַּנְפֵי הַכְּרוּבִים: כִּי הַכְּרוּבִים פֹּרְשִׂים כְּנָפַיִם אֶל־מְקוֹם הָאָרוֹן וַיָּסֹכּוּ הַכְּרֻבִים עַל־

ח הָאָרוֹן וְעַל־בַּדָּיו מִלְמָעְלָה: וַיַּאֲרִכוּ הַבַּדִּים וַיֵּרָאוּ רָאשֵׁי הַבַּדִּים מִן־הַקֹּדֶשׁ עַל־פְּנֵי הַדְּבִיר

ט וְלֹא יֵרָאוּ הַחוּצָה וַיִּהְיוּ שָׁם עַד הַיּוֹם הַזֶּה: אֵין בָּאָרוֹן רַק שְׁנֵי לֻחוֹת הָאֲבָנִים אֲשֶׁר הִנִּחַ

י שָׁם מֹשֶׁה בְּחֹרֵב אֲשֶׁר כָּרַת יְהוָה עִם־בְּנֵי יִשְׂרָאֵל בְּצֵאתָם מֵאֶרֶץ מִצְרָיִם: וַיְהִי בְּצֵאת

יא הַכֹּהֲנִים מִן־הַקֹּדֶשׁ וְהֶעָנָן מָלֵא אֶת־בֵּית יְהוָה: וְלֹא־יָכְלוּ הַכֹּהֲנִים לַעֲמֹד לְשָׁרֵת מִפְּנֵי הֶעָנָן

12 as the glory of the Lord filled the House of the Lord. Then

13 Solomon said: The Lord said that He would dwell in the fog. I

14 have built You an abode, a place for Your dwelling, forever. The king turned his face and blessed the entire assembly of Israel,

15 and the entire assembly of Israel was standing. He said: Blessed is the Lord, God of Israel, who spoke with His mouth of David

16 my father, and with His hand fulfilled it, saying: From the day that I took My people Israel out of Egypt, I did not choose a city from all the tribes of Israel to build a House for My name to be there, but I chose David to be in charge of My people Israel.

17 It was in the heart of David my father to build a House for the

18 name of the Lord, God of Israel. The Lord said to David my father: Because it was in your heart to build a House for My

19 name, you did well, for it was in your heart. However, you will not build the House; rather, your son who will emerge from

20 your loins, he will build the House for My name. The Lord fulfilled His word that He had spoken, and I have risen in place of David my father, and I have taken my seat on the throne of Israel, as the Lord spoke, and I have built the House for the

21 name of the Lord, God of Israel. I put there a place for the ark, in which there is the Covenant of the Lord, which He made with our fathers when He took them out of the land of Egypt.

Haftara for
Vayikra

On Shabbat Zakhor, the haftara on page 1284 is read. On Shabbat HaHodesh, the haftara on page 1290 is read.

The Destiny of Israel
ISAIAH 43:21–44:23

In this prophecy of reproof delivered by Isaiah, God clarifies to the people that the sacrificial service is not an end in and of itself; rather, it must be accompanied by repentance and the improvement of one's ways. Otherwise, the bringing of offerings is a waste of effort that provides no benefit to God or man. In the second section of the prophecy, the prophet seeks to distance Israel from idol worship by mocking the manner in which people bow down to idols that they themselves have fashioned. He then presents the nation of Israel, which was created by the true God, as a contrast to such individuals.

43 21 This people, I formed for Myself; they will relate My praise. But
22
23 you did not call Me, Jacob, for you wearied of Me, Israel. You did not bring Me the sheep of your burnt offerings and you did not honor Me with your offerings; I have not burdened you with a meal offering and I have not wearied you with frankincense.

24 You did not buy cane for Me with silver, and with the fat of your offerings you did not satisfy Me; rather, you burdened Me with

25 your sins, you wearied Me with your iniquities. I, I, am He who expunges your transgressions for My sake, and your sins I will

26 not remember. Remind Me, let us come together for judgment;

27 relate, you, so that you will be vindicated. Your original ancestor

28 sinned and your advocates transgressed against Me. I profaned the sacred princes, and I gave Jacob to destruction and Israel to

44 1 derisions. Now hear, Jacob My servant, and Israel, whom I have

2 chosen, so said the Lord Your Maker and may your Fashioner from the womb help you: Do not fear, Jacob, My servant and

3 Yeshurun, whom I have chosen. Just as I will pour water on the desiccated and liquids upon dry ground, I will pour My spirit upon your descendants and My blessing upon your offspring.

4 They will grow among the grass, like willows by streams of wa-

5 ter. This one will say: I am the Lord's; that one will call in the name of Jacob and this one will write with his hand to the Lord,

6 and he will name himself with the name of Israel. So said the Lord, King of Israel and its Redeemer, the Lord of hosts: I am

יב כִּי־מָלֵא כְבוֹד־יהוה אֶת־בֵּית יהוה: אָז אָמַר שְׁלֹמֹה יהוה אָמַר לִשְׁכֹּן בָּעֲרָפֶל:

יג בָּנֹה בָנִיתִי בֵּית זְבֻל לָךְ מָכוֹן לְשִׁבְתְּךָ עוֹלָמִים: וַיַּסֵּב הַמֶּלֶךְ אֶת־פָּנָיו וַיְבָרֶךְ אֵת כָּל־קְהַל

יד יִשְׂרָאֵל וְכָל־קְהַל יִשְׂרָאֵל עֹמֵד: וַיֹּאמֶר בָּרוּךְ יהוה אֱלֹהֵי יִשְׂרָאֵל אֲשֶׁר דִּבֶּר בְּפִיו אֵת דָּוִד

טו אָבִי וּבְיָדוֹ מִלֵּא לֵאמֹר: מִן־הַיּוֹם אֲשֶׁר הוֹצֵאתִי אֶת־עַמִּי אֶת־יִשְׂרָאֵל מִמִּצְרַיִם לֹא־בָחַרְתִּי

טז בְעִיר מִכֹּל שִׁבְטֵי יִשְׂרָאֵל לִבְנוֹת בַּיִת לִהְיוֹת שְׁמִי שָׁם וָאֶבְחַר בְּדָוִד לִהְיוֹת עַל־עַמִּי יִשְׂרָאֵל:

יז וַיְהִי עִם־לְבַב דָּוִד אָבִי לִבְנוֹת בַּיִת לְשֵׁם יהוה אֱלֹהֵי יִשְׂרָאֵל: וַיֹּאמֶר יהוה אֶל־דָּוִד אָבִי יַעַן

יח אֲשֶׁר הָיָה עִם־לְבָבְךָ לִבְנוֹת בַּיִת לִשְׁמִי הֱטִיבֹתָ כִּי הָיָה עִם־לְבָבֶךָ: רַק אַתָּה לֹא תִבְנֶה הַבָּיִת

יט כִּי אִם־בִּנְךָ הַיֹּצֵא מֵחֲלָצֶיךָ הוּא־יִבְנֶה הַבַּיִת לִשְׁמִי: וַיָּקֶם יהוה אֶת־דְּבָרוֹ אֲשֶׁר דִּבֵּר וָאָקֻם

כ תַּחַת דָּוִד אָבִי וָאֵשֵׁב ׀ עַל־כִּסֵּא יִשְׂרָאֵל כַּאֲשֶׁר דִּבֶּר יהוה וָאֶבְנֶה הַבַּיִת לְשֵׁם יהוה אֱלֹהֵי

כא יִשְׂרָאֵל: וָאָשִׂם שָׁם מָקוֹם לָאָרוֹן אֲשֶׁר־שָׁם בְּרִית יהוה אֲשֶׁר כָּרַת עִם־אֲבֹתֵינוּ בְּהוֹצִיאוֹ אֹתָם מֵאֶרֶץ מִצְרָיִם:

הפטרת

ויקרא

בשבת פרשת זכור קוראים את ההפטרה בעמ' 1285. בשבת פרשת החודש קוראים את ההפטרה בעמ' 1291.

ישעיה | עַם־זוּ יָצַרְתִּי לִי תְּהִלָּתִי יְסַפֵּרוּ: וְלֹא־אֹתִי קָרָאתָ יַעֲקֹב כִּי־יָגַעְתָּ בִּי יִשְׂרָאֵל: לֹא־הֵבֵיאתָ לִּי | מג כא כב כג

שֵׂה עֹלֹתֶיךָ וּזְבָחֶיךָ לֹא כִבַּדְתָּנִי לֹא הֶעֱבַדְתִּיךָ בְּמִנְחָה וְלֹא הוֹגַעְתִּיךָ בִּלְבוֹנָה: לֹא־קָנִיתָ לִּי | כד

בַכֶּסֶף קָנֶה וְחֵלֶב זְבָחֶיךָ לֹא הִרְוִיתָנִי אַךְ הֶעֱבַדְתַּנִי בְּחַטֹּאותֶיךָ הוֹגַעְתַּנִי בַּעֲוֹנֹתֶיךָ: אָנֹכִי | כה

אָנֹכִי הוּא מֹחֶה פְשָׁעֶיךָ לְמַעֲנִי וְחַטֹּאתֶיךָ לֹא אֶזְכֹּר: הַזְכִּירֵנִי נִשָּׁפְטָה יָחַד סַפֵּר אַתָּה לְמַעַן | כו

תִּצְדָּק: אָבִיךָ הָרִאשׁוֹן חָטָא וּמְלִיצֶיךָ פָּשְׁעוּ בִי: וַאֲחַלֵּל שָׂרֵי קֹדֶשׁ וְאֶתְּנָה לַחֵרֶם יַעֲקֹב | כז כח

מד | וְיִשְׂרָאֵל לַגִּדּוּפִים: וְעַתָּה שְׁמַע יַעֲקֹב עַבְדִּי וְיִשְׂרָאֵל בָּחַרְתִּי בוֹ: כֹּה־אָמַר יהוה | א ב

עֹשֶׂךָ וְיֹצֶרְךָ מִבֶּטֶן יַעְזְרֶךָּ אַל־תִּירָא עַבְדִּי יַעֲקֹב וִישֻׁרוּן בָּחַרְתִּי בוֹ: כִּי אֶצָּק־מַיִם עַל־צָמֵא | ג

וְנֹזְלִים עַל־יַבָּשָׁה אֶצֹּק רוּחִי עַל־זַרְעֶךָ וּבִרְכָתִי עַל־צֶאֱצָאֶיךָ: וְצָמְחוּ בְּבֵין חָצִיר כַּעֲרָבִים | ד

עַל־יִבְלֵי־מָיִם: זֶה יֹאמַר לַיהוה אָנִי וְזֶה יִקְרָא בְשֵׁם־יַעֲקֹב וְזֶה יִכְתֹּב יָדוֹ לַיהוה וּבְשֵׁם יִשְׂרָאֵל | ה

יְכַנֶּה: כֹּה־אָמַר יהוה מֶלֶךְ־יִשְׂרָאֵל וְגֹאֲלוֹ יהוה צְבָאוֹת אֲנִי רִאשׁוֹן וַאֲנִי אַחֲרוֹן | ו

7 first and I am last and besides Me there is no God. Who like me
can proclaim and tell it and order it for Me since My setting of
the world's people? Let them tell them that which approaches
8 and that which will come. Do not be afraid and do not fear;
wasn't it from then that I announced to you and declared, and
you are My witnesses: Is there a God besides Me? There is no
9 rock I do not know. Fashioners of idols, they are all empty and
the objects of their admiration are of no avail; they are their witnesses; they do not see and they do not know, so that they will
10 be ashamed. Who fashioned a god or cast an idol to no avail?
11 Behold, all his colleagues will be ashamed, and the craftsmen,
they are people; let them all gather, stand, be afraid, be ashamed
12 together. An ironsmith with an adze and he works with coal and
fashions it with hammers; he wields it with his strength of arm,
even hungry and having no strength, he does not drink water
13 and he tires. The carpenter stretches a line, marks it with dye,
makes it with planes, and with a compass, marks it; he makes it
like the form of a man, like the splendor of a person, to sit in a
14 house. He cuts cedars for it and takes arbutus and oak; he exerts
himself among the trees of the forest; he plants a fir and the rain
15 makes it grow. It will be for a person for fuel; he takes of it and
is warmed; he burns it and bakes bread; he even makes a god
and prostrates himself; he makes it into an idol and worships it.
16 Half of it he burns in fire; on half of it he eats meat, roasts a roast
and is satiated; he even warms himself and says: Ah, I am warm,
17 I see the flame. Its remainder he makes into a god; his idol, he
worships it and prostrates himself and prays to it and says: Save
18 me, for you are my god. They do not know and they do not
understand, for their eyes are sealed from seeing, their hearts
19 from understanding. He does not reflect in his heart and it has
no knowledge and no understanding to say: Half of it I burned
in fire, and I even baked bread on its coals; I roasted meat and
ate it, and the rest of it I will make into an abomination, I will
20 worship the stock of a tree? He is guided by ashes; a foolish
heart has led him astray and he does not save his soul and does
21 not say: Is there not falsehood in my right hand? Remember
these, Jacob and Israel, for you are My servant; I fashioned you
22 as My servant, Israel, do not abandon Me. I have wiped away
your transgressions like a thick cloud and your sins like a cloud;
23 return to Me, for I have redeemed you. Sing, heavens, as the
Lord has acted; shout, depths of the earth; mountains, break
out into song, forest and every tree in it, for the Lord has redeemed Jacob and in Israel He is glorified.

ז וּמִבַּלְעָדַי אֵין אֱלֹהִים: וּמִי־כָמוֹנִי יִקְרָא וְיַגִּידֶהָ וְיַעְרְכֶהָ לִי מִשּׂוּמִי עַם־עוֹלָם וְאֹתִיּוֹת וַאֲשֶׁר
ח תָּבֹאנָה יַגִּידוּ לָמוֹ: אַל־תִּפְחֲדוּ וְאַל־תִּרְהוּ הֲלֹא מֵאָז הִשְׁמַעְתִּיךָ וְהִגַּדְתִּי וְאַתֶּם עֵדָי הֲיֵשׁ
ט אֱלוֹהַּ מִבַּלְעָדַי וְאֵין צוּר בַּל־יָדָעְתִּי: יֹצְרֵי־פֶסֶל כֻּלָּם תֹּהוּ וַחֲמוּדֵיהֶם בַּל־יוֹעִילוּ וְעֵדֵיהֶם
י יא הֵמָּה בַּל־יִרְאוּ וּבַל־יֵדְעוּ לְמַעַן יֵבֹשׁוּ: מִי־יָצַר אֵל וּפֶסֶל נָסָךְ לְבִלְתִּי הוֹעִיל: הֵן כָּל־חֲבֵרָיו
יב יֵבֹשׁוּ וְחָרָשִׁים הֵמָּה מֵאָדָם יִתְקַבְּצוּ כֻלָּם יַעֲמֹדוּ יִפְחֲדוּ יֵבֹשׁוּ יָחַד: חָרַשׁ בַּרְזֶל מַעֲצָד וּפָעַל
יג בַּפֶּחָם וּבַמַּקָּבוֹת יִצְּרֵהוּ וַיִּפְעָלֵהוּ בִּזְרוֹעַ כֹּחוֹ גַּם־רָעֵב וְאֵין כֹּחַ לֹא־שָׁתָה מַיִם וַיִּיעָף: חָרַשׁ
עֵצִים נָטָה קָו יְתָאֲרֵהוּ בַשֶּׂרֶד יַעֲשֵׂהוּ בַּמַּקְצֻעוֹת וּבַמְּחוּגָה יְתָאֳרֵהוּ וַיַּעֲשֵׂהוּ כְּתַבְנִית אִישׁ
יד כְּתִפְאֶרֶת אָדָם לָשֶׁבֶת בָּיִת: לִכְרָת־לוֹ אֲרָזִים וַיִּקַּח תִּרְזָה וְאַלּוֹן וַיְאַמֶּץ־לוֹ בַּעֲצֵי־יָעַר נָטַע
טו אֹרֶן וְגֶשֶׁם יְגַדֵּל: וְהָיָה לְאָדָם לְבָעֵר וַיִּקַּח מֵהֶם וַיָּחָם אַף־יַשִּׂיק וְאָפָה לָחֶם אַף־יִפְעַל־אֵל
טז וַיִּשְׁתָּחוּ עָשָׂהוּ פֶסֶל וַיִּסְגָּד־לָמוֹ: חֶצְיוֹ שָׂרַף בְּמוֹ־אֵשׁ עַל־חֶצְיוֹ בָּשָׂר יֹאכֵל יִצְלֶה צָלִי וְיִשְׂבָּע
יז אַף־יָחֹם וְיֹאמַר הֶאָח חַמּוֹתִי רָאִיתִי אוּר: וּשְׁאֵרִיתוֹ לְאֵל עָשָׂה לְפִסְלוֹ יסגוד־לוֹ וְיִשְׁתַּחוּ יִסְגָּד־
יח וְיִתְפַּלֵּל אֵלָיו וְיֹאמַר הַצִּילֵנִי כִּי אֵלִי אָתָּה: לֹא יָדְעוּ וְלֹא יָבִינוּ כִּי טַח מֵרְאוֹת עֵינֵיהֶם מֵהַשְׂכִּיל
יט לִבֹּתָם: וְלֹא־יָשִׁיב אֶל־לִבּוֹ וְלֹא דַעַת וְלֹא־תְבוּנָה לֵאמֹר חֶצְיוֹ שָׂרַפְתִּי בְמוֹ־אֵשׁ וְאַף אָפִיתִי
כ עַל־גֶּחָלָיו לֶחֶם אֶצְלֶה בָשָׂר וְאֹכֵל וְיִתְרוֹ לְתוֹעֵבָה אֶעֱשֶׂה לְבוּל עֵץ אֶסְגּוֹד: רֹעֶה אֵפֶר לֵב
כא הוּתַל הִטָּהוּ וְלֹא־יַצִּיל אֶת־נַפְשׁוֹ וְלֹא יֹאמַר הֲלוֹא שֶׁקֶר בִּימִינִי: זְכָר־אֵלֶּה יַעֲקֹב
כב וְיִשְׂרָאֵל כִּי עַבְדִּי־אָתָּה יְצַרְתִּיךָ עֶבֶד־לִי אַתָּה יִשְׂרָאֵל לֹא תִנָּשֵׁנִי: מָחִיתִי כָעָב פְּשָׁעֶיךָ
כג וְכֶעָנָן חַטֹּאותֶיךָ שׁוּבָה אֵלַי כִּי גְאַלְתִּיךָ: רָנּוּ שָׁמַיִם כִּי־עָשָׂה יהוה הָרִיעוּ תַּחְתִּיּוֹת אָרֶץ
פִּצְחוּ הָרִים רִנָּה יַעַר וְכָל־עֵץ בּוֹ כִּי־גָאַל יהוה יַעֲקֹב וּבְיִשְׂרָאֵל יִתְפָּאָר:

Haftara for
Tzav

On Shabbat Zakhor, the haftara on page 1284 is read. On Shabbat Para, the haftara on page 1288 is read. On Shabbat HaGadol, the haftara on page 1292 is read.

A Reproof to Those Who Come to the Temple

JEREMIAH 7:21–8:3, 9:22–23

In connection with the opening command of the *parasha* involving the burnt offering, the *haftara* begins with God's rejection of those burnt offerings brought on His behalf by those Israelites who do not obey His commands. This reproof, which was apparently stated by Jeremiah at either the gates of the Temple or inside the compound, is a continuation of his preceding prophecy. The prophet issues harsh statements to those who have come to the House of God, as he emphasizes that there is no justification for the existence of the Temple and the sacrifices if the people do not listen to the word of God. Jeremiah further predicts a terrible destruction as a result of the crisis of faith among the people and their persistent idol worship, which has become a public social norm conducted alongside the Temple service. The *haftara* skips some verses of retribution that appear in the original text in Jeremiah, and ends the reading with two later verses that teach a moral lesson.

7 21 So said the Lord of hosts, God of Israel: Add your burnt offer-
22 ings to your peace offerings, and eat meat. For I did not speak to your fathers, and I did not command them on the day that I took them out of the land of Egypt with regard to the matters
23 of burnt offerings or peace offerings. Rather, this matter I commanded them, saying: Heed My voice, and I will be your God, and you will be My people, and you will walk in the entire path
24 that I will command you so that it will be good for you. But they did not heed, and they did not incline their ear; they went after their counsels, in the desire of their evil heart, and they faced
25 backward and not forward from the day that your fathers came out from the land of Egypt until this day, and I sent to you all
26 My servants, the prophets, daily, time and again. But they did not heed Me, and they did not incline their ear; they stiffened
27 their neck; they did worse than their fathers. You will tell them all these matters, but they will not heed you; you will call to
28 them, but they will not answer you. You will say to them: This is the nation that did not heed the voice of the Lord their God and did not accept chastisement; faithfulness is lost, and it is
29 removed from their mouths. Shear your hair, and cast it away, and raise a lament on the bare hills, for the Lord has despised
30 and forsaken the generation of His anger. For the children of Judah have performed that which is evil in My eyes – the utterance of the Lord – they placed their detestable items in the
31 house upon which My name is called to defile it. They built the high places of Tofet, which is in the Valley of the Son of Hinom, to burn their sons and their daughters in the fire, which I did

32 not command and it did not enter My mind. Therefore, behold, days are coming – the utterance of the Lord – and it will no longer be said: Tofet and the Valley of the Son of Hinom; rather: The valley of slaughter, and they will bury in Tofet for lack of
33 room. The carcass of this people will be food for the birds of the heavens, and for the animals of the earth, and there will be none
34 to frighten them away. I will eliminate from the cities of Judah and from the streets of Jerusalem the sound of gladness and the sound of joy, the sound of a groom and the sound of a bride, for
8 1 the land will become ruins. At that time – the utterance of the Lord – they will remove the bones of the kings of Judah, the bones of its princes, the bones of the priests, the bones of the prophets, and the bones of the inhabitants of Jerusalem, from
2 their graves. They will spread them out before the sun and the moon, and to the entire host of the heavens, which they loved and which they worshipped, which they followed and which they sought, and to which they prostrated themselves. They will not be gathered and they will not be buried; they will be
3 as dung on the face of the earth. Death will be chosen over life by all the survivors that remain from this evil family, in all the remaining places where I have banished them – the utterance of
9 22 the Lord of hosts. So said the Lord: Let the wise not glory in his wisdom, and let the mighty not glory in his might, let the rich
23 not glory in his riches. Rather, let the one who glories glory in this: Perceiving and knowing Me, for I am the Lord who performs kindness, justice, and righteousness in the land, for these I desire – the utterance of the Lord.

הפטרת

צו

בשבת פרשת זכור קוראים את ההפטרה בעמ' 1285. בשבת פרשת פרה קוראים את ההפטרה בעמ' 1289. בשבת הגדול קוראים את ההפטרה בעמ' 1293.

ירמיה

כב ז כֹּ֣ה אָמַ֞ר יְהוָ֤ה צְבָאוֹת֙ אֱלֹהֵ֣י יִשְׂרָאֵ֔ל עֹלוֹתֵיכֶ֛ם סְפ֥וּ עַל־זִבְחֵיכֶ֖ם וְאִכְל֥וּ בָשָֽׂר: כִּ֣י לֹֽא־דִבַּ֗רְתִּי

כג אֶת־אֲבֽוֹתֵיכֶם֙ וְלֹ֣א צִוִּיתִ֔ים בְּי֛וֹם הוֹצִיאִ֥י אוֹתָ֖ם מֵאֶ֣רֶץ מִצְרָ֑יִם עַל־דִּבְרֵ֥י עוֹלָ֖ה וָזָֽבַח: כִּ֣י אִֽם־ אֶת־הַדָּבָ֣ר הַ֠זֶּה צִוִּ֨יתִי אוֹתָ֤ם לֵאמֹר֙ שִׁמְע֣וּ בְקוֹלִ֔י וְהָיִ֤יתִי לָכֶם֙ לֵֽאלֹהִ֔ים וְאַתֶּ֖ם תִּֽהְיוּ־לִ֣י לְעָ֑ם

כד וַהֲלַכְתֶּ֗ם בְּכָל־הַדֶּ֙רֶךְ֙ אֲשֶׁ֣ר אֲצַוֶּ֣ה אֶתְכֶ֔ם לְמַ֖עַן יִיטַ֥ב לָכֶֽם: וְלֹ֤א שָֽׁמְעוּ֙ וְלֹֽא־הִטּ֣וּ אֶת־אָזְנָ֔ם

כה וַיֵּֽלְכוּ֙ בְּמֹ֣עֵצ֔וֹת בִּשְׁרִר֖וּת לִבָּ֣ם הָרָ֑ע וַיִּֽהְי֥וּ לְאָח֖וֹר וְלֹ֥א לְפָנִֽים: לְמִן־הַיּ֗וֹם אֲשֶׁ֨ר יָֽצְא֤וּ אֲבֽוֹתֵיכֶם֙ מֵאֶ֣רֶץ מִצְרַ֔יִם עַ֖ד הַיּ֣וֹם הַזֶּ֑ה וָאֶשְׁלַ֤ח אֲלֵיכֶם֙ אֶת־כָּל־עֲבָדַ֣י הַנְּבִיאִ֔ים י֖וֹם הַשְׁכֵּ֥ם וְשָׁלֹֽחַ:

כו וְל֤וֹא שָֽׁמְעוּ֙ אֵלַ֔י וְלֹ֥א הִטּ֖וּ אֶת־אָזְנָ֑ם וַיַּקְשׁוּ֙ אֶת־עָרְפָּ֔ם הֵרֵ֖עוּ מֵאֲבוֹתָֽם: וְדִבַּרְתָּ֤ אֲלֵיהֶם֙

כז אֶת־כָּל־הַדְּבָרִ֣ים הָאֵ֔לֶּה וְלֹ֥א יִשְׁמְע֖וּ אֵלֶ֑יךָ וְקָרָ֥אתָ אֲלֵיהֶ֖ם וְלֹ֥א יַֽעֲנֽוּכָה: וְאָמַרְתָּ֣ אֲלֵיהֶ֗ם זֶ֤ה הַגּוֹי֙ אֲשֶׁ֣ר לֽוֹא־שָׁמְע֗וּ בְּקוֹל֙ יְהוָ֣ה אֱלֹהָ֔יו וְלֹ֥א לָקְח֖וּ מוּסָ֑ר אָֽבְדָה֙ הָֽאֱמוּנָ֔ה וְנִכְרְתָ֖ה

כט מִפִּיהֶֽם: גָּזִּ֤י נִזְרֵךְ֙ וְהַשְׁלִ֔יכִי וּשְׂאִ֥י עַל־שְׁפָיִ֖ם קִינָ֑ה כִּ֚י מָאַ֣ס יְהוָ֔ה וַיִּטֹּ֖שׁ אֶת־דּ֥וֹר

ל עֶבְרָתֽוֹ: כִּֽי־עָשׂ֨וּ בְנֵֽי־יְהוּדָ֤ה הָרַע֙ בְּעֵינַ֔י נְאֻם־יְהוָ֑ה שָׂ֣מוּ שִׁקּֽוּצֵיהֶ֗ם בַּבַּ֛יִת אֲשֶׁ֥ר נִקְרָֽא־שְׁמִ֖י

לא עָלָ֣יו לְטַמְּא֑וֹ: וּבָנ֞וּ בָּמ֣וֹת הַתֹּ֗פֶת אֲשֶׁר֙ בְּגֵ֣יא בֶן־הִנֹּ֔ם לִשְׂרֹ֛ף אֶת־בְּנֵיהֶ֥ם וְאֶת־בְּנֹֽתֵיהֶ֖ם בָּאֵ֑שׁ

לב אֲשֶׁר֙ לֹ֣א צִוִּ֔יתִי וְלֹ֥א עָֽלְתָ֖ה עַל־לִבִּֽי: לָכֵ֞ן הִנֵּֽה־יָמִ֤ים בָּאִים֙ נְאֻם־יְהוָ֔ה וְלֹא־יֵֽאָמֵ֨ר ע֤וֹד הַתֹּ֙פֶת֙ וְגֵ֣יא בֶן־הִנֹּ֔ם כִּ֖י אִם־גֵּ֣יא הַהֲרֵגָ֑ה וְקָבְר֥וּ בְתֹ֖פֶת מֵאֵ֥ין מָקֽוֹם: וְֽהָיְתָ֞ה נִבְלַ֣ת הָעָ֣ם

לד הַזֶּ֗ה לְמַֽאֲכָ֛ל לְע֥וֹף הַשָּׁמַ֖יִם וּלְבֶֽהֱמַ֣ת הָאָ֑רֶץ וְאֵ֖ין מַֽחֲרִֽיד: וְהִשְׁבַּתִּ֣י ׀ מֵעָרֵ֣י יְהוּדָ֗ה וּמֵֽחֻצוֹת֙

ח א יְר֣וּשָׁלַ֔͏ִם ק֣וֹל שָׂשׂ֤וֹן וְק֣וֹל שִׂמְחָ֔ה ק֥וֹל חָתָ֖ן וְק֣וֹל כַּלָּ֑ה כִּ֥י לְחָרְבָּ֖ה תִּֽהְיֶ֥ה הָאָֽרֶץ: בָּעֵ֣ת הַהִ֣יא

יוציאו נְאֻם־יְהוָ֗ה ויוציאו [וְיֹצִ֜יאוּ] אֶת־עַצְמ֣וֹת מַלְכֵֽי־יְהוּדָ֣ה וְאֶת־עַצְמ֣וֹת שָׂרָיו֮ וְאֶת־עַצְמ֣וֹת הַכֹּֽהֲנִים֒ וְאֶת֙

ב עַצְמ֣וֹת הַנְּבִיאִ֔ים וְאֵ֖ת עַצְמ֣וֹת יֽוֹשְׁבֵֽי־יְרֽוּשָׁלָ֑͏ִם מִקִּבְרֵיהֶֽם: וּשְׁטָח֣וּם לַשֶּׁ֗מֶשׁ וְלַיָּרֵ֙חַ֙ וּלְכֹ֣ל ׀

צְבָ֣א הַשָּׁמַ֗יִם אֲשֶׁ֨ר אֲהֵב֜וּם וַֽאֲשֶׁ֤ר עֲבָדוּם֙ וַֽאֲשֶׁר֙ הָֽלְכ֣וּ אַֽחֲרֵיהֶ֔ם וַֽאֲשֶׁ֥ר דְּרָשׁ֖וּם וַֽאֲשֶׁ֣ר

ג הִֽשְׁתַּֽחֲו֣וּ לָהֶ֑ם לֹ֤א יֵֽאָֽסְפוּ֙ וְלֹ֣א יִקָּבֵ֔רוּ לְדֹ֛מֶן עַל־פְּנֵ֥י הָֽאֲדָמָ֖ה יִֽהְיֽוּ: וְנִבְחַ֥ר מָ֙וֶת֙ מֵֽחַיִּ֔ים לְכֹל֙ הַשְּׁאֵרִ֣ית הַנִּשְׁאָרִ֔ים מִן־הַמִּשְׁפָּחָ֥ה הָֽרָעָ֖ה הַזֹּ֑את בְּכָ֨ל־הַמְּקֹמ֤וֹת הַנִּשְׁאָרִים֙ אֲשֶׁ֣ר הִדַּחְתִּ֣ים

ט כב שָׁ֔ם נְאֻ֖ם יְהוָ֥ה צְבָאֽוֹת: כֹּ֣ה ׀ אָמַ֣ר יְהוָ֗ה אַל־יִתְהַלֵּ֤ל חָכָם֙ בְּחָכְמָת֔וֹ וְאַל־יִתְהַלֵּ֥ל

כג הַגִּבּ֖וֹר בִּגְבֽוּרָת֑וֹ אַל־יִתְהַלֵּ֥ל עָשִׁ֖יר בְּעָשְׁרֽוֹ: כִּ֣י אִם־בְּזֹ֞את יִתְהַלֵּ֣ל הַמִּתְהַלֵּ֗ל הַשְׂכֵּל֮ וְיָדֹ֣עַ אוֹתִי֒ כִּ֚י אֲנִ֣י יְהוָ֔ה עֹ֥שֶׂה חֶ֛סֶד מִשְׁפָּ֥ט וּצְדָקָ֖ה בָּאָ֑רֶץ כִּֽי־בְאֵ֥לֶּה חָפַ֖צְתִּי נְאֻם־יְהוָֽה:

Haftara for
Shemini

On Shabbat Para, the haftara on page 1288 is read. On Shabbat HaHodesh, the haftara on page 1290 is read.

The Preparation of a Place for the Ark of God

II SAMUEL 6:1–7:17

Like the death of two of Aaron's sons at the inauguration of the Tabernacle, here too the unfortunate turn of events vividly illustrates the inherent dangers of violating the laws of sacred objects. The death of such dignified individuals, while they were occupied with preparing a place for the Divine Presence, was a crucial lesson to the entire people of the great caution, awe, and respect that one must pay to the ark and the Tabernacle (see *Tanḥuma, Beshalah* 21). Furthermore, these incidents teach that those who serve in the Sanctuary must rise above personal emotions. Consequently, in the *parasha* Aaron is commanded to refrain from practices of mourning for his sons while the celebrations for the inauguration of the Tabernacle are ongoing. Similarly, in the *haftara* David himself dances with all his might before the Ark of God when it is finally brought to Jerusalem, without concern for his personal dignity.

After engaging in defensive wars against the Philistines, David turns his attention to another task that was of undoubted importance for the legacy of the monarchy in Israel: The establishment of the Temple. As a first step, he brings up the Ark of the Covenant from its temporary place to the city where it will reside permanently. However, this joyous occasion is cut short by the tragic death of one of the men accompanying the ark, when he treats it in a hasty, careless manner.

6 1 David again gathered all the chosen of Israel, thirty thousand.
2 David and all the people who were with him rose and went
from Baalei Yehuda, to take up the Ark of God from there,
upon which is called the name, the name of the Lord of hosts,
3 who is enthroned upon the cherubs. They mounted the Ark
of God onto a new cart, and they conveyed it from the house
of Avinadav, which was on the hill, and Uza and Ahyo, sons of
4 Avinadav, guided the new cart. They conveyed it from the house
of Avinadav, which was on the hill, with the Ark of God, and
5 Ahyo was walking before the ark. David and the entire house
of Israel were reveling before the Lord with all kinds of juniper
wood, with harps, with lyres, with drums, with timbrels, and
6 with cymbals. They came to the threshing floor of Nakhon, and
Uza extended his hand to the Ark of God and grasped it, since
7 the oxen slipped. The wrath of the Lord was enflamed against
Uza, and God smote him there for the error, and he died there
8 near the Ark of God. David was distressed because the Lord
had inflicted a breach upon Uza, and he called the place Peretz
9 Uza to this day. David feared the Lord on that day, and he said:
10 How can the Ark of the Lord come to me? David did not wish
to move the Ark of the Lord to him, to the City of David, and
11 David diverted it to the house of Oved Edom the Gitite. The
Ark of the Lord remained in the house of Oved Edom the Gitite
for three months, and the Lord blessed Oved Edom and his
12 entire household. It was told to King David, saying: The Lord
has blessed the house of Oved Edom and everything that is his,
due to the Ark of God. David went and took up the Ark of God
13 from the house of Oved Edom to the City of David with joy. It
was when the bearers of the Ark of the Lord walked six paces,
14 he would slaughter a bull and a fatling. And David was dancing
before the Lord with all his might, and David was girded with
15 a linen ephod. David and all the house of Israel were taking up
the Ark of the Lord with shouting and with the sounding of the
16 shofar. It was as the Ark of the Lord was entering the City of
David that Mikhal, daughter of Saul, peered through the window, and she saw King David leaping and dancing before the
17 Lord; and she felt contempt for him in her heart. They brought
the Ark of the Lord, and they set it in its place within the tent
that David had pitched for it; and David offered up burnt of-
18 ferings before the Lord and peace offerings. David concluded
offering up the burnt offerings and the peace offerings, and he
19 blessed the people in the name of the Lord of hosts. He distributed to all the people, to the entire multitude of Israel, from
men to women, to each, one loaf of bread, one portion of beef,
and one raisin cake. The entire people went, each to his home.
Seph. end 20 David returned to bless his household. Mikhal daughter of Saul
came out to meet David, and said: How honorable today was
the king of Israel, who was exposed today before the eyes of
the maidservants of his servants, in the manner that one of
21 the idlers is exposed. David said to Mikhal: Before the Lord,
who chose me over your father and over his entire household
to appoint me ruler over the people of the Lord, over Israel, I
22 will revel before the Lord. And I would be even lowlier than
this, and I would be lowly in my eyes; and with the maidservants of whom you spoke, with them, I would be honored.
23 Mikhal, daughter of Saul, did not have a child until the day of
7 1 her death. It was when the king dwelled in his house and the
Lord had given him respite from all his surrounding enemies,

הפטרת

שמיני

בשבת פרשת פרה קוראים את ההפטרה בעמ' 1289. בשבת פרשת החודש קוראים את ההפטרה בעמ' 1291.

שמואל ב'

ו א וַיֹּסֶף עוֹד דָּוִד אֶת־כָּל־בָּחוּר בְּיִשְׂרָאֵל שְׁלֹשִׁים אָלֶף: וַיָּקָם וַיֵּלֶךְ דָּוִד וְכָל־הָעָם אֲשֶׁר אִתּוֹ
ב מִבַּעֲלֵי יְהוּדָה לְהַעֲלוֹת מִשָּׁם אֵת אֲרוֹן הָאֱלֹהִים אֲשֶׁר־נִקְרָא שֵׁם שֵׁם יְהוָה צְבָאוֹת יֹשֵׁב
ג הַכְּרֻבִים עָלָיו: וַיַּרְכִּבוּ אֶת־אֲרוֹן הָאֱלֹהִים אֶל־עֲגָלָה חֲדָשָׁה וַיִּשָּׂאֻהוּ מִבֵּית אֲבִינָדָב אֲשֶׁר
ד בַּגִּבְעָה וְעֻזָּא וְאַחְיוֹ בְּנֵי אֲבִינָדָב נֹהֲגִים אֶת־הָעֲגָלָה חֲדָשָׁה: וַיִּשָּׂאֻהוּ מִבֵּית אֲבִינָדָב אֲשֶׁר
ה בַּגִּבְעָה עִם אֲרוֹן הָאֱלֹהִים וְאַחְיוֹ הֹלֵךְ לִפְנֵי הָאָרוֹן: וְדָוִד וְכָל־בֵּית יִשְׂרָאֵל מְשַׂחֲקִים לִפְנֵי
ו יְהוָה בְּכֹל עֲצֵי בְרוֹשִׁים וּבְכִנֹּרוֹת וּבִנְבָלִים וּבְתֻפִּים וּבִמְנַעַנְעִים וּבְצֶלְצֶלִים: וַיָּבֹאוּ עַד־גֹּרֶן
ז נָכוֹן וַיִּשְׁלַח עֻזָּא אֶל־אֲרוֹן הָאֱלֹהִים וַיֹּאחֶז בּוֹ כִּי שָׁמְטוּ הַבָּקָר: וַיִּחַר־אַף יְהוָה בְּעֻזָּה וַיַּכֵּהוּ
ח שָׁם הָאֱלֹהִים עַל־הַשַּׁל וַיָּמָת שָׁם עִם אֲרוֹן הָאֱלֹהִים: וַיִּחַר לְדָוִד עַל אֲשֶׁר פָּרַץ יְהוָה פֶּרֶץ
ט בְּעֻזָּה וַיִּקְרָא לַמָּקוֹם הַהוּא פֶּרֶץ עֻזָּה עַד הַיּוֹם הַזֶּה: וַיִּרָא דָוִד אֶת־יְהוָה בַּיּוֹם הַהוּא וַיֹּאמֶר
י אֵיךְ יָבוֹא אֵלַי אֲרוֹן יְהוָה: וְלֹא־אָבָה דָוִד לְהָסִיר אֵלָיו אֶת־אֲרוֹן יְהוָה עַל־עִיר דָּוִד וַיַּטֵּהוּ
יא דָוִד בֵּית עֹבֵד־אֱדֹם הַגִּתִּי: וַיֵּשֶׁב אֲרוֹן יְהוָה בֵּית עֹבֵד אֱדֹם הַגִּתִּי שְׁלֹשָׁה חֳדָשִׁים וַיְבָרֶךְ
יב יְהוָה אֶת־עֹבֵד אֱדֹם וְאֶת־כָּל־בֵּיתוֹ: וַיֻּגַּד לַמֶּלֶךְ דָּוִד לֵאמֹר בֵּרַךְ יְהוָה אֶת־בֵּית עֹבֵד אֱדֹם
וְאֶת־כָּל־אֲשֶׁר־לוֹ בַּעֲבוּר אֲרוֹן הָאֱלֹהִים וַיֵּלֶךְ דָּוִד וַיַּעַל אֶת־אֲרוֹן הָאֱלֹהִים מִבֵּית עֹבֵד אֱדֹם
יג עִיר דָּוִד בְּשִׂמְחָה: וַיְהִי כִּי צָעֲדוּ נֹשְׂאֵי אֲרוֹן־יְהוָה שִׁשָּׁה צְעָדִים וַיִּזְבַּח שׁוֹר וּמְרִיא: וְדָוִד
יד מְכַרְכֵּר בְּכָל־עֹז לִפְנֵי יְהוָה וְדָוִד חָגוּר אֵפוֹד בָּד: וְדָוִד וְכָל־בֵּית יִשְׂרָאֵל מַעֲלִים אֶת־אֲרוֹן
טו יְהוָה בִּתְרוּעָה וּבְקוֹל שׁוֹפָר: וְהָיָה אֲרוֹן יְהוָה בָּא עִיר דָּוִד וּמִיכַל בַּת־שָׁאוּל נִשְׁקְפָה ׀ בְּעַד
טז הַחַלּוֹן וַתֵּרֶא אֶת־הַמֶּלֶךְ דָּוִד מְפַזֵּז וּמְכַרְכֵּר לִפְנֵי יְהוָה וַתִּבֶז לוֹ בְּלִבָּהּ: וַיָּבִאוּ אֶת־אֲרוֹן יְהוָה
יז וַיַּצִּגוּ אֹתוֹ בִּמְקוֹמוֹ בְּתוֹךְ הָאֹהֶל אֲשֶׁר נָטָה־לוֹ דָּוִד וַיַּעַל דָּוִד עֹלוֹת לִפְנֵי יְהוָה וּשְׁלָמִים:
יח וַיְכַל דָּוִד מֵהַעֲלוֹת הָעוֹלָה וְהַשְּׁלָמִים וַיְבָרֶךְ אֶת־הָעָם בְּשֵׁם יְהוָה צְבָאוֹת: וַיְחַלֵּק לְכָל־
יט הָעָם לְכָל־הֲמוֹן יִשְׂרָאֵל לְמֵאִישׁ וְעַד־אִשָּׁה לְאִישׁ חַלַּת לֶחֶם אַחַת וְאֶשְׁפָּר אֶחָד וַאֲשִׁישָׁה

הספרדים מסיימים כאן

אֶחָת וַיֵּלֶךְ כָּל־הָעָם אִישׁ לְבֵיתוֹ: וַיָּשָׁב דָּוִד לְבָרֵךְ אֶת־בֵּיתוֹ וַתֵּצֵא מִיכַל בַּת־שָׁאוּל לִקְרַאת
כ דָּוִד וַתֹּאמֶר מַה־נִּכְבַּד הַיּוֹם מֶלֶךְ יִשְׂרָאֵל אֲשֶׁר נִגְלָה הַיּוֹם לְעֵינֵי אַמְהוֹת עֲבָדָיו כְּהִגָּלוֹת
כא נִגְלוֹת אַחַד הָרֵקִים: וַיֹּאמֶר דָּוִד אֶל־מִיכַל לִפְנֵי יְהוָה אֲשֶׁר בָּחַר־בִּי מֵאָבִיךְ וּמִכָּל־בֵּיתוֹ
כב לְצַוֹּת אֹתִי נָגִיד עַל־עַם יְהוָה עַל־יִשְׂרָאֵל וְשִׂחַקְתִּי לִפְנֵי יְהוָה: וּנְקַלֹּתִי עוֹד מִזֹּאת וְהָיִיתִי
כג שָׁפָל בְּעֵינָי וְעִם־הָאֲמָהוֹת אֲשֶׁר אָמַרְתְּ עִמָּם אִכָּבֵדָה: וּלְמִיכַל בַּת־שָׁאוּל לֹא־הָיָה לָהּ יָלֶד
עַד יוֹם מוֹתָהּ:

ז א וַיְהִי כִּי־יָשַׁב הַמֶּלֶךְ בְּבֵיתוֹ וַיהוָה הֵנִיחַ־לוֹ מִסָּבִיב מִכָּל־אֹיְבָיו:

2 that the king said to Natan the prophet: See now, I am dwelling in a house of cedar, but the Ark of God dwells within the cur-
3 tain. Natan said to the king: Go, do everything that is in your
4 heart, as the Lord is with you. It was on that night that the word
5 of the Lord was with Natan, saying: Go and say to My servant David: So said the Lord: Shall you build Me a House for My
6 dwelling? For I have not dwelled in a house from the day that I took up the children of Israel from Egypt, to this day; I would
7 make my way in a tent and in a Tabernacle. Whenever I made my way among all the children of Israel, did I speak a word to any of the tribes of Israel, whom I commanded to shepherd My people Israel, saying: Why did you not build Me a House
8 of cedar? Now, so you shall say to My servant David: So said the Lord of hosts: I took you from the pasture, from after the
9 sheep, to be ruler over My people, over Israel. I have been with you wherever you went, and I eliminated all your enemies from before you, and I made a great name for you, like the name of
10 the prominent that are in the world. I will make a place for My people Israel, and will plant it, and they will dwell in their place and no longer be disturbed; iniquitous people will not continue
11 to afflict them as in the past and since the day that I appointed judges over My people Israel; but to you I have given respite from all your enemies. The Lord will tell you that the Lord will
12 establish a house for you. When your days are completed and you lie with your fathers, I will set up your offspring after you, who will emerge from your body, and I will establish his king-
13 dom. He will build a House for My name, and I will establish
14 the throne of his kingdom forever. I will be a father to him, and he will be a son to me who, when he commits iniquity, I will rebuke with the staff of men and with the afflictions of the
15 children of men. My kindness will not turn away from him, as I
16 removed it from Saul, whom I removed from before you. Your dynasty and your kingdom will be resolute before you forever;
17 your throne will be established forever. In accordance with all these words, and in accordance with this entire vision, so Natan spoke to David.

ב וַיֹּאמֶר הַמֶּלֶךְ אֶל־נָתָן הַנָּבִיא רְאֵה נָא אָנֹכִי יוֹשֵׁב בְּבֵית אֲרָזִים וַאֲרוֹן הָאֱלֹהִים יֹשֵׁב בְּתוֹךְ
ג ד הַיְרִיעָה׃ וַיֹּאמֶר נָתָן אֶל־הַמֶּלֶךְ כֹּל אֲשֶׁר בִּלְבָבְךָ לֵךְ עֲשֵׂה כִּי יְהוָה עִמָּךְ׃ וַיְהִי
ה בַּלַּיְלָה הַהוּא וַיְהִי דְּבַר־יְהוָה אֶל־נָתָן לֵאמֹר׃ לֵךְ וְאָמַרְתָּ אֶל־עַבְדִּי אֶל־דָּוִד
ו כֹּה אָמַר יְהוָה הַאַתָּה תִּבְנֶה־לִּי בַיִת לְשִׁבְתִּי׃ כִּי לֹא יָשַׁבְתִּי בְּבַיִת לְמִיּוֹם הַעֲלֹתִי אֶת־בְּנֵי
ז יִשְׂרָאֵל מִמִּצְרַיִם וְעַד הַיּוֹם הַזֶּה וָאֶהְיֶה מִתְהַלֵּךְ בְּאֹהֶל וּבְמִשְׁכָּן׃ בְּכֹל אֲשֶׁר הִתְהַלַּכְתִּי
בְּכָל־בְּנֵי יִשְׂרָאֵל הֲדָבָר דִּבַּרְתִּי אֶת־אַחַד שִׁבְטֵי יִשְׂרָאֵל אֲשֶׁר צִוִּיתִי לִרְעוֹת אֶת־עַמִּי אֶת־
ח יִשְׂרָאֵל לֵאמֹר לָמָּה לֹא־בְנִיתֶם לִי בֵּית אֲרָזִים׃ וְעַתָּה כֹּה־תֹאמַר לְעַבְדִּי לְדָוִד כֹּה אָמַר
ט יְהוָה צְבָאוֹת אֲנִי לְקַחְתִּיךָ מִן־הַנָּוֶה מֵאַחַר הַצֹּאן לִהְיוֹת נָגִיד עַל־עַמִּי עַל־יִשְׂרָאֵל׃ וָאֶהְיֶה
עִמְּךָ בְּכֹל אֲשֶׁר הָלַכְתָּ וָאַכְרִתָה אֶת־כָּל־אֹיְבֶיךָ מִפָּנֶיךָ וְעָשִׂתִי לְךָ שֵׁם גָּדוֹל כְּשֵׁם הַגְּדֹלִים
י אֲשֶׁר בָּאָרֶץ׃ וְשַׂמְתִּי מָקוֹם לְעַמִּי לְיִשְׂרָאֵל וּנְטַעְתִּיו וְשָׁכַן תַּחְתָּיו וְלֹא יִרְגַּז עוֹד וְלֹא־יֹסִיפוּ
יא בְנֵי־עַוְלָה לְעַנּוֹתוֹ כַּאֲשֶׁר בָּרִאשׁוֹנָה׃ וּלְמִן־הַיּוֹם אֲשֶׁר צִוִּיתִי שֹׁפְטִים עַל־עַמִּי יִשְׂרָאֵל
יב וַהֲנִיחֹתִי לְךָ מִכָּל־אֹיְבֶיךָ וְהִגִּיד לְךָ יְהוָה כִּי־בַיִת יַעֲשֶׂה־לְּךָ יְהוָה׃ כִּי ׀ יִמְלְאוּ יָמֶיךָ וְשָׁכַבְתָּ
יג אֶת־אֲבֹתֶיךָ וַהֲקִימֹתִי אֶת־זַרְעֲךָ אַחֲרֶיךָ אֲשֶׁר יֵצֵא מִמֵּעֶיךָ וַהֲכִינֹתִי אֶת־מַמְלַכְתּוֹ׃ הוּא
יד יִבְנֶה־בַּיִת לִשְׁמִי וְכֹנַנְתִּי אֶת־כִּסֵּא מַמְלַכְתּוֹ עַד־עוֹלָם׃ אֲנִי אֶהְיֶה־לּוֹ לְאָב וְהוּא יִהְיֶה־לִּי
טו לְבֵן אֲשֶׁר בְּהַעֲוֺתוֹ וְהֹכַחְתִּיו בְּשֵׁבֶט אֲנָשִׁים וּבְנִגְעֵי בְּנֵי אָדָם׃ וְחַסְדִּי לֹא־יָסוּר מִמֶּנּוּ כַּאֲשֶׁר
טז הֲסִרֹתִי מֵעִם שָׁאוּל אֲשֶׁר הֲסִרֹתִי מִלְּפָנֶיךָ׃ וְנֶאְמַן בֵּיתְךָ וּמַמְלַכְתְּךָ עַד־עוֹלָם לְפָנֶיךָ כִּסְאֲךָ
יז יִהְיֶה נָכוֹן עַד־עוֹלָם׃ כְּכֹל הַדְּבָרִים הָאֵלֶּה וּכְכֹל הַחִזָּיוֹן הַזֶּה כֵּן דִּבֶּר נָתָן אֶל־דָּוִד׃

Haftara for
Tazria

On Shabbat HaHodesh, the haftara on page 1290 is read.

Elisha Cures Naaman's Leprosy
II KINGS 4:42–5:19

One of the stories of the miracles wrought by the prophet Elisha, which were performed mostly for anonymous individuals, involves the curing of the Aramean officer Naaman from his leprosy. The healing of Naaman, the commander of the enemy army, restores the honor of Israel. This wondrous cure did not have political consequences alone; it also led Naaman to conclusions about the religious life he should lead. The lepers mentioned in the Bible are generally leaders and renowned figures. It can be suggested that such individuals were more vulnerable to contracting leprosy, as leprosy was considered a Heavenly sign of their excessive pride or that they had infiltrated a domain outside of their authority (see Numbers 12:10; II Kings 5:26; II Chronicles 26:16–23). Another example, according to the Sages, of such an individual who contracted leprosy was Shevna the scribe, a minister in the government of King Hizkiya (*Sanhedrin* 26a). It is likewise stated with regard to King David that he was leprous for six months (see *Yoma* 22b). Since leprosy was considered a disease indicative of improper behavior, sufferers would seek a cure not from doctors but from those who dealt with sacred matters, such as a priest or prophet.

4 42 A man came from Baal Shalisha, and he brought to the man of God bread of the first fruits: Twenty loaves of barley and moist kernels in their husks. He said: Give to the people, and they 43 will eat. His servant said: How shall I place this before one hundred men? He said: Give to the people, and they will eat, for 44 so said the Lord: Eat and leave over. He placed it before them, and they ate, and they left over, in accordance with the word **5** 1 of the Lord. Naaman, commander of the army of the king of Aram, was a great man before his master and highly esteemed, as through him the Lord had granted salvation for Aram. The 2 man was a mighty man of valor, a leper. Aram issued forth in raiding parties; they took a young girl captive from the Land of 3 Israel and she served before Naaman's wife. She said to her mistress: May my master's requests be put before the prophet who 4 is in Samaria; then he will heal him of his leprosy. He came and told his master, saying: This and that spoke the young woman 5 who is from the Land of Israel. The king of Aram said: Come and I will send a letter to the king of Israel. He went and took with him ten talents of silver, and six thousand gold, and ten 6 changes of garments. He brought the letter to the king of Israel, saying: Now, with the arrival of this letter to you, behold, I have sent Naaman my servant to you, and you will heal him of his 7 leprosy. It was when the king of Israel read the letter, he rent his garments, and he said: Am I God, to put to death and to bring to life, that this person sends to me to heal a man of his leprosy? Indeed, for now you know and see that he seeks a pretext 8 against me. It was when Elisha, man of God, heard that the king of Israel rent his garments, he sent to the king, saying: Why did you rend your garments? Let him come to me now, and he will 9 know that there is a prophet in Israel. Naaman came with his

horses and with his chariot, and he stood at the entrance of 10 the house of Elisha. Elisha sent a messenger to him, saying: Go and bathe in the Jordan seven times. Your flesh will return to 11 you, and you will be cleansed. Naaman was incensed. He went and said: Behold, I said to myself: He will come out to me and stand, and he will call in the name of the Lord his God, and 12 he will wave his hand over the area, and heal the leper. Aren't Amana and Parpar, the rivers of Damascus, better than all the water of Israel? Could I not bathe in them, and be cleansed? He 13 turned and went in fury. His servants approached, and spoke with him, and said: My father, had the prophet spoken to you to perform a difficult matter, would you not do it? All the more 14 so, when he said to you: Bathe and be cleansed? He went down and immersed seven times in the Jordan, in accordance with the word of the man of God, and his flesh returned like the flesh 15 of a small lad, and he was cleansed. He returned to the man of God, he and all his camp; he came, stood before him, and said: Behold, now I know that there is no God in all the earth, except in Israel; now please, accept a tribute from your servant. 16 He said: As the Lord, before whom I have stood, lives, I will 17 not accept. He implored him to accept, but he refused. Naaman said: If not, please let there be given to your servant a pair of mules' load of earth, as your servant will no longer present a burnt offering or an offering to other gods, but only to the Lord. 18 For this matter, let the Lord pardon your servant: When my master comes to the house of Rimon to prostrate himself there, and he leans on my hand, and I prostrate myself in the house of Rimon; when I prostrate myself in the house of Rimon, may the 19 Lord pardon your servant for this matter. He said to him: Go in peace. He departed some distance from him.

הפטרת

תזריע

בשבת פרשת החודש קוראים את ההפטרה בעמ' 1291.

ד מב וְאִישׁ בָּא מִבַּעַל שָׁלִשָׁה וַיָּבֵא לְאִישׁ הָאֱלֹהִים לֶחֶם בִּכּוּרִים עֶשְׂרִים־לֶחֶם שְׂעֹרִים מלכים ב׳
מג וְכַרְמֶל בְּצִקְלֹנוֹ וַיֹּאמֶר תֵּן לָעָם וְיֹאכֵלוּ: וַיֹּאמֶר מְשָׁרְתוֹ מָה אֶתֵּן זֶה לִפְנֵי מֵאָה אִישׁ
מד וַיֹּאמֶר תֵּן לָעָם וְיֹאכֵלוּ כִּי כֹה אָמַר יהוה אָכֹל וְהוֹתֵר: וַיִּתֵּן לִפְנֵיהֶם וַיֹּאכְלוּ וַיּוֹתִרוּ כִּדְבַר
ה א יהוה: וְנַעֲמָן שַׂר־צְבָא מֶלֶךְ־אֲרָם הָיָה אִישׁ גָּדוֹל לִפְנֵי אֲדֹנָיו וּנְשֻׂא פָנִים כִּי־בוֹ
ב נָתַן־יהוה תְּשׁוּעָה לַאֲרָם וְהָאִישׁ הָיָה גִּבּוֹר חַיִל מְצֹרָע: וַאֲרָם יָצְאוּ גְדוּדִים וַיִּשְׁבּוּ מֵאֶרֶץ
ג יִשְׂרָאֵל נַעֲרָה קְטַנָּה וַתְּהִי לִפְנֵי אֵשֶׁת נַעֲמָן: וַתֹּאמֶר אֶל־גְּבִרְתָּהּ אַחֲלֵי אֲדֹנִי לִפְנֵי הַנָּבִיא
ד אֲשֶׁר בְּשֹׁמְרוֹן אָז יֶאֱסֹף אֹתוֹ מִצָּרַעְתּוֹ: וַיָּבֹא וַיַּגֵּד לַאדֹנָיו לֵאמֹר כָּזֹאת וְכָזֹאת דִּבְּרָה הַנַּעֲרָה
ה אֲשֶׁר מֵאֶרֶץ יִשְׂרָאֵל: וַיֹּאמֶר מֶלֶךְ־אֲרָם לֶךְ־בֹּא וְאֶשְׁלְחָה סֵפֶר אֶל־מֶלֶךְ יִשְׂרָאֵל וַיֵּלֶךְ וַיִּקַּח
ו בְּיָדוֹ עֶשֶׂר כִּכְּרֵי־כֶסֶף וְשֵׁשֶׁת אֲלָפִים זָהָב וְעֶשֶׂר חֲלִיפוֹת בְּגָדִים: וַיָּבֵא הַסֵּפֶר אֶל־מֶלֶךְ
יִשְׂרָאֵל לֵאמֹר וְעַתָּה כְּבוֹא הַסֵּפֶר הַזֶּה אֵלֶיךָ הִנֵּה שָׁלַחְתִּי אֵלֶיךָ אֶת־נַעֲמָן עַבְדִּי וַאֲסַפְתּוֹ
ז מִצָּרַעְתּוֹ: וַיְהִי כִּקְרֹא מֶלֶךְ־יִשְׂרָאֵל אֶת־הַסֵּפֶר וַיִּקְרַע בְּגָדָיו וַיֹּאמֶר הַאֱלֹהִים אָנִי לְהָמִית
וּלְהַחֲיוֹת כִּי־זֶה שֹׁלֵחַ אֵלַי לֶאֱסֹף אִישׁ מִצָּרַעְתּוֹ כִּי אַךְ־דְּעוּ־נָא וּרְאוּ כִּי־מִתְאַנֶּה הוּא לִי:
ח וַיְהִי כִּשְׁמֹעַ ׀ אֱלִישָׁע אִישׁ־הָאֱלֹהִים כִּי־קָרַע מֶלֶךְ־יִשְׂרָאֵל אֶת־בְּגָדָיו וַיִּשְׁלַח אֶל־הַמֶּלֶךְ
ט לֵאמֹר לָמָּה קָרַעְתָּ בְּגָדֶיךָ יָבֹא־נָא אֵלַי וְיֵדַע כִּי יֵשׁ נָבִיא בְּיִשְׂרָאֵל: וַיָּבֹא נַעֲמָן בְּסוּסָו וּבְרִכְבּוֹ
י וַיַּעֲמֹד פֶּתַח־הַבַּיִת לֶאֱלִישָׁע: וַיִּשְׁלַח אֵלָיו אֱלִישָׁע מַלְאָךְ לֵאמֹר הָלוֹךְ וְרָחַצְתָּ שֶׁבַע־פְּעָמִים
יא בַּיַּרְדֵּן וְיָשֹׁב בְּשָׂרְךָ לְךָ וּטְהָר: וַיִּקְצֹף נַעֲמָן וַיֵּלַךְ וַיֹּאמֶר הִנֵּה אָמַרְתִּי אֵלַי ׀ יֵצֵא יָצוֹא וְעָמַד
יב וְקָרָא בְּשֵׁם־יהוה אֱלֹהָיו וְהֵנִיף יָדוֹ אֶל־הַמָּקוֹם וְאָסַף הַמְּצֹרָע: הֲלֹא טוֹב אבנה וּפַרְפַּר אֲמָנָה
יג נַהֲרוֹת דַּמֶּשֶׂק מִכֹּל מֵימֵי יִשְׂרָאֵל הֲלֹא־אֶרְחַץ בָּהֶם וְטָהָרְתִּי וַיִּפֶן וַיֵּלֶךְ בְּחֵמָה: וַיִּגְּשׁוּ עֲבָדָיו
וַיְדַבְּרוּ אֵלָיו וַיֹּאמְרוּ אָבִי דָּבָר גָּדוֹל הַנָּבִיא דִּבֶּר אֵלֶיךָ הֲלוֹא תַעֲשֶׂה וְאַף כִּי־אָמַר אֵלֶיךָ
יד רְחַץ וּטְהָר: וַיֵּרֶד וַיִּטְבֹּל בַּיַּרְדֵּן שֶׁבַע פְּעָמִים כִּדְבַר אִישׁ הָאֱלֹהִים וַיָּשָׁב בְּשָׂרוֹ כִּבְשַׂר נַעַר
טו קָטֹן וַיִּטְהָר: וַיָּשָׁב אֶל־אִישׁ הָאֱלֹהִים הוּא וְכָל־מַחֲנֵהוּ וַיָּבֹא וַיַּעֲמֹד לְפָנָיו וַיֹּאמֶר הִנֵּה־נָא
טז יָדַעְתִּי כִּי אֵין אֱלֹהִים בְּכָל־הָאָרֶץ כִּי אִם־בְּיִשְׂרָאֵל וְעַתָּה קַח־נָא בְרָכָה מֵאֵת עַבְדֶּךָ: וַיֹּאמֶר
יז חַי־יהוה אֲשֶׁר־עָמַדְתִּי לְפָנָיו אִם־אֶקָּח וַיִּפְצַר־בּוֹ לָקַחַת וַיְמָאֵן: וַיֹּאמֶר נַעֲמָן וָלֹא יֻתַּן־נָא
לְעַבְדְּךָ מַשָּׂא צֶמֶד־פְּרָדִים אֲדָמָה כִּי לוֹא־יַעֲשֶׂה עוֹד עַבְדְּךָ עֹלָה וָזֶבַח לֵאלֹהִים אֲחֵרִים כִּי
יח אִם־לַיהוה: לַדָּבָר הַזֶּה יִסְלַח יהוה לְעַבְדֶּךָ בְּבוֹא אֲדֹנִי בֵית־רִמּוֹן לְהִשְׁתַּחֲוֹת שָׁמָּה וְהוּא ׀
נִשְׁעָן עַל־יָדִי וְהִשְׁתַּחֲוֵיתִי בֵּית רִמֹּן בְּהִשְׁתַּחֲוָיָתִי בֵּית רִמֹּן יִסְלַח־נָא־יהוה לְעַבְדְּךָ בַּדָּבָר
יט הַזֶּה: וַיֹּאמֶר לוֹ לֵךְ לְשָׁלוֹם וַיֵּלֶךְ מֵאִתּוֹ כִּבְרַת אָרֶץ:

Haftara for **Metzora**

On Shabbat HaGadol, the haftara on page 1292 is read.

The Salvation of the City of Samaria

II KINGS 7:3–20

The prospect of death by famine or sword hung over the inhabitants of the city of Samaria, which was besieged by the army of Aram. The king of Israel, Yoram son of Ahav, blamed Elisha for the dire situation, arguing that the prophet had not come to his nation's aid and had even criticized the people (see Rashi and Ralbag; II Kings 6:31). However, when the king comes to the house of the prophet in order to kill him, Elisha prophesies a sudden deliverance, and salvation soon arrives through the agency of lepers who were living outside the city walls. Thus, those who had been ostracized from society and were considered as though they were dead were the very ones who brought the tidings of renewed life to the starving city.

7 3 There were four men who were lepers at the entrance of the
gate. They said one to the other: Why are we sitting here until
4 we die? If we say: Let us enter the city, there is famine in the
city, and we will die there; but if we sit here, we will die. Now
let us go and fall upon the camp of Aram; if they let us live, we
5 will live; and if they put us to death, we will die. They arose at
twilight to go to the camp of Aram. They came to the edge of
6 the camp of Aram, and behold, no one was there. The Lord had
sounded to the camp of Aram the sound of chariots, the sound
of horses, the sound of a great army. They had said to one another: Behold, the king of Israel has hired against us the kings
7 of the Hitites and the kings of Egypt, to come upon us. They
had risen and fled in the twilight, and they had abandoned their
tents, their horses, and their donkeys, the camp as it was, and
8 they had fled for their lives. These lepers came to the edge of
the camp; they entered one tent and ate and drank, and they
carried away from there silver, gold, and garments; they went
and hid them; and they came back, and entered another tent,
9 and carried away from there, and went and hid them. Then they
said one to another: What we are doing is not right. This day is
a day of tidings, and we are silent. If we wait until the morning
light, iniquity will be upon us. Now, let us come and report to
10 the king's palace. They came and they called to the gatekeepers
of the city, and they told them, saying: We came to the camp
of Aram, and behold, there was no one, nor the sound of a
person there; only the horses are tethered and the donkeys are
11 tethered, and the tents are as they were. The guards of the gate
12 called, and they reported in the king's palace. The king arose
at night, and he said to his servants: I will tell you now what
Aram has done to us. They know that we are hungry, and they
departed the camp to hide in the field, saying: When they come
out from the city, we will seize them alive, and we will come
13 into the city. One of his servants answered, and said: Please, let
five of the remaining horses that remain in it be taken; behold,
they are like the entire multitude of Israel that remains in it;
behold, they are like the entire multitude of Israel that has per-
14 ished. Let us send and see. They took two chariots with horses,
and the king sent after the camp of Aram, saying: Go and see.
15 They went after them until the Jordan, and behold, the whole
way was filled with garments and vessels that Aram had cast
away in their haste. The messengers returned and reported to
16 the king. The people came out and looted the camp of Aram.
A se'a of high-quality flour was for a shekel and two se'a of barley was for a shekel, in accordance with the word of the Lord.
17 The king appointed the official on whose arm he leaned to be in
charge of the gate, and the people trampled him at the gate, and
he died, as the man of God had spoken, who spoke when the
18 king came down to him. It was as the man of God had spoken
to the king, saying: Two se'a of barley will be for a shekel, and
a se'a of fine flour for a shekel, at this time tomorrow at the gate
19 of Samaria. The official answered the man of God, and he said:
Behold, if the Lord makes windows in the heavens, could this
thing be? He said: Behold, you will see it with your eyes, but
20 you will not eat from there. It was so for him, and the people
trampled him at the gate, and he died.

הפטרת

מצרע

בשבת הגדול קוראים את ההפטרה בעמ׳ 1293.

ז ג וְאַרְבָּעָה אֲנָשִׁים הָיוּ מְצֹרָעִים פֶּתַח הַשָּׁעַר וַיֹּאמְרוּ אִישׁ אֶל־רֵעֵהוּ מָה אֲנַחְנוּ יֹשְׁבִים פֹּה מלכים ב׳
ד עַד־מָתְנוּ׃ אִם־אָמַרְנוּ נָבוֹא הָעִיר וְהָרָעָב בָּעִיר וָמַתְנוּ שָׁם וְאִם־יָשַׁבְנוּ פֹה וָמָתְנוּ וְעַתָּה
ה לְכוּ וְנִפְּלָה אֶל־מַחֲנֵה אֲרָם אִם־יְחַיֻּנוּ נִחְיֶה וְאִם־יְמִיתֻנוּ וָמָתְנוּ׃ וַיָּקֻמוּ בַנֶּשֶׁף לָבוֹא אֶל־
ו מַחֲנֵה אֲרָם וַיָּבֹאוּ עַד־קְצֵה מַחֲנֵה אֲרָם וְהִנֵּה אֵין־שָׁם אִישׁ׃ וַאדֹנָי הִשְׁמִיעַ ׀ אֶת־מַחֲנֵה
אֲרָם קוֹל רֶכֶב קוֹל סוּס קוֹל חַיִל גָּדוֹל וַיֹּאמְרוּ אִישׁ אֶל־אָחִיו הִנֵּה שָׂכַר־עָלֵינוּ מֶלֶךְ יִשְׂרָאֵל
ז אֶת־מַלְכֵי הַחִתִּים וְאֶת־מַלְכֵי מִצְרַיִם לָבוֹא עָלֵינוּ׃ וַיָּקוּמוּ וַיָּנוּסוּ בַנֶּשֶׁף וַיַּעַזְבוּ אֶת־אָהֳלֵיהֶם
ח וְאֶת־סוּסֵיהֶם וְאֶת־חֲמֹרֵיהֶם הַמַּחֲנֶה כַּאֲשֶׁר הִיא וַיָּנֻסוּ אֶל־נַפְשָׁם׃ וַיָּבֹאוּ הַמְצֹרָעִים הָאֵלֶּה
עַד־קְצֵה הַמַּחֲנֶה וַיָּבֹאוּ אֶל־אֹהֶל אֶחָד וַיֹּאכְלוּ וַיִּשְׁתּוּ וַיִּשְׂאוּ מִשָּׁם כֶּסֶף וְזָהָב וּבְגָדִים וַיֵּלְכוּ
ט וַיַּטְמִנוּ וַיָּשֻׁבוּ וַיָּבֹאוּ אֶל־אֹהֶל אַחֵר וַיִּשְׂאוּ מִשָּׁם וַיֵּלְכוּ וַיַּטְמִנוּ׃ וַיֹּאמְרוּ אִישׁ אֶל־רֵעֵהוּ
לֹא־כֵן ׀ אֲנַחְנוּ עֹשִׂים הַיּוֹם הַזֶּה יוֹם־בְּשֹׂרָה הוּא וַאֲנַחְנוּ מַחְשִׁים וְחִכִּינוּ עַד־אוֹר הַבֹּקֶר
י וּמְצָאָנוּ עָווֹן וְעַתָּה לְכוּ וְנָבֹאָה וְנַגִּידָה בֵּית הַמֶּלֶךְ׃ וַיָּבֹאוּ וַיִּקְרְאוּ אֶל־שֹׁעֵר הָעִיר וַיַּגִּידוּ
לָהֶם לֵאמֹר בָּאנוּ אֶל־מַחֲנֵה אֲרָם וְהִנֵּה אֵין־שָׁם אִישׁ וְקוֹל אָדָם כִּי אִם־הַסּוּס אָסוּר וְהַחֲמוֹר
יא יב אָסוּר וְאֹהָלִים כַּאֲשֶׁר הֵמָּה׃ וַיִּקְרָא הַשֹּׁעֲרִים וַיַּגִּידוּ בֵּית הַמֶּלֶךְ פְּנִימָה׃ וַיָּקָם הַמֶּלֶךְ לַיְלָה
וַיֹּאמֶר אֶל־עֲבָדָיו אַגִּידָה־נָּא לָכֶם אֵת אֲשֶׁר־עָשׂוּ לָנוּ אֲרָם יָדְעוּ כִּי־רְעֵבִים אֲנַחְנוּ וַיֵּצְאוּ
מִן־הַמַּחֲנֶה לְהֵחָבֵה בהשדה לֵאמֹר כִּי־יֵצְאוּ מִן־הָעִיר וְנִתְפְּשֵׂם חַיִּים וְאֶל־הָעִיר נָבֹא׃ בַשָּׂדֶה
יג וַיַּעַן אֶחָד מֵעֲבָדָיו וַיֹּאמֶר וְיִקְחוּ־נָא חֲמִשָּׁה מִן־הַסּוּסִים הַנִּשְׁאָרִים אֲשֶׁר נִשְׁאֲרוּ־בָהּ הִנָּם
כְּכָל־ההמון יִשְׂרָאֵל אֲשֶׁר נִשְׁאֲרוּ־בָהּ הִנָּם כְּכָל־הֲמוֹן יִשְׂרָאֵל אֲשֶׁר־תָּמּוּ וְנִשְׁלְחָה וְנִרְאֶה׃ הֶהָמוֹן
יד טו וַיִּקְחוּ שְׁנֵי רֶכֶב סוּסִים וַיִּשְׁלַח הַמֶּלֶךְ אַחֲרֵי מַחֲנֵה־אֲרָם לֵאמֹר לְכוּ וּרְאוּ׃ וַיֵּלְכוּ אַחֲרֵיהֶם
עַד־הַיַּרְדֵּן וְהִנֵּה כָל־הַדֶּרֶךְ מְלֵאָה בְגָדִים וְכֵלִים אֲשֶׁר־הִשְׁלִיכוּ אֲרָם בהחפזם וַיָּשֻׁבוּ בְּחָפְזָם
טז הַמַּלְאָכִים וַיַּגִּדוּ לַמֶּלֶךְ׃ וַיֵּצֵא הָעָם וַיָּבֹזּוּ אֵת מַחֲנֵה אֲרָם וַיְהִי סְאָה־סֹלֶת בְּשֶׁקֶל וְסָאתַיִם
יז שְׂעֹרִים בְּשֶׁקֶל כִּדְבַר יְהוָה׃ וְהַמֶּלֶךְ הִפְקִיד אֶת־הַשָּׁלִישׁ אֲשֶׁר־נִשְׁעָן עַל־יָדוֹ עַל־הַשַּׁעַר
יח וַיִּרְמְסֻהוּ הָעָם בַּשַּׁעַר וַיָּמֹת כַּאֲשֶׁר דִּבֶּר אִישׁ הָאֱלֹהִים אֲשֶׁר דִּבֶּר בְּרֶדֶת הַמֶּלֶךְ אֵלָיו׃ וַיְהִי
כְּדַבֵּר אִישׁ הָאֱלֹהִים אֶל־הַמֶּלֶךְ לֵאמֹר סָאתַיִם שְׂעֹרִים בְּשֶׁקֶל וּסְאָה־סֹלֶת בְּשֶׁקֶל יִהְיֶה
יט כָּעֵת מָחָר בְּשַׁעַר שֹׁמְרוֹן׃ וַיַּעַן הַשָּׁלִישׁ אֶת־אִישׁ הָאֱלֹהִים וַיֹּאמַר וְהִנֵּה יְהוָה עֹשֶׂה אֲרֻבּוֹת
כ בַּשָּׁמַיִם הֲיִהְיֶה כַּדָּבָר הַזֶּה וַיֹּאמֶר הִנְּךָ רֹאֶה בְּעֵינֶיךָ וּמִשָּׁם לֹא תֹאכֵל׃ וַיְהִי־לוֹ כֵּן וַיִּרְמְסוּ
אֹתוֹ הָעָם בַּשַּׁעַר וַיָּמֹת׃

Haftara for
Aharei Mot

The Judgment of Jerusalem on the Eve of the Destruction

EZEKIEL 22:1–16

This prophecy primarily consists of an extremely harsh reproof of Jerusalem. Ezekiel describes a variety of sins that have become the norm in the city, including transgressions of the more severe type. Ezekiel declares that the only remedy for such a place is for it to be destroyed and its residents dispersed in exile. A similar conclusion is stated at the end of the *parasha* with regard to the impurities of forbidden relations and worshipping the idol Molekh, which cause the land to expel its inhabitants.

In practice, this *haftara* is the least read of all the *haftarot*. When, as in the majority of years, the *parashot* of *Aḥarei Mot* and *Kedoshim* are combined, the *haftara* of the second *parasha*, *Kedoshim*, is read. Even when the *parashot* are separated, and *Parashat Aharei Mot* does not occur on a special Sabbath, such as *Shabbat HaGadol* or Passover, it is nevertheless the custom in many communities not to read the *haftara* of *Aharei Mot* if a unique *haftara* will be read on the following Sabbath of *Kedoshim*. For example, if the New Moon or the day before New Moon falls on that Sabbath, the *haftara* of *Kedoshim*, with its gentler content, is read on the Sabbath of *Aharei Mot*. It is only when each of the Sabbaths are regular that the actual *haftara* of *Aharei Mot* is read on its Sabbath. This occurs roughly once every twenty years.

22 1 2 The word of the Lord was with me, saying: You, Son of man,
will you judge, will you judge the city of bloodshed? Inform it
3 of all its abominations. You shall say: So said the Lord God:
City that sheds blood in its midst, that its time may come, and
4 that crafted idols in it for defilement: Through your blood
that you shed you became guilty, and with your idols that you
crafted you were defiled, and you brought your days near, and
you came to your years; therefore, I rendered you a disgrace to
5 the nations and an object of derision to all the countries. Those
who are near and those who are far from you will deride you,
6 who is defiled of name and great of tumult. Behold, the princes
of Israel, each according to his power, have been among you in
7 order to shed blood. They demeaned father and mother among
you; they engaged in the exploitation of the stranger in your
midst; they mistreated the orphan and the widow among you.
8 That which is sacred to Me you scorned, and My Sabbaths you
9 profaned. Gossipmongers were among you in order to shed
blood; among you they ate upon the mountains; lewdness was
10 performed in your midst. Among you one uncovered the nakedness of the father; the woman with menstrual impurity was
11 raped among you. One committed an abomination with his
neighbor's wife, and one defiled his daughter-in-law with lewdness, and one raped his sister, the daughter of his father, among
12 you. Bribery was taken among you to shed blood; you took
interest and increase; you enriched your neighbors through exploitation, and you forgot Me – the utterance of the Lord God.
13 Behold, I have struck My hand at your ill-gotten gain that you
14 made and at your bloodshed, which were in your midst. Will
your heart endure, will your hands be strong on the days that
15 I will deal with you? I, the Lord, have spoken and acted. I will
disperse you among the nations, and I will scatter you among
16 the lands, and I will eliminate your impurity from you. You will
be profaned by you before the eyes of the nations, and you will
know that I am the Lord.

הפטרת

אחרי מות

כב א ב וַיְהִי דְבַר־יְהוָה אֵלַי לֵאמֹר: וְאַתָּה בֶן־אָדָם הֲתִשְׁפֹּט הֲתִשְׁפֹּט אֶת־עִיר הַדָּמִים וְהוֹדַעְתָּהּ יחזקאל
ג אֵת כָּל־תּוֹעֲבוֹתֶיהָ: וְאָמַרְתָּ כֹּה אָמַר אֲדֹנָי יֱהוִה עִיר שֹׁפֶכֶת דָּם בְּתוֹכָהּ לָבוֹא עִתָּהּ וְעָשְׂתָה
ד גִלּוּלִים עָלֶיהָ לְטָמְאָה: בְּדָמֵךְ אֲשֶׁר־שָׁפַכְתְּ אָשַׁמְתְּ וּבְגִלּוּלַיִךְ אֲשֶׁר־עָשִׂית טָמֵאת וַתַּקְרִיבִי
ה יָמַיִךְ וַתָּבוֹא עַד־שְׁנוֹתָיִךְ עַל־כֵּן נְתַתִּיךְ חֶרְפָּה לַגּוֹיִם וְקַלָּסָה לְכָל־הָאֲרָצוֹת: הַקְּרֹבוֹת
ו וְהָרְחֹקוֹת מִמֵּךְ יִתְקַלְּסוּ־בָךְ טְמֵאַת הַשֵּׁם רַבַּת הַמְּהוּמָה: הִנֵּה נְשִׂיאֵי יִשְׂרָאֵל אִישׁ לִזְרֹעוֹ
ז הָיוּ בָךְ לְמַעַן שְׁפָךְ־דָּם: אָב וָאֵם הֵקַלּוּ בָךְ לַגֵּר עָשׂוּ בַעֹשֶׁק בְּתוֹכֵךְ יָתוֹם וְאַלְמָנָה הוֹנוּ בָךְ:
ח ט קָדָשַׁי בָּזִית וְאֶת־שַׁבְּתֹתַי חִלָּלְתְּ: אַנְשֵׁי רָכִיל הָיוּ בָךְ לְמַעַן שְׁפָךְ־דָּם וְאֶל־הֶהָרִים אָכְלוּ בָךְ
י זִמָּה עָשׂוּ בְתוֹכֵךְ: עֶרְוַת־אָב גִּלָּה־בָךְ טְמֵאַת הַנִּדָּה עִנּוּ־בָךְ: וְאִישׁ ׀ אֶת־אֵשֶׁת רֵעֵהוּ עָשָׂה
יא יב תּוֹעֵבָה וְאִישׁ אֶת־כַּלָּתוֹ טִמֵּא בְזִמָּה וְאִישׁ אֶת־אֲחֹתוֹ בַת־אָבִיו עִנָּה־בָךְ: שֹׁחַד לָקְחוּ־בָךְ
לְמַעַן שְׁפָךְ־דָּם נֶשֶׁךְ וְתַרְבִּית לָקַחַתְּ וַתְּבַצְּעִי רֵעַיִךְ בַּעֹשֶׁק וְאֹתִי שָׁכַחַתְּ נְאֻם אֲדֹנָי יֱהוִה:
יג יד וְהִנֵּה הִכֵּיתִי כַפִּי אֶל־בִּצְעֵךְ אֲשֶׁר עָשִׂית וְעַל־דָּמֵךְ אֲשֶׁר הָיוּ בְּתוֹכֵךְ: הֲיַעֲמֹד לִבֵּךְ אִם־
טו תֶּחֱזַקְנָה יָדַיִךְ לַיָּמִים אֲשֶׁר אֲנִי עֹשֶׂה אוֹתָךְ אֲנִי יְהוָה דִּבַּרְתִּי וְעָשִׂיתִי: וַהֲפִיצוֹתִי אוֹתָךְ
טז בַּגּוֹיִם וְזֵרִיתִיךְ בָּאֲרָצוֹת וַהֲתִמֹּתִי טֻמְאָתֵךְ מִמֵּךְ: וְנִחַלְתְּ בָּךְ לְעֵינֵי גוֹיִם וְיָדַעַתְּ כִּי־אֲנִי יְהוָה:

Haftara for **Kedoshim**

Israel's Revival after Its Downfall

AMOS 9:7–15

This short *haftara*, taken from the concluding passage of the prophecy of Amos, is a continuation of a prophecy about the destruction of the Temple and the two kingdoms that Amos envisioned while Israel and Judah were still living complacently in their land. The prophet warns the people not to rely on the fact that they are God's chosen nation, as this does not mean that He will ignore their sins. On the contrary, God brought Israel out of Egypt so that they should be His holy nation, and if they fail to fulfill their mission, then there is no justification for their special status. The idea that the sanctity of the nation is a direct result of their exodus from Egypt is reiterated on several occasions in the book of Leviticus, e.g., in the verse: "For I am the Lord who brought you up from the land of Egypt to be your God; you shall be holy, as I am holy" (Leviticus 11:45).

However, alongside the reproof and prophecy of retribution, the prophet also promises the people in the name of God that His nation will ultimately be revived, once it has learned the lessons of its downfall.

9 7 Are you not like the children of the Kushites to Me, children of
Ashk. begin Israel – the utterance of the Lord? Did I not take Israel up from
the land of Egypt, and the Philistines from Kaftor, and Aram
8 from Kir? Behold, the eyes of the Lord God are upon the sinful
kingdom, and I will destroy it from upon the face of the earth;
however, I will not destroy the house of Jacob – the utterance of
9 the Lord. For behold, I command, and I will shake the house of
Israel among all the nations, as if it is shaken in a sieve, and not a
10 grain will fall to the ground. By the sword will die all the sinners
of My people who say: The misfortune will not come upon us
11 more quickly. On that day, I will raise the booth of David that
is fallen, and I will repair their breaches; their ruins will I raise
12 and I will build it as in days of old, so that they upon whom
My name is called will inherit the remnant of Edom and all the
13 nations – the utterance of the Lord – who does this. Behold,
days are coming – the utterance of the Lord – and the plow-
man will encounter the reaper, the grape treader the sower of
seed, and the mountains will drip nectar, and all the hills will
14 melt. I will return the captives of My people Israel and they will
build the desolate cities, and they will inhabit them; they will
plant vineyards and drink their wine; they will till gardens and
15 eat their fruits. I will plant them upon their land, and they will
Ashk. not be uprooted from their land that I gave them, said the Lord
end your God.

Reproach for Israel's Conduct in Egypt and in the Wilderness

EZEKIEL 20:2–20

This *haftara* is part of a long sermon of reproach that encompasses the entire history of Israel from its inception. God censures the Israelites' perpetual failure to internalize their special destiny as a holy people devoted only to God. The sins of idolatry and desecration of the Sabbath take center stage in this sermon, and their prohibitions are also the opening commandments and central themes of *Parashat Kedoshim*.

20 2 3 The word of the Lord was with me, saying: Son of man, speak
Seph. to the elders of Israel, and say to them: So said the Lord God:
begin Do you come to seek Me? As I live, I will surely not acquiesce
4 to you – the utterance of the Lord God. Will you judge them,
will you judge, Son of man? Inform them of the abominations
5 of their fathers. Say to them: So said the Lord God: On the day
that I chose Israel, I raised My hand to the descendants of the
house of Jacob and made Myself known to them in the land of
Egypt, and I raised My hand to them, saying: I am the Lord
6 your God. On that day, I raised My hand to them to take them
out of the land of Egypt to the land that I scouted for them,
flowing with milk and honey; it is the most magnificent of all
7 the lands. I said to them: Each man shall cast out the detestable objects of his eyes, and do not defile yourselves with the
8 idols of Egypt; I am the Lord your God. They defied Me and
were unwilling to heed Me; no man cast out the detestable objects of their eyes, and they did not forsake the idols of Egypt;
I said to pour My fury upon them, to spend My wrath upon
9 them within the land of Egypt. But I acted for the sake of My
name, that it not be profaned before the eyes of the nations
in whose midst they were, before whose eyes I made Myself
10 known to them to take them out of the land of Egypt. I took
them out of the land of Egypt and brought them into the wil-
11 derness. I gave them My statutes, and I informed them of My
12 ordinances, which a man shall perform and live by them. I also
gave them My Sabbaths to be a sign between Me and them, to
13 know that I am the Lord, their sanctifier. But the house of Israel
defied Me in the wilderness; they did not follow My statutes,
and they despised My ordinances, which a man shall perform
and live by them, and My Sabbaths they profaned greatly;

הפטרת

קדשים

עמוס
לאשכנזים

ט הֲל֣וֹא כִבְנֵי֩ כֻשִׁיִּ֨ים אַתֶּ֥ם לִ֛י בְּנֵ֥י יִשְׂרָאֵ֖ל נְאֻם־יְהֹוָ֑ה הֲל֣וֹא אֶת־יִשְׂרָאֵ֗ל הֶעֱלֵ֙יתִי֙ מֵאֶ֣רֶץ מִצְרַ֔יִם
ח וּפְלִשְׁתִּיִּ֥ים מִכַּפְתּ֖וֹר וַאֲרָ֥ם מִקִּֽיר׃ הִנֵּ֞ה עֵינֵ֣י ׀ אֲדֹנָ֣י יֱהֹוִ֗ה בַּמַּמְלָכָה֙ הַֽחַטָּאָ֔ה וְהִשְׁמַדְתִּ֣י אֹתָ֔הּ
ט מֵעַ֖ל פְּנֵ֣י הָאֲדָמָ֑ה אֶ֗פֶס כִּ֠י לֹ֣א הַשְׁמֵ֤יד אַשְׁמִיד֙ אֶת־בֵּ֣ית יַעֲקֹ֔ב נְאֻם־יְהֹוָֽה׃ כִּֽי־הִנֵּ֤ה אָֽנֹכִי֙
י מְצַוֶּ֔ה וַהֲנִע֥וֹתִי בְכׇל־הַגּוֹיִ֖ם אֶת־בֵּ֣ית יִשְׂרָאֵ֑ל כַּאֲשֶׁ֤ר יִנּ֙וֹעַ֙ בַּכְּבָרָ֔ה וְלֹא־יִפּ֥וֹל צְר֖וֹר אָֽרֶץ׃ בַּחֶ֣רֶב
יא יָמ֔וּתוּ כֹּ֖ל חַטָּאֵ֣י עַמִּ֑י הָאֹמְרִ֗ים לֹֽא־תַגִּ֧ישׁ וְתַקְדִּ֛ים בַּעֲדֵ֖ינוּ הָרָעָֽה׃ בַּיּ֣וֹם הַה֔וּא אָקִ֛ים אֶת־סֻכַּ֥ת
יב דָּוִ֖יד הַנֹּפֶ֑לֶת וְגָדַרְתִּ֣י אֶת־פִּרְצֵיהֶ֗ן וַהֲרִֽסֹתָיו֙ אָקִ֔ים וּבְנִיתִ֖יהָ כִּימֵ֥י עוֹלָֽם׃ לְמַ֙עַן֙ יִֽירְשׁ֣וּ אֶת־
יג שְׁאֵרִ֣ית אֱד֔וֹם וְכׇל־הַגּוֹיִ֔ם אֲשֶׁר־נִקְרָ֥א שְׁמִ֖י עֲלֵיהֶ֑ם נְאֻם־יְהֹוָ֖ה עֹ֥שֶׂה זֹּֽאת׃ הִנֵּ֙ה
יָמִ֤ים בָּאִים֙ נְאֻם־יְהֹוָ֔ה וְנִגַּ֤שׁ חוֹרֵשׁ֙ בַּקֹּצֵ֔ר וְדֹרֵ֥ךְ עֲנָבִ֖ים בְּמֹשֵׁ֣ךְ הַזָּ֑רַע וְהִטִּ֤יפוּ הֶֽהָרִים֙ עָסִ֔יס
יד וְכׇל־הַגְּבָע֖וֹת תִּתְמוֹגַֽגְנָה׃ וְשַׁבְתִּי֮ אֶת־שְׁב֣וּת עַמִּ֣י יִשְׂרָאֵל֒ וּבָנ֞וּ עָרִ֤ים נְשַׁמּוֹת֙ וְיָשָׁ֔בוּ וְנָטְע֣וּ
טו כְרָמִ֔ים וְשָׁת֖וּ אֶת־יֵינָ֑ם וְעָשׂ֣וּ גַנּ֔וֹת וְאָכְל֖וּ אֶת־פְּרִיהֶֽם׃ וּנְטַעְתִּ֖ים עַל־אַדְמָתָ֑ם וְלֹ֨א יִנָּתְשׁ֜וּ
ע֗וֹד מֵעַ֤ל אַדְמָתָם֙ אֲשֶׁ֣ר נָתַ֣תִּי לָהֶ֔ם אָמַ֖ר יְהֹוָ֥ה אֱלֹהֶֽיךָ׃

יחזקאל
לספרדים

כ ג וַיְהִ֥י דְבַר־יְהֹוָ֖ה אֵלַ֥י לֵאמֹֽר׃ בֶּן־אָדָ֗ם דַּבֵּ֞ר אֶת־זִקְנֵ֤י יִשְׂרָאֵל֙ וְאָמַרְתָּ֣ אֲלֵהֶ֔ם כֹּ֤ה אָמַר֙ אֲדֹנָ֣י
ד יֱהֹוִ֔ה הֲלִדְרֹ֥שׁ אֹתִ֖י אַתֶּ֣ם בָּאִ֑ים חַי־אָ֙נִי֙ אִם־אִדָּרֵ֣שׁ לָכֶ֔ם נְאֻ֖ם אֲדֹנָ֣י יֱהֹוִֽה׃ הֲתִשְׁפֹּ֥ט אֹתָ֛ם
ה הֲתִשְׁפּ֖וֹט בֶּן־אָדָ֑ם אֶת־תּוֹעֲבֹ֥ת אֲבוֹתָ֖ם הוֹדִיעֵֽם׃ וְאָמַרְתָּ֣ אֲלֵיהֶ֗ם כֹּֽה־אָמַר֮ אֲדֹנָ֣י יֱהֹוִה֒
בְּיוֹם֙ בׇּחֳרִ֣י בְיִשְׂרָאֵ֔ל וָאֶשָּׂ֣א יָדִ֗י לְזֶ֙רַע֙ בֵּ֣ית יַעֲקֹ֔ב וָאִוָּדַ֥ע לָהֶ֖ם בְּאֶ֣רֶץ מִצְרָ֑יִם וָאֶשָּׂ֨א יָדִ֤י
ו לָהֶם֙ לֵאמֹ֔ר אֲנִ֖י יְהֹוָ֥ה אֱלֹהֵיכֶֽם׃ בַּיּ֣וֹם הַה֗וּא נָשָׂ֤אתִי יָדִי֙ לָהֶ֔ם לְהֽוֹצִיאָ֖ם מֵאֶ֣רֶץ מִצְרָ֑יִם אֶל־
אֶ֜רֶץ אֲשֶׁר־תַּ֣רְתִּי לָהֶ֗ם זָבַ֤ת חָלָב֙ וּדְבַ֔שׁ צְבִ֥י הִ֖יא לְכׇל־הָאֲרָצֽוֹת׃ וָאֹמַ֣ר אֲלֵהֶ֗ם אִ֣ישׁ שִׁקּוּצֵ֤י
ז עֵינָיו֙ הַשְׁלִ֔יכוּ וּבְגִלּוּלֵ֥י מִצְרַ֖יִם אַל־תִּטַּמָּ֑אוּ אֲנִ֖י יְהֹוָ֥ה אֱלֹהֵיכֶֽם׃ וַיַּמְרוּ־בִ֗י וְלֹ֤א אָבוּ֙ לִשְׁמֹ֣עַ
ח אֵלַ֔י אִ֣ישׁ אֶת־שִׁקּוּצֵ֤י עֵֽינֵיהֶם֙ לֹ֣א הִשְׁלִ֔יכוּ וְאֶת־גִּלּוּלֵ֥י מִצְרַ֖יִם לֹ֣א עָזָ֑בוּ וָאֹמַ֞ר לִשְׁפֹּ֧ךְ חֲמָתִ֣י
ט עֲלֵיהֶ֗ם לְכַלּ֤וֹת אַפִּי֙ בָּהֶ֔ם בְּת֖וֹךְ אֶ֣רֶץ מִצְרָ֑יִם וָאַ֙עַשׂ֙ לְמַ֣עַן שְׁמִ֔י לְבִלְתִּ֥י הֵחֵ֖ל לְעֵינֵ֣י הַגּוֹיִ֑ם
י אֲשֶׁר־הֵ֣מָּה בְתוֹכָ֔ם אֲשֶׁ֨ר נוֹדַ֤עְתִּי אֲלֵיהֶם֙ לְעֵ֣ינֵיהֶ֔ם לְהוֹצִיאָ֖ם מֵאֶ֣רֶץ מִצְרָֽיִם׃ וָאוֹצִיאֵ֖ם
יא מֵאֶ֣רֶץ מִצְרָ֑יִם וָאֲבִאֵ֖ם אֶל־הַמִּדְבָּֽר׃ וָאֶתֵּ֤ן לָהֶם֙ אֶת־חֻקּוֹתַ֔י וְאֶת־מִשְׁפָּטַ֖י הוֹדַ֣עְתִּי אוֹתָ֑ם
יב אֲשֶׁ֨ר יַעֲשֶׂ֥ה אוֹתָ֛ם הָאָדָ֖ם וָחַ֥י בָּהֶֽם׃ וְגַ֤ם אֶת־שַׁבְּתוֹתַי֙ נָתַ֣תִּי לָהֶ֔ם לִהְי֣וֹת לְא֔וֹת בֵּינִ֖י וּבֵינֵיהֶ֑ם
יג לָדַ֕עַת כִּ֛י אֲנִ֥י יְהֹוָ֖ה מְקַדְּשָֽׁם׃ וַיַּמְרוּ־בִ֣י בֵֽית־יִשְׂרָאֵ֣ל בַּמִּדְבָּ֗ר בְּחֻקּוֹתַ֣י לֹא־הָלָ֡כוּ וְאֶת־מִשְׁפָּטַ֣י
מָאָ֡סוּ אֲשֶׁר֩ יַעֲשֶׂ֨ה אֹתָ֤ם הָֽאָדָם֙ וָחַ֣י בָּהֶ֔ם וְאֶת־שַׁבְּתֹתַ֖י חִלְּל֣וּ מְאֹ֑ד וָאֹמַ֞ר לִשְׁפֹּ֤ךְ חֲמָתִ֤י

I said to pour My fury upon them in the wilderness, to anni-
14 hilate them. But I acted for the sake of My name, that it not
be profaned before the eyes of the nations before whose eyes
15 I took them out. I also raised My hand to them in the wilderness that I would not bring them to the land that I gave, flowing
16 with milk and honey, it is the most magnificent of all the lands,
because they despised My ordinances, and they did not follow
My statutes, and they profaned My Sabbaths, as their heart

17 was following their idols. But My eye pitied them, that I not
destroy them, and I did not engender annihilation of them in
18 the wilderness. I said to their children in the wilderness: Do not
follow the practices of your fathers, and do not observe their or-
19 dinances, and do not defile yourselves with their idols. I am the
Lord your God; follow My statutes, and observe My ordinances
20 and perform them. Sanctify My Sabbaths, and they shall be a
sign between Me and you, to know that I am the Lord your God.

Haftara for
Emor

Priests in the Future Temple
EZEKIEL 44:15–31

This *haftara* is taken from the prophecies of Ezekiel that discuss the laws of the priests in the future Temple, specifically their various functions and the priestly gifts to which they will be entitled. A straightforward reading of this passage indicates that the prophet is referring to additional prohibitions that serve to enhance the sanctity of the priesthood, beyond the laws that are expressly stated in the Torah itself. It is unclear whether these additional prohibitions are new instructions that will be instituted at a particular point later in time, or if they were ancient oral traditions that Ezekiel recorded in writing (see Radak, Abravanel, and Malbim throughout Ezekiel chaps. 43–45).

44 15 But the priests, the Levites, sons of Tzadok, who kept the commission of My Sanctuary when the children of Israel strayed
from Me, they shall approach Me to serve Me, and they shall
stand before Me to present to Me fat and blood – the utter-
16 ance of the Lord God. They shall come into My Sanctuary,
and they shall approach My table to serve Me, and they shall
17 keep My commission. It shall be when they come to the gates
of the Inner Courtyard, linen garments they shall don, and no
wool shall be put upon them when they serve inside the gates
18 of the Inner Courtyard and inward. Linen headdresses shall be
on their heads, and linen trousers shall be on their waists; they
19 shall not gird themselves where one perspires. When they go
out to the outer courtyard, to the outer courtyard to the people, they shall remove their vestments in which they serve and
place them in the sacred chambers, and they shall don other
garments, that they should not sanctify the people with their
20 vestments. Their heads they shall not shave, and they shall not
21 grow long hair; they shall trim their heads. No priest shall drink

22 wine when they come to the Inner Courtyard. A widow or a
divorcée they shall not take as wives; rather, they shall marry
virgins from the offspring of the house of Israel or a widow
23 who is the widow of a priest. They shall teach My people; of
that which is between the sacred and the profane and between
24 the impure and the pure they shall inform them. Concerning
a quarrel they shall stand in judgment; according to My ordinances they shall judge it. They shall observe My laws and My
statutes in all My appointed times, and My Sabbaths shall they
25 sanctify. He shall not go near to the corpse of a person to become impure; only for a father, for a mother, for a son, for a
daughter, for a brother, or for a sister who had not been with
26 a man, they may become impure. After his purification, seven
27 days they shall count for him. On the day of his coming to the
Sanctuary, to the Inner Courtyard, to serve in the Sanctuary,
he shall present his sin offering – the utterance of the Lord
28 God. It shall be for them as a heritage; I am their heritage. And
you shall not give them a portion in Israel; I am their portion.

יד עֲלֵיהֶם בַּמִּדְבָּר לְכַלּוֹתָם: וָאֶעֱשֶׂה לְמַעַן שְׁמִי לְבִלְתִּי הֵחֵל לְעֵינֵי הַגּוֹיִם אֲשֶׁר הוֹצֵאתִים
טו לְעֵינֵיהֶם: וְגַם־אֲנִי נָשָׂאתִי יָדִי לָהֶם בַּמִּדְבָּר לְבִלְתִּי הָבִיא אוֹתָם אֶל־הָאָרֶץ אֲשֶׁר־נָתַתִּי
טז זָבַת חָלָב וּדְבַשׁ צְבִי הִיא לְכָל־הָאֲרָצוֹת: יַעַן בְּמִשְׁפָּטַי מָאָסוּ וְאֶת־חֻקּוֹתַי לֹא־הָלְכוּ בָהֶם
יז וְאֶת־שַׁבְּתוֹתַי חִלֵּלוּ כִּי אַחֲרֵי גִלּוּלֵיהֶם לִבָּם הֹלֵךְ: וַתָּחָס עֵינִי עֲלֵיהֶם מִשַּׁחֲתָם וְלֹא־עָשִׂיתִי
יח אוֹתָם כָּלָה בַּמִּדְבָּר: וָאֹמַר אֶל־בְּנֵיהֶם בַּמִּדְבָּר בְּחוּקֵּי אֲבוֹתֵיכֶם אַל־תֵּלֵכוּ וְאֶת־מִשְׁפְּטֵיהֶם
יט אַל־תִּשְׁמֹרוּ וּבְגִלּוּלֵיהֶם אַל־תִּטַּמָּאוּ: אֲנִי יְהוָה אֱלֹהֵיכֶם בְּחֻקּוֹתַי לֵכוּ וְאֶת־מִשְׁפָּטַי שִׁמְרוּ
כ וַעֲשׂוּ אוֹתָם: וְאֶת־שַׁבְּתוֹתַי קַדֵּשׁוּ וְהָיוּ לְאוֹת בֵּינִי וּבֵינֵיכֶם לָדַעַת כִּי אֲנִי יְהוָה אֱלֹהֵיכֶם:

הפטרת

אמר

יחזקאל

מד טו וְהַכֹּהֲנִים הַלְוִיִּם בְּנֵי צָדוֹק אֲשֶׁר שָׁמְרוּ אֶת־מִשְׁמֶרֶת מִקְדָּשִׁי בִּתְעוֹת בְּנֵי־יִשְׂרָאֵל מֵעָלַי הֵמָּה
טז יִקְרְבוּ אֵלַי לְשָׁרְתֵנִי וְעָמְדוּ לְפָנַי לְהַקְרִיב לִי חֵלֶב וָדָם נְאֻם אֲדֹנָי יְהוִה: הֵמָּה יָבֹאוּ אֶל־מִקְדָּשִׁי
יז וְהֵמָּה יִקְרְבוּ אֶל־שֻׁלְחָנִי לְשָׁרְתֵנִי וְשָׁמְרוּ אֶת־מִשְׁמַרְתִּי: וְהָיָה בְּבוֹאָם אֶל־שַׁעֲרֵי הֶחָצֵר
הַפְּנִימִית בִּגְדֵי פִשְׁתִּים יִלְבָּשׁוּ וְלֹא־יַעֲלֶה עֲלֵיהֶם צֶמֶר בְּשָׁרְתָם בְּשַׁעֲרֵי הֶחָצֵר הַפְּנִימִית וָבָיְתָה:
יח יט פַּאֲרֵי פִשְׁתִּים יִהְיוּ עַל־רֹאשָׁם וּמִכְנְסֵי פִשְׁתִּים יִהְיוּ עַל־מָתְנֵיהֶם לֹא יַחְגְּרוּ בַּיָּזַע: וּבְצֵאתָם אֶל־
הֶחָצֵר הַחִיצוֹנָה אֶל־הֶחָצֵר הַחִיצוֹנָה אֶל־הָעָם יִפְשְׁטוּ אֶת־בִּגְדֵיהֶם אֲשֶׁר־הֵמָּה מְשָׁרְתִם בָּם
כ וְהִנִּיחוּ אוֹתָם בְּלִשְׁכֹת הַקֹּדֶשׁ וְלָבְשׁוּ בְּגָדִים אֲחֵרִים וְלֹא־יְקַדְּשׁוּ אֶת־הָעָם בְּבִגְדֵיהֶם: וְרֹאשָׁם
כא לֹא יְגַלֵּחוּ וּפֶרַע לֹא יְשַׁלֵּחוּ כָּסוֹם יִכְסְמוּ אֶת־רָאשֵׁיהֶם: וְיַיִן לֹא־יִשְׁתּוּ כָּל־כֹּהֵן בְּבוֹאָם אֶל־
כב הֶחָצֵר הַפְּנִימִית: וְאַלְמָנָה וּגְרוּשָׁה לֹא־יִקְחוּ לָהֶם לְנָשִׁים כִּי אִם־בְּתוּלֹת מִזֶּרַע בֵּית יִשְׂרָאֵל
כג וְהָאַלְמָנָה אֲשֶׁר־תִּהְיֶה אַלְמָנָה מִכֹּהֵן יִקָּחוּ: וְאֶת־עַמִּי יוֹרוּ בֵּין קֹדֶשׁ לְחֹל וּבֵין־טָמֵא לְטָהוֹר
כד יוֹדִעֻם: וְעַל־רִיב הֵמָּה יַעַמְדוּ לשפט בְּמִשְׁפָּטַי ושפטהו וְאֶת־תּוֹרֹתַי וְאֶת־חֻקֹּתַי בְּכָל־ לְמִשְׁפָּט יִשְׁפְּטֻהוּ
כה מוֹעֲדַי יִשְׁמֹרוּ וְאֶת־שַׁבְּתוֹתַי יְקַדֵּשׁוּ: וְאֶל־מֵת אָדָם לֹא יָבוֹא לְטָמְאָה כִּי אִם־לְאָב וּלְאֵם
כו וּלְבֵן וּלְבַת לְאָח וּלְאָחוֹת אֲשֶׁר־לֹא־הָיְתָה לְאִישׁ יִטַּמָּאוּ: וְאַחֲרֵי טָהֳרָתוֹ שִׁבְעַת יָמִים
כז יִסְפְּרוּ־לוֹ: וּבְיוֹם בֹּאוֹ אֶל־הַקֹּדֶשׁ אֶל־הֶחָצֵר הַפְּנִימִית לְשָׁרֵת בַּקֹּדֶשׁ יַקְרִיב חַטָּאתוֹ נְאֻם
כח אֲדֹנָי יְהוִה: וְהָיְתָה לָהֶם לְנַחֲלָה אֲנִי נַחֲלָתָם וַאֲחֻזָּה לֹא־תִתְּנוּ לָהֶם בְּיִשְׂרָאֵל אֲנִי אֲחֻזָּתָם:

29 They shall eat the meal offering and the sin offering and the guilt
30 offering, and everything proscribed in Israel shall be theirs. The
first of all first fruits of everything, and every gift of everything
from all your gifts, shall be for the priests, and the first of your

kneading basket you shall give to the priest to rest a blessing
31 upon your house. Any carcass or mauled animal, of the birds or
of the animals, the priests shall not eat.

Haftara for
Behar

The Acquisition of a Field, Accompanied by a Message of Redemption
JEREMIAH 32:6–27

This prophecy was issued shortly before Jerusalem fell to Babylonia. The city was under siege, but at the time conditions within its walls were not so terrible. At that stage, with the destruction imminent, Jeremiah is commanded to perform an action that exhibits his confidence in a better future. He must redeem a field from his cousin and guard the deed of sale for a later period, when he can actualize his purchase. The redemption of an inheritance of land from a family relative is one of the central commandments of the *parasha*. Here its performance symbolizes the renewal of the covenant between God and His people as well as the ties between the nation and its land, both of which are also alluded to in the *parasha*.

32 6 Jeremiah said: The word of the Lord was with me, saying:
7 Behold, Hanamel son of Shalum your uncle is coming to you, saying: Purchase for you my field that is in Anatot, as yours is
8 the right of redemption to purchase. Hanamel, my uncle's son, came to me to the Courtyard of the Guard, according to the word of the Lord, and he said to me: Please, purchase my field that is in Anatot, which is in the land of Benjamin, as yours is the right of inheritance, and the redemption is yours; purchase
9 it for you. And I knew that it was the word of the Lord. I purchased the field that was in Anatot from Hanamel, my uncle's son, and I weighed the silver for him, seven shekels and ten
10 of silver. I wrote in the deed, sealed it, called witnesses, and
11 weighed the silver on scales. I took the deed of the purchase, that which was sealed, the laws and the statutes, and that which
12 was unsealed. I gave the deed of purchase to Barukh, son of Neriya, son of Mahseya, before the eyes of Hanamel my uncle and before the eyes of the witnesses who wrote in the deed of purchase, before the eyes of all the Jews who were sitting
13 in the Courtyard of the Guard. I commanded Barukh before
14 their eyes, saying: So said the Lord of hosts, God of Israel: Take these deeds, this deed of the purchase and that which was sealed and this unsealed deed, and place them in an earthen-
15 ware vessel so that they will endure for many days. For so said

the Lord of hosts, God of Israel: Houses, fields, and vineyards
16 will again be purchased in this land. I prayed to the Lord, after I gave the deed of purchase to Barukh son of Neriya, saying:
17 Alas, My Lord God, behold: You made the heavens and the earth with Your great power and with Your outstretched arm;
18 there is nothing that is beyond You, who engages in kindness for the thousands and repays the iniquity of the fathers into the bosom of their children after them. The great, the mighty
19 God, the Lord of hosts is His name, who is great in designs and mighty in deed; whose eyes are open upon all the ways of men, to give each man in accordance with his ways and in accordance
20 with the fruit of his actions; You, who placed signs and wonders in the land of Egypt to this day, and among Israel and among
21 mankind, and made for You a name like this day. You took out Your people Israel from the land of Egypt, with signs and with wonders and with a mighty hand and with an outstretched
22 arm and with great awe. You gave them this land that You took an oath to their forefathers to give them, a land flowing with
23 milk and honey. They came and they took possession of it, but they did not heed Your voice, and they did not follow Your laws; everything that You commanded them to perform they did not perform, and You caused all this evil to befall them.

כט ל הַמִּנְחָה וְהַחַטָּאת וְהָאָשָׁם הֵמָּה יֹאכְלוּם וְכָל־חֵרֶם בְּיִשְׂרָאֵל לָהֶם יִהְיֶה׃ וְרֵאשִׁית כָּל־בִּכּוּרֵי
כֹל וְכָל־תְּרוּמַת כֹּל מִכֹּל תְּרוּמוֹתֵיכֶם לַכֹּהֲנִים יִהְיֶה וְרֵאשִׁית עֲרִיסוֹתֵיכֶם תִּתְּנוּ לַכֹּהֵן לְהָנִיחַ
לא בְּרָכָה אֶל־בֵּיתֶךָ׃ כָּל־נְבֵלָה וּטְרֵפָה מִן־הָעוֹף וּמִן־הַבְּהֵמָה לֹא יֹאכְלוּ הַכֹּהֲנִים׃

הפטרת

בהר

לב ו ז וַיֹּאמֶר יִרְמְיָהוּ הָיָה דְּבַר־יְהוָה אֵלַי לֵאמֹר׃ הִנֵּה חֲנַמְאֵל בֶּן־שַׁלֻּם דֹּדְךָ בָּא אֵלֶיךָ לֵאמֹר ירמיה
ח קְנֵה לְךָ אֶת־שָׂדִי אֲשֶׁר בַּעֲנָתוֹת כִּי לְךָ מִשְׁפַּט הַגְּאֻלָּה לִקְנוֹת׃ וַיָּבֹא אֵלַי חֲנַמְאֵל בֶּן־דֹּדִי
כִּדְבַר יְהוָה אֶל־חֲצַר הַמַּטָּרָה וַיֹּאמֶר אֵלַי קְנֵה נָא אֶת־שָׂדִי אֲשֶׁר־בַּעֲנָתוֹת אֲשֶׁר ׀ בְּאֶרֶץ
ט בִּנְיָמִין כִּי לְךָ מִשְׁפַּט הַיְרֻשָּׁה וּלְךָ הַגְּאֻלָּה קְנֵה־לָךְ וָאֵדַע כִּי דְבַר־יְהוָה הוּא׃ וָאֶקְנֶה אֶת־
הַשָּׂדֶה מֵאֵת חֲנַמְאֵל בֶּן־דֹּדִי אֲשֶׁר בַּעֲנָתוֹת וָאֶשְׁקֲלָה־לּוֹ אֶת־הַכֶּסֶף שִׁבְעָה שְׁקָלִים וַעֲשָׂרָה
י יא הַכָּסֶף׃ וָאֶכְתֹּב בַּסֵּפֶר וָאֶחְתֹּם וָאָעֵד עֵדִים וָאֶשְׁקֹל הַכֶּסֶף בְּמֹאזְנָיִם׃ וָאֶקַּח אֶת־סֵפֶר הַמִּקְנָה
יב אֶת־הֶחָתוּם הַמִּצְוָה וְהַחֻקִּים וְאֶת־הַגָּלוּי׃ וָאֶתֵּן אֶת־הַסֵּפֶר הַמִּקְנָה אֶל־בָּרוּךְ בֶּן־נֵרִיָּה
בֶּן־מַחְסֵיָה לְעֵינֵי חֲנַמְאֵל דֹּדִי וּלְעֵינֵי הָעֵדִים הַכֹּתְבִים בְּסֵפֶר הַמִּקְנָה לְעֵינֵי כָּל־הַיְּהוּדִים
יג יד הַיֹּשְׁבִים בַּחֲצַר הַמַּטָּרָה׃ וָאֲצַוֶּה אֶת־בָּרוּךְ לְעֵינֵיהֶם לֵאמֹר׃ כֹּה־אָמַר יְהוָה צְבָאוֹת אֱלֹהֵי
יִשְׂרָאֵל לָקוֹחַ אֶת־הַסְּפָרִים הָאֵלֶּה אֵת סֵפֶר הַמִּקְנָה הַזֶּה וְאֵת הֶחָתוּם וְאֵת סֵפֶר הַגָּלוּי הַזֶּה
טו וּנְתַתָּם בִּכְלִי־חָרֶשׂ לְמַעַן יַעַמְדוּ יָמִים רַבִּים׃ כִּי כֹה אָמַר יְהוָה צְבָאוֹת אֱלֹהֵי יִשְׂרָאֵל
טז עוֹד יִקָּנוּ בָתִּים וְשָׂדוֹת וּכְרָמִים בָּאָרֶץ הַזֹּאת׃ וָאֶתְפַּלֵּל אֶל־יְהוָה אַחֲרֵי תִתִּי אֶת־
יז סֵפֶר הַמִּקְנָה אֶל־בָּרוּךְ בֶּן־נֵרִיָּה לֵאמֹר׃ אֲהָהּ אֲדֹנָי יֱהֹוִה הִנֵּה ׀ אַתָּה עָשִׂיתָ אֶת־הַשָּׁמַיִם
יח וְאֶת־הָאָרֶץ בְּכֹחֲךָ הַגָּדוֹל וּבִזְרֹעֲךָ הַנְּטוּיָה לֹא־יִפָּלֵא מִמְּךָ כָּל־דָּבָר׃ עֹשֶׂה חֶסֶד לַאֲלָפִים
יט וּמְשַׁלֵּם עֲוֺן אָבוֹת אֶל־חֵיק בְּנֵיהֶם אַחֲרֵיהֶם הָאֵל הַגָּדוֹל הַגִּבּוֹר יְהוָה צְבָאוֹת שְׁמוֹ׃ גְּדֹל
הָעֵצָה וְרַב הָעֲלִילִיָּה אֲשֶׁר־עֵינֶיךָ פְקֻחוֹת עַל־כָּל־דַּרְכֵי בְּנֵי אָדָם לָתֵת לְאִישׁ כִּדְרָכָיו
כ וְכִפְרִי מַעֲלָלָיו׃ אֲשֶׁר־שַׂמְתָּ אֹתוֹת וּמֹפְתִים בְּאֶרֶץ־מִצְרַיִם עַד־הַיּוֹם הַזֶּה וּבְיִשְׂרָאֵל וּבָאָדָם
כא וַתַּעֲשֶׂה־לְּךָ שֵׁם כַּיּוֹם הַזֶּה׃ וַתֹּצֵא אֶת־עַמְּךָ אֶת־יִשְׂרָאֵל מֵאֶרֶץ מִצְרָיִם בְּאֹתוֹת וּבְמוֹפְתִים
כב וּבְיָד חֲזָקָה וּבְאֶזְרוֹעַ נְטוּיָה וּבְמוֹרָא גָּדוֹל׃ וַתִּתֵּן לָהֶם אֶת־הָאָרֶץ הַזֹּאת אֲשֶׁר־נִשְׁבַּעְתָּ
כג לַאֲבוֹתָם לָתֵת לָהֶם אֶרֶץ זָבַת חָלָב וּדְבָשׁ׃ וַיָּבֹאוּ וַיִּרְשׁוּ אֹתָהּ וְלֹא־שָׁמְעוּ בְקוֹלֶךָ ובתרותך וּבְתוֹרָתְךָ
לֹא־הָלָכוּ אֵת כָּל־אֲשֶׁר צִוִּיתָה לָהֶם לַעֲשׂוֹת לֹא עָשׂוּ וַתַּקְרֵא אֹתָם אֵת כָּל־הָרָעָה הַזֹּאת׃

24 Behold, the embankments have come to the city to capture it, and the city has been delivered into the hand of the Chaldeans, who are making war against it due to the sword and the famine and the pestilence, and that which You spoke has happened,
25 and behold, You see. And You said to me, My Lord God:

Purchase the field with silver, and call witnesses, but the city
26 has been delivered into the hand of the Chaldeans. The word
27 of the Lord was with Jeremiah, saying: Behold, I am the Lord, God of all flesh. Is anything beyond Me?

Haftara for
Behukotai

Depend on Man's Relationship with God
JEREMIAH 16:19–17:14

The blessings that stem from the people's loyalty to their covenant with God, and the curses that result from their breach of that covenant, the main topics of *Parashat Behukotai*, are also the subjects of the *haftara*. Furthermore, both readings refer to the link between the nation's behavior and their continued presence in the Land of Israel.

According to the Yemenite custom and that of some other communities, this *haftara* is read on the Sabbath of *Parashat Behar*, as it concludes with the reaffirmation of the covenant at Sinai and a warning about idolatry, both of which are discussed in *Behar*.

16 19 Lord, my strength, my stronghold, and my refuge on the day of trouble, to You nations will come from the ends of the earth, and they will say: It is but falsehood that our fathers inherited,
20 futility, and they are to no avail. Will a person make gods for
21 himself, and they are not gods? Therefore, behold, I am informing them; this time, I will inform them of My hand and My
17 1 might, and they shall know that My name is the Lord. The sin of Judah is written with an iron pen, with a point of crystal; it is engraved on the tablet of their heart and on the horns of your
2 altars. Like the remembrance of their children are their altars and their sacred trees by the flourishing trees, on the lofty hills.
3 Mountains in the field, your wealth, all your treasures, I will deliver as loot; your high places are with sin throughout your bor-
4 ders. You will be expelled, because of you, from your heritage that I gave you, and I will cause you to serve your enemies in the land that you did not know, for you ignited a fire in My nostrils;
5 it will burn forever. So said the Lord: Cursed is the man who trusts in people and makes flesh his strength and whose heart
6 strays from the Lord. He will be like a solitary tree in the desert

and will not see when good comes; he will inhabit the parched
7 places in the wilderness, a salty land and uninhabited. Blessed is the man who trusts in the Lord, and the Lord is his haven.
8 He will be like a tree planted near water, and near a stream it shall spread its roots, and it will not see when heat comes, and its leaves will be flourishing; during a year of drought it will not
9 be concerned, and it will not cease from producing fruit. The heart is deceitful above all, and it is mortally ill; who can know
10 it? I, the Lord, probe the heart, examine kidneys to give to each man in accordance with his ways, in accordance with the fruit
11 of his actions. A partridge collects eggs that it did not lay; one who amasses wealth unjustly, in the middle of his days he will
12 leave it, and at his end he will be reviled. Throne of Glory, ex-
13 alted from the first, is the place of our Temple. Hope of Israel, the Lord, all who forsake You will be ashamed, and those who stray from Me will be written in the earth because they forsook
14 the fount of flowing water, the Lord. Heal me, Lord, and I will be healed; save me, and I will be saved, for You are my praise.

כד הִנֵּה הַסֹּלְלוֹת בָּאוּ הָעִיר לְלָכְדָהּ וְהָעִיר נִתְּנָה בְּיַד הַכַּשְׂדִּים הַנִּלְחָמִים עָלֶיהָ מִפְּנֵי הַחֶרֶב
כה וְהָרָעָב וְהַדָּבֶר וַאֲשֶׁר דִּבַּרְתָּ הָיָה וְהִנְּךָ רֹאֶה: וְאַתָּה אָמַרְתָּ אֵלַי אֲדֹנָי יְהוִה קְנֵה־לְךָ הַשָּׂדֶה
כו בַּכֶּסֶף וְהָעֵד עֵדִים וְהָעִיר נִתְּנָה בְּיַד הַכַּשְׂדִּים: וַיְהִי דְּבַר־יְהוָה אֶל־יִרְמְיָהוּ לֵאמֹר:
כז הִנֵּה אֲנִי יְהוָה אֱלֹהֵי כָּל־בָּשָׂר הֲמִמֶּנִּי יִפָּלֵא כָּל־דָּבָר:

הפטרת

בחקתי

טז יט יְהוָה עֻזִּי וּמָעֻזִּי וּמְנוּסִי בְּיוֹם צָרָה אֵלֶיךָ גּוֹיִם יָבֹאוּ מֵאַפְסֵי־אָרֶץ וְיֹאמְרוּ אַךְ־שֶׁקֶר נָחֲלוּ ירמיה
כ כא אֲבוֹתֵינוּ הֶבֶל וְאֵין־בָּם מוֹעִיל: הֲיַעֲשֶׂה־לּוֹ אָדָם אֱלֹהִים וְהֵמָּה לֹא אֱלֹהִים: לָכֵן הִנְנִי מוֹדִיעָם
יז א בַּפַּעַם הַזֹּאת אוֹדִיעֵם אֶת־יָדִי וְאֶת־גְּבוּרָתִי וְיָדְעוּ כִּי־שְׁמִי יְהוָה: חַטַּאת יְהוּדָה
ב כְּתוּבָה בְּעֵט בַּרְזֶל בְּצִפֹּרֶן שָׁמִיר חֲרוּשָׁה עַל־לוּחַ לִבָּם וּלְקַרְנוֹת מִזְבְּחוֹתֵיכֶם: כִּזְכֹּר בְּנֵיהֶם
ג מִזְבְּחוֹתָם וַאֲשֵׁרֵיהֶם עַל־עֵץ רַעֲנָן עַל גְּבָעוֹת הַגְּבֹהוֹת: הֲרָרִי בַּשָּׂדֶה חֵילְךָ כָל־אוֹצְרוֹתֶיךָ
ד לָבַז אֶתֵּן בָּמֹתֶיךָ בְּחַטָּאת בְּכָל־גְּבוּלֶיךָ: וְשָׁמַטְתָּה וּבְךָ מִנַּחֲלָתְךָ אֲשֶׁר נָתַתִּי לָךְ וְהַעֲבַדְתִּיךָ
ה אֶת־אֹיְבֶיךָ בָּאָרֶץ אֲשֶׁר לֹא־יָדָעְתָּ כִּי־אֵשׁ קְדַחְתֶּם בְּאַפִּי עַד־עוֹלָם תּוּקָד: כֹּה | אָמַר
ו יְהוָה אָרוּר הַגֶּבֶר אֲשֶׁר יִבְטַח בָּאָדָם וְשָׂם בָּשָׂר זְרֹעוֹ וּמִן־יְהוָה יָסוּר לִבּוֹ: וְהָיָה כְּעַרְעָר
ז בָּעֲרָבָה וְלֹא יִרְאֶה כִּי־יָבוֹא טוֹב וְשָׁכַן חֲרֵרִים בַּמִּדְבָּר אֶרֶץ מְלֵחָה וְלֹא תֵשֵׁב: בָּרוּךְ
ח הַגֶּבֶר אֲשֶׁר יִבְטַח בַּיהוָה וְהָיָה יְהוָה מִבְטַחוֹ: וְהָיָה כְּעֵץ | שָׁתוּל עַל־מַיִם וְעַל־יוּבַל יְשַׁלַּח
שָׁרָשָׁיו וְלֹא יִרְאֶ כִּי־יָבֹא חֹם וְהָיָה עָלֵהוּ רַעֲנָן וּבִשְׁנַת בַּצֹּרֶת לֹא יִדְאָג וְלֹא יָמִישׁ מֵעֲשׂוֹת
ט י פֶּרִי: עָקֹב הַלֵּב מִכֹּל וְאָנֻשׁ הוּא מִי יֵדָעֶנּוּ: אֲנִי יְהוָה חֹקֵר לֵב בֹּחֵן כְּלָיוֹת וְלָתֵת לְאִישׁ כִּדְרָכָו
יא כִּפְרִי מַעֲלָלָיו: קֹרֵא דָגַר וְלֹא יָלָד עֹשֶׂה עֹשֶׁר וְלֹא בְמִשְׁפָּט בַּחֲצִי יָמָו יַעַזְבֶנּוּ
יב יג וּבְאַחֲרִיתוֹ יִהְיֶה נָבָל: כִּסֵּא כָבוֹד מָרוֹם מֵרִאשׁוֹן מְקוֹם מִקְדָּשֵׁנוּ: מִקְוֵה יִשְׂרָאֵל יְהוָה כָּל־
יד עֹזְבֶיךָ יֵבֹשׁוּ יסורי בָּאָרֶץ יִכָּתֵבוּ כִּי עָזְבוּ מְקוֹר מַיִם־חַיִּים אֶת־יְהוָה: רְפָאֵנִי יְהוָה וְסוּרַי
וְאֵרָפֵא הוֹשִׁיעֵנִי וְאִוָּשֵׁעָה כִּי תְהִלָּתִי אָתָּה:

Haftara for
Bemidbar

Vision of the Return of the People to the Covenant

HOSEA 2:1–22

This prophecy of Hosea includes a harsh reproof of the nation for its betrayal of God, alongside a vision of the renewal of the covenant and a reconciliation between God and His people (see *Pesaḥim* 87b; Rashi, Hosea 2:1). In order to rekindle the mutual love and establish the people's loyalty to God, the people would have to rid themselves of their dependence on idolatry and their illusions of protection by the powerful neighboring kingdoms. For God's part, He will once again intimately lead His people as He did in the wilderness, through the performance of miracles. Notwithstanding the similarity between the nation's wanderings through the wilderness upon the exodus from Egypt and its future travels through the wilderness, the *haftara* also alludes to the absence of certain features of the earlier journey, such as censuses, borders between the tribes, princes, the presence of environmental threats, and the general hardships of that time.

2 1 The number of the children of Israel will be like the sand of the sea, which cannot be measured and cannot be counted; it will come about that instead of it being said of them: You are not My people, it will be said of them: Children of the living 2 God. The children of Judah and the children of Israel will be assembled together, and they will appoint themselves one head, and they will go up out of the land, for great will be the day of 3 Yizre'el. Say to your brethren: My people; and to your sisters: 4 Recipient of mercy. Contend with your mother, contend, as she is not My wife and I am not her husband; let her remove her licentiousness from before her and her adulteries from between 5 her breasts, lest I strip her naked and present her as on the day of her birth; I will make her like a wilderness and render her 6 like an arid land and kill her with thirst. I will not have mercy 7 on her children, as they are children of licentiousness. For their mother committed licentiousness, she who conceived them acted shamefully; for she said: I will follow my lovers, who give me my bread and my water, my wool and my flax, my oil and my 8 drink. Therefore, behold, I am hedging your way with thorns 9 and I will erect her fence and she will not find her paths. She will pursue her lovers but she will not catch them; she will seek them but will not find them. And she will say: I will go and return to my first husband, as it was better for me then than now. 10 She did not know that I gave her the grain, the wine, and the oil, and lavished upon her the silver and the gold they used for the 11 Baal. Therefore, I will return and take back My grain at its time, and My wine at its appointed time, and I will salvage My wool

12 and My flax which were to cover her nakedness. Now I will reveal her vileness in the eyes of her paramours, and no man 13 will save her from My hand. I will bring all her rejoicing to an end: her festivals, her new moons, her sabbaths, and all her ap-14 pointed times. I will render her vines and her fig trees desolate, of which she said: These are my fee that my paramours gave me; I will make them into a forest, and the beasts of the field shall eat 15 them. I will reckon upon her the days of the Be'alim, to which she burned incense, and donned her earrings and her jewelry and followed her paramours, but Me she forgot – the utterance 16 of the Lord. Therefore, behold, I will seduce her and lead her 17 to the wilderness, and I will speak to her heart. I will give her her vineyards from there and the murky valley as an entrance of hope; she will respond there like in the days of her youth and 18 like on the day of her coming up from the land of Egypt. It shall be on that day – the utterance of the Lord – that you shall call 19 Me my spouse, and you will no longer call Me my husband. I will remove the names of the Be'alim from her mouth and they 20 will no longer be mentioned by their name. I will establish a covenant for them on that day with the beasts of the field, and with the birds of the heavens, and with the crawling creatures of the ground; bow, sword and war will I terminate from the land, 21 and I will have them lie down in security. I will betroth you to Me forever; I will betroth you to Me with righteousness, with 22 justice, with grace, and with mercy. I will betroth you to Me with faithfulness and you will know the Lord.

הפטרת

במדבר

הושע

ב א וְהָיָה מִסְפַּר בְּנֵי־יִשְׂרָאֵל כְּחוֹל הַיָּם אֲשֶׁר לֹא־יִמַּד וְלֹא יִסָּפֵר וְהָיָה בִּמְקוֹם אֲשֶׁר־יֵאָמֵר לָהֶם
ב לֹא־עַמִּי אַתֶּם יֵאָמֵר לָהֶם בְּנֵי אֵל־חָי: וְנִקְבְּצוּ בְּנֵי־יְהוּדָה וּבְנֵי־יִשְׂרָאֵל יַחְדָּו וְשָׂמוּ לָהֶם
ג רֹאשׁ אֶחָד וְעָלוּ מִן־הָאָרֶץ כִּי גָדוֹל יוֹם יִזְרְעֶאל: אִמְרוּ לַאֲחֵיכֶם עַמִּי וְלַאֲחוֹתֵיכֶם רֻחָמָה:
ד רִיבוּ בְאִמְּכֶם רִיבוּ כִּי־הִיא לֹא אִשְׁתִּי וְאָנֹכִי לֹא אִישָׁהּ וְתָסֵר זְנוּנֶיהָ מִפָּנֶיהָ וְנַאֲפוּפֶיהָ מִבֵּין
ה שָׁדֶיהָ: פֶּן־אַפְשִׁיטֶנָּה עֲרֻמָּה וְהִצַּגְתִּיהָ כְּיוֹם הִוָּלְדָהּ וְשַׂמְתִּיהָ כַמִּדְבָּר וְשַׁתִּהָ כְּאֶרֶץ צִיָּה
ו ז וַהֲמִתִּיהָ בַּצָּמָא: וְאֶת־בָּנֶיהָ לֹא אֲרַחֵם כִּי־בְנֵי זְנוּנִים הֵמָּה: כִּי זָנְתָה אִמָּם הֹבִישָׁה הוֹרָתָם
ח כִּי אָמְרָה אֵלְכָה אַחֲרֵי מְאַהֲבַי נֹתְנֵי לַחְמִי וּמֵימַי צַמְרִי וּפִשְׁתִּי שַׁמְנִי וְשִׁקּוּיָי: לָכֵן הִנְנִי־שָׂךְ
ט אֶת־דַּרְכֵּךְ בַּסִּירִים וְגָדַרְתִּי אֶת־גְּדֵרָהּ וּנְתִיבוֹתֶיהָ לֹא תִמְצָא: וְרִדְּפָה אֶת־מְאַהֲבֶיהָ וְלֹא־
תַשִּׂיג אֹתָם וּבִקְשָׁתַם וְלֹא תִמְצָא וְאָמְרָה אֵלְכָה וְאָשׁוּבָה אֶל־אִישִׁי הָרִאשׁוֹן כִּי טוֹב לִי אָז
י מֵעָתָּה: וְהִיא לֹא יָדְעָה כִּי אָנֹכִי נָתַתִּי לָהּ הַדָּגָן וְהַתִּירוֹשׁ וְהַיִּצְהָר וְכֶסֶף הִרְבֵּיתִי לָהּ וְזָהָב
יא עָשׂוּ לַבָּעַל: לָכֵן אָשׁוּב וְלָקַחְתִּי דְגָנִי בְּעִתּוֹ וְתִירוֹשִׁי בְּמוֹעֲדוֹ וְהִצַּלְתִּי צַמְרִי וּפִשְׁתִּי לְכַסּוֹת
יב יג אֶת־עֶרְוָתָהּ: וְעַתָּה אֲגַלֶּה אֶת־נַבְלֻתָהּ לְעֵינֵי מְאַהֲבֶיהָ וְאִישׁ לֹא־יַצִּילֶנָּה מִיָּדִי: וְהִשְׁבַּתִּי
יד כָּל־מְשׂוֹשָׂהּ חַגָּהּ חָדְשָׁהּ וְשַׁבַּתָּהּ וְכֹל מוֹעֲדָהּ: וַהֲשִׁמֹּתִי גַּפְנָהּ וּתְאֵנָתָהּ אֲשֶׁר אָמְרָה אֶתְנָה
טו הֵמָּה לִי אֲשֶׁר נָתְנוּ־לִי מְאַהֲבָי וְשַׂמְתִּים לְיַעַר וַאֲכָלָתַם חַיַּת הַשָּׂדֶה: וּפָקַדְתִּי עָלֶיהָ אֶת־
יְמֵי הַבְּעָלִים אֲשֶׁר תַּקְטִיר לָהֶם וַתַּעַד נִזְמָהּ וְחֶלְיָתָהּ וַתֵּלֶךְ אַחֲרֵי מְאַהֲבֶיהָ וְאֹתִי שָׁכְחָה
טז יז נְאֻם־יְהוָה: לָכֵן הִנֵּה אָנֹכִי מְפַתֶּיהָ וְהֹלַכְתִּיהָ הַמִּדְבָּר וְדִבַּרְתִּי עַל־לִבָּהּ: וְנָתַתִּי
לָהּ אֶת־כְּרָמֶיהָ מִשָּׁם וְאֶת־עֵמֶק עָכוֹר לְפֶתַח תִּקְוָה וְעָנְתָה שָּׁמָּה כִּימֵי נְעוּרֶיהָ וּכְיוֹם עֲלֹתָהּ
יח מֵאֶרֶץ־מִצְרָיִם: וְהָיָה בַיּוֹם־הַהוּא נְאֻם־יְהוָה תִּקְרְאִי אִישִׁי וְלֹא־תִקְרְאִי־לִי עוֹד
יט כ בַּעְלִי: וַהֲסִרֹתִי אֶת־שְׁמוֹת הַבְּעָלִים מִפִּיהָ וְלֹא־יִזָּכְרוּ עוֹד בִּשְׁמָם: וְכָרַתִּי לָהֶם בְרִית בַּיּוֹם
הַהוּא עִם־חַיַּת הַשָּׂדֶה וְעִם־עוֹף הַשָּׁמַיִם וְרֶמֶשׂ הָאֲדָמָה וְקֶשֶׁת וְחֶרֶב וּמִלְחָמָה אֶשְׁבּוֹר
כא מִן־הָאָרֶץ וְהִשְׁכַּבְתִּים לָבֶטַח: וְאֵרַשְׂתִּיךְ לִי לְעוֹלָם וְאֵרַשְׂתִּיךְ לִי בְּצֶדֶק וּבְמִשְׁפָּט וּבְחֶסֶד
כב וּבְרַחֲמִים: וְאֵרַשְׂתִּיךְ לִי בֶּאֱמוּנָה וְיָדַעַתְּ אֶת־יְהוָה:

Haftara for
Naso

The Wondrous Birth of Samson
JUDGES 13:2–25

An angel of God informs a barren woman, Mano'ah's wife, of the future birth of a son, Samson, and the important historical role he will fulfill through his miraculous strength. This story shows how Samson's selection occurred under supernatural circumstances even before his birth.

13 2 There was a certain man from Tzora, from the family of the Danites, whose name was Mano'ah; his wife was barren and 3 had not given birth. The angel of the Lord appeared to the woman and said to her: Behold now, you are barren and have not given birth; but you will conceive, and you will give birth 4 to a son. Now, please beware, and do not drink wine or intoxi-5 cating drink, and do not eat any impurity. For behold, you will conceive and give birth to a son; a razor shall not come upon his head, for the lad will be a nazirite to God from the womb; and he will commence to save Israel from the hand of the 6 Philistines. The woman came and she told her husband, saying: A man of God came to me, and his appearance was like the appearance of an angel of God, very awesome; I did not ask him 7 from where he was, and he did not tell me his name. He said to me: Behold, you will conceive and give birth to a son. Now, do not drink wine or intoxicating drink, and do not eat any impurity, as the lad will be a nazirite to God from the womb until the 8 day of his death. Mano'ah entreated the Lord, and said: Please, my Lord, the man of God whom You sent, let him come again to us, and instruct us what we shall do with the child who will 9 be born. God heeded the voice of Mano'ah, and the angel of God came again to the woman; she was sitting in the field, and 10 Mano'ah her husband was not with her. The woman quickly ran and told her husband; she said to him: Behold, the man who 11 came to me on that day appeared to me. Mano'ah rose, went after his wife, came to the man, and said to him: Are you the 12 man who spoke to the woman? He said: I am. Mano'ah said: Now let your words come: What will be the arrangement for 13 the lad, and his actions? The angel of the Lord said to Mano'ah:

14 From everything that I said to the woman let her beware. She shall not partake from anything produced from the grapevine; she shall not drink wine or intoxicating drink, and she shall not eat any impurity; everything that I have commanded her, she 15 shall observe. Mano'ah said to the angel of the Lord: Please let 16 us detain you, and we will prepare a young goat before you. The angel of the Lord said to Mano'ah: If you detain me, I will not eat of your food. If you wish to prepare a burnt offering, offer it up to the Lord, for Mano'ah did not know that he was the 17 angel of the Lord. Mano'ah said to the angel of the Lord: What is your name so that when your words come to pass we may 18 honor you? The angel of the Lord said to him: Why do you ask 19 my name? It is my mystery. Mano'ah took the goat and the meal offering, and he offered it up on the rock to the Lord; he acted 20 wondrously, and Mano'ah and his wife were watching. It was with the ascension of the flame from upon the altar toward the heavens that the angel of the Lord went up in the flame of the altar. Mano'ah and his wife were watching, and they fell on their 21 faces to the ground. The angel of the Lord did not appear again to Mano'ah or to his wife; then Mano'ah knew that he was an 22 angel of the Lord. Mano'ah said to his wife: We will die, because 23 we have seen God. His wife said to him: Had the Lord wished to kill us, He would not have taken a burnt offering and a meal offering from our hand, and He would not have shown us all these, and He would not have told us tidings like these at this 24 time. The woman bore a son and she called his name Samson; 25 the lad grew and the Lord blessed him. The spirit of the Lord began to move him in the camp of Dan, between Tzora and Eshtaol.

הפטרת

נשא

יג ב ג וַיְהִי אִישׁ אֶחָד מִצָּרְעָה מִמִּשְׁפַּחַת הַדָּנִי וּשְׁמוֹ מָנוֹחַ וְאִשְׁתּוֹ עֲקָרָה וְלֹא יָלָדָה: וַיֵּרָא מַלְאַךְ־ שופטים
ד יהוה אֶל־הָאִשָּׁה וַיֹּאמֶר אֵלֶיהָ הִנֵּה־נָא אַתְּ־עֲקָרָה וְלֹא יָלַדְתְּ וְהָרִית וְיָלַדְתְּ בֵּן: וְעַתָּה
ה הִשָּׁמְרִי נָא וְאַל־תִּשְׁתִּי יַיִן וְשֵׁכָר וְאַל־תֹּאכְלִי כָּל־טָמֵא: כִּי הִנָּךְ הָרָה וְיֹלַדְתְּ בֵּן וּמוֹרָה לֹא־
יַעֲלֶה עַל־רֹאשׁוֹ כִּי־נְזִיר אֱלֹהִים יִהְיֶה הַנַּעַר מִן־הַבָּטֶן וְהוּא יָחֵל לְהוֹשִׁיעַ אֶת־יִשְׂרָאֵל מִיַּד
ו פְּלִשְׁתִּים: וַתָּבֹא הָאִשָּׁה וַתֹּאמֶר לְאִישָׁהּ לֵאמֹר אִישׁ הָאֱלֹהִים בָּא אֵלַי וּמַרְאֵהוּ כְּמַרְאֵה
ז מַלְאַךְ הָאֱלֹהִים נוֹרָא מְאֹד וְלֹא שְׁאִלְתִּיהוּ אֵי־מִזֶּה הוּא וְאֶת־שְׁמוֹ לֹא־הִגִּיד לִי: וַיֹּאמֶר לִי
הִנָּךְ הָרָה וְיֹלַדְתְּ בֵּן וְעַתָּה אַל־תִּשְׁתִּי ׀ יַיִן וְשֵׁכָר וְאַל־תֹּאכְלִי כָּל־טֻמְאָה כִּי־נְזִיר אֱלֹהִים
יִהְיֶה הַנַּעַר מִן־הַבֶּטֶן עַד־יוֹם מוֹתוֹ:
ח וַיֶּעְתַּר מָנוֹחַ אֶל־יהוה וַיֹּאמַר בִּי אֲדוֹנָי אִישׁ הָאֱלֹהִים אֲשֶׁר שָׁלַחְתָּ יָבוֹא־נָא עוֹד אֵלֵינוּ וְיוֹרֵנוּ
ט מַה־נַּעֲשֶׂה לַנַּעַר הַיּוּלָּד: וַיִּשְׁמַע הָאֱלֹהִים בְּקוֹל מָנוֹחַ וַיָּבֹא מַלְאַךְ הָאֱלֹהִים עוֹד אֶל־הָאִשָּׁה
י וְהִיא יוֹשֶׁבֶת בַּשָּׂדֶה וּמָנוֹחַ אִישָׁהּ אֵין עִמָּהּ: וַתְּמַהֵר הָאִשָּׁה וַתָּרָץ וַתַּגֵּד לְאִישָׁהּ וַתֹּאמֶר
יא אֵלָיו הִנֵּה נִרְאָה אֵלַי הָאִישׁ אֲשֶׁר־בָּא בַיּוֹם אֵלָי: וַיָּקָם וַיֵּלֶךְ מָנוֹחַ אַחֲרֵי אִשְׁתּוֹ וַיָּבֹא אֶל־
יב הָאִישׁ וַיֹּאמֶר לוֹ הַאַתָּה הָאִישׁ אֲשֶׁר־דִּבַּרְתָּ אֶל־הָאִשָּׁה וַיֹּאמֶר אָנִי: וַיֹּאמֶר מָנוֹחַ עַתָּה יָבֹא
יג דְבָרֶיךָ מַה־יִּהְיֶה מִשְׁפַּט־הַנַּעַר וּמַעֲשֵׂהוּ: וַיֹּאמֶר מַלְאַךְ יהוה אֶל־מָנוֹחַ מִכֹּל אֲשֶׁר־אָמַרְתִּי
יד אֶל־הָאִשָּׁה תִּשָּׁמֵר: מִכֹּל אֲשֶׁר־יֵצֵא מִגֶּפֶן הַיַּיִן לֹא תֹאכַל וְיַיִן וְשֵׁכָר אַל־תֵּשְׁתְּ וְכָל־טֻמְאָה
טו אַל־תֹּאכַל כֹּל אֲשֶׁר־צִוִּיתִיהָ תִּשְׁמֹר: וַיֹּאמֶר מָנוֹחַ אֶל־מַלְאַךְ יהוה נַעְצְרָה־נָּא אוֹתָךְ וְנַעֲשֶׂה
טז לְפָנֶיךָ גְּדִי עִזִּים: וַיֹּאמֶר מַלְאַךְ יהוה אֶל־מָנוֹחַ אִם־תַּעְצְרֵנִי לֹא־אֹכַל בְּלַחְמֶךָ וְאִם־תַּעֲשֶׂה
יז עֹלָה לַיהוה תַּעֲלֶנָּה כִּי לֹא־יָדַע מָנוֹחַ כִּי־מַלְאַךְ יהוה הוּא: וַיֹּאמֶר מָנוֹחַ אֶל־מַלְאַךְ יהוה מִי
יח שְׁמֶךָ כִּי־יָבֹא דבריך וְכִבַּדְנוּךָ: וַיֹּאמֶר לוֹ מַלְאַךְ יהוה לָמָּה זֶּה תִּשְׁאַל לִשְׁמִי וְהוּא־פֶלִאי: דְּבָרְךָ
יט וַיִּקַּח מָנוֹחַ אֶת־גְּדִי הָעִזִּים וְאֶת־הַמִּנְחָה וַיַּעַל עַל־הַצּוּר לַיהוה וּמַפְלִא לַעֲשׂוֹת וּמָנוֹחַ וְאִשְׁתּוֹ
כ רֹאִים: וַיְהִי בַעֲלוֹת הַלַּהַב מֵעַל הַמִּזְבֵּחַ הַשָּׁמַיְמָה וַיַּעַל מַלְאַךְ־יהוה בְּלַהַב הַמִּזְבֵּחַ וּמָנוֹחַ
כא וְאִשְׁתּוֹ רֹאִים וַיִּפְּלוּ עַל־פְּנֵיהֶם אָרְצָה: וְלֹא־יָסַף עוֹד מַלְאַךְ יהוה לְהֵרָאֹה אֶל־מָנוֹחַ וְאֶל־
כב אִשְׁתּוֹ אָז יָדַע מָנוֹחַ כִּי־מַלְאַךְ יהוה הוּא: וַיֹּאמֶר מָנוֹחַ אֶל־אִשְׁתּוֹ מוֹת נָמוּת כִּי אֱלֹהִים
כג רָאִינוּ: וַתֹּאמֶר לוֹ אִשְׁתּוֹ לוּ חָפֵץ יהוה לַהֲמִיתֵנוּ לֹא־לָקַח מִיָּדֵנוּ עֹלָה וּמִנְחָה וְלֹא הֶרְאָנוּ
כד אֶת־כָּל־אֵלֶּה וְכָעֵת לֹא הִשְׁמִיעָנוּ כָּזֹאת: וַתֵּלֶד הָאִשָּׁה בֵּן וַתִּקְרָא אֶת־שְׁמוֹ שִׁמְשׁוֹן וַיִּגְדַּל
כה הַנַּעַר וַיְבָרְכֵהוּ יהוה: וַתָּחֶל רוּחַ יהוה לְפַעֲמוֹ בְּמַחֲנֵה־דָן בֵּין צָרְעָה וּבֵין אֶשְׁתָּאֹל:

Haftara for
Behaalotekha

Visions of the Prophet Zechariah
ZECHARIAH 2:14–4:7

The candelabrum that Moses was shown on Mount Sinai is clearly related to this vision that Zechariah sees at the time of the construction of the Second Temple, which centers on a candelabrum. The *parasha* and the *haftara* share other themes as well, including the fitness of the priests appointed to perform the sacred service, God's rebuke of those who criticize His chosen ones, and the division and decentralization of the national leadership. The *haftara* recalls the traditional model of leadership in Israel, which was split between the priests, the descendants of Aaron, such as Yehoshua the High Priest, and the political rulers from the house of David, such as Zerubavel.

At the time of this prophecy, the city of Jerusalem is desolate, sparsely inhabited, and surrounded by hostile peoples. The prophet Zechariah, who is probably one of the few to immigrate from Babylonia to Israel with Zerubavel after the declaration of Cyrus, offers words of support to Yehoshua the High Priest and Zerubavel, and perhaps through them to the residents of Jerusalem in general. He encourages the building of the Temple and declares to the people of Jerusalem that in the future the city will be restored to its position of greatness.

2 14 Sing and rejoice, daughter of Zion, for here I come and I will
15 dwell in your midst – the utterance of the Lord. Many nations will accompany the Lord on that day, and they will become My people, and I will dwell in your midst, and you will know that
16 the Lord of hosts sent me to you. The Lord will bequeath his portion to Judah on the sacred land, and He will again choose
17 Jerusalem. Hush, all flesh, before the Lord, for He is roused
3 1 from His abode of sanctity. He showed me Yehoshua the High Priest, standing before the angel of the Lord and the accuser
2 standing on his right to accuse him. The Lord said to the accuser: May the Lord rebuke you, the accuser, and may the Lord who has chosen Jerusalem rebuke you. Is this not a firebrand
3 salvaged from the fire? Yehoshua was clothed in filthy garments
4 and standing before the angel. He responded and said to those standing before him, saying: Remove the filthy garments from upon him. He said to him: Behold, I have removed your iniq-
5 uity from upon you and have clothed you in clean garments. I said: Let them place a pure turban on his head. They placed the pure turban on his head and clothed him with garments and the
6 angel of the Lord was standing. The angel of the Lord warned
7 Yehoshua, saying: So said the Lord of hosts: If you follow My ways, and if you keep My commission and judge My house as well as guard My courtyards, I will set you walking among these

8 standing. Hear now, Yehoshua the High Priest, you and your colleagues who sit before you, as they are men of distinction,
9 for behold, I bring My servant, Zemah. For behold, the stone that I placed before Yehoshua has seven hues on one stone; behold, I am engraving its etching – the utterance of the Lord of hosts – and I will remove the iniquity of that land in one day.
10 On that day – the utterance of the Lord of hosts – each of you will invite his neighbor beneath the vine and beneath the fig
4 1 tree. The angel that spoke with me returned and woke me like
2 a man that is awakened from his sleep. He said to me: What do you see? I said: I saw, and behold, a candelabrum of gold in its entirety, with a bowl on its top and its seven lamps on it. There
3 are seven pipes for each of the lamps that are on its top. Two olive trees are over it, one on the right of the bowl, and one on
4 its left. I answered and said to the angel that spoke with me,
5 saying: What are these, my lord? The angel that spoke with me responded and said to me: Don't you know what these are? And
6 I said: No, my lord. He responded and said to me, saying: This is the word of the Lord to Zerubavel, saying: Not by might, and
7 not by power, but by My spirit, said the Lord of hosts. Who are you, great mountain? Before Zerubavel you will become a plain. He will take out the keystone, with shouts of: Grace, grace, to it.

זכריה

ב יד רָנִּי וְשִׂמְחִי בַּת־צִיּוֹן כִּי הִנְנִי־בָא וְשָׁכַנְתִּי בְתוֹכֵךְ נְאֻם־יְהֹוָה: וְנִלְווּ גוֹיִם רַבִּים אֶל־יְהֹוָה

טו בַּיּוֹם הַהוּא וְהָיוּ לִי לְעָם וְשָׁכַנְתִּי בְתוֹכֵךְ וְיָדַעַתְּ כִּי־יְהֹוָה צְבָאוֹת שְׁלָחַנִי אֵלָיִךְ: וְנָחַל יְהֹוָה

יז אֶת־יְהוּדָה חֶלְקוֹ עַל אַדְמַת הַקֹּדֶשׁ וּבָחַר עוֹד בִּירוּשָׁלָ͏ִם: הַס כָּל־בָּשָׂר מִפְּנֵי יְהֹוָה כִּי נֵעוֹר

ג א מִמְּעוֹן קָדְשׁוֹ: וַיַּרְאֵנִי אֶת־יְהוֹשֻׁעַ הַכֹּהֵן הַגָּדוֹל עֹמֵד לִפְנֵי מַלְאַךְ יְהֹוָה וְהַשָּׂטָן

ב עֹמֵד עַל־יְמִינוֹ לְשִׂטְנוֹ: וַיֹּאמֶר יְהֹוָה אֶל־הַשָּׂטָן יִגְעַר יְהֹוָה בְּךָ הַשָּׂטָן וְיִגְעַר יְהֹוָה בְּךָ הַבֹּחֵר

בִּירוּשָׁלָ͏ִם הֲלוֹא זֶה אוּד מֻצָּל מֵאֵשׁ: וִיהוֹשֻׁעַ הָיָה לָבֻשׁ בְּגָדִים צוֹאִים וְעֹמֵד לִפְנֵי הַמַּלְאָךְ:

ד וַיַּעַן וַיֹּאמֶר אֶל־הָעֹמְדִים לְפָנָיו לֵאמֹר הָסִירוּ הַבְּגָדִים הַצֹּאִים מֵעָלָיו וַיֹּאמֶר אֵלָיו רְאֵה

ה הֶעֱבַרְתִּי מֵעָלֶיךָ עֲוֺנֶךָ וְהַלְבֵּשׁ אֹתְךָ מַחֲלָצוֹת: וָאֹמַר יָשִׂימוּ צָנִיף טָהוֹר עַל־רֹאשׁוֹ וַיָּשִׂימוּ

הַצָּנִיף הַטָּהוֹר עַל־רֹאשׁוֹ וַיַּלְבִּשֻׁהוּ בְּגָדִים וּמַלְאַךְ יְהֹוָה עֹמֵד: וַיָּעַד מַלְאַךְ יְהֹוָה בִּיהוֹשֻׁעַ

ז לֵאמֹר: כֹּה־אָמַר יְהֹוָה צְבָאוֹת אִם־בִּדְרָכַי תֵּלֵךְ וְאִם אֶת־מִשְׁמַרְתִּי תִשְׁמֹר וְגַם־אַתָּה תָּדִין

ח אֶת־בֵּיתִי וְגַם תִּשְׁמֹר אֶת־חֲצֵרָי וְנָתַתִּי לְךָ מַהְלְכִים בֵּין הָעֹמְדִים הָאֵלֶּה: שְׁמַע־נָא יְהוֹשֻׁעַ

הַכֹּהֵן הַגָּדוֹל אַתָּה וְרֵעֶיךָ הַיֹּשְׁבִים לְפָנֶיךָ כִּי־אַנְשֵׁי מוֹפֵת הֵמָּה כִּי־הִנְנִי מֵבִיא אֶת־עַבְדִּי

ט צֶמַח: כִּי הִנֵּה הָאֶבֶן אֲשֶׁר נָתַתִּי לִפְנֵי יְהוֹשֻׁעַ עַל־אֶבֶן אַחַת שִׁבְעָה עֵינָיִם הִנְנִי מְפַתֵּחַ פִּתֻּחָהּ

נְאֻם יְהֹוָה צְבָאוֹת וּמַשְׁתִּי אֶת־עֲוֺן הָאָרֶץ־הַהִיא בְּיוֹם אֶחָד: בַּיּוֹם הַהוּא נְאֻם יְהֹוָה צְבָאוֹת

ד א תִּקְרְאוּ אִישׁ לְרֵעֵהוּ אֶל־תַּחַת גֶּפֶן וְאֶל־תַּחַת תְּאֵנָה: וַיָּשָׁב הַמַּלְאָךְ הַדֹּבֵר בִּי

ב וַיְעִירֵנִי כְּאִישׁ אֲשֶׁר־יֵעוֹר מִשְּׁנָתוֹ: וַיֹּאמֶר אֵלַי מָה אַתָּה רֹאֶה וָיֹּאמַר רָאִיתִי וְהִנֵּה מְנוֹרַת וָאֹמַר

זָהָב כֻּלָּהּ וְגֻלָּהּ עַל־רֹאשָׁהּ וְשִׁבְעָה נֵרֹתֶיהָ עָלֶיהָ שִׁבְעָה וְשִׁבְעָה מוּצָקוֹת לַנֵּרוֹת אֲשֶׁר עַל־

ג רֹאשָׁהּ: וּשְׁנַיִם זֵיתִים עָלֶיהָ אֶחָד מִימִין הַגֻּלָּה וְאֶחָד עַל־שְׂמֹאלָהּ: וָאַעַן וָאֹמַר אֶל־הַמַּלְאָךְ

ה הַדֹּבֵר בִּי לֵאמֹר מָה־אֵלֶּה אֲדֹנִי: וַיַּעַן הַמַּלְאָךְ הַדֹּבֵר בִּי וַיֹּאמֶר אֵלַי הֲלוֹא יָדַעְתָּ מָה־הֵמָּה

אֵלֶּה וָאֹמַר לֹא אֲדֹנִי: וַיַּעַן וַיֹּאמֶר אֵלַי לֵאמֹר זֶה דְּבַר־יְהֹוָה אֶל־זְרֻבָּבֶל לֵאמֹר לֹא בְחַיִל וְלֹא

בְכֹחַ כִּי אִם־בְּרוּחִי אָמַר יְהֹוָה צְבָאוֹת: מִי־אַתָּה הַר־הַגָּדוֹל לִפְנֵי זְרֻבָּבֶל לְמִישֹׁר וְהוֹצִיא

אֶת־הָאֶבֶן הָרֹאשָׁה תְּשֻׁאוֹת חֵן ׀ חֵן לָהּ:

Haftara for **Shelah**

The Spies in Jericho

JOSHUA 2:1–24

Joshua's first major act as leader is to send spies to the land of Canaan. These spies are not sent specifically to strategic locations for the conquest of Jericho. In fact, the two men are not assigned any specific practical task. Rather, their mission is to evaluate the morale and fighting spirit of the local population. None of the inhabitants of the land knew when Israel would enter their territory, or where the Israelites would go once they crossed the Jordan. Presumably, the residents of Jericho did not think that their fortified city would be the first to be attacked. Although Joshua proceeds with the assurance of divine assistance, which would include miraculous intervention, he requires inside information regarding the mindset of the people of Jericho and the other inhabitants of the land in order to properly assess the strength of the resistance he could anticipate (see also commentary of Rabbi Yaakov Fidanque, editor of the books of Abravanel).

2 1 Joshua son of Nun sent two men from Shitim as spies, covertly,
saying: Go see the land and Jericho. They went and they came
to the house of a prostitute; her name was Rahav, and they
2 lodged there. It was said to the king of Jericho, saying: Behold,
men came here tonight from the children of Israel to spy the
3 land. The king of Jericho sent to Rahav, saying: Bring out the
men who came to you, who came to your house, as they came
4 to reconnoiter the land. The woman took the two men and hid
them; she said: Yes, the men came to me, but I did not know
5 from where they were. It was when the gate was about to close
at dark that the men departed; I do not know where the men
went; pursue quickly after them, as you will overtake them.
6 But she took them up to the roof and hid them in the stalks of
7 flax that were arranged for her on the roof. The men pursued
after them toward the Jordan, to the fords, and they shut the
8 gate after them when the pursuers departed after them. As for
them, before they had gone to sleep, she went up to them on
9 the roof. She said to the men: I know that the Lord has given
you the land, and that dread of you has fallen upon us, and that
10 all the inhabitants of the land have melted from before you. For
we have heard how the Lord dried the water of the Red Sea for
you upon your exodus from Egypt, and that which you did to
the two kings of the Emorites, who are beyond the Jordan, to
11 Sihon and to Og, whom you utterly destroyed. We heard and
our hearts melted, and spirit did not remain in any man because
of you, because the Lord your God, He is God in the heavens
12 above, and on earth below. Now, please take an oath to me by
the Lord, since I have done kindness to you, you too will do
kindness to my father's house; provide me with a reliable sign
13 that you will keep alive my father, my mother, my brothers, my
sisters, and everything that is theirs, and save our lives from
14 death. The men said to her: Our lives are instead of yours to die,
if you do not tell of these matters of ours; it shall be, when the
Lord gives us the land, we will act with kindness and truth to
15 you. She lowered them with a rope through the window, as her
16 house was at the side of the wall, and she lived in the wall. She
said to them: Go to the highlands, lest the pursuers encounter you. Hide there three days, until the pursuers return, and
17 then go on your way. The men said to her: We are absolved of
18 this oath of yours that you administered to us. Behold, when
we come into the land, you will tie this cord of scarlet thread
in the window through which you lowered us, and your father,
your mother, your brothers, and your father's entire household
19 you will gather to you, into the house. It shall be, that anyone
who will exit from the doors of your house outside, his blood
shall be on his head, and we will be absolved. But anyone who
will be with you in the house, his blood shall be on our head, if
20 a hand will be upon him. But if you tell of these matters of ours,
we will be absolved of your oath that you administered to us.
21 She said: In accordance with your words, so it is. She sent them
22 and they went and she tied the scarlet cord in the window. They
went and came to the highlands and stayed there three days,
until the pursuers returned; the pursuers sought them along
23 the entire way, but they did not find. The two men returned,
and descended from the highlands, and crossed, and came to
Joshua son of Nun. They told him all that had befallen them.
24 They said to Joshua: For the Lord has given the entire land into
our hands, and also, all the inhabitants of the land have melted
before us.

הפטרת
שלח

יהושע

א וַיִּשְׁלַ֣ח יְהוֹשֻֽׁעַ־בִּן־נ֠וּן מִֽן־הַשִּׁטִּ֞ים שְׁנַֽיִם־אֲנָשִׁ֤ים מְרַגְּלִים֙ חֶ֔רֶשׁ לֵאמֹ֔ר לְכ֛וּ רְא֥וּ אֶת־הָאָ֖רֶץ
ב וְאֶת־יְרִיח֑וֹ וַיֵּ֨לְכ֜וּ וַ֠יָּבֹ֠אוּ בֵּֽית־אִשָּׁ֥ה זוֹנָ֛ה וּשְׁמָ֥הּ רָחָ֖ב וַיִּשְׁכְּבוּ־שָֽׁמָּה: וַיֵּ֣אָמַ֔ר לְמֶ֥לֶךְ יְרִיח֖וֹ לֵאמֹ֑ר
ג הִנֵּ֣ה אֲ֠נָשִׁ֠ים בָּ֣אוּ הֵ֧נָּה הַלַּ֛יְלָה מִבְּנֵ֥י יִשְׂרָאֵ֖ל לַחְפֹּ֥ר אֶת־הָאָֽרֶץ: וַיִּשְׁלַח֙ מֶ֣לֶךְ יְרִיח֔וֹ אֶל־רָחָ֖ב
ד לֵאמֹ֑ר ה֠וֹצִ֠יאִי הָאֲנָשִׁ֤ים הַבָּאִים֙ אֵלַ֔יִךְ אֲשֶׁר־בָּ֣אוּ לְבֵיתֵ֔ךְ כִּ֛י לַחְפֹּ֥ר אֶת־כָּל־הָאָ֖רֶץ בָּֽאוּ: וַתִּקַּ֣ח
ה הָאִשָּׁ֗ה אֶת־שְׁנֵ֧י הָאֲנָשִׁ֛ים וַֽתִּצְפְּנ֑וֹ וַתֹּ֣אמֶר ׀ כֵּ֗ן בָּ֤אוּ אֵלַי֙ הָֽאֲנָשִׁ֔ים וְלֹ֥א יָדַ֖עְתִּי מֵאַ֥יִן הֵֽמָּה: וַיְהִ֨י
הַשַּׁ֜עַר לִסְגּ֗וֹר בַּחֹ֨שֶׁךְ֙ וְהָֽאֲנָשִׁ֣ים יָצָ֔אוּ לֹ֣א יָדַ֔עְתִּי אָ֥נָה הָלְכ֖וּ הָֽאֲנָשִׁ֑ים רִדְפ֥וּ מַהֵ֛ר אַחֲרֵיהֶ֖ם כִּ֥י
ו תַשִּׂיגֽוּם: וְהִ֖יא הֶעֱלָ֣תַם הַגָּ֑גָה וַֽתִּטְמְנֵם֙ בְּפִשְׁתֵּ֣י הָעֵ֔ץ הָעֲרֻכ֥וֹת לָ֖הּ עַל־הַגָּֽג: וְהָֽאֲנָשִׁ֗ים רָדְפ֤וּ
ז אַֽחֲרֵיהֶם֙ דֶּ֣רֶךְ הַיַּרְדֵּ֔ן עַ֖ל הַֽמַּעְבְּר֑וֹת וְהַשַּׁ֣עַר סָגָ֔רוּ אַחֲרֵ֕י כַּֽאֲשֶׁ֛ר יָצְא֥וּ הָרֹדְפִ֖ים אַחֲרֵיהֶֽם:
ח וְהֵ֖מָּה טֶ֣רֶם יִשְׁכָּב֑וּן וְהִ֛יא עָלְתָ֥ה עֲלֵיהֶ֖ם עַל־הַגָּֽג: וַתֹּ֙אמֶר֙ אֶל־הָ֣אֲנָשִׁ֔ים יָדַ֕עְתִּי כִּֽי־נָתַ֧ן יְהוָ֛ה
י לָכֶ֖ם אֶת־הָאָ֑רֶץ וְכִֽי־נָפְלָ֤ה אֵֽימַתְכֶם֙ עָלֵ֔ינוּ וְכִ֥י נָמֹ֛גוּ כָּל־יֹשְׁבֵ֥י הָאָ֖רֶץ מִפְּנֵיכֶֽם: כִּ֣י שָׁמַ֗עְנוּ אֵ֠ת
אֲשֶׁר־הוֹבִ֨ישׁ יְהוָ֜ה אֶת־מֵ֤י יַם־סוּף֙ מִפְּנֵיכֶ֔ם בְּצֵאתְכֶ֖ם מִמִּצְרָ֑יִם וַאֲשֶׁ֣ר עֲשִׂיתֶ֗ם לִשְׁנֵי֙ מַלְכֵ֣י
יא הָֽאֱמֹרִ֗י אֲשֶׁ֤ר בְּעֵ֣בֶר הַיַּרְדֵּ֔ן לְסִיחֹ֖ן וּלְע֑וֹג אֲשֶׁ֥ר הֶחֱרַמְתֶּ֖ם אוֹתָֽם: וַנִּשְׁמַע֙ וַיִּמַּ֣ס לְבָבֵ֔נוּ וְלֹא־קָ֨מָה
ע֥וֹד ר֙וּחַ֙ בְּאִ֔ישׁ מִפְּנֵיכֶ֑ם כִּ֚י יְהוָ֣ה אֱלֹֽהֵיכֶ֔ם ה֤וּא אֱלֹהִים֙ בַּשָּׁמַ֣יִם מִמַּ֔עַל וְעַל־הָאָ֖רֶץ מִתָּֽחַת:
יב וְעַתָּ֗ה הִשָּֽׁבְעוּ־נָ֥א לִי֙ בַּֽיהוָ֔ה כִּֽי־עָשִׂ֥יתִי עִמָּכֶ֖ם חָ֑סֶד וַעֲשִׂיתֶ֙ם גַּם־אַתֶּ֜ם עִם־בֵּ֤ית אָבִי֙ חֶ֔סֶד
יג אֲחִיוֹתַי וּנְתַתֶּ֥ם לִ֖י א֣וֹת אֱמֶֽת: וְהַחֲיִתֶ֞ם אֶת־אָבִ֣י וְאֶת־אִמִּ֗י וְאֶת־אַחַי֙ וְאֶת־אַחְיוֹתַ֔י וְאֵ֖ת כָּל־אֲשֶׁ֣ר
יד לָהֶ֑ם וְהִצַּלְתֶּ֥ם אֶת־נַפְשֹׁתֵ֖ינוּ מִמָּֽוֶת: וַיֹּ֧אמְרוּ לָ֣הּ הָאֲנָשִׁ֗ים נַפְשֵׁ֤נוּ תַחְתֵּיכֶם֙ לָמ֔וּת אִ֠ם לֹ֣א
טו תַגִּ֜ידוּ אֶת־דְּבָרֵ֣נוּ זֶ֑ה וְהָיָ֗ה בְּתֵת־יְהוָ֥ה לָ֙נוּ֙ אֶת־הָאָ֔רֶץ וְעָשִׂ֥ינוּ עִמָּ֖ךְ חֶ֥סֶד וֶאֱמֶֽת: וַתּוֹרִדֵ֥ם
טז בַּחֶ֛בֶל בְּעַ֥ד הַחַלּ֖וֹן כִּ֣י בֵיתָ֔הּ בְּקִ֣יר הַֽחוֹמָ֔ה וּבַֽחוֹמָ֖ה הִ֥יא יוֹשָֽׁבֶת: וַתֹּ֤אמֶר לָהֶם֙ הָהָ֣רָה לֵּ֔כוּ
פֶּֽן־יִפְגְּע֥וּ בָכֶ֖ם הָרֹֽדְפִ֑ים וְנַחְבֵּתֶ֨ם שָׁ֜מָּה שְׁלֹ֣שֶׁת יָמִ֗ים עַ֚ד שׁ֣וֹב הָרֹֽדְפִ֔ים וְאַחַ֖ר תֵּלְכ֥וּ לְדַרְכְּכֶֽם:
יז וַיֹּאמְר֤וּ אֵלֶ֙יהָ֙ הָאֲנָשִׁ֔ים נְקִיִּ֣ם אֲנַ֔חְנוּ מִשְּׁבֻעָתֵ֥ךְ הַזֶּ֖ה אֲשֶׁ֣ר הִשְׁבַּעְתָּֽנוּ: הִנֵּ֛ה אֲנַ֥חְנוּ בָאִ֖ים
בָּאָ֑רֶץ אֶת־תִּקְוַ֡ת חוּט֩ הַשָּׁנִ֨י הַזֶּ֜ה תִּקְשְׁרִ֗י בַּֽחַלּוֹן֙ אֲשֶׁ֣ר הוֹרַדְתֵּ֣נוּ ב֔וֹ וְאֶת־אָבִ֥יךְ וְאֶת־אִמֵּ֛ךְ
יט וְאֶת־אַחַ֗יִךְ וְאֵת֙ כָּל־בֵּ֣ית אָבִ֔יךְ תַּאַסְפִ֥י אֵלַ֖יִךְ הַבָּֽיְתָה: וְהָיָ֡ה כֹּ֣ל אֲשֶׁר־יֵצֵא֩ מִדַּלְתֵ֨י בֵיתֵ֤ךְ ׀
הַח֨וּצָה֙ דָּמ֣וֹ בְרֹאשׁ֔וֹ וַאֲנַ֖חְנוּ נְקִיִּ֑ם וְ֠כֹ֠ל אֲשֶׁ֨ר יִֽהְיֶ֤ה אִתָּךְ֙ בַּבַּ֔יִת דָּמ֣וֹ בְרֹאשֵׁ֔נוּ אִם־יָ֖ד תִּֽהְיֶה־
כ בּֽוֹ: וְאִם־תַּגִּ֖ידִי אֶת־דְּבָרֵ֣נוּ זֶ֑ה וְהָיִ֣ינוּ נְקִיִּ֔ם מִשְּׁבֻעָתֵ֖ךְ אֲשֶׁ֥ר הִשְׁבַּעְתָּֽנוּ: וַתֹּ֙אמֶר֙ כְּדִבְרֵיכֶ֣ם
כב כֶּן־ה֔וּא וַֽתְּשַׁלְּחֵ֖ם וַיֵּלֵ֑כוּ וַתִּקְשֹׁ֥ר אֶת־תִּקְוַ֥ת הַשָּׁנִ֖י בַּֽחַלּֽוֹן: וַיֵּלְכוּ֙ וַיָּבֹ֣אוּ הָהָ֔רָה וַיֵּ֥שְׁבוּ שָׁ֖ם
שְׁלֹ֣שֶׁת יָמִ֗ים עַד־שָׁ֙בוּ֙ הָרֹ֣דְפִ֔ים וַיְבַקְשׁ֧וּ הָרֹדְפִ֛ים בְּכָל־הַדֶּ֖רֶךְ וְלֹ֥א מָצָֽאוּ: וַיָּשֻׁ֜בוּ שְׁנֵ֤י הָֽאֲנָשִׁים֙
כד וַיֵּרְד֣וּ מֵֽהָהָ֔ר וַיַּעַבְרוּ֙ וַיָּבֹ֔אוּ אֶל־יְהוֹשֻׁ֖עַ בִּן־נ֑וּן וַֽיְסַפְּרוּ־ל֔וֹ אֵ֥ת כָּל־הַמֹּצְא֖וֹת אוֹתָֽם: וַיֹּאמְרוּ֙
אֶל־יְהוֹשֻׁ֔עַ כִּֽי־נָתַ֧ן יְהוָ֛ה בְּיָדֵ֖נוּ אֶת־כָּל־הָאָ֑רֶץ וְגַם־נָמֹ֛גוּ כָּל־יֹשְׁבֵ֥י הָאָ֖רֶץ מִפָּנֵֽינוּ:

Haftara for
Korah

Samuel's Historical Address to the People

I SAMUEL 11:14–12:22

After the renewal of the kingdom of Saul, with the consent of all the people, Samuel retires from political leadership. In his last speech to the people, which begins with personal matters, the prophet offers a general historical survey of Israel, and delivers his last spiritual testament with regard to fundamental and moral aspects of the concept of the monarchy.

In the *parasha*, those who rebelled against the concentration of leadership roles in the wilderness were rejected and punished. By contrast, in the *haftara* the people's request for monarchical rule in their land receives a positive response from God, despite the fact that the appointment of a king is contrary to the wishes of Samuel who, according to the tradition of the Sages, was a descendant of Korah (see Malbim). In both cases, the leader at that time testified to his personal integrity and incorruptibility, and his claim was affirmed by a sign from heaven.

11 14 Samuel said to the people: Come, let us go to Gilgal, and renew 15 there the kingdom. The entire people went to Gilgal, and they crowned Saul king there before the Lord in Gilgal; and there they slaughtered peace offerings before the Lord; and Saul and **12** 1 all the men of Israel rejoiced greatly there. Samuel said to all Israel: Behold, I have heeded your voice, to everything that you 2 said to me, and I have crowned a king over you. Now behold, the king is walking before you and I have grown old and gray and my sons are here with you. I have walked before you from 3 my youth to this day. Here I am; testify against me before the Lord, and before His anointed: Whose ox did I take? Whose donkey did I take? Whom did I exploit? Whom did I pressure? From whose hand did I take a bribe to avert my eyes from him? 4 I will return it to you. They said: You did not exploit us, and you did not pressure us, and you did not take anything from the 5 hand of any man. He said to them: The Lord is witness against you, and His anointed is witness this day, that you did not find 6 anything in my hand. They said: Witness. Samuel said to the people: It is the Lord who appointed Moses and Aaron, and 7 who took your fathers up from the land of Egypt. Now stand and I will clarify with you before the Lord all the righteous acts of the Lord that He performed with you and with your fore- 8 fathers. When Jacob came to Egypt, your forefathers called to the Lord, and the Lord sent Moses and Aaron, and they took your forefathers out of Egypt, and he settled them in this place. 9 They forgot the Lord their God, and He delivered them into the hand of Sisera, commander of the army of Hatzor, and into the hand of the Philistines, and into the hand of the king of 10 Moav, and they made war on them. They called to the Lord, and said: We have sinned, for we have forsaken the Lord, and we worshipped the Be'alim and the Ashtarot; but now, deliver

11 us from the hand of our enemies, and we will worship You. The Lord sent Yerubaal, Bedan, Yiftaḥ, and Samuel, and He rescued you from the hand of your enemies around, and you lived in 12 security. You saw that Naḥash, king of the children of Amon, came upon you, and you said to me: No, but a king will reign 13 over us; but the Lord your God is your king. Now, behold the king whom you have chosen, and whom you have requested; 14 and behold, the Lord has placed a king over you. If you will fear the Lord, serve Him, heed His voice, and not defy the directive of the Lord, both you and the king who reigns over you will 15 follow the Lord your God. But if you will not heed the voice of the Lord, and you will defy the directive of the Lord, the hand 16 of the Lord will be against you, and against your fathers. Now stand and see this great thing that the Lord performs before 17 your eyes. Is it not wheat harvest today? I will call to the Lord and He will give thunder and rain, and you will know and see that your wickedness that you have done in requesting a king 18 for yourselves is great in the eyes of the Lord. Samuel called to the Lord, and the Lord gave thunder and rain that day, and 19 all the people greatly feared the Lord and Samuel. The entire people said to Samuel: Pray on behalf of your servants to the Lord your God and we will not die, for we have added evil upon 20 all our sins, to request a king for ourselves. Samuel said to the people: Do not fear; you have performed all this wickedness, but do not turn away from following the Lord, and worship the 21 Lord with all your heart. Do not turn away, for it is following nothingness that is ineffective and cannot bring deliverance be- 22 cause it is nothingness. For the Lord will not forsake His people for the sake of His great name, as the Lord decided to make you His people.

קרח

יא יד וַיֹּ֤אמֶר שְׁמוּאֵל֙ אֶל־הָעָ֔ם לְכ֖וּ וְנֵלְכָ֣ה הַגִּלְגָּ֑ל וּנְחַדֵּ֥שׁ שָׁ֖ם הַמְּלוּכָֽה: וַיֵּלְכ֨וּ כָל־הָעָ֜ם הַגִּלְגָּ֗ל

וַיַּמְלִכוּ֩ שָׁ֨ם אֶת־שָׁא֜וּל לִפְנֵ֤י יְהֹוָה֙ בַּגִּלְגָּ֔ל וַיִּזְבְּחוּ־שָׁ֛ם זְבָחִ֥ים שְׁלָמִ֖ים לִפְנֵ֣י יְהֹוָ֑ה וַיִּשְׂמַ֣ח שָׁ֗ם

שָׁא֛וּל וְכָל־אַנְשֵׁ֥י יִשְׂרָאֵ֖ל עַד־מְאֹֽד: יב א וַיֹּ֤אמֶר שְׁמוּאֵל֙ אֶל־כָּל־יִשְׂרָאֵ֔ל הִנֵּה֙ שָׁמַ֣עְתִּי

ב בְקֹֽלְכֶ֔ם לְכֹ֥ל אֲשֶׁר־אֲמַרְתֶּ֖ם לִ֑י וָאַמְלִ֥יךְ עֲלֵיכֶ֖ם מֶֽלֶךְ: וְעַתָּ֞ה הִנֵּ֥ה הַמֶּ֣לֶךְ ׀ מִתְהַלֵּ֣ךְ לִפְנֵיכֶ֗ם

ג וַֽאֲנִ֤י זָקַ֨נְתִּי֙ וָשַׂ֔בְתִּי וּבָנַ֖י הִנָּ֣ם אִתְּכֶ֑ם וַֽאֲנִי֙ הִתְהַלַּ֣כְתִּי לִפְנֵיכֶ֔ם מִנְּעֻרַ֖י עַד־הַיּ֣וֹם הַזֶּ֑ה הִנְנִ֣י עֲנ֣וּ

בִ֡י נֶ֩גֶד֩ יְהֹוָ֨ה וְנֶ֜גֶד מְשִׁיח֗וֹ אֶת־שׁוֹר֩ ׀ מִ֨י לָקַ֜חְתִּי וַֽחֲמ֧וֹר מִ֣י לָקַ֗חְתִּי וְאֶת־מִ֤י עָשַׁ֨קְתִּי֙ אֶת־מִ֣י

ד רַצּ֔וֹתִי וּמִיַּד־מִ֣י לָקַ֤חְתִּי כֹ֨פֶר֙ וְאַעְלִ֣ים עֵינַ֖י בּ֑וֹ וְאָשִׁ֖יב לָכֶֽם: וַיֹּ֣אמְר֔וּ לֹ֥א עֲשַׁקְתָּ֖נוּ וְלֹ֣א רַצּוֹתָ֑נוּ

ה וְלֹֽא־לָקַ֥חְתָּ מִיַּד־אִ֖ישׁ מְאֽוּמָה: וַיֹּ֨אמֶר אֲלֵיהֶ֜ם עֵ֧ד יְהֹוָ֣ה בָּכֶ֗ם וְעֵ֤ד מְשִׁיחוֹ֙ הַיּ֣וֹם הַזֶּ֔ה כִּ֣י לֹ֤א

ו מְצָאתֶם֙ בְּיָדִ֣י מְא֔וּמָה וַיֹּ֖אמֶר עֵֽד: וַיֹּ֥אמֶר שְׁמוּאֵ֖ל אֶל־הָעָ֑ם יְהֹוָ֗ה אֲשֶׁ֤ר עָשָׂה֙

ז אֶת־מֹשֶׁ֣ה וְאֶֽת־אַֽהֲרֹ֔ן וַֽאֲשֶׁ֧ר הֶֽעֱלָ֛ה אֶת־אֲבֹֽתֵיכֶ֖ם מֵאֶ֣רֶץ מִצְרָ֑יִם: וְעַתָּ֗ה הִֽתְיַצְּב֛וּ וְאִשָּֽׁפְטָ֥ה

אִתְּכֶ֖ם לִפְנֵ֣י יְהֹוָ֑ה אֵ֚ת כָּל־צִדְק֣וֹת יְהֹוָ֔ה אֲשֶׁר־עָשָׂ֥ה אִתְּכֶ֖ם וְאֶת־אֲבֽוֹתֵיכֶֽם: ח כַּאֲשֶׁר־בָּ֣א יַֽעֲקֹב֮

מִצְרָיִם֒ וַיִּזְעֲק֤וּ אֲבֽוֹתֵיכֶם֙ אֶל־יְהֹוָ֔ה וַיִּשְׁלַ֨ח יְהֹוָ֜ה אֶת־מֹשֶׁ֣ה וְאֶֽת־אַֽהֲרֹ֗ן וַיּוֹצִ֨יאוּ֙ אֶת־אֲבֹֽתֵיכֶם֙

ט מִמִּצְרַ֔יִם וַיֹּֽשִׁב֖וּם בַּמָּק֥וֹם הַזֶּֽה: וַֽיִּשְׁכְּח֖וּ אֶת־יְהֹוָ֣ה אֱלֹֽהֵיהֶ֑ם וַיִּמְכֹּ֣ר אֹתָ֡ם בְּיַ֣ד סִֽיסְרָא֩ שַׂר־צְבָ֨א

חָצ֜וֹר וּבְיַד־פְּלִשְׁתִּ֗ים וּבְיַד֙ מֶ֣לֶךְ מוֹאָ֔ב וַיִּֽלָּחֲמ֖וּ בָּֽם: י וַיִּזְעֲק֤וּ אֶל־יְהֹוָה֙ וַיֹּאמְר֣וּ חָטָ֔אנוּ כִּ֤י עָזַ֨בְנוּ֙

יא אֶת־יְהֹוָ֔ה וַנַּֽעֲבֹ֥ד אֶת־הַבְּעָלִ֖ים וְאֶת־הָֽעַשְׁתָּר֑וֹת וְעַתָּ֗ה הַצִּילֵ֛נוּ מִיַּ֥ד אֹֽיְבֵ֖ינוּ וְנַֽעַבְדֶֽךָּ: וַיִּשְׁלַ֤ח

יְהֹוָה֙ אֶת־יְרֻבַּ֣עַל וְאֶת־בְּדָ֔ן וְאֶת־יִפְתָּ֖ח וְאֶת־שְׁמוּאֵ֑ל וַיַּצֵּ֨ל אֶתְכֶ֜ם מִיַּ֤ד אֹֽיְבֵיכֶם֙ מִסָּבִ֔יב וַתֵּֽשְׁב֖וּ

יב בֶּֽטַח: וַתִּרְא֗וּ כִּֽי־נָחָ֞שׁ מֶ֣לֶךְ בְּנֵֽי־עַמּ֗וֹן בָּ֣א עֲלֵיכֶ֔ם וַתֹּ֣אמְרוּ לִ֔י לֹ֕א כִּי־מֶ֖לֶךְ יִמְלֹ֣ךְ עָלֵ֑ינוּ וַֽיהֹוָ֥ה

יג אֱלֹֽהֵיכֶ֖ם מַלְכְּכֶֽם: וְעַתָּ֗ה הִנֵּ֤ה הַמֶּ֨לֶךְ֙ אֲשֶׁ֣ר בְּחַרְתֶּ֔ם אֲשֶׁ֖ר שְׁאֶלְתֶּ֑ם וְהִנֵּ֨ה נָתַ֧ן יְהֹוָ֛ה עֲלֵיכֶ֖ם מֶֽלֶךְ:

יד אִם־תִּֽירְא֣וּ אֶת־יְהֹוָ֗ה וַֽעֲבַדְתֶּ֤ם אֹתוֹ֙ וּשְׁמַעְתֶּ֣ם בְּקוֹל֔וֹ וְלֹ֥א תַמְר֖וּ אֶת־פִּ֣י יְהֹוָ֑ה וִֽהְיִתֶ֣ם גַּם־אַתֶּ֗ם

טו וְגַם־הַמֶּ֨לֶךְ֙ אֲשֶׁ֣ר מָלַ֣ךְ עֲלֵיכֶ֔ם אַחַ֖ר יְהֹוָ֥ה אֱלֹֽהֵיכֶֽם: וְאִם־לֹ֤א תִשְׁמְעוּ֙ בְּק֣וֹל יְהֹוָ֔ה וּמְרִיתֶ֖ם

טז אֶת־פִּ֣י יְהֹוָ֑ה וְהָֽיְתָ֧ה יַד־יְהֹוָ֛ה בָּכֶ֖ם וּבַֽאֲבֹֽתֵיכֶֽם: גַּם־עַתָּ֣ה הִֽתְיַצְּב֗וּ וּרְאוּ֙ אֶת־הַדָּבָ֣ר הַגָּד֣וֹל הַזֶּ֔ה

יז אֲשֶׁ֣ר יְהֹוָ֔ה עֹשֶׂ֖ה לְעֵֽינֵיכֶֽם: הֲל֤וֹא קְצִֽיר־חִטִּים֙ הַיּ֔וֹם אֶקְרָא֙ אֶל־יְהֹוָ֔ה וְיִתֵּ֥ן קֹל֖וֹת וּמָטָ֑ר וּדְע֣וּ

יח וּרְא֗וּ כִּֽי־רָֽעַתְכֶ֤ם רַבָּה֙ אֲשֶׁ֣ר עֲשִׂיתֶ֗ם בְּעֵינֵ֣י יְהֹוָ֔ה לִשְׁא֥וֹל לָכֶ֖ם מֶֽלֶךְ: וַיִּקְרָ֤א שְׁמוּאֵל֙

אֶל־יְהֹוָ֔ה וַיִּתֵּ֧ן יְהֹוָ֛ה קֹלֹ֥ת וּמָטָ֖ר בַּיּ֣וֹם הַה֑וּא וַיִּירָ֨א כָל־הָעָ֥ם מְאֹ֖ד אֶת־יְהֹוָ֥ה וְאֶת־שְׁמוּאֵֽל:

יט וַיֹּֽאמְר֨וּ כָל־הָעָ֜ם אֶל־שְׁמוּאֵ֗ל הִתְפַּלֵּ֧ל בְּעַד־עֲבָדֶ֛יךָ אֶל־יְהֹוָ֥ה אֱלֹהֶ֖יךָ וְאַל־נָמ֑וּת כִּֽי־יָסַ֤פְנוּ

כ עַל־כָּל־חַטֹּאתֵ֨ינוּ֙ רָעָ֔ה לִשְׁאֹ֥ל לָ֖נוּ מֶֽלֶךְ: וַיֹּ֨אמֶר שְׁמוּאֵ֤ל אֶל־הָעָם֙ אַל־תִּירָ֔אוּ

אַתֶּ֣ם עֲשִׂיתֶ֔ם אֵ֥ת כָּל־הָֽרָעָ֖ה הַזֹּ֑את אַ֗ךְ אַל־תָּס֨וּרוּ֙ מֵֽאַֽחֲרֵ֣י יְהֹוָ֔ה וַֽעֲבַדְתֶּ֥ם אֶת־יְהֹוָ֖ה בְּכָל־

כא לְבַבְכֶֽם: וְלֹ֖א תָּס֑וּרוּ כִּ֣י ׀ אַֽחֲרֵ֣י הַתֹּ֗הוּ אֲשֶׁ֧ר לֹֽא־יוֹעִ֛ילוּ וְלֹ֥א יַצִּ֖ילוּ כִּי־תֹ֥הוּ הֵֽמָּה: כב כִּ֠י לֹֽא־יִטֹּ֤שׁ

יְהֹוָה֙ אֶת־עַמּ֔וֹ בַּֽעֲב֖וּר שְׁמ֣וֹ הַגָּד֑וֹל כִּ֚י הוֹאִ֣יל יְהֹוָ֔ה לַֽעֲשׂ֥וֹת אֶתְכֶ֛ם ל֖וֹ לְעָֽם:

Haftara for
Hukat

Yiftah Saves Israel from Amon
JUDGES 11:1–33

Yiftah the Giladite is a mighty warrior who is disinherited by his brothers and who subsequently becomes the leader of a band of landless men. Yiftah comes to the aid of the inhabitants of Gilad by fighting against the Amonites, who have claimed rights to the land of Gilad. Before going out to war, the Giladites offer a peace treaty to the enemy. They also present them with an account of the historical events related in *Parashat Hukat,* to prove that the territory claimed by Amon was not taken by the Israelites from the Amonites themselves, but from Sihon, who forced war upon the Israelites. However, the king of Amon, apparently confident in his superior strength, chooses to fight. At this time of danger, Yiftah utters a vow to God, just as Israel did in the *parasha* before their war with the dwellers of the south who took captives from them (Numbers 21:1). The formula of the vow is identical in both cases: "…took a vow to the Lord, and said: If You will deliver…into my hand" (Numbers 21:2; Judges 11:30). Yiftah defeats the people of Amon, thereby ensuring that they will remain subjugated to Israel for many years. As a consequence of this significant victory, Yiftah ascends to a position of leadership over Gilad.

11 1 Yiftah the Giladite was a valiant soldier; he was the son of a
2 harlot, and Gilad begot Yiftah. Gilad's wife bore him sons; his wife's sons grew, and they banished Yiftah, and they said to him: You shall not inherit in the household of our father, for you are
3 the son of another woman. Yiftah fled from his brothers, and he settled in the land of Tov; idle people gathered to Yiftah,
4 and they ventured out with him. It was some time later, and
5 the children of Amon made war with Israel. It was when the children of Amon made war with Israel that the elders of Gilad
6 went to take Yiftah from the land of Tov. They said to Yiftah: Go and be our chief, and we will make war with the children
7 of Amon. Yiftah said to the elders of Gilad: Didn't you hate me and banish me from my father's house? Why did you come
8 to me now when you are in distress? The elders of Gilad said to Yiftah: For this we have returned to you now: You will go with us, and make war against the children of Amon and you
9 will be our chief, over all the inhabitants of Gilad. Yiftah said to the elders of Gilad: If you restore me, to make war with the children of Amon, and the Lord delivers them before me, I will
10 be chief over you. The elders of Gilad said to Yiftah: May the Lord be witness between us, if we do not so act according to
11 your word. Yiftah went with the elders of Gilad, and the people placed him over them chief and commander; and Yiftah spoke
12 all his words before the Lord at Mitzpa. Yiftah sent messengers to the king of the children of Amon, saying: What is there between you and me that you have come to me to make war in my
13 land? The king of the children of Amon said to the messengers of Yiftah: Because Israel took my land when it came up from

Egypt, from Arnon to the Yabok, to the Jordan; now, restore
14 them peacefully. Yiftah sent messengers again to the king of the
15 children of Amon. He said to him: So said Yiftah: Israel did not
16 take the land of Moav or the land of the children of Amon. For when they came up from Egypt, Israel went in the wilderness to
17 the Red Sea and came to Kadesh. Israel sent messengers to the king of Edom, saying: Please let me pass through your land; but the king of Edom would not heed. They also sent to the king of
18 Moav, but he was unwilling, and Israel dwelled in Kadesh. They went through the wilderness and circled the land of Edom and the land of Moav, and they came from the rising sun to the land of Moav. They encamped beyond the Arnon; but they did not enter the border of Moav, as the Arnon is the border of Moav.
19 Israel sent messengers to Sihon, king of the Emorite, king of Heshbon; and Israel said to him: Please let us pass through your
20 land to our place. Sihon did not trust Israel to pass through his border, and Sihon gathered all his people, and they encamped
21 in Yahatz, and they made war with Israel. The Lord, God of Israel, delivered Sihon and his entire people into the hand of Israel, and they smote them; Israel took possession of the entire
22 land of the Emorites, inhabitants of that land. They took possession of the entire border of the Emorites, from the the Arnon
23 to the Yabok, and from the wilderness to the Jordan. Now the Lord, God of Israel, has dispossessed the Emorites from be-
24 fore His people Israel, would you take possession of it? That which Kemosh, your god, grants you to possess, that is what you may take possession of. All that the Lord our God dispos-
25 sesses for our sake, we will take possession of it. Now, are you

הפטרת

חקת

שופטים

יא א וְיִפְתָּח הַגִּלְעָדִי הָיָה גִּבּוֹר חַיִל וְהוּא בֶּן־אִשָּׁה זוֹנָה וַיּוֹלֶד גִּלְעָד אֶת־יִפְתָּח: וַתֵּלֶד אֵשֶׁת־
גִּלְעָד לוֹ בָּנִים וַיִּגְדְּלוּ בְנֵי־הָאִשָּׁה וַיְגָרְשׁוּ אֶת־יִפְתָּח וַיֹּאמְרוּ לוֹ לֹא־תִנְחַל בְּבֵית־אָבִינוּ כִּי
ג בֶן־אִשָּׁה אַחֶרֶת אָתָּה: וַיִּבְרַח יִפְתָּח מִפְּנֵי אֶחָיו וַיֵּשֶׁב בְּאֶרֶץ טוֹב וַיִּתְלַקְּטוּ אֶל־יִפְתָּח אֲנָשִׁים
ד רֵיקִים וַיֵּצְאוּ עִמּוֹ: וַיְהִי מִיָּמִים וַיִּלָּחֲמוּ בְנֵי־עַמּוֹן עִם־יִשְׂרָאֵל: וַיְהִי כַּאֲשֶׁר־נִלְחֲמוּ
ו בְנֵי־עַמּוֹן עִם־יִשְׂרָאֵל וַיֵּלְכוּ זִקְנֵי גִלְעָד לָקַחַת אֶת־יִפְתָּח מֵאֶרֶץ טוֹב: וַיֹּאמְרוּ לְיִפְתָּח לְכָה
ז וְהָיִיתָה לָּנוּ לְקָצִין וְנִלָּחֲמָה בִּבְנֵי עַמּוֹן: וַיֹּאמֶר יִפְתָּח לְזִקְנֵי גִלְעָד הֲלֹא אַתֶּם שְׂנֵאתֶם
אוֹתִי וַתְּגָרְשׁוּנִי מִבֵּית אָבִי וּמַדּוּעַ בָּאתֶם אֵלַי עַתָּה כַּאֲשֶׁר צַר לָכֶם: וַיֹּאמְרוּ זִקְנֵי גִלְעָד
ח אֶל־יִפְתָּח לָכֵן עַתָּה שַׁבְנוּ אֵלֶיךָ וְהָלַכְתָּ עִמָּנוּ וְנִלְחַמְתָּ בִּבְנֵי עַמּוֹן וְהָיִיתָ לָּנוּ לְרֹאשׁ לְכֹל
ט יֹשְׁבֵי גִלְעָד: וַיֹּאמֶר יִפְתָּח אֶל־זִקְנֵי גִלְעָד אִם־מְשִׁיבִים אַתֶּם אוֹתִי לְהִלָּחֵם בִּבְנֵי עַמּוֹן וְנָתַן
י יְהוָה אוֹתָם לְפָנָי אָנֹכִי אֶהְיֶה לָכֶם לְרֹאשׁ: וַיֹּאמְרוּ זִקְנֵי־גִלְעָד אֶל־יִפְתָּח יְהוָה יִהְיֶה שֹׁמֵעַ
יא בֵּינוֹתֵינוּ אִם־לֹא כִדְבָרְךָ כֵּן נַעֲשֶׂה: וַיֵּלֶךְ יִפְתָּח עִם־זִקְנֵי גִלְעָד וַיָּשִׂימוּ הָעָם אוֹתוֹ עֲלֵיהֶם
יב לְרֹאשׁ וּלְקָצִין וַיְדַבֵּר יִפְתָּח אֶת־כָּל־דְּבָרָיו לִפְנֵי יְהוָה בַּמִּצְפָּה: וַיִּשְׁלַח יִפְתָּח
מַלְאָכִים אֶל־מֶלֶךְ בְּנֵי־עַמּוֹן לֵאמֹר מַה־לִּי וָלָךְ כִּי־בָאתָ אֵלַי לְהִלָּחֵם בְּאַרְצִי: וַיֹּאמֶר מֶלֶךְ
יג בְּנֵי־עַמּוֹן אֶל־מַלְאֲכֵי יִפְתָּח כִּי־לָקַח יִשְׂרָאֵל אֶת־אַרְצִי בַּעֲלוֹתוֹ מִמִּצְרַיִם מֵאַרְנוֹן וְעַד־הַיַּבֹּק
יד וְעַד־הַיַּרְדֵּן וְעַתָּה הָשִׁיבָה אֶתְהֶן בְּשָׁלוֹם: וַיּוֹסֶף עוֹד יִפְתָּח וַיִּשְׁלַח מַלְאָכִים אֶל־מֶלֶךְ בְּנֵי
טו עַמּוֹן: וַיֹּאמֶר לוֹ כֹּה אָמַר יִפְתָּח לֹא־לָקַח יִשְׂרָאֵל אֶת־אֶרֶץ מוֹאָב וְאֶת־אֶרֶץ בְּנֵי עַמּוֹן: כִּי
טז בַּעֲלוֹתָם מִמִּצְרָיִם וַיֵּלֶךְ יִשְׂרָאֵל בַּמִּדְבָּר עַד־יַם־סוּף וַיָּבֹא קָדֵשָׁה: וַיִּשְׁלַח יִשְׂרָאֵל מַלְאָכִים ׀
אֶל־מֶלֶךְ אֱדוֹם ׀ לֵאמֹר אֶעְבְּרָה־נָּא בְאַרְצֶךָ וְלֹא שָׁמַע מֶלֶךְ אֱדוֹם וְגַם אֶל־מֶלֶךְ מוֹאָב שָׁלַח
יח וְלֹא אָבָה וַיֵּשֶׁב יִשְׂרָאֵל בְּקָדֵשׁ: וַיֵּלֶךְ בַּמִּדְבָּר וַיָּסָב אֶת־אֶרֶץ אֱדוֹם וְאֶת־אֶרֶץ מוֹאָב וַיָּבֹא
מִמִּזְרַח־שֶׁמֶשׁ לְאֶרֶץ מוֹאָב וַיַּחֲנוּן בְּעֵבֶר אַרְנוֹן וְלֹא־בָאוּ בִּגְבוּל מוֹאָב כִּי אַרְנוֹן גְּבוּל מוֹאָב:
יט וַיִּשְׁלַח יִשְׂרָאֵל מַלְאָכִים אֶל־סִיחוֹן מֶלֶךְ־הָאֱמֹרִי מֶלֶךְ חֶשְׁבּוֹן וַיֹּאמֶר לוֹ יִשְׂרָאֵל נַעְבְּרָה־נָּא
כ בְאַרְצְךָ עַד־מְקוֹמִי: וְלֹא־הֶאֱמִין סִיחוֹן אֶת־יִשְׂרָאֵל עֲבֹר בִּגְבֻלוֹ וַיֶּאֱסֹף סִיחוֹן אֶת־כָּל־עַמּוֹ
כא וַיַּחֲנוּ בְּיָהְצָה וַיִּלָּחֶם עִם־יִשְׂרָאֵל: וַיִּתֵּן יְהוָה אֱלֹהֵי־יִשְׂרָאֵל אֶת־סִיחוֹן וְאֶת־כָּל־עַמּוֹ בְּיַד
כב יִשְׂרָאֵל וַיַּכּוּם וַיִּירַשׁ יִשְׂרָאֵל אֵת כָּל־אֶרֶץ הָאֱמֹרִי יוֹשֵׁב הָאָרֶץ הַהִיא: וַיִּירְשׁוּ אֵת כָּל־גְּבוּל
כג הָאֱמֹרִי מֵאַרְנוֹן וְעַד־הַיַּבֹּק וּמִן־הַמִּדְבָּר וְעַד־הַיַּרְדֵּן: וְעַתָּה יְהוָה ׀ אֱלֹהֵי יִשְׂרָאֵל הוֹרִישׁ
כד אֶת־הָאֱמֹרִי מִפְּנֵי עַמּוֹ יִשְׂרָאֵל וְאַתָּה תִּירָשֶׁנּוּ: הֲלֹא אֵת אֲשֶׁר יוֹרִישְׁךָ כְּמוֹשׁ אֱלֹהֶיךָ אוֹתוֹ
כה תִירָשׁ וְאֵת כָּל־אֲשֶׁר הוֹרִישׁ יְהוָה אֱלֹהֵינוּ מִפָּנֵינוּ אוֹתוֹ נִירָשׁ: וְעַתָּה הֲטוֹב טוֹב אַתָּה מִבָּלָק

better than Balak, son of Tzipor, king of Moav? Did he provoke
26 a fight with Israel? Did he make war against them? When Israel
lived in Heshbon and in its environs, and in Aroer and in its
environs, and in all the cities that are along the Arnon, for three
27 hundred years, why didn't you recover them at that time? I did
not sin against you, but you are doing me wrong to make war
against me. May the Lord, the Judge, judge today between the
28 children of Israel and the children of Amon. But the king of the
children of Amon did not heed the words of Yiftah that he sent
29 to him. The spirit of the Lord was upon Yiftah, and he passed
through Gilad and Manasseh, and he passed Mitzpe Gilad, and
30 from Mitzpe Gilad he passed to the children of Amon. Yiftah
vowed to the Lord, and he said: If You will deliver the children
31 of Amon into my hand, it shall be that which emerges from the
doors of my house to meet me when I return in peace from the
children of Amon, it shall be for the Lord, and I will offer it up
32 as a burnt offering. Yiftah passed to the children of Amon to
make war against them, and the Lord delivered them into his
33 hand. He smote them from Aroer until your approach to Minit,
twenty cities, and to Avel Keramim, a very great blow, and the
children of Amon submitted before the children of Israel.

Haftara for **Balak**

God's Kindnesses to Israel in the Past and the Future

MICAH 5:6–6:8

The memory of the episode of Balak and Bilam and the related events is cited by the prophet Micah in God's rebuke to Israel. Apart from this obvious connection between the *parasha* and the *haftara*, various phrases in the optimistic passages of the *haftara* echo several of Bilam's blessings to the people. For example, the expression, "like dew from the Lord, like raindrops on vegetation" (5:6), corresponds to "like marigolds planted by the Lord" (Numbers 24:6); the verse, "The remnant of Jacob will be in the midst of many peoples…that does not hope for a man and does not long for the sons of man" (5:6) conveys a similar idea to, "Behold, it is a people that shall dwell alone, and shall not be reckoned among the nations" (Numbers 23:9); the phrase, "like a lion among the animals of the forest" (5:7), brings to mind the formulation, "Behold, a people will rise like a great cat, and like a lion will raise itself" (Numbers 23:24); and lastly, the assurance, "I will eliminate sorcery from your hand and you will not have soothsayers" (5:11) alludes to the declaration: "For there is no divination in Jacob, and no sorcery in Israel" (Numbers 23:23).

5 6 The remnant of Jacob will be in the midst of many peoples like
dew from the Lord, like raindrops on vegetation that does not
7 hope for a man and does not long for the sons of man. The remnant of Jacob will be among the nations, in the midst of many
peoples, like a lion among the animals of the forest, like a young
lion among flocks of sheep, from whom, when he passes, tram-
8 ples and mauls, there is no rescuer. Your hand will be raised
9 over Your foes, and all Your enemies will be eliminated. It shall
be on that day – the utterance of the Lord – that I will eliminate
10 your horses from your midst, and I will destroy your chariots; I
will eliminate the cities of your land and I will destroy all your
11 fortresses; I will eliminate sorcery from your hand and you
12 will not have soothsayers. I will eliminate your idols and your
monuments from your midst, and you will no longer worship
13 the work of your hands. I will uproot your sacred trees from
14 your midst, and I will destroy your enemies. With wrath and
with fury I will take vengeance upon the nations, who did not
6 1 heed. Hear now that which the Lord is saying: Arise, quarrel
2 with the mountains, and let the hills hear your voice. Hear,
mountains, the Lord's quarrel, and the strong foundations of
the earth, as the Lord has a quarrel with His people, and with
3 Israel He will contend. My people, what did I do to you, and
4 how did I exhaust you? Testify against Me. For I took you up
from the land of Egypt and redeemed you from the house of

כו בֶּן־צִפּוֹר מֶלֶךְ מוֹאָב הֲרוֹב רָב עִם־יִשְׂרָאֵל אִם־נִלְחֹם נִלְחַם בָּם׃ בְּשֶׁבֶת יִשְׂרָאֵל בְּחֶשְׁבּוֹן
וּבִבְנוֹתֶיהָ וּבְעַרְעוֹר וּבִבְנוֹתֶיהָ וּבְכׇל־הֶעָרִים אֲשֶׁר עַל־יְדֵי אַרְנוֹן שְׁלֹשׁ מֵאוֹת שָׁנָה וּמַדּוּעַ
כז לֹא־הִצַּלְתֶּם בָּעֵת הַהִיא׃ וְאָנֹכִי לֹא־חָטָאתִי לָךְ וְאַתָּה עֹשֶׂה אִתִּי רָעָה לְהִלָּחֶם בִּי יִשְׁפֹּט
כח יהוה הַשֹּׁפֵט הַיּוֹם בֵּין בְּנֵי יִשְׂרָאֵל וּבֵין בְּנֵי עַמּוֹן׃ וְלֹא שָׁמַע מֶלֶךְ בְּנֵי עַמּוֹן אֶל־דִּבְרֵי יִפְתָּח
כט אֲשֶׁר שָׁלַח אֵלָיו׃ וַתְּהִי עַל־יִפְתָּח רוּחַ יהוה וַיַּעֲבֹר אֶת־הַגִּלְעָד וְאֶת־מְנַשֶּׁה וַיַּעֲבֹר
ל אֶת־מִצְפֵּה גִלְעָד וּמִמִּצְפֵּה גִלְעָד עָבַר בְּנֵי עַמּוֹן׃ וַיִּדַּר יִפְתָּח נֶדֶר לַיהוה וַיֹּאמַר אִם־נָתוֹן
לא תִּתֵּן אֶת־בְּנֵי עַמּוֹן בְּיָדִי׃ וְהָיָה הַיּוֹצֵא אֲשֶׁר יֵצֵא מִדַּלְתֵי בֵיתִי לִקְרָאתִי בְּשׁוּבִי בְשָׁלוֹם מִבְּנֵי
עַמּוֹן וְהָיָה לַיהוה וְהַעֲלִיתִהוּ עוֹלָה׃
לב לג וַיַּעֲבֹר יִפְתָּח אֶל־בְּנֵי עַמּוֹן לְהִלָּחֶם בָּם וַיִּתְּנֵם יהוה בְּיָדוֹ׃ וַיַּכֵּם מֵעֲרוֹעֵר וְעַד־בּוֹאֲךָ מִנִּית
עֶשְׂרִים עִיר וְעַד אָבֵל כְּרָמִים מַכָּה גְּדוֹלָה מְאֹד וַיִּכָּנְעוּ בְּנֵי עַמּוֹן מִפְּנֵי בְּנֵי יִשְׂרָאֵל׃

הפטרת

בלק

מיכה

ה ו וְהָיָה ׀ שְׁאֵרִית יַעֲקֹב בְּקֶרֶב עַמִּים רַבִּים כְּטַל מֵאֵת יהוה כִּרְבִיבִים עֲלֵי־עֵשֶׂב אֲשֶׁר לֹא־
ז יְקַוֶּה לְאִישׁ וְלֹא יְיַחֵל לִבְנֵי אָדָם׃ וְהָיָה שְׁאֵרִית יַעֲקֹב בַּגּוֹיִם בְּקֶרֶב עַמִּים רַבִּים כְּאַרְיֵה
ח בְּבַהֲמוֹת יַעַר כִּכְפִיר בְּעֶדְרֵי־צֹאן אֲשֶׁר אִם עָבַר וְרָמַס וְטָרַף וְאֵין מַצִּיל׃ תָּרֹם יָדְךָ עַל־
ט צָרֶיךָ וְכׇל־אֹיְבֶיךָ יִכָּרֵתוּ׃ וְהָיָה בַיּוֹם־הַהוּא נְאֻם־יהוה וְהִכְרַתִּי סוּסֶיךָ מִקִּרְבֶּךָ
י יא וְהַאֲבַדְתִּי מַרְכְּבֹתֶיךָ׃ וְהִכְרַתִּי עָרֵי אַרְצֶךָ וְהָרַסְתִּי כׇּל־מִבְצָרֶיךָ׃ וְהִכְרַתִּי כְשָׁפִים מִיָּדֶךָ
יב וּמְעוֹנְנִים לֹא יִהְיוּ־לָךְ׃ וְהִכְרַתִּי פְסִילֶיךָ וּמַצֵּבוֹתֶיךָ מִקִּרְבֶּךָ וְלֹא־תִשְׁתַּחֲוֶה עוֹד לְמַעֲשֵׂה
יג יד יָדֶיךָ׃ וְנָתַשְׁתִּי אֲשֵׁירֶיךָ מִקִּרְבֶּךָ וְהִשְׁמַדְתִּי עָרֶיךָ׃ וְעָשִׂיתִי בְּאַף וּבְחֵמָה נָקָם אֶת־הַגּוֹיִם
ו א אֲשֶׁר לֹא שָׁמֵעוּ׃ שִׁמְעוּ־נָא אֵת אֲשֶׁר־יהוה אֹמֵר קוּם רִיב אֶת־הֶהָרִים וְתִשְׁמַעְנָה
ב הַגְּבָעוֹת קוֹלֶךָ׃ שִׁמְעוּ הָרִים אֶת־רִיב יהוה וְהָאֵתָנִים מֹסְדֵי אָרֶץ כִּי רִיב לַיהוה עִם־עַמּוֹ
ג ד וְעִם־יִשְׂרָאֵל יִתְוַכָּח׃ עַמִּי מֶה־עָשִׂיתִי לְךָ וּמָה הֶלְאֵתִיךָ עֲנֵה בִי׃ כִּי הֶעֱלִתִיךָ מֵאֶרֶץ מִצְרַיִם

5 bondage and I sent before you Moses, Aaron, and Miriam. My people, remember now what Balak king of Moav devised, and what Bilam son of Beor answered him, from Shitim to Gilgal, in

6 order to know the righteous acts of the Lord. With what shall I approach the Lord, and bow to God on high? Shall I approach

7 Him with burnt offerings, with year-old calves? Does the Lord desire thousands of rams, with tens of thousands of streams of oil? Shall I give my firstborn for my transgression, the fruit of

8 my belly for the sin of my soul? He told you, man, what is good, and what the Lord demands from you: Only to perform justice, and to love kindness, and to walk humbly with your God.

Haftara for
Pinhas

Read on the Shabbat preceding the Fast of the Seventeenth of Tamuz. If Parashat Pinhas is read after the fast, then the haftara is read for Matot.

Elijah After His Act of Zealousness for God

I KINGS 18:46–19:21

Just as Pinhas acted zealously for God, killing a prince of Israel when the people strayed after Baal Peor, so too Elijah, who some identify with Pinhas himself, slaughters the priests of Baal in the name of God. However, unlike Pinhas, whose zealousness earned him the priesthood, through which he could atone for Israel's sins, Elijah is forced to leave his people and abandon all of human society because of his zealousness. After requesting that his life end in the wilderness, Elijah receives a divine revelation at Mount Horev, on which occasion he is instructed to appoint another prophet to replace him.

18 46 The hand of the Lord was upon Elijah, and he girded his loins,
19 1 and he ran before Ahav until the approach to Yizre'el. Ahav told Izevel everything that Elijah had done and all about how

2 he killed all the prophets by sword. Izevel sent a messenger to Elijah, saying: So may the gods do, and so may they add, for at this time tomorrow I will set your life as the life of one of them.

3 He saw and rose and fled for his life and came to Beersheva,

4 which is in Judah, and he left his servant there. He went one day's journey into the wilderness and came and sat beneath a retama bush and he asked for his life, to die. He said: Enough;

5 now, Lord, take my life, as I am no better than my fathers. He lay down and slept beneath a retama bush and behold, an an-

6 gel was touching him, and said to him: Arise, eat. He looked, and behold, near his head, a cake baked on coals and a cruse of

7 water. He ate and drank, and lay down again. The angel of the Lord returned a second time, touched him and said: Arise and

8 eat, as the way is too great for you. He rose, ate and drank, and walked on the strength of that eating forty days and forty nights

9 until the mountain of God, Horev. He came there into a cave and stayed the night there and behold, the word of the Lord was to him, and He said to him: What are you doing here, Elijah?

10 He said: I have been zealous for the Lord, God of hosts for the children of Israel have forsaken Your covenant; they have destroyed your altars and killed Your prophets by the sword; I

11 alone remain, and they seek my life to take it. He said: Go out, and stand on the mountain before the Lord. Behold, the Lord was passing, and there was a great and powerful wind, smashing mountains and shattering rocks before the Lord. The Lord was not in the wind. After the wind, an earthquake; the Lord

12 was not in the earthquake; after the earthquake, fire; the Lord

13 was not in the fire; after the fire, a faint sound of silence. It was, when Elijah heard, he wrapped his face in his cloak and came out and stood at the entrance of the cave. Behold, a voice came

14 to him, and said: What are you doing here, Elijah? He said: I have been zealous for the Lord, God of hosts, for the children of Israel have forsaken Your covenant, they have destroyed Your

ה וּמִבֵּית עֲבָדִים פְּדִיתִיךָ וָאֶשְׁלַח לְפָנֶיךָ אֶת־מֹשֶׁה אַהֲרֹן וּמִרְיָם׃ עַמִּי זְכָר־נָא מַה־יָּעַץ בָּלָק
מֶלֶךְ מוֹאָב וּמֶה־עָנָה אֹתוֹ בִּלְעָם בֶּן־בְּעוֹר מִן־הַשִּׁטִּים עַד־הַגִּלְגָּל לְמַעַן דַּעַת צִדְקוֹת
ו ז יהוה׃ בַּמָּה אֲקַדֵּם יהוה אִכַּף לֵאלֹהֵי מָרוֹם הַאֲקַדְּמֶנּוּ בְעוֹלוֹת בַּעֲגָלִים בְּנֵי שָׁנָה׃ הֲיִרְצֶה
ח יהוה בְּאַלְפֵי אֵילִים בְּרִבְבוֹת נַחֲלֵי־שָׁמֶן הַאֶתֵּן בְּכוֹרִי פִּשְׁעִי פְּרִי בִטְנִי חַטַּאת נַפְשִׁי׃ הִגִּיד
לְךָ אָדָם מַה־טּוֹב וּמָה־יהוה דּוֹרֵשׁ מִמְּךָ כִּי אִם־עֲשׂוֹת מִשְׁפָּט וְאַהֲבַת חֶסֶד וְהַצְנֵעַ לֶכֶת
עִם־אֱלֹהֶיךָ׃

הפטרת

פנחס

הפטרה לשבת פרשת פנחס שלפני י״ז בתמוז. אם היא חלה אחרי כן, קוראים את ההפטרה הבאה אחריה.

מלכים א׳

יח מו יט א וְיַד־יהוה הָיְתָה אֶל־אֵלִיָּהוּ וַיְשַׁנֵּס מָתְנָיו וַיָּרָץ לִפְנֵי אַחְאָב עַד־בֹּאֲכָה יִזְרְעֶאלָה׃ וַיַּגֵּד
אַחְאָב לְאִיזֶבֶל אֵת כָּל־אֲשֶׁר עָשָׂה אֵלִיָּהוּ וְאֵת כָּל־אֲשֶׁר הָרַג אֶת־כָּל־הַנְּבִיאִים בֶּחָרֶב׃
ב וַתִּשְׁלַח אִיזֶבֶל מַלְאָךְ אֶל־אֵלִיָּהוּ לֵאמֹר כֹּה־יַעֲשׂוּן אֱלֹהִים וְכֹה יוֹסִפוּן כִּי־כָעֵת מָחָר
ג אָשִׂים אֶת־נַפְשְׁךָ כְּנֶפֶשׁ אַחַד מֵהֶם׃ וַיַּרְא וַיָּקָם וַיֵּלֶךְ אֶל־נַפְשׁוֹ וַיָּבֹא בְּאֵר שֶׁבַע אֲשֶׁר
ד לִיהוּדָה וַיַּנַּח אֶת־נַעֲרוֹ שָׁם׃ וְהוּא־הָלַךְ בַּמִּדְבָּר דֶּרֶךְ יוֹם וַיָּבֹא וַיֵּשֶׁב תַּחַת רֹתֶם אחת אֶחָד
וַיִּשְׁאַל אֶת־נַפְשׁוֹ לָמוּת וַיֹּאמֶר ׀ רַב עַתָּה יהוה קַח נַפְשִׁי כִּי־לֹא־טוֹב אָנֹכִי מֵאֲבֹתָי׃
ה ו וַיִּשְׁכַּב וַיִּישַׁן תַּחַת רֹתֶם אֶחָד וְהִנֵּה־זֶה מַלְאָךְ נֹגֵעַ בּוֹ וַיֹּאמֶר לוֹ קוּם אֱכוֹל׃ וַיַּבֵּט וְהִנֵּה
ז מְרַאֲשֹׁתָיו עֻגַת רְצָפִים וְצַפַּחַת מָיִם וַיֹּאכַל וַיֵּשְׁתְּ וַיָּשָׁב וַיִּשְׁכָּב׃ וַיָּשָׁב מַלְאַךְ יהוה
ח ׀ שֵׁנִית וַיִּגַּע־בּוֹ וַיֹּאמֶר קוּם אֱכֹל כִּי רַב מִמְּךָ הַדָּרֶךְ׃ וַיָּקָם וַיֹּאכַל וַיִּשְׁתֶּה וַיֵּלֶךְ בְּכֹחַ ׀
ט הָאֲכִילָה הַהִיא אַרְבָּעִים יוֹם וְאַרְבָּעִים לַיְלָה עַד הַר הָאֱלֹהִים חֹרֵב׃ וַיָּבֹא־שָׁם אֶל־הַמְּעָרָה
י וַיָּלֶן שָׁם וְהִנֵּה דְבַר־יהוה אֵלָיו וַיֹּאמֶר לוֹ מַה־לְּךָ פֹה אֵלִיָּהוּ׃ וַיֹּאמֶר קַנֹּא קִנֵּאתִי לַיהוה ׀
אֱלֹהֵי צְבָאוֹת כִּי־עָזְבוּ בְרִיתְךָ בְּנֵי יִשְׂרָאֵל אֶת־מִזְבְּחֹתֶיךָ הָרָסוּ וְאֶת־נְבִיאֶיךָ הָרְגוּ בֶחָרֶב
יא וָאִוָּתֵר אֲנִי לְבַדִּי וַיְבַקְשׁוּ אֶת־נַפְשִׁי לְקַחְתָּהּ׃ וַיֹּאמֶר צֵא וְעָמַדְתָּ בָהָר לִפְנֵי יהוה וְהִנֵּה
יהוה עֹבֵר וְרוּחַ גְּדוֹלָה וְחָזָק מְפָרֵק הָרִים וּמְשַׁבֵּר סְלָעִים לִפְנֵי יהוה לֹא בָרוּחַ יהוה וְאַחַר
יב הָרוּחַ רַעַשׁ לֹא בָרַעַשׁ יהוה׃ וְאַחַר הָרַעַשׁ אֵשׁ לֹא בָאֵשׁ יהוה וְאַחַר הָאֵשׁ קוֹל דְּמָמָה
יג דַקָּה׃ וַיְהִי ׀ כִּשְׁמֹעַ אֵלִיָּהוּ וַיָּלֶט פָּנָיו בְּאַדַּרְתּוֹ וַיֵּצֵא וַיַּעֲמֹד פֶּתַח הַמְּעָרָה וְהִנֵּה אֵלָיו קוֹל
יד וַיֹּאמֶר מַה־לְּךָ פֹה אֵלִיָּהוּ׃ וַיֹּאמֶר קַנֹּא קִנֵּאתִי לַיהוה ׀ אֱלֹהֵי צְבָאוֹת כִּי־עָזְבוּ בְרִיתְךָ בְּנֵי

altars and killed Your prophets by the sword; I alone remain
15 and they seek my life, to take it. The Lord said to him: Go, return on your way to the wilderness of Damascus; and you will
16 come and anoint Hazael as king over Aram. You shall anoint
Yehu son of Nimshi, as king over Israel; and you shall anoint
Elisha son of Shafat, of Avel Mehola, as prophet in your place.
17 It shall be that he who escapes from the sword of Hazael, Yehu
will put to death, and he who escapes from the sword of Yehu,
18 Elisha will put to death. I will leave seven thousand in Israel,
all the knees that did not kneel to the Baal, and every mouth

19 that did not kiss it. He went from there, and he found Elisha
son of Shafat; he was plowing with twelve pairs of oxen before
him, and he was with the twelfth; Elijah went over to him, and
20 he cast his cloak upon him. He left the oxen, ran after Elijah,
and said: Please, let me kiss my father and my mother, and I
will follow you. He said to him: Go, return, for what did I do to
21 you? He returned from following him and took the pair of oxen
and slaughtered them; in the utensils of the oxen he boiled the
flesh, gave it to the people, and they ate. He rose and followed
Elijah and served him.

Haftara for
Matot

Read on the first Shabbat after the Fast of the Seventeeth of Tamuz.

Jeremiah's First Prophecy
JEREMIAH 1:1–2:3

This *haftara*, which discusses the initiation of Jeremiah into his prophetic career, describes where, when, and how he became a prophet. In addition, it specifies who would be the subjects of his prophecies. Jeremiah is also offered words of encouragement as he takes his first steps on this lonely path. However, already in his early prophetic visions Jeremiah receives hints of the forthcoming destruction of Judah and Jerusalem, a tragedy which the prophet himself would experience firsthand years later.

This is the first of a series of *haftarot* that are connected to the calendar year rather than to the *parasha*. The Sages state that from the start of the reading of Genesis until the Seventeenth of Tamuz, the *haftara* is related to the *parasha*, after which the *haftarot* proceed as follows: There are three *haftarot* of retribution from the Seventeenth of Tamuz until Tisha Be'Av; seven *haftarot* of consolation from Tisha Be'Av to Rosh HaShana; and two *haftarot* of repentance from Rosh HaShana until the festival of Sukkot (Rashi; Radak; *Metzudat Tzion*).

Although the book of Jeremiah is full of reprimands to the nation, some of which are very harsh indeed, his very first prophecy is one of reconciliation, comfort, and love for Israel. The *haftara* concludes with these encouraging verses.

1 1 The words of Jeremiah son of Hilkiyahu, of the priests who
2 were in Anatot in the land of Benjamin, to whom the word of
the Lord was in the days of Yoshiyahu, son of Amon, king of
3 Judah, in the thirteenth year of his reign: It was in the days of
Yehoyakim, son of Yoshiyahu, king of Judah, until the conclusion of the eleventh year of Tzidkiyahu, son of Yoshiyahu, king
4 of Judah, until the exile of Jerusalem in the fifth month. The
5 word of the Lord was with me, saying: Before I formed you in
the belly I knew you, and before you emerged from the womb
6 I sanctified you; a prophet to the nations I set you. I said: Alas,
My Lord God, behold, I do not know to speak, for I am a lad.

7 The Lord said to me: Do not say: I am a lad, for to wherever I
will send you, you shall go, and whatever I will command you,
8 you shall speak. Do not fear them, as I am with you to save you
9 – the utterance of the Lord. The Lord sent His hand forth and
touched my mouth, and the Lord said to me: Behold, I have set
10 My words in your mouth. See, I appointed you this day over the
nations and over the kingdoms, to uproot and to smash and to
11 eradicate and to destroy, to build and to plant. The word of the
Lord was with me, saying: What do you see, Jeremiah? I said: I
12 see a branch of an almond tree. The Lord said to me: You have

ישְׂרָאֵל אֶת־מִזְבְּחֹתֶיךָ הָרָסוּ וְאֶת־נְבִיאֶיךָ הָרְגוּ בֶּחָרֶב וָאִוָּתֵר אֲנִי לְבַדִּי וַיְבַקְשׁוּ אֶת־נַפְשִׁי

טו לְקַחְתָּהּ: וַיֹּאמֶר יְהוָה אֵלָיו לֵךְ שׁוּב לְדַרְכְּךָ מִדְבַּרָה דַמָּשֶׂק וּבָאתָ וּמָשַׁחְתָּ

טז אֶת־חֲזָאֵל לְמֶלֶךְ עַל־אֲרָם: וְאֵת יֵהוּא בֶן־נִמְשִׁי תִּמְשַׁח לְמֶלֶךְ עַל־יִשְׂרָאֵל וְאֶת־אֱלִישָׁע

יז בֶן־שָׁפָט מֵאָבֵל מְחוֹלָה תִּמְשַׁח לְנָבִיא תַּחְתֶּיךָ: וְהָיָה הַנִּמְלָט מֵחֶרֶב חֲזָאֵל יָמִית יֵהוּא

יח וְהַנִּמְלָט מֵחֶרֶב יֵהוּא יָמִית אֱלִישָׁע: וְהִשְׁאַרְתִּי בְיִשְׂרָאֵל שִׁבְעַת אֲלָפִים כָּל־הַבִּרְכַּיִם אֲשֶׁר

יט לֹא־כָרְעוּ לַבַּעַל וְכָל־הַפֶּה אֲשֶׁר לֹא־נָשַׁק לוֹ: וַיֵּלֶךְ מִשָּׁם וַיִּמְצָא אֶת־אֱלִישָׁע בֶּן־שָׁפָט וְהוּא

חֹרֵשׁ שְׁנֵים־עָשָׂר צְמָדִים לְפָנָיו וְהוּא בִּשְׁנֵים הֶעָשָׂר וַיַּעֲבֹר אֵלִיָּהוּ אֵלָיו וַיַּשְׁלֵךְ אַדַּרְתּוֹ אֵלָיו:

כ וַיַּעֲזֹב אֶת־הַבָּקָר וַיָּרָץ אַחֲרֵי אֵלִיָּהוּ וַיֹּאמֶר אֶשְּׁקָה־נָּא לְאָבִי וּלְאִמִּי וְאֵלְכָה אַחֲרֶיךָ וַיֹּאמֶר

כא לוֹ לֵךְ שׁוּב כִּי מֶה־עָשִׂיתִי לָךְ: וַיָּשָׁב מֵאַחֲרָיו וַיִּקַּח אֶת־צֶמֶד הַבָּקָר וַיִּזְבָּחֵהוּ וּבִכְלִי הַבָּקָר

בִּשְּׁלָם הַבָּשָׂר וַיִּתֵּן לָעָם וַיֹּאכֵלוּ וַיָּקָם וַיֵּלֶךְ אַחֲרֵי אֵלִיָּהוּ וַיְשָׁרְתֵהוּ:

הפטרת

מטות

הפטרה לשבת הראשונה שאחרי י"ז בתמוז (פנחס או מטות)

א ב דִּבְרֵי יִרְמְיָהוּ בֶּן־חִלְקִיָּהוּ מִן־הַכֹּהֲנִים אֲשֶׁר בַּעֲנָתוֹת בְּאֶרֶץ בִּנְיָמִן: אֲשֶׁר הָיָה דְבַר־יְהוָה **ירמיה**

ג אֵלָיו בִּימֵי יֹאשִׁיָּהוּ בֶן־אָמוֹן מֶלֶךְ יְהוּדָה בִּשְׁלֹשׁ־עֶשְׂרֵה שָׁנָה לְמָלְכוֹ: וַיְהִי בִּימֵי יְהוֹיָקִים

בֶן־יֹאשִׁיָּהוּ מֶלֶךְ יְהוּדָה עַד־תֹּם עַשְׁתֵּי עֶשְׂרֵה שָׁנָה לְצִדְקִיָּהוּ בֶן־יֹאשִׁיָּהוּ מֶלֶךְ יְהוּדָה עַד־

ד גְּלוֹת יְרוּשָׁלִַם בַּחֹדֶשׁ הַחֲמִישִׁי: וַיְהִי דְבַר־יְהוָה אֵלַי לֵאמֹר: בְּטֶרֶם אֶצָּרְךָ בַבֶּטֶן **אֶצָּרְךָ**

ו יְדַעְתִּיךָ וּבְטֶרֶם תֵּצֵא מֵרֶחֶם הִקְדַּשְׁתִּיךָ נָבִיא לַגּוֹיִם נְתַתִּיךָ: וָאֹמַר אֲהָהּ אֲדֹנָי יְהוִה הִנֵּה לֹא־

ז יָדַעְתִּי דַּבֵּר כִּי־נַעַר אָנֹכִי: וַיֹּאמֶר יְהוָה אֵלַי אַל־תֹּאמַר נַעַר אָנֹכִי כִּי עַל־כָּל־אֲשֶׁר אֶשְׁלָחֲךָ

ח תֵּלֵךְ וְאֵת כָּל־אֲשֶׁר אֲצַוְּךָ תְּדַבֵּר: אַל־תִּירָא מִפְּנֵיהֶם כִּי־אִתְּךָ אֲנִי לְהַצִּלֶךָ נְאֻם־יְהוָה: וַיִּשְׁלַח

י יְהוָה אֶת־יָדוֹ וַיַּגַּע עַל־פִּי וַיֹּאמֶר יְהוָה אֵלַי הִנֵּה נָתַתִּי דְבָרַי בְּפִיךָ: רְאֵה הִפְקַדְתִּיךָ ׀ הַיּוֹם הַזֶּה

עַל־הַגּוֹיִם וְעַל־הַמַּמְלָכוֹת לִנְתוֹשׁ וְלִנְתוֹץ וּלְהַאֲבִיד וְלַהֲרוֹס לִבְנוֹת וְלִנְטוֹעַ: **וַיְהִי**

יא דְבַר־יְהוָה אֵלַי לֵאמֹר מָה־אַתָּה רֹאֶה יִרְמְיָהוּ וָאֹמַר מַקֵּל שָׁקֵד אֲנִי רֹאֶה: וַיֹּאמֶר יְהוָה

13 seen well, for I hasten My word to perform it. The word of the
Lord was with me a second time, saying: What do you see? I
said: A boiling pot I see, and its opening is facing toward the
14 north. The Lord said to me: From the north the evil shall be
15 unleashed upon all the inhabitants of the land. For behold, I
am calling all the families of the kingdoms of the north – the
utterance of the Lord – and they will come, and each man will
place his throne at the entrance of the gates of Jerusalem, and
16 against all its walls around, and against all the cities of Judah. I
will speak My judgments against them for all their evildoing,
that they forsook Me and burned to other gods, and they pros-
17 trated themselves to their handiwork. You shall gird your loins,
you shall arise, and you shall speak to them everything that I

will command you; do not be dismayed because of them, lest I
18 devastate you before them. Behold, I have rendered you today
as a fortified city, an iron pillar, and as bronze walls, against the
entire land, to the kings of Judah, to its princes, to its priests,
19 and to the people of the land. They will battle against you, but
they will not prevail against you, as I am with you – the utter-
2 1 ance of the Lord – to deliver you. The word of the Lord was
2 with me, saying: Go, and proclaim in the ears of Jerusalem, saying: So said the Lord: I have remembered for you the kindness
of your youth, the love of your nuptials, your following Me in
3 the wilderness, in a land not sown. Israel is sacred to the Lord,
the first of His crop, all those who devour it will be guilty, evil
will come upon them – the utterance of the Lord.

Haftara for
Masei

Reproof of the People for Turning to Idolatry and Relying on Foreign Nations
JEREMIAH 2:4–28, 3:4, 4:1–2

This is the second *haftara* in the period of commemoration for the destruction of the Temple. It continues the prophecy of Jeremiah from the previous *haftara*. This section incorporates the main complaints of the prophets against the people of Israel, namely, that they worshipped idolatry and abandoned the path of God. These statements of rebuke, some of which are graphic and extremely vivid, are directed at the entire nation of Israel, including all their tribes and throughout the generations. In this case too the *haftara* concludes with an uplifting message, after the omission of certain harsh passages of reproof.

2 4 Hear the word of the Lord, house of Jacob, and all the fami-
5 lies of the house of Israel. So said the Lord: What injustice did
your fathers find in Me, that they distanced themselves from
6 Me, and they followed futility, and they became futility? They
did not say: Where is the Lord, who brings us up from the
land of Egypt, who leads us in the wilderness, in a land of desert and crater, in a land of waste and the shadow of death, in a
land that no man has crossed, and where no man has dwelled?
7 I brought you into a fruitful land, to eat its fruit and its goodness. You came, and you defiled My land, and My heritage you
8 rendered an abomination. The priests did not say: Where is the
Lord? Those who grasp the Torah did not know Me, and the

shepherds were disloyal to Me, and the prophets prophesied
9 to the Baal and followed that which is of no avail. Therefore,
I will yet quarrel with you – the utterance of the Lord – and
10 with your children's children I will quarrel. For cross the isles
of the Kitites and see, and send to Kedar and observe diligently,
11 and see whether there has been anything like this. Has a nation
exchanged its gods, and they are not gods? But My people has
12 exchanged its glory for that which is of no avail. Be astonished,
the heavens, at this and be agitated, be greatly devastated – the
13 utterance of the Lord – as My people have performed two evils:
They forsook Me, the fount of flowing water, to dig for them cis-
14 terns, broken cisterns, that will not hold water. Is Israel a slave?

יג אֵלַי הֵיטַבְתָּ לִרְאוֹת כִּי־שֹׁקֵד אֲנִי עַל־דְּבָרִי לַעֲשֹׂתוֹ: וַיְהִי דְבַר־יהוה ׀ אֵלַי
יד שֵׁנִית לֵאמֹר מָה אַתָּה רֹאֶה וָאֹמַר סִיר נָפוּחַ אֲנִי רֹאֶה וּפָנָיו מִפְּנֵי צָפוֹנָה: וַיֹּאמֶר יהוה אֵלָי
טו מִצָּפוֹן תִּפָּתַח הָרָעָה עַל כָּל־יֹשְׁבֵי הָאָרֶץ: כִּי ׀ הִנְנִי קֹרֵא לְכָל־מִשְׁפְּחוֹת מַמְלְכוֹת צָפוֹנָה
נְאֻם־יהוה וּבָאוּ וְנָתְנוּ אִישׁ כִּסְאוֹ פֶּתַח ׀ שַׁעֲרֵי יְרוּשָׁלִַם וְעַל כָּל־חוֹמֹתֶיהָ סָבִיב וְעַל כָּל־
טז עָרֵי יְהוּדָה: וְדִבַּרְתִּי מִשְׁפָּטַי אוֹתָם עַל כָּל־רָעָתָם אֲשֶׁר עֲזָבוּנִי וַיְקַטְּרוּ לֵאלֹהִים אֲחֵרִים
יז וַיִּשְׁתַּחֲווּ לְמַעֲשֵׂי יְדֵיהֶם: וְאַתָּה תֶּאְזֹר מָתְנֶיךָ וְקַמְתָּ וְדִבַּרְתָּ אֲלֵיהֶם אֵת כָּל־אֲשֶׁר אָנֹכִי
יח אֲצַוֶּךָּ אַל־תֵּחַת מִפְּנֵיהֶם פֶּן־אֲחִתְּךָ לִפְנֵיהֶם: וַאֲנִי הִנֵּה נְתַתִּיךָ הַיּוֹם לְעִיר מִבְצָר וּלְעַמּוּד
יט בַּרְזֶל וּלְחֹמוֹת נְחֹשֶׁת עַל־כָּל־הָאָרֶץ לְמַלְכֵי יְהוּדָה לְשָׂרֶיהָ לְכֹהֲנֶיהָ וּלְעַם הָאָרֶץ: וְנִלְחֲמוּ
ב א אֵלֶיךָ וְלֹא־יוּכְלוּ לָךְ כִּי־אִתְּךָ אֲנִי נְאֻם־יהוה לְהַצִּילֶךָ: וַיְהִי דְבַר־יהוה אֵלַי לֵאמֹר:
ב הָלֹךְ וְקָרָאתָ בְאָזְנֵי יְרוּשָׁלִַם לֵאמֹר כֹּה אָמַר יהוה זָכַרְתִּי לָךְ חֶסֶד נְעוּרַיִךְ אַהֲבַת כְּלוּלֹתָיִךְ
ג לֶכְתֵּךְ אַחֲרַי בַּמִּדְבָּר בְּאֶרֶץ לֹא זְרוּעָה: קֹדֶשׁ יִשְׂרָאֵל לַיהוה רֵאשִׁית תְּבוּאָתֹה כָּל־אֹכְלָיו
יֶאְשָׁמוּ רָעָה תָּבֹא אֲלֵיהֶם נְאֻם־יהוה:

הפטרת

מסעי

ירמיה

ב ד ה שִׁמְעוּ דְבַר־יהוה בֵּית יַעֲקֹב וְכָל־מִשְׁפְּחוֹת בֵּית יִשְׂרָאֵל: כֹּה ׀ אָמַר יהוה מַה־מָּצְאוּ אֲבוֹתֵיכֶם
ו בִּי עָוֶל כִּי רָחֲקוּ מֵעָלָי וַיֵּלְכוּ אַחֲרֵי הַהֶבֶל וַיֶּהְבָּלוּ: וְלֹא אָמְרוּ אַיֵּה יהוה הַמַּעֲלֶה אֹתָנוּ מֵאֶרֶץ
מִצְרָיִם הַמּוֹלִיךְ אֹתָנוּ בַּמִּדְבָּר בְּאֶרֶץ עֲרָבָה וְשׁוּחָה בְּאֶרֶץ צִיָּה וְצַלְמָוֶת בְּאֶרֶץ לֹא־עָבַר
ז בָּהּ אִישׁ וְלֹא־יָשַׁב אָדָם שָׁם: וָאָבִיא אֶתְכֶם אֶל־אֶרֶץ הַכַּרְמֶל לֶאֱכֹל פִּרְיָהּ וְטוּבָהּ וַתָּבֹאוּ
ח וַתְּטַמְּאוּ אֶת־אַרְצִי וְנַחֲלָתִי שַׂמְתֶּם לְתוֹעֵבָה: הַכֹּהֲנִים לֹא אָמְרוּ אַיֵּה יהוה וְתֹפְשֵׂי הַתּוֹרָה
ט לֹא יְדָעוּנִי וְהָרֹעִים פָּשְׁעוּ בִי וְהַנְּבִיאִים נִבְּאוּ בַבַּעַל וְאַחֲרֵי לֹא־יוֹעִלוּ הָלָכוּ: לָכֵן עֹד אָרִיב
י אִתְּכֶם נְאֻם־יהוה וְאֶת־בְּנֵי בְנֵיכֶם אָרִיב: כִּי עִבְרוּ אִיֵּי כִתִּיִּים וּרְאוּ וְקֵדָר שִׁלְחוּ וְהִתְבּוֹנְנוּ
יא מְאֹד וּרְאוּ הֵן הָיְתָה כָּזֹאת: הַהֵימִיר גּוֹי אֱלֹהִים וְהֵמָּה לֹא אֱלֹהִים וְעַמִּי הֵמִיר כְּבוֹדוֹ בְּלוֹא
יב יג יוֹעִיל: שֹׁמּוּ שָׁמַיִם עַל־זֹאת וְשַׂעֲרוּ חָרְבוּ מְאֹד נְאֻם־יהוה: כִּי־שְׁתַּיִם רָעוֹת עָשָׂה עַמִּי אֹתִי
יד עָזְבוּ מְקוֹר ׀ מַיִם חַיִּים לַחְצֹב לָהֶם בֹּארוֹת בֹּארֹת נִשְׁבָּרִים אֲשֶׁר לֹא־יָכִלוּ הַמָּיִם: הַעֶבֶד

15 Is he born in the house? Why was he subjected to looting? Lion
cubs will roar over him; they raised their voice, and they have
rendered his land desolation; his cities are destroyed, without
16 inhabitants. The people of Nof and Tahpanhes will also crush
17 your head. Is it not this that did it to you, your forsaking of the
Lord your God at the time that He was leading you on the way?
18 Now, what is it for you on the way to Egypt, to drink water of
Shihor? What is it for you on the way to Assyria, to drink wa-
19 ter of the river? Your own evildoing will chastise you, and your
deviations shall reprove you, and know and see that evil and
bitter is your forsaking the Lord your God, and awe of Me is
20 not in you – the utterance of the Lord – God of hosts. For I have
always broken your yoke, snapped your restraints, and you said:
I will not transgress. Yet upon every high hill and under every
21 flourishing tree you saunter, a harlot. I planted you a select vine,
all of it from true seed, and how did you transform into a devi-
22 ant, strange vine for Me? For if you launder with natron, and
use much soap, your iniquity is stained before Me – the utter-
23 ance of my Lord God. How can you say: I was not defiled, after
the Be'alim I did not go? See your way in the valley, know what
you have done, a swift young she-camel meandering her ways.
24 A wild donkey accustomed to the wilderness, she inhaled the
wind in her desire; her lust, who can restrain it? All her seekers
25 will not weary, in her month they will find her. Prevent your
foot from being unshod and your throat from thirst, but you
said: It is hopeless. No, for I have loved strangers, and after
26 them I will go. Like the shame of a thief when he is discovered,
so has the house of Israel been shamed: they, their kings, their
27 princes, and their priests and their prophets. They say to wood:
You are my father, and to stone: You have borne us, for they
have turned their back to Me and not their face, but in the time
28 of their misfortune they will say: Arise, and save us. Where are
your gods that you made for you? Let them arise, if they can
save you in the time of your misfortune, for like the number of
your cities are your gods, Judah.

3 *Ashk. add* 4 Didn't you call to Me from now: My Father, You are the Master
of my youth?

4 *Seph. add* 1 If you will return, Israel – the utterance of the Lord – you will
return to Me, and if you will remove your detestable things from
2 before Me and not wander. You will take an oath: As the Lord
lives, in truth, in justice, and in righteousness, and the nations
will bless themselves by him, and will praise themselves by him.

טו יִשְׂרָאֵל אִם־יְלִיד בַּיִת הוּא מַדּוּעַ הָיָה לָבַז: עָלָיו יִשְׁאֲגוּ כְפִרִים נָתְנוּ קוֹלָם וַיָּשִׁיתוּ אַרְצוֹ

לְשַׁמָּה עָרָיו נִצְּתָה מִבְּלִי יֹשֵׁב: גַּם־בְּנֵי־נֹף וְתַחְפַּנְחֵס יִרְעוּךְ קָדְקֹד: הֲלוֹא־זֹאת תַּעֲשֶׂה־לָּךְ

יז עָזְבֵךְ אֶת־יְהוָה אֱלֹהַיִךְ בְּעֵת מוֹלִכֵךְ בַּדָּרֶךְ: וְעַתָּה מַה־לָּךְ לְדֶרֶךְ מִצְרַיִם לִשְׁתּוֹת מֵי שִׁחוֹר

יט וּמַה־לָּךְ לְדֶרֶךְ אַשּׁוּר לִשְׁתּוֹת מֵי נָהָר: תְּיַסְּרֵךְ רָעָתֵךְ וּמְשֻׁבוֹתַיִךְ תּוֹכִחֻךְ וּדְעִי וּרְאִי כִּי־רַע

כ וָמָר עָזְבֵךְ אֶת־יְהוָה אֱלֹהָיִךְ וְלֹא פַחְדָּתִי אֵלַיִךְ נְאֻם־אֲדֹנָי יְהוִה צְבָאוֹת: כִּי מֵעוֹלָם שָׁבַרְתִּי

עֻלֵּךְ נִתַּקְתִּי מוֹסְרוֹתַיִךְ וַתֹּאמְרִי לֹא אֶעֱבוֹד כִּי עַל־כָּל־גִּבְעָה גְבֹהָה וְתַחַת כָּל־עֵץ רַעֲנָן

כא אַתְּ צֹעָה זֹנָה: וְאָנֹכִי נְטַעְתִּיךְ שֹׂרֵק כֻּלֹּה זֶרַע אֱמֶת וְאֵיךְ נֶהְפַּכְתְּ לִי סוּרֵי הַגֶּפֶן נָכְרִיָּה:

כב כִּי אִם־תְּכַבְּסִי בַּנֶּתֶר וְתַרְבִּי־לָךְ בֹּרִית נִכְתָּם עֲוֹנֵךְ לְפָנַי נְאֻם אֲדֹנָי יְהוִה: אֵיךְ תֹּאמְרִי לֹא

נִטְמֵאתִי אַחֲרֵי הַבְּעָלִים לֹא הָלַכְתִּי רְאִי דַרְכֵּךְ בַּגַּיְא דְּעִי מֶה עָשִׂית בִּכְרָה קַלָּה מְשָׂרֶכֶת

כד דְּרָכֶיהָ: פֶּרֶה ׀ לִמֻּד מִדְבָּר בְּאַוַּת נַפְשָׁהּ שָׁאֲפָה רוּחַ תַּאֲנָתָהּ מִי יְשִׁיבֶנָּה כָּל־מְבַקְשֶׁיהָ לֹא

יִעָפוּ בְּחָדְשָׁהּ יִמְצָאוּנְהָ: מִנְעִי רַגְלֵךְ מִיָּחֵף וגרונך מִצִּמְאָה וַתֹּאמְרִי נוֹאָשׁ לוֹא כִּי־אָהַבְתִּי

כו זָרִים וְאַחֲרֵיהֶם אֵלֵךְ: כְּבֹשֶׁת גַּנָּב כִּי יִמָּצֵא כֵּן הֹבִישׁוּ בֵּית יִשְׂרָאֵל הֵמָּה מַלְכֵיהֶם שָׂרֵיהֶם

כז וְכֹהֲנֵיהֶם וּנְבִיאֵיהֶם: אֹמְרִים לָעֵץ אָבִי אַתָּה וְלָאֶבֶן אַתְּ יְלִדְתָּנוּ כִּי־פָנוּ אֵלַי עֹרֶף וְלֹא פָנִים

וּבְעֵת רָעָתָם יֹאמְרוּ קוּמָה וְהוֹשִׁיעֵנוּ: וְאַיֵּה אֱלֹהֶיךָ אֲשֶׁר עָשִׂיתָ לָּךְ יָקוּמוּ אִם־יוֹשִׁיעוּךָ

בְּעֵת רָעָתֶךָ כִּי מִסְפַּר עָרֶיךָ הָיוּ אֱלֹהֶיךָ יְהוּדָה:

ג ד הֲלוֹא מֵעַתָּה קָרָאתי לִי אָבִי אַלּוּף נְעֻרַי אָתָּה:

ד ב אִם־תָּשׁוּב יִשְׂרָאֵל ׀ נְאֻם־יְהוָה אֵלַי תָּשׁוּב וְאִם־תָּסִיר שִׁקּוּצֶיךָ מִפָּנַי וְלֹא תָנוּד: וְנִשְׁבַּעְתָּ

חַי־יְהוָה בֶּאֱמֶת בְּמִשְׁפָּט וּבִצְדָקָה וְהִתְבָּרְכוּ בוֹ גּוֹיִם וּבוֹ יִתְהַלָּלוּ:

Haftara for
Devarim

Reproof for Corruption and Injustice

ISAIAH 1:1–1:27

Just as Moses opened his final speech to Israel with a rebuke but ended with words of consolation and blessings, so too Isaiah's vision begins with a harsh reproof and concludes with words of comfort. The prophet castigates those who perform empty ritual acts of worship while they conduct their moral and social lives in contradiction to the will of God. The prophet informs them that despite their superficial observance of the festivals and public gatherings, their visits to the Temple, and their bringing of offerings, none of these express their actual religious orientation. He tells them that they must improve their behavior, by restoring justice and righteousness in the land, before God will accept them with love.

This *haftara*, called *Haftarat Hazon*, after its first word, meaning vision, is the third and last of three *haftarot* of retribution. It is always read on the Sabbath before the Ninth of Av. The key term of lament, *eikha*, meaning how, which is also the first word in the book of Lamentations and the name of that book in Hebrew, appears both in Isaiah's reproof and early in Moses' speech in the *parasha*.

1 1 The vision of Isaiah son of Amotz, that he envisioned concerning Judah and Jerusalem, in the days of Uziyahu, Yotam, Ahaz,
2 and Hizkiyahu, kings of Judah. Hear, heavens, and listen, earth, as the Lord has spoken: I have reared children and raised them
3 up, and they have rebelled against Me. An ox knows its owner, and a donkey its master's trough. Israel does not know; My peo-
4 ple does not perceive. Woe! Sinful nation, people laden with iniquity, villainous descendants, corrupting children; they forsook the Lord, they scorned the Holy One of Israel, they have
5 turned backward. For what will you be struck, that you continue
6 straying still? Every head is ill and every heart suffers. From foot to head, there is nothing whole in it; wound, bruise, and fresh blow have not been treated nor bandaged nor softened with
7 oil. Your land is desolation; your cities are burned in fire; your land, strangers devour it in your presence and it is desolation
8 like an upheaval by strangers. The daughter of Zion remains like a booth in a vineyard, like a shed in a field of gourds, like
9 a besieged city. Had not the Lord of Hosts left us a miniscule remnant, we would have been like Sodom, we would have been
10 comparable to Gomorrah. Hear the word of the Lord, leaders of Sodom; listen to the Torah of our God, people of Gomorrah.
11 Why do I need the multitude of your offerings, says the Lord; I am sated with burnt offerings of rams and the fat of fattened bulls; I do not desire the blood of bulls and sheep and goats.
12 When you come to appear before Me, who sought this from
13 your hand, trampling My courtyards? Do not continue bringing a vain meal offering; incense is an abomination for Me; New Moon and Sabbath, convoking convocations, I cannot

14 abide evil and assembly. My soul loathes your New Moons and your festivals; they are a burden for Me; I have wearied of
15 forbearance. And when you spread your hands, I will avert My eyes from you; even when you multiply prayer, I do not hear;
16 your hands are full of blood. Wash, purify yourselves, remove the evil of your actions from before My eyes; cease doing evil.
17 Learn well, seek justice, bolster the oppressed, adjudicate for
18 the orphan, champion the widow. Let us go now and reason together, says the Lord. If your sins will be like scarlet, they will be whitened as snow; if they will be reddened like crimson, they
19 will be like wool. If you are willing and heed, the goodness of
20 the land you will eat. But if you refuse and are defiant, you will be devoured by the sword, as the mouth of the Lord has spo-
21 ken. How did it become a harlot, the faithful city? Filled with
22 principle, justice would abide in it, but now, murderers. Your
23 silver has become dross, your liquor diluted with water. Your princes are wayward and cohorts of thieves; each loves bribery and pursues graft. They will not provide justice for an orphan
24 and the cause of the widow will not come to them. Therefore, the utterance of the Master, the Lord of hosts, the Mighty One of Israel: Woe! I will be relieved of My adversaries and will
25 avenge Myself on My enemies. I will turn My hand against you, and I will refine your dross as with lye; I will remove all your
26 slag. I will restore your judges as at first and your counselors as at the beginning; thereafter, you will be called the city of righ-
27 teousness, the faithful city. Zion will be redeemed with justice and its returnees with righteousness.

דברים

א חֲז֣וֹן יְשַׁעְיָ֣הוּ בֶן־אָמ֗וֹץ אֲשֶׁ֣ר חָזָ֔ה עַל־יְהוּדָ֖ה וִירִוּשָׁלָ֑͏ִם בִּימֵ֨י עֻזִּיָּ֧הוּ יוֹתָ֛ם אָחָ֥ז יְחִזְקִיָּ֖הוּ מַלְכֵ֥י   ישעיה

ב יְהוּדָֽה: שִׁמְע֤וּ שָׁמַ֙יִם֙ וְהַאֲזִ֣ינִי אֶ֔רֶץ כִּ֥י יְהוָ֖ה דִּבֵּ֑ר בָּנִים֙ גִּדַּ֣לְתִּי וְרוֹמַ֔מְתִּי וְהֵ֖ם פָּ֥שְׁעוּ בִֽי: יָדַ֣ע

ג שׁ֚וֹר קֹנֵ֔הוּ וַחֲמ֖וֹר אֵב֣וּס בְּעָלָ֑יו יִשְׂרָאֵל֙ לֹ֣א יָדַ֔ע עַמִּ֖י לֹ֥א הִתְבּוֹנָֽן: ה֣וֹי ׀ גּ֣וֹי חֹטֵ֗א עַ֚ם כֶּ֣בֶד עָוֺ֔ן

ד זֶ֣רַע מְרֵעִ֔ים בָּנִ֖ים מַשְׁחִיתִ֑ים עָזְב֣וּ אֶת־יְהוָ֗ה נִֽאֲצ֛וּ אֶת־קְד֥וֹשׁ יִשְׂרָאֵ֖ל נָזֹ֥רוּ אָחֽוֹר: עַ֣ל מֶ֥ה

ה תֻכּ֥וּ ע֖וֹד תּוֹסִ֣יפוּ סָרָ֑ה כָּל־רֹ֣אשׁ לׇחֳלִ֔י וְכָל־לֵבָ֖ב דַּוָּֽי: מִכַּף־רֶ֤גֶל וְעַד־רֹאשׁ֙ אֵֽין־בּ֣וֹ מְתֹ֔ם פֶּ֥צַע

ו וְחַבּוּרָ֖ה וּמַכָּ֣ה טְרִיָּ֑ה לֹא־זֹ֙רוּ֙ וְלֹ֣א חֻבָּ֔שׁוּ וְלֹ֥א רֻכְּכָ֖ה בַּשָּֽׁמֶן: אַרְצְכֶ֣ם שְׁמָמָ֔ה עָרֵיכֶ֖ם שְׂרֻפ֣וֹת

ז אֵ֑שׁ אַדְמַתְכֶ֗ם לְנֶגְדְּכֶם֙ זָרִים֙ אֹכְלִ֣ים אֹתָ֔הּ וּשְׁמָמָ֖ה כְּמַהְפֵּכַ֥ת זָרִֽים: וְנוֹתְרָ֥ה בַת־צִיּ֖וֹן כְּסֻכָּ֣ה

ח בְכָ֑רֶם כִּמְלוּנָ֣ה בְמִקְשָׁ֔ה כְּעִ֖יר נְצוּרָֽה: לוּלֵי֙ יְהוָ֣ה צְבָא֔וֹת הוֹתִ֥יר לָ֛נוּ שָׂרִ֖יד כִּמְעָ֑ט כִּסְדֹ֣ם

ט הָיִ֔ינוּ לַעֲמֹרָ֖ה דָּמִֽינוּ:   שִׁמְע֥וּ דְבַר־יְהוָ֖ה קְצִינֵ֣י סְדֹ֑ם הַאֲזִ֛ינוּ תּוֹרַ֥ת אֱלֹהֵ֖ינוּ עַ֥ם

י עֲמֹרָֽה: לָמָּה־לִּ֤י רֹב־זִבְחֵיכֶם֙ יֹאמַ֣ר יְהוָ֔ה שָׂבַ֛עְתִּי עֹל֥וֹת אֵילִ֖ים וְחֵ֣לֶב מְרִיאִ֑ים וְדַ֨ם פָּרִ֧ים

יא וּכְבָשִׂ֛ים וְעַתּוּדִ֖ים לֹ֥א חָפָֽצְתִּי: כִּ֣י תָבֹ֔אוּ לֵרָא֖וֹת פָּנָ֑י מִי־בִקֵּ֥שׁ זֹ֛את מִיֶּדְכֶ֖ם רְמֹ֥ס חֲצֵרָֽי: לֹ֣א

יב תוֹסִ֗יפוּ הָבִיא֙ מִנְחַת־שָׁ֔וְא קְטֹ֧רֶת תּוֹעֵבָ֛ה הִ֖יא לִ֑י חֹ֤דֶשׁ וְשַׁבָּת֙ קְרֹ֣א מִקְרָ֔א לֹא־אוּכַ֥ל אָ֖וֶן

יג וַעֲצָרָֽה: חׇדְשֵׁיכֶ֤ם וּמוֹעֲדֵיכֶם֙ שָׂנְאָ֣ה נַפְשִׁ֔י הָי֥וּ עָלַ֖י לָטֹ֑רַח נִלְאֵ֖יתִי נְשֹֽׂא: וּבְפָרִשְׂכֶ֣ם כַּפֵּיכֶ֗ם

יד אַעְלִ֤ים עֵינַי֙ מִכֶּ֔ם גַּ֛ם כִּֽי־תַרְבּ֥וּ תְפִלָּ֖ה אֵינֶ֣נִּי שֹׁמֵ֑עַ יְדֵיכֶ֖ם דָּמִ֥ים מָלֵֽאוּ: רַֽחֲצוּ֙ הִזַּכּ֔וּ הָסִ֛ירוּ רֹ֥עַ

טו מַעַלְלֵיכֶ֖ם מִנֶּ֣גֶד עֵינָ֑י חִדְל֖וּ הָרֵֽעַ: לִמְד֥וּ הֵיטֵ֛ב דִּרְשׁ֥וּ מִשְׁפָּ֖ט אַשְּׁר֣וּ חָמ֑וֹץ שִׁפְט֣וּ יָת֔וֹם רִ֖יבוּ

טז אַלְמָנָֽה: לְכוּ־נָ֛א וְנִוָּכְחָ֖ה יֹאמַ֣ר יְהוָ֑ה אִם־יִֽהְי֨וּ חֲטָאֵיכֶ֤ם כַּשָּׁנִים֙ כַּשֶּׁ֣לֶג יַלְבִּ֔ינוּ

יז אִם־יַאְדִּ֥ימוּ כַתּוֹלָ֖ע כַּצֶּ֥מֶר יִהְיֽוּ: אִם־תֹּאב֖וּ וּשְׁמַעְתֶּ֑ם ט֥וּב הָאָ֖רֶץ תֹּאכֵֽלוּ: וְאִם־תְּמָאֲנ֖וּ

יח וּמְרִיתֶ֑ם חֶ֣רֶב תְּאֻכְּל֔וּ כִּ֛י פִּ֥י יְהוָ֖ה דִּבֵּֽר: אֵיכָה֙ הָיְתָ֣ה לְזוֹנָ֔ה קִרְיָ֖ה נֶאֱמָנָ֑ה

יט מְלֵאֲתִ֣י מִשְׁפָּ֔ט צֶ֖דֶק יָלִ֣ין בָּ֑הּ וְעַתָּ֖ה מְרַצְּחִֽים: כַּסְפֵּ֖ךְ הָיָ֣ה לְסִיגִ֑ים סׇבְאֵ֖ךְ מָה֥וּל בַּמָּֽיִם:

כ שָׂרַ֣יִךְ סוֹרְרִ֗ים וְחַבְרֵי֙ גַּנָּבִ֔ים כֻּלּוֹ֙ אֹהֵ֣ב שֹׁ֔חַד וְרֹדֵ֖ף שַׁלְמֹנִ֑ים יָת֙וֹם֙ לֹ֣א יִשְׁפֹּ֔טוּ וְרִ֥יב אַלְמָנָ֖ה

כא לֹא־יָב֥וֹא אֲלֵיהֶֽם: לָכֵ֗ן נְאֻ֤ם הָֽאָדוֹן֙ יְהוָ֣ה צְבָא֔וֹת אֲבִ֖יר יִשְׂרָאֵ֑ל ה֚וֹי אֶנָּחֵ֣ם

כב מִצָּרַ֔י וְאִנָּקְמָ֖ה מֵאוֹיְבָֽי: וְאָשִׁ֤יבָה יָדִי֙ עָלַ֔יִךְ וְאֶצְרֹ֥ף כַּבֹּ֖ר סִיגָ֑יִךְ וְאָסִ֖ירָה כָּל־בְּדִילָֽיִךְ: וְאָשִׁ֤יבָה

כג שֹׁפְטַ֙יִךְ֙ כְּבָרִ֣אשֹׁנָ֔ה וְיֹעֲצַ֖יִךְ כְּבַתְּחִלָּ֑ה אַחֲרֵי־כֵ֗ן יִקָּ֤רֵא לָךְ֙ עִ֣יר הַצֶּ֔דֶק קִרְיָ֖ה נֶאֱמָנָֽה: צִיּ֖וֹן

כד בְּמִשְׁפָּ֣ט תִּפָּדֶ֑ה וְשָׁבֶ֖יהָ בִּצְדָקָֽה:

Haftara for
Va'ethanan

Words of Consolation
ISAIAH 40:1–26

The Ninth of Av, which commemorates the destruction of the Temple, is followed by a series of seven *haftarot* of comfort that are read on the Sabbaths leading up to Rosh HaShana. All of them are taken from the book of Isaiah.

Isaiah's prophecies of comfort have been a source of consolation and encouragement for the Jewish people over the generations. Among other reasons, this is because they are timeless and make almost no reference to specific events. Rather, they deal with worldwide upheavals on a broad scale. While the first chapters mention the return of Zion from the Babylonian exile several times, in later passages Babylon is not mentioned at all. This notion is supported by the Ramban, who divides the book of Isaiah into three parts: Prophecies that came before the fall of Assyria (chaps. 1–38); prophecies dealing with the exile to Babylonia and the return (39–51:11); and prophecies of comfort for the future redemption (51:12–66:24 ; see *Sefer HaGe'ula* of the Ramban, Chavel edition, vol. 1, p. 268).

This *haftara* opens the prophecies of comfort with four declarations relating to God's promise to comfort and redeem His people. In the first declaration (40:1–2), God commands that His people and His city must be comforted. The second (40:3–5) announces preparations for redemption, and a call to pave a path to God for those He is redeeming as they return from exile. The third declaration (40:6–8) is an instruction to proclaim that God's assurance of comfort and redemption for His people will stand forever. Finally, the fourth declaration (40:9–11) proclaims that a loud voice is heard in Jerusalem, heralding the appearance of God as He gathers in His scattered people.

After these declarations, which convey God's fulfillment of His promise to redeem His people, the prophet speaks of the greatness of God, which is beyond all possible human imagination, description, and estimation, as he stresses to the people that they must place their hopes in Him alone.

40 1 2 Comfort, comfort My people, will say your God. Speak to the heart of Jerusalem and call to it, for its time is completed, for its iniquity is rectified, for it has received double at the hand of the 3 Lord for all its sins. A voice proclaims in the wilderness: Clear the way of the Lord, level in the desert a highway for our God. 4 Every valley will be raised and every mountain and hill will be lowered; the crooked will become straight and the ridges a 5 plain. The glory of the Lord will be revealed and all flesh will see 6 together that the mouth of the Lord has spoken. A voice says: Proclaim, and he says: What shall I proclaim? All flesh is grass 7 and all its grace is like a flower of the field. The grass withers, the flower fades, for the breath of the Lord blows upon it; indeed, 8 the people are grass. The grass withers, the flower fades, but 9 the word of our God will stand forever. Ascend you, herald of Zion, upon a high mountain; raise your voice powerfully, herald of Jerusalem; raise it, do not fear; say to the cities of Judah: 10 Behold, your God. Behold, the Lord God will come mightily and His arm will rule for Him; behold, His reward is with Him 11 and His wage is before Him. Like a shepherd, He will herd his flock; with His arm He will gather lambs and carry them in His 12 bosom, guiding the nursing ewes. Who has measured the waters with His steps and determined the heavens with a span, gauged with a flask the dust of the earth, weighed mountains with a 13 scale, and hills with a balance? Who can determine the spirit of 14 the Lord? Yet He will inform a man of His counsel. With whom did He consult and grant Him understanding, teach Him the

path of justice and teach Him knowledge, inform Him of the 15 way of understanding? Behold, nations may be regarded like a drop from a bucket or like the powder of scales; behold, He will 16 take up islands like dust. Lebanon is not sufficient for kindling 17 and its beasts are not sufficient for burnt offerings. All the nations are as nothing before Him; they are considered by Him as 18 nothing and emptiness. To whom will you liken God, and what 19 likeness will you ascribe Him? An idol is cast by a craftsman, a goldsmith will plate it, and it will have silver chains from an ar- 20 tisan. The collector of contributions will choose a tree that will not rot, he will seek a wise craftsman to prepare an idol that will 21 not topple. Will you not know? Will you not hear? Were you not told from the beginning? Haven't you understood the foun- 22 dations of the earth? It is He who sits over the circle of the earth whose inhabitants are like grasshoppers, who spreads the heavens like a curtain and stretches them like a tent for habitation, 23 who renders princes into nothing; He makes judges of the land 24 like emptiness. It is as though they were not planted, as though they were not sown, as though their trunk had not taken root in the earth. Moreover, one may blow on them and they wither, 25 and a storm will carry them off like straw. To whom would you 26 liken Me that I would be equal? says the Holy One. Raise your eyes on high and see: Who created these? He who brings out their host by number, calling all of them by name; from abundance of might and the exertion of power, not one is missing.

הפטרת

ואתחנן

מ א ב נַחֲמוּ נַחֲמוּ עַמִּי יֹאמַר אֱלֹהֵיכֶם׃ דַּבְּרוּ עַל־לֵב יְרוּשָׁלִַם וְקִרְאוּ אֵלֶיהָ כִּי מָלְאָה צְבָאָהּ כִּי ישעיה
ג נִרְצָה עֲוֺנָהּ כִּי לָקְחָה מִיַּד יְהוָה כִּפְלַיִם בְּכָל־חַטֹּאתֶיהָ׃ קוֹל קוֹרֵא בַּמִּדְבָּר
ד פַּנּוּ דֶּרֶךְ יְהוָה יַשְּׁרוּ בָּעֲרָבָה מְסִלָּה לֵאלֹהֵינוּ׃ כָּל־גֶּיא יִנָּשֵׂא וְכָל־הַר וְגִבְעָה יִשְׁפָּלוּ וְהָיָה
ה הֶעָקֹב לְמִישׁוֹר וְהָרְכָסִים לְבִקְעָה׃ וְנִגְלָה כְּבוֹד יְהוָה וְרָאוּ כָל־בָּשָׂר יַחְדָּו כִּי פִּי יְהוָה
ו דִּבֵּר׃ קוֹל אֹמֵר קְרָא וְאָמַר מָה אֶקְרָא כָּל־הַבָּשָׂר חָצִיר וְכָל־חַסְדּוֹ כְּצִיץ
ז ח הַשָּׂדֶה׃ יָבֵשׁ חָצִיר נָבֵל צִיץ כִּי רוּחַ יְהוָה נָשְׁבָה בּוֹ אָכֵן חָצִיר הָעָם׃ יָבֵשׁ חָצִיר נָבֵל צִיץ
ט וּדְבַר אֱלֹהֵינוּ יָקוּם לְעוֹלָם׃ עַל הַר־גָּבֹהַּ עֲלִי־לָךְ מְבַשֶּׂרֶת צִיּוֹן הָרִימִי בַכֹּחַ
י קוֹלֵךְ מְבַשֶּׂרֶת יְרוּשָׁלִָם הָרִימִי אַל־תִּירָאִי אִמְרִי לְעָרֵי יְהוּדָה הִנֵּה אֱלֹהֵיכֶם׃ הִנֵּה אֲדֹנָי
יא יְהוִה בְּחָזָק יָבוֹא וּזְרֹעוֹ מֹשְׁלָה לוֹ הִנֵּה שְׂכָרוֹ אִתּוֹ וּפְעֻלָּתוֹ לְפָנָיו׃ כְּרֹעֶה עֶדְרוֹ יִרְעֶה בִּזְרֹעוֹ
יב יְקַבֵּץ טְלָאִים וּבְחֵיקוֹ יִשָּׂא עָלוֹת יְנַהֵל׃ מִי־מָדַד בְּשָׁעֳלוֹ מַיִם וְשָׁמַיִם בַּזֶּרֶת תִּכֵּן
יג וְכָל בַּשָּׁלִשׁ עֲפַר הָאָרֶץ וְשָׁקַל בַּפֶּלֶס הָרִים וּגְבָעוֹת בְּמֹאזְנָיִם׃ מִי־תִכֵּן אֶת־רוּחַ יְהוָה וְאִישׁ
יד עֲצָתוֹ יוֹדִיעֶנּוּ׃ אֶת־מִי נוֹעָץ וַיְבִינֵהוּ וַיְלַמְּדֵהוּ בְּאֹרַח מִשְׁפָּט וַיְלַמְּדֵהוּ דַעַת וְדֶרֶךְ תְּבוּנוֹת
טו טז יוֹדִיעֶנּוּ׃ הֵן גּוֹיִם כְּמַר מִדְּלִי וּכְשַׁחַק מֹאזְנַיִם נֶחְשָׁבוּ הֵן אִיִּים כַּדַּק יִטּוֹל׃ וּלְבָנוֹן אֵין דֵּי
יז בָּעֵר וְחַיָּתוֹ אֵין דֵּי עוֹלָה׃ כָּל־הַגּוֹיִם כְּאַיִן נֶגְדּוֹ מֵאֶפֶס וָתֹהוּ נֶחְשְׁבוּ־לוֹ׃
יח יט וְאֶל־מִי תְּדַמְּיוּן אֵל וּמַה־דְּמוּת תַּעַרְכוּ־לוֹ׃ הַפֶּסֶל נָסַךְ חָרָשׁ וְצֹרֵף בַּזָּהָב יְרַקְּעֶנּוּ וּרְתֻקוֹת
כ כֶּסֶף צוֹרֵף׃ הַמְסֻכָּן תְּרוּמָה עֵץ לֹא־יִרְקַב יִבְחָר חָרָשׁ חָכָם יְבַקֶּשׁ־לוֹ לְהָכִין פֶּסֶל לֹא יִמּוֹט׃
כא כב הֲלוֹא תֵדְעוּ הֲלוֹא תִשְׁמָעוּ הֲלוֹא הֻגַּד מֵרֹאשׁ לָכֶם הֲלוֹא הֲבִינֹתֶם מוֹסְדוֹת הָאָרֶץ׃ הַיֹּשֵׁב
כג עַל־חוּג הָאָרֶץ וְיֹשְׁבֶיהָ כַּחֲגָבִים הַנּוֹטֶה כַדֹּק שָׁמַיִם וַיִּמְתָּחֵם כָּאֹהֶל לָשָׁבֶת׃ הַנּוֹתֵן רוֹזְנִים
כד לְאָיִן שֹׁפְטֵי אֶרֶץ כַּתֹּהוּ עָשָׂה׃ אַף בַּל־נִטָּעוּ אַף בַּל־זֹרָעוּ אַף בַּל־שֹׁרֵשׁ בָּאֶרֶץ גִּזְעָם וְגַם
כה נָשַׁף בָּהֶם וַיִּבָשׁוּ וּסְעָרָה כַּקַּשׁ תִּשָּׂאֵם׃ וְאֶל־מִי תְדַמְּיוּנִי וְאֶשְׁוֶה יֹאמַר קָדוֹשׁ׃
כו שְׂאוּ־מָרוֹם עֵינֵיכֶם וּרְאוּ מִי־בָרָא אֵלֶּה הַמּוֹצִיא בְמִסְפָּר צְבָאָם לְכֻלָּם בְּשֵׁם יִקְרָא מֵרֹב
אוֹנִים וְאַמִּיץ כֹּחַ אִישׁ לֹא נֶעְדָּר׃

Haftara for **Ekev**

Zion Has Not Been Abandoned

ISAIAH 49:14–51:3

This *haftara* deals with the consolation of the people of Israel upon the ingathering of its exiles. When God fights for Israel and redeems His nation, the entire world will change: Former enemies will cease their hostilities, while the land and its returning children will be revitalized. Later in this prophecy, Isaiah sharpens his tone, as he clarifies to the people that their exile from the land is a punishment for their deeds and not an arbitrary decree. This fundamental idea also appears in the second section of *Shema*, which is in *Parashat Ekev*.

Alongside its words of consolation and encouragement for Zion, this *haftara* also describes the role of the prophet, with all the difficulties that this position entails. The content of Isaiah's prophecies is often highly unpopular, as he states matters that his listeners do not wish to hear. However, the prophet's hardships do not undermine his confidence. He does not break down or bemoan his fate; on the contrary, he disparages his obtuse audience, and instead of worrying about what is in store for him, he urges them to take heed of their own impending doom.

49 14 Zion said: The Lord has forsaken me and my Master has forgot-
15 ten me. Can a woman forget her baby or from being merciful
to the child of her womb? These too may forget, but I will not
16 forget you. Behold, I have engraved you upon My palms; your
17 walls are before Me always. Your children will hasten; your de-
18 molishers and your destroyers will depart from you. Raise your
eyes around and see: All of them have gathered, have come to
you. As I live – the utterance of the Lord – that you will don all
19 of them like jewelry and you will tie them like a bride. For your
ruins and your desolation and your destroyed land you will
now crowd with inhabitants, and your destroyers will be dis-
20 tanced. The children of your bereavement will yet say in your
ears: The place is crowded for me, make way for me that I may
21 sit. You will say in your heart: Who bore me these? As I am
bereaved and lonely, exiled and astray. And these, who raised
them? Behold, I remained alone; these, from where are they?
22 So said the Lord God: Behold, I will raise My hand to nations
and I will hoist My banner to peoples; and they shall bring your
sons in their garments, and your daughters will be carried on
23 shoulders. Kings will be your caregivers, and their princesses
your wet nurses; they will prostrate themselves to you, faces to
the ground, and they will lick the dust of your feet. And you will
know that I am the Lord, of whom those who long for Me will
24 not be ashamed. Can plunder be taken from the mighty, or the
25 captives of the victorious escape? For so said the Lord: Even
the captives of the mighty may be taken and the plunder of the
powerful may escape; with your rivals I will contend and your
26 children will I save. I will feed your oppressors their own flesh;
like sweet wine their blood will intoxicate them. And all flesh
will know that I the Lord am your Savior and your Redeemer,
50 1 the Mighty One of Jacob. So said the Lord: Where is the scroll
of your mother's severance with which I sent her away, or to
whom among My creditors did I sell you? Behold, for your
iniquities you were sold and for your transgressions was your
2 mother sent away. Why did I come and there is no man, I called
and there is no one to answer? Is My hand insufficient for redemption? Is there no strength in Me to rescue? Behold, with
My rebuke I dry the sea, I render rivers wilderness; their fish
3 will reek from no water and die of thirst. I clothe the heavens
4 with blackness and I make sackcloth their garment. The Lord
God has given me a skilled tongue to know to give timely advice to the tired; He rouses me each morning, He rouses my
5 ear to hear skillfully. The Lord God opened my ear and I did
6 not rebel, I did not retreat backward. I gave my body to the
smiters and my cheeks to the pluckers; I did not hide my face
7 from humiliation and spittle. And the Lord God will help me;
therefore, I was not humiliated; therefore, I made my face like
8 a flint and I know that I will not be ashamed. My vindicator is
near, who will contend with me? Let us stand together; who
9 is my adversary? Let him approach me. Behold, the Lord God
will help me; who is he that will condemn me? Behold, all of
10 them will wear out like a garment, a moth will eat them. Who
among you fears the Lord, hears the voice of His servant, who
walked in darkness and there was no light for him? Let him
11 trust in the name of the Lord and rely on his God. Behold, all
of you are igniters of fire, lighters of sparks; go in the flame of
your fire and in the sparks that you kindled. This was for you
51 1 from My hand; you will lie in suffering. Listen to Me, pursuers
of justice, seekers of the Lord; look to the rock from which you
were hewn and to the hole of the pit from which you were dug.
2 Look to Abraham your father and to Sarah your originator; for
3 as one I called him and I blessed him and multiplied him. For
the Lord will comfort Zion; He will comfort all her ruins; He
will render its wilderness like Eden and its desert like a garden
of the Lord. Gladness and joy will be found in it, thanksgiving
and the sound of music.

הפטרת

עקב

מט יד טו וַתֹּאמֶר צִיּוֹן עֲזָבַנִי יְהוָה וַאדֹנָי שְׁכֵחָנִי: הֲתִשְׁכַּח אִשָּׁה עוּלָהּ מֵרַחֵם בֶּן־בִּטְנָהּ גַּם־אֵלֶּה ישעיה
טז יז תִשְׁכַּחְנָה וְאָנֹכִי לֹא אֶשְׁכָּחֵךְ: הֵן עַל־כַּפַּיִם חַקֹּתִיךְ חוֹמֹתַיִךְ נֶגְדִּי תָּמִיד: מִהֲרוּ בָּנָיִךְ מְהָרְסַיִךְ
יח וּמַחֲרִבַיִךְ מִמֵּךְ יֵצֵאוּ: שְׂאִי־סָבִיב עֵינַיִךְ וּרְאִי כֻּלָּם נִקְבְּצוּ בָאוּ־לָךְ חַי־אָנִי נְאֻם־יְהוָה כִּי
יט כֻלָּם כַּעֲדִי תִלְבָּשִׁי וּתְקַשְּׁרִים כַּכַּלָּה: כִּי חָרְבֹתַיִךְ וְשֹׁמְמֹתַיִךְ וְאֶרֶץ הֲרִסֻתֵךְ כִּי עַתָּה תֵּצְרִי
כ מִיּוֹשֵׁב וְרָחֲקוּ מְבַלְּעָיִךְ: עוֹד יֹאמְרוּ בְאָזְנַיִךְ בְּנֵי שִׁכֻּלָיִךְ צַר־לִי הַמָּקוֹם גְּשָׁה־לִּי וְאֵשֵׁבָה:
כא וְאָמַרְתְּ בִּלְבָבֵךְ מִי יָלַד־לִי אֶת־אֵלֶּה וַאֲנִי שְׁכוּלָה וְגַלְמוּדָה גֹּלָה ׀ וְסוּרָה וְאֵלֶּה מִי גִדֵּל הֵן
כב אֲנִי נִשְׁאַרְתִּי לְבַדִּי אֵלֶּה אֵיפֹה הֵם: כֹּה־אָמַר אֲדֹנָי יֱהוִה הִנֵּה אֶשָּׂא אֶל־גּוֹיִם
כג יָדִי וְאֶל־עַמִּים אָרִים נִסִּי וְהֵבִיאוּ בָנַיִךְ בְּחֹצֶן וּבְנֹתַיִךְ עַל־כָּתֵף תִּנָּשֶׂאנָה: וְהָיוּ מְלָכִים אֹמְנַיִךְ
וְשָׂרוֹתֵיהֶם מֵינִיקֹתַיִךְ אַפַּיִם אֶרֶץ יִשְׁתַּחֲווּ־לָךְ וַעֲפַר רַגְלַיִךְ יְלַחֵכוּ וְיָדַעַתְּ כִּי־אֲנִי יְהוָה אֲשֶׁר
כד כה לֹא־יֵבֹשׁוּ קֹוָי: הֲיֻקַּח מִגִּבּוֹר מַלְקוֹחַ וְאִם־שְׁבִי צַדִּיק יִמָּלֵט: כִּי־כֹה ׀ אָמַר יְהוָה
גַּם־שְׁבִי גִבּוֹר יֻקָּח וּמַלְקוֹחַ עָרִיץ יִמָּלֵט וְאֶת־יְרִיבֵךְ אָנֹכִי אָרִיב וְאֶת־בָּנַיִךְ אָנֹכִי אוֹשִׁיעַ:
כו וְהַאֲכַלְתִּי אֶת־מוֹנַיִךְ אֶת־בְּשָׂרָם וְכֶעָסִיס דָּמָם יִשְׁכָּרוּן וְיָדְעוּ כָל־בָּשָׂר כִּי אֲנִי יְהוָה מוֹשִׁיעֵךְ
נ א וְגֹאֲלֵךְ אֲבִיר יַעֲקֹב: כֹּה ׀ אָמַר יְהוָה אֵי זֶה סֵפֶר כְּרִיתוּת אִמְּכֶם אֲשֶׁר שִׁלַּחְתִּיהָ
אוֹ מִי מִנּוֹשַׁי אֲשֶׁר־מָכַרְתִּי אֶתְכֶם לוֹ הֵן בַּעֲוֹנֹתֵיכֶם נִמְכַּרְתֶּם וּבְפִשְׁעֵיכֶם שֻׁלְּחָה אִמְּכֶם:
ב מַדּוּעַ בָּאתִי וְאֵין אִישׁ קָרָאתִי וְאֵין עוֹנֶה הֲקָצוֹר קָצְרָה יָדִי מִפְּדוּת וְאִם־אֵין־בִּי כֹחַ לְהַצִּיל
ג הֵן בְּגַעֲרָתִי אַחֲרִיב יָם אָשִׂים נְהָרוֹת מִדְבָּר תִּבְאַשׁ דְּגָתָם מֵאֵין מַיִם וְתָמֹת בַּצָּמָא: אַלְבִּישׁ
ד שָׁמַיִם קַדְרוּת וְשַׂק אָשִׂים כְּסוּתָם: אֲדֹנָי יֱהוִה נָתַן לִי לְשׁוֹן לִמּוּדִים לָדַעַת
ה לָעוּת אֶת־יָעֵף דָּבָר יָעִיר ׀ בַּבֹּקֶר בַּבֹּקֶר יָעִיר לִי אֹזֶן לִשְׁמֹעַ כַּלִּמּוּדִים: אֲדֹנָי יֱהוִה פָּתַח־לִי
ו אֹזֶן וְאָנֹכִי לֹא מָרִיתִי אָחוֹר לֹא נְסוּגֹתִי: גֵּוִי נָתַתִּי לְמַכִּים וּלְחָיַי לְמֹרְטִים פָּנַי לֹא הִסְתַּרְתִּי
ז מִכְּלִמּוֹת וָרֹק: וַאדֹנָי יֱהוִה יַעֲזָר־לִי עַל־כֵּן לֹא נִכְלָמְתִּי עַל־כֵּן שַׂמְתִּי פָנַי כַּחַלָּמִישׁ וָאֵדַע
ח ט כִּי־לֹא אֵבוֹשׁ: קָרוֹב מַצְדִּיקִי מִי־יָרִיב אִתִּי נַעַמְדָה יָּחַד מִי־בַעַל מִשְׁפָּטִי יִגַּשׁ אֵלָי: הֵן אֲדֹנָי
י יֱהוִה יַעֲזָר־לִי מִי־הוּא יַרְשִׁיעֵנִי הֵן כֻּלָּם כַּבֶּגֶד יִבְלוּ עָשׁ יֹאכְלֵם: מִי בָכֶם יְרֵא
יְהוָה שֹׁמֵעַ בְּקוֹל עַבְדּוֹ אֲשֶׁר ׀ הָלַךְ חֲשֵׁכִים וְאֵין נֹגַהּ לוֹ יִבְטַח בְּשֵׁם יְהוָה וְיִשָּׁעֵן בֵּאלֹהָיו:
יא הֵן כֻּלְּכֶם קֹדְחֵי אֵשׁ מְאַזְּרֵי זִיקוֹת לְכוּ ׀ בְּאוּר אֶשְׁכֶם וּבְזִיקוֹת בִּעַרְתֶּם מִיָּדִי הָיְתָה־זֹּאת
נא א לָכֶם לְמַעֲצֵבָה תִּשְׁכָּבוּן: שִׁמְעוּ אֵלַי רֹדְפֵי צֶדֶק מְבַקְשֵׁי יְהוָה הַבִּיטוּ אֶל־צוּר
ב חֻצַּבְתֶּם וְאֶל־מַקֶּבֶת בּוֹר נֻקַּרְתֶּם: הַבִּיטוּ אֶל־אַבְרָהָם אֲבִיכֶם וְאֶל־שָׂרָה תְּחוֹלֶלְכֶם כִּי־
ג אֶחָד קְרָאתִיו וַאֲבָרְכֵהוּ וְאַרְבֵּהוּ: כִּי־נִחַם יְהוָה צִיּוֹן נִחַם כָּל־חָרְבֹתֶיהָ וַיָּשֶׂם מִדְבָּרָהּ כְּעֵדֶן
וְעַרְבָתָהּ כְּגַן־יְהוָה שָׂשׂוֹן וְשִׂמְחָה יִמָּצֵא בָהּ תּוֹדָה וְקוֹל זִמְרָה:

Haftara for
Re'eh

Comfort for Desolate and
Impoverished Zion
ISAIAH 54:11–55:5

In this message of consolation, Zion, which refuses to accept comfort, is informed that God has sworn to maintain an eternal bond with her, to build her in splendor with precious stones, and to widen her former borders. This prophecy of reassurance includes a call to Israel to return and seek God, and a promise that God will come to the nation's assistance and usher in the final redemption. In this section, the redemption is depicted as a time of the bestowal of an abundance of goodness upon Israel, the ingathering of its exiles, and the transformation of the entire world into a wonderful, joyful place.

54 11 Afflicted, storm-tossed one, she has not been comforted; behold, I will set your flagstones with carbuncle and lay your foun-
12 dation with sapphires. I will make your windows of chalcedony, your gates of ruby, and your entire border of precious stones.
13 All your children will be disciples of the Lord and the peace of
14 your children will be abundant. With righteousness you will be established; distance yourself from exploitation, for you need
15 not fear, and from ruin as it will not come near you. Behold, one who is not with Me will be afraid; whoever resides with you will
16 fall in with you. Behold, I created the smith who fans the fire of coal and produces a tool with his labor, and I created the de-
17 stroyer to cause harm. Any weapon crafted against you will not succeed and any tongue that will rise against you in judgment will be condemned. This is the heritage of the servants of the Lord and their just deserts from Me – the utterance of the Lord.

55 1 Ho, everyone thirsty, go to water, and one who has no silver, go purchase and eat; go purchase wine and milk without silver
2 and without cost. Why do you weigh our silver for no bread and your exertion for no satisfaction? Heed Me and eat well,
3 and your soul will delight in fatness. Incline your ear and go to Me; take heed and your soul will live, and I will establish with
4 you an eternal covenant, the enduring grace of David. Behold, I have set him a witness for the peoples, a prince and commander
5 to the peoples. Behold, you will call a nation that you do not know, and a nation that has not known you will run to you, for the sake of the Lord your God and for the Holy One of Israel, as He glorified you.

Haftara for
Shofetim

Solace and Encouragement
ISAIAH 51:12–52:12

In the words of consolation delivered in this *haftara*, which is rich in poetic repetition, the prophet reassures those who worry over their fate, infusing them with confidence and hope for a new world. This *haftara* juxtaposes prophecies that were directed at the people returning from exile in Babylonia with passages that refer to the future, final redemption, which will not be followed by any more exiles.

51 12 It is I, I who am your Comforter; who are you, that you fear
13 mortal man and a person who will be rendered to grass? You forgot the Lord your Maker, who spread the heavens and laid the foundation of the earth; you feared continually all day due to the fury of the oppressor, when he prepares to destroy. But
14 where is the fury of the oppressor? The wanderer will quickly be released. He will not die in the destruction, and his bread
15 will not be lacking. And I am the Lord your God, who maintains the sea though its waves rage; the Lord of hosts is His
16 name. I placed My words in your mouth and with the shadow of My hand I have covered you, to plant the heavens and to lay the foundation of the earth and to say to Zion: You are My peo-
17 ple. Awaken, awaken, arise, Jerusalem, who has drunk from the hand of the Lord the cup of His fury; the goblet of the cup of
18 stupefaction have you drunk and drained. There is no one to guide her from all the children she bore, and there is no one
19 holding her hand from all the children she raised. Your experiences are these two; who will be moved for you? Pillage and
20 destruction, famine and the sword; who will comfort you? Your children have fainted; they lie at the head of every street, like

הפטרת

ראה

נד יא יב עֲנִיָּה סֹעֲרָה לֹא נֻחָמָה הִנֵּה אָנֹכִי מַרְבִּיץ בַּפּוּךְ אֲבָנַיִךְ וִיסַדְתִּיךְ בַּסַּפִּירִים׃ וְשַׂמְתִּי כַּדְכֹד ישעיה
יג שִׁמְשֹׁתַיִךְ וּשְׁעָרַיִךְ לְאַבְנֵי אֶקְדָּח וְכָל־גְּבוּלֵךְ לְאַבְנֵי־חֵפֶץ׃ וְכָל־בָּנַיִךְ לִמּוּדֵי יְהוָה וְרַב שְׁלוֹם
יד טו בָּנָיִךְ׃ בִּצְדָקָה תִּכּוֹנָנִי רַחֲקִי מֵעֹשֶׁק כִּי־לֹא תִירָאִי וּמִמְּחִתָּה כִּי לֹא־תִקְרַב אֵלָיִךְ׃ הֵן גּוֹר יָגוּר הִנֵּה
טז אֶפֶס מֵאוֹתִי מִי־גָר אִתָּךְ עָלַיִךְ יִפּוֹל׃ הֵן אָנֹכִי בָּרָאתִי חָרָשׁ נֹפֵחַ בְּאֵשׁ פֶּחָם וּמוֹצִיא כְלִי
יז לְמַעֲשֵׂהוּ וְאָנֹכִי בָּרָאתִי מַשְׁחִית לְחַבֵּל׃ כָּל־כְּלִי יוּצַר עָלַיִךְ לֹא יִצְלָח וְכָל־לָשׁוֹן תָּקוּם־אִתָּךְ
נה א לַמִּשְׁפָּט תַּרְשִׁיעִי זֹאת נַחֲלַת עַבְדֵי יְהוָה וְצִדְקָתָם מֵאִתִּי נְאֻם־יְהוָה׃ הוֹי
כָּל־צָמֵא לְכוּ לַמַּיִם וַאֲשֶׁר אֵין־לוֹ כָּסֶף לְכוּ שִׁבְרוּ וֶאֱכֹלוּ וּלְכוּ שִׁבְרוּ בְּלוֹא־כֶסֶף וּבְלוֹא
ב מְחִיר יַיִן וְחָלָב׃ לָמָּה תִשְׁקְלוּ־כֶסֶף בְּלוֹא־לֶחֶם וִיגִיעֲכֶם בְּלוֹא לְשָׂבְעָה שִׁמְעוּ שָׁמוֹעַ אֵלַי
ג וְאִכְלוּ־טוֹב וְתִתְעַנַּג בַּדֶּשֶׁן נַפְשְׁכֶם׃ הַטּוּ אָזְנְכֶם וּלְכוּ אֵלַי שִׁמְעוּ וּתְחִי נַפְשְׁכֶם וְאֶכְרְתָה
ד ה לָכֶם בְּרִית עוֹלָם חַסְדֵי דָוִד הַנֶּאֱמָנִים׃ הֵן עֵד לְאוּמִּים נְתַתִּיו נָגִיד וּמְצַוֵּה לְאֻמִּים׃ הֵן גּוֹי
לֹא־תֵדַע תִּקְרָא וְגוֹי לֹא־יְדָעוּךָ אֵלֶיךָ יָרוּצוּ לְמַעַן יְהוָה אֱלֹהֶיךָ וְלִקְדוֹשׁ יִשְׂרָאֵל כִּי פֵאֲרָךְ׃

הפטרת

שפטים

נא יב יג אָנֹכִי אָנֹכִי הוּא מְנַחֶמְכֶם מִי־אַתְּ וַתִּירְאִי מֵאֱנוֹשׁ יָמוּת וּמִבֶּן־אָדָם חָצִיר יִנָּתֵן׃ וַתִּשְׁכַּח ישעיה
יְהוָה עֹשֶׂךָ נוֹטֶה שָׁמַיִם וְיֹסֵד אָרֶץ וַתְּפַחֵד תָּמִיד כָּל־הַיּוֹם מִפְּנֵי חֲמַת הַמֵּצִיק כַּאֲשֶׁר כּוֹנֵן
יד טו לְהַשְׁחִית וְאַיֵּה חֲמַת הַמֵּצִיק׃ מִהַר צֹעֶה לְהִפָּתֵחַ וְלֹא־יָמוּת לַשַּׁחַת וְלֹא יֶחְסַר לַחְמוֹ׃ וְאָנֹכִי
טז יְהוָה אֱלֹהֶיךָ רֹגַע הַיָּם וַיֶּהֱמוּ גַּלָּיו יְהוָה צְבָאוֹת שְׁמוֹ׃ וָאָשִׂם דְּבָרַי בְּפִיךָ וּבְצֵל יָדִי כִּסִּיתִיךָ
יז לִנְטֹעַ שָׁמַיִם וְלִיסֹד אָרֶץ וְלֵאמֹר לְצִיּוֹן עַמִּי־אָתָּה׃ הִתְעוֹרְרִי הִתְעוֹרְרִי קוּמִי
יְרוּשָׁלִַם אֲשֶׁר שָׁתִית מִיַּד יְהוָה אֶת־כּוֹס חֲמָתוֹ אֶת־קֻבַּעַת כּוֹס הַתַּרְעֵלָה שָׁתִית מָצִית׃
יח יט אֵין־מְנַהֵל לָהּ מִכָּל־בָּנִים יָלָדָה וְאֵין מַחֲזִיק בְּיָדָהּ מִכָּל־בָּנִים גִּדֵּלָה׃ שְׁתַּיִם הֵנָּה קֹרְאֹתַיִךְ
כ מִי יָנוּד לָךְ הַשֹּׁד וְהַשֶּׁבֶר וְהָרָעָב וְהַחֶרֶב מִי אֲנַחֲמֵךְ׃ בָּנַיִךְ עֻלְּפוּ שָׁכְבוּ בְּרֹאשׁ כָּל־חוּצוֹת

an aurochs in a trap; they are full of the fury of the Lord, the
21 rebuke of your God. Therefore, now hear this, afflicted and
22 drunken, but not from wine: So said your Master, the Lord,
and your God who will battle for His people: Behold, I have
taken from your hand the cup of stupefaction; the goblet of the
cup of My fury, you will not continue to drink it any longer.
23 I will place it into the hand of your oppressors, who said to
your soul: Bow and we will pass; you placed your body like the
52 1 ground and like the street for the passersby. Awaken, awaken,
don your strength, Zion; don the garments of your splendor,
Jerusalem, the holy city, as the uncircumcised and the impure
2 will not continue to come among you any longer. Shake off the
dust, arise and sit, Jerusalem; open the restraints on your neck,
3 captive daughter of Zion. For so said the Lord: You were sold
4 for naught and you will not be redeemed for money. For so said
the Lord God: My people went down to Egypt at first to re-
5 side there, and Assyria exploited them for nothing. And now,
what is here for Me – the utterance of the Lord – for My people
was taken for naught? Its rulers glorify themselves – the utterance of the Lord – and always, all day, My name is blasphemed.
6 Therefore, My people will know My name; therefore, on that
7 day they will know that I am He who speaks; here I am. How
pleasant are the feet of the herald on the mountains, announcing peace, heralding good tidings, announcing salvation, who
8 says to Zion: Your God reigns. The voice of your lookouts, they
raise voice, together they sing, for with actual eyes they will see
9 the return of the Lord to Zion. Break out and sing together,
ruins of Jerusalem, as the Lord has comforted His people; He
10 has redeemed Jerusalem. The Lord has bared His holy arm before the eyes of all the nations, and all the ends of the earth will
11 see the salvation of our God. Turn aside, turn aside, come out
from there; do not touch impurity; come out from its midst;
12 cleanse yourselves, bearers of the vessels of the Lord. For you
will not come out in haste and you will not go in flight, for the
Lord will go before you and the God of Israel will be your rear
guard.

Haftara for **Ki Tetze**

Visions of Ultimate Increase

ISAIAH 54:1–10

This specific prophecy of comfort is particularly suitable for *Parashat Ki Tetze*, which relates to the relationship between husbands and wives and their families, including separations and the establishment of new ties. The *haftara* mentions these issues as well, which are used as metaphors for the relationship between God and Israel.

At the start of the Second Temple period, only a small number of Jewish exiles returned to the Land of Israel from Babylonia, and they rebuilt the land themselves. However, the Jewish settlement was dispirited and miserable. The prophet foresees that when the future redemption occurs, the community remaining in the land will grow and broaden. He calls for the opening of the cities of Israel to welcome the returning exiles from the lands of their dispersal.

54 1 Sing, barren one, who did not give birth; burst into song and rejoice, she who did not go into labor, for the children of the desolate are more than the children of the married woman, said the
2 Lord. Expand the place of your tent and spread the curtains of
your dwellings, do not spare; extend your cords and reinforce
3 your stakes. For you will spread out to the right and the left; and
your descendants will inherit nations and they will settle deso-
4 late cities. Do not fear, for you will not be shamed; do not feel
humiliated, for you will not be disgraced; for you will forget the
shame of your youth and you will not remember the disgrace of
5 your widowhood any longer. For your Husband is your Maker,
the Lord of hosts is His name, and your Redeemer is the Holy

כא כְּתוּא מִכְמָר הַמְלֵאִים חֲמַת־יהוה גַּעֲרַת אֱלֹהָיִךְ׃ לָכֵן שִׁמְעִי־נָא זֹאת עֲנִיָּה וּשְׁכֻרַת וְלֹא
כב מִיָּיִן׃ כֹּה־אָמַר אֲדֹנַיִךְ יהוה וֵאלֹהַיִךְ יָרִיב עַמּוֹ הִנֵּה לָקַחְתִּי מִיָּדֵךְ אֶת־כּוֹס
כג הַתַּרְעֵלָה אֶת־קֻבַּעַת כּוֹס חֲמָתִי לֹא־תוֹסִיפִי לִשְׁתּוֹתָהּ עוֹד׃ וְשַׂמְתִּיהָ בְּיַד־מוֹגַיִךְ אֲשֶׁר־
נב א אָמְרוּ לְנַפְשֵׁךְ שְׁחִי וְנַעֲבֹרָה וַתָּשִׂימִי כָאָרֶץ גֵּוֵךְ וְכַחוּץ לַעֹבְרִים׃ עוּרִי עוּרִי לִבְשִׁי
עֻזֵּךְ צִיּוֹן לִבְשִׁי ׀ בִּגְדֵי תִפְאַרְתֵּךְ יְרוּשָׁלִַם עִיר הַקֹּדֶשׁ כִּי לֹא יוֹסִיף יָבֹא־בָךְ עוֹד עָרֵל וְטָמֵא׃
ב ג הִתְנַעֲרִי מֵעָפָר קוּמִי שְּׁבִי יְרוּשָׁלִָם התפתחו מוֹסְרֵי צַוָּארֵךְ שְׁבִיָּה בַּת־צִיּוֹן׃ כִּי־כֹה התפתחי
הִתְפַּתְּחִי
ד אָמַר יהוה חִנָּם נִמְכַּרְתֶּם וְלֹא בְכֶסֶף תִּגָּאֵלוּ׃ כִּי כֹה אָמַר אֲדֹנָי יֱהֹוִה מִצְרַיִם
ה יָרַד־עַמִּי בָרִאשֹׁנָה לָגוּר שָׁם וְאַשּׁוּר בְּאֶפֶס עֲשָׁקוֹ׃ וְעַתָּה מַה־לִּי־פֹה נְאֻם־יהוה כִּי־לֻקַּח
ו עַמִּי חִנָּם מֹשְׁלָו יְהֵילִילוּ נְאֻם־יהוה וְתָמִיד כָּל־הַיּוֹם שְׁמִי מִנֹּאָץ׃ לָכֵן יֵדַע עַמִּי שְׁמִי לָכֵן בַּיּוֹם
ז הַהוּא כִּי־אֲנִי־הוּא הַמְדַבֵּר הִנֵּנִי׃ מַה־נָּאווּ עַל־הֶהָרִים רַגְלֵי מְבַשֵּׂר מַשְׁמִיעַ
ח שָׁלוֹם מְבַשֵּׂר טוֹב מַשְׁמִיעַ יְשׁוּעָה אֹמֵר לְצִיּוֹן מָלַךְ אֱלֹהָיִךְ׃ קוֹל צֹפַיִךְ נָשְׂאוּ קוֹל יַחְדָּו יְרַנֵּנוּ
ט כִּי עַיִן בְּעַיִן יִרְאוּ בְּשׁוּב יהוה צִיּוֹן׃ פִּצְחוּ רַנְּנוּ יַחְדָּו חָרְבוֹת יְרוּשָׁלִָם כִּי־נִחַם יהוה עַמּוֹ גָּאַל
י יְרוּשָׁלִָם׃ חָשַׂף יהוה אֶת־זְרוֹעַ קָדְשׁוֹ לְעֵינֵי כָּל־הַגּוֹיִם וְרָאוּ כָּל־אַפְסֵי־אָרֶץ אֵת יְשׁוּעַת
יא אֱלֹהֵינוּ׃ סוּרוּ סוּרוּ צְאוּ מִשָּׁם טָמֵא אַל־תִּגָּעוּ צְאוּ מִתּוֹכָהּ הִבָּרוּ נֹשְׂאֵי כְּלֵי יהוה׃
יב כִּי לֹא בְחִפָּזוֹן תֵּצֵאוּ וּבִמְנוּסָה לֹא תֵלֵכוּן כִּי־הֹלֵךְ לִפְנֵיכֶם יהוה וּמְאַסִּפְכֶם אֱלֹהֵי יִשְׂרָאֵל׃

הפטרת

כי תצא

נד א רָנִּי עֲקָרָה לֹא יָלָדָה פִּצְחִי רִנָּה וְצַהֲלִי לֹא־חָלָה כִּי־רַבִּים בְּנֵי־שׁוֹמֵמָה מִבְּנֵי בְעוּלָה אָמַר ישעיה
ב יהוה׃ הַרְחִיבִי ׀ מְקוֹם אָהֳלֵךְ וִירִיעוֹת מִשְׁכְּנוֹתַיִךְ יַטּוּ אַל־תַּחְשֹׂכִי הַאֲרִיכִי מֵיתָרַיִךְ וִיתֵדֹתַיִךְ
ג ד חַזֵּקִי׃ כִּי־יָמִין וּשְׂמֹאול תִּפְרֹצִי וְזַרְעֵךְ גּוֹיִם יִירָשׁ וְעָרִים נְשַׁמּוֹת יוֹשִׁיבוּ׃ אַל־תִּירְאִי כִּי־לֹא
תֵבוֹשִׁי וְאַל־תִּכָּלְמִי כִּי לֹא תַחְפִּירִי כִּי בֹשֶׁת עֲלוּמַיִךְ תִּשְׁכָּחִי וְחֶרְפַּת אַלְמְנוּתַיִךְ לֹא תִזְכְּרִי־
ה עוֹד׃ כִּי בֹעֲלַיִךְ עֹשַׂיִךְ יהוה צְבָאוֹת שְׁמוֹ וְגֹאֲלֵךְ קְדוֹשׁ יִשְׂרָאֵל אֱלֹהֵי כָל־הָאָרֶץ יִקָּרֵא׃

6 One of Israel, the God of the entire world He will be called. For as a wife forsaken and aggrieved of spirit the Lord called you, and as the wife of one's youth she will be despised, said your

7 God. For a brief moment I forsook you, and with great mercy I

8 will gather you. In an outburst of rage, I concealed My face from you for a moment, but with eternal grace I will have mercy on

9 you, said your Redeemer, the Lord. For this is for Me like the waters of Noah; as I took an oath that the waters of Noah would no longer pass over the earth, so I took an oath that I would not

10 be furious with you, nor would I rebuke you. For the mountains will move and the hills will collapse, but My grace will not move from you and the covenant of My peace will not collapse, said the One who has mercy on you, the Lord.

Haftara for
Ki Tavo

The Light of the World from Zion
ISAIAH 60:1–22

The entire prophecy in this *haftara* deals with the comforting of Zion, as it poetically depicts the redemption of Israel. The darkened, abandoned, and impoverished Zion will become a source of wondrous light for the whole world. Zion will be crowded with people, full of bounteous goodness, and protected from all enemies. The gentile nations will seek the holiness of Zion as they come to participate in the sacred service, and will thereby be enlightened through the light of Zion.

60 1 Arise, shine, for your light has come and the glory of the Lord

2 has shone upon you. For behold, the darkness will cover the earth and peoples, a fog; but upon you the Lord will shine and

3 His glory will be seen upon you. Nations will walk by your

4 light, and kings by the glow of your shining. Lift your eyes all around and see, they are all assembling and coming to you; your sons are coming from afar and your daughters are car-

5 ried on the side. Then you will see and be radiant, and your heart will thrill and swell; for a multitude like the sea will be turned upon you, the power of the nations will come to you.

6 A herd of camels will cover you, the young camels of Midyan and Ephah; all of them will come from Sheba; they will carry

7 gold and frankincense and herald the praises of the Lord. All the flocks of Kedar will be gathered to you, the rams of Nevayot will serve you; they will be offered up for the propitiation of My

8 altar and I will make splendid the House of My splendor. Who

9 are these who fly like a cloud and like doves to their cotes? For the lands of the sea will long for Me with the ships of Tarshish in the lead, to bring your children from afar, their silver and their gold with them, and for the name of the Lord your God and for the Holy One of Israel, because He has glorified you.

10 Foreigners will build your walls and their kings will serve you, as in My anger I struck you, and in My favor I have had mercy

11 on you. Open always your gates; day and night they will not be closed, to bring to you the wealth of the nations and their kings

12 led. For the nation and the kingdom that will not serve you will

13 perish, and the nations will be destroyed. The glory of Lebanon will come to you: Juniper, ash, and boxwood together, to make splendid the place of My Temple and the place of My feet will I

14 honor. The sons of your tormenters will come to you bent over; all those who have cursed you will prostrate themselves at your feet and will call you: City of the Lord, Zion of the Holy One

15 of Israel. Instead of your being forsaken and hated, with no one passing through, I will designate you for eternal glory, gladness

16 for generations. You will nurse the milk of the nations, and from the breast of kings will you nurse, and you will know that I, the Lord, am your Savior, and your Redeemer is the Mighty One

17 of Jacob. Instead of bronze I will bring gold; instead of iron I will bring silver; instead of wood, bronze; and instead of stones, iron; I will appoint your officials for peace and tax collectors for

18 righteousness. No longer will villainy be heard of in your land, robbery and ruin within your borders; you will call your walls

19 salvation and your gates, praise. The sun will no longer be for light for you by day, and the glow of the moon will not illuminate for you; the Lord will be for you an eternal light and your

20 God will be your splendor. Your sun will no longer set and your

ז כִּי־כְאִשָּׁה עֲזוּבָה וַעֲצוּבַת רוּחַ קְרָאָךְ יהוה וְאֵשֶׁת נְעוּרִים כִּי תִמָּאֵס אָמַר אֱלֹהָיִךְ: בְּרֶגַע

ח קָטֹן עֲזַבְתִּיךְ וּבְרַחֲמִים גְּדֹלִים אֲקַבְּצֵךְ: בְּשֶׁצֶף קֶצֶף הִסְתַּרְתִּי פָנַי רֶגַע מִמֵּךְ וּבְחֶסֶד עוֹלָם

ט רִחַמְתִּיךְ אָמַר גֹּאֲלֵךְ יהוה: כִּי־מֵי נֹחַ זֹאת לִי אֲשֶׁר נִשְׁבַּעְתִּי מֵעֲבֹר מֵי־נֹחַ

י עוֹד עַל־הָאָרֶץ כֵּן נִשְׁבַּעְתִּי מִקְּצֹף עָלַיִךְ וּמִגְּעָר־בָּךְ: כִּי הֶהָרִים יָמוּשׁוּ וְהַגְּבָעוֹת תְּמוּטֶינָה וְחַסְדִּי מֵאִתֵּךְ לֹא־יָמוּשׁ וּבְרִית שְׁלוֹמִי לֹא תָמוּט אָמַר מְרַחֲמֵךְ יהוה:

כי תבוא

ישעיה

ס א קוּמִי אוֹרִי כִּי בָא אוֹרֵךְ וּכְבוֹד יהוה עָלַיִךְ זָרָח: כִּי־הִנֵּה הַחֹשֶׁךְ יְכַסֶּה־אֶרֶץ וַעֲרָפֶל לְאֻמִּים

ב וְעָלַיִךְ יִזְרַח יהוה וּכְבוֹדוֹ עָלַיִךְ יֵרָאֶה: וְהָלְכוּ גוֹיִם לְאוֹרֵךְ וּמְלָכִים לְנֹגַהּ זַרְחֵךְ: שְׂאִי־סָבִיב

ג עֵינַיִךְ וּרְאִי כֻּלָּם נִקְבְּצוּ בָאוּ־לָךְ בָּנַיִךְ מֵרָחוֹק יָבֹאוּ וּבְנֹתַיִךְ עַל־צַד תֵּאָמַנָה: אָז תִּרְאִי

ה וְנָהַרְתְּ וּפָחַד וְרָחַב לְבָבֵךְ כִּי־יֵהָפֵךְ עָלַיִךְ הֲמוֹן יָם חֵיל גּוֹיִם יָבֹאוּ לָךְ: שִׁפְעַת גְּמַלִּים תְּכַסֵּךְ

ו בִּכְרֵי מִדְיָן וְעֵיפָה כֻּלָּם מִשְּׁבָא יָבֹאוּ זָהָב וּלְבוֹנָה יִשָּׂאוּ וּתְהִלֹּת יהוה יְבַשֵּׂרוּ: כָּל־צֹאן קֵדָר

ז יִקָּבְצוּ לָךְ אֵילֵי נְבָיוֹת יְשָׁרְתוּנֶךְ יַעֲלוּ עַל־רָצוֹן מִזְבְּחִי וּבֵית תִּפְאַרְתִּי אֲפָאֵר: מִי־אֵלֶּה כָּעָב

ח תְּעוּפֶינָה וְכַיּוֹנִים אֶל־אֲרֻבֹּתֵיהֶם: כִּי־לִי אִיִּים יְקַוּוּ וָאֳנִיּוֹת תַּרְשִׁישׁ בָּרִאשֹׁנָה לְהָבִיא בָנַיִךְ

ט מֵרָחוֹק כַּסְפָּם וּזְהָבָם אִתָּם לְשֵׁם יהוה אֱלֹהַיִךְ וְלִקְדוֹשׁ יִשְׂרָאֵל כִּי פֵאֲרָךְ: וּבָנוּ בְנֵי־נֵכָר

י חֹמֹתַיִךְ וּמַלְכֵיהֶם יְשָׁרְתוּנֶךְ כִּי בְקִצְפִּי הִכִּיתִיךְ וּבִרְצוֹנִי רִחַמְתִּיךְ: וּפִתְּחוּ שְׁעָרַיִךְ תָּמִיד

יא יוֹמָם וָלַיְלָה לֹא יִסָּגֵרוּ לְהָבִיא אֵלַיִךְ חֵיל גּוֹיִם וּמַלְכֵיהֶם נְהוּגִים: כִּי־הַגּוֹי וְהַמַּמְלָכָה אֲשֶׁר

יב לֹא־יַעַבְדוּךְ יֹאבֵדוּ וְהַגּוֹיִם חָרֹב יֶחֱרָבוּ: כְּבוֹד הַלְּבָנוֹן אֵלַיִךְ יָבוֹא בְּרוֹשׁ תִּדְהָר וּתְאַשּׁוּר

יג יַחְדָּו לְפָאֵר מְקוֹם מִקְדָּשִׁי וּמְקוֹם רַגְלַי אֲכַבֵּד: וְהָלְכוּ אֵלַיִךְ שְׁחוֹחַ בְּנֵי מְעַנַּיִךְ וְהִשְׁתַּחֲווּ

יד עַל־כַּפּוֹת רַגְלַיִךְ כָּל־מְנַאֲצָיִךְ וְקָרְאוּ לָךְ עִיר יהוה צִיּוֹן קְדוֹשׁ יִשְׂרָאֵל: תַּחַת הֱיוֹתֵךְ עֲזוּבָה

טו וּשְׂנוּאָה וְאֵין עוֹבֵר וְשַׂמְתִּיךְ לִגְאוֹן עוֹלָם מְשׂוֹשׂ דּוֹר וָדוֹר: וְיָנַקְתְּ חֲלֵב גּוֹיִם וְשֹׁד מְלָכִים

טז תִּינָקִי וְיָדַעַתְּ כִּי אֲנִי יהוה מוֹשִׁיעֵךְ וְגֹאֲלֵךְ אֲבִיר יַעֲקֹב: תַּחַת הַנְּחֹשֶׁת אָבִיא זָהָב וְתַחַת

יז הַבַּרְזֶל אָבִיא כֶסֶף וְתַחַת הָעֵצִים נְחֹשֶׁת וְתַחַת הָאֲבָנִים בַּרְזֶל וְשַׂמְתִּי פְקֻדָּתֵךְ שָׁלוֹם וְנֹגְשַׂיִךְ

יח צְדָקָה: לֹא־יִשָּׁמַע עוֹד חָמָס בְּאַרְצֵךְ שֹׁד וָשֶׁבֶר בִּגְבוּלָיִךְ וְקָרָאת יְשׁוּעָה חוֹמֹתַיִךְ וּשְׁעָרַיִךְ

יט תְּהִלָּה: לֹא־יִהְיֶה־לָּךְ עוֹד הַשֶּׁמֶשׁ לְאוֹר יוֹמָם וּלְנֹגַהּ הַיָּרֵחַ לֹא־יָאִיר לָךְ וְהָיָה־לָךְ יהוה

כ לְאוֹר עוֹלָם וֵאלֹהַיִךְ לְתִפְאַרְתֵּךְ: לֹא־יָבוֹא עוֹד שִׁמְשֵׁךְ וִירֵחֵךְ לֹא יֵאָסֵף כִּי יהוה יִהְיֶה־לָּךְ

moon will not be gathered in, as the Lord will be for you an
21 eternal light; the days of your mourning will be completed. And
your people, they are all righteous, they will inherit the land forever, the scion of My planting, My handiwork, to be adorned in

22 splendor. The smallest will become a thousand and the youngest a mighty nation; I am the Lord; at its time, I will hasten it.

Haftara for
Nitzavim

Also read when Nitzavim and Vayelekh are read together.

Tidings of the Future Redemption
ISAIAH 61:10–63:9

The background for the following prophecies of comfort is the state of despondency and desolation of Jerusalem and the rest of the land. The prophet speaks words of consolation and foresees that all this despair will come to an end. These passages are apparently referring to the final redemption that will occur in the distant future (see Ramban's *Sefer HaGe'ula*, Mossad HaRav Kook edition, p. 268; Radak, Isaiah 63:1). The prophet predicts the salvation of Israel and Jerusalem, as well as God's vengeance upon their enemies.

Here, in the last of the seven *haftarot* of God's words of comfort to Israel, it seems that Zion finally agrees to be comforted and shows signs of joy and hope. With this optimistic perspective, the *haftarot* of the year are thereby concluded.

61 10 I will be gladdened in the Lord, my soul will exult in my God, as He has clothed me with the garments of salvation, with a robe of triumph has He cloaked me, like a groom who exhibits splendor and like a bride who bedecks herself with her orna-
11 ments. For like the earth produces its growth and like the gar-
den sprouts its seeds, so the Lord God will sprout strength and
62 1 praise before all the nations. For the sake of Zion, I will not be silent and for the sake of Jerusalem I will not be still, until its rightness emerges as a glow and its salvation will blaze like a
2 torch. Nations will see your rightness and all kings your glory; you will be called a new name that the mouth of the Lord will
3 designate. You will be a crown of splendor in the hand of the
4 Lord and a royal mitre in the palm of your God. Forsaken will no longer be said of you, and desolate will no longer be said of your land; rather, you will be called, My desire is for her and your land, wedded; for the Lord desires you and your land
5 will be wed. Just as a young man weds a maiden, so your sons will wed you; and like the gladness of a groom with a bride,
6 so your God will be glad with you. On your walls, Jerusalem, I appointed guards; all day and all night, they will never be silent.
7 Those who remind the Lord, do not be quiet, and do not afford Him quiet until He establishes and until He places Jerusalem to
8 be an accolade in the land. The Lord took an oath by His right hand and by His mighty arm: I will no longer give your grain as food for your enemies, and foreigners will not drink your wine

9 for which you labored. Rather, its harvesters will eat it and will praise the Lord, and its gatherers will drink it in the courtyards
10 of My sanctuary. Pass, pass through the gates, clear the way of the people; pave, pave the highway, clear the stones, raise
11 a banner over the peoples. Behold, the Lord has announced to the ends of the earth: Say to the daughter of Zion: Behold, your Savior has come; behold, His reward is with Him and His
12 recompense before Him. They will call them: Holy people, redeemed of the Lord; and you will be called: Sought after, a
63 1 city not forsaken. Who is this, coming from Edom, red-clothed from Botzra, resplendent in His attire, striding in His abundant
2 strength? I speak with justice, potent to save. Why is there red on Your attire, and are Your garments like one treading in a
3 winepress? I have trodden the winepress alone and from the peoples there was no man with Me; I trod them in My wrath and I trampled them in My fury; and their lifeblood splashed
4 against My garments, and I sullied all My attire. For it was a day of vengeance in My heart, and the year of My redemption
5 has come. I looked and there was no helper, and I inquired and there was no supporter; My arm brought Me salvation and My
6 fury supported Me. I trampled peoples in My wrath and made them drunk with My fury, and I poured their lifeblood to the
7 earth. The mercies of the Lord I will mention; the praises of the Lord, in accordance with everything that the Lord has bestowed upon us and the great goodness for the house of Israel

כא לְאוֹר עוֹלָם וְשָׁלְמוּ יְמֵי אֶבְלֵךְ: וְעַמֵּךְ כֻּלָּם צַדִּיקִים לְעוֹלָם יִירְשׁוּ אָרֶץ נֵצֶר מַטָּעוֹ מַעֲשֵׂה

כב יָדַי לְהִתְפָּאֵר: הַקָּטֹן יִהְיֶה לָאֶלֶף וְהַצָּעִיר לְגוֹי עָצוּם אֲנִי יְהוָה בְּעִתָּהּ אֲחִישֶׁנָּה:

הפטרת

נצבים

הפטרה לפרשת נצבים גם כשנצבים וילך מחוברות.

סא י שׂוֹשׂ אָשִׂישׂ בַּיהוָה תָּגֵל נַפְשִׁי בֵּאלֹהַי כִּי הִלְבִּישַׁנִי בִּגְדֵי־יֶשַׁע מְעִיל צְדָקָה יְעָטָנִי כֶּחָתָן יְכַהֵן ישעיה

יא פְּאֵר וְכַכַּלָּה תַּעְדֶּה כֵלֶיהָ: כִּי כָאָרֶץ תּוֹצִיא צִמְחָהּ וּכְגַנָּה זֵרוּעֶיהָ תַצְמִיחַ כֵּן ׀ אֲדֹנָי יְהוִה

סב א יַצְמִיחַ צְדָקָה וּתְהִלָּה נֶגֶד כָּל־הַגּוֹיִם: לְמַעַן צִיּוֹן לֹא אֶחֱשֶׁה וּלְמַעַן יְרוּשָׁלִַם לֹא אֶשְׁקוֹט

ב עַד־יֵצֵא כַנֹּגַהּ צִדְקָהּ וִישׁוּעָתָהּ כְּלַפִּיד יִבְעָר: וְרָאוּ גוֹיִם צִדְקֵךְ וְכָל־מְלָכִים כְּבוֹדֵךְ וְקֹרָא לָךְ

ג שֵׁם חָדָשׁ אֲשֶׁר פִּי יְהוָה יִקֳּבֶנּוּ: וְהָיִית עֲטֶרֶת תִּפְאֶרֶת בְּיַד־יְהוָה וּצְנִוף מְלוּכָה בְּכַף־אֱלֹהָיִךְ: וצנוף

ד לֹא־יֵאָמֵר לָךְ עוֹד עֲזוּבָה וּלְאַרְצֵךְ לֹא־יֵאָמֵר עוֹד שְׁמָמָה כִּי לָךְ יִקָּרֵא חֶפְצִי־בָהּ וּלְאַרְצֵךְ

ה בְּעוּלָה כִּי־חָפֵץ יְהוָה בָּךְ וְאַרְצֵךְ תִּבָּעֵל: כִּי־יִבְעַל בָּחוּר בְּתוּלָה יִבְעָלוּךְ בָּנָיִךְ וּמְשׂוֹשׂ חָתָן

ו עַל־כַּלָּה יָשִׂישׂ עָלַיִךְ אֱלֹהָיִךְ: עַל־חוֹמֹתַיִךְ יְרוּשָׁלִַם הִפְקַדְתִּי שֹׁמְרִים כָּל־הַיּוֹם וְכָל־הַלַּיְלָה

ז תָּמִיד לֹא יֶחֱשׁוּ הַמַּזְכִּרִים אֶת־יְהוָה אַל־דֳּמִי לָכֶם: וְאַל־תִּתְּנוּ דֳמִי לוֹ עַד־יְכוֹנֵן וְעַד־יָשִׂים

ח אֶת־יְרוּשָׁלִַם תְּהִלָּה בָּאָרֶץ: נִשְׁבַּע יְהוָה בִּימִינוֹ וּבִזְרוֹעַ עֻזּוֹ אִם־אֶתֵּן אֶת־דְּגָנֵךְ עוֹד מַאֲכָל

ט לְאֹיְבַיִךְ וְאִם־יִשְׁתּוּ בְנֵי־נֵכָר תִּירוֹשֵׁךְ אֲשֶׁר יָגַעַתְּ בּוֹ: כִּי מְאַסְפָיו יֹאכְלֻהוּ וְהִלְלוּ אֶת־יְהוָה

י וּמְקַבְּצָיו יִשְׁתֻּהוּ בְּחַצְרוֹת קָדְשִׁי: עִבְרוּ עִבְרוּ בַּשְּׁעָרִים פַּנּוּ דֶּרֶךְ הָעָם סֹלּוּ

יא סֹלּוּ הַמְסִלָּה סַקְּלוּ מֵאֶבֶן הָרִימוּ נֵס עַל־הָעַמִּים: הִנֵּה יְהוָה הִשְׁמִיעַ אֶל־קְצֵה הָאָרֶץ

יב אִמְרוּ לְבַת־צִיּוֹן הִנֵּה יִשְׁעֵךְ בָּא הִנֵּה שְׂכָרוֹ אִתּוֹ וּפְעֻלָּתוֹ לְפָנָיו: וְקָרְאוּ לָהֶם עַם־הַקֹּדֶשׁ

סג א גְּאוּלֵי יְהוָה וְלָךְ יִקָּרֵא דְרוּשָׁה עִיר לֹא נֶעֱזָבָה: מִי־זֶה ׀ בָּא מֵאֱדוֹם חֲמוּץ

ב בְּגָדִים מִבָּצְרָה זֶה הָדוּר בִּלְבוּשׁוֹ צֹעֶה בְּרֹב כֹּחוֹ אֲנִי מְדַבֵּר בִּצְדָקָה רַב לְהוֹשִׁיעַ: מַדּוּעַ

ג אָדֹם לִלְבוּשֶׁךָ וּבְגָדֶיךָ כְּדֹרֵךְ בְּגַת: פּוּרָה ׀ דָּרַכְתִּי לְבַדִּי וּמֵעַמִּים אֵין־אִישׁ אִתִּי וְאֶדְרְכֵם

ד בְּאַפִּי וְאֶרְמְסֵם בַּחֲמָתִי וְיֵז נִצְחָם עַל־בְּגָדַי וְכָל־מַלְבּוּשַׁי אֶגְאָלְתִּי: כִּי יוֹם נָקָם בְּלִבִּי וּשְׁנַת

ה גְּאוּלַי בָּאָה: וְאַבִּיט וְאֵין עֹזֵר וְאֶשְׁתּוֹמֵם וְאֵין סוֹמֵךְ וַתּוֹשַׁע לִי זְרֹעִי וַחֲמָתִי הִיא סְמָכָתְנִי:

ו וְאָבוּס עַמִּים בְּאַפִּי וַאֲשַׁכְּרֵם בַּחֲמָתִי וְאוֹרִיד לָאָרֶץ נִצְחָם: חַסְדֵי יְהוָה

אַזְכִּיר תְּהִלֹּת יְהוָה כְּעַל כֹּל אֲשֶׁר־גְּמָלָנוּ יְהוָה וְרַב־טוּב לְבֵית יִשְׂרָאֵל אֲשֶׁר־גְּמָלָם כְּרַחֲמָיו

that He bestowed upon them in His mercy and in His many
8 kindnesses. He said: Indeed, they are My people, children, they
9 will not play false; and He was their Savior. In all their troubles
He was troubled, and the angel of His presence saved them; in
His love and in His compassion He redeemed them; and He
took them and raised them up all the days of old.

Haftara for
Shabbat Shuva

Read on the Shabbat between Rosh HaShana and Yom Kippur (Vayelekh or Haazinu).

Repentance

HOSEA 14:2–10; JOEL 2:11–27; MICAH 7:18–20

The *haftara* opens with the conclusion of the book of Hosea, which calls on the people to return to God. The prophet declares that only by cleaving to Him will they find a cure for their ills; salvation will sprout from Him alone. The *haftara* continues with other passages of comfort and reconciliation from the books of Joel or Micah, or both, depending on the custom of the particular community.

HOSEA

14 2 Return, Israel, to the Lord your God, for you have stumbled
3 in your iniquity. Take words with yourselves and return to the
Lord; say to Him: Forgive all iniquity, and accept good, and we
4 will substitute our lips for bulls. Assyria will not save us; we will
not ride on a horse and we will no longer say to our handiwork:
5 Our gods; for it is in You that an orphan will find mercy. I will
heal their mischief; I will love them gratuitously, for My wrath
6 has turned from them. I will be like the dew to Israel; it will
blossom like the lily and it will strike its roots like the Lebanon.
7 Its branches will spread, and its beauty will be like the olive tree,
8 its fragrance like the Lebanon. Those who dwell in its shade will
return; they will give life to grain and they will blossom like
9 the vine; its repute will be like the wine of Lebanon. Ephraim:
What have I to do with idols anymore? I have responded and
I will gaze upon them; I am like a lush juniper, from Me your
10 fruit is found. Who is wise and will understand these, understanding and will know them? For the ways of the Lord are
straight, and the righteous will walk in them, and transgressors
will stumble on them.

JOEL

Some Ashk. add

2 11 The Lord projected His voice before His army, for His camp is
very great, for the executor of His word is mighty, for the day
12 of the Lord is great and very awesome; who can bear it? Even
now – the utterance of the Lord – return to Me with all your
13 heart, with fasting, with weeping, and with lamentation. Rend
your heart, and not your garments, and return to the Lord your
God, as He is gracious and merciful, slow to anger, abounding
14 in kindness, and reconsiders harm. Who knows? Perhaps He
will relent and reconsider, and leave a blessing after it, a meal
Most Ashk. add
15 offering and a libation to the Lord your God. Sound the sho-
16 far in Zion, set a fast, convene an assembly; gather the people,
sanctify the congregation, assemble elders, gather children, and
those who suck at breasts; let the groom emerge from his cham-
17 ber, and the bride from her canopy. Let the priests, servants of
the Lord, weep between the hall and the altar and let them say:
Pity your people, Lord, and do not give over Your inheritance
to disgrace to have the nations rule over them. Why should they
18 say among the peoples: Where is their God? The Lord was zeal-
19 ous for His land, and He had compassion for His people. The
Lord answered and said to His people: Behold, I am sending
you the grain and the wine and the oil, and you will be satisfied
20 with it. I will not render you a disgrace among the nations. I
will distance the northerner from you, and I will banish him to
an arid and desolate land, its face toward the eastern sea, and its
rear toward the western sea; its stench will arise, because it has
21 exceeded in its actions. Fear not, land; exult and rejoice, for the
22 Lord has exceeded in His actions. Fear not, animals of the field,
as the oases have grown grass, for the tree has borne its fruit,
23 the fig tree and the vine have yielded their riches. Children of
Zion, be glad and rejoice in the Lord your God, as He has given
you the early rain in charity, and He brings down for you the
24 early rain and the later rain, in the first. The threshing floor will
25 be full of grain, and the vats will overflow with wine and oil. I
will repay you for the years that were eaten by the desert locust,

ח ט וּכְרֹב חֲסָדָיו: וַיֹּאמֶר אַךְ־עַמִּי הֵמָּה בָּנִים לֹא יְשַׁקֵּרוּ וַיְהִי לָהֶם לְמוֹשִׁיעַ: בְּכָל־צָרָתָם ׀
לֹא צָר וּמַלְאַךְ פָּנָיו הוֹשִׁיעָם בְּאַהֲבָתוֹ וּבְחֶמְלָתוֹ הוּא גְאָלָם וַיְנַטְּלֵם וַיְנַשְּׂאֵם כָּל־יְמֵי עוֹלָם: לו

הפטרה

לשבת שובה

הפטרה לשבת שבין ראש השנה ליום הכיפורים (וילך או האזינו).

יד ב ג שׁוּבָה יִשְׂרָאֵל עַד יהוה אֱלֹהֶיךָ כִּי כָשַׁלְתָּ בַּעֲוֺנֶךָ: קְחוּ עִמָּכֶם דְּבָרִים וְשׁוּבוּ אֶל־יהוה אִמְרוּ הושע
ד אֵלָיו כָּל־תִּשָּׂא עָוֺן וְקַח־טוֹב וּנְשַׁלְּמָה פָרִים שְׂפָתֵינוּ: אַשּׁוּר ׀ לֹא יוֹשִׁיעֵנוּ עַל־סוּס לֹא נִרְכָּב
ה וְלֹא־נֹאמַר עוֹד אֱלֹהֵינוּ לְמַעֲשֵׂה יָדֵינוּ אֲשֶׁר־בְּךָ יְרֻחַם יָתוֹם: אֶרְפָּא מְשׁוּבָתָם אֹהֲבֵם נְדָבָה
ו ז כִּי שָׁב אַפִּי מִמֶּנּוּ: אֶהְיֶה כַטַּל לְיִשְׂרָאֵל יִפְרַח כַּשּׁוֹשַׁנָּה וְיַךְ שָׁרָשָׁיו כַּלְּבָנוֹן: יֵלְכוּ יֹנְקוֹתָיו וִיהִי
ח ט כַזַּיִת הוֹדוֹ וְרֵיחַ לוֹ כַּלְּבָנוֹן: יָשֻׁבוּ יֹשְׁבֵי בְצִלּוֹ יְחַיּוּ דָגָן וְיִפְרְחוּ כַגָּפֶן זִכְרוֹ כְּיֵין לְבָנוֹן: אֶפְרַיִם
י מַה־לִּי עוֹד לָעֲצַבִּים אֲנִי עָנִיתִי וַאֲשׁוּרֶנּוּ אֲנִי כִּבְרוֹשׁ רַעֲנָן מִמֶּנִּי פֶּרְיְךָ נִמְצָא: מִי חָכָם וְיָבֵן
אֵלֶּה נָבוֹן וְיֵדָעֵם כִּי־יְשָׁרִים דַּרְכֵי יהוה וְצַדִּקִים יֵלְכוּ בָם וּפֹשְׁעִים יִכָּשְׁלוּ בָם:

ב יא וַיהוה נָתַן קוֹלוֹ לִפְנֵי חֵילוֹ כִּי רַב מְאֹד מַחֲנֵהוּ כִּי עָצוּם עֹשֵׂה דְבָרוֹ כִּי־גָדוֹל יוֹם־יהוה וְנוֹרָא יואל
יב יג מְאֹד וּמִי יְכִילֶנּוּ: וְגַם־עַתָּה נְאֻם־יהוה שֻׁבוּ עָדַי בְּכָל־לְבַבְכֶם וּבְצוֹם וּבִבְכִי וּבְמִסְפֵּד: וְקִרְעוּ (יש אשכנזים שמוסיפים מכאן)
לְבַבְכֶם וְאַל־בִּגְדֵיכֶם וְשׁוּבוּ אֶל־יהוה אֱלֹהֵיכֶם כִּי־חַנּוּן וְרַחוּם הוּא אֶרֶךְ אַפַּיִם וְרַב־חֶסֶד
יד וְנִחָם עַל־הָרָעָה: מִי יוֹדֵעַ יָשׁוּב וְנִחָם וְהִשְׁאִיר אַחֲרָיו בְּרָכָה מִנְחָה וָנֶסֶךְ לַיהוה אֱלֹהֵיכֶם:
טו טז תִּקְעוּ שׁוֹפָר בְּצִיּוֹן קַדְּשׁוּ־צוֹם קִרְאוּ עֲצָרָה: אִסְפוּ־עָם קַדְּשׁוּ קָהָל קִבְצוּ זְקֵנִים אִסְפוּ עוֹלָלִים (רוב האשכנזים מוסיפים מכאן)
יז וְיֹנְקֵי שָׁדָיִם יֵצֵא חָתָן מֵחֶדְרוֹ וְכַלָּה מֵחֻפָּתָהּ: בֵּין הָאוּלָם וְלַמִּזְבֵּחַ יִבְכּוּ הַכֹּהֲנִים מְשָׁרְתֵי יהוה
וְיֹאמְרוּ חוּסָה יהוה עַל־עַמֶּךָ וְאַל־תִּתֵּן נַחֲלָתְךָ לְחֶרְפָּה לִמְשָׁל־בָּם גּוֹיִם לָמָּה יֹאמְרוּ בָעַמִּים
יח יט אַיֵּה אֱלֹהֵיהֶם: וַיְקַנֵּא יהוה לְאַרְצוֹ וַיַּחְמֹל עַל־עַמּוֹ: וַיַּעַן יהוה וַיֹּאמֶר לְעַמּוֹ הִנְנִי שֹׁלֵחַ לָכֶם
כ אֶת־הַדָּגָן וְהַתִּירוֹשׁ וְהַיִּצְהָר וּשְׂבַעְתֶּם אֹתוֹ וְלֹא־אֶתֵּן אֶתְכֶם עוֹד חֶרְפָּה בַּגּוֹיִם: וְאֶת־הַצְּפוֹנִי
אַרְחִיק מֵעֲלֵיכֶם וְהִדַּחְתִּיו אֶל־אֶרֶץ צִיָּה וּשְׁמָמָה אֶת־פָּנָיו אֶל־הַיָּם הַקַּדְמֹנִי וְסֹפוֹ אֶל־הַיָּם
כא הָאַחֲרוֹן וְעָלָה בָאְשׁוֹ וְתַעַל צַחֲנָתוֹ כִּי הִגְדִּיל לַעֲשׂוֹת: אַל־תִּירְאִי אֲדָמָה גִּילִי וּשְׂמָחִי כִּי־הִגְדִּיל
כב יהוה לַעֲשׂוֹת: אַל־תִּירְאוּ בַּהֲמוֹת שָׂדַי כִּי דָשְׁאוּ נְאוֹת מִדְבָּר כִּי־עֵץ נָשָׂא פִרְיוֹ תְּאֵנָה וָגֶפֶן
כג נָתְנוּ חֵילָם: וּבְנֵי צִיּוֹן גִּילוּ וְשִׂמְחוּ בַּיהוה אֱלֹהֵיכֶם כִּי־נָתַן לָכֶם אֶת־הַמּוֹרֶה לִצְדָקָה וַיּוֹרֶד לָכֶם
כד כה גֶּשֶׁם מוֹרֶה וּמַלְקוֹשׁ בָּרִאשׁוֹן: וּמָלְאוּ הַגֳּרָנוֹת בָּר וְהֵשִׁיקוּ הַיְקָבִים תִּירוֹשׁ וְיִצְהָר: וְשִׁלַּמְתִּי

the migratory locust, the Moroccan locust, and the caterpillar,
26 My great army that I sent among you. You will eat, eating to
satisfaction, and you will praise the name of the Lord your God,
who has acted with you wondrously, and My people will not be
27 ashamed forever. You will know that I am in the midst of Israel,
and I am the Lord your God, and there is no other, and My
people will not be ashamed forever.

MICAH 7

Seph. and some Ashk. add

18 Who is God like You, bearing iniquity and overlooking transgression for the remnant of His inheritance? He does not main-
19 tain His wrath forever, because He desires kindness. He will
again have mercy upon us; He will suppress our iniquities and
20 You will cast all their sins into the depths of the sea. You will
give truth to Jacob, kindness to Abraham, as You took an oath
to our forefathers from days of old.

Haftara for **Haazinu**

The haftara is read on the Shabbat between Yom Kippur and Sukkot. On Shabbat Shuva, the haftara on page 1268 is read.

The Song of David

II SAMUEL 22:1–51

This song was composed during David's final, relatively serene years, when he could settle back and reflect upon his life. In this song, David pours out his soul, as he reflects on his remarkable life in its entirety, in which miracles were constantly wrought for him. In the merit of his righteousness, God repeatedly came to his aid in minor matters as well as important issues. He was also assisted by other people and forces of nature. All David could do in response was to give thanks to God, who had chosen him, placed His name specifically upon him, and elevated him to his current status.

The topics of faith in God, divine salvation, and vengeance upon one's enemies feature in both the song of *Ha'azinu*, which refers to the entire nation throughout history, as well as in the song of David, which focuses on the life of one individual selected to lead the people.

22
1 David spoke to the Lord the words of this song on the day that
the Lord delivered him from the hand of all his enemies, and
2 from the hand of Saul. He said: The Lord is my rock, my for-
3 tress, and my deliverer. God who is my rock, I take shelter in
Him, my shield, and the glory of my salvation, my stronghold,
4 and my refuge; my savior, You save me from villainy. Praised, I
5 call the Lord, and from my enemies I am saved. For the waves
of death encompassed me; the unbridled torrents frightened
6 me; the cords of the abyss surrounded me; the snares of death
7 preceded me. In my distress, I called the Lord and to my God
I called; He heard my voice from His Temple and my cry was
8 in His ears. The earth erupted and quaked, the foundations of
the heavens trembled; they erupted, because He was incensed.
9 Smoke rose in His nostrils, and fire would devour from His
10 mouth; coals blazed from Him. He bent the heavens and de-
11 scended, and fog was beneath His feet. He rode on a cherub
12 and flew; He was seen on the wings of the wind. He placed
darkness around Him as screens, a heap of water, thick clouds
13 14 of the skies. From the aura before Him blazed coals of fire. The
Lord will thunder from the heavens, and the Most High will
15 project His voice. He sent his arrows and scattered them, light-
16 ning, and confounded them. The channels of the sea became
visible; the foundations of the world were exposed, by the re-
17 buke of the Lord, by the gust of the breath of His nostrils. He
18 sent from on high; took me, drew me out of vast waters; He
delivered me from my mighty foe, from my enemies, for they
19 overpowered me. They confronted me on the day of my calam-
20 ity, but the Lord was a support for me. He took me out into
21 the open; He extricated me, because He desired me. The Lord
rewarded me in accordance with my righteousness; in accordance with the cleanliness of my hands He recompensed me.
22 For I kept the ways of the Lord, and I did not deviate from my
23 God. For all His ordinances are before me, and His statutes I
24 will not stray from them. I was wholehearted toward Him, and
25 I protected myself from my iniquity. Therefore the Lord recompensed me in accordance with my righteousness, in accordance

לָכֶם אֶת־הַשָּׁנִים אֲשֶׁר אָכַל הָאַרְבֶּה הַיֶּלֶק וְהֶחָסִיל וְהַגָּזָם חֵילִי הַגָּדוֹל אֲשֶׁר שִׁלַּחְתִּי בָּכֶם׃
כו וַאֲכַלְתֶּם אָכוֹל וְשָׂבוֹעַ וְהִלַּלְתֶּם אֶת־שֵׁם יהוה אֱלֹהֵיכֶם אֲשֶׁר־עָשָׂה עִמָּכֶם לְהַפְלִיא וְלֹא־יֵבֹשׁוּ
כז עַמִּי לְעוֹלָם׃ וִידַעְתֶּם כִּי בְקֶרֶב יִשְׂרָאֵל אָנִי וַאֲנִי יהוה אֱלֹהֵיכֶם וְאֵין עוֹד וְלֹא־יֵבֹשׁוּ עַמִּי לְעוֹלָם׃ רוב אשכנזים מוסיימים כאן
ז יח מִי־אֵל כָּמוֹךָ נֹשֵׂא עָוֺן וְעֹבֵר עַל־פֶּשַׁע לִשְׁאֵרִית נַחֲלָתוֹ לֹא־הֶחֱזִיק לָעַד אַפּוֹ כִּי־חָפֵץ חֶסֶד מיכה
יט כ הוּא׃ יָשׁוּב יְרַחֲמֵנוּ יִכְבֹּשׁ עֲוֺנֹתֵינוּ וְתַשְׁלִיךְ בִּמְצֻלוֹת יָם כָּל־חַטֹּאתָם׃ תִּתֵּן אֱמֶת לְיַעֲקֹב חֶסֶד הספרדים וחלק מהאשכנזים מוסיפים
לְאַבְרָהָם אֲשֶׁר־נִשְׁבַּעְתָּ לַאֲבֹתֵינוּ מִימֵי קֶדֶם׃

הפטרת

האזינו

הפטרה לשבת שבין יום הכיפורים לסוכות. בשבת שובה קוראים את ההפטרה בעמ׳ 1269.

שמואל ב׳

כב א וַיְדַבֵּר דָּוִד לַיהוָה אֶת־דִּבְרֵי הַשִּׁירָה הַזֹּאת בְּיוֹם
הִצִּיל יְהוָה אֹתוֹ מִכַּף כָּל־אֹיְבָיו וּמִכַּף שָׁאוּל׃
ב ג וַיֹּאמַר יְהוָה סַלְעִי וּמְצֻדָתִי וּמְפַלְטִי־לִי׃ אֱלֹהֵי
צוּרִי אֶחֱסֶה־בּוֹ מָגִנִּי וְקֶרֶן יִשְׁעִי מִשְׂגַּבִּי
ד וּמְנוּסִי מֹשִׁעִי מֵחָמָס תֹּשִׁעֵנִי׃ מְהֻלָּל
ה אֶקְרָא יְהוָה וּמֵאֹיְבַי אִוָּשֵׁעַ׃ כִּי אֲפָפֻנִי מִשְׁבְּרֵי־
ו מָוֶת נַחֲלֵי בְלִיַּעַל יְבַעֲתֻנִי׃ חֶבְלֵי
שְׁאוֹל סַבֻּנִי קִדְּמֻנִי מֹקְשֵׁי־
ז מָוֶת׃ בַּצַּר־לִי אֶקְרָא יְהוָה וְאֶל־
אֱלֹהַי אֶקְרָא וַיִּשְׁמַע מֵהֵיכָלוֹ
ח קוֹלִי וְשַׁוְעָתִי בְּאָזְנָיו׃ ותגעש
וַתִּרְעַשׁ הָאָרֶץ מוֹסְדוֹת הַשָּׁמַיִם
ט יִרְגָּזוּ וַיִּתְגָּעֲשׁוּ כִּי־חָרָה לוֹ׃ עָלָה
עָשָׁן בְּאַפּוֹ וְאֵשׁ מִפִּיו
י תֹּאכֵל גֶּחָלִים בָּעֲרוּ מִמֶּנּוּ׃ וַיֵּט
שָׁמַיִם וַיֵּרַד וַעֲרָפֶל תַּחַת
יא רַגְלָיו׃ וַיִּרְכַּב עַל־כְּרוּב וַיָּעֹף וַיֵּרָא

יב עַל־כַּנְפֵי־רוּחַ׃ וַיָּשֶׁת חֹשֶׁךְ סְבִיבֹתָיו
יג סֻכּוֹת חַשְׁרַת־מַיִם עָבֵי שְׁחָקִים׃ מִנֹּגַהּ
יד נֶגְדּוֹ בָּעֲרוּ גַּחֲלֵי־אֵשׁ׃ יַרְעֵם מִן־שָׁמַיִם
טו יְהוָה וְעֶלְיוֹן יִתֵּן קוֹלוֹ׃ וַיִּשְׁלַח
טז חִצִּים וַיְפִיצֵם בָּרָק ויהמם׃ וַיֵּרָאוּ אֲפִקֵי וַיָּהֹם
יָם יִגָּלוּ מֹסְדוֹת תֵּבֵל בְּגַעֲרַת
יז יְהוָה מִנִּשְׁמַת רוּחַ אַפּוֹ׃ יִשְׁלַח מִמָּרוֹם
יח יִקָּחֵנִי יַמְשֵׁנִי מִמַּיִם רַבִּים׃ יַצִּילֵנִי
מֵאֹיְבִי עָז מִשֹּׂנְאַי כִּי אָמְצוּ
יט מִמֶּנִּי׃ יְקַדְּמֻנִי בְּיוֹם אֵידִי וַיְהִי
כ יְהוָה מִשְׁעָן לִי׃ וַיֹּצֵא לַמֶּרְחָב וַיִּתְגָּעַשׁ
כא אֹתִי יְחַלְּצֵנִי כִּי־חָפֵץ בִּי׃ יִגְמְלֵנִי
יְהוָה כְּצִדְקָתִי כְּבֹר יָדַי יָשִׁיב
כב לִי׃ כִּי שָׁמַרְתִּי דַּרְכֵי יְהוָה וְלֹא
כג רָשַׁעְתִּי מֵאֱלֹהָי׃ כִּי כָל־מִשְׁפָּטָו
כד לְנֶגְדִּי וְחֻקֹּתָיו לֹא־אָסוּר מִמֶּנָּה׃ וָאֶהְיֶה
כה תָמִים לוֹ וָאֶשְׁתַּמְּרָה מֵעֲוֺנִי׃ וַיָּשֶׁב יְהוָה לִי

26 with my cleanliness before His eyes. With the kind You act
27 kindly; with the genuinely valiant one You act genuinely; with
the innocent You act innocently; and with the perverse You
28 act tortuously. The humble people You save; and Your eyes
29 look down upon the haughty. For You are my lamp, Lord, and
30 the Lord illuminates my darkness. For with You I will pursue
31 a troop; with my God I will leap over a wall. God, His way is
perfect; the word of the Lord is pure; He is a shield for all who
32 take refuge in Him. For who is God, other than the Lord, and
33 who is a rock, other than our God? God is my mighty fortress;
34 He has perfectly opened my way. He steadies my feet like the
35 hinds', and on my heights He will set me. He trains my hands
36 for war, and my arms bend a bow of bronze. You have given me
Your shield of salvation, and Your response has made me great.
37 You would broaden my steps beneath me, and my feet did not
38 falter. I would pursue my enemies and would destroy them; I
39 would not return until their annihilation. I annihilated them
and crushed them, and they will not arise; they fell beneath
40 my feet. You girded me with might for battle; those who rose

41 against me You subdued under me. My enemies, you had them
turn their backs to me; those who hate me, I eradicate them.
42 They would plead, but there is no savior, to the Lord, but He
43 did not answer. I pulverized them like the dust of the earth; I
44 flattened them, trampled them like clay of the streets. You delivered me from the quarrels of my people, would protect me
to be the head of nations; a people whom I did not know serve
45 me. The sons of the foreigner would lie to me; upon their ear's
46 hearing, they obey me. The sons of the stranger would wither,
47 they would break out from their enclosures. The Lord lives, and
48 blessed be my rock; exalted is God, rock of my salvation, God
49 who grants me vengeance, subjects peoples beneath me, extri-
cates me from my enemies, and You would lift me over those
who rise against me; from the villainous man You would rescue
50 me. Therefore, I will thank You among the nations, Lord, and
51 to Your name I will sing. He is a tower of salvation for His king
and performs kindness to His anointed, to David and to his descendants, forever.

כו כְּצִדְקָתִ֑י כְּבֹרִ֖י לְנֶ֣גֶד עֵינָֽיו׃

עִם־חָסִ֖יד תִּתְחַסָּ֑ד עִם־גִּבּ֥וֹר תָּמִ֖ים תִּתַּמָּֽם׃

כז עִם־נָבָ֖ר תִּתָּבָ֑ר וְעִם־עִקֵּ֖שׁ תִּתַּפָּֽל׃

כח וְאֶת־עַ֥ם עָנִ֖י תּוֹשִׁ֑יעַ וְעֵינֶ֥יךָ עַל־רָמִ֖ים תַּשְׁפִּֽיל׃

כט כִּֽי־אַתָּ֥ה נֵירִ֖י יְהוָ֑ה וַֽיהוָ֖ה יַגִּ֥יהַּ חָשְׁכִּֽי׃

ל כִּ֥י בְכָ֖ה אָר֣וּץ גְּד֑וּד בֵּאלֹהַ֖י אֲדַלֶּג־שֽׁוּר׃

לא הָאֵל֙ תָּמִ֣ים דַּרְכּ֔וֹ אִמְרַ֥ת יְהוָ֖ה צְרוּפָ֑ה מָגֵ֣ן ה֔וּא לְכֹ֖ל הַחֹסִ֥ים בּֽוֹ׃

לב כִּ֣י מִי־אֵ֖ל מִבַּלְעֲדֵ֣י יְהוָ֑ה וּמִ֥י צ֖וּר מִֽבַּלְעֲדֵ֥י אֱלֹהֵֽינוּ׃

לג הָאֵ֥ל מָֽעוּזִּ֖י חָ֑יִל וַיַּתֵּ֥ר תָּמִ֖ים דרכו דַּרְכִּֽי

לד מְשַׁוֶּ֥ה רַגְלָ֖יו כָּאַיָּל֑וֹת וְעַ֥ל בָּמֹתַ֖י יַעֲמִדֵֽנִי׃

לה מְלַמֵּ֥ד יָדַ֖י לַמִּלְחָמָ֑ה וְנִחַ֥ת קֶֽשֶׁת־נְחוּשָׁ֖ה זְרֹעֹתָֽי׃

לו וַתִּתֶּן־לִ֖י מָגֵ֣ן יִשְׁעֶ֑ךָ וַעֲנֹתְךָ֖ תַּרְבֵּֽנִי׃

לז תַּרְחִ֥יב צַעֲדִ֖י תַּחְתֵּ֑נִי וְלֹ֥א מָעֲד֖וּ קַרְסֻלָּֽי׃

לח אֶרְדְּפָ֥ה אֹיְבַ֖י וָאַשְׁמִידֵ֑ם וְלֹ֥א אָשׁ֖וּב עַד־כַּלּוֹתָֽם׃

לט וָאֲכַלֵּ֥ם וָאֶמְחָצֵ֖ם וְלֹ֣א יְקוּמ֑וּן וַיִּפְּל֖וּ תַּ֥חַת רַגְלָֽי׃

מ וַתַּזְרֵ֥נִי חַ֖יִל לַמִּלְחָמָ֑ה תַּכְרִ֥יעַ קָמַ֖י תַּחְתֵּֽנִי׃

מא וְאֹ֣יְבַ֔י תַּ֖תָּה לִּ֣י עֹ֑רֶף מְשַׂנְאַ֖י וָאַצְמִיתֵֽם׃

מב יִשְׁע֖וּ וְאֵ֣ין מֹשִׁ֑יעַ אֶל־יְהוָ֖ה וְלֹ֥א עָנָֽם׃

מג וְאֶשְׁחָקֵ֖ם כַּעֲפַר־אָ֑רֶץ כְּטִיט־חוּצ֛וֹת אֲדִקֵּ֖ם אֶרְקָעֵֽם׃

מד וַתְּפַלְּטֵ֖נִי מֵרִיבֵ֣י עַמִּ֑י תִּשְׁמְרֵ֙נִי֙ לְרֹ֣אשׁ גּוֹיִ֔ם עַ֥ם לֹא־יָדַ֖עְתִּי יַעַבְדֻֽנִי׃

מה בְּנֵ֥י נֵכָ֖ר יִתְכַּחֲשׁוּ־לִ֑י לִשְׁמ֥וֹעַ אֹ֖זֶן יִשָּׁ֥מְעוּ לִֽי׃

מו בְּנֵ֥י נֵכָ֖ר יִבֹּ֑לוּ וְיַחְגְּר֖וּ מִֽמִּסְגְּרוֹתָֽם׃

מז חַי־יְהוָ֖ה וּבָר֣וּךְ צוּרִ֑י וְיָרֻ֕ם אֱלֹהֵ֖י צ֥וּר יִשְׁעִֽי׃

מח הָאֵ֕ל הַנֹּתֵ֥ן נְקָמֹ֖ת לִ֑י וּמֹרִ֥יד עַמִּ֖ים תַּחְתֵּֽנִי׃

מט וּמוֹצִיאִ֖י מֵאֹֽיְבָ֑י וּמִקָּמַ֣י תְּרֽוֹמְמֵ֔נִי מֵאִ֥ישׁ חֲמָסִ֖ים תַּצִּילֵֽנִי׃

נ עַל־כֵּ֛ן אוֹדְךָ֥ יְהוָ֖ה בַּגּוֹיִ֑ם וּלְשִׁמְךָ֖ אֲזַמֵּֽר׃

נא מגדיל מִגְדּ֖וֹל יְשׁוּע֣וֹת מַלְכּ֑וֹ וְעֹֽשֶׂה־חֶ֗סֶד לִמְשִׁיח֛וֹ לְדָוִ֥ד וּלְזַרְע֖וֹ עַד־עוֹלָֽם׃

Haftara for
Vezot HaBerakha

Picking Up Where the Torah Leaves Off
JOSHUA 1:1–18

This *haftara* is a direct continuation of the concluding passages of the Torah, read on Simhat Torah. Joshua, who was Moses' assistant, is appointed as the highest leader of the people. From here onward, the responsibility for the entire leadership rests upon his shoulders, with the transfer of authority to him already implemented in Moses' lifetime. At the start of Joshua's independent rule, God addresses him directly, offering guidance and encouragement. He assures him that he will succeed in crossing the Jordan River, and he will enter and conquer the Land of Israel. Joshua's function is not merely political or military. He is commanded to remain in constant contact with God and to wholly cleave to His Torah.

To a great extent, Joshua's leadership role was forged when he was Moses' minister and assistant, as he already executed Moses' commands during the first war against Amalek (Exodus 17:8–16). Always at Moses' side, Joshua was the one chosen to complete his master's mission. For this reason, statements of Moses himself are cited on several occasions in the book of Joshua (see 8:31–35, 11:12–23, 23:6). Moses' words and prophecy are at the basis of all the events described in this book, while their realization in practice was the task imposed upon Joshua, his successor and the people's new military leader (see Ralbag, 1:1).

1 1 It was after the death of Moses servant of the Lord, the Lord 2 said to Joshua son of Nun, Moses' attendant, saying: Moses My servant is dead; now you and this entire people, arise, cross this Jordan to the land that I am giving to them, to the 3 children of Israel. Every place that your foot will tread, I have 4 given it to you, as I spoke to Moses. From the wilderness and this Lebanon to the great river, the Euphrates River, the entire land of the Hitites to the Great Sea, toward the setting sun, will 5 be your borders. No man will stand against you all the days of your life; just as I was with Moses, so I will be with you; I will 6 not neglect you and I will not forsake you. Be strong and courageous, as you will bequeath to this people the land that I took 7 an oath to their fathers to give them. Just be very strong and courageous, to take care to act in accordance with the entire Torah that Moses My servant commanded you; do not deviate from it right or left so that you will be accomplished wherever 8 you will go. This book of the Torah shall not depart from your mouth, and you shall ponder it day and night, so that you will take care to act in accordance with everything that is written in it, as then you will succeed on your way, and then you will 9 be accomplished. Truly I have commanded you: Be strong and courageous, do not break and do not be alarmed, as the Lord *Seph.* 10 your God is with you wherever you will go. Joshua commanded *end* 11 the officers of the people, saying: Pass through the midst of the camp, and command the people, saying: Prepare for yourselves provisions, for in three more days you are crossing this Jordan, to go and to take possession of the land that the Lord your God 12 is giving you to take possession of it. To the Reubenites, and to the Gadites, and to half the tribe of Manasseh, Joshua said, 13 stating: Remember the matter that Moses servant of the Lord commanded you, saying: The Lord your God is granting you 14 repose, and He has given you this land. Your wives, your children, and your livestock will inhabit the land that Moses gave you beyond the Jordan, but you shall cross, armed, before your 15 brethren, all the valiant soldiers, and you shall help them until the Lord grants your brethren repose, like you, and they too take possession of the land that the Lord your God is giving them, and you return to the land of your possession and take possession of it, which was given to you by Moses the servant 16 of the Lord, across the Jordan, toward the rising sun. They answered Joshua, saying: Everything that you commanded us we 17 will do, and to wherever you send us we will go. Just as we always heeded Moses, so we will heed you; only, may the Lord 18 your God be with you, as He was with Moses. Any man who disobeys you and does not heed your words in everything that you command him, will be put to death; just be strong and courageous.

וזאת הברכה

א א וַיְהִ֗י אַחֲרֵ֛י מ֥וֹת מֹשֶׁ֖ה עֶ֣בֶד יְהוָ֑ה וַיֹּ֤אמֶר יְהוָה֙ אֶל־יְהוֹשֻׁ֣עַ בִּן־נ֔וּן מְשָׁרֵ֥ת מֹשֶׁ֖ה לֵאמֹֽר: מֹשֶׁ֥ה   יהושע

ב עַבְדִּ֖י מֵ֑ת וְעַתָּה֩ ק֨וּם עֲבֹ֜ר אֶת־הַיַּרְדֵּ֣ן הַזֶּ֗ה אַתָּה֙ וְכָל־הָעָ֣ם הַזֶּ֔ה אֶל־הָאָ֕רֶץ אֲשֶׁ֧ר אָנֹכִ֛י נֹתֵ֥ן

ג לָהֶ֖ם לִבְנֵ֥י יִשְׂרָאֵֽל: כָּל־מָק֗וֹם אֲשֶׁ֨ר תִּדְרֹ֧ךְ כַּֽף־רַגְלְכֶ֛ם בּ֖וֹ לָכֶ֣ם נְתַתִּ֑יו כַּאֲשֶׁ֥ר דִּבַּ֖רְתִּי אֶל־מֹשֶֽׁה:

ד מֵהַמִּדְבָּר֩ וְהַלְּבָנ֨וֹן הַזֶּ֜ה וְֽעַד־הַנָּהָ֧ר הַגָּד֣וֹל נְהַר־פְּרָ֗ת כֹּ֚ל אֶ֣רֶץ הַחִתִּ֔ים וְעַד־הַיָּ֥ם הַגָּד֖וֹל מְב֣וֹא

ה הַשָּׁ֑מֶשׁ יִהְיֶ֖ה גְּבוּלְכֶֽם: לֹֽא־יִתְיַצֵּ֥ב אִישׁ֙ לְפָנֶ֔יךָ כֹּ֖ל יְמֵ֣י חַיֶּ֑יךָ כַּֽאֲשֶׁ֨ר הָיִ֤יתִי עִם־מֹשֶׁה֙ אֶהְיֶ֣ה

ו עִמָּ֔ךְ לֹ֥א אַרְפְּךָ֖ וְלֹ֥א אֶעֶזְבֶֽךָּ: חֲזַ֖ק וֶֽאֱמָ֑ץ כִּ֣י אַתָּ֗ה תַּנְחִיל֙ אֶת־הָעָ֣ם הַזֶּ֔ה אֶת־הָאָ֕רֶץ אֲשֶׁר־

ז נִשְׁבַּ֥עְתִּי לַאֲבוֹתָ֖ם לָתֵ֣ת לָהֶֽם: רַ֩ק חֲזַ֨ק וֶֽאֱמַ֜ץ מְאֹ֗ד לִשְׁמֹ֤ר לַעֲשׂוֹת֙ כְּכָל־הַתּוֹרָ֗ה אֲשֶׁ֤ר צִוְּךָ֙

ח מֹשֶׁ֣ה עַבְדִּ֔י אַל־תָּס֥וּר מִמֶּ֖נּוּ יָמִ֣ין וּשְׂמֹ֑אול לְמַ֙עַן֙ תַּשְׂכִּ֔יל בְּכֹ֖ל אֲשֶׁ֥ר תֵּלֵֽךְ: לֹֽא־יָמ֡וּשׁ סֵפֶר֩

הַתּוֹרָ֨ה הַזֶּ֜ה מִפִּ֗יךָ וְהָגִ֤יתָ בּוֹ֙ יוֹמָ֣ם וָלַ֔יְלָה לְמַ֙עַן֙ תִּשְׁמֹ֣ר לַעֲשׂ֔וֹת כְּכָל־הַכָּת֖וּב בּ֑וֹ כִּי־אָ֛ז תַּצְלִ֥יחַ

ט אֶת־דְּרָכֶ֖ךָ וְאָ֥ז תַּשְׂכִּֽיל: הֲל֤וֹא צִוִּיתִ֙יךָ֙ חֲזַ֣ק וֶֽאֱמָ֔ץ אַֽל־תַּעֲרֹ֖ץ וְאַל־תֵּחָ֑ת כִּ֤י עִמְּךָ֙ יְהוָ֣ה אֱלֹהֶ֔יךָ

י בְּכֹ֖ל אֲשֶׁ֥ר תֵּלֵֽךְ:   וַיְצַ֣ו יְהוֹשֻׁ֔עַ אֶת־שֹׁטְרֵ֥י הָעָ֖ם לֵאמֹֽר: עִבְר֣וּ ׀ בְּקֶ֣רֶב הַֽמַּחֲנֶ֗ה

יא וְצַוּ֤וּ אֶת־הָעָם֙ לֵאמֹ֔ר הָכִ֥ינוּ לָכֶ֖ם צֵדָ֑ה כִּ֞י בְּע֣וֹד ׀ שְׁלֹ֣שֶׁת יָמִ֗ים אַתֶּם֙ עֹֽבְרִים֙ אֶת־הַיַּרְדֵּ֣ן הַזֶּ֔ה

יב לָבוֹא֙ לָרֶ֣שֶׁת אֶת־הָאָ֔רֶץ אֲשֶׁר֙ יְהוָ֣ה אֱלֹֽהֵיכֶ֔ם נֹתֵ֥ן לָכֶ֖ם לְרִשְׁתָּֽהּ:   וְלָרֽאוּבֵנִ֣י

יג וְלַגָּדִ֗י וְלַחֲצִי֙ שֵׁ֣בֶט הַֽמְנַשֶּׁ֔ה אָמַ֥ר יְהוֹשֻׁ֖עַ לֵאמֹֽר: זָכוֹר֙ אֶת־הַדָּבָ֔ר אֲשֶׁ֨ר צִוָּ֥ה אֶתְכֶ֛ם מֹשֶׁ֥ה

יד עֶבֶד־יְהוָ֖ה לֵאמֹ֑ר יְהוָ֤ה אֱלֹֽהֵיכֶם֙ מֵנִ֣יחַ לָכֶ֔ם וְנָתַ֥ן לָכֶ֖ם אֶת־הָאָ֥רֶץ הַזֹּֽאת: נְשֵׁיכֶ֣ם טַפְּכֶ֗ם

וּמִקְנֵיכֶם֮ יֵשְׁב֣וּ בָּאָרֶץ֒ אֲשֶׁ֨ר נָתַ֤ן לָכֶם֙ מֹשֶׁ֔ה בְּעֵ֖בֶר הַיַּרְדֵּ֑ן וְאַתֶּם֩ תַּעַבְר֨וּ חֲמֻשִׁ֜ים לִפְנֵ֣י אֲחֵיכֶ֗ם

טו כֹּ֚ל גִּבּוֹרֵ֣י הַחַ֔יִל וַעֲזַרְתֶּ֖ם אוֹתָֽם: עַ֠ד אֲשֶׁר־יָנִ֨יחַ יְהוָ֥ה ׀ לַֽאֲחֵיכֶם֮ כָּכֶם֒ וְיָרְשׁ֣וּ גַם־הֵ֔מָּה אֶת־

הָאָ֕רֶץ אֲשֶׁר־יְהוָ֥ה אֱלֹהֵיכֶ֖ם נֹתֵ֣ן לָהֶ֑ם וְשַׁבְתֶּ֞ם לְאֶ֤רֶץ יְרֻשַּׁתְכֶם֙ וִֽירִשְׁתֶּ֣ם אוֹתָ֔הּ אֲשֶׁ֣ר ׀ נָתַ֣ן

טז לָכֶ֗ם מֹשֶׁה֙ עֶ֣בֶד יְהוָ֔ה בְּעֵ֥בֶר הַיַּרְדֵּ֖ן מִזְרַ֥ח הַשָּֽׁמֶשׁ: וַֽיַּעֲנ֣וּ אֶת־יְהוֹשֻׁ֔עַ לֵאמֹ֑ר כֹּ֤ל אֲשֶׁר־צִוִּיתָ֙נוּ֙

יז נַעֲשֶׂ֔ה וְאֶֽל־כָּל־אֲשֶׁ֥ר תִּשְׁלָחֵ֖נוּ נֵלֵֽךְ: כְּכֹ֤ל אֲשֶׁר־שָׁמַ֙עְנוּ֙ אֶל־מֹשֶׁ֔ה כֵּ֥ן נִשְׁמַ֖ע אֵלֶ֑יךָ רַ֠ק יִֽהְיֶ֞ה

יח יְהוָ֤ה אֱלֹהֶ֙יךָ֙ עִמָּ֔ךְ כַּאֲשֶׁ֥ר הָיָ֖ה עִם־מֹשֶֽׁה: כָּל־אִ֞ישׁ אֲשֶׁר־יַמְרֶ֣ה אֶת־פִּ֗יךָ וְלֹֽא־יִשְׁמַ֧ע אֶת־

דְּבָרֶ֛יךָ לְכֹ֥ל אֲשֶׁר־תְּצַוֶּ֖נּוּ יוּמָ֑ת רַ֖ק חֲזַ֥ק וֶאֱמָֽץ:

הספרדים
מסיימים כאן

Haftara for
Rosh Hodesh Eve

David's Last Flight from the House of Saul, and His Farewell to Yonatan

I SAMUEL 20:18–42

The first verse of this *haftara* includes the phrase "tomorrow is the new moon." While this is clearly a central reason this passage was chosen to be read on the eve of the New Moon, some suggest that other ideas in the passage are thematically related to the New Moon as well. David's many temporary periods of hiding and his covenant of everlasting survival allude to the uniqueness of the nation of Israel as the eternal people of God, despite all the blatant and concealed hardships it must endure. One of the signs of this special status is the manner in which Israel sets its calendar and festivals in accordance with the waxing and waning of the moon. This analogy is hinted in the verse: "This month is for you" (Exodus 12:2); the passage of the months themselves symbolizes Israel.

20 18 Yonatan said to him: Tomorrow is the New Moon, and you will 19 be remembered because your seat will be empty. Wait three days, lie very low, and come to the place where you hid on 20 the day of the incident, and remain near the Ezel stone. I will shoot three arrows to the side, as though shooting at a target. 21 Behold, I will send the lad: Go, find the arrows. If I say to the lad: Here are the arrows; they are on this side of you; take them and come, then peace is with you and there is no concern, as 22 the Lord lives. But if I say this to the boy: Behold, the arrows 23 are beyond you, go, for the Lord has sent you away. But with regard to the matter of which we spoke, I and you, behold, the 24 Lord is between me and you forever. David concealed himself in the field. It was the New Moon, and the king sat to the meal 25 to eat. The king sat on his seat, as at other times, on the seat near the wall; Yonatan rose, and Avner sat at Saul's side, but David's 26 place was empty. Saul did not say anything that day, as he said: 27 It is incidental; he is impure, as he is not purified. It was on the next day, the second day of the month, and David's place was empty. Saul said to Yonatan his son: Why did the son of Yishai 28 not come to the meal, both yesterday and today? Yonatan an- 29 swered Saul: David requested of me to go to Bethlehem. He said: Please let me go, as there is a family feast offering for us in the city, and my brother, he commanded me; now, if I found favor in your eyes, please let me get away and see my broth- 30 ers. Therefore, he did not come to the king's table. Saul's wrath was enflamed at Yonatan, and he said to him: Son of a perverse, rebellious woman! Don't I know that you choose the son of Yishai to your own shame, and to the shame of your mother's 31 nakedness? For all the days that the son of Yishai lives upon the earth, you and your kingdom will not be established. Now, 32 send and take him to me, as he is deserving of death. Yonatan answered Saul his father, and he said to him: Why should he 33 be put to death? What did he do? Saul cast his spear at him to smite him. Yonatan knew that it was settled with his father to 34 put David to death. Yonatan arose from the table in enflamed wrath, and he did not eat food on the second day of the month, as he was sad over David, because his father had humiliated 35 him. It was the morning and Yonatan went out to the field at the 36 time appointed with David, and a small lad was with him. He said to his lad: Run now, find the arrows that I am shooting. The 37 lad ran, and he shot an arrow to go beyond him. The lad came to the place of the arrow that Yonatan shot, and Yonatan called 38 after the lad, and said: Isn't the arrow beyond you? Yonatan called after the lad: Quickly, hurry, do not stand. Yonatan's lad 39 gathered the arrows and he came to his master. The lad did not know anything; only Yonatan and David knew the matter. 40 Yonatan gave his weapons to his lad, and he said to him: Go, 41 bring it to the city. The lad was gone, and David rose from the south side, and he fell on his face to the ground and prostrated himself three times. Each kissed the other, and each wept with 42 the other, until David was overcome. Yonatan said to David: Go in peace, for we have taken an oath, both of us, in the name of the Lord, saying: The Lord shall be between me and you, and between my descendants and your descendants, forever.

שבת ערב ראש חדש

שמואל א' כ יט וַיֹּאמֶר־לוֹ יְהוֹנָתָן מָחָר חֹדֶשׁ וְנִפְקַדְתָּ כִּי יִפָּקֵד מוֹשָׁבֶךָ: וְשִׁלַּשְׁתָּ תֵּרֵד מְאֹד וּבָאתָ אֶל־

כ הַמָּקוֹם אֲשֶׁר־נִסְתַּרְתָּ שָּׁם בְּיוֹם הַמַּעֲשֶׂה וְיָשַׁבְתָּ אֵצֶל הָאֶבֶן הָאָזֶל: וַאֲנִי שְׁלֹשֶׁת הַחִצִּים

כא צִדָּה אוֹרֶה לְשַׁלַּח־לִי לְמַטָּרָה: וְהִנֵּה אֶשְׁלַח אֶת־הַנַּעַר לֵךְ מְצָא אֶת־הַחִצִּים אִם־אָמֹר אֹמַר

כב לַנַּעַר הִנֵּה הַחִצִּים ׀ מִמְּךָ וָהֵנָּה קָחֶנּוּ ׀ וָבֹאָה כִּי־שָׁלוֹם לְךָ וְאֵין דָּבָר חַי־יְהוָה: וְאִם־כֹּה אֹמַר

כג לָעֶלֶם הִנֵּה הַחִצִּים מִמְּךָ וָהָלְאָה לֵךְ כִּי שִׁלַּחֲךָ יְהוָה: וְהַדָּבָר אֲשֶׁר דִּבַּרְנוּ אֲנִי וָאָתָּה הִנֵּה

כד יְהוָה בֵּינִי וּבֵינְךָ עַד־עוֹלָם: וַיִּסָּתֵר דָּוִד בַּשָּׂדֶה וַיְהִי הַחֹדֶשׁ וַיֵּשֶׁב הַמֶּלֶךְ עַל־אֶל־

כה הַלֶּחֶם לֶאֱכוֹל: וַיֵּשֶׁב הַמֶּלֶךְ עַל־מוֹשָׁבוֹ כְּפַעַם ׀ בְּפַעַם אֶל־מוֹשַׁב הַקִּיר וַיָּקָם יְהוֹנָתָן וַיֵּשֶׁב

כו אַבְנֵר מִצַּד שָׁאוּל וַיִּפָּקֵד מְקוֹם דָּוִד: וְלֹא־דִבֶּר שָׁאוּל מְאוּמָה בַּיּוֹם הַהוּא כִּי אָמַר מִקְרֶה

כז הוּא בִּלְתִּי טָהוֹר הוּא כִּי־לֹא טָהוֹר: וַיְהִי מִמָּחֳרַת הַחֹדֶשׁ הַשֵּׁנִי וַיִּפָּקֵד מְקוֹם

דָּוִד וַיֹּאמֶר שָׁאוּל אֶל־יְהוֹנָתָן בְּנוֹ מַדּוּעַ לֹא־בָא בֶן־יִשַׁי גַּם־תְּמוֹל גַּם־הַיּוֹם אֶל־הַלָּחֶם:

כח כט וַיַּעַן יְהוֹנָתָן אֶת־שָׁאוּל נִשְׁאֹל נִשְׁאַל דָּוִד מֵעִמָּדִי עַד־בֵּית לָחֶם: וַיֹּאמֶר שַׁלְּחֵנִי נָא כִּי זֶבַח

מִשְׁפָּחָה לָנוּ בָּעִיר וְהוּא צִוָּה־לִי אָחִי וְעַתָּה אִם־מָצָאתִי חֵן בְּעֵינֶיךָ אִמָּלְטָה נָּא וְאֶרְאֶה

ל אֶת־אֶחָי עַל־כֵּן לֹא־בָא אֶל־שֻׁלְחַן הַמֶּלֶךְ: וַיִּחַר־אַף שָׁאוּל בִּיהוֹנָתָן וַיֹּאמֶר לוֹ

לא בֶּן־נַעֲוַת הַמַּרְדּוּת הֲלוֹא יָדַעְתִּי כִּי־בֹחֵר אַתָּה לְבֶן־יִשַׁי לְבָשְׁתְּךָ וּלְבֹשֶׁת עֶרְוַת אִמֶּךָ: כִּי כָל־

הַיָּמִים אֲשֶׁר בֶּן־יִשַׁי חַי עַל־הָאֲדָמָה לֹא תִכּוֹן אַתָּה וּמַלְכוּתֶךָ וְעַתָּה שְׁלַח וְקַח אֹתוֹ אֵלַי כִּי

לב בֶן־מָוֶת הוּא: וַיַּעַן יְהוֹנָתָן אֶת־שָׁאוּל אָבִיו וַיֹּאמֶר אֵלָיו לָמָּה יוּמַת מֶה עָשָׂה:

לג וַיָּטֶל שָׁאוּל אֶת־הַחֲנִית עָלָיו לְהַכֹּתוֹ וַיֵּדַע יְהוֹנָתָן כִּי־כָלָה הִיא מֵעִם אָבִיו לְהָמִית אֶת־

לד דָּוִד: וַיָּקָם יְהוֹנָתָן מֵעִם הַשֻּׁלְחָן בָּחֳרִי־אָף וְלֹא־אָכַל בְּיוֹם־הַחֹדֶשׁ הַשֵּׁנִי

לה לֶחֶם כִּי נֶעְצַב אֶל־דָּוִד כִּי הִכְלִמוֹ אָבִיו: וַיְהִי בַבֹּקֶר וַיֵּצֵא יְהוֹנָתָן הַשָּׂדֶה

לו לְמוֹעֵד דָּוִד וְנַעַר קָטֹן עִמּוֹ: וַיֹּאמֶר לְנַעֲרוֹ רֻץ מְצָא נָא אֶת־הַחִצִּים אֲשֶׁר אָנֹכִי מוֹרֶה הַנַּעַר

לז רָץ וְהוּא־יָרָה הַחֵצִי לְהַעֲבִרוֹ: וַיָּבֹא הַנַּעַר עַד־מְקוֹם הַחֵצִי אֲשֶׁר יָרָה יְהוֹנָתָן וַיִּקְרָא יְהוֹנָתָן

לח אַחֲרֵי הַנַּעַר וַיֹּאמֶר הֲלוֹא הַחֵצִי מִמְּךָ וָהָלְאָה: וַיִּקְרָא יְהוֹנָתָן אַחֲרֵי הַנַּעַר מְהֵרָה חוּשָׁה אַל־

לט תַּעֲמֹד וַיְלַקֵּט נַעַר יְהוֹנָתָן אֶת־הַחֵצִי וַיָּבֹא אֶל־אֲדֹנָיו: וְהַנַּעַר לֹא־יָדַע מְאוּמָה אַךְ יְהוֹנָתָן הַחִצִּים

מ וְדָוִד יָדְעוּ אֶת־הַדָּבָר: וַיִּתֵּן יְהוֹנָתָן אֶת־כֵּלָיו אֶל־הַנַּעַר אֲשֶׁר־לוֹ וַיֹּאמֶר לוֹ לֵךְ הָבֵיא הָעִיר:

מא הַנַּעַר בָּא וְדָוִד קָם מֵאֵצֶל הַנֶּגֶב וַיִּפֹּל לְאַפָּיו אַרְצָה וַיִּשְׁתַּחוּ שָׁלֹשׁ פְּעָמִים וַיִּשְּׁקוּ ׀ אִישׁ אֶת־

מב רֵעֵהוּ וַיִּבְכּוּ אִישׁ אֶת־רֵעֵהוּ עַד־דָּוִד הִגְדִּיל: וַיֹּאמֶר יְהוֹנָתָן לְדָוִד לֵךְ לְשָׁלוֹם אֲשֶׁר נִשְׁבַּעְנוּ

שְׁנֵינוּ אֲנַחְנוּ בְּשֵׁם יְהוָה לֵאמֹר יְהוָה יִהְיֶה ׀ בֵּינִי וּבֵינֶךָ וּבֵין זַרְעִי וּבֵין זַרְעֲךָ עַד־עוֹלָם:

Haftara for
Rosh Hodesh

The Future Reward and Punishment
ISAIAH 66:1–24

Alongside a rebuke to those who act improperly and thereby distance themselves from God, the last section of the book of Isaiah also depicts the revelation of God. The future redemption is not portrayed merely as a series of gifts, salvations, and consolations, but also as a time of recompense. Consequently, the prophecy includes a depiction of both the reward for those who follow the upright path and the punishment that awaits evildoers. The *haftara* concludes with a prophecy that in the future all peoples will ascend to the Temple for the Sabbaths and the New Moons.

66 1 So said the Lord: The heavens are My throne and the earth is My footstool; what house could you build for Me and what 2 place could be My resting place? My hand made all these and all these came into being – the utterance of the Lord – but to this I will look, to the poor and the depressed and fervent for 3 My word. He who slaughters an ox, smites a man; he who offers a sheep, beheads a dog; he who presents a meal offering, it is blood of a swine; he who burns frankincense, bestows wickedness. They too chose their ways and their soul desires 4 their abominations. I too will choose their exploits and I will bring their fears upon them, because I called and none answer, I spoke and they did not hear. They performed that which is 5 evil in My eyes and chose that which I did not desire. Hear the word of the Lord, those who are fervent for His word: Your brethren, those who hate you, those who ostracize you, said: For the sake of my name the Lord will be glorified, but we will 6 see your joy and they will be ashamed. The sound of a din is from the city, a sound from the Sanctuary; the Lord pays rec- 7 ompense to His enemies. Before she begins labor, she will give 8 birth; before a pang comes, she will deliver a male child. Who has heard something like this? Who has seen something like these? Will a land complete labor in one day? Is a nation born at one time? For Zion has labored and has also given birth to her 9 children. Will I set the birthing stool and not cause birth, said the Lord? Will I, who causes birth, prevent it, said your God? 10 Rejoice with Jerusalem and all who love it be happy with it; all 11 who mourn for it be gladdened in gladness with it, so that you may nurse and be satisfied from the breast of its consolation, 12 so that you may suck and delight from the aura of its glory. For so said the Lord: Behold, I will direct peace to her like a river and the wealth of the nations like a flowing stream, and you will nurse; you will be borne on the side and dandled on the knees.

13 Like a man whose mother comforts him, so will I comfort you; 14 and in Jerusalem you will be comforted. You will see and your heart will be gladdened and your bones will flourish like grass; and the hand of the Lord will be known to His servants and He 15 will rage at His enemies. For behold, the Lord will come in fire and His chariots like a storm to assuage His anger with wrath 16 and His rebuke with flames of fire. For the Lord will judge all flesh with fire and with His sword, and the slain of the Lord will 17 be many. Those who prepare themselves and purify themselves for the gardens after the one in the center, eaters of the flesh of swine, detestable things, and mice, will perish together – the 18 utterance of the Lord. And as for Me, their actions and their thoughts are coming to be, to gather all the nations and the 19 tongues that will come and see My glory. I will place a sign upon them and I will send their survivors to the nations, to Tarshish, Pul, and Lud, drawers of the bow, Tuval and Yavan, the distant lands of the sea that have not heard of My fame and did not see 20 My glory, and they will tell My glory among the nations. They will bring all your brethren from all the nations as a gift to the Lord, on horses and in chariots and in coaches and on mules and on camels, to the mountain of My holiness, Jerusalem, said the Lord, when the children of Israel bring the gift in a pure 21 vessel to the house of the Lord. And from them too will I take as 22 priests and as Levites, said the Lord. For just as the new heavens and the new earth that I will make will remain before Me – the utterance of the Lord – so your descendants and your name will 23 remain. It shall be that on each and every New Moon and on each and every Sabbath all flesh will come to prostrate them- 24 selves before Me, said the Lord. They will emerge and they will see the corpses of the people who betray Me, as their worm will not die and their fire will not be extinguished and they will be a disgrace for all flesh.

הפטרת

שבת ראש חודש

ישעיה

סו א כֹּה אָמַר יְהֹוָה הַשָּׁמַיִם כִּסְאִי וְהָאָרֶץ הֲדֹם רַגְלָי אֵי־זֶה בַיִת אֲשֶׁר תִּבְנוּ־לִי וְאֵי־זֶה מָקוֹם

ב מְנוּחָתִי: וְאֶת־כָּל־אֵלֶּה יָדִי עָשָׂתָה וַיִּהְיוּ כָל־אֵלֶּה נְאֻם־יְהֹוָה וְאֶל־זֶה אַבִּיט אֶל־עָנִי וּנְכֵה־

ג רוּחַ וְחָרֵד עַל־דְּבָרִי: שׁוֹחֵט הַשּׁוֹר מַכֵּה־אִישׁ זוֹבֵחַ הַשֶּׂה עֹרֵף כֶּלֶב מַעֲלֵה מִנְחָה דַּם־חֲזִיר

ד מַזְכִּיר לְבֹנָה מְבָרֵךְ אָוֶן גַּם־הֵמָּה בָּחֲרוּ בְּדַרְכֵיהֶם וּבְשִׁקּוּצֵיהֶם נַפְשָׁם חָפֵצָה: גַּם־אֲנִי אֶבְחַר בְּתַעֲלֻלֵיהֶם וּמְגוּרֹתָם אָבִיא לָהֶם יַעַן קָרָאתִי וְאֵין עוֹנֶה דִּבַּרְתִּי וְלֹא שָׁמֵעוּ וַיַּעֲשׂוּ הָרַע

ה בְּעֵינַי וּבַאֲשֶׁר לֹא־חָפַצְתִּי בָּחָרוּ: שִׁמְעוּ דְּבַר־יְהֹוָה הַחֲרֵדִים אֶל־דְּבָרוֹ אָמְרוּ אֲחֵיכֶם שֹׂנְאֵיכֶם מְנַדֵּיכֶם לְמַעַן שְׁמִי יִכְבַּד יְהֹוָה וְנִרְאֶה בְשִׂמְחַתְכֶם וְהֵם יֵבֹשׁוּ: קוֹל שָׁאוֹן

ו מֵעִיר קוֹל מֵהֵיכָל קוֹל יְהֹוָה מְשַׁלֵּם גְּמוּל לְאֹיְבָיו: בְּטֶרֶם תָּחִיל יָלָדָה בְּטֶרֶם יָבוֹא חֵבֶל

ז לָהּ וְהִמְלִיטָה זָכָר: מִי־שָׁמַע כָּזֹאת מִי רָאָה כָּאֵלֶּה הֲיוּחַל אֶרֶץ בְּיוֹם אֶחָד אִם־יִוָּלֵד גּוֹי

ח פַּעַם אֶחָת כִּי־חָלָה גַּם־יָלְדָה צִיּוֹן אֶת־בָּנֶיהָ: הַאֲנִי אַשְׁבִּיר וְלֹא אוֹלִיד יֹאמַר יְהֹוָה אִם־אֲנִי

ט הַמּוֹלִיד וְעָצַרְתִּי אָמַר אֱלֹהָיִךְ: שִׂמְחוּ אֶת־יְרוּשָׁלַ͏ִם וְגִילוּ בָהּ כָּל־אֹהֲבֶיהָ

י שִׂישׂוּ אִתָּהּ מָשׂוֹשׂ כָּל־הַמִּתְאַבְּלִים עָלֶיהָ: לְמַעַן תִּינְקוּ וּשְׂבַעְתֶּם מִשֹּׁד תַּנְחֻמֶיהָ לְמַעַן

יא תָּמֹצּוּ וְהִתְעַנַּגְתֶּם מִזִּיז כְּבוֹדָהּ: כִּי־כֹה ׀ אָמַר יְהֹוָה הִנְנִי נֹטֶה־אֵלֶיהָ כְּנָהָר

יב שָׁלוֹם וּכְנַחַל שׁוֹטֵף כְּבוֹד גּוֹיִם וִינַקְתֶּם עַל־צַד תִּנָּשֵׂאוּ וְעַל־בִּרְכַּיִם תְּשָׁעֳשָׁעוּ: כְּאִישׁ אֲשֶׁר

יג אִמּוֹ תְּנַחֲמֶנּוּ כֵּן אָנֹכִי אֲנַחֶמְכֶם וּבִירוּשָׁלַ͏ִם תְּנֻחָמוּ: וּרְאִיתֶם וְשָׂשׂ לִבְּכֶם וְעַצְמוֹתֵיכֶם כַּדֶּשֶׁא

יד תִפְרַחְנָה וְנוֹדְעָה יַד־יְהֹוָה אֶת־עֲבָדָיו וְזָעַם אֶת־אֹיְבָיו: כִּי־הִנֵּה יְהֹוָה בָּאֵשׁ יָבוֹא וְכַסּוּפָה

טו מַרְכְּבֹתָיו לְהָשִׁיב בְּחֵמָה אַפּוֹ וְגַעֲרָתוֹ בְּלַהֲבֵי־אֵשׁ: כִּי בָאֵשׁ יְהֹוָה נִשְׁפָּט וּבְחַרְבּוֹ אֶת־כָּל־

טז בָּשָׂר וְרַבּוּ חַלְלֵי יְהֹוָה: הַמִּתְקַדְּשִׁים וְהַמִּטַּהֲרִים אֶל־הַגַּנּוֹת אַחַר אֶחָד בַּתָּוֶךְ אֹכְלֵי בְּשַׂר אַחַת

יז הַחֲזִיר וְהַשֶּׁקֶץ וְהָעַכְבָּר יַחְדָּו יָסֻפוּ נְאֻם־יְהֹוָה: וְאָנֹכִי מַעֲשֵׂיהֶם וּמַחְשְׁבֹתֵיהֶם בָּאָה לְקַבֵּץ

יח אֶת־כָּל־הַגּוֹיִם וְהַלְּשֹׁנוֹת וּבָאוּ וְרָאוּ אֶת־כְּבוֹדִי: וְשַׂמְתִּי בָהֶם אוֹת וְשִׁלַּחְתִּי מֵהֶם ׀ פְּלֵיטִים

יט אֶל־הַגּוֹיִם תַּרְשִׁישׁ פּוּל וְלוּד מֹשְׁכֵי קֶשֶׁת תֻּבַל וְיָוָן הָאִיִּים הָרְחֹקִים אֲשֶׁר לֹא־שָׁמְעוּ אֶת־

כ שִׁמְעִי וְלֹא־רָאוּ אֶת־כְּבוֹדִי וְהִגִּידוּ אֶת־כְּבוֹדִי בַּגּוֹיִם: וְהֵבִיאוּ אֶת־כָּל־אֲחֵיכֶם ׀ מִכָּל־הַגּוֹיִם ׀ מִנְחָה ׀ לַיהֹוָה בַּסּוּסִים וּבָרֶכֶב וּבַצַּבִּים וּבַפְּרָדִים וּבַכִּרְכָּרוֹת עַל הַר קָדְשִׁי יְרוּשָׁלַ͏ִם אָמַר

כא יְהֹוָה כַּאֲשֶׁר יָבִיאוּ בְנֵי יִשְׂרָאֵל אֶת־הַמִּנְחָה בִּכְלִי טָהוֹר בֵּית יְהֹוָה: וְגַם־מֵהֶם אֶקַּח לַכֹּהֲנִים

כב לַלְוִיִּם אָמַר יְהֹוָה: כִּי כַאֲשֶׁר הַשָּׁמַיִם הַחֳדָשִׁים וְהָאָרֶץ הַחֲדָשָׁה אֲשֶׁר אֲנִי עֹשֶׂה עֹמְדִים לְפָנַי

כג נְאֻם־יְהֹוָה כֵּן יַעֲמֹד זַרְעֲכֶם וְשִׁמְכֶם: וְהָיָה מִדֵּי־חֹדֶשׁ בְּחָדְשׁוֹ וּמִדֵּי שַׁבָּת בְּשַׁבַּתּוֹ יָבוֹא כָל־

כד בָּשָׂר לְהִשְׁתַּחֲוֺת לְפָנַי אָמַר יְהֹוָה: וְיָצְאוּ וְרָאוּ בְּפִגְרֵי הָאֲנָשִׁים הַפֹּשְׁעִים בִּי כִּי תוֹלַעְתָּם לֹא תָמוּת וְאִשָּׁם לֹא תִכְבֶּה וְהָיוּ דֵרָאוֹן לְכָל־בָּשָׂר:

וְהָיָה מִדֵּי־חֹדֶשׁ בְּחָדְשׁוֹ וּמִדֵּי שַׁבָּת בְּשַׁבַּתּוֹ יָבוֹא כָל־בָּשָׂר לְהִשְׁתַּחֲוֺת לְפָנַי אָמַר יְהֹוָה:

Haftara for the
First Shabbat of Hanukkah

On the second Shabbat of Hanukkah, the haftara on page 1282 is read..

Zechariah's Lamps
ZECHARIAH 2:14–4:7

Zechariah's prophecies are among the most exotic and esoteric in the entire Bible. The passages read in this *haftara* depict a collage of cryptic images, some of which Zechariah himself has difficulty comprehending. They focus on various aspects of God's redemption of the Jewish people, both in the Second Temple period and in the Messianic Era. One of these visions involves the candelabrum and its lamps, which is why this is a *haftara* for Hanukkah (Levush, *Oraḥ Ḥayyim*, 684). Furthermore, these visions focus on the national leadership, both political and priestly, which is another connection to the Maccabees and Hanukkah.

2 14 Sing and rejoice, daughter of Zion, for here I come and I will 15 dwell in your midst – the utterance of the Lord. Many nations will accompany the Lord on that day, and they will become My people, and I will dwell in your midst, and you will know that 16 the Lord of hosts sent me to you. The Lord will bequeath his portion to Judah on the sacred land, and He will again choose 17 Jerusalem. Hush, all flesh, before the Lord, for He is roused **3** 1 from His abode of sanctity. He showed me Yehoshua the High Priest, standing before the angel of the Lord and the accuser 2 standing on his right to accuse him. The Lord said to the accuser: May the Lord rebuke you, the accuser, and may the Lord who has chosen Jerusalem rebuke you. Is this not a firebrand 3 salvaged from the fire? Yehoshua was clothed in filthy garments 4 and standing before the angel. He responded and said to those standing before him, saying: Remove the filthy garments from upon him. He said to him: Behold, I have removed your iniq- 5 uity from upon you and have clothed you in clean garments. I said: Let them place a pure turban on his head. They placed the pure turban on his head and clothed him with garments and the 6 angel of the Lord was standing. The angel of the Lord warned 7 Yehoshua, saying: So said the Lord of hosts: If you follow My ways, and if you keep My commission and judge My house as well as guard My courtyards, I will set you walking among these

8 standing. Hear now, Yehoshua the High Priest, you and your colleagues who sit before you, as they are men of distinction, 9 for, behold, I bring My servant, Zemah. For behold, the stone that I placed before Yehoshua has seven hues on one stone; behold, I am engraving its etching – the utterance of the Lord of hosts – and I will remove the iniquity of that land in one day. 10 On that day – the utterance of the Lord of hosts – each of you will invite his neighbor beneath the vine and beneath the fig **4** 1 tree. The angel that spoke with me returned and woke me like 2 a man who is awakened from his sleep. He said to me: What do you see? I said: I saw, and behold, a candelabrum of gold in its entirety, with a bowl on its top and its seven lamps on it. There are seven pipes for each of the lamps that are on its top. 3 Two olive trees are over it, one on the right of the bowl, and 4 one on its left. I answered and said to the angel that spoke with 5 me, saying: What are these, my lord? The angel that spoke with me responded and said to me: Don't you know what these are? 6 And I said: No, my lord. He responded and said to me, saying: This is the word of the Lord to Zerubavel, saying: Not by might, 7 and not by power, but by My spirit, said the Lord of hosts. Who are you, great mountain? Before Zerubavel you will become a plain. He will take out the keystone, with shouts of: Grace, grace, to it.

הפטרת

שבת ראשונה של חנוכה

ב יד רָנִּי וְשִׂמְחִי בַּת־צִיּוֹן כִּי הִנְנִי־בָא וְשָׁכַנְתִּי בְתוֹכֵךְ נְאֻם־יהוה: וְנִלְווּ גוֹיִם רַבִּים אֶל־יהוה זכריה
טו בַּיּוֹם הַהוּא וְהָיוּ לִי לְעָם וְשָׁכַנְתִּי בְתוֹכֵךְ וְיָדַעַתְּ כִּי־יהוה צְבָאוֹת שְׁלָחַנִי אֵלָיִךְ: וְנָחַל יהוה
טז אֶת־יְהוּדָה חֶלְקוֹ עַל אַדְמַת הַקֹּדֶשׁ וּבָחַר עוֹד בִּירוּשָׁלָםִ: הַס כָּל־בָּשָׂר מִפְּנֵי יהוה כִּי נֵעוֹר
ג א מִמְּעוֹן קָדְשׁוֹ: וַיַּרְאֵנִי אֶת־יְהוֹשֻׁעַ הַכֹּהֵן הַגָּדוֹל עֹמֵד לִפְנֵי מַלְאַךְ יהוה וְהַשָּׂטָן
ב עֹמֵד עַל־יְמִינוֹ לְשִׂטְנוֹ: וַיֹּאמֶר יהוה אֶל־הַשָּׂטָן יִגְעַר יהוה בְּךָ הַשָּׂטָן וְיִגְעַר יהוה בְּךָ הַבֹּחֵר
ג בִּירוּשָׁלָםִ הֲלוֹא זֶה אוּד מֻצָּל מֵאֵשׁ: וִיהוֹשֻׁעַ הָיָה לָבֻשׁ בְּגָדִים צוֹאִים וְעֹמֵד לִפְנֵי הַמַּלְאָךְ:
ד וַיַּעַן וַיֹּאמֶר אֶל־הָעֹמְדִים לְפָנָיו לֵאמֹר הָסִירוּ הַבְּגָדִים הַצֹּאִים מֵעָלָיו וַיֹּאמֶר אֵלָיו רְאֵה
ה הֶעֱבַרְתִּי מֵעָלֶיךָ עֲוֺנֶךָ וְהַלְבֵּשׁ אֹתְךָ מַחֲלָצוֹת: וָאֹמַר יָשִׂימוּ צָנִיף טָהוֹר עַל־רֹאשׁוֹ וַיָּשִׂימוּ
ו הַצָּנִיף הַטָּהוֹר עַל־רֹאשׁוֹ וַיַּלְבִּשֻׁהוּ בְּגָדִים וּמַלְאַךְ יהוה עֹמֵד: וַיָּעַד מַלְאַךְ יהוה בִּיהוֹשֻׁעַ
ז לֵאמֹר: כֹּה־אָמַר יהוה צְבָאוֹת אִם־בִּדְרָכַי תֵּלֵךְ וְאִם אֶת־מִשְׁמַרְתִּי תִשְׁמֹר וְגַם־אַתָּה תָּדִין
ח אֶת־בֵּיתִי וְגַם תִּשְׁמֹר אֶת־חֲצֵרָי וְנָתַתִּי לְךָ מַהְלְכִים בֵּין הָעֹמְדִים הָאֵלֶּה: שְׁמַע־נָא יְהוֹשֻׁעַ
הַכֹּהֵן הַגָּדוֹל אַתָּה וְרֵעֶיךָ הַיֹּשְׁבִים לְפָנֶיךָ כִּי־אַנְשֵׁי מוֹפֵת הֵמָּה כִּי־הִנְנִי מֵבִיא אֶת־עַבְדִּי
ט צֶמַח: כִּי ׀ הִנֵּה הָאֶבֶן אֲשֶׁר נָתַתִּי לִפְנֵי יְהוֹשֻׁעַ עַל־אֶבֶן אַחַת שִׁבְעָה עֵינָיִם הִנְנִי מְפַתֵּחַ פִּתֻּחָהּ
י נְאֻם יהוה צְבָאוֹת וּמַשְׁתִּי אֶת־עֲוֺן הָאָרֶץ־הַהִיא בְּיוֹם אֶחָד: בַּיּוֹם הַהוּא נְאֻם יהוה צְבָאוֹת
ד א תִּקְרְאוּ אִישׁ לְרֵעֵהוּ אֶל־תַּחַת גֶּפֶן וְאֶל־תַּחַת תְּאֵנָה: וַיָּשָׁב הַמַּלְאָךְ הַדֹּבֵר בִּי
ב וַיְעִירֵנִי כְּאִישׁ אֲשֶׁר־יֵעוֹר מִשְּׁנָתוֹ: וַיֹּאמֶר אֵלַי מָה אַתָּה רֹאֶה ויאמר רָאִיתִי וְהִנֵּה מְנוֹרַת וָאֹמַר
זָהָב כֻּלָּהּ וְגֻלָּהּ עַל־רֹאשָׁהּ וְשִׁבְעָה נֵרֹתֶיהָ עָלֶיהָ שִׁבְעָה וְשִׁבְעָה מוּצָקוֹת לַנֵּרוֹת אֲשֶׁר עַל־
ג ד רֹאשָׁהּ: וּשְׁנַיִם זֵיתִים עָלֶיהָ אֶחָד מִימִין הַגֻּלָּה וְאֶחָד עַל־שְׂמֹאלָהּ: וָאַעַן וָאֹמַר אֶל־הַמַּלְאָךְ
ה הַדֹּבֵר בִּי לֵאמֹר מָה־אֵלֶּה אֲדֹנִי: וַיַּעַן הַמַּלְאָךְ הַדֹּבֵר בִּי וַיֹּאמֶר אֵלַי הֲלוֹא יָדַעְתָּ מָה־הֵמָּה
ו אֵלֶּה וָאֹמַר לֹא אֲדֹנִי: וַיַּעַן וַיֹּאמֶר אֵלַי לֵאמֹר זֶה דְּבַר־יהוה אֶל־זְרֻבָּבֶל לֵאמֹר לֹא בְחַיִל וְלֹא
ז בְכֹחַ כִּי אִם־בְּרוּחִי אָמַר יהוה צְבָאוֹת: מִי־אַתָּה הַר־הַגָּדוֹל לִפְנֵי זְרֻבָּבֶל לְמִישֹׁר וְהוֹצִיא
אֶת־הָאֶבֶן הָרֹאשָׁה תְּשֻׁאוֹת חֵן ׀ חֵן לָהּ:

Haftara for the
Second Shabbat of Hanukkah

The Vessels of the Temple
I KINGS 7:40–50

King Solomon prepares the vessels for his Temple, with assistance from his ally, King Hiram of Tyre, who supplies both craftsmen and material. Like the *haftara* of the first Shabbat of Hanukkah, this one also deals with the candelabra and lamps, together with other sacred vessels, and therefore it is read on Hanukkah (Levush, *Oraḥ Ḥayyim*, 684).

7 40 Hiram made the basins, the shovels, and the bowls, and Hiram
completed all the labor that he performed for King Solomon in
41 the House of the Lord: Two pillars; the two orbs of the capitals
that were atop the pillars; the two screens to cover the two orbs
42 of the capitals that were atop the pillars; the pomegranates, four
hundred for the two screens, two rows of pomegranates for
each screen, to cover the two orbs of the capitals that were atop
43 44 the pillars; the ten bases and the ten lavers on the bases; the
45 one sea and the twelve oxen beneath the sea; the pots, the shovels, the bowls, and all these vessels that Hiram crafted for King
Solomon in the House of the Lord were of burnished bronze.
46 The king cast them on the Jordan plain, in an excavation in the
47 ground between Sukot and Tzaretan. Solomon refrained with
regard to all the vessels, due to the exceedingly great quantity;
48 the weight of the bronze was not quantified. Solomon crafted
all the vessels that were in the House of the Lord: The golden
49 altar; the gold table upon which is the showbread; the candelabra, five on the right and five on the left before the inner sanctum, of pure gold; the flowers, the lamps, and the tongs of gold;
50 the jugs, the musical instruments, the bowls, the ladles, and the
pans of pure gold; the hinge sockets for the doors of the inner
house, the Holy of Holies, and for the doors of the House, the
Sanctuary, of gold.

Haftara for
Parashat Shekalim

King Yeho'ash and the Temple Treasury
II KINGS 11:17–12:17

King Yeho'ash, who had been hidden throughout his childhood in the Temple, commits himself to its repair and maintenance as an adult. He instructs the priests that the half-shekels each adult male was obligated to give to the Temple for the purchase of public offerings, as well as personal donations to the Temple, should be allocated to the repair of the neglected Temple structure.

11 17 Yehoyada made a covenant between the Lord, the king, and the
Seph. begin people, to be the people of the Lord, and between the king and
18 the people. All the people of the land went to the house of the
Baal and smashed it; they thoroughly shattered its altars and its
images and killed Matan, priest of the Baal, before the altars.
19 The priest installed appointees over the House of the Lord. He
took the leaders of hundreds, the Karites, the infantry, and all
the people of the land, and they brought the king down from
the House of the Lord and came via the gate of the infantry to
20 the king's palace, and he sat on the royal throne. All the people
of the land rejoiced, and the city was quiet; they put Atalyahu
12 1 to death by the sword in the king's palace. Yeho'ash was seven
Ashk. begin 2 years old when he became king. In the seventh year of Yehu,
Yeho'ash became king. He reigned forty years in Jerusalem, and
3 his mother's name was Tzivya of Beersheba. Yeho'ash did that
which was right in the eyes of the Lord all his days, as Yehoyada
4 the priest instructed him. However, the high places were not
discontinued; the people continued sacrificing and burning

שבת שנייה של חנוכה

| מלכים א' | ז | מז וַיַּעַשׂ חִירוֹם אֶת־הַכִּירוֹת וְאֶת־הַיָּעִים וְאֶת־הַמִּזְרָקוֹת וַיְכַל חִירָם לַעֲשׂוֹת אֶת־כָּל־הַמְּלָאכָה |

אֲשֶׁר עָשָׂה לַמֶּלֶךְ שְׁלֹמֹה בֵּית יְהוָה: עַמֻּדִים שְׁנַיִם וְגֻלֹּת הַכֹּתֶרֶת אֲשֶׁר־עַל־רֹאשׁ הָעַמּוּדִים

מא שְׁתָּיִם וְהַשְּׂבָכוֹת שְׁתַּיִם לְכַסּוֹת אֶת־שְׁתֵּי גֻּלֹּת הַכֹּתָרֹת אֲשֶׁר עַל־רֹאשׁ הָעַמּוּדִים: וְאֶת־

מב הָרִמֹּנִים אַרְבַּע מֵאוֹת לִשְׁתֵּי הַשְּׂבָכוֹת שְׁנֵי־טוּרִים רִמֹּנִים לַשְּׂבָכָה הָאֶחָת לְכַסּוֹת אֶת־שְׁתֵּי

גֻּלֹּת הַכֹּתָרֹת אֲשֶׁר עַל־פְּנֵי הָעַמּוּדִים: וְאֶת־הַמְּכֹנוֹת עָשֶׂר וְאֶת־הַכִּיֹּרֹת עֲשָׂרָה עַל־

מד הַמְּכֹנוֹת: וְאֶת־הַיָּם הָאֶחָד וְאֶת־הַבָּקָר שְׁנֵים־עָשָׂר תַּחַת הַיָּם: וְאֶת־הַסִּירוֹת וְאֶת־הַיָּעִים

מה וְאֶת־הַמִּזְרָקוֹת וְאֵת כָּל־הַכֵּלִים הָאֹהֶל אֲשֶׁר עָשָׂה חִירָם לַמֶּלֶךְ שְׁלֹמֹה בֵּית יְהוָה נְחֹשֶׁת | הָאֵלֶּה |

מו מְמֹרָט: בְּכִכַּר הַיַּרְדֵּן יְצָקָם הַמֶּלֶךְ בְּמַעֲבֵה הָאֲדָמָה בֵּין סֻכּוֹת וּבֵין צָרְתָן: וַיַּנַּח שְׁלֹמֹה אֶת־

מז כָּל־הַכֵּלִים מֵרֹב מְאֹד מְאֹד לֹא נֶחְקַר מִשְׁקַל הַנְּחֹשֶׁת: וַיַּעַשׂ שְׁלֹמֹה אֵת כָּל־הַכֵּלִים אֲשֶׁר

מח בֵּית יְהוָה אֵת מִזְבַּח הַזָּהָב וְאֶת־הַשֻּׁלְחָן אֲשֶׁר עָלָיו לֶחֶם הַפָּנִים זָהָב: וְאֶת־הַמְּנֹרוֹת חָמֵשׁ

מט מִיָּמִין וְחָמֵשׁ מִשְּׂמֹאל לִפְנֵי הַדְּבִיר זָהָב סָגוּר וְהַפֶּרַח וְהַנֵּרֹת וְהַמֶּלְקַחַיִם זָהָב: וְהַסִּפּוֹת

נ וְהַמְזַמְּרוֹת וְהַמִּזְרָקוֹת וְהַכַּפּוֹת וְהַמַּחְתּוֹת זָהָב סָגוּר וְהַפֹּתוֹת לְדַלְתוֹת הַבַּיִת הַפְּנִימִי לְקֹדֶשׁ הַקֳּדָשִׁים לְדַלְתֵי הַבַּיִת לַהֵיכָל זָהָב:

פרשת שקלים

| מלכים ב' | יא | יא וַיִּכְרֹת יְהוֹיָדָע אֶת־הַבְּרִית בֵּין יְהוָה וּבֵין הַמֶּלֶךְ וּבֵין הָעָם לִהְיוֹת לְעָם לַיהוָה וּבֵין הַמֶּלֶךְ |
| הספרדים מתחילים כאן | | |

וּבֵין הָעָם: וַיָּבֹאוּ כָל־עַם הָאָרֶץ בֵּית־הַבַּעַל וַיִּתְּצֻהוּ אֶת־מִזְבְּחֹתוֹ וְאֶת־צְלָמָיו שִׁבְּרוּ הֵיטֵב

יט וְאֵת מַתָּן כֹּהֵן הַבַּעַל הָרְגוּ לִפְנֵי הַמִּזְבְּחוֹת וַיָּשֶׂם הַכֹּהֵן פְּקֻדֹּת עַל־בֵּית יְהוָה: וַיִּקַּח אֶת־שָׂרֵי

הַמֵּאוֹת וְאֶת־הַכָּרִי וְאֶת־הָרָצִים וְאֵת | כָּל־עַם הָאָרֶץ וַיֹּרִידוּ אֶת־הַמֶּלֶךְ מִבֵּית יְהוָה וַיָּבוֹאוּ

כ דֶּרֶךְ־שַׁעַר הָרָצִים בֵּית הַמֶּלֶךְ וַיֵּשֶׁב עַל־כִּסֵּא הַמְּלָכִים: וַיִּשְׂמַח כָּל־עַם־הָאָרֶץ וְהָעִיר שָׁקָטָה

וְאֶת־עֲתַלְיָהוּ הֵמִיתוּ בַחֶרֶב בֵּית מֶלֶךְ: | בֶּן־שֶׁבַע שָׁנִים יְהוֹאָשׁ בְּמָלְכוֹ: בִּשְׁנַת־ | הָאשכנזים האשכנזים מתחילים כאן הַמֶּלֶךְ |

יב [יב] שֶׁבַע לְיֵהוּא מָלַךְ יְהוֹאָשׁ וְאַרְבָּעִים שָׁנָה מָלַךְ בִּירוּשָׁלִָם וְשֵׁם אִמּוֹ צִבְיָה מִבְּאֵר שָׁבַע: וַיַּעַשׂ

ד יְהוֹאָשׁ הַיָּשָׁר בְּעֵינֵי יְהוָה כָּל־יָמָיו אֲשֶׁר הוֹרָהוּ יְהוֹיָדָע הַכֹּהֵן: רַק הַבָּמוֹת לֹא־סָרוּ עוֹד

5 incense at the high places. Yeho'ash said to the priests: All the consecrated money that is brought to the House of the Lord, the silver passed from each man, the silver of the valuation of persons, all silver that it would enter the heart of any man to

6 bring to the House of the Lord shall be taken from them by the priests, each from his acquaintance, and they maintain the repair of the House, wherever any need for repair will be found.

7 It was in the twenty-third year of King Yeho'ash, the priests did

8 not maintain the repair of the House. King Yeho'ash summoned Yehoyada the priest and the priests, and said to them: Why are you not maintaining the repair of the House? Now, do not take silver from your acquaintances; rather, you shall give it to the

9 repair of the House. The priests acceded not to take money from the people and not to maintain the repair of the House.

10 Yehoyada the priest took a chest, bored a hole in its lid, and placed it near the altar on the right as one comes into the House of the Lord; the priests who were the doorkeepers put there all

11 the money that was brought to the House of the Lord. It was, upon their seeing that the money in the chest was abundant,

that the king's scribe and the High Priest came up and collected and counted the silver that was found in the House of the Lord.

12 They gave the silver that was tallied into the hands of the workmen who were appointed in the House of the Lord, and they disbursed it to the carpenters and the builders who were work-

13 ing in the House of the Lord and to the masons and the hewers of stone, and to purchase timber and quarried stone to maintain the repair of the House of the Lord, and for any outlay for the

14 House to maintain it. But cups of silver, musical instruments, bowls, trumpets, all vessels of gold, or vessels of silver would not be crafted for the House of the Lord from the silver that was

15 brought to the House of the Lord, as they would give it to the workmen, and they maintained with it the House of the Lord.

16 They did not require an accounting from the men by whose hand they gave the silver to give to the workmen, as they acted

17 with trustworthiness. The silver of guilt offerings and the silver of sin offerings would not be brought to the House of the Lord; it was for the priests.

Haftara for
Parashat Zakhor

Saul's War against Amalek
I SAMUEL 15:1–34

The additional Torah reading for Parashat Zakhor is the passage in which Israel is commanded to expunge the memory of Amalek from under the heavens. In this *haftara* we read about how Saul, Israel's first king, is instructed by the prophet Samuel to make war on Amalek and utterly destroy them. Though Saul triumphs in the war, he fails to fully carry out his mission.

15
Seph. begin
Ashk. begin

1 Samuel said to Saul: The Lord sent me to anoint you as king over His people, over Israel; now, heed the sound of the words

2 of the Lord. So said the Lord of hosts: I have remembered that which Amalek did to Israel, that it situated itself on the

3 way when it came up from Egypt. Now, go and smite Amalek and utterly destroy everything that it has and do not spare it; you shall put to death from man to woman, from infant to

4 suckling, from ox to sheep, from camel to donkey. Saul summoned the people, and he counted them in Tela'im, two hundred thousand infantrymen, and ten thousand men of Judah.

5 Saul came to the city of Amalek, and he raided in the ravine.

6 Saul said to the Kenite: Go, withdraw, and go down from the midst of the Amalekites, lest I destroy you with them, as you performed kindness for all the children of Israel when they

ה הָעָם מְזַבְּחִים וּמְקַטְּרִים בַּבָּמוֹת: וַיֹּאמֶר יְהוֹאָשׁ אֶל־הַכֹּהֲנִים כֹּל כֶּסֶף הַקֳּדָשִׁים אֲשֶׁר יוּבָא
בֵית־יְהוָה כֶּסֶף עוֹבֵר אִישׁ כֶּסֶף נַפְשׁוֹת עֶרְכּוֹ כָּל־כֶּסֶף אֲשֶׁר יַעֲלֶה עַל לֶב־אִישׁ לְהָבִיא בֵּית
ו יְהוָה: יִקְחוּ לָהֶם הַכֹּהֲנִים אִישׁ מֵאֵת מַכָּרוֹ וְהֵם יְחַזְּקוּ אֶת־בֶּדֶק הַבַּיִת לְכֹל אֲשֶׁר־יִמָּצֵא שָׁם
ז בָּדֶק: וַיְהִי בִּשְׁנַת עֶשְׂרִים וְשָׁלֹשׁ שָׁנָה לַמֶּלֶךְ יְהוֹאָשׁ לֹא־חִזְּקוּ הַכֹּהֲנִים אֶת־בֶּדֶק
ח הַבָּיִת: וַיִּקְרָא הַמֶּלֶךְ יְהוֹאָשׁ לִיהוֹיָדָע הַכֹּהֵן וְלַכֹּהֲנִים וַיֹּאמֶר אֲלֵהֶם מַדּוּעַ אֵינְכֶם מְחַזְּקִים
ט אֶת־בֶּדֶק הַבָּיִת וְעַתָּה אַל־תִּקְחוּ־כֶסֶף מֵאֵת מַכָּרֵיכֶם כִּי־לְבֶדֶק הַבַּיִת תִּתְּנֻהוּ: וַיֵּאֹתוּ הַכֹּהֲנִים
י לְבִלְתִּי קְחַת־כֶּסֶף מֵאֵת הָעָם וּלְבִלְתִּי חַזֵּק אֶת־בֶּדֶק הַבָּיִת: וַיִּקַּח יְהוֹיָדָע הַכֹּהֵן אֲרוֹן אֶחָד
וַיִּקֹּב חֹר בְּדַלְתּוֹ וַיִּתֵּן אֹתוֹ אֵצֶל הַמִּזְבֵּחַ בימין בְּבוֹא־אִישׁ בֵּית יְהוָה וְנָתְנוּ־שָׁמָּה הַכֹּהֲנִים מִיָּמִין
יא שֹׁמְרֵי הַסַּף אֶת־כָּל־הַכֶּסֶף הַמּוּבָא בֵית־יְהוָה: וַיְהִי כִּרְאוֹתָם כִּי־רַב הַכֶּסֶף בָּאָרוֹן וַיַּעַל סֹפֵר
יב הַמֶּלֶךְ וְהַכֹּהֵן הַגָּדוֹל וַיָּצֻרוּ וַיִּמְנוּ אֶת־הַכֶּסֶף הַנִּמְצָא בֵית־יְהוָה: וְנָתְנוּ אֶת־הַכֶּסֶף הַמְתֻכָּן
עַל־יַד עֹשֵׂי הַמְּלָאכָה הפקדים בֵּית יְהוָה וַיּוֹצִיאֻהוּ לְחָרָשֵׁי הָעֵץ וְלַבֹּנִים הָעֹשִׂים בֵּית יְהוָה: הַמֻּפְקָדִים
יג וְלַגֹּדְרִים וּלְחֹצְבֵי הָאֶבֶן וְלִקְנוֹת עֵצִים וְאַבְנֵי מַחְצֵב לְחַזֵּק אֶת־בֶּדֶק בֵּית־יְהוָה וּלְכֹל אֲשֶׁר־יֵצֵא
יד עַל־הַבַּיִת לְחָזְקָה: אַךְ לֹא יֵעָשֶׂה בֵּית יְהוָה סִפּוֹת כֶּסֶף מְזַמְּרוֹת מִזְרָקוֹת חֲצֹצְרוֹת כָּל־כְּלִי
טו זָהָב וּכְלִי־כָסֶף מִן־הַכֶּסֶף הַמּוּבָא בֵית־יְהוָה: כִּי־לְעֹשֵׂי הַמְּלָאכָה יִתְּנֻהוּ וְחִזְּקוּ־בוֹ אֶת־בֵּית
טז יְהוָה: וְלֹא יְחַשְּׁבוּ אֶת־הָאֲנָשִׁים אֲשֶׁר יִתְּנוּ אֶת־הַכֶּסֶף עַל־יָדָם לָתֵת לְעֹשֵׂי הַמְּלָאכָה כִּי
יז בֶאֱמֻנָה הֵם עֹשִׂים: כֶּסֶף אָשָׁם וְכֶסֶף חַטָּאוֹת לֹא יוּבָא בֵּית יְהוָה לַכֹּהֲנִים יִהְיוּ:

הפטרת

פרשת זכור

שמואל א׳

האשכנזים
מתחילים כאן

טו א וַיֹּאמֶר שְׁמוּאֵל אֶל־שָׁאוּל אֹתִי שָׁלַח יְהוָה לִמְשָׁחֳךָ לְמֶלֶךְ עַל־עַמּוֹ עַל־יִשְׂרָאֵל וְעַתָּה
ב שְׁמַע לְקוֹל דִּבְרֵי יְהוָה: כֹּה אָמַר יְהוָה צְבָאוֹת פָּקַדְתִּי אֵת אֲשֶׁר־עָשָׂה עֲמָלֵק
ג לְיִשְׂרָאֵל אֲשֶׁר־שָׂם לוֹ בַּדֶּרֶךְ בַּעֲלֹתוֹ מִמִּצְרָיִם: עַתָּה לֵךְ וְהִכִּיתָה אֶת־עֲמָלֵק וְהַחֲרַמְתֶּם
אֶת־כָּל־אֲשֶׁר־לוֹ וְלֹא תַחְמֹל עָלָיו וְהֵמַתָּה מֵאִישׁ עַד־אִשָּׁה מֵעֹלֵל וְעַד־יוֹנֵק מִשּׁוֹר וְעַד־שֶׂה
ד מִגָּמָל וְעַד־חֲמוֹר: וַיְשַׁמַּע שָׁאוּל אֶת־הָעָם וַיִּפְקְדֵם בַּטְּלָאִים מָאתַיִם אֶלֶף רַגְלִי
ה ו וַעֲשֶׂרֶת אֲלָפִים אֶת־אִישׁ יְהוּדָה: וַיָּבֹא שָׁאוּל עַד־עִיר עֲמָלֵק וַיָּרֶב בַּנָּחַל: וַיֹּאמֶר שָׁאוּל אֶל־
הַקֵּינִי לְכוּ סֻּרוּ רְדוּ מִתּוֹךְ עֲמָלֵקִי פֶּן־אֹסִפְךָ עִמּוֹ וְאַתָּה עָשִׂיתָה חֶסֶד עִם־כָּל־בְּנֵי יִשְׂרָאֵל

came up from Egypt. The Kenites withdrew from the midst of

7 the Amalekites. Saul smote the Amalekites from Havila as you

8 come to Shur, which is before Egypt. He apprehended Agag, king of the Amalekites, alive, and he utterly destroyed the en-

9 tire people by sword. Saul and the people spared Agag, the best of the flocks and the cattle, the second best, the fatted sheep, and all that was good, and they did not wish to destroy them; but all property that was wretched and contemptible; that they

10 utterly destroyed. The word of the Lord was with Samuel, say-

11 ing: I regret that I crowned Saul as king, because he turned from following Me and did not fulfill My words. Samuel was

12 distressed and he cried out to the Lord all night. Samuel arose early to meet Saul in the morning; it was told to Samuel, saying: Saul came to Carmel, and behold, he is establishing for himself a monument, and he turned and passed, and descended to

13 Gilgal. Samuel came to Saul, and Saul said to him: Blessed are

14 you to the Lord; I have fulfilled the word of the Lord. Samuel said: What is this sound of the flocks in my ears, and the sound

15 of the cattle that I hear? Saul said: They brought them from the Amalekites; for the people spared the best of the flocks and the cattle in order to slaughter them for the Lord your God, and the

16 rest we utterly destroyed. Samuel said to Saul: Stop, and I will tell you that which the Lord said to me this night. He said to

17 him: Speak. Samuel said: Although you are small in your eyes, you are the head of the tribes of Israel, and the Lord anointed

18 you as king over Israel. The Lord sent you on the way, and He said: Go and utterly destroy the sinners, Amalek, and make war

19 against them until you annihilate them. Why did you not heed the voice of the Lord, and you fell upon the spoils, and did that

20 which is evil in the eyes of the Lord? Saul said to Samuel: So I heeded the voice of the Lord, and I went on the way that the

Lord sent me, and I brought Agag, king of Amalek, and I utterly

21 destroyed Amalek. The people took from the spoils, flocks, and cattle, the best of the proscribed, to slaughter to the Lord your

22 God in Gilgal. Samuel said: Does the Lord desire burnt offerings and sacrifices, like heeding the voice of the Lord? Behold, to obey is better than a good sacrifice, and to heed than the fat

23 of rams. For the sin of sorcery is defiance and sin and house idols are stubbornness. Because you despised the word of the

24 Lord, He has despised you as king. Saul said to Samuel: I have sinned, for I violated the directive of the Lord and your words,

25 because I feared the people, and I heeded their voice. Now please, forgive my sin, and return with me, and I will prostrate

26 myself before the Lord. Samuel said to Saul: I will not return with you, as you despised the word of the Lord, and the Lord

27 has despised you from being king over Israel. Samuel turned

28 to go, but he seized the edge of his tunic, and it tore. Samuel said to him: The Lord has torn the kingdom of Israel from you today, and has given it to your counterpart, who is better than

29 you. Indeed, the Eternity of Israel will not lie and will not re-

30 gret, as He is not a man to regret. He said: I have sinned; now, please, honor me before the elders of my people and before Israel, and return with me, and I will prostrate myself before

31 the Lord your God. Samuel returned following Saul, and Saul

32 prostrated himself before the Lord. Samuel said: Bring to me Agag king of Amalek. Agag went to him falteringly. Agag said:

33 Indeed, the bitterness of death is at hand. Samuel said: Just as your sword rendered women childless, so shall your mother be childless among women. Samuel slashed Agag before the Lord

34 in Gilgal. Samuel went to Rama, and Saul went up to his house in Givat Shaul.

ז בַּעֲלוֹתָם מִמִּצְרָיִם: וַיָּסַר קֵינִי מִתּוֹךְ עֲמָלֵק: וַיַּךְ שָׁאוּל אֶת־עֲמָלֵק מֵחֲוִילָה בּוֹאֲךָ שׁוּר אֲשֶׁר

ח עַל־פְּנֵי מִצְרָיִם: וַיִּתְפֹּשׂ אֶת־אֲגַג מֶלֶךְ־עֲמָלֵק חָי וְאֶת־כָּל־הָעָם הֶחֱרִים לְפִי־חָרֶב: וַיַּחְמֹל

ט שָׁאוּל וְהָעָם עַל־אֲגָג וְעַל־מֵיטַב הַצֹּאן וְהַבָּקָר וְהַמִּשְׁנִים וְעַל־הַכָּרִים וְעַל־כָּל־הַטּוֹב

י וְלֹא אָבוּ הַחֲרִימָם וְכָל־הַמְּלָאכָה נְמִבְזָה וְנָמֵס אֹתָהּ הֶחֱרִימוּ: וַיְהִי דְּבַר־יהוה

יא אֶל־שְׁמוּאֵל לֵאמֹר: נִחַמְתִּי כִּי־הִמְלַכְתִּי אֶת־שָׁאוּל לְמֶלֶךְ כִּי־שָׁב מֵאַחֲרַי וְאֶת־דְּבָרַי לֹא

יב הֵקִים וַיִּחַר לִשְׁמוּאֵל וַיִּזְעַק אֶל־יהוה כָּל־הַלָּיְלָה: וַיַּשְׁכֵּם שְׁמוּאֵל לִקְרַאת שָׁאוּל בַּבֹּקֶר

יג וַיֻּגַּד לִשְׁמוּאֵל לֵאמֹר בָּא־שָׁאוּל הַכַּרְמֶלָה וְהִנֵּה מַצִּיב לוֹ יָד וַיִּסֹּב וַיַּעֲבֹר וַיֵּרֶד הַגִּלְגָּל: וַיָּבֹא

יד שְׁמוּאֵל אֶל־שָׁאוּל וַיֹּאמֶר לוֹ שָׁאוּל בָּרוּךְ אַתָּה לַיהוה הֲקִימֹתִי אֶת־דְּבַר יהוה: וַיֹּאמֶר

טו שְׁמוּאֵל וּמֶה קוֹל־הַצֹּאן הַזֶּה בְּאָזְנָי וְקוֹל הַבָּקָר אֲשֶׁר אָנֹכִי שֹׁמֵעַ: וַיֹּאמֶר שָׁאוּל מֵעֲמָלֵקִי הֱבִיאוּם אֲשֶׁר חָמַל הָעָם עַל־מֵיטַב הַצֹּאן וְהַבָּקָר לְמַעַן זְבֹחַ לַיהוה אֱלֹהֶיךָ וְאֶת־הַיּוֹתֵר הֶחֱרַמְנוּ:

טז וַיֹּאמֶר שְׁמוּאֵל אֶל־שָׁאוּל הֶרֶף וְאַגִּידָה לְּךָ אֵת אֲשֶׁר דִּבֶּר יהוה אֵלַי הַלָּיְלָה וַיֹּאמְרוּ לוֹ דַּבֵּר: וַיֹּאמֶר שְׁמוּאֵל הֲלוֹא אִם־קָטֹן אַתָּה בְּעֵינֶיךָ רֹאשׁ שִׁבְטֵי

יז וַיֹּאמֶר

יח יִשְׂרָאֵל אָתָּה וַיִּמְשָׁחֲךָ יהוה לְמֶלֶךְ עַל־יִשְׂרָאֵל: וַיִּשְׁלָחֲךָ יהוה בְּדָרֶךְ וַיֹּאמֶר לֵךְ וְהַחֲרַמְתָּה

יט אֶת־הַחַטָּאִים אֶת־עֲמָלֵק וְנִלְחַמְתָּ בוֹ עַד־כַּלּוֹתָם אֹתָם: וְלָמָּה לֹא־שָׁמַעְתָּ בְּקוֹל יהוה וַתַּעַט

כ אֶל־הַשָּׁלָל וַתַּעַשׂ הָרַע בְּעֵינֵי יהוה: וַיֹּאמֶר שָׁאוּל אֶל־שְׁמוּאֵל אֲשֶׁר שָׁמַעְתִּי בְּקוֹל יהוה וָאֵלֵךְ בַּדֶּרֶךְ אֲשֶׁר־שְׁלָחַנִי יהוה וָאָבִיא אֶת־אֲגַג מֶלֶךְ עֲמָלֵק וְאֶת־עֲמָלֵק הֶחֱרַמְתִּי:

כא וַיִּקַּח הָעָם מֵהַשָּׁלָל צֹאן וּבָקָר רֵאשִׁית הַחֵרֶם לִזְבֹּחַ לַיהוה אֱלֹהֶיךָ בַּגִּלְגָּל: וַיֹּאמֶר

כב שְׁמוּאֵל הַחֵפֶץ לַיהוה בְּעֹלוֹת וּזְבָחִים כִּשְׁמֹעַ בְּקוֹל יהוה הִנֵּה שְׁמֹעַ מִזֶּבַח טוֹב לְהַקְשִׁיב

כג מֵחֵלֶב אֵילִים: כִּי חַטַּאת־קֶסֶם מֶרִי וְאָוֶן וּתְרָפִים הַפְצַר יַעַן מָאַסְתָּ אֶת־דְּבַר יהוה וַיִּמְאָסְךָ

כד מִמֶּלֶךְ: וַיֹּאמֶר שָׁאוּל אֶל־שְׁמוּאֵל חָטָאתִי כִּי־עָבַרְתִּי אֶת־פִּי־יהוה וְאֶת־דְּבָרֶיךָ

כה כִּי יָרֵאתִי אֶת־הָעָם וָאֶשְׁמַע בְּקוֹלָם: וְעַתָּה שָׂא נָא אֶת־חַטָּאתִי וְשׁוּב עִמִּי וְאֶשְׁתַּחֲוֶה לַיהוה:

כו וַיֹּאמֶר שְׁמוּאֵל אֶל־שָׁאוּל לֹא אָשׁוּב עִמָּךְ כִּי מָאַסְתָּה אֶת־דְּבַר יהוה וַיִּמְאָסְךָ יהוה מִהְיוֹת

כז מֶלֶךְ עַל־יִשְׂרָאֵל: וַיִּסֹּב שְׁמוּאֵל לָלֶכֶת וַיַּחֲזֵק בִּכְנַף־מְעִילוֹ וַיִּקָּרַע: וַיֹּאמֶר אֵלָיו שְׁמוּאֵל קָרַע

כח יהוה אֶת־מַמְלְכוּת יִשְׂרָאֵל מֵעָלֶיךָ הַיּוֹם וּנְתָנָהּ לְרֵעֲךָ הַטּוֹב מִמֶּךָּ: וְגַם נֵצַח יִשְׂרָאֵל לֹא

כט יְשַׁקֵּר וְלֹא יִנָּחֵם כִּי לֹא אָדָם הוּא לְהִנָּחֵם: וַיֹּאמֶר חָטָאתִי עַתָּה כַּבְּדֵנִי נָא נֶגֶד זִקְנֵי־עַמִּי

ל וְנֶגֶד יִשְׂרָאֵל וְשׁוּב עִמִּי וְהִשְׁתַּחֲוֵיתִי לַיהוה אֱלֹהֶיךָ: וַיָּשָׁב שְׁמוּאֵל אַחֲרֵי שָׁאוּל וַיִּשְׁתַּחוּ

לא שָׁאוּל לַיהוה: וַיֹּאמֶר שְׁמוּאֵל הַגִּישׁוּ אֵלַי אֶת־אֲגַג מֶלֶךְ עֲמָלֵק וַיֵּלֶךְ אֵלָיו אֲגַג

לב מַעֲדַנֹּת וַיֹּאמֶר אֲגָג אָכֵן סָר מַר־הַמָּוֶת: וַיֹּאמֶר שְׁמוּאֵל כַּאֲשֶׁר שִׁכְּלָה נָשִׁים חַרְבֶּךָ כֵּן־תִּשְׁכַּל

לג מִנָּשִׁים אִמֶּךָ וַיְשַׁסֵּף שְׁמוּאֵל אֶת־אֲגָג לִפְנֵי יהוה בַּגִּלְגָּל: וַיֵּלֶךְ שְׁמוּאֵל הָרָמָתָה

לד וְשָׁאוּל עָלָה אֶל־בֵּיתוֹ גִּבְעַת שָׁאוּל:

Haftara for
Parashat Para

A Prophecy of Purity and Rejuvenation of Israel
EZEKIEL 36:16–38

The ritual purification from the impurity imparted by a corpse by means of spring water is the topic of the section read from the Torah in preparation for Passover, the Festival of Freedom. The prophet Ezekiel uses this theme as a metaphor for the purification of the people's transgressions and the spiritual renewal of the nation returning to its land. The *haftara* stresses that the revival of the people and their land is performed by God, who acts for the sake of His name, not due to the righteousness of Israel. The feelings of shame and regret, which the children of Israel experience when they are made aware of this fact, are important factors for the rejuvenation process itself.

36 **16 17** The word of the Lord was with me, saying: Son of man, the house of Israel dwelled in its land, and they defiled it with their way and with their exploits; their way was like the impurity of a 18 menstruating woman before Me. I poured My fury upon them for the blood that they had shed upon the land, and with their 19 idols they had defiled it. I dispersed them among the nations, and they were scattered through the lands; in accordance with their way and in accordance with their exploits I judged them. 20 They came to the nations to which they came, and they profaned My holy name when it was said of them: These are the 21 people of the Lord, and they went out from His land. I pitied My holy name, which the house of Israel had profaned among 22 the nations to which they came. Therefore, say to the house of Israel: So said the Lord God: Not for your sake am I acting, house of Israel; rather, for My holy name, which you have pro- 23 faned among the nations to which you came. I will sanctify My great name that was profaned among the nations, which you profaned among them, and the nations will know that I am the Lord – the utterance of the Lord God – when I am sanctified 24 through you before their eyes. I will take you from the nations and gather you from all the lands, and I will bring you to your 25 land. I will sprinkle pure water upon you, and you will be purified; from all your impurities and from all your idols I will pu- 26 rify you. I will give you a new heart, and a new spirit I will place within you; I will remove the heart of stone from your flesh, 27 and I will give you a heart of flesh. And I will place My spirit within you, and I will act so that you will follow My statutes,

28 and My ordinances you will observe and perform. You will dwell in the land that I gave to your fathers, and you will be My 29 people, and I will be your God. I will save you from all your impurities. I will call for the grain, and I will increase it. I will not 30 bring famine upon you. I will increase the fruit of the tree and the produce of the field so that you will no longer be subject to 31 the disgrace of famine among the nations. You will remember your evil ways and your exploits that were not good, and you will loathe yourselves for your iniquities and for your abomi- 32 nations. Not for your sake am I acting – the utterance of the Lord God – let it be known to you; be ashamed and humiliated 33 because of your ways, house of Israel. So said the Lord God: On the day that I purify you from all your iniquities, I will cause 34 the cities to be inhabited, and the ruins will be rebuilt. And the land that had been made desolate will be tilled, instead of hav- 35 ing been desolation before the eyes of every passerby. They will say: This land that had been made desolate has become like the Garden of Eden, and the ruined, desolate, and destroyed cities 36 have been inhabited and fortified. The nations that will remain all around you will know that I, the Lord, rebuilt the destroyed,

Seph. end

37 planted the desolate; I, the Lord, have spoken and acted. So said the Lord God: Concerning this too, I will acquiesce to the house of Israel, to perform for them; I will multiply them, like 38 the flock, with men. Like the consecrated flock, like the flock of Jerusalem on its festivals, so will the ruined cities be filled with the flocks of men, and they will know that I am the Lord.

פרשת פרה

יחזקאל

לו
יז וַיְהִי דְבַר־יְהֹוָה אֵלַי לֵאמֹר: בֶּן־אָדָם בֵּית יִשְׂרָאֵל יֹשְׁבִים עַל־אַדְמָתָם וַיְטַמְּאוּ אוֹתָהּ בְּדַרְכָּם וּבַעֲלִילוֹתָם כְּטֻמְאַת הַנִּדָּה הָיְתָה דַרְכָּם לְפָנָי: וָאֶשְׁפֹּךְ חֲמָתִי עֲלֵיהֶם עַל־הַדָּם אֲשֶׁר־שָׁפְכוּ

יח עַל־הָאָרֶץ וּבְגִלּוּלֵיהֶם טִמְּאוּהָ: וָאָפִיץ אֹתָם בַּגּוֹיִם וַיִּזָּרוּ בָּאֲרָצוֹת כְּדַרְכָּם וְכַעֲלִילוֹתָם

יט שְׁפַטְתִּים: וַיָּבוֹא אֶל־הַגּוֹיִם אֲשֶׁר־בָּאוּ שָׁם וַיְחַלְּלוּ אֶת־שֵׁם קָדְשִׁי בֶּאֱמֹר לָהֶם עַם־יְהֹוָה

כ אֵלֶּה וּמֵאַרְצוֹ יָצָאוּ: וָאֶחְמֹל עַל־שֵׁם קָדְשִׁי אֲשֶׁר חִלְּלֻהוּ בֵּית יִשְׂרָאֵל בַּגּוֹיִם אֲשֶׁר־בָּאוּ

כא שָׁמָּה: לָכֵן אֱמֹר לְבֵית־יִשְׂרָאֵל כֹּה אָמַר אֲדֹנָי יְהֹוִה לֹא לְמַעַנְכֶם אֲנִי עֹשֶׂה בֵּית

כב יִשְׂרָאֵל כִּי אִם־לְשֵׁם־קָדְשִׁי אֲשֶׁר חִלַּלְתֶּם בַּגּוֹיִם אֲשֶׁר־בָּאתֶם שָׁם: וְקִדַּשְׁתִּי אֶת־שְׁמִי הַגָּדוֹל

כג הַמְחֻלָּל בַּגּוֹיִם אֲשֶׁר חִלַּלְתֶּם בְּתוֹכָם וְיָדְעוּ הַגּוֹיִם כִּי־אֲנִי יְהֹוָה נְאֻם אֲדֹנָי יְהֹוִה בְּהִקָּדְשִׁי

כד בָכֶם לְעֵינֵיהֶם: וְלָקַחְתִּי אֶתְכֶם מִן־הַגּוֹיִם וְקִבַּצְתִּי אֶתְכֶם מִכָּל־הָאֲרָצוֹת וְהֵבֵאתִי אֶתְכֶם

כה אֶל־אַדְמַתְכֶם: וְזָרַקְתִּי עֲלֵיכֶם מַיִם טְהוֹרִים וּטְהַרְתֶּם מִכֹּל טֻמְאוֹתֵיכֶם וּמִכָּל־גִּלּוּלֵיכֶם

כו אֲטַהֵר אֶתְכֶם: וְנָתַתִּי לָכֶם לֵב חָדָשׁ וְרוּחַ חֲדָשָׁה אֶתֵּן בְּקִרְבְּכֶם וַהֲסִרֹתִי אֶת־לֵב הָאֶבֶן

כז מִבְּשַׂרְכֶם וְנָתַתִּי לָכֶם לֵב בָּשָׂר: וְאֶת־רוּחִי אֶתֵּן בְּקִרְבְּכֶם וְעָשִׂיתִי אֵת אֲשֶׁר־בְּחֻקַּי תֵּלֵכוּ

כח וּמִשְׁפָּטַי תִּשְׁמְרוּ וַעֲשִׂיתֶם: וִישַׁבְתֶּם בָּאָרֶץ אֲשֶׁר נָתַתִּי לַאֲבֹתֵיכֶם וִהְיִיתֶם לִי לְעָם וְאָנֹכִי

כט אֶהְיֶה לָכֶם לֵאלֹהִים: וְהוֹשַׁעְתִּי אֶתְכֶם מִכֹּל טֻמְאוֹתֵיכֶם וְקָרָאתִי אֶל־הַדָּגָן וְהִרְבֵּיתִי אֹתוֹ

ל וְלֹא־אֶתֵּן עֲלֵיכֶם רָעָב: וְהִרְבֵּיתִי אֶת־פְּרִי הָעֵץ וּתְנוּבַת הַשָּׂדֶה לְמַעַן אֲשֶׁר לֹא תִקְחוּ עוֹד

לא חֶרְפַּת רָעָב בַּגּוֹיִם: וּזְכַרְתֶּם אֶת־דַּרְכֵיכֶם הָרָעִים וּמַעַלְלֵיכֶם אֲשֶׁר לֹא־טוֹבִים וּנְקֹטֹתֶם

לב בִּפְנֵיכֶם עַל עֲוֺנֹתֵיכֶם וְעַל תּוֹעֲבוֹתֵיכֶם: לֹא לְמַעַנְכֶם אֲנִי־עֹשֶׂה נְאֻם אֲדֹנָי יְהֹוִה יִוָּדַע לָכֶם בּוֹשׁוּ וְהִכָּלְמוּ מִדַּרְכֵיכֶם בֵּית יִשְׂרָאֵל:

לג כֹּה אָמַר אֲדֹנָי יְהֹוִה בְּיוֹם טַהֲרִי אֶתְכֶם מִכֹּל עֲוֺנוֹתֵיכֶם וְהוֹשַׁבְתִּי אֶת־הֶעָרִים וְנִבְנוּ הֶחֳרָבוֹת:

לד וְהָאָרֶץ הַנְּשַׁמָּה תֵּעָבֵד תַּחַת אֲשֶׁר הָיְתָה שְׁמָמָה לְעֵינֵי כָּל־עוֹבֵר: וְאָמְרוּ הָאָרֶץ הַלֵּזוּ

לה הַנְּשַׁמָּה הָיְתָה כְּגַן־עֵדֶן וְהֶעָרִים הֶחֳרֵבוֹת וְהַנְשַׁמּוֹת וְהַנֶּהֱרָסוֹת בְּצוּרוֹת יָשָׁבוּ: וְיָדְעוּ

לו הַגּוֹיִם אֲשֶׁר יִשָּׁאֲרוּ סְבִיבוֹתֵיכֶם כִּי אֲנִי יְהֹוָה בָּנִיתִי הַנֶּהֱרָסוֹת נָטַעְתִּי הַנְּשַׁמָּה אֲנִי יְהֹוָה

דִּבַּרְתִּי וְעָשִׂיתִי: כֹּה אָמַר אֲדֹנָי יְהֹוִה עוֹד זֹאת אִדָּרֵשׁ לְבֵית־יִשְׂרָאֵל לַעֲשׂוֹת

לח לָהֶם אַרְבֶּה אֹתָם כַּצֹּאן אָדָם: כְּצֹאן קָדָשִׁים כְּצֹאן יְרוּשָׁלַם בְּמוֹעֲדֶיהָ כֵּן תִּהְיֶינָה הֶעָרִים הֶחֳרֵבוֹת מְלֵאוֹת צֹאן אָדָם וְיָדְעוּ כִּי־אֲנִי יְהֹוָה:

הספרדים
מסיימים כאן

Haftara for
Parashat HaHodesh

The Laws of Taxes, Offerings, and Inheritance as They Relate to the Prince and the Building of the Temple

EZEKIEL 45:16–46:18

The Tabernacle of Moses was inaugurated on the first day of Nisan, the first month. According to Ezekiel's prophecies, the future Temple will be inaugurated on that same date. The first of Nisan represents priority and renewal in all matters of the sacred service and the Kingdom of Israel. At the center of the prophecy stands the prince, who is the senior figure among the people. It should be noted that it is unclear from the context whether this prince is the supreme political leader, a king, or the High Priest. The prophecy deals with the formalization of the relationship between the prince and the people in various areas: The orderly arrangement of the government in the realms of law and finance, the funding and responsibility for bringing communal offerings, and the nature of the visits of the prince and the people to the Temple.

45 16 All the people of the land shall take part in this gift for the
Ashk. 17 prince in Israel, and upon the prince shall be the burnt offer-
begin ings and the meal offerings and the libations on the festivals,
on the New Moons and on the Sabbaths, on all the appointed
times of the house of Israel; he shall offer the sin offering and
the meal offering, the burnt offering and the peace offering, to
Seph. begin 18 atone for the house of Israel. So said the Lord God: In the first
month, on the first of the month, you shall take an unblemished
19 young bull, and you shall cleanse the Sanctuary. The priest shall
take of the blood of the sin offering, and he shall place it on
the gatepost of the House, and on the four corners of the stratum of the altar, and on the gatepost of the gate of the Inner
20 Courtyard. So you shall do on the seventh of the month for the
person who acted unwittingly, and for the ignorant, and you
21 shall atone for the House. In the first month, on the fourteenth
day of the month, there shall be the paschal lamb for you, a fes-
22 tival of seven days; unleavened bread shall be eaten. The prince
shall offer on that day a bull as a sin offering for himself and for
23 all the people of the land. For the seven days of the festival he
shall offer a burnt offering to the Lord, seven bulls and seven
rams unblemished for each day, for the seven days, and a goat
24 for each day as a sin offering. He shall offer a meal offering: An
ephah per bull and an ephah per ram, and oil, a hin per ephah.
25 In the seventh month, on the fifteenth day of the month, during
the festival, he shall offer like these, for the seven days: like the
sin offering, like the burnt offering and like the meal offering,
46 1 and like the oil. So said the Lord God: The gate of the Inner
Courtyard that faces eastward shall be closed for the six days of
work, but on the Sabbath day it shall be opened, and on the day
2 of the New Moon it shall be opened. The prince shall come by
the way of the Hall of the Gate from without, and he shall stand
by the gatepost of the gate, and the priests shall offer his burnt
offering and his peace offering, and he shall prostrate himself
at the threshold of the gate and depart, but the gate shall not
3 be closed until the evening. The people of the land shall prostrate themselves at the entrance of that gate on the Sabbaths
4 and on the New Moons before the Lord. The burnt offering
that the prince shall present to the Lord on the Sabbath day
5 shall be six unblemished sheep and an unblemished ram; and
a meal offering of one ephah for the ram, and for the sheep, a
meal offering of the gift of his hand; and oil, a hin per ephah.
6 On the day of the New Moon it shall be an unblemished bull,
7 and six sheep and a ram; they shall be unblemished. And an
ephah for the bull and an ephah for the ram he shall offer as a
meal offering, and for the sheep according to that for which his
8 means suffice, and oil, a hin per ephah. When the prince comes,
by way of the Hall of the Gate he shall come, and by its way
9 he shall depart. But when the people of the land come before
the Lord at the appointed times, he who comes by way of the
north gate to prostrate himself shall depart by way of the south
gate, and he who comes by way of the south gate shall depart
by way of the north gate; he shall not return by way of the gate
10 through which he came; rather, he shall depart opposite it. And
the prince, he shall come in their midst when they come, and
11 when they depart he shall depart. On the festivals and at the
appointed times the meal offering shall be an ephah per bull
and an ephah per ram; and for the sheep, the gift of his hand;
12 and oil, a hin per ephah. When the prince offers a gift offering, a burnt offering or a peace offering as a gift offering to the
Lord, one shall open for him the gate that faces eastward, and
he shall offer his burnt offering and his peace offering as he does
on the Sabbath day, and he shall depart and one shall close the
13 gate after his departure. An unblemished sheep in its first year
you shall offer as a burnt offering for the day to the Lord; every
14 morning you shall offer it. And a meal offering you shall offer
with it every morning, one-sixth of an ephah, and oil, one-third
of a hin, to moisten the fine flour, a meal offering to the Lord,
15 an eternal ordinance continually. They shall offer the sheep and

הפטרת

פרשת החודש

יחזקאל
האשכנזים
מתחילים כאן
הספרדים
מתחילים כאן

מה טז כָּל הָעָם הָאָרֶץ יִהְיוּ אֶל־הַתְּרוּמָה הַזֹּאת לַנָּשִׂיא בְּיִשְׂרָאֵל: וְעַל־הַנָּשִׂיא יִהְיֶה הָעוֹלֹת
וְהַמִּנְחָה וְהַנֵּסֶךְ בַּחַגִּים וּבֶחֳדָשִׁים וּבַשַּׁבָּתוֹת בְּכָל־מוֹעֲדֵי בֵּית יִשְׂרָאֵל הוּא־יַעֲשֶׂה אֶת־
יח הַחַטָּאת וְאֶת־הַמִּנְחָה וְאֶת־הָעוֹלָה וְאֶת־הַשְּׁלָמִים לְכַפֵּר בְּעַד בֵּית־יִשְׂרָאֵל: כה

אָמַר אֲדֹנָי יֱהֹוִה בָּרִאשׁוֹן בְּאֶחָד לַחֹדֶשׁ תִּקַּח פַּר־בֶּן־בָּקָר תָּמִים וְחִטֵּאתָ אֶת־הַמִּקְדָּשׁ:
יט וְלָקַח הַכֹּהֵן מִדַּם הַחַטָּאת וְנָתַן אֶל־מְזוּזַת הַבַּיִת וְאֶל־אַרְבַּע פִּנּוֹת הָעֲזָרָה לַמִּזְבֵּחַ וְעַל־
כ מְזוּזַת שַׁעַר הֶחָצֵר הַפְּנִימִית: וְכֵן תַּעֲשֶׂה בְּשִׁבְעָה בַחֹדֶשׁ מֵאִישׁ שֹׁגֶה וּמִפֶּתִי וְכִפַּרְתֶּם
כא אֶת־הַבָּיִת: בָּרִאשׁוֹן בְּאַרְבָּעָה עָשָׂר יוֹם לַחֹדֶשׁ יִהְיֶה לָכֶם הַפָּסַח חָג שְׁבֻעוֹת יָמִים מַצּוֹת
כב יֵאָכֵל: וְעָשָׂה הַנָּשִׂיא בַּיּוֹם הַהוּא בַּעֲדוֹ וּבְעַד כָּל־עַם הָאָרֶץ פַּר חַטָּאת: וְשִׁבְעַת יְמֵי־הֶחָג
כג יַעֲשֶׂה עוֹלָה לַיהֹוָה שִׁבְעַת פָּרִים וְשִׁבְעַת אֵילִים תְּמִימִם לַיּוֹם שִׁבְעַת הַיָּמִים וְחַטָּאת
כד שְׂעִיר עִזִּים לַיּוֹם: וּמִנְחָה אֵיפָה לַפָּר וְאֵיפָה לָאַיִל יַעֲשֶׂה וְשֶׁמֶן הִין לָאֵיפָה: בַּשְּׁבִיעִי
כה בַּחֲמִשָּׁה עָשָׂר יוֹם לַחֹדֶשׁ בֶּחָג יַעֲשֶׂה כָאֵלֶּה שִׁבְעַת הַיָּמִים כַּחַטָּאת כָּעֹלָה וְכַמִּנְחָה
וְכַשָּׁמֶן:

מו א כֹּה־אָמַר אֲדֹנָי יֱהֹוִה שַׁעַר הֶחָצֵר הַפְּנִימִית הַפֹּנֶה קָדִים יִהְיֶה סָגוּר שֵׁשֶׁת
ב יְמֵי הַמַּעֲשֶׂה וּבְיוֹם הַשַּׁבָּת יִפָּתֵחַ וּבְיוֹם הַחֹדֶשׁ יִפָּתֵחַ: וּבָא הַנָּשִׂיא דֶּרֶךְ אוּלָם הַשַּׁעַר מִחוּץ
וְעָמַד עַל־מְזוּזַת הַשַּׁעַר וְעָשׂוּ הַכֹּהֲנִים אֶת־עוֹלָתוֹ וְאֶת־שְׁלָמָיו וְהִשְׁתַּחֲוָה עַל־מִפְתַּן הַשַּׁעַר
ג וְיָצָא וְהַשַּׁעַר לֹא־יִסָּגֵר עַד־הָעָרֶב: וְהִשְׁתַּחֲווּ עַם־הָאָרֶץ פֶּתַח הַשַּׁעַר הַהוּא בַּשַּׁבָּתוֹת
ד וּבֶחֳדָשִׁים לִפְנֵי יְהֹוָה: וְהָעֹלָה אֲשֶׁר־יַקְרִב הַנָּשִׂיא לַיהֹוָה בְּיוֹם הַשַּׁבָּת שִׁשָּׁה כְבָשִׂים תְּמִימִם
ה וְאַיִל תָּמִים: וּמִנְחָה אֵיפָה לָאַיִל וְלַכְּבָשִׂים מִנְחָה מַתַּת יָדוֹ וְשֶׁמֶן הִין לָאֵיפָה: וּבְיוֹם
ו הַחֹדֶשׁ פַּר בֶּן־בָּקָר תְּמִימִם וְשֵׁשֶׁת כְּבָשִׂים וָאַיִל תְּמִימִם יִהְיוּ: וְאֵיפָה לַפָּר וְאֵיפָה לָאַיִל
ז יַעֲשֶׂה מִנְחָה וְלַכְּבָשִׂים כַּאֲשֶׁר תַּשִּׂיג יָדוֹ וְשֶׁמֶן הִין לָאֵיפָה: וּבְבוֹא הַנָּשִׂיא דֶּרֶךְ אוּלָם
ח הַשַּׁעַר יָבוֹא וּבְדַרְכּוֹ יֵצֵא: וּבְבוֹא עַם־הָאָרֶץ לִפְנֵי יְהֹוָה בַּמּוֹעֲדִים הַבָּא דֶּרֶךְ שַׁעַר צָפוֹן
ט לְהִשְׁתַּחֲוֺת יֵצֵא דֶּרֶךְ־שַׁעַר נֶגֶב וְהַבָּא דֶּרֶךְ־שַׁעַר נֶגֶב יֵצֵא דֶּרֶךְ־שַׁעַר צָפוֹנָה לֹא יָשׁוּב
דֶּרֶךְ הַשַּׁעַר אֲשֶׁר־בָּא בּוֹ כִּי נִכְחוֹ יֵצֵאוּ: וְהַנָּשִׂיא בְּתוֹכָם בְּבוֹאָם יָבוֹא וּבְצֵאתָם יֵצֵאוּ: יצא
יא וּבַחַגִּים וּבַמּוֹעֲדִים תִּהְיֶה הַמִּנְחָה אֵיפָה לַפָּר וְאֵיפָה לָאַיִל וְלַכְּבָשִׂים מַתַּת יָדוֹ וְשֶׁמֶן הִין
יב לָאֵיפָה: וְכִי־יַעֲשֶׂה הַנָּשִׂיא נְדָבָה עוֹלָה אוֹ־שְׁלָמִים נְדָבָה לַיהֹוָה וּפָתַח לוֹ אֶת־
הַשַּׁעַר הַפֹּנֶה קָדִים וְעָשָׂה אֶת־עֹלָתוֹ וְאֶת־שְׁלָמָיו כַּאֲשֶׁר יַעֲשֶׂה בְּיוֹם הַשַּׁבָּת וְיָצָא וְסָגַר
יג אֶת־הַשַּׁעַר אַחֲרֵי צֵאתוֹ: וְכֶבֶשׂ בֶּן־שְׁנָתוֹ תָּמִים תַּעֲשֶׂה עוֹלָה לַיּוֹם לַיהֹוָה בַּבֹּקֶר בַּבֹּקֶר
יד תַּעֲשֶׂה אֹתוֹ: וּמִנְחָה תַעֲשֶׂה עָלָיו בַּבֹּקֶר בַּבֹּקֶר שִׁשִּׁית הָאֵיפָה וְשֶׁמֶן שְׁלִישִׁית הַהִין לָרֹס
טו אֶת־הַסֹּלֶת מִנְחָה לַיהֹוָה חֻקּוֹת עוֹלָם תָּמִיד: וְעָשׂוּ אֶת־הַכֶּבֶשׂ וְאֶת־הַמִּנְחָה וְאֶת־הַשֶּׁמֶן יעשׂו

the meal offering and the oil every morning as a continual burnt
Seph. end 16 offering. So said the Lord God: If the prince gives a gift to one
of his sons, it is his inheritance, it shall be for his sons; it is their
17 portion by inheritance. If he gives a gift from his inheritance to
one of his servants, it shall be his until the year of liberty and it
shall return to the prince; however, his inheritance shall be for
18 his sons. The prince shall not take from the inheritance of the
people to dispossess them from their portion; from his portion
he shall bequeath to his sons so that My people will not be dis-
Ashk. end persed, each from his portion.

Haftara for **Shabbat HaGadol**

Toward the Great Day of the Lord

MALACHI 3:4–24

Malachi's last prophecy, which concludes all the books of the Prophets, contains words of reproof and encouragement in preparation for the "great and awesome day of the Lord" (3:23) at the end of days. This *haftara* does not relate to the reading of the Torah portion of a particular Sabbath, but to the calendar date, the eve of the festival of Passover. The first and last redemptions share themes that are expressed in the *haftara*: Unyielding judgment and punishment alongside God's passing over and His mercy; a service of God that is clearly linked to the redemption; the continuous tradition over the generations; and the relationship between fathers and sons.

In addition, the prophet encourages the people to give their dues of *teruma* and tithes to the priests and Levites respectively, and he speaks of the blessing they will receive if they perform this duty. This topic is suitable both for the beginning of the harvest season and for the eve of Passover, which is the designated time for the removal of the previous year's tithes from one's house, to be given to those who are entitled to them.

3 4 The offering of Judah and Jerusalem will be pleasant to the
5 Lord, as in the days of old and as in former years. I will approach you for judgment and I will be a swift witness against
the sorcerers, against the adulterers, against the takers of false
oaths, against the exploiters of the wages of the hireling, the
widow, and the orphan, and the perverters of justice against
6 the stranger; they do not fear Me, said the Lord of hosts. For I
the Lord did not change, and you, sons of Jacob, did not perish.
7 From the days of your forefathers you deviated from My statutes, and you did not observe them. Return to Me, and I will return to you, said the Lord of hosts, but you say: For what should
8 we return? Can a man rob God, as you rob Me? But you say:
9 How have we robbed You? It is the tithes and the gifts. You are
10 cursed with the curse, yet you rob Me, the entire nation. Bring
all the tithes to the storehouse, and let it be food in My house.
Test Me now with this – the utterance of the Lord of hosts – if
I will not open for you the windows of heaven, and pour out
11 an endless blessing for you. I will rebuke the devourer for you,
and he will not destroy the fruits of your land, and the vine will
not lose its fruit for you in the field prematurely, said the Lord
12 of hosts. All the nations will praise you, as you will be a desired
13 land, said the Lord of hosts. Your words have been harsh against
Me, said the Lord; but you say: How have we spoken against
14 you? You said: It is vain to worship God and what is the profit
in our keeping His commission and that we have walked in the
15 dark because of the Lord of hosts? Now we praise criminals;
also, the wicked are built up; they also test God and escape.
16 Then those who fear the Lord spoke one to another and the
Lord listened and heeded; a book of remembrance was written
before Him for those who fear the Lord, and those who think of
17 His name. They will be Mine, said the Lord of hosts, on the day
that I make as a distinction; I will have compassion on them,
18 just as a man has compassion on his son who serves him. You
will return and see the difference between the righteous and the
wicked, between one who serves God and one who does not
19 serve Him. For behold, the day is coming, burning like a furnace, and all the criminals and all the doers of wickedness will
be straw; the day that is coming will burn them, said the Lord
20 of hosts, so that it will not leave of them root or branch. But
the sun of righteousness will shine for those who fear My name
with healing in its rays and you will emerge and grow fat like
21 fattened calves. You will crush the wicked, for they will be ashes

טז בַּבֹּקֶר בַּבֹּקֶר עֹלַת תָּמִיד: כֹּה־אָמַר אֲדֹנָי יְהֹוִה כִּי־יִתֵּן הַנָּשִׂיא מַתָּנָה לְאִישׁ
                                  הספרדים מסיימים כאן

יז מִבְּנֵיו נַחֲלָתוֹ הִיא לְבָנָיו תִּהְיֶה אֲחֻזָּתָם הִיא בְּנַחֲלָה: וְכִי־יִתֵּן מַתָּנָה מִנַּחֲלָתוֹ לְאַחַד מֵעֲבָדָיו

יח וְהָיְתָה לּוֹ עַד־שְׁנַת הַדְּרוֹר וְשָׁבַת לַנָּשִׂיא אַךְ נַחֲלָתוֹ בָּנָיו לָהֶם תִּהְיֶה: וְלֹא־יִקַּח הַנָּשִׂיא מִנַּחֲלַת
הָעָם לְהוֹנֹתָם מֵאֲחֻזָּתָם מֵאֲחֻזָּתוֹ יַנְחִל אֶת־בָּנָיו לְמַעַן אֲשֶׁר לֹא־יָפֻצוּ עַמִּי אִישׁ מֵאֲחֻזָּתוֹ:   *האשכנזים מסיימים כאן*

הפטרת
שבת הגדול

ג וְעָרְבָה לַיהֹוָה מִנְחַת יְהוּדָה וִירוּשָׁלָ͏ִם כִּימֵי עוֹלָם וּכְשָׁנִים קַדְמֹנִיּוֹת: וְקָרַבְתִּי אֲלֵיכֶם לַמִּשְׁפָּט   *מלאכי*
וְהָיִיתִי ׀ עֵד מְמַהֵר בַּמְכַשְּׁפִים וּבַמְנָאֲפִים וּבַנִּשְׁבָּעִים לַשָּׁקֶר וּבְעֹשְׁקֵי שְׂכַר־שָׂכִיר אַלְמָנָה

ו וְיָתוֹם וּמַטֵּי־גֵר וְלֹא יְרֵאוּנִי אָמַר יְהֹוָה צְבָאוֹת: כִּי אֲנִי יְהֹוָה לֹא שָׁנִיתִי וְאַתֶּם בְּנֵי־יַעֲקֹב

ז לֹא כְלִיתֶם: לְמִימֵי אֲבֹתֵיכֶם סַרְתֶּם מֵחֻקַּי וְלֹא שְׁמַרְתֶּם שׁוּבוּ אֵלַי וְאָשׁוּבָה אֲלֵיכֶם אָמַר
יְהֹוָה צְבָאוֹת וַאֲמַרְתֶּם בַּמֶּה נָשׁוּב: הֲיִקְבַּע אָדָם אֱלֹהִים כִּי אַתֶּם קֹבְעִים אֹתִי וַאֲמַרְתֶּם

ט בַּמֶּה קְבַעֲנוּךָ הַמַּעֲשֵׂר וְהַתְּרוּמָה: בַּמְּאֵרָה אַתֶּם נֵאָרִים וְאֹתִי אַתֶּם קֹבְעִים הַגּוֹי כֻּלּוֹ: הָבִיאוּ
אֶת־כָּל־הַמַּעֲשֵׂר אֶל־בֵּית הָאוֹצָר וִיהִי טֶרֶף בְּבֵיתִי וּבְחָנוּנִי נָא בָּזֹאת אָמַר יְהֹוָה צְבָאוֹת

יא אִם־לֹא אֶפְתַּח לָכֶם אֵת אֲרֻבּוֹת הַשָּׁמַיִם וַהֲרִיקֹתִי לָכֶם בְּרָכָה עַד־בְּלִי־דָי: וְגָעַרְתִּי לָכֶם
בָּאֹכֵל וְלֹא־יַשְׁחִת לָכֶם אֶת־פְּרִי הָאֲדָמָה וְלֹא־תְשַׁכֵּל לָכֶם הַגֶּפֶן בַּשָּׂדֶה אָמַר יְהֹוָה צְבָאוֹת:

יב וְאִשְּׁרוּ אֶתְכֶם כָּל־הַגּוֹיִם כִּי־תִהְיוּ אַתֶּם אֶרֶץ חֵפֶץ אָמַר יְהֹוָה צְבָאוֹת: *חזקו*

יד חָזְקוּ עָלַי דִּבְרֵיכֶם אָמַר יְהֹוָה וַאֲמַרְתֶּם מַה־נִּדְבַּרְנוּ עָלֶיךָ: אֲמַרְתֶּם שָׁוְא עֲבֹד אֱלֹהִים וּמַה־בֶּצַע

טו כִּי שָׁמַרְנוּ מִשְׁמַרְתּוֹ וְכִי הָלַכְנוּ קְדֹרַנִּית מִפְּנֵי יְהֹוָה צְבָאוֹת: וְעַתָּה אֲנַחְנוּ מְאַשְּׁרִים זֵדִים

טז גַּם־נִבְנוּ עֹשֵׂי רִשְׁעָה גַּם בָּחֲנוּ אֱלֹהִים וַיִּמָּלֵטוּ: אָז נִדְבְּרוּ יִרְאֵי יְהֹוָה אִישׁ אֶל־רֵעֵהוּ וַיַּקְשֵׁב
יְהֹוָה וַיִּשְׁמָע וַיִּכָּתֵב סֵפֶר זִכָּרוֹן לְפָנָיו לְיִרְאֵי יְהֹוָה וּלְחֹשְׁבֵי שְׁמוֹ: וְהָיוּ לִי אָמַר יְהֹוָה צְבָאוֹת

יח לַיּוֹם אֲשֶׁר אֲנִי עֹשֶׂה סְגֻלָּה וְחָמַלְתִּי עֲלֵיהֶם כַּאֲשֶׁר יַחְמֹל אִישׁ עַל־בְּנוֹ הָעֹבֵד אֹתוֹ: וְשַׁבְתֶּם

יט וּרְאִיתֶם בֵּין צַדִּיק לְרָשָׁע בֵּין עֹבֵד אֱלֹהִים לַאֲשֶׁר לֹא עֲבָדוֹ:   כִּי־הִנֵּה הַיּוֹם בָּא בֹּעֵר
כַּתַּנּוּר וְהָיוּ כָל־זֵדִים וְכָל־עֹשֵׂה רִשְׁעָה קַשׁ וְלִהַט אֹתָם הַיּוֹם הַבָּא אָמַר יְהֹוָה צְבָאוֹת אֲשֶׁר

כ לֹא־יַעֲזֹב לָהֶם שֹׁרֶשׁ וְעָנָף: וְזָרְחָה לָכֶם יִרְאֵי שְׁמִי שֶׁמֶשׁ צְדָקָה וּמַרְפֵּא בִּכְנָפֶיהָ וִיצָאתֶם

כא וּפִשְׁתֶּם כְּעֶגְלֵי מַרְבֵּק: וְעַסּוֹתֶם רְשָׁעִים כִּי־יִהְיוּ אֵפֶר תַּחַת כַּפּוֹת רַגְלֵיכֶם בַּיּוֹם אֲשֶׁר אֲנִי

under the soles of your feet on the day that I am preparing, said
22 the Lord of hosts. Remember the Torah of Moses My servant,
which I commanded him at Horev for all of Israel, statutes and
23 ordinances. Behold, I am sending Elijah the prophet to you

before the coming of the great and awesome day of the Lord.
24 He will return the heart of the fathers to the children, and the
heart of the children to their fathers, lest I come and smite the
land with utter destruction.

כב עָשֹׂה אָמַר יהוה צְבָאֽוֹת: זִכְר֕וּ תּוֹרַ֖ת מֹשֶׁ֣ה עַבְדִּ֑י אֲשֶׁר֩ צִוִּ֨יתִי אוֹת֥וֹ בְחֹרֵב֙

כג עַל־כָּל־יִשְׂרָאֵ֔ל חֻקִּ֖ים וּמִשְׁפָּטִֽים: הִנֵּ֤ה אָֽנֹכִי֙ שֹׁלֵ֣חַ לָכֶ֔ם אֵ֖ת אֵלִיָּ֣ה הַנָּבִ֑יא לִפְנֵ֗י בּ֚וֹא יֹ֣ום

כד יהוה֙ הַגָּד֣וֹל וְהַנּוֹרָ֔א: וְהֵשִׁ֤יב לֵב־אָבוֹת֙ עַל־בָּנִ֔ים וְלֵ֥ב בָּנִ֖ים עַל־אֲבוֹתָ֑ם פֶּן־אָב֕וֹא וְהִכֵּיתִ֥י

אֶת־הָאָ֖רֶץ חֵֽרֶם:

הִנֵּ֤ה אָֽנֹכִי֙ שֹׁלֵ֣חַ לָכֶ֔ם אֵ֖ת אֵלִיָּ֣ה הַנָּבִ֑יא לִפְנֵ֗י בּ֚וֹא יֹ֣ום יהוה֙ הַגָּד֖וֹל וְהַנּוֹרָֽא:

Book of Genesis

Bereshit

1. Isaiah 34:11; Jeremiah 4:23.
2. Isaiah 45:7.
3. See, e.g., Jeremiah 6:4; Ezekiel 30:18; Amos 5:20; Job 3:4.
4. See Isaiah 43:13, and commentary ad loc.
5. See *Bereshit Rabba* 3:7.
6. See *Responsa of Rav Avraham ben HaRambam* 43.
7. *Ḥagiga* 12a; see Rashi.
8. *HaKetav VehaKabbala*; see Ibn Ezra and Sforno, verse 1.
9. See I Kings 7:23.
10. See Isaiah 27:1; Psalms 74:13–14; *Bava Batra* 74b; *Bereshit Rabba* 7.
11. See Ezekiel 29:3; Job 40.
12. See commentary on Leviticus 11:2.
13. Ibn Ezra; Ramban.
14. Ramban.
15. See *Pirkei deRabbi Eliezer* 11.
16. See Rashi, verse 29; Rashi, *Sanhedrin* 57a; *Tosafot, Sanhedrin* 56b; see also Rabbi Eliyahu Mizraḥi and *Gur Arye*, verse 29; Rabbi Menaḥem Azarya of Fano, *Ḥikkur HaDin* 3:21.
17. *Ḥullin* 60b.
18. *Sanhedrin* 38b; *Bereshit Rabba* 8:1.
19. See Onkelos.
20. See II Kings 19:12; Ezekiel 27:23.
21. Onkelos.
22. Rashi; *Zohar* 1:125a.
23. *Yalkut Shimoni, Bereshit* 22; *Megilla* 11a.
24. See, e.g., 31:21; Joshua 24:2; II Samuel 10:16; see also *Ḥizkuni*.
25. See, e.g., Joshua 24:2; I Kings 5:4; Ezra 8:36; *Avot deRabbi Natan* 47; *Bereshit Rabba* 42:8.
26. See Ramban.
27. See *Berakhot* 61a.
28. See Rashi, based on *Pirkei deRabbi Eliezer* 12; *Responsa of the Rashba* 60.
29. See Onkelos; *Targum Yonatan*; *Bereshit Rabba*; Ibn Ezra.
30. See *Ḥizkuni*; *Akedat Yitzḥak*; Alsheikh; introduction to the Ra'avad's *Sha'arei Kedusha*; *Responsa of the Rashba* 1:60.
31. See *Kohelet Shlomo* 7, *Responsa of Rav Hai Gaon*.
32. See *Berakhot* 40a.
33. See Rashi; Ramban; Rashi, *Avoda Zara* 5b.
34. See Sforno; Ba'al HaTurim.
35. See Rashi; *Ḥizkuni*; *Meshekh Ḥokhma*.
36. Rabbi Samson Raphael Hirsch.
37. See *Responsa of the Radbaz* 257.
38. See, e.g., I Samuel 4:4; Ezekiel 10.
39. See, e.g., *Tikkunei Zohar* 108a; *Sefer HaPelia*.
40. *Tanḥuma, Bereshit* 9; see also *Bereshit Rabba* 22; Ibn Ezra.
41. See, e.g., I Kings 18:38.
42. See Ibn Ezra.
43. *Bereshit Rabba* 22:5; see Ibn Ezra and Sforno, verse 3.
44. See Rashi; Ibn Ezra; Ramban.
45. *Gittin* 57b; *Eikha Rabba Petiḥta* 23; *Devarim Rabba* 2:25.
46. See Leviticus 5:1, 22:9; Deuteronomy 22:26; I Samuel 28:10; Zechariah 14:19.
47. See *Bemidbar Rabba* 7:5; *Devarim Rabba*, Lieberman, ed., *Va'ethanan*, s.v. *az*; *Targum Yonatan*; Ibn Ezra.
48. Ibn Ezra; Ramban.
49. Onkelos; *Targum Yonatan*; Rashi.
50. See *Bereshit Rabba* 22:2; *Sanhedrin* 38b, 58b.
51. Ramban.
52. See Onkelos.
53. *Bereshit Rabba* 23:3.
54. *Tanḥuma, Bereshit* 11.
55. See Radak; Malbim.
56. See Numbers 24:17.
57. Rashbam; Ibn Ezra.
58. *Sifrei, Devarim* 43; *Bereshit Rabba* 23:7; *Targum Yonatan*.
59. See Rambam, *Sefer HaMadda, Hilkhot Avoda Zara* 1:1.
60. See, e.g., *Berakhot* 61a; *Vayikra Rabba* 14:1.
61. Isaiah 14:14; see *Shela, Hakdamat Toldot Adam* 3.
62. See *Targum Yonatan*; *Zohar* 2:167b.
63. See, e.g., 6:9, 17:1; Deuteronomy 13:5; I Samuel 2:30; Psalms 116:9.
64. See Onkelos.
65. See, e.g., *Bereshit Rabba* 25:1; *Zohar* 1:56b.
66. I Kings 2.
67. See *Targum Yonatan*.
68. See, e.g., *Tanḥuma, Bereshit* 11; Rashi; Rashbam.
69. Rashi; Ramban; *Sanhedrin* 69b; *Tanḥuma, Toledot* 23; Rashi, *Avoda Zara* 9a.
70. Onkelos; Rashi; Ibn Ezra; Radak; Rabbeinu Baḥya; see *Sifrei, Bemidbar* 86; *Bereshit Rabba* 26:5.
71. See Job 1:6; I Samuel 28:13; Zechariah 12:8; *Pirkei deRabbi Eliezer* 22; *Zohar* 1:37a.
72. Rav Se'adya Gaon.
73. Rashi; see *Targum Yonatan*; *Zohar* 1:58a.
74. See Rabbi Samson Raphael Hirsch; *Torah Shelema* 47; *Da'at Zekenim*; *HaKetav VehaKabbala* 338.
75. See Deuteronomy 3:11; *Targum Yonatan*, Deuteronomy 3:11.
76. See, e.g., Mishna *Berakhot* 9:5; *Avot deRabbi Natan* 14; *Berakhot* 61a–b; see *Sefer Mitzvot Katan* 53.
77. See Rashi; Ibn Ezra; Ramban.
78. Rav Se'adya Gaon.
79. *Sanhedrin* 108a.

Noah

1. See *Sanhedrin* 108a; *Midrash Rabba* and *Tanḥuma*.
2. See, e.g., Onkelos.
3. See Psalms 29:10; see also Mishna *Sanhedrin* 10:3; *Yalkut Shimoni, Bereshit* 61.
4. Ramban.
5. See, e.g., *Sanhedrin* 108a.
6. *Tanḥuma* 58:5; Rashi, verse 14.
7. See the dispute between Rabbi Yehoshua and Rabbi Eliezer, *Rosh HaShana* 11b, and Rashi ad loc.
8. See *Ḥullin* 139b; Rashi; Onkelos.
9. *Kiddushin* 13a.
10. See *Rosh HaShana* 12a.
11. Rashi, 8:22; see *Bereshit Rabba* 25:2.
12. See *Targum Yonatan*.
13. *Ḥizkuni*.
14. Onkelos; *Targum Yonatan*; see Ibn Ezra; *Bekhor Shor*; Ramban.
15. See *Bereshit Rabba* 34; *Keli Yakar*.
16. See 9:7; Exodus 1:7.
17. Jerusalem Talmud, *Berakhot* 3:5.
18. See 1:30, and the commentaries.
19. *Sanhedrin* 56b; Rambam, *Sefer Shofetim, Hilkhot Melakhim* 9:1.
20. Exodus 21:29; Rambam, *Sefer Nezikin, Hilkhot Nizkei Mammon*, from 10:1 onward.
21. See Onkelos; Radak.
22. See Radak.
23. *Hagigah* 16a; see Ezekiel 1:28.
24. See *Bereshit Rabba* 36:3; Rashi; Sforno.
25. *Tanḥuma* 58:21; Ibn Ezra, Genesis 9:21; see *Sanhedrin* 70a.
26. See Leviticus 20:17.
27. See also verse 24.
28. See Ramban, verse 18.
29. See *Targum Yonatan*; Ibn Ezra.
30. See *HaKetav VehaKabbala*.
31. Ezekiel 38:2.
32. See *Yoma* 10a.
33. See Isaiah 23:1.
34. See Onkelos, Numbers 24:24; *Targum Yonatan*, Jeremiah 2:10 and Ezekiel 27:6.
35. *Eiruvin* 53a; see *Bereshit Rabba* 42:4.
36. See Ramban; Samuel David Luzzatto.
37. See Rabbi Samson Raphael Hirsch.
38. See *Targum Yonatan*; Samuel David Luzzatto.
39. Jonah 1:2; see Rashi; Rabbi Samson Raphael Hirsch.
40. Jeremiah 44:1; Ezekiel 29:14; see Isaiah 11:11.
41. See *Sanhedrin* 69b.
42. See Ramban; Rashi, *Avoda Zara* 9a.
43. Job 1:1; Jeremiah 25:20; Lamentations 4:21.
44. I Kings 10; Isaiah 60:6; Psalms 72:10.
45. See also commentary on Isaiah 40:4.
46. See Ba'al HaTurim.

Lekh Lekha

1. Ibn Ezra.
2. See Ramban; see also 13:4.
3. See Radak; Passover Haggada.
4. See Deuteronomy 11:10–12.
5. *Ḥizkuni*.
6. With regard to Sarai's character and beauty, see *Bava Batra*

58a; *Tanḥuma, Lekh Lekha* 5.
7. *Bereshit Rabba* 41:3.
8. Radak; others translate "to the east"; see Samuel David Luzzatto.
9. See commentary on 10:10.
10. Onkelos.
11. *Targum Yonatan*; Ibn Ezra; see also Onkelos.
12. See Rashi; Deuteronomy 2:10.
13. Rashi; Deuteronomy 2:11.
14. See Ramban, Deuteronomy 2:10, who identifies the Horites with the Hivites.
15. II Chronicles 20:2.
16. *Nidda* 61a.
17. See Radak.
18. See Joshua 19:47; Judges 18:29.
19. Psalms 76:3.
20. *Nedarim* 32b; *Bereshit Rabba* 56:10.
21. Ramban.
22. See, e.g., Exodus 6:8, Numbers 14:30; Ezekiel 20:6; Daniel 12:7; Psalms 106:26.
23. Onkelos; Ibn Ezra.
24. See Rashi.
25. Ibn Ezra.
26. *Geon HaGe'onim* 44, citing Rav Se'adya Gaon.
27. See also Exodus 19:18.
28. Numbers 34:5; Joshua 15:4.
29. See *Yalkut Shimoni* 78; *Tanna deVei Eliyahu Rabba* 18.
30. *Bereshit Rabba* 45:4; Rashi.
31. See commentary on I Samuel 1:6.
32. Radak.
33. *Bereshit Rabba* 5:10; see Ibn Ezra; Ramban.
34. See, e.g., 26:24; Exodus 3:6; I Kings 18:36; Psalms 47:10.
35. *Shevuot* 13a; Rambam, *Sefer HaMadda, Hilkhot Teshuva* 8:1; Ramban, *Sha'ar HaGemul*.

Vayera

1. See *Shevuot* 35b.
2. Ramban; Abravanel.
3. *Bekhor Shor*; Ibn Ezra.
4. See, e.g., Numbers 3:6; Deuteronomy 1:38; I Kings 17:1; Isaiah 6:2.
5. See Ibn Ezra.
6. See Rashbam; Rabbeinu Baḥya; Judges 6:14.
7. See *Bava Metzia* 87a.
8. See *Targum Yonatan*; Ramban.
9. See Ramban.
10. See Radak; Rashbam.
11. See Rashi.
12. See the essay by Rav Aharon Lichtenstein: "Does Jewish Tradition Recognize an Ethic Independent of Halacha," in Marvin Fox (ed.), Modern Jewish Ethics (Columbus, 1975) pp. 52–88, reprinted in Menachem Kellner (ed.), Contemporary Jewish Ethics (New York, 1978), pp. 102–119.
13. Rambam, *Guide of the Perplexed*, 2:42
14. *Sanhedrin* 109a; see Ramban.
15. Rambam, *Sefer Shofetim, Hilkhot Melakhim* 9:5; see *Sanhedrin* 57b–58a.
16. Ramban.
17. See, e.g., Judges 15:1; I Samuel 2:21.
18. See Rashi, 17:19.
19. See I Samuel 1:24; Rashbam.
20. Ramban; Ibn Ezra; Sforno; Radak.
21. See *Midrash HaGadol*.
22. See chap. 15; Jeremiah 34:18–19.
23. *Bereshit Rabba* 44:5; *Sanhedrin* 89b.
24. See Ramban.
25. Ibn Ezra.
26. Rashbam; see *Avot* 5:6.
27. See *Bereshit Rabba* 44:5; *Sanhedrin* 89b.
28. Ba'al HaTurim.

Hayei Sarah

1. See Rashi; *Bereshit Rabba* 58:1.
2. Ibn Ezra; see also *HaKetav VehaKabbala*.
3. See Ramban.
4. See *Ḥizkuni*.
5. *Bereshit Rabba* 60:8.
6. See Ibn Ezra; Radak.
7. See *Tzeror Hamor*.
8. See *HaKetav VehaKabbala*.
9. *Avot deRabbi Natan* 40; see Rashi.
10. See *Ḥullin* 95b.
11. Ramban.
12. See *Midrash Sekhel Tov*.
13. Radak; Ibn Ezra.
14. Ibn Ezra.
15. See Isaiah 21:13.
16. Ibn Ezra.
17. See Onkelos; *Targum Yonatan*; Ramban.
18. See Sforno, verse 2.
19. See commentary on 10:7.

Toledot

1. See Ibn Ezra.
2. See Rashi; *Ḥizkuni*; Radak.
3. See Radak.
4. See *Targum Yonatan*; Rashi; Rashbam.
5. Rashi; Ibn Ezra.
6. See Rashbam; Ibn Ezra.
7. See Isaiah 29:8; Psalms 63:2.
8. See Rashbam and Ramban, verse 31.
9. See Rashbam, verse 31; see also 26:30.
10. See Rashbam, 41:10; Maharit, I Samuel 21:14.
11. See Radak here and I Samuel 21:12; *Bekhor Shor*, Numbers 27:7.
12. See Ibn Ezra.
13. See Ezra 4:6.
14. See Rav Se'adya Gaon.
15. See *Bereshit Rabba* 65:1.
16. Ibn Ezra.
17. See Rashi.
18. Ramban.
19. See Onkelos; Rashbam; Ibn Ezra; see also II Samuel 14:9.
20. See *Ḥizkuni*, verse 19; see also *Tanḥuma, Toledot* 11; Rashi, verses 21–22.
21. *Ta'anit* 29b; Rashi.
22. Ibn Ezra.

Vayetze

1. *Bereshit Rabba* 70:8; Rashi; *Targum Yonatan*.
2. See above 24:50; commentary on 25:20; Rabbeinu Baḥya, and Ramban ad loc.
3. See *Bereshit Rabba* 70:12; Ramban; Rabbi Samson Raphael Hirsch.
4. *Aggadat Bereshit*, verse 13; see Rashi.
5. See Rashi; Rashbam; *Ḥizkuni*.
6. See Rashbam; *Tosafot*; Ramban, verse 9.
7. See Ibn Ezra ad loc.; Esther 2:7.
8. Rashbam; *Ḥizkuni*; see Rashi; Rabbi Samson Raphael Hirsch.
9. See, e.g., *Seder Olam Rabba* 2.
10. See Onkelos.
11. See *Seder Olam Rabba*; Ramban.
12. See Ramban.
13. Sforno; Rabbi Samson Raphael Hirsch.
14. See Rabbi Samson Raphael Hirsch.
15. Rabbi Samson Raphael Hirsch.
16. See *Tanḥuma, Vayetze* 24.
17. See Judges 17:5; I Samuel 19:13; Zechariah 10:2.
18. See Ibn Ezra; Ramban.
19. Ramban.
20. See Rashi as to why Jacob used the word "fear," rather than "God."
21. See Onkelos; *Targum Yonatan*, verse 48.
22. See Sforno.
23. See Rashbam.
24. Joshua 21:36; II Samuel 2:8.

Vayishlah

1. Ibn Ezra.
2. See Judges 20:6.
3. Verses 1–2; see *Bereshit Rabba* 75:4; Rashi.
4. See Ramban.
5. See Rashi.
6. Judges 13:22, see also, e.g., 6:22–23.
7. Rashi; Rashbam.
8. Ibn Ezra.
9. Exodus 17:15.
10. Ezekiel 48:35.
11. See, e.g., Judges 14:3; I Samuel 17:26.
12. Ibn Ezra.
13. See, e.g., 23:10; Deuteronomy 25:7; II Samuel 19:9; Ruth 4:1–11.
14. See Rashi, verse 16.
15. See *Targum Yonatan*; Samuel David Luzzatto.
16. See Rambam, *Sefer Shofetim*, *Hilkhot Melakhim* 9:14; Sforno.
17. *Bekhor Shor*.
18. Rashbam; see Rav Se'adya Gaon; Sforno.
19. 31:13, and Ramban ad loc.; *Da'at Mikra*.
20. Rav Se'adya Gaon; Ramban, 28:18; see Ibn Ezra.
21. See 21:31; 26:33; Ramban.
22. See Rashi; Ramban.
23. See Exodus 15:6.
24. See I Samuel 10:2.
25. See Rashbam.
26. Onkelos; see 14:5; Deuteronomy 2:10–11; Ramban; see also Jerusalem Talmud, *Berakhot* 8:5; *Zohar*, *Vayishlah* 178a.
27. *Pesaḥim* 54a.
28. See Ramban.
29. See, e.g., Lamentations 4:21; Job 1:1, and Ibn Ezra ad loc.
30. Deuteronomy 33:5; Rashbam; Ibn Ezra.
31. Numbers 22:5.
32. See *Targum Yonatan*; Ibn Ezra.
33. See Abravanel.
34. Onkelos.
35. See Ibn Ezra.

Vayeshev

1. See Jerusalem Talmud, *P'ea* 1:1.
2. See Rashbam and *Ḥizkuni*, 41:5.
3. Ramban.
4. *Ḥizkuni*.
5. See Ramban.
6. See Rashbam; Sforno, 42:22.
7. See Sforno.
8. Rashi.
9. See Ibn Ezra.
10. Ibn Ezra.
11. Rashi; Rashbam.
12. Rashi.
13. Rashbam.
14. See Amos 2:6.
15. See Rashbam; Ramban, verse 25.
16. See commentary on Isaiah 56:5.
17. Onkelos; Rav Se'adya Gaon; Rashbam.
18. See Ibn Ezra, 10:25.
19. *Bereshit Rabba* 85:10; Rashi, verse 24.
20. *Bereshit Rabbati*.
21. Deuteronomy 25:6.
22. See Rashi; Ramban.
23. See II Samuel 14:2.
24. See Ibn Ezra; see also *Sota* 10a.
25. See *Sanhedrin* 57–58, and Rashi ad loc.; see also Ramban, Rashba, and Ritva, *Yevamot* 97b–98a.
26. See, e.g., *Yevamot* 38a.
27. See Rashbam.
28. See 29:17; commentary on 37:3.
29. See Rashbam; Ibn Ezra; *Yoma* 35b.
30. See *Bemidbar Rabba* 14:6; Rashbam.
31. See *Bereshit Rabba*.
32. See *Sota* 36b; *Bereshit Rabba* 87; *Yalkut Shimoni*; Rashi.
33. See commentary on 21:9.
34. *Bereshit Rabba* 99; see Rashi, verse 1.
35. See Onkelos.
36. See *Lekaḥ Tov*; *Midrash HaGadol*.
37. Radak; see Rashbam; Rabbi Samson Raphael Hirsch.
38. Ramban; see Radak; Rabbi Samson Raphael Hirsch.
39. *Berakhot* 55b; see Rashi, verse 5.

Miketz

1. Rav Yeshaya of Trani; see *Da'at Zekenim*; *Ḥizkuni*.
2. *Bereshit Rabba* 89:6; Rashi.
3. Rashbam; see Rashi, Exodus 31:3.
4. Onkelos; Rashi.
5. Rashbam; Radak.
6. See Ibn Ezra.
7. *Sifrei*, *Devarim* 1; Ibn Ezra.
8. See Rashbam; Sforno.
9. See Rav Se'adya Gaon; Ramban.
10. Ibn Ezra.
11. See Sforno; *Or HaḤayyim*.
12. 37:26; see also I Chronicles 5:2: "For Judah prevailed above his brothers."
13. See Rashi, 37:25.
14. See Ibn Ezra, 37:25.
15. See Ibn Ezra.
16. See Rashi; Ramban.
17. See Sforno.

Vayigash

1. See Rashi.
2. See Ramban.
3. See 42:24, and commentary ad loc.
4. Onkelos; see also Rashi; Ibn Ezra.
5. See commentary on 42:24.
6. Rashi.
7. See Ramban, verse 27.
8. See Rav Se'adya Gaon; Rabbi Yom Tov Miyyuni.
9. Ramban; Ibn Ezra; see also 37:35, and commentary ad loc.
10. See Ibn Ezra.
11. See *Targum Yonatan*; *Sota* 13a.
12. See Numbers 26:42–43.
13. Rashbam; Ibn Ezra.
14. See Judges 9:5, and Radak ad loc.
15. *Bereshit Rabba* 95:4; Rashi.
16. Rashbam; *Akedat Yitzḥak*.
17. See Rashi.
18. See Leviticus 13:6–7 for a similar usage of the term "second."

Vayhi

1. See Ramban.
2. See commentary on 35:19.
3. See *Ba'alei Tosafot*, citing Rabbi Ovadya Bartenura.
4. Onkelos; Rashi; Ibn Ezra.
5. Rashbam.
6. Ibn Ezra.
7. Rashbam.
8. Onkelos; Rashi.
9. See Rashi; *Ḥizkuni*.
10. See Joshua 20:7, 24:32.
11. Ibn Ezra.
12. See *Ḥizkuni*.
13. Rashi; see Rabbeinu Bahya.
14. See Ibn Ezra.
15. See Onkelos; Rashi.
16. See, e.g., Jeremiah 15:17; Psalms 89:8, 111:1.
17. See *Bereshit Rabba* 99:7.
18. *Bereshit Rabba* 99:8; Rashi.
19. See Onkelos; *Targum Yonatan*; Rashi; Rashbam.
20. See Onkelos; Rashi; *Bereshit Rabba* 99.
21. See *Bemidbar Rabba* 13:17; *Megilla* 6a; *Hazon Ish*, *Shevi'it* 3:27.
22. Onkelos.
23. Rashbam; Ramban.

24. See Ibn Ezra.
25. Rashi; *Sota* 10a.
26. See Ramban.
27. Rashi.
28. Deuteronomy 33:20; see Joshua 4:12.
29. Based on *Bekhor Shor*.
30. See Ibn Ezra; Ramban.
31. See Rashi.
32. See Radak.
33. See Rashi; Rashbam; Radak.
34. See Onkelos; Rashi; Rashbam.
35. See commentary on Isaiah 1:24.
36. See Rashbam.
37. II Samuel 23:3; Isaiah 30:29.
38. Rashi.
39. Radak.
40. Rashbam.
41. See Rashi.
42. See Rashi; Ibn Ezra; Sforno; *Ha'amek Davar*.
43. See Rashi; *Bekhor Shor* here, and Numbers 20:29.
44. See Rashi.
45. Rashi; Ibn Ezra.
46. See Rashi; Abravanel; *Midrash Tanḥuma* 96:7.
47. *Devarim Rabba* 5:15; see Rashi; *Da'at Zekenim*; *Ḥiddushei HaRim, Parashat Vayeshev*.

Book of Exodus

Introduction to Exodus

1. 25:8; see *Or HaḤayyim*; *Alsheikh*.

Shemot

1. See 3:22; *Ha'amek Davar*.
2. Rabbi Samson Raphael Hirsch.
3. See Ramban; *Bekhor Shor*; *Akedat Yitzḥak*.
4. *Sota* 11a; Rashi.
5. See *Sota* 11b.
6. Ibn Ezra.
7. See *Bekhor Shor*; Ibn Ezra, short commentary on Exodus.
8. See *Sota* 12a.
9. *Sota* 12a.
10. See Rabbeinu Baḥya; Ramban.
11. See Deuteronomy 34:7; see also Rambam, *Guide of the Perplexed* 2:45.
12. See Rambam, *Guide of the Perplexed* 2:45.
13. *HaKetav VehaKabbala*.
14. Onkelos.
15. See *Tzeror HaMor*.
16. *Bekhor Shor*.
17. *Bekhor Shor*.
18. *Bekhor Shor*; see I Kings 19:13; Isaiah 6:2.
19. See Ibn Ezra.
20. See Genesis 32:31; Judges 6:22–23, 13:22.
21. *Shemot Rabba* 3:6.
22. *Berakhot* 9b; Rashi.
23. Rashbam; see Onkelos.
24. *HaKetav VehaKabbala*.
25. Ibn Ezra; Sforno.
26. Rashbam.
27. Genesis 15:14.
28. Rav Se'adya Gaon; Samuel David Luzzatto; *HaKetav VehaKabbala*.
29. Ramban.
30. See Rashi; Ibn Ezra; Rabbeinu Baḥya.
31. See Jerusalem Talmud, *Nedarim* 3:9.
32. *Nedarim* 31b–32a; Rashi; Ibn Ezra; Rashbam.
33. Rashi; Ibn Ezra.
34. Rashi, Numbers 11:16; see *Shemot Rabba* 5:20.
35. See commentary on Jeremiah 12:1.
36. Rashbam.

Va'era

1. See Ibn Ezra; Ramban; Sforno; *Adderet Eliyahu*.
2. See also *Or HaḤayyim*.
3. See Ramban 6:12.
4. Genesis 50:26.
5. See Numbers 16.
6. See Leviticus 10:4; Numbers 3:30.
7. See Numbers 1:7, 2:3, 7:12–17.
8. *Sota* 43a; *Bava Batra* 109b–110a; Rashi.
9. Numbers 25:31.
10. Ibn Ezra.
11. See Rashi; *Bekhor Shor*.
12. Psalms 90:10.
13. See *Bekhor Shor*.
14. *HaKetav VehaKabbala*.
15. Ibn Ezra.
16. Ibn Ezra.
17. *Shemot Rabba* 9:11; Onkelos; Rashi.
18. *Targum Yonatan*; Rashi; Rashbam; Ibn Ezra.
19. See Onkelos.
20. Rashi; Ibn Ezra.
21. See Rashi.
22. See Rashi; *Bekhor Shor*.
23. Rashi.
24. See *Ḥizkuni*.
25. Rashbam; Ibn Ezra; see *Targum Yonatan*.
26. See *Targum Yonatan*; Rashi.
27. Rashi.
28. Onkelos.
29. See Ibn Ezra; Rashbam.
30. See *Responsa of the Ge'onim*, Assaf, p. 245.

Bo

1. See *Targum Yonatan*; Ibn Ezra.
2. *Targum Yonatan*; Rashi.
3. See Ibn Ezra, citing Rav Moshe HaKohen; *Or HaḤayyim*.
4. Rabbeinu Baḥya.
5. Onkelos; Ibn Ezra.
6. *Shemot Rabba* 14:1; see Rashi; Ibn Ezra.
7. See *Keli Yakar*.
8. See *Shemot Rabba* 14:3; Rashbam.
9. Onkelos; Rashbam.
10. Rambam, *Guide of the Perplexed* 1:28.
11. *Bekhor Shor*.
12. *Rosh HaShana* 22a; Rabbeinu Baḥya.
13. See *Pesaḥim* 61a, and Rashi ad loc.
14. *Pesaḥim* 86a.
15. See Isaiah 1:13, and Rashi ad loc.; see also Ramban, Leviticus 23:2, and commentary ad loc.
16. See, e.g., *Megilla* 7a; Jerusalem Talmud, *Beitza* 5b.
17. See *Pesaḥim* 43a.
18. Translation based on Onkelos; Rashi.
19. See Rashi.
20. *Ha'amek Davar*.
21. See Sforno; see also Rashi, Genesis 37:11.
22. See Rashi; Ramban.
23. *Mekhilta*.
24. See Rashi.
25. See *Sefer HaḤinnukh* 16.
26. Rashi; Ramban.
27. Rabbi Menaḥem ben Shimon, Jeremiah 31:5.
28. See 23:15; Deuteronomy 16:1.
29. See *Pesaḥim* 91a, 120a.
30. Numbers 18:15.

Beshalah

1. See Ibn Ezra; *Ḥizkuni*.
2. See Rashbam; Ramban.
3. See Genesis 50:24–25.
4. See Deuteronomy 1:33; *Menaḥot* 95a.
5. Rashi.
6. Rashi.
7. See Numbers 14:33–34.
8. See *Sota* 30b.
9. Isaiah 12:2; Psalms 118:14.
10. See Rashi; Rashbam.
11. See Ibn Ezra, long commentary on Exodus; *Adderet Eliyahu*.
12. See Rashi.
13. See Onkelos; Ibn Ezra, long commentary on Exodus ad loc. and 15:13.
14. See Rashi.
15. Rashbam.
16. See Deuteronomy 32:22; Jeremiah 15:14.
17. See *Targum Yonatan*; Rashi; Rashbam; Ibn Ezra.
18. See Onkelos.
19. Translation based on Onkelos; Rashi; Ibn Ezra.
20. See Judges 11:34; I Samuel 29:5; Psalms 150:4.
21. Genesis 16:7.
22. *Mekhilta*; *Sanhedrin* 56b; see Rashi here and 16:23.
23. See *Yoma* 75b.
24. *Mekhilta*; Rashbam; *Bekhor Shor*.
25. Rashi; Rav Se'adya Gaon.
26. Radak.
27. See Ramban.
28. See Sforno, verse 16.
29. Rav Se'adya Gaon.
30. See Rashi, 15:25.
31. See *Shabbat* 118b.
32. Rashi.
33. See Numbers 1.
34. *Bekhor Shor*; *Ḥizkuni*.
35. Ibn Ezra; *Bekhor Shor*.
36. Onkelos; Rashi.
37. See, e.g., 6:8; Genesis 14:22.
38. See *Shevuot* 38b; Rashi, Genesis 24:2.

Yitro

1. See Joshua 2:9–11; I Samuel 4:7–8.
2. Rashi, based on *Mekhilta*; see *Bekhor Shor*.
3. *Bekhor Shor*, 2:22.
4. *Bekhor Shor*.
5. See Rashi; *Bekhor Shor*; *Mekhilta deRashbi* 18:6.
6. Onkelos; *Sota* 11a.
7. See *Bekhor Shor*.
8. See *Targum Yonatan*; *Bava Metzia* 30b.
9. Rabbi Yehoshua in the *Mekhilta*; Rashbam; *Bekhor Shor*.
10. See *Shemot Rabba* 30:10; Rashi, Deuteronomy 1:15.
11. *Ḥizkuni*.
12. See *Bekhor Shor*; the expressions in 40:2; I Samuel 20:34; Ezekiel 46:1–6; II Kings 4:23; *Shabbat* 86b; commentary on Exodus 12:2.
13. Leviticus 19:2.
14. See Rambam, *Guide of the Perplexed* 1:18.
15. *Mekhilta*; Rashi.
16. Based on Rav Se'adya Gaon and Rashi.
17. See Rashi.
18. Onkelos; Rashi; Rashbam; *Bekhor Shor*.
19. See Rashbam; *Bekhor Shor*; Ibn Ezra, long commentary on Exodus.
20. See Ibn Ezra, verse 17.
21. See Deuteronomy 5:5.
22. 34:28; Deuteronomy 4:13, 10:4.
23. 20:2–14; Deuteronomy 5:6–18, with small changes.
24. See verses 15–18; Deuteronomy 5:19–24; see also *Bekhor Shor*.
25. Rav Ḥasdai Crescas, in the beginning of *Or Hashem*; Abravanel.
26. Rambam, *Sefer HaMitzvot*, positive commandment 1.
27. See Rambam, *Guide of the Perplexed* 1:54.
28. Deuteronomy 7:9.
29. See *Yoma* 86a.
30. See *Sha'arei Teshuva* 3:158, 4:16.
31. See *Pesaḥim* 106a.
32. See *Mekhilta deRashbi* 20:8; *Shabbat* 119a, 113a.
33. Genesis 2:1–3.
34. See Genesis 2:3.
35. See Ramban.
36. See *Bekhor Shor*.
37. See Rashi.
38. See *Or HaHayyim*.
39. Rashi; see Rambam, *Guide of the Perplexed* 3:24.
40. See *Bekhor Shor*; Sforno; Rabbi Isaac Samuel Reggio.
41. *Sanhedrin* 39a.
42. Mishna *Middot* 3:4.
43. Deuteronomy 27:5.
44. See *Sifra*; Rashi.

Mishpatim

1. See Ramban.
2. See Rashi; Rashbam.
3. See Ibn Ezra.
4. Deuteronomy 15:12–15.
5. See *Kiddushin* 21b.
6. See Leviticus 25:39–41; *Kiddushin* 21b.
7. See also *Adderet Eliyahu*.
8. *Kiddushin* 14b; Rashi.
9. See *HaKetav VehaKabbala*; Samuel David Luzzatto; see also Abravanel, II Samuel 14:13.
10. *Adderet Eliyahu*.
11. *Kiddushin* 18b–19a.
12. See *Targum Yonatan*; Rashi; Rashbam; see also *Ketubot* 47b.
13. *Mekhilta*, *Masekhta deNezikin* 3; Rashi; Rashbam.
14. See *Adderet Eliyahu*.
15. Numbers 35:6–29; Deuteronomy 4:41–43.
16. See I Kings 2:28–34.
17. Rambam, *Guide of the Perplexed* 3:39; *Adderet Eliyahu*.
18. See Rav Se'adya Gaon.
19. See *Sanhedrin* 86a; Rashi, Exodus 20:12.
20. See, e.g., I Samuel 3:13; II Samuel 16:5–13; Jeremiah 26:6.
21. Deuteronomy 27:16.
22. *Targum Yonatan*; Ramban.
23. See *Targum Yonatan*; Rashi; Ibn Ezra, long commentary on Exodus.
24. Rashi; see 21:12; see also *Bava Batra* 50a–b.
25. See Genesis 42:4, 38.
26. See *Sanhedrin* 79a; Rashi; Ibn Ezra, long commentary on Exodus.
27. See *Bava Kamma* 41a.
28. See *Bava Kamma* 41a.
29. See *Sanhedrin* 15b; *Targum Yonatan*; Rashi; Ramban; *Bekhor Shor*; *Adderet Eliyahu*; see also commentary on Leviticus 24:21.
30. See *Mekhilta*; Rashi.
31. See *Bava Kamma* 54b.
32. *Bava Kamma* 49b–50a; Rashi; Ibn Ezra.
33. *Adderet Eliyahu*.
34. *Bava Kamma* 10b.
35. Rashi.
36. See Rashi, Leviticus 26:41.
37. See *Bava Kamma* 23b; *Yevamot* 64b–65a.
38. *Sanhedrin* 72a; Rashi.
39. Ra'avad, *Sefer Nezikin*, *Hilkhot Geneiva* 9:8; Rav Se'adya Gaon; Rashbam; Ibn Ezra; Gra.
40. *Bekhor Shor*.
41. Translation based on Rashi; Rashbam; Ibn Ezra.
42. See *Bava Kamma* 6b–7a; Rashi.
43. Rashbam.
44. Onkelos; *Targum Yonatan*; Rashi; Rashbam.
45. *Adderet Eliyahu*.
46. Rashbam; *Bekhor Shor*; Ibn Ezra; *Adderet Eliyahu*.
47. *Bekhor Shor*; *Adderet Eliyahu*.
48. See *Targum Yonatan*; Rav Se'adya Gaon; Ibn Ezra.
49. See Rashi; Ramban.
50. See Genesis 23:16; Rav Se'adya Gaon.
51. Rambam, *Guide of the Perplexed* 3:37.
52. See Leviticus 18:23; see also *Sanhedrin* 54b.
53. See *Adderet Eliyahu*.
54. See Rashi; Ramban; *Adderet Eliyahu*.
55. See *Bava Metzia* 58b.
56. Psalms 68:6.
57. See Rashi; *Bekhor Shor*.
58. See Rashbam.
59. See Leviticus 19:14.
60. See *Sefer HaḤinnukh* 69.
61. See *Ḥizkuni*; Sforno.
62. See 13:2, 13; see, however, Sforno.
63. *Targum Yonatan*.
64. See Rashi; *Pesaḥim* 118a.
65. See *Sanhedrin* 27a and the commentaries on this verse.
66. Exodus 20:13; see also *Mekhilta*.
67. See Rashi; *Bekhor Shor*.

68. See Deuteronomy 32:36; Nehemiah 3:8.
69. *Mekhilta*.
70. See *Pesaḥim* 63a–64a.
71. See *Pesaḥim* 59b, 71a; Rashi; Rashbam.
72. See Rashi; *Targum Yonatan*; Sforno.
73. See Rashbam; *Bekhor Shor* here and 34:26; Ramban, Deuteronomy 14:21; see also commentary on 34:26.
74. See *Ḥullin* 113a–114a; Rambam, *Sefer HaMitzvot*, negative commandments 186,187.
75. See Ibn Ezra, long commentary on Exodus.
76. Based on Rashbam, Ibn Ezra, and Ramban.
77. See Numbers 11:16; Mishna *Sanhedrin* 1:6.
78. Rashbam; *Ḥizkuni*.
79. Translation based on Ibn Ezra, long commentary on Exodus; *Ḥizkuni*; see Ramban.
80. Onkelos; *Targum Yonatan*; Rashi; see Rosh.
81. See Leviticus 17:11; Deuteronomy 12:23.
82. Similar to the basins mentioned in 27:3; see also Song of Songs 7:3.
83. See Rashbam; Ibn Ezra, short commentary on Exodus.
84. See Onkelos; Ibn Ezra, short commentary on Exodus.
85. *Targum Yonatan*; Rashi; see Jerusalem Talmud, *Sukka* 4:3.
86. See Ibn Ezra; *Bekhor Shor*.
87. Rav Se'adya Gaon; Rashbam.
88. Lamentations 4:7.
89. See *Menaḥot* 43b.
90. See Isaiah 41:9.
91. Rashbam; Ibn Ezra; Ramban.
92. See *Yoma* 4b; Rashi; Ibn Ezra.

Teruma

1. See *Bemidbar Rabba* 4:5; Rashi.
2. See Numbers 31:22.
3. See Rashi.
4. See *Yoma* 72b.
5. Rashi.
6. See Ezekiel 10.
7. See Rashi.
8. See above, verses 14–15; Numbers 4:7–8.
9. See Leviticus 24:7, and Onkelos ad loc.; *Menaḥot* 97a.
10. Rashi.
11. See *Bekhor Shor*.
12. Rashi.
13. See Rashi; Ibn Ezra.
14. See *Yoma* 52a.
15. Onkelos; Rav Se'adya Gaon; see Rashi, Numbers 8:2.
16. See Rashi; *Megilla* 21b; *Responsa of the Rivash*; Numbers 8:2.
17. See *Yevamot* 4b; Ibn Ezra, Exodus 25:4.
18. See Jerusalem Talmud, *Shekalim* 8:2; *Yoma* 72b, and Rashi and Ibn Ezra ad loc.
19. See Sforno, 40:18.
20. Rashi.
21. See *Adderet Eliyahu* on *Pekudei*.
22. See *Shabbat* 28, and Rashi ad loc.
23. See *Targum Yonatan*; Ibn Ezra; *Shabbat* 98b, and Ran ad loc.; Rabbeinu Gershom Meor HaGola, *Ḥullin* 17b.
24. *Targum Yonatan*; *Sukka* 45b.
25. See *Targum Yonatan*; *Pesikta Zutreta*.
26. See Rashi.
27. Rashi; see Ramban.
28. See Rashbam.
29. See Rashi.
30. See, e.g., *Zevaḥim* 54a.
31. See Rashi; Rashbam.
32. See Rashi; *Zevaḥim* 62a.
33. Sforno.
34. *Yoma* 71b; Rashi; Rambam, *Sefer Avoda*, *Hilkhot Kelei HaMikdash* 8:14.
35. See Rashi; Ibn Ezra.

Tetzaveh

1. See *Menaḥot* 86a.
2. Rashi.
3. Rashi; see Onkelos.
4. See Rashi.
5. See *Targum Yonatan*; Rashbam.
6. Rashi.
7. See Rashi; *Ḥizkuni*.
8. See Rambam, *Sefer HaMitzvot*, negative commandment 86; Rambam, *Sefer Avoda*, *Hilkhot Kelei HaMikdash* 9:10.
9. See *Targum Yonatan*; Rashi.
10. *Bekhor Shor*.
11. Rashi; Rashbam; *Bekhor Shor*, verse 6.
12. Ramban; Rambam, *Sefer Avoda*, *Hilkhot Kelei HaMikdash* 9:3.
13. See *Zevaḥim* 88a; see also Ibn Ezra.
14. See Onkelos.
15. Onkelos.
16. Rashi, based on *Yoma* 72a.
17. *Targum Yonatan*.
18. See Ramban, verse 31.
19. *Zevaḥim* 88b; see Onkelos and Rashi, verse 33.
20. 29:6, 39:30; Leviticus 8:9.
21. See *Kiddushin* 66a.
22. *Pesikta Zutreta*; see Ibn Ezra, long commentary on Exodus.
23. See *Shevuot* 9b; *Zevaḥim* 23a; *Menaḥot* 25a.
24. See Jerusalem Talmud, *Yoma* 7:3.
25. See Ibn Ezra.
26. See Rashbam, verse 4.
27. Rashi.
28. Ramban, verse 35; see *Meshekh Ḥokhma*.
29. See Leviticus 22:17–25.
30. See *Menaḥot* 78a.
31. Leviticus 8:26.
32. See Rashbam.
33. See Ibn Ezra.
34. See *Targum Yonatan*; Rashi; II Kings 5:10, 14.
35. Ibn Ezra.
36. See Ramban.
37. See *Ḥagiga* 16b.
38. See *Tamid* 30b; *Zevaḥim* 53b; Rashi; see also Leviticus 1:5.
39. See *Tamid* 31a.
40. See Rashi; see also Leviticus 8:26.
41. Rashi; see Rav Se'adya Gaon; Ibn Ezra.
42. Rashi.
43. Rashi.
44. Rashi; see *Yoma* 5a.
45. See Rashi.
46. See, e.g., above, 12:10; Leviticus 7:15.
47. Onkelos.
48. See *Bekhor Shor*; *Adderet Eliyahu*.
49. See Rashi, 12:5.
50. See *Baraita deMelekhet HaMishkan*; Rambam, *Sefer Avoda*, *Hilkhot Beit HaBeḥira* 1:7.
51. *Pesaḥim* 59a.
52. Ibn Ezra; see Rashi.
53. See Leviticus 16:18–19.

Ki Tisa

1. See Rashi, verse 15.
2. See *Bekhor Shor* and *Adderet Eliyahu*, 38:25.
3. See *Bekhorot* 5a.
4. Rashi.
5. See Song of Songs 4:14; Rashbam.
6. See Ramban.
7. See Rashi; *Karetot* 5a.
8. See Ibn Ezra, long commentary on Exodus.
9. Rashi; see *Zevaḥim* 83b.
10. Rashbam.
11. *Karetot* 6b.
12. See Onkelos; Rashi; Rashbam.
13. See Ibn Ezra; Ramban.
14. See Rav Se'adya Gaon; Sforno; 33:17.
15. *Pirkei deRabbi Eliezer* 44.
16. See Numbers 4:6–15; Rashi and Ibn Ezra here and 39:1.
17. Numbers 15:32–36.
18. See *Targum Yonatan*; Ibn Ezra.
19. Rashbam, 25:16.
20. See *Shabbat* 89a; Rashi.
21. Rashi; see Isaiah 8:1.
22. See Ibn Ezra.
23. See *Bereshit Rabba* 53:11; Rashi.
24. *Berakhot* 32a; see *Targum Yonatan*; Rashi.
25. *Berakhot* 32a.
26. Abravanel.
27. See Ramban; *Bekhor Shor*.
28. See Rashi.
29. See Ramban.
30. See Sforno.
31. See *Tanḥuma* 19; Rashi, 32:4.
32. Rashi; Rambam's Commentary on the Mishna, *Kelim* 21:1.
33. See Rashbam; Ibn Ezra.

34. See *Meshekh Ḥokhma*; *Minḥa Belula*.
35. See Psalms 69:29, 139:16; Isaiah 4:3; *Rosh HaShana* 16b.
36. See commentary on 33:2; Daniel 10:20.
37. See Ibn Ezra.
38. See *Sanhedrin* 102a; Rashi.
39. Rashi.
40. See *Shabbat* 88a; *Tanḥuma*, *Shelah* 13; *Shemot Rabba* 51:8; *Targum Yonatan*; Rashi; Ibn Ezra, long commentary on Exodus, 33:6.
41. *Akedat Yitzḥak*.
42. See Numbers 3:38.
43. See Rashi; Ibn Ezra; *Bekhor Shor*.
44. Rashi.
45. See, e.g., Genesis 15:12; Job 4:12–16; Daniel 10:8.
46. See Numbers 8:9; 12:6–8.
47. Rambam, *Guide of the Perplexed* 1:54.
48. See Rashi; Rashbam; *Bekhor Shor*; Ramban.
49. See Rashi.
50. See Rashi and Ramban, 33:12.
51. See Rashi; Ibn Ezra; Ramban; Rambam, *Sefer HaMadda*, *Hilkhot Yesodei HaTorah* 1:10; Rambam, *Guide of the Perplexed* 1:54.
52. See *Sifra*, *Vayikra* 1:5; *Bemidbar Rabba* 14:22.
53. See Rambam, *Guide of the Perplexed* 1:37–38, 54.
54. See *Berakhot* 7a; *Bekhor Shor* here and 20:5; Radak, Jeremiah 31:28.
55. See *Da'at Zekenim*; *Ha'amek Davar*.
56. 33:4; see *Bekhor Shor*; *Derashot HaRan* 4.
57. See commentary on 13:4.
58. Ibn Ezra.
59. Rashbam; Ibn Ezra.
60. See *Pesaḥim* 63a–64b; Rav Se'adya Gaon.
61. See Deuteronomy 26:1–11.
62. Rashbam; *Ḥizkuni*.
63. See 34:1; Deuteronomy 10:2–4.
64. Rashi.
65. See Ramban; *Ha'amek Davar*.
66. Ramban.

Vayak'hel

1. See Ezekiel 16:10; *Bekhor Shor*.
2. See Numbers 4:4–14.
3. 40:34–38; Leviticus 9:23–24.
4. Leviticus 10:1–7.
5. See II Kings 19:28; Ezekiel 29:4.
6. See Ramban.
7. Ibn Ezra.
8. See Rashi.
9. See Rashi; *Shabbat* 28a.
10. See *Targum Yonatan*; Ibn Ezra, long commentary on Exodus; *Shabbat* 98b, and *Ḥiddushei HaRan* ad loc.
11. *Targum Yonatan*; *Sukka* 45b.
12. See Rashi, 26:31.
13. See *Yoma* 72b.
14. Rashi.
15. Ibn Ezra.
16. See Ezekiel 10; commentary on 25:18.
17. See Rashi, 25:18.
18. See Rashi and Rashbam, 25:25–26.
19. See Rashi; Ibn Ezra.
20. See, e.g., *Zevaḥim* 54a.
21. See Ibn Ezra, long commentary on Exodus, 30:25.
22. See Sforno.
23. See, e.g., *Zevaḥim* 54a.
24. See Sforno, 27:10; *Bekhor Shor*, 27:17.

Pekudei

1. See Ramban.
2. See 37:1; *Zohar* 2:214:2.
3. See *Bekhorot* 5a.
4. See Ramban.
5. See Rashi, 31:10.
6. See Ramban.
7. See 28:30 and Rashi, Ibn Ezra, and Ramban ad loc.
8. See Rambam, *Sefer HaMitzvot*, negative commandment 86; Rambam, *Sefer Avoda*, *Hilkhot Kelei HaMikdash* 9:10.
9. Onkelos.
10. Rambam, *Sefer HaMitzvot*, negative commandment 88.
11. See Ramban, 28:31.
12. See Onkelos and Rashi, 28:33.
13. See *Yoma* 12a–b; Rambam, *Sefer Avoda*, *Hilkhot Kelei HaMikdash* 8:1 and *Sefer Zera'im*, *Hilkhot Kilayim* 10:32.
14. Ibn Ezra; *Ḥizkuni*.
15. See *Bemidbar Rabba* 12:15.
16. See *Shemot Rabba* 52:4; Sforno.
17. See Leviticus 1:1, and Rashi ad loc.; Ramban.

Book of Leviticus

Introduction to Leviticus

1. See, e.g., Mishna *Megilla* 3:5 and *Menaḥot* 45b.
2. See *Pesaḥim* 6b.
3. See Ramban, Exodus 40:2; Numbers 7:1; *Bekhor Shor*, Leviticus 1:2; *Responsa of the Rosh* 13:21.

Vayikra

1. See Exodus 24:15–16, 25:22; see also Rashbam; *Bekhor Shor*.
2. See Numbers 7:89, 12:4, 14:10; Joshua 18:1.
3. Exodus 30:28, 31:9; Leviticus 4:10.
4. *Da'at Zekenim*.
5. See Rashbam; *Bekhor Shor*; see also Jeremiah 6:20, and commentary on Leviticus 22:19.
6. See Ibn Ezra; *Ḥizkuni*.
7. See Judges 16:29; II Kings 18:21.
8. See *Bekhor Shor*; Mishna *Para* 1:2; *Rosh HaShana* 10a.
9. *Yoma* 27a.
10. See Exodus 27:3; Numbers 7:13.
11. Mishna *Tamid* 4:1; *Zevaḥim* 53b.
12. See 6:5; *Eiruvin* 63a.
13. See Onkelos; Ibn Ezra; Rashbam; Ramban.
14. See Rav Se'adya Gaon; Ibn Janaḥ.
15. Ibn Ezra; Ramban.
16. Rashi; *Sifrei*, *Pinhas* 143.
17. See Rashi and Ramban; *Zevaḥim* 65a, and commentaries ad loc.
18. See Mishna *Zevaḥim* 6:6.
19. See *Menaḥot* 74b–75a.
20. See *Sifra*; *Menaḥot* 13a–b, 106b.
21. See *Menaḥot* 60b; *Ḥizkuni* 23:13.
22. See *Menaḥot* 74b–75a for a discussion of the exact manner in which the oil was smeared on the wafers.
23. See *Menaḥot* 63a.
24. *Menaḥot* 74b–75a.
25. See Rashi; Rav Se'adya Gaon.
26. See *Menaḥot* 60a–61a; see also *Bekhor Shor* 6:7.
27. See Rashi; Deuteronomy 8:8; II Chronicles 31:5.
28. See Deuteronomy 26:2; *Targum Yonatan*, and Rashi here.
29. See *Sifra*; *Menaḥot* 68b.
30. See 23:9–14; *Sifra*, and Rashi ad loc.; *Menaḥot* 68b, 84a; see also Ibn Ezra.
31. See Mishna *Menaḥot* 6:1.
32. See *Ḥullin* 49; Ralbag.
33. See *Responsa of Rabbi Menahem Azarya of Fano* 113.
34. See Rabbi Samson Raphael Hirsch.
35. See Onkelos; Rashi; *Sifra*.
36. See *Sifra*; Abravanel.
37. See Rashi.
38. See *Menaḥot* 90b.
39. See *Sifra*, *Dibbura deNedava* 14:18.
40. Rashi, verse 7; see Ramban.
41. See *Pesaḥim* 96b; see also introduction to Exodus 40.

42. See *Eiruvin* 65a.
43. See Mishna *Horayot* 3:4.
44. See Rashi; *Meshekh Ḥokhma*.
45. See *Yoma* 36a; *Ḥizkuni*.
46. See *Sifra*; *Sifrei*, *Beha'alotekha* 6; *Meshekh Ḥokhma*, Numbers 8:3.
47. Exodus 30:9–10.
48. *Zevaḥim* 51a.
49. See *Sifra*; Rabbeinu Baḥya.
50. See Numbers 35:24–25; Joshua 20:6; see also commentary on Leviticus 8:5.
51. See commentary on verse 2.
52. Mishna *Horayot* 1:1–5.
53. See Ibn Ezra; *Horayot* 11b; Ramban, Exodus 22:27.
54. Rashbam.
55. See 3:9, *Targum Yonatan*, and Rashi ad loc.
56. Rashi.
57. See Onkelos.
58. *Karetot* 10b.
59. *Bekhor Shor*.
60. See *Sifra* 4:10; *Rosh HaShana* 16b; Rashi and Ibn Ezra, Leviticus 11:8; Rambam, *Guide of the Perplexed* 3:47.
61. See 7:20, 15:31, 22:3–16; Numbers 5:1–4, 9:6, 19:20; see also Ramban; *Shevuot* 6b–7b.
62. See *Shevuot* 5a, 14b.
63. See, e.g., Mishna *Shevuot* 4:3.
64. See, e.g., *Shevuot* 25b.
65. See Ibn Ezra, verse 4.
66. See Rav Se'adya Gaon; Ibn Janaḥ.
67. *Ḥullin* 19b.
68. See *Zevaḥim* 65b–66a.
69. See Rashi, Leviticus 1:15; *Zevaḥim* 64b; compare with Rashi, *Menaḥot* 2b, 97b.
70. See *Menaḥot* 6a–b.
71. See commentary on 2:2.
72. See Rashbam 27:3; Ibn Ezra 27:2.
73. See *Menaḥot* 77a; *Karetot* 26b; see also commentary on Exodus 39:26.
74. Mishna *Zevaḥim* 5:5.
75. See Sforno.
76. See Ramban.
77. See *Sifra*; Rav Se'adya Gaon; Ibn Ezra.
78. See Numbers 5:7, and Rashi ad loc.; *Targum Yonatan*; Rabbeinu Baḥya.
79. Sforno; see Mishna *Bava Kama* 9:12.
80. Mishna *Zevaḥim* 5:5.

Tzav

1. See *Zevaḥim* 56a, 98a.
2. See Exodus 29:39–42.
3. Rashi; see *Yoma* 23b; Onkelos; Rashbam.
4. See *Yoma* 23b.
5. See *Zevaḥim* 18a–b; *Yoma* 23b; Ramban.
6. See *Yoma* 68b; *Kaftor VaFeraḥ* 6.
7. See 14:40–45; *Bekhor Shor*.
8. See Ibn Ezra.
9. See Exodus 29:38–46; Numbers 28:1–5.
10. See Ibn Ezra; Onkelos.
11. See *Zevaḥim* 46b.
12. See *Menaḥot* 55a–56a.
13. See *Yoma* 34a.
14. See *Menaḥot* 50b–51b, 78a.
15. See *Menaḥot* 50b.
16. Rashi; *Sifra*.
17. See Rashi; *Menaḥot* 75b.
18. See Rashi.
19. See Rashi.
20. See 7:15–17; Rashi.
21. See *Pesaḥim* 30b.
22. See *Zevaḥim* 97a.
23. See *Zevaḥim* 14a.
24. See *Zevaḥim* 54b–55a.
25. 5:15, 14:12; Numbers 6:12.
26. *Shekalim* 18a; *Zevaḥim* 103a; Ramban.
27. See *Targum Yonatan*; Rashi; Rambam, *Sefer Avoda*, *Hilkhot Ma'aseh HaKorbanot* 9:19; see also 6:14.
28. See *Pesaḥim* 120b.
29. *Sifra*; Rashi.
30. See 11:23–15:33; Numbers 19:14–22; Deuteronomy 23:11–12.
31. See *Pesaḥim* 23b.
32. See *Karetot* 21a.
33. See 17:10–14; *Bekhor Shor*, and *Meshekh Ḥokhma* ad loc.; Rabbi Samson Raphael Hirsch.
34. See *Ha'amek Davar*; *Bekhor Shor*, 1:3.
35. See *Bekhor Shor*, Numbers 8:11.
36. See *Yevamot* 87a.
37. See Ramban.
38. *Targum Yonatan*.
39. Exodus 28–29; see Ramban.
40. *Targum Yonatan*; Rashi, Exodus 29:4; see II Kings 5:10, 14.
41. See Exodus 28:30, and commentary ad loc.
42. See commentary on Exodus 28:40.
43. *Targum Yonatan*.
44. See 6:19; Rashi.
45. See *Sifra*; *Tosefta*, *Para* 1:1; *Zevaḥim* 7b.
46. See verse 33; Exodus 29:29.
47. See Rav Se'adya Gaon; Ibn Ezra.
48. See Exodus 29:34; Ramban.
49. See Ibn Ezra, verse 33; Ramban; Rabbi Samson Raphael Hirsch; *Tosafot*, *Sukka* 43b.

Shemini

1. Ibn Ezra; see *Yoma* 3b, 51b.
2. *Bekhor Shor*.
3. See Ibn Ezra; Ba'alei HaTosafot on the Torah; see also 16:14–15; *Yoma* 43b; *Bava Metzia* 107b.
4. Sforno.
5. See Rashi, 10:16, based on *Sifra*; see *Targum Yonatan*.
6. Numbers 6:24–26.
7. See *Sifra*; Jerusalem Talmud, *Ta'anit* 4:1.
8. See *Sifra*; *Bekhor Shor*.
9. See Rav Se'adya Gaon; Ibn Ezra.
10. See also Genesis 17:3, 6–17; Exodus 34:8.
11. See Rashbam.
12. See *Sanhedrin* 52a; *Targum Yonatan*; Rashi, verse 5.
13. See Ramban; Rosh.
14. See *Sanhedrin* 52a.
15. Based on Onkelos; *Sifra*; Rashi, Ibn Ezra.
16. See Ba'al HaTurim.
17. See Onkelos; *Targum Yonatan*; Rav Se'adya Gaon; *Nazir* 4a.
18. See *Nazir* 38a; see also Deuteronomy 16:9, 17:9, 18, 19:17, 33:10; Ezekiel 44:22–23; Malachi 2:7.
19. See *Sifra*, *Shemini* 1:2; Rashi.
20. See Rashi.
21. See Deuteronomy 27:7; *Zevaḥim* 99b, 101a.
22. Based on *Targum Yonatan*; Ibn Ezra; Ramban.
23. See Rav Se'adya Gaon; Ibn Ezra; *Bekhor Shor*.
24. See *Rosh HaShana* 16b.
25. See *Ḥullin* 66; *Bekhor Shor*.
26. See Rabbeinu Baḥya; *Minḥa Belula*.
27. *Ḥullin* 63b.
28. See *Ḥullin* 62, and *Tosafot* ad loc.; *Ḥullin* 63a, 64a; *Responsa of the Radbaz*.
29. See Onkelos; Rashi; *Ḥullin* 63a.
30. See *Pesikta Zutreta Shemini* 11:16; *Responsa of the Rosh* 20:20.
31. *Sifra*; Rashbam.
32. See Rashi; *Targum Yonatan*; see also *Shemirat Shabbat KeHilkhata*, chap. 27, note 154, citing Rabbi Shlomo Zalman Auerbach.
33. See *Ḥullin* 25a.
34. See Jerusalem Talmud, *Terumot* 11:2.
35. See *Pesaḥim* 16; Rambam, *Sefer Tahara*, *Hilkhot Tumat Okhalin*, chap. 1.
36. See *Eiruvin* 104b; Rashi.
37. See *Makhshirin* 6:4; *Tosefta*, *Teharot* 10:4.
38. See *Ḥullin* 71a; *Nidda* 42b; see also *Ḥizkuni*; Rabbi Samson Raphael Hirsch.
39. See *Ḥullin* 67b.
40. Exodus 19:6.

Tazria

1. See Rashbam.
2. *Kinnim* 2:1.
3. See Ibn Ezra; *Ḥizkuni*; Ramban.
4. See *Arakhin* 3a.
5. See *Nega'im* 1:1.
6. See *Nega'im* 4:3; *Ḥizkuni*.
7. *Sifra*; Rashi; *Shevuot* 6b.
8. See *Megilla* 8b.
9. See Rambam, *Sefer Tahara*, *Hilkhot Tumat Tzara'at* 1:11;

Meshekh Ḥokhma.

10. See *Sifra;* Rambam; Rambam, *Sefer Tahara, Hilkhot Tumat Tzara'at* 3:4.
11. See *Nega'im* 6:8; Rambam, *Sefer Tahara, Hilkhot Tumat Tzara'at* 5:4.
12. *Nega'im* 1:2.
13. *Ha'amek Davar.*
14. See Abravanel.
15. See *Ḥizkuni.*
16. See Rashi; Ramban.
17. See *Nega'im* 10:5.
18. Rashi; Ramban; see *Nega'im* 10:5.
19. See *Sifra; Ḥizkuni.*
20. See Rashi.
21. See *Nega'im* 10:10; Rabbi Shimshon of Saens.
22. Rashi; *Moed Katan* 15a; see Leviticus 10:6, 21:10.
23. Rashi; Ibn Ezra; *Moed Katan* 15a.
24. See Rambam, *Sefer Tahara, Hilkhot Tumat Tzara'at* 13:1, 4.
25. See *Shabbat* 28a.
26. See *Zevaḥim* 95a.
27. See Rav Se'adya Gaon; Rashbam.
28. Rabbi Samson Raphael Hirsch.
29. Rav Se'adya Gaon; Ibn Ezra.
30. Rashi, based on Onkelos.

Metzora

1. See *Bekhor Shor; Ḥizkuni;* Ralbag; Sforno.
2. See *Sota* 16b; Ibn Ezra; Ramban; *Ḥazon Ish; Nega'im* 11:10.
3. See Rashi; *Nega'im* 14:6 ; and see Sifra.
4. See *Sifra*, and commentaries ad loc.; *Nega'im* 14:1.
5. See *Nega'im* 14:1 and Rambam's commentary on the Mishna.
6. See *Ḥizkuni.*
7. See II Kings 5:10, 14.
8. Rashi; *Nega'im* 14:2.
9. *Bava Batra* 9b.
10. See *Sota* 16a.
11. See *Sefat Emet, Sota* 16a, citing Ramban.
12. *Menaḥot* 61a.
13. Based on Rashi.
14. *Meshekh Ḥokhma.*
15. See commentary on 8:23.
16. See Ibn Ezra; *Nega'im* 14:10.
17. See *Sanhedrin* 71a.
18. See Rambam, *Sefer Tahara, Hilkhot Tumat Tzara'at* 16:10; Rambam, commentary on the Mishna, *Nega'im* 12:5.
19. *Nega'im* 12:5; *Sifra*; Rashi.
20. See *Tosafot*, Ran, and Rosh, *Nedarim* 56b; Rashi, *Ḥullin* 10b; *Mishne LaMelekh*, Rambam, *Sefer Tahara, Hilkhot Tumat Tzara'at* 14:5.
21. See *Bekhor Shor* 6:4.
22. See Onkelos; Rashi.
23. See also *Tosefta, Nega'im* 6:4, Rambam, *Sefer Tahara, Hilkhot Tumat Tzara'at* 15:2; *Mishna Aḥarona, Nega'im* 12:6.
24. See *Nega'im* 13:9.
25. Rashi.
26. See *Sifra; Nidda* 56a.
27. Rashi, based on *Sifra.*
28. See *Zavim* 2:4.
29. See Rashi, based on *Torat Kohanim*; Rashbam; Ibn Ezra; Ramban.
30. See 11:32; Numbers 31:23.
31. See *Mikvaot* 1:8; *Para* 6:5, 8:8.
32. See *Nidda* 72b–73a.
33. See Rashi.
34. Ibn Ezra.
35. See *Ḥizkuni.*
36. See *Nidda* 33a; *Sifra*; Rashi.
37. See Rashi; *Bekhor Shor.*
38. See *Sifra*; Rambam's Introduction to Order *Teharot* 9.

Aharei Mot

1. See Leviticus 10:1; Numbers 3:4; see also *Tanḥuma, Aharei Mot* 7.
2. See *Sifra.*
3. Rav Se'adya Gaon; Rashi; Rashbam.
4. Rashi; *Bekhor Shor.*
5. See *Vayikra Rabba* 21; Gra; *Meshekh Ḥokhma.*
6. Mishna *Yoma* 6:1; see also *Aleh Yona* 359.
7. See *Yoma* 36b; *Megilla* 20b.
8. See *Shevuot* 13b–14a.
9. See *Yoma* 39a.
10. Sforno.
11. See *Targum Yonatan*; Rashi; *Shevuot* 14a.
12. *Sifra; Pesaḥim* 75b.
13. See *Responsa of the Rosh* 13:21; *Peri Tzaddik, Aharei Mot* 2.
14. See Exodus 25:22, and Rashi ad loc.; *Sifra, Aharei Mot* 5.
15. See *Yoma* 53b, 55a; see also the Yom Kippur liturgy describing the Yom Kippur Temple service.
16. *Sifra.*
17. See Rav Se'adya Gaon.
18. See Rashi; Ibn Ezra.
19. Ibn Ezra; *Ḥizkuni.*
20. See *Yoma* 44a.
21. See 4:7; Exodus 30:9–10.
22. See *Sifra*; Rashi; Rashbam.
23. See *Sifra* and Rashi, verse 8.
24. Ibn Janaḥ; Rashbam; *Bekhor Shor*; Rambam, *Guide of the Perplexed* 3:46.
25. *Pesaḥim* 26a; *Yoma* 12b, 24a, 60a; Jerusalem Talmud, *Yoma* 7:3.
26. See *Vayikra Rabba* 21:10.
27. See *Yoma* 74b; *Sifra*; Ibn Ezra.
28. See *Sifra*; Rambam, *Sefer HaMadda, Hilkhot Teshuva* 1:3–4.
29. See 23:26–32; Exodus 31:15.
30. See Ibn Ezra.
31. Rashi.
32. See *Sifra.*
33. See Ramban.
34. *Sifra.*
35. For birds, see 11:13–19 and Deuteronomy 14:11–18; for beasts, see Deuteronomy 14:4–5.
36. See *Sifra*; *Ḥullin* 84a.
37. See Ramban, 22:8.
38. *Sifra.*
39. See 11:8 and 15:31, and commentary ad loc.; Rambam, *Sefer HaMitzvot*, positive commandment 109.
40. *Sifra.*
41. See Ramban.
42. See Genesis 42:9; I Samuel 20:30; Isaiah 47:3; *Targum Yonatan* and Ibn Ezra, verse 6.
43. See *Makkot* 5b.
44. See Ibn Ezra; Rashbam; *Bekhor Shor*; Ramban; *Yevamot* 23a.
45. See Rashi; *Yevamot* 3a.
46. See *Yevamot* 22b; *Responsa Yakhin UBoaz* 36.
47. See *Sota* 43b.
48. See commentary on II Samuel 13:13.
49. See *Targum Yonatan.*
50. See Onkelos.
51. See Malbim, Ezekiel 16:43.
52. See *Shabbat* 13a–b.
53. See *Bava Metzia* 59.
54. See Rashi; Ibn Ezra; Ramban; II Samuel 12:30; Jeremiah 19:5; *Sanhedrin* 64.
55. See Deuteronomy 12:29–31; see also *Responsa Yakhin UBoaz* 105 and commentary on Jeremiah 7:31.
56. See verse 29; 20:10–21; *Sifra*; *Yevamot* 84b.
57. See Genesis 19; Isaiah 24:5; Jeremiah 16:18, and Radak ad loc.; Ezekiel 36:17–19.
58. See Ibn Ezra; Rashi, verse 4; Ramban, verse 6; *Yoma* 67b.
59. See *Bekhor Shor*, verse 29.
60. See Numbers 35:33; Deuteronomy 11:10–21; Ezekiel 36:16–21; Ramban here and Genesis 19:5.
61. See 19:20, 21:7; Deuteronomy 7:3, 23:2–4.
62. See, e.g., Rambam, *Sefer HaMadda, Hilkhot Teshuva* 8:1; Ramban, *Torat HaAdam, Sha'ar HaGemul.*
63. See *Moed Katan* 5a; *Yevamot* 21a.

Kedoshim

1. This division of the book into sections is evident in the *Sifra*, the halakhic midrash on Leviticus.
2. See Rashbam; Ibn Ezra; *Vayikra Rabba* 24:5.
3. Several commentators have attempted to explain the structure of this *parasha*, and the order of the laws it presents. See for example Rabbi Samson Raphael Hirsch, Rabbi David Tzvi Hoffman, and *Sefer HaParshiot.*
4. Exodus 19:6.
5. See *Sifra*; Rashi; *Yevamot* 5b.
6. *Ḥizkuni.*
7. Rashi; Ramban.
8. Rashbam.
9. See Rashi; Rashbam; *Zevaḥim* 29a.
10. See Genesis 26:20.

11. See Deuteronomy 24:14; Malachi 3:5; *Sifra*; Rambam, *Sefer Nezikin, Hilkhot Gezeila VaAveda* 1:4.
12. See Rashi; Rabbeinu Baḥya; Abravanel; *Bava Metzia* 58b.
13. See *Sifra*; Rambam, *Sefer HaMadda, Hilkhot Deot* 7:2.
14. See *Sifra*.
15. See Ibn Ezra; *Ḥokhmat Shlomo, Bava Metzia* 61b.
16. *Ḥizkuni*; Ibn Ezra.
17. See Rambam, *Sefer HaMadda, Hilkhot Deot* 6:5; Rambam, *Sefer HaMitzvot* 302; *Sefer HaḤinnukh* 238.
18. See *Sifra, Kedoshim* 2:4; Numbers 31:2.
19. See Abravanel.
20. See *Keritut* 11a.
21. See 26:41; Genesis 17:11–25; Exodus 6:12; Jeremiah 6:10; Ezekiel 44:9.
22. See Ramban.
23. See Rashi; Ramban; Deuteronomy 20:6; Jeremiah 31:5; *Ma'aser Sheni* 5:2; *Rosh HaShana* 31b; Jerusalem Talmud, *Pe'a* 7:5.
24. See Rashi.
25. See Rashbam; Ramban; Rambam, *Guide of the Perplexed* 3:46; see also I Samuel 14:36.
26. *Sanhedrin* 65b–66a; Ibn Ezra.
27. See Deuteronomy 14:1; *Makkot* 20b–21a.
28. See Ramban.
29. See Rashi.
30. See Rashi; *Bava Metzia* 58b.
31. See commentary on 18:21.
32. See *Sanhedrin* 44b–45b.
33. See Ibn Ezra; see also *Shevuot* 13a; Rashi; Maharsha.
34. See commentary on 19:31.
35. Rabbi Eliezer of Metz, *Sefer Yere'im* 272.
36. See *Sanhedrin* 65a, and commentaries ad loc.
37. Exodus 20:11.
38. See Rashi.
39. See Onkelos; Ibn Ezra.
40. See *Sanhedrin* 54a–55a.
41. See Exodus 34:13.
42. See Ibn Ezra.
43. See also Ezekiel 22:8–11.
44. See Rashi.

Emor

1. See Rashbam; Ramban.
2. Rav Se'adya Gaon; *Ḥizkuni*.
3. *Sifra*; Rashi.
4. See Ibn Janaḥ; *Ḥizkuni*; *Adderet Eliyahu*; *Bekhor Shor*, verse 1.
5. See, e.g., Jeremiah 16:6; Ezekiel 7:18.
6. 19:27–28; see also Deuteronomy 14:1.
7. See also *Bekhor Shor*; Abravanel; Rambam, *Sefer HaMadda, Hilkhot Avoda Zara* 12:7.
8. See *Yevamot* 88b; Jerusalem Talmud, *Bikkurim* 5:5; Rambam, *Sefer Avoda, Hilkhot Kelei HaMikdash* 4:1–2; *Sefer HaMitzvot*, positive commandment 32.
9. See Rashi; *Sanhedrin* 50b.
10. See *Sanhedrin* 50b, and Rashi ad loc.
11. See Abravanel.
12. See Rashi; Ibn Ezra; Ramban; *Meshekh Ḥokhma*.
13. See *Sifra*; *HaKetav VehaKabbala*.
14. See *Sifra*; Rashi; Ramban; *Bekhorot* 43b.
15. See *Sifra*; *Bekhorot* 43b–44a.
16. See *Targum Yonatan*; Rashi; *Bekhorot* 38a.
17. See Rashi; *Bekhorot* 41a.
18. See *Targum Yonatan*; Rashi; *Bekhorot* 44b.
19. Rashi; Ibn Ezra.
20. *Sifra*; Rashi; *Bekhorot* 43b.
21. See *Ḥizkuni*; Rabbi Samson Raphael Hirsch.
22. See Rashi.
23. See Rashi.
24. See Rashi; Rashbam; *Zevaḥim* 45b.
25. See 17:15; Ramban.
26. See Rashi.
27. See Ibn Ezra; *Meshekh Ḥokhma*.
28. See Rashi.
29. See Ibn Ezra; 10:14–15; Numbers 18:11–19; *Yevamot* 68a.
30. See Ibn Ezra; Abravanel.
31. See Numbers 6:13 for another example of this unusual self-reflexive use of the term; see also *Sifrei*, Numbers 6:13; *Meshekh Ḥokhma* here.
32. See Rashi, verse 19.
33. See Rashi; Ibn Ezra.
34. *Sifra*.
35. See Rashi; *Bekhorot* 38a, 39a, 41a.
36. See *Bekhorot* 38a–40a; *Torah Temima*.
37. See *Bekhorot* 41a.
38. See Ibn Ezra.
39. See Rashi; Ramban; Rabbi Samson Raphael Hirsch; *Bekhor Shor*; *Ḥizkuni*; *Temura* 7b.
40. See Rashi; *Bekhorot* 39b.
41. See Rashi; *Ḥagiga* 14b.
42. Numbers 28–29.
43. See Ramban; Joel 1:14.
44. See Ramban; Abravanel.
45. See Ramban, 23:2.
46. See commentary on 23:2.
47. See *Sifra*.
48. Exodus 12:2.
49. See *Ha'amek Davar*; Numbers 33:3; *Tosafot, Kiddushin* 37b; *Beur HaGra, Shulḥan Arukh, Yoreh De'a* 399:9.
50. See *Bekhor Shor*, verse 4.
51. See *Bekhor Shor*; *Menaḥot* 63b.
52. See Exodus 9:31–32; *Menaḥot* 68b.
53. See commentary on 1:3, 22:19; Introduction to chap. 2.
54. See *Menaḥot* 65b–66a.
55. See Rashi, *Karetot* 4b.
56. Rashi.
57. See *Menaḥot* 64b, 66b.
58. See Onkelos; *Meshekh Ḥokhma*.
59. See commentary on 2:1.
60. See, e.g., Numbers 15:1–13, 28:12–14.
61. See *Menaḥot* 45b.
62. See *Rosh HaShana* 16a; see also *Resisei Laila* 50–51.
63. Numbers 29:1–6.
64. Rashbam; *Bekhor Shor*.
65. See Numbers 30:14; *Yoma* 74b.
66. See 16:3–29; Numbers 29:7–11.
67. See commentary on 22:9.
68. Numbers 29:12–34.
69. Numbers 28:9; see *Ḥizkuni*; Ramban, verse 2.
70. See *Da'at Zekenim*; Sforno.
71. See *Bekhor Shor*.
72. See Ramban; *Sukka* 35a; *Rambam's Introduction to the Mishna*.
73. See *Sukka* 32a.
74. See *Sukka* 32b.
75. See *Sukka* 33b–34a.
76. See *Sukka* 41a.
77. See, e.g., *Sukka* 6b, 11b–12a.
78. See 16:29, 17:15; Exodus 12:18; see also *Sukka* 28b.
79. See *Sifra*.
80. See Onkelos; Rav Se'adya Gaon; Rashi, Numbers 8:2.
81. See *Sifra*; *Ḥizkuni*.
82. See Rav Se'adya Gaon.
83. See *Sifra*; Rashi.
84. See commentary on Exodus 31:8.
85. Exodus 25:29.
86. See *Menaḥot* 98a; *Ḥizkuni*.
87. Rashi.
88. See Rashi; Ramban.
89. See I Samuel 3:13, and Rashi and Radak ad loc.; I Kings 21:10.
90. See Ramban.
91. See Rashi; *Sanhedrin* 56a.
92. See *Targum Yonatan*; commentary on 19:14.
93. See *Targum Yonatan*; Numbers 9:8, 12:6–8.
94. See *Sifra*; *Ḥizkuni*; *Adderet Eliyahu*.
95. See *Sanhedrin* 78b.
96. See Rav Se'adya Gaon; Ramban; *Bava Kamma* 83b–84a.
97. See Rashi; Ibn Ezra.
98. Exodus 21:12, 24.

Behar

1. Onkelos; Rashbam; *Ḥizkuni*; Ramban.
2. See Rav Se'adya Gaon.
3. See Deuteronomy 15:1–9.
4. See Rashi; Exodus 19:13.
5. See Exodus 3:1.
6. See *Bava Metzia* 106a.
7. Based on Ramban and Sforno.
8. See *Sifra*.
9. Based on Onkelos and Rashi; *Arakhin* 31a.
10. *Ḥizkuni*.
11. See Rashi; Ibn Ezra.
12. See Numbers 35:2.
13. See *Bekhor Shor*; see also *Arakhin* 33b.
14. See Rashi; *Bekhor Shor*.
15. Rashi; see *Kiddushin* 22a.
16. See commentary on Numbers 12:7.
17. See Rashi; Rambam, *Sefer Kinyan, Hilkhot Avadim* 1:5.
18. See *Sifra*.
19. See Rav Se'adya Gaon; *Bekhor Shor*.

Behukotai

1. See *Or HaHayyim*.
2. See Rashi.
3. See *Sifra*.
4. See *Sifra;* Rashi; Ramban.
5. See Numbers 11:29; Ezekiel 36:20; Zephaniah 2:10.
6. *Bekhor Shor*; *Ḥizkuni*.
7. See also Ezekiel 36:9; Judges 6:14; II Kings 13:23.
8. See, e.g., 20:3–6; Jeremiah 21:10; Ezekiel 14:8.
9. See Rashbam; Genesis 4:15, 24; I Samuel 2:5; Isaiah 4:1, 30:26; Jeremiah 15:9; Psalms 79:12; *Responsa of the Rambam* 271.
10. See Ezekiel 24:21; *Targum Yonatan*; Rashi.
11. See Jeremiah 14:19.
12. See *Avot deRabbi Natan* 38; *Tanḥuma, Behar* 1.
13. See *Makkot* 24a.
14. See *Bava Batra* 97a.
15. See *Temura* 4b.
16. See Rashi; Rashbam; *Temura* 32b–33a.
17. See *Arakhin* 14a.
18. See Onkelos; Rashi; *Bekhorot* 50a.
19. See *Bekhorot* 5a; see also commentary on Exodus 38:26.
20. See also Exodus 13:1, 12, 15, 34:19; Numbers 8:17, 18:15; Deuteronomy 15:19.
21. See Ramban.
22. Ibn Ezra; see Exodus 34:20; *Bekhorot* 11a.
23. See Rashi; *Bekhor Shor*; Ramban; see also *Arakhin* 6b.
24. See Numbers 21:2–3; Deuteronomy 2:34.
25. See Deuteronomy 14:22; *Karetot* 4b; *Bekhorot* 54a; Jerusalem Talmud, *Bikkurim* 1:3.
26. See Deuteronomy 14:22–27.
27. See *Bekhorot* 58b.

Book of Numbers

Bemidbar

1. See *Adderet Eliyahu*.
2. Ibn Ezra.
3. See Rashi.
4. Rashbam.
5. Ibn Ezra, verse 49.
6. See Onkelos.
7. See *Pesaḥim* 68a.
8. See Sforno; Ramban, 1:47.
9. *Bekhor Shor*.
10. Leviticus 10:1–2.
11. See *Bekhor Shor* and *Ḥizkuni*, here and 8:9.
12. See Mishna *Zevaḥim* 14:4; Rashi, Exodus 19:22.
13. Exodus 12:29, 13:2, 12–13, 22:28, 34:19–20.
14. See Rashi; *Shabbat* 135b.
15. See Rashi.
16. Rav Se'adya Gaon.
17. Rashi.
18. Ibn Ezra.
19. See Rashi; *Tosafot, Bekhorot* 4a.
20. Exodus 30:13; Leviticus 27:25.
21. See Rav Eliezer of Beaugency, Ezekiel 9:1.
22. See Rashi; Ibn Ezra; Ramban.
23. Sforno.
24. Rav Se'adya Gaon; Rashi; Ibn Ezra.
25. See *Ḥizkuni*; see also Rav Yosef Kara, Rav Yeshaya of Trani, and Malbim, I Samuel 6:19; Song of Songs 1:6, and Rashi ad loc.

Naso

1. See Ibn Ezra; *Bekhor Shor*; Sforno; see also II Chronicles 30:17, 35:14.
2. See Rabbi Samson Raphael Hirsch.
3. See Abravanel.
4. See *Bemidbar Rabba* 6.
5. See Leviticus 13–14.
6. See Leviticus 15.
7. See Ibn Ezra; *HeKetav VeHaKabbala*.
8. Leviticus 5:14–25.
9. Leviticus 7:14, 7:31–34, 22:14, 27:19–23; Numbers 18:20.
10. See *Or HaHayyim*.
11. See Rashi; *Bekhor Shor*.
12. *Sifrei*; Rashi; see *Ḥizkuni*; Rabbi Isaac Samuel Reggio.
13. Ibn Ezra.
14. Exodus 30:17–21.
15. See *Sota* 7a.
16. See Rashi.
17. See Rashi; Rav Se'adya Gaon; *Ḥizkuni*.
18. See Rashi; *Bemidbar Rabba* 8:19.
19. See Mishna *Sota* 3:4–5.
20. *Bekhor Shor*.
21. Rashi.
22. Rashi 6:2.
23. See *Nazir* 34b.
24. See Leviticus 21:1–12.
25. See Ibn Ezra; Rav Se'adya Gaon; *Or HaHayyim*.
26. See Rashbam.
27. See *Targum Yonatan*; Rashi; *Bemidbar Rabba* 10:17.
28. See Mishna *Temura* 7:4.
29. See Rashi.
30. See *Hullin* 49a. Interestingly, this interpretation is stated by Rabbi Yishmael, who was a priest himself and who heard it from his ancestors.
31. Leviticus 9:24.
32. Exodus 18:13–26.
33. See *Bemidbar Rabba* 12:17; Rambam, Mishna *Kelim* 18:2.
34. Exodus 25:1–7.
35. See Sforno; *Ha'amek Davar*.
36. See *Sifrei*.

Behaalotekha

1. See Exodus 27:20–21; Leviticus 24:1–4.
2. See Rashi.
3. See *Targum Yonatan*; Rashi; *Megilla* 21b.
4. See *Responsa of the Rivash* 410.
5. See Rashbam; *Hizkuni*; *Bekhor Shor*.
6. See *Ha'amek Davar*; *Ḥizkuni*.
7. See Malbim.
8. *Bekhor Shor*.
9. *Bekhor Shor*; see Rashi; Ramban.
10. See Shabbat 34b; Rashi, Ramban, and Ibn Ezra, Exodus 12:6.
11. See *Pesaḥim* 96a.
12. See Sforno.
13. Exodus 33:11.
14. See Ramban.
15. See Exodus 19:16, 20:18, 40:34.
16. Ramban.
17. See Sforno.
18. Exodus 13:21; Deuteronomy 1:33; *Menaḥot* 95a; Ibn Ezra; *Pa'ane'aḥ Raza* here.
19. Ramban.
20. See *Menaḥot* 28b; Rashi, 10:2; *Bemidbar Rabba* 15:15; *Bekhor Shor*, Deuteronomy 31:28.
21. Rashi.
22. See *Sifrei*; Rashi; Ibn Ezra; *Tanḥuma, Yitro* 4.
23. See Ibn Ezra.
24. See Ramban; Sforno.
25. See *Targum Yonatan*; Ibn Ezra.
26. See Isaiah 30:15.
27. See Onkelos; *Targum Yonatan*.
28. See Ramban.
29. See *Sifrei*.
30. See *Akedat Yitzḥak*.
31. See *Yoma* 75a.
32. See Ibn Ezra.
33. Ibn Ezra.
34. Rashi; *Sifrei, Behaalotekha* 37; *Sanhedrin* 17a.
35. See Ibn Ezra; Rashbam.
36. Onkelos; Rashbam.
37. Ibn Ezra.
38. *Moed Katan* 16b.
39. See commentary on Genesis 37:28.
40. See *Nega'im* 2:1; Ibn Ezra.

41. See Rashi; *Sifrei, Bemidbar* 99; see also Rambam, *Sefer HaMadda, Hilkhot Yesodei HaTorah* 7:6.
42. See Ibn Ezra.

43. See *Sifrei, Bemidbar* 100; see also *Tzeror Hamor*.
44. See Ramban.
45. See Rabbeinu Baḥya; *Tzeror Hamor; Shabbat* 97a.

46. Rashi; Rashbam.
47. See II Kings 5:11.
48. See Sforno.

Shelah

1. Ibn Ezra.
2. Joshua 14:7.
3. See Joshua 17:14–18.
4. See *Sota* 34a, based on Deuteronomy 1:36; Joshua 14:8–14; Judges 1:20; see also Ibn Ezra; Rashbam; *Ha'amek Davar*; Ezekiel 14:1, and Rav Eliezer of Beaugency ad loc.
5. Malbim.
6. See, e.g., Exodus 3:8.
7. See Ramban.
8. See Genesis 6:4; Deuteronomy 9:2.
9. Based on Onkelos; Rashi.
10. Based on *Or HaḤayyim.*

11. See *Sota* 35a, and Maharal ad loc.
12. Exodus 34:6–7; *Da'at Zekenim.*
13. See Rav Se'adya Gaon; Rashi.
14. See *Berakhot* 7a; Ramban; Radak, Hosea 2:15.
15. See also Rashi.
16. See Ramban.
17. See Rashi; Ibn Ezra.
18. See *Megilla* 23b.
19. Rashi.
20. Rashbam.
21. See Rashi.

22. See Sforno; Rabbi Samson Raphael Hirsch.
23. See *Sota* 35a, and Rashi ad loc.
24. See 21:3, and *Bekhor Shor* ad loc.
25. See *Karetot* 8b–9a.
26. Rav Se'adya Gaon.
27. *Sifrei.*
28. *Sifrei;* Rashi; *Horayot* 8a.
29. Exodus 20:2–3.
30. See Rashi; *Karetot* 7b.
31. Exodus 31:14.
32. See Rashi; Rashbam.

Korah

1. Based on Rav Se'adya Gaon; Rashbam; Ibn Ezra.
2. Based on Rashi.
3. See Ramban; Sforno.
4. See, e.g., Exodus 3:8, 13:5.
5. See *Akedat Yitzḥak.*
6. Based on Rashbam; *Bekhor Shor.*
7. Ramban.
8. Based on Ramban; Abravanel.
9. Ibn Ezra; *Bekhor Shor.*
10. Genesis 3:19.

11. Leviticus 10:1; see also Numbers 3:4.
12. See Rashi; Ibn Ezra; Sforno.
13. See Ramban.
14. See Rashi; *Tanḥuma, Aharei Mot* 8.
15. Leviticus 10:11; Numbers 3:4.
16. Ibn Ezra; see *Tamid* 26b; Rambam, *Sefer Avoda, Hilkhot Beit HaBeḥira* 8:4.
17. *Bekhor Shor.*
18. See Rashi; *Sota* 15a.
19. Leviticus 6:9, 19, 7:6.
20. See Leviticus 7:14, 32, 34.

21. See Rashi; *Bekhorot* 53b.
22. See Leviticus 22:11; Mishna *Zevaḥim* 5:6.
23. See Mishna *Terumot* 11:9; *Sifra, Emor* 5.
24. Exodus 13:13.
25. See *Bava Batra* 90a; see also commentary on Numbers 3:47.
26. See II Chronicles 13:5.
27. See *Ḥullin* 133b; Rambam, *Sefer Zera'im, Hilkhot Bikkurim* 1.
28. See Rav Se'adya Gaon; *HaKetav VehaKabbala;* see also *Ḥizkuni; Bekhor Shor.*
29. See Rav Se'adya Gaon; Rashi.
30. Based on Ibn Ezra; *Ḥizkuni.*

Hukat

1. See Zechariah 2:4; Lamentations 3:53.
2. See *Shabbat* 27b–28a, and *Tosafot* ad loc.
3. See Rashi; *Ha'amek Davar.*
4. See 13:23–27; Deuteronomy 8:8.
5. See, e.g., Exodus 14:16.
6. See 17:25; Ibn Ezra.
7. See Rashi; *Bemidbar Rabba* 19:9.
8. *Bekhor Shor;* see Ibn Ezra; Rashi.
9. Ramban; see Rashbam.
10. Based on Rav Se'adya Gaon.
11. Leviticus 10:3.
12. See, e.g., Genesis 36:1, 8, 9.
13. Rashi.

14. Ibn Ezra; see Abravanel, Judges 13:1.
15. Rashbam.
16. Ibn Ezra.
17. Rabbi Samson Raphael Hirsch.
18. 33:38–39.
19. Rashi; *Bekhor Shor.*
20. See Rashi.
21. See Rashi; *Tanḥuma, Ḥukat* 42.
22. See Rashi; *Rosh HaShana* 3a.
23. See Ramban.
24. Rashi.
25. See Jerusalem Talmud, *Rosh HaShana* 3:9; Rashi.
26. See Rashi.

27. Based on Ibn Ezra; Ramban.
28. Exodus 15:1.
29. Rashbam.
30. Rashbam.
31. Ibn Ezra.
32. See Genesis 32:23–24.
33. See commentary on Isaiah 28:14.
34. See *Ḥizkuni.*
35. See Rashi; Rav Se'adya Gaon.
36. See Rashbam; Ibn Ezra; Rabbi Samson Raphael Hirsch.
37. See Deuteronomy 3:8.
38. Deuteronomy 3:11.

Balak

1. Deuteronomy 2:9.
2. See Ramban; *Bemidbar Rabba* 20:4.
3. Rashi; Rashbam.
4. *Targum Yonatan; Ḥizkuni.*
5. See *HaKetav VehaKabbala.*
6. See Rashi; Ibn Ezra; Ramban; *Ḥizkuni.*
7. See Rashi; *Bemidbar Rabba* 10:8.
8. See Rashbam.
9. See Ibn Ezra.

10. See Ramban.
11. See *Sota* 34a.
12. Onkelos; Rav Se'adya Gaon; Rashi.
13. *Targum Yonatan; Bemidbar Rabba* 20:18; see *Sota* 10a.
14. See also I Samuel 10:12; Isaiah 14:4; Micah 2:4.
15. See Onkelos; Ibn Ezra.
16. *Bekhor Shor;* Samuel David Luzzatto.
17. Rabbeinu Baḥya, based on Onkelos.
18. See Rashi.

19. Onkelos; Rashi; Rashbam.
20. See Rashi; Ibn Ezra.
21. See Onkelos; Rav Se'adya Gaon; Rashi.
22. See, e.g., Genesis 17:3; Ezekiel 1:28.
23. Rashi; *Bekhor Shor;* see also Jeremiah 50:17.
24. See Rav Se'adya Gaon; Ibn Ezra.
25. See Rashi.
26. Ibn Ezra.
27. Ramban.

28. See Rashi; Ibn Ezra; Ramban.
29. Rashi; Rav Se'adya Gaon; Ibn Ezra.
30. See I Samuel 15:6; Rashi.
31. Rashi.
32. See Onkelos; *Targum Yonatan*.
33. See Genesis 10:4.
34. See Rashi.
35. See 25:14 and onward.
36. See Rashi; *Ḥizkuni*.

Pinhas

1. See commentary on 26:53.
2. See Rashi.
3. Genesis 46:16.
4. See Genesis 46:12; I Chronicles 2:3.
5. See Genesis 46:21; Rashi.
6. See commentary on Genesis 46:15.
7. See *Sifrei*; Ramban.
8. See *Bava Batra* 115a–b; Ramban.
9. See Rashi, Numbers 20:26, 33:38; *Berakhot* 8a.
10. See commentary on 20:13.
11. Sforno.
12. See commentary on Exodus 28:30.
13. Rashi; Ibn Ezra; see also Joshua 14:1.
14. See Rabbi Samson Raphael Hirsch.
15. See Joel 1:14; see also commentary on Leviticus 23:2.
16. See *Megilla* 7b.
17. Leviticus 23:3.
18. See commentary on Leviticus 23:7.
19. See *Shevuot* 2a.
20. Rashi.
21. See Leviticus 23:10–20.
22. See Leviticus 16.
23. Deuteronomy 16:8.
24. See also Ramban, Leviticus 23:36.

Matot

1. See *Nedarim* 79a; Rambam, *Sefer Hafla'a, Hilkhot Nedarim* 12:1–11.
2. See, e.g., *Bekhor Shor*; Ramban.
3. See Deuteronomy 20:1–4.
4. See Rashi.
5. Rav Se'adya Gaon; others suggest that this commandment was given even before they set out to war.
6. See Rav Se'adya Gaon; Rashi; Ibn Ezra.
7. See *HaKetav VehaKabbala*.
8. See Ramban, verse 49.
9. See Ibn Ezra.
10. See *Ḥizkuni*.
11. Joshua 1:14.
12. See Ramban; Jerusalem Talmud, *Bikkurim* 1:8; *Ha'amek Davar*, Deuteronomy 1.
13. See commentary on Joshua 13:30.
14. See Rashi; Ramban.

Masei

1. Deuteronomy 1:46.
2. See also Exodus 12:12.
3. See Exodus 14:2.
4. See Exodus 15:23–25.
5. Genesis 46:27.
6. See commentary on 13:21.
7. Exodus 17:8.
8. Based on Ba'al HaTurim.
9. See *Targum Yonatan*.
10. See Deuteronomy 2:8.
11. See Rashi.
12. See *Ta'anit* 30b.
13. See Rashi.
14. See Ra'avad, *Bava Batra* 117a, 122a; see also Ramban, Numbers 26:5.
15. Based on Rav Se'adya Gaon.
16. See Rashi; *Gittin* 8a.
17. See Rashi.
18. See Rashbam.
19. Onkelos; see commentary on 13:21.
20. Rashi; see commentary on II Kings 14:25.
21. See *Nedarim* 81a; Rashi.
22. See Ramban.
23. See Joshua 20–21; I Samuel 22:9–19.
24. *Makkot* 9b.
25. Translation based on *Sifrei*; Rashi.
26. Rabbi Samson Raphael Hirsch.
27. *Sanhedrin* 45b.
28. See Rashi; *Targum Yonatan*.
29. See Rashi.
30. See Rav Se'adya Gaon; Ramban.
31. See *Targum Yonatan*.
32. See Leviticus 25:10.Numbers

Book of Deuteronomy

Devarim

1. Rabbi David Tzvi Hoffman; see also *Adderet Eliyahu*.
2. See *Zohar*, *Pinhas* 232a; see also Yalkut HaReuveni.
3. See *Yevamot* 4a.
4. Rashbam.
5. See Ibn Ezra; *Bekhor Shor*.
6. Rashi.
7. See Numbers 34:4.
8. Gra; see also *HaKetav VehaKabbala*.
9. See Joshua 9:10, 12:4, 13:12, 31.
10. See Rashi; Ramban.
11. Onkelos.
12. *Bekhor Shor*; see Exodus 2:21; II Samuel 7:29.
13. See *Ḥizkuni*; Rashi; Ramban.
14. *Bekhor Shor*.
15. See Numbers 13:27–33; see also verse 28.
16. Numbers 20.
17. See Rabbeinu Baḥya, Numbers 13:2; Abravanel, Numbers 20:1; see also commentary on 3:26 and Numbers 20:13.
18. See Rashi; Rashbam; Ibn Ezra; *Bekhor Shor*.
19. Ibn Ezra.
20. See Genesis 36:8–30.
21. See Rashi; Rashbam; Genesis 15:13–19; Obadiah 1:19.
22. See Genesis 42:1–3.
23. Rashi; see Hosea 3:2.
24. See Hosea 13:5, and Rav Yeshaya of Trani ad loc.
25. See *Bekhor Shor*.
26. See 23:8; Numbers 20:14; Malachi 1:2; Obadiah 1:10.
27. See Genesis 36:20–30.
28. See *Targum Yonatan*, Numbers 21:12.
29. See Jeremiah 50:24; Daniel 11:25.
30. See Genesis 10:14.
31. See Judges 11:12–27.
32. *Sefer Shofetim*, *Hilkhot Melakhim* 6:1.
33. See Rashi; Rashbam.
34. See Rashi; commentary on Joshua 15:3.
35. Rav Se'adya Gaon.
36. See II Kings 15:25.
37. See Ramban.
38. See *Eiruvin* 48a.
39. See Exodus 17:9–10.

Va'ethanan

1. See Radak, Zechariah 10:10.
2. *Ḥizkuni*.
3. Numbers 25; Deuteronomy 4:3.
4. Numbers 25.
5. See *Shabbat* 88a.
6. See *Sanhedrin* 99b.
7. Rashi; Onkelos.
8. See II Kings 18:4.
9. Genesis 1:17–18.
10. See Rashi; Rashbam; *Avoda Zara* 55a; *Tosafot, Sanhedrin* 63b; *Oraḥ Ḥayyim* 156:1.
11. See Rashbam.
12. Numbers 20:9–13; see also Psalms 106:32.
13. Ibn Ezra; *Ḥizkuni*.
14. See Ibn Ezra; Ramban; Sforno.
15. See Rashi; Numbers 5:12–14, 25:11; Song of Songs 8:6.
16. *Targum Yonatan*.
17. See Genesis 32:30; Exodus 33:20; Judges 13:22.
18. Rashi.
19. See Rav Se'adya Gaon; Rashi.
20. See Ibn Ezra; *Ḥizkuni*; Sforno.
21. See Rashi.
22. Abravanel.
23. Numbers 35:9–28.
24. Rabbi David Tzvi Hoffman.
25. *HaKetav VehaKabbala*; *Da'at Mikra*.
26. Rashi; see Rabbeinu Baḥya.
27. Ibn Ezra; *Ḥizkuni*; Sforno.
28. See Exodus 19:12, 20:16.
29. Rav Ḥasdai Crescas, in the beginning of *Or Hashem*; Abravanel.
30. Rambam, *Sefer HaMitzvot*, positive commandment 1.
31. See commentary on Ezekiel 18; Radak, Ezekiel 18:5; *Berakhot* 7a.
32. See Rambam, *Guide of the Perplexed* 1:54.
33. See commentary on Exodus 20:7.
34. Rashi; *Shabbat* 87b.
35. See Exodus 16:29.
36. Genesis 2:1–3.
37. Rashi.
38. See *Bekhor Shor*, Exodus 20:11.
39. See Rashi.
40. See *Onkelos*; Rashi; *Ḥizkuni*; *Sanhedrin* 17a.
41. See Ramban; *Avoda Zara* 4b.
42. See Rashbam.
43. See *Bekhor Shor*.
44. See Rashi.
45. Ibn Ezra.
46. See *Shabbat* 57b; Rav Se'adya Gaon; *Bekhor Shor*.
47. *Kiddushin* 36a.
48. Rashi.
49. Ramban.
50. *Bekhor Shor*.
51. See Exodus 17:6–7; Rashi, Exodus 17:8.
52. See Ramban.
53. See Ibn Ezra.
54. *Ḥizkuni*.
55. Sforno; Ibn Ezra.
56. Onkelos.
57. See Genesis 34:9; I Samuel 18:21.

Ekev

1. Rashi.
2. See Rav Se'adya Gaon.
3. See Exodus 23:27–29.
4. See Rashi and Ibn Ezra.
5. Onkelos.
6. *Ḥizkuni*.
7. *Ha'amek Davar*.
8. See Rambam, *Guide of the Perplexed* 3:24.
9. See *Targum Yonatan*; Rashi, Exodus 34:26; Rashbam and Ibn Ezra, Leviticus 2:11.
10. Ibn Ezra.
11. See Exodus 16:4, 19; Numbers 21:5.
12. Onkelos; Ibn Ezra.
13. Based on Abravanel.
14. *Ḥullin* 90b.
15. See Ramban.
16. See Ramban, 4:9.
17. See Exodus 32:32.
18. See Numbers 11.
19. See Exodus 17.
20. See Numbers 11.
21. Rashi; *Ḥizkuni*; Rabbi Samson Raphael Hirsch.
22. Mishna *Zevaḥim* 14:4; Jerusalem Talmud, *Megilla* 1:11; *Bemidbar Rabba* 4:6; see Exodus 32:26.
23. See Rashi; Ibn Ezra; *Adderet Eliyahu, Ki Tisa*.
24. See Ibn Ezra, Joel 2:13.
25. See Isaiah 1:1–17; Malachi 1:6–13.
26. See Psalms 113:5–6.
27. Rashi.
28. See Ramban, Exodus 13:16; commentary on Ezekiel 24:17.

Re'eh

1. See Rashi; *Sota* 32a.
2. See *Sota* 33b.
3. See Rashi.
4. See *Avoda Zara* 46a; commentary on II Samuel 11:21.
5. See Rashi; Rashbam; Ramban.
6. Ramban.
7. See Mishna *Zevaḥim* 14:5–9.
8. See commentary on Leviticus 17:4.
9. Leviticus 17:14.
10. See also commentary on Leviticus 3:17; Rambam, *Guide of the Perplexed* 3:46.
11. Verses 15–16; *Ḥizkuni*; Ibn Ezra; as stated above, the Sages expounded the earlier verses as referring to consecrated animals that became disqualified for the altar.
12. Rashi.
13. See *Bekhor Shor*; *Ḥizkuni*; see also Judges 8:19; Song of Songs 8:1.
14. See *Bekhor Shor*, 21:21.
15. See Rashi; *Bekhor Shor*.
16. See *Midrash Tanna'im*; Tractate *Kutim*, 1:12.
17. Vilna Gaon; Rabbi Samson Raphael Hirsch.
18. See *Sifrei*; *Yalkut Shimoni, Behar* 667.
19. See *Bekhor Shor*; Ramban; Rashbam, Exodus 23:19.
20. *Sifrei*; Rashi; *Bekhorot* 53b.
21. See *Sifrei*; *Sefer HaḤinnukh* 360.
22. See *Ḥizkuni*.
23. Rabbi Samson Raphael Hirsch.
24. See Rashbam.
25. See Ramban, verse 11.
26. See Rambam, *Sefer Zera'im, Hilkhot Mattenot Aniyyim* 7:1–7.
27. See *Bava Batra* 9b; Rambam, *Sefer Zera'im, Hilkhot Mattenot Aniyyim* 10:4–5.
28. See Exodus 22:2; *Kiddushin* 14b; Rashi.
29. See Isaiah 16:14; *Kiddushin* 17a, and *Tosafot* ad loc.; Ibn Ezra; Rashbam.
30. See *Pesaḥim* 70b; Jerusalem Talmud, *Pesaḥim* 6:1; *Sifrei*.
31. See *Pesaḥim* 115b–116a.
32. Exodus 12:10.
33. *Sifrei*.
34. See Leviticus 23:8.

Shofetim

1. See Rashi and Ibn Ezra; Rambam, *Sefer HaMadda, Hilkhot Avoda Zara* 6:6; see also Joshua 24:26.
2. See Leviticus 22:21–25.
3. See *Sifrei, Devarim* 147.
4. See Rabbi Samson Raphael Hirsch.
5. Sforno.
6. See 8:19; Exodus 22:19.
7. See *Sanhedrin* 45a.
8. Ibn Ezra; Rashbam.
9. Rashi.
10. See *Targum Yonatan*; Rashi.
11. See Ralbag, II Samuel 20:23.
12. See Micah 5:9.
13. See Mishna *Sanhedrin* 2:4; Onkelos; *Targum Yonatan*.
14. See Ibn Ezra.
15. Malachi 1:7.
16. See *Ḥullin* 134b.
17. See Rashi.

18. See Rashi; *Sukka* 55b–56a.
19. See Ramban.
20. See Rashi.
21. See Rashi, Leviticus 19:26.
22. Ibn Ezra.
23. See *Sanhedrin* 65a.
24. See Onkelos; Ramban.
25. See *Targum Yonatan* and *Ḥizkuni*, verse 14.
26. See Rashi.
27. 5:20–28; Exodus 20:15–18.
28. See Rashi; *Makkot* 10a.
29. See *Makkot* 9b.
30. See Rashi; *Makkot* 7b.
31. See similar uses of the term in I Samuel 21:6 and Jeremiah 51:14.
32. See Genesis 15:18.
33. See *Makkot* 10b.
34. See Exodus 21:14; Numbers 35:31.
35. See Rashi; *Shevuot* 30a.
36. See Mishna *Avot* 1:18.
37. See *Sota* 42a; *Nazir* 47b.
38. Translation based on Ibn Ezra; see also Ramban.
39. See Leviticus 19:24 and the sources cited in the commentary ad loc.
40. See also commentary on I Samuel 8:10.
41. See Numbers 33:55.
42. See Onkelos; Rashi.
43. Rashi.
44. Rashbam; see Ibn Ezra.
45. See *Targum Yonatan*; Rashi; *Sota* 44b.
46. See Mishna *Para* 1:1.
47. See *Sota* 46a.
48. See *Sota* 45b; Rashi; *HaKetav VehaKabbala*.
49. Based on Rambam, *Sefer Nezikin, Hilkhot Rotze'aḥ* 9:2; Abravanel.
50. See Rashi; *Sota* 46b.
51. Numbers 35:33.

Ki Tetze

1. *Sifrei*; Rashi.
2. See *Yevamot* 48a; Ramban.
3. See Rashi; *Kiddushin* 21b; *Yevamot* 48a.
4. *Bekhor Shor*.
5. See Rashi; Ramban.
6. See Rav Se'adya Gaon; Ibn Ezra.
7. *Sanhedrin* 71b.
8. See *Bekhor Shor*.
9. See *Targum Yonatan*; Rashi; *Sanhedrin* 46b.
10. See Ibn Ezra; Ramban; Joshua 8:29, 10:26–27; Ezekiel 39:12.
11. See I Samuel 9:25; II Samuel 11:2; Isaiah 22:1.
12. Rashbam.
13. Onkelos; Rashi.
14. Ibn Ezra here, and Hagai 2:12.
15. See *Kiddushin* 39a.
16. Ibn Ezra.
17. See Rashbam; *Bekhor Shor*.
18. See Leviticus 21:18; I Kings 12:11; *Ketubot* 46a.
19. Verse 29; *Ketubot* 10a; Rambam, *Guide of the Perplexed* 3:49.
20. See *Ketubot* 39b.
21. *Sifrei*; *Ketubot* 46a.
22. *Sanhedrin* 42b.
23. See *Ketubot* 45b.
24. See Ramban.
25. See Sforno.
26. Genesis 29:21; see also Joel 1:8.
27. Exodus 20:13.
28. See *Ketubot* 41b.
29. See *Ketubot* 39b.
30. See Rashi; *Yevamot* 75b.
31. See *Midrash Tanna'im*, as well as the following verse.
32. See *Kiddushin* 69a.
33. Numbers 23–24.
34. See Malachi 1:2.
35. See Genesis 45–47.
36. Based on Ramban; *Bekhor Shor*; *Ḥizkuni*; *Pesaḥim* 68a; Radak, Jeremiah 41:9; see also commentary on Numbers 5:3.
37. Onkelos; *Targum Yonatan*.
38. See *Targum Yonatan*; Rashi.
39. *Targum Yonatan*.
40. See Rashi; *Gittin* 45a.
41. See Ibn Ezra; *Meshekh Ḥokhma*; II Kings 23:7; Hosea 4:14; Ibn Ezra, Hagai 2:12.
42. See *Temura* 30b.
43. Ibn Ezra; Rashbam.
44. See above, 12:5–6; Leviticus 23:38; *Rosh HaShana* 4.
45. See Onkelos; Rashi; *Bava Metzia* 87b, 92a.
46. See Leviticus 21:7.
47. Rabbi Joseph Kimḥi; Rabbi Samson Raphael Hirsch.
48. See *Bekhor Shor*; Ramban; Sforno; Rabbi Samson Raphael Hirsch.
49. *Targum Yonatan*; see Ibn Ezra.
50. Rashi; *Sota* 44a.
51. 20:4; Rashi; *Sota* 44a.
52. See Onkelos; Rashi; 21:14, and Ibn Ezra and Ramban ad loc.; *Sanhedrin* 88b.
53. Leviticus 13–14.
54. Numbers 12:1–16.
55. See *Targum Yonatan*; Rashi; *Bava Metzia* 114b.
56. Ibn Ezra; Radak, II Samuel 21:1.
57. *Ta'anit* 8b.
58. See 22:4; Genesis 24:64; II Kings 5:21.
59. *Makkot* 22b.
60. Rabbi Samson Raphael Hirsch.
61. See, e.g., *Makkot* 16b.
62. See Sforno; *Makkot* 22b–23a.
63. See *Bava Metzia* 91a.
64. See Jerusalem Talmud, *Yevamot* 1:1.
65. See Ramban; Ramban, Genesis 38:8; *Yevamot* 24a.
66. See *Yevamot* 44a.
67. *Sifrei*; Rashi.
68. Rabbi Samson Raphael Hirsch.
69. See Exodus 21:18–25.
70. See *Sifrei*.
71. 19:21; Exodus 21:24.
72. See *Bava Kamma* 28a, 86b.
73. See *Bava Batra* 89b.
74. See Exodus 17:8–16.
75. Rashi citing *Sifrei*; *Bekhor Shor*; Ibn Ezra.
76. *Ḥizkuni*, citing *Mekhilta*, *Beshalaḥ*.

Ki Tavo

1. See *Kiddushin* 37b.
2. See Rashi; *Targum Yonatan*; *Sukka* 47b.
3. See Ibn Ezra; *Ḥizkuni*; Sforno.
4. See Rashi; *Sifrei*, *Ki Tavo* 301; Passover Haggadah.
5. Ibn Ezra.
6. See *Targum Yonatan*.
7. See Rashi; Jerusalem Talmud, *Ma'aser Sheni* 5:5.
8. See 14:22–27; Leviticus 27:30.
9. See Ibn Ezra; Ramban.
10. See *Targum Yerushalmi*; *Da'at Zekenim*.
11. Exodus 19:5.
12. Exodus 19:6.
13. See Joshua 8:30–35.
14. See Exodus 20:22.
15. See *Ḥizkuni*; see also *Sefer HaParshiyot*.
16. See commentary on 11:29.
17. See Rashi, 27:12; *Sota* 37a; Joshua 8:33.
18. Jerusalem Talmud, *Sota* 7:4.
19. See Rashbam.
20. See *Bekhor Shor*.
21. See *Responsa of the Rambam* 273.
22. Leviticus 19:14.
23. See *Targum Yonatan*; Rashi.
24. See Ibn Ezra.
25. See *Sanhedrin* 53a.
26. See *Ḥizkuni*, 27:19.
27. See also commentary on Leviticus 20:17 and Ezekiel 22:11.
28. See *Targum Yonatan*; Rashi; *Pirkei deRabbi Eliezer* 52.
29. See Jerusalem Talmud, *Sota* 7:4; see also *Ha'amek Davar*.
30. See Ibn Ezra.
31. See Psalms 144:14.
32. *Targum Yonatan*; Rashi.
33. Rashi; see I Kings 8:37.
34. See Exodus 9:9–11.
35. See 4:28; Jeremiah 16:13; Rabbi Samson Raphael Hirsch; see also *Avoda Zara* 8a.
36. Rashi.
37. See Rashbam; Ibn Ezra; Rabbi Samson Raphael Hirsch.
38. Onkelos.
39. Onkelos; Rashi.
40. See *Gittin* 58a.
41. See Onkelos; *Targum Yonatan*; Rashi.
42. See *Bekhor Shor* 29:15.
43. Onkelos.

Nitzavim

1. See Ramban.
2. See, e.g., Genesis 24:41; Ezekiel 17:16.
3. See *Targum Yonatan*; Rashi.
4. See Rashi; *Bekhor Shor*.
5. See Rashbam.
6. See Genesis 18:20–19:29.
7. See Rashi; Rabbeinu Baḥya; commentary on 4:19.
8. See *Targum Yonatan*; Rashi.
9. Onkelos.
10. See Ramban; Sforno.
11. See *Bekhor Shor*.

Vayelekh

1. *Bekhor Shor*.
2. See Rashi; *Rosh HaShana* 11a.
3. See Ibn Ezra; Numbers 27:17; Joshua 14:11; I Samuel 18:13.
4. Rashi; see also *Bekhor Shor*; Sforno.
5. Rashi, 34:7.
6. See Onkelos, *Targum Yonatan*.
7. See *Sota* 41b.
8. *Bekhor Shor*; *Ḥizkuni*.
9. *Bekhor Shor*.
10. See Rashi; Radak, Ezekiel 17:5.
11. See Ibn Ezra; Rabbi Samson Raphael Hirsch; Radak, II Samuel 17:28, Jeremiah 19:4, Ezekiel 17:5; Responsa of the Rashba 1:134.
12. See Joshua 1.
13. See *Bava Batra* 14a.

Haazinu

1. See *Ḥizkuni*; *HaKetav VehaKabbala*.
2. See Rashi; Ibn Ezra; *Or HaḤayyim*.
3. See II Samuel 3:33; Jeremiah 17:11; Abravanel.
4. Rashbam.
5. See Genesis 10.
6. Exodus 1:5; Deuteronomy 10:22; see Rashi and *Targum Yonatan* here; *Bemidbar Rabba* 9:14.
7. See *Bekhor Shor*; Rashbam.
8. See Rashi; Ibn Ezra; Sforno.
9. See *Sifrei, Haazinu* 314; Rashi; *Mekhilta*, Exodus 19:4.
10. Translation according to Ibn Ezra.
11. See Rashi; Ibn Ezra.
12. See, e.g., Ezekiel 27:6, 39:18; Amos 4:1.
13. 33:5, 26; see commentary on Isaiah 44:2.
14. See Onkelos; Ibn Ezra.
15. Rav Se'adya Gaon; *Ḥizkuni*.
16. See Rashi; Ibn Ezra.
17. See Onkelos; *Targum Yonatan*.
18. See *Pesaḥim* 111b.
19. See Ibn Ezra.
20. See Rashi; *Ha'amek Davar*.
21. See Rashi; Ramban.
22. Ibn Ezra; *Adderet Eliyahu*.
23. See Rashi.
24. See Ibn Ezra.
25. See Rashi; Ibn Ezra.
26. See Onkelos; Rashi; Rashbam; *Ḥizkuni*.
27. Rashi; see Exodus 23:5; I Samuel 9:17; Nehemiah 3:8.
28. Rashi.
29. *Ḥizkuni*.
30. See Exodus 6:8; Ezekiel 20:15, 42; Isaiah 62:8.
31. See, e.g., Judges 8:19; I Samuel 19:6.
32. Rashi.
33. See *Targum Yonatan*.
34. See 32:14.
35. *Ḥizkuni*.
36. See Ibn Ezra; see also Numbers 35:33.
37. See Numbers 13:16; Ibn Ezra.
38. Numbers 27:12–14.
39. See Rav Se'adya Gaon; Ibn Ezra.
40. See Numbers 27:12; Deuteronomy 3:27.
41. See Numbers 20:1–13.

Vezot HaBerakha

1. See Rashbam; Ramban.
2. See Exodus 19:18.
3. Rashbam; Sforno.
4. See Onkelos; Rashi; Ramban.
5. See Rashi.
6. See, e.g., Jeremiah 18:18; Ezekiel 24:24, and Radak ad loc.
7. See Rashi; Ramban; *Rosh HaShana* 32b.
8. See *Targum Yonatan*; Ibn Ezra; Ramban; *Midrash Tanna'im*; *Pe'er HaDor Teshuvot HaRambam* 225; *Responsa of Rav Se'adya ibn Denan*.
9. See Genesis 49:4.
10. See *Or HaḤayyim*.
11. See Ramban.
12. See Judges 1:2, 20:18; II Samuel 1:18; Jerusalem Talmud, *Horayot* 3:5.
13. See Exodus 17:6–7; Numbers 20:12–13.
14. See, e.g., Exodus 32:26–28; *Bemidbar Rabba* 1:12.
15. See 17:9, 18, 19:17, 21:5; Leviticus 10:8–11; Ezekiel 44:22–23; Hagai 2:11; Malachi 2:7.
16. See Onkelos.
17. See Rashi; *Zevaḥim* 54b.
18. See Rashi.
19. Exodus 3:2; Onkelos; *Targum Yonatan*; Rashi.
20. See I Kings 12; Judges 4:5; commentary on Genesis 48:19.
21. See *Bereshit Rabba* 31:13.
22. See Rashi.
23. See Genesis 48:13–19.
24. See *Targum Yonatan*; Rashi; Rashbam; Ramban.
25. Genesis 49:13; see also Joshua 19:16.
26. See Ibn Ezra; Ramban; *Ḥizkuni*.
27. See I Chronicles 12:33; Rashi.
28. Rashi.
29. See Isaiah 19:18; Jonah 1:10–16.
30. See *Targum Yonatan*; Rashi; *Megilla* 6a.
31. Rashi; *Bekhor Shor*; *Bereshit Rabbati* 49:19.
32. Rashi; *Sota* 13b.
33. Abravanel.
34. See Rashi; Ibn Ezra; *Bemidbar Rabba* 13:20.
35. See Rashi; *Sifrei, Vezot HaBerakha* 355; Judges 18.
36. See *Sifrei, Vezot HaBerakha* 355.
37. See Rashi; *Sifrei, Vezot HaBerakha* 355.
38. See *Menaḥot* 85b.
39. Rashi.
40. See Rashi; Ibn Ezra; *Ḥizkuni*.
41. See Ramban; Rashi.
42. Rashi.
43. Onkelos.
44. See Ibn Ezra.
45. See Ibn Ezra; Rabbi Samson Raphael Hirsch.
46. See Sforno.
47. Ibn Ezra.
48. Rashi; *Ḥizkuni*; see Isaiah 57:11.
49. See *Or HaḤayyim*; *Sifrei, Pinḥas* 135.
50. See Joshua 19:47.
51. See Onkelos; *Ḥizkuni*.
52. See Ibn Ezra; *Sifrei, Naso* 32; Radak, Ezekiel 34:2.
53. See Rashi; *Targum Yonatan*; *Sota* 9b.
54. See Numbers 20:29.
55. *Targum Yonatan*.

GENESIS

p38 left image © Patche99z; **p38** right image © Ronald Saunders; **p162** © tato grasso; **p166** lower right image © Eitan f; **p166** upper right image © Vinayaraj; **pp166** upper left image © Dedda71; **pp204** left image © Eitan Amiel et al., Shelef Oren; **p274** © Le.Loup.Gris; **p312** © Wellcome Collection;

EXODUS

p288 © Travelers in the Middle East Archive/TIMEA; **p290** © pjt56; **p294** © Michael Westhoff; **p306** © Didier Descouens, Muséum de Toulouse; **p308** right image © Whiteghost.ink; **p324** © KostaMumcuoglu; **p328**© Darkone; **p334** © AtelierMonpli; **p340** © **courtesy of the Temple Institute**; **p344** © Benjamin Shafir; **p366** © Traumrune; **p474** © Ján Svetlík; **p376** © David Turner (Novalis); **p424** Gideon Pisanty (Gidip); **p430** left images © H. Zell; **p430** upper right image © JMK; **pp434–436** all images © HaRav Menachem Makover, courtesy of *Harenu Bevinyano*; **pp442–448** all images © HaRav Menachem Makover, courtesy of *Harenu Bevinyano*; **p450** upper image © HaRav Menachem Makover, courtesy of *Harenu Bevinyano*; **pp454–462** all images © **courtesy of the Temple Institute**; **p470** © HaRav Menachem Makover, courtesy of *Harenu Bevinyano*; **p474** left image © Temple Mount Sifting Project; **p474** right image © HaRav Menachem Makover, courtesy of *Harenu Bevinyano*; **p476** upper image © Simon A. Eugster; **p476** lower image © Alessandra Perugi; **p478** left image © Tigerente; **p478** right image © Mauro Raffaelli; **p486** © Walters Art Museum; **p510–512** all images © HaRav Menachem Makover, courtesy of *Harenu Bevinyano*; **p514** upper right image © **courtesy of the Temple Institute**; **p514** center image © Deror Avi; **p516** left image © **courtesy of the Temple Institute**; **p516** right image © HaRav Menachem Makover, courtesy of *Harenu Bevinyano*; **p522** all images © **courtesy of the Temple Institute**; **p530** © HaRav Menachem Makover, courtesy of *Harenu Bevinyano*;

LEVITICUS

p544 center right image © Paco Gómez; **p544** lower right image © Peter Presslein; **p552** © HaRav Menachem Makover, courtesy of *Harenu Bevinyano*; **p578** © **courtesy of the Temple Institute**; **p582** © **courtesy of the Temple Institute**; **p584** right image © Mimicki; **p584** left image © Paul Bischoff; **p592** right image © Marion Wacker; **p594** lower left image © RSPCA WOAW; **p594** lower center left image © Derkarts; **p594** lower center right image © Natural England; **p594** upper right image © Thomas Kohler; **p596** upper left image © Juan Lacruz; **p596** upper center image © Yathin sk; **p596** upper right image © Ed Dunens; **p596** center left image © Доктор рукиноги; **p596** middle center image © Stig Nygaard; **p596** center right image © Dave Curtis; **p596** lower left image © Ferran Pestaña; **p596** lower right image © Jörg Hempel; **p598** upper left image © Ian; **p598** upper second-to-left image © محمد الفلسطيني; **p598** upper second-to-right image © Aparajita Datta; **p598** upper center left © MOCHO-DOS-BANHADOS; **p598** upper center right image © Steve Garvie; **p598** upper right image © Piotr J; **p598** lower left image © Natan Slifkin; **p598** lower second-to-left image © Arjan Haverkamp; **p598** lower center image © Rushen; **p598** lower second-to-right image © Umberto Salvagnin; **p598** lower right image © Michael Pennay; **p600** upper center left image © Yevgeny Kudinov; **p600** upper center right image © Michael Höhne; **p600** lower right image © GlebK; **p600** lower left image © Derek Keats; **p600** lower center image © Klara Matusevich (Klaram); **p616** © Ein Yael Living Museum; **p618** left image © Patche99z; **p618** right image © Benjamin Shafir; **p618** center image © Spodek M, Ben-Dov Y; **p624** © Institute for the Study of the Ancient World; **p628** right image © Hanay; **p628** left image © Clara Amit, Yoram Lehmann, Yael Yolovitch, Miki Koren, and Mariana Salzberger, courtesy of the Israel Antiquities Authority; **p660** right image © Meena Kadri; **p690** upper left and lower left images © Eliyahu Misgav; **p692** © HaRav Menachem Makover, courtesy of *Harenu Bevinyano*; **p698** © Eliyahu Misgav; **p708** © Mark Nesbitt;

KOREN

Steinsaltz Center